PERSONALITIES OF AMERICA

Personalities

of

America

Third Edition

published by:

the **American Biographical Institute**

5126 Bur Oak Circle, Post Office Box 31226, Raleigh, North Carolina 27622 USA.

Library of Congress Catalog Card Number 79-51997
International Standard Book Number 0-934544-28-X

Printed and bound in the United States of America
by
BookCrafters, Chelsea, Michigan, U.S.A.

Table of Contents

Preface   vii

ABI Biographical Titles   viii

Delineative Information   ix

Biographical Codes   ix

Table of Abbreviations   x

Biographies   1

Addendum   586

Young Personalities   589

Appendix I   xvii
    Editorial Advisory Board
    The American Biographical Institute

Appendix II   xxiii
    Roster of Life and Annual Members
    The American Biographical Institute
     Research Association

Preface

The American Biographical Institute proudly presents the Third Edition of PERSONALITIES OF AMERICA, recognizing thousands of outstanding individuals from across the nation. Each edition of PERSONALITIES OF AMERICA is different in the sense that the Institute feels a responsibility to update every entry that is selected for more than one edition. Also indicating its uniqueness as compared to previous editions, the Third Edition honors many new individuals whose accomplishments are most deserving of the recognition.

Following the main body of biographical entries is a section devoted to young Americans. These youths have demonstrated great talents and goals in areas of educational studies and extracurricular activities, community projects, and a multitude of professions. These young people are paving the way for the youth of tomorrow and represent a bright future for all other Americans.

Copies of PERSONALITIES OF AMERICA will be placed in all state libraries across the United States as well as in leading institutions of higher education, and public and private libraries. This distribution policy ensures the biographer, genealogist, and general researcher of an authoritative and up-to-date source of reference on leading Americans. Other titles published by the Institute are distributed in the same manner.

The American Biographical Institute is entering into its third decade of biographical publishing with a worldwide reputation for its sincerity to highlight, in an everlasting book form, the achievements of men and women of today. The individuals included in the Third Edition of PERSONALITIES OF AMERICA can claim this honor because of their long list of achievements. On behalf of the Governing Board of Editors and the entire editorial staff, I congratulate all of the individuals whose biographies appear on the following pages.

J. M. Evans

J. M. Evans
Editorial Director
THE AMERICAN BIOGRAPHICAL INSTITUTE, INC.

ABI
Biographical Titles

Directory of Distinguished Americans
International Directory of Distinguished Leadership
Community Leaders of America
Young Community Leaders of America
Community Leaders of the World
Notable Americans
Two Thousand Notable Americans
Personalities of America
Personalities of the South
Personalities of the West and Midwest
Five Thousand Personalities of the World
The Book of Honor
International Book of Honor

Delineative Information

Individual biographical entries are arranged according to standard alphabetical practice, and information for publication is consistently and uniformly presented in the categorical order as below. Coding symbols are clarified below as well.

Editors of the Institute make all attempts to edit accurately the information furnished by each biographee. In the rare event of an error by the publisher, the sole responsibility of the publisher will be to correct such in the subsequent edition of this publication.

Editorial evaluation is the ultimate determinant of publication selection. Admission in this series is based on the value of achievement or recognized outreach of endeavor.

Nomination sources for the Institute's publications are received from personal recommendations of the Institute's National Board of Advisors, National Educational Advisory Board, Governing Board of Editors, Media Research Department and Board of Directors. Recommendations are filed by nationwide universities and colleges; national, state and local professional organizations; service and civic organizations; businesses; and individuals. Mailing lists have never been bought or sold. Neither nominees or nominators are placed under any financial obligation. Nominees are contacted for their personal submissions of biographical materials, and it is these credentials that are editorially reviewed by the Governing Board of Editors upon receipt. Inclusion in an *ABI* publication series is based on merit.

Biographical Codes

oc/	Occupation	fam/	Family
b/	Birth	ed/	Education
h/	Home Address	mil/	Military Service
ba/	Business Address	pa/	Professional Activities
m/	Married-Wife or Husband	cp/	Civic & Political Activities
c/	Children	r/	Religious Activities
p/	Parents	hon/	Honors
sp/	Spouse's Parents		

Table of Abbreviations

AA	Associate of Arts
AAAS	American Association for the Advancement of Science
AAC	Army Air Corps
AAF	Army Air Force
AAHE	American Association of Higher Ed
AAHPER	American Association of Health, Physical Education and Recreation
AART	American Academy of Radiology Technicians
AASA	American Academy of School Administrators
AAUA	American Association of University Administrators
AAUP	American Association of University Professors
AAUW	American Association of University Women
AB	Bachelor of Arts
ABA	American Bar Association
Acad	Academy, Academic
Acct	Accountant
Acctg	Accounting
Achmt	Achievement
ACLU	American Civil Liberties Union
Activs	Activities
Addit	Additional
Adj	Adjunct
Adm	Administration, Administrative
Admr	Administrator
Adv	Advisory
Advmt	Advancement
Advr	Advisor
Advtg	Advertising
Aeronaut	Aeronautical
AESP	Association of Elementary School Principals
AF	Air Force
AFB	Air Force Base
AFCW	American Federation of Colored Women
Affil	Affiliate, Affiliation
Agri	Agriculture
Agst	Against
Agt	Agent
Agy	Agency
AIA	American Institute of Architects
Ala	Alabama
Alt	Alternate
Am	American, America
AM	Master of Arts
AMA	American Medical Association
AME	African Methodist Episcopal
Am Inst EE	American Institute of Electrical Engineers
Am Soc CE	American Society of Civil Engineers
Am Soc ME	Am Soc of Mechanical Engineers
Anal	Analysis, Analyst
Anesth	Anesthesiologist
ANG	Army National Guard
Anniv	Anniversary
AP	Associated Press

APGA	American Personnel and Guidance Association
Apr	April
Apprec	Appreciate, Appreciation
Approp	Appropriations
Appt	Appointment
Appt'd	Appointed
Apt	Apartment
ARC	American Red Cross
Arch	Architect, Architecture
Ariz	Arizona
ArM	Master of Architecture
Ark	Arkansas
Art	Article, Artillery
ASAS	American Society for the Advancement of Science
ASCAP	American Society of Composers, Authors, and Publishers
ASHA	American Speech and Hearing Association
Assessmt	Assessment
Assn	Association
Assoc	Associate
ASSP	Associaton of Secondary School Principals
Asst	Assistant, Assistance
Astronom	Astronomy, Astronomical
Ath	Athlete, Athletic
Atl	Atlantic
Att'd, Att'g	Attended, Attending
Atty	Attorney
Aug	August
AUS	United States Army
Auth	Authority
Aux	Auxiliary
A-V	Audio-Visual
Ave	Avenue
AWC	American Women Composers
Awd	Award
Awd'd	Awarded
BA	Bachelor of Arts
Bach	Bachelor
Balto	Baltimore
Bapt	Baptist
B Agr	Bachelor of Agriculture
B Arch	Bachelor of Architecture
Bat	Batallion
BBA	Bachelor of Business Administration
BBB	Better Business Bureau
BC	Bachelor of Chemistry
BCE	Bachelor of Chemical Engineering
Bch	Beach
BCL	Bachelor of Civil Law
Bd	Board
BD	Bachelor of Divinity
BDS	Bachelor of Dental Surgery
BE	Bachelor of Education, Engineering
BEE	Bachelor of Electrical Engineering
BF	Bachelor of Finance
B'ham	Birmingham
Bibliog	Bibliography, Bibliographical
Bicent	Bicentennial
Biog	Biography
Biol	Biology, Biological
Bk, Bkg, Bkr	Bank, Banking, Banker
Bkkpg	Bookkeeping

Bkkpr	Bookkeeper
Bklyn	Brooklyn
Bldg	Building
Bldr	Builder
BLit	Bachelor of Literature
BLS	Bachelor of Library Science
Blvd	Boulevard
BM	Bachelor of Medicine
BMus	Bachelor of Music
BPd, BPe	Bachelor of Physical Education
BPW	Business and Professional Women
Br	Branch
Brit	Britain, British
BS	Bachelor of Science
BSA	Boy Scouts of America
BSc	Bachelor of Science
BSED	Bachelor of Science in Education
BT, BTh	Bachelor of Theology
Bultn	Bulletin
Bur	Bureau
Bus	Business
Cal	California
Cand	Candidate
Capt	Captain
Cardiovas	Cardiovascular
Cath	Catholic
Cav	Cavalry
CB	Bachelor of Surgery, Citizen Band
CC	Country Clb
CDA	Catholic Daughters of America
CE	Chemical Engineer
CEC	Council for Exceptional Children
Cert	Certificate, Certification
Ch	Church
Champ(s)	Champion(s)
Chapt	Chapter
Chatta	Chattanooga
ChD	Doctor of Chemistry
Chd	Children
ChE	Chemical Engineer
Chem	Chemical, Chemist
Chiro	Chiropractic
Chm	Chairman
Chperson	Chairperson
CIA	Central Intelligence Agency
Cinc	Cincinnati
Cir	Circle
Cit	Citation
Clb	Club
Clin	Clinic, Clinical
Clk	Clerk
Cmdr	Commander
Cnslg	Counseling
Cnslr	Counselor
Co	County
CO	Commanding Officer
CoChm	Co-Chairman
C of C	Chamber of Commerce
Col	College, Collegiate, Colonel
Com	Committee
Comdg	Commanding
Comm	Commission
Com-man	Committeeman
Commend	Commendation

Commr	Commissioner	Div	Division, Divinity	Ft	Fort
Commun	Community	DLit, DLitt	Doctor of Literature, Letters	Ftball	Football
Communs	Communications			FTC	Federal Trade Commission
Com-wom	Committeewoman	DLS	Doctor of Library Science	Furn	Furniture
Conf	Conference	DMD	Doctor of Dental Medicine	FWB	Free Will Baptist
Cong	Congress	DMus	Doctor of Music		
Congl	Congressional	DO	Doctor of Osteopathy	Ga	Georgia
Cong of P's & T's	Congress of Parents and Teachers	Doct	Doctoral	GA's	Girls' Auxiliary
		Dr	Drive, Doctor	GE	General Electric
Congreg	Congregational	DS, DSc	Doctor of Science	Gen	General
Conserv	Conservation	DTh/DTheol	Doctor of Theology	Geneal	Genealogy, Genealogical
Conslt	Consultant	DVM	Doctor of Veterinary Medicine	Geo	George
Consltg	Consulting			Geog	Geography, Geographical
Consol	Consolidated			Geol	Geological
Constit	Constitution	E	East	Gov	Governor
Constrn	Construction	Ec	Economics	Govt	Government
Cont'd	Continued	Ecol	Ecology	Govtl	Governmental
Cont'g	Continuing	Ed	Education	Grad	Graduate, Graduated
Contbr	Contributor	EdB	Bachelor of Education	GSA	Girl Scouts of America
Contbtg	Contributing	EdD	Doctor of Education	Gtr	Greater
Conv	Convention	Edit	Editorial	Guid	Guidance
Coop	Cooperation	EdM	Master of Education	Gyn	Gynecology
Coor	Coordinator, Coordinating	Ednl	Educational		
Corp	Corporation	Edr	Educator	Hd	Head
Corr	Corresponding, Correspondence	EE	Electrical Engineer	Hdqtrs	Headquarters
		Elect	Electrical, Electric Electronics	Hgts	Heights
Cosmetol	Cosmetology, Cosmetologist			Hi	Hawaii
		Elem	Elementary	Hist	History
Coun	Council	Emer	Emergency	Histn	Historian
Creat & Success Person-alities	Creative and Successful Personalities of the World	Employmt	Employment	Hlth	Health
		EMR	Educable Mentally Retarded	Hon	Honor, Honorable
CPA	Certified Public Accountant			Hort	Horticulture
Cpl	Corporal	EMT	Emergency Medical Technician	Hosp	Hospital
CPR	Cardio-Pulmonary Resuscitation			HPER	Health, Physical Education and Recreation
		Ency	Encyclopedia		
Crim	Criminal	Eng	English	HS	High School
CSB	Bachelor of Christian Science	EngD	Doctor of Engineering	HUD	Housing and Urban Development
		Engr	Engineer		
Ct	Court	Engrg	Engineering	Hwy	Highway
Ctl	Central	Entomol	Entomology		
Ctr	Center	Envir	Environment, Environmental	Ia	Ia
Cult	Cultural			IBM	International Business Machines
Curric	Curriculum	Epis	Episcopal		
		Equipmt	Equipment	IEEE	Institute of Electrical and Electronic Engineers
DAC	Daughters of the American Colonists	Est	Establish		
		Establishmt	Establishment	Ill	Illinois
DAR	Daughters of the American Revolution	ETO	European Theater of Operations	Inc	Incorporated
				incl	Include
Daugh	Daughter	Eval	Evaluation	incl'g	Including
DAV	Disabled American Veterans	Evang	Evangelical	Indep	Independent, Independence
		Exam	Examination	Indiv	Individual
DC	District of Columbia	Examr	Examiner	Indpls	Indianapolis
DCL	Doctor of Canon Law	Exc	Exchange	Indust	Industry
DD	Doctor of Divinity	Exec	Executive	Inf	Infantry
DDS	Doctor of Dental Surgery	Ext	Extension	Info	Information
Dec	December			Ins	Insurance
dec	Deceased	FAA	Federal Aviation Agency	Insp	Inspector
Def	Defense	Fac	Faculty	Inst	Institute
Deg	Degree	Fam	Family	Instn	Institution
Del	Delegate	F&AM	Free and Accepted Mason	Instnl	Institutional
Dem	Democrat	FBI	Federal Bureau of Investigation	Instr	Instructor
Denom	Denomination, Denominational			Instrn	Instruction
		FCC	Federal Communications Commission	Intell	Intelligence
Dept	Department			Intells	Intellectuals
Delinq	Delinquent, Delinquency	FDA	Federal Drug Administration	Intl	International
Dermatol	Dermatology, Dermatologist			Intercont	Intercontinental
		Fdg	Founding	Intergovtl	Intergovernmental
Desc	Descendant	Fdn	Federation	Interpret	Interpretation
Devel	Development	Fdr	Founder	Invest	Investigation
DIB	Dictionary of International Biography	Feb	February	Investmt	Investment
		Fed	Federal	IOOF	Independent Order of ODD FELLOWS
Dic	Dictionary	Fest	Festival		
Dipl	Diploma	FFA	Future Farmers of America	IPA	International Platform Association
Dir	Director, Directory				
Dis	Disease	FHA	Future Homemakers of America	IRA	International Reading Association
Dist	District				
Dist'd	Distinguished	Fin	Finance	IRS	Internal Revenue Service
Distn	Distinction	Foun	Foundation	Isl	Island
		Frat	Fraternity		

Jan	January	MDiv	Master of Divinity	NJ	New Jersey
JCD	Doctor of Canon Law	MDS	Master of Dental Surgery	NIH	National Institute of Health
JD	Doctor of Law	Mdse	Merchandise	No	Northern
jg	Junior Grade	Me	Maine	NO	New Orleans
Jour	Journal, Journalism	Mech	Mechanical	Nom	Nominee
Jr	Junior	Med	Medical, Medicine	Nom'd	Nominated
Jt	Joint	MEd	Master of Education	Nom'g	Nominating
Jud	Judicial, Judiciary	Mem	Member	NM	New Mexico
Judic	Judicature	Meml	Memorial	NSA	National Security Agency
Jul	July	MENC	Music Educators National Conference	NSAC	National Society for Autistic Children
Jun	June	Merch	Merchant	Nsg	Nursing
Jurisd	Jurisdiction	Metall	Metallurgical	NSF	National Science Foundation
Jurisp	Jurisprudence	Meth	Methodist	Num	Numerous
J of P	Justice of the Peace	Metro	Metropolitan	NW	Northwest
Juv	Juvenile	Mfg	Manufacturing	NY	New York
Juv Delinq	Juvenile Delinquent	Mfr	Manufacturer	NYC	New York City
		Mgmt	Management		
K	Knights	Mgr	Manager	OAS	Organization of American States
Kgn	Kindergarten	Mil	Military		
K of C	Knights of Columbus	Min	Minister, Ministry	Ob	Obstetrics, Obstetrician
K of G	Knights of the Garter	Minn	Minnesota	Occup	Occupation, Occupational
K of P	Knights of Pythias	Misc	Miscellaneous	OCS	Officer Candidate School
Ks	Kansas	Miss	Mississippi	Oct	October
Ky	Kentucky	Mkt	Market	OD	Doctor of Optometry
		Mktg	Marketing	OES	Order of Eastern Star
La	Louisiana	Mng	Managing	Ofc	Office
LA	Los Angeles	Mo	Missouri	Ofcl	Official
Lab	Laboratory	mo, mos	Month, Months	Ofcr	Officer
Lang	Language	Mod	Modern	OLC	Oak Leaf Cluster
Laryngol	Laryngological	Mont	Montana	Opports	Opportunities
LB	Bachelor of Letters	MPd	Master of Pedagogy	Opthal	Opthalmology
LCA	Lutheran Church of America	MPE	Master of Physical Education	Optom	Optometry, Optometrist
LD	Learning Disabilities	MS, MSc	Master of Science	Orch	Orchestra
Ldg	Leading	MS	Multiple Sclerosis	Org	Organization
Ldr	Leader	Mt	Mount	Org'd	Organized
Ldrship	Leadership	Mtl	Mental	Orgnl	Organizational
LDS	Latter Day Saints	Mtly	Mentally	Orgr	Organizer
Leag	League	Mtn	Mountain	Orient	Orientation
Lectr	Lecturer	Mun	Municipal	Orig	Original
Legis	Legislative, Legislature, Legislator, Legislation	Mus	Museum	Ornithol	Ornithology
		MusB	Bachelor of Music	Ortho	Orthopedic, Orthopedist
LHD	Doctor of Humanities	Mut	Mutual	Outstg	Outstanding
LI	Long Island	Mvt	Movement		
Lib	Library			Pa	Pennsylvania
Libn	Librarian			Parliamentn	Parliamentarian
Lic	License	N	North	Path	Pathology, Pathologist
Lic'd	Licensed	NAACP	National Association for the Advancement of Colored People	PdB	Bachelor of Pedagogy
Lit	Literary, Literature			PDM	Master of Pedagogy
Lit(t)B	Bachelor of Literature, Letters	NAHPER	National Association of Health, Physical Education and Recreation	PE	Physical Education
Lit(t)D	Doctor of Literature, Letters			PeD	Doctor of Pedagogy
		NAm	North America	Perf	Performance
LLB	Bachelor of Laws	NASA	National Aeronautical and Space Administration	Period	Periodical
LLD	Doctor of Laws			Perm	Permanent
Ln	Lane, Loan	Nat	National	Pers	Personnel
Lng	Learning	N Atl	North Atlantic	Pgh	Pittsburgh
Lt	Lieutenant	Nat Reg	National Register of	PharB	Bachelor of Pharmacy
Ltd	Limited	Prom Ams	Prominent Americans	PharD	Doctor of Pharmacy
Lttrs	Letters	Nav	Naval	Pharm	Pharmacy, Pharmacist, Pharmacology
Luth	Lutheran	NBC	National Broadcasting Company		
LWC	League of Women Composers	NC	North Carolina	PharmM	Master of Pharmacy
LWV	League of Women Voters	NCNW	National Council of Negro Women	PhB	Bachelor of Philosophy
Lwyr	Lawyer			PhD	Doctor of Philosophy
		NCPGA	North Carolina Personnel and Guidance Association	Phil	Philosophy
MA	Master of Arts			Phila	Philadelphia
Mag	Magazine	NCTE	National Council of Teachers of English	Philharm	Philharmonic
MAgr	Master of Agriculture			Photo	Photography
Maj	Major	NCTM	National Council of Teachers of Math	Photog	Photographer
Mar	March			Phy	Physical
MArch	Master of Architecture	ND	North Dakota	Phys	Physician
Mat(s)	Material(s)	NE	Northeast	Physiol	Physiologist
Math	Mathematics	NEA	National Education Association	Pk	Park
MB	Bachelor of Medicine			Pkwy	Parkway
MBA	Master of Business Administrator	Neb	Nebraska	Pl	Place
Mbrship	Membership	Neurol	Neurology, Neurological	Placemt	Placement
MC	Master of Ceremonies	NG	National Guard	PO	Post Office
MCL	Master of Civil Law			PodD	Doctor of Podiatry
Md	Maryland	NH	New Hampshire	Polit	Political, Politics
				Pop	Population

PR	Puerto Rico
Pract	Practice
Precnt	Precinct
Predoct	Predoctoral
Premed	Premedical
Pres	President, Presidential
Presb	Presbyterian
Presby	Presbytery
Preven	Prevention
Prin	Principal
Prob	Problem
Prod	Product
Prodn	Production
Prodr	Producer
Prof	Professor
Profl	Professional
Prog	Program, Progress
Proj	Project
Prom	Prominent
Prot	Protestant
Protem	Pro tempore
Psycho	Psychology, Psychologist
Psychi	Psychiatry, Psychiatrist
PTA	Parents and Teachers Association
PTO	Pacific Theater of Operations, Parents and Teachers Organization
Pt-time	Parttime
Pub	Publish, Publication
Pub'd	Published
Pubr	Publisher
Pvt	Private
QMC	Quartermaster Corps
Qtr(s)	Quarter(s)
Qtrly	Quarterly
Que	Quebec
Radiol	Radiology
RAF	Royal Air Force
RCAF	Royal Canadian Air Force
Rd	Road
Rdg	Reading
Real Est	Real Estate
Rec	Recreation
Rec'd	Received
Recog	Recognition
Reg	Regional, Region
Reg'd	Registered
Rehab	Rehabilitation
Rel	Religion
Relats	Relations
Rep	Representative
Repub	Republican
Res	Research
Reschr	Researcher
Resv	Reserve
Retard	Retarded, Retardation
Ret'd	Retired
Rev	Reverend
RN	Registered Nurse
RR	Rural Route, Railroad
Rt	Route
Rts	Rights
Rwy	Railway
S	South
SF	San Francisco
SAR	Sons of the American Revolution
Sask	Saskatchewan
Savs	Savings
Savs & Ln	Savings and Loan
SB	Bachelor of Science
SCA	Speech Communication Association
ScD, SD	Doctor of Science
Sch	School
Sci	DScience
Scis	Sciences

Scist(s)	Scientist(s)
ScM	Master of Science
SDA	Seventh-Day Adventist
Sec'dy	Secondary
Sect	Section
Secy	Secretary
Sel	Selective
Sem	Seminar, Seminary
Sept	September
Ser	Service
Sev	Several
Sgt	Sergeant
SI	Staten Island
SJD	Doctor of Judicial Science
SM	Master of Science
So	Southern
Soc	Society
Sociol	Sociology
Spch	Speech
Spec	Special, Specialist
Spkg	Speaking
Spkr	Speaker
Sprgs	Springs
Sq	Square
Sqdrn	Squadron
Sr	Senior
SS	Sunday School
S/Sgt	Staff Sergeant
St	State, Street, Saint
Sta	Station
Stab	Stabilization
Stat	Statistic, Statistician
STB	Bachelor of Sacred Theology
STD	Doctor of Sacred Theology
Subcom	Subcommittee
Subst	Substitute
Sum	Summer
Supr Ct	Supreme Court
Supt	Superintendent
Supvn	Supervision
Supvr	Supervisor
Surg	Surgeon, Surgery
Symp	Symposium
Symph	Symphony
Sys	System
TB	Tuberculosis
Tchg	Teaching
Tchr	Teacher
Tech	Technical, Technician
Technol	Technology, Technologist
Temp	Temporary
Terr	Terrace
ThD	Doctor of Theology
Theol	Theology
TMR	Trainable Mentally Retarded
Tnd	Trained
Tng	Training
Tnr	Trainer
Tour	Tournament
Trans	Transportation
Treas	Treasurer
T&T	Telephone & Telegraph
TV	Television
Twp	Township
U	United
UDC	United Daughters of the Confederacy
UF	United Fund
UN	United Nations
UNESCO	United Nations Educational, Science and Cultural Organization
UNICEF	United Nations International Childrens Emergency Fund
UMW	United Methodist Women

Univ	University
UPI	United Press International
US	United States
USA	United States Army
USAAC	United States Army Air Corps
USAAF	United States Army Air Force
USAF	United States Air Force
USAFR	United States Air Force Reserve
USAR	United States Army Reserve
USASC	United States Army Signal Corps
USCG	United States Coast Guard
USMC	United States Marine Corps
USMM	United States Merchant Marine
USN	United States Navy
USNR	United States Naval Reserve
USPHS	United States Public Health Service
USS	United States Ship
USSR	Union of Soviet Socialist Republic
VA	Veterans Administration
Va	Virginia
Val	Valley
Var	Various
VBS	Vacation Bible School
VChm	Vice Chairman
Vet	Veteran, Veterinarian
VFW	Veterans of Foreign Wars
VI	Virgin Islands
VMD	Doctor of Veterinary Medicine
Voc	Vocational
Vol	Volunteer
VP	Vice President
Vt	Vermont
W	West
w	With
WAC	Women's Army Corps
Wash	Washington
WAVES	Women's United States Naval Reserves
Wed	Wednesday
Wel	Welfare
WHO	World Health Organization
Wis	Wisconsin
Wk	Week
Wkr	Worker
Wkly	Weekly
Wkshop	Workshop
Wm	William
WOW	Woodmen of the World
WSCS	Women's Society of Christian Service
WVa	West Virginia
W/W	Who's Who
W/W Fin & Indust	Who's Who in Finance and Industry
W/W MW	Who's Who in the Midwest
Wyo	Wyoming
Yg	Young
Ygst	Youngest
YMCA	Young Men's Christian Association
YMHA	Young Men's Hebrew Association
Yr	Year
Yth	Youth
YWCA	Young Women's Christian Association
Zool	Zoology, Zoologist, Zoological

A

AARON, MERICK ROY oc/Supervisor of Science, Financial Executive; b/May 22, 1947; h/104 Ward Street, Westbury, NY 11590; ba/Cedarhurst, NY; p/Harry and Gertrude S Aaron, Carle Place, NY; ed/BA 1969, MS 1971, Long Isl Univ; Cert Adv Studies 1973, Profl Dipl 1974, Hofstra Univ; EdD, Nova Univ, 1982; pa/Dist Supvr of Sci, Lawrence Public Schs, 1980-; Pres, GNS Investmt Fund, NYC, NY, 1971-; VP, Mervic Enterprises, Huntington, NY, 1978-; Supvr of Sci 1972-80, Tchr of Sci 1969-72, Carle Place, Public Schs, NY; Adj Prof, Nassau Commun Col (1973-) & Syracuse Univ (1974-83); Pres, NY St Sci Supvrs Assn, 1982-83; Pres, Naussau Co Sci Supvrs Assn, 1979; Exec Bd, Nat Sci Supvrs Assn, 1983-; cp/Trustee, Carle Place Bd of Ed, 1981-; Pres, Kiwanis Clb Westbury-Carle Place, 1982-83; Ofcr Meadowbrook Lodge F & AM, 1982-; hon/Author of *Psychol, A Behavioral Sci*; "Students Tchg Sci in the Elem Sch"; Phi Theta Kappa Hon Soc Awd, 1982; Outstg Contbns to Sci Ed in Nassau Co, NCSSA, 1981; Edr of Yr, Carle Place Public Schs, 1975 & 1977; W/W: in E, in World, in Fin & Indust; Personalities of E.

AARONSON, MARC ARNOLD oc/Astronomer; b/Aug 24, 1950; h/7825 North Camino de Maximillian, Tucson, AZ 85704; ba/Tucson, AZ; m/Marianne Gabrielle Kun; c/Laura, Jamie; p/Simon and Rena Aaronson, LA, CA; sp/Andrew and Agnes Kun, LA, CA; ed/BS, CA Tech Inst, 1972; MA 1974, PhD 1977, Harvard Univ; pa/Assoc Prof 1983-, Res Assoc 1977-83, Univ AZ; Am Astronom Soc; Astronom Soc of Pacific; Sigma Xi; Intl Astronom Union; hon/Over 90 Papers Pub'd in Profl Sci Jours; van Biebroeck Awd, Univ AZ, 1980; Bok Prize, Harvard Univ, 1983; Pierce Prize, AAS, 1984.

ABARAVICH, MARGARET MARY oc/Educator; b/Feb 15; h/3051 South 50th, Milwaukee, WI 53219; ba/Milwaukee, WI; m/Vincent C; c/Vincent P Barr, Margaret A Atwell, Patric J; p/James and Margaret McCormick (dec); sp/William and Anne Abaravich (dec); ed/BA Ed, Univ WI Milwaukee, 1980; pa/Staff Mem, Pleasant View Sch for Multi Handicapped/Deaf, 1973-; VPres, WI Telecommun Org; WI Reg'd Interpreters for Deaf; WI Assn for Deaf; Nat Assn for Deaf; cp/Charter Pres, WI's 1st Deaf Lioness Clb; Secy Chapt 7, Intl Cath Deaf Org; Ldr, CSA; Num Grass Root Orgs for Deaf Awareness, Understanding & Improvement; r/Cath; hon/Pres, Gtr Milwaukee Lioness Clb, 1980; Pres, St John's Scholarship Com, 1978; Milwaukee Co Commr for Handicapped; Listed in WI Wom, Gifted Heritage.

ABBASY, IFTIKHARUL HAQUE oc/Surgeon; b/Oct 28, 1935; h/905 Burr Oak Ct, Oak Brook, IL 60521; ba/Villa Park, IL; m/Kare Gaye; c/Shameen Ara; p/Mumtaz Begum Abbasy, Pakistan; sp/Mr and Mrs Kharpur, Pakistan; ed/MBBS, 1961; FRCS(C), 1973; Dipl, Am Bd of Abdominal Surg, 1973; Dipl, Am Bd of Surg, 1974; pa/House Phys, Civil Hosp, Karachi, Pakistan; House Phys & Surg, St Olave's Hosp, London, England; Sr House Surg of Casualty Dept,

E Meml Hosp, London, England; Rotating Intern, Swedish Covenant Hosp, Chgo, IL; Residency Surg, Michael Reese Hosp, Chgo, IL; AMA; IL Med Assn; Dupage Co Med Soc; Am Col of Surgs; Royal Col of Surgs; Pan Pacific Surg Soc; r/Islam; hon/W/W in MW; Men & Wom of Distn; DIB.

ABBOTT, MITCHEL T oc/Professor; b/Jun 6, 1930; h/5812 Fontaine Street, San Diego, CA 92120; m/Florine L; c/Valerie Michele, Mark Nelson, Chester Bruce; p/Chester and Judith Abbott (dec); ed/BS Chem 1957, PhD Biol Chem 1962, Univ CA-LA; mil/AUS, 1951-53; pa/Postdoct Fellow, Biochem Dept, NY Univ Med Sch, 1963-64; Vis'g Sci, Roche Inst of Molecular Bio, Nutley, NJ, 1972-73; Prof Chem, San Diego St Univ, 1964-; Am Soc of Biol Chems; AAAS; hon/Contbr, Over 30 Articles to Profl Sci Jours & Books; Recip, Basic Res Grants from NIH, 1965-83; W/W in Frontier Sci & Technol.

ABBOTT, ROBERT DEAN oc/Professor; b/Dec 19, 1946; h/7357 57 Northeast, Seattle, WA 98115; ba/Seattle, WA; m/Sylvia Patricia; c/Danielle, Matthew; p/Charles D and Billie J Abbott, Atwater, CA; ed/BA, CA Wn Univ-San Diego, 1967; MS 1968, PhD 1970, Univ WA Seattle; pa/Assoc Prof Psych, CA St Univ-Fullerton, 1970-75; Asst to Full Prof Ednl Psych, Univ WA, 1975-; Am Psychol Assn, 1968; Psychometric Soc, 1968-; Am Ednl Res Assn, 1975-; Am Stats Assn, 1973-; Nat Coun on Measurement in Ed, 1974-; r/Christian; hon/Author of 2 Books, 1980 & 1983; Over 50 Articles Pub'd in Profl Jours, 1968-; CA St S'ship, 1964-67; W/W.

ABDALLAH, SHAABAN AHMED oc/Research Associate; b/Oct 7, 1947; h/718 East Foster Avenue #4, State College, PA 16802; ba/State College; p/Ahmed and Hanem Abdallah, Sohag, Egypt; ed/BS in Aerospace Engrg, Cairo Univ, 1970; BS Math, Cairo Univ, 1973; MS Aerospace Engrg 1976, PhD Aerospace Engrg 1980, Univ of Cinc; pa/Instr, Sch of Engrg, Cairo Univ, Egypt, 1970-1975; Res Asst, Dept of Aerospace Engrg, Univ of Cinc, OH, 1975-1980; Res Assoc, Applied Res Lab, PA St Univ, 1981-; Mem, AIAA; Grad Student Assn, Pres 1977-1978; r/Moslem; hon/Author of Num Profl Pubs; Rec'd Hon Awd Assuit Univ, Assuit, Egypt, 1966; W/W in E.

ABDEL-GHANY, MOHAMED oc/Professor and Department Head; b/Mar 24, 1940; h/24 Peach Grove, Cottondale, AL 35453; ba/University, AL; c/Tamara, Sonya; p/Ibrahim Abdel-Ghany (dec); sp/Esha Hassanen, Cairo, Egypt; ed/BS, Univ Cairo, 1962; MS, IA St Univ, 1972; PhD, Univ MO, 1974; pa/Instr, Inst of Nat Planning, Cairo, Egypt, 1962-65; Res Asst, Univ MO, 1972-74; Asst Prof Fam Ec, Univ of NC-Greensboro, 1974-78; Assoc Prof & Hd of Consumer Scis, Univ AL, 1978-82; Prof & Hd Consumer Scis, Univ AL, 1982-; Dir 1977-79, Am Coun on Consumer Interests; Am Ec Assn; Chm of Res Sect 1984-86, Am Home Ec Assn; Assn for Consumer Res; Inst of Nutrition; VP 1975-77, NC Consumer Res Foun; AL Home Ec Assn, Chm Res Com 1981-84; hon/Num Res Articles in Areas of Consumer Studies & Fam Ec Pub'd in Sci Jours; Sigma Xi; Omicron Nu;

Gamma Sigma Delta; W/W in S & SW.

ABEL, RICHARD WAYNE oc/Communications Consultant; b/Jul 4, 1941; h/1089 Miramar Street, Laguna Beach, CA 92651; ba/Same; p/John William and Olive Mae Bickmore Abel; ed/BFA, Cornell Univ, 1963; MFA, Univ HI, 1966; Advtg Trainee, Persons Advtg, NYC, 1963-64; Campaign Dir, Am Cancer Soc, SF, 1966-67; Theatre Instr, Occidental Col, LA, 1967-69; Pres & Owner, Comm/Cord, LA, 1969-72; Dir, Communs Tran Corp, El Segundo, CA, 1972-74; Communs Conslt, Laguna Bch, CA, 1974; Ptnr, Abel/Naugler Communs, Dana Pt, CA, 1983-; cp/Co-Fdr, Secy & Bd of Dirs, Nautical Heritage Mus; Fdr, Heritage Player; Conslt, Packard 43rd Congl Dist Write-in Campaign, Capt CA, Ofcl Tallship Ambassador, St of CA.

ABELAR, INA MAE oc/Physics Supervising Instructional Support Technician; b/Jul 18, 1926; h/1833 Benedict Way, Pomona, CA 91767; ba/Pomona, CA; c/Debora Jean Arcoverde, Michelle Elain Prostler, Randolph Lee; p/Merritt Lyle Cameron (dec), Leeta May (Worthen) Cameron, Salem, OR; ed/BA, CA St Polytechnic Univ, 1978; pa/Lumber Estimater, Keith Brown Bldg Supply, Salem, OR, 1946-48; Whiting-Mead Bldg Supply, Vernon, CA, 1949-51; Trojan Lumber Co, Burbank, CA, 1952-55; Bkkpr, Jerry Kalior Bkkpr Sys, N Hollywood, CA, 1959-66; Supvg Equip Tech II, Dept of Physics, CA St Polytechnic Univ, Pomona, CA, 1979-; Campus Staff Coun, Mem 1970-83, 1984-87, Chm, 1977-78; Mu Phi Epsilon, Mem 1978-, Pres 1983-85; r/Mem, Upland Christian Ch; hon/Outstg Staff, CA St Polytechnic Univ, 1983-84; W/W: in W, of Wom; of Contemp Achmt.

ABELL, LeRON EVELYN oc/Researcher and Writer; b/Dec 31, 1912; h/1209 Murray Avenue, Tifton, GA 31794; ba/Same; m/C Stanley Abell (dec); p/Elbert D and Mary E Paulk (dec); sp/Stanley Walker and Tobitha Abell (dec); ed/Att'd Univ of Houston, Houston, TX, 1952-56; MT (ASCP); Cont'g Ed, Univ GA 1960, GA St Univ 1967; pa/Chief, J D Hosp Blood Bk, Houston TX, 1950; Chief Technologist, Diagnostic Hosp of Houston, Houston, TX, 1956; Chief Bacteriology & Mycology, Tchg Hosp, Univ of FL, 1959; Devel'd Tchg Prog for Clin Lab Assts, Clarkesville, GA, 1960; Devel'd Med Diagnostic & Res Labs, Atlanta, GA, 1962; Am Soc of Med Technologists, 1963; Assoc Mem, Am Soc of Clin Pathol, 1977; cp/Mem, Nat Assn Ret'd Fed Employees; Am Legion Aux; OES; DAR; UDC; Pine Garden Club; r/Bapt; hon/Author: *Simple Technique for Blood Cholesterol 1959, Med Technol Retraining in 6 Mos, 1970; Mem Steering Com, Listen, Look & Learn;* W/W in W.

ABELL, WILLIAM LAWRENCE Jr oc/Sculptor; b/Apr 5, 1945; h/924 Meadowbrook Road, Crest Park, CA 92326; ba/PO Box 232, Crest Park, CA 92326; m/Pamela Sue; c/Mark Aaron; p/William Lawrence Abell Sr, Oxnard, CA; sp/Pat and Gloria Davis, Reseda, CA; ed/AA, CC, Glendale Col, 1971; pa/Designer, Artist, Sculptor, Self-Employed; Mem, Bd of Dirs, Fine Arts Assn; San Bernardino Co Mus; Pasadena Soc of Artists; r/Christian;

hon/Author of Num Profl Pubs.

ABELOFF, ABRAM JOSEPH oc/ Surgeon; b/Mar 19, 1900; h/150 East 77th St, New York, NY 10021; ba/New York, NY; m/Gertrude Theresa Kopsch; c/Tobias Samuel; p/Samuel and Rebecca Esther Rogow Abeloff; ed/AB 1922, MD 1926, Columbia Univ; mil/AUS, Hosp Cmdr; pa/Intern, Presb Hosp, NYC, 1926-27; Surg Intern, Lenox Hill Hosp, NYC, 1927-29; Res Asst, Inst Pathol, Univ Freiburg, Germany, 1929; Surg Ser, Frankfurt Univ, Germany & Univ Vienna, Austria, 1930; Adj Surg, Beth Israel Hosp, NYC, 1930-37; Assoc Surg, Neuorol Hosp, NYC, 1930-33; Asst Adj Surg 1930-36, Att'g Surg Clin 1930-36, Chief of Clin 1936-42, Adj Att'g Surg 1936-46, Assoc Surg 1946-54, Att'g Surg 1954-65, Consltg Surg 1965-, Att'g in Charge of Surg Ser 1971, Lenox Hill Hosp; Surg, Lexington Sch for Deaf, 1947-68; Assoc Clin Prof Surg, NY Univ Sch of Med, 1947-; AMA; NY Co & St Med Socs; NY Acad of Med; NY Surg Soc; cp/Trustee, Columbia Univ, 1959-65; Dir, Mem of Adm & Exec Com, Am Jewish Joint Dist Com, 1948-; Trustee & Treas, Past Pres, Phys Female MYC Pres, 1956-57; Trustee, Col of Phys & Surg Alumni Assn; Life Mem, NY Hist Soc; Bd Mem, Metro Mus of Art; Mem, Crolier Clb; Num Other Orgs & Coms; r/Jewish; hon/AUS Legion of Merit; Dist'd Ser Cross of St of NY; Cit for Meritorious Ser Unit, Lawson Gen Hosp; Dist'd Achmt Awd, Stuyvesant HS, 1965; Fdn Medal for Dist'd Columbia Univ Alumni Ser, 1963; Silver Medal, P & S Alumni Assn, 1969; Diplomate, Am Bd of Surg; Fellow, Am Col Surgs & Brazilian Col of Surgs.

ABER, MARGERY V oc/Professor; b/ Feb 15, 1914; h/511 Michigan Avenue, Stevens Point, WI 54481; ba/Stevens Pt, WI; p/Earle J Aber, Waterford WI; ed/ BM, Oberlin Col, 1937; MA, Columbia Univ, 1946; Att'd NY Univ; Att'd Wayne St Univ, 1938-63; Att'd CO Univ, 1963; Studied w Shinichi Suzuki, Japan, 1967-1984; Att'd Univ WI Madison, 1963; Att'd Oakland Univ & Rochester Univ, 1965; Att'd Univ HI, 1979; pa/ Tchr, Detroit Public Schs, 1937-67; Pt-time Fac, Wayne St Univ, 1947-59; Univ WI Extended Sers, 1968-73; Univ WI Wausau Affil, 1972-73; Univ WI Marshfield Affil, 1978-79; Assoc Prof (1967-) & Dir (1974-), Am Suzuki Talent Ed Ctr, Univ WI Stevens Point, 1967-; Am String Tchrs Assn; Bd Mem 1971-78 & 1981-, Suzuki Assn Am; Dir, Am Suzuki Inst, 1971-; cp/Concert Mistress, WI Symph Orch, 1967-84; Affil, 1st Am-Japan Tour to China, 1983; r/Prot; hon/Editor: ASTEC Newslttr, 1974-; Suzuki Jour, 1982; Kappa Gamma, 1977; Pi Kappa Lamda, 1974; Hall of Fame, Wash Point HS, Racine, WI, 1976; 1st Dist'd Ser Awd, Suzuki Assn Am, 1980; Worlds W/W of Wom in Ed.

ABERCRUMBIE, P ERIC oc/University Administrator; b/Jun 14, 1948; h/ 1625 Asmann, #6, Cincinnati, OH 45221; ba/Cincinnati, OH; c/Paul E; p/ Margaret Nelson; ed/BA 1970, MA 1971, En KY Univ; pa/Adv Spec, Princeton City Sch Dist, 1971-72; Resident Cnslr 1972-73, Spec Sers Cnslr 1973-75, Assoc to Assoc VProvost for Minority Progs & Sers 1975-, Univ Cinc; cp/Omega Psi Phi Frat Inc;

NAACP; Omicron Delta Kappa; Gtr Cinc Dr Martin Luther King Jr Coalition; r/Bapt; hon/Articles in Omega Psi Phi Pub, 1976 & 1979; Univ Cinc Alpha Phi Alpha Frat; Dr Martin Luther King Jr Awd of Excell, 1980; Univ Cinc U Black Fac & Staff Assn Awd of Excell, 1981; Omicron Delta Kappa, 1974, 1982; Outstg Yg Men in Am.

ABEY, BERNARD EARL JR oc/Industrial Engineer; b/Aug 9, 1947; h/4013 Shelley Court, Virginia Beach, VA 23452; ba/Virginia Bch, VA; m/Betty Bowers; p/Bernard E Abey Sr, Weems, VA; sp/Mrs Virginia Bowers, Norfolk, VA; ed/BS Indust Engrg, 1970; MS Opers Res, 1977; pa/Sr Engr, CACI Inc, 1981-; Sr Analyst, Aron Fashions, 1978-81; Orgnl Analyst, Commonwlth of VA, 1974-78; Nat Soc Profl Engrs; VA Soc Profl Engrs; AIIE.

ABILDSKOV, J A oc/Medical Researcher, Professor; b/Sep 22, 1923; h/1506 Canterbury Drive, Salt Lake City, UT, 84108; m/Mary Helen McKell; c/Becky, Alan, Mary, Marilyn; p/John Abildskov (dec); Annie Abildskov, Salem, UT; ed/BA 1944, MD 1946, Univ of UT; mil/USAR, 1954-56; pa/Instr Med, Tulane Univ, 1948-54; Asst, Assoc & Prof Med, SUNY, 1956-68; Prof Med, Univ of UT, 1968-; Assn Am Phys; Am Soc for Clin Investigation; Wn Soc for Clin Investigation; Wn Assn Phys; r/ LDS; hon/Author, Over 150 Articles Pub'd in Profl Sci Jours; Univ of UT Dist'd Res Awd, 1976; W/W: in W, in Frontier Sci & Technol; Dir of Med Specs.

ABLES, BILLIE S oc/Clinical Psychologist, Professor; b/Jul 14, 1925; h/1600 Elkchester, Lexington, KY 40510; ba/ Lexington, KY; m/Alan S Church; c/ Scott, Amy; p/Mary T Talantis, Knoxville, TN; ed/AB 1946, MA 1949, Univ AL; PhD, Purdue Univ, 1954; pa/ Postdoct Fellow Child Psych, The Menninger Foun, 1956-57; Asst Prof, Washburn Univ, 1957-60; Chief Psychol, Fam Ser & Guid Ctr, Topeka, KS, 1960-64; Asst Prof Psychi, Dept Psychi 1966-71, Assoc Prof Psychi & Psych 1971-78, Clin Psychol & Prof Psychi 1978-, Univ KY Med Ctr; Am Psychol Assn; KY Psychol Assn; Am Orthopsychi Assn; Acad Psychols in Marital & Fam Therapy; AAUP; Am Acad Psychotherapists; r/Prot; hon/Author & Co-Author of Books: Multiple Personality: Etiology, Diagnosis & Treatment 1982, Therapy for Couples 1977; Sigma Xi, Purdue Univ, 1958; KY Bd of Psych Appt, 1981-85; Intl Dir of Dist'd Psychotherapists; W/W: of Am Wom, in S & SW.

ABOLINS, MARIS A oc/Physics Professor; b/Feb 5, 1938; h/220 Loree Drive, East Lansing, MI 48823; ba/E Lansing, MI; m/Frances; c/Mark, Krista; p/Arvids and Olga Abolins, Sumner, WA; sp/J Morrill Delano, Puyallup, WA; ed/BS Physics, Univ WA Seattle, 1960; MS 1962, PhD 1965, Univ CA San Diego; pa/Res Asst, Univ CA San Diego, 1960-65; Physicist, Lawrence Berkeley Lab, 1965-68; Assoc Prof 1968-73, Prof 1973-; MI St Univ; Vis'g Rschr, CERN, Geneva, Switzerland, 1967-77; Vis'g Rschr, CEA, Saclay, France, 1977; Phi Beta Kappa, 1958; Am Phy Soc, 1960; Exec Com, Div of Particles & Fields, Am Phys Soc; AAAS; Exec Com 1981-84, Chm 1982-83, Fermi Lab Users; hon/ Author, Over 100 Tech Articles & Book

Chapts Pub'd; G M Nat S'ship, 1956-60; Grad, magna cum laude, 1960.

ABRAHAMSON, WARREN G oc/ Professor; b/Mar 26, 1947; h/153 Mountain View Road, Lewisburg, PA 17837; ba/Lewisburg, PA; m/Christy Raye; c/ Jill Raye; p/Warren and Alice Abrahmson, Ludington, MI; sp/Donald and Joyce Harmon, Scottville, MI; ed/BS Botany, Univ MI Ann Arbor, 1969; MA Biol 1971, PhD Biol 1973, Harvard Univ; pa/David Burpee Prof of Plant Genetics 1983-, Assoc Prof Biol 1979-83, Asst Prof Biol 1973-79, Bucknell Univ; Res Assoc 1976-, Res Fellow 1980-81, Archbold Biol Sta, FL; Vis'g Asst Prof Biol, MI St Univ, 1976; Biol Tutor 1972-73, Tchg Fellow Biol 1969-72, Harvard Univ; Mem 1973-, Coun 1980-81, Chp Ecol Sect 1980-81, VChp Ecol Sect 1979-80, Botanical Soc Am; Mem 1977-, Chapt Pres 1982-84, Prog Chp 1978-80, Nat Audubon Soc; Ecol Soc Am, 1972-; Nat Wildlife Fdn, 1979-; Phi Sigma, 1969-; Soc for Study of Evolution, 1973-; Num Others; hon/ Author & Co-Author, Over 50 Articles Pub'd in Profl Sci Jours incl'g: Am Jour Botany, Ecol, Bull Torrey Bot Clb, Others; Nat Audubon Soc Wm Dutcher Awd for Outstg Ser to Audubon Cause at Reg Level (Mid-Atl), 1984; Class of 1956 Lectrship for Inspirational Tchg, Bucknell Univ, 1982-83; Lindback Awd for Dist'd Tchg, Bucknell Univ, 1975-76; Bradley-Moore-David Awd, Outstg Sr in Botany, Univ MI, 1969; Am Men & Wom in Sci.

ABRAIRA, CARLOS oc/Physician; b/ Mar 25, 1936; ba/Hines, IL; m/Rosa; c/ Daniel, Irene; p/Jose B and Maria Abraira, Buenos Aires, Argentina; ed/ BS Nat Col 1953, MD Med Sch 1961, Univ Buenos Aires, Argentina; pa/Chief Endocrinology 1972-, Asst Chief 1970-72, Hines VA Hosp; Prof Med, Loyola Univ, 1983-; Assoc Prof Med 1978-, Asst Prof Med 1970-78, Lincoln Sch of Med, Univ IL; Att'g Phys, M Reese Hosp, Chgo, 1969-70; Mem Bd of Dirs 1978-, Chair Profl Progs Com 1979-, Am Diabetes Assn of No IL; Coor, Diabetes Prog, MW Clin Conf, Chgo Med Soc, 1979-; hon/Author of 39 Pubs in Clin Med; Co-Author Book Chapt, "Diabetes Mellitus," 1980; Co-Editor, "Lrng to Be Your Diabetes Mgr," 1981; Fellow, Am Col of Phys, 1976; Allstate Foun Grant Awd, 1966; The Sugar Foun Inc Grant Awd, 1983; Dir of Med Specs; W/W in Frontier Sci & Technol.

ABRAM, ALENE JAMES oc/Educator; b/Aug 6, 1915; h/612 Highland Court, Upland, CA 91786; m/J Tilden; c/Janice Amundson; p/Frank S James (dec); Anna M James, Grass Valley, CA; sp/Achille Abram (dec); ed/BA Spanish 1936, MA 1938, Univ CA Berkeley; Postgrad Study, Claremont Grad Sch, Claremont, CA; pa/Rdr Spanish Dept, Univ CA Berkeley, 1937-38; Jr High Tchr, Grass Val, CA, 1938-39; HS Tchr, Spanish & Latin: Monterey, CA 1939-42; Chowchille, CA 1942-45; Chaffey HS 1945-47; Covina HS 1947-50; Tchr 1958-72 & Chm Fgn Lang Dept 1962-72, Chino HS; Spanish Tchr, Don Lugo HS, Chino, CA, 1972; Madera Co Rep of CA Tchrs Assn, 1943; Secy Pomona Val Br, AAUW; CA S'ship Advr, 1948-50; Others; cp/Pres 1955, Parliamentn & Musician 1983, Ontario,

CA Post 112, Am Legion Aux; Claremont Grad Sch Alumni Coun, 1976-; Num Others; r/Meth; hon/Phi Beta Kappa, 1936; Levi Strauss Scholar, 1935; Phoebe A Hearst Scholar, 1936; Inter Am Scholar, 1946; Sigma Delta Pi, 1936; Pi Sigma, 1937; Named to Tchrs to Freedoms Foun, 1966; Delta Kappa Gamma, 1973; Commun Ldrs Am; DIB; Intl Book of Hon.

ABRAMS, BARBARA oc/Career and Life Planning Specialist; b/Apr 16, 1942; h/13902-9B Yorba Street, Tustin, CA, 92680; ba/Tustin, CA; p/Mr and Mrs Nathan Abrams (dec); ed/BS Psych, NY Univ, 1964; pa/Secy-Nat Accounts Mgr For 6 Sts in 5 Yrs, McKesson Drug Co; Career & Life Planning Spec, 1984-; Mem: Wom in Mgmt; Nat Spkrs Assn; Am Soc for Tng & Devel; cp/Nat Coun of Jewish Wom; We Can; hon/Pub'd Article for *Am Druggist Mag*, 1978; Featured in Article, *LA Times*, 1984; Prod'd & Copyrighted 4 Motivational Progs for Bus & Commun; Sales Rep of Yr Awd, McKesson Drug Co, 1978.

ABRAMS, HERBERT LEROY oc/ Professor and Department Chairman; b/Aug 16, 1920; h/433 Walnut Street, Brookline, MA 02146; ba/Boston, MA; m/Marilyn Spitz; c/John, Nancy; p/ Morris Abrams, Long Isl, NY; ed/BA, Cornell Univ, 1941; MD, SUNY-Downstate Med Ctr, 1946; AM, (Hon Deg) Harvard Univ, 1968; pa/Intern, Long Isl Col Hosp, Bklyn, NY 1946-47; Asst Resident Med, Montefiore Hosp, Bronx, NY, 1947-48; Resident Radiol, Stanford Univ Hosp, San Francisco, CA, 1948-51; Res Fellow, Nat Cancer Inst, 1950-51; Instr, Asst Prof, Assoc Prof Radiol 1951-61, Dir Div Diagnostic Radiol 1960-67, Prof Radiol 1961-67, Vis'g Prof Radiol 1980-81, Stanford Univ Med Sch, Stanford, CA; Philip H Cook Prof Radiol 1967-, Chm Dept Radiol 1967-80, Harvard Med Sch, Boston; Radiol-in-Chief, Peter Bent Brigham Hosp, Boston, 1967-80; Radiol-in-Chief, Sidney Farber Cancer Inst, Boston, 1970-; Chm Dept Radiol, Brigham & Wom's Hosp, Boston, 1980-; Vis'g Prof & Spec NIH Fellow, Dept Radiol, Univ Lund, Sweden, 1959-60; Spec Res Fellow, Nat Heart Inst, 1960; Sr Fellow Cardiovas Res Inst, Univ CA Med Sch, San Francisco, 1973-74; Henry J Kaiser Sr Fellow, Ctr for Adv'd Study in Behavioral Scis, Stanford, 1980-81; Edit Bd 1965-, Edit Exec Com 1977-, *Investigative Radiol*; Editor, *Contemp Surg*, 1970-76; Bd of Editors, AMA, *Archives of Surg*, 1974-79; Editor-in-Chief, *Cardiovas & Interventional Radiol*, 1977-; Editor-in-Chief, *Jour Cont'g Ed in Radiol*, 1978-80; Editor-in-Chief, *Post Grad Radiol*, 1980-; Pres, N Am Soc Cardiac Radiol, 1978-79; Mem Public Policy Subcom, Ch Coun Affairs Com, Prog Chm 1972-75 & Mem Coun on Cardiovas Radiol 1979-80, Bd of Dirs 1978-79, Am Heart Assn; Pres 1977-78, Inst Radiologic Sci Com 1977-, Assn of Univ Radiols-Soc of Chm Acad Radiol Depts; Exec Com & Adv Com, Inter-Soc Comm for Heart Disease Resources; Com on Efficacy Studies, Am Col of Radiol; Am Col Cardiol; Am Col Radiol; Am Soc Nephrol; Am Roentgen Ray Soc; Assn of Am Med Socs; Inst of Med, Nat Acad of Sci; Fdg Mem, Nat Acad of Pract in Med; Num Others; cp/Over 50 Postgrad Lectures at Num Nat & Intl

Univs, Socs, Coms, Orgs & Assns 1962-84; Num Others; hon/Over 180 Articles Pub'd in Profl Med & Sci Jours; Over 30 Books & Book Chapts Pub'd; Phi Beta Kappa; Cornell Univ S'ship; Woodford Meml Prize; 94' Meml Prize; Editor, *Cornell Jour Opinion*; Mem, Cornell Student Coun; Joanna Szerlip Prize; Phi Epsilon Pi Awd for Scholastic Achmt; Alpha Omega Alpha.

ABRAMS-SMITH, PAULA oc/Psychologist; b/Nov 22, 1951; h/4828 Bussendorfer Road, Orchard Park, NY 14075; m/James Theodore; p/Arnold and Naomi Abrams, Chicago, IL; sp/ Theodore and Nelma Smith, Kinston, NC; ed/Cert Alliance Francaise, Inst Montesano, Switzerland, 1968; BA, Univ of WA, 1972; MS, 1974 Early Childhood/Spec Ed, 1974; PhD, NWn Univ, 1977; Master Student at Large/ Explorative Geog, Univ of Chgo, 1978; Exec Tng Prog, Harvard Bus Sch of Buffalo, 1980-1981; pa/Res Asst, Lab Techn, Dept of Pathol, Univ of Chgo Hosp, 1967-68; Tchr Simultaneous Lang & Indiv Therapy Progs w Austistic & Handicapped Chd, 1972-73; Prog Supvr 1974-78, Dysfunctioning Child Ctr, Michael Reese Hosp & Med Ctr; Prog Coor, Spec Ed Progs, Abraham Lincoln Ctr, 1973-74; Assoc Editor, *Sch Psych Intl Jour*,1980-; Asst Adj Prof, Dept of Devel Psych, SUNY-Buffalo, 1981-; Res Psychol/Mgr Child Res Progs 1978-83, Corp Conslt 1983-, Fisher Price Toys Dept of R&D; Am Psychol Assn; NY Acad of Sci; NY Metro Assoc of Applied Psych; cp/4-H Conslt; CPR Instr, ARC; Scuba Instr, Nat Assn of Underwater Instrs; Coach, W Side Rowing Clb; hon/Author, *Chd's Perceptions of Outer Space* w G Vogt of NASA, 1983; Phi Delta Kappa Scholastic Hon; Proj Ocean Search Participant, Cousteau Soc, 1979; NASA Edrs Shuttle Conf, 1981-82; 1st Place Nat Champ-'ship, Nat Wom's Rowing Assn Competition, 1971; Swiss Govt Silver Medal, Skiing 1969; W/W: of Am Wom, in E.

ABRASH, BRUCE MARVIN oc/ Numismatist; b/May 5, 1940; ba/560 Broad Hollow Road, Melville, NY 11747; m/Catherine Faith Collins; c/ Alex, Ross, Douglas, Lara; p/Louis and Rachel Abrash; ed/Att'd SUNY-Buffalo, 1958-62; pa/Pres, Numismatic Funding Corp; Pres, The Old Roman Nat Coin Exch, 1964; Chm Bd, Numismatic Enterprises Corp, 1975; Pres, Brasher Mint; Pres, Adco Assoc Inc, 1983; Direct Mktg, Advtg & Numismatic Innovator; Life Mem Am, Numismatic Assn; Life Mem Canadian Numismatic Assn; Life Mem, Intl Numismatic Soc; Lit Bus-man Assn; r/Jewish; hon/Numismatic Authenticator, US Govt; Nom'd to US Assay Comm; Bd Govs, Inst Numismatics & Philatelic Studies; W/W: in W, in World of Fin.

ABSOLOM, DARRYL ROBIN oc/ Biomedical Researcher, Professor; b/ Dec 12, 1954; h/44 Charles Street, West, Toronto, Ontario, Canada M4Y1R7; ba/ Toronto, Ontario, Canada; p/Mr and Mrs George Dalziel Absolom, Pinetown, S Africa; ed/BSc 1973, BSc (Hons) 1974, PhD 1977, Univ Cape Town; mil/ 1972-73; pa/Res Asst Prof 1979-83, Res Assoc Prof 1983-, St Univ NY-Buffalo; Assoc Prof, Univ Toronto, 1983-; Cancer Sci, Roswell Park Meml Inst, Buffalo, 1978-79; Sci, Hosp for Sick

Chd, Toronto, 1982-; Editor, *Molecular Immunol*, 1983; Edit Advr: *Immunol Commun Jour*, 1980-; *Preparative Biochem Jour*, 1980-; *Biol Dispersions & Surfaces Jour*, 1983-; Mem, Intl Surface Sci Grp; Am Soc Artificial Internal Organs; NY Acad Sci; Am Chem Soc; Others; r/Cath; hon/ Author, Over 129 Articles & Papers Pub'd in Sci Jours; S'ship Awardee, 1977; Ontario Heart Foun F'ship, 1978-82; Canada Heart Foun Sr F'ship, 1983; W/W in Frontier Sci & Technol.

ACCAD, EVELYNE oc/Professor; b/ Oct 6, 1943; h/504 West Illinois, Urabana, IL 61801; ba/Urbana, IL; p/Fuad and Suzanne Accad, Beirut Lebanon; ed/ AA, Beirut Col for Wom, 1965; BA, Anderson Col, 1967; MA, Ball St Univ, 1978; PhD, IN Univ, 1973; pa/Instr (pt-time), Anderson Col, 1967-68; French & Eng Tchr, Cnslr, Internat Col, Beirut, 1968-70; Asst Prof 1974-79, Assoc Prof, Univ IL, Urbana; Mem, African Lit Assn; MLA; Mem, Wom's Caucus for MLA; Arab Am Univ Grads; Nat Wom's Studies Assn; Mid E Studies Assn; hon/Author of Books: *Veil of Shame: The Role of Wom in Mod Fiction of N Africa & the Arab World*, 1978; *Montjoie Palestine! or Last Yr in Jerusalem*, 1980; *L'Excise*, 1982; *Indiv Rebellion & The Context of Culture*, 1983; Articles & Reviews Pub'd; Delta Kappa Gamma Intl Edrs Awd, 1978; Ct for Adv'd Studies Fellow, 1978-79; Recip Spec Recog Awd, IL Arts Coun, 1979; Fulbright Awd, 1983-85.

ACHTARIDES, THEODOROS ANTONIOU oc/Assistant Professor of Naval Architecture; b/Jul 30, 1948; h/ 1437 Anderson Avenue, Fort Lee, NJ 07024; ba/Memorial University of Newfoundland, St John's, Newfoundland, Canada; p/A and V Achtaridou, Athens, Greece; ed/BA Math, summa cum laude, Augustana Col, Sioux Falls, SD, 1968; MS Nav Arch Marine Engrg 1972, OE Ocean Engrg 1973, MA Inst of Technol (MIT); PhD, Nav Arch, Univ of Newcastle-upon-Tyne, England, 1979; mil/Hellenic Army Signal Corps, 1980; pa/Tchg Asst 1968-69 & 1970-73, Res Fellow 1969-70, Res Asst 1972, MIT; Res Engr, Am Bur of Shipping, NY, NY, 1973; Ridley Res Fellow in the Facs of Sci & Applied Sci 1974-77, Demonstrator 1974-78, Univ of Newcastle-upon-Tyne, England; Asst Prof of Ocean Engrg, SIT, 1981-83; Conslt'g Assoc, C R Cushing & Co Inc, 1983; Fellow, Hellenic Inst of Marine Technol; Mem, Royal Inst of Nav Arch; Inst of Marine Engrs; Soc of Nav Archs & Marine Engrs; Marine Technol Soc; Soc for Underwater Technol; Soc of Sigma Xi; Underwater Assn; Assn Technique Maritime Et Aeronautique; Nat Soc of Profl Engrs; r/Greek Orthodox; hon/Author of Num Profl Papers; Intl W/W in Engrg; W/W: in Engrg, in World.

ACKEN, BRENDA T oc/Executive; b/ Mar 16, 1947; h/628 Parkway, Bluefield, WV 24701; ba/Bluefield, WV; p/Murl and Pauline Thomas, Princeton, WV; ed/BS in Bus, Concord Col, 1973; CPA; pa/Sr Acct, Higgins & Gorman, Attys & CPAs, 1968-74; Corp Ofcr, Bd Dirs, S Atl Coal Co Inc, Race Fork Coal Corp, Permac Inc, REP Aviation Inc, Bakertown Coal Co Inc, REP Sales Inc; Comptroller, Tri-Sts Sales Co; Trustee, 3 Pension Plans, 1974-; VP, Bluefield Hlth Sys Inc; Secy-Treas, S Atl Coal Co

Inc; VChm Bd Dirs, Bluefield Commun Hosp; WV Soc CPAs, So Chapt Pres 1976-77, St Bd Dirs 1978-, Pres-Elect 1982-83; Pres, WV Soc of CPAs, 1983-84; Indust Com, Am Inst CPAs, 1981-84; Am Wom's Soc of CPAs; Am Soc of Profl & Exec Wom; Nat Assn of Accts; Nat Coal Assn Internal Audit Subcom; Taxation Com, VA Coal Assn; cp/Quota Clb of S Bluefield; E Area Dir, Quota Intl, 1983-85; Chm, Devel & Growth Com, Quota Intl Inc, 1984-85; Graham HS Bus Adv Coun; Concord Col Adv Bd, 1984-88; Mem Adv Bd of the Bluefield Salvation Army, 1979-83; Lt Gov of 1st Dist of Quota Intl Inc, 1979-80; Gov of 1st Dist of Quota Intl Inc, 1980-81; Mem of Mus Sub-Com of the Pocahontas Coalfield Cent Celebration; Participant in Var C of C Activs on Behalf of the Cos; Appt'd to By-Laws Com of Quota Intl Inc, 1981-1982; Appt'd to Ser Com of Quota Intl Inc, 1982-83, Mem Selective Ser Bd; hon/ Outstg Chapt Pres, WV Soc CPAs, 1976-77; Outstg Com Chm as Chm Public Relats Com of CPAs, 1978-79; 1st Wom VP, WV Soc CPAs, 1981-82; Recip Public Ser Awd, WV Soc of CPAs, 1983; Personalities of S; W/W: of Wom, in S & SW; 2000 Notable Ams; The Biogl Roll of Hon; Dir of Dist'd Ams; Intl Book of Hon; Other Biogl Listings.

ACKERMAN, DANIA FELICIA oc/ Professor; b/Jun 23, 1947; ba/Providence, RI; p/Arthur S Ackerman (dec); Zeida S Ackerman, New York, NY; ed/ AB, Cornell Univ, 1968; PhD, Univ MI, 1976; pa/Asst Prof Phil 1974-79, Assoc Prof Phil 1979-, Brown Univ; Vis'g Assoc Prof Phil, Univ CA-LA, 1976; Hon Vis'g Lectr, Univ St Andrews, Scotland, 1983; ACLU, 1979-; hon/ Author, Over 12 Articles Pub'd in Profl Jours incl'g: *Philosophical Studies, Canadian Jour of Phil, MW Studies in Phil, SD Review, AZ Qtly, Jour of Phil*, Others; Phi Beta Kappa, 1967; AB summa cum laude in Phil & 1st in Class, Cornell Univ, 1968; Fellow at Ctr for Adv'd Behavioral Scis; W/W: in E, of Am Wom.

ACKERMAN, DIANE oc/Author; b/ Oct 7, 1948; h/126 Texas Lane, Ithaca, NY 14850; p/Sam and Marcia (Tischler) Fink; ed/BA Eng, PA St Univ, 1967-70; MFA Creat Writing 1971-1973, MA Eng 1974-76, PhD Eng 1976-78, Cornell Univ; pa/Vis'g Writer, Wash Univ-St Louis, Sprg 1984; Vis'g Writer, OH Univ, Athens, Fall 1983; Vis'g Writer-in-Residence, Col of Wm & Mary, 1982-83; Asst Prof, Univ Pgh, 1980-; Bd of Dirs, Assoc'd Writing Progs, 1982-85; Lit Panel, NY St Coun on the Arts, 1980-83; Adv Bd, The Planetary Soc, 1980-; Poetry Panel, PA Arts Coun, 1980; Poetry Panel, CAPS, 1978-79; Mem, P E N AOPA; hon/ Author of 3 Volumes of Poetry: *Lady Faustus* 1983, *Wife of Light* 1978, *The Planets: A Cosmic Pastoral*, 1976; Author of Prose Memoirs: *Twilight Of The Tenderfoot* 1980, *On Extended Wings* 1985; The Pushcart Prize VIII: *Best of the Small Presses*, 1983-84; *Black Warior Review* Poetry Prize, 1981; CAPS F'ship, 1980; NEA F'ship, 1976-77; Abbie Copps Poetry Prize, 1974; W/W in E; Contemp Authors; Intl W/W in Poetry.

ACKERMAN, RALPH EMIL oc/Professor; b/Aug 21, 1921; h/124 Sunset Drive, Box 29, Edinboro, PA 16412; ba/ Edinboro, PA; m/Eileen Dotta; p/Meyer

and Frieda Ackerman (dec); sp/Alvin and Wilma Dotta; ed/BS Ed 1948, MEd 1949, OH Univ; PhD, Univ of Cinc, 1960; mil/ AUS, 3½ Yrs; pa/Bio Tchr & Dept Chm, Kingsport City Sch, 1949-54; Sci & Math Tchr, Glastonbury Sch CT, 1954-61; Prof Psychol, Edinboro Univ, 1961-; Am Psychol Assn; Am Ed Res Assn; Pres Acad Div, PA Psychol Assn; Local Pres, Phi Delta Kappa; PA Ed Assn; Nat Ed Assn; cp/Rotary Intl; Mason; r/Prot; hon/Contbr to Several Books; Articles in *TN Tchr; Nat Sec'dy Sch (Admr) Prin Bull*; Grad w Hons; Psi Chi; Kappa Delta Pi; W/W in E; Am Men in Govt.

ACKERMANN, NORBERT J JR oc/ Executive; b/Jul 3, 1942; h/12220 Bluff Shore Drive, Knoxville, TN 37922; ba/ Knoxville, TN; m/Cathryn Graber; c/ Dori, Nancy, Andy, Jill; p/Norbert J Ackerman, Chamblee, GA; sp/John and Ruth Graber, Knoxville, TN; ed/BS Nuclear Engrg 1965, MS Nuclear Engrg 1967, PhD Nuclear Engrg, 1971; pa/Hd Fast Reactor Measurements Methods Devel Grp 1968-71, Hd Reactor Controls Devel Sect 1971-76, Instrumentation & Controls Div, Oak Ridge Nat Lab; Dir Spec Instrumentation Grp, 3 Mile Isl Recovery Oper, 1976; Pres & Chm of Bd, Technol for Energy Corp, 1975-; Bd of Dirs, TN Technol Foun, 1982-; cp/Bd of Dirs & Pres, Jr Achmt, Knoxville, 1983-84; Bd of Dirs & Pres, Gtr Knoxville C of C, 1984-85; SE Conf Football Ofcl, 1972-; hon/Num Articles Pub'd in Field of Nuclear Power Plant Surveillance & Diagnostics & Spec Nuclear Measurement Sys; Fellow, US Atomic Energy Comm; Herman Hickman Fellow, Univ TN; Outstg Alumnus, Univ TN Col of Engrg, 1974; W/W: in Fin & Indust, in Technol Today; Intl W/ W in Engrg.

ACOSTA-RAMOS, JOSÉ A oc/ Assistant Superintendent of Schools; b/ Oct 30, 1937; h/RR 886 B333, Sabana Grande, PR 00747; ba/Mayaquez, PR; ed/BA, UIA, PR, 1963; MPHE, Univ of PR, 1965; EdD, Lehigh Univ, 1978; cp/ Asst Prof, La Montana Reg Col, 1981-82; Assoc Dean of Acad Affairs, La Montana Reg Col, 1979-82; Dir Curric Design Div, Dept of Public Instrn, 1979; Supt of Sch, S Mayaguez Sch Dist, 1978; Asst Supt of Sch, Mayaguez Sch Dist, 1969-1977; Sch Hlth Supvr, Las Marias Sch Dist, 1964-1969; Pt-time Prof, Inter Am Univ Grad Prog in Ed, 1974-77, l981-82; Phi Delta Kappa; NCSS; NASSDSE, Mem of Bd of Dirs 1979; ASCD; ASCD-PR, VP 1983-84; cp/George Wash Masonic Lodge Mem; r/Christian; hon/Last Deg, Ancient & Accepted Scottish Rite of Freemasonry, 1975; Alternate Selection to 1982 Fulbright Sum Sem on India's Gt Books; 2 Yr S'ship Grant from the Supr Coun of the 33rd Numismatics; Author of Num Profl Pubs; W/W in S & SW.

ACRIVOS, ANDREAS oc/Professor; b/Jun 13, 1928; h/788 Cedro Way, Stanford, CA 94305; ba/Stanford, CA; m/Juana; p/Athanasios and Anna Acrivos, Athens, Greece; ed/B Chem, Syracuse Univ, 1950; MS 1951, PhD 1954, Univ MN; pa/Instr & Assoc Prof Chem, Univ CA-Berkeley, 1954-62; Prof Chem Engrg, Stanford Univ, 1962-; Fellow, AIChE; Am Phy Soc; Am Chem Soc; Nat Acad Engrg; r/Greek Orthodox;

hon/Author, Over 100 Articles Pub'd in Profl Sci Jours; Guggenheim F'ship, 1959 & 1976; Colburn Awd 1963, Profl Prog Awd 1967, of the AIChE; Elect to Nat Acad Engrs, 1977.

ACRIVOS, JUANA L VIVÓ oc/ Professor; b/Jun 24, 1928; h/788 Cedro Way, Stanford, CA 94305; ba/Stanford, CA; m/Andreas; p/Adolfo Vivó and Lilia Azpeitia; sp/Athanasios and Anna Acrivos; ed/PhD Phy Chem, Univ MN, 1956; pa/Lctr Chem, Univ MN, Sum 1961; Asst Prof 1963, Assoc Prof 1967, Full Prof 1972, San José St Univ; Dir, NATO Adv'd Study Inst, Cambridge, England, 1983; Sabbatical Leave at Cavendish Lab, 1970, 1977 & 1983; Vis'g Sci Stanford Univ, 1971-75; Res Prof'ship at San José St Univ, 1968 & 1974; Adv Edit Bd, D Reidel Pub Co, 1980-; Adv Bd to Laser Lab at Stanford, Univ CA-Berkeley Facility, 1979-; Referee to: *Jour of Chem Physics, Jour Am Chem Soc, Jour Phy Chem*, 1965-; r/Cath; hon/Author & Co-Author, Over 30 Articles Pub'd in Profl Sci Jours & Books; Over 20 Papers Presented to Var Nat & Intl Profl Sci Orgs & Assns; Elected Vis'g Fellow Commoner, Trinity Col, Cambridge, England, 1983-84; Grad Fellow, Inst of Intl Ed, 1951-52; Exceptl Merit Ser Awd 1984, Univ Fellow 1975, Dean's Awd for Exemplary Res, 1976, Pres Scholar 1982, San José St Univ; Dist'd Acad Achmt, Phi Kappa Phi, 1980.

ACZEL, JANOS DEZSÓ oc/Professor; b/Dec 26, 1924; h/97 McCarron Crescent, Waterloo, Ontario N2L 5M9, Canada; ba/Ontario, Canada; m/Susan Kende; c/Catherina Boivie, Julie More; p/Dezso and Iren Aczel (dec); ed/BA 1946, MA 1947, PhD 1947, Univ Budapest; Habil 1952, DSc 1961, Hungarian Acad of Scis; pa/Asst Prof, Univ Szeged, 1948-50; Assoc Prof & Dept Hd, Tech Univ, Miskolc, 1948-50; Assoc Prof, Prof & Dept Hd, L Kossuth Univ (Debreccen, Hungary), 1950-65; Prof, Univ of Waterloo, 1965-; Vis'g Prof, Res Fellow, Conslt, Sev Univs & Res Insts in Australia, Austria, Germany, Italy, Japan, Nigeria & US; Royal Soc of Canada, Coun Mem, Com Mem, Chm (Convener) Math Div 1973-74; Chm Editorial Com, Acad of Sci, 1976-78; Editor, *Math Reports*, 1978-; Canadian Math Soc, Coun Mem 1971-73; Bolyai Math Soc, Bd Mem 1960-63; Univ Waterloo Senate, 1969-71; hon/Author Over 200 Articles & Books; M Beke Awd, 1961; Awd of Hungarian Acad of Scis, 1962; Dist'd Prof, Univ Waterloo, 1969; Fellow, Royal Soc of Canada, 1971; W/W: in Am, in World; World W/ W of Sci; Canadian W/W; Am Men & Wom of Sci; 2000 Men of Achmt; Hungarians in Am.

ACZEL, SUSAN KENDE oc/Mathematician; b/Jun 22, 1927; h/97 McCarron Crescent, Waterloo, Ontario N2L 5MG, Canada; ba/Same; m/János D; c/Cathy Boivie, Julie More; p/Lajos and Iren Kende (dec); sp/Dezso and Iren Aczel (dec); ed/BA, Univ of Budapest, 1948; MA, Univ of Szeged, Hungary, 1950; pa/Asst Prof & Hd Dept of Student Affairs, Univ of Miskolc, 1950-53; Hd of Cultural Dept, City of Debrecen, Hungary, 1953-55; Res Assoc, Univ of Waterloo, Ontario, 1965-70; Res Assoc, Axel, Waterloo, Ontario 1981; r/Rom Cath; hon/Contbr to Var Math Jours;

DIB; Intl W/W; W/W of Am Wom; World W/W of Wom.

ACZEL, THOMAS oc/Researcher; b/ Dec 18, 1932; h/8003 Duffield Lane, Houston, TX 77071; ba/Baytown, TX; m/Mollie G; c/Joseph I, Stephen M, Elisabeth Anne, Bettina Vera; p/Joseph and Elizabeth Aczel (dec); sp/Aaron and Bessie Goodman, Houston, TX; ed/ Baccalaureate (Classical), Lyceum Dante Alighieri, Trieste, Italy, 1949; PhD Scis, Univ of Trieste, Italy, 1954; pa/Tech Conslt, Aquila Refinery, Trieste & Rome, Italy, 1955-58; Res Chem 1959, Sr Res Chem 1963, Res Spec 1966, Res Assoc 1969, Sr Res Assoc 1976-, Sci Advr 1983-, Exxon (formerly Humble Oil Co); Mem 1959-, Chm Chem Ed Com 1967-71, Dir 1969-70 & 1976-77, Chm Cont'g Ed Com 1979-80, Adv Coun 1980-82, Chm Elect 1983, Chm 1984, SE TX Sect, Am Chem Soc; Secy 1978-79, VChm 1980-81, Chm 1982-83, ASTME-14; Chm 1972-, Res Div IV Sect 7, ASTMD-2; Dir, Am Soc for Mass Spectrometry, 1982-83; Fellow, AIChE; Mem, NY Acad of Scis; cp/ Dir, Baytown Symph, 1976-77; Dir, Friends of Sterling Mun Lib, Baytown; r/Jewish; hon/Author, Over 60 Articles in Profl Sci Jours & 7 Book Chapts; Profl Awd, Baytown Soc of Chems & Chem Engrs, 1967; Awd for Best Paper, Am Chem Soc Nat Meeting, Mpls, 1969; Profl Awd, SE TX Sect, Am Chem Soc, 1978; W/W in S & SW; Am Men of Sci.

ADAIR, JOHN CLAY oc/Executive; b/Aug 20, 1933; h/632 Tudor Lane West, Mobile, AL 36608; ba/Daphne, AL; m/Carole Joyce Ward; c/Susan Elizabeth, Steven Clay, Robert Ward; p/ Charles J and Leona (Sexton) Adair (dec); sp/Clarence and Aarah Ward, Mobile, AL; ed/BS 1956, MBA 1965, Univ of Tulsa; ad/AUS, 1956-57, Capt; pa/Adm Asst, Sinclair Res Inc, Tulsa, 1953-63; Econ, Standard Oil Co (IN), Tulsa, 1963-65; Dept Hd, Gt No Oil Co, St Paul, 1965-71; Grp VP, Marion Corp, Mobile, 1971-; Pres, Marion Pipeline Co Inc, 1976-; Mem, Am Petro Inst; cp/Mobile Area C of C; hon/W/W in World Oil & Gas; En Petro Dir.

ADAIR, JOHN G oc/Professor; b/Dec 19, 1933; h/14 Tunis Bay, Winnipeg, Manitoba, Canada R3T 2X1; ba/Winnipeg, Canada; m/Carolyn Johnson; c/ Leslie Kyle, Colin Glenn, Heidi Janelle, Joel Channing; p/C G Adair, Coaldale, CO; sp/Erma Johnson, Mitchell, SD; ed/ BS 1954, MS 1956, Trinity Univ, TX; PhD, Univ IA, 1965; mil/USAF, 1956-57; pa/Prof Psych, Univ of Manitoba, 1965-; Vis'g Prof, Univ Toronto, 1978; Vis'g Assoc Prof, Univ CO, 1971-72; Prof, Univ of IA, 1964-65; Prof, Dakota Wesleyan Univ, 1959-63; Pres, Canadian Psychol Assn, 1979-80; Pres, Soc Sci Fdn of Canada, 1983-84; Pres, Assn for Advmt of Sci in Canada, 1982-84; Am Psychol Assn; Soc for Social Studies of Sci; hon/Author of Book, *The Human Subject*, 1973; Author, Over 30 Articles on Soc Nature of Behavioral Res in Profl Sci Jours; Recip, C J Robson Dist'd Psychol in Manitoba Awd, 1980.

ADAMS, ANNE MOREL MAYO oc/ Social Worker; b/Mar 25, 1931; h/8227 Pine Tree Lane, Lake Clark Shores, FL 33406; ba/W Palm Bch, FL; m/Charles B; c/Michelle Morel Zanartu (Mrs

Antonio); André Morel; p/Edward L and Kate Hammond Mayo (dec); sp/A B and Doreen Adams (dec); ed/Laurel Sch for Girls, 1949; Att'd Skidmore Col, 1949-51; BA Sociol, Univ WI, 1951-53; Att'd Bridgewater St Tchrs Col toward MA in Ed; pa/Soc Wkr, Summit Co Welfare Dept, Akron, OH, 1969-70; Soc Wkr, Medina Co Welfare Dept, Medina, OH, 1970-72; Soc Wkr, Div Fam Sers, Chds Sers, W Palm Bch, FL, 1972-73; Conslr, Repub Pers, Nashville, TN, 1973; Soc Wkr, Adult Protective Ser Wkr, HRS, W Palm Bch, FL, 1974-; Ct Apptd "Layperson" for Guardianship Exam Proceedings, St of FL; Mem, FL Assn for Hlth & Soc Sers, 1981-; Instr, Gerentology, FL Atl Univ, Boca Ratan; Num Wkshops & Sems; Others; cp/ Public Spkg Engagements for HRS Progs; Soc Wkr Vol, Soc for Crippled Chd, OH, 1953-57; Vol Secy, Cuyahoga Co Nsg Home, Cleveland, OH, 1953-56; Pilgrim Ch Nursery Sch Tchr, Cleveland, 1967-68; Guarantor, Lakewood Civic Art Gallery, 1968; Steering Com, Cotillion Clb of the Palm Bchs, 1984; Assn of Univ Wom; LWV Alpha Chi Omega; Palm Bch Hist Soc; Others; r/ Prot; hon/W/W in S & SW.

ADAMS, DAVID WAYNE oc/ Semi-Retired; b/May l5, 1948; h/42319 Green Mountain Drive, Lebanon, OR 97355; m/Holly Jane; c/David Wayne, Christopher Shane, & Cassandra Lynn; p/David and Marjorie Adams, Drain, OR; sp/Elizabeth J Kelly (dec); ed/ Supvn, Linn Benton Commun Col; mil/ AUS; pa/Mem of Exec Bd of Am Fdn of St, Co & Mun Employees 1973-75; r/Pentecostal.

ADAMS, DONALD ROBERT oc/ Professor; b/Aug 3, 1937; h/812 Onyx Circle, Ames, IA 50010; ba/Ames, IA; m/Carol Gene; c/Shawn Ryan, Robert James; p/Nellie May Adams, Cottonwood, CA; sp/Ludwig and Mary Gribler; AB Zool 1960, PhD Anatomy 1970, Univ CA-Davis; MA Biol, Chico St Univ, 1967; pa/Biol Tchr, Malangali Govt Sec'dy Sch, Malangali, Tanganyika, E Africa, 1962-64; Asst Prof, Dept Vet Anatomy, MI St Univ, 1970-74; Assoc Prof, Dept Vet Anatomy, Col of Vet Med, IA St Univ, 1974-; Am Assq of Anatomists; Am Assn Vet Anatomists; hon/Author & Co-Author, Articles Pub'd in Profl Sci Jours incl'g: *Embryol, Jour Anatomy*; Author of Book: *Canine Anatomy: A Systemic Study*; Norden Dist'd Tchr, 1982.

ADAMS, EDWIN CARROLL oc/ Electrical Engineer; b/Aug 9, 1927; h/ 8744 Acorn Lane, Sandy, UT 84092; ba/ Salt Lake City, UT; m/Lillian; c/Donald Edward, Nancy Jean; p/Edward and Esther Adams (dec); sp/Nickolas and Katherine D Uebel; ed/BSEE, IL Inst of Technol, 1955; mil/USN, 1945-46; Engrg Asst, IL Testing Labs, Chgo, 1949-51; Devel Engr, Motorola Inc, Chgo, 1951-57; Sr Engr, Cook Res Labs, Morton Grove, IL, 1957-60; Proj Engr, Zenith Radio Corp, Chgo, 1960-65; Engrg Mgr, Sierra Res Corp, Buffalo, NY, 1965-79; Engrg Mgr, Thermal Tech Lab, Buffalo, NY 1979-80; Prin Engr, Sperry Corp, SLC, UT, 1980-; IEEE; AIAA; Assn for Unmanned Vehicle Sys; r/Presb; hon/US Patentee: Doppler Target Simulator, 1967; W/W; W/W in W.

ADAMS, ERNEST DEAN oc/Micro-

biologist; b/Jun 22, 1940; h/8670 Bristlecone Drive, San Antonio, TX 78240; ba/Lackland AFB, TX; m/Sharon Ann Leahey; c/Mariah Anne, Ernest Dean III; p/Oma Launa Gray Adams, Chickasaw, AL; sp/Marie Richards Leahey (dec); ed/ Att'd Univ of AL, 1958-61; BS Microbiol, Univ of AZ, 1964-65; Med Tech Intern, USAF Wilford Hall Med Ctr, 1965-66; MS Microbiol, Temple Univ, 1971-73; mil/USAF, 1961-; pa/Med Lab Spec, 6510 USAF Hosp, Edwards AFB, CA, 1961-63; Chief Clin Lab Sers, 806 Med Grp, K I Sawyer AFB, MI, 1966-70; Asst Chief Clin Lab Sers, UASF Hosp, Clark AB, Philippines, 1970-71; Chief Clin Lab 1973-76, Chief Clin Lab Sers 1976-77, USAF Reg Hosp, Maxwell AFB, AL; Conslt, Jackson Hosp, Montgomery, AL, 1974-77; Dir Clin Microbiol, Wilford Hall, USAF Med Ctr, Lackland AFB, TX, 1977-; Med Mycological Soc of Ams; Soc of Armed Forces for Med Lab Scis; Am Soc for Microbiol; TX Br of Am Soc for Microbiol; S TX Assn of Microbio̊l Profls; r/Bapt; hon/ Author & Co-Author, Articles Pub'd in Profl Sci Jours incl'g: *Jour Endodontics, Jour Clin Microbiol, Am Jour Med Tech*; Chief Biomed Sci Corps Badge, 1981; USAF Outstg Unit Awd, 1964, 1969 & 1979; USAF Commend Med for Meritorious Ser, 1977; Meritorious Ser Medal, 1984; Appt'd Mil Conslt to AF Surg Gen, 1984; Beta Beta Beta; Num Others; W/ W in S & SW.

ADAMS, GEORGE G oc/Professor; b/Sept 12, 1948; h/30 Beaufort Road, #30, Jamaica Plain, MA 02130; ba/ Boston, MA; m/Janet; p/George and Sally Adams (dec); sp/Albert and Dorothy Magenheim; BS Mech Engrg, Cooper Union, 1969; MS Mech Engrg 1972, PhD Mech Engrg 1975, Univ CA-Berkeley; pa/Assoc Prof, NEn Univ, Boston, 1979-; Asst Prof, Clarkson Coll, 1975-79; Vis'g Scholar, Univ CA-Berkeley, 1979; Vis'g Sci, IBM Research Lab, 1978-79; Mem, ASME; Soc of Engrg Sci; Am Acad of Mechs; Am Soc Engrg Ed; r/En Orthodox; hon/ Author, Over 20 Articles in Profl Sci Jours; NSF F'ship, 1970-73; Tau Beta Pi; Pi Tau Sigma; W/W in Frontier Sci & Technol.

ADAMS, HOLLY JANE oc/Waitress; b/Dec l, 1955; h/42319 Green Mountain Drive, Lebanon, OR 97355; m/David W; c/David Wayne, Christopher Shane, Cassandra Lynn; p/Elizabeth J Kelly (dec); sp/David and Marjorie Adams, Drain, OR; pa/Waitress, Tom Tom Restaurant; cp/Writer of Lttrs & Petitions Regarding Due Process; r/ Pentecostal.

ADAMS, MARGARET B oc/Anthropologist, Museologist; b/Apr 29, 1936; h/363 Hillcrest Avenue, Pacific Grove, CA 93950; p/Kathleen B Adams; ed/BA Anthropol & Art Hist/Museology, San Jose St Univ, CA, 1971; MA Anthropol, Univ of UT, SLC, 1973; pa/Pres, Mus of Monterey Col, CA, 1974-; Instr, Monterey Peninsula Col, 1973-83; Tchr & Museol, Univ CA-Santa Cruz, CA, 1972-74; Tchr & Museol, UT St Mus of Fine Arts, SLC, 1972; Museol, Civic Art Gallery, San Jose, CA, 1971; Museol, Milton H DeYounge Meml Mus, SF, CA, 1970; Am Anthropol Assn; Am Archaeol Assn; Monterey Hist & Art Assn; Pacific Grove Art Ctr; AAAS; Am Indian Ed Assn; CA Indian

Ed Assn; cp/Dir, Am Indian Info Ctr, Monterey Co (Vol), 1973-; r/Epis; hon/ Editor of Mus Catalogs: *Chronology of Pueblo Indian & Old World Events, Am Indian Tribal Arts,* Spider Wom's Daugh-Navaho Weavers; Author of Misc Articles on Indian Art in *Indian Am* Mag; Panel Mem "Minorities in Sci" of AAAS, 1972-74; Book Reviewer "Proj Media" of Am Indian Ed Assn, 1973-77; Book Reviewer on Indians for *Monterey Herald,* 1974-; W/W: in Am Wom, in W, of Wom; Ohoyo Dir of Profl Am Indian Wom.

ADAMS, RENÉE REACIE oc/Career Counselor; b/Dec 24, 1956; h/827A Daffaodil Court, Fort Gordon, GA 30905; ba/Augusta, GA; m/Charles Michael; p/John F Wiggins (dec); Mrs John F Wiggins, Sidney, OH; sp/Mr and Mrs Raymond T Adams, Tuskegee, AL; ed/BS Social Wk 1978, MA Col Student Pers 1980, Bowling Green St Univ; pa/ Commun Coor Right to Read Prog Jan-May 1978, Peer Cnslr Student Devel Prog Apr-Dec 1978, Grad Asst Peer Cnslr Student Devel Prog Sep 1979-Aug 1980, Bowling Green St Univ; Cnslr, GA Mil Col, 1982; Cnslr 1982, Career Cnslr 1982-, Paine Col, GA; Mem: GA Col Pers Assn; GA Pers & Guid Assn; r/Bapt; hon/Grad Asst- 'ship, 1979; Dean's List 1978, "Ms Congeniality," Ms Bronze Pageant 1976, Longfellow S'ship 1975; Featured in *Bowling Green St Univ Alumni News,* 1976.

ADAMS, ROY DOUGLAS oc/ Research Scientist; b/Mar 7, 1944; h/8 Meadow Street, Houghton, MI 49931; ba/Houghton, MI; m/Fiona B; c/Lynn D and Alison D; p/Ronald and Edna Adams, Lymington, Hants, England; sp/ Tom and Nancy Clark, Aberdeen, Scotland; ed/BSc Forestry, Univ of Aberdeen, Scotland, 1966; MF Wood & Pulp Sci, Univ of Brit Columbia, Canada, 1969; PhD Engrg Sci, WA St Univ, 1981; pa/Sr Res Sci 1981-, Res Sci 1975-81, Inst of Wood Res, MI Technol Univ; Acting Instr & Res Asst, Univ of ID, 1969-71; Chm 1984, Ofcr (Past 6 Yrs), Upper MS Val Sect of Forest Prods Res Soc; Mem, Univ Sen, MI Technol Univ, 1978-84; cp/Pres, Copper Country Ski Clb, 1983-85; hon/Author, Num Pubs on Composite Wood Prods; Holder of 5 US Patents in Wood Engrg Res.

ADAMS, WILLIAM EUGENE oc/ Executive; b/Oct 18, 1930; h/4306 Arlington Drive, Royal Oak, MI 48220; ba/Ferndale, MI; m/Fiona Drollinger; c/ Eric W, Barbara A; p/Mr and Mrs Elmer W Adams, Berea, OH; sp/Freda Drollinger, Clawson, MI; ed/BA Mech Engrg, OH St Univ, 1955; pa/Engr San Bernadino, CA 1955-58, Proj Engr Ferndale, MI 1958-67, Prod Applications Engr 1967-70, Res Advr 1970-74, Dir Auto Res 1974-76, Mgr Det Res Labs 1976-, w Ethyl Corp; Mem, Soc Automotive Engrs; Mem, Engrg Soc Detroit; r/Presb; hon/Author, Num Tech Papers for Soc Automotive Engrs & Am Petro Inst, Others; Horning Meml Awd, Soc Auto Engrs, 1964; W/ W in Am; Other Biogl Listings.

ADAMS, WILLIAM HAMPTON oc/ Archaeologist; b/Nov 23, 1948; h/ 1421-B North Mount Vernon Avenue, Williamsburg, VA 23185; ba/Williamsburg, VA; p/William R Adams, Ellettsville, IN; ed/AB, IN Univ, 1970; MA

1972, PhD 1976, WA St Univ; pa/Mus Curator 1971-74, Asst Prof 1976-77, WA St Univ; Vis'g Prof, Univ of KY, 1977-78; Sr Archaeol, Consltg Firm, 1978-81; Asst Res Sci, Univ of FL, 1981-84; Sr Staff Archaeol, Colonial Wmsburg Foun, 1983-; Pres, Soc for Hist Archaeol, 1983-85; Am Anthropological Assn; Soc for Am Archaeol; Soc of Profl Archaeologists; Soc for Post-Medieval Archaeol; hon/Author, Num Articles Pub'd in Profl Jours incl'g: *Ethnohist* 1973, *NARN* 1975 & 1977, *Hist Archaeol* 1974, 1976 & 1985, *N Am Archaeologist* 1979 & 1983, *Am Anthropologist* 1983 & 1984, *Am Antiquity* 1984.

ADAMS, WINSLOW HEATH JR oc/ Mutual Funds Executive; b/Feb 12, 1937; h/130 East Sheridan Place, Lake Bluff, IL 60044; ba/39 South LaSalle Street, Chicago, IL 60603; m/M Carroll Stevens; c/Richard Warren, Tracy Lee; p/Winslow Heath Adams (dec); Elizabeth Swett (Mrs Richard L Kenney), Chatham, MA; sp/George W Stevens, Phila, PA; ed/BA, Wesleyan Univ, 1961; pa/Field Underwriter, Mut of NY, 1961-66; Asst Mgr, Life Dept, Starkweather & Shepley, 1966-67; Asst Dir Devel, Lake Forest Col, 1967-72; VP 1972-79, Dir 1975-79, Francoeur & Co; Reg Mgr, Lord, Abbett & Co, 1979-81; Reg VP, McNeil Securities Corp, 1981-82; Reg VP, Griffin Securities Corp, 1982-83; Reg VP, J & W Seligman & Co, 1983-; Pres, Chgo Wholesalers Assn, 1983; Intl Assn for Fin Planning, 1984-; Securities Indust Assn, 1983-; cp/ Pres 1968-72, Class Agt 1981-, Wesleyan Univ Alumni Clb Chi; Pres, Lake Bluff Town & Tennis, 1973; Chm, Lake Bluff Progressive Party, 1975-79; Trustee, Lake Forest/Lake Bluff Hist Soc, 1982-83; Lake Bluff Mowers, 1974-; r/ Prot; hon/W/W in Fin & Indust.

ADAMSON, TERRENCE BURDETT oc/Attorney; b/Nov 13, 1946; h/140 Jett Forest Court Northwest, Atlanta, GA 30327; ba/Atlanta, GA; c/Terrence Morgan; p/S B and Lois Adamson, Calhoun, GA; ed/BA 1968, JD 1973, Emory Univ; mil/USAR, 1969-73; pa/ Reporter, *Atlanta Constit,* 1969-71; Law Clk to Hon Griffin Bell, US Ct Appeals, 5th Jud Circuit, 1973-74; Assoc 1974-77, Ptnr 1980-, Hansell & Post Attys; Henry Luce Scholar, Ishii Law Ofc, Tokyo, Japan, 1975-76; Spec Asst to Atty Gen of US, 1977-79; Dir of Public Affairs & Chief Spokesman, Dept Justice, 1978-79; Bd of Trustees, The Asia Foun, SF, 1984-; ABA; Am Judic Soc; r/Prot; hon/Author, Num Law Reviews, Newspaper & Mag Articles & Book Reviews; Omicron Delta Kappa, 1973; Order Baristers, 1973; Order Coij, 1973; W/W in Am.

ADDANKI, SAM oc/Professor; b/ Mar 7, 1932; h/1739 Blue Ash Place, Columbus, OH 43229; ba/Columbus, OH; m/Sathyavathi; c/Rathna, Usha, Sheila; p/Perayya Rachuri and Vijayawada Addanki, India; pa/Assoc Prof, OH St Univ, 1970-; Am Bd Clin Chem; Am Inst Chems; Am Soc Billogical Chems; Am Fed Clin Res; cp/Toastmasters Intl; Nat Spkrs Assn; r/Hindu; hon/Author of Books: *Diabetes Breakthrough* 1982, *Renewed Hlth* 1982; Also Pub'd 20 Res Papers on Cancer, Heart Attack, Diabetes & Nutrition; Diplomate, Am Bd Clin Chem; Cert Profl Chem; Intl W/ W of Intells.

ADELLA, FRANK oc/Marriage and Family Counselor; b/Oct 19, 1936; h/ 6212-L North Hills Drive, Raleigh, NC 27609; ba/Raleigh, NC; m/Harriet Thurman; c/Gregory, Keith, Melissa, Amanda, Carol, Joseph; p/George and Martha Adella (both Dec); sp/Henry and Alice Thurman (both Dec); ed/BS Hist, Univ of NC-Chapel Hill, 1957; MS Marriage & Fam Cnslg, Univ of SC-Columbia, 1960; PhD Marriage & Fam Cnslg, Univ of CA-LA (UCLA), 1974; pa/Tchg Asst, Univ of SC, Columbia, SC, 1957-60; Cnslr, Forestgreen HS, Columbia, SC, 1960-62; Marriage & Fam Cnslr, Marriage & Fam Sers Inc, LA, CA, 1962-76; Marriage & Fam Cnslr, Pvt Pract, Raleigh, NC, 1976-; Mem: Am Assn for Marriage & Fam Therapists; Am Pers & Guid Assn; Wake Co Cnslg Assn; Nat Ed Assn; AAAS; Am Businessmen's Assn; AMA; NC & En Psychol Assn; Am Assn of Sex Therapists; cp/Vol Marriage & Fam Cnslr, Local HELP Hotline; Soc for the Prevention of Cruelty to Animals; Smithsonian Instn; SAR; Rotary Intl; Com to Aid Immigrants; Raleigh C of C; NC JCs; Active in Var Fundraising Campaigns for Local Orgs incl'g: March of Dimes, ARC, Muscular Dystrophy Assn, Am Heart Assn; Others; Cnslr & SS Tchr, First Meth Ch; r/Meth; hon/ Author, Num Articles in Profl Jours & Mags incl'g:"Promenade Your Partner," 1983; "Undoing Unto Others," 1981; "Open Your Eyes & Listen" 1979; Others; Book in Progress; Cert for Vol Efforts, March of Dimes, 1981; Grad w Hons, Univ of CA-LA; Employee of the Day, WQDR, 1982; Cert of Appreciation, Am Heart Assn; Others.

ADELMAN, IRMA oc/Professor; b/ Mar 14, 1930; h/10 Rosemont Avenue, Berkeley, CA 94708; ba/Berkeley, CA; p/Jacob Max Glicman and Raissa Etinger (dec); ed/BS Bus Adm 1950, MA Ec 1951, PhD Ec 1955, Univ CA-Berkeley; pa/Prof Agr & Resource Ec 1979-, Lectr & Instr 1955-58, Univ CA-Berkeley; Prof Ec, Univ MD, 1972-79; Cleveringa Chr, Leiden Univ, Netherlands Inst Adv'd Study, 1977-78; Fellow, Ctr Adv'd Study in Behavioral Scis 1970-71, Acting, Vis'g & Asst Prof 1960-62, Stanford Univ; Prof Ec, NWn Univ, 1966-72; Assoc Prof Ec, Johns Hopkins Univ, 1962-66; Mem, Soc Sci Assem & Nat Acad Scis, 1976-79; Fellow, Am Acad Arts & Scis; Order Bronze Tower, Govt S Korea, 1971; VPres, Am Ec Assn, 1979-80; r/Jewish; hon/Editor, *Economic Growth & Resources* Volume 4: *Nat & Intl Policies,* 1979; Author, 7 Books on Ec Devel; Over 70 Articles Pub'd in Profl Jours; Phi Beta Kappa, 1950; Fellow, Econometric Soc, 1968; 100 GI Economists Since Keynes; Contemp Authors; W/W: in Ec, in Am, in World; Intl Biog of Scholars; Men of Sci; 2000 Wom Achmt; Other Biogl Listings.

ADELMAN, SAUL JOSEPH oc/Professor; b/Nov 18, 1944; h/1434 Fairfield Avenue, Charleston, SC 29407; ba/ Department of Physics, The Citadel, Charleston, SC 29409; m/Carol Jeanne; c/Aaron Solomon, Barry Eshkol, David Eli; p/Benjamin and Kitty Adelman, Silver Spring, MD; sp/David Sugerman; Betty Sugerman (dec); ed/BS Physics, Univ MD, 1966; PhD Astronomy, CA Inst of Technol, 1972; pa/NRC/NAS Res Assoc, NASA, Goddard Space Flight

Ctr, 1972-74; Asst Prof Astronomy, Boston Univ, 1974-78; Asst Prof Physics 1978-83, Assoc Prof Physics 1983-, The Citadel; NRC-NASA Res Assoc, Goddard Space Flight Ctr, 1984-85; Am Astronom Soc; Intl Astronom Union; Optical Soc Am; Royal Astronom Soc; Astronom Soc Pacific; Brit InterPlanetary Soc; hon/Co-Author, *Bound For The Stars*, 1981; Over 75 Articles Pub'd in Profl Sci Jours; Phi Beta Kappa; Phi Kappa Phi; Sigma Pi Sigma; Sigma Xi; Am Men & Wom in Sci; Contemp Authors; W/W in S & SW.

ADELSTONE, JEFFREY ALAN oc/ Tax Specialist/Accountant; b/Feb 15, 1947; h/8231 East 3rd Place, Tucson, AZ 85710; ba/Tucson, AZ; m/Ruth Wilcox; c/Kimberley, Stacey, Toni; p/James Adelstone, Tucson, AZ; Joyce Adelstone, Tucson, AZ; sp/Frances A Wilcox, Tucson, AZ; ed/BS, Univ of AZ, 1969; mil/Univ AZ, 1971; pa/Tchr, Tucson Public Schs, 1969-72; Tax Spec/ Acct, Self-Employed, 1970-; Instr, Pima Commun Col Pt-Time, 1971-78; Tax Law Instr, Brodsky Sch of Real Est, Pt-Time, 1981; St VP, AZ Soc of Practicing Accts, 1983-84, Pres 1984-85; Assoc St Dir, Nat Soc of Public Accts, 1983-84; Pres, Tucson Chapt, AZ Soc of Practicing Accts, 1982-83, 1983-84; St Treas, AZ Soc of Practicing Accts, 1981-82; Dir, AZ Soc of Enrolled Agts, St Bd, 1978-79; Dir, AZ Soc of Practicing Accts, Tucson Chapt Bd, 1981-82, 1982-83; Dir, AZ Soc of Practicing Accts, St Bd, 1981-82, 1982-83; hon/ Author of Num Profl Pubs; W/W in W.

ADERHOLD, VICTOR W oc/Radio Station Manager; b/Mar 28, 1941; h/ 4308 Sage Oak Court, Jacksonville, FL 32211; ba/Jacksonville, FL; m/Jane; c/ Blair; p/Mrs Harvey J Aderhold, Atlanta, GA; sp/Mrs H B Flowers, Pensacola, FL; ed/AB Jour, Univ of GA, 1964; mil/AUS, 1966-68, 1st Lt; pa/ Radio Announcer 1958-65, Radio Sales 1968-74, WPLO Atlanta; Radio Sales Mgr, WKLS Atlanta, 1974-79; Radio Gen Mgr, WFYV Jacksonville, 1979-; Sigma Delta Chi Jour Frat; Bd of Dirs, Jacksonville Advtg Fedn, 1979-82; Affil Bd of Dirs, NBC "The Source" Netwk, 1951-; cp/Mem, S-side Bus-men's Clb, Jacksonville, 1979-; r/Bapt; hon/Bronze Star, Ser in Viet Nam; W/W: in Am, in SE.

ADHAV, RATNAKAR SHANKAR oc/Executive; b/Oct 30, 1927; h/119 Slade Drive, Longwood, FL 32750; ba/ Sanford, FL; m/Nalini Sadashiv Satpute; c/Sanjay, Geeta, Shailesh; p/Shankar Dhondo and Shevantabai Adhav, Poona, India; sp/Sanashiv Shamboji and Saraswati Bai Sadashiv Satpute (dec); ed/BSc 1949, MSc 1952, Poona Univ, India; PhD, Gujarat Univ, India, 1958; pa/Pres, Quantum Technol Inc, 1969-; Mgr Res & Devel, EDO (Canada) Ltd, 1963-69; Res Physicist, Canadian Civil Ser, 1960-63; Lectr in Physics, Bombay Ednl Ser 1952-58; Optical Soc of Am; Chm, St Lawrence Intl Subsection, IEEE; r/Hindu; hon/Author Num of Profl Pubs; Two Patents; Postdoct Fellow, Canadian NRC, 1958-60; W/W.

ADKINS, PATRICIA GUYNES oc/ Educator; b/Aug 23, 1949; h/609 La Cruz, El Paso, TX 79902; ba/El Paso, TX; m/Fitzhugh L Adkins Jr (dec); c/ Patricia A Ainsa, F Lee Adkins III; p/ James T Guynes (dec); Margaret Brady

Guynes (dec); sp/Mr and Mrs Hugh L Adkins, El Paso, TX; ed/BA, Univ of TX, 1960; MA, TX Wom's Univ, 1962; PhD, Univ of CO-Boulder, 1966; pa/Prof, Univ of TX-El Paso, 1961-69; Dir Early Childhood Ed, Reg XIX Ed Ctr, 1970-; Pres, Assn Child & Lrng Devel (ACLD) of El Paso 2 Terms, 1970-72 & 1972-74; cp/Jr Leag El Paso, 1955-; Bd of Dir: GSA; YWCA; Epilepsy Assn El Paso; Others; r/Epis; hon/Author of Books: *Spch for Bilingual Spanish Student* 1962, *Structured Experiences for Devel Lrng* 1972, *A Priceless Playground for Exceptl Chd* 1974; Num Pub'd Articles; Force Awd, Univ of TX, 1960; Outstg Contbn Awd, ACLD, 1973; Dir Am Scholars; Personalities of S; W/W: of Wom, Among Authors & Journalists.

ADLER, CHARLES SPENCER oc/ Psychiatrist; b/Nov 27, 1941; h/955 Eudora Street #1607, Denver, CO 80220; ba/Same; m/Sheila Morrissey; p/ Benjamin and Anne Greenfield Adler, Whitestone, NY; sp/John E Morrissey (dec); Margaret Morrissey, Aurora, CO; ed/BA, Cornell Univ, 1962; MD, Duke Univ Med Sch, 1966; Intern, Tucson Hosps Med Ed Prog, 1966-67; Psychi Residency, Univ CO Med Ctr, 1967-70; mil/USNR, Lt; pa/Pvt Pract in Psychi & Psychosomatic Med (Denver), 1970-; Staff Psychi, Bethesda Commun Mtl Hlth Ctr (Denver), 1970-73 (pt-time); Co-Fdr, Applied Biofeedback Inst (Denver), 1972-75; Chief, Div of Psychi, Rose Med Ctr (Denver), 1982-; AMA; Am Psychi Assn; Am Assn for Study of Headache; Am Acad of Psychoanal; Biofeedback Soc of CO, Pres 1978; Biofeedback Soc of Am, Chm Nat Ethics Com 1983-, Chm Nat Task Force on Autogenic Therapy, Others; Adv Bd, Duke Univ Ctr for Aging & Human Devel, 1983-; Bd Dirs, Muscular Dystrophy Assn of Am, No CO Chapt 1971-77; Diplomat, Am Bd of Psychi & Neurology; hon/Author *We Are But a Moment's Sunlight*, Num Profl Articles; Awd of Recog, Nat Migraine Foun, 1981; Elected Fellow, Am Psychi Assn, 1983; Elected to Sci Assoc Status, Am Acad of Psychoanal, 1982; W/W in W; Dir of Am Med Specialists.

ADLER, HELMUT E oc/Professor; b/ Nov 25, 1920; h/162-14 86th Avenue, Jamaica, NY 11432; ba/New York, NY; m/Leonore Loeb; c/Barry Peter, Beverly Sharmaine, Evelyn Renee; p/Paul and Lola Eiseman (Offenbacher) Adler; sp/ Leo and Elsie Loeb; ed/BS 1948, AM 1949, PhD 1952, Columbia Univ; mil/ AUS, 1942-46; Prof Psych 1964-, Assoc Prof 1957-64, Asst Prof 1953-57, Instr 1950-53, Yeshiva Univ, NY; Sci Staff 1952-55, Lectr 1955-60, Columbia Univ; Res Assoc 1969-84, Res Fellow 1955-69, Am Mus Nat Hist; Res Assoc, Mystic Marinelife Aquarium, Mystic CT, 1976-; Fellow, Am Psychol Assn; Fellow, NY Acad Scis; Mem: AAUP; EPA; ABS; Sigma Xi; Psi Chi; Others; r/Jewish; hon/Author of Book, *Fish Behavior*, 1975; Co-Author of Books: *Bird Behavior*, 1969; *Bird Life*, 1969; Translator, G T Fechner's: *Elements of Psychophysics*, 1966; Co-Editor, *Past, Present & Future of Comparative Psych*, 1973; Sect Editor & Contbr, *Ency Judaica*, 1972; Num Articles Pub'd in Profl Jours & Book Chapts; Adv Com 1972-, VChm 1976-77, Ch 1978-80, Psych Sect of NY Acad Sci; Secy Gen, Sect of Exptl Psych & Animal

Behavior, Intl Union Biol Sci, 1972-; W/ W in E; Am Men & Wom Sci.

ADLER, KENNETH PAUL oc/Opinion Research Specialist; b/Sep 20, 1922; h/8721 Susanna Lane, Chevy Chase, MD 20815; ba/Washington, DC; m/ Alice Cecilia; c/Marc David, Steven Aaron, Anita Emmeli, Deborah Diane; p/Eric D Adler (dec); Irene Adler, Holywood, FL; sp/Morris and Mollie Sprafkin (dec); ed/BA, Syracuse Univ, 1948; MA 1950, PhD 1956, Univ Chgo; mil/AUS, 1943-46; pa/Sr Res Spec 1983-, Chief Wn Europe Res 1979-83, Dept Chief Audience & Attitude Res 1977-78, Mgr Radio Res 1975-76, Reg Res Ofcr (Europe) 1971-75, Dept Chief Res Ser 1969-71, Reg Res Ofcr (Asia) 1966-69, Chief Media Res 1963-66, Ofc of Res, USIA; Asst Prof, Univ Chgo, 1952-57; Sr Res Ofcr, CBC/Radio Canada, 1957-62; Sec-Treas, Am Assn for Public Opinion Res, 1982-84; Exec Coun, World Assn for Public Opinion Res, 1982-; r/Jewish; hon/Author, Num Articles in Var Jours incl'g: *Public Opinion, Public Opinion Qtly, Quill, Studies in Public Commun, The Annals*; Chapt in Book on "Successor Generation," 1983; Grad magna cum laude, Syracuse Univ; W/W: in Am Sci, in Wash.

ADLER, KRAIG KERR oc/Professor; b/Dec 6, 1940; h/Box 149, Woodland Road, Bedford, NY; ba/Ithaca, NY; m/ Dolores P; c/Todd David; p/Mr and Mrs William C Adler, Columbus, OH; ed/ BA, OH Wesleyan Univ, 1962; MS 1965, PhD 1968, Univ MI-Ann Arbor; pa/Asst Prof Biol, Univ Notre Dame, 1968-72; Assoc Prof Biol 1972-80, Prof Biol 1980-, Chm Sect Neurobiol & Behavior 1976-79, Cornell Univ; Res Assoc, VA Hosp, 1983-84; Asst Prof of Med, Univ of MN, 1983-84; Secy, Assn of VA Scists, 1983-84; Assoc Prof, Dept of Med, NY Med Col, 1984-; Pres, Soc for Study Amphibians & Reptiles, 1982; Animal Behavior Soc; Am Soc Naturalists; Sigma Xi; hon/Author, Over 96 Pub'd Papers & Editor of 2 Collections on Biol Amphibians & Reptiles; Baer Meml Lectr, Milwaukee Pub Mus, 1977; Hefner Lectr, Miami Univ, 1980; Anderson Meml Lectr, Rutgers Univ, 1982; Dist'd Scholar, China Prog, US Nat Acad Sci, 1984-85; Elected Fellow, AAAS & Acad Zool (India); Am Del, 16th Intl Ethological Cong, Vancouver, Brit Columbia, 1979; Am Del, 1st Herpetological Cong, Socialist Sts, Budapest, 1981; Vis'g Fellow, Univ of Cambridge, England, 1985; Secy-Gen, World Cong of Herpetology, 1982-; Men of Achmt; W/W: in Am, in Technol Today; Am Men & Wom Sci.

ADLER, KURT HERBERT oc/Maestro, Opera Director, Conductor; b/Apr 2, 1905; h/P O Box 1446 Ross, CA 94957; ba/SF, CA; m/Nancy M; c/ Ronald, Kristin, Sabrina, Roman Curtis; p/Ernst Adler and Ida BoBauer (dec); sp/ Harry E Miller (dec); Elizabeth Schwenk; pa/Gen Dir Emeritus 1981-, Chorus Dir & Conductor 1943-49, Asst to Gen Dir 1949-53, Artistic Dir 1953-57, Gen Dir 1957-81, SF Opera; Conductor, Max Reinhardt Theater, Vienna, 1925; Asst to Arturo Toscanini, Salzburg Festival, 1936; Conductor, Vienna Volksoper & Throughout En Europe, 1936-38; Conductor, Chgo Opera, 1938-43; Num Other Nat Intl Conducting Engagements in USA,

Europe, Australia, China, Philippines; Launched: The SF Opera Auditions, 1954; The Merola Opera Prog, 1957; Sprg Opera Theater, 1961; Wn Opera Theater, 1966; Brown Bag Opera, 1974; SF/Affil Artists-Opera Prog (now Adler F'ship Prog), 1977; The Am Opera Proj, 1979 & SF Opera Summer Fest, 1981; Policy Panel Mem, Opera/Musical Theater Prog, NEA Music Prog, 1978-80; Appt'd Mem, Nat Coun on Arts; Life Mem, Nat Inst for Music Theater; Mem, Intl Assn Opera Dirs; cp/Num Memorable Perfs Featuring Outstg Performers (Leontyne Price, Renata Tebaldi, Mario del Monaco, Beverly Sills, Elisabeth Schwarskopf, Gwyneth Jones, Karl Ridderbusch, Teresa Berganza, Placido Domingo, Luciano Pavarotti, Sherill Milnes, Others) & Important Operas incl'g: *Aida, Madame Butterfly, Cosi fan tutte, Tristan und Isolde, Die Meistersinger von Nürnberg, Fidelio, Carmen, La Forza del Destino*, Num Others; r/Luth; hon/Conductor of Recordings: *O Holy Night* w Luciano Pavorotti; *Leona Mitchell w Kurt Herbert Adler: An Operatic Ptnrship, Verismo Arias* w Maria Chiara, *Adler at the Opera, Romantic Operatic Duets* w Renata Scotto & Placido Domingo; Recip Num Hons incl'g: Berkeley Fellow 1979 & Berkeley Cit 1976, Univ CA-Berkeley; Hon DMus, Univ of Pacific & Univ of SF; 1st Cultural Ldr to Receive SF's St Francis of Assisi Awd, 1973; Hon Mem, Am Fdn Musicians & Intl Alliance Theatrical Stage Employees; Merit Awd, Am Fedn TV & Radio Artists, 1981; Num Distns from Fgn Govts; W/W; Num Other Biogl Listings.

ADLER, LEONORE LOEB oc/Professor; b/May 2, 1921; h/162-14 86th Avenue, Jamaica, NY 11432; ba/Rockville Ctr, NY; m/Helmut E; c/Barry Peter, Beverly Sharmaine, Evelyn Renee; p/Leo and Elsie (Laemle) Loeb (dec); sp/Paul Adler and Lola Eiseman (Offenbacher) (dec); ed/BA, Queens Col, 1968; PhD Exptl Soc Psych, Adelphi Univ, 1972; Prof Psych & Dir, Inst for Cross-Cultural & Cross-Ethnic Studies, Molloy Col, 1980-; Adj Asst Prof, Dept Psych, Soc & Anthropol, Staten Isl Col, CUNY, 1974-80; Adj Asst Prof, Dept Psych, York Col, CUNY, 1979-80; Adj Asst Prof, Dept Psych, Queens Col, CUNY, 1979-80; Res Asst, Dept Animal Behavior & Mammalogy, Am Mus Nat Hist, 1956-84; Res Assoc, Mystic Marinelife Aquarium, Sums 1976-; Fellow, NY Acad Scis; Mem: Am Psychol Assn; En Psychol Assn; Intl Assn Cross-Cultural Psych; Soc Cross-Cultural Res; Assn Wom Sci; Sect Animal Behavior & Sociol, Animal Behavior Soc; Soc Advmt Soc Psych; Coun Rep 1981-84, Pres Div Soc Psych 1978-79, 1980-82, 1984-85, NY St Psychol Assn; Treas, Intl Coun Psychols, 1983-85; Mng Editor, Intl Org for Study Grp Tension; Mng Editor, *Intl Jour Grp Tensions*, 1978-84; Monitor, Psi Chi; cp/Org, Chaired & Presented Papers at Num Nat & Intl Sci Meetings; Others; r/Jewish; hon/Author & Editor of Books: *Cross Cultural Res At Issue* 1982, *Issues in Cross-Cultural Res* 1977; Co-Editor: *Lang, Sex & Gender: Does "La Difference" Make a Difference?* 1979, *Comparative Psych At Issue* 1973; Contbr, Num Book Chapts & Over 50 Sci Articles Pub'd; Dist'd Contbn of Decade Awd, Intl Org for Study Grp Tensions, 1981; Medallion, Div Soc Psych, NY St Psychol Assn, 1984; Plaque for Outstg Achmt,

Com on Wom's Issues, NY St Psychol Assn, 1984; W/W: of Am Wom, in E, in Frontier Sci & Technol Am Men & Wom Sci.

ADRIEN, NICOLAS GEFFRARD oc/Consultant, Independent Contractor; b/May 6, 1938; h/403 Elmwood Avenue, Maplewood, NJ 07040; m/Vivianne T; c/Claude T, Huguette M L, Florence I; p/Maxilia Adrien, Jamaica, NY; sp/Carmen Thrasybule, Queens Village, NY; ed/BSCE, Univ Haiti, 1961; MS Sanitary Engrg 1967, MEng Environ Planning 1968, Harvard Univ; pa/Civil Engr & Instr, Haiti & Mali, 1961-66; Res Asst & Cnsltg Engr US, 1966-71 & 1974-79; Engr, World Hlth Org, 1971-74; Conslt, Indep Contractor, 1979-; Diplomate, Am Acad Envir Engrs; Mem, Am Soc Civ Engrs; Am Water Wks Assn; UN Roster Conslts; r/Cath; hon/Author, Num Tech Articles, Book Reviews & Engrg Reports; W/W: in E, in MW.

AFKARI, ELIZABETH ANN (TAYLOR) oc/Instructor; b/Jul 3, 1932; h/27 Cue Court, Apt 3D, Owings Mills, MD 21117; ba/Baltimore, MD; c/Semene Anne; p/Pearl Frye Taylor, N Smithfield, RI; ed/AAS, 1951; Dipl Nsg, 1956; BS, Nsg, 1958; EdM, Nsg Ed, 1967; pa/Staff Nurse, Hd Nurse, Supvr & In-Ser Ed Supvr for Var Agys; Asst Dir Nsg, Staff Devel, Sinai Hosp Balto, 1977-80; Instr Nsg, Univ of MD, 1980-; ANA; MD Nurses Assn; Am Soc Hlthcare, Ed & Tng; r/Epis; hon/Pi Lambda Theta, 1958; Kappa Delta Pi, 1958; W/W of Am Wom; Intl W/W of Commun Ldrs; Intl Biog; Commun Ldrs Am; Other Biogl Listings.

AFSHAR, SIROOS K oc/Computer Engineer; b/Jul 3, 1949; h/10 Constitution Court, Manalapan, NJ 07726; ba/Lincroft, NJ; m/Simin; c/Pedram, Afsheen; p/Bagher Afshar (dec); Mastooreh Afshar, Tehran, Iran; sp/Abdolhosein (dec); Fatemeh, Tehran, Iran; ed/BSEE, 1972; MSE, 1976; PhD, 1979; pa/Elect Design Engr, Nat Iranian Oil Co, 1972-74; Res Asst, Univ Of MI, 1976-79; Asst Prof, LA St Univ, 1979-82; Tech Staff, AT&T Info Sys, 1982-; IEEE; ACM; SIAM; r/Islam; hon/Author of Tech Articles Pub'd in Sci Books & Jours; Eta Kappa Nu; Tau Beta Pi; Phi Kappa Phi.

AGARD, E THEODORE oc/Radiological Physicist; b/Aug 15, 1932; h/8600 Hide-Away Lane, Centerville, OH, 45459; ba/Dayton, OH; m/Joyce E; c/Noel, Ian, Wendy, Linda; p/Samuel Agard (dec); Pearl Doris Agard, Christ Church, Barbados; sp/Courtney A and Clarice Phillips, Barbados; ed/BSc Physics & Math, Univ of W Indies (Jamaica), 1956; MSc Physics, Univ of London, 1958; PhD, Univ of Toronto (Canada), 1970; Cert Radiol Physics, Am Bd Radiol, 1982; pa/Asst Physicist, MA Gen Hosp, 1959-63; Lectr, Univ of W Indies (Trinidad), 1963-72; Dir Med Physics Prog, PR Nuclear Ctr, 1972-76; Radiation Physicist, Kettering Med Ctr, Dayton, OH, 1976-84; Prof, Kettering Col for Med Arts, 1979-83; Mem, Intl Relats Com 1974-77 & Public Ed Com 1980-84, Am Assn Physicists in Med; Pres PR Chapt 1976, Cinc Radiation Soc Chapt 1980-81, Chm Affirmative Action Com 1980-81, Hlth Phys Soc; Dir, Miami Val Alt Energy Assn, 1980-81; Radiol Soc N Am; Am Col Radiol; cp/Sen, Univ of W Indies, 1971-72; Rep, of PR Nuclear Ctr to Com N44 of Am Nat Studies Inst, 1972-76; Conslt in Radiol Physics to VA, 1973-76 & 1978-84;

r/Christian; hon/Author, Over 15 Sci Articles Pub'd in Profl Jours; 1st Class Hons in BSc Deg, 1957.

AGARWAL, DWARIKA PRASAD oc/Research Scientist, Director; b/Sep 3, 1942; h/13 Stonehedge Lane, Attleboro, MA 02703; ba/Attleboro, MA; m/Constance Snyder; c/Meena Elizabeth, David James; p/Mrs Madho Lal Agarwal, Indore, India; sp/Mr and Mrs J Kenneth Snyder, York, PA; ed/BTech, Indian Inst of Technol, Bombay, 1965; PhD, Univ of PA Phila, 1973; pa/Jr Sci Ofcr, Def Metall Res Labs, Hydesabad, India, 1965-67; Res Engr, Carnegie-Mellon Univ, Pgh, 1973-75; Mgr Mats Res, Wms Gold, Buffalo, 1975-83; Dir, Phy Metall, Leach & Garner Co, Attleboro, 1983-; Pres, Indian Students Assn, Univ of PA, 1969-70; hon/Holder of 3 US Patents in Field; Nom'd, Inventor of Yr Awd, Niagara Frontier, 1980; Recip, 2nd Place Awd, Inventor of the Yr, Niagara Frontier, 1983; W/W in E.

AGENT, JERRY PEYTON oc/Instructor; b/May 31, 1949; h/6 Brandywine Court, Jackson, MS 39212; ba/Raymond, MS; m/Don Willard; c/Charles Peyton; p/Liston and Ollie Maragaret Jones Peyton, Raymond, MS; ed/AA, Hinds Jr Col, 1969; BS, Univ of So MS, 1971; MEd 1972 & Addit Grad Wk, Univ of MS; pa/Spch & Drama Instr, Holmes Jr Col, Goodman, MS, 1972-73; Spch & Theatre Instr, Hinds Jr Col, Raymond, MS, 1973-; Secy 2 Yrs, Fac Welfare Com 2 Yrs, Chm 1 Yr, Hinds Jr Col Ed Assn; MS Jr Col Fac Assn, 6 Yrs; MS Spch Communs Assn, 10 Yrs; So Spch Communs Assn, 9 Yrs; cp/Fac Sponsor, Phi Theta Kappa; Raymond Presb Wom in the Ch; Conducted Public Spkg Clin for HS Students in Future Bus Ldrs of Am, 2 Yrs; r/Presb; hon/Kappa Delta Pi; Phi Theta Kappa; Phi Kappa Phi; Pi Kappa Delta; Delta Psi Omega; Outstg Yg Wom Am.

AGGREY, O RUDOLPH oc/Consultant, US Ambassador, Ret'd; b/Jul 24, 1926; h/1257 Delaware Avenue, Southwest Washington, DC 20024; ba/Same; m/Francoise F; c/Roxane R; p/Mr and Mrs J E K Aggrey (dec); sp/Mr and Mrs Georges Fratacci (dec); ed/BS, Hampton Inst, 1946; MS, Syracuse Univ, 1948; Fellow, Harvard Univ Ctr for Intl Affairs, 1964-65; Hon LLD, Livingstone Col, 1977; pa/News Reporter, 1948-49; Public Relats, 1947 & 1950; US VConsul, Lagos & Nigeria, 1951-53; USIS Ofcr, Lille & Paris, 1953-60; Dept Public Affairs Ofcr for Africa 1964-65, Dir W African Affairs 1970-73, Dept of St; French Br Chief, Voice of Am, 1966; USIS Ofcr, Kinshasa, Zaire, 1966-68; Prog Mgr, USIA Motion Picture & TV Ser, 1968-70; US Ambassador, Senegal, The Gambia, Romania, 1977-81; Res Prof of Dipl, Georgetown Univ, 1981-83; St Dept Ofc of Res & Anal for Soviet Union & En Europe, 1983-84; Mem, Fed City Clb; Assn Black Am Ambassadors; Mem, NC Soc of Prodigal Son; Grand Ofcr, Senegalese Nat of Lion; Hon Mem, French Acad of Jazz; hon/Author, Articles Pub'd in Var Newspapers & Mags incl'g: *Quill & Scroll, Col & Univ Bus, Our World*; Philiss Wheatley S'ship Cup, Hampton Inst, 1946; Hampton Inst Alumni Awd, 1961; USIA Meritorious Awd 1955 & Superior Ser Awd 1960; Pres Meritorious Awd, 1984; Syracuse Univ Chancellor's Awd, 1984; W/W: in Am, in E; Dic Am Negro Biog; Other Listings.

AGOGINO, GEORGE A oc/Professor, Museum Director; b/Nov 18, 1920; h/ 1600 South Main, Portales, NM 88130; ba/Portales, NM; m/Mercedes; c/Alice, Karen; p/Andrew and Buleah Agogino (dec); sp/Herbert Merner (dec); Majory Merner, San Jose, CA; ed/BA Anthropol 1949, MA Sociol 1951, Univ NM; PhD Anthropol, Syracuse Univ, 1958; Postdoct F'ship (Wenner-Gren) Harvard Univ 1961-62; mil/USASC, 1943-46; pa/Asst Prof, Syracuse Univ, 1958; Asst Prof, Univ of SD, 1954; Asst Prof, Univ of WY, 1960-61; Assoc Prof, Baylor Univ, 1962; Assoc Prof 1963, Prof 1967-, En NM Univ; Dir, Blackwater Drawing Mus, 1968-; Fellow: AAAS; Am Anthropol Assn; Am Soc Phy Anthropols; Royal Anthropol Soc Great Brit & Ireland; Others; r/Prot; hon/Author, Over 200 Articles & Monographs Pub'd in Profl Jours incl'g: *Nat Geog Soc, Earth Sci, Am Antiquity, Archaeol,* Others; Hon Doct, Inst Arts & Scis, Rome, Italy; W/W: in W & SW, in Am Ed, Authors & Jours; Other Biogl Listings.

AGRAWAL, PIYUSH CHANDRA oc/ Supervisor; b/Jun 26, 1936; h/10600 Southwest 73 Court, Miami, FL 33156; ba/Miami, FL; m/Sudha; c/Seema, Sukrit, Akhil; p/Ram Chandra and Chameli Kiran Agrawal (dec); sp/Laxmi Narain and Sarla Bhagwandevi Bansal, Agra, India; ed/BS, Agra Univ, 1955; BEd, Delhi Univ, 1958; MSc, Agra Univ, 1963; MS 1972, EdS 1978, EdD 1979, SUNY-Albany, NY; pa/Supvr for Math Progs, Dade Co Public Schs, Miami; Dir, Metric Ed Progs, Reg Planning Ctr, Albany, NY, 1977-78; UNESCO Expert, Liberia 1971-76, Tanzania 1968-70; Gen Chm, Nat Conf & Annual Meeting, US Metric Assn, 1982; Mem, Adv Bd, Global Ed, 1981-; VP, Merrick Investmt Inc, 1981-; Pres, Assn of (Asian) Indians in Am, FL Chapt, 1982-; r/Hindu; hon/ Author of Num Profl Pubs; Mem, FL House Spkr's Task Force on Math, Sci & Computer Ed; Mem, Com for FL St Ed Dept's Prog Eval; W/W in S & SW.

AGUIRRE, BENIGNO EMILIO oc/ Sociologist; b/Oct 25, 1947; h/1204 Goode, Col Station, TX 77840; ba/Col Sta, TX; m/Lauriece Elaine; c/Carlos Agustin, Benigno E Jr; p/Carlos V and Rita Maria Aguirre, Hialeah, FL; sp/Roy and Lissi Chitwood, Valdosta, GA; ed/BA, FL St Univ, 1970; MA, Tulane Univ; PhD, OH St Univ, 1977; pa/Staff Mem, Disaster Res Ctr, OH St Univ, 1975-77; Assoc Prof, Dept Sociol, TX A&M Univ, 1977-; Am Sociol Assn; Soc for Study of Soc Probs; Latin Am Studies Assn; Nat Coun on Fam Relats; hon/Author, Over 30 Articles Pub'd in Profl Jours incl'g: *Am Jour of Sociol, Intl Jour of Aging & Human Devel, Jour of Marriage & Fam, Jour Sociol & Social Welfare, Ethnicity,* Others; Papers Presented at Assn Meetings; Fulbright-Hayes Lectureship, Universidad de la Republica, Montevideo, Uruguay, 1981; Fulbright-Hayes Lectureship, San Simon Univ, Cochabamba, Bolivia, 1980; Sum S'ship, Dept Latin Am Studies, Tulane Univ, 1971; Dept Hlth, Ed & Welfare Predoct Res F'ship, 1976; Phi Kappa Phi, 1976; W/W.

AGUS, ZALMAN S oc/Physician, Professor; b/Apr 3, 1941; h/334 Roosevelt Drive, Cherry Hill, NJ 08002; ba/Philadelphia, PA; m/Sondra; c/David, Joel, Michael; p/Rabbi and Mrs Jacob B Agus, Balto, MD; sp/Mrs Mildred LeBow,

Cherry Hill, NJ; ed/AB, Johns Hopkins Univ, 1961; MD, Univ of MD, 1961; (Hon) MA, Univ of PA, 1979; mil/USAF, 1971-73, Maj; pa/Residency, Internal Med, Univ of MD, 1965-68; Fellow Nephrology 1968-71, Asst Prof Med 1973-79, Assoc Prof Med 1979-, Univ of PA; Chief, Renal-Electrolyte Sect, Hosp of Univ of PA, 1979-; Chm, Sch Bd, Solomon Schecter Day Sch of San Antonio, 1972-73; Chm, Sch Bd, Harry B Kellman Acad, 1979-81; r/Jewish; hon/ Author, Over 100 Articles Pub'd in Sci Jours on Renal & Electrolyte Metabolism, Physiol & Disease; AOA, 1965; Housestaff Tchg Awd, 1972; Res Career Devel Awd, NIH 1976-81; ASCI, 1983; W/W: in E, in Am Jewry.

AHERN, MAUREEN oc/Gallery Director; h/Rural Route 1, Box 211, Eaton Road, Swanzey, NH; ba/Keene, NH; m/ William J Knorr; p/M Jeanne Ahern, Salem MA; sp/Mr and Mrs Edwin Knorr, Albany, NY; ed/BFA Painting, Univ of MA-Amherst, 1969; MFA, St Univ NY-Albany, 1972; pa/Director, Thorne-Sagendorf Art Gallery, Keene St Col, NH, 1981-; Acting Curator 1980-81, Asst Curator Exhibits Dept 1975-80, Instr Painting & Drawing Harmanus Bleeker Ctr 1975-79, Albany Inst Hist & Art; Curator 1979, Instr Drawing & Design 1972, St Univ of NY-Albany; Art Dir, Jewish Commun Ctr Boston, 1969; Undergrad Tchg Resident, Univ of MA-Amherst, 1968; Contemp Art Conslt, Rockefeller Empire St Plaza Art Collection, 1979-; Num Lectr, Conslt & Juror Positions; Mem: N Eng Mus Assn; Col Art Assn; NH Visual Arts Coalition; Am Assn St & Local Hist; Am Assn Mus; W/W in E.

AHMED, ALICE PEARCE oc/ Research Associate; b/Sep 15, 1934; h/410 Blue Spring Road, Princeton, NJ 08540; ba/Princeton, NJ; m/S Bashee Ahmed; c/ Ivy Amina; p/Clay Pearce (dec); Ivy Pearce, KY; sp/S Muhammed Hussain and K Amina Ahmed, India; ed/BS, Wn KY Univ, 1957; MA, Murray St Univ, 1965; EdD Cand, Univ of TN; pa/Bus & Ofc Ed Tchr, Warren Co Bd of Ed, Bowling Green, KY, 1971-81; Instr, Bus Ed & Ofc Adm, TN Technol Univ, Cookeville, TN, 1966-68; Bus & Ofc Edn Tchr, Davies Co HS, Owensboro, KY, 1957-66; Mem, NEA; KY Ed Assn; Pres 1976-77, VPres 1975-76, Secy 1974-75, Treas 1973-74, 3rd Dist Ed Assn; Mu Chapt, Delta Pi Epsilon, Univ of TN, 1967-; cp/Secy, Fac Wives Clb, Wn KY Univ, 1977; Dir, Mission Friends, 1st Bapt Ch, Bowling Green, KY, 1974-77; r/Bapt; hon/Co-Editor of Books: *Cookbook of Fac Favorites,* 1977; *Technol & Growth,* 1983; Personalities of Am; World W/W of Wom.

AHMED, NAHED K oc/Professor, Hospital Member; b/Sep 29, 1945; h/4228 Belle Meade Cove, Memphis, TN 38117; ba/Memphis, TN; m/Mohamed Said; c/ Tamer, Sonya; p/Ahmed Ibrahim and Safie Ibrahim Khalil, Cairo, Egypt; sp/ Mohamed Said Ahmed (dec); Aziza Labib, Maady, Egypt; ed/MS, Cairo Univ, 1970; PhD, Univ of TN Ctr for Hlth Scis, Memphis, 1975; pa/Vis'g Fellow, Balto Cancer Res Ctr, NCI, 1975-77; Res Assoc 1977-79, Asst Mem 1979-, Div Biochem, Clin Pharm, St Jude Hosp, Memphis, TN; Asst Prof Biochem, Univ of TN Ctr for Hlth Scis, 1982-; Am Assn for Cancer Res, 1981-; r/Moslem; hon/Author & Co-Author, Over 17 Articles Pub'd in Sci

Jours incl'g: *Jour Biochem, Cancer, Biochem & Pharm,* Others; 2nd Class Hons, BS Deg, 1966; S'ship for MA, Nat Res Ctr Cairo, Egypt, 1967-70; S'ship for PhD, Univ of TN, 1972-75; Recip ACS Res Grant, 1973; W/W in Frontier Sci & Technol.

AHNER, DAVID HURLEY oc/Physician; b/Apr 29, 1943; h/1139 Dorest Drive, West Chester, PA 19380; ba/ Chadds Ford, PA; m/Conchita Uy de Leon; p/Hurley Thomas Ahner(dec); Elizabeth Show Gade, Newark, DE; ed/ BA, Univ of DE, Newark, 1964; DO, Phila Col of Osteopathic Med, 1965-70; Intern, Tri-Co Hosp, Springfield, PA, 1970-71; Intern, Albert Einstein Med Ctr, Phila, 1971-72; Residency in Psychi, Inst of PA Hosp, Phila, 1972-75; pa/Phys, Commun Ser for Human Growth Inc, 1981-83; Var Positions & Coms, Crozer-Chester Med Ctr, Upland, Chester, PA, 1975-81; Phys: Fair Acres Farm, Glen Riddle-Lima, PA, 1976-; Fairmont Inst, Phila, 1980-; Metro Hosp, Springfield, 1976-; Riddle Meml Hosp, Media, 1977-; Sacred Heart Gen Hosp, Chester, 1977-; Taylor Hosp, Ridley Pk, 1976-; Mem: Am Psychi Assn; PA Psychi Soc; Phila Psychi Soc; Am Oesteopathic Assn; Am Col of Neuropsychis; PA Osteopathic Med Assn; Am Col of Utilization Review Phys; Nat Coun on Alcoholism; Others; hon/Author of "A Transference Cure of an Hysterical Neurosis in Brief Psychotherapy"; The Chapel of 4 Chaplains, Legion of Hon, 1979; Biogl Roll of Hon; Commun Ldrs in Am; Outstg Yg Men of Am; Num Other Biogl Listings.

AHUJA, JAGDISH CHAND oc/Professor; h/9914 Southwest 30th Avenue, Portland, OR 97219; ba/Portland, OR; m/ Sudarshan; c/Naina, Anita; p/Nihal Chand Ahuja, India; Ishwardai (Chhabra) Ahuja (dec); ed/BA 1953, MA 1955, Banaras Univ; PhD, Univ of Brit Columbia, 1963; pa/Prof Math 1969-, Assoc Prof 1966-69, Portland St Univ; Asst Prof Math, Univ Calgary, 1963-66; Lectr Stats 1961-63, Stats Lab Instr 1959-61, Tchg Fellow 1961-63, Tchg Asst 1958-61, Univ of Brit Columbia, Canada; Math Tchr, Ed Dept, Tanzania, 1956-68; Sr Math Tchr, DAV HS, Nairobi, Kenya, 1955-56; Mem: Inst of Math Stats; Am Statl Assn; Referee for Num Sci Jours; Participant in Num Nat & Intl Socs, Confs & Meetings; r/Hindu; hon/Author & Co-Author, Over 25 Articles Pub'd in Profl Math Jours incl'g: *Fibonacci Qtly, Am Stats, Inst Math Stats Bul, Annals Math Stats,* Others; W/W: in W, in Technol Today; Am Men & Wom of Sci.

AIDLIN, SAMUEL SIMEON oc/Consulting Mechanical Engineer; b/Jul 29, 1913; h/5079 Village Gardens Drive, Sarasota, FL 33580; ba/Bradenton, FL; m/ Ruth Baker; c/Stephen Howard; p/Isidore and Mollie Aidlin (dec); sp/Emanuel and Fannie Baker (dec); ed/BME, Col of the City of NY, 1937; MME, Polytech of Bklyn NY & Stevens Inst, 1945; DME, World Univ, 1983; pa/Engrg Draftsman, NY Nav Yard, 1937-39; Secy in Charge of Planning Sect, Raritan Arsenal, Metuchen, NJ, 1939-40; Tech Asst Mech Engr, Gibbs & Cox Inc NYC, 1940-44; Devel Engr, Bendix Aviation Corp, 1944-45; Chief Engr, Specialty Engrg Co, NYC, 1945-47; Consltg Engr, Aidlin Assocs of NYC, 1947-; Consltg Wk Clients Incl: Paragon Oil Co, Kay Mfg Corp, Acme Fire Alarm Co, Watson Labs, Ford Instrument Div of Sperry-Rand, US

Rubber Co, Nat Silver Co, Gen Elect Co, IBM Corp, Num Others; Pres, Kings Co Chapt, NY St Soc Profl Engrs, 1972-73; Pres, Mfg Engrs Coun, 1962-; ASM; ASEE; Bd of Trustees, NYC Commun Col of Applied Arts & Scis, 1950-; Adj Professor, Polytech Inst of Bklyn & Pratt Inst; Others; cp/Secy, Lambda Rho; Chancellor & Cmdr, K of P, 1945-46; Num Others; hon/Author of Books: *Engrg Ec* 1951, *Basic Engrg Mechs & Machine Design* 1952, *Profl Engrg-Ecs & Pract* 1953; Engr of Yr, Nat Soc Profl Engrs, 1973; Pres Coun Awd, NY St Soc Profl Engrs, 1973; Ency Am Biog; W/ W in Engrg.

AIELLO, JOHN R oc/Professor; b/Jun 14, 1946; h/77 Carson Avenue, Metuchen, NJ 08840; ba/New Brunswick, NJ; m/Donna Thompson; c/Lauren Elizabeth; p/John V and Elsie Aiello, Bklyn, NY; sp/Bernard and Rosie Thompson, Old Bridge, NJ; ed/BBA Psych, City Col of NY, 1968; MA Communs, Queens Col, CUNY, 1970; PhD Psych, MI St Univ, 1972; pa/Asst Prof 1972, Assoc Prof Psych 1979-, Rutgers St Univ; Assoc Prof & Dir Doct Prog in Social Psych, Peabody Col, Vanderbilt Univ, Nashville, 1977-79; Orgnl Conslt, 1979-; Fellow, Am Psychol Assn; Fellow, Soc Exptl Social Psych; VP, Inst Nonverbal Communication Res; Mem, En Psychol Assn; hon/Author of *Residential Crowding & Design*, 1979; Over 75 Papers & Articles in Behavioral Sci Jours; Elected Fellow, Am Psychol Assn, 1982; W/W.

AIGNER, DENNIS JOHN oc/Professor; b/Sep 27, 1937; h/16044 Aiglon Street, Pacific Palisades, CA 90272; ba/ LA, CA; c/Mitchell A, Annette N, Anita L, Angela D; p/Herbert L and Della G Aigner, LA, CA; ed/Att'd Univ of CA-LA (UCLA), 1955-58; BS Agri Ec 1959, MA Stats 1962, PhD Agri Ec 1963, Univ of CA-Berkeley; pa/Math Stat, USDA, Forest Ser, Berkeley, 1960-62; Asst Prof Ec 1962-66, Dir Computer Lab, Col Bus Adm 1964-66, Assoc Prof Ec 1966-67, Univ of IL; Assoc Prof Ec 1967-70, Dir Programming & Computation Ser, Data & Computation Ctr for Social Scis 1967-73, Prof Ec 1970-77, Chm Social Sys Res Inst 1971-76, Vis'g Prof Fall 1982, Univ of WI-Madison; Vis'g Prof Ec, Univ of HI, Sum 1970; Vis'g Prof, Ctr for Opers Res & Econometrics (CORE), Universite Catholique de Louvain (Belgium), 1970-71; Resident Conslt, The Rand Corp, Santa Monica, CA, Sprg 1976; Prof Ec 1976-, Co-Dir Modelling Res Grp 1976-79, Acting Chm Dept Ec 1978-79, Chm Dept Ec 1979-, Univ of So CA (USC); Consltg Wk Clients Incl: Elect Power Res Inst, LA Dept of Water & Power, Pacific Gas & Elect Co, So CA Edison Co; Ch of Chp's Grp 1983 & Mem, Am Ec Assn; Mem, Am Statl Assn; Mem, Econometric Assn; Mem Proj Review & Eval, Nat Sci Foun; Co-Editor, *Jour Econometrics*, 1972-; Assoc Editor, *Review Public Data Use*, 1980-; Referee, *Am Jour Agri Ec & The Energy Jour*; Confs Incl: Wn Sts Load Res Grp Elect; Wn Ec Assn; Econometric Soc; Participant, Num Sems at Nat & Intl Univs; hon/Author of 2 Books, 3 Monographs & 3 Reports on Ec; Over 50 Articles in Profl Ec Sci Jours; Fulbright Scholar, Belgium (1970-71) & Israel (May 1983); Elected Fellow, Econometric Soc, 1972; H I

Romnes Fac F'ship, Univ of WI, 1976; Am Statl Assn Vis'g Lectr Prog in Stats, 1980-83; W/W; W/W in Ec.

AIJAZ, SYED MOHAMMAD oc/ Professor; b/Jan 15, 1941; h/2005 Wellington Drive, Pine Bluff, AR 71603; ba/Pine Bluff, AR; m/Salma; c/Asim S; p/S M Isa and Wali-Un-Nesa (dec); sp/ Mohammad A and Razia Rizvi, India; ed/BS, 1963; MS, 1965; PhD Chem, 1973; pa/Postdoct Fellow, Univ of TN Med Ctr & MST Labs, Memphis, 1973-74; Assoc Prof, Edward Waters Col, Jacksonville, FL, 1974-76; Asst Prof, NE MO St Univ, Kirksville, MO, 1976-77; Assoc Prof, Univ of AR-Pine Bluff, 1977-; Mem, Am Chem Soc; cp/ Mem, Muslim Assn of AR; r/Islam; hon/ Author of *Lab Manual Phy Sci*, 1980; Recip, Kellogg Tchg Awd, 1978 & 1979.

AINSLIE, MICHAEL L oc/Executive; b/May 12, 1943; h/3021 Q Street, Northwest, Washington, DC 20007; ba/ Washington, DC; m/Lucy Scardino; c/ Katherine Oxnard, Liza Oxnard, Robbie Oxnard, Michael Loren; p/Mr and Mrs George Ainslie, Kingsport, TN; sp/Mr and Mrs Peter Scardino, Savannah, GA; ed/BA, Vanderbilt Univ, 1965; Corning Foun World Travel Fellow, 1965-66; MBA, Harvard Bus Sch, 1968; McKinsey & Co (on Leave of Absence) Served as Dept Dir, NYC Model Cities, 1968-71; Ofc & Dir, Sea Pines Co Inc, Hilton Head, SC, 1971-73; Pres, Palmas del Mar (subsidiary of Sea Pines Co Inc), PR, 1973-75; VP Adm 1975-77, Sr VP & Chief Operating Ofcr 1977-80, N-ReN Corp, Cincinnati, OH; Pres, Nat Trust for Hist Presv, 1980-; Dir, Nat Bldg Mus; Mem, Design Arts Policy Panel of NEA; Mem Bd of Overseers, Univ of PA Sch of Fine Arts; Mem Exec Coun, Harvard Bus Sch; Mem Alumni Bd, Vanderbilt Univ; Dir, Guest Ser Inc, Wash DC; r/Epis; hon/Corning Foun World Travel Fellow; J Spencer Love Fellow.

AISENBERG, NADYA oc/Writer, Publisher; h/124 Chestnut Street, Boston, MA 02108; ba/Boston, MA; m/ Alan Clifford; c/Margaret Kate, James Oliver; ed/BA, Bennington Col, 1949; MA Eng Lit 1956, PhD Eng Lit 1974, Univ of WI; ba/Dept Eng, Wellesley Col, 1956-69; Dept Eng, Univ of MA-Boston, 1963-64; Dept Eng, Tufts Univ, 1976-78; Ed Dept, Mus of Fine Arts, 1967; WGBH, Nat Pub Radio, Boston, 1961-62; Fdr & Editor, Rowan Tree Press, 1981-; Bd of Dirs, Alliance of Indep Scholars, Cambridge, MA, 1980-; r/Jewish; hon/Author: *A Common Sprg: Crime Novel & Classic* 1981, *Invincible Sum* 1979, *The Justice-Worm* 1981; Editor: *London Crimes* 1982, *The Creative Mind* 1981; Recip, Sum Stipend, NEA for Humanities, 1980.

AITKEN, PETER GIL oc/Neurobiologist, Part-time Photoillustrator; b/Mar 7, 1947; h/2526 Chapel Hill Road, Durham, NC 27707; ba/Durham, NC; m/Kathryn Ann Conte; c/Benjamin Joseph Tapia; p/Hugh Walter and Laura Tapia Aitken, NJ; sp/Joseph Conte (dec); Sadie Conte, NY; ed/BS, Univ of Rochester, 1972; MA, SUNY-Brockport, 1974; PhD, Univ of CT, 1978; pa/Lectr 1978-79, Postdoct Fellow 1979-82, Cornell Univ; Res Assoc, Duke Univ Med Ctr, 1982-; Freelance Photoillustrator, 5 Yrs; AAAS; Sigma Xi; Soc for Neurosci; hon/Num Papers Pub'd in Sci

Jours; Photos Pub'd in Art & Comml Mags; Indiv Res Ser Awd, NIH, 1979-82; S'ship to Ansel Adams Photo Wkshop, 1983; W/W in E.

AKERA, TAI oc/Professor; b/Jul 13, 1932; h/1873 Ridgewood Drive, East Lansing, MI 48823; ba/East Lansing, MI; m/Chiseko; c/Atsushi, Yukako, Chika; p/Jibusuke and Ayako Akera, Tokyo, Japan; sp/Yoshiji and Shizuko Masuda, Tokyo, Japan; ed/MD 1958, Intern 1958-59, PhD 1965, Keio Univ Sch of Med; pa/Postdoct Fellow, Univ of MI, 1962-64; Res Assoc 1959-65, Asst Prof 1965-71, Keio Univ Sch of Med; Vis'g Asst Prof 1967-70, Assoc Prof & Prof 1971-, MI St Univ; Japanese Med Assn; Japanese Pharm Soc; Am Soc for Pharm & Exptl Therapeutics; hon/Author, Over 150 Articles Pub'd in Profl Sci Jours.

AKINS, JAMES E oc/Diplomat, Consultant; b/Oct 15, 1926; h/2904 Garfield Terrace, Northwest, Washington, DC 20008; m/Marjorie Abbott; c/Thomas Andrew, Mary Elizabeth; ed/BS Physics, Akron Univ, 1947; mil/USN, 1944-46; pa/US Fgn Ser, 1954-76; Ambassador, Saudi Arabia, 1973-76; Fgn Affairs Conslt, 1976-; Ptnr, Value Quest, 1981-; Mem, Coun on Fgn Relats, 1972; cp/Mem, Union Leag Clb, NYC; r/ Quaker; hon/Author, Num Articles on Energy & Fgn Relats, 1970-; LLD, Wittenberg Univ, 1978; W/W.

ALALA, JOSEPH BASIL JR oc/Lawyer, Certified Public Accountant; b/Apr 29, 1933; h/1216 South Street, Gastonia, NC 28052; ba/ Gastonia, NC; m/ Nell Powers; c/Sheron Josephine, Tracy Maria, Joseph Basil III; p/Joseph Basil Alala (dec); Wahada Alala, Greensboro, NC; ed/BSBA 1957, JD Sch of Law 1959, Univ of NC-Chapel Hill; mil/AUS, Inf & Mil Police; pa/Lwyr, Mng Ptnr, Garland & Alala, PA, Currently; Assoc, Garland & Eck Attys, 1962; CPA, Arthur Anderson & Co, 1959-62; Mem: Am Judic Soc; ABA; Am Assn Atty-CPAs Inc; NC Bar Assn; Gaston Co Bar Assn; Am Inst of CPAs; NC Assn of CPAs; Nat Assn of Accts; cp/Dir, Gastonia Chapt Rotary Intl; Past Pres & Dir, Jr C of C; Grand K of Malta; Past Mem Bd of Dirs & Pres, Gaston Co Country Clb; Bd of Dirs, Salvation Army Boy's Clb; Past Dir, C of C; Bd of Dirs, Indep Nat Bk; Bd of Dirs, Garrison Commun Foun; Past Dir & Pres, YMCA; Exec Bd, Piedmont Coun of BSA; Bd Advrs, Belmont Abbey Col; Bd of Dirs, Gtr Gastonia Citizens Comm; Past Mem Bd of Trustees & Chm Fin Com, St Michael's Ch; Others; r/Cath; hon/Author & Co-Author, "Fam Tax Planning" & Other Titles in the NC Assn for CPAs Course Series; Bd of Editors, *NC Law Review*; Cont'g Legal Ed Awd, NC Bar Assn; Key Lectr Awd, CPE of NC Assn of CPAs; W/W in S & SW; Outstg Yg Men of Am; Outstg Personalities of S; DIB; W/W: in Fin & Indust, in Am Law, of Intells; Num Other Biogl Listings.

ALBANTIDES, MARGARET oc/Graphic Artist, Proprietor; b/Oct 14, 1942; ba/New York, NY; m/Danny; c/Adam E Rodriguez, Tri Doan; p/Joseph E Bezares, Rio Piedras, PR; ed/Cathedral HS, 1956-57; St Helena's HS, 1957-60; BA, Bernard Baruch Sch of Bus, CUNY, 1960-65; Att'd LaSalle Ext Univ, 1977-; Extra Comml Art Courses: BOCES,

1982-83; Var Sems, Am Mgmt Assn, 1970-; pa/Exec (Propr), The Button Factory, 1981-; Info Asst, E Ramapo Ctl Sch Dist, 1981-; Mgr, Admar's Mdse Co Inc, 1976-81; Sales Rep, Metro Life Ins Co, 1971-76; Bus Mgr, Adm Asst Radiol Dept, Lenox Hill Hosp, 1968-71; Adm Asst, London Records Inc, 1964-68; Mem: (NAHB) Nat Assn of Home-based Bus Wom 1982-83, (AIGA) Am Inst of Graphic Artists 1983, (GAG) Graphic Artists' Guild 1983; Secy 1979-80, NYC (SAM) Soc for Advmt of Mgt, 1962-81; r/Prot; hon/Author of *The Fair Affair*; 1st Place Graphics for NY St Chapt, Nat Schs Public Relats Assn; W/W: in Am Wom, in E, of Wom; Dir of Dist'd Ams; Other Biogl Listings.

ALBERS H ELLIOTT oc/Research Scientist; b/Apr 7, 1953; h/104 Lakeside Drive, Shrewsbury, MA 01545; ba/Shrewsbury, MA; p/Henry H and Marjorie K Albers, Cedar Rapids, IA; ed/BA, Univ of NE, 1974; MS 1978, PhD 1979, Tulane Univ; pa/Res Fellow, Dept Physiol, Harvard Med Sch, 1979-82; Res Assoc 1982-83, Sr Res Assoc 1983-, Worcester Foun for Exptl Biol; Mem, Soc for Neurosci; Mem, Intl Soc for Chronobiol; hon/Author, 20 Articles Pub'd in Sci Jours; Nat Res Ser Awd, 1979; Pub Hlth Ser Grantee, 1982-85; W/W in Frontier Sci & Technol.

ALBERT, LOIS E oc/Archaeologist, Palynologist; b/June 2; h/1610 North Peters, Norman, OK 73019; ba/Norman, OK; m/Abbott H; p/Mr and Mrs Clinton L Wilson, Alva, OK; sp/Mr and Mrs Joseph Albert, Oklahoma City, OK; ed/BS Chem, NWn St Col, Alva, OK, 1960; MS, Biochem, OK St Univ, Stillwater, 1963; MA Anthropol, Univ of OK, Norman, 1974; pa/Chem Lab Tchg Asst, NWn St Col, 1957-60; Res Asst, Univ of CO Med Ctr, Denver, 1962-64; Res Asst, OK Med Res Foun, 1964-66; Res Asst Full-time 1966-70 & Sum 1974 & Pt-time 1970-72, Univ of OK Hlth Sci Ctr; Archaeol Asst, Sum 1971 & 1973, Univ of OK; Clk-Typist, OK Hwy Dept, Sum 1975; Sec I 1975-76, Res Asst I 1976-78, Acting Dir 1978-79, Res Asst 1979-81, Archaeol II 1981-, OK Archaeol Survey, Univ of OK; Editor, *Studies OK's Past*, 1978-79; Proj Dir, Prehist People of OK Film Series Planning Proj, 1979; Co-Prin Investigator, Spiro Mounds Proj, Phase I, 1979; Prin Investigator, Ferndale Bog Proj, 1979-81; Co-Prin Investigator, Red River Survey Proj, 1980-; Co-Prin Investigator, James Fork Creek Watershed Survey Proj, 1981-; Mem: Am Chem Soc, Sigma Xi, Am Assn of Stratigraphic Palynologists, Soc for Am Archaeol, OK Anthropol Soc, OK Acad Scis, AAAS, Soc for Archaeol Scis; hon/Author & Co-Author, Over 30 Sci Articles & Reports Pub'd; Num Papers Presented at Var Assn Meetings; Phi Sigma; W/W: in Am Cols & Univs, in S & SW; Outstg Yg Wom of Am.

ALBERTS, W WATSON oc/Science Administrator; b/Dec 31, 1929; h/9205 Friars Road, Bethesda, MD 20817; ba/Bethesda, MD; m/Marilyn West; c/Allison Christine, Allan Watson; p/Hugo W Alberts (dec); Ruth W Marness, Santa Cruz, CA; sp/T Reginald and Evelyn L West, Sacramento, CA; ed/BA 1951, PhD 1956, Univ of CA-Berkeley; pa/Res Physiol, Med Ctr Univ of CA-SF, 1955-56; Biophysicist, Mt Zion Hosp &

Med Ctr, SF, 1956-72; Grants Assoc, NIH, Bethesda, MD, 1972-73; Spec Asst 1973-74, Hd Res Contracts Sect 1974-75, Asst Dir Contract Res Progs, Extramural Activs Prog 1975-77, Dept Dir Fundamtl Neuroscis Prog 1978-, Nat Inst of Neurol & Communicative Disorders & Stroke; Adm Dir, Smith Kettlewell Inst & Dept Visual Scis, Univ of Pacific, SF, 1977-78; Fellow, AAAS; Mem: Am Physiol Soc, Biophy Soc, IEEE, Soc for Neurosci, Fdn Am Scis, Planetary Soc; r/Prot; hon/Author, Over 40 Papers & Abstracts Pub'd on Neurophysiol; Phi Beta Kappa, 1950; Sigma Xi, 1951 & 1956; Awd of Merit, NIH, 1983; Am Men & Wom of Sci.

ALBINSKI, HENRY STEPHEN oc/Professor, Administrator; b/Dec 31, 1931; h/803 Cornwall Drive, State College, PA 16801; ba/University Park, PA; c/Lawrence, Gillian, Allison; ed/BA 1953, MA 1955, Univ of CA-LA (UCLA); PhD, Univ of MN, 1959; pa/Prof Polit Sci & Dir Australian Studies Ctr, PA St Univ, Currently; Num Past Vis'g Prof'ships; Num Govt & Pvt Consltg Wks; Mem of Num US, Australian, Canadian & New Zealand Profl Assns; hon/Author of 8 Books; Approx 30 Book Chapts; 50 Scholarly Articles & Num Book Reviews & Reports; Recip of Num Grants, F'ships, Appts in US, Australia & Canadian Univs; Num Biogl Listings.

ALBY, JAMES FRANCIS oc/Priest, Educator; b/Jul 16, 1936; h/5607 West Brooklyn Place, Milwaukee, WI 53216; ba/West Allis, WI; m/Jan Lorraine (Peplinski); c/Jonathan James Francis; p/Frank J and Sara S Alby, W Allis, WI; sp/Edward Kenneth Peplinski, Milwaukee, WI; ed/Lincoln HS, 1955; W Allis Voc Sch, 1956; BA 1963, MA Grad Sch of Ed 1964, Gallaudet Co; VA Theol Sem, 1981; pa/Tchr of Deaf, John Marshall HS, 1972-; Asst to Rector, St Peter's Epis Ch, W Allis, 1972-; Tchr, IL Sch for Deaf, 1964-68; Draftsman, Rexnord Co, 1956-59; Mem, Nat & WI Assns of Deaf; Mem, Evang & Cath Mission of Epis Ch; cp/Fdr 1974, Charter Pres 1974-76, Pres 1979-80, Gtr Milwaukee Lions Clb; Liaison, Gtr Milwaukee Lioness Clb, 1980-; Nat Frat Soc of Deaf; Alpha Sigma Pi; r/Epis; hon/Author, "The Ednl Phil of Thomas Hopkins Gallaudet," in *Buff & Blue*, 1963; Num Articles in Periods of the Deaf; Pres's Awd 1976 & 1980, Dist Govs Awd 1975 & 1980, Lions Clb; Awd of Apprec, St Peter's Ch, 1982; W/W: in MW, in Rel; Dir of Epis Clergy; DIB.

ALCORN, TROY GENE oc/Pastor; b/Aug 4, 1930; h/3812 Templeton Gap Road, Colorado Springs, CO 80907; ba/Same; m/Yvonne McCrady; c/Karen L (Havens), Chris A, Gayle M (Haggard), Cynthia J (Morris); p/Mahlon W Alcorn, Colorado Springs, CO; sp/Bob McCrady, Waxahachie, TX; ed/BS, E TX St Univ, 1952; Grad Wk, Indust Col of Armed Forces, 1972-73; mil/USAF, 1952-76, Col; pa/Sr Pastor, Christian Assem Colorado Springs, CO,1977-; Assoc Pastor, Christian Assem Vienna, VA, 1976-77; Cmdr, 1143 Air Base Sqdrn, Pentagon, 1973-76; Cmdr, 18th Survival Squad, Edwards AFB, 1970-72; Line Ofcr, Var Command, Operational & Material Positions, 1952-70; cp/Bd of Dirs, Mission to Am (Humble, TX), 1978-; Bd of Dirs, Commun Care Ctr

(Colorado Springs, CO), 1983-; Adv Bd, The Christian Homes, 1978-; r/Christ Prot; hon/Legion of Merit w OLC; Meritorious Ser Medal; Commend w OLC; W/W: in W, in CO.

ALCORN, WILLIAM LLOYD SR oc/Federal Government Executive; b/May 10, 1927; h/5800 Bucknell Terrace, College Park, MD 20740; ba/Washington, DC; c/Joyce, Janet, Bill, Amy; p/Norman L Alcorn (dec); sp/Daisy A Clites; ed/AA, W VA Univ, 1957; BS Public Adm, Am Univ, 1959; mil/USN 1945-46; AUS, 1950-51; pa/Dir, Security & Safety, Nat Labor Relats Bd, 1960-; Investigator, US Civil Ser Comm, 1956-60; Detective, Wash, DC Police Dept, 1952-56; r/Meth.

ALDERMAN, JAMES E oc/Chief Justice, Florida Supreme Court; b/Nov 1, 1936; h/3058 Carlow Circle, Tallahassee, FL 32308; ba/Tallahassee, FL; m/Jean; c/James Allen; p/B E and Frances Alderman, Ft Pierce, FL; ed/BA 1958, LLB Col of Law 1961, Univ of FL; pa/Judge, 4th Dist Ct of Appeals, FL, 1976-78; Circuit Judge, 19th Jud Circuit, FL, 1973-76; Co Judge, St Lucie Co, FL, 1971-72; Past Pres, St Lucie Co Bar Assn; cp/Past Pres: Ft Pierce-St Lucie Co C of C; St Lucie Co Fair Assn; Ft Pierce Mut Concert Assn; Mem, Ft Pierce Rotary Clb; r/Epis.

ALDERMAN, LOUIS CLEVELAND JR oc/College President; b/Aug 12, 1924; h/Old Chester Road, Cochran, GA 31014; ba/Cochran, GA; m/Anne Augusta Whipple; c/Amelia Anne, Louis III, Fielding D, Jonathan A; ed/AA, S GA Col, 1942; AB, Emory Univ, 1946; MS, Univ of GA, 1949; EdD, Auburn Univ, 1959; mil/AUS, WW II (PTO); pa/Instr Biol 1949-50, Dir & Prof Biol 1951-56, Univ of GA, Rome Ctr; Dir & Instr Biol, Univ of GA, Savannah Ctr, 1950-51; Dir, Univ of GA, Columbus Ctr, 1956-59; Dir, Henderson Col, Univ of KY, 1959-64; Pres, Mid GA Col, 1964-; Past Pres, GA Assn Jr Cols; GAE; NEA; Assn of Higher Ed; Phi Delta Kappa; Phi Theta Kappa; cp/Past Dist Gov, S'ship Com, Bd of Trustees, Student Loan Fund, Rotary Intl; Past Pres, Cochran Rotary Clb; GA Hist Soc; Organizing Pres, Mid GA Chapt, SAR; Order KY Cols; r/Bapt; hon/Author, Articles incl: "In vitro Cultivation of Asian Malaria Parasite, Plasmodium Catheymerium," "50 Yrs as Mid GA Col," "Ed in Am Colonies," "Hist Old Richland Bapt Ch," "Phil, Role & Function of Land Grant Col"; Grad Res Asst'ship, USPHS, 1948-49; Civitan Good Citizenship Awd, 1955; F'ship Fund for Advmt of Ed, Ford Foun, Auburn Univ, 1958-59; Rotary Clb Spec Awd, 1969; Commun Ldrs of Am; Creat & Successful Personalities of World; Am Men of Sci; Pres & Deans of Am Cols & Univs; Other Biogl Listings.

ALDERSHOF, KENT LeROY oc/Management Consultant; b/Jan 13, 1936; h/327 Allison Way, Wyckoff, NJ 07481; ba/Ridgewood, NJ; c/Ann Loraine, Brian Kent, Curtis David; p/Peter R and Margaret M Aldershof, Cedar Rapids, IA; ed/BSEE, IA St Univ, 1959; MSEE, Polytech Inst of NY, 1966; MBA, Harvard Bus Sch, 1965; pa/Pres, Mgmt Strategies Inc, 1980-; Dir, Corp Devel & Planning Div, Am Cyanamid Co, 1972-79; Sr Conslt & Mgr, The Boston Consltg Grp Inc, 1968-72; Fin

Planner, Irwin Mgmt Co Inc, 1965-68; Fin Planner: IBM Corp, RCA Corp, Grumman Corp, 1959-64; Dir, N Am Soc for Corp Planning, NYC; Mem, AF&AM; cp/Trustee, Emma Willard Sch, Troy, NY; Mem, World Future Soc; Mem, Intl Soc for Philosophical Enquiry; r/Prot; hon/Author, *Perspectives on Experience 1970, Parables for Planners 1983*; George F Baker Scholar, 1964; Thayer Awd, Harvard Univ, 1965; Baker Foun Fellow, 1965; W/W: in E, in Computer Graphics; S & P Register of Execs.

ALDRICH, RICHARD J oc/Research Agronomist; b/Apr 16, 1925; h/1715 Woodrail Avenue, Columbia, MO 65201; ba/Columbia, MO; m/June E; c/Judith, Sharon, Jeffrey; p/George and Eva Aldrich (dec); sp/Percy and Ella Ellison (dec); ed/BS, MI St Univ, 1948; PhD, OH St Univ, 1950; mil/1943-46; pa/Agronomist, USDA & Res Spec, Rutgers St Univ, 1950-57; Asst Dir AES, MI St Univ, 1957-64; Assoc Dir AES & Assoc Dean Col of Agronomy 1964-76, Prof Agronomy 1978-80, Res Agronomist, USDA & Prof Agronomy 1981-, Univ of MO-Columbia; Admr & CSRS, USDA, 1976-78; Am Soc Agronomy, 1948-57; WSSA, 1954-57 & 1981-; Pres 1975, Mem 1957-78, Agronomy Res Inst; Chm 1975, Mem Explorer Sta Sect, NASULGC, 1957-78; Sect on Nom'g Com 1974, Mem 1970-, AAAS; r/Prot; hon/Author of Book, *Weed-Crop Ecol: Principles in Weed Mgmt*, 1984; Num Articles Pub'd in Profl Sci Jours; Alpha Zeta, 1948; Phi Kappa Phi, 1947; Sigma Xi, 1950; Gamma Sigma Delta, 1967; Am Men & Wom of Sci; Ldrs in Ed; W/W in Am Col & Univ Adm.

ALDRICH, STEPHANIE RAE oc/Analytical Chemist; b/Jun 26, 1944; h/1215 Earl Road, Michigan City, IN 46360; ba/Chesterton, IN; c/Todd Clifton, Robert LeRoy; p/Steven Paul Hegedus Sr, LaGrange, IL; Fannie Alberta Beck Hegedus (dec); ed/Att'd Purdue Univ, 1972-74; Grad, Varian Inst of Chromatography, Pk Ridge, IL, 1980; pa/Tchr Reality Therapy, Dir of Activs & Rec, Woodview Rehab Ctr, Michigan City, IN, 1972-74; Served Metall Apprenticeship & Sand Control at Josam Mfg, 1977-79; Worked in QC at Manley Bros, 1979, Mgr QC 1981; AAAS; Nat Assn of Female Execs; Mem Chem Engrg Prod Res Panel; r/Luth; hon/Aldrich Method Accepted as 100 % Accurate, 1981; Sev Writings of Free-Verse Poetry Pub'd by *New Worlds Unltd*, 1976-80; W/W Am Wom; Personalities in W & MW.

ALDRICH, THOMAS ALBERT oc/Executive; b/Nov 30, 1923; h/1355 Commons Drive, Sacramento, CA 95825; ba/Sacramento, CA; m/Virginia Peterson; c/Sharon Elaine (Lingis), Pamela Kay (Williams), Thomas Charles; p/John Albert Aldrich (dec); Georgia Opal Hilliard Aldrich, TX; sp/Marenus and Annie Peterson (dec); ed/Att'd TX A&M Univ, 1942-43; Grad, Inst of Meteorology, Univ of Chgo, 1944; Grad, Air War Col, 1960; BA Math 1961, MBA 1968, George Wash Univ; mil/USAF, Maj Gen Ret'd; pa/Command 2nd Lt, USAAF, 1943; Pilot, Meteorologist, 1944-68; Dir War Plans, HQ's, Mil Airlift Command, Scott AFB, IL, 1968; Dept Chief Staff/Plans, 1974-75; Cmdr, 9th Weather Recon-

naissance Wing, McClellan AFB, CA, 1968-69; Cmdr, US Forces Azores, Portugal, 1971-73; VCmdr 1970-71, Cmdr 1973-74, Air Weather Ser, Scott AFB; Cmdr, 22nd AF, Travis AFB, CA, 1975-78; Ret'd, Maj Gen, 1978; VP & Corp Rep, Anheuser-Busch Cos Inc, 1978-; Dir, CA Mfrs Assn; Dir Mktg Intl Corp; Mem, US Brewers Assn; Mem, AF Assn; r/Presb; hon/Dist'd Ser Medal; Legion of Merit w OLC; Meritorious Ser Medal; Order of Merit (Portugal).

ALEJANDRE, EDWARD FIDEL oc/Artist, Preservationist; b/May 18, 1948; h/2307 Wayne Avenue, Los Angeles, CA 90027; ba/Same; p/Fidel Aldama (dec) and Alice Anthony Alejandre, Canoga Park, CA; ed/BA (Spanish) 1971, BA (Art) 1973, CA St Univ; pa/Tchr, Norwalk La Mirada Unified Schs 1973-79, LA Unified Sch Dist 1979-; Creates Pen & Ink Renderings & Paintings to Presv the Architectural Heritage of the US; Nat Trust for Hist Presv; Californians for Presv Action; Hist Soc of So CA; LA Hist Soc; Soc of Architectural Histns; Glendale Art Soc; N Univ Park Commun Assn; LA Conservancy; hon/W/W in W.

ALESCHUS, JUSTINE L oc/Real Estate Broker; b/Aug 13, 1925; h/PO Box 267 Tanglewood Drive, Smithtown, NY 111787; ba/Lake Ronkonkoma, NY; m/John; c/Verdene Jan, Janine Kimberley, Joanna Lauren; sp/Walter and Mildred Lawrence (dec); sp/Mr and Mrs John Aleschus (dec); att'd Rutgers Univ; pa/Dept Sec, Am Bapt Home Mission Soc; Claims Examr, Republic Ins Co; New Home Sales Mgr Damon Homes; Exclusive Broker, Estate Kenneth H Leeds; Past Pres, Nassau-Suffolk Coun of Hosp Auxs, Hon Mem & Past Pres Aux of St John's Epis Hosp, 1975-77; Mem of Comm on Hosp Auxs of the Hosp Assn of NY St, 1984; Bd of Dir, VP, Comm Adv Bd of St John's Epis Hosp, 1984; Treas, W Suffolk Civic Assn; Co-VChm, J&EI; Pres, LI Coalition Sensible Growth; LI Assn; LI Bus Assn; LI Ctr B&P Wom, Smithtown BPW Netwk, Wm's Hlth Alliance, Smithtown Wm's Clb; r/Luth; hon/Hon Mem Aux of St John's Epis Hosp; W/W: of Am Wm, in Real Est Nat.

ALEXANDER, BENJAMIN HAROLD oc/University President; b/Oct 18, 1921; h/3520 Rittenhouse, Northwest, Washington DC 20015; ba/Washington, DC; m/Mary Ellen Spurlock; c/Drew Wilson; Dawn Criket; Bush Manoah Alexander (dec); Annie Willie Alexander; sp/Charles N and Ruby Wilson Alexander; ed/BA Chem, Univ of Cinc, 1943; MS Chem, Bradley Univ, 1950; PhD Chem, Georgetown Univ, 1957; Grants Assoc Tng Prog, NIH, 1967-68; mil/AUS, 1946-47, Tech Sgt; USAR, 1947-65; pa/Pres, Univ of DC, 1982-; Pres, Chgo St Univ, 1974-82; Asst to Chief, Gen Res Support Br, Div Res Resources, NIH, 1971-74; Admr, New Hlth Careers Proj; Spec Asst to Dir for Disadvantaged, Nat Ctr for Hlth Ser Res & Devel, 1968-71; Mem, Joint Bd on Sci Ed, Wash DC, 1958-71; Ednl Com, Urban Leag, Wash DC, 1962-66; cp/YMCA Boys Ldr, Cinc, 1935-43; Active in PTA, Wash DC, 1958-71; Bd Mem, Jackson Pk Hosp, Chgo, 1974; Bd Mem, Chgo S C of C, 1974; r/Meth; hon/Author of Article,

"Will Man Survive His Polluted Envir," 1976; Also Articles in *Vital Spchs of Day*, 1980 & *Sense, Courage & Profl Competency*, 1981; Recip of 13 Commends & 12 Cits, AUS, 1946-47; Cert of Recog, Walter Reed Army Inst, 1967; Am Men of Sci; W/W in Am.

ALEXANDER, ELLA M oc/Management Consultant, Trainer; b/Aug 21, 1947; h/1295 Donnelly Avenue, B8, Atlanta, GA 30310; p/Vera S Kinsey, Atlanta, GA; ed/BA, Clark Col, 1968; MA, Univ WI, 1971; pa/Mgmt Analyst, US Gen Sers Adm, 1078-82; Ednl Coor, GA Dept of Offender Rehab, 1977-78; Equal Opport Spec/Generalist, EEOC, 1975-77; cp/Pres, Bd Dirs, Atlanta Wom's Netwk, 1979-81, Dir, St-wide Netwk, ERA GA, 1978-79; VP, Pubs Dir, Feminist Action Alliance, 1977-79; Chp Coor, Bd Dirs, Proposition Theater Co, 1979; hon/Author *Task & Intratask Differences in Vocab Perf*; Outstg Yg Wom of Am.

ALEXANDER, LENORA COLE oc/Federal Government Official; b/May 9, 1935; h/3020 Brandywine Street, Northwest, Washington, DC 20008; ba/Washington, DC; m/T M Sr; p/Susie Stamper Cole, Buffalo, NY; ed/BS, SUNY, 1957; MEd 1969, PhD 1974, SUNY-Buffalo; pa/Dir of Wom's Bur, US Dept Labor, Wash, DC, 1981-; VP Student Affairs, Univ of DC, 1978-81; VP Student Life, The Am Univ, Wash, DC, 1974-77; Dir Coop Col Ctr 1972, Asst to VP Student Affairs 1968-Feb 1972 & Jul 1973, Res Asst 1968-69, SUNY-Buffalo; Tchr, Bd of Ed, Chgo, 1961-68; Tchr, Ctl Sch Dist # 1, Lancaster, NY, 1957-61; Mem Bd of Dirs, Legal Aid Soc of Wash, DC, 1975-77; Mem Bd of Dirs, Wash Opport for Wom, 1974-76; cp/Mem Bd of Dirs, DC C of C, 1979-81; Commr, DC Rental Accommodations Comm, 1978-79; r/Prot; hon/Dist'd Alumni Awd, SUNY-Buffalo, 1983.

ALEXANDER, MELTON LEE oc/Attorney; b/Jan 4, 1927; h/2044 Cedarcrest Drive, Birmingham, AL 35214; ba/Birmingham, AL; m/Beverly Ann Lankford; c/Melton Lee II, Susan Denise, Craig Alan, Richard Roy; p/Richard Lincoln Alexander and Marie Owens (dec); sp/Eloise Lankford, Lipscomb, AL; ed/AB 1950, LLB Sch of Law 1954, Univ of AL; mil/AUS (Paratroops) 1944-46; AUS, 1951-53, Capt Inf & Co Cmdr; pa/Spec Agt Cleveland, OH & Wash DC 1954-66, Spec Agt Supvr B'ham 1962-66, FBI; Atty, Asst US Atty, 1st Asst US Atty Chief Prosecutor, Chief Crim Div N Dist of AL, US Dept Justice, 1966-82; Mem, Nat Bd of Advrs; Mem, Nat Security Coun; cp/Mem, Assn of AUS; Mem, Anglo-Am Soc; r/Bapt; hon/Phi Beta Kappa, 1950; Farrah Order Jurisp, 1951; Edit Bd, *Atlanta Law Review*; Bronze Star Medal; Combat Inf Badge; Sr Parachutist Badge; Atty Gen's Outstg Ser Awd, 1969 & 1982; Dir's Hon Awd, US Secret Ser, 1982; Outstg Ser Awd, FBI, 1969; W/W: in Am, in S & SW, in AL.

ALEXANDER, PATRICIA MULLINS oc/Professor; b/Oct 28, 1947; h/703 Chalet Court, College Station, TX 77840; ba/College Station, TX; c/John Franklin II; p/William C and Rose A Mullins, Alexandria, VA; ed/BA Elem Ed, Bethel Col, 1970; MEd Elem & Early Childhood Ed (Rdg Spec), James Madison Univ, 1979; PhD Rdg Ed, Univ of MD-Col Pk, 1981; pa/Asst Prof Ednl Curric & Instrn 1981-, Proj Coor for Dean's Grant Proj, Col of Ed 1981-, TX A&M Univ; Pt-time Instr 1979-80, Grad Asst 1980-81, Univ of MD; Instr Exceptl Students Rdg & Math Lab 1977-79, Sci Tchr (1973-74) & Lang Arts Rdg Tchr (1974-77) Grade 5 Woodstock Mid Sch, Shenandoah Co Public Schs, VA; Phy Sci Tchr Grades 7 & 8, St Thomas More Sch, Arlington, VA, 1970-71; Mem: Am Ednl Res Assn; Col Rdg Assn; IRA; Nat Rdg Conf; Nat Assn for Gifted Chd; Phi Delta Kappa; r/Cath; hon/Author, Over 16 Articles Pub'd in Profl Ednl Jours incl'g: *Jour Rdg Behavior, Jour Ednl Res, Nat Rdg Conf Yrbook, Rdg Psych*, Others; BA summa cum laude, Bethel Col, 1970; Outstg Yg Female Scholar Nom, Col Ed, TX A&M Univ, 1982; W/W: in Am Cols & Univs, of Am Wom.

ALEXANDER, ROBERT J oc/Professor; b/Nov 26, 1918; h/944 River Road, Piscataway, NJ 08854; ba/New Brunswick, NJ; m/Joan P; c/Anthony R, Margaret A Brixton; p/Ralph S Alexander, Hightstown, NJ; Ruth J Alexander (dec); sp/George and Augusta Powell (dec); ed/BA 1940, MA 1941, PhD 1950, Columbia Univ; mil/USAF, 1942-45; pa/Bd of Ec Warfare, Jan-Apr 1942; Ofc of Inter Am Affairs, 1945-46; Prof, Rutgers St Univ, 1947-; Mem, Am Ec Assn; Mem, Am Studies Assn; Mem, Mid Atl Coun of Latin Am Studies, Inter Am Assn for Democracy & Freedom; hon/Author, 27 Books & Over 700 Articles Pub'd; Ofcr of Order of Condor of the Andes (Bolivia), 1962; W/W in E; Am Men of Sci.

ALEXANDER, SHARON KAY oc/Medical Technologist, b/Aug 10, 1953; h/316 Glasgow Street, Pottstown, PA 19464; m/Mitchell H; c/Christopher Mitchell; p/Clyde William (dec) and Jewell (Gibbons) Campbell; Rosamond Alexander, Marion, IL; ed/AS w hons, John A Logan Jr Col, 1973; BA Microbiol, So IL Univ, 1975; Postgrad Studies, 1975-76; pa/Lib Asst, John A Logan Jr. Col, 1973; Med Asst, Secy, Dr Hugh D McGowan (Carbondale, IL), 1973-77; Secy, Container Stapling Corp, 1977; Co-Asst Ofc Mgr, Am Investmt, 1977; Med Transcriptionist, Marion Meml Hosp, 1977-78; Med Technologist, Herrion Hosp, 1978-83; Med Technologist, Paoli Meml Hosp, 1984-; So IL Med Technol Ed Grp; S Ctl Assn for Clin Microbiol; Assoc Mem, Am Soc of Clin Pathols; hon/IL St Scholar, 1971-72, Phi Theta Kappa; W/W: Amg Am HS Students, of Am Wom, of Wom.

ALEXANDER, STEVE oc/Management Consultant; b/Jun 29, 1951; h/4158 Balboa Way, San Diego, CA 92117; ba/San Diego, CA; m/Lynette; p/Alexander D and Anne M Szymanski, Santa Barbara; ed/BA Behavioral Sci, Merrimack Col, N Andover, MA, 1975; MA Behavioral Sci, US Intl Univ, San Diego, CA, 1978; Completed Num Other Profl Courses; Mgmt Conslt, Self-Employed, 1981-; Exec Dir, CA Assn of Marriage & Fam Therapists, 1980-82; Assoc Dir, San Diego Fam Inst; Conslt, Media Liaison, Aseltine Sch; Dir Communs & Asst Dir Social Action Projs, Merrimack Col; Mem Commun Chapt, Nat Mgmt Assn, 1982-; Mem, Pers Mgmt Assn, 1982-; Mem San Diego Chapt, Soc for Advmt of Mgmt, 1982-; Mem, Am Soc

Assn Execs, 1979-82; Mem, APGA, 1979-82; Mem, San Diego Mtl Hlth Assn; Num Other Profl Assn Mbrships; cp/Gov Appt to Bd of Behavioral Examrs, 1982-; Gov's Coun on Wellness & Phy Fitness, 1982-; Dept Mayor Appt to Telecote Canyon Adv Com, 1982-; Neighborhood Coor, San Diego Commun Alert Prog, 1982-; Mem Fin Com, Aseltine Sch Bd of Dirs, 1981-; Mem Bd of Dirs, Uptown Commun Planners, 1982-; Mem Prog Review Panel, U Way, 1982-; Mem, Commun Cong, 1976-; Mem, Mensa Soc; Mem (1981-) & Dir (1983-), Dem Profl Clb; Mem, Gtr San Diego C of C, 1982-; Mem, Clairemont Town Coun, 1983-; Num Other Civic Positions; hon/Scroll of Hon, CA Assn of Marriage & Fam Therapists, 1982; Vol of Yr Awd, San Diego Dem Party, 1982; Good Ser Awd, BSA Troop 988, 1978; Outstg Achmt Awd, Merrimack Col, 1975; Outstg Yg Men in Am, US JCs, 1982; W/W: in CA, in W, in Am & Indust, Personalities of W & MW; Other Biogl Listings.

ALEXANDER, SUSAN REED oc/Study Manager, Economic Analyst; b/Mar 3, 1941; ba/Houston, TX; p/Andrew Stirling and Betsy Reed Miller Alexander; ed/AB Math, Sweet Briar Col, 1963; Grad Wk, Golden Gate Univ, 1977-79; MBA Fin, Univ of Houston, 1984; pa/Adm Asst, Earl & Wright Constrn Engrs, SF, 1965-72; Programmer, Analyst (SF) 1972-79, Ec Analyst (Houston) 1979-81, Study Mgr, Ec Analyst (Houston) 1981-, Bechtel Petro Inc; cp/Mem, Jr Leag of SF Inc, 1965-74; Mem, Lifemaster, Am Contract Bridge Leag, 1974; hon/W/W of Am Wom.

ALEXANDER, WILLIAM NEBEL oc/Dental Educator; b/May 22, 1929; h/300 Forest Point Drive, Brandon, MS 39042; ba/Jackson, MS; m/Lorraine Michaela; c/Kathleen, Gregory, Christopher, Jeffrey, Steven; p/William H and Ida M Alexander; sp/Elmer Berg (dec); Mary Berg, Brandon, MS; ed/Pre-Dentistry, St Vincent Coll, 1949; DDS, Univ of Pgh, 1953; Cert, Walter Reed Army Hosp, 1954; Cert in Oral Med, Univ of PA, 1961; MSEd, Jackson St Univ, 1982; mil/AUS, 1953-78, Col; pa/Intern, Walter Reed Army Hosp, 1953-54; Dental Ofcr & Chief Clinician, US Forces Austria & Italy, 1954-57; Cmdg Ofcr, Dental Det, Ft Kiley, KS, 1957-60; Chief Oral Med Ser, Letterman Army Hosp, SF, 1961-66; Chief Clinician & Conslt, AUS Europe, 1966-69; Cmdg Ofcr, 257th & 499th Med Det, Vietnam, 1969-70; Dir, Gen Dental Residency, Ft Hood, TX, 1970-74; Chm, Dental Ed, Madigan Army Med Ctr, 1974-75; Prof & Dir, Patient Adm, Univ of MS Sch of Dentistry, 1978-; Am Dental Assn, 1953-; AAAS, 1960-; Fellow, Am Col of Dentists, 1966-; Fellow & Diplomate, Am Bd of Oral Med, 1969-; Intl Assn Dental Res, 1978-; Am Acad Oral Pathol, 1972-; Chapt Pres, Omicron Kappa Upsilon, 1953-; US Power Sqdrn, 1964; r/Rom Cath; hon/Author, Over 25 Jour Articles & Abstracts; Author of Books: *Users Guide to Prob Oriented Dental Record*, 1980; *Lab Med for Dentists*, 1980; Contbg Author & Co-Editor, *GINN: Oral Hlth of the Elderly*, 1984; Omicron Kappa Upsilon, 1953; Phi Kappa Phi, 1982; Am Col of Dentists, 1966; Sigma Xi, 1980; 3 Army Commend Medals;

Bronze Star, 1970; Legion of Merit, 1978; W/W: in World, in Frontier Sci & Technol.

ALEXEFF, IGOR oc/Professor; b/Jan 5, 1931; h/2790 Turnpike, Oak Ridge, TN 37830; ba/Knoxville, TN; m/Anne I (Fabina); c/Alexander, Helen; p/Tamara (Tchirkow) Alexeff; ed/BA, Harvard Univ, 1952; MS, Univ of WI, 1955; PhD 1959, Postdoct Study 1959-60, Univ of Zurich (Switzerland); pa/Elect Engr, Westinghouse Res Lab, 1952-53; Elect Engr, Oak Ridge Nat Lab, 1960-70; Prof Elect Engrg, Univ of TN, 1971-; Vis'g Profships: Japan, India, S Africa, Brazil; Mem & Num Ofcs, IEEE; Secy-Treas Plasma Div, Am Phy Soc; Sigma Xi; Mensa; r/E Orthodox; hon/Author, Over 100 Articles Pub'd in Tech Jours; Holder of 4 US Patents (1 Pending) in Field; Fellow: Am Phy Soc; IEEE; Recip, Weinberg Prize, Oak Ridge Nat Lab; W/W: in World, in Am, in S & SW.

ALFORD, GLYNN HERMAN oc/Consultant in Process Control; b/Jan 14, 1926; h/10 East Levert, Luling, LA 70070; ba/Luling, LA: m/Ruth Mae Gavin; c/Cathy Ruth Alford Davis, Ronald Glynn, Kevin Randolph; p/Homer Sherman Alford, Vero Bch, FL; Tinie Estelle Clark Alford (dec); ed/BSEE 1955, MSEE 1956, GA Tech; mil/USNR; pa/Asst Film Dir, Evening Star Broadcasting Co (Wash DC), 1950-53; Instrument Engr, E I duPont de Nemours & Co (Victona, TX) 1956-57; Chemstrand Corp (Pensacola, FL), 1957-61; Sr Devel Engr, Monsanto Co (Chocolata Bayou, TX), 1961-67; Sys Grp Supvr, Prin Engrg Spec, Monsanto, 1977-82; Conslt in Measurement & Controls, 1982-; Instrument Soc of Am; cp/Repub; Neighborhood Watch; Former BSA Ldr; r/Bapt; hon/Author Num Profl Pubs; HS Valedictorian, 1943; Louis-Allis Sr S'ship, 1954-55; FL & GA Power Sys Analysis F'ship, 1955-56; Tehg F'ship, GA Tech, 1954-55; Monsanto Co Achmt Awd, 1979, 1981; Eta Kappa Nu; W/W S & SW.

AL-HIBRI, AZIZAH Y oc/Editor; b/Jan 14, 1943; h/1810 South Rittenhouse Square, Apartment 1504, Philadelphia, PA; ba/Philadelphia, PA; p/Yahia M T El-Hibri, Beirut, Lebanon; Yusra M Al-Midani (dec); ed/BA Phil, Am Univ of Beirut, 1966; MA Phil, Wayne St Univ, 1968; PhD Phil 1975, JD Law Sch 1985, Univ of PA; pa/Editor-in-Chief: *HYPATIA: A Jour of Feminist Phil*, & *Jour of Comparative Bus & Capital Mkt Law*, 1984-; Sum Assoc, Davis Polk & Wardwell, 1984; Sum Intern for Judge Louis H Pollak, US Dist Ct, Jul-Aug, 1983; Sum Intern for Judge Wm F Hall Jr, US Magistrate, Jun-Jul, 1983; Vis'g Assoc Prof, Wash Univ-St Louis, 1981-82; Assoc Prof, TX A&M Univ, 1975-83; Mem, ABA; Mem, Am Soc Intl Law; Pres So Div (1977-79), Soc Wom in Phil; Mem Coor Coun (1981-82), Nat Wom Studies Assn; hon/Author of Book, *Deontic Logic: A Comprehensive Appraisal & a New Proposal*, 1978; Editor, *Wom & Islam*, 1982; Co-Editor, *Technol & Human Affairs*, 1981; Num Articles incl'g: "Reproduction, Mothering & the Origins of Patriarchy," in *Mothering: Essays in Feminist Theory*, 1984; Strengthening Grant (Title) 1981, Strengthening Grant Mini-Grant (Title XII) 1980, Sum

Res Grant 1978, Mini-Grant 1977, Philip S Harper Grant 1981, TX A&M Univ; W/W of Am Wom; Intl W/W of Wom.

ALLAN, LARRY oc/Photographer, Lecturer; b/Apr 28, 1940; h/PO Box 99585, San Diego, CA 92109; ba/Same; m/Jalma Barrett; p/Mr and Mrs Albert Allan (dec); sp/Mr and Mrs James Connolly Barrett (dec); ed/Grad Profl Photo, NY Inst of Photo, 1960; pa/Photojour, *Pueblo Chieftain* & *Salt Lake Desert News*; News Photog, CBS/TV; VP, *Photo World Mag*; Freelance Profl Photog; Owner & Photog, Allan/The Animal Photogs; Photo Lectr, Allan/Ideas; Dir of Photo, The Photographic Inst; Mem, Profl Photogs of Am; Mem, Profl Photogs of CA; Bd of Dirs 1980-81, Editor *The San Diegan* 1982-, Profl Photogs of San Diego Co; Mem, Am Soc of Mag Photogs; Mem, Soc for Photographic Ed; Mem, Photo Admrs; Mem, Photo Mktg Assn; cp/Mason, Scottish Rite, Shrine; Vol Sgt, Animal Rescue Resv, San Diego Humane Soc; hon/Author, Articles & Photos Pub'd in Num Profl Mags incl'g: *Petersen's Photo-Graphic Mag, The Profl Photog Mag, The Rangefinder Mag, Photo Jour* (France), *Art Dirs' Index, Am Showcase, Photog's Mkt,* Others; Assoc Fellow, Royal Photographic Soc (Gt Brit).

ALLAN, ROGER DEMUTH oc/Executive; b/Oct 12, 1933; h/2801 Adams Mill Road, Northwest, Washington, DC 20009; ba/Washington, DC; c/Theresa Joan, Susan Marie; p/Stuart E Allan (dec); Clara D Allan, Des Moines, IA; ed/BA Jour, Univ of Notre Dame, 1957; Att'd Law Sch, George Wash Univ, 1962-63; mil/AUS, Discharged 1956; pa/Pres & Owner, Roger D Allan (Public Relats/Affairs) Co, 1984-; VP Corp Sect, E Bruce Harrison Co, 1979-83; Dir Hwy Div 1973-79, Dir Public Relats 1963-66, Associated Gen Contractors; Dir Public Relats, Elect Industs Assn, 1968-73; Acct Exec, Ketchum, McLeod & Grove, 1967-68; Writer, US C of C, 1966-67; Public Relats Asst, Nat Assn Rltrs, 1961-63; Dir Public Relats, The Homestead, 1959-61; News Reporter, *Covington Virginian*, 1957-59; Pres Nat Capital Chapt, Public Relats Soc of Am, 1979; Chm, Wash Road Gang (Trans Lobbyiests), 1979; cp/Pres Potomac Val Chapt, Myasthenia Gravis Foun, 1983-84; r/Rom Cath; hon/Monthly Columnist: Comml Trade Pub on Energy & Envir Issues; Comml Trade Pub on Home Remodeling; Contbr to *Funk & Wagnalls Ency*; Author of Num Other Articles; W/W: in Wash, in S & SW.

ALLARD, MARVEL JUNE oc/Professor of Psychology, Consultant to Research and Development Companies; h/24 Curtis Street, Auburn, MA; ba/Worcester, MA; p/Adrian C and Marvel G Allard, Grosse Pointe, MI; ed/AB, MA, PhD, MI St Univ; ca/7 NSF F'ships, 1959-64; MI St Univ, 1958-66; Proj Dir & Res Sci, Am Univ, 1966-67; Prin Staff & Sr Staff, Opers Res Inc, 1967-70; Res Conslt (Pvt), 1970-; Prof, Psych, Worcester St Col, 1973-; Am Psychol Assn; hon/Author, Over 20 Res Articles; 4 Undergrad S'ships; 7 NSF F'ships; 1 SCD Assoc'ship; 1 Scholastic Prize; Dist'd Ser Awd, Worcester St Col, 1981; W/W: Am Men & Wom of Sci; Wom in Ed; Intl Wom in Sci; Am Wom, E; Notable Ams; Registry of Wom in Sci.

ALLEN, ARIS T oc/Physician; b/Dec 27, 1910; h/1323 Magnolia Avenue, Annapolis, MD 21403; ba/Annapolis, MD; m/Faye W; c/Aris T Jr, Lonnie W; p/James and Marietta Allen (dec); ed/MD; mil/USAF, Capt; pa/Pvt Med Pract, Annapolis Over 33 Yrs; Mem & Pres, Anne Arundel Gen Hosp Staff; Mem: Anne Arundel Co Med Staff; Am Acad Fam Phys; AMA; Monumtl Med Soc; Past VPres, Med-Chirurgical Fac St of MD; Bd of Dirs, MD Acad Fam Phys; cp/Past Mem, Anne Arundel Bd of Ed; Chm, Repub MD St Ctl Com; Com of Bicent Comm; Past Bd of Dirs: BSA & (Life Mem) NAACP, Anne Arundel Co Commun Col; Gtr Annapolis C of C; Elected Mem, MD St Sen; Elected MD St Legis, 1966; Elected MD St Legis Minority Whip, 1967-68 & 1970-73; Paul Harris Fellow, Rotary Intl, 1978; Anne Arundel Co Brs, NAACP Awd, 1976; Humanitarian Awd, Frontier Intl, 1977; Awd of Merit, Monumtl Med Soc; Alpha Phi Alpha Frat Awd, 1973; Alumni Achmt Awd, Howard Univ; Others; W/W: in Am, in World, Among Black Ams, in En Am Polits.

ALLEN, BELLE oc/Executive; b/Aug 1; ba/Chgo, IL; m/William Karp (dec); p/Isaac and Clara (dec); sp/Harry Karp (dec); Sadie Karp; ed/Humanities, Univ of Chgo; pa/Pres, Wm Karp Consltg Co Inc, 1979-; Pres, Belle Allen Communs, 1961-; VPres & Treas, Cultural Arts Surveys Inc, 1965-79; Conslt & Dir, Am Diversified Res Corp, 1967-70; Mem, IL Gov's Grievance Panel for St Employees, 1979-; Nom, Consumer Advr Coun, Bd of Govs, Fed Resv Sys, 1979; Mem, Adv Gov'g Bd, IL Coalition on Employmnt of Wom, 1979; Conslt, IL Comm on Technol Prog, 1965-67; Conslt, The City Clb of Chgo, 1962-65; Mem (By Invitation), AAAS, 1981-; Bd of Dirs, Chp Mbrship Com, Affirmative Action Assn, 1981-; Mem, Indust Relats Res Assn, 1981-; Mem, Soc of Pers Admrs, 1979; cp/Mem, Sarah Siddons Soc, 1981-; hon/Editor & Contbr, Over 65 Articles & Papers in Profl & Bus Pubs, Jours, Comm Reports & Manuals; Plus Book: *Opers Res & Mgmt of Mtl Hlth Sys*; Selected as Ref Source, Am Bicent Res Inst, Lib of Human Resources, 1973; Spec Communs Prog, The White House, 1961; Dist'd Ser Awd, Outstg Ser, Publicity Clb of Chgo, 1968; Cit for Outstg Ser, U Cerebral Palsy Assn of Chgo, 1954; W/W: of Am Wom, in Fin & Indust; Num Other Biogl Listings.

ALLEN, BERTHA LEE oc/Clinical Social Worker; b/Mar 28, 1908; h/Route 9, Box 796, Lucedale, MS 39452; ba/Same; p/Charles Hamilton and Winnie McLeod Allen (dec); ed/BA, MS Univ for Wom, 1932; Att'd Univ AL 1936, LA St Univ 1937, MS St Univ 1939, Univ MS 1940; MSW, Tulane Univ, 1949; pa/5th Grade Tchr, Rocky Creek (Lucedale, MS), 1932-33; Tchr, HS Eng & Latin, Libn, Agricola (MS), 1933-36; Tchr, Tchula (MS), 1936-44; Child Welfare Wkr, MS Dept of Public Welfare, 1944-48; Caseworker, Columbia (MS) Tng Sch, 1949-50; Casework Supvr, Chief Social Wkr, O Sawatomie (KS) St Hosp, 1950-51; Dir of Casework, MS Chd's Home Soc, 1952-54; Casework Supvr, Child & Fam Ser, 1954-58; Supvr of Casework Pract, Fam Cnslg Ctr (Mobile, AL), 1958-65; Casewkr, ARC Disaster Sers, Hurricane Betsy (New Orleans), 1965; Casewkr, Fam Ser Soc (New Orleans), 1965-66, Jewish Fam & Chd's Ser (New Orleans), 1966-71; Willow Wood, New Orleans Home for Jewish Aged, 1971-73; Pvt Pract, New Orleans, Lucedale, Mobile, 1969-; Conslt, Wilmer Itall & Prot Chd's Home (Mobile) 1954-65, YWCA Teen-age Com (Mobile) 1962, Providence Nsg Home (New Orleans) 1973-77, Willow Wood New Orleans Home for the Jewish Aged 1974; MS Ed Assn; PTA MS, 1932-44: MS Conf of Social Work, 1944-54; Charter Mem & Secy, MS Mt HLTH Assn, 1953-54; Mobile Coun of Social Agys, Casework Com 1954-58, Inter-agy Planning Com 1958-62, In-ser Tng Com 1963-65; Bd Dirs, Mulherin Home for Spastic Chd (Mobile), 1958-59; Fam Ser Assn of Am, SEn Planning Com 1964-65; Assn of Maternity & Adoption Agys, Secy 1969-70; Am Assn of Psychi Social Wkrs, 1952-55; NASW, Charter & Gold Card Mem 1955-; ACSW, 1955-; LA Soc for Clin Social Wkrs, 1955-; IPA, 1968-69; cp/Oakliegh Gdn Clb, 1964-65; hon/20th Cent Soc Awd for Superior S'ship, 1926, 1927, 1928; Eta Sigma Phi, 1931-32; Cit for Excell of S'ship, MS Univ for Wom, 1931; Cit & Awd for 25-Yrs of Social Work, Jewish Fam & Chd's Ser, 1969; W/W: in S & SW, of Am Wom, of Wom; Nat Social Dir; Royal Blue Book of Ldrs of Eng Spkg World; 2000 Wom of Achmt, Personalities of S; DIB.

ALLEN, DENIS McGEE oc/Radiologic Engineer; b/Jun 2, 1944; h/Star Route 1762, Eagle River, AK 99577; ba/Anchorage, AK; p/Don Allen, Chgo, IL; Joan Drangas (dec); ed/Att'd Univ of MN, 1963; Att'd Palomar Col, 1964; Att'd Chapman Col, 1965; BA Eng Lit, Univ of IL (Chgo), 1969; MSEd, Chgo St Univ, 1978; mil/USMC, 1962-66; pa/Tchr of Eng, Rdg & Color TV Ser, Indust Skills Ctr, Chgo Bd of Ed, 1969-80; Chief Engr, KSKA-FM Anchorage Public Radio, 1980-83; Adj Prof, Univ of AK, 1980-83; Radiologic Engr, Cancer Therapy Ctr, Providence Hosp, Anchorage, 1983-; Mem: Am Fdn of Tchrs; Soc of Broadcast Engrs; IEEE; Am Radio & Relay Leag; Chgo Tchrs Union; AAAS; Amateur Radio Satellite Corp; Exptl Aircraft Assn; Intl Aerobatic Clb; r/Rom Cath; hon/Author of Poems Pub'd in Lit Mags & Book, *Beyond Poems*, 1970; Other Pubs; Gave Poetry Rdg, Chgo Mus Contemp Art, 1969; DXCC, Am Radio Relay Leag, 1974; W/W: in Engrg, in W & MW, of Intells; Commun Ldrs of Am.

ALLEN, DON L oc/University Dean; b/Mar 13, 1934; h/303 Longview Drive, Sugar Lane, TX 77478; ba/Houston, TX; m/Winnifred Rouse; c/Don Jr, Michael, Susan; p/William A Allen, Elon Col, NC; Gena D Allen, Burlington, NC; ed/MS & DDS; pa/Dean, Univ TX Dental Br-Houston, 1984-; Dean Col of Dentistry, Univ of FL-Gainesville; Pres, Intl Col of Dentists, 1982; Pres, Am Assn of Dental Schs, 1983; Pres, So Conf of Dental Deans & Examrs, 1984; Mem: Intl Assn for Dental Res; Am Dental Assn; Am Acad of Periodontology; r/Prot; hon/Omicron Kappa Upsilon, 1968; Am Col of Dentists, 1973; Intl Col of Dentists, 1974; W/W in Hlth Care; Dist'd Ldrs in Hlth Care; Men & Wom of Distn.

ALLEN, GARY CURTISS oc/Professor; b/Jul 18, 1939; h/6961 Mayo Boulevard, NO, LA 70126; ba/NO, LA; m/Ruth Lee Mayeux; c/Adrienne Lucille, Christopher Gary; p/Mrs H L Allen, Tigard, OR; sp/Mrs L J Mayeux, Crowley, LA; ed/BS Chem, Stanford Univ, 1961; MA Geol, Rice Univ, 1963; PhD Geochem, Univ of NC-Chapel Hill, 1968; pa/Prof 1978-, Assoc Prof 1972-78, Univ of NO; Pres, Sunbelt Assocs Inc, 1978-; Asst Prof, LA St Univ-NO, 1968-72; Hd of Geochem & Petrochem Res Sect, VA Div of Mineral Resources, 1966-68; Mem: Am Chem Soc; Geochem Soc; Geol Soc of Am; Mineralogical Soc of Am; Sigma Gamma Epsilon; (Pres 1977-78), Univ of NO, Sigma Xi; hon/Author of Num Articles on Geol, Mineralogy & Geochem Pub'd in Sci Jours; NASA Res Fellow, Univ of NC-Chapel Hill, 1963-66; W/W in S & SW; Am Men & Wom of Sci.

ALLEN, GARY IRVING oc/Government Official, Neurophysiologist; b/Apr 7, 1942; h/965 Knollwood Road, White Plains, NY 10603; ba/Same; m/Elaine I; c/Michelle Irene, Elisa Joy, Scott Jeremy; p/Ralph W and Lois M Allen, Lockport, NY; ed/BSEE, Cornell Univ, 1965; PhD Physiol, SUNY-Buffalo, 1969; pa/Asst Prof 1971-76, Dir 1975-76, Lab of Neurobiol, Dept Physiol, SUNY-Buffalo; Lectr, Vis'g Scholar Dept Physiol & Anatomy 1976-79, Dir Intl Student Min Devel Base Campus Crusade for Christ 1976-79, Univ of CA-Berkeley; Dir UN Min, Christian Embassy, Campus Crusade for Christ, 1979-83; Adj Asst Prof, Dept Physiol, NY Med Col, 1981-; Pres, Christian Mission for UN Commun, 1983-; Mem: Am Physiol Soc; Soc for Neurosci; Intl Brain Res Org; Asia Soc; Am-Nepal Soc; Am Sci Affil; Metro NY Exec Coun, 1983-; r/Christian; hon/Co-Author of Article, "Cerebrocerebellar Communs Sys," in *Physiol Review*, 1974; Plus Num Other Articles in Sci Jours incl'g: *Exptl Brain Res, Brain Res, Jour of Physiol*, Others; Am Men & Wom of Sci; Men of Achmt; W/W: in E, in Frontier Sci & Technol; Commun Ldrs of Am; Num Other Biogl Listings.

ALLEN, GARY K oc/Aerospace Engineering Consultant; b/Jun 27, 1944; h/15710 Southeast 46 Way, Bellevue, WA 98006; ba/Bellevue, WA; m/Catherine; c/Matthew, Sarah; p/Howard W Allen (dec); Ethel M Allen, Painted Post, NY; sp/William J and Edith W Reardon, Orchard Pk, NY; ed/BSCE, Clarkson Col of Technol, 1962-66; MBA, Nat Univ, San Diego, 1976-77; pa/Conslt, Adv'd Design, RHO Co Inc, 1979-84; Lead Engr, Preliminary Design Spec, ROHR Industs Inc, 1974-79; Sr Structural Anal Engr, Boeing Corp, 1966-73; Mem: AIAA, 1976-84; Nat Adv Bd, Am Security Coun, 1970-76; r/Luth; hon/Co-Author, Num Flight Cert & Tech Proposal Documents; Pride in Excell Awd, 1980; W/W in E.

ALLEN, HOWARD P oc/Executive; ed/BA, Pomona Col; JD, Stanford Univ Law Sch; pa/Pres & Bd of Dirs 1980-, Exec VP 1973-80, Sr VP 1971-73, VP 1962-71, Joined 1954, So CA Edison; Asst Dean & Asst Prof Law, Stanford Univ, 1951-54; Mem: US Supr Ct Bar; Am Judic Soc; ABA; CA St, LA Co, SF Bar Assns; Trustee & Mem of Exec Com, Pomona Col; Nat Prot Co-Chm,

Nat Conf of Christians & Jews; VChm of Bd, Exec Com of LA Olympic Organizing Com, 1983-84; Bd of Dirs, So CA Rapid Transit Dist; Bd Mem, CA St Univ & Col Foun; VP of Chancellor's Assocs & Mem Law Sch Bd of Visitors, Stanford Univ; Mem, Bd of Dirs for Num Cos incl'g: CA Fed Savs & Ln, Republic Corp, ICN Pharms Inc, PSA Inc, Pacific SW Airlines, Computer Scis Corp, MCA Inc, Associated So Investmt Co, Mono Power Co, Pacific Coast Elect Assn, CA Coun for Envir & Ec Balance, Others; cp/St Chm, Californians for Schs, Proposition 1, 1974; Chm, LA Citizens Com for Schs, Propositions A, B & C, 1975; Chm, Proposition 5, 1976; Mem 1971-79, Chm 1971-72, LA Co Election Comm; Chm U Crusade Campaign of En Metro-San Gabriel Val Area, 1975-76; Dir 1969-81, Pres 1978, Chm 1979, LA Area C of C; Num Others; r/Prot; hon/Phi Beta Kappa; Mem, Mayor's Select Com, LA Olympics.

ALLEN, JERRY MICHAEL oc/Aerospace Technologist; b/Jan 19, 1940; h/117 Huxley Place, Newport News, VA 23606; ba/Hampton, VA; m/Carolyn Jolene; c/Michael, Scott, Kellie; p/William H Allen, Forest City, NC; sp/Horace L Harris, Forest City, NC; ed/BS Aerospace Engrg, NC St Univ, 1962; MS Aeospace Engrg, Univ of VA, 1967; pa/Aerospace Technol, Langley Res Ctr, 1962-; Assoc Fellow, AIAA; cp/Mem, Glendale Rec & Civic Assn; Mem, Centre Ct Raquet Clb; r/So Bapt; hon/Author, Over 45 Articles & Tech Reports Pub'd in Sci Jours & Presented at Meetings; Math & Physics Awds, Gardner-Webb Col, 1961; Apollo Achmt Awd, NASA, 1970; Sustained Superior Perf Awd, NASA, 1980; Assoc Fellow, AIAA, 1981; W/W: in Frontier Sci & Technol, in Technol Today, in Aviation & Aerospace; Men of Achmt; Personalities of S; Other Biogl Listings.

ALLEN, JOHN ELDRIDGE oc/Historian, Federal Government Official, Retired; b/Sep 11, 1911; h/7339 South West 82 Street, Apartment 2, South Miami, Florida 33143; m/Mary Edwards; c/Mark E; p/Arthur and Annie Willis Allen (dec); sp/Marvin and Alma Glassco Edwards (dec); ed/BBA, Univ Miami, 1934; MA, George Wash Univ, 1937; mil/USN, 1942-46, Lt Cmdr; pa/Aide, Exec Br, US Govt, 1935-59; Tech Analyst, NSA, Army & Defense Depts, 1948-57; cp/Asst Exec Dir, Lincoln Sequicent Comm, Nat Archives 1958-59; Housing Asst, Univ Miami 1963-74; Com Mem, Nat Lincoln Sequicent Dinner Com Commemoration of 200th Anniv Birth of Marquis de Lafayette, Lafayette Pk, Wash, 1957; Mem Dedication Assembly, Pres Truman Spoke accepting Equestrian Statues Gift from Italy to US, Arlington Bridge Plaza, Wash 1951; Com Mem Opening Ceremonies Grp, Freedom Train Exhib of Am, Union Sta, Wash 1947; Mem Dramatic Presentation of 25-Yr Hist of Arts Clb of Wash 1941; r/Meth; hon/Histn & Editor *Allen Personal Papers & Hist Jours* 1973; Lttr of Apprec & Gratification from the Dir, Nat Security Agy, Wash, 1955; Apprec Soc, Norfolk, VA; Apprec Cert from Canon Treas of York Minster, Mother Ch since 627 AD of N England 1982;

Apprec Cert from Am Biogl Inst l981; Dipl of Hon from Adv Bd Inst, W/W in Commun Ser, London 1973; W/W in Am.

ALLEN, JOHNNY MAC oc/Educator and Public Relations; b/Aug 25, 1937; h/3348 Del Aire Place, Del City, OK 773115; ba/Midwest City, OK; m/Hughanne; c/Anthony Marc, Nichole Julianna, Andrea Danielle; sp/Chester Maxwell, Midwest City, OK; ed/BS 1978, MA 1979; Doct Cand, OSU; AUS 1959-1961; pa/Prog Dir TV News, WX, Sports Anchor, KLOE Radio-TV, 1962-67; Public Ser Dir, Announcer, KBAT Radio, 1967-68; Music Dir News, Anchor, WX, Sports, Announcer, KLOE Radio-TV, 1968-68; Prodn Dir, Announcer, KAKE Radio-TV, 1968-69; Asst Prodn Dir, Announcer, KTOK Radio, 1969-1972; Music Dir, Announcer, KLEC Radio, 1972-73; News Dir, Announcer, KOCY-KXXY-FM Radio, 1973-77; News Dir, Announcer KFNB-FM Radio, 1978-79; News Dir, Instr, KGOU-FM Radio, Univ of OK 1979-1980; Contract Announcer, KWTV-Channel 9, 1974-; Coor, Public Relations Instr, Oscar Rose Jr Col, 1980-; Kappa Tau Alpha; Phi Delta Kappa; Alpha Ipsilon Rho; Sigma Delta Chi, The Soc for Prof Journalists; Public Relats Soc of Am; OK Higher Ed Alumni Assn; Bd Mem, OK Assn of Commun & Jr Col; Instnl Rep to the Coun for the Advmt & Support of Ed; Mem of the Nat Ednl Press Assn; Nat Commun Journ Assn; Elected to the Bd of Dirs of the Del City C of C 1983; Appt'd, CoChm of the MW City C of C Public Image Comm; Appt'd by the MW City Coun to the MW City Tree Bd; r/Cath; hon/Author, Num Profl Pubs; Outstg Achmt Awd from the Univ of OK Chapt of Alpha Epsilon Rho; Bronze Derrick Awd for Best Public Relats Campaign in St of OK for 1981; W/W in S & SW.

ALLEN, JOYCE SMITH oc/Hospital Librarian; b/Aug 1, 1939; h/4908 LeMans Drive, Number X2, Indianapolis, IN 46205; ba/Indpls, IN; m/Jim F; c/Shani J; p/Harold W and Mary E Smith, Teaneck, NJ; ed/BA, Howard Univ, 1961; MLS, Atlanta Univ, 1966; CAS, Univ of IL, 1974; pa/Ref Libn, Med-Dental Lib, Howard Univ, 1966-73; Lib Mgr, Meth Hosp of IN Inc, 1978-; Beta Phi Mu, Lib Hon Soc; Pres, Ctl IN Hlth Sci Lib Consortium, 1974-75; Pres, IN Hlth Sci Lib Assn, 1980-81; Bd of Dir, MW Hlth Sci Lib Netwk, 1974-75; Exec Com, IN Coop Lib Ser Auth, 1976-77; cp/Adv Bd, IN Voc Tech Col, 1979-; r/Bapt; hon/Author Num Profl Pubs; Beta Phi Mu 1967; Ctr for Ldrship Devel, Inc Minority Bus & Profl Achiever Recog Award 1981.

ALLEN, JUDITH oc/College Administrator; b/Dec 13, 1938; h/23 Southworth Street, Williamstown, MA 01267; ba/Williamstown, MA; p/Mrs Roland L Studley, Needham, MA; ed/BA Liberal Studies, 1970; MEd, 1975; Att'd Inst of Exec Mgmt, 1979; pa/Asst to Pres, Wms Col, 1979-; Dir of Admissions & Fin Aid 1976-79, Dir of Fin Aid 1970-76, Regis Col; Mem Bd of Dirs, N Eng Ed Loan Mktg Assn, 1981-; Mem Exec Bd 1976-, VPres 1978-81, MA Higher Ed Assist Corp; hon/Pres, MA Assn of Student Fin Aid Admrs,

1973-75; W/W of Am Wom.

ALLEN, LAYMAN E oc/Professor; b/ June 9, 1927; ba/Ann Arbor, MI; m/ Christine R Patmore (dec); 2nd Emily C Hall; c/Layman G, Patricia R, Phyllip L Hall, Kelly C Hall; ed/Att'd Wash & Jefferson Col, 1946-47; AB Public & Intl Affairs, Princeton Univ, 1951; MPA, Harvard Univ, 1952; LLB, Yale Univ, 1956; mil/USNR, 1945-46; pa/Instr 1958, Sr Fellow & Lectr 1958-59, Asst Prof 1959-63, Assoc Prof 1963-66, Yale Univ Law Sch; Assoc Prof Law 1966-71, Res Sci Mtl Hlth Res 1966-, Prof Law 1971-, Univ of MI; Chm Jurimetrics Com 1961-62, Chm Tchg Methods Com 1968-69, Assn of Am Law Schs; Chm Elect Data Retrieval Com 1966-67, Mem Coun of Sect on Sci & Technol, ABA; VP, N Am Simulation & Gaming Assn; Assn for Symbolic Logic; AMIN-TAPHIL; AAAS; Nat Assn of Tchrs of Math; Am Ednl Res Assn; Num Others; Editor: *Jurimetrics Jour, Jour of Legal Ed, Jour of Conflict Resolution, Simulation/Gaming/ News*, Others; Var Consltg Positions; cp/ Chm Social Action Com, Unitarian Soc of New Haven; Mem, (HOME) Housing Opports Made Equal, Com of Human Relats Coun, New Haven; Trustee, Ctr for Study of Responsive Law; Spec Task Grp Mem w US Gen Acct Offc; hon/ Author: Over 40 Articles Pub'd in Jours; Over 37 Videotapes; Over 27 Books & Book Chapts; Var Games, Puzzles, Reviews; Fellow, Ctr for Adv'd Study in Behavioral Scis; Ford Foun F'ship, Social Scis Res Coun F'ship; Felix S Cohen Prize for Best Essay on Legal Phil, Frances Kellor Prize for Best Essay on Arbitration, Benjamin Scharps Prize for Most Meritorious 3rd Yr Essay, Yale Law Sch.

ALLEN, MICHAEL DAVID oc/Doctor of Chiropractic, Doctor of Naturopathy; b/Jul 24, 1953; h/24992 Express, Laguna Hills, CA 92653; ba/Lake Forest, CA; m/Kristina Marie; c/Matthew Steven; p/Bernard K and Heidi H Allen, Corona, CA; sp/Leo J and Jackie C Suffia, Cayucos, CA; ed/AA 1973; BA 1973; DC 1977; Dr of Naturopathy 1977; pa/Assoc Chiro/Naturopathic Phys, Swan Clin of Natural Healing, 1977-78; Assoc Chiro/Naturopathic Phys, Hlth Tng Ctr (San Diego, CA), 1978; Clin Dir, Chiro/Naturopathic Phys, Serra Natural Healing Clin, 1978-81; Clin Dir, Serra Natural Healing Clin, 1981-; cp/Intl Col of Applied Kinesiology; Am Chiro Assn; CA Chiro Assn; Orange Co Chiro Assn; AR Chiro Assn; Am Naturopathic Assn; Council on Nutrition of the Am Chiro Assn; Nat Iridology Res Assn, Exec Bd Chm; Profl Mem, Touch for Hlth Foun; Intl Col of Applied Nutrition; Nat Academy of Res Biochems; W Coast Res & Pub'g Co; Exec Bd Pres, Saddleback Val C of C; r/Epis; hon/Author, Num Profl Pubs; Dean's List Grad, Citrus Commun Col, 1973; Dean's List Grad, LA Col of Chiro, 1977; Hlth & Immortality, World Plan Exec Coun, 1982; W/W Orange Co.

ALLEN, ROBERT ERWIN oc/Medical Research Official; b/Oct 9, 1941; h/8 Jeb Stuart Court, Potomac, MD 20854; ba/ Washington, DC; m/Roma Leah; c/ Jennifer Kay; p/Mr and Mrs Rusty Walker, Lufkin, TX; sp/Mrs Roma McKenney, Memphis, TN; ed/BA, Stephen F Austin Univ, 1963; PhD, Vanderbilt Med Sch, 1968; pa/Br Chief,

Biotechnol Br, NASA, 1968-76; Exec Secy to NIAMDD, NIH, 1976-78; Spec Asst to Dir Med Res, VA, 1978-; cp/ Parish Staff Coun, U Meth Ch, 1978-; r/Meth; hon/Author of 8 Articles Pub'd on NASA Space Flight Expts, 1969-76; Skylab Achmt Awd & Grp Achmt Awd, NASA', 1974; Spec Achmt Awd, VA, 1980.

ALLEN-NOBLE, ROSIE ELIZA-BETH oc/Administrator in Health Careers Program; b/Jun 22, 1938 h/377 South Harrison Street 4K, East Orange, NJ 07018; ba/Upper Montclair, NJ; c/ Antoinette Celine Monica Noble; p/ Ulysses Grant Allen (dec); ed/BS, Albany St Col, 1960; MS Zool, Atlanta Univ, 1967; cp/Public Sch Tchr, 1960-70; Instr, Spellman Col, 1965-67; Instr & Asst Prof, Rutgers Univ, 1970-76; Vis'g Asst Prof, Seton Hall Univ, 1971-77; Fairleigh Dickinson Univ, 1976-1980; Asst Prof & Coor Med Tech Prog, Univ Med & Dental of NJ; Adj Instr & Ed Conslt 1971-; Admr, Montclair St Col, 1980-; AAUW; AAUP; AFT; Soroptomists Intl; AAAS; NJ Black Edrs; SESS; NAMME; Wom Admrs in Voc Ed; Alpha Kappa Alpha Sorority, Inc; Nat Cong of PTA; NJ Col & Univ Coalition on Wom's Ed; r/Cath; hon/ Author of Article "Succeeding" Pub'd in *Comment* 1982 & *Power* 1982; Dean's List 1959-67; Highest Ranking Sophomore & Jr 1957-59; Highest Ranking Grad Biol Maj 1960; Grad cum laude 1960; Grad w Hons 1967; Merit Awd 1982; W/W in Am Cols & Univs.

ALLENTUCH, ARNOLD oc/Academic Administrator; b/Dec 4, 1930; h/ 49 Fairview Street, Huntington, NY 11743; ba/Newark, NJ; m/Harriet Ray; c/Simon Irving, Sarah Doris; p/Norman Allentuch, Worcester, MA; sp/Lena Ray; ed/BS Mech Engrg, Worcester Polytech Inst, 1953; MS Applied Mechs, Cornell Univ, 1959; PhD Applied Mechs, Polytech Inst of NY, 1962; mil/ USN, 1956-57; pa/Res Assoc, Polytech Inst of NY, 1962-63; Preceptor, Columbia Univ, 1963-64; Asst Prof, Cooper Union, 1964-66; Assoc & Full Prof 1966-71, Assoc VPres Res & Grad Studies 1971-, Newark Col of Engrg/ NJ Inst of Technol; Mem Commun Adv Bd, Ednl Opport Prog, St of NJ & NJ Inst of Technol; Past VChm Bd of Dirs & Past Chm Projs Com, NJ Energy Res Inst; Com on Minorities Task Force, Nat Res Coun, Nat Acad of Engrg; Chp, NJ Univ Res Coor Coun; Mem & Chm, Ed Com, Univ HS Adv Bd; Mem, St Task Force on Grad Studies & Res; Mem Bd of Dirs, Pres's & Exec Coms, Marine Scis Consortium; Chp, Res Adv Coun, Public Ser Elect & Gas Res Corp; Steering Com Reg II, Nat Coun of Univ Res Admrs, 1979-80; Chp, Res Communs Com, Hlth Scis Grp; Num Others; cp/Mem & 1st Ch of Bd, Ferry St Foun; Co-Chp Envir Com, Coun for Res & Devel, St of NJ; Mem, Gov of NJ's Sci Adv Coun; Others; hon/Author, Over 15 Articles Pub'd in Profl Jours & Over 20 Res Reports.

ALLER, JAMES C oc/Program Director; h/9111 Deer Park Lane, Great Falls, VA 22066; ba/Washington, DC; m/ Mary B; c/Charles C, James D, Robert C, Mary S, Cynthia Jane Kelly; sp/ Charles C Bramble, McLean, VA; ed/ BS, Nav Acad, 1942; MA 1949, MES 1954, Harvard Univ; DSc, George Wash

Univ, 1968; mil/USN, 1942-62, Cmdr; pa/Prog Dir- Quantum Elect, Waves & Beams Prog, NSF, 1975-; Sr Assoc, Ketron Inc, 1873-75; Assoc Prof, George Wash Univ Med Sch, 1970-73; Prof, Nav War Col, 1968-70; F'ship, Public Hlth Ser Lab, 1967-68; Profl, Ctr for Nav Anal, 1963-67; Fellow, AAAS; Sr Mem, IEEE; Mem, WORMSC; Mem, NY Acad of Scis; r/Prot; hon/Author of Books: *The Pract of Clin Engrg*, 1977; *Status of Ultrasound Diagnostic Imaging Standards in US*, 1980; *The Biosaline Concept*, 1979; Author of Res Paper, "Sys Anal of Opers Data from A Multiphasic Screening Ctr," 1969; Meritorious Ser Awd 1980, Spec Achmt Awds 1978 & 82, NSF; Ctr for Nav Anal F'ship, 1967-68; Others; Am Men & Wom of Sci.

ALLEY, WILLIAM J oc/Executive; b/ Dec 27, 1929; h/2014 Illini Road, Springfield, IL 62704; ba/Springfield, IL; m/Deborah Bunn; c/Susan, Patricia, Sarah, Pamela Larson, Brayton; p/W H Alley (dec); Opal Cater Alley; ed/Durant HS, 1947; AA, NE OK A&M Col, 1949; BBA 1951, JD Sch of Law 1954, Univ of OK; mil/USNR, 1947; USAF, 1954-56; pa/Atty, OK St Ins Bd, 1956-57; Asst VPres 1957-59, VPres 1959-60, VPres & Agy Dir, 1960-66, Dir 1961, Sr VPres Mktg 1966-67, Pioneer Am Ins Co; VPres 1967-69, Sr VPres & Agy Dir 1969-74, Exec VPres 1974-76, Pres & CEO 1976-, Chm of Bd 1977-, Franklin Life Ins Co; Sr VPres Strategic Planning CLU, 1983; Bd of Dirs: Am Coun of Life Ins; IL Life Ins Coun; cp/Mem: Tavern Clb (Chgo); Sangamo Clb; Illini Country Clb; Springfield Racquet Clb; r/Presb; hon/Author of Num Articles in Ins Pubs; W/W: in Ins, in Fin & Indust, in Am, in World; Standard & Poor's Register.

ALLNUTT, FRANKLIN LLOYD oc/ Publisher, TV Producer; b/Apr 16, 1940; h/Box 879, Evergreen, CO 80439; ba/ Same; m/Ruth Cutler; c/Garrett Franklin, Theodore William, Lara Ruth; p/ William Lloyd Allnutt (dec); G G Allnutt, Peoria, IL; ed/BA Radio-TV-Film, Denver Univ, 1965; Pub Relats Courses at Univ CA-LA (UCLA), 1966; mil/USNR, Parachute Rigger 3rd Class; pa/Owner, Publisher & Editor, Frank Allnutt Co (*Books for Better Living Mag*), Evergreen, CO, 1981-; Exec Dir & TV Prog Prodr, Charles Blair Foun, Denver, CO, 1980-81; Owner & Mgr, Allnutt Advtg, Lake Arrowhead, CA, 1979-80; Gen Mgr & Editor, Here's Life Publishers Inc, San Bernadino, CA, 1976-79; Pres & Prodr, Christian Resource Communs Inc, Orange, CA, 1975-76; Owner & Mgr, Franklin L Allnutt Public Relats & Advtg, Newport Bch/El Toro, CA, 1969-75; Var Public Relats Positions w Walt Disney Prodns, 1963-69; Mem: The Am Film Inst; Christian Booksellers Assn; Christian Min Mgt Assn; Evang Christian Publishers Assn; Nat Writers Clb; Past Mem, Public Relats Soc of Am; r/Prot; hon/Author, Co-Author & Editor/ Publisher of 12 Books incl'g: *The Force of Star Wars*, 1983; *Salvation for a Doomed Zoomie* w John Galvin, 1983; *The Holy Spirit* w Bill Bright, 1980; *In Search of Superman*, 1980; Others; Prodr & Host for 6 TV Shows incl'g: "The Omen & the Antichrist," 1981; "War & Peace, " 1981; "God's Smuggler," 1976; Others; Prodr & Dir of Film, "A Visit w Corrie (ten Boom)," 1976; Ath Awd for 4 Yrs & Competed in NCAA Nat Champ-'ships (Swim Diver), Univ of Denver; 3 Books on Bestsellers Lists; Num W/ W & Other Biogl Listings.

ALLOCCA, JOHN ANTHONY oc/ Med Res Sci; b/Aug 17, 1948; h/234-05 Avenue 133, Rosedale, NY 11422; ba/ Deer Park, NY; c/Jennifer, Jerry; p/ Dorothy (Aulicino) Allocca, Rosedale, NY; ed/AAS, SUNY-Farmingdale, 1972; BA, SUNY-Old Westbury, 1975; MS, Poytech Inst of NY, 1979; DSc, Pacific Wn Univ, 1981; pa/Admr, Hofstra Univ, 1967-71; Psychotherapist, Creedmore St Hosp, 1975-76; Biomed Engr, Doll Res Inc, 1971-77; Res Sci, Albert Einstein Col of Med, 1977-78; Res Conslt, LI Col Hosp, 1979-80; Res Sci, Tech Dir Pulmonary Labs, Mt Sinai Med Ctr, 1980-82; Res Sci, Langer Biomech Grp Inc, 1983-; Mem: IEEE; Assn Advmt of Med Instrumentation; AAAS; Am Assn Physicists in Med; NY Acad of Scis; Radiol & Med Physics Soc of NY; Alumni Assn of Mt Sinai Med Ctr; hon/ Author & Co-Author of 4 Pub'd Books; 1 Jour Article in *Med Elect*, 1982; Designed, Devel, Invented Num Elect-Med Instruments in Field; W/W in Fronteir Sci & Technol.

ALLOWAY, DAVID NELSON oc/ Educator; h/1303-B, Troy Towers, Bloomfield, NJ 07003; ba/New York, New York; ed/AB, Muhlenberg Col, 1950; MA, Columbia Univ, 1955; PhD, NY Univ, 1965; LLD, London Univ, 1981; mil/AUS 1946-47; AUSR 1948-51; pa/Tchr, Sr HS, Millville, NJ, 1950-52; Tchr 1954-57, Chm Social Studies Dept 1955-57, Pennsbury Sr HS, Yardley, PA; Num Prof & Adm Positions, Montclair St Coll, Upper Montclair, NJ, 1957-82; Adj Assoc Prof 1978-82, Prof Liberal Arts 1982-, The Col of Ins, NYC; Vis'g Prof: Fairleigh Dickinson Univ, 1959; Wn IL St Univ, 1964 & 1966; IN St Univ of PA 1965; Adj Prof: Fairleigh Dickinson Univ, 1960-64; Seton Hall Univ, 1961-62; Pres Fac Coun 1974-75, Parliamentn Fac Sen 1975-77, Chm All Col Coor Coun 1975-76, Chm Col-wide Com on Instnl Reorg 1975-77, Chm Col Governance Constit-Writing Comm 1974-75, Montclair St Col; Mem, Com on Citizenship, Nat Coun for Social Studies, 1972-74; Pres 1970-72, NJ Coun for Social Studies, 1959-73; Pres 1969-71, Mid Sts Coun for Social Studies, 1959-73; Mem Comm on Citizenship 1970-72, Mem Nat Comm on Racial & Ethnic Slurs in US Textbooks 1969, Nat Coun for Social Studies, 1954-72; Intl Sociological Assn, 1967-; Am Sociological Assn, 1965-; Am Hist Assn, 1952-; Am Acad of Polit & Social Sci, 1970-; Life Mem, NEA, 1959; AAUP, 1972-; AAAS, 1969-; Num Others; cp/Co-Fdr & Exec Dir 1968-71, Mem 1971-79, Gtr Montclair Urban Coalition; Chm, Spec St Study Comm on Housing Probs of Minorities in NJ, 1978; Dir, Ctr for NJ Studies, St Dept of Ed (NJ), 1959-65; Chm, Co Charter Study Comm (Essex), 1971-72; Spec Rep for NJ St Col Facs, 1975-76; Chancellor-Gen, Accademia delle Scienze di Roma for US, 1981-; Reg Chancellor, Metro NY Area Royal K of Justice, 1982-; Hon Counsul-Gen for NY, Polish Govt in Exile, 1982-; Am Pres, Ordre de St-Georges de France, 1980-; Am Pres, Ordre de Civisme et

Renovation de France, 1980-; Num Others; Chm of 5 Reg Sems on Urban Unrest, 1968; Presenter of 6 Keynote Addresses, 1959-80; hon/Author & Co-Author: 4 Ref Wks; 6 Monographs; 2 Ency Articles; Over 20 Jour Articles, Proceedings, Reviews, Manuals; Co-Editor: *Am Ethnic Grps: The European Heritage* (47 Volumes), 1980; Spec Issue of *Jour of Human Relats*, 1972; Recip of 3 Awds, Accademia delle Scienze di Roma, 1980; Gold Medal Awd, Movimento Universale Fraternita Umana, 1980; Grand' Croix et Haute Dignitaire, Chevalerie de St-Georges de France, 1980; K Grand Cross, Order of Sacred K of Mt Sinai, 1981; Num Other Intl Hons; Resource Person in Criminol Cit, Acad of Criminol, 1982; Human Resource of US Cit, Am Heritage Res Assn Inc, 1975; Resolution of Commend For Accomplishments, NJ St Legis, 1980; Num Other Nat Hons & Awds; DIB; Intl Scholars Dir; Men & Wom of Dist; Commun Ldrs of Am; Contemp Authors; Outstg Edrs in Am; W/W: in Commun Ser, in E, in US; Num Other Biogl Listings.

ALLUISI, EARL ARTHUR oc/Chief Scientist; b/Jun 11, 1927; h/15211 Sandia, San Antonio, TX 78232; ba/ AFHRL/CCN, Brooks AFB, TX 78235; m/Mary Jane Boyle; c/John C, Jean E, Paul D J, Janet A; p/Humbert P (dec) and Elizabeth M (Dini) Alluisi; ed/BS Psych, Col of Wm & Mary, 1949; MA Psych 1950, PhD Psych 1954, OH St Univ; mil/AUS, 1944-47, Sgt Inf; AUS Med Res Lab, Psych Div, Ft Knox, KY, 1st Lt MSC & Res Psychol 1950-53; Capt MSC & Hd Envir Factors 1957-58; pa/Chief Sci 1983-, Chief Sci on Assignment from Old Dominion Univ under Title IV-Intergovtl Pers Act of 1970 1979-83, AF Human Resources Lab, Brooks AFB, TX; Univ Prof of Psych 1974-83, Dir 1974-83, Perf Assessmt Lab, Psych Dept, Old Dominion Univ, Norfolk, VA; VP Planning & Instnl Res 1971-74, Assoc Dean of Grad Sch 1970-71, Sabbatical Leave 1969-70, Dir Perf Res Lab 1968-72 Res Prof Perf Res Lab 1968-74, Exec Ofcr for Planning & Devel 1967-69, Acting Coor of Sponsored Progs 1967-69, Asst Dean for Res at Grad Sch 1966-67, Prof of Psych 1963-74, Univ of L'ville, KY; Assoc Sci, Human Factors Res Lab, Lockeed-GA Co, Marietta, GA, 1961-63; Lectr, Sch of Psych, GA Inst of Technol, Atlanta, GA, 1961-63; Asst to Assoc Prof of Psych, Dept of Psych, Emory Univ, Atlanta, GA, 1959-61; Sr Psychol & Hd Engrg Psych, Ec Res Div, Stanford Res Inst, Menlo Park, CA, 1958-59; Sr Engrg Psychol, Lockheed Aircraft Corp, Sunnyvale, CA, 1958; Lectr Univ Col, Dept of Psych, Univ of L'ville, KY, 1957-58; Res Assoc & Lectr Lab of Aviation Psych 1954-57, Univ Fellow Dept of Psych 1953-54, OH St Univ, Columbus, OH; Vis'g Instr, Dept of Psych, Col of Wm & Mary, Wmsburg, VA, Sums 1953 & 1954; Fellow, AAAS; AF Assn; Active in Am Psychol Assn (Fellow); GA Psychol Assn; Active in Human Factors Soc (Fellow); Intl Assn Applied Psych; Intl Soc Chronobiol; Num Others; cp/L'ville HELP Org, Steering Com, 1965; Woodrow Wilson Nat F'ship Foun, Region VII Com, 1965-67; Mem Bd of Dirs 1967-74, VChp 1971-72, Chp 1972-74, KY Civil

Liberties Union Inc; Others; hon/Phi Beta Kappa, 1949; Psi Chi, 1953; OH St Univ Fellow, 1953-54; Alpha Psi Delta, 1954; Life Mem, Soc of Sigma Xi, 1955; Jerome H Ely Awd of Human Factors Soc, 1970; Franklin V Taylor Awd of Soc of Engrg Psychols, 1971; Phi Kappa Phi, 1972; Num Biogl Listings.

ALM, JAMES oc/Director of Training and Human Resource Development; b/ May 6, 1937; h/5800 Rose Avenue, LaGrange, IL 60525; ba/Chicago, IL; p/ Mrs B J A Alm, Chgo, IL; ed/BA Eng Lit, Cornell Univ, 1959; mil/Sub Ser; pa/ CNA Claim Negotiator, 1962-64; Org Devel Spec, Allstate Ins, 1964-80; Dir Tng & H R Devel, Midas Intl, 1980-; Ofcr, Chgo Org Devel Assn, 1981-82; Ofcr, IL Tng Dir Assn, 1962-64; Chm Publicity & Promotion, MW Hypnosis Conv, 1976; Am Soc Tng & Devel; Am Soc Pers Adm; Human Res Planning Soc; Org Devel Inst; Assoc Psychol Type; Am Name Soc; cp/USS Nautilus (SS(N)571) Nat Mus Com; Adv Bd, ARC, 1983-84; Lectr, Mus of Contemp Art, Chgo; Spec Advr, Crusade of Mercy, 1964-65; Adv Bd, Broader Urban Involvement & Ldrship Devel, 1965; r/ Meth; hon/Editor, *Remedial Rdg for HS Students*, 1956; *Lttrtalk*, Editor, 1974; *Getting Things Done* (in press), Peter Simpson, Editor; *Applied Photoanal* (in press), Robert Akeret; "1st Annual TA Conf on Orgnl Applications: Spec Report," *Behavioral Sci Newslttr*, Mar 1975; Reviewed Tng & Devel Mats for "The Informer"; "Photoanal/Body Lang" (Cassette), 1982; Num Public Presentations; Pres Unit Cit & Nav Expeditionary Medal; W/W: MW, Fin & Indust; Men of Achmt; Dir of Dist'd Ams.

ALMANZA, HELEN PLUMMER oc/ College Professor; b/Aug 4, 1939; h/ 2206 Meadowbrook, Austin, TX 78703; ba/Col Sta, TX; m/Albert; c/Albert Boone, Katherine Elizabeth; p/Ethel Black Plummer; sp/Manuel Almanza; ed/BA, Spch Pathol 1960, MA, Audiology 1970, PhD, Ed Adm 1980, Univ of TX-Austin; pa/Vis'g Asst Prof, TX A&M Univ, 1981-; Conslt & Proj Dir, Ed Ser Ctr, Reg XIII, 1971-81; Spch Pathol, Brown Sch, 1970; Tchg Asst in Dept of Spch, Univ of TX-Austin, 1968-69; Spch Pathol, Jordanton ISD, 1966-68; Tchr, El Paso Pre-Sch for Deaf & Hard of Hearing, 1963-65; Spch Pathol, Austin ISD, 1960-62; Num Adv Positions; ASHA; ACLD; CEC; ASCD; TSTA; cp/Num Pvt Wkshops & Consultations on Nat Level; Num Presentations at Nat Convs & Confs; r/Meth; hon/Author "Recruiting & Retaining Ednl Pers in Rural TX," *Nat Rural Proj Newslttr*, 1980; "Where Are We Going? Reflections on Mainstreaming," in *Shared Responsibility for Handicapped Students: Advocacy & Programming*, Philip Mann (Editor), 1976; "Curric Adaptations & Modifications for Culturally Diverse Handicapped Chd," *Exceptl Chd*, 1980; Num Other Articles & Curric Pubs; Calcasieu S'ship, 1956; Sigma Alpha Eta, 1958; RSA F'ship, 1969; EPDA F'ship, 1970; Outstg Yg Wom of Am, 1974; Phi Delta Kappa, 1976; Phi Kappa Phi, 1977; TED Ser Awd for Outstg Tng Presentation, Coun for Exceptl Chd, 1978; W/ W in Am.

ALPER, MICHAEL FREDERICK oc/ Paralegal; b/Jan 24, 1954; h/367 Milltown Road, Springfield, NJ 07081; ba/ Irvington, NJ; p/Harold and Anne Alper, Springfield, NJ; ed/Jonathon Dayton Reg HS, 1972; BA Polit Sci, Rutgers, The St Univ, 1976; Broker Assoc Cert, Profl Sch of Bus, 1978; pa/Paralegal, 1981-; Law Clk, Commodities Asst Corp, 1980-81; Law Clk, Wildes & Weinberg, 1979-80; Broker Assoc, IMA Rity Corp, 1977-79; Publisher, Mike Alper's *Newsline*; cp/Appt'd Mem, Union Co Elderly & Handicapped Trans Bd; Standardbearer, Michael F. Alper Civic Assoc; Steering Com Mem, Jewish Fdn of Ctl NJ; Westfield JCs; Springfield Kiwanis; Del, NJ Dem St Com Conv; r/Jewish; hon/Cert of Apprec, Dem Nat Com, 1982; Cit for Dist'd Ser, Jewish Fed of Ctl NJ, 1983; Outstg Yg Men of Am.

ALPETER, V RAY oc/Executive; b/ Apr 4, 1931; h/ 7943 Colony Lane, Lenexa, KS 66215; ba/Shawnee Mission, KS; p/Frank And Clara Alpeter; ed/BS, Bus Adm, Univ of OR, 1953; pa/ Sys Advr, TWA, 1955-64; Sys Advr, McDonnell/Douglas, 1964-70; Mr Payroll/Pers, Borg Warner, 1970-74; Conslt, 1974-78; Pres/Owner, AD REM Consltg Ser Inc, 1978-; Am Soc Profl Conslts, 1981-83; Hon Mem, Am Payroll Conslts Assn, 1983; Contbg Editor, *Payroll Exch*, 1983/84; cp/US Congl Adv Bd, 1983; Charter Mem, Aviation Hall of Fame, 1981; hon/Author, "Insuring Compliance w Regulation Affecting Payroll," *Adv'd Mgmt Jour*, 1983; "Fed Regulations," *Payroll Exch*, 1983; "Developing an Automated Human Resource Sys," *Am Mgmt Assn*, 1980; "Improving Automated Payroll Sys," *Am Mgmt Assn*, 1980; "Evaluating Bus Application Software Packages," *Am Mgmt Assn*, 1982; NASA, Silver Snoopy Awd, 1969; Marquis W/W.

ALSPAUGH, THOMAS ATKINS oc/ Environmental Expert; b/Sep 18, 1925; h/2003 Mimosa Drive, Greensboro, NC 27403; ba/Greensboro, NC; m/Peggy Johnston; c/Thomas A Jr, Martha West, John Curtis; p/Mr & Mrs Everett C Alspaugh, Greensboro, NC; sp/Henry W Johnston (dec); Mrs Henry W Johnston, Greensboro, NC; ed/BS, Chem, Univ of NC-Chapel Hill, 1949; MS, Public Hlth, Univ of NC Sch of Public Hlth, 1951; mil/USNR, 1943-46; pa/Mgr Water & Air Resources 1972-, Supt Water & Wastes 1965-72, Supvr Water & Wastes Plants 1959-65, Res Chem 1958-59, Chem 1953-58, Cone Mills Corp; Chem, Mobile Lab, OH Dept of Hlth, 1951-53; Am Chem Soc; Water Pollution Control Assn; Am Assn of Textile Chems & Colorists; NC Piedmont Waste Operators Assn; Air Pollution Control Assn; Mem, NC Textile Mfrs Assn; Mem Envir Presv Com, Chm Water Subcom, CoChm Opers Subcom for Res Grant on 1983 Treatment Guidelines, Am Textile Mfrs Inst Inc; Mem, Sanitary Engrg Technol Curric Com, NC Tech Schs; VChm 1973-74, Chm 1974-75, NC Piedmont Water Plant Operators Assn; Num Others; cp/Guilford Co Envir Affairs Com; Yadkin-Pee Dee River Citizens Adv Com; Piedmont Triad Coun of Govts Reg Com on Envir Affairs; Mem, Adv Com, NC Water Resources Res Inst; Leag of Wm Voters Hazardous Waste Com; Com Chm, Cub Scout Pack 157 & 160; Num Others; r/Meth; hon/

Author & Co-Author, Num Pubs on Textile Waste Res, Water Reuse, Opers of Textile Waste Disposal Facilities; Co-Winner, Indust Waste Medal for Best Paper WPCA, 1959 & 1963; W/W: in Am, in Hlth Care, in SW.

ALSUP, REBA oc/Author; b/Aug 21, 1904; h/Owensville Road, Calvert, TX 77834; ba/Calvert, TX; m/Rodney Jackson (dec); p/Charles Thomas Rushing Sr (dec); ed/Att'd Rice Inst, 1922-23; Att'd SWn Univ, 1923; BA 1927, MA 1930, Baylor Univ; Att'd Columbia Univ, 1929; BS, Lib Sci, LA St Univ, 1941; Att'd Univ of CO, 1956; Att'd Univ of Houston, 1956, 1957, 1958; Golden Dipl, 1980, Sum Sch Cert of Grad, 1982, Baylor Univ; mil/WAC, Corporal; pa/Clrm Tchr, HS Eng & Spanish, Jones Prairie (TX) 1925-26, Branchville (TX) 1927-28, Lorena (TX) Fall 1928, Corsicana (TX) Sprg 1929, Waco (TX) 1929-31, Aldine (TX) Sprg 1934-Fall 1940; Sch Libn, Houston, TX, 1941-43 & 1945-63; NO Archdiocese, Metairie, LA, 1965-70; Pres, Houston Sch Libns, 1960-61; cp/Secy, Robertson Co Hist Comm, 1979; Pres, Wom of the Yr, Calvert C of C, 1980; r/Meth; hon/ Author, "Calvert Diary" 1983, "Hidden Diary" (in Preparation), "Old Families of Calvert"; Notable Wom of TX; World Biogl Hall of Fame; Personalities of S.

ALTHOFF, JAMES L oc/Executive; b/ Jun 9, 1928; h/ 508 N Green St, McHenry, IL 60050; ba/McHenry, IL; m/ Joan; c/Tim, Betsy, Tod, Katy, Patti, Jim Jr, Karyn; p/William H and Eleanor Althoff (dec); pa/Exec, Althoff Industries; Pres Sch Bd, Dist 156, Bd of Govs, St Univs; Mem, Law Enforcement Comm, Bd of Ed Dist 156; cp/McHenry Twp Fire Protection Dist, Bradley Univ.

ALTIER, WILLIAM JOHN oc/Management Consultant; b/Jul 22, 1935; h/ R D 4, Doylestown, PA 18901; ba/ Buckingham, PA; m/Mileen B; c/William C, Dwight D; p/William J (dec); Gertrude S, Stroudsburg, PA; sp/L Miles Bower (dec); Sarah R Bower, Blain, PA; ed/BA Lafayette Col, 1958; MBA, PA St Univ, 1962; pa/Pres, Princeton Assoc Inc, 1976-; Assoc 1964-68, Gen Mgr of Princeton Res Prin Div & Sr Assoc 1970-76, Kepner-Tregoe, Inc; Dir of Mktg, Comstock & Wescott, Inc, 1969-70; Sr Assoc, Applied Synergetics Ctr, 1968-69; Plant Mgr, Oak Industs, McCoy Electronics Div, 1960-64; Cert Mgmt Conslt, Inst of Mgmt Conslts; Am Mgmt Assn; VP, Prod Dev & Mgmt Assn; cp/VChm, ARC, Bucks Co; Probational Vol Sers; r/Presb; hon/Author, Several Articles Pub'd in *Bus Horizons* & *Mgmt Review*; W/W: in Fin & Indust, in E.

ALTIERO, NICHOLAS JAMES oc/ Associate Professor; b/Sep 22, 1947; h/ 2696 Lake Lansing Road, East Lansing, MI 48823; ba/East Lansing, MI; m/Amy Jean; c/Elizabeth Claire; p/Nicholas and Fanny Altiero, Niles, OH; sp/Wilbur and Kathryn Johnson, East Lansing, MI; ed/ BS, Aerospace Engrg, Univ of Notre Dame, 1969; MSE Aerospace Engrg 1970, MA Math 1971, PhD Aerospace Engrg 1974, The Univ of MI; pa/Assoc Prof, Dept of Metallurgy, Mechs & Mats Sci 1979-, Asst Prof, Dept of Metallurgy, Mechs & Mats Sci 1975-79, MI St Univ; Postdoct Scholar & Lectr, Dept of Aerospace Engrg 1974-75, Res Asst & Tchg Fellow 1969-74, The Univ

of MI; Res Asst, Dept of Aerospace Engrg, Univ of Notre Dame, 1968-69; Vis'g Prof, Istituto di Scienza e Tecnia delle Costruzioni, Politecnico di Milano, Milan, Italy, Jul-Dec 1981; Vis'g Prof, Lehrstuhl und Institut fur Technishe Mechanik, Technischen Hochshule Aachen, Aachen W Germany, Jan-Sep 1982; Am Acad of Mechs; Am Soc of Mech Engrg; Intl Soc for Computational Methods in Engrg; Sigma Xi, The Sci Res Soc; Soc of Engrg Sci; Tau Beta Pi Hon Engrg Soc; hon/Co-Author, "The Formation of Chips in the Penetration of Elastic-Brittle Mats," (w D L Sikarskie), *Jour of Applied Mechs*, 1973; "Some Exptl Observations on the Initiation & Propagation of Fracture in Elastic-Brittle Mats Subjected to Compressive Stress Fields," (w D L Sikarskie), *Devels in Mechs*, 1975; "Chip Formation in Anisotropic Rock" (w D L Sikarskie), *Rock Mechs*, 1977; "An Effective Boundary-Integral Approach for the Mixed Boundary-Value Prob of Linear Elastostatics" (w S D Gavazza), *Applied Math Modelling*, 1979; "A New Numerical Method For The Anal of Anisotropic Thin-Plate Bending Probs" (w B C Wu), *Computer Methods in Applied Mechs & Engrg*, 1981; "An Integral Equation Approach to Fracture Propagation in Rocks" (w G Gioda), *Rivista Italiana di Geotecnica*, 1982; Num Other Pubs; Fullbright Scholar, 1981; Von Humboldt Fellow, 1982; W/W: in Technol Today,in the MW, in Frontier Sci & Technol; Ldg Conslts in Technol.

ALTMAN, STEVE oc/Photographer; b/Dec 23, 1944; h/79 Grand Street, Margate City, NJ 07302; ba/Same; p/ Mrs Louis Feldman, Margate City, NJ; ed/BA 1967, Att'd Grad Studies in Jour, Am Univ; mil/AUS, 1969-71; pa/Comml Photog, 1980-; Instr, *Time-Life Lrng* Photo Wkshops, 1979-80; Instr, Beginning & Adv Photo, Dallas Commun Col & Eastfield Col, 1972-76; ASMP; IABC; Fdg Mem, Adelphi Soc, Am Univ; hon/ Contbr of Articles to *Time*, *Newswk*, *Nations Bus*, *Time-Life Books*, *Black Star*, *Time-Life Lrng*, *Fortune*; Contbr to Books *A Zoo For All Seasons* & *The Smithsonian Book of Invention*; IABC Silver Inkwell, 1980; Best Photo U Way, 1980; Chief Del World Jewish Yth Conf, 1963.

AL-TURKI, MOHAMMED SALEH oc/Administrative Attache; b/Sep 26, 1951; h/5300 Columbia Pike #908, Arlington, VA 22204; ba/Washington, DC; ed/Att'd King Abdulaziz Mil Acad; BS, Bus Adm, Jeddah Univ; mil/Saudi Arabia Land Forces, 9 yrs; pa/Diplomatic Adm Attache, Armed Forces Ofc, w Saudi Arabia Embassy; Saudi Arabia Army Mobility Prog-Am Corps of Engrs; Dept of Culture & Ed; r/Muslim.

ALUISI, JAMES VINCENT oc/Sheriff; b/Nov 22, 1945; h/14103 Rectory Lane, Upper Marlboro, MD 20772; ba/ Upper Marlboro, MD; p/Francis J and Carmella A, District Heights, MD; ed/ Att'd Prince George's Co, MD Police Acad, 1967; Att'd Bureau of Narcotics & Dangerous Drugs Enforcement Sch, 1968; Att'd FBI Law Enforcement Ofcrs In-Ser Tng Sch, 1973; Att'd MD Police Tng Comms Adm Ofcrs Sch, 1975; Att'd Univ of MD Public Admrs Sch, 1978; Nat Sheriff's Inst, Univ of So CA, 1979; Att'd Secret Ser VIP Protection

Sch, 1981; AA, Sec'dy Ed, Prince George's Commun Col, 1982; Att'd USAF 29th Nat Security Forum at Air War Col, 1982; Att'd FBI Nat Acad, 1983; pa/Prince George's Co Sheriff's Dept, 1967-1978; Elected Sheriff & Took Ofc, 1978; Re-elected 2nd term Sheriff, 1982; Mem, Correctional Adv Bd; MD St Sheriff's Assn; Nat Sheriff's Assn; Prince George's Bd of Trade; Intl Assn of Chiefs of Police; Nat Rifle Assn; FOP; cp/Prince George's Co Lodge OSIA; Prince George's CoC of C; Upper Marlboro C of C; Mem, 1982 Gtr Wash Chapt Telethon Com for MDA; VChm, 2 Rivers Dist, Nat Capitol Area Coun BSA, Fin Com; CoChm, Prince George's Co Viet Nam Vets Meml Com; K of C; r/Cath; hon/Articles for Law Enforcement Newlttrs; Legion of Valor, Am Law Enforcement Ofcrs Assn, 1978; Law Enforcement Ser Awd, FOP Lodge #9; VFW Post 482 Outstg Citizen of Yr, 1980; White House Commendation for Vets Prog, 1980; DAV Dept of MD Cit for Outstg Ser, 1981; Num Others; W/ W in Wash.

ALVARES, OLAV F oc/Associate Professor; b/Nov 1, 1939; h/2015 Morning Dove Lane, San Antonio, TX 78232; ba/San Antonio, TX; m/Dorthea; c/ Bryan, Stacy; p/Diva Noemia Alvares, Aldona Goa, India; sp/Oliver and Pearl Johnson (dec); ed/BDS, Dental Deg, Univ of Bombay, 1961; MS, Periodontics, Univ of Detroit, 1963; PhD, Pathol, Univ of IL, 1971; pa/USPHS Spec Postdoct Fellow, Royal Dental Col, Copenhagen, Denmark, 1971-72; Asst Prof, Col of Dentistry, Univ of IL, Chgo, 1972-74; Res Assoc Prof, Sch of Dentistry, Univ of WA, Seattle, 1974-81; Assoc Prof, Dental Sch, Univ of TX, San Antonio, 1981-; Vis'g Prof, Univ of Benin, Nigeria, Jan 1982; Mem, Am Assoc Dental Res, 1965-; Fellow, Am Acad Oral Pathol, 1967-; Secy 1981-83, Chm-Elect 1983-84, Chm 1984-85, Oral Biol Sect of Am Assoc Dental Schs; Dir, Salivary Gland Res Grp, Intl Assoc Dental Res, 1983-84; Mem, Spec Grants Review Com, Nat Inst of Hlth, 1981-85; r/Rom Cath; hon/Mem, Sigma XI, 1977; Mem, Omicron Kappa Upsilon, 1980; Res Career Dev Awd, NIH, 1976-81; Tchg Awds, Sch of Dentistry, Univ of WA, 1975, 1978, 1979, 1981; W/W: in Frontier Sci & Technol, in W & SW.

ALVAREZ, EVERETT JR oc/Administrator; b/Dec 23, 1937; h/1919 Sunrise Drive, Rockville, MD 20854; ba/Washington, DC; m/Thomasine Ilyas; c/Marc Ilyas, Bryan Thomas; p/Everett and Sally Alvarez, Santa Clara, CA; ed/ BSEE, Univ of Santa Clara, 1960; MS, Nav Postgrad Sch, 1976; JD, George Wash Univ, 1982; mil/USN, 1960-80; pa/Aviator, Nav Ofcr, 1960-80; Dept Dir, Peace Corps, 1981-82; Dept Admr, Vets Adm, 1982-; VFW, 1973-; Am Legion; DAV; Mil Order of Purple Heart; Bohemian Clb; Tailhook Assn; ABA; cp/Num Lectrs & Spchs on POW Experience (was Longest Held Am POW in N Viet Nam, Aug 5, 1964- Feb 12, 1973); r/Cath; hon/Silver Star; Legion of Merit; Dist'd Flying Cross; Hon Doct of Public Ser, 1982; Polit Appt by Pres Reagan.

ALVAREZ-MAYOL, LYSETTE oc/ Assistant Professor; b/Feb 7, 1934; h/ PO Box 1028 Adjuntas, Puerto Rico 00601; ba/Ponce, PR; m/Antonio J

Mayol; c/Antonio J Mayol II, Javier J Mayol; p/Joaquin Alvarez Colon and Eva M de Alvarez, Rio Piedras, PR; sp/ Concepcion C Vda Mayol, Ponce, PR; ed/BA, Ed & Eng, Univ of PR, 1955; MA Ed, Adm & Supvn, Inter-Am Univ of PR, 1978; Currently Doct Cand Higher Ed, NY Univ, NYU Residence Ctr, & Inter-Am Univ of PR, Santurce, PR; pa/ Asst Prof, Inter-Am Univ of PR, 1981-; Instr, Music & Ed, Inter-Am Univ of PR, 1976-1981; Music Tchr, Dept of Ed, Elem & Sec'dy Levels, Adjuntas, PR, 1966-75; Part-Time Instr, Music, Guayama Reg Col, 1966-75; Eng Tchr, Wash Irving Sch, Dept of Ed, Ajuntas, PR, 1962-65; Eng Tchr, SU Yahueca Sch, Dept of Ed, Adjuntas, PR, 1959-1960; Eng Tchr, Padre Rufo Elem Sch, Dept of Ed, Santurce, PR, 1958-59; Lib Asst, Univ of PR, Rio Piedras, PR, 1956-57; Eng Tchr, Dept of Ed, Rio Piedras, PR, 1955-56; Soprano Soloist, Coral Polifonica de Ponce; Soloist & Dir, Coral de Camara Augusto A Rodriguez; MENC; SATB; TEMA; BPW; Sociedad Puertorriquena de Directores de Coro; Musical Heritage Soc; Coro Sinfonico de PR; Phi Delta Kappa; Num Others; cp/Org'd & Dir'd SATB Chorus in Guayama Reg Col; Org'd, TEMA; Pres, BPWC of Adjuntas, PR, 1966-68; Num Others; r/Cath; hon/"Tchrs Enthusiasm & Student Achmt in Col," 1982; "The Coming of the Post-Indust Soc"; "A Venture in Soc Forecasting & The Ed Establishment," 1980; "The Evolution of Tchr Power & its Effect on Policy-Making in Ed," 1980; "Curric & Its Conflicting Conceptions: Classical Point of View vs Change & Innovation," 1979; Num Poems Pub'd in Bltns & Newspapers; Recog Cert of the Circle of Future Social Wkrs of the Inter-Am Univ of PR, Ponce Reg Col, 1982; Cert of Recog for Outstg Coop in Music, Commonwealth of PR, 1980; Cert in Recog of Outstg Wk in Ldrship Sem of the Prog of Soc Wk, Dept of Ed, Ponce Reg Ofcs, 1973; Plaque for Dedication to Music & Yth, Rotary Intl Clb of Adjuntas, 1971; Num Others.

ALVARIÑO de LEIRA, ANGELES (ANGELES ALVARIÑO oc/Research Biologist; b/Oct 3, 1916; h/7535 Cabrillo Avenue, La Jolla, CA 92037; ba/La Jolla, CA; m/Eugenio Leira-Mansso; c/ Angeles; p/Antonio Alvariño-Grimaldos and Carmen Gonzalez Diaz-Saavedra de Alvariño (dec); ed/BS summa cum laude, Scis & Lttrs, Univ of Santiago de Compostela, 1933; MS w Hons, Univ of Madrid, 1941; Cert Doct, Univ of Madrid, 1951; DSci (PhD) summa cum laude, Univ of Madrid, 1967; Postgrad/Postdoct, 1948-52; pa/ Fishery Res Biologist, Dept of Sea Fisheries, Spain, 1948-52; Biologist, Oceanographer, Spanish Inst of Oceanography, Madrid, 1952-57; Biologist, Scrips Instn of Oceanography, Univ of CA-La Jolla, 1958-69; Res Biologist, US Dept of Commerce, Nat Marine Fisheries Ser, SW Fisheries Ctr, 1970-; Assoc Prof, San Diego St Univ, 1978-; Vis'g Prof, Univ Nacionale (Mexico) & Univ Fed Parana (Brazil); Vis'g Prof, Nat Politechnic Inst of Mexico, Ctr of Res & Adv Studies of Merida, Yucatan, Mexico, 1982-; Assoc Rschr, Univ of San Diego, 1982-; Other Former Positions; Lectr at Univs & Oceanic Instns; Dir of PhD Theses; Supvr of Oceanic Res

in US & Abroad; Fellow, Am Inst Fishery Res Biologists; San Diego Mus of Nat Hist; Am Mus of Nat Hist; Marine Biologists of UK; CA Acad of Scis; Sigma Xi; Num Others; hon/ Author, Over 90 Papers, Books & Book Chapts; Discoverer of 20 New Oceanic Animals, 11 Chaetognatha & 9 Siphonophorae; Brit Coun Fellow, 1953-54; Fulbright F'ship, 1956-57; NSF Grants, 1958-69; Biogl Listings; Num Others.

ALY, OSMAN MOHAMAD oc/Environmental Specialist; b/Oct 15, 1932; h/ 1254 Ollerton Road, West Deptford, NJ 08066; ba/Camden, NJ; m/Aida Kamel; c/Maggy O, Sherry O, Sherif O; p/ Mohamad M Aly (dec); Monira M Aly, Cairo, Egypt; ed/BS 1953, MS 1958, Cairo Univ; PhD, Rutgers Univ, 1964; pa/Dir, Tech Sers (Conslltg Engrg Subsidiary) 1971-81, Mgr, Envir Quality 1970-, Campbell Soup Co; Res Assoc Rutgers Univ, 1968-70; Asst Prof Nat Res Ctr (Cairo), 1965-68; Mem, Envir Res Adv Panel, Nat Food Processors Assn, 1979-; Standards Methods Com, Am Water Works Assn, 1979-; St Panel of Sci Advrs, St of NJ, 1981-; Am Chem Soc, 1972-; r/Moslem; hon/Author or Co-Author, Over 40 Sci Pubs on Water & Wastewater Pollution; Others.

AMAN, MOHAMMED M oc/Educator & Academic Administrator; h/4020 West Mequon Road, Mequon, WI 53201; ba/Milwaukee, WI; m/Mary Jo; c/David; p/Mohammed Aman, Cairo, Egypt; Fathia Ali al-Maghrabi (dec); sp/ Mr and Mrs Ronald Parker, Portsmouth, OH; ed/BA Cairo Univ, 1961; MS Columbia Univ, 1965; PhD Univ of Pgh, 1968; pa/Dean & Prof, Sch of Lib & Info Sci, Univ of WI, Milwaukee, 1979-; Dean & Prof, Grad Lib Sch, LI Univ, CW Post Ctr, NY 1976-79; Dir & Prof Div of Lib & Info Sci 1973-76, Assoc Prof of Lib & Info Sci 1971-73, Asst Prof 1969-71, St John's Univ; Asst Prof of Lib & Info Sci, Pratt Inst, Bklyn, NY; Chm, Intl Relats Round Table, Chm of Intl Relats Com, Am Lib Assoc; Coun of Deans & Dirs, Chm of Intl Ed Com, Assn of Lib & Info Sci Ed; Am Soc for Info Sci; Egypt-Am Scholar Assoc; MidE Studies Assoc; r/Moslem; hon/Cataloging & Classification of Non-Wn Lib Mats, 1981; Arab Serials & Periods: A Subject Bibliog, 1979; Internal & Comparative Libnship, 1976; Online Databases, 1983; W/W: in Am, in the MW, in Computer Sci Ed; Men of Achmt; DIB.

AMAR, AMAR DEV oc/Production Systems Educator; b/Oct 10, 1946; h/ 124 Christie Street, Edison, NJ 08817; ba/South Orange, NJ; m/Sneh Lata; c/ Harpriye Amar Juneja, Januj Amar Juneja; p/Prem D and Kaushlya Shakir, Chandigarh, India; sp/Agya R and Shayama Chopra, Chandigarh, India; ed/BS, Prodn Engrg w Hons, Punjab Univ; MS, Indust & Mgmt Engrg, MT St Univ, 1973; MBA, Baruch Col, 1980; M Phil 1980, PhD 1980, CUNY; pa/ Engr, Orisun Machine Tools, Chandigarh, India, 1966-67; Asst Prof, Prod Engrg, Punjab Engrg Col, Chandigarh, 1969-72; Asst Engr, Teledyne Pacific Indust Controls, Oakland, CA, 1972; Indust Engr, Vornado-Store Decor, Garfield, NJ, 1973-76; Internal Mats Mgmt Conslt, Arkwin Industs, Westbury, NY, 1977; Asst Prof 1978-83, Dir Mgmt Dev Ctr 1981-83, Montclair St Col, Upper Montclair, NJ; Proj Assoc

Res Foun of CUNY NYC, 1980-82; Assoc Prof, Seton Hall Univ, S Orange, NJ; Sr Mem, IIE; Mem ORSA; Mem, TIMS; Acad Liaison SHU APICS Chapt; Mem, Fac Senate MSC, 1978-83; r/ Hindu; hon/Res Articles in Areas of Prodn/Opers Mgmt; Merit List for BS in Prodn Engrg, Punjab Univ, 1969; W/ W in Frontier Sci & Technol; Nom'd for W/W in World.

AMBACH, GORDON, MAC KAY oc/Commissioner of Education, University President; b/Nov 10, 1934; h/Box 528, 33 Fiddlers Lane, Newtonville, NY 12128; ba/Albany, NY; m/Lucy DeWitt Emory, c/Kenneth Emory, Alison Repass, Douglas Mac Kay; p/Russell Ambach, Brookline, MA; ed/BA, Yale Univ, 1956; MA Grad Sch of Ed 1957, CAS 1966, Harvard Univ; mil/AUS Resv, 1957-63; pa/Pres, Univ of St of NY, 1977-; Commr of Ed, St of NY, 1977-; Former Asst Prog Planning Ofcr, Asst Legis Spec & Exec Secy for Higher Ed Facilities Act Task Force, w US Ofc of Ed (Wash DC); Mgr Staff Sem on USOE Report, "Equality of Ednl Opport," Harvard Univ Grad Sch, 1966-67; Former Spec Asst to Commr James E Allen Jr, Long Range Planning, Dept of Ed; Mem, Gov's Cabinet; Mem, 18 St Bds & Comms incl'g: NY St Sci & Technol Foun, NY St Hlth Planning Comm, NY St Comm on Hwy Safety, NY St Higher Ed Ser Coop Bd, NY St Bd for Historic Presv; Num Others; cp/ Pres, Coun of Chief St Sch Ofcrs, 1984-85; Bd Dirs: Lincoln Ctr Inst, Nat Comm on Libs & Info Sci, Saratoga Perf'g Arts Ctr, Nat Dance Hall of Fame; Others; hon/Dist'g Public Ser Awd, Indep Student Coalition, 1982; W/W in Am; Men of Achmt; Other Biogl Listings.

AMBRE, JOHN JOSEPH oc/Associate Professor; b/Sep 14, 1937; h/1210 Walden Lane, Deerfield, IL 60015; ba/ Chgo, IL; m/Anita; c/Susan, Peter, Denise, Mathew; p/Frederick and Cecilia Ambre, Naperville, IL; sp/Richard and Beatrice Sievert, Peoria, AZ; ed/BS, Notre Dame Univ, 1959; MD, Stritch Sch of Med, Loyola Univ, 1963; MS Pharm/Toxology 1970, PhD 1972, Univ of IA; mil/Med Corp, Capt; pa/Res/Med, Mayo Clin, 1966-68; Fellow/Clin Pharm/Toxology, Univ of IA, 1968-72; Prof of Med, Univ of IA, 1972-78; Med Dir, CBT Labs, 1978-83; Prof of Med, NWn Univ Med Sch, 1980-; Toxicology Conslt, MetPath Inc & Abbott Labs; Am Soc for Clin Pharm & Therapeutics; The NY Acad of Scis; Am Soc for Pharm & Exptl Therapeutics; Am Fdn for Clin Res; Am Assoc for Clin Chem; Am Assoc for the Advmt of Sci; Others; r/ Cath; hon/Over 40 Sci Articles in Profl Jour; Contbr of Chapt to Book; Co-Editor of Book; Co-Author of Book on Toxicology & Therapeutic Drug Monitoring; NIH/NIGMS F'ship Awd, Clin Pharm, 1968-72; Clin Investigatorship, US Vets Adm, 1973-76; W/W: in the MW, in Frontier Sci & Technol; Am Men & Wom of Sci.

AMERICA, FRANCINA H oc/Nurse Audiologist; b/Feb 18, 1937; h/1260 Evergreen, Bronx, NY 10472; ba/New York, NY; m/Sammie; c/Adrienne; p/Mr and Mrs O H Hudmon, New York, NY; sp/Lillian Goldman, Atmore, AL; ed/ RN, Howard Univ Hosp, 1959; BS, CUNY, 1978; MA, City Col of NY, 1979;

pa/Nurse, NY Hosp, 1959-60; Med Coor, City Col of NY, 1960-; ANA; ASHA; City Col Alumni Assn; City Col Black Alumni Assn; r/Prot; hon/Grad cum laude, 1978.

AMES, A E LYN oc/Health Care Administrator, Nursing; b/Apr 25, 1949; h/5020 Laurel Canyon Boulevard, North Hollywood, CA 91607; ba/Pasadena, CA; p/Betty A Ames, Bushnell, IL; ed/AA, Santa Fe City Col, 1976; Cert'd Hlth Care Admr, UCLA, 1980; BS/BA, summa cum laude, Univ of Redlands, 1982; RN, Pasadena City Col, 1985; MBA Cand, CA St Univ-LA, 1986; pa/Team Ser Ldr, Plastic & Reconstructive Surg, Univ of FL, 1973-78; Assoc Dir of Mats Mgmt, Cedars-Sinai Med Ctr, 1978-81; OR Charge Nurse, St Luke Hosp, 1981-83; Labor & Delivery, Val Presb Hosp, 1983-; Chapt Pres Assn of Surg Technols Inc, 1975-78; Am Soc for Hosp Purchasing & Mats Mgmt; Am Soc for Hosp Ctr Ser Pers; Bd of Dirs, Student Nurses' Assn of CA; Lectr, So CA Nsg Diagnosis Assn; cp/OES; Intl Order Rainbow for Girls; hon/Contbr to *OR Tech* Mag, *Point of View/Ethicon* Pub, *Ctl Ser Tng Manual*; OMD Hon Soc PCC; Student Nurses' Assn of CA Scholar; Mildred Porter Powell Nsg Scholar; Grand Cross of Color, Intl Order of Rainbow Girls; W/W: in W, in Am Nsg.

AMES, FRANK ANTHONY oc/Producer & Principal Percussion, National Symphony; b/Oct 12, 1942; h/1235 Potomac St, Northwest, Washington, DC 20007; ba/Same; m/Annette Ruth; c/Kristin Susan; p/Camille O'Brien Ames, Clinton, NJ; sp/Earl and Ruby Beck; ed/HS at Linsley Inst; BM, Eastman Sch of Music; MFA, Carnegie-Mellon Univ; pa/Pgh Symph, 1965; Balto Symph, 1966; Nat Symph, 1968-; Fdr & Exec Dir, 20th Century Consort, 1975-; Fdr & Exec Dir, Millenium Inc, 1979-; Fdr, Martha's Vineyard Music Fest, 1978-; Pres, Potomac Prods; hon/Prodr of Recordings, 20th Century Consort Volumes I & II; Co-Prodr of "Naughty Marietta" & "Rose Marie"; W/W: in Am, in World.

AMHERD, NOEL A oc/Research Scientist; b/Dec 12, 1940; h/1742 Austin Avenue, Los Altos, CA 94022; ba/ Fremont, CA; m/Charlene; c/Alicia, Keven; ed/BS, Physics, AZ St Univ, 1963; MS, Aerospace Engrg Scis, Univ of CO, 1968; PhD, Aeronautics & Astronautics, Univ of WA, 1973; pa/ Mgr, Energy Sys, Titan Sys Inc. 1983-; Sr Proj Mgr, Adv'd Power Sys Div, Elect Power Res Inst, 1975-1983; Prof, Aerospace & Mech Scis Dept, Princeton Univ, 1973-75; Mem, Tech Staff Space Sys Div, Hughes Aircraft Co, 1963-67; Bd of Editors, *Jour of Fusion Energy*, 1979-; Am Nuclear Soc; Am Phy Soc Assn for the Advmt of Sci; hon/Author of "Viewpoints on Fusion-Fission Hybrid Sys," *Atomkernenergie Kerntechnik*, 1984; Sigma Xi; W/W: in the W, in Technol.

ANASTASIADIS, SOTIRI SOKRATIS oc/Mechanical Engineer & Economist; b/Jan 19, 1933; h/4670 Hollywood Boulevard #302, Los Angeles, CA 90027; ba/Los Angeles, CA; p/Sokratis and Anastasia Anastasiadis (dec); ed/BS, Mech Engrg, Tech Univ of Constantinople, 1955; MS Mech Engrg 1960, PhD Mech Engrg 1961, Tech Univ of Berlin; PhD, Nuclear Engrg, Columbia Univ, 1968; pa/Chief Scist & Chief Engr, Soan

Co, LA, 1977-; Prin Nuclear & Process Engr, The Ralph M Parsons Co, Pasadena, 1974-1977; Nuclear Engr Supvr, Gibbs & Hill Inc, NY, 1972-74; Nuclear Anal Grp Ldr, Sargent & Lundy Engrs, Chgo, 1970-72; Nuclear Engrg Grp Ldr, Consol Edison Co of NY, NY, 1968-70; Consltg Engr, Am Standards Testing Bur Inc, NY, 1966-68; Sr Nuclear Engr, Nat Lead Co, NY, 1964-66; Res Engr, Columbia Univ, NY, 1962-64; Mech Engr for Others in Turkey & Germany, 1956-62; Mem, Am Nuclear Soc, 1962-; Mem, Columbia Engrg Assn, 1962-; Mem, AAAS, 1972-; Mem, Soc for Advmt of Mgmt, 1972-; Mem, Hellenic-Am C of C, 1982-; cp/Mem, Nat Geog Soc, 1972-; Mem, The Soc for the Presv of the Greek Heritage, 1972-; Mem, Hellenic Inst Inc, 1972-; Mem, Krikos Inc, 1972-; St Adv, US Congl Adv Bd, 1982-; Hellenic Univ Clb of So CA, 1984-; r/Greek Orthodox; hon/Author of Articles: "Modern High Efficiency Power Plant" 1961, "Criticality Control By Neutron Absorbing Plates" 1966, "The Direct Rdg of Shielding Requirements for Any Source & Any Shielding Mat" 1970, "With Zero Cash Investmt & Zero Investmt Risk, How To Make Multiples of $10,000 in the Stock Mkt w Unique Option Methods" 1984, "Profits Up to 160% per Month w Zero Risk Showing Unique Option & Index Stock Market Methods" 1984, Others; The Cultural Doct in Nuclear Sci, World Univ, 1982; Full S'ships in Constantinople & Berlin; Grad w Hons; Men of Achmt; Intl W/ W of Intells; Am Hellenic W/W in Bus & the Professions; The Intl Book of Hon; Num Other Biogl Listings.

ANBAR, MICHAEL oc/Professor & Department Chairman; b/Jun 29, 1927; h/181 Halwill Drive, Buffalo, NY 14226; ba/Buffalo, NY; m/Ada; c/ Rani, Ariel; ed/MS 1950, PhD 1953, Hebrew Univ; pa/Assoc Dean Applied Res Sch of Med 1983, Exec Dir Hlth-Care Instrument & Device Inst 1983, Prof & Chm Dept of Biophy Scis 1977, Prof Dept of Dental Mats 1977, SUNY-Buffalo; Prof Dept of Biophysics, Roswell Pk Mem Inst, Buffalo; Am Chem Soc; Biophys Soc; Am Assn Mass Spectrometry; Am Assn for Advmt of Sci; Am Assn for Clin Chem; Assn of Am Med Cols; NY Acad of Sci; hon/Over 200 Articles Pub'd; Sigma Xi, UNESCO S'ship; NAS & NRC F'ships.

ANCIELLO, MICHAEL SALVATORE oc/Professor; b/Apr 16, 1940; h/ 38 Yankee Circle, Westfield, MA 01086; ba/Westfield, MA; m/Lucille A; c/ Michael John, Christopher Nicholas; p/ Mr & Mrs Nicholas J Anciello, Belmont, MA; sp/Mrs Lucille F McLellan, Milton, MA; ed/AB & AM 1966, Cert in Russian & En European Studies 1968, Boston Col; PhD, St Louis Univ, 1974; pa/Assoc Acad Affairs, Westfield St Col, 1982-; Hist Prof, Boston St Col, 1968-82; Tchg Fellow, St Louis Univ, 1969-70; Tchg Asst 1965-66, Tchg Asst Russian & En European Ctr 1966-68, Boston Col; Tchr, The Winchendon Sch, 1962-63; Phi Alpha Theta; Am-Italian Hist Assn; NEn Slavic Assn; New Eng Ctr for Italian Studies; E European Res Ctr; Am-Roumanian Acad of Arts & Scis; Am Hist Assn; r/Cath; hon/Pub'd "Britains En Policy & the Roumanian Principalities from 1829-1856," 1974;

Num Book Reviews for *Am Hist Review*, *Cath Hist Review*, Others; Elected Mem, The Romanian Acad of Arts & Scis, 1981; Elected Fellow, E European Res Ctr Hellenic Col, 1981; Fellow Orgr & Treas, New Eng Ctr for Italian Studies Pine Manor Col; W/W in E; Dir of Am Scholars.

ANDEREGGEN, ANTON oc/Professor; b/May 20, 1936; h/7273 Southwest Nevada Terrace, Portland, OR 97219; ba/Portland, OR; m/Liselotte; c/Desiree, Dino; p/Joseph and Anna Andereggen, Switzerland; sp/Hans Blank, Switzerland; ed/Brevet, Academie Militaire Suisse, Berne, 1960; Certificat d'etudes & Diploma, Universite de Geneve, 1962; BA, Monmouth Col, NJ, 1968; PhD, Univ of CO, 1973; pa/Assoc Prof, Lewis & Clark Col, 1977-; Asst Prof, Univ of Portland, 1973-77; Tchg Asst, Univ of CO, 1969-73; Tchr & Cnslr, Rumson Country Day Sch, 1965-68; Tchr & Cnslr, Morristown Prep Sch, 1963-65; Chapt Pres 1978-79, Bd Mem 1979-82, Am Assn of Tchrs of French; Mod Lang Assn of Am; Philological Assn of Am; Pacific NW Coun on Fgn Langs; Rocky Mtn Mod Lang Assn; Confdn of OR Fgn Lang Tchrs; World Affairs Coun of OR; hon/Pub'd Article in *Etude philologique du Jugement Dernier (Lo Jutgamen General), drame provencal du XVe siecle*, Edited by Joseph P Williman, 1983; *Blueprint for Crisis Preparedness*, 1981; Outstg Edr of Am, 1973-74; Fulbright Fellow; DIB.

ANDERL, STEPHEN oc/Roman Catholic Priest; b/Jul 13, 1910; h/2214 Peters Drive, Apt 309, Eau Claire, WI 54703; ba/Same; p/Henry A Anderl and Katherine Schneider (dec); ed/McDonell Mem HS, 1928; BA 1932, MDiv 1974, St John's Univ; PhD, World Univ, 1982; pa/Curate: Sts Peter & Paul Parish, Wisconsin Rapids, WI, 1936-37; Holy Trinity Parish, LaCrosse, WI, 1937-40; VPrin, Guid Cnslr, Instr in Latin & Sociol at Aquinas HS, LaCrosse, 1937-49; Pastor, Sacred Heart Parish, Sprg Val, 1949-52; Pastor, St Michael's Parish, Hewitt, 1952-53; Pastor, St Mary's Parish, Durand, 1953-82; Vicar Forane of Durand Deanery, 1953-82; Mem, Diocesan Bd of Ed; Exec Bd, Cath Soc Agy; Diocesan Clergy Pers Bd, 3 terms; Vicar Gen for Religious, 15 Yrs; Com for Cont'd Ed of the Clergy; Diocesan Chaplain for Boy Scouts & Girl Scouts, 12 Yrs; Exec Secy, Diocesan CYO & Sodality of Our Lady; Faithful Friar & Fdr of Pope John XXIII 4oGen Assem K of C, 1946-80; Am Acad of Rel; Christian Writers Assn; WI Acad of Arts & Lttrs; Num Others; cp/Civilain Chaplain at Ft McCoy, WW II; Chaplain World Jamboree 1967, Nat Jamboree 1969 & 1973, of BSA; Bd of Dirs, Chippewa Val Coun BSA; Bd of Dirs, Indian Waters Girl Scout Coun; Fdr & Exec Bd, W Ctl WI Commun Action Agy; Gov's Comm on Chd & Yth, 3 Terms; WI St Com on Mtl Hlth & Retard Planning; Moderator of USO Clb; WI Geneal Soc; WI Hist Soc; Chippewa Val Hist Soc; Num Others; hon/Author of *Technique of the Cath Action Cell*, (translated into Korean), 1943; *Rel & Cath Action*, 1955; *Adult Christians*, 1955; *Thy Will Be Done*, 1960; *Parish of the Assumption*, 1960; Contbr to Num Other Cath Pubs; Domestic Prelate by Pope John XXIII, 1962; St George Awd, 1970; Silver Beaver Awd, 1968; St Ann Awd,

1982; Cit from WCap for Outstg Ser to the Poor, 1972; Cit from USO for Outstg Ser to the Nat, 1950; Cit from Pepin Co Min Assn for 'Ecumenism', 1982; Cit from the K of C Coun 2422 for 28 Yrs of Ser as Chaplain; Cit from St Mary's Parish, Durand for 29 Yrs of Ser as Pastor; Others; W/W: in Rel, in Cath World, in MW; Am Cath W/W; Intl Biogl Assn; WI Men of Achmt; Book of Hon; Num Other Biogl Listings.

ANDERLE, RICHARD JOHN oc/Mathematician; b/Oct 8, 1926; h/Box 3436 College Station, Fredericksburg, VA 22402; ba/Dahlgren, VA; m/Fay Antoinette Leitch (dec); p/Joseph and Jennie Anderle (dec); ed/BA, Math, Bklyn Col, 1948; Grad Wk, Math & Physics, Am Univ & George Wash Univ, 1956-70; pa/Mathematician Exterior Ballistics Br 1948-59, Hd Exterior Ballistics Div 1959-60, Hd Astronautics & Geodesy Div 1960-80, Res Assoc to Hd Strategic Sys Dept 1981-, Nav Surface Weapons Ctr; Lctr, Am Univ, 1964-65; Pres Geodesy Sect, Chm Audit Com, Am Geophy Union, 1980-82; Secy Space Techniques Sect 1979-83, Pres Adv'd Space Technol Sect 1983-87, Intl Assn of Geodesy; AAAS; Am Soc of Photogrammetry; Am Cong on Surveying & Mapping; IEEE; AIAA; Inst of Navigation; NY Acad of Scis; Div of Dynamic Astronomy of Am Astronom Soc; cp/Coun-man 1963-65, Treas 1963-64, Fin Secy 1976-, Christ Luth Ch; r/Lutheran; hon/Over 50 Contbns to Texts, Jour, Meetings Proceedings; Over 30 Agy Reports; Nav Superior Accomplishment Awd, 1960; Nav Surface Weapons Ctr John A Dahlgren Awd, 1978; Hon DSc, OH St Univ, 1981; Am Geophy Union, 1981; Am Corres'g Astronomer Royal Belgian Observatory, 1984; Am Men of Sci; W/W: S & SE, Govt; Ldrs in Am Sci; Num Other Biogl Listings.

ANDERS, SARAH FRANCES oc/Professor; b/Jan 5, 1927; h/111 Mary Street, Pineville, LA 71360; ba/Pineville, LA; p/Mr & Mrs Edward E Anders (dec); ed/AB, Social Scis, LA Polytechnic Univ; MRE, Theol & Music, So Bapt Theol Sem; MA Sociol, PhD Sociol, FL St Univ; Postdoct, Urban Planning, Rennselaer Polytechnic Inst; Postdoct, Hist of Behavioral Scis, Univ of NH; Sabbatical, Wom's Studies, Vanderbilt Univ; pa/Grad Fellow 1952-53, Asst Dir Res Lab 1953-55, FL St Univ; Prof & Chp, Dept of Sociol, Mary Hardin-Baylor Col, 1955-62; Prof & Chp Dept of Sociol 1962-, Acting Dean 1972-73, Holds Herman and Norma Walker Chair, 1981, LA Col; Num Guest Lectrships; Fellow, Am Sociological Assn; Ofcr, LA Coun on Fam Relats; Mem, SWn Social Sci Assn; Mem, SWn Sociological Assn; Del-at-Large, AAUW; Staley Foun Lctr; Past Pres, TX Coun on Fam Relats; Past Pres, SWn Rel Res Coun; Past Mem, Gov's Comm on Chd & Yth; Staff, 1st Bapt Ch, Marshall, TX, 1945-46; Dir of Music & Ed, 1st Bapt Ch, Quincy, FL, 1948-52; Dir of Ed, 1st Bapt Ch, Gadsden, AL, 1952-53; Others; cp/Bd Mem: Fam Cnslg Agy, Alexandria-Pineville Renaissance, Chds Receiving Ctr for Pre-Delinqs, Alexandria-Pineville Mtl Hlth & Child Guid Clin; Former Chm of Bd, Cenla Commun Action Prog, 1965-66; Former Ofcr & Bd Mem, Alexandria-Pineville YWCA;

Campus Sponsor, Alpha Chi & Sociol Clb; CoChp, Arab-Israeli Relief Fund, 1968; Bible Tchr of Col Students, 25 Yrs; Spkr & Lectr at Num Confs, Schs, Clbs, Wkshops; Others; r/So Bapt; hon/Num Profl Articles Pub'd: "Rel Behaviour of Ch Fams," *Marriage & Fam Living* 1955, "Rel Beliefs of Students in a Ch-Related Col" *The Edr* 1959, "Rel Variables & the Role of the Clergy among Mtl Patients," *The Jour of Pastoral Care* 1965, "New Dimensions in Ethnicity & Childrearing Attitudes," *Am Jour of Mtl Deficiency* 1968, "Woms Role in the So Bapt Conv & Its Chs as Compared w Selected Other Denoms," *Review & Expositor* 1975, "Moral Issues in the Woms Liberation Mvt," in *Issues in Christian Ethics* ed by Paul Simmons 1980, Others; Plus Num Articles in Denoml Periods; Pub'd Books: *Christian Freedom for Wom... & Other Human Beings* 1975, *Wom Alone: Confident & Creat* 1976; Also Num Book Chapts & Cassettes; Danforth Assoc, 1977-; Dist'd Alumna Awd, So Bapt Theol Sem, 1978; Dist'd Ser Awd, Christian Life Comm, SBC, 1978; Hilda Simon Awd & Charles Freeman Awd, LA Assn of Social Wkrs, 1982; Alumna Awd for Excell Tchg, 1973; Nat Sci Fellow, 1965, 1968, 1972-73; Piper Prof of TX, 1959; Sigma Delta Pi; Gamma Epsilon; Phi Kappa Phi; Others; W/W: Among Am Wom, in Am Ed, Among Authors & Jours, in Commun Ser; Outstg Edrs of Am; 2,000 Wom of Distn; Other Biogl Listings.

ANDERSEN, BARBARA LEE oc/Professor; b/May 2, 1957; h/RR #6 Box 144N Iowa City, IA 52240; ba/Iowa City, IA; m/John Terrance Cacioppo; p/Edgar and Gladys Anderson, Elgin, IL; sp/Cyrus and Mary Catherine Cacioppo, Swisher, IA; ed/BS 1973; MA 1978; PhD 1980; pa/Psych Fellow, Neuropsychi Inst (UCLA), 1979-80; Asst Prof Psych, Univ of IA, 1980-; Lic'd Psychol (IA); Mem: Am Psychol Assn, Soc of Behavioral Med, MWn Psychol Assn; r/Luth; hon/*Behavior Modification: Behavioral Approaches to Human Probs*, 1979; Num Jour Articles; BS w High Hons & Distn in Psych; Psi Chi; Phi Kappa Phi; Sigma Xi; W/W in Frontier Sci & Technol.

ANDERSEN, DAVID CHRISTIAN oc/Corporate Director of Public Relations; b/Dec 16, 1948; h/5367 Redfield Road, Dunwoody, GA 30338; ba/Atlanta, GA; m/Nancy Ellen Emery-Andersen; c/Elizabeth Emery, Kristen Ellen; p/Harold and Marguerite Elizabeth Andersen, L'ville, KY; sp/John and Elizabeth Emery, Bloomfield Hills, MI; ed/BA, Univ of KS, 1971; pa/*Eagle & Beacon* Newspaper, 1970; Profl Spkr 1971-72, Commun Affairs Sect 1972-1973, Mgr *Previews of Progress* 1973-75, Public Affairs Sect 1975-77, News Release Sect, 1977-78, SE Reg Rep 1978-82, Public Relats Staff, Gen Motors Corp; Corp Dir of Public Relats, Cox Cable Communs, Inc 1982-; Soc of Profl Jours, Sigma Delta Chi; Public Relats Soc of Am; Cable TV Adm Soc; hon/Nat Col Register; Outstg Yg Men of Am; Men of Achmt; W/W: in Am Cols & Univs, in S & SW, in Auto Indust, in Cable TV.

ANDERSEN, MARK E oc/Concert Organist, Vocalist, Flutist; b/Feb 15, 1947; h/3410 Bonneville Drive, Charlotte, NC 28205; ba/Charlotte, NC; p/

Edd and Susan Welsh, Lumberton NC; ed/E Carolina Univ; BA, Am Conservatory; MA, NEn Sem; PhD, Conservatiore National de Paris, France; pa/ Pres, Andersen & Maddox, Inc; Am Guild of Organists; Nat Flute Assn; Brit Flute Soc; hon/Num Titles of Music; Author *An Artists Guide of Alto & Bass Flute*; First Pl, Intl Composers Competition; 1st Pl, Paris Yth Opera Competition; 1st Pl, Mozart Fest; Dir of Distn Am; Intl W/W in Music.

ANDERSEN, RICHARD oc/Author; b/Dec 27, 1946; 2708 Southeast Tolman Street, Portland, OR 97202; ba/Same; m/Deborah; p/Arnold Andersen; sp/ Isabel Kraus; ed/BA, MA, PhD; pa/ Writer-in-Residence Michael Karolyi Foun, Vence, France, 1983-84; Fulbright Prof of Am Lit, Univ of Bergen, Norway, 1982-83; Prof of Humanities, Boston Univ, 1977-82; cp/Vence Basketball Team; hon/Pub'd Books: *William Goldman*, 1979; *Robert Coover*, 1981; *Straight Cut Ditch*, 1979; *Muckacuck*, 1980; Num Articles on Ed & Lit; Fulbright Profship; Writer-in-Residence; W/W in Am; Contemp Authors; Men of Achmt.

ANDERSON, ANN M CASSAGNE oc/Professor; b/Apr 19, 1944; h/5920 Memphis Street, New Orleans, LA 70124; ba/New Orleans, LA; m/Robert B; p/Mrs C J Moseley, NO, LA; ed/BS Microbiol/Med Technol, Loyola Univ, 1966; MS Microbiol 1968, PhD Microbiol 1971, LA St Univ Med Ctr; pa/Asst Prof 1974, Assoc Prof 1976, Grad Fac 1976-, Intl Hlth Fac 1977-, Now Assoc Prof Envir Hlth Sci Tulane Univ Sch of Public Hlth & Tropical Med, Tulane Univ; APHA; Am Soc for Microbiol; Soc Envir Geochem & Hlth; Soc Exptl Biol & Med; The Biodeterioration Soc; cp/ LA Engrg Soc-Aux; Tulane Med Intl Clb; Chds Carnival; Orleans Clb; PEU, NO Opera Guild; r/Cath; hon/Over 50 Pub'd Jour Articles on Envir Hlth Scis; DHEW Grantee, 1974-82; Pres, LA Engrg Soc-Aux; Pres, Tulane Med Intl Clb; Mem, Sigma Xi & Delta Omega; Hon Col, Govs Staff, St of LA; W/W: in S & SW, of Am Wom, of Wom.

ANDERSON, DAVID POOLE oc/ Journalist; b/May 6, 1929; h/8 Inness Road, Tenafly, NJ 07670; ba/New York, NY; m/Maureen; c/Stephen, Mark, Mary Jo, Jean-Marie; p/Robert P and Josephine Anderson (dec); sp/John and Mary Young (dec); ed/BA, Holy Cross Col, 1951; pa/Sportswriter, *Bklyn Eagle*, 1951-55; Sportswriter, *NY Jour-Am*, 1955-66; Sportswriter, *NY Times*, 1966-; hon/Author: *Countdown to Super Bowl* 1969, *Sugar Ray* (w Sugar Ray Robinson) 1970, *Always On The Run* (w Larry Csonka & Jim Kick) 1973, *Poncho Gonzalez* 1974, *Frank, The 1st Yr* (w Frank Robinson) 1976, *Sports Of Our Times* 1979, *The Yankees* 1979; Editor, *The Red Smith Reader*, 1981; The Pulitzer Prize, 1981.

ANDERSON, DAVID THOMAS oc/ Scientist; b/May 24, 1950; h/1106 Shorewood Boulevard, Madison, WI 53705; ba/Madison, WI; m/Pamela Jane; ed/BSEE 1974, MSEE 1975, PhD, Plasma Physics, 1984, Univ WI-Madison; pa/Proj Mgr IMS Spec 1980-84, Asst Dir of Torsatron Stellarator Lab 1984-, Staff Sci 1984-, Univ of WI; Mem: Sigma Xi, IEEE, APS; hon/ Articles Pub'd: "3 Dimensional MHD Equilibria in Toroidal Stellarators," *Physics Review* 1975, "Neutral Beam Injection Calculations in Torsatrons," *Nuclear Fusaion* 1980; Others; Contbr, Over 45 Papers; Plus 4 Invited Papers to APS; Bacon F'ship, 1976; IEEE Nuclear & Plasma Scis Grad Student of The Yr, 1976; Grand Prize *Design News* Excell in Design Contest, 1982.

ANDERSON, DAVID WALTER oc/ Physicist, Professor; b/Jun 18, 1937; h/ 7419 South Maplewood, Tulsa, OK 74136; ba/Tulsa, OK; m/Jane L; c/ Bonnie J, Brian D; p/Mr and Mrs Walter O Anderson (dec); sp/Mr and Mrs Harold Friedland, St Louis Pk, MN; ed/ BS, Hamline Univ, 1959; PhD, IA St Univ, 1965; pa/Postdoct Fellow, IA St Univ, 1965; Var Profl Positions in Physics Dept, Univ of OK, 1966-82; Prof of Radiological Scis (Radiol Physics), Univ of OK Hlth Sci Ctr, 1975-82; Dir of Radiological Physics/Prof of Radiol, City of Faith Med & Res Ctr, 1982; Am Assn of Physicists in Med, Radiation Res Soc; Am Phy Soc; Am Col of Radiol; Soc of Nuclear Med; Soc of Magnetic Resonance Imaging; r/U Meth; hon/Author, *Absorption of Ionizing Radiation*, 1984; Pub'd Over 45 Articles in Sci Jours, 1962-84; Grad summa cum laude, Hamline Univ, 1959; AEC Postdoct F'ship IA St Univ, 1965; Cert in Radiological Physics Am Bd of Radiol, 1975; W/W in S & SW; Am Men & Wom of Sci.

ANDERSON, EDMUND H oc/Geophysicist; b/Jan 8, 1924; h/Route 4, 140 Barbara Lane, Midland, TX 79701; ba/ Midland, TX; m/Mary J; c/John, Gail, Robert, Steven, Kay, Chris; p/E J Anderson, Camden, AR; sp/Mr and Mrs Roy L Jorgensen, Houston, TX; ed/ BSEE, TX A&M Univ, 1948; MS Math 1964, PhD Math 1967, LA St Univ; mil/ USASC, 1943-46; pa/Geophysicist, Shell Oil Co, 1948-62; Grad Student, LA St Univ, 1962-67; Tchr & Rschr, Univ of ND, MS St Univ, LA St Univ, 1967-81; Geophysicist, El Paso Exploration Co, 1981-; Am Math Soc; AAUP; MS Acad of Sci; hon/Pub'd: "Two Spheres Which Avoid I^3 if I^3 Contains a P-OD," "The Equivalence of The Uncountably Many Closed Sets Property And The Least Upper Bound Property of the Real Nums," 8 Others; Tau Beta Pi, 1948; Phi Kappa Phi, 1967; Sigma Xi, 1969; Am Men of Sci; W/W in Technol Today.

ANDERSON, EDWARD LEE oc/ Physician, Medical Director; b/May 22, 1950; h/5550 Columbia Pike #942, Arlington, VA 2204; ba/Arlington, VA; m/Pamela; p/LeRoy and Brenda Taylor Anderson, Arlington, VA; ed/BS Biol 1972, MD Sch of Med 1976, Georgetown Univ; Residency in Internal Med, The Wash Hosp Ctr, Wash DC, 1976-79; pa/Med Dir, C & P Telephone Co of VA, 1979-; Am Col of Phys, 1980-; Phi Beta Kappa, 1972-; Sigma Xi, 1972-; AMA, 1980; VA Med Soc, 1980-; The Arlington Co Med Ctr, 1980-; r/Epis; hon/The Biol Medal, Georgetown Univ, 1972; Diplomate, Am Bd of Internal Med, Nat Bd of Med Examrs; W/W in Wash DC; Marquis Am Med Spec Dir.

ANDERSON, ERIC EDWARD oc/ Executive, Psychologist; b/Jan 24, 1951; h/7316 Cornelia Drive, Edina, MN 55435; ba/Edina, MN; m/Florence Kaye; c/Cara Elizabeth; p/Charles and Elizabeth Anderson, Ft Myers, FL; sp/Esther Kaye, New York, NY; ed/BA Univ of MN, 1973; MA Grad Sch of Theol 1977, PhD Grad Sch of Psych 1978, Fuller Theol Sem, CA; pa/Pres, Kiel Profl Sers Inc, 1984-; Grp VP, Kiel Profl Sers Inc, 1983-84; Asst Prof, Hlth Psychol, Univ of MN, 1979-83; Postdoct Intern Univ of MN, 1978-79; Am Psychol Assn; MN Psychol Assn; Gerontological Soc of Am; cp/Rotary Intl; r/Congl/Jewish; hon/Pub'd Articles in Num Pfl & Sci Jours; Phi Beta Kappa; Am Acad of Achmt; W/W: in Am Col & Univs, in MW, in Frontier Sci & Technol, in World, in Am; DIB; Other Biogl Listings.

ANDERSON, EVANS LELAND oc/ Professor; b/Sep 26, 1914; h/4650 60th Street, San Diego, CA 92115; ba/San Diego, Ca; m/Virginia E (dec); c/Anita Elaine; p/Mr and Mrs C M Anderson, Upsala, MN; sp/Mr and Mrs V Steinberger, Forest City, IA; ed/Dipl, St Cloud St Col, 1934; BA, Gustavus Adolphus Col, 1938; MA, Univ of MN, 1939; EdD, Univ of Denver, 1951; mil/ AUS, 1942-46; pa/Elem Tchr, Upsala, MN, 1935-37; Dir of Tchr Tng, Waldorf Col, Forest City, IA, 1939-42; Psychol Res & Pers, AUS, 1942-46; Assoc Prof, St Cloud St Col, MN, 1946-54; Prof, San Diego St Univ, 1954-; Am Psychol Assn; CA St Employees Assn; NEA; CA Tchrs Assn; cp/Am Legion; Kiwanis; r/ Luth; hon/Pub'd Text Manual: *Successful Tchg, A Prob-Solving Approach*; Selected Articles on Ed; Tchg Fellow, Univ of Denver; Phi Kappa Delta; Pi Gamma Mu; Psi Chi.

ANDERSON, FLORA MAE oc/ Departmental Aide; b/Oct 14, 1951; h/ 1106 North Williams Street, Bay City, MI 48706; ba/Bay City, MI; c/Marsha Little; p/Jerome and Marie Badour, Essexville, MI; ed/HS Dipl, Bay City All Sts, 1969; Exec Secy, Saginaw Bus Inst, 1977; pa/Bay City Public Schs, 1970-72; Clerical Aide & Dept Aide, Dept of St, MI Secy of St Br Ofc, 1977-; Chapt Pres 1980-81, Adult Dirs 1979, Bay Co Chapt #762 of Parents w/o Ptnrs; VP, Awds & Protocol 1982-83, VP, Prog & Ed 1984, Mid-MI Reg Coun of PWP; cp/ Bay Co Participant, Expanding Horizons in Ldrship, 1980-81; Bd of Dir 1982-84, & Chm Walk America 1983, 1984, Bay Co March of Dimes; Num Other Commun Ser; r/Cath; hon/Single Parent of Yr for Mid-MI Reg Coun #96, Parents w/o Ptnrs.

ANDERSON, GERALD RICHARD oc/Guidance Counselor; b/Jan 26, 1941; h/3145 Berry Road, Northeast, Washington, DC 20018; ba/Washington, DC; c/Gerald Richard Jr, Shelley Yvonne, Kwame Gerald; p/Alice Tucker, Las Vegas, NE; ed/BA Soc Wk, Fed City Col, 1974; MS PE 1976, 27 Semester Hours toward MA Guid & Cnslg 1976-78, Howard Univ; MA Adult Ed 1980, MA Cnslg & Mtl Hlth 1982, The Univ of the DC; mil/AUS, 1963-65; pa/Laborer, Walter Reed Army Med Ctr, 1966-67; Janitor, 1967-68; Truck Driver, 1968-71; Purchasing Agt, 1971-73; Laundry Supvr, 1973-74; Soc Ser Asst, 1974-75; Supply Clk, 1975-76; Rec Spec, 1976-79; Guid Cnslr, 1979-; Mem, Nat Assn of Black Soc Wkrs, 1971-75; Mem Bd of Dirs, DC Metro Interagy Coun on Fam Planning, 1980-82; Mem, UDC Alumni Assn; Mem, ALPA NU Chapt of Alpha Delta Mu Natl Soc Wk Hon Soc at Univ of the DC, 1979; Mem,

APGA, 1981; Mem, En HS Alumni, 1980; hon/Soc Wkr Hon Soc, 1979; Outstg Perf Awd Laborer 1968, Superior Perf Awd as Driver 1969, Superior Perf Awd 1980 & Exceptl Perf Awd 1981 as Guid Cnslr, Walter Reed Army Med Ctr; W/W in E.

ANDERSON, GORDON WOOD oc/Research Physicist; Electronic Engineer; b/Mar 8, 1936; h/1320 North Carolina Avenue, Northeast, Washington, DC 20002; ba/Washington, DC; m/Gillian B; p/Gordon H Anderson (dec); Mrs Avis H Anderson, Hendersonville, NC; sp/Mr and Mrs Robert S Bunshaft, Newton Ctr, MA; ed/BSEE, Cornell Univ, 1959; MS Physics 1961, PhD Physics 1969, Univ of IL-Urbana-Champaign; pa/Res Physicist 1971-, Nat Res Coun Res Assoc 1968-70, Nav Res Lab, Wash DC; Conslt, Planning & Human Sys Inc, Wash DC, 1978-79; Ford Foun Fellow, Res Asst, Tchg Asst, Univ of IL-Urbana-Champaign, 1959-69; Instr, Tougaloo Col, Tougaloo, MS, 1965; Am Phy Soc; Institute of Electrical & Electronic Engineers; AAAS; Found for Sci & Handicapped; Fdn of Am Scis; Union Concerned Scis; cp/Bd of Dirs 1979-, Epilepsy Foun Am; Pres 1976-78, Fdg Mem Bd of Dirs 1972-73, 1974-, Epilepsy Foun for Nat Capital Area; Fdg Mem Bd of Dirs 1981-, VP 1982-83, Wash DC Sers for Indep Living; Univ of IL Alumni Assn; Cornell Clb of Wash DC; Capitol Hill Restoration Soc; ACLU; Amnesty Intl; NOW; Envir Def Fund; Sierra Clb; Friends of the Earth; Oesterreichischer Alpenverein; Alpine Clb of Canada; Others; r/Epis; hon/Contbr of Num Articles; *Jour of Applied Physics, Jour of The Electrochem Soc, Jour of Chem Physics,* Others; Presenter of Num Papers at Profl Confs; Author, Book Chapt; Nat Res Coun Res Assoc-ship 1969-79; Nat Sci Foun Grantee 1963; Navy Spec Achmt Awd 1983; Patentee in Field; Sloan Foun Nat S'ship; Cornell Nat S'ship; Wms Col Book Awd; Sigma Xi; Tau Bet Pi; Eta Kappa Nu; Ford Foun F'ship; W/W: in E, in Technol Today; Am Men & Wom of Sci; Resource Dir of Handicapped Scis.

ANDERSON, JACK GARNER oc/Executive; b/Apr 21, 1922; h/28 Winged Foot Road, Dover, DE 19901; ba/Frederica, DE; m/Patricia Menacher; c/Judy Miller, Jack L, James G, William J, Richard P, Jerald R, Mark L, Donald B; p/Wilfred John and Ruth A Garner (dec); ed/BS, USAF Tech, 1950; BS Chem Engrg, Univ of L'ville, 1943; mil/USAF, 1954-54, Maj, Ret'd; pa/VP Mktg, Hoffman Electronics Corp, LA, 1954-60; VP, Gen Dynamics Electronics, NY, 1960-61; VP, Kollsman Instrument Corp, Elmhurst, NY, 1961-68; Exec VP Kaman Corp, Broomfield, CT, 1968-72; Pres 1972-83, Chm of Exec Com 1983-, ILC Industs Inc; Am Rocket Soc; EIA; NSIA; Nat Aeronaut Assn; AFA Assn; Nat Aviation Clb; Aviation Hall of Fame; cp/Aero Modelers Clb; Fellow Radio Club; Am Mgmt Assn; Kent Co Amateur Radio Clb; Dover Rotary; hon/Grad'd cum laude, USAF Tech, 1950; Aviation Hall of Fame.

ANDERSON, JoANN MARIE oc/Program Director Employee Assistance and Rehabilitation; b/Feb 26, 1937; h/9557 Pine Cluster Circle, Vienna, VA 22180; ba/Washington, DC; ed/BS,

Sociol & Psychol, Amhurst Col, 1955; MA, Communs, Univ of Hartford, 1956; pa/Dir Employee Ast Prog & Rehab Sers 1983-, Mgr Employee Asst Prog 1975-82, AMTRAK; Dir of Public Relats 1971-75, Public Relats Conslt 1967-72, Fairfax Co Alcohol Safety Action Prog; TV Interviewer Hostess, ZBM-TV, Bermuda, 1959-66; Chp, RR Pers Assn-EAP; Mem, Nat Fedn of Press Wom; VA Press Wom; Assn of Labor/Mgmt Adm & Conslts; Nat Assn of Alcoholism Cnslrs; Public Relats Soc of Am; Alcohol & Drug Progs of N AM; Am Coun of RR Wom; Wom in Trans; Nat Assn of RR Passengers; cp/Bd of Trustees: Woms Home, Arlington, Coun on Alcoholism for Fairfax Co; r/Cath; hon/Author of Instrs Manual for EAP Tng Wkshop, 1979; Amtrak Pres's Achmt Awd, 1981; Amtrak Employee of the Yr, 1981; YWCA's Acad of Wom Achievers, 1980; Num 1st Place Awds from VA Press Wom Writing Competition; W/W of Am Wom; DIB.

ANDERSON, JOE LEWIS SR oc/Industrial Relations Specialist; b/Mar 18, 1948; h/2465 Flint Hill Road, Vienna, VA 22180; ba/Arlington, VA; m/Angeles Webb; c/Joe L Jr, Jeffrey L, April N; p/Mr and Mrs Leroy Anderson, Charlotte, NC; sp/Mr and Mrs Wilson Webb, Charlotte, NC; ed/BS, Ec, NC A&T St Univ; mil/AUS, 1971-73, Resv 1973-, Maj; pa/Indust Relats Spec Wash DC 1980-, EO Progs Asst Rochester, NY 1979-80, Indust Relats Spec Distbn Div Rochester 1976-79, Employmt Spec Rochester 1973-75, Mgmt Trainee Rochester 1970-71 & Part of 1973, Eastman Kodak Co; Resv Ofcrs Assn; Civil Affairs Assn; cp/Urban Leag; NAACP; Mem Adv Com: Univ of the DC, VA Employmt Comm, Joseph P Kennedy Inst; Mayor's Com on the Handicapped, Wash DC; Omega Psi Phi Frat; Charter Mem & 1st Pres (Rochester Chapt) NC A&T St Univ Alumni Assn; r/Bapt; hon/Alpha Kappa Mu Hon Soc 1969-70; Omicron Delta Epsilon Hon Soc in Ec 1967-70; Dist'd Mil Grad 1970; W/W Among Students in Am Cols; Outstg Yg Men of Am.

ANDERSON, JOHN FORD oc/Trust Investment Officer; b/Aug 12, 1933; h/9638 Kensington Parkway, Kensington, MD 20895; ba/Washington, DC; m/Katherine Ruhl; c/Katherine Marguerite, Elizabeth Scott; p/Harry Ford and Marguerite Weaver Anderson (dec); ed/BS, The Univ of the S, 1957; Att'd NY Inst of Fin, 1958; Att'd Am Inst of Bkg, 1960-62; pa/Stock Broker, Ferris & Co, 1958-59; Securities Anal, Securities Trading, Mktg & Opers, Riggs Nat Bk of Wash DC, 1959-; Past Mem & Treas Org of Instl Traders; Past Mem & VPres Cashiers Assn of Bks & Brokers; cp/Dir & Treas, Rockville Musical Theatre Inc, 1979-; Mem, Soc of Mayflower Descendants; Treas & Vestry, Christ Ch Kensington, 1972-74; Loaned Exec to the DC U Way, 1980; Mason & Mem of Several Masonic Orders 1977-; r/Epis; hon/ W/W of Wash DC.

ANDERSON, JUDITH JAN oc/Graduate Student; b/May 15, 1955; h/5271 Sorrento Dr, Boise, ID 83704; ba/Caldwell, ID; p/Mr and Mrs Dale V Anderson, Boise, ID; ed/AA, Cottey Col, 1975; BS, Univ of ID, 1977; MA, Col of Idaho, 1984; pa/Van's Catering Co, 1977; Jr HS Tchr Meridian Sch Dist,

1978-83; Receptionist KTVB, 1981-; Hall Dir Col of ID, 1983-84; Meridian Ed Assn; PEO; cp/Chapt Ofcr, Kappa Alpha Theta; Phi Upsilon Omicron; Phi Beta Kappa; Job's Daughs; r/Meth; hon/Nom'd Outstg Sr Univ of ID, 1977; Outstg Pledge Kappa Alpha Theta, 1976; PEO S'ship, 1973-74; Mary Hall Niccols S'ship, 1975-77; W/W in W.

ANDERSON, JUDY M oc/Attorney; b/Aug 14, 1948; h/3255 Jett Ferry Court, Dunwoody, GA 30338; m/George K; p/Leonard Fred (dec); M M Mattox, Jay, FL; sp/Mr and Mrs Preston Anderson, Carryville, FL; ed/BS Troy St Univ, 1969; JD 1978, LLM 1979, Atlanta Law Sch; pa/Regulatory Compliance Atty 1981-, Sr Contracts Atty 1980-81, Sn Co Sers Inc; Fin Sers Mgr Am Hosp Supply Corp, 1972-80; ABA; GA St Bar Assn; Statutory Revisions Com; Elect Woms Roundtable; VPres/Pres Elect & Bd of Dirs, GA Exec Woms Netwk; Bd of Dirs, Polit Action Com, Sn Co Sers Inc; cp/Bd of Trustees, Atlanta Chapt Leukemia Foun; r/Bapt; hon/W/W in GA.

ANDERSON, KENNETH ROY oc/Naval Officer/Admiral's Aide; b/Mar 3, 1954; h/5977 Memory Lane, San Diego, CA 92114; ba/San Diego, CA; m/Monica Sharrell; c/Marian Kathleen, Karmen Dionne, Kendra Monique; p/Nathaniel and Mary Anderson, Phila, PA; ed/BS, Polit Sci, US Nav Acad; mil/USN, Lt; pa/Surface Warfare Ofcrs Sch, 1977; Asst Force Gunnery/Logistics Ofcr Comsurfpac, 1978-79; M Div Ofcr, MPA, Navigator, Pers Ofcr, USS Gridley 1979-81; Flag Aide, Cmdr Nav Tng Ctr, 1981-; cp/Editor of *Israelite Scroll,* 1978-79; Selected to Lead Inc, 1982-83; Asst Tchr, In Depth Bible Ed Class, Gtr Israelite CO CIC, San Diego; Sales Mgr, AL Williams Org; r/Pentecostal; hon/Pub'd Article in *Phila Daily News,* 1971; Maxwell Awd, 1972; *Phila Inquirer* Player of the Wk 1971; 1st Team All-Public, All Scholastic, All Area in Football, 1971-72; Hon Mention Sunkist All-Am, 2nd Team All St, 1971-72; MVP City Champ'ship Game, 1970.

ANDERSON, KIM EDWARD oc/Corporate Director; b/Nov 6, 1950; h/5201 North Hills Boulevard, North Little Rock, AR 72116; ba/Little Rock, AR; m/Rebecca C; c/Kristin L, Courtney L; p/Mr and Mrs K E Anderson, El Reno, OK; sp/Georgia Cogwell; ed/BS, E Ctl St Univ, 1972; MS 1973, PhD Cand, OK Univ; pa/Environmtl Engr, OK Hlth Dept, 1971-72; Indust Hygienist, Johnson Space Ctr, NASA, 1973-74; Sr Industl Hygienist, US Dept of Labor, Occupl Safety & Hlth Admn, 1974-78; Corp Dir Envir & Occupl Safety & Hlth, A O Smith Corp, 1978-; Asst Prof Univ of AR & Univ of Ctl AR, 1979-; Pres AR Sect 1979, Toxicology Com 1978-81, Wkroom Envir Exposure Level Com 1979-81, Am Industl Hygiene Assn; VPres 1981, Pres 1982, AR Sect Am Soc of Safety Engrs; CoChm Welding Safety & Hlth Com 1980-81, Am Welding Soc; Bd of Dirs 1978-, Chm Industl Envir Com 1979-81, Chm Hazardous Waste Com 1981-, AR Fedn of Water & Air Users Inc; r/Meth; hon/Author of *Fundamtls of Industl Toxicology,* 1980; Article Pub'd in *Pers Admr,* 1983; US Public Hlth Ser Fellow, 1972-73; AK Frontiers of Sci Scholars, 1972-73; Skylab Med Team Achmt Awd, 1974;

23

W/W in the S & SW.

ANDERSON, LEONARD LOUIS oc/ Biochemist; b/Sept 20, 1934; h/353 Hayward Street, Bridgewater, MA 02324; ba/Stoughton, MA; m/M Bernadette; c/Christine, Eric, Lauren; p/ Everett F and Concetta Anderson, Brockton, MA; sp/Bernard and Rosalie Judge (dec); ed/AB, Harvard Univ, 1956; MA, Boston Univ, 1963; DSc, Sussex Univ, 1974; mil/AUS, 1957-59; pa/ Biochem, Gen Foods, Boston, 1956-57; Biochem, Boston Univ Med Sch, 1959-60; Biochem, MA Gen Hosp, 1960-63; Biochem, Tufts Univ, 1963-66; Biochem, Lahey Clin Foun, 1966-79; Biochem, Goddard Med Assocs, 1979-81; Clin Rschr & Gen Supvr, Biostat Lab, 1981-84; Lab Dir, N Eng Sinai Hosp, 1984-; Field Archeologist 1979-80, MA Archeological Soc; cp/ Coach 1980-84, Bridgewater Yth Soccer Assn; r/Cath; hon/Cont'd Chapt to Book on Cancer Chemotherapy; Pub'd Res Papers on Cancer Chemotherapy & Immunotherapy in Num Jours: *Nature*, *Cancer Res*, *Annals of Surg*, *Clin Res*; Sigma Xi; NY Acad of Scis; Am Fdn for Clin Res; W/W in E.

ANDERSON, LILLIE MAE oc/Social Worker; b/Apr 15, 1918; h/Route 5, Box 166, Columbia, SC 29203; ba/Columbia, SC; m/Calvin R Goff; p/Julius and Lillie Hardy (dec); ed/BA, magna cum laude, Benedict Col, 1959; Postgrad, Howard Univ, 1960-61; MSW, Atlanta Univ, 1969; Postgrad, Univ of SC, 1975 & 1978; Att'd So Reg Inst, 1976; Att'd Univ of AL, 1980; pa/Beautician, Columbia, SC, 1938-45; File Clk, Ofc Dependency Benefits, Newark NJ, 1945-46; Grp Ldr, Utility Elect Corp, E Newark, NJ, 1946-52; Owner & Propr, A & W Store, Columbia, 1952-56; Grp Wkr, Bethlehem Commun Ctr, Columbia, 1959-60; Soc Wkr, SC Mtl Hlth, Columbia, 1960-63 & 1966-68; Pilgrim St Hosp, 1963-66; Supvr, Columbia Housing Auth, 1969-71; Mem, Nat Assn of Soc Wkrs; St of SC Bd of Soc Wk Registration; Richland & Lexington Cos Soc Wk Assn; Pres 1973, Soc Wk Clb; cp/Zeta Phi Beta; Alpha Kappa Mu; Cath Charity Bd; r/Rom Cath; hon/ Alpha Kappa Mu Hon Soc, 1959; Cert of S'ship, 1959; W/W: Among Students, of Wom, of Am Wom.

ANDERSON, LLOYD H oc/Architect; b/Oct 21, 1945; h/12791 West Jewell Circle, Lakewood, CO 80228; ba/ Same; m/Linda Jane Proctor; c/Scott Dirk, Tadari Ciel; p/Willard H and Edith Rymph (dec) Anderson, San Diego, CA; sp/Mr and Mrs W O Proctor, Tulsa, OK; ed/BA, Arch, Univ of CO, 1970; Archl & Prod Designer, Charles Deaton Assocs, 1967-71; Chief Design Arch, Bur of Reclamation, US Dept of the Interior, Denver CO, 1971-76; Ptnr, Deaton-Anderson Design, Denver, CO, 1975-; Dir of Design, Zuhair Fayez & Assocs, Jiddah, Saudi Arabia, 1976-78; Pvt Pract, Intl Design & Consltg, Lakewood, CO, 1978-; hon/Designed Over 40 Comml, Govtl, Rel, Mil & Pvt Projs in Saudi Arabia & Jordan; Designed Others in US; Patentee in Furn Design & Bldg Prods; Emerson Meml Prize, Nat Inst for Archl Ed, 1965; DIB; W/W in W; Men of Achmt; Biog Intl; CO W/W.

ANDERSON, LLOYD LEE oc/Professor; b/Nov 18, 1933; h/1703 Maxwell Avenue, Ames, IA 50010; ba/Ames, IA; m/JaNelle R; c/Marc C, James R; p/Mrs Clarence Anderson, Zearing, IA; sp/Mr and Mrs Everett Hall, Hinton, IA; ed/ BS 1957, PhD 1961, IA St Univ; mil/ AUS, 1953-55; pa/Lalor Foun Fellow, Station de Physiologie Animale, Jouy-en-Josas, France, 1963-64; NIH Postdoct Fellow 1961, Asst Prof 1961-65, Assoc Prof 1965-71, Prof of Animal Sci 1971-, IA St Univ, Ames IA; Sect Editor of Endocrinology & Metabolism, *Jour of Animal Sci*, 1983-86; Mem Reproductive Biol Study Sect, NIH, 1984-88; r/Meth; hon/Pub'd Res Articles in Neuroendocrine Regulation of Growth & Reprodn in Farm Animals; Agri Hon; Gamma Sigma Delta; Res Hon, Soc of Sigma Xi; Postdoct Fellow; Lalor Foun Fellow.

ANDERSON, LORIN WILLARD oc/ Professor; b/May 21, 1945; h/4437 Willingham Drive, Columbia, SC 29206; ba/Columbia, SC; m/Jo Anne Craig; c/ Christopher Craig, Nicholas Craig; pa/ Mr and Mrs Willard Anderson, Keewatin, MN; sp/Mr and Mrs Edward B Craig III, Shelbyville, TN; ed/AB, Macalester Col, 1967; AM, Univ of MN, 1971; PhD, Univ of Chgo, 1973; pa/Jr HS Math Tchr, Esko, MN, 1967-69; Sr HS Math Tchr, Burnsville, MN, 1969-71; Asst Prof 1973-76, Assoc Prof 1976-81, Prof 1981-, Univ of SC; Mem, Am Ednl Res Assn, 1971-; Nat Coun of Measurement in Ed, 1971-; Assn for Supvn & Curric Dev, 1976-; cp/Mem, St Michael & All Angels Church, 1979-; r/Epis; hon/Author of Books: *Mastery Lrng in Clrm Instrn*, 1975; *Assessing Affective Characteristics in the Schs*, 1981; *Time & Sch Lrng: Theory, Res, & Pract*, 1983; Pres's Awd for Emerging Yg Rschr, 1980; Outstg Tchr Awd, 1978; Susan Colver Rosenberger Prize for Constructive Study & Orig Res, 1976; W/W in S & SW; Commun Ldrs & Noteworthy Ams; Ldrs in Ed.

ANDERSON, MARJORIE E A oc/ Executive Director; h/3 Sawyer Place, Plymouth, MA 02360; ba/Plymouth, MA; p/Marian F Amado, Plymouth, MA; ed/Massasoit Commun Col; S En MA Univ, 1974-76; pa/Exec Dir, Parting Ways, The Mus of Afro-Am Ethnohist Inc, 1976-; Mem, Am Assn of Mus; Mem, African Am Mus Assn; Mem, The Assn for the Study of Afro-Am Life & Hist; Mem, MA Cultural Alliance; MA Bicentennial Comm; Plymouth Bicentennial Comm; Plymouth Arts Lottery Comm; Participant: Nat Coun of Artists, N Eng Assn of Mus, Weeksville Afro-Am Conf, RI Black Heritage Soc, CT Afro-Am Hist & Cultural Soc, The Am Assn for St & Local Hist, Assn for the Study of Afro-Am Life & Hist, N Eng Coun for Black Studies; cp/Num Commun Lectrs incl'g: Plymouth Rotary Clb, Plymouth Public Lib, Pilgrim Soc Lectr Series, Univ of MA, Stoughton Human Rights Grp, Plymouth Area Leag of Wom Voters, Plymouth Bay GSA, Others; Plymouth Fair Housing Com; MA Coun for Chd; Plymouth Affirmative Action Comm; Assoc Mem, Dem Town Com; Del to Nat Dem Conv, 1980; S En MA Univ Alumni Assn; r/Cath; hon/Bethel A M E Recog Awd; MA Tchrs Assn Human Relats Awd, 1983; W/W: in Am Wom, of Black Ams, in Am Civic Wom, in E; The Registry of Am Achmt; Other Biogl

Listings.

ANDERSON, MARY JORGENSEN oc/Mathematician; b/Oct 31, 1937; h/Route 4, 140 Barbara Lane, Midland, TX 79701; ba/Midland, TX; m/Edmund H; c/Carolyne Gail Calvert, Gary Steven Calvert, Christopher Lewis Calvert; p/Mr and Mrs R L Jorgensen, Houston, TX; ed/BS Math 1965, MS Math-Topology 1968, PhD Math-Partial Differential Equations 1979, LA St Univ; pa/Engrg Tech, LA Dept of Hwys, 1957-60; Instr 1970-76, Asst Prof 1978-81, MS St Univ; Mathematician 1982-84, Reviewer of Var Math Reviews 1984-, Superior Oil Co; Am Math Soc; Assoc for Wom in Math; MS Acad of Scis; r/Epis; hon/Articles Pub'd in *Jour of Integral Equations* 1982 & 1981, *Jour of MS Acad of Sci* 1980, *Jour of Nonlinear Anal* 1980; Phi Delta Kappa; Pi Mu Epsilon; W/W in Am Wom; Personalities of S.

ANDERSON, REBECCA COGWELL oc/Instructor; b/Jun 28, 1948; h/5201 North Hills Boulevard, North Little Rock, AR 72116; ba/Conway, AR; m/ Kim Edward; c/Kristin Lain, Courtney Lynn; p/Alvy Lynn Cogwell (dec); Georgia Earles Cogwell, Cabot, AR; sp/ Kermit and Zeta Anderson, El Reno, OK; ed/BS 1972, MSE 1976, Univ of Ctl AR; Studied at Univ of AR, Marquette Univ & Univ of OK Hlth Sci Ctr Pursuing PhD; pa/Instr, Univ of Central AR, 1977-; Indust Hygiene Conslt, AR Dept of Labor, 1976-77; Indust Hygienist, US Dept of Labor OSHA, 1975-76; Claims Developer, VA Reg Ofc, 1973-75; Tchr, Pulaski Co Spec Sch Dist, 1972-73; AEA, NEA, AAUW, 1972-73; AR Public Hlth Assn, 1973-76; Am Indust Hygiene Assn, Am Cong of Govt Indust Hygienists, 1975-80; Bd of Dir, AR Indust Hygiene Assn, 1977-79; ETA Sigma Gamma, Am Alliance of Hlth, PE, Rec & Dance, AR Alliance of HPER&D, AR Sch Hlth Assn, 1977-; cp/ Vol, ARC & Am Heart Assn; Co-Ldr, GSA; hon/Pub'd Articles in Profl Jours incl'g: *The Pers Admr* 1979, *Prfl Safety* 1981, *Occupl Hlth Nsg* 1981; Others; Marquette Univ S'ship, 1982; Gamma Beta Phi Hon Soc, 1970; W/W.

ANDERSON, ROBERT SIMPERS oc/Immunologist/Immunotoxicologist; b/Jan 4, 1939; h/12795 Buttercup Court, West Friendship, MD 21794; ba/Aberdeen Proving Ground, MD; m/Lucy A Macdonald; c/Robert S Jr, Donald P; p/ Paul A Anderson (dec); Ella T S Anderson, Phila, PA; sp/F A Macdonald (dec); Emily H Macdonald (dec); ed/BS, Drexel Univ, 1961; MS, Hahnemann Med Univ, 1968; PhD, Univ of DE, 1971; pa/Postdoct Fellow, Univ of MN, 1970-73; Lab Head 1973-82, Adjunct 1982-, Sloan-Kettering Inst for Cancer Res, Rye, NY; Asst Prof, Sloan-Kettering Div, Cornell Univ Grad Sch of Med Scis, NY, 1975-82; Immunologist, Res Div, CRDC, Aberdeen Proving Ground, 1982-; Am Assn of Immunologists; Intl Soc of Devel & Comparative Immunol; NY Acad of Scis; Phila Physiological Soc; Soc for Invertebrate Pathol; cp/Am Entomological Soc; Am Soc of Zoologists; r/Epis; hon/Over 45 Reports on Orig Res in Sci Jours; 8 Book Chapts; Others; Exceptl Perf Awd, Dept of the Army, 1984; W/W: in E, in Frontier Sci & Technol.

ANDERSON, ROGER CLARK oc/ Professor; b/Oct 30, 1941; h/14 McCormick Boulevard, Normal, IL 61761; ba/ Normal, IL; m/Mary Rebecca; c/John Allen, Nancy Lynn; p/Virginia S Anderson, Stevens Point, WI; sp/Kenneth and Ruth Blocher, Greenville, OH; ed/ BS, WI St Col, 1963; MS 1965, PhD 1968, Univ of WI-Madison; pa/Asst Prof Botany, So IL Univ, Carbondale, IL, 1968-70; Asst Prof Botany & Dir of Arboretum, Univ of WI-Madison, 1970-73; Assoc Prof Bio, Ctl St Univ, Edmond, OK, 1973-76; Prof of Biol, IL St Univ, Normal, IL, 1976-; cp/Pres, So IL Audubon Soc, 1970; Secy & Mem of Miller Pk Zool Soc, 1980-82; Chm, McLean Co Pk & Rec Adv Coun, 1982-84; Mem, Pklands Foun Bd, 1983-84; r/Unitarian-Universalist; hon/ Over 43 Articles Pub'd in Sci Jours, 1966-83; Contb'd 2 Book Chapts 1974 & 1982; 1 Book, *Envir Bio*, 1970; Kappa Delta Phi, 1962; BS, magna cum laude, 1963; Davis F'ship, Univ of WI, 1968; McMullen Lectr Monmouth Col, 1982; Roger Wilson Lectr, Miami Univ, Oxford, OH, 1984; Personalities of S; W/W: in MW, in Technol Today.

ANDERSON, ROLPH ELY oc/Professor; b/Aug 27, 1936; h/106 Avonbrook Road, Wallingford, PA 19086; ba/ Philadelphia, PA; p/Eugene J and Susannah Anderson, Buchanan, MI; ed/BA 1958, MBA 1964, MI St Univ; PhD, Univ of FL, 1971; mil/USN-Ret'd, Capt, SC; pa/Prof & Hd Dept of Mktg, Drexel Univ, 1975-; Chm, Dept of Bus Mgmt, Old Dominion Univ, 1971-74; New Prod Devel Mgr, Quaker Oats Co, 1964-67; Pres, SE Am Inst for Decision Scis, 1978; Secy, Acad of Mktg Sci, 1984-85; VP for Programming, Am Mktg Assn, Phila Chapt, 1984-85; Co-Chp Intl Conf, Am Mktg Assn, 1978; Sales & Mktg Execs; Others; cp/NRA; r/Meth; hon/Author of Books, *Multivariate Data Anal*, 1979; *Sales Mgmt*, 1983; Pub'd Num Articles in Profl Jours; W/W: in Am, in E, in S.

ANDERSON, RON J oc/Physician/ Chief Executive Officer; b/Sept 6, 1946; h/1022 Wind Ridge, Duncanville, TX 75317; m/Sue Ann Blakely; c/Sarah Elizabeth, Daniel Jerrod, John Charles; p/Ted J Anderson (dec); Ruby A Benjamin, Chickasha, OK; ed/BS, Pharm, SWn Univ of OK 1969; MD, Med, Univ of OK, 1973; Internal Med Bd Cert, Internship & Residency at Univ of TX Hlth Sci Ctr, Parkland VA Hosps, Dallas, 1977-76; pa/CEO 1982-, Acting Med Dir 1981-82, Med Dir Ambulatory Care-Emer Ser 1979-82, Chm of TX St Bd of Hlth, Jr Active Att'g, Pkland Meml Hosp; Assoc Prof Internal Med 1981-, Asst Dean Clin Affairs 1979-82, Asst Prof of Internal Med 1976-81, Asst Prof Sch of Allied Hlth 1976-81, Univ of TX Hlth Sci Ctr at Dallas; Adj Assoc Prof 1982-83, Adj Asst Prof Med Sch 1981-82, Uniformed Ser Univ of the Hlth Scis; Fellow, Am Col of Phys; AMA; Dallas Co Med Soc; Kappa Psi Pharm Frat; Soc for Res & Ed in Primary Care Internal Med; Advr, TX Assn of Phys Assts; Am Soc of Internal Med; Num Past & Present Profl Coms incl'g: Chm Med Records Com 1980-82, Chm Utilization Review Com 1980-82, TX Hosp Assn 1982-, Gerontolog & Geriatric Med 1980-, Num Others; Num Symposia Presentations to: Pkland VA Hosp Resident's Confs, Am Col of

Surgs Nat Trauma Symp, Dept of Internal Med UTHSC, Nat Med Assn, Chds Med Ctr, Others; r/Baptist; hon/ Author & Co-Author, Num Articles & Abstracts Pub'd in Profl Jours incl'g: *Am Jour of Med, Primary Cardiology, Dallas Med Jour, Hosp Formulary, Excerpta Medica, Clin Res*, Others; Pub'd Num Symposia Presentations & Tch Manuscripts; Rho Chi, 1968; Alpha Omega Alpha, 1973; W/W: in Col & Univs, in S & SW; Personalities of Am; DIB; Other Biogl Listings.

ANDERSON, THEODORE WILBUR oc/Professor; b/Jun 5, 1918; h/746 Santa Ynez Street, Stanford, CA 94305; m/ Dorothy Fisher; c/Robert Lewis, Janet Lynn Yang, Jeanne Elizabeth; ed/AA, North Park Col, 1937; BS Math, NWn Univ, 1939; MA Math 1942, PhD Math 1945, Princeton Univ; pa/Asst Math, NWn Univ, 1939-40; Instr Math 1941-43, Res Assoc Nat Def Res Com 1943-45, Princeton Univ; Res Assoc, Cowles Comm for Res in Ec, Univ of Chgo, 1945-46; Instr 1946-47, Asst Prof Math Stats 1947-50, Assoc Prof Math Stats 1950-56, Prof Math Stats 1956-67, Chm Dept of Math Stats 1956-60 & 1964-65, Act'g Chm Dept of Math Stats, 1950-51 & 1963, Columbia Univ; Prof Stats & Ec, Stanford Univ, 1967-; Num Profl Positions incl'g: Res Conslt, Cowles Foun for Res in Ec 1946-60, Conslt, Rand Corp 1949-66, Dir, Ofc of Nav Res Proj, Dept of Math Stats Columbia Univ 1950-68 & Dept of Stats Stanford Univ 1968-82, Prin Investigator, Nat Sci Foun Proj, Dept of Ec, Stanford Univ 1969-; Pres 1963, Abraham Wald Meml Lectr 1982, Inst of Math Stats; VP, Am Stat Assn, 1971-73; Exec Com Mem, Conf Bd of the Math Scis, 1963-64; Res Visitor, Tokyo Inst of Technol, 1977; Fellow, Ctr for Adv'd Study in the Behavioral Scis, 1957-58; Vis'g Scholar, Ctr for Adv'd Study in the Behavioral Scis, 1972-73, 1980; Mem, Exec Com, Conf Bd of the Math Scis, 1963-64; Wesley C Mitchell Vis'g Prof of Ec, Columbia Univ, 1983-84; Others; Fellow: AAAS, Am Stat Assn, Econometric Soc, Royal Stat Soc; Mem: Am Math Soc, Bernoulli Soc for Math Stats & Probability, Intl Stat Inst, Phi Beta Kappa, Others; hon/Author & Co-Author of *AN Intro to Multivariate Stat Anal* 1958 (2nd Edition 1984), *The Stat Anal of Time Series* 1971, *A Bibliog of Multivariate Stat Anal* (w Somesh Das Gupta & George P H Styan) 1972, *Into Stat Anal* (w Stanley L Sclove) 1974, *An Intro to the Stat Anal of Data* (w Stanley L Sclove) 1978; Pub'd Over 100 Articles in Stat Jours; Editor, *Annals of Math Stats*, 1950-52; Guggenheim Fellow, Univ of Stockholm & Univ of Cambridge, 1947-48; Sherman Fairchild Dist'd Scholar, CA Inst of Technol, 1980; Fellow, Am Acad of Arts & Sci, 1974; Mem, Nat Acad of Scis, 1976; Others; W/W: in Am, in World; Am Men & Wom of Sci; Contemp Authors; DIB; Other Biogl Listings.

ANDERSON, TRUDY B oc/Professor; b/Nov 23, 1947; h/2953 Paddock Plaza, Omaha, NE 68124; ba/Lincoln, NE; m/Eugene U. p/John J and Cathern Bohrer, Omaha, NE; ed/BA, Creighton, Univ, 1970; MA, Univ of NE Omaha, 1974; PhD, Univ of NE Lincoln, 1981; pa/Asst Prof of Sociol, E TX St Univ-Texarkana, 1983-; Vis'g Asst Prof

Sociol 1982-83, Tchg Asst 1977-78 & 1979-81, Undergrad Prog Asst 1978-79, Univ of NE Lincoln; Adj Instr, Bellevue Col, 1975-78; Am Sociological Assn; MW Sociological Soc; hon/Pub'd Articles in Profl Jours: *Res On Aging* 1981, *N Eng Sociologists* 1982, *Jour of Marriage & the Fam* 1984; Happold Res Grant, 1981; W/W of Wom.

ANDERSON, URSULA M oc/Physician; b/Cheshire, UK; h/310 West Walnut Street, Carbondale, IL; ba/So IL Univ, Carbondale, IL; m/Lino H Dominguez Montenegro; ed/MB ChB, Liverpool, 1952; MHCS, LRCP, London, 1952; Dipl Pub Hlth, 1954; Dipl Child Hlth, 1957, UK; Dipl Am Bd of Pediatrics, 1963; Fellow, Am Acad of Pediatrics, 1964; pa/Chief, Div Commun Hlth, Dept Pediatrics Hosp for Sick Chd, Toronto, 1969-73; Assoc Prof Pediatrics, Univ of Toronto, 1969-75; Med Cons, Maternal & Child Hlth, Reg IV, US HEW, 1976-1982; Clin Assoc Prof Pediatrics, Cons Nat Per-Natal Assn, Emory Univ, Atlanta, 1976; Med Dir, Interagy Progs for Mothers & Chd, HCFA; Prof, So IL Univ, 1982-; AMA; Woms Med Assn; Pan-Am Hlth Assn; APHA; hon/Pub'd Num Articles in Profl Jours; Pub'd a Collection of Poems.

ANDERSON, WARREN M oc/Majority Leader, New York State Senate/ Attorney; b/Oct 16, 1915; h/34 Lathrop Avenue, Binghamtom, NY 13905; ba/ Binghamton, NY; m/Eleanor S; c/ Warren David, Lawrence C, Richard S, Thomas B; p/Floyd E Anderson (dec); Edna S Anderson, Binghamton, NY; ed/ BA, Colgate Univ, 1937; JD, Albany Law Sch, 1940; mil/Served EM, 1943-44 & Lt Judge Advocate Gen Dept, 1945-46; pa/Asst Atty, Broome Co, NY, 1940-42; Assoc 1949-52, Ptner 1952-, Firm Hinman, Howard, & Kattell; Mem 1953-, Pres Pro Tem & Maj Ldr 1973-, NY St Senate; cp/Binghamton Clb; Ft Orange Clb, Albany; r/Presb; hon/ Colgate Univ LLD, 1982; Albany Law Sch LLD, 1979; Hartwick Col LLD, 1976; Col of New Rochelle LLD, 1979; Fordham Univ LLD, 1980; Union Col LLD, 1981; W/W: in Am, in E, in Am Law.

ANDREW, CLIFFORD GEORGE oc/ Professor Neurology/Neuroscientist; b/ Sep 10, 1946; h/474 Old Orchard Circle, Point Field Landing on the Severn, Millersville, MD 21108; ba/Baltimore, MD; m/Louise Briggs; c/Galen Michael, Amalie Linnea; p/Eugene Ashton and Anna Louise Hanish Andrew, Florissant, MO; sp/Eugene LeRoy Briggs, High Point, NC; Elizabeth Brockman Miller, Greensboro, NC; ed/AB, Columbia Col, 1968; PhD 1974, MD 1975, Med Sci Trng Prog, Duke Univ Med Sch; pa/ Med Internship, Duke Hosp, 1975-76; Neurol Residency 1976-79, Neuromuscular F'ship 1979-80, Neurol Asst Prof 1980-, Johns Hopkins Hosp; Diplomate, Am Bd of Psychi & Neurol, 1981; AAAS; Am Acad of Neurol; Soc for Neurosci; Am Soc of Neurochem; Phys for Soc Responsibility; Columbia Chems; cp/ Pres, Severn River Assn; Chesapeake Bay Foun; Save Our Streams; r/Presb; hon/Num Articles Pub'd in Profl Jours: *Jour of Biol Chem, Sci*; Patentee in Field; Columbia S'ship, 1964-68; Avalon S'ship, 1968-75; Game Recip Tchr Investigator Devel Awd NINCDS, 1980-; Muscular Dystrophy Assn Basic

Res Grantee, 1980-.

ANDREWS, DALE C oc/Attorney; b/ Jan 11, 49; h/3127 Rittenhouse Street, Northwest, Washington, DC 20015; ba/ Washington, DC; m/Patricia M Black; p/Ruth K Andrews, Ballwin, MO; sp/ Calvin L Black, Vincennes, IN; ed/BA Sociol, The George Wash Univ, 1971; JD, Wash Col of Law, The Am Univ, 1976; pa/Sys Anal, McDonnell Douglas Automation Co, 1971-73; Sr Res Assoc, The Am Univ, 1974-76; Law Clk, The Hon Austin L Fickling, 1976-77; Assoc, Galland, Kharasch, Calkins & Short, PC, 1977-82; Assoc 1982-84, Ptnr 1984-, Short, Klein & Karas, PC; Lectr, Wash Col of Law, The Am Univ, 1981-83; Sigma Phi Epsilon; Maritime Adm Bar Assn; ABA; DC Bar Assn; cp/ The Jefferson Isl Clb; Intl Aviation Clb; hon/Assoc Editor, *The Am Univ Law Review*, 1975-76; Del, DC Jud Conf, 1980-82; Outstg Yg Men in Am.

ANDREWS, ERNEST CHARLES oc/ General Surgeon; b/Jul 5, 1930; h/PO Box 374 Goldthwaite, TX 76844; ba/ Goldthwaite, TX; m/Nelda; c/Charlotte (Mrs Rahim Dokht), Leatrice (Mrs John Bailey); p/Ernest and Vesta Andrews (dec); sp/Delos Harris (dec); Lily Harris, Dublin, TX; ed/AA, Tarleton Col, 1948; BA, Univ of TX, 1950; MD, Univ of TX Med Br, 1958; Surg Residency, Univ of TX-San Antonio, 1969; mil/AUS, 1950-54; pa/Gen Pract, Fredericksburg (TX) 1960-65; Gen Surg Pract, Weathorford (TX) 69-70; Gen Surg Pract, Grand Prairie (TX) 1970-79; Gen Surg, Tawam Hosp, Al Ain, Abu Dhabi, UAE, 1979-81; Gen Surg, Kaiser Prudential Permanente Assn of TX, Dallas, 1981; Gen Surg Pract, Goldthwaite (TX) 1982-; AMA; TX Med Assn; Tri-Col Med Assn; So Med Assn; Am Bd of Surg; Am Col of Surgs; Austin Surg Assn; Intl Col of Surgs; Am Soc of Abdominal Surgs; Sigma Xi Res Assn; r/Luth; hon/Num Articles Pub'd in Profl Jours, 1957-1982; Borden Res Awd, 1958; W/W in S & SW; Dir of Med Specs.

ANDREWS, HUGH ROBERT oc/ Research Officer; b/Apr 29, 1940; h/66 Rutherford Avenue, Deep River, Ontario, Canada, KOJ1PO; ba/Chalk River, Ontario, KOJ1JO; m/Josephine Dawn Kennedy; c/John Matthew, Elizabeth Louise; sp/J L Kennedy, Deep River, Ontario; ed/BSC, Univ of New Brunswick, 1962; AM 1963, PhD 1970, Harvard Univ; pa/Res Offcr, Nuclear Physics Br, Chalk River Labs, 1971-; Canada Assn of Physicists; Am Phy Soc; Sigma Xi; Canadian Nuclear Soc; r/ Anglican; hon/Author & Co-Author, 90 Papers in Profl Jours in Nuclear Physics & Other Fields; Rutherford F'ship, Royal Soc Canada, 1968; Frank Knox F'ship, Harvard Univ, 1963 & 1964; Beaverbrook Scholar, Univ of New Brunswick, 1958-62; Am Men & Wom of Sci; W/W in Frontier Sci & Technol.

ANDREWS, J ROBERT oc/Radiation Researcher; b/Jun 10, 1906; h/4428 Volta Place, Northwest, Washington, DC 20007; ba/Washington, DC; m/ Catherine F Kapikian; c/William B, J Robert Jr; p/William Baird and Anna Gable Doyle; ed/PhB, Brown Univ, 1928; MD, Wn Resv Univ, 1932; DSc, Univ of PA, 1946; pa/Chief, Radiation Br, Nat Cancer Inst, 1955-64; Prof & Dir, Radiation Oncology, Georgetown Univ Med Ctr, 1964-74; Head, Radia-

tion Sect, Wash VA Hosp, 1964-1975; Radiation Res Soc; Am Assn for Cancer Res; Am Radium Soc; Radiol Soc of N AM; Am Roentgen Ray Soc; AMA; hon/ Author of *The Radiobiol of Human Cancer Radiotherapy*, Volume I (1968), Vol II (1978); Pub'd Over 80 Articles in Profl Sci & Med Jours.

ANDREWS, JEAN CAROL oc/Logistics & Energy Planner/Technical Writer/ Editor; b/Aug 16, 1929; h/6800 Granby Street, Bethesda, MD 20817; ba/Falls Church, VA; m/Peter Gibson; c/Richard Gibson, Patricia Susan; p/Mr and Mrs John F Fitzgerald, Williamsburg, VA; sp/ Peter G Andrews, Bethesda, MD; ed/ AB, Brown Univ, 1950; MA, Columbia Univ, 1951; MA, Urban & Reg Planning, George Wash Univ, 1981; pa/Logistics Planner, Zimmerman Assoc Inc, 1983-; Sr Logistician, INTEX Inc, 1981-83; Sr Assoc, CACI Inc, 1976-81; Res Dir, Housing Guid Coun, 1971-76; Instr, Eng Dept, Col of Wm & Mary, 1965-71; Acct Exec, Gordon Schonfarber Assoc Inc, 1953-54; Head Eng Dept, St Dunstan's Sch, 1951-53; Mem Nat Capital Area Chapt 1980-, Mem NCAC Energy Com 1981-, Chp Energy Planning Div 1983-, Am Planning Assn; Am Inst of Cert Planners, 1981; AICP NCAC Devel Com, 1981-; r/Prot; hon/Writer & Editor, *Energy Planning Netwk*, Qtly Newslttr of Energy Planning Div of Am Planning Assn, 1982-; Co-Editor, *Guide to Taxation, Public Fin & Relat'd Lit* (Volume 2) 1976, *The Papers & Gums of US Postage Stamps 1847-1909*, 1983; W/W in the E.

ANDREWS, MARY LOU oc/Systems Engineer; b/Oct 17, 1935; h/4020 West Whitehall Road, Pennsylvania Furnace, PA 16865; ba/St Col, PA; c/Judy Lynn Edighoffer, Tammy Lee Harkness; p/Earl and Carolyn Drust Andrews, Hillsdale, MI; ed/BS, MI St Univ, 1956; MA, PA St Univ, 1965; pa/Sys Engr 1981-, & 1978-80, HRB Singer Inc; Prof Bus Adm & Computer Sci, Hillsdale Col, 1980-81; Instr & Res Asst 1967-77, Instr 1960-66, PA St Univ; Prof Stats, CA St Univ-Hayward, 1966-67; Instr Stats, MI St Univ, 1958-59; Am Math Soc; Soc of Industl Applied Math; Assn of Computing Machinery; Am Stat Assn; Math Assn of Am; r/Rom Cath; hon/ Author of *Stats Lab Manual* 1966, *Course Outline for Stats 200* 1977; Pub'd Article, "The Generalized Hyperbolic Secant Distbn," *Jour of the Am Stat Assn*, 1968; Pi Mu Epsilon, 1956; Kappa Delta Pi, 1956; Tau Sigma, 1956; Sigma Delta Pi, 1966; Sigma Zeta, 1981; Dairy Queen, 1953; W/W: of Wom, in Frontier of Science & Technol; DIB.

ANDREWS, SUSANNAH SMITH oc/Clinical Psychologist & Consultant; b/Mar 15, 1949; h/757 East Scenic Drive, Pass Christian, MS 39571; ba/ Gulfport, MS; m/Kent; c/Nathan Walter; p/Sydney Allen Smith (dec); Frances Smith Darden, Poindexter, MS; sp/ Walter Irving Andrews, Lincoln City, OR; Catherine Pemberton Andrews (dec); ed/BA Psych, Vassar Col, 1970; MS Clin Psych, San Jose St Univ, 1973; PhD Clin Psych, CA Sch of Profl Psych, 1975; pa/Child Wkr, Head Start Proj, Jackson, MS, 1968; Child Care Wkr, Zonta's Chd Ctr, San Jose, CA, 1970-71; Student & Tchg Asst, Fremont Union HS, Sunnyvale, CA, 1971; Psychol Asst & Child Care Wkr, Peninsula Chd Ctr,

Palo Alto, CA, 1971-72; Genetic & Fam Cnslg, MidPeninsula Sicle Cell Anemia Foun, Stanford, CA, 1971-72; Res w Mtly Retarded, Agnews St Hosp, San Jose, CA, 1971-72; Psych Internship 1972, Play Therapy Internship Child & Fam Clin 1971-72, CA St Univ; Clin Psych Internship, Fam Ser Assn, San Diego, CA, 1972-73; Adolescent Cnslr, SE Involvement Prog, San Diego, CA, 1973-74; Prog Dir, Drug Diversion Prog, Fam Ser Assn, El Cajon, CA, 1974; Tchg Asst 1972, Tchg Asst 1973-74, CA Sch of Profl Psych; Clin Psych Internship 1974-76, Orgl Behavior Res Mtl Hlth Unit 1976, Mercy Hosp, San Diego, CA; Pvt Clin Pract, Psych & Guid Ctr, San Diego, CA, 1975-76; Prog Chief 1975-78, Clin Psychol 1977-78, San Louis Obispo Commun Mtl Hlth Ctr; Orgl Devel Conslt, 1973-; Tchr, San Louis Obispo Ctr for Psychol Sers, 1977-80; Pvt Pract in MS, 1983-; Pt-time Prof, Univ of So MS, 1983-; Mem: Am Psychol Assn, MS Psychol Assn, CA St Psychol Assn; Bd Mem & Co-Fdr, ANRED-Anorexia Nervosa & Related Eating Disorders, Ctl CA Coast; San Diego Soc of Clin Hypnosis; Staff Mem at Gulfport Meml, Biloxi Reg, Garden Park Hosps; cp/Bd of Dirs & V, Am Cancer Soc, Harrison Co; Patron, Gulf Coast Arts Coun; Choir Mem, Trinity Epis Ch; r/Epis; hon/Author, "Effects of Combat & Mil Experience on Personality & Attitude," *Jour of Mil Sci*; Regular Newspaper Column, "Pract Psychol," in *NE MS Daily Jour*; Several Musical Compositions Copyrighted; Invitation to Daisy Chair, Vassar Col, 1970; Commend 1972, CSPP-SD 1973, San Jose St Univ; Invitation to be Del to China for People To People; W/W in Am Wom.

ANDREWS, THEODORA ANNE oc/ Librarian/Professor; b/Oct 14, 1921; h/ 2209 Indian Trails Drive, PO Box 2362, West Lafayette, IN 47906; ba/West Lafayette, IN; c/Martin Harry; p/Harry F Ulrey, Lafayette, IN; M Grace Ulrey (dec); ed/BS, Purdue Univ, 1953; MS, Univ of IL, 1955; pa/Asst Ref Lib 1955-56, Pharm Libn/Asst Prof/Assoc Prof 1956-71, Prof Lib Sci/Pharm Libn 1971-79, Prof Lib Sci/Pharm, Nsg & Hlth Scis Libn 1979-, Purdue Univ; Vis'g Lectr Sum Sessions: Syracuse Univ, Univ of IL, IN St Univ, 1958-71; Bd of Dirs 1966-69, Secy of Bd of Dirs 1966-68, Chm Pharm Div 1970-71, Pres IN Chapt 1962-63, Spec Libs Assn; Chm Pharm Grp, Med Lib Assn, 1960-61; Treas Purdue Chapt, AAUP, 1977-; Am Assn of Cols of Pharm; Am Lib Assn; r/Bapt; hon/Author, *Bibliog of the Socioeconomic Aspects of Med* 1975, *Bibliog of Drug Abuse, incl'g Alcohol & Tobacco* 1977, *Bibliog of Drug Abuse Supplement 1977-80* 1981, *Bibliog on Herbs, Herbal Med, "Natural" Foods, & Unconvtl Med Treatment* 1982; Pub'd Num Articles in Profl Jours; John H Moriarity Awd for Dist'd Libn, IN Chapt, Spec Libs Assn, 1972; W/W: Am Wom, in Lib Sci & Info Sers, of Wom; Men & Wom of Distn; IN Authors & Their Books.

ANDRICHUK, JOHN MICHAEL oc/ Independent Geologist; b/Jul 4, 1926; h/ 209 Varsity Estates Bay, Northwest, Calgary, Alberta T3B 2W5; ba/Calgary, Alberta; m/Ollie June; c/Carol Linda, Janet Brenda, Craig Spencer; p/Doris Prostebby, Vancouver, British Columbia; sp/Mary Solodky, Calgary, Alberta; ed/BS 1946, MS 1949, Univ of Alberta; PhD, NWn Univ, 1951; pa/Geologist, Gulf Oil Corp, 1951-54; Geologist, A W McCoy Assoc, 1954-56; Conslitg & Indep Geologist, Andrichuk & Edie, 1956-; Am Assn of Petro Geol; Geol Soc Am; Canadian Soc of Petro Geol; Assn Profl Engrs, Geologists & Geophysicists of Alberta; Councillor 2 Yrs, Soc Ec Paleontologists & Mineralogists; hon/ Author of 10 Maj Sci Articles for Profl Jours, Mainly: *Bltn of Am Assn Petro Geologists*; Pres's Awd, Am Assn of Petro Geologists, 1959; Medal Awd, Alberta Soc of Petro Geologists, 1959; Am Men of Sci; W/W in Oil.

ANEMA, DURLYNN C oc/Professor/ Executive Director; b/Dec 23, 1935; h/ 1728 West Vine Street, Lodi, CA 95240; ba/Stockton, CA; m/Charles J; c/Charlynn Ann, Charles Jay Jr, Richard F; p/ Durlin L Flagg and Carolyn L Owen (dec); sp/Charles J and Helen Anema (dec); ed/BA 1968, MS 1977, CA St Univ-Hayward; ED, Univ of the Pacific, 1984; pa/Asst Prof Communs 1984-, Exec Dir CCAE 1984-, Dir Lifelong Lrng 1981-84, Univ of the Pacific; VPrin, Lodi Unified Sch Dist, 1977-80; VPrin 1976-77, Dean of Girls 1975-76, Hayward Unified Sch Dist; Bd of Dirs, Val Commun Cnslg, 1981-; Pres & Mem, Lib Trustees, San Leandro, 1970-75; cp/Pres, Monroe PTA, San Leandro, 1961-62 & 1966-67; Yth Ldr, Grace Presb Ch, Lodi, 1981; r/Presb; hon/Author: *Get Hired*, 1979; *Don't Get Fired*, 1978; *Sharing An Apt*, 1982; *CA Yesterday & Today*, 1983; Phi Kappa Phi, 1984; Life Mbrship, PTA, 1966; W/W: in W, Among Am Col & Univ Students.

ANGEL, THOMAS MICHAEL oc/ Diving Executive; b/Apr 16, 1939; h/25 Mary Hughes Court, Houma, LA 70363; ba/Houma, LA; m/Bette Jean Miller; c/Nicole Lee, Tommie Jean, Martine Renée; p/Joseph Vincent and Mary Lucille (Stock) Angel (dec); sp/Leo Miller, Dillonvale, OH; Alberta (Howell) Miller (dec); ed/Mt Pleasant HS, 1957; BS Manned Submersibles, Cath Univ of Am, 1975; Att'd Mgmt Courses 1980 & 1981-82, Am Mgmt Assn; mil/ USN, Sea Bees; pa/Sr VP, Sonat Sub Sea Sers Inc, 1984-; VP & Mgr, Santa Fe Underwater Sers Inc, 1980-; VP & Mgr, Santa Fe Diving Sers Inc, 1973-80; Mgr Diving Sers, Floor Ocean Sers, 1970-73; Tech Com for Underwater Sys & Vehicles, Am Bur of Shipping; Bd of Advrs, FL Inst of Technol & Santa Barbara City Col; Dir & Past Pres, Assn of Diving Contractors; Mem, Am Petro Inst; cp/C of C; r/Cath; hon/Pub'd Articles, "Saturation Diving, A Tool for Underwater Welding & Cutting" 1967, "How Accurate Record-Keeping Can Assist in Reducing Decompression Sickness" 1975; Hon Fac Mem, FL Inst of Technol; W/W in S & SW.

ANGELO, GAYLE-JEAN oc/ Research and Development Analyst, Instructor; b/Nov 27, 1951; h/113 Butler Avenue, Wakefield, MA 01880; ba/ Gloucester, MA; p/John W and Josephine M Angelo, Wakefield, MA; ed/BA w Hon Physics, 1975; MEd Curric & Instrn: Math & Sci, 1978; MS Applied Stats, 1984; mil/USAF, 1980-82; Air NG, 1982-84; pa/Res & Devel Analyst, Varian/Extrion, 1984-; Res Assoc, Columbia Univ, 1982-83; Res Sci, USAF

Rocket Propulsion Lab, 1980-82; Math Instr, Cerro Coso Commun Col & Golden Gate Univ, 1980-82; Res & Tchg Asst, Columbia Univ, 1978-80; Hd of Sci Dept, Girls Cath HS, 1977-78; Asst Physicist, Dana Res Ctr, NEn Univ, 1975-76; Asst Clin Chem, Boston Med Lab, 1971-73; AAAS; Am Assn of Physics Tchrs; Am Phy Soc; Am Stat Assn; Assn for Wom in Sci; Inst of Mgmt Scis; Nat Coun of Math Tchrs; Nat Sci Tchr Assn; NY Acad of Scis; Opers Res Soc of Am; Sch Sci & Math Assn; Soc for Col Sci Tchrs; Am Mensa Ltd; r/Cath; hon/Ednl: Kappa Delta Pi, Phi Delta Kappa; Sci: Sigma Pi Sigma, Sigma Xi; W/W of Am Wom.

ANGEVINE, GEORGE B oc/Executive; b/Jun 26, 1918; h/625 Pine Road, Sewickley, PA 15143; ba/Pittsburgh, PA; m/Margaret Muse; c/Paula A Craig, Sheryl Jane, Katherine Lewis, Barbara Braud; p/Lewis Jame and Eugenia A Angevine (dec); sp/Albert and Margaret Muse; ed/BA, Rutgers Univ, 1940; LLB, Univ of Pgh Law Sch, 1948; mil/USAF, 1941-45, Capt; pa/Ptnr, Thorp, Reed & Armstrong, 1948-62; VChm, Nat Steel Corp, 1963-; ABA; PA Bar Assn; MI Bar Assn; Allegheny Bar Assn; Am Iron & Steel Inst; cp/Dir, Allegheny Trails Coun of BSA; Nat Kidney Foun of Wn PA; Allegheny C of C; Rolling Rock Clb.

ANGINO, ERNEST EDWARD oc/ Professor; b/Feb 16, 1932; h/1215 West 27th Street, Lawrence, KS 66044; ba/ Lawrence, KS; m/Margaret; c/Cheryl Ann, Kimberly Ann; p/F M Angino, Winsted, CT; sp/R Lachat, Winsted, CT; ed/BS Mining Engrg, Lehigh Univ, 1954; MS Geol 1958, PhD Geochem 1961, Univ KS; mil/AUS, 1955-57; Signal Corp; pa/Instr 1961-62, Prof & Chm Dept Geol 1972-, Univ KS; Asst Prof Oceanography, TX A&M Univ, 1962-65; Chief, Geochem Sect, KS Geol Survey, 1965-70; Assoc St Geol, 1970-72; Pres, Soc Envir Geochem & Hlth, 1978-79; Secy, Geochem Soc, 1970-76; Treas, Intl Asn Geochem & Cosmochem, 1980-; Soc of Ec Paleontologists & Mineralogists; Geol Soc of Am; KS Geological Soc; Am Assn of Petro Geols; AAAS; Served on Num Other Nat, Indust & Acad Coms, Surveys & Couns; 10 Yrs of Conslitg Wk in Field; Other Res Progs; pa/City Commr 1983, Mayor 1984, Lawrence, KS; r/Cath; hon/Author, Num Books in Field incl'g: *Atomic Absorption Spectrometry in Geology* (w G K Billings) 1967 & 72, *Geochem of Subsurface Brines* (w G K Billings) 1969, *Geochem of Bismuth* (w D T Long, Editors) 1979, Others; Over 100 Articles in Profl Jours Incl'g: *Geol*, *Envir Geol*, *Mod Geol*, *Jour of Sedimentary Petrology*, *Mineralogical & Geol Chem*, *Chem Abstracts*, Others; Sigma Xi; Angino Buttress (Mtns), Antarctica 78 14'S, 160 45'E, 1967; Antarctic Ser Medal of DOD for Antarctic Res, 1969; NSF F'ship Radiochem, ORNL, 1963; Am Men of Sci; W/W in MW; DIB.

ANGLE, SHARON (SHARI) A oc/ Certified Legal Assistant; b/Sep 8, 1946; h/410 5th Avenue Southeast, Miami, OK 74354; ba/Miami, OK; c/David Scott; p/Bernie R and Thelma L (Wilmoth) Pennington, Miami, OK; ed/Cert Legal Asst, Paralegal Inst, Phoenix, AZ, 1979; Att'd NEn OK A&M Col, 1980-81; pa/Bkkpr, Burtrum Motor Co, 1964-65; Serv Rep 1966-67, Bus Ofc

Supvr 1968-69, Gen Telephone Co; Secy to Dir of Adult Ed, Rock Val Commun Col, Rockford, IL, 1969-73; Secy/Bkkpr, J R Hall Jr Atty at Law, 1973-75; Legal Secy, Hall, Stockwell & Wooley Attys, 1975; Legal Secy, Garrette, Stockwell & Miller Attys, 1976-78; Cert Legal Asst 1978-81 & 1981-, Garrette & Stockwell Attys; Ins Rep, Insuror's Nationwide Ser Inc, 1981; Adult Ed Instr, NE OK Area Vo-Tech School, 1980; Secy/Treas 1977-78, VPres 1978-79, Pres 1979-80, Hi-Noon Bus & Profl Wom's Clb; Secy/ Dir, Ray-Son Inc & Maverick Enterprises; Adv Bd, NEn OK A&M Col for Cert Legal Asst Curric, 1980-81; r/Prot; hon/W/W in Am Wom.

ANOUCHI, ABRAHAM Y oc/Executive; b/Oct 3, 1930; h/701 Knollwood Drive, Pittsburgh, PA 15215; ba/Pittsburgh, PA; c/Yoel S Anouchi; p/Shlomo M (dec); ed/BS, Elect Engrg, IN Inst of Technol, 1954; MSEE, Harvard Univ, 1956; mil/Israel Def Force, 1948-51; pa/ VP Res & Engrg, U Technols-Bacharach, 1976-; Chief Engr, E G & G Envir Div 1971-76; Chief Engr, Flow Corp, 1963-70; Sr Mem, Instruments Soc of Am; Mem, IEEE; cp/Bd of Trustees, Yg People's Synagogue; r/ Jewish; hon/Pub'd Tech Articles in Profl Jours on Circuits & Instruments, 1958-80; 6 US Patents in Electronics & Transducers.

ANSAH-ABOAGYE, EDWARD oc/ Diplomat; b/Feb 27, 1940; h/6207 Adelaide Drive, Bethesda, MD 20817; ba/Washington, DC; m/Kate; c/Clement, Linda, Sylvia; p/Peter Ansah (dec); Yaa Fio, Kibi, Ghana; sp/Sam and Salome Amo-Baah, Kibi, Ghana; ed/ Diplome d'Etudes Francaises, Univ of Bordeaux, France, 1965; BA, French, Univ of Ghana, 1966; Diploma in Public Adm, 1967; pa/Min Cnslr, Embassy of Ghana, Wash DC, 1981-; Dept Consul Gen, Ghana Mission, NY, 1981; Cnslr (Lome) 1975-79, Cnslr (Algiers) 1974, Ghana Embassy; Mem, Diplomatic Corps; Mem, Consular Corps of Wash DC; Fellow, Intl Consular Acad; Mem, IPA; Ghana's Repr, Commonwlth Royal Overseas Leag, Wash DC; Ghana's Olympic Attaché, LA; r/Prot; hon/ Guest Spkr 3rd Tidewater Sem & Cert of Hon, VA Bar Assn (Intl Law Sect), 1982; Diplomatic List; W/W in Wash DC.

ANSCHUTZ, LUCY ANN oc/Student; b/Apr 10, 1961; h/PO Box 190, Russell, KS 67665; p/Willis Anschutz, Dorrance, KS; MaryAnna Anschutz, Russell, KS; ed/Dorrance HS, 1979; BA 1983, MS Cand Clin Psych, Ft Hays St Univ; pa/Undergrad Asst Dept Psych 1983-84, Secy Biol Dept, 1979-80, Ft Hays St Univ; Dir, Crisis Intervention Hotline; cp/Dorrance HS: Volleyball, Basketball, Band, Choir; Ft Hays St Univ: VPres, Grad Assn of Student Psychols, 1983-84; Debate, Forensic Team; Treas, Mortar Bd, 1982-83; French Clb; Sen & Appropriations Com, Student Govt Assn; Treas 2 Yrs, Resident Hall Assn; RHA Exec Coun; McMindes Hall Coun; Hays Cnslrs Assn; VFW Aux; r/Luth; hon/Psi Chi; Phi Kappa Phi; Nat Residence Hall Hon; Intl Ambassador to Europe, 1980; Nat 4-H Cong, 1980; KS St 4-H Achmt Awd; St People-to-People & Rec Awds; Rep, Rogg Trophy for Public Spkg; 3rd Yr

Grad Am Yth Foun Ldrship Conf, 1980-82; Rep, Ft Hays St Univ to Nat Assn of Cols & Residence Halls, 1980-82; Asst Editor, "Maude's Morsels"; W/W in Am Cols & Univs; Intl Yth of Achmt; Commun Ldrs of Am.

ANSLEY, NINA McCABE oc/Fashion Director; b/Jul 26, 1918; h/815-A Northwest Huckle Drive, Silverdale, WA 98310; ba/LA, CA; c/Janis Ansley-Ungar; p/Rex and Ruth (Hillsman) McCabe; sp/Troy Ansley (dec); Anne Ansley; ed/Jour Maj 2 Yrs, Mary-Hardin Baylor Col, 1937-39; Grad Cert, Univ of Sci & Phil, Waynesboro, VA, 1959; Num Univ Ext Courses for Writers & Photogs, Univ of CA-LA; Att'd SAM Sem for Wom Execs; pa/Fashion Copywriter, Neiman-Marcus, Dallas, 1950-55; Acct Supvr of Woms Accts, Don L Baxter Inc (Advtg Agy), Dallas, 1955-66; Public Relats Dir, Security World Publishing Co, LA, 1967-70; Fashion Dir, Merle Norman Cosmetics, LA, 1980-; Lectr in Fashion Field; Fashion Grp Inc, 1956-; Color Mktg Grp, 1982-; Dallas Press Clb, 1956-66; Dallas Advtg Leag, 1960-66; cp/Dallas Chapt, UN Assn, 1956-66; Fac Lectr, The Mtl Shop, LA 1980-; Clb Francaise d'Amerique, 1983-; r/Epis; hon/Author of Hist Novel *The Crucible & The Cross* (1979), Which Won 2nd Place in Nat Writers Clb Book Contest, 1980; Num Mag Articles incl'g: "Teke to Teke," in *Camera Life*, 1980; Intl W/W: of Intells, of Am Wom.

ANTAL, MICHAEL JERRY JR oc/Professor; b/May 18, 1947; h/357 Opihikao Place, Honolulu, HI, 96825; ba/Honolulu, HI; m/Ann Gorsuch Slaughter; c/Dickinson James, Rachel Caroline; p/Michael Jerry Antal, Lawrenceville, NJ; sp/Lovelace Gorsuch Slaughter, Balto, MD; ed/AB Physics & Math, Dartmouth Col, 1969; MS Applied Physics 1970, PhD Applied Math 1973, Harvard Univ; mil/USAR, Capt; pa/Staff Mem, Los Alamos Sci lab, 1973-75; Asst Prof, Princeton Univ, 1975-81; Coral Industs Dist'd Prof of Renewable Energy Resources, Univ of HI, 1982-; Chm, Gov's Task Force on Alt Trans Fuels, 1984; r/Christian Sci; hon/Pub'd Over 50 Articles in Profl Sci Jours; summa cum laude w High Distn in Physics & Math, 1969; Am Men & Wom of Sci.

ANTHONY, DONALD BRUCE oc/Music Instructor/Lecturer/Writer; b/Aug 8, 1936; h/463 Melville Avenue, Palo Alto, CA 94301; ba/Same; m/Marie Davilla; p/Donald Elliot and Arvella Coffin Anthony; sp/Mildred Davilla, SF, CA; ed/BA Music, Oberlin Col, 1958; MA Music 1959, PhD Music 1968, Stanford Univ; pa/Pvt Music Instr, Palo Alto, 1960-; Lectr Music Theory, Stanford Univ, 1966-68; Lectr Avante Garde Music, Sacramento St Col, 1968; Lectr Music Hist, SF Conservatory of Music, 1969-70; Pres of Bd, Soc for the Perf of Contemp Music, 1961-70; hon/Num Poems Pub'd in *Carousel Qtly*, *Impact*, *The Spirit That Moves Us*, *Bird Effort*, *The N Am Mentor Mag*, *The Poet*.

ANTON, WILLIAM TERRENCE oc/Major, AUS; b/Jul 7, 1948; h/7324 Better Hours Court, Columbia, MD 21045; ba/Ft Leavenworth, KS; m/Sue Erlenkotter; c/Susan; p/Andrew and Patricia Anton, McLean, VA; sp/Richard and Elizabeth Erlenkotter, San Rafael, CA;

ed/BS Ed, Univ of NE, 1970; MEd, NC St Univ, 1974; EdD, George Wash Univ, 1984; mil/AUS, 1970-; pa/AUS, 1970-, Maj; Nat Cmdr, Pershing Rifles, 1969; Cmdr, Benjamin Lincoln Camp, Heroes of '76, 1980; cp/Pres, Chapt 515 Nat Sojourners, 1980; Sr Warden, Scottish Rite, Seoul, Korea, 1980; Jr Warden, MacArthur Lodge #183, 1980; Pi Kappa Alpha, 1968; r/Rom Cath; hon/Omicron Delta Kappa, 1969; Phi Alpha Theta, 1969; Kappa Delta Pi, 1969; Phi Delta Kappa, 1981; W/W in Freemasonry.

ANTONACCIO, MICHAEL JOHN oc/Executive; b/Mar 26, 1943; h/915 Sycamore Lake Drive, Evansville, IN 47712; ba/Evansville, IN; m/Patricia; c/Nicholas; p/Mario and Frances Antonaccio, Yonkers, NY; sp/George and Mary Jane, Summit, NJ; ed/ BS Pharm, Duquesne Univ, 1966; PhD Pharm, Univ of MI, 1970; pa/Sr Sci I 1970-72, Sr Sci II 1972-73, Sr Stafff Sci 1973-75, Mgr Cardiovas Pharm 1975-77, Geigy/ CIBA Geigy Pharms; Dir Pharm, Squibb Inst of Med Res, 1977-81; VPres New Drug Discovery 1981-83, Chm Cardiovas Proj Team 1981-83, Schering Corp; VPres Cardiovas Res & Devel, Bristol-Myers Co, 1983-; Am Pharm Assn, 1963; AAAS, 1966; NY Acad of Sci, 1971; Am Heart Assn, 1974; Am Soc of Pharm & Exptl Therapeutics, 1975; Phila Physiological Soc, 1975; Soc of Neurosci, 1977; Intl Soc of Hypertension, 1978; Intl Soc of Heart Res, 1978; Intl Soc of Immunopharm, 1982; cp/Fellow, Coun for High Blood Pressure, 1978; Fellow, Coun on Circulation 1980, Del of Coun for High Blood Pressure Res 1982, Am Heart Assn; Guest Lectr on Profl Topics at Over 45 Nat/Intl Cols & Symps; hon/Author & Co-Author, Over 100 Profl Abstracts in Field; Fdg Editor, *Clin & Exptl Hypertension*; Editor of Book, *Cardiovas Pharm*, 1977 & (2nd Edition) 1984; Serves on Edit Bd & Reviews for Num Profl Jours incl'g: *Clin & Exptl Hypertension*, *Neuropharm*, *Drug Devel Res*, *Blood Vessels*, Num Others; NY St Regents S'ship, 1961; Acad S'ships from Duquesne Univ, Fordham Univ, Purdue Univ, Univ of Buffalo, Univ of Pgh; Bernard Schiller Awd for Excell in Humanities, 1966; James L Strader Awd for Intell & Maturity, 1966; Harry Goldblatt Awd in Cardiovas Res, 1981; RHO CHI Hon Pharm Soc, 1965; Am Men & Wom of Sci; W/W in Frontier Sci & Technol.

ANTONSON, BRIAN ALBERT oc/Educator/Administrator; b/Jun 28, 1948; h/32427 Diamond Avenue, Mission, British Columbia, Canada V2V 1M2; ba/Burnaby, Brittish Columbia, Canada; m/Susan Audrey; c/Jeremy Leigh, Kristin Terryl; p/Al and Elsie Antonson, Burnaby, Brit Columbia; sp/ John and Margaret Scrivener, Burnaby, Brit Columbia; ed/Dipl of Technol Broadcast Communs, Brit Columbia Inst of Technol, 1969; pa/Prodr 1969-70, Prodr 1970-74, Prodn Dir 1974-77, Radio Sta CKNW, New Westminster, BC; Prodn Dir Radio Sta CJOB, Winnipeg, Manitoba, 1970; Instr Radio Prog, Prog Hd Radio Prog, Asst Dept Hd, Broadcast Communs Dept, Brit Columbia Inst of Technol, Burnaby, 1977-; Co-Owner, Antonson Publishing Ltd, 1972-80; cp/Public Relats Dir, The Mission Heritage Assn, 1981-; Scoutmaster, Boy Scouts of Canada,

1969-74; r/Luth; hon/Author, "In Search of a Legend: Slumach's Gold," 1972; Editor, *Canadian Frontier*, 1974-80; Pub'd Num Non-Fiction Articles; Recip of Awds for Comml Prodn Excell, 1970-77.

ANTOS, JOHN JEFFREY oc/Executive; b/Jan 13, 1949; h/771 Willow Vine Court, #222, Dallas, TX 75230; ba/ Dallas, TX; m/Lana Ethelyn Antos; p/ Frank and Estelle Antos, Cicero, IL; sp/ Eve and Leo Uryasz, Arlington Hgts, IL; ed/BS, Univ of IL, 1971; MBA, Univ of Chgo, 1976; pa/Controller, Hi-Line Elect Co, 1984-; Pres, Bellatrix Inc, 1980-84; Sr Conslt, W A Golomski & Assoc, Chgo, 1977-80; Fin Anal & Conslt, Marsh & McLennon, Chgo, 1975-77; Conslt, Antos & Assoc, Cicero, 1973-75; Asst Sales Mgr, S Wn Co, Nashville, 1968-73; Fdr, Yg Execs Clb, Chgo; Palm Bch Round Table; Nat Assn of Accts; Am Soc of Quality Control; Intl Assn of Fin Planners; TACA; hon/ Cert Mgmt Acct, 1980; Real Est Broker, TX & FL; Outstg Yg Man of the Yr; W/W: in Fin & Indust, in S & SW; Personalities of the S; Men of Achmt; Intl Dir of Dist'd Ldrship; Registry of Am Achmt; Biogl Roll of Hon; 2,000 Notable Ams.

ANWYLL, B JEAN oc/Executive; b/ Oct 10, 1936; h/535 Sugartown Road, Berwyn, PA 19312; ba/Philadelphia, PA; p/James Anwyll (dec); Martha Anwyll, Holyoke, MA; ed/BA Phil, Mt Holyoke Col, 1958; PMD, Harvard Grad Sch of Bus Admn, 1978; pa/Res Assoc, Gen Dynamics•Corp, 1956-1960; Edit Dir, Itek Corp, 1961-64; Prog Dir, Bolt Beranek & Newman, 1961-64; Ednl Sys Conslt, Litton Industs, 1965; Consumer Prod Publicity Dir, Polaroid Corp, 1966-79; Pres, McKinney/Mid-Atl, 1979-; Local & Nat Bd Positions since 1974, VP Profl Devel 1983-, Am Wom in Radio & TV; Dir Del, Public Relats Soc of Am, 1982-85; Bus Woms Netwk, 1982-; cp/Mktg Com, Gtr Phil C of C, 1982-83; hon/Accredited, Pub Relats Soc of Am, 1980; PR News Golden Key Awd, 1982; W/W: Among Bus & Profl Wom, in E.

APESOS, JAMES oc/Plastic Surgeon; b/Mar 16, 1948; ba/5692 Far Hills Avenue, Dayton, OH 45429; m/Elizabeth Ann; c/Amanda, Clay, John; p/John and Helen Apesos, Habertown, PA; sp/ W & Elizabeth Richardson, Coral Gables, FL; ed/Att'd The Acad of the Prot Epis Ch, 1962-66; BA, The Univ of PA, 1970; MD, Georgetown Univ, 1974; pa/Residency, Surg, Hosp of the Univ of PA, 1974-76; Residency, Gen Surg, So IL Univ, 1976-79; Residency, Plastic & Maxillofacial Surg, Univ of VA, 1979-81; Asst Prof Plastic Surg 1981-84, Dir Microsurg Res & Tng Lab 1981-84, Univ of KY; Att'g Surg, VA, Lexington, KY, 1982-84; Assoc Staff Phys, Cardinal Hill Hosp & Rehab Ctr, Lexington; Att'g Phys, Shriner's Hosp for Crippled Chd, Lexington; Assoc Clin Prof of Surg, Wright St Univ; Chief & Prog Dir, Plastic Surg, Wright St Affil'd Hosps; Dayton Surg Soc, 1984-; Bd Cert'd, Am Bd Surg, 1983; Bd Cert'd, Am Bd Plastic Surg, 1983; Am Soc of Plastic & Reconstructive Surg, 1984; Dir, Plastic Surg Res Labs, Cox Heart Inst; Chief of Plastic Surg, Chd's Hosp, 1984; Conslt in Plastic Surg, Wright Patterson AFB, 1984; AMA, 1977; KY

Med Assn, 1981-; Fayette Co Med Soc, 1981; Sigma Xi, 1979; Sci Res Soc of Am, 1979; Alpha Epsilon Delta Hon Soc, 1967; r/Greek Orthodox; hon/Over 16 Pubs & Presentations: "Tensile Strength in Ischemic Wounds" 1968-70, "Pulsed Electromagnetic Field Currents & Peripheral Nerve Healing" 1981, "Stat Methods in Anal of Burn Victims" 1980, "Intra Operative Photog Utilizing a Fiberoptically Illuminated Boom Camera" 1982; Recip, NIH Basic Res Support Grant; Univ of KY Phys Ser Plan Grant; Davis & Geck Am Cyanamid Corp Grant; W/W Biogl Dir.

APIRION, DAVID oc/Professor, Scientist; b/Jul 17, 1935; h/6415 Alamo, Clayton, MO 63105; ba/St Louis, MO; c/Jonathon, Michael, Allison; p/Shlomo and Golda Apirion; ed/MSc Hebrew Univ, 1960; PhD Glasgow Univ, 1963; Postdoct Fellow, Harvard Univ, 1964-65; mil/Israeli Army, 1953-55; pa/Asst Lectr, Glasgow Univ, 1963; Res Fellow Harvard Univ, 1964-65; Asst Prof 1965-70, Assoc Prof 1970-78, Prof 1978-, Wash Univ-St Louis; The Am Soc for Microbiol; AAAS; Genetics Society of Am; The Am Soc of Biol Chems; The Am Soc for Cell Biol; r/Jewish; hon/Author, Over 160 Pub'd Articles in Sci Jours; Editor of Book, *Processing of RNA*, 1984; The Tuvia Kashnir Prize, 1960; The Alexander Milman Prize, 1961; The Sir Maurice Bloch Awd, 1962; Lady Davis Vis'g Prof, 1980; Nat Acad of Sci Exch, 1980; W/W in Am Sci.

APLIN, CHARLES O'NEAL oc/Educator; b/Jun 14, 1943; h/516 Justine Avenue, Ft Walton Beach, FL 32548; ba/Ft Walton Beach, Fl; m/Joy Hardwick; c/Michelle, Kevin; p/Rebecca Aplin, Eufaula, AL; sp/Mr and Mrs Jack Hardwick, Shorterville, AL; ed/AA, Wallace Commun Col, 1967; BS, Troy St Univ, 1969; MEd, Univ of W FL, 1974; EdS 1976, EdD 1979, FL St Univ; pa/Chm Math Dept, Ft Walton Bch HS, 1969-83; Math Prog Coor, Okaloosa Dist Schs, 1983; Adj Asst Prof Math, Troy St Univ, 1980-; Adj Assoc Prof Math & Ed, St Leo Col, 1982-; Assn of Supvn & Curric Devel; NCTM; FL Coun of Tchrs of Math; cp/Mem, Alpha Lodge 172 F&AM; r/Bapt; hon/"Supvr Role Expectations of the HS Dept Chp as Perceived by Prins, Tchrs, & Chps," *Dissertation Abstracts*, 1979; Inducted, Phi Kappa Phi Hon Soc, 1969; Ft Walton Bch HS Tchr of Yr, 1979-80; W/W in S & SW.

APPELL, GERALD F oc/Project Engineer; b/Jun 9, 1942; h/11805 Earnshaw Court, Brandywine, MD 20613; ba/Rockville, MD; m/Marika; c/Stephen, Michael; p/Frank and Evelyn Appell, Waldorf, MD; sp/John and Teresa Jorbach, Woodhaven, NY; BS Mech Engrg, 1964; pa/Mech Engr, Nav Oceanographic Ofc, 1964-70; Proj Engr, Nat Oceanographic Instrumentation Ctr, 1970-76; Proj Engr, Nat Oceanic & Atmospheric Adm, 1976-; VChm Tech Com, IEEE; Marine Technol Soc; r/Luth; hon/Over 30 Articles in Profl Tech Pubs; W/W in Sci & Engrg.

APPEL-MOSESOF, RHODA SARA oc/Board of Education Supervisor; b/Oct 24, 1920; h/203 Ivy Street, Newark, NJ 07106; ba/Newark, NJ; m/Louis Mosesof; ed/BS, NJ Col for Wom, 1940; MEd, Rutgers Univ, 1949; Att'd Postgrad Study: Univ of So CA 1969,

Montclair St Col, NY Univ, Mgmt Inst Lib 1979, Others; pa/Supvr NJ Stwide Lib Proj for Dept of Libs & AV Ser 1941-42, Dir Dept of Libs & AV Ed 1969-82, Bd of Ed Newark, NJ; Libn, Nat Tng Sch for Boys, Br of Prisons, US Dept of Justice, 1944-46; Libn, Newark, NJ, Public Schs, 1946-69; Supvr Div of Fine Arts & Media, 1982-; Adj Staff (Sums), Rutgers Univ & Kean Col; Pres, Newark Sch Libns Assn, 1954-55; Dir, Chds Book Coun, 1976-78; Secy, Newark Assn Dirs & Supvrs, 1976-81; VP, NJ Sch Media Assn, 1971-73; Pres Evening Div Essex Co Sect, NCJW, 1958; Dir Newark Clb of Zonta; r/Judaism; hon/Pub'd Articles in *Lib Jour*; Prepared Bibliogs for Newark Sch Dist; Contbr NDEA Bibliog on Math, Sci & Fgn Langs for US Ofc of Ed; Num Commends for Sers as Pres & Dir of Profl & Soc Orgs; W/W in E.

APPLBAUM, RONALD LEE oc/University Administrator/Professor; b/Dec 14, 1943; h/1320 Tulip Circle, McAllen, TX 78504; ba/Edinburg, TX; m/Susan Stone; c/Lee David; p/Irwin Applbaum, Bakersfield, CA; Marion Applbaum, Buena Park, CA; sp/Irving and Gertrude Stone, Cypress, CA; ed/BA 1965, MA 1966, CA St Univ-Long Bch; PhD, PA St Univ, 1969; pa/Asst Prof 1969-73, Assoc Prof 1973-77, Full Prof 1977-82, Assoc Dean of Lttrs 1976-77, Dean of Humanities 1977-82, CA St Univ-Long Bch; VP for Acad Affairs & Prof Communs, Pan Am Univ, 1982-; Chp Ed Div, WSCA, 1972; Chapt Ofcr 1973-78, Chapt Pres 1976-77, Phi Kappa Phi; Charter Mem (Pan Am Univ), 1982-83; cp/Bd of Dirs: Temple Israel (LB 1982); B'nai B'rith (McAllen, TX) 1983-84; hon/Author of Books: *Bus & Profl Spkg Book* 1983, Orgnl Communs 1981, *Public Communication* 1978, Process of Grp Communication 1979, Persuasive Communication 1975; Pub'd Over 25 Articles in Profl Jours, 1972-; Outstg Yg Man in Am, 1976.

APPLEBERRY, JAMES B oc/University President; b/Feb 22, 1938; h/1240/ 1440 Center Street, Marquette, MI 49855; ba/Marquette, MI; m/Patricia Ann Trent; c/John Mark, Timothy David; p/James Earnest and Bertha Viola (Lane) Appleberry (dec); sp/Ryland and Lucille (Neer) Trent, Waverly, MO; ed/BA 1960, MA 1963, Ed Spec 1967, Ctl MO St Univ; PhD, OK St Univ, 1969; pa/Pres, No MI Univ, 1983-; Pres, Pittsburg St Univ, 1977-83; Dir of Planning & Prof of Adm, Founs & Higher Ed 1975, Asst to Chancellor 1976-77, Univ of KS; Asst Prof 1968-71, Assoc Prof 71-75, Prof 1975-77, Hd Dept of Adm & Higher Ed 1973-77, OK St Univ; Asst Dir of Field Sers 1964-67, Interim Admr of Br Campus in Independence, MO, Ctl MO St Univ; Tchr 1960-62, Prin 1962-64, Knob Noster Public Schs, Knob Noster, MO; Abstracter for *Ednl Adm Abstracts*, 1971-77; Am Assn for Higher Ed; Am Ednl Res Assn; Nat Ed Assn; Nat Conf of Profs of Ednl Adm; Appt'd by US Dept of Ed: VChp & Mem, Adv Coun to Nat Ctr for Ednl Stats; Chp of Com on Res & KS St Rep; Am Assn of St Cols & Univs; Mem, Policies & Purposes Com, Am Assn of St Cols & Univs; Mem, Am Coun on Ed Comm on Ldrship Devel & Acad Adm; Mem, Adv Com for the Coop Instl Res Prog; Del, Sin-Am Sem on Higher

Ed; Adv Com & the Maj Res Univs Adv Com, Nat Ctr for Higher Ednl Mgmt Sys; Num Other Govtl Appts; cp/Bd of Dirs: Mt Carmel Med Ctr; First St Bk & Trust Co of Pittsburg; Mid-Am Ec Devel Org; Pres Elect, Pittsburg Rotary Clb; Bd of Dirs & Chp of Ambassadors Clb, Pittsburg Area C of C; AF Assn; Bd of Dirs, Hiawathaland Coun, BSA; City Clb of Lansing; Detroit Ath Clb; Gtr MI Foun, Bd of Govs; Marquette Area C of C; Marquette Co Ec Devel Task Force; Marquette Ec Clb; Marquette Gen Hosp Bd of Trustees; Marquette Golf & Country Clb; Marquette Rotary Clb; Num Spkg Presentations; Num Others; r/Bapt; hon/Num Articles Pub'd in Profl Jours incl'g: *Ednl Adm Qtly*, *Jour of Exptl Ed*, *Change & Innovation*; Over 20 Profl Paper Topic Presentations to Confs, Sems, Assns & Bd Meetings; 1st Grad Fellow, Ctl MO St Univ; Pi Delta Kappa; Phi Kappa Phi; Phi Sigma Phi; Kappa Mu Epsilon; Alpha Kappa Psi; W/W: in Am, Among Authors & Jours, Among Students in Am Cols & Univs; Notable Ams; Ldrs in Ed; Num Other Biogl Listings.

APPLEGARTH, PAUL VOLLMER oc/Executive; b/Apr 21, 1946; h/2155 Edgecourt Drive, Hillsborough, CA 94010; ba/SF, CA; m/Linda D; c/Katharine Davis, Caroline Elizabeth; p/Mr and Mrs Wm F Applegarth, Atlanta, GA; sp/Mr and Mrs Norman H Davis; ed/BA, Yale Univ, 1968; MBA Bus Sch 1974, JD Law Sch 1974, Harvard Univ; mil/AUS, 1968-70, Ofcr; pa/Sr VP & Dir Investmt Bkg Grp N Am, Dir Proj Fin 1983-, Bk of Am; The World Bk, 1974-83; Pres, Langley Oaks Homeowners Assn; Exec Com, World Bk Staff Assn; MA Bar Assn; DC Bar Assn; Dir, McLean Citizens Assn; cp/ 1974 Class Com, Harvard Law Sch; r/ Rom Cath; hon/White House Fellow, 1981-82; Baker Scholar, Harvard Bus Sch, 1974; J Spencer Love F'ship; Outstg Yg Men of Am.

APPLEMAN, WAYNE DOUGLAS oc/Chief of Management and Staff Development; b/Jul 8, 1937; h/6819 Coachlite Way, Sacramento, CA 95831; ba/Sacramento, CA; m/Penny Ann; c/ Todd Douglas, Scott Douglas; p/W Ross Appleman, Laguna Hills, CA; Alberta M Appleman (dec); sp/Wilbur A and Gladys W Sears (dec); ed/BA Psych, OH Wesleyan Univ, 1959; Grad Study in Law & Bus, OH St Univ, 1961; mil/AUS, 1960-61; pa/Chief Mgmt & Staff Devel 1984-, Mgr Quality of Wklife 1981-82, Mgr Tng Policy 1978-81, Mgr Instrnl Design 1975-78, Mgr Mgmt Devel Sers 1972-75, Coor Reg Tng Ctr 1971, St of CA; Pres, Appleman & Assoc, 1982-; Asst Dir Tng & Devel, Wetterau Foods, 1969; Mgr Manpower Dev, The Vendo Co, 1968; Dir of Tng, Am Investmt Co, 1966-68; Pers Staff Wk, Nationwide Ins Co, 1961-66; Asst Reg VPres, Admr, Chapt Co-Fdr, Pres & VPres, Am Soc for Tng & Devel, 1975-84; Chapt Fdr & Pres, Chm Nat Com, Intl Assn of Quality Circles, 1983-84; Mgmt & Supvn Adv Com Chm, Sierra Col, 1977-80; Guest Lctr, CA St Univ at Sacramento, Univ of CA at Davis, Univ of CA at Berkeley; cp/Chm, U Way, 1973-76; Ch Elder, 1979-82; r/Presb; hon/Contbg Author to *Going Public: Quality Circles in the Public Sector*, IAQC Press, 1984; Am Soc for Tng & Devel

Torch Awd for Dist'd Contbn to the Profession & Soc, 1978; W/W: in the W, in CA; Personalities in the W & MW; Anglo Am Acad; Dir of Dist'd Ams.

AQUADRO, CHARLES FREDERICK oc/Geneticist; b/Jul 16, 1953; h/812 Chalice Street, Durham, NC 27705; ba/Research Triangle Park, NC; m/Gwen Sholl; c/Christine Anne, Brian Sholl; p/Lawrence and Anne Aquadro, Chadds Ford, PA; sp/Calvin and Nancy Sholl, Lunenburg, MA; ed/BS Biol, St Lawrence Univ, 1975; MS in Zool, Univ of VT; PhD in Genetics, Univ of GA, 1981; pa/Staff Fellow 1981-84, Sr Staff Fellow 1984-, Lab of Genetics, Nat Inst of Envir Hlth Scis, NIH; Genetics Soc of Am; Society for the Study of Evolution; Am Soc of Mammologists; hon/Author & Co-Author, Over 20 Articles Pub'd in Sci Jours; Author of Book, *Canoeing the Brandywine, A Naturalist's Guide,* (2nd ed, rev), 1981; NIH Traineeship in Genetics, 1978-81; Theodore Roosevelt Meml Awd of the Am Mus of Nat Hist, 1979; High Hon in Biol, St Lawrence Univ, 1975; Omicron Delta Kappa, 1975; W/W in Frontier Sci & Technol; Personalities of S.

AQUINO-BERMUDEZ, FEDERICO oc/Professor; b/Jul 18, 1923; h/273 Graphic Boulevard, New Milford, NJ 07646; ba/NYC; m/Lillian Sepulveda-Carmona; c/Beatriz, Diana, Frederico; p/Enrique Aquino and Ana Bermudez (dec); Jun Sepulveda and Eugenia Carmona (dec); ed/Ctl Eve HS, 1948; BS, Univ of PR, 1952; MA Tchrs Col, Columbia Univ, 1956; Profl Dipl, Fordham Univ, 1969; EdD, Univ of MA, 1975; mil/AUS, 1943-46, S/Sgt; pa/Prof & Chm Dept of PR Studies, The City Col of NY, 1969-; Conslt/Evalr, Urban Ed Inc, NYC, 1973-75; Dir Public Sch 6, Bronx Minn Sch 1969, Bilingual Tch Sch & Commun Relats 1963-68, Sub Aux Tch 1957-63, NYC Bd of Ed; Conslt NCCJ, NY Reg, 1963-69; NY Acad of Sci; Acad of Polit Sci; AAUP; Am Acad of Polit & Soc Scis; Bd of Dirs, Nat Col Adv Ser; Edit Bd of *Minority Voices;* Past Mem, Adv Coun for the Asian Am Assem for Policy Res, 1977-79; ASPIRA of NY, 1957-70; Bd of Dirs, Nat PR Forum, 1957-73; Others; W/W in E.

ARAGONA, GUYLAINE R oc/Executive, Assistant Researcher; b/Jul 31, 1954; h/4 Brimstone Hill Road, Amherst, NH 03031; ba/Manchester, NH; m/Ronald J; c/Ronald J Jr, Danielle Vita Valente, Jason Bryant Palmer, Shani Jamie Valente, Bradford Ashley Hamilton, Conan Michael Christopher Valente; p/Mr and Mrs Armand P Magella Rouleau, Auburn, NH; sp/Paul and Marie Antoinette Aragona, Westerloo, NY; ed/NH Tech Inst of Hlth Sci, 1982; pa/Asst Res 1983-, Asst to Chief of Staff 1983-, R J Aragona Chiro Spinal Biomechanics Res Lab; Asst to Exec Dir, Dept of Ed, R J Aragona Coop Chiro Hlth Ctr, 1983-; Curator, R & G Aragona Gallery of Infinite Unparalleled Expressions of Perceptive Art, 1983-; VPres & Treas, R J Aragona Publishers Inc. 1983-; Exec Controller, En Gypsum "76" Inc, 1976-81; Mem Patient Ed Sub Com 1976-, Exec Bd Mem, B J Palmer Chiro Phil Res Com Inc; Mem, Assn for the Hist of Chiro; Exec Mem, Selectron Intell Sys, Res Inst of Am; Others; cp/Sr Rep Mem for St

Gov of NH; YMCA; Manchester, NH Bldg Expansion Prog, 1982; Sustaining Mem, NH Assn of Chief of Police, 1979-; r/Cath; hon/Commun Ldrs of Am Awd, 1982; Biogl Roll of Hon, 1982; Awd of Merit, 2000 Notable Ams; Intl Book of Hon; Life Patron & Nat Advr, ABIRA.

ARAVE, CLIVE WENDELL oc/Animal Scientist; b/May 12, 1931; h/1460 East 2100 North Logan, UT 84321; ba/Logan, UT; m/Carley McMurtrey; c/Wendy, Stephanie, Joe, Christine, Lorraine, James; p/Joseph Clarence and Rhoda Elvera Peterson Arave (dec); sp/Annie McMurtrey, Shelley, ID; ed/BS 1956, MS 1957, UT St Univ; PhD, Univ of CA-Davis, 1963; mil/AUS, 1951-53, Sgt; pa/Asst Mgr, Lavacre Farms, Modesto, CA, 1957-59; Asst Prof, CA St Univ-Chico, 1963-65; Asst Prof 1965-83, Assoc Prof 1984-, UT St Univ-Logan; Vis'g Prof, Purdue Univ, 1972-73; Vis'g Sci, Ruakura Agri Res Ctr, Hamilton, New Zealand, 1980-81; Chm Hlth Com, Am Dairy Sci Assn, 1977; Mem, N Ctl Reg Dairy Mgmt Com 1983-; Mem, N Ctl Reg 131, Animal Care & Behavior Com, 1983-; cp/Pres, N Logan Lions Clb, 1973-74; r/LDS; hon/Author, Over 70 Articles & Abstracts Pub'd in Sci Jours incl'g: *Jour of Dairy Sci, Applied Animal Ethology;* Phi Kappa Phi, 1956; Nat Sci Foun US-New Zealand Coop Res Grant, 1980; W/W in W, in Technol Today; Ldg Conslts in Technol.

ARAYA, PEDRO ALFONSO oc/Engineering & Management Consultant; b/Jan 19, 1927; ba/Wilmington, DE & Buenos Aires, Argentina; m/Esther E Roussillion; c/Carla Francesca; p/Francisco Araya y Benett; ed/BS Mech Engrg, Chilean Nav Col, 1943; BA, Univ of Chile, 1945; MS Industl & Mgmt Engrg, Columbia Univ, 1963; mil/Chilean Navy, Lt; pa/Airlines Oper, Civil Aeronautics Admn, Wash DC, 1946-47; Var Tech & Mgmt Positions w Rubber & Plastic Indust, 1949-53; Gen Magr Bottling Opers Venezuela 1959-61, Industl Mgmt Conslt Mexico, Mid Am, & Columbia 1961-63, Mid E Reg Mgr & Asst Area Mgr for the Mid E, N Africa & S W Asia (HQ's Beirut) 1963-67, Mktg Mgr for S Am (HQ's Buenos Aires) 1968-69, The Coca-Cola Export Corp; Sr Corp Conslt for Prod & Opers, The Coca-Cola Co, Atlanta, GA, 1970-82; Chm, Bd of Dirs & Pres, Global Growth & Devel Corp, Wilmington, DE, 1973-; Pres, Compañia Argentina de Crecimiento y Desarrollo, SACIF, Buenos Aires, 1975-; AAAS; Sr Mem, AIIE; Inst Envir Sci Soc; Na Arch & Marine Engrs; Am Chem Soc; IEEE; Soc for the Advmt of Mgmt; Res Soc of Japan; Nat Soc of Corp Planning; Gen Sys Res; Nat Soc of Profl Engrs; Am Mktg Assn; Assoc of Computer Machinery; Num Others; cp/Buenos Aires Lawn Tennis Union; Others; hon/Contbr of Num Articles Pub'd in Profl Jours; Prodr of Num Corp Orgnl & Tng Manuals; W/W in Fin & Indust; Intl Bus-Men's W/W; Intl W/W in Commun Ser; Men of Achmt; Personalities of Am; Commun Ldrs & Noteworthy Ams; Num Other Biogl Listings.

ARBELBIDE, SYLVIA JEAN oc/Geologist; b/Jun 7, 1951; h/364 Goldco Circle, Golden, CO 80403; ba/Denver, CO; p/Ollie Marion Arbelbide (dec);

Betty Lou Arbelbide; ed/Att'd Boise St Col, 1969-71; BS Geol Sci, Univ of WA, 1973; pa/Underground Geol, Magma Copper Co, Superior, AZ, 1973-75; Area Geol Golden, CO 1975-77, Dist Geol Canon City, CO 1977-78, St Ofc Geol Denver, CO 1978-80, Bur of Land Mgt; Phy Sci, Bur of Mines, Denver, CO, 1980-; Assn for Wom Geoscis, 1981-; CO Sci Soc, 1976-; Wom in Mining, 1983-; Am Inst of Mining Engrs, 1976-; cp/Mem, Jefferson Symph, 1977-; NOW, 1981-; CO Nat Abortion Rgts Action Leag, 1981-; Leag of Wom Voters, 1983; hon/Co-Author of Sci Articles Pub'd in Profl Jours: "Preliminary Geologic Map of The McCarthy Gulch Quad, CO," "Aluminum Availability- Market Economy Countries," "Availability of Domestic Lead & Zinc"; Unit Cit for Excell Ser, 1982; Unit Cit for Foothills Envir Statement, 1977; W/W of Am Wom.

ARCEMENT, BILLY P oc/Manager of Technical Services; b/Jun 3, 1939; h/108 Magnolia Drive, Donaldsville, LA 70346; ba/Donaldsville, LA; m/Ernestine V; c/Stacie, Corey, Patrick, Mary; p/Herman and Isabelle Arcement; sp/Ernest and Marie Veron (dec); ed/BS Phy Ed 1961, Postgrad Cert as Guid Cnslr 1973, Nichols St Univ; MEd Admn & Supvn, LA St Univ, 1965; mil/AUS, 1961-62 (Active Duty) & 1962-65; pa/Sci Tchr & Coach, Assumption HS, 1962-64, Sc Tchr & Coach, Donaldsville HS, 1965-69; Chem, Triad Chem Co, 1969-73; Chief Chem 1973-80, Mgr of Tech Sers 1980-, Melamine Chems Inc; Pres 1980-81, Div Pres 1982-83, Gtr Baton Rouge Intl Mgmt Coun (IMC); Tech Assn of the Pulp & Paper Indust, 1977-; cp/Nat Spkrs Assn, 1980-; Bd of Dirs, Donaldsville Area C of C, 1980-; Elected Mem, Ascension Parish Sch Bd, 1982; r/Cath; W/W: in S & SW, Among Am Cols & Univs.

ARCHBOLD, NORMA PARRISH oc/Executive; b/Feb 15, 1938; h/451 North Winston, Palatine, IL 60635; ba/Elmwood Pk, IL; m/(dec); c/Camerson A, Jennifer Anne, Jeffrey Thomas, C Michael; p/Henry K Parrish (dec); Ruth F Parrish, New Hartford, MO; sp/Vernon Archbold, Libertyville, IL; ed/BA Eng Lit, Univ of MO, 1959; MA Ed, Loyola Univ, 1975; pa/Pres, Appletree Sys Inc, 1981-; Assoc Engr, Wn Elect, 1978-81; OLMC, Div of Rel Ed, 1975-78; St Mary's, Div of Rel Ed, 1971-75; Indep Computer Conslts Assn; hon/*Duncan Fam Register,* 1967; W/W of Am Wom.

ARCHER, CARL MARION oc/Executive; b/Dec 16, 1920; h/304 South Endicott, Spearman, TX 79081; ba/Spearman, TX; m/Mary Frances (Peggy) Garrett; c/Mary Frances, Carla Lee; p/Robert Barton Archer (dec); Gertrude Lucille Archer; sp/Mr and Mrs E G Garrett; ed/Att'd Univ of TX- Austin; pa/Pres, Anchor Oil, 1959-; Pres, Carl M Archer Farms, 1960-; Gen Mgr, Speartex Grain, 1967-; Gen Mgr, Speartex Oil & Gas Co, 1974-; Dir, Panhandle Bk & Trust Co of Borger, TX; Dem Co Chm, 1969-; Mem, TX Grain Dealers Assn; Mem, Nat Grain Dealers Assn; Mem, TX Indep Prodrs & Royalty Owners Assn; Mem, Panhandle Prodrs & Royalty Owners Assn; Mem, Am Petro Landmen Assn; Mem, Nat Bkrs Assn; cp/Mem, Ch of Christ; hon/W/

30

W in Fin & Indust; Dun & Bradstreet.

ARCHER, FRANK WILSON oc/Management Consultant; b/Mar 13, 1913; h/4336 Foeburn Lane, L'ville, KY 40207; ba/L'ville, KY; m/Laura Macmaster; c/Gary W, Stephen R; ed/BA, Wn Resv Univ, 1934; MBA, Univ of L'ville, 1976; pa/Pres, Mgmt Devel Assoc of KY, 1978-; Mktg Assignments, Gen Elect Co, 1934-78; Nat VPres, Pres & Dir L'ville Chapt, Am Mktg Assn; Hon Life Mem, Advtg Clb of L'ville; Am Soc for Tng & Devel; Execs Clb of L'ville; r/Meth; hon/Co-Author of Text Book, *Retail Mgmt*; Num Articles Pub'd in Profl Jours incl'g: *Jour of Mktg, Mktg News, Mkt Mag*; Man of the Yr, Nat Assn of Retail Dealers of Am, 1978; Mktg Man of the Yr, L'ville Chapt of Am Mktg Assn, 1974; Silver Beaver Awd, BSA; KY Col; W/W in S & SW.

ARDEN, DANIEL DOUGLAS oc/Petroleum Geologist; b/Sept 24, 1922; h/4141 Loire Drive, Kenner, LA 70065; ba/NO, LA; m/Mary Moore; c/Dana, Daniel D (V), Nancy, Laurie; ed/AB 1948, MS 1949, Emory Univ; PhD, Univ of CA-Berkeley, 1961; mil/USAF, 1942-46 & 1951-53; pa/Asst Prof, B'ham-So Col, 1949-51; Geol/Exploration Mgr, Var Petro Cos: Socal, Sohio, Signal, 1954-70; Prof & Chm Dept Geol & Physics, GA SWn Col, 1970-82; Staff Geol, LA Land & Exploration Co, 1982-; Geol Soc of Am; Geophy Union; Am Inst of Profl Geols; r/Epis; hon/Author & Editor, Over 50 Pub'd Articles in Profl Jours; Prof Emeritus, GA SWn Col; W/W in S & SW.

ARDEN, JOHN RÉAL oc/Attorney; b/Aug 17, 1944; h/23 Sandra Road, Easthampton, MA 01027; ba/Northampton, MA; m/Margot Elkin; c/Michael John-Réal, Stephen Patrick, Catherine Elizabeth; p/Mr and Mrs Sylvan S Arden, Holly, MI; sp/Mr and Mrs Philip Elkin, Phila, PA; ed/AA Sci Engrg, Flint Commun Col; BSEE, MI St Univ; JD Law Sch, Univ of Notre Dame; pa/John R Arden, Atty at Law, 1974-; Adj Prof Greenfield Commun Col, 1978; Adj Prof Wn N Eng Sch of Law, 1977; Tax Atty, The Res Grp, 1974; Res & Edit Asst, Dr Ronald A Anderson, 1973; Assoc Atty, Atty Donald Conway, 1972-73; Mgmt Trainee Prog, Gen Motors Divs, 1964-69; cp/Chm 1977-80, Fin Com 1976-80, Town of Southampton, MA; Mem Bd of Dirs, 1977-80, Hampshire Commun Action Comm; Dem Cand for Cong, 1st MA Congl Dist, 1982; r/Cath; hon/MI Alpha Chapt, Tau Beta Pi, 1964; Gamma Zeta Chapt, Eta Kappa Nu; Moot Court, Univ of Notre Dame Law Sch, 1970; W/W: in Fin & Indust, in World.

AREF, HASSAN oc/Professor; b/Sept 28, 1950; ba/Providence, RI; m/Susanne; c/Michael, Thomas; ed/Cand Sci, Univ of Copenhagen, 1975; PhD, Cornell Univ, 1980; pa/Asst Prof Engrg 1980-84, Assoc Prof Engrg & Applied Physics 1984-, Brown Univ; Assoc Editor, *Jour of Fluid Mechs*, 1984-; Mem, Am Phy Soc, Div of Fluid Mechs; Mem, Soc for Indust & Applied Math; Mem, Am Acad of Mechs; Mem, NY Acad of Sci; hon/Author & Co-Author, Over 18 Articles Pub'd in Profl Jours incl'g: *Jour of Fluid Mechs, Phy Fluids*, Others; NATO F'ship, 1975; Cornell Grad F'ship, 1976-79; W/W in Frontier Sci & Technol.

ARENAS, ANDREA-TERESA oc/Director; b/Nov 1, 1951; h/321 West Newhall #8, Waukesha, WI 53186; ba/Waukesha, WI; p/Glen and LaVerne Lowery; ed/BA Profl Communs & Computer Studies, Alverno Co, 1982; Att'g Urban Ed PhD Prog, Univ WI-Milwaukee; pa/Asst to Mgr, Prudential Ins Co, 1969-70; Ethnicity Coor & Assessment Ctr Coor, Alverno Col, 1981-83; Asst Dir, La Casa de Esperanza, 1983-; Co-Editor, *Alpha*, 1980-81; Co-Editor, *La Guardia*, 1981-82; Editor, *Inside Alverno*, 1982-; VPres, FOCUS Communs, 1983-; Host, *Nuestro Lateno*, Channel 10, PBS, 1984; Ex-oficio, WI Hispanic Coun on Higher Ed, 1983-; Appt'd to Gov's Hispanic Adv Coun, 1983-; Num Others; cp/Promotion Asst for St-wide Conf "New Horizons: The Hispanic Fam"; Num Guest Spkg Appearances; Planning Com Mem & Public Relats Dir, "Looking for the Best: a Career Day for Hispanic Yth"; Planned Parenthood Commun Adv Com; Presenter at Num Wkshops; Num Others; r/Cath; hon/Author of Article "Latina Feminists," Pub'd in *La GUARDIA*, 1980; Pub'd Poetry in *Nat Assn of Chicano Studies Proceedings* & *Wom of Color*, 1984; Prodd & Host of Weekly TV Show, *Mural Latina*, 1983-; Schumann Foun S'ship, 1980; Designated a Wingspread Scholar, 1980; Grad w Hons, 1982; Nat Deans List, 1982; Commun Ser Awd from Organazion Puertorriquena, 1982; Outstg Yg Wom in Am, 1983; Planned Parenthood Ser Awd, 1983; La Colectiva Outstg Latina Col Grad Awd, 1983; 2nd Place Winner for Poetry in 10th Annual Nat Chicano Lit Competition, Univ of CA-Irvine, 1984; Commun Ser Awd, U Commun Ctr, Milwaukee, 1984.

AREY, WILLIAM GRIFFIN JR oc/Executive; b/Feb 18, 1918; h/2700 Virginia Avenue, Northwest, Washington, DC 20037; ba/Washington, DC; m/Louise Craft; c/William Griffin III, John Gordon Craft; p/William Griffin and Catherine Roberts Arey (dec); sp/Jack G and Louise Turner Craft (dec); ed/AB, Univ of NC-Chapel Hill, 1939; mil/AAC, 1942-45, 1st Lt; pa/Co-Publisher & Editor, Cleveland Times Publishing Co, Shelby, 1941-48; Public Affairs Ofcr Bogota, Columbia 1948-51 & Panama, Republic of Panama 1951-53, US Dept of St; Public Relats Ofcr, Panama Canal Co, 1954-62; Dir of Travel Promotion 1963-67, Dept Dir 1967-70, Exec Ofcr 1970-73, Exec Dir 1973-76, US Travel Ser, US Dept of Commerce; Asst Exec VPres & Corp Secy, Nat Trust for Hist Presv, 1976-84; VPres, Intl Union of Ofcl Travel Orgs, 1968; Dir, Pacific Area Travel Assn, 1972; cp/Sigma Nu Frat; Pres (Shelby) 1947 & VPres (Panama) 1961, Rotary Intl; Nat Press Clb; Cosmos Clb; r/Meth; hon/Recip, Silver Medal Awd, US Dept of Commerce, 1973; W/W in E.

ARGUESO de ACEVEDO, OLGA MARIA (MERIOLD) oc/Spanish Supervisor; b/Jun 25, 1925; h/1858 Marginal, Santa María, Río Piedras, PR 00927; ba/Santurce, PR; m/Ricardo Acevedo Defillo; c/Ricardo Luis Acevedo Argueso, Pablo Enrique Acevedo Argueso, Miold del Pilar Acevedo de Valdés; p/Luis Argueso (dec); Niní Rotger do Argueso; sp/Francisco Acevedo and Pilar Defelló; ed/BA, Ed, 1946; MEd,

1972; pa/Basic Spanish Tchr, Univ of PR, 1949-51; Spanish Tchr (All Grades from Elem to Superior) in Public & Pvt Schs, 1957-71; Sch Prin: Labra, Ctl, Einstein, Barbosa, Baldoriots, Elzaburg & Bueso Schs, 1971-75; Spanish Supvr for Underprivileged Chd, 1975-78; Sch Prin, Bueso, 1978-82; Mem: Tchrs Assn of PR; Assn for Supvn & Curric Devel; Ateneo de PR; Edt Bd of Ed Ed Mag, *El Sol*; r/Cath; hon/Author of Games, Poems & Exercises for Chd, Pub'd in *El Sol*, 1979; *Remedial Prog for Under Achievers from 2nd to 6th Grade*, 1977; Carolina Sch Dist, 1975; Dorado Sch Dist, 1976; Distrib Ed Clb of Am, 1978; ARC, 1967; COSMIF Teen Clb, 1968; W/W in S & SW.

ARINOLDO, CARLOS GUY oc/Psychologist; b/Sep 21, 1948; ba/2 Sunbury Lane, Stony Brook, NY 11790; m/Linda Diana; c/Brandon Carlo; p/Daniel and Isabella Arinoldo, New Hyde Pk, NY; sp/Irene Wickstein, Bklyn, NY; ed/BA Psych, Pace Univ, 1971; MA Psych, John Jay Col of Crim Justice, 1974; PhD Psych, Univ of GA, 1979; pa/Cnslg Psychol, Dallas St Correctional Inst, Dallas, PA, 1975-76; Psychol, Mississippi Bend Area Ed Agy, Clinton, IA, 1979-81; Psychol, Brookhaven Meml Hosp Med Ctr, Patchogue, NY, 1981-; Psychol, Brookhaven Hlth Ctr-E, Shirley, NY, 1981-; Am Psychol Assn; Nat Assn of Sch Psychols; r/Cath; hon/Author of Articles: "Black-White Differences in the Gen Cognitive Index of the McCarthy Scales & in Full Scale IQ's of Wechsler's Scales," *Jour of Clin Psychol* 1981, "Concurrent Validity of McCarthy's Scales," *Perceptual & Motor Skills* 1982, Others; W/W in E.

ARKIN, L JULES oc/Executive; b/Mar 19, 1929; h/250 North Hibiscus Drive, Miami Beach, FL 33139; ba/Miami, FL; c/Richard, Gary; ed/Emory Univ; LLB, Univ of Miami; mil/USNR-Ret'd, Lt Cmdr; pa/Ptner, Meyer, Weiss, Rose & Arkin, Attys at Law, 1957-; Dir 1967 & Pres 1980, Fin Fed Savs & Ln Assn, 1967-80; ABA; FL Bar Assn; Dade Co & Miami Bch Bar Assns; cp/Past Pres, Gtr Miami Jewish Fdn; Past Pres, Trustee & Former Mem Bd of Govs, Miami Bch C of C; Life Trustee & Past VPres Bd of Trustees, Mt Sinai Hosp of Gtr Miami; Mem, & Past Pres, Miami Bch Kiwanis Clb; Others; r/Jewish; hon/Pres's Ldrship Awd, Gtr Miami Jewish Fdn, 1967; Outstg Civic Ldr of Miami Bch, Civic Leag of Miami Bch, 1971; Silver Medallion Awd, Nat Conf of Christians & Jews, 1979.

ARMBRECHT, WILLIAM HENRY oc/Lawyer; b/Nov 1, 1908; h/112 Pinebrook Drive West, Mobile, AL 33608; ba/Mobile, AL; m/Katherine Little; c/William H III, Katherine A Brown, Anna Bell A Bru, Conrad P II, Clara L; p/Wm H and Anna Bell Armbrecht (dec); sp/Con R and Clara R Little (dec); ed/Att'd Spring Hill Col, 1927-29; LLB, Univ of AL, 1929-32; pa/Atty w Armbrecht, Jackson, DeMouy, Crowe, Holmes & Reeves, Mobile, AL, 1932-; Pres & Dir, AL, TN & Nn RR Co, 1950-70; Dir, Title Ins Co of Mobile, 1970-74; Dir, Sn Industs Corp, 1958-79; Dir, 1st Bk Grp-AL, 1973-79; Dir, Pt Clear Inc & Diamondhead Corp, 1979-; Pres, Mobile Bar Assn, 1954; Chm of Bd, 1st Nat Bk of Mobile, 1969-74; Others; cp/Dir, Mobile Founs for Public Higher Ed,

1962-74; Dir, Mobile Area C of C, 1954-75; Others; r/Epis; hon/Dir Emeritus, 1st Nat Bk of Mobile; W/W: in Am, in Fin & Indust, in S & SW, in Am Law, in AL; DIB; Personalities of the S; Standard & Poor's Register of Corps, Dirs, & Execs; Other Biogl Listings.

ARMIJO, JACQULYN D oc/Interior Designer; b/Jul 2, 1938; h/509 Chamiso Lane, Northwest, Albuquerque, NM 87107; ba/Same; m/Marshall L (dec); c/John Marshall, Christy Lynn, Michael Lawrence; p/Vi Martin and Iris Cook, Gilmer, TX; sp/Mr and Mrs Joe Armijo; ed/Att'd N TX St Univ & Univ of NM-Albuquerque; pa/Profl Model for 17 Yrs; Affil w St Farm Ins Co for 5 Yrs; Interior Designer, for the Past 24 Yrs; Mem, Am Soc of Interior Design; cp/Soc Chm for Symph Wom; Judge, Jr Miss Pageant; Soc Chm, Las Amapolas Garden Clb; Mem, Little Theater; Com Wom, Same Old Town Com; Chm, Hist Com of Albuquerque; Num Public Lectrs; Others; r/Cath; hon/Num Design Wks Pub'd in Newspapers, Mags & Books, 1965-75; Host for Duke Ellington on His Visit to Albuquerque; Brought Bob Hope to City for Arthritis Foun; Appt'd Mem, Armand Hammer Col of SW Beneficiaries.

ARMITAGE, RICHARD LEE oc/Assistant Secretary of Defense for International Security Affairs; b/Apr 26, 1945; h/9113 Glenbrook Road, Fairfax, VA 22031; ba/Washington, DC; m/Laura Alice Samford; c/Beth, Lee, Jenny, Paul, Chris; p/Leo Holmes and Ruth H Armitage (dec); ed/HS Dipl, St Pious HS; BS, US Nav Acad; mil/USN, 1963-73; pa/Def Attache Ofc, Saigon, Viet Nam, 1973-75; Conslt 1975-76, Dept Asst Sec of Def for E Asia & Pacific 1981-83, Asst Secy of Def for Intl Security Affairs 1983-; Dept of Def; Ptnr, Agt/Export, Bangkok to Wash DC, 1976-78; Adm Asst, US Senate (Bob Dole), 1978-79; Self-Employed, Fairfax, VA, 1979-80; Campaign Wkr 1980, Transition Team Wkr & Fgn Policy Advr 1980-81, Pres Reagan; r/Cath; hon/Tran Hung Dao, Saigon Chapt, Viet Nam, 1973.

ARMON, DALE DIANE oc/Executive; b/Aug 13, 1936; h/1500 Lee Boulevard, Berkeley, IL 60163; ba/Pet Rescue Incorporated, 151 North Bloomingdale Road, Bloomingdale, IL 60108; p/Dr Godfrey H Kurtz (dec); Ida Kurtz (dec); ed/BA, Univ of So CA; MA, Univ of CA LA; pa/Fdr & Pres, Pet Rescue Inc, 1973-; Fin Conslt, Mut Fund Assocs, 1969-72; Exec Salesperson, Elite Inc, 1968-71; Conslt, Patricia Stevens Col, 1965-68; Pres, Valor & Assocs Public Relats, 1960-63; Profl Fashion & TV Model, 1958-65; Author, Lectr & Newspaper Columnist; Editor & Publisher of Pet Rescue Pub, *Paw Prints*; Nat Ldr in Animal Welfare, Wildlife Conserv & Envir Protection; Fdr of 1st Unique & Innovative No-Kill, Minimum Cage Sanctuary for Orphaned Pets; cp/Commr, Bloomingdale Old Town, 1977-81; hon/Num Articles Pub'd in *Paw Prints*; Wom of the Yr, Public Relats Coun, 1961; Humanitarian of the Yr, Atlanta (GA) Humane Soc, 1976.

ARMS, KAREN G oc/Director, Professor; b/Oct 5, 1941; h/505 Schocalog Road, Akron, OH 44320; ba/Kent, OH; m/Walter E; c/Denise Arms Williams, Deborah L; p/Lamar and Dorothy

Gardner, Elletsville, IN; sp/Gilbert and Blanche Arms, Maryville, MO; ed/BS, NW MO St Univ, 1957; MS, Univ of Akron, 1971; PhD, Kent St Univ, 1974; pa/Dir Sch of Fam & Consumer Studies 1980-, Asst Dean Col of Fine & Profl Arts 1976-80, Asst Prof/Coor Div of Indiv & Fam Devel 1974-76, Pt-time Instr 1973-74, Grad Asst 1972-73, Kent St Univ; Pt-time Lctr, Univ of Akron, 1970-72; Adhoc Com on Student Liability Ins, Budget Com of Nat Coun 1982, Assn of Admrs of Home Ecs in St Univs & Land-Grant Cols, 1980-; Secy 1980-81, Ch 1981-82, OH Admrs of Home Ecs; Mem Pubs Com 1982-85, Nat Assn of Wom Deans, Admrs & Cnslrs; Secy 1979-81, Pres Elect 1982, Pres 1983, OH Assn for Wom Deans, Admrs & Cnslrs; Am Home Ecs Assn; OH Home Ecs Assn; Roundtable Discussion Ldr & Affil Congs Planning, Nat Coun on Fam Relats; Pres 1977-79, VPres & St-wide Conf Prog Ch 1976-77, OH Coun on Fam Relats; Am Voc Assn; OH Voc Assn; Num Others; cp/Bd of Trustees, 1st U Meth Ch, 1979-; Num Spkg Engagements & Wkshops; Others; r/Prot; hon/Contbr of Chapts to Books, *Modern Perspectives in the Psych of Mid Age*, 1981; *Bldg Fam Strengths*, 1980; Author of Num Articles Pub'd in Profl Jours incl'g: *Gerontology & Gerontology Ed*, *Resources in Ed, Ednl Horizons*, Others; Over 13 Conv Papers Presented, 1975-82; Lifetime Mem, Kappa Omicron Phi; Omicron Delta Kappa; Pi Lamda Theta; Lifetime Mem, Pi Omega Pi; Kappa Delta Pi; W/W: of Am Wom, of Wom in Ed; Commun Ldrs & Noteworthy Ams.

ARMSTRONG, ALMETTA oc/Math Teacher; b/Aug 18, 1933; h/Route 2, Box 128, Candor, NC 27229; ba/Mt Gilead, NC; p/Mr A C Armstrong (dec); Mrs R B Armstrong, Candor, NC; ed/AB, Shaw Univ, 1953; MA, NC A&T St Univ, 1957; Addit Study at NC St Univ; pa/Tchr, Wadesboro, NC, 1958-68; Tchr, Raleigh Public Schs, 1968-72; Tchr, Montgomery Co Sch, 1972-83; Pres Montgomery Co 1980, Acting VP 1975-79 Dist 8, NCAE; Mem, St Human Relats Coun; Mem, St Inmate Labor Comm; cp/Mem, Sandhills Mtl Hlth Bd; Mem, Drug Abuse Adv Bd; St Platform Dem Com; St Unity Campaign; Chm, Resolutions & Elections Com & Dist 8 Com to Elect Pres Carter in NC; Key Indiv in Gov Hunt Election, 1980; r/Bapt; hon/Miss Shaw Univ Nat Alumni Queen, 1969; Outstg Dedication Sers from Black Ldrship Caucus 1981, NAACP 1980, & Shaw Univ 1979; Nat Coun on Status of Wom; The World's W/W of Wom; W/W: in Am Polits, of Wom in Am.

ARMSTRONG, ANNE L oc/Executive; b/Dec 27, 1927; h/Armstrong Ranch, Armstrong, TX 78338; m/Tobin; c/John Barclay, Katharine A, Sarita S, Tobin Jr and James L; p/Armant and Olive (Martindale) Legendre; ed/Foxcroft HS, 1945; BA, Vassar Col, 1949; pa/Chm, Pres's (Reagan) Fgn Intell Adv Bd, 1981-; US Ambassador to Great Brit, 1976-77; Cnslr to the Pres, Cabinet Rank to Pres's Nixon & Ford, 1973-74; Bd of Dirs: Boise Cascade Airways, 1st City BanCorp of TX, Gen Foods, Gen Motors, Halliburton; Chm of Adv Bd, VChm of Exec Bd, Ctr for Strategic & Intl Studies, Georgetown Univ, 1977-;

Citizen Regent, Bd of Regents, Smithsonian Instn, 1978-; Bd of Trustees, So Meth Univ, 1977-; Vis'g Com, John F Kennedy Sch of Govt, Harvard Univ, 1978-; CoChm, Bob Hope USO Ctr Campaign, 1979-; rel/Epis; hon/Hon LLD: Bristol Univ, England (1976), Wash & Lee Univ (1976), Wms Col (1977), St Mary's Univ (1978), Tulane Univ (1978); Repub Wom of the Yr Awd, 1979; Texan of the Yr, 1981; Gold Medal, Dist'd Ser to Humanity, Nat Inst of Soc Scis, 1977; 2000 Notable Ams.

ARMSTRONG, DANIEL W oc/Professor, Consultant; b/Nov 2, 1949; h/Lubbock, TX 79424; ba/Lubbock, TX; m/Linda M; c/Lincoln T, Ross A; p/Robert E and Nila L Armstrong, Ft Wayne, IN; sp/Kenneth and Phyllis Todd; ed/BS, Washington & Lee Univ, 1972; MS 1974, PhD 1977, TX A&M Univ; pa/Prof Chem, Bowdoin Col, 1978-80; Prof Chem, Georgetown Univ, 1980-83; Prof Chem & Chm of Analytical Chem Div, TX Tech Univ, 1983-; Am Chem Soc; Sigma Xi; Smithsonian Assoc; Host of "Univ Forum Radio Show," (WASH-FM) on Var Sci Topics, 1981-83; Over 50 Spkg Presentations & Lectrs at Var Univs & Profl Symps, 1969-; hon/Author & Co-Author, Over 40 Articles Pub'd in Sci Jours incl'g: *Precambrian Res, Jour Molecular Evolution, Jour Am Chem Soc, Jour Chromtography Sci, Jour Chem Ed, Macromolecules*, Others; Phi Lambda Upsilon, 1975; Edit Bd of *Jour of Liquid Chromotography*, 1983; Am Men & Wom of Sci; Dir of World Rschrs.

ARMSTRONG, ELLIS LEROY oc/Consulting Engineer; b/May 30, 1914; h/3709 Brockbank Drive, Salt Lake City, UT 84124; ba/Salt Lake City, UT; m/Florine Clark; c/Ellis Bruce, Dale Clark, Larry Leroy, Elaine, Diane Kay, David Kent; p/Leroy S and Mae Wood Armstrong (dec); BSCE, UT St Univ, 1936; Postgrad, CO St Univ; EngrD, Newark St Col, 1966; DSc (honoris causa), So UT St Col, 1972; pa/Design, Constrn Projs in Wn US 1936-45, Asst Reg Dir 1968-69, US Bur Reclamation; Supvr, Design Sect on Dam & Hwy Wk, Engrg Ctr, Denver, CO, 1945-47; Supvr, Trenton Dam Proj, NE, 1948-52; Engr Egyptian-Am Rural Improvement Comm & Spec Conslt to Egyptian Govt on High Aswan Dam Proj, Cairo, 1953; Proj Engr & Dept Proj Mgr, St Lawrence Power & Seaway Proj, Power Auth, NY St, 1954-57; Dir of Hwys, UT, 1957-58; US Commr of Public Roads, Dept of Commerce, Wash DC, 1958-61; Pres, Better Hwys Info Foun, 1961-62; Sr Ptnr, Porter, O'Brien & Armstrong Conslt Engrs, 1962-68; Pres, Armstrong Assocs, Engrs & Conslts, SLC, 1968-; Adj Prof Civil Engrg, Univ of UT, 1976-; Vis'g Prof Public Policy-Energy, Brigham Yg Univ, 1980-; Adj Prof Civil Engrg, UT St Univ, 1978-84; US Commr of Reclamation, Dept of Interior, Wash DC, 1969-73; VP URS Sys Corp, 1973; Exec Bd, Pres US Com 1972-80, Intl VP 1980-84, Intl Water Res Assn; Num Others; cp/Mem Exec Com, US Com Large Dams World Power Conf; Chm, US Nat Com World Energy Conf, 1971-73; Chm US Interagy Com on Excavation Technol, 1971-73; Chm, OECD Intl Conf on Tunneling, 1970; Chm Del to USSR on High Voltage Power Generation & Transmission, 1972; Conslt Hydropower, US Dept of

Energy, 1977-80; Chm Adv Bd, Col of Engrg, Univ of UT, 1978-83; Am Water Works Assn; Life Mem, Am Road Bldrs Assn; Rotary Intl; SLC C of C; Num Others; r/LDS; hon/Author & Editor of 3 Books & Contbr of Num Articles on Design, Constrn & Mgmt of Public Wks; Hon Chm, US Nat Com on Tunneling Technol; Nat Hon Mem (Pres UT Sect 1976-77), Royce J Tipton Awd 1970, Pres Awd 1981, ASCE; Nat Hon Mem, Am Public Wks Assn; Nat Hon Mem, Am Waterworks Assn; Phi Kappa Phi; Nat Hon Mem, Chi Epsilon; Recip Dist'd Ser Awd, UT St Univ, 1959; Profl Engr of Yr, UT St, 1969; US Public Wks Man of Yr, 1971; James R Talmage Sci Achmt Awd, Brigham Yg Univ, 1975; Num Others; Intl W/W: in Engrg, in Am, in World.

ARNAUDO, DAVID LLOYD oc/ Special Assistant to Director; b/May 23, 1942; h/ 413 South Fairfax Street, Alexandria, VA 22314; ba/Rockville, MD; m/Patricia S Alexander; c/Juliet; p/ Michael Arnaudo (dec); Thelma Geddes Arnaudo, Berkeley, CA; sp/Barton Alexander, Washington, DC; Marian Alexander, Toledo, OH; ed/BA Ec; MA Public Adm; Law Sch; CPA; pa/Spec Asst to Dir, Ofc of Child Support Enforcement; Dir, Fam Asst Studies; Dir, Income Maintenance Eval, HHS; Assoc Dir: Industl Studies, Cost of Living Coun, Price Comm, Ofc of the Pres; Staff: Ofc of Policy Devel, Ofc of the Secy of Commerce, Ec Devel Adm, Upper Gt Lakes Reg Comm; VChm, Alexandria Bd of Arch Review; Mem, Am Soc for Public Adm; Mem, Wash Economists Clb; cp/Exec Bd & Mem, Nat Capitol Area U Way; Exec Mem, U Way of Alexandria; Bd Mem, Alexandria Vol Bur; Bd Mem, Hopkins House Assn; Mem, Nat Trust for Hist Presv; r/Epis; hon/Pub'd Var Profl Reports & Res Studies; Nom for Sr Exec Ser Internship; Meritorious Perf Awd; Outstg Perf Awd.

ARNAUDO, PATRICIA SUSAN oc/ Housing Executive; b/Jan 3, 1943; h/413 South Fairfax Street, Alexandria, VA 22314; ba/Washington, DC; m/David LLoyd; c/Juliet Gordon; p/Marian Alexander, Toledo, OH; sp/Thelma Arnaudo, Berkeley, CA; ed/BA 1964, MPA 1965, Doct Student 1970-71, Univ of MI; pa/Prog Analyst, Dept HEW, 1966-69; Res Assoc, Consltg Firm, 1969-70; Prog Develr 1970-75; Sr Prog Analyst 1975-76, Dept Dir Prog Mgmt Div, Chief Sect 8, Mgmt Br 1976-78, Dir Existing Housing 1979-81, Dept Dir Ofc of Indian Housing 1981-82, Acting Dir Ofc of Indian Housing 1982-, HUD, Wash DC; Low-Income Housing Coalition; Am Soc of Public Admrs; Nat Assn Housing & Redevel Ofcrs; cp/ Hopkins House Assn; Old Town Civic Assn; r/Epis; hon/Pub'd Var Profl Reports in: Welfare in Review 1967, HEW Brochure 1969, Intl City Mgrs Qtly Jour 1974, Others; Recip Cert of Spec Achmt 1977, Cert of Merit 1979, Cert of Superior Ser 1980, HUD; Recip Planning Awd, City of Alexandria, 1977; W/ W of Am Wom.

ARNETT, PENELOPE PRATT oc/ Professor; b/Mar 4, 1948; h/106 Oakhurst Drive, North Augusta, SC 29841; ba/Aiken, SC; m/Jerry Lorris; c/Andrea, Jay; p/Ray and Nancy Pratt, North, Augusta, SC; sp/Lucille Lay, Jackson-

ville Bch, FL; ed/Dipl in Nsg, Fairview Gen Hosp Sci of NSg 1969; BSN 1974, MSN 1975, Med Col of GA; AS, DeKalb Commun Col, 1981; mil/USANC, 1968-71, 1st Lt; pa/Hd RN, Lakewood Hosp, Lakewood, OH, 1969; Team Ldr, St Joseph Hosp, 1971-74; Pvt Duty Registry, 1974-75; Hd RN, Med Col of GA, 1974-75; Instr, Clemson Univ, 1975-76; Asst Prof, Univ of SC-Aiken, 1976-; Mem 1980-, Secy 1981-82 & 1982-83, N Augusta Unit, Am Cancer Soc; Sigma Theta Tau, 1975-; 10th Dist GA Nurses Assn; Nat Arthritis Foun; r/Cath; hon/Co-Author of Article, "Clin Eval Criteria in Assoc, Baccalaureate, Master's & Cont'g Ed Nsg Progs in the S,"Advances in Nsg Sci, 1982; W/W in S & SW; Personalities in S; DIB; Commun Ldrs of Am.

ARNEY, WILLIAM RAY oc/Professor; h/526 North Rogers Street, Olympia, WA 98502; ba/Olympia, WA; m/ Deborah Henderson; c/John Arthur; p/ John Wilson and Grace Kuhn Arney, Aurora, CO; sp/Arthur D Henderson (dec); Florence L Henderson, Manitou Springs, CO; ed/BA Sociol 1971, MA Sociol 1972, PhD in Soc 1974, Univ CO-Boulder; pa/Assoc Prof Sociol, Dartmouth Col, 1974-81; Fac Mem Sociol, The Evergreen St Col, 1981-; Am Stat Assn; Am Sociological Assn; r/Ch of Christ; hon/Author & Co-Author of Books, Power & the Profession of Obstetrics, 1982; Med & The Mgmt of Living: Taming The Last Gt Beast w Bernard J Bergen, 1984; Pub'd Articles in Profl Jours; Phi Beta Kappa, 1971; Univ Fellow, Univ CO, 1972; W/W in W; Contemp Authors.

ARNEZ, NANCY LEVI oc/Department Chairman; b/Jul 6, 1928; h/3122 Cherry Road, Northeast, Washington, DC 20018; ba/Washington, DC; p/Mrs Ida R Washington, Baltimore, MD; ed/ AB Eng, Morgan St Col, 1949; MA English 1954, EdD Ed Admn 1958, Columbia Univ; pa/Eng Tchr 1949-57, Hd Eng Dept 1958-62, Balto Public Schs; Asst Admissions Ofcr Tchrs Col, Columbia Univ, 1957-58; Prof & Dir, Ctr for Inner City Studies, NEn IL Univ, 1962-66; Dean, Dept Chm Sch of Ed, Howard Univ, 1974-; Mem 1957-63: NEA; MD St Tchrs Assn; Assn Student Tchg; Pub Sch Tchrs Assn; NCTE; Mem 1963-69: AAUP; ASCD; IL Ed Assn; Mem 1972-: African Heritage Student Assn; Ofcr, The Assn of African Hist; Assn for Study of Psych & Sociol; Issues; AAUW; AASA; PDK; Nat Alliance of Black Sch Edrs; r/Presb; hon/ Author of Maj Res Study: The Besieged Sch Supt, 1981; Author of 16 Books & Manuals; Contbr of 5 Book Chapts; Pub'd Over 100 Articles in Profl Jours; Awd'd 2 Million Dollars in Res Funds, 1968-; Hon at "Meet Author" Series, Ellis' Bookstore, Chgo, 1969; PDK 1981, Dist'd Res Prof 83, Howard Univ; PDK, City Col, NY, 1981; Listed in Num W/ W Pubs.

ARNOLD, BILL R oc/Director, Professor; b/Oct 24, 1949; h/1522 Castille, Edinburg, TX 78539; ba/Edinburg, TX; m/Sharon Thompson; c/Nathan Wm; p/ Roy W and Selma F Arnold, TX City, TX; sp/Ralph B and Louise Thompson, TX City, TX; ed/BA Psych, Univ of Houston, 1971; MA Clin Psych 1973, PhD Cnslg Psych 1976, N TX St Univ; pa/Dir & Assoc Prof Human Sers Prog,

Pan-Am Univ, 1978-; Psychol (Pvt Pract), McAllen, TX, 1978-; Psychol (Pvt Pract), Denton/Ft Worth, TX, 1976-78; Rehab Psychol, TX Rehab Comm, Ft Worth, 1976-78; Adj Prof 1977, Res Asst 1975-76, N TX St Univ; Asst Dir, Help House Inc, Denton, 1974-75; Secy & Treas, Rio Grande Val Psychol Assn, 1982-84; Edit Bd, Jour of Nat Org of Human Ser Edrs, 1982-84; Am Psychol Assn, 1976-; TX Psychol Assn, 1976-; Assn for Advmt of Behavior Therapy, 1976-; TX U Fac, 1982-; r/Meth; hon/Author of Num Articles Pub'd in Profl Jours incl'g: Resources in Ed, 1982; Catalog of Selected Documents in Psych, 1980; Rehab Cnslg Bltn, 1978; Res in Mtl Helth & Behavioral Scis, 1973; Others; Cert of Apprec, 2nd Pan-Am Conf on Rehab, 1981; S TX Hlth Sys Agy, 1982; W/W in S & SW.

ARNOLD, JOHN DAVID oc/Senior Management Counselor; b/May 14, 1933; h/15 Reservoir Road, Wayland, MA 01778; ba/Waltham, MA; m/Dorothea DeFeyo; c/Derek, Keith, Craig; p/ Israel and Edith Gordon Arnold; ed/BA, Harvard Univ, 1955; mil/AUS, 1955-57, 1st Lt; pa/Prodn Supvr & Dealer Ser Mgr, Arnold Stretch Mates Corp, 1957-59; Asst Dir of Manpower & Orgnl Devel, Polaroid Corp, 1959-63; Dir of Intl Opers, Kepner-Treger & Assocs, 1963-68; Fdr & Pres, John Arnold ExecuTrak Sys, 1968-; Execu-Trak Ltd, Waltham, MA, 1968-; Mem Bd of Dirs, Shawmut Commun Bk, Framingham, MA, 1981-; Cnslr & Conf Ldr for 142 "Fortune 500" Cos & Smaller Entrepreneural & High Tech Orgs; hon/Author of Books: Make Up Your Mind 1978, The Art of Decision-Making 1980, Shooting the Exec Rapids 1981, How to Make the Right Decisions (w Bert Tompkins) 1982, Trading Up: A Career Guide--Getting Ahead w/o Getting Out 1984, How to Protect Yourself Agst a Takeover 1985; Contbr of Num Articles to Newspapers, Mags & Jours incl'g: Bd Rm Report, Fin Exec, Fortune, Mergers & Acquisitions, The Wall St Jour, Others; Recently Completed TV Series Pilot, "Decision Point,"; W/W in E.

ARNOLD, SHEILA oc/State Legislator; b/Jan 15, 1929; h/1058 Alta Vista Drive, Laramie, WY 92070; ba/ Cheyenne, WY; m/George; c/Michael, Peter; sp/Mrs Thurman Arnold, Laramie, WY; pa/Mem: Legis Mines, Minerals & Industl Devel Com, Agri, Public Lands & Water Com, Select Water Devel Com, WY Ho of Reps, 1977-; Mem of Bd 1st Interst Bk of Laramie, 1983-; Mem, WY St Land Use Adv Com, 1975-79; cp/Past Pres, Laramie C of C; Past Pres, Univ of WY Fac Woms Clb; Zonta; Laramie Woms Clb; Past Pres, Jane Jefferson Dem Woms Clb; Past VChm, Albany Co Dem Ctl Com; Dem St Com Wom, 1978-80; r/Epis; hon/C of C Top Hand Awd, 1977; W/W: in W, of Am Wom, in Am Polit.

ARNOLD, WAYNE oc/Court Counselor; b/Feb 18, 1944; h/PO Box 162 Crossnore, NC 28616; ba/24th Judic Dist, Newland, NC; m/Sharon Johnson; c/Andrea Dawn, Eric; p/Mr and Mrs Kenneth Arnold, Newland, NC; sp/Mrs Doyle Hutchison, Crossnore, NC; ed/ Wn Piedmont Commun Col, 1973; BA Sociol 1973, Addit Studies in 1977, Appalachian St Univ; Att'd Wn Carolina, 1975; MA Crim, IN St Univ, 1977;

NC Justice Acad, 1978; Addit Studies w NC Dept of Justice, 1979; mil/USAF, 1963-67, Air Police; pa/Court Cnslr, 1973-76; Constrn Estimator 1969-70, Constrn Ofc Mgr 1967-68, SEn/Juno Constrn Co, Charlotte, NC; Pers Recruiter Mgr, TRW Inc, Newland, NC, 1973; Pt-time Instr, Mayland Commun Col, 1978-79; Grad Asst, IN St Univ, 1976-77; cp/Treas 1979-81, Chaplin 1979-82, Bd of Dirs 1979-81, Avery Ctl Rescue Squad; r/Presb; hon/ Gardner-Webb Col Hon Roll, 1970-72.

ARNSTEIN, SHERRY R oc/Executive; b/Jan 11, 1930; h/2500 Virginia Avenue, Northwest, Apartment 417-S, Washington, DC 20037; ba/Washington, DC; m/George R; sp/Mrs Elizabeth Neuburger, LA, CA; ed/BS, Univ of CA-LA; MS Communs, Am Univ; Att'd Sum Session, Sys Dynamics, MA Inst of Technol; pa/VPres Govt Relats, Nat Hlth Coun, 1978-; Sr Res Fellow, Dept of Hlth & Human Sers, 1975-78; Self Employed Conslt on Public Policy, Maj Clients incl: Arthur D Little Inc, OSTI & Nellum & Assoc, Acad for Contemp Probs, Boise Cascade, Volt Inc, Others, 1968-75; Chief Citizen Participation Advr, Model Cities Adm (HUD), 1967-68; Spec Asst to the Asst Sec of Dept of Hlth Ed & Welfare, 1965-67; Staff Conslt, Pres's Com on Juv Delinquency (Johnson), 1963-65; Wash Editor, *Current Mag*, 1961-63; cp/Adv Grp on Sci & Public Policy: AAAS; Steering Com Mem, Hlth on Wed Netwk; Vis'g Lectr, Carnegie Mellon Univ & Trans Res Inst; Edit Bd Mem: *Technol Assessmt Update, The Bureaucrat, Public Adm Review*; r/Prot; hon/Editor of Several Pubs in Govt Relats Handbook Series, 1979-84; Editor of Num Pubs of Wash Report Series, 1983-84; Author of Book, *Perspectives on Technol Assessment*, 1975; Author of Num Articles Pub'd in Profl Jours incl'g: *The Internist 1978, IEEE Transactions on Sys, Man & Cybernetics 1977, Jour of Clin Engrg 1977, Jour of Am Inst of Planners 1969, Public Adm Review 1972, Others*; W/W: in Wash, in Technol Today, of Wom; W/Where Among Writers.

ARONSON, MARGOT R oc/Consultant; b/Apr 5, 1942; h/14111 Bauer Drive, Rockville, MD 20853; c/Jeffrey Richard, Stephanie Louise, Alexandra Elisabeth; p/Stuart S Richardson (dec); Elisabeth B Richardson; ed/BA, Barnard Col, 1964; MA, Columbia Univ, 1967; Att'g MSW Prog, Univ of MD Sch of Social Wk; pa/Indep Conslt, 1981-; Dir Info Collection & Exch, Peace Corps, 1975-81; Mng Editor, *Sawaddi Mag*, Bangkok, 1972-74; Writer & Univ Tchr, 1968-72; Prog Coor 1977, CoChp 1978-79, Exec Bd 1980-83, Interagy Fgn Area Studies & Crosscultural Roundtable; Exec Adv Bd for Intl Inst 1981, Design Com for Intl Symp 1982, Am Soc for Tng & Devel; Soc for Intercultural Ed, Tng & Res; cp/Adv Bd Mem for Pks & Rec Depts of Montgomery Co; Exec Bd, Editor, Newslttr, Montgomery Co Assn for Chd w Lrng Disabilities; Spkr at Local, Nat, Intl Confs; Num Other Commun Activs; r/ Jewish; hon/Pub'd Articles, *Look E Mag, Orients Mag, NY Sunday Times*; Column for *Bangkok World*, 1973; Editor, *Peace Corps Prog & Tng Jour*, 1974.

ARONSON, SHEPARD G oc/Physician; ba/1085 Park Avenue, New York, NY 10128; ed/BA, Md Med Sch, Cornell Univ; Intern, Jewish Hosp, Bklyn, NY; Externship Surg Pathol, NY Hosp & Cornell Univ Med Ctr; mil/Chief of Surg Ser at Santa Tomas Hosp, Manilla; pa/Assoc Vis'g Phys, Bellevue Hosp; Asst Clin Prof Internal Med at Med Sch, Conslt Internal Med to Inst Phy Med & Rehab at Med Ctr, Asst Att'g Phys at Hosp, NY Univ; Att'g Phys, NY Infirm-Beekman Downtown Hosp; Att'g Phys, Docts Hosp; Chief Endocrine Clin, NY Univ Hosp; Chief Diabetes Clin, Stuyvesant Polyclin; Chief Dept Metabolic Diseases Diabetes Clin, Good Samaritan Hosp, NYC; Past Pres, Soc Internal Med Col of NY; Mem Bd of Censors, Bd Dirs, Chm Medicare Peer Review (7 Yrs), Chm Public Relats Com (3 Yrs), Chm Liaison Com w NY Cos Reg'd Nurses Assn, NY Co Med Soc; Mem, Disciplinary Com, 1st Jud Dept Appellate Div, Supr Ct NY St; Chm Criteria Com, Internal Med of NY Co Sers Review Org; Assoc, Am Col of Legal Med; Life Mem, Am Col of Phys & Pan-Am Med Assn; cp/Charter Mem & 1st Chp of Bd (NY Chapt), NOW; Mem, Med Adv Bd Com of Planned Parenthood of NY; Mem Bd Dirs, NY Diabetes Assn; Num Lectrs on Med Topics; hon/Num Med Articles Pub'd in Profl Jours; Bronze Star, Purple Heart & 5 Battle Stars.

ARONSON, STANLEY MAYNARD oc/Physician, Educator; b/May 28, 1922; h/PO Box 136, Rehoboth, MA 02769; ba/Providence, RI; m/Betty E; c/Susan, Lisa, Sarah; p/Eliah and Leonora Aronson (dec); sp/Fred and Louise Ellis (dec); ed/BS, Col of The City of NY, 1943; MD, Col of Med, NY Univ, 1947; MA, Brown Univ, 1971; MPH, Sch of Public Hlth, Harvard Univ, 1980; mil/AUS, 1942-46; pa/Prof Pathol, Downst Med Ctr, SUNY, 1954-70; Prof of Med Sci & Fdg Dean of Med 1970-80, Prof of Med Sci 1981-, Brown Univ; Other Profships at Yale Univ, Dartmouth Col, Columbia Univ; Num Med Profl Orgs & Bds; r/Hebrew; hon/Author of 6 Med Textbooks; Over 250 Articles Pub'd in Profl Sci & Med Jours; Vis'g Profships: Canada, Mexico, England & US; W/W.

ARORA, PRINCE KUMAR oc/Immunologist; b/Nov 15, 1947; h/9514 Lindale Drive, Bethesda, MD 20817; ba/ Bethesda, MD; m/Kit-Ying Barbara Chin; p/Khem Kumari and Manohar Lal Arora, Denver, CO; ed/BSc w Hons 1970, MSc w Hons 1973, Panjab Univ, Chandigrah, India; PhD Immunol, MI St Univ, 1978; pa/Grad Res Asst, MI St Univ, 1976-78; John E Fogarty Intl Vis'g Fellow, Nat Cancer Inst, 1978-82; NIH Staff Fellow, Lab of Molecular Genetics, NICHD, 1982-, NIH, Bethesda, MD; Mem, Sigma Xi; Am Assn Immunologists; Am Soc for Microbiol; r/Hindu; hon/Author & Co-Author, Over 15 Pub'd Articles in Profl Jours incl'g: *Jour Infectious Diseases, Nature, Jour Immunol, Cellular Immunol*; Others; Over 7 Abstracts Presented at Meetings of FASEB (Am Assn Immunologists); Nat Merit Scholar, India; Merit Scholar, Gold Medalist, Merit Certs, Panjab Univ, India; Merit Scholar, Min of Hlth & Fam Planning, India; Jr Res Fellow, Indian Coun of Agri Res, New Delhi; W/W.

ARRANTS, SHIRLEY oc/Artist; b/ Mar 3, 1941; h/238 Trinkus Lane, Bigfork, MT 59911; ba/Same; c/Troy, Trace, Chance; p/Philip Micon Elton, Arlington, WA; Velma Corban, Bigfork, MT; ed/Att'd Flathead Co HS, Kalispell, MT, 1955-58; Dipl, La Jolla Sr HS, La Jolla, CA, 1959; pa/Self Employed Artist w Num Pvt Shows incl'g: Sedona, AZ, 1980; Kalispell, MT, 1980; Tuscon, AZ, 1981; Des Moines, IA, 1981; Chgo, IL, 1982; Maui, HI, 1982; Govs Mansion, Helena, MT, 1984; Wks in Galleries: Flathead Lake Gallery, Bigfork, MT; J Harkin & Assocs, Spokane, WA; Call of Wild Gallery, Dallas, TX; Eagle Gallery, Sun Val, ID; Am Art Intl Ltd, Portland, OR; The Drummond Gallery, Hayden Lake, ID; VPres, Am Artists of Rockies Assn, 1981; Non Mem Juror 1982 & 1983 Annual Exhbn in NYC, Pastel Soc of Am; hon/Best of Show: Wn & Wildlife Nat Art Show, Yakima, WA; Ellensburg Wn Art Show, Ellensburg, WA, 1980; Soroptimist Wn Artists Show, Missoula, MT, 1980 & 1983; Artists' Invitational, Kalispell Art Show, Kalispell, MT, 1983; Blackfoot Val Art Show, MT, 1983; Hon Purchase Awd, Wn Art Assn, Ellensburg, WA; Artist for Reg Govs Conf, Kalispell, MT, 1983; Am Artists of Renown; Contemp Wn Artists.

ARRECHE, CANDY ANN oc/Attorney & Notary; b/Jul 7, 1954; h/Hato Rey Plaza, Apartment 19 F, Hato Rey, PR 00918; ba/Nuevo, PR; p/Cándido C Arreche (dec); Olga Holdun Arreche, Orlando, FL; ed/BA Hist & Fgn Langs, FL Technol Univ, 1974; JD, Inter-Am Univ, 1976; pa/Donor Recruiter 1974-76, Exec Dir 1978-81, PR Commun Blopd Ctr, Santurce; Law Clk, Calderon Rosa Silva ad Vargas, San Juan, 1975-76; Atty, Coop Devel Corp, San Juan, 1977; Law Clk, Jud Studies Ctr, 1978; Pvt Pract, 1978; Head of Own Law Firm, 1983-; ABA; PR Bar Assn; Intl Bar Assn; FL Assn of Blood Bks; Am Assn of Blood Bks; cp/BBB; C of C of PR; Alumnus, FL Technol Univ; Rosacrucian; r/Cath; hon/Author of "Hepatitis: A Medico-Legal Prob"; Golden Book Awd 1970, Hon Student Awd 1971, Deerborne Priv Sch; Key to City of Coral Gables, FL, 1971; W/W of Am Wom.

ARRINGTON, LEONARD JAMES oc/Research Historian; b/Jul 3, 1917; h/ 2236 South 2200 East, Salt Lake City, UT 84109; ba/Provo, Utah; m/Harriet Ann Horne; c/James, Carl, Susan; p/ Noah and Edna Corn Arrington (dec); sp/Lyman Merrill Horne, SLC, UT; Myrtle Swainston Horne (dec); ed/BA, Univ ID, 1939; Grad Wk, Univ NC-Chapel Hill, 1939-41, 1949-50 & PhD Ec, 1952; mil/AUS, 1943-46; pa/ Prof Ec, UT St Univ, 1952-72; Ch Hist 1972-78, Dir Hist Div 1978-80, Ch of Jesus Christ, LDS; Dir, Joseph Fielding Smith Inst for Ch Hist, Brigham Yg Univ, 1980-; Pres, Wn Hist Assn, 1968-69; Pres, Mormon Hist Assn, 1965-66; Pres 1981-82, Pacific Coast Br, Am Hist Assn; Mem Com 1976-77, Org of Am Hists; r/LDS; hon/Author of Books: *Gt Basin Kingdom: An Ec Hist of LDS, 1830-1900* 1958, *The Mormon Experience* 1979, *Bldg The City of God* 1976; Hon DHL, Univ ID, 1977; Hon HHD, UT St Univ, 1982; Dist'd Ams; W/W & W/W in W; Intl W/W.

ARROW, KENNETH J oc/Professor; b/Aug 23, 1921; h/580 Constanza Street, Stanford, CA 94305; ba/Stanford, CA; m/Selma; c/David M, Andrew S; p/Harry I and Lillian Arrow (dec); sp/ Albert Schweitzer and Eleanor Atwood (dec); ed/BSc Soc Sci, The City Col of NY, 1940; MA 1941, PhD 1951, Columbia Univ; mil/ASAAC, 1942-46, Capt; pa/Res Assoc, Cowles Comm for Res in Ec, 1947-49; Asst Prof Ec, Univ Chgo, 1948-49; Acting Asst Prof Ec & Stats 1948-49, Assoc Prof & Prof Ec, Stats & Opers Res 1950-68, Jean Kenney Prof Ec & Prof Opers Res 1979-, Stanford Univ; Prof Ec 1968-74, James Bryant Conant Univ Prof 1974-79, Harvard Univ; Pres 1958, Econometric Soc; Pres 1972, Am Ec Assn; Pres 1981-82, Wn Ec Assn; Pres 1972, Inst of Magmt Scis; VPres 1979-81, Am Acad Arts & Scis; Nat Acad of Scis; Brit Acad; Am Phil Soc; Finnish Acad Arts & Scis; Chm Sect K 1982-83, AAAS; r/Jewish; hon/ Author of Books: *Social Choice & Indiv Values* 1951 & 1963, *Aspects Theory of Risk-Bearing* 1965, *Essays on Theory Risk-Bearing* 1971, *Limits of Org* 1974; Co-Author: *Studies in Math Theory of Inventories* 1958, *Studies in Linear & Non-linear Programming* 1958, *A Time Series Anal of Interindust Demands* 1959, *Public Investmt, The Rate of Return, & Optimal Fiscal Policy* 1971, *Gen Competitive Anal* 1971, *Studies in Resource Allocation Processes* 1977; John Bates Clark Medal, Am Ec Assn, 1957; Nobel Meml Prize in Ec Sci, 1972; Num Hon Degs.

ARROYO, ANGEL M oc/Poet and Journalist; h/76 Pinehurst Avenue, Apartment 32, New York, NY 10033; m/Carmen López; c/Alma, Angelina; p/ Manuel Arroyo Pagán and Asunción Correa (both dec); pa/Poet & Journalist, San Juan, PR & New York; Traffic Mgr: w Lanman & Kempt-Barclay & Co, NY; Mundet Cork Corp, NY; Moxey Savon-Lawrick & Co, NY; Others; During Spanish Civil War, was an Activ Jour for the Repub of Spain Agnst Francisco Franco; During WW II, He was a Civil Ser Wkr w US Post Ofc; Also Employed as a Translator; cp/ Active in Num Social, Polit, Civic & Lit Activs; hon/Author, Num Poems & Articles Pub'd in Books, Jours & News-papers; Listed in Contemp Poets of PR.

ARTIS, MARSHA MARIE oc/Student; b/Nov 3, 1949; h/PO Box 22263, Savannah, GA 31403-2263; ba/Same; ed/MBA, 1983; BBA, Mktg/Mgmt, 1980; pa/Sys Engr, IBM, 1980; cp/Peace Corps, Student Strategy Coor 1979-80; City of Savannah Dem Exec Com, 1978-82; Yg Dems of GA; Phi Beta Lambda; r/St John Bapt Ch; hon/ Student Govt Assn Awd, 1978; Awd for Acad Excell, 1977-80; W/W Among Students in Am Univs; Intl Yth in Achmt.

ARTUSHENIA, MARILYN JOANNE oc/Physician; b/Feb 16, 1950; h/142-43 Bayside Avenue, Flushing, NY 11354; ba/Elmhurst, NY; p/Gregory Artushenia Jr (dec); ed/AB, Boston Univ, 1970; MD, Hahnemann Med Col, 1974; Intern 1974-75, Resident Med 1975-77, Fellow Nephrology 1977-79, Mt Sinai Hosp, NYC; Fellow Nephrology 1977-79, Res Fellow Endocrinology 1979-80, Bronx VA Hosp; pa/Res Conslt Endocrinology, Bronx VA Hosp, 1980-81; Asst Att'g Phys Med & Psych, Elmhurst Gen Hosp, 1980-; Instr Med, Mt Sinai Hosp, 1980-; Instr Basic Cardiac Life Support, Reg Med Sers

Coun NYC, 1980-; Provider Adv'd Cardiac Life Support, NY Heart Assn, 1981; Med Staff, Hillcrest Gen Hosp, 1982-; AMA, 1973-; Am Col Phys, 1975-; AAAS, 1977-; NY Acad Scis, 1977-; Med Soc of Co Queens, 1982-; Med Soc St NY, 1982-; r/Prot; hon/ Co-Author of Abstract for Meeting of Am Soc Nephrology, "Maintenance of Acid-Base Balance in Adrenalectomized Rats w Dexamethasone," 1981; Phi Beta Kappa, 1970; Alpha Omega Alpha, 1973; W/W in E.

ARUNKUMAR, KOOVAPPADI A oc/Researcher & Designer of High Powered Lasers; b/Jun 19, 1949; h/ 15622 Hillview Lane, Granada Hills, CA 91344; ba/Chatsworth, CA; m/Radha; c/ Amiethab A; p/K S & Jaya Ananthas-ubramony, Bapatla, India; sp/R & Minaxi Vasudevan, Bangalore, India; ed/BSc Physics 1969, MSc Solid St Physics 1971, Univ of Kerala, India; PhD Magneto-Optics, Indian Inst of Technol, Madras, 1976; PhD Applied Physics, Univ of Hull, England, 1979; pa/Sr Engr, Apollo Lasers Inc, Chatsworth, CA, 1984-; Asst Res Prof Dept of Elect Engrg, 1983-84, Sr Res Assoc Dept of Elect Engrg 1980-82; Vis'g Asst Prof Dept of Physics 1979-80, Univ of KY; Am Phy Soc; Optical Soc Am; Sigma Xi; Eta Kappa Nu; r/Hinduism; hon/Author, Over 20 Sci Articles & Profl Symp Papers Pub'd; Jours & Profl Orgs incl: *Jour Pure & Applied Phys, Jour Phys, Chem & Solids, Spectroscopy Lttrs, Review Sci Instruments,* Intl Soc for Optical Engrg, Am Phy Soc, Others; Best Spkr Awd, 1965-68; Res S'ship Awd, Indian Inst Technol, Madras, 1971-72; Jr Res F'ship, Coun for Sci & Indust Res, 1972-75; Commonwlth S'hip, Govt of UK, 1975-79; W/W: Frontier; Sci & Technol, in World; Personalities of Am; Person-alities of S; Others.

ARVEDON, MAELYN N oc/Loss Prevention Specialist; b/Nov 21, 1954; h/19 Franclaire Drive, West Roxbury, MA 02132; ba/Boston, MA; m/David K; p/Samuel and Sandra Sigal, West Roxbury, MA; sp/Arthur and Marion Arvedon,Chestnut Hill, MA; ed/BA Psych, Boston Col, 1976; MBA, Boston Univ, 1981; pa/Teller, Asst Hd Teller, Hd Teller, Customer Ser Rep, Audit Asst, Loss Preven Spec (1981-), Mut Bk for Savs (formerly Suffolk Franklin Savs Bk); Nat Assoc Female Execs; Savs Bk Wom of MA; MA Police Fraudulent Check Assn; cp/Advr, Jr Achmt, 1982-83; Advr to Comm to Elect Frank Rich Gov of MA; Old Girls Netwk; r/ Jewish; hon/Recip Num Ins Sales Awds; Cert in Life Ins, MA St; W/W: Am Wom, Among Students in Am Cols & Univs.

ARVIDSON, RAYMOND E oc/Professor; b/Jan 22, 1948; h/1612 Forest-view Ridge Lane, Ballwin, MO 63011; ba/St Louis, MO; m/Eloise; c/Tim, Lars; ed/BA, Temple Univ, 1969; MSc 1971, PhD 1974, Brown Univ; pa/Res Assoc, Brown Univ, 1973; Asst Prof 1974-78, Assoc Prof 1978-84, Prof 1984-, Dept Earth & Planetary Scis, Wash Univ-St Louis; Secy Planetary Div, Am Geophy Union, 1984-86; AAAS; Secy Planetary Geol Div, Geol Soc of Am, 1984-86; The Planetary Soc; Chm, NASA Earth Observr Sys, Data Panel, 1984-; Chm, NASA Planetary Cartography Wkg Grp, 1984; Chm, Com on Data Mgmt & Computation, Space Sci Bd, Nat Acad

Of Sci, 1981-84; Dir, Wash Univ/NASA Reg Planetary Image Facility; Chm, Extraterrestrial Scis Com, Am Soc of Photogrammetry, 1978-80; Num Other Profl Mbrships; cp/9 Thesis Advrships; Num Invited Profl Spkg Presentations; hon/Author & Co-Author of Books, Over 50 Articles in Profl Sci Jours incl'g: *Jour Geophy Res, Nature, Ec Geol, Icarus, Sci,* Num Others; Assoc Editor, *Jour of Geophy Res,* 1981-; Assoc Editor, Cambridge Univ Press, 1983-; NASA Traineeship, 1969-71; Fellow, McDonnell Ctr for Space Scis, Wash Univ-St Louis, 1975-; Mem, Viking Lander Imaging Flight Opers Team, 1975-82; Num Vis'g Profships.

ASANTE, KARIAMU WELSH oc/ Choreographer; b/Sep 22, 1949; h/59 Ashland Avenue, Buffalo, NY 14222; ba/Buffalo, NY; m/Molefi Kete; c/ Kasina Eka, Daudi Jackson, Molefi Khumalo; p/Harvey Farabee, NC; Ruth Hoover, NYC; ed/BA 1971, MA 1974, SUNY-Buffalo; Doct Cand, NY Univ; pa/Fulbright Prof, Univ of Zimbabwe, 1981-82; Artistic Dir, Ctr for Positive Thought, 1971-81; Choreographer, Kariamu & Co, 1971-81; Artistic Dir, Nat Dance Co of Zimbabwe, 1981-82; Vis'g Asst Prof, Temple Univ, 1985; Cong of Res in Dance; Laban Inst; Dance Notation Bur; hon/Author of Volume of Poetry, *Textured Wom, Cowrie Shells & Beetle Sticks,* 1978; Contbr of Article to Jour of Black Studies, Spec Edition on Dance, 1984; Other Articles Pub'd; Creat Artist Public Ser Awd, 1974 & 1978; NEA F'ship for Art Choreography, 1973; NY St Coun on the Art Choreography F'ship, 1984; Outstg Commun Ser Awd, Arts Devel Sers, Buffalo, 1981; Wm Wells Brown Awd, Afro-Am Hist Assn of Niagra Frontier, 1981; Outstg Wom of Yr, NAACP, Cinc, OH, 1981; W/W in Black Am.

ASCENSÃO, JOÃO L oc/Professor; b/Jul 6, 1948; h/2604, 37th Ave 80, Minneapolis, MN 55406; ba/Minneapolis, MN; p/João F and Maria A Ascensão, Lisbon, Portugal; ed/MD, Univ of Lisbon Med Sch, 1972; pa/Rotating Intern 1972-74, Resident Internal Med 1974-76, Univ Hosp Santa Maria, Lisbon; Fellow, Clin Immunol & Immunohematology, Dept Med Meml Sloan-Kettering Cancer Ctr, 1974-76; Vis'g Res Fellow, Sloan-Kettering Inst, NY, 1974-76; Resident Dept Med 1977-78, Fellow Hematology/Oncology Dept Med 1979-81, Instr Med 1981-82, Asst Prof Dept Med 1983-, Med Sch, Univ of MN, Mpls; Res Assoc, VA Med Ctr, Mpls, 1983-; Fellow, Dept Med, Med Sch, Cornell Univ, 1976; Fam Pract for Portuguese Nat Hlth Ser, 1973-74; Mem, Mbrshp Com (1983-), Intl Soc for Exptl Hematology, 1976; Chm, White Cell Proliferation I (1983), Am Soc of Hematology, 1980; Secy, Assn of Scis at VA, 1983-; Portuguese Soc of Immunol, 1977; Am Fedn for Clin Res, 1980; AAAS, 1981; Fellow, Am Col of Phys, 1982; Am Soc of Clin Oncology, 1983; hon/Author & Co-Author, Over 20 Articles Pub'd in Profl Sci Jours incl'g: *N Eng Jour of Med, Leukemia Res, Exptl Hematology, Am Jour of Med,* Others; Edit Bd, *Exptl Hematology,* 1980-82; F'ship, Instituto de Alta Cultura, Med Sch, Lisbon, 1974-76; F'ship, J M Foun, 1976.

ASHE, OLIVER RICHARD oc/Assistant for Administration; b/Nov 25, 1933;

h/10600 Vale Road, Oakton, VA 22124; ba/Washington, DC; m/Helen Curtin; c/ Mary Patricia, Pauline, Margaret, Kathleen, Oliver Jr, Caroline, Cecilia; p/ Paul and Mary Ashe, Oakton, VA; sp/ Patrick and Mary Curtin, Washingtonville, NY; ed/BS, Georgetown Univ, 1955; MBA, Hofstra Univ, 1970; PhD, SWn Univ, 1982; mil/AUS, 1955-65, Capt; pa/Reg Pers Dir Mariott Corp, 1965-68; Hd Career Mgmt & Dept Dir, Nav Resale Sys, 1968-76; Spec Asst to Secy Nav 1976-81, Asst for Adm 1981-, Ofc of Secy of Nav; Assn of Former Intell Ofcrs; Am Mgmt Assn; Div Chm, Combined Fed Campaign; Fairfax Hosp Assn; r/Rom Cath; hon/Author of Chapt in *Volunteerism*, 1970; Outstg Fed Ser Awds, 1975, 1976 & 1977; Army Commend Medal, 1961 & 1963; Dist'd Mil Grad, Georgetown Univ, 1955; W/ W: in World, in Am, in Fin & Indust, of S; Other Biogl Listings.

ASHLEY, IRVIN E JR oc/Executive Director; b/Jan 18, 1939; h/Route 1, Box 84- F, Dexter, NM 88201; ba/Roswell, NM; m/Sylvia Anne; c/Mark Edward, James Tod; p/Irvin Ester Ashley (dec); Mary Helen Woodard Ashley; ed/BS 1960, MEd 1966, Univ AR; Phy Therapy Cert, Med Ctr Baylor Univ, 1964; DEd, Univ IL, 1969; mil/USMC, 1960-63; pa/ Res Asst, Voc Ed, Univ AR, 1965-66; Instr & Res Assoc, Voc Ed, Univ IL, 1966-69; Dir Voc Ed & Hlth Voc Tech, En NM Univ, 1969-70; Rehab Spec 1970-72, Exec Dir 1972-, NM Rehab Ctr, Roswell, NM; Nat Rehab Assn; Exec Bd, SEn NM Univ Hlth Ed Coun; Phi Delta Kappa; Am Registry Phy Therapists; Surveyor, Comm of Accreditation of Rehab Facilities; cp/Rotary Clb; r/Bapt; hon/Admr of Yr, 1971; Nat Student Nurse Assn, 1971; En NM Univ Roswell Campus Cert of Recog as CARF Surveyor, 1977; W/W: in Hlth Care, in the W, in Commun Ser, in Fin & Indust; Men of Achmt; Num Other Biogl Listings.

ASHMEAD, HARVE DeWAYNE oc/ Executive; b/Jun 6, 1944; h/304 South Mountain Road, Fruit Heights, UT 84037; ba/Clearfield, UT; m/Eugele Baird; c/Stephen DeWayne, Jilane Michelle, Brett Shane, Angelique Racquelle, Heide Eugele; p/Harvey and Allez Ashmead, Kaysville, UT; sp/ Oliver and Francis Baird, Clinton, UT; ed/BS, Weber St Col, 1969; PhD, Pacific Inst, 1970; PhD, Donsbach Univ, 1981; pa/Ch of Jesus Christ LDS (Paris, France), 1963-66; VP (Ogden) 1966-71, Exec VP (Clearfield) 1971-82, Pres (Clearfield) 1982-, Albion Labs Inc; Bd of Dirs: Kovac Lab, Candies of Am, Stanbrook Lab, Air Travel, Albion Intl, Rhondell Lab, 1981-; Adj Prof, Weber St Col, 1984; Others; Nutritional Conslt, 1981-; AAAS, 1982-; Am Col of Nutrition, 1981-; Am Assn Applied Health Scis, 1981-; Bd of Dirs & Treas, Intl Acad Nutritional Conslts, 1981-; Am Soc Animal Sci, 1979-; Delta Sigma Pi, 1969-; Intl Inst of Nat Health Scis, 1981-; cp/Pres, PTA, 1973 & 1975; Adv Bd, BSA; Bd Dirs, Clearfield C of C, 1977-79; Advr, Weber Co Sch Dist, 1977; Bd Dirs, Donsbach Univ, 1981-; Adv Bd, Weber St Col, 1983-; Advr, Fruit Hgts City, 1982; r/LDS; hon/ Author of Books: *Chelated Mineral Nutrition* 1981, *Chelated Mineral Nutrition in Plants, Animals & Man* 1982, *A New Era*

in *Plant Nutrition* 1982, *Mineral Absorption Mechanisms* 1981, *Intestinal Absorption of Metal Ions & Chelates* 1984, Others; Num Articles Pub'd in Profl Sci Jours incl'g: *Mod Vet ·Pract, Jour of Applied Nutrition, World Hlth & Ecol News, Bestways, Hlth Food Bus, Jour of Plant Nutrition*, Others; Contbg Editor, *Bestways*; Sterling Scholar; S'ship; Reg, Nat and Intl Sci Fair Awds; Grad, magna cum laude, Donsbach Univ, 1981; W/W in W.

ASHMORE, HENRY LUDLOW oc/ Executive Director (Interim); b/1920; h/ PO Box 52066, Atlanta, GA 30355; ba/ Atlanta, GA; m/Clarice Langston; c/ Randan, Jerri; p/John Henry and Nursie Whaley Ashmore (dec); sp/John Howard and Willie Sumner Langston (dec); ed/ BAE 1942, MAE 1948, DEd 1950, Univ of FL; mil/USAF, 1942-46, 1st Lt; pa/ Prin, St Marks Sch, 1946-47; Grad Student, Univ FL, 1942-50; Coor of Student Tchg, GA So Col, 1950-54; Pres, Pensacola Jr Col, 1954-64; Pres, Armstrong St Col, 1964-82; Assoc Exec Dir Comm on Cols, Secy, Exec Coun, Chm Com on Spec Purpose Instns, So Assn of Cols & Schs, 1982-; Pres, FL Assn of Cols & Univs; Pres, FL Public Jr Col Assn; Pres, Assn of Public Instns of Higher Lrng of S; Bd of Dirs, So Assn of Jr Cols; Adm Comm Mem, Am Assn of Jr Cols; Mem, Fed Nat Com on Fgn S'ships; Mem Kellogg Com, Devel Jr Cols Admrs; cp/Dir, FL Nat Bk of Pensacola; Pres, Profl Assoc, Pensacola; Dir, Safeway Auto Clb Inc, Atlanta; Dir, The Citizens & So Bk of Chatham Co; Pres, U Fund, Pensacola; Pres, Escambia Co Commun Coun; VPres, Gulf Coast Coun BSA; Pres, Retirement Village, Pensacola; Bd Dirs, C of C, Savannah; Num Others; r/Bapt; Chm Deacons, 1st Bapt Ch Pensacola & Savannah; hon/ Author, Over 10 Articles Pub'd in Profl Jours incl'g: *Juco Review, The Jr Col Jour, Jour Tchr Ed, Ed Admrs & Supvrs*, Others; Contbr of Humorous Articles to Comml Mags; Grad F'ship, Univ FL, 1947-50; Phi Kappa Phi; Phi Delta Kappa; Kappa Delta Pi; Phi Theta Kappa; Alpha Nat Omega; Hall of Fame, Nat Jr Col Ath Assn; Hon Life Mem, Toastmasters Clb; W/W: in Am Ed, in SE, in Am.

ASHTON, NANCY LYNN oc/Professor; b/Apr 20, 1950; h/PO Box 85, Port Republic, NJ 08240; ba/Pomona, NJ; c/Hilarie Chanda; p/Louise Wickware, Lyme, NH; ed/BA Psych, Smith Col, 1972; MA Soc Psych 1974, PhD Soc Psych 1976, Univ FL; pa/Asst Prof, Kearney St Col, NE, 1976-77; Asst Prof 1977-82, Assoc Prof 1982, Stockton St Col, NJ; Am Psychol Assn; En Psychol Assn; Soc for Advmt Soc Psych; Soc for Psychol Study Soc Issues; AAAS; Num Consltg Positions; Others; cp/Bd of Trustees 1979-84, Pres 1982-83, Atl Co Woms Ctr; Mediator, Commun Justice Inst; Pres 1978-79, Atl Co Chapt, NOW; hon/Author & Co-Author, Over 20 Pub'd Articles, Papers & Reports; Jours incl: *Stats for Psych, Perceptual & Motor Skills, Psych Reports, Bltn of Psychonomic Soc*, Others; Sigma Xi, 1972; Psi Chi, 1980; Outstg Yg Wom Am; W/W: in E, in Wom.

ASHWORTH, SARA ELIZABETH oc/Educational Consultant; b/Oct 7, 1946; h/115 Carlton Avenue, Trenton, NJ 08618; ba/Same; p/Jame Kenneth Ashworth (dec); Kathryn Stoker Ashworth, Wildwood, FL; ed/BA, Blue Mt

Col, MS, 1968; MA, Univ of MS, 1969; EdD, Temple Univ, 1984; pa/Ednl Conslt, 1980-; Prog Coor, Ctr on Tch, 1972-80; Instr, Co Col of Morris, 1970-72; Instr, NW MS Jr Col, 1969-70; Num Wkshops, Presentations & Lctrs; Assn Supvn & Curric Devel; Am Ednl Res Assn; hon/Co-Author (w Muska Mosston), *From Command to Discovery: Sci & Art Tchg*, 1984; Title IV-C Grant 8 Yrs; Recip, Nat Validation Awd for Outstg Success in Ednl Devel, 1978; US Patentee; W/W in E.

ASIMOV, ISAAC oc/Writer, Educator; b/Jan 2, 1920; h/10 West 66th St, New York, NY 10023; ba/Same; m/Janet Jeppson; c/David, Robyn; p/Judah and Anna Rachel Asimov (dec); sp/John R and Rae K Jeppson (dec); ed/BA Chem, 1939, MA Chem, 1941; PhD Chem 1948, Columbia Univ; mil/AUS, 1945-46, Corporal; pa/Instr 1949-51, Asst Prof 1951-55, Assoc Prof 1955-79; Prof 1979-, Dept of Biochem, Boston Univ Sch of Med; hon/Author: 310 Books, Over 300 Short Stories, Over 2,000 Non-Fiction Essays; W/W in Am.

ASKINAS, MITCHEL RAYMOND oc/Executive; b/Mar 13, 1946; h/14 East 4th St, New York, NY 10012; ba/New York, NY; m/Myrna Ram; p/Mr and Mrs Irving Askinas, Great Neck, NY; sp/Mr and Mrs Louis Ram, Quebec Province, Canada; ed/BA Fin, NY Univ Sch of Bus, 1964-68; Att'd Adelphi Grad Sch of Bus, 1968-70; pa/Sr VP Fin, Adm Ins, Glen Oaks Industs Inc, 1970-82; hon/Elected, NY Univ Student Hall of Fame, 1968; W/W in Risk Mgmt.

ASKREN, LAURA MARCY oc/Civic Leader; b/Jun 2, 1909; h/3677 Shadow Lane, Atlanta, GA 30319; c/Edward L III, Mrs Frank C Moore; p/Frank Lucius and Ella Marcy (dec); ed/BS, KS St Col, 1936; cp/Pres, YWCA; Pres, AAUW; Pres, Ch Wom U; Pres, Fulton Co Med Aux; VPres, Metro Atlanta Mtl Hlth Assn; Pres, Atlanta YWCA, 1981-83; Moderator, Ctl Congregational Ch, 1983-84; Pres, Assocs of Emory Sch of Nsg, 1982-83; r/U Ch of Christ; hon/ Atlanta Wom of Yr Civic Ser, 1965; Vol of Yr Mtl Hlth Assn, 1979; Life Deacon, Ctl Cong Ch, 1981.

ASLAM, MUHAMMAD oc/Staff Research Associate; b/Apr 4, 1943; h/ 933 Bienville Street, Davis, CA 95616; ba/Davis, CA; m/Riffat; c/Affifa, Aniqa, Adeel; p/Barkat Ali (dec); sp/M Jamil Ahmad, Sargodh, Pakistan; BSc Agri 1963, MSc Agri 1965, W Pakistan Agri Univ, Lyallpur, Pakistan; PhD, Univ CA-Davis, 1970; pa/Lectr, Dept of Agronomy, Univ of Agri, Faisalabad, 1971-73; Postdoct Fellow, Biol Dept, McMaster Univ, Hamilton, Ontario, Canada, 1974-75; Res Assoc, Crop Sci Dept, Univ of Guelphi, Ontario, 1975-77; Postgrad Plant Physiol Plant Growth Lab 1977-79, Staff Res Assoc Dept Agronomy & Range Sci 1980-, Univ CA-Davis; Vis'g Fellow (Nat Scis & Engrg Res Coun Canada) at Crop Sci Sect, Agri Canada Res Sta, Harrow, Ontario, 1979-80; Am Soc Plant Physiols; Am Soc Agronomy; Am Soc Crop Sci; r/Islam; hon/Author & Co-Author, Over 24 Articles Pub'd in Profl Sci Jours incl'g: *Plant Physiol, Canada Jour Botany, Plant Sci Lttrs*, Others; Assoc Mem, Sigma Xi, 1969-70; Vis'g F'ship, Nat Sci & Engrg Coun Canada, 1979-80.

ASPER, ISRAEL HAROLD oc/Executive; b/Aug 11, 1932; h/1063 Wellington Crescent, Winnipeg, Manitoba, Canada R3N OA1; ba/Winnipeg, Manitoba; m/Ruth Miriam Bernstein; c/David, Leonard, Gail; ed/BA 1953, BL 1957, ML 1964, Univ of Manitoba; pa/Called to Bar of Manitoba, 1957; Mem Law Firm, Drache, Meltzer, Essers, Gold & Asper, 1957-59; Sr Ptnr, Asper & Co, 1959-70; Sr Ptnr, Bucwald, Asper, Henteleff, 1970-77; Chm of Bd & Chief Exec Ofcr, CanWest Capital Corp, 1977-; VChm Na-Churs Plant Food Co; Dir: Wn Approaches Ltd; John Alden Life Ins Co; Blazer Firs Sers Co; Macleod-Stedman Inc; Air Canada; Canadian Bar Assn; Canadian Tax Foun; Manitoba Bar Assn; Manitoba Law Soc; Manitoba Assn of Rights & Liberties; Appt'd Queens Coun, 1975; Chm Policies for Devel Com, Manitoba Govt Comm on Targets for Ec Devel, 1967; Ldr, Liberal Party, Manitoba, 1970-75; Mem, Manitoba Legis Assem, 1972-75; Num Others; cp/Bd Dirs, the Assocs of Fac of Adm Studies, Univ of Manitoba; Mem & Prov Chm (Manitoba) Campaign Com, Canadian Coun Intnl Law; Bd Mem, Canadian S'ship Trust; Bd Mem, Winnipeg Jewish Commun Coun; Carleton Clb; Canadian Clb; Num Other Bd Mbrships; r/Jewish; hon/ Author of Natly Syndicated Column on Taxation, 1966-77; Editor-in-Chief of "Isaac Pitblado Series on Cont'g Legal Ed," 1960 & 1961; Other Writings; Univ of Manitoba Alumni Awd, Outstg 25 Yr Grad, 1979; Num Lectr & Spkg Invitations in Canada.

AST, RAYMOND JOHN oc/College Administrator; b/Sep 4, 1918; h/74 Woodland Avenue, Verona, NJ 07044; ba/Upper Montclair, NJ; m/Doris A Paynter (dec); c/Richard J; r/Raymond J and Mercita A (dec); sp/Horace J and Jessie Paynter (dec); ed/BS Ed, SUNY-Buffalo, 1939; Postgrad Study, SUNY-Albany, 1939-40; MS Ed 1940, Doct Cand Adult Ed, Tchrs Col 1946-55, Columbia Univ; mil/AUS, 1943-46; pa/ Adm Dir Adult Cont'g Ed Ctr 1970-, Dir Adult Ed Resource Ctr 1966-68, Field Dir, NJ Ctr Ec Ed 1965-66, Montclair St Col, NJ; Proj Dir, NJ Dept Ed, ABE Lrng Ctr, 1968-70; Bd Dirs, Intl Coun for Adult Ed, 1973-77; Bd Mem (1970-), Pres 1972-73, Coalitiion of Adult Ed Org in US; Exec Com 1964-72, Pres 1970-71, Adult Ed Assn, USA; Exec Com 1949-64, Pres 1962-63, Assn for Adult Ed in NJ; r/Christian; hon/Co-Author of Books, *Curricular-Instrnl Mats & Related Media for Disadvantaged Adult in the 1970's* 1970, *Guidelines for ABE Lrng Ctrs* 1970; Outstg Ser Awd, Coalition of Adult Ed Assn in US, 1972; Meritorious Ser Awd, Adult Ed Assn of US, 1972; US Del UNESCO World Conf on Adult Ed, Tokyo; W/W: in Am, in World; Commun Ldrs; DIB.

ASTIN, ALEXANDER W oc/Professor; b/May 30, 1932; h/2681 Cordelia Road, Los Angeles, CA 90049; ba/Los Angeles, CA; m/Helen S; c/John Alexander, Paul Allen; p/Allen V and Margaret M Astin, Bethesda, MD; ed/AB, Gettysburg Col; MA 1956, PhD 1958, Univ of MD; mil/USPHS, 1958-60, Lt Cmdr; pa/Dir of Res, Am Coun on Ed, 1965-73; Dir of Res, Nat Merit S'ship Corp, 1960-64; Dept Chief, Psych Res Unit, VA Hosp, Balto, MD, 1959-60;

Fellow, Am Psychol Assn; Fellow, AAAS; Num Others; r/Non-Denom; hon/Author 150 Articles & 15 Books; Recent Books Incl: *Minorities in Am Higher Ed*, 1982; *Maximizing Ldrship Effectiveness*, 1980; *4 Critical Yrs*, 1977; Fellow, Ctr for Adv'd Studies in Behavioral Scis, 1966-67; Num Awds for Outstg Ser in Res Area: Am Ed Res Assn 1983, Am Col Pers Assn 1978, APGA 1965; W/ W in Am; Contemp Authors; Other Biogl Listings.

ATEMA, JELLE oc/Professor; b/Dec 9, 1940; h/10 Quissett Avenue, Woods Hole, MA 02543; ba/Woods Hole, MA; ed/Cand & Doct, Univ of Utrecht, Netherlands, 1962 & 1966; PhD, Univ MI, 1969; pa/Res Asst, Univ Utrecht, 1961-66; Res Assoc, Univ MI, 1966-69; Asst Sci, Woods Hole Oceanographic Inst, 1969-74; Assoc Prof, Boston Univ Marine Biol Prog, 1974-84; Prof, Boston Univ, 1984-; AAAS; Am Soc Zool; Animal Behavior Soc; Assn of Chemoreception Scis; European Chemoreception Res Org; Soc Neuro Sci; Marine Bio Labs; hon/Author, Over 85 Pub'd Sci Articles, Reports & Book Chapts; Fellow, AAAS, 1977.

ATKINS, CHARLES GILMORE oc/ Associate Dean; b/Jul 4, 1939; h/6 Riverview Drive, Athens, OH 45701; ba/Athens, OH; c/Robert, Karla, James; p/Howard B and Bernice Atkins (dec); ed/BA, Albion Col, 1961; Att'd Univ MI Med Sch, 1960-62; MS, En MI Univ, 1962-63; PhD, NC St Univ, 1969; mil/ USAR, 1981-, Maj, MSC; pa/Assoc Dean Col of Osteopathic Med 1976-, Assoc Prof Zool & Biol Med Sci 1974-, Dir Willed Body Prog 1976-77, Dir Appalachian Life Sci Col Tng Prog 1972-74, Asst Prof Zool & Microbiol 1969-74, OH Univ, Athens, OH; Genetics Soc Am; AAUP; Assn of Am Med Cols; AAAS; cp/Rotary Intl; Nat Eagle Scout Assn; r/Presb; hon/Author & Co-Author of Articles Pub'd in Profl Jours: *Jour Invert Pathol* 1978, *Jour Med Ed* 1983; W/W: in MW, in Frontier Sci & Technol, in Hlth Care.

ATKINS, CHESTER G oc/State Senator; b/Apr 14, 1948; h/1540 Monument Street, Concord, MA 01742; ba/Boston, MA; m/Corrine Hobbs; c/Dean, Casey; p/Henry Hornblower and Karkilie Withington Atkins; ed/BA Polit Sci, Antioch Col, 1970; pa/Rep, MA Ho of Reps, 1971-72; Chm Com on Public Ser 1975-78, Chm Com on Ethics 1977-78, VChm Com on Hlth Care 1977-79, Chm Sen Com on Ways & Means 1979-84, MA St Senate; Chm, Dem St Com, 1977-84; Mem, Dem Nat Com; cp/Clark Univ Sch of Mgmt Vis'g Com; Com to Visit the Mus of Comparative Zool, Harvard Univ; r/Unitarian; hon/ Co-Author of Book, *Getting Elected*, 1973; Co-Author of Article, "Psycho-Surg & the Role of Legis," *Boston Univ Law Rev*, 1974; Other Writings; Awd of Hon, MA Early Intervention Consortium Inc, 1982; Cert of Recog, MA Cultural Alliance, 1982; MA Conserv Coun Awd, 1982; MA Ofc of Deafness Awd, 1982; MA Bar Assn Legis of the Yr, 1983; Envir Lobby of MA, 1984.

ATKINSON, EVELYN ROREX oc/ Architect; b/Dec 29, 1931; h/3201 29th Street, Lubbock, TX 79410; ba/Same; m/ Atmar L; c/Penny Atkinson Redmon, Charles Michael; ed/BA Arch, TX Technol Inst, 1955; pa/TX Technol Col

Dept of Landscaping & City of Lubbock Pks Dept, 1953-55; Atcheson, Atkinson & Cartwright, Archs & Engrs, 1955-69; Atcheson, Atkinson, Cartwright & Rorex, Archs & Engrs, 1969-74; Atkinson & Atkinson, Archs, 1974-; AIA, 1958; Treas, Lubbock Chapt AIA, 1966; TX Soc Archs, 1959-; cp/W TX Watercolor Assn, 1973-; Bd of Dirs, Lubbock Cultural Affairs Coun, 1971-76; TX Fine Arts Assn, 1973-; r/Meth; hon/AIA Awd Outstg Grad in Arch, 1955; Awd of Merit, SWn Bell Telephone Co (for Porter Exch Bldg, Lubbock), 1969; W/ W in S & SW; 2000 Wom of Achmt.

ATKINSON, REGINA ELIZABETH oc/Social Services Director; b/May 13, 1952; h/525½ Southwest 10th Street, Belle Glade, FL 33430; ba/Belle Glade, FL; p/Samuel and Virginia Griffin, New Bern, NC; ed/BA Sociol, Univ of CT, 1974; MSW Clin Social Wk in Comprehensive Hlth, Atlanta Univ Sch of Social Wk, 1978; pa/Social Ser Dir, Glades Gen Hosp, 1981-; Med Social Wkr & Hosp Coor, Glades Commun Hlth Ctr, 1978-81; Social Wk Intern, Grady Meml Hosp, 1977-78; Social Wk Intern, Atlanta Residential Manpower Ctr, 1976-77; Clerk Typist, Bethlehem Steel Corp, 1976; Res Asst Ctr for Black Studies 1974, Clerk Typist 1970, Univ CT; Lead Paint Proj Asst, United Newhallville Org, 1970-74; Soc for Hosp Social Wk Dirs; FL Public Hlth Assn Inc; Glades Area Assn for Retarded Citizens; Nat Assn of Black Social Wkrs Inc; Nat Assn of Social Wkrs Inc; The Nat Caucus on The Black Aged; The Chds Home Soc FL; FL Assn for Hlth & Soc Sers; Commun Action Coun; Num Profl Wkshops, Sems & Confs; cp/NAACP; r/Bapt; hon/Panel Discussion Mem, "Needs of Target Pop" Nat Wkshop on Nutrition & Social Wk in Primary Care Sers, 1981; Task Force Mem, "Sers for Spec Pops" Nat Ad Hoc Com to Devel a Guid for Social Wk Ser in Primary Care Projs, 1981; W/W in S & SW.

ATTALLAH, ABDELFATTAH M oc/ Professor, Immunologist; b/Feb 2, 1944; h/5919 Beech Avenue, Bethesda, MD 20817; ba/Bethesda, MD; ed/BSc, Alexandria Univ, Egypt; DEA, Paris Univ, Paris, France, 1971; PhD, George Wash Univ, Wash DC, 1974; pa/Chief of Immunol, OBRR, Ctr for Drugs & Biologics, FDA, 1978-; Res Sci, Nav Med Res Inst, 1976-78; Res Assoc, Res Foun of Chd's Nat Med Ctr, 1974-76; Chem, WHO, Alexandria, Egypt, 1968-69; Adj Prof, George Wash Univ & Georgetown Univ; Am Assn of Immunols; Tissue Culture Assn; The NY Acad of Scis; AAAS; The Am Soc for Microbiol; Intl Soc for Interferon Res; Assn of Egypt-Am Scholars; hon/Co-Author & 10 Sci Books; Over 60 Sci Articles; Yg Investigators Competition Awd, So Soc for Pediatric Res, 1976; Postdoct Res Assoc, 1976; Nat Res Coun, Nat Acad Scis, 1976; Sigma Xi; Adj Prof, Georgetown Univ & George Wash Univ; W/ W: in Frontier Sci & Technol, in Wash, in World; Men of Achmt; Intl W/W of Contemp Achmt; Intl Book of Hon; Biogl Roll of Hon; 2,000 Notable Ams.

ATTIA, SABRY M oc/Manager; b/ Apr 25, 1927; h/19777 East Ida Lane, Grosse Pointe Woods, MI 48236; ba/ 23915 East Jefferson, St Clair Shores, MI 48080; m/Serria; c/Mervat, Mona,

Madiha, Mayssa; ed/BSW, Cairo Sch of Social Wk; Dipl, Inst Nat Planning; MSW 1973, Doct Cand 1983-, Wayne St Univ; MPA, Univ of Detroit, 1979; pa/Dist Mgr, Asst to Dist Mgr, Wayne Co Med Sers Adm; Social Ser Prog Spec, Ctl Adm of Wayne Co Dept Social Sers; Prog Dir, The CYO; Unit Mgr, Henry Ford Hosp, Detroit; Social Planning Coor; Social Wk Instr; Pvt Pract in Social Wk, 1980-; Others; cp/Nat Assn of Social Wkrs Inc; MI Soc for Clin Social Wkrs; Am Hosp Assn; Acad of Cert'd Social Wkrs; Egyptian Social Wkrs Assn; Brit Coun of Social Wk Ed; Others; cp/Detroit City Planning Comm; Mayor's Com for Human Resource Devel; Boys Clb of Metro Detroit; Yth Neighborhood Clb; Num Others; r/Moslem; hon/W/W in W & MW, in Am; Men of Achmt.

ATTINGER, ERNST O oc/Professor; b/Dec 27, 1922; h/Route 1, Box 277, Crozet, VA 22932; ba/Charlottesville, VA; m/Francoise M L; c/Christophe, Nathalene, Juelle; p/Ernst and Martha Attinger (dec); sp/Raymond and Marie Daubige (dec); ed/BA, 1941; MD, 1947; MS Biomed Instrumentation, 1961; PhD Biomed Engrg, 1965; pa/Asst Prof Med, Tufts Sch of Med; Assoc Prof Physiol, Univ PA; Res Dir, Presby Univ PA Med Ctr; Chm Biomed Engrg, Univ VA, 1976-; Biomed Engrg Soc; IEEE, Am Phy Soc; AAAS; Sigma Xi; cp/Jeffersonian Wine Grape Growers Assn; r/Prot; hon/Author of Books: *Pulsatile Bloodflow*, 1964; *Global Sys Dynamics*, 1970; *Biomed Engrg in Dentistry*, 1977; Fellow, IEEE, 1978; Pres & Bd of Visitors Res Prize, 1976; W/W: in Am, in Technol.

ATWATER, JOHN SPENCER oc/Physician; b/Oct 12, 1913; h/2625 Howell Mill Road, Northwest, Atlanta, GA 30327; ba/Atlanta, GA; m/Virginia Zipplies; c/John Spencer Jr, Paul Carleton, Elizabeth Atwater Drewicz; p/Carleton Wm and May Spencer Atwater (dec); sp/Paul and Bertha Zipplies (dec); ed/AB, Denison Univ, 1935; MD, John Hopkins Sch of Med, 1939; MS in Med, Grad Sch Univ of MN, 1944; FACP, Am Col of Phys, 1948; Att'd Others; mil/MC, USNR, Lt, 1944-46; pa/Staff Mem 1946-, Pres 1962, Num Other Positions, GA Bapt Hosp; Mem Consltg Staff 1972-, Other Positions, Crawford W Long Meml Hosp; St Joseph's Infirm, 1946-59; Staff Mem 1967-73, Other Positions, Atlanta Hosp; Conslt Gastroscopy, Grady Meml Hosp, 1946-54; Conslt, Robert T Jones Meml Hosp, Canton, GA, 1962-80; Conslt, Cobb Gen Hosp, Austell, GA, 1968-72; Consltg Staff, Piedmont Hosp, 1977-; Courtesy Staff 1980-, Other Positions, W Paces Ferry Hosp; Instr Med, Univ of MN Sch Med, 1943-44; Instr Med 1946-54, Clin Assoc Med, Emory Univ Sch Med, 1954-; Conslt, Internal Med, St Dept Ed, GA, 1948-82; Conslt Internal Med, VA Reg Ofc, Atlanta, 1948-70; Other Consltg Positions; Diplomate, Am Bd of Internal Med & Am Bd of Gastroenterology, 1947; Fellow, Chm & Mem Num Coms, AMA, 1946-; Treas & Exec Com Mem (1962-73), Chm & Mem Num Coms, Med Assn GA, 1946-; Mem, Atlanta Med Ctr, 1966-; Chm & Mem Num Coms, Med Assn Atlanta, 1946-; Chm & Twice Secy, Gastroenterology Sect, So Med Assn, 1946-; Am Col Phys; Am

Gastroenterological Assn; NY Acad of Sci, 1959-61; Am Heart Assn; Nat Rehab Assn, 1959-68; Num Others; cp/Bds of Dirs: Atlanta Boys Clb, Atlanta Girls Clb, Res Inst of Atlanta, Am Bk of Atlanta, Peoples Am Bk Atlanta, 1st GA Bk, So Gen Ins Co, Stuyvesant Ins Co, Jersey Ins Co NY, Mohawk Ins Co, GAC Corp, The Atlanta Ballet Inc, John Hopkins Alumni Assn, Kiwanis Clb Atlanta, C of C, SAR, Atlanta City Clb, Phoenix Soc, Phi Gamma Delta, Nu Sigma Nu, Num Others; r/Bapt; hon/Author & Co-Author, Over 20 Articles Pub'd in Med Sci Jours; Presenter Num Papers to Var Profl Assns; Cert of Apprec, Fulton Co Med Soc, 1960 & 1963; Cert Dist'd Ser, Med Assn Atlanta, 1975; Aven Citizenship Awd, 1961; Lttr Apprec 1969, Cert Apprec 1970 & 1975, Cert Dist'd Ser 1972 & 1976; Cert Apprec, AMA, 1977; Num Others; W/W: Important in Med, in Allerology, in S & SW, in GA; Am Men in Med; Num Other Biogl Listings.

ATWOOD, JOAN D oc/Director of Marriage and Family Counseling; b/Sep 15, 1943; h/542 Lakeview Avenue, Rockville Centre, NY 11570; ba/Hempstead, NY; m/William R; c/Debra, Barbara, Lisa, Janine, Brian; p/Louis and Helen Armagno, Maspeth, NY; ed/PhD, SUNY-Stony Brook, 1981; MSW, Adelphi Univ, 1984; MA in Sociol 1977, MA in Psych 1975, BA in Psych, SUNY-Stony Brook; AA, Suffolk Commun Col; pa/Dir of Marriage & Fam Cnslg, Hofstra Univ; Prof of Psych, SUNY-Farmingdale, 1973-84; Res Assoc, Dept of Psychi 1975-78, Adj Prof of Psych, Dept of Psych 1974-75, SUNY-Stony Brook; AAMFT; AASECT; SIECUS; Assn for Behavior Therapists; Soc of Wom in Soc; Clin Sociologists; NASW; r/Rom Cath; hon/Pubs, *Making Contact to Human Sexuality* 1982, "Vasocongestive Response in Women" 1976, "Masturbation in Col Yth" 1983; Phi Alpha Sigma Hon Soc, 1972; Suffolk Commun Col; Dean's List, 1973; Nom'd for Excell in Tchg, 1973-82; Nom'd for Elena Coronard Awd for Outstg Wom; W/W in Sci & Technol.

AUBRY, WILLIAM EDWARD oc/Family Psychologist; b/Jul 1, 1939; h/P O Box 12491 El Cajon, CA 92020; ba/Same; m/Jeri Anita; c/Allison, Dawn, Kristie, Michael; p/BB and Dorothy Aubry, Corvallis, OR; m/Mary Ball, Chico, CA; ed/BS 1961, EdM 1963, OR St Univ; EdD, Univ AZ, 1970; Att'd Num Others for Postdoct Study; pa/Pt-time Cnslr, VA, Tucson, AZ, 1963-65; Cnslr, AZ Div Voc Rehab, 1965-66; Conslg Psychol 1966-76, Lctr Dept Sociol, Anthropol & Social Welfare 1972-76, Humboldt St Univ, Arcata, CA; Pvt Pract Marriage, Family & Child Conslg, 1969-; Pvt Pract Psychol, 1972-; Field Supvr & Prof MA Progs in Marriage, Fam & Child Conslg 1974-79, Assoc Prof Cnslr Ed 1977-79, Adj Prof 1979-80, Univ SF; Conslt & Fam Therapist, 1980-; Exec Dir, Profl Psych Sers, 1981-; Fac Mem, The Profl Sch for Humanistic Studies, 1981-; Conslt, Personal Profile Conslts, 1982-; Am Psychol Assn; Acad Psychols in Marriage, Fam & Sex Therapy; Am Assn Marriage & Fam Therapists; Am Soc Clin Hypnosis; Bd Mem & Chm Coms, CA Assn of Marraige & Fam Cnslrs;

Co-Fdr & Pres, No CA Soc Indiv Psych; Others; r/Prot; hon/Author of Articles Pub'd in *Marriage & Fam Cnslrs Qtly* & Other Profl Jours; Presenter of Papers to Profl Assns; Kappa Delta Pi; Diplomate, Am Bd of Fam Psych; W/W in W.

AUERBACH, ROGER MICHAEL oc/Education Official; b/Mar 21, 1946; h/3434 Northwest Franklin Court, Portland, OR 97210; ba/Portland, OR; p/George Auerbach (dec); Mrs Helene Janice Siegal Sparber, Maywood, NJ; ed/BA, Alfred Univ, 1968; JD, Sch of Law, Boston Univ, 1971; pa/MA Comm Agnst Discrimination, Legal Counsel's Ofc, 1969-71; Atty, US Dept HUD, Boston, 1971-72; Mgr, Boston Food Coop Inc, 1973; Buyer & Orgr, N Eng Fedn of Coops, 1973-74; Rschr, OR Student Public Interest Res Grp, 1975-76; Pres, OR Fdn of Tchrs, 1977-84; VPres, OR St Indust Union Coun, 1980-; Exec Bd, Multnomah Co Labor Coun, 1981-; Pres, NW OR Hlth Sys; Commun Relats Com; cp/Jewish Fdn Portland, 1982-; OR Symp Assn; r/Jewish; hon/Most Outstg Sr Awd, Alfred Univ, 1968; BPOE Ldrship Awd, 1964; W/W: in W, in Am Cols & Univs; Outstg Yg Men of Am.

AUERBACH, VICTOR H oc/Professor & Director; b/Oct 2, 1928; h/1244 Hoffman Road, Ambler, PA 19002; ba/Philadelphia, PA; m/Helen M; p/Leo and Goldie Auerbach, Bklyn, NY; sp/Peter and Demetra Matalas (dec); ed/AB, Columbia Univ, 1951; MA Med Scis 1955, PhD Biochem 1957, Harvard Univ; pa/Instr, Univ WI Med Sch, 1957-58; Asst Prof 1958-64, Assoc Prof 1964-68, Res Prof Pediatrics (Biochem) 1968-, Temple Univ; Dir Enzume Lab, St Christopher's Hosp for Chd, 1958-; Dir, Dept of Labs, 1976-; Pres, Temple Univ Fac Sen, 1974-75; Pres, Child Hlth Assocs Inc, 1975-81; Ch & Mem, Num Univ & Hosp Comms; Mem Num Nat & Intl Profl Socs & Orgs; hon/Author of Num Papers in Profl Jours & Chapts in Textbooks; F'ships: Eli Lilly & Co, 1952-53; Arthur Lehman 1953-54; Andelot 1954-55; Arthritis & Rheumatism Foun 1954-56; Recip of Num Grants from NIH, 1958-80; Am Men & Wom in Sci; W/W: in E, in Technol Today, in Frontier Sci & Technol.

AUGENBLICK, JOHN GILBERT oc/Education Consultant; b/May 5, 1947; h/2099 Ivy Street, Denver, CO 80207; ba/Denver, CO; m/Frances Green; c/John Edward, Edward Gilbert; p/Mr and Mrs Gilbert L Augenblick, Maplewood, NJ; sp/Mr and Mrs Edward J Green Jr, Lakewood, NY; ed/BS, MA Inst of Technol, 1969; MA, Tchrs Col, Columbia Univ, 1974; EdD, Univ of Rochester, 1981; pa/Pres, Augenblick, Van De Water & Assocs, 1983-; Dir, Ed Fin Ctr, Ed Comm of the Sts, 1977-83; Res Dir, NJ Comm on Fin Post Sec'dy Ed, 1976-77; Tchr, Wilton Public Schs, 1969-72; Bd Dirs, Am Ed Fin Assn, 1983-86; Mem Adv Bd Nat Equity Proj, Ed Law Ctr, NJ, 1982; hon/Author Num Articles Pub'd in Profl Jours incl'g: *Jour of Ed Fin, Ednl Considerations, The Book of the Sts*, Others; Author of Num Papers & Reports for Profl Assns & Comms; W/W in W.

AUGUSTINE, JANE oc/Poet, Writer, Professor; b/Apr 6, 1931; h/Box 981, Stuyvesant Sta, New York, NY 10009; ba/Brooklyn, NY; m/Michael D Heller;

c/Marguerite Morley, Thomas Morley, Jefferson Morley, Patrick Morley; p/ Marguerite Augustine Radloff, Napa, CA; sp/Philip "Pete" and Martha Heller (dec); ed/AB, Bryn Mawr Col, 1952; MA Eng Lit, Wash Univ-St Louis, 1965; PhD, CUNY Grad Ctr, NY (in Progress); pa/Instr, Pratt Inst, 1977-; Mem Fac, The New Sch, 1977-; NYU-SCE, 1975-77; John Jay Col, NY, 1971-73; Webster Col, St Louis, 1965-67; Wash Univ-St Louis, 1960-65; Mem, The Poetry Soc of Am; Fem Writers' Guild; MLA; Past Edit Bd of *Alpha*; r/Buddhist; hon/Author of Articles in *Paideuma*, *Sagetrieb*, *McGill's Critical Surv of Poetry*, *Contemp Poetry*; Author of 1 Volume of Poems; Num Poems Pub'd in Lit Mags; CAPS F'ship in Poetry, NY St Coun on the Arts, 1976 & 1979; 7 Col Conf Scholar, Bryn Mawr, 1948-52; Browning Soc of CA Poetry Prize, 1947; Intl W/W Among Wom.

AULENBACH, DONALD BRUCE oc/Professor; b/Mar 7, 1928; h/24 Valencia Lane, Clifton Park, NY 12065; ba/Troy, NY; m/Marie P Wertz; c/ Louise M Trakimas, Bruce D, Nancy J Baker, Brent T; p/Henry I and Mildred C Schlasman Aulenbach (dec); sp/ William A Wertz (dec); Mary Mohr Wertz, Palmerton, PA; ed/BS Chem, Franklin & Marshall Col, 1950; MS Sanitation 1952, PhD Sanitation 1954, Rutgers Univ; pa/Chem & Bacteriologist, DE Water Pollution Comm, 1954-60; Prof Envir Engrg, Rensselaer Polytechnic Inst, 1960-; Bd of Dirs 1977-79, Capital Dist Chapt Secy & Treas 1965-67 & 1969-76, Bd of Dirs 1980-84, NY Water Pollution Control Assn; Am Chem Soc; Water Works Assn; Treas NE NY Chapt, Hlth Physics Soc, 1973-75; Assn Envir Engrg Profs; Hudson River Envir Soc; Nat Water Well Assn; Am Soc Limnology & Oceanography; Nat Soc Pfl Engrs; r/Prot; hon/Author, Over 85 Pubs & 5 Book Chapts; Editor, 1 Book; Sigma Xi Res Soc, 1954; Diplomate, Am Acad Envir Engrg, 1980; NY Water Pollution Assn Ser Awd, 1983; NYWPCA Brigham Awd for Extraordinary Ser, 1984; Am Men & Wom of Sci; Commun Ldrs in Am; DIB; Men of Achmt; Personalities of Am; W/W in S.

AULICK, C MARK oc/Professor; b/ Jul 25, 1952; h/PO Box 5861 Shreveport, LA; ba/Shreveport, LA; m/Nona S; c/ Amber Rae Bentrup; p/Frances Aulick Garrard, Orlando, FL; sp/T D Sewell, Coushatta, LA; ed/BS Math, Stetson Univ, 1975; MS Applied Math, FL St Univ, 1977; PhD Computer Sci, Duke Univ, 1981; pa/Instr, Stetson Univ, 1977-78; Pt-time Instr, Duke Univ, 1979-80; Asst Prof, LA St Univ Shreveport, 1981-; Assn for Computing Machinery, 1980-; Soc for Industl & Applied Math, 1981-; IEEE, 1984; Omicron Delta Kappa, 1975; r/Bapt; hon/Co-Author of Article, "Isolating Error Effects in Solving Ill-Posed Probs," *SIAM Jour on Algebraic & Discrete Methods*, 1983; AHEPA S'ship, 1970; Outstg Sr in Math, 1975; Univ F'ship, 1975; LSU's Outstg Fac Awd, 1984; W/ W in S & SW.

AULL, JOHN LOUIS oc/Biochemist; b/May 7, 1939; h/1029 Cumberland Drive, Auburn, AL 36830; ba/Auburn, AL; m/Judy; c/Amber, Ashley; p/Louis E and Helen L Aull, Raleigh, NC; sp/

Major and Pauline Capps, Raleigh, NC; ed/AB, Chem, Univ NC-Chapel Hill, 1964; PhD, Biochem, NC St Univ, 1972; mil/USN, 1964-67, Lt; pa/Asst Prof 1974-80, Assoc Prof 1980-, Auburn Univ; Am Soc Biochems; Am Chem Soc; r/Prot; hon/Author & Co-Author, Over 20 Articles & Papers Pub'd in Profl Sci Jours incl'g: *Jour Biol Chem*, *Biochem*, *Biochem, Biophysics, Acta*, Others; Sigma Xi; Phi Lambda Upsilon; Mem, Grad Fac; W/W in Sci & Technol.

AURELIAN, LAURE oc/Scientist; b/ Jun 17, 1939; h/3404 Bancroft Road, Baltimore, MD 21224; ba/Baltimore, MD; m/Irving I Kessler; c/Amalia Deborah; p/George and Stella Aurelian, Balto, MD; sp/Mrs Anne Kessler, Bloomfield, CT; ed/MSc, Tel Aviv Univ, Israel, 1962; PhD, The Johns Hopkins Univ, 1966; pa/Prof Dept Pharm, Univ MD, 1982; Sr Assoc Dept Biophysics 1983, Assoc Prof Comparative Med 1974-82, Assoc Prof Biophysics 1974-82, Asst Prof Comparative Med & Microbiol 11669-74, Johns Hopkins Univ; Past Pres AAUP; ASM; AAAS; AAI; Soc Exp Biol Med; AACR; hon/ Author, Over 100 Articles in Profl Sci Jours & Num Book Chapts Pub'd; Dist'd Yg Sci Awd, MD Acad of Scis, 1970; Boss of Yr Awd, Hunt County Chapt ABWA, 1977; Hon Mem, D A Boyles Soc Gyn & Oncol, Brit Columbia, Canada; W/W: in Am Wom, in Am Men & Wom of Sci; Personalities of S; Dist'd Ldrs in Hlth Care.

AUST, STEVEN DOUGLAS oc/Professor; b/Mar 11, 1938; h/251 Noble Road, Williamston, MI 48895; ba/East Lansing, MI; m/Anne E; c/Teresa Lee, Brian Edward; ed/BS Agri, 1960; MS Nutrition, 1962; PhD Dairy Sci, 1965; pa/Prof Biochem, MI St Univ, 1967-; Chm, MI Toxic Substances Control Comm, 1981-83; MI Soc of Toxicology; Am Soc of Biol Chems; Am Soc for Pharm & Envir Therapeutics; r/ Non-Denom; hon/Author, Over 70 Articles in Profl Sci Jours & 20 Book Chapts Pub'd; USHPS Postdoct F'ship, 1966; New Zealand Facial Eczema F'ship, 1975.

AUSTAD, LORRAINE BLANCHE oc/Space Planning/Interior Designer; b/ Jun 21, 1947; ba/31755 South Coast Highway, #306, South Laguna, CA 92677; c/Paul K; p/Willard E and Phyllis L Baldwin, Las Vegas, NV; ed/BA in Art/ Design, Univ of CA-Irvine, 1970; Undergrad Study in Arch, AZ St Univ; pa/Model Home Coor w Ldrship Housing Sys Inc, 1971-73; Interior Designer, Laura Merlo & Assocs, 1973-76; Interior Designer, Fleetwood Enterprises, 1977-80; Chief Designer, Dunes Hotel, & Proj Mgr, Sheraton Hotel, 1980-81; Interior Designer, Golden Nugget Hotels, 1981-82; Conslt to Space Planning & Interior Designer of Hotels, Restaurants & Comml Design, Conslt for Le Clarion Hotel for Ashkenazy, 1982-; ASID, 1970-; Color Mktg Grp, Chp 1978-; r/Luth; hon/Accepted w Hons at AZ St Univ; One of Top 25 Acad Students in HS; W/W in W.

AUSTEN, WILLIAM GERALD oc/ Physcicain, Chief of Surgical Services, Professor; b/Jan 20, 1930; h/163 Wellesley Street, Weston, MA 02193; ba/ Boston & Cambridge, MA; c/Karl, W Gerald, Christopher, Elizabeth; ed/BS, MA Inst of Technol (MIT), 1951; MD,

Harvard Med Sch, 1955; Cert, Am Bd of Surg, 1962; Cert, Am Bd of Thoracic Surg, 1964; mil/Surg, USPHS, 1961-62; pa/Intern 1955, Asst Resident in Surg 1956-59, Resident E Surg Ser 1960-61, Chief of Surg Cardiovas Res 1963-70, Vis'g Surg 1966-69, Chief of Surg Sers, 1969-, MA Gen Hosp; Sr Registrar in Surg, Kings Col Hosp, London, England, Apr-Aug 1959; Hon Sr Registrar for Thoracic Unit, Gen Infirm, Leeds, England, Sep 1959-Jan 1960; Surg, Clin of Surg, Nat Heart Inst, Bethesda, MD, 1961-62; Assoc in Surg 1963-65, Assoc Prof Surg 1965-66, Prof of Surg 1966-74, Edward D Churchill Prof Surg 1974-, Harvard Med Sch; Mem: Allen O Whipple Surg Soc; The Am Surg Assn; The Halsted Soc; Intl Cardiovas Soc; N Eng Surg Soc; NY Acad of Scis; Soc of Univ Surgs; Others; Num Com Positions w: NIH; Am Col of Surgs; Am Surg Assn; MIT; The Am Heart Assn; MA Heart Assn; Assn of Am Med Cols; Am Bd of Surg; Am Col of Cardiol; hon/ Author, Num Books & Articles Pub'd in Profl Jours; Edit Bd Mem, Num Profl Pubs; Markle S'ship in Acad Med; Outstg Yg Men Awd, Boston, 1965; Pres, Assn for Acad Surg, 1970; Hon Mem, Panhellenic Surg Soc, 1973; Hon Mem, Dutch Cardiol Soc, 1974-; Pres, Am Heart Assn, 1977-78; Paul Dudley White Cardiac Awd, MA Heart Assn, 1981; Louis Mark Meml Lecture Awd, Am Col of Chest Phys, 1981; Life Mem, Corp, MIT, 1982; Others; Num Spkg Presentations & Vis'g Prof'ships; Intl Book of Hon.

AUSTIN, CHARLES LOUIS oc/Government Deputy Director; b/Jan 26, 1948; h/5757 Heritage Hill Drive, Alexandria, VA 22310; ba/Washington, DC; m/Beverly; p/Mr and Mrs Louis C Austin, Zenith, WA; sp/Mrs Ellenor Velasquez, Twin Falls, ID; ed/BA, Univ of Puget Sound, 1970; MBA, Golden Gate Univ, 1975; mil/USAF, 1970-76; pa/Dept Dir DMSPA 1983-, Dept Dir Policy & Progs Sys Acquisition HQAFSC 1981-83, Sr Analyst of Contracts HQAFSC 1978-79, Pilot & Analyst USAF 1970-76, Ofc of Secy, Dept of Def; Chief, Prog Control & Info Sys Strategic Petro Resv 1979-81, Analyst FFTF 1967-78, Dept of Energy; r/Prot; hon/Air Medal, 1974; Meritorious Sr Medal, 1983; Spec Achmt Awds: 1981, 1982 & 1983; W/W; Personalities of Am.

AUSTIN, LESLIE JAMES oc/Home Builder; b/Feb 4, 1941; h/1943 Hyannis Court, Atlanta, GA 30337; ba/Atlanta, GA; m/Lynda Sue Hammons; c/Lyndsey, Leslie; p/Mrs Rose M Austin, North Mankato, MN; ed/BA Arch 1969, MA Planning 1970, Univ KS; MBA, Harvard Univ, 1972; pa/Exec VPres, Sea Pine Co, Hilton Head Isl, SC, 1972-74; Div Mgr, Ryan Homes Inc, Columbus, OH, 1975-77; Pres, Austin Contrn & Devel Inc, Hilton Head Isl, 1978-83; Gen Mgr, John Wieland Homes, 1984-; Pres, Home Bldrs of Hilton Head Isl, 1980-81; Nat Bd of Dirs, Nat Home Bldrs Assn, 1981-83; Mem, Urban Land Inst; r/Bapt; hon/Hon Mention, 1982 Bldrs Choice Design & Planning Competition, *Better Homes & Gardens & Bldr Mag*.

AUSTIN, LORA EVELYN oc/Medical Technologist; b/Sep 6, 1926; h/10707 Moorpark Street, Toluca Lake, CA 91602; ba/North Hollywood, CA; p/ Carlton and Florence E Tyson Austin

PERSONALITIES OF AMERICA

(dec); ed/BA Olivet Col, 1948; MT
(ASCP) Butterworth Hosp, 1950; MS,
CA St Univ-Dominquez Hills, 1981; mil/
USMC Resv, 1957-60; pa/Staff, Butter-
worth Hosp, Grand Rapids, MI,
1949-52; Lab Supvr (1970-) So CA
Permanente Med Grp, LA, 1952-; Adj
Fac, CA St Univ-Dominquez Hills,
1974-; Am Soc of Clin Pathols; Am Soc
for Med Technols; Cert Lab Sci w Nat
Cert Agy; cp/Asst Ldr LA, CA, GSA,
1970-81; Ldr Campfire Girls Grand
Rapids, MI, 1949-52; Smithsonian Assn;
Nat Wildlife Fdn; Nat Rifle Assn; CA
Rifle & Pistol Assn; Olivet Col Alumni
Assn; r/Prot; hon/Recip Dist'd Alumni
Awd, Olivet Col, 1978; W/W in Am
Wom.

AUSTIN, MICHAEL HERSCHEL oc/
Attorney; b/Nov 7, 1896; h/47 Richards
Road, Columbus, OH 43214; ba/Colum-
bus, OH; m/Inez; p/Michael Green and
Willie Catherine Roberson Austin (dec);
ed/Att'd 1915-18, LLB 1922, Univ of
MS; Att'd Akron Univ, 1919; Att'd
1919-21, LLB 1923, JD 1970, OH St
Univ; mil/Coast Artillery, WW I; pa/Sch
Tchr, Rural MS; Law Pract in OH since
1924; Ptnr, Pfeiffer & Austin, 1927-30;
Atty, Farmers Home Adm, 1963-70;
Atty, Franklin Co, OH, 1965-69; Secy,
Columbus Lwyrs Clb, 1931-32; Mem:
ABA, OH Bar Assn, Columbus Bar
Assn; Am Judic Soc; cp/Pres, Big 4 Vets
Coun, 1956-57; Columbus Real Est Bd;
C of C; OH St Univ Alumni Assn; Post
Cmdr 1953-54, Dist Cmdr 1955-56, St
Treas 1958-64, Am Legion; IPA; Tru-
man Lib Assn; Mason; hon/Cross of
Hon, UDC, 1944; Exec & Profl Hall of
Fame, 1966; Wisdom Awd, 1970; Sr
Coun for 50 Yrs Pract, Columbus Bar
Assn 1972 & OH Bar Assn 1974; Outstg
Legionnaire, 1967; Hon at 50 Yr Ban-
quet, Am Legion Lancaster, OH; Golden
Ser Cert, OH St Univ Alumni Assn;
Others; W/W: in OH, in MW, in Com-
merce & Indust, in World; DIB.

AUTEN, MELVIN R oc/Psychologist;
b/Sep 5, 1944; h/Rout 1, Box 712, Ada,
OK 74820; ba/Tecumseh, OK; m/Carol;
c/Krista; p/Luciel Brown, Ada, OK; sp/
Leona Owen, Tulsa, OK; ed/BS, 1967;
MEd 1970; EdD 1980; mil/Army NG;
pa/Psychol, Dept Human Sers, St of
OK, 1978-; Cnslr, US Govt, 1979-76;
Public Sch Tchr, 1967-70; Am Psychol
Assn; Conslg Psychols Assn; OK Psy-
chol Assn; cp/Kiwanis Intl, 1970; r/Bapt;
hon/Psi Chi Nat Hon Soc in Psych, 1976.

AUTREY, CASSIUS E oc/Pastor; b/
Sept 17, 1904; h/2511 West Strong
Street, Pensacola, FL 32505; ba/Same;
m/Aline H; c/Jarry, R Carroll; p/E A and
Rose Lee Yates Autrey (dec); ed/BA
1924, DD 1960, LA Col; ThM & ThD,
NO Bapt Theol Sem, 1934; pa/Pastor,
Tullos LA, 1928-34; Pastor, Temple
Bapt Ch, 1934-37; Pastor, 1st Bapt Ch,
1937-41; Pastor, 1st Bapt Ch, W Mon-
roe, LA, 1941-48; Dir, Evangelism, LA
Bapt Conv, 1948-52; Prof of Evange-
lism, SW Bapt Theol Sem, 1955-60; Dir,
Evangelism, So Bapt Conv, 1960-70;
Prof of Evangelism, NO Bapt Theol
Sem, 1970-72; Pastor, Univ Bapt Ch
SLC, 1977-82; Dir of Sem & Prof,
Golden Gate Sem, Mill Val, CA,
1978-81; hon/Author of Books: *Basic
Evangelism* (Pub'd in Eng, Arabic, Japa-
nese & Chinese) 1959, *Renewals of Old
Testament* 1960, *You Can Win Souls* 1961,
Evangelism in Book of Acts 1962, *Evangelistic*

Sermons 1963, *Theol of Evangelism* (Pub'd
in Eng & Spanish) 1964; Author of Num
Articles for Nat Pubs; Taught "Jr"
Terms for Golden Gate Sem, Mill Val,
CA & Portland, OR; Spoke 3 Times at
So Bapt Conv; Spoke Twice at Bapt
World Alliance, 1965.

AUVENSHINE, ANNA LEE oc/
Teacher, Reading Specialist; b/Nov 27,
1938; h/PO Box 13, Ranger, TX 76470;
ba/Ranger, TX; m/William Robert Auv-
enshine; c/Karen Lynn, William Lee; p/
D C Banks (dec); Mrs Lois Banks, Waco,
TX; sp/Mr and Mrs E H Auvenshine,
West, TX; ed/BA 1959, MA 1968, EdD
1978, Baylor Univ; Postgrad Study, CO
St Univ, 1970-71; Postgrad Study, Univ
of No CO, 1971-72; pa/Math & Eng
Tchr, Waco ISD, Lake Air Jr HS,
1959-63; Eng Instr, Baylor Univ, 1963;
Math & Eng Tchr, Ranger ISD, Ranger
HS, 1964; Math & Eng Tchr, Canyon
ISD, Canyon Jr HS, 1964-66; Math
Tchr, Canyon ISD, Canyon HS,
1968-70; Math & Eng Tchr, St Vrain
Sch Dist, Erie HS, 1970-71; Eng & Rdg
Tchr, Thompson Sch Dist, Loveland
HS, 1971-72; Est'd Rdg Prog 1972, Instr
& Rdg Prog Dir 1972-, Chm Humanities
Div 1978-82, Ranger Jr Col; Pres
1980-82, VPres 1978-80, Beta Upsilon
Chapt, Delta Kappa Gamma; Pres
1980-81, VPres 1979-81, Secy 1974-75
& 1982-83, Ranger Jr Col Fac Org; Mem
Pfl Devel Com 1974-79, VChm Profl
Devel Com 1976-77, Mem Resolutions
Com 1979-80 & 1982-83, TX Jr Col
Tchrs Assn; Parliamentn, Ranger PTA,
1978-79; Intl Rdg Assn; Assn for Supvn
& Curric Devel; Others; cp/Trustee
1979-, VPres Bd of Trustees 1980-82,
Pres Bd of Trustees 1982-, Ranger ISD;
Commun Chm, Publicity Chm & Troop
Ldr, Ranger GSA Assn; Secy, Eastland
Co Heart Assn, 1975-77; Ch Sch Supt
1979-81, Organist 1974-77, Others, 1st
U Meth Ch, Ranger, TX; Pres, 1947 Clb
(Ranger Woms Clb), 1977-78; r/U Meth;
hon/Cert of Apprec, TX Jr Col Tchrs
Assn, 1979; Achmt Awd, Beta Upsilon
Chapt, Delta Kappa Gamma, 1980; Ser
Awds, Ranger Jr Col, 1977 & 1982; W/
W in S & SW.

AUVENSHINE, WILLIAM ROBERT
oc/College Administrator; b/June 21,
1937; h/412 Corsicana Street, Hillsboro,
TX 76645; ba/Hillsboro, TX; m/Anna
Banks; c/Karen, Lee; p/E H Auvenshine,
Waco, TX; sp/Lois Banks, Waco, TX; ed/
AS, Arlington St Jr Col, 1957; BS, TX
Christian Univ, 1959; MS, W TX St
Univ, 1967; EdD, Univ of No CO, 1973;
pa/Pres, Hill Jr Col, 1984-; Dean of
Student Pers Sers, Ranger Jr Col,
1972-84; Cnslr, Loveland, CO, 1970-72;
Mgr & Pt-Owner, Megert Music Co,
Amarillo, TX, 1964-70; Band Dir,
Ranger, TX, 1957-64; Pres, TX Assn for
Student Deans, 1982-83; cp/Dist Govr,
Lions Clb, 1977-78; Pres, Ranger U
Fund, 1976; Pres, Ranger Indust Foun,
1979; Lay Ldr, Ranger U Meth Ch,
1982-83; r/U Meth; hon/Man of Yr,
Ranger C of C, 1964; Outstg Alumni
of W TX St Univ, 1983; Outstg Edrs
of Am; W/W in TX.

AUVIL, MICHELLE ANNE oc/
Mother & Housewife; b/Jul 28, 1959;
h/PO Box 310, Stanton, ND 58571; m/
Wayne K; c/Brooke Erin; p/Elizabeth
Jane Kelly (dec); sp/Mr and Mrs Gerald
Auvil, Seattle, WA; ed/HS Dipl; pa/
Waitress, Tom-Tom, Albany, OR,

1977-82; r/Christian; hon/Asst Coor for
Inter-St Petition Drive to Retain Con-
stitl Rgt of "Due Process of Law"
Regarding Infractions Imposed by
Enactment of "The Tax & Fiscal Respon-
sibility Act of 1982".

AVASTHI, PRATAP SHANKER oc/
Physician; b/Jan 15, 1936; h/4908
Brenda, Northeast Albuquerque, NM
87109; m/Pushpa; c/Surabbi, Smita,
Swati; p/K S and A B Avasthi, Hardoi,
India; ed/BS 1958, MD 1962, King
George Med Col, Lucknow, India; pa/
Prof Med 1984-, Assoc Prof Med
1979-84, Asst Prof Med 1972-79, Univ
NM-Albuquerque; Chief Renal Sect
1977-, Staff Phys 1972-, VAMC, Albu-
querque, NM; Asst Prof Med 1971-72,
Pool Ofcr 1970-71, All India Inst of Med
Scis, New Delhi, India; Med Adv Bd; NM
Kidney Foun; Facility Rep VAMC ESRD
Netwk VI Inc; AOA; Am Fdn for Clin
Res; Am Heart Assn-Kidney in Cardi-
ovas Diseases; Am Soc Nephrology; Intl
Soc of Nephrology; Sigma Xi; r/Hindu;
hon/Author, Over 26 Abstracts &
Presentations; Over 26 Articles in Sci
Jours & 2 Book Chapts Pub'd.

AVEDISIAN, ARCHIE HARRY oc/
Executive; b/June 22, 1928; h/9832
Meadowcroft Lane, Gaithersburg, MD
20879; ba/Washington, DC; m/Gloria;
c/Debra, Anthony; p/Harry Avedisian
(dec); Charlotte Avedisian, Paducah,
KY; sp/Frank Rogers (dec); Lucy Rogers,
Binghamton, NY; ed/BS Ed 1951, MA
Org & Adm in Ed 1954, Courses toward
PhD 1954-, Boys Clbs Am Exec Tng
1964, NY Univ; Supvn & Mgmt, Nat
Grad Univ, 1976; Fin Mgmt & Resour-
ces, Tandem Tng Assocs, 1976; mil/
USAR, Ret'd; pa/Exec VPres, Boys &
Girls Clbs Gtr Wash DC, 1972-; Exec
Dir, Boys Clbs Seattle & King Co,
1967-72; Exec Dir, Santa Rosa Boys Clb,
CA, 1960-67; Exec Dir, Columbia Pk
Boys Clb, IL, 1959-60; Exec Dir, Boys
Clb E St Louis, IL, 1956-59; Prog Dir,
Flatbush Boys Clb, Bklyn, NY, 1953-56;
Phy Dir, Jamestown Boys Clb, NY,
1955-53; Sum Prog Dir, Binghamton
Boys Clb, NY, 1951; Chm & Mem Num
Coms w Boys Clbs of Am in Var Areas
of US; Num Ofcs & Coms w Boys Clb
Profl Assn; Nat Soc Fund Raisers; Chp
& Com Mbrship, Gtr Wash Soc of Assn
Execs; Nat Capital Spkrs Assn; Num
Others; cp/Touchdown Clb Wash DC;
Montgomery Village Golf Clb, Gai-
thersburg; Rotary Clb Intl; NAACP; Jr
C of C; Lions Clb; Others; r/Rom Cath;
hon/Author, Articles in Boys Clb Profl
Assn; Paul Harris Fellow Awd, Rotary
Intl, 1983; Yth Ser Awd, Boys & Girls
Clbs of Metro Detroit, 1982; Dist'd Ser
Awd, Boys Clb Profl Assn, 1982; Bronze
Keystone w Ser Bar/2 Stars, Boys Clb
of Am, 1980; H Roe Bartle Am Human-
ities Recruiting Awd, 1979; Num Oth-
ers; W/W in Wash DC; Outstg Yg Men
in Am.

AVERY, BYLLYE YVONNE oc/Pro-
ject Director; b/Oct 20, 1937; h/1131
Portland Avenue, Southeast, Atlanta,
GA 30316; ba/Atlanta, GA; c/Wesley
Lee, Sonja Yvonne; p/Mrs L Alyce M
Ingram, Jacksonville, FL; ed/AB Psy-
chology, Talladega Col, 1959; MEd,
Univ FL, 1969; pa/Spec Ed Tchr, Duval
Ct Schs, Jacksonville, FL, 1966-68; Hd
Tchr, Child Psych, SHANDS Tchg
Hosp, 1970-75; Co-Fdr, Gainesville,
Wom's Hlth Ctr, 1974-78; Co-Fdr,

40

Birthplace, 1978-80; Dir, Black Wom's Hlth Proj, 1980-; Action VChp Bd of Dirs, Nat Wom's Wlth Netwk; hon/ Co-Author of Article, "Contrasts in Birthing Place Hosp & Birth Center," in *Birth Control & Controlling Birth.*

AWALT, SUSAN GRAVES oc/Materials Management Director; b/Aug 4, 1953; h/3576 Windmill Drive, Virginia Beach, VA 23456; ba/Virginia Beach, VA; p/John Robert and Audrey Gleason Graves, Newport News, VA; ed/BS Nus Adm & Mgt, Christopher Newport Col, 1981; pa/Account Exec, Tampa Neighbor Newspaper, 1973-74; Placement Mgr, Olsten's Temp Ser, 1974-75; Prod Dealer, Evans & Assocs, 1976-77; Dir Mats Mgmt, Patrick Henry Hosp, 1977-81; Mats Mgr, Westminster-Canterbury, 1981-; Reg Chp, VA Hosp Shared Sers Corp, 1981-82; Secy-Treas, Hlth Care Purchasing Soc of VA, 1981-83; VA Peninsula Bus & Profl Wom's Clb, 1979-80; r/Methodist; hon/Top Salesperson Awd, Evans & Associates, 1977; W/W in South & Southwest.

AWERBUCH, SHIMON oc/State Government Office Chief; b/May 9, 1946; ba/Albany, NY; ed/BS Bldg Sci 1968, MS Urban-Envir Studies 1969, PhD Urban & Envir Studies 1975, Rensselaer Polytechnic Inst; pa/Chief Ec & Policy Studies, Utility Intervention Ofc, Consumer Protection Bd 1980-, Policy Analyst, Gov's Ec Devel Bd 1976-77, NY St Exec Dept, Albany, NY; Mng Ptnr & Co-Fdr, Tibbits Assocs & Pres, Tibbits Devel Corp, 1977-80; Dir Policy Anal & Planning Proj, NY St Ed Dept, 1975-76; Sr Conslt, Mgmt Consltg Ser, Ernst & Whinney, Wash DC, 1974-75; Com Counsel, Standing Com on Envir Conserv, NY St Assem, 1971-73; Planning Analyst, Planning & Devel Agy, Cohoes, NY, 1971-73; Proj Assoc 1971-73, Res Asst Ctr Urban Envir Studies 1968-69, Rensselaer Polytechnic Inst; Opers Res Analyst & Asst Chief of Staff, HQ's USAF, The Pentagon, 1969-71; Mem, Mgmt Sci Steering Com, Akm Soc for Public Adm, 1975-76; Inst Mgmt Sci; Sigma Xi Sci Res Soc;Num Other Com & Org Mbrships; hon/Author & Co-Author Book & Book Chapts: *Policy Eval for Commun Devel: Decision Tools for Local Govt* 1976, "Computer Applications in Public Wks," in *Urban Public Wks Adm* 1976, "A Goal Setting & Eval Model for Commun Devel," in *Rdgs in Sys Engrg* 1977, "Nuclear Cancellations: Ec & Legal Bases for Allocating Losses," in *Awd Papers in Public Utility Ecs & Regulations* 1982; Over 20 Articles & Reports Pub'd in Profl Jours & Presented to Var St Agys, Univs, Nat & Intl Orgs; W/W: in E, in Fin & Indust.

AWTRY, JOHN H oc/Lawyer, Insurance Executive; b/1897; m/Nell Catherine Jacoby; c/Nell Catherine (Gilchrest) (dec); ed/LLB 1921, JD, Univ TX Sch of Law; mil/AUS, Col Ret'd; pa/AUS WW I; Law Pract, Pres, Counsel & Mem of Bd of Dirs of Num Ins Firms, 1942-47; Fgn Claims Comm & Gen Staff, 12 Army Grp (No France & Germany), AUS WW II, 1942-45; Maj/Atty, Chief of Fgn Claims Div, Jud Adv Gen Corp, Wash DC, 1945; Gen Staff & Chief of War Frauds Unit Ofcs of Under Secy War & Asst Secy of Army, 1946-49; Mem War Crimes Staff & Chief Contract & Procurement Div, Cmdg Gen Staff of European Command, Heidelberg, 1949; Mem Army Panel, Armed Sers Bd of Contract Appeals, Ofc of Asst Secy of Army, Wash; Ret'd & Promoted Full Col by Orders of Pres of US, 1953; Admitted to Bar: All Cts in TX, US Supr Ct, US Ct Mil Appeals, US Ct of Claims; Mem, Am, TX, Dallas & Fed Bar Assns; Pres, Nat Exch Clb, 1933-35; Past Pres, TX Exch Clb; Past Pres & Life Mem, Dallas Exch Clb; Fed Grand Jury Assn; Jud Adv Assn; Mil Order of WWs; Life Mem, 12th AUS Grp Assn; AUS Ret'd Ofcrs Assn; Disabled Ofcrs Assn; Num Others; cp/ Order of Lafayette; Leisure Worlder of the Mo; Royal Arch, 320 Scot Rite, Mason; C of C; Pres, Nat Civic Clb; Bkrs of Am; Num Spkg Engagements; Others; r/Bapt; hon/Bronze Star & 3 Battle Stars, 1944; Legion of Merit, 1945; Name Placed in Ct of Hon, Nat Exch Clb, 1966; Others.

AXLINE, STANTON G oc/Physician; b/Jul 11, 1935; h/845 20th Street, #201, Santa Monica, CA 90403; ba/Beverly Hills, CA; c/Thomas Allen, Sheryl Lynne; p/Raymond and Merle Axline, Columbus, OH; ed/BA 1956, MD 1960, OH St Univ; mil/USAF, 1965-67; pa/ Intern, Univ of CO Med Ctr, Denver, 1960-61; Resident Internal Med 1961-63, Fellow Infectious Diseases 1963-65, Asst Prof Internal Med 1969-76, Stanford Univ; Res Sci, USAF, San Antonio, 1965-67; Assoc Prof 1976-83, Chief of Infectious Diseases Sect, Dept of Internal Med 1976-82, Univ AZ-Tucson; Assoc Chief of Staff for Res, VA Med Ctr, Tucson, AZ, 1976-82; Chief Operating Ofcr, Med Res Dir, Meditech Pharms Inc, Bevely Hills, 1982-; Am Soc Cell Biol; Am Assn Immunols; Infectious Disease Soc of Am; AMA; LA Co Med Assn; hon/ Author, Over 55 Articles Pub'd in Profl Sci Jours & Books; Mem Adv Conslt Com on Infectious Diseases to Chief Med Doct, VA, Wash DC, 1974-79; Mem Adv Coun of Nat Inst for Allergy & Infectious Diseases, Bethesda, MD, 1979-83; Phi Beta Kappa, 1956; Alpha Omega Alpha, 1960.

AYALA, FRANCISCO JOSE oc/ Professor; b/Mar 12, 1934; h/747 Plum Lane, Davis, CA 95616; c/Francisco Jose, Carlos Alberto; p/Francisco Ayala and Soledad Pereda (dec); ed/MA 1963, PhD 1964, Columbia Univ, NY; pa/Prof Genetics 1974-, Dir Inst of Ecol 1977-81, Assoc Prof Genetics 1971-74, Univ CA-Davis; Asst Prof Genetics 1967-71, Res Assoc 1964-65, Rockefeller Univ, NY; Asst Prof, Providence Coll, RI, 1965-67; Pres, Soc for Study of Evolution, 1980; Coun Mem 1977-79, Secy 1974-77, Am Soc of Naturalists; Genetics Soc of Am; Ecological Soc of Am; Am Genetics Assn; Am Inst Biol Scis; Nat Acad of Scis; Am Acad of Arts & Scis; hon/Author of Books: *Evolving: Theory & Processes of Organic Evolution* 1979, *Evolution* 1977, *Molecular Evolution* 1976, *Studies in Phil of Bio* 1974, *Mod Genetics* 1984; Author, Over 300 Articles Pub'd in Profl Sci Jours; Mem, Nat Acad of Scis, 1981; Mem, Am Acad Arts & Scis, 1977; Medal of the Col de France, 1979; Fellow, AAAS, 1967; Fellow, CA Acad of Natural Scis, 1079; Mem, Am Phil Soc, 1984; W/W: in Am, in W; Commun Ldrs of Am; Contemp Authors; Other Biogl Listings.

AYISI, ERIC OKYERE oc/Professor; b/Sep 26, 1926; h/32 D Cambridge Apts, 5109 Goldsboro Drive, Hampton, VA 23605; ba/Williamsburg, VA; m/ Dorothy Evelyn; c/Kathleen Judith, Ruth Margaret Doddrell; p/Kofi Ayisi (dec); Mercy Adebra, Ghana; sp/ Mathew and Hebe Nayler (dec); ed/Gen Cert of Ed (Adv Levels) Brit Constit 1951, Ecs 1954, Ec Hist 1955, Hist 1955, BA Sub Ecs 1960, BSc Sociol & Athropol 1961, PhD Social Change, Sch of Ec's 1965, Univ of London; pa/Headmaster, Meth Elem Sch, Ghana, 1940-43; Preacher, Catechist, Ghana 1943-45 & Lagos, Nigeria 1945-50; Fac Mem, Univ Ghana, 1965-74; Fulbright Prof, Curric Conslt, Ramapo, Mahwah, NJ & Bloomfield Col, 1972-73; Dist'd Fulbright Lectr in Humanities, Dillard Univ, NO, 1973-74; Prof Rel & Phil, Fisk Univ, Nashville, 1973-74; Fulbright Scholar in Residence, Intl Studies Consort, Old Dominion Univ, VA Commonwlth Univ, Norfolk St & Hampton Inst, 1974; Vis'g Prof, Hampton Inst, 1974-78; Lectr, Christopher Newport Col, 1979-81; Vis'g Assoc Prof Anthropol, Col of Wm & Mary, 1980; Guest Lectr at Num Cols & Univs; Commr of Inquiry, Nat Liberation Coun, Govt Ghana, 1966-68; Nat Adv Coun Wkrs Brigade, Ghana, 1966-72; Sum F'ship, Nat Endowment Humanities, Univ FL Gainesville, 1980; Mem, Ghana Meth Conf, 1965-; Mem, Ghana Sociol Assn; Brit Sociol Assn; Intl African Inst, UK; African Studies Assn; Fellow, Royal Anthropol Inst; Intl Polit Sci Assn; Current Anthropol Assoc; Am Acad Polit & Social Sci; r/Meth; hon/Author of Books: *An Intro to Study of African Culture*, 1980; *The Polit Instns of Akwapims*, 1972; *Kinship & Local Commun of Akwapims*, 1972; Author Num Articles in Profl Jours; W/W in S & SW.

AYRES, MARY ALLEN oc/Government Official; b/Jun 23, 1924; h/2400 Virginia Avenue, Northwest, Apt C802, Washington, DC 20037; ba/Washington, DC; p/Frank H Ayres (dec); Marion Kellogg Ayres, Wenatchee, WA; ed/BA, Stanford Univ, 1946; Att'd Univ WA; pa/Reporter, *Wenatchee Daily World*, 1948-50; Reporter, *Wash Post*, 1951-52; Reporter, US Fgn Ser, Dept of St, 1950-51; Mem Edit Staff, *Changing Times*, also Editor *Fam Guide*, Kiplinger Wash Editors, 1952-61; Editor, Bur Labor Stats, 1952-61; Editor, Bur Labor Stats, Manpower Adm, US Dept Labor, 1962-67; Public Info Spec, Bur Indian Affairs, US Dept Interiour, 1967-75; Writer & Editor, Bur Labor Stats, 1975-; Tchr, Jour Dept; Past Treas, Govt Info Org; Mem, Publicity Com, Nat Capitol YWCA, 1982; Mem, Treas & Dir 1975-80, Nat Assn Govt Communicators; Am News Wom's Clb; Am Ec Assn; Nat Pres Clb (Wash DC); cp/Stanford Univ Alumni Assn; Kappa Kappa Gamma; Epis Clb; r/Epis; hon/Sigma Epsilon Sigma, 1948; High S'ships at Univ WA.

AZRIN, NATHAN H oc/Psychologist, Professor; b/Nov 26, 1930; h/5151 Bayview Drive, Ft Lauderdale, FL 33308; ba/Ft Lauderdale, FL; m/Victoria B; c/Rachel D, Michael A, David T, Richard L; p/Harry and Esther Azrin (dec); ed/BA 1951, MA 1952, Boston Univ; PhD, Harvard Univ, 1956; mil/ AUS, 1956-58; pa/Prof, So IL Univ, 1959-80; Res Dir, Anna Mtl Hlth Ctr,

1958-80; Prof, Nova Univ, 1980-; Past Pres, MidWn Psychol Assn; Assn of Behavior Anal; Assn for Advmt of Behavior Therapy; FL Assn for Behavior Anal; r/Jewish; hon/Author of Books, *Job-Clb*, 1981; *Token Ec*, 1958; *Toilet Tng*, 1974; Phi Beta Kappa, 1951; Sigma Xi, 1954; W/W in Am; Other Biogl Listings.

AZUMI, KOYA oc/Professor; b/Nov 23, 1930; h/378 West Hudson Avenue, Englewood, NJ 07631; ba/Newark, NJ; m/Jann; c/Eric, Elise; p/T and M Azumi, Tokyo, Japan; sp/C and R Eckert, Belleville, IL; ed/BA, Haverford Col, 1955; PhD, Columbia Univ, 1966; pa/ Instr 1965-67, Prof Sociol 1977-, Rutgers Univ; Asst Prof, NY Univ, 1967-70; Asst Prof, Univ WI, 1970-72; Vis'g Asst Prof & Res Assoc, Columbia Univ, 1972-77; Am Sociol Assn; En Sociol Soc; Intl Sociol Assn; Assn for Asian Studies; hon/Author of Books: *Higher Ed & Bus Recruitment in Japan*, 1969; *Orgnl Sys* (w Jerald Hage), 1972; Author of Num Articles & Book Chapts incl'g: "Japanese Soc: a Sociol View," in A Tiedmann's *An Intro to Japanese Civ*, 1974; Others; Fulbright Scholar to Japan, 1969-70.

AZZAM, RASHEED M A oc/Professor; b/Mar 9, 1945; h/7301 Cranbrook Drive, New Orleans, LA 70128; ba/New Orleans, LA; m/Fatemah M A Elmorsi-; c/Reem, Omar; ed/BSEE, Cairo Univ, Egypt, 1967; PhD Elect Engrg, Univ NE Lincoln, 1971; pa/Dist'd Prof Elect Engrg 1982-, Prof 1981-82, Assoc Prof 1979-81, Univ NO; Assoc Prof Res in Engrg & Med 1974-79, Postdoct Fellow 1972-74, Univ NE; Sigma Xi Sci Res Soc; Soc of Photo-Optical Instrumentation Engrs (SPIE); Optical Soc of Am; r/ Muslim; hon/Author of Book, *Ellipsometry & Polarized Light* (1971), Translated into Russian 1981; Co-Editor, *Proceedings of 3rd & 4th Intl Confs on Ellipsometry* 1976 & 1980; Over 100 Papers Pub'd in Profl Sci Jours; Dist'g Prof Elect Engrg, Univ NO, 1982; Fellow, Optical Soc Am, 1977; Cits for Dist'd Ser, SPIE, 1976 & 1977; W/W: in Engrg, in Technol Today, in S & SW; Other Biogl Listings.

B

BABCOCK, MICHAEL W oc/Associate Professor of Economics; b/Dec 10, 1944; h/720 Harris, Manhattan, KS 66502; ba/Manhattan, KS; m/Virginia L; c/John S, Karen E; p/Bruce and Virginia Babcock, Ottawa, IL; sp/Wayne and Ruby Brooks, Columbia, MO; ed/BSBA, Drake Univ, 1967; MA 1971, PhD 1973, Univ of IL; mil/AUS, 1969-71; pa/Tchg Asst, 1968-71; Res Asst 1972, Univ of IL; Asst Prof Ec 1972-79, Assoc Prof Ec 1979-, KS St Univ; Mem: Trans Res Forum; Am Agri Ec Assn; MO Val Ec Assn; Mid-Continent Reg Sci Assn; Soc Reg Sci Assn; KS Ec Assn; cp/Manhattan Optimist Clb; hon/Author, Over 35 Res Papers & Articles Pub'd in Govt Pubs & Profl Jours incl'g: *Regulation*; *TX Bus Review*; *Proceedings of Trans Res Forum*; *Jour of Ec*; *KS Bus Review*; Others; Over 14 Paper Presentations at Profl Org Meetings, 1972-83; Co-Investigator, *Rail Wheat Efficiency Study*, Fed RR Adm Grant, 1976-78; Co-Investigator, *Improving Prodn Area Logistics for Wheat*, US Dept of Agri Grant, 1980-81; Co-Investigator, *Devel of a Rail Deregulation Monitoring Prog: A KS Study*, US Dept of Agri, 1984-85; Beta Gamma Sigma, 1967; Omicron Delta Epsilon, 1968; W/W: in W & MW, of Intells; Men of Achmt; DIB; Dir, Dist'd Ams; Other Biogl Listings.

BABERO, BERT BELL oc/Parasitologist; b/Oct 9, 1918; h/2202 Golden Arrow Drive, Las Vegas, NV 89154; m/Harriett King Babero; c/Bert Jr, Andras; ed/BS 1949, MS 1950, PhD 1957, Univ of IL; mil/AUS, 1943-46; pa/Parasitologist, USPHS, Arctic Hlth Res Ctr, AK, 1950-54; Res Asst Parasitologist, Univ of IL, 1954-57; Prof & Ch Dept Zool, Ft Val St Col, GA, 1957-60; Parasitologist, Fed Em Sci Skeme, Lagos, Nigeria, W Africa, 1960-62; Parasitologist, Baghdad Med Sch, Iraq, 1962-65; Parasitologist, Univ of NV-Las Vegas, 1984-; Fellow, Tropical Med, LA St Univ Sch of Med; Pres, Rocky Mtn Conf of Parasitologists, 1978; Coun Mem, Am Soc of Parasitologists, 1981-; cp/NAACP; Commr, NV St Equal Rts Comm, 1967-68; r/Prot; hon/Author, Over 100 Sci Pubs on Parasites of Animals & Man in Num Profl Jours; Life Time Mem, Rocky Mtn Conf of Parasitologists, 1950; Man of Yr Awd, NAACP, 1969; W/W in W; Am Men of Sci.

BABICH, ALAN F oc/Computer Scientist; b/Nov 21, 1943; h/27431 Osuna, Mission Viejo, CA 92691; ba/Costa Mesa, CA; p/Mr and Mrs John Babich, Baden, PA; ed/BS Physics, Carnegie Inst of Technol, 1965; MS 1966, PhD Elect Engrg 1972, Carnegie-Melon Univ; pa/Computer Sci, Mgmt Sys Anal, Sr Programmer, Burroughs Corp, 1971-79; Large Sys Arch, Basic Four, 1979-83; Sys Arch, File Net Corp, 1983-; Mem: IEEE; Assn for Computing Machinery; Sigma Xi; Mensa; hon/Author of "Significant Event Simulation," *Comm of the Assn of Computer Machinery*, 1975; "Proving the Total Correctness of Parallel Progs," *IEEE Transactions on Software Engrg*, 1979; Mem, Nat Champ 10 Man Speed Star Sky Diving Team, 1974-76; World Champs 1975 & World Record Holders 1974 & 1975; Parachuting Hall of Fame,

1976; W/W: in CA, in W, in Technol Today.

BABLES, MARILYN MARIE oc/Lab Technician; b/Nov 21, 1954; h/1968 North 32nd Street, Kansas City, KS 66104; ba/Kansas City, KS; p/Leon Bables, Kansas City, KS; ed/AA, KS Commun Col, 1976; BA, Pk Col, 1979; Bus Mgmt Course, 1979; KS Real Est Cert, 1980; MO Real Est Cert, 1981; pa/Lab Tech, Bayvet Labs, 1978-79; QC Lab Techn, Bd of Public Utilities, 1979-; Pres, Bables Investmt Properties; Kaw Val Med Soc Hlth Careers Clb; Am Water Wks Assn; AAUW; Nat Assn for Female Execs; Pres, Women in Bus; hon/Nat Social Registry of Prom Students & Grads; W/W in Am Univs & Cols; Outstg Yg Wom in Am; Personalities of W & MW.

BACH, MARILYN LEE oc/Scientist, Administrator, Policy Analyst; b/Apr 24, 1937; h/644 Goodrich Avenue, St Paul, MN 55105; ba/Mpls, MN; c/David, Peter, Wendy; p/Ida M Brenner, Lynn, MA; ed/BS, Simmons Col, Boston, MA, 1958; PhD, NY Univ Sch of Med, 1966; pa/Spec Asst to VPres for Hlth Scis 1983-, Assoc Prof Med Sch & Sch Public Hlth 1978-, Univ of MN; Assoc Prof Sch of Med, Univ of WI, 1975-78; Edit Bd 1974-77, Symp Com, Transplantation Soc; Chp Nom'g Com 1978, Com on Status of Wom 1982-, Am Assn Immunols; AAAS; r/Jewish; hon/Author, Over 100 Articles Pub'd in Profl Sci Reports & Jours incl'g: *Immunol Today*; *Ednl Record*; *Higher Ed & Nat Affairs*; *Clin Res*; *Transplantation Soc Proceedings*; Num Others; Over 20 Profl Spkg Presentations at Univs & Org Meetings; Gold Medal Awd, Am Inst of Chems, 1958; Fdrs Day Awd, NY Univ, 1967; Mem, Nat Adv Allergy & Infectious Disease Com, 1974-77; Fellow Sci & Public Policy, Brookings Instn, 1981-82; Others; W/ W in Frontier Sci & Technol; Am Men & Wom of Sci.

BACHIREDDY, VEERARAGHAVE REDDY oc/Agronomist; b/Jun 8, 1946; h/211 Kenilworth Parkway, Baton Rouge, LA 70808; ba/Baton Rouge, LA; m/Sunitha; c/Archana, Arpana, Anitha; p/Srinivas and Padma, India; sp/Keshava and Manikya, India; ed/BSc Agri 1967, MSc Agri 1970, PhD 1978; pa/Instr in Agronomy, Andhra Pradesh Agri Univ, 1970; Res Asst in Agronomy, Univ of AR, 1973-77; Postdoct Res Assoc 1978, Asst Prof & Prin Res Investigator 1979-, Plant & Soil Sci Dept, So Univ; Am Soc of Agronomy; Crop Sci Soc of Am; Am Phytopathological Soc; Soc of Nematologists; So Assn of Agri Sci; Louisiana Acad of Sci; hon/16 Res Pub in *Agronomy Abstracts*, *Crop Sci*, *Jour of Nematology*, *Phytopathol*, *So Univ Res Bltn*, *Proceedings of Louisiana Acad of Sci*, *Indian Jour of Agronomy*, *Jour of Res*; Gamma Sigma Delta, the Hon Soc of Agri 1977; Best Tchr Awd 1979; Cert'd Profl Agronomist & Crop Sci 1981; 3 Federally Funded Res Grants 1979-82 & 1982-87.

BACHMAN, BECKY SHEPARD oc/High School English Teacher; b/Nov 11, 1924; h/3102 Briargrove Lane, San Angelo, TX 76904; ba/Wall, TX; m/Francis D; c/Ronald, Dianne, Richard, Robert; ed/BA, 1968; pa/Tchr, San Angelo ISD, 1968-78; Tchr, Wall ISD, 1979-; Mem: NEA, TSTA, 1969-; AAUW, 1976-; Delta Kappa Gamma,

1976-; cp/Philharm Soc, 1974-; Choir Mem 1952-, SS Tchr 1954-, 1st Bapt Ch; r/Bapt; hon/Alpha Chi, 1967; Alpha Mu Gamma, 1966; Delta Sigma Pi, 1967; Kappa Delta Pi, 1967; Tchr of Yr, Wall ISD, 1983; W/W.

BACIGALUPA, ANDREA oc/Liturgical Artist/Designer; b/May 26, 1923; h/626 Canyon Road, Santa Fe, NM 87501; ba/Santa Fe, NM; m/Ellen Williams; c/Gian Andrea, Pier Francesca, Ruan Saire, Chiara Domenica, Daria Concessa; p/Henry and Maria Bacigalupa (dec); sp/John and Paula Williams (dec); ed/BFA, MD Inst of Fine Arts, 1950; Postgrad Study, Accademia di Belli Arti, Florence, Italy, 1950-51; mil/AUS, ETO, WW II; pa/Owner & Artist, The Studio of Gian Andrea, Santa Fe, NM; Chm, Art & Arch Com, Liturgical Comm, Archdiocese of Santa Fe, 1978-; Chm Art & Arch Com, Bldg Comm, Diocese of Amarillo, 1979-; r/Rom Cath; hon/Author of 4 Books: *Jour of an Itinerant Artist*; *A Good & Perfect Gift*; *The Song of Guadalupana*; *Saints & Saints' Days*; Num Articles & Features in: *The Santa Fe New Mexican*; *Santa Fe Reporter*; *Liturgical Arts Qtly*; Others; 1st Prize, Sculpture, Santa Fe Co, Art in Public Places, 1979; Top Awd, Ft Worth Chapt AIA for Design of St Lawrence Cathedral, Amarillo, 1975; W/W: in Am Art, in W, Am Artist of Renown.

BACIN, WILIAM FREDRIC "BILL" "DOCTOR JAZZ" oc/Jazz Writer; Singer, Historian, Editor; b/Jun 14, 1923; h/Box 1225 Kerrville, TX 78029; mil/USN Air, 1943-45; pa/1st HS Vocalist of TV, NY Worlds Fair, 1940; Trombonist w Dance & Jazz Bands, 1939-43; Vocalist w Dance & Jazz Bands, 1940-; Writer since 1941; Jazz Concert Prodr, 1961-68; Dir, Jazz Portion of TV Series KNXT, 1963-68; Editor, *The Jazzologist*, 1963-; Commentator, Jazz & Swing Radio Shows: KIEV Glendale CA, KYMS Santa Ana CA, WWL NO LA, KERV Kerrville TX, 1963-74; Vocalist, "Tishomingo Blues," "If I Could Be w You 1 Hour Tonight," OR Jazz Band-1004, 1970; Vocals, "Capt Billy's Whiz Bang Band," LOJ-8414, 1984; Pres, NO Jazz Clb of CA, 1963-; Mbrships in Over 92 Jazz Socs Throughout the World; hon/Author of Books: *Famous Jazz People Who Have Known Me*, 1983; Pub'd in: *The 2nd Line* Mag, NO; *De Stem* Newspaper, Breda, Holland; *All That Jazz*, Ingram, TX; Num Other Jazz & Music Soc Bltns, Newlttrs & Mags; Key to City & Hon Citizenship, NO, 1966; Gold Watch Apprec Awd, NO Jazz Clb of CA, 1966; Apprec Plaque, NO Jazz Clb & Mus, 1964; Num Hon Life Mbrships incl'g: NO Jazz Clb of CA; Osaka (Japan) Jazz Soc; Dixieland Jazz Soc of San Diego; San Antonio Jazz Soc; Soc for Presv of Dixieland Jazz (Montclair, CA; Napoleon Clb; Potomac River Jazz Clb; Sydney (Australia) Jazz Clb, NO Jazz Clb; Num W/W & Other Biogl Listings.

BACK, NATHAN oc/Professor; b/Nov 30, 1925; h/295 Middlesex Road, Buffalo, NY 14216; ba/Buffalo, NY; m/Toby Ticktin; c/Ephraim Eli, Aaron Issar, Adina, Rachel Tzvia, Sara Deborah; p/Joseph and Freda Back (dec); sp/Israel and Sarah (dec); ed/BSc Biochem, PA St Univ, 1948; MSc 1953, PhD 1955, Pharm, Grad Sch of Phila Col Pharm & Sci; mil/USN, 1944-46, Phm

43

3/c; pa/Assoc Prof 1961-63, Prof Pharm 1963-, SUNY-Buffalo; UN Sci Expert, Israel, 1976-77; Dir Sch of Pharm & Prof Pharm, Hebrew Univ, Israel, 1969-71; Cancer Res Scist 1955-58, Sr Res Scist 1958-61, Roswell Pk Meml Inst, Buffalo; cp/Pres, Kadimah Day Sch, Buffalo, 1959-66; Mem, Jewish Fdn of Buffalo, 1960-70; r/Jewish; hon/Author of 10 Books, 1 Lab Manual & 250 Manuscripts in Pharm, Biochem & Biomed Scis; E K Frey Awd for Basic Res, 1966; Fellow, Royal Acad of Med; Italian Pharm Soc; NY Acad of Scis; Rho Chi; Sigma Xi.

BACON, H ANITA D oc/Educational and Vocational Advisor; h/558 Storrs Road, Mansfield Center, CT 06250; ba/ Storrs, CT; c/Scott Dressen, Mitchell Wright; p/Harry and Helen Dreesen, Mansfield Center, CT; ed/AA, Larson Jr Col, 1948; BA, En CT St Univ, 1968; MA, Univ of CT, 1971; pa/Admr/Cnslr, Ofc of Student Pers, Mansfield St Col, 1971-74; Asst to the Dean, Ofc of Student Affairs, 1974-78; Career Coun, Non-Degree Student Advr, Bach of Gen Studies Degree Prog, Storrs Campus Coor, Univ of CT, 1978-; Mensa; AAUW; Nat Univ Ext Assn; Am Assn of Cnslg & Devel, Div of: Am Col Pers Assn, Nat Voc Guid Assn; Grad Student Coun, Univ of CT, 1968-69; Advr, Zeta Tau Alpha, 1971-74; Secy, Mansfield Bus Assn, 1978-79; cp/Cand, Town of Mansfield Town Coun, 1983; Commr, Mansfield, CT Housing Auth, 1983-; Plaque Citing Public Wk w CT Puerto Rican Cultural Exhibit, 1970; Justice of the Peace, Town of Mansfield, Elected 1984-; hon/Pub'd Short Story "The Prayer," in *Dimensions*, 1968; Phi Kappa Phi; Charter Mem, Beta Sigma Chapt, Pi Lambda Theta Hon Soc; Advr, Beta Omega Chapt, Alpha Sigma Lambda Hon Soc; Zeta Tau Alpha Frat; W/W: in E, of Wom, of Intells.

BACON-BERCEY, JUNE oc/International Meteorologist, TV Journalist, Training Officer, Public Information Officer; h/160 Bella Vista Drive, Hillsborough, CA 94010; ba/San Francisco & Redwood City, CA; m/George W Brewer; c/Dawn-marie, Dail St Claire; p/James Griffin (dec); Cherrye MaSalles Griffin (dec); sp/Mr and Mrs George Wilson Brewer (dec); ed/BA Meteorology & Math 1954, MA Meteorology 1955, Univ of CA-LA; MPA, Univ of So CA, 1979; pa/Tng Ofcr, Weathercasters in No & Ctl CA, 1983-; Public Info Spec & Chief TV Sers, Nat Oceanic & Atmospheric Admin (NOAA), Wash DC, 1979-83; Opers Meteorologist & Broadcaster, NOAA's Nat Weather Ser, Wash DC, 1975-79; Lectr, Num Orgs, 1974-75; TV Meteorologist, News Correspondent, Morning Hostess, NYC & Buffalo, 1965-74; Conslt, Atomic Energy Comm, NYC, 1964-65; Engr, Sperry Rand Corp, 1962-64; Meteorologist, Communicator, NOAA's Nat Weather Ser, Wash DC & NYC, 1956-64; Mem: Wom in Sci & Engrg; VChm, Am Meteorological Soc, Wash DC; VChm, Am Meteorological Soc, No CA; Chm, Am Meteorological Soc, No CA; Com on Minorities, Am Geophys Union; NY Acad of Scis; Am Assn for Public Adm; Past Mem, Nat Ad Hoc Com, Wom in Atmospheric Sci; cp/Past Bd Mem (Elected 3 Times), Nat Bd of Wom & Minorities; Past Bd of Dirs, Nat

Legal Guild; r/Rom Cath; hon/Author of Num Articles Pub'd in Profl Jours; *Earth Sci Book*, 1983; *Heath Sci Book*, 1983; Smithsonian Exhbn (SITES), 1983; Fed Fellow, US Civil Ser Comm, 1978-79; Cer of Recog, US Dept of Commerce, NOAA, 1978; Apprec & Recog Awds, Nat GSA, 1978; Cert of Apprec, Morris Brown Col, Atlanta, 1977; Wom of Yr Awd, Operation PUSH, 1975; *Ladies Home Jour Awd*, 1974; Nat Press Clb Awd, 1974; Seal of Approval for TV Weather-casting Excell, Am Meteorological Soc, 1972; Cert of Apprec, Public Broadcasting Sys, 1972; Ambassadorship Cand to Luxembourg, 1964; The June Bacon-Bercey S'ship for Wom in Atmospheric Sci Estab'd, Am Geophys Union; Others; W/W: of Am Wom, in Sci & Technol, in Earth Scis; Contbns of Black Wom to Am; Appt'd by Gov, St of CA, to Adv Com, 1984-88; Other Biogl Listings.

BADER, WILLIAM BANKS oc/Executive; b/Sep 8, 1931; h/7421 Saville Court, Alexandria, VA 22306; ba/ Arlington, VA; m/Gretta Lange Bader; c/Christopher, Katherine, John, Karl; ed/BA, Pomona Col, 1953; Att'd Univ of Munich, 1953-54; MA 1960, PhD 1964, Princeton Univ; Att'd Univ of Vienna, 1961-62; mil/USN, 1955-58, Bombardier/Navigator, Air Intell Ofcr/ Photo Interpreter; USNR, Capt (Ret'd); pa/VPres, SRI Intl, Wash, 1981-; Staff Dir 1978-81, Staff Mem 1966-69, US Sen Fgn Relats Com; Asst Dept Under Secy of Def for Policy, 1976-78; Fellow, Woodrow Wilson Intl Ctr for Scholars, Smithsonian Inst, 1974-75; Prog Ofcr & European Rep, The Ford Foun, 1969-74; Fgn Ser Ofcr, Dept of St, 1965-66; Ctr for Intl Studies, Princeton Univ, 1964; Ofc of Nat Estimates, CIA, 1962-64; Legis Ref, Libn of Cong, 1954-55; r/Cath; hon/Author of Books: *Austria Between E & W: 1945-55*, 1966; *The US & the Spread of Nuclear Weapons*, 1968; Author of Var Chapts in Books & Articles in Jours incl'g: *Adelphi Papers*; *The Future of Intl Legal Order*; *Nav War Col Review*; Others; W/W.

BADGETT, WYNELLA B oc/Nursing, Higher Education Administration; b/Feb 11, 1932; h/602 Holiday Circle, Pineville, LA 71360; ba/Pineville, LA; m/ Charles B; c/Lynn Ann, Sharon Lee, David Messick; Grandchd: Rebecca Lynn, Christopher Todd, Nicole, Jessica, David Charles; p/Mr and Mrs Wendell Bramblett, Manchester, TN; ed/Dipl, Bapt Meml Hosp, Memphis, 1953; BSN, The Univ of TN, Col of Nsg, Memphis, 1968; MSN, Univ of MD-Balto, 1970; EdD, Univ of TN-Knoxville, 1982; pa/ Staff Nsg Positions, 1953-59; Team Ldr, Neurol, NIH, Bethesda, MD, 1959-61; Nsg Supvr & Coor, Inservice, Chd's Hosp, Wash DC, 1962-65; Coor Nsg Ldrship Dept Baccalaureate Deg Nsg 1970-76, Asst Prof 1979-80, Acting Chm Dept Baccalaureate Deg Nsg & Assoc Prof 1976-80, E TN St Univ; Assoc Prof 1980-82, Chm & Assoc Prof Dept of Nsg, LA Col, Pineville, LA, 1982-; Mem: LA St Nurses Assn; E TN Univ Hon Soc of Nsg; TN Acad of Hlth; Adv Com, Ctl LA Am Cancer Soc & Ctl LA Am Lung Assn; Phi Delta Kappa; Nat Leag for Nsg; ANA; cp/ People-to-People Intl; r/Bapt; hon/ Author of Var Nsg Res Papers; Author of Article Pub'd in *Vital Signs* of TN

Nurses Assn, 1979; Caughlin-Saunders Ch of Nsg, 1984; Dept of Hlth & Human Resources, Wom's Advocacy Bur, LA Talent Bk for Wom, 1983; Cert of Outstg Achmt in Hlth & Safety, 1982; Outstg Edr of Am in Recog on Contbns to Advmt of Higher Ed & Ser to Commun, 1976; Others; W/W of Wom in Ed; Outstg Edrs of Am.

BADHAM, ROBERT E oc/Congressman; b/Jun 9, 1929; h/3859 North River, Arlington, VA 22207; ba/Washington, DC; m/Anne C; c/Robert Jr, William, Sharron, Phyllis, Jennifer; p/Byron J Badham Jr, Los Angeles, CA; Bess Kissinger Badham (dec); sp/Richar G and Phyllis Barto Carroll, Santa Ana, CA; ed/Grad, Beverly Hills HS, 1947; Att'd Occidental Col; AB, Stanford Univ, 1951; mil/USN Ofcr Cand Sch; Korean War, Opers Ofcr USS Walton; pa/VPres, Hoffman Hardware Co, LA, CA, 1954-69; Mem, CA St Legis, 1963-76; Mem, US Ho of Reps, 1977-; Mem: Am Soc Arch Hardware Conslts, 1955-69; CA Repub Ctl Com & Chm Targeting Com, 1963-; Chm Repub Study Com, 1982; Repub Nat Campaign Com, 1982-; Repub Policy Com, 1979-; r/Luth; hon/Author of Num Pubs & Articles; Man of Yr, Costa Mesa C of C, 1963; Watchdog of Budget, 1978, 1980, 1982 & 1984; Guardian of Small Bus, 95th-98th Cong; W/W: in W, in Polit.

BAER, FERDINAND oc/Professor; b/ Aug 30, 1929; h/12501 White Drive, Silver Spring, MD 20904; m/Karen K; c/Darvis, Robin, Jason, Gavin; p/Julius and Leonie Baer (dec); sp/John and Mary Klein; ed/BS 1950, MS 1954, PhD 1961, Univ of Chgo; pa/Asst Prof 1961-65, Assoc Prof 1965-71, CO St Univ; Prof, Univ of MI, 1972-77; Prof & Chm Dept Meteorology, Univ of MD, 1977-; Dir, Coop Inst for Climate Studies (Univ of MD & NOAA), 1983-; Mem: Fellow, Am Meteorological Soc; Fellow, Royal Meteorological Soc; Am Geophy Union; Japanese Meteorological Soc; AAAS; Canadian Meteorological Soc; Wash Chapt Bd Mem 1979-83, Am Recorder Soc; Bd Mem on Atmosphere & Climate, Nat Res Coun, 1982-85; Univ of MD Rep to UCAR; Mem, NCAR Adv Coms; hon/Author, Over 50 Pubs in Am & Fgn Sci Jours; Num Contbns to Books; WMO Expert to India, 1966; Res Fellow, GFDL/NOAA, 1968-69; Vis'g Prof, Univ of Stockholm, 1974-75; Vis'g Prof, Frei Univ of Berlin, 1975; Mem Sci Del to China, 1981; Var W/W; Am Men of Sci.

BAGGETT, WILLIAM (BILLIE) oc/ Instructor; b/Dec 5, 1949; h/West 1621 9th Avenue, Spokane, WA 99204; ba/ Spokane, WA; m/Kathryn Hearst; c/ Debra; p/Louis and Deborah Baggett (both Dec); sp/Harold and Harriet Hearst, Cheney, WA; ed/BA Gonzaga Univ, 1970; MA Ed, En WA Univ, 1972; pa/Tchg Asst, En WA Univ, 1970-72; Eng Tchr, Gonzaga Prep Sch, Spokane, 1972-78; Instr, Elem & Sec'dy Ed, Spokane Falls Commun Col, Spokane, 1978-; Mem: Nat Ed Assn; cp/Girl Scout Ldr; March of Dimes Vol; CDA; r/Cath; hon/Appreciation for Outstg Yth Ldrship, Gonzaga Prep Sch, 1978.

BAHILL, S LARRY oc/Pima County Director of Elections; b/Dec 10, 1943; h/3542 North Wilson, Tucson, AZ 85719; ba/Tucson, AZ; m/Carol Anne;

c/Nathaniel, Natalie, Nicholas; p/Stephen and Tracey Bahill, Tucson, AZ; sp/Ken and Phyllis Skelley, Tempe, AZ; ed/BS, No AZ Univ, 1969; MED 1970, Law 1971, MED 1976, Univ of AZ; mil/USNR, Enlisted 11 Yrs, Ofcr 13 Yrs; pa/Dir of Elections, Pima Co, 1981-; AZ St Rep, 1973-81; House Minority Ldr, 1977-81; Instr Govt, Pima Col, 1973-; Subst Tchr; Hlth Edr; cp/2nd VPres 1979-83, Legis Advr 1983-, Assn for Retard Citizens; 2nd VPres 1981-82, MS Soc, 1979-82; Bd of Trustees, Tucson Residence Foun, 1981-; K of C, 1973-; Am Legion, 1973-; Bd of Dirs, AZ Boys St, 1984-; Legis Advr, St of AZ, 1976-; r/Cath; hon/Legis of Yr, 1977; Outstg Legis, 1978; Barrier Buster Awd, Paralyzed Vets of Am, 1980; Phi Alpha Theta; Personalities of W & MW; W/W in Govt; Commun Ldrs of Am.

BAHNER, CARL TABB oc/Professor; b/Jul 14, 1908; h/PO Box 549 Jefferson City, TN 37760; ba/Bluefield, VA; m/Catharine Garrott; c/Thomas Maxfield, Mary Catharine Bahner Day, Frances Jane Bahner Hendricks; p/G L and Augusta M Bahner (dec); sp/E P J and Eula M Garrott (dec); ed/AB Phy Sci, Hendrix Col, 1927; MS Organic Chem, Univ of Chgo, 1928; PhD Industl Organic Chem, Columbia Univ, 1936; ThM, So Bapt Theol Sem, 1931; Grad Study, Yale Univ, 1931-32; pa/Hd Physics Dept, Union Univ, 1935-37; Hd Chem Dept 1937-67, Coor of Res 1967-73, Carson-Newman Col; Assoc Prof, Walters St Commun Col, 1973-78; Prof Chem, Bluefield Col, 1979-; Conslt, TN Val Auth, 1941-45; Oak Ridge Nat Labs, 1948-79; Oak Ridge Inst of Nuclear Studies 1950-56; Res Chem, Roswell Pk Meml Inst 1956 & Chester Beatty Res Inst 1957; Mem: Fellow, AAAS; Am Assn for Cancer Res; Fellow, Am Inst of Chems; Chm E TN Sect 1951, Am Chem Soc; Fellow, Pres 1951, TN Acad of Sci; Pres 1972, TN Inst of Chems; Alpha Chi; Phi Lambda Upsilon; Sigma Pi Sigma; Sigma Xi; r/Bapt; hon/Author & Co-Author, Over 75 Pubs in Profl Sci Jours; Holder of Over 16 US Patents in Field; FL Awd, 1964; Mfg Chems Awd for Excell in Tchg, 1967; Jefferson City Man of Yr Awd, 1969; Algernon Sydney Sullivan Awd, 1969; T I C Hon Scroll, 1975; So Chem Awd, 1977; Dist'd Ser Awd, Walters St Commun Col, 1978; Var Listings in W/W; Am Men of Sci.

BAHR, HOWARD MINER oc/Professor; b/Feb 21, 1938; h/180 East 4320 North, Provo, UT 84604; ba/Provo, UT; m/Rosemary Frances Smith; c/Bonnie Louise, Howard McKay, Rowena Ruth, Tanya Lavonne, Christopher Joseph, Laura Lee, Stephen Smith, Rachel Marie; p/A Francis and Louie Jean Miner Bahr, Orem, UT; sp/B H and Arrena Ruth Crawford Smith, Yakima, WA; ed/BA, Brigham Yg Univ, 1962; MA 1964, PhD 1965, Univ of TX-Austin; pa/Proj Dir "Homelessness: Etiology, Patterns & Consequences" 1965-68, Vis'g Lectr Sum 1968, Proj Dir "Disaffiliation Among Urban Wom" 1968-71, Bur of Applied Res, Columbia Univ; Assoc Prof Sociol & Assoc Rural Sociologist 1968-72, Chm Dept Rural Sociol 1971-73, Prof Sociol & Rural Sociologist 1972-73, WA St Univ, Pullman; Co-Investigator, Midtown III Proj, NSF,

Ctr for Proj Effectiveness Studies 1976-80, Vis'g Prof Sociol 1976-80, Univ of VA; Dir Fam & Demographic Res Inst 1977-83, Prof Sociol 1974-, Brigham Yg Univ; Mem: Am Sociological Assn; Assoc Editor 1978, Nat Coun on Fam Relats; Assoc Editor 1978, Mbrship Com 1975-78, Rural Sociol Soc; SWn Social Sci Assn; Soc for Sci Study of Rel; Pubs Com 1982, Pacific Sociological Soc; Tocqueville Soc; r/Mormon; hon/Author & Co-Author of 9 Books incl'g: *Social Sci Res Meths*, 1984; *Divorce & Remarriage: Probs, Adaptations & Adjustments*, 1983; *All Faithful People: Change & Continuity in Medtown's Rel*, 1983; *Life in Large Fams: Views of Mormon Mothers*, 1982; *The Sunshine Widows*, 1980; *Skid Row: An Introduction to Disaffiliation*, 1973; Others; Editor of 4 Books incl'g: *Indian Ams Today: Social Sci Perspectives*, 1983; *Pop, Resources & the Future: Non-Malthusian Perspectives*, 1972; Others; Num Articles Pub'd in Profl Jours; Recip, Karl G Maeser Res & Creat Arts Awd, Brigham Yg Univ, 1979; W/W: in Am, in W; Am Men & Wom of Sci; Commun Ldrs of Am; DIB.

BAHR, JANICE M oc/Professor; b/Feb 14, 1935; h/1915 Winchester, Champaign, IL 61820; ba/LaCrosse, WI; p/Frank Bahr, LaCrosse, WI; ed/BA, Viterbo Col, LaCrosse, WI, 1964; MSc Zool 1968, PhD Physiol 1974, Univ of IL-Urbana; pa/Biol Instr, Viterbo Col, 1968-70; Endocrine Trainee Dept Physiol 1970-72, Predoct Fellow Dept Physiol 1972-74, Res Assoc Dept Animal Sci 1974, Asst Prof Dept Animal Sci 1974-79, Assoc Prof Dept Animal Sci 1979-, Univ of IL-Urbana; Mem: Poultry Sci Assn; Sigma Xi; Endocrine Soc; Sigma Delta Epsilon; Soc for Study of Reprodn; NY Acad of Sci; Am Soc for Animal Sci; AAAS; hon/Author, Over 12 Articles Pub'd in Book Chapts incl'g: *Brit Poultry Sci*, 1983; *Factors Regulating Ovarian Function*, 1983; *GYN Endocrinology*, 1980; *Physiol & Control of Parturition in Domestic Animals*, 1979; *Ovarian Follicular & Corpus Luteum Function*, 1979; Others; Over 50 Articles & Abstracts Pub'd in Assn Proceedings & Profl Jours incl'g: *Endocrinology; Biol Reprodn; Jour Reprodn & Fertilization; Jour Animal Sci; Proceedings of Soc for Study of Reprodn*; Others; W/W in Am Wom.

BAIANU, ION C oc/Professor; b/Aug 18, 1947; h/402 East George Huff Drive, Urbana, IL 61801; ba/Urbana, IL; m/Kimiko Saito; c/Stephen, Christinna; p/C Baianu (dec); Simionica Baianu, Craiova, Romania; sp/T Saito, Tokyo, Japan; ed/MSc Biophysics 1967, DPhysics 1976, Univ of Bucharest; PhD Biophysics, Univ of London, England, 1974; Postdoct Study, The Cavendish Lab, Univ of Cambridge; pa/Asst Prof Biophysics & Elect 1968-71, Assoc Prof Biophysics & Biochem, Univ of Bucharest, Romania; Postdoct Res Fellow, (SRC UK) Phy Chem Dept, Leeds Univ; Res Assoc, The Cavendish Lab Cambridge, 1977-80; Res Assoc (NSF) 1980-82, Asst Prof 1982-, Phy Chem Dept, Univ of IL-Urbana; Mem: Agri & Food Chem Div, Am Chem Soc; Am Soc for Photobiol; Intl Soc Magnetic Resonance (ISMAR); Biophysics Soc (US); FASEB; Brit Biophy Soc; Sigma Xi; Soc for Math Biol Inc; European Phy Soc (Geneva); Int of Physics (London); hon/Author of 1 Book Translation; 3 Book

Reviews; Over 75 Sci Articles Pub'd in Profl Jours incl'g: *Physics & Phy Chem; Biophysics*; Others; Biophysics Awd for Structural Studies of Biol Membranes, Min of Ed, Bucharest, 1971-74; Men of Achmt; W/W in Commonwlth.

BAILEY, ARTHUR oc/Social Security Representative; ba/SSA, 2021 South Flower Street, Los Angeles, CA 90007; p/William H Bailey; sp/Winifred Townsend; ed/Carnegie Inst of Technol, Pgh Acad, Dept of Interior Mgmt Training Prog 1955-1956; mil/USAF, 1945-46; pa/Contract Spec, NASA, 1966-68; Social Ins Rep 1968-74, Social Security Rep 1974-, Social Security Adm; Dir of Public Relats 1976-78, Advr to Pres 1979-80, Parliamentn 1980-, cp/Black Porsche, Inc; Profl Singer, Downtown Chorale, 1948-56; Actor, Pgh Playhouse, 1958-59; Porsche Clb of Am, 1976-; hon/Prepared Wkly News Releases for 9 Papers, 1974-80; Write Monthly Column for *LA Sentinel*, *Wave Pubs & Porsche Mag*, 1980-; Sustained Superior Perf Awd, US Corps of Engrs, 1960-61; Outstg Perf Awd, Social Security Adm, 1976; W/W Among Black Ams; Men of Achmt, DIB.

BAILEY, CAROLYN FAULKNER oc/Computer Programmer; b/Nov 6, 1942; h/3503 Castle Ridge Road, Montgomery, AL 36116; ba/Montgomery, AL; p/Martin and Sylvania Faulkner, Montgomery, AL; ed/BS Bus Adm/Computer Sci & Mgmt, Univ of AL, 1980; MS Pers Mgmt, Troy St Univ, 1981; Postgrad, Auburn Univ-Maxwell; pa/Edit Asst, Air War Col, Maxwell AFB, 1972-75; Computer Tech, US Govt, Gunter AFS, 1975-82; Invest Mgr, 1970-; Pres, Federally Employed Wom, 1977-81; Bd Mem, AAUW, 1981-; El Matador Con Assn; Univ of AL Alumni Assn; Planning Board Mgmt Wkshops/Sems, 1979-82; cp/Nat Security Coun; Leag of Wom Voters; Cottage Hill Historic Assn; Okaloosa Isl Improvement Assn; Alpha Xi Delta; Beta Gamma Phi Hon Soc; Vol Coun, Montgomery Area Mtl Hlth Crisis Line; hon/Pub Articles: "The Mgmt Consltg Process," "The Productivity Game," "Testing: St-of-the-Art," "Wom, Today & Tomorrow," "Real Est--the Real Asset," "Phy Fitness, A Mgmt Issue,"; Beta Gamma Phi Scholastic Hon Soc, 1981; W/W: in S & SE, in Am Wom; Personalities of S.

BAILEY, DALLAS B oc/Professor, Administrator; b/Feb 16, 1937; h/84 Barbour Street, Buckhannon, WV 26201; ba/Buckhannon, WV; m/Annette Bond; c/Kenneth Bruce, Jeffrey Kent; p/Mrs Pearl Bailey, Huntington, WV; sp/Mrs Paul Bond, Lost Creek, WV; ed/BA, Salem Col, 1959; MA 1961, PhD 1966, Kent St Univ; MSW, WV Univ, 1980; pa/Student Affairs Staff, Kent St Univ, 1959-66; Dean of Residence Hall Progs & Asst Prof, IL St Univ, 1966-72; Prof & Dept Chm Sociol 1972-73, Pres 1973-78, Salem Col; Sabatical Yr, 1978-79; VPres & Dean of Students, Prof Sociol, WV Wesleyan Col, 1979-; Mem: Num Acad & Ser Orgs; cp/Mem: Rotary; Adm Bd, Chm Pastor/Parrish Relats Com, U Meth Ch; Choir, Madrigal Singers of Clarksburg; Comm on Rel & Race Relats; r/U Meth; Omicron Delta Kappa, WV Wesleyan, 1981; Doct of Hum Ser, Honoris Causa, Salem Col, 1978.

BAILEY, ELIZABETH ELLERY oc/

Administrator; b/Nov 26, 1938; h/220 Schenley Road, Pittsburgh, PA 15217; ba/Pittsburgh, PA; c/James Lawrence, William Ellery; p/Irving W Raymond (dec); Henrietta D Raymond, York Harbor, ME; ed/BA Ec, Radcliffe Col, 1960; MS Computer Sci Option, Stevens Inst of Technol, 1966; PhD Ec, Princeton Univ, 1972; pa/Dean Grad Sch Industl Adm, Carnegie-Mellon Univ, 1983-; VChm 1981-83, Acting Chm 1981, Commr 1977-83, Civil Aeronaut Bd; Supvr Ec Anal Grp & Res Hd Ec Res Dept 1973-77, Sr Tech Aid, Assoc Mem & Mem Tech Staff 1960-73, Bell Labs; Adj Asst & Adj Assoc Prof Ec, NY Univ, 1973-77; Mem: Corp Bd, Standard Oil of OH (SOHIO), 1984-; Corp Bd, PA Power & Light, 1983-; Bd of Trustees, Princeton Univ, 1978-82; Corp Vis'g Com, Alfred P Sloan Sch of Mgmt, MIT, 1983-85; Adv Bd Ctr for Ec Policy Res, Stanford Univ, 1983-85; VPres 1985, Exec Com 1981-83, Hd Com on Status of Wom in Ec Prof 1980-82, Am Ec Assn; Exec Coun of Fedn of Orgs for Profl Wom, 1980-82; Res Ad Com, Am Enterprise Inst Ctr for Study of Govt Regulation, 1980-; Bd of Editors, Var Profl Jours; Bd of Trustees, Presb Univ Hosp, Pgh, PA, 1984-; Others; cp/VPres Bd of Trustees & Fdg Mem, Harbor Sch for Chd w Lrng Disabilities, Red Bank, NJ, 1969-72; Others; hon/Author & Editor of 3 Books incl'g: *Deregulating the Airlines: An Ec Anal*, 1974; *Ec Theory of Regulatory Constraint*, 1973; Author, Over 35 Articles, Book Chapts & Reports Pub'd in Sci Books, Assn Proceedings, & Profl Jours incl'g: *Am Ec Review*; *Jour of Polit Economy*; *Bell Jour of Ecs*; *Studies in Public Regulation*; *Yale Jour of Regulation*; *Jour of Ec Lit*; *Jour Industl Ec*; Others; magna cum laude, Radcliffe Col, 1960; Prog Design Trainee Awd, Bell Labs, 1964-66; Doct Support Awd, Bell Labs, 1970-72; Prize Paper Awds, 11th & 12th Annual Confs on Public Utility Valuation, Ames, IA, 1971-72.

BAILEY, MARY ETTA oc/Food Service Director; b/Jun 23, 1947; h/PO Box 387, Rainsville, AL 35986; ba/Fort Payne, AL; m/Bob Lee; c/Sallie Josephine, Mary Elizabeth; p/Walter and Elizabeth, Rainsville, AL; sp/Augustus and Ora Lee, Rainsville, AL; ed/AA 1968, BS 1973, Jacksonville St Univ; Dietetic Internship, Univ of AL Med Ctr, 1973; pa/Therapeutic Dietitian, Huntsville Hosp, 1971-72; Food Ser Dir, Bapt Med Ctr, 1974-; Editor 1975-77, Secy 1977-78, Pres Elect & Pres 1979-80, Nom Com 1981, AL Dietetic Assn; Am Dietetic Assn St Adv Com, 1980; Affil Chm, Am Diabetes Assn; cp/ Bd Mem, DeKalb Diabetes Assn; Chm, DeKalb Co Red Cross Disaster Food Unit; Mem, DeKalb Co Board of Ed; Frequent Lectr to Commun & Civic Grps; hon/Num Articles for Area Newspapers on Nutrition & Hlth; Student Govt Assn Rep; Pres, Alpha Eta Epsilon; Outstg Dietetic Intern, 1973; AL Outstg Yg Dietitian, 1975; Am Dietetic Assn Outstg Yg Dietitian, 1975; W/W Among Students in Am Jr Cols; Outstg Yg Wom of Am; World W/W of Wom.

BAILEY, ROBERT L oc/Insurance Company Manager; b/Oct 9, 1938; h/ 687 Blairshire Circle, Winter Park, FL 32792; ba/Orlando, FL; m/Lorrie W; c/ Tonya; p/Earl and Florence Bailey,

Decatur, GA; sp/Daisy Wade, Codele, GA; ed/Att'd GA St Univ, 1956-59; pa/ 21 Yrs Claim Wk, Wausau Ins Co; Orlando Claim Mgr's Coun; Atlanta Claims Assn; Orlando Arbitration Comm; hon/Num Spchs in Ref to Invasion of Privacy Issues, Proper Coor w Legal & Claim Activs in Ins Indust; Instr, Pers Relats & Employee Motivation, Smith Hughes Voc Sch; W/W in S & SE.

BAILEY, WILLIAM JOHN oc/ Research Professor; b/ Aug 11, 1921; h/6905 Pineway, University Park, MD 20782; ba/College Park, MD; m/Mary Caroline; c/Caroline, John, Barbara; p/ Admiral Ross and Erva Bailey (dec); ed/ BChem, Univ of MN, 1943; PhD, Univ of IL, 1946; pa/Arthur D Little Postdoct Fellow, MA Inst of Technol (MIT), 1946-47; Asst Prof 1947-49, Assoc Prof 1949-51, Chem, Wayne St Univ; Res Prof Chem, Univ of MD, 1951-; Conslt to Num Pvt Corps; Mem: Pres 1975, Dir 1973 & 1977-82, Chm of Bd 1979 & 1981, Chm Div Polymer Chem 1968, Chm Nat Res Coun Com on Macromolecules 1968-77, Am Chem Soc; VPres, 1st Chem Cong of N Am Continent, 1975; Pres, Chem Soc of Wash, 1961; Exec Bd, Com of Sci Soc Pres, 1975-77; Co-Chm, US/Japan Polymer Symp, 1980; Am Inst of Chems; Alpha Chi Sigma; Wash Acad of Scis; Am Oil Chems Soc; AAUP; AAAS; Edit Bd Mem, Num Profl Jours; Num Other Org Positions; r/Unitarian; hon/Author & Co-Author, Over 200 Tech Articles; Author of 2 Books; Holder of 6 US Patents in Field; 1st Fatty Acid Prodrs Res Awd, 1955; Gulf Oil Foun Res Awd, 1971; Hon Scroll, DC Inst of Chems, 1975; Hillebrand Prize, Am Chem Soc, 1984; Phi Beta Kappa; Sigma Xi; Phi Kappa Phi; Phi Lambda Upsilon; Pi Mu Epsilon; W/W: in Am, in Engrg, in World; Other Biogl Listings.

BAILLIE, MARY HELEN (ORR) oc/ Executive; b/Aug 18, 1926; h/3471 Northeast 17th Terrace, Fort Lauderdale, FL 33334; ba/Fort Lauderdale, FL; c/William Jr, Carol; p/Paul Clydus and Laurie Easterling Orr; ed/Carolina Bus Col, 1946; pa/Controller, George I Clarke, Inc, 1953-57; Controller, DuBose-Reed Const Co & W Carroll DuBose, Inc, 1970-74; Asst Controller, H B Fuller Co, 1975-76; Pres, M H Baillie & Assoc, Inc, 1977-; Dir, Nat Assn of Accts, 1977-79, 1982; Secy/Dir, FL Assn of Accts, 1977-79; Treas/Dir, Woms' Exec Clb, 1978-80, Intl Assn of Financial Planning; Tower Forum; cp/Dir, Ft Lauderdale Co of C, 1979; hon/W/W in S & SW.

BAIN, ROBERT ADDISON oc/Professor; b/Sep 20, 1932; h/G-9 Ridgewood Apartments, Carrboro, NC 27510; ba/Chapel Hill, NC; c/Susan Elizabeth Bain McClanahan, Robin Anne, Michael Addison; p/Ernest Addison Bain (dec); Gail Bain Sexson, Mattoon, IL; ed/BS, En IL Univ, 1954; AM 1959, PhD 1964, Univ of IL; pa/ Tchr, Lanphier HS, Springfield, IL, 1954-58; Pt-time Reporter, *IL St Jour*, Springfield, 1954-58; Tchg Asst, Univ of IL-Urbana, 1958-64; Prof Eng, Univ of NC-Chapel Hill, 1964-; Mem: Pres 1970-71, NC-VA Col Eng Assn; Exec Com 1971-74, Conf on Col Composition & Commun; Comm on Comp

1976-79, NCTE; Exec Com 1980-, SEn Conf on Eng in 2-Yr Col; S Atl Mod Lang Assn; r/Bapt; hon/Co-Editor, *Colonial & Federalist Am Writing*, 1966; *H L Davis*, 1974; *The Writer & the Worlds of Words*, 1975; *So Writers: A Biogl Dict*, 1979; BS w Hons, 1954; Editor, *En St News*, 1953; Editor, *Green Caldron*, 1962-64; Tanner Awd for Excell in Undergrad Tchg, 1976; Vis'g Lectr, Univ of Salamanca, Spain, Sum 1982; W/W; W/W in Am; Dict of Am Scholars.

BAINUM, PETER M oc/Professor, Program Director; b/Feb 4, 1938; h/9804 Raleigh Tavern Court, Bethesda, MD 20814; ba/Washington, DC; m/Carmen Cecilia Perez; c/David P; p/Charles J Bainum, Scottsdale, AZ; Mildred T Salyer (dec); sp/L Mariano Perez, Cucuta, Columbia; ed/BS Aerospace Engrg, TX A&M Univ, 1959; SM Aeronaut & Astronautics, MA Inst of Technol (MIT), 1960; PhD Aerospace Engrg, The Cath Univ of Am, 1967; pa/ Sr Engr, Martin-Marietta, 1960-62; Staff Engr, Fed Sys Div, IBM, 1962-65; Sr Staff Engr, Applied Physics Lab, Johns Hopkins Univ, 1965-69; Conslt, 1969-72; Adj Asst Prof 1967-69, Assoc Prof 1969-73, Prof 1973-, Dir Grad Studies 1974-84, Howard Univ; VPres, WHF & Assocs Inc, 1977-; Dir of Intl Progs 1984-, Exec VPres 1982-84, 1st VPres 1980-82, VPres Tech 1978-80, VPres Pubs 1976-78, & Fellow, Am Astronautical Soc; Assoc Fellow, AIAA; VChm Astrodynamics Com, (IAF) Intl Astronautical Fdn; Fellow, Brit Interplanetary Soc; hon/Author of Num Articles Pub'd in Assn Proceedings & Profl Jours incl'g: *AIAA Jour*; *Jour Spacecraft & Rockets*; *Jour Brit Interplanetary Soc*; *ACTA Astronautica*; Others; Intl Acad of Astronautics, 1985; Outstg Res Awd 1981, Grad Sch Outstg Fac Awd 1980, Exemplary Res Awd 1976, Howard Univ; NASA/ASEE Sum Fac F'ship, 1970-71; SAE Teetor Awd, 1971; W/W: in Engrg, in World; Am Men & Wom of Sci; Men of Achmt; DIB.

BAIRD, JAMES CATCHINGS JR oc/ Legal Advisor; b/Sep 12, 1904; h/ Running Knob Hollow Road, Sewanee, TN 37375; ba/Same; m/Mary Louis; c/ Anne B Chatoney (Mrs B J Jr), James III, Henry; p/James and Mary Long Baird (dec); ed/BS; LLD; mil/AUS, Mil Intell, WW II, Capt; pa/Legal Advr, Karatana Inc, Currently; Ch Conslt; Admr; Fund-raising Activs; cp/Civic Clb; EQB; r/Epis; hon/Phi Delta Phi; Dist'd Ser Awd (Fgn Awd), Dept of St, 1954-63; W/W in Am.

BAKER, BONNIE TAYLOR oc/ County Historian; b/Jan 6, 1909; h/201 Flora Lane, Alma, GA 31510; ba/Alma, GA; m/Fred; p/Nick and Flora Taylor, Bacon Co, GA; ed/Att'd S GA Col, Yg Harris Col, SEn Univ Sch of Acctg; pa/ Sch Tchr; Sect Chief, Securities & Exch Comm; Sect Chief & Sys Anal, Civil Ser Comm; Lic Ofcr, Dept of Commerce; Asst Exec Dir, Housing Auth; Co-Fdr & Dir, Hist Soc; Histn; The Pilot Clb; Ret'd Tchrs of Bacon Co; Editor, *The Securities & Exch Comm Newslttr*; cp/ The John Floyd Chapt, DAR; Wom's Aux, Am Legion & VFW; r/Adm Bd, Alma U Meth Ch; hon/Author Num Pubs; *The ABC's of Fam Trees, A Guide to Geneal Res*, *Hist of Camp Ground Meth Ch*, *Bacon Co, GA*, *Hist of Pine Grove Meth Ch*, *Bacon Co, GA*, *"Bacon Bits"*, *A Look Backward* into Bacon Co's Past, A Short Hist of Bacon Co, GA, Taylor-Tuten & Allied Fams, A Geneal, Marked Graves in Bacon Co Cemeteries as of 1969, except the Rose Hill Cemetery of Alma, GA, Lee's of Bacon Co, descendants of James & Cinderella Sellars Lee's 13 chd; 2 Certs of Awds from the Dept of Comm, 1947; Liston Elkin Awd for Commun Ser for SE GA, 1982; W/W: in S & SW, of Am Wom; Intl Register of Profiles.

BAKER, CLAIRE J oc/Poet, Playwright, Secretary; b/Sep 27, 1927; h/2451 Church Lane #47, San Pablo, CA 94806; ba/Emeryville, CA; p/Walter Henry Baker, Walnut Creek, CA; ed/Grad, Greenbrier Jr Col; pa/Secy, Workmen's Compensation Ins Div & Resource for Cancer Epidemiology, St of CA, 18 Yrs; Secy, Diablo-Alameda Br, Nat Leag of Am Pen Wom, 1983-84; Secy, Poetry Org for Wom, 1983-84; Bd of Dirs: INA Coolbrith CR & Alameda Poets, 1983-84; Poetry Soc of Am; CA Writers Clb; Bay Area Poets Coalition; Nat Leag of Am Pen Wom; Others; cp/Promoter, Poetry Landmarks; Co-Sponsor, Intl Peace Poems Contest; Judge, Chm of Contests, Coor of Wkshops & Lectrs; Orig Poetry & Slides Prog, Entitled "Touchings"; hon/Author 3 Books: Touchings; Dear Mother; Space On Ch Lane; Author of Several Plays incl'g: "Kim"; Co-Author Books (w Mary Rudge) incl'g: Collage of Wild Leaves; 2 Plays "Arrangements," & "Kim" Perf'd & Videotaped; Public Showing by Laney Col, 1983; Won Triton Medal for Poem "Old Man," 1976; W/W: of Wom, in Poetry.

BAKER, CON JACYN oc/Research Plant Pathologist; b/Jul 23, 1948; h/ 10773 Cordage Walk, Columbia, MD 21044; ba/USDA, Beltsville, MD; m/ Jane W; c/Frank H, Connie L; p/Con and Ethel Baker (dec); sp/Frank and Virginia Krantz, Ellicott City, MD; ed/BS Biochem, Univ of WI, 1969; PhD Plant Pathol, Cornell Univ, 1978; mil/USMC, 1970-72; pa/Res Asst, Cornell Univ Dept of Plant Pathol, 1978-79; Res Assoc, Univ of WI Dept of Plant Pathol, 1979-81; Res Assoc 1981-82, Res Plant Pathol 1982-, USDA, ARS, Beltsville, MD; Mem 1973-, Mem Disease Physiol Com 1984, Am Phytopathol Soc; Sigma Xi; Phi Kappa Phi; r/Epis; hon/Author & Co-Author, Over 25 Articles Pub'd in Profl Sci Jours; NSF Awd, Sum 1965; NIH Trainee, 1979; Phi Kappa Phi, 1971; Sigma Xi, 1978; Am Men & Wom of Sci; W/W in Frontier Sci & Technol.

BAKER, H KENT oc/Professor; b/ Nov 13, 1944; h/5816 Edson Lane, Rockville, MD 20852; ba/Washington, DC; m/Linda A; p/Ruby L Baker, Chesapeake, VA; sp/Mr and Mrs Jack Weitzel, Hersey, PA; ed/BSBA, Georgetown Univ, 1967; MBA 1969, DBA 1972, MEd 1974, Univ of MD; MS 1979, PhD 1983, The Am Univ; CFA, 1978; CMA, 1979; pa/Prof Fin, The Am Univ, 1975-; Asst Prof Fin, Georgetown Univ, 1972-75; Asst to Dean, Univ of MD, 1969-72; Mem: Bd of Dirs, The Am Univ Employee's Fed Credit Union, 1979-82; Am Fin Assn; Am Mgmt Assn; En Fin Assn; Fin Mgmt Assn; Wash Soc of Investmt Anals; cp/Chm of Bd, Chds TV Intl, 1979-; r/Meth; hon/Author, Over 100 Articles in Profl Jours incl'g: Harvard Bus Review; The Fin Review; Jour of Bk Res; Fin Mgmt; Others; Alpha Iota Delta; Alpha Sigma Nu; Beta Gamma Sigma; Danforth Assocs; Fin Mgmt Assn Hon

Soc; Phi Alpha Alpha; Phi Delta Kappa; Phi Kappa Phi; W/W: in E, in Fin & Indust.

BAKER, HERBERT GEORGE oc/ Professor; b/Feb 23, 1920; h/635 Creston Road, Berkeley, CA 94708; ba/ Berkeley, CA; m/Irene; c/Ruth Elaine; ed/BSc 1941, PhD Botany 1945, Univ of London; pa/Res Chem & Asst Plant Physiol, Hosa Res Labs, England, 1940-45; Botany Lectr, Univ of Leeds, England, 1945-53; Prof Botany, Univ of Gold Coast, 1954-57; Prof Botany 1957-, Dir of Univ Botanical Gardens 1957-69, Univ of CA-Berkeley; Pres, CA Botanical Soc, 1964; Pres, Soc for the Study of Evolution, 1969; Pres, Botanical Soc of Am, 1979; Pres 1983-84 Pacific Div, AAAS; Fellow, Am Acad of Arts & Scis, 1984; VPres 1964-69, Intl Assn of Botanical Gardens; hon/Author of Book, Plants & Civilization, 1964, 1971, 1978 (Translated into Spanish & Japanese); Series Editor of Botanical Monographs; Co-Editor, The Genetics of Colonizing Species; Over 162 Sci Papers Pub'd in Profl Jours; Dist'd Tchr Awd, Univ of CA, 1971; Mert Awd, Botanical Soc of Am, 1980; Fellow, Assn for Tropical Biol, 1982; W/W: in World, in Am, in W, in Frontier Sci & Technol.

BAKER, JOE BENNY oc/Minister; b/ Sep 18, 1948; ba/Garland, TX; m/Donna Lee; c/Cathy, Andrew, Jonathan, Tiffany; p/Mary Wilson, Corinth, MS; sp/ Bill Woods, Plainview, TX; ed/BA, Lubbock Christian Col, 1974; MA, Pepperdine Univ, 1980; MA, Abilene Christian Univ, 1982; mil/USN, 1967-71; pa/Min of Yth, 1974-1980; Asst to the Pres, MI Christian Col, 1975; Min of Yth & Staff Admr, 1980-; cp/ Chm, Citizen Yth Comm; r/Ch of Christ; hon/W/W in SW.

BAKER, JOHN FRANKLIN oc/Executive, Chairman of the Board; b/Oct 25, 1918; h/686 Wallace Drive, Wayne, PA 19087; ba/Philadelphia, PA; m/Edna Dole; c/Dole, Sandra Cressman; p/ Joseph and Almeda Baker, Ironton, OH; sp/John and Mary Dole, Ironton, OH; ed/BS Indust Engrg, OH St Univ, 1944; pa/Ptnr, Worden & Risberg, 1956-64; Pres, J Franklin Baker & Assoc, 1965-; Mem, AIIE; Reg'd Profl Engr, St of OH; Bd of Dirs: Dill Prods Co; Pequea Fishing Tackle Co; Concord Chem Co; Empress Hosiery Corp; Duby Corp; Bernville Mfg Co; Harley Chem Co; cp/ Repub Fin Comm, Chester Co, PA; Bd Mem, Ctl Bapt Ch; Union Leag of Phila; Masonic Lodge #198; Columbus Commandery #69; OES, Radnor Chapt 527; hon/Over 50 Profl Reports to Indust; Dist'd Ser Awd, Grandview Civic Assoc, 1956; Dist'd Alumni Awd, Dept of Indust Engrg, OH St Univ, 1975; Meritorious Ser Awd, Col of Engrg, OH St Univ, 1978; W/W: in E, in Am, in Fin & Indust.

BAKER, JOHN H oc/Electronics Engineer; b/Aug 1, 1917; h/6605 McCallum Street, Philadelphia, PA 19119; ba/ Philadelphia, PA; m/Lila M; c/Daisy P, Mildred E, John III; p/Joseph F and Pauline E Baker (dec); sp/Florence and Bonnie Black (dec); ed/BSc, Jackson Col, 1960; Att'd Univ of HI; Certs from: George Wash Univ; Villanova Univ; Temple Univ; Others; pa/Radio Mech 1942, Radio Engr 1945, Supvr Elect Engr 1952, Hd Spec Applications Sec Elect 1956, Pearl Harbor Nav Shipyard;

Spec Advr, US Embassy, Tokyo, Japan, 1957; Hd Metrology Lab 1960, Hd Undersea Warfare Div 1972, Dept EE O Ofcr 1974, Phila Nav Shipyard; Mem: IEEE; Nat Assn of Techs; Nav Civilian Admrs Assn; NAACP; Nat Assn Securities Dealers; Civil Air Patrol; cp/ Toastmasters Intl; U Supr Coun (33rd Deg Masons); Alt Mem, Mayor's Yth Comm, Phila; r/Presb; hon/Author of "Multiple Procedures on Precision Measurements in Elects"; US Nav Meritorious Civilian Awd, 1946.

BAKER, JOHN STEVENSON oc/ Author; b/Jun 18, 1931; ba/PO Box 16007, Minneapolis, MN 55416; p/ Everette B and Ione M Baker; ed/BA cum laude Ponoma Col, Claremont Cols, 1953; Univ of CA Sch of Med, 1957; pa/Nu Sigma Nu; Pub'd Poems; Fiction: The Diary of Sesso-Vesucci, Trace; Mister Carcoleotes, The Human Voice Qtly; Articles: "Comml Sources for Hart Crane's The River," WI Studies in Contemp Lit; "Brief on Hart Crane & The Artists of Tech," Trace; "LeRoi Jones, Secessionist & Ambiguous Collecting," & "Criteria for 1st Printings of LeRoi Jones," The Yale Univ Lib Gazette; Misc: Review of The Shape of Content, Design Qtly; Cliches, Trace; Psych: The Jour of Aesthetics & Art Crit; Dir Exhbn & Author of Catalog for Mpls Inst of Arts; Co-Author: "Electrógrams During Hypoxia in Hlthy Men," "Electrograms During Hypercapnia," Pub'd in Archives of Neurol; "A Stat Anal of 1 Yr of EEG in an Active 226 Bed Gen Hosp" & "An EEG Anal of 99 Hd Injuries in a 226 Bd Gen Hosp," Abstracts of Papers Electroencephalography & Clin Neurophysiol; hon/1st Prize, Jennings Eng Prize, 1950, Pomona Col, Claremont Cols; Dist'd Ser Awd, 1976, MN St Hort Soc; Donations: Brahms Recordings to Bennington Col; Wild Plants to MN Landscape Arboretum; Num Others.

BAKER, LILLIAN oc/Editor, Layout Artist, Author, Historian; b/Dec 12, 1921; h/15237 Chanera Avenue, Gardena, CA 90249; ba/Gardena, CA; m/ Roscoe Albert; c/Wanda G, George Riley; ed/Grad Cert, Famous Writers Sch; Col Course Credits: Univ of CA-LA; LA Harbor Col; Var Ext Courses, Wkshops & Sems Credits; 4 Wking S'ships, Art Students Leag; Sum S'ship, Univ of NM; Misc Course Credits, El Camino Col; pa/Fdr & Editor, Intl Clb For Collectors of Hatpins & Hatpin Holders, 1977-; Profl Author, Layout Artist, Editor, Freelance Writer for Newslttr, Points & Semi-annual, Pictorial Jour; S Bay Chm for S I Hayakawa's US Senate Campaign, 1976; Fashion Show Dir, & Dist Dir, Emmons Jewelry Co, Newark, NY St (for W Coast), 1952-60; Columnist & Contbr, Gardena Val News, CA, 1964-76; Continuity Writer, WINS (NY), 1945-46; Profl Pub'd Author, 1964-; Editor & Layout Artist, Neighborhood Watch Newslttr, 1983-; Mem: The Nat Writers Clb; The Nat Leag of Am Pen Wom; Former Pres & Fdg Mem, The Torrance Art Grp; Fdrs, S Bay Art Assn; Co-Fdr, Ams for Hist Accuracy; Life Mem, Art Students Leag, NYC; Fdg Mem, The Nat Hist Soc (Gettysburg, 1970) & The Nat Trust for Historic Presv (Decatur House, Wash, DC 1968); cp/W Coast Chm, The Com for Equality for All Draftees; Num Orgnl, Polit, TV & Radio Spkg Appearances; hon/Author of Num Books, Articles & Poetry Pub'd incl'g: *Creat & Collectible Miniatures*, 1984; *Insider Newslttr*, 1983-84; *Hatpins & Hatpin Holders: An Identification & Value Guide*, 1983; *War-Torn Wom*, 1981; *Art Nouveau & Art Deco Jewelry*, 1981 & 1983; *100 Yrs of Collectible Jewelry: 1850-1950*, 4th Printing 1983; Others; *The Concentration Camp Conspiracy: A 2nd Pearl Harbor* 1981, was Awded Conf of CA Hist Socs Awd (Scholastic Category) for Book & Contbns to CA Hist, 1983; Testimony of Hist Significance Presented before 2 US Senate Subcoms which Influenced the Change in Legis, Thus Saving US Taxpayers Over 9 Billion Dollars.

BAKER, PETER MITCHELL oc/High Technology Executive; b/Jul 18, 1939; h/Marina Del Rey, CA 90292; ba/Same; m/Evelyne C Baker; p/George & Clarisse Baker, Dorset, England; sp/Jacques & Yvette Giraud, Boulogne, France; ed/ N HC Elect & Control Sys, 1960; BSc Physics, Univ of London, 1963; pa/Sr Physicist, Itek Corp, 1966-69; Sr VPres, Micronetics Inc, 1969-74; Physics & Math Tchr, Nairobi, Kenya, 1975-77; Pres & CEO, Quantrad Corp, Torrance, CA, 1977-; Treas & Dir, Laser Inst of Am; Mem Elect Mfg Coun, Chm Laser & Electro Optics, Soc of Mfg Engrs; Num Intl Sems & Papers on Optics in Space; Applications of Laser Sys, Automation & Productivity; W/W in Fin & Indust.

BAKER, RAYMOND E (MIKE) oc/ Executive; b/Sep 24, 1947; h/125 Maple St, Brookfield, MO 64628; ba/Brookfield, MO; m/Carol Warnock; c/Ashley, Brooke; p/R E and Helen Baker (dec); ed/BA, Westminster Col; pa/VPres 1969-76, Pres 1976-85, Pepsi-Cola Bottling Co; Former Treas, Pres, MO Pepsi-Cola Assn; Dir, MO Soft Drink Assn; Chm Com, Nat Peps-Cola Assn; cp/Pres, Brookfield C of C 1972-73; Pres, Brookfield Country Clb, 1977-78; Pres, Brookfield Rotary Clb, 1978-79; Del, Dem Nat Conv; r/Presb, Treas & Ruling Elder; hon/Outstg Yg Man of Am; W/W: in MO, in Am Polits, in MW, in Fin & Indust.

BAKER, ROBERT HART oc/Orchestra Music Director; b/Mar 19, 1954; h/ 129 Evelyn Place, Asheville, NC 28801; ba/Greenwich, CT; p/Lee Baker (dec); Jeanne Baker, Whitestone, NY; ed/AB cum laude, Harvard Col, 1974; MM 1976, MMA 1978, Yale Sch of Music; pa/Music Dir, CT Philharm Orch; Conductor, Asheville Symph; cp/ ASCAP; IDRS; Harvard Clbs of NY & Wn NC; Am Symph Orch Leag; hon/ Contemp Music Prog'g Awd, ASCAP, 1981; McCord Book Prize, Harvard Col, 1974.

BAKER, VICTOR RICHARD oc/ Professor; b/Feb 19, 1945; h/6164 East Paseo Cimarron, Tucson, AZ 85715; ba/ Tucson, AZ; m/Pauline Marie; c/Trent Heaton, Theodore William; p/Victor A Baker (dec); sp/Herbert Heaton; ed/BS, Rensselaer Polytech Inst, 1967; PhD, Univ of CO, 1971; mil/USAR, Capt; pa/ Geophysicist, US Geol Surv, Denver, 1967-69; City Geol, Boulder, CO 1969-71; Asst Prof Geol Scis 1971-76, Assoc Prof 1976-81, Univ of TX-Austin; Prof Geoscis 1981-, Prof Planetary Scis 1982-, Univ of AZ; Sigma Xi; AAAS; Am Geophy Union; Intl Assn of Sedimentologists; Fellow 1976-, VChm Planetary Geol 1984, Com For Geol & Public Policy 1980-83, Geol Soc of Am;

hon/Author of Book, *The Channels of Mars*, 1982; Editor; *Catastrophic Flooding*, 1981; *Surficial Geol*, 1981; *The Channeled Scabland*, 1978; *Paleohydrology & Sedimentology of Lake Missoula Flooding*, 1973; Fulbright-Hays Sr Res Scholar, Australian Nat Univ, 1979-80; W/W: in W, in Am Men & Wom of Sci, in Frontier Sci & Technol; Contemp Authors.

BAKER, WILLIAM OLIVER oc/ Chairman of the Board, AT&T Bell Labs (Retired); b/Jul 15, 1915; h/Spring Valley Road, Morristown, NJ 07960; ba/ Murray Hill, NJ; m/Frances Burrill; c/ Joseph; p/Harold & Helen Stokes Baker (dec); sp/(dec); ed/BS, Wash Col, 1935; PhD Phy Chem, Princeton Univ, 1938; Over 20 Hon Doct Degs from Num Univs; pa/Ret'd Chm of Bd, AT&T Bell Labs; Trustee: Chm, Rockefeller Univ; Chm, Andrew W Mellon Foun; Carnegie-Mellon Univ; Bd of Overseers, Col of Engrg & Applied Sci, Univ of PA & Princeton Univ; The Harry Frank Guggenheim Foun; The Fund for NJ; Gen Motors Cancer Res Foun; The Newark Mus; The Charles Babbage Inst; Dir: Annual Reviews Inc; Coun on Lib Resources; Summit & Elizabeth Trust Co; Summit Bancorp; Johnson & Johnson; Hlth Effects Inst; Gen Am Investors; Num Other Affils; Fellow: Am Phy Soc; Am Inst of Chems; The Franklin Inst; Mem: Am Chem Soc; Am Phil Soc; Dirs of Industl Res; Industl Res Inst; Sigma Xi; Omicron Delta Kappa; Phi Lambda Upsilon; Hon Mem, The Chems' Clb NY; Num Other Orgs & Coms; cp/Cosmos Clb of Wash DC; Princeton Clb of NWn NJ; Num Others; hon/Author & Contbr, Over 100 Profl Books & Jours incl'g: *The Random House Ency*; *Annual Review of Mats Sci*; *Jour Am Chem Soc*; *Jour Chem Physics*; *Jour Applied Physics*; Num Others; Over 20 Lectr Presentations; Num Other Spkg Presentations; Holder of 13 Patents in Field; Nat Security Medal, 1981; Sarnoff Prize, Armed Forces Communs & Elects Assn, 1981; Jefferson Medal, NJ Patent Law Assn, 1981; Vanevar Bush Awd, NSF, 1981; Madison Marshall Awd 1980, Willard Gibbs Medal 1978, Parsons Awd 1976, Am Chem Soc; Industl Res Man of Yr Awd, 1973; Gold Medal, Am Inst of Chems, 1975; Num Others Awds; W/W: in Am, in World, in Fin & Indust, in Engrg; Num Other Biogl Listings.

BAKSHI, PRADIP M oc/Professor; b/ Aug 21, 1936; h/122 Florence Road, Waltham, MA 02154; ba/Chestnut Hill, MA; m/Hansika; c/Vaishali, Ashesh; ed/ BSc, Bombay Univ, 1955; AM 1957, PhD 1962, Harvard Univ; pa/Postdoct Fellow, Harvard Univ, 1963; Res Physicist, AF Cambridge Res Labs, 1963-66; Sr Res Assoc 1966-68, Vis'g Assoc Prof 1968-70, Dept of Physics, Brandeis Univ; Res Assoc Prof 1970-75, Res Prof 1975-, Dept of Physics, Boston Col; hon/ Author of Var Articles Pub'd in Profl Sci Jours; W/W: in E, in Frontier Sci & Technol.

BALASSA, BELA oc/Professor, Consultant; b/Apr 6, 1928; h/2134 Wyoming Avenue, Northwest, Washington, DC 20008; ba/Baltimore, MD; m/Carol Anne; c/Mara, Gabor; p/George Balassa, Budapest, Hungary; sp/Samuel Levy, Camarillo, CA; ed/Diplomkaufmann, Acad for Fgn Trade, Budapest, 1946-48; Doct iuris rerumque politicarum, Univ

of Budapest, 1946-51; MA Ec 1959, PhD Ec 1959, Yale Univ; pa/Asst & Assoc Prof, Yale Univ, 1959-67; Prof Polit Economy, Johns Hopkins Univ, 1967-; Conslt, World Bk, Wash DC, 1966-; Conslt, Intl Orgs, Devel Country Govts, 1966-; Pres 1970-71 & 1979-80, Assn of Comparative Ec; hon/Author of 12 Books incl'g: *Change & Challenge in the World Economy*; *Devel Strategies in Semi-Industl Countries*; *European Ec Integration*; *Theory of Ec Integration*; *The Hungarian Experience in Ec Planning*; Prix Rossi, Institut de France, Paris, 1981; Bernhard Harms Prize, Inst of World Ec, Kiel, 1984; W/W: in Am, in Ec.

BALASUBRAHMANYAN, VRIDDAACHALAM K oc/Astrophysicist; b/ Nov 11, 1926; h/9333 Wellington Street, Seabrook, MD 20706; ba/Greenbelt, MD; m/B Saroja; c/B Ravishankar; B Raghu; ed/PhD Physics, 1961; pa/ Fellow, Tata Inst of Fundamtl Res, Bombay, India, 1962-; Res Res Assoc, NSF, 1962-65; Astrophysicist, NASA, Godard Spaceflight Ctr, 1965-; Mem: Am Phy Soc; Am Geophy Union; r/ Hindu; hon/Author, Over 50 Papers on Cosmic Ray Composition & Solar Sys Physics Pub'd in Profl Sci Jours; W/W in Sci.

BALDERSTON, JEAN MERRILL oc/ Psychotherapist, Poet; b/Aug 29, 1936; h/1225 Park Avenue, New York, NY 10028; ba/Same; m/David; p/Frederick and Helen Merrill, Saco, ME; ed/BA, Univ of CT; MA, EdD, Columbia Univ; pa/Psychotherapy, Pvt Pract, 1971-; Univ Tchg Psychol 1965-71: Douglass Col for Wom; Rutgers Univ; Montclair St Col; Hunter Col; Queens Col; Columbia Univ; Edit Staff, *NY Qtly*, 1971-76; Mem: Am Psychol Assn; Am Assn Marriage & Fam Cnslrs; Poets & Writers; The Poetry Soc of Am; Emily Dickinson Soc; AmScandinavian Foun; Am Scandinvaian Soc; r/Prot; hon/ Author of Poems Pub'd in Num Lit Mags & Anthologies; W/W: in NE, in Commun Ser, of Am Wom, DIB.

BALDOCK, EDGAR C oc/Child Therapist; b/Oct 23, 1902; h/2260 Maywood Avenue, San Jose, CA 95128; ba/San Jose, CA; m/Agnes M; c/Alan, Mrs Joan Williamson; ed/Grad, Tchr's Tng Col, 1923; BA, Ec & Ed, Univ of New Zealand, 1929; Grad Study Course Wk for MA, Univ of IA, 1937; Grad Wk at George Warren Brown Sch of Social Wk, 1938; MSW, Univ of Denver, 1946; MEd Cand, OR St Univ; mil/Territorials, New Zealand; pa/Pupil Tchr, Beckenham Sch, Christchurch, New Zealand, 1920-21; Asst Master, Phillipstown Sch, Christchurch, New Zealand, 1924-26; Sr Asst Master, Primary Dept, Motueka Dist HS, Motueka, Nelson, New Zealand, 1927-28; Asst Master, Kariori Sch Wellington, 1929; Hd Tchr, Maraenui Native Sch, Bay of Plenty, New Zealand, 1930-33; Hd Tchr, Oruanui Native Sch, Taupo, New Zealand, 1934-36; Boys' Welfare Ofcr, Ed Dept, Wellington, New Zealand, 1929; Visitor, St Louis Social Security Comm, 1938; Epidemiologist & Case Wkr, Provincial Clin for Control of VD, Vancouver, BC, Canada, 1938-40; Dist Secy Case Wkr, 1st Intake Secy, Big Brothers, Toronto, Canada, 1942-43; Supt Frazer Detention Home, 1943-46; Cnslr, Cnslg & Testing Bur, OR St Col, 1946-47; Case Wkr, Home of Benevolence, San Jose, CA, 1948-; Mem: Am Assn of Social Wkrs; Kappa Delta Pi, Nat Ednl Hon Soc; Com on Agy Function, Coun of Social Agys, San Jose; Assoc Mem, Intl Assn for Child Psychi & Allied Professions; Num Others; hon/ Author of Num Articles incl'g: "The Therapeutic Relatship & Its Ramifications in Child Psychotherapy"; "Before a Child Sees the Cnslr"; "If Your Child is in Therapy"; "Chd in Therapy"; "In the Dark"; Others Pub'd in Profl Jours: *the Brit Jour of Psychi Social Wk; Understanding the Child; The Ednl Courier; VD Info*; Others; Kappa Delta Pi, OR St Univ; Fellow, Royal Soc of Hlth (England); W/ W: in W, in Commun Ser; DIB; Men of Achmt; Other Biogl Listings.

BALDONADO, ARDELINA ERIKA oc/Professor; b/May 18, 1936; h/1808 Dobson, Evanston, IL 60202; ba/Chicago, IL; m/Alfredo; c/Rozelda-Fredelyn, Bradshaw-Mark, Erika-Gina; p/Jovita and Rosalino Albano (dec); sp/Jacinto and Maria Baldonado; ed/BSN, 1959; MS, 1965; PhD, 1982; pa/Instr, Passarant Meml Hosp, 1965-70; Chm, Curric & Level II Fac, St Francis Hosp Sch Nsg, 1972; Nsg Instr, Univ of IL, 1973-; Course Coor, Level I & II, Loyola Univ Sch of Nsg, 1982; Assoc Prof, Loyola Univ, 1984; Mem: Am Ednl Res Assrs; ANA; ANA Coun of Nurse Rschrs; Philippine Nurses Assn; Res on Wom Edrs; Nat Leag for Nsg; cp/Cath Wom's Guild; IL Parents; PTA; r/Cath; hon/ Author of Book, *Cancer Nsg: A Holistic Multidisciplinary Approach*, 1978 & 1982; Author of Var Articles incl'g: "Creat Tchg & Lrng"; "Accountability: Issues & Solutions"; Others; Valedictorian, 1955; College Scholar, 1956-58; University Scholar, 1955; Sigma Theta Tau; W/W: in Am Nursing, in Frontier Science & Technology.

BALDWIN, JOAN BOLLING oc/ Government Policy Administrator; b/ Aug 31, 1930; h/1309 Trinity Drive, Alexandria, VA 22314; ba/Washington, DC; m/Donald Winston; c/Winston Monroe, Elizabeth Bolling, Alan Henry; p/Henry Cecil Bolling (dec); Nelle M Bolling, Norton, VA; sp/Robert J Baldwin (dec); Sabra R Baldwin, Key West, FL; ed/AB, Hollins Col, 1953; MA, Univ of VA, 1955; pa/Press & Res Asst, Senator Len B Jordan (Repub, ID), 1962-64; Res Asst, Repub Nat Com, 1964; Polit Res, James N Juliana Assoc, 1965-69; Legis Asst, Senator James B Pearson (Repub, KS), 1969-71; Spec Asst to Asst Secy of Hlth Ed & Welfare, 1971-73; Pre-profl Staff Mem & Dept Dir, GOP Policy Com, 1973-; cp/Treas, "The Twig," Jr Aux of Alexandria Hosp; Mem, Senate Staff Clb; r/Anglican; hon/Author, Num Articles Pub'd in *The Congl Record*; Others; Contbr, Parts of 1980 Repub Party Platform; W/W: in Am Wom, in Wash; Congl Staff Dir.

BALDWIN, JOHN DAVID oc/Professor; b/Jun 24, 1941; h/5050 East Camino Cielo, Santa Barbara, CA 93105; ba/Santa Barbara; m/Janice I; p/ Mr and Mrs Herman Baldwin, Cinc, OH; sp/Walter Whiteside, Santa Barbara, CA; ed/BA 1963, PhD 1967, The Johns Hopkins Univ; pa/Asst Prof 1967-72, Assoc Prof 1972-78, Prof 1978-, Dept Sociol, Univ of CA-Santa Barbara; hon/Author of 3 Books: *The Gt Upward Force; Behavior Principles in Everyday*

Life; Beyond Sociobiol; Num Articles & Chapts; Prof of Yr, The Univ Affils, 1981-82; Prof of Yr, Mortar Bd Soc, 1982-83.

BALFOUR, LINDA FRIER oc/Administrator; b/Mar 29, 1944; h/203 Northwood Drive, Chapel Hill, NC 27514; ba/ Chapel Hill, NC; m/Robert F Hill Jr; c/ James Burton; p/Robert Henry and Ina Loyce (Riley) Frier, Franklin, TX; sp/ Robert F and Antilee (Dinkins) Hill, High Point, NC; ed/BBA, SWn Univ, 1966; Postgrad Study: NC St Univ, 1968; Univ of NC-Chapel Hill, 1982; pa/ Dir of Data Collection & Reporting 1972-, Social Res Assoc 1977-78, Soc Res Asst 1973-77, Univ of NC Sys; Statl Anal 1968-73, Secy 1967-68, NC Bd of Higher Ed; Tchr, Franklin HS, 1966-67; Mem Exec Com 1978-82, NC Assoc Instnl Res; Mem, NC St Employees Assn; cp/Mem Exec Com 1983-, Nat Foun of Ileitis & Colitis; hon/Pub'd Articles in: *Statl Abstracts of Higher Ed in NC*, 1967-; *Higher Ednl Oppors in NC*, 1967; W/W of Am Wom.

BALINSKY, DORIS oc/Professor; b/ Dec 3, 1934; h/3003 Oakwood Road, Ames, IA 50010; ba/Ames, IA; m/John Boris (dec); c/Andrew Paul, Martin George; p/Else Goldschmidt, London, England; sp/Boris I Balinsky, Johannesburg, S Africa; ed/BSc 1955, BSc Hons 1956, Univ of Witwatersrand, Johannesburg, S Africa; PhD, Univ of London, 1959; pa/Hd Enzyme Unit, S African Inst for Med Res, Johannesburg, S Africa, 1960-76; Sr Res Assoc, Columbia Univ Col of Phys & Surgs, NY, 1975-76; Adj Assoc Prof, Adj Prof Biochem, IA St Univ, IA, 1976-; Mem: Am Soc Biol Chems; Am Assn Cancer Res; Sigma Xi; Iota Sigma Pi; hon/ Author of 81 Articles Pub'd in Profl Sci Jours; Rebecca Lurie Brown Prize (Botany), 1975; AAUW Postdoct Fellow, 1968-69; Witwatersand Coun of Ed Fellow, 1957-59; W/W in Frontier Sci & Technol.

BALL, ROBERT J oc/Professor; b/ Nov 4, 1941; ba/Dept European Langs & Lit, Univ of HI, Honolulu, HI 96822; p/William and Pauline Ball, Floral Park, NY; ed/BA, Queens Col, 1962; MA, Tufts Univ, 1963; PhD, Columbia Univ, 1971; pa/Prof of Classics, 1983-; Col of Arts & Scis Fac Senates; Fdr & Chm, Soc Augustan Poetry (Am Philological Assn); Chm Classics Div, Univ of HI; hon/Author of 2 Books: *Tibullus The Elegist: A Crit Survey*, 1983; *The Classical Papers of Gilbert Highet*, 1983; Excell in Tchg Awd, Univ of HI, 1979; Excell in Tchg Awd, Am Philological Assn, 1981.

BALL, ROBERT MONTAGUE qc/ Surveyor; b/Jan 4, 1933; h/140 Colonial Drive, Perkiomenville, PA 18074; ba/ Schwenksville, PA; m/Barbara Jean; c/ John, Gidget, Robert, Ronald, Mary; p/ John D and Genevieve T Ball (dec); sp/ John and Louise Sills, Brownsville, TN; ed/Assoc in Engrg, PA St Univ, 1962; mil/USMC, 1952-55; pa/Proj Supvr Photogrammetric Engrg, Aero Ser Corp, Phila, PA, 1955-63; Chief Field Opers, Mgr Property Plat Div, A W Martin Inc, King of Prussia, PA, 1963-66; Mgr Field Survey Dept, Treas of Corp, F X Ball Assoc Inc, Schwenksville, PA, 1966-; Mem: WV Land Surveyors Assn; Surveying & Mapping Soc of GA; Fellow, Am Cong of Surveying & Mapping; cp/Dir, Lower Perkiomen

Val Ftball Assn; Dir, St Pius X Ath Assn; r/Rom Cath; hon/Reg'd Profl Surveyor: PA, WV & GA; Reg'd Sewage Enforcement Ofcr, PA; Cert of Attainment in Commun Planning, Public Ser Inst of PA; W/W in E.

BALLARD, GEORGE HENRY III oc/ Executive; b/Aug 23, 1952; h/1001 East Sedgwick Street, Philadelphia, PA 19150; ba/Philadelphia, PA; m/Debra Louise Harris; c/Sean, George IV; p/ George Jr and Nancy Ballard, Phila, PA; sp/Robert and Rose Chapman, Phila, PA; ed/BS Ec, The Wharton Sch, Univ of PA, 1974; pa/Asst to Economists, Fed Resv Bk of Phila, 1969-74; Prog Acct, Gen Elect Co, 1974-77; Dir Fin, U Way Agy, PCCA, 1977-78; Asst Treas, Chief Exec Ofcr, Am Bapt Chs in USA; Mem: Intl Platform Assn; The Wharton Sch Clb; Bd Mem, Rel Conv Mgrs Assn; Audit Com, Nat Coun of Chs; Fin Resource Grp, World Coun of Chs; r/ Bapt; hon/W/W: Among Am HS Students, in Fin & Indust, in World; Outstg Yg Men of Am.

BALLARD, MARGUERITE CANDLER oc/Hematologist; b/Jun 20, 1920; h/3092 Argonne Drive, Northwest, Atlanta, GA 30305; ba/Atlanta, GA; m/ George Speights Jr; p/Asa Warren and Hattie Lee West Candler (dec); sp/ George Speights Sr and Willie Maude Benton Ballard (dec); ed/AB, Vassar Col, 1942; MS 1943, MD 1948, Emory Univ; mil/USPHS; pa/Career Ofcr & Med Dir, USPHS, Ctrs for Disease Control, Atlanta, GA, 1954-; r/Epis; hon/Atlanta's Wom of Yr in the Professions, 1972; Meritorious Ser Medal, USPHS, 1977.

BALLARD, PATRICIA MAE oc/ Administrator; b/Jun 13, 1945; h/Route 1, Berea, KY 40403; ba/Berea, KY; p/ Alonzo Wilson and Fannie Louise Ballard, Berea, KY; ed/BA, Berea Col, 1967; pa/Social Wkr, Dept Ec Security, KY St Govt, 1968-74; Field Ofc Supvr, Cabinet for Human Resources, Dept of Social Sers, Berea, KY, 1974-; Mem: KY Human Sers Assn, 1979-; Nat & KY Fdns of BPW, 1980-; Chp Legis Com 1982-, Berea BPW Clb; Adv Bd, Prospect House Chds Home, 1982-; Madison Co Salvation Army Emer Ser Unit, 1980-; Adv Bd, MEPCO Home Hlth Agy, 1981-; Adv Bd, Berea Col Students for Appalachia, 1979-80; Human Relats Com, KY River Foothils Devel Coun, 1980-82; Adv Com, Open Concern Clothing, 1973-74; Adv Bd, Nat Title XX & KY Title XX; Num Others; cp/ VPres, Berea Area Ch Wom U; Past Pres Yth Dept, New Liberty Bapt SS Conv, 1961-63; Bd of Dirs, Mtn Maternal Hlth Leag, 1979-81; Instnl Rep, BSA, 1971-76; Prog Dir, Trans Vol & Rec Vol, Ctl Commun Ctr, Berea, 1969-78; Others; r/Bapt; hon/Hon Secy, St Commonwlth of KY, 1983; W/W of Am Wom; Outstg Yg Wom of Am.

BALLARD, ROBERT DUANE oc/ Scientist; b/Jun 30, 1942; h/538 Hatchville Road, Hatchville, MA 02536; ba/ Woods Hole, MA; m/Marjorie C; c/Todd Alan, Douglas Matthew; p/Chester and Harriette Ballard; ed/BS Chem/Geol, Univ of CA-Santa Barbara, 1960-65; Oceanography, Univ of HI, 1965-66; Marine Geol & Geophysics, Univ of So CA, 1966-67; PhD Marine Geol & Geophysics, Univ of RI, 1970-74; mil/ US Army, 1965-67; USN, 1967-70; pa/ NSF S'ship, Scripps Inst of Oceanography, 1959; Deep Submersible Engrg 1961, N Am Aviation, Ocean Sys Opers, 1966-67; Res Assoc Ocean Engrg Dept, Deep Submergence Grp 1969-74, Asst Sci Geol & Geophysics Dept 1974-76, Assoc Sci Geol & Geophysics Dept 1976-78, Assoc Sci Ocean Engrg Dept 1978-79, Assoc Sci Ocean Engrg Dept 1980-83, Sr Sci & Ldr Deep Submergence Lab, Ocean Engrg Dept 1983-, Woods Hole Oceanographic Instn; Pvt Conslt, RSC Industs Inc, Wash DC, 1970-71; Vis'g Scholar Geol Dept 1979-80, Consltg Prof Geol Dept 1980-81, Stanford Univ; Pvt Conslt, Benthos Inc, N Falmouth, MA, 1982-83; Dir, OEMC, 1982-; Pres, Deep Ocean Search & Survey Inc, 1983-; Conslt Dept Chief Nav Opers for Submarine Warfare, 1984-; Conslt, Marine Bd Nat Res Coun, Comm on Engrg & Tech Sys, 1984-; Mem: Geol Soc of Am; Marine Technol Soc; Explorers Clb; Am Geophys Union; r/Prot; hon/Author & Co-Author, Over 40 Articles & Sci Papers Pub'd in Profl Jours; Num Pop Articles; Author of Book, *Exploring Our Living Planet*, 1983; Co-Author of Book, *Photo Atlas of Mid-Atl Ridge Rift Val*, 1977; Recip, Sci Awd, Underwater Soc of Am, 1976; Compass Dist'd Achmt Awd, Marine Technol Soc, 1977; Newcomb Cleveland Prize, AAAS, 1981; Cutty Sark Sci Awd & *Sci Digest*, 1982; W/W: in E, in Frontier Sci & Technol; W's Where Among Writers; Am Men & Wom of Sci; Contemp Authors.

BALLHAUS, WILLIAM FRANCIS JR oc/Research Director; b/Jan 28, 1945; ba/Moffett Field, CA; m/Jane Kerber Hamblet; c/William Louis, Michael Frederick, Benjamin Joel, Jennifer Angela; p/William Francis and Edna A Ballhaus, Yorba Linda, CA; sp/Frank O and Lillian M Kerver, Los Altos, CA; ed/BSME 1967, MSME 1968, PhD Engrg 1971, Univ of CA-Berkeley; mil/ USAR, 1968-76, Capt; pa/Dir 1984-, Dir of Astronautics 1980-84, Chief Applied Computational Aerodynamics Br 1979-80, NASA-Ames Res Ctr, Moffett Field, CA; Res Sci, US Army Aviation Res & Devel Command & NASA-Ames Res Ctr, 1971-79; Fellow, Mem Bd of Dirs, AIAA; Mem, Am Astronautical Soc; Pi Tau Sigma; Fellow, Royal Aeronaut Soc; Bd of Govs, Nat Space Clb; r/Cath; hon/ Author of 39 Sci Articles (on Computational Fluid Dynamics) Pub'd; H Julian Allen Awd for Outstg Paper Pub'd by Ames Research Center Staff Mem, 1977; Lawrence Sperry Awd, AIAA, 1980; Arthur S Flemming Awd for Outstg Government Service, 1980; W/ W in Technology Today.

BALLINGER, PAMELA ROSE WERDER oc/Education Coordinator, Psychologist; b/Oct 28, 1947; h/154 Bayberry Road, Versailles, KY 40383; ba/Frankfort, KY; m/Wayne; c/Shari L & Tobey L; p/John J Werder Jr (dec); Edna M Werder, Jeffersontown, KY; sp/ Johnnie & Beulah Ballinger, Richmond, KY; BS 1969, MS 1971, Psych, Murray St Univ; PhD Exptl Psych, TX Tech Univ, 1975; pa/Support Sers/Tng Coor, Div of Mtl Retard, Dept for Mtl Hlth & Mtl Retard, Cabinet for Human Resources, Frankfort, KY, 1981-; Prog Dir, Lrng & Habilitation Sers, En St Hosp, Lexington, 1977-81; Devel Disabilities Dir, Cave Run Comprehensive Care Ctr, Morehead, KY, 1976-77; Staff

Psych, Univ of KY Human Devel Prog, 1975-76; Res Asst 1972-74, TX Tech Univ; Res Asst, Murray St Univ, 1969-71; Previous Tchg Experience; Am Assn on Mtl Deficiency: Treas 1977 & 1978, Pres-elect 1979, Pres 1980, Nom'g Com & Mbrship CoChm 1981, KY Chapt; Exec Com 1980, Nom'g Com 1980, Chp Psych Div 1981 & 1982, SEn Reg; Mem: Am Psychol Assn; Nat Assn for Retarded Citizens; Lic'd Psychol, KY Bd of Psychols; Participant in Over 10 Profl Wkshops; hon/Author & Co-Author, Over 12 Papers & Articles Pub'd in Profl Jours; W/W: in S & SW, in Am Wom, in Am, of Wom; Dir Dist'd Ams; Personalities of Am.

BALTER, ALAN N oc/Musician; Music Director, Conductor; b/Mar 17, 1945; h/327 Dumbarton Road, Baltimore, MD 21212; ba/Memphis, TN; p/ Mr and Mrs Sidney H Balter, Roslyn Hgts, NY; ed/BA Math 1966, BMus 1966, Oberlin Col; MMus, Cleveland Inst of Music; pa/Prin Clarinet, Conducting Asst, Atlanta Symph, 1967-75; Music Dir, Atlanta Chamber Orch, 1971-75; Dir Orch Prog, Conducting Prog of Clarinet Dept, SF Conservatory of Music, 1975-79; Exxon Arts Endowment Conductor, Balto Symph, 1979-82; Assoc Conductor, Balto Symph, 1982-84; Music Dir, Akron Symph, 1983; Mus Dir, Memphis Symph, 1984-; Pvt Clarinet Tchr, 1965-; Mem: Conductors Guild, 1981-; Intl Clarinet Soc, 1979-; Bd of Dirs 1981-, Clarinetwk; Am Symph Orch Leag, 1977-; Am Fedn of Musicians; hon/ Author of *Self-Expression & Conducting: The Humanities*, 1978; Prodr, Music Dir, Conductor, TV Concert for Yg People, 1982; Recip, MD Chd's Prog Awds Com Awd, 1982; Awd Grant, NEA, 1966; 1st Prize, Intl Concours of Conductors, 1976; Exxon Arts Endowment Conducting Fellow, 1979; W/W: in Am Music, in Am.

BAMBURG, JAMES R oc/Professor; b/Aug 20, 1943; h/2125 Sandstone Drive, Ft Collins, CO 80524; ba/Ft Collins, CO; c/Eric, Leslie; p/Leslie H Bamburg (dec); Rose A Bamburg; ed/ BS Chem, Univ of IL-Urbana, 1965; PhD Biochem, Univ of WI-Madison, 1969; Proj Assoc, Univ of WI, 1968-69; Postdoct Fellow, Stanford Univ Med Sch, 1969-71; Asst Prof 1971-76, Assoc Prof 1976-81, Prof 1981-, Interim Chm Dept Biochem 1982-, CO St Univ; Vis'g Prof, MRC Lab Molecular Biol, Cambridge, England, 1978-79; Mem: Am Soc Bio Chems; Am Soc Cell Biol; Am Chem Soc; Intl Soc Neurochem; Sigma Xi; Gamma Alpha; hon/Author, Over 50 Papers & Articles Pub'd in Profl Jours; Over 20 Abstracts Pub'd; W H Peterson Predoct Fellow, 1968; Nat MS Soc Postdoct Fellow, 1969-71; J S Guggenheim Meml Fellow, 1978-79; NIH Study Sect, 1980-85; W/W.

BAME, SAMUEL J oc/Experimental Physicist; b/Jan 12, 1924; h/164 Dos Brazos, Los Alamos, NM 87544; ba/Los Alamos, NM; m/Joyce Fancher; c/Karen Joyce, Dorthe Ann, Barbara Joan; p/ Samual J Bame Sr (dec); sp/Carleton C Fancher (dec); ed/BS, Univ of NC-Chapel Hill, 1947; PhD, Rice Univ, 1951; mil/AUS, 1943-46; pa/Staff Mem 1951-81, Lab Fellow 1981-, Los Alamos Nat Lab; Mem: Fellow, AAAS; Am Astronom Soc; Fellow, Am Geophy

Union; Fellow, Am Phy Soc; hon/ Author & Co-Author Over 200 Space Sci Papers Pub'd; 1 of 1,000 Contemp Scists Most Cited, 1965-78; Phi Beta Kappa, UNC, 1947; NASA Grp Achmt Awds, 1979; Los Alamos Dist'd Perf Awd, 1980; W/W in Sci; Am Men & Wom in Sci.

BANDURSKI, BRUCE LORD oc/ Advisor; b/Jun 28, 1940; h/800 South Saint Asaph Street #203, Alexandria, VA 22314; p/Stanley Alexander Bandurski and Virginia VanRensselaer Hinckley; ed/BS w hons, Hons Col, MI St Univ, 1962; pa/On Secondment as Advr (Transboundary Monitoring Netwk) to US Sect, Intl Jt Comm, US & Canada; Former Positions incl: Fed Civil Ser as Mail Carrier, Smokechaser, Lookout, Pk Ranger, Sci Ref Anal, Intell Opers Spec, Survey Data Anal, Intell Opers Spec, Outdoor Rec Planner, Watch Dir & Dpty/Acting Mission Dir for US Man-in-the Sea Prog, Envir Review Ofcr, Coor of Fed Rec Fee Prog, Natural Resource Spec, Envir Spec, HQs Ofc Br Chief for Envir Planning & Coor, Nat Envir Policy Act Ofc; Fac Mem, USDA Grad Sch Evening Prog, 1968-; Charter Mem, Metro Wash Chapt, Ecol Soc of Am; cp/Pres, Outdoor Ethics Guild (advocating sys approach to probs of ecomgmt); hon/ Outstg Yg Men of Am, Men of Achmt, Intl W/W of Intells, DIB, Personalities of Am, Commun Ldrs of Am, Commun Ldrs of World.

BANDY, ANASTASIUS CONSTANTINE oc/Professor Emeritus; b/Aug 9, 1920; h/9 Appletree Court, Philadelphia, PA, 19106; m/Anastasia Kertiles; p/Constantine A Bandy and Paraskeve Drobonik; ed/AB, La Salle Col, 1951; AM 1954, PhD 1961, Univ of PA; pa/ German Instr, Villanova Univ, 1957-58; Acting Instr Classics 1959-60, Asst Prof Classics 1960-67, Assoc Prof 1967-71, Prof 1979-81, Univ of CA; Mem: Am Inst of Archaeol; Am Philological Assn; Am Soc of Papyrologists; Mod Greek Studies Assn; N Am Patristic Soc; US Nat Com for Byzantine Studies; r/ Greek Orthodox; hon/Author of 2 Books: *The Greek Christian Inscriptions of Crete*, 1970; *Ionnes Lydus: On Powers or the Magistracies of the Roman St*, 1983.

BANE, BERNARD MAURICE oc/ Publisher; b/Nov 23, 1924; h/854 Massachusetts Avenue, Cambridge, MA 02139; ba/Boston, MA; p/Julius and Rhoda (Trop) Bane (dec); ed/Att'd NEn Univ, 1946-48 & NEn Law Sch, 1948-49; pa/Sales & Mdsg, 1949-55; Sales & Mdsg, Ivy Leag Mixer Enterprise, Boston, 1955-65; Author & Publisher, The BMB Pub Co, 1965-; cp/Mem: Notary Public of MA, 1976-; Am Soc of Notaries, 1977-; r/Jewish/Hebrew; hon/Author & Publisher: *The Bane in Kennedy's Existence*, 1967; *Is Pres John F Kennedy Alive...and Well?*, 1973 & 1981; W/W: in Fin & Indust; in World; Men of Achmt; Personalities of E.

BANERJEE, KALI S oc/Professor; b/ Sep 1, 1914; h/1019 Stormont Circle, Baltimore, MD 21227; ba/Catonsville, MD; m/Niti; c/Deb K, Swapna Mukherjee; p/Heramba Ch and Raja Bala Banerjee (dec); sp/Kali M and Bibha Bati Chakraborty (dec); ed/BA Math 1935, MA Math 1937, PhD Stats 1950, Calcutta Univ; pa/Dpty Dir Stat, Statl Bur W Bengal, India, 1951-62; Addit Dir,

Devel & Planning, W Bengal Govt, 1966-68; Vis'g Assoc Prof, Cornell Univ, 1962-63; Vis'g Prof, KS St Univ, 1964-66 & 1968-69; Prof 1969-79, H Rodney Sharp Dist'd Prof 1975-79, Univ of DE; Sr Conslt, Aberdeen Proving Ground, 1979-80; Vis'g Prof, Univ of MD-Balto Co, 1980-; VPres, Calcutta Statl Assn; Assoc Editor, *Communs in Stats;* Var Others; r/Hindu; hon/Author, Over 90 Sci Res Articles Pub'd in Num Intl Profl Jours; Author of 3 Monographs; Fellow, Royal Statl Soc, London; Fellow, Am Statl Assn; Fellow, Inst of Math Stats; Fellow, AAAS; Mem by Secret Ballot, Intl Statl Inst; Excell in Tng Awd, 1972; Dist'd Sci Awd, Sigma Xi, 1975; Dist'd Prof, Univ of DE, 1975; Fulbright Travel Grant, 1962; NSF Grants 5 Times, 1964-74; Num Biogl Listings.

BANGART, GARY LEE oc/Aerospace Program Management; b/Oct 1, 1934; h/1146 Doon Court, Sunnyvale, CA 94087; ba/Sunnyvale, CA; m/Shirley Anne Young; c/Kurt Vaughn, Glenn Eric; p/David Robert Bangart, Culbertson, MT; Etta Mae Harvey, Bremerton, WA; sp/Henry Maxwell and Marie Smith, Palm Springs, CA; ed/BSEE, CA St Univ-San Jose, 1973; mil/USAF, 1953-57; pa/Elect Res Tech, Boeing, 1957-59; Field Engr/Atlas Site Mgr, RCA Ser Co, 1959-61; Sr Reliability Engr 1961-65, Res Spec 1965-71, Prog Engrg Mgr 1974-75 & 1978-79, Chief Sys Engr Adv'd Devel 1975-77 & 1978-80, Asst Prog Mgr 1980-84, Prog Mgr 1984-, Lockheed Missiles & Space Co, Space Sys Div; Mem: IEEE; Am Mgmt Assn; cp/Am Radio Relay Leag; PTA; YMCA; CA St Univ-San Jose Alumni Assn & Engrg Alumni Assn; Bd of Dirs, Homesteaders 4-H Ranch, 1983-; hon/YMCA Yth Ldrship Awd, 1975; W/W.

BANGS, CAROL JANE oc/Writer; b/Jun 22, 1949; h/624 Lincoln Street, Port Townsend, WA 98368; ba/Port Townsend, WA; m/Jim Heynen; c/Emily Jane Heynen, William Geoffrey Heynen; p/MaryEllen Berry, Lake Oswego, OR; ed/BA, Portland St Univ, 1970; MA 1972, PhD 1977, Univ of OR; pa/Col & Univ Tchg since 1975: Univ of OR; Boise St Univ; Wn WA Univ; Bellevue Commun Col; Peninsula Col; Univ of WA; Num Rdgs, Lectrs & Wkshops; Dir, Lit Progs, Centrum; Dir, WA St Future Prob Solving Prog; Chp, Port Townsend City Arts Comm, 1980-82; Mem: MLA, 1974-; Philological Assn of Pacific Coast; Associated Writing Progs; WA Assn of Edrs of Talented & Gifted; hon/Author of 2 Books of Poetry: *The Bones of the Earth,* 1983; *Irreconcilable Differences,* 1978; Num Articles, Poems & Reviews in Mags & Lit Jours, 1972-; NDEA Title IV F'ship for Grad Studies, Univ of OR, 1971-74; W/W in Am Wom.

BANK, HARVEY L oc/Professor; b/Feb 13, 1943; h/1315 Winchester Drive, Charleston, SC 29407; ba/Charleston, SC; m/Ellen; c/Daniel, Laura; p/Myron and Ruth, Bklyn, NY; sp/Sol and Lilian Shield (dec); ed/BA, Hunter Col, CUNY, 1960-65; MA Cand, NY Univ, 1966-68; PhD, Univ of TN, 1968-72; Postdoct Fellow, Duke Univ, 1972-73; pa/Assoc Prof Pathol 1979-, Asst Prof Pathol 1974-79, Assoc 1973-74, Med Univ of SC; Conslt, Envir Protection Agy, 1979-; Guest Investigator, NIEHS,

1972-73; Sr Tech Dept Biol, Rockefeller Univ, 1967-68; Tech, Lamont Geol Observatory, 1965-67; Prin Investigator Anal Electron Microscopy Facility 1974-, Coor Vis'g Sci Series for MCBP Prog 1978-, Chm Student Housing Com 1979-, Others Coms, Med Univ of SC; Mem: Var Com Positions 1977-, Soc for Cryobiol; Am Soc for Cell Biol; Biophy Soc; Electron Microscopy Soc of Am; Chm Rusca Awd Com 1979-, SE Soc for Electron Microscopy; Var Positions 1975-, Sigma Xi (Charleston Clb); AAAS; Microbean Anal Soc; hon/Author, Over 46 Sci Papers & Articles Pub'd in Profl Jours; Predoct Traineeship, NIH, 1968-69; Postdoct F'ship, NIH, 1972-74; Smith, Kline & French Fellow, 1973-75; W/W in SE.

BANKS, MELINDA LUELLA oc/Hair Stylist (Semi-Retired); b/Mar 6, 1920; h/810 North Minnesota, Wichita, KS 67214; ba/Same; m/Riley Banks Jr; c/Pembrook G Love; p/Gordon and Ruby (Foreman) Newsome (both dec); sp/Mr and Mrs Riley W Banks Sr (both dec); Grad, HS; Att'd W Univ; Instrs Course, Beautician Sch; Real Est Courses, W St Univ; pa/Beautician, Shop Owner, 23 Yrs, Ret'd; cp/Mem: Ch of Christ, 48 Yrs; Wichita, KS BU Beautician Clb Nat; Bd Mem, YWCA, 3 Yrs; 2nd 3 Yr Term as 1st & only Black Bd Mem, KS Chapt of Arthritis Foun; NAACP; Black Hist Soc; Nat Treas of Ladies Aux of 9th & 10th Cavalry (US Army); r/Ch of Christ; hon/Support of Christian Ed Cert, 1981; Has Toured 48 US Sts (except AK & RI); Cruise of Caribbean, 1983; Listed in *Logan Co Vol I, Hist Book in Guthrie, OK.*

BANKS, SHARON ELIZABETH oc/Navy Nurse Corps Lieutenant; b/Apr 5, 1950; h/1750 East Ocean Boulevard, Apartment 101, Long Beach, CA 90802; ba/Long Beach, CA; p/Mr and Mrs Robert Davis, Pgh, PA; ed/BS Nsg 1974, M Nsg 1980, Univ of Pgh; mil/USN; pa/Critical Care Nurse, Presb Univ Hosp, Pgh, 1974-79; Relief Supvr Critical Care Div, Critical Care Instr 1979-80, Critical Care Edr 1980-82, Docts Med Ctr, Modesto, CA; Critical Care Nurse, LaVina Hosp, Altadena, CA, 1982; Critical Care Nurse, Lt, USNR, 1984; Mem: Critical Care Nurses Assn; Female Execs; ANA; Nat Leag for Nurses; cp/CPR Instr, Am Heart Assn; r/Christian; W/W in W.

BANKSTON, GORDON DEWEY oc/Artist, Syndicated Cartoonist; b/Oct 10, 1932; h/3813 Springdale, Odessa, TX 79752; ba/Odessa, TX; c/Debra Dolores, Gary Gordon; p/Lee Dewey and Gurtha (Threadgill) Bankston, Abilene, TX; ed/Grad, Monahans HS, 1950; Att'd Hardin Simmons Univ, 1950-51; Att'd N TX Univ, 1951-53; mil/USNG, 1949-58; pa/Pumper Chevron Oil Co Monahans & Kermit (TX), Owner City Sign Ser, 1955-74; Artist of Oil Field Paintings, 1958-74; Syndicated Cartoonist, "The Oil Patch," 1958-82; Pres, Gordon Bankston Enterprises Inc, 1966-; cp/W TX Rehab for Crippled Chd; W TX C of C; Monahans & Odessa C of C; Kappa Alpha Frat; Num Public Spkg Presentations; r/Bapt; hon/Author & Artist of Cartoon Books: *Red in the Oil Patch,* 1970; *The Oil Patch,* 1974; *Yep, It's the Oil Patch,* 1982; The Gordon Bankston Collection Estab'd in His Name, Petro Hist & Res Ctr, Univ of WY-Laramie, 1976-; Intl

Platform Assn; Rec'd Num Lttrs & Comments on Art Wk From Many Famous Govt, Art & Hollywood Personalities; W/W: of S & SW; Intl Biogl Roll of Hon; Men of Achmt; Dict of Dist'd Ams; Num Other Biogl Listings.

BANNON, KATHLEEN ANGELA oc/International Arts Management-Government; b/Jan 19, 1947; ba/Washington DC; p/Angela Bannon, Washington, DC; ed/Arts Tng, Col-Conservatory of Music, Cinc, OH, 1955-63; Nat Mus Acad, Interlochen, MI, 1962-63; HS Dipl w Hons, Wash Sch of Ballet, 1964; BA Commns, Am Univ, 1970; pa/Intl Prog Ofcr 1977-, F'ship Prog Ofcr 1972-77, Nat Endowment for the Arts, Wash DC; Prodn Coor, Wolf Trap Park/Perf Arts, Wash DC, 1971-72; Asst Nat Coor, Call For Action, Wash DC, 1970-71; Dance Fac, Intl Sch, Ecole Francaise, Sidwell Friends, Am Univ, 1967-72; Solo Dancer, Harkness Ballet, NY, 1964-67; Dir Bd, Interam Music Friends, Wash DC, 1984; Mem, Fgn Policy Assn, 1980-; Alliance Francaise, 1982-; Phi Kappa Phi, 1970-; Zonta Intl, 1978-81; Am Wom in Radio & TV, 1970-74; Am Guild of Musical Artists, 1964-69; r/Cath; hon/Author of Var Articles Pub'd in: *Cleveland St Law Review; USIA World;* Chevalier, Order of Danneborg, Danish Govt, Copenhagen, Denmark, 1983; Awd-Nordic, Coun of Mins, Copenhagen, Denmark, 1982; Del, White House Del, UNESCO Conf on Cultural Policy, Mexico City, 1982; Chevalier, Order of Leopold II-King of Belgium, Brussels, Belgium, 1980; W/W: in E, in Wash, in Govt; Intl Book of Hon; DIB; 5,000 Personalities of World.

BANWART, GEORGE J oc/Professor; b/Sep 15, 1926; h/262 Highgate Avenue, Worthington, OH 43085; ba/Columbus, OH; m/Sally F; c/Deborah, Geoffrey; p/Mr and Mrs George W Banwart (dec); sp/Mrs Harold Foss, Dearborn, MI; ed/BS 1950, PhD 1955, IA St Univ; mil/AUS, WW II; pa/Prof Food Microbiol, OH St Univ, 1969-; Res Microbiol, US Dept Agri, Beltsville, MD, 1965-69; Assoc Prof, Purdue Univ, Lafayette, IN, 1962-65; Hd Egg Prods, USDA, Wash DC, 1957-62; Asst Prof, Univ of GA-Athens, 1955-57; Mem: Inst of Food Technols, 1950-; Am Soc for Microbiol; Soc Applied Microbiol; r/Prot; hon/Author of Book, *Basic Food Microbiol,* 1979; Over 100 Articles Pub'd or Presented; W/W in MW; Men & Wom in Sci.

BAPNA, MAHENDRA SINGH oc/Professor, Consultant; b/Sep 8, 1939; h/711 North Jefferson Street, Hinsdale, IL 60521; ba/Chicago, IL; m/Prabha Bhandari; c/Manish, Mitali; p/Lal and Chagan Bai Bapna (both dec); sp/Chandra Singh and Nazar Kunwar Bhandari, Bhilwara, India; ed/BSc, Rajasthan Univ, 1957; BSc Metallurgy, Banaras Hindu Univ, 1961; MS Mats Sci, Marquette Univ, 1964; PhD Mats Sci, NWn Univ, 1969; pa/Asst Prof, Loyola Univ, Maywood, IL, 1970-73; Postdoct Fellow, NWn Univ 1973-74; Asst Prof Biomats 1974-77, Assoc Prof & Dir Biomats 1977-83, Prof & Dir Biomats 1983-, Univ of IL Col of Dentistry, Chgo; Mem: Am Soc for Metals; Intl Assn of Dental Res; Am Assn of Dental Res; Sigma Xi; Am Acad of Dental Mats; r/Jain; hon/Author,

Over 30 Res Papers & Articles in Profl Jours; Univ Scholar, 1955-57; Murphy Fellow, 1966-68; Fellow, Am Acad of Dental Mats; W/W in Frontier Sci & Technol.

BARANOV, ANDREY I oc/Botanist; b/Oct 17, 1917; h/18 Locke Street, Apartment 2, Cambridge, MA 02140; ba/Cambridge, MA; m/Nina M; c/Elena; p/Ippolit G and Vrvara M Baranov (dec); sp/Mikhail G and Anna I Shcherbakov (dec); ed/LLB, Harbin Law Sch, 1938; Att'd Univ of WA, 1960-61; MS, NEn Univ, 1973; pa/Res Fellow, Harbin Reg Mus; Academia Sinica (Inst of Forestry & Soil Sci); Herbarum Asst, Arnold Arboretum of Harvard Univ; Bibliog Resr, World Life Res Inst; Indep Res on Taxonomy of Far-En Plants & on Medicinal Plants (Primarily Ginseng) & Their Uses in Mod Soviet Med & Traditional Med of Far-En Nations; cp/Bd of Advrs, Inst for Traditional Med & Preventive Hlth Care, 1979; Assoc Mem, Sigma Xi, 1973-; Coun Mem, N Eng Bot Clb, 1974; Am Fern Soc; Intl Assn for Plant Taxonomy & Nomenclature; Botanical Soc of Am; r/Russian Orthodox; hon/Author, Over 100 Articles & Monographs on Plant Taxonomy & Ethnobotany Pub'd in Profl Jours, 1942-83; Author of: *Basic Latin for Plant Taxonomists*, 1971; *Studies in the Begoniaceae (Phytoligia Memoirs IV)*, 1981.

BARANOWSKI, TOM oc/Professor; b/Dec 3, 1946; h/1706 Church Street, Galveston, TX 77550; ba/Brooklyn, NY; c/Tanya Elise, Todd Michael; p/Joseph Baranowski; Vera Willard; ed/AB Polit, Princeton Univ, 1968; MA Social Psych 1970, PhD Social Psych 1974, Univ of KS; mil/Alternative Ser, 1971-73; Assoc Prof, Depts Pediatrics (Div Sch Hlth & Commun Pediatrics) & Preventive Med & Commun Hlth (Div Sociomed Scis), Univ of TX Med Br, Galveston, 1980-; Asst Prof Dept Commun Med, Coor Div Consumer Ed, Clin Asst Prof Dept Behavioral Med & Psychi 1979-80, Res Assoc (Div Consumer & Cont'g Ed) Dept Commun Med 1976-78, WV Univ Med Ctr, Charleston, WV; Res Sci, Hlth Care Study Ctr, Battelle Human Affairs Res Ctrs, Seattle, WA, 1974-76; Res Assoc/Evalr & Acting Dir Planning & Eval, KS Reg Med Prog, KC, KS, 1971-73; Tchg Asst, Univ of KS, 1973-74 & 1970-71; Vol So Kennebec Val Augusta ME 1968-69, Assoc Manzano NM Sum 1967, VISTA; Intern, NJ Ofc of Ec Oppor, Sum 1966; Investigator, Prin Investigator & Co-prin Investigator, 11 Res Projs, 1969-84; Mem: Spec Ad Hoc Study Sect, Preventive Cardiol Sect, External Review Br, NIH-NHLBI, 1983-; Prog Com, Public Hlth Ed Sect 1983-, Task Force on Reimbursement 1980-82, Stats Sect, Food & Nutrition Sect, APHA; Coun on Epidemiology, Am Heart Assn; TX Heart Assn, 1983-; Var Divs, Am Psychol Assn; Task Force on Hlth Psychol & Behavioral Med, Interam Soc of Psych; Nat Ctr for Hlth Ed; Soc for Advmt of Social Psych; SWn Psychol Assn; SWn Soc for Res in Human Devel; Num Coms & Positions, Univ of TX Med Br; Num Consltg Positions; Manuscript Reviewer, Var Profl Jours; Num Spkg Presentations, Wkshops & Confs; Others; cp/Chp Field Com, Bd of Dirs, Galveston Yth Soccer Clb, 1983-; Asst Coach (12 Yr Olds) 1982, Asst (9-10 Yr

Olds) 1981, Bay Area Soccer Leag; Coach (9-10 Yr Olds), Kanawha Val Soccer Leag, 1979; hon/Author of Num Books, Book Chapts, Articles & Other Writings Pub'd in Profl Jours & Sci Pubs; Cit, Am Diabetes Assn, 1980; USPHS F'ship, Univ of KS, 1969-71; Dean's List, 1967; Acad S'ship, Princeton Univ, 1964-68; NY St Regents S'ship Awd, 1964; W/W: in S & SW, in Biobehavioral Scis, in Frontier Sci & Technol, of Contemp Achmt; Men of Achmt; Num Other Biogl Listings.

BARBOUR, THOMAS oc/Actor, Writer; b/Jul 25, 1921; h/60 Perry Street, New York, NY 10014; ba/Same; p/Mrs Herbert S Burling, Hightstown, NJ; ed/AB, Princeton Univ, 1943; MA, Harvard Univ, 1948; mil/Am Field Ser, Mid E, N Africa, Wn Europe, 1942-45; pa/Eng Instr, Emerson Col, Boston, MA, 1948-50; Lectr Playwriting & Theatre Arts, Columbia Univ, NY, 1960-61; Freelance Actor & Writer, 1950-; Mem: Actors' Equity Assn; Screen Actors Guild; Am Fedn of TV & Radio Artists; Epis Actors Guild; Assoc Mem, Dramatists Guild; The Players: VPres, Plays For Living; Chm, Polaris Repertory Co; cp/Corres'g Secy, Former Pres, Perry Street Block Assn; r/Epis; hon/Author of 5 Plays incl'g: *A Little Brown Bird*, 1954; *The Smokeweaver's Daugh*, 1959; Num Articles, Poems Pub'd in Mags & Jours incl'g: *The Hudson Review*; McCosh Prize in Phil, Princeton Univ, 1946; Hilltop Theatre Awd (Playwriting), 1954.

BARDARSON, DOT oc/Artist; b/Dec 27, 1932; h/Box 636, Seward, AK 99664; ba/Seward, AK; m/Linnie; c/Dori, Blaine, Rolf; p/Capt and Mrs Vernon E Day, Seattle, WA; sp/Gertrude Bardarson, Seattle, WA; ed/Att'd MD Inst; AA, Lasell Col, 1953; Att'd Univ of WA, 1954-55; Studied w: Tsutakawa, Betts, Chi, Sheets, Whitney; pa/Artist; Bd Men, AK St Coun on Arts, 1976-82; Chm Visual Arts Com, Pres of Resurrection Bay Art Guild, 1978-80; Mem, MW Watercolor Soc; NW Watercolor Soc; AK Watercolor Soc; AK Artists Guild; Port City Players; Allied Artists of Am; cp/Comms: 1% Public Art, AK, 1978 & 1984; Collections: Atl Richfield Fine Arts Collection, 1982; Sheldon Jackson Col, 1978; Juror: Kenai Peninsula Show 1978; Pratt Mus, 1983; hon/Pub'd in *AK Jour*, 1982; *AK Mag*, 1981; *AK Wom*, 1978; Winner of 3 Best of Shows, 1973, 1973 & 1976; Critic's Choice, AK Watercolor Soc, 1982; Purchase Awd, AK Contemp Art Bk, 1978 & 1979; 5 St-wide Juried Hon Mentions, 1978, 1979, 1980, 1982; 2nd Place Peninsula Juried Art, 1983; 2 Peninsula Juried Art Hon Mentions, 1984; Purchase Awd in St-wide Show, 1979; All AK Juried Show, 1977, 1979, 1982, 1984, 1985; Puget Sound Country Juried Show, 1984; NW Watercolor Annual Show, 1984; A Little Erotic, Rochester, NY, 1985.

BARDIN, C WAYNE oc/Biomedical Scientist; b/Sep 18, 1934; h/1148 Fifth Avenue, New York, NY 10028; ba/New York, NY; m/Dorothy T Krieger; c/Charlotte E, Stephanie F; p/James A and Nora I Bardin, Yokum, TX; ed/MS 1962, MD 1962, Col of Med, Baylor Univ; BA Biol, Rise Univ, 1975; mil/USPHS; pa/VPres Pop Coun, Dir Ctr for Biomed Res, NYC, 1978-; Adj Prof, Rockefeller

Univ, NYC, 1978-; Prof Med, Chief Div of Endocrinology 1972-78, Assoc Physiol 1970-78, Assoc Prof Med 1970-72, The Milton S Hershey Med Ctr of PA St Univ; Consltg Phys, Lebanon VA Hosp, Lebanon, PA, 1970-78; Sr Investigator 1967-70, Clin Assoc 1964-67, Endocrinology Br, Nat Cancer Inst; Inter & Asst Resident Med, NY Hosp, Cornell Med Ctr, NY, 1962-64; Num Univ Coms incl'g: Fac Adv Com on Animal Care, Rockefeller Univ, 1981-83; Chm, Intl Com for Contraception Res of the Pop Coun, 1978-; Bd of Sci Cnslrs 1980-83, Chm Bd 1982-83, NICHD; Public Affairs Com, Soc for Study of Reprodn, 1977-78; Am Assn of Phys; Am Fdn Clin Res; Am Physiological Soc; Am Soc of Andrology; Am Soc for Clin Investigation; Endocrine Soc; NY Acad of Sci, Alpha Omega Alpha; Num Other Coms & Orgnl Positions; Edit Bd Mem Var Profl Jours incl'g: *Vitamins & Hormones*, 1981-; *Jour of Steroid Biochem*, 1981-; *Contraception*, 1981-; *Intl Jour of Andrology*, 1977-; Others; r/Prot; hon/Author, Over 250 Sci Articles & Books on Endocrinology, Reprodn, Hormone Action & Contraception; Serono Awd for Outstg Contbn to Field of Male Reproductive Endocrinology, Am Soc of Andrology, 1984; Decorated Cmdr, Order of Lion of Finland, 1984; Num Other Awds & Lectrships.

BARDIS, PANOS DEMETRIOS oc/Professor, Editor, Author; b/Sep 24, 1924; h/2533 Orkney, Ottawa Hills, Toledo, OH 43606; ba/Toledo, OH; m/Donna Jean; c/Byron Galen, Jason Dante; ed/BA, Bethany Col, 1950; MA, Notre Dame Univ, 1953; PhD, Purdue Univ, 1955; pa/Instr to Assoc Prof Sociol 1955-59, Assoc Prof Sociol 1959-62, Albion Col; Prof Sociol, Toledo Univ, 1963-; Editor & Book Review Editor, *Intl Social Sci Review*, 1982-; Edit Advr: Am Biogl Inst, 1980-; *Jour of Sociol Studies*, 1979-; *Renaissance Universal Jour*, 1982; *Social Inquiry*, 1981-; *S African Jour of Sociol*, 1971-; *Synthesis, The Interdisciplinary Jour of Sociol*, 1973-; Edit Conslt: *Col Jour of Ed*, 1973-; *Society & Culture*, 1972-; Book Review Editor 1974-, & Edit Bd 1965-, *Harshana Intl*; Asst Am Editor & Book Review Editor, *Indian Jour of Social Res*, 1965-; Assoc Editor: *Indian Psychol Bltn*, 1965-; *Intl Jour of Contemp Sociol*, 1971-; *Intl Jour of Sociol of the Fam*, 1970-; *Jour of Polit & Mil Sociol*, 1972-; *Lit Endeavour*, 1981-; *Poetry Intl*, 1982-; *Revista del Instituto de Ciencias Sociales*, 1965-; Assoc Editor 1968-, Book Review Editor 1981-, *Intl Review of Hist & Polit Sci*; Co-editor, *Intl Review of Mod Sociol*, 1972-; Edit Bd, *Jour of Ed*, 1965-; Am Editor, *Sociol Intl*, 1967-; Editor-in-Chief & Book Review Editor, *Intl Jour on World Peace*, 1983-; Mem: Acad of Am Poets, 1982-; Accademia Tiberina, 1982-; Alpha Kappa Delta, 1954-; Fellow, AAAS, 1960-; AAUP, 1955-; Mem 1979-, Pubs Com 1983-, Awds Com 1983-, ABI; Bd of Advrs, Am Soc for Neo-Hellenic Studies, 1969-; Fellow 1953-, Mbrship Com 1966-71, Am Sociol Assn; Conf Intl de Sociologie de la Rel, 1969-; Coun of Social Sci Jour Editors, 1979-; Democritos, 1973-; Edit Advr, Free Press Intl, 1980-; Acad Adv Bd, Georgetown Univ Inst, 1981-; Mem 1980-, Assoc Trustee 1982-, Chm Task Force on the Fam 1982-, Global Cong of World's Rels; Grp for the Study of

Sociols, 1967-; Ernest Groves Fund Com, Groves Conf, 1977-; Hellenic Profl Assn of Am Intl, 1981-; Mem 1981-, Adv Bd on Profl, Ednl & Govtl Matters, 1982-; Chm 1982-, Trustee 1982-, Biogl, Credential Upgrading & Acad Referral Subcom; Fellow 1969-, Chm of Mbrship Com 1970-, Coor for USA 1974-, Exec Com 1982-, Institut Intl de Sociologie; Adv Coun, Int for Mediterranean Affairs, 1968-; Hon Assoc, Inst for the Study of Plural Societies, Univ of Pretoria, S Africa, 1974-; Fellow, Intercontinental Biogl Assn, 1976-; Intl Assn of Fam Sociol, 1976-; Fdg Life Fellow, Intl Col of Proctors & Preceptors, 1982-; Life Fellow, Intl Inst of Arts & Lttrs, 1966-; Hon Advr, Intl Pers Res, 1971-; Intl Sci Comm on the Fam, 1969-; Mem 1970-, Res Com on Social Change 1972-, Res Com on Sociol of Ed 1972-, Res Com on Fam Sociol 1974-, Intl Sociol Assn; Kappa Delta Pi, 1975-; KRIKOS, 1975-; cp/Adv Coun for Acad Affairs, 1977-; Adv Mem, Marquis Biogl Lib Soc, 1973-; Bd of Trustees, Marriage Mus, 1969-; Adv Bd, Minority Alliance Intl, 1981-; Mod Greek Soc, 1973-; Bd of Dirs, Nat Acad of Ec & Polit Sci, 1959-; Conslt, Nat Assn on Standard Med Vocab, 1963-; Nat Coun on Fam Relats, 1953-; Nat Soc of Lit & the Arts, 1975-; Nat Soc of Pub'd Poets, 1976-; Profl Mem, Nat Writer's Clb, 1963-; Active Mem, NY Acad of Scis, 1963; Adv Bd, New World Communs, 1980-; N Ctl Sociol Assn, 1972-; OH Coun on Fam Relats, 1959-; OH Soc of Poets, 1976-; Life Mem, Phi Kappa Phi, 1972-; Pi Gamma Mu, 1959-; Fdg Mem 1979-, Gt Lakes Coor 1983-, Exec Com 1983-, Profs World Peace Acad; Royal Asiatic Soc, 1982-; Sigma Xi, 1979-; Assoc, Smithsonian Instn, 1977-; Fellow, World Acad of Scholars, 1976-; World Alliance of Civil Rts, 1981-; World Poetry Soc Intl, 1980-; Chief of Intl Bd & Mem of Gov'g Body (Rep'g N Am), World Univ, 1981-; hon/Pub'd Wks: *Atlas of Human Reproductive Anatomy*, 1983; *Evolution of the Fam in the W*, 1983; *Global Marriage & Fam Customs*, 1983; *Studies in Marriage & the Fam*, 1975, 2nd Edit 1978; *The Fam in Changing Civilizations*, 1969; *Ency of Campus Unrest*, 1975; *Ivan & Artemis*, 1975; *Hist of the Fam*, 1975; *The Future of the Greek Lang in the US*, 1976; *Nine Oriental Muses*, 1983; *Hist of Thanatology*; *Phil, Rel, Psych & Sociol Ideas Concerning Death from Primitive Times to the Present*, 1981; Co-Editor: *Poetry Americas*, 1982; *The Fam in Asia*, 1978; Recip, Couphos Prize; Winner, Seminario de Investigacion Historica y Arqueologica Awd, Museo de Historia, Barcelona, Spain, 1975; Outstg Achmt in Ed, Bethany Col, 1975; Outstg Tchg Awd, Toledo Univ, 1975; Outstg Jour Awd, ABI, 1982; Poetry Awd, *Hoosier Challenger Mag*, 1983; Listed in Num W/W & Other Biogl Listing.

BARDT, BARBARA F (WHITE) oc/ Entrepreneur; b/Feb 13, 1944; h/10608 Sweetbriar Parkway, Silver Spring, MD 20903; ba/Chevy Chase, MD; p/Rose Katz, Rockville, MD; ed/BA Eng Lit 1967, MA Eng Lit 1979, Univ of MD; MA Clin Psych, Antioch Col, 1979; Bibliotherapist Intern, St Elizabeth's Hosp, 1978-79; Postgrad Study, Cath Univ, Cath Univ, 1979; Doct Wk, Am Univ, 1980-81; pa/Spec Ed Tchr, 1977-78; Owner, "As Time Goes By,"

Vintage Clothing Boutique, 1974-77; Owner, S'ship Search Fin Aid Cnslg, 1977-81; Owner, Wom Cnslg Wom (Cnslg Pract), 1981-82; Owner, Phoney Alibi Tape Cassette Prods, 1982-; Mem: Assn for Humanistic Psych; Am Psych Assn; Am Assn of Marriage & Fam Therapists; Am Pers & Guid Assn; hon/ Author of Booklets & Articles Relating to Cnslg; 5 Grad S'ships, 1969; W/W in E.

BAREISS, LYLE EUGENE oc/Aerospace Engineer; b/Nov 4, 1945; h/8031 East Phillips Circle, Englewood, CO 80112; ba/Denver, CO; m/Chris Elizabeth; p/Godfrey M and V Edith Bareiss, Encampment, WY; sp/George and Betty Bartlett, Riverton, WY; ed/BSME Aerospace Engrg, Univ of WY, 1969; Postgrad, Industl Mgmt, CO St Univ; pa/ Dept Mgr Mech Mats Engrg 1984-, Supvr Spacecraft Contamination & Laser Effects Technol 1980-, Staff Engr Shuttle Payload Contamination Integration 1977-80, Shuttle/Spacelab Contamination Anal 1973-77, Skylab Prog Sys Engr 1969-73, Martin Marietta Aerospace; Mem: Nat Thermophysics Tech Com 1980-84, AIAA; Sigma Tau; Sigma Alpha Epsilon; Odd Fellows, Omicron Delta Kappa; r/Presb; hon/ Author, Over 50 Reports & Tech Papers Pub'd in Profl Jours incl'g: *AIAA Jour of Spacecraft & Rockets*; *AIAA Progress in Thermophysics*; NASA Skylab Awd; Tech Author Awds, 1974, 1975, 1979, 1984; Operational Perf Awd, 1982; NASA New Technol Awds, 1977, 1982, 1985; W/W: in W, in World, in Frontier Sci & Technol.

BARELA, GUILLERMO G oc/Financial Consultant; b/Apr 23, 1952; h/2220 Lester Avenue, Bakersfield, CA 93304; ba/Bakersfield, CA; p/Lucia and Basilio Barela y de Villaverde; BS/BA, MBA, CA St Col; Depl, Mortgage Bkg Inst; Depl (Russian, Rumanian) Fgn Lang Inst; Cert, Univ of Istanbul; Dipl, Univ of Barcelona; pa/Lectr Sociol & Psych 1970-71, Lectr Psych 1975-76, Univ of CO, Interpreter (Russian, Bulgarian, Turkish, Arabic, Spanish, Portuguese, Italian, German, Danish), US Govt; Sr VPres, Cook Rltrs, 1976-80; Mng Ptnr & Sr Conslt, Corp Real Est Conslts, 1980-; Mem: Nat Assn of Rltrs; CAR; BBR; Farm & Land Inst; Mortgage Bkg Inst; Am Psychol Assn; Am Mgmt Assn; cp/Kiwanis; r/Jewish; hon/Author of Books: *UMAS*; *Univ of CO Proton-Proton Exch*; *How to Study*; *Curanderismo*; *Devel of 15th Cent Spanish*; Co-Author of Books: *Kern River Val*; *Status & Needs (volume 3)*; Num Other Articles; Outstg Unit Cit, USAF, 1973-75; Nom'd Outstg Meritorious Ser, USAF, 1973; Outsg Yg Man of Am, 1982.

BARKER, COLIN G oc/Professor; b/ Aug 3, 1939; h/2527 East 26th Place, Tulsa, OK 74114; ba/Tulsa, OK; m/ Yvonne I; c/Conan N; p/Mr and Mrs George Barker, Plymouth, England; sp/ Mr and Mrs Norman Meredith, Birmingham, England; ed/BA 1962, DPhil 1965, Oxford Univ; pa/Prof, 1969-; Sr Res Chem, Exxon Prod Co, Houston, 1967-69; Res Fellow, Univ TX-Austin, 1965-67; Mem: Am Assn Petro Geols (AAPG); Assoc Editor, *AAPG Bltn*; Chm Organic Geochem Div 1978-79, Geochem Soc; Assoc Editor, *Geochem Soc Jour*; Tulsa Geol Soc; hon/Author of 1 Book & 35 Tech Papers; Matson Awd 1978

& 1982, Dist'd Lectr 1980-81, Am Assn Petro Geols.

BARKER, ELLIOTT SPEER oc/Conservationist, Game Warden (Retired); b/ Dec 25, 1886; h/343 Palace Avenue, Santa Fe, NM 87501; ba/Same; m/Ethel Margaret; c/Roy E, Mrs Florence (B) Giers, Dorothy E (B) Elmore; p/Squire L and Priscilla Jane Barker; HS and Sophia Rebecca Arnold; ed/Dipl, HS, 1905; Hon LLD, NM St Univ, 1976; pa/ Photog for John Phillips, 1906 & 1907; Home Ranch, 1908; US Forest Ranger: Jemez Nat Forest, Pecos Nat Forest, Carson Nat Forest, 1909-1913; Dept Forest Supvr 1914, Forest Supvr 1915-19, US Forest Ser, Taos, NM; Pvt Rancher, 1909-1929; Wildlife & Predator Mgr, Vermejo Pk, 1930-31; St Game Warden, St of NM, 1931-53; Orgr & Bd of Dirs 1936, Dist Rep 12 Yrs, Nat Wildlife Fedn; Served 5 Yrs on St Pers & Water Pollution Bds, 1954-70; Hunting Guide, 1953-75; Mem 1915-, Exec Secy 1953, NM Game Protective Assn (NM Wildlife Fedn); 2 Term Pres, Wn Assn St Game & Fish Commrs; Pres, Intl Assn Game & Fish Commrs, 1935; cp/NG Ofcr & Dept US Marshall, 1917; Pres, Taos Br of NRC, 1917; Appt'd to Spec Com "Find a Way to Give Wildlife a Better Break" by Franklin Roosevelt; Rep (Conductor) of 34 Ten Day Wilderness Trail Rides in Var Sts, 1953-76; r/Meth; hon/Author of Books: *When The Dogs Bark Treed*, 1946; *Beatty's Cabin*, 1956; *Wn Life & Adventures*, 1971; 2 Booklets of Poetry; Others; Orgr, Nat Wildlife Fedn; Donated "Smokey Bear" to US Forest Ser; Agent for Purchase of Land for Elliott S Barker Girl Scout Camp; Elliot S Barker Wildlife Area Named in His Hon by NM St Game Comm; Recip, NM Public Ser Awd, 1982; Num Other Certs & Awds.

BARKER, TIMOTHY oc/Professor; b/Oct 21, 1946; h/8 Gary Road, Norton, MA 02766; ba/Norton, MA; m/Gloria; c/Eric; p/Roy C Barker, Brewster, MA; sp/Kenneth Landon, El Cerrito, CA; ed/ AB, Swarthmore Col, 1969; PhD, Univ of CA-Santa Cruz, 1974; pa/NDEA Fellow 1969-72, Res Asst 1973-74, Univ of CA-Santa Cruz; Prof Astronomy, Wheaton Col & Bridgewater St Col, 1974-; Mem: Planetary Soc; Astronom Soc of Pacific; Am Astronom Soc; hon/ Author of 11 Articles incl'g: "The Ionization Structure of Planetary Nebulae IV NGC 6853," *Astrophy Jour*, 1984; Recip, 5 NASA Res Grants & 2 Astronom Soc Res Grants, 1980-; W/W in Frontier Sci & Technol.

BARKMEIER, WAYNE WALTER oc/ Dental Research Scientist; b/Mar 29, 1944; h/2 Crossley Drive, Dover, DE 19901; ba/Milford, DE; m/Carolyn A; c/ Kimberly, Jennifer, Wayne Jr; p/Walter H and Virginia R Barkmeier, Exeter, NE; sp/Leonard A and Bernetta M Johnsen (dec); ed/Att'd Univ of NE, 1962-65; DDS, Univ of NE Col of Dentistry, 1965-69; Cert, USAF Med Ctr, Keesler (Rotating Dental Internship) AFB; MS, Univ of TX Hlth Sci Ctr-Houston, 1973-75; mil/USAF, (Active) 1969-78, (Resv) 1978-; pa/Dental Res Sci, L D Caulk Co, 1982-; Asst Prof, Creighton Univ, 1978-82; Chief of Operative Dentistry, USAF Hosp Chanute, 1975-78; Gen Dentist, Whiteman AFB, 1972-73; Gen Dentist, Karamursel (Turkey) Air Sta, 1970-72; Mem: Am

Dental Assn; Kent Sussex Dental Soc, DE; DE Dental Soc; Acad of Operative Dentistry; Intl Assn for Dental Res; Am Assn for Dental Res; Del to Coun of Facs 1980-82, Am Assn of Dental Schs; Omicron Kappa Upsilon; Am Prosthodontic Soc; r/Cath; hon/Author of Num Articles in Profl Dental Jours; Regent S'ship, Univ of NE, 1967-68; Hon List, Univ of NE, 1969; Grad w Distn, Univ of NE, 1969; Omicron Kappa Upsilon, 1969; Quintessence Awd for Orig Article, 1977; W/W in Frontier Sci & Technol.

BARLEY, LINDA ROSE oc/Professor; b/Apr 16, 1947; h/83-39 116th Street, Apartment 3A, Kew Gardens, NY 11418; ba/Jamaica, NY; p/Mr and Mrs L A Barley, Ventura, CA; ed/BA Hlth Ed, Gerontology, St Francis Col, 1973; MS, CUNY, 1975; DEd, Columbia Univ, 1980; pa/Asst Prof, York Col of CUNY, 1981-; Dept Hd, Cath Med Ctr of Bklyn & Queens, 1975-81; Dept Hd, Hlth & Hosp Corp, 1970-75; Sci Tchr Grades 5-8, Sacred Hearts of Jesus & Mary, 1965-70; Mem: Profl Ad Coun, Vis'g Nurse Ser of NY, 1980; Queensboro Lung Assn, 1980; Bd of Dirs & Secy, Queens Hlth Manpower Consortium, 1975-80; SE Queens Consortium of Sers for Elderly, 1975-; Adv Bd, Commun Ser Soc, 1978-; cp/Cert Basic Cardiac Life Support Instr, Am Heart Assn & St Vincent's Inst of Emer Care; r/Rom Cath; hon/Author of "Drug Compliance & the Elderly," *Intl Dissertation Abstracts*, 1980; Edit Comment, *Geriatric Conslt*, 1983; Var Other Articles; Deans List, 1975, 1977, 1978, 1980; W/W in Wom.

BARLOW, WALLACE DUDLEY oc/Engineer; b/Feb 11, 1909; h/6210 Massachusetts Avenue, Bethesda, MD 20816; ba/Same; m/Theresa Gilson; c/Elizabeth Lynton, Douglas Atherton, Christopher Lincoln; ed/BS, MS, VA Polytech Inst & St Univ; mil/AUS, 8 Yrs, Maj; pa/Field Geol, Brit S Africa Co; Asst to Secy of War Stimson, 1940; Asst to Donald Nelson, War Prodn Bd, 1941-42; Profl Staff, Interior Com of US Senate; Mats Engr & Industl Engr, Ofc of Nav Mat, 1951-75; CEO, Barlow Intl, Reg'd Profl Engrs, 1975-; Mem: Am Inst Mining Engrs, 1928-; cp/Chm, Wash Grp of Explorers Clb; r/Presb; hon/Author of *US Life Lines*, 1943; *Labor Content of US Industs*, 1981.

BARLOWE, AMY oc/Violinist/Violist; b/Jan 20, 1952; h/19 Highland St, West Massapequa, NY 11758; ba/Salem, OR; ed/BM, MM, Juilliard Sch of Music, NY, 1970-76; Att'd Meadowmoor Sch of Music, Westport, NY, 1969-76; Att'd Scotia Music Fest, Nova Scotia, Canada, 1981; pa/Pvt Instr; Tchg Fellow, Meadowmount Sch of Music; Fdr/Dir, Pre-Col Div in Music, Asst Prof Violin 1976-82, Assoc Prof Violin 1982-, Sum Yth Music Camp, Willamette Univ; Orch Experience Incl: Asst Concertmaster, Juilliard Pre-Col Orch; Isaah Jackson Juilliard Theatre Orch; Co-Concert Master, Salem Symph; Concertmaster, Virtuoso Ensemble; Queensborough Symph & Chamber Orch; NY String Orch; Am Yth Perfs, Nat Yth Orch; Num Others; Solo Recitals Incl: Juilliard Sch; Bronx Mus of Arts; Massapequa Public Lib; Great Neck Wom's Guild; Marshfield HS, Coos Bay, OR; Blue Mtn Commun Col; Camerata Musica; Por-

tland Art Mus; Num Others; Solo Appearances Incl: Vieuxtemps Concerto # 5 w David Garvey Piano, Meadowmount Sch of Music; Vitali Chaconne w Sandra Rivers Piano, Carnegia Recital Hall; Bach Concerto for Oboe & Violin w Salem Symph, OR; Basically Beethoven Series, Willamette Univ, OR; Num Others; Chamber Music Perfs Incl: Tully Hall, NY; Sacramento, CA; Portland Lib, OR; Reed Col, OR; Poncho Theatre, Seattle, WA; Whitman Col, Walla Walla, WA; Scotia Music Fest, Nova Scotia, Canada; Willamete Univ, Salem, OR; Num Others; cp/Featured on PM Mag TV; Perfs on WNYC, WFUV & KSLM Radio; Recording w OR Piano Trio, Univ So CA Sound Studios; hon/Author of Book, *A Guide For Enjoyable Listening*, 1983; Author of Articles "String Thing on a Shoestring," *ASTA Jour*, 1983; "Gen Ed for the Love of Music," *Jour of Gen Ed*; Sabbatical, Willamette Univ, 1983; Selected for 1st Annual Chamber Music Fest NW, OR Piano Quartet, 1981; Adjudicator, OR St Univ Hons Competition, 1981-83; Adjudicator, OR Music Tchrs Assn Competitors, 1974-76; Adjucator, Seattle Yg Artists Music Fest; Full S'ship Oberlin Conservatory, Eastman Sch of Music & Tanglewood, 1969-70; NW Area Grant, 1982; Friday Music Clb Medal, 1969; Helena Rubinstein Foun S'ship, Juilliard, 1975; Massapequa Symph S'ship, 1970; Great Neck Symph Awd; Num Others; W/W in Am Music; Yg Commun Ldrs; Intl Yth in Achmt; Intl W/W in Music.

BARNARD, GEORGE HUGH (dec Sep 4, 1984) oc/Former Lawyer & Tax Specialist; b/Jun 14, 1909; h/Formerly of 200 East Chestnut Street, Chgo, IL 60611; ba/Chgo, IL; p/Julius and Martha Barnard (dec); ed/Att'd Morgan Pk Mil Acad & Elgin Acad; PhB 1930, JD 1931, Univ of Chgo; Att'd NY Univ Inst of Fed Taxation & Univ of Miami Inst on Fed Taxation; mil/USN, Cmdr; USNR, Ret'd; pa/Ptner, Barnard & Barnard Atty's, 1932-84; Former Mem: Exec Clb, Chgo; Chgo & IL Bar Assns; ABA; Govs Comm on Equal Rts of Wom; Nav Leag; cp/Taven Clb, Chgo; Belmont Yacht Clb; Yachting Clb of Am; Coor of Yachting, Pan-Am Games Comm; 100 Com, Cook Co; hon/Bronze Star & Commend Ribbons, USN; Nav Order US; 50 Yr Awd, IL St Bar Assn; W/W in MW; Notable Ams; Book of Hon; Nat Social Dir.

BARNES, DALPHNA RUTH oc/Infection Control Coordinator; b/May 11, 1933; h/20319 Belleau Wood Drive, Humble, TX 77338; ba/Houston, TX; m/Alvine Burnell; c/David Lynn, Jeanne Michele Barnes-Boxley; p/Raymond V Boatright, Springdale, AR; sp/Mr and Mrs T B Barnes; ed/AA Nsg, Texarkana Col, 1966; BA Psych, Univ of Houston, 1974; mil/USN, WAVE Corps, 1957-58; Ofc Nurse 1966, Staff Nurse 1967-68, Little York Hosp, Houston; Staff Nurse, Psychi Hosp, Houston, 1968; Intensive Care Nurse, Hermann Hosp, Houston, 1968-69; Ofc Nurse & Therapist 1969, Staff Nurse to Infection Control Ofcr 1970-77, Pkway Hosp, Houston; Infection Control Coor, Houston NW Med Ctr, 1977-; Mem: Pres Houston Chapt, Assn for Practitioners in Infection Control; Adv Bd 1980-82, Bd of Dirs

1982, 2nd VPres 1983, Houston Hospice; Fdr & Facilitator, Cancer Interaction Grp, 1980-; VPres N Harris Chapt, Am Cancer Soc, 1980-81; cp/Num Public Spkg Presentations; r/Assem of God; hon/Author of Poem "And All Through the Night," *Am Jour of Nsg*, 1967; Recip Sword of Hope Awd, Am Cancer Soc, 1979-82; Wm L Benson Meml Awd, TX Soc of Infection Control Practitioners, 1980; W/W of Am Wom.

BARNES, GEORGE LEWIS oc/Plant Pathologist; b/Aug 21, 1920; h/424 North Donaldson, Stillwater, OK 74075; ba/Stillwater, OK; m/Phyllis June; c/William, Jeffrey, Gregory, Susan; p/Harold B Barnes, Royal Oak, MI; sp/Mrs William Dollarhite, Lansing, MI; ed/BS Biol Scis 1948, MS Botany 1950, MI St Univ; PhD Plant Pathol, OR St Univ, 1953; mil/AUS, Air Corp, 1942-45; pa/Res Asst & Instr, OR St Univ-Corvalis, 1950-53; Sr Sci, Olin Matheson Chem Corp, Columbus, OH & Port Jefferson, NY, 1953-58; Asst Prof, Assoc Prof, Prof, OK St Univ-Stillwater, 1958-; Mem: Am Phytopathol Soc, 1950-; cp/Cubmaster & Asst Scoutmaster, BSA, 1960-65; Former Bd Mem & Pres, Town & Gown Theatre, 1964-; r/Unitarian; hon/Author, Over 59 Jour Articles & 20 Abstracts; Other Pubs; Sigma Xi; Phi Kappa Phi.

BARNES, HUBERT LLOYD oc/Professor; b/Jul 20, 1928; h/213 East Mitchell Avenue, State College, PA 16803; ba/Univ Park, PA; m/Mary W; c/Roy M, Catherine P; p/George L Barnes, Woburn, MA; sp/Malcolm Westergaard (dec); ed/BS, MA Inst of Technol (MIT), 1950; PhD, Columbia Univ, 1958; pa/Resident Geol, Peru Mining Co, 1950-52; Lectr, Columbia Univ, 1952-54; Postdoct Fellow, Carnegie Instn of Wash, 1956-60; Asst Prof, Full Prof, PA St Univ, 1960-; Mem: Fellow, Geol So Am; Fellow, Mineralogical Soc Am; Councilor, Soc Ec Geol, 1981-83; Pres, Geochem Soc, 1983-85; AAAS; Am Geophy Union; Mineralogic Assn of Canada; r/Prot; hon/Author, *Uranium Prospecting*; Editor, *Geochem of Hydrothermal Ore Deposits*; Author & Co-Author, Over 82 Tech Papers; N L Britton Scholar, Columbia Univ, 1955-56; Guggenheim Fellow, Univ of Goettingen, 1966-67; C F Davidson Lectr, St Andrews, 1971; Thayer Lindsley Lectr for Soc Ec Geol, 1980-81; Nat Acad Sci Exch Sci, Moscow, 1974; Crosby Lectr, MIT; W/W; Am Men of Sci.

BARNES, JAMES J oc/Professor; ed/BA, Amherst Col, 1954; BA, New Col, Oxford, 1956; PhD, Harvard Univ, 1960; DHL, Col of Wooster, 1976; pa/Hist Instr, Amherst Col, 1959-62; Asst Prof Hist 1962-67, Assoc Prof Hist 1967-76, Prof Hist 1976-, Dept Chm & Hadley Prof 1979-, Wabash Col; Mem: Am Hist Assn; Conf on Brit Studies; So Hist Assn; Res Soc for Victorian Periods; Soc for Values in Higher Ed; Assn of Am Rhodes Scholars; Soc for Histns of Am Fgn Relats; Bd of Trustees 1982, IN Hist Soc; Montgomery Co Hist Soc; MW Victorian Studies Assn; The Bibliogl Soc; The Nat Book Leag; The Dominions F'ship Trust; Bodley's Am Friends; The U Oxford & Cambridge Univ Clb; cp/Crawfordsville Commun Action Coun, 1966-69; Crawfordsville

Commun Day Care Com, 1966-67; IN Adv Com, St Rehab Sers for Blind, 1979-81; Crawfordsville Lit Soc, 1980-; MW Conf of Brit Studies; Vestry, St John's Epis Ch; r/Epis; hon/Author of 4 Books incl'g: *Free Trade in Books: A Study of the London Book Trade since 1800*, 1964; *Hitler's Mein Kampf in Britain & America: 1930-39*, 1980; Others; Author, Over 30 Articles, Reviews & Paper Presentations incl'g: "Thomas Aspinwall: 1st Transatl Lit Agt," *Papers of the Bibliogl Soc of Am*, 1984; "Depression & Innovation in the Brit & Am Book Trade, 1819-1939," *Books & Soc in Hist*, 1983; "Bancroft, Motley, Parkman & Prescott: A Study of Their Success as Histns," *Lit & Hist*, 1977; "Why a Hist of the Book Trade?" 1965; "Why 19th Cent Am Produced Some Famous Histns," 1966; Others; Phi Betta Kappa, 1954; Rhodes S'ship, 1954-56; Woodrow Wilson F'ship, 1956-57; Kent F'ship, 1958; Great Lakes Cols Assn Tchg F'ship, 1975 & 1976; Fulbright S'ship, 1978; Recip Num Res Grants incl'g: Social Sci Res Coun; Wabash Col; Am Coun of Learned Socs; Am Phil Soc.

BARNES, LINDA ERNESTINE ROBERTS oc/Insurance Broker, Business Mangager; b/Jan 18, 1951; h/3776 East 153rd Street, Cleveland, OH 44128; ba/Cleveland, OH; m/W Marvin; c/Courtney Ernestine; p/Frank Roberts (dec); Helen Roberts, Cleveland, OH; ed/Att'd Fisk Univ, 1969-71; Att'd Cuyahoga Commun Col, 1971-73; BS Biol, Kent St Univ, 1976; pa/Ins Broker, Protected Homes Mut, 1980-; Bus Mgr, L & M Auto Clin & W M B Assocs, 1975-; NY Life Inst Co, 1978-81; Bus Mgr, Marco Assocs, 1976-78; Mem: Investmts Chp 1979-81, Delta Sigma Theta; cp/JCs, 1979-80; Vol, YWCA, 1977-; Life Underwriter Polit Action Com, Phyliss Wheatley, 1977-; Mem, Millionaires Clb, 1977-; r/Rel Sci; hon/ Outstg Ldrship Awd, Cuyahoga Commun Col, 1980; Delta Sigma Theta, 1980-82; 5 Yr Vol Pin, ARC; W/W in Am Wom.

BARNES, MARGARET A oc/Consultant, Mathematical Statistician; b/Feb 8, 1939; h/PO Box 586, Lanham, MD 20706; ba/Lanham, MD; m/Benjamin Barnes; ed/BS Math & Ed, NY Ctl Univ, 1958; Grad Studies Theory of Probability, Am Univ, 1962; Contract Tng, OH St Univ, 1973; MA Stats & Measurement, Univ of MD-Col Pk, 1975; pa/Co Pres, 1978-83; Math Stat, 1962-77; Tchr, 1958-61; Appt'd Commr, MD St Accident Fund, 1979-89; Adv Bd, Prince George's St Bk; Adv Bd, Interst Gen Corp; cp/Alpha Kappa Alpha; r/Bapt; hon/Author of "Estimation & Projection of Var Pop Grps for Hlth Planning," 1976; "The Effect of Personal Descriptive Words in Lrng," 1975; Others; Orig Painting: "The Modified Yellow Hat"; Most Outstg Student in Math, 1958; Success to Ser Awd, Johnston Co Schs, 1977; W/W: of Wom, in the World, in Fin & Indust, Num Other Biogl Listings.

BARNES, MARK LANDRY oc/Secret Service Agent; b/Oct 5, 1950; h/11318 Northwest 15th Court, Pembroke Pines, FL 33026; ba/Miami, FL; m/Susan Clark; c/Isaac Alexander; p/Mr and Mrs Chester W Barnes, L'ville, KY; sp/Mr DeLair A Clark, Orlando, FL; ed/BS Police Adm, Univ of L'ville, 1976; MS

Crim Justice, Univ of So MS, 1982; mil/ AUS, 1969-71; pa/Correctional Ofcr, Jefferson Co Jail, 1972-73; Police, Patrolman, Jefferson Co, 1973-78; Spec Agt, US Treas Dept (ATF), 1978-82; Spec Agt, US SS, 1982-; Mem: Nat Rifle Assn, 1972-; cp/Delta Upsilon Frat, 1968-; Sons of Confederate Vets, 1979-; r/Presb; hon/Omicron Chapt, Alpha Phi Sigma, Nat Police Sci Hon Frat, 1975; W/W in S & SW.

BARNES, MELVER RAYMOND oc/ Theoretical Scientific Researcher; b/ Nov 15, 1917; h/Route 1, Box 424, Linwood, NC 27299; ba/Same; p/Oscar Lester and Sarah Albertine (Rowe) Barnes (dec); ed/Dipl, Tyro HS, 1935; BA Chem, Univ of NC-Chapel Hill, 1947; Att'd Courses in Math, Physics & Chem at Following Univs: McCoy Col, Johns Hopkins Univ; Univ of UT; Univ of CA-LA; Dipls in Elects & Computers: Radio Elects TV Schs & Capitol Radio Engrg Inst; mil/AUS, 1942-45; pa/Chem, Pgh Testing Labs, Greensboro, NC, 1948-49; Chem, NC St Hwy & Public Wks Comm, Raleigh, NC, 1949-51; Chem, Edgewood Arsenal, Edgewood, MD, 1951-61; Chem, Dugway Proving Ground, Dugway, UT, 1961-70; Pvt Sci Res, Linwood, NC 1970-; Mem: The Am Chem Soc; The Am Phy Soc; AAAS; NY Acad of Scis; World Univ Round Table; Intl Platform Assn; The Am Defense Preparedness Assn; Soc of Am Mil Engrs; UN Assns of US; Nat Space Inst; Intl Biogl Assn; ABIRA; r/Christian; hon/Author of Num Tech Papers; Hon Doct Theoretical Physics, World Univ, 1981; W/W: in W, in S & SW, of Intells; DIB; The Book of Hon; Dict of Dist'd Ams; The Biogl Roll of Hon; Num Other Biogl Listings.

BARNETT, SARA MARGARET oc/ Health Occupations Education Coordinator; b/Aug 6, 1941; h/100 Pioneer, Texarkana, TX 75501; ba/Texarkana; m/Herman H; c/Gregory Lynn, Lori Elizabeth; p/Grady and Mary Mills, Texarkana, TX; sp/Homer and Nannie Crisp Barnett; ed/BS Med Tech, Univ of TX-Arlington, 1963; MS Biol Ed, Univ Ctl AR, 1968; PhD Voc Ed, E TX St Univ, 1984; pa/Med Tech, Wadley Reg Med Ctr, Texarkana, 1963-65, 1976-77; Biol Tchr, Texarakana ISD, 1965-69; Med Tech, Collom & Carney Clin, Texarkana, 1970-72; Biol Tchr, Liberty-Eylau ISD, 1972-76; Biol Tchr & Hlth Occups Coor, Texarakana ISD, 1977-; Mem: TX Ed Foun Chm, AAUW; Pres, Lambda Zeta & Ceremonials Chrm, Delta Kappa Gamma; Phi Delta Kappa; ASCP; AVA; THOA; TSTA (Life); PTA (Life); NEA; CTA; AR Acad of Sci; NAHOT; cp/Num Spkg Presentations in Field; r/Meth; hon/Author of Book, *Med Lab Asst, 1981; Author of Article, "A Study of Herbaceous, Vascular Plants from Selected Sites in Faulkner Co, AR," in Proceedings of AR Acad of Sci, 1969; Martin-Lowrance Scholar, Delta Kappa Gamma, 1981; Tchr of Yr, Texarakana ISD, 1982-83; Tchr of Yr, Liberty-Eylau, 1976; AAUW Ed Foun Named Gift, 1975; W/W: of Am Wom, in TX.*

BARNEY, JAMES EARL II oc/Manager, Analytical Chemist; b/Sep 1, 1926; h/64 Cold Spring Road, Avon, CT 06001; ba/Farmington, CT; m/Patricia Leonard; c/Alan Earl, Anne Louise; p/ J Earl Barney, Topeka, KS; ed/BS Chem

1946, PhD Anal Chem 1950, Univ of KS; pa/Sci, Oak Ridge Nat Labs, 1946-47; Grp Ldr, Standard Oil Co (IN), 1950-60; Sr Sci, Spencer Chem Co, 1960-62; Sect Mgr, MW Res Inst, 1962-69; Mgr, Stauffer Chem Co, 1969-; Mem: Chm KC Sect, Am Chem Soc, 1965; cp/KC Mus Com, 1966-69; Pres, Farmington C of C, 1983-; Rotary Intl; BSA; hon/Author, 35 Papers in Field of Anal Chem; Adv Com, *Anal Chem Jour*, 1962-64; AOAC Referee of Yr, 1973; W/W in E; Am Men of Sci.

BARNHART, RAY A oc/Federal Highway Administrator; b/Jan 12, 1928; h/327 Wren's Way, Falls Church, VA 22046; ba/Washington, DC; m/Jacqueline; c/Mallory Rousselot, Whitney Ziegler; p/O E Barnhart (Alice), Houston, TX; ed/AB, Marietta Col, 1950; MA, Univ of Houston, 1951; mil/AUS, 1946-47; pa/Fac Mem, Marietta Col, 1951-55; Underground Utilities Constrn, Houston, 1956-78; Barmore Ins Agy, Pasadena, TX, 1978-81; Fed Hwy Admr, 1981-; Mem: Pasadena (TX) City Coun, 1965-69; TX St Legis, 1973-74; Commr, TX Hwys & Public Trans Dept, 1979-81; Bd of Dirs, TX Turnpike Auth, 1979-81; cp/Chm, Harris Co Repub Party; Co-Chm, Texans for Reagan, 1976; Chm, Repub Party of TX, 1977; r/Prot.

BARÓN, AUGUSTINE JR oc/Clinical Psychologist; b/Mar 13, 1950; h/ 2507 Rae Dell Avenue, Austin, TX 78704; ba/Austin, TX; p/Augustine Barón Sr (dec); Christine Barraza Barón, El Paso, TX; ed/Dipl, Jesuit HS, El Paso, 1968; BA, Loyola Univ, 1972; MA 1974, PhD Psych 1977, Univ of IL-Urbana-Champaign; pa/Psych Intern Ft Logan Mtl Hlth Ctr, Denver, 1975-76; Staff Psychol 1976-, Prog Dir for Tng 1981-, Cnslg-Psychol Ser Ctr, Univ of TX-Austin; Mem: Am Pers & Guid Assn; Am Psychol Assn; Nat Hispanic Psychol Assn; SWn Psychol Assn; hon/ Author of *The Utilization of Mtl Hlth Ser by Am-Ams: A Critical Anal*, 1979; Editor, *Explorations in Chicano Psychol*, 1981; Num Articles Pub'd in Profl Jours; Hon S'ship, Loyola Univ; 1st Prize, Psi Chi Res Paper Competition, SWn Psychol Assn; Univ Fellow, Loyola Univ; Ford Foun F'ship, Univ of IL; Delta Epsilon Sigma Nat Scholastic Honor Society; Dobro Slovo Nat Hon Soc in Slavic Studies; Psi Chi Psychology Nat Honor Society; W/W in South & Southwest.

BARON, ROBERT ALAN oc/Professor; b/Jun 7, 1943; h/690 Cardinal Drive, Lafayette, IN 47905; ba/West Lafayette, IN; m/Sandra Faye; c/Jessica Lynn; p/ Bernard and Ruth Baron, Bklyn, NY; ed/BS, Bklyn Col, 1964; MA 1967, PhD 1968, Univ of IA; pa/Asst Prof, Univ of SC, 1968-71; Assoc Prof 1971-75, Prof 1975-, Purdue Univ; Vis'g Prof, Princeton univ, 1977-78; Prog Dir, NSF, 1979-81; Vis'g Fellow, Oxford Univ, 1982; pa/Am Psychol Assn; Acad of Mgmt; Intl Soc for Res on Aggression; Soc of Exptl Soc Psych; hon/Author of 14 Books incl'g: *Social Psych* 4th ed, 1984; *Behavior in Orgs*, 1983; *Human Aggression*, 1977; *Understanding Human Relats*, 1985; Fellow, Am Psychol Assn; Vis'g Fellow, Oxford Univ; MCL Awd in Tchg Excell, Purdue Univ, 1984; W/W in MW.

BARONE, FRANK C oc/Gastrointestinal Pharmacologist; b/Jul 5, 1949; h/ 2861 Eagleville Road, Audubon, PA

19407; ba/Phila, PA; m/Diane; c/Adam, Amy; p/Frank & Sophie Barone, Syracuse, NY; sp/Donald & Vivian Osborne, Liverpool, NY; ed/AA, 1971; BA, 1973; PhD, 1978; pa/Res Asst Prof, Syracuse Univ, 1978-82; Postdoct Sci 1982-83, Assoc Sr Investigator 1983-, Smith Kline & French Labs; Mem: Am Physiol Soc; Soc for Neurosci; AAAS; hon/Co-Author of Article in *Am Jour Physiol*, 1984; Co-Author of Book Chapt in *Gastrointestinal Motility*, 1984; Recip, NIH USPHS Traineeship, 1973.

BARR, WARREN PAUL oc/Optometrist; b/Dec 9, 1955; h/640 The Village, Suite 308, Redondo Beach, CA 90277; ba/Hermosa Beach, CA; p/Paul C and Betty Patricia (Warnack) Barr; ed/AA, El Camino Col, 1976; BS 1978, OD 1980, So CA Col of Optom; pa/Visual Electrophysiol Clin, Chd's Hosp, San Diego, 1979-80; Outpatient Clin, LA VA, 1980; Brentwood VA Neuropsychol Hosp, 1980; Las Vegas Low Vision Clin, 1980; Pvt Pract, Hermosa Bch, CA; Mem: AOA; COA; COVD; OEP; APHA; Dir Dept of Profl Affairs, Chm Spkrs Bur, Peer Review Coms, So Bay Optometric Soc; cp/Repub; hon/ Author, Articles Pub'd in *Jour of Am Optom Assn & Review of Optom*; Res on "Effect of Ethanol on the Visual Evoked Cortical Potential in Man"; W/W in CA.

BARRAGA, NATALIE CARTER oc/ Professor Emeritus; b/Oct 10, 15; h/ 1215 Larkwood Drive, Austin, TX 78723; ba/Austin, TX; c/Karen Jeanne; p/Grovie and Bascom Carter (dec); ed/ BS, N TX St Univ, 1938; MEd, Univ of TX-Austin, 1957; EdD, George Peabody Col for Tchrs, 1963; pa/Prof Spec Ed 1971-, Assoc Prof 1966-71, Asst Prof 1963-66, Univ of TX-Austin; Instr, Peabody Col, 1961-62; Tchr Home & Fam Living, TX Sch for the Blind, 1952-61; Tchr, Public Schs TX, 1938-48; Mem: Coun for Exceptl Chd, 1952-; Assn for Ed of Visually Handicapped, 1952-; Fellow, Am Acad Optom, 1965-; Phi Kappa Phi, 1967-; Alpha Chi, 1938; Kappa Delta Pi, 1938; Pi Lambda Theta, 1956; Chapt Pres, Delta Kappa Gamma, 1980-82; Bd of Dirs, Am Foun for the Blind, 1976-82; hon/Author, 3 Books: *Visual Handicaps & Lrng*, 1983; *Source Book on Low Vision*, 1980; *Increased Visual Behavior in Low Vision Chd*, 1964; Author, 3 Monographs & Over 25 Articles; Others; Apollo Awd, Am Optometric Assn, 1979; Tchg Excell, 1966; Shotwell Meml Awd, Assn for Ed & Rehab of Blind & Visually Impaired, 1984; Carel Koch Awd for Ldrshp in Interprof Affairs, Am Acad of Optom, 1983; Dist'd Ser, Low Vision Sec, Am Optom Assn, 1984; W/W: of Wom, of Am Wom, in US, in TX; Outstg Edrs of Am; Other Biogl Listings.

BARRÉ, CHARLES HOWARD oc/ Executive; b/Aug 8, 1922; h/1822 Windsor Place, Findlay, OH 45840; ba/ Findlay, OH; m/Mary Frances Wiseley Smithson; c/Herby C, John B; p/Aubertin Hypolite Barré (dec); Edna Josephine Barré, Findlay, OH; sp/Frank T Wiseley (dec); Mary Wiseley, Findlay, OH; ed/ BS, LA St Univ, 1943; Adv'd Mgmt Prog, Harvard Univ, 1965; pa/Chief Chem 1948-55, Coor Mfg 1955-58, Plant Mgr 1958-65, Plymouth Oil Co, Texas City, TX; Mng Dir, Deutsche Marathon Petro GmbH, Munich, W Germany, 1967-71; Mgr of Spec Prod

Sales 1965-67, VPres Refining 1971-82, Dir 1977-, Dir & VPres 1983-, Marathon Petro Co, Findlay, OH; Mem: Chm Supvry Bd, Deutsche Marathon Petro GmbH, Munich, W Germany, 1977; Dir, Compania Iberica Refinadora de Petroleos, SA-Madrid, Spain, 1977-83; Dir, Citizens Savs & Ln Assn, Tiffin, OH, 1972-; Pres, Marathon Oil Foun, Findlay, OH, 1977-; Dir 1972-, VPres 1975-78, Nat Petro Refiners Assn; Gen Com 1971-, VChm 1975-76, Chm 1977-78, Dept of Am Petro Inst; cp/25 Yr Clb, Am Petro Inst, 1978-; Chm of Bd, SF Plantation Foun, Garyville, LA, 1976; LSA Foun, Baton Rouge, LA, 1978-; r/Cath; hon/Cert of Apprec, Am Petro Inst, Wash DC, 1979; Verdienstorden, St of Bavaria, W Germany, 1982; W/W: in MW, in Am, in World, In Fin & Indust.

BARRETT, BERNARD M JR oc/ Plastic & Reconstructive Surgeon; b/ May 3, 1944; ba/6655 Travis Street, Houston, TX 77030; m/Julia Mae Prokop; c/Audrey Blake, Bernard Joseph, Beverly Frances, Julie Blaine; p/ Dr and Mrs Bernard Barrett, Pensacola, FL; sp/Mr and Mrs Lester Prokop, Houston, TX; ed/BS, Tulane Univ, 1965 MD, Univ of Miami Sch of Med, 1969; Diplomat, Am Bd of Plastic Surg, 1977; Fellow Am Col of Surgs, 1978; mil/USN, Lt Cmdr; pa/Pres, Plastic & Reconstructive Surgs, PA, 1975-; Dir, Am Phys Ins; Dir, API Life Ins Co; Pres, Amerivision Ed TV; Mem: Am Soc of Plastic & Reconstructive Surgs; Am Col of Surgs; TX Soc of Plastic Surgs; Harris Co Med Soc; Fdr, TX Inst of Plastic Surg, Houston, TX; Dir, Plastic Surg Ednl Foun, Chgo, IL; hon/Author of Textbook: *Manual of Patient Care in Plastic Surg*, 1982; Surg Exch S'ship, The Royal Col of Surgs, Guy's Hosp, London, England, 1968; Outstg Surg Intern, Meth Hosp, TX Med Ctr, 1969-70; W/W: in Am, in S & SW; Men of Achmt.

BARRETT, HOLLY JUNE oc/Writer, Retired College Counselor; b/Jun 16, 1928; h/750 Willis Street, Bristol, CT 06010; c/Heather Anne Harris, Laurel Jan Barrett, Jonathan Todd Harris; Steve Craig Harris, Holly June Harris; p/R C Barrett (dec); Ethel Benton Carrington Barrett, Bristol, CT; ed/BA, CT Col for Wom, 1950; MA, AZ St Univ, 1966; AA, Leeward Col, 1982; Grad Wk: Univ Ca-LA; Univ of MO; Univ of HI; pa/Cnslr-Instr, Leeward Col (HI), 1969-84; Spec Edr, Kauai HS, 1968-69; Spanish Tchr, Kapaa HS, 1967-68; Cnslr, Paradise Val HS, 1965-67; Eng Tchr, Wash Sch Dist (Phoenix, AZ), 1964-65; Prescott HS, 1962-63; Publicity Writer, Stephens Col, 1961; Mem: Y-Teen Asst Dir, New London, YWCA, 1950-51; AAUP; AACD; cp/Kappa Delta Pi; Delta Sigma Theta; NAACP; Others; r/Prot; hon/ Pub'd Film: "The Use of Paraprofls in Cnslg," Innovations, 1970; Elected to Kappa Delta Pi, 1964; W/W in W.

BARRETT, JALMA oc/Freelance Writer and Editor, Director; b/Apr 27, 1945; ba/San Diego, CA; m/Larry Allan; p/Mr and Mrs James Conolly Barrett, Norwich & Bklyn, NY; sp/Mr and Mrs Albert Allan, NY; ed/AA, Edgewood Pk Col, 1964; pa/Freelance Writer, 1969-; Edit Dir, The Photographic Inst, 1982-; hon/Author of "How to Take Portraits of Your Pet" w Larry Allan, *Petersen's*

Photographic Mag, 1982; Num Articles in *Dog Fancy* & *Cat Fancy* Mags incl'g: "The Pembroke Welsh Corgi: Royal Favorite Is a Ct Jester," 1983 & "Little Orphan Sandy," 1980; "Unique Animal Rescue Resv Saves Horses' Lives," *Horse Illustrated*; "Exch Homes for Your Next Vacation," *Ladies Home Jour*; Num Others.

BARRETT, JAMES THOMAS oc/ Microbiologist, Immunologist; b/May 20, 1927; h/901 Westport Drive, Columbia, MO 65203; ba/Columbia, MO; m/ Barbro Anna-Lill Nilsson; c/Sara Joann, Robert Wayne, Annika Lill, Nina Marie; p/Alfred W and Mary M Taylor Barrett, Columbia, MO; ed/BA, 1950; MS, 1951; PhD, 1953; pa/Prof 1967-, Assoc Prof 1959-67, Asst Prof 1957-59, Sch of Med, Univ of MO; Asst Prof Bacteriology & Parasitology, Sch of Med, Univ of AR, 1953-57; Res Asst 1952-53, Grad Asst 1951-52, Dept Bacteriology, St Univ of IA; Mem: Am Assn of Immunols; AAAS, 1958; Sigma Xi, 1953; Am Soc for Microbiol, 1951; hon/Author of 2 Books: *Textbook of Immunol* 4th Edition, 1983; *Basic Immunol & its Med Application* 2nd Edition, 1980; Author, Over 50 Articles in Profl Jours incl'g: *Infect Immunol*; *Biochim Biophys Act*; *Tissue Reactions*; *Jour Clin Microbiol*; Others; Fulbright Scholar, Sch of Med, Univ of Repub, Montevideo, Uruguay, 1984; Vis'g Prof & Conslt Sponsored by Scis & Engrs for Ec Devel of NSF 1979, Exch Prof 1974, Sch of Med, Univ of Lagos, Nigeria; Fogarty Sr Intl F'ship, Ludwig-Maxmillians Universitat, NIH, 1977-78; Guest Lectr, Chinese Acad of Sci, Taipai, Taiwan, 1969; Exch Prof, US & Romanian Nat Acads of Sci, 1971; NIH Spec Fellow 1963-64, Sabbatical Leave Res 1970-71, Dept of Immunol, Sch of Med, Univ of Goteborg, Sweden; W/W: in MW, in Frontier Sci & Technol; Commun Ldrs & Noteworthy Ams; Am Men & Wom of Sci; DIB.

BARRETT, RICHARD JOHN oc/ Nuclear Engineer; b/Mar 28, 1945; h/ 7501 Mill Run Drive, Derwood, MD 20855; ba/Bethesda, MD; m/Margaret McNevin; c/Robert, Kathleen; p/Margaret O Barrett, W Pittson, PA; sp/ Evelyn McNevin, Pittson, PA; ed/BS Physics, Univ of Scranton, 1967; PhD Nuclear Physics, Univ of VA, 1973; pa/ Postdoct Fellow, Case Wn Resv Univ, 1972-75; Staff Sci, Los Alamos Nat Lab, 1975-82; Nuclear Engr, US Nuclear Regulatory Comm, 1982-; Mem: Am Nuclear Soc; cp/Bd Mem, Redland Mid Sch PTA; r/Rom Cath; hon/Author of Articles Pub'd in Profl Jours incl'g: *Phy Review*; *Nuclear Physics*; *Nuclear Instrument & Methods*; Num Tech Papers & Reports Presented at Intl Confs; W/W in Frontier Sci & Technol; Am Men & Wom of Sci.

BARRIGA, OMAR O oc/Professor; b/ Mar 1, 1938; h/2315 Fishinger Road, Columbus, OH 43221; ba/Columbus, OH; m/Ines O; c/Omar A, Alvaro G; p/Simon and Elvira Barriga, Santiago, Chile; sp/Mario and Maria, Santiago, Chile; ed/BA 1956, DVM 1963, Univ of Chile; MS 1971, PhD 1973, Univ of IL; pa/Asst Prof, Med Sch, Univ of Chile, Santiago, 1964-68; Asst Prof, Dept Pathobiol, Univ of PA, Phila, 1973-79; Assoc Prof, Dept Pathobiol, OH St Univ, Columbus, 1979-; Mem: Am Soc Parasitologists; Am Soc Tropical Med & Hygiene; Am Soc Profl Hlth &

Preventive Med; r/Cath; hon/Author of Books, *The Immunol of Parasitic Infections*, 1981; Over 50 Sci Articles & Chapts in 3 Books; Vis'g Prof, Univ of Nat Mexico; Vis'g Prof, Univ of Porto Alegre, Brazil; Vis'g Prof, Univ of Dominican Republic.

BARRIGER, JOHN W IV oc/Director of Special Services; b/Aug 3, 1927; h/155 Melrose Avenue, Kenilworth, IL 60043; ba/Chicago, IL; m/Evelyn Dobson; c/John W V, Catherine B; p/John Walker Barriger III (dec); Elizabeth Chambers Thatcher Barriger; sp/David S and Nell Catherine Brundige Dobson (dec); ed/BS, MA Inst of Technol (MIT), 1949; CT, Yale Grad Sch of Ec, 1950; mil/USN, 1946, Seaman 1st Class; USAR, 1951-56, 2nd Lt 713 Ry Batt; pa/Dir Spec Sers, Santa Fe So Pacific Corp, 1983-; Positions w Santa Fe Rwy: Asst to Pres (Chgo) 1979-83, Asst VP of Fin (Chgo) 1977-79, Mgr of Staff Studies & Planning (Chgo) 1970-77, Supt of Trans (Chgo) 1965-68, Trainmaster (Carlsbad, El Paso, Winslow, LA) 1953-65, Trans Insp (Amarillo) 1952-53, Traveling Car Agt (Chgo) 1950-52; Mgr Trans Controls Div, Sylvania Info Sys, Waltham, MA, 1968-70; Mem: Mem 1950-, Dir 1958-68, Am Assn RR Supts; Am Rwy Engrg Assn, 1950-; AAR Treas Div, 1976, Data Sys Div 1968, N Eng RR CLb, 1968-71; Pacific Rwy Clb, 1958-71; Mem 1971-, Chm 1971-76, Rwy Planning Ofcrs Assn; Trans Res Bd, 1974-; Trans Res Forum, 1965-; Mem 1965-, Pres 1979-80, Wn Rwy Clb; Ec Clb of Chgo, 1975-; Exec Clb of Chgo, 1950-; Newcomen Soc, 1950-; Dir, St Louis Mercantile Lib Assn; Trustee, John W Barriger III RR Lib, St Louis; cp/Vis'g Com Dept of Civil Engrg, MIT, 1972-75; Chm MIT Mgmt Conf, Chgo, 1974; Pres MIT Clb of Chgo, 1972-73; Pres, MIT Clb of LA, 1964-65; Dir, MIT Alumni Assn, 1968-72; MIT Awds Com, 1978-80; MIT Corp Devel Com, 1980-; Trustee Village of Kenilworth, 1978-; Chm, Streets, Sanitation & Public Wks, Village of Kenilworth; Delta Kappa Epsilon, MIT & Yale Univs; Kenilworth Yacht Clb, 1972-; MI Shores Clb, 1975-; Union Leag Clb of Chgo, 1967-; Commodore, Kenilworth Yacht Clb; Santa Fe Employee Campaign Chm 1978-79 & 1984, Coalitions Com 1980-, U Way Crusade of Mercy; r/Rom Cath; hon/Author of "The Indust Perspective: Mixing Corp Goals w Public Investmt Critieria," 1975; "Res Needs for Long-Range Planning," 1975; MIT Bronze Beaver Awd, 1975; Employee Campaign Chm of Yr Awd, U Way Crusade of Mercy, 1979; W/W: in MW, in Am, in Fin & Indust; Social Register.

BARRON, CONNIE oc/Restauranteur; b/Apr 16, 1928; h/5016 Airport Hwy, Toledo, OH 43615; ba/Same; m/Darrell Holman; c/Diana Linda Wetzel, Dora Marie Ponce, Daniel Lee; p/Alejos and Ventura Cavazos, Toledo, OH; sp/Reese and Margaret Barron (dec); ed/HS Dipl; w/Loma Linda Restaurant, 1955; Loma Linda Restaurant, Ann Arbor, 1971; Connie Barron Restaurant, 1979; Don Alejos Restaurant, 1979; Casa Barron Restaurant, 1979; Fdr, Wom Bus Owners Assn, 1980; 1st VPres, BPW Clb; hon/Gold Medal Winner, Ballroom Dancing in USA, 1979 & 1980; Nom'd Wom of Yr, 1983; W/W of Wom; DIB.

BARRON, SAUL oc/Professor, Consultant; b/Feb 24, 1917; h/249 Troy-Del-Way, Buffalo, NY 14221; ba/Buffalo, NY; m/Phyllis; c/Elaine Susan Mendelow, Martin Mitchell, Dean Samuel; ed/BSChE, Lafayette Col, 1941; MSChE 1948, PhD Chem Engrg 1954, OH St Univ; mil/USAF, 1943-46 & 1951-52, Capt; pa/US Govt Mech Engr, Wright-Patterson, OH, 1946-54; Staff Engr, Martin-Marietta, 1954-56; Sr Sci, AVCO, 1956-57; Dir of Res, Thiokol Corp, 1958-60; Dir of Res, Bell Aerospace, 1960-64; Prof Chem, SUNY-Buffalo, 1964-; Mem: Tau Beta Pi; Sigma Xi; Phi Lambda Upsilon; Treas 1977 & 1978, VChm 1979, Chm-elect 1980, Chm 1981-82, WNYACS; Adv Coun, Villa Maria Col, 1976-; r/Jewish; hon/Author of Textbook, *Chem for Everyone*, 1984; Over 110 Articles in Profl Jours & 20 Other Tech Pubs; Valedictorian, Southard Public Sch, 1930; Vis'g Prof, Hebrew Univ, 1982; Fellow, Chem Engrg Dept, OH St Univ, 1953 & 1954; W/W in E; Am Men & Wom of Sci.

BARROWS, JOHN FREDERICK oc/Assistant Director Research; b/Dec 26, 1928; h/2254 Ferndell Road, Cazenovia, NY 13305; ba/Syracuse, NY; m/Carol Jane; c/John Edward, Peter Scott, Timothy Allen; p/Elon and Bernice Barrows, Syracuse, NY; sp/Jane Roser, Plymouth, MI; ed/BSME 1951, MSE 1959, PhD 1962, Univ of MI; pa/Proj Engr, Allison Div of Gen Motors Corp, 1951-58; Asst Prof Mech Engrg, Univ of MI, 1961-62; Asst Prof Mech Engrg, Cornell Univ, 1962-67; Chief Aerodynamicist Res Div 1967-70, Chief Engr Res Div 1970-78, Asst Dir Res Div 1978-, Carrier Corp; cp/Layldr, Cazenovia Meth Ch; Pres, Cazenovia Civic Clb, 1976; r/Prot; hon/Author of Book Chapt & Var Articles Pub'd in Profl Jours incl'g: *Trans of ASME*; *Jour of Engrg Ed*; *ASME Jour*; Gen Motors Fellow, 1961; Sigma Xi; Phi Kappa Phi; Pi Tau Sigma; W/W in E; Am Men of Sci.

BARRY, JOHN R oc/Professor; b/Jul 2, 1921; h/189 Spruce Valley, Athens, GA 30605; ba/Athens, GA; m/Marian; c/Judith, David, Elizabeth; p/Stanley R Barry (dec); sp/Clarke Combs, Zanesville, OH; ed/BA, Hamilton Col, 1942; MA, Syracuse Univ, 1943; PhD, OH St Univ, 1949; mil/USAF, 1943-46; pa/Prof Psych, Univ of GA, 1966-; Prof Psych, Univ of FL, 1962-66; Assoc Prof Psych, Univ of Pgh, 1955-61; Asst Dir, Dept Clin Psych, Sch Aviation Med, Randolph Field, TX, 1951-55; Cnslr & Asst Prof, Univ of IL-Chgo, 1949-51; VA Clin Psych Intern, Chillicothe VA Hosp & Columbus VA Mtl Hygiene Clin, OH, 1946-49; Others; Mem: Am Psychol Assn, 1947-; Mem 1962-, Pres 1972, Div of Rehab Psych, APA; Pres 1964, Mem 1955-, Div of Conslltg Psych, APA; Exec Bd, Univ of GA Gerontology Ctr, 1978-; SEn Psychol Assn; AAAS; Soc for Personality Assessment; Am Assn Cnslg & Devel; GA Pers & Guid Assn; Phi Delta Kappa; NY Acad of Sci; Sigma Phi Omega; Conslt, Num Pvt Cos & Public Agys; Conslltg Editor, *Jour of Gerontology*, 1977-; Num Others; cp/Pers Athens Chapt 1982, Mem 1967-, Torch Clb; Mem, Kiwanis Clb; r/Prot; hon/Author, Over 250 Res Papers, Sci Articles & Reports Pub'd in Books, Assn Proceedings & Profl Jours incl'g: *So Jour of Gerontology*; *Rehab Cnslg*; *Acad Psych Bltn*;

Rehab Psych News; *Pers & Guid Jour*; *Conslltg Psych Bltn*; *Eval & Prog Planning*; *The Cnslg Psychol*; *Jour Applied Psych*; Num Others; Cert of Apprec, Nat Proj on Cnslg Older People, Am Pers & Guid Assn, 1981; Spec Issue Dedication, *Jour of Rehab*, 1981; Cert of Apprec, Public Offender Cnslg Assn, 1978; Phi Delta Kappa Ser Key, 1973; Cert of Merit, GA Psychol Assn, 1972 & 1982; Pres Cit for Devel of USAF Airplane Mechs Aptitude Test Battery, 1944; W/W: in S & SW, in GA, Among Writers, in Commun Ser, in Frontier Sci & Technol; Am Men & Wom of Sci; Intl Scholars Dir; 2000 Notable Ams; Num Other Biogl Listings.

BARSKY, ARNOLD MILTON oc/Nuclear Engineer; b/Jun 21, 1953; h/RD 3 Charlton Road, Ballston Lake, NY 12019; ba/Schenectady, NY; m/Dawn Ann; c/Rebecca Marie, Adam Matthew; p/Murray H and Doris Barsky, Morton Grove, IL; sp/Byron and Rosalee Terry, Neenah, WI; ed/BS Physics 1975, BS Astronomy 1975, Univ of IL; MS Nuclear Engrg, Univ of WI, 1977; pa/Exch Student, Energieonderzoek Centrum Nederland, Holland, 1975; Nuclear Opers Engr, Gen Elect Knolls Atomic Power Lab, Schenectady, NY, 1978-81; Nuclear Refueling Engr, Windsor, CT, 1981-83; Chief Refueling Engr, W Milton, NY, 1984; Mem: Am Nuclear Soc; r/Jewish; hon/Author of "Neutron Selfshielding of Activation Detectors Using Total Cross Sect Values from the ENDF/B -IV Lib," 1975; Hon Grad, Univ of IL, 1975; Westinghouse Sci Talent Search Hons Grp, 1971; NASA Sci Contest Winner, 1971; Humble Oil Future Scis S'ship, 1971; Eagle Scout, 1967; W/W in Frontier Sci & Technol.

BARTA, OTA oc/Professor; b/Aug 18, 1931; h/5034 Sout Chalet Court, Baton Rouge, LA 70808; ba/Baton Rouge, LA; m/Vera D; c/Marketa, Tomas; p/Otakar Barta (dec); Ludmila Bartova, Ostrava, Czechoslovakia; sp/Peter and Alzbeta Dadak, Brno, Czechoslovakia; ed/Mediciniae Veterinariae Doctorus (MVDr), 1955; Candidatus Scientiarum (CSc), 1963; Doct of Phil (PhD), 1969; pa/Lectr & Asst Prof, Univ of Vet Med, Brno, Czechoslovakia, 1954-61; Sci, Ctl Res Inst for Animal Husbandry, Prague-Uhrineves, Czechoslovakia, 1961-64; Sci, Inst for Vet Med Res, Brno, Czechoslovakia, 1964-67; Res Assoc, Ontario Vet Col, Univ of Guelph, Ontario, Canada, 1967-69; Asst Prof, Assoc Prof, OK St Univ, Stillwater, OK, 1969-75; Prof, Sch of Vet Med, LA St Univ (LSU), Baton Rouge, 1975-; VPres 1979-80, Pres 1981, Am Assn Vet Immunols; Am Assn Immunols; World Assn of Vet Microbiols, Immunols & Specs in Infectious Diseases; r/Cath; hon/Author, Over 60 Articles in Profl Jours, 1955-; Author of 11 Textbooks & Lab Manuals; Editor, *Lab Techniques of Vet Clin Immunol*, 1984; Chaire Francqui Internationale, Foun Francqui, Bruxelles, Belgium, 1979; Silver Medal, Universite de Liege, Belgium, 1979; Fulbright Sr Lectrship, France, 1981.

BARTELO, DENNISE MASLAKOWSKI oc/Reading And Special Education Specialist; b/Oct 16, 1954; h/PO Box 5054, Weirs Beach, NH 03246; ba/Rochester, NH; p/Henry Maslakowski, Forestville, NY; Harriette Maslakowski (dec); ed/BA Elem Ed & Spec Ed 1976, MA Rdg 1979, Incarnate Word Col; Doct Cand Curric & Instrn, VA Polytech Inst & St Univ; pa/Ed Instr, Univ of Houston, Victoria, TX, 1980 & 1983; Instr in Ed, Plymouth St Col, Plymouth, NH; Rdg/Spec Ed Spec, Spaulding HS, Rochester, NH, 1982-83; Rdg Spec, Charles Co, MD, 1979-82; Title I Rdg Tchr, San Antonio Sch Dist, 1977-79; Grad Asst, Incarnate Word, 1979; Gifted Resource Tchr, Trinity Univ, TX, 1978-79; Elem Tchr (Grade 5), St Paul's Sch, TX, 1975-77; Mem: IRA; NCTE; NH Coun of Tchrs of Eng; Coun of Exceptl Chd; Tchrs of Eng as a 2nd or Other Lang; r/Cath; hon/Author of "Functional Writing, Rdg, Spkg Activs," in *Non-Native & Non-Dialect Students*, 1982; "Functional Writing for ESOL Students," 1983; "Elaborating Curric for the Gifted," 1981; "Effect of Silent Rdg on Rdg Achmt," 1980; Outstg Tchr, Charles Co, MD, 1982; Jr Miss, 1971; Dunkirk-Fredonia Murray Fire Dept Queen, 1970; NY Regents S'ship; Wm Bookstaver S'ship, 1972; W/W in E.

BARTHOLOMEW, GARY RAY oc/College President; b/Jul 3, 1947; h/1001 Platte Avenue, York, NE 68567; ba/York, NE; m/Gwen; c/Stacey, Raymond; p/Mrs Ray Bartholomew, Littleton, CO; ed/AA, York Col, 1967; BA, Harding Univ, 1969; MBA, Univ of Denver, 1971; mil/USAFR, Lt; pa/Pres 1978-, Asst to Pres 1976-78, York Col, NE; Asst Prof Bus Adm, Harding Univ, 1971-76; Staff Acct, Arthur Anderson CPA Firm, 1969-70; Mem: Secy, NE Indep Col Foun, 1982; NE Soc of CPA's, 1977; Am Inst of CPA's, 1973-78; cp/York Co Crusade Chm, Am Cancer Soc, 1982; City of York Airport Zoning Bd, 1979-; Newcomen Soc of Am, 1978-; York C of C, 1978-; Chaplain, Rotary Intl, 1978-; r/Ch of Christ; hon/Var Hon LLD's from: OK Christian Col, 1982; Pepperdine Univ, 1982; Harding Univ, 1982; Lubbock Christian Col, 1983; W/W in MW; Men of Achmt; Outstg Yg Men of Am.

BARTKE, ANDRZEJ oc/Department Chairman; b/May 23, 1939; h/Rural Route 2, Box 157, Makanda, IL 62958; ba/Carbondale, IL; m/Rose; p/Gustaw and Jadwiga Bartke, Krakow, Poland; ed/MSc Biol (Zool), Jagiellonian Univ, Poland, 1962; PhD Zool (Genetics), Univ of KS, 1965; pa/Chm Dept Physiol, So IL Univ Sch of Med, Carbondale, 1984-; Prof Depts of OB & GYN & Anatomy 1982-84, Assoc Prof 1978-82, Univ of TX Hlth Sci Ctr-San Antonio; Sr Sci 1972-78, Staff Sci 1969-72, Fellow Tng Prog in Reproductive Physiol 1967-69, Worcester Foun for Exptl Biol, Shrewsbury, MA; Asst Prof Dept of Genetics, Jagiellonian Univ, Poland, 1965-67; Vis'g Sci, Inst for Cancer Res, Phila, PA, 1965; NIH Trainee, Dept Zool, Univ of KS, Lawrence, 1962-64; Mem: VPres 1984-85, Soc for Study of Reprodn; Pres, Am Soc of Andrology, 1983-84; Endocrine Soc; Soc for Endocrinology (UK); AAAS; Sigma Xi; Soc for Study of Fertility (UK); r/Rom Cath; hon/Author, Over 150 Res Pubs; Var Book Chapts & Abstracts; Mem Edit Bd, *Biol of Reprodn*, 1978-82; Dir, Soc for Study of Reprodn, 1979-81; Mem Reproductive Biol Study Sect, NIH, 1977-81; Mem Coun, Am Soc Andrology, 1976-78; Admiral Ralph Earle Awd,

Worcester Engrg Soc, 1973; Res Career Devel Awd, NICHD, 1972-77; Recip Num Grants, NICHD, NIDA, NSF; W/W in Frontier of Sci & Technol; Am Men of Sci.

BARTLEY, S HOWARD oc/Psychologist, Professor, Writer; b/Jun 19, 1901; h/117 North Highland, Apartment 716, Memphis, TN 38111; ba/Memphis, TN; m/Leola B; c/S Howard Jr, Jeanne Antoinette, Katherine Joyce; p/Edward G Bartley (dec); sp/James McCLure Bevis (dec); ed/BS, Greenville Col (IL), 1923; MA 1928, PhD 1931, Univ of KS; pa/Psych & Physiol Tchr, Miltonvale Wesleyan Col, 1924-25; Asst Instr to Instr in Psych, Univ of KS, 1926-31; Fellow Nat Res Coun Dept Opthal Res 1931-33, Res Assoc Psych & Biophysics Lab of Neurophysiol 1933-42, Wash Univ Med Sch (St Louis); Asst Prof Physiol Optics 1942-45, Prof of Res of Visual Scis 1945-47, Dir Dartmouth Eye Inst's Res for Ofc of Sci Res & Devel WW II, Dartmouth Eye Inst (Dartmouth Med Sch); Prof Psych 1947-71, Dir Lab for Study of Vision & Related Sensory Processes 1966-71, Emeritus Prof 1971-, MI St Univ; Dist'd Vis'g Prof Dept Psych 1972-74, Dist'd Res Prof 1974-, Memphis St Univ; Mem: Am Psychol Assn; Am Physiol Soc; Am Acad of Optom; MWn Psychol Assn; Opt Soc of Am; Am Col Sports Med; AAAS; Soc Exptl Psychols; Sigma Xi; Phi Sigma; Beta Sigma Kappa; So Soc Phil & Psych; r/Prot; hon/Author of 8 Books incl'g: *Intro to Perception*, 1980; *Perception in Everyday Life*, 1972; *The Human Organism as a Person*, 1967; *The Mech & Mgmt of Fatigue*, 1965; *Principle of Perception*, 2nd Edition 1969; Others; Author, Over 278 Articles Pub'd in Profl Jours, Handbooks, Encys; Nat Res Coun Fellow, 1931-32 & 1932-33; Dist'd Prof Awd, MI St Univ, 1960; Sr Sigma Xi Awd for Meritorious Res, MI St Univ, 1962; Apollo Awd, Am Opt Assn, 1970; Prentice Hall Medal, Am Acad Optom, 1972; Am Men of Sci; Ldrs in Am Sci; Commun Ldrs of Am; Dir Ednl Specs; Notable Ams; DIB; Num W/W & Other Biogl Listings.

BARTLIT, JOHN RAHN oc/Chemical Engineer; b/Jun 1, 1934; h/113 Monte Rey North, Los Alamos, NM 87544; ba/Los Alamos, NM; m/Nancy R; c/Jennifer R, John Reynolds; p/Mr and Mrs Fred Bartlit, Flossmoor, IL; ed/BSChE, Purdue Univ, 1956; MSE, Princeton Univ, 1957; DEngrg, Yale Univ, 1963; pa/Instr, Yale Univ, 1961-62; Staff Mem 1962-, Assoc Grp Ldr 1983, Los Alamos Nat Lab; cp/St Chm, NM Citizens for Clean Air & Water Inc, 1971-; hon/Author, Num Tech Papers on Chem Engrg & on Envir; Outstg Citizen Achmt Awd, Rocky Mt Ctr on Envir, 1973; Technol Utilization Awd, NASA/AEC, 1970.

BARTON, GLADYS HOLLANDER oc/Art Director, Advertising; b/Dec 9, 1938; h/245 Everit Aveneue, Hewlett Harbor, NY 11557; ba/Melville, NY; m/Lawrence A; c/Hugh, Ann, Jamie, Laura; p/Miriam Reiman Hollander, Bklyn, NY; sp/Ceil Baron, Deerfield Bch, FL; ed/Grad, HS of Music & Art, NYC, 1956; BFA, Pratt Inst, NYC, 1960; pa/Graphic Designer, R Danzer Studio, 1960; Art Dir, Clairol Inc (Div of Bristol-Meyers), 1961; Sr Art Dir, VPres, Wunderman, Ricotta & Kline

(Div of Yg & Rubicam), 1974; Creat Supvr, VPres, Benton & Bowles Direct Inc, 1981-84; Assoc Creat Dir, Greenstone & Rabasca Advtg; VPres, Art Dirs Clb of NY; Mem: Type Dirs Clb of NY; Nat Assn Female Execs; Allied Bd of Trade; Nat Soc of Interior Designers; hon/Author of Var Articles & Interviews in Advtg Trade Papers & Mags; Recip of Awds from: The Art Dirs Clb of NY, 1979-; Type Dirs Clb of NY, 1975; Direct Mktg Assn, 1979-80; Design Awds, 1980; Creativity, 1977 & 1980 & 1982; Effie Awd, 1979-; W/W of Am Wom.

BARTON, JERRY L oc/Executive; b/Nov 7, 1937; h/1103 Evergreen Road, Anchorage, KY 40223; ba/Louisville, KY; m/Patricia Hollis; c/Lee, Hollis, Stuart, Bill; p/Harry Barton, Hogansville, GA; sp/Mr and Mrs Jim Hollis (dec); ed/Att'd GA St Univ, 1955-57; Deg in Bus Adm, Univ of CA, 1967-68; pa/Genuine Parts Co, 1955-73; VPres Mktg, Gen Genuine Parts Co, 1974-77; Pres, Beck & Gregg Industs (Div of Gen Parts), 1977-80; Pres & Chm of Bd, Belknap Inc, 1980-; Bd of Dirs, Potter Industs; Bd of Dirs, KFC Nat Purchasing Coop Inc; Bd of Dirs, Hillerich & Bradsby Co Inc; Bd of Trustees, Bellarmine Col; Yg Pres's Org; Nat Wholesale Hardware Assn; So Hardware Assn; cp/Bd of Dirs, L'ville C of C; r/Meth; hon/Hardware Mdser of Yr, 1981; Campaign Chm, W/W May, 1982.

BARTON, WILLIAM L oc/Minister, Program Director; b/Aug 25, 1924; h/Route 4, Box 204 Ocean Springs, MS 39564; ba/Ocean Springs, MS; m/Jean L; c/Manly, Virgil, Billy Jr, Michael; p/Manly L Barton (dec); Mrs Addie Barton, Ocean Springs, MS; ed/BA, Toccoa Falls Bible Col, 1948; pa/Pastor: Bay View Hgts Bapt Ch, Mobile, AL, 3 Yrs; 1st Bapt Satsuma, AL, 7 Yrs; Jackson Ave Bapt Ch, Pascagoula, MS, 7 Yrs; Ft Bayou Bapt Ch, 1 Yr; Interim Pastor of 21 Chs in Jackson, George & Harrison Cos from 1966-1980; Exec Dir, Homes of Grace: for Alcoholic Men 1965-, for Wom 1967-, for Chd 1969-, for Sr Citizens 1975-; Pres, Min Assn at Toccoa Falls Bible Col; Pres, Jackson Co Min Assn; Pres, So Dist of Intl Union of Gospel Missions; Others; cp/Pres, Gautier Rotary Clb, 1983-84; Pres, Pascagoula Civitan Clb, 1984-85; Dist Chaplain, MS Civitan Clb, 1983-84; Others; r/Bapt; hon/Outstg Citizen of Jackson Co, MS, 1966; Others.

BARTSCHT, WALTRAUD ERIKA oc/Educator, Germanist; b/Oct 16, 1924; ba/Univ of Dallas, Irving, TX 75061; m/Heri Bert; c/Martin Donald; p/Bruno and Edith Gutensohn, Munich, Germany; sp/Richard and Emma Bartscht, Luedenscheid, Germany; ed/Dipl, Deutsche Meisterschule fuer Mode, Munich, Germany, 1949; MA, So Meth Univ, 1966; PhD Cand, Univ of TX-Dallas; pa/Fashion Designer, Munich, 1949-52; Fashion Designer, LA & Dallas, 1953-65; German Instr 1966-69, Asst Prof German 1969-80, Assoc Prof & Chm Univ Dept Fgn Langs 1980-, Univ of Dallas; Mem: TX Fgn Lang Assn; So Ctl Mod Lang Assn; Reg Chm 1972-75, Am Assn of German Tchrs; TX German Heritage Soc; Fdg Mem, Dallas Goethe Ctr; r/Luth; Pubs/Translator, Goethe's "Das Maerchen," 1972; Num Poems Translated, Reviews

& Articles Pub'd in Jours incl'g: *Rice Univ Studies*; *Constantin Review*; *Schatzkammer*; *Translation Reveiw*; *Dragonflies*; Others; hon/Textile Artwks in Perkins Chapel, So Meth Univ & St Paul's Luth Ch, Brenham, TX.

BARZUN, JACQUES M oc/Author, Literary Consultant; b/Nov 30, 1907; ba/New York, NY; m/Marguerite; c/ James Lowell, Roger Martin, Isabel; p/ Henri and Anna-Rose Barzun; ed/Lycée Janson de Sailly; AB, MA, PhD, Columbia Univ; pa/Positions w Columbia Univ: Instr, 1929-37; Asst Prof, 1938-42; Assoc Prof, 1942-45; Prof Hist, 1945-60; Seth Low Prof of Hist, 1960-67; Univ Prof of Hist, 1967-75; Dean of Grad Facs, 1955-58; Dean of Facs & Provost, 1958-67; Univ Prof Emeritus; Spec Advr on Arts, 1967-75; Lit Conslt, Charles Scribner's Sons, 1975-; Dir, Macmillan Inc, 1965-75; Trustee, NYU Soc Lib; Dir, Coun for Basic Ed; Dir, Peabody Inst; Adv Coun Univ Col at Buckingham; Dir, Am Friends of Cambridge Univ; Mem: Am Acad of Arts & Scis; Pres 1972-75, 1977-78, Am Acad & Nat Inst of Arts & Lttrs; Am Hist Assn; Friends of Columbia Univ Libs; Phi Beta Kappa; Corres'g Mem, MA Hist Soc; hon/Num Pubs; Decorated Legion of Hon; Am Coun of Learned Socs Res Fellow, 1933-34; George Polk Meml Awd, 1967; Fellow, Royal Soc of Arts; Extraordinary Fellow, Churchill Col, Cambridge, 1961-; W/W: in E in World, in Am; Contemp Authors.

BASSETT, ELIZABETH EWING oc/ Director, Publications & Communications; b/Jul 22, 1937; h/332 East 19th Street, New York, NY 10003; ba/New York, NY; p/Ben and Eileen Bassett, Larchmont, NY; ed/AA, Bradford Jr Col; Addit Study: NY Univ & The New Sch; pa/1957-63: Adm Asst-Girl Friday, Time Inc; Life Mag; Chesebrough-Ponds Inc; Ferro, Mogubgub & Schwartz; L & L Animation; 1963-64: Staging Asst & Stage Mgr, NY St Pavilion, NY World's Fair; 1965-72: Reporter/Editor, AP, NY; 1972-77: Freelance Fgn Correspondent in Africa & MidE for AP, *Scholastic Mags*, *Newswk*, ABC Radio & TV, Voice of Am, UNICEF; *MidE Mkts*, *Newsday*; 1978-: Editor-in-Chief & Dir, Pubs & Communs, World Envir Ctr, NY; Mem: Sigma Delta Chi; Soc Profl Jours; Fgn Press Assn, Cairo; Lectr: Am Univ in Cairo 1977, Rutgers Univ 1978, Columbia Univ 1981, LI Univ 1983; hon/Author, Num Pubs in Mags, Jours & Newspapers; Author, *The Growth of Envir in the World Bk*, 1982; Jour Awd for Edit Excell, Best Non-Profit Org Newslttr, Newslttr Assn of Am, 1980; W/W in E; Foremost Wom in Communs.

BASSIN, ALEXANDER oc/Professor; b/Aug 4, 1912; h/2312 Domingo Drive, Tallahassee, FL 32304; ba/Tallahassee, FL; m/Ann; c/Barry, Roy; ed/BA, Bklyn Col, 1934; MA 1951, PhD 1957, NY Univ; mil/AUS, Corp of Engrs, 1943-46; pa/Social Wkr NYC, 1938-43; Probation Ofcr & Dir of Res, 1946-58; Dir of Grp Therapy, Baro Psychi Clin 1958-68; Prof Criminology, FL St Univ, 1968-; Pres, NY Chapt, Am Soc of Grp Psychotherapy & Psychodrama, 1962-66; Pres Bd of Dirs, DISC Village Therapeutic Commun, 1971-; Bd of Govs, Daytop Village Inc, 1966-; hon/Author of Book, *The Reality Therapy Reader*, 1976;

Articles Pub'd in: *Psych Today*; *Jour of Drug Issues*, *Fed Probation*; Others.

BAST, ROSE ANN oc/Chairperson and Professor; b/Sep 10, 1934; h/2900 North Menomonee River Parkway, Milwaukee, WI 53222; ba/Milwaukee, WI; p/Lester and Bernice Bast, Cuba, MO; ed/BS, Notre Dame Col, 1960; MS 1963, PhD 1966, Univ of OK; pa/Tchr, St John Elem Sch, Burlington, IA, 1954-56; Tchr, St Augustine Elem Sch, Breese, IL, 1956-58; Tchr, Sacred Heart HS, NO, 1958-61; Grad Tchg Ass, Univ of OK, 1961-63; Fac of Notre Dame Col, St Louis, 1966-77; Chp & Assoc Prof Dept of Biol 1977-, Mem Fac Senate 1977-80, Chp 1979-80 & Secy 1978-79 Curric & Devel Com, Mt Mary Col; Chapt Fac Advr, Beta Beta Beta; Sigma Xi; Phi Sigma; AAAS; Am Inst Biol Sci; WI Sci Tchrs Assn; Mem, Sch Sisters of Notre Dame; r/Rom Cath; hon/ Author of Var Lectrs: "The Brain: Its Role in the Lrng Process," 1981; "The Aging Brain," 1981-82; Author of Article Pub'd in *Growth*, 1968; Valedictorian of Sr Class, 1952; BS cum laude, 1960; Mem, NY Acad of Sci, 1980; W/ W: of Am Wom, in Ed; 2000 Notable Ams; Dir Dist'd Ams.

BASTURA, BERNARD ALEX oc/ Museum Curator; b/Jul 13, 1933; h/440 Washington Street, Middletown, CT 06457; ba/Middletown, CT; p/Andrew and Mary (Kaminska) Bastura; ed/Dipl, HS; mil/AUS; pa/Fdr & Curator, Submarine Lib/Mus, Middletown, CT; Mem, US Submarine Vets of WW II, 1968; cp/Middletown JCs, 1965; Acad of Country Music, CA, 1976; r/Cath; hon/ Author of Book, *Hist of US Submarine Vets of WW II*; Author of Num Articles on Submarines Pub'd in Var Pubs; hon Life Mem, US Submarine Vets of WW II, 1968; Num Meritorious Ser Awds, US Submarine Vets of WW II Chapts, 1966-83; Hon Cmdr, Submarine Meml Assn, Hackensack, NJ, 1976-; Hon Mem, USS Flasher Chapt, NY, 1980-; Hon Assoc Mem of Acad of Country Music, CA, 1975-; Hon Crew Mem, USS Cavalla (SS-244), 1964; Nom'd for Jefferson Awds, by TV Sta WTNH-TV, New Haven, CT, 1983; Featured on "PM Mag" TV Show on Channel 3 Hartford, CT.

BATES, BARBARA JEANNE oc/ Educator, Speaker, Motivator, Coordinator for Living History Programs; h/ 3000 Valley Forge Circle, King of Prussia, PA 19406; ba/Erdenheim, PA; c/Brenda; ed/BS Ed, 1950; MS Lib Sci 1951, Tchg Cert for PA, 1953; pa/ Co-Fdr, Global Ed Motivators, Erdenheim (suburban Phila), PA, 1981-; Fdr, Pres, Coor & Media Dir, Betsy Ross Living Hist Presentations, 1982; Lib Coor, Springfield Sch Dist, 1971-82; Prison Libn, Kulani Correctional Facility, 1976; Libn, Lansdowne-Aldan Sch Dist, 1962-71; Libn, AUS Dependents Schs, Germany, 1955-62; Libn, Free Lib of Phila, 1951-54; Wkend Libn in Charge of Ref, Phila Commun Col, 1977-80; Mem: NEA; PA Lib Assn; PA Ednl Assn; Friends of Libs, USA; Intl Sch Libs Assn; Nat Soc Studies Assn; Nat Lib Assn; World Future Soc; cp/ ARC Disaster Action Tm, 1983-; r/Prot; hon/Chapel of the 4 Chaplains Awd, 1982; PA Lib Assn Publicity Awd, 1969; Del, Gov's Conf on Libs & Info Sers, 1979; George Wash Hon Medal, Free-

doms Foun, Val Forge, PA, 1982.

BATESKO, MARYLEE oc/Professor; b/Jun 8, 1936; h/2119 Vermont Avenue, Toms River, NJ 08753; ba/Lakewood, NJ; m/Ronald Joseph; c/Ronald Jack, Richard John; p/Leona Binns; sp/John Batesko (dec); ed/BA, Trenton St Col, 1968; MA, Kean Col, 1972; EdD, Rutgers Univ, 1982; pa/Prof Ed 1983-, Assoc Prof 1979-83, Asst Prof 1976-79, Instr 1974-76, Georgian Ct Col; NJ St Dept of Ed, 1972-76; Clrm Tchr, 1966-72; Mem: Zeta Chapt, IRA; NJ Rdg Assn; Pres, Delta Kappa Gamma; ASCD; r/Epis; hon/Author of Papers Presented at Conf for Wom (Rutgers) & Intl Conf for Literacy Vols.

BATISTE, PEARL EDGERLY oc/ Educator; b/Dec 9, 1930; h/2509 Tulare Avenue, El Cerrito, CA 94530; m/ Berwick; c/Michael, Keith, Ronald, Elissa, Ingrid, Patrik; p/Erris Edgerly (dec); Pearl Armelin Edgerly; sp/John and Silvia Batiste (dec); ed/BA, CA St Univ-SF, 1975; MA Ed, Univ of SF, 1978; MS Sch Adm 1979, PhD 1983, Pepperdine Univ; pa/Dir Cnslg Dept, Amrick Advt, Oakland, CA, 1976-77; Public Relats Dir, SF Ed Dept, 1977-78; Fashion Model & Instr, Barbozon Modeling Agy & Sch, 1975-76; Prog & Proj Coor, Oakland Public Sch, 1976; Mem: Nat Assn for Wom Deans, Admrs & Cnslrs; Nat Exec Sales Org; Profl Wom Exec Corp; ABPW Assn; Nat Alliance Bus Assn; r/Cath; hon/Author of "The Black Wom"; "Re-entry Prog for Wom"; The Influence of African Culture on Am Fashion"; Deans List; W/W: in W, in Am; Intl W/W.

BATTERSBY, HAROLD RONALD ERIC oc/Educator; b/Nov 16, 1922; h/ Box 80, Groveland Station, NY, 14462; ba/Blake D 114, Linguistics, SUNY-Geneseo, NY 14454; m/Betty Yertchenig O'Hannesian; p/Battersby, Eric Samuel John (dec); Lilian Susan Darnell Battersby, Surrey, England; ed/BA, Mod Near En Studies, Univ of Toronto, 1960; PhD (Altaic & Uralic Studies), IN Univ, 1969; mil/RAFVR, 1939-46; pa/ Prof Anthropology & Linguistics, SUNY-Geneseo; Res Altaic Studies; Dept Anthropol & Linguistics; Dir, Linguistics Prog 1978-; Mem: Chm, Com of Linguistics; Curric Com, Fac Adv Com Indep Study Linguistics 1970-71, Profl Standards & Ethics Com 1972-73, Num Other Univ Positions; Sect Editor for Altaic & Uralic Studies, *Jour of Ultimate Reality & Meaning*, The Inst for Ency of Ultimate Reality & Meaning, Regis Col, Univ of Toronto, 1981-; 1947-55: Former Fgn Correspondent, *Surrey Times*; Past Adv Dir & Editor, *Turkish Post*; Former Eng Instr, Istanbul Univ Med Fac; Translator; Asst Mgr, City of Toronto, 1955-60; Others; F'ships & Mbrships Incl: Am Anthropol Assn; Linguistic Soc Am; Royal Anthropol Inst Great Brit & Ireland; Royal Asia Soc; Am Oriental Soc; Hakluyt Soc; Intl Soc Oriental Res; Inst Ency Human Ideas Ultimate Reality & Meaning; Armenian Gen Benevolent Union of Am; Brit Inst of Archaeol at Ankara; NY Coun on Linguistics; Others; r/Epis; hon/Author, Over 150 Items Pub'd incl'g: "The Uzbeks & Their Ideas of Ultimate Reality & Meaning"; Others; Nat Trust Awd, Mod Near En Studies, Toronto, 1958-60; NDEA F'ship, Univ of IN, 1969; Recip Grants,

Geneseo Foun, 1973, 1977 & 1978-79; Num Other Fgn & Domestic Hons; Num W/W & Other Biogl Listings.

BATTISTICH, VICTOR ANTHONY oc/Research Psychologist; b/Sep 9, 1952; h/775 Hickory Avenue, Tracy, CA 95376; ba/Devel Studies Ctr, 130 Ryan Ct, Suite 210, San Ramon, CA; m/Martha Susan Montgomery; c/Sarah; p/Carl and Marian Battistich, Sacramento, CA; sp/William and Shirley Montgomery, Saline, MI; ed/BA, CA St Univ-Sacramento, 1974; MA 1976, PhD 1979, Personality-Social Psych, MI St Univ; pa/Sr Res Assoc, Ctr for Eval & Assessment, Dept of Psych, MI St Univ, 1978-79; Vis'g Asst Prof, Dept of Psych & 1st Col, Cleveland St Univ, 1979-80; Sr Res Assoc, Devel Studies Ctr, San Ramon, CA, 1981-; Mem: AAAS; Am Psychol Assn; Intl Assn for Study of Coop in Ed; MWn Psychol Assn; Wn Psychol Assn; Soc for Personality Assessment; Soc for Personality & Social Psych; Soc for Psychol Study of Social Issues; hon/Author, Over 25 Pub'd Articles, Res Paper Presentations & Tech Reports; BA w Highest Hons, CA St Univ, 1974; Phi Kappa Phi, 1976; W/W: in W, in Frontier Sci & Technol.

BATTS, NATHALIE C oc/Librarian; b/Nov 3, 1918; h/21 Claremont Avenue, New York, NY 10027; ba/New York, NY; m/Walter Maitland Petrie (dec); p/Frank C Chlan & Bertha M Prager (dec); sp/Walter Batts & Emma Lakin (dec); ed/AB, Col of Notre Dame (MD), 1940; BS 1946, MS 1966, Lib Ser, Columbia Univ; MA Ec, Mt Holyoke Col, 1951; pa/Jr Asst, Enoch Pratt Free Lib, Balto, MD, 1942-45; 1st Asst Circulation Dept 1945-49, Order Libn 1949-51, Mt Holyoke Col Lib, So Hadley, MA; Asst Ref Libn Columbia Univ Bus Lib 1951-55, Ref Libn 1955-62, Serials Cataloger 1962-, Columbia Univ; Mem: Am Lib Assn; Am Ec Assn; Am Numismatic Assn; Secy/Treas 1968-69, NY Tech Sers Libns; Dir, Columbia Univ Sch of Lib Ser Alumni Assn; Beta Phi Mu, 1966-; Charter Mem, Past Pres, Past VPres, Past Treas, Nu Chapt, Beta Phi Mu (Intl Lib Hon Soc); r/Cath; hon/Compiler, *Org Charts*, 1953; Editor, *The Dewey Decimal Classification: Outlines & Papers*, 1968; Editor, *Lib Ser News*, 1972-; MLS w Hons, Columbia Univ Sch of Lib Ser, 1966; Elected to Beta Phi Mu, 1966; W/W: in Lib & Info Sers, of Am Wom, in E, of Wom; DIB.

BAUER, CHARLES RONALD oc/Physician; b/May 16, 1943; h/14650 Southwest 69th Avenue, Miami, FL 33158; ba/Miami, FL; m/Rita Ehnes; c/Charles Jr, Kristen, Gabrielle; p/Charles and Ann Kalmar Bauer; ed/BS, Iona Col, 1965; MD, Univ of WVA, 1969; pa/Neonatologist, Assoc Prof of Pediatrics, Univ of Miami; Bd of Dirs, S FL Perinatal Netwk; Am Acad Pediatrics, AMA; FL Soc Neonatal Perinatologists; FL Med Assn; cp/Bd of Dirs & Exec Com Dade-Monroe Chapt, Nat Foun March of Dimes; r/Rom Cath; hon/Author of "Corticosteroids & Lung Maturation," in *Gyn & Ob*, 1981; Author, Over 26 Articles Pub'd in Profl Jours, 1972-; Outstg Tchg Awd, Am Acad Pediatrics; W/W in S & SW; "The Best Docts in The US".

BAUER, K JACK oc/Professor; b/Jul 30, 1926; h/9 Riding Club Road, Troy, NY 12180; ba/Troy, NY; m/Dorothy; c/

Eric Day, Neil Fairbanks, Anne Crain; p/Charles A and Isabelle F Bauer; sp/C Forbes and Elizabeth D Sargent; ed/AB, Harvard Univ, 1948; MA 1949, PhD 1953, IN Univ; pa/Archivist, US Nat Archives, 1954-55; Histn, USMC, 1955-57; Histn, USN, 1957-61; Asst Prof, Morris Harvey Col, 1961-65; Assoc Prof 1965-70, Prof 1970-, Hist, Rensselaer Polytech Inst; Mem: Trustee 1958-61 & 1979-, Am Mil Inst; VPres 1981-83, Bd Mem 1985-, N Am Soc for Oceanic Hist; cp/Bd Mem, Friends of Troy Public Lib, 1971-; Bd Mem, Troy Chromatic Concerts Inc, 1980-83; r/Epis; hon/Author of 3 Hist Books: *The Mexican War 1846-1848*; *Ships of the Navy 1775-1969*; *Surfboats & Horse Marines*; Editor & Co-Editor of 4 Hist Books: *Ports of the W*; *New Am St Papers: Nav Affairs*; *Soldiering*; *Am Secys of the Navy*; John Lyman Awd, 1982.

BAUER, RAYMOND G oc/Sales Executive; b/Jun 19, 1934; h/132 Maple Avenue, Haddonfield, NJ 08033; ba/Haddonfield, NJ; m/Jayne Whitehead; ed/AA, Monmouth Col, 1955; BBA, Univ of Miami, FL, 1958; mil/USAF, 1959-64; pa/Owner & Sales Exec, Ray Bauer Assocs (Mfrs Reps Co), 1974-; Div Mgr, R J Reynolds Tobacco Co, Winston-Salem, NC, 1959-68; Mid Atl Mgr, US Envelope Co, MA, 1968-74; Mem: Am Mgmt Assn; Lambda Chi Alpha; Lambda Sigma Tau; Smithsonian Assocs; AF Assn; Am Security Coun; Ofcr, USAF Aux; US Senatorial Clb; Am Conservative Union; Am Tax Reduction Movement; Monmouth Col & Univ of Miami Alumni Assns; Intl Platform Assn; cp/Iron Rock Swim & Country Clb; Arrowhead Racquet Clb; Friends of Haddonfield Lib; Haddonfield Civic Assn; r/Hons Incl Var Co Sales, Mgmt & Ath Awds; Var Biogl Listings.

BAUM, BERNARD oc/Chemist, Executive; b/Sep 21, 1924; h/44 Kirkwood Road, West Hartford, CT 06117; ba/Enfield, CT; m/Evelyn; c/Joanne; p/Samuel and Esther Baum (dec0; ed/BS, Univ of Lowell, 1947; MA 1949, PhD 1950, Chem, Clark Univ; mil/AUS, 1944-46; pa/Chemist, Sherwin Williams, 1950-53; Res Assoc, Union Carbide, 1953-62; Grp Ldr, Allied Chem, 1962-64; Dir of Res Cast Nylon Dept, Budd Co, 1964-67; VPres Mats Res & Devel, Springborn, 1967-; Mem: Am Chem Soc (ACS); Soc of Plastics Engrs (SPE); SAMPE; r/Jewish; hon/Author 2 Books, 6 Book Chapts & 60 Article Pubs; Holder of 25 Patents in Field; Sigma Xi; Men of Sci.

BAUM, CARL EDWARD oc/Electromagnetic Theorist; b/Feb 6, 1940; h/5116 Eastern, Southeast, Unit D, Albuquerque, NM 87108; ba/Albuquerque; p/George Theodore Baum (dec); Evelyn Monica Bliven, Coventry, RI; ed/BS Engrg 1962, MS Elect Engrg 1963, PhD Elect Engrg 1969, CA Inst of Technol; mil/USAF, 1962-71; pa/Capt, AF Weapons Lab, NM, 1963-71; Sr Sci, Electromagnetics, AF Weapons Lab, NM, 1971-; Advr, Num AUS, Navy, AF & Tri-ser Agys on EMP Matters; US Rep, Exchanging EMP Info to Fgn Countries; Mem: Dir & Pres, SUMMA Foun; NM Acad of Sci; Fellow, IEEE, 1984-; Co-Chm, Joint Tech Com of Nuclear Electromagnetic Pulse for IEEE Antennas & Progagation Soc & IEEE Electromagnetic Compatability Soc, 1978-;

Appt'd Dist'd Lectr, Antennas & Propagation Soc, 1977-78; Chm, Albuquerque Joint Chapt IEEE of Antennas & Propagation Microwave Theory & Techniques, & Electromagnetic Compatability Socs, 1977; Elected to Comms B & E of US Nat Com, Intl Union of Radio Sci; US Del to Gen Assem of Union of Radio Sci: Lima Peru 1975, Helsinki Finland 1978, Wash DC 1981; Florence, Italy, 1984; Pres, Electromagnetics Soc; Life Fellow, Intl Biogl Assn, 1976; Life Fellow, Am Biogl Assn, 1979; r/Cath; hon/Composer of 9 Musical Compositions (Sacred), 1981-84; Author of 4 Book Chapts & 15 Res Articles Pub'd in Profl Jours incl'g: *Proceedings of the IEEE*; *IEEE Transactions on Antennas & Propagation*; *IEEE Transactions on Electromagnetic Compatability*; *Jour of Math Physics*; *Electromagnetics*; Mem Nat Hon Soc 1956-58, Valedictorian & Other Acad Medals 1958, Christian Brothers Acad, Syracuse, NY; Wheaton Ftball Trophy 1961-69, Sloan S'ship 1959-62, Tau Beta Pi 1960-61, Honeywell Undergrad Awd in Engrg 1962, Soc of Mil Engrs Awd 1962, Dist'd AFROTC Grad 1962, Sigma Xi 1962, CA Inst of Technol; AF Commend Medal 1969, AF Res & Devel Awd 1970, AF Nom to 10 Outstg Yg Men of Am 1971, USAF; W/W: in W, in Technol Today of Intells; Men of Achmt; DIB; Commun Ldrs of Am; Book of Hon; Num Other Biogl Listings.

BAUMGARDNER, JAMES LEWIS oc/Professor, Administrator; b/Jan 26, 1938; h/PO Box 523 Jefferson City, TN 37760; ba/Jefferson City, TN; c/Ellen Lorena, James Michael; p/Katherine Baumgardner, Columbia, SC; ed/AA, Bluefield Col, 1957; BA, Carson-Newman Col, 1959; MA 1964, PhD 1968, Univ of TN-Knoxville; mil/AUS, 1959-62; pa/Asst Prof 1964-67, Assoc Prof 1967-73, Prof 1973-, Chm Hist & Polit Sci Dept 1974-, Carson-Newman Col; Ordained So Bapt Min: Served as Pastor or Interim Pastor of Var E TN So Bapt Chs; Mem: AM Hist Assn; Org of Am Histns; So Hist Assn; Acad of Polit Sci; So Bapt; hon/Author of Articles & Book Reviews in Var Profl Jours; W/W: in S & SW, in Am, in Rel; Personalities of S.

BAUMGARTEN, REUBEN L oc/Professor; b/Nov 19, 1934; h/22 Eagle Road, Edison, NJ 08820; ba/Bronx, NY; m/Iris M; c/Lainie Nicole, Steven Craig; p/Sonia Baumgarten, Bronx, NY; sp/Dorothy Lesson, Yonkers, NY; ed/BS, The City Col of NY, 1956; MS 1958, PhD 1962, Univ of MI; pa/Instr, Prof 1968-, Chm Chem Dept, (Hunter Col) Herbert H Lehman Col, 1962-; Mem: Am Chem Soc; AAUP; Sigma Xi; Phi Lambda Upsilon; r/Jewish; hon/Author of Textbook, *Organic Chem: A Brief Survey*, 1977; Author of Num Sci Articles Pub'd in Profl Jours; BS Deg cum laude, The City Col, 1956.

BAUNACH, PHYLLIS JO oc/Statistician; b/Jul 29, 1947; h/12203 Winder Place, Ft Washington, MD 20744; ba/Washington, DC; m/Randall E Knack; p/Edward L Baunach (dec); Josephine C Baunach, Richfield Springs, NY; ed/BA, Univ of Rochester, 1969; PhD Psych, Univ of MN, 1974; Att'g as Cand for JD, George Wash Univ; pa/Res Sci, Gov's Comm on Crime Control &

Preven, St Paul, MN, 1974; Correctional Res Spec, Nat Inst of Law Enforcement & Crim Justice, Wash, DC, 1976; Stat, Bur of Justice Stats, Wash, DC, 1982-; Mem: Bd of Dirs 1981-82, Mem 1975-, Chp Div on Wom & Crime 1982, Am Soc of Crim; Am Correctional Assn, 1972-; Am Psychol Assn, 1974-; Phi Beta Kappa, 1969-; cp/George Wash Univ Nat Law Ctr Moot Ct Bd, 1984-; Treas, MN S Dist, Evang Luths in Mission, 1975; Subst Dir 1979-, Assisting Dir 1979-84, Assisting Dir 1984-, Our Savior's Luth Ch Choir; r/Luth; hon/Author, *Mothers in Prisons*, Pub'd by Transaction Inc, 1985; Over 20 Articles & Book Chapts in Profl Crim Justice Pubs incl'g: *Judge, Lwyr, Victim, Thief: Wom, Gender Roles & the Justice Sys*, 1982; *Mtl Hlth Sers in Local Jails*, 1982; *Criminol, Qtly Jour of Corrections; Crime & Corrections*; Others; HS Valedictorian, 1965; Phi Beta Kappa; Class Marshall; Clark Foun S'ship; NIS S'ships; AAUW Yg Scholar Awd, 1982; Outstg Perf Awd, US Dept of Justice, 1979, 1981, 1982 & 1983; Overall 1st Place & Best Argued & Best Unargued Memls 1984, Tm Mem to Rep Sch in Reg Competition, Mar 1985, George Wash Univ Nat Law Ctr Jessup Intl Law Moot Ct Competition; W/W: in E, of Am Wom.

BAWA, KAMALJIT S oc/Professor; b/Apr 7, 1939; h/42 Bacon Road, Belmont, MA 02178; ba/Boston; m/Tshering; c/Sonia, Ranjit; p/Rajinder and Dwarki Bawa; sp/Tashi and Pema Wangdi; ed/BS 1958, MS 1962, PhD 1967, Panjab Univ, Chandigarh, India; pa/Prof 1981-, Assoc Prof 1977-81, Asst Prof 1974-77, Dept Biol, Univ of MA-Boston; Res Fellow, Gray Herbarium, Harvard Univ, 1973-74; Charles Bullard & Maria Moors Cabot Res Fellow, Gray Herbarium & Harvard Forest, Harvard Univ, Cambridge, MA, 1972-73; Postdoct Res Assoc & Instr, Col of Forest Resources, Univ of WA, Seattle, WA, 1967-72; Grad Res Asst, Botany Dept, Panjab Univ, Chandigarh, India, 1962-67; Mem: La Selva Adv Com of Org for Tropical Studies, 1977-; Edit Bd, *Jour of the Arnold Arboretum*, 1980-; N Eng Botanical Clb; Soc for Study of Evolution; Ecol Soc of Am; Assn for Tropical Biol; Soc of Am Naturalists; Intl Soc of Tropical Ecol; hon/Author, Over 50 Articles, Res Papers, Book Chapts & Reviews in Jours & Profl Pubs incl'g: *Handbook of Exptl Pollination Biol; Evolution Biol; Tropical Rain Forest Ecosys; Am Jour Botany; Ecology; Evolution*; Others; Maria Moors & Charles Bullard F'ships, Harvard Univ, 1972; NSF Grantee, 1970, 1975-79, 1983-1985; Smithsonian Instn Grantee, 1975 & 1982; Chancellor's Awd for Dist'd S'ship, 1981; W/W in Frontier of Sci & Technol.

BAXTER, BILL L oc/Professor; b/Aug 31, 1931; h/6991 North Beech Tree Drive, Milwaukee, WI 53209; ba/Milwaukee, WI; m/Helen J; c/Brooke C, Becque M; p/Harley R Baxter, Atlantic, IA; ed/BA 1956, MA 1966, Univ of IA; mil/USAFR, Ret'd Maj; pa/Public Affairs Ofcr, USAF, 1952-67; Dir of Public Relats, IA Wesleyan Col, 1967-73; Dir of Public Relats Mktg, WI Auto Racing Inc, 1973-77; Asst Prof Jour, Univ of MS, 1977-78; Asst Prof Jour & Public Relats, Univ of OK, 1978-83; Assoc Prof, Marquette Univ, 1984-; Mem: Pres 1981 OKC Chapt, Nat Accredita-

tion Bd 1981-83, Public Relats Soc of Am; hon/Author of 54 Pubs (incl'g 2 Books) in Field of Public Relats & Public Relats Ed, 1978-; SW Edr of Yr, Public Relats Soc of Am, 1980.

BAXTER, WILLIAM F oc/Assistant Attorney General (Antitrust Division); b/Jul 13, 1929; ba/Washington, DC; ed/AB 1951, JD 1956, Stanford Univ; pa/Asst Atty Gen, Antitrust Div, US Dept of Justice, Wash, DC, 1981-; Prof Law 1960-81, Asst Prof 1956-58, Stanford Law Sch; Mem, Pres's Task Force on Antitrust Policy, 1969; Conslt & Proj Dir, FAA Study on Legal & Ec Aspects of Aircraft Noise, 1966-68; Joint Com on Adm Law, AALA & APSA, 1962-64; Vis'g Prof Law, Yale Univ, 1964-65; Pvt Law Pract, Covington & Burling, Wash, DC, 1958-60; Conslt to Var Pvt Corps & Govt Agys incl'g: Citicorp; Nat Retail Merchs Assn; Fed Resv Bd; The Brookings Instn; Visa; Exxon; Am Petro Inst; Northrop; Hoffman-LaRoche; Others; hon/Author, Var Books; Articles in Profl Jours incl: *Retail Bkg in Electronic Age: The Law & Ec of Electronic Funds Transfer*, 1977; *People or Penguins, An Optimum Level of Pollution*, 1974; *Jour of Law & Ec; Stanford Law Review*; Others.

BAYER, MARGRET H JANSSEN oc/Research Scientist; ba/The Institute for Cancer Research, Philadelphia, PA 19111; m/Manfred E; c/Ada-Helen, Thora; ed/MS, Univ of Hamburg, W Germany, 1958; PhD, 1961; Dr Rer Nat Habil, 1976; pa/Res Assoc 1962-76, Sr Res Assoc 1977-, Inst of Cancer Res, Phila, PA; Res Assoc Biol, Univ of Hamburg, 1958-61; Mem: Am Soc Microbiol; Am Soc Plant Physiol; NY Acad Sci; Intl Assn Plant Tissue Culture; hon/Author, Over 40 Res Pubs & Articles Pub'd in Profl Jours 1961-, incl'g: *Jour Am Soc Microbiol; Plant Physiol Lttrs; Proceedings of Nat Acad of Sci*; Others; Fellow, Deutsche Forschungsgemeinschaft, 1958-61; Damon Runyon Fellow, 1962-64; Habilitation, 1976; Grantee, NSF, 1980; Vis'g Prof, Univ of Hamburg, 1975; Lectr, Univ of PA, 1980.

BAYER, RAYMOND GEORGE oc/Tribologist, Engineer; b/Jun 9, 1935; h/4609 Marshall Drive West, Binghamton, NY 13903; ba/Endicott, NY; m/Barbara Sartini; c/Joseph, Matthew, Mary, Karen; p/Adam and Caroline Bayer (dec); sp/Eurgen Sartini; Lillian Story; ed/BS Physics, St John's Univ, 1956; SM Applied Math, Brown Univ, 1959; pa/Tech Positions to Sr Engr, Sr Engr Mgr Mats Applications Dept, IBM Corp, Endicott, NY, 1959-; Mem: Mbrship Secy 1980-81, Secy Com on Erosion & Wear 1982-83, Am Soc for Testing & Mats; Secy Planning Com 1982-83, Prog Chm 1984-85, for Intl Conf on Wear of Mats; ASME; AAAS; r/Rom Cath; hon/Co-Author of *Handbook of Analytical Design Procedures for Wear*, 1964; Editor of 3 ASTM Books on Wear Testing, 1976-82; Over 50 Tech Papers; Cert of Apprec, ASTM's Com on Erosion & Wear, 1983; Outstg Contbn Awds, IBM, 1965 & 1972; Am & Wom of Sci.

BAYGENTS, ANNA MARY oc/College Instructor, Dental Assistant; b/Jul 13, 1926; h/PO Box 506 Poplar Bluff, MO 63901; ba/Poplar Bluff, MO; m/Roy Emerson (dec); c/Ralph George (dec); Steven Warren, Edris Marie Beck, Roy

E Jr, William Michael, Jeffrey Thomas, Timothy Gregory, Patricia Joy Scheer; p/George Francis AuBuchon and Bertha Louise Franck (dec); sp/Thomas Fullwood Baygents and Iva Mae Partney (dec); ed/Dipl, Poplar Bluffs HS, 1944; AA, 3 Rivers Commun Col, 1984; pa/Cert'd Dental Asst, A L Bomer DDS, 1944-68; Bkkpr, Baygents Ser, 1968-78; Owner & Bkkpr Baygents Ser, 1978-83; Instr, Dental Assisting, 3 Rivers Commun Col, 1972-; Mem: Treas 1963-68, 8th Dist Trustee 1960-63, Am Dental Assts Assn; Pres, MO Dental Assts Assn, 1957; MO Dental Assisting Edrs; Hlth Occup Div, MO Vocation Assn; MO Assn of Commun & Jr Cols; cp/Organizing Bd Mem, Secy-Treas, Wilhaven Residence for Mtl Handicapped Adults, 1980-; Mem 1958-61, Secy 1960-61, Butler Co U Fund; Pres 1981-82, 1985; Butler Co Coun for Retarded Chd; Organizing Bd Mem, Chapt Treas 1980-83, Chapt Chaplain 1983-86, DAR; Geneal Soc; BSA; GSA; Others; r/Cath; hon/Author of Articles Pub'd in: *Jour of Am Dental Assts Assn; CAL Mag; LeMonde Dentaire*; DAR Hist Awd, 1940; HS Salutatorian, 1944; Achmt Awd, Am Dental Assts Assn, 1967; Coop Awd 1974, Achmt Awd 1976, MO Dental Assts Assn; W/W in MW; Personalities of W & MW; Dir Dist'd Ams; Intl Biog of Wom; 2000 Notable Ams.

BAYS, ROBERT EARL oc/Academic Administrator; b/Apr 8, 1921; h/56 Lake Park, Champaign, IL 61821; ba/Urbana, IL; m/Cleis Armour; c/Deborah Lynn, Rebecca Ann; p/J W and Bertie Cole Bays (dec); ed/BS, Emporia St Univ, 1946; MA, Tchrs Col, Columbia Univ, 1949; PhD, George Peabody Col, 1953; mil/USN, 1942-45; pa/Instr, Wichita Univ, 1946-49; Asst Prof to Prof 1949-69, Dir Sch of Music 1965-69, George Peabody Col; Chm Dept of Music 1969-74, Univ of TX; Dir Sch of Music, Univ of IL, 1974-; Prin Horn, Wichita Symph Orch, 1946-49; Prin Horn, Nashville Symph Orch, 1949-65; Mem: Pres 1979-82, VPres 1976-79, Mem Grad Comm 1970-76, Nat Assn of Schs of Music; VPres 1974-76, Col Music Soc; Pres 1967-69, So Div, Music Edrs Nat Conf; Acad Music Adv Panel, Ofc of Cultural Presentations, Intl Communs Agy, 1974-79; hon/W/W in Am.

BAZERMAN, MAX HAL oc/Professor; b/Aug 14, 1955; h/996 Centre Street, Jamaica Plain, MA 02130; ba/Cambridge, MA; m/E Marla Felcher; p/William and Rose Bazerman; sp/Bernard and Toby Felcher; ed/BS Ec, The Wharton Sch, Univ of PA, 1976; MS Orgnl Behavior 1978, PhD 1979, Grad Sch of Industl Adm, Carnegie-Mellon Univ; pa/Prof, Sloan Sch of Mgmt, MIT, 1983-; Asst Prof, Dept of Orgnl Behavior, Sch of Mgmt, Boston Univ, 1981-83; Asst Prof, Dept of Mgmt, Grad Sch of Bus Adm, Univ of TX-Austin, 1979-80; Instr, The Grad Sch of Industl Adm, Carnegie-Mellon Univ, 1977-79; Conslt, Num Pvt Corps, Govt Agys & Univs, 1977-; Mem: Acad of Mgmt; Acad of Mgmt Task Force on Outstg Contbns in Org & Mgmt Theory; En Acad of Mgmt; Am Psychol Assn; The Orgnl Behavior Tchg Soc; Contb'g Editor & Reviewer for Profl Jours; hon/Author of Var Books, Book Chapts & Over 40 Articles & Conf Reports in

Profl Jours incl'g: *Res in Orgnl Behavior; Am Psychol; Human Judgment in Managerial Decision Making; Bargaining Inside Orgs; Orgnl Behavior & Human Perf; Jour of Conflict Resolution; Proceedings of En Acad of Mgmt;* Num Others; Recip, NSF Grant, 1981-83; Cattell Awd in Res Design, Am Psychol Assn Div 14, 1982; Columbia Univ Paper Prize, 1982; Boston Univ Sch of Mgmt Res Grants, 1981 & 1982; W/W in Frontier Sci & Technol.

BEACH, JOHNSTON oc/Professor, Army Officer; b/Apr 21, 1945; h/3036A Stony Lonesome, West Point, NY 10996; ba/West Point, NY; m/Maureen B; c/Brandon, Amy, Emily; p/Charles A W Beach (dec); Eleanor J Beach, Catskill, NY; sp/Mrs Catherine Brandow, Leeds, NY; ed/BA, Univ of Rochester, 1967; MA 1969, PhD 1975, Univ of ME; mil/AUS, 1969-73 (Enlisted); 1973- (Ofcr); Maj; pa/Chief Psych Ser, Walson Army Hosp, Ft Dix, NJ, 1975-77; Psych Instr, Acad of Hlth Scis, Ft Sam Houston, TX, 1977-81; Assoc Prof Psych, US Mil Acad, W Pt, NY, 1981-; Mem: Am Psych Assn; Assn for Advmt of Psych; Fellow, Inter-Univ Sem on Armed Forces & Soc; r/Prot; hon/Author of 4 Articles: "Psychi Casualties of Combat: An Instrnl Prog For Paraprofls," 1982; "Selected Variables in Predicting Success in Tng Mtl Hlth Paraprofls, 1980; Prediction of Behavioral Sci Spec Course Non-Completers," 1979; "Stress Mgmt in 2 Divergent Mil Tng Settings," 1978; W/W in E.

BEACHAM, WOODARD DAVIS oc/Physician, Gynecologist; b/Apr 10, 1911; h/Route 1, Wood Leaf Cove #6, PO Box 69, Madison, MS 39110; ba/NO, LA; p/Woodard D and Ida (Felder) Beacham (dec); ed/BA 1932, BS 1933, Univ of MS; MD, Tulane Univ, 1935; pa/Intern, Resident Ob-Gyn, Charity Hosp of LA, NO; Prof Clin Gyn & Ob 1949-81, Prof Emeritus 1981-, Tulane Univ Sch of Med; Ob & Gyn, Pres Staff 1961, So Bapt Hosp; Past Pres Surg Staff, Charity Hosp, NO; Conslt: Beacham Meml Hosp, Magnolia, MS; Meth Hosp; Hotel Dieu Sisters Hosp, NO; Med Pract, Spec in Ob & Gyn 1940-75, Spec in Gyn 1975-; Assoc Staff, Tulane Med Ctr Hosp, 1977; Mem: Liaison Com w Intl Fed Gyn & Ob 1973-, Am Col Obs & Gyns; Chm Intl Relats Com, 10th World Cong Gyn & Ob; Lectr in Field; Pres, Beacham Corp, 1964-79; Bd of Dirs 1974, Exec Com 1977, Intl House, NO; Diplomate, Am Bd Ob-Gyn; Fellow, Gov 1955-63, 2nd VPres 1972-73, Adv Coun Gyn & Ob 1963-67, Pres LA Chapt, Am Col of Surgs; Coun Mem 1959-60, Am Gyn Soc; VPres 1970-71, Am Assn Obs & Gyns; Am Gyn & Ob Soc; 1st Pres 1951-52, Am Col Obs & Gyns; Pres 1967, So Gyn & Ob Soc; Chm Sect Ob & Gyn 1957-58, AMA; Chm Sect Ob 1949, Coun Mem 1961-63, 2nd VPres 1972, 1st VPres 1973, So Med Assn; Fdr & Dir, Intl House; Orleans Parish Med Socs; Past Pres, NO Grad Med Assn; Past Pres, NO Gyn & Ob Soc; 1st Pres, Conrad G Collins Ob & Gyn Soc, Tulane Univ; Asst Secy 1950-52, Ctl Assn Obs & Gyns; Charter Assoc Mem, Am Fertility Soc; Dir 1970-71, Secy 1971-73, Pres 1976-77, Tulane Med Alumni Assn; Corres'g Fgn Mem, Sociedad Peruana De Ob & Gyn; Hon Mem, Sociedad Paraguaya De Gyn &

Ob; Royal Soc Med; Dir 1962-65, Past Pres NO Chapt, Univ of MS Alumni Assn; Hon Mem, Phillippine Ob & Gyn Soc; AAAS; Fdg Mem, So Soc Cancer Cytology; Pan Am Cancer Cytology Soc; Assn of Profs Gyn & Ob; Sigma Xi; Alpha Omega Alpha; Sr Nat Pres 1969-73, Exec Trustee 1973-, Phi Chi; Beta Theta Pi; cp/Plimsoll; NO Country Clb; Circumnavigators; r/Meth; hon/Author, (w Robert J Crossen & Dan W Beacham) *Synopsis of Gyn,* 5th ed; (w Dan W Beacham) 9th ed, 1977; 10th Edition, 1982; Editor, for "Gyn & Ob," *Stedman's Med Dict,* 23rd Edition; Contbr, Num Articles in Field to Tech Med Jours; W/W: in Am, in S & SW; Am Men & Wom of Sci; Other Biogl Listings.

BEAGLES, RUTH HARRIGAN oc/Professor; b/Jun 19, 1933; h/Box 172, Christiansted, Saint Croix, VI 00820; ba/Saint Croix, VI; c/Edith, John; p/Mildred F Harrigan, Saint Croix, VI; sp/(dec); ed/BS, Hampton Inst, 1954; MA, NY Univ, 1957; Sch Adm, Univ Hartford, 1974-75; pa/Sch Admr, St Croix Schs, 1954-70; Prin, Pearl B Larsen Elem Sch, 1971-78; Hd Ma, St. Dunstan's Epis Sch, 1978-82; Asst Prof of Ed, Col of VI, 1982-; cp/FTA, 1952-54; Mng Ed, *The Hampton Script,* 1953; Pres, Hampton Inst Alumni Assoc, 1975-80; Secy, 4th Constl Conv, 1979-80; Pres Ch Coun, Luth Ch, 1982-83; Mem Gov Com on Missions & Goals, CVI; Coastal Zone Mgmt Com; Com on Status of Wom; Lectr on VI Creole Lang in Relats to Clrm Tchg; r/Luth; hon/ W/W Am Col & Univ, 1954; Tchr of Yr, St Dunstan's Epis Sch, 1966; Wom of Yr, St Dunstan's Epis Sch, 1974.

BEAMAN, MARGARINE GAY-NELL oc/Scrap Metal Accountant and Consultant; b/Feb 26, 1941; h/1406 Wilshire Boulevard, Austin TX 78722; ba/Austin, TX; m/Robert W Beaman; c/(Stepsons): Richard, Ronald, (Fosterdaugh) Lorena; p/Ryland and Margaret Geistweidt, Mason, TX; sp/Rayond Beaman (dec); ed/Att'd TX Luth Col 1 Yr; Cert in Acctg Univ MI-E Lansing, Hotel-Motel Short Course, Univ Houston; pa/Auditor & Salesperson, Driskill Hotel 1960-69; Pt-time, Bond's TV Sales & Ser, 1961-66; Pt-time to Full-time, Nixon-Clay Commun Col, 1960-74; Dir & Subst Tchr, TX Legis, 1969-72; VP & Owner, Beaman Metal Co, 1974-; Acct & Conslt, 1974; Hotel-Motel Dirs Intl Intl Secy, 1964, Tres, 1966, Dist Secy, 1967, Local Pres, 1965, Secy, 1968; cp/St Recording Secy, 1981-82; Local Pres, 1974-76; Secy, 1971; Treas, 1972-74; Dist Pres, 1978-80; TX Fdn BPW; Pres, 1979, Corres'g Secy, 1981; TXFW; Dist Pres, 1983-86; EWI Chp; Braille Sign for Blind Ser Proj Chp; Austin Jr Wom's Fdn; Zonta Intl; r/Luth; hon/ Gov's & Mayor's Outstg Awd for Braille Idea Put to Work, 1980; Austin Wom of Yr, 1964; Cert'd Consumer Credit Exec, 1965.

BLAMER, JoANN JEAN oc/Personnel Manager; b/Jun 15, 1939; h/5729 Portsmouth, Chino, CA 91710; ba/Cucamonga, CA; m/Michael Ray; c/Steven Dean Pease, Donald Lee Newman, Karey Lee (Newman), Davidofsky & (Step-chd) Christopher Michael & Shelli; p/William Columbus Dennis (dec); Neva Belle (Randolph) Delzell, Seymour, MO; sp/Jeneva N Smith, La Verne, CA; William Beamer, Montclair,

CA; ed/Att'd Univ of Nev; Student Chaffey Col, CA; Att'd Courses & Sem by Dun & Bradstreet, Keye Prod Ctr & Merch & Mfr Assoc pa/Exec Sec'y, Aerojet-Gen Corp, 1960-63 & 1964-67; Exec Secy, Pan Am World Airways (NRDS), 1963-64; Exec Secy, Clark Co Sch Dist, 1967-68; Pers & Safety Asst, Survival Sys, 1969-71; Pers Mgr, Hooker Industs, 1971-74; Pers Mgr & Exec Secy, Harvest Rec Vehicles, 1975-76; Asst Terminal Mgr, CMD Trans, 1978-80, Pers Mgr, Schlosser Forge Co, 1980-; Mem: Merch's & Mfr's Assoc; Pers & Indust Relats Assoc; Nat Assoc of Female Execs; cp/Past Pres & Treas, Current Mem, Chino HS Band Boosters; Guest Spkr, Ontario Comm Hosp; r/Prot.

BEAMER, PARKER REYNOLDS (dec Mar, 1984) oc/Former Pathologist, Educator, Director of Resident Training; b/Jul 27, 1914; h/Formerly of 1040 Erie Street, Oak Park, IL 60302; ba/Oak Park, IL; m/Mary Jo Scovill; c/Jo Beamer Zurbrugg, Mary Susan, Grant Scovill; p/Powhatan Reynolds and Bessie Louise Poole Beamer (dec); sp/Hiram Thompson and Edith E Stewart Scovill (dec); ed/AB w High Hons 1935, MS 1937, PhD 1940, Univ IL; MD cum laude, Wash Univ-St Louis, 1943; mil/Med Corps Resv, Cmdg Ofcr & Chief Microbiol, Serology & Parasitology Divs, Antilles Gen Med Lab, San Juan, PR; 1945-47 1st Lt to Lt Col; pa/Asst in Bacteriology & Immunol, Univ IL, 1935-39; Asst in Pathol 1941-43, Asst Prof Pathol 1943-49, Wash Univ Sch of Med; Dir & Prof Microbiol & Immunology & Assoc Dean 1951-53, Bowman Gray Sch of Med; Microbiol & Assoc Pathol, NC Bapt Hosp, 1949-53; Conslt in Pathol, VA Reg Ofc, Winston-Salem (NC) & VA Hosp (Mtn Home, TN), 1950-53; Prof Pathol 1953-65, Dept Chm 1960-65, IN Univ Sch of Med; Pathol, IN Univ Med Ctr Hosps, 1953-65; Chief Pathol, Dir Pathol & Labs, LA Co-Univ So CA Med Ctr, 1965-69; Prof Pathol, 1970-80, Prof Emeritus, 1980-84, Univ Hlth Scis/ Chgo Med Sch; Assoc Pathol & Dir Resident Tng, W Suburban Hosp Med Ctr, Oak Park, IL, 1980-84; Clin Prof Pathol Loyola Univ Stritch Sch of Med, 1981-84; Former Mbships: Alpha Omega Alpha, Sigma XI; Fellow, Col Am Pathols, Am Soc Clin Pathols; Fdg Fellow Assn Clin Scis; Am Assn Pathols; AMA; Soc Exptl Biol & Med Gamma Alpha; Phi Chi; Kiwanis Intl; World Med Assn; Chgo Inst Med; Chgo Pathol Soc; NY Acad Sci; Assn Am Med Col; AAUP; Exec Coun, Wash Univ Med Ctr, 1972-76 & 1978-79; Mem 1949-53, Pres 1951-53, NC Soc Bacteriologists; r/ Bapt; hon/Co-Author (w F I Volini) *Principles of Basic & Surg Pathol, W Fundamentals of Exptl Pathol;* Author, 250 Articles in Var Am & Fgn Jours; Co-Author, *Principles of Human Pathol,* 1959; *Microscopic Pathol,* 1965; Contbr to 5 Med Books, 1952, 1955, 1977, 1979, 1981; Consltg & Contbg Editor *Stedman's Med Dict* 1961, 1966, 1972, 1976, 1982; Editor-in-Chief 1956-65, Bd of Editors 1953-55 & 1966-76, *Am Jour Clin Pathol;* Fdg Editor-in-Chief, *Survey of Pathol in Med & Surg* 1964; Editor for Pathol, *Current Med Digest,* 1959-68; Co-Editor, *Microbiol-Immunol* Series, 1973; Bronze Tablet for Mil & Scholastic Excell, Univ

IL, 1935; Alpha Omega Alpha Hon Med Soc, 1943; 3 WW II Medals, 1945, 1946; Gold Medal for Meritorious Res, NC Med Soc, 1950; Outstg Fac Mem Plague, IN Univ Med Ctr, 1961; Tchg Awd from Residents IN Univ Med Ctr, 1964; Commemoration & Apprec Plaque LA Co-Univ So CA Med Ctr, 1969; 3 Intl Symp Awds for Meritorious Res on Leukemia & Lymphoma, 1973, 1975, 1979; Charter Mem w Medal of Merit, Pres Task Force, 1981; Dipl w Spec Competence Cert in Microbiol & Immunol, 1950; Trustee 1962-69; Life Trustee Awd for Dist'd Ser 1970, Am Bd Pathol; Chancellors Com of 500, Wash Univ-St Louis, 1968; Jackson Johnson Scholar & Fellow, Wash Univ Sch of Med, 1939-41; W/W: in MW, in Am, in World; Nat Cyclopaedia of Am Biog; Am Men & Wom of Sci; Dir of Med Specs.

BEAMER, WILLIAM FRED oc/Bigfoot Investigator; b/Apr 2, 1938; h/PO Box 285, Canoga Park, CA 91305; ba/ Same; m/Sharon Kaye; ed/BS Nuclear Engrg, NC State Univ, 1960; MBA, Univ of NC, 1962; pa/Engr, Atomics Intl, 1962-68; Pres, Beamer Expeditions for Bigfoot, CA, 1947-; Orgr & Dir, Res Expeditions for Bigfoot in CA & OR, funded by Participating Vol's; cp/Am Soc of Primatologists, Intl Primatological Soc, Intl Soc of Cryptozool; hon/ Eagle Scout Badge, 1952.

BEAN, MAURICE DARROW oc/ Ambassador, Government Advisor; b/ Sep 9, 1928; h/341 Sequoia Drive, Maxwell AFB, AL 36112; ba/Maxwell AFB, AL; m/Dolores Winston; c/Laura L Young, Linda D Burke, James W Boone, Jennifer J Boone, Karen M; p/ Everett T Bean, Lynwood, CA; Vera M Bean (dec); sp/Charles E and Laura M Winston (dec); ed/BA, Howard Univ, 1950; MA, Haverford Col, 1954; Cert, Sch of Adv'd Intl Studies, Johns Hopkins Univ; Att'd Georgetown Univ Sch Law; pa/St Dept Advr to Cmdr, Air Univ, 1980-; Diplomate-in-Residence, Case Wn Resv Univ, 1979-80; US Ambassador to Burma, 1977-79; Sr Fgn Ser Insp, 1976-77; Dept Chief of Mission, Am Embassy Monrovia, Liberia, 1973-76; US Consul Ibadon, Nigeria, 1971-73; Country Dir, US Dept of St, 1966-71; Dir, Peace Corps, Philippines, 1964-66; Mem: Assn Black Am Ambassadors; The Urban Leag; Neighbors Inc; cp/ Mem: Omega Psi Phi; Royal Bangkok Sports Clb; Bd of Dirs Paramount Theatre for Perf'g Arts; r/Meth; hon/ Meritorious Ser Cit, Intl Coop Adm, 1955; Superior Hon Awd, US St Dept, 1977; Benjamin Hooks Awd, NAACP, 1980; W/W: in Am, Among Black Ams, in Govt, in World.

BEARD, JAMES TAYLOR oc/Professor; b/Oct 1, 1939; h/412 Westmoreland Court, Charlottesville, VA 22901; ba/ Charlottesville, VA; m/Kathryn Lee; c/ Rosemary Ann, James David; p/James R Beard, Maryville, TN; sp/Lota Lee, Charlottesville, VA; ed/BME, Auburn Univ, 1961; MS 1963, PhD 1965, OK St Univ; pa/Res Engr, Oak Ridge Nat Labs, Sum 1963; Res Asst, OK St Univ, 1964-65; Asst Prof 1965-69, Assoc Prof 1969-, Asst Provost 1972-77, Univ of VA; Ptnr & Treas, Assoc Envir Conslts, Charlottesville, 1971-; Res Engr, Bartlesville Petro Res Ctr, Sum 1968; Mech Engr, US EPA, Sum 1979; Cert Profl

Engr, VA, 1967-; Mem & Ch, VA Air Conserv Comm, 1970-73; Mem & Treas, Charlottesville Housing Fund, 1976-81; EPA Course Dir & Lectr on Air Pollution Control in US & Mexico, 1972-83; r/Presb; hon/Author & Co-Author, Over 85 Tech Papers, Jour Articles & Reports in Fields of Heat Transfer, Solar Energy Thermal Perf & Combustion; Algernon Sydney Sullivan Awd, Auburn Univ, 1961; Phi Kappa Phi, 1961; Pi Mu Epsilon, 1960; Pi Tau Sigma, 1960; Tau Beta Pi, 1960; Sigma Xi, 1966; Am Men & Wom of Sci; W/ W: in Technol Today, in Frontiers of Sci & Technol, in S & SE.

BEARISON, DAVID J oc/Developmental and Clinical Psychologist; b/Feb 22, 1944; ba/New York, NY; ed/BA, PA St Univ, 1965; MA 1968, PhD 1973, Clark Univ; pa/Assoc Prof Psych, Grad Sch & Univ Ctr & Sr Res Assoc, Ctr for Adv'd Study in Ed (CASE), CUNY, 1973-; Mem Bd of Dirs, Jean Piaget Soc; Mem: Am Psychol Assn; Soc for Res in Child Devel; AAUP; NY Acad of Scis; hon/Author of Num Pubs in Profl Psych Jours incl'g: Devel Psych, Child Devel, Human Devel, Genetic Epistemologist, Others; Plus Several Book Chapts; Edit Bds: Sex Roles: A Jour of Res, 1975-; Human Devel, 1978-; Genetic Epistemologist, 1980-; Jour of Applied Devel Psychol, 1983-; Res & Clin Fellow, Harvard Med Sch & Chds Hosp Med Ctr, 1981-82; Fellow, Merrill-Palmer Inst, 1965-66; Am Men & Wom of Sci; W/W in E.

BEASON, ROBERT CURTIS oc/ Educator; b/May 12, 1946; h/7673 Dutch Street Road, Mt Morris, NY 14510; ba/Geneseo, NY; m/Delena L Sloane; c/Zachary Adam Sloane; p/ Eugene M and Lida J Beason, Seattle, WA; sp/Robert and Loraine Sloane, Holcomb, NY; ed/BA, Bethany Nazarene Col, 1968; MS, Wn IL Univ, 1970; PhD, Clemson Univ, 1976; mil/USAF, 1970-74; Res Sci, USAF, 1970-74; Res Asst, Clemson Univ, 1974-76; Res Biol, US Forest Ser, 1976; Vis'g Lectr, Univ of CA-Irvine, 1977; Vis'g Prof, Wn IL Univ, 1977-78; Asst Prof, SUNY-Geneseo, 1978-; Mem: AAAS; Am Ornithol Union; Animal Behavior Soc; Assn Tropical Biol; Cooper Ornithol Soc; Ecol Soc of Am; Sigma Xi; Soc Study of Evolution; Wilson Ornithol Soc; hon/Author of Num Pubs in Profl Jours incl'g: Auk, IBBA News, Condor, Jour of Wildlife Mgmt, Nature, Others; Recip, Nat Sci Foun Grant, 1981; Recip, NIH Traineeship, 1983; W/W: in Am, in Fronteir Sci & Technol.

BEATTY, JEWELL L BARNETT oc/ Retired Educator; b/Mar 20, 1917; h/801 Northeast 20th Street, Oklahoma City, OK 73105; m/Harold Beatty; c/Harold Edwin, Clarence Herman; p/William F and Lucy M Barnett (dec); sp/Scott and Lessie Beatty (dec); ed/BS 1935; MS, 1943; pa/Prin & Elem Sch Tchr, Rural Lincoln Co, OK Schs, 1935-43; HS Eng & Drama Tchr & Girl's Basketball Coach, S Stroud OK HS, 1943-56; Tchr & Conslr, Dunbar HS, Okmulgee, OK, 1957-61; Rdg Spec, Eng Tchr & Yrbook Sponsor, OKC Sch Sys, 1961-78; Grand Supvr of Yth OK Grand Chapt OES, 1948-56; Orgr & Sponsor, "Zels," Zeta Phi Beta Yth, 1961-68; Orgr & Sponsor, Xinos (Yth) Phi Delta Kappa Nat Sorority Inc; Reg Supvr, Yth OK Fedn of Clbs; NTU Art Assn Inc; cp/Co-Chm,

OK Afro-Am Hall of Fame, 1982; Yth Dir & Dir of Drama 1961-84, St John Bapt Ch; r/Missionary Bapt; hon/ Author of St John Jour: A 50 Yr Hist, 1970; St John Dir: A Pictorial Handbook, 1979; St John Yrbook & Dir, 1984; Orig Drama Progs: "He Died But He Rose Again," & "Jesus Lives," 1979-81; Recip of Plaques for Outstg Contbn to Yth Devel, 1965 & 1979; Retirement Banquet for Outstg Perf as Tchr, 1979; Nom'd OK Afro-Am Hall of Fame, 1983.

BEATTY, KEITH G oc/Research Biochemist; b/Jul 1, 1947; h/Atlanta, GA; p/Roy P and Bonniejean M Beatty, Atlanta, GA; ed/BS Chem, Purdue Univ, 1969; MS Biochem 1976, PhD 1982, Univ of GA; mil/USAF, 1969-71, Ofcr; pa/Res Biochem, Louis Pasteur Univ, Strasbourg, France, 1982-; Res Asst, Travis Lab in Biochem, Univ of GA-Athens; r/Prot; hon/Author of Articles Pub'd in Profl Jours incl'g: Jour of Biol Chem, Jour of Lab & Clin Med, Jour of Analytical Biochem; W/W: in GA, in SW; Men of Achmt.

BEATY, TERRI H oc/Statistical Geneticist; b/Mar 28, 1951; h/15 Thurkill Court, Cockeysville, MD 21030; ba/ Baltimore, MD; m/Narlin B; c/Narlin B Jr; p/Mrs Marie Hagan, Austin, TX; sp/ Mr and Mrs N B Beaty, Charles Groves, TX; ed/BA 1972, MA 1974, Univ of TX; PhD, Univ of MI, 1978; pa/Asst Prof, Dept of Epidemiology, Johns Hopkins Univ, 1980; Postdoct Scholar, Div of Endocrinology & Metabolism, Univ of MI, 1978-79; hon/Author of Num Articles in Profl Sci Jours; Outstg Yg Wom of Am (MD), 1981; Phi Beta Kappa, 1972; W/W.

BEAVER, BONNIE VERYLE oc/Veterinary Educator; b/Oct 26, 1944; h/ Route 3, Box 354, College Station, TX 77840; ba/TX A&M Univ, College Sta, TX; m/Larry J; p/Gladys Gustafson; sp/ Mr and Mrs C J Beaver; ed/BS 1966, DVM 1968, Univ of MN; MS, TX A&M Univ, 1972; pa/Instr 1969-72, Asst Prof 1972-76, Assoc Prof 1976-82, Prof 1982-, Dept Vet Anatomy, TX A&M Univ; Instr, Univ of MN, 1968-69; Chm Ednl Comm for Fgn Vet Grads 1981-84, Coun on Ed, 1980-, Other Com Mbrships, Am Vet Med Assn, 1964-; Dir 1980-, Other Com Mbrships, TX Vet Med Assn, 1970-; Pres 1972-76, Other Ofcs, Wom's Vet Med Assn, 1964-80; Am Vet Neurol Assn, 1973-; Animal Behavior Soc, 1974-; Secy-Treas 1972, Brazos Val Vet Med Assn, 1969-; Pres 1975-80, Mem Exec Bd, 1975-, Am Soc Vet Ethology, 1975; Num Other Vet Assns; Chm 1983-, Mem 1968-, MN Alumni Assn; cp/VPres 1975, Chm Animal Experimentation Com 1975-84, Brazos Val Sci & Engrg Fair; Bd of Dirs 1976, VPres 1977-82, Brazos Unit of Am Cancer Soc; Brazos Co Ext Horse Com, 1982-; hon/Author & Co-Author of 5 Books; Over 50 Articles, Papers & Reports in Profl Vet Jours; Mem: Sigma Epsilon Sigma; Nat Pres 1979-81 & Other Ofcs, Eta Chapt Pres 1975-76 & Other Ofcs, Phi Zeta; Bd of Dirs 1975-76 & Other Ofcs, Phi Delta Gamma; Gamma Sigma Delta, 1977-; Phi Sigma, 1981-; Citizen of Wk, Bryan, TX Press, 1981; Outstg Wom Vet of 1982, Assn for Wom Vets, SLC, UT, 1982; Plaque for Contbn of Wom Vets to Profession, CA Vet Med Assn, SF,

1973; Personalities of S; DIB; Outstg Yg Wom of Am; W/W: in TX, of Am Wom.

BECK, JOHN ROBERT oc/Professor; b/Sep 8, 1953; h/Rural Route #2, Box 154, West Lebanon, NH 03784; ba/ Hanover, NH; m/Sharon Dombkowski; c/John Benjamin, Stefan Andrew; p/ John Edward Beck, Chatham, NJ; Maralyn Smith Beck (dec); ed/AB, Dartmouth Col, 1974; MD, Johns Hopkins Univ, 1978; pa/Resident in Pathol, Dartmouth-Hitchcock Med Ctr, 1978-80; Adj Asst Prof Med Tech, Univ of NH, 1978-82; Clin Fellow in Med Decision Making, N Eng Med Ctr, 1981; Instr Pathol, Tufts Univ Sch of Med, 1981-82; Asst Prof Pathol, Dartmouth Med Sch, 1982-; Mem: Am Assn for Med Sys & Informatics; Soc for Med Decision Making; Am Fedn for Clin Res; AAAS; Acad of Clin Lab Phys & Scis; Am Assn Pathols; Col of Am Pathols; Edit Bd, *Med Decision Making*; cp/Elder, Dartmouth Area Christian F'ship, 1978-; r/Evang Christian; hon/Author of Articles: "The Markov Process Med Prognosis," w S G Pauker in *Med Decis Making*, 1983; "The Role of New Lab Tests in Clin Decision Making," in *Clin Lab Med*, 1982; 50 Other Articles & Abstracts; Yg Investigator Awd, ACLPS, 1979, 1980 & 1981; Koennecke Awd, Johns Hopkins Univ, 1978; Phi Beta Kappa, Dartmouth Col, 1974; Men of Achmt; W/W in Frontier Med & Technol.

BECKMAN, JAMES WALLACE 'BIM' oc/Executive; b/May 2, 1936; h/ Drawer 2350, Crestline, CA 92325; ba/ LA, CA, 90057; m/Phyllis; c/Magda; p/ Wallace Beckman (dec) Mary Louise White, La Selva Bch, CA; ed/BA, Princeton Univ, 1958; PhD Ec & Behavior Sci, Univ of CA, 1973; mil/USMC, 1958-67, Maj; pa/Conslt US Sen, 1955; Conslt CA St Legis, 1967-68; Conslt to Public Agys & Pvt Firms (Intl & Domestic), 1969-77; Conslt to CA St Gov's Ofc, 1977-80; VPres, Mktg Exec & Ec Conslt, Goldwell Investmts Inc, 1980-; Mem: Am Ec Assn; Ofcr 1982-84, Am Mktg Assn; Nat Assn of Bus Economists; Am Statl Assn; Fellow, Soc for Applied Athropol; cp/Commonwlth Clb of CA; r/Presb; hon/Various Articles Pub'd in Profl Jours; Fellow, NIMH, 1971-72; W/W: in W, in Fin & Indust.

BEDA, GAYE ELISE oc/Artist, Printer; b/Feb 12, 1955; h/317 2nd Avenue, New York, NY 10003; ba/Same; p/Mr and Mrs Alfred C Beda, Cortland, OH; ed/BA, Col of Wooster, OH, 1977; Att'd Art Student Leag of NY, 1978-81; Att'd Sch of Visual Arts, NYC, 1981-82; pa/ Self-Employed Artist, 1980-; Printer, Barnes Press, 1978-80; Solo Shows: Lakeview HS, Cortland, OH, 1973; Col of Wooster, OH, 1976; Grp Shows: Trumbull Co Art Guild, OH, 1974; Col of Wooster, OH, 1973-77; Cork Gallery NYC, 1984; Mem, Printing Wom of NY, 1979-; Bd Mem, Wom in the Arts Foun, NYC, 1983-; r/Meth; hon/Author & Illustrator of Book; NHS, 1977; Comm'd Wk of Murals, Mesopotamia Ct House, 1976-77; Wall Murals: Smithville Jt Voc Sch & Col of Wooster, OH, 1976-77.

BEDELL, ELIZBETH REED oc/Academic Administrator; b/Jun 2, 1947; 1218 Terrace Street, Tallahassee, FL 32303; ba/Tallahassee, FL; m/George C; p/Aido Reed (dec); sp/Chester Bedell

(dec); Edmonia Bedell, Jacksonville, FL; ed/BA, Univ of FL, 1969; MS 1974, PhD 1977, FL St Univ; pa/Acad Admr, St Univ Sys of FL, 1979-; Prof, Boston Univ, 1978-79; Asst Prof, FL St Univ, 1977-78; Mem: Zonta; Am Soc of Clin Hypnosis; cp/FL St Univ Lady Seminole Boosters; FL Human Relats Comm; Jacksonville Commun Relats Comm; r/ Epis; hon/Bryn Mawr Sum Inst for Wom in Higher Ed Adm, 1982; Rudolf Driekers Sum Inst, Zurich, Switzerland, 1979; W/W of Am Wom.

BEDELL, THOMAS ERWIN oc/Professor; b/Dec 21, 1931; h/120 Wonderly Lane, Philomath, OR 97330; ba/Corvallis, OR; m/Gretchen B Bencene; c/ Shelley Bedell-Stiles, Kristin Bedell-DePillis, Robin McWalters; p/H Erwin and Muriel C Bedell, Santa Cruz, CA; sp/Addie Watson, Zephyr Hills, FL; ed/ BS, CA St Polytech Col, 1953; MS, Univ of CA-Berkeley, 1957; PhD, OR St Univ, Corvallis, 1966; mil/AUS, 1953-55; pa/Prof Rangeland Resources 1976-, Co Ext Agt 1973-76, Asst Prof Range Mgmt 1966-70, OR St Univ; Ext Range Mgmt Spec, Univ of WY, 1970-73; Farm Advr, Univ of CA, 1957-63; Bd of Dirs 1982-85, Num Com Mbrships & Pres Pacific NW Sect 1978, Soc for Range Mgmt; Am Soc Animal Sci; Am Soc Agronomy; Phi Kappa Phi; r/Prot; hon/Author of Num Articles & Bltns on Range Mgmt, 1966-; Fellow, Soc for Range Mgmt, 1980; Cert Range Mgmt Conslt, 1981-; Am Men of Sci.

BEEKMAN, STANLEY oc/Podiatrist; b/Aug 27, 1951; h/13601 St James Avenue, Cleveland, OH 44135; ba/ Cleveland, OH; m/Marion; c/Amy; p/ David and Sylvia Beekman, Bklyn, NY; sp/James and Marion Kiefer, Cleveland, OH; ed/BS, City Col of NY, 1972; DPM, NY Col of Podiatric Med, 1976; pa/Asst Prof 1978-82, Assoc Prof 1982-, Cleveland Foot Clin; Team Podiatrist, Cleveland Indians, 1982-; Pres, N C Orthotic Lab, 1982; Conslt, N Coast Bobsled Team, 1981; Conslt, SE Running Clb, 1979; OH Podiatry Assn, 1979; Am Podiatry Assn, 1979; Diplomate, Am Bd of Podiatric Ortho, 1981; Am Col of Podopediatrics, 1979; Am Col Podiatric Sports Med, 1982; Am Med Joggers Assn, 1980; r/Jewish; hon/Author: "Relatship of Calcaneal Varus to Tight Hamstrings," *Current Podiatry*, 1976; "Supranalleolar Tenotomy of the Flexor Digitorum Longus," *Archives of Podiatric Med & Surg*, 1980; Awd of Excell in Ortho, 1976; W/W in MW.

BEGO, GIOVANNI oc/Government Official (Italy); b/Jan 22, 1922; h/c/o Prag R1 Longview Road, Wading River, NY 11792; ba/Trieste, Italy; m/Pancotti Maria; c/Daniella, Mirella, Maria, Marina; p/Rocco Bego (dec); sp/Maria Buble (dec); ed/PhD, Bus Adm, Rome Univ; pa/Chief Inspector, Internal Revenue, Trieste, Italy, Over 20 Yrs; Comptroller, Intl Ctr of Nuclear Physics Theoric of Miramar (UNESCO) Trieste, Italy; r/Cath; hon/Author of 15 Books, 3 at Lib of Cong, Wash, DC; Latest Book, *Reagan: Una Svolta Per Il Mondo*; Num Awds; Apprec from Mr & Mrs Reagan.

BEHNKE, LOIS A oc/Educator; b/ Aug 2, 1938; h/500 East 7th Street, Kinsley, KS 67547; ba/Offerle, KS; p/ Otto H Stach (dec); Kathryn Stach, Kinsley, KS; ed/Dipl, Kinsley HS, 1956;

AA, St John's Col, Winfield, KS, 1958; BS, Concordia Tchrs Col, Seward, NE, 1962; Att'd Univ of SD, 1963-64; pa/ Elem Tchr, Monroe, MI, 1958-60; Elem Tchr, Maplewood, MO, 1962; Elem Tchr, Wilroads Gardens, KS 1962-63 & 1968-69; Elem Tchr, Wayne, MI, 1964-68; Elem Tchr, Evart, MI, 1969-72; Elem Tchr, Offerle, KS, 1972-85; Pres 1981-82, K-O NEA; cp/Mem, Royal Neighbors of Am; Organist & Mem, Luth Ch (LCMS) Kinsley, KS; Mem OK Chorale.

BEHRMANN, MARION POLLY oc/ Special Educator; b/Nov 24, 1925; h/115 Lake Road, Framingham, MA 0170l; ba/ Same; m/John W Behrmann; c/James Piper, Judith I Richarson, Charles Roberts, Roland Augustus; p/Marjory R Piper, Framingham, MA; ed/BS Ed & Rec Ldrship, Univ of MA, 1947; Att'd Spec Ed Courses at Var Cols & Univs, 1965-77; pa/Lectr & Conslt, for Num N Eng Col & Univs, the Assn for Chd w Lrng Disabilities (ACLD) & Over 200 Sch Sys in MA, 1967-; Instr, Leag of Wom Voters Paraprofls, 1974; Spec Edr, Resource Ctr, Wellesley, MA, 1973-; Tchr, Clark Univ, 1973; Coor Lrng Disabilities, Framingham Mid Schs, 1971-73; Master Tchr, Framingham St Col, Sum Inst for Lrng Disabilities, 1971; Tchr & Diagnostician, Liberty Coun of Schs, 1970-71; Remedial Rdg & Lrng Disabilities Tchr, Framingham, 1966-71; Master Tchr, Am Intl Col, Sum Inst for Lrng Disabilities, 1968-69; Supvr, Lrng Disabilities for Rdg Res Inst, 1966; Kgn Dir, Tchr, Tutor, Camp Dir, Other Spec Ed Positions, 1948-65; Conducted Num Lectrs, Confs, Radio-TV Progs & Wkshops, 1966-; r/ Prot; hon/Author of 5 Books incl'g: *Why Is It Always Me?*, 1980; *Num & Lttr Dice*, 1978; *Activs for Devel Visual Perception*, 1974; Others; Co-Author of 4 Books incl'g: *Parents As Playmates*, 1981; *Excel I, II*; Others; Editor, *Day Care Mag*; Num Articles Pub'd in Profl Spec Ed Jours; Adv Bd Mem 1973-79, Bd of Dirs 1968-72, (MACLD); Treas, MA Coun for Exceptl Chd, 1974-75; Participant, HEW Conf on Technol for Chd, 1972; MA Mother of Yr, 1979; MACLD Awd for Outstg Contbn to Field, 1970; Phi Kappa Phi; W/W: in Am Cols & Univs, in Outdoor Ed, of Am Wom, in Ed, in Lrng Disabilities.

BEIER, ERNST G oc/Professor; b/Jun 26, 1916; h/44 West 3rd Street #607, Salt Lake City, UT 84101; ba/Salt Lake City, UT; m/Frances; c/Paul, Lisa; p/Paul and Hanna Beier (dec); sp/Frank and Olga Redlich (dec); ed/BA, Amherst Col, 1940; PhD, Columbia Univ, 1949; mil/ AUS, 1943-45; pa/Asst Prof Dept Psych, Syracuse Univ, 1948-53; Prof Dept Psych, Univ of UT, 1953-; Chm Intl Relats, Am Psychol Assn, 1973; Chm Conv Bd 1979, Coun of Reps 1972-82, Pres 1969, Rocky Mt Psychol Assn; Pres, UT Psychol Assn, 1959; Pres Elect, DIU Psychotherapy, 1983; VPres, Psi Chi, 1981; hon/Author of Books: *The Silent Lang of Psych*, 1966 & 1984; *People Rdg*, 1976; Over 90 Articles Pub'd in Profl Jours; Am Bd of Profl Psych, 1961; Dist Ser Awd, Div 29, Am Psychol Assn, 1983; Dist Ser Awd, UT Psychol Assn, 1983; Hon Doct, CA Schs of Profl Psych, 1984; W/W in W.

BEKEY, GEORGE ALBERT oc/Institute Director, Professor; b/Jun 19, 1928;

h/4645 Encino Avenue, Encino, CA 91316; ba/LA, CA; m/Shirley White; c/ Ronald Steven, Michelle Elaine; p/Mr and Mrs Andrew Bekey; ed/BSEE, Univ of CA-Berkeley, 1950; MS Engrg 1952, PhD Engrg 1962, Univ of CA-LA (UCLA); mil/USASC, 1954-56; pa/Dir Robotics Inst 1983-, Prof Elect Engrg, Biomed Engrg & Comp Sci 1968-, Assoc Prof 1964-68, Asst Prof 1962-64; Orgr & Co-Dir, Sys Simulation Lab (Engrg Computer Lab), 1962-66, Chm Elect Engrg-Sys Dept 1970-72 & 1978-82; Orgr & Dir Biomed Engrg Inst 1972-75, Univ of So CA (USC); Grp Ldr, Sect Hd & Sr Staff Engr, TRW Sys, LA, 1958-62; Computer Ctr Mgr, Beckman Instruments, LA, 1956-58; Tchg Asst & Res Engr, Sch of Engrg, Univ of CA-LA (UCLA), 1950-54; Editor, *IEEE Jour of Robotics & Automation*; Mem Edit Bd: *Math Bioscis*; *Math & Computers in Simulation*; *Transactions of Soc for Computer Simulation*; Mem: Soc for Computer Simulation; AAAS; Others; hon/Author: 3 Books & 8 Book Chapts; Over 100 Tech Articles & Papers Pub'd in Jours & Presented at Num Confs & Assn Meetings; Elected Fellow, IEEE, 1972; Dist'd Fac Awd, Univ of So CA, 1976; Sigma Xi Nat Lectr, 1976-77; Num Nat Sci Foun Res Grants; Num Biogl Listings.

BELCHER, LINDA JOYCE ROBINSON oc/Circuit Design Worker; b/Aug 24, 1949; h/1913 South Valentine, Little Rock, AR 72204; ba/Little Rock, AR; m/ James Artis Belcher; c/Ernest Robinson, Clifton Jhamal, Joycelyn Lanelle; p/ Ernest and Mary Janice Brown Robinson, N Little Rock, AR; sp/George Lee Belcher (dec); Mattie Jane Kolen Belcher, Warren, AR; ed/BA Social Sci, AR Bapt Coll, 1982; Att'd Grad Wk Courses at Quachita Bapt Univ; pa/ Comml Dept Jr Clk 1971, Plant Dept 1973, Acctg Dept 1973, Comptrollers Dept 1975, Engrg Dept 1978, Netwk Dept, CPC Design, 1983-, SWB Telephone Co; cp/Mem: Urban Leag; NAACP; AR Bapt Alumni; Past Mem, ATA; r/Bapt; hon/Outstg & Dedicated Ser Awd as Dir of Inspirational Choir, 1972-79; Ch Music & Choral Dir Wkshop Cert, 1977-78; Cert of Significant Achmt in Ch Music, 1982 & 1983; Cert of Merit, 1983; Co Contact Com Cert, 1983; Cert of Recog Highest Awd for Ch Music Dept, 1983; 12 Yrs Perfect Attendance, SWB Telephone Co, 1982; 2nd Pl Forms, 3rd Pl Kumite, MidS Pro Am Champships, 1974; 1st Pl Kata, Dunbar Karate Champships, 1977; 3rd Pl Kata, 1st PL Kumite, Pine Bluff Pks & Rec, Karate Invitation, 1981.

BELL, BRITTON oc/Executive; b/Jun 18, 1948; h/1569 South Carriage Lane, New Berlin, WI 53151; ba/Brookfield, WI; c/Scott Elbert; p/Elbert Pinckley Watts (dec); Betsy G Watts, Waukesha, WI; ed/St Catherine of Siena Grade Sch, Oak Park, IL, 1962; Dipl, Oak Park & River Forest HS, 1966; BA Bus Mgmt & Profl Communs, Alverno Col, Milwaukee, WI, 1981; pa/Pres & Mgmt Conslt, Profl Mgmt Sers, Brookfield, WI, 1979-84; Pres & Mgmt Conslt, The Britton Bell Co, Brookfield, WI, 1983-; Sys Analyst & Designer, Reynolds & Reynolds Co, Dayton, OH, 1977-79; Law Ofc Admr, John W Cusack, SC, Waukesha, WI, 1974-77; Pers Asst, RTE Corp, Waukesha, WI, 1973-74; Ofc Sers Coor, Shell Oil Co, Detroit, MI,

1969-71; Acctg Asst, Am Mut Reins Co, Chgo, IL, 1967-69; Mem: Nat Assn of Accts; Nat Assn; for Female Execs, 1980-; Acad of Mgmt, 1979-; Alverno Profl Alumnae Assn, 1981-; cp/NOW; Local Election Coms; Bd Mem, Coachlight Village Town Assn; Coor, Fund Raising PubCrawl for Florentine Opera, 1983; Spkr & Sem Ldr, Univ of WI Law Sch; r/Rom Cath; hon/Author of 2 Booklets: *Law Pract Mgmt*, 1982; *Financial Mgmt: Key to Successful Pract*, 1983; W/W of Am Wom.

BELL, CAROLYN SHAW oc/Economist; b/Jun 21, 1920; h/167 Clay Brook Road, Dover, MA 02030; ba/Wellesley, MA; m/Nelson S; c/Tova Maria Solo; p/ Clarence E Shaw (dec); Grace W Shaw; ed/AB, Mt Holyoke Col, 1941; PhD, Univ of London, 1949; pa/Ofc of Price Adm, USA, 1941-44; London Sch of Ec, 1946-47; Social Sci Res Coun 1953-, Wellesley Col, 1950-; Self-Employed Conslt, 1967-; Mem: ACLA; AAUP; Exec Com, Chp, CSWEP, Adv Com to Census, Nom'g Com, w Am Ec Assn; Trustee, TIAA; JCEE; UNA; AAUW; Boston Ec Clb; Exec Bd 1983-, En Ec Assn; Assn for Evolutionary Ec; Others; r/Prot; hon/Author of 5 Books & 80 Articles in Field of Law, Ec & Public Policy; Shirley Farr F'ship, AAUW, 1960; Phi Beta Kappa, 1940; Dist'd Sers, AES, 1973; Hon Deg, Babson Col, 1983; W/W: in Ec, in Am Wom; Dict Intl Ec; Am Men & Wom of Sci; Other Biogl Listings.

BELL, CHARLOTTE RENÉE oc/ School Psychologist; b/Jan 23, 1949; h/ 2307 Laurel Street, Columbia, SC 29204; ba/Same; c/David A; p/Willie and Victoria Williams, Denver, CO; ed/BA Sociol, Dillard Univ, NO, LA, 1970; MA Voc Rehab Cnslg 1973, EdD Psych, Cnslg & Guid 1976, Univ of No CO; pa/Pvt Pract, 1983-; Prin Res Investigator, SC St Col, 1978-83; Cert Sch Psychol, Cherry Creek Schs, CO, 1976-78; Cert Sch Psychol, Aurora Public Schs, CO, 1973-76; GED Instr, Collran Civilian Job Corps Ctr, CO, 1970-72; Conslitg Psychol, SC Dept of Social Sers, 1980-84; Conslt, Ednl Comm of the Sts, 1978; Fellow, Am Psychol Assn; Mem, Phi Delta Kappa; Mem, Alpha Kappa Alpha Sorority; Co-Chp Nat Testing Com, Assn of Black Psychols, 1981; Mem, Am Assn of Sex Edrs, Cnslrs & Therapists; Mem, SC Psychol Assn; Mem, Altrusa Intl; VPres, Adlerian Soc, 1982; Mem, Eval Netwk; cp/Fdr & Chp, Orangeburg (SC) Commun Residents for Mtlly Retarded Adv Bd, 1980-83; VChp, Orangeburg Mtl Hlth Assn, 1983; Fdr & Chp, Citizens Agnst Sexual Assault, 1979; Bd Mem, SC Black Adoptions Steering Com, 1981-; Bd Mem, Yg Vols in Action Adv Bd, 1983; Mem Spkrs Bur, Big Sisters & Big Brothers Inc, Columbia, SC, 1984; r/Epis; hon/Author of Book, *Added Dimensions in Fitness*, 1984; Author of Article: "Understanding Adolescent Behavior," 1980; Gubernatorial Appt, SC Chd's Case Resolution Comm, 1984; W/W: in W, in Frontier Sci & Technol.

BELL, GETHA GINA oc/Free Lance Writer; b/Sep 23, 1913; h/2980 Holiday-Lake Lanier, Buford, GA 30518; ba/Same; m/James Paul Harris, Sr (dec); c/James Paul Harris Jr; p/E Robert and Emma Clark Bell (dec); sp/ James Harris (dec); ed/Jour Maj, TX A&I

Univ, 1934; pa/Soc Editor, *Bay City & TX Daily Tribune*, 1934-42; *Houston, Chronicle*, 1943-44; *Midland Reporter Telegram*, 1944-52; Asst to Publisher, *SF Chronicle-Dislay*; Advr to Pres, Collectors Art Gallery, Atlanta, GA, 1964-68; Hist Resr & Free Lance Writer, 1968-; Lifetime Mem, Am Newspaper Guild; r/Epis; hon/Author, Num Articles in Var Pubs; Author of 2 Books incl'g: *Bells in USA & Allied Fams 1650-1977*; Intl W/ W; Other Biogl Listings.

BELL, KEITH F oc/Psychologist; b/ Aug 8, 1948; h/3101 Mistyglen Circle, Austin, TX 78746; ba/ Same; m/ Dorothy D; c/Kirsten Clarice, Keena Paige, Bridger Korbett; p/Jerry and Evelyn Bell, Baton Rouge, LA; sp/ Robert Dillon (dec); Elizabeth Dillon, St Thomas, Virgin Isls; ed/AB Psych, Kenyon Col, 1970; MA 1971, PhD 1974, Cnslg Psych, Univ of TX-Austin; mil/ USN; pa/Pvt Pract in Sports Psych, 1981-; Pt-time Pvt Pract Sports Psych, 1975-81; Cnslg Psych, Austin Commun Col, 1979-81; Adj Prof Psych, St Edwards Univ, Austin, 1979; Prof Psych, Park Col, Bergstrom AFB, Austin, 1979; Asst Prof Psych, SW TX St Univ, 1978-79; Clin Dir, Day Treatment Ctr at Austin-Travis Co Mntl Hlth Retard Ctr, 1976-77; Postdoct Fellow Commun Psych, Cnslg-Psychol Sers Ctr, Univ of TX-Austin, 1974-75; Intern Clin-Cnslg Psych, Mtl Hlth Sect, Univ of TX-Austin Student Hlth Ctr, 1973-74; VA Traineeship, VA Ctr, Temple, TX, 1973; Res Assoc, Hogg Foun Mtl Hlth, Austin, 1972-73; Coach: Longhorn Aquatics Masters, Austin, 1979-80; St Croix Dolphins Age Grp Clb, 1977; Austin Aquatic Clb, 1975-76; Men's Swim Team 1972-77, Wom's Swim Team 1975-76, Univ of TX-Austin; Wheaton Col, IL, 1971; Mem: Am Psychol Assn; Am Swim Coaches Assn; N Am Soc for Psych of Sport & Phy Activity; hon/Author of 5 Books on Sport Psych, 1980-84; Author, Over 50 Articles & Papers in Jours incl'g: *Swimmers*; *Coach*; *Swim Swim*; *A Sci Approach to Sport of Swimming*; Others; US Nat Champ, 400 IM, 1981; Canadian Nat Champ, 200 M, 400 M, 1500 M Freestyle & 200 M IM All Am, 1979 & 1980; Capt 1970, All Am 1967, 1969 & 1970, Kenyon Col; W/W in S & SW.

BELL, MICHAEL S oc/Art Administrator; b/Jul 4, 1946; ba/San Francisco, CA; m/Michele; c/Mercury, Justin, Ororah, Shannon; p/Alpha More Russell, Joplin, MO; sp/Jack Ellis, Albuquerque, NM; ed/BFA, CA Inst of Arts, 1970; MFA, Univ of KY, 1972; Addit Course Wk; mil/USAF; pa/Asst Dir, SF Arts Comm, 1984-; Curatorial Asst, SF Mus of Mod Art, 1982; Dir, Midland Art Coun, MI, 1980; Registrar & Cataloguer 1976, Curatorial Asst w CETA Prog (OMAR) 1975, The Oakland Mus; Studio Artist, SF, Mill Val, Oakland, Berkeley, 1972-74; Tchg Fellow, CA Inst of Arts, 1970; Mem Documentations Com, Mod Art Com, Fine Arts Com, w Intl Coun of Mus; Mem Curators Com, Am Assn of Mus; Trustee, The Mexican Mus, SF, 1983-; Bd of Dirs & Treas, Project Sculpture/ Public Sites, SF, 1983; Adv Bd Mem, Chm Curatorial Planning Com, SF Arts Comm Gallery; Num Other Positions; cp/Frequent Lectr, Conslt & Jurist; r/

Epis; hon/Author, Num Pub'd Articles in Jours incl'g: *Art in Soc*; *The Crafts Report*; *Intermedia*; *Artwk*; Others; Full S'ships: CA Inst of Arts, 1970; Mus Mgmt Inst, 1979; ALI-ABA Course, 1981; Gertrude B Murphy Awd of Merit for Promotional Lit, 1974; Archives of Am Art; W/W: in W, in Am Art; Dir of Am Poets; Other Biogl Listings.

BELL, ROGER ALISTAIR oc/Astronomy Professor; b/Sep 16, 1935; h/706 Quaint Acres Drive, Silver Spring, MD 20904; ba/Univ of MD, College Park, MD; m/Sylvia Anne; c/Alistair Michael, Andrew Christopher; p/Mrs I M Bell, Victoria, Australia; sp/Mrs H Gandine, Northampton, England; ed/BSc, Univ of Melbourne, 1957; PhD, Australian Nat Univ, 1961; PhD, (Honoris Causa), Uppsala Univ, 1982; pa/Lectr, Adelaide Univ, 1962; Asst Prof 1963-69, Assoc Prof 1969-76, Prof 1976, Univ of MD; Prin Res Fellow, Royal Greenwich Observatory, 1969-70; Prog Dir, Nat Sci Foun, 1981-84; Mem: AAUP; Intl Astronom Union; Am Astronom Soc; Royal Astronom Soc; r/Anglican; hon/Author, Over 80 Sci Papers Pub'd; Hon Deg, Uppsala, 1982; J Clarence Karcher Lectr, Univ of OK, 1977; W/W in E.

BELL, RUBY TATE oc/Educator; b/Aug 8, 1931; h/6 Northgate Ct, Willingboro, NJ 08046; ba/Philadelphia, PA; m/2nd, William H Jr; 1st, Rudolph L Bratcher; c/David A Bratcher, Stephen A Bratcher; p/Clevester V Tate (dec); Ruby Robinson Tate, Phila, PA; sp/William H Bell Sr (dec); Julia Odom Bell Boykin, Phila, PA; ed/BEd, Cheyney St Univ, 1953; MEd, Antioch Univ, 1973; EdD Cand, Temple Univ 1978-; pa/Phila Sch Dist: Tchr, Wm Dick Sch, 1954-69; Ld Tchr/Team Ldr, R R Wright Sch, 1969-71; Rdg Spec, Coor, Dept Chp, Acting VPrin, E W Rhodes Mid Sch, 1971-83; Dist 6 Chapt I Rdg Coor, 1983-; Ednl Conslt; Pres, Vel Bell Inc; Ednl Sers Corp; Editor & Publisher, Learn at Home Pub; Chp, Ed Comm, 1973-; Mem, Phila Assn of Sch Admrs; Mem, Intl Rdg Assn; Mem, Keystone Rdg Assn; Mem, DVAEYC; Mem, Black Wom's Ednl Alliance; Kappa Delta Pi; Bd of Dirs, 2nd Macedonia Day Care Ctr; hon/Author of Phila Sch Dist Tchr's Guides for TV Rdg Prog Series, 1973-77; Contbr, Capital Cities TV Rdg Prog Series, 1977-79; Publisher & Editor: *Lrng to Listen: Listening to Learn*, 1979; *Rdg Test Pract for Parents & Chd*, 1981; *Test Pract Pull-Outs*, 1983; *Rdg Pract Booklet*, 1983; Cheyney St Univ Ath Hall of Fame, 1981; W/W of Am Wom.

BELLA, DANTINA CARMEN oc/Director; b/May 11, 1922; h/1029 Clermont Drive, South Bend, IN 46617; ba/South Bend, IN; m/Salvatore J; c/Theresa Maria Bella Dietiker, Joseph Salvatore, Jennifer Marie; ed/MA, Alfred Univ, 1952; MS Adm, Univ of Notre Dame, 1973; pa/Rehab Cnslr, RI Dept of Ed, 1942-46; Admissions Cnslr, Boston Univ, 1946-49; Asst to Dean, Col of Ceramics, Alfred Univ, 1949-53; Dir of Pupil Pers, Marian HS, Mishawaka, IN, 1968-74; Psychol 1975-80, Dir 1980-, Forever Lrng Inst; Textbook Conslt, SBCom Schs, 1974-77; cp/Bd of Dirs, Cath Social Ser, 1968-; Pres, S Bend Comm on Status of Wom, 1975-78; Mem, Career Planning, YWCA, 1974-77; r/Rom Cath; hon/Author of Articles: "Sexism in Text-

books," 1975; "Portrayal of Wom in Textbooks," 1977; "Older Wom & Their Needs," 1977; Prodr, Local TV Prog on Polit Issues, 1977-1980; Grad cum laude, 1944; Beta Gama Sigma Hon Soc, 1973; W/W in MW.

BELLAN, JOSETTE ROSENTWEIG oc/Research Scientist; b/May 9, 1946; h/3744 Valley Lights Drive, Pasadena, CA 91107; ba/Pasadena, CA; m/Paul Murray Bellan; c/Norbert Henry, Leon Marcel, Steven Edward; p/Naftali Leizer (dec); Sara (Scvartz) Rosentweig ; sp/Ruben and Ruth Bellan, Canada; ed/Baccalaureate 1964, MS 1969, AEA 1969, in France; MA, 1972; MS, 1972; PhD, 1974, in USA; pa/Mem Res Staff, Princeton Univ, 1974-77; Staff Sci, S A I, 1977-78; Engrg Spec, Boeing Aerospace Co, 1978-80; Mem Tech Staff, Jet Propulsion Lab, 1980-; Mem: AIAA; ASME; The Combustion Inst; Mem Tech Com on Combustion & Heat Transfer in Fires, ASME; Ad Hoc Math Modeling Com on Fire Res; Mem Tech Com on Propellants & Combustion, AIAA; hon/Author of 10 Jour Pubs & Num Reports; Bourse du Troisieme Cycle, 1969-62; Amelia Earhart F'ship Awd, 1971-74; Certs of Recon, NASA, 1983, 1984; W/W: in W, in Am, in Aerospace Sers, of Wom; Other Biogl Listings.

BELLMAN, SAMUEL IRVING oc/Professor; b/Sep 28, 1926; h/1012 Lake Forest Drive, Claremont, CA 91711; ba/Pomona, CA; m/Jeanne Lisker; c/Joel Ethan, Jonathan David; p/Max Bellman (dec); Bessie Bellman, Richardson, TX; sp/Hyman Lisker (dec); Sonia Lisker (dec); ed/BA, Univ of TX, 1947; MA, Wayne St Univ, 1951; PhD, OH St Univ, 1955; pa/Instr, Fresno St Col, 1955-57; Asst Prof, Cal St Polytech Col, SLO, 1957-59; Asst Prof & Prof, Cal St Polytech Univ, Pomona, 1959-; Vis'g Prof, Univ of So CA, 1968; Vis'g Exch Prof, Portsmouth Polytech, England, 1975-76; Mem, Am Studies Assn; Mem, Rocky Mtn MLA; r/Jewish; hon/Author of Books: *The "New Wom" in the Space Age*, 1966; *Marjorie Kinnan Rawlings*, 1974; *Constance Mayfield Rourke*, 1981; Editor: *The Col Experience*, 1962; *Survey & Forecast*, 1966; Author of Num Essays, Articles & Poems Pub'd in Profl Jours & Mags; Dir of Am Scholars; Contemp Authors; W/W in W; The Writers Dir 1984-86; Gt Writers of the Eng Lang: Poets.

BELTZNER, GAIL ANN oc/Music Specialist; b/Jul 20, 1950; h/959 Tilghman Street, Allentown, PA 18102; p/Conon Nelson and Lorraine Ann (Carey) Beltzner; ed/BS Music Ed, West Chester St Col, 1972; Postgrad Study: Kean St Col, Temple Univ, Westminster Choir Col, Lehigh Univ; pa/Music Tchr, Drexel Jr HS, 1972-73; Music Spec, Allentown, PA Sch Dist, 1973-; Participant in Proj Ecesis, The Sch & Commun Devel Lab Task Force, The Commun Resource Fest & Cultural Fair of Tchr Corps; Exec Com & Sec Music Prog, Allentown Fedn of Tchrs; Mem, Music Edrs Nat Conf; Mem, Music Edrs Assn; Mem, Am Orff-Schulwerk Assn; Mem, Soc for Gen Music; Mem, Am Assn Music Therapy; Mem, Intl Soc Music Ed; Mem, Assn for Supvn & Curric Devel; cp/Mem, Allentown Art Mus Aux; Mem, Lenni Lenape Hist Soc; Former Mem, Lehigh Val Arts Coun; Mem, Lehigh Co Hist Soc; Kappa Delta

Pi; Phi Delta Kappa; Alpha Lambda; r/Luth; hon/Swope Meml S'ship, 1971; Presser Foun S'ship, 1972; W/W: in Am Cols & Univs, in E.

BELLUGI, URSULA oc/Director; ba/San Diego, CA; ed/BA, Antioch Col, 1952; EdD, Harvard Univ, 1967; pa/Dir Lab for Lang & Cognitive Studies 1970-, Res Prof 1981-, Assoc Res Prof 1974-81, Res Assoc 1969-74, Mem 1968-69, The Salk Inst for Biol Studies; Adj Prof 1977-, Adj Assoc Prof 1970-76, Adj Asst Prof 1969-70, Dept of Psych, Univ of CA-San Diego; Adj Prof, San Diego St Univ, 1982-; Vis'g Prof, Consiglio Nationale delle Recerche, Rome, Italy, 1981; Vis'g Asst Prof, Dept Psych, Rockefeller Univ, 1969; Vis'g Lectr Linguistics Inst 1968, Asst Prof & Res Fellow 1967-68, Sr Res Asst, 1964-67, Harvard Univ; Bd of Trustees, Sr Fac Mem, Chm Com on Biol & Lang, Chm Sem Com, w The Salk Inst; Assoc & Adv Bd Mem: Prog in Cognitive Sci, Ctr for Human Info Processing, Ctr for Res in Lang Acquisition, Univ of CA-San Diego Communicative Disorders Panel, Nat Inst of Neurol & Communicative Disorders & Stroke; Tech Com on Lang & Cognitive Devel, Linguistic Soc of Am; Nat Adv Com on Ed of Deaf, Dept of Hlth, Ed & Welfare; Mem Var Panels & Coms: NIH; Am Psychol Assn; Intl Linguistic Assn; Intl Assn for Study of Child Lang; Am Assn Applied Linguistics; Psychonomic Soc; Soc for Res in Child Devel; Soc for Neurosci; Brit Brain Res Assn; European Brain & Behavior Soc; cp/Mem Edit Bds: *Jour of Child Lang*; *Jour of Applied Linguistics*; *Jour of Spch & Hearing Disorders*; *Sign Lang Studies*; *Jour of Human Commun*; Others; Ad Hoc Reviewer for Num Assns & Jours; Num Confs & Over 40 Invited Presentations; hon/Co-Author 1 Book, *The Signs of Lang* w E S Klima, 1979; Co-Editor 3 Books; Author & Co-Author, Over 75 Articles & Book Chapts on Sign Lang, Linguistics, Lang Devel & Psych; Recip of 14 Res Grants; Recip, Most Outstg Book in Behavioral Scis, Profl & Scholarly Pub Div, Assn of Am Publishers, 1979.

BEMAK, FRED PAUL oc/Professor, Mental Health Consultant; b/Oct 23, 1948; h/35 Gray Street, Amherst, MA 01002; ba/Keene, NH; m/Adrienne; c/Amber, Lani; p/Walter and Ruth Bemak, Lisbon, Portugal; sp/Simon and Trudy Stavis, Everett, MA; ed/BA, Boston Univ, 1970; EdD, Univ of MA, Amherst, 1975; pa/Assoc Dir Masters Deg Prog, Antioch N Eng Univ Grad Sch, Keene, NH, 1982-; Clin Dir, Wn MA Teg Consortium, Univ of MA Med Sch, Worcester, 1980-82; Adj Asst Prof, Univ of MA, Amherst, 1980-; Self-Employed Mtl Hlth & Orgnl Conslt for Num Public Agys & Pvt Progs; Interim Chief Psychol, Wing Meml Hosp, Palmer, MA, 1979; Reg Proj Dir, MA Reg I Adolescent Treatment Prog, Northampton, 1977-79; Interim Proj Dir, Gateway Proj, Taunton, 1977; Acting Proj Dir 1974-75, Asst Dir 1973-74, Dir of Cnslg 1971-73, Casewkr 1970-71, Upward Bound Proj, Univ of MA-Amherst; Dir Commun Sers Coun, Boston Univ, 1969-70; Other Adj Fac Positions; Mem: Am Psychol Assn; Am Orthopsychl Assn; Ptnrs of the Ams; Inter-Am Assn of Psychols; Intl Coun of Psychols; hon/Author of Book Chapt, "A Pathway of Principles, Values & Morality: Deinstitutionalizing Chronic Mtl Hlth Clients," in *Applications of Psych to Schizophrenia,* 1983; Author of Tng Manual, 1981; Intl Exch of Experts F'ship, World Rehab Fund, 1982; Vis'g Psychol, Am Psychol Assn, 1982; Nat Mtl Hlth Ctr Spotlight; Vis'g Scholar, Antioch Univ, 1984; W/ W in E.

BENADE, LEONARD EDWARD oc/ Virologist; b/Nov 13, 1944; h/971 Park Avenue, Harndon, VA 22070; ba/Rockville, MD; m/Mary Pat Larsen; c/Tina Marie; p/Mr and Mrs Leo E Benade, Annandale, VA; sp/Mr and Mrs James W Larsen, Lafayette, CA; ed/BA Chem, Univ of VA, 1966; MPh Biochem 1971, PhD Biochem 1971, George Wash Univ, DC; pa/Chem, CIA, Wash, DC, 1971-73; Sr Biochem, Envir Control Inc, Rockville, MD, 1974-75; Lctr in Biol, No VA Commun Col, Alexandria, VA, 1974-77; Sr Analyst, JRB Assocs, McLean, VA 1975-76; Postdoct Fellow, Frederick Cancer Res Ctr (MD), 1977-79; Sr Staff Sci, Meloy Labs, Springfield, VA, 1979-81; Res Sci, Lab of Tumor Virus Genetics, Nat Cancer Inst, Bethesda, MD, 1981; Dept Hd, Dept Molecular Biol, Microbiol Assn, Bethesda, MD, 1982; Dept Hd, Dept Virology, Am Typeculture Collection, Rockville, MD, 1982-; Mem: AAAS; Am Soc for Microbiol; NY Acad of Sci; Foun for Adv Ed in Scis; hon/Author & Contbr, Num Articles in Profl Books & Jours; NSF Traineeship, 1963; Miller Scholar, 1965-66; Phi Beta Kappa, 1966; Alpha Epsilon Delta, 1966; Phi Sigma, 1966; NASA Fellow, 1966-68; USPHS Fellow, 1969-71; W/W: in S & SW, in Fronteir Sci & Technol; Am Men of Sci.

BENDER, BRENDA ANNE WILKIE oc/Educator; b/Apr 9, 1943; h/Route 3, Box 155, Moore, SC 29369; ba/Woodruff & Spartanburg, SC; c/Jacqueline Michele, John Joseph III; p/Lorenzo Belton Wilkie (dec); Gerladine Wilkie Wilson, Chesnee, SC; ed/AA, Spartanburg Jr Col, 1964; BA, Augusta Col, 1969; MEd, PhD, Univ of SC; pa/Adj Prof, Limestone Col Mgmt Prog, 1983-; Adj Prof, Spartanburg Meth Col, 1979-; Tchr, Woodruff Public Schs, 1980-; Instr, Converse Col, 1978; Tchr, Spartanburg City Schs, 1973-78; Tchr, Spartanburg Co Schs, 1971-73; Tchr, SC Public Schs, Barnwell, 1969-70; Fac Rep, NEA; Mem, SC Ed Assn; Mem, Alpha Delta Kappa; cp/Dir, Spartanburg Meth Col Alumni Coun; Former Bd Mem & Co-Chm of Mbrship, Spartanburg Commun Concert Assn; SS Tchr, St Paul's Cath Ch; r/Cath.

BENDER, DAVID R oc/Special Library Director; b/Jun 12, 1942; h/44 Strawberry Hill #11K, Stamford, CT 06902; ba/New York, NY; c/Robert, Scott, Lori Jo; p/John R Bender; Mary Bender (dec); ed/BS Ed, Kent St Univ, 1960-64; MS Lib Sci, Case Wn Univ, 1965-69; PhD, OH St Univ, 1969-77; pa/Exec Dir, Spec Libs Assn, 1979-; Chief, Sch Lib Media Sers Br, MD St Dept of Ed, 1972-79; Lectr, Rutgers Univ, Sum 1978; Pt-time Vis'g Prof, Towson St Univ, MD, 1976; Res Assoc, Sch Lib Ser, OH St Univ, 1970-72; Conslt, Sch Lib Ser, OH Dept of Ed, 1969-70; S HS Libn, Willoughby, OH, 1964-68; Others; Mem Foun Bd of Dirs, Am Soc of Assn Execs, 1982-84; Chm 1982-84, Chm Elect 1981-82, Coun of Nat Lib & Info Assns; Mem Nat Adv

Bd, Ctr for the Book, Lib of Cong, 1983-; Secy, Sect for Social Sci Libs, Intl Fdn of Lib Assns & Instns; Mem Pres's Comm, Am Lib Assn, 1976-77; Served on Num Coms of Am Assn of Sch Librs & Yg Adult Sers Div, ALA; Accreditation Com, Assn of Ednl Communs & Technol, 1976; Served on 2 Task Force Progs, Nat Commm on Libs & Info Sci; Var Positions w St Sch Lib Media Supvrs Assn; Var Positions w Coun on Lib Technol; Exec Bd, MD Ednl Med Org, 1976-79; Num Positions w MD Lib Assn; Mem, Beta Phi Mu; Mem, Kappa Sigma; Nat Adv Bd Mem, ERIC Clearinghouse on Info Resources, 1981-83; Num Consltg Positions & Others; r/ Epis; hon/Author, Over 30 Books, Articles & Media Presentations Pub'd incl'g: *Lrng Resources & the Instrnl Prog in Commun Cols,* 1980; *Lib Media Progs & the Spec Learner,* 1981; "The Impact of Technols on Libs: Response," 1982; "Spec Lib & the Future of Info," 1983; Recip, 3 Grants; Mbrship & Distd Ser Awd; MD Ednl Media Org, 1980; W/ W: in Am, in E; ALA Yrbook; Men of Achmt; Contemp Authors.

BENDER, DOUGLAS RAY oc/Personnel Administration; b/Jul 23, 1953; h/4214 Chateau Drive, Greensboro, NC 27407; ba/Eden, NC; m/Belinda Juanita Lipscomb; c/Douglas Ranier, Danitra Charee, Nathaniel Frederick, Kevin Dante; p/Fred Douglas and Herma Marie Bender, Pachuta, MS; sp/Joe Nathan (dec); Rozellion Lipscomb, Cedar Rapids, IA; ed/BS, Alcorn St Univ, 1975; Univ of NC-Greensboro, 1978-80; NC A&T St Univ, 1982-; pa/ w Miller Brewing Co: Benefits Analyst 1975-76, Corp Benefits Coor 1976-77, Corp Recruiting Admr 1977-78, Milwaukee, WI; Pers Rep 1978-80, Industl Relats Rep 1980-82, Reidsville, NC; Labor Relats Rep, Trenton, OH, 1982-; Mem: Am Mgmt Assn; Am Soc Tng & Devel; Am Soc Safety Engrs; Am Soc Per Admr; Am Soc Pers Adm Pers Admr Mag; cp/Adv Bd, PEOPLE Prog, Rockingham Commun Col, 1978-; Adv Bd, Adult Ed Prog, Rockingham Commun Col, 1979-; Adv Bd Rockingham Co Voc Tech Schs, 1979-; Indust Co, Chp Alcorn St Univ, Col/ Indust Cluster Prog, 1981-82; NAACP; Charter Mem, Rockingham Co Pers Assn; Random Woods Commun Assn; r/Bapt; hon/Outstg Commun Ser Awd, NAACP, 1980; Nat Assn for EO in Higher Ed Dist'd Alumni Awd, 1982; Accredited Pers Mgr, ASPA, 1982; W/ W in S & SW; Personalities of S.

BENDER, HARVEY ALAN oc/Geneticist, Professor; b/Jun 5, 1933; h/1512 Belmont Avenue, South Bend, IN 46615; ba/Notre Dame, IN; m/Eileen T; c/Leslie Carol, Samuel David, Philip Michael; p/Oscar I Bender (dec); Effie G Bender, Euclid, OH; sp/Samuel Teper (dec); Sonia Teper, Bchwood, OH; ed/ AB Chem, Adelbert Col, Case Wn Resv Univ, Cleveland, 1954; MS 1957, PhD 1959, NWn Univ, Evanston; pa/US Public Hlth Postdoct Fellow, Univ of CA-Berkeley, 1959-60; Asst Prof Biol 1960-64, Assoc Prof Biol 1964-69, Prof Biol 1969-, Sr Staff Mem Radiation Lab, 1961-, Adj Prof Law, 1974-, Dir Master's Prog & Biol Sum Prog, 1970-73; Dir NSF/URP Prog in Biol, 1979-81; Dir No IN Reg Genetics Ct, Meml Hosp of S Bend, 1979-, Dir Human Genetics

Prog, 1982-, Univ of Notre Dame; Num Vis'g Profships & Consltg Positions; Fellow, AAAS; Mem: Am Assn on Mtl Deficiency; AAUP; Am Inst of Biol Scis; Am Soc of Human Genetics; Genetics Soc of Am; IN Acad of Sci; Radiation Res Soc; Reg Lectr 1977-, Bd of Dirs Nat Exec Com 1983-84, Nat Dir-at-large 1980-86, Others Ofcs, Sigma Xi; Soc of Devel Biol; Soc for Values in Higher Ed; Num Coms w Univ of Notre Dame; Danforth Foun Assoc, 1979-85; Others; cp/Mem, St IN Genetics Adv Com, 1982-; Alumni Admission Adv Coun, Case Wn Resv Univ, 1967-; At-large Mem, Yale Univ Task Force on Genetics & Reprodn, 1973-; Instnl Review Bd, Meml Hosp S Bend, 1981-; Nat Lectr, Am Chem Soc, 1977-; hon/ Author & Co-Author, Over 60 Articles & Sci Papers Pub'd in Jours incl'g: *Am Jour of Med Genetics; Making Med Decisions; Am Jour of Clin Dysmorphology;* Others; Mem, XI (The Hague) & XII (Tokyo) Intl Cong of Genetics, Genetics Soc of Am, 1963 & 1968; Mem, XII Intl Cong of Entomol, Entomol Soc of Am, London, 1964; Cross-Disciplinary F'ship (Biomed Ethics), Soc for Values in Higher Ed, Yale Univ, 1973-74; W/W.

BENDER, MYRON L oc/Professor; b/ May 20, 1924; h/2514 Sheridan Road, Evanston, IL 60201; ba/Evanston, IL; M/ Muriel Schulman Bender; c/Alec Robert, Bruce Michael, Steven Pat; p/ Averam and Fannie Leventhal Bender (dec); ed/BS 1944, PhD 1948, Purdue Univ; Postdoct Fellow, Harvard Univ, 1948-49; Postdoct Fellow, Univ of Chgo, 1949-50; pa/Chem, Eastman Kodak Co, 1944-45; Instr, Univ of CT, 1950-51; Instr 1951-53, Asst Prof 1953-58, Assoc Prof 1958-60, IL Inst of Technol; Assoc Prof 1960-62, Prof 1962-, NWn Univ; Mem: Am Chem Soc; The Chem Soc London; Phi Lambda Upsilon; Sigma XI; AAAS; AAUP; Am Soc of Biol Chems; r/Jewish; hon/Author of 5 Books & 18 Monographs; Over 205 Articles Pub'd in Sci Jours; Mem, Nat Acad of Sci, 1968-; DSc (honoris causae), Purdue Univ, 1969; Phi Beta Kappa, 1970; MW Awd, Am Chem Soc, 1972; The Blue Book; Intl W/W in World Jewry; W/W in MW; Intl W/W.

BENDICK, MARC JR oc/Economist; b/Aug 20, 1946; h/4201 MA Avenue, Northwest, Washington DC 20016; ba/ Washington, DC; m/Mary Lou Egan; p/ Marc and Lucile Bendick, LA, CA; sp/ Charles and Julia Egan, Cleveland, OH; ed/BA Ec, Univ of CA-Berkeley, 1968; PhD Ec, Univ of WI, 1975; pa/Economist, McDonnell Douglas Corp, 1968-70; Financial Analyst & Proj Mgr Nika Corp, 1973-75; Res Economist & Prog Dir, Urban Inst, 1975-; Mem: Am Ec Assn; Am Public Welfare Assn; Bd of Trustees, World Neighbors Inc; Conslt w Num Pvt Corps & Govt Agys; hon/Author of *Housing Vouchers for the Poor,* 1980; Num Monographs & Articles Pub'd in Profl Jours on Ec & Public Policy; Phi Beta Kappa, 1968; W/W in E.

BENDURE, LEONA JENSEN oc/ Private Piano Teacher; b/Sep 27, 1912; h/711 Euclid, Lawton, OK 73501; ba/ Same; m/Lloyd K Bendure (dec); c/ Lorene B Teed (Mrs Dan), Donald Wesley; p/James and Nettie Folley Jensen (dec); ed/BMus 1934, BMus Ed 1937, Univ of KS; Grad Wk, MWn Univ,

Wichita Falls, TX; pa/Pvt Piano Tchr, 1938- 1984; Music Ed Tchr, Grove, KS, 1937-38; VPres 1983-84, Past Pres, Secy & Treas, Local Music Tchrs Assn of OK Music Tchrs Assn (OMTA); Bd of Dirs & Cultural Chm 1983-84, AAUW; Mem, Pi Kappa Lambda Nat Hon Music Frat; Secy, Mu Phi Epsilon, 1932-34; Mem, Mu Phi Epsilon Alumni, Wichita Falls, TX; cp/Mem, Comm on Missions of Centenary U Meth Ch, 1982-84; 2nd & 3rd VPres, Fine Arts Chp & Bd of Dirs 1983-85, Lawton Wom's Forum; Pres, Entre Nous Study Clb; Pianist, BPW Clb; r/Meth; hon/Howard Taylor Piano S'ship, Univ of KS, 1930-34; Mu Phi Epsilon S'ship; Recip of 5 Other Univ S'ships; Num Biogl Listings.

BENEDEK, ELISSA P oc/Forensic Psychiatrist, Professor; b/Sep 28, 1936; h/3607 Chatham Way, Ann Arbor, MI 48105; ba/Ann Arbor, MI; m/Richard S; c/David, Joel, Sarah, Dina; ed/Pre-Med 1956, MD 1960, Univ of MI; Addit Grad Tng; pa/Dir of Tng & Res, Ctr for Forensic Psychi, 1980-; Instr Psychi 1965-72, Clin Asst Prof Psychi 1972-76, Clin Assoc Prof Psychi 1977-79, Clin Prof Psychi 1979-, Univ of MI; Instr, En MI, Univ 1965-66; Clin Assoc Prof Psychi, MI St Univ, 1976-; Clin Prof Psychi, Wayne St Univ, 1982; Num Vis'g Prof'ships in N Am, 1972-85; Examr, (Adult Psychi 1972-), (Child Psychi 1976-), Am Bd of Psychi & Neurol; Conslt, Nat Inst on Mtl Hlth Probs of Inpatient Wom, 1980-; Num Others Consltg Positions; Edit Bd, *Am Jour of Am Acad of Child Psychi*, 1977-; Num Other Edit Bd Positions; Spec Proj w US Secret Ser at Inst of Med, 1981-; Bd of Dirs 1979-81, Mem Com on Psychi & Law 1975-, Grp for Advmt of Psychi; Com on Adolescence 1973-, Prog Com 1978-, Other Past Com Mbrships, Am Acad of Child Psychi; Com on Spec Interest Grps 1976-, Other Past Com Mbrships, MI Soc of Neurol & Psychi; VPres, 1984, Fellow 1973-, Bd Liaison to Am Acad of Child Psychi 1980-, Bd Liaison to Comm on Jud Action, 1982-, Comm on Malpract Ins 1983-, Num Other Comm Mbrships, Am Psychi Assn; Bd of Trustees 1983-, Fellow 976-, Other Positions, Am Col of Psychis; Mem, AMA, 1980-; Mem, Assn of Psychi & Law, 1975-; Num Other Profl Activs; cp/Bd Mem & Hlth Chm, Beth Israel Nursery Sch; Mem, Hadassah; Mem, Lwyrs Wives, Ann Arbor; Vol: King Sch & Clague Jr HS, Ann Arbor; hon/Author & Co-Author of 5 Books & Over 20 Book Chapts; Over 30 Articles Pub'd in Profl Psychi Jours; Over 20 Reviews & 17 AV Ednl Mats; Over 125 Abstracts, Papers & Panel Discussion Presentations; TV & Radio Appearances; Jr Hons, Univ of MI; W/W: in Am Wom, in MW, of Wom; Other Biogl Listings.

BENGELLOUN, ALI oc/Ambassador; b/Aug 17, 1927; h/2900 Cleveland Avenue, Northwest, Washington, DC 20008; ba/Washington, DC; m/Jacqueline; c/Ibrahim, Abela Laraki; ed/LLD, Law Sch, Univ of Paris; pa/Atty, 1950-55; Cabinet Dir, Min of Justice of Morocco, 1955; VPres Constitnl Coun; Pres Nat Acctg Offc; Prof Sch of Law & Moroccan Sch of Adm; Ambassador E & P of Morocco to US, Canada & Mexico, 1962; Chm of Nat Phosphates, 1965; Min of Justice of Morocco, 1967;

Ambassador at UN, 1976; Ambassador of Kingdom of Morocco to US, 1977-; Mem, Chevy Chase Clb; r/Moslem; hon/Decorated, Commandeur de l'Ordre du Trône.

BENJAMIN, STEPHEN ALFRED oc/Veterinary Educator; b/Mar 27, 1939; h/1454 Lakeshore Drive, Fort Collins, CO 80525; ba/Fort Collins, CO; m/Barbara; c/Jeffery, Karen, Kristine, Susan, Douglas, Eric; p/Dorothy Fabricant, Forest Hills, NY; sp/Jane Larson; ed/AB, Brandeis Univ, 1960; DVM 1964, PhD 1968, Cornell Univ; pa/Asst Prof Comparative Med, PA St Univ Col of Med, Hershey, 1967-70; Pathol, Lovelace Inhalation Toxicol Res Inst, Albuquerque, NM, 1970-77; Prof Pathol & Radiation Biol 1977-84, Dir Collaborative Radiol Hlth Lab 1977-84, Col of Vet Med & Biomed Scis, CO St Univ; Mem: Am Col of Vet Pathols; Am Vet Med Assn; Am Assn of Pathols; Intl Acad of Pathol; Radiation Res Soc; Am Assn for Lab Animal Sci; AAAS; r/Jewish; hon/Author of Num Sci Articles & Book Chapts Pub'd; Phi Zeta, 1964; Phi Kappa Phi, 1967; W/W in Frontier Sci & Technol.

BENN, PHYLISS ASHMUN oc/Lawyer; b/Aug 26, 1924; h/1001 Maple Avenue, LaPorte, IN 46350; ba/LaPorte, IN; m/Donald W; c/David W, Martha Ann, Ruth Louise, Robert Samuel; p/Van S and Margaret Fiege Ashmun (dec); sp/George W and Mattie L Benn (dec); ed/BA, Univ of WI, 1946; JD, Valparaiso Univ, 1975; pa/Self-Employed Lwyr, 1979-; Assoc, Smith & Smith Attys, 1975-79; Edit Asst, Towndan Pub Co, 1964-71; City Editor, *Niles Daily Star*, (MI), 1946-47; Chm 1980-82, LaPorte Human Rts Comm, 1973-82; Secy 1981-82, LaPorte City Bar Assn; ABA; LaPorte Co & IN Bar Assns; Br Pres 1958-59, St Bd 1960-63, AAUW; cp/Bd Mem 1978-82, Secy 1982, LaPorte U Fund; Dem Precnt Com-person, 1974-; Del, Dem Nat Conv, 1976; r/Prot; hon/Phi Beta Kappa, 1946; Phi Kappa Phi, 1946; W/W of Am Wom.

BENNETT, FRANK WEST oc/Financial Consultant; b/Dec 5, 1923; h/Route 1 Brevard Road, Arden, NC 28704; ba/Asheville, NC; m/Martha Moore; c/Frank Whitfield; Robert Lawrence; Rieley Benford, Stuart St John; p/Mr and Mrs Walter Newton Bennett (dec); sp/Mr and Mrs Phillip S Moore (dec); ed/Att'd FBI Sch, 1942; Att'd George Wash Univ, 1942-43; AB Jour & Geol, Univ of NC, 1950; MA Ec & Fin, Sussex Univ of Technol, England, 1975; Cert'd Financial Planner, 1972; mil/AUS 1943-45, 208 Combat Engr; Allied Airborne (ETO); pa/Chem, Am Mfg Co, Chattanooga, TN, 1950-52; Geol Engr, US Geol Survey, 1953-60; Dist Mgr, Liberty Life Ins, Asheville, 1968; Cert'd Financial Planner, Financial Ser Corp Intl, 1968-72; Financial Conslt, Investmt Mgmt & Res Inc, 1972-; Mem: Intl Assn of Fin Planners, 1970-; NC Assn of Life Underwriters; Curator 1953, So Appalachian Mineral Soc; Nat Assn Security Dealers; NC Ins Assn; Nat Speleology Assn; cp/Mem, Million Dollar Round Table; Chm CD 1952, JCs; Mem, Carolina Mtn Clb; r/Meth; hon/Author of "A Guide to Better Electro-Plating," 1952; "NAGI: Mysteries of Gt Smokey Mtns," 1975; "The

Grey Curtain," 1984; Other Articles & Poetry in Var Profl Mags; Bronze Medal (Decathlon) 1942; Berlin Olympic Games, 1945; Other Univ of NC Sports Awds; Million Dolar Roundtable, 1967; Dale Carnegie Awds; Decorated ETO; 5 Bronze Stars; Dist'd Man of Yr Awd, 1965-66; Excell in Financial Planning Awd, 1974-80; Num Others; W/W in Fin & Indust.

BENNETT, JOHN SCOTT oc/Professor; b/Feb 22, 1955; h/1346 Campbell #16, Jackson, TN 38301; ba/Jackson, TN; p/Mr and Mrs Harold C Bennett, Brentwood, TN; ed/BMus, Stetson Univ, 1977; MMus 1979, Currently Doct Cand, Eastman Sch of Music; Postgrad Study, Hochschule für Musik, Cologne, W Germany, 1980-81; German Dipl, Humboldt Inst, W Germany, 1981; pa/Organist, Univ of Rochester, 1978-80; Prof Organ & Theory, Union Univ, 1981-; Mem: Music Tchrs Nat Assn, 1982-83; Am Guild of Organists, 1982-; Col Music Soc, 1982-; Phi Mus Alpha Frat, 1982; Bd of Dirs, Jackson Symph, 1983; r/Bapt; hon/Chosen Recitalist, 11th Annual Mgmt Symp, St Gall, Switzerland, 1981; Rotary Foun Scholar, 1981; Outstg Yg Men of Am.

BENNETT, LAWRENCE ALLEN oc/Program Director; b/Jan 4, 1923; h/8380 Greensboro Drive, 311 The Rotonda, McLean, VA 22102; ba/Washington, DC; m/Beth J; c/Yvonne I Solis-Lantz, Glenn L; p/Walter and Eva Bennett (dec); sp/G L and Lulu Thompson (dec); ed/BA, Fresno St Col, 1949; MA 1954, PhD 1968, Claremont Grad Sch; mil/AUS, 1942-45 & 1949-50; pa/Psych Supvr, CA Med Facility, 1955-60; Dept Supvr of Clin Psych 1960-67, Chief of Res 1967-76, CA Dept of Corrections, Sacramento; Dir, Ctr for Study of Crime Delinq & Corrections, So IL Univ, 1976-79; Dir, Ofc of Prog Eval, Nat Inst of Justice, Wash, DC, 1979-; Mem: Chm 1970, CA St Interdeptmtl Res Coor Coun, 1967-76; Mem of Bd, CA Crime Technol Res Foun, 1970-75; Bd of Dirs, Am Justice Inst, Sacramento, 1970-79; Juv Adv Bd, St of IL, 1977-79; r/Unitarian; hon/Co-Author of Book, *Cnslg in Correctional Envirs*, 1978; Author, Num Book Chapts on Instnl Violence & Other Correctional Res Topics; Mem, Safer CA Com, 1974; Bronze Star w OLC; W/W: in E, in Frontier Sci & Technol; Men of Achmt.

BENNETT, THOMAS LEROY oc/Professor; b/Sep 25, 1942; h/213 Camino Real, Fort Collins, CO 80524; ba/Fort Collins, CO; m/Jacqueline Beekman; c/Dean, Shannon, Brian, Laurie; p/Thomas Bennett (dec); Gertrude Bennett, Santa Fe, NM; sp/Jack and Margaret Beekman, Santa Paula, CA; ed/BA 1964, MS 1966, PhD 1968, Univ of NM; pa/Prof Psych, & Dept Physiol & Biophysics, CO St Univ, 1970-; Asst Prof Psych, CA St Univ-Sacramento, 1968-70; Mem: Am Acad Behavioral Med; Am Psychol Assn; Psychosmic Soc; Sigma Xi; Rocky Mtn Psychol Assn; Intl Neuropsychol Soc; cp/Elder, Timothy Presb Ch; r/Presb; hon/Author & Co-Author of 5 Books on Psych incl'g: *Intro to Physiol Psych*, 1982; Num Articles & Book Chapts Pub'd; Diplomate, Am Acad Behavioral Med; NASA Fellow, 1965-68; Ford Foun Fellow, 1962-65; W/W in Am; Men & Wom of Sci; Intl

Scholar's Dir.

BENNETT, WILLIAM F oc/University Administrator; b/Jan 23, 1927; h/ #9 Brentwood Circle, Lubbock, TX; 79416; ba/Lubbock, TX; m/Audrey; c/ Linda Kay, William F Jr; p/Minnie E Bennett, Austin, TX; ed/BS Soils, OK St Univ, 1950; MS 1952, PhD 1958, Soil Fertility, IA St Univ; pa/Ext Area Agronomist 1952-54, Ext Agronomist 1954-57, IA St Univ; Soil Chem, TX A&M Univ, 1957-63; Chief Agronomist, Elcor Chem Corp, 1963-68; Prof Agronomy 1968-, Assoc Dean Col of Agri Scis 1970-, TX Tech Univ; Mem: Soil Sci Soc Am; Am Soc Agronomy; r/Prot; hon/Co-Author of 3 Books incl'g: *Food & Fiber For Changing World*, 1982; *Crop Sci & Food Prodn*, 1983; W/W: in S & SW, in Frontier Sci & Technol.

BENNETT, WILLIAM JOHN oc/ Chairman, National Endowment for Humanities; b/Jul 31, 1943; h/5619 Western Avenue, Northwest, Washington DC 20015; ba/Washington, DC; m/ Mary Elayne; p/Francis and Nancy Bennett (dec); sp/Clarence and Dorothy Glover, Charlotte, NC; ed/BA, Williams Col, MA, 1965; PhD, Univ of TX-Austin, 1970; JD, Harvard Law Sch, 1971; pa/Pres & Dir 1979-81, Exec Dir 1976-79, Nat Humanities Ctr; Assoc Prof, Univ of NC-Chapel Hill, 1979-81; Assoc Prof, NC St Univ, Raleigh, 1977-81; Asst to Pres 1972-76, Assoc Dean & Asst Prof 1971-72, Boston Univ; Acad Adm Intern Prog, ACE, 1975-76; Vis'g Asst Prof, Univ of WI, 1973; Spkr & Instr, Boston Policy Acad, 1975; Projs Chm, Nat Humanities Fac, 1973-75; Tutor, Harvard Univ, 1969-71; Asst Prof, Univ of TX, 1970; Asst Prof, Univ of So MS, 1967-68; Instr, Gov's Sch, 1966; Mem: UNESCO, 1983; Wilson Ctr, 1982; Pres's Comm on Arts & Humanities, 1982; Nat Acad of Ed. 1980-81; Comm on Future of S, 1970-81; Comm on Basic Res in Behavioral & Soc Scis, 1980-81; Inst for Ednl Affairs, 1978-81; Am Soc Polit & Legal Phil, 1976-81; So Ednl Communs Assn, 1978-79; Soc for Values in Higher Ed, 1977-78; Nat Humanities Fac, 1967-79; Panelist, Nat Endowment for Humanities, 1973-77; r/Cath; hon/Author, Over 45 Articles in Var Profl Jours, 1973-; Hon DLitt, Gonzaga Univ, 1982; Hon HHD, Franklin Col, 1982; Hon DHL, Univ of NH, 1982; Hon LLD, Wms Col, 1983; W/W in Am.

BENSON, GENEVA (NEVA) oc/ Watercolor Artist; b/Sept 6, 1931; h/ 1832 Northwest 34, Oklahoma City, OK 73118; m/Billy E; c/Jeffrey Paul, Gregory Blake, Michael Scott, Anthony Jay; p/Roy Timberlake (dec); Lillie M Timberlake, Lexington, OK; sp/Carl Benson (dec); Ardell Benson, Piedmont, OK; ed/Att'd 3 Yrs OK St Univ, 1949-51; pa/Location Record Clk (Drafter), SWn Bell, 1951-56; Housewife & Mother, 1956-; Started Art Career in Var Media, 1975-; Piano Tchr, 1947-50; Mem: OK Watercolor Assn, 1980-; OK Mus of Art, 1978-; Bus & Profl Wom Assn, 1951-59; cp/Wom's Gridiron, 1953-65; YBA Instr; Vol for Num Local & Nat Charity Drives; r/Bapt.

BENTLEY, CHARLES R oc/Professor; b/Dec 23, 1929; h/5618 Lake Mendota Drive, Madison, WI 53705; ba/ Madison, WI; m/Marybelle (Goode); c/ Molly Clare, Raymond Alexander; p/

Raymond and Janet Everest Bentley (dec); ed/BS Physics, Yale Univ, 1950; PhD Geol, Columbia Univ, 1959; pa/Res Asst 1952-55, Geophysicist 1955-56, Columbia Univ; Traverse Seismologist & Co-Ldr 1956-58, Traverse Ldr 1958-59, IGY Antarctic Progs, Arctic Inst of N Am; Proj Assoc 1959-61, Asst Prof 1961-63, Assoc Prof 1963-68, Prof 1968-, Univ of WI-Madison; Mem: Sci Com Intl Antarctic Glaciological Proj (IAGP), 1979-; Alt US Del, Sci Com for Antarctic Res (SCAR), 1981-; US Nat Rep, Wkg Grp on Solid Earth Geophysics of SCAR, 1982-; Chm Polar Res Bd 1981-, Geophysics Res Forum 1981-, Nat Acad of Sci; Chm 1979-, Bd of Assoc Editors of Am Geophysical Union (AGU) Antarctic Res Series, 1974-; Corres'g Editor, *Jour of Glaciology*; hon/ Author & Co-Author, Over 100 Articles, Reports & Papers Pub'd in Profl Jours incl'g: *Annals of Glaciology*; *Antartic Jour of US*; *Geophysics Res Lttrs*; Others; Num Book Chapts; Co-Author, *Radioglaciology*, Pub'd in Moscow, 1983; Nom'd Yg Man of Yr, Nat Jr C of C, 1963; Sr Postdoct F'ship, Nat Sci Foun, MIT, 1968-69; Bellingshausen-Lazarev Medal 1971, 25th Anniv Medal of Soviet Antarctic Expeditions 1981, Soviet Acad of Sci; W/W; Men of Achmt; Am Men & Wom of Sci.

BENTLEY, ERNEST L oc/Minister, College Field Representative; b/Nov 28, 1914; h/8305 South Burchfield, Oak Ridge, TN 37830; ba/Cookeville, TN; m/ Martha L (Caldwell); c/Pearl Dean Pafford, Ernest L Jr, Anne Stroupe; p/ K O Bentley (dec); sp/Frank Caldwell (dec); ed/Dipl, Lauderdale Co HS, TN; Att'd Ext Classes, Univ of TN, 1945-60; pa/Safety Insp, Proctor & Gamble Corp, 1940-44; Safety Insp, Ford, Bacon & Davis Inc, 1944-45; Safety Engr, TN Eastman Corp, 1945-47; Cert Safety Profl, Union Carbide Corp, 1947-76; Field Rep, E TN Sch Preaching & Missions, 1977-80; Field Rep, TN Bible Col, 1980-; Mem: Am Soc Safety Engrs; Am Indust Hygiene Assn; r/Ch of Christ; hon/Author of Regular Articles in TN Bible Col Newslttr; Dist'd Ser Awd, TN Bible Col, 1981; W/W in S & SW.

BENTZEL, CHARLES HOWARD oc/ Financial Executive; b/Jul 30, 1926; h/ 28637 Dapper Dan, Boerne, TX 78006; ba/San Antonio, TX; m/Wandalee Baer; c/Brent, Alan, Leslie; p/Reece Emory and Idel Burton; ed/BA 1952, BS 1962, Univ of Balto; D Comml Sci, London Inst Applied Res, 1973; pa/VPres & Chief Financial Ofcr, Roblin Industs Inc NYC, 1968-69; VPres, Dir Fin & Controller, ITT & Subsidiaries, NYC & Abroad, 1969-76; VPres & Chief Financial Ofcr, Trane Co, WI, 1976-79; Financial Ofcr, Iscott, Trinidad, 1980-82; Pres, CEO & Dir, Severance Res Lab, San Antonio, 1982-; Dir, Data Terminals Corp; Bd of Dirs, YMCA (WI), 1976-79; Mem, Intl Assn Fin Execs Insts; Dir, Brazilian Fin Execs Inst; Hon Life Mem, Fin Execs Inst; Mem, Am Acctg Assn; Mem, Nat Assn Accts; Mem, Intl Treas Assn; cp/NY Ath Clb; Marco Polo Clb; Fair Oaks Golf & Country Clb; Mason; hon/Contbg Author, *The Mod Accts Handbook*, 1973.

BENZINGER, RAYMOND BURDETTE oc/Attorney, Professor; b/Apr 29, 1938; h/5509 Ivor Street, Spring-

field, VA 22151; ba/Arlington, VA; m/ Patricia Anne Kate; c/Raymond Howard, Susan Raye; p/William Patrick Benzinger, Pgh, PA; sp/Frederick Kate, Oklahoma City, OK; ed/BS, Carnegie Inst of Technol, 1962; JD 1971, LLM 1973 Georgetown Univ Law Ctr; pa/ Asst Dir Engraving & Printing, Nat Geog Soc, 1962-71; Law Clk, Philip Nichols Jr, US Ct of Claims, 1971-72; Trial Atty, US Dept of Justice, 1972-78; Vis'g Prof Law, Intl Sch of Law, 1978-79; Prof Law, George Mason Univ Sch of Law, 1979-; Mem, Georgetown Univ Spkrs Bur, 1970-; Dept Master of Rolls 1971, Supreme Justice 1975-76, Dept VChancellor 1973-82, Delta Theta Phi Law Frat; r/Prot; hon/Bus Editor, *Law & Policy in Intl Bus*, 197-71; Nat Outstg Law Prof, Delta Theta Phi Law Frat, 1978; W/ W in S & SW.

BERDECIA, LUIS A oc/Professor; h/ Urb San Cristóbal, A-5 Barranquitas, PR 00618; ba/Barranquitas, PR; m/Irma Falcón; c/Irma Maricelli, Luis Antonio, Rafael Enrique; p/Enrique Berdecia (dec); sp/Maria Rodriguez, Barranquitas, PR; ed/AA Elem Ed 1961, BA Sec'dy Ed Eng 1966, Univ of PR; MA Higher Ed Eng & Linguistics, NY Univ, 1969; pa/Elem Tchr, 1960-64; Sr HS Eng Tchr, 1964-65 & 1966-68; Jr HS Eng Tchr, 1965-66; Zone Supvr Eng, 1968-69 & 1970-76; Job Corps Eng Tchr, 1968-69; Gen Supvr Job Corps, 1976-77; Evening Sch Eng Tchr, 1964-70; Pt-time Prof Eng & Ed 1971-76, Instr Eng & Linguistics 1976-78, Asst Prof Eng & Linguistics 1978-, IAU Barranquitas Reg Col, PR; Mem: NEA; Bilingual Ed Assn; TESOL; Alumni Assn NY Univ; PR Tchrs Assn; cp/Mem, Nat Wildlife Assn; r/Cath; hon/W/W in S & SW.

BERDY, JACK M oc/Executive; b/Dec 3, 1946; h/72 Stony Ridge Road, Saddler River, NJ 07458; ba/Fort Lee, NJ; m/ Alice Kessler; c/Kimberly, Sherry; p/ Bernard and Mary Goldberg Berdy (dec); ed/Biol Maj, Att'd Univ of MD, 1966; pa/Applications Spec, IBM/SBC, NYC, 1966-67; Sr Sys Analyst, Univac Intl, Coppenhagen, Denmark, 1967-69; Pres, Fdr, Chm of Bd, CEO, On-line Software Intl Inc, 1969-; Nat Chief, Indiance Princesses Prog, YMCA; Spkr & Chm, of Profl Sems & Assns: ADAPSO & INTERFACE Confs; cp/ Appt'd Spec Police, Wyckoff, NJ, 1976-79; Appt'd Aux Police, NYC, 1969-71; hon/Recip, Meritorious Ser Awd, NYC; Certs of Apprec: Am Mgmt Assn; IEEE; Data Communs; Intl Conf Mems Assn; Computer Mgmt Mem of ADAPSO Inc/Developer of Computers to Fail Safe Sys.

BERENDZEN, RICHARD oc/University President; b/Sep 6, 1938; h/3300 Nebraska Avenue, Northwest, Washington DC 20016; ba/Washington, DC; m/ Gail Anita Edgar; c/Deborah Berendzen, Natasha; p/Mr and Mrs Berendzen, Dallas, TX; sp/Mr and Mrs Edgar, Ludlow, MA; ed/BS, MA Inst of Technol, MA 1967, MD 1968, Harvard Univ; pa/Pres & Prof Physics 1980-, Provost 1976-79, Dean Col of Arts & Scis 1974-76, The Am Univ; Conslt: to Am Coun on Ed & Nat Acad of Scis, 1973-74; Acting Dept Chm 1971-72, Fac Mem 1965-72, Boston Univ; Lectr, Harvard Univ, 1964-66; Bd Mem: Bus Coun for Intl Understanding; Linda Pollin Inst for Med Crisis Cnslg; Am

Univ; Assn of Am Cols; Planetary Soc; cp/Fed City Coun; Madison Nat Bk; Wom in Govt Relats; Coms for Proj Hope; Nat Aquarium; 40th Anniv of USO; hon/Author of 3 Books incl'g: *Man Discovers the Galaxies*, 1976; *Ed in & Hist of Mod Astron*, 1972; Author, Over 150 Articles & Reviews Pub'd in Var Profl Jours & Mags; Fellow, AAAS; Fellow, Wash Acad of Scis; Hon JD WV Wesleyan, 1979; Hon LHD, Bridgewater Col, 1983; Hon LLD, Kean Col, 1984; Selected Top 100 Yg Ldrs of Acad, *Change Mag*, 1978; W/W: in Am, in E, in Am Ed; Am Men & Wom of Sci.

BERG, DAVID oc/Writer & Artist; b/ Jun 12, 1920; h/14021 Marquesas Way, #307C, Marina Del Rey, CA 90291; m/ Vivian Lipman; c/Mitchel Ian, Nancy Anne Iva; p/Morris I and Bessie Friedman Berg (dec); sp/Benjamin Lipman; Mary Regelson (dec); ed/Att'd: Pratt Inst; Cooper Union; New Sch of Social Res; Iona Col; Col of New Rochelle, Univ of WI; mil/20th AF, WW II, Sgt, Chem Warfare Tech; AUS, Correspondent; pa/Writer & Artist, *Death Patrol*, Will Eisner, 1940-41; Writer & Artist, *Capt Marvel*, Fawcett Pub Co, 1942; Writer, Artist & Editor, *Combat Kelly Timely Mag*, 1941-56; Writer & Artist, *Archie Comics*, MLJ Pub Co, 1948-50; Writer & Artist, *Mad Mag*, EC Pub Co, 1956-; Writer & Artist, Signet Books, NAL, 1963-; Writer & Artist, Warner Books, Warner Communs, 1973-; Creat Conslt, NBC TV Spec, S Ilson Prodn, 1982; Mem: Nat Cartoonist Soc; Intl Platform Assn; Authors Leag; Writers Guild of Am, West; ZOA; cp/ Dem Party; Scoutmaster, Field Commr & Nat Com Tri-Faith, BSA, 1949-; Bd Mem, City of New Rochelle, NY GSA, 1962; Bd Mem, New Rochelle, B'nai B'rith, 1959-78; Num Mayor's Coms, New Rochelle, 1950-70; Little Leag Coach, New Rochelle, 1962-63; Col Lectr, US & Canada, 1969-74; Judge, Local Miss Am Contest, New Rochelle, 1962-67; VPres, Marina Del Rey Lodge, 1982; r/Hebrew; hon/Author of 10 *Mad's Dave Berg Looks...* Book Series & 4 Other Books, 1964-; Author of Textbook Chapt & Various Articles, 1970-; B'nai B'rith Yth Sers Awd, 1978; David Berg Day, Westchester Co & City of New Rochelle, NY, May 7, 1978; Named to Chair of Gt Cartoonists, Univ of CA-LA (UCLA) Student Body, 1975; Hon ThD, Reconstructionist Rabbinical Col; W/W: in Am, in World; Contemp Authors; Commun Ldrs & Noteworthy Ams; The World Ency of Comics; DIB; Other Biogl Listings.

BERG, M MAJELLA oc/College President; b/Jul 7, 1916; h/Marymount Col of VA, 2807 North Glebe Road, Arlington, VA 22207; ba/Same; p/Gustov Peter and Mary Josephine Berg; ed/BA, Marymount Col, 1938; MA, Fordham Univ, 1948; DHL (Hon), Georgetown Univ, 1970; pa/Pres 1960-, Registrar 1957-58, Marymount Col of VA, Registrar, Marymount Col, Tarrytown, NY 1958-60, Prof Classics & Registrar, Marymount Col, Manhattan, 1948-57; Registrar, Marymount Sch, NY, 1943-48; VPres 1972-73, Secy of Exec Com 1974, Coun of Indep Cols in VA; AAUW; Chm of Arbitration Panel 1967, Arlington Sch Bd & Arlington Ed Assn; Arlington Com, No VA Commun Col; Bd of Dirs, VA Foun for Indep Cols,

1982-; Diocese of Arlington's Evang Comm, 1979-; Bishop's Pastoral Coun, 1979-83; Exec Com, Sister Coun, 1978-; cp/Exec Com, Arlington Citizen Participation Coun; Exec Com, Arlington Chorus; Mem, Arlington Com of 100; Mem, Leag of Wom Voters; Day Care Com Mem, Arlington Hlth & Welfare Coun, 1967-69; Bd of Dirs, Arlington C of C, 1983; Bd of Dirs, HOPE, 1983; r/Cath; hon/W/W: in Am Ed, of Am Wom; Am Cath W/W Among Authors & Jours; Ldrs in Ednl Pres & Deans of Am Cols; Num Other Biogl Listings.

BERG, PATRICIA E oc/Molecular Biologist; b/Sep 17, 1943; h/7355 Broken Staff, Columbia, MD 21045; ba/ Bethesda, MD; m/Paul S Lovett; c/ Bridget K; p/Clifford Emerson (dec); ed/ AB, Univ of Chgo, 1965; PhD, IL Inst of Technol, 1973; pa/Postdoct Fellow, Univ of Chgo, 1973-78; Dir of Genetic Engrg, Bethesda Res Labs, 1978-80; Expert 1980-83, Sr Staff Fellow 1983-, Lab of Molecular Hematology, NHLBI, NIH, Bethesda, MD; Mem: Sigma Xi; Am Soc for Microbio; AAAS; cp/MD Master Swim Team; r/Prot; hon/Author & Co-Author, Num Articles in Sci Pubs incl'g: *Molecular Cell Biol*; *Jour Bacteriology*; *Proceedings of Nat Acad of Sci*; Others; HS Valedictorian & Nat Merit S'ship Finalist, 1961; Univ of Chgo S'ship, 1961-65; IL St S'ship, 1965; Predoct Fellow, NIH, 1969-72; W/W in Frontier Sci & Technol.

BERGER, HOWARD MARTIN oc/ Executive; b/Aug 31, 1927; h/2108 Via Fernandez, Palos Verdes Estates, CA 90274; ba/Torance, CA; m/Barbara Diane; c/Terri Ann, Patricia Jeanne, Lisa Diane; p/Frederick S Berger (dec); Milicent Berger; sp/Alfred and Ruth Lubin, Arcadia, CA; ed/BSE 1948, BS Math 1948, Univ of MI; MS 1949, PhD 1954, CA Inst of Technol; mil/AUS, 1946-47; pa/Pres & Chm of Bd, Robotix Corp, 1981-; Pres, Turbine Elec Corp, 1983-; Chief Financial Ofcr, Keats-Manhattan Inc, 1980-; Chief Financial Ofcr, Justin-Time Sers Inc, 1980-; VPres, Logistics Technol Intl Ltd, 1980-81; Presl, Mil Opers Res Soc, 1966-67; Pres-Elect, Wash Opers Res Coun, 1969; Chm, Mil Applications Sec, Opers Res Soc of Am; Dir, NATO Conf on Oper Res in Strategic Duel, The Hague, Netherlands, 1966; r/Jewish; hon/Author of Articles in Pubs: *Opers Res*, 1971; *Digital Simulation*, 1967; *Jour Applied Mechs*, 1955; W/W: in W, in Indust & Fin.

BERGESON, MARIAN oc/Assemblywoman; b/Aug 31, 1927; h/1721 Tradewinds, Newport Beach, CA 92660; ba/Sacramento, CA; m/Garth; c/ Garth Jr, James, Julie, Nancy; ed/BA Ed, Brigham Yg Univ; Grad Study, Univ of CA-LA (UCLA); pa/Legis, CA St Assem; Elem Sch Tchr; Mem, Newport Bch City Sch Bd of Ed, 1964-65; Mem, Newport-Mesa Unified Sch Dist Bd of Ed, 1965-77; Pres & Reg Dir, CA Sch Bds Assn; Ofcr & Dir Orange Co Sch Bds Assn; Bd of Advrs, CA YMCA Model Legis/Ct; Bd of Dirs, CA Elected Wom's Assn for Ed & Res; cp/Adv Bd, Radio Sta KBIG; Rear Commodore, Odyssean Yacht Clb; Adv Bd, Ctr for Sutton Movement Writing, Oasis Sr Citizens; Govt Relats Com, Orange Co Arts Alliance; r/Mormon; hon/Public Ser Awd, CA Spch-Lang-Hearing Assn,

1983; Outstg Public Ofcl, Orange Co Chapt Am Soc for Public Adm, 1983; Outstg Achmt in Commun & Ed, Mardan Ctr of Ednl Therapy, 1981; Dist'd Ser Awd, Brigham Yg Univ, 1980-81; Wom of Outstg Achmt Awd, Newport Harbor Zonta Clb, 1981; CEEED Awd, 1980; Commun Ser Awd, AAUW, 1976; Life Mbrship & Cont'g Serv Awd of PTA, 1975; Num Other Commun Ser Awds; W/W of Am Wom.

BERGMAN, JANICE JOAN oc/Nursing Home Director; b/Jan 6, 1938; h/713 Castle, Seneca, KS 66538; ba/Seneca, KS; m/Paul H; c/Janel Ann, Jolene Marie Blair, Jennifer Lynn; p/Alban M and Angela P Haug, Seneca, KS; Joseph H Bergman (dec); Mrs Elizabeth Bergman, Baileyville, KS; ed/Dipl Nsg, Marymount Col, Salina, KS, 1959; Cert Voc Tchr, KS St Dept of Ed, 1976; Cert, KS St Nurses Assn Cont'g Ed Prog, 1978; KS St Col of Pittsburg, 1976; Cert Gerontological Nurse 1975-80, ReCert 1980-85, ANA; pa/Co-Owner & Dir Nsg Sers, Crestview Manor Nsg Home, Seneca, KS, 1968-; Gerontological Nsg Conslt Hlth Occups Voc Div 1976-77, Rschr Hlth Occups Progs Oct-Nov 1976, St-wide Dir CETA Hlth Occups Prog Feb-Sep 1976, KS St Dept of Ed; Asst Dir Nsg Sers, N KC Meml Hosp, KC, MO, 1963-67; Asst Dir Nsg, McCleary, Thornton, Minor Hosp, Excelsior Sprgs, MO, 1962-63; Charge Nurse Surg & Psychi Units, St Mary's Hosp, KC, MO, 1960-62; Staff Nurse, Seneca Hosp, Seneca, KS, 1959; Item Writer, ANA Gerontological Cert Exams, 1976-77; KS Del, ANA Biennial Conv, Honolulu, HI, 1978; Exec Com Mem 1978, Secy Exec Com 1980-82, VChp Exec Com 1982-84, ANA Div on Gerontological Nsg Pract; Reviewer, Profl Exam Ser (PES), 1979-80; ANA Gerontological Exec Com Rep, Task Force on Credentialing in Nsg, 1980-82; Ad Hoc Advr & Nat Observer 1981, ANA Eval Com 1982-, White House Conf on Aging; Book Reviewer, *Geriatric Nsg*, 1981-; Prog Planning Com, ANA Gerontological Nurse of Yr Awd, 1982; Edit Adv Bd: *Geriatric Nsg, Am Jour of Care for The Aging*, 1982-; Guest Spkr, Ross Labs Spkrs Bur, Columbus, OH, 1982-; Gerontological Cert Bd, ANA, 1982-; Mem, ANA Inc, 1973-; ANA Coun of Nsg Home Nurses, 1979-; Nat Fed of BPW Clb Inc, 1968-; Num Other Local, St & Nat Com Mbrships & Appts; r/ Rom Cath; hon/Author of *Instrument for Determination of Qualified Nsg Home Aides in KS*, KS St Dept of Ed, 1976; "Articulation & Integration of 90-Hour Nurse Aide Course for Adult Care Homes," in *Articulation & Integration of Voc Hlth Occups Curricula By Clin Sers Perf'd in Pract of The Occup*, KS St Dept of Ed, 1977; Author of Other Articles Pub'd in Profl Jours incl'g: *Geriatric Nsg, ANA Coun of Nsg Home Nurses Newslttr*; One of 1st 99 Profl Nurses in the Nation to be Recog for Excell in Nsg Pract, 1975; Recog in "Lamps Still Aglow," a Hist of KS Nsg, 1976; Hon Recog Awd, KS Nurses Assn, 1980; Cert of Ser Awd, ANA, 1982; Outstg Yg Wom of Am; W/W: of Am Wom, Among Contemp Nurses.

BERGQUIST, JAMES WILLIAM oc/ Mathematician; b/Apr 23, 1928; h/4705 Daleridge Road, La Cañada, CA 91011; ba/Pasadena, CA; m/Madonna Therese Dunham; c/Catherine, James, Mary,

Brian, Thomas, John, Timothy, Joseph, Ann, Bob, Paul; p/Albin and Lucille (Morrison) Bergquist; sp/Frank and Catherine (McGrath) Dunham; ed/BS Engrg, IA St Univ, 1950; MS 1955, PhD 1963, Univ of So CA (USC); mil/ROTC; pa/Computer Analyst, IA Hwy Comm, 1948; Analog Computers, Lockheed Aircraft, 1951-54; Computer Analyst, Gilfillan Brothers, 1956-57; Computer Analyst, IBM, 1957-; Mem: Am Math Soc; Math Assn of Am; Reg Pres, Soc for Industl & Applied Math; cp/VPres, Sierra Clb of Pasadena; Chm Sch Bd Coms, La Cañada, CA; r/Rom Cath; hon/Author of "Difference Sets & Congruences," Univ of So CA, 1963; Num Other Papers on Computing & Math; Num Excell Awds, IBM; Golden Apple Awd, La Cañada Schs; W/W: in W, in Computers, in Fin & Indust, in Frontier Sci & Technol.

BERGSTEN, C FRED oc/Economist; b/Apr 23, 1941; h/4106 Sleepy Hollow Road, Annandale, VA 22003; ba/Washington, DC; m/Virginia Wood; c/Mark David; p/Mr and Mrs Carl A Bergsten, Plattsburg, MO; sp/Mr and Mrs Jess Graham, St Louis, MO; ed/AB, Ctl Meth Col, 1961; MA 1962, MALD 1963, PhD 1969, Fletcher Sch of Law & Diplomacy; Dir, Inst for Intl Ec, 1981-; Sr Assoc, Carnegie Endowment for Intl Peace, 1981; Asst Secy of the Treasury for Intl Affairs, 1977-81; Sr Fellow, Brookings Instn, 1972-76; Asst for Intl Ec Affairs, Nat Security Coun, 1969-71; Fellow, Coun on Fgn Relats, 1967-69; Intl Economist, Dept of St, 1963-67; Mem: Trilateral Comm; Coun on Fgn Relats; Wash Inst of Fgn Affairs; Am Economic Assn; Nat Economics Clb; r/Meth; hon/Author of 12 Books incl'g: *The US & the World Economy*, 1983; *The World Economy in the 1980's*, 1981; *The Intl Economic Policy of the US*, 1979; Others; Exceptl Ser Awd, Dept of Treas, 1980; Dist'd Ser Awd, Dept of St, 1965; 200 Yg Am Ldrs, *Time Mag*, 1974; W/W: in Am, in World.

BERGSTROM, GARY CARLTON oc/Professor; b/May 12, 1953; h/Gaslight Village Apartments, Ithaca, NY 14850; ba/Ithaca, NY; m/Frances Brach; p/Robert and Virginia Bergstrom, Park Ridge, IL; sp/John and Nell Brach, Orchard Park, NY; BS Microbiol 1975, MS Plant Pathol 1978, Purdue Univ; PhD Plant Pathol, Univ of KY, 1981; pa/Grad Tchg Asst 1975-76, Grad Res Asst 1976-78, Purdue Univ; Grad Res Asst, Univ of KY, 1978-81; Asst Prof, Cornell Univ, 1981-; Mem & Chm of Ext Com, Am Phytopathol Soc, 1984; Mem, NY Forage & Grasslands Coun; r/Presb; hon/Author of Num Sci Articles Pub'd in Profl Jours & Mags; Gamma Sigma Delta, 1977; W/W in Frontier Sci & Technol.

BERGSTROM, ROBERT CARLTON oc/Professor Emeritus; b/Aug 20, 1925; h/639 North Babetta Avenue, Park Ridge, IL 60068; m/Virginia Mae; c/Gary Carlton, Bradley James, Neil Reid; p/Carl H and Ethel (Hill) Bergstrom (dec); sp/Jens Jensen; ed/BS 1950, MS 1954, NWn Univ; Postgrad Study, Univ of Chgo, 1960-61 & 1967-69; mil/AUS, 1944-46, Combat Inf, Germany; pa/Sci Tchr, Morton HS, 1950-53; Geol Instr 1953-63, Assoc Dean Admissions & Records 1964-74, Prof of Geog & Geol 1974-84, Prof Emeritus 1984-,

Morton Col; Mem: IL St Acad of Sci; Sigma Xi; Nat Assn of Geol Tchrs; Soc of Vertebrate Paleontology; cp/BSA Scoutmaster; Explorer Advr; Cub Scout Ldr; 15 Yrs Brotherhood Mem, Order of Arrow, BSA; r/Luth; hon/Contbr, *Ency Brittanica World Atlas*; Sci Fac F'ship, Nat Sci Foun, 1960-61; W/W in MW.

BERK, AMY J oc/Managing Editor; b/Jan 9, 1952; h/1606 East 50th Place #2A, Chicago, IL 60615; ba/Chicago, IL; p/Rudolph and Ginger Kean Berk, Ambler, PA; ed/AB Biol, Oberlin Col, 1973; MA Tchg Sec'dy Sch Biol, Univ of Chgo, 1975; pa/Mng Editor 1983-, Prod Devel Editor 1982-83, Am Soc of Clin Pathols Press; Edit Coor, *The Jour of Am Dental Assn*, 1981-82; Editor, CBE Envir Review, 1979-82; Freelance Writer & Editor, 1979-81; Edit Assoc, Univ of Chgo Cancer Res Ctr, 1976-79; Sci Tchr, Akiba-Schechter Jewish Day Sch, 1974-76; Tchr, Med Editing Courses; Num Spkg Presentations, for Chgo Wom in Pub'g (CWIP), 1979-; Mem: Am Med Writers Assn, 1979-; Chgo Book Clin, 1982-; Freelance Com Co-Chp 1980-81, Jobvine Chp 1983-85, Chgo Wom in Pub'g (CWIP); Wom in Mgmt, 1983-; cp/Mem: Sierra Clb; Phys for Social Responsibility; Union of Concerned Scis; Chgo Area Runners Assn; hon/Author, Over 31 Reviews & Articles in Jours & Mags incl'g: *Current Energy & Ecol*; *Current Hlth*; *CBE Envir Review*; *CWIP News*; Others.

BERK, KAREN oc/Executive; b/Mar 29, 1943; h/10400 Ashton Avenue #8, Los Angeles, CA 90024; ba/Los Angeles, CA; p/Harry and Minerva Sternberg, LA, CA; ed/Dipl, Fairfax HS, 1960; BA, Univ of CA-LA (UCLA), 1964; pa/VPres, Dir of Policy Planning & Eval, Pvt Indust Coun, City of LA, 1984-; Chief Prog & Sys Anal Div 1980-84, Chief Prog Eval Sect 1976-80; Adm Asst to Dept Dir Opers 1974-76, Employmt Devel Dept, St of CA; Mem: Intl Assn of Pers in Employmt Security; Sacramento Jewish BPW; cp/Mem: Nat Coun of Jewish Wom; Encorps-Symph Support Grp; Sustained Superior Accomplishment Awd, Employmt Devel Dept, St of CA, 1980; W/W: in Sacramento, in Am Wom, in W.

BERKOVITZ, LEONARD DAVID oc/Professor; b/Jan 24, 1924; h/1131 Hillcrest Road, West Lafayette, IN 47906; ba/West Lafayette, IN; m/Anna; c/Dan, Kenneth; p/Judea Berkovitz (dec); Esther Berkovitz; sp/Eugene Whitehouse (dec); Elizabeth Whitehouse; ed/BS 1946, MS 1948, PhD 1951, Univ of Chgo; mil/USAAF, 1943-46; pa/AEC Postdoct Fellow, Stanford Univ, 1951-52; Res Fellow, CA Inst of Tech, 1952-54, Mathematician, Rand Corp, 1954-62; Prof Math 1962-, Dept Hd 1975-80, Purdue Univ; Mem: Am Math Soc; Math Assn of Am; Soc of Industl & Applied Math; Mng Editor, *SIAM Jour on Control*, 1981-; Assoc Editor, *Jour Optimization Theory & Application*; hon/Author of Book, *Optimal Control Theory*, 1974; Author of Num Tech Papers & Articles in Math Jours; Phi Beta Kappa, 1946; Am Men of Sci; W/W: in Am, in MW.

BERLINCOURT, MARJORIE ALKINS oc/Administrator; b/Jun 2, 1928; h/7844 Langley Ridge Road, McLean, VA 22102; ba/Washington, DC; m/Ted Gibbs; c/Leslie Ellen (Berlincourt) Yale;

p/Herbert John Alkins (dec); Ellen Phypers, Ontario, Canada; sp/Weldon and Gladys Berlincourt (dec); ed/BA Classics, Univ of Toronto, 1950; MA Classics 1951, PhD 1954, Yale Univ; pa/Edit Dir, Tech Pubs, Rocketdyne, 1956-59; Lectr Classics, Univ of So CA, 1959-61; Assoc Prof Classics, CA Luth Col, 1961-67; CA St Univ-Northridge, 1967-71; Prof Metro St Col, Denver, 1971-72; Prog Dir Sum Sems & F'ships 1972-78, Dept Dir Res Div 1978-84, Div of St Progs 1984-; NEH; Mem, Am Assn Ancient Histns; r/Epis; hon/ Author of *De Surprise en Surprise*, 1953; *Entrez Petits Amis*, 1954; *Victory as a Coin Type*, 1973; Contbr of Num Articles to Profl Jours; Vis'g Lectr, Georgetown Univ, 1972; Recip, CA Fac Res Awd, 1970; Sterling Fellow, Yale Univ, 1950-53; DIB; W/W Among Am Wom.

BERLYNE, GEOFFREY MERTON oc/Nephrologist, Researcher; b/May 11, 1931; h/Lawrence, NY; ba/Brooklyn, NY; m/Ruth Selbourne; c/Jonathan, Benjamin, Suzannah; p/Charles and Miriam Berlyne (dec); sp/Henry and Sulamith Selbourne, Manchester, England; ed/MB Chem Biol 1954, MRCP 1956, Univ of London; MD, 1966, Univ of Manchester; FRCP, 1969, London; FACP, 1977; FACN, 1979; mil/Israel Army Med Corps, 1972-76, Resv Ofcr; pa/Instr to Reader, Univ of Manchester Fac of Med, 1957-70; 1969-76: Chief Renal Sect, Soroka Hosp Israel; Prof Med & Life Scis, Ben Gurian Univ of Negev Israel; Prof Med St Univ of NY & Chief Renal Sect Bklyn VA Hosp, 1976-; Pres, Israeli Nephrological Soc, 1970-74; r/Jewish; hon/Author: *Course in Renal Disease* 5 Edits, 1967-78; *Course in Body Fluids*, 1981; Over 200 Articles in Profl Sci Jours; Guest of Hon, Japanese Renal Soc & Physiol Soc, 1980; Edit Bd Mem, Num Jours; Editor, *Nephron*; Contbns to Nephrology & Renal Physiol; W/W in Am, in Sci, in Frontier Sci & Technol.

BERMACHER, HEIDI oc/Executive; b/Aug 11, 1946; h/250 East 87th Street, New York, NY 10028; ba/New York, NY; p/Sonny and Miriam Bermacher, Livingston, NJ; ed/BA Eng Lit, CW Post Univ, 1968; MA Psych, Seton Hall Univ 1974; pa/VPres Mktg (Key Client Credit Acct, Travelers Cheques, Lodging & Trans, Retail Ser Establishments, Green Card, Gold Card), Shearson/Am Express, 1978-; Acct Supvr, Mktg Equities, NY, 1976-78; hon/Kappa Delta Pi Hon Soc, Seton Hall Univ, 1978.

BERMAN, MARLENE OSCAR oc/Professor; b/Nov 21, 1939; h/115 Cotton Street, Newton, MA 02158; ba/Boston, MA; c/Jesse Berman; p/Paul Oscar (dec); Evelyn Oscar Weizenblut, N Miami, FL; ed/BA, Univ of PA, 1961; MA, Bryn Mawr Col, 1964; PhD, Univ of CT, 1968; Postdoct Study, Harvard Univ, 1968-70; pa/Res Psych, Boston VA Med Ctr, 1970-; Prof Neurol & Psych 1982-, Dir Lab Neuropsychol 1981-, Assoc Prof Neurol 1975-82, Boston Univ Sch of Med; Mem, Sigma Xi, 1970-; Intl Neuropsychol Soc, 1975-; Mem 1969, Fellow 1980, Div 6 Prog Chp 1977, Div 6 Secy-Treas 1980-83, Mem-at-large & Exec Com 1981-84, Am Psychol Assn; r/Jewish; hon/Author of "Brain," in *Ency Psych*, 1984; "Comparative Neuropsychol & Alcoholic Korsakoff's Disease," in *Neuropsychol of Memory*,

1984; "Bimanual Tactual Discrimination in Aging Alcoholics," *Alcoholism: Clin & Exptl Res*, 1983; Num Other Articles Pub'd in Profl Jours; Nat Lectr, Sigma Xi, 1980 & 1981; USDHHS Res Career Sci Awds, 1976-81 & 1981-86; VA Clin Investigator Awd, 1973-76; Am Men & Wom of Sci; W/W: in Am Wom, in E, in Sci & Technol.

BERMAN, MURIEL MALLIN oc/Executive; h/20 Hundred Nottingham Road, Allentown, PA 18103; m/Philip I; c/Nancy, Nina, Steven; ed/Deg Phil, Muhlenberg Col; Deg Comparative Rel & Hist, Cedar Crest Col; Att'd Music Apprec & Art Hist, Univ of Pgh Grad Sch; Att'd Carnegie Tech Univ; PhD, PA Col of Optometry; 4 Hon Degs; pa/Ins Underwriter, LLoyd's of London, 1974-; VPres, Hess's Dept Stores Inc; Secy & Mem of Bd, Philip I Berman/DBA Fleetways; Secy-Treas & Mem of Bd, Philip & Muriel Berman Foun; Participant in Var US St Dept Activs incl'g: Del to Intl Wom's Yr Conf, Mexico City, 1975; Participant in Num UN Coms, Bd Mbrships & Delegations; Mem of Num PA St Bds & Coms incl'g: PA Humanities Coun, 1979-; Participant in Num Art Activs: The Berman Circulating Travelling Art Exhbns; Art in US Embassies Prog; Art Select Com w Nat Endowment for Arts, Muhlenberg Col; Carnegie-Berman Coll Art Slide Lib Exchg; Hadassah-Israel Art Show; Num Ednl Instn Activs incl'g: Mem Bd of Regents, Intl Ctr for Univ Tchg of Jewish Civilization, 1982-; Mem: Pres, Jewish Pub Soc of Am; Art Collector's Clb of Am; Friends of Whitney Mus; Archives of Am Art, Smithsonian; Mus of Mod Art; Am Fdn of Art; Jewish Mus; Life Patron, PA Acad of Fine Arts; Metro Mus; Lehigh Co Hist Soc; Life Mem, PA Hist Soc; Num Others; cp/Mem, Leag of Wom Voters; Del & Mem Platform Com, Dem Nat Conv, 1972 & 1976; Rep PA in Harrisburg in US Electoral Col; Mem of Bd of Trustees for Num Orgs; Lectrs on Art, World Travel, Wom's Issues, The UN; r/Jewish; hon/Wom of Valor Cit, Bonds for Israel, 1974; Dist'd Daugh of PA, 1982; Hazlett Awd for Outstg Ser to Arts in PA; Outstg Citizen Awd, BSA, 1982; Myrtle Wreath Awd, PA Reg of Hadassah; Outstg Wom Awd, Allentown YWCA, 1973; Num Others; W/W: in Am Art, of Am Wom, in E; Royal Blue Book; Nat Social Dir; Israel Honorarium.

BERNARDEZ, TERESA oc/Professor; b/Jun 11, 1931; h/835 Westlawn, East Lansing, MI 48823; ba/East Lansing, MI; c/Diego; ed/BA, Liceo #1 de Senoritas, Buenos Aires, Argentina, 1948; MD, Sch of Med, Univ of Buenos Aires, 1956; Residency Psychi, The Menninger Sch of Psychi, Topeka, KS, 1957-60; pa/Staff Psychi, C F Menninger Meml Hosp, 1960-65; Staff Psychi, Menninger Foun, 1965-71; Asst Prof 1971-73, Assoc Prof 1974-79, Prof 1979-, Col of Human Med, Dept of Psychi, MI St Univ; Fellow, Am Psychi Assn, 1982; Fellow, The Menninger Foun, 1979; Examr, Am Bd of Psychi & Neurol, 1979 & 1982; Bd of Dirs, Am Grp Psychotherapy Assn, 1980-83; Bd of Dirs, MI St Univ, Fac Wom's Assn, 1982-85; Mem, Amnesty Intl/USA, Phys Hlth Com; hon/Author of "The Female Therapist in Relation to Male

Roles," in *Changing Male Roles: Theory & Therapy*, 1982; "Wom's Grps," in *Varieties of Short Term Therapy Grps*, 1983; Phys's Recog Awd, AMA, 1970; Tchr's Recog Awd, The Menninger Sch of Psychi, 1971; Peace Awd, Pawlowski Foun, 1974; 1st Ldrship Wkshop Awd, The AMWA, 1977; Dist'd Fac Awd, Fac Wom's Assn, MI St Univ, 1982; DIB; W/W: of Wom, in Commun Ser; 2000 Wom of Achmt.

BERNEY, ROBERT E oc/Professor; b/Sep 13, 1932; h/Northwest 1585 Turner Drive, Apartment 11, Pullman, WA 99163; ba/Pullman, WA; m/Marilyn; c/Michael, Peter, Marybeth, Timothy; p/William E and Dorothy Berney, Walla Walla, WA; sp/Horace A and Fervid Trimble, Kent, WA; ed/BA 1954, MA 1960, WA St Univ; MS 1962, PhD 1963, Univ of WI-Madison; mil/AUS, 1954-58, 1st Lt Ranger-Airborne; pa/Prof Ec 1972-, Assoc Prof Ec 1968-72, Asst Prof Ec 1966-68, WA St Univ; Chief Economist, US Small Bus Adm, Wash, DC, 1978-80; Sr Acad Resident in Public Fin, Adv Com on Intergovtl Relats, Wash, DC, 1973-74; Asst Prof, AZ St Univ, 1964-66; Res Ofcr, Royal Comm on Taxation, 1963-64; Mem: Chm Univ Grad Studies Com 1983-, Fac Sen Steering Com 1983, Col Tenure Com 1981-, Wash St Univ; Exec Bd of Dirs, WA Public Power Supply Sys, 1983-; Am Ec Assn, 1960-; Nat Tax Assn, 1966-; Wn Tax Assn, 1982-; hon/Author of Num Articles Pub'd in Profl Jours incl'g: *Jour of Fin, Land Ec, Nat Tax Jour, Annals of Reg Sci, Am Jour of Small Bus, Wn Ec Jour*, Others; Sr Acad Resident in Public Fin, 1973-74; Spec Achmt Awd, US Small Bus Adm, 1980; Beta Gamma Sigma, 1953; Phi Kappa Phi, 1953; Alpha Kappa Phi S'ship Key, 1954; W/W in W; Intl Scholars Dir; Am Men & Wom of Sci; Men of Achmt; Who's Where Among Writers.

BERNEY, STUART ALAN oc/Pharmacology Consultant; b/Aug 28, 1945; h/5562 Ridge Road, Joelton, TN 37080; ba/Same; m/Mary Helen; c/Elizabeth June, Joshua Forrest; p/Morris Michael Berney; Esther Selk Berney (dec); sp/Harry R and Edna J; ed/BS Pharm, Albany Col of Pharm, 1969; PhD Pharm, Vanderbilt Univ, 1974; pa/Lectr, Dept of Pharm, Univ of Toronto, 1975-76; Res Assoc Instr Dept of Pharm 1976-78, Res Asst Prof Dept of Psychi 1978-82, Vanderbilt Univ; Conslt in Pharm, Joelton, TN, 1982-; Mem: AAAS; Sigma Xi; Soc of Nerosci; Am Pharm Assn; TN Pharm Assn; Mtl Hlth Assn of TN; Mid TN Soc of Pharm; hon/Author & Co-Author, 3 Abstracts & 9 Articles Pub'd in Sci Jours incl'g: *Communs in Pyschopharm, European Jour of Pharm, Jour of Clin Psychi, Intl Pharmopsychi*, Others; Res F'ship Awd, NIDA, 1975-77; W/W in Sci & Technol.

BERNINGER, VIRGINIA WISE oc/Psychologist; b/Oct 4, 1946; h/6 Northgate Road, Wellesley, MA 02181; ba/Boston, MA; m/Ronald William; p/Oscar and Lucille Wise, Neffsville, PA; sp/Bill and Betty Berninger, Livonia, MI; ed/BA Psych, Elizabethtown Col, 1967; MEd Rdg & Lang, Univ of Pgh, 1970; PhD Psych, Johns Hopkins Univ, 1981; pa/Asst Prof Rehab Med, Tufts Univ Sch of Med, 1983-; Mem Spec & Sci Staff, N Eng Med Ctr, 1983-; Instr Psych, Harvard Med Sch, 1981-83; Res

Assoc, Chd's Hosp, Boston, 1980-83; Edr in Var Public Schs: Phila, PA 1967-68; Baldwin-Whitehall, PA 1969-72; Frederick, MD 1972-75; Balto, MD 1975-76; Pvt Clin Conslt Org, Wise Words, 1983-; hon/Contbr of Var Articles to Profl Jours; Student Res Awd, MD Psychol Assn, 1980; W/W in Frontier Sci & Technol.

BERNS, ELLEN MARSHA SCHIMMEL oc/Interior Designer, Architect, Fine Artist, Instructor; b/Oct 3, 1948; h/1365 York Avenue, 35 H, New York, NY; ba/New York, NY; p/Milton Oscar Schimmel (dec); Mrs Ruth Mildred Mall Schimmel, Dallas, TX; ed/Att'd Univ of OK, 1966-68; BA Art Hist & Art, Univ of TX-Austin, 1968-70; 3 Yr Adv'd Cert Interior Design, 2 Yr Applied Arts & Scis Cert Interior Design, 1 Yr Wk toward Applied Arts Deg Fashion Design, El Centro Col, Dallas, TX, 1975-78; Att'd Masters 3 Yr Sum Prog, Parsons Sch of Design & Bank St Col, NYC, 1977-79; Indep Study at Nat Acad of Design & Art Students Leag, NYC, 1980-82; pa/Artist & Designer, Ellen S Berns Design Assocs, 1984-; Artist & Designer, Swanke Hayden Connell Archs, NY, 1981-84; Instr Var Terms, Parsons Sch of Design-Midtown Campus, NYC, 1982-84; Instr, 92nd St YHCA, NYC, Sprg 1980; Instr, El Centro Col, Dallas, TX, 1973-74 & Sprg 1978; Artist & Designer, Ellen S Berns Interiors, 1974-78; Artist & Designer, Sylvan Garret Showroom, 1978; Artist & Designer, Peter Wolf & Assocs, 1975; Lectr 1973-74, Display Artist & Fashion Coor 1971-73, Neiman Marcus; Designer, Apparel Mart/Trade Mart, 1972; Designer, Sanger Harris, 1972; Num Freelance Design Wks, 1980-; Profl Mem, Ednl Com Mem 1981-83, NYC Metro Chapt, Am Soc of Interior Designers, 1980-; Assoc Mem, Wom in Design, NYC, 1982-83; Assoc Mem, AIA, 1984-; cp/Designer: Cert Awd for Parsons Exhbn Given by Wom in Design, 1982; Var Projs for Marble Col Ch, NYC, 1980-83; hon/Exhbns: Fine Art Represented, Szoke-Koo Gallery, NYC, 1984; Wom in Design at Keystone, 1983; Judith Selkowitz Fine Art Gallery, NYC, 1982; Wom in Design at Parsons, 1982; Suzanne's Gallery, NYC, 1980; Parsons Sch of Design Student Exhib, 1979; Dallas Mus of Fine Arts, 1977 & 78; Att'd Sprg Sem, Nat Acad Sch of Fine Arts, NYC, 1982; Recip, Am Watercolor Soc S'ship, 1982; W/W: of Am Wom, in E; Personalities of Am.

BERNSTEIN, CAROL oc/Professor; b/Mar 20, 1941; h/2639 East 4th Street, Tucson, AZ 85716; ba/Tucson, AZ; m/Harris; c/Beryl, Golda, Benjamin; p/Benjamin and Mina Adelberg (dec); sp/Hannah Bernstein, Tucson, AZ; ed/BS Physics, Univ of Chgo, 1961; MS Biophysics, Yale Univ, 1964; PhD Genetics, Univ of CA-Davis, 1967; pa/Postdoct Fellow, Lab of Stephen Wolfe, Univ of CA-Davis, 1967-68; Res Assoc Dept of Microbiol 1970-77, Adj Asst Prof Dept of Microbiol 1977-81, Res Assoc Prof Dept of Micrbiol & Immunol 1981-, Univ of AZ; Pres of AZ St Conf 1983-85, Pres of Univ of AZ Chapt 1983, AAUP; Mem, Genetics Soc of Am; Mem, Biophysics Soc; Mem, Am Soc for Microbiol; Mem, Am Soc for Virology; Mem, Am Wom in Sci; r/Jewish; hon/Author, 19 Articles Pub'd in Profl Sci

Jours, 1970-; Recip of Grants: NSF, 1975-79; NIH Grant, 1979-82; W/W in Am Wom; Am Men & Wom of Sci & Technol.

BERNSTEIN, ELLIOT R oc/Professor; b/Apr 14, 1941; h/908 Pitkin Street, Fort Collins, CO 80524; ba/Fort Collins, CO; m/Barbara; c/Jephta Robin, Rebecca Ann; p/Leonard H Bernstein and Geraldine Roman (dec); sp/Alexander Wyman (dec); ed/AB, Princeton Univ, 1963; PhD Chem & Physics, CA Inst of Tech, 1967; pa/Postdoct Fellow, Univ of Chgo, 1967-69; Asst Prof Dept of Chem, Princeton Univ, 1969-75; Assoc Prof 1975-80, Prof 1980-, Dept of Chem, CO St Univ; Dir, Condensed Matter Scis Lab, CO St Univ, 1982-; Conslt, Los Alamos Sci Lab 1975-; Vis'g Sci, Brookhaven Nat Lab, 1971-75; Mem: Am Chem Soc; Am Phy Soc; Sigma Xi; Panel Mem, NSF, 1976 & 79; Org Com, X Molecular Crystals Symp, 1977, 1980 & 1982; Num Invited Spkg Engagements & Sems, 1972-; hon/ Author & Co-Author, Over 70 Articles Pub'd in Profl Sci Jours incl'g: *Jour of Chem Physics, Molecular Physics, Phy Review*; NSF Sum Fellow, 1961 & 1962; Woodrow Wilson Fellow, 1963 & 1964; Enrico Fermi Postdoct Fellow, 1967-69; Recip of US Patent in Field.

BERNSTEIN, HARRIS oc/Professor; b/Dec 12, 1934; h/2639 East 4th Street, Tucson, AZ 85716; ba/Tucson, AZ; m/Carol; c/Beryl, Golda, Benjamin; p/Hannah Bernstein, Tucson, AZ; sp/Benjamin & Mina Adelberg (dec); ed/BS Biol, Purdue Univ, 1956; PhD Genetics, CA Inst of Technol, 1961; pa/Postdoct Fellow, Yale Univ, 1961-63; Asst Prof, Univ of CA-Davis, 1963-68; Assoc Prof 1968-74, Prof 1974-, Univ of AZ; Mem: Am Soc of Biol Chems; Am Soc of Microbiol; Genetics Soc of Am; AAUP; AAAS; r/Jewish; hon/ Author, Over 60 Articles in Profl Sci Jours; Recip, Nat Inst of Hlth Res Grant, 1983-87; Elected Fellow, Am Acad of Microbiol, 1981; Am Men & Wom in Sci.

BERNSTEIN, ISADORE A oc/Researcher, Professor; b/Dec 23, 1919; h/1200 Arlington Boulevard, Ann Arbor, MI 48104; ba/Ann Arbor, MI; m/Claire; c/Amy Lynne; p/William J and Rosa Bernstein (dec); ed/AB, Johns Hopkins Univ, 1941; PhD Biochem, Wn Resv Univ, 1952; mil/1941-46; pa/Res Assoc 1951-52, Sr Instr 1952-53, Wn Resv Univ; Res Assoc Inst Indust Hlth 1953-56 & 1959-70, Instr Biochem, Asst Prof, Assoc Prof, Prof Dept Dermatol 1954-71, Assoc Prof Dept Indust Hlth 1961-70, Res Assoc Inst Envir Indust Hlth 1970-78, Prof Dept Biol Chem 1971-, Prof Envir Indust Hlth 1970-, Assoc Dir Res Inst Envir Indust Hlth 1978-, Dir Toxicol Prog 1983-, Univ of MI; Mem: Sigma Xi; Am Chem Soc; Am Soc Microbiol; Am Soc Biol Chems; Mem Bd of Dirs 1967-72, VPres 1973-74, Soc Invest Dermatol; Rad Res Soc; NY Acad Scis; Fellow 1975-, Am Assoc Adv Sci; APHA; Am Soc Cell Biol; AAUP; Soc Toxicol; Am Col Toxicols; Charter Mem, Soc Envir Toxicol Chems; Mem, Nat Envir Coun, NIH, PHS DHHS, 1984-87; r/Hebrew; hon/ Author, Over 156 Articles, Papers, Abstracts & Book Chapts; Editor of 4 Sci Books; Co-Recip, Taube Intl Meml

Awd, Res Psoriasis, 1959; Stephen Rothman Meml Awd, Soc Invest Dermatol, 1981; Dist'd Fac Achmt Awd, Univ of MI, 1981; W/W in Am; Am Men & Wom in Sci.

BERNSTEIN, SHELLY COREY oc/Pediatric Hematologist, Oncologist; b/May 4, 1951; h/129 Oakdale Road, Newton Highlands, MA 02161; ba/Boston, MA; m/Nancy J Levy; p/Mr and Mrs Maurice H Bernstein, Lincolnwood, IL; sp/Mrs Betty Levy, Sun City, AZ; ed/AB 1973, PhD Com on Genetics 1978, MD Pritzk Sch of Med 1980, Univ of Chgo; pa/Vis'g Sci, Whitehead Inst, Dept of Biol & Ctr for Cancer Res, MIT, 1983-; Res Fellow, Dept of Pediatrics, Harvard Med Sch, 1982-; Clin Fellow Pediatric Hematology, Chd's Hosp Med Ctr & Dana-Farber Cancer Inst, Boston, 1983-; Mem: AMA; Sigma Xi; MA Med Soc; Am Soc of Human Genetics; Genetics Soc of Am; r/Jewish; hon/ Author of Num Articles in Profl Sci Jours & Book Chapts; F'ship to Cameroun, ITT, 1976-77; Med Alumni Prize, Univ of Chgo, 1980; Nat Res Ser Awd, 1975-78 & 1983-84; MacArthur Foun F'ship, 1984-89; W/W in Frontier Sci & Technol.

BERNSTEIN, STELLA MAINE oc/Businesswoman; b/Oct 3, 1936; ba/Kensington, MD; m/Paul; c/Julie, Mark, Ellen, Jeffrey; p/Benjamin Striner (dec); Isabella Striner; sp/Hyman and Freda Bernstein; ed/AA cum laude, Marjorie Webster Jr Col; pa/Co-Owner P & S Assoc Inc, 1980-; Oral Hist Interviewer; Commun & Civic Vol; pa/Mem, Kensington Bus & Profl Org; Mem, Nat Coun of Career Wom; cp/Past Pres, Jewish Home Retard Chd, 1963; Past Pres, Shaare Tefila Synagogue PTA, 1968-70; Past Pres & Life Mem, Brandeis Nat Wom's Com, 1975-77; Past Pres Gtr Wash Chapt, Ser Guild of Wash, 1978-80; Past Pres, Gtr Wash Chapt, Am Soc of Tech, 1980-82; VPres & Life Mem, Zionist Org of Am-Brandeis Dist, 1982-84; VPres, Wash Chapt, Am Israel Cult Foun, 1982-84; Treas, Jewish Coun for Aging; Bd Mem: Jewish Coun for Aging; Jewish Social Ser Agy; Am Israel Cult Foun; Wom's Perf'g Arts Soc Wash; Jewish Commun Ctr; Nat Coun of Jewish Wom Wash; Mem: Kensington C of C; Jewish Hist Soc; Wom's Com Nat Symph; Life Mem: Hadassah; Nat Chd's Ctr; Hebrew Home for Aged; r/Jewish; hon/Outstg Achmt Awd, Ser Guild of Wash, 1974-75 & 1980-81; W/W in Am Wom.

BERRESFORD, BRADY SCOTT oc/Safety Manager; b/Jul 28, 1940; h/503 South Richey #102 Pasadena, TX 77506; ba/Houston, TX; m/Patricia Powers; c/Terri L, Kelly M, Kimberly A; p/Max H Berresford; Edna M (White) Berresford (dec); sp/Genevieve Powers, Syracuse, NY; ed/Field Indust Safety & Hlth, San Jacinto Col, 1983; mil/USAF, 1958-78; pa/Medic & Safety Supvr, Brown & Root, Inc, Houston, 1978-81; Safety Mgr, Am Rice Inc, Houston, 1981-82; Safety Mgr, KRI Constrn, Houston, TX, 1983-; Owner, Berleather (Custom Leather Craft); Mem, Am Soc of Safety Engrs; W/W in S & SW.

BERRY, JAMES F oc/Professor; b/Dec 22, 1947; h/946 Ashland Avenue, River Forest, IL 60305; ba/Elmhurst, IL; m/Cynthia M; c/Jennifer L, Andrea L; p/James F Berry (dec); Joyce M Berry; sp/

Joseph C and Bea M Valukas; ed/BS 1970, MS 1973, FL St Univ; PhD, Univ of UT, 1978; mil/USAR, 1971-78; pa/Tchg Asst, FL St Univ, 1970-73; Chem, FL Dept of Agri, 1973-74; Tchg Fellow, Univ of UT, 1974-78; Asst Prof 1978-84, Assoc Prof 1984-, Elmhurst Col; Res Assoc, Carnegie Mus of Natural Hist (Pgh), 1983-; Mem: Am Soc of Zools; Soc for Study of Evolution; Soc of Sys Zool; Animal Behavior Soc; Am Soc of Ichthyologists & Herpetologists; Herpetologist's Leag; Soc for Study of Amphibians & Reptiles; Over 30 Paper & Lectr Presentations; r/Rom Cath; hon/ Author & Co-Author, Over 20 Articles, Papers & Book Chapts in Sci Books & Jours (1973-) incl'g: "A Re-Anal of Geog Variation & Systematics in Yellow Mud Turtle Kinosternon flavescens (Agassiz)," *Annals of Carnegie Mus Natural Hist*, 1984; Phi Kappa Phi, 1977; Phi Sigma, 1970; Sigma Xi, 1976; Fac Study Grant Awd, Elmhurst Col, 1979-80, 1980-81 & 1983-84; W/W in MW, in Frontier Sci & Technol; Am Men & Wom in Sci; Am Fac Dir.

BERRY, LEMUEL JR oc/Dean of Music School; b/Oct 11, 1946; h/PO Box 338, Montgomery, AL 36109; ba/Montgomery, AL; m/Christine Elizabeth; c/Lemuel III, Cyrus James; p/Lemuel and Ethel Berry, Burlington, NJ; sp/James and Lillian Elliott, Edenton, NC; ed/BA, Livingston Col, Salisbury, NC, 1969; MA 1970, PhD 1973, Univ of IA; pa/Chp Dept of Music 1973-76, Chp Div of Humanities 1973-75, Fayetteville St Univ, NC; Chp Dept of Music 1976-83, Chp Dept of Music & Art 1981-83, Langston Univ, OK; Dean Sch of Music, AL St Univ, 1983-; Mem: Nat Pres, Kappa Kappa Psi Band Frat, 1983-85; Nat Pres, Assoc of Minority Profs, 1983-85; Nat Assn of Jazz Edrs; Music Edrs Nat Assn; Coun for Res in Music Ed; AL Music Edrs; Assn of Concert Bands; Am Choral Dirs Assn; Nat Assn of Col Wind & Percussion Instruments; r/AME Zion; hon/Author, Books: *Biogl Dict of Black Musicians & Educ*, Volume I 1978, Volume II 1984; *Afro-Am Resource Guide & Dir: A Source Book*, 1979; *Perspectives in Jazz*, 1984; Over 50 Articles Pub'd; German Acad Res Scholar, 1981; Outstg Edr of Am; Outstg Yg Men of Am; W/W in Am, in Music.

BERRY, MICHAEL A oc/Physician; b/Jun 2, 1946; h/8810 Hydethorpe Drive, Houston, TX 77083; ba/Houston, TX; m/Mary Frances; c/Jennifer Alice, Michael David; p/Charles A Berry, Houston, TX; sp/Jack S Cauthen; ed/BS, TX Christian Univ, 1968; MD, Univ of TX SWn Med Sch, 1971; MS Preventive Med, OH St Univ, 1977; mil/USAF, Maj, Flight Surg; pa/Preventive & Aerospace Med Conslts, 1982-; Chief Flight Med, NASA/JSC, Houston, 1977-81; Flight Surg, USAF: England 1975-76, Spain 1972-75, Cmdr 401st Air Transportable Hosp 1974, European Radar Site Phys 1974-75; Mem: AMA; Fellow, Aerospace Med Assn, 1969-; Spare Med Br (ASMA); Soc of USAF Flight Surgs; Soc of NASA Flight Surgs; Fellow, Am Col of Preventive Med, 1978-; Harris Co Med Soc; TMA; Intl Acad of Aviation & Space Med; r/Meth; hon/Author & Co-Author, Over 15 Reports, Articles & Book Chapts on Aerospace Med Pub'd in Sci Books & Jours; Spec Awd for Approach & Landing Test Prog 1978,

Spec Achmt Awd 1980, LBJ Space Ctr Awd 1981, Grp Achmt Awd 1981, 1st Shuttle Flight Achmt Awd 1981, NASA; Julian Awd of ASMA, 1979; W/W: in S & SW, in Aviation & Aerospace.

BERRYMAN, KARAN ANN oc/Library Director; b/Jun 26, 1956; h/111 West Harris Street, Cuthbert, GA 31740; ba/Cuthbert, GA; p/John R and Wilda F Berryman, Cuthbert, GA; ed/AA cum laude, Andrew Col, 1975; BS Ed, Auburn Univ, 1977; MLS, Univ of NC-Chapel Hill, 1979; pa/Hd of Ref Sers, Flagler Col, St Augustine, FL 1984-; Dir of Pitts Lib 1980-84, Prof Eng 1979-80, Andrew Col, Cuthbert, GA; Sponsor, Omega Tau Lambda; Co-Sponsor, Phi Theta Kappa; Mem, SE Lib Assn; Am Lib Assn; GA Lib Assn; cp/Geneal Soc of Old Muscogee Co; Phi Kappa Phi; Phi Theta Kappa Alumni Assn; Twigg Garden Clb; r/Bapt; hon/Author of Var Articles in Nat Orgnl Periods; Miss Andrew Col, 1975; Phi Theta Kappa Nat Alumni Hall of Fame, 1978; Sponsor of Yr; Andrew Col, 1981 & 1982; Outstg Yg Wom of Am; W/W in S & SW.

BERTA, JOSEPH MICHEL oc/Professor; b/May 5, 1940; h/55 Ver Planck Street, Geneva, NY; m/Pamela J; c/Michele L; p/Mr and Mrs Andrew P Berta, Santa Barbara, CA; sp/Mr and Mrs Jackson Nichols, Searsport, ME; ed/BA Music 1962, MA Musicology 1965, Univ of CA-Santa Barbara; Postgrad Study, Vienna, Austria, 1965-66; pa/Prof Music, Hobart & Wm Smith Cols, Geneva, NY, 1971-; Prof Music, Allan Hancock Col, Santa Maria, CA, 1969-71; Prof Music, Prairie View A&M Col, Prairie View, TX, 1967-69; Mem: Am Musicological Soc; Col Music Soc; NY St Sch of Music Assn; Intl Clarinet Soc; Clarinetwk Intl Inc; AAUP; Nat Assn Col Wind & Percussion Instrs; MENC; Pi Kappa Lambda; cp/Pres, Rotary Clb of Geneva, 1984; Campaign Chm, Geneva U Way, 1984; Past Pres, Finger Lakes Torch Clb; Past Pres, Geneva Concerts Inc; r/Rom Cath; hon/Perf'd as Soloist w Buffalo Philharm & Rochester Philharm Orchs; Num Recitals in US; Music Reviewer, *The Finger Lakes Times* Newspaper; Sum Res Grants, Hobart & Wm Smith Cols, 1981 & 1984; Recip, Pillsbury Foun Grant for Grad Study in Vienna, Austria, 1965-66; W/W of Musicians; Men of Achmt; Commun Ldrs of Am; Noteworthy Ams; Men & Wom of Distn; Others.

BERTSCH, THOMAS M oc/Professor; b/Aug 11, 1942; h/641 North Blue Ridge Drive, Harrisonburg, VA 22801; ba/Harrisonburg, VA; m/Faythe E; c/Debra F; p/Mr and Mrs H A Bertsch, FL; sp/Mr and Mrs A J Vranek, FL; ed/BS 1965, MS 1968, No IL Univ; PhD, LA St Univ (LSU), 1977; pa/Mktg Res Conslt, 1980-; Assoc Prof Mktg, James Madison Univ, 1975-; Asst Prof, McNeese St Univ, 1973-75; Asst Prof, Nicholls St Univ, 1972-73; Tchg Asst, LA St Univ, 1970-72; Instr & Coor, Cont'g Bus Ed, Clarion St Col, 1968-70; Bd of Dirs 1983-, Mbrship Chm 1984, VA Social Sci Assn; Article Reviewer for 2 Profl Jours & 6 Mktg Assns; cp/Coun Rep 1981, Muhlenberg Ch; r/Luth; hon/Author, Num Articles, Cases & Book Entries in Mktg & Mgmt Pubs; Profl Devel Awds, VSSA, 1982 & 1983;

Res Grant, AAL, 1983-84; Instl Res Grant, James Madison Univ, 1982-83; Beta Gamma Sigma; Sigma Iota Epsilon; Commun Ldrs of Am; Personalities of S.

BESCHE-WADISH, PAMELA P oc/Director, Teacher; h/PO Box 1261, Chinook, MT 59523; ba/Chinook, MT; ed/BS, Newcastle-upon-Tyne Univ, 1969; MA, Wayne St Univ, 1976; pa/Dir & Tchr, ESEA Title I, Chinook Public Schs, 1978-80; Lectr, Clin Placement Supvr, Tutor, Admr/Curric Planner, Col of Spch Scis, London, England, 1976-77; Vis'g Lectr, Post Dipl Br, Nat Hosps for Nervous Diseases, Hampstead, London, England, 1976-77; Spch Pathol/Psychol Eval, Conslt & Lrng Disabled Remedial Therapy, Chinook Public Schs, 1971-73; Sr Spch Clinician & Supvr for Grad Students, MT St Univ, 1971; Ctr Dir, Easter Seal Spch & Hearing Ctr, Billings, MT, 1970; Spch Pathol Conslt, Camp for Mtly Retarded Chd, ESEA Title VI Supt of Public Instrn, Helena, MT, 1970; Spch Pathol, Univ of MT-Missoula, 1970; Easter Seal Spch & Hearing Ctr & Butte Hdstart Prog, 1969-70; Glenrose Sch Hosp (Edmonton, Canada), 1969; Insp & Exec Ofcr, Min of Hlth & Social Security, Bedford England, 1962-65; Asst Sci Mistress, Convent of the Holy Ghost Sch, 1960; Tech Asst, Biochem Lab, Unilevers Res Dept, 1959-60; Intl Neuropsychol Soc; MT Assn Sch Psychols; Secy Iota Chapt, Delta Kappa Gamma, 1980-82; Master, Col of Spch Therapists (England); MT Spch & Hearing Assn; Brit Chiropody Assn; Assn for Supvn & Curric Devel; CEC; cp/Mother Advr 1980-81, OES Line Ofcr 1972-80, Matron of Chinook Chapt 1980-81, Grand Com Mem Grand Chapt of MT 1981-82, Grand Sentinel Grand Chapt of MT, Order of Rainbow for Girls; Inst of Adv'd Motorists; Welcome Wagon; hon/Grad Asst S'ship, Wayne St Univ Spch Pathol Dept, 1975; Univ Bursary, Newcastle-upon-Tyne Univ, 1968; Co Maj S'ship England, 1965; Lic'ship, Surg Sch of Chiropody, England, 1964; Gen Cert E, Adv'd Level (Physics, Chem, Zool, Botany) & S'ship Level (Use of Eng), Univ of Cambridge, 1959; Sch Sci Prize 1959, Hd Girl in Sch Awd 1959, Sch Math Prize 1956, Bedford, England; Rel Knowledge Theol Cert, 1957; 11+ S'ships for Grammar Sch Students, England, 1950; Brit Inst Adv'd Motorists Awd; Grade & Tchg Certs in Ballet; Medals & Certs in Highland Dance Competitive Fests; W/W: of Wom, of Intells, of Contemp Achmt; Intl Register of Profiles; 5000 Personalities of the World; Intl Book of Honor.

BESNER, ADELE oc/Psychologist; b/Apr 29, 1956; h/2831 Southwest 87th Avenue, Davie, FL 33328; ba/Fort Lauderdale, FL; m/Philip Martin; p/Jack and Hana Besner, Dania, FL; ed/BMus 1977, MMus Music Therapy 1979, Univ of Miami; PsyD, Sch of Profl Psych, Nova Univ, 1983; pa/Staff Psychol (Chd & Adolescent), Nova Univ Clin, 1983-; Psych Intern, S FL St Hosp, 1982-83; Dir Music Therapy Prog, Biscayne Med Ctr, 1978-79; Mem: Am Psychol Assn; FL Psychol Assn; Nat Assn Music Therapy; Broward Co Mtl Hlth Assn; cp/Mem Exec Bd of Dirs, Hostile Inc (Adolescent Shelter Home).

BESTOR, CHARLES L oc/Professor, Department Head; b/Dec 21, 1924; h/19 Birchcroft Lane, Amherst, MA 01002; ba/Amherst, MA; m/Ann Elder; c/Charles Elder, Geoffrey Grant, Phillip Russell, Leslie Ann, Wendy Lynn, Jennifer Lee; p/Arthur Eugene and Jeannette Lemon Bestor (dec); sp/Hugh Gray and Mary Biddle Elder (dec); ed/Att'd Yale Univ, 1943-44; BA, Swarthmore Col, 1946; BS, Juilliard Sch of Music, 1951; MMus, Univ of IL, 1952; DMA, Univ of CO, 1974; mil/USN, 1941-46, Lt; pa/Hd & Prof, Dept of Music & Dance, Univ of MA, 1977-; Hd, Dept of Music, Univ of UT, 1975-77; Chm, Dept of Music, Univ of AL, 1971-73; Dean, Col of Music, Willamette Univ, 1967-71; Asst Prof, Univ of CO, 1959-64; Asst Dean, Juilliard Sch of Music, 1951-55; Mem: Grad Comm, Nat Assn of Schs of Music, 1978, 1984-; Nat Coun, Col Music Soc, 1974-78; Nat Coun, Nat Assn of Composers, 1978-; Nat Bd, Snowbird Arts Foun, 1977-; Bd, Leroy J Robertson Foun, 1977-; cp/Bd, Springfield Jr Symph, 1977-; Music Panel, MA Coun Arts & Humanities, 1980-; Spec Conslt, Joint Comm on Reorg of Higher Ed, MA, 1979-80; hon/Music Compositions: "Lord Unto Thee" & "Unto Thee Do I Lift Up My Soul" for A Capella Choir, Pub'd by Elkan Vogel; Piano Sonata (Serenus Records), Recorder Suite, Suite for Winds & Trumpets from Music to Play "J.B.", "A Wind in the Willows" for Flute, Concerto Grosso for Percusssion & Orch, Little Suite for Beginning Strings, "Music for the Mtn" for Orch, Pub'd by General Music; Improvisation I & II for Instruments & Tape, Pub'd by Media Press; Vars for Oboe & Tape w Viola, Orion Recordings; Overture to a Romantic Comedy for Orch, Pub'd by G Schirmer; hon/Phi Beta Kappa; Pi Kappa Lambda; Nat Patron, ODK & Theta Alpha Phi; Phi Beta; W/W: in Am, in World; DIB.

BETHEL, LEONARD LESLIE oc/Professor, Department Chairman and Pastor; b/Feb 5, 1939; h/146 Parkside Road, Plainfield, NJ 07060; ba/New Brunswick, NJ; m/Veronica Bynum; c/Amiel Wren; Kama Lynn; p/Mrs Anna Bethel Young, Phila, PA; sp/Mrs Charlene Bynum, Stamford, CT; ed/BA Polit Sci, Lincoln Univ, PA, 1961; MDiv, Sch of Theol, Johnson C Smith Univ, NC, 1964; MA Theol, New Brunswick Theol Sem, NJ, 1971; DEd, Rutgers Univ, 1975; pa/Pastor, Wash U Presb Ch, Reading, PA, 1964-67; Dir of Student Ctr 1967-68, Asst Chaplain 1967-69, Dir Cnslg ISE 1968-69, Lincoln Univ, PA; Cnslr Urban Univ Dept 1969-70, Instr, Assoc Prof 1971-82, Dept Chm Rutgers Col, 1980-, Team Chaplain Kirkpatrick Chapel 1980-82, Num Acad Coms, Rutgers Univ; Supply Pastor, Christ Reformed Ch, NJ, 1972-79; Pastor, Bethel Presb Ch, 1982-; Bd of Trustees, Rutgers Prep Sch, 1971-; Mem, New Brunswick Theol Sem Alumni, 1971-; Mem, Assn for Study of Afro-Am Life & Hist (ASALH), 1973-; Mem, Black Presby U, 1973-74; Mem, African-Am Inst, 1973-; Afro-Ams tp Presv the Slave Castles, 1973-; Dept Rep, AAUP, 1977-; Mem, Phi Delta Kappa, 1975-; Mem, Intl Platform Forum, 1977-; Mem, Presby of New Brunswick, 1978-; Mem Bucks

Co Chapt, NAACP, 1978-; Num Others; cp/Num Spkg Presentations; Bd of Dirs: Armat Sch of Graphic Arts, 1980-81; Theatre Forum, Sci Sch & Urban Stage, Plainfield, NJ, 1980-81; Num Others; r/Presb; hon/Author of Books: *La Citadelle: Layle Lane, Her Life & Times*, 1980; *Educating African Lárs: Mission in Am*, 1980; Author of Articles, "The Survival of the Black Theol Sem," *Argus Mag*, 1965; "Background for Evangelism: The Condition of Black Student Today," *Reformed Review*, 1970; Author of "The Am Revolutionary Period & Black Ed," in *Ed Conformity, Liberation: 25th Annual Conf of ISA*, 1977; Maj Contbr & Co-Editor, *Rdgs in Africana Studies*, 1973; Phi Delta Kappa, 1975; Phi Beta Sigma, Lincoln Univ, 1961; Paul Robeson Fac Awd, 1978; NAFEO Pres Cit, Lincoln Univ, 1981; Dist'd Ed & Commun Sers Awd, Frontiers Intl, 1981; Fac & Adm Ser Awd, Omega Psi Phi; W/W; Commun Ldrs of Am.

BETHELL, M ELOISE oc/Painter, Teacher; b/May 7, 1934; h/PO Box 4202, Wilmington, NC 28406; ba/ Same; c/ Mikhael Bethell Wilkinson; p/Mrs William Craig Pinckney Bethell, Wilmington, NC; ed/BA, Converse Col, 1954; Postgrad Study Incls: NY Univ, 1961; Portland St Col, 1959; Instituto Allende, Guanajuato, Mexico, 1958 & 1965 & 1966; Insts of Fine Arts, Bellas Artes Mus Sch in Mexico City, 1959 & in San Miguel Allende, GTO, Mexico, 1966-74; Académie de la Grande Chaumie²re, Paris, France, 1954-56 & 1960; pa/Fine Arts Teacher: NYC, Paris, San Miguel Allende, 1953-60; Sum Acad of Fine Arts, Aley, Lebanon, 1960; Dir of Arts & Crafts, Ft Clark Sprgs, TX, 1974-75; Instr of Watercolor & Drawing, Fine Arts Ctr, Roanoke, VA, 1976; Instr of Oil, Watercolor & Drawing, Cultural Arts Coun, Vinton, VA, 1976-78; Instr of Watercolor, Pastel & Charcoal, Roanoke Co, VA, 1977-78; Instr & Owner, Bethell Studio of Fine Art, Roanoke, VA, 1976-78; Instr & Owner, Bethell Studio of Fine Art, Wilmington, NC, 1978-; Mem: Artist's Equity; Watercolor Soc of NC; Am Watercolor Soc; Wilmington Art Assn; cp/Artist in Residence, Deacon Gallery, Wilmington, NC, 1979-81; Instr, SEn Commun Col, Brunswick Co, NC, 1979-80; Num Wkshops; hon/Num Reprints of Wk Pub'd in: *Jet Mag*, *NY Post*, *Coronet*, *EPOS*, *The Friendly World*, *Kauri*, Others; 6 Spec Editions Pub'd; Plus: *Mexico: A Landscape in People*, 1984; *Watercolor Can Be Easy*, 1982; *Sea Series*, 1982; Studied w Ignaccio Aguirre, Pablo O'Higgins, James Pinto, Fred Samuelson; Over 20 Nat, Intl & Local One Person Shows, 1950-; Over 10 Nat, Intl & Local Two Person & Grp Shows, 1956-; 14 Juried & Awd Exhibs; Num Wks in Public & Pvt Collections incl'g: Gallery Chapultepec, Mexico City; Larry Aldrich, NYC; B H Wragge, NYC; W/W in S & SW; Personalities of S; Artist/USA, 1979-.

BETIN, JOHN W oc/Architect; b/Jul 14, 1914 (Riga, Latvia); h/5959 East Northwest Highway #3002, Dallas, TX 75231; ba/Dallas, TX; m/Erika Betin (dec); c/John, Irene, Barbara, Richard; p/ John & Emma Betin, Vancouver, BC, Canada; ed/Univ of Riga, Latvia, 1933-44; Univ of TX-Austin, 1965; So Meth Univ (SMU), 1968-69; pa/Wk w Var Arch Firms in Dallas, TX, 1950-;

Spec Assignment Arch, US Army Corps of Engrs, NO, LA, 1965; Currently, Self-Employed Arch, Dallas, TX; Mem: Arch GS-11, 12, Wash DC; TX Soc of Archs; Assoc Mem, AIA, Wash DC; r/ Epis; hon/Naturalized US Citizen, 1955; Fellow, Intl Biogl Assn, Cambridge, England, 1984; Medal of Merit, Repub Pres Task Force, 1982; Father: Betins, Janis (Riga, Latvia), Goldsmith-Silversmith, Recipient of Grand Prix, 1937 World's Fair, Paris, France; Grand Prix, 1939 World's Fair, Brussels, Belgium.

BETTER, JENNIFER REESE oc/Development Engineer; h/512 Cambrian Way, San Ramon, CA 94583; ed/BA 1967, Adv'd Rdg, Lang & Ldrship Prog 1980-81, PhD Computer Ed 1981-, Univ of CA-Berkeley; Standard Credential, CA St Univ-Sacramento, 1968; MA Ed, Univ of SF, 1975; pa/Devel Engr, Hewlett Packard, 1984-; Instr Computer Ed, Univ of CA-Santa Cruz, 1984-; Curric Coor, Cupertino Union Sch Dist, 1980-84; Writing Proj Resource Tchr 1979-80, Rdg Spec 1976-79, Clrm Tchr 1968-76, San Juan Unified Sch Dist; Num Tchg Curric & Instrn Topics as Tchr Ed Instr, 1971-; Num Presentations on Rdg & Writing Devel, 1973-; Mem: Com for Tchr Effectiveness 1981; Com for Computer Ed, 1984-; Nat Dir, Exemplary Computer Ed Proj, 1984; Sr Author, Software Documentation-Int Corp, 1983-84; Bd of Dirs, Peoples Computer Co, 1983-; Edit Bd, *Jour of Computer, Rdg & Lang Arts*, 1983-; St of CA Exemplary Computer Ed Proj Dir, 1983-84; Adv Coms: CA St Computer Curric Com; Intl Coun for Computers in Ed- Legal & Moral Ethics; Rep at Large 1981, Ctl Reg, CA Assn for Tchrs; NCTE; CA Coun Social Studies; CA Coun Tchrs of Math; Ad Hoc Com for Curric, Assn of CA Sch Admrs; Assn for Supvn & Curric Devel; Phi Delta Kappa; Pi Lambda Theta; cp/Pub Chp 1975-76, Author, *Old Sacramento Tabloid* 1975; Profl Pres 1976-77, Jr Leag of Sacramento, 1971-; Bd of Dirs, Jr Leag of Palo Alto, 1984; Phi Beta Phi Alumnae, 1968; Vol Coor, KVIE Auction, 1968; Old Sacramento Docent, 1974-76; hon/ Co-Author, *Cooking to Kids*; *Kgn Instrument for Diagnostic Screening*; Author, *Food for Thought: A Turn-on to Cooking & Other Things Too*; Resp Envir Tchr Awd, San Juan Unified Sch Dist, 1971; Nat Awd for Outstg Elem Tchr of Yr, 1974; Nat Awd for Outstg Wom of Yr, 1978.

BETTES, WILLIAM H oc/Aeronautical Engineer; b/Jun 2, 1928; h/409 Alzado, Monterey Park, CA 91754; ba/ Pasadena, CA; m/Valerie A; c/Linda, David, Kimberly, Brian, Keith; p/William and Rosella Bettes (dec); sp/Edward and Lillian Hamilton (dec); ed/Cert'd Aeronaut Engrg, Northrop Aeronautics Inst, 1956; BS Aeronaut Engrg, Northrop Inst of Technol, 1961; MS, Aeronaut Engrg, CA Inst of Technol, 1963; mil/AUA, Korean War; pa/Test Proj Engr, So CA Coop Wind Tunnel, 1956-60; Supvr 1960-61, Asst Dir 1961-63, Dir 1963-65, Galeit 10 Rt. Wind Tunnel, CA Inst of Technol; Dir Exptl Facilities 1965-76, Mgr Grad Aeronaut Labs 1976-, CA Inst of Technol; Conslt, Over 30 Pvt Cos & Govt Agys, 1976-; Mem: Chm Aerodynamic Com on Truck & Bus Fuel Economy, Soc of Automotive Engrs,

1954-60; Am Rocket Soc, 1955-57; Am Inst of Aeronautics & Astronautics, 1956-; Fdg Mem & Chm, Subsonic Aerodynamic Testing Assn, 1965-67; r/ Prot; hon/Author of "Aerodynamic Testing of High Perf Land-Borne Vehicles: A Critical Review," *AIAA Jour*, 1968; "The Influence of Wind Tunnel Solid Boundaries on Automotive Test Data," *BHRA Fluid Engrg*, 1973; Co-Author of 3 Other Studies; W/W in W.

BETTS, DORIS oc/Fiction Writer, Teacher; b/Jun 4, 1932; h/Route 3, Box 157-A, Pittsboro, NC 27312; ba/Chapel Hill, NC; m/Lowry M; c/LewEllyn, David, Erskine; ed/Public Schs, Statesville, NC, 1938-50; Univ of NC-Greensboro, 1950-53, Univ of NC-Chapel Hill (UNC), 1954; pa/ Pt-time Lectr 1966, Assoc Prof 1974, Prof 1978, Alumni Dist'd Prof 1980-, Dir Freshman Eng Prog 1970-77. Dean UNC Hons Prog 1977-80, Dept of Eng, Univ of NC-Chapel Hill; Vis'g Lectr Creat Writing, Duke Univ, 1971; Instr, Ext Course, UCLA-Daivs, 1973; Elected Chm, UNC Fac, 1982-85; Chp, Dept Search Com, 1983; Search Com, UNC Affirmative Action Ofcr; Nom'g Com, Assn of Wom Fac; Bd Mem, UNC Fac Clb; Adv Bd, Student Union; Bd of Govs, UNC Press; Dir, NC Fellows Prog, 1975-76; Chm, Undergrad Advising Com, 1978; Arts & Scis Dean Search Com, 1978; Gen Col Tutorial Sers Com, 1973; Freshman Orient Wk & Planning, 1973, 1978, & 1979; Self Study Com, 1973; Mem, Freshman Com, 1970-72; Editor, *Yg Writer at Chapel Hill*, 1967; Num Other Univ of NC-Chapel Hill Activs; Reporter, Reviewer & Other Jour Employmt; Other Previous Employmt; Mem: AAUP; SAMLA; CCCC: NCTE; NC Writers' Conf; Staff Mem, Num Univ Writers' Confs; Num Others; cp/Bd of Dirs, The Arts Sch, 1983-; Bd of Dirs, Orange Co Wom's Ctr, 1982; Bd of Dirs, Carolina Study Ctr, 1981-; Mem, Chatham Arts Coun, 1981-; Caroliniana Soc, 1981-; Adv Com on Lit, NC Arts Coun, 1981-82; Mem 1978-79, CoChm 1979-80, Chm 1980-81, Lit Panel of NEA; Mem, Nat Humanities Fac, 1978-; Mem Bd of Dirs, Assn Writing Progs in Am Cols & Univs, 1975-77; Num Univ & Assn Spkg Presentations; Judge for Num Lit Contests; Num Rdgs From Own Wk; Other Civic Activs; r/Presb; hon/ Author, Over 9 Books incl'g: *Heading West*, 1981; *Beasts of the So Wild*, 1973; *The River to Pickle Bch*, 1972; *The Astronomer & Other Stories*, 1966; *The Scarlet Thread*, 1965; Short Stories in Over 20 Anthologies incl'g: *The Best Short Stories*; *40 Best Short Stories From Mademoiselle*; *Best Little Mag Fiction*; Short Stories in Num Mags incl'g: *Redbook*; *Red Clay Rdr*; *Carolina Qtly*; *Cosmopolitan*; *MA Qtly Review*; *VA Qtly Review*; Others; Poetry Pub'd in Num Mags incl'g: *So Poetry Review*; *Am Poet*; *Beloit Poetry Jour*; *Descant*; *Voices Intl*; Others; Articles Pub'd in Num Mags & Jours; Recip, Phi Beta Kappa Awd, UNC-Greensboro, 1953; *Mademoiselle Col Fiction Contest*, 1953; UNC-Putnam Book Prize, 1954; Guggenheim F'ship Creat Writing, 1958-59; Sir Walter Raleigh Awd, Best Fiction Book (NC) 1958, 1965 & 1973; Tanner Awd for Tchg 1973, Pogue Leave 1978, UNC-Chapel Hill; John Dos Passos

Awd, Longwood Col; Dist'd Ser Awd for Wom, Chi Omega; Katherine Carmichael Tchg Awd, 1980; Others; W/ W: in S & SW, of Am Wom, in Am; Wom in Communs; Contemp Authors; DIB; Dict Lit Biog; Intl Wom in Ed.

BETTS, EUGENE KÖHLER oc/Pediatric Anesthesiologist; b/Jun 2, 1942; h/ 108 Rock Rose Lane, Radnor, PA 19087; ba/Philadelphia, PA; m/Martha O; c/ Donald R, Douglas E, Daniel K, Anne-Marie; p/Dr and Mrs Reeve H Betts, Asheville, NC; sp/Mr and Mrs E A Overstreet Jr, Bedford, VA; ed/BS, Dickinson Col, 1964; MD, Bowman Gray Sch of Med, Wake Forest Univ, 1968; mil/AUS, 1972-74, Maj; pa/House Ofcr in Anesthesia, NC Bapt Hosp, Winston-Salem, NC, 1968-72; Anesth, AUS Gen Hosp, Saigon, Viet Nam & AUS Med Ctr, Ft Gordon, GA, 1972-74; Pediatric Anesth, Chdn's Hosp of Phila, PA, 1974-; Num Hosp & Adm Appts at Chd's Hosp of Phila, 1974-; Var Tchg Appts, Univ of PA; Over 10 Nat & Intl Vis'g Prof'ships; Over 20 Nat & Intl Lectr Presentations; Num Hosp Dept Lectrs; Mem: Assn of Pediatric Anesths of Gt Brit & Ireland; AMA; Am Soc of Anesths; Intl Anesth Res Soc; Soc of Critical Care Med; Am Acad of Pediatrics; PA Med Soc; PA Soc of Anesths; Phila Soc of Anesths; r/Prot; hon/ Author & Co-Author, Over 30 Papers, Abstracts, Reports & Reviews in Profl Sci & Med Jour; Phys Recog Awd, AMA, 1971-85; Recip, Bronze Star, 1973; Nicolas Copernicus 500th Anniv Awd, Med Acad, Krakow, Poland, 1982; W/ W.

BEUTLER, LARRY E II oc/Professor, Psychologist; b/Feb 14, 1941; h/2249 East Edison, Tucson, AZ 85719; ba/ Tucson, AZ; m/M Elena; c/Jana Lynne, Kelly Jo, Ian David, Gail Lei; p/Mr and Mrs Edward Beutler, Idaho Falls, ID; sp/ Mr and Mrs John Oro, Houston, TX; ed/BS 1965, MS 1966, UT St Univ; PhD, Univ of NE-Lincoln, 1970; pa/Asst Prof Med Psych, 1970-71, Duke Univ; Asst Prof Psych, Stephen S Austin St Univ, 1971-73; Assoc Prof Psychi, Baylor Col of Med, 1973-79; Prof Psychi & Psych, Univ of AZ, 1979-; Mem: Pres, Cont'g Profl Devel, Div 12, Am Psych Assn; hon/Author of Books, *Eclectic Psychotherapy*, 1983; *Spec Probs of Chd & Adolescents*, 1978; Author of Num Articles in Profl Jours; Fellow, Intl Acad of Eclectic Psychotherapy; Fellow, Am Psychol Assn; Am Bd of Profl Psych; W/W in W; Intl Dir of Dist'd Psychotherapists.

BEVELACQUA, JOSEPH JOHN oc/ Safety Review Engineer; b/Mar 17, 1949; h/19 Merion Lane, Hummelstown, PA 17036; ba/Three Mile Island, Middletown, PA; m/Terry Sanders; c/ Anthony Joseph, Jeffrey David, Megan Elizabeth, Peter Joseph, Michael David; p/Frank and Lucy Bevelacqua, Clarksville, PA; sp/Jack and Ann Sanders, Butler, PA; ed/BS, CA St Univ, 1970; MS 1974, PhD 1976, FL St Univ; mil/ USAF; pa/Sr Safety Review Engr, GPU Nuclear, 3 Mile Isl Nuclear Generating Sta, Middletown, PA, 1983-; Chief Physicist-Laser Isotope Separation USDOE, 1978-83; Sr Engr 1976-78, Engr 1973, Radiation Shield Design/ Anal, Westinghouse-Bettis Atomic Power Lab; Mem: Divs of Nuclear Physics, Biol Physics, Particles & Fields, Astrophysics & Atomic Physics, Am

Phy Soc, 1976-; Am Nuclear Soc, 1983-; Hlth Physics Soc, 1983-; AAAS, 1969-72; AAPT, 1970-72; c/Repub Pres Task Force, 1981-; Repub Senatorial Com, 1983-; Oak Ridge Sportsman's Clb, 1983-; r/Luth; hon/Author, Over 42 Articles on Nuclear & Math Physics Pub'd in Profl Jours; Von Humboldt F'ship Awd, Univ of Hamburg, 1976; Outstg Perf Awd, DOE, 1982; Sigma Pi Sigma, 1970; BS summa cum laude, 1970; W/W in Frontier Sci & Technol.

BEVERSLUIS, LINDA ANNE oc/ Executive; b/Apr 22, 1954; h/41 Walray Avenue, North Haledon, NJ 07508; ba/ Same; p/John and Anne BeversLuis, North Haledon, NJ; ed/Dipl, En Christian HS; pa/Secy, Ofc of Public Defender, Paterson, NJ, 1972; Res Asst, US Sen Select Com on Pres Campaign Activs, 1973; Personal Secy, Cong-man John E Hunt, US Ho of Reps, 1973-74; Staff Asst to Pres Gerald Ford, The White House, 1974-77; Dir of Scheduling, Former Pres & Mrs Gerald Ford, Palm Sprgs, CA, 1977-78; Dir of Scheduling, Robert Schuller, Garden Grove, CA, 1978; Dir of Spec Projs, Word Records, Waco Records, Waco, TX, 1979; Spec Proj Asst, Billy Graham Evang Assn, Mpls, MN, 1980; Pres, Beversluis, McKee & Assocs Inc & Snowshoe Entertainment Inc, N Haledon, NJ, 1981-; Writer for Var Mags & Newspapers; cp/Guest Spkr for Num Polit, Rel & Civic Orgs; Mem, Passaic Co Yg Repubs; Mem, Friends of Jesus Follow-up Staff; Exec Com, No NJ John Wesley White Crusade; Vol Asst at 21 Billy Graham Crusades; r/ Prot; hon/Featured in Mag Articles: *Christian Life Mag*, *Solo Mag*, *Decision Mag*; Elected NJ Girl's St Nat Hon Soc, 4 Yrs HS; Placed 8th in St of NJ Spelling Bee; 1st Hon Female Mem Plaque, The Pres's Own, US Marine Band; DIB; Dir Dist'd Ams; W/W of Wom.

BEVILL, TOM oc/US Congressman; b/Mar 27, 1921; h/3827 North Military Road, Arlington, VA 23207; ba/Washington, DC; m/Lou Betts; c/Susan Betts, Donald Herman, Patricia Lou; p/Herman and Fannie Lou Fike Bevill (dec); ed/BS, Univ of Al, 1943; LLB , Univ of Al Sch of Law, 1948; mil/AUS, 1943-46, Lt Col; USAR (Ret'd), 1946-66; pa/Mem, US Ho of Reps, 1967-; Chm, Energy & Water Devel Subcom on Approps, 1977-; Mil Constrn Subcom on Approps, 1981; Atty at Law, 1948-66; Mem: ABA; AL Bar Assn; House Dem Steering & Policy Com, 1973-74 & 1980-84; Nat Dem Adv Coun for Elected Ofcls, 1972-76; Nat Dem Conv Com on Rules, 1976; Maj Whip at Large, 1974-; cp/Mem, Lions Clb; Bd of Trustees, Walker Col; Mason; Shriner; r/ Bapt; hon/Eminent Ser Awd, AL Rural Elect Assn, 1981; Awd of Apprec, Coosa AL River Devel Assn, 1977; Sesquicent, Hon Prof, Hon LLD, Univ of AL, 1981; Rhineland Campaign Ribbon w Battle Star; AUS Commend Ribbon; ETO Ribbon w Bronze Star.

BHALLA, VINOD K oc/Professor; b/ Aug 4, 1940; h/3741 Westlake Drive, Augusta, Georgia 30907; ba/Augusta, GA; m/Madhu B; c/Niti, Jyotti, Varun K; p/Lal Chand and Shanti Devi Bhalla (dec); sp/Mr and Mrs Gopal S Sarin, Agra, India; ed/BS 1962, MS 1964, St Johns Col, Agra, India; PhD, Nat Chem Lab, Poona, 1968; Res Assoc, Univ of

GA-Athens, 1969-72; Res Assoc, Emory Univ, Atlanta, 1972-74; pa/Asst Prof 1974-78, Assoc Prof 1978-82, Prof 1982-, Dept of Endocrinology, Med Col, of GA, Augusta; Mem: Am Soc of Biol Chems; Endocrine Soc; Soc for Study Reprodn; Soc for Complex Carbohydrates; Am Chem Soc; NY Acad of Sci; Am Fertility Soc; Am Soc of Adrology; r/Hinduism; hon/Author of Several Pub'd Sci Papers & Chapts on Male Reprodn Sys; Ad Hoc Mem, Endocrinology Study Sect; Mem Edit Bd, *Biol Reprodn*; Num Sci Spkg Presentations, Wkshops & Confs; Gordon Res Conf; Res Grantee, NIH & Nat Sci Foun; Reviewer, Var Sci Jours; W/W: in GA, in Frontier Sci & Technol.

BHATTACHARYA, SYAMAL KANTI oc/Biomedical Scientist, Educator; b/Feb 13, 1949; h/3750 Marion Avenue, Memphis, TN 38111; ba/ Memphis, TN; m/Keka Ghoshal; c/ Sumoulindra T, Julie, Syamal Dave; p/ Sudhir Chandra and Prabhabati B Bhattacharya; sp/Muraru Mohan and Binapani B Ghoshal; ed/BSc Hons 1968, BA Eng Lit 1969, Univ of Calcutta; MS, Murray St Univ, 1976; AM, Wash Univ-St Louis, 1978; PhD, Memphis St Univ, 1979; Postdoct Res, Univ of TN Ctr Hlth Scis, Memphis, 1979-81; Diplomate, Am Bd Bioanal; pa/Instr Chem, Netaji Shikshyatan, Calcutta, India, 1968-69; Sr Instr Chem, Bhabanath Instn, Calcutta, India,1969-70; Res & Devel Chem, Swastik Household & Industl Prods Pvt Ltd, Bombay, India, 1970-74; Sr Res Tech, Wash Univ Med Sch & St Louis Chd's Hosp, St Louis, 1976-77; Res Assoc 1979-80, Instr Med 1980-82, Dir Surg Res Labs 1982-, Dir Chem & Nutrient Data Output Lab 1982-, Instr Surg 1983-84, Asst Prof 1984-, Univ of TN Ctr Hlth Scis, Memphis; Conslt Clin Chem: Univ of TN Wm Bowld Hosp, Memphis 1982-; City Hosps Memphis, 1982-; Bapt Meml & Affil Hosps, 1983-; Le Bonheur Chd's Med Ctr, 1984-; Meth Hosp, 1984-; VA Hosp, 1984-; Cert'd Profl Chem, 1980-; Fellow, Am Inst Chems; Indian Chem Soc; Indian Instn Chems; Am Col Nutrition; Chartered Chem 1981-, Royal Soc Chem; Am Fed Clin Res; NY Acad Sci; AAAS; Am Chem Soc; Am Oil Chems Soc; Pres's Hon Roll, 1974-79; Couns on Arteriosclerosis & Basic Sci, Am Heart Assn; Phi Kappa Phi Acad Hon Soc; Sigma Xi Sci Res Soc; Chartered Mem, World Olympiads Knowledge, Athens; Adv Bd Mem, Nat Cert Comm Chem & Chem Engrg, Wash DC, 1983-; cp/Mem, Univ of TN Fac Clb; r/Hinduism; hon/Res in Mineral Metabolism in Muscular Dystrophy & Other Neuromuscular Diseases incl'g Dementia, Hypertrophic Cardiomyopathy & Acute Pancreatitis; Application of Calcium Channel Blocking Drugs, A- & B- Adrenergic Receptor Modulating Agts, & Surg Procedures to Ameliorate These Conditions by Inhibiting Intracellular Calcium Shift through the Leaky Plasma Membranes; Nutritional Assessmts in Critical Care Patients & Those on Hyperalimentation & Total Parenteral Nutrition; Author & Co-Author, Over 65 Pubs in Profl Sci Jours, Nat & Intl Conf Proceedings; Indian Nat Scholar, Govt India, New Delhi, 1965-69; Dir Public Instrn Merit Scholar, W Bengal Govt, Calcutta,

1965-69; Govt India Scholar, Min of Ed, 1974-75; Grad Tchg Asst, Murray St Univ, 1974-76; Res/Tchg Fellow, Wash Univ-St Louis, 1976-78; Pres Res Fellow, Memphis St Univ, 1978-79; Nat Res Ser Awd in Med, NIH, 1979-81; Res Grantee: Muscular Dystrophy Assn Am; Am Heart Assn; NIH; W/W: in Am, in World, in Frontier Sci & Technol; Am Men & Wom of Sci; Outstg Men & Wom from India in N Am; Other Biogl Listings.

BHATTACHARYYA, ASHIM K oc/ Professor; b/Jul 9, 1936; h/1156 Elmeer Avenue, Metairie, LA 70005; ba/New Orleans, LA; m/Bani; c/Rupa, Gopa; p/ V N (dec) and Asha Bhattacharyya, Calcutta, India; sp/Mr T K Chatterjee (dec); Mrs P Chatterjee (dec), W Bengal, India; ed/BS, 1957; MS, 1959; PhD, 1965; pa/Assoc Prof of Pathol & Physiol 1980-, Assist Prof Pathol & Physiol 1975-80, LA St Univ (LSU) Med Ctr; Res Sci 1974-75, Assoc Res Seci 1970-74, Postdoct Fellow 1969-70, Univ of IA Col of Med; Postdoct Fellow, Univ of MN, 1966-68; Lectr Physiol, Krishnath Col, Berhampore, W Bengal, India, 1964-65; Mem: Am Physiol Soc; Am Heart Assn; Intl Althero Soc; Am Soc Clin Nutrition; Am Inst Nutrition; Soc Exptl Biol Med; Sigma Xi; AAAS; NY Acad of Sci; r/Hinduism; hon/Author, Over 30 Sci Articles, Reviews in Profl Jours; Contbr, 1 Textbook Chapt on Genetic Diseases; W/W: in S & SW, in Frontier Sci & Technol; Am Men & Wom of Sci.

BHATTACHARYYA, SHANKAR P oc/Professor; b/Jun 23, 1946; h/2803 Normand Drive, College Station, TX 77840; ba/Col Sta, TX; m/Carole Jeanne; c/Krishna Lee, Mohadev, Sona Lee; p/ Mr N K and Mrs H N Bhattacharyya (dec); Howard and Mary Colgate; ed/ BTech, Indian Inst of Technol, Bombay, India, 1967; MS Elect Engrg 1969, PhD Elect Engrg 1971, Rice Univ, Houston, TX; pa/Asst Prof 1971-72, Assoc Prof 1972-75, Prof 1976-80, Chm Dept Elect Engrg 1979-80, Fed Univ, Rio De Janeiro, Brazil; Assoc Prof 1980-84, Prof 1984-, Dept Elect Engrg, TX A&M Univ, Col Sta, TX; r/Hindu; hon/Author, Over 40 Sci Papers in Field of Automatic Control; Govt of India Scholar, 1962-67; Nat Sci Foun F'ship, 1967-68; Rice Univ F'ship, 1968-71; NRC-NASA Res Fellow, 1974-75; W/W in Frontier Sci & Technol.

BHUSHAN, BHARAT oc/Tribologist; b/Sep 30, 1949; h/6500 North Pontatoc Road, Tucson, AZ 85744; ba/ Tucson, AZ; m/Sudha; c/Ankur, Noopur; p/Narain Dass and Devi Vati, Jhinjhana, India; sp/Jagdish Saran and Shakuntla Devi, Bareilly, India; ed/BE Mech Engrg, Birla Inst of Technol & Sci, Pilani, India, 1970; MS Mech Engrg, MIT, 1971; MS Mechs 1973, PhD Mech Engrg 1976, Univ of CO-Boulder; MBA Mgmt, Rensselaer Polytech Inst, Troy, NY, 1980; Conslt, Automotive Specs, Denver, CO, 1973-76; Phy Tribologist, Engrg Sci, Prog Mgr, Tribology Ctr of R & D Div, Mech Tech Inc, Latham, NY, 1976-80; Res Sci, Adv'd Engrg & Anal Dept, Technol Sers Div, SKF Industs Inc, King of Prussia, PA, 1980-81; Adv Engr, Adv'd Tribology Dept, GPD Tucson Devel Lab, IBM Corp, 1981-; Mem: Chm Lubrication Fundamentals Com 1982-, Hons &

Awds Com 1984-, Am Soc of Lab Engrs (ASLE); Chm Wear Com 1983-, Res Com on Tribology 1984-, ASME; ASME/ASLE Tribology Conf Planning Com, 1984-; Nat Soc Phys Engrs; SESA; NY Acad of Scis; Tau Beta Pi; Sigma Xi; IEE; AIME; ASCE; AIME; cp/Pres, India Students Assn, Boulder; Bd of Dirs, Hindu Temple Soc & Tri-City India Assn, Albany, NY; Mem, Intl Humanist Soc; r/Hindu; hon/Author 3 Books; Pub'd Over 60 Tech Papers, 40 Tech Reports in Field of Tribology; Var Pubs in IBM *Tech Disclosure Bltn*; Holds 4 US Patents; Recip, Henry Hess Awd, ASME, 1980; Recip, Alfred Noble Prize, 1981; Recip, Burt L Newkirk Awd, ASME, 1983; GPD Achmt Awd, IBM Corp, 1983; George Norlin Awd, Univ of CO Alumni Assn, 1983; W/W: in E, in World, in Engrg, in Technol Today; Am Men & Wom in Sci; Men of Achmt; DIB; Dir World Acad/Industl Resrs 1980's Res Subjects- 20,000 Items; Commun Ldrs of Am; Other Biogl Listings.

BIANCHERIA, AMILCARE oc/Managing Engineer; b/Apr 28, 1929; h/1014 Old Gate Road, Pittsburgh, PA 15235; ba/Pittsburgh, PA; c/Christine; p/Annibale Biancheria (dec); Aggrepina Biancheria, Worcester, MA; ed/AB Chem 1952, MA Phy Chem 1954, PhD Phy Chem 1957, Clark Univ, Worcester, MA; pa/Sr Engr 1957-60 & 1962-65, Fellow Engr 1965-67, Mgr Mats Applications 1967-68, Mgr Fuels Irradiation 1968-80, Mgr Fuel Anal 1980-, Westinghouse Elect Corp, Pgh, PA; Sr Engr, Nuclear Mats & Equip Corp, 1960-62; Mem: NY Acad of Sci; Am Chem Soc; Am Nuclear Soc; cp/Area Gov 1967, Toastmaster Intl; Mem, Nat Spkrs Assn; Mem, Am Ceramic Soc; Mem, Nat Hist Soc; Bd of Dirs 1970-72, Blackridge Civic Assn; r/Cath; hon/Author of Over 50 Sci Articles Pub'd in Profl Jours incl'g: *Jour Am Chem*; *Procedures Am Nuclear Soc*; Others; Num 1st Place Awds, Toastmaster Spch Contests; Hons in Chem, Clark Univ, 1952; W/W: in Frontier Sci & Technol, in Profl Spkg.

BIBBONS, EMMA PEARL oc/ Teacher; b/Jan 26, 1923; h/1835 Blanchard Road, Shreveport, LA 711107; ba/ Shreveport, LA; m/Jeffrey C (dec); c/M J Gregory, Michael, Gerald Godfrey; p/ Joseph and Rose Hall Lover (dec); sp/ Simon and Evelyn Bibbons (dec); ed/BS, AL St Univ, 1944; BA, Grambling St Univ, 1954; MA, Prairie View A&M Col, 1977; pa/Tchr, Colman Col, 1947-51; Tchr, Phoenix City, AL, 1944-47; Tchr, Dallas, TX, 1952-54; Tchr, Shreveport, LA, 1954-; Secy, Nat Phi Delta, 1979-81; Pres 1982-84, Sect Dir 1984-, Nat Assn Univ Wom; cp/Secy, Peoples Voters Leag, 1944-77; Secy, LA Human Relats, 1954-58; Area Secy, YWCA, 1954-56; Lay Spkr Dir, 1971-82; r/U Meth; hon/ Author of Var Articles in *Nat Assn of Univ Wom Jour*, 1980-82; W/W in Meth.

BICK, RODGER LEE oc/Physician, Reseacher; b/May 21, 42; h/4101 Country Clb Road, Bakersfield, CA 93306; ba/Bakersfield, CA; m/Marcella; c/ Michelle LeAnne, Shauna Nicole; p/Jack A and Pauline E Bick; ed/MD, Univ of CA-Irvine, 1970; Intern/Residency, Kern Med Ctr, Bakersfield, CA, 1971-72; F'ship Hematology/Med, Oncology UCLA Ctr for Hlth Sci, LA, CA & Bay Area Hematology Oncology

Med, Grp, Santa Monica, CA, 1974-76; Coagulation/Hematology Fellow, Hyland Labs, Costa Mesa, CA, 1967; pa/ Staff Hematology/Oncology, Bay Area Hematology Oncology Med Grp, Santa Monica, CA, 1976-77; Med Dir, San Joaquin Hematology Oncology Med Grp & CA Coagulation Labs, Bakersfield, CA, 1977-; Adj Clin Fac, Wesley Med Ctr & Univ of KS, Wichita, KS; Adj Prof Med Physiol, Specialized Ctr for Thrombosis Res, Wayne St Univ, Detroit, MI; Asst Prof Med (Hematology/Oncology), Dept Med, UCLA Ctr for Hlth Sci, LA, CA; Mem: Intl Soc Haematology; Intl Soc Thrombosis & Haemostasis; Am Heart Assn; Am Assn Clin Res; Am Col of Phys; Am Assn of Blood Bks; Am Soc Clin Pathols; Am Soc Hematology; Fdg Fellow, Am Soc Coagulationists; Conslt, Am Tobacco Res Coun; Nigerian Haematology Soc; Fed Am Scis; Am Cancer Soc; hon/ Author, Over 100 Med/Sci Pubs in Profl Jours incl'g: *Am Jour Clin Pathol*; *Jour AMA*; *Thrombosis Res*; *Yrbook of Cancer*; Contbg Author to Num Med Text Books; Author, *Disseminated Intravascular Coagulation & Related Syndromes*; Co-Editor, *Semis in Thrombosis & Hemostasis*; Deans List & Hon Student, Univ of CA-Berkeley, 1964-65; Hons Day Awd for Outstg Res, Univ of CA-Irvine, 1968 & 1969; Vincent P Carroll Awd, Contbg Most to Med Res, 1970.

BICKFORD, KATHRYN WISHTISCHIN oc/Artist, Insurance Representative; b/Feb 13, 1936; h/175 Portsmouth Avenue, Stratham, NH 03885; m/Fred; c/Robert Wishtischin, Bill, Judy Wishtischin, David Wistischin; p/Mr and Mrs DeFazio, Ocala, FL; sp/Mr and Mrs Bickford, Amesbury, MA; ed/ Moore Inst, Phila, PA; Harper Col, ILL; Wn CT St Univ; Warren Bus Sch; John Hancock Life Ins Co; pa/Owner, Image Mgmt (Art Consltg Firm), 1979-; Finan Adv & Rep, John Hancock Life Ins, 1983; Mem, NH Life Underwriters, 1983; Dir, Ponperauy Val Art Leag, 1980; Dir & Advr, Richter Art Leag, 1981; VPres, SCAN Art Assn, CT, 1979; Charter Mem, Newtown Bus Wom's Clb; Mem, Zonta, 1984-; Reg'd Rep, The Nat Assn of Securities Dealers; Lic'd, St of NH; cp/Mem, Portsmouth C of C, 1983; Del, Gubernatorial Conv of CT, 1982; r/Rom Cath; hon/Pubs in *Danbury News Time*; *NY News Times*; Num Others; Nat Sales Awd, Assn of Life Underwriters; Hon Clb Mem for Sales in Ins, 1983; Recip of Num 1st, 2nd & 3rd Prizes for Paintings in Profl Arts Exhibs.

BIEBER-MOSES, JEANETTE J oc/ Professor; ba/Billings, MT; m/Norton H Moses; ed/BS Bus Ed 1960, MS Sec'dy Clrm Tchg (Bus) 1961, No St Col, Aberdeen, SD; EdD Adult Higher Ed, MT St Univ, 1978; pa/Instr to Prof 1961-, Ch Dept Bus Ed & Ofc Adm 1979-83, Acting Dir (1975) Coor (1973-74) Affirmative Action Prog, En MT Col, Billings; Grad Tchg Asst, MT St Univ, 1975-76; Co-Fdr, The Ofc Drs; Mem: Col-wide Rank & Tenure Com, Ch, Unit Rank & Tenure Com, Grad Fac Com, Grad Com, En MT Col; Treas 1984-, Ch WBEA Planning Com 1984-87, Wn Bus Ed Assn; Rep, Nat Assn Bus Tchr Ed, 1984-; Mbrship Dir for Wn Reg, Mt Bus Ed Assn, 1979-82; Mem Steering Com, New Directions for Bus Ed, 1979-82; Pres, MT Bus Ed Assn,

1975-77; Pres, Nat Soc of Profs EMC, 1973-74; Pres Zeta Chapt, Alpha Delta Kappa, 1970-82; Charter Mem, Ofc Sys Res Assn; Am & MT Voc Assn; AAUP; AAUW; Life Mem, Nat Ed Assn; Minerva Chapt, Order of En Star, Aberdeen; Num Presentations, Var Univ Wkshops & Profl Confs; hons/ Author of *User's Guide to SuperScripsit Word Processing & the Scripsit Dict: for TRS-80 Fam of Micros*, 1984; Co-Author of Article in *NABTE Review*, 1981; Editor: *New Directions for Bus Ed*, 1980; *Wn News Exch*, 1978-79; Contbr, *NBEA Yrbook*, 1973; Outstg Wom of Am Cit, 1973; Ser Awd, SPURS, 1965-70.

BIELAWSKI, EDWARD LEONARD oc/Clinical Psychologist; b/Jan 20, 1954; h/644 Carmalt St, Dickson City, PA 18519; ba/Scranton, PA; p/Edward Bielawski and Tessie Bielawski (both dec); ed/BS Ednl Psych, Univ of Scranton, 1975; MA Commun Cnslg, Marywood Col, 1977; pa/Psych Asst, Unit Prog Dir, Qualified Mtl Retard Profl, Apple Creek Devel Ctr, Apple Creek, OH, 1977-79; Outpatient Psychotherapist, Hazelton Mtl Hlth Mtl Retard Ctr, Hazelton, PA, 1979-80; Psychol, Referral Coor, Allied Sers, Intermediate Care Fac for Mtly Retarded, Scranton, PA, 1980-; Pvt Pract Clin Psych, Dickson City, PA, 1982-; Mem: Assn for Advmt Behavior Therapy; Am Psychol Assn; PA Psychol Assn; Profl Affairs Com, NE PA Psychol Assn; Am Assn on Mtl Deficiency; cp/Secy 1974-75, VChm 1976-77, Dickson City Zoning Hearing Bd; Judge of Elections, Ward 1, Dist 1, Dickson City, PA, 1975-79; r/Cath; hon/Lic'd by PA Bd of Psychol Examrs; W/W in E.

BIERLY, EUGENE WENDELL oc/Atmospheric Science Director; b/Sept 11, 1931; h/5806 Conway Road, Bethesda, MD 20817; ba/Washington, DC; m/Charlotte S; c/Eugene, Pamela, Jeannine; p/Eugene Woodring Bierly and Charlotte Henrietta Edgerton (both dec); sp/George J Sima & Elizabeth Oldfield (both dec); ed/AB, Univ of PA, 1953; Cert, Nav Postgrad Sch, 1954; MS 1957, PhD 1968, Univ of MI; mil/USN, 1953-56; pa/Div Dir Atmospheric Scis 1979-, Hd Climate Dynamics Sect 1975-79, Hd Ofc of CD 1974-75, Global Atmospheric Res Prog 1971-74, Prog Dir Meteorology 1966-71, NSF; Meteorologist, AEC, 1963-66; Lect 1961-63, Asst Res Meteorologist 1960-63, Asst Civil Engr Dept 1956-60, Univ of MI; Mem: AAAS; Pres 1984, Am Meterological Soc; APCA; Royal Meteorological Soc; Am Polit Sci Assn; Am Geophy Union; r/Presb; hon/Author, Over 25 Articles in Profl Jour on Atmospheric Diffusion & Applications of Meteorology; Editor of 2 Books incl'g: *Patterns & Perspectives in Envir Scis*, 1972; Congl Fellow, 1971; Fellow, AAAS; Fellow, Am Meteorological Soc; Sigma Xi; Pres Meritorious Exec, SES; W/W in E; Am Men & Wom of Sci.

BIGGS, NANCY GENE CHISHOLM oc/Curriculum Development Consultant; b/Sep 28, 1923; h/1330 Brookfield, Memphis, TN 38119; ba/Memphis, TN; m/Jack C; c/Charles Coleman Shoaf III, Raynor Genevieve Shoaf, Robert James Burnett, John Alexander Burnett; p/ Raynor H and Genevieve Tarrant Chisholm (both dec); sp/Helen B Biggs, Memphis, TN; ed/BS 1961, MA 1962,

EdD 1969, Memphis St Univ; pa/Curric Conslt 1982-, Math Conslt 1971-82, Jr & Sr HS Tchr 1961-71, Memphis City Schs; Instr: Memphis St Univ; MI St Univ; Christian Brothers Col; cp/Pres, 20th Cent Clb (Gen Fedn); r/Bapt; hon/ Editor of 9 Books for Individualized Math, & *Mathactivs*, Memphis City Schs; Edited, *NCSM Newslttr*, 1979-81; Contbr, *Hist of Lauderdale Co*; Wom's Awd Highest Acad Avg 1961, 1st Wom Doct, Memphis St Univ; W/W in S & SW.

BIGLER, RODNEY E oc/Nuclear Medical Physicist; b/Mar 15, 1941; h/ 303 East 71st Street, 2H, New York, NY 10021; ba/New York, NY; m/Louise Ann; c/Ronald, Julie; p/Vance Bigler (dec); Mildred Bigler, Brentwood, CA; sp/Louis and Ann Calabrese, Mt Vernon, NY; ed/Att'd Multnomah Col, 1962-63; BS, Portland St Col, 1966; PhD Nuclear Physics, Univ of TX-Austin, 1971; mil/AUS, 1959-62; pa/Tchg Asst, Portland St Col, 1966-67; Tchg Asst 1967-68, Res Asst 1968-71, Univ of TX; Res Assoc 1971-73, Assoc 1973-82, Asst Mem 1982-84, Sloan-Kettering Inst; Res Collaborator, Chem Dept (1973-79) Med Dept (1983-) Brookhaven Nat Lab; Asst Prof 1974-84, Assoc Prof 1984-, Cornell Univ Med Col; Att'g Physicist, NY Hosp-Cornell Med Ctr, 1984-; Mem: Am Assn of Physics Tchrs, 1966-; Sigma Pi Sigma, 1967-; Nuclear & Biol Divs, Am Phy Soc, 1970-; AAAS, 1971; NY Acad of Sci, 1972-; Radiol & Med Physics Soc NY, 1972-; Am Assn of Physicists in Med, 1973-; Sigma Xi, 1973-; Soc Nuclear Med, 1974-; Hlth Physics Soc, 1976-; Radiation Res Soc, 1979-; Num Other Appts & Positions; Num Nat Spkg & Paper Presentations at Univs & Assn Confs; r/Mormon; hon/ Author & Co-Author, Over 50 Article & Res Pubs incl'g 3 Book Chapts; Over 50 Pub'd Abstracts; Sigma Xi; Sigma Pi Sigma; W/W: in E, in Sci & Technol.

BILLIG, ROBERT M oc/Psychotherapeutic Administrator; b/May 21, 1948; h/10 Park Terrace East, New York, NY 10034; ba/New York, NY; p/ Pearl Billig, New York, NY; ed/BA, McKendree Col, 1968; MS, Ft Hayes KS St Col, 1969; MSW, Sch of Social Wk, Marywood Col, 1974; Addit Study, Inst for Psychotherapies & Ackerman Inst; pa/Psychi Social Wkr, Staten Isl Devel Ctr, 1975-76; Psychi Social Wkr, Bklyn Devel Ctr, 1976-78; All Psychi Social Wkr 1979-83, Clin Psychotherapeutic Social Wk Admr, Commun Support Sys 1983-, Bellevue Psychi Hosp; Mem: NY St Soc of Clin Social Wk Psychotherpists Inc; Nat Registry Hlth Care Providers in Clin Social Wk; Nat Assn Social Wkrs; cp/Secy-Treas, Neighborhood Block Coalition; Yg Ldrship Ed Com, U Jewish Appeal; Zionist Org of Am; Am Mensa Ltd; r/Jewish; hon/Cert Social Wkr: NY St, Acad Cert'd Social Wkrs, NASCW, 1977; Hon Bd of Advrs, ABI; W/W: in E, of Intells; Personalities of E; Commun Ldrs of Am; 2000 Notable Ams; Mem of Achmt; Biogl Roll of Hon; Dir Clin Social Wkrs; Num Other Biogl Listings.

BILLIMEK, THOMAS EWALD oc/ Professor; b/Sep 12, 1945; h/8914 Melinda Court, San Antonio, TX 78240; ba/San Antonio, TX; m/Sharon Ann; c/ Susan Ann, John Thomas, Sarah Beth; p/Ewald P and Emelie H Billimek, Helotes, TX; sp/R L and Betty Pugh, San Antonio, TX; ed/BA Psych, St Mary's

Univ, 1968; MA Psych, Trinity Univ, 1971; mil/USAR, 1968-; pa/Prof Psych, San Antonio Col, 1972-; Psychometrist, San Antonio Goodwill Industs, 1970-71; Mem: Am Psychol Assn; SWn Psychol Assn; TX Psychol Assn; Bexar Co Psychol Assn; AAUP; AAAS; TX Jr Col Tchrs Assn; Civil Affairs Assn; Resv Ofcrs Assn; Assn of US Army; r/Cath; hon/Contbg Editor, *Rdg About Psych & You*, 1979; W/W in S & SW.

BILLINGS, CHARLES REEMS oc/ Clinical Psychologist; b/Apr 5, 1943; ba/ Larkspur, CA; m/Naomi Singer; c/Paul Reems, David Aaron; p/Von D and Nina Eloise (Sanders) Billings (both dec); ed/ AA Lib Arts, Col of Marin, 1963; BA Psych 1965, MA Psych 1967, MA Ednl Adm 1971, SF St Univ; PhD Psych, CA Sch of Profl Psych, Berkeley, CA, 1974; Addit Study & Postdoct Tng at Num Other Univs; pa/Dir Student Cnslg Sers 1982-, Assoc Prof 1981-, Chp Dept Cnslg Psych 1978-, Psychol Conslt to Student Sers 1980-81, Asst Prof 1978-80, Dir Cnslg Prog 1973-78, Instr 1970-78, Dominican Col of San Rafael; Conslt Fac 1982-, Core Psych Fac 1975-76, Contract Psych Instr 1975, CA Sch Profl Psych; Psychol, Alice Jackson & Assocs, SF, 1977-78; Dir Pupil Pers Sers & Spec Ed 1975-78, Dist Psychol 1974-75, Psych Intern 1972-74, Sch Psychol 1970-72, Shoreline Unified Sch Dist, Tomales; Pres, Equinox Sys Inc, San Rafael, 1974-78; Psychol, Stanley, Barber, Southand, Brown & Assocs, SF, 1976-77; Col Instr & Lectr, Sonoma St Col, 1969-70; Sch Psych for Num CA Schs; Num Pvt Clin & Consltg Pract Clients: Marriage, Fam & Child, Art Therapy, Ednl Psych, Indiv Psych, 1968-; Courtesy Med Staff, Marin Gen Hosp, 1982-; Num Referral Panel Mbrships, 1979-; Cmmr, Var CA St Bd of Examrs Licensing Comms; VPres & Bd Mem, Marin Chapt CA Assn of Marriage & Fam Therapists; Num Com Mbrships & Chmships, Dominican Col San Rafael; Num Task Force Mbrships & Num Other Com Mbrships; cp/Mem: Acad of Psychols in Marital, Sex & Fam Therapy; Am Art Therapy Assn; Am Psychol Assn; Am Psychol Assn Div of Psychotherapy; CA Assn Marriage & Fam Therapists; CA St Psychol Assn; CA St Psych Assn Div of Clin Psych; Marin Chapt CA Assn Marriage & Fam Therapists; Marin Co Psychol Assn; Psi Chi Hon Soc; Num Wkshops & Orgnl Presentations; Others; hon/Author, Over 12 Psychol Pubs, 1974-; Hon Bd Mem, Am Bd of Fam Psych; Most Outstg Res Awd & Cert of Merit for Contbns to Conv, CA Assn Sch Psychols & Psychometrists, 1976; Cert of Apprec, Marin Co Career Ed Prog, Marin Co Schsl; Nom'd Dist'd Tchg Psych, Am Psych Fdn; W/W: in W, in CA, in Frontier Sci & Technol; Commun Ldrs of Am; Noteworthy Ams.

BILON, JOHN JULIUS oc/Professor, Director; b/Jul 25, 1926; h/970 Star Crest Drive, Harrisonburg, VA 22801; ba/Harrisonburg, VA; m/Dorothy T; c/ John David, Lawrence Francis, Stephen Paul; p/John and Katherine Bilon (both dec); sp/Frank and Elizabeth Taylor (both dec); ed/BS Hotel & Restaurant Adm 1949, MS Hotel & Restaurant Adm 1957, Cornell Univ; mil/AUS, 1944-46 & 1951-75, Col; pa/Asst Hotel Mgr, Falls Hotel, Newberry, MI,

1949-50; AUS Assignments Incl: Clb Mgr, Restaurant Mgr, Gen Mgr Hotels, Bat Cmdr, Asst Chief Staff Supply, Dir of All AUS Clbs Worldwide, 1951-75; Prof & Dir Hotel & Restaurant Mgmt Prog, Sch of Bus, James Madison Univ, Harrisonburg, VA, 1976-; Mem, Eta Sigma Delta, Intl Hospitality Mgmt Hon Soc; Mem, Ye Hosts, Hotel & Restaurant Adm Hon Soc; cp/Pres, Harrisonburg Rotary Clb Intl, 1984; Chm Adm Bd, Asbury U Meth Ch, 1979-85; r/U Meth; hon/Author of Article on Clb Mgmt in *Hotel & Restaurant Mgt*, 1984; Article on Hospitality Indust, in *Ency Profl Mgmt*, 1984; Other Articles for Num Hospitality Indust Pubs; Dist'd Ser Awd, VA Hotel & Motel Assn, 1982; Legion of Merit 1970 & 1975, Plus 16 Other Mil Awds, AUS; Cert Hotel Admr, 1983; Dir Dist'd Ams.

BILOTTO, GERARDO oc/Neurophysiologist; b/Sep 21, 1948; h/28-7th Street, Bayville, New York, NY 11709; ba/New York, NY; m/Sandra; p/Giuseppe and Violetta, Locust Valley, NY; sp/Eileen, Bayville, NY; ed/AAS, Ferris St Col, 1968; BS, NY Inst of Technol, 1970; MS Bioengrg 1972, MPhil 1976, PhD Physiol 1978, Columbia Univ; pa/ Dir of Indep Living Res, Human Resource Ctr, Albertson, NY 1978-79; Postdoct Res Fellow, Rockefeller Univ, NYC, 1979-81; Sr Res Assoc, Liberty Mut Ins Co Res Ctr, 1981-84; Res Assoc, Dept Ortho Surg, Chdn's Hosp, Boston, 1981-; Res Assoc, Dept Ortho Surg, Harvard Med Sch, 1981-; Assoc Res Scist, Columbia Univ, 1984-; Mem: Soc for Neurosci; Intl Assn for Study of Pain; AAAS; IEEE & IEEE (Engrg in Med & Biol Soc); Sys, Man & Cybernetics Soc; NY Acad of Sci; hon/Author of Articles in *Brain Res; Exptl Brain Res;* Postdoct Indiv F'ship, NIH, 1979-82; Mem, Sigma Xi; BS, magna cum laude, NY Inst of Technol, 1970; W/W: in Frontier Sci & Technol, in World.

BINGHAM, JINSIE SCOTT oc/Executive; b/Dec 28, 1935; ba/PO Box 494, Greencastle, IN 46135; m/Richard Innes (2nd); c/Douglas Scott Wokoun, Richard Frank Wokoun; p/Roscoe Gibson Scott and Alpha Edith Robinson; ed/Att'd: DePauw Univ, 1952-53; NWn Univ, 1953; Coe Col, 1953-54; pa/Receptionist, IN HO of Reps, 1959; Receptionist, Avon Prods, 1961-64; Sales Mgr, Radio Sta WXTA, 1969-77; Owner, Pres & Gen Mgr, WJNZ Radio, 1977-; Exec Secy, IN Yg Dems, 1958-60; Pres Hoosier Chapt 1979-82, Mem, Am Wom in Radio & TV, 1977-; Mem, Wom in Communs; Wom's Press Clb of IN; Nat Fed Press Wom; Pres 1976-77 & 1979-80, Greencastle Fedn BPW, 1970-; IN Dem Edit Assn; VPres for FM, IN Broadcasters Assn, 1982; Mem, Indianapolis Netwk of Wom in Bus, 1977-; Corp Secy, Bd Mem, Main St Greencastle Inc, 1983-86; Nat Assn of Wom Bus Owners, 1984-; Indianapolis Press Clb, 1984-; cp/Co-Chm, Greencastle Gaelic Fest, 1983-86; Charter Mem, Greencastle Civic Leag, 1984-; Com Ch, Legis Awareness Sem, 1978-; Commun Host, Hoosier Hospitality Days, 1981-; Pres 1982, Bd Mem 1979-83, Greencastle C of C; Mem, IN St C of C; Mem, Putnam Co Action Com for Ec Strength, 1979-; Mem, Commun Resources Coun, 1982-; Order of En Star #255, Greencastle; Life Mem &

Hon Queen (1951), Intl Order of Job's Daughs; 2 Term Pres 1966-68, Ladies Aux VFW Post #1550; Ladies Aux Am Legion Post #58; Pres Tippecanoe Chapt 1981, St VPres 1982, Daughs of 1812; Washbauurn Chapt, DAR; Num Others; r/1st Christian Ch, Disciples of Christ; hon/Outstg Citizen, Greencastle JC's, 1981; Communs Sem, DePauw Univ, 1980; W/W in MW.

BINGHAM, ROSIE PHILLIPS oc/ Psychologist; b/Apr 12, 1949; h/5520 NW 23 Terrace, Gainesville, FL 32606; ba/Gainesville, FL; p/Jake and Savanah Phillips, Memphis, TN; ed/BA Sociol, Elmhurst Col, 1971; MA Ed 1973, PhD Cnslg Psych 1977, OH St Univ; pa/ Psychol, Univ of FL, 1978-; Prof & Admr, OH Dominican Col, 1975-78; Mgr, Bell Sys, Chgo, 1971-72; 2nd VPres 1982-, Delta Sigma Theta Inc (Ocala Alumni); Corres'g Secy 1983, Altrusa Clb of Gainesville; Profl Topic Presentations: OH St Univ Cnslrs Conf, 1975; Am Pers & Guid Assn, 1976; cp/ Mem, Leag of Wom Voters, 1979-; r/ Prot; hon/Author & Co-Author, Var Articles Pub'd in Profl Jours incl'g: *Jour of Voc Behavior; Cnslg Blacks; Pers & Guid Jour;* Others; Outstg Yg Profl, Am Col Pers Assn, 1982; Outstg Yg Wom of Am; W/W in S & SW.

BINGHAM, WALTER D oc/Pastor; b/Jun 3, 1921; h/3608 Dumesnil Street, Louisville, KY 40211; ba/Louisville, KY; m/Rebecca T; c/Gail Elaine; p/Willie Sr and Lena Allen Bingham (both dec); sp/ George E and Lolla B Taylor (both dec); ed/AB, Talladega Col, 1945; MDiv, Div Sch, Howard Univ, 1948; pa/Prof Rel, Jarvis Christian Col, 1948-57; Pastor, Pine St Christian Ch, Tulsa, OK, 1957-61; Pastor, 3rd Christian Ch, L'ville, KY, 1961-; Moderator, Christian Ch (Disciples of Christ) in US & Canada, 1971-73; Currently Chp Bd of Dirs, Coun on Christian Unity, Christian Ch (Disciples of Christ) in US & Canada; r/Disciples of Christ; hon/Hon Degs: DD, Christian Theol Sem; LHD, Drury Col; LLD, Transylvania Univ.

BINNION, JOHN EDWARD oc/ Business Editor, Consultant; b/Jul 14, 1918; h/704 North 1st Street, Crowell, TX 79227; ba/Crowell, TX; m/Doris Lee Campbell; c/Margaret Anne, John Edward II, Mary Virginia, Dianna Lee; p/Roy Cecil Binnion (dec); Johnnie Mary (Garner) Binnion, Long Bch, CA; ed/ AA, Chaffey Col, 1936; BBA, Univ of TX-Austin, 1944; MA, NM Highlands Univ, 1951; MBA, Univ of Denver, 1972; EdD, OK St Univ; CPA, (TX & OK) CAM Intl; Lic'd Preacher, U Meth Ch; mil/AUS, 1940-44; pa/Pres TEAMS, 1981-; Prof & Assoc Dean, Col of Bus, Cleveland St Univ, 1972-81; Nat Dir Ed, Lear Siegler, Inc, 1968-72; Prof Bus Ed & Dir Doct Progs, Col of Bus, TX Tech Univ, 1965-68; Prof Bus Ed, Univ of Denver 1955-65; Assoc Prof Bus, SWn (OK) St Univ, 1953-55; Asst Prof Bus, NM Highlands Univ, 1951-52; Mem: Adm Mgmt Soc; Am Inst of CPAs; TX & OK Soc of CPAs; Beta Gamma Sigma; Beta Alpha Psi; Delta Pi Epsilon; Phi Delta Kappa; Kappa Kappa Psi; Nat Bus Ed Assn; Nat Assn for Bus Tchr Ed; Var Positions w Num Orgs; cp/Mem, Rotary Intl; Past Nat Cmdr, Mil Order of Purple Heart; Num Others; r/Meth; hon/ Author of 3 Books on Bus Ed; Editor: *Wn Bus Review,* 1958-62; *CO Study Guides*

in Bus Ed, 1955-65; *The Purple Heart Mag,* 1980-; Awd Excell in Tchg Bus & Ec, Nat Fdn Indep Bus, 1979; Awd of Merit, Assn of Indep Cols & Schs, 1978; Diamond Merit Awd, Adm Mgmt Soc, 1980; 2 Awds, Freedom Foun; W/W: in Am, in World.

BIRK, THOMAS ALLEN oc/Executive; b/Aug 27, 1953; h/5601 Domingo Road Northeast, Albuquerque, NM 87108; ba/Albuquerque, NM; m/Constance Sorensen; p/Mr and Mrs Allen S T Birk, Bellevue, NE; sp/Mrs Lil Sorensen, Gering, NE; ed/Att'd US Mil Acad, 1972-74; BA Broadcast Jour, Univ of NE-Lincoln, 1976; Currently MA Cand Human Relats, Webster Univ; mil/ AUS, 1971-74; pa/Staff Announcer & Acct Exec KOTD Radio, Plattsmouth, NE, 1974; Acct Exec KFMQ-FM, Lincoln, NE, 1974-79; Gen Sales Mgr KAMX/KFMG, Albuquerque, NM, 1979-82; Pres & Gen Mgr KFMG Inc, Albuquerque, NM, 1982-; Mem, Albuquerque Radio Broadcaster Assn, 1982-84; Freelance Conslt, Real Est Advtg, 1978-79; cp/Mem, Big Brothers & Big Sisters of Albuquerque, 1982-84; Guest Lectr, Univ of NE-Lincoln & Lincoln Sch of Commerce, 1976-79; r/ Epis; hon/Alpha Epsilon Rho Hon Jour Soc, 1976; W/W in W.

BIRKENMEIER, THOMAS JOSEPH oc/Executive; b/May 2, 1947; h/8 Frontenac Estates, St Louis, MO 63131; ba/ St Louis, MO; c/Mathew Lawrence, Elizabeth Dorr, Kurt Collins; p/Mrs L J Birkenmeier, St Louis, MO; ed/Att'd: St Louis Univ, 1966-67; Wash Univ-St Louis, 1967-69; Wharton Fin Mgmt Sem; pa/Copywriter, Ralston Purina, 1967; Copy Chief 1967-68, Creat Dir 1968-70, VPres Creat Sers 1970-72, Exec VPres 1972-78, Stozz Advtg; Ptnr & Exec VPres, Birkenmeier, Fraser, Vorderstrasse & Lashly, 1978-; cp/ Mem: Univ Clb, St Louis; Racquet Clb, St Louis; VPres, Fair Inc; Devel Bd, St Louis Chdn's Hosp; r/Cath; hon/ Created Radio Prog: "The Greatest Baseball Game Never Played," Broadcast on Armed Forces Radio; Lectr: Univ of MO; Wash Univ-St Louis; Maryville Col; Planetarium Prog Bd.

BIRKIMER, DONALD LEO oc/Technical Director; b/Sep 6, 1941; h/1291 Seybolt Avenue, Camarillo, CA 93010; ba/Port Hueneme, CA; m/Edith Marie Lowe; c/Mark Austin, Thomas Edgar, Julie Lee; p/Mr and Mrs Edgar E Birkimer, Parma Hgts, OH; sp/Mrs Francis G Lowe, Cincinnati, OH; ed/ BSCE, OH Univ, 1963; MS 1965, PhD 1968, Univ of Cinc; PMD, Harvard Grad Sch Bus, 1973; pa/Civil Engr, Wright-Patterson AFB, 1963-64; Res Civil Engr, US Army Corp of Engrs, 1964-68; Res Structural Engr, Battelle, 1968-69; Acting Chief, Constrn Mats Br, US Army Constrn Engrg Res Lab, 1969-71; Asst Dir, Nav Surface Weapons Ctr, 1971-75; Tech Dir, Coast Guard R & D Ctr, 1975-81; Tech Dir, NCEL, 1981-; cp/Mem, Rotary Intl; Order of the Elks; r/Rom Cath; hon/ Author of Books: *The Effects of Temperature on Concrete; Polymerized Lightweight Structural Elements;* Author, Over 30 Nat & Intl Pubs in Sci & Engrg; Dist'd Alumnus, Univ of Cinc, 1984; Wason Medal, Am Concrete Inst, 1973; Reg'd Profl Engr, Chi Epsilon Hon Frat, 1967; Meritorious Unit Commend Awd, Coast Guard,

1976; W/W: in World, in Am, in Govt, in Engrg; Am Men & Wom of Sci; Intl Book of Hon; Other Biogl Listings.

BIRKITT, JOHN CLAIR oc/Technical Manager; b/Aug 20, 1941; h/32536 Ortega Highway, El Cariso Village, Lake Elsinore, CA 92330; ba/Newport Bch, CA; m/Linda Ann Aylmer; c/ Andra, Robert, Lowell, Daniélle; p/Clair Willis Birkitt (dec); Helene Blanche (Gille) Birkitt, Fullerton, CA; sp/William Stanley and Phyllis Jane (King) Aylmer, Rancho Santa Fe, CA; ed/BS Aerospace Engrg, CA St Polytech Univ, 1969; mil/ USMC, 1959-65; pa/Proj Engr, Aerojet Mfg Co, Fullerton, CA, 1969-74; Engr, TRW Def & Space Sys Grp, Redondo Bch, CA 1974-79, Plant Mgr Adv'd Ground Sys Engrg, Long Bch, CA 1979-80, Test Conductor, TRW's Capistrano Test Site, San Clemente, CA 1975-83; Tech Mgr, Ford Aerospace & Communs Corp, Newport Bch, CA, 1983-; Mem, AIAA; Intl & Nat Mgmt Assn; Am Def Preparedness Assn; cp/ Engr, VPres, Treas & Tng Ofcr, El Cariso Vol Fire Assn, 1978-; Mem, Nat Assn of Watch & Clock Collectors; Mem, Musical Box Soc; hon/Author of Pubs on Aerospace & Def Sys Engrg; Commend, Nav Sea Sys Command, 1983; Commend, Dept of AF Elect Warfare Div, 1982; Commends, Dept of Nav, High Energy Laser Proj, 1978, 1981 & 1982; Cert of Apprec Patriotic Civilian Ser, Dept of Army, 1979; Commend AF Mat Sci Div, 1977; Commend, Dept of AF Intell & Reconnaisance Div, 1976; Commend, TRW Sys Grp Minuteman Prog Ofc, 1975; W/ W: in W, in Frontier Sci & Technol, in Aviation & Aerospace.

BIRKITT, LINDA ANN AYLMER oc/ Physical Therapist; b/Feb 8, 1946; h/ 32536 Ortega Highway, El Cariso Village, Lake Elsinore, CA 92330; m/ John C; c/Andra, Robert, Lowell, Daniélle; p/William Stanley and Phyllis Jane (King) Aylmer, Santa Fe, CA; sp/ Clair Willis Birkitt (dec); Helene Blanche (Gille) Birkitt, Fullerton, CA; ed/BS CA St Plytech Univ, 1963-69; Att'd, Univ of MO at Munich W Germany, 1967-68; MA, Univ So CA, 1973; pa/Staff Phy Therapist, Val Presb Hosp, Van Nuys, CA, 1973-75; Chief Therapist, Ingleside Mtl Hlth Ctr, Rosemead, CA, 1975-79; Lectr, Santa Monica City Col, 1976-79; Asst Chief Phy Therapist, Alhambra CA Commun Hosp, 1979-81; Pvt Pract Phy Therapy, San Juan Capistrano, CA 1981-; Mem, Spkrs Bur, 1976-79; Mem, AAUW; Mem, Nat Assn Female Execs; cp/Vol Fire Fighter, El Cariso Vol Fire Assn, 1979-; Mem, San Juan Sch PTA; r/Epis; hon/Author of Article on Phy Therapy; W/W: in W, of Am Wom.

BIRNBAUM, LUCIA CHIAVOLA oc/Historian; b/Jan 3, 1924; h/349 Gravatt Drive, Berkeley, CA 94705; m/ Wallace; c/Naury, Marc, Stefan; p/Kate C Chiavola, Kansas City, MO; sp/Harry Birnbaum, Pgh, PA; ed/AB 1948, MA 1950, PhD 1964, Univ of CA-Berkeley; pa/Wom's Ctr Res Assoc 1982-83, Lectr 1963-64, Univ of CA-Berkeley; Fac, Feminist Inst, 1982-; Asst Prof, SF St Univ, 1964-69; Mem Exec Coun, Am Italian Hist Assn, 1978-; Steering Com, Feminist Inst, 1982; Num Paper Presentations at Orgnl Confs; cp/VPres, Berkeley Area PTA; Platform Com, Peace & Freedom Party, 1967; Num

Guest Lectures; r/Judeo-Christian; hon/ Author of Var Articles Pub'd in *Stanford Italian Review*; Jour of Wom & Rel; Am Hist Assn Newlttr; Others; Var Reviews; Quill & Scroll Awd, Univ of KS City, 1943; Soroptimist F'ship, Univ of CA-Berkeley, 1955; W/W: of Wom, in W; Dir of Wom Hists; Dir Am Scholars.

BIRNBAUM, MICHAEL HENRY oc/ Professor; b/Mar 10, 1946; h/1001 Devonshire Drive, Champaign, IL 61821; ba/Champaign, IL; m/Bonnie Gail; c/Melissa Anne, Kevin Michael; p/ Mr and Mrs Eugene D Birnbaum; sp/ Mr and Mrs Sidney Bruck; ed/BA Math & Psych 1968, MA Psych 1969, PhD Psych 1972, Univ of CA-LA (UCLA); pa/Tchg & Res Asst 1968-69, NDEA Title IV Fellow 1969-72, Acting Asst Prof 1972, Vis'g Asst Prof 1974, Univ of CA-LA; NIMH Postdoct Scholar, Univ of CA-San Diego, 1972-73; Asst Prof Psych, KS St Univ, 1973-74; Asst Prof Psych 1974-76, Assoc Prof Psych 1976-82, Chm Div Measurement & Industl Psych 1979-80, Prof Psych 1982-, Res Prof Survey Res Inst Sum 1983, Univ of IL-Urbana-Champaign; Mem of Num Acad Coms at Univ of IL-Urbana-Champaign, 1978-; Mem: Am Psychol Assn; AAAS; Judgment & Decision Making Grp; Psychonomic Soc; Psychometric Soc; Soc for Math Psych; Phi Beta Kappa; Psi Chi; Phi Eta Sigma; Sigma Xi; Over 40 Profl Sci Paper Presentations at Assn Confs & Meetings; Edit Consltg for Num Profl Jours; cp/Current Pres, Ring 236, Intl Brotherhood of Magicicians; hon/ Author & Co-Author, Over 50 Pubs in Profl Jours incl'g: *Jour of Exptl Psych, Human Pereception & Perf; Jour Personality & Soc Psych; Jour Applied Psych; Mod Issues in Perceptual Psych; Am Jour Psych*; Others; Woodrow Wilson Hon F'ship, 1968; Other F'ships; Fac Awd Dist'd Tchg 1969, Alumni Assn Dissertation Awd 1972, Psych Dept Res Awd 1968, Univ of CA-LA; Arthur Patch McKinley Awd, Phi Beta Kappa, 1968; W/W: in W & MW, in Frontier Sci & Technol.

BIRO, STEVEN G M oc/Attorney; b/ Aug 17, 1943; h/291 Vine Road, Stamford, CT 06905; ba/New York, NY; m/ S Guzin Biro-Altiok; c/Sinan Geoffrey; p/Dr George G Biro (dec); sp/Nuri Altiok (dec); ed/BA Polit Sci, Columbia Col, Columbia Univ, 1965; MA Polit Sci, Univ of WA, 1966; Nuclear Engr, USN Nuclear Power Engrg Prog, 1968; JD, Fordham Univ Sch of Law, 1974; mil/ USNR, 1967-74, Lt; pa/Propr of Firm, Steven G M Biro Atty at Law, NY & CT, 1982-; Ptnr, Hill & Co, The Sultanate of Oman & U Arab Emirates, 1979-81; Assoc, Winthrop, Stimson, Putnam & Roberts, NY, 1976-77; Law Clk, Hon T J Meskill, US Ct of Appeals, 2nd Circuit, 1975; Law Clk, Justice Joseph S Longo, Supr Ct of CT, 1975; Law Clk, Justice Louis Shapiro, Supr Ct of CT, 1974; Mem: NY, CT, FL, Fed & Intl Bar Assns; Admitted to Pract, US Supr Ct; Circuit Cts of Appeal for DC, 2nd Circuit NY; CT; FL; US Ct of Intl Trade; US Tax Ct; US Dist Cts for CT, So Dist of NY, En Dist NY; Secy Com on Nuclear Technol & Law 1977-79, NYC Bar Assn; Reporter, Com on Application of Technol to Law 1978-79, NYC Lwyrs Assn; hon/Author of Var Articles Pub'd in *Mid E Ec Digest Spec Report on Oman, 1980; NY St Bar Jour*,

1980; *Legal Res*, 1980; Others; Law Sch S'ship, Ny St S'ship Awd, Class VPres Student Bar Assn, Case Notes Editor *Fordham Urban Law Jour*, Fordham Univ Sch of Law; NY St Regents S'ship Awd, Col S'ship, Dean's List, Columbia Univ; IMH F'ships.

BIRSTEIN, SEYMOUR J oc/Executive; b/May 1, 1927; h/7354 Cardigan Circle, Atlanta, GA 30328; ba/Atlanta, GA; c/Diane Birstein; p/Harry and Golde Birstein (dec); ed/BS, NY Univ, 1947; MS, MT St Univ, 1949; Doct Studies, Bklyn Polytech Inst; Addit Study, w Mil & Cornell Univ; pa/Pres, SJB Assocs Inc (Consltg, Res & Devel Technol Firm), 1977-; Chief Aerosol Interaction Br & Prog Mgr, USAF Geophys Res Labs, Bedford MA, 1951-76; Res Chem, Air Reduction Co, Murray Hill, NJ, 1949-50; Fellow, Am Inst of Chems; Mem, Am Chem Soc; Mem, Am Meteorological Soc; Mem, Sigma Xi; r/Hebrew; hon/Author & Co-Author, Over 25 Sci Papers & Articles Pub'd in Profl Jours incl'g: *AF Survey in Geophysics; Jour Meteorology; CIRADS Proceedings*; Others; Holder of 2 US Patents in Field; Am Men & Wom of Sci; W/W in S & SW.

BISHOP, CAMILLA L oc/College Administrator; h/2129-A Woodland Circle Northeast, Olympia, WA 98506; ba/Lacey, WA; c/Jared Morris; p/Roy H Bishop, Redondo, WA; Bess B Polee, Pullman, WA; ed/BA Fgn Lang/Ed 1971, MA Cnslg 1973, Currently PhD Cand, WA St Univ; pa/Res & Tchg Asst 1972-73, Residence Hall Dir 1976-79, WA St Univ; Cnslr, Lewis & Clark St Col, 1973-76; Asst Dir Housing, N TX St Univ, 1979-81; Dir Housing, Linfield Col, 1981-83; Dir Campus Life, St Martin's Col, 1983-; Nat Dir Body Mem Comm III, Am Col & Pers Assn, 1982-; Nat Mbrship Com 1981-82, Nat Prog Com 1982-, Assn of Col & Univ Housing Ofcrs Intl; Prog Com 1981-82, NW Col Pers Assn; hon/W/W in W.

BISHOP, ROBERT CHARLES oc/ Museum Director; b/Aug 25, 1938; h/ 213 W 22nd Street, New York, NY l00ll; ba/New York, NY; p/Charles Bishop, Readfield, ME; Muriel Bishop (dec); ed/ PhD Am Culture, Univ of MI, 1975; pa/ Picture Editor, Am Heritage Pub Co, NY; Mgr Pubs, Henry Ford Mus, MI; Dir, Mus Am Folk Art, NY; Mem, Opport Resources, NYC; Mem, Nat Trust for Hist Presv; Bd of Dirs, ISALTA, NYC; cp/Mem, Koreshan Unity, Estero, FL; Mem, Grove House, Coconut Grove, FL; hon/Author, Co-Author, Designer & Editor, Over 30 Books on Am Folk Art & Collecting; Plus Over 80 Catalogues & Pamphlets for Var Mus; W/W: in E, in Am; Contemp Authors; 2000 Notable Ams; Art Bibliogs.

BISSELL, MICHAEL GILBERT oc/ Clinical Pathologist; b/Mar 5, 1947; h/ 5840 South Stony Island Avenue, Apartment 3F, Chicago, IL; ba/Chicago, IL; m/Sherrie Lynne Lyons; c/Cassandra, Grahame; p/Henry and Margaret Benefiel, Casa Grande, AZ; sp/Harold and Edna Lyons, Pacific Palisades, CA; ed/BS Math & Chem, Univ of AZ, 1969; MD 1975, PhD Neurobiol, 1977, Stanford Univ; MPH, Univ of CA-Berkeley, 1978; pa/Resident Clin Pathol, VA Med Ctr, Martiniez, CA, 1978-81; Sr Staff Assoc Fellow, Lab Neurochem, NIMH,

Bethesda, MD, 1981-84; Asst Med Dir Clin Chem, Univ of Chgo Med Ctr, Chgo, IL, 1984-; Mem: AAAS; APHA; Col Am Pathols; Tissue Culture Assn; Am Assn Clin Scis; Am Assn Clin Chem; hon/Author of *A Hlth & Safety Eval of 400KV Powerline*, 1982; Plus Num Articles in Var Sci Mags incl'g: *Nature*; *Sci: Intl Jour Biomet*; Silver Medal, 1st World Conf on Human Respiration, CICTISIER, Montevideo, Uruguay, 1981; Men of Achmt; W/W in Frontier Sci & Technol.

BITTERS, ROBERT GEORGE NELSON oc/Executive; b/Feb 22, 1932; h/5440 Quakertown Avenue, Woodland Hills, CA 91364; m/Mary Louise; c/Bruce Gordon, Paula Kay (dec); p/Arthur John and Dorothy May Bitters (dec); ed/BSBA, Univ of Cinc, 1953; Att'd Upper Div Course, LA Pierce Col, Woodland Hills, CA, 1964; mil/AUS, 1953-55; pa/Exec VPres 1979, VPres & Div Mgr 1976-78, QA Dir 1972-75, Netwks Elect Corp; QA Dir 1965-71, Mat Mgr 1961-64, Adv'd Communs Inc; Mat Control Mgr, Ramo-Woolridge Corp, 1957-61; Mem: Intl Platform Assn; US Congl Adv Bd; Soc Plastics Engr; Am Chem Soc; Nav Leag of US; Am Property Mgmt Assn; Am Mgmt Assns; Am Def Preparedness Assn; Am Soc QC; Soc Mfg Engrs; AIAA; USN Inst; r/Bapt; hon/Author of UN Res Reports on Low Cost Mass Food, Housing & Trans to Reduce Starvation & Suffering; Corp Ranked #13 in 50 Fastest Growing Cos in LA Co, 1981; Ranked #3 in CA 100 Fastest Growing Cos, 1982; W/W: in W, in CA; 5000 Personalities of World.

BIVENS, JANET A oc/Executive Assistant; b/Nov 19, 1939; h/1944 Rock Cut Place, Conley, GA 30027; ba/Atlanta, GA; m/F Wayne; c/Anthony Wayne, Mark Allen, David Glenn; p/Nelson Leroy Liston (dec); sp/Forrest G Bivens (dec); ed/Dipl, Ripley HS, 1957; AA Secy Sci, Clayton Jr Col, 1980; Att'g GA St Univ-Atlanta; pa/Exec Asst, CBI/Equifax, 1968-; Pres Atlanta Chapt, Profl Secys Intl, 1983-84; Past Pres, Equifax Employees Activs Clb; Mem, Spkrs Bur of Atlanta; Mem, Pres's Coun, Atlanta; r/Meth; hon/Voted Most Outstg Den Mother, Atlanta, 1970; 3 Yrs S'ship Awd for Reg Nurses Tng, 1957; Most Outstg Secy Student Ripley HS Awd, 1956.

BLACK, LAURELL LAURENT b/Dec 13, 1959; h/318 W Alpine Street, Santa Ana, CA 92707; p/Santa Ana, CA; ed/AA Bus Adm, Lib Arts, Santa Ana Col, 1982; BA Mgmt, Sonoma St Univ, 1984; cp/Publicity Chm, Am Mktg Assn; St-wide Ednl Rts Netwk, NAACP, 1984; hon/Editor, Fdr, *The Black Student's Voice*, Sonoma St Univ; W/W Among Students in Am Cols & Univs.

BLACK, LOUIS ECKERT oc/Executive; b/Sept 6, 1942; h/3530 St John Avenue, Jacksonville, FL 32205; ba/Jacksonville, FL; m/Susan H; p/Louis E and Leonie Y Black, Jacksonville, FL; sp/Mr and Mrs William H Harrell, Indian Harbor Bch, FL; ed/BA Col of Wooster, 1965; MAT, Univ of FL, 1966; pa/Chm Dept Fgn Lang, Ribault Jr HS, Jacksonville, FL, 1967-69; Field Claims Rep, State Farm Ins, 1969-70; Acct Exec, Hayden, Stone Inc, 1970-74; Pres, Avondale Travel Bur, 1974-; Mem, Am Soc of Travel Agts; Adv Bds, EA & Pan

Am Airlines; Adv Bd, Norwegian Carribean Cruises; cp/Mem: Rotary Clb Intl; Jacksonville Qtrback Clb; River Clb; SKAL Clb; FL & GA Ftball Ofcls; So Assn Basketball Ofcls; Ponte Vedra Clb; r/Epis; hon/Recip, CREST Awd, Creat Retail Excell in Selling & Travel, 1981, 1982 & 1983; W/W: in S & SW, in Am, in Fin & Indust; Dir Dist'd Ams; Biogl Roll of Hon.

BLACK, PERCY oc/Professor; b/Jan 6, 1922; h/29 Cross Hill Avenue, Yonkers, NY 10703; ba/Pleasantville, NY; m/Virginia; c/Deborah, David, Elizabeth, Jonathan; p/Ovid Black (dec) Mrs Rose Black, Richmond, VA; sp/Fred and Geneva Arne (both dec); ed/BSc, Sir George Wms Col, 1944; MSc, McGill Univ, 1946; PhD, Harvard Univ, 1953; mil/Canadian Ofcrs Tng Corps (COTC), 1942-44; pa/Instr Social Sci, Univ of KY, 1948-49; Secy Com on Race Relats, Univ of Chgo, 1949-50; Res Fellow Child Psych, Univ of MN, 1950-51; Asst Prof Psych, Univ of New Brunswick, 1951-53; Prin & Dir Res, Social Attitude Survey, 1955-67; Prof Psych, Pace Univ, 1967-; Mem: AAAS, 1948-; Am Psych Assn, 1948-; NY Acad of Sci, 1984-; r/Jewish; hon/Author of Books, *The Mystique of Mod Monarchy*, 1953; *Societies Around the World*, 1953 & 1956; Psi Chi Awd, 1953; W/W in E; Am Men of Sci; Other Biogl Listings.

BLACKBURN, DAVID THOMAS oc/Executive; b/Oct 20, 1927; h/Route 1, Box 218A, Rayle, GA 30660; ba/Atlanta, GA; m/Diana Mills; c/David Gregory, Stephen Mills, Charles Edward; ed/Att'd Univ of Tokyo, 1946-47; BS Jour, So Meth Univ, 1953; mil/AUS, Japan after Invasion, WW II; pa/Performer, Starlight Operettas, Dallas, TX, 1948-49; Asst Mgr, St Fair Music Hall, Dallas, TX, 1951-55; Mgr, Lubbock, TX Auditorium-Coliseum, 1956-61; Dir Public Relats 1961-65, VPres Public Relats 1965-71, Six Flags Over TX; VPres Show Prodns, Six Flags Corp, 1971-; Prodr of Num Live Entertainment Shows; Mem & Dir, TX Public Relats Assn, 1965-66; Mem, Dallas Press Clb & Dallas Advtg Clb; Charter Mem & Bd of Dirs, Discover TX Assn; cp/Mem, Rotary Clb & SW Rotary Clb Lubbock, TX, 1956-61; Bd of Dirs, Lubbock Symph Orch; Mem, TX Tourism Assn; Mem, Wash, GA Little Theater; Restoration of Hist Kettle Creek Manor, Wilkes Co, GA; Num Others; r/Bapt; hon/Featured in Var Articles Pub'd in: *The Flag Post*; *Live Show Review*; *Sky: Delta Mag*.

BLACKBURN, WILL R oc/Professor; Physician; b/Nov 4, 1936; h/67 Magnolia Avenue, Fairhope, AL 36532; ba/Mobile, AL; m/Hope Hutchins; ed/BS, Univ of OK, 1957; MD, Tulane Univ Col of Med, 1961; mil/UASF; Prof, Col of Phys & Surgs, Columbia Univ, 1961-64; Prof, Univ of CO Col of Med, 1964-66; Prof, Armed Forces Inst Pathol, 1966-68; Phys, Wom's & Chdn's Hosp, Bangkok, Thailand, 1966-68; Prof, PA St Univ Sch Med, 1968-74; Prof, Univ of So AL Col of Med, 1974-; Mem: Teratology Soc; Soc for Pediatric Res; Soc for Exptl Biol & Med; Am Assn Pathols; Dysmorphology Grp; Pediatric Pathol Clb; Intl Acad Pathol; Nat Perinatal Soc; r/Meth; hon/Author of Num Articles in Med Jours & Contbr to Num Med Sci Books; W/W; W/W in

Frontier Sci & Technol; Am Men of Sci.

BLACKLOW, NEIL RICHARD oc/Professor; b/Feb 26, 1938; h/144 Summer Street, Weston, MA 02193; ba/Worcester, MA; m/Margery; c/John A, Peter D; p/Leo Blacklow, Belmont, MA; Clara Blacklow (dec); sp/Charles And Gertrude Brown, Newton, MA; ed/BA, Harvard Univ, 1959; MD, Columbia Univ, 1963; mil/USPHS, 1965-68; pa/Sr Sci, NIH, Bethesda, MD, 1969-71; Assoc Prof Med, Boston Univ Sch of Med, 1971-76; Prof Med, Molecular Genetics & Microbiol, Univ of MA Med Sch, 1976-; Mem: Am Soc for Clin Invest; Am Assn for Immunols; Infectious Deseases Soc of Am; Am Col of Phys; cp/Harvard Musical Assn; hon/Author, Over 100 Articles in Field of Infectious Diseases; Assoc Editor, *Reviews of Infectious Diseases*, 1982-; Edit Bd, *Infection & Immunity*, 1981-.

BLACKMON, FLOYD F oc/Broker, Executive; b/Jul 4, 1912; h/PO Box 1341, Orangeburg, SC 29115; ba/Orangeburg, SC; m/Amy; c/Floyd F III; ed/ALP, 1954; CCE, 1977; GRI, 1978; CRPA, 1980; CRS, 1982; mil/USAF, Lt Col; pa/Gen Mgr Stores in En US, K-Mart, 1940-63; Pharm, Arnolds Pharm, 1963-67; Exec, Orangeburg C of C & Orangeburg Co Devel Bd, 1967-77; Propr, Floyd Blackmon Rlty Inc, 1977-; Chm, Retail Merchs Assn (Hazelton, PA & Bridgeport, CT), 1960-62; cp/Pres, Kiwanis Clb, Bridgeport, CT, 1963; Pres, SC C of C Execs, 1972-73; Chm & Spkr, US C of C, 1962-63; r/Prot; hon/Man of Yr Awd, Bridgeport, CT, 1964; Spec Awd, USAF, 1964; W/W in SC; Num Other Biogl Listings.

BLACKWELL, VELMA L oc/College Administrator; b/Apr 38, 1939; h/2206 Carver Street, Tuskegee, AL 36088; ba/Tuskegee, AL; p/Mr and Mrs David E Blackwell (both dec); ed/BS Tuskegee Inst, 1956; MEd, Temple Univ, 1967; PhD, FL St Univ, 1973; Addit Postgrad Study; pa/Tchr, Mobile Public Sch Sys, 1956-65; Instr, FL St Univ, 1973; Instr Dept Student Pers Sers (AL) 1968, Assoc Dir Ofc Fed Relats (Wash, DC) 1973-77, VPres for Devel (Wash DC & NYC) 1977-, Tuskegee Inst; Conslt, Var Ed Agys; CoChm, Commun Relats Com, Black Instns Pioneering Adult Ed, Tuskegee Inst; Fdr, Macon Co Chapt, Nat Coalition of 100 Black Wom; Mem, Comm on Higher Ed & Adult Learner, Am Coun on Ed; Mem: Nat Fundraising Execs; Nat Adult Ed Assn; Am Pers & Guid Assn; Nat Assn Wom Deans & Cnslrs; NEA; Phi Delta Kappa; AAUP; AAUW; Nat Adult Ed Identification; Prog For Advmt Wom in Higher Ed; VChm, St Pers Bd (AL); cp/Num Spkg Presentations; hon/Author of "An Experience in Autonomous Lrng," *Adult Ed Ldrship Jour*, 1971; "Race Relats in UK," FL St Univ, 1972; "Power & Ldrship," FL St Univ, 1973; Others; Mem, Ednl Brain Trust, Congl Black Caucus, 1976; Dist'd Cit, U Negro Col Fund; Black Exec Exch Cit, Nat Urban Leag; Achmt Cit, Omega Psi Phi Frat; Nat Think Tank for Adult Ed, 1973; Outstg Yg Wom of Am; Intl W/W of Intells; Commun Ldrs & Noteworthy Ams; W/W of Wom; DIB.

BLAESE, LOIS PATIENCE oc/Executive; b/Jan 23, 1937; h/PO Box Columbus, NJ 08022; ba/Columbus, NJ; m/

Donald F; c/Monique, Donald Jr, Nic-cole; p/Louis Frank and Erma (Mott) Lamp'l; sp/Frank W and Marie (Dei-chert) Blaese; ed/Att'd Public Schs; pa/ Div Mgr, Beeline Fashions, Bensonville, IL, 1963-73; Secy & Treas, Accurate Screw Machine Prodn Co, Div of Blaese Enterprises, Columbus, NJ, 1973-; VPres 1979-, Mem 1976-, Mansfield Twp Bd of Ed; Mem, NJ Sch Bds Assn; cp/Liaison to NJ Motion Picture & TV Comm, for Mansfield Twp; Mem Chapt Deborah, Mansfield Twp; Mem Ladies Aux, Franklin Fire Co; Mem Hist Soc, Mansfield Twp; Coor, Miss Columbus, NJ Contest; r/Meth; hon/W/W: in E, in A, of Am Wom.

BLAIR, JEAN DODDS oc/Typist; b/ Mar 27, 1919; h/2242 US Alt 19, Lot 149, Palm Harbor, FL 33563; ba/Largo, FL; m/Lloyd Joseph Blair; c/Paul Joseph Blair (dec); Joan Eileen (Blair) Morrell; p/Keith Alexander and Emma Broeffle Dodds (both dec); sp/Frank John and Bessie Snyder Blair (both dec); ed/Grad, Gouverneur HS, Gouverneur, NY, 1934; Grad, Sch of Commerce, Water-town, NY, 1936; pa/Tissue Wrapper, Rushmore Paper Mills, Natural Dam, NY, 1936-38; Mender, Hosiery Mills, Gouverneur, NY, 1938-39; Window Trimmer & Clk, JC Penney Co, Gou-verneur, NY, 1949-57; Dept Mgr, WT Grant Co, Gouverneur, NY, 1957-63; Acting Libn, Rdg Rm, Gouverneur, NY, 1963; Asst to Editor 1963-65; Editor 1967-72, *Tribune Press*, Gouverneur, NY; Prescription Dept Typist, Eckerd Drugs, Clearwater, FL, 1972-76; Unit Secy, Anclote Psychi Ctr, Tarpon Sprgs, FL, 1976-77; Prescription Dept Typist, Eckerd Drugs, Largo, FL, 1977-; Mem, St Lawrence Val Chapt, Sigma Delta Chi Soc Profl Jours; Gouverneur Grange 303; St Lawrence Co Ponoma Grange; r/Rom Cath; hon/Author of "Our Home At Last" (1967) & "Recess Time" (1973), *The Qtly*, St Lawrence Co, NY Hist Assn Mag; "Jewels," *Sunshine Mag*, 1974; Feature Articles in Num Newspapers incl'g: *Clearwater Sun; The Ldr; Dunnedin Times; Tribune Press; Water-town Daily Times; St Lawrence Plain-Dealer; Ogdensburg Jour; Massena Observer; Courier-Freeman*; Others; Good Citizen Awd, Silas Wainwright Post 6338, VFW, Gouverneur, NY, 1972; W/W: of Am Wom, of Wom; Intl W/W of Intells; Intl Book of Honor; Dir Dist'd Ams; DIB.

BLAKE, BRIAN F oc/Professor, Consultant; b/Aug 26, 1942; h/34200 Lake-view Drive, Solon, OH 44139; ba/ Cleveland, OH; m/Ann Marie; c/Kristin, Eric, Sean, Kevin; p/Andrew A Blake (dec); Mary A (White) Blake, Edison, NJ; ed/AB, St Peter's Col, 1964; MS 1966, PhD 1969, Purdue Univ; pa/Asst Prof Psych 1969-72, Assoc Prof 1972-73, St John's Univ; Asst Prof 1973-75, Assoc Prof 1975-79, Prof 1979-81, Purdue Univ; Prof Psych, Cleveland St Univ, 1981-; Pres, Decision Dynamics Inc, Cleveland, OH, 1981-; Mem: Am Psy-chol Assn; Am Mktg Assn; En Psychol Assn; MWn Psychol Assn; Sigma Xi; r/ Rom Cath; hon/Author, Over 125 Jour Articles, Book Chapts, Tech Reports & Presentations to Scholarly Socs; Awd of Excell, USDA, 1977; W/W: in MW, in Frontier Sci & Technol.

BLAKE, DUDLEY BENEDICTUS oc/ Executive; b/Jan 28, 1920; h/1619 Morningside Drive, Orlando, FL 32806;

ba/Sanford, FL; m/Marilyn Luntz; c/ Charles Roger, Russell Phillip, Geoffrey Robert, Christopher Luntz, Matthew Field; ed/Att'd Columbia Univ; mil/ Capt, Adjutant Gen Dept, 1942-46; pa/ Pres, U Solvents of Am Inc, 1969-82; Pres, Blake Paint Corp, 1950-68; Pres, FL Paint & Coatings Assn, 1963-64; cp/ Pres, Ctl FL Chapt, Am Diabetes Assn, 1982-83; Mem Bd of Dirs, Ctl FL Civic Theatre, 1964-70; W/W in FL.

BLAKE, JAMES FREDERICK JR oc/ Naval Logistician; b/Nov 21, 1933; h/ 7930 Bayberry Drive, Alexandria, VA 22306; ba/Arlington, VA; m/Barbara Darkis; c/Susan Lynn (Blake) Crabb, James Frederick III; p/James Frederick Blake (dec); Alpha (Snipes) Blake, Hillsborough, NC; sp/Frederick Ran-dolph Darkis (dec); Mildred Morris Darkis, Durham, NC; ed/BS, Univ of NC-Chapel Hill, 1955; MS, Rensselaer Polytech Inst, 1967; PMD 24, Harvard Bus Sch, 1972; Nav War Col, 1974; mil/ USN, 24 Yrs; pa/Comm'd Ensign 1955, Var Positions 1955-78, Asst Chief of Staff Supply & Finan Mgmt, Cmdr Nav Surface Force, US Atl Fleet, 1978; Ret'd Capt, 1978; Logistician 1978-81, Mgr Logistics Scis Dept 1981-82, Mgr Logis-tics Sci Dept Grp, 1982-; cp/Mem, Harvard Bus Sch Clb, Wash DC; r/ Meth; hon/Nav Commend Medal; Two Nav Awds, 1970 & 1978; W/W in S & SW.

BLAKE, KAY ANN oc/Nurse; b/Feb 1, 1950; h/3222 Elma Drive, Midland, TX 79707; ba/Midland, TX; m/Kenneth Noel; p/John Ruskin and Elizabeth (Green) Porter, Shamrock, TX; sp/John Wesley (Jr) and Helen (Hise) Blake, Shamrock, TX; ed/Att'd Amarillo Col, 1968-69; Nrsg Deg, Amarillo Co of Voc Nsg, 1970-71; pa/Nurses Aide, Sham-rock Gen Hosp, 1968-69; Nurse, Labor & Delivery, NW TX Hosp, Amarillo, TX, 1971-76; Pvt Scrub Nurse, TX Tech Un Sch of Med, Amarillo, 1972-73; Dir of Nurses, Leisure Lodge Inc, Midland, 1977-; Labor & Delivery Charge Nurse, Midland, 1977-; Mem, NA of Ob & Gyn; r/Ch of Christ; W/W of Wom in Am.

BLAKE, MARGARET PEYTON oc/ Regional Accountant; b/Jul 10, 1941; h/ 312 Paulette Street, Houma, LA 70360; ba/Houma, LA; m/Charles C; c/Charles Jr, Virginia Lynn; p/Mr and Mrs Liston Peyton, Raymond, MS; sp/L C Blake (ded); Mrs Elva C Blake, Leakesville, MS; ed/AD, Hinds Jr Col, 1959; BS, Univ of So MS, 1961; VTIE, LA St Univ (LSU); Computer Sci, Nicholls St Univ, 1979-80; pa/Jr Auditor, Slay & Slay CPA, 1960-62; Ofc Mgr, L B Letcher Ins, 1964-66; Acct & Pers Ofcr, S LA Voc Tech Inst & St of LA, 1969-84; Reg Acct, Houma Reg 3 Voc-Tech Ctr, 1984-; Mem, Pers Mgmt Assn of Ter-rebonne Parish; Treas, Mtl Hlth Assn; cp/Adm Bd & Fin Com, 1st Meth Ch, 1982-85; H L Bourgeois Band Boosters, LA St Pers Coun; Terrebonne Parish Coun on Nsg Home Care; Secy, Ever-green Band Boosters, 1979-81; U Meth Wom; Ldrs Coun, BSA; Den Mother, CSA; r/Meth.

BLAKE, MARILYN LUNTZ oc/Exec-utive; b/Dec 6, 1922; h/1619 Morning-side Drive, Orlando, FL 32806; ba/ Sanford, FL; m/Dudley Benedictus; c/ Charles Roger, Russell Phillip, Geoffrey Robert, Christopher Luntz, Matthew Field; p/Charles Thurston and Vera

Dorothy (Field) Luntz (both dec); sp/ Florence B Blake (dec); ed/Grad, Scars-dale HS, 1940; Att'd Bennington Col, 1940-42; pa/Dir of Woms Activ, WHBC, Canton, OH, 1943-44; VPres, Blake Paint Corp, Sanford, FL, 1955-68; Freelance Documentary Film Writer, Orange Co Bd of Ed & FL St Dept of Ed, 1969-78; Exec VPres, U Solvents of Am Inc, Sanford, FL, 1969-; Mem, Quota Intl Inc; cp/Intl Pres 1981-82, 1st VPres 1980-81, Intl Treas 1978-79, S Area Dir 1976-78, Gov Dir 27 1974-76, Bd of Dir 1981-, Am Diabetes Assn; Bd of Dir, Am Cancer Soc of Orange Co, 1978-79; Bd of Dir: Orange, Seminole, & Osceola Cos Easter Seal Soc, 1975-76; Author, Over 36 Films incl'g: "Media in Action," 1974; Nat Paint & Coatings Awd for Contbn to Indust, 1967; Nat Film Indust Cindy Awd for Documen-tary Film "Gateway to Tomorrow," 1969; W/W in S & SW.

BLAKE, TERRI (THERSEA LANDS BLALACK) oc/Author; b/Sep 10, 1903; ba/570 N Rossmore Avenue, Holly-wood, CA 90004; m/Russell E Blalack (dec); c/Russell E, David E, Ronald R; p/Fran and Anna Lands (both dec); ed/ Att'd Orange Coast Col, 1963-64; Att'd LA City Col, 1965; pa/Real Est Devel-oper, Hollywood, CA, 1953-62; Actress in Var Motion Pictures, 1955-62; TV Hostess, "Take a Break w Terri Blake," Dayton, OH, 1966; Spkr, Var Grps & Orgs, 1966-78; Prodr, USO Shows, VA, 1955-59; Choreographer for Night Clb Act, 1983; cp/Started Campaign for Nat Grandparents Day, 1968 (Signed into Law Sep 5, 1979); Started Campaign Agnst Mandatory Retirement; Mem, Nat Repub Com; Bd of Dir & in Charge of Publicity, Hollywood Wilshire Symph Assn; Pres LA Br, Nat Leag Am Pen Wom, 1974-76; Order of En Star; Thursday Morning, Newport Bch, CA; hon/Author of Book, *You Can Do It Too*, 1970 & 1979; Recip, Mayor's Commun Ser Awd, LA, 1972; Commun Ser Awd, LA, 1972; Commun Ser Awd, New Neighbor Clb, Dayton, OH, 1971; World's Most Glamorous Grand-mother, Holywood C of C, 1957; Ever Ythful Sr Inspiration of Yr, Gtr NY Citizens Soc, 1972; Wom of Yr, Intl Authors Guild, 1973; Pin-Up Grand-mother, Am Legion, Oceanside, CA, 1979; White House Honoree as Fdr of Grandparents Day Sept 7, 1979; Plaque for Entertaining Vets, CA Legis, 1981; Pres's Cit & Wom of Achmt Awd, Nat Leag Am Pen Wom, 1981; 1st Prize, Intl Poetry Soc, 1969 & 1977; Honored by Congl Record for Retirement Legis, 1975 & 1978; 1st Grandmother Fea-tured in *Playboy Mag*, Aug, 1982; Num Other Hons.

BLAKENEY, ANNE BACON oc/ Occupational Therapist; b/Mar 16, 1947; h/Route 1, 29 Birnam Wood, Chapel Hill, NC 27514; ba/Chapel Hill, NC; m/Michael Louis; c/Ruth Ellen, Kathleen; p/David Ray Bacon (dec); Ruth Ann Bacon, Knoxville, TN; sp/Mr and Mrs T O Blakeney, Baton Rouge, LA; ed/BS, Univ of TN, 1969; MSOT, Boston Univ, 1974; mil/USPHS, 1976-77; pa/Rec Wk in S Korea & US Army Hosp Ft Polk, LA, ARC, 1969-71; Staff Occupl Therapist, USPHS Hosp, Carville, LA, 1975-77; Instr 1978-81, Asst Prof 1982-, Med Allied Hlth Professions, Univ of NC-Chapel Hill;

Mem Com of St Assn Pres, Mem Rep Assem, Am Occupl Therapy Assn, 1974-; VPres, Pres, LA Occupl Therapy Assn; Cont'g Ed Com, AOTA Rep, NC Occupl Therapy Assn; Mem, Ctr for Neurodevel Studies; Mem, World Fedn of Occupl Therapists; r/Christian; hon/ Author of "Static Splinting & Temperature Assessment of Insensitive Hand," in *Rehab of Hand*, 2nd Edition, 1982; "Exploring Sensory Integrative Dysfunction in Process Schizophrenia," *Am Jour Occupl Therapy*, 1983; W/W of Am Wom.

BLAKUT, MITCHELL ANTHONY oc/Engineering Supervisor; b/Feb 15, 1921; h/5725 North Marmora, Chicago, IL 60646; ba/Northbrook, IL; m/Helen; c/Mary (Blakut) Robak, Charles Blakut, p/Anna Blakut, Mundelein, IL; sp/Mr and Mrs John G Mikos (both dec); ed/ Grad HS, 1939; Att'd 2 Yr Col; mil/AUS, Inf S/Sgt, 1944-46; pa/QC Engrg Supvr, B & H Home Video, Present; QC Engr Mgr, A B Dick Co, 1952-58; Sr Process Engr & Toolmaker, Skilsaw Inc, 1954-58; Sr Process Engr, Pioneer Tool & Engrg, 1958-61; Sr Mfg Engr, Pyle Nat, 1961-64; QC Mgr, Bell & Howell, 1964; Life Mem, Am Soc of QC Cert'd Mfg Engrs, 1967; Reg'd Profl Mfg Engr, CA, 1979; cp/Order of Arrow (18 Yrs), Asst Scoutmaster, BSA; Commr, Confrat Christian Doct, Chgo Area Cath Arch Diocese; r/Cath; hon/Supvr Master Cert, 1967; Adv'd Supvr Tech Awd, 1979; W/W: of W & MW, in Commun Ser; Intl Book of Hon; Commun Ldrs of Am; Men of Achmt; Personalities of Am; Personalities of W & MW.

BLANCHARD, ROBERT OSBORN oc/University Dean; b/Jul 5, 1939; h/2 Meserve Road, Durham, NH 03824; ba/ Durham, NH; m/Ellen L; c/Lori A, Gregory S; p/Nelson and Luella Blanchard, Cumberland Ctr, ME; ed/AAS, So Main Voc Tech Inst, 1959; BS, Univ of ME-Gorham, 1964; MEd 1969, PhD 1971, Univ of GA; mil/Air NG; pa/Jr HS Sci Tchr, Northbrook, ME & Windsor, CT, 1964-67; Postdoct Fellow, Univ of GA, 1971-72; Asst Prof & Chm Dept Bot & Plant Pathol 1972-76, Assoc Prof 1977-, Assoc Dean of Resident Instrn 1982-, Prof 1984-, Univ of NH; Chm NE Sect 1984, Nat Resident Instrn Com on Org & Policy; Mem: Sigma Xi; Gamma Sigma Delta; Phi Sigma; Alpha Zeta; Mycological Soc of Am; Botanical Soc of Am; Am Phytopath Soc; NE Forest Pest Coun; cp/Grange, 1953-; JCs, 1965-67; Oyster River Yth Assn, 1973-; r/Cath; hon/Author, Over 60 Articles in Profl Jours; Author of Textbook on Tree Diseases; 25 Yr Dist'd Ser Awd, Grange, 1978; Fac Merit Awd, Univ of NH, 1979; JC of Mo, 1966; Outstg Airman Awd, 253rd Comm Grp, 1962; W/W: in E, in Frontier Sci & Technol.

BLANCK, ANDREW R oc/Executive; b/Feb 7, 1925; h/89 Prospect Place, Rutherford, NJ 07070; ba/Rutherford, NJ; m/Edna H Ruppert; c/Elaine Lois, Evelyn Joyce; p/Andrew G Blanck (dec); ed/BA, NY Univ, 1950; MA, Polytech Inst of Bklyn, 1953; ScD, Sussex Inst Technol, 1959; pa/Proj Engr, Centro Res Labs, 1950-53; Tech Ser Engr, Celanese Corp of Am, 1953-56; Chief Applications Lab & Chief Elect Lab, W R Grace & Co, 1956-58; Proj Coor, AUS Res Ctr, 1958-65; Fdr, Pres & Tech Dir,

Rutherford Res, 1956-; Fac Mem, NY Univ Sch Cont'g Ed, 1968-; Num Chm & Com Mbrships: ASIM; IEEE; ACCHCE; ACIL; Others; r/Bapt; hon/ Author, *Glossary of Plastics Indust*, 1973; Author, Over 100 Articles & Tech Papers; Keynote Spkr, Conf on Elect Insulation, London, 1963; Am Men of Sci; W/W: in E, in Elect, Specifying & Purchasing; Other Biogl Listings.

BLANK, FRANKLIN oc/Freelance Writer; b/Oct 19, 1921; h/5477 Cedonia Avenue, Baltimore, MD 21206; ba/ Baltimore, MD; m/Annette Evelyn Chotin; p/Louis J and Anna (Liefer) Blank (both dec); sp/Solomon and Frances Chotin (both dec); ed/BA Bus Adm, SEn Univ, 1956; AA, Univ of Balto, 1966; Grad Wk, Dept of Agri, Wash, DC, 1960; Writing Sem, *Writer's Digest*, 1981; Mass Communs (Jour), Col of Notre Dame, Balto, MD, 1983; Cont'g Ed Jour & Public Relats, Towson St Univ, 1984; mil/USAAF, 1942-46; AF Resvs, 1946-49; pa/Profl Writer; Washington-Based Stringer for Var Newspapers; Mem: Authors Guild; Nat Writers Clb; Life Fellow, Intl Biog Assn; Foun Cong & Adv Bd Mem (MD St Com), Am Security Coun, 1984; Intl Platform Assn; Am Fedn Govt Employees; Blood Donor Assur Grp, ARC; Univ of Balto Alumni Assn; Assoc Jewish Charities & Welfare; cp/Petition Ldr, Vote Agnst SALT II, Am Security Coun, 1980; Petition & Team Ldr for Employees, Social Security Adm, 1983; Sponsor, Adopt-A-Fam, City of Balto, MD; r/Jewish; hon/Author of Fiction Play, "Struggle for an Unknown Cause," *Jour Irish Lit*, 1976; Author of Articles: "Despite Wash," 1982; "Med Evac Helicopter-MD Style," 1982; "Charlie Magicop," a Grit Fam Newspaper Feature, 1979; Num Edit Lttrs to Reg Newspapers & Labor Union Pubs; Aided *Emer Mag* as Recip, Maggie Awd for Best Wn Pub, 1982; 11th Place Hon Mention for "Angel of Mercy," *Writer's Digest* Writing Competition, 1980; Cert Awd 1961, Superior Awd 1963, US Postmaster Gen; Spec Recog Awd, Am Security Coun Edn Foun-Pentagon Ed Ctr, 1979; Spec Achmt Awd, Social Security Adm, 1982; Lightweight Boxing Medal, 1942; Rifleman's Shooting Medal; Am Theatre Ribbon; WW II Victory Medal; Asia PTO Ribbon; Good Conduct Medal; W/W: Authors & Writers, of Intells; DIB; Men of Achmt; Intl Book of Hon.

BLASH, HOSEZELL oc/School Principal; b/Dec 12, 1939; h/PO Box 272, Jeffersonville, GA 31044; ba/Danville, GA; m/Rosa Shines; c/Kimberly Michelle, Rajyumar DeShawn, Kendra Marguita; p/Mr and Mrs Roosevelt Black, Dry Br, GA; sp/Mr and Mrs Willie Shines (both dec); ed/BS, 1968; MEd, 1974; mil/USAF; USN; pa/Attendant & Hlth Ser Tech, Col St Hosp, 1975; Elem Sch Prin, 1975-76; Prin, S Elem Sch, Danville, GA, 1976-; Treas, Twiggs Co Assn of Edrs, 1977-; Secy, Twiggs Co Public Lib, 1982; Advr, Twiggs Co Neighborhood Ctr, 1969-70; Chm Prog Com 1977-, & Num Other Coms, S Elem Sch; Chaplain, Phi Beta Sigma Frat, 1960; cp/Financial Secy 1977-, Secy Deacon Bd 1982, Chm Mem's Day Prog 1981, Mt Olive Bapt Ch; VPres 1981, SS Tchr 1960-, VSupt of SS 1981-, Mt Olive Ch Mission; Coor, BSA, 1978-;

Jr Wardman, Masonic Lodge, 1975; Vol, Heart Fund, 1979; Vol Wkr, Var Election Campaign Coms, 1980; Num Others; r/Bapt; hon/Author of Poem "The Optimist & The Pessimist," 1978; Author of Songs: "Why Keep Hesitatin'," 1976; "I Gonna Sing Sunshine," 1977; Lt Col, Aide De Comp Cert from George Busbee, Gov of GA; Outstg Yg Men in Am; W/W in S & SW.

BLAUER, AARON CLYDE oc/Professor, Botanist; b/Apr 26, 1939; h/295 North 300 East, Box 16-5, Ephraim, UT 84627; ba/Ephraim, UT; m/Geaneen Whittle; c/Alan Clyde, Robert Darrell, Lucille, Anthony Henry, Elizabeth, Amy Geaneen; p/Henry William and Lucile Woodbury Blauer (both dec); sp/Darrell Eugene Whittle, Oakley, ID; Rettie Elizabeth Gorringe (dec); ed/BS 1964, MS 1965, Brigham Yg Univ; Postgrad Study: Cornell Univ, 1965-66; Univ of AL, Sum 1973; pa/Botany Lab Instr, Brigham Yg Univ, 1962-64; Forest Range Tech, Uintah Nat Forest, UT, Sums 1963 & 1964; Instr 1966-71, Asst Prof 1971-78, Assoc Prof Biol 1978-, Snow Col, Ephraim, UT; Range Res Tech Sum 1967 & 1973, Botanist Sum 1974-, Inter-mt Forest & Range Expt Sta, Ogden, UT; Mem: AM Horticultural Soc; Botanical Soc of Am; Am Inst of Biol Sci; Nat Sci Tchrs Assn; NY Acad of Scis; AAAS; UT Assn Acad Profls; cp/Chm, Repub Voting Dist, 1970; Del, Repub St Conv, 1970; Mem, Ephraim City Beautification Com; Emer Med Tech, 1977-78; Merit Badge Coun 1966-, Scout Master 1978, Scout Com Mem 1978-83, Unit Commr 1982-, BSA; Num Others; r/Served as Bishop, Currently High Councilor, LDS (Mormon); hon/Author of Num Botanical Sci Articles incl'g: "Growth Perf Comparisons Among 18 Accessions of Fourwing Saltbush (Atriplex canescens) at 2 Sites in Ctl UT," 1983; "Site Influence on Frequency of Male & Female Flowers for Some Monoecious Plant Species," 1981; Others; hon/3 Yr Nat Def Edn Act F'ship to Brigham Yg Univ, 1964; Outstg Male Student 1964, Dean's Scholar List Srs Top 10% Col of Agri & Bio Scis 1964, Nat Sci Foun F'ship 1965, Brigham Yg Univ; Phi Etta Sigma; Beta Beta Beta; Sigma Xi; Phi Kappa Phi; Shell Foun F'ship in Plant Sci, Cornell Univ, 1965-66; Tchr of Yr, Snow Col, 1967, 1972 & 1977; People-to-People Intl Botanical Sci Del to Repub of S Africa, 1984; W/W in W.

BLAYLOCK, WILMA FRANCES oc/ Educator, Curriculum Consultant; b/ Jan 28, 1940; h/1171 Marcia Road, Memphis, TN 38117; ba/Memphis, TN; p/William C and Lema L Blaylock, Memphis, TN; ed/BA, Blue Mtn Col, 1962; MEd, Duke Univ, 1974; pa/Tchr, Memphis City Schs, 1962-70; Exch Tchr, from Memphis to Am Sch in Guatemala, 1967; Instrnl Conslt 1970-82, Curric Conslt 1982-, Memphis City Schs; Mem: Assn for Supvn & Curric Devel; IRA; TN Rdg Assn; Exec Bd, W TN Rdg Assn, 1976-77; Nat Assn for Ed Yg Chd; Memphis City Schs Admrs Assn; VPres 1970-72, Pres 1972-74, TN St Hist 1978-80, Lambda Chapt, Alpha Delta Kappa; r/Meth; hon/ Contbg Author: *One, Two, Three, Go!*, 1978; *For the Little Ones*, 1980; *Home is a Lrng Place*, 1980; Awd for Excell in Developing Curric for Newspaper in

Clrm Prog, 1979; W/W in S & SW.

BLAYTON, DORIS ADA oc/ Teacher, Attorney; b/Oct 19, 1922; h/ 1235 Martin Luther King Jr Drive, Southwest, Atlanta, GA 30314; ba/ Atlanta, GA; p/Mr and Mrs Jesse B Blayton (both dec); ed/AB, Spelman Col, 1943; Att'd Univ of Chgo, 1943-44 & 1945; LLB, JD, John Marshall Law Sch (Chgo), 1949; MBA 1962, MA Ed 1974, Atlanta Univ; pa/Admitted to IL Bar, 1950; Admitted to GA Bar, 1951; Instr, GA St Industl Col, Savannah, 1944-45; Instr, AR A&M Col for Negroes, 1966-67; Tchr, Blayton Sch of Acct & Blayton Bus Col, 1943-77; Pvt Pract; Staff, J B Blayton Co, CPA, 1943-76; Tchr, Public Schs of Atlanta, 1973-; Mem: Gate City Bar Assn; Black Wom's Law Assn; Nat Coun Negroes Wom; YWCA; NAACP; U Negroes Col Fund; NBA; NANBPW; NTE; AAE; SCLC; r/Christian Bapt; hon/High Hons, Spelman Col, 1943; Res, Asst, Univ of Chgo; W/W: Am Wom, of Wom; DIB; Personalities of the S.

BLEDSOE, CARL B "BEV" oc/ Speaker of the House, CO State Legislature; b/Oct 6, 1923; h/PO Box 516, Hugo, CO 80821; ba/Denver, CO; m/ Alice; c/Robert Carl, Thomas Beverly, Christopher Joel; p/Carl and Josie Bledsoe (both dec); p/Owner, C B Bledsoe Ranch, NW of Wild Horse, CO, 1949-; Mem, CO St Legis, 1972-; Secy 2 Yrs, Cheyenne Co Rep Ctl Com; Secy 1958-62, Lincoln Co Stockmen's Assn; Pres, Cheyenne Co Farm Bur, 1962-64; 2nd VPres & Chm of Bd 1965, 1st VPres 1966, Pres 1967, CO Cattlemen's Assn; Mem, Com on Ednl Endeavor; Mem, CO St Fiscal Policy Com, 1968; Mem, CO St Bd of Vet Med, 1968-72; Appt'd Mem & Elected Mem, CO St Ho of Reps, 1972; VChm, Ho of Reps Com on Labor & Bus Affairs, 1973-74; VChm 1973, Chm 1976, Ho of Reps Legis Audit Com; Chm, Ho of Reps Fin Com, 1979-80; Spkr of Ho of Reps, 1981-82 & Re-elected 1983-84; cp/Secy 6 Yrs, Pres 2 Yrs, Kit Carson Sch Bd; Mem Bd of Dirs, CO Housing Inc; Mem, St Bd of Equalization, 1983-; Mem, Gov's Task Force on Ed, 1983-; VChm, Wn Reg, Coun of St Govts, 1983-; r/Prot; hon/ Alpha Zeta; CO Assn of Sch Bds Hon Rol; 1968; Life Mem, Lincoln Co Stockmen's Assn; Ser Awd as Chm of Audit Com; Legis Awd, CO Lib Assn, 1981; Hon Marine Corps Leag Mem; W/W in W; Men of Achmt.

BLEDSOE, JOSEPH CULLIE oc/ Professor; b/Sep 16, 1918; h/260 Burnett St, Athens, GA 30605; ba/Athens, GA; m/Adele Berryman; c/Joseph Christian, Gisela (Bledsoe) Bunch; p/James Arthur and Elizabeth Denney Bledsoe (both dec); sp/Mack M and Frances Christian Berryman (both dec); ed/AB 1939, MS 1940, Univ of GA; PhD, Vanderbilt Univ, 1952; mil/AUS, AGD 1942-46, PTO 3 Yrs, Capt; pa/Rating Examr, US Civil Ser Comm (Reg Ofc), 1940-42; Pers Conslt, AUS, Asia PTO, 1942-46; Ednl Psych, Air Univ, Maxwell AFB, 1946-47; Asst Prof 1948-56, Assoc Prof 1956-60, Prof 1960-83, Univ of GA; Mem: Am Psychol Assn; Am Ednl Res Assn; Psi Chi; En Ednl Res Assn; GA Ednl Res Ass; Num Com Positions

& Fac Gov'g Bd, Univ of GA Coun; r/ Bapt; hon/Author of *Essentials of Ednl Res*, 1963 & 1972; *Study Guide in Statl Inference*; Over 100 Articles & Reports Pub'd in Profl Jours & Pubs; Jesse Jones Fellow in Ed, 1947-48 & 1951-52; 1st Recip Awd of Excell in Tchr Ed, Kappa Delta Pi, 1964; Fellow, Am Psychol Assn, 1971; W/W in S; Am Men of Sci; Intl Writers; Other Biogl Listings.

BLEJER, HÉCTOR P oc/Physician; b/ Dec 17, 1933; h/4477 Wilshire Boulevard, LA, CA 90010; ba/Beverly Hills, CA; p/Luís E and Zoraida P Blejer, LA, CA; ed/ Att'd Bishop's Col Sch, Lennoxville, Québec, Canada, 1947-51; BSc Biol 1954, MD & CM Med Surg 1958, McGill Univ, Montréal, Canada; DIH Industl Hlth, Univ of Toronto, Ontario, Canada, 1963; pa/Pvt Pract, LA, CA, 1979-; Dir, Occupl Hlth Dept, The City of Hope Med Ctr, Duarte, CA, 1976-78; Dept Dir Div of Field Studies & CLin Invest, Nat Inst Occupl Safety & Hlth, USPHS, DHEW, Cinc, OH, 1975; Head So CA Bur of Occupl Hlth & Envir Epidemiology, CA St Dept of Public Hlth, LA, CA, 1965-74; Mem: Am Acad Occupl Med, 1977-; Am Col Preventive Med, 1969-; Am Occupl Med Assn, 1966-; Am Mem 1966-80, Hon Mem 1980-, Am Conf Govtl Industl Hygienists; CA Med Assn, 1982-; LA Co Med Assn, 1982-; Mem 1970-, Councellor 1975-77, Soc for Occupl & Envir Hlth; Alpha Delta Phi, 1953-; Num Others; hon/ Author, Over 300 Pub'd Sci Articles, Book Chapts, Bltns, Res Reports & Monographs; F'ships: Am Col Preventive Med, 1969; Am Occupl Med Assn, 1970; Am Acad Occupl Med, 1980; Cert Commend, St of CA Merit Awd Bd, 1969; W/W in W; Am Men of Sci; Intl W/W in Commun Ser.

BLINCOE, CLIFTON oc/Professor; b/Nov 21, 1926; h/1041 University Terrace, Reno, NV 89503; ba/Reno, NV; m/Bertha Fisher; c/Clyde, Allen, Carl; p/C R Blincoe (dec); sp/Mrs J P Fisher; ed/BS Chem, 1947; MA, 1948; PhD, 1955; pa/Asst Prof, Univ of MO, 1947-55; Prof, Univ of NV, 1956-; Mem: Biophy Soc; Am Chem Soc; Am Soc of Animal Sci; Soc for Computer Simulation; Soc of Chem Indust (London); NY Acad of Scis; Int Soc of Quantum Biol; hon/Author, Over 50 Sci Articles; Fulbright Lectr in Biochem, Univ of Dublin, Eire, 1969-70; Travel F'ship for Trace Mineral Res, 1974; W/W in W; Am Men of Sci; Other Biogl Listings.

BLIZNAKOV, EMILE GEORGE oc/ Scientist; b/Jul 28, 1926; h/189 Ledges Road, Ridgefield, CT 06877; ba/Ridgefield, CT; p/George P and Paraskeva Bliznakov (both dec); ed/MD, Acad of Med, Fac of Med, Sofia, Bulgaria, 1953; pa/Dir Reg Sta for Hygiene & Epidemiology, Chief Dist Dept Hlth, Pirdop, Bulgaria, 1953-55; Staff Scist Microbiol Res Inst Epidemiology & Microbiol, Min of Public Hlth, Sofia, 1955-59; Vis'g Scist, Gamaleya Res Inst Epidemiology & Microbiol, Acad Med Scis, Moscow, 1958-59; Sr Staff Scist & Prof Life Scis 1961-81, Dir Pers 1968-74, VPres 1974-76, Pres 1976-81, N Eng Inst, Ridgefield, CT; Exec Dir Res & Devel, Libra Res, 1981-83; Pres, Scist & Dir, Lupus Res Inst, Rockville, MD, 1981-; Dir, Child Safety Corp; Conslt, Num Industl, Pharm, & Public Relats Firms; Mem: AMA; Am Fedn Clin Res; Fellow,

Royal Soc Tropical Med & Hygiene (London); Am Soc Microbiol; NY Acad Scis; Am Col Toxicology; Am Soc Neurochem; Inter-Am Soc for Chemotherapy; Reticuloendothelial Soc; Bioelectromagnetic Soc; AAAS; r/En Orthodox; hon/Author, Over 80 Sci Articles, Res Reports & Papers Pub'd in Profl Jours & Presented at Orgnl Meetings; W/W: in Am, in Frontier Sci & Technol; Am Men & Wom in Sci; Other Biogl Listings.

BLOCK, ROBERT MICHAEL oc/ Endodontist, Researcher; b/Oct 15, 1947; h/1322 Woodkrest Drive, Flint, MI 48504; ba/Flint, MI; m/Anne M; p/ Dr and Mrs W D Block, Ann Arbor, MI; sp/Mr and Mrs W B Marshall, Greencastle, PA; ed/BA, DePauw Univ, 1969; DDS, Univ of MI, 1974; Gen Pract Resident 1974-75, Cert in Endontics 1975-77, Univ of CT; MS Pathol, Med Col of VA, VA Commonwlth Univ, 1978; Diplomate, Am Bd of Endodontics, 1982; pa/Gen Pract Resident Univ Hlth Ctr 1974-75, Res Assoc Dept Endodontics 1975-78, Univ of CT-Farmington, CT; Vis'g Sr Sci, Nat Med Res Inst, Bethesda, MD, 1976-78; Endodontic Resident Clin Col 1975-78, Instr Pathol Dept 1977-78, Med Col of VA, VA Commonwlth Univ, Richmond, VA; Res Assoc, McGuirge VA Hosp, Richmond, VA, 1977-78; Endodontist & Pulp Biol Res, Flint, MI, 1978-; Mem 1975-, Res Com 1978-81, Am Assn of Endodontists; St Bd Exam Com 1983-84, MI Assn of Endodontists; Mem Pulp Biol Sect, Intl & Am Assn of Dental Res Mem, ADA; MI Dental Assn; Genesee Dist Dental Soc; Ralph Sommer Endodontic Study Clb; VChm 1980-84, Lapeer Dental Study Clb; hon/ Author & Co-Author, Over 100 Sci Articles, Textbook Chapts & Res Papers in Profl Pubs; HEW Sum Res F'ships 1970 & 1971, NIH; Am Student Dental Assn Preventive Dentistry Awd 1973, Jonathan Taft Soc 1973-74, Univ of MI; Edward P Hatton Awd, Intl Assn of Dental Res, 1977; Meml Res Awd, Am Assn of Endodontists, 1977; W/W: in the World, in Frontier Sci & Technol.

BLOCK, WALTER DAVID oc/ Research Director, Professor; b/Oct 16, 1911; h/1335 Glendaloch Circle, Ann Arbor, MI 48104; ba/Ann Arbor, MI; m/ Thelma L; c/Robert M, Margery E; p/ Samuel and Minah Block (both dec); ed/ BSEE, Univ of Dayton, 1933; MS Biol Chem 1934, PhD Biol Chem 1938, Univ of MI; pa/Instr Biol Chem 1939-44, Asst Prof Bio Chem 1944-48, Assoc Prof Bio Chem 1948-67, Prof Human Nutrition & Biol Chem 1967-81, Prof Emeritus 1981-, Univ of MI; Res Dir, Caylor-Nickel Res Fdn, 1981-; Clin Dir, Caylor-Nickel Hosp Labs, 1984-; Conslts Positions w Univ of MI, Caylor-Nickel Fdn & Var Govt Agys, 1947-78; Mem: Nat Mbrship Com, Soc of Exptl Bio & Med, 1975-78; Mem of Gov's Mtl Hlth Comm, St of IN, 1968-70; Am Inst of Nutrition; Am Soc for Biochem; r/Jewish; hon/Co-Author, "Monograph on Metabolism, Pharm & Therapeutic Uses of Gold Compounds," 1956; Var Book Chapts, Reviews & Symp Papers; Over 120 Sci Articles Pub'd in Profl Jours incl'g: *N Eng Jour of Med*; *Am Jour Clin Nutrition*; *Ecol Food & Nutrition*; *Jour of Biomechs*; *Archives of Internal Medicine*; Other Pubs; W/W;

Am Men of Science.

BLODGETT, ELSIE GRACE oc/Executive, Businesswoman; b/Aug 2, 1921; h/2285 West Mendocino Street, Stockton, CA 95204; m/Charles; c/Carolyn Doyel, Charleen Bier, Lyndon; p/Charles Ishmal and Naoma Florence Worthington Robison; ed/Att'd Warrensburg St Tchrs Col (MO), 1939-40; BA, Fresno St Col, 1953; pa/Tchr, Schs in MO & CA, 1940-42 & 1947-72; Owner & Mgr, Rental Units, 1965-79; Exec Dir, San Joaquin Co Rental Property Assn Inc, 1970-81; Ptnr, Key W Property Mgmt & Owner, Crystal Sprgs Hlth World, 1980-; Editor, News Bltn; Bd of Dirs, Stockton BBB; St Treas Wom's Div, Nat Apt Assn, 1977-79; CA Ret'd Tchrs Assn; cp/Repub Party; Zonta; PTA; GSA; BSA; Bd of Dirs, Stockton Goodwill Industs; r/Meth; hon/Named w Husband as Mr & Mrs Apt Owner of San Joaquin Co, 1977; Personalities of W.

BLOM, JoANN E oc/Marketing/Distributive Education Coordinator; b/Jun 11, 1945; h/45 Mohawk Trail, West Melford, NJ 07480; ba/West Melford, NJ; m/Neil Blom; c/Joy Blom; p/Mr and Mrs Alfred Ruberto, Medland Pk, NJ; sp/Mrs Tina Blom, Ramsey, NJ; ed/Att'd Lab Inst of Mdsg, 1966; BA, Montclair St Col, 1974; Mktg/Distrib Ed Coor, W Melford HS, 1974-; Asst to Mds Mgr, Sealfon's, 1969-71; Asst Buyer, De Pinna, 1967-68; Ex Trainee, Bloomingdales, NYC, 1966-67; Mem: MJ Mktg/Distrib Ed Coors Assn; No Mktg/Distrib Ed Coors Assn; W Melford Ed Assn; NEA; Epsilon Delta Epsilon; r/Cath; hon/Nom'd W Melford Tchr of Yr, to NJ Ed Assn, 1982-83; Nom'd Princeton Tchr Awd, 1982-83; W/W in E.

BLOOM, HAROLD oc/Professor; b/Jul 11, 1930; h/179 Linden Street, New Haven, CT 06511; ba/New Haven, CT; m/Jeanne Gould; c/Daniel, David; p/William Bloom (dec); ed/BA, Cornell Univ, 1951; PhD, Yale Univ, 1955; pa/Fac Mem 1955-, Currently Sterling Prof of Humanities, Yale Univ; r/Jewish; hon/Author of 16 Books incl'g: The Anxiety of Influence, 1973; A Map of Misreading, 1975; Agon, 1982; Freud: Transference & Auth, 1983; Hon DHL, Buston Col, 1974; Hon Doct, Yeshiva Univ, 1976; Num W/W & Other Biogl Listings.

BLOOM, MIRIAM K oc/Psychoanalyst; b/Dec 22, 1920; h/2240 Linden Avenue, Boulder, CO 80302; ba/Same; m/Louis R; c/Robert, Fredi, Steven, Debra; ed/BS 1941, MA 1955, Univ of IL; ABP, CA Grad Inst; pa/Psychoanal, Pvt Pract, 1969-; Fdr & Dir, CO Ctr for Mod Psychoanal Studies Inc, 1982-; Sch Psychol, Public Schs in NY & CO, 1955-81; Coor, Prog for Emotionally Disturbed Chd, Longmont, CO, 1978-81; Tchr, Public Schs in IL & NY, 1940-55; Mem: Nat Assn for Accredetation of Psychoanal; Am Psychol Assn; CO Psychol Assn; CO Soc of Sch Psychols; r/Jewish; hon/Co-Author, "The Feeling Avoider," in Guidance, 1972; "Mod Psychoanal in Fam Therapy," in Fam Therapy, 1973; W/W: in Am Wom, in W.

BLOSSER, PATRICIA ELLEN oc/Professor; b/Apr 17, 1931; h/2606 Brandon Road, Columbus, OH 43221; ba/Columbus, OH; p/Mabel E Blosser, Columbus, OH; ed/BA, The Col of

Wooster, 1953; MA, Univ of No CO, 1956; MA Liberal Studies, Wesleyan Univ, CT, 1962; PhD, OH St Univ, 1970; pa/Prof 1970-, Tchg & Res Assoc 1967-69, Col of Ed, OH St Univ; Sci Tchr, Shaker Hgts Schs, OH, 1961-67; Sci Tchr, Glencoe Schs, IL, 1959-61; Sci Tchr, Wooster Schs, 1955-56; Sci Tchr, Margaretta Twp Schs, OH, 1953-55; Bd Mem & Reg Dir, NSTA; NARST; Pres, AETS, 1976-77; Pres, OH St Univ Chapt, Phi Delta Kappa, 1976-77; ASCD; ATE; AERA; Tch Ed Sect Editor, Sci Ed, 1978-81; Bd Mem & Jour Editor, Sci Ed Coun of OH; r/Prot; hon/Author, Crit Review of the Role of Lab in Sci Tchg, 1981; Review of Res in Tchr Behavior in Sci Clrms & Related Content Areas, 1973; Handbook of Effective Questioning Techniques, 1973; Editor: Invests in Sci Ed, 1978-; SECO Jour, 1983-; Jennings Master Tchr; Margaret L White F'ship, Delta Kappa Gamma, 1967 & 1969; W/W: of Wom, of Am Wom, of Wom in Ed; Ldrs in Ed.

BLOSSER, PATRICIA O oc/Executive; b/Feb 21, 1932; ba/27 West 150 North Avenue, West Chicago, IL 60185; m/Robert M; c/Daniel, Robert, Thomas, Kimberly, Vonnie; p/Issac & Loretta Equedt (both dec); sp/Walter & Sara Blosser, Naples, FL; pa/Owner & Pres, Paw Print Ltd, 1966-; Pres, Adv'd Acoustical Ceilings Inc, 1975-; Fdr 1971, Secy-Treas 1971-73, Nat Assn of Pet Cemeteries; Pres 1973-75, Exec Dir 1975-82, Adv Coun Mem 1971-83, Intl Assn of Pet Cemeteries; Fdg Bd of Dir & Secy 1975-79, Conv & Meeting Planner 1975-80, Am Bding Kennels Assn; Editor & Pub, New & Views, 1971-81; Mem, Nat Bd of Dirs of Profl Animal Disposal Adv Coun; cp/Charter Mem, Wheaton, IL Chapt ABWA; Noble Grand, Whitbeck Rebecca Lodge, 1953-54; hon/Num Awds incl'g: Participation Awd, Key Stone St Assn of Human Cemeteries; Bronze Plaque for Devoted Ser & Patricia Blosser S'ship Fund, Intl Assn of Pet Cemeteries; Pet Cemetery of Yr Awd; Cert Kennel Owner Awd; Others; Num Radio & TV Appearances; Featured in Num Newspaper & Mag Articles.

BLOSSEY, ERICH CARL oc/Professor; b/Jun 10, 1935; h/261 West Kings Way, Winter Park, FL 32789; ba/Winter Park, FL; m/Elizabeth Diane; c/Christina, Elizabeth, Butch; p/Erich Fredrick Blossey, Mt Dora, FL; sp/Mr and Mrs Gordon T Frye, Bartonsville, VT; ed/BS, OH St Univ, 1957; MS, IA St Univ, 1959; PhD, Carnegie Mellon Univ, 1963; pa/Prof, Rollins Col, 1965-; Intern, Wabash Col, 1964-65; Postdoct Fellow, Syntex, SA Mexico), 1963-64; Postdoct Fellow, Stanford Univ, 1962-63; Local Subsect Chm 1981-82 & 1971-72, Am Chem Soc; Mem, Royal Inst of Chem; AAAS; Chm Rollins Col Chapt 1971-72, AAUP; NY Acad of Scis; Sigma Xi; Phi Lambda Upsilon; Sierra Clb; Audubon Soc; hon/Author of Symp Meeting Papers & 19 Sci Articles Pub'd in Var Profl Jours; Author of PSI Study Guide for Organic Synthesis, 1977; Solutions Manual for Organic Chem, 1977; Co-Editor, Solid Phase Synthesis, 1975; Arthur Vining Davis Fellow, 1978-79; AG Bush Prof of Sci, 1981-84.

BLOUNT, EVELYN oc/Education Executive; b/Oct 20, 1942; ba/Woman's Missionary Union, SBC, 100 Missionary Ridge, Highway 280 East, Birmingham,

AL 35243-2798; p/Willie Brown Blount (dec); Ouida Pool Blount, Winder, GA; ed/BS, Wom's Col of GA, 1964; MRE, So Bapt Theol Sem, L'ville, KY, 1969; pa/Tchr, Blue Mtn Col, MS, 1964-66; Tchr, Berkmar HS, Gwinnett Co, GA, 1966-67; Grp Ldr, Long Run Bapt Assn Ctr, L'ville, 1967-68; Adult Ed Conslt, Bapt Tabernacle Ch, L'ville, 1968-69; Min Ed, 1st Bapt Ch, Auburn, AL, 1969-70; Acteens Dir, Wom's Missionary Union of GA, 1970-73; Yth Dept Supvr 1973-74, Field Sers Dept Dir 1974-79, Asst to Ed Div Dir 1979-80, Nat Enlargement Plan Dir 1980-83, Prog Devel Spec 1983-, Wom's Missionary Union, So Bapt Conv; Cnslr, Camp Crestridge, NC, 1964-65; Asst Dir, YMCA Camps GA, 1966 & 1967; Dir, YMCA Camp, Richmond, VA, 1968; VPres 1978, Mem 1973-, So Bapt Social Sers Assn; Mem, Bapt Wom Mission Support Ch, 1982-83; Mem, Mtn Brook Bapt Ch, 1973-; r/So Bapt; hon/Author of Tchrs Guide for Code E, 1973; Co-Author, Yth Min Missions Projs, 1978; Article in Volume IV, Ency of So Bapts; Article on Wom's Mission Union, in Bapt Prog; Num Others in Wom's Mission Union Period; W/W: in Am Cols & Univs, of Wom, in S & SW; Outsstg Yg Wom of Am.

BLUE, FAYE COPE oc/Businesswoman; b/Aug 5, 1936; h/404 Fayetteville Avenue, Bennettsville, SC 24572; ba/Bennettsville, SC; m/Herbert M; c/Lisa Blue Freeman, Herbert Mark, Lona Noel, Faye Anne; p/Murray Lee Cope; Lois Turner Cope (dec); sp/Thomas Marshall and Livie Henslee Blue (dec); ed/Grad, Bennettsville, HS, 1954; pa/Employee 1954-55, Buyer 1980-, Marnat Packaging Co; Employee, J P Stevens Co, 1955-59; Housewife, 1959-68; Employed in Fed Prog, US Dept of Labor, 1969-75; Exec Dir, Bennettsville, Housing Auth, 1975-79; cp/Charter Mem, Secy-Treas 1979-80, Pres 1980-81, Tail Twister 1981-82, Lion Tamer 1982-83, Bd of Dirs 2 Yrs, Bennettsville Lions Clb; hon/Contbr to Scottish Blue Fam Book.

BLUMSTEIN, JAMES F oc/Professor of Law; b/Apr 24, 1945; h/2113 Hampton Avenue, Nashville, TN 37215; ba/Nashville, TN; m/Andree Sophia Kahn; p/Mr and Mrs David Blumstein, Bklyn, NY; sp/Ludwig W Kahn, Scarsdale, NY; ed/BA Ec, Yale Col, 1966; MA Ec, Yale Univ, 1970; LLB, Yale Law Sch, 1970; pa/Currently Spec Advr to Chancellor for Acad Affairs & Prof Law, Assoc Prof Law 1973-76, Asst Prof Law 1970-73, Vanderbilt Univ; Sr Res Assoc, Vanderbilt Inst Public Policy Studies; Dir 1972-74, Assoc Dir 1970-72, Vanderbilt Urban & Reg Devel Ctr; Vis'g Prof Hlth Law & Scholar-in-Residence, Dartmouth Med Sch, 1976-78; Vis'g Assoc Prof Law & Policy Scis, Duke Law Sch & Duke Inst of Policy Scis & Public Affairs, 1974-75; Pre-law Advr 1968-69 & Sr Pre-law Advr 1969-70, Ofc of Yale Col Dean; Asst in Instrn (under Prof Charles L Black Jr), Yale Law Sch, 1969-70; Pt-time Instr Ec, New Haven Col, 1967-68; Secy, ABA Sect of Legal Ed & Admissions to Bar, 1982-83; Chm Subcom on St & Local Taxation, Com on Corp Law & Taxation, ABA Sect of Corp, Bkg & Bus Law, 1983-; Num Adm & Com Chmships/Mbrships, Vanderbilt Univ; Conslg Positions, Num Pvt

Corps, Univs, St, Local & Nat Agys; Over 30 Lectrs, Presentations & Orgnl Confs; Num Others; cp/Edit Bd, *Jour of Hlth Politics, Policy & Law*, 1981-; 2nd Level Review Bd, *Land Use & Envir Law Rev*, 1983-; 2nd VChp Sect on Local Govt Law 1976-78, Sect Nom'g Com 1983-84, Sect Coun Mem 1980-, Assn Am Law Schs; Panel Mem, Am Arbitration Assn, 1977-; Mem, Publisher's Adv Bd, *Nashville Banner*, 1982-; Mem, Ldrship Nashville, 1977-; Num Others; hon/ Co-Editor of 3 Books: *The Urban Scene in the Seventies*, 1974; *Growing Metropolis: Aspects of Devel in Nashville*, 1975; *Growth Policy in the Eighties*, 1979; Author, Over 20 Maj Articles in Profl Pubs & Law Jours incl'g: *VA Law Review; TX Law Review; Circulation; Vanderbilt Law Review; NWn Law Review; Yale Law Jour*; Others; Num Op-ed Pieces, Other Articles & Reports; Num Litigation Cases; Bates Jr Fellow, Jonathan Edwards Col, Yale Univ, 1968-69; Editor, *Yale Law Jour*; Co-Fdr & Editor, *Yale Review of Law & Social Action*; Paul J Hartman Awd for Outstg Prof, Vanderbilt Univ, 1982; Univ Res Coun Awds, 1979-80, 1973-74 & 1971-72; Commonwlth Fund Hlth Res Fellow, Ctr for Study of Hlth Policy, Duke Inst of Policy Sci & Public Affairs, 1974-75; Ford Foun/Rockefeller Foun Pop Prog Grant, 1970-73; Outstg Yg Man of Yr, 1971; W/W: in Am Law, in Ed, of Intells, Contemp Achmt; Dir Am Scholars; Commun Ldrs of World; Num Other Biogl Listings.

BLYSTONE, FRANK LYNN oc/ Executive; b/Aug 28, 1935; h/8320 East Hinsdale Drive, Englewood, CO 80112; ba/Denver, CO; m/Patricia Louise; c/Jon Franklin, Ryan Taylor; p/Frank Edgar Blystone (dec); Reta Lee Blystone, Brea, CA; sp/John Allen Baker (dec); Teresa P Baker, Bakersfield, CA; ed/AA, Fullerton Col, 1955; BA, Whittier Col, 1957; Grad Study, George Wms Col, Chgo, 1958; mil/AUS, 1958-60 & 1961-62; pa/Gen Exec, YMCA of Kern Co, Bakersfield, 1963-70; Owner, Blystone Enterprises, 1970-74; Mgr Spec Projs & Corp Devel, Banister Pipelines Am (Trans AK Pipeline Proj), 1974-78; Pres & CEO, Bandera Land G Inc, 1983-; Chm, Contracting Corp, 1979-; Chm, Merit Fin Corp, 1980-; Pres & CEO, Tri-Val Oil & Gas Corp, 1981-; Pres, Merit Courier Corp, 1982-; cp/Mem, Libertas Lodge 466 F & A M; r/Prot; hon/Alumni Achm Awd, George Wms Col, 1972; Alumni Achmt Awd, Whittier Col, 1982; W/W: in W, in Fin & Indust, in CA, in World.

BLYSTONE, ROBERT VERNON oc/ Cell Biologist; b/Jul 4, 1943; h/2635 Worldland, San Antonio, TX 78217; ba/ San Antonio, TX; m/Donna Joan Moore; c/Daniel Vernon; p/Ed Blystone, Prescott, AZ; Cecilia Blystone, El Paso, TX; sp/Mr and Mrs C W Moore, El Paso, TX; ed/BS, Univ of TX-El Paso, 1965; MA 1968, PhD 1971, Univ of TX; pa/ Pt-time Instr, Univ of TX-El Paso, 1965; Asst Prof 1971-76, Assoc Prof 1976-84, Prof Biol 1984-, Chm Dept of Biol 1984-, Dir, Elect Microscopy Labs 1971-, Trinity Univ; Mem: Am Inst for Biol Sci, 1965-; AAAS, 1965-; TX Soc Elect Micro, 1968-; Elect Micro Soc Am, 1971-; TX Acad of Sci, 1973-; Am Soc Zool, 1981-; AAUP, 1982-; Am Soc Cell Biol, 1983-; cp/Dir 1974, 1975 & 1984, VPres 1976, Alamo Reg Sci Fair; hon/

Author of Num Sci Articles Pub'd in Profl Jours incl'g: *Proceedings of Elect Micro Soc Am; TX Soc of Elect Micro Jour; Am Zoo*; Others; Outstg Prof, Trinity Univ, 1982; Fellow 1978, Hon Life Fellow 1979, TX Acad of Sci; Am Men & Wom of Sci; W/W in Frontier Sci & Technol.

BOAL, JAN LIST oc/Professor; b/Oct 20, 1930; h/1126 Clifton Road, Northeast, Atlanta, GA 30307; ba/Atlanta, GA; m/Bobby Snow; c/Robert Kelly, Emily Ann (Mrs James Wert), Virginia List (Mrs Douglas Jamieson); p/Mr and Mrs Jan Boal (both dec); sp/Mr and Mrs Robert P Snow (both dec); ed/BME 1975, MS Math 1954, GA Inst of Technol; PhD Math, MIT, 1959; pa/ Instr, MIT, 1954-60; Asst Prof 1960-62, Assoc Prof 1962-69, Univ of SC; Prof & Chm 1969-77, Prof 1977-, GA St Univ; cp/Mem & Deacon 1975-, VChm of Deacons 1984, Druid Hills Bapt Ch; Mem, Sanctuary Choir, 1975-; Mem, Lions Clb, 1982; r/Bapt; hon/Author, Over 7 Articles in Profl Math Jours incl'g: *Jour of Math & Physics; The Math Tchr; GA Coun of Tchrs of Math Reflections; 2 Yr Col Math Jour; Math Mag*; Others; Danforth Grad Fellow & Gerard Swope Gen Elect F'ship, 1953; 1st Hon Grad, Brierian Cup & Phi Kappa Phi Cup, GA Inst of Technol, 1954; Blue Key Hon Soc 1965, Russell Outstg Tech Awd 1966, Univ of SC; NSF AID Conslt, Sum Inst Prog India, 1967 & 1968; Interviewer & Reader, Danforth Grad F'ship Prog, 1973-77; Mem Vis'g Coms, So Assn of Schs & Cols, 1972-; Omicrom Delta Kappa; GA Reg Coor for Annual HS Math Exam, 1979-; W/W: in GA, in Technol Today; Men of Achmt; Intl Dir of Biog.

BOALS, GORDON FORBES oc/ Clinical Psychologist; b/Feb 11, 1943; h/ 5-F Reler Lane, Somerset, NJ 08873; ba/ North Brunswick, NJ; p/Mr and Mrs Gordon P Boals, McLean VA; ed/AB, Denison Univ, 1964; PhD Ec, Princeton Univ, 1970; PhD Clin Psych, Rutgers Univ, 1979; pa/Asst Prof Ec, Rutgers Univ, 1969-72; Intern Clin & Commun Psych, Rutgers Med Sch, 1974-75; Sr Clin Psych, Middlesex Commun Mtl Hlth Clin 1979-84; Pvt Pract Psych, 1981-; Conslt g Psych, Fam Ser Agys of Middlesex Co & Scotch Plains, 1982-; Field Supvr, Grad Sch of Applied & Profl Psych, 1982-; Mem: Am Psych Assn; NJ Psychol Assn; NJ Grp Psychotherapy Assn; Assn for Transpersonal Psych; hon/Author of Book, *The Ec Anal of Book Publishing*, 1970; Author of Var Articles Incl'g: "Toward a Cognitve Reconceptualization of Meditation," 1978; "Psychotherapy Outcome in a Univ-based Tng Clin," 1981; "The Reliability, Validity & Utility of 3 Data Modes in Assessing Marital Relat'ships," 1982; Others; Phi Beta Kappa; Woodrow Wilson Fellow, 1964-65; Danforth Fellow, 1964-69; W/W in E.

BOARMAN, ANTHEA MARY oc/ Attorney, Commission Director; b/Nov 26, 1944; h/194 Castlewood Drive, Lexington, KY 40505; ba/Lexington, KY; c/Colin Luke Simmons, Cherise E Bishop; p/Lewis W and Ruth Barnes, Morehead, KY; ed/AB Phil, Tulane Univ; Linguistics Studies at Morehead St Univ; JD, Univ of KY Law Sch; pa/ Pvt Law Pract, Gilliam, Bush & Boarman, 1967-69; Fayette Co Juv Trial Commr, 1969-70; Dir Ky Child Advo-

cacy Coun, 1970-73; Dir, Prison Trial Unit, KY Public Defender, 1973-74; Dir, Urban Co Human Rts Comm, 1976-; Mem, KY Coun of Juv Ct Judges, 1970-72; VPres, KY Legal Aid & Defender Assn, 1971-73; Gen Counsel 1979-, Mem 1977-, Nat Assn Human Rts Wkrs; Bd Mem, Intl Assn Ofcl Human Rts Agys, 1979-; r/Epis; hon/ Author of "Programmed for Failure," *ADIT*, 1970; Contbr, Banks-Baldwin KY Revised Statutes & KY Pract (Fam Law) 1968-70; Outstg Yg Wom of Am; W/ W: in KY in Am Law, in Wom of World; Personalities of S.

BOATRIGHT, TONY JAMES oc/ Aerospace Engineer; b/Sep 13, 1954; h/ 2204 Pike Court, Cocoa, FL 32926; ba/ Kennedy Space Ctr, Fl; p/James Benjamin & Ethel Boatright, Douglasville, GA; ed/BS Space Scis 1979, MS Space Tech 1984, FL Inst of Technol; pa/Lead Engr, Cargo Elect Integration & Test, Lockheed Space Opers Co, Kennedy Space Ctr, Feb 1984-; Sys Engr, Space Shuttle Launch Opers Div, Rockwell Intl, Kennedy Space Ctr, Nov 1982- Feb 1984; Sr Engr, Planning Res Corp, Kennedy Space Ctr, Mar 1979-Nov 1982; Mem Adj Fac, Dept of Physics & Space Sci, FL Inst of Technol, 1980-; Mem 1972-, Editor & Coun Mem Cape Canaveral Chapt 1982, AIAA; Men: Am Aerospace Ed Assn, 1983-; The Planetary Soc; Astronom Soc of Pacific; cp/ Mem, Repub Pres Task Force, 1982-; hon/Creator of Var Illusts & Cartoons in: *OMNI Mag; Nat Space Inst Newslttr; AIAA Student Jour; INFOSPACE Aerospace Newslttr*; Awd, GA Soc of Profl Engrs, 1972; Aerospace Res Awd 1972, 1st Shuttle Flight Achmt Awd 1981, NASA; Spacelab I Turnover Medal, NASA/ European Space Agy, 1982; Superior Perf Awd, Rockwell Intl, 1983; Outstg Yg Men of Am, 1983; W/W: in Frontier Sci & Technol, Among Am HS Students.

BOAZ, MARTHA T oc/Dean Emeritus, Professor; h/1849 Campus Road, Los Angeles, CA 90041; ed/BS, Madison Col, 1935; BS Lib Sci, George Peabody Col, 1937; MA Lib Sci 1950, PhD Lib Sci 1955, Univ of MI; pa/Dean & Prof Grad Sch of Lib Sci 1955-79, Assoc Prof Lib Sci 1953-55, Res Assoc Ctr for Study of Am Experience 1979-81, Univ of So CA (USC); Critic, Eng Tchr, Sch Libn, Bridgewater, VA, 1935-37; Latin & Eng Tchr, Sch Libn, Jeffersontown, KY, 1937-40; Asst Libn, Madison Col, Harrisonburg, VA, 1940-49; Assoc Prof Lib Sci, Univ of TN, 1950-51; Instr Lib Sci, Univ of MI, 1951-52; Libr, Public Ser Dept, Pasadena Public Lib, CA, 1952; Chm Intell Freedom Com 1964-66, Pres Lib Ed Div 1968-69, Num Other Com Chmships & Mbrships, Am Lib Assn; Pres 1962-63, Chm Coun of Deans 1977-78, Num Other Coms, Assn of Am Lib Schs; Pres 1962, Mem Bd of Dirs CA Soc of Libns 1975-77, Chm Res Com 1976-77, Num Other Coms, CA Lib Assn; Num Com Mbrships, Univ of So CA; cp/Mem Bd of Dirs, LA Lib Assn, 1970-; Mem, Mayor's Blue Ribbon Com on Ctl Lib LA, 1976-78; Num Others; hon/Author & Editor, Over 10 Books incl'g: *Strategies for Meeting the Info Needs of Soc in Yr 2000; Issues in Higher Ed & the Professions in the 1980's; Current Concepts in Lib Mgmt*; Others; Author of Num Articles, Book

Chapts, Surveys & Abstracts incl'g: "The Am Lib Spec in an Underdeveloped Country," *Jour of Ed for Libnship*, 1967; "Censorship," *Ency of Lib & Info Sci*, 1970; "The Future of Lib & Info Sci Ed," *Jour of Ed for Libnship*, 1978; "Passage to Pakistan," Wilson Lib Bltn, 1964; "Res and "Futures Res" in Lib/Info/Sci/ Communs," *Ednl Res Qtly*, 1980; "The Uses of Dissent," *Saturday Review*, 1961; Compiled Var Abstracts for Basis of *Lib Sci Dissertations*, 1963; Planned & Moderated "The Living Lib," TV Prog, (Univ of So CA Video-Cassette); Others; US AID Rep, Libs in Pakistan, 1962; US St Dept Rep (Cultural Affairs Ofc), Libs in Vietnam, 1966; Recip, Sesquicent Awd 1967, Alumnus in Residence Awd 1971, Univ of MI; Vis'g Scholar, Univ of GA, 1969; Sr Scholar in Residence, US Ofc of Ed Proj, US Intl Univ, 1972-73; Honored Scholar, CA Luth Col, 1974; Recip, Nat Beta Phi Mu Awd for Dist'd Ser to Lib Ed, 1974; Num Others; W/W: in Am, in Lib Sci, in Am Ed, in W; Pres & Deans of Am Cols & Univs; Biogl Dir of Libns in US & Canada; Other Biogl Listings.

BOAZ, NOEL THOMAS oc/Paleoanthropologist; b/Feb 8, 1952; h/43 Monroe Avenue, Staten Island, NY 10301; ba/New York, NY; m/Dorothy D; p/ Elena M Robertson, Martinsville, VA; sp/Mr and Mrs H P Dechant, San Pablo, CA; ed/BA, Univ of VA, 1973; MA 1974, PhD 1977, Univ of CA-Berkeley; pa/ Lectr Anthropology, Univ of CA-LA, 1977-78; Asst Prof Anthropology, NY Univ, 1978-; Dir, Intl Sahabi Res Proj, 1976-; Dir, Semliki Res Expedition, 1982-; Mem: Am Assn of Phy Anthropologists; Com on Hist & Hons, Am Anthropological Assn; AAAS; Fellow, Royal Anthropological Inst; Soc of Vertebrate Paleontology; Fellow, Explorers Clb; r/Epis; hon/Author of 1 Textbook, 9 Reviews, & Over 25 Sci Articles Pub'd in Profl Jours; Editor of 3 Volumes; Grantee: NSF, Nat Geographic Soc; Hon Mention, Rolex Awd, 1981; Pres Fellow, NY Univ, 1981; Fulbright Fellow, 1983-84; W/W: in World, in Frontier Sci & Technol; Am Men & Wom of Sci.

BODDINGTON, CRAIG THORNTON oc/Editor, Outdoor Journalist; b/ Dec 11, 1952; h/16044 Knapp Street, Sepulveda, CA 91343; ba/LA, CA; p/E M Boddington Jr, Kansas City, KS; ed/ BA, Univ of KS, 1974; mil/USMC, 1974-78, Capt (Inf Ofcr); USMCR, 1978-, Maj; pa/VPres, Intl Hunting Conslts Ltd, 1978; Editor: *Hunting Mag* 1983-, *Guns & Ammo Spec Pub* 1979-, Petersen's Pub Co; Mem, Nat Rifle Assn; Mem, Ducks Unltd; Mem, Amateur Trapshooting Assn; Bd of Dirs 1979-, Pres 1981-82, LA Chapt Safari Clb Intl; Chm Americas Subcom, Safari Clb Intl; r/Presb; hon/Author of Articles Pub'd in Num Maj Jours; Author of Column & Monthly Feature in *Hunting Mag*; Editor: Num Newsstand Books & Pubs; Hardcover Edition of *Am- The Men & Their Guns Who Made Her Gt*; Mem, All-Am Trapshooting Tm, 1969-70; Eagle Scout, 1967; Vigil Hon Mem, Order of Arrow, 1969; W/W in W; Intl W/W of Contemp Achmt.

BODENHEIMER, PETER oc/Astronomer, Professor; b/Jun 29, 1937; h/222 Columbia Street, Santa Cruz, CA 95060; ba/Santa Cruz, CA; m/Dori; c/

Daniel, Debora; p/Edgar Bodenheimer, Davis, CA; Brigitte Bodenheimer (dec); ed/AB, Harvard Univ, 1959; PhD, Univ of CA-Berkeley, 1965; pa/Res Assoc, Princeton Univ, 1965-67; Asst Prof & Assoc Astronomer 1967-70, Assoc Prof & Assoc Astronomer 1970-76, Prof & Astronomer 1976-, Chm Bd of Studies in Astronomy & Astrophysics 1975-78 & 1982-83, Univ of CA-Santa Cruz; Mem: Intl Astronom Union; Royal Astronom Soc (UK); Am Astronom Soc; r/Jewish; hon/Author of Num Res Reports & Sci Articles in Profl Jours; W/W in Frontier Sci & Engrg.

BODILY, DAVID M oc/Professor; b/ Dec 16, 1933; h/2651 Cecil Drive, Salt Lake City, UT 84124; ba/Salt Lake City, UT; m/BethAlene J; c/Robert, Rebecca, Timothy, Christopher; p/Levi Delbert and Norma Bodily, Lewiston, UT; sp/ Lavern and Bessie Judy, Mormon, ID; ed/BA Chem 1959, MA Chem 1960, Brigham Yg Univ; PhD Phy Chem, Cornell Univ, 1964; pa/Res Assoc, NWn Univ, 1964-65; Asst Prof Chem, Univ of AZ, 1965-67; Asst Prof, Assoc Prof, Prof Fuels Engrg 1967-, Assoc Dean Col of Mines 1983-, Univ of UT; Chm SLC Sect 1975, Mem, Am Chem Soc; Mem: Sigma Xi; Am Inst of Mining, Metall & Petro Engrs; Catalysis Soc; r/LDS (Mormon); hon/Author of Var Pubs in Profl Jours; W/W: in Am, in W; Men of Achmt; Personalities of W & MW.

BOEHME, RICHARD WILLIAM oc/ Librarian; b/Jul 13, 1936; h/23 Oriole Avenue, Framingham, MA 01701; ba/ Framingham, MA; m/E Hannah Shearer; William R Boehme (dec); Ruth M Boehme, Auburn, NY; sp/William C and Winona Shearer, Cortland, NY; ed/ BA 1961, MA 1964, SUNY-Buffalo; MLS, Univ of Pgh, 1965; pa/Lib Trainee, Univ of Pgh, 1963-65; Asst Col Libn, SUNY-Cortland, 1965-71; Assoc Libn, Framingham St Col, 1971-; Mem: Assn of Col & Res Libs; N Eng Lib Assn; MA Lib Assn; On-line AV Catalogers; Paleontological Res Instn; Paleontoligical Soc; Phi Beta Mu; Sigma Xi; Soc of Vertebrate Paleontology; N Eng Microcomputer Grp; Am Soc for Info Sci; cp/Adirondack 46'rs; Appalachian Mtn Clb; N Eng 4000; NH 46; NE 111; Trout Unltd; U Fly Tyers; Bass Anglers Sportsman Soc; r/Prot; hon/Biogl Dir of Libns in US & Canada; Commun Ldrs of Am; Dir of Dist'd Ams; W/W in E; Men of Achmt; Commun Ldrs of World; DIB.

BOENHEIM, MARION oc/University Administrator, Professor; b/Aug 27, 1946; ba/6000 S Street, Sacramento, CA; c/Laura Renee; p/Fred Boenheim, FL; Irene Shwetz, CA; ed/BA Psych, Univ of MI, 1968; MA Psych Cnslg, En MI Univ, 1969; EdD Adm, Univ of MA-Amherst, 1976; pa/Dir Progs for Adult Students, Coor of Math 1983-, Sr Adm Anal & Assoc Prof 1974-78, CA St Univ-Sacramento; Dir Human Relats 1980-83, Assoc VPres 1978-79, Univ of CA; Asst to VChancellor Adm 1972-74, Assoc Dean 1971-72, Univ of MA-Amherst; Exec VPres, CA Wom in Higher Ed, 1982-84; Treas 1981-84, Advr to St Bd, Fac Wom's Assn; Gov's Task Force on the Status of Wom (MA); Treas, AK & CA Arts Coun; AAUW; Conslt, US Civtl Rts Comm; Am Assn of Higher Ed; NASPA; Dir, Am Col Pers Assn; Dir, Am Inst of Res; r/Jewish;

hon/Author of Var Articles incl'g: "Fac Unions"; "Unionism in Academia"; "Listening Grps: Wave of the Future?"; "Laws & Their Impact on Higher Ed"; Exxon Foun F'ship, 1976; US St Dept Rep to Japan; Wom's Advocate Exceptl Achmt Awd, 1983; Advr to Assem Spkr of CA, 1982-84; Vol Activist Awd, 1984; Outstg Yg Wom of Am; Dir of Dist'd Ams.

BOFF, KENNETH RICHARD oc/ Engineering Research Psychologist; b/ Aug 17, 1947; h/3314 Village Court, Dayton, OH 45432; ba/ Wright-Patterson AFB, OH; m/Judith Marion; c/Cory Asher; p/Victor and Ann Boff, Bklyn, NY; sp/Murray and Daisy Schoer, Woodbourne, NY; ed/BA 1969, MA 1972, Hunter Col (CUNY); MPhil 1975, PhD 1978, Columbia Univ; mil/NY Army NG; pa/Staff, Columbia Univ, 1976; AF Human Resources Lab, 1977-80; Engrg Res Psych, AF Aerospace Med Res Lab, 1980-; Mem: Human Factors Soc; Am Psychol Assn; Assn for Res in Vision & Ophthal; Num Orgnl & Univ Addresses & Spkg Presentations; hon/Author & Co-Author, Over 15 Res Reports & Sci Articles Pub'd in Profl Jours incl'g: *Supplement to Invest Ophthal & Visual Sci*; *Perception & Psychphysics*; *Proceeding of Nat Aerospace & Elects Conf*; Others; Grad F'ship, Columbia Univ, 1972-76; Rank Prize Travel Grant, London, England, 1984; Outstg Perf Rating w Quality Step Increase, 1982; Sustained Superior Perf Cash Awds, 1981-83; W/W: in MW, in Frontier Sci & Technol.

BOGGESS, ROBERT K oc/Teacher, Researcher; b/Apr 26, 1945; h/2108 Charlton Lane, Radford, VA 24141; ba/ Dept of Chem, Radford Univ, Radford, VA 24142; m/Susan Scott Boggess; c/ Teresa Elaine, Brian Michael; p/Mrs Thomas C Boggess Sr, Rich Creek, VA; sp/S D Scott, Marion, VA; ed/BS Chem, Emory & Henry Col, Emory, VA, 1967; PhD Chem, Univ of AL, 1973; pa/Res Assoc, VA Polytech Inst & St Univ, 1984-85; Prof Chem 1984-, Assoc Prof 1978-84, Asst Prof 1977-78, Radford Univ; Asst Prof, Thomas Moore Col, KY, 1974-77; Res Assoc, Univ of VA, 1972-74; Mem, Am Chem Soc; hon/ Author, Over 20 Sci Res Articles in Profl Pubs; Res Grantee: Jeffress Foun, 1984-85; ACS-PRF, 1979-81, 1981-84; NSF, 1981; Res Corp, 1976-78.

BOGGS, GEORGE JOHNSON oc/ Psychophysicist; b/Mar 2, 1949; h/1909 Stearns Hill Road, Waltham, MA 02154; ba/Waltham, MA; p/Margaret Boggs Dillon, Beckley, WV; ed/BS 1972, MA 1974, Marshall Univ; PhD, Purdue Univ, 1981; pa/Staff Psychol, Nicholas Co Mtl Hlth Ctr, 1974-75; Dir Psychol Sers, Cabell Co Bd of Ed, 1975-77; Res Asst, Purdue Univ, 1977-81; Sr Mem Tech Staff, GTE Labs, 1981-; Mem: Acoustical Soc of Am; NY Acad of Scis; Am Psychol Assn; IEEE; Assn for Computing Machinery; Mensa; hon/ Author, Num Res Papers, Conf Proceedings & Sci Articles on Psychphysics & Engrg Psych Pub'd in Profl Jours; Elected to Sigma Xi, 1977; Sr Fulbright Res Fellow, 1984-85; W/W in Frontier Sci & Technol.

BOGNER, FRED K oc/Professor; b/ Jul 7, 1939; h/9516 Bridlewood Trail, Spring Valley, OH 45370; ba/Dayton, OH; m/Mary L; c/Fred C, Sharon L; p/

Fred W Bogner (dec); Esther V Bogner, Mansfield, OH; sp/Harold and Ruth Reynolds, Mansfield, OH; ed/BS Civil Engrg 1961, MS Engrg Mechs 1964, PhD Engrg Mechs 1967, Case Inst of Technol; pa/Mem Tech Staff, Bell Telephone Labs, 1967-69; Res Engr 1969-84, Prof & Chm Dept Civil Engrg & Engrg Mechs 1984-, Univ of Dayton; Mem: Am Soc of Civil Engrs; AIAA; Am Soc Engrg Ed; Soc Engrg Sci; Am Acad Mechs; hon/Author of Var Articles in *AIAA Jour* incl'g: "Finite Element Vibration Anal of Damped Structures," 1982; Am Men & Wom of Sci; Commun Ldrs & Noteworthy Ams; Mechs of Composite Mats Dir; Notable Ams in Bicent Era.

BOGOFF, BRENDA ANN oc/Artist; b/Apr 11, 1941; h/20 Doctor Frank Road, Spring Valley, NY 10977; m/Stanley A; c/Rickie Sue, Jodie J, Mindie M; p/Herman and Blanche Greenberg (dec); sp/Jacob and Celia Bogoff (dec); pa/Chief of Pharm, Spring Val Gen Hosp, 1959-61; Currently, Wking Artist; Mem, Art Dirs Leag; Dir Ctl Park S Outdoor Art Exhib; r/Hebrew; hon/Features on WNEW-TV; WABC-TV News; *The Jour News*; *Reporter Dispatch*; *News Times*; Art Wk has Appeared on Num TV Progs & Written About in Num Newspapers; Num Awds & Certs From Art Shows & Galleries; W/W: in E, of Wom; Commun Ldrs of Am; Dir of Dist'd Ams.

BOHACHEVSKY, IHOR OREST oc/Mathematician; b/Sep 7, 1928; h/829 Pine Street, Los Alamos, NM 87544; ba/Los Alamos, NM; m/Ulana Mary; p/Daniel and Rostyslava, McLean, VA; sp/Constantine and Myroslava, Queens, NY; ed/BA Aero Engrg 1956, PhD Applied Math 1961, NY Univ; mil/AUS, Korea, 1951-53; pa/Res Sci, Adj Assoc Prof, NYU, 1961-63; Res Engr, Cornell Aero Lab, Buffalo, 1963-66; Prin Res Sci, Sr Staff, Avco-Everett Res Lab (MA), 1966-68; Tech Staff, Bellcomm Inc, Wash, 1968-72; Tech Staff, Bell Lab Inc, Murray Hill, NJ, 1972-75; Staff, Los Alamos Nat Lab, 1975-; Mem: Am Nuclear Soc; NY Acad of Sci; AIAA; Soc Industl & Applied Math; Sigma Xi; Tau Beta Pi; r/Cath; hon/Author, Approx 50 Articles Pub'd in Sci & Tech Jours; US Patentee: Beam Heated Linear Theta-Pinch Device for Producing Hot Plasma; Recip, W Bryans Medal in Engrg Mechs, NY Univ, 1956; Apollo Achmt Awd, NASA, 1969; Cert of Recog, AT&T, 1969; Fellow, NSF, 1956, 1957, 1958 & 1959; Am Men of Sci; W/W: in Technol Today, in W, in Aviation & Aerospace, in Frontier Sci & Technol.

BOHLANDER, ROBERT W oc/Professor; b/Jun 26, 1952; h/1355 Chase Road, Shavertown, PA 18708; ba/Wilkes-Barre, PA; m/Yvonne S; c/Nathan R; p/William W Bohlander, Wmsport, PA; Louella Bohlander (dec); sp/Michael and Julia Stefanick, Wmsport, PA; ed/BA Psych, Lebanon Val Col, 1974; MA Psych 1980, PhD Psych 1981, Univ of Rochester; pa/Instr, Univ of Rochester, 1977-79; Asst Prof Psych, Wilkes Col, 1979-; Mem: PA Psychol Assn; En Psychol Assn; Am Psychol Assn; Optic Soc Am; AAUP; Am Inst of Physics; Sigma Xi; Phi Alpha Epsilon; Psi Chi; cp/Asst Chief, Jackson Twp Vol Fire Dept; VPres, Jackson Twp Vol Ambulance Assn; r/Luth; hon/

Author, Num Sci Papers & Articles Pub'd in Profl Jours & Presented at Psychol Confs; Rush Rhees Fellow, Univ of Rochester, 1974-78; Pres S'ship, 197-74; Apprec Awds, Lions & Kiwanis Clbs; Recip, Var Res Grants; W/W: Among Am Col Students, in E.

BOHLMANN, DANIEL ROBERT oc/Financial Planner, Invester, Attorney; b/Apr 28, 1948; h/Vista Las Palmas, 1022 Friar Court, Palm Springs, CA 92262; ba/Same; m/Sylvia-Maria Martha; p/Mr and Mrs Walter Richard Bohlmann, Milwaukie, OR; sp/Mrs Renate Yelvington, Stockton, CA; ed/Dipl, Clackamas HS, 1966; Pre-law, Multnomah Jr Col, 1969; BS Polit Sci & Bus Adm, Lewis & Clark Col, 1970; JD, NWn Sch of Law, 1974; mil/USAR, 1967; pa/Bohlmann & Bohlmann Investmt Trust, 1962-; Blitz Weinhard Brewery, 1966-70; Fdr & Investor, Gen Computer Software, 1980-; Fdr & Co-Finder, Petro Ltd; Owner, SunW Energy Inc; Owner, Gem-Con Inc; Owner, Hopps Body & Paint Shop Inc, 1976-80; CEO & Dir Promotions & Investmts, Atlas Intl Ltd, 1979-; Overseeing Intl Promotions & Investmts, NBC-KCHV FM-93 Social Prog; Notary Public, OR, 1978; Fin Advr, US Pres Task Force, 1981-84; Subcom Mem, OR Bd of Ed, 1973-75; Bus Adv Bd, US Senate, 1981-83; Mem: Am Mgmt Assn; US Envir Coun; Phi Theta Kappa; OR St Bar Assn; ABA; OR & Am Trial Lwyrs Assn; Am Judic Soc; Phi Alpha Delta; Intl Assn Fin Planners; Desert Est Planning Coun; Nat Fdn Indep Bus-men; Others; cp/Bd of Dirs, Williamette Dem Soc, 1979-81; Precinct Com-man, OR, 1976-78-80; Desert Mus; Palm Springs Elks Clb; Am Legion, Palm Springs; Portland, Palm Springs, Indio, Rancho Mirage, Cathedral City & Desert Hot Springs, C of C; Comml Clb; Smithsonian Nat Assoc; US Antique & Collectors Automobile Assn; Desert Classic Car Assn; Am Film Inst; Beverly Hills Coun, Nav-Leag of the US; Columbia River Yacht Clb; Others; r/Luth (MO Synod); hon/Author of "Polit Ramifications Concerning US Agri Adjustment Act," 1970; "Tax Shelter & Investmt Guide," 1979; "Advtg Sales for Profit," 1980; Others; Appt by Gov to OR Bd of Ed, 1973; Elected as Precinct Com-person, 1976-80; Repub Pres Task Force; Outstg Benefactor, Elks Nat Foun, 1979-80; W/W: in Am Law, in Fin & Indust, of Intells; Outstg Yg Men of Am.

BOHLMANN, SYLVIA-MARIA MARTHA oc/International Model, Promotions & Investor; b/Mar 18, 1953; h/Vista Las Palmas, 1022 Friar Court, Palm Springs, CA 92262; ba/Same; m/Daniel Robert; p/Renate Yelvington, Stockton, CA; sp/Mr and Mrs Walter Richard Bohlmann, Milwaukie, OR; ed/BA, Algeimeines Bus Univ, W Germany, 1970; AA, Delta Col, 1973; Dipl, Am Mgmt Assn; pa/QC Supvr, Safeway Stores Inc, 1972-76; Sales Dir, Del Monte Co, 1976-78; Pres, Atlas Intl Ltd, 1979-; Overseeing Intl Promotions & Investmts, NBC-KCHV FM-93 Social Prog; Mem: ABWA; Am Mgmt Assn; Comml Clb; Nat Fedn Indep Bus-men; Others; cp/US & Palm Springs C of C; Living Desert Resv; Benefactor, Meow & Bark; Vol, Bob Hope Desert Classic; Palm Springs Desert Mus; Tiempo De Los Ninos; Palm Springs Wom's Press

Clb; Loaves & Fishes; OR Arts Coun; Willamette Dem Soc; US Antique & Collectors Automobile Assn; Palm Sprgs Models Guild; Am Film Inst; Others; r/Luth; hon/Author of "Discovering Yourself," 1983; "Inside Palm Springs," 1983; "Developing the Female Mystic," 1979; Others; Mrs Palm Sprgs, CA, 1983-84; Outstg Mktg Perf in Pacific NW, Am Mgmt Assn Chapt Exec, 1979; US Senate Task Force, 1982-84; US Pres Task Force, 1982-84; Superior Sales Perf, Hilshire Co; Am Sales Achiever, Pacific NW Bell; 1st Place Decathlon, W German Jr Olympics, 1966; Apprec Awd, CA Am Legion, 1983; Top 10 Bus Achievers of Pacific NW; Outstg Fund Raiser Awd, 1980-82; Others; Outstg Yg Wom of Am; W/W: of Intells, of Wom, in Fin & Indust.

BOHN, DENNIS ALLEN oc/Audio Electronic Engineer; b/Oct 5, 1942; h/Boc 401 Kingston, WA 98346; ba/Mountlake Terrace, WA; c/Kira Michelle; p/Iris Mulvaney, Hemet, CA; ed/BSEE 1972, MSEE 1974, Univ of CA-Berkeley; mil/USAF, 1960-64; pa/Engrg Tech, Gen Elect Co, San Leandro, CA, 1964-72; Res & Devel Engr, Hewlett-Packard Co, Santa Clara, CA, 1973; Application Engr (Audio), Nat Semiconductor Corp, Santa Clara, CA, 1974-76; Engrg Mgr, Phase Linear Corp, Lynnwood, WA, 1976-82; VPres Engrg, Rane Corp, Mountlake Terrance, WA, 1982-; cp/Vol, Suicide & Crisis Ctr, Berkeley (1972-74) & Santa Clara (1974-76); hon/Columnist, *Polyphony Mag*, 1981-; Editor, "We Are Not Just Daffodils," 1975; Tech Editor & Author, *Audio Handbook*, 1976; Contbr of Poetry to *Reason Mag*; Contbr Num Articles to Var Tech Jours; Am Spirit of Hon Medal, USAF, 1961; Mat Achmt Awd, Chem Rubber Co, 1962-63; W/W in W.

BOHNING, ELIZABETH E oc/Professor; b/Jun 26, 1915; h/PO Box 574 Newark, DE 19715-0574; ba/Newark, DE; m/William Harvey; c/Barbara B Young, Margaret B Anderson; ed/BA, Wellesley Col, 1936; MA 1938, PhD 1943, Bryn Mawr Col; pa/Pt-time Instr, Bryn Mawr Col, 1939-40; Tchg Asst, Stanford Univ, 1940-41; Hostess, Grinnell Col, 1941-42; Fac Mem, Middlebury Sum Sch of German, 1956 & 1958; Instr 1942-46, Asst Prof 1946-57, Assoc Prof 1957-67, Prof 1967-, Chm Dept Lang & Lit 1971-78, Univ of DE; Former Gen Secy of Nat Contest, ExecCom & Chapt Pres, Am Assn of Tchrs of German; Former Pres, Delta Phi Alpha; Trustee 1970-80, Mid Sts Assn of Cols & Schs; Former Pres, Mid Sts Assn of Fgn Lang Tchrs; Soc for German-Am Studies; Am Coun for Study of Austrian Lit; cp/Pres, DE Coun for Intl Visitors; VChm 1981-82, DE Humanities Coun; r/Epis; hon/Author of 1 Book; Over 30 Articles of Lit & Pedagogical Subjects Pub'd in Profl Jours; Awd for Excell in Tchg, Lindback & Alumni Assn, 1962; Cert of Merit, Goethe House & AATG, 1982; Tchr of Yr, DE Coun on Tchg of Fgn Langs, 1984; W/W: in Am, of Am Wom; Dir of Am Tchrs; Intl Book of Hon; Commun Ldrs of Am.

BOISSEVAIN, MATTHIJS GIDEON JAN oc/Consultant; b/Apr 24, 1916; h/216 Prospect Hill Road, Noank, CT 06340; ba/Boston, MA; m/Helen Fisk (dec); c/Robert, Romelia Bayer, Pamela

Wilkinson, Kimberley Buck, Lance, Mia; p/Ethel S Knobloch; sp/Antony Fisk (dec); ed/BSME 1938, Completed Course Wk for PhD 1942, MIT; MS Adm Sci, Hartford Grad Ctr of Rensselaer Polytech Inst, 1979; pa/Instr, MIT, 1938-42; Engr 1942-43, Conslt 1981-, Stone & Webster Engrg Corp; Chief Engr, L Lasher & Co, 1943-46; Asst Dir Warehousing & Trans, Stop & Shop, 1946-49; Asst Prof, Pratt Inst, 1949-51; Chief Test Engr, Asst Oper Mgr, Asst to VPres Nuclear Engrg, Mgr Adv'd Technol, Div Prod Assurance, Gen Dynamics Elect Boat, 1951-82; Chm, N Stonington Bd of Ed, 1956-68; Dir, Nat Campground Owners Assn, 1981; Pres, CT Campground Owners Assn, 1975-76; Pres, Computer Country Corp, 1982-; Pres, Highland Orchards Resort Pk Inc, 1970-; cp/Chm, Republican Town Com, 1978-79; Lions Clb; Mason; Elks Clb; r/Christian Sci; hon/Author of "Comparison of Power Plant Heater Arrangements," *Mech Engrg*; "How Evaporation Hook-up Affects Heat Rate Power"; Patentee in Field; W/W: in World, in Fin & Indust, in E.

BOLANDER-OLSON, CHRISTINE JUMES oc/Retired Entertainer, Athlete; b/Mar 1, 1913; h/222 East Pearson, Chicago, IL 60611; m/Ralph Bolander-Olson (dec); p/George N and Veronica Stukowsky Jumeś (dec); sp/Oscar Rinald Olson and Agnes M Bolander (dec); ed/Grad, Carl Schurz HS, 1929; Att'd, Heald Bus Col, Sacramento, CA, 1962; pa/Theatrical Career from Age 5; Dancer/Choreographer, Var Sch Progs, 1918-29; Dancer: Alice Bradford Revue, 1930-31; DeRonda & O'Dear Prodns, 1931-32; Dance Tm: Christine & Comyns, 1932-33; Heller & JuMez, 1934-35; DeCarlos & JuMeś, 1935-36; Entertainer, TV Theatre, Chgo World's Fair/Cent of Progress, 1934; Photg's Model, 1930-36; Num Night Clb & Hotel Appearances, 1930-36; Water Ballet & Long Distance Swimmer, Lake MI, 1945-51; Jour, *Chgo Am News*, 1961; *SF Chronicle News*, 1962; Lay Evang, 1970-78; Judge, Arts & Crafts Shows, 1980-81; Spkrs Bur; Am Newspaper Guild; cp/Mayfair Wom's Aux, Poster Design, 1927; Student Guard Marshall, Carl Schurz HS, 1929; Num Fund Raising Activs; Judge, Spectrum Art Guild & Albany Pk Fair, 1980-81; Mem, Medinah Ath Clb, 1944-46; r/Charismatic; hon/World's 1st Miss TV (under Name of Christine James), World's Fair/Cent of Progress, 1934; Winner, Jantzen Bathing Beauty Contest, Chgo, 1933; Miss Cent of Progress Beauty Contest, 1934; Chgo Hist Soc; W/W of Wom; Personalities of Am; DIB; Intl Book of Hon; Foremost Wom of 20th Cent; Other Biogl Listings.

BOLDEN, THEODORE EDWARD oc/Dentist, Educator; b/Apr 19, 1920; h/29 Montague Place, Montclair, NJ 07042; ba/Newark, NJ; m/Dorothy M Forde (dec); p/Mary E Bolden, Montclair, NJ; sp/Adelaide F Forde, Houston, TX; ed/AB 1941, Hon LLD 1981, Lincoln Univ; DDS, Meharry Med Col, 1947; MS 1951, PhD 1958, Univ of IL-Chgo; mil/USA; DC USA, 1942-43; 1951-53; pa/Instr, Operative Dentistry, Pedodontics & Periodontia, Sch Dentistry, Meharry Med Col, Nashville, 1948-49; Prof Dentistry, Chm Dept Oral Pathol

& Oral Med 1962-69, Dir Res Sch Dentistry 1962-73, Assoc Dean Sch Dentistry 1967-74, Prof Dentistry, Chm Dept Oral Pathol 1962-77, Asst in Oral Pathol Sch Dentistry 1949-51, Univ IL-Chgo; Res Fellow in Dentistry 1949-51, Instr Pathol 1955-57, Asst Prof Dept Oral Diagnosis & Pathol Sch Dentistry 1957-60, Seton Hall Col Med & Dentistry; Assoc Prof 1960-62, Prof Gen & Oral Pathol, Col Med & Dentistry NJ 1977-, Acting Chm Dept 1979-80, Dean NJ Dental Sch 1977-78, CMDNJ-NJ Dental Sch-Newark; Diplomate, Am Bd Oral Med; Am Bd Oral Pathol; Fellow, Am Acad Oral Pathol; Mem, Intl Assn Dental Res; NE Soc of Periodontists; NY Acad of Sci; V Chm Sect Pathol 1969-70, Am Assn Dental Schs; Pres 1968-70, Capital City Dental Soc; Stat 1977-, TN Dental Assn; Soc for Study of Negro in Dentistry; Nat Alliance Black Sch Edrs; Sigma Xi; Omega Psi Phi; Kappa Sigma Pi; Omicron Kappa Upsilon; cp/Conslt Dentistry, VA Hosps: Tuskegee, AL, 1962-; Nashville, TN, 1968-77; Bklyn, NY, 1979-; Conslt Dentistry, Hlth, Ed & Wel, 1979-80 & 1980-81; Trustee, St Paul Bapt Ch, Montclair, NJ, 1959-70; Commr, Urban Redevel, Town of Montclair, 1960-62; Chm, Adv Hlth Com, Town of Montclair, 1959-60; Co-Chm Crusades 1981-82 & 1982-83, Mem Steering Com Newark Unit 1980-81, Med VPres & Bd Mgrs 1981, Interim Chm Exec Com Trustee NJ Div 1982, Am Cancer Soc; r/Bapt; hon/Author, Over 130 Res Articles Pub'd in Sci Jours & 7 Books incl'g: *Dental Hygiene Exam Review Book*, 4th Edition, 1982; "A Symp on Diagnosis & Treatment of Oral Cancer," 1973; Editor, *Qtly of Nat Dental Assn*, 1975-; Recip of Plaque & Cit, Meharry Med Col, 1971; Dentist of Yr, Nat Dental Assn, 1977; Plaque, Conn Black Caucus Dentists, 1979; Cit, Neighborhood Coun Fed Credit Union, 1974; Golden State Dental Assn, 1974; PATCH, 1979; Newark Div Nat Coun Negro Wom, 1979; Others; W/W in Am.

BOLDT, ELIHU A oc/X-ray Astronomer, Administrator; b/Jul 15, 1931; h/10 Lakeside Drive, Greenbelt, MD 20770; ba/Greenbelt, MD; m/Yvette; c/Adam, Abigail, Jessica; p/Joel Boldt (dec); Yetta Boldt; sp/David and Sol Benharroch; ed/BS 1953, PhD 1958, MIT; pa/Asst Prof, Rutgers Univ, 1958-64; Guest Staff Mem, Ecole Polytechnique, Paris, 1960-62; Adj Prof, Univ of MD, 1980-; Fellow & Exec Com Div of Cosmic Physics 1978-80, Am Phy Soc; Mem: Am Astronom Soc; Intl Astronom Union; hon/Author of "The Cosmic X-ray Background," in *Comments on Astrophysics*, 1981; Num Other Sci & Res Articles Pub'd; Lindsay Meml Awd, Goddard Space Flight Ctr, 1977; Outstg Sci Achmt, NASA, 1978.

BOLINGER, CAROL DARLENE oc/Medical Technologist; b/Jan 2, 1950; h/Rural Route Box 520, Brazil, IN 46834; ba/Terre Haute, IN; p/Mildred Bolinger, Brazil, IN; ed/BS, Med Technol, IN St Univ, 1971; pa/Med Tech Staff 1971-81, Ednl Coor 1981-83, Staff Med Tech Spec in Hematology 1983-, Terre Haute Med Lab; Reg'd Med Tech & Mem, Am Soc Clin Pathols; Mem, Am Soc for Med Technol; Mem & Dist Dir, IN Soc for Med Technol; r/Prot; hon/Co-Writer & Tech Advr, Ednl Videotape on Phlebot-

ony, an IN St Univ AV, 1982; Grad magna cum laude, IN St Univ; Outstg Ser Awd, Am Soc for Med Technol (Omicron Sigma), 1982; W/W of Am Wom.

BOLINO, AUGUST C oc/Professor; b/Sep 30, 1922; h/11411 Lund Place, Kensington, MD 20895; ba/Washington, DC; m/Thora J; c/Bradlee A, Douglas K, Jacquelyn R, Gregory N; p/Nicholas Bolino, Revere, MA; Rose Bolino (dec); sp/Krisjan Johnson (dec); Dora Cheever, Seattle, WA; ed/BBA 1948, MBA 1949, Univ of MI; Grad Study in Ec, Univ of WA, 1950-52; PhD Ec, St Louis Univ, 1957; mil/USAF, 1942-45; pa/Instr Stats, Univ of WA, 1950-51; Instr Bus & Ec, ID St Univ, 1952-55; Asst & Assoc Prof Ec, St Louis Univ, 1955-62; Lectr, Univ of MD, 1963; Adj Prof Ec, Am Univ, 1964-66; Assoc Prof Ec 1966-69, Prof Ec 1970-, Cath Univ; Conslt & Other Previous Employmnt, Var Pvt Cos & Govt Agys, 1950-81; Chief Div Ec Anal Automation, Ofc Manpower Automation Tng, US Dept of Labor, 1962-64; Dir Eval & Manpower Devel & Utilization Progs Br, US Ofc Ed, Dept of Hlth, Ed & Wel, 1964-66; Mem: Ec Hist Assn; En Ec Assn; Alpha Kappa Psi; Others; cp/VPres, Ellis Isl Restoration Comm; Over 10 Papers Presented at Orgnl Meetings; Others; r/Rom Cath; hon/Author of 4 Books incl'g: *The Ellis Isl Source Book*, 1984; *Career Ed: Contbns to Ec Growth*, 1973; *Manpower & the City*, 1969; Author of 4 Monographs & Over 17 Articles Pub'd in Var Mags & Jours incl'g: *Ec Synthesis*; *The Bridge*; *Jour Ec Issues*; *Qtly Review Ec & Bus*; *Am Jour Ec & Sociol*; Others; Dist'd Ser Awd, Bronze Deg 1949, Silver Deg 1960, Alpha Kappa Psi, Profl Frat of Commerce; Res Fellow, Bur of Bus, Univ of MI, 1949; Res Asst James Ford Bell Foun, Univ of MN, 1957; Grant-in-Aid Res, Am Phil Soc, 1969; Res Grant, US Manpower Adm, 1971-72; W/W: in E, in S & SW; Am Ec Assn Handbook; Am Men of Sci; Am Authors Today; DIB; Writers Dir; Other Biogl Listings.

BOLLER, BRUCE RAYMOND oc/Educator; b/Jan 22, 1940; h/Sunset Lane, Rural Dist 1, Oak Ridge, NJ 07438; ba/Bronx, NY; m/Susan S; c/John, Janet; p/Raymond Edward, Alice M; sp/Albert E and Harriet S Saunders; ed/BS, Iona Col, 1961; MS, Univ of Pgh, 1964; PhD, CUNY, 1970; pa/Res Assoc Instr, City Col, CUNY, 1970-73; Asst Prof Physics, Baruch Col, NYC, 1973-75; Assoc Prof Physics, SUNY Maritime Col, Bronx, 1975-; Hon Chm Student Br Am Nuclear Soc 1981-, Chm Radiation Safety Com 1979-, Plus Num Other Com Chmships & Mbrships, SUNY-Maritime Col; Mem: Am Geophy Union; Am Nuclear Soc; Am Assn Physics Tchrs; cp/Cubmaster, Cub Pack #49, Milton, NJ, 1975-77; hon/Co-Author of 3 Res Articles w Harold Stolov, Pub'd in *Jour of Geophy Res*, 1970, 1973 & 1974; Univ Awd, SUNY, 1978.

BOLLWAGE, J CHRIS oc/City Council Member; b/Dec 7, 1954; h/1029 North Avenue, Elizabeth, NJ 07201; p/Frank and Jeanne, Elizabeth, NJ; ed/BA Ec, Kean Col of NJ; pa/Inward Traffic Clk, Sealand Ser, 1978-80; Acct Revenue Clk, PRMMI, 1980-81; Traffic Coor, Keer Steamship, 1981-; Elected City Coun Mem, Elizabeth, NJ, 1982-;

cp/Elizabeth & Union Co Dem Com, 1979-; Pres, N Elizabeth Yth Baseball, 1972-; Pres, Chiodo Assn, 1976-77; Elected Mem, Blessed Sacrament Parish Coun, 1977-; r/Rom Cath.

BOLTON, DOUGLAS JOHN oc/Curriculum Coordinator; b/Oct 20, 1953; h/North Village Apts #123, 2515 Culver Rd, Rochester, NY 14609; ba/Rochester, NY; p/Robert & Claire Bolton, Hamburg, NY; ed/BS Sec'dy Social Studies, SUNY-Cortland, 1975; Cert of Study, Common Mkt Prog, Col of Europe, Brugge, Belgium, 1974; MEd Sec'dy Instrn 1978, EdD Curric Devel & Instrn Media 1981, SUNY-Buffalo; pa/Curric Coor, East Irondequoit Ctl Schs, 1983-; Adm Asst, Addison Ctl Schs, 1982-83; Adm Asst, Hamburg Ctl Schs, 1981; Curric Spec, Rush Henrietta Ctl Schs, 1980-81; Asst Elem Prin, Frontier Ctl Schs, 1980; Instr & Supvr of Student Tchrs, Ofc of Tchr Ed, SUNY-Buffalo, 1979-81; Mem: Assn for Supvn & Curric Devel; NY St Assn for Supvn & Curric Devel; Wn NY Assn for Supvn & Curric Devel; Nat Coun for Social Studies; NY St Coun for Social Studies; Org for Am Hists; John Dewey Soc; Nat Humanistic Ed Ctr; Sagamore Inst; Assn for Humanistic Ed; Assn of Sch Bus Ofcls; Adv Coun for Reg Early Childhood Dir Ctr; Corning Career Devel Coun; Sch Admrs Assn of NYS; cp/Participant, Irondequoit Presb Ch, 1983-; Mem, Steuben Co Adv Coun Reg Early Childhood Dir Ctr, 1982-83; Mem Bus Ed Com & Chm Futures Subcom, Corning E Steuben Reg, 1982-83; Mem, Addison Kiwanis, 1982-83; Instr & Coach, Corning Commun Col, 1982-83; Rehab Cnslr, Tonawanda YMCA, 1981; Asst Ath Tnr, SUNY-Buffalo, 1979; AAU Track & Field Coach, 1978-79; Participant, Geneva-Waterloo Finger Lakes Men's Basketball Div, 1977-78; Track & Field Coach, Syracuse Chargers, 1975-76; Others; r/Meth; hon/Author of Num Ednl Articles Pub'd in Profl Jours incl'g: *NY St Coun for Social Studies Newslttr*; *Social Sci Record*; *Wn NY Assn for Supvn & Curric Devel Report*; *Sch Admrs Assn of NY Jour*; *Addison Newslttr*; *Addison Post*; Tchr of Yr & Coach of Yr, W Genesee Ctl Schs, 1976; Coach of Season, Geneva City Public Schs, 1976; 1st Place, Gen Motors Intercol Bus Understanding Contest 1978, Grad Asst in Tchr Ed Dept 1979, SUNY-Buffalo; Cert'd Notary Public, 1982-; Phi Delta Kappa; Kappa Delta Pi; Phi Alpha Theta; Pi Sigma Alpha; W/W: in E, in Am.

BOLTON, JAMES DENNIS oc/Engineer; b/Apr 24, 1952; h/503 Aurora Street, Lancaster, NY 14086; ba/Lockport, NY; m/Mary R; c/Andrew Toby; p/Robert K and Claire Bolton, Hamburg, NY; sp/Robert and Florence Rightmyer, Ithaca, NY; ed/BSME 1975, MSME 1976, Purdue Univ; Lic'd Profl Engr, NY St; mil/NROTC; pa/Prod Engr 1976-80, Buyer 1980-82, Sr Buyer 1982-83, Sr Mfg Engr 1983-, Harrison Radiator Div; Career Guid & Student Contest Chm Buffalo Sect 1977-79, Am Soc Mech Engrs; Mem, Soc Automotive Engrs, 1971-; Mem, Soc Mfg Engrs, 1983-; cp/Choir Mem, Ch Bd, Wesleyan Ch of Orchard Pk; r/Christian; hon/Pi Tau Sigma; Eagle Scout, Leag & Country Awd, BSA; 3rd Place, Reg VI Student Paper Contest, Am Soc Mech Engrs,

1975; Dir of Dist'd Ams.

BOLTON, ROGER EDWIN oc/Professor; b/Nov 23, 1938; h/30 Grandview Drive, Williamstown, MA 01267; ba/Fernald House, Williamstown, MA; m/Julia Carolyn Gooden; c/Christopher Andrew, Jonathan Hughes; p/Oscar and Edna Bolton, Dover, PA; sp/Merrill and Mary Gooden, Newark, DE; ed/AB, Franklin and Marshall Col, 1959; MA 1961, PhD 1964, Harvard Univ; pa/Instr Ec, Harvard Univ, 1964-66; Asst Prof 1966-69, Assoc Prof 1969-74, Prof Ec 1974-, Wms Col; Assoc Staff Mem, Brookings Instn, 1965-68; Vis'g Prof: Wellesley Col 1977 & Univ of PA 1981-82; Sr Ec (Pt-time), Curran Assocs, 1973-75; Mem & Rep to AAAS 1980-, Am Ec Assn; Mem: AAAS; Reg Sci Assn; Assn for Public Policy Anal & Mgmt; cp/Mem 1983-, VChm 1984-, Planning Bd, Town of Wmstown, 1983-; Mem 1979-81 & 1982-, Clk 1983-, Reg Planning Comm, Berkshire Co; r/Prot; hon/Editor: *Def Purchases & Reg Growth*, 1966; *Def & Disarmament*, 1966; Co-Author *Reg Diversity*, 1981; Author of Num Papers & Articles on St & Local Fin, Reg Ec, Solid Waste Mgmt, Multireg Ed Modeling & Fin Higher Ed in US; AB, summa cum laude, 1959; Phi Beta Kappa, 1958; Pi Gamma Mu, 1958; Woodrow Wilson & Danforth F'ships for PhD, 1961-64; W/W: in E, in Am.

BOMGARDNER, WILLIAM EARL oc/Executive, Editor; b/Jan 28, 1925; h/56 Maple Avenue, Hershey, PA 17033; ba/Hershey, PA; m/Jean Ebersole; c/Barbara B Elliot, Susan; ed/AA Bus, Hershey Jr Col, 1946; BS Bus, Susquehanna Univ, 1947; mil/USAAF, 1943-45, 1st Lt; pa/Supvr Clerical Div A & H, CT Gen Life Ins Co, Hartford, 1947-54; Salesman, CT Mut Life Ins Co, Hartford, 1954-55; Public Acct, Hershey, PA, 1955-62; Exec Dir, Antique Automobile Clb of Am, 1959-; Editor, *Antique Automobile Mag*, 1970; Mem: Soc of Automotive Histns; Am Soc of Assn Execs; PA Soc of Assn Execs; Phi Mu Delta; Treas, Derry Twp Sch Bldg Auth, 1973-79; cp/Lions Clb; Masons; Shriners; Royal Order of Jesters; Pres, Hershey Shrine Clb, 1979; Pres, Zembo Golf Clb, 1981; Pres, Zembo Shepherds Unit, 1981-82; Pres, Zembo Antique & Classic Car Unit, 1979; r/Meth; hon/Editor, *Antique Automobile Mag*, 1970; Air Medal w 4 OLC; Dist'd Flying Cross; Charles E Duryea Cup, Antique Automobile Clb of Am; W/W in Am.

BOND, THOMAS JEFFERSON JR oc/Trust Services Officer; b/Aug 27, 1936; h/PO Box 1301, Vienna, VA 22180; ba/Washington, DC; m/Wilma M; c/T Jefferson III, Mrs Julia B Franklin; p/Thomas J Bond (dec); Clara Chisam Bond, Soddy, TN; sp/Keller B McCrary (dec); Lee Reid McCrary, Old Hickory, TN; ed/BS, TN Tech Univ, 1958; MA, Vanderbilt Univ, 1959; mil/AUS, 1960; pa/Instr, Univ of TN-Chattanooga, 1959-63; Instr, Univ of L'ville, 1963-64; Fish & Wildlife Ser 1964-81, Bur of Indian Affairs 1981-, Dept of Interior; Tng Dir, Refuge Mgrs Acad, Arden Hills, NM, 1968-69; Docent 1972-77, CoChm Wkend Ednl Prog 1974-76, Nat Mus Am Hist & Smithsonian Instn; Guest Lectr, Univ of NM, 1970; Mem, NRA; Past Mem, AAUP; Past Mem, Am Soc of Tng Dirs; Mem, Nat Wildlife Fdn; Wildlife Soc;

Am Forestry Assn; Conslt, Biol Scis Curric Study; Mem Career Oppor & Tng Com 1968-69 & 1973-74, Fish & Wildlife Ser; Dept of Interior Rep to Upper MS River Basin Comm, 1978; Task Force Mem, Dept Org for NEPA Compliance, 1978; Task Force Mem, Bur Indian Affairs Re-org, 1982; cp/Treas, Clans of Scotland, USA, 1979-80; Property Mgr 1982, Boom Com 1983-85, Potomac Corral of The Wnrs; Pres, DC Soc SAR, 1985; Pres, IDRA Rod & Gun Clb, 1983; Mem, Fairfax Co Arbitration Comm, 1974-; Var Ch Ofcs & Coms, Wesley U Meth Ch, Vienna, VA; r/Meth; hon/Author & Co-Author of Var Govt Agy Reports, 1969-79; Book Reviewer, *Chattanooga Times*, 1961-76; Mensa; Beta Beta Beta; W/W in Tng; Personalities of S.

BONDS, NADINE CELESTE oc/Telecommunications; b/Nov 20; h/6120 Foxwood Lane, Indianapolis, IN 46208; ba/Westfield, IN; m/Richard Thomas; c/Marcel Tyrone, Rodney Darnell; p/Thomas J and Mable N (Hines) Perry, Indianapolis, IN; sp/William T and Marian D Bonds, Indianapolis, IN; ed/Att'd IN St Univ, 1969-73; BA Psych, Purdue Univ, 1983; Internal Telecommuns 1983, Curric Developer 1980-82, Tng Admr 1978-79, GTE MWn Telephone Opers; Adm Sales Mgr 1977-78, Ofc Opers Supvr 1974-76, Allstate Ins Co; Mem: Am Mgmt Assn; Am Soc for Pers Adm; NAACP; Netwk Dir Statonians Inc, Nat Assn Female Execs; Fellow, Fred Pryor Mgmt Inst; Editor *Carousel* 1982, Treas 1983, Intl Assn for Pers Wom; cp/Pres 1984-86, VPres 1978-82, Chm Registration 48th Ctl Reg Conf 1982, Sec 43rd Ctl Reg Conf 1977, Alpha Mu Omega Chapt of Alpha Kappa Alpha Sorority; Mem, Urban Leag; r/U Meth; hon/Var Articles in *Carousel* for Intl Assn Pers Wom, 1982 Issues; Mem of Yr Alpha Mu Omega Chapt 1980, Advr of Yr Ctl Reg 1979, Alpha Kappa Alpha Sorority Inc; Advr of Yr, Ctl IN Jr Achmt, 1977; W/W: Among Am Wom, in Ctl Reg.

BONFANTE, LARISSA oc/Professor; h/50 Morningside Drive, New York, NY 10025; ba/New York, NY; m/Leo Ferrero Raditsa; c/Alexandra Bonfante-Warren; p/Giuliano and Vittoria Bonfante, Rome, Italy; sp/Nina Ferrero and Bogdan Raditsa, NYC; ed/BA, Barnard Col, 1954; MA, Univ of Cinc, 1957; PhD, Columbia Univ, 1966; pa/Instr, Asst Prof, Assoc Prof, Prof & Chm Classics Dept, NY Univ, 1963-83; Fgn Mem, Istituto di Studi Etruschi, 1973-; Exec Com Mem, Archaeol Inst of Am, 1981-84; hon/Author of 3 Books incl'g: *The Etruscan Lang*, 1983; Editor, Several Books of Essays; Translator, Book of Plays; Author of Num Articles & Reviews Pub'd in Scholarly Jours; Gt Tchr Awd, NY Univ, 1983; Num Biogl Listings.

BONHOMME, DENISE oc/Educator; b/Jan 20, 1926; h/1220 Tasman Drive, Number 420, Sunnyvale, CA 94089; ba/San Jose, CA; p/Rene Louis and Jeanne Anna (Giroud) Bonhomme (dec); c/Claire Helen Quebedeau, Norman Ray Quebedeau; ed/Baccalauréat Phil, Académie de Lille, France, 1943; MA Lit, Univ of OR, 1969; pa/Var Secy Positions, Austin, TX, 1949-64; Instr, Prof French Lang & Lit, Mt Angel Col, OR, 1964-72; Ofc Wkr in Monterey, CA & Tchr in

Seaside & Monterey, 1972-77; Prog Secy, Elec Power Res Inst, Palo Alto, CA, 1977-80; Pt-time French Instr, Mission Commun Col, Santa Clara, CA, Fall 1981; Secy & Word Processor, Nat Semiconductor, Santa Clara, CA, 1981-1983; Legal Secy, Pillsbury, Madison & Sutro, San Jose, CA, 1983-; hon/ Author: *The Esoteric Substance of Voltairian Thought*, 1975; *Le Collier Symbolique d'Alfred de Vigny*, 1968; W/W Among Wom; Contemp Authors; DIB; Other Biogl Listings.

BONILLA-SAN MIGUEL, SANDRA IVONNE oc/Social Work Therapist, Administrator; b/May 23, 1944; 1214 Howell Creek Drive, Winter Springs, FL 32708; m/Manuel; p/Isidoro Bonilla Ortiz (dec); Flora Carrero-Bonilla (dec); ed/BA, St Joseph's Col, NYC, 1966; MSSW, Columbia Univ Sch of Social Wk, NYC, 1970; pa/Dir Substance Abuse Div & Sanford Br Ofc, Seminole Co Mtl Hlth Ctr, Altamonte Springs, FL, 1978-81; Coor & Supvr Inmate Treatment Sers St Penitentiary & Minimum Custody Prisons, Dept of Addiction Control Sers, Govt of PR, Zarzal & Naguabo, PR, 1974-77; Social Wk Therapist, Chd's Aid Soc; Sr Social Wk Therapist, Traveler's Aid Soc, PR; Soc Sers Caseworker, PR Migration Div, NYC; Mem: Intergovtl Com for Re-org of PR St Penitentiary, 1975; Col of PR Social Wkrs; Nat Assn Social Wkrs; FL Coun on Mtl Hlth; VChm, Pres's Minority Adv Coun, Univ of Ctl FL; r/Rom Cath; hon/Manhattan Borough Pres's Awd, NYC, 1959; Cardinal Spellman Yth Awd, NYC, 1960; F'ship Scholar, Columbia Univ, 1968; Cert of Merit, Dept of Addiction Control Sers, PR, 1976; Cert of Apprec, Seminole Co Sch Vol Prog, 1981.

BONOMA, THOMAS V oc/Professor; b/Sep 18, 1946; h/45 Drum Hill Road, Concord, MA 01742; ba/Boston, MA; m/Elaine McElhattan; c/Thomas, Matthew, Jonathan, Benjamin; p/Emil A Bonoma, Rocky River, OH; sp/K E McElhattan, Pgh, PA; ed/AB Psych, OH Univ, 1968; MS Psych, Univ of Miami, Coral Gables, FL, 1969; PhD Social Psych, SUNY-Albany, 1972; pa/Assoc Prof Bus Adm 1981-, Vis'g Assoc Prof Bus Adm 1979-81, Harvard Bus Sch; Assoc Prof Bus Adm & Psych, Univ of Pgh, 1975-79; Sr Res Sci, Inst for Juv Res, Chgo, 1972-75; Mem: Am Mktg Assn; Am Psychol Assn; Assn for Consumer Res; Bd Mem of 5 Cos; r/ Epis; hon/Author of 5 Books: *Mng Mktg*, 1984; *Segmenting the Industl Mkt*, 1983; *Psych for Mgrs*, 1981; *Exec Survival Manual*, 1978; *Conflict, Power & Influence*, 1973; Sr Fulbright-Hayes Awd, 1978; Doct Dissertation Grant, US Arms Control & Disarmament Agy, 1972; Blue Key Nat Hon, 1968; Var W/W.

BOOK, JOHN K oc/Businessman; b/ Jun 26, 1950; h/PO Box 840, Winchester, KY 40391; ba/Same; m/Betty L; c/ Michelle Dunn, Marie Dunn; p/Vern R Book and Pearl I Alford, Winchester, KY; sp/Mr and Mrs Ray Christy, Winchester, KY; ed/AA Higher Acctg & Bus Adm, KY Bus Col, Lexington, 1974; pa/Store Owner, Kenny's Signs & Bus Sers, 1977-; Irvin Industs, Lexington, 1973-75; A O Smith, Mt Sterling, KY, 1972-73; Lexington Army Depot, KY, 1968-70; cp/Cand: Sch Bd 1976 & 1978; City Commr 1977, 1979,

1981 & 1983; r/Bapt; hon/KY Col, 1973; Notary Public, St-at-large, KY, 1981; W/ W in S & SW; Personalities of S.

BOOKSTEIN, ABRAHAM oc/Professor; b/Mar 22, 1940; h/5445 South, East View Park, Chicago, IL 60615; ba/ Chicago, IL; m/Marguerite; p/Alex Bookstein; sp/Lindley Vickers; ed/BS, City Col of NY, 1961; MS, Univ of CA-Berkeley, 1966; PhD Physics, Yeshiva Univ, NY, 1969; MA Lib Sci, Univ of Chgo, 1970; pa/Prof Grad Lib Sch & Dept Behavioral Scis, Univ of Chgo, 1971-; Mem: Assn for Computing Machines; Am Soc for Info Sci; hon/ Co-Author of Books: *Prospects for Change in Bibliographic Control*, 1977; *Opers Res: Implications for Libs*, 1972; Author, Over 50 Articles in Profl Jours; Mem Bd of Editors: *Lib Qtly*, 1980-; *Info Processing & Mgmt*, 1980-; Bd of Trustees, *Rel Index*, 1984; Awardee, NSF Grant; Num Nat & Intl Vis'g S'ships; Am Men & Wom of Sci; Intl Authors & Writers W/W; Num Other Biogl Listings.

BOON, DONALD JACKSON oc/ Allergist, Medical Consultant; b/May 9, 1937; h/4509 Oahu Northeast, Albuquerque, NM 87111; ba/Albuquerque, NM; m/Cheryl Yvonne; c/Sharon Marie, Diana Jean; p/Clifton U Boon, Aurora, IL; sp/L Robert Sladek, Albuquerque, NM; ed/BS, Purdue Univ, 1959; MS & MD, Univ of IL Med Ctr, Chgo, 1963; Residency Pediatrics, Univ of OK, 1968-71; Cert, Am Bd Pediatrics, 1971; mil/AUS Med Corp, 1964-67, Capt; pa/Currently: Allergist, Pvt Pract, Albuquerque, NM; Res Fellow, Human Ecol Res Foun, Chgo, IL; Mem: Albuquerque Bernalillo Co Med Assn; NM Med Soc; NM Chapt, Am Lung Assn; N AM Soc for Pediatric Gastroenterology; Am Acad Allergy; Christian Med Soc; AAAS; NM Acad of Sci; Am Phys Poetry Assn; r/U Meth; hon/Author of Num Pub'd Poems incl'g: "Beautiful," "Rally Cry of the Balloonist," & "The Balloon Chase Crew"; Clin Asst Prof, Univ of NM Med Sch; Cert'd Lay Spkr, Ctl U Meth Ch, Albuquerque; W/W in W & MW; Dir Dist'd Ams; Book of Hon; Men of Achmt; Dir Med Specs; Am Men & Wom of Sci; Other Biogl Listings.

BOOTH, G GEOFFREY oc/Professor; b/Jan 13, 1942; h/102 Downing Road, DeWitt, NY 13214; ba/Syracuse, NY; m/Kathryn M; c/Christopher, Timothy, James; ed/BBA 1964, MBA 1966, OH Univ; PhD, Univ of MI, 1971; Fin Analyst, Ford Motor Co, 1966-67; Fin Sys Analyst, Dow Chem Co, 1967; Asst Prof 1970-74, Assoc Prof 1974-79, Res Dir 1974-81, Prof & Dept Chm 1979-81, Univ of RI; Prof & Dept Chm, Syracuse Univ, 1981-; Ec & Fin Conslt; Num Pvt Instns & Legal Firms, 1968-; Editor of Pubs 1973-76, VPres Prog 1976-77, Pres 1979-80, Trustee 1980-; En Fin Assn; Dir, Fin Mgmt Assn 1979-80; Editor of Pubs 1978-81, Pres 1978-79, N Eng Bus & Ec Assn; Mem: Am Ec Assn; Am Fin Assn; So Fin Assn; hon/Author, Over 80 Articles, Papers & Monographs in Ec & Fin Pub'd in Profl Jours incl'g: *Jour of Reg Sci*; *Jour of Monetary Ec*; *Rivista Internazionale Di Scienze Economiche E Commerciali*; *Jour of Bkg & Fin*; Others; Beta Gamma Sigma, 1966; Phi Kappa Phi, 1968; Contbns Chronicled in *Fin Mgmt*, 1981; Hon Lifetime Mem, N Eng Bus & Ec Assn, 1982; W/W: in E, in Conslitg; Am Men & Wom of Sci;

Commun Ldrs & Noteworthy Ams; Outstg Yg Men of Am; Num Other Biogl Listings.

BOOTHE, ROASLIE J oc/Executive; b/Jun 15, 1938; h/103-16 Matthieu Lane Northeast, Aurora, OR 97002; ba/ Portland, OR; m/Thomas; c/Linda Boothe Johnson, Saundra Adelle; p/ Edna Adelle Johnson, NY; sp/Murtice Boothe, Richmond, VA; ed/BS, Bklyn Col, 1960; Att'd MS Prog Behav Sci, Johnson Sch of Profl Arts, Jamaica, NY, 1962; pa/Pres & Fdr, The House of Exodus Alcoholism Drug/Mtl Hlth Ednl Treatment Ctr of USA, 1978-; Fam Therapist, Yaun Yth Care Ctr, 1974-76; Co-Prodr, TV Prog "Our World Too," 1973-74; Admr, Med Lab, Portland, OR, 1970-73; Bacteriologist, NY, 1957-69; Mem: UGN: Leag of Wom Voters; Nat Ed for Tchrs; Nat Consumer Info Ctr; r/Meth; hon/Author of Poetry incl'g: "Going Out My Child," Poem Dedicated to Martin Luther King Jr wich Hangs in White House & Martin Luther King Center, Atlanta; Mgmt Awd for Yth Sers; Recip, N/NE Portland Mtl Hlth Plaque; Cert of Excell for Yth Progs, St of OR Dept of Labor; W/W.

BORCHERDT, EDWARD RAHR JR oc/Entrepreneur; b/Jul 12, 1930; h/2828 Wisconsin Avenue, Northwest, Washington DC 2007; ba/Washington, DC; m/Wendy; c/Kimberley Borcherdt Bolt, Edward Rahr III; sp/Mrs Stuart Meek Hawley, Atherton, CA; ed/Grad, The Taft Sch, Watertown, CT, 1949; AB, Stanford Univ, 1953; MBA, Stanford Univ Grad Sch of Bus, 1957; mil/USMC, 1953-60, Ret'd Capt; pa/Crown Zellenbach, LA, 1958-59; Fry Conslts, LA, 1960-66; Pres, Borcherdt & Co, LA, Wash DC & Seoul, Korea, 1966-; Former Pres, Stanford Clb of LA; Mem, Stanford Bus Sch Assn, LA Co; cp/ Trustee, Devil Pups Inc (USMC Yth Prog); Former Sr Warden, All Sts Epis Ch, Beverly Hills, CA; r/Epis; hon/Pres Appt to Bd of Visitors, US Nav Acad, 1981-84; W/W: in W & E, in World.

BORDALLO, RICARDO JEROME oc/Governor; b/Dec 11, 1927; h/Office of Governor, PO Box 2950, Agana, Guam 96910; ba/Same; m/Madeleine Zeien; c/Deborah; p/Baltasar and Josefina Bordallo, Tamuning, Guam; ed/ Att'd Univ of SF; pa/1st Term 1974-78, 2nd 4 Yr Term 1982-86, Gov of Guam; Owner, Nat Automotive Parts Assn, Guam, 1974-84; Owner, Guan Intl Ins Co, 1974-84; Housing & Apt Bldg Investmts, 1974; Real Est Devel, 1974; Former Pubr, *Guam Pacific Jour Daily Newspaper*, 1966; Chm & Bd of Dirs, Fam Fin Co Inc Gen Ins Agy, 1959-74; Other Past Bus Positions; Senator, 4th-10th Guam Legis, 1956-70; Other Legis Experience; cp/Chm, Dem Party Guam, 1971-73; Dem Party Nom Isls, 1970; Del: Nat Dem Conv SF, 1984; Nat Dem Conv NYC, 1976; Nat Dem Conv Chgo, 1968; Legis Ldrs Conf, PR, 1965; Nat Legis Conf, Atl City, 1964; Others; Mem, Num Guam Legis Coms, 1956-70; Mem: Guam' C of C, AT Assn Guam; Nav Leag; Lions Clb; SKOL; Bd of Dirs & Chm, ARC; Yg Mens Leag; Spanish Clb; Tourist Comm; Rehab Ctr; Marianas Assn Retarded Chdn; Liberation Day Com; r/Cath; hon/Lifemem, Nat Geog Soc; Mem, Soc Intl Devel; Mem, Intl Platform Assn; Hon Mem, Kiwanis Agana Clb of Guam; W/W: in Am, in

91

Am Polits; Men of Achmt; Intl Biographic Ctr, Cambridge, England.

BORDERS, WILLIAM D oc/Archbishop; b/Oct 9, 1913; ed/Att'd St Meinrad Sem, IN, 1935; Att'd Notre Dame Sem, NO, 1936-40; MS Ed, Notre Dame Univ, S Bend, IN, 1947; mil/AUS Chaplain Corps, 1943-46, Maj; pa/Assoc Pastor, Sacred Heart Parish, Baton Rouge, NO, 1940-43; Assoc Pastor, Our Lady of Prompt Succor, Westwago, LA; Assoc Pastor, Our Lady of Lourdes, NO, 1947-48; Asst Chaplain 1948-57, Chaplain 1959-64, Christ the King Chapel, LA St Univ (LSU); Pastor, Holy Fam Ch, Port Allen, LA, 1957-59; Rector, St Joseph Cathedral, Baton Rouge, LA, 1964-68; Bishop, Diocese of Orlando, 1968-74; Archbishop, Archdiocese of Balto, 1974-; Chm Ed Com & Mem Adm Bd, US Cath Conf; Mem Adm Com, Bishops Welfare Emer Relief Com, Bishops' Com on Moral Values, Nat Conf of Cath Bishops; Chm, ad hoc Com of Bishops & Cath Col Pres; Chm, Ad Hoc Com for Bicent of US Hierarchy; Mem, Bishops Com on Laity; cp/Creator & Orgr of Num Couns, Bds, Ednl Progs & Sers; r/Cath; hon/Mem, of 3 Wk Tour of Peoples Repub of China, 1981.

BORNSTEIN, MARC H oc/Professor; b/Nov 23, 1947; ba/New York, NY; m/Helen G; p/Mr and Mrs G Bornstein, Waltham, MA; ed/BA, Columbia Col, 1969; MS 1973, PhD 1974, Yale Univ; pa/Prof Psych & Human Devel, NY Univ, 1983-; Adj Prof Psychi 1983-, Dir of Res Tng Ctr for Transcultural Human Devel 1981-, NY Univ Sch of Med; Prof Invité, Laboratoire de Psychologie Expérimentale, Centre National de la Recherche Scientifique, Paris, 1984; Child Clin Fellow, Child & Fam Ctr, Inst for Behavior Therapy, NY, 1981-82; Vis'g Fellow, Univ Col, London, 1978-79; Postdoct Res Fellow 1974-75, USPHS Trainee 1971-72, Yale Univ; Vis'g Sci, Max-Planck-Institut für Psychiatrie, Munich, 1974; Other Previous Univ Appts; Mem: AAAS; Am Psychol Assn; NY Acad of Scis; Sigma Xi; Soc for Res & Child Devel; Intl Conf on Infant Studies; Conslt, Var Profl Jours, Nat Founs & Univs; hon/Editor of 5 Books incl'g: Devel Psych: An Adv'd Text, 1984; Author & Co-Author: Over 20 Book Chapts; Over 50 Sci Res Articles Pub'd in Profl Psych Jours; Over 80 Scholarly Reviews; Res Career Devel Awd, NIH, 1983; JS Guggenheim Fellow, 1984; B R McCandless Yg Sci Awd, Am Psych Assn, 1978; C S Ford Cross-Cultural Res Awd, Human Relats Area Files, 1972; W/W: in E, in Frontier Sci & Technol.

BORSOS, TIBOR oc/Immunologist; b/Mar, 12, 1927; h/4703 Edgefield Road, Bethesda, MD 20814; ba/Frederick, MD; m/Ruth Moser; c/Michael B, David J; p/Edmund Borsos-Nachtnebel (dec); Anna Borsos (dec); ed/BA Chem, Cath Univ of Am, 1954; ScD Path-Biol, Johns Hopkins Univ, 1958; pa/Res Assoc 1958-62, Asst Prof 1960-62, Dept of Microbiol, Johns Hopkins Sch of Med; Sr Sci 1962-66, Sect Chief 1966-, Assoc Lab Chief 1971-, Lab Chief 1981-, Nat Cancer Inst; Mem, Am Assn of Immunols, 1959-; hon/Author, Over 200 Pubs on Immunol; Co-Author (w H J Rapp) of Book, Molcecular Basis of Complement Action, 1970; Sr Exec Ser Awd, 1981; W/W in Govt; Am Men of Sci.

BOSE, SAM C oc/Executive; b/Jul 28, 1953; h/7101 Farralone Avenue, #156, Canoga Park, CA 91303; ba/Canogo Park, CA; p/Amresh and Renuka Bose, SLC & Calcutta; ed/BSEE 1973, MSEE 1974, Polytech Inst of Bklyn; PhD Engrg, Univ of CA-LA (UCLA), 1980; pa/Pres & CEO, Applied Sci Analytics Inc, Canoga Park, 1982-; Staff Sci, Litton Guid & Control Sys, Woodland Hills, CA, 1976-82; Mem Tech Staff, Computer Scis Corp, Mtn View, CA 1974-76; Mem: IEEE; AIAA; Am Geophy Union; Intl Fedn Automatic Control; Reviewer for IEEE, AIAA & AGU Jours; Author, Over 30 Profl Sci Articles & Assn Res Papers Pub'd; Eta Kappa Nu; Tau Beta Pi; Sigma Xi; Danforth Foun Fellow; Spec Grad F'ship, Undergrad S'ship & Best Grad Sr Awd, Polytech Inst of Bklyn; Rotary Foun S'ship; Sum Student F'ship, Woods Hole Oceanographic Instn; Student Paper Awd, Sigma Xi; Outstg Doct Cand Awd, UCLA; W/W in W.

BOSEKER, BARBARA JEAN oc/Professor; b/Dec 2, 1944; ba/Moorhead, MN; m/Dale Leslie Sutcliffe; p/Alice Boseker, Milwaukie, WI; ed/Exch Student, Univ of Nigeria-Naukka, 1966; BS Sec'dy Ed 1968, MA Anthropol 1971, Cert in African Studies 1972, PhD Ed 1978, Univ of WI-Madison; pa/Chem Lab Tech, Allen-Bradley Corp, Milwaukee, WI, 1963; Coor, Neighborhood Yth Corp, Madison,, 1970; Prog Devel Spec, Tchr Corps, Madison, 1976-77; Asst Prof Ed, Occidental Col, LA, CA, 1978-80; Asst Prof Ed, Moorhead St Univ, 1980-; Mem: NEA; Am Assoc Cols for Tchr Ed; Moorhead St Univ Fac Advr for Student MN Ed Assn; Former Mem, African Studies Assn; Former Mem, NCTE; Pres Moorhead St Univ Chapt, Phi Kappa Phi; cp/Vol Fundraiser, Prairie Public TV (PBS); r/Christian Science; hon/Contbr of Num Articles to Profl Jours; Conslt, Inst of Latin Am Studies, Univ of TX-Austin, 1980; Phi Kappa Phi; Pi Lambda Theta; Kappa Delta Pi; Sigma Tau Delta; Sigma Epsilon Sigma; Mortar Bd; Nat Def Ed Act Lang F'ships, 1970-75; Num F'ships & S'ships; W/W: of Wom, of Am Wom.

BOSKEY, ADELE LUDIN oc/Scientist; b/Aug 30, 1943; h/4 Winding Way, North Caldwell, NJ 07006; ba/New York, NY; m/James B; c/Elizabeth Rona; p/Benjamin and Anna Ludin, Marlboro, NJ; sp/Loeser Boskey, West Orange, NJ; Grace Boskey (dec); ed/BA, Barnard Col, 1964; PhD, Boston Univ, 1970; pa/Instr, Col of Liberal Arts, .Boston Univ, 1969-70; Editor, Cambridge Data File, 1970-71; Postdoct Trainee 1971-73, Asst Sci 1973-75, Assoc Sci 1975-, Dir Ultrastructural Biochem Lab 1984, The Hosp for Spec Surg; Asst Prof Biochem 1975-79, Assoc Prof 1979-, Cornell Univ Med Col; Exec Com & Mem-at-large, Ortho Res Soc, 1981-82; Prog Com, Am Soc Bone & Mineral Res, 1982-83; Pres Mineralized Tissue Grp, Intl Assn Dental Res, 1985-86; Author, Over 50 Articles in Sci Res Jours incl'g: Calcified Tissue Int; Dist'd Res in Ortho, Kappa Delta, 1979; Career Devel Awd 1975-80, Res Grant 1973, NIH-NIDR; BMRC Grant, 1984; W/W: in Am, in Sci.

BOSKEY, JAMES B oc/Professor; b/Mar 27, 1942; h/4 Winding Way, North Caldwell, NJ 07006; ba/Newark, NJ; m/Adele; c/Elizabeth Rona; p/L M Boskey, West Orange, NJ; sp/Benjamin and Anne Ludin, Marlboro, NJ; ed/AB, Princeton Univ, 1964; JD, Univ of MI, 1967; LLM,

London Sch of Ec & Polit Sci, 1972; pa/Instr, IN Univ Law Sch, 1967-68; Asst Prof, Cleveland St Univ Law Sch, 1968-70; Asst Prof Law 1971-73, Assoc Prof 1973-77, Prof 1977-, Seton Hall Law Sch; Mem, ABA & NJ Bar Assn; Mem, Govs Com, Chdn Ser Planning, 1983-84; Mem, Assn for Chd of NJ, 1978-; cp/Treas, Suburban Jewish Sch, 1983-; hon/Co-Author of Book, Tchg About Aging, 1982; Editor, Child Abuse Manual, 1977; Author of Var Articles in Profl Jours.

BOSSERT, MICHAEL H oc/Executive; b/Apr 21, 1948; h/2943 Rambling Drive, Dallas, TX 75228; ba/Dallas, TX; m/Frances D; c/Melody Leigh, Stephanie Denise; p/Mr and Mrs W L Bossert, Tampa, FL; sp/Mr and Mrs William Ambagais, Kingsley, PA; ed/BA Geog, IN Univ of PA, 1970; MA Urban Affairs, VA Polytech Inst, 1976; mil/AUS, 1970; pa/Assoc Watch Ofcr, CIA, 1972-74; Assoc Duty Ofcr, White House, Wash, DC, 1974-76; Dist Mgr, Public Ser Co of OK, 1976-79; Mgmt Analyst, Ctl & SW Sers, 1979-81; VPres of Land & Adm, Ctl & SW Fuels Inc, 1981-; Mem, AIIE, 1980-; r/Rom Cath; hon/Author "Citizen Participation in Local Govt of Falls Ch, VA," 1975; "Low Income Housing Anal for Wash DC," 1974; Deans List, IN Univ of PA, 1969-70; Rec'd Real Est Sales License (St of TX), 1982; W/W in S & SW.

BOST, RAYMOND MORRIS oc/Administrator; b/Aug 18, 1925; h/7333 Germantown Avenue, Philadelphia, PA 19119; ba/Philadelphia, PA; m/Margaret Vedder; Timothy Lee, Penelope Ruth, Peter Raymond, Jonathan Otto; p/Mrs Loy R Bost Sr, Maiden, NC; sp/Mrs Otto Vedder, Phila, PA; ed/Att'd The Citadel; BA 1949, DD 1976, Lenoir-Rhyne Col; MA 1959, PhD 1963, Yale Univ; mil/USMC, 1943-47; USAR (Chaplain); pa/Pastor, Nativity Luth Ch, Spartanburg, SC, 1952-53; Pastor, Holy Trinity Luth Ch, Raleigh, NC, 1953-57; Campus Luth Pastor, Yale Univ, 1957-59; Acad Dean 1966-67, Pres 1968-76, Lenoir-Rhyne Col; Prof Ch Hist & Dir Field Ed, Luth Theol So Sem, 1960-66; Pres 1976-, Luth Theol Sem-Phila; cp/Mem, Yale Clb of NYC; Mem, Rotary Intl; r/Luth; hon/Author & Contbr of Articles to 5 Books incl'g: Essays & Reports of The Luth Hist Conf, 1980; W/W in Am.

BOSTLEY, SISTER JEAN R oc/Librarian; b/Sep 26, 1940; ba/Pittsfield, MA; p/G Kenneth and Malvina M Bostley, Greenfield, MA; ed/BA, Col of Our Lady of the Elms; MLS, St Univ of NY-Albany; pa/Mem, Sisters of St Joseph of Springfield, MA, 1958-; Tchr, Sacred Heart Acad, Worcester, MA, 1961-63; Tchr & Libn, St Thomas the Apostle Sch, W Springfield, MA 1963-69; Libn, St Joseph Ctl HS, Pittsfield, MA, 1969-; Mem, Am Lib Assn; VChm 1979-81, Chm 1981-83, Past Chm 1983-, HS Libs Sect of Cath Lib Assn; Secy 1977-81, N Eng Chapt, Cath Lib Assn; Mbrship Devel Com, Cath Lib Assn, 1981-85; Mem, Wn MA Media Coun; r/Rom Cath; hon/Resr for Book Joyous Ser: A Hist of Sisters of St Joseph of Springfield, 1883-1983; Reg Reporter 1983-, Author of Chm's Annual Report 1983, Editor "Salvation Hist Since Pius IX: A Review of Lit," Clare S Dowd, 1980; Others; Cath Lib World; "Chm's Message" for 6 Issues of HS Libs Sect, Cath Lib Assn Newslttr, 1981-83; W/W: in E, of Wom; Other Biogl Listings.

BOSWORTH, BRUCE LEIGHTON oc/Educator; b/Mar 22, 1942; h/PO Box 1162 (6170 South Bemis Street), Littleton, CO 80160; c/David, Timothy, Paul, Reuben, Sheri; p/John Wayman and Alice Elizabeth Rodgers Bosworth, East Aurora, NY; ed/BA Elem Ed/Psych, Univ of Denver, 1964; MA Sch Adm 1970, Postgrad Study in Spec Ed 1970-77, Univ of No CO; EdD Social & Ednl Change in Spec Ed, Walden Univ, 1984; pa/Elem Tchr 1964-67 & 1970-81, Littleton, CO Public Schs; Bldg Prin, East Smoky Sch Div #54, Valleyview, Alta, CO; Pres Bd of Dirs & Lower Sch Tchr, Chatfield Sch, 1981-; cp/Secy 1974-76, Mem 1970-77, Littleton Lions Clb; Mason, 1963-; York Rite/Shriners, 1979-; Englewood, Colorado City C of C, 1984-; r/Meth; hon/ W/W in W.

BOTBOL, JOSEPH MOSES oc/Geologist; b/Oct 7, 1937; h/9 Inkberry Lane, North Falmouth, MA 02556; ba/Woods Hole, MA; m/Sandra Lynn; c/Moses Joseph; p/Mr and Mrs Melvin J Botbol, Milton, MA; ed/BS Geol, St Lawrence Univ, 1959; MS 1961, PhD 1968 Geol Engrg, Univ of UT; pa/Minerals Spec, US Bur of Mines, 1966-67; Geochem Exploration, Geostats, Computer Applications w Br of Exploration Res 1967-72; Resource Modelling, Computer Methods w Ofc of Resource Anal 1972-79; Chief Computer Applications Sect w Br of Atl Geol 1979-, US Geol Surv; Fellow, Wash Acad of Scis; cp/Mem, Nat Rifle Assn; Mem, Falmouth Rod & Gun Clb; r/ Jewish; hon/Author, Over 35 Articles in Profl Jours; Patentee in Field; Grad w Hons, 1959; Pres Cit for Mgmt Improvement, 1978; Cash Awd for GRASP Sys Design, 1978; W/W in E.

BOUCHER, BETTY JANE oc/Secretary, Bookkeeper; b/Oct 16, 1944; h/3008 Joyce Lane, Memphis, TN 38116; ba/ Memphis, TN; p/Mr and Mrs C R Boucher, Memphis, TN; ed/Acctg Deg, Draughon's Bus Sch, 1964; pa/Accts Record Clk, Philco Finan Co, Div of Ford Motor Co, 1964-65; Cashier, Wonder Snack Foods 1965; Corp Secy & Bookkeeper, C R Boucher Constrn Co Inc, 1965-; Pres 1975-76 & 1978-79, VPres 1974-75, Treas 1980-81, Bd of Dirs 1976-78, 1979-80 & 1981-82, Mem Num Coms, Memphis Chapt 13, Nat Assn of Wom in Constrn; Mem Var Reg V Coms 1978-, Nat Assn Wom in Constrn; Pres 1980-82, Record Secy 1979-80, 1st VPres 1978-79, 2nd VPres 1982-83, Treas 1975-78, Num Other Coms, Quota Clb of Memphis; Bd of Dir 1981-82, Record Secy 1982-83, Wom's Exec Coun of Memphis; Chm Public Affairs Coun, Memphis, 1982-83; Bd of Dirs 1978-82, Treas 1982-83, WAGES Inc; Mem, Nat Assoc Female Execs Inc; Del, Memphis Jobs Conf, 1981; cp/Mem, Bethel Grove Chapt, OES, TN; r/Bapt; hon/Jessie Ramsey Awd for Ser, Quota Clb of Memphis, 1979; WIC of Yr, Memphis Chapt 13, Nat Assn of Wom in Constrn, 1981; Hon Mem, Memphis City Coun, 1981; Nom'd 1982 Bus Wom of Yr Awd, Wom's Exec Coun; W/W: of Am Wom, of S & SW, in Fin & Indust; Personalities of S.

BOUCHER, FREDERICK CARLYLE oc/Legislator; b/Aug 1, 1946; ba/Abingdon, VA; ed/BA, Roanoke Col, 1968; JD, Univ of VA Sch of Law, 1971; pa/Assoc, Milbank, Tweed, Hadley & McCloy, NY, 1971-73; Assoc, Penn, Stuart, Eskridge

& Jones, Abingdon, VA, 1974-78; Atty, Boucher & Boucher Law Firm, 1978-82; Mem, VA St Senate, 1975-82; Mem, US Ho of Reps, 1982-; Mem, VA ST Crime Comm; Chm, Oil & Gas Subcom of VA Coal & Energy Comm; Mem, LA & Justic Com of Nat Conf of St Legis; cp/Mem Bd of Dirs, 1st VA Bk-Damascus; r/Meth; hon/Recip, Outstg Yg Bus-man Awd, Abingdon JCs, 1975; W/W in S & SW.

BOUDOULAS, HARISIOS oc/Professor; b/Nov 3, 1935; h/4185 Mumford Court, Columbus, OH 43220; ba/Columbus, OH; m/Olga Paspati; c/Sophia, Konstantinos; p/Konstantinos and Sophia Boudoulas, Velvendo-Kozani, Greece; ed/MD 1959, Doct Dipl Fac of Med 1967, Univ of Salonica, Greece; Bd of Internal Med & Bd of Cardiol, Greece, 1967; Dipl, Edn Coun Fgn Med Grads, USA, 1970; Dipl, Fedn Licensing Exam, 1975; Med Lic St of OH & St of MI, 1975; pa/Resident Internal Med, Red Cross Hosp, Athens, 1960-61; Resident in Internal Med & Cardiol Units & Lectr, 1st Med Clin, Univ of Salonica, Greece, 1961-75; Postdoct Fellow 1975, Asst Prof of Med Div of Cardiol 1975-78, Div Cardiovas Non-Invasive Res Labs 1978-80, Assoc Prof of Med 1978-80, Prof of Med 1980-82 & 1983-, Dir Cardiovas Res Div 1983-, OH St Univ; Prof of Med, Dir Clin Cardiovas Res, Acting Dir Div of Cardiol, Wayne St Univ, 1980-82; Chief Cardiovas Ctr 1980-82, Prof of Pharm 1982-, VA Med Ctr, Allen Pk, MI; Acting Chief Sect of Cardiol, Harper-Grace Hosps, Detroit, MI, 1982; Mem: AAAS, 1982; Detroit Ht Clb, 1981; MI Heart Assn, 1981; Am Col of Phys, 1979; Ctl Soc Clin Res, 1979; Am Col Angiology, 1979; Am Col Clin Pharm, 1978; Coun on Clin Cardiol, 1978; Am Fedn Clin Res, 1976; Greek Com Agnst Hypertension, 1973; Greek Heart Assn, 1973; Am Col Cardiol, 1973; Am Heart Assn, 1972; Royal Soc Med, London, 1969-71; Med Assn of Salonica, 1966; Num Other Mbrships; cp/Over 150 Presentations at Nat & Intl Univs & Orgnl Meetings; hon/Author, Over 150 Articles & 60 Abstracts Pub'd in Profl Med Jours & Textbooks; Dist'd Res Investigator, Ctl OH Heart Chapt, Am Heart Assn, Columbus, 1983; W/W: in Am, in World, in MW; Men of Achmt; Other Biogl Listings.

BOULPAEP, EMILE L oc/Professor; b/ Sep 15, 1938; h/Burnt Swamp Road, Woodbridge, CT 06525; ba/New Haven, CT; m/Elisabeth J Goris; p/Henri J Boulpaep and Eulalie J de Croes-Boulpaep (dec): sp/R C L Goris, Brasschaat, Belgium; ed/BS 1958, MD 1962, Lic'd Med Sci 1963, Univ of Louvain; mil/Belgium AF, 1966-68; pa/Asst 1962-66, Instr & Chief Asst 1966-68, Univ of Louvain; Asst Prof Physiol, Cornell Univ Med Col, 1968-69; Asst Prof Physiol 1969-72, Assoc Prof Physiol 1972-79, Prof & Chm Dept Physiol 1979-, Yale Univ Sch of Med; Dir 1971-, Pres 1977-, Belgium Am Ednl Foun; Dir, Fondation Universitaire, Belgium, 1977-; Dir, Fondation Francqui, 1977-; Dir, Belgium Soc of Benevolence, NY, 1980-; Dir, Universitas Ltd, 1982-; hon/Author, Over 125 Pubs in Sci Jours; Mem, Royal Acad of Med, Belgium, 1983; Overseas Fellow, Churchill Col, Cambridge Univ, UK, 1978-; K Order of Crown, Belgium, 1979; Cmdr, Order of Leopold II, Belgium, 1980; Prix des Alumni, Fondation Universitaire, Bel-

gium, 1973; W/W: in Am, in Frontier Sci & Technol.

BOULTON, SHAUNA DEE oc/Elementary School Teacher; b/May 29, 1949; h/1516 Glen Arbor, Salt Lake City, UT 84105; ba/Salt Lake City, UT; p/Melvin and Afton Lillie (Davidson) Boulton, SLC, UT; ed/BS Elem Ed 1971, MEd & Elem Mtly Handicapped Ed Cert 1981, Univ of UT; pa/Tchr, Habilitation Ctr for Multiple Handicapped, SLC, 1971-73; Tchr, Hartvigsen Sch for Multiple Handicapped, SLC, 1973-79; Tchr, Wm Penn Elem Sch, SLC, 1979-83; Tchr, E Mill Creek Elem, SLC, 1983-; Mem: NEA; UT Ed Assn; Granite Ed Assn; Assn for Supvn & Curric Devel; W/W in W.

BOUMA, ARNOLD H oc/Scientist; b/ Sep 5, 1932; h/1318 Austin Colony Drive, Richmond, TX 77469; ba/Houston, TX; m/Mechelina H; c/Mark A, Nils R, Lars O; ed/BS, Univ of Groningen, The Netherlands, 1956; MS Geol & Sedimentology 1959, PhD Sedimentology 1961, Univ of Utrecht, The Netherlands; mil/ Artillery, Dutch Army, 1st Lt; pa/Lectr, Univ of Utrecht, 1961-66; Fullbright Postdoct F'ship, Scripps Inst, Oceanography, La Jolla, CA, 1962-63; Assoc & Full Prof Oceanography, TX A & M Univ, 1966-75; Geol Menlo Park, CA 1975-79, Geol-in-charge Corpus Christi, TX 1979-81, US Geol Surv; Sr Sci 1981-82, Mgr 1982-83, Chief Sch 1983-, Gulf Res & Devel Co; Mem: Am Assn Petro Geols; Soc Ec Paleontologists & Mineralogists; Geol Soc Am; Int Assn Sedimentologists; Dutch Geol & Mining Soc; AAAS; Editor-in-Chief, *Geo-Marine Lttrs*; hon/ Author, Over 140 Sci Pubs incl'g 2 Books; Editor & Co-Editor of Num Papers & Abstracts; Num Reports & Reviews; Am Assn Petro Geols, 1982-83; Dist'd Lectr; W/W.

BOURGEOIS, DAVID RICHARD oc/ Manager; b/Oct 8, 1938; h/6 Currier Drive, Framingham, MA 01701; ba/ Millerica, MA; m/Marsha C; c/Derek S; p/Joseph and Inez Bourgeois, Waltham, MA; sp/Paul and Angelia Wing (dec); ed/ BSEE, NEn Univ, 1977; mil/USN; pa/Sr Design Engr, Boston Digital, 1972-76; Sr Design Engr, Incoterm, 1976-77; Proj Ldr 1978, Mgr 1979-, Honeywell; Pt-time Instr, NEn Univ, 1982-; r/Cath; hon/ Patentee in Field; Tech Excell Awd, Honeywell, 1980; W/W in E; Dir of Dist'd Ams.

BOURGEOIS, PATRICK LYALL oc/ Professor & Associate Dean; b/Mar 17, 1940; h/6915 General Haig Street, New Orleans, LA 70124; ba/New Orleans, LA; m/Mary Hallaron; c/Daniel Patrick, Margaret Mary; p/Eugene and Una Bourgeois (dec); sp/Daniel Hallaron (dec); Gladys Hallaron; ed/AA, St Joseph Sem Col, 1960; BA 1962, MA 1964, Notre Dame Sem; MA, Notre Dame Univ, 1965; PhD, Duquesne Univ, 1970; pa/Instr Theol, Duquesne Univ, 1965-67; Lectr, Mt Mercy Col, Pgh, Fall 1967; Instr 1968-70, Asst Prof 1970-73, Assoc Prof 1973-78, Prof 1978-, Dean of Commun Curric 1982-, Loyola Univ, NO, LA; r/ Cath; hon/Author of Books, *Ext of Ricoeur's Hermeneutic*, 1976; *Can Caths Be Charismatic?*, 1976; Co-Author of Books, *Pragmatism & Phenomenology: A Phil Encounter*, 1980; *Thematic Studies in Phenomenology & Pragmatism*, 1984; Outstg Yg Men of Am; W/ W: in Ed, in S & SW; DIB; Personalities of S.

BOURNE, PETER G oc/United

Nations Assistant Secretary General; b/ Aug 6, 1939; h/2119 Leroy Place, Washington, DC 2008; ba/New York, NY; m/ Mary King; p/Geoffrey Bourne, Atlanta, GA; sp/Luther King, Spottsylvania, VA; ed/MD, Emory Univ, 1962; MA, Stanford Univ, 1969; mil/AUS, 1964-67, Capt; pa/ Asst Secy Gen UN, 1979-; Spec Asst for Hlth Issues to the Pres, The White House, 1977-79; Pres, Global Water, 1979-82; Dept Campaign Mgr, Carter Pres Campaign, 1975-77; Pres, Foun for Intl Resources, 1974-78; Fellow, Royal Soc of Med, 1972-; Mem, Am Psychi Assn, 1966-; Pres, Am Assn for World Hlth, 1983-; Bd Mem, Save the Chd Fedn, 1984-86; cp/Alt Del, Dem Nat Conv, 1972; r/Epis; Author of Books, *Water Resource Devel*, 1984; *Men, Stress & Vietnam*, 1969; *Alcoholism: Progress in Res & Treatment*, 1973; Others; Author of Over 100 Articles Pub'd; Public Ser Awd, Chinese Am Assn, 1978; Nat Assn St Drug Abuse Auths, 1974; W/W in Polit; Am Men & Wom in Sci; Other Biogl Listings.

BOVA, V ARTHUR JR oc/Attorney, Consultant; b/Apr 25, 1946; h/5604 Cresta Luna Court, Northeast, Albuquerque, NM 87111; ba/Albuquerque, NM; m/Breda Murphy; c/Kate Murphy; p/Vincent A and Janie (Pope) Bova, Pgh, PA; sp/Theresa Murphy, NJ; ed/BA Bus Adm, Alma Col, 1968; MPA, OH St Univ, 1972; JD, OK City Univ, 1975; mil/Air NG, 1969-75; pa/Mktg & Sys Rep, Computer Sys Div of RCA, Cinc & Dayton, OH, 1968-70; Res Anal, Res Atlanta, 1972-73, Assoc, Threet, Threet, Glass, King & Maxwell, Albuquerque, NM, 1976-78; Ptner, Lill & Bova, Public Accts, Albuquerque, NM, 1978-81; Single Pract, 1981-; Mem & Adv'd Grad Nat Col Advocacy, Assn of Trial Lwyrs of Am; Adv'd Diplomate, Ct Pract Inst; ABA; NM Bar Assn; NM Trial Lwyrs Assn; Intl Assn of Financial Planners; Nat Org SS Claimants Reps; Albuquerque Bar Assn; Phi Alpha Delta; cp/Toastmasters; Bare Bulls Ltd; Millionaires Tip Clb; Albuquerque Bus Assn; r/Presb; hon/Pacesetters Awd, OH St Univ, 1972; Outstg Yg Men's Awd; W/W: in Am Cols & Univs, in W, in Am Law, Contemp Achmt; Personalities of W & MW.

BOVARD, DAVID LAWRENCE oc/ Mission Founder, Director and Pastor; b/ Apr 8, 1934; h/Rural Dist 1, Box 469, McGary Road, New Wilmington, PA 16142; ba/New Castle, PA; m/Cecilia M; c/Joyce Ann (Bovard) Ulrich, Joan Marie, John David, James Alan; pa/Field Secy, Indep Faith Mission, 1959-68; Fdr & Dir, Indep Gospel Missions, 1969-; Record Secy, Assoc'd Mission, 1959-; Com on Evang 1976-; Exec Com 1983, Intl Coun of Christian Chs; Chm Dept Missions & Bd Mem, Faith Bapt Bible Inst Col & Sem, 1980-; Pastor, Victory Bapt Ch; Ext Nat & Intl Missionary Travel; Started Num Mission Stas & Fields; Ldr, Missionary Tours & Wk Projs in Fgn Countries; cp/ Mem, Zoning Bd of Neshannock Twp, New Castle, PA, 1982-; r/Bapt; hon/ Author, Num Rel Articles Pub'd & Distributed Intly incl'g: "Multitudes in the Val of Decision," "Who Cares Enough?" & "Wasted Yrs."

BOW, STEPHEN T oc/Executive; b/ Oct 20, 1931; ba/San Francisco, CA; m/ Kathy O'Connor; c/Sandra, Carol, Deborah, Clara; p/Mr and Mrs Stephen T Bow Sr, Elizabethtown, KY; sp/Mr and Mrs Grover O'Connor, Dayton, OH; ed/

Att'd Lindsey Wilson Col; BA Sociol, Berea Col, 1953; pa/Num Positions w Metro Life Ins Co: Agt, Lexington, KY, 1953-55; AM, Steel City, AL, 1955-58; FTI, S Ctl, 1958-59; TFS, S Ctl, 1959-60; DSM, Frankfort, KY, 1960-64; DSM, Lexington, KY, 1964-66; Exec Asst Field Tng, 1966-67; RSM No Jersey, 1967-72; Agy VPres, Canadian Home Ofc, 1972-76; VPres, MWn Home Ofc, 1976-78; Sr VPres, MWn Home Ofc, 1978-; Mem: NALU; Dayton LUA; Dayton CLU; Past Mem: Gama; Ottowa LUA; VPres, Lexington CLU; cp/Mem Bd & Chm Audit Com, Dayton Power & Light Co; Mem Bd, Duriron Co Inc; Bd Mem, Wright St Univ Foun; Bd of Trustees, Berea Col; Adv Bd, OH Univ Ct for Ec Ed; Bd Mem, Dayton Philharm Assn; Nat Corp Com, U Negro Col Fund; Mem, Area Progress Coun; Civic Adv Coun & Chm Govt Relats Com, Kettering Med Ctr; r/Meth; hon/Author of Var Ins Pubs.

BOWDEN, CHARLES MALCOLM oc/Research Physicist; b/Dec 31, 1933; h/ 716 Versailles Drive, Huntsville, AL 35803; ba/Redstone Arsenal, AL; m/Lou Marguerite (Tolbert); c/David Malcolm, Steven Mark, Melissa Gail; p/Charles Edward and Emma Stevens (Hoover) Bowden (dec); sp/Clyde and Marguerite Theresa Tolbert; ed/BS Physics, Univ of Richmond, 1956; MS Physics, Univ of VA, 1959; PhD Physics, Clemson Univ, 1967; pa/Res Physicist, US Nav Res Lab, Wash DC, 1959-61; Instr Physics, Univ of Richmond, 1961-64; Res Physicist, US Army Missile Lab, Redstone Arsenal, 1967-; Mem: Am Phy Soc; AAAS; Am Optical Soc; Sigma Pi Sigma; Sigma Xi; cp/VChm Deacon Coun 1981, Chm Pastor Search Com 1981-82, U Bapt Ch; Mem, Huntsville Ath Clb; r/Bapt; hon/ Author, Over 60 Articles in Profl Res Jours & Books; Editor of 2 Key Ref Wks in Field; NASA Fellow, Clemson Univ, 1965-67; Oak Ridge Nat Lab Grad F'ship, 1965; Paul A Siple Awd, 1st Prize, US Army Sci Conf, W Point, NY, 1978; US Army Missile Res & Devel Command Sci & Engrg Awd, 1977; Sci Achmt Awd, US Army Sci Conf, W Point, NY, 1980; Outstg Perf Awd, 1980; Resr of Yr, Huntsville Chapt, Sigma Xi, 1982; W/W in S & SW; Commun Ldrs & Noteworthy Ams; DIB; Men & Wom of Sci; Men of Achmt; Other Biogl Listings.

BOWDEN, MARY LUCAS WILLI-AMS oc/Music Teacher; b/Jan 16, 1928; h/1609 Baltimore Road, Alexandria, VA 22308; ba/Same; m/Warren Franklin; c/ Pamela Victoria; p/Thomas and Maude Williams (dec); sp/James and Irene Bowden (dec); ed/BS, Ed, 1948; Grad Wk in Ed, 1948-49; 6 Yrs Piano & Music Theory w Joanne Raulin, Alexandria, VA, 1968-74; 1 Yr Music Comp w Robert Dumm, 1975; pa/Music Tchr, Alexandria VA, 1968-; cp/Mem & Patrolwom, Neighborhood Watch, 1981-; r/Meth; hon/Var Lib Exhibit Pubs on Music: "The Old Ch Modes," "The Maj Chinese Modes," "W Indian Music," "A Fam of Music Modes (w 3 Subfams); Cert of Merit, Neighborhood Watch, 1983; W/W: of Am Wom; in Music.

BOWEN, DONALD DEANE oc/Professor; b/Jan 18, 1934; h/5533 South Toledo Avenue, Tulsa, OK 74135; ba/ Tulsa, OK; m/Pauline Marie; c/Michael, Edward, Thomas, Matthew; p/Mr and Mrs H H Gebhart, Rio Rondo, NM; sp/ Mr and Mrs D A Yeneri, Pompano Bch,

FL; ed/AB, Brown Univ, 1956; MBA, Univ of CA-LA, 1962; MPhil 1968, PhD 1971, Yale Univ; pa/Prof of Mgmt, Univ of Tulsa, 1975-; Asst Prof Mgmt, Univ of Pgh, 1969-75; Num Other Previous Positions in Indust; Mem: Acad of Mgmt; Am Psychol Assn; Orgnl Behavior Tchg Soc; En Psychol Assn; Fellow, PA Psychol Assn; Intl Assn of Applied Psych; cp/Over 15 Profl Topic Presentations at Univs & Orgnl Meetings; Edit Bd Mem, *Exch: The Orgnl Behavior Tchg Jour*; Others; hon/ Co-Author of 2 Books on Mgmt & Behavior; Author & Co-Author, Over 14 Articles Pub'd in Profl Jours incl'g: *The Orgnl Behavior Tchg Jour*; *Jour Applied Behavior Sci*; Others; Phi Beta Kappa, 1956; Beta Gamma Sigma, 1961; Sgt at Arms 1980-, Mem 1976-, Phi Gamma Kappa; W/W: in E, in S & SW; Am Men & Wom of Sci.

BOWEN, LINDA CAROLYN POLSTON oc/Professor; b/Sep 1, 1944; h/815 Churchill Drive, Chapel Hill, NC 27514; ba/Chapel Hill, NC; m/Chester Edward; c/Stephen Todd, Bradley Scott, Geoffrey Edward; p/James Olon and Lottie Myrl Polston, Chamblee, GA; sp/Chester Bowen (dec); Agnes Bowen, Columbus, GA; ed/BBA 1967, MPA 1971, PhD Acctg 1972, GA St Univ; CPA, in NC & GA; pa/Audit Sr, Peat, Marwick, Mitchell & Co, 1967-69; Asst Prof Acctg, Oglethorpe Univ, 1972-74; Asst Prof Acctg 1974-78, Assoc Prof Acctg 1978-, Univ of NC-Chapel Hill; St Mbrship Chm, Am Acctg Assn; Mem, NC Assn of CPA's; Mem, Am Inst of CPA's; Bd of Dirs, Chm of Fin Com, Wesley Foun; Fac VPres, Beta Alpha Psi (Nat Acctg Soc); Beta Gamma Sigma; r/Meth; hon/Author of Var Articles incl'g: "Social Responsiveness of the Acctg Prof," *CPA Jour*, 1978; Others; Outstg Edrs of Am, 1974; Tanner Tchg Awd, Univ of NC, 1978-79; Tchg Awd, Oglethorpe Univ, 1973-74; Nat F'ship, Am Acctg Assn, 1970-71; W/W: in Am Wom, in GA, in Am Univs & Cols.

BOWEN, PAUL TYNER oc/Professor; b/Sep 2, 1953; h/3220 Caddo Lane, Norman, OK 73069; ba/Norman, OK; m/ Barbara Jean Amstutz; c/Ashlea Harbison; p/Dr and Mrs I W Bowen III, Barnesville, GA; sp/Mr and Mrs Paul A Amstutz, Seneca, SC; ed/BS Chem, Mercer Univ, 1975; MS Engrg Sys 1976, PhD Engrg 1982, Clemson Univ; pa/Asst Prof, Sch of Civil Engrg & Envir Sci, Univ of OK, 1982-; Mem: Water Pollution Control Fedn, 1977; Am Water Wks Assn, 1978; Envir Chem Div, Am Chem Soc, 1974; Envir Engrg Div, ASCE, 1982; Assn Envir Engrg Profs, 1982; Intl Assn on Water Pollution Res & Control, 1983; hon/Author of Articles Pub'd in *Proceedings of ASCE Nat Conf on Envir Engrg*, 1983 & *Water Sci & Technol*, 1984; Gamma Sigma Epsilon Chem Soc, 1974; Beta Beta Beta Biol Soc, 1974; Chi Epsilon Civl Engrg Soc, 1976; Sigma Xi Nat Res Soc, 1982; W/W in Frontier Sci & Technol; Outstg Yg Men of Am.

BOWEN, RAFAEL LEE oc/American Dental Association Director; b/Dec 27, 1925; h/16631 Shea Lane, Gaithersburg, MD 20877; ba/Gaithersburg, MD; m/ Rosalie Jean McCarty; c/Cheryl Lynn, Heather Jean; p/William Tyler Bowen and Naomi Ruth Carroll; Warsaw, VA; ed/ DDS, Univ of So CA (USC), 1953; mil/ US Army Med Corps; pa/Pvt Pract Dentistry, San Diego, CA, 1953-55; Res Assoc, Am Dental Assn Res Unit at Nat

Bur Standards, 1956-69, Assoc Dir 1970-83, Dir 1983-, Am Dental Assn Hlth Foun Res Unit at Nat Bur Standards; Var Com Mbrships, Am Dental Assn; Mem Dental Mats Grp, Intl Assn for Dental Res; Mem: Am Assn for Dental Res; Fdn Dentaire Internationale; MD Dental Soc; So MD Dental Soc; Fellow, Am Col of Dentists; Sigma Xi; Omicron Kappa Upsilon; Edit Review Bd: *Jour Dental Res*; *Jour Am Dental Assn*; *Jour Biomed Mats Res*; hon/Author, Over 100 Sci Pubs; 12 Patents Issued on Synthetic Dental Mats, 1962-83; Mitch Nakayama Meml Awd for Dist'd Contbns to Dentistry, Japanese Sect, Pierre Fauchard Acad, 1984; Mbrship, Omicron Kappa Upsilon, 1982; Clemson Univ Awd, 1982; Hollenback Meml Prize, Acad of Operative Dentistry, 1981; Callahan Meml Awd, OH Dental Assn, 1976; Wilmer Souder Awd, Dental Mat Grp of Intl Assn for Dental Res, 1973; Cert of Apprec, US Dept of Commerce, 1971; Outstg Polymer Res, Am Acad for Plastics Res in Dentistry, 1969; W/W: in US, in E, in MD, in Frontier Sci & Technol; Dir Dist'd Ams; DIB; Men of Achmt; Num Other Biogl Listings.

BOWERS, JANETTE LAWHON oc/ Self-Employed, Direct Sales; Retired Educator; b/Nov 13, 1933; h/Drawer 1440, Alpine, TX 79830; ba/Same; m/ Richard E; c/Connie, Clay, Cole, Kelly, Casey, George; ed/BS, Sam Houston St Univ, 1954, MA, Sul Ross St Univ, 1970; Grad Wk: Sam Houston St Univ & Univ of Houston; pa/Elem PE Tchr, Pasadena, ISD; Jr HS PE Tchr, Cypress-Fairbanks, ISD; Hlth & PE Instr 1968-75, Dir Adult & Cont'g Ed 1975-83, Sul Ross St Univ; Pres 1980, Mem 1975-, TX Assn for Commun Ser & Cont'g Ed; Bd of Trustees 1974-82, Secy 2 Yrs, Alpine ISD; cp/ Mem 1967-, Pres 1970-71, Pilot Clb of Alpine; Gov of TX Dist 1981-82, Projs Coor 1983-84, Dir 1984-86, Pilot Clb Intl; Mem 1967-, Pres 1980-81 & 1983-85, Am Cancer Soc, Alpine Unit; Dist I Dir 1970-74 & 1982-84, TX Div Bd of Dirs 1976-, Area I VPres 1984-85, St Yth Agnst Cancer Chm; Elder, 1st Presb Ch; Fdr & Chm of Bd, Sunshine House (Alpine Sr Ctr), 1976-; Mem 1967-, Girl's St Chm 1975-84, Am Leg Aux; Delta Kappa Gamma, 1974-83; Mem 1975-, Pres 1980-81, TX Assn for Commun Ser & Cont'g Ed; Mem 1977-, Pres 1983-85, Daughs of the Repub of TX; Charter Mem, VPres 1984, UDC; Hon Mem, Am Assn of Ret'd Persons, Chapt 2100; Hon Mem, Sr Citizen's Clb of Alpine; VPres 1974-77, Bicent Chm 1976, Alpine C of C; Num Yrs Wking w: GSA; Brownies; Cub Scouts; Little Leag; Buck Boosters; Band Boosters & Ch Yth Grps; r/Presb; hon/Outstg Vol in TX; Finalist, Nat Vol Activist Awd, 1977; Outstg Citizen of Alpine, 1976; Outstg Wom of Alpine, 1981; W/W: in Sul Ross Fac, of Am Wom, in Am, in World, in Commun Ser; Personalities of S; Notable Ams; Commun Ldrs of Am; Men & Wom of Am; Notabel Wom of TX; DIB; Intl Dir of Dist'd Ldrship; Num Other Biogl Listings.

BOWLES, FRANCES MARIE oc/Executive, Businesswoman; b/Feb 5, 1938; h/ 1061 Parkwood, Madisonville, KY 42431; ba/Sebree, KY; m/James E; c/Robert Wayne, Michael Ray, Benjamin Earl; p/ Mr and Mrs Jessie Raymond Walker, Paducah, KY; ed/ Grad, Reidland HS, 1955; Grad, Murray St Univ, 1957; pa/ Collection Correspondent & Ofc Supvr,

Sears, Paducah, KY, 1957-65; Credit Mgr, Jeans Dept Store, Paducah, 1965-67; Mgr & Estimator, Slay Plumbing & Heating, Paducah, 1967-72; Ofc Mgr, Amick & Helm CPA Ofc, Madisonville, KY, 1972-74; Mgr Arch Mgmt Corp & Exec Asst to Pres of Affil Cos, 1974-82; Pt-owner & Operator of Sebree Dock Inc & HBH Mgmt Sers Inc, 1982-; Mem, Jr Wom's Clb, 1966-67; Secy & Treas, Beta Sigma Phi, 1972-75; Secy & Treas, Plumbing & Piping Contractors Assn, 1969-72; VPres, Pres Elect & Pres, Madisonville Chapt, Nat Secys Assn Intl (PSI), 1973-; Mem, Nat Assn Exec Secys, 1977-; Mem, Nat Assn for Female Execs, 1978-; cp/Vol Wkr: Heart Fund, Cancer Soc & U Way, 1976-; Active in Martha Layne Collins Campaign for Gov, 1983; r/Bapt; hon/Outstg Yg Wom of Am, 1973; Secy of Yr, Madisonville Chapt, Nat Sceys Assn, 1976; KY Col, 1978; W/W of Am Wom.

BOWMAN, CLEMENT WILLIS oc/ Executive; b/Jan 7, 1930; h/2112 Huron Shores Drive, Rural Route #5, Sarnia, Ontario, Canada N7T 7H6; ba/Sarnia, Ontario; m/Marjorie Elizabeth Greer; c/ Elizabeth Ann, John Clement; p/Clement Willis Bowman (dec); sp/Albert Ernest Greer (dec); ed/BASc 1952, MASc 1958, PhD 1961, Univ of Toronto, Ontario; pa/ Res Engr, Dupont of Canada, Kingston, Ontario, 1953-57; Res Mgr, Syncrude Canada Ltd, Edmonton, Alberta, 1963-69; Res Engr, 1960-63, Chems Res Mgr 1969-72, Petro Res Mgr 1972-75, Imperial Oil Ltd, Sarnia, Ontario; Chm, Alberta Oil Sands Technol & Res Auth, Edmonton, Alberta, 1975-84; VPres Res Div, ESSO Petro Canada, Sarnia, Ontario, 1984-; Dir, Alberta Res Coun, Edmonton, Alberta, 1979-; Pres, Chem Inst of Canada, 1982-83; Pres, Canadian Soc for Chem Engrg, 1974-75; hon/ Author, Over 40 Articles Pub'd in Profl Sci Jours & Assn Conf Proceedings; Meritorious Ser Medal (25 Yrs), Univ of Toronto Alumni Assn, 1977; Queen's 25 Yr Jubilee Medal, 1977.

BOWMAN, JODI A oc/Geologist; b/ May 17, 1952; h/4923 Imogene, Houston, TX 77096; ba/Houston, TX; m/Artur W Krueger; p/Edward L and Billye J Bowman, Houston, TX; sp/Werner and Charlotte Krueger (dec); ed/BA Art Hist, Trinity Univ, 1974; BS Geol, Univ of Houston, 1977; pa/Geol, Anderson & Bowman, 1974-80; Indep Geol, 1980-; VPres, Edward L Bowman Inc, 1982-; Mem: Houston Geol Soc; Am Assn of Petro Geols; Assn of Wom in Geosci; The Petro Clb of Houston; r/Luth; hon/ Outstg Yg Wom of Am.

BOWMAN, NORMAN HOWARD oc/ Journalist, Author & Newspaper Editor; b/Jul 24, 1919; h/935 Thornton Way, San Jose, CA 95128; ba/Same; m/Virginia A; c/Judith, Robert, Karen; p/Norman H and Jennie D Bowman (dec); sp/Cleo Richey, Campbell, CA; Ruby Richey (dec); mil/ USASC, 1941-45; pa/Jour. *Gilroy Dispatch*, 1938-41; *Los Gatos Times*, 1946-48; *San Jose Mercury News*, 1948-78; Pres, Local 98 The Newspaper Guild, 1968; Hon Mem, San Jose Real Est Bd, 1963-; Editor, *CA Legionnaire*, Am Legion Dept of CA, 1982-; cp/Adjutant 1980, San Jose Post 89, Am Legion; r/Meth; hon/Newspaper Columnist, "Bus As Usual," 1953-78; Author of Book, *Publicity in Print- for Unpaid Reporters*, 1974; Co-Author, *The Grandparenting Book*, 1982; Num Awds for Reporting Excell,

1960-78; Editor, "The Barrage," Class II Newslttrs, 4th Place (Nat) The Am Legion, 1981 & 1982; Class IV Edit Excell, (Nat) The Am Legion, 1983; W/W: in Am, in World; Men of Distn.

BOWSHER, ARTHUR LEROY oc/ Geologist; b/Apr 29, 1917; h/2707 Gaye Drive, Roswell, NM 88201; ba/Artesia, NM; m/Ruth-E; c/Donna Jean (A) DeMar, Jane (B) Drake, Anne (B) Atkinson, Arthur L Jr, Dale C; p/Dallas & Sallie Bowsher, Pampa, TX; sp/Beulah Webber, Forsythe, MO; ed/BS PE, Univ of KS, 1941; 3 Yrs Grad Study, Univ of Tulsa; mil/AUS Civil Engrg Corp, Capt; Curator, US Nat Mus, 1947-52; Geol, US Geol Surv, 1952-57 & 1978-81; Geol, Sinclair Oil & Gas Co, 1957-69; Geol, Arco, 1969-70; Geol, Aramco, 1970-78; Geol, Yates Petro Corp, 1981; Mem, AAPG, 1942; Pres, Univ of Tulsa Geol Clb, 1939; Pres, Sigma Gamma Epsilon, 1946; Sigma Xi; Geol Soc of Am; cp/Pres, Exch Clb, Redwood City, 1980; Pres, Roswell Geol Soc, 1984; hon/Author, Over 40 Pubs in Profl Jours; Woodbadge 1962, Silver Beaver 1978, BSA; W/W in Am Sci; W Knows & What.

BOX, BENTON HOLCOMB oc/ Administrator; b/Jan 31, 1931; h/107 Carteret Court, Clemson, SC 29631; ba/ Clemson, SC; m/Sallie Yates; c/Benton Holcomb Jr, John William, Jane Ellen (B) Bishop; p/James A and Gay Holcomb Box (dec); sp/Adlai Robin Yates, Clemson, SC; Gladys Collins Yates (dec); ed/BS 1957, MF 1959, LA St Univ (LSU); DF, Duke Univ, 1967; mil/USAF, 1951-55; pa/Res Assoc, Asst Prof, Assoc Prof, Forestry Dept & Spec, Coop Ext Ser, LA St Univ, 1957-72; Exec VPres, So Forest Inst, 1972-77; Conslt, 1977-78; Dean, Col of Forest & Rec Resources, Clemson Univ, 1978-; Mem: Soc of Am Foresters; SC Forestry Assn; Am Forestry Assn; Forest Farmer Assn; Nat Rec & Pk Assn; SC Res & Pk Soc; cp/Chm of Bd, Clemson Sertoma Clb; Deacon, 1st Bapt Ch, Clemson, SC; r/Bapt; hon/Author, Over 40 Articles on Forestry & Related Subjects in Profl Pubs, 1959-81; W/W in S & SW.

BOX, JOHN HAROLD oc/Architect; b/Aug 18, 1929; h/2111 Highgrove, Austin, TX 78703; ba/Austin, TX; m/ Eden; c/Richard, Kenneth, Gregory, William, Kate; p/E O and Mary Emma (Haynes) Box; ed/B Arch, Univ of TX-Austin, 1950; mil/AUS Civil Engrg Corp, Lt; USNR; pa/Apprentice, O'Neil Ford Arch, San Antonio, 1948; Designer, Broad & Nelson Archs, Dallas, 1954-56; Assoc, Harrell & Hamilton, Dallas, 1956-57; Ptner, Pratt, Box & Henderson Archs, Dallas, 1957-84; Fdg Dean, Sch of Arch, Univ of TX-Arlington, 1971-76; Dean, Sch of Arch, Univ of TX-Austin, 1976-; Pres Dallas Chapt 1967, Nat Dir 1975-78, Fellow, AIA; VPres Commr Ed & Res 1971, Design Awds 1964-66, TX Soc of Archs; cp/Chm, Design of City Task Force Goals for Dallas, 1968-70; Chm, Design Com, Gtr Dallas Planning Coun, 1969; Bd of Dirs, Dallas Chamber Music Soc, 1960-76; VPres, Save Open Space, 1970; Bd of Dir, Austin Hist Ctr, 1984-; Bd of Dirs, Austin Symph Orch, 1982-; Bd of Dirs, Laguna Gloria Art Mus, 1984-; hon/Co-Author, *Prairies Yield*, 1962; "Goals for Dallas Proposals for Design of City," 1970; Co-Recip, Enrico Fermi Meml Arch Competition, 1957; Grand Prize, Homes for Better Living

PERSONALITIES OF AMERICA

Competition, 1959; Grantee, Arch Foun, 1957; W/W: in Am, in SW.

BOYAJIAN, BEN K oc/Materials Scientist; b/Jun 20, 1947; h/309 Alderman Road, Charlottesville, VA 22903; ba/ Charlottesville, VA; pa/Dental Lab Tech, Chemodent Labs, 1976-83; Chem, Salem Col & WV Univ, 1969-75; Mts Sci, Chemodent Co, 1980-83; Mem: Am Dental Lab Assn; Am Chem Soc; Am Soc of Metals; Soc of Am Inventors; cp/C of C; hon/Holder of 2 US Patents in Field; Outstg Jr in Chem, Salem Col, 1972; Outstg Yg Men of Am, 1977.

BOYD, ANN LEWIS oc/Professor, Research Scientist; b/Nov 15, 1944; h/ 8821 Indian Springs Road, Frederick, MD 21701; ba/Frederick, MD; c/Kathryn Ann; p/Mrs Fletcher Lewis, Shreveport, LA; ed/BS 1965, MS 1968, NWn Univ; PhD, LA St Univ (LSU), 1971; pa/Postdoct Res, Dept of Virology, Baylor Col Med, 1971-73; Res Sci, NCI-Frederick Res Facility, 1973-; Assoc Prof Biol, Hood Col, 1980-; Mem: Am Soc Microbiol; Am Soc Virology; Am Tissue Culture Assn; NY Acad of Sci; Phi Kappa Phi; Mem Bd Frederick Chapt, Sigma Xi; cp/Vestry, Harriett Chapel Epis Ch; Tnr, Penn Laurel GSA; r/Epis; hon/Author & Co-Author, Over 20 Res Articles Pub'd in Sci Books & Profl Jours; Num Abstracts & Paper Presentations at Orgnl Meetings; Dist'd Tchr Awd, Hood Col, 1983-84; Del, People-to-People Intl for Tissure Culture to Europe, 1984; W/W: in Am Men & Wom of Sci, in Frontier Sci & Technol.

BOYD, HARRIET MARTIN oc/Certified Public Accountant and Certified Financial Planner; b/Apr 10, 1948; h/ 12735 Grand Cross Lane, Houston, TX 77072; ba/Houston, TX; c/Jennifer, Julie; p/Harry R Martin (dec); Bess Martin, Uvalde, TX; ed/BS, Stephen F Austin St Univ, 1970; pa/Asst Controller, Surfcote Pipe Coating Inc, Houston, TX, 1971-77; Pvt Pract CPA, 1978-; Dir, Med Ctr Prosthetics Inc; Mem: CPA; AICPA; TX Soc CPA; AWSCPA; Charter Mem, Houston AWSCPA; IAFP; Beta Alpha Psi; Past Treas, Braewood Glen CIA; W/W in Houston, in S & SW.

BOYD, JESSIE MAE oc/Teacher; b/ Dec 16; h/4809 Colorado Avenue, Northwest, Washington, DC 20011; ba/ Northeast, Washington, DC; m/Thomas J; p/James and Pinkie M Jackson (dec); sp/ Elijah and Josie Boyd (dec); ed/BA, Washburn Univ, 1947; MS, KS St Col-Pittsburg, 1952; Grad Study, Howard Univ 1957-59 & Trinity Col (DC) 1979; pa/Tchr, Prince Frederick, MD Public Schs, 1948-49; Tchr, Burnie, MO 1951-52; Cnslr 1954-56, Social Wkr 1956-57, Supv Cnslr 1959-63, Acting Chief Cnslr 1963-64, Public Schs, Dept of Public Wel (Dept of Human Resources); Tchr, Wash DC Public Schs, 1964-; cp/Mem: Rock Creek Neighborhood Leag; Wom's Aux of Howard Univ Hosp; VPres 1971-73, Corres'g Secy 1982-, Sigma Wives; Record Secy 1967-71, Ward 4 Dems; Transafrica; Afracare; DC Wom's Polit Caucus; Outreach Ser Clb; Coun of Exceptl Chd; Asst Secy 1971-81, Nat Coun Negro Wom; 2nd VPres, Friendship Social Clb, 1982-; Mem, Sodality of Our Blessed Lady; Corres'g Secy 1979-80 & 1982-, Gtr Wash DC Life Mems Guild; hon/Author of "A Study of Segragation in Negro Ed & Efforts to Secure Racial Integration in Ed," 1953;

Employee of Mo, 1961; Cit & Stipend, Govt of DC, Dept of Public Wel, 1962; Outstg Perf Awd, Div of Spec Ed, Wash DC Public Schs, 1979-80 & 1980-81.

BOYD, JOSEPH A JR oc/Florida State Supreme Court Chief Justice; b/Nov 16, 1916; h/2210 Monaghan Drive, Tallahassee, FL 32308; ba/Tallahassee, FL; m/ Anilouise Stripling; c/Joanne Goldman, Betty Jean Jala, Joseph Robert, James Daniel, Jane Nan; p/Joseph Arthur and Esther Puckett Boyd; ed/Att'd Piedmont Col & Mercer Univ Law Sch; JD, Univ of Miami Law Sch, 1948; LLD, Piedmont Col, 1963; Lic'd to Pract Before Supr Ct of US, Cts of FL, DC & Other Fed Cts; Grad, NY Univ's Sr Appellate Judges Sem; mil/USMC, WW II; pa/City Atty, Hialeah, 1951-58; Law Pract, City of Hialeah, 1948-68; Elected Mem 1958-68, Chm 1963, VMayor 1967, Dade Co Comm; Elected Justice, Supr Ct of FL, 1968-; Dir, St Assn Co Commrs, 1964-68; ABA; Tallahassee Bar Assn; Am Judic Soc; Pres, Hialeah-Miami Sprgs Bar Assn, 1955; cp/Pres, Hialeah-Miami Sprgs C of C, 1956; Pres & Orgr, Tallahassee Northside Lions Clb, 1979; Com to Organize New FL Clbs, Lions Intl; St Cmdr, Am Legion, 1953; Trustee, Piedmont Col; Scottish Rite Masons; 33rd Deg York Rite Masons, Shrine; Phi Alpha Delta Law Frat; Soc of Wig & Robe; Iron Arrow Hon Soc, Univ of Miami; Alpha Kappa Psi Bus Frat; VFW; BPOE; Moose; Tallahassee Tiger Bay Clb; Juror, Freedoms Foun Awds at Val Forge, PA, 1971 & 1973; r/1st Bapt Ch of Tallahassee; Dir, Gtr Miami Coun of Chs, 1962-66; hon/ Author, Num Law Review Articles Pub'd incl'g: Univ of Miami Law Jour; Nova Univ Law Jour; Nat Top Hat Awd, BPW Clbs of US, 1957.

BOYD, KAREN J BARTOS oc/Sales Administrator; b/Sep 6, 1956; h/3464 Wells Avenue, Fremont, CA 94536; ba/ 1000 16th Street, San Francisco, CA 94107; m/Bruce A; p/Beverly J Bartos, Iowa City, IA; sp/Exie W Boyd, Beechgrove, IN; ed/BA Chem Engrg, Univ of IA, 1978; MBA, Gov's St Univ, 1982; pa/ Intern, Eli Lilly, Sum 1976, 1977 & 1978; Constrn Engr, Amoco Chems Corp, 1979; Reg Process/Proj Engr, Chem Coatings Div Mobil Chem Co, 1979-82; Conslt, KB Enterprise, 1982-83; Chem Coatings Sales Admr, SCM Glidden Coatings & Resins, 1983-; Mem: Beta Sigma Phi; Alpha Chi Sigma; AIChE; Tau Beta Pi; Omicron Delta Kappa; r/Luth; Author of Book, IA & You, 1977; Cert of Achmt, 1977-78; Scholastic All-Am; W/ W: Among Students in Am Cols & Univs; Among Am Wom.

BOYER, PAUL SLAYTON oc/Professor; b/Feb 11, 1942; h/Sand Spring Road, Morristown PO, NJ 07960; ba/Madison, NJ; m/Marian Dehmel; c/Virginia Ann, Charles W; p/Paul K Boyer (dec); Martha S Boyer, Tucson, AZ; ed/AB Geol, Princeton Univ, 1964; PhD Geol, Rice Univ, 1970; pa/Asst Prof, Franklin & Marshall Col, Lancaster, PA, 1969-71; Asst Prof & Prof, Fairleigh Dickinson Univ, Madison, NJ, 1971-; Mem: Am Assn Petro Geols; Nat Assn Geol Tchrs; Past Pres Local Chapt, AAUP; Paleontology Assn (London); Paleontology Soc; Paleontological Res Inst; cp/Harding Twp Bd of Hlth; Harding Twp Envir Comm; Mem, Rep Co Com; r/Epis; hon/Author, Over 20 Sci Papers, Abstracts & Ency Articles Pub'd; Cum Laude Soc, 1964; Bausch &

Lomb Sci Awd, 1964; Nat Merit S'ship, 1960-64; NASA F'ship, 1964-66; Ldrship Hon Soc, 1984; Am Men & Wom of Sci.

BOYER, RICHARD E oc/Attorney; b/ Sep 3, 1944; h/19 Wellesley Road, Nashua, NH 03062; ba/Nashua, NH; m/ Karen; c/Holly, Matthew; p/Jeannie Ford, Maneadero, BCFA Mexico; sp/William and Louise Johnson, Falmouth, NH; ed/ BGS, Univ of NE, 1969; JD, Univ of ME Sch of Law, 1972; mil/Ofcrs Cand Sch, Comm'd AUS, 1965, Lt; pa/Atty, Smith, Welts & Currier, Nashua, NH, 1972-76; Atty, Lesieur & Boyer, Nashua, NH, 1976-79; Atty, Boyer Profl Assn, 1979-; NH St Sen, 1981-; Depty Dem Ldr, 1983-86; Chm Senate Judiciary Com, 1983-86; St Rep, 1979-80; Depty Whip, 1981-82; Chm, NH St Dem Party, 1981-82; cp/Pres & Dir, Nashua Boys Clb, 1981; Trustee, Daniel Webster Col, 1982-; r/Meth.

BOYKAN, MARTIN oc/Professor; b/ Apr 12, 1931; h/10 Winsor Avenue, Watertown, MA 02172; ba/Waltham, MA; m/Susan Schwalb; c/Rachel, Deborah; p/Matilda Boykan, NYC, NY; sp/Judge and Evelyn Schwalb, NYC, NY; ed/BA, Harvard Univ, 1951; MMus, Yale Univ, 1953; pa/Asst Prof, Assoc Prof & Prof Music, Brandeis Univ, 1957-; Mem, Am Music Ctr; Mem Edit Bd, *Perspectives of New Music*; r/Jewish; hon/Author, Num Musical Compositions incl'g: "Psalm 128 For A Cappella Chorus," 1965; "Piano Trio," 1976; "Concerto For 13 Players," 1971; "String Quartet #1," 1967; "String Quartet #3," 1974; "Elegy for Soprano & 6 Instruments," 1982; Jeunesse Musicales, 1967; Fromm Foun, 1976; Martha Baird Rockefeller Grant, 1975; NEA Grant, 1983; Leag ISCM Nat Winner, 1983; Guggenheim Foun, 1984; W/W: in Music, in Am, in E.

BOYLAN, DAVID RAY JR oc/Educator, Administrator; b/Jul 22, 1922; h/1516 Stafford Street, Ames, IA 50010; ba/ Ames, IA; m/Juanita Rose Sheridan; c/ Sharon Rae, Gerald Ray, Elizabeth Anne, Lisa Dianne; p/Mr and Mrs David R Boylan Sr, Boulder, CO; sp/Mr and Mrs N W Sheridan, Kansas City, MO; ed/ BSChE, Univ of KS, 1943; PhD Chem Engrg, IA St Univ, 1952; pa/Instr, Univ of KS, Lawrence, 1942-43; Design Field & Proj Engr, Gen Chem Co, Camden, NJ, 1943-47; Sr Engr, Am Cyanamid, Linden, NJ, 1947; Plant Mgr, Arlin Chem Co, Elizabeth, NJ, 1947-48; Asst Prof 1949-55, Assoc Prof 1955-56, Prof 1956-, Assoc Dir 1959-66 & Dir 1966-70 Engrg Res Inst, Dean Col Engrg 1970-, IA St Univ, Ames, IA; Mem, Am Chem Soc; Mem, Am Soc Engrg Ed; Mem, IA Engrg Soc; Mem, Nat Soc Profl Engrs; r/Prot; hon/Author of 24 Pubs on Fertilizer Processes & Fluid Flow Porous Media; Patentee in Field; r/Prot; hon/Reg Dir Reg 7, US Dept of Trans Nat Def Exec Resv, 1981; Fellow, AIChE, 1973; Fellow, AAAS, 1981; W/W: in Am, in MW, in Frontier Sci & Technol.

BOYLE, JOHN S oc/Director of Public Relations and Fund Raising; b/May 10, 1945; h/139 Wellington Road, Elmont, NY 11003; ba/Harrison, NY; p/William F and Mae A (Peets) Boyle, Ft Covington, NY; ed/AA, Wadhams Hall Col, 1964; BA Niagara Univ, 1966; Cert in Public Relats Mgmt, NY Univ, 1975; pa/Cultural Enrichment Coor 1971-73, Dir of Public Info 1973-77, Lincoln Hall, Lincolndale, NY; Dir of Public Relats & Fund Raising,

96

St Vincent's Hosp, Harrison, NY, 1977-; Mem: Mtl Hlth Assn; Westchester-Fairfield Chapt, Public Relats Soc of Am; Westchester Co Assn; Am Soc for Hosp Public Relats; No Metro Chapt, Hosp Public Relats Assn; r/Rom Cath; hon/Contbr, *Long Isl's Nightlife Mag*; Dist'd Ser Medal, Westchester-Fairfield Chapt, Public Relats Soc of Am, 1983; W/W: in E, in Public Relats Profls (Hlth Care).

BOYLE, MICHAEL DERMOT oc/ Research Scientist; b/Jan 4, 1949; h/1809 Southwest 44th Avenue, Gainesville, FL 32608; ba/Gainesville, FL; m/Carla E; c/ Klerow Andrew, Sarah Irene; p/Mr Dermot Boyle (dec); Mrs Dermot Boyle, Laughton, England; sp/Mr and Mrs William Colville, Helensburgh, Scotland; ed/BSc Biochem, Univ of Glasgow, Glasgow, Scotland, 1971; PhD Biochem, Chester Beatty Res Inst, Belmont, Sutton, Surrey, England, 1974; Fellow (Immunol), Nat Cancer Inst, Bethesda, MD, 1974-76; pa/Expert 1976-80, Vis'g Sci 1980, Humoral Immunity Sect Lab Immunobiol, DCBD, Nat Cancer Inst, NIH, Bethesda, MD; Assoc Prof, Dept Immunol & Med Microbiol & Dept Pediatrics, Univ of FL Col Med, Gainesville, 1981-; Mem: Foun for Advmt of Ed in Scis, 1976-; Am Assn of Immunols, 1977-; Am Assn for Cancer Res, 1977; SEn Immunol Conf, 1982-; Fac Sen, Univ of FL, 1983-; Assoc Editor, *Molecular & Cellular Biochem, 1983-*; r/Prot; hon/Author, *Over 50 Sci & Res Articles Pub'd in Profl Jours & Books; Studentship, Inst of Cancer Res, 1971-74; W/W in Sci & Technol.*

BOYTER, SCOTT M oc/University Administrator; b/Jun 19, 1947; h/331 North 875 East, Orem, UT 84057; ba/ Provo, UT; m/Sherrie Lynn; c/Laura, Tonia, Diana; p/Reside in Cedar City, UT; sp/Reside in Bountiful, UT; ed/Att'd So UT St Col, 1965-67; Grad, AUS Fin Sch, Ft Harrison, IN, 1972; BS 1973, MS Cand, Brigham Yg Univ; mil/AUS, 1971-, Br Chief & Platoon Sgt, 395th Financial Sect, Ft Douglas, UT; pa/Adm Asst Col of Fine Arts & Communs 1973-76 & 1982-, Adm Mgr Dept of Music 1976-82, Pt-time Instr Dept of Info Mgmt 1979, Exec Asst to ASBYU Pres 1970-71, Brigham Yg Univ; Financial Secy, OH-WV Mission, Ch of Jesus Christ of LDS, Columbus, OH, 1969; Exec Asst to ASSUSC Pres, So UT St Col, 1966-67; Mem: Am Mgmt Assn, 1978-; Adm Mgmt Soc, 1979-; Brigham Yg Univ Mgmt Soc, 1982-; UT Pers Assn, 1972-73; cp/Am Philatelic Soc, 1981-; Postal Commemorative Soc, 1979-; Profl Bus Assn, 1972-73; Key Clb Intl, 1964-65; r/LDS (Mormon); hon/AUS Achmt Medal, 1982; Outstg Grad Awd in Adm Mgmt, Brigham Yg Univ, 1973; AUS Spirit of Am Awd, Ft Leonard Wood, MO, 1972; Pres Awd for Outstg Contbn to Student Govt, So UT St Col, 1967; Outstg Yg Men of Am, 1979; Prominent Men & Wom of Provo, 1982.

BRAATZ, JAMES ANTHONY oc/ Research Biochemist; b/Jul 17, 1943; h/ 4510 Yates Road, Beltsville, MD 20705; ba/Columbia, MD; m/Geraldine Lee; c/ James Anthony III, Ronald Chester, Mary Janet; p/James A Braatz (dec); Janet Early, Balto, MD; sp/Chester Jakubowski (dec); Mary Jakubowski, Balto, MD; ed/BS Chem 1968, PhD Biochem 1973, Johns Hopkins Univ; mil/MD Air NG; pa/Sr Res Biochem, W R Grace & Co, 1984-; Hd Biochem Sect BRMP, NC 1981-84, Staff

Fellow 1973-81, NIH; Mem: Am Soc Biol Chems; Am Chem Soc; AAAS; r/Rom Cath; hon/Author of Num Res Pubs & Book Chapts; Patentee in Field; Jr Staff F'ship 1973, Sr Staff F'ship 1975, Expert 1979, Appt'd HD Biochem 1981, NCI; Elected Mem, Am Soc Biol Chems, 1981; W/W in Frontier Sci & Technol.

BRABANT, SARAH CALLAWAY oc/ Professor; b/Nov 18, 1932; h/149 Memory Lane, Lafayette, LA 70506; ba/ Lafayette, LA; m/Wilmer MacNair; c/ Jennie Crowell, Enoch Callaway, Anne Delebart; p/Enoch and Jennie Crowell Callaway (dec); ed/BS 1967, MA 1968, Memphis St Univ; PhD, Univ of GA, 1973; pa/Instr Sociol, Memphis St Univ, 1968-70; Asst Prof Anthropology, LA St Univ, Sums 1973-74; Asst Prof Sociol 1973-77, Assoc Prof Sociol & Anthropology 1977-83, Prof 1983-, Univ of SWn LA; Mem: Am Sociol Assn; Mid-S Sociol Assn; SWn Sociol Assn; Others; cp/Pres & Bd of Dirs, Faith House; Bd of Dirs, U Christian Outreach; Patient Advr, Univ Med Ctr; Adv Bd, Rape Crisis Ctr; Former Mem 1977-80 & Pres 1977-79, Mayor's Comm on Needs of Wom; Others; r/Epis; hon/Author of Articles in Var Pubs incl'g: *Jour of Col Student Pers*; *Sex Roles*; *Mid-S Folklore*; *LA Folklore Misc*; *Attakapas Gazette*; *ACM SIGUCCS Newslttr*; Num Book Reviews & Other Contbns; Res Awd, Am Pers & Guid Assn, 1977; Martin Luther King Jr Humanitarian Ser Awd, Lafayette Coun on Human Relats, 1978; Dist'd Prof Awd, Univ of SWn LA, 1980; Others; Am Men & Wom of Sci; W/W: of Wom, in S & SW; Other Biogl Listings.

BRACEY-LIGGINS, SHEILA ANN oc/ Senior Umbrella Analyst/Manager; b/ Nov 11, 1946; h/570 Varsity Road, South Orange, NJ 07079; ba/New York, NY; m/ James A Liggins; p/Leon F and Leona C Bracey, Trenton, NJ; sp/Altheus Liggins (dec); Louise Liggins, East Orange, NJ; pa/Sr Umbrella Analyst/Mgr, Continental Ins Cos, NYC, 1980-; Supvg Re-Ins Underwriter, Am Intl GP, NYC, 1975-80; Underwriter, Hartford Ins GP, NJ, 1971-75; Mem: Phi Gamm Nu; Assn of Profl Bus Wom; No NJ Chapt, Ctl St Univ Alumni Assn; Am Soc of Notaries; r/Bapt.

BRADEN, VERLON PATRICK oc/ Author, Automotive Writer, Producer, Photographer; b/Jul 8, 1934; h/1049 North Richman Avenue, Fullerton, CA 92635; ba/Torrance, CA; m/1st, Marie Elsie Kobrehel (dec); 2nd, Cheryl Marie Olson; c/(by 1st Marriage) Mark Patrick, Leslie Marie; (by 2nd Marriage) Mary Kathryn; p/Verlon Lee Braden (dec); Mary Virginia Presson; sp/1st, Peter and Elsie M Kobrehel; 2nd, Marie Kathryn (Lopp) West and Craig Greenhalgh Olson; ed/BA Eng & Ed, WN MI Univ, 1956; MA Eng Lit, Univ of IA, 1956-57; PhD Cand, St Univ of IA, 1957-58; pa/ Cert'd Sec'dy Ed Tchr, MI Tchr & Prison Social Wkr & Probation Ofcr St of MI, 1959-67; Writer/Mgr: Bill Sandy Co, Communico, Maritz Communs, Bob Thomas & Assocs, Dancer Fitzgerald Sample Inc 1969-; Editor, *The Alfa Owner*, 1980-; Mem, Am Soc of Tng & Devel; cp/Mem: Alfa Romeo Owners Clb; Am Abarth Register, Scuderia del Portello (Ofcl Alfa Factory Racing Clb); r/Prot; hon/Author of 2 Books: *The 365 GTB/ 4 Daytona Ferrari*, 1982; *Abarth*, 1983; Author of "Viva Alfa," in *Auto Qtly* ; W/ W in W; Men of Achmt.

BRADLEY, LAURENCE ALAN oc/ Clinical Psychologist; b/Sep 13, 1949; h/ 2016 Gaston Street, Winston-Salem, NC 27103; ba/Winston-Salem, NC; m/Elizabeth W; c/Sean C Sullivan, Samantha Ann-Wright Sullivan; p/Irving and Jeanne Bradley, Novelty, OH; sp/James and Nancy Wrenn, Columbia, SC; ed/BA Psych 1971, PhD Psych 1975, Vanderbilt Univ; pa/Assoc Prof & Hd Sect on Med Psych 1982-, Asst Prof & Hd Sect Med Psych 1980-82, Bowman Gray Sch of Med; Asst Prof, Dept Psych, Fordham Univ, 1977-1980; Asst Prof Dept Psych, Univ of TN-Chattanooga, 1976-77; Intern, Duke Univ Med Ctr, 1975-76; Mem: Am Psychol Assn; En Psychol Assn; SEn Psychol Assn; Intl Assn for Study of Pain; En Pain Assn; Am Pain Soc; Fellow, Soc for Personality Assessment; Soc of Behavioral Med; hon/Co-Editor of Books, *Coping w Chronic Disease: Res & Applications*, 1983; *Med Psych: Contbns to Behavioral Med*, 1981; Phi Beta Kappa, 1971; Sigma Xi, 1979; W/W in S & SW; Personalities of S.

BRADLEY, WALTER GEORGE oc/ Professor; b/Sep 1, 1937; h/Sunset Cliff, Burlington, VT 05401; ba/Burlington, VT; m/Jeanne Baker; c/Guy Andrew, Russell Stuart, Miles Dominic, Shoshana Amy; p/Ernest and Amy Bradley; ed/BA 1959 BSc 1961, MA, BM & BCh 1963, DM 1970, Oxon; MRCP 1966, FRCP 1976, London; Wellcome Sr Res Fellow 1969-71, Sr Lectr Neurol 1971-74, Prof Exptl Neurol 1974-77, Univ of Newcastle-upon-Tyne, England; Prof & VChm Neurol, Tufts N Eng Med Ctr, 1977-82; Prof & Chm Dept Neurol, Univ of VT, 1982-; Mem: Am Acad Neurol 1977-; Soc Neurosci, 1978-; Am Neurol Assn, 1978-; Assn Univ Profs of Neurol, 1982-; Am Assn Electromyography & Electrodiagnosis, 1983-; hon/Author of 2 Books; Over 160 Sci Articles, Book Chapts, Reviews Pub'd in Profl Sci Jours; Radcliffe Travelling F'ship, 1968; Fullbright F'ship, 1968.

BRADSHAW, JAMES PHILIP oc/ Retired Associate Professor Emeritus, Author and Editor; b/May 22, 1919; h/ 2306 Southwest 13th Street, Apartment 1210, Gainesville, FL 32608; p/Jennie Bevill Bradshaw, Gainesville, FL; ed/AB 1939, AM 1940, Univ of FL; MSLS 1951, Profl Study at Tchrs Col 1951-53, Columbia Univ; mil/AUS, 1941-46, USASC, Med Corps; pa/Hd Eng Dept, Hernando HS, Brooksville, FL, 1940-41; Instr to Assoc Prof, Adm Asst to Chm, Interim Chm Eng Dept, Univ Col, Univ of FL, 1946-72; Assoc Prof Eng Dept Col of Arts & Scis, Univ of FL, 1972-77; Assoc Prof Emeritus (Ret'd), 1978-; Author & Editor, Harcourt Brace Jovanovich, NYC, 1960-; Mem: Eng-Spkg Union, 1966-; Coun Tchrs Eng, 1948-; NCTE 1952-; Conf on Col Composition & Commun, 1952-; S Atl MLA, 1950-; MLA, 1972-; hon/Author, "Surv of the Bard Col Lib," 1952; Author of Books: *The Meaning in Rdg*, 1960, 1964 & 1968; *The Modern Essay*, 1965, 1969 & 1973; *Col Eng: the 1st Yr*, 1960, 1964, 1968, 1973, 1982; *Imaginative Lit*, 1968, 1972, 1978, 1982; Co-Author: *Word Study 9*, 1959; *Commun Arts*, 1960; r/Presb; hon/Mem, Admissions Writing Test Panel, Col Entrance Exam Bd, Ednl Testing Ser, 1965-72; Mem, Univ Pres's Com on Student Awds, Prizes & Grants; Mem, Search Com for Dean of Univ Col, Univ of FL, 1965, 1972; Men of Achmt;

Intl W/W in Ed.

BRADSHAW, JEANIE BOK DONG oc/Homemaker, Organization Officer; b/Apr 9, 1944; h/Box 108, BYU-H, Laie, HI 96762; ba/Same; m/James R; c/Scott, Lisa, Jonathan, Mibi; p/In Jong Chung, Honolulu, HI; sp/Mr and Mrs LaVel Bradshaw, Beaver, UT; ed/Att'd Brigham Yg Univ-HI, 1970-; Att'd Univ of HI, 1980-; pa/Self-Employed, Home Beauty Conslt, 1970-; Pres, Laie, HI St Relief Soc; Mem: HI Bus Ed Assn; Wn Bus Ed Assn; Nat Bus Ed Assn; Pres, Laie Elem PTA, 1983-84; cp/Presented Num Sems on Dress, Grooming & Attitude, BYU-HI, 1981-82; Num Lectrs on Personal Motivation & Attitude, 1980-; Mem, LDS Ch, 1980-; Ordinance Wkr, HI LDS Temple, 1970-; r/LDS; hon/Commun Ser Recog, LDS Korean Commun, Seoul, Korea, 1975; LDS Commun Ldr Recog, LDS Wom, Laie, HI, 1982; Outstg Yg Wom of Am, 1979.

BRADSHAW, JERALD S oc/Professor; b/Nov 28, 1932; h/1616 Oak Lane, Provo, UT 84604; ba/Provo, UT; m/Karen; c/Donna Maree, Melinda Caroline; p/Sherwin Bradshaw, Cedar City, UT; sp/Donna Lee, Provo, UT; ed/BS, Univ of UT, 1955; PhD Chem, Univ of CA-LA (UCLA), 1963; mil/USNR, Ret'd; pa/Res Chem, Chevron Res, 1963-66; Asst Prof 1966-69, Assoc Prof 1969-74, Prof 1974-, Acting Dept Chm 1984-, Brigham Yg Univ; Chm Local Sect, Am Chem Soc, 1971; Adv Bd Mem, Intl Soc of Heterocyclic Chem, 1982-84; Bd of Editors, *Jour of Heterocyclic Chem*; cp/Pres 1978, Lt Gov 1983-84, Kiwanis Clb; r/LDS; hon/Author, Over 114 Articles Pub'd in Profl Sci & Chem Jours; Prof of Yr 1974, Maeser Tchg Awd 1982, Brigham Yg Univ; Nat Acad of Sci Exch Prof in Yugoslavia, 1972-73; Am Men & Wom of Sci; W/W in W.

BRADY, BENNETT MANNING oc/Government Official, Mathematician; b/Apr 11, 1943; h/9501 Kingsley Avenue, Bethesda, MD 20814; ba/Washington, DC; m/Roscoe O; c/Roscoe Owen Jr, Randolph Owen; p/Mr and Mrs William E Manning, Stuart, VA; sp/Mrs Roscoe O Brady, Coronado, CA; ed/AB, Vassar Col, 1965; Fulbright Fellow, 1965-66; MA, Univ of CA-Berkeley, 1968; Att'd George Wash Univ, 1972; pa/Opers Res Anal, HQs, USAF, 1968; Sr Mgmt Conslt, Ernst & Ernst, 1968-70; Res Assoc, Pres Comm on Fed Stats, 1970-71; US Intl Statl Liaison, Ofc of Mgmt & Budget, 1971-78; Spec Asst to Commr of Labor Stats, Bur of Labor Stats, Wash, 1978--79; Dir, Ofc of Prog Coor & Eval, 1979-; Chm: Interagy Com on Statl Policy 1971-78, Fed Com on Fgn Trade Stats 1971-74, Fed Com on Intl Stats 1971-78; Secy, Fed Com on Standard Metro Statl Areas, 1977-78; Rapporteur, Ec Comm for Europe's Sem on Stats of Coming Decade, 1976; Mem: Am Math Soc; Opers Res Soc of Am; Adv Com on Statl Policy 1971-77, Am Statl Assn; Mbrship Chm 1971, Profl Opports Chm 1984, Wash Opers Res Coun; Wash Statl Soc; cp/Pres 1983-84, 1st VPres 1983, Metro Intl Toastmistress Clb; Wash Vassar Clb; r/Presb; hon/Author, Co-Author & Editor of 10 Articles Pub'd in Var Profl Jours & Books; Phi Beta Kappa Prize 1st in Class & Mem, Vassar, 1965; Nat Sci Foun F'ship, 1966-68; Fulbright F'ship,

1965-66; NASA F'ship in Planetary Physics, 1964; Hon Soc Mem, Univ of CA-Berkeley, 1968; W/W: of Am Wom, in S & SE, in Am.

BRADY, CARL FRANKLIN oc/Executive; b/Oct 29; h/510 "L" Street, Anchorage, AK 99501; ba/Anchorage, AK; m/Carol Elizabeth Sprague; c/Carl F Jr, Linda Brady Farr, James K; ed/Grad, HS, 1937; mil/Army Air Corps, 1943-46; pa/Ptnr, Economy Helicopters, Yakima, WA, 1947-60; Pres, ERA Helicopters Inc, Anchorage, AK, 1960-; Pres, ERA Aviation Ctr, 1977-; Exec VPres, Rowan Cos Inc, 1973-; Dir, AK Pacific Bk, AK Pacific Bancorp, 1968-; Mem, AK Ho of Reps, 1965-66; Mem, AK St Senate, 1967-68; Pres 1953-57, Mem, Helicopter Assn Intl; cp/Pres, Anchorage C of C, 1963 & 1964; Fdr & Dir, Commonwlth N; Mem, Nat Adv Com on Oceans & Atmosphere, 3 Yr Term 1981-84; r/Meth; hon/Lawrence D Bell Awd, 1976; W/W: in W, in Am, in World.

BRADY, LUTHER W JR oc/Professor; b/Oct 20, 1925; h/316 Delancey Street, Philadelphia, PA 19102; p/Gladys L Brady, Bethesda, MD; ed/AA 1944, AB 1946, MD 1948, George Washington Univ; Intern, Jefferson Med Col Hosp, Phila, 1948-49; mil/USN, Med Ofcr, 1950-53, Lt; pa/Residencies: US Nav Med Sch, US Nav Hosp, Duke Univ Med Sch, Jefferson Med Col Hosp, Hosp of Univ of PA, 1951-56; F'ships: Nat Cancer Inst, Am Cancer Soc, 1954-59; Assoc Radiol, George Wash Univ, Wash DC, 1952-53; Asst Instr Radiol, Jefferson Med Col Hosp, Phila, 1954-55; Asst Instr 1955, Instr 1956-57, Assoc 1957-59, Radiol, Univ of PA, Phila; Asst Prof Radiol, Col of Phys & Surgs, Columbia Univ, NYC, 1959; Asst Prof Radiol, Harvard Med Sch, Boston, 1962-63; Assoc Prof Radiol 1959-62, Prof Radiol 1963-70; Prof & Chm Dept of Radiation Oncology & Nuclear Med 1970-, Hahnemann Univ, Phila; Prof Clin Oncology, Hylda Cohn/Am Cancer Soc, 1975-; Mem of Num Com Chmships & Mbrships at Hahnemann Univ; Num Chmship & Mbrship Positions w Profl Orgs: AMA; Med Soc of St of PA; Phila Co Med Soc; Am Col of Radiol; Col of Phys of Phila; Radiol Soc of N Am; PA Radiol Soc; Am Roentgen Ray Soc; Am Radium Soc; Assn of Univ Radiols; Radiation Res Soc; Phila Roentgen Soc; Am Cancer Soc; Am Fedn Clin Res; Am Bd of Radiol; Am Soc of Clin Oncology; Am Fedn of Clin Oncologic Socs; Soc of Chm of Acad Radiation Oncology Progs; Soc of Chm of Acad Radiol Depts; Am Assn for Cancer Res; Assn of Pendergrass Fellows; Intl Skeletal Soc; James Ewing Soc; Intl Clb of Radiotherapists; Others; Mem, Corp of PA Blue Shield, 1975-; Editor & Assoc Editor: *Am Jour Clin Oncology*; *Investigative Radiol*; *Applied Radiol*; *Am Jour Roentgenology*; *Cancer*; *Intl Jour Radiation Oncology, Biol & Phys*; *Gynecologic Oncology*; *Skeletal Radiol*; Pres, Intl Cong of Radiation Oncology, 1985; Conslt for Num Hosps, 1967-; cp/Var Coms & Positions, Phila Mus of Art; PA Acad of the Fine Arts; Univ of PA Mus; Assn of Artists Equity of Phila; Com for Restoration of Thomas Eakins House; Merion Cricket Clb; Racquet Clb of Phila; Union Leag of Phila; Bd of Dirs: Welcome House; Settlement Music Sch; Phila Art Alliance; Others; r/Epis; hon/

Co-Editor for Num Pubs: *Wiley Series in Diagnostic & Therapeutic Radiol*; *Appleton Cent Croft Books in Nuclear Med*; *Cancer Mgmt Series*; Author & Co-Author, Over 300 Med Sci Articles, Res Papers, Reports Pub'd in Profl Jours & Book Chapts, 1952-; Annual Honoree, PA Radiol Soc, 1980; Janeway Lectrship, Am Radium Soc, 1980; Erskine Lectrship, 1979; Elsa Pardee Lectrship, 1979; Mark Blum Lectrship, 1977; Grubbe Awd, Chgo Radiol Soc, 1977; Hon Mem, Phi Lamda Kappa & Alpha Omega Alpha, Hahnemann Med Col Chapt; Hylda Cohn/Am Cancer Soc Prof of Oncology, 1975-; Num Others.

BRAGMAN, RUTH SUSAN oc/Professor; b/Dec 9, 1947; h/1429 Oak Manor #9, Memphis, TN 38119; p/Benjamin and Miriam Bragman, Boca Raton, FL; ed/BS, Univ of WI, 1969; MEd, Univ of TX, 1973; PhD, Univ of MD, 1980; pa/Tchr/Vol, Sherut La'Am, Tel Aviv, Israel, 1969-1971; Rec Therapist, Austin St Sch, Austin, TX, Fall 1972; Acad Asst PE for Handicapped 1971-1973, Intern in Adaptive PE 1972-1973, Univ of TX; Hd Motility Tchr, Diagnostic Spec Ed Sch at Tidewater Rehab Inst, Norfolk, VA, 1973-76; Water Safety Instr Tnr, ARC, Norfolk, VA, 1975-76; Adaptive PE Tchr, Alternative Sch, Wash DC, 1977; Grad Asst in Rec 1976, Grad Asst in Spec Ed 1977-80, Intern in Arts for Handicapped 1979-80, Univ of MD; Proj Coor, Nat Com Arts for Handicapped, Wash, DC, 1980; Asst Prof, Dept Spec Ed & Rehab, Memphis St Univ, 1980-; Mem: Am Ednl Res Assn; Am Psychol Assn; Am Voc Assn; Coun for Exceptl Chd; Eval Netwk; Mid-S Ednl Res Assn; Nat Coun on Measurement in Ed; cp/Asst, Cardiac Preven & Rehab Prog, Jewish Commun Ctr, Norfolk, VA, 1974-75; Fdr & Ldr, Handicapped GSA Troop, Norfolk, 1974-75; Com Mem & Exec Com, Spec Olympics, Norfolk, 1974-76; Com Mem, Arts for Handicapped Prog, Univ of MD, 1979-80; Com Mem, Fam Life Com, Jewish Commun Ctr, Memphis, TN, 1981-; Com Mem, Ad Hoc Com on Arts for Handicapped Chd, St of TN, 1981-; Mem, St Monitoring Team for Spec Ed, Dept of Ed, St of TN, 1981; Steering Com, Spec Ed Alliance, Memphis, TN, 1982-; Over 20 Spkg & Res Paper Topic Presentations to Num Profl Assns & Orgs; hon/Author & Co-Author, Over 20 Articles Pub'd in Profl Jours incl'g: *Jour Applied Rehab*; *Jour Res in Voc Ed*; *Jour of Lrng Disabled*; *Jour Mtl Retard*; *Am Annals of Deaf*; *Alberta Jour of Ed Res*; *Resources in Ed*; *Mid-S Ednl Assn, The Res*; *Therapeutic Rec Jour*; Others; Fac Res Grant, Memphis St Univ, 1982; Outstg Paper, Mid-S Ednl Res Assn, 1980; F'ship 1979-80, Grad Asstship Spec Ed 1977-78 & 1978-79, Grad Asstship in Rec 1976-77, Univ of MD; Grad Study Grant in PE for Handicapped, Univ of TX, 1971-72 & 1972-73; Grad w Distn, Univ of WI; Phi Kappa Phi; Phi Lambda Theta; W/W in S & SW.

BRAITO, RITA MURPHY oc/Sociologist; b/Mar 3, 1930; h/1043 South Clarkson, Denver, CO 80209; ba/Denver, CO; p/Frederick E & Glenwood Murphy Braito (dec); ed/BS, San Jose St Univ, 1956; MA, Univ of CO-Boulder, 1958; MA, Univ of WA, 1967; PhD, Univ of MN, 1970; pa/Asst to Assoc Prof, Dept

Sociol, Univ of Denver, 1973-; Asst Prof Sociol, IA St Univ, 1970-73; Res Assoc & Instr, Univ of MN, 1968-70; Res Asst & Tchg Asst, Univ of WA, 1963-68; Instr, Univ of CA-LA, 1960-62; Instr, Univ of CO, 1958-60; Mem Bd of Dirs, Hospice of Metro Denver, 1982-84; Chm Nom'g Com, Sociols for Wom in Soc, 1976; Mem Bd of Dirs, Soc for Study of Social Probs, 1975-78; Others; hon/Num Pubs in Profl Sociol Jours, Books & Assn Reports; Recip, Nat Inst Mtl Hlth Tng Grant, 1963; Registry of Wom in Sci; Num W/W in W & Other Biogl Listings.

BRAKE, EDWARD THOMAS oc/ College Administrator; b/Jun 16, 1942; h/2011 Ferry Avenue, Apartment U-16, Camden, NJ 08104; ba/Philadelphia, PA; p/Mr and Mrs E T Brake, Springfield, MO; ed/BS & Dipl in Voice Perf, SW MO St Univ, 1964; MS, So IL Univ, 1966; pa/Dean of Admissions/Student Affairs, Phila Col of Perf'g Arts, 1976-; Dir of Fin Aid, Trenton St Col, 1970-76; Dean of Student Affairs, Bethany Col (Lindsborg, KA), 1966-70; Secy, NJ Assn of Student Fin Aid Admrs, 1973-76; VPres & Bd of Dirs, Phila Boys Choir, 1980-; Chm Bd of Dirs, PCPA ACT 101 Prog, 1979-80; Bd of Dirs, JUBA Contemp Dance Co of Phila; r/ Prot; hon/Serv Awd, Trenton St Col, 1977; Outstg Yg Man of Yr Awd, US JCs, 1977; Recog Awds, Bethany Col & Phila Boys Choir, 1966-83; Man of Yr, Phila Boys Choir, 1976-78; Soloist w Phila Symph Orch, 1974; W/W in E.

BRAME, EDWARD GRANT JR oc/ Polymer Spectroscopist; b/Mar 20, 1927; h/13 North Cliffe Drive, Wilmington, DE 19809; ba/Wilmington, DE; m/ Grade Adolphsen; p/Mr and Mrs Edward Brame (dec); sp/W F Adolphsen (dec); ed/BS, 1948; MA, 1950; PhD, 1957; mil/USNR; pa/Res Chem, Corn Prods Refining Co, 1950-53; Res Chem 1957-67, Sr Res Chem 1967-79, Res Assoc 1979-, Du Pont Co; Chm, En Anal Sump, 1967; Pres Soc for Applied Spectroscopy, 1978; cp/Pres, Civic Assn, 1968; r/Luth; hon/Editor of Qtly Jour, *Applied Spectroscopy Review*; Editor-in-Chief of Books Series, *Practical Spectroscopy*; Spectroscopist of Yr Awd, DE Val Sect, Soc for Applied Spectroscopy, 1983; W/W; Men & Wom of Sci.

BRAÑA, LEJO CATEDRAL oc/Manager; b/Feb 8, 1938; h/7121 Cecil Street, Houston, TX 77030; ba/Houston, TX; m/Concordia M Barrameda; c/Desiree Ann; p/Salvador and Rosalia C Braña, Philippines; ed/BSChE, Mapua Inst of Technol, Manila, 1957; Cert'd Profl in Packaging, Soc of Packaging & Handling Engrs, 1975; pa/Tech Packaging Mgr, Riviana Foods, Houston, TX, 1973-; Res & Devel Mgr, Intl Packaging Inc, Manila, 1971-72; Package Engr, S C Johnson & Son Inc, Racine, WI, 1969-71; Proj Ldr Package Res & Devel, Hunt Wesson Foods Inc, 1967-69; Sect Hd, Packaging & Plastics Machinery, Edward Keller Ltd, Manilla, 1963-67; Packaging Devel Tech, Procter & Gamble Philippine Mfg Corp, Manilla, 1958-63; Mem: Soc of Packaging & Handling Engrs; Packaging Inst Am; Inst of Packaging UK; Soc of Plastics Engrs; Packaging Engr & Adv Bd, TX A & M Univ; cp/Advr, Filipino Assn of Metro Houston; Advr, TX Assn of Mapua Alumni; Bd Mem, CPU Alumni

Assn of TX; r/Bapt; hon/Author of "Tests Point Way to Peak Plastic Bottle Perf," *Package Engrg Mag*, 1978; Patentee in Field; W/W in S & SW.

BRANCH, RAYMOND LEE oc/ Administrator; b/Jul 3, 1928; h/615 East Maywood, Wichita, KS 67216; ba/ Haven, KS; m/Idaline; c/Joan L Roberts; Pamela L Gilyard; Pamela J Whitaker; Bonnie F Marshall; sp/Aline Harrison, San Antonio, TX; ed/BS Hlth Care Adm, 1980; mil/USAF, 1947-74; pa/Admr, Spec Care Devel Ctr (Mtly Retarded & Develmtly Disabled), 1982-; Admr, Medicalouge S of KC, 1981-82; Admr, Stafford Nsg Home, 1980-81; Mem: Am Col of Nsg Home Admrs; Am Assn Mtl Deficiencies; Am Mgmt Assn; r/Bapt; hon/W/W in MW; Men of Achmt; Commun Ldrs of Am; Personalities of W & MW.

BRANDON, BILLIE oc/Attorney, Professor; b/Jul 8, 1949; h/3501 Susan Lewis Drive, Erlanger, KY 41018; ba/ Highland Heights, KY; m/Ronald E Abrams; c/Chad Everett Say; p/Everett & Eunice Brandon, Grove City, PA; ed/ BA Sociol, Slippery Rock St Col, 1971; JD, Salmon P Chase Col of Law, 1978; pa/Asst Prof 1980-, Affirmative Action Coor 1978-80, Sr Adm Ofcr 1972-78, No KY Univ; Mem: Num Com Positions, No KY Univ; ABA, KY & Campbell Co Bar Assns; Am Bus Law Assn; Am Assn for Higher Ed; Del to Nat Assem 1981, Nat Wom's Studies Assn; N Ctl Wom's Studies Assn; Nat Assn of Affirmative Action, Slippery Rock St Col Alumni Assn; Coor Alumni Celebration 1980, Chase Col of Law Alumni Assn; cp/Bd of Dirs 1979-, & Other Coms, No KY Commun Action Comm; Bd of Dirs 1979-, & Other Coms, No KY Leag of Wom Voters; Bd of Dirs 1978-, & Others Coms, No KY Wom's Polit Caucus; St Planning Com, Am Coun on Ed/Nat Identification Prog, KY, 1979-; Charter Mem, No KY Wom Lwyrs Assn, 1981; NOW, 1981-; hon/ Author & Co-Author, Over 25 Articles Pub'd in Profl Jours incl'g: "Riding the 3rd Wave: Guidelines for Staying on Top of ADEA Complaints," in *Pers Admr*, 1983; "Innovations in Tchg Bus Law," in *Jour of Legal Studies in Ed*, 1983; Author & Co-Author Var Grants & Paper Presentations; Appt'd Vis'g Team, So Assn of Cols & Schs, 1981; Order of the Curia, Chase Col of Law, 1978; S'ship Awd, Ednl Profl Devel Act, 1971-72; Pi Gamma Mu, 1969; Outstg Yg Wom of Am; W/W: of Wom, in Am Law.

BRANNIGAN, GARY G oc/Professor, Clinical Psychologist; b/Mar 22, 1947; h/53 Leonard Avenue, Plattsburgh, NY 12901; ba/Plattsburgh, NY; m/Linda; c/Marc, Michael; p/George T Brannigan, Bridgeport, CT; Ann Brannigan (dec); sp/John Baker, Trumbull, CT; Lottie Baker (dec); ed/BA, Fairfield Univ, 1969; MA 1972, PhD 1973, Psych, Univ of DE; Intern Clin Psych, Devereux Foun, Devon, PA, 1972-73; pa/Asst Prof 1973-75, Assoc Prof 1976-82, Prof Psych 1982-, SUNY-Plattsburgh; NDEA F'ship 1969-70, Tchg Asstship 1970-72, Univ of DE; Fellow, Soc for Personality Assessment; Mem, Am Psychol Assn; Mem, Assn for Retarded Chd; Mem, Clinton Co Mtl Hlth Assn; Dir 1975-80, Univ of NY Psychol Sers Clin; Consltg Editor: *Jour of Genetic Psych*,

1984-; *Genetic Psych Monograph*, 1984-; Var Consltg Positions, 1974-; cp/Elks Clb; hon/Author, Co-Author: 2 Books & 2 Book Chapts; Over 40 Articles in Profl Psych & Ednl Jours; Num Local, St & Nat Orgnl Paper Presentations; Psi Chi; Outstg Yg Men of Am; Am Men & Wom of Sci; W/W: in E, in Frontier Sci & Technol.

BRANOVAN, LEO oc/Professor Emeritus; b/Apr 17, 1895; h/3201 North 48th Street, Milwaukee, WI 53216; ba/ Milwaukee, WI; m/Pearl Branovan; c/ Rosalind Branovan Turner; ed/BSEE, Univ of WI, 1924; MS Math, Univ of Chgo, 1927; Pt-time Grad Study Applied Math, Columbia Univ, 1935-38; pa/ Engr, Gen Elect Co, Ft Wayne, 1924-26; Instr & Conslt Math, Univ of MN, 1927-31; Conslt Math, J P Goode Co, Chgo, 1932-34; Conslt Math, NYC, 1935-38; Conslt Math, Bklyn Polytech Inst, 1939-44; Instr to Prof Math 1944-770, Prof Emeritus Math 1970-, Marquette Univ, Milwaukee, WI; Mem: Am Math Soc; Am Soc Engrg Ed; AAAS; AAUP; WI Acad Arts, Lttrs & Scis; Num Fgn Math Assns; hon/Author of "Umbilics on Hyperellipsoids in 4 Dimensions," Res on "Global Differential Geometry"; Pi Mus Epsilon, 1946; Pres Hon Coun 1979; Qtr Cent Clb, 1969; Fellow, Am Biogl Inst, England; Num W/W; WI Men of Achmt; DIB; Others.

BRANSON, FARREL A oc/Botanist; b/May 3, 1919; h/906 24th Street, Golden, CO 80401; ba/Denver, CO; m/ Lydia Constance Tuttle; c/Steven Arthur, Kirk Allen; ed/BS 1942, MS 1946, Botany, Ft Hays St Univ; PhD Botany, Univ of NE, 1952; mil/USNR, 1952-46, LT; pa/Instr, Ft Hays St Univ, KS, 1947; Asst Prof, MT St Univ, Bozeman, 1951-57; Res Botanist, US Geol Surv, Denver, CO, 1957-; Fellow, AAAS, 1967-; Assoc Editor, *Soc for Range Mgmt Jour*, 1965; r/Unitarian; hon/ Author & Co-Author, Over 50 Ecol Papers; Sr Author of Textbook, *Rangeland Hydrology*, 1981; Hon Awd for Superior Ser, US Dept of Interior, 1981; AAAS, 1968; Sigma Xi, 1952; Am Men & Wom of Sci; DIB; W/W in Sci.

BRANTLEY, CINDY oc/Assistant Manager; b/Dec 13, 1963; h/PO Box 1850, Kingsland, GA 31548; ba/Same; p/Pauline Brantley, Kingsland, GA; ed/ Dipl, Coffee HS, 1982; Att'd So GA Col, 1983; Att'd Turnabout Modeling Sch, 1983; pa/Asst Mgr, Country Girl Mobile Homes, 1983-; Model, 1983-; Past Mem: Anchor Clb, VOT, FHA & Student Coun, Coffee HS; r/Bapt; hon/Hon Roll, Jr High & HS; Chosen from Top Modeling Agys in NY & Germany to Model, 1983; Photos in Var Newspapers incl'g: *Coffee Co Prog*; *SE Georgian*; *Douglas Enterprize*; *Ft Pierce Newspaper*.

BRASHIER, EDWARD MARTIN oc/ Technical Consultant; b/Sep 30, 1954; h/PO Box 841, Livingston, AL 35470; m/Deborah Warren; c/Shannon Elise, Edward Martin II, Joseph Lee II; p/Mr and Mrs Martin Lee Brashier, Jacksonville, FL; sp/Mr and Mrs W E Warrens, Woodbine, GA; ed/AS Chem/Biol, Jones Jr Col, 1974; BS Chem/Biol, Univ of MS, 1976; pa/Tech Dir, Am Envir Protection Corp, 1982-; Chief Chem 1979-80, Tech Mgr 1980-82, Chem Waste Mgmt Inc; Chem, Nilok Chems Inc, Div of Hilton Davis Chem, 1978-79; Lab Tech, Agri Prods Div, Union Carbide Corp,

1977-78; Safety Coor, FL Machine & Foundry, 1976-77; Mem: Am Chem Soc; Am Soc Safety Engrs; Instrument Soc of Am; Am Water Wks Assn; Industl Hygiene Assn; Assn of Anal Chems; Nat Assn Envir Profls; Am Inst of Chems; r/Meth; hon/Author of Var In-house Tech Pubs; Cert'd Envir Profl, NAEP, 1982; Cert'd Safety Profl, ASSE, 1982.

BRAUN, PHYLLIS CELLINI oc/Professor; b/Jan 19, 1953; h/30 Hanover Road, Newtown, CT 06470; ba/Fairfield, CT; m/Kevin F; c/Ryan Christopher; p/Mr and Mrs Rudolph Cellini, Trumbull, CT; sp/Mr and Mrs Theodore Braun, Newtown, CT; ed/BS Biol, Fairfield Univ, 1975; PhD Microbiol, Georgetown Univ Sch of Med & Dentistry, 1978; pa/Postdoct Fellow, Dept Molecular Biol, Univ of CT Sch of Med, 1978-79; Instr 1979-80, Asst Prof 1980-84, Assoc Prof 1984-, Dept of Biol, Fairfield Univ; Mem: Am Soc for Microbiol; Assn for Wom in Sci; AAAS; r/Rom Cath; hon/Author of Book, *Ltd Proteolysis*, 1979; Author, Var Articles Pub'd in Profl Jours incl'g: *Jour of Bacteriology*; *Jour of Gen Virology*; *Jour of Shellfish Res*; W/W in Frontier Sci & Technol; Dist'd Ldrs in Hlth Care.

BRAY, HAROLD V JR oc/Clinical Psychologist; b/Aug 28, 1946; h/APO, New York, New York 09360; ba/Same; m/Suzanne J; p/Mr and Mrs H V Bray Sr, Kansas City, MO; sp/Mr and Mrs J H Couch, Escondido, CA; ed/AB, Westminster Col, Fulton, MO, 1971; MEd, Univ of MO-Columbia, 1973; PhD, US Intl Univ-San Diego, CA, 1981; Addit Ed: Harvard Med Sch & Univ of MD, 1982; pa/Clin Psychol & Dir, US Army Mtl Hlth Clin, Fed Repub of Germany, 1982-84; Psychol, VA, SF, CA, 1980-82; Mem: Am Psychol Assn, 1981-; ABA, 1981-; Phi Alpha Delta, 1981-; cp/Repub Pres Task Force, 1982-; Repub Sen Com 1982-; Congl Adv Bd, 1983; r/Prot; hon/Psi Chi; W/W in W; 2000 Notable Ams; Personalities of W & MW.

BRAY, JACQUELINE LANGLOIS oc/Art Director; b/Apr 20, 1932; h/10721 Oldfield Drive, Reston, VA 22091; ba/Reston, VA; m/Roy William Gaines; c/Leslie Marie Kitchings, Judith Mae Johnson, David Edward Stevens, Laura Ann Louett; p/Irving Charles and Margaret Stone Langlois, Aiken, SC; ed/MS, Col of Art & Design, Univ of MN, 1951-55; Addit Study: Univ of Copenhagen, Denmark, 1962; Cornell Univ, 1964-65; George Mason Univ, 1976-77; pa/Med Illustr for Textbooks & Comml Artist, Univ of MN, 1953-55; Tech Illustr, Battelle, Richland, WA, 1966-68; Artist for City Planning Dept, Richland, WA, 1968-70; Pvt Comml Art Studio & Tchr at Mead Hall, Aiken, SC, 1970-75; Illustr & Designer, Potomac Res Inc, VA, 1977-78; Graphic Arts Conslt, Xerox Corp, Leesburg, VA, 1978-79; Art Dir, Centec Corp, Reston, VA, 1979-; Mem: Industl Graphics Intl; Nat Assn Female Execs; hon/Illustr of Chds Book, *The Magic Machine*, 1978; Martha Gold Scholar, 1952; W/W of Am Wom.

BRAZER, WYNONA MARIE oc/Budget Director; b/Mar 6, 1937; h/240 Dolores, Apartment 236, San Francisco, CA 94103; ba/Oakland, CA; c/Ronald, Kenneth, Gregory, Jeffory, Samuel, Nancy; p/Perry Moler (dec); Katherine

Moler, Columbus, MT; ed/Dipl, Rapelve HS, 1955; AA, Olympic Commun Col, 1971; BA, Portland St Univ, 1977; pa/Budget Dir, Am Cancer Soc, 1983-; Acctg Mgr, U Cerebral Palsy, 1980-83; Asst Controller, Harsh Investmt Corp, 1979; Portland Metro Steering Com, 1974-78; Acct, The Old Spaghetti Factory Inc, 1973-74; Bkkpr, Acme Signs Inc, 1972-73; Bkkpr, GAM Distributing Co, 1972; Ofc Mgr, Dennys Music, 1971-72; Gen Clk, GN & NP RR, 1955-63; Mem: Am Bus Wom Assn; Nat Assn for Female Execs; The C of C for Wom; r/Cath; hon/W/W of Am Wom.

BRAZIEL, JAMES HARRISON III oc/Physician, Anesthesiologist, Professor; b/Jun 13, 1950; h/1707 Cherry Circle, Anniston, AL 36201; ba/Augusta, GA; m/Debran Keith Taylor; p/Mr and Mrs H Braziel Jr, Lyons, GA; sp/Mr and Mrs L James Taylor, Augusta, GA; ed/BA Pharm, Univ of GA, 1974; MD 1978, Residency Tng 1981, Med Col of GA; mil/AUS NG; pa/Clin Instr 1981-82, Asst Prof 1982-83, Dept Anesth, Med Col of GA; Staff Anesth, NE AL Reg Med Ctr, Anniston, AL, 1983-; Mem (1979-): AMA; Am Soc of Anesths; GA Soc of Anesths; Intl Anesthesia Res Soc; Theta Kappa Psi; Chaplain, Phi Delta Chi, 1973-74; r/Christian; hon/Mem (1973-74): Rho Chi; Omicron Delta Kappa; Blue Key; Am Farmer Deg, FFA; Gridiron Soc, Univ of GA; W/W in S & SW.

BREAKIRON, LEE ALLEN oc/Astronomer; b/Jul 26, 1948; h/5248 Monroe Drive, Springfield, VA 22151; ba/Washington, DC; m/Patricia J McDonough; c/Jason Lance; p/Philip L Breakiron, Alexandria, VA; Margaret E (Jensen) Breakiron (dec); sp/Robert L and Nora B (Murray) McDonough; ed/BA, Astronomy, Univ of VA, 1970; MS 1973, PhD 1977, Astronomy, Univ of Pgh; pa/Tchg Asst & Grad Res, Univ of Pgh, 1971-76; Postdoct Res Fellow, Wesleyan Univ, 1976-80; Spec Asst, NSF, 1980-; Mem, Am Astronom Soc; Mem, Sigma Xi; hon/Author, Var Res Papers Pub'd in Jours incl'g: *The Astronom Jour*; *Pubs of Astronom Soc of Pacific*; *The Astrophy Jour Supplement*; *Icarus*; Recip, Zaccheus Daniel F'ship, 1972-76; W/W: in E, in S, in Frontier Sci & Technol, in Wash, DC.

BREIDENBACH, STEVEN THEODORE oc/Research Psychologist; b/Jun 30, 1953; h/4858 Tinasa Way, San Diego, CA 92124; ba/9233 Balboa Avenue, San Diego, CA, 92123; m/Cherie Elizabeth Johnson; p/Mr and Mrs T M Breidenbach, Aberdeen, SD; sp/Mr and Mrs Neil A Johnson, Aberdeen, SD; ed/BA Psych 1975, MA 1977, PhD 1979, Human Factors/Applied Exptl Psych, Univ of SD; pa/Tech Spec, Cubic Corp, 1984-; Res Psych, Nav Pers Res & Devel Ctr, 1983-84; Pvt Conslt, 1983-; Assoc Sci, Dunlap & Assocs W Inc, 1979-83; Grad Res Asst, Univ of SD Human Factors Lab, 1975-77 & 1978-79; Pers Mgmt Spec, Pers Div, St of WY, 1977-78; Tech Advr, *Tng Technol Jour*, 1983-; Mem: Human Factors Soc; Am Psychol Assn; Soc for Applied Lrng Technol; r/Rom Cath; hon/Author of Articles Pub'd in *Tng Technol Jour* & *Perception & Motor Skills*; Over 20 Tech Reports; Num Paper Presentations at Human Factors Soc Annual Meetings; Others; Eta Sigma Phi; Deans List, Univ

of SD; W/W in W.

BREIMYER, HAROLD FREDERICK oc/Professor Emeritus, Economist; b/Apr 13, 1914; h/1616 Princeton Drive, Columbia, MO 65203; ba/Columbia, MO; m/Rachel E; c/Frederick S; p/Fre Breimyer (dec); sp/Alfred B Styles (dec); ed/BS 1934, MS 1935, OH St Univ; Att'd Univ of CA; PhD, Am Univ, 1960; mil/USNR 1942-45, Lt Cmdr, Ret'd; pa/Economist, Agri Adjustment Adm, Bur of Agri Ecs & Agri Mktg Ser, US Dept of Agri, 1936-59; Staff Ec for Agri, US Coun Ec Advrs, 1959-61; Staff Economist, Agri Mktg Ser, 1966; Prof of Agri Ecs, Univ of MO-Columbia, 1966-84; cp/Pres 1961, Bd of Ed 1959-62, Montgomery Co, MD; Pres, Columbia, MO Coun of Chs, 1974-76; Lions; r/Meth; hon/Author of 3 Books: *Indiv Freedom & the Ec Org of Agri*, 1965; *Ecs of the Prod Mkts of Agri*, 1976; *Farm Policy: 13 Essays*, 1977; Superior Ser Awd, US Dept of Agri, 1954 & 1959; Cent Awd, Col of Agri, OH St Univ, 1970; Fellow, Am Agri Ecs Assn, 1973; Fac-Alumni Awd, Univ of MO-Columbia, 1975; W/W in Am.

BREMER, RONALD ALLAN oc/Editor; b/May 2, 1937; h/PO Box 16422, Salt Lake City, UT 84116; ba/Bountiful, UT; c/Ronald Allan, Ruby Katrina, Rebecca Elizabeth, Serena Sue, Lorrie Lou, Jennie Joyce, Elizabeth Ellen, Hans Joseph, Adam Erik, Rachel Suzanna; p/Mr and Mrs Carl L Bremer, Bellflower, CA; ed/Att'd: LA Trade Tech; Cerritos Col; Am Univ; Brigham Yg Univ; pa/Res Spec, Geneal Soc, 1969-72; Profl Geneal & Lectr, 1973-; Editor, *Geneal Digest*, 1982-; Fdr, Fedn of Geneal Socs, 1975; Fdr, Assn of Geneal Editors, 1983; cp/Mem, German Harmonie Chorus, 1982-; Fdr, Wholistic Soc, 1983; r/Mormon; hon/Author of 2 Books: *The Compendium of Hist Sources*; *The World's Funniest Epitaphs*; Author of Num Articles for Geneal Pubs; Hon Citizen of TX, 1975; W/W in W.

BRENCHLEY, JEAN ELNORA oc/Director of Biotechnology; b/Mar 6, 1944; h/238 Waring Avenue, State College, PA 16801; ba/University Park, PA; p/Mr and Mrs J Edward Brenchley, Canton, PA; ed/BS, Mansfield Univ, 1965; MS, Univ of CA-San Diego, 1967; PhD, Univ of CA-Davis, 1970; Postdoct Study, MIT, 1971; pa/Asst & Assoc Prof, PA St Univ, 1971-77; Prof of Biol, Purdue Univ, 1977-81; Res Dir, Genex Corp, 1981-84; Dir of Biotechnol, PA St Univ, 1984-; Mem: Am Soc for Microbiol; Am Soc of Biol Chems; Am Chem Soc; Genetics Soc of Am; Soc of Industl Microbiol; AAAS; hon/Author, 67 Sci Articles Pub'd in Profl Jours; Editor, *Applied & Envir Microbiol*, 1981-; Edit Bd, *Jour of Bacteriology*, 1974-83; Mem Bd of Trustees, BIOSIS, 1983-; Am Men & Wom of Sci.

BRENDEL, KLAUS oc/Professor; b/Jun 14, 1933; h/3231 North Manor Drive, Tucson, AZ 85715; ba/Tucson, AZ; m/Barbara; c/Sabine, Katrin, Caroline; p/Erich and Eva Brendel, Berlin, Germany; ed/Studies in Chem, Biochem & Bacteriology, Free Univ of Berlin, 1952-62; DSc, Free Univ of Berlin, 1962; pa/Prof of Pharm & Toxicology 1976-, Assoc Prof 1970-76, Univ of AZ; Assoc Prof Pharm, Duke Univ, 1970; Asst Prof, Estab'd Investigator of Am Heart Assn, Duke Univ, 1967-70; hon/PhD summa cum laude, 1962; NATO Postdoct Res F'ship, 1963-64; Investigatorship, Am Heart Assn, 1967-72; Personalities of W & MW; Num Other Biogl Listings.

BRENEMAN, DAVID WORTHY oc/College President; b/Oct 24, 1940; h/136 Thompson Street, Kalamazoo, MI 49007; ba/Kalamazoo, MI; m/Judith; c/Erica, Carleton; p/Muriel Breneman, Washington, DC; sp/Mildred Dodge, Santa Fe, NM; ed/BA, Univ of CO-Boulder, 1963; PhD, Univ of CA-Berkeley, 1970; pa/Amherst Col, 1970-72; Nat Acad of Scis, 1972-75; The Brookings Instn, 1975-83; President, Kalamazoo Col, 1983-; Mem, Am Ecs Assn; Bd of Dirs, NCHEMS; Bd of Dirs, AAHE; Bd of Dirs, Woodrow Wilson Nat F'ship Foun; r/Epis; hon/Author of Books: Fin'g Commun Cols, 1981; Public Policy & Pvt Higher Ed, 1978; The Coming Enrollment Crisis, 1982; Phi Beta Kappa, 1962; Danforth Fellow, 1963; Woodrow Wilson Fellow, 1963; NDEA Fellow, 1967; W/W in E.

BRENKER, THOMAS CLARKSON oc/Executive; b/Apr 1, 1944; h/314 East 41st Street, New York, NY 10017; ba/New York, NY; p/Frederick Joseph Brenker (dec); Murilla Beatrice Clarkson, Massapequa, NY; ed/BA, The Am Univ, 1968; Postgrad Study, Georgetown Univ; mil/USNG, 1966-72, 1st Lt; pa/Mem Communs Staff, Sen James L Buckley, NY, 1966-72; Public Relats Dir, Goodwill Industs, NYC, 1975-76; Dir Mktg & Communs, Atwood Richards Inc, NYC, 1976-78; Pres, Expogrp Inc, NYC, 1978-; Bd of Dirs: Intergrp; Bradshaw, Caffrey, Dillon & Smith; Fdr & Exec Dir, Mexican Food & Beverage Bd, NYC; Mem: Public Relats Soc of Am; Publicity Clb of NY; Advtg Clb of NY; cp/ARC; St Bartholomew's Commun House; Fraunces Tavern Mus; Social Clbs; Empire St Soc; Bd of Mgrs & Communs Com, SAR; Legion of Valor, Medal of Hon Soc; St Bartholomew Clb; Yg Pres Org; Union Leag; r/Epis; hon/Author of "The Brenker's Since The German Reformation, 1539-;" W/W in E; The Hereditary Register of US of Am.

BRENNER-TOURTELOT, ELIZABETH F oc/Geologist; b/Jan 8, 1941; h/734 East Morse Street, Dillon, MT 59725; ba/Dillon, MT; c/John Brenner Tourtelot, Frances Grace Tourtelot; p/John S (Jack) Brenner, (dec); Frances F Brenner, Dillon, MT; ed/BA Geol, Wellesley Col, 1962; pa/Edit Clk 1962-63, Phy Sci Tech 1963-67, Geol 1967-78, US Geol Surv, Denver, CO; Conslt Geol & Pres, X-Min Co, Dillon, MT, 1979-; Mem: Am Inst Profl Geols; Soc Ec Geols; Geol Soc of Am; Assoc Editor, Rocky Mtn Assn Geols; AAAS; MT Geol Soc; WY Geol Soc; NM Geol Soc; CO Sci Soc; Past Pres, Tobacco Root Geol Soc; NW Mining Assn; Past Pres Local Chapt, MT Mining Assn; Assn Wom Geols; Beaverhd Ch Comm; Past Mem Wom Geosci Com, Am Geol Inst; cp/VPres, Dillon Toastmistress Clb; r/Epis; hon/Author & Co-Author, Over 30 Res Papers & Tech Articles Pub'd in Profl Jours & Orgnl Guidebooks; W/W of Am Wom.

BRESEE, WILMER EDGAR oc/Executive; b/Mar 8 1910; h/160 East Street, Oneonta, NY 13820; ba/Oneonta, NY; m/Esther Bartow; p/Lynn H Bresee and Mary Temple White (dec); sp/Stanley E Bartow and Maude Bedfors (dec); ed/AB, Hamilton Col, 1932; Att'd, NY Univ Sch of Retailing, 1932; Att'd, Harvard Univ Sch of Overseas Adm, 1944; mil/AUS, Mil Police, 1943-44; AF, 1944-46; pa/Mdse Mgr & Advtg Mgr 1932-43, Mdse Mgr 1946-66, Dir 1932-, Pres 1967-73, Chm of Bd 1973-, Bresee's Oneonta Dept Store Inc; Dir & Secy of Chestnut & Dietz Land Co Inc; Dir & Vhm of Exec Com, Preferred Mut Ins Co, 1966-; Reg Bd Mem, Key Bank, Oneonta, 1963-82; cp/Pres 1950-51, Rotary Clb; Past Master, F & AM, 1936; Dist Dept Grand Master, 1946-47; Grand Hist, 1960-62; 1964-; Sr Grand Warden, F & AM, 1962-63, Illustrious Master, R & SM, 1940; Dept Grand Master, R & SM, 1954; HP, RAM, 1943 & 1947; Otsego Commdry, 76 KT; Shrine, Utica; AASR, 33nd Deg Mason, 1965; hon/Author of Masonic Trails of Early NY, 1984; Along Masonic Trails, 1961; Trails From the E, W & S, 1963; Var Articles in New Age, Masonic Fam Mag & Philalethes Mag; Phi Beta Kappa, Hamilton Col, 1931; Eta Mu Pi, 1932; Paul Harris Fellow, Rotary Intl, 1973; DHL, Hamilton Col, 1981; W/W: in E, in Fin & Indust; Commun Ldrs & Noteworthy Ams.

BRICKER, HERSCHEL LEONARD (dec May 20, 1984) oc/Former Professor Emeritus; b/May 22, 1905; h/Formerly of 1 Middle Street, Farmington, ME 04938; ba/Orono, ME; m/Cecelia Kohl; c/Gary Robert; p/Augustus Melvin and Mary Ella (Taylor) Bricker (dec); sp/Christian William and Althea (Walker) Kohl (dec); ed/AB, Coe Col, 1928; Rockefeller Foun Grant to Study Theatre & Directing Methods on Broadway, Cleveland Play House, Pasadena Playhouse & Univ of WA, 1936-37; DFA, Colby Col, 1978; DFA, Univ of ME-Orono, 1983; pa/Instr to Prof 1928-70, Dir of Theatre 1937-70, Univ of ME; Mem, War Depts Civilian Adv Com on Entertainment, WW II; Co-Chm Entertainment, AUS Gen Hosps; Hd Theatre Br, AUS Shrivenham Am Univ, England, 1945; Theatre Conslt, AUS Forces in Europe & Dir of Army Day Show, Vienna, 1946-47; Fdr & Dir, Camden Hills Theatre (Sch) for Col & Univ Students in US, 1947-56; ME Masque Theatre Tour for ATA-USO, AUS in W Germany & No Italy, 1960; MW Masque Theatre Tour for US St Dept, India, E & W Pakistan, 1962; Prof Theatre, Univ of ME-Farmington, 1970-75; Prin Fdr & Exec Dir, The Arts Inst of Wn ME, 1973-76; Pres 1944-45 & Mem, Am Theatre Assn; Elected Mem, Nat Theatre Conf, 1940; Mem, St of ME Arts & Humanities Comm, 1965-68; r/1st Congregl; hon/Author of Our Theatre Today, 1936; Num Articles Pub'd in Mags incl'g: Nayta; Mondales; Theatre Qtly Jour; Coe Col Awd of Merit, 1978; Dist'd Ser Awd, Univ of ME-Farmington, 1977; DIB; W/W: in Ed, Contemp Achmt; Am Scholars; Men of Achmt.

BRIDGES, ALAN LYNN oc/Information Resource Management Executive; b/Oct 10, 1950; h/2754 Pine Hill Drive, Kennesaw, GA 30144; ba/Marietta, GA; p/E Paul and Beuna L Bridges, Kennesaw, GA; ed/BS Physics 1972, MS Physics 1974, Postgrad Studies 1975-78, GA Inst of Technol; pa/Asst Res Sci, Engrg Expt Sta, GA Inst of Technol, 1975-78; Asst Prod Mgr, Humphrey Inst, San Leandro, CA, 1978-79; Conslt, Gen Motors, Intl Resource Devel, Rubin Legal Clins & Via Video, 1979-83; Prin Spec Engr, Elects Res & Devel Dept, Lockeed-GA, 1983-; Pres & Fdr, EJC W, Very Extra Spec Res Sys, Atlanta, 1979-; VPres Engrg, Rand Space Co, Champlee, GA, 1984-; Coor, Adv'd Concepts Flight Sta Simulator Prog, NASA, 1984-; Mem, IEEE; ACM; DSA; SPIE; AIAA; NMA; cp/Editor, Atlanta Ham, Atlanta Radio Clb, 1975-76; Bd of Dirs, Kennehoochee Radio Clb, 1976-79; hon/Author, Over 60 Tech Reports, Articles & Conf Papers Pub'd in Profl Jours & Org Pubs; Contbg Editor, Computer Technol Review, 1983-; Sigma Pi Sigma; Num Others; W/W: in S & SW, in Frontier Sci & Technol; in Computer Graphics.

BRIDGES, DONALD NORRIS oc/Nuclear Engineer; b/Aug 13, 1936; h/1002 Longleaf Court, North Augusta, SC 29841; ba/Aiken, SC; m/Charlene Kiser; c/Denise B McMillan, David Lynn, Daryl Dean, Donna Michelle; p/Mr and Mrs T F Bridges, Shelby, NC; sp/Mr and Mrs Z J Kiser, Shelby, NC; ed/BCE 1958, MS 1960, NC St Univ; MSNE 1968, PhD 1970, GA Inst of Technol; mil/USN, 1962-66; USNR, Capt; pa/Civil Engr, Du Pont Co, Savannah River Plant, 1960-62; Nuclear Engr, AEC, Savannah River Plant, 1970-74; Nuclear Engr, NRC, Wash DC, 1974-76; Nuclear Engr, Chief Reactors Br, Dept of Energy, Savannah River, 1976-; Soc Am Mil Engrs; Am Nuclear Soc; cp/Cmdr, Resv Nav Constrn Battalions, Atl Fleet Resv Assn; Resv Ofcr Assn; SS Tchr, 1st Bapt Ch, NA; r/Bapt; hon/Author of 2 Articles Pub'd in Nuclear Sci & Engrg; Tau Beta Pi, Phi Kappa Phi, Sigma Xi, Chi Epsilon; AEC Spec F'ship, 1966-70; Reg'd Engr, St of NC.

BRIGGS, HILTON MARSHALL oc/President Emeritus; b/Jan 9, 1913; ba/Brookings, SD; m/Lillian D; c/Dinus Marshall, Janice B Remmele; p/John Weaver and Ethel Briggs (dec); sp/Tryggvi and Hall Erider Dinusson (dec); ed/BS, IA St Univ, 1933; MS, ND St Univ, 1935; PhD, Cornell Univ, 1938; pa/Asst Prof 1936-41, Assoc Prof 1941-45, Prof 1945-50, Assoc Dean of Agri & Assoc Dir Agri Expt Sta 1949-50, OK St Univ; Dean of Agri Esp Sta 1950-58, Univ of WY; Pres 1958-75, Dir Fgn Progs 1978, Pres Emeritus & Dist'd Prof Agri 1975-, SD St Univ; Sec 1947-50, VPres 1951, Pres 1952, Am Soc Animal Sci; Com on Animal Nutrition, Nat Res Coun, 1951-57; Exec Com 1943-48, Pres 1948, Continental Dorset Clb; Dir 1970-76, Dir for Life 1976-, Am Sdown Breeders Assn; Dir 1948-49, Comm on Cols & Univs of N Ctl Assn So Agri Dirs; r/Meth; hon/Author of Book & Book Chapts: Mod Breeds of Livestock; "Feed Sect," in Ency Chem Technol; "Cattle Sect," in World Book Ency; Author of Approx 40 Jour Articles Pub'd in Profl Jours & Assn Bltns; Fellow, Am Soc Animal Sci; AAAS; Nat 4-H Clb Alumni Achmt Awd, 1959; Outstg SD Citizen, SD Press Assn, 1975; Others; W/W: in Am, in World, in Ed; Am Men & Wom of Sci; DIB.

BRIGGS, NANCY E oc/Communications Consultant, Professor; b/1944; ba/Long Beach, CA; m/Rodney A; c/Eric,

Nicole; ed/BA Spch Communs, Theatre & Rel, Augustana Col, SD, 1966; Addit Study, Univ of CA-Berkeley; MA, PhD Spch Communs, Univ of So CA (USC), 1970; pa/Prof Spch Communs, CA St Univ-Long Bch, 1970-; Conslt, LA Free Public Theatre, 1977-; Discussion Ldr, Joy Bible Study, Covenant Ch, Rolling Hills Ests, CA, 1982-83; Rltr, CA Real Est Bd, 1980; Ednl Conslt, Fountain Val Sch, Dist on Spch Activs, 1975-78; Conslt, Newport USD on Statement of Ed Principles on Spch Commun, 1973-75; Conslt, Intraleisure Inc, Redondo Bch, CA, 1969-71; Instr, CA St Univ-Dominguez Hills, 1968-70; Instr, Univ of So CA, 1966; Mem: Wn Spch Commun Assn; Spch Commun Assn of Am; Intl Communs Assn; Author, Over 40 Articles, Reports & Conv Papers Pub'd in Profl Jours & Orgnl Pubs; r/Luth; hon/Recip of 6 Res Grants, 1970-82; Var Guest Appearances on Romper Rm, 1981 & 1982; Mem, Intl Platform Assn, 1981; Pres & Outstg Wom of Yr in S Bay Area, Am Luth Ch Wom, Palos Verdes, 1980; Outstg Yg Wom of Am Awd, 1980; Alpha Lambda Delta; NDEA F'ship, 1966-70; Miss SD Career Girl, 1965; Miss SD Runner-up, 1965; Champ, Pi Kappa Delta Wom's Nat Debate, 1965; Bd of Advrs, Am Biogl Inst; Num Others; W/ W: of Intells, of Am Wom, of Wom, in Am Ed; DIB; 2000 Notable Ams; Dir of Am Scholars; Intl Book of Hon; Num Other Biogl Listings.

BRIGGS, VERNON MASON JR oc/ Professor; b/Jun 29, 1937; h/332 Winthrop Drive, Ithaca, NY 14850; ba/ Ithaca, NY; m/Martijna A; c/Vernon III, Kees; ed/BS Ec, Univ of MD, 1959; MA Ec 1960, PhD Ec 1965, MI St Univ; pa/ Asst Instr, Ec, MI St Univ, 1960-64; Asst Prof to Prof Ec, Univ of TX-Austin, 1964-78; Prof Labor Ec & Human Resource Studies, Cornell Univ, 1978-; Mem: Am Ec Assn; Industl Relats Res Assn; Assn for Evolutionary Ec; r/Cath; hon/Co-Author of 5 Books: *The Negro & Apprenticeship*, 1967; *Chicanos & Rural Poverty*, 1973; *The Chicano Wkr*, 1977; *Employmnt, Income & Wel in the Rural S*, 1980; *Labor Ec: Wages, Employmnt & Trade Unionism*, 1980 & 1984; *Immigration Policy & the Am Labor Force*, 1984; Jean Holloway Awd for Tchg Excel, Univ of TX-Austin, 1974; W/W in Am.

BRILL, THOMAS B oc/Professor; b/ Feb 3, 1944; h/101 Tanglewood Lane, Newark, DE 19711; ba/Newark, DE; m/ Patricia; c/Barbara, Russell; p/Kenneth and Priscilla Brill, Webster Groves, MO; sp/Marion and Marjorie, Highland Park, IL; ed/BS, Univ of MT, 1966; PhD, Univ of MN, 1970; pa/Asst Prof 1970-74, Assoc Prof 1974-79, Prof 1979-, Univ of DE; Vis'g Prof, Univ of OR, 1977; Mem: Am Chem Soc; Sigma Xi; Phi Kappa Phi; Phi Lambda Epsilon; r/Epis; hon/Author of Book, *Light: It's Interaction w Art & Antiquities*; Over 90 Articles in Profl Chem Jours; Sigma Xi Nat Lectr, 1984-87; NDEA Title IV F'ship, 1966-69; W/W: in Sci & Technol, in Technol Today, in Frontier Sci & Technol.

BRILLINGER, DAVID R oc/Professor; b/Oct 27, 1937; ba/Statistics Dept, Univ of CA, Berkeley, CA, 94720; m/ Lorie S; c/Jef A, Matthew D; p/Austin C Brillinger (dec); Winnifred E Brillinger; sp/Frederick and Priscilla Silber; ed/

BA, Univ of Toronto, 1959; MA 1960, PhD 1961, Princeton Univ; mil/Canadian Nav Resv; pa/Lectr Math, Princeton Univ, 1962-64; Mem Tech Staff, Bell Labs, 1962-64; Lectr, Rdr Stats, London Sch of Ec, 1964-69; Prof Stats, Univ of CA-Berkeley, 1969-; Mem: Am Statl Assn; AAAS; Inst Math Stats; Intl Statl Inst; Seismological Soc of Am; ca/ Author of *Time Series: Data Anal & Theory*, 1975; Over 90 Articles & Papers; hon/ Guggenheim Fellow, 1975-76 & 1982-83.

BRINKLEY, JOEL GRAHAM oc/ Newspaper Reporter; b/Jul 22, 1952; h/ 2224 39th Place Northwest, Washington, DC 20007; ba/Washington, DC; p/ David and Ann Brinkley, Washington, DC; ed/AB Eng & Jour, Univ of NC-Chapel Hill, 1975; pa/Reporter, AP, Charlotte, NC, 1975; Reporter, *Richmond News Ldr*, 1975-78; Reporter 1978-82, Editor 1983, *The Courier-Jour*, L'ville; Wash Correspondent, *The NY Times*, 1983-; Mem, Soc of Profl Jours, 1981-; Investigative Reporters & Editors, 1981-; hon/Author of Var Newspaper & Mag Articles; Pulitzer Prize for Intl Reporting, 1980; Grand Prize, Investigative Reporters & Editors Inc, 1982; Hdliner Awd for Public Ser Reporting (1st Prize), Nat Hdliners Clb, 1983; Nat Press Clb & Nat Consumer Reporting Awds, 1981 & 1983; Wm S Miller Awds, 1983; Roy W Howard Awds, Scripps-Howard Foun, 1981 & 1982; Runner-up, Pulitzer Prize, Investigative Reporting, 1982; Penney-Missouri Consumer Reporting Awd, 1982; Clarion Awd, 1982; Num Society of Professional Journalists Awds, 1981-83; Num Others; W/W: in S & SW, in Am; Contemp Authors; Other Biogl Listings.

BRINSON, DONALD EDWARD oc/ Data Processing Manager; b/Sep 6, 1953; h/308 Draper Drive, Midwest City, OK 73110; ba/Midwest City, OK; p/Merwyn Glen and Mildred Colleen (Good) Brinson, Ponca City, OK; ed/ BSc, Univ of OK, 1980; pa/Var Positions w Sta KGOU, Norman, OK, 1971-73; Lab Instr, ELS Lang Ctr, Norman, OK, 1972-74; Computer Programmer, Oscar Rose Jr Col, 1974-78; Sys Programmer, OK Tax Comm, Oklahoma City, OK, 1978-80; Dir Computing Sers, Rose St Col, Midwest City, 1980-; Mem, Assn for Computing Machinery; Prog Chm 1982, Pres 1983, Ctl OK Chapt, Hewlett-Packard Intl Users Grp; cp/Co-Fdr, Prog Chm 1978, Pres 1979, Single Adult Persons; r/Meth; hon/W/ W: in S & SW, in Frontier Sci & Technol, of Contemp Achmt; Personalities of S.

BRISCOE, DIANE-FROST ASBURY oc/Executive; b/Jan 8, 1945; h/408 Sycamore Drive, Decatur, GA 30030; ba/Atlanta, GA; p/Philip and Mary Louise Asbury Briscoe, Annapolis, MD; ed/La Colline, Ecole des Langues, La Tour-de-Peilz, Vaud, Switzerland, 1963; BS, Univ of GA, 1971; pa/Adm Asst to Pres, Airclaims Inc, Wash DC, 1966-68 & 1971-72; Adm Asst to Claims Mgr 1972-75, Claims Rep & Ofc Mgr 1975-79; Asst VPres 1979-81, VPres 1981-, Rowedder Aviation Adjustment Ser Inc, Atlanta, GA; Mem: Atlanta Claims Assn Inc; Intl Info/Word Processing Assn; Secy 1978, Pres 1979 & 1980, Comptroller 1981 & 1982, Dana Marie Condominium Assn Inc; Coress'g

Secy 1978-79, Reg III Chm Mag Com (Reg Editor, *Today's Ins Wom*) 1979-80, Chm Ins Com 1980-81 & 1982-83; CoChm Public Relats Com 1977-78, Spch Class Instr 1982, Atlanta Assn of Ins Wom Inc; cp/The Nat Soc of Colonial Dames of Am, St of MD; 1st Saturday Chm Nearly New, The Jr Leag of Atlanta, 1977-81; r/Epis; hon/Author of Var Articles Pub'd in *Atlanta Ins Wom* & *Today's Ins Wom*; Reg III VR Ed Awd, Nat Assn of Ins Wom, 1978; Assoc in Mgmt Designation, Ins Inst of Am, 1979; CPIW/AIM Designation, Nat Assn of Ins Wom, 1980; W/W: in S & SW, of Am Wom.

BRITT, GEORGE G JR oc/Executive, Political Consultant; b/May 19, 1949; h/ 906 South 60th Street, Philadelphia, PA 19143; ba/Philadelphia, PA; p/George Sr and Mary Britt, Philadelphia, PA; ed/BA Polit Sci, Cheyney St Col, 1972; Att'd Georgetown Univ Law Sch, 1976; pa/ Chm, W Phila Commun Devel Prog, 1970-73; Chm, Nat Assn of PR Yth, 1973-; Mgmt Conslt & Owner of Firm, George Britt Jr & Staff; Mem: ASPA; Interracial Ec Devel Forum; Assn MBA Execs; U Minority Enterprises Assn; Chm, Intl Ec Devel Forum; Ch, Coun for EOE Bd; cp/Former Cand, Mayor of Phila & US Cong; Mem, SW Human Relats Coun; Edison HS Commun Adv Com; Mem, Dem Nat Com; Others; r/ Bapt; hon/Del to White House Conf on Small Bus, 1980; Hon KY Col; Hon Citizen of MN, TX, AR, AL, KY, WV; W/W: in E, in Fin & Indust.

BRITWETZ (BRITVEC), STANISLAUS JOSEPH oc/Professor; b/Feb 16, 1930; h/PO Box 247, Orono, ME 04473; ba/Orono, ME; ed/BSc, London Univ, 1957; PhD, Cambridge Univ, 1960; F'ship, Harvard Univ, 1964; Habilitation, Univ of Stuttgart & DSc, Univ of Zagreb, 1972 & 1974; pa/Prof Engrg Mech & Civil Engrg, Univ of ME, 1983-; Vis'g Prof, Univ of CO-Boulder, 1979-83; Conslt, Martin-Marietta Aerospace Corp, 1978-82; Privatdozent, Prof Univ of Stuttgart, Germany, 1972- 78; Prof Engrg Mech & Civil Engrg, Univ of Zagreb, Yugoslavia, 1974-79; Assoc Prof Applied Mechs & Mech Engrg, Univ of Pgh, 1966-72; Gordon McKay Lectr on Structural Mechs, Harvard Univ, 1964-65; Asst Prof Civil Engrg & Structural Mechs, Cornell Univ 1960-64; Selwyn Col, Cambridge Univ 1957-60; Mem: ASCE; Am Soc Mech Engrs; NY Acad of Scis, 1973; Sigma Xi, 1961; r/Rom Cath; hon/Author of *The Stability of Elastic Sys*, 1973; *Nonlinear Dynamics of Elastic Bodies*, 1979; Author of Num Articles & Sci Papers on Structural Stability Pub'd in Profl Sci Jours, 1960-; Maj Co Awd for Outstg S'ship, London, 1956; Aluminum Devel Assn of Great Brit F'ship, Cambridge Univ, 1957-60; Var Biogl Listings.

BROADNAX, PIER ANGELI oc/ Nurse; b/Sep 9, 1955; h/140-F Tide Mill Lane, Hampton, VA 23666; ba/Hampton, VA; p/Mr and Mrs Herbert Broadnax Jr, Covington, VA; ed/BS Nsg, 1977; MS Nsg, 1983; pa/Staff Nurse, Univ Hosp, Augusta, GA, 1977; Staff Nurse & Asst Hd Nurse, Wash VA Med Ctr, 1978-80; Staff Nurse, Hampton VA Med Ctr, 1980-; Mem: ANA, 1981-; VA Nurses Assn, 1981-; Charter Mem, VA Soc Profl Nurses, 1983; r/Bapt; hon/W/ W in Am Cols & Univs.

BROADWATER, JOHN DAVID oc/ Underwater Archaeologist; b/Dec 21, 1943; h/177 The Maine, Williamsburg, VA 23185; ba/Yorktown, VA; m/Sharon Thompson; c/Jennifer Noelle, April Renee; p/William Clinton and Dorothy Goodloe Broadwater, Middlesboro, KY; sp/Herbert and Mildred Thompson, Duncanville, TX; ed/BSEE, Univ of KY, 1966; MA Am Studies, Col of Wm & Mary, in Progress; pa/Planning Engr, Wn Elect Co, 1967-72; VPres, Marine Archaeol Res Sers Inc, 1972-77; Sr Underwater Archaeol, VA Hist Landmarks Comm, 1978-; Dir, Yorktown Shipwreck Archaeol Proj, 1978-; Hon Life Mem, Inst of Nautical Archaeol; Mem, Public Info & Action Com, Soc for Hist Archaeol; Coun VA Archaeols; Archaeol Soc VA; Instr Emeritus, Profl Assn Diving Instrs; hon/Author of *Kwajalein, Lagoon of Found Ships*, 1971 & 1972; "Diving Sect," in *The Explorers Ltd Source Book*, 1973 & 1977; Var Articles Pub'd in Profl Jours incl'g: *Intl Jour Nautical Archaeol*; *Sea Frontiers*; Num Others; Lectr & Instr, Col of Wm & Mary.

BROADWELL, RICHARD DOW oc/ Professor; b/Nov 4, 1945; h/10401 Grosvenor Place #1010, Rockville, MD 20852; ba/Baltimore, MD; p/Robert and Dorothy Jane (Dow) Broadwell, Naperville, IL; ed/BA, Knox Col, 1967; MS 1971, PhD 1974, Univ of WI-Madison; pa/Staff Fellow, Lab of Neuropathol & Neuroanatomical Scis, NINCDS, NIH, 1974-80; Asst Prof Div Neuropathol, Dept Pathol 1980-84, Assoc Prof Div Neurosurg, Dept Surg & Dept Pathol 1985, Hd Lab Exptl Neuropathol & Hd Lab Neuro-Oncology, Univ of MD Sch of Med; Mem: Neurosci Soc; Am Soc of Cell Biol; Histochem Soc; Chesapeake Soc for Electron Microscopy; r/Presb; hon/Author Num Articles on Neurocytolgy, Blood-Brain Barrier & Enzyme Cytochem Methodologies Pub'd in Profl Sci & Med Jours; Merit Scholar, NSF, 1966-67; Japanese Soc Promotion of Scis F'ship, 1979-80; Grantee, NINCDS/ NIG, 1982-; W/W: Frontier Sci & Technol, Am (E), World.

BROBST, JOYCE ELAINE oc/ Teacher; b/Sep 17, 1946; h/2111 Fairview Avenue, Reading, PA, 19606; ba/ Reading, PA; p/Clyde H Brobst (dec); Sarah L Brobst, Bloomsburg, PA; ed/BS Biol 1968, MEd Biol 1969, Bloomsburg Univ; MS Ed, Marywood Col, 1977; Sec'dy Sch Guid, Kutztown Univ, 1978-; pa/Biol Tchr 1968-, Sci Dept Chp 1977-, Antietam Sch Dist, PA; Mem: Nat Assn of Biol Tchrs, 1968-; Nat Sci Tchrs Assn, 1968-; Antietam Ed Assn, 1968-; PSEA, 1968-; En Reg Del, PSEA, 1971; NEA, 1968-; Nat Wildlife Fedn, 1968; Thespian Soc, 1964; Beta Sigma Phi, 1971-; Assn Supvn & Curric Devel, 1978-; r/ Luth; hon/Nolde Forest Envir Ct Awd for Achmt & Ser to Sch, Commun & Commonwlth of PA, 1977; Outstg Yg Ed Awd, Antietam Val JCs, 1976; Finalist, Biol Tchr of Yr, 1976; Finalist, PA's Outstg Tchr of Yr, 1975; Girl of Yr, Beta Sigma Phi, 1973, 1975 & 1982; Zeswitz Music Awd, 1964; Others; Outstg Yg Wom of Am; Outstg Yg Sec'dy Ed of Am; W/W in W.

BRODERICK, JOHN J oc/Radio Astronomer, Educator; b/Oct 14, 1940; h/2810 Wellesley Court, Blacksburg, VA 24060; ba/Blacksburg, VA; m/ Sandy; c/Rosemarie, Jack, Cynthia Hassler, Matthew Hassler; p/Mrs Margaret Broderick, Locustdale, PA; sp/Mr and Mrs Loyd Bussey, Port Moody, BC, Canada; ed/BS Physics, PA St Univ, 1962; MA 1964, PhD 1970, Physics, Brandeis Univ; mil/AFROTC, 2 Yrs; pa/ Res Assoc, Nat Radio Astronomy Observatory, 1969-71; Res Assoc, Nat Astronomy & Ionosphere Ctr, 1971-74; Asst Prof 1974-80, Assoc Prof 1980-, VA Tech; Mem: Intl Astronom Union; Intl Radio Sci Union; Am Astronom Soc; Sigma Xi; VA Acad of Sci; r/Rom Cath; hon/Author, Over 30 Sci Pubs in Field of Radio Astronomy; W/W: in S & SW, in Frontier Sci & Technol; Am Men of Sci; Registry of Brodericks in Am.

BROHN, FREDRICK HERMAN oc/ Biochemist; b/Mar 6, 1940; h/1370 Circle Drive West, Baldwin, NY 11510; ba/New York, NY; m/Margaret Sue; c/ Karl, Philip, Adam, Keith, Margaret, Caroline; p/Wiliam H Brohn, Ridgeway, PA; Ottilia Caroline Brohn (dec); sp/W Karl & Marge Standley, Grosse Pointe Woods, MI; ed/BS, Univ of MI, 1965; PhD, Wayne St Univ, 1972; pa/Lectr, Oakland Commun Col, MI, 1971-72; Postdoct Fellow 1972-75, Res Assoc 1975-77, Rockefeller Univ; Asst Prof, NY Univ Sch of Med, 1977-84; cp/VPres 119th NY Vol Hist Assn, 1983-84; hon/ Author of Num Articles in Sci Jours on Biochem & Parasitology; Phi Lambda Upsilon, 1968; Sigma Xi, 1976; W/W in Frontier Sci & Technol; Am Men & Wom of Sci.

BROMMER, GERALD F oc/Artist, Author; b/Jan 8, 1927; h/11252 Valley Spring Lane, North Hollywood, CA 91602; ba/Same; m/Georgia E; p/Edgar and Helen Brommer (dec); ed/BS Ed, Concordia Col, 1948; MA, Univ of NE, 1955; pa/Tchr, St Paul's Sch, No Hollywood, CA, 1948-55; Art Instr, Dept Chm, Luth HS, LA, 1955-77; Self-employed, 1977-84; Mem: Pres 1962 & 1983, 1st VPres 1982, Nat Watercolor Soc; W Coast Watercolor Soc; Nat Arts Clb, NY; Rocky Mtn Nat Watermedia Soc; Artists Equity; r/Luth; hon/Author of 11 Books incl'g: *Careers in Art*, 1984; *Discovering Art Hist*, 1981; *Art of Collage*, 1978; *Drawing*, 1978; *Landscapes*, 1977; *Art in Your World*, 1977; Others; Num Articles Pub'd in Art Jours; Alumni of Yr 1974, NE Crest of Christ Awd 1981, Concordia Col; W/ W: in Am Art, in CA, in W; Contemp Authors; Am Artists of Renown; Other Biogl Listings.

BRONSON, SHIRLEY GERENE oc/ Financial Manager, Feminist Consultant; b/Oct 15, 1936; h/8640 Gulana Avenue, #J-1012, Playa Del Ray, CA 90291; ba/Los Angeles,CA; m/Bobby Ed; c/Richard Ed, David Dee, Daniel Lee, Robert Edward; p/Dee Lawrence Green (dec); Mrs Velma Geneva (Smith) Green, Roswell, NM; sp/Ed Nathanel Bronson (dec); Dorothy (Brownlowe) Bronson-Westmoreland, North Little Rock, AR; ed/BA 1975, MBA 1977, Golden Gate Univ; pa/Fed Wom's Prog Mgr 1973-74, Asst to Comptroller 1974-76, Record's Mgmt Ofcr 1976-77, AF Flight Test Ctr, Edwards, CA; Prog/ Budget Anal 1977-81, Fin Mgr 1981-, Fed Wom's Prog Mgr, AF Space Div, LA, CA; Contract Tchr, Pacific Christian Col, CA, 1977; Data Processing Mgr: Nav COMSUBPAC, HI; Data Processing Div, Page Aircraft, HI; Wn Elect, Nashville, TN; Nat Assn Female Execs; LA Chapt, Am Soc Mil Comptrollers; Pres Antelope Val Chapt, Fed Employed Wom Inc, 1976 & 1977; Fed Wom's Prog Com, LA Fed Exec Bd; LA Chapt, AF Assn; cp/Histn & Libn Gamma Alpha Tau Chapt 1970-72, Pres Omicron Chapt 1973-74, Beta Sigma Phi; VPres 1972-73, Parliamentn & Recording Secy 1972-74, Lancaster City Coun, Beta Sigma Phi; VPres, So CA Chapt, Icelandic/Am Clb, 1976 & 1977; Task Force Mem, UN Decade for Wom, 1977; CA Del, Nat Wom's Conf, 1977; Citizens for Incorp of Lancaster, CA, 1977; hon/Author of Horizon's W 80, AF Conf Cmdr's Conf Article, "Space Div is # 1 Fed Wom's Prog," 1980; Author of 2 Fed Wom's Prog Films; Dist'd EOE Awds, HQ's Space Div, LA AF Sta, CA, 1979-82; Dist'd Public Ser Awd, Fed Exec Bd, 1981; Mgr of Yr Awd, Dept of AF Fed Wom's Prog, 1980; Mgr of Yr Awd, AF Sys Fed Wom's Prog, 1979; Spec Recog Awd 1976, Spec Achmt Awd 1971 & 1976 & 1982, AF Flight Test Ctr Fed Wom's Prog; Num Others; W/W: of Am Wom; Personalities of W & MW; Dir Dist'd Ams; Other Biogl Listings.

BRONZATI, ARLINE L oc/Professor; b/Mar 26, 1936; h/505 East 79th Street, New York, NY 10021; ba/Bronx, NY; m/Bertram; c/Robin, Susan; p/Ida Cohen, Bklyn, NY; ed/BA, Hunter Col, 1956; MA 1958, PhD 1966, Psych, Columbia Univ; pa/Lectr, Hunter Col, 1958-65; Res Asst Psychi 1958-67, Instr 1965-67, Finch Col; Asst Prof to Prof, Herbert H Lehman Col, 1967-; Conslt, NYC Transit Auth, 1977-; Pres, NY St Chapt Wom's Equity Action Leag, 1974-76; Secy, Phi Beta Kappa Assn of NY, 1972-; Ch, Noise Com, Coun on Envir NYC, 1984-; Pres Lehman Col Chapt, Sigma XI, 1980-81; Ch, Mayor's Subway Watchdog Comm NYC, 1970-74; Mem, Transit Ser Characteristics Com, Trans Res Bd, Nat Acad of Scis, 1977-; Others; hon/Author, Over 25 Pubs in Psych, Sociol & Ed Jours; Phi Beta Kappa, 1956; Sigma Xi, 1976; Psi Chi, 1956; Phi Sigma, 1956; Kappa Delta Pi, 1959; Outstg Bklyn Wom, Bklyn Chapt, NOW, 1974; Reg Cert of Apprec for Achmts in Protection of Envir, US EPA Reg 2, 1976; W/W: in Frontier Sci & Technol, of Am Wom, in E.

BROOK, BENJAMIN NATHAN oc/ Social Welfare Consultant; b/Jan 31, 1913; h/2542 Avenue San Valle, Tucson, AZ 83715; ba/Same; m/Elizabeth; c/Robert Henry, Mark Dahiel; ed/AB 1934, MA 1936, NY Univ; MSW, Columbia Univ, 1949; EdD, Univ of AZ, 1972; pa/Exec VPres, Tucson Jewish Commun Coun; Asst Prof Sociol, CA St Univ-LA; Lectr, Public Adm, Univ of AZ; Conslt, Weizmann Inst of Sci & Res; Pres, AZ Conf Social Welfare; cp/Pres, U Way Profl Assn; VPres, Parents U; Treas, Commun Food Bk; Chm, Commun Devel Block Grant Prog; Referee, Pima Co Juv Ct; Others; r/Hebrew; hon/ Author of "Role of Overseas Vol Agys Following WW II Relief Wk"; "Budget & Allocation Processes of U Way"; Commendare Awd, Italian Govt, 1947; Citizen Awd, City of Tucson, St of AZ, 1965; Profl of Yr Awd, 1975; W/W: in W, in Israel; Men of Achmt.

BROOKE, JOHN A oc/Executive; b/ May 9, 1934; h/111 West Wesminster, Lake Forest, IL 60045; ba/Lake Forest, IL; m/Georgia E; c/Elizabeth, Cynthia, John E, Katherine, Martha; p/William L Brooke (dec); Virgina Brooke Boyd, Oak Park, IL; sp/George & Florence Eisermann, Oak Park, IL; ed/Grad, Culver Mil Acad, 1953; BS, Cornell Univ Sch of Hotel Adm, 1957; mil/AUS, 1957-59, 2nd Lt; pa/Pres, Brooke Inns Inc, 1964-; Dir of Sales, Topeka Inn Mgmt Inc, 1963; Innkeeper & Mgr of Var Holiday Inns owned by Topeka Mgmt Inc, 1960-63; Food & Beverage Mgr, Hotel Cornhusker, Lincoln, NE, 1959-60; Num Ofc Positions, Am Hotel & Motel Assn; Pres 1981, Chm of Bd 1982, Pres Intl Assn of Hotel Inns 1973, Chgo Hotel & Motel Assn, IL Hotel & Motel Assn; cp/Lake Forest Sch Bd Mem; Elder, 1st Presb Ch; Mem, Social Chm 1982, Chgo Chapt, Yg Pres OrgPast Pres, Cornell Soc of Hotelmen; Mem, Cornell Univ Coun 6 Yrs; Former Trustee, Goodwill Industs Chgo.

BROOKER, ALAN EDWARD oc/ Clinical Neuropsycholgist; b/Jan 26, 1949; h/206 Emory Drive, Vacaville, CA 95688; ba/Travis AFB, CA; m/Mary Naglee; c/Jeffrey Alan, Jarrod Russell; p/Mrs Margaret Gorman Simpson (dec); sp/Elizabeth B Naglee, Marysville, CA; ed/BA, Chapman Col, 1971; MS, CA St Univ-Sacramento, 1975; PhD, KS St Univ, 1977; Clin Psych Intern, Wright-Patterson USAF Med Ctr, 1977-78; Med Psych Residency, OR Hlth Sci Ctr, 1981-82; mil/USAF, 1968-73 & 1973-, Maj; pa/Dept Combat Crew Cmdr, Malmstrom AFB, MT, 1972-73; Voc Rehab Cnslr, St of CA, Auburn, CA, 1973-77; Chief Psychol Testing, USAF Reg Med Ctr, Wiesbaden, W Germany, 1978-81; Clin Neuropsychol Ofcr, David Grant USAF Med Ctr, Travis AFB, CA, 1982-; Mem: Am Psychol Assn; Fellow, PA Psychol Assn; Intl Neuropsychol Soc; AF Soc of Clin Psychols; Diplomate, Am Bd of Profl Psychol Inc; Diplomate in Profl Psychotherapy, Intl Acad of Profl Cnslg & Psychotherapy Inc; r/Rom Cath; hon/ Author of Num Articles Pub'd in Profl Jours incl'g: *Psychol Reports*; *Mil Med*; *Perceptual & Motor Skills*; *Cognitive Rehab*; *USAF Med Ser Digest*; *Jour of Nervous & Mtl Disease*; Mil Psych Awd (Div 19), 1981; Am Psychol Assn, 1981; Meritorious Ser Medal; Humanitarian Ser Medal, 1981; AF Achmt Medal, 1982; Awd of Merit, CA Dept of Rehab, 1984; W/W in W, Frontier Sci & Technol.

BROOKS, JUDITH ANNE oc/USO Executive; b/Jul 14, 1940; h/228 South Country Club Road, Tucson, AZ 85716; ba/Box 743 FPO, Seattle, WA 98773; p/ Ralph D Brooks Jr, Tucson, AZ; BA Hist & Govt, Univ of ME, 1962; Cert TEFL, Univ of MI, 1964; ba/Pacific Area Exec, Okinawa, Japan, 1979-; Exec Dir: Naples, Italy 1978-79, Wiesbaden, Germany 1977-78, USO Sattahip & USO U-Tapao, Thailand 1967-75; Airport USO Lounge Dir, SF Intl Airport 1975-76; USO World HQs, Wash DC; Sr Cnslr & Resident Ldr, Poland Sprg Job Corps Ctr, Poland Sprng, ME, 1966-67; Peace Corps Vol (Iran), Peace Corps, Wash DC, 1964-66; Mem: Nat Assn for Female Execs; Intl Mil Rec Assn; Armed Forces Rec Br, Nat Rec & Pk Assn; hon/Extensive Fgn Travel;

W/W in W.

BROOM, VERNON H oc/State Supreme Court Justice; b/Jan 16, 1924; h/PO Box 50, Columbia, MI 39429; ba/ Jackson, MI; m/Clemetine Broom; c/ Judy B Brock; Susan B Herron; p/John Calvin and Bertha Broom (dec); sp/Neal and Ida Johnson (dec); ed/BBA 1948, LLD 1948, Univ of MI; mil/AUS, 1943-45, Inf Div, ETO; pa/Dist Atty, 1952-64; Atty, Columbia Mun Schs, 1966-67; Circuit Judge, 1971-72; MI Supr Ct Justice, 1972-; cp/Mem: VFW; Am Legion; DAV; SAR; Lions Clb 1949-71; r/Bapt; hon/Pres, Marion Co C of C, 1968; Purple Heart, 1944; Bronze Star Medal, 1944; W/W in Am.

BROOMFIELD, ANN LOUISE oc/ Comptroller; b/Jun 2, 1943; h/PO Box 5187, Tucson, AZ 85703; ba/Tucson, AZ; m/Robert William; c/Mary Louise; p/Harold E and Betty A Sanders, Palmdale, CA; sp/Joel V and Evelyn O Weaver Bloomfield (dec); ed/AA Liberal Arts 1973, AA Bus Adm 1984, Pima Col; Cert'd Constrn Assoc Deg in Constrn Mgmt, 1983; pa/Comptroller & Ofc Mgr, Borderland Constrn Co Inc, 1982-; Civil Engrg Tech & Maintenance Anal, AZ Dept of Trans, 1975-82; Engrg Secy, Ofc Mgr & Asst Prod Coor: A & J Mfg, H P Foley, Abscoa Ind, Northrop Corp, 1966-75; Tucson Chapt Mem 1976-, Pres 1983-85, Nat Assn of Wom in Constrn; Mem, Profl Secys Intl, 1975-; cp/Bd of Dirs, Big Brothers/Big Sisters, 1982-83 & 1983-86 (w Big Sisters 5 Yrs); Life Mem, Nat Wildlife Fedn; Life Mem, Ldr 13 Yrs, GSA; Life & Charter Mem, Wom in Nat Rifle Assn; Allocation Com 1984-85, Fall Campaign Commerce & Indust II Sect Ch 1983, U Way; r/Epis; hon/Phi Theta Kappa, 1981-; W/W in W; Intl W/W of Intells; Intl Book of Hon; Dir of Dist'd Ams; World Biogl Hall of Fame; Intl Dir of Dist'd Ldrship; Biogl Roll of Hon.

BROPHY, MARY O'REILLY oc/ Scientist, Researcher; b/Aug 3, 1948; h/ 5954 Smith Road, North Syracuse, NY 13212; Syracuse, NY; m/Robert H; c/ Robert, Sara, Lena; p/Luke and Regina O'Reilly, Mineola, NY; sp/Robert and Madeline Brophy, Glendale, NY; ed/BS 1970, MS 1972, PhD Human Anatomy 1979, Univ of MI; pa/Res Assoc, Syracuse Res Corp, 1984-; Adj Asst Prof 1984-, Res Asst Prof 1982-84, Postdoct Fellow & Instr 1979-82, Upstate Med Ctr; Mem: Tissue Culture Assn 1974-; Co-Fdr, Pregnancy Cnslg Ctr, Moscow, ID, 1974-75; r/Christian; hon/Author of "Changes in Uterine Morphology which Accompany the Devel of Preneoplastic & Neoplastic Mammary Lesions," *Scanning Electron Microscopy Jour*, 1984; "The Breasts," *Atlas of Human Reprodn by Scanning Electron Microscopy*, 1982; NIH Predoct F'ship, 190-73 & 1975; AAUW F'ship, 1977-78; Recip of Grant, Hendricks Fund for Med Res, 1983-84.

BROTHER BLUE (HILL, HUGH MORGAN) oc/Storyteller, Teacher; b/ Jul 12, 1921; h/30 Fernald Drive, Cambridge, MA 02138; ba/Cambridge, MA; m/Ruth Ina Edmonds; p/George E Hill (dec); Beatrice Hill, Cleveland, OH; sp/William Edmonds (dec); Florence J Edmonds, Pittsfield, MA; ed/AB, Harvard Col, 1948; MFA, Yale Drama Sch, 1953; PhD, Union Grad Sch, 1953; Ordained Min, 1981; mil/AUS; pa/ Self-employed; Partial Listing incl:

Continuity Writer, "Shakespeare at Yale," *Omnibus* TV Prog, 1953; Storyteller, *The Spiders Web*, WGBH-FM, Boston, 1974-81; Instr, Storytelling, Salem St Col, MA, 1976; Storyteller, *Playmates/Schoolmates*, Westinghouse Broadcasting Co, from WBZ-TV, Boston, 1976; Resident Storyteller, Habitat Forum, UN Nongovtl Orgs Conf, Vancouver, BC, Canada, 1976; Field Ed Supvr, Harvard Div Sch, 1976-78; Informal Wkshops in Storytellings, Harvard Univ, 1977-83; Adj Fac, Lesley Col, Cambridge, MA, 1977-82; Resident Storyteller, New Age Cong, Florence, Italy, 1978; Am Acad of Psychotherapists Annual Meeting, Cinc, OH, 1979; Am Imagery Conf, NY, 1981; Co-Star in Film, *Knightriders*, 1981; Others; Mem: Am Fdn of TV & Radio Artists; Screen Actors Guild; Bd of Dirs, Public Media Foun; Bd Mem, Cambridge Oral Hist Ctr, MA; Sch Vols for Boston; hon/ Author, Num Stories; Blevins-Davis Awd for Playwriting, Yale Drama Sch; 1952; Corp for Public Broadcasting 1975 Local Prog Awd & Spec Cit for Outstg Solo Perf; Walt Whitman Intl Media Competition for Poetry on Sound Tape, 1976; MA Dental Soc Awd for Contbns to Dental Hlth Mo, 1982; Best of Boston Awd for Best Street Perf, from *Boston Mag*, 1982; Tribute from 21st Congl Dist, St of OH, US Ho of Reps, 1983; Cong Cert of Achmt & Awd as Boston's Crown Prince of Street Performers, 1983; Men of Achmt.

BROTHERS, JOYCE DIANE oc/ Psychologist; h/1530 Palisades Avenue, Ft Lee, NJ 07024; ba/New York, NY; m/ Milton; c/Lisa, Robin; p/Morris K and Estelle Rapoport Bauer; ed/BS Cornell Univ, 1947; MA 1950, PhD 1953, Columbia Univ; pa/Asst Psychol, Columbia Univ, 1948-52; Instr, Hunter Col, 1948-52; Ress Proj Ldrship, UNESCO, 1949; Co-Host, *Sports Showcase TV Prog*, 1956; Num TV Prog Appearances: "Dr Joyce Brothers" 1958-63, "Conslt Dr Brothers" 1960-66; "Ask Dr Brothers" 1965-75; Hostess TV Syndication, "Living Easy w Dr Joyce Brothers," 1972-75; Columnist: N Am Newspaper Alliance, 1961-71; Bell-McClure Syndicate, 1963-71; *Good Housekeeping Mag*, 1962-; King Features Syndicate, 1970-; Other Appearances: Radio Sta WNBC, 1966-70; NBC Radio Prog "Emphasis," 1966-75 & "Monitor," 1967-75; WMCA, 1970-73; ABC Reports, 1966-67; NBC Radio Netwk News Line, 1975-; News Analyst, Metro Media TV, 1975-76; News Correspondent: TVN Inc, 1975-76; KABC-TV, 1977-82; WABC-TV, 1980-82; Spec Feature Writer: Hearst Papers; UPI; cp/CoChm Sports Com, Lighthouse for Blind; Door-to-Door Chm, Jewish Fdn Philanthropies, NYC; Fund Raising Com, Olympic Fund; People-to-People Prog; Sigma Xi; hon/Author of 6 Books incl'g: *10 Days to a Successful Memory*; *Woman*; *The Brothers Sys for Liberated Love & Marriage*; *Better Than Ever*; *How to Get Whatever You Want Out of Life*; *What Every Wom Should Know About Men*; $64,000 Winner, "$64,000 Question" TV Prog, 1956; $70,000 Winner, "$64,000 Challenge" TV Prog, 1957; Mennen Baby Foun Awd, 1959; Newhouse Newspaper Awd, 1959; Am Acad Achmt Awd; Deadline Awd, Sigma Delta Chi, 1971; Pres's Cabinet Awd, Univ of Detroit,

1975; Profl Wom of Yr, Dist 1 BPW Clbs, 1968; Num Others; W/W of Am Wom.

BROTHERTON, NAOMI oc/Artist, Instructor; h/4808 Oak Trail, Dallas, TX 75232; ba/Dallas, TX; m/Henry Lemuel Brotherton Jr; c/Betty Ruth B Crudden, Robert James; p/Hunter Smith Macon (dec) and Vernon Smart Macon, Dallas, TX; sp/Henry Lemuel and Ruth Glass Brotherton (both dec); ed/BA, Baylor Univ, 1941; Addit Study: Art Students Leag & Art Career Sch, NYC; Att'd Num Wkshops; pa/Free Lance Comml Artist Over 20 Yrs; Artist & Tchr Over 22 Yrs; Pres, SWn Watercolor Soc, 1967-68; Pres, Artists & Craftsmen Associated, Dallas; TX Watercolor Soc; OK Watercolor Assn; r/Epis; hon/ Co-Author, Variations in Watercolor, 1981; Var Awds in Num Exhbns; W/W: in Am Art, of Am Wom; Notable Wom of TX; Other Biogl Listings.

BROWER, ANN M oc/Controller for Newspaper (Ret'd); b/Nov 26, 1924; h/ 103 West Cedarville Road, Pottstown, PA 19464; ba/Pottstown, PA; m/Francis T; c/Patricia Brower Boles, Karen Brower MacNeill, Richard A; ed/Dipl, Pottstown HS, 1942; Grad, Pottstown Bus Sch, 1944; Att'd Ford Mktg Inst, 1966; pa/Bkkpr-Secy, Levin's Dept Store, Pottstown, 1943-48; Payroll Clk/ Bkkpr, The Mercury, Pottstown, 1948-52 & 1966-73; Ofc Mgr 1974-79, Controller 1979-83, Ret'd, Peerless Pub'g Inc, Pottstown; Mem: Nat Assn Female Execs; cp/N Coventry Fire Co Aux; Treas, Indep Day Ltd, 1978-84; Fund Raiser, Cub Scouts, BSA, 1969-; CCD Tchr, St Thomas More Ch, 1983-84; Pres, Leisure Hour Clb, 1984; Treas, Jameson Evangelistic Assn, 1983-84; r/Rom Cath; hon/Montgomery Co Spelling Champ, 1938-40; W/ W of Am Wom.

BROWMAN, CARL P oc/Clinical Polysomnographer, Psychologist; b/Jul 4, 1947; h/7710 Circle Crest Road, Louisville, KY 40222; ba/Louisville, KY; m/Cathleen A; ed/BS, Roosevelt Univ, 1973; MS 197, PhD 1978, St Louis Univ; mil/AUS, 1967-69; pa/Res Asst, Sleep Lab, St Louis Univ, 1975-77; Postdoct F'ship, Sleep Disorder Ser & Res Ctr, Rush-Presb-St Lukes Med Ctr, Chgo, 1978-79; Asst Dir, Sleep Disorders Ctr, SUNY-Stony Brook, 1979-83; Dir, Sleep Disorders Ctr, Humana Hosp Audubon, L'ville, 1983-; Mem: AAAS; Am Psychol Assn; MWn Psychol Assn; NY Acad of Scis; Sleep Res Soc; Soc for Neurosci; Jefferson Co Med Soc; r/ Meth; hon/Author, Over 50 Sci Articles & Papers on Sleep & Sleep Disorders; Franklin Hon Soc, Roosevelt Univ, 1972; BS Deg w Hons, 1973; Psi Chi, 1975; Sigma Xi, 1982; W/W in E.

BROWN, ALBERTA MAE oc/Nurse, Instructor; b/Nov 11, 1932; h/1545 North Hancock Street, San Bernadino, CA 92411; ba/LA, CA; m/Norman Brown; c/Charon L Oates, Steven A McCrory, Carole Y McCrory; p/Sylvester C Angel; Malinda Mason-Angel (dec); sp/Seaborn and Leslie Brown, Milwaukee, WI; ed/Lic'd Voc Nurse, Anelope Val Col, 1961; Cert'd Respiratory Therapist, San Bernadino Val Col, 1967; AA Nsg, LA Val Col Sch of Nsg, 1975; BS (Reg'd Nurse), CA St Univ-Dominguez Hills, 1981; pa/ Nurse-aid, LVN & Respiratory Thera-

pist: St Bernadine's Hosp 1965-69; Good Samaritan Hosp 1969-70, Midway Hosp 1973-81; LVN, Respiratory Therapist, Acting Dept Hd Allergy Nurse, Respiratory Instr, Wadsworth VA Hosp, 1970-; Mem: Am Assn of Respiratory Therapy; Eta Phi Beta; CPR Instr, Am Heart Assn; cp/Past Pres, Corres'g Secy, Socialites Inc of San Bernadino; OES; r/Bapt; hon/Patentee in Field for Disposable/Replacable Tubing for Stethoscope; Outstg Perf Awd, VA Hosps; Nat Hon Soc; W/W: of Am Wom, in the World.

BROWN, BONITA STARLIPER oc/ Administrator; b/May 26, 1942; h/ Route 1, Box 181, Stephenson, VA 22656; ba/Winchester, VA; m/Richard F; c/Elizabeth Catherine, Christopher Franklin; p/Howard P Starliper (dec); ed/RN Grad, Winchester Meml Hosp Sch of Nsg, 1963; Postgrad, Lord Fairfax Commun Col; BA Cand, Prog Bus Mgmt, Mary Baldwin Col; pa/Ofc Nurs, Drs George & James Troxel, Gen Pract, Winchester, VA, 1963-66; Admr-in-Tng, VA St Prog, 1976-77; Nsg Supvr 1973-76, Orientation Coor 1977-78, Asst Admr & Dir of Nsg 1978-81, Nsg Home Admr 1981-, Shawnee Sprgs Nsg Home, Beverly Enterprises; Mem: Hlth Care Div 1982-, Nat Fire Protection Assn; Nsg Manpower Com 1981, Ed & Tng Com 1982, Public Relats Com 1983, VA Hlth Care Assn; Employee Adv Com, VA Employmnt Comm, 1980-; Adj Fac Med to AD Nsg Prog, Shenandoah Col, 1978-; Nsg Craft Adv Com, Dowell J Howard Voc Sch, 1977-79; Adv Com, Nsg Asst Prog, James Rumsey Voc Sch, 1979-81; Am Col of Nsg Home Admrs, 1980-; Nat Leag of Nsg, 1980-; cp/Winchester/Frederick C of C, 1981-; Winchester Wom's Civic Leag, 1980-; Winchester BPW, 1982-; Winchester JC-ettes, 1964-66; VPres & Pres, Appt'd St Public Relats Dept for PA Fedn of Wom's Clbs, Carlisle Jr Civic Clb, 1970-71; r/Bapt; hon/W/W of Am Wom.

BROWN, CARLTON E oc/Professor; b/Jun 12, 1948; h/111 Towler Drive, Hampton, VA 23666; ba/Norfolk, VA; m/T Laverne Ricks; c/Kwame Masa'il, Jamila Chinyelu Damali; p/Mr and Mrs Edward Brown, Littleton, MA; sp/Mr and Mrs Sidney F Ricks Sr, Hampton, VA; ed/BA Eng & Afro-Am Studies 1972, EdD Multicultural Ed 1979, Univ of MA; pa/Hd Tchr, Cnslr, Prog ESI Springfield, MA, 1970-73; Prog Planning Spec, Tchr Corp, Univ of MA, 1974-77; Prog Devel Spec, Tchr Corp, Univ of NH, 1977-79; Dir Discipline Res Proj 1979-81, Asst Prof Ed 1979-, Old Dominion Univ, Norfolk; Mem: ASCD, 1979-; NVEA, 19790-; NERA, 1978; NAACP, 1978-; r/Baha'i; hon/Author of 2 Booklets: Needs Assessment, 1978; Systematic Ad Hocism, 1978; Author of Articles: "Disciplinary Alternatives for Urban Sch Dists," 1980; "Black Student Views of Sch Discipline," 1982; W/W: Among Students, in S & SW; Outstg Yg Men of Am.

BROWN, DALE SUSAN oc/Program Manager; b/May 27, 1954; h/Apartment 104, 4570 Mac Arthur Boulevard, Washington, DC 20007; ba/Washington, DC; p/Bertram and Joy Brown, Philadelphia, PA; ed/BA, Antioch Col; pa/Prog Mgr 1982-, Public Info Spec

1979-82, Pres's Com on Employmnt for Handicapped; Ofc Mgr, Am Occupl Therapy Assn, 1977-79; Pres, Nat Netwk of Lrng Disabled Adults, 1981; r/Jewish; hon/Author of Book, Steps to Indep for People w Lrng Disabilities, 1980; Author of Articles : "Lrng to Wk," (1983) & "Rehabilitating the Lrng Disabled Adult," (1982), Am Rehab; Over 50 Articles Pub'd in Disabled USA Mag.

BROWN, EDGAR CARY oc/Professor; b/Apr 14, 1916; h/163 Valley Road, Concord, MA 01742; ba/MIT, Cambridge, MA 02139; m/Margaret Durham; c/Rebecca, Gretchen, Elizabeth, Robert; p/Verne Brainard and Ruth Cary Brown (dec); sp/Robert Durham (dec); Mary Edwards Durham; ed/BS, Univ of CA-Berkeley, 1937; PhD, Harvard Univ, 1948; pa/Tchg Fellow, Univ of CA-Berekly, 1937-39; Economist, US WPB, 1940-41; Tchg Fellow, Harvard Univ, 1941-42; Economist, US Treasy, 1942-47; Prof Ec 1947-, Hd of Ec Dept 1965-83, MIT; Vis'g Prof Ec: Yale Univ 1953-54; Univ of Chgo 1963-64; Stanford Univ 1983; Vis Scholar, Hoover Instn, 1983; Mem: Am Ec Assn; Nat Tax Assn; Acting Editor, Nat Tax Jour, 1958-59; hon/Author of 5 Books: Financing Def, 1951; Depreciation Adjustments for Price Changes, 1952; Stabilization Policies, 1963; Studies in Ec Stabilization, 1967; Paul Samuelson & Mod Ec Theory, 1984; Author of Num Articles Pub'd in Jours & Mags; Phi Beta Kappa, 1936; Beta Gamma Sigma, 1936; Am Acad of Arts & Scis, 1967-; Guggenheim Fellow, 1957; Ford Foun Fac Res Fellow, 1956-57; W/W in Am; Blue Book; Men of Sci.

BROWN, EDWARD FRENCH oc/ Retired Air Force Officer, Adjunct Instructor in Political Science, Lecturer on Ancient Chinese Art and Culture; b/July 9, 1910; h/12008 Golden Gate Avenue, Northeast, Albuquerque, NM 87111; ba/Albuquerque, NM; m/Charlott Holz Sommer; c/Jessica DeMichel Lynes (Mrs Bruce Cleveland); Monica Ruth Sommer (Mrs Charles N Mastin); Suzanne French (Mrs Charles F Luker); p/Carleton French and Teresa McCormick Brown (dec); sp/George and Johanna Vogelsang Holz (dec); ed/ Staunton Mil Acad, 1928; Univ of Toronto, 1933; US Army Air Corps Ofcrs' Tng Coprs, 1942; Cmd & Gen Staff Sch, 1946; George Wash Univ AF Cmdrs' Course, 1956; BA, Univ of Albuquerque, 1974; MA, Univ of NM, 1976; PhD, Clayton Univ, 1983; mil/US Army Air Corp, 1941-43, 1st Lt to Capt; 14th AF, 1943-45, Maj; Mil Advr in China until 1948; Dir of Sers & Supply Air Proving Ground Command, Eglin AFB, FL, 1949; USAF Inst of Technol, Wright-Patterson AFB & Clevite Inc, Cleveland, OH, 1949-50; Chief Component Div, Aircraft Prodn Resources Agy, Wright-Patterson AFB, 1950-52, Lt Col; Spec Asst to the Hon W Averell Harriman, Dir for Mutual Security, Exec Ofc of the Pres, Wash DC & Paris, 1952, 1953; After Change in Adm, Perf'd Same Duties for the Hon Harold Stassen, Exec Ofc of the Pres, Wash DC & Paris, 1954-56; Assoc Dir of Trade Controls w NATO 1956; Chief of Prodn Equip, Ofc of Dept Chief of Staff for Materiel, HQs USAF, Pentagon, 1956; Spec Assignment, Aerospace Tech Intell Ctr, Wright-Patterson AFB, Dayton

OH, NYC, Wash DC, World-wide, 1957-66, Full Col; Ret'd Because of Disability, 1966; pa/Pres, Colmar Intl Corp, NYC, 1966-69; Jr Salesman, Salesman, Sales Supvr, Dist Mgr, Br Mgr, SCM Corp, 1928-42; Mem, Gov's Comm on Probation, Parole & Crime Preven, Providence, RI, 1937-39; Chp, Albuquerque Comm on Fgn Relats, 1978-79; C-Chm, NM Com for Ratification of Panama Canal Treaty, 1978; Mem, NM Com for Ratification of SALT II Treaty, 1978-79; Mem: The Am Acad of Polit Sci; Assn for Asian Studies; Ctr for Study of Pres, 1973-75; Citizens for Am Way; Asia Soc; Disabled Ofcrs & Ret'd Ofcrs Assn; Others; cp/ Fdg Mem 1975 & 1st Pres 1975-77, Maxwell Mus Assn of Anthropology, Univ of NM; Dir & Chm of Fund Raising 1973-74, Albuquerque Mus Assn; Num Others; hon/Author of *Polits of China* in Univ of NM's DIALOGUE Series, 1976; *An Hist Memoir of Chinese-Am Relations (1943-48), 1983; Num Articles & Lectrs on Ancient Chinese Art & Culture, 1976-; Pres Unit Cit (WW II China), 1945; AF Commend Medal for Intl Polit-Mil Affairs, 1966; Asiatic-Pacific Campaign Medal w 3 Battle Stars, 1944-45; Pao Ting Spec Breast Order, from Chinese Pres Chiang Kai-shek, 1947; Chien Yuan Medal from Min of Def, 1944; Mao Chi Medal from Chinese AF, 1944; Var Commend Lttrs; DIB.*

BROWN, ERIC REEDER oc/Professor; b/Mar 16, 1925; h/PO Box 335, Wonder Lake, IL 60097; ba/North Chicago, IL; m/Chloe Ledbetter; c/Carl, Christopher, Amy Elizabeth, Dianne, Eric Jr, Daniel, Christine Virginia; p/ Harold McDaniel and Helen Seitz Brown (dec); sp/Durward Ledbetter, Prescott, AZ; ed/Cert'd Engr, USCG Acad Sch, 1943; BS 1949, MS 1951, Syracuse Univ; MD, Univ of Rochester, 1953; PhD, Univ of KS, 1957; DSc, Quincy Col, 1966; mil/USCG, 1942-46; USAF MC, 1952-Ret'd, 1982 BG; pa/ Instr, Univ of IL Med Sch, 1957-59; Dept Pathol, Univ of MN, 1959-61; Hektoen Inst, 1961-64; Dept Microbiol, NWn Univ Med Sch, 1964-67; Prof & Dept Microbiol Chm 1967-82, Prof Microbiol 1982-, Chgo Med Sch; Industl Col of Armed Forces, 1952-59; Nat Def Univ, 1981; Mem, Am Soc Microbiol, 1950-; Fellow, Am Inst Chems, 1968-;; Fellow, APHA, 1970; Fellow, Inst of Med, 1969; Phi Beta Kappa, 1949; Sigma Xi, 1956; Fellow, Am Acad Microbiol; Life Mem, AF Assn; Ret'd Ofcrs Assn; Mil Order of World Wars; Royal Soc of Hlth, 1966; cp/Dominion of Golden Dragon; Life Mem, VFW & DAV; r/Epis; hon/Author, Over 210 Articles, Papers & Chapts in 4 Textbooks, 1955-84; Meritorious Ser Awd, 1982; Exceptl Ser to Nation, 1982; Purple Heart, Nav Cross & Bronze Star, 1944; Fellow & Cash Awd, Leukemia Soc, 1966; W/W in Am.

BROWN, GARY R oc/Attorney; b/ Nov 11, 1947; h/PO Box 778, Estes Park, CO 80517; ba/Estes Park, CO; m/Kelly Ann; c/Julie Marie, Phillip Ross; p/F Ross and Leona Brown, Estes Park, CO; sp/ Ted and Jan Haines, Gresham, OR; ed/ BA, Lewis & Clark Col, 1969; JD, Univ of Denver Law Sch, 1973; mil/Army NG, 14 Yrs; pa/Law Clk, Clarence L Batholic Atty, Denver, CO; Pvt Pract Atty, Denver & Estes Pk, Co, Current; Pt-time US Magistrate, Dist of CO w

Jurisd Over Rocky Mtn Nat Pk, Current; Mem: ABA; CO, Denver & Larimar Co Bar Assns; cp/Presiding Ofcr (32nd Deg Mason), Rocky Mtn Consistory, Highlands Masonic Lodge, 1983; Dir 1984-86, Mem 1982-, Rotary Clb of Estes Pk; W/W: in W, in Am Law.

BROWN, HELEN GURLEY oc/ Editor-in-Chief, *Cosmopolitan Mag*; b/Feb 18, 1922; h/1 West 81st Street, New York, NY 10024; ba/224 West 57th Street, New York, NY 10019; m/David Brown; p/Ira M and Cleo (Sisco) Gurley (dec); ed/Student, TX St Col for Wom, 1939-41; Att'd Woodbury Col, 1942; pa/ Exec Secy: Music Corp Am, 1942-45; Wm Morris Agy 1945-47; Copywriter, Foote, Cone & Belding Advtg Agy, LA, 1948-58; Advtg Writer, Acct Exec, Kenyon & Eckhardt Advtg Agy, Hollywood, CA, 1958-62; Editor-in-Chief, *Cosmopolitan Mag*, 1965-; Edit Dir, Cosmopolitan Intl Edits; Mem: Authors Leag of Am; Am Soc Mag Editors; AFTRA; Eta Upsilon Gamma; hon/ Author of 7 Books incl'g: *Sex & the Single Girl*, 1962; *Sex & the Ofc*, 1965; *Outrageous Opinions*, 1966; *Having It All*; Others; Recip, Francis Holmes Achmt Awd for Outstg Wk in Advtg, 1956-59; Dist'd Achmt Awd, Univ of So CA Sch of Jour, 1972; Spec Awd for Edit Ldrship, Am Newspaper Wom's Clb Wash, DC, 1972; Dist'd Achmt Awd in Jour, Stanford Univ, 1977; Named 1 of 25 Most Influential Wom in *US World Almanac*, 1976-81; Num Biogl Listings.

BROWN, HERBERT CHARLES oc/ Professor Emeritus; b/May 12, 1912; h/ 1840 Garden Street, West Lafayette, IN 47906; ba/West Lafayette, IN; m/Sarah Baylen; c/Charles Allan; p/Charles and Pearl Gorinstein Brown (dec); ed/Chgo City Jr Cols, 1935; BSc 1936, PhD 1938, Univ of Chgo; pa/Instr, Univ of Chgo, 1939-43; Asst & Assoc Prof, Wayne St Univ, Detroit, 1943-47; Prof 1947-59, R B Wetherill Res Prof 1959-78, Wetherill Res Prof Emeritus 1978-, Dept of Chem, Purdue Univ; Mem: Nat Acad of Sci; Am Acad of Arts & Sci; Hon Fellow, The Chem Soc (London); Phi Beta Kappa; Phi Lambda Upsilon; Sigma Xi; Alpha Chi Sigma; Chm Purdue Sect 1955, Am Chem Soc; cp/Bd of Govs, Hebrew Univ; r/Judaism; hon/Author of 4 Books: *Hydroboration*, 1962; *Boranes in Organic Chem*, 1972; *Organic Synthesis*, 1975; *The Nonclassical Ion Prob*,1977; Over 900 Articles & Papers Pub'd in Profl Sci Jours; Recip, Gold Medal, American Institute of Chemists, 1985; The Perkin Medal, Soc of Am Indust Chems, 1982; Priestley Medal, Am Chem Soc, 1981; Inducted into Nobel Hall of Sci, Mus of Sci & Indust, Chgo, 1980; Recip, The Nobel Prize in Chem, 1979; Hon Fellow, Royal Inst of Chem, 1978; Life Fellow, Am Inst of Chems, 1978; Nat Medal of Sci, 1969; Hon Docts from Var Univs; Num Other Nat & Intl Awds; Les Prix Nobel, 1979; The Blue Book; Intl Yrbook & Statesman's W/W; W/W in World Jewry & Num Other Biogl Listings.

BROWN, JACK ELLIOTTE oc/ Administrator; b/Jun 12, 1933; h/618 Cardinal Street, Bluefield, VA 24605; ba/Bluefield, VA; m/Mary Jean; c/Lisa Dawn (Brown) Moore, Jill Wilson; sp/ Lucille Wilson, Cadiz, KY; ed/BA, Georgetown Col, 1958; MDiv, So Bapt Theol Sem, 1961; MA, Ball St Univ,

1972; EdD Wn MI Univ, 1981; mil/ USMC, 1951-54; AUS, 1961-79, Ret'd LTC; pa/Pastor, Emmanuel Bapt & Kiddville Bapt Chs, KY, 1956-61; AUS Chaplain, 1961-79; Dean of Students, Bluefield Col, VA, 1979-; Mem: Mil Chaplains Assn 1962-79; So Bapt Assn for Student Devel, 1979-; Ret'd Ofcrs Assn, 1979-; AUS Assn, 1971-; cp/Lions Clb, 1984-; r/Bapt; hon/Author of Num Articles for Mil, Rel & Profl Pubs; Legion of Merit; Bronze Star; Num Other Mil Decorations.

BROWN, JAMES NELSON JR oc/ Executive; b/Apr 17, 1929; h/47 Pinho Avenue, Carteret, NJ 07008; ba/New York, NY; m/Lila Barbara Watt; c/ Constance Ellen Brown Buttacavole, Nelson Arthur, Richard John; p/James Nelson and Agnes Mary (Cummins) Brown (dec); sp/Arthur L Watt, Burlington, IA; Clara H (Wemmie) Paxson, Burlington, IA; ed/BS Bus Adm, Drake Univ, 1956; mil/AUS, 1947-52, Sgt; pa/ Sr Acct, Arthur Andersen & Co, NYC, 1956-61; Asst VPres & Dir of Internal Auditing, Phibro-Salmon Inc, NYC, 1961-; Mem: Am Inst of CPAs, 1967-; NJ Soc of Cert'd CPAs, 1967-; Inst of Internal Auditors, 1965-; cp/Elks Clb, Carteret, NJ; Am Legion, Carteret, NJ; Am Mgmt Assn; Com Chm 1976-77, Com Mem 1973-75, Cub Scouts Pack 88, Com Chm BSA Troop 88, Carteret, NJ, Com Mem 1977-; r/Rom Cath; hon/ CPA, 1976; Cert'd Internal Auditor, 1973.

BROWN, JOSEPH S oc/Executive; b/ Dec 3, 1943; h/2995 Botanical Square, Bronx, NY 10458; ba/New York, NY; m/Beverly Brown; c/Kareen, Jamal; p/ Austin S Brown, Bklyn, NY; Ruby M Reid, Beacon, NY; sp/Mary Odell Hoffler, Elizabeth City, NC; ed/BS Social Studies Ed, Elizabeth City St Univ, 1966; MA Hist, Ed Adm, NC Ctl Univ, 1968; pa/Dir 1981-, Ed/Tng Ofcr 1979-81, NYC Minority Bus Devel Ofc & Locally Based Enterprise; Sr Staff Conslt, H B Reynolds Assocs, 1975-78; Pers/Planning Anal, NYC Dept of Gen Sers, 1977-79; Admr, NYC Bd of Ed/ Harlem HS, 1975-76; Fdg Mem & VPres, Alliance of Minority Bus Orgs; Mem: Coun for Concerned Black Execs; Nat Assn of Hlth Ser Execs; New Harlem 10-K Com; Omega Psi Chi; Affil Mem, Urban Bkrs Coalition; r/prot; hon/Cert of Apprec, Ec Devel Coun of NY Inc, 1981-82; Citizenship Awd, NYS Assem-man Louis Nine, 1977; Jr Achmt Awd, 1975; Cert of Recog, Nat Alliance of Bus-men, 1973; Outstg Yg Men in Am.

BROWN, KATHLEEN E oc/Manager; b/Feb 17, 1949; h/1320 Northwest, 43 Terrace, Lauderhill, FL 33313; ba/ Pompano Beach, FL; p/David J and Shirley K Brown, Sheboygan Falls, WI; ed/BS, Univ of WI, 1972; MBA, Nova Univ, 1983; pa/Treatment Plant Mgr BCUD 1980-, Treatment Plant Operator BCUD 1975-80, Water QC Tech 1974-75, City of Ft Lauderdale, FL; Aluminum Smelter, ALRECO, 1973-74; Proj Spec 1972-73, Res Asst 1968-72, Univ of WI; Mem: Am Water Wks Assn, 1977-; Chm Reg 7 Distbn & Collection Sem, FL Water & Pollution Control Operators Assn, 1974-; cp/OES, 1977-; Nat Assn Female Execs, 1981-; Squire, FL Renaissance Guild Inc, 1982; hon/ Author of "Pathol & Endocrinologic

106

Changes Associated w Porcine Agalactia," 1970; "The Effect of Pentobarbital on Amino Acid & Urea Flux in the Isolated Dog Brain, 1973; Dean's List, Univ of WI, 1970; Operator of the Mo, BCUD, Jan 1978; Nat Dean's List, 1981-82; W/W in S & SW.

BROWN, LAURENCE WATSON oc/ Safety Manager; b/Feb 3, 1937; h/40 Bartman Road, East Brunswick, NJ 08816; ba/Staten Island, NY; m/Joan Lee Reier; c/Helen Kay, Laurence Watson, Howard Vernon; p/Howard Gambrill and Lula Nichols (Biddison) Brown (dec); sp/Vernon Dilworth and Lottie Eileen (Watkins) Reier, Clermont, FL; ed/BS, Univ of MD, 1959; MBA, Univ of MO, 1968; mil/USAF, 2nd Lt to Maj; pa/Command Missile Safety Ofcr, Hickman AFB, HI, 1969-71; Chief Opers Missile Sqdrn, Minot AFB, ND, 1971-74; Safety/Fire Coor 1974-77, Risk Control Supvr 1977-81, Safety Mgr 1981-, Nav Resale & Ser Support Ofc, Ft Wadsworth, SI, NY; Mem: Am Soc of Safety Engrs; Nat Safety Mgmt Soc; Nat Fire Protection Assn; Nat Retail Merchs Assn; r/Meth; hon/Cert'd Safety Profl; Cert'd Hazard Control Mgr; Assoc in Risk Mgmt; W/W in E.

BROWN, LESTER R oc/Executive; b/ Mar 28, 1934; h/2032 Belmont Road, Northwest, Washington, DC 20009; ba/ Washington, DC; c/Brian, Brenda; p/ Calvin C Brown and Delia Smith, Bridgeton, NJ; ed/BS Agri Sci, Rutgers Univ; MS Agri Ec, Univ of MD; MPA, Harvard Univ; pa/Pres & Sr Rschr, Worldwatch Inst, 1974-; Sr Fellow, Overseas Devel Coun, 1969-74; Admr, Intl Agri Devel Ser, 1966-69; Policy Advr, Sec of Agri, USDA, 1964-66; Intl Agri Economist (Policy), USDA Ec Res Ser, 1959-64; Mem: Coun on Fgn Relats; Bd Mem, US Com for UNICEF; Bd of Dirs, Overseas Devel Coun; cp/ Mem, Cosmos Clb; hon/Author of 7 Books: *Man, Land & Food; Seeds of Change; World Without Borders; In the Human Interest; By Bread Alone; The 29th Day; Building a Sustainable Soc*; Christopher Awd, for *By Bread Alone*, 1980; Ecologia Firenze Prize for *The 29th Day*, 1981; A H Boerma Awd, FAO for Writings on World Food Prob, 1981; Spec Conserv Awd, Nat Wildlife Fedn, 1982; Recip Superior Ser Awd, Dept of Agri, 1965; Arthur S Flemming Awd, 1 of 10 Outstg Yg Men in Fed Ser, 1965; Num Others; W/W; Outstg Yg Men in Am.

BROWN, LINDA LEE oc/Technology Supervisor; b/Oct 29, 1955; h/Box 114, Wright, WY 82732; ba/Wright, WY; ed/ AS Drafting Tech, Amarillo Col, 1975; Jour & Eng Credits, W TX St Univ, Canyon, TX, 1977; BSBA 1984, MA Cand in Bus Mgmt, Cent Univ, Beverly Hills, CA; pa/Sr Lead Drafter 1977-; Permits Coor 1980, Thunder Basin Coal Co, Black Thunder Mine, Atl Richfield Co; Dir, WY Div, Atl Richfield's Spkr's Bur, for Thunder Basin Coal Co, 1984-; Drafter Pioneer Natural Gas Co 1975-76, Drafter Amarillo Oil Co 1976-77, Pioneer Corp, Amarillo, TX; Freelance Drafter, Panhandle Steel Bldgs, Amarillo, 1974-75; Freelance Drafter, Harris & Patterson Engrs, Amarillo, 1974-75; Ygest Mem & 1st Wom Mem, Bd of Dirs, Nat Secy of the Bd, Am Inst for Design & Drafting; Mem, Nat Assn of Female Execs; Ocean Res & Ed Soc, Gloucester, MA (Wrote

Grant Application for ORES to ARCO Foun); hon/Author of 2 Books: *God Was Here, But He Left Early*, 1976; *A Gift of Wings*, 1980; Pub'd in Num Poetry Anthols; Var Profl Articles Incl: "Wom of the Yr in Drafting Indust," *Plan & Print Mag*, 1980; "Project Planning," *Plan & Print Mag*, 1981; Others; Grand Prize Winner for Painting "Energy," the Powder River Arts Coun, 1979; W/W of Am Wom; The World W/W of Wom; Num Other Biogl Listings.

BROWN, LOUIS DANIEL oc/Attorney at Law; b/Aug 31 1908; h/3850 Dublin Avenue, Los Angeles, CA 90008; ba/Los Angeles, CA; m/Felice; c/Lawrence Louis, Ronald Stamper, Carole Felice; p/Louis Thomas and Ella Rose Kelly Brown (dec); sp/Lawrence J and Dora F Stamper (dec); ed/AA, Univ of SF; AB, Stanford Univ; LLB, JD, SWn Univ; mil/Med Corp; St NG; pa/Pres, Romer, O'Connor & Co, 1939-72; Ptner, Romer, Brown Attys, 1944-68; Ptner, Romer, Brown, Miller, Murphy, 1968-72; Atty & Cnslr at Law, Sole Pract, 1972-; Mem: CA St Bar Assn; LA Co Bar Assn; ABA; Am Judic Soc; LA Lwyrs Clb; Lic'd to Pract in US Supr Ct; US Ct of Claims; Dept of Justice-Immigration; cp/LA Chapt, Univ of SF Alumni Assn; Pres, Stanford Univ Alumni Assn; SWn Univ Alumni Assn; Univ of CA-Hastings Law Sch Alulmni Assn; Borrego Sprgs C of C; Pres & Zone Chm, Intl Lions Clb; Elks Clb; La Quinta Dessert Clb; BSA; Univ of SF, Stanford Univ & SWn Univ Law Socs; r/Rom Cath; hon/Author of Num Articles on Legal Aspects of Credit for Nat Assn of Credit Petro Assn; Var Articles for Lions Clb Bltn; Others for Consumer Credit Assn; Cert of Apprec, St Guard of CA Med Corp, WW II; Cert of Apprec for Serving 3 Yrs as Judge Pro Tem, LA Mun Ct; W/W: in W, in CA, in Commun Ser; Men of Achmt; DIB; Other Biogl Listings.

BROWN, MARK H JR oc/Resort Owner; b/Mar 10, 1926; h/PO Box 154, Ludlow, UT 05144; ba/Same; m/Josephine (Jo); c/Mark III, Josephine, Deborrah, John; p/Mar H Brown Sr (dec); Ruth (Shunkweiler) Brown, Patton, PA; ed/ BA 1950, MA 1951, Univ of Pgh; CLU, US Amphibious Assault Forces, S Pacific, 1943-46; pa/Adjuster, Claims Mgr, Spec Agt, Liability Assurance Corp, 1950-59; Agt, Dist Mgr, Agy Mgr, Equitable Life Assurance Soc of UT, 1959-70; Gen Agt, Lincoln Nat Life, 1970-73; Mgr, Canada Life Assurance Agy, 1973-84; Owner, Operator, Echo Lake Inn Resort, 1979-; Bd of Dirs, Profl Life Underwriters, 1974-77; Bd of Dirs, Gen Agts & Mgrs Assn, 1976-78; Nat Assn Chm, Canada Life Gen Agts & Mgrs Assn, 1974-77; cp/Mem, Edgewood, PA Sch Bd; Past Pres, Rotary Intl, Wilkinsburg, PA; Mem, Pgh Ath Assn; Fellows Clb; Edgewood Country Clb; Woodstock Country Clb; r/Rom Cath; hon/Pres Unit Cit, WW II; 5 Combat Stars, WW II; Num Profl Insurance Bus Awds.

BROWN, MAUDE NORRIS oc/ Administrator; b/Jun 17, 1927; h/310 Tiffany Circle, Garner, NC 27529; ba/ Research Triangle Park, NC; m/Robert William; c/Donna Rose, Robert William; p/Alma Moore Norris, Clayton, NC; sp/ Nettis Stamey, Brevard, NC; ed/Kings

Bus Col, Raleigh, NC, 1944-45; pa/Sec to Pres, Raleigh Bonded Warehouse Inc, 1946-58; Acting Ofc Mgr, Fed Crop Ins, 1958-61; Ofc Mgr, Allied Chem Corp, 1961-69; Adm Sec Mgr 1973-77, Grants & Projs Costs Admr 1977-, Burroughs Wellcome Co; Secy & Mem Bd of Dirs, Burroughs Wellcome Employees Credit Union, 1975-78; r/So Bapt; hon/W/W in Am Wom; Personalities of S.

BROWN, NATALIA TAYLOR oc/ Contract Specialist; h/PO Box 14263, St Louis, MO 63178; ba/St Louis, MO; m/ Edward; p/Gentry and Olivia Webb Taylor (dec); sp/Edward and Ora Brown, Coffeeville, MS; ed/Grad, Hubbard Bus Col, 1949; BS BA, St Louis Univ, 1983; pa/Contract Spec, 1969-; cp/ Charted Mem, Iota Chapt, Gamma Phi Delta Sorority Inc; Ladies Aux, K of Peter Claver; Urban Leag Metro St Louis; YWCA; Life Mem, NAACP; Nat Ofc of Black Caths Laity; r/Rom Cath; hon/Dipl w Hons, Hubbard Bus Col, St Louis, 1949; Elizabeth Garner Meml Awd, Gamma Phi Delta, 1966; Sustained Superior Perf Awd, AUS, St Louis, 1964; W/W of Am Wom.

BROWN, NEDRA THOMPSON oc/ Director of Institutional Development; b/Feb 10, 1945; h/801 10th Avenue, Conway, SC 29526; ba/Conway, SC; m/ James W; c/Emma Catherine, Emerson Elliott; p/Mr and Mrs Ben L Thompson, Conway, SC; sp/Mr and Mrs W H J Brown, Aynor, SC; ed/BA Eng, Univ of SC, 1967; MA Eng, NC St Univ, 1971; pa/Tchr, Horry Co Schs, 1967-74; Div Hd 1974-82, Dir Instnl Devel 1982-, Horry-Georgetown Tech Col, Conway, SC; Mem: SC Tech Ed Assn; NCTE; Nat Coun for Resource Devel; cp/Bd of Dirs & Pres, Theatre of the Repub; Secy, Fine Arts Clb, 1982-83; r/Meth; hon/Outstg Edr, Horry-Georgetown Tech Col, 1981-82.

BROWN, PATRICIA BUFORD oc/ Executive Director; b/Aug 3, 1938; h/ PO Box 33 Zamalek, Cairo, Egypt; ba/ Same; c/Andrew James, Allison Paige; p/Mildred Wainwright Newsome; ed/ AA, 1957, BA 1976, MBA, 1978; Exec Dir, Am C of C in Egypt, 1983-; VPres Sales, Freedom Dranel, 1981-82; Dist Mgr, Victor Temp Sers, 1979-80; Admr, Wn St Univ, 1967-79; Bd of Govs, San Jose C of C; Chm, Wom in Bus; PA Prof Wom's Netwk; Bd of Dirs, Big Brothers/ Big Sisters; hon/W/W in Am Wom.

BROWN, ROBERT L JR oc/Educator; b/May 25, 1936; h/1219 West Emory, L-7, Dalton, GA 30720; ba/Dalton, GA; p/Robert Lee and Florine C Brown, Cartersville, GA; ed/BA, Morehouse Col, 1957; MAT, Purdue Univ, 1966; mil/AUS, 1959-61, Mil Police Corps, Adjutant Gen Corps, Overseas Duty, Bordeaux, France; pa/Tchr of French, Latin, Eng & Gifted, Dalton HS for 20 Yrs; Chm Lang Arts Dept, Dalton HS, 1972; Tchr, Emory HS 5 Yrs; Dalton Public Schs, 1962-; Tchr, Henderson HS, 1961-62 & 1957-59; Mem: Assn for Supvn & Curric Devel; NEA; GAE; Dalton Assn Edrs; Liaison Ofcr GA Chapt 1968, Assn Tchrs French; Secy-Treas 7th Dist 1968-69, Classical & Mod Fgn Lang Assn; NCTE; GA Coun Tchrs of Eng; Phi Delta Phi Nat French Hon Soc; Phi Beta Sigma Frat; cp/Treas 1979, Past Mem Bd of Dirs, Dalton Little Theatre; Whitfield-Murray Hist Soc; Child Parent Care; Juv Ct; Creat Arts Guild; Mtl Hlth Assn; Dalton-Whitfield Day Care Ctrs Inc; Atlanta Assessment Proj, 1982; St Com for Oral & Written Commun Guide, 1980; Criterion Ref Test Proj, 1979; Gov's Hons Prog for Gifted Instr in Communs, 1977-81; Interviewer of Students in Eng & Drama, 1977; Dir, HS Musicals & Chd's Theatre; VChm, Big Brother Assn, Dalton, 1969; r/Bapt; hon/Author, "Simulations & Lit" & "The Goose Bumps" (on Drama); *The Eng Cnslr*; W/ W in S & SW.

BROWN, ROBERT WILLIAM oc/ Analytical Chemist; b/Dec 31, 1954; h/ 1511 Brookhollow Drive, Baton Rouge, LA 70810; ba/St Gabriel, LA; m/ Deborah McFarland; c/Kelly Renee, Robin Kathleen; p/Robert Eugene and Eleanor Alice Brown, Scottsmoor, FL; sp/Joel U and Velma O McFarland, Columbia, MD; ed/BS Chem, Univ of FL, 1975; Att'd MS Prog, Rutgers Univ, 1976-79; MA Cand, LA St Univ (LSU), 1980-; pa/USDA Chem, Univ of FL, 1976-77; Chem & Res Chem, Am Cyanamid, 1977-79; Devel Chem & Sr Devel Chem, Ciba-Geigy, 1979-; Mem: Am Chem Soc, 1976; Anal Div of Am Chem Soc; Assn of Anal Chems; Baton Rouge Anal Discussion Grp; r/Bapt; hon/Grad w Hons, Univ of FL, 1975; W/W in S & SW.

BROWN, SHERRI RUTH oc/Dentist; b/Mar 14, 1953; h/Rural Route 1, Clay, KY 42404; ba/Louisville, KY; p/Mr and Mrs Sammy Brown, Clay, KY; ed/BS, MI Univ for Wom, 1975; Cert in Med Tech, Univ of L'ville, 1976, DMD, Univ of L'ville Sch of Dentistry,1983; pa/Med Tech Supvr in Hematology, Hopkins Co Hosp, 1976-79; Gen Prac Resident Dentistry, Med Col of GA, Augusta, 1983-84; Mem: Student Rep 1980-81, KY Assn for Wom Dentists; Acad Gen Dentistry; Am Student Dental Assn; Am Soc Clin Pathols; Beta Beta Beta; Lambda Tau; Pi Tau Chi; r/So Bapt; hon/ W/W: in Am Cols & Univs, of Am Wom.

BROWN, VALERIE A oc/Psychoth- erapist, Educator; b/Feb 28, 1951; h/250 North 19th Street, Kenilworth, NJ 07033; ba/Same; p/William J and Ade- laide (Krasa) Brown, Kenilworth, NJ; ed/BA, C W Post Col, 1972; MSW, Hunter Col Sch of Social Wk, 1975; CSW, NY St, 1975-; pa/Pvt Pract in Psychotherapy, Supvn & Consultation, 1979-; Sr Psychi Social Wkr, Runnells Hosp, Berkeley Hgts, NJ, 1980-; Fieldwk Prof, NY Univ, 1980-; Field Supvr, Fairleigh Dickinson Univ, 1981-; Sr Psychi Social Wkr, Co-Admr-in-Chief, Saturday Clin, Essex Co Guid Ctr, E Orange, NJ, 1975-80; Conslt, Passaic Drug Clin, Passaic, NJ, 1977-80; Mem: NASW; NJ Assn of Clin Social Wkrs; NJ Assn of Wom Therapists; Am Soc for Tng & Devel; Am Soc Clin Social Wkrs; r/Prot; hon/Author of *What is Psychotherapy*, 1982; Psych Fellow, LI Univ, 1972 Silberman Scholar, 1973-75; Psi Chi; Pi Gamma Mu; Sigma Tau Delta; Intern, Metro Conslt Ctr, 1974-75; Intern, Greenwich House Cnslg Ctr, 1973-74; W/W of Am Wom.

BROWN, WAYNE S oc/Engineer; b/ Mar 19, 1928; h/1630 Arlington Drive, Salt Lake City, UT 84103; ba/Salt Lake City, UT; m/Joyce F; c/Karen B Brews- ter, Diane B Whittaker, Gary W, Don R, Janet B Sorensen; p/Cleveland W

Brown (dec); sp/Fay Fechser, Provo, UT; ed/BS Mech Engrg, Univ of UT, 1951; MS Mech Engrg, Univ of TN, 1953; PhD, Stanford Univ, 1960; mil/USMC, 1946-47; pa/Chm, UT Innovation Ctr, SLC, UT, 1980-; Prof Mech Engr 1964-, Dean Col of Engrg 1973-78, Univ of UT; Mem, Gov's Adv Coun on Sci & Tech- nol, 1982-; cp/Bd of Govs, SL Area C of C, 1983-; Bd of Dirs 1978-82, VPres Campaign 1981, SL U Way; r/LDS (Mormon); hon/Author, Num Articles Pub'd in Tech Jours; Fellow, ASME, 1983; W/W in W; Num Other Biogl Listings.

BROWNE, MICHAEL LEON oc/ Insurance Commisioner; b/Sep 2, 1946; h/840 Carpenter Lane, Philadelphia, PA 19119; ba/Harrisburg, PA; m/Elizabeth Owen; c/Sarah Skelton; p/Ernest J and Jane Heisig Browne, Beaumont, TX; ed/ AB, Princeton Univ, 1968; JD, Univ of PA Law Sch, 1974; mil/USMC, 1968-71, Capt; Inf Ofcr in Vietnam, 1969; pa/PA Ins Commr, 1980-; Ptner 1979-80, Assoc 1977-78 & 1974-75, Dilworth, Paxson, Kalish, Levy & Kauffman, Phila, PA; Spec Asst to US Secy of Trans & Dept Under Secy US Dept of Trans, 1975-77; Law C lk, Judge Raymond J Broderick, US Dist Ct for En Dist of PA; Chm, Gov's Task Force on Hlth Care Cost Containment, 1980-; Bd of Dirs, *Jour of Ins Regulation*; Mem Exec Bd, *Commonwlth of PA*; Mem, *Gov's Ec Devel Com of Cabinet*; Mem: ABA, Phila & PA Bar Assns; cp/Mem, W Mt Airy Neighbors Assn; r/Epis; hon/Spec Achmt Awd 1975, Outstg Achmt Awd 1977, US Secy of Trans; Bronze Star Medal.

BROWNE, SHIRLEY ANNETTE oc/ Anesthesiologist; b/May 26, 1952; ba/ 4010 J, Highway 6 South, Houston, TX; p/Williams B and Mildred S Browne, TX; ed/BS, Lamar Univ, 1974; MD 1977, Residency 1981, Univ of TX Med Sch-Houston; pa/Asst Anesth & Instr in Anesth, MD Anderson Hosp & Tumor Inst, 1981-83; Anesth, Alied Gen Hosp, 1983-; Mem: Am Soc of Anesths; TX Soc of Anesths; TX Gulf Coast Soc of Anesths; Intl Anesth Res Soc; AMA; TX Med Assn; Harris Co Med Soc; Soc of Critical Care; Am Med Wom's Assn; hon/Phys Recog Awd, AMA, 1981 & 1983; W/W in S & SW, of Wom; Personalities of S.

BROWNING, HAZEL GAY oc/Asso ciate Executive Director, North Carol ina Nurses Association; b/May 29, 1950; h/4305 Sunbelt Drive, Raleigh, NC 27612; ba/Raleigh, NC; c/Lauran Shel ton; p/Mr and Mrs Daniel R Gay, Fountain, NC; BSN 1972, MS Rehab Cnslg 1976, MSN Nsg 1979, E Carolina Univ; pa/Staff Nurse, Pitt Meml Hosp, Greenville, NC, 1972-73; Ofc Nurse, Dr David Pearsall, Greenville, NC, 1973; Instr 1973-77, Asst Prof 1977-80, E Carolina Univ; Asst Prof 1980-84, Duke Univ, Durham, NC; Assoc Exec Dir, NC Nurses Assn, 1982-; Mem: Nom'g Com 1979-81 & Secy 1981-83 Maternal- Child Hlth Div on Pract, VChm & Mem Exec Com Baccalaureate & Higher Deg Forum 1981-83, NC Nurses Assn, 1979-; Mem, Dist 13 NC Nurses Assn; ANA; Beta Epsilon Chapt, Sigma Theta Tau; Nat & Triangle Chapts, Nurses Assn of Am Col of Ob Gyn; Reg Mem Planning Com for 1981 Dist IV Conf, Mem Adv Coun 1981-85, Chp Publicity Com for 1982-84 Sect

Confs, Chm Registration Com 1984-85 Sec Confs, St Legis Ch 1984-85, NC Nurses Assn of Am Col of Ob Gyn; Carolina Soc of Assn Execs; Mem Spkr's Bur, Ross Labs, NC Dist; Conducted Num In-service & Commun Prenatal Ed Progs; r/Presb; hon/Charter Mem, Rho Lambda Nat Hon Frat; Guest Spkr, Pinning Ceremony, E Carolina Univ Sch of Nsg, 1980, 1985; Guest Spkr, Recog Ser, Duke Univ Sch of Nsg, 1982; W/ W of Am Wom.

BRUBECK, DAVID WARREN oc/ Musician, Jazz Pianist, Composer; b/Dec 6, 1920; h/221 Millstone Road, Wilton, CT 06897; ba/San Francisco, CA; m/Iola Marie Whitlock; c/David Darius, Michael, Christopher, Catherine, Daniel, Matthew; p/Howard Peter Brubeck (dec); ed/BA, Univ of Pacific, 1942; Postgrad Wk, Mills Col; mil/AUS, 1942-46, ETO; pa/Pianist w Dance Bands & Jazz Combos, Formed Own Trio & Octet, 1946; Formed Dave Brubeck Quartet, 1951-67; World Tours w Var Musicians, Ldr of Quartet w sons Darius, Chris & Dan, 1967-; Mem: NARAS; Fellow of Morse Col, Yale Univ; Duke Ellington Fellow, Yale Univ; cp/Adv Bd, Westport-Weston Arts Coun; r/Cath; hon/Composer Over 250 Songs; 90 Recordings; Com- positions Incl: "Points on Jazz" (Ballet); "Elementals" (Orch); "The Light in the Wilderness" (Oratorio); "Gates of Justice" (Cantata); "Truth" (Cantata); "They All Sang Yankee Doodle" (Vari- ations for Orch); "La Fiesta de la Posada" (Folk Cantata); "Glances" (Ballet); "Beloved Son" (Oratorio); "To Hope" (Mass); "Variations of Pange Lingua" (Chorus & Orch); Has Rec'd Num Hon Docts: Fairfield Univ, Univ of Pacific, Univ of Bridgeport, Mills Col; W/W.

BRUCE, A JERRY oc/Professor; b/Feb 24, 1942; h/1800 Greenbriar Elkins Lake, Huntsville, TX 77340; ba/Hunts- ville, TX; m/Betty Bryant; c/Gregory A, Scott B; p/Amos Bruce, Muscle Shoals, AL; sp/Kyle Bryant, Huntsville, TX; ed/ BA, Anderson Col, 1964; MS 1968, PhD 1972, Univ of GA; pa/Vis'g Instr Psych, Troy St Univ, 1970; Asst Prof Psych 1970-74, Assoc Prof Psych 1974-80, Prof 1980-, Chm Div Psych & Phil 1975-, Sam Houston St Univ; Mem: Am Psychol Assn; TX Psychol Assn; Soc for Res in Child Devel; r/Prot; hon/Author of Var Articles Pub'd in Profl Jours incl'g: *Devel Psych*, 1974; *Jour Ednl Studies*, 1981 & 1983; Outstg Yg Men of Am, Jr C of C, 1977.

BRUCE, JAMES TAYLOR oc/Ocea- nographer; b/Oct 21, 1953; h/5913 Halsey Road, Rockville, MD 20851; ba/ Rockville, MD; p/Alfred C and Sheila D Bruce J, Guilford, CT; ed/BS Biol, Nasson Col, 1976; Grad Cert Oceanic Ed, Univ of VA, 1983; pa/Oceano- grapher, Nat Oceanic & Atmospheric Adm, 1976-; Resident Hall Cnslt, Nas- son Col, 1974-75; Spar Bldr, Kenyon, ME, 1973-74; Boatyard Wkr, Bruce & Johnson's Marina, 1969-71; USCG Aux Instr, 1983-84; Mem: Intl Oceanic Foun; Marine Technol Soc; Oceanic Soc; r/ Epis; hon/Co-Author of *Puget Sound Approaches Circulatory Surv*, NOS Oceano- graphic Survey Report # 3; *Cook Inlet Circulatory Surv: 1973-75*, NOS Oceano- graphic Survey Report #4; Outstg Perf Ratings, NOAA/NOS, 1980, 1981 & 1984; Recip Unit Cit, NOAA/NOS,

1981; W/W: Among Students in Am Univs & Cols, in Frontier Sci & Technol.

BRUCE-SPRINGER, CHERYL LYNN oc/Program Director, Instructor; b/Feb 17, 1954; h/East 3517 Bridgeport, Spokane, WA 99207; ba/Spokane, WA; m/Mark H Springer; c/Megan Christan, Melissa Mary; p/Mr and Mrs Ralph E Bruce, Orchards, WA; sp/Mr and Mrs Harold Springer, Spokane, WA; ed/AA, So CA Col of Optom, 1974; AA, Spokane Falls Commun Col, 1973; BA, En WA Univ, 1984; pa/Optometric Tech Prog Dir & Instr, Spokane Commun Col, 1979-; Optician, Lund Optical, 1976-77; Optometric Tech, Robert Kettenhofen, 1974-75; Optometric Tech & Ofc Mgr, Ralph E Bruce, 1969-73; Mem: Para-optometric Sect, Am Optometric Assn; Assn of Higher Ed; WA Ed Assn; VPres 1980-81, Assn of Para-optometric Ed Prog; Optometric Ext Prog Foun; r/LDS; hon/W/W in W.

BRUHN, JOHN GLYNDON oc/University Dean; b/Apr 27, 1934; h/7521 Beluche, Galveston, TX 77551; ba/Galveston, TX; p/Margaret Bruhn, Phoenix, AZ; ed/BA 1956, MA 1958, Univ of NE; PhD, Yale Univ, 1961; mil/USAR, 1957-63; pa/Resr, NE Psychi Inst, Univ of NE Sch of Med, 1958; Resr, New Haven Co Jail Proj on Psychi, Legal & Sociol Probs of Juv Offenders, CT Dept of Mtl Hlth, 1958-59; Instr Sociol, So CT Col, New Haven, 1960-61; Res Sociol, Grace-New Haven Commun Hosp Psychi Out-patient Clin, NIMH Proj, 1960-61; Resident Freshman Cnslr, Yale Univ, 1960-61; Res Sociol, Dept of Psychol Med, Univ of Edinburgh, Scotland, 1961-62; Instr Sociol, OK City Univ, 1963; Instr in Med Sociol 1962-63 & Asst Prof 1963-64 Dept of Psychi & Behavioral Scis, Asst Prof Preven Med & Public Hlth & Res Sociol Nat Heart Inst Grant on Coronary Heart Disease Dept of Med 1964-67, Assoc Prof Sociol in Med Dept of Med & Assoc Prof Sociol 1967-72, Assoc Prof Human Ecol Sch of Hlth, Prof & Chm Dept Human Ecol Sch of Hlth 1969-72, Univ of OK Med Ctr; Assoc Dean for Commun Affairs 1972-81, Prof Preven Med & Commun Hlth 1972-, Acting Dean Sch Allied Hlth Scis 1979, Dean Sch Allied Hlth Sci & Spec Asst to Pres for Commun Affairs 1981-, Univ of TX Med Br-Galveston; Prof Human Ecol, Univ of TX Sch of Public Hlth, Houston, TX, 1975-; Mem: Coor Bd & Allied Hlth Ed Adv Com, TX Col & Univ Sys, 1982-84; Bd of Advrs, TX Acad of Phys Assts, 1981-82; Bd Advrs, The Foun of Thantology, NYC, NY, 1979-; Conslt Dept of Mtl Hlth & Mtl Retard, Commonwlth of VA, 1975; Pres & Dir, Totts Gap Inst of Human Ecol, Bangor, PA, 1975-77; Standing Com on Public Policy & Resolutions 1974, Task Force on Funding 1973-74, So Br APHA; Dir of Planning & Eval, Area Hlth Ed Ctr, Univ of TX Med Br-Galveston, 1972-75; Edit Bd Mem 1979-, Assoc Editor 1980-, *Hlth Values: Achieving High Level Wellness;* Prin Investigator on Num Grants Progs, 1968-; Am Sociol Assn; Fellow, Royal Soc of Hlth; Am Orthopsychi Assn; Am Psychosomatic Soc; AAUP; Num Other Profl Orgs; cp/Bd Mem, Galveston Co Commun Orch, 1979-; Bd Mem, Friends of Rosenberg Lib, 1980-81; Bd Mem, Galveston Co Heart Assn, 1980; Bd Mem, Galveston Co Cancer Soc,

1979-80; Ctl Res Review Com, Am Heart Assn TX Affil, 1982-83; Hlth Promotion Adv Coun, Hlth Sys Agy, Houston, TX, 1979-80; Num Other Commun Activs; r/Luth; hon/Author Co-Author of 5 Books incl'g: *Med Sociol: An Annotated Bibliog 1972-82;* Num Book Chapts & Reviews; Over 120 Articles & Res Papers Pub'd in Profl Jours; Over 40 Res Paper Presentations; Career Devel Awd, Nat Heart Inst, 1968-69; Danforth Assoc, 1973-; Awd for Outstg Adm from Fac, Sch Allied Hlth Scis, Univ of TX Med Br-Galveston, 1981 & 1982; Alpha Kappa Delta; Sigma Xi; W/W: in Am, in S & SW, in TX, in Commun Ser; 2000 Notable Ams; DIB; Dist'd Ldrs in Hlth Care; Men of Achmt; Outstg Edrs in Am; Num Other Biogl Listings.

BRUNALE, VITO JOHN oc/Aerospace Engineer; b/Jul 2, 1925; h/459 Bronxville Road, Bronxville, NY 10708; ba/Farmingdale, NY; m/Joan Florence; c/Stephen John; p/Donato and Ann Wool Brunale (dec); sp/Victor Montuori (dec); Grace Bartlett Montemurro, Bronx, NY; ed/AAS, Stewart Aeronaut Inst, 1948; BSAE, Tri-St Univ, 1958; MSME, Univ of Bridgeport, 1966; DSc, NV Inst of Technol, 1973; mil/USAF, 1943-45, Tech Sgt, POW Germany; pa/Res Engr, Norden Lab, 1948-55; Instr Engrg, Tri-St Univ, 1955-58; Engrg Conslt, U Aircraft, 1958-67; Engrg Div Conslt 1967-73, Chief Mech Engr Diagnostic/Retrieval Sys 1973-75, Res Engr Mech Anal 1975-77, Singer Aerospace Co; Conslt, Loural Corp & Ferron Assocs, 1977-; Engrg Tech Mgr, Fairchild Repub, 1977-; VPres, Lithoway Corp, 1967-70; Engrg Conslt, Engrg Mechs & Adv'd Math, Maj Aerospace Corps; Mem, Inst of Envir Sci, 1959-; Mem, 1948-: AIAA; AF Assn; USN Inst; Am Ordnance Assn; Nat Space Inst; AAAS; Nat Mgmt Assn; Chm Membrship Com 1976-77, Reg'd Profl 1948-, Engrg Soc; cp/Asst Scout Master Troop 16, BSA; K of C; r/Cath; hon/Author, Var Articles Pub'd in Profl Jours incl'g: *Envir Scis Jour; Prod Engrg; Aviation Wk;* Author of *Energy Tech,* Ofc of Nav Res, 1973; *Gimbal Structures,* 1959; Num Other In-house Co Documents; Fairchild Achmt Awds, 1979-83; Selected as Engrg Expert by US Govt to Participate in NSF Grant; Lect Awd 1948, Aircraft Design Awd 1948, Mbrship Awd 1973, AIAA; Norden Cost Reduction Awd, 1966; Singer Achmt Awd, 1964; W/W: in Aviation, in E, in Aviation & Aerospace.

BRUNER, RALPH CLAYBURN oc/Executive; b/Apr 22, 1921; h/3316 East 76th Street, Tulsa, OK 74136; ba/Tulsa, OK; m/Cicely Louise Fidler; c/Martha Ellen, David Ralph; p/Mr and Mrs Ralph S and Macil G Bruner (dec); sp/Percy Fidler, Jenks, OK; ed/BA Chem, CA St Univ-Fullerton, 1965; pa/Pres, Metlab Testing Sers Inc, 1976-; Mgr Labs, Rockwell Intl, 1965-76, Chief Chem Labs, Autonetics, 1959-65; Supvr Metall 1952-57, Sr Res Engr 1947-52, N Am Aviation; Mem: Am Soc Metals; Am Foundrymen's Soc; Am Welding Soc; Nat Assn of Corrosion Engrs; ASME; r/Rom Cath; hon/Author of Num Presentation Papers to Nat Tech Soc Meetings; Holder of 3 Patents in Field; W/W: in the World, in Frontier Sci & Technol.

BRUNS, PETER JOHN oc/Professor;

b/May 2, 1942; h/106 Hampton Road, Ithaca, NY 14850; ba/Ithaca, NY; p/Dr Hans Bruns, Syracuse, NY; ed/AB Zool, Syracuse Univ, 1964; PhD Cell Biol, Univ of IL, 1969; pa/Asst Prof Genetics 1969-74, Assoc Prof Genetics 1975-82, Prof Genetics 1982-, Chm Sect of Genetics & Devel 1980-, Assoc Dir Biotechnol Inst 1984-, Cornell Univ; Vis'g Sci, Biol Inst of Carlsberg Foun Denmark, 1977-78; Tchg Staff, European Milecular Biol Org Cours, Copenhagen, Denmark, 1977; Mem: Bd of Reviewers, *Jour of Protozool;* AAAS; Soc of Protozools; Genetics Soc of Am; Biomed Scis Study Sect, NIH, 1980-; hon/Author, Over 45 Sci Papers & Abstracts; John Simon Guggenheim Meml Foun Fellow, 1977-78; Orgr, Conf on Ciliate Macroucleus, 1977; Co-Orgr, 1st Cold Sprg Harbor Meeting on Ciliate Molecular Biol, 1984; W/W: in E, in Frontier Sci & Technol; Am Men & Wom of Sci; DIB; Other Biogl Listings.

BRUTLAG, DOUGLAS LEE oc/Professor, Consultant; b/Dec 19, 1946; h/4 Aliso Way, Menlo Park, CA 94025; ba/Stanford, CA; m/Simone C Manteuil; c/Pauline, Benjamin; p/Minehart and Cora Lee Brutlag, Albuquerque, NM; sp/Pierre and Odette Manteuil, Paris, France; ed/BS, CA Inst of Technol, 1968; PhD Stanford Univ, 1972; pa/Res Sci, Commonwlth Sci & Industl Res Org, Canberra, Australia, 1972-74; Asst Prof 1974-80, Assoc Prof 1980-, Stanford Univ; Fdr & Dir, Intellicorp Inc (formerly IntelliGenetics Inc) 1981-; Assoc Investigator, NIH Bionet Nat Resource, 1984-89; Mem: Fdn of Am Socs for Exptl Biol, 1974-; Am Soc of Biol Chems, 1974-; Cell Biol Study Sect 1978, Molecular Cytology Study Sect 1979, Genetics Study Sect 1982-, NIH; cp/Over 15 Invited Nat & Intl Profl Org Presentations; r/Author, Over 40 Articles Pub'd in Symp Pubs & Profl Jours incl'g: *Nucleic Acids Res; Biochem; Jour Molecular Biol; Cell;* Others; Var Book Chapts; George W Green Awd for Creat S'ship, 1968; PhD w Gt Distn, 1972; Andrew W Mellon Foun F'ship, 1974-76; Basil O'Connor Nat Foun Yg Investigator Awd, 1975-78; Henry & Camille Dreyfus Tchr-Scholar Grant, 1979-84; NIH Sr Fogarty Intl Fellow, 1981-82; W/W: in CA, in W, in Frontier Sci & Technol.

BRYAN, DAVID BARCLAY oc/Attorney at Law; b/Aug 30, 1933; h/2163 Ahaku Place, Honolulu, HI 96821; ba/Honolulu, HI; c/Michael David, John Frederic; p/Frederck C Bryan (dec); Florence H Becker, Los Angeles, CA; ed/BA, Duke Univ, 1955; JD, Univ of CA-Berkeley, 1958; pa/Indiv Law Pract, 1979-; Atty & Ptnr, Heen, Kai & Dodge/Kai, Dodge & Evensen, 1969-79; Dept Prosecuting Atty, City & Co of Honolulu, 1965-68; Asst to Mgr, Pers Dept, HI Elect Co, 1964-65; Asst to Pres, Civil Air Transport & Acting Dir Pers Air Asia, 1961-64; Labor Relats Mgr, HI Air, 1960-61; Mem: ABA; HI Bar Assn; Am Trial Lwyrs Assn; Assn of Immigration & Nationality Lwyrs; cp/Pres 1980-82, Exec Com Mem 1975-80, Muscular Dystrophy Assn; Trustee & Dir, Alliance Francaise, 1976-; Outrigger Canoe Clb, 1970-; Oahu Country Clb; r/Epis; hon/W/W: in Am Law, in W; Ldrs of HI.

BRYAN JANE C oc/Technical Trainer; b/Sep 29, 1925; h/4750 Gainsborough Drive, Fairfax, VA 22032; ba/Bethesda, MD; c/Elizabeth, Carolyn, James; p/Langdon and Rhoda Trego Campbell (dec); ed/AB Art & Psych, Case Wn Resv; Cert'd Life Underwriter; pa/Tech Instr, Elect Data Sys Corp, Bethesda, MD, 1983-; Tech Tng Admr 1980-84, Programming Anal 1976-80, Prudential Ins Co, Houston, TX; Fellow, Life Mgmt Assn Inst; Soc Cert'd Data Processors; AAUW; cp/Past Bd Trustees, Union Co Psychi Clin; Past Ofcr & Trustee, Summit Art Ctr; cp/DAR; LWV; r/Presb; hon/Chi Beta Phi; Recip Var Awds Juried St & Local Art Shows; W/W in S & SW.

BRYAN, LESLIE AULLS oc/Transportation Economist; b/Feb 23, 1900; h/34 Fields East, Champaign, IL 61821; ba/Champaign, IL; m/Gertrude C Gelder; c/Leslie A Jr, George G; p/Daniel B Bryan and Anna R Aulls (dec); sp/Frederick T Gelder and Edith L Brown (dec); ed/BS 1923, MS 1924, JD 1939, Syracuse Univ; PhD, The Am Univ, 1930; Hon DSc, SWn Col, 1972; mil/USAF, Col, Ret'd; pa/Professor, SWn Col, 1924-25; Instr to Franklin Prof of Trans, Syracuse Univ, 1925-46; Pres, Seneca Flying Sch, 1944-45; Dir Aviation, St of NY, 1945; Prof Mgmt & Dir Inst of Aviation 1946-68, Prof Emeritus 1968-, Univ of IL; Pres 1955-56, Am Assn of Airport Execs; Chm, Pres Eisenhower's Gen Facilities Planning Grp, 1957; Pres Arrowhd Coun 1954-60, BSA; Mem, Pres Kennedy's Com on Nat Aviation Goals, 1961; r/Prot; hon/Author of 13 Books incl'g: *Fundamtls of Aviation*, 1959; *Traffic Mgmt in Indust*, 1952; *Air Trans*, 1949; *Water Trans*, 1939; Others; Over 300 Articles Pub'd; Brewer Trophy, 1953; Dist'd Ser Med, CAP, 1954; Arents Medal, 1955; Dist'd Public Ser Awd, FAA, 1965; Elder Statesman of Aviation, 1966; Minute Man Awd, SAR, 1976; Dist'd Ser Medal, Nat Huguenot Soc, 1976; W/W: in Am, in World, in Aviation; Am Men of Sci; Num Other Biogl Listings.

BRYANT, BETTY L oc/Nursing Instructor; b/Sep 3, 1929; h/Rural Route 1, Bloomingdale, IN 47832; ba/Danville, IL; m/Bobby L; c/Taunnie L, Gregry L; Christopher L; p/Odus Ratcliff (dec); Latitia Ratcliff, Rockville, IN; sp/Milton and Lula Bryant (dec); ed/Lic'd Pract Nurse, Ivy Tech Col, 1972; BS Nsg, IN St Univ, 1980; MA Cand, IN Univ; pa/Nurse Aide, IN St Sanitorium, Rockville, IN, 1968-70; Lic'd Pract Nurse, Vermillon Co Hosp, Clinton, IN, 1972-79; Asst Admr, Lee Alan Bryant Hlth Care Facility, Rockville, 1979-80; Dir Nsg Ser 1980-82, Conslt Gerontology Prog 1981-82, Cont'g Ed Conslt 1981-82, Asst Instr Anatomy, Physiol & Sci Dept 1979-80, Asst in Sociol Dept 1982, IN St Univ-Terre Haute; Jr & Sr Med Serg Nsg Instr, Lakeview Med Ctr, Danville, IN, 1982-; Mem: IN Assn of Quality Assurance Profession; IN St Univ Alumni Assn; cp/Secy, Wom's Soc Christian Ser, 1960-62; Ldr, BSA, 1961-62; Meth Yth F'ship Ldr, 1969-70; Ch Camp Cnslr, 1968-70; Precinct Com Person, 1968-72; Diabetes Screener, 1979-; r/Prot; hon/W/W of Am Wom; World Wom's W/W.

BRYANT, BETTYE COBB oc/Reading Consultant; b/Mar 3, 1935; h/810 Clear Lake Avenue, West Palm Beach, FL 33401; ba/West Palm Beach, FL; m/B Carleton; c/Carleton Russell, Carla Shay; p/Elanor Elixa Cobb (dec); sp/Annie P Bratcher; ed/BS, AL St Col, 1954; MEd, FL A&M Univ, 1962; EdD, S FL Atl Univ, 1978; pa/Eng Tchr, AL Industl Sch, Mt Meigs, AL, 1954-56; Secy 195657, Pharm Libn 1957-62, FL A&M Univ; Eng Tchr, Edison Jr Col, 1962-63; Eng Tchr, Palm Bch Co Sch Bd, 1963-66; Rdg Tchr, 1966-74; Title I Conslt, 1974-; Mem: IRA; Bd of Dirs 1976-79, FL St Rdg Assn; Pres 1974-75, Palm Bch Co Rdg Assn; Assn for Supvn & Curric Devel; FL Assn for Supvn & Curric Devel; r/Cath; hon/Author of "Let's Talk So that Parents Can Understand Us," *FL Rdg Qtly*, 1977; W/W in SE.

BRYANT, EDWARD ALBERT oc/Art Museum Director; b/Jul 23, 1928, Lenoir, NC; h/1400 Marron Circle Northeast, Albuquerque, NM 87112; ba/Albuquerque, NM; m/Tamara Thompson; c/Adam Edmond Thompson, Mary Emmaline; p/Edmond Henry Bryant (dec); sp/Shelton Emmaline Bryant (dec); ed/AB 1950, MA 1955, Univ of NC-Chapel Hill; Postgrad Study: Univ Italiana per gli Stranieri, Perugia, 1954; Univ di Pisa, 1954-55; Univ di Ravenna, 1955; NC St Univ, 1956; Columbia Univ, 1958; pa/Fellow, Bklyn Mus, 1957-58; Gen Curator, Wadsworth Atheneum, Hartford, CT, 1959-61; Assoc Curator, Whitney Mus of Am Art, 1961-65; Dir Art Gallery & Asst Prof, Univ of KY-Lexington, 1965-68; Dir Picker Art Gallery 1968-80, Prof Art 1980, Chm Dept Fine Arts 1976-77, Colgate Univ; Prof Art & Dir Art Mus 1980-, Univ of NM; Mem: Col Art Assn of Am, 1970-; Adv Panel, Inst of Arch & Urban Studies, NYC, 1976-79; Sculpture Panel, NEA Art in Public Places, Albuquerque, NM, 1980; Visual Arts F'ship Panel, AZ Comm on Arts, Phoenix, 1981; hon/Author of Num Books incl'g: *Joseph Pennell's NY Etchings; Jason Seley; Drawing by Robert Broderson; Jack Tworkov*; Num Articles Pub'd in Jours Incl: *Arts; Artspace; Art in Am; Art News*; others; Exhibns Incl: Jack Tworkov Retrospective, Whitney Mus, 1964; Graphics 1968, Univ of KY Mus; Contemp Italian Drawings & Collage (AFA); Num Others; Fulbright Fellow, 1954-55; Spec Res Grant, Colgate Univ, 1969-70 & 1976; Grantee, NEA, 1974-75; W/W: in Am, in W, Contemp Authors.

BRYANT, EMILY MARSHBURN oc/Educator (Retired); b/Sep 9, 1919; h/1714 North Payson Street, Baltimore, MD 21217; ba/Baltimore, MD; m/Leon D (dec); c/Leon Douglas Jr; p/William and Violet Marshburn (dec); sp/Fred and Ada Bryant (dec); ed/Cert, Coppin Tchrs Col, 1940; BS Ed, Morgan Univ, 1947; MA Early Childhood Ed, NY Univ, 1954; Grad Study: Univ of MD & Johns Hopkins Univ; pa/Tchr, Balto City Public Schs, 1942-81; Student Instr, NY Univ, 1951-53; Tchr & Curric Coor, 1973-81; Prin, Sum Sch, 1976; Mem Math Book Selection Com; Grade Chm; Demo Tchr; Supervising Tchr; Orgr & Conductor of Tutorial Prog in Rdg, 1961-73; Wkshop Ldr; Mem: NEA; PSTA; MSTA; Treas 1963-64, Nat Coun Negro Wom; Chm Ed Com 1968-70 & Exec Com 1965-70, MD Leag of Woms Clbs; Basilews 1968-70, Reg Treas 1967-71, Sigma Gamma Rho Sorority Inc; cp/Pres, WANA, 1969-71 & 1977-78; Layldr & Trustee 1982, Douglas Meml Commun Ch; Mayor's Vol Coun; Meals on Wheels; r/Meth; hon/Outstg Serv Sigma Wom of Yr, 1967; Outstg Balto City Tchr Awd, 1978; Sigma Awd for 39 Yrs of Outstg Ed & Commun Ser, 1981; Stewardship to Ch Awd, 1950, 1960, 1970, 1980 & 1981.

BRYANT, FRANKLIN DELANO oc/Chem Engr; b/Jan 30, 1934; h/303 Softwood Drive, Duncanville, TX 75137; ba/Dallas, TX; m/Mary Sue; c/Franklin Delano II, Durlon Laroi, Shoshana Renee; p/James Thomas Bryant (dec); Hessie Bryant, Bridgeport, TX; sp/Roy L and Amy Floy Brooks, Dallas, TX; ed/BS Chem, 1956; MS Chem, 1965; mil/AUS, 1956-58; pa/Chem Engr, Vought Corp, 1958-59 & 1966-; Fac, SWn A & G Coll, 1959-63; Fac, TX St Univ, 1963-66; Bd of Dirs, World Electroless Nickel Soc; Am Electroplaters Soc; Alpha Chi Sigma; Duncanville City Elect Bd; r/Assem of God; hon/Author of Var Articles on Plating in Profl Jours; Valedictorian, 1952; Pres's Awd, Vought Corp, 1968; W/W in SW.

BRYANT, JACQUELINE EOLA oc/Educator; h/3845 North Ingleside Drive, Norfolk, VA 23502; ba/Virginia Beach, VA; p/James T Bryant (dec); Wincie J Bryant, Norfolk, VA; pa/Eng Tchr, Balto City Public Schs, 1971-75; Curric Develr, Conslt, Tutorial Proj, Norfolk Com for Improvement of Ed, 1975; Curric Conslt, Develr 1976-78, Tchr & Dept Chp Eng 1979-, Instrnl Spec Lang Arts K-12 1984-, VA Bch City Public Schs; Team Tchr, St Leo's Col, VA Bch, 1977-78; Mem: Pres 1978, VA Bch Assn of Tchrs of Eng; Pres 1985, VA Assn of Tchrs of Eng; Dir 1985, NCTE; PTA; Edit Bd, *VA Eng Bltn*; Adv Bd, Scholastic Pubs Inc, 1980-81; r/Rom Cath; hon/Columnist, "The Needle's Eye"; Outstg Yg Wom In Am; W/W of Am Wom.

BRYANT, SYLVIA LEIGH oc/Poet, Editor-Publisher, Free Lance Writer; b/May 8, 1947; h/Rt 5, Box 498-A, Madison Heights, VA 24572; ba/Lynchburg, VA; p/Mr and Mrs Hudley Bryant, Madison Heights, VA; ed/Cultural Doct in Lit, World Univ, 1981; pa/Poet, 1976-; Free Lance Writer; Editor-Publisher, *The Anthology Soc*, 1979-; Pub'd in *Adventures in Poetry Anthology*, 1978; *The Poet*, 1978 & 1979; *Adventures in Poetry Mag*, 1978-80; *Am Poet*, 1979-80; *IBC Mag*, 1980; *Mod Images*, 1979-80; *Hoosier Challenger*, 1979-84; *The Anthology Soc*, 1979, 1980, 1982-83; *Animal World*, 1981; *Premier Poets*, 1980; *Quickenings Mag*, 1981-84; *Laurel Leaves*, 1980; *The Durango Herald*, 1980; *Born of the Beauty of Storm & Calm*; Mem: India; Fellow, Intl Acad of Poets; Intl Biogl Assn; Hon Mem, Anglo-Am Acad; Accademia Leonardo Da Vinci; Intl Poet Laureate, Stella Woodall Poetry Soc Intl; Am Poets F'ship Soc; U Poets Laureate Intl (Philippines); Num Others; r/Bapt; hon/Poet Laureate Intl, 1979; Gold Medal & Cert of Merit, Accademia Leonardo Da Vinci, 1980; Rep, St of VA in *Poet*, Mar Issue, 1981; Hon Mem, Edit Adv Bd, ABI, 1980-; W/W in Poetry; Lit Hall of Fame; Commun Ldrs of Am; Anglo-Am W/W; DIB; Num Other Biogl Listings.

BRYON, TAMSEN TAYLOR oc/ Medical Anthropologist; b/Dec 13, 1943; h/84 Sumpwams Avenue, Babylon, NY 11702; ba/Stony Brook, NY; m/Robert Findlay Stevenson; c/ Gregg, Tamsen, Experience Robinson, Alix, Talor English Alden Bryon; ed/ Dipl, Colegio Americano, Guadalajara, Jalisco, Mexico, 1960; BS, SUNY-Stony Brook, 1981; pa/VPres Corp Graphics, Pty Ltd, Sydney, Australia, 1969-76; Prog Coor, FREE, 1977; Res Asst, World Hunger Prog 1977-78, Med Athropol 1978-, SUNY-Stony Brook; Mem: Am Wom in Sci; Am Public Hlth Assn; Am Anthropological Assn; Am Med Anthropological Assn; Hastings Inst; cp/Mem: Comm on Hunger & Malnutrition, Suffolk Co; Nassau/Suffolk Hlth Sys Agy; Pres 1977-, Suffolk Co Coun; Suffolk Co Exec; r/Rom Cath; hon/ Recip, NSF F'ship, 1983-85; W/W of Wom.

BRYSON, FRED WYLIE oc/Professor, Consultant; b/Jul 7, 1922; h/3504 Villanova, Dallas, TX 75225; m/Vivian Hintze; c/Mark Hintze; p/Charles Wilburn and Millie Lee Wylie Bryson (dec); sp/Mr and Mrs J Fred Hintze; ed/BA, Bethel Col, 1943; MA, Scarritt Col, 1954; EdD, N TX St Univ, 1964; pa/HS Tchr, 1943-45; Pastor of Var Chs, 1943-45; Tchr, Colegio American, Cali, Columbia, S Am, 1945-47; Acting Pres, Bethel Col, 1975; Fac Mem 1947-52, Dir of Student Ctr, Assoc Dean of Students & Dean of Student Life 1952-67, Academic Dean 1967-75, Dean of Sum Sessions 1970-75, Dean of Univ 1975-76, Prof of Ed 1976-, So Meth Univ; Mem: Am Psychol Assn; Am & Guid Assn; Nat Assn of Student Pers Admrs; SW Assn of Student Pers Admrs; TX Assn of Student Per Admrs; Phi Delta Kappa; Blue Key Nat Hon Frat; TX Psychol Assn; Dallas Psychol Assn; cp/Pres, Dallas UN Assn; Moderator, Gen Assem, Cumberland Presb Ch; Chm, Com on the Min; Moderator, Presby & TX Synod; Chm of Trustees, Bethel Col, Trustee, Presb Hosp, Dallas; Dir, Ctr for Pastoral Care, Dallas; r/ Presb; hon/Fulbright Lectr, Univ of San Marcos, Lima, Peru; Cert'd Psychol; Conslt, Goals for Dallas Prog; Hon DHL, Baker Univ, 1978; Hon DD, Bethel Col, 1981.

BUCHANAN, DONALD D oc/Executive; b/Oct 13, 1935; h/4603 Bayshore Boulevard, Tampa, FL 33611; ba/ Tampa, FL; m/Eleanor L Opie; c/Scott Alan, Karen Lynn; p/Donald H Buchanan (dec); Reba L Buchanan; sp/Lona Opie, Denver, CO; ed/Att'd Univ of Denver, 1953-57; Grad, Univ of CO Grad Sch Bkg, 1963; Adv'd Mgmt Prog, Harvard Univ, 1979; pa/Employee 1956-70, VPres & Sr Trust Ofcr 1970, Sr VPres & OPS Div Exec 1970-75, U Bk of Denver; Employee 1975-79, Exec VPres & Trust Grp Exec 1979-83, NCNB Nat Bk-Charlotte; Pres, NC NB Nat Bk of FL-Tampa, 1983-; NCNB Corp Exec, 1983; Exec VPres, NCNB Nat Bk of NC, 1983; cp/Trustee, Univ of Tampa, 1984; Bd of Govs, FL Orch; Dir, Tampa Clb, 1984; FL Coun of 100; Nat Bd of Dirs, Campfire Girls; r/Meth; hon/W/W: in Am, in S & SW.

BUCHANAN, ROSE MAY oc/Chemical Lab Supervisor; b/Jun 26, 1947; h/ PO Box 294, Bluefield, WV 24701; ba/ Bluefield, WV; p/Ambrose and Lacie

Buchanan, Falls Mills, VA; ed/RBA, Bluefield St Col, 1981; MBA Cand, WV Col of Grad Studies, Currently; pa/Lab Technol, Clinch Val Clin, 1966-71; Lab Technol, Bluefield Sanitarium Clin, 1971-79; Chem Supvr & Lab Technol, Bluefield Commun Hosp, 1979-; Reg'd Med Technol, Am Soc Clin Pathols, 1983; Previously CLA & MLT, Am Soc Clin Pathols; Med Technol, Am Med Technols, 1983; r/Bapt; hon/RBA cum laude, 1981; W/W of Am Wom.

BUCHHOLZ, DONNA M oc/Project Manager; b/May 27, 1950; h/451 Highland Avenue, West Chicago, IL 60185; ba/Abbott Laboratories, Abbott Park, IL; m/William E Hourigan; p/Arthur and Doris Buchholz, Chicago, IL; sp/Richard and Hazel Hourigan, Glen Ellyn, IL; ed/ BS Biol Scis, Quincy Col, 1972; MS 1975, PhD 1978, Microbiol/Immunol, Univ of IL at the Med Ctr; pa/Med Technol, Univ of IL Med Ctr, 1972-73; Postdoct Appointee Div of Biol & Med Res, Argonne Nat Lab, 1978-80; Res Info Sci 1980-82, Proj Mgr Res Mgmt & Devel 1982-, Abbott Labs; Mem: Am Assn of Immunols; Am Soc for Microbiol; Councilor 1981-82, IL Soc for Microbiol; Soc for Industl Microbiol, Chapt Pres 1983-84, Reg Nom'g Com Chm 1983-85, Sigma Xi; AAAS; Nat Sci & Engrg Exploring Com; cp/Citizens Adv Com, Du Page Airport; Du Page Art Leag; W Chgo Energy Comm; r/ Rom Cath; hon/Author, 10 Res Articles & 4 Book Reviews Pub'd in Profl Jours incl'g: *Envir Res*; *Proceedings Hanford Life Scis Symp*; *Cellular Immunol*; *Sci Books & Films*; Others; IL St Scholar, 1968-72; Sigma Xi Grad Student Res Awd, 1978; Pres Awd, Abbott Labs, 1984; W/W: in MW, of Am Wom, in Frontier Sci & Technol; Am Men & Wom of Sci.

BUCK, ROSS WORKMAN oc/Professor; b/Aug 16, 1941; 63 Cedar Swamp Road, Storrs, CT 06268; ba/ Storrs, CT; m/Marianne Jenney; c/Ross William, Maria Lenore, Nancy Jenney, Theodore Reed; p/Ross W Sr and Ruth Isabel Hadley Buck (dec); sp/Eleanor Jenney, Meadville, PA; ed/BA Psych, Allegheny Col, 1963; MA Social Psych, Univ of WI-Madison, 1963; PhD Social Psych, Univ of Pgh, 1970; pa/Res Assoc, Univ of Pgh Med Sch, 1967-70; Asst Prof Psych, Carnegie-Mellon Univ, 1970-74; Asst, Assoc, Full Prof, Communs Scis & Psych, Univ of CT, 1974-; Mem: Fellow & Mem Div of Personality & Social Psych, Am Psychol Assn, 1967-; Intl Communs Assn, 1979-; Intl Soc for Res on Aggression, 1984; En Psychol Assn; MWn Psychol Assn; r/Soc of Friends; hon/Author of 2 Books, *Human Motivation & Emotion*, 1976; *The Communication of Emotion*, 1984; Over 40 Book Chapts & Articles Pub'd in Profl Jours; Fellow, Am Psychol Assn, 1984; Overseas Edit Bd, *Brit Jour of Social Psych*, 1984-; Edit Bd, *Jour of Personality & Social Psych*, 1981-; W/W: in E, in Frontier Sci & Technol; Am Men & Wom of Sci; Comm Ldrs & Noteworthy Ams.

BUCKALEW, LOUIS WALTER oc/ Professor, Researcher; b/Apr 21, 1944; ba/Normal, AL; p/L W Buckalew Jr (dec); Maryruth Buckalew, Orlando, FL; ed/ BA, GA So Col, 1967; MS, Univ of So MS, 1969; Doct Study, Howard Univ, 1978-79 & 1982-83; mil/AUS, 1969-70, Vietnam; pa/Asst Prof Psych 1975-83, Assoc Prof Psych 1983-, Dir Inst for

Drug/Alcohol Res 1975-, AL A&M Univ; Res Assoc Sums 1981 & 1982, Assoc Sum 1983, USAF Aerospace Med Res Lab; Consltg Psychol, Buckalew & Davis Assocs, 1973-75; Instr Psych, SC St Col, 1970-73; Adm Spec Engr Opers AUS, 1969-70; Grad Res Asst, US Civil Def Res, Univ of GA, 1967; r/Epis; hon/ Author-Editor, 4 Books; Contbr to 3 Books, 12 Profl Org Presentations, 48 Sci Jour Articles in 19 Different Jours; Bronze Star & Army Commend Medal, 1970; White House Fellow, Reg Finalist, 1980; Psi Chi Nat Hon Soc, 1967; Kappa Delta Pi Nat Hon Soc, 1978; Sigma Xi Sci Res Soc; AL Acad of Scis; USAF Sum Fac Res Awd, 1981 & 1982; NSF Profl Devel Awd, 1978; NSF Grad Res Traineeship, 1982; Pres, Achmt Awd, Nat Repub Com, 1982; Mu Omega Chapt Awd, Kappa Delta Pi, 1980; W/W: in S & SW, of Intells; Outstg Yg Men of Am; Am Registry of Sci; DIB; Men of Achmt; 2000 Notable Ams; Num Other Biogl Listings.

BUCKMAN, MAIRE TULTS oc/ Physician; b/Sep 25, 1939; h/2415 Vista Larga, Northeast, Albuquerque, NM 87106; ba/Albuquerque, NM; c/Sabrina, James; p/Kate Tults, Albuquerque, NM; ed/Att'd Univ of CA-LA, 1957-59; Completed Course Wk, Sch of Med, Friedrich-Wilhelm Univ, Bonn, W Germany, 1963; MD, Univ of WA Sch of Med, 1966; Diplomate Cert, Nat Bd of Med Examrs, 1967; mil/US Army Med Corp; pa/Intern, Santa Clara Hosp, San Jose CA, 1966-67; Capt w AUS Med Corps, Gen Dispensary, Frankfurt, W Germany, 1967-68; Resident Endocrinology & Metabolism 1971-72, NIH Spec F'ship Awd 1972-74, Instr Med 1973-74, Asst Prof Med 1974-80, Assoc Prof Med 1980-, Univ of NM Med Sch, Albuquerque; Mem: Am Col of Phys; Am Fdn for Clin Res; The Endocrine Soc; Wn Soc for Clin Res; Pacific Coast Fertility Soc; AAAS; Reviewer: *Clin Endocrinology & Metabolism*; *Jour Endocrinological Investigation*; Chp, Endocrine-Metabolism-Nutrition Res Sem, 1978-83; Assoc Chief of Nuclear Med (Dir, VA Radioimmunoassay Lab), 1979-; Res Conf Com 1984-, Other Previous Coms, VAMC; Others; hon/Author & Co-Author, Over 40 Articles in Profl Sci Jours; 6 Book Chapts; Over 40 Abstracts & Res Paper Presentations; Sandoz Lab Multictr Cyclic Mastodynia Study Grant, 1982-84; Lilly Res Lab Multictr Pergolide Study Grant, 1981-82; Merit Review Awd, VA, 1980-82; Chosen to Chair 2 Sessions, 62nd Annual Meeting, The Endocrine Soc, Wash DC, 1980; NM Chapt, Am Heart Assn Grant-in-Aid, 1980-81; Spkr, 64th Annual Meeting, Am Med Wom's Assn, 1979; 1st Prize, 4th Annual Housestaff Res Forum, Univ of NM Sch of Med, 1973; VA Career Devel Prog Awd, 1974-80; Mosby S'ship Book Awd for Scholastic Excell, Sr Yr Med Sch, 1966; Num Others; Var Biogl Listings.

BUDZINSKY, ARMIN ALEXANDER oc/Investment Banker; b/Nov 25, 1942; h/4510 Shetland, Houston, TX 77027; ba/Houston, TX; m/Pamela Plimmer; c/Andrea Budzinsky; p/Alexander Wladimir, Cleveland, OH; Maria Gisella Budzinsky (dec); sp/Ralph and Elsie Plimmer, Springfield, MO; ed/AB, John Carroll Univ, 1964; MA, Rutgers

Univ, 1969; MBA, Univ of Chgo, 1974; pa/Instr, Cleveland St Univ, 1969-72; Financial Conslt, Citibk, NA, 1974-76; Corp Fin, Dean Witter & Co, 1976-77; VPres, Merrill, Lynch, White, Weld Capital Mkts Grp, 1977-; Mem: Indust Adv Com to Minerals Interests Subcom, N Am Securities Admrs Assn; Oil Investmnt Inst; Alumni Assn Bd of Dirs, Univ of Chgo Grad Sch Bus; hon/ Author of Var Articles Pub'd in: *Houston Chronicle*; *The Am Oil & Gas Reporter*; *Oil & Gas Investor*; W/W: in S & SW, in World, in Fin & Indust; Personalities of S.

BUEDING, ERNEST oc/Professor Emeritus; b/Aug 19, 1910; h/4001 Roundtop Road, Baltimore, MD 21218; ba/Baltimore, MD; m/Raya; c/Robert; ed/Att'd Univ of Frankfurt (Main) Med Sch, 1930-33; Predoct Fellow, Institut Pasteur, Paris, 1933-35; MD, Univ of Paris, 1936; mil/Conslt, Ofc Res & Devel; pa/Asst Biochem, Univ of Istanbul, Turkey, 1936-38; Res Fellow, Dept of Med, Col of Med, NY Univ, 1939-44; Asst & Assoc Prof Pharm, Wn Resv Univ, 1944-54; Prof Pharm & Dept Chm, LA St Univ, 1954-60; Prof Pathobiol, Sch of Hygiene & Public Hlth, Exptl Therapeutics, Sch of Med 1960-81, Prof Emeritus 1981-, The Johns Hopkins Univ; Mem: Fellow, Am Acad Arts & Scis, 1979; Am Soc Parasitology, 1972; Assoc Mem, Brit Pharm Soc, 1963; Brit Biochem Soc, 1951; Fellow, AAAS, 1948; Am Chem Soc, 1948; Am Soc Pharm & Exptl Therapeutics, 1948; Am Soc Biol Chems, 1946; Chm US Schistosomiasis Del to People's Repub China, US Nat Acad of Scis, 1975; Comm on Parasitology, Armed Forces Epidemiological Bd, 1953-72; Conslt to Surg Gen, Dept of Army, 1973-; Mem Var Coms, World Hlth Org; Edit Bd Mem, Var Profl Jours; Others; cp/Fdr & Past Pres: Cleveland Chamber Music Soc; NO Friends of Music; Shriver Hall Concert Series (Johns Hopkins Univ); hon/Author, Over 250 Articles Pub'd in Profl Jours; Chamber Music Am Nat Ser Awd, 1984; 1st Theodor Weicker Meml Awd in Pharm & Exptl Therapeutics, 1978; Paul Ehrlich Awd, Frankfort, W Germany, 1985; Vis'g Fulbright Prof Pharm, Univ of Oxford, Eng, 1959; Guggenheim Fellow, Univ of Oxford, Eng, 1963; W/W; W/W in Sci; Am Men of Sci; Ldrs in Am Sci; DIB.

BUFORD, EVELYN CLAUDENE oc/ Sales Manager; b/Sep 21, 1940; h/100 Kenneth Lane, Burleson, TX 76028; ba/ Ft Worth, TX; m/William Joseph; c/ Vincent Shilling Jr, Kathryn Lynn Vassar (Mrs Chris A Vassar); p/Claude and Winner Evelyn Hodges, Burleson, TX; sp/Thelma Buford, Utica, MS; ed/ Att'd Hill Jr Col, 1975-76; pa/Gen Sales Mgr/Comml Div 1964-83, Corp Secy 1977-, Imperial Printing Co; Employee 1973-77, Asst to Admr 1981-82, Tarrant Co Hosp Dist, Ft Worth; Mem: Am Mgt Assn; Ways & Means Dir 1983-84, Exec Wom Intl; Nat Assn Femal Execs; cp/Pres's Clb of TX; Repub Party; r/ Meth; hon/W/W of Am Wom; Personalities of S.

BUFORD, THOMAS O oc/Professor; b/Nov 17, 1932; h/104 Abingdon Way, Greenville, SC 29615; ba/Greenville, SC; m/Delores Phife; c/Russell Warren, Anna Louise; p/Mr and Mrs R W Jambura, Shreveport, LA; ed/BA, N TX St Univ, 1955; BD, SWn Theol Sem,

1958; PhD, Boston Univ, 1963; pa/Asst to Pastor, Tremont Temple Bapt Ch, Boston, MA, 1961-62; Chm Dept Phil, KY So Col, 1962-68; Assoc Prof Phil 1968-69, Prof Phil & Chm Dept of Phil 1969-, Furman Univ; Pres 1980-82, Pres Elect 1979-80, Mem-at-large Exec Com 1976-77, S Atlantic Phil of Ed Soc; Pres 1982-83, VPres 1981-82, Secy-Treas 1981-82 & 1972-73, SC Soc of Phil; Exec Com, Personalistic Discussion Grp, Wn Div, Am Phil Assn; Soc Christian Phils; Fellow, Phil of Ed Soc; Chm, Student Essay Contest, SC Soc for Phil, 1970-72; Mem Griffiths Awds Com, So Soc for Phil & Psych, 1978; cp/SS Tchr, 1st Bapt Ch, Greenville, SC; Pres, PTA, Eastside HS, Greenville; r/Bapt; hon/Author of Book, *Personal Phil: The Art of Living*, 1983; Editor-Co-Editor 4 Books incl'g: *Phil for Adults*, 2nd Ed, 1983; *Towards a Phil of Ed*, 1969; Others; Author of Var Articles in Bltns & Jours; Alpha Chi, 1954-55; Phi Mu Alpha, 1975-; Dept F'ship & Asst to Chm Dept of Phil, Boston Univ, 1958-60; Res Stipend, Nat Endowment for Humanities, 1972; W/W in S & SE; Contemp Authors; Dir Am Phils.

BUGG, WILLIAM MAURICE oc/ Professor, Department Head; b/Jan 23, 1931; h/5113 Yosemite Trail, Knoxville, TN 37919; ba/Knoxville, TN; m/Marian Sly; c/Susan Theresa, Thomas Maurice, Linda Ann, David William; p/Maurice Angel Bugg (dec); Abbie Ruth Bugg, Oak Ridge, TN; sp/Thomas and Ollie Sly (dec); ed/AB Physics, Wash Univ-St Louis; PhD, Univ of TN; mil/AUS Artillery, 1952-54; pa/Asst Prof 1959, Assoc Prof 1964, Prof Physics 1961, Acting Hd Physics Dept 1968, Hd Physics Dept 1969-, Univ of TN; Mem: Sigma Pi Sigma; Fellow, Am Phy Soc; Exec Coun, Pres 1979, SEn Sect, Am Phy Soc; r/Rom Cath; hon/Author, Over 70 Articles in Profl Jours; Recip, Physics Prize, 1948.

BUGGS, DWAYNE ANDRÉ oc/Vocal Music Tchr; b/Sep 24, 1954; h/7441 San Diego, Apartment 4, St Louis, MO 63121; ba/St Louis, MO; p/Overton Joe and Faye Evelyn Buggs; ed/BA Vocal Music & Piano, LA Polytech Univ, 1975; MMus Music Ed & Piano, So IL Univ-Edwardsville, 1977; pa/Vocal Music Tchr, Normandy Sch Dist, 1977-; Min of Music, St James African Meth Epis Ch, St Louis, MO, 1977-; Instr Piano, St Louis Commun Col-Forest Pk, 1981-; Mem: Phi Mu Alpha Sinfonia Music Frat; Nat Assn Negro Musicians; MENC; MMEC; NEA; MNEA; NTA; Appt'd MO Conf Choir Music Dir, Bishop of 5th Epis Dist for African Meth Epis Ch, 1983; St Louis New Betterment Prog, 1983; r/Prot; Selected to Perf on LA Tech Music Camp Recording Album, 1970; Invited to Perf, MO Music Ed Conf at Tan-tar-ra, 1983; Outstg Yg Men of Am.

BUJTAS, MARK STEVEN oc/Executive; b/Aug 24, 1952; h/3379 Route 46, Parsippany, NJ 07054; ba/Fairfield, NJ; m/Cornelia E; p/Andrew E and Anneliese Bujtas; ed/BSME, Newark Col of Engrg, NJ Inst of Technol; pa/Asst Engr, US Machine Co, Cedar Grove, NJ, 1974; Proj Engr 1975, Chief Engr 1977, Fluorocarbon Co, Pine Brook, NJ; VPres, Bermag Corp Intl, Fairfield, NJ, 1983; Assoc Mem, AMSE, 1979; Mem, Soc of Mfg Engrs, 1980; Structural Bearing Com, Am Concrete Inst, 1982;

Engr-in-tng, NJ Cert, 1984; Cert'd Mfg Engr, 1982; W/W in Frontier Sci & Technol.

BULL, COLIN BRUCE B oc/Educator; b/Jun 13, 1928; h/4187 Olentangy Boulevard, Columbus, OH 43214; ba/ Columbus, OH; m/Diana Gillian Garrett; c/Nicholas, Rebecca, Andrew; p/ George Ernest and Alice Matilda (Collier) Bull (dec); sp/W Basil and Doris E Garrett (dec); ed/BSc 1948, PhD 1951, Birmingham Univ (Eng); mil/Sci Wk of Nat Importance; pa/Geophysicist, Chief Sci, Brit N Greenland Expdn, 1952-56; Sr Lectr Physics, Victoria Univ, Wellington, New Zealand, 1956-61; Assoc Prof Geol 1962-65, Prof & Dir Inst Polar Studies 1965-69, Chm Dept Geol 1969-72, Dean 1972-, OH St Univ; Vis'g Fellow Geophysics, Australian Nat Univ, Canberra, 1960; Vis'g Scholar, Cambridge Univ (Eng), 1969; Vis'g Prof, Nat Inst Polar Res, Tokyo, Japan, 1983; US Rep Wkg Grp on Glaciology 1974-, Secy 1978-, Sci Com Antarctic Res; Bd of Govs 1966-72, Fellow, Arctic Inst N Am; Coun Mem 1974-78, Intl Glaciological Soc; Mem, Am Geophys Union; Fellow, Geol Soc Am; Royal Soc Arts; hon/Author of Num Articles Pub'd in Profl Jours incl'g: *Geophysics*; *Glaciology*; Others; Recip, Polar Medal, Queen Elizabeth, 1954; US Antarctic Ser Medal, 1974; Phi Beta Kappa; W/W: in Am, in Frontier Sci & Technol.

BULLARD, JOHN WESLEY JR oc/ Production Superintendent; b/Jun 12, 1928; h/519 Helen St, Lake Charles, LA 70601; ba/Lake Charles, LA; m/Sula Jones; c/Christine, Steven, Kenneth; p/ John W Sr and Earlah Edge Bullard (dec); sp/Olney and Sula Gault Jones (dec); ed/ Att'd Univ of SWn LA; mil/USN, 1945-49; pa/Surveyor & Landman, Precision Exploration, 1952-54; Offshore Pumper, Pure Oil Co, 1954-60; Prodn Suppt, Conoco Inc, 1960-; Mem: Am Petro Inst; LA Archaeol Soc; Acad Model Aeronauts; cp/Bd of Govs, SW LA Campground Assn, 1977-80; Am Radio Relay Leag; 32nd Deg Mason & K Templar; SW LA 2-Meter Clb; r/ Meth; hon/KY Col, 1982; W/W in SW.

BULLAS, LEONARD R oc/Professor; b/Dec 8, 1929; h/10781 Shedden Drive, Loma Linda, CA 92354; ba/Loma Linda, CA; m/Rosemary G; c/Roslyn, Graham; p/Raymond Bullas, Adelaide, Australia; Arum Bullas (dec); sp/Roy Ekdahl, New Plymouth, New Zealand; Emma Ekdahl (dec); pa/Instr Microbiol, Univ of Adelaide, 1953-58; Res Asst, MT St Univ, 1959-62; Asst Prof 1962-70, Assoc Prof 1970-80, Prof Micriobiol 1980-, Loma Linda Univ; Vis'g Prof, Univ of Louvain, Belgium, 1973; Vis'g Prof, European Molecular Biol Lab, Heidelberg, Germany, 1982; Mem: Sigma Xi; Am Soc for Microbiol; Genetics Soc of Am; r/ 7th-day Adventist; hon/Author of Num Articles Pub'd in Profl Jours incl'g: *Jour Bacteriology*; *Jour of Virology*; *Molecular & Gen Genetics*; Others; Basic Sci Investigator of Yr, Sch of Med, Loma Linda Alumni Assn, 1975 & 1981; Basic Sci Fellow, 1981; Var W/W & Other Biogl Listings.

BUNNER, ALAN NEWTON oc/ Astrophysicist, Manager; b/Jan 11, 1938; ba/Danbury, CT; m/Barbara Lin Ames; c/Andrew Ames, Anne Elizabeth; p/William John Kelvin Bunner (dec); Freda Helen Newton Bunner, Owen

Sound, Ontario, Canada; ed/BA, Univ of Toronto, 1960; MS 1966, PhD 1967, Cornell Univ; pa/Instr & Res Assoc, Cornell Univ, 1966-67; Assoc Sci, Dept of Physics, Univ of WI, 1967-79; Sr Staff Sci, Mgr Future Astronomy Progs, Perkin-Elmer, 1979-; Mem: Tech Com on Space Scis, AIAA; Am Astronom Soc; Comm on Astronomy from Space, Intl Astronom Union; Others; hon/Author, Over 50 Pubs on Astrophysics & Space Astronomy; Skylab Achmt Awd, NASA, 1974; Co-Chm, Brookhaven Conf on Soft X-ray Optics, 1981; W/ W in Frontier Sci & Technol.

BUNTÉ, DORIS oc/State Representative; b/Jul 2, 1933; h/161 Townsend Street, Dorchester, MA 02121; ba/ Boston, MA; c/Yvette, Harold, Allen; ed/EdM, Harvard Univ, 1982; Doct Cand, Univ of MA-Amherst, Currently; pa/Commr, Boston Housing Auth, 1969-75; St Rep, MA Ho of Reps, 1973-; Mem: MA Legis Black Caucus; MA Caucus Wom Legis; Black Polit Task Force; Dem Nat Convs Del, 1972, 1976 & 1980; Elector, Electoral Col, Pres Election, 1976; Nat Order Wom Legis; cp/Exec Bd, NAACP; Roxbury Multi-ser Ctr; r/Cath; hon/Author of "Child Advocacy: A Dependency Cycle is not the Goal," Dept of Hlth, Ed & Welfare, 1977; "Address to City Missionary," 1973; SCFNHC, Commun Ser Awd, 1983; Roger Baldwin Awd, MA CLU Foun, 1983; Cert of Apprec, MA Citizens Agnst Death Penalty, 1983; Annual Commun Awd, Action for Boston Commun Devel, 1983; Cert of Apprec, Roxbury 1st Inc, 1983; MA Leag Commun Hlth Ctrs Awd, 1981; MA Skycap Assn Cert, 1981; NASW Awd, 1980; 3rd Nail Awd, 1980; Notary Public, Commonwlth of MA, 1976; Var Biogl Listings.

BUNZA, LINDA HATHAWAY oc/ Writer, Editor, Composer; b/Feb 23, 1946; h/14002 N 48th Way, Scottsdale, AZ 85254 & RD #2 Box 409, Brown Road, Harvard, MA 01451; ba/Same; m/ Geoffrey J; c/Stephen Christopher, Matthew Peter; p/John H Fisher, Hartford, CT; Mrs Richard C Hathaway, Wethersfield, CT; sp/Mr and Mrs H Bunza, Bklyn, NY; ed/AB, Bates Col, 1968; MA, Hartford Sem Foun, 1971; PhD Cand, Syracuse Univ, Currently; pa/Dir Brockway Lib & Coor of Residence Hall Libs, Syracuse Univ, 1971-74; Editor, *Harvard Ednl Review,* Cambridge, MA, 1974-75; Writer, Editor, Soc for the Arts, Rel & Contemp Culture, NY, 1974-78; Mng Editor, *The Andover Rev,* Philips Acad, Andover MA, 1976-80; Free Lance Writer & Editor, Conslt in Humanities, Lectr, 1980-; Mem: Nat Soc of Lit & Arts; Col Art Assn; MLA; Soc for Arts, Rel, Contemp Culture Inc; Am Acad Rel; Bd of Advrs, Intl Ctr for Rel & Human Experience; Bd of Consltg Eds & Assoc Editor, *Anima Mag,* Nat Wildlife Fdn; hon/Author of *Nikos Kazantzakis: Journey of a Dialectical Imagination; Theories of Modern Art I, II, III;* Editor-in-Chief, *Rennaissance Mag,* 1963-64; Contbr, Articles in Humanities to Num Profl Jours & Newspapers; Gold Quill Lit Awd, 1963; Nat Hon Soc, 1964; DIB; W/W: of Wom, of Intells; Other Biogl Listings.

BURBANK, HOWARD DONALD oc/Clergyman; b/Dec 20, 1918; h/19980 Lomo Ranchos Road, Volcano, CA 95689; ba/Washington, DC; m/Helen Greavu; c/MaryAnn Carol Burbank Roberts, Donna Jean Burbank Lindsay; p/Bester Pierce and Carrie Ella Woodward Burbank (dec); sp/Cornell Greavu and Mary Dobre (dec); ed/Adelphian Acad; Lansing (MI) Bus Col; LaSalle Ext Univ; pa/Pastor of Chs: Howell & Grand Rapids, MI, 1939-46; Dir Pubs Dept, MI Conf 7th-day Adventists, Lansing, MI, 1946-48; Gtr NY Conf, NYC, 1949-53; Pastor, 7th-day Adventists Tabernacle, Battle Creek, MI, 1953; Dir Laymen's Activs & Disaster Relief, MI Conf, 1954-61; SEC, TX Conf Corp, Ft Worth, 1961-65; SEC SWn Union Conf Corp, Dallas, 1965-70; Dir Pubs, 7th-day Adventists Chs in Europe & N Africa, 1970-73; Exec Dir, 7th-day Adventist World Ser, Wash, DC, 1974-80; Exec Com, Gen Conf 7th-day Adventists; Bd of Dirs, CARE, Ch World Ser; Am Coun Vol Agys for Fgn Ser; Interch Med Asst Corp; Rep Adv Com US Aid; White House Comm on Refugees; cp/Lions Clb; r/7th-day Adventist; hon/Author of Num Articles & Prodr of Films on World Disaster & Vol Relief; W/W: in Am, in World.

BURCHELL, CHARLES R oc/Psychologist, Journalist; b/Nov 24, 1946; ba/2346 Laurel Street, New Orleans, LA 70130; c/Kimberly Yvonne; p/Mr and Mrs Charles B Burchell, Baton Rouge, LA; ed/BA, So Univ, 1968; MA 1971, PhD 1980, LA St Univ (LSU); pa/Team Ldr, Adolescent Ser Ctr, Orleans Parish Sch Bd, 1981-; Dir, Comprehensive Cnslg Ctr, So Univ, 1977-78; Mng Editor/Anchor Reporter, WJBO Radio, 1978-81; Reporter/Anchor, WXOK Radio, 1978; Anchor Reporter/Prodr, WRBT-TV, 1971-79; Mem: Am Psychol Assn; LA Psychol Assn; SEn Psychol Assn; Pres-Elect NO Chapt, Assn of Black Psychols, 1982; Past Pres, Nat Assn of Black Jours, 1981; Baton Rouge Press Clb; r/Cath; hon/Author of Num Articles & Reports; W/W in Black Am.

BURDETTE, WALTER JAMES oc/ Surgeon; b/Feb 5, 1915; h/239 Chimney Rock Road, Houston, TX 77024; ba/ Houston, TX; c/Susan, William J; p/ James Sidney and Ovazene Weatherred Burdette (dec); ed/AB, Baylor Univ, 1935; AM 1936, PhD 1938, Univ of TX; MD, Yale Univ, 1942; Intern, Johns Hopkins Univ, 1942-43; Residency, New Haven Hosp, 1943-46; pa/Asst Anatomy Yale Univ, 1938-42; Instr Surg 1946-49, Asst Prof 1949-53, Assoc Prof 1953-55, LA St Univ; Prof & Chm Dept Surg, Univ of MO, 1955-56; Prof Clin Surg, St Louis Univ, 1956-57; Prof & Hd Dept Surg, Univ of UT, 1957-65; Prof Surg & Assoc Dir Res, Univ of TX-Houston M D Anderson Hosp & Tumor Inst, 1965-72; Prof Surg, Univ of TX Med Sch-Houston, 1971-79; Adj Prof, Col of Pharm, Univ of Houston, 1978-; NO: Vis'g Surg Charity Hosp, Conslt Touro Infirm, Vis'g Surg So Bapt Hosp; Oak Ridge: Conslt Inst of Nuclear Studies Hosp; Columbia: Surg-in-Chief Univ Hosps; St Louis: Chief of Surg VA Hosp, St Louis Univ Surg Ser; SLC: Surg-in-Chief Gen Hosp; Chief Surg Conslt VA Hosp; Houston: Chief Sect of Exptl Oncology M D Anderson Hosp, Conslt Hermann Hosp, Conslt Pavilion Hosp, Conslt St Luke's Hosp, Conslt TX Chdn's Hosp; Staff Mem St Joseph's Hosp, Staff Mem Pk Plaza Hosp; Pres, Genetics Soc of UT; VPres, Bd of Dirs, Am Assn for Cancer Res; Treas, Soc of Clin Surg; Res Adv Coun, Am Cancer Soc; Genetics Study Sect, NIH; USA Nat Com, Intl Union Agnst Cancer; Com on Carcinogenesis, Nat Adv Cancer Coun; Task Force on Carcinoma of Large Intestine, Nat Cancer Inst; Num Others; cp/Surg Gen's Com on Smoking & Hlth; Transplantation Com, Nat Acad of Sci; Edit Bd, *Cancer Res;* Guest Editor, *Surg Rounds;* Exec Com, Yale Alumni in Med; Sigma Xi; Beta Beta Beta; Alpha Epsilon Delta; Alpha Omega Alpha, Nu Sigma Nu; Num Lectrs at Intl & Nat Insts, Med Schs & Univs; Num Others; r/Christian; hon/Editor of 7 Books incl'g: *Viruses Inducing Cancer;* Author of 3 Books incl'g: *Invertebrate Endocrinology & Hormonal Heterophylly;* Co-Author, "Report of Adv Com to Surg Gen of Public Hlth Ser on Smoking & Hlth"; Over 200 Articles & Papers in Sci & Med Jours; Gibson Lectr in Adv'd Surg, Oxford Univ; AEA Dist'd Alumnus of Yr, Baylor Univ, 1983; Rockefeller Travel F'ship, Soviet Union, Czechoslovakia, Poland, 1958; Num Others; W/ W: in World, in Am, in Frontier Sci & Technol, in S & SW; Am Men of Sci.

BURDICK, GLENN ARTHUR oc/ University Dean; b/Sep 9, 1932; h/1005 Curlew Place, Tarpon Springs, FL 33589; ba/Tampa, FL; m/Joyce M Huggett; c/Stephen Arthur, Randy Glenn; p/M E Boyce, Meridian, ID; sp/E M Trainer, Tarpon Springs, FL; ed/BS 1958, MS 1959, GA Tech Inst; PhD, MA Inst of Technol, 1961; mil/USAF; pa/ Dean Col of Engrg 1979-, Prof 1968-, Accident Reconstrn 1965-, Assoc Prof 1965-68, Univ of S FL; Sr Mem Res Staff, Sperry Microwave, 1961-65; Res Physicist, MIT, 1961; Instr, GA Tech Inst, 1956-59; Sr Mem, IEEE; Pres 1974, ISHM-Internat; Mem: AAAS; AREA; AAR; NY Acad of Sci; Sigma Xi; Phi Kappa Phi; Sigma Pi Sigma; Tau Beta Pi; Omicron Delta Kappa; cp/Tampa Bay Fgn Affairs Com; Rotary Intl; Pres, Clearwater Tennis Clb, 1967 & 1970; Var HS Lectrs, 1961-; Conslt to Local Attys, 1964-; r/Prot; hon/Author, 20 Res Papers, Articles & Presentations Pub'd in Profl Jours & Org Reports; Engr of Yr, FL Chapt IEEE, 1981; IEEE Engr of Yr-FL, 1980; USF Fac Hon Guard; NSF Fellow, 1958-61; Woodrow Wilson Scholar; W/W: in Frontier Sci & Technol, in Engrg, in Technol Today; Outstg Floridians.

BURFORD, MARY ANNE oc/Medical Technologist, Lab Manager; b/Aug 24, 1939; h/1509 West Buckingham Drive, Muncie, IN 47302; ba/Muncie, IN; c/Sarah Elizabeth, Shawn Anthony, Joseph Paul Jr, Daniel Aaron; p/Mr and Mrs A J Elsken, Ft Smith, AR; ed/BS Biol, Benedictine Col, 1961; Med Technol, St Mary's Hosp, 1962; Med Tech (ASCP), Am Soc Clin Pathols, 1962; pa/ Evening Supvr Clin Labs & Blood Bk, St Vincent's Infirm, Little Rock, AR, 1962-65; Med Tech, Holt-Krock Clin, Ft Smith, AR, 1966-68; Clin Chem, Ball Meml Hosp, Muncie, IN, 1971-72; Supvr, Pathol Assoc, Muncie, IN, 1972-73; Chief Tech, OB-GYN Inc, Muncie, IN, 1975-; Assoc Mem, Soc of Clin Pathols, 1972-; Am Assoc of Clin Chems, 1980-; Am Soc for Microbiol, 1981-; Altrusa Clb of Muncie, 1982-; cp/ Chm Liturgical Life, 1979-; Lector,

113

1977-; Eucharistic Min, 4 Yrs; r/Cath; hon/Author of Articles in Profl Jours incl'g: *Lab Med; Diagnostic Med;* A-1 Cont'g Ed Awd, 1981-84; W/W of Am Wom.

BURGEI, THOMAS JOHN oc/Educator; b/Dec 26, 1947; h/2439 Dolphin Drive, San Jose, CA 95124; ba/San Jose, CA; m/Nancy Noble; c/Sara Elizabeth, Rachel Alyssa; p/John and Mildred Burgei, Rome City, IN; sp/Carl and Geraldine Noble, Greenwood, IN; ed/ Att'd St Joseph's Col (IN), 1966-67; BA, IN Univ, 1970; MA Elem Ed 1976, MA Adm Sers 1980, San Jose St Univ; pa/ Spch Therapist 1970-79, Sum Sch Prin 1973-76, Asst Sum Sch Admr 1977, Sum Sch Admr 1978, Resource Tchr 1979-80, Elem Prin 1980-83, Intermediate Sch Prin 1983-, Oak Grove Sch Dist; Mem: Buddy Prog, 1970-71; Oak Grove Tchrs Assn, 1970-80; CA Tchrs Assn, 1972-80; NEA, 1972-80; Am Spch/Hearing Assn, 1970-83; VPres 1983, Pres 1984, Mem 1980-, Oak Grove Mgmt Assn; Assn CA Sch Admrs, 1980-84; Assn Supvn & Curric Devel, 1981-84; Kettering Foun's IDEA Prog, 1982-84; r/Cath; hon/Author, "Normative Study of Sentence Memory Subtest of Detroit Test of Lrng Aptitude for 11, 12, 13 Yr Olds in Oak Grove Sch Dist"; Grad w Hons, 1970 & 1976; W/W in W; Outstg Yg Men of Am.

BURGER, CHRISTIAN PIETER oc/ Professor; b/Dec 29, 1929; h/1724 Meadowlane Avenue, Ames, IA 50010; ba/Ames, IA; m/Marie Mundy; c/Marie Elise, Christian David, Robert Johann; ed/BSc Mech Engrg, Univ of Stellenbosch, S Africa, 1952; PhD Mech Engrg, Univ of Capetown, S Africa, 1967; pa/ Engr, Mobil Oil Co, S Africa, 1955-62; Sr Lectr, Univ of Capetown, 1962-71; Prof Dept Engrg Sci & Mechs, IA St Univ, 1971-; Chm Paper's Review Com 1979-82, Exec Com 1982-, Soc for Exptl Stress Anal; Editor, *Jour Exptl Mechs,* 1979-82; r/Epis; hon/Author of Num Review & Tech Articles in Profl Jours & Symp Volumes; R E Peterson Awd, Soc for Exptl Stress Anal, 1973 & 1976.

BURGESS, ANNIE PEARL oc/Cytotechnologist; b/Oct 10, 1945; h/Route 2, Box 35, Belden, MS 38826; ba/Tupelo, MS; c/Terree Terrinda, Kimetta Arlinda, Leander Marcellus; p/Jerome Ratliff (dec); Bernice Ratliff, Belden, MS; ed/Att'd Malcolm X Jr Col, 1972-73; Att'd Roosevelt Univ, 1973-75; Att'd Univ Hlth Sci Chgo Med Sch, 1975; AA, Kennedy-King Jr Col, 1975; Cert, Mt Sinai Sch of Cytotechnol, 1975; Cand, Univ of MS, 1981-; CT (ASCP), 1975; CT (IAC), 1980; C1Sp (CT), 1980; pa/ Catalog Writer, Sears Roebuck & Co, 1972; Ser Reg, IL Bell Tel Co, 1973-74; Cytotechnol, Mason-Barron Labs, 1975-76; Cytotechnol, N MS Med Ctr, 1976-; Mem: Fdg Ofcr/Secy-Treas 1980-81, Secy-Treas 1981-82, Pres-elect 1982-83, Pres 1983-84, MS Soc of Cytopathol; Mem 1977-, Treas 1981-82, Nom'g Com Chm 1982-83, Pres-elect 1983-84, Pres 1985, Sci Assem Chp of Cytolgoy 1980-85, MS St Soc for Med Technol; Am Soc for Med Technol, 1977-; Am Soc of Cytology, 1976-; Am Soc of Cytotechnol, 1979-; IL Soc of Cytology, 1975-; Am Acad of Cytology, 1983-; Am Soc Clin Pathols (ASCP), 1976-; cp/Pres Adults Grp 1982, VPres Yg Adults Grp

1981-82, Mem 1976-, Lane Chapel CME Ch; r/Meth; hon/Author of Var Res Symp Presentation Papers for: Am Soc for Med Technols & MS Soc Med Technols; Cert of Apprec & Recog of Contbn to Soc, MS Soc for Med Technol, 1981 & 1982; W/W: of Am Wom, in the World.

BURGIO, JANE oc/Secretary of State for New Jersey; ba/Department of State, State House, CN-300, Trenton, NJ 08625; m/John P Burgio; c/John E, James Burgio; ed/Att'd Rutgers the St Univ; Att'd Newark Sch of Fine & Industl Design; pa/Arts, Decorating & Design Positions; St Assem-wom, NJ St Assem, 1973-81; Secy of St, St of NJ, 1982-; Mem: Nat Assn of Secys of St; Nat Conf of St Legis; cp/Trustee, for Support of Free Public Schs; BPW Clb; Hackensack Meadowlands Cultural Study Comm; Trustee, St Barnabas Hosp Devel Com, Trustee, Planned Parenthood of Essex Co; Trustee, Caldwell Col; Trustee, Rider Col; Num Other Local Civic, Ednl & Cultural Activs; hon/Alumni Recog Awd, Univ Col, Rutgers; Hist Awd, NJ Leag of Hist Socs; Cert, NJ Humane Soc; Num Other Awds & Certs from Bus, Polit, Art & Civic Orgs.

BURGOYNE, MARIANNE HARDING oc/Teaching Fellow; b/Jun 22, 1948; h/1637 Damon Way, Salt Lake City, UT 84117; ba/Salt Lake City, UT; m/Robert H; p/Edward Bailey Harding (dec); Lurean Stevens Harding, Craig, CO; sp/Sidney E and Beatrice Holmes Burgoyne (dec); pa/Model, Pvt Modeling & Dancing Instr, SLC, 1969; Stewardess Tng, U Airlines, Chgo, IL, 1972; Tchr, Bryant Intermediate Sch, SLC, 1972-78; Eng & Debate Tchr, E Sr HS, SLC, 1978-79; Tchg Asst 1979-81, Tchg Fellow 1981-, Eng, Univ of UT; Mem: UT Ed Assn 1972-79; NEA, 1972-79; Chp Eng Dept, Bryant Intermediate Sch, SLC, UT; cp/Mem: UT Opera Guild; Dem Party; hon/Author of Poem Pub'd in *Am Poetry Anthol,* 1982; Pi Delta Phi; Life Mbrship, Societe d'Honneur Francaise; Rep to Dept Meetings & to Col of Humanities Coun 1980-81; Clarice Short Tchg Awd, 1981-82; Tchg Cnslr, 1982-83; W/W of Am Wom.

BURGOYNE, ROBERT H oc/Psychiatrist, Department Chairman; b/Nov 22, 1920; h/1637 Damon Way, Salt Lake City, UT 84117; ba/Salt Lake City, UT; m/Marianne Harding; c/Diane Burgoyne Pond, Robert H II, John D, Elizabeth; p/Sidney E and Beatrice Holmes Burgoyne (dec); sp/Edward B Harding (dec); Lurean Stevens Harding, Craig, CO; ed/BS Physics, UT St Univ, 1942; MD, Cornell Univ Med Col, 1950; Psychi Residency, Univ of So CA, 1962; pa/Staff Mem Radar Res, MIT, 1942-45; Chem & Math HS Tchr, 1945-46; Gen Med Pract, ID, 1952-59; Gen Pract Psychi, 1962-; Chm & Dir Dept of Psychi, LDS Hosp, 1964-; Clin Assoc Prof Psychi, Univ of UT, Presently; Mem: AMA; UT St Med Assn; SL Co Med Soc; Am Psychi Assn; Secy 1972-73, Pres-elect 1973-74, Pres 1974-75, UT Psychi Assn; ASCAP; hon/ Author, Book Chapt in *Primarily for Parents;* Song Lyric "Encircle the Child"; Var Articles in Jours & Mags incl'g: *Jour of Operational Psychi; Dialogue;* the LDS *Instr;* Others; HS Valedictorian, 1938;

Phi Kappa Phi, 1942; Bausch & Lomb Sci Awd, 1938.

BURISH, THOMAS G oc/Professor; b/May 4, 1950; h/625 Brook Hollow Road, Nashville, TN 37205; ba/Nashville, TN; m/Pamela Jean; c/Mark Joseph, Brent Christopher; p/Bernard and Donna Burish, Peshtigo, WI; ed/AB Psychol, Univ cf Notre Dame, 1972; MA Psych 1975, PhD Clin Psych 1976, Univ of KA; pa/Asst through Assoc Prof 1976-, Dept Chm 1984-, Vanderbilt Univ; Mem Div 12, Mem & Co-Chm Div 38 Res Com 1981-84; Asst Coor Adv'd Wkshop Prog 1974, Spec Asst Ed & Tng Bd 1975, Mem 1978-, Chm 1979-, Com on Prog Innovation, w Am Psychol Assn; Biofeedback Soc of Am; Biofeedback Soc of TN; cp/Pres, St Ann's Sch Bd; r/Rom Cath; hon/Author & Co-Author, Over 40 Articles Pub'd in Book Chapts & Profl Jours incl'g: *Am Jour Clin Biofeedback; Jour Consltg & Clin Psych; Annals of Internal Med; Jour Social Psych; Clin Neuropsych;* Others; NSF Undergrad Res Participation F'ship, 1971; Phi Beta Kappa, 1972; Grad summa cum laude, Univ of Nortre Dame, 1972; NIMH F'ship in Clin Psych, 1972-76; David Shulman Meml Awd for Excell in Clin Psych, Univ of KS, 1975; Sum Res F'ship 1978, Madison Sarratt Awd for Excell in Undergrad Tchg 1980, Vanderbilt Univ; W/W: in S & SW, in Frontier Sci & Technol, in Biobehavioral Scis; Am Men & Wom of Sci.

BURKE, JAMES H oc/Financial Planner; b/Nov 28, 1926; h/1157 Candlelight Way, Cupertino, CA 95014; ba/ Los Gatos, CA; m/Frankie C; c/Catherine L (Burke) Braga, Jason C; ed/Att'd Univ of CA; JD, Hastings Col of The Law, 1955; CFP, Col for Fin Planning, 1983; mil/AUS Airborne, 1945-46; pa/ Gen Pract of Law, Sacramento, CA, 1955-69; Gen Pract of Law, San Jose, CA 1970-79; Gen Financial Planning (Taxation), Los Gatos, CA, 1979-; Mem: CA Bar Assn, 1955-; ABA, 1955-; Hastings Thurston Hon Soc, 1955-; Intl Assn of Financial Planners, 1981-; cp/ Elks Lodge, 1959-; Toastmasters #31, 1982-; Num Spkg Presentations on Tax Matters; Others; hon/Var Profl Pubs.

BURKHARDT, MARY ELIZABETH oc/Executive; b/Feb 21, 1945; h/715 Ascot Court, Hoffman Estates, IL 60194; ba/Schaumburg, IL; p/Betty Hiza, Pampano Bch, FL; ed/BA, Math/ Ed; MS, Math Stats; MBA, Mktg; pa/ Fin Anal, Mkt Res Anal, Lipton Co, 1969-73; USA-Mkt Res Mgr, Coca-Cola Co, 1973-75; New Prods Mgr, Frito-Lay Inc, 1975-77; Residential Mkt Planning, GTE Ser, 1978-82; New Technol, Citicorp, 1983-; Local Pres, Am Mgmt Assn; Local Pres & Nat Dir, Am Mktg Assn; Nat Secy, Mkt Res Assn.

BURKHART, CRAIG GARRETT oc/ Dermatologist; b/Apr 15, 1951; h/2241 Orchard Road, Toledo, OH 43606; ba/ Toledo, OH; m/Anna Kristiina; c/ Kristiina Maria, Craig Nathaniel, Heidi Rebecca; p/Garrett Giles and Mary Kathleen Burkhart, Toledo, OH; ed/BA, Univ of PA, 1972; MD, Med Col of OH, 1975; Intern 1976, Residency & Fellow in Dermatol 1976-79, Univ of MI Hosps; MSc Ed, Univ of Toledo, 1983; pa/Hd Dermatol, Med Col of OH, 1979-; Med Pract (Dermatol), 1982-; Editor-in-Chief, *Jour of Dermatol,* 1980-; Edit Bd, *Jour of Current Adolescent Med,* 1980-; Edit

Adv Bd, OH St Med Jour, 1982-; Mem: AMA; OH St Med Assn; Sci Invest & Res Com, MI Dermatologic Assn; Am Acad of Dermatol; Mbrship & Ser Comm, Toledo Acad of Med; Dermatol Foun; Soc of Investigative Dermatol; Trustee on Bd of Dirs, U Chapts & Toledo Area Chapt, Phi Beta Kappa Grad Assn; Trustee on Bd of Dirs, Med Col of OH; Industl Hygiene Masters Prog Adv Com, Univ of Toledo; Gt Lakes Med Review; cp/Toledo Zoo; Toledo Mus; Toledo Symph; r/U Meth; hon/Author of Num Articles in Profl Jours; Conslt to Var Jours; Phi Beta Kappa; W/W: in Am, in World.

BURKHOLDER, JAMES ALFRED JR oc/Plans Chief; b/Jun 23, 1944; h/5620 Old Farm Terrace, Colorado Springs, CO 80917; ba/Osan AFB, Korea; c/ James A III; p/James Burkholder Sr, Bonners Ferry, ID; ed/BS Eng & Spch, Univ of ID, 1967; MPA Public Adm, Boise St Univ, 1977; USAF Air Command & Staff Col, 1980; mil/USAF, 1967-; pa/Pilot Tng, Vance AFB, OK, 1968; 225 Missions in F-4 Aircraft, Vietnam, 1969; Sqdrn Pilot & Scheduler, Holloman, AFB, NM, 1970-71; Chief Standardization Eval Div, Shaw AFB, SC, 1972-74; Wing Chief Wing Tng Div, RAF, Lakenheath, England, 1977-79; Air Ofcr Cmdg Cadet Sqdrn 14 1980-82, Chief Mil Tng Div 1982-84, USAF Acad; Chief, Contingency Plans, Air Component Command, Osan AFB, Korea, 1984-85; Mem: Am Legion, 16 Yrs; Life Mem, AF Assn; Am Soc for Tng & Devel; Theta Chi; Orders & Medals Soc; Am Soc of Mil Insignia Collectors; r/Meth; hon/Author, Var Articles in Books & Profl Jours incl'g: *Concepts of AF Ldrship*; *Air Univ Review*; *Jour of Profl Mil Ethics*; *Airman Mag*; Dist'd Flying Cross, 1969; 13 Air Medals, 1969; 3 Meritorious Ser Medals, 1984, 1979 & 1974; AF Commend Medal, 1977; George Wash Hon Medal, Freedoms Foun, 1975; Master Pilot Rating; Sr Parachutist Rating; W/W in W.

BURLAGA, LEONARD FRANCIS oc/Astrophysicist; b/Oct 1, 1938; h/1328 Dickey Drive, Gambrills, MD 20715; ba/ Greenbelt, MD; m/Catherine Mary; c/ Anna Marie, David Ryan; p/Edward and Helen Burlaga, Superior, WI; ed/BS, Univ of Chgo, 1960; MS 1962, PhD 1966, Univ of MN; pa/Tchng Asst to Res Assoc, Univ of MN, 1960-66; Astrophysicist, Goddard Space Flight Ctr, NASA, 1966-; Mem: Am Geophy Soc; Am Phy Soc; Intl Astronom Union; Chm Solar Wind & Interplanetary Magnetic Field Div, Intl Assn of Geomagnetism & Aeronomy, 1979-83; r/ Cath; hon/Author, Over 80 Res Papers Pub'd in Profl Jours; Exceptl Sci Achmt Medal, NASA, 1979.

BURMAN, CEARA SUE (WITH-ROW) oc/Owner, Administrator; b/Apr 23, 1941; h/2346 Cedarwood, Maumee, OH 43537; ba/Toledo, OH; p/Woodrow W and Garnet Wagner Withrow, Arcadia, OH; ed/BA, Heidelberg Col, 1963; Bowling Green St Univ, 1964; Grad Studies: Univ of Dayton 1966, Univ of UT 1967, Univ of Toledo 1980; MA, Univ of Toledo, 1969; pa/Owner, Admr, Intl Lang Sers (Translation/Interpretation), 1982-; Tchr, Old Ft Local Schs, 1962-63; Chm Fgn Lang Dept, Pt Clinton City Schs, 1963-68; Spanish Tchr, Maumee City Schs, 1969-76;

Coor, ESL, Penta Co JVS, 1977-78; Bilingual Conslt, 1979-; Instr, Owens Tech Col, 1981; Dir, Intl Info Specs, 1981; Mem: Netwk Dir 1979-, Nat Assn Female Execs, 1977-; Charter Mem, Pres 1985, The Exec Netwk; The Am Translators Assn, 1981-; AATSP, 1966-77; ACTFL, 1977-79; Num Ednl & Other Orgs; cp/Toledo Area C of C; Toledo Area Intl Trade Assn; BD Mem, 1st Call for Help; Host, Area Rep 1969-75, Yth for Understanding; W/W: in MW, of Am Wom; 2000 Notable Ams.

BURMEISTER, JOHN LUTHER oc/ Professor, Consultant; b/Feb 20, 1938; h/1 Carriage Lane, Newark, DE 19711; ba/Newark, DE; m/Doris Aileen Crawford; c/Lisa Anne, Jeffrey Scott; p/ Luther John and Frieda May (Tielmann) Burmeister (dec); s/Kenneth Milton and Doris (Pease) Crawford, Tyrone, PA; ed/BS Chem, Franklin and Marshall Col, 1959; PhD Chem, NWn Univ, 1964; pa/ Lab Asst, Bakelite Co, Bloomfield, NJ, 1956 & 1957; Res Chem, Union Carbide Plastics Co, Bound Brook, NJ, 1959 & 1960; Tchg Asst 1959-60, AEC Res Fellow 1960-63, NWn Univ, Evanston, IL; Instr Inorganic Chem, Univ of IL-Urbana, 1963-64; Asst Prof 1964-69, Assoc Prof 1969-73, Prof 1973-, Assoc Chm 1974-, Univ of DE, Newark, DE; Num Com Positions w Am Chem Soc & DE Sect of Am Chem Soc; Royal Soc of Chem; Intercol Student Chem; Edit Bd, *Inorganica Chimica Acta*, 1967-; Edit Bd, *Synthesis & Reactiv in Inorganic & Metalorganic Chem*, 1970-; Conslt, Num Pvt Corps, Nat Panels & Sci Pubrs; Referee, Num Chem Jours; Others; cp/ Ruling Elder, Chm Christian Ed Com, Del to New Castle Presby Meetings, Hd Christiana Presb Ch, Newark, DE; Avon S'ship Com, 1975-76; Bd of Dirs 1977-79, Pres 1977-79, Covered Bridge Farms Maintenance Corp; r/Presb; hon/ Author & Co-Author, Over 90 Res Papers & Articles Pub'd in Profl Jours & Symp Reports incl'g: *Organometallics*; *Inorganic Chem*; *Synthesis Reactiv in Inorganic & Metalorganic Chem*; *Inorganica Chimica Acta*; Others; Phi Lambda Upsilon; Sigma Xi; Phi Kappa Phi; Omicron Delta Kappa; Union Carbide Corp Scholar 1955-59, AFROTC Acad Achmt Awd 1956, Franklin & Marshall Col; Gelewitz Awd, NWn Univ, 1963; Lindback Foun & DE Alumni Assn Excell in Tchn Awds 1968 & 1979, Fac Sum Res F'ships 1965 & 1970, Instrn Grant 1973, Univ of DE; Silver Anniv Catalyst Awd for Excell in Chem Tchg, Chem Mfrs Assn, 1981; Lectr, Mid Atl Reg, Sigma Xi, 1981-83; Vis'g Scholar in Residence, CA St Univ-Sacramento, 1983; White House Fellow Nom, 1969; W/W: in Am Men of Sci; Outstg Edrs of Am; Dict of Intl Biog; Num Other Biogl Listings.

BURNHAM, LEAH LUCILLE oc/ Medical Technologist; b/Jul 31, 1947; ba/ Tucson, AZ; m/Frederick R II; c/Russell Adam; p/Mr and Mrs Dresden G Taylor, St Thomas Village, AZ; sp/Roderick D Burnham (dec); H Gayle Cranney Burnham, Carmel, CA; ed/Att'd Luth Hosp Sch of Med Technol, 1968-69; BS, Millikin Univ, 1969; MS, Univ of VT, 1972; pa/Sr Tech, Clin Toxicology, Univ of AZ Hlth Sci Ctr, 1974-; Ed Coor, Sch of Med Technol, Tucson Med Ctr, Tucson, 1972-74; Grad Tchg Fellow, Univ of VT, 1970-72; Gen Technol,

Lake Forest Hosp, Lake Forest, IL, 1970; Blood Bk Technol, Luth Hosp, Cleveland, OH, 1969-70; Mem: Wkshop Com, Am Soc Clin Pathols (ASCP); Wkshop Com, Am Soc Med Technols (ASMT); hon/Author of Articles Pub'd in *Annals of Internal Med*; Theses Pub'd, 1972 & 1982; MT (ASCP), 1969; SC (ASCP), 1981; W/W of Am Wom.

BURNS, ANNE M oc/Teacher, Nursing Assistant; b/Apr 13, 1921; h/1 Sheila Lane, Smithfield, RI 02917; ba/Providence, RI; p/James B and Annie (Hagan) Burns; ed/MA, Univ of CT, 1965; PhB, Providence Col, 1964; pa/Tchr, Providence Sch Dept, Providence, RI, 1961-; Nsg Asst, RI Hosp, Providence, RI, 1972-; Mem: Providence Tchrs Union; Am Fdn of Tchrs; cp/RI Hist Soc; Cath Wom's Clb; r/Cath; hon/Article on Op-Ed Page of *NY Times*, 1980; Secy of RI Del, Dem Nat Conv, 1980; Chosen by BBC to Rep Kennedy Dels for Film about 1980 Dem Nat Conv; W/W of Am Wom.

BURNS, SANDRA KAYE oc/Attorney; b/Aug 9, 1949; h/12126 Forestwood Circle, Dallas, TX 75234; ba/ Dallas, TX; c/Scott; p/C W & Bert Burns; ed/BS, Univ of Houston, 1971; MA 1972, PhD 1975, Univ of TX-Austin; JD, St Mary's Univ Sch of Law, San Antonio, TX, 1978; pa/Contracted Oil & Gas Atty, to ARCO, Dallas, TX, 1985; Contracted Oil & Gas Atty, to Humble Exploration, Dallas, TX, 1984; House Counsel, 1st Intl Oil & Gas Inc, Dallas, 1983; Indep Atty, 1981-82; Contracted Oil & Gas Atty, to Repub Energy Inc, Bryan, TX, 1981 & 1982; Lectr, Dept of Mgmt & Dept of Ed, TX A&M Univ, 1981; Intl Legal Conslt, Colombotti & Assocs of London, Aberdeen, Scotland, 1980; Sen Com Clk-Counsel, Sen St Affairs Com, St of TX, Austin, 1978; Legis Aide, Wm T Moore, TX Sen, Austin, 1978; Instrnl Devel Asst, Ofc Ed Resource, Univ of TX Hlth Sci Ctr, San Antonio, 1976-77; Col Lectr, Our Lady of the Lake Col, San Antonio, 1975; Prof, Var Depts: Child Devel/Fam Life & Home Ec, Tchr Ed, Col of Nutrition, Textiles & Human Devel, TX Wom's Univ, Denton, 1974-75; Grant Supvr, Reg XIII Ed Ser Ctr, Austin, 1973-74; Num Others; Mem: ABA; Am Petro Inst; Delta Theta Phi; St Bar Assn of TX; r/Meth; hon/Dissertation, "The Relatship of Pupil Self-concept to Tchr-Pupil Dyadic Interaction in Kgn"; Kappa Delta Pi; Phi Delta Kappa; Phi Kappa Phi; Phi Lambda Theta; W/W: in Am Law, of Wom, of Intells; DIB; Intl Book of Hon; Dir Dist'd Ams; Commun Ldrs of Am; Num Other Biogl Listings.

BURNS-BLAGMON, DJUANA PHAE oc/Public Health Analyst; b/Oct 4, 1944; h/9801 Justina Court, Lanham, MD 20706; ba/Washington, DC; m/ Nieri; p/James Venice Burns (dec); Cleopatra Diamond Burns, Little Rock, AR; ed/Att'd Univ of AR-Little Rock, 1965; BSc Zool, Howard Univ, 1966; USDA Grad Sch, 1970; Addit Ed: ASCP, HI, Boston, Las Vegas, LA; Intl Soc Hematology, Paris & Montreal; mil/ USAR, Maj; pa/Clin Lab Sci Spec, Medicaid Prog, DC Dept of Public Hlth, 1978-81; Med Technol Supvr, 1969-77; Cardiopulmonary Res Technol, Hosp for Sick Chd, 1969; Res Technol, Wash Hosp Ctr, 1968-69; Histotechnol, Georgetown Univ Med Sch, 1966-68; Mem: Am Soc of Clin Pathols; AAUW; Am Inst Biol Scis; APHA; Recording Secy, DC Hlth Ctr Technols; cp/DC Dept of Rec Showmobile-Dancer, 1967-68; Charity Modeling Clb; Pitcher, DC Softball Team, 1975-79; r/Meth; hon/ Author of "Plant Cell Wall Deposition & Its Influence on Cytodifferentiation & Tissue Function," *Biosci Mag*, 1967; Sustained Excell in Job Perf, 1979-82; Cert of Recog for Outstg Ser in Christian Ed Wkshop, 1983; W/W of Am Wom.

BURRIS, LESLIE oc/Laboratory Director; b/Sep 1, 1922; h/206 Douglas Avenue, Naperville, ILL 60540; ba/ Argonne, ILL; m/Mary Elizabeth Bush; c/Susan Elizabeth Burris Madeira, James Leslie, Kathryn Lorraine Burris Turner; p/Nellie Varney Burris, Concordia, KS; sp/James Harlan and Helen Richardson Bush (dec); ed/Grad, Canon City HS, 1939; BSChE, Univ of CO-Boulder, 1943; MSChE, IL Inst of Technol, 1956; pa/Anal Chem, Monsanto Chem Co, Monsanto, IL, 1943-45; Nuclear Engr, Monsanto Chem Co, X-10 now Oak Ridge Nat Lab, Oak Ridge, TN, 1945-48; Nuclear Chem, Tracerlab Inc, Boston, MA, 1948; Nuclear & Alternative Devel, Dir Dir, Argonne Nat Lab, 1948-; Mem: AIChE, 30 Yrs; Am Nuclear Soc; Res Soc of Am; Chrm, Argonne Combined Appeal, 1982 & 1983; cp/Bd Mem, Bd Pres 6 Yrs, Elem Sch Dist #78, 1961-72; Chm Adv Com, Naperville Elect Dept, 1973-75; Twice Chm, U Way/Crusade of Mercy; r/Meth; hon/Author & Co-Author, Over 40 Pubs in Profl Jours, Reports & Books incl'g: *Atomic Energy Review*; *Nuclear Engrg Handbook*; Holder of 4 Patents in Field; Fellow, AiChE, 1979; W/W: in MW, in Frontier Sci & Technol.

BURRIS, MARTIN JOE oc/Professor; b/Mar 30, 1927; h/2503 Spring Creek Drive, Bozeman, MT 59715; ba/Bozeman, MT; m/Helen Ada Storey (dec); c/Emilie Jane Burris Dohleman, Lucy Ellen, Martin Joe Jr, Ruth Ada; p/ Sheridan A and Nellie H Burris (dec); sp/Walter L and Lucy F Storey (dec); ed/ BS Agri 1949, MS Animal Breeding 1951, Univ of NE; PhD Genetics, OR St Univ, 1953; mil/AUS, 1945-46; pa/ Asst Prof, Univ of AR-Fayetteville, 1953-54; Assoc Prof, VA Agri Expt Sta, Front Royal, 1954-57; Res Admr, Coop Sts Res Ser, USDA, Wash DC, 1957-66; Vis'g Prof, Purdue Univ, W Lafayette, IN, 1964-65; Assoc Dir MT Agri Expt St 1966-80, Prof A & R Sci 1980-, MT St Univ; Mem: Genetics Soc of Am; Am Soc of Animal Sci; cp/BPO Elks; r/Meth; hon/Author of Num Articles in Agri Sci Jours; USDA Com of 9; Am Men of Sci.

BURROUGHS, WALTER LAUGHLIN oc/Journalist, Editor; b/Aug 21, 1901; h/260 Cagney Lane, Apartment 313, Newport Beach, CA 92663; ba/ Costa Mesa, CA; m/1st, Hazel Georgia Sexsmith (dec); 2nd, Lucy Bell; c/Toni (Mrs Philip Schuyler Doane); p/William S and Bertha Laughlin Burroughs (dec); ed/BA, Univ of WA, 1924; Postgrad Study, Univ CA-Berkeley, 1925-28; mil/ AUS, 1942-45, Col; pa/Dir Pubs, Univ of CA-Berkeley, 1925-28; Gen Mgr, N Pacific Gravure Co, Seattle, 1928-30; Gen Mgr, Crocker Union Lithogrpah & Pub Co, LA, 1930-41; Co-Fdr, Bantam Books, LA, 1938; Indep Book Pubr, w

Merle Armitage, 1938-42; Pacific Coast Rep, H W Kaster & Sons Advtg Agy, LA, 1941-42; Exec VPres, Eldon Industs, LA, 1946-62; Corp Pres Pub 1948-65, Chm of Bd 1965-68, *Orange Coast Daily Pilot*, Newport Bch, Coasta Mesa & Huntington Bch, CA; Pres, Orion Mgmt Corp; Chm Bd of Dirs Emeritus, Chdn's Hosp Orange Co; Mem Exec Com, Trustee, Chd's Hosp Orange Co Foun; Trustee, Jefferson Trust; Wn World Med Foun, Irvine, CA; Nat Pres, Sigma Delta Chi; cp/Bohemian Clb (SF); Jonathan Clb (LA); Newport Harbor Yacht Club; Irvine Coast Country; Rotary; hon/Hon'd w Late E J Power for Role in Bringing Univ of CA to Irvine w Dedication of Fdrs Ct on Campus, 1978; Num Others; Num Biogl Listings.

BURRUS, CHARLES ANDREW (JR) oc/Research Physicist; b/Jul 16, 1927; h/ 62 Highland Avenue, Fair Haven, NJ 07701; ba/Holmdel, NJ; m/Barbara Donlevy; c/Drew, Bonnie, John; p/ Charles A Burrus (dec); Velma M Burrus, Shelby, NC; sp/Mr and Mrs Gerald Dunlevy, Glouster, OH; ed/BS Physics, Davidson Col, 1950; MS Physics, Emory Univ, 1951; PhD Physics, Duke Univ, 1955; mil/USNR, 1945-46; pa/Res Assoc, Physics Dept, Duke Univ, 1954-55; Mem Tech Staff, AT&T Bell Labs, 1955-; Mem: Am Phys Soc; AAAS; IEEE: Optical Soc of Am; Phi Beta Kappa; Sigma Xi; Sigma Pi Sigma; r/ Meth; hon/Author & Co-Author, Over 115 Tech Jour Articles on: Millimeter & Sub-millimeter-wave Spectroscopy (1954-59); Var MM-Wave Semiconductor Diodes (1960-69); Technicaues & Semiconductor Devices for Lightwave Communs, Small-area High-radiance Light-emitting-diodes "Burrus Diodes", (1970-79); Long-wavelength Lasers, LEDs & PIN Photodetectors, & Effects of Hydrogen & Deuterium in Optical Fibers (1980-); Fellow, AAAS, 1976; Fellow, APS, 1975; Fellow, IEEE, 1974; Fellow, OSA, 1979; David Richardson Medal, OSA, 1982; Dist'd Tech Staff Awd, Bell Labs, 1982; W/W: in E, in Engrg, in Technol Today, in Frontier Sci & Technol, in Contemp Achmt; Ldrs in Elects; Am Men & Wom of Sci; Num Other Biogl Listings.

BURRY, KENNETH ARNOLD oc/ Physician; b/Oct 2, 1942; h/8630 SW Pacer Drive, Beaverton, OR 97005; ba/ Portland, OR; m/Katherine A Johnson; c/Michael Curtis, Lisa Bray; p/Frederick H Burry, Laguna Niguel, CA; sp/ Romayne Johnson; ed/BA, Whittier Col, 1964; MD, Univ of CA-Irvine, 1968; mil/ AUS, 1969-71, Capt; pa/Sr Res Fellow, Univ of WA, 1974-76; Asst Prof OB-GYN 1976-80, Assoc Prof OB-GYN 1980-, OR Hlth Sci Univ; Dir, OR Reproductive Res & Fertility Prog, 1982-; Fellow, Am Col OB-GYN; Am Fertility Soc; NY Acad of Sci; The Endocrine Soc; Am Fedn for Clin Res; AAAS; Soc of Reproductive Endocrinology; 6 Profl Soc Presentations; r/Prot; hon/Author, Over 25 Articles, Abstracts, Reviews & Res Papers Pub'd in Profl Jours & Assn Proceedings incl'g: *Fertility & Sterility*; *Am Jour of OB-GYN*; Others; Lange Book Awd, 1966; Med Hon Soc, 1968; Pres Cit, Multnomah Med Soc; Mil Awds Incl: Viet Nam Campaign w Oak Leaf; Flight Surgs Medal; Bronze Star Medal; Army Com-

mend w OLC; Air Medal w 2 O/S Bars; Combat Med Badge; Num Others; Var W/W & Other Biogl Listings.

BURSEY, MAURICE MOYER oc/ Educator, Chemist; b/Jul 27, 1939; h/101 Longwood Place, Chapel Hill, NC 27514; ba/Chapel Hill, NC; m/Joan; c/ John, Sara; p/Reginald P Bursey, Baltimore, MD; sp/Frank W Tesarek (dec); ed/BA 1959, MA 1960, PhD 1963, Johns Hopkins Univ; pa/Lectr Chem, Johns Hopkins Univ, 1963; Prof, Purdue Univ, 1964; Asst Prof 1966, Assoc Prof 1969, Prof Chem 1974, Univ of NC-Chapel Hill; Mem: Am Chem Soc; Secy-Treas 1972-73, Chm-elect 1974, Chm 1975, Councilor 1976-, NC Sect Am Chem Soc; Grand Master of Ceremonies (3rd Nat VPres) 1980-82, Grand Col Alchemist (2nd Nat VPres) 1982-, Grand Prof Alchemist (1st Nat VPres) 1984-, Alpha Chi Sigma; Mem of Bd 1983-, Chapel Hill Hist Soc; r/Rom Cath; hon/Author of 4 Books & Over 200 Articles in Profl Jours; A P Sloan F'ship, 1969; Tanner Awd 1974, R J Reynolds Industs Leave 1983-84, Univ of NC-Chapel Hill; Soc of Scholars, Johns Hopkins Univ, 1982; W/W: in S & SW, in Frontier Sci & Technol; Personalities of S.

BURT, DAVID R oc/Professor; b/Oct 28, 1943; h/327 East 30th Street, Baltimore, MD 21218; ba/Baltimore, MD; p/Clifton H and Ruth E Burt, Millburn, NJ; ed/AB Biophysics, Amherst Col, 1965; PhD Biophysics, Johns Hopkins Univ, 1972; pa/Assoc Res Sci Biophysics, Johns Hopkins Univ, 1972-73; Postdoct Fellow Pharm, Johns Hopkins Sc of Med, 1973-76; Asst Prof 1976-82, Assoc Prof Pharm 1982-, Univ of MD Sch of Med; Mem: Soc for Neurosci; Endocrine Soc; Am Soc for Pharm & Exptl Therapeutics; Am Soc for Neurochem; NY Acad of Scis; AAAS; hon/Author, Over 60 Res Articles Pub'd in Profl Jours & Book Chapts; Gen Motors Nat S'ship 1961-65, Phi Beta Kappa; Sigma Xi, 1965; Nat Inst Neurol Communicative Disorders & Stroke F'ship, 1974-76; W/W in Frontier Sci & Technol.

BURTON, CURTBERT oc/Residence Hall Director; b/Jan 4, 1947; h/1600 Cresthaven Avenue, Orlando, FL 32805; ba/Savannah, GA; m/Carol J Chambers; c/Cornelius; p/Mr and Mrs L C Watts, Orlando, FL; ed/BS, Bam Ed, 1973; pa/Dir of Housing 1974-75, Dir of Residence 1975-, Savannah St Col; Mem: So Col Pers Assn; Nat Assn Col & Univ Residence Halls; Savannah St Col Nat Alumni Assn; Alpha Phi Omega; Soc Col Jours; GA St Dir 1982-83, Phi Beta Sigma; cp/NAACP; Prince Hall F & A Mason; BSA; YMCA; r/Bapt; hon/Sidney A Jones Human Relations Awds, 1972-73; YMCA Mbrship, 1973-74; Nat Alumni Apprec, 1978-82; W/W in S & SW.

BUSCH, ROBERT HENRY oc/ Research Geneticist, Professor; b/Oct 22, 1937; h/2485 Galtier Circle, St Paul, MN 55113; ba/St Paul, MN; m/Mavis Ann Bushman; c/Shari Lynn, Todd William; p/Henry and Lena Busch (dec); sp/Helen Bushman, Rippey, IA; ed/BSc Agronomy 1959, MSc Plant Breeding 1963, IA St Univ; PhD Plant Breeding & Genetics, Purdue Univ, 1967; mil/IA NG; pa/Res Assoc, IA St Univ, 1961-63; Grad Res Instr, Purdue Univ, 1966-67; Asst Prof to Prof, ND St Univ, 1967-77;

Res Plant Geneticist, USDA-ARS, Univ of MN, St Paul, 1978-; Assoc Editor 1976-78, Crop Sci Soc of Am; Secy 1978-, Sprg Wheat Improvement Com, Nat Wheat Improvement Com; r/Meth; hon/Author, Over 60 Profl Sci & Popular Articles on Wheat; Phi Kappa Phi; Sigma Gamma Delta; Sigma Xi; W/W: in MW, in Frontier Sci & Technol.

BUSH, BARNEY F oc/Fiction Writer, Poet; b/Aug 27, 1946; h/Stannard Rd #1, Greensboro Bend, VT 05842; ba/Same; c/Phil Dayne; p/Ownly and Ruth Evangeline Bush, Herod, IL; ed/BA Humanities, Ft Lewis Col, 1972; MA Fine Arts, MA English, Univ of ID, 1980; pa/Instr, Milwaukee Area Tech Col, 1978-79; Instr, Inst of Am Indian Arts, Santa Fe, NM, 1971-72; Dir & Instr, Inst of So Plains, Hammon, OK, 1972-73; Spec, Native Am Studies, Univ of WI-Milwaukee, 1973-74; Instr, NM Highlands Univ, Las Vegas, 1975-76; Ed Conslt, Num Cols, Assns & Orgs; Writer-in-Residence: Vermont Arts Coun, 1983-84; ALPS (Alternative Lrng Progs in Schs) NY St Coun on the Arts, 1982-84; OK St Arts Coun, 1980-83; IL Arts Coun, 1980-83; Jackson Hole, WY, 1980; Vis'g Artist/Writer, NC St Coun on the Arts, 1983-84; Num Poetry Rdgs & Perfs; Num Lectrs, in Am Indian Arts, Lit & Ed; Mem: Poets & Writers, NYC; Rio Grande Writer's Assn, Albuquerque; Conservatory of Am Lit, So Thomaston, ME; Nat Soc of Poets; Nat Indian Ed Assn; Ed Conslt, Nat Indian Yth Coun; Fdg Mem, Native Am Studies Devel Assn; cp/Pres 1970-72, Native Am Student Assns at Univ of ID & Ft Lewis Col; Chm of Bd, Indian Commun Sch, Milwaukee, WI, 1977-78; Bd Mem, So Ute Commun Action Prog, Ignacio, CO, 1971-72; Others; hon/Author of Books: *Running The Gauntlet*; *Inherit The Blood*; *Petroglyphs*; *My Horse & A Jukebox*; *Longhouse Of The Blackberry Moon*; Contbr, Wks in Num Anthologies incl'g: *The Remembered Earth*; *Songs From This Earth On Turtle's Back*; *The First Skin Around Me*; *Puerto Del Sol*; *Brother Songs*; *Blue Beech*; *The Nation Within*; *Poetry For A Nuclear Free Culture*; *Moraine II*; *Abraxas*; *Artists for Survival*; Wks in Num Jours & Qtlys incl'g: *Beloit Poetry Jour*; *Denver Qtly*; *Suntracks*; *Live Writers!*; *Indian Am*; *Concerning Poetry*; Others; Wks in Num Mags incl'g: *Kenning View Mag*; *Scree*; *AZ Hwys*; *Quetzal*; *Milwaukee Mag*; *Ekran*; *Riverrun*; Others; Wks in Num Newspapers incl'g: *Akwesasne Notes*; *No Tribes News*; *Drumbeats*; *Ams Before Columbus*; *Shawnee Nation News*; Others; Recordings: *Two Native Am Poets*: *Barney Bush, Joy Harjo*; Recip, Pen Am Awd, NYC, 1983; Writer's Grant, NEA, 1981-82; Narrator Documentary Film, "N Am Indians Today," for Am & Italian Ednl TV; Narrator of Film, Am Indian Students, Concordia & VA Union Cols; Grand Awd for Poetry, Scottsdale Nat Indian Arts Exposition, 1976; Biogl Film "Commmuns," Ednl TV Channel 10, Milwaukee, WI; Num Radio & TV Interviews; Lit Editor for Num Poetry Mags; Num Awds for Art, Jewelry & Photo; Intl Biog of Poets; Men of Achmt; Other Biogl Listings.

BUSHBAUM, MARIANNE LUCILLE oc/Clinic Director; b/Jun 10, 1923; h/14230 Chestnut Drive, Minneapolis, MN 55344; ba/Minneapolis, MN; m/Richard Leonard; c/Holly, Timmi Li, Kimla, Jill, Joan, Dirk, Laurie; ed/Att'd

Univ of MN, 1942-48 & 1975-76; Cert'd Chem Dep, Fam Cnslg, St Mary's Jr Col, 1977; World Traveler: China, Japan, Taiwan, Hong Kong & Samua, 1946-52; pa/Self-employed Designer of Handbags, "Bush Bags," 1964-68; Chem Dep Cns!r, Park View TX Ctr, Mpls, 1977-78; Cnslr 1978, Asst Dir 1979-80, Dir 1982-84, Parkview Pain Clinic, Mpls, MN; Mem: MW Pain Soc; Assn of Humanistic Psych; Assn Rehab Providers; Chapt Pres, Am Field Ser, Eden Prairie, MN, 1965-66; cp/Rosicrucian; Intl Platform Assn; r/Prot; hon/Designed "Discover Am" Handbag for Ladybird Johnson & Presented it at White House During Her Campaign, 1967; W/W: of Am Wom, of Wom, in MW; Biogl Roll of Honor.

BUSHNELL, JIM L oc/Agronomy Extension Specialist; b/Apr 7, 1946; h/2060 North 1400 East, Logan, UT 84321; ba/Logan, UT; m/Carolyn Sue; c/Sheree, Michelle, Staci, James Lee, Susan, Mark Ralph, Joshua Nathan; p/Lola D Bushnell, Meadow, UT; sp/Mr and Mrs Ralph Memmott, Filmore, UT; ed/BS 1970, MS 1972, Brigham Yg Univ; PhD Agronomy, OH St Univ, 1976; mil/AUS, 12 Yrs, Trans, Artillery & Qtrmaster Brs, Capt; pa/Res Spec, Chevron Chem-Ortho Res Dev, 1976-78; Millard Co Agt 1978-81, Ext Spec-Agronomy 1981-85, Assoc Prof Plant Sci 1985-, UT St Univ; Mem: Wn Soc of Crop Sci; Nat Mbrship Com Mem, Am Soc of Agronomy; Epsilon Sigma Phi; Wn Alfalfa Improvement Conf; Nat Alafalf Improvement Conf St Ext Spec Assn; Chm Profl Relats Com, Student Recruitment & S'ship Com, Plant Sci Prog Devel, Ext Ser, Crop Sci Soc of Am; cp/70's Pres, Elders Quorum Pres, YMMIA Pres, Varsity Scout Ldr, Ward Clk, LDS; Party Del, Co Conv; r/LDS; hon/Author & Co-Author, Over 20 Articles Pub'd in Profl Jours & Assn Reports incl'g: *Report of UT Agri Expt Sta*; *UT Farmer Stockman*; *Wn Soc of Crop Sci Proceedings*; Others; Recip Var Cash Grants; Farm S'ship, Wn Reg Ext Winter Sch, Tucson, 1981; Rookie of Yr, UT St Univ, Ext Spec Assn, 1983; Personalities of W & MW.

BUSHNELL, ROBERT HEMPSTEAD oc/Solar Energy Consultant; b/May 11, 1924; h/502 Ord Drive, Boulder, CO 80303; m/Martha D; c/Helen, Orson; p/John Bushnell (dec); sp/Alfred Dicks, Southbury, CT; ed/BSc Engrg Physics 1947, MSc Physics 1948, OH St Univ; PhD Meteorology, Univ of WI, 1962; mil/USNR, 1944-46; pa/Physicist, The Hoover Co, N Canton, OH, 1948-50; Engrg Spec, Goodyr Aircraft Corp, Akron, OH, 1950-56; Engr, Radio Corp of Am, Camden, NJ, 1957-58; Res Meterorologist, Nat Ctr for Atmospheric Res, Boulder, CO, 1962-74; Self-employed Consltg Engr, Solar Energy, 1974-; Mem: AAAS; Am Meteorology Soc; Am Soc of Heating, Refrigerating & Airconditioning Engrs; Intl Soc Energy Soc; Treas 1975-79, Metric Pract Com 1978, Chrm 1982, US Metric Assn; hon/Author of Num Articles & Papers Pub'd in Profl Jours incl'g: *Jour Meteorology*; *Jour Geophysics Res*; *Jour Applied Meteorology*; *Solar Energy*; Others, 1958-82; Tau Beta Pi, 1947; Sigma Pi Sigma, 1948; Sigma Xi; Fellow, Univ Corp for Atmosphere Res, Univ of WI, 1960-61; Am Men of Sci.

BUSHNELL, WILLIAM RODGERS oc/Plant Physiologist; b/Aug 19, 1931; h/1555 Oak Avenue, St Paul, MN 55112; ba/St Paul, MN; m/Ann Holcomb; c/Thomas, John, Mary; p/John and Dyllone Bushnell (dec); sp/Arden and Etholin Holcomb (dec); ed/BA, Univ of Chgo, 1951; BS 1953, MS 1955, OH St Univ; PhD, Univ of WI, 1960; pa/Plant Physiol, Agri Res Ser, US Dept of Agri, 1960-; Asst Prof 1966, Assoc Prof 1972, Prof 1973-, Dept of Plant Pathol, Univ of MN; Mem: AAAS; Am Phytopathol Soc; r/Unitarian; hon/Author of Num Res Pubs in Sci Jours; Co-Editor of Books: *The Cereal Rusts Vol I & II*, 1984; *Plant Injection: The Physiol & Biochem Basis*, 1982; Predoct Fellow, NSF, 1957-60; Alexander von Humboldt Sr US Sci Awd, 1984; Fellow, Am Phytopathol Soc, 1984; W/W.

BUSKE, NORMAN oc/Consulting Scientist; b/Oct 11, 1943; ba/Davenport, WA; m/Linda Susan Josephson; p/G E Buske, Stamford, CT; ed/BA 1964, MA Physics, 1965, Univ of CT; MS Oceanography, Johns Hopkins Univ, 1967; Adit Adv'd Courses: Johns Hopkins Univ & Univ of RI; pa/Oceanographer, Ocean Sci & Engr Inc, 1968-71; Prin, Sea-test Co, 1972-76; Sr Sci Engr, Van Gulik & Assocs, 1976-77; Dir Res, Pacific Engr Corp, 1977-78; Prin, Search Tech Sers, 1978-; Mem: AAAS; ASME; ASTM; IEEE; NY Acad of Sci; NSPE; MTS; NFPA; SAE; Greenpeace; PSR; hon/Author of Var Res Papers Pub'd by ASME; Holder of Patents on High-speed Internal Pressure Engine; W/W in Frontier Sci & Technol.

BUSS, EDWARD G oc/Professor, Geneticist; b/Aug 28, 1921; h/1420 S Garner Street, State College, PA 16801; ba/University Park, PA 16802; m/Dorothy; c/Ellen, Norman; p/George E Buss (dec); Kathryn Buss Wohler, King City, MO; sp/Robert B and Allie B Arvidson (dec); ed/BS, KS St Col, 1943; MS 1949, PhD 1956, Purdue Univ; mil/AUS (Airborne Inf), 1943-46, Capt; pa/Grad Res & Grad Tchg Asst 1946-49, Instr 1955-56, Purdue Univ; Asst Prof & Acting Hd 1949-55, Dept of Poultry Husbandry 1950-55, CO A&M Col; Assoc Prof 1956-65, Prof 1965-83, Prof of Agri 1983-, PA St Univ; Mem: AAAS; Exec Com, Am Inst for Biol Sci; Am Genetic Assn; Am Soc of Zools; Genetics Soc of Am; Poultry Sci Assn; Soc for Study of Reprodn; Worlds' Poultry Sci Assn; Coun Mem, AGA; r/Unitarian; hon/Author, Num Articles Pub'd in Profl Jours incl'g: *Poultry Sci*; *Jour of Heredity*; *Genetics*; *Comparative Biochem & Physiol*; *Am Jour of Physiol*; Others; Phi Eta Sigma, 1980; Correspondence Estero-Societa Italiana per il Progresso della Zootechnica, 1972; Am Men & Wom of Sci; W/W in Frontier Sci & Technol.

BUTLER, ALTA FLEMING oc/Educator; b/Jan 7, 1951; h/5 Laurel Road, Weston, MA 02193; ba/Boston, MA; m/David E; c/Molly Fleming; p/Edward L and Jeanne M Fleming, NJ; sp/Edward and Catherine Butler, NJ; ed/BS, Syracuse Univ, 1973; MS, 1978; pa/Dir Arts & Crafts, Hunterdon (NJ) St Sch, 1970-72; Hd Tchr, 1st Presb Ch Nursery Sch, NYC, 1973-75; Resr, Bk Street Col, NYC, 1974-75; Dir, Union Theol Sem Day Care Ctr, NYC, 1975-79; Instr, Quinsigamond Commun Col, Worcester, MA, 1980-82; Prog Developer, Citizen Involvement Tng Proj, Univ of MA-Amherst, 1981-82; Instr, Supvr, Wheelock Col, Boston, MA, 1982-; Ednl Conslt, 1981-; Mem: Nat Assn for Ed of Yg Chd; Assn for Supvn & Curric Devel; NOW; NE Coalition of Ednl Ldrs; cp/Warren Commun Theatre; Del, MA Conf of U Ch of Christ; r/U Ch of Christ; hon/ Author of Article, "Scratchy is Dead," *Tchr Mag*, 1978; Eta Pi Upsilon, 1972; Phi Kappa Phi, 1973; Omicron Nu, 1973; W/W in E.

BUTLER, FREDRICK MYRON oc/ Executive; b/Apr 28, 1935; h/45 Warmwood Way, Hillsborough, CA 94010; ba/ Spartanburg, SC; m/Karen; c/Michael Fredrick, Mark Kenneth, Christy Anne; p/MF and Leila Butler, Salem, OR; sp/ Charles and Viberta Briggs, San Diego, CA; ed/BS Ec & Engrg, Univ of OR, 1958; mil/AUS, 1958-59, 1st Lt; pa/Pres, Tyger Const Co, 1984-; Bus & Field Engrg Experience: Briones Dam 1961, Purchasing Agt Emigrant Gap Hwy 1962, Bus Mgr at Emigrant, Briones & Buena Vista Pumping Plant 1964, Asst Bus Mgr Heavy Constrn Div 1965, Bus Mgr 1967 & Equip Mgr 1967-82 Mica Dam BC Canada, Proj Mgr Cochiti Dam NM 1972-74, Proj Mgr New Melones Dam & Powerhouse CA 1974-79, Gen Mgr Israeli AB 1979-82, VPres Constrn Co 1982-83, VPres Constrn 1983-84, Guy F Atkinson Co of CA; Mem: Soc of Am Mil Engrs; cp/Rotary Clb; r/ Christian; hon/Author of Articles on Projs & Aspects of Constrn in Num Trade Mags incl'g: *Engrg News Record*; Merit Awd, Portugal; Merit Awd, Israel, 1982.

BUYSE, MARYLOUISE oc/Clinical Pediatric Geneticist; b/Jun 17, 1946; h/ 61 Winthrop Street, Newton, MA 02165; ba/Boston, MA; m/Carl N Edwards; p/Mr and Mrs George J Buyse, New York, NY; sp/Mrs Cecile P Edwards, Needham, MA; ed/BA, Hunter Col, 1966; MD, The Med Col of PA, 1970; Inter, Univ of MI Med Ctr, 1970-71; Residency (Pediatrics 1971-73, Postgrad F'ship (Human & Clin Genetics) 1973-75, Univ of So CA Med Ctr; pa/Clin Geneticist, Tufts-N Eng Med Ctr, 1976-; Dir, Cystic Fibrosis Ctr, 1975-82; Dir, Myelodysplasia Clin, 1976-80; Med Dir 1978-82, Dir 1982-, Ctr for Birth Defects Info Sers; Mem: Teratolgy Soc; MA Med Assn; Am Acad of Pediatrics; Chm Public Relats Com, Am Med Wom's Assn; Am Soc of Human Genetics; NY Acad of Sci; AAAS; hon/Author, Num Articles Pub'd in Profl Jours; Editor-in-Chief, *The Birth Defects Compendium*; Editor, *Jour of Clin Dysmorphology*; W/W in Am Wom.

BUZZO, MARGARET MINNIE WALKER (MARGE) oc/Artist; b/Nov 28, 1927; h/4620 Santa Lucia Drive, Woodland Hills, CA 91364; ba/Canoga Park, CA; m/Frank Ross; c/Yvonne Marie (B) Oster, Wayne Bennette; p/ Harold Styles and Mollie (Whitman) Walker (dec); sp/Amador and Merced Buzzo (dec); ed/AA, Long Bch City Col, 1950-52; Addit Studies, Art Ctr Sch of

Design, LA, CA, 1956-58; pa/Artist, Owner, Marge Buzzo Art Ser, 1972-; Artist, Owner, Margie Ditto Creations, 1982-84; Charter Mem, Bd of Dirs 1983-84, Zonta Intl of San Fernando Val, CA; Charter Mem, Intl Art Guild, Van Nuys, CA, 1982-84; VPres, W Val Artists Assn, 1972-73; r/Cath; hon/ Illustrated 13 Chd's Books; Over 34 Illusts Pub'd in Var Pubs, 1972-; Wk in Invitational Exhibit, Centre Intl dé Art Contemporaire de Paris, Francis, 1984; Paintings in Permanent Collection, of Burbank Public Lib; Desi Awd Winner for Book Illust, 1980; Nat Artists Dir; Intl Artists Dir; Art Guide Intl; Artists USA, Desi Awds; W/W in W.

BYRD, CAROLE F oc/Administrator; b/Mar 5, 1944; ba/Oak Ridge, TN; c/Eric Michael; p/Frank D and Mary N Faulkner, Knoxville, TN; ed/BS Communs/Public Relats, Univ of TN, 1985; pa/Adm Ofcr & Pers Admr, Comparative Animal Res Lab, Oak Ridge, TN, 1979-; Printing Design Clk Div Y-12 Plant 1977-79, Asst Supvr Tech Pubs Dept 1966-73, Union Carbide Corp, Oak Ridge, TN; Ofc Mgr, Barber & McMurry Inc Archs, Knoxville, TN, 1973-77; Mem: ABWA; Nat Assn for Female Execs; Gamma Beta Phi; r/Bapt; hon/Wom of Achmt 1980, Dean's List (Consistently), Univ of TN; W/W of Am Wom.

BYRD, JACK CLIFFORD oc/Executive; b/Dec 27, 1928 (dec Aug 3 1983); h/2030 Forest Manor Drive, Kingswood, TX 77339; ba/Houston, TX; m/ Juanita Ann Byrd (dec); c/Rachel Ann, Scott Clifford, Glen David; p/Otis C and Truce T Byrd (dec); sp/David J and Ollie H Smelley Jr (dec); ed/Oil Acctg, Tyler Comml Col, 1950; BBA, Baylor Univ, 1956; mil/AUS, 1952-54; pa/Oil Acct, Killam Oil Co, Laredo, TX, 1950-52; Jr Internal Auditor, Humble Oil & Refining Co (Exxon), 1956; Asst Controller 1965, Proj Mgr Clear Lake City & Bayport Industl Devel 1965, VPres 1965, Proj Mgr Kingswood 1968-81, VPres Residential Div & Overseer of Var Devels 1981-83, for Friendswood (a Subdiv of Exxon); Mem: TX CPA's; TX Forestry Assn; Sam Houston Resource Conserv & Devel Proj; the Zool Soc; Urban Land Inst; cp/Houston C of C; Fest Chm, Humble Bicent Com, 1976; Dir, NE Hosp; Flaming Arrow Dist Chm, Sam Houston Coun, BSA, 1974; Bd of Govs, Kingswood Country Club; Past Pres Nassau Bay Bapt Ch, 1979; Clear Lake Lodge # 1417; AF & AM of Seabrook; r/Bapt; hon/Jack C Byrd S'ship Estab'd Kingswood HS.

BYRD, JAMES JACKSON SR oc/ Executive, Scientist; b/Sep 16, 1928; h/ 806 Percheron Drive, Bear, DE 19701; ba/Bear, DE; m/Betty Owens; c/James Jackson Jr, Eleanor Sue, Diana Lee, Robert, Patricia Anne; p/James Orris Byrd, Temperanceville, VA; Mae Alice Byrd (dec); sp/Paul D Owens, Wilmington, DE; Beulah Owens (dec); ed/ BSChE, Univ of DE, 1957; pa/Proj Insp, St of VA, 1948-53; Eletron Microscopist, EI, DuPont de Nemours & Co, Wilmington, DE, 1953-57; Engr, Lab

Mgr, RCA, Camden, NJ, 1957-63; Chm of Bd, DE Sci Labs Inc, Bear, DE, 1964-; Mem: US Congl Adv Bd; Electron Microscope Soc; cp/Repub; r/Bapt; hon/ Author of Num Articles in Profl Pubs; Patentee in Field; W/W in E.

BYRD, LARRY DONALD oc/ Research Professor, Behavioral Pharmacologist; b/Jul 14 1936; h/1026 Viking Drive, Stone Mountain, GA 30083; ba/ Atlanta, GA; m/Corrinne; c/Kay, Lynn, Renée, Andrew; p/Donald T Byrd (dec); Mildred Byrd, Salisbury, NC; sp/Marshall Williams (dec); Betty Williams, Greenville, NC; ed/AB 1961, MA 1964, E Carolina Univ; PhD, Univ of NC-Chapel Hill, 1968; Postdoct Fellow, Harvard Med Sch, 1967-70; mil/AUS, Spec Sers, 1954-57; pa/Tchg Fellow 1962-63, Instr 1963-64, Psych, E Carolina Univ; Tchg Asst 1964-66, Res Asst 1965-67, Exptl Psych, Univ of NC-Chapel Hill; Res Fellow Pharm 1967-70, Instr Psychobiol 1970-73, Prin Assoc Psychi 1973-74, Harvard Med Sch; Assoc Sci Psychobiol Lab 1969-74, Prin Assoc Div Psychobiol 1974, N Eng Reg Primate Res Ctr; Lectr, Dept Psych, GA Inst of Technol, 1975-; Psychobiol & Chm Div Primate Behavior Yerkes Primate Res Ctr 1974-79, Lectr Dept Psych 1974-81, Assoc Res Prof & Chm Div Primate Behavior Yerkes Reg Primate Res Ctr 1979-80, Assoc Res Prof & Chief Div Behavioral Biol Yerkes Reg Primate Res Ctr 1980-82, Adj Prof Dept Psych 1981-, Assoc Prof Dept Pharm 1981-, Res Prof & Chief Div Behavioral Biol Yerkes Reg Primate Res Ctr 1982-, Emory Univ; Pres, Behavioral Pharm Soc, 1984-86; Pres Div 28 (Psychopharm Div), Am Psychol Assn, 1982-83; Pres, Atlanta Area Chapt, E Carolina Univ Alumni Assn, 1982-83; Bd of Dirs 1970-78, VPres 1975-76, Soc for Exptl Anal of Behavior; Mem, Clin, Behavioral & Psychosocial Res Rev Com 1982-85, Chp 1984-85, Nat Inst on Drug Abuse; Am Soc Pharm & Exptl Therapeutics; AAAS; SEn Psychol Assn; Atlanta Area Chapt, Soc for Neurosci; Am Soc of Primatologists; Conslt Editor, *Am Jour Primatology*, 1980-83; Editor, *Psychopharm Newslttr*, 1976-82; Assoc Editor 1970-76, Edit Bd 1969-79, *Jour of Exptl Anal of Behavor*; Others; hon/Author, Over 40 Res Articles Pub'd in Profl Jours incl'g: *Sci*; *Jour Pharm & Exptl Therapeutics*; *Life Scis*; Others; Woodrow Wilson F'ship Nom, 1962; Outstg Alumnus Awd, E Carolina Univ, 1977; Phi Sigma Pi; Others; W/ W: in S & SW, in Frontier Sci & Technol; Intl Dir Pharms & Pharmacologists; Men of Achmt; DIB; Num Other Biogl Listings.

BYRNE, JOHN PATRICK oc/Administrator; b/May 25, 1929; h/7679 Waverly Mountain, Littleton, CO 80127; ba/ Golden, CO; m/Dolores Ann Meyer; c/ John Patrick Jr, David Michael, Richard Terrence, Kevin Francis; p/George Arnold & Opal Vere Byrne, Lakewood, CO; sp/William Anthony Meyer (dec); Marion Dolores Meyer, Randallstown, MD; ed/BS, Johns Hopkins Univ, 1958; MBA, Univ of MI, 1961; Grad, Army

War Col, 1971; mil/AUS, 1949-78, Col; pa/Dir Disaster Emer Sers, St of CO, 1979-; Dir of Emer Preparedness, City & Co of Denver, 1978-79; Cmdr, Rocky Mtn Arsenal, Denver, 1975-78; Var Command & Logistics Mgmt Staff Assignments w AUS, 1949-78; Pres, Nat Emer Mgmt Assn, 1983-; Bd of Advrs, Emer Med Techs, CO, 1980-; Dir, St Vincent De Paul Stores, Denver, 1979-; Secy-Treas, CO Civil Def Assn, 1978-80; Secy, Gallant Pelham Chapt, Assn of AUS, 1969-70; cp/Mil Affairs Com, Denver C of C, 1975-; Denver Rotary Clb; Denver Execs Clb; Pres, Brookland Ests Citizens Assn, Alexandria, VA, 1963-65; r/Rom Cath; hon/Phi Kappa Phi; Beta Gamma Sigma; Delta Sigma Pi; Hon Mem, Bd of Dirs, Mile High Chapt, ARC, 1984-; W/W in W; CO W/W.

C

CABELL, HARRIET WILLIMON oc/ Professor, Program Director; h/83 Arcadia Drive, Tuscaloosa, AL 35404; ba/Tuscaloosa, AL; m/Ben; c/Benjamin, Kennedy, Charles; p/Mrs Ruby S Willimon, Greenville, SC; ed/BS, Col of Wm & Mary, 1953; MA Spch Therapy 1954, Grad Wk Spec Ed 1966, Grad Wk Human Devel 1968, EdS Curric & Res 1971, EdD Adm of Higher Ed 1979, Univ of AL; pa/Spec Conslt, B'ham-So Col, 1979-80; Assoc Prof, Hd Dept & Dir of External Deg Prog, New Col 1979-, Joint Appt, New Co & Sch of Hom Ec 1975-76, Instr Dept of Human Devel & Fam Life, Sch of Ec 1968-75, Univ of AL; Mem: Coun for Advmt of Exptl Lrng; AL Assn Cont'g Edrs; AL Assn of Admrs; Am Assn of Higher Ed; Nat & AL Assns Ed Yg Chd; Am Home Ec Assn; Delta Kappa Gamma; The Alliance: Assn for Alternative Deg Progs for Adults; cp/Tuscaloosa Jr Leag; Past Pres, Belle Arts Study Clb; Past Pres, Delta Delta Delta; Past Mem Ofcl Bd & Other Activs, 1st Meth Ch; Past Pres, The Kettledrum; The Arcadia Clb; UDC; Advr, Univ Theatre; Past Bd of Dirs, Tuscaloosa Commun Theatre; Charter Mem, Past Pres, Fantastics Dance Clb; Masquers Dance Clb; Jesters Dance Clb; r/Meth; hon/Contb'g Author to a Handbook for Distance Lrng & a Textbook on Child Devel; Elected in Nat Election to Bd of Trustees for 3 Yr Term 1979, Elected to Exec Bd 1980, CAEL; Advr, Alliance; Tuscaloosa BPW, 1979; Danforth Assoc, 1978; Kappa Delta Pi, 1975; Outstg Edr, 1973; Outstg Mem, Tuscaloosa Assn for Retarded Chd, 1967; Phi Beta Kappa, 1954; Wom of Achmt.

CACUCI, DAN GABRIEL oc/ Nuclear Scientist and Applied Mathematician, Researcher and Educator; b/ May 16, 1948; h/1939 Stonebrook Drive, Knoxville, TN 37923; ba/Oak Ridge, TN; p/Gabriel D Cacuci, Las Vegas, NV; Malvina Preda, Bucharest, Romania; ed/MS 1973, Master of Phil 1977, PhD 1978, Columbia Univ; pa/ Nuclear Engrg Assoc III, Brookhaven Nat Lab, 1975-76; Lead Engr, EBASCO Sers Inc, 1976-77; Grp Ldr & Sr Sci, Oak Ridge Nat Lab, 1977-; Assoc Editor, *Nuclear Sci & Engrg*, 1984-; Am Nuclear Soc (Secy, Nat Planning Com, 1983-); NY Acad of Sci; AAAS; Sigma Xi; hon/ Hon Assoc Prof, Dept of Nuclear Engrg, Univ of TN-Knoxville, 1983-; ORNL Spec Recog Awd, 1982; Merriman Meml Awd, Columbia Univ, 1977; Cit for Outstg Achmts in Grad Wk, Columbia Univ, 1973; W/W: in Frontier Sci & Tech, in World, in S & SW.

CADY, HENRY LORD oc/Professor; b/Jul 6, 1921; h/24 Minquil Drive, Newark, DE 19713; ba/Newark, DE; m/ Priscilla S; c/Sharon Anne, Christopher Scott, Jonathan Lord; p/George L Jr and Myrtle L Cady (dec); sp/George L and Mildred Scott, Camden, ME; ed/BA, Middlebury Col, 1947; Westminster Choir Col, 1947-48; MA Tchrs Col, Columbia Univ, 1952; PhD, Univ of KS, 1962; mil/USAF, 1942-45, Pfc to Capt; pa/Music Instr, Pembroke Country Day Sch, 1948-55; Prof & Hd Music Dept, Wm Jewell Col, 1955-62; Asst Prof 1962-66, Assoc Prof 1966-70, Prof 1970-75, Sch of Music, OH St Univ;

Prof & Chm Dept of Music 1975-80, Prof 1980-, Univ of DE; Mem: MENC; Dir 1970-72, Col Music Soc; Pres-Elect 1984-86, Pres 1986-88, Dir 1976-81, DE Mus Edrs Assn; AAUP; Exec Com, DE Chapt Intl Torch Clbs, Secy/Treas 1984-85, VP 1985-86, Pres 1986-87; Phi Mu Alpha Sinfonia; Pi Kappa Lamda; Bd Dir, DE Symph Orch Assn, 1976-81; hon/Editor, *Contbns to Music Edns*, Vols 1-4; Conslt'g Editor, *IA Studies in Psych of Music*, Vols 6-10; Over 40 Articles on Sociol, Psych, Music Ed & Higher Ed in Profl Pubs; W/W in E; Ldrs in Ed; Nat Reg Ed Resrs.

CADY, JOHN FRANK oc/History Writer, Professor Emeritus; b/Jul 14, 1901; h/45 Mapplewood Drive, Athens, OH 45701; ba/Athens, OH; m/Vivian Thomas; c/John Thomas, Susan Grace, George Franklin; p/J Frank and Katie Hall Cady (dec); ed/AB, DePauw Univ, 1923; AM, Univ of Cinc, 1924; PhD, Univ of PA, 1929; mil/Civilian Ofc of Strategic Sers, 1943-45; pa/Hist Instr, Univ of ME, 1925-26; Hist Prof, Marshall Coi, Huntington, WV, 1929-30; Prof Hist 1930-35, Dean 1938-43, Franklin Col of IN; Ofc Strategic Sers, Wash DC, 1943-45; Dept of St, 1945-49; Prof Hist 1949-72, Prof Emeritus 1972-, OH Univ; Prof Hist, Judson Col, Burma, 1935-38; Prof Hist, Thammasat Univ, Bangkok, 1967-68; Mem: Am Hist Assn; Assn of Asian Studies; OH Hist Soc; r/Bapt, Meth; hon/Author, Over 40 Pubs on Hist Subjects incl'g: *Contacts in Burma: 1935-49*; *The US & Burma: Post-War SE Asia*; *SE Asia: Its Hist Devel*; *The Roots of French Imperialism in En Asia*; *The Bapt Ch in IN*; Others; Recip of Hon Degs: DePauw Univ; Franklin Col; OH Univ; Acad of Hist; Cert of Merit, Ofc Strategic Sers, 1945; Dir Dist'd Ams.

CAETANO, DONALD FRED oc/ Sociologist, Research Analyst; b/Nov 22, 1940; h/2507-4 Harbor, Ventura, CA 93001; ba/Ventura, CA; m/Suzan; p/Edith Caetano, Bakersfield, CA; sp/ Albert Fortier, Bakersfield, CA; ed/BA, 1965; MA, 1968; PhD, 1971; mil/AUS, 1959-62; pa/Sociol, Res Anal, St Compensation Ins Fund, 1978-83; Sociol, CA St Col-San Bernadino, 1973-78; Sociol, Univ of IA, 1971-73; Sociol, CA Polytech Univ-San Louis Obispo, 1969-70; Mem: Am Sociol Assn, 1970-83; r/Rom Cath; hon/Author of Var Articles in Profl Jours incl'g: *Jour of Hlth & Social Behavior*; *Jour of Ob & Gyn*; *Jour of Communs*; W/W in W.

CAGLIERO, ENRICO oc/ Researcher; b/May 18, 1955; h/6333 La Jolla Boulevard, Number 173, La Jolla, CA 92037; ba/San Diego, CA; p/Giovanni and Teresa Cagliero, Torino, Italy; ed/BS, Liceo Scientifico G Segre, 1973; MD, Univ of Torino, 1979; pa/ Clin Clk in Endocrinology 1976-79, Med Resident 1979-80, Univ of Torino; Res Fellow, Retinopathy Unit, Royal Postgrad Med School, Univ of London, 1980; Res Fellow, Univ of CA-San Diego, 1981-; Societa Italiana Di Diabetologia; EASD; AAAS; NY Acad of Sci; r/Cath; hon/Author, Num Articles in Field; Grant Recip, Societa Italiana Di Diabetologia & Consiglio Nazionale Delle Ricerche; W/W in World.

CAIN, J(AMES) ALLAN oc/Department Chairman, Professor; b/Jul 23, 1935; h/Rural Route 1, Box 788, West Kingston, RI 02892; ba/Kingston, RI; c/

Geoffrey Carleton, Trevor Bradley; p/ James Herbert and Margaret Ivy (Moore) Cain (dec); ed/BSc Geol & Chem, Univ of Durham (England), 1958; MS Geol 1960, PhD Geol 1962, NWn Univ; mil/Royal AF, 1953-55; pa/ Geol Instr 1961, Asst Prof Geol 1962-66, Case Inst of Tech & Wn Resv Univ; Assoc Prof Geol 1966-71, Prof Geol 1971-, Chm Geol Dept 1967-, Acting Assoc Dean Col of Arts & Scis, Univ of RI, 1983-84; Hon Res Assoc, Harvard Univ, 1973; cp/VChm Bd of Trustees, Kingston Lib, 1970-78; VPres, Providence Opera Theatre, 1978-79; Mem, Richmond Conserv Comm, 1983-86; hon/Author, Over 30 Res Articles in Profl Jours & Co-Author, 3 Books: *Geol: A Synopsis Part I Phy Geol*; *Part II Hist Geol*; *Envir Geol*; *Sigma Xi*, 1961; *Fellow, Geol Soc of Am*; *Recip, NSF Res Grant, 1964-68*; W/W in E; Am Men & Wom of Sci; DIB.

CAIN, JAMES DOUGLAS JR oc/ Intelligence Specialist; b/Jul 4, 1946; h/ PO Box 1702, APO, New York, NY 09021; ba/APO, New York, NY; m/Joyce Dilworth; p/Mr and Mrs James D Cain, Spring Hill, FL; sp/Mr and Mrs A W Dilworth, Baltimore, MD; ed/BS Polit Sci, SUNY-Albany, 1980; MSc Intl Relats, Troy St Univ, 1981; BA Hist, Univ of MD, 1982; PhD Polit Sci, Univ of S Africa, 1984; mil/AUS, 1965-73, Mil Intell Ofcr; pa/Fgn Ser Ofcr, Dept of St, 1973-74; Intell Opers Spec, Dept of Def, 1974-; Instr, Univ of MD, 1982-; Freelance Conslt in Hist, 1983-; Mem: Intl Polit Sci Assn, 1981-; APSA, 1980-; Am Ec Assn, 1980-; Mid E Inst, 1981-; Assn for Asian Studies, 1980-; US-China People's Friendship Assn, 1972-; Intl Ctr for Asian Studies, 1984; cp/VFW, 1968-; Masons, 1971-; OES, 1971-; Vietnam Vets of Am, 1982-; MN Chippewa Tribe, 1967- Nat Coun of Am Indians, 1979-; Dem Abroad, 1982-; r/ Prot; hon/Author *The China Market; Pipedream or Reality; Images of Green* in Progress; Alpha Sigma Lamda; Phi Alpha Theta; Pi Sigma Alpha; Fellow, Intl Ctr for Asian Studies; Bronze Star w OLC; Vietnamese Cross of Gallantry w Palm; Chinese Min of Def Ser Medal.

CAINE, PHILIP DAVID oc/Deputy Commandant of Cadets, Professor; b/ Jul 3, 1933; h/19060 Pebble Beach, Monument, CO 80132; ba/Colorado Springs, CO; m/Doris E; c/Barbara Lynn (C) Wagenfuhr, Virginia Lee (C) Tonneson; Jennifer Louise; p/Mr and Mrs C M Caine; sp/Mr and Mrs Harry Johnson; ed/BA Social Sci, Denver Univ, 1955; MA Asian Hist 1964, PhD US Diplomatic Hist 1966, Stanford Univ; Nat War Col, 1978; mil/USAF, 1955-, Col; pa/Dpty Commandant for Mil Instrn 1980-, Prof & Hist Dept Hd 1978-80, Prof & Acting Hist Dept Hd 1976-77, Assoc Prof, Prof, Dept Hd Hist Dept 1970-76, Asst Prof Hist 1966-69, Instr 1963-64, USAF Acad, Colorado Sprgs, CO; Prof Intl Studies, Nat War Col, Ft McNair, Wash DC, 1977-78; Dept Chief, Acting Chief, Proj CHECO, HQ's 7th AF, Saigon, Rep of Vietnam, 1969-70; AFIT PhD Prog 1964-66, AFIT MA Prog 1961-63, Stanford Univ; Instr Pilot & Flight Examr 1959-61, Mission Pilot 1957-59, Mather AFB, CA; Student, Primary Pilot Tng, Hondo AB, TX & Basic Pilot Tng, Vance AFB, OK, 1956-57; Dist'd AFROTC Grad, Univ of

Denver, 1955; Mem: AF Assn; Order of Daedalians; Soc for Histns of Am Fgn Relats; Am Soc for Tng & Devel; Chm & Mem, Num USAF Acad Coms & Projs; cp/Bd of Mgrs, Mem Exec Swimming Com, Rocky Mtn AAU; Bd of Govs, Woodmoor Country Clb; Pres, CO Sprgs Swim Team Booster Clb; Nat AAU Swimming Ofcl; Others; r/Prot; hon/Author, Var Reports, Book Chapts, Reviews & Articles Pub'd in Jours incl'g: *Mil Review; Air Univ Review; Dict of Am Hist; Proceedings of 1st Citadel Conf on War & Diplomacy; The Am Hist Review; World Hist in Lib Mil Ed; CHECO Reports (Classified);* Co-Author of Book, *Commando Hunt III;* Other Pubs & Presentations; Bronze Star; Meritorious Ser Medal; AF Commend Medal; AF Outstg Unit Awd; Nat Def Ser Medal; Vietnam Ser Medal; AF Longevity Ser Awd Ribbon; Small Arms Expert Marksman Ribbon; Vietnamese Cross w Device; Rep of Vietnam Campaign Medal.

CALABRIA, SEBASTIAN SAM oc/Reading Supervisor; b/Jun 6, 1949; h/15 Clover Street, Nutley, NJ 07110; m/Elisa Tramaglini; c/Melissa Beth, Marc Sebastian; p/Sebastian S and Concetta (DeCicco) Calabria, Belleville, NJ; sp/Anthony and Geraldine Tramaglini, Belleville, NJ; ed/BA 1971, MA Rdg & Lang Arts, Jersey City St Col; Cert Course Wk, Kean Col, 1981; pa/Rdg Tchr, Abington Ave Sch, Newark, NJ, 1970-75; Rdg Tchr, Norwood, NJ Public Sch, 1975-79; Rdg Supvr, Reynolds Sch, Upper Saddle River, NJ, 1979-; Owner & Coor, Small Wonder Sch, Upper Saddle River, NJ, 1981-; Mem: IRA; Assn for Supvn & Curric Devel; Phi Delta Kappa; r/Rom Cath; hon/W/W in E.

CALAPAI, DELIA oc/Concert Pianist, Artist, Teacher; b/Mar 8, 1928; h/3003 Van Ness Street, Northwest, Washington, DC 20008; ba/Same; ed/Study w Olga Samaroff, Phila Conservatory; Juilliard Sch of Music; 6 Yrs Study w Artur Schnabel, 1943-49; pa/Concert Perfs in US, Canada & Europe; Series of Concerts in London; Tchg in NYC, London, Paris, Wash DC; Artist Fac, Cath Univ, Univ of KS, Ithaca Col; Master Classes & Lectrs in England, Scotland, Juilliard Sch of Music, IN Univ, Royal No Col Music-Manchester England, Phila Col of Perf'g Arts, Cath Univ, Broadcast Series Celebrating Artur Schnabel's 100th Birthday, WGMS Radio-Wash, DC, 1982, & Num Others; Mem: Col Music Soc; Music Tchrs Nat Assn; European Piano Tchrs Assn; Beethoven Soc; Recording Schubert, "Piano Sonata, A Maj Posthumous, D" Orion Release; hon/Author of Articles, "Schnabel & Schubert," Pub'd in *Clavier Mag,* US-1983, *Piano Jour,* London-1981, & *Chopin Mag,* Tokyo-1984; "The Electrofying Artur Schnabel," *Music Jour,* 1969; "A Visit w Rubinstein", *Clavier Mag,* 1985; Martha Baird Rockefeller Awd, 1961; World W/W of Wom; Intl W/W of Intells; W/W Among Wom, Among Intells, in Mus; Outstg Wom of 20th Cent.

CALDER, ROBERT MAC oc/Aerospace Design Engineer; b/Oct 16, 1932; h/530 South 700 East, Kaysville, UT 84037; ba/Magna, UT; m/Yoshiko Iemura; c/Suzanne, Alex, Irene, John; p/E Harold and Sydney G Calder, Bountiful, UT; sp/Einosuke and Yukiko

Iemura, Japan; ed/BS 1956, UT Sec'dy Tchg Cert 1956, MS 1967, Univ of UT; Att'd Univ of WA, UT St Univ, Univ of IA; mil/USAF, 1956-70, Capt; pa/Tchr, UT Public Schs, 1958-82; VP, Sydney Corp, 1958-82; Sr Design Engr, Aerospace Div, Hercules Inc, 1979-; Conslt in Field, 1960-; Owner, RMC Enterprises, 1983-; UT Ed Assn; NEA; cp/World Jamboree Participant 1947, Scoutmaster, Webelos, Boy Scouts, Nat Jamboree Troop 1973, Mem 1960-75, BSA; Vol Instr, UT St Hunter Safety & Survival Prog, 1964-74; St Advr, US Congl Adv Bd, 1982-; AIAA; Nat Rifle Assn; Am Qtr Horse Assn; Oratorio Soc of UT; Sustaining Mem, Repub Nat Com; Treas 1980, Ed VP 1981, Pres 1982, Hercules Toastmasters Clb; r/LDS; hon/W/W in W.

CALDWELL, JAMES D oc/Executive; b/Jun 25, 1928; h/Box AF, Snowflake, AZ 85937; ba/Same; m/Dixie F; c/Clay, Mark, Jill, Jackie, Bret, Janet, Julie, Ben, Tom; p/Dahl and Una Caldwell, Alberta, Canada; sp/Virgil (dec) and Gerda Flake, Mesa, AZ; ed/BS, Brigham Yg Univ, 1957; MS, Univ of NE, 1960; pa/Fieldman, Univ of NE, 1958-60; Jackson & Kroutwou, 1960-62; Animal Resr, Univ of NV, 1962-64; Pres & Owner, Snowflake Pig Farm Inc, 1966-; AZ Livestock & Sow Bd; AZ Pork Prodr Assn Bd; Lectr, Pig Raising; r/Church of Jesus Christ of LDS; hon/AZ Farm Fam of Yr, 1973; W/W: in World, in W, in Fin & Bus.

CALDWELL, JESSE BURGOYNE III oc/Attorney; b/May 18, 1949; h/PO Box 186, Gastonia, NC 28052; ba/Same; m/Gloria Cline; c/Jesse B IV; p/Dr and Mrs Jesse B Caldwell, Gastonia, NC; ed/AB 1971, JD 1973, Univ of NC-Chapel Hill; pa/Ptnr of Roberts, Caldwell & Planer, 1973-77; Asst Public Defender, 27-A Jud Dist; Sole Practitioner, Jesse B Caldwell III, Atty at Law, 1980-83; Ptnr, Caldwell & Planer, 1983-; Mem Task Force on Battered Wom, 1977-79; Bd of Dirs, Cherryville Comprehensive Day Care Ctr, 1978-80; Bd of Dirs, Crisis Asst Min of Gastonia, 1978-82, Pres 1983-; Pres 1979-81, Bd of Dirs 1978-82, Little Theatre of Gastonia; Bd of Dirs 1979-84, First VP 1980-81, Pres 1982-83, Gaston Commun Action; Bd of Dirs 1979-, VP 1980-, Horizon House Drug Action Ctr; Bd of Dirs, Pioneer Coun, Girl Scouts, 1981-; Mem Task Force on Commun Based Alt, 1981-; Bd of Dirs 1981-, Pres 1982-84, Shepherds Way; Gaston Co Coun on Status of Wom, 1982-83; Gaston Co Pvt Indust Coun, 1980-83; Mem ABA; Mem NC Bar Assn; Mem NS St Bar; Mem NC Acad of Trial Lwyrs; Mem 27-A Bar, Sec 1976-77, Treas 1981-82; r/Meth; hon/Gastonia Jr Wom's Clb Commun Ser Awd, 1981; Indiv Commun Vol Ldr Awd, Gaston Co Vol Assn, 1982; W/W: in Am Law, in S & SW.

CALDWELL, NANCY LOUISE oc/Nurse, Officer; b/Dec 16, 1939; h/2415 8th Street Northwest, Minot, ND 58701; ba/MacDill AFB, FL; m/Douglas Lorimer; p/Goldie M Johnson, Argyle, WI; ed/RN, Sparks Sch of Nsg, Ft Smith, AR, 1960; BSN, TX Christian Univ, 1976; MA Cand in Nsg, Univ of OK; mil/USAF, 1963-, Col; pa/OR Nurse, Madison Gen Hosp, Madison, WI 1960-61; Evening Supvr & Hd Nurse, Sparks Meml Hosp, Ft Smith, AR,

1961-63; Charge Nurse, Supvr, Infection Control Nurse, Chief Nurse, Var USAF Hosps, 1963-; Clin Conslt in Infection Control to Surg PACAF; Mem: Pres, Misawa Chapt, AF Assn, 1982-83; Assn for Practitioners in Infection Control; Assn of OR Nurses; Assn of Mil Surgs of US; Sigma Theta Tau; r/Luth; hon/Author of "Infection Control, " in *Med Ser Digest,* 1980; Grad magna cum laude & w Nsg Hons, TX Christian Univ, 1976.

CALE, LETTIE BEASLEY oc/Educator; b/May 7, 1935; h/1924 West Ashland, Phoenix, AZ 85009; ba/Phoenix, AZ; m/Charles E; c/Dana, Michael, Timothy, Kathleen; p/William L and Emma I Beasley (dec); sp/Glenn and Dorothy Harris Cale, Bucklin, KS; ed/BS, AZ St Univ, 1957; M Home Ec Ed, Univ of AZ, 1969; pa/Tchr (5th Grade), Holbrook, AZ, 1957-59; Tchr (5th Grade) Flagstaff, AZ, 1959-61; Tchr (Kgn), Tucson, AZ, 1962-63; Tchr (Home Ec, Biol), Pinetop-Lakeside, AZ, 1963-67; Asst Supvr Home Ec, AZ Dept of Ed, 1968-77; Spec, Adult Commun Ed, AZ Dept of Ed, 1977-; Mem: AZ Commun Ed Assn; AZ Sch Adm Inc; Am Voc Assn; AZ Voc Assn; Nat Commun Ed Assn; Toastmasters Inc; AZ Adult Ed Assn; Nat Coun St Ed Agy Commun Ed; cp/Chm of Bd, Nat FHA, 1975-76; Chm, Yth Ldrship Prog, AZ Toastmasters, Intl; Pres for 3 Terms, Capitol Clb, T I; r/Prot; hon/Editor, *Displaced Wkrs Progs: Guidelines for Instrn & Oper,* 1983; Author, *Adm Perspectives,* 1982; *Reaching the Hard-to-Reach Parent,* 1981; *Guidelines for Tng Vol Coors in Commun Ed,* 1980; Nat Dist'd Ser Awd, FHA, 1977; AZ Commun Edr of Yr, 1983; Dist'd Ser Awd, AZ Toastmasters, 1983; W/W in W.

CALFEE, WILLIAM H oc/Artist, Sculptor; h/7206 45th Street, Chevy Chase, MD 20015; pa/Instr, Phillips Gallery; Chm Art Dept 1946, Currently Emeritus Prof, Am Univ, Wash DC; Mural Teacher, Centre D'Art, Port-au-Prince, Haiti, 1949; Guest Assoc Prof of Painting, Univ of CA-Berkeley, 1951; Instituted Kensington Wkshop w Patricia Friend, 1978; Co-Fdr, Jefferson Place Gallery Where Some Mems of Washington Color Sch 1st Exhibited; Initiated Watkins Meml Collection & Arranged Var Exhibs incl'g: Tradition & Experiment in Mod Sculpture, Am Univ; Created 8 Murals & 2 Sculptures, Sect of Fine Arts, US Treas Dept; Has Completed Var Comm'd Wks in Wash DC & MD Area; hon/Wks in Var Collections incl'g: Root Collection, Metro Mus of Art, NYC; Nat Collection of Fine Arts, Wash DC; Corcoran Gallery of Art, Wash DC; Honolulu Art Acad; The Phillips Gallery; Edward Bruce Meml Collection; Selden Rodman Collection; Andrew S Keck Collection; Nat Acad of Scis, Wash DC; Num 1 Man Shows incl: Santa Barbara Mus of Art & Travelling Show; Balto Mus; Corcoran Gal of Art; Syracuse Mus of Fine Arts; Phoenix Art Mus; OK Art Ctr; Wehye Gallery; Graham Gallery; Jefferson Place Gallery; Franz Bader Gallery; Watkins Gallery of Am Univ; Univ of MD Sch of Arch; Plum Gallery; Retrospective at Nat Acad of Scis; Grp Shows incl: Carnegie Intl; Metro Mus of Art; Nat Archives; Phillips Gallery;

Nat Acad of Scis; Zabriski Gallery; Ext Travels incl: Turkey, Greece & Egypt; Hon PhD, Am Univ, 1979.

CALHOUN, ERNESTINE ABNEY oc/Editor of Family Books; b/Jan 14, 1923; h/615 39th Avenue, North, Nashville, TN 37209; ba/Nashville, TN; m/Walter (dec); c/Thomas Charles, Paulette; p/Tommie and Ollie Hilliard Abney (dec); ed/BS Elem Ed, Jackson St Col, 1958; MA Christian Ed, Scarritt Col, 1974; pa/Tchr, Meridian Public Schs, Meridian, MS, 1958-70; Editor, *The Kindergartner*, U Meth Publishing House, 1970-72; Editor, Chd's Books, Abingdon Press, 1972-; Mem: Chd's Book Coun; Am Lib Assn; NCTE; IRA; Assn of Childhood Ed Intl; Wom's Nat Book Assn; Black Meth for Ch Renewal; r/U Meth; hon/W/W: in Lib Info, in Am Wom, Dist'd Ams.

CALIO, ANTHONY JOHN oc/Administrator; b/Oct 27, 1929; h/10112 S Glen Road, Potomac, MD 20854; ba/Washington, DC; m/Cheryll Madison; p/Mrs Mary Calio, Phila, PA; sp/Mrs Carl Keller Madison, Potomac, MD; ed/BA Physics 1953, Att'd Grad Sch 1953-54, Univ of PA; Att'd Grad Sch, Carnegie Inst of Technol, 1956-59; Stanford Univ Grad Sch Bus, Sloan Fellow, 1975; mil/AUS,1954-56, Army Chem Corps, Ft Dietrich, MD; pa/Dpty Admr 1981-, Nat Oceanic & Atmospheric Adm, Dept of Commerce, Wash DC; Assoc Admr for Space & Terrestrial Applications 1977-81, Dept Assoc Admr for Space Sci 1975-77, Asst Dir of Planetary Exploration 1967-68, Chief of Instrumentation & Sys Integration 1965-67, NASA HQ's; Dir of Sci & Applications, NASA Johnson Space Ctr, Houston, TX, 1968-75; Chief of Res Engrg, NASA Elects Res Ctr, Boston, MA, 1963-65; Exec VPres & Opers Mgr, Mt Vernon Res Co, Alexandria, VA, 1961-63; Chief of Nuclear Physics Sect, Am Machine & Foundry Co, Alexandria, VA, 1959-61; Assoc Sci, Westinghouse Atomic Power Div, Pgh, PA, 1956-59; Mem: Fellow, AIAA; Fellow, Am Astronautical Soc; Am Geophy Union; The Conf Bd; Bd of Govs, Nat Space Clb; Hd of US Del, Intl Negotiations for Space Search & Rescue Devel & Var Joint Space Projs; cp/Cosmos Clb; hon/Pres Rank of Dist'd Execs, 1980; Dist'd Ser Medal 1973 & 1981, Exceptl Sci Achmt Medal 1971, Exceptl Ser Medal 1969, NASA; Hon DSc, Wash Univ-St Louis, 1974; Nom'd by Pres Reagan for Adm Position, 1981; W/W: in Am, in E, in Frontier Sci & Technol; Am Men & Wom of Sci; Notable Ams.

CALK, MARILYN GRACE BLEDSOE oc/Executive Assistant; b/Apr 20, 1947; h/7096 East Euclid Drive, Englewood, CO 80111; ba/Englewood, CO; m/George D Jenkins; c/Jason Alan; p/F P Bledsoe, Littleton, CO; ed/BMusEd, Univ of CO, 1969; Grad, Jones Real Est Salesman, 1982; pa/Sales Asst, Trane Co, 1976-79; Mktg Asst 1980-81, Asst to Pres 1982-83, John Madden Co; cp/Co-Chm, PR Wom & Bus Conf, 1982-83; Coor, Mus of Outdoor Arts, 1982-83; Dir, Greenwood Plaza Christmas Lighting Prog, 1981-83; Den Mother, CSA Pack 436, 1983; Team Mother, Bruins' Ftball, 1982; hon/DTC JC's Dist'd Ser Awd, 1982; Outstg Yg Wom of Am.

CALKIN, ABIGAIL BURGESS oc/Principal; b/Jun 30, 1941; h/631 Lane Street, Topeka, KS 66606; ba/Topeka, KS; m/Robert Barry Giese; c/Seth McKenzie Koch; p/Ruth Witmer Hunt, Savannah, GA; sp/Eleanor B Giese, Lakeview, OR; ed/BA, Univ of CO, 1963; MA, Univ of OR, 1969; PhD, Univ of KS, 1979; pa/Cnslr, Wallace Village for Chd, 1959-62; Tchr, Chd's Hosp Sch, 1965-67; Prog Coor, Chd's Hosp Sch, 1968-70; Instr, Seattle Pacific Col, 1969; Res Asst, Univ of OR, 1970-72; Instr, OR Col of Ed, 1970, 1972-75; Sch Psychol, 1977-78; Asst Prin, Capital City Sch, 1978-82; Asst Prof, KS St Univ, 1980-83; Prin, Capital City Sch, 1982-; KS Assn of Sch Psychol, Pubs Chp 1978-79; U Sch Admrs of KS, 1979-81; Bd of Editors, *The Behavior Anal*, 1980-81; Bd of Editors, *Jour of Precision Tchg*, 1981-; Topeka Chamber Theatre, 1982-; Assn for Behavior Anal, 1980-; Coun for Exceptl Chd Mbrship, 1967-70, 1979-; Secy, Student Coun for Exceptl Chd, 1967-68; Bd Mem, Univ of OR YWCA, 1971; Adv Bd Mem, Mt Hood Commun Col Nsg Prog, 1971-73; KS Assn of Sch Psychol, 1977-79; r/Soc of Friends; hon/Num Pubs; Elks Foun F'ship, 1966; USOE F'ship Grant, 1967-68; The Compendium, Persons of Eminence in Spec Ed; Outstg Tchrs in Exceptl Ed; W/W: Child Dev, Am Wom; Personalities of W & MW; Intl W/W in Commun Ser.

CALLAHAN, ERRETT H JR oc/Experimental Archaeology Consultant; b/Dec 17, 1937; h/3412 Plymouth Place, Lynchburg, VA 24503; ba/Same; m/Linda Abbey; c/Timothy Callahan; p/Errett and Mary Callahan, Lynchburg, VA; sp/Paul and Gerri Abbey, Richmond, VA; ed/BA, Hampden-Sydney Col, 1960; MFA, VA Commonwlth Univ, 1973; MA 1978, PhD 1981, Cath Univ of Am; mil/NG, 1960-66; pa/Conslt, Cahokia Mounds Mus, E St Louis, IL, 1982; Conslt, Lithic Technol & Exptl Archaeol, Lejre Res Ctr, Lejre, Denmark, 1979-81; Conslt, Lithic Technol & Exptl Archaeol, Flevopolder, Floriadia Projs, Amsterdam, Holland, 1978-81; Fdr & Dir, Piltdown Prodns, Lynchburg, VA, 1974-; Mus Designer, Pamunkey Indian Mus, Pamunkey Indian Tribe, 1977-80; Instr, Dept Anthropology, Cath Univ of Am, Wash DC, 1976-80; Instr, Dept of Sociol & Anthropology, VA Commonwlth Univ, Richmond, VA, 1971-77; Mem: Am Anthropological Assn; Soc for Am Archaeol; Coun of VA Archaeols; En Sts Archaeol Fedn; Archaeol Soc of VA; Sigma Xi; hon/Fdr & Editor, *Flintknappers Exch*, 1978-82; Author: *The Old Rag Report: A Pract Guide to Living Archaeol*, 1973; *Pamunkey Housebldg: An Exptl Study of Late Woodland Constrn Technol in the Powhatan Confederacy*, 1979; Other Articles in Var Jours incl'g: *Archaeol in En N Am*; Grantee, Pamunkey Indian Tribe, 1977; Recip, Grant from Danish-Am Coun w Lejre Res Ctr, 1981; W/W in S & SW; Personalities of S; Men of Achmt; Dir of Dist'd Ams.

CALLAHAN, SISTER MARY VINCENT oc/Professor; b/Jul 2, 1922; h/4701 North Charles Street, Baltimore, MD 21210; ba/Same; p/Mr and Mrs Vincent T Callahan (dec); ed/BA, Col of Notre Dame, Balto, MD, 1943; MS 1945, PhD 1966, Cath Univ of Am,

Wash DC; pa/Mem, Tchg Rel Commun, the Sch Sister of Notre Dame, 1943-; Tchr Math & Chem, Inst of Notre Dame HS, Balto, 1944-45; Tchr Math & Chem, Notre Dame Prep HS, Balto, 1946-48; Tchr Chem & Physics, St Savious HS, Bklyn, NY, 1950-54; Chem Instr 1948-50, Asst Prof to Prof Chem 1954-82, Col of Notre Dame, Balto; Lectr 1983-, Vis'g Prof Chem, Sum Sch 1965-, Cath Univ of Am; Mem: Chm Ednl & Safety Affairs, Chesapeake Sect, Am Chem Soc; Soc Applied Spectroscopy; Sigma Xi; Delta Epsilon Sigma; Kappa Gamma Pi; r/Rom Cath; hon/Author of *Infrared Spectral Study of Dipeptides*, 1966; Winthrop F'ship for MS, Cath Univ, 1943-45; Alumnae S'ship, Col of Notre Dame, 1941-42; NSF Fac F'ships for PhD, Cath Univ, 1959 & 1961; Am Men & Wom of Sci.

CALLAN, PATRICK M oc/Education Administrator; b/Oct 7, 1942; ba/Sacramento, CA; p/Marc Callan (dec); Mary Callan, Capitola, CA; ed/BA Hist 1964, MA Hist 1966, Univ of Santa Clara; Grad Study Am Hist, Univ of CA-LA & Irvine, 1968-71; mil/USAR, 1964-70, 2nd Lt; pa/Dir, CA Post-sec'dy Ed Comm, 1978-; Spec Conslt, Assem Ways & Means Com, CA St Legis, 1981; Exec Dir, WA St Coun for Post-sec-dy Ed, 1975-78; Dir, MT Comm on Post-sec'dy Ed, 1973-74; Staff Dir, Joint Legis Com on Master Plan for Higher Ed, CA St Legis, 1971-73; Tchr, Elem Sch, 1964 & 1965; Instr, Univ of MD, Far E Div, 1966 & 1967; Instr, Grad Sch of Ed, Syracuse Univ, 1974; Fac, Univ of CA Mgmt Inst, 1979-83; Fac, Inst of Ednl Mgmt, Harvard Grad Sch of Ed, 1982 & 1983; Num Conslttg Positions; Mem: Chm, Wn Inter-st Comm for Higher Ed; CA Public Broadcast Comm; CA Student Loan Auth; Adv Coun of Pres, Assn of Gov'g Bds; Adv Coun, Proj on Expanding Reg Coop in Grad & Profl Progs; Wn Tech Manpower Coun; Adv Panel, Nat Inst of Ed Proj; Nat Adv Com, Policy Conf on Post-sec'dy Progs for Disadvantaged, 1982 & 1983; Pres, St Higher Ed Exec Ofcrs Assn, 1981-82; Num Others; cp/Bd of Dirs, Eleanor McClatchy Ctr for Perf'g Arts, Sacramento; Bd of Trustees, Stanford Homes Foun; Others; hon/Author, Over 20 Papers, Reports, Adresses & Articles in Jours incl'g: *CA Jour*; *Critical Choice in Wn Higher Ed*; *New Directions for Higher Ed*; *CA Fin Report*; *AGB Reports*; *Ednl Record*; *WICHE Reports*; *AZ Post-sec'dy Ed in 80's Background Report for the AZ Acad Town Hall on Post-sec'dy Ed*; Others; Recip, Univ of Santa Clara Nobili Medal, 1964; Named by *Change Mag* as 1 of "Top 100 Yg Ldrs of the Acad," 1978; Outstg Yg Men of Am Awd, 1977, 1978; W/W: in W, in CA, in Sacramento; Men of Achmt; Other Biogl Listings.

CALLAWAY, HOWARD HOLLIS oc/Executive; b/Apr 2, 1927; h/3131 East Alameda Avenue, Apartment 2103, Denver, CO 80209; ba/Denver, CO; m/Elizabeth Walton; c/Betsy C Considine, Howard Hollis Jr, Edward Cason, Virginia Hand Martin, Ralph Walton; p/Cason J Callaway Sr (dec); Virginia Hand Callaway, Hamilton, GA; sp/Ralph Walton Sr, Hamilton, GA; ed/Att'd GA Inst of Technol, 1944-45; BS Mil Engrg, US Mil Acad W Point, 1949; mil/AUS, 1949-51, Lt Inf; pa/Chm, Crested Butte Mtn Resort, 1977-; Pres,

Callaway Mgmt Grp, 1982-; Mgr, Pres Ford's Campaign, 1975-76; Secy of AUS, 1973-75; CEO Interfin Inc, 1970-77; Pres, Callaway Gardens, 1953-70; Mem of US Cong, Rep from GA, 1965-66; cp/St Chm, CO Repub Party, 1981-; Bd Men, Chief Exec Org, 1976-; Mem, World Bus Coun, 1958-; Rotary Clb, 1982-; r/Epis; hon/Medal of Dist'd Public Ser, Dept of Def, 1975; Combat Inf Badge; 3 Campaign Ribbons; Korea Pres Unit Cit; W/W: in Am Politics, in S & SW, in W, of Contemp Achmt, in Am; Men of Achmt; Intl Biogl Ctr; Men & Wom of Distn; Notable Ams; Other Biogl Listings.

CALLIER, M ALICE oc/Educational Supervisor K-9; b/Jul 10, 1937; h/4000 Colemere Circle, Dayton, OH 45415; ba/Dayton, OH; m/M Ernest; c/Myron Ernest; p/Frank and Mary Dowe (dec); ed/BS, Ctl St Univ, 1962; MEd, Wright St Univ, 1970; Doct Cand, OH St Univ, 1977; pa/Tchr, Penn Hill Sch Dist, 1962-63; Lang Arts Resource 1968-71, Rdg/Lang Arts Supvr 1971-, Dayton City Schs; Bd of Dirs, Wittenberg Univ, 1982-85; Dir, Coop Lang Arts Writing Proj, Tchr Tng Model, 1980-82; cp/ASCD; IRA; Pres, Dayton Area Rdg Coun, 1972-73; OAESA; DSMA; Pi Lambda Theta; Phi Delta Kappa; Alpha Kappa Alpha Sorority, Inc; r/Luth; hon/Author of Num Profl Pubs.

CAMERON, CAROLINE STEELE oc/Fiscal Specialist; b/Apr 5, 1955; h/5630 Willow Drive, Durham, NC 27712; ba/Durham, NC; m/Keith R; c/Christina; p/Mr and Mrs Harold Steele, Medford, OR; sp/Mr and Mrs W Cameron, Brookings, OR; ed/BS summa cum laude, So OR St Col, 1976; pa/Planning Aide for Medford, OR, 1976; Bkkpr, Stark's, 1977-78; Patient Relats Rep 1979-81, Fiscal Spec 1981-, Duke Univ Med Ctr; Assoc Staff, Campus Life, 1974-76; cp/Area Coor, Conservative Caucus of Rogue Val, OR, 1977-78; Co-Chm, Durham Co Right to Life, 1981-; Mem Congl Clb of NC, 1982-; Mem Yg Repub of NC, 1983-; Mem Wash Legal Foun, 1981-; Mem Conservative Caucus, 1979-; r/Christian; hon/So OR St Col Friendship Awd, 1977; Outstg Wom Grad, 1977; St S'ship Comm, OR Scholar, 1973; Outstg Yg Wom of Am; World W/W of Wom.

CAMERON, DOUGLAS GEORGE oc/Emeritus Professor Medicine; b/Mar 11, 1917; h/227 Portland Avenue, Montreal, Quebec, Canada H3R1V3; ba/Montreal, Canada; m/Jeanne; c/George, Janes, Heather, Bruce, Nancy, Marian; p/G L Cameron (dec); sp/Mr L M Thompson, N Sidney, Nova Scotia; ed/BS 1937, Rhodes Scholar 1940, Univ of Saskatchewan; MD, CM, McGill Univ, 1940; Internship, Montreal Gen Hosp, 1940; BS Med Sci, Univ of Oxford, 1948; mil/Royal Canadian Army Med Corps, 1941-46, England, N Africa, Italy, NW Europe, Lt Col; pa/Phys-in-Chief 1957-80, Conslt in Med 1980-, Other Positions, Montreal Gen Hosp; Prof Med 1957-80, Emeritus Prof 1980-, Other Positions, McGill Univ; Conslt in Med at Var Hosps incl'g: Barrie Meml Hosp, Ormstown, Quebec; Brome-Missiquoi-Perkins Hosp, Sweetsburg, Quebec; Douglas Hosp, Verdun, Quebec; Reddy Meml Host, Montreal, Quebec; Montreal Chest

Hosp Ctr, Montreal, Quebec; Med Conslt, The Montreal Chd's Hosp, Montreal; Other Hon Conslt Positions; Num Vis'g Prof'ships; Mem: Fellow, Am Col of Phys; Bd of Dirs: Canadian Assn of Rhodes Scholars; Nutrition Today Soc; Chm'ships Incl: Bd of Examrs, the Royal Col of Phys & Surgs of Canada; Com on Med Ed, Canadian Med Assn; Med Adv Com, Cancer Res Soc; Gov, Am Col of Phys; Pres Positions incl: Pres, The Royal Col of Phys & Surgs of Canada, 1978-80; L'Assn Médicale de la Province de Québec; Canadian Soc for Clin Invest; Montreal Physiol Soc; Osler Reporting Soc; Montreal Medico-Chirurgical Soc; Canadian Assn of Profs of Med, 1978; Num Other Com Positions & Assn Mbrships; r/Prot; hon/Author, Over 70 Reports, Book Chapts & Articles in Profl Jours incl'g: *Experientia Supplementum; Transactions of Assn of Am Phys; Canadian Med Assn Jour; Nova Scotia Med Bltn; Canadian Jour of Public Hlth; Annals of Royal Col of Phys & Surgs of Canada;* Others; Conslt in Med, The Montreal Gen Hosp, 1982; Prof Emeritus, McGill Univ, 1982; Sr Mem, Canadian Med Assn, 1982; Hon Conslt in Internal Med, Douglas Hosp Ctr, 1982; Dixon Meml Lectr, Dalhousie Univ, 1981; Hon Fellow, Royal Australian Col of Phys, 1980; Hon Fellow, Royal Col of Phys Glasgow, 1980; Ofcr, The Order of Canada, 1979; Recip, The Queen's 25th Anniv Medal, 1977; Lectrships: Univ of Toronto; Univ of Wn Ontario; Mercy Hosp, Pgh; Cent Medal Canada; Mil Cross, Royal Canadian Regiment.

CAMERON, NINA RAO oc/District Counsellor for Immigration Service; b/Apr 28, 1925; h/441 East 20th Street, New York, NY 10010; ba/New York, NY; c/Scott Cameron; p/Paul P Rao, NYC; ed/BA, Manhattanville Col of Sacred Heart, 1945; BA Law, Bklyn Law Sch, 1950; Hon Doct in Law, Mexican Acad of Intl Law, Univ of Mexico, 1968; pa/Dist Counsel, US Immigration Ser, 1968-; Law Asst, to Supr Ct Justice St of NY, 1967; Dir, UN & Consular Corp Com of City of NY & Asst Com of Public Events Chief of Protocol, NYC, 1958-65; Asst Dir of Commerce, NYC, 1958-65; Pvt Law Pract, 1966 & 1955-56; Atty Advr, Dept of Justice-INS, US Naturalization Examr, 1952-54; Mem: Bas Assn of City of NY-Grievance Com, 1972-75; Formerly w Spec Com to Coop w the Inter-Am Bar Assn; Past Mem of Bd of Dirs & Judiciary Com, Wom's Bar Assn of NY; Legions of Merit-Chief of Protocol & Mem Bd of Dirs, Am Soc of Italy; cp/Mem Bd of Dirs, Co Symph Orch of Westchester; Co-Chm, Intl Debutante Ball; r/Cath; hon/Exceptl Perf Cert, Dept of Justice Atty from US Atty Gen, 1982; Amita Aws, Wom of Outstg Achmt of Italian Ancestry, 1956; Vespucci Awd, Outstg Achmt of Italian Ancestry, 1957; Silver Tray, Soc of Fgn Consuls, 1961; Guest of Hon & Recip of Gold Watch, Soc of Fgn Consuls, 1963; Num Decorations from Fgn Govts incl: Ecuador, Italy, Repub of Germany, Nicaragua, Taiwan (Nationalist China); W/W: of Am Am, in E; Nat Social Dir; Royal Blue Book; Commun Ldrs of Am; Personalities of Am; Notable Ams.

CAMERON, SARAH ANN MAZIQUE oc/Nurse; b/Oct 6, 1954; h/

425 College Street, Natchez, MS 39120; ba/Natchez, MS; c/Kendrick Cavanaugh Cameron; p/Mr and Mrs W C Mazique, Natchez, MS; ed/AA, Natchez Jr Col, 1974; BS Biol, Jackson St Univ, 1977; Course Wk toward MS, OH St Univ, 1978; Hours toward MS 1981, BS RN 1983, Alcorn St Univ; pa/Musician for Var Chs, Childhood to Present; Lab Asst, Kinwood Gen Hosp, W Davison-Detroit, MI, 1978-79; Instr Gen Biol & Phys Sci, Asst Choir Dir & Student Govt Sponsor, Natchez Jr Col, 1979-83; Staff Nurse, RN Nsg Supvr, Jefferson Co Hosp, Fayette, MS, 1983; RN Staff Nurse, Jefferson Davis Hosp, Natchez, MS, 1984-; Mem Zeta Delta Omega Chapt, Alpha Kappa Alpha; Bd Mem, Emer Med Benevolent Assn; Yg People's Orgl Union, Natchez Jr Col; Jackson St Univ Alumni Assn; Past Mem: Choir, Bapt Student Union, at Natchez Jr Col; Choir, Chorale, Opera So Prodns, Beta Beta Beta, Alpha Chi, Phi Kappa Phi, Gamma Rho Chapt Alpha Kappa Alpha, at Jackson St Univ; MS Student Nurses Assn, at Alcorn St Univ; cp/Voices of Hope of Natchez, MS; Org for Ednl & Social Improvement; r/Bapt; hon/Phi Kappa Phi; Alpha Chi; Beta Beta Beta; W/W Among Students in Am Cols & Univs.

CAMP, LOUISE PHIFER oc/Farmer, Housewife; b/Mar 22, 1912; h/701 Oleander Avenue, Bakersfield, CA 93304; ba/Same; m/Wofford Benjamin; c/Addie Louise Wise Segars; George William Wise; Sarah C Cory; p/Louisa and Charles McKnight Phifer, Gaffney, SC; ed/BA, BMus 1933, Converse Col; pa/Min of Mus, Bapt Evang Meetings in NC, SC & GA, 1929-34; Voice Tchr, Limestone Col, 1932; Orgr & Dir, Choral Grps in NC, SC & GA, 1935-55; Soloist, St John's Meth Ch, 1953-55; Soloist, Presb Ch, 1934-55; Farmer, Edgefield Co, SC, 1945-77; Dir, Bank of Trenton, 1945-78; Co-Fdr, Trenton Dev Corp, 1950; Secy, W B Camp Inc, 1956-; Nat Assn Bk Wom & Farm Bur in SC & CA; Pres, Pro Am, 1958-59; Dir, Kern Co, Music Assn, 1957-59; Co-Fdr, Louise Phifer Camp Foun, Limestone Col, 1957; Co-Fdr & Dir, Kern Co Free Enterprise Assn, 1960; Orgr & Pres, Wom's Div, Kern Co Chapt, Freedoms Foun at Val Forge, 1969; Nat Trustee, Freedoms Foun at Val Forge, 1974-; Trustee, SC Foun of Indep Col Inc, 1973-; Bd of Trustees, Limestone Col; Dir, John & Beverly Stauffer Foun, 1973; VChm, Rel Heritage of Am, 1980-; AAUW; DAR; UDC; PEO; Bakersfield Wom Clb; Bakersfield Garden Clb; Presb Ch; Philharm Assn; Dir, Gospel Music Assn & Nat Campaign Chm, Gospel Music Hall of Fame, Res Lib & Mus, 1978-81; Nat Chm, Decade of Confidence Campaign, Limestone Col, 1980-; hon/Outstg Cotton Grower of SC, SC Agri Ext Ser, 1954; Outstg Alumna Awd, Limestone Col, 1956; Awd, Freedoms Foun at Val Forge, 1973; Hon Dr Humanities, Limestone Col, 1977; Order of K Hospitallers of St John, 1979; Hon Alumnus, Clemson Univ, 1982.

CAMP, WILIAM G oc/Professor; b/Oct 20, 1946; h/2200D Foxridge Apartments, Blacksburg, VA 24061; ba/Blacksburg, VA; c/Mary Elizabeth, William Grantley; p/Mr and Mrs W G Camp, Rockmart, GA; ed/BSA, 1968;

MEd, 1970; PhD, 1977; mil/AUS, 1970-72; Army NG, Currently; pa/Voc Agri Tchr, 1972-75; Voc Supvr, 1975-78; Asst Prof Agr Ed, Purdue Univ, 1978-80; Asst Prof Agri Ed, VA Polytech Inst & St Univ, 1980-; Mem: Am Voc Assn; VA Voc Assn; Nat Voc Agri Tchrs Assn; VA Voc Agri Tchrs Assn; NG Assn of US; hon/Author of Var Res, Practical & Profl Jour Articles; Curric Mats & Textbooks; Var Paper Presentations; Phi Delta Kappa, 1980; Omicron Tau Theta, 1981; Gamma Sigma Delta, 1981; Phi Kappa Phi, 1970; Scabbard & Blade, 1970; Outstg Yg Men of Am.

CAMPANIZZI, CHARLES VANDORA oc/Educator; b/Mar 24, 1938; h/100 Faculty Drive, West Liberty, WV 26074; ba/West Liberty, WV 26074; m/Judy Dell Saffell; c/Barry and Cory; p/Vandora "Duke" and Elizabeth Campanizzi, Flushing, OH; sp/Herman (dec) and Hazel Saffell, New Philadelphia, OH; ed/BS, Muskingum Col, 1960; MA, WV Univ, 1964; MS, Radford Col, 1968; pa/Tchr 1960-67, Prin 1964-67, Flushing HS; Assoc Prof of Psych 1968-, Chm of Psych Dept 1970-79, W Liberty St Col; Pt-time Conslt & Tchr, 1969-; Am Psychol Assn; cp/Wheeling, WV Crisis Hotline; r/Prot; hon/Profl Pub in Progress; W/W in S & SW.

CAMPBELL, CHARLES ALTON oc/Executive; b/Mar 10, 1944; h/10 Canterbury Place, Southwest, Rome, GA 30161; ba/Rome, GA; m/Alla Traber; c/Christine Beensen, Elizabeth Traber, Charles Traber; p/Rayford M and Celecia Campbell, Brunswick, GA; sp/Eugene E Traber (dec); Elizabeth A Traber, Madison, GA; ed/BIE, GA Inst of Technol, 1966; MBA, Harvard Bus Sch, 1973; mil/USN, Civil Engr Corps, 1967-69; pa/Gen Sales Mgr, Nat Homes Corp, Thomson, GA, 1973; Asst to Pres & Chm, Knox Rlty & Investmt, 1973-74; Mgr Opers Projs-Knox Div Camak Lumber Opers Thomson GA 1974-75, Mgr Opers Wood Prods Grp NYC 1975-77, Dir Chems Devel NYC 1977-79, Dir Oper Planning & Control NW Reg Opers Seattle WA 1979-80, ITT Rayonier; Pres & CEO, Fox Mfg Co, 1980-81; Pres, Camtec Inc, 1981-; cp/Mem, Coosa Country Clb, Rome, GA; r/Epis; hon/Author of "Computers & Decisions," Plywood & Panel World, 1983; W/W: in S & SW, in Fin & Indust, of Contemp Achmt; Men of Achmt; Dir of Dist'd Ams; Biogl Roll of Hon; DIB; 2000 Notable Ams.

CAMPBELL, CLIFTON PAUL oc/University Professor, and Executive; b/Jul 5, 1938; h/1420 Moorgate Drive, Knoxville, TN 37922; ba/Univ TN, Knoxville, TN, & Wilmington, DE; m/Linda Lee; c/Scott Alan and Douglas Eric; p/Clifton and Kathleen Campbell, Knoxville, TN; sp/Rhuama and Edward Reavis, Winston-Salem, NC; ed/BS, CA Univ of PA, 1964; MEd, 1968, EdD 1971, Univ of DE, 1973-75; mil/USNR, 1955-, CDR; pa/Dean of Instrn, DE Tech Col, 1975-76; Ed Spec, US Dept of Labor, Riyadh, Saudi Arabia, 1976-78; Tng Advr, EG & G InterTech, Dammam, Saudi Arabia, 1978-83; Prof Voc Tech Ed, 1983-; VP, DTA Assoc, 1983-; cp/Nav Resv; Mason; Shriner; Nat Sojourners; Am Soc for Tng & Devel; Am Voc Assn; Am Indust Arts Assn;

Nat Assn of Indust & Tech Tchr Edrs; Nat Assn for Trade & Indust Ed; Am Coun on Indust Arts Tchr Ed; r/Presb; hon/Author Num Profl Pubs; Cert of Apprec, 1981; Outstg Res Awd, 1975, Am Indust Arts Assn; Cert of Apprec, 1969, Iota Lambda Sigma; W/W: World, E, Indust Arts Tchr Ed; 2,000 Notable Ams; Men of Achmt; Intl W/W Contemp Achmt; Prom Tng & Devel Profls.

CAMPBELL, EVELYN LOUISA MOORE oc/Marketing Representative; b/Aug 1, 1951; h/3414 Carriage Hill Circle T4, Randalstown, MD 21133; ba/Baltimore, MD; c/Evelyn Louisa Alyshe; p/Arthur (dec) and Evelyn Moore, Mt Vernon, NY; ed/BA, Manhattanville Col, 1973; Cert, Urban Leag Data Processing Ctr, 1976; pa/Tchr, Mt Vernon Bd of Ed, 1978-74; Sys Mktg Rep, Control Data Corp, 1976-; cp/ACM; NAACP; NCNW; Mem Student Fac Com of Manhattanville Col, 1978; Co-Chm of Gospel Choir of Manhattanville, 1971-73; Civil Def Cadets Supvr, 1968-70; Pres of MYF, 1967; Ch Sch Tchr, 1967-70; Voter Registration Dr, 1969, 71, 74; Canvassing Internal & External; r/U Meth; hon/Sys Mktg Rep of the Mo, 1979; Profl Mktg Awd, 1982; SEn Winners Cir, 1979; Br Net Revenue Ldr; 4 Yr S'ship Awd, 1969-74; Hon Student, Urban Leag Data Processing Ctr.

CAMPBELL, GEORGE JR oc/Physicist; b/Dec 2, 1945; h/149 Livingston Avenue, New Brunswick, NJ 08901; ba/Holmdel, NJ; m/Mary Schmidt; c/Sekou, Gankai; p/Lillian Campbell, Phila, PA; sp/Harvey N Schmidt, Phila, PA; ed/BS Physics, Drexel Univ, 1968; PhD Physics, Syracuse Univ, 1977; pa/Enrgr Res, Intl Harvester Co, 1966-68; Sr Fac, Mkumbi Intl Col, 1969-71; Fac, Syracuse Univ, 1977; Satellite Transmissions, Bell Telephone Labs, 1977-; cp/Mem Bd of Trustees, Rantan Val YMCA, 1979-83; Bd of Dirs 1978-, VChm 1980-81 & 1983, Urban Leag of Gtr New Brunswick; Allocations Panel, U Way of Ctl Jersey, 1981-; Commun Bd of Advrs, Cook Col, Rutgers Univ, 1978-; hon/Author of Var Articles in Profl Jours incl'g: Jour Math Physics; Phy Review; AIAA Communs Satellite Sys Conf; Guggenheim Scholar, 1963-67; Physics Hon Soc, 1966; Sum Fellow, Syracuse Univ, 1973-75; Num Other Civic Hons; W/W in E.

CAMPBELL, GLORIA MAE oc/Fabric and Interior Designer; b/Dec 19, 1925; h/9414 216th Street Southwest, Edmonds, WA 98020; ba/Same; m/John Malcolm; c/Moira Mary, Morna Selma; p/Jacob L Pete, Ely, MN; sp/Alexander Campbell (dec); ed/BFA 1950, MFA 1951, Sch of Art Inst of Chgo; pa/Interior Designer, Glass-Huebner Assocs, Chgo, 1951-52; Textile Designer, Cannon Mills, NYC, 1952-54; Free Lance Designer, NYC 1954-65 & Edmonds, WA 1965-; Pres Pacific NW Chapt, Nat Home Fashions Leag, 1980-82; Assoc Mem, Illuminating Engrs Soc; Handweavers Guild of Am; Am Tapestry Alliance; cp/Secy 1972-74, Pres 1978-80, Seaview Weavers Guild; r/Prot; hon/Daniel D Vandergrift S'ship, Art Inst of Chgo, 1947-48; Joseph S Snydacker S'ship, Art Inst of Chgo, 1948-49; Zeta Chapt, Delta Phi Delta; W/W: of Wom, of Am Wom; DIB; Personalities of W & MW.

CAMPBELL, JOHN CLYDE III oc/Executive; b/Dec 3, 1944; h/6809 Edmonstone Avenue, Richmond, VA 23226; ba/Glenn Allen, VA; m/Maureen Theresa (Butler); c/John C IV, Justin W; p/John and Dorothy (McKenna) Campbell (dec); sp/Joseph and Josephine Butler (dec); ed/BA 1967, MBA 1969, MA 1984, SUNY-Buffalo; mil/AUS, 1969-72, Capt; pa/VA Rep-at-Large, Am Cancer Soc, 1972-73; VA Sales Rep, Metro Life Ins Co, 1973-78; Dir for Long-Range Devel, Am Heart Assn, 1978-; Mem, Soc for Heart Assn Staff; cp/Fdg Chm, Richmond Area Alliance, 1975; Pres, Duntreath Assocs, 1980; Chm Scouting Prog St Bridgets & Cubmaster, BSA, 1981-; Chm 1981-82, Dir 1982-, Richmond Area Inter-Clb Coun; Civitan; JC's; r/Cath; hon/Author of Articles in Profl Jours incl'g: The Jour; Life Ins Selling; Fund Raising Mgmt; F'ship Awd, Soc of Heart Assn Profl Staff, 1982-84; 1st Yr Awd & Spoke Awd, JC's, 1974; Past Secy Awd, Richmond Civitan, 1979-80; AUS Commend Medal, 1972; W/W in S & SW.

CAMPBELL, JOHN GOOCH oc/Surgeon; b/Jun 13, 1940; h/3506 East 66th Street, Tulsa, OK 74136; ba/Tulsa, OK; m/Linda; c/Darin P Ramey; p/G Raymond and Mary M Campbell, OKC, OK; sp/Philip Edens (dec) and Louise Norcom, OKC, OK; ed/AB, Westminster Col, 1962; MD, Univ of OK, 1966; mil/USAF, 1968-70, Flight Surg; pa/Pres, Assn Ear, Nose & Throat of Tulsa, OK; Pres, OK Acad Otolaryngology, 1980-81; AMA; OK St Med Assn; ACS; AAFPRS; AAO-HNS; ASHNS; So Med Assn; Tulsa Co Med Soc; Pres, Tulsa Otolaryngologic Soc, 1979-80; r/Presb; hon/Book Reviewer, Am J of Otolaryngology; Diplomate, Am Bd of Otolaryngology; Clin Assoc Prof, Univ of OK; W/W in S & SW.

CAMPBELL, JOHN MORGAN JR oc/Executive; b/Jan 17, 1947; h/4316 Northridge, Norman, OK 73069; ba/Norman, OK 73069; m/Linda; c/Mark and Jennifer; p/J Campbell, Norman, OK; sp/Lydia Norie, Norman, OK; ed/BS Ec, BS Polit Sci, 1969; MS Stats, 1971; PhD, Ec Stats, 1974; pa/Res Assoc, Univ of Chgo, 1975-77; Assoc Prof, DePaul Univ, 1975-77; Assoc Prof, FL St Univ, 1977-81; Pres/CEO, John M Campbell & Co, 1981-; cp/Econometric Soc; Am Ec Assn; Soc of Petro Engrs; Am Stat Assn; Soc for Risk Anal; hon/Author Num Profl Pubs; Omicron Delta Epsilon; W/W: in S & SW, in Energy, in Technol Today.

CAMPBELL, WILLIAM PEYTON oc/Brigadier General, USA, (Retired); SCORE Counselor; b/Jul 8, 1896; h/Route 1, Box 123, Searcy, AR 72143; ba/Same; m/Kathleen Williams; c/Harriet Theresa C King; p/William A and Harriet (Gabbert) C (dec); ed/BSA, Univ of AR, 1917; AMP, Harvard Univ, 1952; Army Fin Sch; VMI; Chem Warfare Sch; Cavalry Sch; Indust Col of Armed Forces; mil/USA, 1917-1953; pa/Asst Mil Attache, London, England, 1941-42; Fin Rep HQ, ETO, London, England, 1942-43; Advr Adm Fin Peruvian Army, Lima, Peru, 1945-47; Chief Army Audit Agy, 1948-50; Mem Gen Staff Corps, USA, Wash, DC, 1949-53; Appt'd Brigadier Gen, USA, 1951; Asst Chief of Fin, AUS, Wash, DC, 1951-53; Exec Asst to Pres Harding Col, Search, AR,

1953-66; On Bd Armed Forces Relief & Benefit Assn, 1950-51; Cnslr, SCORE; cp/Ret'd Ofcrs Assn, 1953-; Nat Assn Uniformed Sers, 1970-; Mil Order World Wars, 1979-; Hon Mem Army Non-Comm'd Ofcrs Assn, 1971-; Chm, Migratory Labor Com, St of AR, 1970; Kappa Alpha; Alpha Psi Omega; Omicron Delta Alpha; Brotherhood of St Andrew, Epis Lay Order; Epis Ch Lay Rdr, 1954-; Ser Corps of Ret'd Execs, 1967-; Am Legion, 1953-; Disabled Am Vets, 1953-; Mil Order of the Purple Heart; r/Epis; hon/Named "SCORE Cnslr of the Yr", 1973, Small Bus Adm, Wash, DC; 5 Geo Wash Hon Medals from Freedom's Foun "For Outstg Achmt in Bringing About a Better Understanding of Am Way of Life", 1954-60; 1975 Annual Americanism Awd, AR Am Legion; Mil Decorations from Peru, Philippine Isls, Nepal, France, Chile; 9 Mil Decorations incl'g US, Legion of Merit, Bronze Star, Commend Ribbon W5 OLC, Purple Heart, 14 Ser Medals; UN, 2 Ser Medals, Order of Lafayette, US Gen Staff Insignia, Conspicious Ser Cross of NY; Author, "Machine Gunners Note Book", 1931; Co-Author, "World War Procurement & Industl Mobilization", 1939; Co-Author, "Here's How by Who's Who", 1965; Contbr, *Cavalry Jour*; Contbr, *Army, Nav & Air Force Jour*, *Nat Paper Trade Assn Qtrly*, *Christian Crusade*, *Nat Ed Prog's Freedom Forum*, 1962; Editor, "Prayer Corner" of *AR Legionnaire*; W/ W Am Ed; Commun Ldrs of Am.

CANALIZO, ALBERT EUGENE II oc/Executive, Civic Worker; b/Dec 26, 1943; h/6578 Louis XIV, New Orleans, LA 70124; ba/Brooklyn, NY; m/Marilyn Suzanne Belanger; c/Donna Lynn; p/ Albert Eugene Sr and Alene (McElroy) Canalizo, NO, LA; sp/Julius P and Stella (Rhodes) Belanger, Houma, LA; ed/BS, LA St Univ, 1964; MBA 1968, Postgrad Study in Law, Tulane Univ; Att'd Adv'd Mgmt Prog, Harvard Univ, 1975; Att'd Columbia Univ Bus Sch, 1976; mil/LA St Mil Dept, 1972-74, Col; pa/Mgr VSI Credit Corp Div 1974-76, VPres Dir Mktg & Human Resources 1976-82, US Industs Inc; Pres, Canalizo & Assocs, 1981-; Co-Fdr, Texas, Lakeshore Yeshiva Sch, 1970-81; Notary Public, 1970-; cp/Metro Mus of Art; Am Mus of Nat His; NY Hist Soc; Agudah Israel World Org; House of Sages, Am Cancer Soc; Am Jewish Com; B'nai B'rith Metro Conf; Bd of Jewish Ed; BSA; Chd Aid Soc; Conf of Pres of Maj Jewish Org; Fdn of Jewish Philanthropies Gtr NY Fund; Jewish Bd of Fam & Chd Sers; Jewish Child Care Assn of NY; Metro NY Coor Coun on Jewish Poverty; Nat Soc for Autistic Chd; NY Soc for Preven of Cruelty to Chd; Save Russian Jewery; U Jewish Appeal, Edna Gladney Home; Ohel Chd's Home; Asthmatic Chd's Foun; Maimonides Med Ctr; NY Coun for Humanities; NY Geneal Soc; Soc CA Pioneers; Bikur Cholim; Harvard Bus Sch Clb; r/Jewish; hon/Author & Contbr of Num Articles to Profl Pubs; Bus-man of Yr, BBB, 1973; Ldr of Yr, C of C; Aid de Camp, Gov of LA, 1972-74; Lemann-Stern Fellow, 1975-76; Mgr of Yr, US Industs, 1976; W/W in World, in Am.

CANCRO, MICHAEL PAUL oc/ Research Immunologist, Educator; b/

Oct 28, 1949; h/56 N Hillcrest Road, Springfield, PA, 19064; ba/Philadelphia, PA; m/Jamie Arlene Robinson; c/Robin Elizabeth; p/Ciro A and Florence L (Meekima) Cancro, Silver Spring, MD; sp/James P and Marjory McCoy Robinson, Charleston, WV; ed/BS Zool, 1973; PhD Zool, 1976; Postdoct Study, 1976-78; pa/Res Assoc, LCB NIH; Postdoct Trainee, Asst Prof Pathol 1979, Assoc Prof Pathol 1984-, Univ of PA; Mem: AAAS; Am Assn of Immunols, 1980; Am Soc Zools, 1980; cp/ Scoutmaster, BSA; hon/Author of Num Sci Articles Pub'd in Profl Jours; Berwick Tchg Awd, Univ of PA, 1984; AAE F'ship, 1980; Awardee, NIH & ACS Grants.

CANNADY, HERMAN REGINALD SR oc/Archbishop; b/Mar 30, 1937; h/ 34 Morris Street, Yonkers, NY 10705; ba/Yonkers, NY; m/Ruth Agnes Hutner; c/Herman R Cannady Jr, Brian D Cannady; p/Maguerite Bruton, New Rochelle, NY; sp/Ruth Hutner, Yonkers, NY; ed/BA Theol, MA Rel Ed, Grad Theol, ThD, DD: Am Bible Sem, IL; Forge Inst, PA; Am Bible Sem, FL; NY Jewish Theol Sem Inst for Rel Studies; Ch of Christ Bible Inst, NY; Evang Tchr Tng Assn, IL; PhD Sacred Lttrs, Am Wesleyan Col, IN; pa/Currently: Archbishop & Moderator, New Covenant Ch of the Holy Spirit, Nat & Intl; Chancellor, Christ Theol Sem; Pres, En Theol Consortium Fac of Arts & Scis, Currently; Pres, Evang Synod, Nat & Intl; Fdr, 301 Devel Foun of New Covenant J; Fdr & Pres: Neo-Covenant Energy Sales Corp, New Covenant Devel & Mfg Corp, Neo-Covenant Trans Corp; Fdr & Prin, Epic Intl (Advtg) Inc; Assoc & Bd Mem, Agri Teams Inc; Prin, Taft Enterprises; Num Lectr Engagements; Chaplain for Var Orgs; Num Others Secular & Rel Orgs; Past: Pres, Ch of Christ Bible Inst, NY; Dir Public Relats, Dir Rel Ed Pastor, Chm Westchester & Wn NY St Diocese, Other Positions, w Ch of Christ; VPres & Pres, Interdenom Min Alliance of New Rochelle, NY; Mem Exec Com, Chm World Hunger Com, Interrel Coun of New Rochelle; Adj Prof, Shaw Div Sch Sem w/o Walls, Raleigh, NC; Num Others; cp/Current: Mem, Yonkers Anti-Crime Roundtable, NY; Mem, Clergy of Yonkers; Fdr & Chm of Bd, Gilead Med Ctr, Yonkers; Fdr & Chm of Bd, Universal Improvement Assn; Bd of Dirs, Yonkers Day Care Ctr Inc; Trustee, West-chester-Rockland Guardians Assn; Num Spkg Presentations; Num Other Previous Activs; r/Evang-Liturgical, Ethiopian Orthodox; hon/Author of Num Sermons, Lectrs & Articles in Jour Pubs; Proclamation Awds 1976, 1981 & 1982, Ofc of Mayor of Yonkers; Hon in Issue of *Westchester Spotlight*, 1984; K Cmmdr of Grace, Ambassador-at-large Extraodinary, K of Malta, Order K Hospitallers of St John of Jerusalem, 1982; Plaque of Recog & Apprec, Deliverance Bible Inst, 1979; Plaque of Recog, Ofcl Bd & Standing Coms, Archbishop's Chapel, 1976; Apprec Awd, Commun Bible Inst, 1982; Humanitarian Awd, Nat Black Police Assn, 1981; Dean of Col, Fellow, Am Wesleyan Col; Chancellor's Chain, Ch of Christ Bible Inst, 1973; Black Arts Awd, NY Metro Area, 1973; Armor Bearers

Yg People's Union, St of NY.

CANNON, GARLAND oc/Professor; b/Dec 5, 1924; h/805 Hawthorn, College Station, TX 77840; ba/College Station, TX; m/Patrica Richardson; c/Margaret, India, Jennifer, William; ed/BA Eng 1947, PhD Linguistics 1954, Univ of TX; MA Eng, Stanford Univ, 1952; mil/ USMC, WW II; pa/Assoc Prof Eng, CUNY, 1963-66; Prof Eng & Linguistics, TX A&M Univ, 1966-; Vis'g Prof Humanities, Univ of MI, 1970-71; Vis'g Prof Eng & Linguistics, Kuwait Univ, 1979-81; Mem: Am Dialect Soc; Linguistic Soc of Am; MLA; Pres, S Asian Lit Assn, 1979-84; r/Prot; hon/Author of Books incl'g: *Sir Wm Jones, Orientalist*, 1982; *Oriental Jones*, 1964; Editor, *Lttrs of Sir Wm Jones*, 1970; *Hist of Eng Lang*, 1972; *Integrated Transformational Grammar of Eng*, 1978; Num Res Articles Pub'd in Profl Jours; Dist'd Res Awd, TX A&M Univ, 1972; Book of Yr Awd, *London Sunday Telegraph*, 1970; W/W: in S & SW, of Authors; Dir Am Scholars; Contemp Authors; Other Biogl Listings.

CANNON, (FARR) VIVIAN MARRIE oc/Career Education Coordinator; b/Sep 17, 1946; h/2965 Oro Blanco Street, Colorado Springs, CO 80917; ba/Colorado Springs, CO 80903; m/ Edward E; c/Angela Renee, Aelaina Joy; p/Mr and Mrs Ruben H Farr, Colorado Springs, CO; sp/Lavonia Cannon, SF, CA; ed/BA 1972, MA 1978, Adams St Col; Att'd CO St Univ, 1980; Att'd Univ of WI, 1983; pa/Ft Carson, 1964-67, USAF Peterson Field & USAF Acad; Supvr, Pueblo Deversified Ind, 1967-68; Travel Coor, Ball Brothers Res Corp, 1968-70; Tchr, Martin Luther King Elem Sch, 1972-77; Spec Needs Tchr, Sabin Jr HS, 1977-80; Tchr, Doherty HS, 1980-82; Coor of Career Ed, Diagnostic & Spec Lrng Ctr, 1983-; Yth Conslt, Dir Ch Yth Grp, 1972-; cp/El Paso City Black Caucus-Ed Chm, 1982-83; NAACP, 1976-; John Adams Sch PTA, 1976-84; Black Edrs of Dist #11, Chm Career Ed, 1980-84 & Corp. Sect; Am Voc Assn, 1981-; Secy 1982-83, Pres-elect 1983-84-85, CO Voc Assn; Iota Beta Omega Chapt of Alpha Kappa Alpha, 1972-, Ivyleaf Reporter; Ofcr, 1982-83-84, Magnolia Chapt, OES, 1982-; CO Springs Tchrs Assn, 1977-; NEA, 1977-; r/Bapt; hon/ Devel'd 1st Career Exploration Activity for Minority Students in CO Springs; Maj Lutz Outstg Wkmanship, 1967; Rev M E Ford Christian Ed, 1979; Sch Dist #11 Recog, 1983; W/W in W.

CANONICO, DOMENIC A oc/Engineering Director; b/Jan 18, 1930; h/3 Big Rock Road, Signal Mountain, TN 37377; ba/Chattanooga, TN; m/Colleen Margaret Jennings; c/Judith Canonico Asreen, Mary Carol, Angel Edward, Domenic Michael, Catherine Anne; p/ Angelo Anthony and Anna Contratto Canonico; ed/BS Metall Engrg, MI Tech Univ, 1951; MS Metall Engrg 1961, PhD Metall Engrg 1963, Lehigh Univ; mil/ USAF, Korean Police Action; pa/Grp Ldr Pressure Vessel Technol Lab Metals & Ceramics Div, Oak Ridge Nat Lab, Union Carbide Corp, Oak Ridge, TN, 1965-81; Dir Metall & Mats Lab, Combustion Engrg Inc, Chatta, TN, 1981-; Mem: ASME; Am Welding Soc; Fellow, Am Soc for Metals; Sigma Xi; r/Cath; hon/Author of Articles in Var Pubs incl'g: *Welding Jour*; *Alloys for the 80's*;

PERSONALITIES OF AMERICA

Lincoln Gold Medal, Am Welding Soc, 1980; Dist'd Ser Awd NE Sect, Am Welding Soc, 1978; Rene D Wasserman Awd for Best Paper on Brazing, 1977; Adams Lectr, Am Welding Soc, 1983; Others; W/W: in S & SW, in Engrg, in Frontier Sci & Technol; Other Biogl Listings.

CANTOR, PAMELA CORLISS oc/Psychologist; b/Apr 23, 1944; ba/Chestnut Hill, MA; m/Howard L Feldman; c/Lauren Jaye, Jeffrey Lee; p/Alfred and Eleanor Cantor, Floral Park, NY; sp/Samuel and J Feldman, Plainfield, NJ; ed/BS cum laude, Syracuse Univ, 1965; MA 1967, PhD 1972, Columbia Univ; NIMH Fellow, Johns Hopkins Univ Med Sch, 1969-70; Postdoct Fellow, Harvard Univ, 1973-74; pa/Assoc Prof, Boston Univ, 1970-80; Pvt Pract, Clin Psych, 1972-; Bd of Dirs, Am Assn of Suicidology, 1968-; Am Psychol Assn; Bd of Dirs, Samaritans of Boston, 1979-; MA Psychol Assn; Am Orthopsychiatric Assn; hon/Author *Understanding a Child's World: Rdgs in Infancy Through Adolescence*; Num Articles & Chapts; Yg Contbrs Awd, Am Assn of Suicidology, 1979; App'd to St-wide Adv Bd, Ofc for Chd by Gov of MA; W/W: in E, in Frontier Sci & Technol, Wom.

CANTÚ, VIRGINIA DOLORES oc/State Social Service Program Specialist; b/Jan 11, 1948; h/1803 East Anderson, Apartment 2154, Austin, TX 78752; ba/Austin, TX; p/Mr and Mrs Emilio Severo Cantú(dec); ed/Att'd Del Mar Col, 1965-68; Ext Courses, Univ of TX, 1967-68; Sum Sessions, Pan Am Univ, 1966-69; BMus, TX A&I-Kingsville, 72; Grad Study, TX A&I-Laredo, 1972-73; St Edwards Univ, 1978; pa/Prog Spec, Day Care/Child Devel, TX Dept of Human Resources, St Ofc, Austin, 1979-; Child Devel Spec, TX Dept of Human Resources, Edinburg, TX, 1978-79; Cnslr, Col Asst Migrant Prog, Pan Am Univ, Edinburg, 1978; Trainee, Gulf Coast Broadcasting Co, Corpus Christi, TX, 1976-77; Parent Involvement, Social Sers, Vol Sers, Recruitment Coor, Hd Start Prog, Corpus Christi, 1974-77; Others; Mem: Nat Assn for Ed of Yg Chd, TX & Local Affils; Nat & TX Tchrs of Eng to Spkrs of Other Langs; So Assn for Chd Under 6; Alumni, Delta Omicron Intl Music Frat; Bd of Dirs, VPres Commun Ser 1979-80, VPres of Prog 1980-81, Mexican Am BPW of Austin; cp/Mex Am Dems, 1979-81; 2nd VPres/Treas 1974-78, YWCA; So TX Planned Parenthood, 1976-77; Bd of Dirs, Coastal Bend Child Abuse Coun, 1976-78; Others; r/Rom Cath; hon/Author of a Book of Songs, Poetry, Others; Apprec Awd as Conslt to Fam Life Ed Grp, Bd of Trustees Nueces Co MHMR Commun Ctr; Apprec for Outstg Ser To Yg Chd, Dallas Assn for Ed of Yg Chd, 1980; Apprec Awd for Outstg Ser in Commun Theatre, Austin, 1981; Grant for Poetry Manuscript, TX Writer's Circuit, 1981; Other Hons; W/W in S & SW.

CAPORALE, LYNN HELENA oc/Professor; b/Sep 3, 1947; ba/Washington, DC; p/Ralph Jr and Stella Caporale, Bklyn, NY; ed/BS, Bklyn Col of CUNY, 1967; PhD, Univ of BA-Berkeley, 1973; pa/Postdoct Fellow, NYU Med Ctr, 1973-74; Assoc Resr, Sloan-Kettering Inst for Cancer Res, 1975-76; Res Assoc

1976-77, Adj Asst Prof 1978, The Rockefeller Univ; Asst Prof Biochem, Georgetown Univ, 1978-; cp/Del, Dem Pres Nom'g Conv, 1972; hon/Author of Num Articles in Sci Jours; Phi Beta Kappa; Sigma Xi; Am Inst of Chems; Medal from Bklyn Col, 1967; Woodrow Wilson Fellow; Recip, Res Grants from NIH, 1978-.

CAPPELLI, LOUIS JOSEPH oc/Executive; b/Feb 17, 1931; h/20 Pasadena Road, Bronxville, NY 10708; ba/New York, NY; m/Virginia; c/Louis, Craig, Cheryl, Michael, Stephen; ed/BBA, City Col of NY, 1958; mil/AUS, 1951-53, Sgt; pa/Dir & Exec VPres, Standard Fin Corp; Dir & Exec VPres, Sterling Bancorp; Executive VPres, Sterling Nat Bnk; Mem: Dir, Nat Comml Fin Conf; Fin-men's Clb; NY Credit & Fin Mgmt Assn; cp/St Joseph's Parish Coun, Cardinal's Com of Laity; BSA; Yonkers Commun Relats Bd; Tuckahoe Union Free Sch-Budget Adv Com; r/Cath; hon/Author, Var Articles in Profl Jours incl'g: *Am Bkr; Credit & Fin Mgmt.*

CAPUTO-MAYR, MARIA-LUISE oc/Educator; h/160 East 65th Street, Apartment 2 C, New York, NY 10021; ba/Philadelphia, PA; m/Lucio Caputo; c/Giorgio Caputo; p/Leopoldine and Emil Mayr, Austria; sp/Checchina and Giuseppe Caputo, Italy; ed/Tch Lics for German, Italian, Eng; Interpreters & Translators Degs, 1963 & 1964; PhD, Univ of Vienna, 1966; pa/Asst for German Burlington Girl's Sch, 1965-66; Asst Lectr, German-Italian, Barking Reg Col, 1966-67; Prof of German, Temple Univ, 1968-; Fdr, Exec Dir, Past Pres, Kafka Soc of Am; MLA; AATG; Interpreters Assn; cp/Exec Secy, Am Coun for the Study of Austrian Lit; r/Luth; hon/Author Num Profl Pubs; Editor, *Newslttr of the Kafka Society of Am,* 1977-; Orgr & Fund-Raiser, Scholarly Projs.

CARALLARO, MARION LOUISE oc/Professor; b/Jul 15, 1954; h/149 Grayson Avenue, Mercerville, NJ 08619; ba/Trenton, NJ; m/Richard Karl Fromuth; c/Michael Carallaro Fromuth; p/Salvatore and Ruth Carallaro, Glen Ridge, NJ; sp/Harry and Esther Fromuth, Trevose, PA; ed/BA, Univ of DE; MA 1978, PhD 1980, OH St Univ; pa/Prof & Coor Gerontological Cnslg Cert Prog, Trenton St Col, 1981-83; Cnslg Psych & Lectr in Psych, Muhlenberg Col, 1980-81; Mem: Am Psychol Assn; Am Per & Guid Assn; Assn of Wom in Psych; Gerontological Soc of NJ; cp/DAR; r/Rom Cath; hon/Author of Article in *Gerontology & Geriatrics Edr;* Sigma Phi Omega, 1982; Grant Recip, OH St Univ Ofc of Wom's Studies, 1979; Phi Beta Kappa, 1976; Phi Kappa Phi, 1975; W/W in E; Outstg Yg Wom of Am.

CARBAJAL, ULYSSES MEJIA oc/Eyes, Ears, Nose & Throat Specialist; b/Aug 10, 1922; h/3209 Ridgewood Trail, Berrien Springs, MI 49103; ba/Berrien Springs, MI; m/Jovita; c/Dwight, Ritchie, Jan, Eugene; p/Crisanto and Candida Carbajal (dec); sp/Pete and Marcelina dela Cruz, Glendale, CA; ed/Pre-Med 1947, MDiv 1977, Philippine Union Col; MD, Manila Ctl Univ, 1952; MTh 1980, EdD 1983, Andrews Univ; PhD Cand, Fuller Theol Sem; Cert'd, Am Bd of Ophthal, 1956; Resident Ophthal, Eye & Ear Hosp,

Chds Hosp, Univ of CA-LA Med Ctr, 1953-56; pa/Med Staff 1953, Chief Eye Sect Surg Dept 1960-77, Manila Sanitarium & Hosp; EENT Surg, Santa Fe Coast Lines Hosp, 1957-60; EENT Surg, Unity Hosp, Buchanan, MI, 1979-; Pres, P C Berrien Springs, 1979-; Mem: Pres 1970-71, Mem Coun of Elders 1974-77, Philippine Med Assn; Pres 1973-, Philippine Bd of Med Specs; Secy, Philippine Hosp Assn, 1974-76; Secy, Assn of Cols & Schs of Nsg, 1975-77; Advr, Assn of Philippine Ophthal, 1979-; cp/Pres, Philippine Choral Conductors Assn, 1974-; r/7th Day Adventist; hon/Author of Books incl'g: *PMA Story,* 1975; *My Beloved Country 1st,* 1973; Others; Over 65 Sci Articles Pub'd in Profl Jours incl'g: *Phil Jour of Ophthal; Am Jour Ophthal; Archives of Ophthal; EENT Mnthly; Mod Med;* Num Others; HS Valedictorian, 1941; MD w Hons, 1952; MA Rel, 1977; 1st Prize, Roche Instrument Contest, 1972; 1st Prize, Abbott Res Awd, 1976; Awd of Distn, MCU & PUC, 1967; W/W in World.

CARENS, MARILYN E oc/Stockbroker; b/Sep 30, 1944; h/15 Leighton Road, Wellesley, MA 02181; ba/Chestnut Hill, MA; m/Edward M; c/Kelley M, Mark J, Heidi E; p/Edward Daily, Reno, NV; Mary Daily (dec); sp/Mr and Mrs George Carens, Jr, East Dennis, MA; ed/BA cum laude, Regis Col, 1965; MBA, Babson Col, 1977; pa/S Korean Lectr, 1969-75; Xerox Corp, 1978-80; E F Hutton & Co, 1980-; Boston Bus Wom Assn, 1980-; cp/Longwood Cricket Clb, 1958-; r/Christian; hon/W/W Among Wom in Am.

CAREW, JAMES L oc/Professor; b/May 2, 1945; h/2047 Dogwood Road, Charleston, SC 29407; ba/Charleston, SC; m/Gail; c/Sarah; p/Ernest W and Joyce M (Andrews) Carew; ed/AB, Grown Univ, 1966; MA 1969, PhD 1978, Univ of TX-Austin; pa/Asst Prof Geol, Wms Col, Williamstown, MA, 1972-75; Asst Prof Geol, Rennsselaer Polytech Inst, Troy, NY, 1975-77; Marine Sci, Williams/Mystic Prog, Mystic Seaport Mus, CT, 1977-80; Pt-time Vis'g Asst Prof, CT Col, New London, 1978-79; Adj Prof Geol, Murray St Univ, Murray, KY, 1979-; Vis'g Asst Prof, Univ of S FL, 1981; Assoc Prof Geol, Col of Charleston, 1981-; Mem: Geol Soc of Am; Soc of Ec Paleontologists & Mineralogists; Paleontolgical Soc; Carolina Geol Soc; Am Mus of Nat Hist; Smithsonian Instn; Intl Assn for Study of Fossil Cnidaria; Bahamas Nat Trust; Num Col Com Mbrships; cp/Pres, Forest Lakes Civic Clb, 1982-84; Num Commun Lectrs & Spkg Engagements; hon/Author, Over 40 Profl Org Presentations, Book Chapts, Articles in Profl Jours; Recip, Num Res Grants & F'ships; Sigma Xi; Phi Kappa Phi; Sigma Gamma Epsilon; W/W in Frontier Sci & Technol.

CAREW, LYNDON BELMONT JR oc/Professor; b/Nov 27, 1932; h/Collamer Circle, Shelburne, VT 05482; ba/S Burlington, VT; m/Lynn Harrington; c/Leslie, Audre; p/Lyndon B Carew (dec); Myrtle Louella Carew, Pinellas Pk, FL; sp/Edwin C and Herol M Harrington, Wilbraham, MA; ed/BA, Univ of MA, 1955; PhD, Cornell Univ, 1961; pa/Prof Animal Scis & Prof Human Nutrition & Foods 1969-, Sci Prog Mgr Intl Nurtrition Proj 1980-82,

126

Univ of VT; Dir, Poultry Res, Hess & Clark Div of Richardson-Merrell, 1966-69; Dir, Colombian Poultry Prog & Animal Nutrition Lab, Rockefeller Foun, Bogota, 1961-65; Res Asst 1955-61, Res Assoc 1965-66, Cornell Univ; Mem: Pres 1976-81, 1984-, VT Nutrition Coun; Am Inst of Nutrition; Endocrine Soc; Soc Exptl Biol & Med; Assoc Editor 1978-, Poultry Sci Assn; World's Poultry Sci Assn; Animal Nutrition Res Coun; Nutrition Ed Soc; AAAS; Nat Assn Col Tchrs of Agri; Sigma Xi; Gamma Alpha; Phi Kappa Phi; Ptnrs of the Americas; cp/VCham, Shelburne Conserv Com, 1970-73; hon/ Author, Over 160 Articles in Profl Sci Jours; Carrigan Outstg Tchg Awd, Univ of VT, 1981; George V Kidder Outstg Fac Awd, Univ of VT, 1983; W/W in E, in Frontier Sci & Technol; Men of Achmt; Intl Book of Hon; Other Biogl Listings.

CAREY, JAMES JOSEPH oc/Executive; b/Apr 9, 1939; h/The Capital Yacht Clb, 100 Water Street Southwest, Washington DC 20024; ba/Washington, DC; c/Lynn Margaret, Sarah Ann; p/ Ruth Carey Johnson, Berlin, WI; ed/ BSBS 1960, MBA 1972, NWn Univ; mil/ USNR, 1961-, Capt; pa/VCham, Fed Maritime Comm, 1983-85; Fed Maritime Commr, 1981-84; Intl Bus Devel Mgr 1979-81, Mgmt Conslt 1978-79, Telemedia Inc, Chgo; Mgmt Conslt 1978-79, Pres & CEO 1976-78, Coor Graphics, Waukegan, IL; Exec VPres 1974-76, Pres & CEO Chgo Offset Corp 1972-74, Total Graphic Communs, Addison, IL; Sr Acct Exec, I S Berlin Press, Chgo, 1966-72; Mem: Nat Pres 1979-81, Nat VPres Legis 1977-79, The Bluejackets Assn; Nat Adv Com, Nat Exec VPres 9th Dist 1979-80, Nat Bd of Dirs 1977-79, Nat VPres 1977-79, Pres Gt Lakes IL 1969-73, Nav Resv Assn; Nat Adv Bd, Am Security Coun; Nat VPres, Nat Bd of Dirs, Reg Dir Gt Lakes Reg 1979-81, US Nav Sea Cadet Corps; Bd of Dirs Lake Co IL 1977-81, Nat Bd of Dirs 1979-80, Nat Bd of Dirs 1968-72, Zeta Psi Frat of N Am; Pres, Ofcrs Ser Clb; Num Others; cp/Capitol Hill Clb; Jefferson Isls Clb; Capital Yacht Clb; Ofcrs & Fac Clb, US Nav Acad; Mem Repub Nat Com & Num Other Com Activs, Repub Party; Others; r/Cath; h/Author, Var Articles incl'g: "Maritime Regulation for the Benefit of All Am," in *Shipmate*, 1982; "The 4th Arm of Def," 11th Dist Newslttr of Nav Resv Assn; Others; MENSA; INTERTEL; Triple 9 Soc; Intl Soc of Phil Enquiry; 2 Nav Commend Medals; Awd of Merit, Nat Meritorious Ser Awd, Nav Resv Assn; Num Others; DIB; W/W: of Intells, of Contemp Achmt, in Am, in Wash DC; More W/ W & Other Biogl Listings.

CARGILE, MARY CHASTEEN oc/ Manager; b/Apr 24, 1939; h/PO Box 420441, Atlanta, GA 30342; ba/Atlanta, GA; c/William Henry Nichols III; p/Mrs Ralph Chadwick, Beaufort, NC; ed/ Att'd Duke Univ, 1959; AA, GA St Univ, 1962 & 1979; pa/Secy & Real Est Agt, Economy Homes; Exec Secy & Asst Ofc Mgr, Lloyd A Fry Roofing Co, 1961-62; Data Processing 1966-74, Equip Locator 1974-80, So Rwy Sys; Sales Analyst, Hal Eason Assoc, 1974-80; Gen Mgr, Christmas SE, Inc, 1980-; Conslt to Small Bus Firms & Minority Grps, 1968-; Nat

Assoc for Female Execs, 1974-; GA Coun for Notaries Public, 1982-; Rwy Wom of Am, 1974-; r/Meth; hon/ Author Atlanta Constit, "Understanding the Interracial Fam" 1973; Local Newspaper Articles; Danforth Foun Awd, 1957; Rennoc Corp Sales Awd, 1980; Miss Down E Carteret Co, 1955; Miss Dairy Princess, 1957; W/W: of Am Wom, in S & SW; World W/W of Wom; Personalities of S.

CARIS, JOHN CLAYTON oc/Business Consultant; b/Sep 5, 1929; h/106 Logo Virginia, Puerto Corona, Jalisco, Mexico; ba/Dallas, TX; m/Fan Benno; c/ Wendy Lee, John Randolph; p/Mildred W Cares, Farmers Br, TX; ed/BS Physics, Case Inst of Technol, 1951; PhD Physics, Univ of CA-Berkeley, 1960; mil/USAF, 1952-56, Flying Ofcr; pa/Res Sci, Venture Anal, Asst Venture Mgr, E I duPont, Wilmington, DE, 1960-68; Sr Invesmt Anal, Laird, Bissell & Meeds Inc, Wilmington, DE, 1968-69; Dir Corp Devel Planning, Univ Computing Co, Dallas, TX, 1969-72; Bus Strategist, Mktg Mgr for New Venture, TX Instruments Inc, Dallas, 1972-75; Fdr, Pres & Chm: Isis Conslt'g Grp Inc, Dallas, 1975-; Isis Devel Inc, Dallas, 1977-; Isis Corp, Dallas, 1978-; Isis Intl Inc, Dallas, 1981-; Isis Internacional SA de CV, Guadalajara, Mexico, 1982; Mem: Entrepreneurship Inst; N Am Soc for Corp Planning; World Future Soc; cp/Coun Mem Circle 10, BSA; Brookhaven Country Clb; r/Prot; hon/Author of 14 Tech Articles in Profl Pubs, 1956-61; Author of Book for Mexican Govt; Patentee in Phy Optics; Tau Beta Pi; Sigma Xi; Others; W/W in SW.

CARLSON, ERMA WOOD oc/Educator, Librarian (Retired); b/Mar 3, 1896; h/4747 Sunset, La Crescenta, CA 91214; m/Carl E (dec); p/Mr and Mrs W W Wood (dec); ed/Deg, SD St Normal Sch; BS, MN Univ; Gregg Bus Sch; BLS, Drexel Inst; pa/Eng Tchr, Fergus Falls, MN; Libn, Baytown, TX; Org'd Col Lib in Baytown; hon/Author "The Everlasting Light" (Chronological Arrangement of King James Version of the Bible); "The Manifestation of God's Law of Abundance"; Carnegie Awd for Excel, Baytown Lib; W/W of Intells; Intl Book of Hon; Men & Wom of Distn.

CARLSON, NANCY L oc/Counseling Program Director; b/Dec 15, 1936; ba/Kingston, RI; p/Stanley H Carlson (dec); Elizabeth Carlson, Ludlow, PA; ed/BS, Edinboro St Univ, 1954; MA, OH Univ, 1964; PhD Cnslg Psych, Univ of KS, 1970; pa/Dir Cnslg & Career Sers, Univ of RI, 1978-; Dir Cnslg, SUNY-New Paltz, 1975-78; Sr Cnslg, Asst Prof, Univ of MD-Col Pk, 1970-74; Cnslr, Univ of KS, 1966-70; Prog Advr, Univ of WI, 1964-66; Asst Dean of Wom, Edinboro St Col, 1959-64; Mem: Am Psychol Assn; Am Pers & Guid Assn; Com Positions w Am Col Pers Assn; Com Positions w Assn of Univ & Col Cnslg Ctr Dirs; RI Psychol Assn; cp/Kent Co Mtl Hlth Com; Hlth Planning Bd, Ulster Co; Num Spkg Engagements; hon/Author, Num Profl Presentations, Articles in Profl Jours incl'g: *Per & Guid Jour*; Danforth Grantee, 1961 & 1962; Diplomate in Cnslg Psych, Am Bd of Profl Psych; W/W: Among Wom, in E, in S.

CARLSON, REYNOLD ERLAND oc/ Educator (Retired); b/Sep 7, 1912; h/

Rokeby, 3901 Harding Road, Nashville, TN 37205; ba/Nashville, TN; m/Patricia P; c/Marie Louise Roehm; ed/BS 1936, MA 1937, NWn Univ; PhD, Harvard Univ, 1946; mil/USAF, 1942-45; pa/Asst Prof of Ec, Johns Hopkins Univ, 1940-48; Ec Conslt, UN, 1946-47; Ec Commn, 1948; Assoc Prof of Ec, Dir of Inst of Brazilian Studies, Vanderbilt Univ, 1949-53; Economist Joint Brazilian-US Devel Commn, Inst Inter-Am Affairs, Rio de Janeiro, 1951-52; Sr Economist Wn Hemisphere Op, World Bk, 1953-58; Prof Ec, Dir Grad Prog Ec Devel, Vanderbilt Univ, 1958-63; Adj Prof, 1978-79; Vis'g Prof, Grinnell Col, 1979-80; Franklin Pierce Col, 1980-81; Cons Ford Foun, 1959-61; Rep in Rio de Janeiro, 1961-65; Assoc Dir Latin Am Prog, 1965-66; US Ambassador to Colombia, 1966-69; Rep Ford Foun in Buenos Aires, 1969-72; Reg Prog Adv, Lima, Peru, 1972-75; cp/Mem Am Econ Assn; Phi Beta Kappa; Delta Sigma Pi; r/Prot; hon/Author; Cruzeiro Do Sul, Brazil; W/W: in Am, in World.

CARLSON, RICHARD WARNER oc/Mortgage Banker, Lecturer, Journalist; b/Feb 10, 1941; h/7956 Avenida Alamar, La Jolla, CA 92037; ba/San Diego, CA; m/Patricia Caroline Swanson; c/Roberta Hunt, Tucker McNear, Buckley Peck; p/Warner and Ruth Carlson (dec); mil/Col, St Mil Resv; pa/ Sr VP, San Diego Fed; Former Awd-Winning Jour & TV Anchorman; Former Staff Reporter; UPI (SF); Capitol Bur (Sacramento); Investigative Reporter, KGO-TV, SF 1966-70;' News Anchorman 'AM' Show, 1967-69; Polit Editor, Hd Investigative Unit KABC-TV's Flagship Sta. LA 1971-75; Anchorman KFMB-TV, San Diego 1975; Other Profl Activs; Dir Cal Gen Mortgage Ser Co; Dir Del Mar News Press, Inc, CA C of C; San Diego C of C; VP Dir Mem Exec Com; Sigma Delta Chi; San Diego Press Clb; Co-Fdr A I Liebling Soc; VP Repub Bus & Profl Clb; Dir Motion Picture & TV Bur San Diego; cp/Appt by Pres Reagan to Peace Corps Adv Coun, 1982; The City Clb; Senate Repub Adv Com Citizens for Open Space, Former Chm; Fin Adv Com Jr Leag San Diego, Inc; Mem Var Charitable Orgs & Social Clbs; Trustee, La Jolla Country Day Sch; Dir, La Jolla Chamber Music Soc; r/Epis; hon/ Author *Wom in San Diego's Hist*; Num Articles; San Diego Press Clb Awds; Best Documentary, Investigative Reporting; LA Press Clb Grand Awd, Investigative Reporting; George Foster Peabody Broadcasting Awd; Several "Emmy" Awds; Several "Golden Mike" Awds; Nat Hdliners Awd, Hunter's Point Riot Coverage; San Diego St Col Broadcasting Awd, Best Documentary Film; Num Assoc'd Press TV & Radio Awds; W/W: in W, in Fin & Indust.

CARLTON, FRAN STEWART oc/ State Legislator; b/Jan 19, 1936; h/1250 Henry Balch Drive, Orlando, FL 32810; ba/Orlando, FL; m/Ernest E; c/Lynne, Julie; p/Daniel James and Delma Stewart; sp/Nellie Carlton; ed/AA, Univ of FL, 1956; BS, Stetson Univ, 1959-65; pa/ Fac Mem, Stetson Univ, 1959-65; Host of Natly Syndicated TV Show: "The Fran Carlton Show," 1963-; Mem FL Ho of Reps, 1976-; VCham Appropriations Com, 1980-; Chm Tourism Subcom, 1979-; cp/Pres-Elect, Univ of FL Nat

Alumni Assn; Gov's Coun on Phy Fitness & Sports; Nat Conf of St Legis; Adv Bd, Univ of Ctl FL Inst of Tourism Studies; So Dist of Nat Rec & Pk Assn; Sr Citizens Adv Bd of Sea World; Num Others; hon/Author of *A Time for Fitness*, 1978; Writer of Newspaper Column on Fitness: *Orlando Sentinel & Today*, 1972-74; Outstg Legis of Yr, Orlando Area Tourist Trade Assn, 1979; Orange Co Clrm Tchrs Assn, 1977; FL PTA, 1980; Dist'd Alumni, Stetson Univ, 1974; Others; W/W: of Wom in Polits, in Am Polits.

CARMODY, SANDRA ELLEN oc/ Curriculum Consultant; b/Jun 14, 1944; h/5945 West Vegas Drive, Las Vegas, NV 89108; ba/Las Vegas, NV 89101; c/ Theresa Ellen, Patrick William; p/Victor and Jeanette Murphy, Las Vegas, NV; ed/BA, Nazareth Col, 1971; MEd, Univ of NV-Las Vegas, 1980; St of NV Tchr Cert, K-6; St of NV Admr Cert, K-12; St of NV Cnslr Cert, K-12; pa/Tchr of Grade 4, Sch of the Good Shepherd, 1966-67; Tchr of Grade 3, St Christopher's Cath Sch, 1972-73; Tchr of Grade 1, St Anne's Cath Sch, 1973-74; Tchr of Graces 2 & K 1974-78, Tchr of Grade K 1978-79, Lois Craig Elem Sch; Dance & Body Movement Resource Tchr, Comprehensive Fine Arts Proj, ESEA Title IV-C, Clark Co Sch Dist; Tchr of PE to Deaf Students, Ruby Thomas Elem Sch, 1981-83; Curric Conslt, Generalist & Elem PE/ Dance, Clark Co Sch Dist, 1979-; cp/ AAHPERD; SW Dist AAHPERD, Dance Div, 1981; Nat Dance Assn; NAHPERD, Dance Chm, 1981; ASCD; Allied Arts Coun, Dance Div Chm, 1978-79; Yg Audiences, Inc Adv Bd; IRA; NEA; NSEA; r/Rom Cath; hon/Author *Dance/ Body Movement Procedural Guide* (Grades 1-6); *Sec'dy Dance Curric Syllabi: Dance Awareness, Survey of Dance, Dance II; Elemen Phy Ed/Movement/Dance Curric Guide* (Grades 1-6); Dean's List, Univ of NV; W/W in W.

CARNEY, BARBARA JOYCE oc/ Consultant; b/Nov 6, 1942; h/2020 Lincoln Park West, Chicago, IL 60614; ba/Chicago, IL; c/Michael, Michelle; p/ Maurice D (dec) and Celia B. Sachnoff, LA, CA; ed/BA cum laude, Univ of CA-LA, 1960-64; MEd, Nat Col of Ed, 1966-68; pa/Tchr, N Suburban Chgo Sch Sys, 1965-68; Mfrs Rep, Shardon Mktg, Inc, 1976-78; MWn Reg Sales Mgr, Superscope, Inc, 1978-80; Nat Spec Mkts Sales Mgr, Ronco, Inc, 1980-81; Exec Search Conslt, Womack & Assocs, Inc, 1982-; cp/Nat Assn for Female Execs; Am Soc of Profl & Exec Wom; AAUW; VP & Com Chp, Local Chapt Leag of Wom Voters, 1968-76; Bd of Dirs, N Shore Mtl Hlth Assn, 1975-76; Wom in Mgmt; hon/W/W: MW, Am Wom; Pres, Jr Wom Hon; Election Bd; Sorority Pres & Hall of Fame; Miss White Stag, 1959; Hons in Hist, Univ of CA; Student Jud Bd; Prytanean Wom Ser Hon.

CARNICERO, JORGE E oc/Executive; b/Jul 17, 1921; h/3949 52nd Street, Northwest, Washington DC 20016; ba/ McLean, VA; m/Jacqueline Damman; c/ Jacqueline C Duchange, Jorge J; sp/Mr and Mrs George Damman, Oradell, NJ; ed/Aeronaut Engr, Rensselaer Polytech Inst, 1945; pa/Chief Engr, Dodero Airlines, Argentina, 1945; Engr, Flota Aerea Mercante, Argentina, 1945-46;

VPres, Air Carrier Ser Corp, Wash DC, 1946; Exec VPres 1947-55, Chm of Bd & Dir 1955-, Dynalectron Corp (Formerly CA En Aviation); Mem: Sch of Fgn Ser Bd of Visitors, Georgetown Univ; Rensselaer Coun, Rensselaer Polytech Inst, Troy, NY; Assoc Fellow, Royal Aeronaut Soc, England; Bd of Trustees, Pan Am Devel Foun, Wash DC; r/Cath; hon/W/W: of Intl Yr Book & Statesmen, in Fin & Indust.

CAROSELLI, PATRICIA ANN oc/ Executive; b/Feb 21, 1954; h/608 Montana Avenue, Santa Monica, CA 90403; ba/Los Angeles, CA; p/Patrick R and Elvira J Caroselli, Rochester, NY; ed/ Att'd Fgn Study Leag's European Arts Wkshop, Austria, France, Italy & Germany, 1971; BA Psych, SUNY-Buffalo, 1975; MBA Mktg, Univ of CT, 1979; pa/VPres of Prodn, Blake Edwards Entertainment; Has Worked on Var Films incl'g: "10," "S.O.B.," "Victor/ Victoria," "Trail of Pink Panther," "Curse of Pink Panther," "The Man Who Loved Wom"; Assoc Prodr, "Mickey & Maude," w Dudley Moore, 1979-84; Asst Proj Dir, Grey's Advtg Mktg Res Dept, 1977-79; Mem: Wom in Film; The Am Film Inst; Assn of MBA Execs; ACLU; Advtg Clb of LA; cp/Oper CA's World Disaster Relief Prog; Former Mem, NOW; CT Comm on Arts; hon/Var Photographic Wks Pub'd; Num Reports; S'ship, Nat Hon Soc, Grad cum laude, Univ of CT Sch of Bus Adm; W/W.

CARPENTER, JOHN RANDELL oc/ Writer, Translator, Editor; b/Apr 14, 1936; h/1606 Granger Avenue, Ann Arbor, MI 48104; ba/Ann Arbor, MI; m/ Bogdana Chetkowski; c/Michael Randell, Magdalena Maria Anna; p/Mr and Mrs F I Carpenter, Walnut Creek, CA; sp/Józef and Zelazna Chetkowski, Warsaw, Poland; ed/BA, Harvard Col, 1958; Doct d'Université, Cit Mention Tres Honorable, Sorbonne, Univ of Paris, 1966; mil/USAF Resv; pa/Translator & Editor, 1967-74; Freelance, 1982-83; Poet-in-Residence, 1975-76; Tchr, 1977-80; Fellow, NEA: Poetry, 1976-77; Translation, 1980-81; Mem: Poets & Writers Inc; Am Lit Translators Assn (ALTA); hon/Author, Translator, Editor: *Gathering Water*, 1978; *Selected Poems of Zbigniew Herbert*, 1977; *Egret*, 1980; *Chd, Poetry & Space*, 1984; *Report from the Besieged City*, 1984; Witter Bynner Poetry Translation Awd, Poetry Soc of Am, 1979; Ists & Continents Translation Awd, 2nd Prize, 1979; Dir Am Poets & Fiction Writers; Contemp Authors; W/W in Poetry, of Contemp Achmt.

CARPENTER, NORMA R oc/Representative (Retired); b/Dec 27, 1910; h/ 3704 Tangiewood Lane, Davidsonville, MD 21035; m/Jarrott Elmo Brogdon and Maurice C Carpenter; c/Jennie Brogdon, Jarrott Brogdon, Linda Sands, Paul Carpenter, Joanne Judkins; p/Leslie and Melissa Rowe (dec), Davidsonville, MD; ed/BA, Univ of MD, 1931; Tchrs Cert; pa/Prof Asst, Census Bur, 1940-42; Corres Hyattsville Indep, 1942-44; Subst Tchr, 1946-55; Exec Secy, Heart Assn, 1956-63; Ser Rep, C & P Tel Co, 1963-69; cp/Secy, Histn, Anne Arundel Co Ext Homemakers; VP, Secy, U Dem Wom Clubs; Local & Dist Pres, Fed Wom Club; Local & Dist Pres, U Meth Wom; Nat Leag of Am Pen Wom; r/U Meth; hon/Author; Plaque for Meritor-

ious Ser, Am Heart Assn, 1963; 3 Life Mbrships, U Meth Wom; DIB; Personalities of S; World W/W of Wom; Intl Reg of Profiles.

CARR, DANIEL BARRY oc/Medical Reseacher; h/4 Greenough Circle, Brookline, MA 02146; ba/Boston, MA; m/Justine Meehan; c/Nora Elizabeth, Rebecca Ann; p/Andrew Joseph Carr (dec); Florence Carr, City Isl, NY; ed/ BA Physics, Columbia Col, 1968; MA Physics 1970, MD Col of Phys & Surgs 1976, Columbia Univ; pa/Intern & Jr Resident, Internal Med, Presb Hosp, NY, 1976-78; Sr Resident, Internal Med 1978-79, Clin & Res Fellow Endocrinology 1979-82, Clin Assoc Phys Gen Clin Res Ctr 1982-84, Clin Asst Med 1982-, Staff Mem Endocrine Assocs 1983-, Fellow Anesth 1984-, MA Gen Hosp; Instr Med 1982-84, Asst Prof Med 1984-, Fellow Anesth 1984-, Harvard Med Sch; Mem: Diplomate, Am Bd of Internal Med, 1979; Encocrinology & Metabolism Subspec Bd, 1981; Am Fedn for Clin Res, 1982; Clin Ligand Assay Soc, 1983; The Endocrine Soc, 1983; Soc for Neurosci, 1983; hon/Author of Num Res Reports, Reviews, Book Chapts, Articles in Jours & Profl Pubs; Alpha Omega, 1976; Titus Munson Coan Res Awd, Columbia Col of Phys & Surgs, 1976; Doland Fellow, Am Phil Soc, 1980; W/W: in Frontier Sci & Technol, in World.

CARR, GEORGE L oc/Professor; b/ Dec 11, 1927; h/2 Gifford Lane, Chelmsford, MA 01824; ba/Lowell, MA; m/ Phyllis A Wenger; c/Cynthia Louise, George Lawrence, Melinda Susan; p/ Wiliam G and Florence M Carr, Towson, MD; sp/Irwin S Wenger (dec); Allegra V Wenger, Lebanon, PA; ed/BS 1949, MEd 1959, Wn MD Col; PhD, Cornell Univ, 1969; mil/AUS, CMLC, 1951-53; pa/Bd of Ed, Balto Co, MD, 1948-51 & 1953-62; Prof Physics, Cornell Univ, 1963-64; Prof Physics, Wn MD Col, 1965-66; Prof Physics, Univ of Lowell, 1966-; Mem: Am Phy Soc, 1981-; Am Assn of Physics Tchrs, 1960-; Am Geophy Union, 1968-; Nat Sci Tchrs Assn, 1957-; NY Acad of Scis, 1961-; r/Meth; hon/Co-Author of Books: *Gen Exptl Physics*, 1982; *Secrets of the Nucleus*, 1967; *PSSC Physics*; MD St Senatorial Scholar, 1944-48; Shell Merit Fellow 1958, Resident 1961-63, Cornell Univ; W/W in E, in Technol; Am Men & Wom of Sci; Intl Dict of Scholars.

CARR, KENNETH WILSON JR oc/ Executive; b/Jul 12, 1934; h/Route 4, Highway 96, Franklin, TN 37064; ba/ Nashville, TN; m/Mary Ann H; c/James Douglas, Richard Stuart, Kenneth William; p/Kenneth Wilson and Erna Branch, Richmond, VA; sp/William Power and Lucille Hackett, Richmond, VA; ed/VPI, 1953-56; Univ of VA, 1957; Aetna Casualty Safety Engrg Sch, 1961; CE Courses, 1962-82; pa/Safety Engrg Rep 1960-65, Supt Engrg Dept 1970-82, Mgr Agy Devel & Mktg, Aetna Casualty & Surety; cp/Masons; ARC; JC's; Profl Mem, Am Soc of Safety Engrs, Reg VP 1976-79, Chapt Pres 1968-69; Vets of Safety; Fed Safety Coun; Reg'd Profl Engr; Intl Cert Hazard Control Mgr; r/ Meth; hon/Designed & Taught Indust & Constrn Safety Courses, Old Dominion Univ & Tidewater Commun Col, 1970-77; Outstg Vol Awd, ARC, 1977; Outstg JC, 1956; W/W in S & SW.

CARRENO, MARY JANE oc/Educator; b/Jun 26, 1938; h/4907 Indian Hills Drive, Racine, WI 53406; m/Jesse; c/Susan, David, Sandra, Nancy; ed/BS, 1976; MEPD, 1978; MEd, 1981; pa/Girl's Ath Dir, Prairie Sch, 1970-78; Adj Lectr, Univ of WI-Parkside, 1979-; Tchr, Racine Unified Schs, 1980-; Chp 1980-81, VP and Mem of Bd of Dirs 1981/82, WI Assn of Hlth, PE, and Rec; r/Cath; hon/Author *Mexican Dance Book*; Phi Delta Kappa.

CARSON, WILLIAM MORRIS oc/Manager; h/PO Box 967, Riyadh, Saudi Arabia; ba/Riyadh, Saudi Arabia; m/Arlene Fay H; c/Anthony Lunt, Karen Tracy, Adrien Lee, Lincoln Bruce; p/Edward Carson and Frances Powell (dec); sp/Eva Lampe, Quakertown, PA; ed/BS magna cum laude, Columbia Univ, 1950; MA, Johns Hopkins Univ, 1951; Grad Res Wk, Univ of Chgo, 1953-54; London Sch of Ec; mil/USN, 1943-45; pa/Chief Tng Sect, UN Devel Prog, 1972-74; Mgr, Mgmt Devel, GTE Sylvania Tng Sys, 1974-75; Dir of Tng, Ingersoll-Rand Constrn Sers, 1977-79; Dir of Consltg Servs & Sr Advr Manpower Planning, IHRDC, 1979-83; Gen Mgr, ITECO Div of Saudi Tng Servs, 1983-; The Acad of Mgmt; Org Devel Inst; Nat Assn for Adult & Cont'g Ed; Am Soc of Profl Conslts (NY); Assn of Internal Mgmt Conslts; Soc for Applied Anthropology; r/Christian; hon/Co-Author, *Manpower Planning & Devel: The Developing World*; "Tng is not Enough"; Fellow, Mid E Inst, 1951; Twice Ford Foun Fellow; AID Outstg Ser Awd, 1959; W/W in E; Am Men of Sci.

CARTER, BETSY L oc/Editor; b/Jun 9, 1945; h/339 East 18th Street, New York, NY 1003; ba/New York, NY; m/Malcolm N; p/Mr and Mrs Rudy Cohn, Bal Harbour, FL; sp/Mr and Mrs Arno Lamm, Newton, MA; ed/BA, Univ of MI, 1967; pa/Edit Asst, Air & Water News, McGraw Hill, 1967-68; Editor, The Am Security & Trust Mag, *The Shield*, 1968-69; Edit Asst, *The Atl Monthly*, 1969-70; Rschr, Asst Editor, Assoc Editor, *Newswk*, 1971-80; Sr Editor, Exec Editor, Sr Exec Editor, *Esquire*, 1980-; W/W & W/W of Am Wom.

CARTER, DEAN oc/Professor; b/Apr 24, 1922; h/1011 Highland Circle, Blacksburg, VA 24060; ba/Blacksburg, VA; m/Rosina McDonnell; c/Frances, Katherine, Clement, J Thomas, Mary G; p/Mary C Carter, Blacksburg, VA; sp/Mrs Paul McDonnell, Memphis, TN; ed/Att'd Corcoran Sch of Art, 1940-43; AB, Am Univ, 1947; MFA, IN Univ, 1948; Postgrad Studio of Zadkine, Paris, 1948-49; mil/AUS AF, 1943-46, India & China; pa/Instr, Oguinquit Sch of Art, ME, 1941-42; Grad Asst, IN Univ, 948; Prof Sculpture 1950-, Hd Dept of Art 1967-79, VA Polytech Inst & St Univ; Mem: Pres, Univ Clb, 1957; Pres, SEn Col Art Assn, 1977; VPres 1966-68, So Sculptors Assn; St Rep 1965, Am Crafts Coun; So Highlands Handicraft Guild; Col Art Assn; cp/Pres, Blacksburg Reg Art Assn, 1960 & 1961; r/Meth; hon/Wks in Var Public Collections: Wachovia Bk & Trust; 1st Colony Life Ins Co; Roanoke Meml Hosp; Drs Clin Annandale, VA; Providence Bldg; 7 Corners, VA; Bk of VA; VPI & St Univ; St Joseph's Prep Sch, Phila; Sleicher Awd, Am Univ; Purchase Awd, Cranbrook Mus of Art, 1949; Purchase Awd, Wichita Art Assn, 1955; Cini F'ship, Venice, 1964; W/W in Am.

CARTER, DELORES COPPEDGE oc/Acting Principal; b/Jul 5, 1937; h/3510 Jeff Road, Landover, MD 20785; ba/Washington, DC; m/Raymond L Jr; c/Raymond A, Wanda T, David L; p/George and Elouise Coppedge, Washington, DC; sp/Raymond and Gertrude Carter; ed/BS, DC Tchrs Col, 1961; MAT, Trinity Col, 1974; pa/Elem Tchr & Team Ldr, 1961-73; Pt-time Instr, 1969-81; Adm Asst, 1973-74; Local Sch Open Space Coor, 1974-77; Reg Open Space Coor, 1977-79; ESEA Title IVC Proj Coor/Dir, 1979-82; Wkshop Ldr/Conslt, 1973-; Acting Prin, J F Cook/Slater-Langston Elem Sch, 1982-; Sec 1981-82, Treas 1982-83, ASCD, Wash Chapt; Nat Assn of Elem Sch Prins; cp/Sec 1973, Fox Ridge Civic Assn; Phi Delta Kappa Ed Frat, Am Univ Chapt; NCNW; r/Rom Cath; hon/Co-Author, "Staff Devel Prog Eval- Application of a Peer Supvn Model 1;" Outstg Ldrs in Elem & Sec'dy Ed; Outstg Open Space Coor, 1977.

CARTER, DELORIS JUANITA oc/Social Worker; b/Oct 23, 1948; h/149 Passaic Street, Hackensack, NJ 07601; ba/Hackensack, NJ; p/Clarence and Martha Alease; ed/BSW, 1977; MSW, 1980; pa/Social Wkr, Div of Yth & Fam Sers, 1980-.

CARTER, FRANCES TUNNELL oc/Editor; b/May 21; h/2561 Rocky Ridge Road, Birmingham, AL 35243; ba/Birmingham, AL; m/John T; c/Wayne, Nell; p/David A and Mary Annie McCutcheon Tunnell (dec); sp/Mr and Mrs John F Carter (dec); ed/AA, Wood Jr Col, 1942; Elem Cert, Blue Mtn Col, 1942; BS, Univ of So MS, 1946; MS, Univ of TN, 1947; EdD, Univ of IL, 1954; Addit Study; pa/Editor, Acteen/GA Prods, Wom's Missionary Union, SBC, B'ham 1983-; Instr Charm Classes, Rocky Ridge Commun Sch, 1976-; Vis'g Prof, Hong Kong Bapt Col, 1963-66; Asst Prof 1956-57, Assoc Prof 1957-63, Prof 1963-, Samford Univ Sch of Ed & Dept of Home Ec; Hd Dept Home Ec, Clarke Meml Col, 1950-56; Hd Dept Home Ec, E Ctl Jr Col, 1948-49; Hom Ec & Art Instr, Wood Jr Col, 1947-48; Var Elem & HS Tchg Positions in MS; Num Coms & Ofc Positions: AL Assn of Tchr Edrs; Assn for Childhood Ed; Nat Assn for Ed of Yg Chd; So Assn for Chd Under 6; AL Assn of Yg Chd; AL Ed Assn; NEA; St Adv Com on Early Childhood Ed; Am Home Ec Assn; Pres 1980-85, Other Positions, Kappa Delta Epsilon; Kappa Delta Pi; Kappa Omicron Phi; Phi Delta Kappa; Num Other Orgs; cp/Num Coms & Ofc Positions: Dir of Public Affairs, S E Reg, Civil Air Patrol, 1980-; Dawson Meml Bapt Ch; B'ham Wom's C of C; DAR; B'ham BPW Clb; AAUW; Wom's Civic Clb; Samford Univ Wom's Clb; AL St Poetry Soc; Jefferson Co Hist Soc; Nat Leag of Am Pen Wom; Wom's Chapt Freedom Foun; Num Other Activs; r/Bapt; hon/Author of 4 Chd's Books: *Ching Fu & Jim*, 1978; *Sharing Times* 7, 1971; 'Tween-age Ambassador, 1970; *Sammy in the Country*, 1960; Num Curric Units; Over 54 Articles Pub'd in Profl Jours; 28 Poems Pub'd; Songs, Textbook Draft; Other Pubs; Honoree at Convocation, Univ of AL-B'ham, 1977; B'ham Wom of Yr, 1977; W/W: in Am Cols & Univs, in Am Wom, in S & SW; Contemp Authors; Num Other Biogl Listings.

CARTER, HARRIET VANESSA oc/Administrative Assistant; h/7320 Biscayne Boulevard, Miami, FL 33138; p/Gerard F MD and Eugenia Carter, Miami, FL; ed/BA magna cum laude, Tulane Univ, 1969; MEd, Univ of IL at Urbana, 1971; Att'd Newcomb Col, Monterrey, Aix-en-Provence & Nice, Univ of Montreal, Univ of Vienna, Univ of Madrid; pa/Tchg Fellow, Univ of IL, 1969-71; Tchr, King Philip HS, 1971-76; Tchr, Closter HS, 1977-78; HS for Gifted Chd, 1978-81; Adm Asst to Clin Dean of a Med Sch & PR Coor, 1981-; Editor of Med Sch Newslttr, 1981-; Mod Lang Assn; Tchrs of Spanish & Portuguese; Nat Fdn of Bus & Profl Wom, Yg Careerist Chm, 1980-81; Co-Chm, AAUW; cp/World Trade Coun of Palm Bch Co; Phi Delta Kappa; Phi Beta Kappa; Coun for Intl Visitors of Gtr Miami; Alliance Francaise of Dade Co; Caribbean Tourism Assn; hon/Author "Air Pollution & Hazardous Noise"; Scholars & Fellows Prog; Lib Prize; Dir, Sigma Delta Pi; Admissions Com; F'ship by Austrian Govt; 2000 Wom of Achmt; Personalities of S; Commun Ldrs of Am; DIB; IBA Biog Dir; World W/W of Wom; Men & Wom of Distn; Reg of Palm Bch Co; 5000 Personalities of World.

CARTER, JOHN MARSHALL oc/Educator/Writer; b/Apr 6, 1949; h/517 Dumaine Street, Eden, NC 27288; ba/Eden, NC; m/Suzon Grogan; c/Alyson; p/Howard and Virginia Carter, Eden, NC; sp/Robert and Ollie Grogan, Eden, NC; ed/BA, Elon Col, 1971; MA, Univ NC-Greensboro, 1975; PhD, Univ IL, 1982; pa/Instr, Eden City Schs, 1980-83; Instr, Univ IL, 1978-80; Supvr, Cumberland Co Schs, 1977-78; Instr/Coach, Fayetteville Acad, 1975-76; NEA; NCTE; cp/Medieval Acad Am; Am Hist Assn; Nat Coun Social Studies; N Am Soc Sport Hist; Am Mil Inst; ASCAP; hon/Author of Nine Verse Volumes incl'g *Wampus Cats & Dan River Rimes*; Six Prose Volumes incl'g *Ludi Medi Aevi, Studies in the Hist of Medieval Sport*; Draper-Gullander-Largent Hist Prize, Univ NC, 1975; Swain Hist Prize, Univ IL, 1980, 1981, 1982; St Nicholas Prize, Univ CA-LA, 1982; W/W in S & SW; Outstg Yg Men Am; Men Distn.

CARTER, MILDRED BROWN oc/Executive Assistant to Corporation President; b/Feb 22, 1927; h/2180 Elaine Drive, Bountiful, UT 84010; ba/Salt Lake City, UT; m/Richard Bert; c/Paul, Mark, Janis, David; p/Eddie Washington Brown (dec); sp/Richard Bert Carter; ed/Real Est, Univ WA, Seattle, 1965; PACE Sem Dale Carnegie Ldrship Course; Am Mgmt Assn Sem, 1978; mil/USO, WWII; pa/FBI, 1943-52; Jr HS Secy & Registrar, Bellevue Sch Dist, 1966-75; Asst to Exec VP, Bonneville Intl Corp, 1975-83; cp/Beta Sigma Phi; Woms Cent Clb; Soc of Former FBI Wom; Soroptimist; PTS Mbrship Chm & Treas; Red Cross Vol; hon/HS Salutatorian, 1943; Winner, SC St-wide Contests in Algebra, 1942, 1943; Winner, SC Dist Bkkpg Contest, 1943.

CARTER, RICHARD BERT oc/Historian; b/Dec 2, 1916; h/2180 Elaine Drive, Bountiful, UT 84010; ba/Same; m/Mildred Brown; c/Paul, Mark, Janis, David; p/Richard Bert Sr and Lula

Selena Jones Carter (dec); sp/Eddie Washington (dec) and Hester Lessie Lee Poston Brown; ed/BA, WA St Univ, 1939; Grad Wk, Georgetown Univ Law Sch, Brown Univ, Brigham Yg Univ; mil/USAR, 1st Lt Mil Intell; pa/Ofcr Mgr, Elect Prods Conslt, 1939-40; Spec Agt & Communi-ofcl, FBI, 1940-75; Assoc Dir, Stakes & Missions Ofc; Public Communs Dept, Ch of Jesus Christ of LDS; Soc of Profl Jours; Pi Sigma Alpha; cp/Scabbard & Blade; Profl Photogs of Am; Phi Delta Theta; IPA; Bd Mem, Salvation Army; Past Pres, Toastmasters; Bd Mem, U Way; Bd Mem, Coun VP Fin, Coun Commr, BSA; hon/Editor, Biogs of Mems, SLC Chapt, Sons of UT Pioneers, 1980; Eagle Scout 1931, Silver Beaver 1964, Vigil Hon 1970, BSA; Engraved Saber as Cmdr of ROTC Co-Winning WA St Univ Regimental Competition, 1939; Nat Media-Man-of-the-Month, Morality in Media, 1976; World W/W; Notable Ams; Men of Achmt; DIB.

CARTER-DIXON, ROSALIE GRACE oc/Education Consultant; b/Oct 30, 1932; h/1198 Chestnut Street, Newton, MA 02164; ba/Westport, CT; m/John M Dixon III; c/Kwame DuBois Dixon; p/Oscar and Sletha Carter, Newton, MA; sp/John M (dec) and Anna Mae Dixon, Champagne, IL; ed/BS, Tufts Univ, 1955; MAEd, Salem St, 1965; Att'g CAGS Prog, Univ of MA; pa/1st Grade Tchr, 1955-65; Hd Start Tchr, 1967; Hd Start Dir, 1967-80; Proj Dir 1980-82, Field Opers & Monitor of Measures Proj 1982-, Early Chdhood Ed Conslt 1980-, Mediax Assoc; cp/Nat Bd Mem, Nat Hd Start Assn, 1976-; Fin Com 1978-, Choir Mem 1971-, Yth Coun 1980-, Bd of Christian Ed 1974-81, Myrtle Bapt Ch; Proj IMPACT, MA Dept of Public Welfare VP 1978-79; N Eng Bd Rep to Nat Hd Start Assn, 1976-81; City of Newton Commun Devel Adv Com, 1980-; St Tng Ctr Adv Grp, 1974-78; Life Mem, NAACP; CDA Umbrella Career Devel Com, Wheelock Col; Bd Mem, MA Assn for Child Devel, 1976; Exec Bd Mem, N Eng Hd Start Dirs Assn, 1971-76; Bd Mem, MA Chd's Lobby, 1971-72; Chm, N Eng Hd Start Dirs Assn, 1971-72; Chm, MA Assn of Child Devel Dirs, 1970-71; Mem, Lowell YWCA Bd of Dirs, 1968-71; App'd to Gov's Com on Child Devel, 1969; r/Bapt; hon/Author "Good Parenting"; NAACP Cert of Apprec; World W/W of Wom.

CARTEY, WILFRED G O oc/Professor; b/Jul 19, 1931; h/21 Claremont Avenue, New York, NY 10027; ba/New York, NY; p/Samuel and Ada Cartey (dec); ed/BA, Univ Col of W Indies, 1955; MA 1956, PhD 1964, Columbia Univ; pa/Dist'd Prof 1979-, Prof Dept Black Studies 1977-79, Prof Comparative Lit 1969-72, City Col, CUNY; Dist'd Prof Martin Luther King Ch, Bklyn Col, CUNY, 1972; Adj Prof Eng & Comparative Lit 1969, Assoc Prof Comparative Lit 1963-69, Spanish Instr Columbia Col 1957-62, Columbia Univ; Var Nat & Intl Vis'g Prof'ships; cp/Num Spkg Presentations; hon/Author of 4 Vols of Poetry: *Red Rain; Suns & Shadows; Water of My Soul; House of Blue Lightning*; Editor of 6 Books incl'g: *Whispers From A Continent; Black Images; Palavar; The Africa Reader Vol I & II*; Lit Editor, *African Forum*, 1967-68; Other Pubs; Awd from Black Student

Union, Essex Commun Col, 1975; Awd of Hon & Cit of Merit, Mid Sts Coun for Social Studies for *Black Images*, 1973; Dist'd Prof Martin Luther King Chr, CUNY, 1972; Mem, Black Acad of Arts & Lttrs, 1971; Fulbright Travel Grant, 1955-59; Bernard Van Leer Foun F'ships, 1955-56; Open W Indian Univ S'ship, 1951-56; W/W in World.

CARTLEDGE, DAVID LLOYD oc/Executive; b/Jul 9, 1923; h/4610 Sylvan Drive, Columbia, SC 29206; ba/Columbia, SC; m/Emily Thomas R; c/David T, Terry Lane C Parker; p/Joseph Z (dec) and Ida Lou B Cartledge, Edgefield, SC; sp/Rufus R and Lola D Radford (dec); ed/BS, Univ of SC, 1947; mil/Army Intell, 1943-46; pa/Field Rep, SC Retirement Sys, 1946-48; Underwriter, Seibels Bruce & Co, 1948-71; Ins Conslt to Devel of Policy Mgmt Sys, 1971-77; Underwriting VP, Seibels Bruce Grp, 1977-; VP and Dir, KY Ins Co; VP & Dir, Nautilus Scuba Supply Indust; Co-fdr, Past Pres & Dir, The One Hundred Corp; Guest Instr, Col of Bus Adm, Univ of SC; cp/Personal Application Com, Acord Corp, 1975-80; Personal Property Com, Ins Ser Ofc, 1980-; Palmetto Pond Hon Order of Blue Goose Intl; Univ of SC Alumni Assn & Gamecock Clb; Execs Clb; President, 1980, Past Masters Clb; Worshipful Master, 1971, Acacia Lodge of Ancient Free Masons; Am Leag Post #6; Pres 1965, Dir to Present, Downtown Optimist Clb; Pres 1972, Chaplain of SC Dist 1974, Columbia Toastmasters Clb; r/Bapt; hon/Awd Life Mbrship, Downtown Optimist Clb, 1980; Commun Ser Awd, Downtown Optimist Clb, 1977 & 1979; Past Master Cert, Acacia Lodge, 1971; Cert of Outstg Ser, Acacia Lodge, 1977, 1980 & 1981; Competent Toastmaster Awd, Toastmasters Intl, 1972; Able Toastmasters Awd, 1973; ETO Ribbon w 3 Battle Stars, 1943-46; W/W in S & SE.

CARTWRIGHT, PRINCE JR oc/Attorney; b/Aug 31, 1948; h/9430 Rentur Drive, Houston, TX 77031; ba/Houston, TX; m/Rayola Brown; p/Prince (dec) and Beula Mae Cartwright, Dallas, TX; sp/Mr and Mrs Enoch Brown, Bay City, TX; ed/BA 1970; JD 1975; mil/AUS, 1972; pa/Computer Run Messenger Ctl Supply, Jefferson-Davis Hosp, 1968-70; Pers Mgmt Spec, 1970-72, AUS; Postal Clk, US Postal Ser, 1973-78; Atty in Pvt Pract, 1977-; cp/NAACP; YMCA; Bd of Dir, TSU Alumni Assn; Treas, Thurgood Marshall Sch of Law Alumni Assn; Trustee, Antioch Bapt Ch; r/Bapt; hon/US JC's Outstg Yg Man of Am Awd, 1979 & 1982.

CARUCIO, FRANK THOMAS oc/Professor; b/Sep 7, 1935; h/3823 Edinburgh Road, Columbia, SC 29204; ba/Columbia, SC; m/Gwendelyn Geidel; c/Nicholas Charles, Christina Marie; p/Nicholas & Genovetta Caruccio (dec); sp/Augustus and Elizabeth Geidel, Lowville, NY; ed/BS, City Col of NY; MS 1963, PhD 1964, PA St Univ; mil/AUS Signal Res & Devel Unit; pa/Res Asst 1961-67, Postdoct Fellow 1967-69, PA St Univ; Asst Prof Geol,SUNY-New Paltz, 1969-71; Assoc Prof Geol 1971-81, Prof Geol 1981-, Univ of SC; Mem: Fellow, Geol Soc of Am; Am Geophy Union; Sigma Xi; Nat Water Well Assn; Am Water Resources; Water

Pollution Control Fedn; Soc Envir Geochem & Hlth; r/Epis; hon/Author, Over 40 Articles in Jours, Book Chapts, Reports in Profl Pubs; Mem Com on Ground Water Resources, Coal Mining Nat Res Coun/NAS, 1979-83; Beijer Inst, Royal Swedish Acad of Scis, 1983-85.

CARVALHO, JULIE ANN oc/Government Program Analyst; b/Apr 11, 1940; h/Reston, VA 22090; ba/Washington, DC; m/Joao M P; c/Alan, Dennis, Melanie, Celeste, Joshua; p/Daniel H Schmidt (dec); Elizabeth G Schmidt; ed/BA 1962, PhD Human Devel 1973, Univ of MD; MA Social Psych, George Wash Univ, 1966; PhD Cand Public Adm & Public Policy Anal, VI Polytech Inst & St Univ, 1978-; Addit Study; pa/Prog Anal Res & Eval Br 1978-, Legis Anal Legis Anal Br Policy Planning & Res Div 1977-78, Ofc of Civil Rts, DHHS & DHEW; Equal Oppor Spec, Ofc of Secy, DHEW, 1973-77; Prog Anal/Spec 1970-73, Ed Prog Spec Nat Ctr Ednl Res & Devel 1969-70, US Ofc of Ed; Ed & Tng Anal, Computer Applications Inc, 1967-68; Res Assoc, Univ Res Corp, 1967; Social Sci Res Anal, Mtl Hlth Study Ctr, NIMH, 1963-67; Num Other Positions; Pres, VPres, Bd of Dirs, Fairfax Co Assn for Gifted, 1978-80; Interdeptl Task Force on Minority Wom, 1977-78; VChr Handicapped Employees Com, Office of Civil Rts, 1977-; Nat Wom's Agenda of Wom's Action Alliance; Alliance for Child Care; Treas, Bd of Dirs, HEW Employees Assn; Bd of Dirs, Penthouse Nursery Inc; Editor, Fed Employed Wom Newslttr; Num Other Activs; r/Christian; hon/Author & Editor, Over 50 Govt Reports, Bltns & Articles in Profl Jours & Var Pubs; Commends: Secy of DHEW; The US Commr of Ed; Spec Asst to Pres, Dept Comr of Ed; The Dir of Wom's Bur, Div Dirs in DHEW, the Acting Dir of Wom's Action Prog, The Dept Dir of Civil Rts; Others; Nom'd High Ser Awds, Nat Fed Employed Wom, 1977; Psi Chi; Phi Alpha Theta; Wash Jr Acad of Scis; Merit S'ship Commend; W/W: in E, of Wom, of Am Wom, in Commun Ser; Wom's Orgs & Ldrs Dir; Num Other Biogl Listings.

CARVER, GEORGE BRYAN oc/Police Official, Purchasing Agent; b/Sep 30, 1935; h/Apartment 802, 6129 Leesburg Pike, Falls Church, VA 22041; ba/Washington, DC; m/Marjorie Lee C; p/Bryan and Virginia Carver, Hot Springs, VA; sp/William L and Carrie M Crabill (dec); ed/FBI Nat Acad Cert, 1974; BA, George Wash Univ, 1975; mil/AUS, 1969-1970, 1962; pa/Appt'd 1960, Re-appt'd 1962, Sgt 1967, Lt 1971, Capt 1973, Tng Dir 1976, Purchasing Agt 1981-, US Capitol Police; Intl Assn of Chiefs of Police; VP 1975-76, Pres, 1976-77, DC Chapt FBI Nat Acad Assoc; Frat Order of Police Fed Lodge #1; cp/Nat VP 1965-66, Nat Pres 1966-67, Greenbrier Mil Sch Alumni Assn; VA Mil Inst Alumni Assn; George Wash Univ Alumni Assn & Heroes, Inc; Franklin Mint Collectors Soc & Am Bicent Commemorative Soc; r/Prot; hon/Hon KY Col; Fellow of Acad of Police Sci, Nat Law Enforcement Acad; Hon Admiral in TX Nav; Meritorious Cert, Frat Order of Police; The Old Guard Cert of Achmt; Intl W/W of Intells; Men of Achmt; 2000 Notable

Am; Intl Book of Honor; 5000 Personalities of the W; Others.

CARVER, STEVEN H oc/Director of Motion Pictures; b/Apr 5, 1945; h/1010 Pacific Avenue, Venice, CA 90291; p/ Murray and Frances Carver, Queens, NY; ed/HS Music & Art; BFA, Univ of Buffalo; MFA, Washington Univ; Am Film Inst, Ctr for Adv'd Studies; pa/Dir of Num Motion Pictures incl'g *Lone Wolf McQuade, Capone, Big Bad Mama, Syndrome, Johnny Got His Gun, An Eye for An Eye, Moonbeam Rider, The Arena, World's Greatest Lover;* Florissant Val Col, Metro Ednl Coun in Arts, Tchg Positions; Num Still Photo Positions; hon/*The Tell-Tale Heart,* Cine Golden Eagle Awd, Cork Film Fest Winner, Time-Life Ednl Distbn; *More Than One Thing,* NY Fest Bronze Awd, Nat Ednl TV-Hon Mention; *Syndrome,* SF Fest Bronze Medal, Chgo Film Fest Gold Medal; Wks in Personal Collection of Edward G Robinson, William Bernoudy, L'ville Mus, Springfield Mus, Phila Eagles Ftball Team; One Man Art Shows in Schweig Gallery, Norton Gallery, Steinberg Mus, Univ of Buffalo.

CARWILE, WALTER DeWITT JR oc/ Assistant Manager and Assistant Director; b/Mar 13, 1922; h/Highway 460, Thaxton, VA 24174; ba/Bedford, VA; m/Kathryn W; c/Kathie C Johnson, Cynthia C Causer, Gwynne C Robinson; p/Walter Carwile and Hessie Mae Finch, Rustburg, VA; sp/Rev Floyd J and Annie Mae L Wingfield, Thaxton, VA; ed/AB, Lynchburg Col; Addit Courses; mil/WW II; pa/Pilot Life Ins Co, 1950-52; N & W Mfg Co, Inc, 1953; Acctg Staff, Grt Am Indust, 1954-55; Asst Mgr-Asst Dir, Elks Nat Home & Hosp, 1955-; cp/ Dist Dir, Am Cancer Soc, 1981-82; Cert'd Admr Homes for Adults, Mem C of C; Thaxton Ruritan Club; Gideons Intl; Past Trustee, Lynchburg Lodge of Elks; VFW, Mil Order of Purple Heart; hon/Decorated Purple Heart, WW II; W/ W in S & SW.

CASAS, GUILLERMO oc/Educator; b/Apr 19, 1931; h/550 South Brentwood Drive, Mt Laurel, NJ 08054; ba/ Camden, NJ; m/Guillermina; c/Rey, Rene; ed/BS 1962, MEd 1966, Temple Univ; PhD, Union Grad Sch, 1978; mil/ AUS Mil Attache, 1951-60; pa/Spanish Instr, HS & Col, 1963-72; Burlington City Supvr of Bilingual Ed, Public Schs of Camden, 1973-74; Dir, Bilingual Ed Progs, Camden Bd of Ed, 1974-; Secy, PR Devel Corp; Am Assn of Spanish Tchrs; Am Assn Bilingual Edrs; cp/Pres Bd of Trustees, 1st Spanish Bapt Ch; 32nd Deg Mason; Blue Lodge & Shriner; Legion of Honor; Mem Pres Reagan's Task Force; r/Bapt; hon/Author, *The Writings of Rafael Arevalo, Retorno, Ocho Encuentros, Visiones de Primavera;* Mil Cross, Antonio Narino by Colombian Govt, 1951; Contbn to the Ed of the Hispanic Child, 1975; W/W in E.

CASATI, LAWRENCE WILLIAM III oc/Pastor; b/Sep 3, 1953; h/2126 Elsmere Avenue, Dayton, OH 45406; p/ Lawrence W II and Gloria Ann D Casati, Findlay, OH; ed/BA, Univ of Dayton, 1974; MA Theol, MA Biblical Studies, Athenaeum of OH, Mt St Mary's Sem in Cinc; Addit Studies; pa/Yth Coor, Queen of Apostles Ch, 1974-1975; Dir of HS Rel Ed 1976-79, Jr HS Rel Tchr 1977-79, Precious Blood Ch; Deacon, Holy Spirit Ch, 1981; Deacon for St

Mary's Byzantine Ch & Rel Tchr for St Mary's Sch, 1981-1982; Notary Public, St of OH, 1978-; Pastor, Sts Cyril & Methodius Orthodox Ch, 1983-; cp/Univ of Dayton Alumni Assn; Sons of Italy in Am, Chaplain of John Pirelli Lodge; Fellow of the Octavian Soc; Mem of Heraldry Soc-USA; Am Numismatic Assn; F'ship of St Alban & St Sergius; Montgomery Co Hist Soc; The Augustan Soc, Inc; r/E Orthodox; hon/Author, "What's on Your Mind?", "The Anaphora of St John Chrysostom as an Expression of Faith".

CASCIO, ANGELINA GIOVINO oc/ Histotechnologist; b/Jun 13, 1930; h/ 2765 20th Place West, Birmingham, AL 35208; ba/Birmingham, AL; p/Sam and Josephine Giovino, Birmingham, AL; ed/BS 1951, BA 1952, B'ham So Col; Histotechn 1960, Histotechnologist 1980, Am Soc of Clin Pathologist; Fellow, Royal Soc of Hlth, 1971; pa/ Histology Tech 1952-56, Res Asst to Dr Robert Mowry 1956-60, Chief Histotechnologist 1960-, Univ of AL Hosp; Am Chem Soc, 1950; Am Soc of Clin Pathol, 1970; Am Soc of Med Technol, 1975; Reg of Med Technol, 1978; AL Soc for Histotechnol, 1974; Nat Soc for Histotechnol, 1971; r/Rom Cath; hon/ Nat Histotechnologist of Yr, 1981; Fellow, Royal Soc of Hlth, England, 1971.

CASE, STUART oc/Public Relations Director; b/Nov 12, 1941; h/Rural Route 1, Box 32A, Hampton, CT 06247; ba/ W Hartford, CT; m/Lenore Bank; c/ David Adam; p/Mrs Frank Seivert, Ridge, NY; sp/Mr and Mrs Harry Bank, Bronx, NY; ed/AB, Columbia Co, Columbia Univ, 1962; MA, New Sch for Social Res, NYC, 1965; pa/Cost Editor, *Engrg New-Record,* McGraw Hill Inc, NYC, 1962-64; Mng Editor, *Constrners Mag,* Chatham, NJ, 1964-66; News Editor, Alumni Editor, Pubs Editor, Univ of CT, Storr, CT, 1966-82; Dir of Public Relats, St Joseph Col, W Hartford, CT, 1982-; cp/Mem 1980, Secy 1981-, Zoning Bd of Appeals, Hampton, CT; r/Jewish; hon/Author of Num Pubs; W/W in E.

CASELLA, RUSSELL CARL oc/Theoretical Physicist; b/Nov 6, 1929; h/1485 Dunster Lane, Potomac, MD 20854; ba/ Washington, DC; m/Marilyn Smith; c/ Sheryl M, Cynthia L (Casella) Conturie; p/Rosaria and Lena Casella, Framingham, MA; sp/Edward and Catherine Smith (dec); ed/BS, MA Inst of Technol (MIT), 1951; MS 1953, PhD 1956, Univ of IL-Urbana; pa/Physicist, USAF Cambridge Res Ctr, 1951-52; Physicist, MA Inst of Technol Labs, Sum 1953; Res Assoc, Univ of IL, 1956-58; Physicist, IBM Watson Res Ctr, 1958-65; Physicist, Nat Bur of Standards, 1965-; Mem: Am Phy Soc; Sigma Xi; hon/Author, Num Sci Articles in Profl Pubs, 1956-; US Dept of Commerce Silver Medal Awd for Outstg Res, 1973; W/W in E.

CASEY, WILLIAM R oc/Executive; b/ Jun-15, 1922; h/310 Lake Street, Rouses Point, NY 12979; ba/Rouses Point, NY; m/Carlyn Temple; c/Richard T; p/ William R and Clare (Gordon) Casey (dec); sp/Carl B and Loretta M Temple, Bel Air, MD; ed/Grad, Phillips Acad; Att'd Amherst Col, 1940-42;; BS, US Nav Acad, 1945; mil/USN, 9 Yrs; pa/ Sales Exec, John-Manville Corp, until

1953; Treas, Exec VPres & Pres 1953-76, Chm of Bd & CEO 1976-, The Myers Grp Inc; Mem: Past Pres, Current Chm, Nat Customs Brokers & Forwarders Assn; Industy Sector Adv Com (ISAC) for Sers; NCITD Computerization Com; NY Dist Export Coun; cp/Past Dir, Champlain Val Phys Hosp; Past Trustee, Plattsburgh St Univ Foun; Past Dir, Thousand Isl Pks Comm; r/ Rom Cath; hon/Author, Num Articles in Trans Indust Trade Pubs; Led US Del to FIATA Conv, Dublin, Ireland, 1981; W/W: in Fin & Indust, in World.

CASPERSON, LEE WENDEL oc/ Professor; b/Oct 18, 1944; h/2571 Westwood Boulevard, Los Angeles, CA 90064; ba/Los Angeles, CA; m/Susann Diane Lunnam; c/Jule Diane, Janet Marie, Robert James; p/Mr and Mrs R O Casperson, Clackamas, OR; sp/Mr and Mrs R L Lunnam, Santa Monica, CA; ed/BS, MA Inst of Technol (MIT), 1966; MS 1967, PhD 1971, CA Inst of Technol; pa/Asst Prof Engrg & Applied Sci 1971-76, Assoc Prof Engrg & Applied Sci 1976-80, Prof 1980-, Univ of CA-LA (UCLA); Vis'g Prof Physics, Univ of Auckland, New Zealand, 1981; Conslt, Var Labs; Mem: Sigma Xi; Optical Soc of Am; Sr Mem, IEEE; AAAS; Eta Kappa Nu; hon/Author, Over 80 Res Articles Pub'd in Sci Jours; IEEE Cent Medal, 1984; W/W in W; Men of Achmt.

CASSARA, BEVERLY BENNER oc/ Dean, Professor; b/Aug 2, 1922; h/ 10421 Courthouse Drive, Fairfax, VA 22030; ba/Washington, DC; m/Ernest; c/Shirley, Catherine, Nicholas; ed/AB, 1947; MEd, 1954; EdD, 1970; pa/Dir Adult Ed, Goddard Col, Plainfield, VT, 1966-70; Prof Adult Ed 1970-, Dean Grad Studies 1973-, Univ of DC; Mem: Ch, Intl Assocs in Adult Ed, 1981-83; VChm Bd of Trustees, Beacon Col, 1981-83; Bd of Dirs 1976-79, Ch Com on Wom 1980-83, Coun of The Grad Schs in US; Grad Record Exam Bd, 1975-79; Exec Com, Conf of Deans of Black Grad Schs; hon/Sr Editor, *Lifelong Lrng: The Adult Yrs,* 1977-80; Editor, *Am Wom: The Changing Image,* 1962; Author of Num Book Chapts & Articles; Vis'g Res Prof, Univ of Siegen, W Germany, 1982; Fulbright-Hayes Sr Res F'ship, W Berlin, W Germany, 1975-76; Featured in WRCTV, NBC Prog "A Wom Is"; W/ W of Am Wom; Num Other Biogl Listings.

CASSIDY, MICHAEL E oc/Legislative Staff; b/Sep 15, 1955; h/PO Box 173 Newry, PA 16665; ba/Harrisburg, PA; p/Louis and Frances Cassidy, Atglen, PA; ed/Att'd PA St Univ; pa/Exec Dir, Labor Relats Com, PA Ho of Reps, 1978-; Mem, Ho of Reps, 1977-78; Mem, PA Dem St Com, 1980-; Del, Dem Conv, 1984; cp/Former Mem, Newry Borough Coun; SAR; Grange; AOH; r/ Rom Cath; hon/Eagle Scout, BSA, 1973; Fac Awd, Altoona Campus, PA St Univ; W/W in Am Polits.

CASTELLANOS, JULIO J oc/Banking Advisor; b/Mar 7, 1910; h/510 East 85th Street, Apartment 5-D, New York, NY 10028; ba/New York, NY; m/Irene Machado; c/Julio J, Maria C, Ana M, Carlos E; p/Manuel DeJesus and Virginia (dec); sp/Luis (dec) and Genoveva Machado, Washington, DC; ed/BA & LittB, De La Salle Col, 1927; JD, Tulane Univ, 1933; DCL, Univ of Havana, 1934;

Fed Resv Sys Examr Sch, 1964; pa/ Admitted to Havana Bar, 1934; Tax Commr 1935, Legal Advr 1936-59, City of Havana; Sr Ptnr, Lopez-Munoz & Castellanos, 1946-59; Secy Gen, Banco De La Construccion; Analyst of Credits, Morgan Guaranty Trust Co of NY, 1960-63; Exmr, Fed Resv Bk of NY, 1963-66; VP, Marine Midland Bk, 1966-71; Fdr Orgr & Sr VP, 1st WI Intl Bk, 1971-76; Pres, Pan Am Nat Bk, 1976; Exec Rep, Banco De Intercambio Reg, 1976-80; Pres, Banco Del Estado Holding Co, Inc, 1982-; Advr, Banco De Reservas De La Republica Dominicana, 1982-; Rep, Banco Del Estado, 1978-; Dir, Corporacion Financiera Del Norte, 1936-71; Bkg Advr, Reid & Priest, 1983-; Rep, Banco Hipotecario Dominicano, 1983-; cp/Dir, Colombian Am Assn, 1982-; Mem, NY C of C & Indust; NY Ath Clb; India House; r/Cath; hon/ Author of Profl Pubs; Retirement Recog Dipl, 1st WI Intl Bk, 1976; Public Recog Dipl, Dr Guillermo Belt, Former Mayor of Havana, 1979.

CASTENSCHIOLD, RENÉ oc/Executive; b/Feb 7, 1923; h/Lee's Hill Road, New Vernon, NJ 07976; ba/Florham Park, NJ; m/Martha Naomi; c/Gail F, Frederick T, Lynn C Jones; p/Tage (dec) and Juno Castenschiold, Green Village, NJ; ed/BEE, Pratt Inst, 1944; pa/Design Engr, Gen Elect Co, 1946-47; Sr Prod Engr, Am Transformer Co, 1947-50; Lectr, NJ Inst of Tech, 1967-79; Exec Engrg Mgr, Automatic Switch Co, 1951-; Chm, US Tech Adv Grp for the Intl Electrotech Comm (Geneva, Switzerland), 1981-; Mem, Indust Adv Coun of Underwriters Labs Inc, 1973-; cp/Dir of Civil Def 1966-70, Chm of Bd of Adjustment 1975-76, Chm of Planning Bd, 1982-, Harding Twp; Trustee, Wash Assn of NJ, 1984-; IEEE Standards Bd, 1983-; r/Epis; hon/Author Num Profl Pubs; Fellow, IEEE, 1979; Dist'd Alumni Bd of Visitors, Pratt Inst, 1979; Reg'd Profl Engr in NY & NJ; Holder of 9 Patents; W/W: in Engrg, in Fin & Indust, in World, in Tech Today, in E; Am Men & Wom in Sci; Intl W/W in Engrg.

CASTER, WILLIAM OVIATT oc/Professor; b/Dec 7, 1919; h/155 Devonshire Drive, Athens, GA 30606; ba/Athens, GA; m/Lora Joos; c/Charles Alfred, Arthur Bruce, John David, Donald Martin; p/Charles A And Rena O Caster (dec); ed/BA, Univ of WI, 1942; MS 1944, PhD 1948, Univ of MN; pa/Biochems, Nutrition Br, USPHS, 1951-63; Asst Prof Pshysiol Chem, Univ of MN Med Sch, 1963-70; Assoc Prof Nutrition, Univ of GA, 1970-; Mem: MN St Adv Com on Atomic Devel Probs, 1957-59; Adv Bd on Qtrmaster Res & Devel, 1959-63; Chm, Int-Instnl Com on Nutrition for GA, 1969-72; GA St Comm on Hunger & Malnutrition, 1972; Long-Range Planning Com, Am Inst of Nutrition, 1973-77; Councilor, Soc for Envir Geochem & Hlth, 1979-82; Pres, GA Nutrition Coun, 1982-83; r/Meth; hon/Author, Over 160 Sci Pubs incl'g: 70 Res Jour Articles & 34 Chapts, Reviews; Spec Res Fellow, Nat Heart Inst, 1956-61; Outstg Edr Awd, 1972.

CASTIGLIA, NOEL FRANCIS oc/Executive; b/Dec 25, 1937; h/917 Blue Ridge Drive, Annapolis, MD 21401; ba/Springfield, VA; m/Ann Anderson; c/Tria Marie, Carla Victoria; p/Alba Deleo

Castiglia, Westport, CT; sp/Mr and Mrs Norman Grahe, Baltimore, MD; ed/BSEE, BA 1959, Univ of CT, 1959; Postgrad EE, Univ of Bridgeport; Postgrad Bus, USC; Raytheon Engrg & Advance Mgmt Progs, 1976 & 1978; MA Cand, 1984; pa/Pt-time Jr Engr, Reeves Instrument Co; Design Engrg Positions, Electronic Specialty Co; Owner/Mgr, Intl House of Pancakes, 1966; Reg Mgr, Raytheon Co, 1972; Dir of Bus Devel, Litton Amecom, 1979; VP Engrg 1981, Pres 1983, Raven Inc; cp/Sigma Alpha Epsilon; IEEE 1962; AOA 1964; AOC 1967; RPV Assn 1978; Dem Co Com, Fairfax, VA 1974; r/Meth; hon/Num Profl Pubs; Nat Hon Soc 1952.

CASTILLO, GUADALUPE MARIA oc/Teacher; b/Mar 12; h/223 Santa Maria Drive, San Bruno, CA 94066; ba/San Bruno, CA; p/Doroteo and Josefa Reyes Castillo (dec); ed/AA, SF Jr Col; BA, SF St Univ; Grad Study, Univ CA-Berkeley, SF St Univ; Civil Rts Insts, Univ CA-Berkeley; pa/Jr HS Tchr (Biling/Bicultural), Oakland Unified Sch Dist; Clrm Tchr & Cnslr, Jefferson Elem Sch Dist, CA; Clrm Tchr & Fgn Lang Dept Chwom, Patterson, CA; OEA, Orgr & Fdr Chicano Caucus; CA Tchrs Assn, Fdr Chicano Caucus; NEA, Fdg Mem Chicano Caucus; Mem Nat Task Force on Testing (Wash DC); Assn Mexican Am Edrs Inc, Pres Oakland Chapt 1969, Regl VP 1970, Mem St Exec Bd, Other Activs; Others Profl Activs; cp/Co-Fdr, Lupe Lib; Fdr/Pres, Bertita St Block Clb; SF Comm on Status of Wom, Coor'g Com, Pre-Screening Com on Talent Bank, Resource Talent Bk Task Force; Wom for Racial & Ec Equality; Concilio De Mujeres, Pres; Challenged Safeway Corp & Permanently Closed One-Block Long Bertita St w Steel Barricade w Support of SF Ofcls; Bd Mem, Commun of Outer Mission; Mem, Com to Save Alemany Emer Hosp; r/Cath; hon/Awd for Contbn to Ed, Assn Mexican Am Edrs Inc; Awd by NEA Pres John Ryor for Contbn to Ed in Field of Testing; Pub'd Author; Mexican-Am Dir; Notable Ams; Personalities of Am; Personalities of S.

CASTILLO, LUCY NARVAEZ oc/Real Estate Broker; b/Jun 25, 1943; h/6450 Milk Wagon Lane, Miami Lakes, FL 33014; ba/Miami Beach, FL; c/Sylvia, Boris; p/Jose N (dec) and Teresa Sanchez Narvaez, Miami Lakes, FL; ed/St Peters Col, 1971; Embry-Riddle Univ, 1977; PhD, Kensington Univ, 1981; pa/Sales Agt, Globe Travel Bur, 1967; Asst Supvr of Files, Franklin Nat Bk, 1968; Corp Secy, Castillo Med Assoc, 1972-76; Mgr, Bell Med Grp Med Clin; Pres, Lunar Enterprises Inc Import-Export Co, 1976-78; Real Est Broker, Watson Rlty Inc; Mem, Daytona Bch Bd of Rltrs; cp/Mem, Logos, Life & Light; Mem, Lincoln GPO Repub Clb; r/Christian; hon/Pub'd Author; Awd of Merit "Challenge to Am", 1979; W/W Am Wom.

CASTLE, KATHRYN oc/Professor; b/Jan 20, 1948; h/30 Preston Circle, Stillwater, OK 74074; ba/Stillwater, OK; m/Douglas B Aichele; c/Adam Douglas Aichele, Clin Philip Aichele; p/Lorene Bentley, Shawnee, OK; sp/Philip and Gladys Aichele, Stillwater, OK; ed/BA, 1970; MA, 1971; EdD, 1975; pa/Assoc Prof 1979-, Asst Prof 1975-79, OK St Univ; Instr Early Childhood Ed,

Univ of VA, 1973-75; Mem: Gov'g Bd of So Assn on Chd Under 6; Gov'g Bd, Nat Assn of Early Childhood Tchr Edrs; Fac Sponsor, OK St Univ Assn for Chd Ed Intl; NAEYC, SWSRHD; ACEI OACEI; OACUS; OAEYC; Phi Delta Kappa; Author of Book: *The Inf & Toddler Handbook*; Var Articles in Profl Jours incl'g: *Jour of Contemp Psych*; *Jour of Genetic Psych*; Outstg Tchr of Yr, Col of Ed, 197-78; "Up & Coming," *OK Monthly*, 1979; Yg Ednl Ldr, Phi Delta Kappa, 1981; W/W of Am Wom; Notable Ams; Outstg Yg Wom in Am.

CASTOR, WILLIAM STUART JR oc/Chemical Consultant; b/May 23, 1926; h/111 Schuyler Road, Allendale, NJ 07401; ba/Allendale, NJ; m/Marilyn Anne Hughes; c/Jon Stuart, Richard Lee, Suzanne Marie, Cynthia Anne; p/William Stuart and Ruth Williams Castor (dec); ed/BS 1947, PhD 1950, NWn Univ; mil/USNR, 1944-46; pa/Res & Devel Chem 1950-55, Asst Dir of Pigments Tech Ser 1955-56, Asst Plant Mgr 1957-58, Dir White Pigments Res & Devel 1958-61; Tech Dir of Pigments Div 1961-68, Dir Prod Devel of Ctl Res Div 1969-72, Am Cyanamid Co; Conslt, 1973-74; Devel Mgr 1974, Mgr Pigments & Chems Res 1975-79, Mgr Res & Devel Tech Ser 1980-81, Dir of Res & Devel 1982-83, Gulf-Wn Industs, Natural Res Grp; Par/Tec Labs, 1984-; cp/No Highlands Regl Bd of Ed, Allendale, NJ, 1967-73; NJ St Bd of Ed, Needs Assessment Adv Coun, 1972-73; Am Chem Soc; Oil & Colour Chems Assn; Soc of Chem Indust; Others; r/Epis; hon/Num Profl Pubs; Elected Pres, Assn of Res Dirs, New York, 1977-78; Awd'd US & Fgn Patents for Improved Titanium Dioxide Pigments & Processes, 1965-67; W/W in E; Am Men & Wom of Sci.

CATE, RODNEY L oc/Professor; b/Dec 8, 1950; h/4738 Augusta, Wichita Falls, TX 76302; ba/Wichita Falls, TX; m/Charlene; c/Stephanie Cate, Christina Cate; p/Mr anf Mrs Rex L Cate, Novice, TX; sp/Laneta Baskerville, Ft Worth, TX; ed/BS, Tarleton St Univ, 1973; PhD, AZ St Univ, 1977; pa/Tchg Res Asst, Tarleton St Univ, 1969-73; Tchg & Res Assoc, AZ St Univ, 1973-77; Postdoct Scholar, Univ of CA-LA, 1977-78; Asst Prof Chem 1978-83, Assoc Prof Chem & Grad Biol 1983-, MW St Univ; Mem: Local Sect Secy-Treas 1981, Chm-elect 1982, Chm 1983, Am Chem Soc; Sigma Xi; AAAS; TX Acad of Sci; Planetary Soc; Beta Beta Beta; Gamma Sigma Epsilon; Phi Eta Sigma; r/Meth; hon/Author, Num Articles in Profl Jours incl'g: *Jour Phy Chem*; *Biochem Biophy Res Commun*; *Archives Biochem Biophys*; *Toxicon*; Others; Outstg Student Awd, 1973; Robert A Welch Foun S'ship, 1972-73; Grad Student F'ship, AZ St Univ, 1975; NIH/NSF Postdoct S'ship, 1977-78; W/W in Frontier Sci & Technol; Other Biogl Listings.

CATTANEO, JACQUELYN A KAMMERER oc/Artist; Instructor; b/Jun 1, 1944; h/210 East Green, Gallup, NM 87301; ba/Same; m/John Leo; c/John Auro, Paul Anthony; p/Ralph J (dec) and Gladys A Kammerer, Gallup, NM; sp/Auro (dec) and Nellie Cattaneo, Gallup, NM; ed/Att'd TX Wom Univ, 1962-64; Master Art Classes: Frederick Taubes, Ben Konis, Geo Cherepov,

Sergei, Bongart, Daniel Greene; pa/ Tchr of 1st Pvt Art Classes in Gallup, NM, 1965-77; Sponsor, Public Art Shows & Competitions in Gallup, NM, 1965-79; Judge, Art Competitions; Currently Portrait Artist; cp/Charter Mem, Gallup Area Arts & Crafts Coun; Charter Mem, Intl Fine Arts Guild; Charter Mem, Am Portrait Soc; Perm Collections incl: Zuni Arts & Crafts Ed Bldg, Univ of NM, C J Wiemar Collection, McKinley Manor; hon/Num Articles; Num Grp Shows; Artists USA; Guide to Contemp Am Art; Personalities of W & MW; World W/W of Wom; Dir Am Portrait Artists.

CAVE, WILLIAM THOMPSON JR oc/Professor; b/Oct 17, 1942; h/9 Ten Eyke Circle, Pittsford, NY 14534; ba/ Rochester, NY; m/Jacqueline; c/Catherine, John, Christopher; p/Mr and Mrs W T Cave, Rockville, MD; sp/Mrs H McWilliams, Appleton City, MO; ed/ BA, Kenyon Col, 1963; MD, Yale Univ, 1967; mil/MC USAR, 1969-72, Maj; pa/ Resident 1967-69, Fellow Endocrinology 1972-75, Instr & Assoc Prof 1975-77, Univ of VA Hosp; Asst Prof 1977-83, Assoc Prof 1983-, Univ of Rochester; Mem: Endocrine Soc; Am Thyroid Assn; Am Diabetes Assn; Am Assn for Cancer Res; NY Acad of Scis; Soc for Exptl Biol & Med; Fellow, Am Col of Phys; r/Epis; hon/Author of Articles in Profl Jours incl'g: Cancer Res; Endocrinology; Jour Nat Cancer Inst; Sigma Xi; Commend Medal, USAR.

CAVIGGA, MARGARET MADDOX oc/Quilt Collector & Historian, Art Consultant; b/Oct 31, 1924; h/119 N Mansfield Avenue, Los Angeles, CA 90036; ba/Los Angeles, CA; m/Albert Anthony; p/Mr T C and Coctabelle Peterson Maddox (dec); sp/Mr and Mrs Albert Cavigga, Jeanette, PA; ed/Att'd: So Meth Univ, 1943; Univ of MO-Columbia, 1945; BA Art, Psych & Sociol, LA St Univ, 1946; Postgrad Study in Art: Univ of CA-LA, 1949-53; CA St Univ-Northridge, 1950-60; pa/ Public Sch Tchr, LA, 1953-72; Master Tchr, Tchr Tng Prog, 1954-72; Tour Conductor, Clb Universe-Unitours, LA, 1960-73; Owner, Operator, The Margaret Cavigga Quilt Collection, LA, 1973-; Appraiser, Am Quilts & Americana; Lectr on Collecting Textiles & Collectibles; Curator, Num Hist Quilt Exhibns, US & Abroad; Num TV & Radio Appearances; Mem: Bd Dirs, Wom in Design, LA; Decorative Arts Coun; LA Co Mus; Costume & Textile Coun; LA Cou Mus; ASID Affil LA, Am Soc of Interior Designers; Craft & Folk Art Mus; NY Folk Art Mus; Hancock Pk Hist Soc; Smithsonian Inst; Nat Trust Hist Presv; cp/Repub of LA; Repub of CA; r/Meth; hon/Author of Books, Am Antique Quilts Eng & Japanese Edits, 1981; Quilt Connoisseurship, 1982; More Am Than Apple Pie, 1984; Var Articles in Num Mags incl'g Early Am Life; Hobbies; The Best Report; An Am Quilt Collection; Featured in Other Mags; LA Co Mus Civic Awd Recip, LA Co Supr, 1981; Awd, Mayor of LA, 1981; Awd, Mayor of Santa Monica, 1982; Awd, Gov of CA, 1982; Recip, Senate Resolution, State of CA Senate, 1982; W/ W in W.

CAWS, MARY ANN oc/Professor; b/ Sep 10, 1933; h/140 East 81st Street, New York, NY 10028; ba/New York,

NY; m/Peter James; c/Hilary, Matthew; p/Mrs Harmon C Rorison, Wilmington, NC; ed/BA, Bryn Mawr Col, 1954; MA, Yale Univ, 1956; PhD, KS, 1962; pa/Asst Prof to Prof: Univ of KS; Sarah Lawrence Col; Barnard Col; Hunter Col; Prof, Exec Ofcr Comparative Lit PhD Prog 1976-, Exec Ofcr French PhD Prog 1979-, Grad Sch, CUNY; Pres, MLA, 1983-84; hon/Editor, Dada/Surrealism; Author of Num Books incl'g: Surrealism & the Lit Imagination, 1970; Andre Breton, 1972; The Eye in the Text: Essays Mannerist to Mod, 1981; The Poetry of Dada & Surrealism, 1971; The Inner Theatre of Recent French Poetry, 1972; The Surrealist Voice of Robert Desnos, 1977; Rene Char, 1978; The Presence of Rene Char, 1976; Metapoetics of the Passage: Architextures in Surrealism & After, 1982; Translator of Books by: Breton, Char, Reverdy & Tzara; Hon DLH, Union Col, 1983; Guggenheim Fellow, 1972; Fulbright Fellow, 1972; NEH Fellow, 1978; ACLS Grant, 1981; Ofcr, Palmes Acadmiques; W/W in Am Wom; Dict of Am Scolars.

CAZEAUX, ISABELLE ANNE-MARIE oc/Professor; b/Feb 24, 1926; h/ 415 East 72nd Street, New York, NY 10021; ba/Bryn Mawr, PA; p/ Marie-Anne Fort Cazeaux, New York, NY; ed/BA, Hunter Col, 1945; MA, Smith Col, 1946; MLS 1959, PhD Musicology 1961, Columbia Univ; Premiere Médaille, Conservatiore National de Musique, Paris, 1950; Licence d'Enseignement, Ecole Normale de Musique, Paris, 1950; pa/Sr Music Cataloguer & Hd Music & Phonorecords Cataloguing, NY Public Lib, 1957-63; Fac, Bryn Mawr Col, 1963-; Alice Carter Dickerman Prof & Chm Music Dept Fac of Musicology, Manhattan Sch of Music, 1969-82; Vis'g Prof, Douglass Col, Rutgers Univ, 1978; Mem: Coun 1968-70, Com on Status of Wom in Musicology 1974-76, Am Musicological Soc; Société Francaise de Musicologie; Intl Musicological Soc; Cataloguing & Bibliog Coms, Asst Chm NY Chapt, Music Lib Assn; Col Music Soc; Intl Assn of Music Libs; AAUP; r/ Rom Cath; hon/Author of 3 Books incl'g: French Music of the 15th & 16th Cents; Others; Recip F'ships & S'ships: Smith Col; Columbia Univ; Inst of Intl Ed; Grant from Martha Baird Rockefeller Fund for Music, 1971-72; Grant from Herman Goldman Foun, 1980; W/W in Music; New Grov Dict of Music & Musicians.

CEBRIK, MELVIN L oc/Executive; b/ Mar 19, 1947; h/20 Kimberly Court, Ramsey, NJ 07446; ba/New York, NY; m/Elizabeth Ann; c/Kimberly, Kristta; p/Michael and Melvina Cebrik, Nutley, NJ; sp/Louis and Anna Mae Recchione, Hawthorne, NJ; ed/AB, Colgate Univ, 1968; MBA w Distn, NY Univ, 1970; Adv'd Profl Cert in Fin, 1975; pa/Asst Secy, Chem Bk of NYC, 1970-76; Dir of Planning, Bradford Nat Corp of NYC, 1976-78; VP, The Chase Manhattan Bk of NYC, 1978-; Exec VP & Dir, Wn Hemisphere Life Ins Co; VP and Dir of Bd, Chase Agy Ser Inc; Chief Rep, Consumer Credit Ins Assn; hon/Kappa Mu Epsilon, 1967; Beta Gamma Sigma, 1970; W/W in E; Am Bkr Dir of US Bkg Execs.

CECCONI-BATES, AUGUSTA NORMA oc/Composer, Music Educator; b/Aug 9, 1933; h/Toad Harbor, 816

Shaw Drive, W Monroe, NY 13167; ba/ Syracuse, NY; m/Robert N Bates; ed/ BA 1956, MA 1960, Syracuse Univ; pa/ F'ship, Scuola Italiana, Middlebury Col, 1956; Libn, Syracuse Univ, 1957; Music Tchr, Public Schs, 1958-; Prof, Maria Regina Col, 1964-65; Composer-in-Residence, VT Music & Arts Ctr, Sums 1977-; Bd of Dirs, Syracuse Soc for New Music; cp/Oswego Co Coun on the Arts; Assoc Life Mem, ABI; Life Mem, Assn of Concert Bands Inc; VT Music & Arts Ctr; Centro Italiano; Pro Art, Syracuse; Sigma Alpha Iota; Phi Sigma Iota; MENC; NYSSMA; hon/Musical Compositions incl: "Willie Was Different" (Based on an Illust'd Story by Norman Rockwell); "We Have A Dream" Cantata for Soloists & Orch; "Something Songs Unrelated"; Petite Ragtime Rhapsody" (for Ian Hobson, Pianist); "War is Kind"; "The Ship of the World"; Intl W/W of Music; Register of Profiles; Book of Hon; Other Biogl Listings.

CEDAR, PAUL A oc/Pastor; b/Nov 4, 1938; h/1771 East Orange Grove, Pasadena, CA 91104; ba/Pasadena, CA; m/Jean Helen; c/Daniel, Mark, Deborah; p/C B Cedar, Duluth, MN; sp/Margaret Lier, Aberdeen, SD; ed/BS, No St Col, 1960; MDiv, No Bapt Theol Sem, 1967; DMin, Am Bapt of the W, 1973; Att'd Univ of IA, Wheaton Grad Sch, CA St Univ; pa/Minister, 1960-63 and 1965-67; Crusade Assoc for Billy Graham Evangelistic Assn, 1964-65 and 1967-69; Pastor, Yorba Linda, CA, 1969-73; Exec Pastor, First Pres Ch of Hollywood, 1975-80; Pres, Dynamic Communs, 1973-; Sr Pastor, Lake Ave Congreg Ch, 1981-; cp/Secy 1979-80, Pastor of Hollywood, CA, 1978-80; Rotary Clb of Pasadena, CA, 1981-; Life Mem, Pi Kappa Delta; r/Congreg; hon/ Author Becoming a Lover, 7 Keys to Maximum Communication, The Communicator's Commentary; Bible Rdg Awd, Am Bible Soc; W/W in CA.

CEGLES-COMSTOCK, KATHLEEN ANNE oc/Physical Therapist; b/ Jun 15, 1953; h/12 Ferncliff Beach, Erie, PA 16505; ba/Erie, PA; m/John Daniel Comstock; ed/BS, FL Intl Univ, 1976; pa/Chief Phy Therapist, Barlow Hosp in LA, 1976-78; Chief Phy Therapist, Shriners Hosp for Crippled Chd in Erie, 1978-80; Coor of Phy Therapy, Home Hlth Ser of Erie Co, 1980-82; Co-owner, Hlth Consltg Assoc Inc of Erie, 1981-; Assn of Fitness Dirs; AAUW; Am Col of Sports Med; Am Phy Therapy Assn; ARC; Am Running & Fitness Assn; CA Thoracic Soc; PA Phy Therapy Assn; Profl Adv Bd; Respiratory Care Assem; cp/Nat Ctr Hlth Ed, Charter Assoc; Erie Co Polit Assem for Wom; Lifetime Mem, FL Intl Univ Alumni Assn; ZONTA Clb of Erie II; r/Cath; hon/Cert Fitness Instr from Am Col of Sports Med, 1982; W/W of Am Wom.

CELLINI, WILLIAM QUIRINO JR oc/Electrical Engineer and Operations Research Analyst; b/Mar 12, 1951; h/ 2111 Jefferson Davis Highway, Apartment 1012-S, Arlington, VA 22202; p/ Mr and Mrs Quirino Cellini, Ardmore, PA; ed/BSEE, Drexel Univ, 1974; MBA, Univ of Pgh, 1975; Hon Discharge, Army Engr Ofcrs Basic Sch, 1976; MSEE Cand, George Wash Univ, 1977-82; mil/USAR, 2nd Lt, 1975-76; pa/Res Asst, Franklin Inst Res Labs,

1973; Elect Engr & Sys Anal, Adv'd Marine Enterprises, 1977-79; Assoc of Solar Elect Power Sys, PRC Energy Anal Co, 1979-80; Res Anal of Energy Sys, Presearch Inc, 1980-81; Elect Engr, Gauthier, Alvarado & Assoc, 1981; Sys Anal, Harry Diamond Lab, 1981-82; Elect Engr & Oper Res Anal, J J Henry Co Inc, 1982; Elect Engr & Oper Res Anal, Sys & Applied Sci Corp, 1982-83; Mem: IEEE; Nat Soc of Profl Engrs; Soc of Am Mil Engrs; Am Soc for Engrg Ed; Am Mgmt Assn; Assn of MBA Execs; Assn of the Army; AAAS; Assoc Energy Engrs; Friends of Kennedy Ctr; Nat Trust Hist Presv; USOS; Smithsonian Instn; Nat Italian Am Foun; Intl Platform Assn; cp/Life Mem, Alpha Phi Omiega; Cath Yd Adults Clb; Arlington Diocese, Parish Rep Coor, 1980-81; PA Newman Alumni Assn; Others; r/Cath; hon/Num Profl Pubs; High Ranking Positions as Sr Yr Army ROTC Cadet; Assoc, ABI; Zeta Theta Alumni Assn; Others; Intl Reg of Profiles; Intl W/W of Intells; Men of Achmt; W/W in S & SW; Other Biogl Listings.

CEURVELS, WARREN STEVEN oc/Administrator; b/Mar 30, 1944; h/RR 2, Box 1089, Highland Lakes, NJ 07422; ba/Upper Montclair, NJ; m/Denise A Saladini; c/Frank; p/Frank and Evelyn Ceurvels, Newark, DE; sp/Vincent and Viola Saladini, Clifton, NJ; ed/BA, Newark St Col, 1967; MA, Montclair St Col, 1969; EdD, Rutgers Univ, 1983; pa/Indust Arts Tchr, Gov Livingston Regl HS, 1965-68; Tng Supvr, Ohaus Scale Corp, 1969; Pers Anal, Montgomery Co Public Schs, 1969-70; Dir, Adult Ed Resource Ctr, Montclair St Col, 1970-; Reg III Rep, Adult Basic Ed Comm of USA, 1979-81; Mem, Am Assn of Adult Cont'g Ed, 1970-; Assn of Adult Ed, 1970-; cp/Lake Commun Property Owners Assn, Barry Lakes, NJ; r/Cath; hon/Author Profl Pubs; W/W in E.

CHADDA, KUL DEEP oc/Cardiologist; b/Aug 14, 1943; h/235 Saddle Lane, Muttontown, NY 11791; ba/New Hyde Park, NY; m/Usha Nath; c/Rishi, Manu; p/Moti Chadda (dec); Saraswati Chada, India; ed/Pre-med, Ewing Christian Col, Allahabad, 1961; MD, Maulana Azad Med Col, Univ of Delhi, 1966; NY St Med License, Am Bd of Internal Med, 1974; Subspec Cardiovas Disease, Am Bd of Internal Med, 1977; pa/LIJ-HMC Acting Phys-in-Charge Adult Cardiology, Hd Cardiac Catheterization & Electrophysiol, 1981-; Assoc Prof Med, SUNY-Downstate, Bklyn, 1978-; LIJ-HMC Sect Co-Hd Invasive Cardiology & Incharge of Electrophysiol, 1979-; Dir of Cardiopulmonary Labs, Maimonides Med Ctr, Bklyn, 1976-79; Att'g Phys Univ Hosp Downst Med Ctr, Bklyn, 1978-; Asst Att Cardiologist, Maimonides Med Ctr, Bklyn, 1976-79; Other Previous Positions; Mem: Fellow, Am Cols of Phys, Cardiology, Nutrition, Angiology, Chest Phys; Fellow, Coun of Clin Cardiology, Am Heart Assn; Fellow, Soc for Cardiac Angiography; Fellow, The NY Cardiological Soc; Nassau Chapt, Mbrship Com 1980-81, Res Com 1980-82, NY Heart Assn; Am Soc Internal Med; Am Fedn for Clin Res; Med Soc Co of Kings & Acad of Med; N Am Soc Pacing & Electrophysiol; hon/Author of 31 Res Paper Presentations; 58 Article Pubs in Profl Jours; Num

Abstracts; hon/Cert of Apprec, Nassau Chapt Am Heart Assn, 1981; 2nd Best Paper Presentation Awd, Am Col of Phys, 1976; VPres, Assn of Intern & Residents, Mt Sinai Hosp Sers, Elmhurts, NY, 1971-72; M M Dhar S'ship, Univ of Delhi, 1961-66; Social Scis Assn Cert of Merit 1960-61, 1st w Distns Pre-med Class 1960-61, Ewing Christian Col; Cert, Delhi St Postgrad Tchrs Clb, 1959; Res & Pubs & Radiation Safety Com, Mt Sinai Hosp Sers, Elmhurst, 1975-76; Recip, Num Res Grants.

CHAFETZ, MORRIS EDWARD oc/Executive; b/Apr 20, 1924; h/3129 Dumbarton Street, Northwest, Washington, DC 20007; ba/Washington, DC; m/Marion Donovan; c/Gary, Marc, Adam; p/Isaac and Rose Chafetz, Worcester, MA; sp/William and Molly Donovan, Lawrence, MA; ed/MD, Tufts Med Sch, Boston, MA, 1948; Intern, US Marine Hosp, Detroit, MI, 1948-49; Resident Psychi, St Hosp, Howard, RI, 1949-51; Fellow Neurophysiol, Instituto Nacional de Cardiologia, Mexico, 1951-52; Clin Res Fellow Psychi, MA Gen Hosp, 1952-54; Res Fellow Psychi, Harvard Med Sch, 1952-54; mil/AUS, 1944; Psychi, US Coast Guard, 1952; pa/Mem, Pres Comm on Drunk Driving, Chm Com on Ed & Preven, 1982-; Pres, Morris Chafetz & Assocs, 1980-; Clin Prof Psychi & Behavioral Sci, Med Univ of SC, 1980; Adj Prof, Ctr for Metro Affairs & Public Policy, The Col of Charleston, 1979-; Pres, Hlth Ed Foun, 1976-; Prin Res Sci, The Johns Hopkins Univ Ctr for Metro Planning & Res, 1975-; Chm of Bd, Hlth Insts, 1977-82; Dir, Nat Inst on Alcohol Abuse & Alcoholism, Alcohol, Drug Abuse & Mtl Hlth Adm, 1971-75; Acting Dir, Div of Alcohol Abuse & Alcoholism, Nat Ist Mtl Hlth, 1970-71; Dir Clin Psychi Sers 1968-70, Dir Acute Psychi Sers 1961-68, Dir Alcohol Clin 1957-68, Clin Asst in Psychi to Psychi 1954-70, MA Gen Hosp; Asst Psychi to Assoc Clin Prof Psychi, Harvard Med Sch, 1954-70; Mem: DC Mayor's Adv Task Force on Drunk Driving, 1982-; Conslt, Pan Am Hlth Org, 1972-; Corres'g Mem, Inst for Study & Preven of Alcoholism, Zagreb, 1971; Sigma Xi; Am Orthopsychi Assn; AAAS; Edit Bd Mem & Advr to Var Jours incl'g: *Med Insight; Mtl Hlth Digest; Psychi Opinion; Jour of Studies on Alcohol;* Others; Num Other Org Coms & Activs; hon/Author, Over 140 Articles in Profl Jours; 14 Books on Alcohol Related Topics; Author of Newspaper Column; Nat Lectr, Sigma Xi, 1978-79; Public Ser Awd, Alcohol & Drug Probs Assn of N Am, 1975; Mr Airy Gold Medal Awd for Dist'd Ser to Psychi, 1974; Fellow, Royal Col of Hlth, 1974-; Intl Film & TV Fest of NY Gold Medal, 1972; Bronze Recog Plaque, Tilton Bldg, MA Gen Hosp, 1970; Louis & Amelia Block Lectr, Mt Zion Hosp & Med Ctr, SF, CA, 1969; Moses Greeley Parker Lectr, 1969; Maudsley Bequest Lectr, Univ of Edinburgh, Scotland, 1965; Num Biogl Listings.

CHAFFEE, JEAN COCHRAN oc/Educator; h/7711 Ravensridge, St Louis, MO 63119; ba/St Louis, MO; c/Clinton Jared; p/Georgia Cochran, Corpus Christi, TX; ed/RDH, Univ of TX, 1969; BA, Dominican Col, 1975; MSHP, SW TX Univ, 1977; pa/Clin Coor, Wharton

Jr Col, 1975-76; Dental Hygienist, J R Alexander DDS, 1976-77; Dept Chp, St Louis Commun Col, 1977-; Am Dental Hygiene Assn; MO Assn of Commun & Jr Cols; cp/Sigma Phi Alpha, 1984-; Am Acad Hist Dentistry, 1984-; Spkr's Bur, 1977-; MO Botanical Gardens, 1977-; Wom Commerce Assn; Arts & Ed Coun of St Louis; Parents w/o Ptnrs; r/Epis; hon/W/W: in TX, Am Wom; Dir Dist'd Ams; Outstg Yg Wom of Am, 1978.

CHAGALL, DAVID oc/Writer, Researcher, TV/Radio Personality; b/Nov 22, 930; h/PO Box 85; Agoura, CA 91301; ba/Los Angeles, CA; m/Juneau Joan Alsin; p/Harry and Ida Coopersmith Chagall (dec); ed/BA, PA St Univ; 1952; Lisc Lit Gen, Sorbonne, Univ of Paris, France, 1954; pa/Pubr, *Inside Campaigning,* 1983-; Contbg Editor, *LA Mag;* VPres, SCB Res, LA, 1981-; Mktg Res Proj Dir, Aug Assocs, LA, 1964-74; Mktg Res Assoc, Chilton Co, Phila, 1962--63; Pub Relats Staff, AEI-Hotpoint Ltd, London, 1961-62; Sci Editor, *Jour of IEE,* London, 1959-61; Other Previous Positions; Mem: Acad Polit & Social Sci; Judic Soc; Mark Twain Soc; Author's Guild; Am Acad of Polit & Social Sci; SW Social Sci Assn; Fund For Animals; cp/Repub Nat Com; r/Deist, Millenium House Congreg, ULC; hon/Author of 5 Books: *The New Kingmakers,* 1981; *Summer of Love,* 1973; *The Spieler For The Holy Spirit,* 1973; *Diary of a Deaf Mute,* 1972; *The Cent God Slept,* 1964; Num Short Stories, Articles, Reviews & Columns in Nat Mags & Jours, 1968-; Carnegie Awd, 1964; Nat Book Awd Nom for Fiction, 1972; Nom for Pulitzer Prize in Lttrs, 1973; Winner, Dist'd Hlth Jour Awd, 1978; Univ of WI Poetry Awd, 1970; Pres Achmt Awd, 1982; W/W: in Am, in W, in World.

CHAKRABARTI, SUBRATA KUMAR oc/Marine Research Director; b/Feb 3, 1941; h/191 East Weller Drive North, Plainfield, IL 60544; ba/Plainfield, IL; m/Prakriti; c/Sumita, Prabal; p/Asutosh and Shefal Chakrabarti, Calcutta, India; sp/Santosh and Bijali Bhaduri, Malda, India; ed/ISc, Presidency Col, 1959; BSME, Jadavpur Univ, 1963; MS 1965, PhD 1968, Univ of CO; PE, St of IL, 1971; pa/Asst Engr, Trainee, Kuljian Corp, Calcutta, 1963-64; Asst Engr, Simon Carves Ltd, Calcutta, 1964; Instr, EDEE Dept, Univ of CO, 1965-66; Hydrodynamicist, 1968-70; Hd Anal Crp, 1970-79,; Dir 1979-, Chgo Bridge & Iron Co; Fellow, Mem W/W Pub Com, ASCE; Fellow, AAS; Edit Bd, Applied Ocean Res; Sigma Xi; Tech Reviewer: ASCE, ASME, NSF, AWC, SPE; Assoc Editor: *Jour ERT; ASME Jour;* hon/Author, Over 80 Tech Pubs in Sci & Engrg Jours Intlly; Proceedings of Offshore Technol Conf, Civil Engrg in Ocean, Riser Anal; Intl Symp Ocean Engrg & Ship Handling, Sweden; Gold Medal Jadavpur Univ, 1963; Scholastic Cit, Univ of CO, 1968; James Croes Medal, ASCE, 1974; Freeman F'ship, ASCE, 1979; W/W: in Engrg, Technol Today, Intl Dir of Engrg Anal; Men of Achmt; Other Biogl Listings.

CHAKRABARTY, ANANDA MOHAN oc/Professor; b/Apr 4, 1938; h/206 Julia Drive, Villa Park, IL 60181; ba/Chicago, IL; m/Krishnac; c/Kaberi, Asit; p/Satya Das and Sasthi Bala

Chakrabarty (dec); sp/N C and Sulata Chakraverty, Calcutta, India; ed/MS, 1960; PhD, 1965; pa/Staff Mem, Gen Elct Res & Devel Ctr, Schenectady, NY, 1971-79; Prof, Univ of IL-Chgo, 1979-; Mem: Am Soc for Microbiol; Am Soc of Biol Chems; Soc of Indust Microbiol; r/Hindu; hon/Editor of 2 Books, *Genetic Engrg*, 1979; *Biodegradation & Detoxification of Envir Pollutants*, 1982; Sci of Yr, Indust Res, 1975; Am Chem Soc Public Affairs Awd, Chgo, 1984; W/W in Am.

CHALMERS, DAVID BAY oc/Chief Executive Officer; b/Nov 17, 1924; h/908 Town and Country Boulevard, Houston, TX 77024; ba/Houston, TX; c/David B Jr; p/Dorrit Bay Chalmers, Denver, CO; ed/BA, Dartmouth Col, 1947; Tuck Sch Bus, Dartmouth Col; Harvard Bus Sch Adv'd Mgmt Prog, 1966; mil/USMC, Lt 1943-45, 1st Lt Korean War 1949-50; pa/Pres, Canadian Occidental Petro Ltd, Pres & CEO, Petrogas Processing Ltd, 1968-73; VP Occidental Petro Corporation, 1967-68; Var Managerial Positions incl'g: VP, Tenneco Oil Co, 1951-55; cp/US C of C; Indep Petro Assn Am; Nat Petro Refiners Assn; Am Petro Inst; Am Petro Refiners Assn; TX Indep Petro & Royalty Owners Assn; Houston C of C; r/Epis; hon/Pub'd in *Leaders Mag*; Elected to 25 Yr Clb of Petro Indust, 1976; Intl Press, Europe Contemp Personalities; Two Thousand Notable Ams; Canadian W/W; Denver Social Register; Dir of Dist'd Ams.

CHAMBERS, CAROLYN SILVA oc/Executive; b/Sep 15, 1931; h/PO Box 640 Pleasant Hill, OR 97455; ba/Eugene, OR; m/Richard A; c/William, Scott, Elzabeth, Clark, Silva; p/Julio and Elizabeth Silva (dec); ed/BA, Univ of OR, 1953; pa/Pres, Chambers Cable Communs Inc, 1983-; Treas, VPres/Treas, Exec VPres/Treas, Liberty Communs Inc, 1960-83; VPres, R A Chambers & Assocs, 1979-; Acct, KASH Radio, 1967-68; Secy/Treas, Bd Mem, Pres, McKenzie River Motors; Univ of OR Alumni Ofc, 1953-54; Bus Mgr, Advtg Mgr, *OR Daily Emerald*; Mem: VPres, Pres, Ed Com Chp, Conv Chp, OR Cable Communs Assn; Bd Mem, 1980 Conv Chp, Conv Panelist, CA Cable TV Assn; Fin Com, Chp of Elect & By-laws, Nat Cable TV Assn; Treas, VPres, Pres, Nat Chapt Wom in Cable; 1983 Conv Chp, Pacific NW Cable Communs Assn; Cable TV Pioneers; Commun Antenna TV Assn; Dir, Portland Br OR-Pacific Devel Corp; cp/Sacred Heart Med Foun; Bd of Trustees, Univ of OR Foun; Bd, Treas, Dir Search Com, Eugene Symph; Adv Com, Eugene Hearing & Spch Ctr; Alton Baker Pk Comm; Chp, Pleasant Hill Sch Bd; Treas, Bd, Mgr of Thrift Shop, Jr Leag of Eugene; Ch Budget Com, Treas, Chwom Guild, Epis Ch; hon/Kappa Alpha Theta; Gamma Alpha Chi; Sigma Delta Chi; Idel Kaitz Awd, Nat Cable TV Assn, 1983; Pioneer Awd, Univ of OR; W/W in Fin & Indust; Men & Wom of Distn.

CHAMBERS, JOAN LOUISE oc/University Librarian; b/Mar 22, 1937; h/7019 Caprice Way, Riverside, CA 92504; ba/Riverside, CA; m/Donald R; ed/Cert, Univ of Edinburgh, Scotland, 1957; BA, Univ of No CO, 1958; MLS, Univ of CA-Berkeley, 1970; pa/Univ Libn, Univ of CA-Riverside, 1981-; Asst

Univ Libn, Univ of CA-San Diego, 1979-81; Chm Fac Sen 1977-78, Libn 1970-79, Univ of NV-Reno; Public Sch Tchr & Libn, St of CA, 1958-70; Mem: Var Ofc Positions, Am Lib Assn, 1970-; Am Soc for Info Sic, 1980-; CA Lib Assn, 1972-; Univ of CA Press Assocs, 1981-; cp/Sierra Clb, 1968-; Audubon Soc, 1981-; Univ of CA-Riverside: Friends of Lib; Botanic Gardens; Mus of Photo & Ath Booster, 1981-; hon/Author of Var Articles & Reviews in Jours incl'g: *The Jour of Acad Libnship*; *Lib Res*; *Microform Review*; *Energy & NV*; Acad Lib Mgmt Internship, Duke Univ, Coun on Lib Resources, 1978-79; Acad Lib Conslt Trainee, Wash DC, Assn Res Libs, 1981; Sr Fellow, UCLA, 1982; W/W in Lib & Info Scis.

CHAN, ARTHUR WING KAY oc/Research Scientist, Professor; b/Jun 24, 1941; h/94 Gaslight Trail, Williamsville, NY 14221; ba/Buffalo, NY; m/Shirley Pou; c/Alvin Mark; ed/BSc 1966, PhD 1969, Australian Nat Univ; pa/Postdoct Fellow 1969-71, Res Assoc 1971-73, Wash Univ-St Louis; Res Sci III 1974-76, Res Sci IV 1976-79, Res Sci V 1979-, Res Inst on Alcoholism; Res Asst Prof 1974-81, Res Assoc Prof 1982-, SUNY-Buffalo; Mem: Sigma Xi, 1974-; Res Soc on Alcoholism, 1976-; Am Soc of Pharm & Exptl Therapeutics, 1978-; Bd of Dirs, NY St Res Foun for Mtl Hygiene Inc, 1979-80; Exec Com, NY St Coun of Res Scis, 1980-; r/Cath; hon/Author of Over 40 Res Articles & Abstracts in Profl Jours incl'g: *Jour of Thoracic Cardiovas Surg*; *Pharm, Biochem Behavior*; Others; Final Yr Hons S'ship 1966, Postgrad Res S'ship 1966-69, Australian Nat Univ; W/W: in E, in Am Men & Wom of Sci, in Frontier Sci & Technol.

CHAN, FREDERICK MAN HIN oc/Architect; Real Estate Developer; b/Jun 17, 1947; h/3505 South Figueroa Street, Number 555, Los Angeles, CA 90071; ba/Los Angeles, CA; p/William Chak Yan and Nancy Sui Yin Tse Chan, Ontario, Canada; ed/BArch, Univ of CA-Berkeley, 1969; MArch, Harvard Univ, 1974; pa/NY St Urban Devel Corp, 1973-74; Devel Mgr Commun Land Devel, Min of Housing of Toronto, Canada, 1974-78; Pres, Nu W Real Est Investmt Corp, 1978-; Treas, Pearl City Investmts Corp, 1978-; Pres, SW New Horizons Corp, 1982-; Ontario Assn of Arch; Intl Coun of Shopping Ctrs; Urban Land Inst; Am Planning Assn; The Asia Soc; LA HQ City Assn; Town Hall of CA; LA C of C; Am Mgmt Assn; Chinese C of C (Dir); cp/Marina City Clb; hon/Co-author *Investmnt in CA Real Est by Residents of the Far E*.

CHAN, PAK HOO oc/Professor; b/Apr 11, 1942; h/635 Jackson Street, Albany, CA 94706; ba/SF, CA; m/Helen S Chu; c/Tammy Yuen-Wah, Olivia Yee-Wah, Goldie Yan-Wah; p/Sik-Kee and Hong-King Leung Chan; sp/Chun-Hwa and Juping Huang Chu; ed/BS, Chinese Univ of Hong Kong, 1964; MA 1970, PhD 1972, Univ of CA-LA; pa/Assoc Adj Prof 1983-, Assoc Res Biochem 1980-83, Asst Res Biochem 1975-80, Univ of CA-SF; Postdoct Fellow, Stanford Univ, 1974-75; Postdoct Fellow, Univ of CA-Berkeley, 1972-74; Mem: Univ Ad Hoc Review Com, 1981-; Univ Hearing Com, 1979; Conslt, Clin Res Fellows, 1975-; Adv

Cnslt, NIH-NINCDS, 1984; Ad Hoc Reviewer, Var Sci Jours, 1977-; hon/Author of Books: *Brain Edema Symp*, 1982; *Neural Membrane Symposium*, 1983; *Princeton-Wmsburg Ischemic Symp*, 1984; *Handbook of Neurochem*, 2nd Ed 1984; New Haven S'ship Awd, Yale Univ, 1964; NIH Grantee, 1978-; W/W: in World, in Frontier Sci & Technol.

CHAN, ROSALIE Y oc/Medical Technologist; b/Apr 26, 1938; h/13437 Doolittle Drive, San Leandro, CA 94577; ba/Berkeley, CA; m/Tom; c/Jane W; p/Mr and Mrs Shong-ching Lau, Philadelphia, PA; sp/Lum-oy Chan, Visalia, CA; ed/BS, 1960; Postgrad, CA St Univ, 1970; pa/Tchr, Chinese Commun Ctr, Oakland, CA, 1961-63; Res Asst, Univ of CA-Berkeley, 1967-68; Sr Med Technol, Kaiser Permanente Med Grp, Berkeley, CA, 1972-; Mem, Am Soc of Clin Pathol, 1974-; Real Est Broker, 1978-; hon/Mem, US Congl Adv Bd, 1983; W/W of Am Wom.

CHAN, WAI-YEE oc/Molecular Geneticist, Professor; b/Apr 28, 1950; h/8725 Raven Avenue, Oklahoma City, OK 73132; ba/Oklahoma City, OK; m/May-Fong; c/Connie Hai-Yee, Joanne Hai-Wei; p/Kui Chan and Fung-Hing Wong, Hong Kong; sp/Fung-Cheung Sheung and Chui-Wan Cheung, Hong Kong; ed/BSc, Chinese Univ of Hong Kong, 1974; PhD, Univ of FL, 1977; pa/Tchg Asst, Univ of FL, 1974-77; Staff Res Assoc 1978-79, Asst Prof 1979-82, Assoc Prof 1982-, Univ of OK; Staff Affil, OK Chd's Hosp, 1979-; Conslt, Med Ser, VA Med Ctr, 1981-; Co-Sci Dir, St of OK Tchg Hosps, 1982-; Mem: Am Soc of Biol Chems; Am Inst of Nutrition; Soc for Pediatric Res; The Biochem Soc; Nutrition Soc; NY Acad of Sci; Am Soc of Human Genetics; cp/Rotary Clb, 1982-; hon/Editor, *Metabolism of Trace Metals in Man, Volumes I & II*, 1984; Num Sci Articles in Profl Jours & Var Book Chapts; S'ship for Chem 1972-74, S'ship for Biochem 1973-74, The Chinese Univ of Hong Kong; F'ship to NATO ASI Meeting, NATO, 1979; NIH Grantee, 1983-86; W/W in S & SW; Am Men & Wom of Sci.

CHANCE, JANE oc/Professor; b/Oct 26, 1945; h/12510 Ashling Drive, Stafford, TX 77477; ba/Houston, TX; m/Paola Passaro; c/Antony Damian Passaro, Therese Chance Nitzsche; p/D W Chance, Albuquerque, NM; sp/Antonio Passaro, Italy; ed/BA, Purdue Univ, 1967; AM Eng 1968, PhD Eng 1971, Univ of IL-Champaign; pa/Lectr & Asst Prof, Univ of Saskatchewan, Canada, 1971-73; Asst Prof Eng 1973-77, Assoc Prof Eng 1977-80, Prof Eng 1980-, Rice Univ; Mem: Secy-Treas, Rice Chapt, AAUP, 1975-76; Italy in Am Assn, 1980-; Dir, Scientia, Rice Univ, 1983-84; PEN, Author's Guild; MLA; SCMLA; Medieval Acad of Am; Poets & Writers; New Chaucer Soc; Intl Assn for Neo-Latin Studies; r/Cath; hon/Author, *The Genius Figure in Antiquity & the Mid Ages*, 1975; *Tolkien's Art: A Mythology for England*, 1979; Editor, *Studies in Medievalism: The 20th Cent*, Volume 2, #1, 1982; Co-editor, *Approaches to Tchg Sir Gawain & the Green Knight*, 1984; NEH F'ship, 1977-78; Hon Res Fellow, Univ Col London, 1977-78; Guggenheim Fellow, 1980-81; Scientia, 1981-; W/W: in S & SW, of Am Wom; Contemp Authors; Dict of Am Poets; Other Biogl Listings.

CHANDLER, DAVID RALPH oc/ Psychologist, Counseling Center Director; b/Sep 20, 1940; h/77 Sear Street, Metuchen, NJ 08840; ba/New Brunswick, NJ; m/Beverly Helen Francis; c/ William Francis; p/William S and Janet Carncross Chandler, Auburn, CA; sp/ Walter and Eleanore Francis, Seven Lakes, NC; ed/BA, Antioch Co., 1963; MA 1968, PhD 1970, Psych, Univ of MI; pa/Asst Dir, Cnslg & Placement Ser 1970-76, Dir Cnslg Ctr 1976, Rutger Col; Mem: Am Psychol Assn; Am Pers & Guid Assn; cp/Exec Com 1977-81, Secy 1981-83, Country Dance & Song Soc of Am; Mem 1974-, Squire 1982, Greenwich Morris Men; hon/W/W in E.

CHANDLER, KARLYN DOROTHY oc/Supervisor of Computer Operations; b/Mar 28, 1943; h/1119 Bessica Street (Rear), Pittsburgh, PA 15221; ba/ Pittsburgh, PA; m/James R; c/Tina Marie; p/Theresa O McClenny Scott, Pgh, PA; sp/Mr and Mrs Riley Chandler, Pgh, PA; ed/Cert, Intl Data Processing Inst, 1967; AA, Allegheny Commun Col, 1979; Currently Att'g Point Pk Col; pa/Dir Rschr, R L Polk Co, Cleveland, OH, 1966; Keypunch Oper, Higbee Co, 1968-69; Keypunch Oper 1970-76, Sr Keypunch Oper 1976-80, Fin Projs Clerk 1980, Supvr of Computer Oper 1980-, Westinghouse Elect Co; Mem, Nat Assn for Female Execs Inc; r/Bapt; hon/W/W in Am Wom.

CHANDRA, ASHOK K oc/Computer Scientist; b/Jul 30, 1948; h/1601 Summit Street, Yorktown Heights, NY 10598; ba/Yorktown Heights, NY; m/ Mala; c/Ankur, Anuj; p/Harish and Sushila Chandra, New Delhi, India; sp/ Yogendra Nath and Sushma Gupta, Lucknow, India; ed/BTech, Indian Inst of Technol, Kanpur, 1969; MS, Univ of CA-Berkeley, 1970; PhD, Stanford Univ, 1973; pa/Res Staff 1973-, Mgr Theoretical Computer Sci 1981-83, Mgr Exploratory Computer Sci 1984-, IBM Thomas J Watson Res Ctr, Yorktown Hgts, NY; Tech Adv Ofc of VPres & Chief Sci, IBM, Armonk, NY, 1983-84; Mem: Assn of Computing Machinery; Soc of Indust & Applied Math; Editor, *Jour on Computing*, SIAM, 1982-; hon/ Contbr to Num Profl Jours; Patentee in Field; Recip Pres Gold Medal, Indian Inst of Technol, 1969; Outstg Innovation Awd 1980, Invention Achmt Awds 1977 & 1981, IBM; W/W in Frontier Sci & Technol.

CHANG, STEPHEN S oc/Professor, Department Chairman; b/Aug 15, 1918; h/29 Gloucester Court, East Brunswick, NJ 08816; ba/New Brunswick, NJ; m/ Lucy Ding; ed/BS, Nat Chi-Nan Univ, Shanghai, China, 1941; MS, KS St Univ, 1949; PhD, Univ of IL, 1952; pa/Res Assoc, Univ of IL, 1952-55; Res Chem, Swift & Co, 1955-57; Sr Res Chem, A E Staley Co, 1957-60; Assoc Prof 1960-62, Prof 1962-, Chm Food Sci Dept 1977-, Rutgers Univ; Mem: Pres 1970, VPres, Secy, Am Oil Chems Soc; Fellow, Inst of Food Technols; Am Chem Soc; Hon Pres, Intl Soc for Fat Res, 1980; Sigma Xi; Phi Lambda Upsilon; Phi Tau Sigma; Assoc Editor, *Jour of Am Oil Chems Soc*; r/Meth; hon/Author, Over 100 Sci Res Articles in Profl Jours; Nicholas Appert Medal, Inst of Food Technols, 1983; Lipid Chem Awd, Am Oil Chems Soc, 1979.

CHANG, WILLIAM oc/Executive; b/

Sep 15, 1926; h/1612 Via Barcelona, Palos Verdes Estates, CA 90274; m/ Margaret Tao; c/Mark, Kris; p/ Chi-Pang Chang and I-Lan, Wu (dec); ed/BS, Univ of Detroit, 1953; MS, Univ of Wichita, 1957; PhD Cand, Bklyn Polytech Inst, 1959; Att'd MA Inst of Tech, 1958; pa/Pres, Argonaut Prods Corp, 1960-65; MTS, Rockwell Intl Space Sys; Pres and Chm, All Am Investmt Corp; Adv Bd, Intl Trade, US Dept of Commerce; Secy, Chinese Engrs & Scis Assn; Adv Bd, Far E Nat Bk; Dir, Chinese ANA; cp/Pres, Org of Chinese Am; VP, So CA Chinese Bus-man's Assn; Exec Dir, Asian Am Repub Nat Assn; Lions Intl; r/Cath; hon/W/W in CA; Personalities of W & MW.

CHANG, WINSTON W oc/Professor; b/Aug 1, 1939; h/139 Old Farm Circle, Williamsville, NY 14221; ba/ Buffalo, NY; m/Shanyong; c/David, Jacqueline; p/Tsan-chin and Shio-fong Chang, Taipei, Taiwan; sp/Chin-chi Kuo, Taipei, Taiwan; ed/BA, Nat Taiwan Univ, 1962; MA 1966, PhD 1968, Univ of Rochester; mil/China Marine Corps, 1962; pa/Asst Prof Ec 1967-70, Assoc Prof Ec 1970-78, Prof Ec 1978-, SUNY-Buffalo; Vis'g Res Prof, Inst of Ec, Academia Sinica, Taipei, Taiwan, 1982; Mem: Am Ec Assn; Econometric Soc; r/Christian; hon/Author of Num Articles in Profl Jours incl'g: *Qtly Jour of Ec; Metroeconomica; Jour of Intl Ec; Intl Ec Review; Am Ec Review*; Num Others; Chancellor's Awd for Excell in Tchg, SUNY-Buffalo, 1975; NSF Res Grant, 1969.

CHANG, Y AUSTIN oc/Professor, Department Chairman; h/3701 Deerpath Road, Middleton, WI 53562; ba/ Madison, WI; m/P Jean; c/Vincent D, Lawrence D, Theodore D; ed/BSCE 1954, PhD Metallurgy 1963, Univ of CA-Berkeley; MSCE, Univ of WA, Seattle, 1955; pa/Chem Engr, Stauffer Chem Co, Richmond, CA, 1956-59; Postdoct Res Assoc, Univ of CA, 1963; Metall Engr, Aerojet-Gen Corp, Sacramento, CA, 1963-67; Assoc Prof, Chm, Assoc Dean, Univ of WI-Milwaukee, 1967-80; Prof 1980-, Chm Dept of Met & Min Engrg 1982-, Univ of WI-Madison; Mem: Trustee 1981-84, Milwaukee Chapt Chm 1976-77, Am Soc for Metals; Bd Mem, AIME, 1978-80; Chm for Var Tech Coms for Am Soc for Metals & the Met Soc of AIME; cp/Bd Mem, Goodwill Residential Inc, Milwaukee, 1979-80; Pres, WI Chapt of Org of Chinese Ams; Mem, Gov's Adv Coun on Minority Initiative, 1980-83; r/Prot; hon/Author & Co-Author, Over 100 Pubs incl'g 2 Books & Editor of 2 Books; Fellow, Am Soc for Metals, 1978; Outstg Instr Awd, Univ of WI-Milwaukee, 1972; Sigma Xi; Tau Beta Pi; Phi Tau Phi; W/W: in Am, in World, in Engrg; Num Other Biogl Listings.

CHANT, DAVIS RYAN oc/Executive; b/Dec 15, 1938; h/PO Box E, Milford, PA 18337; ba/Milford, PA 18337; m/Judy; c/Tamara, Holley; p/B Ryall and Miriam C, Milford, PA; sp/ Eleanor Gahm, Kansas City, MO; ed/ BA, Belmont Abbey Col, 1960; Real Est Courses, Univ of Rochester, PA St Univ, Hofstra Univ, Univ of PR; pa/US Gypsum Co, 1960-62; Pres, Davis R Chant Inc, Rltrs of Milford, 1962-; Pres,

Davis R Chant Assoc of Lords Val, PA; Pres, Davis R Chant Inc of NJ; Pres, Davis R Chant Inc of FL; Mem, Nat PA & NJ Rltrs Assn; NY Rltrs Assn; Pike Co Chapt of Nat Assn of Home Bldrs; Fdr/Past Pres, Pike-Wayne Bd of Rltrs; Am Right of Way Assn; PA Vacation Land Devel Assn; Sullivan Co & DE Co Bds of Rltrs; Pike Co, Wayne Co & Port Jervis C of C; NEn Soc of Farm Mgrs & Rural Appraisers; Pike-Wayne Co Bd of Rltrs (Past Pres); Monroe-Pike Bldrs Assn; Urban Land Inst; Nat Inst of Farm & Land Brokers; Pocono Mtn Vacation Bur; Intl Inst of Valuers; Am Chapt of Intl Real Est Fdn; Conslt, Time Sharing Indust; Mem, Nat Time Share Coun HQ; cp/Lions Clb; Charter Dir, Commun Assn Inst of Am; r/Prot; hon/Num Profl Pubs; Nat Assn of Rltrs Awd, 1971.

CHANTILES, VILMA LIACOURAS oc/Writer/Editor, Home Economist; b/ Aug 11, 1925; h/13 Circle Road, Scarsdale, NY 10583; ba/Same; m/Nicholas; c/Dean Nicholas, James Lea, Maria Nicole; p/James Peter Liacouras (dec); Stella Lagakos Liacouras, Phila, PA; sp/ Constantinos and Helen Chantiles (dec); ed/BA, Drexel Univ, 1947; MA 1970, Currently in Grad Sch of Arts & Scis, NY Univ; pa/Writer: *The NY Ethnic Food Mkt Guide & Cookbook*, 1983; *The Food of Greece*, 1979 & 1981; Home Economist: Freelance Contbr, *Fam Circle & Redbook* Test Kitchens; Food Editor: *The Athenian Mag*, 1975-; Instr: Deree-Pierce Col, Athens, Sum, 1979; Herbert Lehman Col, 1971 & 1977; NY Univ, 1973; Mem: NY Chapt, Hom Economists in Bus; Am Home Ec Assn, 1969-; Embroiderer's Guild of Am, 1972-; cp/Mbrship Secy, Westchester Choral Soc, 1969-; r/Greek Orthodox; hon/Author of Var Books; Contbr: *The Good Cook*, Time-Life, 10 Volumes, 1978-83 & *The Great Cook*, Random House, 8 Volumes, 1977; Articles in Num Newspapers & Mags; A Average, NY Univ, 1970; 1st Hons Grad Class, Drexel Univ, 1947; Grad Asstship, Syracuse Univ, 1947; Omicron Nu; Pi Epsilon; W/W: in E, of Am Wom; Contemp Authors.

CHAPMAN, ELEANOR HOWELLS oc/Senior Administrative Assistant; b/ Feb 19, 1938; h/6475 Dawnridge Drive, Houston, TX 77035; ba/Houston, TX; c/Laura Ann; p/John L (dec) and Callie N Howells, Durham, NC; ed/Att'd Croft Secretarial & Acctg Sch; Univ of NC-Chapel Hill; pa/Bkkpr & Secy-Receptionist, Ricca, Nelson and Gantt, 1958-60; Legal Secy, Haywood, Denny & Miller, 1961-62; Secy to Dir of Cytology Lab, Dept of Pathol of Duke Med Ctr, 1962-63; Secy, Noble Truck Leasing, 1963-64; Secy, Pgh Plate Glass Co, 1964-65; Secy in Dept of Biophysics 1966-67, Housestaff Secy in Dept of Pathol 1967, Dept Secy in Dept of Pathol 1967-68, Med Col of VA; Adm Secy & Asst Ofc Mgr, Ofc of Chief Med Exmr for St of NC, 1968-70; Adm Secy in Dept of Zool 1970-73, Adm Asst in Dept of Chem 1973-74, Univ of NC-Chapel Hill; Adm Secy, Div of Neurol, Duke Univ Med Ctr, 1974-77; Acting Adm Asst 1977, Adm Asst 1978-81, Sr Adm Asst 1981-, Dept of Neurol, Baylor Col of Med; Exec Com Mem 1978-, Secy 1980-81, Treas 1984-, Houston Gulf Coast Chapt of Muscular Dystrophy Assn; Attendant, Adult

Muscular Dystrophy Patients, 1978-; Vol, Muscular Dystrophy Chd's Progs, 1978-; Vol, Muscular Dystrophy Fund Raising Progs, 1978-; Secy, Neurol A Study Sect of Nat Inst of Neurol & Communicative Disorders & Stroke, NIH, 1979-82; Mem Bd of Dirs, Houston Area Parkinson's Soc, 1981-; cp/ Beta Sigma Phi; Houston Gulf Coast Chapt Muscular Dystrophy Assn; Houston Area Parkinson's Disease Soc; Myasthenia Gravis Soc; hon/W/W of Am Wom, Personalities of S.

CHAPMAN, HARRY SAMUEL oc/Engineer; b/May 11, 1936; h/603 Hickory Hill - L Road, Oxford, PA 19363-2259; ba/Avondale, PA; m/Grace Ann; c/Matthew Harry, Pamela Grace; p/Karl and Gertrude Chapman, S Wallingford, VT; sp/Harry and Louise Biermann, Alloway, NJ; ed/BC, Univ of VT, 1959; Att'd Patent Inst, Fairleigh Dickson, Kent St Univ, NY Univ, Temple Univ; mil/AUS, 1960; USAR, 1960-66; pa/Pres, Ideal Design Co, 1960-67; Plant Mgr, Fluorodynamics Inc, 1964-67; VP & Co-Fdr, Chapman Indust, 1967-74; Tech Mgr, Carborundum, 1974-79; Engrg Mgr, Kennecott, 1979-82; Mgr Application Engrg, Standard Oil of OH, 1982-; cp/Sch Bd, 1973-76; Chm Pastor-Parish Relats Com, 1981-83; Ch Adm Bd, V Chp, 1975-83; BSA, Cubmaster, Asst Scoutmaster, 1974-83; Past Pres, Fdr, S Wallingford Yth Commun Ctr; Dir, Chapman Indust; Former Mem, Joint Com for the Voc-Tech Sch, So Chester Co, PA; Dir, VT Maple Sugar Makers Assn; Mem, Tech Assn of the Pulp & Paper Indust; Former Mem, Soc of Plastics Indust; ASME; PA Farmers Assn; Aircraft Owners & Pilots Assn; r/Prot; hon/Num Profl Pubs; Gold Key Hon Soc, 1957; Capt USAR, 1966; Scouters Key, BSA, 1981; Comml & Instrument Pilot Certs; W/W in E.

CHAPMAN, JANET G oc/Professor; b/May 26, 1922; h/223 Gladstone Road, Pittsburgh, PA 15217; ba/Pittsburgh, PA; m/John W; c/Hazel Perry; p/Carter and Florence Goodrich (dec); sp/John and Hazel Chapman (dec); ed/BA, Swarthmore Col, 1943; MA 1951, PhD 1963, Columbia Univ; pa/Anal, Nat War Labor Bd, 1943; Economist, Bd of Govs of Fed Res Sys, 1945-46; Conslt, The Rand Corp, 1949-69; Assoc Prof 1964-67, Prof 1967-, Chm Dept of Ec 1978-, Dir of Russian & E European Studies 1970-83, Univ of Pgh; Mem: Am Ec Assn; Bd of Dirs, Am Assn for Advmt of Slavic Studies, 1974-79; Ec Com 1977-78, VPres 1982, Pres 1983, Assn for Comparative Ec Studies; Com on F'ships to Am Wom, AAUW, 1975-78; hon/Author of Var Articles incl'g: "Are Earnings More Equal Under Socialism: The Soviet Case, w Some US Comparisons," 1979; "Recent Trends in Indust Wages," 1979; "Equal Pay for Equal Wk?," 1977; Others; NY St F'ship, AAUW, 1948-49; Am Coun of Learned Socs Grant, 1973; NSF Grant, 1973-74; Nat Coun for Soviet & E European Res, 1982-83; W/W: in Am, in Russian Studies & Culture, of Wom.

CHAPMAN, JIMMY CARL oc/Superintendent of ISD; b/May 18, 1946; h/2903 North Murco, Mineral Wells, TX 76067; ba/Mineral Wells, TX; m/Lynda Kay; c/Christopher Brandon; p/Carl and Iba Chapman, Austin, TX; sp/Willis and

Vivian McVey, Austin, TX; ed/BMusEd 1968, PhD 1972, Univ of TX-Austin; pa/ Tchr 1971-74, Prin 1974-79, Austin ISD; Asst Supt for Curric & Instrn, Huntsville ISD, 1979-81; Supt, Bellville ISD, 1981-83; Supt, Mineral Wells ISD, 1983-; VP 1978-79, Pres 1979-80, Founs of Ed Adm; AASA; IRA; Am Assn for Supvr & Curric Devel, TX Assn for SCD; cp/Univ TX Chapt VP 1978-79, Pres Elect 1979-80, Phi Delta Kappa; r/ Meth; hon/Profl Pubs; Ed Speeches; W/ W in S & SW.

CHAPMAN, WEAKLY oc/Pastor; Director; b/Aug 30, 1935; h/466 Gerard Street, Grenada, MS 38901; ba/Same; m/Mary Lee; c/Wanda, Victor, Fenton, Kenneth; p/E Weakly and Lily Bell Chapman, St Tougaloo, MI; sp/Earl and Pearl Sanders, Rolling Fork, MS; ed/ CLEP, Tulane Univ, 1967; BTh, Ctl Ctr Sem, 1970; MDiv, Turner Theol Sem, 1973; mil/US Army Airborne, 1955-58; pa/Confectioner, Ford Candy Co, 1958-66; Operating Forman, 1964-66; Hd Start Dir, 1966-67; Ins Agt, 1967-70; Adm, Go Retardation Ctr, 1970-76; Prof, 1978-; Pastor, AME Ch, 1955-; cp/ Trustee & Secy, Grant Rd Water Assn, 1966-71; Commun Orgr, Tougaloo, MS, 1966-68; NAACP, Instr of Adult Ed & Constit of MS, 1963-65; r/Meth; hon/Rel Articles; Outstg Participation in GA Juv Justice Assn, 1975; Dir, Christian Ed NE W MS Annual Conf, 1983.

CHAPPELL, ANNETTE M oc/ Administrator; b/Oct 31, 1939; ba/ Towson, MD; p/Joseph J Chappell (dec); Annette Harley Chappell, Silver Spring, MD; ed/AB 1962, MA 1964, PhD 1970, Univ of MD-Col Pk; pa/Den Col of Liberal Arts 1982-, Dean Human & Social Scis 1977-82, Spec Asst to Pres & Aff Actn Ofcr 1974-77, Eng Dept: Asst Prof 1969-72, Assoc Prof 1972-79, Prof 1979-, Towson St Univ; Instr Eng, Univ of MD-Col Pk, 1966-69; Mem: VPres 1980, Pres 1981, Exec Wom's Coun of MD; cp/Pres 1977-79, Balto Co Comm for Wom; Bd Men, Pres 1980-82, Sekval Assault/Domestic Violence Ctr; Ed Com Chm 1982, Symp Moderator 1980-82, Balto Co C of C; r/Epis; hon/ Author, Var Articles in Jours: *Signs; Shakespeare Qtly; Studies in Eng Lit;* Book Reviews in *Ms; Balto Sunday Sun;* AB w Hons & Spec Hons in Eng, 1962; W/ W: in E, of Wom, Personalities of S; Num Other Biogl Listings.

CHAPPELL, CHARLES RICHARD oc/Scientist; b/Jun 2, 1943; h/2803 Downing Court, Huntsville, AL 35801; ba/Marshall Space Flight Ctr, AL; m/ Barbara Harris; c/Christopher Richard; p/Gordon T and Winn O Chappell, Montgomery, AL; sp/James W and Barbara W Harris, Austin, TX; ed/BA, Vanderbilt Univ, 1965; PhD, Rice Univ, 1968; pa/Res Sci 1968-72, Staff Sci 1972-74, Lockeed; Chief Magnetospheric Physics Br 1974-80, Chief Solar Terrestrial Physics Div 1980-84, Mission Sci for Spacelab Mission 1 (STS-1) 1976-, NASA/Marshall Space Flight Ctr; Mem: Am Geophy Union; Intl Assn of Geomagnetism & Aeronomy; r/ Meth; hon/Author, Over 100 Sci Pubs in Var Geophy Jours, 1968-; Over 50 Invited Lectrs incl'g: Nobel Symp, 1982 & Cong of Space Res, 1984; Phi Eta Sigma, 1962; Phi Beta Kappa, 1965; John Underwood Awd for Best Physics

Student, 1965; Alfred P Sloan S'ship, 1961-65; Trainee F'ship 1965-68, Med for Exceptl Sci Achmt 1981, Outstg Perf 1984, NASA; W/W in Sci & Technol.

CHAPPELL, GARY ALAN oc/Software Manager, Graphics; b/Jan 24, 1954; h/2220 Homestead Court, Apartment 204, Los Altos, CA 94022; ba/ Saratoga, CA; p/J Earl and Eunice M Chappell, Independence, MO; ed/BS Computer Sci & Chem, Univ of MO-Rolla, 1976; Grad Prog Chem, Stanford Univ, 1976-77; pa/Graphics Programmer, Lawrence Livermore Lab, CA, 1977-79; Prin Investigator Res & Devel, Def & Space Sys Grp, TRW, Redondo Bch, CA, 1979; Prod Mgr, Comtal Image Processing Inc, Pasadena, CA, 1979-80; Mgr User Interface Devel, Tymshare Inc, Cupertino, CA, 1980-82; Software Mgr, Graphics, Qubix Graphic Sys, Saratoga, CA, 1982-; Mem: Assn Computing Machinery; Soc Info Displays; Am Chem Soc; MENSA; W/ W: in CA, in Frontier Sci & Technol.

CHAPPELL, LORA LEE oc/Sales Representative; b/Jul 18, 1923; h/1104 Ellis Avenue, Jackson, MS 39209; ba/ Jackson, MS; m/Everett Mitchell; c/Lora Nell Chappell Tillery, Norman Verell, Jarvis Mitchell; p/Clyde Jarvis and Mamie Ross Lee (dec); ed/Grad, Petal HS, 1941; Grad, Spencer's Bus Col, NO, LA, 1942; pa/E M Chappell Co (Mfg Agy), 1962-; US Govt: MS Induction St, Jackson, MS, 1951-52; Supply Div, Res Br, Brookley AFB, Mobile, AL, 1943-45; tp/Num Coms & Positions incl'g: Pres: Jackson Public Sch Bd of Trustees 1979-80; So Reg Sch Bd Assn, 1976-77; MS PTA, 1975-77; Jackson City PTA Coun, 1968-70; Whitfield Elem PTA Univ, 1966-68; Hardy Jr HS PTA Univ, 1959-61; Coms w Nat PTA; Conslt: US Ofc of Ed, 1976 & NSF, 1975; Chm Jackson Mun Bond Election 1972, Adv Coun 1972-76, Arts Ctr-Planetarium; Num Other Commun Activs; r/Calvary Bapt Ch: Tchr, HS Yth SS & Tng Union, 20 Yrs; Tchr, Adult SS Class; Pres, WMU; Vacation Bible Sch Tchr & Supt; Dir Older Singles SS Dept, 1980-; hon/ St Life Mbrship, MS PTA, 1974; Life Mbrship, Nat PTA, 1975; MS Outstg Lady Sch Bd Mem, 1975; MS Vol Activist, 1976; Hon Mem: Tau Chapt, Zeta St, Delta Kappa Gamma Soc Intl; Personalities of S.

CHAPPELL, ROBERT P oc/Dentist, Dental Educator; b/Nov 28, 1918; h/415 East 79th Terrace, Kansas City, MO 64131; ba/Kansas City, MO; m/Penelope A; p/William Chappell, CA; Nellie Chappell (dec); sp/Paul E Nelson, Blue Springs, MO; Dorothy Nelson (dec); ed/ BS 1948, DDS 1950, Univ of IL; mil/ AUS, Coast Artillery Corp, 1941-42, 2nd Lt; ETO, 1944-45; AUS Resv, 1946-52; USAF Dental Corp, 1952-67, Lt Col; pa/Pvt Dental Prac, St of IN, 1950-52; Gen Dentistry, USAF, 1952-55; Instr Sch of Aviation MEd, Gunter AFB, AL, 1955-59; Chief of Dental Sers, Var AF Dental Clins, England & US, 1959-67; Asst Prof Sch of Dentistry Dept of Removable Prosthodontics 1967-70, Asst Prof Dept of Comprehensive Dentistry 1970-72, Assoc Prof & Chm Dept of Dental Mats 1972-80, Prof & Chm Dept of Dental Mats 1980-, Univ of MO-Kansas City; Mem: Am Assn of Dental Schs; Intl Assn of Dental Res; Secy 1984-85,

Kansas City Chapt, Am Assn of Dental Res; Intl Col of Oral Implantology; Am Acad of Dental Mats; Life Mem, Mil Order of World Wars; Life Mem, The Ret'd Ofcrs Assn; cp/Assoc Mem, The Smithsonian Instn & Audubon Soc; The Friends of Art (Nelson Art Gallery), Friends of the Zoo; City Lyric Opera, in Kansas City, MO; r/Unity; hon/Author, Articles in Profl Jours incl'g: *Jour of Prosthetic Dentistry; Jour of Oral Implantology; MWn Dentist; Jour of Dental Ed;* Contbr of Implant Photos, in *Treatment Planning: A Pragmatic Approach;* Num Lab & Tng Manuals, Videotapes, Slide Progs & Computer Progs for AF & Univ of MO; Elected to Rho Chapt, Omicron Kappa Upsilon Hon Dental Frat, 1971; Fellow, Intl Col of Oral Implantologists, 1979; Fellow, Acad of Dental Mats, 1983; W/W in Frontier Sci & Technol.

CHARLESWORTH, EDWARD ALLISON oc/Psychologist; Author; b/Mar 23, 1949; h/11803 Moorcreek, Houston, TX 77070; ba/Houston, TX; m/Robin Rupley; p/Albert Ernest and Wilma Nadine Charlesworth (dec); sp/Ralph and Rae Rupley, Houston, TX; ed/BS with honors, Psych, 1974; MS, Clin Psych, 1978; PhD, Clin Psych, 1980; pa/ Intern in Clin Psych 1978-79, Postdoct Fellow in Clin Psych 1979-80, Baylor Col of Med; Fac & Staff Psychol, Baylor Col of Med & The Meth Hosp, 1980-82; Dir of Willowbrok Psychol Assoc, 1982-; Pres of Stress Mgmt Res Assoc Inc, 1977-; Am Psychol Assn, 1980-; TX Psychol Assn, 1981-; Harris Co Biofeedback Soc, 1982; Houston Psychol Assn, 1982; Am Acad of Behavioral Med, 1982; r/Presb; hon/Author, *Stress Mgmt: A Conceptual & Procedural Guide, Stress Mgmt: A Comprehensive Guide to Wellness,* Other Profl Pubs; NIMH Traineeship Grant, 1975-77; Dipl of the Am Acad of Behavioral Med, 1982.

CHASE, ANTHONY GOODWIN oc/ Lawyer; b/Feb 15, 1938; h/2404 Wyoming Avenue, Northwest, Washington, DC 20008; ba/Washington, DC; m/ Mary Costa; c/Betsy, Whitney, Samuel, Joseph; p/Mr and Mrs Goodwin Chase, Tacoma, WA; sp/Hazel Costa, Washington, DC; ed/BA, Univ of WA, 1960; JD, Georgetown Univ Law Ctr, 1967; mil/ USMC Capt; pa/Nat Bk Examr & Adm Asst to Comptroller of Currency, Treas Dept, 1962-67; Counsel to Chm of Bd and Pres, Am Security & Trust Co, 1967-69; Fed St Coor, St of WA, 1967-69; Assoc, Comfort Dolack, Hansler & Billett, 1967-69; Asst to Secy of Commerce, Dept of Commerce, 1969-70; Gen Counsel 1970-71, Dpty Adm 1971-73, Small Bus Adm; Ptnr, Brownstein, Zeidman, Schomer & Chase, 1973-78; Ptnr, Tufo, Johnston, Zuccotti & Chase, 1978-80; Ptnr, Drinker, Biddle & Reath, 1980-82; Mng Ptnr, Trammell, Chase, Lambert & Martindale, Cnslrs-at-Law, 1982-; ABA; Fed Bar Assn; DC Bar Assn; WA St Bar Assn; PA St Bar Assn; Adm Conf of the US; Nat Devel Com of Georgetown Univ; Secy to Nat Adv Com on Bkg Policies & Practs; Dir & Fin Advr, Students of Georgetown Univ; Adv Com to the Securities & Exch Comm on Indust Issuers; Fed Adv Coun on Reg Ec Devel; Dir, Diplomat Nat Bk; Dir, VSE Corp; Dir & Mem of Exec Com, Digital Switch Inc; Dir & Chm of Loan Com, The Reservoir Grp Inc; cp/Ch of

Fin Com, St Columbia's Epis Ch; Union Leag Clb; Nat Lwyrs Clb; Mid-Ocean Clb; r/Epis; hon/Author Num Profl Pubs; Outstg Yg Man of Yr Awd, US Jr C of C, St of WA, 1968; Fed Silver Medal for Meritorious Ser, 1970; Fed Gold Medal for Dist'd Ser, 1971; Dist'd Ser to Am Small Bus Awd, Nat Assn of Small Bus Investmt Co, 1972; Outstg Ser to Am Small Bus Commun Awd, Nat Small Bus Assn, 1974; W/W in Am; Social List of WA.

CHASE, JOHN WILLIAM oc/Biochemist, Biologist, Educator; b/May 30, 1944; h/90 Perth Avenue, New Rochelle, NY 10804; ba/Bronx, NY; m/ Anne Christine W; c/Kristen Lynnette, Kimberly Anne; p/John W and Ethel A Chase, Venice, FL; sp/Charles H and Alvilda J Wright, Linthicum, MD; ed/ AB, Drew Univ, 1966; PhD, Johns Hopkins Univ, 1971; Postdoct Fellow, Harvard Univ, 1975; pa/Asst Prof of Molecular Biol 1975-81, Assoc Prof of Molecular Biol 1981-, Albert Einstein Col of Med; Am Soc of Biol Chem, 1982-; Am Soc of Microbiol, 1976-; r/ Prot; hon/Est'd Investr, Am Heart Assn, 1978-83; Sinsheimer Scholar Awd, 1980; F'ships & Res Grants, Am Cancer Soc & NIH, 1971-; W/W: in E, in Frontier Sci & Technol; Am Men & Wom of Sci.

CHASE, MERRILL WALLACE oc/ Professor Emeritus; b/Sep 17, 1905; h/ 500 East 63rd Street, NYC, NY 10021; ba/NYC, NY; m/1st, Edith Steele Brown (dec); 2nd, Cynthia Pierce; c/by 1st Marriage: Nancy C Cowles, John Wallace; p/John Whitman and Bertha Wallace Chase (dec); sp/Howard Castner and Leila Hambury Pierce (dec); ed/AB 1927, ScM 1929, PhD 1931, Brown Univ; pa/Instr, Brown Univ, 1931-32; Staff Mem, Rockefeller Inst for Med Res, 1932-65; Prof Immunol & Microbiol & Hd Lab of Immunol & Hypersensitivity, Rockefeller Univ, 1956-79; Mem: Phi Beta Kappa, 1926; AAAS, 1927; Am Soc for Microbiol; Pres 1956-57, Am Assn of Immunols; Harvey Soc; NY Acad of Sis; Am Assn of Lab Animal Sci; r/Unitarian; hon/Editor, w C A Williams, *Methods in Immunol & Immunochem, Volumes I-V,* 1967-76; Fellow 1952, Dist'd Sci Awd 1969, Am Acad of Allergy; Fellow, Am Col of Allergists, 1958; Von Pirquet Medal, NE Allergy Assn, 1963; Hon Mem, NY Allergy Soc, 1971; Am Acad Arts & Scis, 1974; Nat Acad of Scis, 1975; Hon Doct of Med, Univ of Munster, 1974; ScD, Brown Univ, 1977.

CHASTAIN, GARVIN oc/Psyhology Educator, Research Director; b/Feb 23, 1945; h/3500 Tulara Drive, Boise, ID 83704; ba/Boise, ID; m/Jean; c/Ross Calvert; p/Garvin D Jr and Bertha P Chastain, Ft Worth, TX; ed/PhD, Univ of TX-Austin, 1976; pa/Hd Computer Instrn, Durhams Col, Austin, TX, 1976-77; Res Sci, Human Resources Res Org, Ft Hood, TX, 1977-78; Asst Prof Psych 1978-82, Assoc Prof & Dir Perceptual Res Labs 1982-, Boise St Univ; Mem: Univ Pres, Phi Kappa Phi, 1983; Bd of Dirs 1982-, Univ Scholastic Assn; ID Com of Corres of Creation/Evolution; Am Psychol Assn; Psychonomic Soc; Psi Chi; AAAS; cp/Rocky Mtn Reg VPres 1978-82, Bd of Dirs 1982-, Freedom from Rel Foun; hon/ Author, Num Sci Articles on Perception in Profl Psych Jours; Recip, Alumni Assn Awd for Scholarly Excell, Boise St Univ,

1979; W/W: in W, in Sci & Technol.

CHAU, ALFRED S Y oc/Chemist, Professional Artist; b/Nov 20, 1941; h/ 664 Ramsgate Road, Burlington, Ontario L7N 2Y3, Canada; ba/Burlington, Ontario, Canada; m/Lindy May; c/ Andrew T M; p/Mr and Mrs Yat-Lun Chau, Calgary, Alberta, Canada; sp/Mr and Mrs Y Lim, Vancouver, Brit Columbia, Canada; ed/BSc, Univ of BC, 1961; MSc, Carleton Univ, 1966; pa/Chem, Agri Canada, 1965-70; Hd of Organic Lab 1970-73, Hd of Spec Ser 1973-80, Hd of Quality Assurance & Methods Sect 1980-, Envir Canada; Assn of Ofcl Anal Chem, Mem & Gen Referee; Fellow, Chem Inst of Canada; cp/Fellow, IBA; hon/Author Num Profl Pubs; Caledon Awd for Chem, 1980; Collectors' Choice Awd, Ontario Soc for Artists, 1981; W/W.

CHAVE, KEITH E oc/Professor; b/Jan 18, 1928; h/4935 Mana Place, Honolulu, HI 96816; ba/Honolulu, HI; m/Edith Hunter; c/Alan D, Warren T; p/Earnest J and Winnifred Carruthers Chave (dec); sp/Phelps and Edith Hunter, CA; ed/PhB 1948, MS 1951, PhD 1952, Univ of Chgo; pa/Res Geochem, CA Res Corp, La Habra, CA, 1952-59; Asst, Assoc, Full Prof, Lehigh Univ, 1959-67; Prof Oceanography, Univ of HI, 1967-; Mem: Pres, Palau Marine Res Inst; Fellow, AAAS; Sigma Xi; Am Geophys Union; Am Soc Limnology & Oceanography; Goechem Soc; hon/Author, Over 50 Articles in Profl Sci Jours, 1952-; Sr US Sci, A Von Humboldt Stiftung, Kiel, W Germany, 1974.

CHEAL, MARYLOU oc/Psychobiologist; h/127 East Loma Vista, Tempe, AZ 85282; ba/Tempe, AZ; m/James; c/ Thomas James, Catheryn Leda, Robert David; p/Marion Louis Fast; Leda Eleanor Shaw Martin (dec); sp/James Archie Cheal; ed/BA, Oakland Univ, Rochester, MI, 1969; PhD, Univ of MI, 1973; pa/Res Investigator Dept Zool 1973-75, Res Investigator Dept Oral Biol Sch of Dentistry 1975-76, Lectr Dept Psych 1973-76, Univ of MI, Ann Arbor; Charles A King Fellow, McLean Hosp, Harvard Med Sch, 1976-77; Asst Psychol 1977-81, Assoc Psychol 1981-83, McLean Hosp, Belmont, MA; Lectr Dept Psych, Harvard Med Sch, 1977-83; Fac Res Appt, Dept Psych, AZ St Univ, 1983-; Mem: AAAS, 1969-; Am Psychol Assn, 1981-; Assn for Wom in Sci, 1977-; En Psychol Assn, 1976-; Assn for Chemorecption Schis, 1979-; Soc for Neurosci, 1974-; Sigma Xi, 1972-; Steering Com, SWn Comparative Psychol Assn, 1984-; Steering Com, Wom in Neurosci, 1982-; Intl Soc for Comparative Psych, 1984-; hon/Author, Over 60 Res Articles Pub'd in Profl Sci Jours; Pvt Res Grant, 1981-; Biomed Res Support Grant, McLean Hosp, 1976-78, 1979-81; Scottish Rite Schizophrenia Res Prog, 1977-79; NIMH, 1977-78; Howard Univ & Rockefeller Foun Awd, 1980; Charles A King F'ship, 1976-77; Dept Hon in Psych, Oakland Univ, 1969; W/W in E; Am Men & Wom in Sci.

CHEEK, JAMES EDWARD oc/University President; b/Dec 4, 1932; h/8035 16th Street, Northwest, Washington, DC 20012; ba/Washington, DC; m/ Celestine Juanita; c/James Edward Jr, Janet Elizabeth; p/King Virgil and Lee Ella Cheek (dec); sp/Lewis J and Lela Bennett Williams (dec); ed/BA, Shaw

Univ, 1955; MDiv, Colgate-Rochester Div Sch, 1958; PhD, Drew Univ, 1962; mil/USAF, 1950-51; pa/Pres, Howard Univ, Wash DC, 1969-; Pres, Shaw Univ, Raleigh, NC, 1963-69; Asst Prof New Testament & Hist Theol, VA Union Univ, Richmond, VA, 1961-63; Vis'g Instr Christian Hist, Upsala Col, E Orange, NJ, Sum 1960; Instr Wn Hist, Union Jr Col, Cranford, NJ, 1959-61; Tchg Asst Hist Theol, Drew Theol Sch, Madison, NJ, 1959-60; Mem: Am Acad of Rel; AAUP; Am Soc of Ch Hist; Nat Assn of Biblical Instrs; Nat Soc of Lit & the Arts; Rel Res Assn; Soc for Biblical Lit & Exegesis; Am Coun on Ed; Am Foun for Negro Affairs; Am Mgmt Assn Inc; Col Entrance Exam Bd; Spec Conslt to Pres of US on Black Cols & Univs, 1970; Pres Comm on Campus Unrest, 1970; Bd of Fgn S'ships, 1970-74; Alpha Theta Nu; Alpha Phi Alpha; Num Others; Bd of Dirs: Continental African C of C, USA; 1st Am Bk, NA; Joint Ctr for Polit Studies; Nat Assn for Equal Oppor in Higher Ed; Bd & Adv Com, Capital Area Div, UN Assn; People U to Save Humanity (PUSH); Num Others; Bd of Trustees: Wash Ctr for Metro Studies; NY Inst of Technol; Inst of Intl Ed; Consortium of Univs of Wash Metro Area; Num Others; Bd of Advrs: AAAS; St Advr DC, Am Arts Assn; Assn for Integration of Mgmt Inc; Inst for Study of Ednl Policy; Nat Coun for Black Studies; Nat Urban Leag & Booker T Wash Foun; Num Others; Bd of Editors: *The Jour of Rel Thought*; Black Forum Inc; hon/12 Hon Docts from Num Univs incl'g: Duke Univ; Univ of NC; NY Inst of Technol; Bucknell Unv; Univ of MD; Trinity Col; Shaw Univ, 1970-82; Others; Colagate-Rochester Grad Fellow, 1958; Lilly Foun Fellow, 1958 & 1959; Rockefeller Doct Fellow, 1960; Recip, Pres Medal of Freedom, 1983; Sigma Pi Sigma; Alpha Kappa Delta; Phi Delta Kappa; W/W: in Am, Among Black Ams, in Am Ed; Num Other Biogl Listings.

CHEESMAN, DAVID R oc/Public Relations, Artist, Writer; b/Mar 5, 1938; h/PO Box 25132, Chicago, IL 60625; ba/Chicago, IL; m/Kathleen; c/David R Jr, Donna K Ramos; p/Charles and Irma Cheesman, Fort Worth, TX; ed/Att'd Wright Col; mil/IL NG, 1957-63; pa/PIO Photography, IL NG, 1957-63; Freelance Artist, Oils, Watercolors, Engravings, w Num One-Man Shows, 1958-; Writer of Feature Stories for Newspapers & Mags, 1965-; Est'd Lincoln Sq Art Fair, 1971 (Chm 1971-83); Lectr on Etching & Engraving, 1972-; Newspaper Columnist, 1973-; Public Relats Exec, MOTRA Transmissions, 1976-; Author, "Gemini 7 & 6 Rendezvous," 1967; Feature Writer for *Logic*, 1969-74; Columnist for *Culture Corner*, 1973-; Hon Life Mem, Swedish Artist of Chcgo, Pres, 1973-78; cp/Dir, Ravenswood Conserv Comm, 1976-79; Dir, BUILD, 1976-78; Chm Am Topical Assn, Reg & Dist VP & Dir Info Sers, 1965-71; hon/Awd for Outstg Sers, Andersonville C of C, 1978; Gold Medal for Painting, 1968; Silver Awd for Art, 1969; Num Bronze Awd Medals; Intl Dir of Arts, Men of Achmt; Personalities of Am; DIB; Artists USA; Intl Dir of Arts & Artists.

CHEIN, ORIN NATHANIEL oc/Professor; b/Aug 29, 1943; h/60 Ivy Lane, Cherry Hill, NJ 08002; ba/Phila, PA; m/Carrie; c/Adam, Jason; p/Isidor Chein (dec); Norma Chein, NYC, NY; sp/John and Susan Graham, Cherry Hill, NJ; ed/BA 1964, MS 1966, PhD 1968, NY Univ; pa/Asst Prof Math 1968, Assoc Prof Math 1971, Prof Math 1980-, Temple Univ; Mem: Math Assn of Am, 1965-; Am Math Soc, 1968-; cp/Exec Bd 1979-, Pres 1981-, Cherry Hil Soccer Clb; r/Jewish; hon/Author of Monograph, *Moufang Loops of Small Order*, 1978; Author of 3 Books incl'g: *Math: Problem Solving Through Recl Math*, 1980; Num Reviews & Articles in Profl Jours incl'g: *Jour of Recl Math*; *Archiv der Mathematik*; *Communs on Pure & Applied Math*; *Acta Mathematica*; *Transaction of Am Math Soc*; Others; Grad summa cum laude 1964, Fdrs Day Awd 1964, NY Univ; Coop Grad Fellow 1964-66, Grad Fellow 1966-68, NSF; Hon Fellow, Woodrow Wilson Foun, 1964-65; Outstg Scholar of Yr, Tau Delta Phy Frat, 1964; Elected Mem, Phi Beta Kappa, 1964; Num Others; W/W in E; Am Men of Sci.

CHELF, RALPH LOWELL oc/State Official; b/Jan 17, 1926; h/561 Menominee Trail, Frankfort, KY 40601; ba/Frankfort, KY; m/Helen; c/Alan Douglas; p/Elbert B and Lennie Chelf (dec); sp/Lee and Gladys Greer, Casey Creek, KY; ed/ Att'd Univ of WI & Univ of KY; Completed Col Level GED Requirements; mil/Sr Chief Elects Tech, USN, 1944-63; pa/Field Engr, Lockheed Elects, 1963-65; Mgr Computer Sys Devel 1965-76, Staff Asst in Ofc of Mgmt Info Ser 1976-78; Dpty Hd of Ofc of Mgmt Info Ser 1978-80, Dir of Div of Facilities Mgmt 1980-, KY Dept of Ed; ASBO; AEDS; cp/Masonic Lodge; r/Prot; hon/W/W in S & SW.

CHEN, KAO oc/Consulting Electrical Engineer; b/Mar 21, 1919; h/11 Barone Road, West Orange, NJ 07052; ba/Bloomfield, NJ; m/May Yee Yoh; c/Jennifer H, Arthur B, Carlson S; p/C S Chen and W C Hsu (dec); sp/B J Yoh and J R Ku (dec); ed/BSEE with honors, Jiao Tong Univ, 1942; MSEE, Harvard Univ, 1948; Adv'd Grad Studies, Poly Inst of Bklyn, 1952; pa/Relay Spec, Am Gas & Elect Corp, 1950-52; Proj Ldr, Ebasco Corp, 1953-55; Sr Proj Engr 1956-67, Fellow Engr 1968-83, Westinghouse Elect Corp; Fellow Engr, N Am Philips Lighting Corp, 1983-; Chm, IEEE Power Sys Anal Com, 1970-73; Chm, IEEE-IAS N Jersey Chapt, 1981-82; Indust Applications Soc Dept V Chm, 1981-84, Chm 1985-; Chm, Prodn & Application of Light Com, 1983-84; Reg'd Profl Engr in NY & NJ; cp/4 Orange Cub Scouts Exec, 1966-70; hon/Author of 66 Profl Pubs; IEEE Soc Prize Paper Awds, 1981, 1983; IEEE Fellow, 1983; IEEE, Cent Medal, 1984; Fdn of Brit Indust Scholar, 1945-47; W/W: in E, in Commerce & Indust, in Am; DIB; Intl W/W Engrg; Nat Reg of Prominent Am; Intl Reg of Profiles.

CHEN, KIEN HAI oc/Physician; b/May 23, 1937; h/51 Warren Road, West Orange, NJ 07052; ba/New York, NY; m/Fu Mei; c/Richard, Humphrey, Christopher; p/Jon Bei Yeh; sp/Tong Chou and Chiu Chi Lai; ed/MD, Nat Taiwan Univ Med Col, 1964; mil/AF; pa/Chief, Spinal Cord Injury Ser, BA Med Ctr, E Orange, NJ, 1972-76; Pres, KFC Corp, 1979-; Mem: Fellow, Am Acad of Fam Phys, 1983; Fellow, Am Geriatric Soc, 1983; World Med Assn; AMA, 1983; Bd of Dirs, Taita Ting-Fu Foun 1981-; NY Acad of Sci, 1983; Secy 1979-81, Pres 1981-83, Bd of Dirs 1983, Nat Taiwan Univ Med Col Alumni Assn; WV Med Inst; cp/VPres 1978-80, Pres 1980-84 Parents Assn, Chm Exec Com 1983, Spec Com Reformed Ch in NY, Taiwan Union Christian Ch, NY; r/Christian; hon/Author of Books, *Am Spoken Eng; Specialty Bd Exams*; Num Articles; Dist'd Ser Ldrship Awd, Dist'd Ser Awd, Nat Taiwan Univ Med Col Alumni Assn; W/W in E, in Am, of Intells; Commun Ldrs of Am; Other Biogl Listings.

CHEN, SHIH-TA oc/Banker; b/Sep 30, 1945; h/8A Borrett Mansion, 7/F, 8 Bowen Road, Hong Kong; ba/Hong Kong; m/Lilian Hsiao-Mei; c/Te-Kuang, Te-Ming; p/Chih-Ping and Lilleo Wong Yung-Chieh (dec) Chen, Berkeley, CA; sp/Ming-Chang (dec) and Chin Liang Fung Oung; ed/BA w hons, Univ of CA-Berkeley, 1966; MA 1969, PhD 1973, Cornell Univ; MBA, Harvard Univ, 1972; pa/Staff Ofcr, Citibank N A NY, 1973-76; Mgr 1976-78, Asst VP 1979-80, VP 1980-, Citibank N A Hong Kong; cp/Dir & Pres, Harvard Bus Sch Assn of Hong Kong; Pres, Harvard Clb of Hong Kong; Am Clb of Hong Kong; Taipei Bkrs Clb; Royal Hong Kong Golf Clb; Royal Hong Kong Jockey Clb; Fgn Correspondent Clb of Hong Kong; Ladies Rec Clb; Taipei Intl Bus-man's Clb; Asia Soc of NY; Dir of Mgmt for Exec Devel Course, Chinese Univ of Hong Kong; Coor Com for Mgmt Devel Programme for Social Welfare Agcy Execs for Hong Kong Coun of Social Ser; hon/Author Profl Pubs; W/W: in W, of Brit Commonwlth, of Intells; Men of Achmt; 5000 Personalities of W; DIB; Commun Ldrs of W.

CHEN, TAI-CHU oc/Columnist; b/Jan 2, 1922; h/1040 Mandana Boulevard, Oakland, CA 94610; m/Shulan; c/Victor; p/Tze-fan and Tuan-ho Chen (dec); sp/Hou-ching and Hui-ching Huang (dec); ed/BA, Yenching Univ, 1943; MA, Columbia Univ, 1945; PhD, London Univ, 1948; pa/Ambassador to Australia, 1951-59; Ambassador to Liberia, 1961-65; Prof of Intl Law & Relats, Soochow Univ, 1966-70; Dpty Ambassador to WA, 1971-79; Res Fellow, George Wash Univ, 1980-; Columnist, Wash Times; cp/Pres, Formosan Assn Public Affairs, 1984-85; Bd Mem, Sino-Am Cultural Soc, 1971; Bd Mem, The Intl Clb of Wash, 1971; hon/Author, *China Frontier Problems, a Diplomatic History, Inside Russia*; Decorated by Australian Govt, the Liberian Govt & the Govt of the Republic of China.

CHEN, TAN SUN oc/Research Scientist; b/Sep 16, 1935; h/7914 Viola Street, Springfield, VA 22152; ba/Suitland, MD; m/June; c/Felix, Norman, Victor; p/Neon Tong (dec) and Yeh Zang; sp/Sheng T (dec) and Shui-chi; ed/MS, Univ of OK, 1966; PhD, Purdue Univ, 1972; mil/ROTC; pa/Postdoct Fellow, Purdue Univ, 1972-73; Res Assoc, CO St Univ, 1973; Res Scist, NESS/NOAA, Dept of Commerce, 1973-; Am Meteorological Soc; cp/Pres, Taiwanese Assn, Wash DC Chapt, 1977; Pres, Taiwanese Assn of Am, 1979-80; Pres, World Fdn of Taiwanese Assn, 1980-; Advy Bd, Ctr for Devel Policy at Wash DC, 1980-; hon/Profl Pubs; Member, Sigma Xi,

1972; Outstg Awd by NOAA, 1981; Awd for Superior Perf in Res Meteorology, 1982; Outstg Awd as Pres of World Fdn of Taiwanese Assn by Houston Chapt, 1982.

CHEN, WAI-FAH oc/Professor, Administrator; b/Dec 23, 1936; h/1021 Vine Street, West Lafayette, IN 47907; ba/West Lafayette, IN; m/Lily; c/Eric, Arnold, Brian; p/Yu-Chao Chen, Chgo, IL; sp/H C Hsuan, Taipei, Taiwan; ed/ BSCE, Cheng-Kung Univ, 1959; MSCE, Lehigh Univ, 1963; PhD, Brown Univ, 1966; mil/ROTC; pa/Prof & Hd Structural Engrg, Sch of Civil Engrg, Purdue Univ, 1976-; Prof Civil Engrg, Lehigh Univ, 1966-75; Mem: Chm Coms on Structual Connections & Properties of Mats, ASCE; Chm Structural Stability Res Coun Task Grp on Columns, Exec Com, SSRC; hon/Author of Books, *Plasticity in Reinforced Concrete*, 1982; *Constitutive Equations for Engrg Mats*, 1982; Num Articles in Profl Jours; Var Awds, James F Lincoln Welding Foun, 1972, 1974 & 1981; US Sr Sci Awd, Alexander Von Humboldt Foun, 1984; W/W: in MW, in Technol Today, in Frontier Sci & Technol.

CHENG, LESLIE YU-LIN oc/Neurologist, Psychiatrist (Semi-Retired); b/May 27, 1905; h/9129 Bonny Brook, San Antonio, TX 78239; m/Elissa Chen-Chu Chin; c/Alfred, B Jane, C Joan Cheng Mok, Joyce K, Elaine Cheng Lin, Marian Cheng Chamberlin; p/James H and Mary Chou Cheng (dec); sp/Teh Chang and Tong-Fu Cheng (dec); ed/MD, 1928; pa/Vis'g Prof Neurol & Psychi, Nat Def Med Ctr & Nat Yangming Med Col, Taiwan, Repub of China, 1978-81; Clin Prof Psychi Col Human Med 1971-73 & 1975-78, Prof 1973-75, Chm Dept Undergrad Psychi 1973-75, MI St Univ; Med Dir, Genessee Co Commun Mtl Hlth Sers 1975-76; Fdr, Supt, Med Dir Broadview Ctr, Cleveland, OH, 1966-72; Clin Dir, KS Neurol Inst, Topeka, KS, 1960-65; Clin Asst Prof Psychi, Univ of WA, Seattle, 1958-59; Clin Dir, No St Hosp, Sedro Wooley, WA, 1958-59; Staff Psychi, Chief Tuberculosis Sect, Chief Neurol Ser, Topeka St Hosp, Topeka, KS, 1950-58; Supt, Taiwan Provincial Mtl Hosp, 1949-50; Dir, Nat Neuro-psychi Inst, Nanking, China, 1947-49; Ctl Hosp, Canton, China, 1946-47; Chm, Neuro-psychi Dept U Univs Chengtu, Szechuan, China 1938-46; Pract Med, Spec in Neurol & Psychi, 1933-; Resident, Psychopathic Hosp, Boston, USA, 1932-33; Other Residencies & Internships; Mem: Mem, AMA, 1950-78; Life Mem, Chinese Med Assn, 1947-; Life Fellow, Am Psychi Assn; Fellow, Am Acad of Neurol; Am Child Neurol Soc; cp/Rotary Intl; Pres, Chengtu Rotary Clb, 1945-46; Parma Rotary Clb, 1970-71; Sr Active, 1972-; Mem, Var Masonic Lodges Intly; r/U Meth; hon/ Author of 2 Chinese Textbooks on Neurol & Psychi, 1982; Bronze Hope Chest Awd, Nat MS Assn, 1963; Diplomate, Am Bd of Psychi & Neurol; Cert'd: in Psychi, 1957; in Neurol, 1959; in Child Neurol, 1969; W/W: in MW, in World; Commun Ldrs of Am; DIB.

CHENNAULT, ANNA CHAN oc/ Executive; b/Jun 23, 1925; h/2510 Virginia Avenue, Northwest, Washington, DC 20037; ba/Washington, DC; m/ Claire Lee (dec); c/Claire A, Cynthia L;

p/Y W Chan (dec); Bessie Jeong Chan; ed/BA; pa/Pres, TAC Intl, 1976-; VChm, Pres's Export Coun, 1981-; Bd of Dirs: Nat Aeronaut Assn; USA-ROC Economic Coun 1976-; Wash Crossing Foun, 1977-; Communs Corp of Am, 1975-77; DC Nat Bk, 1972-; CoChm, Aviation & Trans Com, 1976; Bd of Trustees, People-to-People Intl, 1976-; Mem, US C of C, 1976-; Coun on Trends & Perspectives, 1976-; Intl Policy Com, 1976-; CoChm, US Coun for SE Asian Trade & Investmt, 1973-; VPres Intl Affairs; The Flying Tiger Line Inc, 1968-76; Num Other Positions; Mem: Nat Coun of Fgn Policy Assn; IPA; Flying Tiger Assn; An Newpaper Wom's Clb, Wash DC; Aero Clb of Wash DC; Nat Leag Am Pen Wom; Writers' Assn of Free China; Others; cp/USAF Wives Clb, Wash DC; Friends of Chung-ang Univ; Nat Press Clb; DC Repub Com; Repub Nat Fin Com; Leag Repub Wom of DC; Fdg Mem, Cent Clb; Nat Repub Heritage Grps; Num Other Civic Activs; r/Cath; hon/Author & Translator, Num Books & Articles in Eng & Chinese incl'g: *The Ed of Anna; A Thousand Sprgs; Chennault & the Flying Tigers; Dict of New Simplified Chinese Characters*; Others; Hon Fellow, Aerospace Med Assn; Repub of Yr, DC; Repub Fdn 1st Annnual Awd; Awd of Hon, Chinese-Am Citizens Alliance; Lady of Mercy Awd; Chosen 1 of Am's 75 Most Important Wom, *Ladies Home Jour*; Freedom Awd, Free China Assn; Num Hon Doct Degs from Var Univs; Num Biogl Listings.

CHERBERG, JOHN A oc/Lieutenant Governor; b/Oct 17, 1910; h/515 Howe Street, Seattle, WA 98109; ba/Olympia, WA; m/Elizabeth (Betty) Walker; c/ James Walker Cherberg, Kay Cherberg Cohrs, Barbara Cherberg Tonkin; p/ Fortunato Cherberg and Annie Rand Cherberg (dec); sp/Robert Gile Walker and Marie Katherine Heilig; ed/BA Ec 1933, Grad Col of Ed Life Tchg Dipl 1934, Univ of WA; pa/Lt Gov, St of WA, 1957-; Chm, Nat Conf of Lt Govs, 1968-69; Ftball Coach, Univ of WA, 1946-56; Tchr of Var Subjects, Queen Anne HS, Seattle, 1938-46; Tchr Var Subjects & Ftball Coach, Cleveland HS, Seattle, 1934-38; Chm: WA St Data Processing Auth; Senate Rules Com; Joint Legis Com on Intl Bus & Tourism; Mem: St Fin Com; St Capitol Com; St Patrol Retirement Bd; Hlth Care Facilities Auth; Energy Fair Comm 1983; WA St Patrol Meml Foun; St Oil & Gas Conserv Com; cp/AUS Assn; Hon Life Mem, WA St Assn of Broadcasters; Hon Life Mem, Seattle Fdn of Tchrs; Hon Life Mem, WA St Coun of Firefighters; Nat Assn of Ftball Coaches; Nat & WA Ed Assns; Am Fdn of TV & Radio Artists; Mfrs Rep Clb; Elks; Moose; Sigma Nu Frat; Dem; Num Other Orgs & Activs; r/Cath; hon/King Carl XVI Gustaf Swedish Medal; Norwegian-Am C of C Man of Yr; Liberty Awd, Conf of 7th Day Adventists, 1979; Italian Legion of Merit Awd; Police Ofcrs 1st Class Cities Awd; Cert of Merit WARC; Chm Fund Raising Com, Spec Olympics; Hon Firefighter; Hon Chief, Yakima Indian Nation; VFW Achmt Awd; Num Others; W/W: in W, of Contemp Achmt.

CHERMOL, BRIAN HAMILTON oc/ Psychologist; b/Jun 24, 1944; h/102

Artillery Post Road, Fort Sam Houston, TX 78234; ba/Houston, TX; m/Annie Laurie; c/Sherry L, Laurie Ann; p/John and Esther Chermol, Lionville, PA; ed/ BA magna cum laude, Psych, 1970; MA, Psych, 1972; PhD, Clin Psych, 1977; mil/ Lt Col 0-5, AUS, 1962-; pa/AUS Ofcr, 1963-70; Psych Instr, Univ of SC, 1973-75; Psych, VAH, 1976-77; White House/Army Hon Guard, Wash Dept Conslt, 1977-78; Chief of Psych Ser, Army Aeromed, 1978-79; Chief Mtl Hlth Dept, USAAMC, Ft Rucker/Conslt US Helicopter Tm, 1979-81; Chief Behaviorial Sci Spce Br, AHS, Ft S Houston, TX, 1981-; Am Psychol Assn; Am Soc of Clin Hypnosis; APA Div: Mil Psych, Psychol Hypnosis, Clin Psychol; Assn for the Advmt of Psych; r/Prot; hon/Num Profl Articles; Phi Kappa Phi Honor Society, 1970-; Psi Chi, 1970; Silver Star, Bronze Star w/V (3), Merit Ser Medal; W/W in S & SW.

CHERRY, PHILIP oc/State Department Foreign Service; b/Aug 14, 1931; h/9422 Locust Hill Rd, Bethesda, MD 20814; ba/Washington, DC; m/Barbara Clay; c/William Clay, John Bradford, Bettine Marguerite, James Douglas; p/ Harry Cherry, Phila, PA; sp/Earle Clay, Tarpon Springs, FL; ed/BS, Temple Univ, 1956; LLB, Univ of PA Law Sch, 1959; Att'd The Hague Acad of Intl Law, 1958; mil/USN, 1949-53; pa/US St Dep Fgn Ser: Salisbury, Rhodesia, 1962-64; Nairobi, Kenya, 1964-67; New Delhi, India, 1971-74; Dacca, Bangladesh, 1974-77; Lagos, Nigeria, 1977-81; cp/ Kenwood Golf & Country Clb, Bethesda, MD; W/W in E.

CHIANG, THOMAS CHI-NAN oc/ Educator; b/Jan 20, 1945; h/528 Coventry Lane, West Chester, PA 19380; ba/ Philadelphia, PA; m/Marilyn Chih-Hsin; c/Stephen Benjamin; p/Ming-Chu & Hsieuh-Hwa Chiang (dec); sp/Chien-Ho and Kui-Chen Lee, Taipei, Taiwan; ed/ BA, The Nat Chung-Hsing Univ, 1967; MA, Univ of HI, 1973; PhD, PA St Univ, 1981; mil/Marines; pa/Money Mkts Spec, Hua-Nan Comml Bk, 1968-70; Res Fellow of Intl Fin, The Coun for Intl Ec Coop & Devel, 1970-71; Asst Prof of Ec, PA St Univ, 1980-81; Asst Prof of Fin, Drexel Univ, 1981; Am Ec Assn; Am Fin Assn; Nat Assn of Bus Ec; Atl Ec Soc; Wn Fin Assn; cp/Phi Kappa Phi; hon/Num Profl Pubs; E-W Ctr F'ship, 1971-73; Charles V Donohue Awd, 1977; Ervin P Hexner Awd, 1978; W/W in E.

CHIAPPELLI, FRANCESCO oc/Mental Retardation Researcher; b/Jun 11, 1953; h/10969 Coventry Place, LA, CA 90064; ba/LA, CA; m/Gloriela María; c/ Gioia Elvira María; ed/BA Biol 1975, MA Ed 1981, PhD Cand, Univ of CA-LA; pa/Mtl Retard Res Ctr; Neuropsychi Inst; Univ of CA-LA; Mem: MY Acad of Scis; Other Profl Assns; cp/St Paul the Apostle Parish; r/Cath; hon/Author of Several Articles in Profl Jours; W/ W: in W, of Contemp Achmt.

CHIARENZA, CARL oc/Artist, Professor; b/Sep 5, 1935; h/14 Maple Street, Arlington, MA 02174; ba/Boston, MA; m/Heidi Katz; c/Suzanne, Jonah, Gabriella; p/Mary Chiarenza, Rochester, NY; sp/A & A Katz, LA, CA; ed/ AAS 1955, BFA 1957, Rochester Inst of Technol; MA 1959, AM 1964, Boston Univ; PhD, Harvard Univ, 1973; mil/ AUS, 1960-62; pa/Lectr 1963-64, Instr

1964-68, Asst Prof 1968-72, Univ Prof 1972-73, Assoc Prof 1973-80, Prof 1980-, Acting Chm 1973-74, Chm 1976-81, Boston Univ; Harnish Vis'g Prof of Art, Smith Col, 1983-84; Dir, Soc for Photographic Ed, 1968-73; Trustee, Visual Studies Wkshop, 1975-; Adv Trustee, Friends of Photo, 1980-83; Dir, Photo Resource Ctr, 1977-; Adv Coun, Intl Ctr of Photo; Former Editor, *Contemp Photog* during 1960's; Num Lectrs & Wkshops; hon/Author of Book & Book Chapts incl'g: *Aaron Siskind: Pleasures & Terrors*, 1982; "Notes Toward an Integrated Hist of Picturemaking," 1982; Num Other Articles; Num Photographs Pub'd; Wks in 22 One-man Shows, Over 135 Grp Exhibns & Wks in Collections incl'g: Intl Mus of Photo; Fogg Art Mus; Princeton Univ Mus; Yale Univ Art Gallery; Houston Mus of Fine Arts; Ctr for Creat Photo; Worcester Art Mus; Mpls Inst of Arts; Carl Siembab Gallery; Susan Harder Gallery; Arthur Stanley Katz; Recip, 2 Danforth Tchr Grants; Recip Kress Foun Res Grant; Var Artist's F'ships: MA Arts & Humanities Foun, Nat Endowment for Arts; W/W in E, in Am, in Am Art.

CHILCOTE, THOMAS FRANKLIN oc/University President; b/May, 25, 1918; h/Box II, Emory, VA 24327; ba/Emory, VA; m/Margaret Mossor; c/Wayne Leslie, Deborah Jean; p/Thomas F Chilcote Sr (dec); sp/Mrs Henry C Mossor, Drexel Hill, PA; ed/Att'd Taylor Univ, 1936-38; BA, Univ of Pgh, 1938-40; Att'd Wn Theol Sem, 1940-41; MDiv, Boston Univ Sch of Theol, 1941-43; pa/Pastor: McCandless Ave Meth Ch, Pgh, PA, 1939-42; Walnut Ave Meth Ch, Roxbury MA, 1941-43; Cresson Meth Ch, PA, 1943; 1st Meth Ch, Chattanooga, TN 1948-55; News Editor, *The Christian Advocate*, 1943-45; Mng Editor, *New Life Mag*, 1945-48; Supt, Abingdon Dist Meth Ch, VA, 1955-58; Sr Min: 1st Meth Ch, Maryville, TN, 1958-62; Fountain City Meth Ch, Knoxville, TN, 1962-68; 1st Meth Ch, Oak Ridge, TN, 1968-71; 1st Broad St, U Meth Ch, Kingsport, TN, 1971-73; Pres, Emory & Henry Col, Emory, VA, 1973-; Ordained Clerical Mem, Holston Conf, U Meth Ch; Mem, World Meth Confs, Oxford & Oslo, 1951 & 1960; Mem, Uniting Conf of U Meth Ch, 1969; r/U Meth; hon/Author of 3 Books: *God's 21*, 1983; *Quest For Meaning*, 1972; *The Excell of Our Calling*, 1958; DD, Univ of Chattanooga, 1955; KY Col, 1973; W/W: in Am, in World.

CHILDERS, JOHN STEPHEN oc/Director of Testing, Professor; b/Aug 10, 1946; h/1101 Johnston Street, Greenville, NC 27834; ba/Greenville, NC; m/Beth Austin; c/John Stephen Jr. Amy Suzanne; p/Earl S and Norma H Childers, Elizabeth City, NC; sp/O S and Grace Austin, Poplar Branch, NC; ed/BA 1968, MA 1972, E Carolina Univ; EdD, NC St Univ, 1983; pa/Psychol, Coastal Plain Metl Hlth Ctr, Greenville, NC, 1969-71; Mtl Hlth Instr, Pitt Tech Inst, Greenville, NC, 1971-72; Dir of Testing, Asst Prof Psych, E Carolina Univ, 1972-; Mem: Am Psychol Assn; SEn Psychol Assn; cp/Civitans; Greenville Sports Clb; E Carolina Univ Pirate Clb; r/Meth; hon/Author of Num Articles in Profl Jours, 1977-; Co-Editor, *SEn Test Ctr Pers Newslttr*, 1972-; W/W in

W & SW; Personalities of S.

CHILDERS, NEIDA GENEIEVE oc/Registered Nurse Supervisor; b/Dec 18, 1940; h/Route 5, Box 17F, Hartselle, AL 35640; ba/Decatur, AL; m/Bobby Ray; c/Susan Ann, Bobby Ray Jr, Betty Lynn; p/Louis Bebo (dec), Phyllis Francis, St Petersburg, FL; sp/Robert (dec), Mae Childers, Falkville, AL; ed/Assoc Deg Nsg, 1975; Att'd John C Calhoun Jr Col & St Bernard Col; Grad of Dale Carnegie Course; pa/Long Distance Oper & Overseas Oper, IL Bell Telephone Co, 1956-57; Blue Print Proof Rdr, Wn Elect, 1965-66; Patient Care Asst, Huntsville Hosp, 1974-75; ICCU Nurse, Pineview Hosp, 1975-78; Assistance Dir & Dir of Nsg, Flint City Nsg Home, 1978-80; Convelescent Ctr Supvr, 1980-; ANA; AL St Nsg Assn; cp/Am Heart Assn; r/Bapt.

CHILDRES, MARY R oc/Senior Business Administrator for Continuing Education; b/Apr 13, 1936; h/838 Crowden Drive, Cincinnati, OH 45224; ba/Cincinnati, OH; m/Robert W Greene; c/Margie, Janet, John, Darrell; p/Simon (dec) and Mary Childres, Cincinnati, OH; ed/AS 1973, BS 1976, Univ of Cinc; pa/Clerk-typist, Hamilton Co Welfare Dept, 1954-59; Secy & Med Transcriber, VA Hosp, 1965-66; Secy to Ofc Mgr, Mutl Benefit Life Ins Co, 1965-66; Secy to Pres, KY St Univ, 1966-68; Nutrition Prog Asst, WV Univ, 1969-70; Secy to Asst Dean of Evening Col 1970-71, Secy to Hd Dept of Biol Sci 1971-72, Secy to Summer Sch 1973-75, Secy to VP for Cont'g Ed & Metro Ser 1975-76, Adm Asst to Dir of Cont'g Ed 1976-78, Sr Bus Adm for Ofc of VProvost for Cont'g Ed & Metro Ser 1978-83, Sr Bus Adm for Cont'g Ed, 1983-, Univ of Cinc; Adv Coun, Univ of Cinc Evening Col Alumni Assn; Career Advr in Bus & Mgmt, Univ of Cinc Alumni Assn; Chm, Cornelius Van Jordan S'ship Fund, Univ of Cinc; Chm, Dr William D Smith Awd of Excell Fund, Univ of Cinc; Treas, U Black Assn of Fac, Adm, & Staff, Univ of Cinc, 1978-83; Charter Mem & Co-Fdr of Frankfort, KY Chapt of Nat Secys Assn (Intl), 1968; Co-fdr & Orgr, Gamma Sigma Sigma Nat Ser Sorority, KY St Univ, 1967; Mem, Mid-Level Mgrs Assn, Univ of Cinc; Mem, Intl Spkrs Platform; Mem, Nat Adv Bd of ABI; Fin Chp, Nat Univ Cont'g Ed Assn Conf, 1982; Mem, Am Entrepreneurs Assn; Mem, U Black Assn of Fac, Adm & Staff, Univ of Cinc; r/Ch of God; hon/Author *Handbook of Ofc Procedures*; Awd of Perseverance, Cinc Fdn of Colored Women's Clbs, 1954; Mem, Delta Tau Kappa Intl Social Sci Hon Soc, 1975-; Dean's Lists, Univ of Cinc Evening Col; Cover Girl, *Pride Mag*, 1971; W/W: Among Am Wom, of Wom of World, in Fin & Indust; Personalities: of Am, of W & MW; Dir of Dist'd Ams.

CHILDRESS, JAMES ROBERT (BOB) JR oc/Rancher, Businessman; b/Nov 3, 1942; h/Box 1249, Ozona, TX 76943; ba/Ozona, TX; m/Ann; c/Charles Ira, Clay James; p/James R Childress (dec); Mrs James R Childress, Ozona, TX; sp/Mr and Mrs R L Pennington, Atlanta, GA; ed/Att'd SW TX St Univ; mil/AUS, 6 mos; USAR, 6 Yrs; pa/Pres, TX Mohair Comodity Bd; Secy-Treas, 1st VPres, Pres, Mohair Coun of Am; Pres, 1st VPres, Inter-Nations Mohair

Coun, London; Pres, Mohair Grower Grp (Rep'g Growers From Around World); US Border Collie Assn; cp/Crockett Co Hosp Bd; Crockett Co Pk Bd; Pres, Ozona Roping Clb; Bd of Dirs, S TX Paint Horse Assn; r/Bapt.

CHILTON, W E III oc/Publisher; b/Nov 26, 1921; ba/Charleston, WV; m/Elizabeth Easley Early; c/Susan Carroll; p/W E Jr and Louide Schoonmaker Chilton; ed/BA, Yale Univ, 1950; mil/AUS & USAAC, 1941-45; pa/Mem, WV House of Dels, 1953-60; Del-at-large, Dem Nat Conv, 1960 & 1964; Dem Nat Platform Com, 1964; Bd of Trustees: Morris Harvey Col, 1967-79; Univ of Charleston, 1979-82; Bd of Dirs, So Newspaper Pubrs Assn, 1981; cp/Mem, Edgewood Country Clb; Glade Sprgs Country Clb; hon/Pubr, *The Charleston Gazette*; Contbr, *The Nation*; Hon HHD, WV St Col, 1966; Elijah Parish Lovejoy Awd for Freedom of Spch & Press & Hon JD, Colby Col, 1982; 1st Vis'g Prof of Jour, WV Univ, 1969; Vis'g Profl, Wm Allen White Sch of Jour, Univ of KS, 1982.

CHIN, HONG WOO oc/Physician, Educator, Researcher; b/May 14, 1935; h/1096 Chinoe Road, Lexington, KY 40502; ba/Lexington, KY; m/Soo J; c/Richard Y, Helen H, Kisik; p/Jik Hyon & Woon Kap Chin (dec); sp/Il Chae Chung (dec); Bong Sun Kim, Seoul, Korea; ed/MD Col of Med 1962, Phd Postgrad Sch 1974, Seoul Nat Univ; mil/Korean Nav, 1967-70, Lt Cmdr; pa/Intern & Resident Internal Med, Seoul Red Cross Hosp, 1962-67; Res in Radiation Oncology, McGill Univ, Royal Victoria Hosp & Montreal Gen Hosp, 1975-78; Staff Phys Dept Internal Med, Assoc Chm, Seoul Res Cross Hosp, Korea, 1970-74; Prof Radiation Oncology, Phys-in-Charge Sect of Neuro-radiation-oncology, Univ of KY, Currently; Coun Mem, Pan Am Med Assn; Mem: AMA; NY Acad of Scis; Am Col of Radiol; AAAS; Am Soc Therapeutic Radiol Oncology; Others; r/Cath; hon/Author of 2 Monographs, *Medulloblastoma, I & II*; Articles in *Current Probs in Cancer* & Num Other Sci Jours; Sigma Xi, 1980; W/W: in S & SW, in World, in Frontier Sci & Technol.

CHIN, LINDA G oc/Research Nurse; b/Jul 13, 1958; h/51-31 Simonson Street, Elmhurst, NY, 11373; ba/New York, NY; p/Sing Quon and So Keen Yee Chin, New York, NY; ed/BA 1980, MA 1982, NY Univ; pa/Sr Res Nurse in Parkinson Disease; ANA; NYS Nurses Assn; Neurosurg Nurses Assn; cp/Pres, Campaign Wkr for Manhattan Borough; Vol, ARC; r/Prot; hon/Title II S'ship, USPHS, 1980-81; SEHNAP S'ship, NY Univ, 1978-80; Martin Luther King Jr S'ship, 1976-78; Regents S'ship, 1976-80; Dean's List; Yg Commun Ldrs; Intl Yth in Achmt.

CHIN, PAUL LEE oc/Human Resources Development Consultant, Vocational Rehabilitation Counselor; b/Jul 17, 1949; h/78 Floral Street, Newton, MA 02161; ba/Brookline, MA; m/Christine L; p/Tong G (dec) and Ngook L Chin, Boston, MA; sp/Joe and May Young (dec) Lee, Boston, MA; ed/BS, Univ of MA-Boston, 1977; MEd, Antioch Univ, 1981; mil/AUS, 1968-70; pa/Jr Field Engr/Draftsman, Franchi Constrn Co Inc, & Raymond Intl Constrn Co Inc, 1971; Conslt/Staff Tnr/

Area Prog Dir/Cnslr, ABCE Inc, 1971-73; Asst Exec Dir/Prog Dir/Sr Cnslr, Chinatown Boys' Clb, 1971-73; Agy Dir/Sr Cnslr, Proj Listen/Boys' Clbs of Boston & Charlestown, 1971-76; Human Resources Devel &d Ldrship Tng Cnslt, Self-employed, 1976-; Employmt Spec/Voc Rehab Cnslr/Disability Examr, MA Rehab Comm, 1976-; Am Pers & Guid Assn; Assn for Non-White Concerns in Pers & Guid; Am Mtl Hlth Cnslrs Assn; Assn for Spec in Grp Wk; Am Rehab Assn; Assn for Humanistic Psych; Am Arbitration Assn; Nat Employmt Cnslrs Assn; Assn for Humanistic Ed & Devel; Pacific-Asian/Am Mtl Hlth Ctr Assn; Nat Assn of Non-White Rehab Wkrs; Nat Assn of Social Wkrs; cp/Exec Bd of Dirs & Chm of Yth Affairs Com, Chinese Ed Devel Coun; Chinese Mtl Hlth Team Adv Com, Tufts NE Med Ctr; Exec Bd Mem, Boston Teen Ctr Alliance; Chinatown Adv Com, ABCD Inc; Multi-Ser Ctr Adv Com, Chinese-Am Civic Assn; Pers Com & Prog Eval Com, Quincy Sch Commun Coun; Reg VI Coun Mem, MA Ofc for Chd; Design & Constrn Sub-Com, August Moon Fest Planning Com; Chinatown Adv Com, Boston Police Dept; Prog Eval Com & Pers Com, Bayside Coun for Chd; Coun Mem, S-End Inter-Agy Coun; Design Sub-Com, Chinatown Bicent Com; Design & Ceremonies Com, Pagoda Pk Planning; Resources Mixer Planning Com, Boston Chds' Mus; hon/Author, *Boston's Chinatown A Hist 1976, Psychol Effects of Frustration & Aggression on the Personal Field of the Vietnam Veteran: an Anthological Study 1981;* W/W in E.

CHIN, SUE SUCHIN oc/Artist; h/PO Box 1415, San Francisco, CA 94101; ba/San Francisco, CA; p/William W and Soo-Up S Chin; ed/Grad of CA Col of Arts, Mpls Art Inst, & Schaeffer Design Ctr; Studied w Yasuo Ku-niyo-shi and Rico LeBrun; pa/Exhibs: LA Co Mus of Art 1975-78, CA Mus of Sci & Indust 1975-78, Capricorn-Asunder 1972, Peace Plaza, Japan Ctr, Kaiser Ctr; One-Wom Show, Lucien Labaudt Gallery, 1975; Photojour for the "All Together Now" Art Show on KPIX-TV, "E W News," & KNBC "Sunday Show;" Fdg VP, Asian Wom Artist, 1978-81; Secy-Treas, CA Chinese Artists, 1978-81; Dir & CoChm, Japanese Am Arts Coun, 1978-82; SF Wom Artists; Artists in Print; SF Graphics Guild, Chinatown Coun on Perf'g & Visual Arts; Chinese Cultural Ctr Galleries; cp/Psychic Counsel; Wom Psychics; Healers of SF; Pacific Asian-Am Wom Bay Area Coalition; Fellow, IBA; hon/Chm, "ESP Full Moon Monthly Fair"; Editor, *Psychic News;* St Del to Pan Asian Wom's Conf, 1980; Hon, AFL-CIO Labor Studies Ctr, 1976; Bicent Awd, LA Co Mus of Art, 1975-78; 1st Awd, Asian Wom Artists, 1978-81; W/W: in W, of Am Wom, in CA; World W/W of Wom; DIB; Personalities of W & MW.

CHINN, KENNETH SAI-KEUNG oc/Research Chemist; b/Dec 20, 1935; h/499 Country Club Drive, Stansbury Park, UT 84074; ba/Dugway, UT; m/Marie L; c/Stephen A; p/Edward K Chinn (dec); Sinn-Tai (Zan) Chinn, Honolulu, HI; sp/Mrs Kit-Ying Lee, Hong Kong; ed/BS 1957, Postgrad Study 1957-59, Wash Univ-St Louis;

mil/AUS, 1959-61; pa/Res Chem, AUS Med Res & Nutrition Lab, Denver, CO, 1959-68; Res Biochem, USN Med Res Ctr, Taipei, Taiwan, 1968-74; Res Chem, AUS Dugway Proving Ground, UT, 1974-; Mem: Am Nutrition Soc, 1965-; CO-WY Acad of Sci, 1966-; SE Asian Min of ED Org, 1969-; r/Christian; hon/Author of 2 Books; Author, Over 50 Sci Articles in Profl Jours; Outstg Awd, AUS Med Res, 1966; Outstg Awd, USN Med Res, 1971; Outstg Awd, AUS Dugway Proving Ground, 1983; Spec Achmt Awd, AUS Test & Eval Comm, 1983; W/W: in World, in Frontier Sci & Technol.

CHISHOLM, WILLIAM DEWAYNE oc/Contracts Manager; b/Mar 1, 1924; h/1364 Hercules Avenue South, Clearwater, FL 33546; ba/Clearwater, FL; m/Esther Troehler; c/James Scott, Larry Alan, Brian Duane; p/Dr James and Evelyn Chisholm (dec); sp/Frederick and Lena Troehler (dec); ed/BSChE 1949, BS Indust Engrg 1949, Univ of WA; MBA, Harvard Univ, 1955; mil/Elect Tech, USN, 1944-46; pa/Chem, Unit Ldr & Tech Rep, Coca-Cola Co, 1949-59; Proj Admr 1959-61, Mktg Admr 1961-64, Contracts Wk Dir 1964-66, Contracts Mgr 1966-73, Contracts Supvr 1973-75, Sr Contracts Mgmt Rep 1975-80, Prin Contract Mgmt Rep & Wk Dir 1980-82, Contracts Mgr of Profl Devel & Mgmt Pract 1982-, Honeywell Inc; Adj Fac FL Inst of Tech, 1976-; Instr Pinellas Co Bd of Public Instr Adult Ed Prog in Contract Adm, 1969-74; Nat Dir 1976-77 & 1967-69, Suncoast Chapt Pres 1975-76, VP 1970-75, Nat Contract Mgmt Assn, 1966-; Am Soc for Tng & Devel, 1981-; Budget Adv Com, City of Clearwater, 1983-; John Calvin Foun Bd of Trustees 1974-82, VP 1974-80; cp/VP 1980-81, Dir 1982-83, Secy-Treas 1983-84, Pres 1984-85, Breakfast Optimist Clb of Clearwater, 1980-; r/Presby; hon/Author, "Return on Assets Considerations for Contract Admrs;" CPCM, 1974; Fellow Mem, Nat Contract Mgmt Assn, 1975; Commr to 196th Gen Assem of Presb Ch, 1984; W/W: in S & SW, in Aviation & Aerospace; Men of Achmt; Dir of Dist'd Ams; Personalities of S; Intl Book of Hon; Biographical Roll of Hon; Commun Ldrs of World; Intl W/W: of Intells, of Contemp Achmt; 2000 Notable Ams; 5000 Personalities of World; DIB.

CHISHOM, ANDREW J oc/Executive; b/Oct 17, 1942; h/202 Holiday Road, Columbia, SC 29201; ba/Columbia, SC; m/Lottie; c/Mark André, Wendi; p/Mr and Mrs Junious Chishom, Augusta, GA; sp/Mr and Mrs Clyde Screen, Bath, SC; ed/BA, Univ of MD-Col Pk, 1969; MA 1972, PhD 1975, Univ of GA; Addit Study: Harvard Univ Grad Sch of Ed, 1980; Luth Sem, 1980; mil/ASAF, E-5; USNR, Lt Cmdr; pa/Spec Asst to Pres, Prof Dept Crim Justice 1979-, Dept of Justice Transition Team Mem LEAA Policy Anal, Pres Transition 1979, Asst Prof Dept Crim Justice 1975-77, Univ of SC; Assoc Min, Ridgewood Bapt Ch, 1979-; US Marshal, US Marshal Ser, Dist of SC; Instr, Dept of Correctional Rehab, Univ of GA, 1973-75; Coor, Ofc of Gov St of SC, 1972-73; Coor Vol Ser, Dept of Probation, St of GA, 1971-72; Field Dir, Urban Leag, Ed Advmt Prog, Greenville, SC, 1970-71; Chm Bd: Co & City of

Greenville Commun Org for Drug Control, 1970-71; Juv Placement Ofcr, Juv Placement U Aftercare, St of SC, 1969-70; Prog Planner, Metro Police Dept Commun Relats Div, Wash DC, 1968-69; Adm Aide, Ho of Reps Cong-man Robert Stephens Ofc, 10th Dist, GA, 1967; Chm, UN Days Prog Gov's Ofc St of SC, 1979; Mem: Chm, Nat Assn for Equal Oppor in High Ed; Police Foun, 1978-; Police Exec Res Forum, 1977-; So Assn of Crim Justice Edrs, 1975-; Fdr 1973, Exec Chm 1974-76, Mem, Nat Assn of Blacks in Crim Justice; Nat Coun on Crime & Delinq, 1973-; CoChm Am Correctional Assn, 1972-; Num Other Orgs; cp/Chm Race Relats Com; Chm, Crime Prev Com; Bd of Dirs, Commun Relats Coun; Chm, Goals & Objectives Com, SC Legal Aid Prog; Bd of Dirs, Columbia Voc Rehab Ctr; Chm, Commun Crime Prev Annual Banquet; Chm, Citizens Com Studying Methods of City Coun-men Election; Spec Task Force on Budget Allocation Reform, 1977; U Way; Chm, 73rd Breakfast Clb, 1977-; Coach, Pop Warner Ftball; Num Other Commun Activs; r/Bapt; hon/Author of "Surviving Reaganomics During the Eighties," 1981; "Can Black Col Students Survive Fed Ednl Cutbacks," 1981; Num Other Articles & Paper Presentations; Commun Care's Outstg Citizen Awd, 1981; Outstg Palmetto Law Enforcement Assn Awd for Achmts in Ed, 1981; Outstg Ser in Crime Preven, 1981; Key to City of Little Rock, AR, 1981; Key to City of Kansas City, MO, 1981; Outstg Commun Awd, Zeta Zeta Frat, 1981; Outstg Commitment & Contbn Plaque, Nat Assn of Blacks in Crim Justice 6th Annual Conf, Phila, 1979; Dept of Justice Spec Achmt Awd, from US Atty Gen Griffin Bell, 1978; Key to City of Columbia, SC, 1977; Outstg Humanitarian Awd, Polit Action Com, St of SC, 1977; Andy Chishom Day, Greenville, SC, 1971; Num Other Awds & Hons; Men of Achmt; DIB; Commun Ldrs of Am; Book of Hon; W/W in Black Am & Num Other W/W Listings.

CHISUM, GLORIA TWINE oc/Research Psychologist; b/May 17, 1930; h/4120 Apalogen Road, Phila, PA 19144; ba/Warminster, PA; m/Melvin J; p/Chauncey D Twine (dec); Nadine D Twine, Muskogee, OK; sp/Mr and Mrs Melvin J Chisum Sr (dec); ed/BS 1951, MS 1953, Howard Univ; PhD, Univ of PA, 1960; pa/Lectr in Psych, Univ of PA, 1957-68; Res Psychol, 1960-65; Mgr, Vision Lab, 1965-81; Mgr, Life Scis Res Grp, Nav Air Devel Ctr, 1981-; Mem: Treas 1981-, En Psychol Assn; Fellow, Am Psychol Assn; Optical Soc of Am; Sigma Xi; Fellow, Aerospace Med Assn; AAAS; NY Acad of Scis; Bd Mem, Global Interdependence Ctr; World Affairs Coun; Com on Fgn Affairs; Dir, PSFS; Dir, Fischer & Porter Co; Trustee, Univ of PA; cp/Dir, Phila Orch Assn; Gov, En PA Chapt, Arthritis Foun; Life Mem, NAACP; Urban Leag of Phila; r/Meth; hon/Author of 79 Sci Pubs & Reports; Patentee in Field; Longacre Awd, Aerospace Med Assn, 1979; Sci Achmt Awd, Freedom Day Assn, 2980; Hon Doct Sci, Med Col of PA, 1981; Dist'd Daugh of PA, 1981; Alumni Awd, Univ of PA, 1982; Doct Sci, Ursinus Col, 1981; DHL, York Col,

1982; Alumni Achmt Awd, Howard Univ, 1983; W/W: of Am Wom, in E; Am Men & Wom of Sci; DIB.

CHMIELINSKI, EDWARD ALEXANDER oc/Electronics Company Executive; b/Mar 25, 1925; ba/238 Water Street, Naugatuck, CT 06770; m/Elizabeth Carew; c/Nancy, Elizabeth, Susan Jean; p/Stanley and Helen Chmielinski; ed/BS, Tulane Univ, 1950; Postgrad Study, Univ of CO, 1965; mil/USN, 1943-46; pa/VP, Gen Mgr, Clifton Prods, Litton Industs, Colorado Springs, 1965-67; Pres, Memory Prods Div, Litton Industs, Beverly Hills, 1967-69; Pres, Bowmar Instruments Canada, 1969-73; Gen Mgr, Leigh Instruments, Ontario, 1973-75; Pres & Dir, Liquidometer Corp, Tampa, 1975-; ASME; Am Mgmt Assn; Am Mfrs Assn; IEEE; Sales Exec Clb NY; cp/Naugatuck C of C; Pres Coun; Pres Assn; Pres, Acad Water Bd, Colorado Springs, 1963-65; Bd Dirs, U Way, Colorado Springs, 1965-67; AF Assn; Navy Leag; hon/Tau Beta Pi; Omicron Delta Kappa; W/W: in Fin & Indust, in World, in E.

CHNUPA, PEGGY A oc/Educator; b/June 10, 1952; h/1419 Mississippi Place, Hobart, IN 46342; ba/Hobart, IN; c/Kathleen Ann; p/John C and Dessie Robinson, Hobart, IN; ed/BS Elem Ed, IN Univ-Bloomington, 1974; MS Elem Ed 1978, EdS in Ed Adm, IN St Univ, 1983; pa/Tchr Grades 1 & 4 1974-80, Asst Elem Curric Coor 977-79, Adm Intern 1979-80, Dir Spec Sers 1980-82; Dir of Curric & Instrn 982-, Hobart Twp Commun Sch Corp; Mem: Secy 1977-78, VPres 1978-79, Hobart Twp Tchrs Assn; Assn for Supvn & Curric Devel, 1978-; IASCO, 1979-; Phi Delta Kappa, 1980-; IN Univ Alumni Assn, 1981-; Secy 1982-83, BB/BS of NW IN; cp/Secy 1975-76, VPres 1976-77, PTA; r/Luth; hon/Author of "Formative Eval: The Neglected Eval Tool," *IN St Univ Bltn*, 1982; W/W in MW; Outstg Yg Wom of Am.

CHO, SOUNG MOO oc/Engineering Management, Education; b/Oct 1, 1937; h/1051 Vail Road, Parsippany, NJ 07054; ba/Livingston, NJ; m/Ki Sun Kim; c/Rose, Richard, Karen, Gace, Christopher, Andrew; p/Song-Nyung Cho (dec) Mi-Ok Cho, Seoul, Korea; sp/Nyung-Han and Sun-Myung Kim, LA, CA; ed/BA, Seoul Nat Univ, 1960; MS 1964, PhD 1967, Univ of CA-Berkeley; pa/Resr, Korean Atomic Energy Res Inst, 1960-61; Res Asst/Spec, Univ of CA-Berkeley, 1962-67; Engrg Spec, Garrett Corp, LA, CA, 1967-69; Staff Conslt, Energy Technol Engrg Ctr, Div of Rockwell Intl, Canoga Pk, CA, 1969-73; Engrg Mgr 1973-80, Dept Dir Engrg 1980-84, Dir of Engrg Sers 1984-, Foster Wheeler Energy Applications Inc; Adj Prof, Fairleigh Dickinson Univ, Teaneck, NJ, 1975-83; Adj Prof, Stevens Inst of Technol, Hoboken, NJ, 1978-; Conslt & Lectr, Var Univs, Utilities & Profl Socs; Mem 1968-, Nuclear Engrg Div Exec Com 1982-, Chm Nuclear Heat Exchanger Com 1980-82, ASME; Mem, Am Nuclear Soc, 1969-; hon/Author Num Engrg Articles Pub'd in Profl Jours; Var Book Reviews; Referee, Var Profl Jours; Recip, Republic of Korea Pres Awd, 1960; Fulbright Travel Scholar, 1962; W/W in Frontier Sci & Technol.

CHOE, WON-GIL oc/Electronics

Company Executive; b/Apr 24, 1932; h/11 Cowell Lane, Atherton, CA 94025; ba/Sunnyvale, CA; m/Mirang Wonne, PhD; c/Iliad, Christopher, Charlotte; p/Chan-Sang and Sook Ja Shim Choe (dec) sp/Dr Heung-Kyun Wonne, Seoul Korea; ed/BSEng, AZ St Univ, 1960; MSIE 1962, PhD 1975, Stanford Univ; pa/Supvr of Prodn, Fairchild Semiconductor Corp, 1962-65; Mgr of Mfg Engrg, Memorex Corp, 1964-66; Mgr of Prodn, Signetic Corp, 1966-68; VP Oper, Dole Electronics Sys, 1968-71; Exec VP, Vacu-Blast Corp, 1971-75; Pres, Tronic Corp, 1975-79; Dir, Applied Mat Inc, 1979-80; Pres, EEI Inc, 1980-82; Pres, Video Logic Corp, 1982-; hon/Author Profl Pubs; W/W in W.

CHOI, ED SUNGKYU oc/Investment Counsel; b/Mar 16, 1931; h/1046 South Dunsmuir Avenue, Los Angeles, CA 90019; ba/Los Angeles, CA; m/Ae Soon; c/Mike, Jerry, David, Julie; ed/Att'd Korean Mil Acad, 1950; BA, VA Unino Univ, 1960; MA, Univ of CA-LA, 1962; pa/Fin Anal, 1st CA Co; Investmt Advr, Reg w Sec Under Investmt Advrs Act of 1940; LA Fin Anal Soc; hon/Author of Securities Res Reports; Devel/Inventor, Math Formulas Used in Calculating Securities Margin Accts; Ygst Lt Col in Korean Army.

CHOPRA, NAITER MOHAN oc/Professor, Researcher; b/Nov 23, 1923; h/1803 Red Forest Road, Greensboro, NC 27411; ba/Greensboro, NC; m/Santosh; c/Kiran, Ashok, Hersh, Siddharth; p/H L Chopra, New Delhi, India; sp/P N Dhanda, Rajasthan, India; ed/BSc 1944, MSc 1945, Univ of Punjab; PhD, Univ of Dublin, 1955; pa/Prof Chem, Dir Tobacco & Pesticide Res 1967-, Assoc Prof Chem 1965-67, NC A&T St Univ, Greensboro; Res Ofcr, Canada Dept of Agri, 1957-65; Mem: Dir, CNC Sect, Am Chem Soc, 1970-72; Pres, India Assn, Greensboro, NC, 1972; Pres, Hindu Soc of NC, Greensboro, 1979-82; NC St Tobacco Res & Extension Fac; r/Hindu; hon/Author, Var Pubs on Tobacco & Pesticide Res; Recip Govt of Tire Res Grant, 1954-55; Res Grant, Coun For Tobacco Res USA, 1967-71; USDA- SEA/CR Res Grants, 1972-; Am Men & Wom of Sci; W/W in S; Other Biogl Listings.

CHOU, IRIS LI-YIN oc/Counsul of CCNAA; b/Jan 11, 1951; h/41-40 Union Street, #10H, Flushing, NY 11355; ba/New York, NY; p/Chuen-chi Chou and Shen-Chen Jen, Taiwan, Rep of China; ed/BA, Nat Chengchi Univ, 1974; MA, Am Univ, 1981; pa/Sr Staff, Min Fgn Affairs, 1975-78; Third Secy in Chinese Embassy, 1978-80; Asst in Wash DC, CCNAA, 1980-82; Secy (Consul) in New York, CCNAA, 1982-; hon/W/W of Am Wom.

CHOU, TSU WEI oc/Professor; b/Jun 2, 1940; h/15 Kenwick Road, Hockessin, DE 19707; ba/Newark, DE; m/Viviam M S Lo; c/Helen H H, Vivian H C, Evan H H; ed/BS Civil Engrg, Nat Taiwan Univ, 1963; MS Mats Sci, NWn Univ, 1966; PhD Mats Sci, Stanford Univ, 1969; pa/Asst Prof 1969, Assoc Prof 1973, Prof 1978, Univ of DE; Vis'g Prof, German Aerospace Res Establishment-Koln, 1983; Liaison Sci, US Ofc of Nav Res-London, 1983; Vis'g Prof, Nat Comm for Investigation of Space, Argentina, 1981; Vis'g Prof, Univ of Witwatersrand, S Africa, 1977; Sr

Vis'g Res Fellow, Brit Sci Res Coun, 1976; Vis'g Sci, Argonne Nat Lab, 1975-76; hon/Author of Book, *Composite Mats & Their Use in Structures*, 1975; Over 100 Papers Pub'd in Tech Jours; Sr Vis'g Res F'ship, Brit Sci Res Coun, 1976; Frederic Gardner Cottrell Res Corp F'ship, 1970-71; Ford Foun F'ship, Stanford Univ, 1966-67; Walter P Murphy F'ship, NWn Univ, 1964-65; Am Men & Wom of Sci; W/W: in E, in Technol; Intl Dir to Geophy Res; Other Biogl Listings.

CHOUDHURI, HIRAN C oc/Professor of Cell Biology; b/Mar 1, 1924; h/104 Davignon Road, Dollard des Orneaux, Quebec H9B2H1, Canada; ba/Zarla, Nigeria; m/Monica; c/Hirak; p/Julada P and Saraju Choudhuri (dec); sp/Narendra K Majumder (dec); Nalini Majumder, Calcutta, India; ed/MSc, Calcutta Univ; PhD, London Univ; PhD, Edinburgh Univ; pa/Potato Spec, Govt of W Bengal & Prof of Agri Botany; Jt Dir Agri Res; Jr Dir Agri Ext; Jt Dir Agri Mktg; Agri Spec, Govt of En Nigeria; Tchg Fellow, McGill Univ; Rdr Dept of Biol Scis, Prof Cell Biol, Chm Res & Conf Attendance Com Bio Scis 1979-, Ahmadu Bello Univ, Zaria, Nigeria; Mem: FRSE; FBSE; FIGS; FIPS; Am Genetical Soc; AAAS; Am Potato Assn; Genetical Soc of Canada; Soc of Cell Biol; Assn of European Potato Res; Others; r/Hindu; hon/Author, 63 Pub'd Papers in Intl Sci Jours; Author, "Potato in W Bengal,"; Postdoct F'ship, Nat Res Coun of Canada; Carnegie Trust Res Grant for Pub in Transactions of Royal Soc of Edinburgh; Invited Participant, Decennial Review Conf on Cell Tissue & Organ Culture, Lake Placid, NY, 1976; W/W of Intells; DIB; Other Biogl Listings.

CHOULES, JOHN MAYNARD oc/Chief Engineer; b/May 28, 1934; h/5363A Harris Street, Dugway, UT 84022; ba/Dugway, UT; c/Jack Mark, David Victor, Karen Diane, Dale William, Nancy Coral, Stacy Lynn, Grant Aldon, Ryan Trent; p/George Choules (dec); sp/Esther Ebbers, SLC; ed/BSCE, UT St Univ, 1956; Electron CS, NRI, 1984; pa/Chief Engr, Hawthorne Co, 1983-; Real Est Develr, Choules Devel Co, 1983; Site Constrn Mgr, Prowswood Inc, 1981-83; cp/Ch Dist Counselman, Saudi Arabia, 1979-1980; Toast Master, Dist Lt Gov, Orange Co, CA, 1977-78; Scout Master; Missionary; Tchr; r/Mormon; hon/Civic Ser Awd, Bechtel Corp for Wk in Nuclear Campaign, 1976; W/W in W.

CHOUN, ROBERT JOSEPH JR oc/Educator; b/Aug 17, 1948; h/818 Clover Park Drive, Arlington, TX 76013; ba/Arlington, TX; m/Jane Willson; p/Robert J and Mildred F Choun, Trumbull, CT; sp/William H and Dorothy T (dec) Willson, Barnegat, NJ; ed/AA, Luther Col, 1969; BA, Gustavus Adolphus Col, 1971; MRE cum laude, Trinity Div Sch, 1974; MA summa cum laude, Wheaton Col, 1979; DMin summa cum laude, Faith Evang Sem, 1980; Postgrad Study, N TX St Univ, 1978-; pa/Min of Ed, Pantego Bible Ch, 1975-; Adj Prof of Ed, Dallas Theol Sem, 1977-; Ed Cnslt, Gospel Light Pubs, 1977-; Am Mgmt Assn, 1980-; TX SS Assn; TX Assn for Ed of Yg Child, 1981-; ICL, Voc Staff Conf; Pioneer Min, Bd of Review & Christian Ed Adv Comm,

1980-; Steering Co for Lang Acquisition Skills, Fleming H Revell Pub Co, 1982-; Assn of Christian Schs (Sem Ldr), 1978-; Assn for Curric Devel, 1978-; Ed Chm, Sch Bd, Pantego Christian Acad, 1975-; SW Chinese Bible Org, Conf Spkr; r/Bible Ch; hon/Author of Columns; Kappa Delta Pi; Phi Delta Kappa; W/W in S & SW.

CHOW, GREGORY CHI-CHONG oc/Professor; b/Dec 25, 1919; h/30 Hardy Drive, Princeton, NJ 08540; ba/Princeton, NJ; m/Paula K; c/John S, James S, Jeanne M; p/Tin-Pong and Pauline Chow, Hong Kong; ed/BA Ec, Cornell Univ, 1951; MA 1952, PhD 1955, Ec, Univ of Chgo; Asst Prof, MA Inst of Technol, Cambridge, MA, 1955-59; Assoc Prof 1959-62, Vis'g Prof 1964-65, Cornell Univ, Ithaca, NY; Staff Mem, Mgr Ec Models, IBM Res Ctr, Yorktown Hgts, NY, 1962-70; Adj Prof, Columbia Univ, NYC, 1965-71; Lectr, Academia Sinica (Chinese Acad of Scis) & Taiwan Univ, 1966; Vis'g Prof, Harvard Univ, 1967; Prof Ec & Dir of Econometric Res Prog 1970-, Class of 1913 Prof of Polit Ec 1979-, Princeton Univ; Mem: Exec Com, Inst of Stats, Academia Sinica, 1981-; Chm, Am Ec Assn Com on Exchanges w People's Republic of China; Conslt, IBM Corp; Chief Editor in Ec, *Sci & Technol Review*, (Chinese); Edit Bd, *Economic Perspectives: Annual Survey of Ec*, 1978-; Edit Bd, *Academia Ec Papers*, 1970-; Pres, Soc for Ec Dynamics & Control, 1979-; Intl Prog Com, IFAC/IFORS; Co-Editor, *Jour of Ec Dynamics & Control*, 1978-; Ints of Math Stats; Am Ec Assn; Num Others; hon/Author of 5 Books incl'g: *The Chinese Economy*, 1984; *Econometrics*, 1983; Co-Editor, *Evaluating the Reliability of Macro-ec Models*, 1982; Contbr of Jour Articles & Book Chapts to Num Intl Profl Pubs; Fellow: Econometric Soc; Am Statl Assn; W/W: in E, in Am, in World, in Ec, in Fin & Industry; Men of Achmt; Other Biogl Listings.

CHRÉTIEN, LaVERNE ARDRA oc/Social Worker; b/Dec 24, 1916; h/1034 South Orlando Avenue, Los Angeles, CA 90035; ba/Los Angeles, CA; p/Robert L and Annie Mable Williams (dec); ed/BS cum laude, Huston Tillotson Col, 1938; MSW, Atlanta Univ Sch of Social Wk, 1949; Postgrad Studies, Smith Col Sch for Social Wk, 1958-59; pa/Child Welfare Wkr, Chgo, 1948-59; Sch Social Wkr, Cook Co Sch Dist, 1959-69; Med Social Wkr, Schwab Rehab Hosp, 1969-71; Prog Spec, Sickle Cell Anemia, Co of LA Hlth Social Wk, LAC/USC Med Ctr, 1981-; Pres, E Val Commun Coor Coun of N Hollywood, 1980-82; Chm of Chgo Area Sch Social Wk Coun, Nat Assn of Social Wk, 1968-69; cp/Pres, Nat Assn of Col Wom, Chgo Br, 1966-68; r/U Meth; hon/"Sickle Cell Anemia;" Meritorious Ser to the Col, Moraine Val Commun Col, 1967, 1970 and 1971; Valuable Ser in Promoting Hlth Awareness Among Citizens of Our Commun, Hollywood Hlth Fair Planning Com and LA City Col, 1972; Outstg Ser and Sense of Civic Responsibility to N Hollywood C of C, 1981; Outstg Ldrship in Promoting Coop Among Organizations and Individuals in Making the Commun a Better Place in Which to Live, LA Co Supvrs, 1981; W/W Among Black Wom in CA.

CHRISTENBERRY, MARY ANNE oc/Educator; b/Apr 30, 1932; h/1533 Craig Street, Augusta, GA 30904; ba/Augusta, GA; m/David B Bell; p/A L and Mattie S (dec) Christenberry, Knoxville, TN; ed/BA, Wake Forest Col, 1954; MA, Geo Peabody Col for Tchrs, 1956; EdS 1971, PhD 1974, GA St Univ; pa/Dir of Christian Ed, Smithwood Ch, 1954-55; Tchr, Kgn & 1st Grade of Pomona, CA 1956-57, Burbank, CA 1959-61, Beverly Hills, CA 1961-69; Instr & Dept Chm, Child Devel Prog, Atlanta Area Tech Sch, 1970-73; Asst, Assoc & Full Prof, Augusta Col, 1954-; Editor & Writer, Gospel Light Pub, 1959-64; Soc for Res in Child Devel; Assn for Chd Ed; Nat Assn on Yg Child; Mid-S Ed Res Assn; Assn Tchr Edr; GA Assn on Yg Chd; GA Early Chd Ed/Child Devel Higher Ed Assn (Pres 1981-82); GA Supporters for the Gifted; Nat Early Chd Ed Higher Ed Assn; cp/Jean Piaget Soc; Delta Kappa Gamma; Phi Delta Kappa; Mensa; r/Bapt; hon/Author, *Games Graffiti, How to Make a Creat Cocoon, Why Didn't Anyone Ever Tell Me That Chd are Like That?*, Profl Articles; Delta Kappa Gamma Intl F'ship, 1973-74; Fullbright-Hays F'ship to India, 1981; W/W in S & SW.

CHRISTENSEN, C LEWIS oc/Executive; b/Jun 3, 1936; h/2948 Country Club Dr, Colorado Springs, CO 80909; ba/Colorado Springs, CO; m/Sandra; c/Kim, Brett; p/Raymond H Christensen, Colorado Springs, CO; ed/BS, Univ of WY, 1959; mil/1st Lt, USAF, 1959-62; pa/Mgmt Trainee, Gen Mills, 1959; 1st Lt, USAF Malmstrom AFB, 1959-62; Mgmt Trainee 1962-63, Data Communs Mgr 1964-66, Dist Mktg Mgr 1970-73, Mtn Bell; Sem Ldr 1966-68, Mktg Supvr 1968-70, Am T&T; Land Planning & Devel 1973, Exec VP 1975-77, Village Assocs; VP, Cimarron Corp, 1974-75; Pres & Gen Mgr, Briargate Mgmt Co, 1977-; Chm of Bd 1981, Bd of Dirs 1976-82, Chm of City-Co Liaison Com 1982-, Colorado Springs C of C; cp/Bd of Dirs, Colorado Springs Homebldrs Assn, 1975-81; Bd of Dirs, Citizens Goals, 1980-; Bd of Dirs, Colorado Coun on Ec Ed, 1978-80; Chancellors Adv Bd, Univ of CO-Colorado Springs, 1979-; Bd of Dirs, Pikes Peak Coun of BSA, 1980-; r/Presb; hon/W/W in Fin & Indust.

CHRISTENSEN, LUELLA GRACE oc/Payroll Clerk (Retired); b/Nov 27, 1910; h/5111 28th Avenue South, Minneapolis, MN 55417; m/John E Christensen (dec); c/Ramona L Foley, Marlene J Strachota, Carol J Rogers; m/James H and Rosie M Holland (dec); sp/Lars and Hannah Christensen (dec); ed/Att'd Univ of MN Col of Home Ec, 1930-31; pa/Stenographer, MN Farm Bur Fdn & Land O' Lakes Creameries, 1930-31; Machine Adj, Twin City Ordinance, 1942-45; Div Mgr, Sears Roebuck & Co, 1946-52; Payroll Clerk, Jensen Printing Co & Holden Printing Co, 1953-75; cp/Sq Dance Fdn of MN Inc; r/Presb; hon/Num Columns; Salutatorian of Pine City HS, 1930.

CHRISTENSEN, MARY LUCAS oc/Director of Virology; b/Oct 18, 1937; h/900 North Lake Shore Drive, Apartment 1905, Chicago, IL 60611; ba/Chgo, IL; p/Kermit Christensen, St Louis, MO; Margaret Isabelle Lucas Christensen (dec); ed/BA 1959, MS 1961,

Bacteriology, Univ of IA; PhD Microbiol, NWn Univ Med Sch, 1974; pa/Res Virologist, Wyeth Labs, Phila, PA, 1961-65; Res Virologist, Abbott Labs, N Chgo, 1965-68; Chief Clin Virology Lab, Univ Med Ctr 1969-71, Res Fellow, Nat Cancer Inst 1974-78, Asst Prof Pathol & Pediatrics, Med Sch 1978-, NWn Univ; Dir Virol, The Chd's Meml Hosp, Chgo, 1978-; Mem: Gamma Phi Beta; Am Soc for Microbiol; IL Soc for Microbiol; APHA; AAAS; Pan-Am Grp for Rapid Viral Diagnosis; Am Med Wom's Assn; Tissue Culture Assn; Univ of IA Alumni Assn; NWn Univ Alumni Assn; r/Epis; hon/Author of 2 Books, *Basic Lab Procedures in Diagnostic Virology*, 1977; *Microbiol for Nsg & Allied Hlth Students*, 1982; Contbr, Num Articles to Profl Sci Jours; Iota Sigma Pi; W/W: in W,in Frontier Sci & Technol; Other Biogl Listings.

CHRISTIAN, GARY DALE oc/Professor, Consultant; b/Nov 25, 1937; h/7827 Northeast 12th Street, Medina, WA 98195; ba/Seattle, WA; m/Suanne Coulbourne; c/Dale Brian, Carol Jean; p/Roy Christian (dec); sp/Edna A Gonier, Eugene, OR; ed/BS Chem, Univ of OR, 1959; MS 1962, PhD 1964, Univ of MD; pa/Res Anal Chem, Walter Reed Army Inst of Res, Wash DC, 1961-67; Asst Prof 1967-70, Assoc Prof 1970-72, Univ of KY, Lexington; Prof Chem 1972-, Univ of WA; Vis'g Prof, Univ Libre de Bruxelles, Brussels, Belgium, 1978-79; Vis'g Prof, Univ of Geneva, Switzerland, 1979; Mem: Chm Puget Sound Sect, Am Chem Soc, 1983; Mbrship Chm 1982, Nom'g Chm 1985, Pacific NW Chm 1979-80, Soc for Applied Spectroscopy; Canadian Spectroscopy Soc; r/Prot; hon/Author of 3 Books incl'g: *Anal Chem*, 3rd Edition, 1980; *Instrumental Anal*, 1977; Over 200 Pubs in Profl Jours; Fullbright-Hays Scholar, 1978-79; Medal, Universite de Bruxelles, 1978; Hon Cert of Res, Univ of Ghent, 1979; Fellow, Am Inst of Chems; W/W: in Am, in Sci, in S & SW, of Intells, in Frontier Sci & Technol; Other Biogl Listings.

CHRIST-JANER, ARLAND F oc/Art School President; b/Jan 27, 1922; h/Royal Street Andrew, Apartment 401, 555 Gulfstream Avenue, Sarasota, FL 33577; ba/Sarasota, FL; m/Sally Johnson; p/William Henry and Bertha Wilhelmina Bechman Christ-Janer (dec); ed/BA, Carleton Col; BD, Yale Div Sch; ID, Univ of Chgo Law Sch; mil/USAAC, 1943-46, Pvt to Capt; pa/Pres, Ringling Sch of Art & Design, Sarasota, 1984-; Pres, Stephens Col, Columbia, MO, 1975-83; Pres, New Col, Sarasota, FL, 1973-75; Pres, Col Entrance Exam Bd, NYC, NY, 1970-73; Pres, Boston Univ, Boston, 1967-70; Mem: Trustee & Chm Ednl Policy Com, Carleton Col; Acad Affairs Com, New Col; Trustee, Stephens Col; Dir, Am Republic Ins Co of NY; Phi Beta Kappa; Cent Assn, NYC; Am Acad Arts & Scis; Cleveland Conf; Intl Assn Univ Pres; Japan Intl Christian Univ-Men's Com; cp/Columbia C of C; Missourians for the Equal Rts Amendment; Bd of Dirs, Mus Assocs, Univ of MO; US People's Fund for UN Inc; Nat Coun Wilberforce Univ's Pres Devel Coun; Newcomen Soc N Am; Rotary Clb, Columbia; hon/LLD: Coe Col; CO Col; Carleton Co; LHD: Monmouth Col; Curry Col; Var Biogl Listings.

CHRISTOPHER, DOLORES LEE oc/ Manager of International Accounts; b/ Feb 5, 1940; h/101-125 West 147 Street, New York, NY 10039; ba/New York, NY; p/Ernest (dec) and Ethel Christopher, New York, NY; ed/AAS, Borough Manhattan Commun Col, 1970; BA, Fordham Univ, 1978; pa/Pers/ Postal Clk, US Postal Service, 1965-73; Shop Steward, Am Postal Wkrs Union, 1974-77; Ad-Hoc EEO Cnslr, 1977-; Jr Acct 1976-77, Supvr of Settlement Sect 1977-81, Mgr 1981-, Intl Accts Ctr of the US Postal Ser; cp/Bd of Dirs, Borough Manhattan Commun Col, Mem/V Chp 1964; Bd of Dirs, Esplanade Gardens Coop 1967-75 Parliamentn, V Chp, Treas; Fordham Univ Alumni Assn, 1978-; Mem of Urban Studies Assn, Fordham Univ, 1977-78; Nat Assn for Female Execs Inc, 1978-; r/Rom Cath; hon/Ser Awd, Borough Manhattan Commun Col, 1965; Ser Awd, Esplanade Gardens Assn, 1974; Cert of Apprec, Esplanade Gardens Assn, 1975; Good Standing Awd for Profl & Career Goals, 1981; W/W of Am Wom.

CHRISTOPHER, THOMAS WELDON oc/Law Professor; b/Oct 8, 1917; h/7 Pinehurst Drive, Tuscaloosa, AL 35401; ba/Tuscaloosa, AL; m/Evelyn Montez Hawkins; c/Thomas Heflin; p/ William Arthur and Ruby Thomas Christopher (dec); ed/AB, Wash & Lee Univ, 1939; LLB 1948, LLD 1978, Univ of AL; LLM 1950, JSD 1957, NY Univ; pa/Dean, Univ of NM Sch of Law, 1965-71; Dean 1971-81, Prof Law 1981-, Univ of AL Sch of Law; Mem: ABA; Assn Am Law Schs; Food & Drug Law Inst; hon/Author: Cases & Mats on Food & Drug Law, 2nd Edition, 1973; Constitl Questions in Food & Drug Laws, 1960; Co-Author: GA Procedure & Pract w Leverett & Hall, 1957; Spec Fed Food & Drug Laws w Dunn, 1954; Contbr, Num Articles to Legal Jours.

CHUGH, YOGINDER P oc/Educator, Researcher; b/Oct 6, 1940; h/1618 Tina Drive, Murphysboro, IL 62966; b/ Carbondale, IL; m/Evangeline N; c/ Anjeli, Shirmilee, Pauline; p/Atma Ram and Dharam Devi (dec); sp/Ruben and Luz Negron, Santa Isabel, PR; ed/BS, Banaras Hindu Univ, 1961; MS 1968, PhD 1971, PA St Univ; pa/Res Asst, PA St Univ, 1965-70; Res Engr, IIT Res Inst, 1971-73; Planning Engr, AMAX Coal Co, 1974-76; Prof, So IL Univ, 1977-; Soc of Mining Engrs, 1966-; cp/Rotary Clb of Carbondale, 1981-; r/Hindu; hon/ Num Profl Pubs; Pubs Bd Awd, Soc of Mining Engrs, 1982; W/W in Engrg; Am Men & Wom of Sci; Dir of Dist'd Ams.

CHUN, CONNIE C oc/State Representative, Attorney; b/Jun 2, 1928; h/ 1429 Uila Street, Honolulu, HI 96818; ba/Honolulu, HI; m/Hing Hua; c/May L'ynne, Jerrold, June, Hingson, Joy, Daven; ed/RN, Manila Sanitarium & Hosp, 1953; BS Nsg, Loma Linda Univ, 1958; MPH 1972, JD 1978, Univ of HI; pa/St Rep 30th Dist, HI, 1981-; Atty-at-Law, 1978-; VChm House Com on Hlth, 1983-; Mem: House Coms on Fin, Human Sers, Housing & St Gen Planning, 1983-; Other Previous Coms; Hlth Planner, Rehab Hosp of Pacific, 1970-72; Asst Dir Nsg, St Francis Hosp, 1968-70; Dir Nsg, Golden Gate Hosp, SF, CA, 1960-68; cp/ABA; HI Bar Assn; APHA; HI Nurses Assn; ANA; Chm, Honolulu Police Comm, 1979-80; Num

Other Commun Activs; hon/ Co-Author: HI St Hlth Facilities Plan, 1975; Master Plan Rehab Hosp of Pacific, 1976; Author of Article, "Peer Review & Cont'g Legal Ed," HI Bar Jour, 1978; Fulbright Scholar, 1956; W/W: in Polits, of Am Wom; HI's Eminent Fillipinos.

CHUNG, DEBORAH D L oc/Professor; b/Sep 12, 1952; h/3812 Henley Drive, Pittsburgh, PA 15213; ba/Pittsburgh, PA; m/Lan K Wong; p/Leslie and Rebecca Chung, Don Mill, Ontario, Canada; sp/K H Wong (dec); ed/BS Engrg & Applied Sci, 1973; MS Engrg Sci, 1973; SM Mats Sci, 1975; PhD Mats Sci, 1977; pa/Asst Prof Metall Engrg, Carnegie-Mellon Univ, 1977-82, Assoc Prof Metall Engrg & Mats Sci 1982-, Carnegie-Mellon Univ; Mem: Chm of Pubs 1983, N Am Thermal Anal Soc; cp/Choir Dir, Chinese Pgh Ch, 1980-; r/Christian; hon/Author, Var Articles in Profl Jours incl'g: Mats Sci Res Bltn; Jour Electrochem Soc; Hardy Gold Medal, Am Inst of Mining, Metall & Petro Engrs, 1980; Ladd Awd, Carnegie-Mellon Univ, 1979; W/W in Engrg; Am Men & Wom of Sci.

CHUNG, KEA SUNG oc/Corporation Executive; b/Jan 2, 1935; h/2126 Mott-Smith Drive, Honolulu, HI 96822; ba/Honolulu, HI; m/Ok Soon; c/Hee Sung, Yun Hee, Jaeh Hoon, Juneho; p/ Tae In Chung (dec); ed/Grad Dipl, Kyung Nam Hing Sch, 1953; BS, Ctl MS St Univ, 1957; Hon Doct in Bus Mgmt, CA Intl Univ; pa/Pres, Korea Tourist Bur Inc; Pres, Polynesian Fair Inc; Pres, House of Kea; Pres, Voice of Korea-HI; HI Rep, Korean Natt Tourism Corp; Pres Korean Press Clb of HI; Chm, Temple Constrn, Korean Buddhist Temple DAE WON SA; cp/Past Pres, Korean C of C of Honolulu; Past Dir, HI C of C; Past Dir, Korean Bus-men's Assn of HI; Past Dir, Korean Ath Assn of HI; Past Pres, Korean Commun Coun of HI; Pres, Lay Persons Assn of DAE WON SA Temple of HI; Am Soc Travel Assns; Intl Air Trans Assn; Pacific Area Travel Assn; hon/ Merit Ser Awd, Min Comm & Indust, Repub of Korea, 1978; Merit Ser, Min Public Info & Culture, Repub of Korea, 1982; Men of Achmt.

CHURCH, IRENE ZABOLY oc/Personal Services Executive; b/Feb 18, 1947; h/8 Ridgecrest Drive, Chagrin Falls, OH 44022; ba/Pepper Pike, OH; c/Irene Elizabeth, Elizabeth Anne; p/ Bela Paul William and Irene Chandas Zaboly, Chagrin Falls, OH; ed/Grad of Public Schs, 1965; pa/Pers Recruiter, Champ Pers, 1965; Secy, Tech Sales Co, 1966-68; Pers Recruiter, Brunswick Pers, 1968-70; Chm of Bd, Pres, Oxford Pers Div, A Pers Ser Inc, 1973-; Chm of Bd, Pres, Oxford Temporaries Inc, 1979-; Mem: Num Positions, The Gtr Cleveland Assn of Pers Conslts Inc, 1973-; Num Positions, The OH Assn of Pers Conslts Inc, 1973-; Var Positions, Nat Assn of Pers Conslts Inc, 1973-; Nat Assn of Temporary Sers, 1980-81; Intl Platform Assn, 1982-; cp/Euclid C of C, 1973-81; Var Positions, The Federated Ch, U Ch of Christ, Chagrin Falls, 1980-; Gtr Cleveland Growth Assn, Coun of Small Enterprises, 1980-; ABWA, 1980-; BBB, 1973-81; Ldr, Lake Erie Girl Scout Coun, 1980-81; Num Other Commun Activs; r/Prot; hon/ Cert'd Pers Conslt, 1975; Vi Pender

Awd for Outstg Contbns, 1977; Commun Ldrs of Am; Book of Hon; Intl Book of Honor; Dir of Dist'd Ams; Num W/ W & Other Biogl Listings.

CHURCH, RICHARD DWIGHT oc/ Electrical Engineer; Corporation Executive; b/Jun 27, 1936; h/54 Ithaca Road, Candor, NY 13743; ba/Candor, NY; m/ Vernice Naomi Ives; c/Joel, Benjamin; p/Dwight P Church (dec); sp/Carmeta E Church (dec); ed/BEE, Clarkson Col of Technol, 1963; mil/USAF, 1955-59; pa/Sr Elects Engr, Magnetic Labs, Apalachin, NY, 1980-82; Prin Engr, 1969-; Pres/Chm of Bd 1968-, ASL Sys Inc, Candor, NY; Sr Assoc Elects Engr, IBM, Oswego, NY, 1963-69; cp/Bd of Dirs/Treas, Candor Commun Clb, 1970-78; Pres, Candor Coin Clb, 1978-80; Rep & Mem, Candor Fire Co, 1972- NY Assn of Fire Chiefs, 1978-; r/Candor Congreg Ch, Treas/Trustee 1972-82; hon/Co-Author, "Career Oriented Problems of Sec'dy Math", 1968; US & Canadian Patents; Dr Carl Michel Awd, Clarkson Col of Technol, 1960; Mem 1967 & 1969 US Team to World Champ'ships White Water Canoeing; W/W: in E, of Intells.

CHURCHILL, PETER D oc/Commercial Photographer, Writer, Business Consultant; b/Jun 23, 1940; h/PO Box 276, Sunset Beach, CA 90742; c/Mark, Christina, Michelle; p/Clarence H and Vivian B Drown (dec); ed/BA, Univ of Pacific, 1963; CA Tchg Credential, 1964; MA, CA St Univ, 1971; JD, Am Col of Law, 1978; pa/Sales Tng Mgr, Hallmark Cards Inc, 1967-77; Assoc, Purcell Rlty, 1977-78; Nat Sales Tng Coor, Nissan Motor Corp, 1978-80; Reg Sales Mgr, Burns Intl Security, 1980-82; Owner, Peter Churchill & Assocs, 1982-; Owner, Churchill Pictures, 1982-; Am Mgmt Assn; Am Soc of Tng & Devel; Photographic Soc of Am; Assoc Photogs Intl; Am Film Inst; Am Soc of Mag Photogs; cp/Aircraft Owners & Pilots Assn; Nat Assn of Underwater Instrs; hon/"Song of a Man;" Silver Awd, Intl Film & TV Fest for "Datsun-The Front Runner," 1980; Gold Awd, Houston Intl Film Fest & US Indust Film Fest for "A Matter of Pride," 1981; Exhibitor, Intl Photo Exhibn, LA Co Fair for B/W "Wn Rivers-WA," 1983; W/W in W.

CHUTE, DOUGLAS LAWRENCE oc/Neuroscientist; b/Aug 22, 1947; h/59 Bledlow Manor Drive, Scarborough, Ontario, Canada M1E 1B1; ba/Scarborough, Ontario, Canada; m/Margaret Elizabeth Bliss; c/Jesse Robert, Deborah Evans, Andrew Lawrence; p/A L and Helen E Reid Chute, Loretto, Ontario, Canada; sp/Mr and Mrs C L Bliss, Houston, TX; ed/BA, Univ Wn Ontario, 1969; MA 1971, PhD 1973, Univ of MO; Cert Psych, Ontario, 1980; pa/Res Fellow, NASA Space Sci Ctr, 1972-73; Asst Prof, Univ Houston Dept Psychol, 1973-77; Asst Dean Social Sci 1976-77, Lectr, Univ Otago New Zealand, 1977-80; Dir Neurosci, Univ Toronto, 1980-; Assoc Clin Prof Psychi, McMaster Univ, 1980-; APA; CPA; OPA; MPA; Soc for Neurosci; So Ontario Neurosci Assn; Sigma Xi, Exec; Nat Acad Neuropsychol; Am Bd of Profl Neuropsychol; Soc for Stimulus Properties of Drugs; Canadian Assn Neurosci; cp/Boy Scouts of Canada; hon/Num Articles Pub'd; Fidelity Ins Awd; Outstg Res in

CIALLELLA, EMIL A JR oc/Library Director; b/Jul 1, 1943; h/78 Arnold Street, East Providence, RI 02915; ba/Central Falls, RI; m/Carol Ann Cunniff; p/Emil A Ciallella, Barrington, RI; Italia DiBiase Ciallella (dec); sp/Francis D Cunniff (dec); Mary E Sanclon (dec); ed/BA, Providence Col, 1965; MA, Assumption Col, 1967; MLS, Univ of RI, 1971; mil/AUS, 1967-69; pa/Asst Ref Libn, Barrington Public Lib, RI, 1971-74; Lib Dir, Ctl Falls Free Public Lib, RI, 1974-; Mem: RI Lib Assn; N Eng Lib Assn; A Lib Assn; RI Hist Soc; Lib Conslt; Fund Raising/Grants Conslt; r/Cath; hon/Author of Article "RI," in *Am Lib Assn Yrbook*, 1976-83; W/W: in E, in Lib & Info Sers.

CICARELLI, JAMES S oc/University Dean; b/Aug 24, 1941; h/75 Harriet Street, Allegany, NY 14706; ba/St Bonaventure, NY; m/Julianne; c/Jill, David; p/Pasquale and Jelsumina Cicarelli, New Haven, CT; sp/Elaner Belmore, Middletown, CT; ed/BA 1963, MA 1964, PhD 1968, Ec, Univ of CT; pa/Dean Schof Bus Adm, St Bonaventure Univ, 1983-; Chm Dept of Ec, Assoc Prof Ec 1980-83, Asst to Assoc Prof Ec 1970-80, SUNY-Oswego; Vis'g Assoc Prof Ec, Renselaer Polytech inst, 1981-82; Mem: Pres, NY St Ec Assn, 1983-84; cp/Pres, Oswego Racquet Clb, 1978-80; hon/Author of 2 Books: *Ec: Macroeconomic Principle & Issues*, 1978; *Ec: Microeconomic Principle & Issues*, 1978; Author of 1 Monograph & Num Articles Pub'd in Profl Jours; BA w Hons, 1963; Nat Def Act F'ship, 1963-66; W/W in E.

CIOTOLA, CARL JOSEPH oc/Respiratory Therapist; b/May 3, 1951; ba/5757 North Dixie Highway, Ft Lauderdale, FL 33334; p/John Dominic and Mildred Ciotola, Glenburnie, MD; ed/Att'd Johns Hopkins Univ, 1972-73; Att'd Univ of MD, 1975; Att'd Commun Col of Balto, 1976-77; AS, Broward Commun Col, 1983-84; mil/AUS, 1970-76; pa/Examr, FBI, 1970-77; Unit Mgr, St Agnes Hosp, 1977-79; Asst Dir Resp Therapy, Thomas Wilson Hosp Ctr, 1978-81; Dept Dir, Univ of MD Rehab Ctr, 1981-83; Therapist, N Ridge Hosp, 1983-84; Mem: MD-DC Respiratory Therapy Assn; Am Assn of Respiratory Therapy; FL St Respiratory Assn; r/Rom Cath; hon/Outstg Civic Ldr, 1980; Owner of "Best of Breed," Gtr Naples Dog Clb, 1984.

CISSIK, JOHN HENRY oc/Aerospace Physiologist; b/Aug 18, 1943; h/12316 Marlowe Place, Ocean Springs, MD 39564; ba/Keesler, AFB, MS; m/Dorothy Paulette Allen; c/John Mark; p/John Peter and Gladys Lucille Morre Cissik, McGregor, TX; sp/Mrs John Allen, Paris, TX; ed/BA 1965, MA 1967, Univ of TX-Austin; PhD, Univ of IL, 1972; mil/USAF, Biomed Scis Corp, 1967-, Lt Col; pa/Aerospace Physiol, Dept of Med, USAF Med Ctr, Keesler AFB, MS, 1980-; Chief Spec Procedures Lab; Course Dir, USAF Cardiopulmonary Lab Tng Course; Mem or Chm Edit Bd for Sev Profl Jours; Mem Var Coms of Profl Assns; AART; ATS; NSCPT; ASAHP; cp/Evans Presch Coms; Evans PTA; Am Heart Assn; hon/USAF Merit Ser Medal, 1980; W/W in MW; Book of

Hon; DIB.

CITRENBAUM, CHARLES MICHAEL oc/Psychologist; b/Jan 24, 1945; ba/Baltimore, MD; m/C J Golden; c/Anna, Robert; p/Louis and Dorothy Citrenbaum, Balto, MD; sp/Eli and Rose Golden, Margate, FL; ed/BA 1966, PhD 1975, Univ of MD; MA, E Carolina Univ, 1970; pa/Hd Psych Dept, Correctional Inst for Wom, 1968-70; Hd Psych Dept, Receptin Diagnostic Ctr of MD Penitentiary, 1970-71; Dir, Prince George's Co Drug Treatment Ctr, 1971-72; Dir of Clin & Profl Sers, Prince George's Co Addictions Prog, 1972-74; Asst Prof of Social Work & Commun Planning, Univ of MD, 1974-80; Pt-time Instr of Evening Col, Johns Hopkins Univ, 1982-; Adj Asst Prof of Psych, Loyola Col, 1974-; Priv Pract Clin Psych, 1978-; Am Psychol Assn; Balto Assn of Consltg Psychols, Pres 1979; Fellow, MD Psychol Assn; MD Soc of Clin Hypnosis; hon/Co-Author *Irresistible Communication: Creat Skills for Hlth Profls*, Other Chapts of Books; W/W in E.

CIVJAN, SIMON oc/Educator; b/May 25, 1920; h/5734 Indigo Street, Houston, TX 77096; ba/Houston, TX; m/Velta Lilia; c/Ralph Haime, Neal Gabriel; p/Haim and Sonia Rivka (dec); sp/Janis and Emilia Jansons (dec); ed/BChE w hons, Univ of FL, 1944; DDS, Univ of MD, 1954; MS, Georgetown Univ, 1963; mil/US Army, 1944-80, COL; pa/Dental Ofcr & Chief Clin, US Army Dental Corps, 1954-63; Chief Div of Dental Mats, US Army Inst of Dental Res, Wash DC 1963-73; Cmdr/Dir, US Army Inst of Dental Res, 1973-74; Cmdr, 464th Med Detachmt, Vogelweh, Germany, 1974-75; Dept Cmdr for Dental Activs, US Army Med Dept Activ, Landstuhl, Germany 1975-77; Dept Cmdr & Chief, Roll Dental Clin, US Army Dental Activ, Ft Leonard Wood, MO 1977-79; Prof Physics & Dental Mats, Univ of TX-Houston, 1979-; Fellow, Am Col of Dentists, 1970; Fellow, Intl Col of Dentists, 1972; Am Dental Assn; Am Assn of Dental Schs; Assn of Mil Surgs of US; Intl Assn for Dental Res; Dental Mats Grp of Intl Assn for Dental Res; Acad of Dental Mats; Fdn Dentaile Intl; Author Profl Pubs; Holder of US Patent, 1972; r/Jewish; hon/Concerned Patient Care Awd, Ft Leonard Wood, 1978; US Army Legion of Merit, 1974; US Army Legion of Merit, 1st OLC, 1979; W/W: in Frontier Sci & Technol, World; Personalities of S; Intl W/W of Contemp Achmt.

CLACK, DICK SCOTT oc/International Trade Executive; b/Nov 13, 1927; h/PO Box 22367, Honolulu, HI 96822; ba/Honolulu, HI; c/Michael Bruce, Meiling Jade; p/Clyde W Clack (dec); Tink B Clack, Sedan, KS; ed/BS, OK St Univ, 1952; Postgrad, Hokkaido Univ, Sapporo, Japan, 1953-54; Univ of HI, 1979; AUS Info Sch, 1956; Dept of Def Lang Sch, 1958-69; mil/AUS, 1945-70; pa/Asst VP, Makaha Surfside Devel Co, Honolulu, 1970-72; Pres, D Clack Inc Public Relats Conslts, 1972-74; VP, PCO Inc, 1974-76; Exec Trustee, HI Army Mus Soc, 1976-78; VP, Dir Mktg Traders Pacific Ltd, 1979-81; Chm Bd Dirs, Makaha Surfside Assn, 1975-78; Dir Great Pacific Mortgage Co, 1972-74; Dir, 2211 Ala Wai Assn, 1976-78; Owner, C & S Imports, 1980-;

Dir VP, Societe Tahitienne de Devel Agri Indust & Touristique, Pirae, Tahiti, 1982-; Intl Rep, COPABAM, Moorea, Tahiti, 1982; VP & Dir, Pacific Trade & Devel Inc, 1983-; Pres, Intl Real Est Exch Inc, 1983-84; cp/Mil Order of World Wars; VFW, Chief of Staff, HI Dept, 1973; Assn of AUS, Exec Com HI Chapt 1966-; Pacific Reg Conserv Ctr, Bd Dirs 1978; Assn of St & Local Hist Socs, 1976; War Mus of Canada; Aloha Coun, BSA; HI Army Mus Soc, Chm Fdg Com 1965, Trustee 1965-; Rotary Clb of W Honolulu, Dir Public Relats 1974 & 1979, Dir Intl Ser 1980; Rotary Intl Dist 500; Honolulu Press Clb, Chm Num Coms; Advrs Clb, Honolulu, 1982; Blue Water Mem, Cook Isl Game Fishing Clb; hon/Legion of Merit, 1970; 4 Awds of Army Commend; Num Campaign Medals; Vietnam Pres Cit; Hon Mem, City Coun Kumagaya, Japan, 1954; Cert of Commen, Gumma Prefectural Govt, Japan 1955, Saitama Prefectural Govt, Japan 1955; OK Col, 1957; AR Traveler, 1962; LA Col, 1963; Hon Citizen of NO, 1964; Listed in Hist of Blakemore Fam in Am; W/W: in W, in Fin & Indust; Personalities of Am; Men of Achmt.

CLANCY, WILLIAM CHARLES oc/Professor of Criminal Justice; b/Oct 11, 1923; h/200-12 34 Avenue, Bayside, NY 11361; ba/New York, NY; m/Grace T McArdle; c/Brian W, William E, Marie T Hamilton, Grace A Fodera, Thomas J; p/Marie E Clancy, Queens, NY; sp/Grace A McArdle, Santa Clara, CA; ed/AAS, CCNY, 1961; BS summa cum laude 1966, MA 1973, John Jay Col of Crim Justice; mil/USAAF, 1943-45; pa/Police Ofcr 1947-55, Sgt 1955-60, Lt 1960-67, NYC Police Dept; Coor, Police Sci Col Prog, Baruch Col, CUNY, 1960-65; Registrar/Dir of Admissions 1965-73, Assoc Prof 1973-, John Jay Col; Vis'g Prof Police Staff Col, Bramshill, England, 1978; Am Acad of Profl Law Enforcement; Acad Crim Justice Sers; Crim Justice Edrs of NY St; cp/John Jay Col Alumni Assn, 1st Pres 1966-67; r/Rom Cath; hon/Author Articles "Does Am Need A Bramshill?" 1979, "Student Attrition" 1980; Six Battle Stars, USAAF; Bronze Plaque Fac Awd, John Jay Student Coun, 1979; Bronze Plaque Awd, Fire Sci Soc, 1973; W/W: in E, in Intells.

CLARE, GEORGE oc/System Safety Engineer; b/Apr 8, 1930; h/817 North Bowen Road, Arlington, TX 76012; ba/Dallas, TX; m/Catherine Saidee Hamel; c/George Christopher; p/George W and Hildegard M Clare (dec); sp/Catherine M Hamel, Arlington, TX; ed/Att'd Univ of TX at Arlington, Univ of So CA, Univ of WA; mil/USN, 1948-63; pa/Enlisted USNR, 1947; Ensign 1951, Naval Aviator 1951, USN 1948-1963; Cmdr 1968, CO of Res Unit 1969, USNR Ready Res 1963-1971; Sys Safety Engr 1963-1980, Sr Sys Safety Engrg Spec 1980-83, Mgr Sys Safety, 1983-, Vought Missiles & Adv'd Prods Div; Assn of Nav Aviation; The Mil Order of the World Wars; The Ret'd Ofcrs Assn; Am Inst of Aeronauts & Astronauts; Sys Safety Soc; Intl Soc Air Safety Investigators; Intl Prod Safety Mgmt; The Am Def Preparedness Assn; Am Security Coun; cp/Repub Nat Com; Nat Repub Senatorial Com; Nat Repub Congl Com; Nat Polit Action Com; Citizens for the Repub; Repub

Party of TX; Tarrant Co Repub Party Assn; NRA; TX Rifle Assn; r/Rom Cath; hon/Cert'd Proj Safety Mgr; Air Medal w Gold Star, 1952; Vought Pres Awd, 1968; W/W in S & SW; Jane's W/W in Aviation & Aerospace.

CLARK, BARBARA oc/Manager of Compensation; b/Sep 18, 1940; h/894 Commonwealth Avenue, Venice, CA 90291; ba/Los Angeles, CA; p/Cyrus L (dec) and Anna G M Clark, Venice, CA; ed/AA, Santa Monica Col, 1960; BA with honors, Univ of CA-LA, 1962; MA, CA St Univ, 1982; p/Compensation Asst 1960-68, Compensation Anal 1968-70, Sys Devel Corp; Compensation Anal 1970-72, Res Admr 1972-74, Mgr of Compensation 1974-, Automobile Clb of So CA; Am Compensation Assn; Nat Assn of Female Execs; cp/CA Inst of Tech Mgmt Discussion Grp; So CA Mormon Choir, 1968-81 & Assoc Accompanist, 1976-81; LA Co Mus of Art Assn; r/Mormon; hon/Author Num Profl Pubs; W/W in W.

CLARK, BRIAN THOMAS oc/Mathematical Statistician; b/Apr 7, 1951; h/5554 Shawnee Drive, Sierra Vista, AZ 85635; ba/Atlanta, GA; p/Paul H and Martha Lou Clark, Cave Creek, AZ; ed/BS cum laude, No AZ Univ, 1973; Postgrad Studies: W Coast Univ 1975-76 & AZ St Univ 1980-82; pa/Math Aide, Phoenix, AZ Ctr for Disease Control, 1979-83; Math Stat, Atlanta, GA Ctr for Disease Control, 1983-; Am Stat Assn; Biometric Soc; r/Luth; hon/Co-Author "The Prev of Hepatitis B w Vaccine;" Ctrs for Disease Control Grp Profl Awd, 1982; W/W in W.

CLARK, CHRISTINE KAY oc/State Regent, OK St DAR; b/Feb 8, 1910; h/309 West Keetoowak, Tahlequah, OK 74464; m/Everett R (dec); c/Charles and Stella Kay (dec); ed/BS, TX N St Univ, 1952; MEd, Univ of NH, 1967; pa/Elem Tchr in TX, PA & NH, 1952-65; Rdg Spec, Oyster River Sch Dist, 1965-71; cp/DAR; Magna Charta Dames; Mayflower Soc; Jamestown Soc; Daughs of 1812; DAC; Colonial Dames of the 17th Cent; N Eng Wom; Indian Territory Hist & Gen Soc; Pres, Local Fed Wom Clb; Pres, Geneal Soc; Pres, UMW; r/Meth.

CLARK, CORNELIA ANNE oc/Lawyer; b/Sep 15, 1950; h/7 Winstead Court, Franklin, TN 37064; ba/Nashville, TN; p/William H and Cornelia E Clark, Franklin, TN; ed/BA 1971, JD 1979, Vanderbilt Univ; MAT, Harvard Univ, 1972; pa/Tchr, Atlanta Public Schs, 1972-73; Tchr, Arlington Schs, 1973-76; Atty, Farris, Warfield, & Kanaday, 1979-; Asst Franklin City Atty, 1979-; cp/V Chm, Williamson Co Dem Party, 1980-; Secy-Treas, Williamson Co Assn of Public Water & Waste Water Sys, 1981-; Pers Com, Nashville YWCA, 1980-; Heritage Foun; Kappa Alpha Theta; CABLE Clb; Williamson Co Vanderbilt Clb; Harvard Clb of Nashville & Mid TN; r/U Meth; hon/Profl Pubs; Nat Merit Scholar, 1968; Pres Scholar, 1968; Mark Scholar, 1978-79; Articles Editor, Vanderbilt Law Review, 1978-79; Phi Delta Kappa, 1971-72; W/W in S & SW.

CLARK, FREDRICH oc/Executive; b/Mar 30, 1944; h/3454 Charity Lane, Toney, AL 35773; ba/Huntsville, AL; c/Kimberly A, Sheri Lyn; p/Bernice Clark, Marmaduke, AR; ed/BSEE, Univ of AR,

1967; MSEE 1970, PhD 1979, Univ of AL-Huntsville; pa/Engrg Mgr, IBM, 1967-79; Owner/Mgr, CAS Inc, 1979-; IEEE; cp/Tau Beta Pi; AUSA; AUC; Eta Kappa Nu; r/Meth; hon/Profl Pubs; W/W.

CLARK, KEITH COLLAR oc/Music Teacher, Principal Trumpeter (Retired); b/Nov 21, 1927; h/8828 Crest Lane, Ft Myers, FL 33907; m/Marjorie Park; c/Nancy Joy Kleppinger, Sandra Lynn Masse, Karen Jean, Beth Anne Barnard; p/Harry H Clark (dec); Mrs Bethyl June Collar Clark, Grand Rapids, MI; sp/Curtis M Park (dec); Mrs Mary Rogers Park, Tampa, FL; ed/Pvt Study: Pattee Evenson, Eastman, 1943; Clifford P Lillya, Univ of MI, 1944-45; Lloyd Geisler, Nat Symph Orch, 1947-48; Armanda Ghitulla, Boston Symph Orch, 1974; mil/AUS, 1946-66; pa/Trumpet, Grand Rapids Symph Orch, 1943-46; Solo Cornetist, AUS Band, Wash DC, 1947-66; Tchr, Wash Bible Col, 1947-53; Tchr, Montgomery Col, MD, 1964-66; Assoc Prof, Houghton Col, NY, 1966-80; Conductor, Houghton Col Symph Orch, 1966-78; Conslt, Dict of Am Hymnology, 1980-81; Mem: VPres 1974-76, Nat Sch Orch Assn; Pres, Nat Ch Music F'ship 1967-69; Trumpet Guild; Life Mem, Hymn Soc of Am; Life Mem, Hymn Soc of Gt Brit & Ireland; Life Mem, Ch Music Soc; Sonneck Soc; Exec Bd, SW FL Symph Bd; Am Symph Orch Leag; r/Bapt; hon/Author of Book: A Selective Bibliog for the Study of Hymns, 1980; Var Articles in Profl Jours incl'g: NSOA Bltn; The Instrumentalist; Jour Intl Trumpet Guild; Selected to Sound "Taps" for Funeral of Pres John F Kennedy, 1963; Soloist, NBC-TV "Today" Prog w Dave Garroway, 1956; Guest Conductor, Buffalo Philharm, 1969; Clark Hymnology Lib, CBN Univ, Virginia Bch, VA; W/W in S & SW; Other Biogl Listings.

CLARK, LARRY DALTON oc/Civil Engineer, Land Surveyor; b/May 12, 1942; h/4224 Spruce Hills Drive, Cedar Falls, IA 50613; ba/Waterloo, IA; m/Janice Martina Kettleson; c/Tamara Dayrie, Laura Janelle, Jennifer Lynette, Daniel Jerod; p/Christina Hittel, Alberta Canada; ed/BS, 1971; pa/Resident Constrn Engr, IA Dept of Trans, 1971-79; Engr, Black Hawk Co, 1979-; Nat Soc of Profl Engrs, Dir; ASCE; Am Cong of Surveying & Mapping; cp/Dir, Sertoma; r/Luth; hon/Am Asphalt Inst Awd, Sigma Tau; W/W: in MW, in Technol.

CLARK, MARK WILLIAM oc/Physical Educator, Sport Sociologist; b/Jul 19, 1945; h/15 September Drive, Missoula, MT 59802; ba/Missoula, MT; m/Reiko Watanabe; c/Midori Kristen, Saori Jane; p/Herbert P and Elsa M Clark, Sacramento, CA; sp/Tokio and Nobuko Watanabe, Toyama, Japan; ed/BA 1973, MA 1976, PE, Univ of CA-Berkeley; PhD Ed, Stanford Univ, 1980; mil/USN, 1964-70; pa/Assoc Prof, Sch of Ed/HPE Dept, Univ of MT-Missoula, 1981-; Asst Prof, PE Dept/Sociol Dept, Hofstra Univ, Hempstead, NY, 1977-81; Instr, Dept Ath, PE & Rec, Stanford Univ, 1977; Mem: Am Alliance for Hlth PE, Rec & Dance; Am Sociol Assn; Am Assn for Leisure & Rec; Intl Soc for Comparative PE & Sport; N Am Soc for the Sociol of Sport; The Assn for the Anthropological Study of Play; Phi

Delta Kappa; No Rocky Mtn Ednl Res Assn; r/Prot; hon/Author, Co-Author & Editor, Num Articles & Book Chapts Pub'd in Profl Jours incl'g: Jour of PE, Rec & Dance; Others; Over 30 Assn Conf Paper Presentations; Cert of Apprec, Am Assn for Leisure & Rec, 1983; W/W in W.

CLARK, MARY ALICE oc/Epilepsy Research Specialist; b/Jan 7, 1946; h/38715 2nd Street East, Palmdale, CA 93550; c/Heather E, Anthea M; p/Reginald and Betty Smith, Canton, NY; ed/RN, Royal Victoria Hosp Sch of Nsg, 1966; EEG Cert, Univ of CA-LA, 1975; BSPA, St Joseph's Col, 1983; Grad Sch, Univ of CA-LA Sch of Public Hlth, 1983-; pa/Staff Nurse, Montreal Neurol Inst, 1966-67; Team Ldr, Hd Nurse, EEG Nurse Spec, UCLA Neuropsychi Inst, Reed Neurol Inst, 1967-78; Epilepsy Nurse Spec, Wadsworth Vets Hosp, 1978-83; Bd Dirs & Prof Advy Bd, CA Epilepsy Soc; APHA; cp/Royal Victoria Hosp Alumnae Assn; U Meth Ch; Antelope Val Commun Concert Assn; Antelope Val Corvette Clb; W Sts Corvette Coun; r/Meth; hon/Pubs; Nat Hon Soc; Spec Perf Awd, 1982; W/W: in W & MW, of Am Wom, of Intells; Personalities of Am; 5000 Personalities of World; DIB; Other Biogl Listings.

CLARK, MERRY MAUREEN oc/Editor, Journalist; h/220 E 54th Street, New York, NY; ba/New York, NY; p/Mrs Mabel M Clark, Austin, TX; ed/BJ, Univ of TX, 1969; MS Communs, Shippensburg Col, 1974; pa/Editor, Sunday Wom Mag, 1982-; Entertainment Editor on Air, WAXY-106 FM, Ft Lauderdale, FL, 1980-81; Assoc Editor, Miami Mag, 1980-81; On Air Personality, Celebrity Editor, "Good Morning," WABC-TV, NYC, 1980; Editor, NY Mag, 1975-78; Gen Assignment Reporter, Harrisburg Patriot News, Harrisburg, PA, 1971, 1972-74; Editor, The Daily Texan, Student Newpaper, Univ of TX, 1968-69; hon/Author of Num Articles in Newpapers & Mags incl'g: Travel & Leisure Mag; Club Living/Holiday; Miami Mag; En Review; Num Others; Pacemaker Awd, The Daily Texan, 1969.

CLARK, RICHARD EDWIN oc/Educator; b/Feb 3, 1934; h/5111 Westbard Avenue, Bethesda, MD 20816; ba/Bethesda, MD; m/Barbara; c/Todd E, Karen L, John U Detjen, Paul F Detjen, C Warren Detjen; p/Edwin M (dec) and Eleanor M Clark, St Louis, MO; sp/Robert L (dec) and Amy Knight, Clayton, MO; ed/BSE, Princeton Univ, 1956; MS, Univ of VA, 1962; MD, Cornell Univ Med Col, 1960; mil/Med Corps, USNR, 1967-68, Lt Cmdr; Cmdr of Med Corps, 1968-69; pa/Asst Prof Mat Sci, Sch of Engrg & Applied Sci 1967-69, Mem Inst Adv Studies 1967-69, Univ of VA; Asst Prof Surg & Biomed Engrg 1969-73, Assoc Prof Surg & Biomed Engrg 1973-76, Prof Surg & Biomed Engrg 1976-83, WA Univ; Chief, Surg Br, Nat Heart, Lung & Blood Inst, NIH, 1983-; Am Assn for Thoracic Surg; Am Col of Cardiol; Am Col of Chest Phys; Am Col of Surgs; Am Heart Assn; AMA; Am Soc for Artificial Internal Organs; Am Surg Assn; Assn for Acad Surg; Assn for the Advmt of Med Instrumentation; Intl Cardiovas Soc; Muller Surg Soc; Soc of Thoracic Surgs; Soc of Univ Surgs; Soc of Vascular Surg; So Surg Assn; So Thoracic Surg Assn;

PERSONALITIES OF AMERICA

Surg Infection Soc; r/Prot; hon/Profl Pubs; Nav Order of Merit, Venezuela; Several Res F'ships.

CLARK, RUTH oc/Executive; b/Oct 16, 1942; h/425 East 58th Street, Sutton Place, NY 10022; ba/New York, NY; p/ William and Pauline Cheek (dec); ed/ Grad, Geo Wash HS; pa/Owner, Fdr & Pres, Clark Unltd Pers-Employmt Agy, 1974-; Mgr Data Processing Dept, Am Express Co, NYC; Keypunch Operator, City of NY; Mem: NY Assn Temp Sers; Nat Assn Temp Sers; Wom Bus Owners of NY; Wom's Forum; Nat Assn of Female Execs; Others; cp/Bd Mem, March of Dimes, 1973-81; The Edges Grp; Num Spkg Presentations; Other Activs; hon/Author of Articles in Var Mags incl'g: *Money Mag; New Wom Mag; Jet Mag; USA Today* Newspaper; *NY Daily News;* Var Appearances on TV Shows; Bus Wom of Yr Awd, Nat Assn of Negro BPW Clbs, 1978; Role Model Awd, New Future Foun, 1979; Pacesetter Awd, New Dawn Ldrship for Wom Assn, 1980; Cecilia C Saunders Awd for Outstg Entrepeneurship, Harlem YWCA, 1982; W/W in Black Am, of Am Wom; Other Biogl Listings.

CLARK, WILLIAM MERLE oc/Baseball Scouting Supervisor; b/Aug 18, 1932; h/3906 Grace Ellen Drive, Columbia, MO 65201; ba/Same; m/Dolores Pearl; c/Patrick Sean, Michael Seamus, Kelly Kathleen, Kerry Maureen, Casey Connor; p/Merle William and Beulah Wilson Clark (dec); ed/BJ, Univ of MO, 1958; mil/AUS, 1951-54, Korea (1 Yr); pa/Baseball Scouting Supvr, Cinc Reds; CoFdr, Nat Corr Rec Assn; AAU Weightlifting Com 20 Yrs; Originated Nat Masters Prog for Lifters 40-Over; Sports Ofcl 28 Yrs; Past Pres, MO Val AAU; MO Sportswriters Assn; Columbia Ofcls Assn; r/Unitarian-Universalist Ch; hon/Editor, *Bluebird,* Pub of Audubon Soc of MO; John Pike Awd for Contbn to Prison Rec; Columbia Bowling Hall of Fame, 1984; MO Val AAU Fed Hall of Fame, 1984.

CLARKE, JOYCE ANNE oc/Scientist; b/Sep 17, 1947; h/955 Via Zapata #11, Riverside, CA 92507; ba/Lawrenceville, VA; m/Frank Ogawa; p/F Clarke, Sheffield, England; sp/Ethel Ogawa (dec); ed/BA, 1968; MA, 1972; PhD, 1974; pa/Res Assoc, Doe Plant Res Lab, 1976-78; Assoc Biochem, Univ of CA, 1979-82; Conslt, Tissue Culture, 1982-84; Asst Prof, Dept of Natural Sci, St Paul's Col, 1984-; Am Soc Plant Physiols, 1976-; cp/Anglo-Am Friendship Clb, Pres 1980-; Brit Film Inst Assn, 1981-; Jojoba Soc of Am, 1983-; r/Ch of England; Epis; hon/Profl Pubs; Phi Beta Kappa Intl S'ship, 1972-73; Sigma Xi, 1973.

CLARKE, KAY K oc/Executive; b/ Nov 22, 1938; h/31 Main Street, Farmington, CT 06032; ba/Hartford, CT; m/Logan; c/Katherine, Christopher; p/ William Horace and Charline Knight, Osceola, MO; sp/Logan and Marion Clarke, Honolulu, HI; ed/AB Eng, Univ of NC-Chapel Hill, 1960; MS Stats 1962, PhD Course Wk Completed, NC St Univ; pa/VPres Mktg & Investmt Prods, Indiv Fin Sers, CIGNA Corp, Hartford, CT, 1982-; VPres Corp Mktg & Communs, CT Gen Life Ins Co, 1979-82; VPres ADL Impact Sers 1978-79, Stat Conslt 1963-67, Arthur D Little Inc, Cambridge, MA; Sr VPres

& Dir of Retail Bkg, Shawmut Bk of Boston MA, 1976-78; Sr VPres & Dir of Mktg, Shawmut Corp, Boston, 1974-78; VPres & Dir Mktg, Nat Shawmut Bk, 1973-74; Owner of Mgmt Conslg Firm, Mazuy Assocs, 1972-73; Dir of Mktg & Bus Planning, Transaction Technol Inc, Subsidiary of Citicorp, 1970-72; Mgr Mktg Planning & Anal 1969-70, Mgr Mktg Res 1968-69, Mktg Res Proj Mgr 1967-68, Polaroid Corp; Lectr, Amos Tuck Grad Sch of Bus Adm, Dartmouth, 1964; Mem: The Hartford Inst of Crim & Social Justice Bd, 1982-; Corp Adv Bd, Hartford Nat Bk & Trust Co, 1980-; Corporator, Hartford Hosp, 1981-; Corporator, Inst of Living, 1981-; Regent, Univ of Hartford, 1982-; Trustee, Hartford Art Sch, Univ of Hartford, 1982-; Trustee, The Aeroflex Foun 1973-; Overseer, Amos Tuck Grad Sch of Bus Adm, Dartmouth, 1979-; Dir, Mgt Compensation & Audit Coms, McGraw-Hill Inc, 1976-; Num Others; cp/Dir, Goodmeasure Inc, 1981-; Dir, Ecec Com, Chp Mktg Com, Gtr Hartford Arts Coun, 1979-; Num Other Civic Activs; hon/Columist, *Am Bkr;* Contbr, Num Profl Jours incl'g: *Harvard Bus Review; US Investor/En Bkr; IEEE Transaction of Elect Computers; Annals of Math Stats;* Others; Num Spkg Presentations, Radio & TV Appearances; Dist'd Alumni Awd, Univ of NC, 1982; Wom '76 Awd for Achmt in Bus, Boston YMCA; Phi Beta Kappa; Phi Kappa Phi; Exec in Residence, Dartmouth Col & Amos Tuck Grad Sch of Bus; Exec in Residence, Wheaton Col; W/W: in Am, in E, of Am Wom, in Fin & Indust; DIB; Other Biogl Listings.

CLAUSI, ENRICO ANTHONY oc/ Major, United States Army; b/Dec 26, 1947; h/HHC 2AD FWD, APO New York 09355; ba/Garlstedt, West Germany; m/Mary Eugenia Stanley; c/ Catherine Marie; p/Mr and Mrs E F Clausi, Chgo, IL; sp/Mr and Mrs T L Stanley, Jr, Alexandria, LA; ed/BA, Loyola Univ, 1970; Num Ofcr Courses, AUS, 1970-79; mil/AUS, 1970-, Major; pa/AUS Exec Ofcr, Ft A P Hill, VA, 1971-72; AUS Adj, 20th Gen Support Grp, Korea, 1972; AUS Cmdr, HHC 20th Support Grp, Korea, 1972-73; AUS Bat Opers Ofcr, Ft Ord, CA, 1973-74; AUS Cmdr for HQ Detachmt, Pers Control Facility, Ft Ord, CA, 1974-75; AUS Logistics/Trans Ofcr, Ft Ord, CA 1975-76; Dir Indust Opers & Acting Insp Gen, US Mil Commun, Bamberg, Germany, 1977-79; Trans Movements/ Mobilization Ofcr Readiness Grp, Redstone, 1980-; Sr Trans Advr, 1983-84; Div Trans Ofcr 2nd Armored Div Forward, 1984; Assn of AUS; Am Def Preparedness Assn; r/Rom Cath; hon/ AUS Pubs; Hon Lt Col, Aide de Camp, St of AL; Hon Col, Aide de Camp, St of FL; Hon Mem TN St Ho of Reps; AUS Meritorious Ser Medal, 1979, 1984; Army Commend Medal, 1976; Nat Def Medal, 1970; Armed Forces Expeditionary Medal, 1972; Army Ser Ribbon, 1981; Army Overseas Ribbon, 1979; Expert Inf, 1975; Army Achmt Medal, 1984; Dir Dist'd Ams; Personalities of S; W/W in S & SW.

CLAXTON, LARRY DAVIS oc/ Genetic Toxicologist; b/Jun 17, 1946; h/ 5121 Huntingdon, Raleigh, NC 27606; ba/Research Triangle Park, NC; m/ Betty Reed; c/Meredith Jill, Matthew

Reed; p/Carl W and Margaret D (dec) Davis, Chattanooga, TN; ed/BS, Mid TN St Univ, 1968; MS, Memphis St Univ, 1971; PhD, NC St Univ, 1980; Att'd Univ of TN Sch of Med; pa/Res Asst Biol Div, Oak Ridge Nat Lab, 1971-72; Biologist, Mutagenesis Br, Nat Inst Envir Hlth Sci, 1972-77; Res Biologist in Genetic Toxicology Div, EPA, 1977-; Adj Asst Prof in Sch of Public Hlth, Univ of NC; Pres, Genotoxicity & Envir Mutagen Soc, 1983-85; Edit Bd Mem, Envir Mutagenesis, 1981-85; Critical Issues Subcom, Envir Mutagen Soc, 1983-84; Task Grp Chm, ASTM, 1983-84; Advr, *Egyptian Jour of Genetics,* 1982-85; AAAS; Genetic Soc of Am; Genetic Toxicology Assn; Soc for Risk Anal; r/Ch of Christ; hon/Num Profl Pubs; EPA Sci & Technol Achmt Awd; EPA Outstg Perf Rating; EPA Bronze Medal; Gamma Beta Phi Hon Soc; Beta Beta Beta Biol Hon Soc; W/ W in Frontier Sci & Technol.

CLAY, MARIA C oc/Director of Training and Development; b/Feb 26, 1950; h/421 Ridgefield Road, Chapel Hill, NC 27514; ba/Chapel Hill, NC; m/ Thomas H; p/Pablo and Concepcion Castillo, Washington, DC; sp/Faye Clay, Greenville, NC; ed/BA, MEd, E Carolina Univ; Pursuing PhD, Org Dev at Univ of NC-Chapel Hill; pa/Asst to VP of Intl Rel, ARC, 1973-75; Tng Cnslt 1976-78, Dir of Tng & Devel 1978-, NC Meml Hosp; Am Soc of Tng & Devel, Chapt Pres 1981, Bd Mem 1978-82, Inst Com 1980-; Chapel Hill C of C, Com Chair, 1980 & 81; DC Yth Coun, 1974-75; AO Univ Advr (E Carolina Univ & NC St Univ) 1975, 1978; r/Cath; hon/Profl Pubs; W/W: in S & SW, in Am Cols & Univs.

CLAYTON, JAMES LEONARD oc/ Electronics Company Executive; b/Mar 8, 1945; ba/Huntsville, AL; m/Judith Terry; c/Gregory James; p/Leonard Clayton, St Petersburg, FL and June Dow, St Petersburg, FL; sp/William O and Ida M Terry, Hartselle, AL; ed/AA, St Petersburg Jr Col, 1965; BSEE, Univ of S FL, 1968; pa/Assoc Engr, Elect Communs Inc, 1966-68; Mgr, Printer Elects, SCI Sys Inc, 1968-77; Fdr & VP 1977-78, Pres 1978-, Phoenix Microsys Inc; r/Prot; hon/W/W in S & SW; Men of Achmt.

CLAYTON, MABEL SORENSEN NOALL oc/Educator; b/Nov 1, 1908; h/ 1646 South 1500 East, Salt Lake City, UT 84105; ba/Same; m/Albert E Noall (dec); 2nd, C Comstock Clayton (dec); c/Ruth Noall Dickson, David W Noall, Roger Noall; p/Soren G Sorensen (dec); ed/AB, Univ of UT, 1929; EdD, Univ of So CA, 1957; EdM, Boston Univ, 1957; pa/Asst Prof Spch & Ednl Psych, Univ of UT, 1947-56; Dir of Sec'dy Rdg Clin, Assoc Prof, Boston Univ, 1957-63; Sr Ednl Conslt, Sci Res Assocs; Curric Devel in Lang Arts & Content Fields, U-SAIL Proj, 1971-77; cp/1st UT Treas, Chapt Pres, AAUW; Bd Mem, Repertory Dance Theater; Bd Mem, Assn of Improvement of Retard Chd; Advr, UT St Assn of Music Clbs; CoChm, Ticket Sales, UT Symph, 1970-71; Hon Tour Sponsor, UT Symph S Am Tour, 1971; Paperback Book Com, NCTE; hon/Var Profl Pubs; Plaque w UT Seal, Awd'd by Gov Rampton for Ser to Arts in UT, 1971.

CLAYTON, WILLIAM HOWARD

148

oc/College President; b/Aug 16, 1927; h/54 Adler Circle, Galveston, TX 77550; ba/Galveston, TX; c/Jill, Greg; ed/BS, Bucknell Univ, 1949; PhD, TX A&M Univ, 1956; mil/Royal Canadian AF, 1940-43; USAF, 1943-45; pa/Pres Moody Col 1977-, Provost Moody Col Marine Scis & Maritime Resource 1974-77, Dean Col Marine & Maritime Resources 1971-74, Assoc Dean Col Geoscis 1970-71; Prof Oceanography 1965-, Prof Meteorology 1965-, Prin Investigator TX A&M Res Foun 1956-65, Num Other Positions & Univ Coms, TX A&M Univ; Other Profl Positions; Mem: Gulf Univs Res Consortium; Trustee, TX A&M Univ Sys, 1971-; Chm, Am Meteorological Soc, 1977-79; Am Geophy Union; Simulation Coun; Sigma Phi Epsilon; Other Frat Orgs; cp/Galveston Marine Affairs Coun; Former Mem Bd of Dirs, Galveston C of C; Bd of Dirs, Bk of W; Commr Police & Fire Dept Civil Ser Bd, City of Galveston; Bd of Dirs, Galveston UF; Other Civic Activs; r/Prot; hon/ Author of Num Pubs; Num Biogl Listings.

CLEARY, DOROTHY C G oc/Computer Analyst; b/Sep 20, 1942; h/D3 Greenbriar Court, Clifton, NJ 07012; ba/Nutley, NJ; p/John G Cleary; Helen J Cleary, Clifton, NJ; ed/BA, Newark St Col, 1973; pa/Mgr, Tech Lib of Mgmt Info Ser, 1973-77; Ed Skill Spec, 1977-81; Records Retention Computer Anal, 1981-; Loan Ofcr, Credit Union, 1973-; VP, Tri-St Info Mgmt Ed, 1978-79; Bd of Dirs, TIME, 1979-; Spec Lib Assn; Am Soc Info Sci; Am Soc Tng and Devel; NJ Computers Tng Grp; Data Processing Libn/Documentation Assn; Assn of Records Mgrs & Admrs; r/Rom Cath; hon/Featured in Article by "Info & Records Mgmt"; W/W of Am Wom; World W/W of Wom; Am Reg Series.

CLEAVER, CLAIRE MARIE oc/Executive; b/Mar 4, 1943; h/174 Popodickon Drive, Boyertown, PA 19512; ba/Same; p/Mr and Mrs Edward Cleaver, Temple, PA; ed/BA, PA St Univ, 1966; Masters Equivalency, PA Dept of Ed, 1973; Dale Carnegie Mgmt Cert, 1980; Grad Studies at Albright Col, Cedar Crest, W Chester Univ, PA St Univ; pa/12th Grade Eng Tchr, Daniel Boone Area HS, 1966-78 (Dept Chm, 1971-76); Sales Rep, Metro Life Ins Co, 1978-79; Dir of Field Devel, Creat Expressions, Div of Caron Int, 1979; Nat Sales Dir, 1980; VP of Sales, Communs & Tng, 1980; Fdr & Pres, CONCEPTS by Claire Inc. 1981-; Nat Assn of Female Execs; Am Mgmt Assn; Berks Co C of C; Direct Selling Assn; AAUW; Nat Alliance of Homebased Bus Wom; Nat Spkrs Assn; PA Jr Miss Inc (Bd of Dirs 1972-80, Pres 1978-79, VP/S'ship 1982); r/Rom Cath; hon/Profl Pubs; Spec Recog Awd, PA Jr Miss Inc, 1976; W/W of Am Wom.

CLEGG, SUE WALL ROBERSON (Jun 4, 1904 to Sep 10, 1984) oc/Former Realtor; h/Formerly of 2800 Woodley Road NW, Washington, DC 20008; m/ Charles M (dec); c/Charles M Jr (dec), Eleanor C Holloway, Myles S; p/John and Florence Roberson (dec); ed/AB, Wom Col, Univ of NC-Greensboro; Grad Study, Georgetown Univ, 1954-56; r/Meth Epis; hon/Correspondent, Reese Reveille Newspaper, 1956-62; W/W of Am Wom; Nat Social

Dir.

CLEMENTS, MICHAEL REID oc/ Engineering Executive; b/Apr 23, 1943; h/95 West Sunset Circle, Rexburg, ID 83440; ba/Rexburg, ID; m/Genay Shumway; c/Tamara, Michelle Genay, Reid Michael, Sean David, Scott Russell, Tiffani Lynn; p/Reed W (dec) and Phyllis Marie Hoopes Clements, Rexburg, ID; sp/Ross and Ilene L Shumway, Mesa, AZ; ed/AA, Ricks Col, 1965; BES, Brigham Yg Univ, 1968; Postgrad, Stanford Univ, 1968-69; pa/Engr, IBM, 1968-69; Sr Engr, Multi-Access Sys Corp, 1969-70; Mgr Sys Devel, Amdahl Corp, 1970-75; Mgr, Elect Design & Data Sys, 1975-77; Dir Computer Devel 1977-78, Corp VP Engrg 1978-82, Chief Tech Ofcr & Corp VP Adv'd Devel 1982-, Amdahl Corp; IEEE; Am Mgmt Assn; Tau Beta Pi; r/Ch of Jesus Christ of LDS; hon/Profl Pubs; Holder of 6 Patents for Computer Design; W/W in W.

CLEVELAND, PEGGY RICHEY oc/ Cytotechnologist; b/Dec 9, 1929; h/ Route 1, Box 393, Lanesville, IN 47136; ba/Louisville, KY; m/Peter L (dec); c/ Pamela C Litch, Paula C Bertloff, Peter L Jr; p/C F "Pat" (dec) and Alice Richey, Tampa, FL; sp/Paul L and Frances (dec) Cleveland, L'ville, KY; ed/Cert in Cytotechnol, Univ of L'ville & Univ of TN, 1956; Reg CT, Am Soc Clin Pathols, 1959; Reg CT, Intl Acad of Cytology, 1972; BHlthSci Cytotechnol, Univ of L'ville, 1983; pa/Cytotechnol, Cancer Survey Proj, Field Invest Res Br NIH, 1956-59; Cytotechnol Supvr, Parker⋅ Cytology Lab, 1959-75; Mgr, Cytology Lab, Am Biomed Lab, 1976-78; Mgr, Cytology Dept, Nat Hlth Lab, Inc, 1978-; Am Soc of Clin Pathols; Am Soc of Cytology; Intl Acad of Cytology; Univ of L'ville Cytotechnol Advy Com; Clin Instr, Cytotechnol, 1960-; Grp Facilitator, Mgmt Sem, 1983; cp/Horsemans Benevolent & Protective Assn; r/Cath; hon/Nat Hon Soc, 1946; Am Cancer Soc Awd, 1968; World's W/W of Wom; W/ W of Am Wom.

CLEVELAND, WILLIAM T oc/Educator and Union Leader; b/Apr 6, 1946; h/290 State Street, Albany, NY 12210; ba/Delmar, NY; p/Francis Err (dec) and Viola Clara H Cleveland, Watkins Glen, NY; ed/BA 1968, MA, St Univ of NY-Albany; Postgrad Studies, Univ of VA & Claremont Grad Sch; pa/Tchr Assoc, Social Sci Ed Consortium, 1979-80; Social Studies Tchr, Bethlehem Ctl HS, 1968-79, 1980-; NEA (Dir 1976-78, 1981-85; Rep Assem 1973-85); NEA/NY (Dir 1976-79, 1981-85); Bethlehem Ctl Tchrs Assn (Pres 1973-84); Nat Coun Social Studies (Dir 1979-81, House of Dels 1972-81, Chm Carter Woodson Awd Com, 1979-82); NY St Coun for Social Studies (Pres 1978-79); Assn Curric & Supvn Devel; Nat Indian Ed Assn; cp/Dem Com-man, Albany Co, 1975-78; Chm, Guilderland Dem Com, 1976-78; r/Presby; hon/NEH Fellow, 1976-78; Phi Delta Kappa; W/W in E; Commun Ldrs of World.

CLIFFORD, CLARK M oc/Sr Partner, Attorney; b/Dec 15, 1906; h/ 9421 Rockville Pike, Bethesda, MD 20814; ba/Washington, DC; m/Margery Pepperell Kimball; c/Margery Pepperell (Mrs William H Lanagan Jr), Joyce Carter (Mrs Granville A Burland), Randall (Mrs Edward I Wight); p/Frank

Andrew and Georgia (McAdams) Clifford; ed/LLB, Wash Univ-St Louis, 1928; mil/USNR, 1944-46, Capt; Nav Aid to Pres of US, 1946; pa/Assoc, Holland, Lashly & Donnell, St Louis, MO, 1928-33; Ptnr, Holland, Lashly & Lashly, 1933-37; Ptnr, Lashly, Lashly, Miller & Clifford, 1938-43; Spec Coun to Pres of US, 1946-50; Sr Ptnr, Clifford & Miller, Wash DC, 1950-68; Secy of Def, Wash DC, 1968-69; Sr Ptnr, Clifford & Warnke (& Predecessor), Wash DC, 1969-; Mem: Dir, Knight-Ridder Newspapers Inc; Chm of Bd & Dir, 1st Am Bkshares Inc; c/St Louis Racquet Clb; Burning Tree; Metro; Chevy Chase Clbs (Wash DC); hon/ Recip, Medal of Freedom.

CLIFFORD, MARGARET LOUISE oc/Coordinator of Elderly Services; b/ Dec 13, 1920; h/223 North Central Street, Winter Garden, FL 32787; ba/ Orlando, FL; c/Daniel Thomas Davis, Kelly Owen Davis; p/Thomas Saxon and Beatrice Clifford (dec); ed/AB, Chapman Col, 1946-50; MS, San Diego St Univ, 1969-72; PhD, Union Grad Sch, 1975-76; mil/USN, 1943-45, RM2/c; pa/ USN WAVES Radioman 2nd Class, Communs Dept, Nav Air Sta, St Louis MO, 1943-45; Elem Sch Tchr: Hanford, Cuyama, Blythe & LaMesa-Sprg Val, CA, 1950-68; Columnist, Daily Midway Driller, Taft, CA, 1955; Owner/Operator, Marge Davis Sch of Dance, Blythe, CA, 1961-64; Coun, Fam Sers Assn, San Diego, CA, 1971-72; Dir Child Guid Clin, Psychol Belleview Psychi Hosp, Dance Instr Jamaica Public Schs, US Peace Corps, Kingston, Jamaica, W Indies, 1973-76; Psychol, Apalachee Commun Mtl Hlth Sers, Quincy, FL, 1977-80; Coor Elderly Sers, Beth Johnson Commun Mtl Hlth Ctr, Orlando, FL, 1980-; Mem: Am Psychol Assn, 1980-; FL Coun on Aging, 1980-; Am Assn of Ret'd Persons, 1980-; Am Pers & Guid Assn, 1980-82; Mem & Var Positions, FL Coun for Commun Mtl Hlth, 1977-; Nat Tchrs Assn, 1950-55; CA Tchrs Assn, 1950-55; BPW Clb, Blythe, CA, 1963-64; Others; cp/Pres, Chapman Col Rec Assn, Orange, CA, 1948-49; Mem 1958-65, Pres 1962-64, Wom's Soc for Christian Ser, Meth Ch, Blythe, CA; Orgr & Pres Exec Bd, Widowed Person Ser of Orange Col, FL, 1981-; Adv Bd 1981-, Secy 1982, Orange Co Citizen's Coun on Aging; Adv Bd for Wellness Prog, Valencia Commun Col, Orlando FL, 1980-81; Other Civic Activs; r/Prot; hon/Author, "A Study of the Use of Bender Gestalt Visual Motor Test & Draw-a-Person Test w Jamaican Chd," & "Fam Life of the Wking Class Jamaican," 1977; 14 Articles on Aging Pub'd in Var Newspapers & Bltns, 1980-; W/W in S & SW.

CLIFTON, MERRITT ROBIN oc/ Writer, Editor, Publisher, Environmentalist; b/Sep 18, 1953; h/Box 10 Brigham, Quebec, Canada J0E 1J0; ba/ Richford, VT; m/Pamela June Kemp; p/ Jack and Phyllis Clifton, Berkeley, CA; sp/Edward Kemp and Lorna Ham, Brigham, Quebec; ed/BA Creat Writing, San Jose St Univ, 1974; pa/Editor & Pubr, SAMISDAT, Mag & Press, 1973-; Contbg Editor, Small Press Review, 1975-; Correspondent & Contbg Editor, Num Other Mags & Newspapers; Mem: End of The Line; Quebec Press Coun; Tau Delta Phi (Devil's Advocate Emeritus);

Soc for Am Baseball Res; Am Homebrewers Assn; cp/Oxford Area Baseball Assn; Brome Lake Runners' Assn; hon/ Author: Novels: *24 X 12*; *A Baseball Classic*; *Betrayal*; Non-Fiction: *Freedom Comes From Human Beings*; *Disorg'd Baseball*; *On Small Press As Class Struggle*; *Lrng Disabilities: What The Publicity Doesn/t Tell*; 4 Others; Poetry: *Live Free Or Die!*; *From An Age of Cars*; *Vindictment*; *From The Golan Hgts*; Num Other Chapbooks, Pamphlets & Wks in Var Small Presses & Mags; Editor of Bibliog, *Those Who Were There: Writings By Vietnam Veterans About The War*, 1984; Story-of-Yr Selection, Centre for Investigative Jour, 1980; Cit for Dist'd Envir Coverage, Alternative Media Conf, 1981; Story-of-Yr Hon Mention, Assn Quebec Reg Eng Media, 1983; Others; W/W: in Am Cols & Univs, in Poetry; Dir of Editors & Pubrs; Other Biogl Listings.

CLINARD, HELEN HALL oc/Consultant, Trainer, Author; b/Mar 9, 1931; h/3290 High Cliffs Road, Pfafftown, NC 27040; ba/Same; m/David Elwood Clinard; c/Julia Shelton, William Wake Shelton, Perri Hall Shelton, Ann Cooper; p/John Perry and Daisy Hall, Oxford, NC; sp/David Elwood and Ella Clinard, Winston-Salem, NC; ed/BFA, Univ of NC-Greensboro, 1953; Postgrad Study, Wake Forest Univ; pa/Exec Dir, Effectiveness Tng & Consltg, 1976-; Conslt, Num Bus Corps, Govt, Profl & Civic Orgs, Pvt Indivs; Past Sr Instr, Effectiveness Tng Inc, CA; Mem: Pres Piedmont Chapt, Am Soc for Tng & Devel (ASTD), 1979; Nat Chp, Profl Human Resource Devel Conslts Spec Interest Grp of ASTD, 1979; Reg IV Coor of Intl Div, ASTD, 1981; Pres, Assn for Benefit of Child Devel, Winston-Salem, NC, 1970-76; cp/Num Spkg Presentations; r/Epis; hon/Author of Book, *Succeeding W People*, 1984; Author of Tng Manual, *Mng Effective Relat'ship*; Author of Articles Pub'd in *Brit Assn for Comml & Industl Ed Jour*, 1978; Other Articles on Interpersonal Skills Tng in *Tng & Devel Jour*, 1981; Intl Tnr of Yr Awd, Intl Div of Am Soc for Tng & Devel, 1981; W/W in S & SW.

CLINE, RAY STEINER oc/Educator, Writer; b/Jun 4, 1918; h/3027 North Pollard Street, Arlington, VA 22207; ba/ Washington, DC; m/Marjorie Wilson; c/ Judith M Fontaine, Sibyl W Halper; p/ Charles and Ina May Steiner Cline (dec); ed/AB, 1939, MA 1941, PhD 1949, Harvard Univ; pa/Govt Res: OSS 1942-45, AUS 1946-49; Dept Dir for Intell 1962-66, CIA, 1949-69; Dir Intell & Res, St Dept, 1969-72; Adj Prof & Subst Sr Assoc Strategic & Intl Studies, Georgetown Univ; r/Prot; hon/Author, Num Wks & Articles incl'g: *World Power Trends & US Fgn Policy for the 1980's*, 1980; *The CIA: Reality is Myth*, 1982; Dist'd Intell Medal & Career Intell Medal, US Govt.

CLINTON, JANET oc/Magician; b/ Jan 30, 1939; h/Hollybriar Point, Norfolk, VA 23518; ba/Same; m/Richard A Goldbach; c/Kristen R Goldbach, Richard C Goldbach; p/Francis W and Ruth A Clinton, Norfolk, VA; ed/BA magna cum laude, Tufts Univ; pa/Magic Perf on TV, 1947; Offered 2 Wkly TV Series, 1949; 1st Lady Invited to Perf on Stage of Magic Cir of London, 1958; Fdr, Chd's Entertainment Bur, 1975; Magical Conslt, C Terry Clines "Switch-

witch", 1976; Soc of Am Magicians, 1967-; Intl Brotherhood of Magicians, 1966- (VP of VA 1979-80, Pres 1980-81); Life Mem, Profl Entertainers of NY, 1972-; Magigals Intl; Magicians Alliance of En St; Clowns of Am Inc; Chgo Round Table of Magicians; r/Prot; hon/Subject of Several Articles; Profl Pub; 1st Prize in 2 Intl Magic Conv Contests; "Stage Magician of the Yr," VA Intl Brotherhood of Magicians, 1980-81; Blue Book of NY.

CLOUDT, FLORENCE RICKER oc/ President and General Manager; b/Jul 12, 1925; ba/Atlanta, GA; c/Norman Sandford Pottinger, Margaret Halliday Pottinger Bromley; p/Norman Hurd Ricker (dec); Sallie Lee Ricker, Newton Square, PA; ed/BFA, Sophie Newcomb Col, 1946; Courses in Chd Ed, Univ of MD, 1956-58; pa/Tchr, Kgn, Montgomery Co Sch Sys, MD, 1956-60; Tchr, Nat Cathedral Sch, Wash DC, 1960-62; Fdr 1963, Mgr 1963-78, Florence Pottinger Interiors; VP 1970-78, Pres 1978-, Focal Point Inc, Atlanta, GA; cp/ Nat Trust for Hist Presv; Victorian Soc of Am; Hist House Assn of Am; Atlanta Hist Soc; Bd Dirs, Atlanta Presv Ctr Ways & Means Com; Trustee, Atlanta Landmarks; Dir Public Relats, Theater Atlanta, 1966; Past Pres, Yg Matron's Cir, Tallulah Falls Sch, 1951-52; Bd Dir, Charlotte, NC Jr Leag, 1953-55; Wom Bus Owners (Bd Dir, 1983); Sustainer & Advr, Atlanta Jr Leag, 1983; hon/ Wrote & Prod'd Awd-Winning Monthly TV Show in Wash DC; Selected by *Atlanta Mag* as One of 100 Contemp Atlantans Whose Influence was Being Felt & More was Expected, 1977; Atlanta Presv Ctr Outstg Ser Awd, 1983; W/W: Among Students in Am Univs & Cols, in S & SW; Personalities of S.

CLOUGH, SUSAN S oc/Executive Assistant, Secretary; b/Mar 11, 1945; h/ 2440 Virginia Avenue, Apartment D-805, Northwest, Washington, DC 20037; ba/Rosslyn, VA; c/Carol Ann, Douglas Michael; p/Arthur and Mary Sebesta, Haworth, NJ; ed/Att'd Fresno City Col, 1963; pa/Spec Asst to Pres, Secy, Galler Automation Industs, Rosslyn, VA, 1982-; Personal Asst & Secy to Pres (Jimmy Carter) of US, The White House, Wash DC, 1977-81; Asst News Secy, Gov George Busbee, Atlanta, GA, 1976; Asst to News Secy, Gov Jimmy Carter, Atlanta, GA, 1971-76; Legal Secy to Sr Ptnr Specializing in Fed Tax Law, Sutherland, Asbill & Brennan, Atlanta, GA, 1968-71; Secy, US Civil Ser, Ft Bragg, NC, 1965-68; Mem: Mensa, 1970; cp/Atlanta Ski Clb, 1969-72; r/Epis; hon/Secy of Yr, Manpower, 1970; Outstg Yg Wom, 1978; Commend for Outstg Perf, US Spec Warfare Ctr & Sch, Ft Bragg, 1966-67; W/W: in Am, of Am Wom, in Govt.

COASH, JEAN H oc/Contracting Officer Technical Representative; b/ Aug 29, 1923; h/1285 South Milwaukee, Denver, CO 80210; ba/Denver, CO; p/ Colonel and Helen R Coash (dec); ed/ BSBA, Univ of Denver, 1955; mil/USN, 1944-47; pa/Internal Auditor 1979-80, Info Sys Devel Mgr 1975-79, WI Power & Light; Proj Sys Anal, Blue Cross Blue Shield of Kansas City, 1972-75; Proj Sys Anal, McDonald Douglas, 1966-72; Sys Anal, Def Indust Supply, 1963-66; Data Processing Mgr, AF Acct'g Fin, 1952-62;

Vet Adm, 1947-52; Contracting Ofcr Tech Rep; VP, DPMA, 1952-75; Dir, ASM, 1970-75; V Chm, TIMS/ORSA, 1975-80; EDP Auditors, 1979-80; cp/ VP, Rocky Tops Square Dance Clb, 1980-81; hon/Monthly Articles, DPMA and ASM; DPMA 5 Yr Outstg Contbn Spec Awd, 1972; ASM Chm of the Yr, 1975.

COATES, DONALD R oc/Professor; b/Jul 23, 1922; h/Box 268A, RD #3, Endicott, NY 13760; ba/Binghamton; m/ Jeanne G; c/Cheryl D Erickson, D Eric, Lark J Williams; p/Frank Jefferson and Harriet Evelyn (Ferriso) Coates (dec); sp/Wilbur Grandison (dec); ed/BA, Col of Wooster, 1944; MA 1948, PhD 1956, Columbia Univ; mil/USN, 1943-46; pa/ Asst Prof & Chm Dept Geol, Earlham Col, Richmond, IN, 1948-51; Proj Chief, US Geol Survey, Tucson, AZ, 1951-54; Prof Dept Geol 1954-, Chm Dept Geol 1954-63, SUNY-Binghamton; Mem: Pres, NT St Geol Asn, 1962-63, & 1981-82; Enri Mgmt Coun of Broome Co, 1975-77; r/Meth; hon/Author or Editor: *Envir Geomorphology & Landscape Conserv (Volumes I, II & III)*, 1972-74; *Glacial Geomorphology*, 1974; *Coastal Geomorphology*, 1972; *Urban Geomorphology*, 1976; *Geomorphology & Engrg*, 1976; *Thresholds in Geomorphology*, 1980; *Envir Geol*, 1981; Sustained Superior Perf Awd, NSF, 1964; Ralph Digman Awd for Best Tchr, Nat Assn of Geol Tchrs, 1972; Am Men & Wom of Sci; Ldrs in Am Sci; W/W: in E, in Ed; DIB.

COBAUGH, STEPHEN MARCUS oc/Art Director/Account Executive; b/ Nov 6, 1955; h/746 Turnpike Road, Elizabethtown, PA 17022; ba/Harrisburg, PA; p/Charles M and Shirley A Cobaugh, Elizabethtown, PA; ed/BA, Millersville Univ, 1977; MA, IN Univ of PA, 1979; pa/Asst Res Anal, Senator Richard A Snyder, 1980-82; Art Dir, Senate Repub Communs Ofc, Senate of PA Chm, Elizabethtown Area Repub Com, Repub Com-man, West Donegal Twp, 2nd Dist, 1982-84; Intl Pres, US Space Ed Assn; IBA; Am Topical Assn, Space Unit; Intl Assn of Space Philatelists; Aerospace Ed Assn; Friendship Fire & Hose Co; L-5 Soc; Millersville Univ Alumni Assn; IN Univ of PA Alumni Assn; Aviation/Space Writers Assn; Hellenic Profl Assn of Am; cp/Pres, Iota Beta Sigma; VP, Pi Delta Epsilon; Pres, Col Repubs; Artist, *SNAPPER* Wkly Newspaper; r/Prot; hon/Teen of the Wk Awd, *Lancaster New Era* Newspaper, 1973; Rotary Student of the Mo, Elizabethtown Rotary Clb, 1973; J Warren Bishop Meml Awd for S'ship, Ldrship & Americanism, Elizabethtown JC's, 1973; PA Teen Age Repub of the Mo, 1974; Person Contb'g Most to WMSR Awd, MSC, 1975; WMSR Exec Coun Awd, MU, 1976; WMSR Sta Mgr's Awd, MU, 1976; Mbrship's Choice Awd, US Space Ed Assn, 1976; WIXQ Exec Coun Awd, MU, 1977; Mem of the Yr Awd, US Space Ed Assn, 1977; Mbrship's Choice Awd, US Space Ed Assn, 1977; WIXQ Ser Awd, Highest Communs Awd at MU, 1977; Mbrship's Choice Awd, US Space Ed Assn, 1978; Intl Authors & Writers W/W; Jane's W/W in Aviation & Aerospace; Men of Achmt; DIB; Intl W/W of Intells; 2000 Notable Ams.

COBB, CAROLYN ANN KNOPP oc/Staff Specialist, Data Systems; b/Feb 21, 1950; h/6520 Galewood Court, St

Louis, MO 63129; ba/St Louis, MO; m/ Richard Joseph; c/Richard Joseph Jr; p/ Vincent A Knopp (dec); Margaret E Knopp, St Louis, MO; sp/Joseph W and Sylvia L Cobb, Houston, TX; ed/BA, Harris Tchrs Col, 1973; MA, Webster Col, 1975; pa/Math Tchr, St Louis Public Schs, 1973-74; Programmer, Gen Am Life Ins Co, 1974-75; Programmer, Mercantile Trust Co, NA, 1975-78; Programmer/Anal, MO Pacific RR, 1979-81; Data Base Admr & Asst Staff Mgr 1981-83, Staff Spec Data Sys 1983-, SWn Bell Telephone Co; Assn for Sys Mgmt; Data Processing Mgmt Assn; Charter Mem, Assn for Wom in Computing; cp/St Paul's U Ch of Christ; St Paul's Ath Com-Fin Chm; St Paul's Co-ed Softball Coach; St Paul's Co-ed Volleyball Coach; St Paul's T-Ball Asst Coach; St Paul's Choir; St Paul's Adult F'ship; Grace U Ch of Christ; Yth Grp Ldr; Drop-In Ctr Advr; Data Processing Explorer Post Advr; BSA, Yg Repubs; Kappa Delta Pi; r/U Ch of Christ; hon/ Editor, *Fundamentals of Data Communs & Netwking*, for Netwking Resources Ltd; Ronald Winters Meml S'ship; Adv Bd S'ship; Ldrship Conf; W/W: Among Students in Am Cols & Univs, of Am Wom; 2000 Notable Ams; Other Biogl Listings.

COBB, STEVE oc/Legislator (Democrat), Businessman; b/Dec 5, 1942; ba/ State Capitol, Honolulu, HI 96813; ed/ BA Jour, CA St Univ-LA; mil/AUS, 1966-70; Lt Col, USAR; pa/Bk of HI, 1970-72; Mktg, Loans, Pacific Resources Inc, 1976-; Precnt Pres, St Dem Conv Del, 1972; Elected to St House, 1972; Re-elected to St House, 1974 & 1976; Elected to Senate, 1978; Re-elected to Senate, 1982 & 1984; Elected, Senate Majority Floor Ldr: 1981, 1982, 1983, 1984; cp/Oahu Chapt #3, DAV; Kahala Commun Assn; Waialae Nui Val Commun Assn; Citizens Agnst Noise; 22nd Commun Assn; Advr, Big Brothers; Chm, Consumer Protection & Commerce Com, 1979-84; Vietnam Vets of HI LdrshipProg, 1983-; Vietnam Vets of Am, 1984; hon/Vet of the Yr, Honolulu Kiwanis, 1970; Personalities of W.

COCHRAN, SHIRLEY ANN COOL oc/Ohio Assistant Attorney General; b/ Apr 18, 1953; h/2897 Liberty Bell Lane, Reynoldsburg, OH 43068; ba/Columbus, OH; m/Mitchell S; p/Harry B and Ruth S Cool, Akron, OH; sp/Carl and Rose Cochran, Canton, OH; ed/Dipl, Kenmore HS, 1971; BA 1974, JD 1979, Univ of Akron; oc/Asst Atty Gen, St of OH, 1979-; Atty; Mem: Yg Lwyrs & Crim Law Sects, ABA; Yg Lwyrs Exec Com 1981-, OH Bar Assn; Law & Mtl Disabilities Com Chp 1982-83, Yg Lwyrs Com, Columbus Bar Assn; Delta Theta Phi; Columbus Alumni Senate Ofcr; Univ of Akron Sch of Law Dean's Clb; hon/Outstg Reg Student, Delta Theta Phi; W/W Among Students in Am Univs & Cols; Other Biogl Listings.

COCHRANE, JOHN ALEXANDER oc/Lawyer; b/Mar 29, 1922; ba/St Paul, MN; m/Carolyn Ann; c/John A Jr, Catherine Ann, Elizabeth; p/John and Deborah Cochrane (dec); ed/BSL 1957, LLB 1958, DJ 1958, Wm Mitchell Col of Law; Att'd Oxford Univ & Univ of MN; pa/Marine Engr, Bethlehem Steel Corp, 1943-53; Indust Engr, US Air Conditioning Corp, 1953-55; Pres, Met

Gas Ser Corp, 1955-58; Sr Ptnr, Cochrane & Bresnahan, 1958-; Soc of Nav Arch & Marine Engrs; Delta Theta Phi; Mem Ethics Com 1966-67, Ramsey Co Bar Assn; Chm 1960-61, Mem 1961-67, Admiralty Law Com, MN St Bar Assn; Inter-Am Bar Assn; Pres 1967-69, Crim Cts Bar Assn of MN; Maritime Law Assn of US; Pres 1968-69, MN Trial Lwyrs; Mem, Bd of Dirs 1967-69, Nat Assn of Def Lwyrs in Crim Cases; Am Judicature Soc; r/Prot; hon/Admitted to MN Bar 1958, ICC Bar 1959, US Supr Ct Bar 1963; W/W: in MW, in Am Law.

COCKREL, ROBERT LEE oc/President and Chief Executive Officer; b/Nov 27, 1936; h/PO Box 148, Manchester, TN 37355; ba/Same; m/Carolyn June; c/Vicki D, Angela D, Monica R; p/Floyd M and Opal Cockrel, Metropolis, IL; sp/ E Faye Baker; ed/BS, 1968; mil/USAF; USCGR; pa/Unit Mgr 1971-74, Dist Retail Supvr 1974-78, USS Agri Chem; VP & Gen Mgr, Johnson City Chem Co, 1978-81; Pres & CEO, C & S Trading Co Inc, 1981-; TN Plant Food Ed Assn, 1974-; Past Pres, Mem Bd of Dirs; Rotary Intl, 1981-; U Comml Travelers, 1970-; E TN Intl Comm Clb, 1979-; cp/ Manchester C of C, 1981-; Res Ofcr Assn, 1979-; Masonic Lodge, 1964; CO of USCGR Unit, 1974-; r/Meth; hon/ Agronomy Student Awd, Am Soc of Agronomy, 1967; TPFEA Past Pres Awd, 1981.

COE, BENJAMIN PLAISTED oc/ Executive Director; b/Aug 24, 1930; h/ 314 Paddock Street, Watertown, NY 13601; ba/Watertown, NY; m/Margaret Jane Butler; c/Benjamin B, Elizabeth C, Mary Susan, Margaret Jane; p/Benjamin and Mary Plaisted (Ricker) Coe; sp/ Edward W and Billie M Butler (dec); ed/ AB, Bowdoin Col, 1953; BSCHE, MA Inst of Technol, 1953; pa/Exec Dir, Temp St Comm on Tug Hill 1973-; Exec Dir, VITA (Vols in Tech Assistance Inc), 1965-73; Process Ec Engr, Silicone Prods Dept, Gen Elect Co, 1953-65; Mem: Chm NE NY Sect 1965, AIChE; Am Soc Public Adm; cp/Rotary Clb; Chm Public Ser Div (Campaign 1982, 1983), U Way; Chm Nat & World Com of Haas Fund 1978-81, Vestry Mem, Warden 1981-, Trin Epis Ch; r/Prot; hon/Author, 10 Articles in Var Profl Jours & Pubs incl'g: *NY St Today; Carolina Planning; Planning News; The Technol Review; Chem Engrg;* Others; Phi Beta Kappa; Tau Beta Pi; Sigma Xi; Exec of Yr, Watertown Chapt, Profl Secys Intl, 1978; W/W: in Am, in World.

COFFEY, JOHN WILLIAM II oc/ Museum Curator; b/Mar 12, 1954; h/ 3264 Mawuoit Road, Brunswick, ME 04011; ba/Brunswick, ME; p/Mr and Mrs John N Coffey Jr, Raleigh, NC; ed/ BA, Univ of NC-Chapel Hill, 1976; MA, Wms Col, 1978; pa/Asst to Dir 1978-79, Acting Dir & Instr in Art 1979-80, Wms Col; Curator of Collections, Bowdoin Col Mus of Art, 1980-; Mem: N Eng Mus Assn; Visual Arts Adv Panel, ME St Comm on Arts & the Humanities; VPres, Bd of Trustees, ME Fest of the Arts; hon/Compiler of 2 Exhibn Catalogues: *4 Artists: James Biederman, Paul Maddrell, Livio Saganic*, Bowdoin Col Mus of Art, 1982; *Am Posters of WW I*, Wms Col Mus of Art, 1978; Phi Beta Kappa, 1976.

COFFEY, MARVIN DALE oc/Educator; b/Apr 25, 1930; h/1018 Clay Street,

Ashland, OR 97520; ba/Ashland, OR; m/Wanda Kirchgestner; c/Susan, Gregory, Lorilee, Mark, Todd; p/Raymond and Agnes Coffey (dec); sp/Philip Kirchgestner, Hermiston, OR; ed/AB 1952, MA 1953, Brigham Yg Univ; PhD, WA St Univ, 1957; Att'd Whitman Col; pa/Instr 1957, Asst Prof 1959, Assoc Prof 1963, Chm Biol Dept 1965-70, Prof Biol 1967-, So OR St Col; Asst Prof, Fresno St Col, 1964-65; Vis'g Prof Entomology: WA St Univ; Brigham Yg Univ; TX A&M Univ; Univ of KY; Registry of Profl Entomologists, Exam'g Bd, 1980-83; cp/Jackson Co Vector Control Dist Bd of Dirs; r/LDS; hon/ Profl Pubs; Beta Beta Beta, 1950; Sigma Xi (Assoc 1953, Full 1956); W/W in W.

COHEN, ALAN SEYMOUR oc/Physician, Rheumatologist; b/Apr 9, 1926; h/54 Winston Road, Newton Centre, MA 02159; ba/Boston, MA; m/Joan Elizabeth Prince; c/Evan Bruce, Andrew Hollis, Robert Adam; p/George I Cohen, Newton Centre, MA; Jennie Cohen (dec); sp/William Prince; Anne Prince (dec); ed/AB, Harvard Univ, 1947; MD, Boston Sch of Med, 1952; mil/USPHS, 1933-55, Asst Surg to Sr Asst Surg, Chronic Disease Div Diabetes Field Res & Tng Unit; pa/Hd Arthritis & Connective Tissue Disease Sect, Evans Dept of Clin Res, Boston Univ Hosp, 1960-; Conrad Wesselhoeft Prof of Med 1972-, Prof Pharm 1974-, Boston U Sch of Med; Chief of Med & Thorndike Meml Lab, Boston City Hosp, 1960-; Dir Arthritis Ctr, Boston Univ, 1977-; Mem: Pres, Am Rheumatism Assn, 1978-79; Bd of Trustees, Arthritis Foun 1976-82; Bd of Trustees 1966-, Pres 1981 & 1982, MA Chapt Arthritis Foun; Gen Med Study Sec, NIAMDD, NIH, 1972-76; Chm Spec Projs Review Grp A, NIADDK, NIH, 1982-84; Past Pres, N Eng Rheumatism Soc, 1966-67; Assn of Am Phys; Phi Beta Kappa; Alpha Omega Alpha; Am Soc for Clin Invest; Harvard Clb of Boston; r/Jewish; hon/ Author of 7 Books incl'g: *Progress in Rheumatology*, Volume I, 1983; *Med Emers: Diagnostic & Mgmt Procedures from Boston City Hosp*, 2nd Edition, 1983; *The Sci & Pract of Clin Med Rheumatology & Immunol*, Volume 4, 1979; Others; Author, Over 400 Articles in Profl Med & Sci Jours; Contbr to 45 Med Sci Books; Gen Alumni Awd for Spec Distn (Silver Medal) 1981, Outstg Alumnus Awd Sch of Med 1975, Boston Univ; Hon Lifetime Mem, Irish Soc of Rheumatology & Rehab, 1981; James H Fairclough Jr, Meml Awd for Distd Ser to MA Chapt of Arthritis Foun, 1981; Hon Mem, Finnish Rheumatism Soc, 1980; The Purdue Frederick Arthritis Awd, 1979; Hon Mem: Brazilian Rheumatism Assn 1978; Spanish Rheumatism Soc 1978; Italian Rheumatism Soc 1977; Num Other Awds; W/W: in Am, in World Med, in Am Jewry, in Technol; Am Men of Sci; Contemp Authors; The Best Docts in US; DIB; Other Biogl Listings.

COHEN, ANITA oc/Attorney; b/Dec 4, 1945; h/4024 Woodruff Avenue, Lafayette Hill, PA 19444; ba/Philadelphia, PA; p/Dr Rosalie A Cohen, Lafayette Hill, PA; ed/BA, Univ of Pgh, 1967; JD, Duquesne Univ, 1970; PA Supr Ct Admission, 1971, PA Superior Ct, 1970; Wn Dist of PA Fed Ct, 1970; Wn Dist, 1978; Legal Ed Courses; pa/ Monitor, Dynamic Broadcasting Sys,

1969-70; Clk in Atty Ofc of Public Def, Allegheny Co, PA, 1969-71; Trial Atty Ofc of DA, Phila Co, 1971-78; Atty, Gen Pract, 1978-; Ser to Ct as Master in Divorce Hearings & Arbitrator for Small Claim Cases; ABA, 1970-; PA Bar Assn, 1970-, Legal Ethics & Profl Responsibility Com, 1984-85; Am Judic Soc, 1973-; Nat DA's Assn, 1971-; cp/ Bd Mem 1980-, Reg Del 1981, Mem Public Affairs Com 1980-, Mem Fin Com 1980, Planned Parenthood of SEn PA; Bd Mem, Girls Coalition of SEn PA, 1980-81; Shomrin and FOP, 1975-; r/ Jewish; hon/Profl Pubs; Nat DA's Assn Cert of Achmt, 4th Nat Inst Narcotics & Dangerous Drugs, 1972; Del of DA Ofc, Nat DA's Assn Nat Conv, 1973; 1969 Qtr Finalist, Appellate Moot Ct; 1970 Semi-Finalist Trial Moot Ct; W/ W Am Law; Dir of Dist'd Ams; Intl Bk of Hon; Commun Ldrs of Am; 2000 Notable Ams.

COHEN, DAVID E oc/Associate Publisher; b/Nov 17, 1950; h/4133 Clayton Avenue, Los Angeles, CA 90027; ba/Los Angeles, CA; m/Barbara Elia; c/Daniel Elia, Dustin Elia; p/Mr and Mrs Philip J Cohen, Longmeadow, MA; sp/Mr and Mrs Albert Elia, Plantation, FL; ed/BA, Windham Col, 1971; Grad Studies, Inst For Comparative Studies of Hist, Phil & Sci; pa/Advt'g Mgr, Advocate Newspapers of N Eng, 1976-79; Assoc Publisher, LA Wkly Newspaper, 1979-; VPres, Hlth Incentives Intl, Vitamin Co, 1982-; Mem, Legis Com, Advt'g Clb of LA; hon/Publisher, LA Wkly 1984 Olympics Visitors Guide; W/ W in W.

COHEN, EDWARD oc/Construction Engineer; b/Jan 6, 1921; h/56 Chestnut Hill, Roslyn, NY 11576; ba/ New York NY; m/1st, Elizabeth Belle (dec); 2nd, Carol Suzanne Kalb; c/ Samuel, Libby, James; p/Samuel and Ida (Tanewitz) Cohen; ed/BS Engrg 1946, MS Civil Engrg 1954, Columbia Univ; pa/Asst Engr, Dept Public Wks, E Hartford, CT, 1942-44; Structural Engr, Hardesty & Hanover NYC, 1945-47 & Sanderson & Porter NYC, 1947-49; Lectr, Arch, Columbia Univ, 1948-51; Positions w Amman & Whitney Constrn Engrs, 1949-; Ptnr 1963-74, Sr Ptnr 1974-77, Mng Ptnr 1977-, VPres in Charge Bldg, Trans, Communs, Mil & Planning Projs, Ammann & Whitney Inc 1963-76, Exec VPres 1976-78, Chm & Chief Exec Ofcr 1978-, VPres Ammann & Whitney Intl Ltd 1963-73; Pres, Safeguard Constrn Mgmt Corp, 1973-; Conslt: Rand Corp, Santa Monica, 1958-72; Dept of Def, 1962-63; Hudson Inst, Croton-on-Hudson, NY, 1967-71; The World Bk; Stanton Walker Lectr, Univ of MD, 1973; Deptl Adv Com, Urban & Civil Engrg, Univ of PA, 1974-; Mem Engrg Coun, Columbia Univ, 1975-; Fellow, Chm Com Long Term Observations 1972-76, VPres Met Sect 1978-79, Pres Elect 1979, Pres 1980, Chm Reinforced Concrete Res Coun 1980-, ASCE; Am Constrn Engrs Coun; Hon Life Mem, Chm Engrg Sect 1977-79, NY Acad of Scis; Hon Mem, Dir 1966-74, VPres 1970-72, Pres 1972-73, Chm on Bldg Code Requirements for Reinforced Concrete 1963-71, Am Constrn Inst; Bridge & Turnpike Assn; Nat Acad Engrg; Am Soc Planning Ofcls; Am Welding Soc; Chm Con Bldg Require-

ments for Design Loads 1968-, Am Nat Standards Inst; Pres Tall Bldgs Coun 1971-, NY Concrete Constrn Inst; Bldg Code Adv Com, NY Assn Constrn Engrs; Dir 1976-, Pres 1978-79, Concrete Indust Bd, NYC; European Concrete Com; Dir 1974-75, Engrs Clb NY; Moles; Sigma Xi; Chi Epsilon; Tau Beta Pi; cp/B'nai B'rith; Mem, Bklyn Bridge Cent Comm; Bd Dirs, Cejwin Yth Camps; Trustee, Hall of Sci, NYC, 1976-; r/Jewish; hon/Editor, Handbook of Structural Concrete; Contbr to Profl Manuals & of Num Articles in Profl Jours; Mem Adv Bd, Jour Resource Mgmt & Tech, 1982-; Recip, Egleston Medal, Columbia Univ, 1981; Spec Advr, The NY St Statue of Liberty Cent Comm; Ernest Howard Awd, ASCE, 1983; Delmar Bloem Awd 1973, Wason Medal 1956, Am Concrete Inst; Laskowitz Aerospace Res Medal, NY Acad of Scis, 1970; Illig Medal Applied Sci, Columbia Univ, 1946; Patriotic Civilian Ser Awd, Dept of Army, 1973; Reg'd Profl Engr in 12 Sts; W/W in Fin & Indust.

COHEN, JAMES SAMUEL oc/Physicist; b/Jul 29, 1946; h/330 Valle del Sol, Los Alamos, NM 87544; ba/Los Alamos, NM; m/Marion Fay; c/Stephen James, Christy Lynn; p/Herman and Jimmie Ruth Cohen, Houston, TX; sp/Waldon E and Alice Daniel, Houston, TX; ed/ BA 1968, MA 1970, PhD 1973, Rice Univ; pa/Staff Mem, Los Alamos Nat Lab, 1972-; Vis'g Assoc Prof, Rice Univ, 1979-80; Am Phy Soc, 1971-; cp/Phi Beta Kappa, 1964-; Sigma Xi, 1967-; r/ Prot; hon/Num Pubs in The Phy Review & Other Physics Jours; H A Wilson Prize in Physics, Rice Univ, 1973; Am Men & Wom Sci; W/W in Frontier Sci & Technol.

COHEN, JOEL RALPH oc/Professor; b/Oct 20, 1926; h/14 Inglewood Avenue, Springfield, MA 01109; ba/Springfield, MA; m/Marilyn Roberts Lezar; c/Robert Neil, Deborah Ellen C Winer, Peter Alan; p/Meyer and Pearl (Mankin) Cohen (dec); sp/Arthur Lezar, Hallandale, FL; ed/BS Bacteriology 1949, MS Chem & Bacteriology 1950, PhD Plant Sci 1975, Univ of MA; mil/MSC-USAR, Active & Resv, 1943-80, Col; pa/Microbiol & Chief Clin Labs, Bay-st Med Ctr, Springfield, MA, 1950-68; Assoc Prof to Prof Biosci, Prof Biol & Hlth Scis, Springfield Col, 1968-; Conslt, VA Med Ctr, Northampton, MA, 1963-; Conslt, Mun Hosp, Springfield, 1980-; Mem: Am Soc for Microbiol, 1949; NY Acad of Scis, 1960-; Am Assn Blood Bks, 1956-; Mem 1949-, Pres 1960-61, Exec Com 1982-, CT Val ASM; cp/Corp Pioneer Val U Fund, 1968-77; Trustee 1962-, VPres 1980-, Sinai Temple, Sprgfield, MA; r/Jewish; hon/Author of Lab Manual; Over 41 Articles Pub'd in Profl Sci Jours & Assn Presentations; Sigma Xi, 1948; Phi Kappa Phi, 1948; Fellow, APHA, 1957; AAAS, 1959; Royal Soc of Hlth, 1965; Am Acad of Microbiol, 1978; Outstg Edr of Am, 1974; W/W in E; Am Men & Wom of Sci; Other Biogl Listings.

COHEN, JOSEPH ARTHUR oc/Lawyer; b/Feb 28, 1928; h/Route 31, RD #2, West Hebron, NY 12865; ba/New York, NY; m/Janice C; c/Susan Lee, Jonathan Andrew, Nancy Elizabeth; p/Benjamin (dec) and Frieda Cohen, New York, NY; ed/BBA, City Col of NY, 1949; LLB, Columbia Univ, 1952; LLM, NY Univ

1958; mil/AUS, 1946-47, Crim Invest Dept; pa/Atty, Armed Forces Textile & Apparel Procurement Agcy, 1952-54; Assoc Atty, Alexander & Ash, 1954-63; Ptnr, Alexander, Ash, Schwartz & Cohen, 1963-; ABA; The Bar Assn of NYC; Maritime Law Assn; NY St Bar Assn; Def Res Inst; Am Trial Lwyrs Assn; St Magistrates Assn; cp/Town Judge, Scarsdale, NY, 1978-83; Scarsdale Aux Police, 1971-78; Merchs Clb; YMCA Ath Clb; Pres, Round Table of Univ of Puget Sound; hon/Profl Pubs & Lectrs; W/W: in Am, in W.

COHEN, LOUIS ALEXANDER oc/ Civil Engineer; b/Apr 1, 1923; h/ 1099-22nd Street NW #405, Washington, DC 20037; ba/Washington, DC; m/ Barbara Z; c/Marc Jocob; p/Sultan G and Bernice A Cohen (dec); sp/Maurice J (dec) and Lillian F Zucrow, Santa Monica, CA; ed/BSCE, Purdue Univ, 1948; MA Cand, Am Univ, 1970; Att'd MS St Univ; mil/AUS, 1943-46; pa/ Engr, IN St Hwy Dept, 1948-52; Engr, Pvt Consltg Firms, 1952-59; Engr, Intl Cooper Adm, 1959-64; Engr, Agy for Intl Devel, 1964-70; Chief Engr, UN Mekong Com, 1970-74; Dep Dir, RED/ Burgkok, 1974-76; Dir, REDSO/Nairobi, 1976-79; Dir, USAID/Botswana, 1979-82; USAID/Wash, 1982-83; Dir, USAID/Somalia, 1983-; Nat Soc Profl Engr; ASCE; Soc Am M I Engrs; Am For Ser Assn; Am Assoc Asian Studies; African Studies Assn, Botswana Soc; Intl Water Resources Assn; Am Water Res Assn; US Com on Large Dams; cp/ Rotary Intl; r/Jewish; hon/Profl Pubs; Dist'd Ser Awd, Govt of Rep of Viet-Nam Min of Public Wks, 1972; W/W: in Engrg, in World, in Govt, in E; Men of Achmt; Dept of St Biogl Data.

COHEN, MARTIN oc/Research Astronomer; b/Jul 27, 1948; h/3801 Laguna Avenue, Oakland, CA 94602; ba/Berkeley, CA; m/Barbara Freda; p/ Harold and Mildred Cohen, Prestwich, England; sp/Theodore and Gloria Freda, Scottdale, AZ; ed/BA 1969, MA 1974, PhD 1972, Cambridge Univ; pa/Postgrad Res Astronomer Step V 1972-74, Asst Res Astronomer Step I 1974-75, Asst Res Astron Step I 1976-77, Asst Res Astronomer Step III 1977-79, Assoc Res Astronomer Step III 1981-83, Assoc Res Astronomer Step V Radiolab 1983-, Astronomy Dept, Univ of CA-Berkeley; Asst Res Astronomer, Univ of Edinburgh, Royal Observatory, Scotland, 1975; NAS/NRC Sr Postdoct Res Assoc 1979-81, Contract Astronomer 1981-, NASA-Ames Res Ctr; r/Jewish; hon/ Thomas Greene Silver Cup Awd, Clare Col, Cambridge Univ, UK, 1969.

COHEN, MICHAEL FREDERICK oc/Psychologist, Dean; b/Oct 29, 1941; ba/1714 Lombard Street, San Francisco, CA 94123; m/Sharna Delaine Eberlein; c/Isa, Alexandra DeLaine, Theodore Nathaniel; p/Joseph Nathaniel Cohen (dec) and Lee Nagler; ed/BA, FL St Univ, 1962; MS 1965, PhD Clin Psych 1968, Univ of WI-Madison; pa/Prog Dir, Commun Wkrs' Prog, Santa Clara Cou Mtl Hlth Dep, San Jose, CA, 1968-71; Chm, Commun Psych Prog, CA Sch of Profl Psych, SF, 1971-75; Pres & Dir of Eval, Inst for the Study of Social & Hlth Issues, SF, 1971-; Dean Grad Sch, Profl Sch of Psych, SF, 1978-; Mem: Am Psychol Assn; Wn Psychol Assn; Soc for Psychol Study of Social Issues; cp/Nat

Woolgrowers Assn; r/Jewish; hon/ Author, *A Sys Approach to Hlth Manpower Utilization,* 1971; *Procedures for the Devel of a Career Oppor Sys: A Tech Manual,* 1973; Num Articles in Profl Jours & Num Paper Presentations; USPHS F'ships, 1965-66; 1966-67; Hlth Ed & Welfare Grantee, 1971-77; Social & Hlth Issues Travel Grant to Asia, 1973-74; W/W in W.

COHEN, MICHAEL PAUL oc/ Mathematical Statistician; b/Jul 8, 1947; h/201 Eye Street, Southwest #V-413, Washington, DC 20024; ba/Washington, DC; p/Herman C Cohen, Orlando, FL; ed/BA, Univ of CA-San Diego, 1969; MA 1971, PhD 1978, Univ of CA-LA; pa/Math Stat, Price Statl Methods Div, Ofc of Price & Living Conditions, Bur of Labor Stats, 1979-; Applied Res on Prices & Price Indexes; Mem: Am Statl Assn; Inst for Math Stats; Am Math Soc; Intl Assn of Survey Stats; Am Assn for Public Opinion Res; Econometric Soc; hon/Author, Articles Pub'd in Profl Jours; Pi Nu Epsilon, 1971; W/W in Frontier Sci & Technol.

COHEN, MORREL HERMAN oc/ Scientific Advisor, Physics; b/Sep 10, 1927; h/1100 Crim Road, Bridgewater, NJ 08807; ba/Annandale, NJ; m/Sylvia Zwein; c/Julie, Robert, Daniel, Lisa; ed/ BS, Worcester Polytech Inst, 1947; MS Physics, Dartmouth Col, 1948; PhD Physics, Univ of CA-Berkeley, 1952; pa/ Mem Fac 1952-81, Assoc Prof Physics 1957-60, Prof 1960-81, Prof Theoretical Biol 1968, Louis Block Prof Physics & Theoretical Biol 1972-81, Mem Com Devel Biol 1973-74, Pubs Bd 1969-70, Univ of Chgo; Acting Dir 1965-66, Dir 1968-71, James Franck Inst; Dir Mats Res Lab, NSF, 1977-81; Mem: Fellow, Coun 1978-82, Chm Solid St Physics Div 1970, Div Councillor 1978-82, Chm Search Com, Treas APS 1984, Am Phy Soc; AAAS; Am Inst Physics; Nat Acad Scis; Nat Lectr, Sigma Xi, 1966; hon/ Fellow, AEC, 1951-52; Guggenheim Fellow, 1957-58; NSF Sr Postdoct Fellow, Rome, 1964-65; Fellow, NIH Spl, 1972-73; Hon DSc, Dartmouth Col, 1973.

COHEN, MYRON LESLIE oc/Consultant in Biomedical and Mechanical Engineering, President, CAS, Inc; b/ Mar 7, 1934; h/401 Three Corners Rd, Guilford, CT 06437; ba/Same; m/Sally C; c/Amy Beth, David Lawrence, Hilary Ann; p/Henry (dec) and Minnie P Cohen, Bklyn, NY; sp/Samuel (dec) and Esta Gilman, Bklyn, NY; ed/BSME, Purdue Univ, 1955; MSE, Univ of AL, 1958; PhD, Polytech Inst of Bklyn, 1966; mil/AUS, 1956-58; pa/Res Engr, Allegany Ballistics Lab, Hercules Inc, 1955-56; Sr Thermodynamics Engr, Rep Aviation Corp, 1958-60; Instr Mech Engrg, Polytech Inst of Bklyn, 1960-66; Asst Prof Mech Engrg, Stevens Inst of Technol, 1966-69; Assoc Prof 1969-77, Prof, 1977-78; Co Dir Med Engr Lab, 1975-78; Prof, Institut fur Biokybernetik und Biomedizinische Technik Universitat Karlsruhe, 1974-75; Dir Res & Devel Hosp Prods, Chesebrough-Pond's Inc, 1978-83; VP, Freshet Press, 1970-78; Pres, CAS Inc, 1975-78; Adj Assoc Prof Surg, Univ of Med & Dentistry of NJ, 1978-; Pres, M L Cohen Assoc, 1983-; Assoc Fellow, NY Acad of Med; ASME, Chm of Standards Com on Med Devices, 1982-83; Assn

for the Advmt of Med Instrumentation; AAUP; Soc for Biomats; Cardiovas Sys Dynamics Soc; Chm, NY Sect 1971-72, AIAA; NY Acad of Sci; cp/VPres, Temple Beth Tikvah, 1980-82; Dir 1973-74, Theodore Gordon Flyfishers; r/Jewish; hon/Profl Pubs; Humboldt Prize, Sr US Sci Awd, 1974; W/W in E.

COHEN, NICHOLAS oc/Professor; b/Nov 20, 1938; h/211 Highland Parkway, Rochester, NY 14620; ba/Rochester, NY; m/Catharina J van der Harst-Cohen; c/Jaime Anne, Jessica Sevin, Misha Thomas, Mark Sebastian; p/Saris and Francis Cohen, Southbury, CT; sp/Arie and Lenie van der Harst, Scheveningen, The Netherlands; ed/ AB, Princeton Univ, 1959; PhD, Univ of Rochester, 1966; Postdoct Scholar, Univ of CA-LA Med Ctr, 1965-67; pa/ Asst Prof Microbiol 1967-73, Assoc Prof 1973-80, Prof Microbiol (Immunol) 1980, Prof Psychi 1982-, Univ of Rochester; Mem, Basel Inst for Immunol, Basel, Switzerland, 1975-76; Vis'g Prof, Agri Univ, Wageningen, Holland, 1982-83; Mem: The Transplantation Soc, 1967; Am Soc of Zools, 1965; Am Assn of Immunols, 1970; Sigma Xi, 1959; Intl Soc of Del & Comparative Immunol, 1978; Chp, Div of Comparative Immunol, Am Soc of Zools, 1977-79; hon/Author, Over 100 Pubs in Res Jours; Editor, 2 Profl Books; cum laude Grad, Princeton Univ, 1959; Donald R Charles Awd in Biol, 1966; Mem Immunobiol Study Sect, NIH, 1976-80; Fulbright Res Scholar, 1982-83; W/W in E; Am Men & Wom of Sci.

COHEN, RONALD ALEX oc/Dentist; b/Sep 16, 1944; h/10717 NW 19th Street, Coral Springs, FL 33065; ba/ Coral Springs, FL; m/Anita S; C/Jill Stacie, Jodi Nicole; p/Joseph (dec) and Rose Cohen, W Palm Bch, FL; sp/George (dec) and Stephanie Liedarson, Coral Springs, FL; ed/AA, Queensborough Commun Col, 1964; BA, Quinnipiac Col, 1968; MS, Adelphi Univ, 1970; DDS, NY Univ Col of Dentistry, 1974-75; pa/Tchr, NYC Bd of Ed, 1968-71; Instr, Col of Dentistry, 1978-80; Dentist, 1974-; Am Dental Assn, 1971-; C of C, 1980-; Am Assn of Periodontics; Am Acad of Oral Med; Acad of Gen Dentistry; cp/Sec of Dem Clb, 1968; Alpha Omega; Alpha Epsilon Pi; r/Jewish; hon/Profl Pubs & Lectr; Fellow, 11th Dist Dental Soc, 1981; Eagle Scout, BSA, 1959; Fellow, Acad of Gen Dentistry, 1980; W/W: in Dentistry, in Frontier Sci & Technol.

COHEN, ROSALIE AGGER oc/Professor; b/Feb 2, 1923; h/4024 Woodruff Avenue, Lafayette Hill, PA 19444; ba/ Philadelphia, PA; c/David, Anita, Michael, Joel, Brian; p/Benjamin and Pauline Kaufman Agger (dec); ed/BA, IN Ctl Col, 1951; MEd Adm, Duquesne Univ, 1958; PhD Sociol, Univ of Pgh, 1967; pa/Res Asst Lng Res & Devel Ctr 1965-67, Asst Prof of Res Grad Sch of Social Wk 1967-69, Assoc Prof Res & Chm PhD & MSW Res Progs Grad Sch of Social Wk 1969-70, Univ of Pgh; Prof, Inst for Adv'd Studies & Sci Res, Vienna, Austria, Sum 1970; Assoc Prof Sociol & Founs of Ed 1970-, Chm Founs of Ed 1974-77, Temple Univ, Phila, PA; Mem: Am Sociol Assn; Assoc Editor, *Jour of Hlth & Social Behavior;* Fellow, Soc for Applied Anthropology; Chm Com

on Standards & Freedom of· Res, Pub & Tchg 1968-72, Session Chm, Orgr Nom'g Com, Mbr Presentor 1968-, Soc for the Study of Social Probls; Am Judic Soc; Com on the Profession 1981-82, Conf Com Mbr 1982 Conf, En Sociol Soc; hon/Author, Over 60 Scholarly Essays in Profl Jours, Chapts in Edited Books, Tech Reports & Presentations at Profl Assn Meetings Incl; Num Book Reviews & Contbr to Num Confs; Ford Foun Intl Dimensions Grants, 1968 & 1970; Study Leave Awd, Temple Univ, 1974; Hlth & Human Sers Res Grant, 1980-81; Outstg Fac Wom, Temple Univ, 1978; W/W: in E, in Am, of Wom; Am Men & Wom of Sci; Num Other Biogl Listings.

COHEN, SAMUEL ISRAEL oc/ Rabbi; Organizational Executive; b/Apr 17, 1933; h/112 Rand Place, Lawrence, NY 11559; ba/New York, NY; m/Mira H; c/Baruch C, Michael N, Miriam R; p/Rabbi Meyer (dec) and Henrietta Cohen; sp/Rabbi Baruch Hager and Miriam Hager Twersky (dec); ed/BA, Bklyn Col, 1955; Mesivta Rabbi Chaim Berlin Rabbinical Acad, 1956; MEd 1959, EDD 1967, Yeshiva Univ; Ordained Rabbi; pa/Exec Dir, LI Zionist Yth Comm, 1957-61; Dir Mbrship Dept, B'nai B'rith, 1961-72; Dir of Org, Am Jewish Cong, 1972-74; Exec Dir, Am Zionist Fdn, 1974-77; Exec VP, Jewish Nat Fund of Am, 1977-; Exec Com, Nat Conf of Jewish Communal Ser, Union of Orthodox Jewish Congregs; Nat Coun for Jewish Ed; Zionist Org of Am; Rel Zionist of Am; r/Jewish; hon/Num Jewish Pubs; Cit of Ser, B'nai B'rith; W/ W: in E, in Israel, in Am Jewry, in World Jewry.

COHN, DANIEL ROSS oc/Physicist; b/Nov 28, 1943; h/26 Walnut Hill Road, Chestnut Hill, MA 02167; ba/Cambridge, MA; m/Joanne Brecker; c/Adam; p/Roy W and Betty B Cohn, Berkeley, CA; sp/Joseph Brecker (dec); Elizabeth Brecker, Willow Grove, PA; ed/AB, Univ of CA-Berkeley, 1966; PhD, MIT, 1971; pa/Staff Mem, Asst Grp Ldr & Grp Ldr, Laser & Plasma Sys Grp, Francis Bitter Nat Magnet Lab 1971-78, Hd Planning & Adv'd Projs, Plasma Fusion Ctr 1978-80, Hd Fusion Sys Div & Sr Res Sci, Plasma Fusion Ctr 1980-, MIT; Mem: Exec Com, Fusion Energy Div; Am Nuclear Soc; hon/Author, Over 70 Jour Articles & Book Chapts on Submillimeter/Millimeter Wave Technol, Laser-Plasma Interactions & Fusion Reactor Design Concepts for Magnetically Confined Plasmas; Phi Beta Kappa, 1966; Sigma Xi, 1971.

COKE, EUGENE C oc/Scientist, Author, Educator, Executive; h/26 Aqua Vist Drive, Ormond Beach, FL 32074; ba/Ormond by the Sea, FL; m/Sally B Tolmie; p/Chauncey Eugene and Edith Redman Coke; ed/BSc Chem, Univ of Manitoba; MSc Organic Chem, Yale Univ; MA Phy Chem, Univ of Toronto; PhD Polymer Chem, The Univ of Leeds; mil/Royal Canadian AF, 1942-46, 2nd Lt to Maj; pa/Phy Chem Lectr, McMaster Univ; Courtauld Res Fellow, Ontario Res Foun; Res Dir 1938-42, Several Exec Res & Devel Posts 1949-59, Courtaulds, Lts, Canada; Dir Res & Devel, Guaranty Dyeing & Finishing Co, 1946-48; Guest Lectr, Sir George Wms Univ, 1949-50; Dir Res & Devel, Mem Exec Com, Hartford Fibres Co Inc, 1959-62; Tech

Dir Textiles, Drew Chem Corp, 1962-63; Dir New Prods 1963-67, Dir Application Devel 1967-70, Fibers Div, Am Cyanamid Co; Pres 1970-78, Chm 1979-, Coke & Assoc Conslts; Vis'g Res Prof, Stetson Univ, 1979-; Chm Coun on Technol, Adv Coun Admissions Com, Dir, Secy, 1st VPres, Pres, Am Assn for Textile Technol; Chm Var Coms, VChm Panorama of Canadian Fabrics & Fashions, Dir, 2nd VPres, 1st VPres, Pres, Canadian Assn of Textile Colorists & Chems; Co-Fdr, 3rd Pres Chem Inst of Canada, Mem Coun, Inst of Textile Sci; Presenter of Symp Papers, Del 1951-57, Dir 1957-59, Textile Tech Fedn of Canada; Fellow, Am Inst of Chems; Fellow, The Textile Inst (Gt Brit); Fellow, Soc of Dyers & Colourists (Gt Brit); Fellow, NJ Acad of Sci; Life Mem, NY Acad of Sci; Fl Acad of Scis; Chem's Clb, NYC; US Metric Assn; cp/Pres, Aqua Vista Corp, 1972-74; Treas, N Peninsula Citizens Com for Incorp, 1972-75; Dir 1972-74 & 1976-78, N Peninsula Coun of Assns; VChm, N Peninsula Adv Bd to Co Coun, 1976-78; Cand, N Peninsula Zoning Comm, 1974; Pres 1972-75, Dir 1976-79, Gtr Daytona Bch Repub Clb; Pres 1975-77, VPres 1978-83, Repub Pres Forum; VChm, The Grp of 10, 1978-; hon/Co-Author, Advances in Textile Processing; Over 150 Pub'd or Confidential Papers; Bronze Medal 1963, Hon Life Mem 1977, Canadian Assn of Textile Colorists & Chems; Bronze Medal, Am Assn for Textile Technol, 1971; Hon Mem Edit Adv Bd 1976-, Hon Mem Nat Bd of Advrs 1982-, ABI; Am Men & Wom of Sci; Ldrs in Am Sci; Men of Achmt; DIB; Nat Social Dir; Royal Blue Book; Commun Ldrs & Noteworthy Ams; Book of Hon; Num W/W & Other Biogl Listings.

COLACHICO, JEANNE MARIE oc/ Equal Employment Specialist, Attorney; Executive; b/Mar 1, 1951; h/109 Mitchell Avenue, Medford, MA 02155; ba/ Boston, MA; p/Mr and Mrs Charles Colachico, Wakefield, MA; ed/BA magna cum laude, Regis Col, 1973; MUA, Boston Univ, 1977; JD, Suffolk Univ Sch of Law, 1981; pa/Asst to Dir of Consumer Protection, MA Atty Gen Ofc, 1972-74; Equal Opport Spec, Def Contract Adm Ser, 1974-; VP, Jackson Intl Inc, Export Trade Co, 1982-; Atty, Pvt Pract, 1981-; MA Bar; Fed Dist Ct Bar; Ct of Appeals Bar; ABA; MA Assn of Wom Lwyrs, 1980; Phi Delta Phi; Delta Epsilon Sigma; EEO Ofcrs's Coun, 1975-; Nat Legis Com 1980, Bd Mem 1978, Federally Employed Wom; Num Others; cp/Chair Wom's Opport Com 1981-, Chair Hispanic Coun 1979-80, BFEB; Interagy Task Force on Sexual Harassment; Num Spkg Presentations & Radio/TV Appearances; Other Commun Activs; r/Rom Cath; hon/Author of Var BFEB Reports; Other Pubs; Nat Hispanic Employmt Prog Awd, US Ofc of Pers Mgmt, 1978; 33rd Annual Arthur S Flemming Awd, US JC's, 1981; Congl Awd for Exemplary Ser to the Public Finalist, 1982; BFEB Ldrship Awd, 1981 & 1982; Others; Outstg Yg Wom of Am; Intells of World; W/W: of Am Wom, in World.

COLBY, BARBARA D oc/Interior Design/Health; b/Dec 6, 1932; h/PO Box 2902, Beverly Hills, CA 90213; ba/Same; c/Lawrence James Streicher; p/Mr and

Mrs Raymond Colby, Chicago, IL; ed/ Wright Jr Col; Chgo Art Inst; Univ of CA-LA; pa/Barbara Colby Ltd, 1977-81; Ptnr, Ambiance Inc, Wholesale Fabric Distbr, 1976-77; Owner, FLS Showroom, 1971-77; Owner, Chromanetics, Color/Light/Design, 1981-; Mem: Intl Platform Assn; Am Soc of Interior Designers; Intl Soc of Interior Designers; Nat Assn for Female Execs; Color Mktg Grp US; Former Bd Mem, Nat Soc of Interior Designers; hon/ Pub'd in CA Design, 1976; Winning Design Entry, CA Design Competition, Lucite Cube, 1976; W/W in W; 2000 Notable Ams; DIB.

COLE, ADELAIDE MEADOR oc/ Professor; b/Jun 6, 1923; h/968 Mary Lee Avenue, New Castle, IN 47362; ba/ Muncie, IN; m/James Lewis; c/John Aden Hunter, W Alexendra Hunter, Mary Adelaide Hunter, Tanya Sean; p/ Vollmer A and Josephine Ratliff, Muncie, IN; sp/Lloyd L Cole (dec); Mabel T Col, New Castle, IN; ed/AB, Marshall Univ, 1946; MA, Duke Univ, 1947; EdD, Tchrs Col, Columbia Univ, 1950; pa/ Prof, Cedarville Col, 1950-51; Assoc Prof, Pan Am Col, 1953-60; Assoc Prof, CA Wn Univ, 1960-61; Assoc Prof, NM Highlands Univ, 1961-65; Prof, Ball St Univ, 1967-; Mem: Phi Epsilon Kappa; Dappa Delta Pi; Pi Lambda Theta; Phi Delta Kappa; Am Alliance for Hlth, PE & Rec; AAUP; IN Assn for Hlth, PE, Rec & Dance; r/Epis; hon/Author of Articles in Profl Jours incl'g: AAHPER Jour; DAR Mag; AAHPER Res Qtly; Others; Outstg Ser Awd, ARC; Mem, Sigma Sigma Sigma; Chm, IN Interagy Res Coun; Rep, Acad Affairs Conf of MWn Univs; W/W: of Am Wom, of Wom in Ed; Ldrs in Ed; DIB.

COLE, CHARLES LEE oc/Marital and Family Therapist, Professor; b/Aug 24, 1944; h/Rural Route 4, Squaw Valley, Ames, IA 50011; ba/Ames, IA; m/Anna L; p/Artie Lee and Margaret E Cole, Ft Worth, TX; sp/Mr and Mrs H C Haire, Southwick, MA; ed/BA, TX Wesleyan Col, 1967; MA, TX Christian Univ, 1968; PhD, IA St Univ; pa/Dir, Marital & Fam Therapy Tng & Assoc Prof, IA St Univ, 1976-; Asst Prof Sociol 1972-76, Dir of Fam Studies Ctr 1973-76, Denison Univ; Asst Prof Sociol, Univ of AR-Little Rock, 1968-70; Res Clin Sociol, NIMH, Clin Res Ctr, Ft Worth, TX, 1967-68; Mem: Pres 1980-82, Secy/ Treas 1977-80, IA Assn for Marriage & Fam Therapy; Pres 1973-75, OH Coun on Fam Relats; VPres 1978-80, IA Coun on Fam Relats; Chm Fam Action Sect & Mem Bd of Dirs, Nat Coun on Fam Relats, 1980-82; Chair, Fam Wellness Conf, 1981-83; Charter Mem, Assn of Couples for Marriage Enrichment; cp/Clk, Ames Monthy Meeting of IA Conserv Rel Soc of Friends; r/Quaker; hon/Author, Over 30 Pub'd Articles in Profl Jours; Over 50 Maj Paper Presentations to Profl Socs & Assns incl'g: Nat Coun on Fam Relats; Groves Conf on Marriage & the Fam; Am Assn for Marriage & Fam Therapy; Am Sociol Assn; Soc for the Study of Social Probs; Others; Outstg Student Awd, Nat Coun on Fam Relats, 1973; Dist'd Ser to Fams Awd, OH Coun on Fam Relats; Dist'd Ser & Ldrship Awd, Outstg Contbns to Profession Awd, IA Assn for Marriage & Fam Therapy; Outstg Commun Ldrs in Am;

Personalities of W & MW.

COLE, HAROLD S oc/Physician, Professor; b/Apr 20, 1916; h/185 East 85th Street, New York, NY 10028; ba/ Same; m/Elizabeth Ann Jurgensen; p/ Morris and Celia Cole (dec); sp/Frederick Jurgensen (dec); Elizabeth Jurgensen, Hartford, CT; ed/BS, Univ of MD, 1937; Grad Study, Princeton Univ, 1938; MD, NY Univ Col of Med, 1942; mil/AUS, 1943-46, Capt; pa/Prof Pediatrics, Prof Commun & Preven Med, NY Med Col, 1965-; Pvt Pract, Pediatrics, Rutherford, NJ, 1948-65; Mem: Fellow, Am Acad of Pediatrics; Am Diabetes Assn; Lawson Wilkens Pediatric Endocrine Soc; hon/Author, Early Diabetes, 1970; Vascular & Neurol Changes in Early Diabetes, 1973; Early Diabetes in Early Life, 1975; magnu cum laude, Univ of MD, 1937; Alpha Omega Alpha; Am Pediatric Soc; Pres, Univ of MD Alumni Clb of Gtr NY, 1968-74; W/W in E.

COLE, MYRON WILLIAM oc/Electronics Engineer; b/Apr 5, 1927; h/6320 Whitesburg Drive S, Huntsville, AL 35802; ba/Redstone Arsenal, AL; m/ Margaret M; c/Myron William III, Amanda Quinn, Katherine Ellen, Richard Martin, Timothy John; p/ Myron W Cole (dec); Nora Quinn Cole Carter, Charleston, SC; sp/Arthur John and Katherine Embry Martin; ed/BSEE, The Citadel, 1949; mil/USMC, 1945-46, 1950-51; pa/Proj Engr, ABMA, Missile Test Equip, 1958-68; Sys Engr, Army RD & E Lab, Aircraft Armament, 1969-73; Res Coor, Army High Energy Laser Lab, 1979-; Sr Mem, IEEE; Chm, Huntsville Sect IEEE, 1976; Nat Soc of Profl Engrs; St Chm Engr in Govt, AL Soc of Profl Engrs, 1969, 1970; Am Nuclear Soc; hon/Profl Pubs; Spec Act of Achmt Awd, Army Missile Lab, 1982; Eminent Engr Awd, Tau Beta Pi, 1982; Profl Achmt Awd, Gtr B'ham Citadel Clb, 1981; Engr of Yr Awd, Huntsville Sect IEEE, 1981; R & D Awd, Dept of Army, 1977; Chm Advmt Com, Chicasaw Dist, BSA.

COLEMAN, JAMES SMOOT oc/ Professor; b/Feb 1, 1919; h/12315 Darlington Avenue, Los Angeles, CA 90049; ba/Los Angeles, CA; m/Ursula Maria; c/James S Jr, Robert L; ed/BA, Brigham Yg Univ, 1947; MA 1948, PhD 1953, Harvard Univ; mil/1941-46; pa/ Prof Polit Sci 1953-67 & 1978-, Dir African Studies Ctr 1960-65, Chm Coun on Intl & Comparative Studies 1978-, Univ of CA-LA; Assoc Dir & Rep in E Africa & Zaire, The Rockefeller Foun, 1967-78; Mem: Comparative Polit Com 1955-65, Bd of Dirs 1962-64, Social Sci Res Coun; Adv Com of Africa, Nat Acad Sci, 1963-65; Coun Am Polit Sci Assn, 1963-65; Bd of Dirs 1959-63, Pres 1963-64, African Studies Assn; VPres, Int Cong of Africanists, 1962-67; Exec Coun, Intl African Inst, 1966-77; Fellow, Am Acad Arts & Scis, 1966-; Num Others; r/Unitarian; hon/Author of 9 Books & Monographs incl'g:Social Scis & Public Policy in the Developing World, 1982; Govt & Rural Devel in E Africa: Essays in Polit Penetration, 1977; Ed & Polit Devel, 1965; The Polits of the Developing Areas, 1960; Num Articles in Profl Jours & Chapts of Books incl'g: African Studies Review; Comparative Ed Review; Politics & Ed; New Sts in the Mod World; Intl Ency of Social Scis; Others; Woodrow Wilson Foun Awd, Am Polit Sci Assn, 1959; Fellow,

Ctr Adv'd Study Behavioral Scis, 1963-64; Elected Fellow, Am Acad Arts & Scis; MBE (Mil Div), Brit Govt; W/ W in W; Am Men & Wom of Sci.

COLEMAN, PATRICIA REGISTER oc/Author; Editor; Creative Director; b/ Nov 1, 1936; h/22 Willow Street, Mystic, CT 06355; ba/Same; m/William Vincent; c/Sarah Angela, Lisa Coleman Greaney; p/Athena Register, Mystic, CT; sp/Ethel Coleman, Mystic, CT; ed/ AA, Univ of GA, 1956; BA, FL St Univ, 1974; pa/Co-Author w Husband, Over 100 Books in Rel Ed, 1970-; Co-fdr & VP, Growth Assoc Min Ser, 1972; Editor, 3 Intl Newslettr, Cath Yth Min; Parish Communs Synthesis, 1980-; Fdg Mem, Friends of St Vincent de Paul, 1979-; Secy Bd of Dirs, Commun Min, Diocese of Norwich, 1981-83; Secy Bd of Dirs, Martin House, 1982-83; r/Rom Cath; hon/Num Rel Pubs; Hon Grad, FL St Univ, 1974; Intl W/W of Wom; Authors in Am.

COLEMAN-REED, JEANNETTE oc/ Administrative Assistant; b/Mar 17, 1935; h/3404C Laclede Avenue, St Louis, MO 63103; ba/St Louis, MO; c/ Curtiss Jr, Anthohy Renard; p/Prince Coleman Sr, Port Gibson, MS; Inez Smith Coleman (dec); ed/BS Urban Adm & Cert in Bus Adm, Wash Univ-St Louis, 1980; Postgrad Studies, Mgmt & Bus Adm, Webster Univ, 1982-83; pa/ Secy to Treas, St Louis Public Schs, 1959-72; Secy to VPres Process & Plants Enviro-Chem Sys Inc, Monsanto Co, 1972-76; Mktg Asst Chow Div, Ralston Purina Co, 1977-81; Adj Fac (Instr) Bus Ed, St Louis Comm Col-Forest Pk, 1980-; Adm Asst to Pres & Secy to Bd of Regents (Col's Gov'g Bd), Harris-Stowe St Col, 1982-; Mem: Fdr, Orgr & Pres, Black Bus Wom U, 1981-83; Locat Dir, Nat Assn of Female Execs, 1982-83; Public Relats Coor, Saturday Rdg Clb, 1981-83; Mem, Roby Wilkins Mbrship Tm, NAACP, 1983; AAUW; Zeta Phi Beta Amicaes; cp/Pride of the W Chapt #99, OES; Friends of Sherwood Forest Camping Ser Inc; Advr, Jr Achmt, 1981-82; Loaned Exec, U Way, l1981; Bd of Dirs, W Side Bapt Ch Fed Credit Union, 1975-79; Num Other Commun Activs; r/Presb; hon/ Rel Editor/Columnist, St Louis Am News, 1978-80; Career S'ship, Wash Univ-St Louis, 1972; U Way Campaign Vol Awd, 1981; Commun Ser Awd, OES, 1982; Outstg Achmt Awd, Sigma Gamma Rho, 1980; W/W in Am Wom.

COLLARD, SNEED B oc/Marine Biologist; b/Jul 11, 1939; h/PO Box 116, Bagdad, FL 32530; ba/Pensacola, FL; m/ Suzanne Spencer; c/Sneed B III, Tyler S, D Gidon, P Heghann; ed/AA, Phoenix Col, AZ, 1960; BA 1965, MA 1966, PhD 1968, Univ of CA-Santa Barbara; Postdoct Study: Harvard Univ, 1969; Woods Hole Oceanographic Instn, 1969; pa/ Mem, Sci Peer Review Com, SUS-Sea World Shark Inst, Currently; Mem Shiptime Com, Chm Adv Com, FL Inst of Oceanogrphy, Currently; Advr, St of FL Dept of Natural Resources, Currently; Assoc Prof Biol, Univ of W FL, Currently; Guest Investigator, Australian Inst of Marine Sci, Queensland, 1981; Proj Dir, US Army Corp of Engrs, 1972-73; Vis'g Lectr, Marine Envir Scis Consortium, Dauphin Isl, AL, Sum 1972 & 1973; Bd of Govs, NW FL Zool Soc, 1971-72; Guest Investigator, The

Hebrew Univ of Jerusalem, Israel, 1969-70; Guest Investigator, Woods Hole Oceanograhic Instn, MA, 1968-69; NSF Postdoct Fellow, Mus of Comparative Zool, Harvard Univ, 1968-69; Asst Prof Zool 1968, NIH Grad Tng Fellow 1965-68, Res Asst Parasitology 1964-65, Tchg Asst Zool 1964, Asst Curator of Fishes 1963, Univ of CA-Santa Barbara; Asst Marine Biol, AC Elects Def Res Lab, Goleta, CA, 1967; Vis'g Investigator, Bur of Comml Fisheries, Honolulu, HI, 1965-66; Res Asst Biol Oceanography, Gen Motors Def Res Labs, Goleta, CA, 1963; Meterological Res Asst, Aerometric Res Inc, Goleta, CA, 1961-63; Mem: Am Soc of Limnology & Oceanography; Am Inst of Biol Scis; Am Soc of Parasitologists; Am Soc of Ichthyology & Herpetology; Assn of SEn Biols; Chm, FL Acad of Scis, 1974-75; Edit Bd, NE Gulf Sci; Participant in Num Expeditions; cp/Biol Clb Fac Advr, 1969-73; Com on Envir, Pensacola C of C; Bd of Govs 1969-72, NW FL Zool Soc; Cnslr, BSA; Envir Advr, Woodland Bayou Homeowners Assn; Envir Advr, FL Dept of Nat Resources; hon/Author, Over 30 Res Articles & Reports Pub'd in Num Profl Sci Jours & Pubs; Over 20 Profl Assn Presentations; Sum Res F'ship, 1974; NSF Postdoct Fellow, 1968-69; USPHS-HIH Grad Tng Fellow, 1965-68; Woodrow Wilson Grad Fellow, 1965; German Sum F'ship, 1965; Gen Motors Asststhip in Marine Biol, 1964; EPIC Scholar, Ford Foun Exptl Prog, 1963-66; Recip, Num Res Grants & Hons.

COLLE, RONALD oc/Research Scientist; b/Feb 11, 1946; h/2133 North Military Road, Arlington, VA 22207; ba/ Washington, DC; m/Judith Ann Zube; ed/BS Chem, GA Inst of Technol, 1969; PhD Nuclear Chem, Rennselaer Polytech Inst, 1972; MS Adm of Sci & Tech, George Wash Univ, 1979; pa/Res Assoc, Univ of MD, 1973-74; Vis'g Res Fellow, St Univ of NY-Albany, 1971-73; Conslt & Res Assoc 1974-76, Res Chem 1976-77, Chem 1977-, Nat Bur of Standards; Mem: Am Phy Soc; Am Chem Soc Div of Nuclear Chem & Tech; hon/Author, Over 25 Res Articles in Field of Exptl Nuclear Physics & Chem; Co-Author, 2 Books; Editor of 1 Book; Phi Lambda Upsilon; Bronze Medal, US Dept of Commerce, 1981; W/W in Technol Today; Am Men & Wom of Sci.

COLLER, RICHARD WALTER oc/ Sociologist, Professor; b/Aug 29, 1925; h/4911 Lani Road, Kapaa, HI 96746; ba/ Lihue, HI; m/Alicia Mabuhay Peruda; c/ Louis, Margarite, Ann, James, Katherine, Susan, William, Mark, Clair, Ruth, Patrick; p/Walter A Coller and Helen F. Kretz (dec); ed/BA 1948, PhD 1959, Univ of MN; MA, Univ of HI, 1951; mil/AUS, 1943-46; pa/Lectr, Univ of the E, Manila, 1951; Instr & Prof Sociol, Univ of the Philippines, Quezon City, Phillippines, 1952-62; Tng Instr, Peace Corps, Hilo, HI, 1962-66; Prof Sociol, Kauai Commmun Col, Lihue, Kauai, HI, 1966-; Mem: Philippine Studies Assn; Assn for the Improvement of Commun Col Tchg; Soc for Applied Anthropology; Am Sociol Assn; r/Cath; hon/ Author, *Barrio Gacao*, 1962; Co-Author, *Filipinos in Rural HI*, 1983; *Sociol in The Philippine Setting*, 1954; W/W in W.

COLLIE, BERTRAM E oc/United Methodist Minister (Retired); b/Jun 15, 1905; h/2013 San Antonio Street, Grand Prairie, TX 75051; m/Cleo Smith; c/Bertram E Jr, Carrington; ed/NY Evening HS, 1930; Att'd Sn Bible Sch, Howard Payne Col, Perkins Sch of Theol, Dale Carnegie Inst; pa/Min, Galilee Bapt Ch, 1953-56; Min, St John's Bapt Ch, 1955-67; Min, Emmanuel U Meth Ch, 1972-75; Min, God's Kingdom U Meth Ch, 1973-77; Funeral Dir; Outreach Conslt, Tyler St U Meth Ch; Exec Dir, We-Care Ed Foun Inc; Exec Dir, Crusade for Christ as a Deterrent for Crime; cp/Num Commun Ser; Life Member, NAACP; r/U Meth; hon/ Recog Awd for Outstg Commun Contrb, Grand Prairie C of C; Civic & Commun Involvement, Dallas Beautician Assn; Recog Awd for Civic Involvement w Commun, Mt Olive Bapt Ch; Cert Awd, N TX Conf for Profl Ser; Outstg Recog, Brothers & Sisters of Love & Charity; Black Repub Awd; Cert of Apprec, Dallas Black C of C; Cert of Apprec, Galilee Bapt Ch; Cert of Apprec, Gov of TX.

COLLIER, ALEXIS CHRISTINA oc/ Professor; b/Jul 10, 1951; h/5015 Hibbs Drive, Columbus, OH 43220; ba/Columbus, OH; p/Samuel Alexander Collier (dec); Belle Robinett Collier, Appalachia, VA; ed/BS Psych, VA Polytech Inst & St Univ, 1973; Grad Tng Psych, Princeton Univ, 1973-74; PhD Psych, Univ of WA, 1976; pa/Asst Prof Psych 1976-82, Assoc Prof Psych 1982-, Grad Fac Status: Level I 1976-77, Level II 1977-81, Level III 1981-, The OH St Univ, Columbus; Mem: Var Dept Coms 1976-, Fac Senate for Col of Arts & Scis 1982-85, Other Univ Coms, OH St Univ; Var Coms, Am Psychol Assn, 1977-; En Psychol Assn; MWn Psychol Assn; Psychonomic Soc; Intl Soc for Devel Psychobiol; Former Mem, AAAS; Former Mem, Animal Behavior Soc; Consltg Editor, *Jour Supplement Abstract Ser*, 1980-81; Occasional Manuscript Reviewer, Var Profl Jours; Alpha Lambda Delta; Mortar Bd Colony; Phi Kappa Phi; Others; cp/Columbus Metro Clb, 1980-; OES, 1982-; YWCA, 1980-; NOW, 1979-; Assoc Mem, Columbus All-Breed Tng Clb, 1983; Bacchanalia Clb, 1982-; Scandinavian Hlth Spa, 1982-; Jr Coun, Columbus Mus of Art; Alumni Assns: VA Polytech Inst & St Univ; Princeton Univ; Univ of WA; Alumnus, Delta Zeta; r/Prot; hon/ Author & Co-Author, Over 20 Articles Pub'd in Profl Jours incl'g: *Physiol Psych*; *Physiol & Behavior*; *Devel Psychobiol*; *Animal Lrng & Behavior*; *The Am Jour of Psych*; *Bltn of Psychonomic Soc*; Over 20 Paper Presentations for Profl Assn Meetings & Confs; Recip, Univ Small Res Grants Prog, OH St Univ, 1977-78; Recip, NIMH Small Grant, Public Hlth Ser, 1980; NSF Undergrad Res Participant, Univ of VA, 1972; F'ship, Col of Social & Behavioral Scis, OH St Univ, 1981; Basic Behavioral Processes Res Review Com, Alcohol, Drug Abuse & Mtl Hlth Adm Public Hlth Ser, NIMH, 1980-84; Invited Paper Colloquium, Univ of MO, 1980; Outstg Sophomore, VA Polytech Inst & St Univ, 1971; Other Hons; W/ W: of Am Wom; The Blue Book of Franklin Co; Outstg Yg Wom of Am.

COLLIER, BARBARA ANN oc/Management Consultant, Speaker, Trainer;

b/Jan 29, 1942; h/3943 GA, San Diego, CA 92103; ba/Same; c/Ross A Deilke; p/Thelma Jakubco, Dallas, TX; ed/BA, Latin, Eng & Ed, 1964; MA, Human Resource Devel, 1981; pa/Sec'dy Latin Tchr: TX, NJ, SC, 1964-68; Supvr, Social Sers, Co of San Diego, 1968-76; Tng Spec, Co of San Diego, 1976-79; Princ, Collier Enterprises, 1979-; Tng, Spkg, Conslt in Mgmt, Supvn, Communs, Currently; Mem: Secy 1981-82, VPres Fin 1982-83, Reg Conf Chp 1982-84, Am Soc for Tng & Devel, San Diego; Bd 1981-83, San Diego Career Guid Assn; Woms Opports Wk, San Diego, 1981; Nat Mgmt Assn Spkrs' Showcase, San Diego, 1982; r/Cath; hon/Wom in Mgmt Column, *Crossrds*, 1981; Var Columns, *Tng Trends*, 1981-; *Career Transitions Guide*, 1981; Helen Reddy Awd, 1981; Apprec Awds, Am Soc for Tng & Devel, 1981-83; Apprec Awd, San Diego Career Guid Assn, 1982-83; W/W: Among San Diego Wom, in Tng & Devel, in W.

COLLIER, GAYLAN JANE oc/Professor and Coordinator; b/Jul 23, 1924; h/2616 South University, Ft Worth, TX 76109; ba/Ft Worth, TX; p/Ben and Narcis Collier (dec); pa/Instr Drama, Univ of NC-Greensboro, 1947-48; Asst Prof & Acting Chp of Drama, Greensboro Col, 1949-50; Asst Prof & Dir of Theatre 1950-57, Assoc Prof 1957-60, Abilene Christian Univ; Assoc Prof & Chm Acting Prog, ID St Univ, 1960-63; Assoc Prof Drama 1963-65, Prof Drama 1965-67, Sam Houston St Univ; Prof Theatre & Coor Acting/Dir, TX Christian Univ, 1967-; Mem, Am Theatre Assn; SW Theatre Conf, TX Ed Theatre Assn; hon/Profl Pubs; Best Actress, Abilene Christine Univ, 1943-44, 1944-45, 1945-46; Dir of Play Selected to Represent US on Tour of Gt Brit; W/W: in Am, in S & SW, of Am Wom; Dir of Am Scholars; Intl Dir of Scholars; Intl W/W in Commun Ser; World W/W of Wom.

COLLIER, RICHARD BANGS oc/Founder, Director and Philosopher; b/Aug 12, 1918; h/PO Box 1256, Tacoma, WA 98401; ba/Tacoma, WA; p/Nelson Martin and Stella Butler Collier; ed/BA, Univ of WA, 1951; mil/Fgn Aid Ofcr (G-14), Civil Aviation, US Embassy, Bangkok, Thailand, 1958-63; USAF, 1955-56, Capt; pa/Fdr & Dir, Pleneurethics Intl, 1963-; Mem: Assn of Supvn & Curric Devel; Acad of Polit Sci; AAAS; Royal Inst of Phil; Life Patron, ABIRA; cp/Nat Adv Bd, Am Secuirty Coun; Repub Senatorial Clb; hon/Author, 13 Volumes on Pleneurethics, 1964-81, incl'g: *Pleneurethic: A Way of Life, Sys of Therapeutics*; Pleneurethic: Its Evolution & Sci Basis; Pleneurethics: A World Class Phil; Recently Pub'd is *Essential Pleneurethic*, 1985; Carnegie F'ship, Univ of WA Grad Sch, 1950-51; W/W: in W, in World; 2000 Notable Ams; Biogl Roll of Hon; World Biogl Hall of Fame; Intl Dir of Dist'd Ldrship; Dir of Dist'd Ams; Personalites of W & MW.

COLLINS, ALVIN oc/Associate Registrar; b/Apr 18, 1934; h/2231 Bartlett Drive, Savannah, GA 31404; ba/Savannah, GA; m/Lucile Lamar; c/Alvin LeRoi; p/Christine Collins, Waycross, GA; sp/Henrietta Lamar, Savannah, GA; ed/BS, 1959; MEd, 1982; mil/AUS, 1954-56; pa/Eng Instr, Chatham Co Bd of Ed, 1964-70; Prog Cnslr

1971-73, Assoc Registrar 1974-, Savannah St Col; cp/Treas 1970-82, Falcon's Inc; Pres 1968-82, Parkwood Pl Commun Assn; Treas 1976-80, Savannah St Col Nat Alumni Assn; VChm, Deacon Bd, Trustee Bd, Pres, Col Pk Bapt Ch; r/Bapt; hon/Profl Pubs; Tchr of Yr, 1965, 1967, 1969; Driver Achmt Awd, 1975; Outstg Deacon, 1980.

COLLINS, ANITA M oc/Research Geneticist; b/Nov 8, 1947; h/1338 Sharlo Avenue, Baton Rouge, LA 70820; ba/Baton Rouge, LA; p/Edmund & Virginia Collins, Kutztown, PA; ed/BSc Zool, PA St Univ, 1969; MSC 1972, PhD Genetics 1976, OH St Univ; pa/Biol Instr, Mercyhurst Col, Erie, PA, 1975-76; Res Geneticist, USDA-ARS Bee Breeding & Stock Ctr Lab, 1976; Mem: AAAS; Am Assn of Profl Apiculturists; Am Genetic Assn; Animal Behavior Soc; Pres-elect 1981, Pres 1982, Exec Com 1979, 1983, 1984, Baton Rouge Chapt, Assn for Wom in Sci; Entomological Soc of Am; En Apicultural Soc of NA Inc; Intl Union of the Study of Social Insects; hon/Author & Co-Author, Over 25 Res Reports, Articles in Profl Jours & Chapts in Books; Mem 1978, Assoc Mem 1972, Sigma Xi; Grad Student Ldrship Awd, OH St Univ, 1974; Cert of Merit, USDA, 1982, 1983; W/W Among Students in Am Cols & Univs.

COLLINS, DONALD F oc/Independant Filmmaker and Director; b/Apr 5, 1936; h/230 Mount Vernon Place, Newark, NJ 07106; p/Harold and Anna Collins, Newark, NJ; ed/BA 1974, MA 1976, Montclair St Col; mil/USN, 1955-59; pa/Psychol/Edr, St Dept of Mtl Hlth, 1978-82; Indep Film Prodr & Dir, 1975-; Prodr/Dir, George Hicks Radio Prog, 1974-76; Actor/Dir, Arundel Opera Theatre, 1970-74; Actor/Dir, Kennebunk Theatre, 1968-70; Mem: Nat Acad of TV Arts & Scis, 1981-; The NY Film Coun, 1981-; Am Film Inst, 1976-; Nat Assn of Black Artists, 1979-83; Black Dirs Guild, 1980-; r/Cath.

COLLINS, DOROTHY DOVE oc/Writer; Musician; b/Oct 1, 1918; h/Collinwood, Maxton, NC 28364; m/Neil Carmichael Jr; c/Neil Carmichael III, Judith C Millar; p/Rhett Pendleton Dove (dec); Blanche H Dove, Rowland, NC; ed/AA, Campbell Col; BA, Univ of NC; pa/Public Relats Dir, Carolina Mil Acad, 1966-72; Assoc Jour, St Andrew's Presby Col, 1972-75; Ch Organist, 1955-65; St Cecelia Music Clb; cp/Org'g Dir, Carolina Col Alumnae Assn Meth Col, Fayetteville, NC; Former Dist Dir, UDC, NC Div; Pres, Campbell Col Friends of Lib; Former Mem Exec Bd, Maxton Cent Comm, Maxton Hist Soc; r/1st Presb Ch, Maxton; Mem, Dir Chd's Choir, 1974-78; Publicity Dir, Cent Yr, 1978; hon/Author *Carolina Echoes - A Hist of Carolina Col*, 1970; *The Collins Connexion*, 1981.

COLLINS, EILEEN LOUISE oc/Economist; b/Dec 15, 1942; h/1301 20th Street, Northwest, Washington, DC 20036; ba/Washington, DC; p/Theodore M Collins, Columbus, OH; Louise Suess Collins (dec); pa/Lectr Ec, Univ of Waterloo, Ontario, Canada, 1971-73; Asst Prof Ec, Barnard Col, NYC, 1975-76; Asst Prof Ecs, Fordham Univ, 1976-78; Ec, Div of Policy Res & Anal, NSF, Wash DC, 1978-; Mem: Fed

Taxation & Fin Com, Nat Tax Assn; Am Ec Assn; Wash Wom Economists; cp/Nat Capitol YMCA; hon/Author of Var Book Chapts, Reports & Articles in Profl Jours Pub'd; Outstg Perf Awds, NSF, 1979, 1981, 1982; Traineeship, NIMH, 1969-71; F'ship, Nat Inst of Public Affairs, 1966-67; Col S'ship, Bryn Mawr, 1960-64; W/W: of Am Wom, in E.

COLLINS, LEONARD oc/Personnel Analyst; b/May 9, 1948; h/1100 Madison Avenue, Shreveport, LA 71103; ba/Shreveport, LA; p/Mrs Ollie Virginia Rayson Collins, Shreveport, LA; ed/BA, Prairie View A&M Univ, 1972; MS, Commonwlth Col of Sci, 1974; pa/Mgr, Fenelon Funeral Home, 1974-78; Supvr of Pers Dept of Public Works 1978-79, Pers Anal 1979-, City of Shreveport; Lic'd Mortician; Pres 1981, Dir 1980, Shreveport Mun Employees Credit Assn; Am Compensation Assn; NW LA Pers Assn; Shreveport Funeral Dirs & Embalmers Assn; Nat Funeral Dirs & Embalmers Assn; LA St Embalmers & Funeral Dirs; cp/Epsilon Nu Delta; Urban Leag; Elks; r/Cath; hon/W/W in S & SW.

COLLINS, MARGARET STRICKLAND oc/Research Director; b/Sep 4, 1922; h/1642 Primrose Road, Northwest, Washington, DC 20012; ba/Washington, DC; c/Herbert L Jr, James Joseph; p/Rollins Walter and Luella Bowling James; ed/BS, WV St Col, 1943; PhD Zool, The Univ of Chgo, 1949; pa/Instr Zool, Howard Univ, Wash DC, 1947-50; Asst Prof 1950-51, Prof 1978-83, Prof (Ret'd), Zool, FL A&M Univ, Tallahassee; Prof Biol, Fed City Col, Wash DC, 1969-78; Dir, Emerson Field Res Sta, Guyana; Res Assoc, Smithsonian Instn; Mem: Bd of Dirs, Nat Assn for So Poor, 1979-; Entomological Soc, Wash DC, 1972-; Pres 1982, Ecol Soc Am; NY Acad of Sci; Earthwatch; AAAS; Entomology Soc Am; IUSSI; hon/Author & Co-Author, Over 20 Res Articles in Profl Jours & Book Chapts on Water Relats, Temperature, Chem Def in Termites; Co-Editor, *Sci & the Question of Human Equality*, AAAS Symp Volume, 1981; Favorite Female Instr, FL A&M Univ, ROTC Dept, 1960 & 1964; Clark Lectrship, Scripps Cols, Claremont CA, 1974; Outstg Title in Sci & Technol for Edited Book, *Lib Jour*, 1981; Featured in TV Pilot, "Spaces"; W/W: of Am Wom, of Frontier Sci & Technol; Am Men & Wom of Sci.

COLLINS, MICHAEL deMAR oc/Landscape Company Executive; b/Oct 26, 1944; h/1065 Fireplace Road, East Hampton, NY 11937; ba/Bridge Hampton, NY; m/Janice M; c/Brendan; p/Mr and Mrs Thomas L Collins, E Hampton, NY; sp/Clarence E Sanders, Bartlesville, OK; ed/AAS, SUNY, 1964; BS, OK St Univ, 1968; pa/Mgr, Whitmore-Worsley Inc, 1969-72; Gen Mgr, The Bayberry Inc, 1972-79; Gen Mgr, Marders, 1979-; cp/Fdg Mem, Am Conifer Soc; The Royal Hort Soc; Sprgs Fire Dept; Nature Conservancy; Sprgs Citizens Planning Comm; r/Presb; hon/Recip, Warren F Purdy Intl Mgmt Awd, 1982; W/W in Fin & Indust; Intl Book of Hon.

COLMAN, ROBERT W oc/Professor, Thrombosis Research Director; b/Jun 7, 1935; h/9 Rose Valley Road, Moylan, PA 19065; ba/Philadelphia, PA; m/Roberta F; c/Sharon V, David S; p/Mr and Mrs

J K Colman, New York, NY; sp/Mrs Esther Fishman; ed/AB, Harvard Univ, 1956; MD, Harvard Med Sch, 1960; Hon MA, Univ of PA Med Sch, 1973; mil/ USPHS, 1962-64; pa/Asst Prof to Assoc Prof, Harvard Med Sch, 1967-73; Assoc Prof to Prof Med & Pathol, Univ of PA Sch of Med, 1973-78; Prof Med, Hd Hematology-Oncology, Dir Thrombosis Res Ctr, Temple Univ Sch of Med, 1978-; Mem: Am Fedn Clin Res; Am Soc Hematology; Fellow, Am Col of Phys; Am Phy Soc; Am Soc Biol Chems; Am Soc Clin Investigation; Am Soc Exptl Pathol; Assn Am Phys; Mem, Intl Com on Hemostasis & Thrombosis; r/Jewish; hon/Author of Over 265 Pubs in Profl Jours; Editor: Textbook on Hemostasis & Thrombosis; Others; Leon Resnick Prize for Outstg Res, Harvard Med Sch; Sigma Xi; Phi Beta Kappa; Alpha Omega Alpha; Career Devel Awd; Editor, *Thrombosis Res*; Edit Bd, *Jour Clin Investigation*.

COLUMBU, FRANCO MARIA oc/ Chiropractor; Actor; b/Aug 7, 1941; h/ Box 415, Santa Monica, CA 90406; ba/ Los Angeles, CA; p/Antonio and Maria, Ollolai, Italy; ed/DC, PhD; pa/ Self-Employed, Chiropractor; Actor; Bodybldr; Num TV Appearances; Num Radio Appearances; Num Movie Appearances; Lectr on Bodybldg & Hlth; Am Chiropractic Assn; ACA Coun on Sports Injuries; CA Chiropractic Assn; Nat Hlth Fdn; Intl Fdn of Bodybldrs; Am Fdn of TV & Radio Artists; Screen Actors Guild; hon/Num Profl Pubs; Bodybldg Titles: Mr Olympia, Mr Universe, Mr World, Mr Intl, Mr Europe, Mr Italy; Powerlifting Title: World Champ, European Champ; Powerlifting World Records: Bench Press- 525 lbs, Squat- 655 lbs, Deadlift- 750 lbs; Weightlifting Records: Snatch- 280 lbs, Jerk- 405 lbs; Boxing: Boxing Champ of Italy (Amateur Div); Subject of Num Newspaper & Mag Articles.

COLVIN, JOE C JR oc/Educator; b/ Jan 12, 1942; h/PO Box 66862 Houston, TX 77266; ba/Houston, TX; p/Joe C Colvin (dec); Lillian Ann Colvin, Austin, TX; ed/BA, Univ of TX-Austin, 1967; MEd, Sam Houston St Univ, 1972; mil/ AUS NG, 1960-66; pa/Sec'dy Tchr, Aldine, ISD, 1967-74 & 1976-79; Supvr Student Tchrs, Univ of Houston, 1974-76; Chp, Aldine Contemp Ed Ctr, 1978-79; Spec Ed, N Forest ISD, Houston, 1980-82; Spec Ed, Houston ISD, 1982-83; Mem: TSTA, NEA, 1967-79; AFT, 1980-82; Cope Dir, HFT, 1982-83; ASCD, 1974-; Phi Alpha Theta, 1972-; Nat Coun for the Social Studies, Houston & TX CSS, 1970-; cp/Houston JC's 1967-70; Conslt, Gtr Houston Closeup Prog, 1981-; r/Epis; hon/Author & Contbr Articles to *Perspectives*; "Students Change & the Ednl Process," 1980; *Student Tchrs Handbook*, 1975; *50 St Energy Curric*, 1978; Alt Del, Dem Conv, 1976 & 1982; Spoke Awd, Houston JC's, 1968; W/W in S & SW.

COLWELL, T C oc/Labor Relations Specialist; b/Jun 23, 1953; h/3091 Chester Grove Road, Upper Marlboro, MD 20772; ba/Bethesda, MD; p/BA, Chatham Col, 1975; JD, Vanderbilt Univ Sch of Law, 1978; pa/Labor Relats Spec, Dept of Nav, Wash DC, 1981-; Labor Relats Spec, Fed Labor Relats Auth, Wash DC, 1980-82; Staff Atty, Atlanta Legal Aid Soc, Atlanta, GA,

1978-80; Mem: Fed Labor Relats Profls, 1980-; Arbitrator, BBB, 1981-; Nat Conf of Black Lwyrs, 1980-; hon/Team Cash Awd for Outstg Case Productivity, Fed Labor Relats Auth, 1981-82.

COMBIER, ELIZABETH IRENE oc/ Communications Executive; b/Jul 11, 1949; h/315 East 65th Street, New York, New York 10021; ba/Same; p/Julia Taschereau, NYC, NY; ed/BA, NWn Univ, 1971; Deg, Johns Hopkins Univ Sch of Adv'd Intl Studies, 1975; Further Studies: Columbia Univ; Meridien Travel Sch; MPS Interactive Telecommuns Prog, NY Univ, 1983; pa/Sales Order Correspondent, Memorex Corp, 1971-72; Mgmt Conslt, DeMares Investmt Co, 1972-74; Prodr, "Cue-on-J"/TV, *Cue* Mag, 1976-77; Pres, Combier Communs (Prod'g Documentary TV), 1977; Pres, Combier Solar Communs & Ecomedia Intl, 1979-; Prod'd Video in Egypt, Israel & Jordon, 1980-83; Editor, *The Bus Initiative Newslttr*, 1983; Mem: Intl Solar Energy Soc; Assn of Indep Video & Film; Solar Lobby; Wom in Film; Intl Radio & TV Soc; French-Am Active; Intl Inst of Communs; Intl Communs Assn; hon/ Author, "Solar-Powered Video," in *Communs & Devel*, 1983; "Computers in Egypt," in *Vita News*, 1983; "Increasing Awareness in 3rd World by Solar Video"; Art Awds, 1975; Nom'd for Marconi Intl F'ship Awd, 1980; W/W: in E, of Am Wom.

COMBS, GERALD FUSON oc/ Administrator; b/Feb 23, 1920; h/10750 Kinloch Road, Silver Spring, MD 20903; ba/Beltsville, MD; m/Lily Ijams; c/ Gerald F Jr, Lawrence L, John W, Gregory L; p/Mr and Mrs Lloyd R Combs, Olney, IL; sp/Mr and Mrs Luther L Ijams (dec); ed/BS, Univ of IL, 1940; PhD Animal Nutrition, Cornell Univ, 1948; mil/AUS, 1941-46, USAR 1946-80, Lt Col (Ret'd); pa/Grad Res Asst in Nutrition 1940-41, Grad Res Fellow in Nutrition 1946-48, Cornell Univ; Nutrition Ofcr, AUS, 1941-46; Asst Hd Nutrition Sect, Ofc of Intl Res, NIH, 1965-66; Chief Intl Staff & Dept Chief Nutrition Prog, HSMHA, Dept Hlth, Ed & Welfare, 1969-71; Nutrition & Food Safety Coor, USDA, 1971-73; Prof & Hd Foods & Nutrition, Sch of Home Ec, Univ of GA, 1973-75; Nutrition Prog Dir, NIADDK, NIH, 1975-83; Asst Dept Admr for Human Nutrition, ARS, USDA, 1983-; Mem: FAO Adv Panel in Animal Nutrition, 1960-70; Wkg Grp on Nutrition & Man in Space Com, Nat Res Coun, 1962-70; Pres, Fdn of Am Socs for Exptl Biol, 1979-80; Bd Mem, Soc of Nutrition Ed; Bd of Trustees, Animal Nutrition Coun; Conslt in Human Nutrition, Interdeptl Com on Nat Def, 1956-69; Liaison Mem for AIN, Nat Res Coun, NAS, 1965-69; Am Inst of Nutrition; APHA; AAAS; Animal Nutrition Res Coun; NY Acad of Scis; Poultry Sci Assn; World Poultry Sci Assn; Nat & Local Chapts, Soc Exptl Biol & Med; Num Other Com Positions & Appts w Orgs; r/Meth; hon/Author, Over 200 Sci Pubs on Nutrition; Bronze Star, AUS, 1945; Res Awd in Poultry Nutrition, Am Feed Mfrs Assn, 1953; Man of Yr Awd in MD Agri, 1959; Alpha Gamma Rho Awd for Outstg Contbns in Tchg & Res, Col of Agri, Univ of MD, 1964; Meritorious Ser Awd, Delmarva Poultry Industs, 1969; Dist'd

Nutritionist Awd, Distillers Res Coun, 1970; Sigma Xi; Alpha Zeta; Phi Kappa Phi; Omicron Nu; Phi Tau Sigma; W/ W: in E, in Frontier Sci & Technol, in Am Ed; Commun Ldrs of the World; Am Men of Sci; Other Biogl Listings.

COMBS, JULIA CAROLYN oc/Oboist, Educator, Professor; b/Jul 11, 1950; h/1123 South Seventh Street, Laramie, WY 82070; ba/Laramie, WY; m/William B Stacy; p/Joe D and Fay M Combs, Bromaugh, MO; sp/Ralph and Marjory Stacy, Middletown, OH; ed/BMus 1972, MMus 1974, Memphis St Univ; Postgrad Study: Cath Univ of Am, 1976-77; DM Cand, N TX St Univ Sch of Music, Currently; mil/AUS, 1975-78, TUSA Band "Pershing's Own"; pa/Oboist, 1971-74; Solo Eng Horn, Memphis Opera Theater, 1971-74; 2nd Oboe, Memphis Symp, 1972-74; Sole E Horn, Norfolk VA Symp, 1974-75; Prin Oboe, Norfolk Opera Theater, 1974-75; Prin Oboe, AUS Chamber Orch, Ft Myer, VA, 1975-78; Asst Prof Oboe, Univ of WY, 1978-; Ooboist, New World Wind Quartet, 1978-; Mem: Intl Double Reed Soc; Phi Kappa Phi; Pi Kappa Lambda; Fdg Mem, Wom in the Arts; MENC; MTNA; NACWPI; AAUW; Sigma Alpha Iota; Alpha Lambda Delta; Union Internationale de la Marionnette; Sonneck Soc; Frequent Guest Clinician & Spkr; r/Prot; hon/Num Annual Solo Oboe & Oboe d'amore Recitals; Chamber Music Perfs, w New World Wind Quartet; Soloist, Wn Arts Music Fest; Cit for Outstg Musical Ser during Bicent, AUS, 1976; John P Ellbogen Awd for Meritorious Clrm Tchg, Univ of WY, 1983; W/W of Am Wom; Personalities of W & MW.

COMBS, WARREN DENT oc/Pastor; b/Dec 19, 1920; h/3409 West 6th Street Road, Greeley, CO 80631; ba/Greeley, CO; m/Marjorie Hutcheson Gates; c/ Larry LeRoy, Warren Elliott, Anna Marjean, Vernon Pledger; p/William Myron and Nettie Lily Weller Combs (dec); ed/BA, Apostolic Bible Col; Att'd Univ of NC-Chapel Hill; pa/Lobbyist, ID St Leg, 1960-73; Full-time Ordained Min; Pastor for 24 Yrs; Evang for 13 Yrs; Author; Asst Supt, Assems of God in ID, 1962-72; cp/Former Mem, Commun Hosp Bd, Nampa, ID; Mem, ID St PTA Bd; Former Lobbyist, ID St Leg; r/Assem of God; hon/Author *Pentecostal Catechism*; *Pentecostal Catechism Enlarged*; World Traveler; W/W in Am, in Rel.

COMEAU, PAUL THEODORE oc/ Professor; b/Sep 21, 1926; h/1023 Avondale Drive, Las Cruces, NM 88005; ba/Las Cruces, NM; m/Ruby J Klindt; c/Stephen P, Michael F, Lisa M MacMillian; p/Laurent H and Leda (Henley) Comeau (dec); sp/Marie Klindt, Rocky Ford, CO; ed/BA, Assumption Col, 1949; MA 1964, PhD French Lang & Lit 1968, Princeton Univ; mil/AUS, 1945-46; USAF, 1950-75, Lt Col (Ret'd); pa/USAF: Intell NCO, 1950-52; Communs Intel Ofcr, NSA, 1952-55; Security Ser, 1955-61; Assoc Prof French, Chief Acad Advr Humanities, USAF Acad, 1964-70; Dir of Curric & Prof Aerospace Studies, AFROTC, 1970-75; Dept Hd, Dept of Fgn Langs 1975-83, Assoc Prof French/Latin 1983-, NM St Univ; Mem: VPres & Pres, NM Chapt, Am Assn of Tchrs of French (AATF), 1980-84; Reviewer, *World Lit Today*, 1981-83; Fac Senate, NM St Univ,

1980-81; cp/Secy/Treas 1976-77, Dir 1977-78, VPres 1978-79, Pres 1979-80, Rotary Clb of Las Cruces; Chm Spec Gifts 1974, Bd of Dirs 1978-80, U Way; r/Rom Cath; hon/Author, *Wkbook for Wheelock's Latin*, 1980; Num Articles in Profl Jours on French Lit, 1966-81; Var Book Reviews, *World Lit Today*, 1980-82; NEH F'ship, French Lit, Univ of Pgh, 1977; Fac Res Grant, French Romanticis, NM St Univ, 1978-81; W/W in W; Dir of Am Scholars.

COMMON, KENNETH DOUGLAS oc/Optometrist; b/Oct 8, 1949; h/126 Bremerton Avenue, Southeast, Renton, WA 98056; ba/Seattle, WA; m/Roxie M; c/Ronni, Paula, Jennifer, Daniel; p/W Kenneth and Ida M Common, Westwood, NJ; sp/James and Mildred Shannon, Lakeside, CA; ed/BA, Rutgers Univ, 1971; OD, N England Col of Optom, 1976; mil/USN, 1976-81; USAFR, 1982-; pa/Staff Optometrist 1976-81, Chief of Ser 1980-81, USN Hosp, Oak Harbor, WA; Owner, SEA-TAC Vision Clin, Seattle, WA, 1981-; Pt-time Optometrist, Pacific Med Ctr, 1982-; Team Optometrist: Seattle Mariners (Baseball), 1983-; Seattle Breakers (Hockey), 1983-; Mem 1972-, Contact Lens Sect 1981-, Am Optometric Assn; Mem 1977-, Contact Lens Com 1983-84, WA Optometric Assn; King Co Optometric Soc, 1981-; Bausch & Lomb Coun on Sports Vision, 1977-; r/Christian; hon/Author, "An Eye Opener For US Cols," *NJ Jour of Optom*, 1974; "Fabry's Disease (Angiokeratoma Corporus Diffusum)," *Optometric Monthly*, 1984; W/W in W.

COMPEL, ROBERT MICHAEL oc/Director of Industrial Relations; b/Nov 21, 1939; h/2810 Alder Court, Abingdon, MD 21009; c/Petra Michaela, Nicole Veronique; p/Marie Compel, Pittsburgh, PA; ed/BS, Univ of MD, 1974; Att'd Univ of Pgh & Duquesne Univ; mil/AUS, 1960-66; pa/Asst Controller & Loss Preven Spec, Montgomery Ward, 1968-70; Safety Engr 1970-71, Asst Mgr of Indust Relats 1971-75, Pantry Pride Stores Inc; Mgr of Indust Relats, Crown, Cork & Seal Inc, 1975-77; Mgr of Indust Relats, Filterite Corp, 1977-79; Pt-time Instr Pers Mgmt, Harford Commun Col, 1977-; Dir Pers & Indust Relats, J H Filbert Inc, 1980-; Trustee, Warehousemen's Local 570 Hlth & Welfare Fund; Trustee, Warehousemen's Local 570 Pension Fund; Am Soc for Pers Adm; Am Soc of Safety Engrs; Pers Admrs Assn of Balto; Bd of Dirs, Epoint Hlth Ctr Inc; Secy, Bd of Dirs, Metro Balto Hlth Care Inc; hon/W/W in E.

COMPTON, DWIGHT SPEIR oc/Educator; b/Feb 15, 1917; h/222 High Street, Valdosta, GA 31601; ba/Valdosta, GA; m/Margaret B; c/Ervyn D, Robert B, John M; p/Mr and Mrs W D Compton (dec); sp/Mr and Mrs Sidney C Bennett (dec); ed/BSEd 1938, MEd 1949, Univ of GA; PhD, FL St Univ, 1977; mil/USAF, 1941-45; pa/HS Tchr, 1938-41; HS Prin, 1945-58; Exec, Field Enterprises, 1958-75; Asst Prof of Ed 1977-81, Assoc Prof of Ed 1981-, USC; Conslt; Lectr; cp/AAWP; Lions, 1954-58 (Pres, 1958); Rotary, 1963-, (Bd of Dirs, 1964 & 1973); Mid GA Scout Comm, 1958-62; VP, GEA, 1956; Local Pres, GEA, 1954-56; GA Bd of Regents, Staff Devel Comm, 1979-; USC Grad Exec

Comm, 1980-82; r/Meth; hon/Author 3 Articles & 2 Monographs; Phi Kappa Phi; Phi Delta Kappa; Kappa Delta Pi; W/W in S & SW.

CONAWAY, JULIA BONDANELLA oc/Professor; b/Jan 1, 1943; h/1040 South Mitchell Street, Bloomington, IN 47401; ba/Bloomington, IN; m/Peter Bondanella; p/Charles B Conaway, Sidney, MT; Marion Rohlff (dec); sp/Frank Bondanella, Buffalo, NY; Dorothy Bondonella, Greensboro, NC; ed/BA, Univ of MT, 1965; Att'd Universite Laval, Sum 1964; MA French, Univ of KS, 1967; Cert d'études in French, Université de Montpellier, Sum 1971; PhD Comparative Lit, Univ of OR, 1973; pa/Pt-time Fr Instr, Univ of OR, Sum 1968, 1969-70; Eng Instr, Wayne St Univ, 1970 73; Asst Prof & Coor Freshman Hons Sem, Hons Div 1974-80, Assoc Prof Hon Div 1980-, Assoc Dir Hon Div 1982-, IN Univ; Mem: MLA; Am Comparative Lit Assn; Am Assn of Tchrs of Italian; Exe Secy 1980-, AAUP of Italian; Nat Col Hons Coun; r/Epis; hon/Author, *Petrarch's Visions & Their Renaissance Analogues*; *Dic of Italian Lit*, 1979; *The Macmillan Dic of Italian Lit*, 1979; Other Articles Pub'd in Profl Jours; Best Ref Wks Awd for *Dic of Italian Lit*, Am Lib Assn, 1979.

CONAGHAN, DOROTHY DELL oc/State Legislator in House of Representatives; b/Sep 24, 1930; h/PO Box 402, Tonkawa, OK 74653; ba/Oklahoma City, OK; m/Brian Francis (dec); c/Lee, Charles, Roger; p/Joe J Miller (dec); Wilhelmina E Swope; ed/Att'd Univ of OK; pa/Mem OK Ho of Reps, 1973-; Minority Caucus Secy, 1977-82; Asst Minority Ldr, 1983-84; Current Mem: Ed, Agri, Public Safety, Penal Affairs Coms & VChm, Higher Ed Com; cp/VChm, Kay Co Repubs, 1961-65; VChm, 6th Congl Dist, Repub Party, 1967-69; Del, Repub Nat Conv, 1968; St Dir, Am Legis Exch Coun, 1980-84; Adv Mem, No OK Col Nsg Sch, 1980-84; Secy, OK St Yg Repubs, 1957; Com Mem, Kay Co Repub Exec; OK Repub St Exec Com, 1967-71; Delphi Study Clb; PEO; Tonkawa C of C; Am Legion Aux; Org of Wom Legis; St Bd Mem, Yg Ams for Freedom, 1981; Cher-Ok-Kan Gateway Assn; Num Other Commun Activs; hon/Beta Sigma Phi; Wom Helping Wom Awd, Soroptomist Clb, 1975; W/W: in Am Polits, of Am Wom, in S & SW; Commun Ldrs of Am; Dir of Dist'd Ams; Num Other Biogl Listings.

CONANT, HOWARD SOMERS oc/Educator, Artist; b/May 5, 1921; ba/Dept of Art, Univ of AZ, Tucson, AZ 85718; m/Florence C Craft; c/Judith Lynne (C) Steinbach, Jeffrey Scott; p/Rufus P and Edith B (Somers) Conant; ed/Att'd, Art Students Leag, NY, 1944-45; BS, Univ of WI-Milwaukee, 1946; MS, Univ of WI-Madison, 1947; EdD, Univ of Buffalo, 1950; mil/USAF, 1943-46, Lt; pa/Art Instr, Asst Hd WI, 1946-47; Asst Prof Art, St Col for Tchrs, Buffalo, 1947-50; Prof Art 1950-55, Dept Art Chm & Chm Art Collection 1955-76, NY Univ; Art Dept Hd, Univ of AZ, Tucson, 1976-; Mem: Intl Art Critics Assn; Nat Assn of Schs of Art & Design; Col Art Assn; Alliance for Arts Ed; Coun, Chm 1962-63, Nat Comm Art Ed; Bd of Govs 1965-72, Pres 1965-68, Inst for Study of Art in Ed;

cp/Art Ed Conslt to NBC-TV & GSA TV Series, 1958-60; Field Rdr & Title III Prog Conslt, US Ofc of Ed; Advr, NY St Coun on Arts, 1962-63; CT Comm on Arts, 1967-68; Conslt, Ford Foun, 1973; Chd's Theater Assn, 1973; Moderator: Wkly TV Prog "Fun to Learn About Art," WBEN-TV, Buffalo, 1951-55; Lectr, St Dept, India, 1964; Dir, Waukesha Co (WI) YMCA Art Prog, 1956-48; Chd's Creat Art Foun 1959-60; Advy Com, Col of Potomac, 1966; Pres, Torch Clb (NYC), 1965-66; hon/Num One Man Shows; Num Grp Exhbns; Author, (w Arne Randall), *Art in Ed*, 1959 & 1963; Co-Author & Co-Editor: *Masterpieces of the Arts*, Volume 4, 1963; *Sem on Elem & Sec'dy Sch Ed in the Visual Arts*, 1965; *Art Ed*, 1964; *Art Wkshop Ldrs Planning Guide*, 1958; *Lincoln Lib of the Arts*, 2 Volumes, 1973; Art Editor, *Intellect*, 1975-78; *USA Today*, 1978-; Assoc Editor, *Arts Mag*, 1973-75; Contbr, Num Articles in Profl Pubs; Recip Medal, Nat Gallery Art, 1966; Dist'd Alumnus Awd, Univ of WI-Milwaukee, 1968; W/W in Am.

CONE, GEORGE WALLIS oc/Attorney; Pharmacist; b/Jul 20, 1945; h/PO Box 233, Walterboro, SC 29488; ba/Walterboro, SC; m/Patricia Ann Stabenow; c/Jennifer Lee, Laura Katherine, David Wallis; p/W Harry and Agnes Hill Cone (dec); sp/Lee D and Daisy W Stabenow, Shawnee Mission, KS; ed/BSPh 1967, JD 1973, Univ of GA; Att'd Clemson Univ; mil/SC Army NG, 1970-76; pa/Clerk 1955-67, Pharm-in-Charge 1967-76, Walterboro Drug Co; Atty & Ptnr, McLeod, Fraser & Unger, Attys at Law, 1976-; SC Bd of Pharm, 1981-; SC Humane Assn, Bd of Dirs 1978-, Treas 1979-; Public Defender Corp of Colleton Co, Bd of Dirs 1978-, Secy 1979-; Colleton Co Bd of Registration, 1982-; SC Pharm Assn 1967-, House of Dels 1975-76, 1977-78, 1979-; 14th Dist Pharm Assn 1967-, VP 1974-75, Pres 1975-76 & 1980-82, Secy 1976-80; Am Pharm Assn 1970-; Am Soc for Pharm Law, 1974-; NARD, 1981-; ABA, 1974-; St Bar of GA, 1973-; SC Bar Assn, 1974-; Colleton Co Bar Assn, 1976-; SC Trial Lwyrs Assn, 1979; cp/Colleton Co Alcohol & Drug Abuse Comm 1979-81, Chm 1980-81; Lowcountry Commun Action Agy, Bd of Dirs, 1980-; Colleton Co SPCA, Pres 1975-77, Bd of Dirs 1975-; Walterboro Sertoma Clb, Treas 1975-76, VP 1976-77, Pres 1977-78; r/Bapt; hon/Notes Editor 1971-72, Reviews & Comments Editor 1972-73, *GA Jour of Intl & Comparative Law*; Outstg Yg Men of Am; W/W in S & SW.

CONELY, GAIL S oc/Corporate Vice President; b/Aug 11, 1947; h/146 West 74th Street, Apartment 4, New York, NY 10023; ba/New York, NY; m/William S; p/Roy J and Sue W Smith, Toccoa, GA; sp/Andrew and Mabel Conely, Gainesville, FL; ed/BBA, GA St Univ, 1976; pa/Staff Acct, Deloite Haskins & Sells, 1976-80; Acct'g Mgr 1980-82, VP 1982-83, Salomon Brothers Inc; VP, FTS Inc, 1983-; Am Inst of CPA's, 1976-; r/Meth; hon/CPA Profl Designation in GA & NY; W/W in E.

CONEY, CHARLES CLIFTON oc/Malacologist; ba/Los Angeles County Museum of Natural History, 900 Exposition Boulevard, Los Angeles, CA 90007; c/Sonia Lorraine; p/Charles H and Sue Coney, Kingsport, TN; ed/BS 1977, MS 1980, E TN St Univ; pa/Biol Instr, Univ of SC, 1980-83; Collection Mgr, Malcology Sect, LA Co Mus of Natural Hist, 1983-; Mem: Am Malacological Union; AAAS; hon/Author of Var Profl Papers on Paesozoic Crinoids & Recent Mollusks; W/W in Frontier Sci & Technol.

CONFINO, SHIRLEY ROSE LEWIS oc/Interior Designer; b/Oct 20, 1940; h/132 Osborne Road, Norfolk, VA 23503; ba/Norfolk, VA; c/Steven Howard; Liza Beth Dara; p/Benjamin Milton and Lena Abrin Lewis (dec); ed/BA magna cum laude, Queens Col, 1977; Cert of Interior Design, NY Sch of Interior Design, 1973; pa/Admr, Aluminum Ltd, 1959-62; Indep Artist, 1963-64; Owner, Ideas Unlimited, 1970-79; Shirley Confino Interiors, 1980-; Tchr, Norfolk Voc HS; Bd of Dirs, Cultural Experiences; Bd of Dirs, Nat Bus & Profl Wom; Co-Fdr, LA Chapt, Dysautonomia Foun, 1972; Org'd & Lectr, Wom in Bus, 1979-83; Am Soc of Interior Designers; cp/VP of Queens Chapt, Cancer Care, 1964-70; Quota Clb, 1980-; Norfolk C of C; World Affairs Coun; hon/Profl Pubs; Hons in Art; Superior S'ship, Queens Col, 1978; W/W of Am Wom.

CONGDON, JILL SUZANNE oc/Technical Support Programmer Analyst; b/Feb 27, 1953; h/8007 Xerxes Avenue South, Bloomington, MN 55431; ba/Minneapolis, MN; s/Vicky Lynn Gardner-Scharping; p/Woodrow F and Gale E Congdon; ed/AA, NWn MI Col, 1973; Res & Devel Spec A, Am Pathols Computer Ctr, 1976; Acct'g Sys Coor, Supervalu Corp HQ, 1980; Tech Support Anal, E W Blanche Co, 1982; Tech Support Programmer Anal, 1st Bk Mpls, 1983; Freelance Tech Conslt; Bd of Dirs, Eberhardt Co as Homeowner Liaison; Bd of Dirs, Pembco Corp as Homeowner Liaison; r/Evang Christian; hon/Guest Spkr, Al-Anon, 1981; Appeared on Today Show, 1964; Nat Hon Soc, 1970; $100,000 Clb in Real Est, 1979.

CONLEY, JAMES FRANCIS oc/Engineer; b/Sep 19, 1948; h/PO Box 730, Highland Lakes, NJ 07422; ba/Little Falls, NJ; p/James F Conley, Howell, NJ; ed/BCE, Villanova Univ, 1974; MS, NJ Inst of Technol, 1976; mil/USN, LCDR, CEC; pa/Sr Engr 1974-78, Chief Engr 1978-80, Water Supply Div of City of Newark, NJ; Pres, Janell Assoc Conslt'g Engrs, 1980-84; Profl Engr; Nat Soc of Profl Engrs; Soc of Am Mil Engrs; Am Water Works Assn; ASCE; Res Ofcrs Assn of US; Nav Res Assn; r/Cath; hon/Profl Pubs; Mem of US Delegation to XIV UPADI, Pan Am Engrg Conf on Food, Energy & Envir; Alumni & Profl Pubs.

CONNELLEE-CLAY, BARBARA GALBRAITH oc/Administrative Staff Member; h/344 Kimberly, Los Alamos, NM 87544; ba/Los Alamos, NM; m/Edward L Clay; c/Alison Stephens, Rebecca Crabtree, Calvin Clay, Larry Clay, Rebecca Owens; p/Herman and Audrey Galbraith (dec); ed/Bach in Univ Studies w hons 1976, MBA 1981, Univ of NM; pa/Fin Budget Spec 1976-, Facilitator of Quality Circles 1982-, Los Alamos Nat Lab; Wom in Sci; Los Alamos Optical Soc; NSA; Past Pres, Wesleyan Ser Guild; Exec Female Inc; Intl Assn of Quality Circles; cp/Chm,

March of Dimes; Girl Scout Ldr for 3 Yrs; Adm Bd, Commun Chest for 2 Yrs; Ed Dir, U Meth Ch; r/Meth; hon/Author "Quality Circles in a Res & Devel Envir;" Dept of Labor Region 8 Coun on Wking Wom Awd, 1983; Blue Key Nat Hon Soc, 1976; W/W in W.

CONNELLY, FRANK JOHN III oc/Educator; b/Oct 13, 1932; h/Box 300a, North Windham, CT 06256; ba/Willimantic, CT; m/Muriel Glaude; c/Christopher Frank; p/Frank J and Loretta A Connelly (dec); sp/Emil (dec) and Primor Glaud, Willimantic, CT; ed/BA, St Francis Col, 1959; MA, City Col of NY, 1966; mil/USN, 1951-55; pa/Lang Arts Spec, The Gilbert Sch, 1963-66; Lang Arts Spec, NYC Bd of Ed, 1966-68; Asst Prof of Phil 1968-81, Assoc Prof of Phil 1980-, En CT St Univ; Pres, En CT St Univ Chapt 1970 of CT St Fdn of Tchrs; Pres, En CT St Univ Local 2137 CSFT-AFT-AFL-CIO, 1970-76; Pres Col & Univ Coun CSFT-AFT-AFL-CIO; St VP in Charge of Polit Activs, CSFT-AFT-AFL-CIO; Local Grievance Ofcr, En CT St Univ Local of CT St AAUP, 1982-; Am Phil Assn, 1968-; r/Judaeo-Christian; hon/Profl Pubs; Rose Ficarra Awd, St Francis Col, 1959; Hons for Cath Action, St Francis Col, 1959; Duns Scotus Hon Soc, St Francis Col, 1958; Outstg Fac Mem, Col Union Bd of Govs, En CT St Univ, 1971; Outstg Fac Mem, Col Union Bd of Govs, 1972; Featured Spkr Ldrship Banquet, En CT St Univ, 1975; Featured Spkr Ldrship Banquet, En CT St Univ, 1977; Awd for Dedication to Class of 1980, En CT St Univ, 1980; W/W in E.

CONNELLY, MICHAEL ROBERT oc/Attorney; b/Oct 28, 1947; h/15606 Treasurer Street, Baton Rouge, LA 70816; ba/Baton Rouge, LA; m/Marilyn Memory; c/Sean Michael, Patrick Devlin; p/Roy E Connelly, NO, LA; Marjorie B Connelly (dec); ed/BA; JD LSU; mil/USAR, Capt; pa/Baton Rouge Bar Assn; Law Day Com; Spkrs Bur; Nat Justice Foun; cp/Nat Dir Citizens Com for the Right to Keep & Bear Arms; Nat Dir Counsel for Inter-Am Security; Former Exec Dir, LA Conservative Union; Former Nat Secy Yg Ams for Freedom; Atty Baton Rouge Right to Life; Alt Del Repub Nat Conv, 1976; Nat Dir 2nd Amendment Foun; Chm, LA Conservative Union, 1981-; Dir, Am Conservative Union, 1981-; LA Repub St Ctl Com, 1979-; Others; r/U Meth; hon/Hon Cert Awd, Freedoms Foun; Geo Wash Hon Medal, Freedoms Foun; Ser Above Self Awd, Baton Rouge Rotary; Yg Ams for Freedom: Outstg Achmt Awd, Advocate of Freedom Awd; Outstg Yg Men of Am.

CONRAD, VIRGINIA JOAN MATTHEWS oc/Educator; b/Jul 10, 1931; h/PO Box 296, 7410 D Street, Chesapeake Beach, MD 29732; ba/Prince Frederick, MD; c/Matthew Mark; p/Blanche Elizabeth W Matthews (dec); Robert Andrew Matthews, Swarthmore, PA; ed/BS, W Chester St Univ, 1954; MA, Villanova Univ, 1960; pa/Tchr, Ridley Twp, PA, 1954-58; Tchr, Upper Merior Twp, PA, 1958-64; Tchr, Long Br, NJ, 1964-65; Tchr, Manalapan-Englishtown, NJ, 1967-68; Tchr, Indian Creek Sch, Crownsville, MD, 1973-74; Freelance Ed Conslt; NEA; Calvert Co Ed Assn; Assn of Supvn & Curric Devel; MD Assn of Supvn & Curric Devel; r/

Christian; hon/Nat Hon Soc; W/W in E.

CONTRERAS, ANDREW oc/Student; b/Jun 4, 1961; h/605 15th, Snyder, TX 79549; ba/Same; p/Santos and Estolia Contreras, Snyder, TX; ed/HS Dipl, 1980; Wn TX Col, 1982; pa/Student; Pt-time Salesman; cp/Judo Clb; Band Capt; VPres, Student Coun; Pres, Reporter, Indust Arts Clb; Soph Class Pres; Jr Hist of Am; Boys' St; Track; Kappa Delta Pi; r/Cath; hon/St Reg Awds, Indust Arts; Medals, Music Competition; Superior & Hon Roll; Citizen of Yr; AFS Excell Student, Nat Hon Soc; Phi Theta Kappa; Yg Texan of Mo; W/W Among Am HS Students.

CONTRERAS, DARLENE ROWELL oc/Rancher; b/Jun 16l 1926; h/507 Buck Avenue, Vacaville, CA 95688; ba/Same; m/John (dec); c/Patricia Chandler, Pamela Davis; p/Myrlen (dec) and Ada Rowell, Vacaville, CA 95688; ed/HS Grad; pa/Ser Rep, Pacific Telephone Co, 1955-66; Bkkpr, Mobile Oil Bulk Plant, 1967-75; Mobile Oil Distbr, 1978-81; Rancher, 1981-; CA Farm Bur Fdn; cp/IPA; Yolo Fliers Country Clb; r/Prot; hon/O & A Mkting News; W/W: in CA, of Am Wom.

CONWAY de MACARIO, EVERLY oc/Research Scientist; b/Apr 20, 1939; h/18 Carriage Road, Delmar, NY 12054; ba/Albany, NY; m/Alberto J L; c/Alex, Everly; p/Delfin E and Maria G (Benatuil) Conway (dec); sp/Alberto C and Maria Elena (Giraudi) Macario, Villa Mercedes, Argentina; ed/PhD Phar, 1960; PhD Biochem, 1962; pa/Res Sci, Lab Med Inst, NY St Dept of Hlth, Albany, 1976-; Vis'g Sci, Brown Univ, Providence, RI, 1974-76; Vis'g Sci, Intl Agy for Res on Cancer, World Hlth Org, Lyon, France, 1973-74; Sr Res Sci, Lab of Cell Biol, Nat Res Coun of Italy, Rome, 1971-73; Res Fellow, Dept of Tomor-biol, Karolinska Inst, Stockholm, Sweden, 1969-71; Hd Lab of Oncology & Immunol, Argentinian Assn Agst Cancer, Buenos Aires, 1966-77; Res Fellow, Nat Acad of Med of Argentina, Buenos Aires, 1962-63; Mem: Scandinavian Soc for Immunol, 1970-; Italian Assn of Immunols, 1973-; French Soc for Immunol, 1974-; Am Assn of Immunols, 1977-; Am Soc for Microbiol, 1982; r/Cath; hon/Author, Over 80 Sci Pubs in Jours & Books; Prof J M Mezzadra Awd, Nat Univ of Buenos Aires, 1969; Winifred Cullis Grant, Intl Fedn of Univ Wom, 1972; Travel Awd, Am Assn of Immmunols, 1977; Gold Medal, Argentinian Assn of Biochem Awd, 1980; Sci Referee for NATO, 1980-83; Chm, Am Assn of Immunols Com, 1980-85; W/W: in E, in Frontier Sci & Technol; Intl Book of Hon; Other Biogl Listings.

COOK, CHARLES WILLIAM oc/Air Force Administrator; b/Sep 27, 1927; h/1180 Delaview Drive, McLean, VA 22102; ba/Washington, DC; m/Virginia Fosness; c/Jennifer C CLark, William O, Amy E; ed/AB, Univ of SD, 1951; MS 1954, PhD 1957, CA Inst of Technol; mil/USAAC, 1944; pa/Hd, Nuclear Physics, Convair, 1957-60; Chief, Ballistic Missile Def Br, Adv'd Res Proj Agy, 1961; Corp Dir, Elect, N Am Aviation, 1962-67; Dept Div Chief, CIA, 1967-71; Asst Dir, Dept of Def, 1971-74; Dept Under Secys Space Sys, USAF, 1974-79; Dept Asst Secy, Space Plans & Policy,

159

USAF, 1979-; Mem: Assoc Fellow, AIAA; Am Phy Soc; Am Inst of Physics; Sigma Xi; Phi Beta Kappa; IEEE; Sigma Pi Sigma; hon/Co-Author of Book, *Origin of the Elements (II) B^{12} C^{12} & the Red Giants;* Co-Author of Var Nuclear Physics Articles & Physics Reviews; Meritorious Civilian Ser 1974, Dist'd Ser 1977, Dept of Def; Coyote Hall of Fame 1967, Dist'd Alumni 1982, Univ of SD; Exceptl Civilian Ser, USAF, 1981 & 1982; W/W: in Am, in World; Other Biogl Listings.

COOK, DAVID HALL oc/Computer Scientist, Systems Sciences Division; b/ Oct 4, 1930; h/6217 Dana Avenue, Springfield, VA 22150; ba/Falls Church, VA; m/Joyce Fralic; c/David II, John; p/ Jennie Hall Cook, Montgomery, AL; sp/ Irene M Fralic, Montgomery, AL; ed/ BBA 1974, MAEd 1977, George Wash Univ; mil/USN, 1947-67; pa/USN: Airman, Mariner, 1947-67; Engr 1967-70, Sr Engr 1971-74, Tchr 1974-77, Sect Mgr 1977-79, Tng Mgr, Control Sys Activity, Computer Sci Corp, 1979-83; Mem: AAAS; Soc for Interdisciplinary Studies; US Nav Inst; Am Soc for Tng & Devel; Qtly Newslttr Editor, Phi Delta Kappa, 1977-81; Editor, *Ed Perspectives* 1977-81, Chapt Pres-Elect 1981, Pres 1982; NY Acad of Sci, 1981-; r/ Prot; hon/BSA Woodbadge, 1967; Am Def Commend & Good Conduct Medals, 1947-67; Meritorious Ser Awd, Def Communs Agy, 1967; Kiwanis Clb Outstg Ser Awd, 1973; USAF Lttr of Apprec, 1976; ABI Cert, 1979, 1980, 1981, 1982; Harvard Sch of Dental Med, Lttr of Apprec, 1981; Nat Bd of Advrs, ABI; W/W in S & SW; Commun Ldrs of Am; Dir of Dist'd Ams; 2000 Notable Ams.

COOK, GILLIAN ELIZABETH oc/ Educator; b/May 14, 1934; h/146 Future Drive, San Antonio, TX 78213; ba/San Antonio, TX; p/Harold T and Helena J Cook (dec); ed/BA w distn, Sir George Wms Univ, 1972; EdM 1973, EdD 1976, Harvard Univ; pa/Tchr, S Norwood Jr Boys Sch, 1956-58; Tchr, Freetown Sec'dy Sch for Girls, 1958-60; Tchr, Colmer's Farm Jr Sch, 1962-63; Tchr, B'ham Chd's Hosp Sch, 1963-66; Tchr, Maclearon Sch, 1966-67; Dept Chp & Eng Tchr, Howard S Billings Reg HS, 1967-72; Assoc Prof of Ed, Univ of TX-San Antonio, 1976-; NCTE; CEE Nom'g Com 1982; CEE Comm on Supvn, 1982-85; Standing Com on Tchr Preparation & Cert, 1979-82; CEE Comm on Tchr Preparation, 1978-81; Phi Delta Kappa: Exec Bd, UTSA Chapt, 1976-80; Exec Bd, Harvard Chapt, 1973-76; Am Ed Res Assn; Assn for Supvn & Curric Devel; ASCD Nat Comm on Supvn, 1983-85; Assn of Tchr Edrs; r/Epis; hon/Profl Pubs; Recip, AMOCO Tchg Proj Awd, 1981; W/W in S & SW.

COOK, HELGA GISELA oc/Executive Assistant; b/Jun 12, 1941; ba/ Pittsburgh, PA; c/Raymond J; p/Albert and Maria Woelk, W Germany; sp/ Raymond and Emily Cook, Pgh, PA; ed/ Att'd Vorbeck Lang Inst; pa/Secy, EDP Div of AUS, 1962-63; Comml Div, Honeywell, 1966-70; Pricing Clk in Mktg 1970-71, Biling Exec Secy in Polyurethane Div 1971-74, Exec Asst to Pres & CEO 1974-81, Exec Asst to Chm & Pres 1981-, Mobay Chem Corp; Am Soc Profl & Exec Wom; NAFE; cp/Chapt

Secy, Beaver-Lawrence-Butler Co Chapt, Muscular Dystrophy Assn, 1973-74; LRPSI Com of Beaver Co Area Voc-Tech Sch, 1983-; Assoc, Merrick Art Gallery; r/Luth; hon/W/W of Am Wom.

COOK, JOHN WILIAM oc/Research Astrophysicist; b/Oct 25, 1946; ba/ Naval Research Lab, Washington, DC 20375; pa/John W Cook (dec); Veda R Cook; ed/BS, MA Inst of Technol, 1967; MA, City Col of NY, 1970; PhD, Dartmouth Col, 1977; mil/AUS, 1969-71; pa/Res Sci, High Altitude Observatory, 1976-78; Res Astrophysicist, Solar Physics Br Space Sci Div, Nav Res Lab, 1978-; Mem: Am Astronom Soc; Solar Physics Div, Nom'g Com 1980, AAS; Intl Astronom Union; r/ Prot; hon/Author, Over 40 Articles, Reports & Abstracts in Jours & Other Profl Sci Pubs; W/W in Frontier Sci & Technol.

COOK, PETRONELLE MARGUERITE MARY (MARGOT ARNOLD) oc/ Author; Lecturer; b/May 16, 1925; h/ 11 High School Road, Hyannis, MA 02601; c/Philip R III, Nicholas E A, Alexandra M L; p/Harry A and Ada W Crouch, Sussex, England; ed/BA (Hons) 1946, Dipl 1947, MA 1950, Oxford Univ; pa/Curator, Sussex Archaeol Soc, 1948-49; Lectr, Univ of MD, 1971; Instr in Anthropology & Archaeol, Cape Cod Commun Col, 1973-; Archaeol Inst of Am; Boston Authors Clb; Nat Writers Clb; N Eng Hist & Geneal Soc; Planetary Soc; r/Epis; hon/Num Pubs; Travelling Scholar, Brit Inst of Archaeol, 1949; Ryerson Fellow of Prehist Archaeol, Univ of Chgo, 1952; Nat Writers Clb Profl Writers Dir; W/W in E.

COOK, ROBERT CROSSLAND oc/ Research Scientist; b/Jun 5, 1947; ba/ Lawrence Livermore National Lab, Livermore, CA 94550; c/Andrew, Daniel; p/Russell C Cook, Francestown, NH; Tensia V Cook (dec); ed/BS, Lafayette Col, 1969; MPh 1971, PhD 1973, Yale Univ; pa/Asst Prof Chem, Lafayette Col, 1973-81; Res Sci, Lawrence Livermore Nat Lab, 1981-; Vis'g Prof, Dartmouth Col, 1980; Mem: Am Phy Soc; Am Chem Soc; Sigma Xi; hon/ Co-Author, Over 12 Articles Pub'd in Profl Chem & Sci Jours; Recip, Num Res Grants; Phi Beta Kappa; Superior Tchg Awd, Lafayette Col Student Govt, 1980; W/W in W, in Technol; Other Biogl Listings.

COOLEY, J F oc/Minister, Educator, Civil Rights Activist; b/Jan 11, 1926; h/ PO Box 5150, North Little Rock, AR 72119; ba/Same; m/Carolyn A Butler; c/Virginia M Cooley Lewis, James F, Gladys M Cooley Taylor, Franklin D, Stephen Lamar; p/James F and Martha Buie Cooley; sp/Eddie and Ruby M Butler, Marion, LA; ed/AB 1953, BD 1956, MDiv 1973, Johnson C Smith Univ; Cultural Doct in Social Sci, World Univ, 1982; Cert Law Enforcement Instr, AR Comm on Law Enforcement Standards & Tng, 1982; 3 hon Doct Degs; mil/AUS, 1944-46, Chaplain, 1st Lt; pa/Min, Grant Chapel Presby Ch, Darien, GA, 1956-57; St Andrews Presby Ch, Forrest City, AR, 1957-69; Tchr, Forrest City Spec Sch Dist # 7, 1957-69; Juv Probation Ofct, St Francis Co, Forrest City, AR, 1959-68; Assoc Juv Judge, St Francis Co, Forrest City, AR, 1963-74; Polit Sci Dir, Min of Ser,

Dean of Men & Acad Dean, Shorter Col, 1969-73; Dept Sheriff, St Francis Co, 1961-62; Justice of Peace, Pulaski Co, 1973-74; Justice of Peace, 1975-76; Hon Dept Circuit Clk of Pulaski Co, 1977; Dept Sheriff Pulaski Co, 1977-80; Chief Legis Prison Aid to St Rep Grover Richardson, 1977-; Constable Dist 3-A, Pulaski Co, Little Rock, 1978-80; Pres, AR Constable's Assn, 1978; Chaplain Corps, Instr for Night Classes, Pulaski Co Correctional Facilities, 1977; Lt 1975, Capt 1977, Chm Recruitment Com on Minorities, Pvt Investigator, N Little Rock Police Dept; Spec Investigator, Prosecuting Atty's Ofc, Pulaski Co, 1975-77; Public Relats Ofcr, Consumer Protection Div, St Atty Gen's Ofc, 1975-81; Spec Dept Sheriff, Pulaski Co, 1981; Vis'g Tchr & Juv Ofcr, St Francis Co Juv Ct, 1963-65; Lt Col (Ret'd), Pulask Co Civil Def Org, 1978; Mem: AR Tchr' Assn; Intl Platform Assn; SANE; Am Security Coun; Nat Com of Black Chmen; Omega Psi Phi; NAACP; Nat Hist Soc; Nat Sheriff's Assn; Vets Org; Urban Leag; AR Law Enforcement Assn; Press Agt; Early Am Soc; Min Alliance of Ctr Little Rock; Juv Correction Assn; Num Other Mbrships & Orgs; cp/Fdr-Exec Dir, Ex-Inmate Mission & Talent Ctr, 1980; Fdr-Editor, *AR Wkly Sentinel;* Fdr-Exec Dir, Co Contact Com Inc, 1977; Notary Public; AR Coun on Human Relats; Com for Peaceful Co-Existence; Welfare Rgts Org; ACORN; St Dem Party; Inspirational Trio; The Nat Conf of Christians & Jews; Nat Black Vets Org Inc; AF & AM Masons; Public Relats Ofcr; Ednl Prog Vol, AR Dept of Correction; Vol Student Recruiter, Shorter Col & Philander Smith Col; Num Other Civic Activs; r/Meth; hon/Author of Wkly Column, *St Wkly News;* Bi-monthly Column Writer & Assoc Editor, *Bapt Vanguard Mag;* Nat Bd of Advrs, ABI; Ser Awd, Cystic Fibrosis Foun 1982; Martin Luther King Awd for Outstg Commun Ser, The Black Commun Develr's Prog, Hoover U Meth Ch, 1983; J F Cooley Day, Little Rock, AR, 1982; AR Cert of Merit & Plaque, 1981; Recip, Num Other Hons & Awds; W/ W: of Am, of Black Clergy, Among Black Ams, in S & SW; Intl Book of Hon; Men of Achmt; Commun Ldrs & Noteworthy Ams; Num Other Biogl Listings.

COOPER, BENJAMIN DAVID oc/ Director of Financial Aid; b/Sep 11, 1953; h/1809 Marion Street, Apartment D-2, Columbia, SC 29201-2527; ba/ Columbia, SC; p/Benjamin and Naomi Cooper, Los Angeles, CA; ed/BA, Univ of Redlands; Att'd Univ of CA-LA; pa/ Plebotomy Tech- LAC/USC Med Ctr, 1975-77; Peer Grp Cnslr, Jarvis Christian Col, 1977-79; Asst Dir of Fin Aid 1980-81, Dir of Fin Aid 1982-, Benedict Col; cp/Life Mem, Alpha Phi Alpha; NAACP; Minority Concerns Comm Scasfaa; Nasfaa; Sasfaa; Dem Party NACDRAO; r/African Meth; hon/ Outstg Yg Men of Am; Beta Kappa Chi Nat Hon Soc.

COOPER, C JAMES JR oc/Attorney at Law; b/Mar 5, 1931; h/2222 East 7th Avenue Parkway, Denver, CO 80206; ba/Denver, CO; m/Rose Marie; c/Julie L, Jill A, James P; p/Clyde & Mary Perry, Elgin, IL; ed/BA 1952, LLB 1955, Univ of Denver; Att'd CO Col, 1948-50; Admitted CO Bar, 1955; pa/Assoc

1955-58, Ptnr 1958-60, Calkins, Rodden and Kramer; Gen Cnsl & Corp Secy, Consolidated Oil & Gas Inc, 1960-64; Ptnr, Rodden, Cooper, Woods & Mitchell, 1964-72; Atty, C James Cooper Jr, Esq, 1972-82; Atty, C James Cooper Jr, P C, 1982-; Am Immigration Lwyrs Assn (Chm of CO Chapt, 1980-81); Intl Bar Assn; Intl Common Law Exch Soc; CO Bar Assn; Denver Bar Assn; Phi Delta Phi; Phi Gamma Delta; cp/32nd Degree Mason; Shriner; r/Epis; hon/ Author & Lectr on Immigration; Bd of Editors, *Transnat Immigration Law Reporter*, Common Law Lwyr; Law Review, 1953-55; Editor, 1954-55; Recip, Outstg Scholastic Award, Nt Law Wk, 1955; Martindale-Hubbell Law Dir; W/W: in Am Law, in Am W.

COOPER, EDGAR R oc/ Editor-Manager; b/Nov 15, 1918; h/ 7822 Linkside Drive, Jacksonville, FL 32216; ba/Jacksonville, FL; m/Berta Mae; c/Edgar Raydell Jr, Susan Blasingame, Deborah; p/Mrs Wayne Cooper, Ft Pierce, FL; ed/AB, Stetson Univ, 1943; BD, So Bapt Theol Sem, 1946; ThM 1947; ThD 1949; pa/Pastor, Mayfair Bapt Ch, 1948-59; Pastor, N Park Bapt Ch, 1959-68; Pastor, N Jacksonvile Bapt Ch, 1968-70; Editor-Mgr, FL Bapt Witness, 1971-; Pres, FL Bapt Pastors' Conf & FL Bapt St Conv, 1966-67; St Bd of Missions, FL Bapt Conv; Trustee, Bapt Bible Inst; Jacksonville Bapt Home for Chd; So Bapt Hosp Comm for 6 Yrs; Trustee, Bapt Med Ctr, 1971-; r/Bapt; hon/Hon DD, Stetson Univ, 1982.

COOPER, PAUL F oc/School District Administrator; b/Apr 12, 1948; h/10 James Avenue, East Norwich, NY 11732; ba/Bethpage, NY; m/Florence M; c/Justin Paul, Christopher Robert; p/ Lewis R and Janice W Cooper, Westbury, NY; sp/John P and Florence Burghardt, Bayside, NY; ed/AS, Nassau CC, 1969; BA, Marshall Univ, 1971; MS, Adelphi Univ, 1975; PD, LI Univ, 1980; pa/Spec Ed Tchr, Levittown UFSD, 1974-79; Asst Dir of Spec Ed, Levittown UFSD, 1979-82; Supvr Pupil Pers Ser, Bethpage UFSD, 1982-; Chm Com on the Handicapped, 1979-; Conslt to Nassau Co BOCES, 1979-80; Conslt to Hempstead Public Schs, 1982; Secy 1982-83, VP & Pres-Elect 1983-84, LI Assn of Spec Ed Admrs; Spec Ed PTA Exec Bd, 1979-; Am Assn of Spec Ed; Assn of NY St Ed for Emotionally Disturbed; Phi Delta Kappa; Coun of Admrs & Supvrs; cp/Oyster Bay-East Norwich Soccer Clb; r/Rom Cath; hon/ Eagle Scout, 1964; Life Mbrship, NY St PTA, 1982; W/W Among Students in Am Jr Col, 1969.

COOPER, RICHARD NEWELL oc/ Professor; b/Jun 14, 1934; h/33 Washington Avenue, Cambridge, MA 02140; ba/ Cambridge, MA; m/Ann Hollick; c/ Mark, Laura; p/Richard Cooper and Lucile Newell; sp/Geraldine and Robert Hollick; ed/AB, Oberlin Col, 1956; MSc, London Sch of Ecs, 1958; PhD, Harvard Univ, 1962; pa/Boas Prof Intern Ec, Harvard Univ, 1981-; Under Secy of St for Economic Affairs, US Dept of St, 1977-81; Prof Intl Ecs 1966-77, Provost 1972-74, Yale Univ; Chm Exec Panel, Chief of Nav Opers, 1982; Dept Asst Secy of St, 1965-66; St Staff Economist, Pres's Coun of Ec Advrs, 1961-63; Mem, Panel Intl Competition in Adv'd Technol, Nat Acad of Scis, 1982-83; Mem,

Trilateral Comm, Coun on Fgn Relats; hon/Author, *The Ec of Interdependence*, 1968; Editor & Contbr, *A World Re-Ordered*, 1973; Author, *Ec Mobility & Nat Economic Policy*, 1974; Editor & Contbr, *The Intl Monetary Sys under Flexible Exch Rate*, 1982; Num Other Pubs; Phi Beta Kappa, 1955; Marshall S'ship (UK), 1956-58; Brookings Instn Fellow, 1960-61; Ford Foun Fac Fellow, 1970-71; Fellow, Ctr for the Adv'd Studies of Behavioral Scis, 1974; LLD, Oberlin Col, 1978; Fellow, Am Acad of Arts & Scis; Fgn Affairs Awd for Public Ser; W/W: in Am, in Govt.

COOVER, HARRY WESLEY oc/ Executive; b/Mar 6, 1919; h/1335 Linville Street, Kingsport, TN 37660; ba/ Kingsport, TN; m/Muriel Zumbach; c/ Harry W III, Stephen R, Melinda Coover Paul; p/Harry Wesley and Anna Rohm Coover (dec); ed/BS Chem, 1941; MS, 1942; PhD, 1944; pa/All Positions w Eastman Kodak Co: Res Chem, Rochester, 1944-49; Sr Res Chem, Kingsport, TN, 1949; Res Assoc, 1954; Div Hd, 1963; Dir of Res, 1965; VPres, 1970; Exec VPres, 1973-81; VPres, 1981-; Mem: AAAS; Am Assn for Textile Technols; Am Chem Soc; Am Inst of Chems; Assn of Res Dirs; Dirs of Industl Res; Pres 1981-82, Past Mem Bd of Dirs, Industl Res Inst; Co Assoc, Intl Union of Pure & Applied Chem; Adv Bd, *Jour of Polymer Sci*; Nat Acad of Engrg; NY Acad of Scis; Soc of Chem Indust; Soc of Plastics Indust Inc; Bd of Trustees, Textile Res Inst; r/Presb; hon/Author, Over 50 Papers; Granted Over 500 Patents in Field; Southerland Prize in Chem, Hobart Col, 1941; So Chem Awd, Am Chems Soc, 1960; Spkr of Yr-NW TN Sect, Am Chem Soc, 1962; Medalist of Industl Res Inst, 1984; Nat Acad of Engrg, 1983; W/W: in Am, in S & SW; Am Men & Wom of Sci; Men of Achmt; Standard & Poor's Register of Corps; Num Other Biogl Listings.

COPE, DAVID F oc/Nuclear Energy Consultant; b/Jun 28, 1912; h/113 Orange Lane, Oak Ridge, TN 37830; ba/ Same; m/Thelma M; c/Jane E C Pierce, Beth H; ed/AB 1933, MS 1934, WV Univ; PhD, Univ of VA, 1952; mil/AUS, Col; pa/Mining Engr, Elker Coal Co, 1936-37; Math Instr 1937-38, Physics Instr, 1946-47, TX A&M Univ; CCC Duty, AUS, 1937-46; Asst Prof Physics, New Mexico A&M Univ, 1947-50; Asst Dir Res & Devel Div & Dir Reactor Div, USAEC Oak Ridge, 1952-66; USAEC Div Reac Dec & Tech, Sr Site Rep Oak Ridge Nat Lab, 1966-74; Spec Assignment, Energy Res & Devel Fed Energy Ofc, 1974; Energy & Nuclear Energy Conslt, 1974-; Chm, Ch & Nuclear Energy Comm, Epis Diocese of TN, 1980 & 1981; cp/Resv Ofcr's Assn: Pres Oak Ridge Chapt, VP St of TN; Mem 1966-, Pres 1977-78, Oak Ridge Rotary Clb; Oak Ridge C of C, Chm New Bus Dev Comm, 1968-69; St Stephen's Epis Ch Sr Warden, 1972 and 1973; Epis Diocese of TN; Gov Nom Rotary Dist 678, 1985-86; r/Epis; hon/Num Profl Pubs; Phi Beta Kappa; Sigma Xi; USAEC-ORO Superior Perf Awd, 1960; AUS Superior Perf Awd, 1962; Am Men of Sci; W/W in S & SW.

COPELAND, MARILYN FRANCES oc/Executive; b/Dec 26, 1931; h/1308 Kevin Road, Wichita, KS 67208; ba/ Wichita, KS; m/John; c/Jo Elaine C

Hansen; David; p/Mr and Mrs Marion Hall, Rich Hill, MO; sp/Iva Copeland, Rich Hill, MO; ed/BS Ed, 1952; Pvt Pilot, 1961; Instrument Pilot, 1965; pa/HS Tchr, Grandview, MO, 1952-56; Dental Edr & Mgr, 1957-84; Mem: Delta Zeta, 1949-; Var Ofcs incl'g Pres of both Chapt Sects, KS & Wichita Dist Dental Aux; Intl Pres, The 99's Inc (Intl Wom's Pilots); hon/Author of Monthly Article Pub'd in *The 99 News*, 1983-84; Salutatorian of Col Grad Class; W/W in Am Cols & Univs.

COPELAND, MELBA PAULINE MERCHANT oc/Director of Concessions and Vending Services; b/Feb 6, 1927; h/102 Magnolia Circle, Box 236, Itta Bena, MS 38941; ba/Itta Benna, MS; m/William Heard (dec); c/Vincent Heard; p/Edward W (dec) and Libby C Merchant; sp/Benton and Vera Copeland (dec); ed/BS 1950; MS 1954; Att'd So IL Univ, Wayne St Univ, MI St Univ, Delta St, MVSU; pa/Tchr, MS Val St Univ, 1956-58; Dietitian, MS Val St Univ, 1958-75; Asst Dir Food Ser, Leake Co Public Schs, 1950-53 & 1954-56; Asst Dir Food Ser, Newton Co, 1953-54; Sub Tchr, Orange Co FL; Tchr, Prentiss Inst, 1956; Oper Mgr for Food Ser 1978-80, Spec Asst to Student Union Dir, Dir of Concessions & Vending & Landromat, 1981-, MS Val St Univ; Food Ser Intl Exec Assn; cp/Zeta Phi Beta; Phi Delta Kappa; OES; Heroines of Jerico; Rust Col Alumni Assn; TN St Univ Alumni Assn; r/U Meth; hon/ Masters Thesis; Meritorious Awd, The Nat Alumni Assn, 1971; Dedication for Dist'd Ser Awd, Food Ser Clb, 1966-67; Cert of Apprec, MS Val St Univ; Phi Delta Kappa, 1975; Zeta Phi Beta, 1977; Cert of Apprec & Recog, MS Val St Univ's J H White Lib, 1978; W/W: in S & SW, in Am, in MS; Dir of Dist'd Ams; Other Biogl Listings.

COPPOLECHIA, DR YILLIAN CASTRO oc/Associate Dean; b/Jul 26, 1948; h/5634 West 17 Lane, Hialeah, FL 33012; ba/Miami, FL; c/Derek; ed/AA, Miami-Dade Commun Col, 1968; MA 1973, EdD 1984, Univ of Miami; pa/ Program Coor 1975-78, Dept Chp 1978-79, Assoc Dean in Div of Biling Studies 1979-, Miami-Dade Commun Col; Mid Sts Accrediting Assn, Higher Ed Comm; Spanish-Am Leag Against Discrimination; FL TESOL; r/Cath; hon/1 of 10 Wom of Yr, Cuban Wom's Clb Inc, 1978; Cert for Merit as Civic Ldr, Miami Cuban Lions, 1978; Cert of Hon, Wom's Com of One Hundred, 1978; Commend, Mayor Stephen Clark of Metro Dade Co, 1977; Commend, Mayor Maurice Ferre of City of Miami, 1977; World W/W of Wom; DIB; Dir of Dist'd Ams.

CORBETT, ALLEN POWELL oc/ Director; Lecturer; b/Apr 17, 1939; h/ 2809 Magnolia Street, Columbia, SC 29204; ba/Columbia, SC; p/Robert and Melba Corbett, Columbia, SC; ed/BS, Am Univ, 1961; MBA, Univ of SC, 1969; CDP, Inst for Cert of Computer Prof, 1979; pa/Summer Fellow, Georgetown Univ Med Ctr, 1960; Med Prog Asst, Med Stat, Med Aide, Fed Aviation Adm, 1961-65; Lectr in Computer Sci, Res Conslt, Sys Anal, Univ of SC, 1965-71; Supvr of Res, SC Employmt Security Comm, 1971-73; Dir & Asst Prof of Man Sci, James C Self Man Sci Ctr, 1973-; Ch of Bd of Dirs 1981-, Chm

161

of Fin Com 1978-81, SC Protection & Advocacy Sys for Handicapped; VP of Midlands Chapt, Assn for Sys Mgmt, 1982-; Res Conslt, Joint Leg Com to Study Probs of Handicapped, 1977-; Omicron Delta Epsilon, 1977-; Rehab Engrg Soc of N Am, 1982-; Assn for Computing Machinery, 1982-; r/Meth; hon/Profl Pubs: Meritorious Ser Awd, SC Rehab Assn, 1979; Chm of Advy Com for Indep Living, SC Voc Rehab Dept, 1979-; W/W in S & SW.

CORBIN, KRESTINE MARGARET oc/Owner of Publishing and Consulting Company; b/Apr 24, 1937; ba/Same; c/ Michelle Marie, Sheri Karin; p/Lawrence and Judie Dickinson, Monte Vista, NV; ed/BS, Univ of CA, 1958; pa/ Columnist, *McClatchy Newspapers*, 1976-81; Asst Prof, Bauder Col in Sacramento, 1974-; Owner, Creat Sewing Co, 1976-; cp/Crocker Art Gallery Assn, 1960-78; Repub Party Elections Com, 1964 & 1968; r/Prot; hon/Profl Pubs; Recip, Omicron Nu Nat Hon Soc; Elected Mem, Intl Fashion Group, Inc; Diploma Di Merito Universita Delle Arti, Italy; W/W: of Am Wom, of Wom.

CORBIN, SCOTT DOUGLAS oc/ Architect; b/Mar 12, 1950; h/408 Cotton Road, Franklin, TN 37064; ba/Nashville, TN; m/Marissa U; c/Kristen L; p/ William Arthur Corbin, Springfield, VA; sp/Nora Breen, Vienna, VA; ed/ BArch, VA Polytech Inst & St Univ, 1973; mil/USAR, 1982, Capt; pa/ Designer/Draftsman, Gresham & Smith Arch, 1973; Proj Coor, 1975-77; Proj Arch, 1974; Sr Proj Arch, 1977; Assoc, 1982; Mid TN Chapt, Am Inst of Arch; cp/Luth Ch of St Andrew; r/ Luth; hon/W/W in S & SW.

CORDOVA-SALINAS, MARIA ASUNCION oc/Dentist, Assistant Professor Physiology; b/May 14, 1941; h/ 948 Equestrian Drive, Mt Pleasant, SC 29464; ba/Charleston, SC; m/Carlos Francisco; c/Carlos Miguel, Claudio Andres, Maria Asuncion; p/Miguel Cordova, Chile, and Maria Asuncion Requena, France; sp/Carlos & Victoria Salinas, Chile; ed/Liceo de Ninas, Chile; BAS 1958, DDS 1964, Univ Chile; Postdoct Fellow, Johns Hopkins Univ, 1973-74; St TN Dental Lic, 1983; pa/ Fac Mem, Univ Chile, 1965-74; Postdoct Fellow, Johns Hopkins Hosp, 1972-74; Vis'g Scist, NY Med Col, 1974; Fac Mem, Dept Pharm, Univ SC, 1975-79; Fac Mem, Dept Physiol, 1980-; cp/Bd Mem, Circulo Hispanoame-Ricano, Charleston; Coor, Amnesty Intl; Bd Mem, Iglesia Hispanica; Am Physiol Soc Mem; Ptnrs of the Ams; r/Cath; hon/ Author of Num Pubs; PAHO/WHO Fellow, 1972-74; Guest of Hon, City of Mayaguez, PR; W/W in Frontier Sci & Technol.

CORELLI, JOHN C oc/Professor; b/ Aug 6, 1930; h/33 Belle Avenue, Troy, NY 12180; ba/Troy, NY; m/Evelyn; c/ John, Carolyn; sp/Dorothy Hostetter, Indianapolis, IN; ed/BS, Providence Col, 1952; MS, Brown Univ, 1954; PhD, Purdue Univ, 1958; pa/Physicist, Knolls Atomic Power Lab, Gen Elect Co, 1958-61; Prof, Nuclear Engrg & Sci, Rensselaer Polytechnic Inst; Mem: Am Phy Soc, 1954-; Am Nuclear Soc, 1976-; Sigma Xi; r/Cath; hon/Author, Over 60 Articles Pub'd in Profl Jours; Spec Fellow, NIH, 1971; W/W: in Am, in E,

in Engrg; Am Men of Sci.

CORLETT, EMMA JEAN oc/Social Work Administrator; b/Aug 4, 1926; ba/ Santa Barbara, CA; m/John Paul (dec); c/Jeanne Marie, Thomas Lee, Jan Louise; p/LeRoy and Luella Massey, Ventura, CA; sp/Lewis and Elba (dec) Corlett; ed/ BA cum laude, NW Nazarene Col, 1965; MSW w hons, Univ of UT, 1972; Nat VP, PO Aux, 1960-63; ID Dept of Public Asst & Mtl Hlth, 1965-70; Dir of Patient & Fam Cnslg, Mercy Med Ctr, 1972-75; Cnslr, US 8th Army, 1975-76; Dir of Social Ser, Kern Med Ctr, 1976-79; Dir of Med Social Ser, Cottage Hosp, 1979-; CA Lic'd Clin Social Wkr; ACSW; NASW; Soc of Hosp Social Wk Dirs, Am Hosp Assn; NASW Reg of Clin Social Wkrs; Santa Barbara Med Social Ser Assn; Cert'd CA Chd's Ser Social Wkrs; Nat Kidney Foun Coun of Nephrology Social Wkrs; Santa Barbara S Coast Coor'g Coun; cp/Adv Bd, Salvation Army of Santa Barbara; Bd of Dirs, Am Cancer Soc, Santa Barbara Chapt; Bd of Dirs, Gerontology Ed Proj; Interagcy Geriatric Task Force; AAUW; r/Prot; hon/Author *Social Wk Values*; Mrs ID, Finalist in Mrs Am Pageant, 1959; Toast Mistress Clb Dist Spch Contest Winner, 1958; Phi Delta Lambda, 1965; Santa Barbara U Way Campaign Coor of Yr, 1981-82; W/W: of Am Wom, of Wom.

CORR, MICHAEL WILLIAM TINGSTROM oc/Asian Medical Phyto-geography, Iconographer, Translator; b/Nov 14; h/511 Lake Washington Boulevard South, Seattle, WA 98144; ba/Seattle, WA; c/Anders Schwartz Childs Corr; p/William John Forestal and Cecilia Genevieve Tingstrom Brodine Corr; ed/BS Math, Antioch Col, 1963; MA Math 1965, MA Geog 1981, PhC Asian Med Phyto-geog 1982, Univ of WA; pa/Self-employed Writer, Translator, Illustrator, 1973-; Lectr in Sci & Lit: Univ of WA Med Sch, Doshisha Univ, Kyoto Univ, NY Univ in Kyoto 1968-76; US Dept of Interior, Antioch Univ 1961-63; Mem: Exec Sey, AAAS, 1969-73; Comm on Envir Alterations, 1969-73; Am Anthropological Assn; Big River Assn; Com for Social Response in Sci; Lib Com; Ethnobiol Assn; Congres Intl De Paleontologie Humaine (Paris & Nice); Mng Editor, AAS-CEI & Scis Inst for Public Info; Elect Power Study Task Force; cp/Rel Soc of Friends; Meditation Hall Instr, Lin'chi Sect of Ch'an Buddhism, 1974; r/Humanist; hon/Author of Num Pubs incl'g: "The Lake Biwa Watershed: Prob of Agri & Indust Pollution," 1981; "Envir Husbandry & the Hist Japanese Village," 1976; "Lotus & Hoe, Labor & The Roshi's Garden," 1976; *To Leave the Standing Grain*, 1977; *Brooming to Paradise*, 1976; *Cape Alava*, 1981; *Energy & Human Welfare* 3 Volumes, 1972-75; Others; Co-Author, Var Foun Grants; Num Writings & Illusts Supported by, Nat Endowment for Arts; NY, MO & WA St Art Comms; Num Pubs Awds; St Fellow in Med Phyto-geog, Univ of WA Grad Sch, 1981-82; Japanese-Eng Translator Awd, (Alcheringa-Ethnopoetics) Boston Univ, 1977; 1st Place, Print Div, Fremont Fair Art Competition, 1982; W/W in Poetry; NY Times Index; US Fed Register.

CORSELLO, LILY JOANN oc/Guidance Director; b/Mar 30, 1953; h/4521 NE 18 Avenue, Fort Lauderdale, FL

33334; ba/Hallandale, FL; p/Rev and Mrs Joseph Corsello, Ft Lauderdale, FL; ed/BA, FL St Univ, 1974; MEd, FL Atl Univ, 1977; pa/Guid Dir, B F James Adult Ctr, 1983-; Guid Cnslr, Lauderhill Mid, 1981-83; Guid Cnslr, Boyd Anderson HS, 1980-81; Eng Lang Arts Instr, Plantation HS, 1974-80; Drama & Communs Instr, John Robert Powers Sch of Modeling, 1978-80; Lectr/Spkr for Singles Confs, The So Bapt Conv, 1980-; Freelance Author, *Christian Single* Mag, 1979-; Life Mem, Lambda Iota Tau; CTA, 1974-80; NEA; Intl Platform Assn, 1982-; APGA; cp/Pilot Intl; Repub Exec Com, Broward Co, 1981; Yg Repubs, 1981; r/So Bapt; hon/Author of "Loneliness: The Hidden Horror," 1981; "The Liberty of Surrender," 1981; "The Close of The Age," 1980 Pub'd in *Christian Single*; Nat Edrs F'ship, 1974-76; DAR Awd, 1968; Lambda Iota, 1974; W/ W: in S & SW, in World, of Wom, of Intells; Dir Dist'd Ams; Other Biogl Listings.

CORSO, JOHN F oc/Professor; b/Dec 1, 1919; h/Cosmos Hill Road, Rural Delivery # 4, Cortland, NY 13045; ba/ Cortland, NY; m/Josephine A Solazzo (dec); c/Gregory Michael, Douglas Jerome, Christine Ann; p/Onofrio and Santa Curro Corso, Oswego, NY; ed/ BEd, St Univ of NY-Oswego, 1942; MA 1948, PhD 1950, St Univ of IA-Iowa City; mil/AUS 1942-46, Coast Artillery Corps, Anti-Aircraft Artillery, Capt; pa/ Chief Sound & Vibration Sect, Psych Br, Army Med Res Lab, Ft Knox, KY, 1950-51; Chief Human Factors Ofc, Rome Air Devel Ctr, Griffiss AFB, Rome, NY, 1951-52; Assoc Prof Psych 1952-57, Prof Psych 1957-62, Dir Human Factors Res Prog 1952-62, PA St Univ; Staff Psych Sys's Sect, US Nav Tng Device Ctr, Port Wash, NY, 1959; Prof Psych & Dir, Dept Psych, St Louis Univ, MO, 1962-63; Prof Psych & Chm Dept 1963-80, SUNY Dist'd Prof Psych 1973-, SUNY-Cortland; Vis'g Res Sci Dept Otolaryngology, Upst Med Ctr, SUNY-Syracuse, 1971-; Mem: Assn of Fam & Conciliation Cts, 1983; Intl Soc of Audiology, 1968; NY Acad of Scis, 1964; Human Factors Soc, 1958; PA Acad of Sci, 1956; AAUP, 1954; Fellow, AAAS, 1954; Acoustical Soc of Ams, 1951; Fellow Divs 3 & 21, Am Psychol Assn, 1951; Sigma Xi, 1949; r/Rom Cath; hon/Author of 2 Books, *Aging Sensory Sys & Perception*, 1981; *The Exptl Psych of Sensory Behavior*, 1967; 6 Book Chapts incl'g: "Auditory Clin Markers of Aging," "Auditory Perception & Communication," "Sensory Processes in Man During Maturity & Senescence," & Var Articles; Spec Res Fellow, Nat Inst of Child Hlth & Human Devel, 1969-70; Cert, 1st US Annual Creat Talent Awds Prog, Am Inst for Res, 1961; Recip Num Res Grants: PA St Univ, SUNY, NSF, NIH, USAF; Other Hons; W/W: in Sci, in World, in Frontier Sci & Technol; Outstg Edrs of Am; DIB; Othery Biogl Listings.

COSTA, JIM oc/California State Assemblyman; b/Apr 13, 1952; ba/ Sacramento, CA; p/Manuel Costa (dec); Lena Costa, Fresno, CA; ed/BS Polit Sci, CA St Univ-Fresno, 1974; pa/Asst to Cong-man B F Sisk, Wash DC, 1974-75; Spec Asst to Cong-man John Krebs, 1975-76; Dist Adm Asst for Assem-man Richard Lehman, 1976-78; Elected CA

St Assem, 1978, 1980, 1982-; Mem: Chm, Water, Pks & Wildlife Com, 1983-84; Chm Resources & Trans Subcom, Mem, Ways & Means Com; Chm 1980-81, Mem 1984-, Housing & Commun Devel Com; Select Com on Utility Perf, Rates & Regulation; CA Debt Adv Bd; cp/Fresno Cabrillo Clb; IDES Men's Lodge; Sigma Alpha Epsilon Frat Alumni; Fresno Co U Dems; Former Big Brother; Other Commun Activs; Outstg Yg Men of Am, US JC's.

COSTLEY, BILL oc/Learning Center Manager; b/May 21, 1942; h/4 Damien Road, Wellesley Hills, MA 02181-3416; ba/Andover, MA; m/Joan Helen Budyk; c/Maya, Alex William; p/William K Costley Sr; Mary Stefania Kulik Costley (dec); sp/Alexander Budyk; Nettie Adriensen Budyk (dec); ed/St John's Prep Sch, 1959; AB, Boston Col, 1963; MFA, Boston Univ, 1968; pa/Med Tech, Univ Med Sch, Boston, 1966; Engrg Period Libn, MIT, Cambridge, 1967; Libn & Book Acquisitioner, NASA, 1967; Assoc Editor, *Inst of Human Scis Review* (now *Human & Soc Change Review*), Boston Col, 1968; Eng Instr, Grahm Jr Col, 1968; Model Cities Prog & City Demonstration Agy Inc Cambridge, Newspaper Editor & Public Info Ofcr, 1969-73; Freelance Writer & Editor, Brookline, MA, 1973-; Conslt, Cambridge Civic Assn & CITY HS Alternative; Sr Tech Writer, Digital Equip Corp, Marlboro, MA, 1976-79; Sr Course Dev, Data Gen Corp, Westboro, MA, 1979-81; Lrng Ctr Mgr, Digital Equip Corp, Andover, MA, 1981-; cp/Fdr, Lynn Voice Collaborative, 1969-; Secy 1981-83, Wellesley Coun for the Arts; Secy; Boston Local, Strng Comm Nat Writers' Union, 1983-; Others; hon/Author of Poetry Books: *Knosh 1 Cir* (Selected Poems 1964-75); *Rag(a)s*, 1978; Num Pubs in Anthols & Mags; Undergrad Prizes, Boston Col, 1962-63; W/W in E; Contemp Authors.

COTTLE, THOMAS JOSEPH oc/Psychologist, Writer; b/Jan 22, 1939; h/12 Beaconsfield Road, Brookline, MA 02146; ba/Needham, MA; m/Kay Mikkelsen; c/Claudia, Jason, Sonya; ed/BA, Harvard Col, 1959; MA 1963, PhD 1968, Univ of Chgo; pa/Lectr in Psych, Harvard Med Sch; Asst Prof & Asst Chm Dept of Scoial Relats, Dir Sum Inst of Sociol & Social-Psych in Assn w Am Negro Cols, Harvard Univ; Fellow, Ctr for Adv'd Study, Univ of IL; Res Assoc & Psychotherapist, Ed Res Ctr & Dept of Psychi, MA Inst of Technol; Res Assoc & Writer, Chd's Def Fund, Wash Res Proj; Attache Staff Mem, Tavistock Clin, London; Visitor, Freud Clin, London; Vis'g Dist'd Prof Psych, Amherst Col; Fellow, Afro-Am Study Ctr, Wesleyan Univ; Sociol Lectr, Boston Univ; hon/Author, Over 25 Books incl'g: *Chd's Secrets*; *Hidden Survivors*; *Black Testimony*; *Getting Married*; Over 500 Articles Pub'd in Profl Jours; Wkly Contbr, WCVB News & "The Good Day Show," Boston; Host, "The Tom Cottle Show," WGBH, PBS, Boston; Wkly Contbr, NBC "Today Show"; Host, "Tom Cottle: Up Close," Metromedia TV; Guggenheim F'ship; Yg Psychol Awd, Am Psychol Assn; Field Foun F'ship; Writer's Awd, Ednl Press Assn; Writer's Awd, The Nat Assn of TV Broadcast Execs; Am Cancer Soc Awd; Psychol Assn Awd; Nom'd For Emmy

Awds; W/W; Commun Ldrs of Am; Other Biogl Listings.

COUCH, LINDA SUE oc/Supervisor of Chemistry Lab; b/Nov 22, 1947; h/775 Hillview Drive, Dayton, VA 22821; ba/Weyers Cave, VA; m/James Vance; c/Christopher Clifton, Emily Sue; p/Frances Bogos, San Antonio, TX; ed/BA, Univ of KY, 1969; MS 1972, PhD 1978, Univ of MA; pa/Lectr & Asst Prof, James Madison Univ, 1972-81; Supvr of Chem Lab, Degesch Am, 1982-; cp/VP 1982, Pres 1983, Dayton Wom Clb.

COUGHLIN, JOHN WALKER oc/Executive, CPA; b/Jul 30, 1927; h/3819 Lee Street, Fairfax, VA 22030; ba/Washington, DC; m/Betty Boyd; c/Victoria, Brian, Anthony; p/John Bernard and Etta Walker Coughlan (dec); ed/BA; BCom; HA; MA War Fin, Univ of Wn Ontario, 1951; PhD Polit Economy, Johns Hopkins Univ, 1955; CPA, MD & Wash DC; mil/AUS, Capt; pa/Acct: Methieson Chem; Interprovincial Pipeline Corp; Province of Alberta; Prof & Chm Acctg Dept, Geo Wash Univ, 1963-67; Prof, Loyola Col, 1968-81; Tchr, Brown Univ & Georgetown Univ; Treas, Fairfax City, 1982; Ptner, CPA Firm, LaFrance, Walker, Jackley & Saville; Mem: Am Inst of CPA's; Nat Assn of Accts; DC Inst of CPA's; Past VPres of Wash Chapt, Soc for Advmt of Mgmt; cp/Past Pres, Toastmaster 888; Past VPres, Jr C of C, Wash DC; Alpha Kappa Psi; r/Cath; hon/Author of 7 Pub'd Books & Over 20 Articles Pub'd in Profl Jours incl'g: *Jour of Accountancy*; *Acctg Review*; *Mgmt Acctg*; *Data Mgmt*; *Adv'd Mgmt*; The Canadian Ofcrs' Tng Corps Meml F'ship; Canadian Soc Sci Res Coun F'ship.

COULTAS, JUNE IRENE oc/Consultant; b/May 5, 1928; h/14 Pine Avenue, Madison, NJ 07940; ba/Trenton, NJ 08625; m/Aldo Bliss; p/Charles O (dec) and Irene E Booth, Peekskill, NY; sp/A B and Annabell Coultas; ed/AA w hons, Larson Col, 1948; BA, Rutgers Univ, 1950; MS w hons, Kean Col, 1954; MA, Univ of UT, 1974; EdD, Univ of Sarasota, 1981; pa/Roselle Public Schs, 1950-63; Summit Public Schools, 1963-74; Conslt in Devel of Basic Skills K-12, NJ Dept of Ed, 1974-; Adv Bd Mem, NJ Network Ed TV; Early Chd Coor Coun Mem; Curric Advr, NJ St Testing Com; Conslt, Agy for Instr TV Math Series, Mid Grades; Conslt, Agy for Instr TV, Lang Arts Series, Grades 7-8; Conslt to Comm on Supvn & Curric Devel in Eng Lang Arts, NCTE; cp/Writing Com, NJ Teen Arts Fest; Chair, Awd Com for NJ Rdg Assn; hon/Profl Pubs; W/W in E.

COUNCILL, WILLIAM THOMAS III oc/Clinical Supervisor and Licensed Professional Counselor; b/May 9, 1950; h/2739 North Center Street, Hickory, NC 28601; ba/Hickory, NC; p/William T Councill Jr, Hickory, NC; ed/BA w hons, Univ of NC-Chapel Hill, 1972; MS, Nova Univ, 1975; pa/Dir of Indust Anal, Traintex Inc, 1972-73; Psychi Aid, S FL St Hosp, 1973-74; Instr 1974, Asst House Parent 1974, Living & Lrng Ctr, Nova Univ; Behavioral Engr, Univ Sch, Nova Univ, 1975; Clin Biofeedback Therapist, Pvt Pract, 1975-76; Dir of Clin for Psychophysiol Med, Pvt Pract, 1976-80; Instr in Psych, Columbia Col, 1978-79; Lic'd Profl Cnslr, Pvt Pract, 1980-82; Clin Supvr, Fam Guid Ctr,

1982-; Past Pres, AL Mtl Hlth Cnslrs Assn, 1982; Past Pres, N AL Parents & Chd Together, 1980-82; Am Mtl Hlth Cnslrs Assn; Am Mtl Hlth Cnslrs Assn; Am Orthopsychi Assn; APGA; AL Pers & Guid Assn; Am Psych Assn; r/Bapt; hon/Globe & Anchor Medal, TX Soc of Sons of Am Revolution, Marine Mil Acad; Orange Key Hon Soc, Univ of Miami; W/W in S & SW.

COURCHENE, JOHN EDWARD oc/Director of Water Quality; b/Feb 13, 1926; h/1622 North 51, Seattle, WA 98103; ba/Seattle, WA; m/Elaine Patricia; c/Mary Anne Chinn; Christopher, Michael; p/Ed and Mary Courchene (dec); sp/J Ray Heath, Seattle, WA; ed/BS 1950, MS 1953, Seattle Univ; mil/USN; pa/Instr 1951-52, Asst Prof 1953-60, Seattle Univ; Dir Water Quality, City of Seattle, 1965-; cp/Am Water Wks Assn, 1960-; Chm, Pacific NW Sect Water Quality Com, 1968-78; Trustee 1978-, Chm 1983, AWWA Water Quality Div; Seattle Mgmt Assn, 1972-; WA St Water Supply Adv Bd, 1969-72; BSA, Com Chm, Dist Commr, 1969-84; r/Cath; hon/Author of Num Pubs incl'g "Emphasizing QC", *Jour AWWA*, 1973, "Roundtable Discussion-What Causes Water Quality to Deteriorate?", *Jour AWWA*, 1980; Am Waterwks Assn Powell-Lindsey Awd, 1978; Am Waterwks Assn, Res Foun, 1980; W/W in W.

COURNIOTES, HARRY J oc/College President; b/Aug 13, 1921; h/Cote Road, Monson, MA 01057; ba/Springfield, MA; m/Annette R Giguere; c/James H II, Gregory H; p/James H Courniotes, Chicopee Falls, MA; sp/Ruth Giguere, Monson, MA; ed/BS, Boston Univ, 1942; MBA, Harvard Univ, 1943; DCS, Wn N Eng Col, 1976; mil/AUS, 1943-46, QMC, 1st Lt; pa/Asst Prof 1946-52, Assoc Prof 1952-58, Prof 1958-69, Dean Sch of Bus Adm 1960-69, VPres 1964-69, Pres, 1969-, Am Intl Col, Springfield, MA; Pract CPA, 1952-; VChm, Bd of Dir, Lifestyle Cos Inc, 1969-76; Mem: Fin Execs Inst; Am Inst of CPA's; Nat Assn of Accts; MA Soc of CPA's; Trustee, Ec Ed Coun, MA, 1971-; Bd of Advrs, N Eng Congl Inst, 1980-; Bd of Dirs, Springfield Ctl Bus Dist, 1976-; Advy Bd, World Affairs Coun 1970-; U Negro Col Fund, 1971-; Bd of Dirs, Jr Achmt Wn MA, 1975-76; cp/Trustee, Springfield Instn for Savings, 1974-; Exec Com, Springfield Adult Ed Coun, 1972-74; Corporator, Springfield Girls Clb, 1970-; Springfield Boys Clb, 1972-; Corporator, Wing Meml Hosp, 1976-; Sponsor, Laughing Brook Proj, MA Audubon Soc; Other Commun Activs; r/Greek Orthodox; hon/Dist'd Ser to Commun Awd, Am Hellenic Progressive Assn, 1969; Ahepan of Yr, Altis Chapt #85, 1983; Achmt Awd, Acct of Yr, Nat Assn of Cost Accts, 1970; Outstg Servant of Public Awd, Springfield TV WWLP, 1983; W/W: in Fin & Indust, in Am Ed, in E; Commun Ldrs of Am; Men of Achmt; Other Biogl Listings.

COURTENAY, WALTER ROWE JR oc/Department Chairman and Professor; b/Nov 6, 1933; h/1040 Southwest 3rd Street, Boca Raton, FL 33432; ba/Boca Raton, FL; m/Francine Saporito; c/Walter R III, Catherine Simpson; Walter R Courtenay, Hilton Hd, SC; sp/Frank Saporito, Miami, FL; ed/BA

Vanderbilt Univ, 1956; MS 1960, PhD 1965, Univ of Miami; pa/Temp Instr 1963-64, Vis'g Asst Prof 1964-65, Biol Scis, Duke Univ; Asst Prof Biol Scis, Boston Univ, 1965-67; Asst Prof 1967-70, Assoc Prof 1970-72, Dept & Prof 1972-, Biol Scis, FL Atl Univ; Mem: Am Fisheries Soc; Am Soc of Ichthyologists & Herpetologists; Biol Soc of WA; Desert Fishes Coun; FL Acad of Scis; Sigma Xi; Soc of Sys Zool; SEn Fishes Coun; r/Presb; hon/Author, Co-Author & Editor, Over 50 Articles in Profl Sci Jours, Popular Articles, Book Chapts & Books; Dist'd Tchr Awd, Fl Atl Univ, 1972-73; Fellow, Am Inst of Fishery Res Biols, 1974; Phi Kappa Phi; W/W in S & SW.

COUSINO, JOE ANN oc/Sculptress; b/Nov 17, 1925; h/3717 Indian Road, Toledo, OH 43606; ba/Above; c/Paule René and Richard Nils; p/George C Bux, Toledo, OH; Lucille C Bux-Kocher (dec); ed/BA, Univ of Toledo, 1947; Postgrad Study: Univ of So IL, 1954; Univ of Mexico, 1946 & 1949; Grad S'ship, Pratt Inst, 1947; pa/Instr, Adult Art Dept, YWCA, 1944-57; Lectr & Instr in Art, YMCA, 1945-57; Feature Artist in Univ Wkshops, 1966-; Bd of Dirs, Cousino Metal Prods, 1960-72; Bd of Dirs, Friends of Univ of Toledo Libs, 1977-83; Trustee 1966-, Pres 1964-66, Fdn of Art Socs; Nat Craftsmen's Coun, 1962-65; Designer Craftsmen Trustee, 1964-66; cp/Mayor's Com of The Arts, Toledo, 1974-78; Fdr & Pres, Toledo Potters Guild, 1951-53; r/Epis; hon/ Over 50 Awds & Prizes in Nat & Reg Juried Shows; One Person Invitational Show, Toledo Mus of Art, 1949; Arndt Art Mus, Elmira, NY, 1977; Over 70 Nat Invitational Exhibns, 1957-; Sculpture Comms in Var Public Pks, Public & Pvt Collections; Wks in Le Salon de Nations a Paris, 1984; W/W: in Am, of Am Artists; Dir of Dist'd Ams; DIB.

COUSINS, BERNICE B oc/ Co-Director, CW Associates; b/Nov 2, 1937; h/4505 Astoria Boulevard, Astoria, NY 11105; ba/Maspeth, NY; c/David Bruce, Jason Bruce; p/August (dec) and Olympia Brigando, Astoria, NY; ed/ BFA, Pratt Inst, 1959; Grad Div Art Ed, 1960; Grad Div CCNY, 1966 ITTP; pa/ Asst to Dean of Lib Sch 1959-60, Coor of Resource Ctr/Arts 1960-61, Pratt Inst; Asst to Dir of Ed Dept, Mus of Modern Art, 1963-72; Tchr of Chd Art Prog; Secy Nat Com on Art in Ed; Tchr, NY City Bd of Ed, 1966-77; Secy to Pres 1975, Dir Cartography & Res 1976, Dir of Cartographic Ser & Mktg 1978-84, Bd of Dirs 1979-80, Dir of Mktg, 1983-84, Am Map Corp; Free-lance Writer; Lectr in Field; Indep Cnslr; U Fdn of Tchrs, 1966-75; Assn for Res & Enlightenment, 1966-; Nat Assn of Female Execs; Nat Soc of Interior Designers, 1956-60; Nat Com on Art in Ed, 1963-72; Nat Hon Soc, 1955; cp/ Am Fdn of Astrologers, 1966-; Astrologers Guild of Am, 1966-75; Fdg Mem, Nat Coun on Geocosmic Res, 1968-; AAUW; Nat Coun for Christians & Jews; hon/Profl Pubs; Nat Social Studies Hon Soc, 1955; Theodore Roosevelt Meml Medallion, 1955; Illuminating Engrg Soc Hon Mention, 1958; W/W of Am Wom.

COUTO, ROBERT oc/Corporate Communications Manager, Administrative Assistant; b/Jun 30, 1946; h/ Merrimack, NH 03054; ba/Nashua, NH; p/Manuel P and M Gilda Couto, New Bedford, MA; ed/Dipl Indust Elects, NE Inst of Industl Technol, 1965; Dipl Gemologist, Gemological Inst of Am, 1978; BS Orgnl Behavior, Lesley Col, 1983; pa/Mktg Sers Coor 1978-79, Mgr Mktg Communs 1979-81, Mgr Corp Communs 1981-, Asst Treas 1982-, Adm Asst to Pres 1982-, Ferrofluidics Corp, Nashua, NH; Asst Mgr 1973-75, Mgr 1975-78, Karten's Jewelers, Nashua, NH; Spec Asst for Projs & Media Relats, US Rep Hastings Keith (R-MA), 1971-73; Radio News Broadcast Jour, WBSM Radio, New Bedford, MA, 1969-71; Elect Tech, QC Tech, Calibration Tech, Spec Task Force for Devel of Computer-controlled Spectrophotometer, Instrument Devel Labs, Attleboro, MA, 1966-69; Mem: Adv Bd 1979-82, Chm Adv Bd 1982-, NH Voc Tech Col; Adv Com to Design Tech Communs Prog, Tech Inst of Concord, NH, 1982; 2 Accreditation Coms 1981, Legis Affairs Com 1983-, So NH Assn of Commerce & Indust; Legis Affairs Com, Bus & Indust Assn, 1981; Bus & Profl Advtg Assn 1979-; Bd of Dirs, No N Eng Bus Profl Advtg Assn, 1980-82; Boston Chapt, Nat Acad TV Arts & Scis, 1981; Num Others; cp/Chm, Whaling City Fest Parade; Chm, 125th Anniv of New Bedford Parade; VChm Ward #1, Repub City Com, New Bedford; Coor, Heart Fund Drive; Friends of Lib; Public Relats Dir, Gtr New Bedford Immunization Prog; Dir Public Reltas, Bd of Dirs, Whaer's Sr Drum & Bugle Corp, New Bedford, MA, 1963-71; Drill Instr, Var Jr Drum & Bugle Corps, SEn MA, 1968-71; Coor, Cancer Crusade, New Bedford; Appt by Gov NH, Task Force for Tourism, 1982; Fin Com, NH Repub St Com, 1983-; Bd of Dirs, Gtr Nashua Girls Clb, 1981; Instr, Rel Classes, 1981; Team Mgr, NH Yth Hockey, 1980; Num Other Commun Activs; r/Rom Cath; hon/Author of "Establishment of an Internal vs External Advtg Agy," 1983; & Other Prog Reports; Contbr, Num Articles to Profl & Trade Jours; Columnist, Var Daily, Wkly & Monthly Pubs in Canada & US, 1965-71; Cert'd Bus Communr, 1981; Ldrship Awd, SAR, 1964; UPI Thom Phillips Awd, 1971; Profl Jour Awd, 1971; Media Dir to Several Pres Cands in NH Pres Primaries; Guest Lectr on Bus Mgmt & Communs, Var Univs, Cols & Profl Assns; Other Hons; W/W in E; Other Biogl Listings.

COVELL, PEGGY oc/Interior Designer, Consultant; b/Jun 27, 1940; h/2704 Meadow Mere E, Atlanta, GA 30341; ba/Atlanta, GA; c/Ted, Tom; p/ Mr and Mrs E K Hessberg, Juno Beach, FL; ed/AA, Boston Univ; PG, Long Bch St & Boston Univ; Att'd NYU Sch of Interior Design; pa/Photo Essays in Design Pubs; Nat Assn of Female Execs; Women Bus Owners; Fashion Grp; Wom's Commerce Clb; Buckhead Bus Assn; cp/Travel Co; hon/Photo Essays; W/W of Am Wom.

COWLES, DARLEEN LOUISE oc/ Composer, Performer, Teacher; b/Nov 13, 1942; h/2143 West Thomas, Chicago, IL 60622; ba/Chicago, IL; c/ Marcelle, Michelle; p/Douglas and Mary Hoover; ed/BM, DePaul Univ, 1966; MM, NWn Univ, 1967; PhD begun, Univ of Chgo, 1974; pa/Lectr, NWn, 1967; Lectr, Elmhurst Col, 1970; Lectr, DePaul Univ, 1972-82; Perf/Mgr, Marcel Duchamp Meml Players, 1975-84; Prof of Music & Dir of Devel Prog, Am Conservatory of Music, 1982-; Chp, Chgo Soc of Composers, 1980-; Music Panel, IL Arts Coun, 1980-83; Chp of Chgo Chapt, Am Wom Composers, 1981-; Am Soc of Univ Composers; Col Music Soc; New Music Chgo; Am Musicological Soc; hon/Num Compositions; Woodrow Wilson F'ship, 1966; Schmidt Foun Awd, 1966; Faricy Awd for Creat Composition, 1967; IL Arts Coun Grant, 1981, 1982, 1983; Meet the Composers Grant, 1982; Anderson, Contemp Am Composers, A Biogl Dic; Cohen, Ency of the World's Wom Composers; World W/W of Wom.

COWLES, PAUL GREGORY oc/ Auditor; b/Mar 3, 1962; h/404 Eastman Street, Apartment #3, Eastman, GA 31023; ba/Eastman, GA; p/Mr and Mrs Marvin Donald Cowles, Fellsmere, FL; ed/AA, Indian River Commun Col, 1982; BS, Bapt Col at Charleston, 1984; pa/Mgmt Trainee, Fellsmere Enterprises Inc, Wayfara Restaurants, 1981-82; Resident Dir 1983-84, Interim Dir of Housing 1984, Bapt Col at Charleston, Charleston, SC; Auditor, Franklin Inc, Eastman, GA, 1984-; Mem: Fin & Budget Com, City of Fellsmere, FL, 1981-82; cp/Pres, Phi Beta Lambda Bus Frat, Indian River Commun Col, 1981-82; Men's House Coun 1982-83, Beta Chi Bus Clb 1983-84, Adm & Org Com for Col Accreditation 1983-84, Staley Lectr Com 1984, Bapt Col at Charleston; r/So Bapt; hon/Deans List of Scholars Fall 1982, Fall & Sprg 1983, Ldrship Awd 1982, Bapt Col at Charleston; Piper Foun S'ship; Rose McFarland Finley Foun S'ship, 1980; W/W Among Students in Am Univs & Cols; Intl Yth in Achmt.

COX, GERALDINE VANG oc/Vice President, Technical Director; b/Jan 10, 1944; h/301 North Beauregard Street #204, Alexandria, VA 22312; ba/Washington, DC; m/Walter George; sp/Mrs M H Cox, Phila, PA; ed/BS 1966, MS 1967, PhD 1970, Drexel Univ; pa/Coor of Envir Progs, Raytheon, 1970-76; Spec Asst Secy Labor, White House Fellow, 1976-77; Envir Sci, Am Petrol Inst, 1977-79; VP, Chem Mfg Assn, 1979-; Pres 1983-85, Bd 1981-83; Wash Bd, Am Rescue Com, Fdn of Org for Prof Wom; Nat Exec VP, 1972-76, Alpha Sigma Alpha; Water Pollution Control Fdn; Chair, Marine Wat Qual Comm, 1972-77; Mem 1980-83, Chair Water Resources, Am Chem Soc Com on Envir Improvement; Co-Chair, Conserv Foun; r/Luth; hon/Profl Pubs; 1975 One of Ten Outstg Yg Wom in Am; Harriet Worrell Awd, 1977; Engrg Achmt Awd; Soc Wom Engrs; Am Men & Wom of Sci; W/W Among Am Wom.

COX, T VIRGINIA oc/Anthropologist; b/Dec 1, 1937; ba/Boise State University, Boise, ID 83725; c/Stacey E; p/Clyde and Thelma M Cox (dec); ed/ BA, San Diego St Col, 1961; MA, Univ of CA-Davis, 1966; PhD, Univ of GA, 1980; pa/Instr 1967-72, Asst Prof 1972-80, Assoc Prof 1980-, Anthropology, Boise St Univ; Mem Com Chair & Prog Chair 1980-, Coun of Anthropology & Ed; Am Anthropological Assn, 1967-; Soc for Applied Anthropology, 1983-; Mem Num Univ Coms, Boise St

Univ, 1967-; cp/Ad Hoc Info Com, Planned Parenthood Inc; Adv Bd, Wom's Ctr for YWCA; ID Indian Ed Com for Devel Unit on Hist of ID Indians, 1979-80; Num Spkg Presentations, 1967-; hon/Author, Var Res & Field Experience Reports; Num Assn Lectures; Fieldwk in US & Oceania.

COZART, MARJORIE LEE oc/Executive Officer; b/Dec 19, 1930; h/1299 Gilpin, Park Towers 5W, Denver, CO 80218; ba/Denver, CO; c/Judith Conway Hawkins, Douglas Jack Conway; p/Ervin and Clementine Oliva, Newton, KS; ed/Att'd Parks Bus Col, Denver Real Est Prep; pa/Property Mgmt Acct, Van Schaack & Co, 1958-63; Ofc Mgr, Computer Listing Ser, 1963-65; Ofc Mgr, Pennant Petro Co, 1965-67; VP, Petro Data Ser, 1967-72; Pres/Owner/Fdr, Oil-Tronix Ltd, 1972-; Am Assn of Petro Landmen; Denver Assn of Petro Landmen; r/Prot; hon/Author & Designer, Sys Software; Bus-wom of Yr, 1983; W/W in W.

CRABTREE, ELIZABETH C oc/Communication Consultant; b/Oct 25; h/306 Woodlawn Avenue, Greensboro, NC 27401; ba/Greensboro, NC; c/Baxter, Charity; p/Ralph (dec) and Helen M Cartwright, Asheville, NC; ed/BA 1971, MEd 1974, Univ NC-Greensboro; EdD in Prog; pa/Instr, McDowell Tech Inst, 1971-72; Instr, Guilford Tech Inst, 1972-; Instr, Univ NC-Greensboro, 1982; Instr, Guilford Col, 1982-; Coor, Personal Dynamics Inst, 1980-; Am Mgmt Assn, 1982-; Nat Assn Female Execs, 1982-; NEA, 1973-; Intl Assn Bus Communicators, 1982-; Am Soc Tng & Devel, 1981-; r/SDA; hon/Author of "Can We Teach Students to Think Clearly?", 1982; Edr of Yr Awd, 1982; World W/W of Wom.

CRACOFT, RICHARD HOLTON oc/Professor, Dean; b/Jun 28, 1936; h/770 East Center Street, Provo, UT 84601; ba/Provo, UT; m/Janice Marie Alger; c/Richard A, Jeffrey R, Jennifer; p/Ralph and Grace White Cracroft (dec); sp/Leo Laraine Alger (dec); Marie Price Alger Harrison, Provo, UT; ed/BA 1961, MA 1963, Univ of UT; PhD, Univ of WI-Madison, 1979; mil/UT NG, 1952-63; pa/Bus Enterprises for the Blind, UT St Dept of Rehab, 1960-61; Tchg Asst, Univ of UT, 1961-63; Tchg Asst, Univ of WI, 1966-69; Instr Eng 1963-66, Asst Prof, Assoc Prof & Prof 1969-, Brigham Yg Univ, Provo; Mem: Phi Kappa Phi; Wn Lit Assn; Am Lit Sect, MLA; NCTE; Assn of Mormon Lttrs; Mormon Hist Assn; r/LDS; hon/Author, *A Believing People: The Lit of the LDS*, 1974; *22 Yg Mormon Writers*, 1975; *Wash Irving: The Wn Wks*, 1975; *Voice from the Past*, 1980; Author, Over 100 Articles in Profl Jours; Owl & Key, Skull & Bones, Univ of UT; Phi Kappa Phi; Medal for Lit, Assn Students of Brigham Yg Univ; W/W: in W, in Am.

CRADDICK, THOMAS R oc/State Representative; Sales Representative; b/Sep 19, 1943; h/3108 Stanolind, Midland, TX 79701; ba/Midland, TX; m/Nadine Nayfa; c/Christi Leigh, Thomas Russell Jr; p/Mr and Mrs Russ F Craddick, Midland, TX; sp/Mr and Mrs Fred Nayfa, Sweetwater, TX; ed/BBA 1965, MBA 1966, TX Tech Univ; pa/Sales Rep, Mustang Mud Inc; Owner, Craddick Properties; Elected St Rep, Nov, 1968; Mem: Ins Com, Penitentiaries Com, Pks

& Wildlife Com, Liquor Regulation Com, Congl & Legis Dists Com, 61st Legis & Spec Sessions; Re-elected St Rep, 1970; Mem: Pks & Wildlife Com, Liquor Regulation Com, Agri Com, Enrolled & Engrossed Bills, Public Hlth Coms; Re-elected, 1972; Mem: Agri & Livestock Com, Ins Com, Natural Resources Com, Sub-com on Oil & Gas, Del to Constitl Conv 1974; Re-elected 1974-; Mem: Chm Com on Natural Resources, Energy Resources Com, Natural Resources Task Force on Intergovtl Relats Con, Nat Conf of St Legis; cp/Dir, Midland Boys Clb; Past Pres Midland Chapt, Former Nat Dir, TX Tech Ex-students Assn; Past Dir, JC's; Past Dir, Downtown Lions Clb; Adv Dir, Clover House in Permian Basin; Bd of Dirs, Comml Bk & Trust; Bd of Dirs, Midland C of C; r/Cath; hon/Dist'd Ser Awd, Midland JCs, 1976.

CRAFTON-MASTERSON, ADRIENNE oc/Real Estate Executive; b/Mar 6, 1926; h/8200 Rolling Road, Springfield, VA 22153; ba/Alexandria, VA; c/Mary Victoria M Powers, Kathleen Joan, John Andrew, Barbara Lynn; p/John Harold and Adrienne Crafton; ed/Att'd No VA Commun Col, 1971-74; oc/Staff Mem, Sen T F Green of RI, 1944-47, 1954-60; Staff Mem, US Senate Com on Campaign Expenditures, 1944-45; Asst Clk, Ho Govt Ops Com, 1948-49; Asst Clk, Ho Campaign Expenditures Com, 1950; Asst Appt Secy, Ofc of Pres, 1951-53; Hubbard Rlty, 1962-67; Owner/Mgr, Adrienne Invest Real Est, 1968-; Mem, No VA Bd Rltrs (Chm Comml & Indust Com); VA Assn of Rltrs; Nat Assn of Rltrs; Am Soc Profl & Exec Wom; Nat Assn of Indust & Ofc Pks; Nat Assn of Female Execs; Intl Invest & Bus Exch; cp/Alexandria Ch of C; Exec Secy, Legis Chm, Richmond Diocesan Coun Cath Wom; IPA; Fdr, Friends of Kennedy Ctr; Nat Hist Soc; Nat Trust Hist Presv; r/Cath; hon/W/W in Am.

CRAIGHEAD, CHARLES DAVID oc/Vice President of Finance & Treasurer; b/Nov 24, 1943; h/1670 Bennie Drive, Cookeville, TN 38501; ba/Cookeville, TN; m/Ava Jean; c/Michael David, Kristin Leigh, Cynthia Elizabeth; p/James and Mildred Craighead, Cookeville, TN; ed/BS, TN Tech Univ; mil/AUS, 1966-69; pa/Plant Acct, Cleveland Woolens, 1965-66; Cost Acct, Pillsbury Farms, 1969-71; Cost Acctg Mgr, Chadborn Hosiery, 1971-73; Acctg Mgr, Gould Inc, 1973-78; Controller 1978-83, VP Fin, TUTCO Inc & Adams Indust Inc; Charter Mem & Past Chapt Pres, Nat Mgmt Assn, 1976-77; Nat Assn of Accts, 1974-; cp/Exec Bd Mem, Mid TN Coun BSA, 1980-; Dist Commr, BSA, 1981-; Deacon Collegeside Ch of Christ, 1977-; U Way Indust Dr Chm & Bd Mem, 1977-79; Cookeville Nat Little Leag, Bd Mem 1981-83, Treas 1983-84; r/Ch of Christ; hon/Outstg Ser Awd, Nat Mgmt Assn, 1978; Gold Awds, U Way, 1978 & 1979.

CRAIN, RICHARD H oc/Businessman; b/Nov 11, 1939; h/Box 771342, Steamboat Springs, CO 80477; ba/Steamboat Springs, CO; p/Mr and Mrs Leslie H Crain, Cooperstown, NY; ed/BS, SUNY-Cortland, 1962; Grad Wk, Adelphi, C W Post, SUNY-Cortland & Oneonta; pa/Instr Phy Ed & Ftball Coach, Shirley Public Schs, 1962-64; Sci

Tchr & Ftball Coach, Cooperstown Public Schs, 1964-66; Sci Instr, Farmingdale Public Schs, 1966-68; Instr, Aspin Ski Corp, 1968-69; Mgr, Ski Mart Aspen, 1968-69; Asst Dir, Ski Sch, 1969-80; Owner/Ofcr, Budget Rent-a-Car; EPSIA Cert'd Ski Profl; RMSIA Cert'd Profl; PSIA Cert'd Profl; RMSIA Examr; RMSIA Bd Dirs; Lic'd Guide, CO Guide & Outfitters Assn; hon/W/W in W; Intl W/W.

CRANE, FRANK MELVIN oc/Executive; b/Jun 10, 1923; h/2625 Woodland Drive, Ft Dodge, IA 50501; ba/Ft Dodge, IA; m/Audrey Mae Kraus; c/Carolyn Marie, Keith William, Suzanne Blanche, Debora Ann; p/Lucas Melvin and Marie Lindquist Crane (dec); sp/Louis Peter and Blanche Robinson Kraus (dec); ed/BS 1948, MS 1949, PhD 1954, Univ of MN; mil/USNR, 1942-46, Nav Air Corps; pa/Inst Animal Sic, Univ of MN, 1948-54; Res Dir 1951-66, Dir of Res & Mktg Agri 1966-70, VPres of Mktg Agri 1970-74, VPres of Res Agri 1974-, Land O' Lakes Inc; Mem: Chm Nutrition Coun 1967-68, Chm Bod of Dirs 1980-81, Am Feed Mfrs Assn (AFMA); cp/Chm, Ft Dodge U Way, 1977-78; Chm Fin Com, 1st U Meth Ch, Ft Dodge; Bd of Dirs, Ft Dodge C of C, 1979-82; Other Commun Activs; r/Meth; hon/Author of 11 Tech Articles Pub'd in Profl Jours; Var Sci Papers Pub'd & Translated into Fgn Langs; Life Mem, Nutrition Coun of the Am Feed Mfrs Assn, 1983; Life Mem, NW Feed Mfrs, 1983; W/W.

CRAWFORD, HERBERT RAYMOND oc/Consulting Engineer; b/Jul 25, 1918; h/13865 Southwest 74th Avenue, Miami, FL 33158; ba/Miami, FL; m/Evelyn McNelly Crawford (dec); c/Jean Crawford Webber; p/Herbert and Mary Frances Crawford (dec); sp/William and Mary McNelly (dec); ed/BME, NC St Univ, 1940; Postgrad Studies, Johns Hopkins Univ 1940-41, NY Univ 1946-47; pa/Preliminary Design Engr, Glenn L Martin Co; Flight Test Engr 1941-54, Dir of Flight Test 1954-57, Dir of Intl Oper 1957-60, Grumman Aircraft Engrg Corp; VP & Gen Mgr, Grumman Intl Inc, 1960-62; Pres, Intercont Corp, 1963-65; Dir of Wash Opers 1965-69, Dir of Airport Proj Devel 1970-72, Sr Proj Dir 1973-79, Mng Dir 1980-, Howard Needles Tammen & Bergendoff; r/Meth; hon/Profl Pubs; Jane's W/W: in Aviation & Aerospace, in S & SW.

CRAWFORD, JAMES F oc/Director of Industrial Relations; b/May 16, 1920; h/1096 Clifton Road, Atlanta, GA 30307; ba/Atlanta, GA; m/Miriam W; c/Cathy, David; p/Frank M and Loie Marie Crawford (dec); ed/AB, Peru Col, 1941; MA, Univ of CO, 1952; PhD, Univ of WI, 1957; mil/USN, 1942-46, Lt jg; pa/Dir Inst of Industl Relats 1981-, Chm Dept Ec 1962-80, Prof Ec 1960-, Assoc Prof Ed 1958-60, Asst Prof Ed 1956-68, GA St Univ; Prog Dir US Dept Prog for German Industl Relats Trainees 1955-56, Instr in Ec 1955-56, Univ of WI; Mem Bd of Dirs, Atlanta Pvt Indust Coun, 1982-; Mem Commun Disputes Settlement Panel, Am Arbitration Assn, 1970-; Reg 3 Ec Stabilization Com, Ofc of Emer Planning, 1970-; Bd of Trustees, GA Coun on Ec Ed, 1972-; Mem Gov's Joint Full Employmt in GA Study Com & Chm of Subcom on Ec Devel for GA, 1976-77; Exec Bd Mem, Gerontology Ctr, GA St Univ; Pres Atlanta Chapt, Num Other Coms, Industl Relats Res Assn, 1978-81; Pres Atlanta Ec Clb, Other Positions & Coms, Affil of Nat Assn of Bus Economists, 1976-77; Soc of Fed Labor Relats Profls; Am Ec Assn; So Ec Assn; Am Soc of Pers Admrs; cp/Mem Num Coms, GA St Univ; Num Presentations at Over 40 Ec Ed Wkshops; Reviewer, Var Profl Pubs; Other Atlanta & GA Activs; hon/ Author of 2 Books, *Rdgs in Mod Ec*, 1977; *Prin of Ec*, 1956; Co-Author, Book, *Automation & Tech Change*, 1963; Author, Over 12 Pub's in Books, Profl Jours & Assn Proceedings incl'g: *Labor Law Jour*; *Proceedings of Industl Relats Res Assn*; *Atlanta Ec Review*; *Urban Am*; Others; Pi Gamma Mu; Kappa Delta Pi; Alpha Kappa Psi; Omicron Delta Epsilon; W/W; Am Men & Wom of Sci; Men of Achmt; Outstg Edrs of Am; DIB; Other Biogl Listings.

CRAWFORD, JIMMIE RAY oc/ Science and Math Teacher of the Hearing Impaired; b/Aug 3, 1946; h/202 Barbour Drive, Morganton, NC 28655; ba/Morganton, NC; m/Patricia Ann; p/ Mr and Mrs Horace Crawford, Waynesville, NC; sp/Mr and Mrs Harold Pitts; ed/BA, Gallaudet Col, 1970; MA, Wn Carolina Univ, 1979; Att'd Brevard Jr Col, Lenoir Rhyne Col; pa/Asst Chem, Dayco So, 1968-70; Sci & Math Tchr, NC Sch for the Deaf, 1970-; Past Pres 1979-81, Charter Mem 1979-, Foothills Deaf Lions; Pres, NC Assn of the Deaf, Morganton Chapt, 1981-83; VP, Gallaudet Col Alumni Assn, Morganton Chapt; Cabinet Mem, Dist 31-B Lions Clb; NC St Employee Assn, Coun on Ed of the Hearing Impaired; cp/504 Landmark Court Case, Crawford vs Univ of NC; r/Bapt; hon/Man of Yr, Foothills Deaf Lions, 1980; W/W in S & SW.

CRAWFORD, NORMA VIVIAN oc/ Staffing Coordinator, House Supervisor; b/Dec 29, 1936; h/604 Yucca Drive, Coppevas Cove, TX 76522; ba/Killeen, TX; m/Arthur B (dec); c/Pamela Jettolene, Desiree Jean C Tritle; p/Mr and Mrs I W Crawford (dec); sp/Henrietta Crawford, Splendora, TX; ed/LVN, Lee Jr Col, 1971-72; RN, Cumberland Co Col, 1977; Att'g Am Tech Univ; pa/ Patrick Henry Hosp, 1972-73; Staff Nurse, Salem Co Nsg Home, 1975-77; Nicholson Nsg Home, 1977; Staff Nurse, ICU Metroplex Hosp, 1977-79; DON Windcrest Nsg Ctr, 1979-83; Staffing Coor, Metroplex Hosp, 1982-; Adv Com, MHMR; cp/Ldr, GSA; Phi Theta Kappa; OES; r/So Bapt; hon/ Valedictorian, HS, 1953; W/W: in Jr Cols, of Am Wom.

CREAMER, ROBERT W oc/Writer, Editor; b/Jul 14, 1922; ba/Sports Illustrated, Time-Life Building, New York, NY 10020; m/Margaret; c/James, Thomas, John, Ellen, Robert; p/Joseph J and Marie W Creamer (dec); ed/Att'd Syracuse Univ & Fordham Univ; mil/AUS, Inf, WW II (Europe); pa/Advtg Copywriter, Grey Advtg Agy, Wm Weintraub Agy, 1946-50; Assoc Ediitor, Collier's Ency & Yr Book, 1950-54; Writer & Editor, *Sports Illustrated* Mag, 1954-; Mem: Authors Guild; Sports Writers Assn; hon/Author & Co-Author 7 Books, *The Quality of Courage* w Mickey Mantle, 1964; *Jocko* w Jocko Conlan, 1967; *Rhubarb in the Catbird Seat* w Red

Barber, 1968; *Babe, The Legend Comes to Life*, 1974; *Stengel, Casey's Life & Times*, 1984; *The Yankees*, 1979; *The Ultimate Baseball Book*, 1979; Author of Num Mag Articles, *Sports Illustrated*, 1954-.

CREIGHTON, JOHN HANCOCK oc/Educator; b/May 19, 1946; h/PO Box 1581 Syracuse, NY 13201; ba/Same; m/ Lyn Marie; c/Jennifer Lyn; ed/BA, Franklin Col, 1969; MS 1983, Doct Cand 1983-, Syracuse Univ; mil/AUS, 1969-74, Capt; pa/Agt, MONY, 1974-76; Grp Rep, Blue Cross/Blue Shield, 1976-78; Prin Ptnr, ECMI Assocs, 1981-; Adj Prof, Syracuse Univ, 1983-; Mem: VPres, ASTD, 1982-; NSA, 1983-; IPA, 1983-; cp/St Ofcr, JC's, 1974-80; r/Epis; hon/Cmdg Gens Awd, 1973; JCI Senator, 1980; Nat Sales Ldrs, 1979; W/W in E; Outstg Yg Men of Am.

CRENSHAW, MARGARET PRICE oc/Minority Chief Counsel, Lawyer; b/ Apr 16, 1945; h/321 East Capitol Street, Southeast, Washington, DC 20003; ba/ Washington, DC; m/Albert Burford; c/ David Ollinger, Caroline Abbey; p/ Warren Charles Price (dec); Lillian S Price, Eugene, OR; sp/Ollinger Crenshaw (dec); Marjorie B Crenshaw, Lexington, VA; ed/BA 1967, MA 1968, Stanford Univ; JD, Georgetown Univ, 1975; pa/Reporter, *Eugene Register-Guard*, 1965-66; Press Asst, Californians for Humphrey, SF, 1968; Newswom, Assoc Press, New Haven, CT, 1969; Press Asst, Rep Jeffery Cohelan, Wash DC, 1969; Res Writer, *Congl Qtly*, Wash DC, 1969-70; Asst Editor, *Wash Post*, 1979-72; Law Clk, Firm of Harrison, Lucey, Sagle & Solter, Wash DC, 1974-75; Legis Counsel, Sen Philip A Hart, Wash DC, 1975-77; Legis Counsel, Sen Paul S Sarbanes, Wash DC, 1977; Assoc, Firm of Brownstein, Zeidman & Schomer, Wash DC, 1977-79; Coun, Sen Subcom on Govt Efficiency & DC, 1978-81; Minority Chief Counsel, Sen Subcom on Govt Efficiency & DC, 1981-; Mem: ABA; DC Bar Assn; Wom's Bar Assn of DC; DC Ct of Appeals; US Ct of Appeals for DC; US Ct of Claims; r/Congregl; hon/Ford Foun F'ship, Stanford Univ, 1967-68; W/ W of Am Wom.

CRIARES, NICHOLAS JAMES oc/ Obstetrician & Gynecologist; b/Apr 2, 1934; h/34 Andover Road, Hartsdale, NY 10530; ba/Same; m/Helen; c/Peter; p/James (dec) and Christina B Criares, Martinsville, NJ; ed/BA, Columbia Col, 1955; MD, St Louis Univ Sch of Med, 1960; DSc, Univ of PA Grad Sch of Med, 1963; mil/USAF, 1960-, Col; pa/ Full-time Att'g Staff, Montefiore/ Morrisania Hosp, 1968-69; Asst Prof of Ob/Gyn, Upstate Med Ctr, 1969-72; Asst Clin Prof of Ob/Gyn, Albert Einstein Col of Med, 1972-; Bronx Co Ob/Gyn Soc; Soc of Urban Phys; AMA; Med Soc of St of NY; Westchester Co Med Soc; Fellow, Am Col of Obs & Gyns; Fellow, Intl Col of Ob/Gyn; Assn of Mil Surgs of the US; Assoc, Am Col of Legal Med; r/Greek Orthodox; hon/ Profl Pubs; Recog Awd, AMA, 1976-83.

CRINO, ESTELLE MARIE oc/Educational Administrator/Artist; b/Mar 30, 1932; h/326 Central Avenue, Silver Creek, NY 14136; ba/Gowanda, NY; m/ Benjamin W (dec); p/Eugene Wade (dec) and Ethel Murphy, Pompton Lakes, NJ; sp/Mary Calabrese and Benjamin (dec)

Crino, Silver Creek, NY; ed/BS, St Bonaventure, 1966; MS 1971, MS 1977, CAS 1978, SUC; EdD, Univ of Buffalo, 1983; Att'd Nazareth Col; NY Cert, K-6, Sch Adm Supvr; pa/Tchr, Franciscan Sister in NY, NJ, MA, FL, 1950-60; Art Meth/Cont, Bishop O'Hern HS, 1964; Arts Methods/Content, St Elizabeth Tchr's Col, 1965-; Arts/Crafts, Buffalo Public Sch, 1968-70; Tchr & Art Instr, Sch 37, 1968-71; Tchr, New City Elem, 1971-72; Tchr, Silver Creek, 1972-79; Prin, Gowanda, NY, 1979-; Chautauqua Co Assn for G/T, Exec Bd Mem 1977-78; Chautauqua Co Assn for the Arts; Phi Delta Kappa; St Adm Assn for NYS; Nat Assn of Elem Sch Prin; Assn of Supvn & Curric Devel; Guild of Allied Artists; Soc for Ed Ldrship; Curric Adv Coun for 9 Dist, 1981-; r/Cath; hon/ Num Art Shows; W/W in E.

CRISP, ANN DILLIE oc/Community College Administrator; b/Nov 27, 1946; h/7970 NW Ridgewood, Corvallis, OR 97330; ba/Albany, OR; p/Ed Dillie, Anderson, IN; ed/BS w hon, Ball St Univ, 1969; MHEc 1975, PhD Student 1975-, OR St Univ; pa/Yth Nutrition Spec, Univ of AK, 1970-73; Spec in Nutrition Ed, OR St Univ, 1975; Parent Ed Coor 1975-77, Dir of Albany Ctr 1977-79, Dir Benton Ctr 1979-, Linn-Benton Commun Col; Corvallis Pres, Zonta Itl, 1982-83; Pres, NW Adult Ed Assn, 1984-85; Secy, OR Home Ec Assn, 1979-81; AHEA; AAACE; Chair, OR Dept of Ed Consumer Homemaking Com, 1978-79; cp/ Benton Co U Way, Secy, 1984-85; Corvallis Chamber Bd, 1979-80; r/ Disciples of Christ; hon/Profl Pubs; Ldrs of 80's, 1982; 1st Citizen Nominee, 1982; Phi Kappa Phi, 1974; Sigma Zeta, 1967; Hons Prog Grad, 1969; Outstg Yg Wom of Am, 1978; W/W Among HS Sr.

CROAT, THOMAS BERNARD oc/ Research Botanist; b/May 23, 1938; h/ 404 Parker, St Louis, MO 63116; ba/ St Louis, MO; m/Patricia; c/Anne, Kevin; sp/Mrs Leola Swope; ed/BA, Simpson Col, 1962; BS 1966, PhD 1967, Univ of KS; mil/AUS, 1956-58, W Germany; pa/Tchr, Charlotte Amalie Public Schs, Virgin Isls, 1962-63; Tchr, Knoxville Public Schs, Knoxville, IA, 1963-64; Asst Instr, Univ of KS, Lawrence, 1966-67; PA Schulze Curator of Botany, MO Botanical Garden, 1967-; Mem: Am Soc of Plant Taxonomists; Assn for Tropical Biol; Intl Soc of Plant Taxonomists; Beta Beta Beta; Nature Conservancy; Botanical Soc of Am; Hon Bd Mem, Intl Aroid Soc; MO Native Plant Soc; r/Cath; hon/Author, *Flora of Barro CO Isl*, 1978; Num Articles in Profl Botanical Jours; Elected to Epsilon Sigma, 1979; Sci Adv Com, Simpson Col, 1982; W/W in Frontier Sci & Technol.

CROCKER, DOROTHY BRIN oc/ Music Therapist, Consultant, Lecturer; b/Jul 29, 1913; h/2206 East Lakeside Drive, Fairfield Bay, AR 72088; m/ Harold Ford; c/Hal Kenneth, Thomas Edward; ed/Att'd St Mary's Col, 1929-31; Att'd Dallas Conservatory of Music, 1931-34; Spec Dipl in Piano & Composition, Wiesemann Sch of Music, 1934-39; pa/Tchr: St Mary's Col; Dallas Conservatory of Music; Wiesemann Sch of Music; Dir of Music & Music Therapy, Shady Brook Schs; Music Therapy 1950-78, Dir of Pre-Sch Music in Piano

Prep Dept 1966-78, So Meth Univ, Dallas, TX; Mem: Pres, Nat Assn Music Therapy, 1955-57; Pres, Dallas Music Tchrs Assn, 1965-66; Nat Chm Music Therapy Activs, Mu Phi Epsilon, 1962-68; Chm Psych Music & Music Therapy, Nat Assn Music Tchrs, 1965-69; VPres, Juilliard Assn; N TX Jr Pianists Guild; Am Soc of Grp Psychotherapy & Psychodrama; r/Epis; hon/ Author of 2 Book Chapts in *Music Therapy*; Author, *Let's Discover Music Series*; Var Piano Pieces & Vocal Arrangements; Num Articles in Profl Jours; Num Poems Pub'd in Var Anthologies; Outstg Music Therapist in USA, Dr E Thayer Gaston, 1960; Acclaimed by Psychi Dr Rudolf Dreikurs; Hon Life Mbrship, Nat Assn Music Therapy, 1978; W/W: of Intells, of Wom, in Mu Phi Epsilon; Men & Wom of Distn; DIB.

CROGHAN, GARY ALAN oc/ Cancer Research Scientist; b/Oct 2, 1954; h/209 Winspear Avenue, Buffalo, NY 14215; ba/Buffalo, NY; m/Ivana Tallerico; p/Catherine and Robert Crogham, Columbia City, IN; sp/Adelaide and Antonio Tallerico, Newburgh, NY; ed/BA, Wabash Col, 1977; PhD, SUNY-Buffalo, 1983; pa/NY St Cancer Res F'ship Awdee, 1977-81; Cancer Res Affiliate 1981-82, Postdoct Res Affil 1982-83, Cancer Res Sci 1983-, Diagnostic Immunol Res & Biochem, Roswell Pk Meml Inst; NY Acad of Sci; AAAS; Am Assn Clin Chem; Am Soc for Microbiol; APHA; Assn Res on Chd Cancers; Assn of Scis at RPMI; Union of Concerned Scis; Sigma Xi; r/Prot; hon/Profl Pubs; DAAD Selection to Visit Germany, 1981; W/W in E.

CROIS, JOHN HENRY oc/Assistant Village Manager; b/Jan 13, 1946; h/ 10233 Karlov, Oak Lawn, IL 60453; ba/ Oak Lawn, IL; p/Henry and Dorothy Crois, Edwardsburg, MI; ed/BA, Elmhurst Col, 1969; MA, Univ of Notre Dame, 1972; pa/Asst Village Mgr, Village of Oak Lawn, IL, 1975-; Intl City Mgmt Assn; IL City Mgmt Assn; Am Soc for Public Adm; Metro Mgrs Assn; IL Assn of Mun Mgmt Assts; Am Ec Assn; r/Cath; hon/W/W in MW.

CROMER, CHARLES MARION oc/ Office Worker, Poet; b/Sep 15, 1943; h/ 3118 Robin Road, Texarkana, TX 75500; p/Mary Cromer, Texarkana, TX; ed/Att'd Letourneau Col, 1962-63; pa/ Ofc Wkr, Friedman Steel Sales, 1981-82; Poetry Soc of TX, 1966-73; Coun in Poetry Soc of TX, 1967; IPA; r/Bapt; hon/Dist 2nd Prize for Spelling, 1961 & 1962; S'ship, Letourneau Col, 1962; DIB.

CROMIE, THETIS R oc/Pastor; b/ Oct 12, 1947; h/1014 East 54th Street, Chicago, IL 60615; ba/Chicago, IL; ed/ BA w hons, Valparaiso Univ, 1969; AM, Univ of Chgo, 1972; DMin, Univ of Chgo, 1981; pa/Chaplain, Augustana Hosp, 1976-; IL SYNOD Com on Spec Missions; Sub-Com on Wom & Men in Ch & Soc; NOW; Luth Wom's Caucus; Inst of Soc, Ethics & Life Sci; Soc for Hlth & Human Value; r/Luth; hon/Profl Pubs; W/W of Am Wom.

CROMWELL, SUE ANDERSON oc/ Management and Program Evaluator; b/ Aug 5, 1934; h/387 Rodney Drive, Baton Rouge, LA 70808; ba/Baton Rouge, LA; m/James William; c/Ted Finley, Pinney Suzette C Johnson; p/Walter C Anderson (dec) and Lillian S Miller, Lake

Charles, LA; sp/Toy and Reba Cromwell, Lake Charles, LA; ed/BA cum laude, McNeese St Univ, 1969; MEd 1975, EdD 1977, LA St Univ; pa/Ed Res Asst, LA St Univ-Baton Rouge, 1976-77; Clrm Tchr, Calcasieu Parish Sch Bd, 1969-70; Tchr/Rdg Spec, E Baton Rouge Parish Sch Bd, 1969-78; Asst Dir of Bur of Accountability 1978-81, Dir of Bur of Mgmt & Prog Anal 1981-, LA Dept of Ed; Am Ed Res Assn; LA Ed Res Assn; Am Assn of Sch Admrs; LA Assn of Sch Edrs; SE Reg Assn of Tchr Edrs; LA Assn of Tchr Edrs; LA Rdg Assn; Capital Area Rdg Coun; LA St Assn of Sch Pers Admrs; LA Sch Supvr Assn; Phi Delta Kappa; Delta Kappa Gamma; Alpha Delta Kappa; SW Ed Devel Lab Org for LA Dept of Ed; Presentor, AERA Conf, 1981 & 1982; Presentor, Mid S Ed Res Assn, 1981; Spkr, Nat Social Studies Coun, 1976; Conslt, Ed Wkshops in Rdg, Social Studies, Pers Eval; Pres, Alpha Delta Kappa, 1980-82; cp/OES; Little Leag Baseball 1962-69, Mother's Aux, 1965; Mother's March on Polio, 1978-79; Aircraft Owners' & Pilot's Assn; Baton Rouge Aircraft Pilots' Assn; hon/Hon Citizen of NO, 1980; W/ W in S & SW.

CRON, GARY LEIGHTON oc/Franchise Owner; b/Nov 5, 1946; h/Route 1, Box 720, Weyers Cave, VA 24486; ba/Harrisonburg, VA; c/Dean Wesley; p/Zelpha Cron, Harrisonburg, VA; ed/ BA, Emory & Henry Col, 1969; pa/Math Tchr, Spotsylvania Co Schs, 1969-71; Owner, 7-Eleven Franchise, 1971-; Profl 7-Eleven Div Adv Coun; 7-Eleven Nat Adv Coun; VA 7-Eleven Franchise Owner's Assn, VP 1983; r/Bapt; hon/ Small Bus Employer of Yr, VA Gov's Adv Coun on Handicapped; 7-Eleven Dist 2571 1983 Commun Involvement Awd.

CRONIN, DAVID oc/Supervisor-Coordinator of Humanities; b/Jul 12, 1923; h/RD, Cilleyville Road, Potter Place, NH 03265; ba/W Canaan, NH; m/ Mary Lou; c/Neal, Bruce; p/Bella Schmarak, New York, NY; sp/Mr and Mrs Emmett Harkenrider, Rexville, NY; ed/BA, Univ of Denver, 1949; MA, Columbia Univ, 1952; CAS, Univ of VT, 1986; Att'd Mexico City Col, Stanford Univ, CA St Univ, Dartmouth; mil/ USAAC, USAAF; pa/Eng-Spanish Tchr, Alamosa/Alameda HS, 1949-52; Hist Regents Tchr, Mepham HS, 1952-53; Eng Tchr, Anacapa Jr HS, 1953-54; Eng-Spanish Tchr, Delhaas HS, 1954-55; Regents Hist Tchr, Massapequa HS, 1957-68; Fact, C W Post Col, L I U, 1966-68; Chm of Social Studies Dept, Dover Jr-Sr HS, 1968-71; Fac, Dutchess Col; Social Studies Regents Tchr, Jasper HS, 1971-73; Fac, SUNY, 1973-74; Prin, Goshen-Lempster, 1974-76; Supvr of Eng Dept, Woodstock HS; Hd of Humanities Dept, Mascoma HS; N Eng Tchr of Eng (Mem Chm, 1981-85); NEA; IRA; cp/Am Legion Cmdr & VCmdr, 1983-85; Planetary Soc, 1982-83; Lector-Reader, Immaculate Conception Ch, 1982-85; Mastersingers of New London, 1983; r/Rom Cath; hon/Profl Author & Lectr; Phi Beta Kappa, 1949; Phi Delta Kappa, 1983; Wm Black Tchg F'ship in Hist & Govt; Newspaper Fund Fellow, 1976; Writing Process Tchg Fellow, 1978.

CRONN, DAGMAR RAIS oc/Atmos-

pheric Chemist; b/Nov 9, 1946; h/Route 2, Box 596, Pullman, WA 99163; ba/ Pullman, WA; m/Robert Stuart Cronn; p/Wesley Edward Rais, Walla Walla, WA; Sarah Margaret Courtney Rais, Walla Walla, WA; sp/Stuart and Marjorie Cronn, Seattle, WA; ed/BS 1969, MS 1972, PhD 1975, Univ of WA; pa/ Assoc Prof & Res Chem, Lab for Atmospheric Res & Dept of Civil Engrg, Col of Engrg, WA St Univ, 1975-; Mem: Air Pollution Control Assn, 1976; Am Chem Soc, 1972; Am Geophy Union, 1979; Am Meteorological Assn, 1980; Am Soc for Mass Spectrometry, 1975; Assn for Wom in Sci, 1978; hon/Author, Over 24 Articles in Profl Sci Jours; W K Kellogg Foun F'ship, 1981-84; Kenote Spkr, Nat Meeting Soc of Wom Engrs, 1983; Sigma Xi, 1979; Grad Fac 1978, Tenured 1982, WA St Univ; NSF Sum Undergrad F'ship, 1969; 4 Yr Welsh Fund S'ship, 1965-68; Nat Merit Scholar, 1965; W/W in Technol Today; Am Men & Wom in Sci; Outstg Yg Wom of Am.

CROSS, JAMES MILLARD oc/Supervisor Special Services; b/Nov 2, 1945; h/428 West Pine Street, Johnson City, TN 37601; ba/Jonesboro, TN; p/Millard (dec) and Edna Cross, Johnson City, TN; ed/BS 1965, MAT 1970, EdS 1975, E TN St Univ; Doct Fellow, Univ of So MS, 1978; mil/AUS, 1966-69, Capt; USAR, 1970-82, Maj; pa/Hdstart Tchr, Asbury Sch, 1965; Elem Tchr Intern, Bristol, TN City Schs, 1970; Spec Ed Tchr, Elizabethton, TN, 1970-71; Wk Study Coor 1971, Supvr of Spec Sers 1979-82, Wash Co Dept of Ed; VP 1972-73, Pres 1973-74, Wash Co Ed Assn; Secy 1973-74, Pres 1974-75, Chapt 217, Coun for Exceptl Chd; Del, TN Ed Assn, 1972-75; Secy-Treas, Watauga Chapt Res Ofcr Assn, 1975-77; Del, Nat Conv for Coun for Exceptl Chd, 1974-75; Mem Bd of Dirs, Upper E TN Edrs Credit Union, 1976-77; Mem Bd of Dirs, Wash Co Assn for Retard Chd, 1979-82; Secy, Watauga Chapt ROA, 1982; Life Mem, Coun for Exceptl Chd; Nat Rehab Assn; ROA; Assn of Mil Surgs of the US; VFW; Coun of Admr of Spec Ed; Am Assn of Sch Admrs; Assn of Supvn & Curric Devel; cp/Mem, Wash Co Repub Exec Com, 1976-82; Nat Rifle Assn; Elks Club, Johnson City Lodge No 825; hon/ Nat Def Ser Medal, 1966; Lttr of Commend, USN, 1967; Army Commend Medal, 1968; Vietnam Ser Medal, 1969; Vietnam Campaign Medal, 1969; Johnson City JC's Outstg Yg Man of Yr, 1975; Resv Components Ser Medal, 1975; Resv Components Achmt Medal, 1976; Cert of Apprec, 820th Sta Hosp, USAR, 1977; Kappa Delta Phi Nat Hon Soc in Ed; Outstg Edrs of Am; W/W in S & SW.

CROWE, DEVON GEORGE oc/Physicist and Engineering Manager; b/Marc 11, 1948; h/PO Box 11755 Tucson, AZ 85734; ba/Tucson, AZ; m/Bonnie Jean; p/Mr and Mrs Frank I Crowe, Tucson, AZ; sp/Mr and Mrs Eugene McPherson, Fairborn, OH; ed/BS 1971, MBA 1977, MS 1980, Univ of AZ; mil/USAF, 1971-74, 1st Lt; pa/Staff Sci 1980-81, Sr Sci 1981-, Mgr Sys Concepts Br 1984-, Sci Applications Inc; Pres, Desert Cat Software Ltd, 1984-; Elects Engr 1978-79, Sr Electr-Optical Engr 1979, Chief Sys Devel & Opers 1979-80, Bell

Tech Opers; Tech Asst 1975, Sr Res Asst 1975-76, Kitt Peak Nat Observatory; Mem: Sr Mem, IEEE; Am Astronomical Soc; Fellow, Brit Interplanetary Soc; Pres-elect Tucson Sect, Optical Soc of Am; Intl Soc for Optical Engrg (SPIE); AAAS; Planetary Soc; hon/Author, *Optical Radiation Detectors*, 1984; Over 100 Pubs in Profl Jours & Tech Reports; W/ W in W.

CROWE, KEVIN DERRYL oc/ Research Director; b/Apr 26, 1954; h/ 4467 Rita Drive, Las Vegas, NV 89121; ba/Las Vegas, NV; p/Melvin and Dora Crowe, New Britain, CT; ed/BS, Glassboro St Col, 1976; MEd 1978, EdD 1983, Univ of NV; pa/Resource Conslt/Tchr, Berlin Public Sch Sys, 1976-77; Res Coor/Psychometrist, Univ of NV, 1977-78; Owner/Dir, Accessibility Unltd, 1979-81; Res Dir, Wink Corp, 1983-; Indust Rehab Therapist, Jean Hanna Clark Rehab Ctr, 1978-; Am Psych Assn; APGA; Coun for Exceptl Chd; Exec Bd Mem, Am Bioptic Drivers Assn; Co-inventor, AMBU-TRAC, 1982; NV St Classification of Psychol V; Diplomate, Nat Assn of Psychotherapists, 1982; Cert'd Sch & Ed Psychol, 1982; Reg'd Rehab Psychol, Am Assn of Med & Therapeautic Spec, 1979; Tchg Cert in Spec Ed, Indust Ed, & Coun, CT, NJ, NV; Reg'd Indust Rehab Therapist, Am Assn of Rehab Therapy, 1979; Cert'd Voc Eval Spec, Nat Comm of Wk Adjustment & Voc Eval Spec, 1982; Cert'd Wk Adjustment Spec, Nat Com of Wk Adjustment & Voc Eval Spec, 1982; Cert'd Handicapped Spec, St of NV Indust Ins Sys, Nat Safety Coun, 1980; hon/Profl Pubs; W/W.

CROWELL, CRAVEN H JR oc/Director of Information; b/Aug 27, 1943; h/ 11429 Hickory Springs Drive, Knoxville, TN 37922; ba/Knoxville, TN; m/ Fredricka Friedli; c/Stephanie K; p/C H Sr and Addie Ailene Cooper Crowell; BA, David Lipscomb Col, 1965; mil/ USMC, 1966; pa/Copy Editor, Reporter 1964-70, City Editor 1970-77, *The Nashville Tennessean*; Asst Metro Editor, *Dallas Times Herald*, 1977; Press Secy, US Sen Jim Sasser, 1977-80; Dir of Info, TVA, 1980-; Mem: Pi Delta Epsilon; Sigma Delta Chi; r/Ch of Christ; hon/ Nat Hdliner Awd for Best Domestic News Reporting, 1969; W/W in S & SW.

CROWLEY, MARY C oc/President and Sales Manager; b/Apr 1, 1915; h/ 10265 Inwood Road, Dallas, TX 75229; ba/Dallas, TX; m/David M (dec); c/ Donald J Carter, Ruth Carter Shanahan; p/Rev and Mrs L G Weaver (dec); ed/Att'd Univ of AR, So Meth Univ; pa/ Rep Ins Co, 1941-46; Purse Furn Co, 1946-50; Stanley Home Prods, 1950-54; Sales Mgr 1954-55, VP 1955-57, World Gift Co; Pres & Sales Mgr, Home Interiors & Gifts Inc, 1957-; cp/Bd of Dirs, Billy Graham Evang Assn, 1974-; Bd of Dirs, Dallas C of C, 1976; Bd of Dirs, Mercantile Nat Bk, 1977; Small Bus Adm, 1980; r/Bapt; hon/Publ Author; Ch Wom of Yr, Rel Heritage of Am; Oscar of Salesmanship, Am Salesmaster Org, 1966; Mature Wom of Year, Altrusa Club, 1969; K of the Royal Way, Direct Selling Assn, 1973; Wom of Yr, Baylor Univ, 1973; 1st Wom Elected to Hall of Fame, Direct Selling Assn, 1975; Mary C Bldg, 1st Bapt Ch of Dallas, 1975; Horatio Alger Award, 1978; DHL, Grand Canyon Col, 1976;

HHD, Dallas Bapt Col, 1979; Sales & Mktg Awd, 1980; W/W: in Dallas/Ft Worth, in TX, in Fin & Indust, of Am Wom, in Am, of World Wom; Intl W/ W of Intells.

CROYLE, BARBARA ANN oc/Manager of Acquisitions-Lands; b/Oct 22, 1949; h/939 Washington, Number 6, Denver, CO 80203; ba/Denver, CO; p/ Charles E Croyle, Hoover, AL; Elizabeth Croyle, Greensboro, NC; ed/BA cum laude, Col of Wm & Mary, 1971; Inst for Paralegal Tng, 1971; JD, Univ of CO Sch of Law, 1975; MBA, Univ of Denver, 1983; pa/Paralegal, Holland & Hart, 1972-73; Law Clk, CO Ct of Appeals, 1976; Assoc, Shaw Spangler & Roth, 1976-77; Title Anal, Landman, Supvr, Mgr, Petro-Lewis Corp, 1977-; ABA; CO Bar Assn; Denver Bar Assn; CO Wom Bar Assn; Exec & Profl Wom Coun; Denver Assn Petro Landman; Nat Assn for Female Execs; cp/Vol Arbitrator, Am Arbitration Assn & BBB; Bd of Dirs, Mediator, Ctr for Dispute Resolution; Vol, Legal Info Ctr at YWCA; Bd of Dirs, Wom & Bus Enterprises Inc; hon/Profl Pub; Cert, Prog for Mgmt Devel; W/W of Am Wom.

CRYAN, JOHN ROBERT oc/Professor of Early Childhood Education; b/Oct 20, 1941; h/4963 Burkewood Court, Sylvania, OH 43560; ba/Toledo, OH; c/ Julie Ann; p/Marjorie C Atkins, Sylvania, OH; ed/BA 1964, MS 1965, PhD 1972, Syracuse Univ; mil/AUS, Capt; pa/Tchr, The Manlius Sch, 1965-66, 1968-69; Asst Prof, Univ of GA, 1972-78; Assoc Prof, Univ of Toledo, 1978-; Former Chapt Treas & Pres Syracuse, Former Treas & Pres Univ of GA, Phi Delta Kappa; Phi Delta Kappa; AERA; Res Com Chm, ACEI; NAEYC; Sponsor, EVAN-G; r/Epis; hon/Num Profl Pubs; NDEA Title IV Fellow, Syracuse Univ, 1969-72.

CUKJATI, JOSEPH FRANK oc/Veterinarian; b/Oct 29, 1936; h/1609 Canyon Oaks, Irving, TX 75061; ba/ Irving, TX; m/Hlen Charlene; c/Joseph John, Julie Ann, Christopher Lee, Curtis Allen; p/Joseph J and Virginia Cukjati, Girard, KS; ed/BS, KS St Univ, 1958; DVM, 1960; mil/USAF, 1960-62, Capt; pa/Assoc Vine Vet Hosp, Chapel Hill, NC, 1962-63; Bogue Animal Hosp, Wichita, KS, 1963-64; Ridglea Animal Hosp, Ft Worth, 1964; Owner: Story Rd Animal Hosp, Irving, TX, 1964-; N Irving Animal Clin, Irving, TX, 1971-; Conslt J & L Ranches, Girard, KS, 1960-75; Bd Secy, Lab Mgmt Sers Inc, Hurst, TX; Am & TX Vet Med Assns; Dir 1970-75, Secy 1973-74, Pres 1976-77, Dallas Co Vet Med Assns; Am Animal Hosp Assn; Am Vet Radiol Assn; cp/Former Mem Bd of Dirs, Prev Cruelty to Animals, Dallas; Irving C of C; KS St Univ Alumni Clb; Alpha Gamma Rho; hon/W/W in S & SW.

CULBERTSON, KATHERYN CAMPBELL oc/State Librarian and Archivist, Attorney; b/Aug 14, 1920; h/ 800 Glen Leven Drive, Nashville, TN 37204; ba/Nashville, TN; p/Robert Fugate (dec); Mary Campbell; ed/BS, E TN St Univ, 1940; BS Lib Sci, Geo Peabody Col Lib Sch, 1942; LLB 1968, JD 1971, YMCA Night Law Sch; pa/St Libn & Archivist, TN St Lib & Archives, 1972-; Dir, Extension Ser, Public Lib of Nashville & Davidson Co, 1961-72; Reg

Libn, TN St Lib & Archives, Johnson City, TN, 1953-61; Libn, Kingsport Public Sch, Kingsport, TN, 1949-51; Ref Libn & Cataloger, Tech Lib US Bur of Ships, Wash DC, 1945-49; Mem: Pres, TN Fedn of BPW Clbs Inc, 1974-75; ABA; TN & Nashville Bar Assns; Am, SEn & TN Lib Assns; Nashville Chapt, Wom's Nat Book Assn; Lib Com, Pres's Com Employmt of the Handicapped, 1966-; Coor, TN Conf on Lib & Info Sers, 1978; Lib Alt to WHCLIS, 1979; AAUW; cp/Zonta Intl; YMCA Alumni Assn; Com Mem, Bicent of Nashville Cent III; DAR; r/Bapt; hon/Author of "Rural Lib Ser," in Volume 7 *Ency of Ed*, 1971; Wom of Achmt, TN BPW Clbs Inc, 1970; one of 5 Wom of Yr, Nashville Banner & Davidson Co BPW, 1979; W/ W: of Am Wom, in S & SW, in Am; Eminent Tennesseans of the 80's.

CULLER, FLOYD LEROY JR oc/ Executive; b/Jan 5, 1923; h/Menlo Park, CA; ba/Palo Alto, CA; m/Della Hopper; c/Floyd Leroy III; p/Floyd L and Ora L Moore Culler (dec); sp/A B and Katherine Sturgill Hopper; ed/BES, Johns Hopkins Univ, 1943; pa/Design Engr 1943-47, Sect Chief Chem Tech Procs Design 1948-53, Dir Chem Tech Div 1954-65, Asst Lab Dir 1965-70, Dept Dir 1970-77, Oak Ridge Nat Lab; Pres, Elect Power Res Inst, 1978-; Mem: Fellow, AIChE; Am Nuclear Soc; Am Inst of Chems; Energy Res Adv Bd, Dept of Energy; US Sci Advy Com, IAEA; Am Chem Soc; AAAS; r/Prot; hon/Ernest O Lawrence Meml Awd, 1965; Atoms for Peace Awd, 1969; Robert E Wilson Awd, AIChE, 1972; Nat Acad of Engrg, 1974; Spec Awd, Am Nuclear Soc, 1977; W/W; W/W in Fin & Indust.

CULLIGAN, JOHN W oc/Executive; b/Nov 22, 1916; h/345 Algonquin Road, Franklin Lakes, NJ 07417; ba/New York, NY; m/Rita; c/Nancy, Mary Carol, Elizabeth, Sheila, John, Neil; p/John J and Elizabeth Culligan (dec); ed/Att'd Seton Hall Univ; UT Univ; Univ of Chgo; Philippine Univ; mil/AUS, 1943-46; pa/VPres 1967-72, Exec VPres 1972-73, Pres 1973-81, Chm of Bd & CEO 1981-, Am Home Prods Corp; Ofc Mgr, Plant Mgr 1949-59, VPres of Opers 1954-64, Pres & CEO 1964-67, Whitehall Labs, Elkhard, IN, Div of Am Home Prods Corp; VPres & Dir, The Proprietary Assn; Dir, Coun on Fam Hlth; Dir, Mgmt Assistance Inc; Regent, Seton Hall Univ; Dir, Am Foun for Pharm Ed; Ec Clb of NY; Bus Roundtable; cp/Dir, Val Hosp Foun; Adv Bd, St Benedict's Prep Sch; Co-Chm, Archbishop's Com of Laity, Newark; NY Ath Clb; K of Malta; Papal K of St Gregory; r/Cath; hon/Dir of Dirs; Poor's Register of Corps, Dirs & Execs; W/W: in E, in Am, in Fin & Indust, in World, in Advtg, in Commun Ser.

CULP, MILDRED LOUISE oc/Personal Marketing Executive; b/Jan 13, 1949; ba/Seattle Tower, Seattle, WA 98101; p/Col William and Mrs Winifred Stilwell Whitfield Culp, Cinc, OH; ed/ BA, Knox Col, 1971; MA 1974, PhD 1976, Univ Chgo; pa/Personal Mktg Exec, Owner, Exec Resumes, 1981-; Num Radio, TV, Newsprint Appearances; Columnist, Seattle Daily Jour of Commerce, 1982-; Planning Com, Managerial Series, 1982; Admissions Advr, Univ Chgo, 1981-; cp/Bd Mem, Alumni Assn Puget Sound Area, 1982-; Mem,

Netwk of Exec Wom, 1981-, Bd Mem 1981-82, Mbrship Com 1982-; hon/ Author of Num Pubs; Var S'ships & Awds; W/W in W; DIB.

CULVER, CHESTER PAUL oc/Pastor; b/Apr 14, 1929; h/Lafayette Street, Whitesville, KY 42378; ba/Murray, KY; m/Freda Marie W; c/Paula Marie; p/ Sidney and Mary Culver (dec); g/ Leonard and Mattie Wells, Brockville, IN; ed/Att'd Georgetown Col of KY, Cumberland Col of KY, Univ of KY, En KY Univ, Liberty Bapt Col, Billy Graham Schs of Evang, 1969, 1973, 1977; mil/AUS, 1954-56, Chaplain's Asst; pa/ Pastor, Corn Creek Bapt Ch, 1950-52; Pastor, Elm Grove Bapt Ch, 1956-58; Pastor, 1st Bapt Ch of Wooten, KY, 1958-63; Pastor, 1st Bapt Ch of Belfry, KY, 1963-67; Pastor, 1st Bapt Ch of Flatwoods, KY, 1967-70; Pastor, Kirksville Bapt Ch, 1970-74; Pastor, E Hamilton Bapt Ch, 1974-76; Pastor, 1st Bapt Ch of Wooton, KY, 1976-77; Pastor, 1st Bapt Ch of Elberfeld, IN, 1977-78; Pastor, Nortonville Bapt Ch, 1978-81; Pastor, Whitesville Bapt Ch, 1982-; Yth Revival Teams, 1945-50; Asst Clk 1958-59, Clk 1959-60, Asst Moderator 1960-61, Moderator 1962-63, Assoc Com 1976-77, 3 Forks Assn, Clk, Pike Assn, 1965-67; Clk, Treas of Greenup Ass'n, 1968-70; Brotherhood Dir of Tates Creek Assn, 1970-74; Yth Dir of SWn Assn, 1974-76; Assoc Com, SWn Assn, 1977-78; Music Com 1978-80, Pastor's Conf Com 1980-81, Little Bethel Assn; KY St Exec Bd, Christian Life Com, 1968-71; Tchr, M C Napier HS, 1962-63; Daily Radio Prog, WHJC, 1963-67; Priv Piano Tchr, 1976-; Secy 1978-79, Pres 1979-81, Nortonville Min Assn; Preaching Missions to Guatemala, Ctl Am, 1980 & 1981, 1985; Pianist, KY Bapt Pastor's Con, 1980; cp/A G Hodges Lodge, #297, 1982; Sunset Lodge, No 915, 1954-79; N W Shaw Lodge, No 608, 1979-; Lancaster Chapt No 56, 1974-; Scottish Rite, 1980-; Advy Bd, Hyden, KY Hosp, 1976-77; PTA Pres, Van Buren Elem Sch, 1974-76; PTA Pres, W B Muncy Elem Sch, 1976-77; PTA Pres, S Hopkins HS, 1980-81; r/S Bapt; hon/KY Col, Gov Combs, 1963; Ser to Yth Plaque, Y Clubs of Belfry HS, 1965; 3 Awds, S Bapt Conv Better Minutes Contest; W/W in Rel; Commun Ldrs & Noteworthy Ams.

CULVER, ROBERT LONZO JR oc/ Real Estate Executive & Insurance Broker; b/Jul 13, 1922; h/644 Forestwood Road, Birmingham, AL 35214; ba/Birmingham, AL; m/Imogene Webb; c/Jeri Dawn; p/Robert L (dec) and Lelma A Culver, Adamsville, AL; sp/Grady D and Cenie H Webb, Gardendale, AL; ed/ Grad Anderson Airplane Sch, Alverson Bus Col, Att'd Univ of AL; mil/AUS, 1944-46; USAF, 1951-52; pa/Secy, US Steel Corp, 1944-; Owner, Propr, Westside Rlty & Ins Co, 1956-76; Pres, Bob Culver Rlty Inc, 1976-; Nat Assn of Rltrs; AL Assn of Rltrs; B'ham Area Bd of Rltrs; Charter Mem, Forestdale C of C; cp/VFW; Worshipful Master, Mason of Adamsville Lodge, 1953-54; r/Bapt; hon/Recip of Awd, Ins Wom of B'ham, 1960; Hon Lt Col, AL St Militia, 1965; Men of Achmt; Intl Platform Assn; W/W: in Fin & Indust, in World, in S & SW.

CUMMINGS, CONSTANCE

PENNY oc/Public Relations; b/Feb 12, 1948; h/5130 Connecticut Avenue NW, Washington, DC 20008; ba/Washington, DC; p/Mr and Mrs Renwick S Cummings, Morristown, NJ; ed/BA, Univ of MD, 1970; pa/Def Indust Sales, Kaiser Indust, 1970-71; Public Relats, Manning, Selvage & Lee, 1971-77; Dir of Public Relats, Sheraton Wash Hotel, 1977-82; Area Dir of Public Relats, Sheraton Corp, 1982-; Former Pres, Am Wom in Radio & TV; Past Bd Mem, Public Relats Soc of Am; Past Pres, Am News Wom's Clb; Advtg Clb of Wash; Communs Adv Com, Howard-Georgetown Univ Comprehensive Cancer Ctr; r/Prot; hon/Profl Pubs; Gold Key Awd for Public Relats, Am Hotel & Motel Assn, 1979; Public Relats Dir of Yr, Sheraton Corp, 1981 & 1982; Pres' Awd, Sheraton Corp, 1978; Outstg Yg Wom of Am; W/W: of Wom, of Am Wom, in E.

CUMMINGS, JEANETTE GLENN oc/Director of Agency on Aging; b/Aug 11, 1949; h/2715 Vernon Drive, Augusta, GA 30906; ba/Augusta, GA; p/Asbery and Euzera Glenn, Brinson, GA; ed/BS, Tuskegee Inst, 1972; MSW, Atlanta Univ, 1973; pa/Dir of Resident Ser, Wesley Homes Inc, 1973-78; Dir, Area Agy on Aging, 1979-; Augusta Wholistic Hlth Care Planning Task Force; Chp, GA Gerontology Soc Planning Sect; Bd Mem, SEn Assn of Area Agys on Aging; Bd Mem, GA Chapt of Nat Assn of Social Wkrs; Bd Mem, GA Gerontology Soc Planning Sec; Bd Mem, SEn Assn of Area Agys on Aging; Bd Mem of GA Chapt, Nat Assn of Social Wkrs; Bd Mem, GA Gerontology Soc; Adv Mem, Med Col of GA Human Genetics Inst; Adv Mem, GA RR Bk Consumer Adv Panel; Adv Mem, August Red Cross; Profl Wom Assn; Nat Assn of Area Agy on Aging; Mem, GA Assn of Area Agys on Aging; Sr Enrichment Assn; GA Conf on Social Welfare; Nat Assn of Female Execs; cp/ Adv Mem, U Way Helpline; Augusta Leag of Wom Voters; Ldrship Augusta Alumni Assn; Augusts Alumnae Chapt of Delta Sigma Theta Sorority; Vol, Hospice Prog, St Joseph's Hosp; r/Non-Denom; hon/1982 Ldrship Augusta Exec Bd; Social Wkr of Yr, Augusta Unit of Nat Assn of Social Wkrs, 1982; Employee of Yr, CSRA Planning Com, 1980; 5 Yrs of Outstg Service to Wesley Homes Inc, 1978; W/W of American Women.

CUMMINGS, MARY T oc/Museum Director; b/May 22, 1951; h/220 East Pine Street, Missoula, MT 59802; ba/ Missoula, MT; m/Thomas A Breitenbucher; pa/P F and Lorayne A Cummings, Mpls, MN; sp/R B and Lorraine Breitenbucher, Mpls, MN; ed/BA Art Hist, Univ of MN, 1973; MA Art Hist, Univ of MI, 1976; MA Arts Adm, IN Univ, 1981; pa/Asst to Curator, Holburne Mus, Bath, England, 1970; Lectr, Mpls Inst of Arts, 1977-78; Lectr, Macalester Col, 1977-78; Asst to Dir, Tweed Mus of Art, 1978-79; Dir, Missoula Mus of the Arts, 1981-; Mem; Pres, MT Art Gallery Dirs Assn, 1982-; cp/Co-Chm, Missoula Cent Com, 1982-84; Artists in Schs/Communs Com, MT Arts Coun 1982-; hon/ Author, *The Lives of the Buddha in the Art & Lit of Asia*, 1982; *Asian Di-Visions: A Contrast of the Art of China & Japan*, 1982;

MT Art Gallery Dirs' Assn Handbook, 1982; Grad summa cum laude, 1973; Recip, IN Univ Arts Adm F'ship, 1976-77; Other Hons.

CUNNINGHAM, GARY WATSON oc/Executive; b/Jan 15, 1943; h/2 Cellini Court, Lake Oswego, OR 97034; ba/ Tigaro, OR; m/Behnaz; c/Erin V, Cameron W, Kelan R; p/Benjamin W and Virginia Marie Cunningham, Beaverton, OR; sp/Abolghossum and Farrah Al Muluk Ghorbani-nik, Tehran, Iran; ed/BA, Univ of Pacific, 1965; MS, En WA Univ, 1971; pa/Peace Corps Conslt, Min of Ednl TV, Medellin, Columbia, 1966-68; Conslt, Min Spec Ed, San Jose, Costa Rica, 1969; Spch Pathol, N Clackamas Sch Dist, Milwaukie, OR, 1973-76; Pres, C C Pubs Inc, Tualatin, OR, 1976-; Bd of Dirs, Oracle Computing Sys Inc, Tualatin, OR, 1983-; Am Spch, Lang, Hearing Assn; Coun for Exceptl Chd; Ptnrs of the Americas; r/Epis; hon/Author, Over 30 Books & 9 Therapy Mats used by Profl Spch Pathols; Patentee in Field; Cert of Apprec, Lyndon B Johnson, 1968; Ednl Grantee, En MT Univ, 1961; Edn Grantee, En WA Univ, 1970 & 1971; W/W in W.

CUNNINGHAM, HARRY NORMAN JR oc/Professor; b/Mar 7, 1935; h/2323 East Grandview Boulevard, Erie, PA 16510; ba/Erie, PA; m/Louise G; c/ Elisa Lynn, John Charles; p/Mr and Mrs Harry N Cunningham, Imperial, PA; sp/ Mr and Mrs Charles W Gittins (dec); ed/BS 1955, MS 1960, PhD 1966, Univ of Pgh; pa/Instr in Biol, Mt Union Col, Alliance, OH, 1959-61; Asst Prof Biol, Thiel Col, Greenville, PA, 1963-67; Asst Prof Biol 1967-72, Assoc Prof 1972-, Behrend Col, PA St Univ; Mem: Am Soc of Mammalogists, 1957-; Ecol Soc of Am, 1957-; PA Acad of Sci, 1977-; r/ U Meth; hon/Author & Co-Author, of 5 Articles Pub'd in Profl Jours incl'g: *Proceedings of PA Acad of Sci*; *Jour of Mammalogy*; *PA Naturalist*; *Nature*; W/W in E; Am Men of Sci; Intl Naturalists Dir & Almanac.

CUNNINGHAM, PATRICIA MARIE REEDY oc/Nurse, Administrator; b/Nov 9, 1940; h/24 West Main Street, Canisteo, NY 14823; ba/Hayward, CA; m/Harold W; c/Marie, David, Wayne, Deborah; p/John W Reedy (dec); Mary Zita Dempsey, Palmyra, NY; sp/ Jesse F Cunningham and Mary Hester Wright (dec); ed/BS 1980, MS 1983, Chapman Col; Cert Nsg Adm, ANA, 1982; pa/Asst Dir Nsg, Cert'd Nurse Admr, Kaiser Foun Hosp, Hayward, CA, 1976-; Emer Dept Charge Nurse, Mercy Hosp, Orlando, FL, 1972-73 & 1974-76; Industl Nurse, Walt Disney World, Orlando, FL, 1973-74; Mem: CA Soc Nsg Sers Admrs; Patient Care Assessment Coun; Nurses' Legis Netwk; r/Cath; hon/Orgl Skills Awd, Chapman Col, 1980; W/W in Am Wom; Personalities of W & MW; 5000 Personalities of World.

CURET, JUAN D oc/University Administrator; b/Dec 24, 1914; h/H-15 Everglads, Park Gardens, Rio Piedras, PR 00926; ba/San Juan, PR; m/Natita Novoa (dec); c/Carmen Myrta, Ruth Nilda; p/Juan Curet and Liboria Cuevas (dec); sp/Donato and Julia Noboa (dec); ed/BS, Univ of PR, 1936; MS 1946, PhD 1948, Univ of MI; pa/Instr, Asst Prof & Prof 1942-77, Chm Dept of Chem

1959-60, Dean of Natural Scis 1960-67, Coor Grad Prog & Res 1975-77, Univ of PR; Prof Chem 1978-, Chm Chem Dept 1979-80, VPres Acad Affairs 1980-, Inter Am Univ of PR; Mem: Chm PR Chapt 1949, Am Chem Soc; VChm 1956-58, PR Col of Chems; Chm 1971-72, PR Tchrs of Sci Assn; r/Meth; hon/Author, Over 12 Res Articles & Reports Pub'd in Profl Chem Jours & Ed Pubs; Guggenheim Fellow (Latin Am), 1947-48; Dist'd Edrs of Am, 1972; PR Col of Chems Awd, 1980; PR Am Chem Soc Awd, 1978; W/W: in SW, in Atoms; Am Men of Sci; Caribbean Personalities.

CURRY, KATHLEEN HENRY HAR-RIS oc/Poet, Lecturer, Housewife; b/May 26, 1918; h/4918 Lake Moor Drive, Waco, TX 76710; m/Jack; c/Henry M Harris, John L Harris; p/Mr and Mrs P L Henry (dec); sp/W H Curry (dec); Mrs W H Curry; ed/Att'd Baylor Univ; pa/Poet Laureate of TX, 1968-69; Dist'd Am Poet Laureate, U Poets Laureate Intl, 1969; Poet Laureate, Waco Fdn of Woms Clb, 1973-75; Poet Laureate, Centro Studi E Scambi, Italy, 1977; Pres Waco Chapt, The Poetry Soc of TX; Mem, U Poets Laureate Intl; r/Meth; hon/Author of 3 Books of Poetry: *Shadows On The Sand*, 1962 & 1967; *Wine of Joy*, 1968; *My Legacy In Song*, 1977; Num Poems, Articles & Short Stories in Num Pubs; Intl Wom of Yr, 1975; Addressed TX Senate, 1969; Hon VPres, Centro Studi E Scambi, 1977; Num Hons & Awds for Poetry & Prose; Hon DLitt, Sovereign Order Alfred the Gt, Hull, England, 1970; Other Hons; W/W in Poetry; TX Wom of Distn.

CURTIS, DOROTHY (DOLLY) POWERS oc/Textile Artist; b/Apr 25, 1942; h/35 Flat Rock Road, Easton, CT 06612; ba/Same; m/John Edwin; c/Kara Aimee, Jason Andrew; p/David C Powers, Mt Vernon, NY; Miriam Harvey Powers (dec); sp/John Curtis (dec); Ruth Curtis, Springfield, PA; ed/BS Ed, PA St Univ, 1963; MA Ed, NY Univ, 1966; Att'd Brookfield Craft Ctr, 1973-78; Haystack Mtn Sch of Crafts, 1977; pa/Sec'dy Sch Tchr: Public Schs Milesburg, PA, 1963-66 & Rye HS, NY, 1966-69; Owner & Artist Contemp Fibers/Textile Studio, Easton, CT, 1971-; Comms & Maj One Person Exhibns Incl: Naperville Corp Ctr, Naperville, IL; The Pindar Gallery, NYC; Midland Arts Coun, MI; Paul Mellon Arts Ctr/Choaste-Rosemary Hall, Wallingford, CT; Westport Town Hall, Westport, CT; Thorpe Intermedia Gallery, NYC; Richard Bergmann, Archs, New Canaan, CT; Waverly Carriage Barn, New Canaan, CT; Design Res, Westport, CT; Silvermine Artist Guild, New Canaan, CT; Others; Gallery & Mus Exhibns: PA St Univ Mus of Art, 1982; Traveling Mus Exhibn 'Art in Craft Media, In the Haystack Tradition,' 1981-83; in CT: Old St House,Hartford; BEL Gallery Westport; Govs Mansion, Hartford; Branchville Soho Gallery, Ridgefield; Greenwich Art Barn; Westport-Weston Arts Coun Invitationals; in NY: BFM Gallery; The Elements Gallery; The Pindar Gallery; Julie's Artisan Gallery; Artist-Craftsmen of NY, Union Carbide Exhib; in Boston: FIBERS, Fed Resv Bk; in Phila: Art Tapestry, Suzanne Gross Gallery; in NH: Univ of NH Galleries;

Num Others; Num Wks in Permanent Collections; Mem: Am Crafts Coun; Artist-Craftsmen of NY; Surface Design Assn; Soc of CT Craftsmen; Silvermine Artist Guild, CT; Westport Arts Coun; Bridgeport Arts Coun; Handweavers Guild of CT; Handweavers Guild of NY; Handweavers Guild of Am; Brookfield Craft Ctr, CT; Num Spkg Presentations & Wkshops; hon/Wks Included in: *Sourcebook of Architectural Ornament*; *Designing for Weaving*; *Double Weave*; *Color Exercises for the Weaver*; *Soft Jewelry*; *Inventive Fiber Crafts*; Others; Feature of Num Favorable Reviews in Profl Pubs incl'g: *The NY Times*; *Art Voices*; *Art N Eng*; *Arts Mag*; *Fiberarts*; *Shuttle, Spindle, Dyepot*; Others; Asst'ship, Haystack Mtn Sch of Crafts, 1977; Best in Show, Soc of CT Craftsmen Exhibn, 1977; Indiv Artist Grant, CT Comm on the Arts, 1976; Merit Awd for Sculpture, Artist-Craftsmen of NY, 1976; Purchase Awd, Marymount Col, Intl Exhibn, 1975; S'ship for Study in Fiber, Soc of CT Craftsmen, 1974; S'ship, Brookfield Craft Ctr, 1974; Weavership, Handweavers Guild of CT, 1973; Honorarium, CT/Percent for Art Juror, 1981; Finalist, Percent for Art Projs, CT, 1982; Westport Cable TV Prog, "Fairfield Exch," 1983; Other Hons; W/W: in E, in Am Wom.

CURTIS, ROGER WILLIAM oc/Artist; Painting Instructor; h/30 Riverview Road, Gloucester, MA 01930; ba/Same; m/Winifred Joan; c/Alan H, Hannah Joan, William A, David P; p/William H and Etta E Curtis (dec); ed/Att'd Burdett Col, Boston Univ; mil/USCG, Ensign; pa/Treas, Patterson Co Inc, 1935-55; Pres 1955-59, Treas 1966-, N Shore Arts; Treas, Guild Boston Artists, 1970-; VP & Treas, Am Artists Profl Leag, MA Chapt; Fdr, N Eng Artists, 1955; Dir, Copley Soc, 1957-60; Owner, Riverview Gal, 1960; Fdr, Burlington Art Assn Inc; Pres, Affiliated Art Assns of MA; hon/Profl Pubs; 'Water of the World' Awd, 1968-70; Gordon Grand Awd, 1972-75-80; AI McCarthy Awds, 1979-81; Meridian Arts & Crafts Awds, 1965-81; W/W: in Am, in E, in World, in Am Art.

CURVEN, ALFRED GUYDON oc/Theatrical Producer, Promotion, Public Relations; b/Feb 13, 1934; h/11 Maple Street, Poultney, VT 05764; m/Joan N DiSarno; c/Patricia, Francys, Christofer; p/Arthur Whitelaw and Leah Ava Curven; ed/BA, NY Univ, 1955; MS, Carnegie-Mellon Univ; DD, Faith Theol Sem, 1968; mil/USAF, 1955-59; pa/VP, Cyclone Adv Agcy, 1959-68; Pres, Cherylaine Records, Infinity Pub Co, Alive Records (BMI), 1959-; Pres, AlCee Pub Co, 1968-; Multi Media Ad Agy, 1968-74; NE Mgmt Grp, 1975-; Media Spec, *Rutland Daily Herald*, 1980-82; Chm of Bd, VT Commun Theatre Inc, 1980-; Pres, Miracle Mtn Theatre Co, 1980-; Promotion Dir, WSCG Radio, 1983-; Actors Equity Assn; Screen Actors Guild; Nat Cartoonists Soc; AFTRA; hon/Num Pubs & Prodns; Recip, AP Awd for Best Spot News Story, 1960; Awd for Best News Photo, IDPA, 1961; Awd for Best Black & White Newspaper Ad Design, N Eng Ad Execs Assn, 1980; W/W in Fin & Indust.

CURVIN, KENYA JOYCE oc/Energy Executive, Composer, Musician; b/Jun

15, 1938; h/Norman, OK; ba/Oklahoma City, OK; m/James Daniel; c/Derek Jerome Sanderson, Gina Rachelle Sanderson, Cimarron Trace Anthony; p/T C Wallace, Edmond, OK; Jean C Wallace, Oklahoma City, OK; sp/B A (dec) and Eugenia Curvin, Norman, OK; pa/New Accts Rep, Fidelity Bk, 1964-68; Geol Asst, GBK Co, 1968-72; Mgr Psych Univ, Queens Hosp, 1972-74; Exec Ofcr & Dir, Standard of Wewoka Inc, 1974; Naturalist, OK Tourism & Rec Dept, 1977-78; Drafting Coor, GADSCO Inc, 1980-; Pres & Dir, Wildcat Mapping Inc, 1980-; VP, Scissortail Oil Co, 1982-; Asst Sect, GBK Co, 1982-; Owner, MW Galaxy Music, 1982-; Ptnr, Tower Mtn, 1983-; Netwk Dir, Nat Assn of Female Execs, 1982-; OK Petro Drafting Assn, 1982-; BBB of OK City, 1983-; cp/Canadian River Pk Assn, 1983-; hon/Num Pubs & Compositions; Miss OKC, 1957; Univ of OK Hon Roll, 1977-78; Awd for Classical Composition, OK Heritage Assn, 1982; W/W in Am Wom.

CUSACK, MARY JO oc/Attorney; b/Mar 3, 1935; ba/50 West Broad Street, Columbus, OH 43215; p/Edward Thomas and Mary (O'Meara) Cusack (dec); ed/AB, Marquette Univ, 1957; JD, OH St Univ, 1959; Admitted to OH Bar, 1959; Admitted to US Supr Ct Bar, 1962; pa/Atty, Industl Comm of OH, 1960-61; OH Dept of Taxation, 1961-65; Ptnr, Cotruvo & Cusack, 1961-; Spec Counsel to Atty Gen, 1971-; Adj Prof Fam & Probate Law, Capital Univ Law Sch, 1971-; Mem: Legis Com, OH Com Status of Wom; ABA; Coun of Dels, Wkr's Compensation Com, OH Bar Assn; Profl Ethics Com, Spkrs Bur, Columbus Bar Assn; Wkr's Compensation Com, OH Acad Trial Lwyrs; Pres, Franklin Co Trial Lwyrs; VPres, Nat Assn of Wom Lwyrs; Fellow, OH St Bar Foun; Past Pres, Wom Lwyrs of Franklin Co; OH Dem Attys; Past VPres, Franklin Co Dem Attys; Past Pres, OH Assn Attys Gen; Nat Panel Arbitrators, Am Arbitration Assn; Chm Bd of Dirs, 1st Assoc Intl VPres, Past Intl Pres, Past Province Dean, Past Province Dir, Fam & Matrimony, Probate, Wkr's Compensation, Kappa Beta Pi; cp/OH St Univ Alumni Assn; Marquette Univ Alumni Assn; Past Secy-Treas, Ctl OH Nat Wom Polit Caucus; Columbus Wom's Polit Caucus; Columbus Metro Clb; Pilot Intl; r/Cath; hon/W/W: in Am Law, in Am Wom.

CUSIMANO, CHARLES V II oc/State Representative, Attorney; b/Nov 25, 1953; h/437 Brockenbraugh Court, Metairie, LA 70005; ba/Metairie, LA; m/Kathy; c/Katie, Cuck, Staci, Krissi; p/Charles V Cusimano, Metairie, LA; sp/Dan Levy, Metairie, LA; ed/BS 1975, Att'd Law Sch 1978, LA St Univ-BR; pa/LA St Rep, Dist 81; Pvt Law Pract; Prec, CVC Inc, Indep Oil & Gas Co; Clk, Chief Dist Judge L DeSonier, 1978-79; Mem: Bd Mem, IPAA; Mineral Law Inst; Civil Law Inst Natural Resources; cp/St Vincent De Paul Soc; Past Pres, Optimist Clb; r/Cath; hon/Phi Kappa Psi; Delta Theta Phi; City & St Wrestling Champ, LA, 1971; W/W in Am Univs & Cols.

CYPKIN, DIANE b/Sep 10, 1948; h/460 Neptune Avenue, Brooklyn, NY 11224; ba/New York, NY; p/Etta Cypkin, Bklyn, NY; ed/BA 1971, MFA 1975, Bklyn Col, PhD Cand, NY Univ; pa/

Profl Singer & Actress for 20 Yrs in more than 35 Stage Prodns; Dir, 3 Muses Theatre & Lenox Theatre; Yiddish Theatre Conslt, Mus City of NY, 1982; Tchr, Queens Col, Adelphi Univ, Herzl Inst; Radio & TV Spokeswom, WEVD, WFRM, WPIX, WYNY; Actors Equity Assn; Screen Actors Guild; Exec Mem, Hebrew Actors Union; Past Treas, Yiddish Artists & Friends; Asst Secy, Yiddish Nat Theatre; Am Theatre Assn; r/Jewish; hon/

Num Articles; 5 Yr Silver Cup for Ser, USO, 1970's; World W/W of Wom.

CYR, DONALD JOSEPH oc/Professor of Art; b/Feb 17, 1935; h/80 Pound Ridge Road, Cheshire, CT 06410; ba/ New Haven, CT; m/Joan Aili; c/Cathy Ann, Bob; p/Donald and Rita Cyr, Latham, NY; sp/John and Aili Helf, Eaton's Neck, NY; ed/BS, SUNY, 1957; MA 1959, EdD 1965, Columbia Univ; pa/Art Tchr, Isl Trees Meml HS, 1957-58; Shop Tchr, Edgewater Public

Schs, 1959-60; NJ St Col, 1960-67; Prof of Art, So CT St Univ, 1967-; Adj Prof of Art, Univ of New Haven, 1974-75; AAUP; Soc of Photographic Ed; Editor, *SPECTRUM*, 1973-76; Bd of Dirs, SPE, 1972-76; r/Cath; hon/Profl Pubs; Vis'g Artists Prog, CT Comm on Arts, 1975 & 1976; Edit Adv Bd, *Arts & Activs Mag*, 1977-79; Fac of Consltg Examrs, CT St Bd of Acad Awds, 1977; DIB; Men of Achmt; Contemp Authors; W/W in E.

D

DACE, TISH oc/University Dean; b/
Sep 13, 1941; ba/Southeastern Massa-
chusetts University, North Dartmouth,
MA 02747; c/Hal, Ted; ed/AB, Sweet
Briar Col, 1963; MA 1967, PhD 1971,
KS St Univ; pa/Dean Col of Arts & Scis,
Num Univ Coms, Prof Eng, SEn MA
Univ, 1980-; Chm Dept Spch & Theatre
1979-80, Assoc Prof Spch, Drama & Eng
1975-80, Asst Prof 1971-74, Assoc
Editor *Jour of Shakespearean Res & Oppors*
1971-75, Var Univ Coms 1971-80, John
Jay Col of Crim Justice, CUNY; Instr
1967-71, Grad Tchg Asst Eng 1965-67,
Grad Tchg Asst Spch 1963-65, Supvr
Tchg Assts & Instrs, 1969-71, KS St
Univ; Theatre Critic, Var Pubs, 1977-;
Mem: Am Theatre Critics Assn; Am Soc
for Theatre Res; Brit Theatre Inst; New
Drama Forum; Exec Com 1980-, Outer
Critics Circle; Theatre Lib Assn; Drama
Desk; Spch Communication Assn; MLA
of Am; Am Theatre Assn; Wom's
Caucus of Mod Langs; Phi Beta Kappa;
Num Spkg Presentations for MLA &
Other Profl Assns; hon/Author of 4
Books incl'g: *Langston Hughes: The Critical
Tradition*; Contbr to 4 Books incl'g: *The
Theatre Student: Mod Theatre & Drama; Gt
Writers of the Eng Lang: Dramatists*; Author
of Num Articles & Reviews, in Num
Pubs incl'g: *NY Theatre Review; The Village
Voice; Toronto Theatre Review; Soho News;
Other Stages; Greenwich Village News*;
Others; Judge, for Tony Awds, 1978-;
Judge, for Joseph Maharam Foun Awds,
1979-; Pi Epsilon Delta; Theta Alpha
Phi; W/W: of Wom, in Ed, in E, in Lib
& Info Sers; Contemp Authors; Dir of
Am Scholars; Commun Ldrs of Am; Dir
Dist'd Ams; DIB; Other Biogl Listings.

DACKOW, SANDRA KATHERINE
oc/Musician and Educator; b/May 19,
1951; h/122-B Shetland Drive, Lakewood, NJ 08701; ba/Slippery Rock, PA;
pa/Nicholas and Katherine (Wengreno-
vich) Dackow, Lakewood, NJ; ed/BM
1973, MMus 1976, Doct Cand, Eastman
Sch of Music, Rochester, NY; pa/Orch
Dir, Studio String Tchr, Slippery Rock
Univ, 1981-; Orch & Band Dir, E
Brunswick, NJ Public Schs, 1976-80;
Orch & Band Dir, Glen Rock, NJ Public
Schs, 1973-76; Conductor, Num Sch &
Fest Musical Orgs; Mem: NJ Unit Secy
1975-79, VPres 1979-81, Editor
1975-80, Am String Tchrs Assn; Histn
1978-80, Bd of Dirs 1979-80, Music Edrs
Assn; PA Chp 1982-, Nat Sch Orch
Assn; Am Fdn of Musicians; MENC; Intl
Soc for Music Ed; Col Music Soc; PA
Music Edrs Assn; hon/Author of Var
Articles in Profl Jours incl'g: *Am String
Tchr; Sch Musician; Tempo; Music Edrs Jour*;
Editor & Writer, *String Tones*, 1975-80;
W/W in E.

DACRE, JACK CRAVEN oc/
Research Toxicologist; h/8218 Yellow
Springs Road, Frederick, MD 21701; ba/
Frederick, MD; m/Jean Rosina; c/Ken-
neth John Craven, Terrence Michael,
Paul Christopher; p/George Craven and
Grace Dacre (dec); ed/BSc 1944, MSc
1946, Univ of New Zealand; PhD 1950,
DSc 1982, Univ of London, England;
mil/Royal New Zealand AF, 1942 &
1944; pa/Supervisory Toxicologist, AUS
Med Bioengrg Res & Devel Lab, Ft
Detrick, Frederick, MD, 1974-; Assoc
Prof Dept Med, Tulane Univ Med Sch,
NO, LA; Res Toxicologist & Hd of Unit,

Toxicology Res Unit of New Zealand
Med Res Coun, Univ of Otago Med Sch,
Dunedin, New Zealand, 1961-70; Mem:
Expert Com Mem & Conslt, World Hlth
Org, Geneva, Switzerland, 1968-; Inter-
agy Propulsion Com, Toxicology
Sub-com of Safety & Envir Wking Grp,
Joint Army-Nav-NASA-AF (JANNAF),
1974-; Biochem Soc, London, 1950-; Soc
of Toxicology, 1968-; r/Ch of England;
hon/Author of Over 100 Papers,
Abstracts, Book Chapts & Tech Reports
in Profl Pubs; Imperial Chem Industs
(ICI) Silver Medal & Prize in Biochem
Toxicology, New Zealand Inst of Chem,
1973; W/W: in E, in Technol; Am Men
& Wom of Sci.

DAHBANY, AVIVAH oc/School Psy-
chologist; b/Jan 3, 1951; h/1425H Oak
Tree Drive, North Brunswick, NJ
08902; ba/Somerset, NJ; ed/BA Psych
1974, MS Clin Sch Psych 1978, City Col
of NY; Adv Cert, Clin Sch Psych, 1978;
pa/Fellow Clin Psych, Albert Einstein
Col Med, 1976-77; Sch Psychol, Adams
Sch, 1977-78; Dir Spec Ed/Sch Psychol,
Dov Revel Veshiva, 1978-79; Sch Psy-
chol, Franklin Twp Public Schs, 1979-;
Adj Instr, Monmouth Col, 1981; Adj
Lectr, City Col of NY, 1977-78; Chp,
Student Cert Task Force; NY St Psychol
Assn; Am Psychol Assn; Nat Ed Assn;
NJ Psychol Assn; r/Jewish; hon/Grad
Student Coun Pres, City Col of NY,
1977-78; W/W in E.

DAHLSTROM, DONALD A oc/
Research Professor; b/Jan 16, 1920; h/
5340 Cottonwood Lane, Salt Lake City,
UT 84117; ba/Salt Lake City, UT; m/
Betty Cordelia; c/Mary Elizabeth,
Donald Raymond, Christine Dora,
Stephanie Lou, Michael Jeffry; p/Mr and
Mrs Raymond E Dahlstrom (dec); sp/
Mr and Mrs Henry G Robertson (dec);
ed/BSCE, Univ of MN, 1942; PhD, NWn
Univ, 1949; mil/USN; pa/Petro & Chem
Engr, Intl Petro Col, Negritos, Peru,
1942-45; Assoc Prof Chem Engrg, NWn
Univ, Evanston, IL, 1946-56; Var Posi-
tions to Sr VPres Res & Devel, Elanco
Process Equip Co, IL & UT, 1953-84;
Res Prof, Univ of UT, 1984-; Mem: Pres
1964, AIChE; VPres 1975-76, Am Inst
of Mining, Metall & Petro Engrs; Am
Chem Soc; Water Pollution Control
Fdn; Others; r/Presb; hon/Author of
Over 100 Tech Pubs & Contbns to
Engrg Handbooks; Mem, Nat Acad of
Engrg, 1975; Named One of 30 Eminent
Engrs of Chem Engrg; Fdrs Awd,
AIChe, 1967; Richards Awd, AIME,
1976; W/W: in Am, in W.

DAIBER, MARGARET ALICE oc/
Retired Secretary; b/Jan 18, 1909; h/256
North Norma Street, Ridgecrest, CA
93555; m/Georg W Daiber, MD; c/
Michael C Schmitt, Robert O Schmitt,
Olga Howard, Nina Green; p/Ira Johnb-
son and Florence Loretta Craig (dec);
pa/Ret'd Fin Secy; cp/St Pres, CA Gdn
Clbs Inc, 1980-82; Past Pres, Kern
Desert BPW; CA Phi Unit of Parlia-
mentns; r/Presb; hon/Wom of Yr, BPW,
Kern Co; Master Flower Show Judge;
Landscape Design Critic.

DALAL, JYOTSNA N oc/Medical
Researcher; b/Oct 14, 1943; h/3316
Oakwood Street, Morganton, WV
26505; ba/Morganton, WV; m/Nar S;
ed/BS Chem & Biol 1963, MD (II) 1984,
WV Univ; pa/Spectroscopist, Atomic
Energy Comm, 1964-68; Data Proces-
sor, Bk of Montreal, 1976-80; Med Resr,

Sch of Pharm, WV Univ, 1981-; Mem:
Am Chem Soc, 1980-82; Am Pharm
Assn, 1981-82; Am Med Student Assn,
1983-84; hon/Author of Var Res Pubs
in Chem, Pharm & Med Res; Phi Kappa
Phi; Golden Key Soc; 1st Prize, Res of
Am Pharm Soc, 1984; Johnson Foun
Awd, 1982; Deans List, Univ of WV;
W/W in Am Univs & Cols.

DALBY, (JOHN) THOMAS oc/Psy-
chologist; b/Feb 25, 1953; h/4 Var-
shaven Place Northwest, Calgary,
Alberta T3A 0E1, Canada; m/Deborah
Lynn; c/Krista Faith, Meagan Carmel,
Brittany Nicole; p/Jack and Marion
Dalby, Oshawa, Ontario; sp/Art and
Vivian Dutton; ed/BA, York Univ, 1975;
MA, Univ of Guelph, 1976; PhD, Univ
of Calgary, 1979; pa/Res Assoc, Univ
of Calgary Med Sch, 1979-82; Clin
Psychol, Calgary Gen Hosp, 1982-;
Sessional Instr, Univ of Calgary, 1984;
Asst Clin Prof of Psychi, Univ of
Calgary, 1984; Psychol Staff, Athabasca
Univ, 1978-; Am Psychol Assn; Cana-
dian Psychol Assn; Psychol Assn of
Alberta; Nat Acad of Neuropsychols;
Am Acad of Behavioral Med; Nat Reg
of Hlth Ser Providers in Psychol; r/Rom
Cath; hon/Profl Publs; F'ship, Hosp for
Sick Chd, Toronto, 1976; Canada Coun
Doct F'ship, 1978; Doct F'ship, Social Sci
& Humanities Res Coun of Canada,
1979; W/W in Frontier Sci & Tech; Am
Men & Women of Sci.

DALEY, VIRGINIA B oc/Retired
Reading Specialist; b/Nov 7, 1918; h/
1340 North Vine Avenue, Ontario, CA
91762; m/John W Daley; c/Virginia J,
Pamela; p/Walter W and Alice K Brown
(dec); ed/BA, Univ of SF, 1953; MA,
Univ LaVerne, 1971; pa/Elem Tchr, CA
Public Schs, 1949-68; Univ CA Ext Tchr,
1973; Rdg Spec & Conslt, Ontario
Montclair Sch Dist, 1968-81; Rdg
Conslt, W-End Child Devel Ctr, 1982-;
PTA; NEA; CTA; NRTA; CRTA; IRA;
Foothill Coun, CRA; cp/Patroness, Asst
Leag Upland; PP, Delta Kappa Gamma;
Sister Cities Comm, Ontario; r/Epis;
hon/Outstg Elem Tchrs of Am, 1974;
W/W in W.

DALLEY, GEORGE ALBERT oc/
Deputy Campaign Manager for Walter
Mondale, Attorney; b/Aug 25, 1941; h/
1328 Vermont Avenue, Northwest,
Washington, DC 20005; ba/Washing-
ton, DC; m/Pearl Elizabeth; c/Jason
Christopher, Benjamin Christian; p/
Cleveland Dalley, Bronx, NY; Con-
stance Joyce Powell Dalley (dec); sp/
Horace and Linda Love, Pembroke
Lakes, FL; ed/BA 1963, MBA & JD 1966,
Columbia Univ; pa/Lwyr; Asst to Pres,
Metro Applied Res Ctr; Assoc Atty,
Strock, Strock & Lavan; Cnslr to Tech
Coms, US Ho of Reps; Dept Asst Secy
of St for JH Orgs; Mem, Civil Aeronauts
Bd; Others; Mem: NY, DC, Fed & US
Supr Ct Bars; AMA; Fed & Nat Bar
Assns; The Coun of Fgn Relats; r/Presb;
hon/Author of Var Reports: *Fed Drug
Abuse Policy*, 1974; *A Guide to The Dem
Del Selection Process*, 1975; Papers & Spchs
on Airline Deregulation; W/W: in Am,
in Black Am; US Lwyrs.

**DALLMEYER, A(LVIN) RUDOLPH
JR** oc/President of Management Con-
sulting Firm; b/Nov 15, 1919; h/861
Bryant Avenue, Winnetka, IL 60093; ba/
Chicago, IL; c/Richard L, R Ford, J Scott,
P Suzanne H; p/Alvin R and Sara L
Dallmeyer (dec); ed/BS, Washington

Univ, 1941; MBA w distn, Harvard Grad Sch of Bus Adm, 1947; mil/AUS, 1941-45, Maj; pa/Exec Asst, Automatic Elect Co, 1947-52; Conslt & Assoc, Booz, Allen & Hamilton, 1952-59; VP, Spencer Stuart & Assoc, 1959-63; VP & Pres, Donald R Booz & Assoc, 1963-77; Pres, Dallmeyer & Co Inc, 1977-; Dir, Fed'd Foods Inc; Dir, Fidel-itone Inc; Dir, Microseal Inc; Dir, Consol Chem Inc; Dir, Harvard Bus Sch Clb of Chgo; Dir, Inst of Mgmt Conslts (Chgo Chapt); Am Mktg Assn; Chgo Assn of Commerce & Indust; Intl Bus Coun Mid Am; Chgo Coun on Fgn Relats; French-Am C of C in US (Chgo Chapt); German Am C of C of Chgo; r/Presb; hon/Profl Pubs; W/W: in Fin & Indust, in MW; Standard & Poor's Register of Dirs & Execs.

DALRYMPLE, SISTER M CHAR-LENE oc/Director of Education; b/Feb 12, 1933; h/Alvernia College, Reading, PA 19607; ba/Same; p/Edward S (dec) and Kathryn C Dalrymple, Shillington, PA; ed/BA cum laude, Col Misericordia, 1959; MA magna cum laude, Cath Univ of Am, 1968; EdD, Temple Univ, 1981; pa/Tchr, St Joseph Sch, 1952-54; Tchr, Divine Child Sch, 1954-58; Little Flower HS, 1959-60; Marymount HS, 1960-61; Tchr & Dir of Student Affairs, La Reine HS, 1961-66, 1968-71; Tchr & Guid Cnslr, St Mary's HS, 1966-68; Prof of Social Sci & Dir of Ed, Alvernia Col, 1971-; Bd of Dirs, PA Coun for Social Studies, 1979-81; Nat Coun for Social Studies; Bd of Advrs of *Social Ed*, 1978-80; Local & Nat Assns of Supvn & Curric Devel; Am Sociol Assn; World Futures Soc; r/Rom Cath; hon/Am Studies S'ship, 1969; Phi Alpha Theta, 1964; W/W in E; World W/W of Wom.

DALVI, RAMESH R oc/College Pro-fessor; b/Nov 8, 1938; h/1243 Ferndale Drive, Auburn, AL 36830; ba/Tuskegee, AL; m/Rekha R; c/Rajan and Samir; p/Rajaram S and Sumitra R Dalvi (dec); sp/Balwant L Jadhav (dec) and Anusaya B Jadhav, Bombay, India; ed/BSc 1962, BSc 1964, MSc 1967, Univ of Bombay; PhD, UT St Univ 1972; Postdoct Fellow, Vanderbilt Univ, 1972-74; pa/Sci Res Ofcr, Bhabha Atomic Res Ctr, 1967-69; Dir of Diagnostic Toxicology Lab, Sch of Vet Med, 1974-; Asst Prof 1974-79, Assoc Prof 1979-82, Prof 1982-, Tus-kegee Inst; Soc of Toxicology; Am Chem Soc; Am Acad of Vet & Comparative Toxicology; Am Col of Vet Physiol & Pharm; Intl Soc for Study of Xenobi-otics; Sigma Xi; AAAS; Inst of Food Technol; Pharm Soc of Japan; hon/Profl Pubs; Diplomate, Am Bd of Toxicology, 1982; W/W in Frontier Sci & Technol; Dir of Occupl Hlth & Safety Spec.

DALY, VEDA J oc/Curriculum Coor-dinator; b/Oct 26, 1945; h/72 Rosseter Street, Dorchester, MA 02121; ba/Roxbury, MA; p/Jean E Patton, Roselle, NJ; ed/BA, Univ of MA, 1974; EdM, Suffolk Univ, 1981; pa/Dist 9 Mid Sch Curric Coor 1982-, Sch-based Curric Coor Charles E Mackey Mid Sch 1981-82, Tchr/Coor 1978-81, Boston Public Schs; Tchr, Sts Peter & Paul Elem Sch, St Thomas, VI, 1977; Adm Asst to Elma Lewis, Elma Lewis Sch of Fine Arts, 1974-76; Adm Asst to Dir Afro-Am Students, Harvard Univ, 1971-74; Mem: Assn for Supvn & Curric Devel; Nat Assn of Female Execs; Am Fdn of Tchrs; Black Edrs Alliance;

NAACP; Conslt, Intl Ed, 1981; Inst for Contemp Art, 1980; hon/Adolescent Issues Proj, Judge Bakers Guid Ctr, Boston, MA, 1983; Boston Home & Sch Assn, 1983.

DAMACHI, NICHOLAS AGIOBI oc/Executive; b/Mar 16, 1953; h/2075 Clifton Avenue, Cincinatti, OH 45219; ba/Cincinatti, OH; p/Justin and Justina Damachi, Obudu, Nigeria; ed/BSIE 1976, MS 1978, OH St Univ; PhD, Univ of Cinc, 1981; pa/Tchr, Sch Bd Mem, Cross-River St, Nigeria, 1972; Sys Engr, Intern Div of Water, City of Columbus, OH, 1977-79; Industl Engrg Conslt, Dosimeter Corp of Am, 1980; Grad Res Assoc 1979, Adj Instr Dept of Mech & Industl Engrg 1979-81, Lectr Mech Engrg Evening Col 1979-81, Adj Asst Prof 1981-82, Asst Prof 1981-83, Asst Prof Evening Col 1981-83, Univ of Cinc; Adj Asst Prof 1983-, No KY Univ; Mng Dir, Lamic Ltd, Nigeria, 1983-; Mng Dir & Mem Bd of Dirs, Lamic Ltd; LBd of Trustees 1981-, Cinc Freestore; AIIE, 1974-; VPres Sers, Cinc Chapt, AIIE, 1982-83; Am Soc of QC, 1980; Charter Mem, Tri-St Human Factors Assn, 1983-; r/Cath; hon/Author of Var Articles & Reports Pub'd in Profl Jours incl'g: *Proceedings of AIIE*; Others; Alpha Pi Mu; Grad Res S'ship, Univ of Cinc, 1978-81; W/W: in W, in World.

D'AMATO, KEITH R oc/Executive Director; b/Jul 28, 1952; h/PO Box 1701, Key West, FL 33040; ba/Key West, FL; p/Henry and Lillian (dec) D'Amato, Paterson, NJ; ed/BA, Newark St Col, 1973; MEd summa cum laude, William Paterson Col, 1978; MA 1980, PhD 1981, CA Sch of Profl Psych; pa/Tchr-Cnslr, Bd of Ed of Paterson, NJ, 1973-78; Sch Psychol Conslt, Fresno Unified Sch Dist, 1979-80; Prog Dir of Adolescent Day Treatment Prog, Agy for Chd & Yth, 1981-83; Chief Psychol, Tidga Co Cts, 1981-83; Exec Dir, Commun Mtl Hlth of Lower Keys, 1983-; Am Psychol Assn, 1978-; PA Psychol Assn, 1982-; Clin Mem, Psychol in Marital, Fam & Sex Therapy, 1982-; Ex-Officio, Task Force on Mtl Hlth, 1983-; hon/Outstg Student, Pres Cit, 1973; W/W in E.

DAMICO, JAMES A oc/Library Director; b/May 22, 1932; h/607 Wood-bine Lane, Hattiesburg, MS 39401; ba/Hattiesburg, MS; m/Kathryn B; c/Andrew, Mark, Matthew; p/Stephen and Astrid Damico, Margate, FL; sp/Valeria Briwa, Colorado Springs, CO; ed/BS, C W Post Col of LI Univ, 1959; MLS, Rutgers Univ, 1961; mil/USN, 1951-55; pa/Dir, Cook Meml Lib, Univ of So MS, 1981-; Assoc Dir, Fondren Lib, Rice Univ, 1977-81; Hd Ref/Info Sers & Scis Libn, Rockefeller Lib, Brown Univ, 1972-77; Sys & Ref Spec & Assoc Res Coor, Univ of Dayton Lib, 1967-72; Mem: Bldg for Col & Univ Libs Com, Am Lib Assn, 1982-84; Chm Long-range Planning, MS Lib Assn, 1983; Spec Libs Assn; r/Rom Cath; hon/Personalities of S.

D'AMICO, VIRGINIA ANN oc/Fun-draiser and Assistant Campaign Direc-tor; b/Apr 26, 1948; h/3000 Greenridge #2010, Houston, TX 77507; ba/Hous-ton, TX; p/Mr and Mrs Samuel D'Amico, St Petersburg, FL; ed/BA, Univ of HI, 1970; MEd, Boston Univ, 1975; Att'd Notre Dame Col of Cleve-land, Ygstown St Univ; pa/Hlth & PE

Instr, St Mary's HS, 1970-73; Tchg Asst, Boston Univ, 1973-74; Psych Instr, Newbury Jr Col, 1974; Intern, Designated Kellogg Fellow, U Way of Am, 1975; Asst Campaign Dir, U Way of Wichita, KS, 1976-78; Campaign Dir, U Way of Wichita, KS, 1979-81; Asst Campaign Dir, Houston U Way, 1982-; Vol, ARC, 1977-82; Am Mgmt Assn, 1977-80; Nat Assn of Female Execs, 1980-82; cp/Sigma Sigma Sigma Soror-ity, Wichita Alumnae Pres, 1979-81; Bd of Dirs, Maize Commun Bldg, 1980-81; Kappa Delta Pi Hon Ed Soc, 1970-80; r/Cath; hon/Profl Pubs; Grad Tchg Asst, Boston Univ, 1973-74; U Way of Am, Intern-Kellogg Fellow; W/W: Among Students in Am Cols & Univs, of Am Wom.

DAMRON, CARINA KAY oc/Ele-mentary Teacher; b/Dec 26, 1942; h/15640 SE Millmain Drive, Portland, OR 97233; ba/Portland, OR; m/William E; p/Mr and Mrs William J Castagneto, Nampa, ID; sp/Mr and Mrs William E Damron, Safford, AZ; ed/Att'd Brigham Young Univ, 1965; Univ of UT; pa/1st Grade Tchr 1965-71, Kgn Tchr, SLC Sch Bd of Ed; Contract Tchr, Sum Sch; Contract Tchr, Hd Start Prog; Subst Tchr, 1976-79; Cent Sch Dist; cp/March of Dimes Dr; U Fund; Am Cancer Assn; Vol, Primary Chd's Med Ctr, 1966, 1967, 1968; Big Sister Prog; Com to Defeat OR Initiative #6; r/LDS; hon/Golden Gleanner Outstg Wom Awd, LDS Ch, 1972; Tchr of Yr, SLC Schs Adm; W/W of Am Wom.

DANA, DEANE oc/Los Angeles County Supervisor; b/Jul 9, 1926; h/1633 Espinosa Circle, Palos Verdes Estates, CA 90274; ba/Los Angeles, CA; m/Doris W; c/Deane III, Dorothy, Diane, Margie; p/Deane and Dorothy Lawson Dana (dec); sp/Agatha Weiler, LI, NY; ed/MSME, Stevens Inst of Technol; mil/USAF, 1st Lt; pa/Dist Mgr, Pacific Telephone Co, 1953-80; Co Supvr, 4th Dist, LA Co, 1980-; cp/Repub Ctl Com of CA; Rotary; Elks; Bd of Dirs, LA Coun BSA; Am Legion; Sierra Clb; Repub Assocs; r/Prot.

DANATOS, STEVEN CLARK oc/Corporate Tax Manager; b/Sep 24, 1951; h/52 Avenue C, Looi, NJ 07644; ba/Edison, NJ; m/Patrice Bianchi; p/Steven and Catherine Clark, Nutley, NJ; sp/Charles and Marie Bianchi, Elmwood Pk, NJ; ed/BS, Montclair St Col, 1975; MBA, Fairleigh Dickinson Univ, 1978; JD, Rutgers Law Sch, 1983; mil/USMC, 1970-72; pa/Corp Tax Mgr, JM Huber Corp, Edison, NJ, 1982-; Corp Tax Mgr, Sandvik Inc, Fairlawn, NJ, 1980-82; Sr Tax Conslt, Liggett Grp Inc, Montvale, NJ, 1979-80; Tax Supvr, Peat, Marwick, Mitchell & Co, Newark, NJ, 1974-79; Mem: Am Inst of CPA's, 1978-; Mem 1977-, Public Relats & S'ship Coms 1978-79, NJ Soc of CPA's; ABA; NJ St Bar Assn, 1979-; Am Assn of Atty/CPA's, 1979-; Adj Prof Acctg & Tax, Fairleigh Dickinson Univ, 1978-79; r/Rom Cath; hon/Lic'd CPA, St of NJ; W/W: in E, Among Am Law Students.

DANCA, JOHN A oc/Educator, Psy-chotherapist; h/1588 Timber Trail, Wheaton, IL 60187; ba/Des Plaines, IL; c/Matthew John; p/John J and Josephine (Bartolotta) Danca, Chicago, IL; ed/BA, De Paul Univ, 1972; MA, Gov's St Univ, 1975; CAS 1978, EdD 1982, No IL Univ; pa/Cnslg Fac, Fenwick, HS, Oak Park,

IL, 1973-75; Cnslg Fac, Psych Instr, Triton Col, River Grove, IL, 1975-78; Assoc Dir, The Ball Foun, Glen Ellyn, IL, 1978-79; Assoc Prof, Oakton Commun Col, Des Plaines, IL, 1979-; Conslt, IL Dept of Ed; Conslt, Am Med Technologists; Conslt, Goodwill Industs Intl, London, Toronto Ontario & Chgo; Adj Fac, The Grad Sch, No IL Univ; Adj Fac, Moraine Val Commun Col; Mem: N Am Assn of Adlerian Psych; Am Psychol Assn; MW Psychol Assn; IL Psychometry Assn; IL Col Pers Assn; IL Guid & Pers Assn; IL Grp Psychotherapy Assn; Phi Delta Kappa; cp/Bd of Dirs, Chgo Bd of Hlth, Div of Mtl Hlth- NW, 1974-75; Lectr, Acad Humanist, IL Coun for the Humanities, 1977; Crusade of Mercy Appeal, Oakton Commun Col, 1983 & 1984; Others; hon/Var Local, Nat & Intl Profl Pubs; Var Local, St, Nat & Intl Presentations; Medal For Outstg Ldrship/Ser, St Rita HS; Ten Intercol Spkg Awds, Phi Kappa Delta; Blue Key Nat Hon Frat, De Paul Univ; Pres Cit, Oakton Commun Col; W/W: Among Students in Am Univs & Cols, in MW, in World; Outstg Yg Men of Am; Men of Achmt; Personalities of Am.

DANFORTH, ARTHUR EDWARDS oc/Financial Consultant; b/Jan 23, 1925; h/Rural Route 3, Box 119 B, Trinity Pass, Pound Ridge, NY 10576; ba/New Canaan, CT; m/Elizabeth W; c/Hillyard Raible, Nicholas Edwards (dec), Jonathan Ingersoll, Elizabeth Wagley, Michael Stowe; p/Arthur Edwards Danforth (dec); sp/Elizabeth R Evans, Nantucket, MA; ed/BA Yale Univ, 1948; Att'd Columbia Univ Midshipman Sch; mil/USNR, 1943-46, Ensign; pa/Invest Bkr, Hayden Miller & Co, 1949-54; Asst VP & Asst Mgr of Bacnos Dirs Br 1959-61, 1st Nat City Bk, 1954-63; Treas, Burge Corp, 1963-65; Sr VP & Treas, Colonial Bk & Trust Co, 1965-70; Chm & CEO, Farmers Bk, 1970-76; Financial Conslt, Danforthgrp, 1976-; Chm, St Savs Bond Div, US Treas Dept, 1975-76; Chm, NCCJ, 1975; cp/V Chm, U Fund; Repub Party; r/Congregationalist; hon/W/W: in Am, in World, Bkg.

DANIEL, ROBERT CARLTON oc/Health Care Executive; b/Dec 26, 1919; h/520 South Ridge, Tallahassee, FL 32303; ba/Tallahassee, FL; m/Ivy Lee; c/Ivy Lenora D Moultrie, Roberta Katherine; p/Frederick Allen and Carrie Emma Daniel (dec); sp/Ivy Lawrence and Katherine Columbia Butler (dec); ed/AA, Univ of Miami, 1942; BS, Univ of FL, 1948; MA, Trinity Univ, 1955; mil/USAF, 1943-64, Col; pa/Exec Ofcr, USAF Hosp in Bavaria, Germany, 1949-52; Spec Conslt, A F Surg Gen in Wash DC, 1952-54; Dir of Adm Sers, Wilford Hall A F Med Ctr, 1954-56; Exec Ofcr, USAF Hosp at Tyndall AFB, FL, 1956-59; Exec Ofcr, USAF Med Ctr at Elmendorf AFB IN AK, 1959-62; Exec Ofcr, USAF Hosp at Hunter AFB, GA, 1962-64; Assoc Dir, Tallahassee Meml Hosp, 1965-79; Exec VP, Tallahassee Mel Reg Med Ctr Inc, 1979-; Am Col of Hosp Admrs, 1969-; Am Hosp Assn; FL Hosp Assn; Am Soc of Hosp Mgmt, 1969-; cp/Civitan Intl, 1965-67; Rotary Intl, 1968-; r/Presb; hon/Preceptor Appt, Grad Sch of Hosp Adm, Univ of MN, 1959-62; Advr, Sch of Nsg, Tallahassee Commun Col & FL A&M Univ, 1970-; Decorated w Legion of Merit,

USAF, 1964; W/W: in Am, in S & SW.
DANIELS, JANICE E oc/Supervisor of Employment; b/Oct 2, 1943; h/525 Holmes Street, Pittsburgh, PA 15221; ba/Pittsburgh, PA; m/LeRoy J Jr; c/Terri, Carol Ann; p/Lawrence and Ugirtha Johnson, Pgh, PA; sp/Roy and Ann (dec) Daniels, Pgh, PA; ed/BS magna cum laude, Point Pk Col, 1976; pa/Secy to VP, Pgh Brewing Co, 1963-66; Adm Secy, Rust Engrg Co, 1970-71; Exec Asst, Allegheny OIC, 1976-78; Supvr of Employmt, Westinghouse Elect Corp, 1978-; Pgh Pers Assn; Westinghouse Foremen's Assn; Bd of Dirs, Allegheny OIC, 1981-; cp/Jr Achmt Advr, 1980; Wilkinsburg Image Com, Wilkinsburg Sch Dist, 1982-83; Chm of Ed Com, Wilkinsburg Chapt NAACP, 1977-78; r/Bapt; hon/Pers Merit S'ship, Point Pk Col, 1976; Recip, Black Achiever Awd, Talk Mag, 1977; W/W of Am Wom.

DANIELS, JERALD EDWARD oc/Laboratory Administrator; b/Mar 24, 1943; h/207 Mine Head Road, Irmo, SC 29063; ba/Columbia, SC; m/Cynthia Rickie H; c/Jay, Dana; p/Jasper Edward and Jessie Mae Daniels, Columbia SC; sp/Wade Hampton and Margaret Steele Hegler, Lancaster, SC; ed/BS, Newberry Col, 1966; MA, Ctl MI Univ, 1978; mil/USAR, 1967-70, 1976-, Capt; pa/Asst Lab Mgr 1970-74, Lab Mgr 1974-82, SC St Hosp; Chief of Lab Ser, SC Dept of Mtl Hlth, 1982-; Pres 1981-82, SC Soc for Med Technol; Am Soc for Med Tech, 1976-; Adv Com, Fed Area Hlth Ed Comm, 1980-; Adv Com, Midlands Tech Col, 1976-; r/Bapt; hon/Profl Pubs; Lectr, SC Soc for Med Technol Fall Conv, 1982; J T Baker Chem Co Nat Mgmt S'ship, 1978; Hycel S'ship Awd, 1977; W/W in S & SW.

DANIELS, LESLIE BETH oc/Administrative Assistant; b/Jul 14, 1951; h/810 South Kolb #49, Tucson, AZ 85710; ba/Tucson, AZ; p/Charles L (dec) and Helen A Daniels, Tucson, AZ; ed/BA, Univ of AZ, 1972; MA, Univ of Phoenix, Att'd Univ of OK, 1983; pa/Dist Coor, Tucson Hlth Fair, 1982 & 1983; Editor, Repub St Com of AZ Newslttr, 1973-74; Copywriter/Radio/TV Prodr, Owens & Assoc, 1972-73; Graphic Artist, 1970-78; Polit Campaign Mgr, 1972-77; Adm Asst to City Mgr, City of Tucson, 1978-; cp/Delta Sigma Pi; r/Meth; hon/Kappa Tau Alpha, 1972; Dean's List, Univ of AZ, 1971-72; W/W of Am Wom.

DANIELS, MADELINE MARIE oc/Writer, Psychotherapist; b/Oct 14, 1948; h/Starwood, RFD #1, East Kingston, NH 03827; ba/East Kingston, NH; m/Peter W; c/Jonathan, Jedediah; p/William and Dorothy Barlow; ed/BA, City Col of NY, 1971; PhD, Union Gad Sch, 1975; pa/Lectr, Westchester Commun Col, Bronx Commun Col, 1973-74; Adj Fac, SUNY, 1974-76; Data Processing Coor, GTE Intl, 1976-78; Lectr, Univ of NH, 1979-; Exec Dir, Crossroads Ctr for Human Integration, 1979-; Am Psychol Assn, 1980-; Intl Coun of Psychol, 1982-; Biofeedback Soc of Am, 1980-; Soc for Psychol Anthropology, 1980-; Am Anthropological Assn, 1971-79; cp/NOW, 1981-; hon/Author; Cert'd Biofeedback Practitioner; W/W of Am Wom.

DANIELSON, PHYLLIS IRENE oc/College President; b/Jan 25, 1932; h/6137 Charnouix, Grand Rapids, MI

49506; ba/Grand Rapids, MI; c/Matthew T; p/Mrs Alta V Norris, Ardmore, OK; ed/BA, 1953; MA, 1960; EdS, 1966; EdD, 1968; Pres, Kendall Sch of Design, Grand Rapids, MI, 1976-; Assoc Prof Ed & Art, IN Univ, 1970-76; Asst Prof, Univ of NC-Greensboro, 1968-70; Asst Prof, Ball St Univ, 1966-67; Public Sch Tchr, MI, 1953-66; cp/Dir, MI Nat Bk, Grand Rapids, 1981-; VPres Commun Relats, C of C, 1978-; Dir, C of C Foun, 1978-; Bd of Dirs, U Way, 1983-; VPres, Ec Clb, 1983-; Dir, John Ball Pk Zoo, 1979-; r/Epis; hon/Author of "Art for the 2nd & 3rd Grades"; Several Ldrship Awds & Recog in Invitational Art Shows; W/W in Am Wom.

DANNA, KATHLEEN JANET oc/Associate Professor of Molecular Biology; b/Aug 21, 1945; h/4020 Greenbriar Boulevard, Boulder, CO 80303; ba/Boulder, CO; m/Richard L Kautz; p/Mr and Mrs William E Danna, Beaumont, TX; sp/Mr and Mrs Ralph Kautz, Seattle, WA; ed/BS, NM Inst Mining & Technol, 1967; PhD, Johns Hopkins Sch Med, 1972; pa/Postdoct Res, Rijksuniversiteit-Gent, Ghent, Belgium, 1972-73; Postdoct Res, MIT, 1973-75; Asst Prof 1975-83, Assoc Prof 1983-, Dept Molecular Biol, Univ CO; Am Soc Virology; Am Soc Microbiol; Am Wom Sci; cp/Johns Hopkins Surg & Med Soc; hon/Author of Num Pubs; Wilson S Stone Meml Awd for Basic Biomed Res, 1973; Res Grants from the Nat Cancer Inst, NSF, W/W: in Frontiers of Sci & Technol, of Am Wom.

DANOFF, DUDLEY SETH oc/Urologic Surgeon; b/Jun 10, 1937; h/1821 Loma Vista Drive, Beverly Hills, CA 90210; ba/Los Angeles, CA; m/Hevda; c/Aurele, Doran; p/Ruth Danoff, Palm Springs, CA; ed/AB, summa cum laude, Princeton Univ, 1959; MD, Yale Univ Sch of Med, 1963; mil/USAF, Major; pa/Adult & Pediatric Urology Pract w Danoff, Holden & Silver Urology Group, LA; Hosp Staffs: UCLA Med Ctr, Cedars-Sinai Med Ctr, Midway Hosp, Brotman Meml Hosp, Temple Hosp, Cent City Hosp, LA New Hosp; Fellow, Am Col of Surgs; Diplomate, Am Bd of Urology; Am Fertility Soc; Sigma Xi; Soc of Air Force Clin Surgs; Am Urologic Assn; Societe Internationale D'Urologie; Am Assn Clin Urologists; LA Urologic Soc; Transplant Soc So CA; LA Co Med Assn; Pres-elect, Dist 1, Bd Govs; AMA; Am Urologic Assn Wn Sect; cp/Pres-elect, Phi Delta Epsilon; Nat Ldrship Cabinet, U Jewish Appeal; Bd of Govs & Chm Exec Com, Am Friends of Hebrew Univ; Am Technicon Soc; Bd Dirs, Guardians of Courage, Am-Israeli Public Affairs Com; r/Jewish; hon/Phi Beta Kappa; Alpha Omega Alpha; Sigma Xi; Magnes Medal, Hebrew Univ of Jerusalem, 1982; W/W: in CA, in W; Men of Achmt; DIB; Men & Wom of Distn.

DANSEREAU, FRED EDWARD JR oc/University Professor; b/Sep 20, 1946; h/60 Groton Drive, Williamsville, NY 14221; ba/Buffalo, NY; p/Catherine and Alfred Dansereau, Drexel Hill, PA; ed/BS, St Joseph's Univ; MA, PhD 1972, Univ of IL; pa/WSF Fellow, Univ of IL, 1968-72; Vis'g Asst Prof, Baruch Col, 1972-73; Assoc Prof, SUNY, 1973-; NY Acad of Sci; Acad of Mgmt; Phi Kappa Phi Hon Soc; Am Psychol Assn; hon/Profl Pubs; W/W: in E, in Am Men &

Wom of Sci.

DANTON, JAMES A oc/Executive; b/ Sep 29, 1938; h/1302 Constitution Drive, Slidell, LA 70458; ba/New Orleans, LA; m/Jewel A (Pat); c/Joseph Mark, Gregory Paul; p/Anna B Whittle, Chalmette, LA; sp/Anita Armstrong, Metairie, LA; ed/GA, Loyola Univ of the S, 1973; mil/USN; pa/Ser Tech/Ser Mgr, Alo Inc, 1959-65; Salesman 1965-73, Sales Mgr 1973-75, Ins of Wausau; VPres, Marshe & McLennan, 1975-80; VPres & Mgr, Oil & Gas Div, Johnson & Higgins, 1980-; cp/Pinewood C of C; Inwood Forest C of C; r/Cath; hon/ Author, Anal of Liabilities & Var Contracts; Blue Key, 1972; Crossed Keys, 1971; Most Valuable BA Student, 1973; W/W in Am Cols & Univs.

DARE, MILTON KING oc/Tour Consultant; b/Mar 28, 1927; h/PO Drawer 1128, Fredericksburg, TX 78624; ba/Fredericksburg, TX; m/ Dorothy Hahn; c/Milton Lee, Mark Edward; p/H E (dec) and Mildred Dare, Kerrville, TX; sp/Herman J and Selma Hahn (dec); ed/BA, SWn Univ, 1949; MTheol, So Meth Univ, 1952; mil/ USNR, 1944-50; pa/Assoc Min, Ervay St UMC, 1951-52; Min, Wesley UMC, 1952-59; Min, 1st UMC of Lockhart, TX, 1959-62; Min, Meml UMC, 1962-72; Dist Supt, UMC of Kerrville, TX, 1972-76; Min, St Andrew's UMC, 1976-82; Tour Conslt, MeierIntl, 1982-; Chaplain, TX St TB Hosp, 1960-62; Pres, Austin Mins, 1965; Bd of Dirs, Wesley Foun, Univ of TX, 1964-71; Dir, Golden Age Home, 1962-66; Dir, Hilltop Vill, 1972-76; cp/Pi Kappa Alpha Frat, 1948; Pres, Caldwell Co U Fund, 1962; Pres, Harris PTA, 1966; Alumni Bd, SWn Univ, 1965-74; r/Meth; hon/ Hon DD, SWn Univ, 1979; W/W in Meth Ch, in Rel.

DARE, MILTON L oc/Director of Development/Public Relations; b/Aug 13, 1954; h/1931 Ridge Park, San Antonio, TX 78232; ba/San Antonio, TX; m/Sandra Wesch; c/Matthew Lee; p/Dr and Mrs Milton K Dare, Fredericksburg, TX; ed/BBA, SWn Univ, 1976; MS, Trinity Univ, 1979; Adm Resident 1977-78, Adm Dir of Clin Oncology Prog 1978-80, Dir of Public Relats, 1979-82, Dir of Devel/Public Relats, 1982-, SW TX Meth Hosp; Conslt, German Prot Hosp Assn, 1982; Public Relats Soc of Am; Am Hosp Assn; Am Soc for Hosp Public Relats; TX Hosp Assn; TX Soc for Hosp Public Relats & Mktg; Intl Assn of Bus Communrs; Nat Assn for Hosp Devel; r/Meth; hon/ Outstg Annual Report, TX Soc for Hosp Public Relats & Mktg, 1981; Awd of Merit, San Antonio Chapt, Intl Assn of Bus Communrs, 1982; W/W in S & SW.

DARLING, CAROL ANDERSON oc/ Professor; b/Apr 13, 1946; h/2436 Lanrell Drive, Tallahassee, FL 32303; ba/Tallahassee, FL; p/Harry A Anderson, Virginia, MN; Eileen L Anderson (dec); ed/BS, Univ of MN, 1968; MS, UT St Univ, 1972; PhD, MI St Univ, 1979; pa/Home Ec Tchr & Dept Chp, Col E Brooke Lee Jr HS, Silver Sprngs, MD & Montgomery Co Public Sch Sys, Rockville, MD, 1968-71; Tchg Asst 1971-72, Instr Fam & Child Devel 1972-73, UT St Univ; Instr Fam & Chd Devel, Dept of Hom Ec, Univ of MN, 1973-76; Res Asst Dept Human Devel Col of Human Med 1976-78, Tchg Asst

Dept Fam & Child Scis, Col of Human Ecol 1978-79, Adm Asst, Dean Asst Dean & Acad Affairs Ofc, Col of Human Ecol 1978-79, MI St Univ; Legis Aide, Ho of Reps, MI St Legis, Lansing, MI, 1977-78; Asst Prof, Dept of Home & Fam Life, Col of Home Ec, FL St Univ, 1979-; Mem: Am Home Ec Assn; FL Home Ec Assn; Nat Coun on Fam Relats; SEn Coun on Fam Relats; FL Coun on Fam Relats; Nat Assn for Ed of Yg Chd; Am Assn of Sex Edrs, Cnslrs & Therapists; Sex Info & Ed Coun of US; FL Netwk for Fam & Parent Ed; FL Ctr for Chd & Yth; Am Psychol Assn Div 34; Fam Resource Coalition; Nat Fam Life Ed Netwk; Omicron Nu; hon/ Author, Co-Author & Editor, Over 15 Articles in Profl Jours & Books incl'g: *Jour of Ob Gyn & Neonatal Nsg; Perceptual & Motor Skills; Jour of Sex & Marital Therapy; Handbook of Marriage & the Fam; MI Fam Sourcebook;* Others; Nat Chapt Excel Awd, Omicron Nu, 1982; Ski-U-Ma Awd for Ser & Ldrship, Univ of MN, 1967; Caleb Dorr Awd for High S'ship, Univ of MN, 1965-68; Num Other S'ships & F'ships; Phi Kappa Phi; Phi Upsilon Omicron; Kappa Omicron Phi; Pi Lambda Theta; Mortar Bd; Chimes; Sigma Epsilon Sigma; W/W: of Wom, of Am Wom; Outstg Yg Wom of Am.

DARLING, WALTER E oc/Chief Executive Officer of Insurance Company; b/Jun 5, 1929; h/107 Hammitt Drive, Normal, IL 61761; ba/Rockford, IL; m/Elizabeth A; c/Kathryn S, John B, Karen A; p/Mr and Mrs J B Darling, Indianapolis, IN; ed/BS, IN Univ, 1952; MBA, St Edward's Univ, 1974; CPCU Designation, 1979; Assoc Mgmt; Assoc Claims; mil/AUS, 1947-48 & 1952-54, Inf Capt; ed/Auto Underwriter, Grain Dealers Mut, 1954-55; Underwriter 1955-58, Underwriter Supvr 1958-61, Mgr 1961-65, Continental Casualty Co; Casualty Spec 1965-70, Underwriter Supt 1970-74, Asst VP Reins 1974-82, St Farm Ins; CEO, Rockford Mutual Ins Co, 1982-; Merit Awd Soc, 1977; Soc of Chartered Property & Casualty Underwriters, 1979; NAMIC Farm Underwriting Com, 1980-84; cp/VP, Bloomington-Normal Swim Clb, 1977-78; Pres, Lake Highlands Garden Clb, 1968-70; Cub Scout Master, 1972-74; Chm, U Fund Am, Austin-Travis Co, 1970; r/Cath; hon/Profl Pub; Scabbard & Blade, Mil Hon, 1952; Alpha Delta Sigma, Ad Hon, 1951; Merit Awd, Ins Ser Awd, 1977.

DARMAN, RICHARD G oc/Assistant to the President of the US; b/May 10, 1943; h/1137 Crest Lane, McLean, VA 22101; ba/Washington, DC; m/ Kathleen Emmet; c/William Temple Emmet, Jonathan Warren Emmet; ed/ BA 1964, MBA 1967, Harvard Univ; Served in Policy Positions in 5 US Cabinet Depts, 1970-77; Fac Mem, Harvard Univ, 1977-81; Prin & Dir, ICF Inc, 1975 & 1977-80; W/W: in Am, in World; Other Biogl Listings.

DARTER, CLARENCE LESLIE JR oc/Professor; b/Jun 18, 1929; h/4606 Del Rio Trail, Wichita Falls, TX 76310; ba/ Wichita Falls, TX; m/Ada Elizabeth Rogers; c/David, Denise, Donna; p/Mr and Mrs Clarence Darter, Childress, TX; sp/Mr and Mrs Paul Rogers, Idalou, TX; ed/BS 1950, EdD 1961, TX Tech Univ; MEd, Trinity Univ, 1955; mil/ USAF, 4 Yrs; pa/Tchr & Coach, Elem

& Sec'dy Level, Roosevelt Schs, 1955-56; Tchr, Cnslr & Prin, Lubbock Public Schs, Jr HS Level, 1956-63; Staff Assoc, Sci Res Assocs, 1963-66; Prof, Dean of Sch of Ed, Dir of Tchr Cert, MWn St Univ, 1966-; Mem: Indiv Devel Ctr Bd; Pres, Wichita Co Sch Master's, 1970-71; VPres, Texama Field Chapt, Phi Delta Kappa; VPres 1976-77, Pres 1977-78, TX Assn of Cols for Tchr Ed; Life Mem, NEA, 1982-83; TX Assn of Col Tchrs; Am Psychol Assn; TX Pers & Guid Assn; r/Ch of Christ; hon/ Author of 2 Ed Res Study Reports & Article in *Res in Ed;* Outstg Edrs of Am; Ldrs in Ed; W/W in S & SW; Personalities of S.

DARWIN, FRED A(RRANTS) oc/ Business Consultant; b/May 28, 1913; h/11805 Neering Drive, Dallas, TX 75218; ba/Dallas, TX; m/Hope Genung Sparks; c/Hope D Beisinger, Fred Arrants; mil/USNR, 1941-46, Cmdr; ed/ BS, US Nav Acad, 1935; MS, Harvard Univ, 1936; Att'd Univ of Chattanooga, 1929-31; pa/Sr Supvr of Traffic Dept, Wn Union Telegraph Corp, 1936-41; Asst Dir of Engrg, Hazeltine Elects Corp, 1946-49; Exec Dir of Com Guided Missiles Res & Devel Bd, Dept of Def, 1949-54; Mgr of Guided Missiles, Crosley Div, Avco Mfg Corp, 1954-56; Mgr of Missile Elects, McDonnell Aircraft Corp, 1956-61; Gen Mgr of Elect Equip Div 1961-63, Asst to Pres 1963-65, Librascope Grp of Gen Precision Inc; Bus Cnslr & Owner, Gen Bus Ser, 1966-; Spl Com Radio Tech Commn for Aeros, Dept St, Dept Nav, 1946; Cons Del, UN Provisional Intl Civil Aviation Org, 1946; IEEE; Aero Weights Engrs; cp/Harvard Grad Soc; E Dallas C of C; Nav Acad Alumni Assn; Alpha Lambda Tau; r/Presb; hon/Recip, Cits from Secy of Nav & USAAF; Profl Pubs; Originator of World Transponder; Inventor, Multiple-Coincidence Mixer Used in Pulse-Train Coding; W/W in S & SW.

DARWIN, WILLIAM DAVID oc/ Chemist; b/Apr 8, 1951; h/3382 Post Road, Lexington, Kentucky 40503; ba/ Lexington, KY; m/Wanda Faye Roberts; p/Arthur D and Irola H Darwin, Scottsboro, AL; sp/H Milton and Doris C Roberts, Monticello, KY; ed/BA, Berea Col, 1974; Grad Studies, En KY Univ, 1973-75; pa/Chem, Revere Copper & Brass Inc, 1973; Chem Instr, En KY Univ, 1973-75; Chem, NIDA Addiction Res Ctr, 1975-; Am Chem Soc, 1977-; AAAS, 1979-; hon/Num Profl Pubs; Tchg Asst, En KY Univ, 1973-75; W/ W in S & SW.

DARZYNKIEWICZ, ZBIGNIEW DZIERZYKRAJ oc/Cell Biologist; b/ May 12, 1936; h/37 Meadow Lane, Chappaqua, NY 10514; ba/Rye, NY; m/ Elizabeth; c/Richard, Robert; p/Boleslaw and Waclawa Darzynkiewicz, Poland; sp/Boleslaw and Wlodzimira Drogowski, Poland; ed/MD w hons, Warsaw Sch of Med, 1960; PhD, Warsaw Sch of Med & Polish Acad, 1966; pa/Sr Asst Prof, Warsaw Sch of Med, 1966-68; Staff Scist, Boston Biomed Res Inst, 1969-74; Res Assoc, Meml Sloan Kettering Cancer Ctr, 1974-78; Assoc Mem, 1978-; Assoc Prof, Cornell Univ Grad Sch of Med Sci; Conslt: USPHS, USDoE, Am Cancer Soc, NSF; Am Cancer Soc Grantee, 1970-72; USPHS Grantee, 1975, 1978, 1980, 1983; r/Rom

Cath; hon/Num Profl Pubs; Edit Bd: *Cytometry, J Histochem Cytochem;* Gold Millenium of Poland Medal Awd, Polish-Am Soc, 1978; Am Men & Wom of Sci; W/W in E.

DAS, J P oc/Center Director, Professor; b/Jan 20, 1931; h/11724- 38A Avenue, Edmonton, Alberta, Canada T6J 0L9; ba/Univ of Alberta, Edmonton, Canada; m/Gita; c/Satya, Sheela; p/ Biswanath Das/Nilamoni Devi, Bhubaneswar, India; sp/Bhuyan R C Dasmohapatra/Tilottama Devi (dec); ed/BA, Utkal Univ, Cuttack, India, 1951; MA, Patna Univ, India, 1953; PhD, Inst of Psychi, Univ of London, 1957; pa/Lectr in Psych, 1953-55; Res Scholar in Psych, 1955-57; Psych Rdr, 1958-63; Kennedy Prof in Psych 1963-64, Vis'g Assoc Prof Psych 1964-65, Univ of CA-LA; Rdr in Psych 1965-67, Res Prof (CSMR) Ctr for Study of Mtl Retard 1968-71, Dir CSMR & Prof Ednl Psych 1972-, Univ of Alberta, Edmonton, Canada; Mem: Fellow, Canadian Psychol Assn; Fellow, Am Psychol Assn Divs 15 & 33; AAAS; Intl Assn for Res In Lrng Disability; r/ Hindu; hon/Author, Over 100 Res Articles in Profl Jours, Book Chapts, Books Pub'd incl'g: *Intl Jour of Psych; Lrng & Cognition in the Mtly Retard; Jour of Lrng Disabilities; Topics in Lang & Lrng Disorders; Cognitive Strategies & Ednl Perf; Brit Jour of Lrng Disabilities; Brit Jour of Devel Psych;* Num Others; Kennedy Foun Prof'ship, 1963; Nuffield Fellow, 1972; Albert J Harris Awd, IRA, 1979; Canadian W/ W; Am Men & Wom of Sci; Intl Scholar's Dir; Contemp Authors.

DAS, MUKUNDA B oc/Professor; b/ Sep 1, 1931; h/1380 Circleville Road, State College, PA 16801; ba/University Park, PA; m/Rama K; c/Lipika Day Roy, Poppy; p/Banamali Das (dec); Mrs Rupmala Das, Khulna, Bangladesh; sp/ Ramesh C Biswas (dec); Mrs Pravabati Durganagar, W Bengal, India; ed/BSc 1953, MSc 1955, Dacca Univ; PhD, London Univ, 1960; DIC, Imperial Col, London; pa/Lectr in Elect Engrg, Imperial Col, London, 1960-62; LSr Sci Ofcr, Pakistan Coun of Sci & Industl Res, Dacca, 1962-64; Prin Sci Staff Mem, G E C Hirst Res Ctr, Middlesex, England, 1965-68; Assoc Prof Elect Engrg 1968-79, Prof 1979-, PA St Univ; Mem: Sr Mem, IEEE, NY; IEEE Electron Devices Grp; PA St Chapt, Sigma Xi; cp/Nat Wildlife Fdn; r/Hinduism; hon/ Author, Over 50 Papers in Sci & Profl Jours; Recip, 4 Patents in Field; Blumlain-Browne-Willan Premium Awd, IEE London, 1968; W/W: in E, in Technol Today, in Engrg; Am Men & Wom of Sci.

DAS GUPTA, AARON oc/Research Mechanical Engineer; b/Nov 20, 1943; h/104 John Street, Perryville, MD 21903; ba/Aberdeen Proving Ground, MD; m/Runu Biswas; c/Elora, Debraj; p/Amita and Krishna Prosad, India; sp/ Bidhubhusan Biswas, India; ed/BTech (Hons), Indian Inst of Tech, 1963; MSME, Tech Univ of Nova Scotia, 1968; PhD, VA Polytech Inst & St Univ, 1975; pa/Design Engr, Kingsport Press, 1973-75; Proj Engr, Stress Anal, Sundstrand Aviation, 1975-76; Res Mech Engr, Blast Dynamics Br, Terminal Ballistics Civ, Ballistic Res Lab, 1976-; ASME, 1976-; SESA, 1976-; AIAA, 1976-; Invited Co-Chm, 19th SES Conf, 1982; Profl Reg'd Engr, 1975-; Am Acad

of Mech, 1978-; Div Chm, Combined Fed Campaign Com, BRL, APG, 1981; r/Hindu; hon/Num Profl Pubs; Sustained High Quality Perf Awd, AUS, 1982; Merit S'ship, 1959-63; DRB Res Fellow, NSTC, 1966-67; NSF Travel Grant to India, 1983; Am Men & Wom of Sci; W/W: in Aviation & Aerospace, in E, in Frontier Sci & Tech.

DATZ, RUTH ELIZABETH oc/Vocal Music Teacher, Musician; b/Jun 10, 1936; h/1564 Barrington, Ann Arbor, MI 48103; ba/Ann Arbor, MI; p/Robert and Ruth Datz, Jeannette, PA; ed/BA, IN Univ of PA, 1958; MS, NY Univ, 1961; Postgrad Studies, PA St Univ, Univ of CO, SUNY; pa/Music Tchr, Middletown Twp, 1958-61; Music Tchr Tyrone, PA, 1961-65; Music Tchr & Dept Chm, Ann Arbor, MI, 1965-; Cnslr, Rec Dir, Dir of Jr Girls Div, Nat Music Camp, 1956-69; Hd Wom's Cnslr, N Eng Music Camp, 1970-72; Flutist, Pit Orch, 1959-61; Conductor, Spec Choirs; MENC; MI Music Edrs Assn; MI Sch Voc Assn, Dist Chm 1978-79; Am Choral Dirs Assn; Nat Assn of Humanities Edrs; cp/Delta Zeta Sorority; Delta Omicron Hon; U Ch of Christ; OES; Jobs Daugh; r/Prot; hon/Delta Omicron Hon, 1957; W/W of Am Wom.

DAVENPORT, WILLIAM RANDOLPH oc/College President; b/Dec 8, 925; h/1604 Lebanon Avenue, Campbellsville, KY 42718; ba/Campbellsville, KY; m/Janet Chambers; C/Elizabeth, Martin, Mary, Susan; p/Jesse M and Helene Davenport (dec); sp/Jesse L and Mason Chambers (dec); ed/AB, Univ of L'ville, 1947; MS 1950, EdD 1955, Univ of AR; mil/USN (Ret'd); pa/Instr, Univ of AR, 1950-55; Prof, Butler Univ, IN, 1955-64; Prof, Univ of MI, 1964-69; Pres, Campbellsville Col, 1969-; Mem, Phi Delta Kappa; cp/Kiwanis Intl; Intl Pres 1971-74, The Gideons Intl; r/So Bapt; hon/Author of *The Constitl Provisions for Ed in AR,* 1955; *Handbook for Student Tchrs,* 1960.

DAVID, EDWARD E JR oc/Executive; b/Jan 25, 1925; h/Box 435, Bedminster, NJ 07921; ba/Annandale, NJ; m/Ann Hirshberg; c/Nancy; p/Edward Emil and Beatrice Liebman David (dec); sp/Julian Hirshberg (dec); Henrietta Hirshberg, Atlanta, GA; ed/BS, GA Inst of Technol; SM, ScD, MIT; mil/USN, Lt jg; pa/Exec Dir Res, Bell Telephone Labs, 1950-70; Sci Advr to Pres of US, The White House, 1970-73; Exec VPres, Gould Inc, Rolling Meadows, IL, 1973-77; Pres, Exxon Res U Engrg Col, Annandale, NJ, 1977-; Mem: White House Sch Coun; US Rep to NATO Sci Com; Nat Acad of Scis; Nat Acad of Scis; NJ Gov's Comm on Sci & Technol; NY Mayor's Comm on Sci & Technol; Exec Com, MIT; Bd of Overseers, Univ of PA; hon/Author of Over 200 Pub'd Papers; Over 600 Spchs; Num Hon Degs incl'g: Stevens Inst of Technol; Polytech Inst of Bklyn; Univ of MI; Carnegie-Mellon Univ; Lehigh Univ; Univ of IL & Chgo Circle; Rose-Hulman Inst of Technol; Univ of FL; Rensselaer Polytech Inst; Rutgers Univ; Recip, NC Awd; Recip, NJ Sci/Technol Medal; Recip, Industl Res Inst Medal.

DAVID, JAMES LEONARD oc/ Executive; b/Jul 13, 1940; h/PO Box 130, Church Point, LA 70525; ba/Church Point, LA; m/Elizabeth Hope F; c/Elisa, William, Jules, Jaimie; p/Kermit and

Aline David, Church Point, LA; sp/M Elizabeth Fleck, Altoona, PA; ed/BS, Univ of SWn LA, 1957; mil/AUS, 1962-65; pa/Cnslr, Evangeline Area Coun Champ Thiswaite, 1960; Ranger, Philmont Scout Ranch, 1960; Lay Missionary, San Jose Mission, 1960; Oiler, Brown & Root, 1961-62; Dispatcher, Dowell, 1966-67; Shift Supvn, Gates Rubber Co, 1967-68; Mgr 1968-75, Pres & Owner 1975-, David's of Ch Point Inc; Menswear Retailers of Am; Am Fashion Assn; Merch Brokers Exch; Intl Investmt & Bus Exch; Ch Point Indust Inducement Com, Chm 1974-75; cp/Mem 1951-70, Scoutmaster 1956-59, Explorer Advr 1969-70, BSA; CAP, 1958-61; Arnold Air Soc, Cmdr 1961-62; AF Assn; Am Legion; Acadia Hlth Planning Coun; Ch Point JCs; Alpha Phi Omega; Fam Life Aposilate, 1974-; Lai Amis De La Famille, 1975-; Acadia Parish Adv Coun for Voc Prog, 1977-; Parish Coun, Pres, Our Lady of The Sacred Heart Ch, 1978-79; Ch Point Cent Com, 1974-75; Bicent Com, 1975-76; Lafayette Computer Clb, 1978-; Nat Fdn of Indep Bus, 1975-; LA Retailers Assn; Lyons Clb, 1980-81; Newman Clb, 1958-61; LA Farm Bur, 1960-; Pre Cana, Dir, Advr, Coun, 1974-; r/Cath; hon/Public Spkr; Eagle Scout, 1960; AF ROTC, Chgo Tribute Awd, 1961; JC of Yr, 1974; W/W in S & SW.

DAVIDSON, CLIFF IAN oc/Professor; b/May 9, 1950; h/5256 Beeler Street, Pittsburgh, PA 15217; ba/ Pittsburgh, PA; m/Megan Graae; c/Ian Emet; p/Sol M and Penny Davidson, Des Moines, IA; sp/Eva Graae, Portland, OR; ed/BS, Carnegie-Mellon Univ, 1972; MS 1973, PhD 1977, CA Inst of Technol; pa/Asst Prof 1977-82, Assoc Prof 1982-, Civil Engrg & Engrg Public Policy, Carnegie-Mellon Univ; Mem: ASCE; Air Pollution Control Assn; Soc of Envir Geochem & Hlth; Soc of Automotive Engrs; Sigma Xi; Tau Beta Pi; Eta Kappa Nu; r/Jewish; hon/Author, Over 30 Articles In Profl Jours & Books; Co-Editor, *Metals in the Air,* 1984; Lincoln T Wk Awd, Fine Particle Soc, 1976; George Tallman Ladd Awd, Carnegie-Mellon Univ, 1980; Outstg Edr Awd, Soc of Automotive Engrs, 1982; W/W in E; Am Men & Wom of Sci.

DAVIES, GEOFFREY oc/Professor of Chemistry; b/Feb 6, 1942; h/17 Farmcrest Avenue, Lexington, MA 02173; ba/ Boston, MA; m/Elizabeth Florence; c/ Warwick Harvey, Russell Howard, Claire Elizabeth; p/Frank and Alice Davies, Derby, UK; sp/Donald and Evelyn Gardner, Coventry, UK; ed/BSc 1963, PhD 1966, B'ham Univ; pa/ Postdoct Fellow, Brandeis Univ, 1966-68; Res Assoc, Brookhaven Nat Lab, 1968-69; Imperial Chem Indust Fellow, Univ of Kent, 1964-71; Asst Prof 1971-77, Assoc Prof 1977-81, Prof 1981-, NEn Univ; Ancient Soc of Col Yths, 1965-; Am Chem Soc, 1967-; Simon W Robinson Lodge AF & AM, 1980-; N Am Guild of Change Ringers, 1971-; r/Epis; hon/Profl Pubs; Excell in Tchg Awd, NEn Univ, 1981; Mgr, Bell Restoration Proj, Old N Ch, 1981-83; W/W in E; Am Men & Wom of Sci.

DAVIES, IVOR KEVIN oc/Psychologist, Professor, Author; b/Dec 19, 1930; h/2447 Rock Creek Drive, Bloomington, IN 47401; ba/Bloomington, IN; m/Shirley Diana Winyard; c/Simon Winyard, Michelle Winyard; p/S H M Davies, Stourbridge, England; sp/L M Winyard, London, England; ed/BA, 1952; MA, 1953; MS, 1954; Dip Ed, 1955; PLD, 1967; mil/Royal AF, Wing Cmdr, Lt Col; pa/Sr Res Ofcr, Brit Min of Def, RAF, 1955-67; Sr Lectr & Chm Dept of Behavioral Sci, RAF Col, Cranwell, UK, 1967-72; Prof, Sch of Ed, Univ of IN, Bloomington, IN, 1972-; Mem: AECT; AERA; ASTD; BPSS; APA; NSPI; r/Cath; hon/Author of 4 Books: *The Mgmt of Lrng*, 1971; *The Org of Tng*, 1973; *Objectives in Curric Design*, 1976; Instrnl Technique, 1981; Over 100 Articles & Monographs; Over 50 Book Chapt Contbns; Fellow: Col of Preceptors, 1980; Brit Psychol Soc, 1983; W/W; Contemp Authors.

DAVIES, JACK NEVILLE PHILLIPS oc/Pathologist, Forensic Medicine Consultant; b/Jul 2, 1915; h/Selkirk, NY; ba/Albany, NY; m/Valerie Elizabeth; c/Antony, Rupert Davis, Nigel Davis; p/David Osborn Davies and Mabel Mapham (dec); sp/Harold Martin and Madeline King (dec); ed/MBChB w distn, Bristol, 1939; MD w distn, Bristol 1948; DSc (Hons), Univ of E Africa, 1968; mil/Emer Med Ser, 1939-44; pa/Fdr Fellow, Royal Col of Pathol, 1963; Brit Royal Infirm, Bristol, 1939-41; Lectr of Physiol & Pharm, Univ of Bristol, 1941-44; Colonial Med Ser, Uganda, 1944-50; Commonwlth Fund Fellow, Duite Univ, 1949-50; Prof of Pathol, Makerere Univ, 1950-61; Rdr in Pathol, London Univ Royal Postgrad Med Sch, 1961-63; Prof of Pathol, Albany Med Col, 1963-; Brit Med Assn, Pres-Uganda Br, 1953; V African Res Com, 1945-61; E African Med Res Coun, 1953-61; Advr, Cancer Res, Dir Genwaal Who, 1973-; r/Epis; hon/Num Profl Pubs; N Persian Forcue Meml Medal, Res in Tropical Med, 1947; Markham Siturrit Triennial Prize, Med Res, 1954; Maude Abbott Lectr, Intl Acad of Pathol, 1960; W/W in World Sci.

DAVIS, ANN E oc/Professor; b/Sep 17, 1932; h/788 West Sharon Road, Cincinnati, OH 45240; ba/Oxford, OH; c/William, Steven; p/Ilona Schwarcz, Cleveland, OH; ed/BA 1954, PhD 1971, OH St Univ, MSSW, Univ of L'ville, 1960; pa/Prof, Miami Univ, Oxford, OH, 1969-; Cnslr, Psychi W Covina Mtl Hlth Ctr, 1964-66; Social Wkr, KY Dept of Mtl Hygiene, 1958-63; Ins Sales, Wash Nat Ins, 1954-56; Mem: Secy, N Ctl Sociol Assn, 1977-80; Secy/Treas 1976-77, Chm Nom Com 1980-83, Assn for Humanist Sociol; Editor, *Ctl Focus*, Newslttr of N Ctl Sociol Assn, 1977-80; hon/Author of *Schizophrenics in the New Custodial Commun*, 1977; 3 Book Chapts & Over 20 Articles Pub'd in Profl Jours; W/W: of Am Wom; Men & Wom of Sci; Num Other Biogl Listings.

DAVIS, ARTHUR W oc/Certified Executive Chef; b/Jul 21, 1914; h/9039 Amberly Circle, San Diego, CA 92126; ba/San Diego, CA; m/Rose; c/Jean D Kagan; p/Sophia and Menno Davis (dec); sp/Juana Martinez, Ashland, OR; ed/AA, Univ of WA, 1932; Dipls: LaSalle Univ, 134; DeVry Tech Inst, 148; R Inst Am, 1950; Nat Baking Sch, 1962; Tchr Cred, UCLA, 1980; mil/USN; pa/Various Internships in WA, ID, OR, CA, 1934-38; Exec Chef, Tiny's Rest,

1939-45; Exec Chef, Angelus Clb, 1946; Chef/Owner, Fox Gold Room, 1947-48; Exec Chef, Exposition Rest, 1949-71; Exec Chef, Fred Harvey Corp, 1972-73; Exec Chief, Royal Inn of San Diego, 1974; Exec Chef, Chatea La Jolla & Culinary Instr, Mesa Col, 1974-; Past Pres, Chefs Assn of Pacific Coast; Past Dir, Cooks Assn of Pacific Coast; Past Dir, Chefs Assn of San Diego; Cooks Union #44, SF, 1943-75; Hon Order of Golden Toque; Am Acad of Chefs; Am Culinary Fdn; Nat Rest Assn; cp/Elks Lodge, San Mateo & San Diego; hon/Profl Pubs; Chef of Yr, Chefs Assn of Pacific Coast, 1969; Chef of Yr, San Diego Chef Assn, 1978; Master Chef de Cuisine, Intl Crab Olympics, 1969; Antonin Careme Medal #20; Dipl of Hon, Golden Toque, 1973; Certs of Hon, Feria De Pescado, 1978-82; Num Culinary Awds in Seattle, SF, LA, Anaheim, Santa Clara, San Diego.

DAVIS, BRIAN KENT oc/Geneticist; b/Dec 2, 1939; h/90 Everdale Road, Randolph, NJ 07869; ba/Morristown, NJ; m/Janet Anne; c/Catherine Marie, Casandra Nicole; p/Preston Davis (dec); Myrtle Davis, Wheatland, WY; sp/Frank Pettingill, Beloit, WI; Mary Pettingill (dec); ed/BA 1962, MA 1963, Univ of WI; PhD, Univ of WA, 1970; pa/Res Fellow, Univ of CA-San Diego, 1970-72; Asst Prof, VA Polytech Inst & St Univ, 1973-80; Asst Prof, Col of Med, King Faisal Univ, Saudi Arabia, 1980-81; Sr Res Geneticist, Allied Corp, 1981-; Mem: Saudi Biol Soc; Envir Mutagen Soc; Genetics Soc of Am; Am Genetic Assn; hon/Author of Num Sci Articles Pub'd in Jours; W/W in Frontier Sci & Technol; Am Men & Wom in Sci.

DAVIS, BRUCE GORDON oc/Retired School Administrator; b/Sep 2, 1922; h/6614 Sharpview, Houston, TX 77074; m/Mary Virginia J; c/Ford Rouquette, Barton Bolling, Katherine Norvell D McLendon; p/Arthur Lee (dec) and Clara Katherine R Davis, Fulton, TX; sp/Stephen F and Irene B Jackson (dec); ed/BA, Univ of TX, 1950; MEd, Univ of Houston, 1965; mil/USMC, 1942-45; AUS, 1951-57, Capt; ed/Tchr, Edison Jr HS, 1950-51; Tchr, Sidney Lanier Jr HS, 1957-60; Tchr, Sidney Johnston Jr HS, 1960-66; Asst Prin 1966-74, Prin 1974-82, Sidney Lanier Jr HS; Ret'd, 1982-; Nat Assn of Sec'dy Sch Prin; TX Assn of Sec'dy Sch Prin; Houston Profl Admrs; Houston Cong of Tchrs; cp/Repub; A F&AM, Rockport Masonic Lodge 323; A&A Scottish Rite (32 Degree), Houston, TX, Consistory; Am Legion Post #52; r/Presb; hon/Pres Unit Cit, Iwo Jima Campaign; Mil Awds; Korean Campaigns; Korean Service Medal w 2 Bronze Service Stars; UN Service Medal; Nat Def Service Medal; ROK Pres Unit Cit; Korean Service Medal w 2 Bronze Service Stars; W/W in S & SW.

DAVIS, CHARLOTTE HEARNE oc/Assistant Dean of Students; b/Feb 26, 1939; h/1150 Granite Drive, Laramie, WY 82070; ba/Laramie, WY; m/Maron D; c/Wendy Marie; p/Frank J (dec) and Annie T Hearne, Laramie, WY; sp/Bonnie Winskowski, West Sacramento, CA; ed/BS w hons 1960, MEd 1964, Univ of WY; Att'd CA St Col; pa/Tchr 1960-65, Cnslr & Dir of Student Activs 1965-66, Glendora HS; Asst Dean of Wom 1966-69, Asst Dean of Students

1969-, Univ of WY; CO-WY Assn of Wom Admrs & Cnslrs-Ofcr; NAW-DAC; WY Pers & Guidance Assn; Phi Kappa Phi-Ofcr; Beta Gamma Sigma; Fac Wom Clb; Fin Advr, Delta Delta Delta; Advr, Mortor Bd; Student Govt Advr; Fin Com, Assn for Retarded Chd, 1975-78; Bd of Dirs, Devel Ctr for Presch Chd, 1974-77; Gov Comm on Devel Disabilities, 1977-79; cp/Newman Ctr Eucharistic Min, 1980; r/Cath; hon/W/W: Among Students in Am Univs & Cols, of Am Wom; Outstg Yg Wom of Am; Outstg Personalities of W & MW; 2000 Wom of Achmt; World W/W of Wom.

DAVIS, DANIEL RICHARD oc/Commissioner of Revenue; b/Jun 9, 1946; h/Sprucewood Route 1, Box 281, Staunton, VA 24401; ba/Staunton, VA; p/Joseph C and Roxana F Davis (dec); ed/Dunsmore Col, 1968; mil/AUS, 1966-68; pa/Acct, Smith's Transfer Corp, 1968-72; Asst Comm of Revenue, Augusta Co, 1972-82; Comm of Revenue, 1982-; VA Assn of Assessing Ofcrs; Nat Assn of Assessing Ofcrs; Local Exec Constitl Ofcrs; W Cential Comm of Revenue Assn; cp/Augusta & Rockbridge Co, VA Hist Soc; Montgomery Co, PA Hist Soc; SAR; Order Stars & Bars; Sons of Confederate Vets; Mayflower Soc; r/Meth; hon/Author, *From Pennsylvania to Rockbridge Co, VA, Songs & Poems.*

DAVIS, ELAINE CARSLEY oc/Professor and Director; b/Apr 15, 1921; h/3800 Menlo Drive, Baltimore, MD 21215; ba/Baltimore, MD; m/Robert Clarke Davis (dec); c/Lisa Corine, Robert Clarke; p/Stanley and Corinne Carsley (dec); sp/Avon and Edith Davis (dec); ed/BS, Coppin St Col, 1942; BS, Morgan St Col, 1943; LLB, Univ of MD, 1950; MEd 1955, PhD 1958, The Johns Hopkins Univ; pa/Tchr, Asst Prin, Curric Supvr & Dir, Ednl Asst to Supt, Balto City Public Schs, 1942-74; Assoc Prof, Assoc Dir, Dir, Div of Ed, The Johns Hopkins, 1974-; Mem: VChm, Chm 1967-73, Bd of Trustees of MD St Cols; Bd of Trustees, Morgan St Col, 1965-67; Bd of Trustees, Goucher Col, 1972-75; VChm 1959-79, MD Coun on Ed; Life Mem, NEA; NOLPE; NCPEA; NASSP; ASCD; AERA; r/Epis; hon/Author of Var Articles Pub'd in Profl Jours incl'g: *Ednl Horizons*; *Instr*; Phi Beta Kappa, 1958; Recip: AAUW, John Hay Whitney, George Peabody F'ships, 1956-67; Dist'd Alumni Awd, Coppin St Col, 1965; Dist'd Alumni of Yr, 1982; Outstg Edrs in Am; DIB; Commun Ldrs & Noteworthy Ams; Personalities of S; W/W Among Black Ams; Num Other W/W.

DAVIS, ELAINE R oc/President and Chief Executive Officer, Home Health Agency; b/Feb 3, 1948; h/Route 3, Loganville, GA 30249; ba/Decatur, GA; c/Kelline, Robert, Tamara; p/James and Doris Rollins; ed/DeKalb Commun Col, 1972-74; pa/Admr, S DeKalb Ctr, 1972-77; Orgl Sys Anal, Hirschfield & Assoc, 1977-79; Pres & CEO, Am Home Hlth Care of GA Inc, 1979-; Fin Chm, Former Chm of Govtl Affairs, GA Assn of Home Hlth Agy, 1980-; Pres, S DeKalb Coalition, 1973-76; Chm, Ct Appt'd Bi Racial Sch Com, 1977-80; hon/Profl Pubs; Quill & Scroll Awd for Creat Writing; Am Press Assn; W/W in Am Polits.

DAVIS, ELEANOR SUTHERLAND oc/Receptionist; b/Sep 11, 1935; h/616 Mountain Avenue, Bedford, VA 24523; ba/Bedford, VA; m/Darrol E; c/Darrol E Jr; sp/Anna D McAllister, Cottage Grove, OR; ed/Att'd Bus Col of Roanoke, VA; pa/Bkkpr, Commonwlth of VA Div of Purchasing & Printing; Receptionist, Elks Nat Home, 1965-; cp/ Bedford Presb Ch; r/Presb; hon/Subject of Newspaper Article.

DAVIS, ELIZABETH JONES oc/ Community Activist; b/Jun 30, 1939; h/ 10233 South Racine, Chicago, IL 60643; ba/Calumet Park, IL; m/Louis; c/Barbara, Dorissa, Stephanie, Dana; p/ George L (dec) and Ruby Jones, B'ham, AL; sp/John and Ella Davis (dec); ed/ LPN, Nat Inst of Nsg, 1968; AA, Central Col, 1977; BA, Roosevelt Univ, 1981; pa/Nurses Asst, Peace Meml Evergreen Pk, 1969-70; Nurses Asst, Christ Commun Hosp, 1970-71; Dept Area Supvr, Flavor Kist Co, 1972-73; Social Ser Wkr, Dept of Chgo Woodlawn Commun Mtl Hlth, 1975-77; Social Ser Wkr, Wom Ser YWCA, 1979-80; Vol Parole Ofcr, Safer Foun, 1979-83; cp/GS Ldr, 1970-74; Vol Tutor, Mt Vernon Elem Sch, 1971-72; Parent Adv Bd Mem, 10 W 32nd St IL Inst of Tech Inroads Pre-Engrg Prog, 1977-81; Congl Dist Ed Task Force, 1981-82; r/U Meth; hon/Author; Outstg Tutoring S'ship to Olive Harvey Col, Chgo Public Sch, 1972.

DAVIS, ELMO W oc/Agricultural Scientist; b/Sep 9, 1920; h/10713 Lancewood Road, Cockeysville, MD 21030; ba/Hunt Valley, MD; m/Jean Ellen; c/ Elmo W Jr, Thomas G, Glen R, Jeanete E; p/Robert and Cora (Herring) Davis (dec); sp/Grant and Dorothy (Goddard) Davis (dec); ed/BS, Univ of ID-Moscow, 1948; MS, Univ of CA-Berkeley, 1949; PhD, Univ of CA-Davis, 1952; Continuous Addit Study, 1960-; pa/Assoc Olerocultuist & Assoc Prof, KS St Univ, 1952-53; Geneticist, USDA, Parma, ID, 1953-57; Horticulturist (Ldr in Onions & Carrot Invest), USDA, Beltsville, MD, 1957-65; Plant Explorer, USDA, Wn Europe, 1959; Dir of Agri Res & Devel, Gilroy Foods, 1966-76; Corp Agri Sci 1976-80, Dir Agri Sci & Technol 1980-82, Agri Sci 1982-, McCormick & Co; Mem: VPres Indust Div 1980-81, Mem 1952-, Am Soc for Horticultural Sci; Intl Horticultural Soc, 1952-; Am Seed Trade Assn; Sigma Xi; r/Presb; hon/Author, Over 15 Res Articles Pub'd in Profl Jours, 1953-; Union Pacific RR S'ship, 1939; Aggeler Musser F'ship, 1948-52; Gold Awd 1969, Sapphire Awd 1974, C P McCormick Co; Fellow, Am Soc for Horticultural Sci, 1979; KY Col, 1979; W/W: in W, in Am; Am Men & Wom of Sci; DIB; Other Biogl Listings.

DAVIS, EVELYN MARGUERITE BAILEY oc/Organist, Music Teacher; h/ RFD #2, Box 405, Rogersville, MO 65742; ba/Springfield, MO; m/James Harvey; p/Philip Edward Bailey and Della Jane Morris; ed/Att'd Drury Col; pa/Soloist, KWTO; Secy, Shea & Morris Co, 1946; Tchr, Third Baptist Ch, 1946-1954; Former Dir of Yth Choir; Composer; Soloist & Asst Organist/ Pianist, Bible Ch, 1969-70; Pianist, Soloist & Bible Tchr, Temple Bapt Ch, 1970-71; Organist, Pianist, Bible Tchr, Vocal Soloist, Dir & Music Arranger, Ch & Yth Orch of St Charles, MO,

1971-84; Pvt Instr, Piano & Organ, 1960-; Organist, Bellview Bapt Ch, 1984-; Nat Guild of Piano Tchrs; Nat Guild of Organists; ABIRA; IPA; Life Fellow, IBA; r/Bapt; hon/Num Compositions; Num Concerts.

DAVIS, HENRY JR oc/Professor; b/ Nov 29, 1922; h/804 Daphne Court, PO Box 717, Daphne, AL 36526; ba/Mobile, AL; p/Henry and Edna Claire Foval Davis (dec); ed/BM, Boston Univ, 1952; MA, LA St Univ, 1965; mil/AUS, WW II, 1943-45; pa/Foreman, Chem Control Lab, Aralac Inc, 1945-47; Dir Rel Ed, Christ Epis Ch, Mobile, AL, 1956-59; Eng Instr 1959-64, Asst Prof 1964-68, Assoc Prof 1969-, Dir Freshman Eng 1966-70, Spring Hill Col, Mobile, AL; Mem: Intl Info/Word Processing Assn; Am Bus Communs Assn; Soc for Tech Commun; Am Soc for Engrg Ed; cp/Bd of Dirs, Mobile Civic Music Assn, 1957-62; Hist Presv Soc, 1966-; r/Epis; hon/Author, 35 Articles on So Lit & So Wom Writers in Var Profl Jours; Others; Croix de Guerre w Palm, 1944; Title III Grantee, 1981 & 1982; W/W in S & SW.

DAVIS, JOHN MIHRAN oc/General Surgeon, Professor; b/Aug 13, 1946; h/ 430 East 63rd Street, New York, NY, 10021; ba/New York, NY; m/Marlene; c/Nicholas; p/Dwight D Davis, Yonkers, NY; Ruth K Davis, Ctl Pk W, NY; ed/ BA, Columbia Col, NY, 1968; MD, Wayne St Univ Sch of Med, 1972; pa/ Intern & Residency, THe NY Hosp 1972-77, Asst Prof Surg 1977-84, Assoc Prof 1984-, Cornell Univ Med Ctr; Mem: The NY Surg Soc; The Med Strollers; The Am Burn Assn; The Assn of Acad Surgs; Fellow, The Am Col of Surgs; Charter Mem, Surg Infection Soc; The Am Fdn of Clin Res Surgs; The NY St Med Soc; The Assn of Surg Edrs; Chirurgio; NY Cancer Soc; Am Soc of Enteral & Parenteral Nutrition; Other Orgs; r/Prot; hon/Author, Var Articles in Profl Jours incl'g: Surg Forum; Circulatory Shock; Annals of Internal Med; Archives of Surg; Andrew W Mellon Tchr Sci Awd, 1983-84, 1984-85; Prin Investigator, Var NIH Grants.

DAVIS, LLOYD EDWARD oc/Professor of Clinical Pharmacology; b/Aug 23, 1929; h/621 West Hill Street, Champaign, IL 61820; ba/Urbana, IL; m/ Carol; c/Mark, Kimberly; p/Robert Q Davis, MD (dec); sp/Jan Neff, Chillocothe, OH; ed/Att'd Univ of Akron, 1947-50; Att'd George Wash Univ, 1953-55; DVM, OH St Univ, 1959; PhD, Univ of MO, 1963; mil/USN, 1950-53; pa/Assoc Prof, Univ of MO, 1959-69; Prof, OH St Univ, 1969-72; Vis'g Prof, Univ of Nairobi, 1972-74; Prof, CO St Univ, 1974-78; Prof, Univ of IL, 1978-; 1st Pres, Am Col of Vet Pharm & Therapeutics, 1976-79; Pres, Phi Zeta, 1982-84; Bd of Revision, USP, 1980-; Spec Conslt, FDA; Num Coms, Am Soc Pharm Exp Therapeutics; Am Soc Clin Pharm & Therapeutics; Others; r/Prot; hon/Profl Pubs; Dist'd Tchg Awd, Univ of MO, 1968; Ph Zeta, 1965; Sigma Xi, 1964; Ser Awd, AAVPT, 1984; W/W; Intl Scholar's Dir; DIB.

DAVIS, LOWELL LIVINGSTON oc/ Thoracic and Cardiovascular Surgeon; b/Dec 14, 1922; h/4267 Marina City Drive, WTS #310, Marina Del Rey, CA; ba/Los Angeles, CA; p/Rev and Mrs Jordan Davis (dec); ed/BS, Morehouse

Col, 1949; MS, Atlanta Univ, 1950; MD, Howard Univ, 1955; mil/USNR (MC), 1972, Captain; pa/Pvt Pract, Thoracic & Cardiovas Surg; FACS; FCCP; FACC; hon/Profl Pubs; W/W in W.

DAVIS, MICHAEL JAY oc/University Research Scientist; b/Mar 3, 1947; h/10121 Northwest 21st Court, Pembroke Pines, FL 33026; ba/Ft Lauderdale, FL; m/Carol Ann; c/Christpher Michael; p/Jay E and Joan R Davis, Aurora, CO; sp/George W and Ann D Freeman, Menlo Pk, CA; ed/BS 1973, MS 1975, CO St Univ; PhD, Univ of CA-Berkeley, 1978; pa/Res Assoc, CO St Univ, 1973-75; Asst Prof Plant Pathol, Rutgers Univ, 1979-81; Asst Prof Plant Pathol, Ft Lauderdale Res & Ed Ctr, Univ of FL, 1981-; Mem: Chm 1984, Mem 1980-84, Bacteriology Com of The Am Phytopathol Soc; Sigma Xi; Am Soc for Microbiol; Am Fdn of Culture Collections; Gamma Sigma Delta; Am Soc for Sugar Cane Technols; hon/Author, Num Articles Pub'd in Var Jours incl'g: Sci; Phytopathol; Plant Disease; Current Microbiol; Jour of Am Soc for Horticultural Sci; Intl Jour of Systematic Bacteriology; W/W: in Am, in Frontier Sci & Technol.

DAVIS, MICHELE STAR oc/Assistant Program Director; b/Dec 31, 1946; h/29 West Tulane Road, Apartment C, Columbus, OH 43202; ba/Columbus, OH; m/Richard D Watman; p/Robert and April Davis, Spencerville, IN; ed/ BA summa cum laude, St Francis Col, 1970; MA 1972, PhD 1979, Purdue Univ; pa/Grad Instr, Purdue Univ, 1970-77; Instr, OH St Univ, 1979-83; Asst Dir of Hispanic Student Progs, OH St Univ, 1983; Fdr & Dir, Teatro Unidad a Spanish-Spkg Theatre Grp, 1980-; Am Assn of Tchrs of Spanish & Portuguese; OH Theatre Affil; OH Commun Theatre Assn; Am Coun of Tchrs of Fgn Lang; MLA; OH Mod Lang Assn; r/ Cosmic; hon/Author Num Pubs; Hermandad Latina & Mecha Awd for Outstg Ser to Hispanic Students, OH St Univ, 1981; W/W of Am Wom; Outstg Yg Wom of Am.

DAVIS, NANCY ELLEN oc/Benefit Analyst; Volunteer Historian; b/Jun 3, 1935; h/235 East Walnut Street, Westerville, OH 43081; ba/Westerville, OH; c/Susan Elaine, Kathi Lynn, Jennifer Ann, Kevin Lee; p/Clarence and Lottie Nidon; ed/Pvt Secy Dipl, Columbus Bus Univ, 1957; Spec Tng, Mus Activ Presentations, Edison Inst, 1979; pa/Pvt Secy to Supvr of Distributive Ed, St of OH, 1956-57; Pvt Secy to Dir, Nsg Sers & Patient Care, 1958-59; Employee Benefit Spec, Aetna Life & Casualty, 1972-73; Borden Inc, 1973-78; Curator, Hanby House, 1979-; Benefit Anal, J W Didion & Assoc; OH Hist Soc; Westerville Hist Soc; Hanby House Clb; Worthington Hist Soc; Nat Trust for Hist Presv; cp/Fres, Child Conserv Leag; Pres of Dorcas Circle, Grace Luth Ch Wom; Sch Levy Com, Stewardship Com for Fin Proj; r/Luth; hon/Num Hist Presentations; Author Hist Articles; World W/W of Wom; Intl Register of Profiles.

DAVIS, PRESTON AUGUSTUS oc/ Director of Small Business Affairs; ba/ Office of Small & Disadvantaged Business Utilization, Administration Building, 14th and Independence Avenue, Southwest, Washington, DC 20250;

fam/Married, 4 Chd; pa/Dir of Small Bus Affairs, US Dept of Agr; Adj Prof, USDA Grad Sch & No VA Commun Col; Phi Delta Kappa; Bd of Dirs, Agri Fed Credit Union; Am Soc for Public Adm; cp/Past Lt Gov, Kiwanis Intl (1st Black in S); Masonic Lodge; Omega Psi Phi; Jr Citizens Corp Supt, Wash DC; hon/Outstg Achmt Awd, Salvation Army; Metro DC Police Boys & Girls Clb Outstg Annual Support Cit; USDA Cert of Merit, 1979; Hall of Fame, WVSC, 1983; W/W: Among Black Ams, in Black Corp Am.

DAVIS, SIDNEY DEWITT JR oc/President of People's Bank; b/Mar 17, 1945; h/417b Simpson Circle, Mendenhall, MS 39114; ba/Mendenhall, MS; m/JoJo; c/Dee, Brad; p/Mr and Mrs Sidney D Davis, Mendenhall, MS; sp/Mr and Mrs O B Munson, Mendenhall, MS; ed/BBA, Univ of MS, 1967; MA, Univ of AL, 1975; Grad, Sch of Bkg of S, LSU, 1972; Grad, Num Bkg Schs; CPA, 1978; pa/Asst Nat Bk Examr in Jackson, MS 1967-69, Adm Asst in Memphis, TN Reg Ofc 1969-71, Nat Bk Examr & Intl Bk Examr in Montgomery, AL 1971-74, US Treas Dept Ofc of Comptroller of Currency; VP 1975, Pres 1980-, People's Bk; Exec Coun Mem, MS Yg Bkrs Assn, 1977-78; Dir, MS Ec Coun, 1981-84; VChm of MS 1st, 1982-83; cp/Pres, Ldrship MS Alumni Assn, 1981-82; Secy-Treas, MS for Quality Ed, 1982; 1st VP, Simpson Co Ec Devel Foun, 1982-83; Treas & Dir, Mendenhall C of C, 1982-83; Past Pres, Simpson Co Country Clb; Mendenhall Tiger Booster Clb; Past VChm, Simpson C Repub Party; Mem of Planning Com, Gov Corp Vol Action Com, 1982; r/Meth; hon/Author; Outstg Yg Men of Am; W/W: in Fin & Indust, in S & SW, in World, Among Am Law Students; Personalities of S.

DAVIS, WELDON A oc/Safety Director and Personnel Manager; b/Nov 19, 1949; h/802 Lincoln Drive, Longview, TX 75604; ba/Longview, TX; m/Sue Milford; c/Pam; p/Ralph E and Dallas Davis, Spartansburg, PA; sp/Simmie and Thelma Milford, Timpson, TX; ed/BA, Le Tourneau Col, 1973; AAS, Kilgore Col, 1982; Att'g Univ of TX; pa/Num Med & Safety Courses Certs; Ath Tnr, Le Tourneau Col, 1967-73; Spec Ed, E TX Treatment Ctr, 1971-72; Massage Class, YMCA, 1973; Oilfield Wkr; Dowell Chem Co, 1973-74; E TX Fire Protection, 1974-75; First Aid, Jordan Ambulance Ser, 1975-76; Mechanic, Cert'd Auto Sales, 1976-77; EMT & Emer Wk, Gladewater Hosp, 1977; Safety Dir, 1st Aid & Indust Relats, SW Steel Casting Co, 1977-; Spkr, Safety Sems; Pres, B & T Safety Supplies & Sers Inc, 1982-; Am Soc of Safety Engrs; E TX Chapt of Am Soc of Safety Engrs; Treas, Mbrship Chm, Exec Com, E TX Chapt of ASSE; TX Chapt, Am Foundry Man's Soc; TX Safety Assn; Nat Safety Coun; Adv Com, Kilgore Col; r/Bapt; hon/Profl Pub; W/W: in Kilgore Col, in S & SW.

DAWES, ROBYN MASON oc/Professor & Department Head; b/Jul 26, 1936; h/2817 Spring Boulevard, Eugene, OR 97403; ba/Eugene, OR; c/Jennifer Hill, Molly McDermott; p/Norman H and Zita H Dawes (dec); ed/AB, Harvard Univ, 1958; MA 1960, PhD 1962, Univ of MI; pa/Res Assoc, Res Psychol, Ann

Arbor VA Hosp, 1962-67; Lectr, Asst Prof, Univ of MI, 1962-67; Res Assoc, VPres, OR Res Inst, 1968-75; Assoc Prof, Prof 1968-, Psych Dept Hd 1981-, Univ of OR; Mem: Pres, OR Psychol Assn, 1984-85; hon/Author, Var Articles Pub'd in Profl Jours; Fellow, Ctr for Adv'd Study in Behavioral Scis, 1980-81; James McKern Cattell Sabbatical Fellow, 1979-80; NSF-USSR Acad of Scists Sci Exch Del, 1979; W/W in W; Am Men & Wom of Sci.

DAWKINS, IMOGENE oc/Income Tax Consultant/Preparer; b/May 8, 1938; h/PO Box 304, 219 Peachtree Street, Edgefield, SC 29824; ba/Same; p/Rebecca S Dawkins, Edgefield, SC; ed/BS, SC St Col, 1960; Grad, Inst of Chd's Lit, 1980; pa/Adm Asst, Greenwood Sch Dist #50, 1960-70; Manpower Devel Spec, US Dept of Labor, 1970-74; Manpower Devel Spec, Ofc of Gov of SC, 1974-76; Magistrate of Edgefield Co, SC, 1980; Owner & Oper, Dawkins Income Tax & Acct'g Ser, 1978-; cp/Alpha Kappa Alpha Sorority; r/Bapt; hon/Author; W/W in Am Wom.

DAY, ARDEN DEXTER oc/Professor of Plant Sciences; b/Mar 16, 1922; h/2909 East Seneca Street, Tucson, AZ 85716; ba/Tucson, AZ; m/Judith C; c/Vickie L, Peggy A Smith, Nancy N; sp/Mr and Mrs Warren Myers; ed/BS, Cornell Univ, 1950; PhD, MI St Univ, 1954; pa/Asst Prof & Asst Agronomist 1954-56, Assoc Prof & Assoc Agronomist 1956-59, Prof & Agronomist 1959-; Assoc Hd of Plant Scis 1977-, Univ of AZ; Fellow, Am Soc of Agronomy, 1975; Crop Sci Soc of Am; Wn Soc of Crop Sci; AAUP; AZ-NV Acad of Sci; cp/Masonic Lodge; VT Green Mtn Clb; Alpha Gamma Rho; Alpha Zeta; r/Meth; hon/Profl Pubs; Cert'd Profl Agronomist, 1981; Cert'd Profl Crop Scis, 1981; Am Men of Sci; W/W: in W, in Am Ed.

DAY, RICHARD WRISLEY oc/Chief Arts Critic, Editor and Wine Columnist; b/Jan 25, 1936; h/338 Beechwood Avenue, Bridgeport, CT 06604 and Rokeby Farm, Barrytown, NY 12507; ba/Bridgeport, CT; m/Michele Carpenter; p/Herbert Britain and Katherine Wrisley (dec) Day, Barrytown, NY; sp/William and Mary Carpenter, Norwalk, CT; ed/BA, Bard Col, 1958; AB, Academia di Minerva, 1957; Att'd Hartwick Col; Opera Studies w John Nichols, 1948-54; Drama Studies w Stewart Bush & Henry Robinson , 1948-54; pa/Arts Critic, Woodstock Review, 1958; Arts Editor & Critic, Landers Newspapers, 1959; Music & Drama Critic, The Post & The Telegram, 1960-71; Wine Columnist 1979-, Arts Editor & Chief Critic 1982-, The Post & The Telegram; Bd of Dirs, CT Grand Opera; Gtr Bridgeport Symph Orch; Music Critic's Assn; Nat Assn of Theater Critics; Film & Dance Critics Assn; Am Archaeol Inst; Les Amis du Vin; Adv Bd, Downtown Cabaret Theater; Num Critiques & Articles, Prin Opera Houses & Music Fests in Wn World; Congl Aide/Trainee, Cong-man W R Williams, 1953-54; hon/won Huneker Awd for Arts Criticism, 1982; W/W; Dic of Am Theater Critics.

DAYAL, SAHAB oc/University Professor of Management; b/Oct 8, 1938; h/3100 South Concourse Drive, Mt Pleasant, MI 48858; ba/Mt Pleasant, MI; m/Ranjna; c/Sapna, Sandeep, Sareeka;

p/Badri (dec) and Girjak Dayal, India; sp/Bela R Mathur, India; ed/MA, Allahabad Univ, 1959; MS, London Sch of Ec, 1968; PhD, Cornell Univ, 1973; pa/Vis'g Lectr, Inst of Social Studies, The Hague, 1972-73; Asst Prof of Ec, SUNY, 1973-74; Sr Lectr in Indust Relats, Univ of New S Wales, Australia, 1974-78; Prof of Mgmt, Ctl MI Univ, 1978-; Univ Fac Senate, 1979-82; Univ Grad Coun, 1980-82; Univ Pers Policies Com, 1979--82; Mgmt Pers Com Chair, 1981-; Acad of Mgmt, 1979-; Indust Relats Res Assn, 1970-; Intl Indust Relats Assn, 1972-; hon/Author, Num Profl Pubs.

DAYAL, VEENA KUMARI oc/Research Director; b/Jan 10, 1949; h/20 Landing Lane, Princeton Junction, NJ 08550; ba/Newark, NJ; m/Bishambar; c/Rajeev, Geeta, Munish; p/Piara Ram & Shanti Duseja, New Delhi, India; ed/MD, GSVM Med Col, Kanpur, India, 1968; MS, Fairleigh Dickinson Univ; PhD, Univ of Med & Dentistry of NJ, 1978; pa/Dir, Thrombosis Res Lab, St Michael's Med Ctr, Newark, NJ, 1983-; Postdoct Fellow, Temple Univ Thrombosis Ctr, 1978-82; Res & Tchg Fellow, Univ of Med & Dentistry of NJ, 1974-78; Other Previous Employmt; Mem: NY Acad of Scis; Sigma Xi; AAAS; r/Hindu; hon/Author & Co-Author, Over 20 Res Articles & Abstracts in Profl Sci Jours; Sol Sherry Awd for Res, 1981; W/W in E.

DE ACEVEDO, OLGA MARIA MERIOLD ARGUESO oc/Spanish Supervisor; b/Jun 25, 1925; h/1858 Marginal, Santa Maria, Rio Piedras, PR 00927; ba/Santurce, PR; m/Ricardo Acevedo Defillo; c/Ricardo Luis Acevedo Argueso, Pablo Enrique Acevedo Argueso, Meriold del Pilar Acevedo de Valdes; p/Luis Argueso (dec); Nini Rotger de Argueso; sp/Francisco Acevelo & Pilar Defello (dec); ed/BA, 1946; MA 1972; pa/Basic Spanish Tchr, Univ of PR, 1949-51; Spanish Tchr, Public & Pvt Schs, 1959-71; Sch Prin at Labra, Central, Einstein, Barbosa, Baldoriots, Elzabura, Bueso, 1971-75; Spanish Supvr, Underprivileged Chd, 1975-78; Sch Prin, Bueso, 1978-82; Tchrs Assn of PR; Assn for Supvn & Curric Devel; Ateneo de PR; Edit Bd, Ed Mag El Sol; r/Cath; hon/Profl Pubs; Carolina Sch Dist, 1975; Dorado Sch Dist, 1976; ARC, 1967; COSMIF Teen Clb, 1968; W/W in S & SW.

DEAL, BORDEN oc/Author; b/Oct 12, 1922; h/1851 Datura Street, Sarasota, FL 33579; ba/Same; c/Ashley, Shane, Brett; p/Borden Lee and Jimmie Anne (Smith) Deal; ed/BA, Univ of AL, 1949; Grad Study, Mexico City Col, 1950; mil/USN, 1942-45; pa/Civilian Conserv Corps; US Dept of Labor, Wash DC; Pub'd Short Story, "Exodus," in Tomorrow Mag, 1948; During 1950-54: Correspondent, Assn Films, NY; Freelance Writer in Mexico; Skip Tracer, Auto Fin Co, B'ham, AL; Telephone Solicitor, Times-Picayune, NO, LA; Copywriter, WKRG & WABB, Mobile, AL; Full-time Author, 1954-; Mem: Authors Guild; Am PEN; TN Squire Assn; Sarasota Writers' Round Table; cp/Num Lectr & Spkg Presentations on Writing & C J Jung; hon/Author, Over 100 Short Stories in Pop & Lit Mags & Anthols; Novels incl: Walk Through the Val, 1956; Dunbar's Cove, 1957; Search for

Surrender, 1957; *Killer in the House*, 1957; *Secret of Sylvia*, 1958; *The Insolent Breed*, 1959; *Dragon's Wine*, 1950; *Devil's Whisper*, 1961; *The Spangled Road*, 1962; *The Advocate*, 1968; *The Loser*, 1964; *The Winner*, 1973; *The Tobacco Men*, 1965; *A Long Way To Go*, 1965; *The Least One*, 1967; *The Other Room*, 1974; *Interstate*, 1970; *Bluegrass*, 1976; *The Legend of the Bluegrass*, 1977; *Adventure*, 1978; *A Neo-Socratic Dialogue on the Reluctant Empire*, 1971; *Greenfield Co; The Platinum Man*; The Novel *Dunbar's Cove*, became the Film, "Wild River," w Montgomery Clift & Lee Remick; *The Insolent Breed*, became the Stage Musical "A Joyful Noise"; Hon Sesquincent Prof, Univ of AL, 1981; John Simon Guggenheim F'ship; MacDowell Colony F'ship; Hon Mention, Am Lib Assn Liberty & Justice Awds for 1st Novel, *Walk Through the Val*; AL Lib Assn Lit Awd; John H McGinnis Meml Awd; Worst Liar of Yr, Sarasota Writers' Roundtable Awd, 1971; Order of KY Cols; W/W of Authors; Men of Achmt; Contemp Authors; Personalities of S; DIB; Other Biogl Listings.

DEAL, PATRICIA EISENBISE oc/ Vocational Administrator; b/Mar 25, 1932; h/8401 Woodlawn Avenue Southwest, Tacoma, WA 98499; ba/ Tacoma, WA; m/Robert L; c/Robert Lee Jr, David Alan, James Edward; p/Jasper Paul (dec) and Mae Eisenbise, Shillington, PA; sp/Warren M Cox Jr, Evansville, IN; ed/BS, Albright Col, 1954; MA, Pacific Luth Univ, 1978; pa/Tchr Aide Instr/Coor 1970-79, Occupl Inf Spec 1979-81, Asst Dir of Elective HS 1982, Dir of Elective HS 1983, Clover Park Voc-Tech Inst; Life Mem, Am Voc Assn, 1980-83; Nat Coun of Local Voc Admrs, 1980-83; Life Mem, WA Voc Assn, 1980-83; Past Pres, Local Univ of WA, 1983; Exec Bd, WA Assn for Career Ed, 1982; Adm Wom in Ed, 1982-83; cp/Bd of Dirs, Singletree Est, 1981-82; r/ Christian; hon/U Way Commun Awd, 1980; W/W of Am Wom.

DEALY, JOHN FRANCIS oc/Professor, Lawyer, Investment Banker; b/May 4, 1939; h/11504 West Hill Drive, Rockville, MD 20852; ba/Washington, DC; m/Nana L; c/Anne L, Marian J; p/ Marie Dealy, Bklyn, NY; sp/William May and Asdee Lane, Hoadley, VA; ed/ BS, Fordham Col, NY, 1957-61; LLB, NY Univ Sch of Law, NY, 1964; mil/ USAF; pa/Assoc, Donovan, Leisure, Newton & Irvine, NY, 1964-; Atty-Advr to Secy of the AF, 1964-67; Gen Coun & Dir of Contracts 1967-68, VPres & Gen Coun 1968-72, VPres Law Devel & Acquisitions 1972-74, Exec VPres & Chief Financial Ofcr 1974-76, Pres & Chief Operating Ofcr, Mem Bd of Dirs & Exec Com 1982-, Fairchild Industs Inc; Chm, Am Satellite Corp, 1976-80; Chm, Space Communs Inc, 1981-82; Coun Mem, Shaw, Pittman, Potts & Trowbridge, 1982-; Dist'd Prof, Georgetown Univ Sch of Bus Adm 1982-; Sr Advr, Drexel Burnham Lambert, 1983-; Bus Exec Fellow, The Brookings Instn, 1982-; Mem: cp/Mem, Ec Adv Coun, Montgomery Co, MD, 1978-; Chm Gov's Ad-Hoc Com on High Technol, St of MD, 1981-83; Bd of Dirs, Nat Assn of Mfrs, 1980-82; High Technol Roundtable, 1983-; Nat Comm on a Free & Responsible Media, 1983-; r/Cath; hon/Author of "Policy Issues & Options for the 1980's," *The Brookings*

Review, 1982.

DE A'MORELLI, RICHARD C oc/ Author, Publisher, Computer Systems Analyst; b/Feb 1, 1952; ba/Spectrum 1 Network, Box 7464, Burbank, CA 91510; m/Rachel; c/David Alexander; p/ Claude C and Rowena (Hurlburt) Hale; sp/Mory and Helen Levin; ed/BA 1972, MLit 1974, Pacifica Col; pa/Pres 1982-, Editor-in-Chief 1981-, Spectrum 1 Netwk Inc; Edit Staff, *The Book of Predictions* by Irving Wallace; Mgn Editor, Globe News Ser, 1977-; Exec Editor, *The Hefley Report, 1978-79; Exec Editor, Probe The Unknown*, 1976-77; r/Non-Denom; hon/Author of *Numerology: The Key to Your Inner Self*, 1972; *Psychic Power: How to Read Your ESP*, 1972; *How to Survive the Future*, 1976; *Psychic Tests For Everyone*, 1976; Author of Var Computer Software; W/ W: in Am, in CA, of Contemp Achmt.

DEAN, KENNETH oc/Architectural Interior Designer, Educator; b/May 10, 1939; h/28807 Flowerpark Drive, Canyon Country, CA 91351; ba/Studio City, CA; m/Linda Elizabeth Benitez; p/ Mr and Mrs Wayne Smith, Panorama City, CA; sp/Mr and Mrs Benitez, Hollywood, CA; ed/Att'd LaSalle Univ, Los Angeles Col, Ottis/Parsons Sch of Design; mil/IL NG; AUS; USAR; pa/ Stage, Film & TV Actor, 1961-70; Interior Designer, 1971-; Edr, 1974-; Journalist, Var Design & City Mags, 1978-; Pres, San Fernando Chapt, Intl Soc of Interior Designers; Am Soc of Interior Designers, Constrn Specifications Inst; Cand, CA St Assem, 1984; r/Cath; hon/Design Room of Mth, 1978; Awd of Merit for Outstg Design, LA Co Fair, 1979; Best Actor Awds, 1960's; W/W in W.

DEAN, LLOYD oc/Counselor; Minister; b/Aug 17, 1930; h/Route 6, Box 498, Morehead, KY 40351; ba/Morehead, KY; m/Arvetta Plant; p/Bert T and Minty Creech Dean, Morehead, KY; ed/ BS 1958; MA 1959; mil/USAF 1953-57; pa/Cnslr, Rowan Co HS, 1970-79; Pastor, U Pentecostal Ch, Hays Crossing 'Cobblestone Ch in the Woods', 1963-; Past Pres: RCPGA, CCEA, EKPGA; Presby Sect N, UPC KY Dist; cp/Rowan Co HS; 4-H Ldr, Histn Clb Ldr; APEBP Ldr; Pres, Rowan Co Hist Soc, 1977-79; Repub; Notary Public; Pastor, Morehead U Pentecostal Ch, 1959-; Editor, KY Dist New, 1957-69; UPC SS Dir, KY 1957-69; UPC Secy & Treas, KY Dist 1969-73; Pres, KY Gourd Assn, 1983-84; Blackford Keychain Assn; Org, Dean & Creech Reunion, 1980; Org, Haldeman Reunion, 1980; Fdr & Pastor, Morehead U Pentecostal Ch, 1959-; hon/Hon Mem, FFA; 4-H Awds; Rowan Co Hist Soc Awd, 1983; Flag Day Observance, Morehead, KY, 1976; Others.

DEAN, RICHARD A oc/Executive; b/ Dec 22, 1935; h/6699 Via Estrada, La Jolla, CA 92-37; ba/San Diego, CA; m/ Sheila Grady; c/Carolyn, Julie, Drew; p/ Anthony and Ann Dean, Savannah, GA; sp/Hugh and Laura Grady, Savannah GA; ed/BME, GA Inst of Technol, 1957; MSME 1963, PhD 1970, Univ of Pgh; mil/AUS, 1957-59, 1st Lt; pa/Therma & Hydraulics Mgr, Westinghouse Corp, 1959-70; Tech Dir LWR Fuel Div 1970-71, Dir LWF Div 1974-76, Gen Atomic Co; VPres, Gulf U Nuclear Fuels, 1971-74; VPres, GA Technols Inc, 1976-; Mem: Past Chm Nuclear Fuels

Technol Subcom, ASME; Nat Planning Com, Am Nuclear Soc; AAAS; Reg'd Profl Engr, CA; r/Cath; hon/Author, Var Articles & Res Papers Pub'd in Profl Jours incl'g: *Am Nuclear Soc Transactions*; *Jour of ASME*; Others; W/W: in Technol Today, in Engrg, in Energy & Nuclear Sci, in Frontier Sci & Technol; Num Other Biogl Listings.

DEANIN, RUDOLPH DRESKIN oc/ Professor; b/Jun 7, 1921; h/Box 466, Westford, MA 01886; ba/Lowell, MA; m/Joan Marie Berkoff; c/Nancy, Alice; p/Zalman Samuel and Sonya Sophie Dreskin Deanin (dec); sp/Carl E and Helen C Berkoff, Norwichtown, CT; ed/ AB, Cornell Univ, 1941; MS 1942, PhD 1944, Univ of IL; pa/Sopec Res Asst, Govt Synthetic Rubber Prog, 1943-47; Gp Ldr, Allied Chem Corp, 1947-60; Dir Chem Res & Devel, DeBell & Richardson Inc, 1960-67; Prof Plastics, Univ of Lowell, 1967-; Mem: Am Chem Soc; Adhesion Soc; Soc of Plastics Engrg; N Eng Soc Coatings Technol; hon/Author of 7 Books & 160 Articles in Sci Pubs; Recip, 36 US Patents in Field; Cornell Tuition S'ship, 1937-41.

DEAVER, AGNES JEAN oc/Business Management; b/Aug 2, 1931; h/3950 Via Real Space #14, Carpinteria, CA 93013; ba/Ventura, CA; p/Russell and Christena Deaver, Mercersburg, PA; ed/Att'd Chambersburg Bus Col 1951, King's Col 1958, Univ of CA 1969; pa/ Secy to Gen Mgr, Cumberland Val Elect Co, 1951-61; Secy to Acting Pres & Public Relats Dir, King's Col, 1961-62; Adm Asst to Bus Mgr, Westmont Col, 1962-64; Adm Asst to Resident Vice Pres, Sentry Ins, 1964-70; Bus Mgmt, Chi Alpha Mgmt Inc, 1970-; Secy/Treas, Chi Alpha Mgmt Inc, W D Mgmt Inc, Am Family Sers Inc, U Fam Assoc Inc; Charter Mem, Santa Barbara Chapt of Nat Secretarial Assn; Cert'd to Teach Num Bus Subjects; r/Prot; hon/W/W of Am Wom; Personalities of W & MW.

DeBAKEY, LOIS oc/Writer, Lecturer, Editor, Communication Expert, Educator; ba/Baylor College of Medicine, 1200 Moursund Avenue, Houston, TX 77030; p/S M and Raheeja Z DeBakey (dec); ed/BA Math, Newcomb Col 1949, MA 1959, PhD Lit & Linguistics 1963, Tulane Univ; pa/Asst Prof Eng, Tulane Univ, 1963-65; Asst Prof Sci Commun 1963-65, Assoc Prof Sci Commun 1965-66, Prof Sci Commun 1966-68, Adj Prof & Lectr Sci Commun 1968-, Tulane Med Sch; Prof Sci Commun, Baylor Col of Med, 1968-; Mem: Bd of Regents 1982-, Biomed Lib Review Com, 1973-77, Nat Lib Med; Nat Adv Coun 1981-, USC Ctr for Cont'g Med Ed; The Usage Panel, *The Am Heritage Dic*, 1980-; Conslt, Legal Writing Com, ABA, 1983-; Com on Cols, Exec Coun 1975-80, So Assn of Cols & Schs; Dic Soc of N Am; Soc for Advmt of Good Eng; Dir, Plain Talk Inc, 1979-; Spec Com on Writing, Coun Basic Ed; Chm Com on Edit Policy 1971-75, Dir 1973-77, Coun of Biol Editors; Com on Tech & Sci Writing, Conf on Col Composition & Commun, NCTE; Awds, Pub, Style & Standards & Ed Coms, Am Med Writers Assn; Conslt, Nat Assn of Standard Med Vocab; AAAS; Assn of Tchrs of Tech Writing; Com of 1000 for Better Hlth Reg; Inst Soc, Ethics & Life Scis; Intl Soc for Gen Semantics; Nat Assn Sci

Writers; Alumni Assn, NIH; Soc for Hlth & Human Values; Soc for Tech Commun; Panel of Judges, Writing Awds for Am Acad of Fam Phys; Edit Bd Mem, Num Profl Jours incl: *Intl Jour of Cardiol*, 1981-; *Core Jours in Cardiol*, 1981-; *Cardiovas Res Ctr Bltn, 1971-*; *Hlth Commun & Biopsychosocial Hlth*, 1981-; Others; r/Epis; hon/Author of *The Sci Jour: Edit Policies & Practs*, 1976; Num Orig Articles on Sci Writing, Med Jour & Literacy; Num Public Spkg Presentations; John P McGovern Awd, Med Lib Assn, 1983; Golden Key, Nat Hon Soc, 1982; Dist'd Ser Awd, Am Med Writers Assn, 1970; Bausch & Lomb Sci Awd for Outstg Acad Per; Phi Beta Kappa; Am Registry Series; Book of Hon; Commun Ldrs & Noteworthy Ams; Personalities of S; DIB; Men of Achmt; Num W/W & Other Biogl Listings.

DeBAKEY, MICHAEL E oc/Cardiovascular Surgeon; b/Sep 7, 1908; h/5323 Cherokee Street, Houston, TX 77005; ba/Houston, TX; m/Katrin Fehlhaber; c/ Michael M, Ernest O, Barry E, Denis A, Olga Katerina; p/Shaker M and Raheeja Zorba DeBakey (dec); BS 1930, MD 1932, MD 1935, Tulane Univ; Certs: Am Bd Surg; Am Bd of Thoracic Surg; Nat Bd Med Examrs; pa/Acad Affils: Instr, Assoc & Asst Prof Surg, Tulane Univ; Pres, Dist'd Ser Prog, Prof & Chm Cora Webb Mading Dept Surg, Baylor Col Med; Clin Profl Surg Univ TX Dental Br 1971-72; Hosp Affils: Dir Nat Heart & Blood Vessel Res & Demo Ctr, Houston; Sr Att'd Surg, Meth Hosp Houston; Surg-in-Chief, Ben Taub Gen Hosp; Edit Bd, Nat & Intl Med Jours incl'g: Hon Chm, *Iranian Cardiovas Jour*; *New Technique for AV Ed for Surgs*; Bd of Govs, Am Acad of Achmt; Pres 1959, Am Assn Thoracic Surg; Fdg Mem, Am Heart Assn; Dir 1966, Assn for Advmt of Med Instrumentation; Bd of Dirs 1968, Bio-Med Engrg Soc; Adv Coun 1968-69, Houston Heart Assn; Pres 1964, Nat Assn on Standard Cryobiol; Pres 1954, Soc for Vascular Surg; Pres 1952, SWn Surg Cong; Com for Preven of Heart Disease, Cancer, Stroke, Am Heart Foun; Hon Sponsor, Draper World Pop Fund; Bd of Advrs, Intl Med Complex of Iran; Adv Bd, Nat Coun Drug Abuse; Ofc of Technol Assessment Hlth Adv Com; Hon Chm, Art Rooney Benefit Dinner; Hon Mem, Associacion Mexicana de Cirugia Cardiovas A C; Awds Chm 1973, Albert Lasker Clin Med Res Jury; Chm 1974, Citizens for Treatment of High Blood Pressure; Sci Adv Com, Intl Heart & Lung Inst; Nat Heart & Lung Adv Coun 1974, NIH; Hon Fellow, Royal Col Surgs, England; Hon Men, Acad of Med Scis, USSR; cp/Press Clb, Houston; Rotary Clb; hon/Hon DSc Hahnemann Med Col & Hosp, Phila, 1973; Baylor Alumni Dist'd Fac Awd, Soc Contemp Med & Surg, 1973; Baylor Alumni Dist'd Fac Awd: Lions Intl Spec Awd; Intl Prize "La Madonnina," NY Univ Med Col of Dentistry Alumni Awd; USSR Acad Sci 50th Anniv Jubilee Medal; Lib Human Resources; Alpha Omega Alpha; Alpha Pi Alpha; Omicron Delta Kappa; Phi Beta Pi; Phi Lambda Kappa; Sigma Xi; Hon LLD; AMA Dist'd Ser & Hektoen Gold Awds; Eleanor Roosevelt Humanities Awd; St Jude Man of Yr & Medal of Freedom Press Awds; TX Med Ctr Medallion, 1972; Am

Col Chest Phys Pres Cit; Michael DeBakey Day, Baylor Col of Med; St Francis Hosp F'ship Awd, Roslyn, NY; Harris Co Dist'd 30-Yr Ser Awd, 1978; Intl Register of Chivalry K Humanity Awd; Honoris Causa, Milan, Italy, 1978; Caja Costarricense de Seguro Social Dipl de Merito, San Jose, Costa Rica, 1979; TX Sci of Yr, TX Acad of Sci, 1979; Dist'd Ser Plaque, TX St Bd of Ed Adv Coun for Tech-Voc Ed in TX, 1079; Am Acad of Achmt 8th Annual Gold Medal for Extraordinary Ser, 1979; Britannica Achmt in Life Awd, 1979 & 1980; Medal of Freedom w Distn Pres Awd, 1969; 5th Intl Symp of Atherosclerosis & Intl Soc of Atherosclerosis Awd for Dist'd Ser, 1979; Indep of Jordan Medal 1st Class, Amman, Jordan, 1980; Merit, Order of the Repub 1st Class, Cairo, Egypt, 1980; ASME Cent Awd, 1980; Sovereign Order of the K Hospitallers of St John of Jerusalem; Denmark Cmdr Cross of Merit, Pro Utilitate Hominum, 1980; St Mary's Univ Marian Hlth Care Awd, 1981; Am Surg Assn Dist'd Ser Awd, 1981; Testimonial Dinner, St Jude Chd's Res Hosp, 1978; W/W: in Am, in World, in Adm Sci, in Commun Ser; Dir Ednl Specs; Intl Scholars Dir; Other Biogl Listings.

DeBAKEY, SELMA oc/Professor, Writer; b/Baylor College of Medicine, 1200 Moursund Avenue, Houston, TX 77030; ed/BA, Newcomb Col, Grad Study, Tulane Univ, NO, LA; pa/Dir, Dept of Med Comm, Alton Ochsner Med Foun 1942-68; Editor, *Ochsner Clin Reports*, 1942-68; Prof Sci Commun, Baylor Col of Med, Houston, TX, 1968-; Editor, *Cardiovas Res Ctr Bltn*, 1971-; Mem, Soc for Tech Commun; hon/ Author of *Current Concepts in Breast Cancer*, 1967; Num Articles on Sci Commun; DIB; The Am Registry; Am Men & Wom of Sci; W/W of Wom; Num Other Biogl Listings.

De BIASE, RAY N oc/Psychotherapist, Researcher; b/Feb 24, 1928; h/126 East 62nd Street, New York, NY 10021; ba/New York, NY; p/Nicholas and Eva (Bruno) De Biase; ed/BS, Columbia Univ, 1955; MS, Hunter Col, NYC, 1977; PhD, NY Univ, 1983; mil/AUS, 1947-50; pa/Sys Anal, CA-TX Oil Co, NYC, 1957-60; Owner, Reycourt Fin Corp, NYC, 1960-75; Res Assoc, Payne Whiney Psychi Clin, Cornel Univ Med Ctr, 1976-; Mem: Am Psychol Assn; Am Grp Psychotherapy Assn; Nat Rehab Cnslg Assn; NY St Psychol Assn; Am Public Hlth Assn; Asst Dir, Substance Abuse Prog; hon/Author of "Psychopathol Observations on Alcoholics," in *Alcoholism: Clin & Exptl Res*, 1977; Awd in Ed, Sys & Procedure Assn, 1953.

DEBREU, GERARD oc/Professor; b/ Jul 4, 1921; ba/Department of Economics, University of CA-Berkeley, CA 94720; m/Francoise Debreu; c/Chantal Debreu Teller, Florence Debreu Tetrault; p/Camille and Fernande (Decharne) Debreu (dec); sp/Madelaine Musset, Maisons-Laffitte, France; ed/ Ecole Normale Supérieure, Paris, 1941-44; Agrégé de l'Université, Paris, 1946; DSc, Université de Paris, 1956; mil/French Army (N Africa, Germany), 1944-45; pa/Res Assoc, Centre de la Recherche Scientifique, Paris, France, 1946-48; Res Assoc, Cowles Comm for Res in Ec, Univ of Chgo, 1950-55; Assoc Prof Ec, Cowles Foun for Res in Ec, Yale

Univ, 1955-61; Prof Ec 1962-, Prof of Ec & Math 1975-, Univ of CA-Berkeley; Mem: Pres, Econometric Soc, 1971; Fellow, Am Acad of Arts & Scis, 1970-; Nat Acad of Scis of USA, 1977-; hon/ Author of 3 Books: *Theory of Value, An Axiomatic Anal of Economic Equilibrium* 1959, Translated into French 1966, Spanish 1973, German 1976, Japanese 1977; *Math Ec; 20 Papers of Gerard Debreu*, 1983; Hon Docts: Univ of Bonn, 1977; Université de Lausanne, 1980; NWn Univ, 1981; Université des Sciences Sociales de Toulouse, 1983; Dist'd Fellow, Am Ec Assn, 1982; Nobel Meml Prize in Ec Scis, 1983; Intl W/W in France.

DeBROSSE, THEODORE A oc/ Geologist, Administrator; b/Jun 25, 1930; h/118 Chatham Road, Columbus, OH 43214; ba/Columbus, OH; m/Betty Lou Johnson; c/Richard A, Myron E, Jeffrey L, Nanette M; sp/Harrison E Johnson, Springfield, OH; ed/BS, Geol, 1955; pa/Staff Geol Div of Geol Survey 1955-65, Tech Asst Div of Oil & Gas 1965-69, Asst Chief Div of Oil & Gas, OH Dept of Natural Resources; Mem: Dist Rep 1962-64, Am Assn of Petro Geols; Pres 1964-65, OH Geol Soc; Pres OH Sect 1971, Am Inst of Profl Geols; cp/Pres, Clintonville Conserv Clb, 1972-73; r/Rom Cath; hon/Author of Var Reports incl'g: *Coal Beds of the Conemaugh Formation in OH*, 1957; *Summary of OH Oil & Gas Devel*, 1969-82; Num Other Short Articles Pub'd in Trade Jours; Energy Conservationist of Yr, Nat Wildlife Fdn, 1975.

De BRUIN, HENDRIK CORNELIS oc/College Administrator; b/Jan 3, 1929; h/1811 Mariyana, Gallup, NM 87301; ba/Gallup, NM; m/Jo Ann; c/Mari, Derek, Julie Watson, Michael Watson, Steve Watson; p/William de Bruin, Whiting, NJ; sp/Mrs Gilbert Buck, Roswell, NM; ed/BA, Montclair St Col, 1951; MEd 1953, PhD 1962, Univ of AZ; mil/AUS, Mil Police, 1946-48; pa/Assoc Dir for Instrn, Univ of NM-Gallup, 1982-; Hd Dept of Ed, The Citadel, 1979-82; Chm Div of Ed, IN Univ-S Bend, 1976-79; Dean Col of Ed, En NM Univ, 1968-76; Col Prof, Sch Tchr, Sch Admr for 30 Yrs; Other Previous Employmt; Num Ofcs & Coms in Profl, Univ & St Orgs; cp/Num Civic Positions & Commun Activs; Sr Deacon, Gallup Lodge of Masons; Inner Guard, Gallup Lodge of Elks; r/Presb; Deacon, Westminister Presb Ch; hon/Author of Over 24 Articles Pub'd in Profl Jours; Num Spkg Presentations; VPres, Pres Elect, Phi Kappa Phi, The Citadel, 1981; Past Pres's Awd, Phi Kappa Phi, 1976; Pres 1974-76, VPres 1971, Charter Mem 1971, Phi Kappa Phi, En NM Univ; Ser Key Awd, Phi Delta Kappa, 1964; Grad Res Asst, Coop Res Proj #1359, 1961; Spoke Awd, Jr C of C, 1957; Westinghouse Sci F'ship, Carnegie Inst of Technol, 1952; Undergrad S'ship, Montclair St Col, 1948-51; W/W in W; Book of Hon; Men of Achmt; Ldrs in Ed; DIB; Num Other Biogl Listings.

DeCELLES, CHARLES EDOUARD oc/Professor of Religious Studies; b/ May 17, 1942; h/923 East, Dunmore Street, Dunmore, PA, 18512; ba/Scranton, PA; m/Mildred Voight; c/Christopher Emanuel, Mark Joshua, Salvador Isaiah; p/Fernand and Stella DeCelles, Holyoke, MA; sp/Salvador and Aurita

Valdez, Union City, CA; ed/BA, Univ of Windsor, Ontario, Canada, 1964; MA, Marquette Univ, 1966; PhD, Fordham Univ, 1970; MA, Temple Univ, 1979; pa/Instr, Dept Theol, Dunbarton Col, Holy Cross, 1969-70; Instr 1970-72, Asst Prof 1972-75, Assoc Prof 1975-80, Prof 1980-, Dept of Rel Studies, Marywood Col, Scranton, PA; Mem: Col Theol Soc of Am, 1970-; Moderator Marywood Chapt 1982-, Theta Alpha Kappa, 1982; cp/Chm, UN Day, City of Scranton, 1974; Bd of Dirs, Scranton UN Assn, 1974-75; Bd of Dir Scranton Chapt 1983-, Pennsylvanians for Human Life; r/Rom Cath; hon/ Author of Book, *Paths of Belief*, 1977; Contbg Author, *Psyche & Spirit*, 1973; Author of Num Articles in Profl Jours, Nat Mags & Newspapers; Var Pamphlets, 1982-83; Cert of Apprec, Nat Coun Cath Bishops, 1976; Dist'd Ser Awd, UN Assn, 1974; Hon Mention, Cath Press Assn of Am Essay Competition, 1975; W/W: in E, in Ed; Commun Ldrs; Dir of Am Scholars; DIB; Other Biogl Listings.

DECHARIO, TONY H oc/Orchestra Manager; b/Sep 25, 1940; h/199 Oak Lane, Rochester, NY 14610; ba/Rochester, NY; m/Gill R; c/Samuel Paul, Rachel Christina, Mary Rebecca, Toni Elizabeth; Edmund Kidd Jr, Todd R Kidd, Kenneth H Kidd; p/Tony and Enid Dechario, Girard, KS; sp/Mary Roby, Rochester, NY; ed/Att'd, Univ of Wichita, 1958-61; BM & Performer's Cert 1962, MM 1963, Eastman Sch of Music; pa/2nd Trombone, KC Philharm, 1963-64; Prin Trombone, Dallas Symph, 1964-65; 2nd Trombone 1965-75, Pers Mgr 1972-75, Gen Mgr 1975-, Rochester Philharm; cp/Treas, Ctr for Dispute Settlement, Rochester, NY; Mem, Rochester Rotary Clb.

DECKER, DOUGLAS LESTER oc/ Professor; b/Mar 20, 1937; h/614 High Street, Petersburg, VA 23803; ba/ Petersburg, VA; p/Lester William Decker, Citrus Hgts, CA; Dorothy Alice Decker (dec); ed/BA Elem Ed 1961, MA Ed, Sch Adm 1968, MA Soc Sci 1969, CA St Univ-Sacramento; EdS Soc Studies Ed, En MI Univ, 1968; MA Curric Devel 1972, EdD Curric & Instrn 1976, Tchrs Col, Columbia Univ; Addit Studies; pa/Assoc Prof, Co-Dir Title IV-C Southside VA Writing Proj, VA St Univ, Petersburg, VA, 1976-; Grad Ed Lectr, Adj Fac, CA Polytech St Univ, San Luis Obispo, CA, 1975-76; Elem Sch Prin, K-6, Model HEP Bilingual, Lucia Mar Unified Sch Dist, Pismo Bch, CA, 1974-76; Elem Sch Prin, K-4, Follow Through Bilingual Model/CA Process Model, Lamont Sch Dist, Lamont, CA, 1972-74; 5th/6th Grade Tchr 1969-70, Exch Spanish Sum Tchr 1964, Exch Art Tchr 1969, Transition Sch Admr 1965, Sacramento City Unified Sch Dist, Sacramento, CA, 1962-670; 5th Grade Tchr, Wash Unified Sch Dist, W Sacramento, CA 1961-62; Num Overseas Sum Study/Travel Experiences; Num Univ & Sch Coms, 1977-; Mem: VA Coun for the Social Studies; Life Mem, Phi Delta Kappa; Life Mem, NEA; VA Ed Assn; Life Mem, The Col Rdg Assn; Chd's Lit Assem, IRA; NCTE; Signal; Gtr Richmond Rdg Coun; Assn for Supvn Curric Devel; Latin Am Studies Assn; Bilingual Ed Assn; Nat Coun for the Social Studies; VA St Rdg

Assn; Nat Assn for Elem Sch Prins; Recording Secy 1981-82, VA Assem on Lit for Adolescent, NCTE; Orgr & Pres 1979-80, Recording Secy 1980-81, VA St Univ Chapt, Phi Delta Kappa; Kappa Delta Pi; VA Assn of Tchrs of Eng; Num Conslt Positions for Var Orgs; Att'd Num Rdg, Curric, Ednl Confs & Wkshops; cp/Secy 1977-78 & 1978-79, Fall Fests Com 1978-81, High Street Assn; PTA 1977-78, Bojoster Clb 1977-78, Gibbons HS; Historic Petersburg Foun; High Street Meth Ch; Foster Parent; r/Meth; hon/Author, Over 20 Articles Pub'd in Profl Jours incl'g: *AZ Eng Bltn; Tchr Corps VSU/Surry Co Newslttr; Phi Delta Kappan; Rdg World*; Co-Editor, *Southside Writing Proj Digest, I, II & III*, 1980-82; Other Writings; Participant in Var Res Grants; Col Sect Cand, NCTE, 1981; Elec Sect Cand, VA Assn of Tchrs of Eng, 1982-; Storytelling Conslt, Southside Early Childhood Assn, 1982; Conslt for NTE Valadation Study for Early Childhood Exam, 1982; Num Others; W/W in S & SW.

DECKER, FRED WILLIAM oc/Government Administrator in Education; b/ Jul 5, 1917; h/1400 South Joyce Street, Apartment A-910, Arlington, VA 22202; ba/Washington, DC; m/Charlotte Eleanor (Menker) Decker; c/ Charlotte Jane, William Allen, Lorraine Ann D Takalo, Rebecca Jane Takalo (Grandchild); p/John William and Emma Sophia (Schlickaiser) Decker (dec); sp/ Earle Lincoln and Charlotte Ann (Manhire) Menker (dec); ed/AE, Multnomah Col, 1937; BS 1940, PhD 1952, OR St Univ; MS, NY Univ, 1943; Grad of Resv Courses: Nat War Col, Air War Col, Air Command & Staff Sch; mil/Reservist, 1937-; WW II Active Duty, 1942-46; pa/ Observer to Forecaster, US Weather Bur, 1937-41; Instr, NY Univ, 1941-44; Instr, Multnomah Col, 1946; Instr to Assoc Prof 1946-81, Emeritus Fac 1981-, OR St Univ; Dept Asst Secy, Ofc of Ed Res & Improvement, US Dept of Ed, 1981-; Mem: Pres & Exec Dir-Editor, Univ Profs for Acad Order; Dist Lt Gov, Toastmasters Intl; Chm OR Sect, Am Assn Physics Tchrs; Chm OR Chapt, Am Meteorological Soc; Am Phy Soc; Am Geophy Union; OR Acad of Sci; AAAS; cp/Scoutmaster, BSA; Citizens of Corvalis, OR; OR Skyline Trail Hikers; r/Luth; hon/Author of *The Weather Wkbook*, 1956-; *Weather Map Study*, 1958-; *Sci Travel Guide*, 1970; Over 85 Articles & Papers Pub'd, 1942-; Editor, *Universitas*, 1975-82; Dist 7 Toastmasters Spch Eval Champ, 1978; AF Commend Medal; Armed Forces Resv Medal w Cluster; W/W: in W, in E.

DECKER, JEAN CAMPBELL oc/ Treasurer and Consultant; b/Mar 10, 1915; h/885 Smith Street, Glen Ellyn, IL 60137; ba/Addison, IL; p/D M and Bertha (Campbell) Decker (dec); ed/ BBA, Univ of Chgo, 1937; pa/Employee 1950-, Asst Treas 1967, Treas 1969-81, Plan Admr & Dir 1976-82, Calco Mfg Co, Addison, IL; Treas, Envir Inc, Haines City, FL, 1971-72; Treas 1971-, Dir 1971-78 & 1982-, Gustafson Enterprises Inc, Addison, IL; cp/Phi Delta Upsilon Sorority, Univ of Chgo, 1934-; Univ of Chgo Alumni Assn, 1937-; Notary Public, St of IL, 1951-87; r/Prot; hon/W/W of Am Wom.

DeCROW, KAREN oc/Attorney, Writer; h/Fir Tree Lane, Jamesville, NY

1078; ba/Syracuse, NY; ed/BS, Medill Sch of Jour, NWn Univ, 1959; Att'd Grad Prog Communs Newhouse Sch of Jour 1967, JD Col of Law 1972, Syracuse Univ; pa/Fashion Editor, Resorts Editor, *Golf Digest*, 1959-60; Editor, *Zoning Digest*, Am Soc of Planning Ofcls, 1960-61; Writer & Author, Ctr for Study of Liberal Ed for Adults, 1961-64; Social Studies & Adult Ed Editor, Holt, Rinehart & Winston Inc, 1965; Textbook Editor, L W Singer Co Inc, 1965-66; Writer, En Reg Inst for Ed, 1967-69; Course Tchr on Wom's Lib, Wom & Law, YWCA, 1972 & 1973; Tchr, Wom & the Law, Onondaga Commun Col, 1974; Atty, Constitl, Sex Discrimination, Lit & Entertainment Law, 1972-; Mem: NY St Bar Assn; No Dist of NY Fed Ct; Onondaga Bar Assn; NY St Wom's Bar Assn; Nat Pres 1974-77, Nat Bd Mem 1968-77, NOW; ACLU; Bd of Trustees, Elizabeth Cady Stanton Foun; Bd of Advrs, Wking Wom's Inst; Nat Cong for Men; Nat Bd Mem, Gay Rights Nat Lobby; Commun Disputes Panel, Am Arbitration Assn; Equal Rts for Fathers; hon/Author, *Sexist Justice*, 1974 & 1975; *The Yg Wom's Guide to Liberation*, 1971; Co-Author, *Univ Adult Ed*, Am Coun on Ed, 1967; Co-Author, *Wom Who Marry Houses: Panic & Protest in Agoraphobia*, 1983; Num Columns & Articles in Var Mags & Newspapers incl'g: *Vogue; Mademoiselle; The Civil Rts Qtly; NY Times; LA Times; Boston Globe; Miami Herald; SF Chronicle; Chgo Sun-Times*; Others; Num Lectr Presentations at Univs, Law Schs, Corp Grps, Med Schs & in US, Canada, Mexico, Greece, Finland & USSR; 200 Future Ldrs of Am, *Time*, 1974; 50 Most Influential Wom in Am, Newspaper Enterprise Assn, 1975; W/W: in Am, of Am Wom, in E, in World; The Writers Dir; Commun Ldrs & Noteworthy Ams; DIB; Other Biogl Listings.

DEDIU, MICHAEL MIHAI SR oc/ Computer Scientist, Mathematician; b/ Nov 6, 1943; h/1242 Cook Avenue, Lakewood, OH 44107-2504; ba/Cleveland, OH; m/Sophia; c/Horace, Michael Ovidiu; p/Ana and Virgil Dediu, Bucharest; ed/PhD 1972; pa/Rschr, Inst of Math, 1967-75; Asst Prof, Univ of Bucharest, 1973-74; Resr, Inst of Physics, Bucharest, 1975-76; Resr, Univ of Torino, 1977-78; Computer Sci & Math, Case Wn Resv Univ, 1978-; Am Math Soc; Math Assn of Am; Soc for Indust & Applied Math; hon/Profl Pubs; F'ship, Nat Coun of Res of Italy, 1977; 25 Invitations at 16 Univs & Res Insts in 7 Countries; W/W: in Frontier Sci, in Mid Am.

DEED, MARTHA LOUISE oc/Certified Psychologist; b/May 1, 1941; h/4774 Harlem Road, Snyder, NY 14226; ba/ Same; c/Mildred Elizabeth Niss; p/ Robert and Louise Deed, Nyack, NY; ed/ BA, New Sch for Social Res, 1964; PhD, Boston Univ, 1969; Cert'd Psych, NY St, 1971; pa/Staff Psychol, Rockland Co Mtl Hlth Clin, 1969-73; Indep Res, Cultural & Psychol Aspects of Pregnancy & Maternity Experience, 1973-75; Indept Pract Psychol, 1972-81; Psychol, Wn NY Inst for Psychotherapies, 1981-83; Pvt Pract, 1983-; Indiv Psychotherapy w Chd, Adults, Couples, Families, 1969-; Conslt to Schs & Public Agys; Am Psychol Assn; APA Divs on Psychotherapy & Wom; NY St Psychol

Assn; NYSPA Div of Clin Psychol; Fellow, Am Orthopsychi Assn; Authors Guild; r/Rel Soc of Friends; hon/F'ships, Boston Univ, 1965-68; Am Friends Ser Com, 1966-69; Grant, Friends World Com, 1968-69; Cert'd Psychol, NY St, 1971-; W/W: of Am Wom. in E.

DEESE, DONALD WOODROW oc/Corporate Financial Officer; b/Oct 27, 1945; h/626 Hatrick Road, Columbia, SC 29209; ba/Columbia, SC; m/Kathryn Nettles; c/Donald Rogers; p/William Boyd and Thelma Lee Deese; ed/Att'd USC, 1965; pa/Auditor, J W Hunt & Co, CPA's, 1968-73; Auditor, T H Montgomery, CPA, 1973-78; Treas, Jim Moore Cadillac Inc, 1978-; Treas, Moore-Hudson Oldsmobile Inc, 1980-; Conslt; Am Inst of CPA's; SC Assn of CPA's; Nat Assn of CPA's; cp/Repub; Summit Clb; r/Meth.

De FILIPPO, RITA MARCELLA oc/Budget Analyst; h/2820 Scott Street, San Francisco, CA 94123; ba/San Francisco, CA; p/Sal and Margaret De Filippo; ed/Att'd LA City Col 1957, City Col of SF 1975, Univ of SF 1976, LaSalle Univ 1968; pa/Asst Ad Dir, Gump's Inc, 1959; Res Stat, Honig-Cooper & Harrington, 1960-61; Salesperson, Landau Rlty, 1962-63; Mgmt Anal, Oakland Army Base, 1978-80; Budget Anal, Dept of Army in SF, 1980-; Am Bus Wom Assn; Am Soc Mil Comptrollers; Assn Wom in Sci; Assn US Army; Nat Fdn Fed Employees; cp/Sierra Clb; hon/Recip, Outstg Perf Awd, Fed Govt, 1979; W/W of Am Wom.

De GENARO, GUY JOSEPH oc/Professor of Management; b/Nov 20, 1921; h/3 Berkshire Rd, Richmond, VA 23221; m/Jennie Jennings; c/Marsha Jean Blakemore; p/Ralph De Genaro (dec); Madeline De Genaro, Hamden, CT; ed/BS, MBA, PhD; mil/USAF, Lt Col; pa/Assoc Prof of Mgmt, VA Commonwlth Univ, 1970-; Chief of Manpower & Org, USAF Maj Command, 1946-70; Glider Pilot, USAF, 1942-46; Acad of Mgmt; VP & Bd Mem, Soc for Advmt of Mgmt; Richmond Pvt Indust Coun; Loaned Exec, U Fund; Am Soc for Tng & Devel; cp/Bd Dirs, VA Affil Am Heart Assn; Soc for Prev of Blindness; hon/Profl Pubs; Outstg of Edrs Am; Dist Ser Awd, SAM, Phi Kappa Phi, Sigma Iota Epsilon, Beta Gamma Sigma, Alpha Kappa Psi; W/W: in Ed, in S & SW; Personalities of S; Men & Wom of Distn; Notable Ams.

DeGHETTO, KENNETH ANSELM oc/Engineering Company Executive; b/Apr 1, 1924; h/42 Cornell Drive, Livingston, NJ 07039; ba/Livingston, NJ; m/Helen Marie Z; c/Donna D MacConnell, Glenn; p/Linda Z DeGhetto, Clifton, NJ; sp/Elsie Zschack, Whiting NJ; ed/BS, USMM Acad, 1948; BME, Rensselaer Polytech Inst, 1950; mil/USMM, 1942-43; USNR, 1943-46, Lt; pa/Engr 1951-64, VP in Milan Italy 1964-67, Dir of Process Plants Div 1967-69, Mng Dir & Chm of Bd 1969-75, Exec VP & Pres 1975-82, Chm of Bd 1982-, Foster Wheeler Corp; ASME, 1960-; Nat Assn of Corrosion Engrs, 1960-; Tau Beta Pi; Sigma Xi; Pi Tau Sigma; r/Luth; hon/Profl Pubs; Standard & Poors Register of Dirs & Execs; W/W in Am.

DeGIDIO, SANDRA FAY oc/Freelance Author and Lecturer; b/Feb 12, 1943; h/230 North Central Avenue #114, Wayzata, MN 55391; ba/Same; p/

Nick and Jovina DeGidio, Cumberland, WI; ed/BA, Mt Senario Col, 1964; MA, Marquette Univ, 1974; Postgrad, Notre Dame Univ, 1979; pa/Elem/Jr HS Tchr, Cath Schs, 1964-70; Assoc Pastor, Webster Area Cath Ch, 1971-73; Dir of Rel Ed/Liturgist/RCIA Dir, Paris Commun of St Joseph, 1973-81; Fac, St Norbert Col Theol Inst, 1982-84; r/Rom Cath; hon/Pub'd Author; Outstg Yg Wom of Am, 1977.

DeGIOVANNI-DONNELLY, ROSALIE F oc/Professor, Researcher; b/Nov 22, 1926; h/1712 Strine Drive, McLean, VA 22101; ba/Washington, DC; m/Edward F Donnelly; c/Edward F Jr, Francis M; p/Frank and Rose DeGiovanni (dec); sp/Edward and Julia Donnelly (dec); ed/BA 1947, MA 1953, Biol, Bklyn Col; PhD, Zool & Microbiol Genetics, Columbia Univ, 1961; pa/Adj Prof Microbiol 1984-, Assoc Prof Lectr 1978-84, Asst Res Prof 1968-78, George Wash Univ Med Ctr; Res Biol, Food & Drug Adm, Wash DC, 1968-; Chief Microbiol Genetics Sect, Bionetics Labs; Res Asst Biochem, Columbia Univ Med Ctr; Mem: AAAS; Am Soc for Microbiol; Sigma Xi; Omicron Chapt, Sigma Delta; Envir Mutagen Soc; NY Acad of Sci; r/Rom Cath; hon/Author & Co-Author, Over 30 Sci Pubs in Profl Jours, 1954-84; Food & Drug Awd of Merit; Am Men & Wom in Sci.

DEHNERT, EDMUND JOHN oc/Professor; b/Feb 15, 1931; h/1121 Harvard Terrace, Evanston, IL 60202; ba/Chicago, IL; m/Donna Marie Wroblewski; c/Mark, Carl, Gregory, Caroline; sp/Estelle Wroblewski, Evanston IL; ed/BA, St Mary of the Lake Univ 1952; MMus, De Paul Univ, 1956; PhD, Univ of Chgo, 1963; pa/Chm Dept of Humanities & Fgn Langs, Truman Col, Chgo, IL, 1964-; Prof of Humanities, City Cols of Chgo, 1970-; Mem: Am Musicological Soc; Am Folklore Soc; Am Soc of Univ Composers; hon/Author, *The Dialectic of Technol & Culture*, 1983; *The Consciousness of Music Wrought by Musical Notation*, 1983; *A Contemp Course in other Humanities*, 1976; *Music as Liberal in Augustine & Boethius*, 1968; F'ship, Nat Endowment for the Humanities for Res in Polish Folklore, 1981-82; Fellow, Nat Humanities Inst, Univ of Chgo, 1976-77; W/W in MW; DIB; Royal Blue Book.

DE HODGINS, OFELIA CANALES oc/Materials Scientist; b/Oct 25, 1944; h/612 Granite Springs Road, Yorktown Heights, NY 10598; ba/Poughkeepsie, NY; m/Martin Garry Hodgins; c/Sidarta Perables Hodgins; p/Fernando Canales Rocha, Mexico City; sp/Leana de Canales, Mexico City; ed/BS, MSBS 1972, MS 1973, Univ of Mexico; MSc, Univ of VA, 1977; Pursuing PhD in Mats Sci & PhD in Engrg Physics at Univ of VA; pa/Jr Rschr 1971-73, Sr Rschr 1973-76, On Leave 1973-76, Nuclear Inst of Mexico; Vis'g Res Fellow, Univ of VA, 1973; Prof of Math, Instituto Freinet de Mexico, 1971-72; Asst Prof of Thermodynamics, Univ of Mexico, 1972-73; Asst Prof of Math, Instituto Politecnico Nacional, 1973-74; Grad Res Asst in Dept of Mats Sci, Univ of VA, 1976-79; Grad Res Asst in Dept of Nuclear Engrg & Engrg Physics, Univ of VA, 1979-; Sigma Xi; Mexican Soc of Physics; Am Soc of Metals; Electron Microscopy Soc of Am; hon/Num Profl

Pubs; Dorothea Buck F'ship Awd, 1975-76; Nat Prize of Science, 1974; S'ship, Mexican Inst of Physics, 1970-72.

De JARNETTE, JAMES EDWARD oc/Psychoanalyst, Family Therapist; b/Mar 22, 1948; h/8535 West Knoll Drive, #215, West Hollywood, CA 90069; ba/Same; p/Charles N and Sara P de Jarnette, Cape Canaveral, FL; ed/BA, Shorter Col, 1970; MA, W GA Col, 1971; PhD, Sussex Col, 1973; Addit Tng; Exec Dir, Mid GA Cnslg Ctr, 1972-78; Psychotherapist, de Jarnette & Assocs, Warner Robins, GA, 1974-78; Psychotherapist, Powers Ferry Psychotherapy Clin, Atlanta, GA, 1976-80; Psychotherapist, Chattahoochee Val Cnslg Ctr, Columbus, GA, 1977-79; Pvt Pract Psychotherapy & Bus Conslt, de Jarnette & Assocs, Beverly Hills, CA, 1979-; Pres & Chm Bd of Dirs, Leonidas Ltd Inc, 1972-80; Bd of Dirs, Alpha-Omega Enterprises Inc, 1978-80; Sr Ptner, de Jarnette, Harrington, Sterrette & Assocs, 1978-80; CEO, Bus Consltg & Mgmt, Sales Sems, Motivation Sems, Stress Mgmt Consltg, Exec Cnslrs of Mgmt, 1978-80; Bd of Dirs, Subliminal Sys Inc, Vis'g Prof Psych, Loyola Marymount Univ, 1981-83; Consltg Psychotherapist & Fam Cnslr, Cath Social Sers, 1981-; Mem: Fellow, Am Orthopsychi Assn; Am Pers & Guid Assn; CA Pers Guid Assn; Nat Chm for Marriage & Fam Cnslg, Am Mtl Hlth Cnslrs Assn; Pres Elect & Pres, GA Mtl Hlth Cnslrs Assn; Intl Soc of Adlerian Psych; Life Mem, Nat Psychi Assn; Intl Platform Assn; Cert Mem, Am Assn for Poetry Therapy; Lic'd: Marriage & Fam Therapy, St of GA; Marriage, Fam & Child Cnslr, St of CA; Hypnotherapy Cert, St of CA; cp/Mensa; Triple Nine Soc; Intertel; hon/Author of Column in Var Newspapers, 1974-76; Num Articles in Profl Jours; Pi Gamma Mu; Sigma Phi Omega; F'ship, Am Acad of Behavioral Sci; Hon Grad, W GA Col & Sussex Col; St of GA Outstg Ser Awd, Dept of Offender Rehab; W/W: in S & SW, in W, in CA.

DE JESUS, JOSEFINA ESTARIS oc/Nursing Research Coordinator; h/1950 Berkshire Drive, Fullerton, CA 92633; ba/Los Angeles, CA; m/Marcelo V Jr; c/Marc Jonathan E, Mary Jo Angelica E; p/Policarpio (dec) and Salud Estaris, Norwalk, CA; sp/Susana (dec) and Marcelo, Philippines; ed/BS, Univ of Redlands, 1983; MA Cand in Mgmt; Att'd Univ of E Philippines; pa/Charge Nurse 1973-75, Nsg Coor 1975-79, Asst Dir of Nsg 1979-83, Nsg Res Coor, 1983-, Cedars-Sinai Med Ctr; ANA; CA Nurses Assn; Philippine Nurses Assn; r/Meth; hon/Profl Pubs; Dean's Gold Medal Awd, 1967; W/W of Am Wom.

DEJNOZKA, EDWARD L oc/Professor; b/May 14, 1927; h/7145 San Salvador Drive, Boca Raton, FL 33433; ba/Boca Raton, FL; m/Mary B; c/Dean, Jeanne, Bruce, Janice; ed/BA, Queens Col, 1949; MA, Tchrs Col, Columbia Univ, 1951; EdD, NY Univ, 1960; mil/AUS, 1945-47; pa/Tchr, Baldwin & Gt Neck, NY, 1949-52; Tchr & Prin, Shoreham, NY, 1952-54; Elem Prin & Asst Supt, Plainedge, NY, 1954-59; Prof of Ednl Adm, NY Univ, 1959-67; Dept Chm, Trenton St Col, 1967-69; Asst Dean, No AZ Univ, 1969-74; Dean of Ed, Univ of NE-Omaha, 1974-78; Prof

Ednl Adm, FL Atl Univ, 1978–; Mem: Phi Delta Kappa; Am Assn of Sch Admrs; Assn for Supvn & Curric Devel; cp/Rotary, 1974–78; hon/Author of Num Articles Pub'd in Ednl Jours; Sr Author, *Am Edrs' Ency*, 1982; W/W in S & SW; Ldrs in Ed.

DeJOIA, RUTH ANN oc/Director of Domestic Relations Section; b/Aug 16, 1927; h/PO Box 248, Meadville, PA 16335; ba/Meadville, PA; m/Joseph F A DeJoia; c/John F, Joanne Marie D Winans; ed/Att'g Penn St Univ, 1976–; pa/Var Lwyrs, Meadville, PA, 1945–56; Clk/Typist, Crawford Co Assessment Ofc, 1956–59; Secy to Chief Adult & Juv Probation Ofcr, 1959–65; Secy, Holiday Inn of Meadville, 1965–66; Asst Innkeeper, 1966–68; Exec Secy, Crawford Co Tourist Assn, 1970–71; Adm Asst, 1971–76, Asst Dir 1977–78, Dir 1978–, Crawford Co Domestic Relats Sec, Court of Common Pleas; Crawford Co Mtl Hlth Assn, 1970–; Crawford Co Commun Coun, 1978–; Child Adv Coun of PA, 1978–80; Wom's Resource Grp Crawford Co Drug & Alcohol Commn, 1980; Dir 1978–81, Secy 1980–81, Domestic Relats Assn of PA; Nat Reciprocal & Fam Sup Enforcement Assn; En Reg Reciprocal & Fam Sup Enforcement Assn; En Reg Coun on Wel Fraud; cp/Past Ofcr, PTA; r/U Ch of Christ; hon/W/W of Am Wom.

DEJOIE, CAROLYN BARNES-MILANES oc/Professor; b/Apr 17; h/ 5322 Fairway Drive, Madison, WI 53711; ba/Madison, WI; c/Deirdre Jeanelle, Prudhomme III, Duan Kendall; p/ Edward F Barnes (dec); Alice Milanes Barnes, NO, LA; ed/MA, Universidad Nacional de Mexico, 1962; MSW, Univ of WI, 1970; PhD, Union Grad Sch, 1976; pa/Instr, So Univ, Baton Rouge, LA, 1962–63; Asst Prof, VA St Col, Norfolk, VA, 1963–66; Asst to Pres, Univ of WI Sys-Madison, 1970–73; Assoc Prof, Univ of WI-Ext, 1973–; Mem: AAUP; AAUW; Nat Assn of Media Wom; Nat Assn of Black Social Wkrs; cp/Num Commun Activs; hon/ Author, *La Clase Humilde de Mexico*, 1962; *Social Adjustment of Inmates in WI Prisons*, 1976; *The Black Wom in Alienation in White Academia*, 1977; *Inequalities Inherent in Crim Justice Sys & Role of Cnslr-Social Wkr*, 1978; *The Univ & Social Ed for Prisoners*, 1979; *Poetry-Just Me*, 1980; *Rdgs from a Black Perspective: An Anthology*, 1984; *Black Wom: Achmt Agnst the Odds*, 1983; Recog Awd, VA St Col, 1965; Fulbright S'ship, US Govt, 1966; Outstg Wom Awd, Zeta Phi Beta Sorority, 1980; W/W in Black Am.

DEKKER, EUGENE E oc/Professor & Department Chairman; b/Jul 23, 1927; h/2612 Manchester Road, Ann Arbor, MI 48104; ba/Ann Arbor, MI; m/Harriet E; c/Gwen E, Paul D, Tom R; p/Peter and Anne Dekker (dec); sp/John J and Jennie Holwerda; ed/AB, Calvin Col, 1949; MS 1951, PhD 1954, Univ of IL-Urbana; mil/USN, 1945–46; USNR, 1946–51; pa/Asst Prof, Univ of L'ville Med Sch, 1954–56; Asst Prof, Assoc Prof, Prof, Assoc Chm, Univ of MI Med Sch, 1956–; Mem: Am Chem Soc; Am Soc of Biol Chems; Am Soc of Plant Physiobiols; Sigma Xi; Phi Lambda Upsilon; r/Prot; hon/Author, Over 60 Sci Articles in Scholarly Jours; Over 10 Chapts in Med-Sci Books; Lederle Med Fac Awd, 1958–61; Amoco Outstg Tchg Awd, The Univ of MI, 1978; Nat Res

Ser Awd For Sr Fellows, 1981–82.

De KOONING, ELAINE MARIE CATHERINE oc/Artist, Writer; h/51 Raynor Street, Freeport, NY 11520; ba/ New York, NY; m/Willem de Kooning; p/Charles F and Mary Ellen O'Brien Fried (dec); ed/Hon DFA, Wn Col, Oxford, OH, 1964; Hon DFA, Moore Col of Art, Phila, PA, 1972; Fellow, RI Sch of Design; pa/Milton & Sally Avery Chair, Bard Col, 1982; Lamar Dodd Chair, Univ of GA, 1976–78; Mellon Chair, Carnegie Mellon Univ, 1969–70; Mem Edit Assoc, *Art News*, 1948–49; hon/Author of Articles, "Originals: Am Wom Artists"; "Wom & Art"; "The Bacchus Series," & Cover, *Arts Mag*; W/ W: in Am, of Am Wom; Other Biogl Listings.

DELANO, JONATHAN WILLIAM oc/Administrative Assistant in Government; b/Apr 8, 1949; h/906 6th Street, Southwest, Washington, DC 20024; ba/ Washington, DC; p/Hubert and June Delano, Pittsburgh, PA; ed/BA, Haverford Col, 1971; 1st Class Hons, Univ of Edinburgh, Scotland, 1969–70; JD, Univ of PA Law Sch, 1974; pa/Adm Asst, US Rep Doug Walgren (PA), Rayburn House Ofc Bldg, Wash DC, 1977–; Atty, Reed, Smith, Shaw & McClay, Pgh, 1974–77; Mem: VPres 1983–84, Bd of Dirs 1980–83, Adm Assts Assn, US Ho of Reps; Allegheny & PA Bar Assns; PA Hist Soc; Wn PA Conservancy; Pgh Hist & Landmarks Foun; r/Epis; hon/Author of Var Newspaper Articles on Congl Ethics & Campaign Fin; Phi Beta Kappa, 1971; Cope F'ship for Grad Studies, 1971; St Andrews S'ship, 1969; Margaret Balfour Keith Awd in Brit Hist, 1970; Am Legion Citizenship Awd, 1964; Var Biogl Listings.

DELATTE, ANN PERKINS oc/Educational Administrator, Project Director; b/Apr 8, 1934; h/2423 Nancy Lane, Northeast, Atlanta, GA 30345; ba/ Atlanta, GA; m/Martine Joseph (dec); c/ Martin David & Michael William; p/ William Donovan Perkins (dec); Lalia Callaway Perkins, Savannah, GA; ed/ AA, Armstrong Col, 1954; BA, Oglethorpe Univ, 1956; MA Eng, NO Univ, 1971; PhD Ednl Ldrship, GA St Univ, 1978; pa/Tchr, Atlanta Public Schs, 1956–59; Tchr, Savannah Public Schs, 1959–60; Res Asst, Am Inst for Res, Pgh, 1962–64; Prog Writer & Staff Tng Coor, NO Public Schs, 1969–71; Dir of Ednl Sers, GA Dept of Offender Rehab, Atlanta, 971–78; Assoc Prof & Acad Dir, GA St Univ, 1978–; Mem: GA Right to Read Adv Coun, 1973; GA St Manpower Planning Coun, 1974; GA Employmt & Tng Coun, 1975; Deptmtl Liaison w Legis Study Com on Correctional Ed, 1975–76; Adv Com on Planning, Implementation & Eval in Juv Justice, Univ of SC Prog w Nat Inst of Corrections & Law Enforcement Adm, 1978–79; Reg Adv Com on Improved Sers to Wom, US Dept of Labor, 1979–80; Task Force on Tng, Ofc of Mgmt Asst, Employmt & Tng Adm, US Dept of Labor, Wash DC, 1980; GA Balance-of-St Planning Coun, CETA, 1982; Fac of Inst of Industl Relats, GA St Univ, 1981–; cp/Trustee, Big Brothers/Big Sisters of Atlanta Inc, 1983; Var Other Commun Activs; r/Prot; hon/ Author & Co-Author, Over 15 Reports & Papers Pub'd in Profl Pubs incl'g: GA

Dept of Corrections/Offender Rehab; *GA Jour of Corrections*; *GA Profl Engr*; *Trend: Mag for Dept of Offender Rehab Pers*; Others; Armstrong S'ship, 1952 & 1953; Jr C of C S'ship 1952; Elks Clb S'ship, 1952; Oglethorpe Univ S'ship, 1954; Wm F Cooper Meml S'ship, 1954 & 1955; Agnes Scott/Emory Univ Jt S'ship, 1957; Lisle F'ship, Intl Org for the Study of Human Relat'ships, Jamaica & CA, 1956 & 1957; Recip of Var Outstg Student Awds: Kiwanis Clb, 1952; JCs, 1952; Jr C of C, 1952; Armstrong Fac, 1954; Omicron Delta Kappa; Outstg Ser Awds: NO Public Schs, 1971; BSA, 1974; NO Chapt, Am Cancer Soc, 1969; Meth Conf of S GA, 1955; YWCA, 1949–52; Intl Assn of Correctional Edrs, 1974; US Dept of Labor Reg Adm, 1979 & 1981; W/W: in S & SW, of Am Wom.

Del CERRO, MANUEL oc/Professor, Medical Researcher; b/Sep 20, 1931; h/ 14 Tall Acres Drive, Pittsford, NY 14534; ba/Rochester, NY; m/Constancia; c/Alicia and Marilu; p/Manuel and Julia del Cerro (dec); sp/Pedro and Maria Nunez, Resistencia, Argentina; ed/BA & BS, Buenos Aires Nat Col, 1951; MD, Univ of Buenos Aires Med Sch, 1958; mil/Argentina Army, 1952, Pvt; pa/ Assoc Prof, Ctr for Brain Res, 1971–79; Assoc Prof Anatomy, 1976–; Assoc Prof Ophthal, Univ of Rochester, 1980–; Prof, Ctr for Brain Res & Ctr for Visual Sci, Univ of Rochester, 1979–; Intl Brain Res Org, 1971–; Assn for Res in Vision & Ophthal, 1977–; Am Assn of Neuropathols, 1974–; Am Assn of Anatomists; r/Rom Cath; hon/Num Prof Pubs; Argentian Nat Res Coun Intl F'ship, 1960, 1969; Univ of Rochester Senate, 1977–80; Mem, Hlth Res Coun, NYS Hlth Planning Com, 1982–; Fellow, Royal Microscopical Soc, 1982–; W/W: in Frontier Sci & Technol, in E, in Am, of Am Men & Wom of Sci.

DELCO, EXALTON ALFONSO JR oc/University Administrator; b/Sept 4, 1929; h/1805 Astor Place, Austin, TX 78721; ba/Austin, TX; m/Wilhelmina Ruth; c/Deborah Diane, Exalton Alfonso III, Loretta Elmirle, Cheryl Pauline; ed/AB; MS; PhD; mil/46th Surg Mobile Army Landstuhl, Germany; pa/ VPres for Acad Affairs 1984–, Former Acad Dean, Huston-Tillotson Col; Mem: Sigma Xi; cp/Bd Mem, Holy Cross Hosp; r/Cath; hon/Stoye Prize, Am Soc Ichthyologists & Herpetologists, 1954.

De LERMA, DOMINIQUE-RENÉ S oc/Musicologist; b/Dec 8, 1928; h/711 Stoney Springs Drive, Baltimore, MD 21210; p/Danie-Robert-Francois de Lerma (dec); ed/BM, Univ of Miami, 1952; PhD, IN Univ, 1958; Addit Study: Curtis Inst of Music; Col of Notre Dame; Berkshire Music Ctr; Univ of OK; pa/Assoc Prof Music, Univ of Miami, 1951–61; Assoc Prof, Univ of OK, 1962–63; Vis'g Prof 1961–62, Assoc Prof 1963–1976, IN Univ; Prof & Grad Music Coor, Morgan St Univ, 1976–; Fac, Peabody Conservatory of Music, 1983–; Mem: Chm Nat Adv Bd, Inst for Res in Black Am Music, Fisk Univ; MD St Arts Coun, 1983–; Bd, Dance Theatre of Harlem, 1975–; Bd, Bklyn Philharm, 1980–; VPres, Black Composers Proj, 1977–; Coun, Col Music Soc, 1980–82; Chm Auditioning Com, Balto Symph Orch, 1982–; Chief Conslt, Black Composers Series, CBS Records, 1975–; Bd, Eubie Blake Cultural Ctr, 1982–; r/Cath;

hon/Author of *Bibliog of Black Music*, 1981-; *Black Music in Our Culture*, 1970; *Reflections on Afro-Am Music*, 1973; Over 900 Articles in Var Pubs; Nat Black Music Caucus, 1982; W/W: in E, in Commun Ser, in Music & Musicians Dir; Biogl Dir of Libns in US & Canada; Other Biogl Listings.

DELGADO DE TORRES, ALMA oc/ Lawyer; ba/May 16, 1913; h/4th Street D 28, Hnas Davila Dev Bayamon, PR; ba/Bayamon; m/Manuel Torres Reyes (dec); c/Manuel; p/Luis Mario Delgado Lugo and Maria Pasapera Tio (dec); sp/ Manuel Torres River and Alfonsa Reyes Perez (dec); ed/Comml Dipl, 1933; BA, Politech Inst, 1937; LLB & JD, Univ of PR, 1940; Addit Studies; pa/Lwyr in Pvt Legal Ofc, 1940-44; Judge, Min Ct 1944-45; Assoc Lwyr, Div of Opinions, Dept of Justice, 1946-47; Mun Judge, 1948-50; Dist Atty 1950-56; Pvt Pract, 1956-65; Dist Judge, 1965-75; Pvt Pract, 1975-; Asst Prof, Inter-Am Univ, 1970-75; PR Bar Assn; Former Secy & VP, Bayamon Lwyrs Assn; Pres, Comm of Public Acts, PR Lwyrs Assn, 1960-70; Inter-Am Lwyrs Assn; Others; cp/Pres, BPW Clb of Bayamon 1970-71; Altrusa Clb; Parents Assn, LaSalle Cath Sch, 1970-74; Others; r/Cath; hon/Pub'd Author; Plaque, PR Bar Assn; Lwyr of Yr, 1970; BSA Awd; Awds from Masonic Lodge, Altrusa; BPWC; Personalities of the Caribbean; W/W in World; 2000 Wom of Achmt; Others.

DELOACH, ROBERT EDGAR oc/ Corporate President; b/Jan 6, 1939; h/ 1207 West 47th Avenue, Anchorage, AK 99505; ba/Anchorage, AK; p/Ollie N DeLoach, Orlando, FL; ed/Att'd Univ of SC, AK Meth Univ, Univ of AK; pa/ Chm, AK Stagecraft Inc, 1982-83; Pres, IATSE Local 770, 1980-; Pres, B G Tax & Acctg, 1983-; Pres, B G Systems Co, 1980-; Intl Assn of Elect Inspectors, 1982-84; cp/Anchorage Commun Theatre, 1954-; Anchorage Theatre Guild, 1978-80; hon/Pub'd Poet; Num Stage Prodns.

DELONG, NANCY GLYN oc/Realtor; Writer; Designer; b/Oct 2, 1946; h/ 4779 Musket Way, Columbus, OH 43228; ba/Columbus, OH; p/Glen A (dec) and Reba Z DeLong, Columbus, OH; ed/BA, OH St Univ, 1969; pa/Exec Dir, Tri-Co Dental Hlth Coun, 1971-76; Reporter, *The Detroit News*, 1970-71; Reporter, *The Columbus Dispatch*, 1965-68; Edit Photog, Contbg Editor, *Amusement Bus*, 1968-73; Prodr, The Oz of Prev, 1971-74; Ptnr, Real to Reel, 1973-77; Pres of Proj Promotion, Glyn Prodn Ltd, 1977-79; Pres, N Glynn & Assoc Inc, 1979-83; Bus Conslt, 1976-; Interior Designer, 1976-; Assoc, Walt Peabody Ad Ser Inc; Profl Boxing Judge; St of MI; Rltr, Cent 21 Pug Pepper & Assoc; r/Cath; hon/Num Pubs; W/W of Am Wom.

DELPHIN, JACQUES MERCY oc/ Medical Doctor; b/Apr 20, 1929; h/8 Garfield Place, Poughkeepsie, NY 12601; m/Marlene M; c/Barthold, Patrick, Beverly, Miriam, Matthew, Janice; p/Alexander and Sonia Bernadin Delphin (dec); sp/Mr and Mrs Louis Harte, West Indies; ed/BS, Lycee Nat Phillipe Guerrier Col, 1949; MD, Fac of Med, Haiti, 1957; pa/Psychi Dir, Day Hosp, Hudson River Psychi Ctr, 1964-69; Psychi Dir Day Hosp 1969-74, Commr at Interim 1974, Supvg Psychi

1980-, Dutchess Co Dept of Mtl Hygiene; Med Dir, St Cabrini Home, 1974-80; Att'g Phys, St Francis Hosp, 1968-; Past Pres, Mid Hudson Br of Am Psychi Assn, 1972-73; Am Psychi Assn, 1965-; r/Cath; hon/Pub'd Poet; Commun Ldrs & Noteworthy Ams; Best Drs in Am; W/W: in NE, Among Black Ams; Men of Achmt; DIB, Intl Register of Profiles.

DEL TORO-ROBLEDO, ILIA oc/ College Professor and Coordinator of Student Teaching; b/Jul 17, 1918; h/506 Parque de las Fuentes, Hato Rey, PR 00918; ba/Rio Piedras, PR; p/Angela Robledo and Gerardo del Toro (dec); ed/ BA, Univ of PR, 1940; MA, NY Univ, 1958; pa/Elem Tchr, 1942-44; Tchr HS Social Studies, St Dept of Ed, 1944-57; Instr HS Social Studies, Col of Ed, Univ of PR, 1957-59; Supvr of Student Tchg, Dept of Curric & Tchg, 1959-70 & 1976-79; Coor, Fam Fin, 1952-69; Coor of EPDA/UR, Univ of PR; Coor of Student Tchg, Col of Ed, Univ of PR; Ofcr, External Resources Col Ed, Univ of PR, 1975-76; Nat Coun for Social Studies, 1957-82; Assn of Supvn & Curric Devel, 1959-82; Assn of Tchr Edrs, 1959-70; NEA; PR Tchrs Assn; Phi Delta Kappa, 1976-82; Delta Kappa Gamma, 1976-82; Future World Soc, 1976; Smithsonian Inst; cp/Girl Scout; Cath Daughs of Am, 1948-60; Casino de PR, 1948-60; r/Rom Cath; hon/Num Profl Pubs; Girl Scout Del to Camp Edith Macy, 1947; PDK Distg Edr Jubilee, 1981; W/W in S & SW.

DeLYNN, JANE oc/Novelist; b/Jul 18, 1946; ba/c/o Jane Rotrosen Agency, 226 East 32nd Street, New York, NY 10016; p/Wilson and Bernice DeLynn, NYC; ed/ BA, Barnard Col, 1968; MFA, Univ of IA, 1970; pa/Author; Fdg Editor, *Fiction*, Resident, MacDowell Colony, 1980; Resident, Edward F Albee Foun, 1981; Participant in Theatre: *The Monkey Opera*, 1982; *Snob's Cabaret*, 1981; *Hoosick Falls*, 1980; Book Reviewer, Kirkus Ser Inc; Dramatists Guild; BMI; PEN; cp/Rdgs of Her Wk at: Manhattan Theater Clb; Ear Inn; St Marks Ch; 3 Lives Bookstore; Franklin Furnace; Stony Brook Univ; Beyond Baroque; Folio Bookstore; Others; r/Jewish; hon/Author of 2 Novels, *In Thrall*, 1982; *Some Do*, 1978 & 1980; Author of Wks Pub'd in Anthologies incl'g: *Knock Knock*, 1981; *A True Likeness*, 1980; *The Poet's Ency*. 1979; *The Stone Wall Book of Short Fictions*, 1974; Num Short Fictions & Essays Pub'd in: *The Paris Review*; *Redbook*; *Pequod*; *Christopher Street*; *Sun*; *La-Bas*; *The World*; *Fiction*; Other Articles in: *Cosmopolitan*; *Viva*; *New Dawn*; *Crawdaddy*; *Wash Post*; *NY Herald*; Phi Beta Kappa, 1968; Book of the Mo Clb Writing F'ship, 1968; Elizabeth Janeway Prize for Writing, 1967 & 1968.

DEMAS, JEAN V oc/Attorney; b/Dec 30, 1940; h/6842 North Kostner, Lincolnwood, IL 60646; ba/Chicago, IL; m/ Emil Athineos; c/Irene L Dallianis; Thomas H Dallianis; ed/BA, NWn Univ, 1962; JD, DePaul Univ Col of Law, 1982; pa/Hist Tchr, Von Steuben HS, 1962-65; Secy-Treas, Ideal Real Est & Inst Brokerage Inc, 1965-72; VPres, Ideal Rlty Co, Realtors, 1972-79; Real Est Conslt, 1979-82; Assoc, Kois & McLaughlin, PC, 1982-; Mem: IL Bar Assn; Chgo Bar Assn; Chgo Coun of Lwyrs; Chair, Chgo Real Est Bd Sales Coun, 1980-81; Dir 1978-80, Pres

1976-77, N Suburban Chgo Land Real Est Bd; Sr Mem, Cert'd Review Appraiser (CRA), Nat Assn of Review Appraisers, 1977; Indep Fee Appraiser (IFA), Nat Assn of Indep Fee Appraisers, 1975; hon/Author, Var Articles in Profl Jours incl'g: *Real Est News Annual Forecast & Review*, 1977 & 1978; N Suburban Chgo Land Real Est Bd Coop Sales Awd, 1967, Side Real Est Bd Coop Sales Awd, 1967, 1968, 1974 & 1975; W/W: in MW, in W, of Am Wom, in Fin & Indust.

DE MEYER, JOSEPH AUGUST oc/ Clinical Director and Adjunct Professor; b/Jun 13, 1950; h/1916 Dresden Drive Southwest, Decatur, AL 35603; ba/ Decatur, AL; m/Elma; c/Robert; p/ Joseph Francois August De Meyer and Constance Maria Van Delft, The Netherlands; sp/Jacob Meijers (dec) and Geraldina Pothoven, The Netherlands; ed/Dr of Clin Psych, St Univ of Leyden, 1969-77; pa/Staff Psychol, Retreat Mtl Hosp, 1977-80; Adj Prof, Am Inst of Psychotherapy, 1981-; Clin Dir, N Ctl AL Mtl Hlth Ctr, 1980-; Am Psychol Assn, 1978-; AL Psychol Assn, 1978-; Netherlands Inst of Psychol, 1977-; hon/ Profl Pubs; Cert, AL St Lic in Psych, 1981; W/W: in S & SW, in World.

DeMILLE, LESLIE BENJAMIN oc/ Fine Artist, Portrait Painter; b/Apr 24, 1927; h/1721 Orchard Drive, Santa Ana, CA 92707; ba/Same; m/Isobel; c/ Lynn, Dan, Malcolm, Rick, Mark; p/ Warren C DeMille (dec); sp/John C Don (dec); ed/Study at: Hamilton Tech Inst; Arts Students Leag, NY; Leon Franks, Laguna Bch, CA; pa/Dir & Instr, Sem for Art Org in US, 1966-76; Fac Mem, Nat Portrait Sem, NY, 1981; Lectr & Demonstrator, NAMTA, Detroit, MI, 1983; Art Dealer, Leslie B De Mille Galleries, Laguna Bch, CA; El Prado Galleries Inc, Sedona, AZ; Mem: Exec Coun, Chm of Credentials, Com for Am Portait Soc, 1983; VPres, Dir & Exec Bd, Death Val 49er's Inc, 1984; Past Dir, Am Inst of Fine Arts; Fellow, Am Artists Prof Leag; Am Portrait Soc; Juror for Num Maj Art Shows; r/Presb; hon/ Portrait Comms incl: Ronald Reagan (Gov of CA), 1967; Pres Richard Nixon, White House, 1970; US 6th Fleet Medit 1972 & Pearl Harbor, HI 1973, Nav Combat Artist; George Barber, Pres & Chm of Bd, Anchor Hocking Co, OH, 1980; Wks in Public Collections incl: Nav Combat Art Gallery, Wash, DC; Whitter Col, CA; Death Val 49er's Inc Permanent Mus Collection; Wks Pub'd in *Wn Painting Today*; *How to Draw Cats & Kittens*; "Portraits in Pastel," PBS-TV Prog, 1981; Awds incl: Best in Show 1971, & Gold Medals 1976, 1979 & 1980, Am Artists Prof Leag, NY; Best in Show 1980, Death Val 49er's Inc; Others; Featured in *SW Art Mag*, 1981; W/W in Am Art; DIB; Contemp Wn Artists; SW Art Pub.

DE MONTEBELLO, PHILIPPE oc/ Director, The Metropolitan Museum of Art; b/May 16, 1936; h/1150 Fifth Avenue, New York, NY 10028; ba/New York, NY; m/Edith Bradford Myles; c/ Marc, Laure, Charles; p/Count Roger de Montebello, New York, NY; ed/BA cum laude, Harvard Col, 1958; MA, NY Univ, 1963; mil/AUS, 2nd Lt, 1956-58; pa/Asst Curator 1963, Assoc Curator 1968, Vice Dir Curatorial Affairs 1974, Acting Dir 1977, Dir 1978-, Metro Mus Art; Dir, Houston Mus Fine Arts,

1969-74; cp/Mem, Edit Bd, *Intl Jour Mus Mgmt & Curatorship*; Mem, Columbia Univ Adv Coun of Depts of Art & Archaeol; Mem, Assn Art Mus Dirs, Wks of Art Com; Mem, Am Assn Mus; Mem, Am Fdn Arts, Exec Com; Mem, NY Univ Inst Fine Arts, Bd Trustees; Mem, Coun Mus & Ed in Visual Arts; Mem, Skowhegan Sch Painting & Sculpture, Adv Com; hon/Author of *Peter Paul Rubens*, 1968; LLD, Lafayette Col 1979, Bard Col 1981, Iona Col 1982; W/W: World, E, Am.

DEMPSEY, JOHN PATRICK oc/ Professor; b/Oct 13, 1953; h/27 Leroy Street, Potsdam, NY 13676; ba/Potsdam, NY; m/Marsha Yvette; c/Mega Constance; p/Basil J and Elizabeth S Dempsey, Pukekohe, New Zealand; sp/ Philip and Clara Shifman, Chgo, IL; ed/ BE, 1974; PhD, 1978; pa/Res, Dept Civil Engrg, NWn Univ, 1978; Asst Prof, Dept Civil & Envir Engrg, Clarkson Univ, Potsdam, NY, 1980-; Mem: ASME; Am Soc of Civil Engrs; Soc of Industl & Applied Math; hon/Author & Co-Author Over 12 Res Articles Pub'd in Profl Jours incl'g: *Jour of Applied Mechs*; *Intl Jour of Engrg Sci*; *Intl Jour Solids Structures*; *Proceedings of 4th ASCE-EMD Spec Conf, Purdue Univ, IN*; *Jour of Elasticity*; W/W.

DEMPSEY, TERRY ALLEN oc/Chaplain (Captain), US Army; b/Aug 14, 1950; h/210 First Street, Hot Springs, AR 71913; ba/APO, New York, NY; m/ Patricia J; c/Stacey R, Ryan T; p/John T (dec) and Kathryn M Dempsey, Hot Springs, AR; sp/Everett G and Erna Vance, Tonasket, WA; ed/BA 1972, MA 1975, MA 1975, Harding Univ; PhD Cand, Univ of MS; mil/AUS, 1978-, Capt; pa/Min, Cypert Ch of Christ, 1975-76; Min, Ch of Christ of Batesville, MS, 1977-78; Brigade Chaplain, 44th Med Brigade at Ft Bragg, NC, 1978-80; Battlion Chaplain, 530th Supply & Serv Bn, 1980-81; Clin Pastoral Ed Resident, Walter Reed Army Med Ctr, 1981-82; Chaplain Ofcr Adv Course, 1982; Bn Chaplain, 1st Bn, 1st Air Def Artillery, W Germany, 1983-; Am Pers & Guid Assn, 1975-; Assn for Rel & Values Issues in Coun, 1978-; Mil Chaplains Assn, 1978-; IPA; Clin Mem, Am Assn for Marriage & Fam Therapy; Cert'd Marital & Fam Therapist, 1981-; r/Ch of Christ; hon/ Army Commend Medal, 1981; Outstg Yg Men of Am; Personalities of S; DIB; W/W: in S & SW, in E.

De NICOLA, PETER FRANCIS oc/ Certified Public Accountant; b/Oct 28, 1954; h/135 Highview Avenue, Stamford, CT 06907; ba/Wilton, CT; p/Louis J and Nancy E De Nicola, Yonkers, NY; ed/BS 1976, MBA 1978, NY Univ; pa/ Tax Acct, Main Hurdman CPAs, 1978-81; Tax Mgr, Gen Signal Corp, 1981-83; Tax Mgr, Emery Air Freight Corp, 1983-; CT Soc of CPAs; Westchester Est Planning Coun; Am Inst CPAs; NY St Soc of CPAs; Tax Execs Inst; Tax Soc of NY Univ; Am Mgmt Assn; Stamford Tax Assn; cp/NY Univ Alumni Assn, NY Univ Commerce Alumni Assn (Dir 1978-); r/Rom Cath; hon/Profl Pubs; F W Lafentz Acctg Awd; W/W: in E, in Bus, in World.

DENNIS, CHERRY NIXON oc/ Artist; Painter; Etcher; b/Sep 2; h/Route 1, Box 655, Lakeview Add, Wagoner, OK 74467; sa/12505 Summer NE,

Albuquerque, NM 87112; m/Thomas L 'Jack' (dec); p/Howard T Nixon (dec); Ida May Piersol (dec); ed/Univ of Tulsa; OK St Univ; Univ N Mexico; pa/Exhbns incl: MWn Exhib (KC, Mo), Nat Watercolor & Print Ann Oakland Art Gallery (Cal), Philbrook Art Ctr (Tulsa, OK), Nat Representational Art Ann, Thomas Gilcrease Inst (Tulsa), SWn Biennial, Mus NM (Sante Fe), Long Bch Art Ann (Cal), Others; St Reg & Nat Juried Shows; Art Instr in Etching & Drawing, Philbrook Art Ctr, 1940-41; cp/Pres, Alpha Rho Tau Art Frat; Pres & Bd Chm, Adah M Robinson Mem Fund, 1967-69; Pub Info Ofcr, Civil Air Patrol, OK Wing 1950-56; r/Christian; hon/ Cert of Apprec, Univ of Tulsa, 1968; Watercolor Awd, Philbrook Art Ctr; Graphic Awds, New Art Leag, 1972; Artist of Mo, Four Hills Gallery, 1976; Hon Life Mem, Alpha Rho Tau Art Frat, 1983; W/W in Am Art; World W/W of Wom; Others.

DENNIS, HERMAN oc/Social Worker; b/Apr 10, 1927; h/143 - 7th Street, Elizabeth, NJ 07201; p/Nathaniel Dennis, Elizabeth, NJ; ed/Att'd Manhattan Sch of Music, Rutgers Univ; mil/ Korean War, 2 Yrs; pa/USPS, 1951-79 (Retired); Union Pres, 15 Yrs; Adv Bd, Salvation Army; NAACP; Urban Leag Union Co, NJ; cp/Committeeman, 5th Ward, 3rd Dist, Elizabeth, NJ; r/Bapt; hon/Pub'd Author; Singer of Nat Anthem for Pres Harry S Truman, 1948.

DENNIS, JOHN M oc/Physician; Radiologist, Medical School Dean; b/Jan 31, 1923; h/803 Huntsman Road, Towson, MD 21204; ba/Baltimore, MD; m/ Mary Helen France; ed/BS 1943, MDD 1945, Univ of MD; pa/Phys (Radiol), Instr, Assoc Prof, Prof & Chm Dept of Radiol, Dean & VChancellor for Hlth Affairs, Univ of MD Sch of Med; VChancellor for Acad Affairs, Univ of MD-Balto; Pres, MD Radiol Soc; Chm of Bd of Chancellors, Pres, Am Col of Radiol (ACR); Trustee, Nat Bd of Med Examrs; Am Bd of Radiol, Mercy Hosp; 1st Chm, Comm on Med Discipline, St of MD; Sci Adv Bd of Conslts, Armed Forces Inst of Pathol; Trustee, Am Bd of Radiol; Chm Ad Hoc Com on Rewriting Med Pract Act, Med & Chirurgical Fac of MD; cp/Pres, MD Div, Am Cancer Soc; Bd of Mgrs, Union Meml Hosp; Bd Mem, Coun of Med Spec Socs; Liaison Com on Cont'g Med Ed; hon/ Gold Medal, Am Col of Radiol; Andrew White Medal, Loyola Col (Balto); Div Awd for Outstg Ser, Am Cancer Soc; Caldwell Medal & Caldwell Lectr, Am Roentgen Ray Soc; 1st Annual E P Pendergrass Lectr, Univ of PA; W/W in MD.

DENNIS, SHARON J oc/Social Service Administrator; b/Apr 22, 1948; h/ 4212 Charley Forest Street, Olney, MD 20832; ba/Washington, DC; m/Richard A D Jr; c/Jessica Rae, Brooke Alexis; p/ Paul F (dec) and Florence A Woolridge, Pendell, PA; sp/Richard Dennis Sr (dec) and Rae Rice, Arlington, VA; ed/BA, Col of Artesia; MA, Ball St Univ; pa/Bus Ser Rep, Mtn St Telephone, 1970-72; Field Registrar, Univ of MD, European Div, 1978-79; Asst Field Dir, ARC in W Germany, 1979-80; Asst Dir of Social Ser, ARC in Wash DC, 1981-; Am Pers & Guid Assn; BPW, Chp of Foun, 1983-84; Nat Assn of Female Execs;

Montgomery Co Commun Mtl Hlth Ctr Adv Bd, V Chp, 1982-; hon/Pres Scholar, 1966-70; Magna cum laude, 1970; Best Supporting Actress, 1970; Top Student in Fine Arts, 1969; Loaned Exec U Way Fall 1983 Campaign; W/W in E.

DENOMMÉ, ROBERT T oc/Professor and Department Chairman; b/May 17, 1930; h/119 Cameron Lane, Charlottesville, VA 22903; ba/Charlottesville, VA; p/George E Denommé Sr and Sarah Richards (dec); ed/AB, Assumption Col, 1952; MA, Boston Univ, 1953; Grad Dipl, Sorbonne, Univ of Paris; PhD, Columbia Univ, 1962; mil/AUS, Signal Corps, Army Security Agy; pa/ Instr French 1960-62, Asst Prof 1962-64, Assoc Prof 1966-70, Prof French 1970-, Dept Chm 1977-, Univ of VA; Asst Prof French, Univ of Chgo, 1964-66; Vis'g Prof French, Univ of Orléans, France, 1978; Mem: Am Assn of Tchrs of French, 1962-; Exec Com 1970-73, Mem 1962-, MLA; Assn Intérnationale des Etudes Francaises, Paris; r/Rom Cath; hon/Author of 4 Books: *Le Conte de Lisle*, 1973; *French Parnassian Poets*, 1972; *19th Cent French Romantic Poets*, 1969; *The Naturalism of Gustave Geffroy*, 1963; Fulbright S'ship, France, 1959; Phi Sigma Iota, 1980; Intl W/W in Poetry; Dir of Am Scholars.

DENTON, CAROL FORSBERG oc/ Training Systems Analyst; b/Mar 5, 1937; h/4222-B Lake Underhill, Orlando, FL 32803; ba/Orlando, FL; m/ Earle L; c/Susan Elizabeth, Kathleen Ann; p/Algot and Isabelle Forsberg (dec); sp/Earle and Merle Denton (dec); ed/BS, Univ of OK, 1959; MAT, Rollins Col, 1970; pa/Cnslr, Univ of OK, 1959; Tchr, Lee Co FL, 1960-61; Cnslr, Univ of FL, 1961-62; Tchr, Seminole Co FL, 1965-69; Tng Sys Anal, Nav Tng Equip Ctr, 1969-; Sigma Xi Resa; cp/Altrusa Clb of Winter Pk, Pres 1978-80 & 1982; Orlando Mayor's Com on Human Relats; Human Factors Soc, Pres 1977; Mid-FL Sailing Clb, Commodore 1980-; r/Presb; hon/Num Profl Pubs; Letseizer Awd, Univ of OK, 1959; Kappa Delta Pi, 1969; Outstg Perf Ratings, 1974, 1980, 1982; W/W: of Am Wom, in S & SW, in Am Cols & Univs.

DENTON, EARLE LEWIS oc/Senior Systems Analyst; b/Mar 16, 1930; h/ 4222-B Lake Underhill Road, Orlando, FL 32803; ba/Orlando, FL; m/Carol Forsberg; c/Susan Elizabeth, Kathleen Ann; p/Earle W and Merle L Denton (dec); sp/Algot and Isabelle Forsberg (dec); ed/BS, USA Command & Gen Staff Col, 1969; MBA, AUS Mgmt Engrg Agy, 1975; mil/AUS, Lt Col; pa/ AUS, Lt Col (Ret), 1952-73; Pres, E L Denton Conslts Inc, 1974-78; Pres & CEO, Tng Technol Inc, 1979-; SOLE; IEEE; Alpha Kappa Psi; Sigma Xi; SAM; Life Mem, Mil Order of Purple Heart; DAV; TROA; AUSA; ADPA; US Cong Adv Bd; V Chm, EEO Com, 1972; cp/ Citrus Clb of Orlando; Rio Pinar Country Clb; Sustaining Mem, Repub Nat Com; r/Presb; hon/Profl Pubs; KY Col, 1973; Hon St Trooper of AL, 1969; Hon Citizen of WV, 1964; Pres Achmt Awd, 1982; Silver Star, 1953; Legion of Merit, 1967 & 1973; 4 Air Medals, 1967; 2 Combat Int Badges; W/W: in S & SW, in Aviation & Aerospace.

DENTON, ROBERT WEBSTER oc/ Physician and Surgeon; b/Dec 2, 1922; h/687 Keough St, Bishop, CA 93514; ba/

Bishop, CA; m/Betty Spaeth; c/Susan D Jensen, William R, Margaret D Brewer; p/William and Vivian Denton (dec); sp/ Edwin and Margaret Spaeth (dec); ed/ Pre-Med, Pnoma Col, Claremont, CA; MS, NWn Univ, 1947; MD, NWn Univ Med Sch, 1947; PhD, Univ of IL, 1950; Intern, Cook Co Hosp, Chgo, 1947; mil/ MAC, US, 1942-46; pa/Phys & Surg, Univ of LIL Sch of MD, 1947-50; Gen Med Pract, Bishop, CA, 1950-; Affil'd w No Inyo Hosp, Bishop, CA, 1950-; Vols in Mission Med Pract, India, Taiwan, Egypt & Nepal, 1976-80; Mem: Bd of Trustees 1969-78, Chief of Staff 1960, No Inyo Hosp, Bishop, CA; Secy & Pres Inyo-Mono Co Med Soc, CA, 1950-60; Med Instr, Fam Pract Preceptor Prog, Univ of CA Sch of Med-Davis, 1975-82; Am Assn of Fam Pract; Am Field Ser Sponsor; cp/Over 30 Yrs: Mason; Lions Clb; Toastmasters Clb; Elder, Bishop Presb Ch; r/Presb; hon/ Author of Num Sci Res Articles in Jours incl'g: *Jour of Applied Physiol*; Others & Pubs of NW Inst of Med Res, Univ of IL; Sigma Xi, 1948.

DENYES, JAMES RICHARD oc/ Industrial Engineer; b/Oct 9, 1948; h/ 1241 Kingsway Drive, Chesapeake, VA 23320; ba/Norfolk, VA; m/Mary Garcin; c/Amy Cheryne, Laura Michelle; p/ Heyward T and Rosalie Denyes, Virginia Bch, VA; sp/Raymon (dec) and Mildred Garcin, Chesapeake, VA; ed/ BS, VA Tech, 1970; pa/Indust Engr, Prodn Control Engr, Distbn Foreman, Allied Chem Corp, 1970-72; QC Engr, Duke Contrn Co, 1972-75; Command Indust Engr, Staff Indust Engr, Hd Mgmt Engrg Dept, Nav Manpower & Mat Anal Ctr, 1975-; Pres, SEn VA Chapt, AIIE, 1980-81, Bd of Dirs, 1977-; cp/Financial Advr, NOW, 1975-76; St Treas 1977-79, Bd of Dirs 1979-80, VA Org to Keep Abortion Legal; Pres, B M Wms PTA, 1982-83; Mem, Standards of Quality Planning Coun, Chesapeake Public Schs, 1982-84; Bd of Trustees, The Improvement Inst, 1982-85; Phi Delta Epsilon, 1968-70; r/Meth; hon/ Outstg Yg Men of Am; W/W in S & SW.

DERAMUS, WILLIAM NEAL III oc/ Executive; b/Dec 10, 1915; h/37 Le Mans Court, Prairie Village, KS 66208; ba/ Kansas City, MO; m/Patricia Howell Watson; c/Patricia Nicholas Fogel, William Neal IV, Jean Watson Wagner, Jill Watson Dean; p/William Neal Deramus II (dec); Lucille Ione (Nicholas) Deramus; sp/Philip Jay and Mildred Watson (dec); ed/AB, Univ of MI, 1936; LLB, Harvard Univ, 1939; mil/Mil Railway Ser, Trans Corps, Maj; pa/ Trans Apprentice, Wabash RR, St Louis, 1939-41; Asst Trainmaster, Wabash RR, 1941-43; Asst to Gen Mgr, Kansas City So Rwy, KC, 1946-48; Asst to Pres 1948, Pres & Dir 1949-57, Chm Exec Com 1954-57, Gt Wn Rwy Co, Chgo; Pres & Dir, MO-KA-TX RR Co, 1957-61; Pres & Dir 1961-66, Pres & Chm 1966-73, Chm of Bd & CEO 1973-81, KC So Rwy; Pres & Dir 1961-66, Pres & Chm 1966-74, Chm of Bd 1974-81, LA & AR Rwy; Pres & Chm 1966-71, Chm & CEO 1971-81, Chm 971-, KC So Industs Inc; Chm 1960-73, Chm Exec Co 1973-80, Mapco Inc, Tulsa, OK; Mem: Bd of Trustees, Former Chm of Bd, KC Art Inst; Hon Dir, Rockhurst Col; VPres, Starlight

Theater Assn; Former Chm, MW Res Inst; Former Pres, Downtown Inc; cp/ Hon Dir, Former Pres, KC Crime Comm; Civic Coun; Bd of Govs, Am Royal; Chm, Perf'g Arts Foun; Gen Chm Fund Campaign, Jr Achmt, 1982; Bd, Friends of the Zoo; Adv Bd, Heart of Am Coun, BSA; r/Prot; hon/Man of Yr, MO C of C, 1979; W/W: in Am, in World, in Railroading.

DERGALIS, GEORGE oc/Artist; Lecturer; Teacher; b/Aug 31, 1928; h/ 72 Oxbow Road, Wayland, MA 01778; ba/Same; m/Margaret; c/Alexis; p/ Demetri and Zinaida Dergalis (dec); sp/ James and Florence Murphey, Oreland, PA; ed/MFA, Accademia delle Belle Arti, 1951; MA, Mus Sch of Fine Arts, 1959; mil/USAF, 1951-55, Hon Discharge; pa/ Artist-Lectr, Mus Sch of Fine Arts, 1961-69; Fac Mem, De Cordova Mus, 1961-; Tchr, Priv Studio, 1969-; Chm Curator of Several Exhibs; VP, Art Chm, Copley Soc of Boston, 1977-78; Lectr, Helicon, Harvard Univ, 1981; cp/ Pres, Alumni Assn, Mus Sch of Fine Arts, 1966-67; Hon Dir, Boston Ballet, 1971; r/Orthodox; hon/Pub'd Author; Bronze Medal for Excell, Prix de Rome, 1951; Boit 1st Prize, 1st Prize Collaborative Design, 1959; James Wm Paige Traveling S'ship, 1959-61; Civilian Merit Awd, 1969; Gold Medal, Accademis Italia delle Arti; Artist-in-Residence, Ptnrs of Ams, 1979; W/W: in E, in Am Art; DIB; Dir of Contemp Prints.

DERICK, DOROTHY BOSK oc/ Executive; b/Apr 29, 1943; h/Evanston, IL; ba/Chicago, IL; p/Clifford Lambie Derick (dec); Dorothy Edith Bosk Derick, N Newton, MA; ed/AB, Mt Holyoke Col, 1965; SM, MIT, 1981; Grad, Nat Grad Trust Sch, NWn Univ, 1976; Cert'd, NEn Univ & Boston Soc of Security Anals, 1971; pa/VPres, The No Trust Co, Chgo, 1982-; Secy 1965-67, Asst Probate Spec 1967-68, Mgmt Trainee 1968-70, Asst Trust Ofcr 1970-74, Trust Ofcr 1974-79, Sr Trust Ofcr & Unit Hd 1979-82, Shawmut Bk of Boston, NA; Mem: Dir, Nat Assn of Bk Wom Inc (NABW), 1978-79; VChm 1978-79 & Trustee 1977-78, NABW Ednl Foun; Clk & Dir, Fabtron Corp, Waltham, MA, 1973-; Intl Soc of Preretirement Planners; The Nat Coun on Aging Inc; Assn of Chgo Bk Wom; The Art Inst of Chgo; cp/Bd of Dirs 1982-, Other Positions, St Chgo Area Com for UNICEF; Trustee 1978-83, Num Other Coms & Positions 1978-, Mt Holyoke Col; Mt Holyoke Clb of Chgo; MIT Clb of Chgo; MIT Fac Clb, Boston, MA; Vestry & Other Coms, Trinity Epis Ch, 1975-82; Bd of Dirs, Metro Chgo Coalition on Aging, 1983-; City of Evanston Comm on Aging, 1983-; Chgo Coun on Fgn Relats; r/Epis; hon/Alfred P Sloan Fellow, 1980-81; 1st Wom to Chair Fin Com, Bd of Trustees, Mt Holyoke Col; Nat Assn of Bk Wom, N Eng Reg S'ship, 1974; W/W: in E, of Am Wom, in Fin & Indust.

DeROSA, ALFONSO MICHAEL oc/ Executive; b/Mar 31, 1943; h/3515 T Street, Northwest, Washington, DC 20007; ba/Washington, DC; c/Christina Beth, Lisa Anne, Michael Andrew, Mathew John; p/Salvatore and Julia DeRosa, Neptune, NJ; ed/BSBA, Georgetown Univ, 1964; MBA, Am Univ, 1966; pa/Acct Exec, Reynolds & Co,

Wash DC; Nat Sales Developer, NYC, 1969-70; Mgr, Reg Instl Dept, Wash DC; VPres, Resident Mgr, Hayden Stone, Wash DC, 1971-73; VPres Resident Mgr, Hornblower, Weeks Hemphill, Noyes (merged w Shearson Loeb Rhoades), Wash DC, 1973; VPres, Shearson/Am Express, 1980; cp/Bond Clb of Wash; Pres, Bd of Govs, Georgetown Univ Alumni Coun; Lay Adv Com, Ctr for Applied Res in the Apostolate; r/Rom Cath; hon/W/W: in E, in Bus & Fin.

D'ERRICO, ALBERT P JR oc/Psychological Consultant; b/Feb 27, 1941; h/ 157 Lake Forest Drive, Elberton, GA 30638; ba/Elberton, GA; m/Alice W White; p/Albert D'Errico, Dallas, TX; ed/AB, 1965; MA, 1968; PhD, 1976; MDiv, 1982; DMin, 1983; pa/Consltg Psychol, 1980-; Adj Prof, Rice Sem, 1981-; Diagnostic Admr, Shelby Co Sheriff's Dept, 1976-80; Psychol, NE LA Univ, 1974-76; St Metric Coor, US Metric Assn, 1983; Mem: Am Psychol Assn; US Metric Assn; cp/Smithsonian Instn; hon/Author of "The Relat'ship Among Conserv, Achmt & Intell in Concrete Operl Chd," 1976; "On The St of Inerrancy," 1982; W/W in Frontier Sci & Technol.

DERRY, MICHAEL L oc/Management Consultant; b/Jul 7, 1949; h/6480 Westmoor, Birmingham, MI 48010; ba/ Farmington Hills, MI; m/Margaret L Sowers; p/Charles L and Samuella D Derry; sp/Raliegh and Elanor Sowers; ed/BA, No MI Univ, 1972; pa/Chm of Bd, M L Derry & Assoc Inc, 1973-; Chm of Bd, Inf Mgmt Corp, 1978-; Am Mgmt Assn; Pres Assn; hon/Profl Pubs; W/W in Fin & Indust.

DESAI, SURESH AMBELAL oc/College Dean; b/Oct 29, 1933; h/101 Osborne Street, Glen Ridge, NJ 07028; ba/Upper Montclair, NJ; m/Rambha S; c/Nirjari, Niraj; p/Ambela and Gajaraben Desai (dec); sp/Navinchandra and Indumati Daulatjada (dec); ed/BA 1954, MA 1956, LLB 1957, PhD 1960, Gujarat Univ, India; MA 1963, PhD 1968, Univ of CA-LA; pa/Dean Sch of Bus Adm 1981-, Chm & Prof Ec 1973-81, Montclair St Col; Assoc Prof Ec, Hanover Col, 1967-73; Asst Prof Ec, M T B Col, Surat, India, 1956-62; Mem: Chp 1981-85, Prog Com Chm 1974-81, Assn of Indian Ec Studies; Orgr & Participant, Num Orgl Confs; r/Hinduism; hon/Author, Co-Author & Editor, Over 14 Books; Num Articles in Area of Ec Devel, Gandhian Ec, Ec in Higher Ed & Public Fin Pub'd in Profl Jours.

DESAI, VEENA BALVANTRAI oc/ Obstetrician & Gynecologyst; b/Oct 5, 1931; h/12 Harborview Drive, Rural Free Delivery #1, Portsmouth, NH 03801; ba/Portsmouth, NH; m/Gandevia Vinay; c/Vijay Vinay Gandevia; p/ Balvantrai P Desai (dec); S B Desai, Bombay, India; ed/MBBS; MD; MRCOG; FACOG; DABOG; FACS; FICS; Hon PhD, World Univ; Dipl, Am Bd Ob & Gyn; Fellow, Am Soc Colposcopy & Cervical Pathol; pa/Att'd Ob & Gyn, Portsmouth Hosp; Courtesy Staff Ob & Gyn, Exeter Hosp; Courtesy Staff Ob & Gyn, Wentworth Douglas Hosp, Dover, NH; Pres, Desai Profl Assn; Mem: NH Med Soc; Portsmouth Med Soc; Am Med Wom's Assn; Nat Soc Lit & Art; Brit Med Assn; B'ham & Midlands Ob & Gyn Soc, UK; IPA; cp/Chm's

Advr, US Congl Adv Bd; Nat Repub Cogl Com, 1981-83; Charter Mem, Pres Task Force, 1983; r/Hindu; hon/Author & Contbr of Articles to Profl Jours; Medal of Merit, Pres Ronald Reagan, 1982; Open Merit Scholar, 1952-57; Phys's Recog Awd, AMA, 1977; Cert of Cont'g Profl Devel, Am Col Ob & Gyn, 1977 & 1979; Others; W/W: of Wom, in Am Wom, of Intells; Intl Register of Profiles; Other Biogl Listings.

DE SANTI, ROGER JOSEPH oc/ Professor; b/Apr 30, 1950; h/PO Box 823, New Orleans, LA 70148; ba/New Orleans, LA; p/Vincent E and Anita J De Santi, Bklyn, NY; ed/BA, St Francis Col, 1972; MEd, Boston Univ, 1973; EdD, IN Univ, 1976; pa/Clin & Asst to Dir, Eden-Baychester Lng Ctr, 1971-72; Clin & Tm Tchg Mem, Horace Man Sch for Deaf, 1972-73; Clin, Boston Univ Spch & Hearing Clin, 1972-73; Res Asst in Spec Ed, Boston Univ, 1972-73; Supvr of Sum Rdg Prog, Monroe Co Sch Corp, 1974; Res Asst in Rdg Ed, IN Univ, 1973-75; Asst Editor *Jour of Rdg Behavior*, IN Univ, 1975-76; Asst Prof Ed 1976-79, Assoc Prof Ed 1979-, Coor of Grad Progs 1979-, Acting Chm Dept of Curric & Instrn 1980, Univ of NO; Am Rdg Forum; Coun for Exceptl Chd; IRA; Nat Rdg Conf; Phi Delta Kapp; Assn of LA Col Tchrs of Rdg; LA Rdg Assn; LA Tchrs Assn; Jefferson Parish Coun of IRA; Orleans Parish Coun of IRA; r/Christian; hon/Num Profl Pubs; Eagle Scout, BSA, 1968; Recip, Lttr of Merit, Pres Lyndon B Johnson, 1968; Vigil Honor, Order of Arrow, BSA, 1970; Cert of Apprec, IRA, 1981; Cert of Apprec, Jefferson Parish Coun of IRA, 1982; W/W in S & SW; Outstg Yg Men of Am.

DESER, STANLEY oc/Professor of Physics; b/Mar 19, 1931; ba/Department of Physics, Brandeis University, Waltham, MA 02254; ed/PhD, 1953; pa/ Ancell Prof of Physics, Brandeis Univ; Mem: Fellow, Am Physicis Soc; Am Acad of Arts & Scis; hon/Author of Num Articles & Papers in Sci Pubs; Hon ScD, Stockholm Univ Cent, 1978; W/ W; Num Other Biogl Listings.

DESOMOGYI, AILEEN ADA oc/ Librarian (Retired); b/Nov 26, 1921; h/ 9 Bonnie Brae Boulevard, Toronto, Ontario, Canada M4J 4N3; m/(dec); p/ Harry Alfred and Ada Amelia Taylor (dec); ed/BA 1941, MA 1943, London; ALA of Brit Lib Assn, 1946; MLS, UWO, 1971; Cert of Proficiency in Archive Mgmt, Carleton Univ, 1969; Dipl in Computer Programming, Career Lng Ctr, Toronto, 1980; mil/WRAC, 1955-56; pa/Libn in Spec & Public Libs, 1943-66; St Instr in Eng, Nat Coal Bd, 1956-57; Libn, Lawson Meml Lib, UWO, 1966-71; Cataloguer, Nat Book Ctr, 1971; Staff Mem, E York, Ontario, Public Lib, 1971-74; Libn, Man 8 Info Servs Lib, Ontario Min of Govt Ser, 1974-78; Libn, Sperry Univac Toronto Ctl Lib, 1980-81; Am Lib Assn; cp/Secy, London Br, Ontario Geneal Soc, 1967-71; E York Hist Soc; hon/Profl Pubs; DIB; W/W: of Am Wom, in Commonwlth, in Lib & Inf Sers, in Commun Ser, of Intells; Contemp Personalities; Am Cath W/W; Men & Wom of Distn; 2000 Notable Ams; Dir of Dist'd Ams.

DES RIOUX, DEENA V oc/Exhibiting

Artist/Acrylic Paint on Canvas; b/Dec 7, 1941; h/251 West 19th Street, New York, NY 10011; ba/New York, NY; m/ Philippe R des Rioux de Messimy; p/Sam and Sophina G Coty, Rockport, MA; sp/ France and Antoine des Rioux de Messimy, La Colle Sur Loup, France; ed/ Figure Drawing, Ecole de la Grande Chaumiere, Paris, 1961; Att'd RI Sch of Design, 1959-1962; Att'd Brown Univ, 1961-62; Att'd La Sorbonne, Paris, 1961 & 1963; pa/Fdr & Dir, Seven at Large, A Diverse Media Artists' Collaborative, 1975-; Exhibns Coor, N Eng & NYC, 1973-; Lectr, Harvard Grad Sch of Design, Cambridge MA, 1976; Package Designer, Fed Distillers Inc, Cambridge, MA, 1966-70; Public Relats Coor 1982-, Exhibns Coor 1981-82, Assn of Artist-Run Galleries, AARG Inc, NYC; Alumni Coun Rep, RI Sch of Design, 1976-80; Exhbns Coor, Wom Exhibiting in Boston (WEB), MA, 1973-75; Exhbns Coor, Boston Visual Artists Union (BVAU), MA, 1974; hon/Collector's Choice-Selections by Ethel Scull, Exhbn, Soho/NYC, 1983; Featured in *Patriot Ledger*, Qunicy, MA, 1978; Critic's Choice in *Boston Globe*, 1975 & 1978; Reviewed in *Christian Sci Monitor*, 1978; Recip, Funding for Exhbn at Boston's Mus of Sci, Boston, MA, 1977-78; Recip, Partial Funding for Exhbn at Art Inst of Boston, 1975; Painting Awd, Cambridge Art Assn, MA, 1973; S'ship, RI Sch of Design, Providence, 1959-61; W/ W: in Am Art, of Am Wom; Am Artists of Renown; DIB; Other Biogl Listings.

DETJEN, GUSTAV H D JR oc/Editor and Publisher; b/Jan 20, 1905; h/154 Laguna Court, St Augustine Shores, FL 32086; m/Marion Louise Kirby; c/ Christine (Mrs Wm H Westendorf), Theodore G, James Y, Louise Harriet (Mrs Thomas Agne); ed/Att'd Pace Col; pa/Treas, Jay Dreher Corp, NYC, 1930-38; Pres, Detjen Corp, Clinton Corners, NY 1938-80; Editor, *The Philatelic Jour*, 1971-; Life Mem, AAAS; Life Mem, NY Acad of Sci; Life Mem, CCNY Soc of Philaticians; F D Rooosevelt Philatelic Soc; Am Philatelic Soc; Am Topical Assn; Editor, *Fireside Chats*; Editor, *JAPOS Bltn*; Pub's in *Philatelic Dir*; Var Other Pubs; W/W.

DEUTSCH, HAROLD CHARLES oc/ Professor; b/Jun 7, 1904; h/1801 Ridgeview Drive, Carlisle, PA 17013; ba/ Carlisle Barracks, PA; m/Marie Frey; c/ Janet, Dorothy, Harold Jr; p/Herman Deutsch (dec); sp/Julia Wettendorf (dec); ed/AB 1924, MA 1925, Univ of WI; MA 1927, PhD 1929, Harvard Univ; pa/Prof Hist, Univ of MN, 1929-72; Ofc of Strategic Sers, 1943-45; Chief of Polit Sub-Div, Europe, Africa, Mid E, Nat War Col, 1948, 1950 & 1972-74; Dir of Studies for Wn Europe, Prof of Mil Hist, US Army War Col, 1972-; Mem: Nat Pres, Phi Alpha Theta, 1941-45; Bd Mem, US Comm on Mil Hist; Chm, Com on Atl Studies, 1970-76; Am Hist Assn; Acad of Indep Scholars; Am Mil Inst; Inter-Univ Sem on Armed Forces & Soc; Other Coms; hon/Author, *Genesis of Napoleonic Imperialism*; *The Conspiracy Agnst Hitler in the Twilight War*; *Lttrs & Diaries of Helmut Groscurth*; *Hitler & His Gens*; *The Hidden Crisis of Jan-Jun 1938*; Other Pubs; Medal of Freedom, 1946; Recip, 2 Fulbright F'ships; Recip of 5 Other F'ships & Var Tchg Awds; W/W in E; Dic of Am Scholars.

DEUTSCH, NINA oc/Musicician; b/ Mar 15; h/410 Hazlitt Avenue, Leonia, NJ 07605; ba/New York, NY; p/Dr and Mrs Irvin Deutsch, NY; ed/BS, Juilliard; MMA, Yale Univ, 1973; pa/Recording Artist, Vox Prodns; Music Conslt, Joe Franklin Show, WOR-TV, 1975-; Exec VP, Intl Symph; Music Critics Assn; Publicity Clb; cp/Bd of Dirs, Metzner Foun for Overseas Relief; Ft Lee Coor Channel 13, 1974; hon/Profl Pubs; NEA Grantee, 1977; 1st Am Invited to People's Rep of China to Perf Am Music for Peace; Tanglewood Fellow, 1966; Recip Awd, Am Music Nat Fdn Music Clbs, 1975; Oberlin Col Scholar; W/W: of Am Wom, in E; DIB.

DEVANEY, JOSEPH JAMES oc/ Physicist; b/Apr 29, 1924; h/4792 Sandia Drive, Los Alamos, NM 87544; ba/Los Alamos, NM; m/Marjorie Ann; c/Kathleen Ann; p/Joseph and Madeline Devaney (dec); sp/Adele and Hume Jones, Williams, CA; ed/Att'd TX Tech Univ, 1943-44; Att'd US Coast Guard Acad, 1944-45; SB 1947, PhD 1950, MIT; mil/AUS, 1942-44; USCG, 1944-45; pa/Res Asst, MIT, 1942, 1946 & 1947; Staff Physicist, Los Alamos Nat Lab, 1950-; Adj Prof Math 1956-59, Adj Prof Physics 1959-70, Univ of NM; Mem: Sigma Xi; Am Phy Soc; Gov's Adv Bd on Air & Water Pollution, 1969-70; Co & St Ctl Com, 1953-71; Co-Fdr & 1st Pres, Anti-Smog Fdn, 1967-; Nat Patrolman, Nat Ski Patrol, 1953-79; cp/ Los Alamos Ski Patrol Ldr, 1962-63; Fdr & 1st Pres, Los Alamos Aero Assn, 1964-; Water Safety/1st Aid Instr, ARC, 1952-79; hon/Author of Num Articles on Nulcear Physics, Laser Fusion, Particle Transport, Air Pollution; Recip S'ships, MIT, 1941, 1942, 1945, 1946 & 1947; AEC Fellow, 1947-50; W/W: in W, in Technol Today, in Frontier Sci & Technol, in Lasers & Quantum Elects, in Govt; Am Men & Wom of Sci; DIB.

DEVEAU, ROGER JOSEPH oc/Professor, Consultant; b/May 14, 1943; h/ 5 Sisson Brook Lane, Westport, MA 02790; ba/North Dartmouth, MA; m/ Jeanine; c/David, Jennifer, Andrea, Laura, Amy; p/Norman Deveau, Westport, MA; Idola Mella, Danielson, CT; sp/Loretta Miller, Fall River, MA; ed/ BS, SEn MA Univ, 1965; MBA, TX A&M Univ, 1967; DEd, Boston Univ, 1976; mil/AUS, 1968-70, Spec 5; pa/ Asoc Prof, SEn MA Univ, 1970-; Master Lectr, Boston Univ, 1977-84; Conslt, Saluti Assocs, 1979-84; Instr/Conslt, Kinyon-Campbell Bus Sch, 1981-84; Vis'g Lectr, Providence Col, 1983-84; Mem: Assn for Sys Mgmt, 1980-; Delta Pi Epsilon, 1974-; AAUP; MA Fdn of Tchrs; cp/Ch Coun, Our Lady of Grace Ch, Westport, MA, 1980-82; r/Cath; hon/Author of "Ec Outlook," in *The Outlook in MA*, 1983; Author of Other Articles & a Career Planning Wkshop.

DE VECCHIO, LOIS LINDLEY oc/ ANC Commissioner of DC; b/Aug 5, 1914; h/4841 Rodman Street, Northwest, Washington, DC 20016; m/Col R G De Vecchio (dec); c/R Lindley, Warren Jahue; p/Philomena and David Jahue De Vecchio (dec); sp/Amelia and A P De Vecchio (dec); ed/BA, Fresno St Univ, 1935; Att'd Student Art Inst, Sophia Univ; Fashion Conslt, Vogue of CA, 1936-40; Freelance Interior Designer, 1960-62; Property Mgr, Shapiro & Dreyfuss Co, 1970-74; Lectr, Demonstrator, Ikebana Cart of Japanese Flower Asso, 1958-; Chm Commr, ANC of Wash DC, 1977-; Pres, Potomac Repub Clb; VChm, DC Repub Ctl Com, 1980-; Repub Cand for DC Coun, 1982; Fdg Mem, Ikebana Intl, 1956; Pres, II, DC Chapt, 1962-64; Co-Fdr of Overseas Sch of Rome, Pres 1947-49; Co-Fdr of Armed Forces Hostess Assn, 1949; Past Pres, VA Wives Clb, 1966-68; Pres, Many Ser Wives Clbs; r/Cath; hon/Profl Pubs; W/W: of Am Wom, in Am Polits.

DEVENING, R RANDOLPH oc/Executive; b/Mar 8, 1942; h/6921 Avondale Court, Oklahoma City, OK 73116; ba/Oklahoma City, OK; m/Susan Willis; c/Jennifer McQueen, Brian Willis, Jason Bolen; p/John I Bolen, Pasadena, CA; sp/Mr and Mrs R E Willis, Delray Beach, FL; ed/AB Intl Relats, Stanford Univ, 1963; MBA, Harvard Univ, 1966; pa/Price Waterhouse & Co, 1963-64; Applied Power Industs Inc, 1966-67; Dir Distbn, Planning & Res 1969-74, Joseph Schlitz Brewing Co; Controller, Fairmont Foods Co, Omaha, NE, 1970-72; Exec VPres, Treas, Ponderosa Sys Inc, Dayton, OH, 1972-74; VPres Fin, Wilson Foods Co, OKC, 1975-79; Exec VPres Fin & Adm, Dir, Fleming Cos Inc, OKC, 1979-; Mem: Adv Dir, Arkwright Boston Ins Co; Fin Exec Inst; cp/Trustee, Casady Sch; Trustee, Ballet OK; W/W: in Am, in SW.

DEVEREUX, WILLIAM P oc/Aerospace Engineering Manager; b/Mar 21, 1923; h/805 Agate Street, Broomfield, CO 80020; ba/Boulder, CO; m/Theodora Anna Desider; c/Lawrence Michael; p/William T Devereux (dec); Mary C Devereux, Bronx, NY; sp/Frank Desider (dec); Marie Desider, Brick Twp, NJ; ed/AB 1946, PhL 1947, Woodstock Col; pa/Tech Tng Engr, Bell Aircraft Corp, Buffalo, NY, 1952-56; Physicist, Farrand Optical Co, Bronx, NY, 1956-59; Physicist, Gen Dynamics/Elect Boat, Groton, CT, 1960-62; Prin Engr, Kollsman Instrument Corp, Syosset, NY, 1962-71; Sr Engr 1971-, Engrg Mgr 1980-, Ball Aerospace Sys Div; Mem: Soc of Photo-optical Instrumentation Engrs (SPIE), 1981-; Optical Soc of Am, 1961-; Dir Rocky Mtn Sect, Optical Soc of Am, 1983-; r/Rom Cath; hon/Author & Co-Author, Over 5 Tech Papers Pub'd in Profl Jours; 4 Papers at Tech Soc Meetings; Holder of 2 Patents on Optical Inventions.

DEVINE, FRANK J oc/Executive Director; b/Jun 30, 1922; h/The Pierre, Apartment 3-I, 185 Prospect Avenue, Hackensack, NJ 07601; ba/New York, NY; m/Barbara Ryan; c/Margaret Rose, Frank J III, Penelope Anne; p/Mr and Mrs Frank J Devine (dec); sp/Mr and Mrs Edward B Ryan (dec); ed/BA, Bus Adm; Addit Study, 1 Yr Study in Intl Ec; 1 Yr Study in Politico-Mil Sci, Nat Air War Col; mil/AUS, 1943-46; pa/US Fgn Ser Ofcr, 1948-77; US Ambassador, El Salvador, 1977-80; Exec Dir, Brazilian-Am C of C, 1981-; Mem: Am Fgn Ser Assn; Sigma Xi; Nat War Col Alumni Assn; r/Rom Cath; hon/Author of Book, *El Salvador: Embassy Under Attack*, 1981; Hons from Govts of Dominican Repub & El Salvador; W/W in Am.

DEVINS, LINDA CLARIECE oc/Professional Artist; b/Sep 23, 1940; h/Route 1, Box 42 E, Mary Esther, FL 32569; ba/Mary Esther, FL; m/Michael Shannon; c/Candace Lynn; p/Louis and Bennie Bestland, Mary Esther, FL; sp/Lucille Devins, Plattsburg, NY; ed/Att'd Plattsburg St Univ; pa/Instr Art Wkshops, SEn & En Seabord, 1971-75; Illus, Editor, USAF, 1972-75; Owner, Art Gallery, 1975-76; Art Dir, City of Ft Walton Bch, FL, 1976-81; Art Show Juror; Conslt; Interior Decorator; Nat Soc of Painters in Casien & Acrylics, 1979-; Nat Leag of Am Penwom (Arts Div), 1979-; Nat Assn of St Art Agys, 1980-; Co-Chm, Sn Artist Coalition, 1979-83; Bd of Dirs, Co Artists & Craftsmen Co-Op, Charter Mem 1978-81; Bd of Dirs & Fdr, "The Artisan" a Co-Op Store; Bd Ofcr, FL Fine Arts Guild, 1973-75; Okaloosa Symph; Stagecrafters; Ft Walton Bch C of C; r/Prot; hon/Comm Wk for Several Well Known People; Wks in Collections; Artist USA; W/W in S & SW.

DeVITO, ALBERT KENNETH oc/Musician, Composer, Editor/Publisher; b/Jan 17, 1919; h/361 Pin Oak Lane, Westbury, NY 11590; ba/Westbury, NY; m/Irene Scally; p/Ralph and Rose (Abronze) DeVito (dec); ed/Att'd Hartford Fed Col, 1939-41; Att'd Columbia Univ, 1950-52; BS 1948, MA 1950, NY Univ; PhD, MWn Univ, 1975; Hon MusD, E NE Christian Col, 1974; mil/AUS, 1942-46, Spec Sers; pa/Mgr, G Schirmer Inc, NYC, 1948-52; Instr, Westbury Public Schs, 1952-55; Author, 11 Chord & Instrn Music Books; Composer: Piano Sonata, Over 15 Chorals, 5 Organ Solos, Over 55 Piano Solos, 2 Vocal Solos, 2 Pop Songs; Author of Instrn Books incl'g: 12 for Chord Organs; 5 Organ Methods Books; 5 Piano Method Books; 1 Music Terms Dic; 2 Piano Arrangements; Compiler of Orig Wks incl'g: 16 Collections for Organ; 11 Collections for Piano; Contbr, Piano Arrangements for Sch Music Instrn Book Series; Lectr & Conslt in Field; Mem: Intl Platform Assn; Inter-contl Biog Assn; Am Choral Dirs Assn; Am Music Ctr; NY St Music Tchr Assn; ASCAP; Screen-Actors Guild; AFTRA; Dramatists Guild; Nat Acad TV Arts & Scis; Assn Musicians Gtr NY; Assn Music Tchrs Leag; MENC; Intl Assn Organ Tchrs; Phi Mu Alpha Sinfonic; Pres, Hon Mem, Piano Tchrs Cong NYC; NY St Sch Music Assn; Dir, NY Fdn Music Clbs; cp/Nat Geog Soc; r/Bd of Dirs, LI Chapt, Spiritual Frontier F'ship; hon/Contbr, Over 35 Articles to Profl Jours; Editor, Contbr, *Tech Control for the Mod Pianist*; Editor, *The Piano Tchrs Art*; Num W/W & Other Biogl Listings.

DeVITO, ANTHONY JOSEPH oc/Assistant Director of Counseling Center; b/Sep 18, 1946; h/2 Brookside Avenue, Pelham, NY 10803; ba/Bronx, NY; p/Rocco and Marie DeVito, Staten Island, NY; ed/BA, Villanova Univ, 1967; MA 1970, PhD 1974, Fordham Univ; pa/Asst Dir Cnslg Ctr, Fordham Univ, 1976-; Conslt in Exptl Design, Stats & Computer Utilization, 1970-; Clin Psych Intern, VA Hosp, Newington, CT, 1975-76; Conslt, Smoking Res Proj Hlth Care Scis Div, George Wash Univ, 1982-; Profl Affil, Hispanic Res Ctr, Fordham Univ, 1979-; Chm & Mem Var Coms, Fordham Univ, 1979-; Reviewer, Var Res Grants & Profl Jours; Mem: En Psych Assn, 1980-; Var Divs, Am Psychol Assn, 1978-; AAAS, 1973-; hon/Author, Co-Author & Editor, Over

16 Articles & Papers Pub'd in Profl Jours incl'g: *Cnslg & Values; The 9th Mtl Measurements Yrbook; Jour of Col Student Pers; Jour Clin Psych; Ednl & Psychol Measurement; Others; Author & Co-Author, Over 15 Papers Presented at Profl Assn Meetings; Tchg Fellow, Fordham Univ, 1970-72; Sigma Xi, 1970-; Chm Intstnl Review Bd, Protection of Human Subjects, Fordham Univ, 1983-; W/W in E; Dir Dist'd Ams; Personalities of E; Comun Ldrs of World; Commun Ldrs of Am.

DeVORE, DALE PAUL oc/Biomedical Research/Biochemist; b/Mar 31, 1943; h/4334 Greenhaven Circle, Vadnais Heights, MN 55110; ba/St Paul, MN; m/Sandra Bernice; c/Mychelle Leigh, Braden Patrick; p/David H (dec) and Anna E DeVore, Belyidere, NJ; sp/Ted and Jane Grebowiec, Kansas City, MO; ed/BS 1966, MS 1972, PhD 1973, Rutgers Univ; pa/Staff Scist, Battelle Mem Inst, 1972-76; Prin Scist, Battelle Mem Inst, 1976-79; Res Spec, 3M-Riker, 1979-81; Res Spec, 3M-Surg Prod, 1981-83; Sr Res Spec/Mgr Collagen Prods Labs, 3M-Surg Prods Div, 1983-; Fac, Univ of MN, 1981-; Am Rheumatism Assn; Intl Assn Dental Res; MW CT Tissue Assn; Sigma Xi; 3M Tech Forum; Chm, Life Sci Chapt; Chair, Spec Progs Comm; cp/Vadnais Heights Planning Com, V-Chm; Vadnais Hgts Lions Clb, 1st VP; r/Prot; hon/Profl Pubs; Alpha Zeta Scholastic Soc, 1965-66; Cir of Tech Excell Awd, 3M, 1984; W/W in Frontier Sci & Technol.

DeVRIES, K LAWRENCE (LARRY) oc/Professor; b/Oct 27, 1933; h/1466 Penrose Drive, Salt Lake City, UT 84112; ba/Salt Lake City, UT; m/Kay McGee; c/Kenneth J, Susan K; p/Fern S DeVries, Ogden, UT; sp/Marvin and Evylen McGee, Springfield, MO; ed/ASCE, Weber St Col, 1953; BSME 1959, PhD 1962, Univ of UT; pa/Asst Prof 1956-69, Assoc Prof 1969-81, Prof 1981-, Dept Chm of Mech & Industl Engrg 1980-81, Assoc Dean Engrg, 1984-, Univ of UT; Dir Polymer Prog, NSF, 1975-76; Mem: UT St Coun for Sci & Technol, 1971-78; Adv Coms, NSF-DMR, 1978-81; Mats Adv Coms, NBS, 1977-80; Num NRC & NAS Coms; r/LDS; hon/Co-Author, Book-Testing & Anal of Adhesives, 1978; Author & Co-Author of 20 Chapts in Books; Over 150 Pubs in Profl Jours & Assn Proceedings; Univ Dist Res Awd 1978, Univ Dist'd Tchg Awd 1983, Univ of UT; Dist'd Ser Awd, UT Acad of Arts & Scis, 1984; W/W: in Am, in World; Other Biogl Listings.

DE WIT, MARGOT A L M oc/Artist, Sculptor/Printmaker; b/Jun 29, 1936; h/4418 Spruce Street, Philadelphia, PA 19104; ba/Glassboro, NJ; m/V S Naiken; p/C A M J de Wit, Amsterdam, Holland; ed/BFA, Acad of Fine Arts, Amsterdam, Holland, 1964; MFA, Ateliers '63, Haarlem, Holland, 1967; Att'd Univ of Amsterdam; Tyler Sch of Art; Phila Col of Art; pa/Art Tchr, Sculture/Printmaking, Glassboro St Co, NJ, 1977-; Art Tchr, Univ City Arts Leag, Phila, 1968-77; Tchr, Printmaking, Abington Art Ctr, Jenkintown, 1974-81; Tchr, Wk w Delinq Yth, Public Sch Sys, Holland, 1962-67; Wkshop Instr: Papercasting, Wellesley Col for Wom, Boston, 1979; Oreland Art Ctr, Willow Grow, 1978; Papercasting, Printmakers Guild-

Cheltenham Art Ctr, Cheltenham; Glassboro St Col, 1979-; Lectr: Dylestown Art Ctr; Abington Art Ctr; Mt Holly Hosp; Isl of Mauritius; Phila Art Alliance; Currator of Num Exhbns, 1979-; Over 16 One Man Shows incl'g: Gallery-de Bleeker, Heemstede, Holland, 1982; Civic Ctr "De Vaart" City of Hilversum, Holland, 1980-81; A J Wood Galleries, Phila, 1979; Walter Thomson Gallery, Amsterdam, Holland, 1978-79; Phila Art Alliance, Phila, 1978; Others; Num Grp Exhbns incl: Lever Brothers Gallery, NY-Dutch Artists in NY, 1982; Kling Gallery, Phila, 1982; Marian Locks Gallery, Phila-Cheltenham Printmakers Guild, 1982; Woodmere Art Gallery, Phila, 1982; Underpass Art Liberties, Phila, 1982; S/300 Sculpture/Tri-cent, Phila Art Alliance, 1982; Art at Fairmount, Fairmount Inst, Phila, 1982; S B K Galleries, Haarlem, Holland, 1979-81; Others; Comms incl: Edition Print: Phila Chapt, Wellesley Col for Wom, 1975; Georgetown Graphics, Wash Print Clb, 1978; Select Pvt & Public Collections incl: Lessing B Rosenwald Collection, Smithsonian Inst, Wash DC; St Joseph Col, Phila; Intl House, Phila; Phila Mus of Art; Ben J D Bernstein, Phila; Lynne Abrahams, Phila; Var Collections in USA, France, Holland; Mem: Chp Sculpture Com 1977-81, Bd of Dirs 1978-81, Phila Art Alliance; Bd of Dirs, Univ City Arts Leag, Phila, 1975-78; Bd of Advrs, Cheltenham Art Ctr, 1979-80; hon/ Awds incl: Woodmere Art Gallery 40th Annual Show, 1980; Perkiomen Val Art Ctr Annual Show, 1977; Stone Harbour Annual Bdwalk Show, 1974; Sculpture Outdoors, Temple Univ Music Fest; Artist in Residence, Glassboro St Col, 1978-81; Purchase Prize, Provident Nat Bk, Phila, 1975; W/W; W/W of Am Art.

DEWITZ, ARDEN VON oc/Artist; b/ Mar 7, 1915; h/5132 White Oak Avenue, Encino, CA 91316; ba/Encino, CA; m/ Amalie Von Dewitz; c/Marlen Demontford; p/Hrolf and Vahkyrien Von Dewitz (both dec); ed/BA, Stickney Sch of Art, 1932; pa/Prof Painting & Drawing, Laguna Bch Sch of Art, 1964; Prof Painting, Anatomy Life Drawing, Marymount Col, 1965-66; Instr Painting & Drawing, LA Bd of Ed, 1960-80; Painting Demo, ABC-TV Prog "Scope & Guidelines," 1966; Painting Demo, CBS-TV Prog, "Form, Space & Vision," 1967; Past Pres, Am Inst of Fine Arts, 1965; Wks in Permanent Collection incl: Laguna Bch Mus of Art; Haus Der Kunst Mus, Munich, W Germany; USN Mus, Wash DC; USCG Mus, Wash DC & FL; Wks in Other Collections; r/Cath; hon/Wks included in: Creat Color Book; Red Barns & Other Scenes; How to Paint Rock's & Surf; A Fun Book on Acrylic Painting Polymer; Am Artist Mag, 1969-72; 1st Purchase Awd, Sacramento St Fair, 1964; Gold Medal, Accademia Italia Delle Artie del Lavoro, 1980; F'ship & Silver Medal, The Am Inst of Fine Art, 1965; Gold Medal, Barnsdall Awd, 1966; W/W: in Art & Antiques, of Intell, in W.

DE YARMIN, RAYMOND WESLEY oc/Museum Curator, Naval Historian, Author; b/May 25, 1924; h/87-825 Farrington Highway, Waianae, HI 96792; ba/Pearl Harbor, HI; m/Constance Marie Fedor; c/Karen Sue,

Richard Michael, Daniel Raymond, Thomas Grady; p/William Franklin de Yarmin, Kingsburg, CA; sp/Frank Fedor, Cardiff-by-the-Sea, CA; ed/BGS, Chaminade Univ, 1981; MPA, Ctl MI Univ, 1983; mil/USN, 1942-77; pa/USN, 1942-77; Mus Curator & Nav Histn, Pacific Submarine Mus, 1979-; Am Mus Assn; HI Mus Assn; Submarine Vets; Sigma Iota Epsilon; Elks (Secy 1983); Fleet Res Assn; Nav Submarine Leag; Intl Submarine Assn (Brit Sect); cp/PA Genealogical Soc; Sierra Clb; r/Epis; hon/Num Pubs; Civilian Employee of Yr, Submarine Base & Nav Base Pearl Harbor, 1983; Hon'd Guest, Submarine Birthday Ball Honolulu, 1982; W/W in W.

DHANIREDDY, RAMASUBBAR-EDDY oc/Professor; b/Jul 8, 1951; h/2 Anamosa Court, Derwood, MD 20855; ba/Washington, DC; m/Brezeetha; c/ Shireeha, Kiran Kumar; p/Pedda Eswarareddy and Veeramma Dhanireddy, India; sp/Subbamma Chinnayyareddy, India; ed/PUC, Sri Venkateswara Arts Col, Tirupate, India, 1968; MBBS, Kurnool Med Col, Kurnool, India, 1974; Cert'd: Am Bd of Pediatrics, 1980; Sub Bd of Neonatal-Perinatal Med, Am Bd of Pediatrics, 1981; mol/USAFR, Capt; pa/Asst Prof Pediatrics, Georgetown Univ Med Ctr, 1982-; Med Staff Fellow, NIH, 1982-84; Asst Prof Pediatrics, LA St Univ Med Ctr, 1980-82; Mem: AMA; Indian Med Assn; Fellow, Am Acad of Pediatrics; Fellow, Am Col of Nutrition; Am Fdn for Clin Res; So Soc for Pediatric Res; r/Hindu; hon/Co-Author of 3 Res Papers Pub'd in Profl Jours incl'g: Jour of Pediatrics; Biol of Neonate; Over 15 Abstracts & Papers Pub'd in Jours & Presented at Profl Assn Meetings; Nat Merit S'ship, 1968-73; St Spec Merit S'ship, 1969; W/W in Frontier Sci & Technol.

DIAMOND, ESTHER E oc/Educational and Psychological Consultant; h/ 721 Brown Avenue, Evanston, IL 60202; ba/Same; m/Ben; c/Ellen D Kolbo, Toby Trupin; ed/BA, Bklyn Col; MA, NWn Univ, 1961; PhD, Loyola Univ, 1968; pa/ Ed & Psychol Conslt, 1973-; Devel Prog Admr 1979-82, Previous Positions incl: Sr Proj Dir, Mgr & Contract Test Devel, Test Devel Sci Res Assocs; Reg'd Psychol, IL; Mem: Fellow, Am Psychol Assn; Bd of Dirs, Am Pers & Guid Assn, 1981-; Past Pres, Assn for Measurement & Eval in Guid; Bd of Dirs, Jt Com on Standards for Ednl Eval; Intl Coun of Psychols; Intl Assn of Applied Psych; Am Ednl Res Assn; hon/Editor, Measurement & Eval in Guid, 1968-74; Staff Mem, Var Psychol & Measurement Jours, 1973-78; Editor of Book, Issues of Sex Bias & Sex Fondness in Career Interest Measurement, 1975; Author of Var Articles in Profl Jours; Fellow, Am Psychol Assn, 1978; Dist'd Profl Ser Awd, Am Pers & Guid Assn, 1978; Hon Mem, Wom Edrs for Res on Wom; DIB; Num W/W & Other Biogl Listings.

DIAZ, MYRIAM oc/Managing Director of Sales; b/Jan 19, 1940; h/84-20 55th Avenue, Elmhurst, NY 11373; ba/New York, NY; m/Nelson; c/Nelson Jr, Ronald, David; p/Anna Laffite and Max Rivas (dec); sp/Emilio Diaz (dec) and Ana Balbas; ed/CPA, Col Manuel Bonilla; Att'd Notre Dame Acad & Cambridge Sch of Bus; pa/Chief For Acct, Embassy Picture Corp, 1961-75; Comptroller

1975-77, Mng Dir/Latin Am Supvr 1977-83, Rizzoli Film Distbrs Inc; Mng Dir of Sales, The World Motion Pictures, 1983-; r/Cath; hon/W/W of Am Wom.

DI BELLA, JOSEPH PATRICK oc/ Insurance Company Executive; b/Mar 15, 1940; h/PO Box 191249, Miami Beach, FL 33119; ba/Miami, FL; m/ Francoise Catherine C; c/Alexandra Chatanay, Melissa Chatanay; p/Cosimo Joseph (dec) and Jessica Antoinette Di Bella, Rome, NY; sp/Jacques Noel and Colette Chatanay, France; ed/BS, USCG Acad, 1962; MBA, Columbia Univ, 1968; mil/USCG, 1962-68, Lt; pa/ Systems Anal 1968-70, Mgr 1971, En Airlines; Commun Prof Bus Mgmt, FL Intl Univ, 1972; Controller, Kimex Intl, 1972; VP 1973-76, Pres 1976-, Gen Ins Co; cp/Sodality of Transfiguration Ch; Rome Civil Def; Rome Block R Clb, VP 1957-58; Rome Hi-Y Clb, Pres 1957-58; K of C; USCG Acad Alumni Assn; Ft Wadsworth Flying Clb, Pres 1965; Venetian Causeway Improvement Assn, Dir 1979; r/Rom Cath; hon/Profl Pubs; Joseph Borden Awd, 1958; BSA Eagle Scout, 1956; Admiral LA Leamy Awd, 1962; USCGA Monogram Awd, 1962; Hawaiian AAU Cert of Merit, 1964; USCG Commandant Commend, 1964; Cert of Apprec, Dade Co Consumer Advocate, 1978; Cert of Recog, FL Secy of St, 1983; W/W.

DiBENEDETTO, ANTHONY T oc/ University Adminstrator; b/Ovt 27, 1933; h/1 Brookside Lane, Mansfield, CT 06250; ba/Storrs, CT; m/Rose Marie Lima; c/Diane, Laura, Thomas, David, Stephen; p/Mathilda DiBenedetto, Yorktown Heights, NY; sp/Carmela Lima, Putnam Lake, NY; ed/BSChE, City Col of NY, 1954; MSChE 1956, PhD 1960, Univ of WI; pa/VPres for Acad Affairs 1981-, VPres for Grad Ed & Res 1979-81, Hd Chem Engrg Dept 1971-76, Univ of CT; Hd Mats Prog, Wash Univ, 1967-71; Prof Chem Engrg, Univ of WI, 1956-66; Chem Engr, Union Carbide, 1954-55; Mem: AIChE; Sigma Xi; Tau Beta Pi; Bd of Dirs Plastics in Bldg Div 1974-78, Soc of Plastics Engrs; hon/Author of Book, The Structure & Properties of Mats, 1967; Num Articles in Profl Pubs; Outstg Edrs of Am; Ednl Ser Awd, PIA, 1973; Profl Devl Awds, NSF, 1975-78; Dist'd Ser Awd, Univ of WI, 1981.

DiBIANCA, VINCENT F oc/Executive Management Consultant; b/Jul 4, 1945; h/Box 23 Amwell Road, Hopewell, NJ 08525; ba/New York, NY; m/Jody; c/Richard, Suzanne, Brandon Williams, Susan Williams; p/Mr and Mrs Vincent J DiBianca, Atlantic City, NJ; sp/Mr and Mrs Edwin T Deal Jr, Ocean City, NJ; ed/BS Commerce & Engrg, Drexel Univ, 1968; MA Mgmt, Bucknell Univ, 1969; pa/Industl Engr, Gen Motors, 1965-68; Mgmt Conslt 1969-77, Ptnr 1977-, Touche Ross & Co; Mem: Co-Fdr & Trustee, The Bus Initiative; Lectr in Field; Am Inst of Decision Scis; Assn for Behavioral Anal, NJ Inst of Technol; Former Dir, The Wiltwyck Sch; Sonsor, Breakthrough Foun; Sponsor, The Hunger Proj; hon/Co-Author of 2 Book Chapts in Transforming Org, 1983; Author, Var Articles Pub'd in Profl Jours incl'g: Mgmt Reveiw; Indust Wk; Others; W/W in Fin & Indust.

DI BONA, LUDMILA CHALAS oc/

Linguist, Graduate Student of Computer Science; b/Nov 21, 1952; h/2737 Paulding Avenue, Bronx, NY 10469; m/Aidano Maurizio; c/Paul; p/Olga and Josef Chalas, Norwalk, CT; sp/Anna and Victor Di Bona, Bronx, NY; ed/BA, Lehman Col, 1975; MA 1976, PhD 1981, Brown Univ; MS, Pace Univ, 1984; pa/Tchg Asst in Russian & Czech, Brown Univ, 1977-78; Tchg Proctor in Russian & Czech, Brown Univ, 1978-79; AAT-SEEL; CAS; LSA; Phi Beta Kappa (Chi Chapt); MLA; Smithsonian Inst; r/Cath; hon/Profl Pubs; NDFL F'ship, 1976-77; Univ Endowment F'ship, 1975-76; World W/W: of Intells, of Wom.

DICK, RICHARD IRWIN oc/Professor; b/Jul 18, 1935; h/115 West Upland Road, Ithaca, NY 14850; ba/Ithaca, NY; m/Delores Den Beste; c/Natalie, Kevin, Laura, Craig; p/Laurence and Lillian Dick, Sibley, IA; sp/Margaret Den Beste, Sibley, IA; ed/BS, IA Univ, 1957; MS, St Univ of IA, 1958; PhD, Univ of IL, 1965; mil/USPHS, 1960-62; pa/Sanitary Engr, USPHS, 1958-60; Design Engr, Clark, Daily & Dietz, 1960-62; Instr through Prof Envir Engrg, Univ of IL, 1962-72; Prof Civil Engrg, Univ of DE, 1972-77; Joseph P Ripley Prof of Engrg, Cornell Univ, 1977-; Mem: Acting Editor, *Jour of Envr Engrg Div* 1979-, ASCE; Water Pollution Control Fdn; Pres 1973, Dist'd Lectr 1980, Assn of Envir Engrg Profs; Gov'g Bd 1974-78, Exec Com 1976-78, Intl Assn on Water Pollution Res & Control; Am Water Wks Assn; Brit Instn of Water Pollution Control; hon/Author, Over 125 Profl Papers; Recip, Harrison Prescott Eddy Medal, Water Pollution Control Fdn, 1968; Thomas R Camp Lectr, Boston Soc of Civil Engrs, 1981; Dist'd Lectr, Assn of Envir Engrg Profs, 1980; Sigma Xi; Phi Kappa Phi; Tau Beta Phi; Chi Epsilon; W/W in Am; Am Men & Wom of Sci; Other Biogl Listings.

DICKENS, KELLI KINGSLEY oc/Dance Instructor; b/Nov 28, 1958; h/16220 Waycross Drive, Biloxi, MS 39532; ba/Biloxi, MS; m/Burk; p/Mellonee Kingsley, Biloxi, MS; sp/Mr and Mrs Gene Dickens, Biloxi, MS; ed/Nat Assn of Dance & Affil'd Artist, 1982; pa/Budget Cnslr, Barclays Fin Ser, 1977-79; Budget Cnslr, Assoc Fin Ser, 1979-80; Owner, Kelli's Steps, Sch of Dance, & Leotard Place, 1980-; NADDA, 1980-83; ASCAP, 1980-83; Pageant Dir, Merchs Assn, 1983; cp/Dir & Perf Arts Cnslr, Biloxi Rec Sr Citizen, 1979; r/Bapt; hon/Mrs MS Contestant, 1983; Dance Olympus Tchrs Achmt, 1980-83.

DICKERSON, LAUREL oc/Instructional Developer/Educator; b/Sep 2, 1943; ba/Gainesville, FL; p/Jayne and Norman Dickerson, Westfield, NY; ed/BA, Park Col, 1966; MA 1973, PhD 1977, MI St Univ; pa/Peace Corps Vol, Colombia, S Am, 1964-66; Mgmt Tech, Dept of Army, 1968-70; Ed Spec, Hlth, Ed & Wel Dept, 1970-72; Asst Prof of Ed, Univ of MD, 1976-77; Asst Prof of Ed, Univ of FL, 1977-; Am Soc for Tng & Devel, 1982-; Assn for Ed Communs & Technol, 1973-; Assn for Supvn & Curric Devel, 1977-82; Div of Instr Devel, Assn for Ed Communs & Technol, 1973-; Nat Assn of Female Execs, 1982-; Phi Delta Kappa, 1974-; Wom in Instr Technol, 1978-; Wom in Instr Technol, 1974-78; FL Assn for Media

in Ed, 1977-78; FL Assn of Supvn & Curric Devel, 1981-; FL Ed Res Assn, 1981-; hon/Num Profl Pubs; Fac Wom's S'ship, MI St Univ, 1974; Cert of Recog, Assn for Ed Communs & Technol, 1977; Outstg Yg Wom; W/W in SE.

DICKEY, JAMES L oc/Poet-in-Residence; b/Feb 2, 1923; h/4620 Lelia's Court, Columbia, SC 29206; ba/Columbia, SC; m/Deborah Dodson; c/Christopher Swift, Kevin Webster, Bronwen Elaine; p/Eugene and Maibelle Swift Dickey (dec); ed/BA 1949, MA 1950, Vanderbilt Univ; mil/USAAF, WW II; USAF, Korea; pa/Eng Instr, Rice Inst, Houston, TX, 1950, 1952-54; Eng Instr, Univ of FL, Gainesville, 1955-56; From 1956-61: Advtg Copywriter, McCann-Erickson, NY; Art Dir, Liller, Neal, Battle & Lindsey, Atlanta; Art Dir, Burke, Dowling, Adams, Atlanta; Poet-in-Residence, Reed Col, Portland, OR, 1963-64; Poet-in-Residence, San Fernando Val St Col, LA, CA, 1964-65; Poet-in-Residence, Univ of WI-Madison 1966 & Milwaukee 1967; Poetry Conslt, Lib of Cong, Wash DC, 1966-68; Poet-in-Residence & Franklin Dist'd Prof, GA Tech Inst, 1968; Poet-in-Residence 1968-, Carolina Prof 1979, Univ of SC; Mem: Am Acad & Inst of Arts & Lttrs; Am Acad of Arts & Scis; hon/Author, Over 38 Lit Wks of Poetry, Essays, Novel incl'g: *Helmet's*, 1962; *Buckdancer's Choice*, 1965; *James Dickey: Poems, 1957-67*; *Babel to Byzantium*, 1968; *Deliverance*, 1970; *Self-Interviews*, 1970; *The Strength of Fields*, 1979; *Falling, May Day Sermon, & Other Poems*, 1981; *Puella*, 1982; *Varmland: Poems Based on Poems*, 1982; *The Ctl Motion: Poems, 1968-79*; Others; Poetry F'ship, *Sewanee Review*, 1954; Union Leag Civic & Arts Foun Prize, *Poetry Magazine*, 1958; Longview Foun Awd, 1959; Vachel Lindsay Prize, *Poetry Magazine*, 1959; Guggenheim F'ship, 1961; Nat Book Awd for Poetry & the Melville Cane Awd of the Poetry Soc of Am, for *Buckdancer's Choice*, 1966; Nat Inst of Arts & Letters Grant, 1966; Pris Medicis, Best Fgn Book of Yr (Paris), for Novel *Deliverance*, 1971; Wrote & Delivered Poem "The Strength of Fields" at Inauguration of Pres Carter, 1977; Levinson Prize for *Puella*, *Poetry Magazine*, 1982; W/W; Contemporary Authors.

DICKEY, JOSEPH W oc/Physicist; Congressional Fellow; b/Feb 26, 1939; h/295 Hillsmere Drive, Annapolis, MD 21403; ba/Annapolis, MD; c/Ellen, William; p/Mrs Joseph L Dickey, Annapolis, MD; ed/BS, Drexel Univ, 1963; MS, Univ of NH, 1965; PhD, Cath Univ of Am, 1973; pa/Res Physicist, DTNSRDC, 1963-80; Supervisory Physicist, DTNSRDC, 1980-83; Congl Sci Fellow, 1983-84; Acoustical Soc of Am; Sigma Xi; MD Acad of Sci; hon/Profl Pubs; 3 US Patents; Am Men & Wom of Sci; W/W in Technol.

DICKMAN, ROBERT LAURENCE oc/Astrophysicist; b/May 16, 1947; h/115 Grantwood Drive, Amherst, MA 01002; ba/Amherst, MA; m/Albertina Catharina Otter; c/Joshua, Ilana; p/Eve Dickman, Plainview, NY; sp/A Otter, Driebergen, Holland; ed/AB 1969, MA 1972, MPhil 1974, PhD 1976, Columbia Univ; pa/Postdoct Res Assoc, Rensselaer Polytech Inst, 1975-77; Tech Staff, The Aeospace Corp, 1977-80; Fac Res Assoc & Observatory Mgr, Univ of MA, 1980-; Mem:

Am Phy Soc; Am Astronom oc; hon/Author, Var Articles & Papers Pub'd in Profl Jours & Profl Soc Proceedings incl'g: *Jour of Astronomy & Astrophysics*; *Sci Am*; Pubs of IEEE; Others; W/W.

DIENER, EUGENIA (EUGENIA DIMER) oc/Free-lance Writer and Translator; b/Jan 7, 1925; h/17 Porter Road, West Orange, NJ 07052; ba/West Orange, NJ; m/Morris; c/Gloria Johnson; p/Paraskeva Bojko and Alexander (dec); sp/Joseph and Minnie (dec); ed/MA Ec, Univ of Muenster, W Germany, 1949; Med Lab Tech, Lyons Med Lab Sch, Newark, NJ, 1954; pa/Model; Lab Tech; Free-lance Translator & Writer; Mem: Intl PEN Clb, 1980-; Secy/Treas, Russian Writers' Clb, NY, 1978; r/Russian Orthodox; hon/Author, Over 100 Short Stories, Travelogues, Essays & Poems Pub'd in Periods (in Russian), 1955-; Author, 3 Books: *Distant Harbors*, 1967; *The View From the 9th Wave*, 1977; *Silent Love*, 1979; Intl W/W in Poetry.

DIFILIPPO, FELIX CARLOS oc/Research Scientist; b/Jul 24, 1943; h/102 Westwind, Oak Ridge, TN 37830; ba/Oak Ridge, TN; m/Nuria Hernandez; c/Ernesto A, Eduardo P; p/Miguel and Angela, Difilippo, Buenos Aires, Argentina; sp/Juan and Josefa Hernandez, Barcelona, Spain; ed/MA Physics 1967, PhD Physics 1978, Balseiro Inst, Univ of Cuyo, Argentina; pa/Aux Prof, Univ of Buenos Aires, Argentina, 1968-69; Res AEC, Argentina, 1968-79; Res Asst Prof, Univ of TN, 1979-83; Staff Mem, Oak Ridge Nat Lab, 1983-; Mem: Am Nuclear Soc; Am Phy Soc; hon/Author of Num Articles Pub'd in Profl Jours & Assn Proceedings, 1970-; Fellow, Intl Atomic Energy Agy, Vienna, 1974; W/W in Frontier Sci & Technol.

DIGHE, SHRIKANT VISHWANATH oc/Research Chief; b/Nov 29, 1933; h/9811 Wildwood Road, Bethesda, MD 20814; ba/Rockville, MD; m/Judith Ginaine; c/Ranjit, Anand; p/Vishwanath G Dighe, Bombay, India; sp/Vincent L Ginaine, St Louis, MO; ed/BSc 1955, MSc 1957, Univ of Bombay; PhD, Univ of Cinc, 1965; MAS, Johns Hopkins Univ, 1977; pa/Res Chem, W R Grace & Co, Clarksville, MD, 1965-71; Res Assoc, The Johns Hopkins Univ Sch of Med, 1971-73; Chem 1973-79, Chief Biopharm Review Br 1980-, Food & Drug Adm; Mem: Am Chem Soc; Fellow, Am Inst of Chems; Sigma Xi; NY Acad of Scis; cp/Troop Com, BSA; r/Hinduism; hon/Author of 12 Pubs in Profl Jours; Recip, 6 US Patents in Field; Petro Res Fund Fellow, Univ of Cinc, 1959-62; Laws Fellow, Univ of Cinc, 1963-64; Commend Ser Awd, FDA, 1978; W/W in E; Am Men of Sci.

Di LELLA, ALEXANDER ANTHONY oc/Professor; b/Aug 14, 1929; ba/Catholic University of America, Washington, DC 20064; p/Alessandro and Adelaide (Grimaldi) Di Lella, Paterson, NJ; ed/BA, St Bonaventure Univ, 1952; STL 1959, PhD 1962, Cath Univ of Am; SSL, Pontifical Biblical Inst, 1964; pa/Entered Franciscan Order (OFM), 1950; Ordained Priest, 1955; Eng Instr, 1956-58; Lectr in Old Testament, Holy Name Col, 1964-69; Asst Prof Semitic Langs 1966-68, Assoc Prof Semitic Langs 1968-76, Assoc Prof Biblical Studies 1976-77, Prof Biblical Studies 1977-, Cath Univ of Am, Wash DC; Book Review Editor 1966-69, Assoc Editor 1969-73 & 1976-79, *Cath Biblical Qtly*; Editor, *Theol Bltn*, 1968-72; Adj Prof

Old Testament, Wash Theol Union, 1969-72; Edit Bd Mem, *Cithara*, 1973; Assoc Editor, *Old Testament Abstracts*, 1978-; Edit Bd Mem, *Studia Biblica* (Brill), 1983-; Mem: Pres 1975-76, Cath Biblical Assn; Pres Chesapeake Bay Sect 1972-73, Soc of Biblical Lit; Am Schs of Oriental Res; Old Testament Sec, Revised Standard Version Bible Com, 1982-; r/Rom Cath; hon/Author, *The Hebrew Text of Sirach: A Text-Critical & Hist Study*, 1966; *Proverbs (The Old Testament in Syriac)*, 1979; Co-Author, "The Book of Daniel" in *The Anchor Bible*, Volume 23, 1978; Translator of Part, *New Am Bible*, 1970; Num Other Biblical Articles in Profl Jours; Fellow, Am Sch of Oriental Res, Jerusalem, 1962-63; Guggenheim Fellow, 1972-73; F'ship, Assn of Theol Schs, US & Canada, 1979-80; Contemp Authors; DIB; Num W/W & Other Biogl Listings.

DILLARD, EILEEN WHITTINGTON oc/Director of Dietary; b/Jan 1, 1921; h/PO Box 746, Sylva, NC 28779; ba/Sylva, NC; m/John Colman (dec); c/Paul John, Teresa Eleanor, Drucilla Lynn D Conn; p/James and Eleanor Whittington; sp/David and Ora Dillard; ed/AA, St Ann's Acad, 1940; mil/Royal AF, 1942-44; pa/Adm Asst, AF, 1942-44; Dir of Dietary, C J Harris Commun Hosp, 1959-; Pres, NC Hosp Food Ser Admrs, 1975; Reg 4 Dir of Hosp Food Ser Admrs of AHA, 1979-80; Dir of NC Hosp Food Ser Adm, 1984-85; r/Epis; hon/Recog Awd, Dist'd Hlth Care Food Ser Adm, 1979; Intl Merit Awd for Hosp Ser, 1975; Asheville Citizen 'Wom of the Wk,' 1961; Personalities of S; World W/W of Wom; DIB.

DILLEHAY, DAVID ROGERS oc/Pyrotechnist; b/Sep 21, 1936; h/107 Ashwood Terrace, Marshall, TX 75670; ba/Marshall, TX; m/Marilyn Heath; c/Janet Lee, David Rogers Jr; p/Thomas J and Rachel Todd Dillehay (both dec); sp/W F Heath (dec); Mrs W F Heath, Marshall, TX; ed/BA Chem, Rice Univ, 1958; PhD Chem, Clayton Univ, 1983; pa/Spec Projs Supvr 1982-, Process Engrg Supvr 1979-82, Sr Engr 1972-79, Chem 1958-72, Longhorn Div, Thiokol Corp, Marshall, TX; Mem: Secy 1980-, Intl Pyrotechnics Soc; Steering Com, Intl Pyrotechnic Sems, 1978-; cp/VPres 1981, Pres 1982, Nat Coun Rep for AR-LA-TX Chapt, Am Def Preparedness Assn; Scoutmaster, BSA, 1972-73; r/Cath; hon/Author of Num Tech Papers Pub'd in Profl Jours & Soc Proceedings; Recip, 3 US Patents in Field; Civic Cit as Image Maker of Marshall, Marshall C of C, 1983; AUS Materiel Command Value Engrg Awd, 1975; W/W: in S & SW; Men of Achmt; Dir Dist'd Ams; DIB; Other Biogl Listings.

DILLINGHAM, MARJORIE CARTER oc/Eductor; b/Aug 20, 1915; h/2109 Trescott Drive, Tallahassee, FL 32312; m/William P; c/William P Jr (dec), Robert Carter, Sharon D Martin; ed/PhD, FL St Univ, 1970; pa/Nat Pres, La Sociedad Honoraria Hispanica; Pres, For Lang Div, FL Ed Assn; Pres, FL Chapt of Am Assn of Tchrs of Spanish & Portuguese; Pres, Alpha Lambda Chapt of Delta Kappa Gamma; Pres, Coor'g Coun of 5 Chapts of Delta Kappa Gamma; Pres, For Tchrs of Leon Co, FL; Phi Kappa Phi; Sigma Delta Pi; Beta Pi Theta; Kappa Delta Pi; Alpha Omicron Pi; Former Tchr at Duke Univ, Univ of GA, FL St Univ, Panama Canal Zone Col, St George's Sch of La Habana, Cuba & Sec'dy Schs in FL; hon/

Winner, Delta Kappa Gamma Intl F'ship for Grad Res; Recipient, Delta Kappa Gamma Local & St of FL S'ships.

DILLON, ROBERT WILLIAM oc/Professor of English Language and Literature; b/May 31, 1942; h/PO Box 524, 970 Wood Street, California, PA 15419; ba/California, PA; m/Susan M; c/Christopher Mark, Christian Randall, Robert William Jr; p/William J (dec) and Catherine M Dillon, Staten Isl, NY; sp/Frances R Ritonia, Monongahela, PA; ed/AB, Fairfield Univ, 1964; MA 1965, PhD 1969, OH Univ; pa/Chm of Dept of Eng 1968-70, Acting Dean of Col of Arts & Sci 1968-70, OH Univ-Lancaster; Grad Asst, OH Univ, 1964-65; Tchg Fellow, OH Univ-Athens, 1967; Instr of Eng 1967-69, Asst Prof of Eng 1969-70, OH Univ-Lancaster, Assoc Prof of Eng 1970-71, Prof of Eng Lang & Lit 1971-, CA Univ of PA; MLA; AAUP; NEA; Am Fdn of Tchrs; PA Assn of Higher Ed; PA St Ed Assn; Assn of PA St Col & Univ Fac; PA Assn of Tchrs of Eng; cp/Scoutmaster, BSA, U Christian Ch; Advr & Trustee, PSI Chapt, PHi Kappa Theta Frat; CA Yth Assn; Past Pres, CA St Col Shotokan Karate Clb; r/Rom Cath; hon/Profl Pubs: Poetry Awd, Fairfield Univ, 1962; Editor-in-Chief, *New Frontiers*, 1964-67; Tchg Merit Awd, CA St Col, 1974; Res Grant, OH Univ, 1968; Intl W/W Ed; Dir of Dist'd Ams; 2000 Notable Ams; Intl Book of Honor.

DILLON, WILTON STERLING oc/Anthropoligist and Educator; b/Jul 13, 1923; h/1446 Woodacre Drive, McLean, VA 22101; ba/Washington, DC; m/Virginia Leigh Harris; c/Wilton Harris; p/Earl Henry Dillon (dec); Edith Holland Canfield, Tulsa, OK; ed/BA, Univ of CA-Berkeley, 1951; PhD, Columbia Univ, 1961; Postgrad Study, Univ of Paris & Univ of Leyden, 1951-52; mil/USAC, 1943-46; pa/Info Spec, Supr Cmdr Allied Powers, Tokyo, 1946-49; Instr, Hobart & Wm Smith Cols, Geneva, NY, 1952-53; Staff Anthropologist, Japan Soc of NY, 1954; Dir of Clearinghouse, Soc for Applied Anthropology, NY, 1954-56; Exec Secy, Phelps-Stokes Fund of NY, 1957-63; Staff Dir, Ofc of Egn Secy, Nat Acad of Scis, 1963-69; Dir of Symps & Sems, Smithsonian Instn, 1969-; Mem: Trustee, Phelps-Stokes Fund, 1975-; Bd of Visitors, Wake Forest Univ, l1976-80; Pres, Anthropological Soc of Wash, 1974; Fellow, Am Anthropological Assn; Secy, Inst for Psychi & Fgn Affairs, 1976-; Adj Prof, Univ of AL, Tuscaloosa, 1975-; r/Epis; hon/Author, *Gifts & Nats*, 1968; Co-Editor, *Man & Beast*, 1971; Editor, *The Cultural Drama*, 1974; Article, "Margaret Mead & Govt," *Am Anthropologist*, 1980; Others; Hon Commr, Intl Yr of the Child, 1979; W/W in Am; Am Men & Wom of Sci; Contemp Authors.

DINABURG, MARY ELLEN oc/Painter; b/Feb 22, 1954; h/3404 Partridge Road, Oklahoma City, OK 73120; ba/Oklahoma City, OK; p/Howard and Selma Dinaburg; ed/BFA, Phila Col of Art, 1972-76; MFA, Pratt Inst, 1977-79; Cooper Union, 1970-72; Art Students Leag, 1967-68; pa/Asst to Dean of Student Affairs & Sub Instr 1972-76, Instr 1976-77, Co-Tchr 1978, Coor of UICA Lecture Series 1978-79, Instr 1977-79, Phila Col of Art; Grad Admissions 1977-78, Undergrad Admissions 1978-79, Pratt Inst; Instr, Grover Cleveland Art Inst, 1979; Hist Sem, OK Art

Ctr, 1979; Lectr & Conslt, OK Mus of Art, 1981; cp/Monthly Lectures, Les Femmes Salon; r/Jewish; hon/Profl Pubs; Num Exhbns; W/W in SW.

DINH, ANTHONY TUNG oc/Chief of Medicine; b/Jan 1, 1938; h/208 Jamescrest Drive, Beckley, WV 25801; ba/Beckley, WV; m/Lisa; c/Andrew; p/Mr and Mrs H B Dinh, Montreal, Canada; sp/Mr and Mrs Q V Tran, Munich, W Germany; ed/MD, Univ of Saigon, 1967; Am Bd of Med Microbiol, 1974; Am Bd of Internal Med, 1981; pa/Asst Prof, Dept of Microbiol & Tropical Med, Fac of Med of Saigon, 1970-75; Asst Prof, SE Asia Sch of Tropical Med, 1974-75; Staff Phys 1981-82, Chief of Med Ser, 1982-, Beckley VA Med Ctr; Am Soc for Microbiol, 1973-; NY Acad of Sci, 1982-; Am Col of Med, 1983-; Am Bd Internal Med; AMA; Am Bd of Med Microbiol; hon/Profl Pubs.

DINKINS, CAROL EGGERT oc/Assistant Attorney General; b/Nov 9, 1945; h/422 Buckingham, Houston, TX 77024; ba/Washington, DC; m/O Theodore Jr; c/Anne, Amy; p/Mr and Mrs Edgar H Eggert Jr, Mathis, TX; sp/O T Dinkins Sr, Livingston, TX; ed/BS 1968, Att'd Sch of Law 1968-69, Univ of TX-Austin; JD, Univ of Houston Col of Law, 1971; pa/Adj Asst Prof of Law, Univ of Houston Col of Law, Houston, 1971-73; Princ Assoc, TX Law Inst of Coastal & Marine Res, Houston, 1971-73; Assoc 1973-80, Ptner 1980-81, Law Firm of Vinson & Elkins, Houston; Asst Atty Gen.US Dept of Justice, WashDC, 1981-; Mem: Houston Law Review Assn, 1978-; Dir, Nat Consumer Bk Bd, 1981-82; Commr, TX Water Conserv Assn; Native Hawaiian Study Comm, 1981-; Chm, Pres's Task Force on Legal Equity for Wom, 1981-; Chm, Gov's Task Force on Coastal Mgmt, 1979-; Chm, Gov's Flood Control Action Grp, 1980; r/Luth; hon/Author, Var Articles in Profl Jours incl'g: *Houston Law Review*; *SW Legal Fund*; *Rice Univ Studies*; W/W: in Am, in Am Polits, in Wash, of Am Wom.

DIONNE, GERALD FRANCIS oc/Research Physicist; b/Feb 5, 1935; h/182 High Street, Winchester, MA 01890; ba/Lexington, MA; m/Claudette Marie; c/Stephen Gerald; p/Louis Philip and Claire Isabel Dionne, Montreal, Canada; ed/BS summa cum laude, Concordia Univ, 1956; BEngrg magna cum laude, 1958, PhD 1964, McGill Univ; MS, Carnegie-Mellon Univ, 1959; pa/Engr I, Bell Canada, 1958; Tchg Asst, Carnegie-Mellon 1958-59; Jr Engr, IBM Corp, 1959-60; Sr Engr, GTE Corp, 1960-61; Res Asst/Lectr, McGill Univ, 1963-64; Sr Res Assoc, Pratt & Whitney Aircraft, 1964-66; Tech Staff, MIT Lincoln Lab, 1966; Sr Mem, IEEE; Am Phy Soc; Sigma Xi; Corp of Profl Engrs of Quebec; r/Cath; hon/Profl Pubs; Lt Gov's Medal, Concordia Univ, 1956; Nat Res Coun of Canada F'ship, 1961-64; W/W: E, Technol Today; Am Men & Wom of Sci.

DISHMAN, RODNEY KING oc/Research Sport Psychologist; b/Feb 4, 951; h/257 Grande, Davis, CA 95616; ba/Davis, CA; m/Sharon Emily; c/Jessic E, Amanda Corinne; p/Willand K and Virginia Lanette Dishman, Strafford, MO; sp/Robert N and Phyllis Eileen Alter, W Plains, MO; ed/BS, SW MO St Univ, 1973; MS 1975, PhD 1978, Univ of WI-Madison; pa/Res Asst 1976, Grad Asst 1973-77, Univ of WI; Vis'g Lectr,

N TX St Univ, 1977; Asst Prof SW MO St Univ, 1978-83; Asst Res Sport Psychol & Assoc Dir Cardiopulmonary Rehab Exercise Prog, Univ of CA-Davis, 1983-; Mem: AAAS; Am Psychol Assn; Fellow, Chair Psychol & Psychi Area 1980, Res Awds Com 1981-84, Am Col of Sports Med; Soc of Behavioral Med; AAHPERO; r/U Meth; hon/Author, Over 20 Articles in Profl Sci Jours; Var Book Chapts; Co-Author, *Essentials of Fitness*, 1980; A J McDonald Awd, SW Mo St Univ, 1973; Res Writing Awd, AAHPERO, 1982; Editor, *Res Qtly for Exercise & Sport*; Editor, *Jour of Sport Psych*; Reviewer, Var Other Profl Jours; W/W: in Am Univs & Cols, in MW.

DISHNO, DUANE ALLAN oc/School District Administrator; b/Oct 26, 1941; h/7652 Concordia Place, Westminster, CA 92683; ba/Huntington Beach, CA; m/ Pauline Amelia; c/Joel Thomas, Chris Edward; p/Thomas C and Nellie M Dishno, Thousand Oaks, CA; sp/Laura Schwandt, Upland, CA; ed/BA, En WA St Univ, 1963; MA, CA St Univ, 1972; EdD, Univ of La Verne, 1984; pa/Lectr, CA St Univ, 1973-74; Coor 1973-75, Lang Anal 1972-73, Rdg Spec 1968-72, Tchr 1963-69, Westminster Sch Dist; Prin 1975-77, Dir 1977-82, Asst Sup 1982-, Huntington Bch City Sch Dist; Assn of CA Sch Admrs; Assn for Supvn & Curric Devel; CA Soc of Ed Prog Auditors & Evalrs; EDUCARE; Orange Co Rdg Assn; Orange Co Admrs of Spec Ed; CA Assn of Compensatory Ed; Conslt, CA St Dept of Ed; Adv Com, CA St Univ & Goldenwest Commun Col; W Orange Co Consort for Spec Ed; W Orange Co Staff Devel; Coop Policy Bd VP; cp/Large Pacific Dist, BSA; r/Cath; hon/W/W in W.

DITTMER, JAMES HAROLD oc/ Retail Food Management Trouble Shooter; b/Jul 9, 1951; h/145 Orchid Lane, Port Orange, FL 32019; ba/Daytona Beach, FL; p/Harold and Petro Dittmer, Barrington, IL; ed/BS, Wn MI Univ, 1974; pa/Public Admr, Dundee Park Dist, 1974-75; VP & Gen Mgr, Interstate GME, 1975-76; Pres & Fdr, J H Dittmer & Co, 1976-; Retail Food Mgmt, Super Food Sers Inc, 1981-82; Retail Food Mgmt, Quality Foods Inc, 1982-; Nat Grocers Assn; Retail Grocers Assn; r/Epis; hon/ Profl Pubs; Eagle Scout Awd, BSA, 1967; Ser Awd, YMCA; Ath Lttrs Awds; AAU, 1972; NCAA Judge; W/W in S & SE.

DIXON, CELESTINE FRAZIER oc/ Retired School Teacher; b/Nov 11, 1908; h/1420 North Davis Street, Pensacola, FL 32503; m/Rev J O Dixon (dec); c/ Barbara D Simpkins; ed/BS, FL A&M Col, 1931; Att'd Tuskeegee Inst, Cornell Univ; pa/Tchr, Delray Bch, FL Palm Bch Co, 1932-33; Escambia Co, WA HS, Pensacola 1932-73; Pensacola, WA HS, 1939-73; Pres, Wom Aux to Bapt Gen St Conv of FL, 1981; VP & Christian Ldr, Nat Bapt SS & BTU Cong of USA Inc, 1945; Coor of Com Wk, Nat Bapt Wom Aux, 1972-; r/Bapt; hon/Pub'd Author.

DIXON, CORA O oc/Labor Relations Specialist; b/Jul 10, 1930; h/2031 38th Street, Southeast, Washington, DC 20020; ba/Washington, DC; p/Cora A O'Neal, Durham, NC; ed/BS, DC Tchrs Col, 1973; MA, George Wash Univ, 1975; pa/Spec Asst to Exec Dir, EEOC, 1974-77; Spec Asst to NY Reg Dir, EEOC, 1977-78; Pers Staffing Spec, EEOC, 1978-79; Labor Relats Spec, EEOC, 1979-; Pre, Correspondence Secy, Recording Secy,

Durhamites; Treas, Corres'g Secy, Alpha Kappa Alpha; VP, Kappa Delta Pi; Supvr of SS, Ch Bd of Ed, Vestry Mem, Trinity Epis Ch; r/Prot; hon/Pub'd Articles; Outstg Student, 1972; magna cum laude, 1973; Wom of Yr, 1976; Outstg Commn Ser, 1978; Outstg Commun Ser, Salvation Army, 1980 & 1982; Merit Pay Awd, 1980 & 1982.

DIXON, LAWRENCE PAUL oc/Insurance Executive; b/Oct 23, 1938; h/35 Bunkerhill Drive, Huntington, NY 11743; ba/Melville, NY; m/Zelen D; c/Laurie Jean, Gregory, Linda, Kenneth; p/Clinton D and Frances M, New York, NY; sp/ Dewey and Zelda (both dec); ed/BS, Fordham Univ; Postgrad Study, Col of Ins; mil/ROTC, 2 Yrs; pa/Sr Underwriting Ofcr, Chubb & Son Inc; Sr VP, Contractors Coverage Corp; Ptnr, Global Planning Corp; Pres, Tiburon Sers Ltd, 1978-; Pres, Dixon Brokerage Inc, 1978-; Subcontractors Trade Assn, Chm of Ins Com; Am Subconstractors Assn, Keynote Conv Spkr; Profl Ins Agts; Indep Ins Agts; Bd of Govs, LaSalle Mil Acad; Pres, Fathers Clb, LaSalle Mil Acad, 1983-84; Chm of Beef-o-Rama, LaSalle Mil Acad, 1982-83; cp/Nat Repub Congl Com, Repub Nat Com; Repub Pres Task Force; US Senatorial Clb; Drug & Chem Clb; Northport Yacht Clb; Soaring Society; W/W: in E, in Fin & Indust.

DIXON, ROBERT MORTON oc/ Research Soil Scientist; b/May 30, 1929; h/1231 East Big Rock Road, Tucson, AZ 85718; ba/Tucson, AZ; m/Sharon Ann Youngblood; c/James Robert, Curtis Gregory, Donna Elaine, Gregory Eric; p/ William Gill Dixon; Vivian Marshall (dec); ed/BS 1959, MS 1960, KS St Univ; PhD, Univ of WI-Madison, 1966; mil/AUS, 1954-56; pa/Agronomy Instr, KS St Univ, 1959-60; Res Soil Sci, US Dept of Agri, (Agri Res Ser Locations: Madison, WI; Sidney, MT; Reno, NE; Tucson, AZ), 1960-; Irrigation Conslt, Ford Foun, Cairo, Egypt, 1967; Agri Conslt, US Dept of St, Agy for Intl Devel, Port-au-Prince, Haiti, 1978; Irrigation Spec, People-to-People Intl, Var Locations in Peoples Repub of China, 1982; Mem: Intl Soc of Soil Sci; Soil Sci Soc of Am; Soil Conserv Soc of Am; Am Geophy Union; Soc for Range Mgmt; Intl Erosion Control Assn; Intl Platform Assn; AZ-NE, Acad of Sci; Am Soc of Agri Engrs; r/Unitarian; hon/Author, Num Tech & Semitech Articles in Profl Jours & Pop Pubs; Recip, US Patent in Field; Sigma Xi; Gamma Sigma Delta; Phi Kappa Phi; Intl Panel to Study Land Imprinting, Nat Acad of Scis; W/W: in W, of Contemp Achmt, in Technol Today; Am Men & Wom of Sci; DIB; Commun Ldrs of Am; Num Other Biogl Listings.

DIXON, WARREN ARTHUR oc/ Architect and Educator; b/Mar 11, 1934; h/1817 Ivan Drive, Tallahassee, FL 32303; ba/Tallahassee, FL; m/Alice Gay Pound; c/Heloise Leonora; p/Coleman Sweeting Dixon (dec); Madie Lea Dixon, Tallahassee, FL; sp/James Hannon Pound Sr, Tallahassee, FL; Heloise Pound (dec); ed/ Att'd FL St Univ, 1952-54; BArch, Univ of FL, 1958; mil/USAR, 1958-64; pa/ Intern at Var Tallahassee Arch Ofcs: Huddleston & Assoc, 1958; Albert Woodward, 1959; James Stripling, 1959-60; Barret, Daffin & Bishop, 1961-63; Arch, Fl Bd of Pks & Hist Memls, 1963-66; Assoc, Robert Maybin & Assocs, Arch, 1966-68; Assoc, Robert Maybin &

Warren Dixon Archs, 1968-71; Warren Dixon Arch, 1971-; Hd Drafting & Arch Technol Dept, Lively Area Voc-Tech Ctr, Tallahassee, FL, 1976-; Mem: Var Chapt Ofc Positions incl'g Pres 1967, FL N Ctl Chapt, AIA, 1964-78; Constrn Specifications Inst, 1981-; r/Prot; hon/Var Arch Wks incl: Providence Plaza Housing for Elderly, Thomasville, GA, 1981; Tallahassee Police HQ's (w Robert Maybin), 1971; Var Ofc Bldgs in Tallahassee, 1968-75; Var FL St Pks Plans & Structures, 1963-66; W/W in S & SW.

DOAK, JANICE ASKEW oc/Banker; b/Jan 15, 1925; h/2814 Ashwood, Houston, TX 77025; ba/Houston, TX; m/Ira Kennedy; c/Barbara Sue, Carolyn Mary; p/Andrew M Askew (dec); sp/Mark Kennedy Doak (dec); ed/BBA, Univ of TX, 1944; 14 Am Inst of Bkg Courses; pa/Bkkpr 1949, Cashier 1960, VP & Cashier 1962, VP 1974, Bk of Houston; Nat Assn of Bk Wom; Past Mem of Bd, Am Inst of Bkg, Houston Chapt; Past Pres, Houston Credit Wom-Intl; Dist Treas, Lone Star Coun Credit Wom-Intl; Past Pres, Houston Charter Chapt, Am Bus Wom Assn; Bd Mem, House Corp for Gamma Upsilon Chapt Alpha Chi Omega; VP, Houston Fdn of Profl Wom; cp/Vol Wkr, St Luke's Hosp, 1973-; Docent w Harris Co Heritage Soc, 1981-; r/Epis; hon/W/W of Am Wom.

DOBBINS, GEORGE C oc/Horticulture Instructor/Consultant; b/Jul 30, 1916; h/7301 Antelope Road, Citrus Heights, CA 95621; ba/Sacramento, CA; c/Barbara, Dan (dec); ed/AB, Univ of CA-Berkeley, 1946; mil/AUS, 1941-46, Field Artillery; pa/Gen Mgr, Oki Nursery, 1958-61; Mgr, Nursery Div Cap, Nursery Co, 1961-66; Horticulture Conslt, Rusch Botanical Gdn, 1978-; Horticulture/For Instr, Am River Col, 1966-; Bd of Dirs, Sacto Tree Foun, 1982-; Exec Bd, Friends of the Univ of CA David Arboretum, 1978-; Pres, Sacto Val Chapt, CNPS, 1971; Pres, Sup Chapt, CAN, 1964; hon/ CAN Ednl Awd, 1971; Bert Kallman Awd, CAN, 1967; W/W in W.

DOBBS, GEORGE ALBERT oc/Retail Corporation Executive; b/Oct 16, 1943; h/PO Box 301, Avondale Estates, GA 30002; p/Albert F and Ruby Lee Dobbs, Decatur, GA; ed/BA 1966, MBA 1972, Cornell Univ; pa/Retail Grocery Mgr, Alterman Foods, 1960-72; Indep Mng Agt, DBA George A Dobbs and Assoc, 1972-78; Retail Mgr, K-Mart Corp, 1978-; Notary Public, GA St at Large, 1976-; DeKalb Bus-man's Assn, 1974-; GA Small Bus Mgrs Assn, 1976; cp/ DeKalb Sheriffs Posse, 1974-77; GA Sheriffs Assn, 1976-; Capital City Clb; Mason; Scottish Rite; Shriner; r/So Bapt; hon/Small Bus Mgr of Yr, DeKalb Bus-man's Assn, 1974; Recog Cert, GA Small Bus Mgrs Assn, 1976; W/W in S & SW.

DOBLER, NORMA MAE oc/State Senator; b/May 2, 1917; h/1401 Alpowa Street, Moscow, ID 83843; ba/Boise, ID; m/Clifford; c/Sharon D Vega, Carol D Harris, Terry L; p/Lester and Bessie Woodhouse (dec); sp/Lee and Minnie Dobler (dec); ed/BS, Univ of ID, 1939; pa/ Secy, Registrar, Univ of ID, 1939-41; Secy, Am Express Co, Seattle, WA, 1943; Secy to Judge S Ben Dunlap, Caldwell, ID, 1945; Lab Tech, Wood Utilization, Univ of ID, 1960-70; Secy to St Ext Forester, 1971-75; St Legis, 1973-; cp/ LWV, St Pres, 1968-71; Moscow C of C;

Conserv Leag; Hon Life Mem, ID Mtl Hlth Asn; Hon Mem, ID Assn of Home Ec; Hon Mem, Delta Kappa Gamma; hon/Ser Cit, ID Comm on Wom's Progs, 1975; Ser Cit, Assoc'd Students of Univ of ID, 1975; Citizen of Yr, ID Chapt Nat Assn of Social Wkrs, 1980; W/W: in Am, of Am Wom.

DOCKETT, DOSHIA C M oc/Head of Music Department; b/Feb 6, 1938; h/113 Wellington Hill Street, Boston, MA 02126; ba/Jamaica Plain, MA; p/James A and Doshia Dockett, Boston, MA; ed/BMus 1961, EdD 1982, Boston Univ; MEd, Boston St Col, 1963; Leag of Wom for Commun Ser; Music Edr Nat Conf; Am Guild of Organists; Am Choral Dirs Assn; Black Edrs Alliance of MA; cp/Tchr 1963-67, Curric Design Spec 1967-69, Music Supvr 1969-79; Curric Coor 1979-81, Boston Public Schs; Hd Music Dept, Jamaica Plain HS, 1981-; cp/Organist & Dir Music, Ebenezer Bapt Ch, 1971-; Organist & Choir Dir for St Paul AME Ch 1962-67, St John's Epis 1967-70; Pres 1980-82, Delta Kappa Gamma Intl; Phi Lambda Theta; NAACP; Handel & Haydn Soc, 1963-81; Alpha Kappa Alpha, 1969-; r/Prot; hon/Profl Pubs; Martin Luther King Jr F'ship Awd, Boston Univ, 1975; Outstg Yg Wom of Am, 1972 & 1975; Apprec Awd, St Mark Congregl Ch, 1972.

DOCKING, ROBERT B oc/Bank Executive; b/Oct 9, 1925; h/Stonebridge, Route 3, Arkansas City, KS 67005; ba/Arkansas City, KS; m/Meredith Gear; c/William Russell, Thomas Robert; p/George Docking (dec); Mary Virginia Blackwell; ed/BS, Univ of KS, 1948; Cert of Grad, Grad Sch of Bkg, Univ of WI; mil/USAAC, 1943-46, Corporal; USAFR, 1946-51, 1st Lt; pa/Credit Analyst, Wm Volker Co, KC, MO, 1948-50; Cashier & Asst Trust Ofcr, 1st Nat Bk, Lawrence, KS, 1950-56; VPres, Union St Bk, Arkansas City, KS, 1956-59; Pres, Union St Bk, Arkansas City, KS, 1959-; Pres, City Nat Bk, Guymon, OK, 1978-; Gov of KS, 4 Terms, 1967-75; Former Mayor & Former City Commr, Arkansas City, KS; Owner, Docking Ins Agy, Arkansas City, KS; Asst Treas & Dir, KS Public Ser Co, Lawrence, KS; Pes & Chm of Bd of Dirs, Union St Bk, Arkansas City, KS; Owner, Docking Devel Co, Oxford, KS; Pres & Dir, City Nat Bk & Trust Co, Guymon, OK; Dir, 4th Nat Bk & Trust Co, Wichita, KS; Dir, 1st KS Life Ins Co, Newton, KS; Dir: Cimarron Investmt Co Inc, Cimarron Ins Co Inc, Cimarron Life Ins Co, Plains Ins Co & Cimarron Fin Co Inc, Cimarron, KS; Mbrships & Ofc Positions in Num Profl Coms & Assns; cp/Mason; Moose Lodge; Elks Lodge; Eagles Lodge; Num Other Orgs & Commun Activs; hon/Num Hon Mbrships; Fred Ellsworth Medallion for Unique & Significant Ser, Univ of KS, 1981; Dist'd Kansan Awd, 1981; Citizenship Awd, Nat Conv of AME U Chs, 1974; Key to Oil Patch Awd, KS Indep Oil & Gas Assn, 1973; Hon Marshall, Dodge City, KS, 1968; Conservator Awd, St of KS, KS Wildlife Assn, 1973; Eagle of Yr, St of KS, 1970; Apprec Awd, Nat Coun on Crime & Delinq, 1973; NY Humanitarian Awd, U Jewish Orgs, 1974; Hope Awd, Student Body, Univ of KS, 1974; KS Man of Yr, *Topeka Capitol Jour* & St Hist Soc, 1968; Yg Man of Yr, KS Jr C of C, 1959; Legion of Hon, Demolay, 1959; Wisdom Awd, Wisdom Soc for Advmt of Knowledge, Lrng &

Res in Ed, 1969; Doct of Law: Washburn Univ, Topeka & Benedictine Col, Atchison, KS; W/W: in Am, in Am Polits, in MW, in Bkg; Commun Ldrs of Am; Men of Achmt; Other Biogl Listings.

DODGE, ARTHUR BYRON JR oc/Executive; b/Jun 13, 1923; h/1142 Marietta Avenue, Lancaster, PA 17303; ba/Lancaster, PA; m/Margaretha Gerbert; c/Arthur Byron III, Andrew Nikolaus; p/Arthur Byron and Marion Cochran Dodge (dec); sp/G N and Helena G Gerbert (dec); ed/BS Ec, Franklin & Marshall Col, Lancaster, PA, 1947; mil/AUS, Inf, 1943-52, Capt; Battlefield Comm, Italy, 1944; pa/Employee 1947-, Dir 1956-, Pres 1981-, Dodge Cork Co Inc; Dir & Secy, Gerbert Ltd, 1979-; Dir & Treas, Intertrade Ltd, 1978-; Mem: ASTM, 1963-; Am Newcom, 1967-; Trustee, St Andrews Sch, Middletown, DE, 1958-; Treas, Cork Inst of Am, 1979-; cp/Pres, Friends of SOS Chd's Villages, 1979-; r/Epis; hon/Cit for Meritorious Ser, Pres's Comm for Employmt of the Handicapped, 1967; Cit of Merit, DAV, 1980; W/W: in W, in Commerce & Indust.

DODSON, RONALD GENE oc/Regional Representative of Audubon Society; b/Aug 2, 1948; h/Wemple Road, Glenmont, NY 12077; ba/Delmar, NY; m/Theresa Jane; c/Kelly Gene, Ronald Eric, Travis Ryan; p/Mr and Mrs Bruce Dodson, Jeffersonville, IN; sp/Mr and Mrs Charles Vowels, Evansville, IN; ed/AS, Vincennes Univ, 1968; BS, Oakland City Col, 1970; BS, IN St Univ, 1973; Postgrad Study in Biol; pa/Biol Tchr, Evansville, IN Sch Sys, 1970-72; Biol Tchr, Henderson, KY Sch Sys, 1972-73; Prodn Supvr, Anaconda Aluminum, 1973-78; Sales Mgr ERA/Real Est, 1978-79; Exec Dir, Operation Commun Pride, Hendersonville, KY, 1979-82; NE Reg Rep, Nat Audubon Soc, 1982-; cp/Bd of Dirs, WNIN Public TV, 1978-82; Pres, KY Audubon Coun, 1979-82; Pres, Henderson KY, Audubon Soc, 1977-79; Bd of Dirs, Henderson C of C, 1979-82; Gov's Coun on Energy, 1979-80; OH River Water Sanitation Comm, 1980-82; Envir Chair, NY Legis Forum, 1982; r/Bapt; hon/Envir Columnist for Henderson, KY *Gleaner*, Daily Newspaper, 2 Yrs; Outstg Yg Man of Am, 1980; W/W in S & SW; Men of Achmt.

DOGBE, KORSI oc/Associate Professor of Sociology; b/Dec 4, 1940; h/533-D East Queen Street, Hampton, VA 23669; ba/Hampton, VA; m/Akosua Tess; c/Kila, Mawuse; p/Yaovi Dogbe, Ghana; sp/Obenewa Asante, Ghana; ed/BA, Univ of Ghana, 1966; MA 1970, MSc 1971, PhD 1973, Univ of So CA; pa/Peace Corps Vol, US Depts of St & Ed, 1967-69; Vis'g Prof, Chapman Col for World Campus Afloat, 1972-73; Lectr in African Sociol & Sociol of Ed, Univ of Cape Coast, 1973-77; Fulbright-Hays Curric Conslt, US Depts of St & Ed for Norfolk St Univ, 1977-78; Assoc Prof of Sociol, Hampton Inst, 1978-; Am Sociol Assn; Intl Sociol Assn; Am Assn of Tchr Edrs; African Studies Assn; Am Coun for the U Nations U; Fellow, African Inst for Study of Human Values; r/Presb; hon/Pub'd Author; Distn in Tchg, 1963; Best Ga Student of Yr, 1962; Best Student of Yr, 1959; W/W in S & SW; Dir of Scholars & Spec in 3rd World Studies.

DOHERTY, GEORGE WILLIAM oc/Psychologist; b/Oct 18, 1941; h/Box 607, Ely, NV 89301; ba/Ely, NV; p/William

Doherty, Wood-Ridge, NJ; Catherine M Doherty (dec); ed/BS, PA St Univ, 1964; MS, MS St Univ, 1977; Att'd Baylor Univ, N TX St Univ; mil/USAF, 1964-68, Capt; pa/Prog Coor, Ec Opports Advmt Corp, 1968-70; Dir of Yth Dev Prog, Ec Opports Advmt Corp, 1970-71; Psychol Cnslr, Cora Ser, 1973-75; Parent Tng Conslt, Cora Ser, 1973-075; Psychol III, Rural Clinics Commun Cnslg Ctr, 1980-; Instr, No NV Commun Col, 1980-; Am Psychol Assn; TX Psychol Assn; Soc for Psychol Study of Social Issues; Inter Am Soc of Psychol; Intl Assn of Applied Psychol; Am Assn for Cnslr Dev; Assn for Cnslr Ed & Supvn; Assn for Measurement in Ed & Guid; Am Mtl Hlth Cnslr's Assn; Biofeedback Soc of Am; Wn Psychol Assn; NV Psychol Assn; Intl Acad of Profl Cnslg & Psychotherapy; Task Force on Commun Cnslg, Assn for Cnslr Ed & Supvn; Task Force on Intl Cnslr Ed & Supvn, Assn for Cnslr Ed & Supvn; Air Force Assn; PA St Alumni Assn; AAAS; Wn Assn of Cnslr Edrs & Supvrs; Cert'd Clin Mtl Hlth Cnslr, Nat Acad of Cert'd Clin Mtl Hlth Cnslrs; Nat Cert'd Cnslr, Nat Bd of Cert'd Cnslrs; r/Cath; hon/Psi Chi, 1970-; Exec Ofcr, Arnold Air Soc, Harry R Armstrong Sqdrn, Penn St, 1963-64; John Henry Cardinal Newman Nat Honor Soc, 1964; W/W in W.

DOLE, ARTHUR A oc/Professor; b/Oct 25, 1917; h/543 Manor Road, Wynnewood, PA 19096; ba/Philadelphia, PA; m/Marjorie W; c/Barbara L, Steven M, Peter L; ed/BA, Antioch Col, 1946; MA 1949, PhD 1951, OH St Univ; Hon MA, Univ of PA, 1973; pa/Cnslr, OH St Univ, 1948-51; Dir, Bur of Testing & Guid, Univ of HI, 1951-60; Asst Prof 1951-60, Assoc Prof 1960-66, Prof Psych 1966-68, Cnslg Psychol, Cnslg & Testing Ctr, 1962-67; Coor Rehab Cnslg 1962-67, Vis'g Scholar Indust Relats Ctr 1965, Univ of MN; Vis'g Prof Psych & Ed, Tchrs Col, Columbia Univ, 1966-67; Prof Ed, Psych in Ed Div 1967-, Coor Psychol Sers Prog 1967-71, Coor Psych in Ed Prog 1976-77, Chm Psych in Ed Div 1982-, Univ of PA; Mem: Fellow, Am Psychol Assn; Intl Coun of Psychols; AAAS; AAUP; Am Ednl Res Assn; Am Pers & Guid Assn; Am Voc Guid Assn; Intl Rehab Assn; Assn Cnslr Edn & Supvn; Am Rehab Cnslg Assn; Sigma Xi; hon/Author, Over 60 Articles Pub'd in Profl Jours incl'g: *Jour of Cnslg Psych*; *Pers & Guid Jour*; *Am Ednl Res Jour*; *Profl Psych*; Num Others; W/W: in Am, in E.

DOLE, MALCOLM JR oc/Economist; b/Apr 24, 1935; h/2221-6 Woodside Lane, Sacramento, CA 95825; c/Malcolm III, Heather McAdie; p/Mr and Mrs Malcom Dole Sr, Los Gatos, CA; ed/BA, NWn Univ, 1957; PhD, Univ of CA-LA, 1974; pa/Res Mgr 1976-, Sr Economist 1973-76, CA Air Resources Bd; Prof, CA St Univ-Northridge, 1967-72; Mem: Am Ec Assn; Wn Reg Sci Assn; cp/Commonwlth Clb; Sheridan Shore Yacht Clb; Bd of Dirs, Sacramento Metro Ski Patrol; N Clb of NWn Univ; hon/Author, *An Ec Theory of Bureaucracy*, 1974; *Omicron Delta Epsilon*, 1967; *Awd of Apprec*, *U Way*, 1979; *Phi Gamma Delta*.

DOLEY, HAROLD E JR oc/Executive Director; b/Mar 8, 1947; h/616 Baronne Street, New Orleans, LA 70113; ed/BA, Xavier Univ, 1968; pa/US Exec Dir, African Devel Bk & Fund, Abidjan, Ivory Coast, 1983-; Dir, Minerals Mgmt Ser, 1982-83; Pres, Doley Securities Inc,

1976-82; Bd Mem, LA St Minerals Bd, 1980-81; Treas, WYES-TV, Public Broadcasting Affil, NO, 1975-81; Ec Instr, So Univ, 1970-77; Asst VPres, Howard, Weil, Labouisse & Fredericks, 1974-76; Mem, NY Stock Exch, 1973-74; Acct Exec, Bache & Co, 1973; Mem, NY Futures Exch.

DOLGIN, STEPHEN MARK oc/Public Administrator; b/Dec 22, 1949; h/27808 Huntwood Avenue #8, Hayward, CA 94544; ba/Richmond, CA; p/David A Dolgin, Concord, CA; Ruth Dolgin, Oakland, CA; ed/BA 1972, MSW 1976, Univ of MN; MBA, Golden Gate Univ, 1982; mil/AUS, 1976-79; USAR, Capt; pa/Social Wkr, Contia Costa Co, 1979-81; Social Wkr, AUS, 1976-79; Capt, USAR Med Ser Corp; Civil Air Patrol Sqdrn Dep Cdr for Cadets, 1977-; Resv Ofcrs Assn, 1973-; Assn of US Army, 1976-; AF Assn, 1977-; Toastmasters, 1983-; Advr Med Explorers, 1977-79; cp/Jewish Lay Ldr, Ft Bragg, 1977-79; r/Jewish; hon/Civil Air Patrol Sqdrn Sr Mem of Yr, 1980; W/W in W.

DOLGUN, ALEXANDER MICKAEL oc/Program Officer; b/Sep 29, 1926; h/12704 Deep Spring Drive, Potomac, MD 20853; ba/Bethesda, MD; m/Irene; c/Andrew; ed/BSc, Moscow St Pub'g & Printing Inst, 1961; M Degree, All-Union Inst of Postgrad Tng for Wkrs of Media, 1965; pa/Chief of Consular Files, Am Embassy, 1943-48; Prisoner in Soviet Hard Labor Camps, 1948-56; Sr Sci Editor & Br Chief, "Meditsyna" Pub'g House, USSR Min of Hlth, 1956-71; Prog Anal, Prog Ofcr, Fogarty Intl Ctr, Nat Inst of Hlth, Dept of Hlth & Human Ser, 1972-; hon/Pub'd Co-Author, *Alexander Dolgun's Story.*

DOLL, WILLIAM E JR oc/Coordinator of Elementary Education Department; b/Jan 29, 1931; h/111 So 4th Street, Fulton, NY 13069; ba/Oswego, NY; m/Mary A; c/William Campbell; p/William E and Anne Moran Doll (dec) sp/Edward Campbell (dec) and Mary Louise Aswell, Santa Fe, NM; ed/BA, Cornell Univ, 1953; MA, Boston Univ, 1960; PhD, Johns Hopkins Univ, 1972; pa/Tchr, Park Sch, 1953-60; Dir of Math, Graland Sch, 1960-64; Hdmaster, Val Sch, 1964-67; Asst/Assoc Prof of Ed 1971-75, Dept Chair 1980-82, Coor Elem Ed 1983-, St Univ of NY; Presentations: Am Assn of Col of Tchr Ed, Am Ednl Res Assoc, Am Ednl Studies Assn; Assn of Supvn & Curric Developers, Conf on Tchr Ed, Curric Theory Conf, John Dewey Soc, Nat Assn of Lab Schs, NY St Foun of Ed Assn, Soc for Prof of Ed, Terman Meml Conf, WI Con on Social Studies; Acad Policies Coun; NY St Foun of Ed Assn; Bd of Dirs, John Dewey Soc, 1979-81; Bd of Dirs, Oswego Coop Nursery Sch, 1981-; r/Cath; hon/Num Profl Pubs; SUNY Grants, 1979 & 1980; W/W in E.

DOMBRO, MARCIA WINTERS oc/Director of Nursing Education; b/Dec 14, 1940; h/9841 Southwest, 123rd Street, Miami, FL 33176; ba/Miami, FL; m/Roy S; c/Rayna, Meryl; p/Mrs Thelma Winters, Phoenix, AZ; sp/Mrs Esther Dombro, Miami Bch, FL; ed/BSN, WA, 1963; MS Adult Ed, FL Intl Univ, 1976; Cert'd CPR Instr, Am Heart Assn, 1982; pa/Dir Dept Nsg Ed, Bapt Hosp of Miami, 1980-; Instr, Univ of Miami Sch of Nsg, 1976-80; Instr Ob, Miami-Dade Commun Col, '1973-74; Instr Ob, City Hosp, Elmhurst, NY, 1968-69; Hd Nsg Home

Care Univ, Bellevue Hosp, NYC, 1966-67; PHN, City of NY, Bur of Nsg, 1965-66; PHN, Seattle-King Co Hlth Dept, Seattle, WA, 1964-65; Ofc Nurse for Pediatrician, Grp Hlth of Puget Sound, Seattle, 1963-64; Childbirth Ed Instr, Cert'd by ASPO & ARC, 1970-83; Mem: NOW; ANA; Nat Leag for Nsg; Am Soc for Psychoprophylaxis in Ob; Am Soc for Hlth, Ed & Tng; r/Jewish; hon/Author of Var Articles incl'g: "The Challenge of the Future in Nsg," 1983, "Therapeutic Uses of Human Figure Drawings in Childbirth Ed," 1980; W/W in Am Wom.

DOME, MICHAEL T oc/Physician Assistant; b/Oct 4, 1953; h/PO Box 319 McQueeney, TX 78123; ba/San Antonio, TX; m/Isabel; p/Mr and Mrs Marcion J Dome, New Braunfels, TX; ed/BA, Upper IA Univ, 1982; AAS, SWn TX St Univ, 1983; mil/USAF, 1972-76; Army NG 1976-; pa/Medic, USAF, 1972-76; Med Supvr, Pan Am World Airways, 1979-80; Medic, Santa Fe Overseas, 1981-82; Phys Asst, Phys Emer Ofc Ctr, 1982-; Mem: Am Acad of Phys Assts; Aerospace Med Assn; Resv Ofcr's Assn; r/Cath; hon/Awd for Acad Excell, SWn TX St Univ, 1979; Grad cum laude, Upper IA Univ, 1983; TX Meritorious Ser Medal, Army NG, 1978.

DOMSTEAD, MARY M oc/Freelance Writer; b/Jul 29, 1928; h/425 North 19th Street, Duncan, OK 73533; ba/Same; m/Billy R E; c/Billy Eugene, June Domstead Wagner; p/Jefferson Wesley and Lucille Elleen Wadley (dec); sp/Royal Edward and Sylvia Domstead (dec); ed/Att'd S OK City Jr Col; pa/Homemaker; Sangamon Greeting Cards K-Mart; Rep for Keepsake Clippines; Freelance Writer; cp/Den Mother, Cub Scouts, 1960; Sponsor, Campfire Girls, 1963; Marlow OK 1967, Harper KS 1968, Duncan OK 1976, Yth Sponsor; Reporter, Wom for Christ, 1979; r/New Testament Christian; hon/Pub'd Author; World W/W of Wom; Intl W/W of Intells; DIB.

DONAHO, JOHN A oc/Company President; b/Sep 9, 1917; h/6600 Deer Park Road, Reisterstown, MD 21136; ba/Baltimore, MD; m/Patricia Maguire; c/Rondi; sp/Luci Maguire, Baltimore, MD; ed/AB, Ctl YMCA Col, 1941; Cert in Public Adm 1942, MA 1943, Univ of Chgo; pa/Asst to Comptroller, Commonwlth Edison Co, 1935-43; Prin, Bur of Budget, Wash DC, 1943-47; VP, Roosevelt Univ, 1947-48; Budget Dir & Act'g City Mgr, Richmond, VA, 1948-52; Conslt to Gov of MD, 1952-54; Pres, John A Donaho & Assoc, 1953-; Conslt to Mayor of Balto City, 1976-; cp/Pres & Dir, Univ Clb of Balto; Dir, U Reisterstown Residents; Pres, Civitan Clb of Richmond, 1951-52; Dir, Civitan Clb of Balto, 1965-80; Pres, Lakeview Clb Inc, 1961; hon/Num Profl Pubs; Fellow, Soc for Advmt of Mgt, 1958; Sen Fellow, Am Soc for Public Adm, 1963; Pres, MD Chapt, Am Soc for Pub Adm, 1955; Pres, Balto Reg Chapt, Soc for Advmt of Mgt, 1972-073; W/W: in E, in Commerce & Indust, Among Jours & Authors; Am Men of Sci; Personalities of S; DIB.

DONAHUE, JACK DAVID oc/Professor; b/Nov 21, 1938; h/1251 Denniston Avenue, Pittsburgh, PA 15217; ba/Pittsburgh, PA; m/Jessie Gilchrist; c/Michael Steven, Jack Kevin; p/Leonard G and Ruth Donahue; sp/Iris M Hertner; ed/BA Univ of IL, 1960; PhD, Columbia

Univ, 1967; pa/Geol Lectr 1965-67, Asst Prof Geol 1967-70, Queens Col of CUNY; Asst Prof Geol 1970-74, Assoc Prof Geol/Anthropology 1974-83, Prof Geol/Anthropology 1983-, Univ of Pgh; Mem: AAAS; AIPG; Cert'd Petro Geol, AAPG; SGPM; Fellow, Geol Soc of Am; IAS; Paleontology Soc; SAA; hon/Author, 2 Books in Field of Geol & Archaeol Geol; Over 55 Articles in Profl Jours.

DONALD, ALEXANDER GRANT oc/Professor; b/Jan 24, 1928; h/4354 Chicora Street, Columbia, SC 29206; ba/Columbia, SC; m/Emma Louise Coggeshall; c/Sandy, Mary Chesnut, Marion Lide; p/Raymond George Donald (dec); sp/Marion Lide Coggeshall (dec); ed/BS, Davidson Col, 1948; MD, Med Univ of SC, Charleston, 1952; Intern, Jefferson Med Col Hosp, Phila, PA, 1952-53; Residency in Psychi, Walter Reed Hosp, Wash DC, 1956-59; mil/AUS, 1953-62; pa/Dir, Mtl Hlth Clin, Florence, SC, 1962-66; Dept Commr, Dept of Mtl Hlth, Columbia, SC, 1966-67; Dir, Wm S Hall Psychi Inst, Columbia, SC, 1967-; Prof & Chm Dept of Neuropsychi 1975-, Dir of Admissions 1982-83, Assoc Dean for Student Affairs 1982-, Univ of SC Sch of Med; Mem: Am Psychi Assn; Pres 1967, SC Dist Br, Am Psychi Assn; So Psychi Assn; Columbia & SC Med Assns; AMA; Am Col of Mtl Hlth Adm; r/Presb; hon/Co-Editor, *Endorphins & Opiate Antagonists in Psychi Res,* 1982; Var Articles in Profl Jours incl'g: *The Psychi Forum; So Med Jour;* Others; Fellow, Am Psychi Assn; Fellow, Am Col of Psychis; Examr, Am Bd of Psych & Neurol Inc, 1969-; Fellow, So Psychi Assn; W/W: in Hlth Care, in World, in Am; Other Biogl Listings.

DONNELLY, BARBARA SCHETTLER oc/Medical Technologist; b/Dec 2, 1933; h/204 Greenbriar Lane, Bedford, TX 76021; ba/Irving, TX; c/Linda Ann, Richard Michael; p/Clarence G (dec) and Irene Elizabeth B Schettler, Sweetwater, TN; ed/AA, TN Wesleyan Col, 1952; BS, Univ of TN, 1954; MT, Broness Erlanger Hosp Sch of Med Technol, 1954; Att'd So Meth Univ, 1980-81; pa/Med Technol, Baroness Erlanger Hosp, 1953-57; Med Technol, St Luke's Epis Hosp, TX Med Ctr, 1957-58 & 1962; Med Technol, Engrg Res & Dev, SCI Systems Inc, 1974-76; Conslt, Hematology Sys 1976-77, Hematology Spec 1977-81, Tech Spec, Microbiol Sys 1981-82, Tech Ser Coor Microbiol, Bio-Chem & Hematology Sys 1982-83, Customer Tng Coor Clin Chem Sys 1983-, Abbott Labs; Am Soc of Clin Pathols; Am Soc for Microbiol; Nat Assn for Female Execs; hon/Pub'd Author; 5 Yr Service Award, Abbott Labs; W/W of Am Women; Personalities: of South, of Am; World W/W of Women; 5000 Personalities of World.

DONNELLY, LORETTA ROBINSON oc/Manager Budgets; b/Jan 24, 1946; h/1588 Little Neck Road, West, Virginia Beach, VA 23452; ba/Roanoke, VA; m/Joseph M Jr; c/Joseph Michael III, Benjamin Trevor; p/Herbert T and Julia H Robinson, Bradford, VA; sp/Joseph M (dec) and Virginia I Donnelly, Roanoke, VA; ed/BS 1970, MBA 1975, VA Polytech Inst & St Univ; Cert'd CPA, VA; pa/Tax Acct 1970-76, Cost Anal 1976-77, Sr Profitability Anal 1977-80, Mgr Budget 1980-, Norfolk & Wn Rwy Co; Part-time Acct'g Instr, VA Wn Commun Col, 1975-76; Am Inst of

CPAs; VA Soc of CPAs; Am Wom's Soc of CPA; Roanoke Netwk for Profl & Managerial Wom; Am Soc of Wom Acct; Jr Achmt Advr; hon/Beta Alpha Psi.

DORN, ROSE MARIE oc/Advertising Executive; b/Jan 23, 1946; h/1522 South Centinela Avenue #202, Los Angeles, CA 90025; ba/Los Angeles, CA; p/Irene Korenak Dorn, Milwaukee, WI; ed/BA, Univ of WI-Milwaukee, 1968; pa/Media Buyer, McCann-Erickson, 1968-74; Sr Media Planner, Eisaman Johns & Laws, 1974-77; Sr Media Supvr, Chiat/Day Advtg, 1977-79; Asst Media Dir, Dailey & Assoc, 1979-; Advtg Indust Emer Fund, 1981-; Demo Pres Campaign, 1972; ERA Amendment; Guest Lectr, Univ of So CA; r/Cath; hon/Salutatorian, HS, 1964; Nat Hon Soc, 1962-64; S'ship to Univ of WI, 1965; W/W in W.

DORNER, SHARON A HADDON oc/ Business Educator; b/Nov 3, 1943; h/28 College Avenue, Upper Montclair, NJ; ba/ Woodcliff Lake; c/Wendy Ann, Meridith Lynn; p/Mr and Mrs William Haddon, Lavallette, NJ; ed/BA 1965, MA 1970, MA 1978, Montclair St Col; EdD, Rutgers Univ, 1982; pa/Bus Tchr, Morris Knolls HS, 1965-70; Adult Ed Tchr, Sussex Voc Sch, 1969-70; Bus Tchr, Katherine Gibbs Sec Sch, 1972-73; Bus Tchr, Co Col of Morris, 1973; Bus Tchr, Leonia HS, 1974-75; Bus Tchr, Montville HS, 1976; Bus Tchr & Adm Intern to Supt, Woodcliff Sch, 1976-; Acct'g, Drew Chem Corp, 1960-70 (Sums); Phi Delta Kappa; Delta Pi Epsilon; Omicron Tau Theta; Kappa Delta Pi; Pi Omega Pi; NECEL; NJCEL; NEA; NJ Ed Assn; Bergen Co Ed Assn; Woodcliff Lake Ed Assn; Nat Bus Ed Assn; En Bus Ed Assn; NJ Bus Ed Assn; Am Voc Assn; NJ Voc Assn; Am Res Assn; Am Voc Res Assn; Assn for Supvn & Curric Devel; Consumers Leag of NJ; cp/ Byram Bd of Ed, 1968-70; Lenape Val Bd of Ed, 1969-72; Essex Co Bd of Elections, 1975-; Sigma Kappa Nat Sorority; OES, 1963-; Daugh of Nile, 1976-; r/Presb; hon/ Author, Profl Pubs; W/W: of Am Wom, in E; World W/W Wom; Dir of Dist'd Ams; 2000 Notable Ams; Intl Book of Hon.

DORON, ZVI J oc/Director of Strategic Planning; b/Feb 11, 1935; h/11 Grist Mill Lane, Westport, CT 06880; ba/ Stamford, CT; m/Beverly; c/Opher, Yael, Uri; p/Paul & Elizabeth Doron, Jerusalem, Israel; ed/BSc 1958, MSc Nuclear Power 1959, Imperial Col, Univ of London; m/ Israeli Army, 1952-54; pa/Dir Strategic Planning Grp W Satellite Communs 1981-, Sr Conslt Corp Planning 1980-81, Dir Planning & Technol Uranium Resources 1977-80, Mgr Strategic Planning Uranium Resources 1976-77, PWR Sys Div 1974-76, Westinghouse Elect Corp; Dir Projs Dept 1972-74, Dir Tech Coor 1970-72, Westinghouse Nuclear Europe; Dept Hd Nuclear Div 1968-70, Sr Rep in US 1966-68, Nordostschwiz, Kraftwerke AG; Israel Atomic Energy Comm, 1959-66; r/Jewish; hon/Contbr, Over 12 Articles to Profl Jours; Grad Study F'ship, Israel Atomic Energy Comm, 1958-59; W/ W: in World, in E, in Fin & Indust, in Am Jewry, in Technol Today; Num Other Biogl Listings.

DORR, DARWIN ALFRED oc/Clinical Psychologist; b/Apr 1, 1940; ba/Highland Hosp, PO Box 1101, Asheville, NC 28802; c/Benjamin Paul, Christopher Joseph; p/ Joseph Frank Dorr (dec); Catherine Joahanna La Rock; ed/BA Psych 1962, MA Psych 1965, Alfred Univ; PhD Clin Psych,

FL St Univ, 1969; Res Assoc & Asst Prof, Clin Psych Tng Prog, Univ of Rochester, Rochester, NY, 1969-72; Asst Prof Clin Psych Tng Prog, Dept Psych, Wash Univ-St Louis, 1973-75; Assoc Prof of Med Psych, Duke Med Sch, 1975-80; Chief Psychol, Highland Hosp Div of Duke Univ Med Ctr, Asheville, NC 1975-80; Chief Psychol, Highland Hosp, 1980-; Mem: Fellow Var Divs, Am Psychol Assn; SEn Psychol Assn; NC Psychol Assn; NY St Cert in Clin & Sch Psych; Mo Cert in Clin Psych; Lic'd Pract Psychol, St of NC; r/Epis; hon/Author, Over 39 Articles & Editor of Var Chapts in Profl Pubs & Books incl'g: *Jour of Rel & Hlth; Wom & Soc; Intl Ency of Ed: Res & Studies; Psychotherapy Theory, Res & Pract; Personality & Indiv Differences; Jour Clin Psych; Am Jour Commun Psych;* Others; Nat Register of Hlth Ser Providers in Psych; W/W: in Ed, in S & SW; Dir of Dist'd Ams.

DORSCH, ROBERTA FUNK oc/Field Director; b/Jul 9, 1943; h/PO Box 358, Ellerslie, MD 21529; ba/Martinsburg, WV; m/Dennis Edward; c/Brenda Jean; p/ Roberta E (dec) and Edward Funk, Baltimore, MD; sp/Rebecca and Baldwin Dorsch, Balto, MD; ed/Att'd Univ of MD & Johns Hopkins Univ Sch of Cytotechnol; pa/Cytoprep Tech, Johns Hopkins Hosp, 1962-68; Cytotechnol, Johns Hopkins Hosp, 1966-69 & 1971-74; Cytotechnol, Meml Hosp at Easton, MD, 1969-71; Cytotechnol, VA Hosp, 1974-76; Cytotechnol, Sacred Heart Hosp, 1976-78; Field Dir, Shawnee Girl Scout Coun; Am Soc of Cytology, 1966-; Am Soc of Clin Pathols, 1966-; MD Assn of Cytotechnols, 1968-; GSA; cp/PTA & Swimming Tchr, Cash Val Sch; Water Ballet Tchr, Cumberland Pks & Rec; Water Ballet Tchr, Frostburg Pks & Rec; Am Cancer Soc; Frostburg Badminton Clb; Ellersue U Meth Ch Yth Activs, 1977; Girl Scout Ldr; Brownie Ldr; Jr Girl Scout Ser Unit Dir; Girl Ldr Tnr; r/Cath; hon/W/W of Am Wom.

DORSET, GERALD H oc/Librarian; b/ Aug 9, 1920; h/45 Tudor City Place, New York, NY 10017; m/Edna Bagley; p/ Stoyan and Teresa Rilsky (dec); ed/LLB, St Clement Univ of Sofia, Law Sch, 1941-45; Att'd La Sorbonne, 1946-47; BA, Univ of MD, 1971; MLS, Cath Univ of Am, 1973; pa/Script-Writer, Voice of Am, NYC, 1948-52; Script-Writer, Radio Free Europe, NYC, 1952-54; Script-Writer, BBC, London, 1955-61; Eng Dept, Univ of HI, 1963-65; Univ of PR, San Juan, 1965-67; Libn, Lib of Cong, Wash DC, 1967-69; Lib, US Book Exch, Wash DC, 1969-73; Mem: ALA; AWU; APA; NY PAS; NYDA; ABA; Am Lib Assn; Am Writers Union; Am Poetry Assn; NY Painters & Artists Soc; NY Drama Assn; Am Book Critics Assn; r/Greek Orthodox; hon/Author of Poetry & Fiction incl'g: *Adventure in Port Rich; Tales of 2 Worlds; Love Lttrs; Hawks & Doves; Time Music; NYC Poems;* Laurel Intl Poetry Awd, 1969; WHP & WEFG Poetry Awd, 1971; Danae Intl Poetry Assn Awd, 1973; Manhattan Col Cert, 1976; Pass Co Col Cert of Awd, 1983; CODA; Dir of Contemp Fiction Writers; Gale Res Series.

DORSON, WILLIAM JOHN oc/Professor; b/May 9, 1936; h/960 East La Jolla Drive, Tempe, AZ 85282; ba/Tempe, AZ; m/Denise E; c/Mark J, Peter G; p/ Josephine Dorson, Nashua, NH; sp/

Estelle Larivee, Redington Bch, FL; ed/ BChE 1958, MChE 1960, Rensselaer Polytech Inst; PhD Chm & Bioengrg, Univ of Cinc, 1967; pa/Prof Engrg 1971-, Assoc Prof 1966-71, AZ St Univ; Instr, Univ of Cinc, 1965-66; Res Engr 1958-65, Coop Engr 1955-58, Gen Elect Co; Mem: Secy/Treas 1984-, Exec Com 1982-, Am Soc for Artificial Internal Organs; AAAS; BMES; ISOTT; AIChE; ASME; Exec Com, AAMI; Renal Disease & Detox Com; Gen Hosp & Pers Use Panel, FDA; Prog Com, ASAIO, 1973-76; Diagnostic Imaging Com 1970-83, Res Com 1967-81, St Luke's Hosp Med Ctr; Others; r/Rom Cath; hon/Author, Over 100 Articles in Profl Jours & Assn Proceedings, Var Books & Book Chapts in Field incl'g: *ASAIO Jour; Proc of AMA Symp on Drinking Water & Human Hlth; Clin Res; Proc of ACEMB;* Others; 1st Place Sci Exhibit, AZ Med Assn, 1973; Men & Molecules Prog, Am Chem Soc, 1971; Sci Exhibit Awd, SAMA-AQUIBB, 1970; Sigma Xi, 1966; Tau Beta Pi, 1957; Phi Lambda Upsilon, 1957; W/W: in Am, in Frontier Sci & Technol, of Contemp Achmt; DIB; Other Biogl Listings.

DOSSETT, BETTY JO oc/Social Insurance Representative (Retired); b/Sep 14, 1931; h/409 North Street, Hattiesburg, MS 39401; c/Linda Gail Dossett David, Mark Richard; p/James Daniel (dec) and Mary Allen Ishee Mooney, Hattiesburg, MS; ed/BS, 1953; MEd, 1972; pa/Social Ins Rep, Social Security Adm of Hattiesburg MS, 1960-66; Social Ins Rep, Social Security Adm of Holiday FL, 1976-78; Social Ins Rep, Social Security Adm of Dallas TX, 1978-83; Bus Conslt, Paul Stephen Lee, Concert Organist, 1976-81; Nat Assn of Female Execs, 1980-81; Nat Bus Ed Assn, 1950-52; cp/Dir of So Bapt Wom Missionary Union Girl's Aux, Whitehaven Bapt Ch, 1967-68; HS Sunday Sch Tchr & Coor, Main St Bapt Ch, 1962-66 and 1969-71; Univ of So MS Alumni Assn, 1962-; Bel Canto Music Clb, 1973-75; r/Bapt; hon/15 Yr Ser Awd, Social Security Adm, 1979; Fed Employee Recog Awd, Tampa Bay Fed Exec Assn, 1977; W/W Am Wom.

DOTSON, ALBERT EUGENE oc/ Retail Executive; b/Mar 2, 1938; h/17901 Southwest 78th Avenue, Miami, FL 33157; ba/Hialeah, FL; m/Earlene Puryear; c/Albert Eugene, Toya Sereta, LaTessa Denesa, Jonathan LaMar, Christa Ver Shona; p/Gred Rowland and Alberta D Dotson; ed/Att'd: Detroit Inst of Technol; Wayne St Univ; Miami-Dade Commun Col; Att'd Var Sears Mgmt Schs, 1970-77; pa/Career w Sears & Roebuck Co: Var Positions, 1956-64; Div Mgr Sewing Machine/Vacuum Cleaner Dept, Highland Pk, IL, 1964-67; Div Mgr Furniture Dept, 1967-68; Hard Lines Sales Supt 1968-69, Operating Supt 1969-71, Grand River, MI; Englewood Store Mgr, Chgo, 1971-73; Mall W End Store Mgr, Atlanta, GA, 1973-76; Westland Mall Store Mgr, Hialeah, FL, 1976-; VPres 1981-83, Treas 1979-81, Pres 1977-79, Dir 1976-77, Westland Mall Merchs Assn; 1st VPres 1970, Booker T Wash Bus Assn; Dir, Atlanta BBB, 1973-76; Num Other Org Mbrships in Detroit, Chgo, Atlanta & Hialeah; cp/Dir, Hialeah-Miami Lakes Rotary Clb, 1977-80; Pres Elect 1982-83, 1st VPres 1981-82, Treas, 1980-81, Secy 1979-80, Dir 1977-79, Hialeah-Miami Sprgs C of C; Dir 1980-82, 3rd VPres 1979-80, Dir

1978-79, NAACP; Dir, 1979-83, Spotlite Clb; Bd Mem, 1980-83, VChm 1979-80, Bd 1978-79, Hialeah-Miami Sprgs YMCA; Pres 1979-80, VPres 1978-79, Bd 1977-78, Miami Palmetto Sr HS All Sports Booster Clb; Sports Adv Bd, Dade Co Public Schs, 1980-83; Adv Bd, FL Meml Col, 1980-83; Co-Chp, Ptnr For Yth, 1981-82; Inst Rep, Detroit Area Coun BSA, 1960-68; Cour Rep 1966-69, Dist Fin Chm 1971-72, VChm 1972-73, Cherokee Coun Chgo; Fin Chm 1974-76, VPres 1976, John H Harland Boys Clb, Atlanta; Bd Dirs, Southtown 1971-72, Chm 1972-73, YMCA, Chgo; Pres Credit Union 1968-71, Bd of Deacons 1962-71, Corinthian Bapt Ch, Detroit; Bd of Deacons, Mt Moriah Bapt Ch, Atlanta, 1973-76; VPres Layman Dept, Progressive Nat Bapt Conv So Reg, 1974-76; Num Other Commun Activs in Detroit, Chgo, Atlanta & Hialeah; r/Bapt; hon/ Tribute for Ser, Booker T Wash Bus Assn, 1971; Awd of Merit, Cherokee Dist, Chgo Area Coun BSA, 1972; Ser Awds, Englewoods Bus-men's Assn; Ser Awds, Southtown Planning Assn; Ser Awds, Englewood Shopping Concourse Comm, 1975; Dist'd Ser Awd, Englewood Bus-men's Assn, 1971-73; Good Guy Awd, Ratio Sta WGRT, Chgo, 1971; Outst'g Ser Aws, Southtown YMCA, 1972; Ldrship Awd, Nat Assn of Mkt Developers, 1975; Spark Plug Awd, Detroit Jr C of C, 1965; VChm 1972, Englewood Concourse Comm Appt by Mayor Daley; Hamtramck Hall of Hon, Hon Life Time Citizen, Hamtramck, MI, 1975; Achmt Awd, Outstg Ser Awd, Mbrship Campaign, Atlanta NAACP, 1975; Outstg Ldrship Awd, John H Harland Boys Clb, 1976; Key to City, Hialeah, FL, 1981; Finalist for "Tony Brown's Black Jour"; W/W in S & SW; 100 Most Influential Friends.

DOTSON, CHERYL L oc/Certified Public Accountant; Manager of Consulting Department; b/Jul 7, 1954; h/206 Plaza Verde Drive E32, Houston, TX 77038; ba/Houston, TX; p/Mr and Mrs S W Dotson, Houston, TX; ed/BBA magna cum laude, Univ of Houston, 1976; pa/Audit Dept 1976-79, Sr Conslt Mgmt Cnslg Dept 1979-82, Mgr of Cnslg Dept 1982-, Peat Mavrick Mitchell & Co CPA's; V Chp, Bd of Dirs, Voc Guid Ser; Delta Sigma Theta; Nat Assn of Black Accts; NAACP; YWCA; TX Soc of CPA's; cp/Asst Treas, Antioch Bapt Ch; r/Bapt; hon/Appointed to Ethics Com of City of Houston by Mayor Kathryn Whitmore; W/W Among Col Students.

DOTY, LYNDA KAY oc/Dir of Show Productions; b/Sep 24, 1950; h/ 7919 Meadow Park Drive, #211, Dallas, TX 75230; ba/Grand Prairie, TX; p/John Vernon Doty (dec); Loraine Doty, Grand Prairie, TX; ed/BA Eng, Univ of TX-Arlington, 1973; Photo Course, Cont'g Ed Dept, So Meth Univ, 1979; pa/Dir of Show Prodns 1983-, Mgr Show Prodns 1978-83, Publicity Mgr 1977-78, Six Flags Show Prodns; Show Opers Mgr, Six Flags Over GA, 1976; Asst Mgr of Pulbic Relats 1973-76, Mgmt Trainee 1972-73, Guest Relats Hostess 1970-72, Live Show Secy 1969, Rider Operator & Foreman 1967-69, Six Flags Over TX; hon/Finalist for Outstg Yg Wking Wom in Am, *Glamour* Mag, 1984; Recip, Dallas Panhellenic S'ship,

1970-73.

DOUGLAS, J FIELDING oc/Toxicologist, Chemical Carcinogenesis; b/Jan 25, 1927; h/Hermitage Farm, Front Royal, VA 22630; ba/Front Royal, VA; m/Rose Terrazzino; c/David Benjamin, Pamela Susan, Jason Terrell; p/Ben and Amelia Fielding Douglas (dec); sp/Ben and Lena Caruso Terrazzino (dec); ed/ BS, Univ of IL, 1948; MS 1950, PhD 1953, Columbia Univ; mil/AUS, 1944-46; pa/Proj Ldr, Johnson & Johnson Co, 1952-58; Dir of Biochem, Carter-Wallace Inc, 1958-74; Pvt Conslt, Var Industs & Govt Agys, 1974-80; Dept Dir, Carcinogenesis Test Prog & Chief of Opers Nat Toxicology Prog, 1980-84; Pres, Sci Sers Inc, 1984-; Mem: Chm Biochem Grp, 1954, Chm Organic Grp 1956, Bd of Dirs 1954-58, NJ Chem Soc; cp/Ch Ofcs incl: Chm, Treas, Ser Ldr, 1956-; hon/Author, Over 75 Sci Articles, 30 Abstracts, 1950-; Book, *Carcinogenesis & Mutagenesis Testing*, 1984; Holder of 2 Patents in Field; BS w High Hons, 1948; USPHS F'ship, 1950-52; Richard Neff Soc Awd, 1970; Achmt Awd, NCI, 1979; W/W in Frontier Sci & Technol; Am Men of Sci.

DOUGLAS, STEVEN C oc/Attorney; b/Sep 2, 1952; h/1112 North Hills Drive, Crossville, TN 38555; ba/Crossville, TN; m/Deborah W; p/Ann C Douglas, Crossville, TN; sp/Mr and Mrs Ben T Welch, Floresville, TX; ed/BA, Maryville Col, 1974; JD, Univ of TN, 1977; pa/ Ptnr, Sabine & Douglas Attys, 1979-; Assoc, Sabine & Warner Attys, 1977-79; Mem: Pres, Cumberland Co Bar Assn, 1980; cp/VPres Govtl Affairs, Gtr Cumberland Co C of C, 1982; VPres, Crossville JCs, 1980; r/Prot; hon/magna cum laude, Maryville Col, 1974; Outstg Local Pres, TN JCs, 1980; W/W in Am Cols & Univs.

DOVERSPIKE, WILLIAM FRED oc/ Clinical Psychologist; b/Dec 22, 1951; h/ 1085 Chartley Drive, Lilburn, GA 30247; ba/Atlanta, GA; m/Lenre' Eidson; p/Mr and Mrs William F Doverspike, Atlanta, GA; sp/Mr and Mrs E Larry Eidson, Stone Mtn, GA; ed/BS, Emory Univ, 1974; MS Psych 1976, PhD Psych 1979, VA Commonwlth Univ; pa/ Pres, Wm F Doverspike PhD PC, 1982-; Psychol, N Atlanta Psychol Assocs, 1982-; Conslitg Psych Staff, Peachtree & Parkwood Mtl Hlth Ctrs & Hosps, 1981-; Allied Profl Staff, W Paces Ferry Hosp, Atlanta, 1981-; Hlth Profl Affil Staff, Peachford Hosp, Dunwoody, GA, 1982-; Allied Profl Staff, Brawner Psychi Inst, Smyrna, Ga, 1982-; Allied Profl Staff, Ridgeview Psychi Inst, Smyrna, 1982-; Psychol, N Dekalb Mtl Hlth Ctr, 1979-82; Pscyhol, NE Conslg Ctr, 1979-; Conslt, Cerebral Palsy Ctr of Atlanta, 1979-81; Psych Intern, GA Mtl Hlth Inst, 1978-79; Fac Mem, VA Commonwlth Univ, 1976-78; Psych Instr, Univ of Richmond, 1977-78; Previous Others; Mem: Policy & Planning Coun, Fin Com, Ins Com & GA Psychols Polit Action Com 1982-; Previous Other Coms, GA Psychol Assn; Profl Adv Bd, Atlanta Med Pers Sers Inc, 1980-; Profl Adv Bd Gwinnett Chapt, Parents w/o Ptnrs, 1980-; Am Psychol Assn; AAAS; Assn for Advmt of Psych; Union of Concerned Scis; Am Soc of Psychols in Pvt Pract; So En Psychol Assn; Biofeedback Soc of GA;

Mtl Hlth Assn of GA; Atlanta Assn for Retarded Citizens; cp/Spkr's Bur, Atlanta Mtl Hlth Assn, 1979-; Num Commun Guest Spkg Presentations, 1974-; r/Bapt; hon/Author & Co-Author, Over 30 Res Articles in Profl Jours & Papers in Assn Proceedings; Nom, Res Excell Awds, SEn Psychol Assn, 1978-1980; Nom, Outstg Yg Men of Am, US JC's, 1980-81; Psi Chi, VA Commonwlth Univ, 1977-78; Gross-Lockheed Acad S'ship Awd, Emory Univ, 1974-76; W/W in S & SW.

DOWD, ANN MARIE oc/Section Head of Histology; b/Oct 17, 1924; h/ 29231 Oak Point Drive, Farmington Hills, MI 48018; ba/Detroit, MI; m/ Thomas Stephen (dec); c/Cynthia Ann Dowd Restuccia, Kevin Thomas; p/ Frank Raymond (dec) and Frances M Ayling Sullivan; ed/BS, Wayne St Univ, 1947; pa/Wom's Hosp, 1946-52; St James Clin Lab, 1960-62; Sup Histology-Pathol Lab, Hutzel Hosp, 1962-72; Sect Hd of Histology, Mt Carmel Hosp, 1972-; Am Soc Clin Pathols; Am Soc Med Technol; MI Soc Med Technol; Nat Soc for Histotechnol; MI Soc Histotechnols; cp/Wayne St Univ Alumni Assn; Smithsonian Assn; Detroit Inst of Arts; Fdrs Soc; r/Cath; hon/Pub'd Author; W/W of Am Wom.

DOWDY, RONALD RAYMOND oc/US Air Force Officer, Director of Air Plans; b/Sep 5, 1944; h/149 Melmar Drive, Prattville, AL 36067; ba/Maxwell AFB, AL; m/Susan; c/Veronica, Richard; p/L H LeVine, Sun City Ctr, FL; sp/ Curtis Beers, Scotts Val, CA; ed/BA, Univ of MD, 1968; MS 1975, EdS 1976, Troy St Univ; mil/USAF, Maj; pa/Dir of Plans, Air Univ Ctr for Aerospace Doctrine, Res & Ed 1982-, Dir of Eval 1981-82, Aircraft Cmdr/Command Post Controller, Charleston AFB, SC, 1976-81; Sect Cmdr, Sqdrn Ofcrs Sch, 1973-76; Instr Pilot T-37, Moody AFB, 1970-73; Aircraft Cmdr, Phan Rang RVN, 1969-70; cp/Order of Daedalians; Secy, Combined Fed Campaign, Var AL Cos, 1981-82; Den Ldr, Cub Scouts, Webelos, 1982; r/Meth; hon/Author, "The Assessment Ctr As a Diagnostic Tool for Profl Devel; W/W: in S & SW, in Am Aviation; Outstg Yg Men of Am.

DOWDY, WILLIAM LOUIS oc/ Technology Commercialization Consultant; b/Dec 3, 1937; h/27 Old Spanish Trail, Portola Valley, CA 94025; ba/ Menlo Pk, CA; c/Mark Allen, John Joseph, Daniel Patrick; p/Eurgene Joseph Dowdy, San Antonio, TX; ed/BS, St Mary's Univ, 1959; MEng, TX A&M Univ, 1964; Technol Comml Conslt, SRI Intl, 1983-; Dir, Lurgi Corp, 1978-83; Mgr 1977-78, Conslt 1977, Elect Power Res Inst; Mng Dir, Rockwell Intl, 1964-76; TX A&M Nuclear Sci Ctr, 1962-64; Engr, Chrysler Corp, 1959-62; Mem: World Future Soc; Am Mgmt Assn; Commwlth Clb of Ca; Nat Com Chm 1973-, Com Mem 1969-72, Conf Chm 1971, AIAA; r/Cath; hon/Author, Over 20 Profl Pubs in Field; Technol Utilization Awd 1968, Apollo Achmt Awd 1969, NASA; W/W: in Aviation, in W, in CA, in Technol Today.

DOWELL, KIMBERLY KAY oc/ Director of Marketing-Banking; b/Mar 5, 1947; h/4289 Putting Green, San Antonio, TX 78217; ba/San Antonio, TX; c/Ryanne Kara; p/Mr and Mrs E M Enos Jr, Tampa, FL; ed/BA, Mercer Univ,

1969; Att'd Univ of FL; Corpus Christi St Univ, Sch of Bk Mktg; pa/Tchr/ Sponsor, Englewood Sr HS, 1969-74; Tchr, Epis HS, 1977-79; Mktg Ofcr 1980-82, Asst VP 1982-83, Alamo Bk; Dir of Mktg, TX Bk, 1983-; TX Bkrs Assn Mktg Coun-Dist II Rep, 1983-85; VChm 1982, Chm 1983, Exec Com 1981-84, Nat Assn of Bk Wom; Publicity Chm, Zonta Intl, 1981-84; cp/Meml Com, Am Heart Assn, 1983-84; Adv Bd Mem, Bus Com for the Arts, 1983-84; Charter Mem, San Antonio Perf'g Arts Assn 'Encore', 1983-84; Southside C of C, 1983-84; San Antonio Advtg Fdn, 1981-83; U Way, Special Accts Recruiter, 1983; Gtr San Antonio Chamber-'Helping Hands' Com, 1983-84; San Antonio Fest-Mktg Com, 1984; Wom in Communs, 1983-84; r/ Epis; hon/Ldrship, San Antonio, 1983-84; Art Show Finalist, Bus Com for the Arts, 1983; Notable Wom of TX.

DOWNS, A CHRIS oc/Developmental Psychologist; b/Nov 28, 1951; h/3737 Watonga Boulevard #31, Houston, TX 77092; ba/Houston, TX; p/Asa Woodrow and Opal House Downs, Mishawaka, IN; ed/BA, IN Univ-S Bend, 1973; PhD, Univ of TX-Austin, 1978; pa/Asst Prof, Moorhead St Univ, 1978-79; Asst Prof 1979-84, Assoc Prof 1984, Univ of Houston-Clear Lake; Am Psychol Assn; SWn Psychol Assn; Soc for Res in Child Dev; MWn Psychol Assn; Wn Psychol Assn; r/Christian; hon/Profl Pubs; Piper Prof Final Nom, Tchg Excell Awd; W/ W: in S & SW, in Frontier Sci & Technol.

DOYLE, ELIZABETH LEWIS oc/ Writer, Lecturer; h/3284 Paris Pike, Lexington, KY 40511; ba/Lexington, KY; m/Walter A; p/Alvin E Lewis, Sacramento, CA; ed/BA Eng & Sci, Univ of CA-Berkeley & MI St Univ; MS Med Jour, MI St Univ; pa/Book Editor, *Apothecary Mag*, Boston, MA; Book Reviewer & Columnist, *Am Druggist Mag*, NYC; Med Jour, Harvard Affil'd Tchg Hosps, Boston, MA; Columnist, *Boston Today Mag*, Boston, MA; Editor-in-Chief, *The Beacon Mag*, Boston; Pres, Doyle Advtg, Lexington, KY; Author; Mem: Intl Assn of Bus Communrs; Bd of Dirs, Soc of the Fellows of the Coun of Arts; cp/Life Mem, Aid to Blind; Bluegrass Land & Nature Trust; Num Spkg Presentations to Var Profl Assns & Commun Orgs; hon/ Author 5 Books, *The Old Lady & The Bkr; Is Going to A Dentist Worth the Trouble It Sometimes Takes?; Momma Miser Finds Elect Solutions to the Probs of Everyday Life; Momma Miser Finds Algebraic Solutions to the Probs of Everyday Life; It Takes All Types*; Num Articles; Recip, Over 60 Awds for Writing & Design in Local, Reg, Nat & Intl Competitions incl'g: Finalist, CLIO Awd, 1981; Theta Sigma Pi; Kappa Delta Pi; Nom, Outstg Yg Wom of Yr, 1981; Featured on Var TV Progs; W/ W: of Wom, in S & SW, of Intells; Other Biogl Listings.

DOYLE, ROBERT JOSEPH oc/Deputy Project Engineer; b/Sep 13, 1936; h/3431 Arcadia Drive, Ellicott City, MD 21043; ba/Glen Burnie, MD; m/Marilyn N; c/William F, Stephen M, Christopher R; p/Frederick S and Catherine D Doyle, Roslindale, MA; sp/Fran Norton, Yarmouth Port, MA; m/ Mary Norton (dec); ed/BSEE, NEn Univ, 1959; MS Engrg Adm, George Wash Univ, 1980; mil/AUS, 1959-60, Signal Corps, 2nd Lt;

pa/Sr Proj Engr, CBS Inc; Asst, Stamford, CT, 1963-72 Dir Engrg, CGR Med Corp, 1972-83; Proj Engr, Def Elects Div, Gould Inc, 1983-; Mem: Sr Mem, IEEE; Am Assn of Phys in Med; NEMA Sub-Com on X-Ray Imaging; cp/Rolling Acres Improvement Assn; Assn to Save the Norwalk Isls; r/Cath; hon/Author, Over 18 Res Articles Pub'd in Profl Jours & Assn Proceedings; W/W.

DOZIER, WELDON GRADY oc/ Corporate Executive; b/Oct 21, 1938; h/ 800 Crestview Drive, Sherman, TX 75090; ba/Denison, TX; m/Pamela Kay; p/Weldon and Dorothy Dozier, Gainesville, TX; sp/Herman and Helen Kerns, Dallas, TX; ed/BA, 1962; pa/Hybrid Computer Mgr, NASA, 1963-69; EDP Mgr, Continental Ins Companies, 1970-72; Dist Sys Mgr, TRW Data Sys Inc Over 14 States, 1973-75; Pres, Property Mktg Inc, 1976-; Sherman C of C; Denison C of C; Am Land Devel Assn; Nat Spkrs Assn; IPA; Toastmasters Intl; Life Sustaining Mem, Repub Nat Com; r/Prot; hon/Pub Author; W/ W in Fin & Indust; Personalities of S.

DRAGON, PAUL K oc/Electronics Engineer; b/Sep 19, 1950; h/2180 Bridle Path, Melbourne, FL 32935; ba/Eau Gallie, FL; m/Gopher Carlson; c/Terrence John; ed/AS, Hillsborough Commun Cl, 1975; AA, St Petersburg Jr Col, 1970; mil/AUS, 1971-73, MP; pa/Sr Customer Engr, Perkin-Elmer, 1975-79; Sr Test Engr, Harris Corp, 1979-82; Design Engr, FL Data, 1982-83; Mgr of Elects Mfg, FL Data, 1983-; Pres, GMTA, 1981-; Pres, FL Herpetological Soc, 1976-77; r/Jewish; hon/Intl W/W of Intells; Men of Achmt.

DRAGUN, JAMES oc/Director of Laboratory Division; b/Jul 29, 1949; h/ 1907-A Shuey Avenue, Walnut Creek, CA 94596; ba/San Francisco, CA; m/ Noelle Dawn; c/Nathan, Heather; p/ Henry and Stella Dragun, Brighton, MI; sp/Donald and Margaret Crouch, Royal Oak, MI; ed/BS, Wayne St Univ, 1971; MS 1975, PhD 1977, Penn St Univ; Post Grad Studies at Univ of CA-Berkeley & NIH; pa/Grad Res Asst, PA St Univ, 1972-77; Sr Soil Chemist, US Envir Protection Agy, 1978-80, 1980-82; Div Dir & Proj Mgr, Kennedy/Jenks Engrs, 1982-; Am Chem Soc, 1971-; Am Soc of Agronomy, 1972-; Soil Sci Soc of Am, 1972-; Soc of Envir Toxicology & Chem, 1983-; hon/Profl Pubs; US EPA Bronze Medal for Dist'd Ser, 1980; PA St Dist'd Ser Awd; Am Men & Wom of Sci; W/ W in W.

DRAKE, RODMAN LELAND oc/ Management Consultant, Managing Director; b/Feb 2, 1943; h/66 East 91st Street, New York, NY 10028; ba/New York, NY; m/Lenir Leme-Lambert; c/ Stephan Rodman, Philip Lambert; p/ Leland Rodman Drake, Colorado Springs, CO; sp/Acyr Lambert, Paulista, Brazil; ed/BA, Yale Univ, 1965; MBA, Harvard Grad Sch of Bus Adm, 1969; mil/AUS, 1965-67, 1st Lt; pa/Mng Dir & CEO 1981-, VPres & Dir 1977-81, Mng Ptnr São Paulo Brazil Ofc 1972-77 Assoc 1969-72, CRESAP, McCormick & Paget Inc, Mgmt Conslts; Cert'd Mgmt Conslt, CMC; cp/Secy, Class of 1965, Yale Univ; r/Epis; hon/Author of Var Articles in Profl Jours incl'g: *Bus Horizons; Chief Exec Mag*; Book Chapt, in *Prod Line Strategies*; Dir: Alliance Intl Fund Inc; The Westergaard Fund Inc Bd; Towers,

Perrin, Forster & Crosby Inc.

DRAPER, THOMAS WILLIAM oc/ Professor; b/Jun 19, 1947; h/3100 Barnock Drive, Provo, UT 84604; ba/ Provo, UT; m/Linda Gordon; c/Thomas Gordon, Janine Louise, Robert Anderson; p/Terry Parshall Draper (dec); Lillian Anderson Draper, Am Fork, UT; sp/R Robert Gordon, Mesa, AZ; ed/BS 1971, MS 1973, Brigham Yg Univ; PhD, Emory Univ, 1976; pa/Asst Prof Fam Scis, Brigham Yg Univ, 1982-; Asst Prof Child Devel & Fam Relats, Univ of NC, 1976-82; Psych Instr, Atlanta Univ Ctr, 1975-76; Res Asst, Ednl Testing Ser, 1973-75; Mem: AAAS, 1976-; Am Psychol Assn, 1973-; Assn of Early Childhood Tchr Edrs, 1977-; Nat Coun on Fam Relats, 1978-; Nat Assn for the Ed of Yg Chd, 1982-; Soc for Res in Child Devel, 1976-; r/LDS; hon/ Co-Author, *See How They Grow*, 1980; Author, Over 21 Res Articles In Profl Jours & Var Book Chapts; Fac Res Excell Awd, Univ of NC, 1979; W/W in S & SW.

DRESCH, STEPHEN P oc/Economist; b/Dec 12, 1943; h/100 McKinley Avenue, New Haven, CT 06515; ba/ Laxenburg, Austria; m/Linda Carol Ness; c/Soren K, Stephanie Elizabeth; Phaedra Augusta, Karl Friedrich Johannes; p/Lester Wilson Reuben and Lenore Steege Dresch, Loudonville, OH; ed/AB, Miami Univ (OH), 1963; MPhil 1966, PhD 1970, Yale Univ; pa/ Tchg Asst Ec, Miami Univ (OH), 1963-64; Ec Instr, So CT St Col, 1968-69; Res Assoc, Nat Bur of Ec Res, 1969-77; Lectr Urban Planning, Rutgers Univ, 1970; Tchg Assoc Ec 1966-67, Dir of Res in Ec of Higher Ed, Res Assoc, Lectr in Ec & Intn for Social & Policy Studies 1972-75, Chm Inst for Demographic & Ec Studies 1975-, Res Scholar Intl Inst for Applied Sys Anal 1983-, Yale Univ; Conslt, Num Nat & Intl Govts, Agys, Acad & Res Instns & Pvt Corps, Founs; Am Ec Assn; AAAS; Fdn of Am Scis; hon/Author, Over 100 Res Articles & Reports Pub'd in Profl Jours & Profl Org Pubs & Books incl'g: *Occupl Earnings & the Returns to Med & Other Profl Tng*, 1984; Others; NSF Grad Fellow, 1964-68; Endowed Chair in Bus Enterprise, Univ of ID, 1982; Mem, Nat Planning Com on Ed Stats, 1982-; W/ W in E.

DRESSLER, FREDERIC MICHAEL oc/Company Executive; b/Sep 23, 1941; h/7213 East Hinsdale Place, Englewood, CO 80112; ba/Denver, CO; m/Betty; c/ Kevin David, Douglas Hays; p/Martin and Anne Dressler, Englishtown, NJ; sp/ Goldie Brown, Delray Beach, FL; ed/BS, Syracuse Univ, 1963; mil/NG, 1963-69; pa/Editor, U Press Intl, 1965-67; Reporter, Edit Dir, KBTV, 1967-74; Exec News Prodr, KMGH-TV, 1974-76; Mgr, Fresno Cable TV, 1977; Div Mgr, Am TV & Communs, 1977-80; VP, Am TV & Communs, 1980-; Pres & CEO, Mile Hi Cablevision, 1982-; Nat Cable TV, 1976-; CO Cable TV Assn, Legis Com, 1983-; cp/Dir & Ofcr, CO Easter Seals Soc, 1980-; Gov's Com on Drug Abuse & Alcoholism, 1971; Rotary Clb of Denver, 1983-; r/Jewish; hon/Dist'd Ser in Jour, Sigma Delta Chi, 1971; Dist'd Ser, Nat Broadcast Edit Assn, 1975; W/W: in W, in Cable Communs.

DRINAN, ROBERT F oc/Professor; b/Nov 15, 1920; ba/Georgetown University Law Center, 600 New Jersey Avenue, Northwest, Washington, DC 20001; ed/BA 1942, MA 1947, Boston Col; LLB 1949, LLM 1950, Georgetown Univ Law Ctr; STD, Gregorian Univ, Rome, 1954; pa/Entered Soc of Jesus, 1942; Ordained Priest, 1953; Prof Law, Georgetown Univ Law Ctr, 1981-; Mem of Cong (4th Dist MA), Ho of Reps, Wash DC, 1971-81; Dean & Prof Law, Boston Col Law Sch, Newton, MA, 1959-70; Vis'g Lectr, Andover-Newton Theol Sem, 1966-68; Vis'g Prof, Univ of TX Law Sch, Austin, 1966-67; Mem: DC Bar Assn, 1950; MA Bar Assn, 1956; US Supr Ct Bar Assn 1955; Vis' g Com, Harvard Univ Div Sch, 1975-78; Chm Adv Com for MA, US Comm on Civil Rts, 1962-70; Chm Com on Adm of Justice 1962-69, VPres 1961-64, MA Bar Assn; Exec Com, Assn of Am Law Schs, 1967-69; Chm Sect on Fam Law, ABA, 1966-67; Chm Com on Fam Law, Boston Bar Assn, 1960-64; Nat Exec Com, Am Judic Soc, 1962-64; Exec Com, N Eng Congl Caucus, 1979-81; Exec Com, Envir Study Conf, 1977-81; Exec Com, House Dem Study Grp, 1977-78; Steering Com, Mbrs of Cong Peace through Law, 1975-76; cp/Pres, Ams for Dem Action; Nat Gov'g Bd, Common Cause; Hon Pres, World Federalists Assn; Exec Com, Bread For the World; Nat Adv Com, US Nat Archives; Bd of Dirs, Lwyrs Com for Intl Human Rts; Bd of Dirs, Coun For A Livable World Edl Fund; Bd of Dirs, Com for Nat Security; Adv Bd, Union of Cons for Soviet Jews; Nat Adv Coun, ACLU; Am Acad of Arts & Scis; Chm, Intl Com for Release of Anatoly Shcharansky; Nat Bd of Trustees, Nat Conf of Christians & Jews; Fdr, Nat Interrel Task Force on Soviet Jewry; r/Cath Priest, Soc of Jesus; hon/Author: Hon The Promise: Am's Commitment to Israel; Vietnam & Armageddon; Democracy, Dissent & Disorder; Rel, The Cts & Public Policy; Editor, The Right to Be Educated; Columnist, Nat Cath Reporter, 1980-; Contbg Editor, Am Mag; Editor-in-Chief, Fam Law Qtly; Contbns to Var Other Jours & Reviews; Recip Num Hon Degs incl'g: Kenyon Col, 1981; Loyola Univ, 1981; Gonzaga Univ, 1981; Villanova Univ, 1977; St Joseph's Col, 1975; LI Univ, 1970; Others; Mem, Var Ofcl Congl Dels to Asia & SE Asia; Mem, Var Pvt & Human Rts Dels to Africa, Soviet Union, Israel, Latin & S Am.

DRISCOLL, JOHN W oc/Training Supervisor; b/May 2, 1942; h/1325 Walker Street, Blackfoot, ID 83221; ba/ Idaho Falls, ID; m/Deanne Y; c/Suzanne, Debra, Charlotte, David; p/John H (dec) and Inez Carter Driscoll, Reidsville, NC; sp/Judson and Marion Yancey, Blackfoot, ID; ed/BEd, 1981; mil/USN, 1960-68; pa/Tng Spec, Gen Physics Corp, 1973-74; Tng Spec 1968-73, Tng & Procedures Supvr 1974-, Argonne Nat Lab; Am Soc for Tng & Devel, 1981-; ID Sect, Am Nuclear Soc, 1975-; Fin Chm 1980-83, VChm 1974-84, Blackfoot Dist BSA; Bishop, Ch of Jesus Christ of LDS, 1983-; r/LDS; hon/Profl Pubs; Grad w High Hons; Dist Awd of Merit, Blackfoot Dist BSA; W/W in W.

DROLL, MARIAN CLARKE oc/ Speech Writer; b/Jan 11, 1931; h/305 University Place, Grosse Pointe, MI 48230; ba/Washington, DC; c/Cynthia E, Stephanie A, Jennifer M, Kristin M;

p/Harold B Clarke; Marguerite G Clarke (dec); ed/BA, George Wash Univ, 1954; pa/Asst Editor, Knight News Ser, 1971; Mgr Media/ Public Relats, McLeod Advtg Co, 1972-77; Edit Coor 1977-80, Public Issues Spec & Spch Writer 1980-, MI Consolidated Gas Co; Ec Clb of Detroit; Jr Leag of Detroit; Public Relats Soc of Am; cp/Bd of Dirs, Presv Way, 1980-82; Public Relats Dir, S'ship Fund for Chd, 1982; Reg Chm, Muscular Dystrophy, 1963; r/Rom Cath; hon/ Contb'g Articles; Alpha Lambda Delta, 1950; W/W of Am Wom.

DROWATZKY, JOHN NELSON oc/ Professor; b/Apr 11, 1936; h/3332 Brantford Road, Toledo, OH 43606; ba/ Toledo, OH; m/Linnea Louise; c/Kara Louise, Katrina Leigh; p/Mark (dec) and Minnie L Drowatzky, Wichita, KS; sp/ Mr and Mrs Kenneth J Swanson, McPherson, KS; ed/BS, Univ of KS, 1957; MS 1962, EdD 1965, Univ of OR; JD, Univ of Toledo, 1979; mil/AUS, 1958-60, Lt; pa/Tchr & Coach, Enterprise Sch S, 1961-62; Dir of PE, The Inst of Logopedics, 1962-63; Tchg Asst, Univ of OR, 1963-65; Asst Prof 1965-68, Assoc Prof 1968-71, Prof 1971-, Dept Chm 1972-76, Univ of Toledo; AAHPERD; Am Acad for PE; OH Assn for HPER; Phi Epsilon Kappa; Phi Delta Kappa; ABA; OH Bar Assn; Toledo Bar Assn; r/Luth; hon/Pub'd Author; Cert of Recog, Lucas Co Assn for MR, 1970; Corpus Juris Secundum Awd for Significant Legal S'ship, 1978; Fellow, Am Acad of PE, 1983; W/W in MW; Men of Achmt.

DROWNS-ALLEN, KAREN SUE oc/ Clinical Psychologist, Professor; b/Mar 12, 1943; ba/Dallas, TX; m/R Michael; c/Brandwyd Michele; ed/BS Psych 1965, MS Clin Psych 1967, Univ of ID-Moscow; PhD Human Devel, Univ of MD-College Pk, 1973; APA Approved Clin Psych Intern, Walter Reed Army Hosp, 1974; mil/US Army Med Corp, 1973-76, Capt; USAR, 1976-82; pa/Assoc Chief of Staff for Ed, VA Med Ctr, Dallas, 1982-; Clin Asst Prof, SWn Med Sch Dept Psych & Sch of Allied Hlth Scis, Univ of TX Hlth Ctr-Dallas, 1982-; Clin Asst Prof Dept Psychi 1981-, Asst Prof & Coor Clin Behavior Neurol, Dept Psychi 1980-81, Asst Prof Dept Fam Med 1979-80, LA St Univ (LSU) Med Sch-Shreveport; Conslt, Sabine Val Mtl Hlth Ctr, Longview/Marshall, TX, 1979-80; Asst Prof, TX Tech Med Sch; R E Thomason Gen Hosp (Psychi), El Paso, TX, 1977-78; Chief of Psych Ser, Dept Psychi & Neurol, Ft Hood, TX, 1974-76; Conslt, Copperas Cove Sch Sys, TX, 1974-76; Psych II, Gt Oaks Ctr, Silver Sprgs, MD, 1971-73; Adj Col Lectr, Howard Commun Col, Columbia, MD, 1971-72; Res Psych, Friends of Psychi Res, Catonsville, MD, 1968-70; Psych I, VA Treatment Ctr for Chd, Richmond, VA, Sum 1967; Lic'd in TX, VA & LA; Mem, Am Psychol Assn, 1976; Mem, TX Psychol Assn, 1976-; Bd of Dirs, Hlth Sci Consortium, Chapel Hill, NC, 1982-; Kappa Alpha Theta, 1962-; hon/Psych Grad Asst, 1965; Tchr of Yr Awd, Howard Commun Col, 1972; Grant Awd to Produce 3 Tng Films: "The Step Behind Series"; 1972; Army Nat Def Ser Med, 1973; W/W: in S & SW, of Am Wom; Personalities of Am; Other Biogl Listings.

DROZDZIEL, MARION J oc/Chief Engineer; b/Dec 21, 1924; h/152 Linwood Avenue, Tonawanda, NJ 14150; ba/Buffalo, NY; m/Rita L Korwek; c/Eric A Drozdziel; p/Stephen and Veronica Drozdziel, Dunkirk, NY; sp/Margaret Korwek, Buffalo, NY; ed/BS, Tri-St Univ, 1947; BSME, Tri-St Unv; Postgrad Studies: Niagara Univ, OH St Univ, Univ of Buffalo; mil/AUS, 1944-47, Crim Invest Div; pa/Structures Engr, Curtiss Wright Corp, 1948; Proj Weight Engr 1949-52, Stress Anal 1952-60, Asst Supvr-Stress Anal 1960-64, Chief-Stress Anal-Propulsion 1964-79, Chief Engr-Stress & Weights 1979-, Bell Aerospace Textron; VChm of Ed, AIAA, 1982-; AF Assn; Am Mgmt Assn; Soc of Reliability Engrs; Am Space Foun; AAAS; Planetary Soc; Intl Soc of Allied Weight Engrs; US Nav Inst; Bell Mgmt Clb; Quarter Cent Clb; Nature Conservancy; Nat Audubon Soc; Cousteau Soc; Am Acad of Polit & Social Sci; Acad of Polit Sci; Union of Concerned Scis; Smithsonian Assoc; r/Cath; hon/ Profl Pubs; Commend, NASA Apollo, 1972; W/W: in E, in Aviation & Aerospace, in Aviation.

DRUM, BRUCE ALAN oc/Visual Scientist; b/May 18, 1947; h/5503 Calhoun Avenue, Alexandria, VA 22311, ba/Baltimore, MD; m/Pamela Joy Neff; c/Rachel Lynne Neff, Kevin Michael Neff; p/Virgil and Clela Drum, Bryan, OH; sp/Reuben and Irene Neff; ed/BSc 1969, PhD 1973, OH St Univ; pa/Tchg Assoc 1969-70, Res Assoc Dept Biophysics 1970-73, Vis'g Res Assoc Inst for Res in Vision 1973, OH St Univ; Postdoct F'ship, Physiol Optics, Johns Hopkins Univ, Balto, Md, 1974; Asst Res Prof 1975-79, Res Sci 1979-83, Sr Res Sci 1983-84, Dept Ophthal, George Wash Univ, Balto, MD, 1981-; Asst Prof Lab Physiol Optics, Wilmer Eye Inst, Johns Hopkins Univ, Balto, MD, 1984-; Investigator, Var NIH Grants & NEI Small Bus Grant; Mem: AAAS; Optical Soc of Am; Assn for Res in Vision & Ophthal; Intl Res Grp for Colour Vision Deficiencies; Intl Perimetric Soc; Psychonomic Soc; Am Soc for Parapsychol Res; Fedn of Am Scis; hon/Author, Over 20 Res Articles & Reports Pub'd in Profl Jours; Over 18 Papers Presented at Var Profl Assn Meetings; NIH Res Grantee, 1975-82 & 1981-84; Postdoct F'ship, Seeing Eye Inc, 1974; Biomed Res Support Grantee, George Wash Univ, 1978-79; W/W in Frontier Sci & Technol.

DRUMMOND, OLIVER LEE oc/ Chief of Police; b/Oct 7, 1947; ba/ Hanford, CA; m/Deborah Louise; c/ Deborah Lee; p/Joseph L Drummond (dec); Ollie Lee Peetz, Manteca, CA; sp/ Dwight Duteau, LA, CA; Jacqueline Clark, Long Bch, CA; ed/BS, CA St Univ, 1974; Adv Grad Cert, Pacific Christian Col, 1979; PhD Cand, Newport Univ, 1980-; mil/Commissioned Ofcr Mil Police Corps, CALARNG/ USAR/CSMR; pa/Police Ofcr, Police Sgt, Police Lt, Gen Investigations Cmdr, Area Cmdr, Santa Ana Police Dept, 1970-82; Chief of Police, Hanford Police Dept, 1982-; Intl Assn of Chiefs of Police; Intl Police Assn; Intl Narcotics Ofcr Assn; Nat Assn of Chiefs of Police; ABA, Crim Justice Sect; CA Peace Ofcrs, Law & Legis Com; CA Police

Chiefs Assn, Tng Com; CA Leag of Cities, Adm Ser Com & Public Safety Com; CA Assn of Police Tng Ofcrs; CA Combat Shooters Assn; CA Assn of Adm of Justice Edrs; Chm, Kings Co Crim Justice Adv Com; cp/Sgt at Arms, Rotary Intl; Adv Bd, Salvation Army; VChm, Kings Co Vol Bur; Co Chm, Better Public Safety Through Court Reform; Alcohol Adv Bd, Kings Co Commun Action Org; Kings Co Sch Attendance Review Bd; Sch Site Coun, Kings River Hardwick Sch Dist; 2nd VP, Chm of Action Com, Pres Clb, Ambassador Corps, Hanford C of C; r/Christian; hon/Hon Doct of Humane Lttrs, Newport Intl Univ, 1979; Hon LLD, Van Norman Univ, 1980; Hon Grad 1970, Outstg Ofcr Awd, Firearms Awd, Phy Ability Awd, 5 Acad Records, Orange Co Sheriff's Acad, 1970; Meritorious Ser, Valor Awd, Santa Ana Police Dept, 1973; Silver Medal, CA Police Olympics-Combat Shooting, 1975; Profl Ser Awd, Santa Ana Police Dept, 1982; City Employee of Yr, Hanford C of C, 1982; Chief of Yr, St of CA, Law Enforcement Mgmt Ctr; W/W: Am Law Enforcement, W; Commun Ldrs of World.

DRYBROUGH, RALPH II oc/Direct Mail Catalog Conslt; b/Jan 28, 1947; h/632 Spring Mill Lane, Indianapolis, IN 46260; ba/Indianapolis, IN; m/Sharon H; c/Ralph III, Andrew A L; p/T R and Nancy N Drybrough, Indianapolis, IN; sp/A K and Elizabeth L Heiligmann, Lake Leelanau, MI; ed/Att'd De Pauw Univ, 1965-67; IN Univ, 1967-69; mil/IN NG, MA Army NG, NY Air NG, 1970-76; pa/Advtg Coor, ITT Pub'g, 1969-72; Advtg Mgr, ITT Pub'g, 1972-74; Prod Mgr, Amsterdam Co, 1974-76; Dir of Mktg, Kole Indust, 1976; Gen Mgr, Magnatag Prods, 1976-78; Pres, Magnacontrol Corp, 1978-79; Pres, Drybrough Lave, Inc, 1980-; Dir Mail Mktg Assn; Dir Mktg Assn of Indianapolis; Indianapolis NFL Com; r/Epis.

DRYFOOS, NANCY P oc/Sculptor; h/45 East 89th Street, New York, NY 10028; ba/New York, NY; m/Donald; p/Richman and Edith Prosfauer (dec); sp/Florence L Warms (dec); ed/Att'd Drew Sem for Yg Wom, Sarah Lawrence Col, Columbia Univ Architectural Sch, Art Students Leag; mil/Red Cross Nurse's Aide; pa/Comm Artist, Silver Prod Mfg Co; Packaging, Purse Pac Drug Co; Drawing & Sculpting Tchr; former Pres, NY Soc of Wom Artists; Chm, Fine Arts Div, Am Jewish Tercentenary; Dir, Am Soc Contemp Artists; Exhibn Chm & Rec Secy, Nat Sculpture Soc; hon/Author; W/W: in Am Artists, in E, of Am Wom; DIB.

DuBOIS, ANDRE oc/Research Professor; b/Mar 16, 1939; h/9210 Bardon Road, Bethesda, MD 20814-4799; m/Marie-Claude Moreau; c/Joel, Lauren; p/Mr T DuBois, Brussels, Belgium; sp/Mr J Moreau, Versailles, France; ed/BS 1959, MD 1963, PhD 1975, Univ of Brussels & Med Sch; mil/Mil Hosp, Brussels; pa/Instr Dept of Anatomy 1965-66, Staff Fellow Dept of Surg Univ Hosp 1969-71, Univ of Brussels; Res F'ship Lab of Clin Sci, NIMH, Bethesda, MD, 1970; NATO F'ship Lab of Clin Sci, NIMH, 1971-75; Vis'g Assoc Lab of Theoretical Biol, Nat Cancer Inst, 1972-73; Vis'g Assoc & Vis'g Sci, Nat

Inst of Arthritis, Metabolism & Digestive Diseases, 1973-75; Instr Dept of Med 1975-76, Asst Prof Dept of Med 1977-78, Assoc Prof Res Dept of Med 1978-, Assoc Prof Res Dept of Surg 1981-, Asst Dir Digestive Diseases Div 1980-, Uniformed Sers Univ of the Hlth Scis, Bethesda, MD; Sr Investigator, Armed Forces Radiobiol Res Inst, Bethesda, MD, 1983-; Adj Assoc Prof Physiol, Georgetown Univ Sch of Med, Wash, DC, 1984-; Mem: Societe Belge de Chirurgie (Belgiun Surg Assn), 1964; Wm Beaumont Soc of Gastroenterology, 1976; Am Fend of Clin Res, 1977; En Gut Clb, 1977; Am Gastroenterological Assn, 1978; Am Physiol Soc, 1981; Am Assn of Acad Surg, 1982; hon/Author, Co-Author & Editor, Over 58 Articles, Over 10 Reviews & Book Chapts, Over 90 Abstracts Pub'd in Profl Jours & Assn Proceedings Pubs incl'g: *Digestive Diseases & Scis; Intl Jour of Obesity; Am Jour Physiol; Metabolism; Gastroenterology; Brain Res Bltn; Jour Clin Invest*; Num Others; van Engelen Prize for Internship, Univ Hosp, Univ of Brussels, 1963; 1st Prize for Sci Paper Presentation, Am Soc of Nuclear Med, 1983; Wm Beaumont Awd for Excell in Clin Res, 1984; W/W in Frontier Sci & Technol.

Du BROFF, DIANA D oc/Counsellor at Law; b/Mar 4, 1909; h/12 West 72nd Street, New York, NY 10023; ba/Same; c/William, Elinoor; ed/BS, LLB, Bklyn Law Sch; pa/Law Pract, The Humanized Law Ctr, Inst for Pract Justice, NYC, 1983-; Law Pract, Fam Law & Supr Cts St of NY, Currently; Assoc'd w Legal Aid Soc, 4 Yrs; Admitted to Pract: US Supr Ct, US Ct of Claims, US Dist Cts So & En Dists NY; Mem: Past Chp Fam Law Com, Bronx Wom's Bar Assn; Past Chp Fam Law Com, Past CoChp Matrimonial Ethics Com, NY St Trial Lwyrs Assn; Fam Law Com, ABA; Matrimonial Panel, Am Arbitration Assn; Diplomate, Am Acad Matriomonial Lwyrs; Legis Sect Fam Law Com, NY St Bar Assn; Am Judges Assn; Fed Bar Coun; Nat Assn Wom Lwyrs; Small Claims Arbitrator; Alumni Dir, Bklyn Law Sch; Former Adj Prof Fam Law, City Col; Pres & Fdr, Nat Org to Insure Support Enforcemt; Num Other Profl Activs; hon/Writer; Wkly Columnist, "Let's Look at the Law"; Other Num Profl Pubs; Mem, Am Soc of Dist'd Persons; Num Biogl Listings.

DUCKETT, CHLOE Z "SANDY" oc/Foreign Service Staff Officer; b/Jun 25, 1925; h/2124 East 1st Street, Tucson, AZ 85719; ba/Miami, FL; c/Lee L, Theo Z; p/Audrey Sandefur, Tucson, AZ; ed/BA, Psych, 1949; MEd Cnslg, 1982; pa/Ofc Mgr, Marsh Aviation, Tucson, AZ, 1946-48; Var Positions, Corps of Engrs, Fairbanks, AK, 1952-54; Adm Asst, Tucson Airport Auth, Tucson, AZ, 1957-74; Fgn Ser Staff Ofcr, 1974-; Mem: Am Assn of Airport Execs; Pres Tucson Clb 1973-74, Altrusa Intl Inc; Mensa; r/Unitarian; hon/Co-Author of Concept Requiring 1st Aid Tng of Apprentice Union Mems Prior to Journeyman Cert; W/W in W.

DUDACK, GAIL MARIE oc/Vice President, Technical Analyst; b/Aug 17, 1948; ba/New York, NY; p/Mr and Mrs John Dudack, Johnson City, NY; ed/BA, Skidmore Col; pa/Res Assoc 1970-73, Asst VP & Tech Anal 1973-75, VP &

Tech Anal 1975-78, Pershing & Co Inc; VP & Tech Anal, Pershing Div of DLJ Inc, 1978-; Financial Anal Fdn; NY Soc of Security Anal; VP 1982-83, Secy 1981-82, Treas 1979-80, Chm of Public Relats Com, 1978-79, Mkt Tech Assn; Fin Wom Assn; Bus Res Adv Coun, US Dept of Labor for Consumer & Prodr Price Indices; Bd of Arbitrators, Nat Assn of Security Dealers, 1979-80; hon/Student Achmt Awd, *Wall St Jour*, 1970; W/W of Am Wom.

DUDARYK, SHARON DIANN SLIMAK oc/Kindergartenn Teacher; Career Counselor, Naval Research; b/Aug 29, 1945; h/2725 Saratoga, Troy, MI 48084; ba/Detroit, MI; c/Jeffrey Michael, Linda Helen, Patricia Marie; p/Mike and Nettie Slimak, Detroit, MI; ed/MEd, Wayne St Univ, 1971; mil/USNR, 1979-, Career Cnslr; pa/Tchr, Detroit Bd of Ed Hdstart, Kgn, 1967 & 1979; Tchr, Van Zile Elem Sch, 1983-; AFT DFT Local 231; AAUW; Nav Leag; AARP; PWP; Girl Scouts; MAAT; WCAAT; TASET; MCAAT; 4-H; Farm Bur of MI; FROC; Birmingham/Bloomfield Art Assn; r/En Orthodox; hon/4-H, 1982; Ed, 1982; W/W of Am Wom.

DUDLEY, VIVIAN GATLIN oc/Public School Teacher; b/Jun 4, 1944; h/440 Washington Street, apartment 12-B, Newark, NJ 07102; ba/Paterson, NJ; m/James K; c/Shelton, Martha, Jacques; p/Milton and Ella Gatlin, Paterson, NJ; ed/BS, Elizabeth City St Univ; Gad, NJ Mil Acad, 1979; mil/NJ Army NG; pa/Tchr, Public Sch #21, 1971-; NY Univ Sch of Ed; Paterson Bd of Ed, 1971-; Chm Bd of Dirs, St Joseph Day Care/Nursery Sch, Newark, 1977-; Mem: NJ Ed Assn, 1971-; Black Edr of Paterson, 1981-; r/Bapt; hon/Outstg Enlisted Female Soldier, 50th Arm Div, St of NJ Army NG, 1980; W/W of Am Wom.

DUERR, JOYCE BLAKNEY GOODWIN oc/Elementary School Principal; b/Mar 10, 1937; h/Potter Hill Road, Westerly, RI 02891; ba/Westerly, RI; m/Clifford; c/Mark Daniel Goodwin, David Carl Goodwin, James Robert Goodwin, Thomas Warren Goodwin, Jonathan Roy Goodwin; p/Hilman Roy Blakney (dec); Sybil Crosby Blakney, Hillsboro, NH; ed/BS, Gordon Col, 1958; MA, Univ of RI, 1972; CAGS, RI Col, 1976; EdD Cand, Boston Univ, 1985; pa/Clrm Tchr, NH, 1960-63, Clrm Tchr, Peabody MA, 1964-66; Clrm Tchr, Hopkinton RI Sch Dept, 1966-71; Rdg Spec, Hopkinton RI Sch Dept, 1971-77; Prin, Westerly RI Sch Dept, 1977-; IRA; Past Pres, RI St Rdg Coun; Past Bd Mem, N Eng Rdg Assn; Past Secy, NE Assn for Supvn & Curric Devel; ASCA; Nat Assn Elem Sch Prin; Secy of RI Chapt, Phi Delta Kappa; r/Bapt; hon/Profl Pubs; W/W in E.

DUFFY, EVELYN GROENKE oc/Nurse Practitioner; b/Mar 30, 1953; h/33 Lathrop Street, Madison, WI 53705; ba/Madison, WI; m/Mark Elton; p/John and Marcy Groenke, Wayne, PA; sp/Arthur and Shirley Duffy; ed/BS, Baylor Univ, 1975; MS, Univ of WI-Madison, 1981; pa/Nurse Practitioner, Ambulatory Care Adult & Aging, VA Hosp, 1981-; Vis'g Nurse, Vis'g Nurse Ser, Madison, 1976-81; Staff Nurse, Surg Intensive Care, OH St Univ Hosp, 1975-76; Mem: Chm

Public Relats Com, Madison Dist Nurse Assn, 1983; Chm Nom'g Com, Nurse Practitioner Coun, WI Nurses Assn, 1982-83; cp/Secy, Calvary Luth Wom; Others; r/Luth; hon/Co-Author, "The Effect of Sex Ed Prog on a Grp of Older Adults," *Proceedings of Am Assn of Sex Edrs, Cnslrs & Therapists,* 1982; Spec Recog for Profl Achmt on Completion of Cert, VA Hosp, 1983; Alpha Lambda Delta; Dean's Hon List; NHS; Sigma Theta Tau; Commun Ldrs of Am.

DUFFY, FRANK HOPKINS oc/Neurologist, Neurophysiologist, Biomedical Engineer; b/Jan 22, 1937; h/49 Harrison Street, Brookline, MA 02146 & Spring Road, Tunbridge, VT 05077; ba/Boston, MA; m/Heidelise Als; c/Lisa G, Stephen W H, Victoria C, Christopher Rivinus; p/Irving and Frances Duffy (dec); sp/Heinrich Als (dec); Elisabeth Als, Ansbach, W Germany; ed/BSE Elect Engrg & Math, Col of Engrg, Univ of MI, 1958; MD, Harvard Med Sch, 1963; mil/AUS, Med Corps, 1968-70, Maj; pa/Assoc in Neurol, Beth Israel Hosp, Boston, 1970-; Assoc in Neurol Chds Hosp, Boston, 1970-; Assoc Prof Neurol, Harvard Med Sch, 1979-; Mem: Pres, En Assn of Electroencephalographers, 1981-82; Am EEG Soc; Am Neurol Assn; Soc for Neurosci; hon/Author, Num Profl Articles in Clin & Neurol & Neurophysiol Res in Profl Jours; Sci of Yr, ACLD, 1982; Mem, US Olympic Equestrian Tm, 1956.

DUGUNDJI, JOHN oc/Professor; b/Oct 25, 1925; h/39 Albert Avenue, Belmont, MA 02178; ba/Cambridge, MA; m/Wraye; c/Elenna Rose, Elise Anthe; p/Basile Dugundji (dec); sp/Walter Polkey (dec); ed/BAE, NY Univ, 1944; MS 1948, ScD 1951, MIT; mil/USN, 1944-46; pa/Res Engr, Grumman Aircraft, 1948-49; Dynamics Engr, Republic Aviation, 1951-56; Prof Aeronautics/Astronautics, MIT, 1957-; Mem: AIAA; Sigma Xi; Tau Beta Pi; r/Greek Orthodox; hon/Author, Var Articles in Profl Jours; W/W in E.

DUKE, ANGIER BIDDLE oc/Executive, Ambassador; b/Nov 30, 1915; ba/560 Lexington Avenue, New York, NY 10022; m/Robin Chandler; p/Angier B Duke (dec); Cordelia Biddle (Mrs T Markoe Robertson); ed/Att'd St Pauls Sch, Concord, NH; Grad, Yale Univ, 1938; mil/USAF, 1941-46, USAF, WW II Europe, Maj; pa/Chm, US-Japan Foun, 1981-; w US Fgn Ser: Consul in Buenos Aires, Argentina, 1949-51; Consul, US Embassy in Madrid, Spain, 1951-52; Ambassador to El Salvador, 1952-53; Ambassador to Spain, 1965-68; Ambassador to Denmark, 1968-69; Ambassador to Morocco, 1978-81; Former Chief of Protocol, The White House & Dept of St under Pres Kennedy & Johnson; Mem: Chm, Appeal of Conscience Foun; Pres, Moroccan-Am Foun; Chm, Spanish Inst, NYC; CoChm, Columbus Quincent Foun of NYC; cp/Pres, Intl Rescue Com, 1954-60; LI St Pk Commr, 1954-60; Commr of Civic Affairs & Public Events, NYC, 1974-77; Pres's Assoc, Duke Univ; Chm World Affairs Coun of LI, Trustee, Southampton Col of LI Univ; Commr, Statue of Liberty/Ellis Isl Cent Comm; Spec Advr, Aspen Inst for Humanistic Studies; Treas, Coun of Am Ambassadors; Dir: Fgn Policy Assn; Am Polit Foun; Oper Crossroads Africa; CONDUCT- Com

on Decent Unbiased Campaign Tactics; hon/Recip, Hans J Morgenthau Meml Awd for Dist'd Ser in Field of Am Fgn Policy, 1981; Recip, Var Decorations of Hon from Govts of Denmark, France, Gt Brit, Greece, Haiti, Spain & Sweden; LLD Honoris Causa, Duke Univ, 1969.

DUMAS, ELNORA JEANETTE oc/Psychotherapist, Social Worker; b/Oct 24, 1938; h/361 Clinton Avenue #5E, Brooklyn, NY 11238; ba/Brooklyn, NY; p/Mr and Mrs Henry Dumas, Elmira, NY; ed/BA 1960, MSW 1962, Howard Univ; pa/Yth Parole Wkr, Warwick St Tng Sch; Casewkr, Commun Ser Soc; Supvr, Foster Home Care, Bur of Child Wel, Dept of Wel; Public Hlth Social Wk Conslt, Maternal & Infant Care Fam Planning Proj; Conslt, Pre-Kgn Hdstart; Supvr, NYC Soc of Meth Ch Hdstart Prog; Supvr, Bronx St Hosp; Supvr, E NY Mtl Hlth Proj; Dir, Proj Teen Aid; Psychotherapist, Pvt Pract; Mtl Hlth Conslt, Addiction & Res Tng Corp (Brownsville Clin); cp/Bd Mem, Commun Bd 2; Bd Mem & Chp of Appts Com, Bklyn Wom Polit Caucus; Vol, Cabrini Hosp; Lambda Kappa Mu Sorority, Gamma Chapt; Coalition of 100 Black Wom; Past Secy, POCA; Asst Secy, Bklyn Psychi Ctrs; VP, Bushwick Mtl Hlth Ctr; Literacy Vol Prog; Vol, Intl Ctr; Vol, Polit Campaigns; r/Cath; hon/Profl Pubs; NY St Cert'd Social Wkr; W/W: of Am Wom, in E.

DUNCAN, JOHNNY L oc/Engineering Supervisor; b/Feb 2, 1939; h/10820 Nelle, NE, Albuquerque, NM 87111; ba/Albuquerque, NM; m/Kerin D; c/Glenn K, David L (dec), Melinda E; p/Lloyd T Duncan (dec); Ruby A Jaggars, Vinita, OK; sp/Robert and Emma Boston, Pryor, OK; ed/AAS, NE OK A&M, 1957; BSEE, OK St Univ, 1962; MSEE, Univ of NM, 1964; mil/USAR, 1956-64; pa/Staff Mem Tech Div 1962-69, Supvr Radiation Effects 1970-74, Test Supvr B61 Nuclear Bomb Prog 1975-77, Test Supvr W80/Cruise Missile Testing 1978-82, Test & Eval Supvr W88/Trident II Testing 1983-, Sandia Labs; Sr Mem, IEEE; Radiation Effects Conf, Session Chm 1973, Awds Com 1974, Fin Chm 1975, Fam Prog Com 1978; Publicity Chm 1979, Secy/Treas Steering Com 1980-83; Adm Com, Nuclear & Plasma Sci Soc, 1983-; hon/Num Nuclear Weapon Test Reports; Boss of Yr, 1973; W/W: in W, in Aviation & Aerospace.

DUNEIER, DEBRA HOPE oc/Certified Gemologist; b/Aug 30, 1954; ba/New York, NY; m/Dana Brad; c/Jamie Troy; p/Anita Arkow; sp/Clyde and Estelle Duneier; ed/Att'd Queens Col; Grad Gemologist, Gemological Inst of Am, 1980; Cert'd Gemologist, Am Gem Soc, 1981; pa/Salesperson 1975, Sales Mgr 1978-, Dir of Loose Stones, VP of Loose Stones Div 1980; In Charge of Colored Stone Sems & Lectrs; Am Gem Soc; So Jewelers Travelers Assn; hon/Sem Ldr in Field; W/W of Am Wom.

DUNIKOSKI, SARAH BEELS oc/Vocal Music Teacher; b/Dec 11, 1947; h/185 Kemp Avenue, Fair Haven, NJ 07701; ba/Rumson, NJ; m/Leonard Karol Jr; p/Kenneth W and Kathryn M Beels, Knox, PA; sp/Leonard K and Helyn K Dunikoski, Cranford, NJ; ed/BMus, Westminster Col, 1969; MEd, PA St Univ, 1970; pa/Vocal Music Tchr, Butler Area Sch Dist, 1970-72; Vocal

Music Tchr, Montgomery Co Sch Dist, 1972-73; Vocal Music Tchr, Rumson Sch Dist, 1974-; Nat Guild of Piano Tchrs, 1966-; NEA, 1970-; MENC, 1968-; Rumson Ed Assn, 1981-; Delta Zeta, 1966-; cp/Chm 1981 & 1982, Recruiting Chm 1983, Gtr Red Bk Area CROP Hunger Walk; Rumson Commun Ed Vol Tchr, 1977-; Wom Org 1980-, Exec Bd 1980-, Presb Ch at Shrewsbury; Ordained Deacon, Presb Ch; r/Presb; hon/Co-Designer of 250th Anniv Commemorative Communion Token, Presb Ch of Shrewsbury; Mu Phi Epsilon, 1969; Kappa Delta Pi, 1969; Sr Achmt Awd, 1969; Outstg Yg Wom of Am, 1982.

DUNLOP, DAVID WALLACE oc/Economist, Professor; b/Jul 6, 1942; h/1800 R Street Northwest, Washington, DC 20009; ba/Boston, MA; p/William and Sarah Dunlop, Pleasant Hill, CA; ed/BS Univ of CA-Berkeley, 1965; MA 1969, PhD 1973, MI St Univ; pa/Vis'g Prof, Sch of Mgt, Boston Univ, 1983-; Vis'g Prof, Dartmouth Med Sch, 1976-; Sr Economist, US Agy for Intl Devel, 1979-83; Vis'g Prof Sch of Public Hlth, Univ of NC, 1979-; Vis'g Prof, Univ of Darea Salaam, 1975 & 1977; Asst Prof, Meharry Med Col, 1972-79; Asst Prof, Vanderbilt Univ, 1972-79; Instr, MI St Univ, 1971-72; Res Anal, Makermere Inst for Social Res, 1969-70; Res Anal, St of MI, 1966-69; Acct, Mannings Inc, 1963-65; Mem: Am Envir Assn; APHA; African Studies Assn; Sr Editor, *Social Sci & Med,* 1976-83; r/Prot; hon/Co-Author of Book, *Hlth, What is it Worth?,* 1979; Author of Var Articles in Profl Jours incl'g: *Social Sci & Med;* MW Univs Consort PhD Res Grant, 1969-70; Luce Vis'g Prof of Envir Studies, Darmouth Col, 1981.

DUNN, CHARLES WILLIAM oc/Educator, Author; b/Nov 30, 1915; h/26 Longfellow Road, Cambridge, MA 02138; ba/Cambridge, MA; m/Patricia Campbell (dec); 2nd Elaine Birnbaum; c/Deirdre, Peter Arthur, Alexander Joseph; p/Peter Alexander and Alberta Mary Margaret (Freeman) Dunn; ed/BA, McMaster Univ, 1938; AM 1939, PhD 1948, Harvard Univ; LLD Honoris Causa, St Francis Xavier, Nova Scotia, Canada, 1983; pa/Asst in Eng 1939-40, Tutor 1940-41, Prof Celtic Langs & Lits, Chm Dept 1963-, Master Quincy House 1966-81, Margaret Brooks Robinson Prof of Celtic Langs & Lits 1967-, Harvard Univ; Humanities Instr, Stephens Col, 1941-42; Eng Instr, Cornell Univ, 1943-46; Eng Instr Univ of Toronto, 1946-50; Asst Prof 1950-55, Assoc Prof 1955-56, Taft Lectr 1956, Univ of Cinc; Prof Eng, NY Univ, 1956-63; Mem: Fellow, Am Acad Arts & Scis; Am Folklore Soc; MLA; Irish Texts Soc; Medieval Acad Am; Early Eng Text Soc; Royal Scottish Country Dance Soc; St Andrews Soc NY; Comunn Gaidhealach (Scotland); Hon Pres 1963, Celtic Union Edinburgh; Maitre, Commanderie de Bordeaux a Boston; Socts' Charitable Soc, Boston; cp/Tavern Clb; Somerset Clb; Odd Volumes Clb Boston; Harvard Clb NYC; Scottish Arts Edinburgh; hon/Author, *Highland Settler: A Portrait of the Scottish Gael in Nova Scotia,* 1953 & 1968; *The Foundling & the Werwolf: A Study of Guillaume de Palerne,* 1960; Editor: *A Chaucer Rdr,* 1952; *Hist of the Kings of Brit*

(*Geoffrey of Monmouth*), 1958; *Chronicles (Froissart)*, 1961; *Romance of the Rose*, 1962; *Lays of Ctly Love*, 1963; Co-Editor, *Mid Eng Lit*, 1973; Contbr, Num Articles & Reviews to Profl Jours; Dexter Fellow, Novia Scotia, Sum 1941; Rockefeller Fellow, Dublin, Edinburgh & Aberystwyth, 1954-55; Guggenheim Fellow, Scotland, Wales & Brittany, 1962-63; Recip, Canada Awd, Fedn Gaelic Socs, 1955.

DUNN, CHARLETA J oc/Professor; b/Jan 18, 1927; h/300 Oak Drive, Friendswood, TX 77546; ba/Houston, TX; m/Roy A; c/Thomas A, Roy E, Sharleta E; p/James A Sisk, Corpus Christi, TX; Ruby Burcham Rice, Amarillo, TX; ed/BS 1951, MEd 1954, W TX St Univ; EdD, Univ of Houston, 1966; Post Doct Clin, Univ of TX Med Br, 1971; pa/Asst Prof Cnslg, Univ of Houston, 1966-70; Psychol, Goose Creek ISD, 1971-74; Prof Psych, TX Wom's Univ, 1974-; Conslt, to 4 ISD in Gulf Coast; Mem: Am Psych Assn; SWn Psych Assn; TX Psych Assn; r/Presb; hon/Author, *World of Wk*, 1970; *Songs of Sharleta*, 1968; 4 Monographs & 36 Articles Pub'd in Profl Jours & Other Pubs; Res Grantee, GUSREDA, 1964-66; Hogg Foun for Mtl Hlth, 1966-70; Reg IV Ed Ser Ct, 1978; ARCA, TX Wom's Univ, 1982; W/W of Wom.

DUNN, CLEO DORIS ALLEN (O'NEAL) oc/Teacher (Retired); b/May 24, 1914; h/701 South Main Street, Mullins, SC 29574; m/Langdon Barmore; c/David Brooks O'Neal Jr, Doris Jean Dunn Gurley; p/Joseph Judson and Sara Barmore Dunn (dec); sp/Larkin Barmore and Sara Barmore Dunn (dec); ed/AB magna cum laude, Winthrop Col, 1935; Att'd Univ of SC, Wn Carolina Univ; Choir Mem & Curator, Heritage Room, Mullins 1st Bapt Ch; pa/Tchr, Ware Shoals SC, 1935-38; Tchr, Mullins & Marion SC, 1938-1976; Ret'd Tchrs Clb; St Chm, Nat Soc Colonial Dames XVII Cent; Registrar, Nat Soc Daughs of Am Colonists, Pedee Chapt; St Historian, Nat Soc Daughs of Colonial Wars; Order of Wash; Nat Soc Magna Charta Dames; SC St Soc NSDAR Dist VI Dir 1979-82 & St VRegent, SC St Soc Nat Soc DAR, 1982-85; Trustee of Tamassee DAR Sch; DAR Palmetto St Ofcrs Clb; NSDAR St V Regents Clb; Charter Mem, Pee Dee Chapt Genealogical Soc; St Corres'g Secy, Chd of Am Revolution; hon/Pub'd Author; Bronze Plaque, SC Geneal Soc, Pee Dee Chapt Fam Awd, 1980; World W/W of Wom; DIB.

DUNN, ERAINA BURKE oc/Community Coordinator; b/Oct 4, 1945; h/15221 Lincoln, Harvey, IL 60426; ba/Harvey, IL; m/James N; c/Kyle Tierre, Jamison Leon; p/Lolita D Moore, Chicago Heights, IL; Marion Burke, Jr, Calumet City, IL; sp/Katherine Dunn, Harvey, IL; ed/BA, Wilberforce Univ, 1968; BC/BS, Acad Sch of Perf'g Arts, 1972; pa/Programmer/Anal, Blue Cross/Blue Shield, 1968-74; Mbrship Conslt, Blue Cross Assn, 1975; Personal Bkr, Wachovia Bk & Trust, 1976; Pers /Benefits Spec, Kimberly-Clark Corp, 1976-78; Commun Coor, Tchr Corp Proj Sch Dist 147, 1980-; cp/Pres Wesley UMC 1980-82, Commun Coun Coor 1980-, U Meth Wom; Coor, W Harvey Block Capts Coalition, 1982-; IL Com-

mun Ed Assn, 1981-; Nat Commun Ed Assn, 1980-; Delta Sigma Theta; World Goodwill, 1971-; r/U Meth; hon/Outstg Vol Ser, BUILD, 1971; Outstg Commun Ser Awd, Sch Dist 147, 1981-82; Vol After Sch Tutorial Prog Awd, 1981-82; W/W of Am Wom.

DUNN, IMA CHARLENE (DEBBIE) oc/Educational Administrator; b/Jan 29, 1941; h/131 West Routt, Pueblo, CO 81004; ba/Pueblo, CO; p/William A and Fern E Gant, Pueblo, CO; ed/AA, Univ of So CO, 1960; BA, Univ of No CO, 1962; MA, Ctl St Univ, 1966; EdD, Univ of No CO, 1973; Att'd Univ of NM, Wn St Col, Fort Hays St Univ; pa/Tchr 6th Grade & Remedial Rdg, Albuquerque Public Sch, 1962-65; Dev Rdg & Rdg Methods, Univ of So CO, 1966-68; Sec'dy Rdg Coor, Pueblo Dist No 70, 1968-71; Spec in Field Experiences, Univ of No CO, 1971-73; Coor of Sec'dy Ed, Pueblo Dist No 70, 1973-74; Dir of Spec Ser, Pueblo Dist No 70, 1974-; Spkr & Conslt in Field, 1966-; NEA; Ctl St Univ Alumni; Assn of Sch Curric Devel; CO Asn of Sch Exec; Coun for Exceptl Chd; Coun for Admrs in Spec Ed; Am Assn for Sch Admrs; Kappa Delta Pi; Phi Delta Kappa; Pi Lambda Theta; IPA; AAUW; r/Prot; hon/Profl Pubs; Outstg: Yg Wom of Am, Commun Ldrs, Bicent Ldrs, Tchrs in Exceptl Ed, Ldrs in N Am; Personalities of W & MW; W/W of W.

DUNSING, MARILYN M oc/University Administrator; b/Feb 19, 1926; h/2208 Staley Road, Champaign, IL 61821; ba/Urbana, IL; ed/MBA 1948, PhD 1954, Univ of Chgo; pa/Dir Sch of Human Resources & Fam Studies 1979-, Hd Dept of Fam & Consumer Ec 1978-79, Assoc Prof & Prof Dept of Fam & Consumer Ec 1962-, Univ of IL-Urbana; Instr, Asst Prof, Assoc Prof, Dept of Home Ec, Univ of CA-Davis, 1954-62; Mem: Policy Bd, *Home Ec Res Jour*, 1976-78; Edit Bd, *Jour of Consumer Affairs*, 1976-80; Ec Advr Bd, US Secy of Commerce, 1976-78; Adv Com, US Secy of Agri, 1962-64; Num Coms, Am Home Ec Assn, US Dept of Agri & IL Home Ec Assn; Sigma Xi; Phi Kappa Phi; Omicron Nu; Sigma Delta Epsilon; Gamma Sigma Delta; Am Ec Asn; Nat Coun on Fam Relats; Am Coun on Consumer Interests; Assn of Admrs of Home Ec; Nat Coun of Admrs of Home Ec; r/Luth; hon/Author, Over 100 Article Pub'd in Profl Jours & Books in Field, 1956-; Other Profl Reports & Pubs; Recip, Paul A Funk Awd, Col of Agri, 1973; Outstg Tchr Awd, Hom Ec Univ of IL-Urbana-Champaign, 1973; Home Ec Alumni F'ship, Univ of Chgo, 1950; Am Men & Wom of Sci; Personalities of W & MW.

DUNSTONE, JOHN JOSEPH oc/Professor, Experimental Psychologist; b/Apr 29, 1939; h/14 Sunset Road, Rural Delivery #2, Moscow, PA 18444; ba/Scranton, PA; m/Patricia Marie Brunori; c/Joan Marie, John Joseph Jr; p/Miriam Dunstone, Scranton, PA; p/Joanna Jackson, Scranton, PA; ed/BS, PA St Univ, 1961; MA 1964, PhD 1966, Univ of MA; pa/Asst Prof Psych, Valparaiso Univ, IN, 1965-66; Res Sci Trans Res Div INTEXT 1969-71, Stat Conslt 1975-80, Appalacia Lab Inc, Charleston, WV; Ast Prof 1966, Assoc Prof 1969, Prof 1974-, Chm Psych Dept 1972-76, Univ of Scranton, PA; Mem:

En Psychol Assn; Am Psychol Assn; NWn Psychol Assn of PA; Assn for Exptl Anal of Behavior; Sigma Xi; AAAS; r/Rom Cath; hon/Author, 6 Res Articles in Profl Jours; 6 Tech Reports; 1 Book Chapt; 2 Paper Presentations at Assn Meetings; Psi Chi, 1961; Sigma Xi, 1964; Outstg Edr of Am; Am Men & Wom of Sci; W/W in E, in Ed; Other Biogl Listings.

DUONG, WENDY NHU-NGUYEN oc/Executive Director of Risk Management; b/Nov 30, 1957; h/11202 Radford Lane, Houston, TX 77099; ba/Houston, TX; m/Andy H Q Tran; p/Nhu D Duong, Houston, TX; ed/BS, So IL Univ, 1978; JD, Univ of Houston, 1983; pa/Copy Rdr, Weekly & Penny Advtg Inc, 1978-79; Commun-Staff Anal, Houston IDS, 1979-82; Exec Dir of Risk Mgmt, Houston IDS, 1982-; ABA; Public Risk & Ins Mgmt Assn; Risk & Ins Mgmt Soc; hon/Profl Pub; S Vietnam Nat Hon Prize in Lit for Wom, 1975; So IL Edit Assn Scholar, 1977; So IL Univ Pres's Scholar & Dean's List, 1975-78; Intl Word/Info Processing Hons List Mem; W/W in SW.

DuPONT, ANN McGEATH oc/College Professor; b/Aug 29, 1944; h/Route 2, Box 315E, San Marcos, TX 78666; ba/Austin, TX; m/Lawrence Edward Jr; c/Diane; p/Alice Graham Bishop McGeath, San Marcos, TX; sp/Joe Everett McGeath (dec); ed/BS, w Highest Hons, Univ of TX-Austin, 1966; MBA, SW TX St Univ, 1975; PhD, TX Tech Univ, 1978; Att'd Sophie Newcomb Col, TX Tech Sch of Law; pa/Federated Dept Stores, 1966-70; Assoc Dry Goods, 1970-72; SW TX St Univ, 1975-77; Univ of TX-Austin, 1978-; Buyer; Store Mgr; Sys Anal; Col Prof; Dir of Mdsg Prog; Am Home Ec Assn; Am Col Retailing Assn; Assn of Col Profs of Textiles & Clothing; Omicron Nu; Phi Upsilon; Phi Alpha Delta Legal Frat; Fashion Grp Intl; Delta Gamma; r/Presb; hon/Profl Pubs; Mbrship Chr, ACPTC; St Adv Coun on Consumer in Voc Homemaking in TX 1981-82; Chm Mdsg Curric Eval Com, Coor Bd; Outstg Yg Wom in Am; W/W of Am Wom.

DUPONT, MARY ANN oc/Secondary Mathematics Curriculum Specialist; h/408 S Mangonia Circle, West Palm Beach, FL 33401; ba/West Palm Beach, FL; m/Wallace Sylvester; c/Tiana LaChelle; p/Otis and Isabell Larry, Tampa, FL; ed/BA, Univ of S FL, 1968; MS, FL St Univ, 1972; pa/Math Tchr & Lng Spec, Hillsborough Co Sch Bd, 1968-71; Instr, FL St Univ, 1971-72; Math Tchr 1978-77, Coor Tchr for Math 1977-78, Sec'dy Math Spec 1978-, Palm Bch Co Sch Bd; Past Dir, FL Coun of Tchrs of Math; Nat Coun of Tchrs of Math; Assn for Supvn & Curric Devel; Phi Theta Kappa; Math Curric Guide Com, St of FL, 1971-72; Learn & Earn Selection Com, 1972; Gen Math Writing Team, St of FL, 1972; FL St Dept of Ed Basic Skills Planning Team, 1977; Coun on Tchr Ed Math Competency Com, 1979; Writer of Proposal Outlining Minimum Essential Competencies for Math Tchrs, FL Coun of Tchrs of Math, 1978; Contracted by Ed Testing Ser to Write & Review Items Specifications, 1980; Reviewer, Proposals Submitted to NSF, 1980; r/Bapt; hon/

Profl Pubs; NSF Acad Yr Recip, FL St Univ, 1972; W/W in S & SE.

DURHAM, JO ANN oc/Artist and Art Patron; b/May 31, 1935; h/4300 Plantation Drive, Fort Worth, TX 76116; ba/Same; m/William E Durham; c/William F, John Lee; p/Judge and Mrs W J Fanning; ed/BS, E TX St Univ, 1956; pa/Art Tchr, 1966-68; Coor for Spec Events (Art Gallery Dir), TX Col of Osteopathic Med, 1978-83; Past Pres, Reg Dir & St Bd Mem, TX Fine Arts Assn; Patron & Sponsor, 'Art in Metroplex'; Co-Chm, Gamma Phi Beta Art Al Fresco; TX Christian Univ Fine Arts Guild; cp/SS Tchr, Wn Hills Bapt Ch & Wn Hills Nsg Home; Former Mem, Waverly Pk Garden Clb; Pres, Jr Wom's Clb Art Dept; Ft Worth Wom's Clb Art Dept; Chm, Sprg Art Show; Pres, Gamma Phi Beta Alumnae; Chm, Gamma Phi Beta Tour of Scott Home; Co-Chm, 'Decorator's Show for Thistle Hill'; Chm of Dedication Ser & Presentation, TX St Hist Marker at Thistle Hill; Chm, Var Art Auctions for Thistle Hill & Com for an Artists Ctr; r/Bapt; hon/Art Works in Pvt Collections; Cert of Apprec, Thistle Hill, 1979; Cert of Awd, TX Fine Arts Assn, 1978-79-80-81; Cert of Apprec, Wn Hills Nsg Home; Gittings Portrait, Scott Theatre as Patron of Arts.

DURIG, JAMES ROBERT oc/Chemist, College Dean; b/Apr 30, 1935; h/3815 Fernleaf Road, Columbia, SC 29209; ba/Columbia, SC; m/Katherine Marlene Sprowls; c/Douglas Tybor, Bryan Robert, Stacey Ann; p/Roberta Mounts, Washington, PA; sp/Mr and Mrs Donald W Sprowls, Claysville, PA; ed/BA 1958, Hon DSc 1979, Wash & Jefferson Col; PhD, MIT, 1962; mil/AUS, Chem Corps, 1963-64; pa/Asst Prof 1962-65, Assoc Prof Chem 1965-68, Prof 1968-70, Ednl Foun Prof Chem 1970-73, Dean Col of Sci & Math 1973-, Univ of SC; Mem: Chm Sub-com on Infrared & Raman Spectroscopy 1975-, Secy 1982 & Mem, Comm on Molecular Spectra & Structure 1978-, Intl Union of Pure & Applied Chems; Pres Alpha Chapt SC, Phi Beta Kappa, 1970; Gov'g Bd 1972-76, Pres 1974-76, Coblentz Soc; Sigma Xi; Blue Key Soc; Am Phy Soc; Am Chem Soc; Soc for Applied Spectroscopy; r/Presb; hon/Author, Over 406 Res Articles, 20 Review Articles & 13 Books in Field; Russell Awd, Univ of SC, 1968; Coblentz Soc Awd for Outstg Res in Molecular Spectroscopy, 1970; Charles A Stone Awd, Piedmont Sect of Am Chem Soc, 1975; So Chems Awd, Am Chem Soc, 1976; Alexander von Humbolt Sr Sci Awd, Gov of W Germany, 1976; Spectroscopy Soc of Pgh Awd, 1981; W/W: in S, in World; Am Men of Si; Other Biogl Listings.

DURLEY, CARRIE BARNES oc/School Counselor; b/Apr 13, 1942; h/727 Doncrest Drive, Channelview, TX 77530; ba/Houston, TX; m/Bose H Jr; c/Sonja (dec); p/Will (dec) and Mary Barnes, Charlotte, NC; sp/Bose Sr and Mattie Durley, Pittsburg, TX; ed/BA cum laude, NC Col, 1964; MEd, Univ of Houston, 1969; pa/Tchr, Brevard Co Schs, 1964-66; Tchr, Houston ISD, 1966-67; Tchr 1967-75, Title I Supvr 1975-77, Asst Prin 1977-82, Cnslr 1982-, Aldine ISD; Part-time Conslt, Reg IV Ed Ser Ctr, 1980-82; TX Per &

Guid Assn; Assn for Supvn & Curric Devel; TX Assn of Sec'dy Sch Prin; Nat Assn of Sec'dy Sch Prin; NCTE; r/Bapt; hon/Co-Editor, NC Col Yrbook, 1963-64; Table Tennis Awd, 1964; W/W in S & SW.

DUSKO, HAROLD GEORGE oc/Military Technology Branch Chief; b/Jul 1, 1942; h/5244 Eastland Drive, New Carlisle, OH 45344; ba/Wright Patterson AFB, OH; m/Janet Lamonby Craig; c/Steven Harold, Christopher David, Jeffrey Craig; p/Harold Richard and Josephine Mary (Goralka) Dusko, Natrona Hghts, PA; sp/James & Adah Craig (dec); ed/BS, Slippery Rock Univ, 1964; MBA, Univ of Dayton, 1970; pa/Cartographer, Aero Chart & Info Ctr, St Louis, MO, 1964-66; Imagery Anal Fgn Tech Div 1966-69, Methods Ofcr Fgn Tech Div 1970-79, Br Chief Fgn Tech Div 1979-, Wright Patterson AFB; Adj Prof Geog, Wright St Univ, 1970-; Mem: Am Soc of Photogrammetry, 1975-; Steering Com for Remote Sensing in OH, 1982-; cp/So OH Forge & Anvil Assn, 1983-; Blacksmith, Carriage Hill Hist Farm, 1982-; Bd of Dirs, New Carlisle Baseball Assn, 1974-78; r/Presb; hon/Author of 2 Manuals: *Lab Exercises in Cartography*, 1975; *Locational Cartography*, 1983; Author, *Digital Image Processing*, 1980; Other Pubs; Outstg Perf Awds, AF Sys Command, Fgn Tech Div, 1975, 1978, 1979; Sustained Superior Perf Awd, 1982, 1983; W/W in Frontier Sci & Technol.

DUTTA, SISIR KAMAL oc/Professor in Molecular Genetics; b/Aug 28, 1928; h/8841 Tuckerman Lane, Potomac, MD 20854; ba/Washington, DC; m/Minati; c/Mahasweta, Basabi; p/Mr and Mrs Krishma K Dutta (dec); sp/Mr and Mrs Roy (dec); ed/MS 1958, PhD 1960, KS St Univ; mil/ROTC; pa/Dir & Chief Res Ofcr, Nat Pineapple Res Inst, 1961-64; Res Assoc & Vis'g Scist, Chgo Univ 1960-61, Rice Univ 1964-65; Asst Prof Biol, TX Sn Univ, 1965-66; Chm Math & Sci Dept, Assoc Prof Biol, Jarvis Col, 1966-67; Prof Molecular Genetics, Dept of Botany, Howard Univ, 1967-; Conslt to UN; Sci Advr to Pineapple Indust of S/E Asian Countries; Collaborator, Rockefeller Univ; NIH; Pasteur Inst; Environ, EPA Res Ctr, Res Triangle Pk, NC; Mbrship; hon/Profl Pubs; Recip, Over 100 Million Dollar Res Grant Awds from Var US Govt Agys & Pvt Founs; Hon Soc; Sigma Xi; Recip Chi; Notable Am of Bicent Era; W/W: in World/USA, in Intl Ed.

DUVE, JOHN LARRY oc/University and Public Administration; b/Sep 14, 1949; h/43 Esplanade, Irvine, CA 92715; ba/Los Angeles, CA; p/Jay and Ada Duve, Columbia, MO; ed/BS, Univ of NE, 1972; pa/Prodn & Engrg Dept, M&M/Mars Co, 1969-70; Engrg Dept, Zenith Radio Corp, 1970-71; Asst to Dir of Public Safety, Univ of NE, 1971-74; Parking & Trans Admr, Univ of NE, 1974-80; Dir, Parking & Trans Ser, Univ of CA-Irvine, 1980-; Reg Trans Mgr, LA Olympic Org Com, 1983; Asst Dir for Olympic Village Adm, LA Olympic Org Com, 1984-; Institl & Mun Parking Cong, 1974-; Univ of CA Handicapped Adv Com, 1980-; Irvine Trans Corridor Adv Bd, 1981-; Assn Col & Univ Security Dirs, 1974-; Former Pres, Triangle Frat, 1971-; Am Mgmt Assn; Nat Assn of Vanpool Operators; r/

Congregl; hon/City of Lincoln Spark Plug Awd, 1980; W/W.

DWYER, MARIE RITA oc/Assistant to Dean of Student Affairs; b/Sep 4, 1915; h/526 Oakwood, St Louis, MO 63119; ba/St Louis, MO; m/John D; c/John D Jr, Joseph, James, Jerome; ed/BA, Notre Dame Col of Staten Isl, 1936; MA 1938, PhD Cand 1944-, Fordham Univ; Diplomes d'Etudes Francaises, Sorbonne, Paris, 1933-37-52; Certificat, Institut de Phore'ique, Paris, 1937-52; Certificat de la Sorbonne, Paris, 1952; pa/Instr, Fordham Univ Sch of Ed, NYC, 1938-42; Instr, Notre Dame Col, NYC, 1939-40; Instr, Col of St Rose, Albany, NY, 1949-53; Instr, Wash Univ-St Louis, 1959-60; Instr, Meramac Commun Col, St Louis, 1968-70; Instr, Webster Col, St Louis, 1966-74; Instr Eng to Fgn Wives 1974-, Asst to Dean of Student Affairs 1982-, Dir Commun Relats Intl Progs 1974-82, St Louis Univ; Mem: Mem 1974-, Past Chm COMSEC Reg 4 1978-79, Registration Com Nat Conv 1980, Nat Assn of Fgn Student Affairs; Life Mem, MO Acad of Sci; Societe Intl de la Linguistique; Ctr Studie Scambi Internaionali; Intl Platform Assn; Consort Secy Fgn Lang Depts, Webster Col, Maryville Col; Beta Kappa Chapt, Pi Delta Phi; Pres 1961-63, MO Mod Lang Assn; Pres 1954-1955, Am Tchrs of French Assn St Louis; VPres 1973, Fgn Lang Assn of MO; Record Secy 1970, Assn of Fgn Lang Tchrs of Gtr St Louis; Secy 1955, La Societe Francaise; VPres 1983-84, Dir 1956-58, Fac Wom's Clb of St Louis Univ; AAAS; Num Others; cp/Num Positions & Coms, Archdiocesan Coun of Laity & Archdiocesan Coun Cath Yth; Pres, Notre Dam Col Alumnae, 1942-43; Pres, Intl Fdn Cath Alumnae, Albany Circle, NY, 1945-49; Pres, K of C Aux, Webster Groves, MO, 1956-57; Pres, Jesuit Mothers' Guild, MO Province, 1963-65; Pres, Cath Woms' Leag, Holy Redeemer Parish, St Louis, 1964-66; r/Cath; hon/MO Acad of Sci; Num Travels to Fgn Countries; W/W: of Am Wom, in MW; DIB; 2000 Wom of Achmt; Am Cath W/W; Other Biogl Listings.

DY-RAGOS, LYDIA SY oc/Business Manager/Managing Partner; b/Apr 17, 1946; h/10106 Northwest 74th St, Kansas City, MO 64152; ba/Kansas City, MO; m/Ramon R; c/R Leonard, Julian B, Philip L, Mark J; p/Mr and Mrs Thomas Sy Ling, Manila, Philippines; sp/Julian (dec) and Marciana Dy-Ragos, Philippines; ed/Col Grad; pa/Credit-Collection, Fam Bus, 1965-68; Controller, Fam Bus, 1968-69; Mktg Res, VA Nat Bk, 1969-70; Bus Mgr & Corp Secy, Ramon R Dy-Ragos MD Inc, 1977-; Mng Ptnr, D T K Investmt Co, 1978-; Mng Ptnr, H D H Investmt Co, 1980-; Pres 1982-83, Co Rep to AMA Aux Conv Ldrship Tng 1981, Mem, 1973-, Clay Co Med Assn Aux; 1st Dist Dir, MO St Med Assn Aux, 1983-85; N KC Meml Hosp Aux, 1981-; Chm, N KC Meml Hosp Ways & Means, 1983-84; Nat Assn for Female Execs, 1982-; cp/Den Mother, Pack #261, 1977-78; Coun Mem & Social Mem, St Theresa Rom Cath Ch, 1978-80; Social Chm 1975, Ways & Means Chm 1981, Filipino Assn of Gtr KC; r/Rom Cath; hon/Apprec Awd, Filipino Assn of Gtr KC, 1981; Recip Recog Cert, Bicent

Ethnic Heritage Commun Plan, 1976; Apprec Cert, St Theresa Rom Cath Ch, 1979; Cert of Spec Tng, Ins Profile Dev in Hlth Care Profession, 1981; W/W of Am Wom.

DYER, GEORGE CARROLL oc/ Retired Vice Admiral, US Navy; b/Apr 27, 1898; h/4 Chase Road, Annapolis, MD 21401; m/Adaline Shick; c/Mary D Corrin, Georgia D Burnett, Virginia D Smith; p/Harry Blair and Georgia Mortimer Dyer (dec) ed/BS, US Nav Acad, 1918; Nav War Col; Nat War Col; Addit Studies; mil/USN, 1915-55; Line Ofcr Submarines, Deep Sea Diver, Submarine Rescue Ship, Destroyer, Mine Layer, Cruiser, Battleship; Staff Cmdr, Destroyers; Staff Cmdr, Battleforce; Staff Cmdr-in-Chief & Chief of Nav Opers; cp/Pres, US Nav Acad Class of 1919; Pres, US Nav Acad Alumni Assn; Cmdr-in-Chief, Mil Order of World Wars; Bd Dirs, Ret'd Ofcrs Assn; Pres, Abenaki Tower & Trail Assn; Soc of the Cinc, St of VA; r/Epis; hon/Pub'd Author; Dist'd Ser Medal; US Legion of Merit; Purple Heart; Cmdr of Brit Empire; Most Exalted Order of White Elephants (Thailand); Cross of Nav Merit, Grt Ofcr (Peru); Mil Order of Merit (Italy); Others.

DYKES, DEWITT SANFORD SR oc/ Design Architect; b/Aug 16, 1903; h/ 2139 Dandridge Avenue, Knoxville, TN 37915; ba/Knoxville, TN; m/Viola Logan; c/Reida B Gardiner; DeWitt S Jr; ed/AB, Clark Col, 1930; BD, Gammon Theol Sem, 1931; STM, Boxton Univ, 1971; pa/U Meth Pastor, 1932-54; Dist Sup (Meth), 1954-55; Field Dir (Architectural), Nat Div of Missions (U Meth Ch), 1956-68; Arch, 1970-; AIA; Interfaith Forum on Rel, Art & Arch; Beck Cultural Exch Ctr; Alpha Phi Alpha Frat; cp/YMCA; U Meth Ch; r/ U Meth; hon/1st Prize, Christology, 1930; S'ship, Boston Univ, 1931; Design Arch in 1982 World's Fair; Outstg Minority Bus Awd, 1979.

E

EADIE, MARGARET LOUISE oc/ Educational and Business Consultant; ba/652 Santa Helena, Solana Beach, CA 92075; m/Robert James Eadie; c/Dr William F II, Lynne Eadie Oddo, Janet Eadie Cohen, Craig Alan; p/Samuel and Elsa Larson, Johnsonburg, PA; ed/BA, Miami Univ, Oxford, OH; MA in Cnslg, Chapman Col, Orange, CA; Adv'd EdM, Univ of So CA, LA; pa/Tchr, Tustin HS, Tustin, CA; Lectr, Sch of Ed & Asst to VP of Cont'g Ed, CA St Univ-Fullerton; Conslt, Ednl & Bus; Assoc Mem, Am Psychol Assn; AAUW; PEO; Delta Delta Delta Sorority; The Hon Assn of Wom in Ed, Univ of So CA; hon/2 Athena Awds from the Panhellenic Assn, 1973; W/W of Am Wom.

EAKIN, THOMAS CAPPER oc/ Sports Promotion Executive; b/Dec 16, 1933; h/2729 Shelley Road, Shaker Heights, OH 44122; m/Brenda Lee Andrew; c/Thomas Andrews, Scott Frederick; p/Frederick William and Beatrice Capper Eakin (dec); ed/BA, Denison Univ, 1956; mil/AUS 1956-58, Spec 4th Class; pa/Pres, TCE Enterprises, Shaker Hgts, 1973-; Dist Mgr, Hitchcock Pub'g Co, Cleveland, OH, 1970-72; Reg Bus Mgr, Chilton Pub'g Co, Cleveland, 1969-70; Other Former Positions; Fdr & Pres, Golf Intl 100 Clb, 1970-; Fdr & Dir: Cy Young Mus 1970-, "TRY" Target/Reach Yth 1971-; Fdr & Pres, OH Baseball Hall of Fame, 1976-; Trustee, Newcomerstown Sports Corp; Hon Dir, Tuscarawas Co Old Timers Baseball Assn; Other Profl Activs; cp/ Trustee, Tuscarawas Co Hist Soc; Bd Dirs, Wahoo Clb; Fellow, IBA; Former Mem, Cleveland Indians Old Timers Com; Adv Bd: Camp Hope, Cuyahoga Hills Boys Sch; Cleveland Coun on Correction; Others; r/1st Bapt Ch of Gtr Cleveland, Bd Mem 1966-69; hon/ Commend, City of New Orleans; Certs of Merit: St of LA, Tuscarawas Co Am Revolution Bicent Comm; Apprec Awd, Am Revolution Bicent Adm; Outstg Alumnus Awd, Phi Delta Theta Alumni Clb; OH Senate Commend Awd; Awd of Achmt, OH Assn Hist Socs; Gov's Awd for Commun Action, OH Gov, 1974; Proclamation Awd, "Thomas C Eakin Day," City of Cleveland, 1974; Num Others; Biogl Listings.

EAKINS, PAMELA S oc/Sociologist; b/Mar 12, 1953; ba/Center for Research on Women, Stanford, CA 94305; m/ Bernhard M Haisch; c/Katherine Stuart Haisch, Christopher Taylor Haisch; ed/ BA 1975, MA 1977, Univ of CO; PhD, Univ of CO-Boulder, 1980; pa/Instr, Univ of CO, 1975-77, 1978-79; Vis'g Sociologist, Netherlands Nat Ctr for Res & Devel in Adult Ed, 1977-78; Lectr & Affil'd Scholar, Ctr for Res on Wom, Stanford Univ, 1982-; Am Sociological Assn; Soc for the Study of Social Probs; Wn Social Sci Assn, Wom's Studies Sect Chair; Sociologists for Wom in Society, Secy of CO Chapt, Treas of Bay Area Chapt; The Birth Place Maternity Clin & Resource Ctr, Pres; hon/Author, *Mothers in Transition* 1983, *Labor of Love* (Forthcoming), *Childbirth: The Sociological Perspective* (Forthcoming); W/W W World W/W of Wom; Am Men & Wom of Sci.

EARLY, GEORGE HUGHES oc/Professor; b/Mar 20, 1920; h/111 Van Buren Boulevard, Terre Haute, IN

47803; ba/Terre Haute, IN; m/Frances Greene; c/George Greene (1970), Jane Hannah E Boswell, Robert Lee, Peter Stone (dec), Martha Scott E Hall; p/N D and Ada Hughes Early (dec); sp/Mrs John D Greene, Terre Haute, IN; ed/ BS, MS St Univ, 1942; MDiv, Princeton Theol Sem, 1956; MS, Purdue Univ, 1968; PhD, Purdue Univ, 1972; mil/ AUS, 1942-46, Staff Ofcr; pa/Bus, 1946-53; Pastor Knoxville TN 1956-60, Columbia TN 1960-66, Oxford IN 1966-68; Clin Dir, Purdue Achmt Ctr for Chd, 1969-72; Prof, Dept of Spec Ed, Sch Ed, IN St Univ, 1972-; Tau Beta Pi; Kappa Mu Epsilon; Moderator, Nashville Presby, U Presb Ch, 1963-64; Contbg Editor, *Growing Child*; Contbg Editor, *Academic Therapy*; r/Presb; hon/ Pub'd Author; Profl Pubs; Bronze Star, AUS, 1945.

EASTLAND, MARY LOU WHITE oc/Company Executive; b/Jul 3, 1939; h/ Gulfport, MS; ba/Gulfport, MS; c/ Charles Lamar Jr, James Denson, Laura Lynette; p/James Dewitt Sr and Mary Belle Barnes White; ed/BSE, Delta St Univ, 1961; Att'd Univ of So MS, 1978; pa/El Paso Public Sch Sys, 1961-62; IRS, 1963-65; Owner, Bresler's 33 Flavors, 1974-77; Sci Instr, Harrison Co Sch Sys, 1978-82; Owner, Top-Flite Pubs, 1982-; cp/YWCA; GSA; Northwood Hills Garden Clb; U Heart Fund Drive; Optimists Clbs of Gulfport & Orange Grove; Orange Grove Yth Assn; Orange Grove Jr C of C; Harrison Ctl HS Parents Booster Clb; Beta Sigma Phi-Nu Delta Chapt, Pres 1968, Fac Advr; OGMS Sci Fair; Rebel Rap; Jr Optimists Clb; r/Prot; hon/Pub'd Author; Pres, Wom Hon Coun, Delta St Univ, 1960-61; Girl of Yr, Beta Sigma Phi, 1968; W/W Am Wom.

EASTMAN, MICHAEL PAUL oc/ Chemistry Educator and Researcher; b/ Apr 14, 1941; h/1308 Madeline, El Paso, TX 79902; ba/El Paso, TX 79968-0509; m/Carol Oden; c/Michael E, Nathaniel L; p/LeRoy Irons (dec) and Virginia Marie Anderson Eastman, Lancaster, WI; ed/BA, Carleton Col, 1963; PhD, Cornell Univ, 1968; pa/Fellow, Los Alamos Nat Lab, 1968-70; Asst Prof 1970-74, Assoc Prof 1970-80, Prof of Chem 1980-, Asst Dean, Col of Sci 1981-, Univ of TX-El Paso; Secy-Treas 1973, Chm 1975, 1983, Alt Cnslr, Rio Grande Val Sect, Am Chem Soc; r/Prot; hon/35 Profl Pubs; Phi Beta Kappa; Sigma Xi, 1963.

EASTON, SUSAN WARD oc/Asst Prof of Church Hist; b/Nov 9, 1944; h/ 555 Sumac Drive, Provo, UT 84604; ba/ Provo, UT; c/Brian, Todd, John; p/ Ethelyn Ward, Long Beach, CA; ed/BA, 1966; MA 1975; EdD 1977; pa/Instr & Asst Prof in Col of Fam Home & Social Sci 1977-80, Asst Prof of Rel Ed 1980-, Brigham Yg Univ; Phi Kappa Phi, 1978-; UT Hist Assn; Mormon Hist Assn; Bd Mem, C of C, Wom Div 1983-84; Assn of Mormon Cnslrs & Profls; r/LDS; hon/Pub'd Author; Sandberg Awd for Rel Res & Writing; B Wes Belnap Awd for Rel Res; Outstg Yg Wom of Am; Prominent Men & Wom of Provo, 1973.

EATON, JAMES ALLEN JR oc/Medical Research Analyst; b/Jan 15, 1946; h/2317 Northeast 75th Terrace, Gladstone, MO 64118; ba/Kansas City, MO; c/James Allen III; p/James Allen and Mary E Eaton, Enid, OK; ed/BS 1969,

MS 1976, KS St Univ, Manhattan, KS; mil/AUS, 1971-73; pa/Adm Asst, Larned (KS) St Hosp, 1970-71; Lab Tech, Hardin Co Hosp, Elizabethtown, KY, 1972-73; Instr, Dept of Anatomy & Physiol, Col of Vet Med, KS St Univ, 1973-76; Med Res Analyst, Law Firm of Shook, Hardy & Bacon, 1976-; Sigma Xi; r/Cath; hon/Author, Papers in Field; Decorated, AUS Commend Medal; Grad Res & Thesis Excell Awd, Sigma Xi, 1976; Recip, Grad Res Excell Awd, Intl Poultry Assn, 1975.

EATON, JOAN TUCKER oc/Associate Director of Scholarships and Financial Aid; Coordinator of Student Counseling; b/Jun 12, 1922; h/6440 Fairfield, Apartment 117, Fort Wayne, IN 46807; ba/Fort Wayne, IN; c/Sara Joan, Nancy E Wilhite, Olney Benjamin, Jeffrey Tucker; ed/MS, IN Univ, 1973; BA cum laude, Midland Luth Col, 1944; pa/Admissions Ofc, Midland Luth, 1944; News Editor for Daily Newspapers in Plattsmouth NE, Wellington KS, & Fremont NE, 1944-46; Univ Public Relats, IL Inst of Technol, 1942-48; Asst Dir of Financial Aids, Univ of Evansville, 1967-69; Asst Dir of Financial Aids, IN-Purdue, 1970-77; Dir of Financial Aid 1977-81, Assoc Dir 1981-, IN Univ-Purdue Univ, 1969-; Nat Financial Aid Assn, 1969-; MW Financial Aid Assn, 1969-; IN Financial Aid Assn; Adm Coun, IN-Purdue Univ, 1972-; OES, 1944-; Fort Wayne Campus S'ship & Financial Aid Adv Com, 1972-; r/ Luth; hon/W/W: of Wom in World, in Am Cols & Univs.

EATON, VIRGINIA FORD oc/High School Teacher and Head of the History Department; b/Dec 3, 1941; h/342 East Jefferson, Kosciusko, MS 39090; ba/ Kosciusko, MS; m/William Howard; c/ Billy, Ginny; p/Mr and Mrs S Hassell Ford, Laurel, MS; sp/Mr and Mrs R F Eaton, Bonneville, MS; ed/BS, MS St Univ Wom, 1962; MA, Univ So MS, 1976; Wkg Spec, MS St Ed; pa/Tchr, Jones Co Schs; Tchr, Laurel City Schs; Tchr, Smith Co Schs; Tchr, Kosciusko City Schs; MS Coun of Social Studies; Delta Kappa Gamma; V Regent, DAR, Samuel Hammonds Chapt; Outreach Dir, First Bapt Ch; Cheerleader Sponsor, KHS, 1977-84; Hd of Social Studies Dept, KHS; r/Bapt; hon/Profl Pub; Outstg Wom of Arts, 1981; Pres, USM Alumni Assn Attala Co, 1981-82; Outstg Am Hist Tchr, Attala Co, 1982; Outstg Am Hist Tchr, Dist III of DAR, 1982; F'ship, Taft Inst of Govt, 1983; Outstg Hist Tchr, Webb Franklin in Congl Record; F'ship to Study Constitl Hist in Austin TX, 1983 by Am Hist Soc; Soloist at St Cnvn Delta Kappa Gamma 1982, DAR Conv, 1984.

EAVES, BURCHET CURTIS oc/ Professor of Operations Research; b/ Nov 25, 1938; h/5 Coyote Hill, Portola Valley, CA 94025; c/Jordon, Lesley; p/Everett and Mary Curtis, Shreveport, LA; ed/BS, Mech Engrg, Carnegie Tech, 1961; MBA, Tulane Univ, 1965; MS in Stat, PhD in Opers Res, Stanford Univ, 1969; mil/AUS, 1st & 2nd Lt, 1961-63; pa/ Acting Asst Prof of Bus, Univ of CA-Berkeley, 1968-70; Asst Prof 1970-72, Assoc Prof 1972-75, Prof 1975-, Opers Res, Stanford Univ; Vis'g Assoc Prof of Ec, Org & Mgmt, Yale Univ, 1975; Am Math Soc; Math Programming Soc; Math Assn of Am; Opers Res Soc of Am; Soc for Indust & Applied Math; The Inst of Mgmt Sci; Assoc Editor of Jours, *Math Programming* 1976-, *Math of Opers Res* 1974-; hon/Pubs, "Finite Solution of Pure Trade Mkts w Cobb-Douglas Utilities" 1984, "Line-Sum-Symmetric Scalings of Square Nonnegative Matrices" Dec 1983, "A Decomposition & Inequality for Line-Sum-Symmetric Matrices" Nov 1983, "A Course in Triangulations for Solving Equations w PL Homotopies" Jul 1983; "Subdivs from Primal & Dual Cones & Polytopes" Jun 1983, "Equivalence of LCP & PLS: Part II" 1983; Num Other Pubs; Beta Gamma Sigma, Tulane Univ, 1965; Sigma Xi, Stanford Univ, 1968; Guggenheim F'ship, 1979-80.

EBERSOLE, J GLENN JR oc/Engineering and Marketing Executive; b/Feb 8, 1947; h/RD 2, Box 305, Manheim, PA 17545; ba/Same; m/Helen W; p/J Glenn Ebersole Sr, Elizabethtown, PA; Marie Christine Ebersole (dec); sp/Mr and Mrs Ellsworth Kistler, Coopersburg, PA; ed/BSCE 1970, MEngr 1973, PA St Univ; pa/Penn DOT, Civil Engr Intern, 1970-71, Asst Dist Design Liaison Engr 1971, Chief Res & Spec Studies Sect, Bur of Traffic Engrg, 1971-76; Asst Chief Engr, Traffic PA Turnpike Comm, 1976-78; Chief Trans Engr, Huth Engrs Inc, 1978-81; Acct Exec, GSGSB, 1981-82; Engrg & Mktg Exec, J G Ebersole Assoc, 1982-; Fdr & Grp Exec, The Renaissance Grp, 1983-; ASCE; Inst of Trans Engrs, Tech Prog Chm, 50th Annual Meeting; NSPE; PSPE; IPA; Past Pres, Am Mktg Assn, Ctl PA Sect, 1982-83; Am Mgmt Assn; cp/Paster Master of Casphia Lodge #551, F&AM, 1983; Alpha Sigma Phi; Phi Eta Sigma; Shriners; TRB Mem of 4 Natl Coms; Rapho Twp Planning Comm, Chm 1971-76; r/Luth; hon/ Num Profl Publs; Gil Shirk Meml Trophy for Outstg Sr Ath, 1965; Best All Around Ath, 1965; Num Sports Awds; W/W: in E, in Fin & Indust.

EBERSPACHER, WARREN A oc/ Historical Aircraft Corporation Executive; b/Jun 8, 1929; h/PO Box 221B, Durango, CO 81301; ba/Same; m/ Nancy; c/Kim, Michael; p/A R Eberspacher, Southern St Paul, MN; ed/Bach of Aeronaut Engrg, Univ of MN, 1952; MBA, Pepperdine Univ, 1972; mil/Ret'd Navy Cmdr; pa/Pres, Hist Aircraft Corp (Present); Self Employed Mgmt Conslt, Von Eberspach Assocs, 1977-; Dept of the Navy, 1952-77; Exptl Aircraft Assn, 1973-; Aircraft Owners & Pilots Assn, 1952-; Am Aviation Hist Soc, 1952-; Cross & Cockade, 1962-; cp/Optimist Intl, 1982-; r/Presb; hon/Author of Articles Pub'd in *INC Mag, Pot Pilot, Fine Scale Modeler, Datamation, AAHS Jour, Aero Album*; W/W: in W, in Engrg; Dir of Dist'd Ams.

ECKENFELDER, W WESLEY JR oc/ Distinguished Professor of Environmental Engineering; b/Nov 15, 1926; h/ 153 Valley Forge, Nashville, TN 37205; ba/Nashville, TN; m/Kathleen Hurley; c/Lawrence, Janice; p/W Wesley Eckenfelder, Ramsey, NJ; ed/BCE, Manhattan Col, 1946; MS, PA St Univ, 1948; MCE, NY Univ, 1954; pa/Asst Prof, Manhattan Col, 1953-65; Pres Hydroscience Ind, 1960-65; Prof, Univ of TX, 1965-70; Bd Chm, Aware Inc, 1975-82, Dist'd

Prof of Envir Engrg, Vanderbilt Univ, 1982-; ASCE; ACS; AICHE; AIC; AEEP; AAUP; Hon Mem, IAWPR; r/Prot; hon/ Profl Pubs; Indust Wastes Medal, WPCF, 1957; Kenneth Alley Medal, NYWPCS, 1957; SOCMA Gold Medal for Envir Chem, 1974; Thomas Camp Medal, WPCF, 1981; W/W in SE.

EDDY, ESTHER MANGONE oc/ Professor of Reading; b/Oct 24, 1923; h/200 Church Street, Newington, CT 06111; ba/Hartford, CT; m/Frank Vincent; c/Chaplain Joshua F, Norah E; p/ Eugene and Onorina Varbella Mangone; ed/BS, Ctl CT St Univ, 1945; MA, Columbia Univ, 1948; Postgrad, Univ of CT, 1966; pa/Col Instr, Ctl CT St Univ, 1945-58; Owner, Dir, Red Rock Nursery Sch, 1958-64; Assoc Prof of Rdg 1968-, Dir of Spec Sers Prog 1978-82, Gtr Hartford Commun Col; Chp, Rdg Coun of CT Commun Cols, 1978-79; Res Chp, CT Assn of Rdg Res, 1971-73; cp/Chp, Bicent Comm, Town of Newington, 1973-77; Pres, Newington Hist Trust, 1975-78; Pres, Newington Hist Soc & Trust, 1978-79; Chp, Diaconate Bd, 1971; r/Congregationalist; Chp, Bd of Trustees, Ch of Christ, Congregational, 1981-83; hon/Chm, "Recommendations for Rdg Progs" (Booklet), 1972; Kappa Delta Pi, 1944; Cert of Ofcl Recog for Outstg Ser in the Observance of the Am Revolution Bicent, CT Comm, 1977; Cert of Commend for Outstg Ser for a Very Successful Bicent Observance, 1976; W/W in E; Notable Ams.

EDELSTEIN, ROSEMARIE HUBLOU oc/Nurse Educator; b/Mar 3, 1935; h/10 Grande Paseo, San Rafael, CA 94903; ba/San Francisco, CA; c/Julie Marie, Lori Therese, Lynn Kathleen, Toni Anne; p/Francis J and Myrtle Hublou, Bismarck, ND; ed/BSN, Col of St Teresa, 1956; Cert, Public Hlth Nsg, 1972; MEd, Holy Names Col, 1977; EdD, Univ of SF, 1981; mil/Med Mil Resv, St of CA, Major; pa/Dir, Instr, Clin Supvr, Voc Nsg Prog, SF Sch for Hlth Professions, 1971-74; Dir, Instr, Clin Supvr, Rancho Arroyo Sch of Voc Nsg, 1974-75; Instr, Voc Nsg Prog, Clin Supvr, Ctr for Hlth Studies, 1975; Intensive Care/Coronary Care Staff Nurse, Kaiser-Permanente Hosp, 1976-77; Dir, Inservice Ed, Ross Gen Hosp, 1977-78; Dir of Nsg Ed & Tng, St Francis Meml Hosp, 1978-81; Assoc Dir of Nsg, Nsg Ed/Staff Dev, St Francis Meml Hosp, 1981-; Am Heart Assn; Asst Dirs of Nsg; Sigma Theta Tau, Alpha Eta Chapt, Univ of CA; r/Rom Cath; hon/Profl Pubs; W/W: of Am Wom, in W.

EDEN, WILLIAM MURPHEY oc/ Radiation Physicist; b/Sep 26, 1928; h/ 2812 Duffton Loop, Tallahassee, FL 32303; ba/Tallahassee, FL; m/Clara May; c/Andrew Mark; p/Rev and Mrs J Fred Eden Jr; ed/AB, Mercer Univ, GA, 1955; MS, Radiological Physics, Univ of Miami, FL, 1964; mil/USN, Hosp Corps, 1948-52; pa/Surg Tech, Macon, GA, 1954-56; Sanitarian, Jones Co, GA 1956-59, Daytona Bch, FL 1960-63; Public Hlth Physicist, Dept of Hlth & Rehabilitative Sers, 1964-84; Radiation Physics Conslt; Hlth Physics Soc, 1965-; Intl Radiation Protection Assn, 1965-; APHA, Fellow 1968; Am Conf of Govtl Indust Hygienists, 1980-; Intl Soc of Photoptical Engrs; Am Assn of Phys-

icists in Med, 1980-; Am Col of Radiol, Physics Assoc 1984; r/Bapt; hon/Pubs, "Radiation Protection Surveys of Cardiovas Labs" Jun 1970, "Hazards to Microwave Repairman" (Proceedings of 2nd Nat Conf of Radiation Control) Apr 1970, "Microwave Oven Repair: Hazard Eval" in *Electronic Prod Radiation & the Hlth Physicist* Jan 1970, "Microwave Oven Study in FL" Nov 1969, "How do Med Facilities Handle Brachytherapy Radiological Emergencies? " Jun 1984; W/W: in Atoms, in Frontier Sci & Technol.

EDERER, FRED oc/Epidemiologist and Biostatistician; b/Mar 5, 1926; h/ 5504 Lambeth Road, Bethesda, MD 20814; ba/Bethesda, MD; m/Hilda; c/ Julian, Judith, Susan; p/Joel and Celia Ederer (dec); ed/BS, Math, City Col of NY, 1949; Postgrad Wk in Biostats, Columbia Univ, 1950-51; MA, Stats, Am Univ, 1959; Postgrad Wk in Biostats, Stanford Univ, 1962; mil/USN, 1944-46; pa/Assoc Dir for Biometry & Epidemiology 1984-, Chief, Ofc of Epidemiology 1974-84, Hd, Sect on Clin Trials & Natural Hist Studies 1971-74, Nat Eye Inst, NIH; Nat Heart, Lung & Blood Inst, NIH, 1964-71; Nat Cancer Inst 1957-64, NIH; Bur of Labor Stats, Dept of Labor, 1955-57; Ofc of Surg Gen, USAF, 1952-55; NYC Hlth Dept, 1950-52; Lectr in Stats, Am Univ, 1965-68; Lectr on Methods of Clin Res, Annual Courses Sponsored by Nat Eye Inst, 1976-; Lectr in Epidemiology, Johns Hopkins Univ, 1977-78; Lectr in Epidemiology, London Sch of Hygiene & Tropical Med, 1980; Fellow, Am Statl Assn; Fellow, Coun on Epidemiology, Am Heart Assn, Com on Criteria in Methods 1970-72; Biometrics Soc, ENAR, Reg Adv Bd 1970-72; Soc for Epidemiologic Res; Intl Epidemiological Assn; Soc for Clin Trials, Bd of Dirs 1979-83; Fellow, Am Col of Epidemiology, Bd of Dirs 1979-81, Chm of Com on Cert 1983-; Nat Diet-Heart Study, Dir of Statl Ctr 1964-67; Diet-Heart Review Panel, 1968-69; Urokinase-Pulmonary Embolism Trial, Dir of Coor'g Ctr, Data Monitoring Com 1968-71; Diabetic Retinopathy Study, Proj Ofcr, Data Monitoring Com 1971-78; Visual Acuity Impairment Survey, Dir 1981-83; Sorbinil Retinopathy Trial, Policy, Data & Safety Monitoring Com 1983-; MN Colon Cancer Control Study, Policy & Data Monitoring Com, 1984-; Edit Bd, *Am Jour of Ophthal*, 1976-; Sect Editor for Epidemiology, *Survey of Ophthal*, 1979-81; Assoc Editor, *Am Jour of Epidemiology*, 1982-; cp/Pres, Gt Oaks Assn, 1973-75; Montgomery Co Assn for Retarded Citizens, Mem, Bd of Dirs 1973-79, Chm of Proj CARRI 1973-75, Chm of Planning Com 1976-79; Trustee, MD Trust for Retarded Citizens, 1981-; r/Jewish; hon/ *Sustained High Quality Wk Perf Awd from Dir of NIH, 1974*; Dept of Hlth, Ed & Wel Superior Ser Awd, 1975; The David Rumbough Sci Awd, Juv Diabetes Foun, 1983; Pubs, "Epidemiologic Assns w Senile Lens Changes" 1983, "Incidence Estimates for Lens Changes, Macular Changes, Open-Angle Glaucoma & Diabetic Retinopathy" 1983, "Jerome Cornfield's Contbns to the Conduct of Clin Trials" 1982; Num Other Pubs in Biostatl & Epidemiologic Res Jours.

EDGAR, C BALDOCK oc/Child Therapist; b/Oct 23, 1902; h/2260 Maywood Avenue, San Jose, CA 95128; ba/San Jose, CA; m/Agnes M; c/Alan, Joan

Williamson; ed/BA, Univ of New Zealand, 1929; MA, Univ of IA, 1937; MSW, Univ of Denver, 1941; MEd Cand, OR St Col; mil/Territorials, New Zealand; pa/Pupil Tchr, Beckenham Sch, 1920-21; Asst Master, Phillipstown Sch, 1924-26; Sr Asst Master, Primary Dept, Motueka Dist HS, 1927-28; Asst Master, Kariori Sch Wellington, 1929; Hd Tchr, Maraenui Native Sch, 1930-33; Hd Tchr, Oruanui Native Sch, 1934-36; Boys' Wel Ofcr, Ed Dept in Wellington, 1929; Visitor, St Louis Social Security Com, 1938; Epidemiologist & Case Wkr, Provincial Clin for the Control of VD, 1938-40; Dist Secy, Big Brothers, 1942-43; Sup of Frazer Detention Home, 1943-46; Cnslr, Cnslg & Testing Bur at OR St Col, 1946-47; Case Wkr, Home of Benevolence, 1948-; Am Assn of Social Wkrs; Kappa Delta Pi; hon/Num Profl Pubs; Fellow, Royal Soc of Hlth.

EDGAR, THOMAS E oc/Professor of Counselor Education; b/Jan 30, 1925; h/419 South Garfield, Pocatello, ID 83204; ba/Pocatello, ID; c/Thomas A; p/Clyde and Opal Edgar; ed/BS in Psych 1950, EdS in Ed 1953, WA St Univ, Pullman; MA in Cnslr Ed 1962, EdD in Cnslr Ed 1965, Univ of WY Laramie; Postdoct Study in Psychotherapy, Alfred Adler Chgo, 1974-75; mil/AUS, 1943-46; pa/Tchr, Clover Pk HS (Eng) 1950-58, Univ Place HS (Eng, Creat Writing, Psych-Cnslr) 1959-62; NDEA Doct F'ship, Univ of WY, 1962-65; Dir, Bur of Ednl Res & Assoc Prof, Ednl Psych, SUNY-Albany; Assoc Prof 1966, Chm, Dept of Ed 1967-68, Fulbright Sr Lectr 1968-69, Prof of Cnslr Ed 1967-, ID St Univ; Rocky Mtn Assn for Cnslr Ed & Supvn; ID Pers & Guid Assn; Assn for Cnslr Ed & Supvn; APGA; N Am Soc for Adlerian Psych; ID Soc for Indiv Psych; Dir, Fam Ed Ctr, ID St Univ, 1975-; Conslt to SE ID Dept of Hlth & Wel Fam Therapy, 1978-79; Conslt to Dist-Wide Parent Ed Prog, Boise Public Schs, 1977-; Conslt to Competency Based Cnslr Ed Proj, NW Reg Ed Lab, 1977-79; Conslt to Boys' Town Ctr, NE, Res Prog in Adlerian Psych, 1977; Conslt in Childhood Devel & Early Childhood Tng to a Proj of the Sociol Dept, ID St Univ, 1977; Keynote Spkr, ID Soc of Indiv Psych, Sprg 1977; Presenter of Adlerian Point of View Along w Albert Ellis & John Krumboltz, Sum 1977; Demo of Life Style Assessment & Keynote Spkr, ID Soc of Indiv Psych, Sprg 1977; Demo of Life Style Assessment, ID Pers & Guid Assn Annual Conf, Fall 1977; Reg Coor for Accreditation, ACES, 1978-80; Mem, Nat Accreditation Com, Assn for Cnslr Ed & Supvn, APGA, 1978-; Consltg Editor, *Cnslr Ed & Supvn*, 1976-78; Conslt to Col of Grad Studies, Beckley, WV, 1978; Mem, Edit Bd, *Pers & Guid Jour*, 1977-81; Life Style Assessment in the Treatment of Depression, ID Soc of Indiv Psych, Sprg 1981; Consltg Editor, *The Indiv Psychol*, 1980-82; Mem, Edit Bd, *Jour of Indiv Psych*, 1982-; Dean's Adv Coun, Col of Ed, 1976-77; Selection Com, Col of Ed, Dean, Mem-at-Large, Bd of Dirs, ID Soc for Indiv Psych, 1977-; Mem, Bd of Dels, Reg I, N Am Soc for Adlerian Psych, 1976-80; Nat Treas, N Am Soc for Adlerian Psych, 1979-80; St Coor, Licensure, ID Pers & Guid Assn, 1980-81; Pres, ID Pers &

Guid Assn, 1981-82; VChm, Nat Bd for Cert'd Cnslrs, APGA, 1982-86; Pres, ID St Univ Chapt, AAUP, 1972-73; hon/Fulbright-Hays Sr Lectr, Philippines, 1967-68; Meritorious Tchr, ID St Univ Awd, 1968-69, 1969-70; Elected Grad Coun Rep; Grad Coor'g Coun, Col of Ed; Dist'd Ser Awd, ID Pers & Guid Assn, 1973-74; Ednl Ldr's Fellow, NW Ednl Lab, 1980; Pubs, "The Can Do It Procedure" 1984, "A Proven Approach to Licensure" 1983, "The Cnslr as Conslt: The Application of Adlerian Consltg Methods in Schs" 1983, "Human Creativity in Adlerian Psych" 1984, "Adlerian Subjective Psych-Philosophic Roots" 1984; Num Other Pubs; W/W in W.

EDINGER, JACK DONALD oc/Clinical Psychologist; b/Jul 24, 1951; h/8312 Polaris Drive, Durham, NC 27503; ba/Durham, NC; m/Wanda Hood; p/Edith and Norman Edinger, Lehighton, PA; sp/Faye and Clifton Hood, Dover, NC; ed/BA summa cum laude, Lafayette Col, 1973; MS 1975, PhD 1977, VA Commonwlth Univ; pa/Staff Psychol, Butner, Fed Correctional Instn, 1977-80; Asst Prof, Div of Behavioral Med, Dept of Psych, Duke Univ, 1980-; Staff Psychol, VA Med Ctr, 1980-; Am Psych Assn; SEn Psych Assn; r/Luth; hon/Num Profl Pubs; Phi Beta Kappa; Psi Chi Honor Soc; Nat Hlth Register of Ser Providers in Psych; W/W: Among Students in Am Univs & Cols, in S & SW.

EDMOND, DOROTHY COLEY oc/Director of Baccalaureate Nursing Program; b/Dec 27, 1927; h/4210 Eaton Creek Road, Nashville, TN 37218; ba/Nashville, TN; m/Joel B; p/Warren J (dec) and Lottie A Coley, Nashville, TN; ed/BS, Fisk Univ, 1952; BSN, Meharry Med Col Sch of Nsg, 1952; PHN Cert, Univ of PA, 1955; MA, Nsg Ed, Tchrs' Col, Columbia Univ, 1959; EdD, George Peabody Col for Tchrs, 1981; Assoc Prof 1981-, Dir of Baccalaureate Nsg Prog 1979-, Asst Prof & Dir of Baccalaureate Nsg Prog 1979-, TN St Univ Sch of Nsg; Asst Prof, Univ of TN-Nashville Div of Nsg, 1974-79; Asst Prof & Dir of Nsg Ed, TN St Univ Sch of Home Ec & Agri, 1966-74; Dir of Inser & Asst to Dir of Nsg Ser, George W Hubbard Hosp, Meharry Med Col, 1962; Pt-time Instr, TN St Univ Dept of Home Ec, 1962-66; Instr, Meharry Med Col, Sch of Nsg, 1960-62; Instr, Tuskegee Inst Sch of Nsg, 1959-60; Sr Staff Nurse, Vis'g Nurse Soc of Phila, 1953-59; Gen Staff Nurse, Epis Hosp of Phila, 1952-53; ANA, 1953-; TN Nurses' Assn, Mem 1960-, Dist #3 Bd of Dirs 1977-79, Ethics Com 1975-80, Bicent Com 1974-76, Spec Com on Ed 1970-72, BACT Sect, Nom'g Com Chm 1970-71, Dist #3 2nd VP 1966-70, Profl Nurse Registry Chm 1966-70, Economic Security Com 1966-68, Nsg Ser Adm Sect Chm 1964-66, Nsg Ser Adm Sect Secy 1962-64; PA Nurses' Assn, Chm of Public Hlth Nurse Sub-Unit, 1953-60; Elected Del, TN Nurses' Assn Conv, 1976 (Nashville), 1972 (Chattanooga), 1963 (Knoxville); Elected Del, ANA Conv 1964, PA Nurses' Assn 1958, Am Nurses Conv 1954; Nat Leag for Nsg, 1953-; TN Leag for Nsg, 1960-; TN Leag for Nsg, Bd of Dirs (Mid-Cumberland Chapt) 1980-, Chm (Mid-Cumberland Chapt) 1975-78, Mbrship Com Chm

1968-70, TB Assn Interorg Com 1963-73; TN Coun for Nsg, Secy 1963-66; Del, TN Nurses Assn Conv, 1976 (Memphis), 1964 (Chattanooga), 1977 (Knoxville); SREB, Nsg Div, June 1973 Wkshop (Disadvantaged Students in Nsg Progs), Feb 1971 Conf for Black Nsg Progs; Coun of Deans & Dirs of Nsg in TN, 1966-74; Assoc Deg Nsg Coun, Treas 1973-74, VChm 1972-73; Delta Sigma Theta Sorority, 1951-; Chi Eta Phi Nsg Sorority, Mem 1953-, Pres 1969-71, Fdr of Alpha Chi Chapt 1963; AAUW, 1966-; Am Assn of Univ Profls, 1966-70; TN Student Nurses' Assn, Student Advr, 1975-76; TN Higher Ed Comm, Comm on Cost Study Anal, Nsg Progs in TN, 1969; TN Mid-S, Reg Med Adv Com 1967-74, Site Visitor 1970; Nat Assn of Negro BPW Clb, 1966-70; Metro Hlth & Hosp Planning Coun, Subcom on Nsg Ed, 1966-67; ARC Nsg Ser Com, 1964-70; Meharry Med Col Nsg Ser Adv Com, 1966-70; So Assn of Cols & Schs, Accreditation Visitor 1970-73; NC Ctl Univ Visit 1970, Angelo St Univ (ADN Prog) 1971, Troy St Univ 1973, USPH-HEW (ADN and BSN Progs, Constrn Grant Conslt); cp/Pace Setters Inc, 1964-; Enchanted Hills Commun Clb, 1975-; hon/Author, "Public Hlth Nurse's Role in the Care of the Congenital Cardiac Child" 1957, "Student Nurse Goes to Col" 1967, "Who Am I?" 1978, "Adm Functioning & Lrng Opports for High Risk Students" 1972, "Innovative Tchg Strategies" 1973; TN St Univ, Cert of Extolment & Distn, Res Day Prog, 1982; Univ of TN, Nashville Devel Grant Recip, 1978-79; Newman Clb Awd, 1952; Delta Sigma Theta, Phila Chapt Ser Awd, 1955; Meharry Yr Book Dedication, 1961; Dorothy Coley Edmond Awd to an Outstg Student Nurse, TN St Univ, 1976; Nat Assn of Negro BPW Clb, Nashville, TN Profl Wom Awd, 1968; Radio WLAC, Wom of the Day Awd, Feb 16, 1971; Mid-S Reg Med Ser Awd, 1974; W/W of Am Wom.

EDMONDS, EDWARD LESLIE oc/Professor Emeritus; b/Mar 15, 1916; h/50 East River Drive, Bunbury, Prince Edward Island, Canada; ba/Charlottetown, Prince Edward Island, Canada; m/Ruth I Auty (dec); c/Ian David Foster, Kirsteen Fiona Hillary; p/Edward Oliver and Olive Foster; ed/BA w Hons in Eng; BA w Hons in Hist; MA; MA in Ed; PhD; mil/War Ser, Maj; pa/Prof & Dean Emeritus, Prof of Ed, Univ of Prince Edward Isl; Provincial Histn, St John Ambulance; cp/Pres, Prince Edward Isl Commonwlth Soc; Pres, Citizens' Coun on Drug Ed; r/Anglican; hon/Misc S'ships; Essay Prizes; K St J; Hon Chief, Micmac Indians.

EDWARDS, ANGELA L oc/Practical Nurse and Clubwoman; b/Oct 23; h/180 South Main Street, #44, Red Bluff, CA 96080; m/Dr H T Edwards (dec); c/Betti Lou Gilliam, James Robert Gilliam (dec), John Harold Gilliam, Glenn Richard Gilliam; p/Betty Persich, Los Angeles, CA; ed/Studies in Italy, Superior Grades; Metro Col, LA; San Mateo Jr Col, Shasta Col Ext; Univ of CA-LA Ext; Current Studies in Higher Divine Phil; Rose-Croix Univ, Esoteric Hierarchy, Rosicrucian Frat Order, AMORC 12 Degs, Circle of Unknown Philosophers, Martinist Fraternal Order AS Deg, Mystic Deg, Superior Deg; pa/Ward

Clk, CA Luth Hosp; Pract Nurse, Santa Fe Hosp; Pract Nurse, St John Hosp, Longview, WA; Executor of Husband's Est & Clin; cp/Hosp Pink Lady; PTA, Chm of Child Psych Class & Hlth Chm; Active in Med Fund Raising Drives; Brownie Scout Ldr; Pres of Home Arts Clb; Westside Grange Clb; Anderson Sen Clb; Nat Geog Soc; Lectr, Parents w/o Partners; Lectr & Talk Show Hostess on Astrology, KBLF & Chico St Univ Radio Stas; Smithsonian Inst, Assoc Mem; Implemented First Aid & Home Nsg in Commun & Sch, Estab'd Scout Tng within Commun; IPA; r/Epis Ch Activs & Bible Studies; Christian Singles, F'ship Mem; hon/Author, Poetry; Hon Mem, ABIRA; Fellow, Intl Biogl Assn; Has Won Many Prizes at Srs/Costumes Dances; Appt'd as Ofcr, 15th Point of En Star, "Electa"; World W/W of Wom; Commun Ldrs of Am; Personalities of the W & MW; Biogl Roll of Hon; Book of Hon; Commun Ldrs of the World; 5,000 Personalities of the World; Dir of Dist'd Ams; Intl W/W of Intells; DIB; Intl Register of Profiles; Men & Wom of Distn.

EDWARDS, DEL M oc/Businessman and Investor; b/Apr 12, 1953; h/3415 South Keaton Avenue, Tyler, TX 75701; ba/Tyler, TX; p/Mr and Mrs Welby C Edwards, Tyler, TX; ed/AA cum laude, Tyler Jr Col, 1974; BBA, Baylor Univ, 1976; pa/Corp Coor, Dillard Dept Stores, 1976-77; Exec VP, W C Supply Co Inc, 1977-; Pres, Walker's Auto Spring, 1978-; VP & Ptnr, W C Sq Shopping Ctr Inc, 1976-; cp/Treas, Jas P Douglas Camp #124, Sons of Confederate Vets, 1977-82; Bd of Dirs 1981, Internal VP 1982-83, Tyler JCs; Patron Mem, E TX Symph Orch, 1978-; Patron Mem, Tyler Civic Theatre, 1978-; Patron Mem, Tyler Area C of C, 1978-; Patron Mem, Smith Co Hist Soc, 1978-; Chm, Rose Garden Trust Fund, 1981-82; r/So Bapt; hon/Pub'd Author; Honor Awd, TX Div, Sons of Confederate Vets, 1978; W/W: in World, in Fin & Indust, in S & SW.

EDWARDS, DONNA O'STEEN oc/Piano Professor; b/Jun 2, 1932; h/3229 Regent Drive, Dallas, TX 75229; ba/Ft Worth, TX; m/Harold Hugh Jr; c/Richard, Margaret, Marianne; p/Mrs Earl Mealer, Irving, TX; sp/Mrs Harold H Edwards Sr, El Paso, TX; ed/BM 1959; MM 1954, So Meth Univ; Dr of Musical Arts, N TX St Univ; pa/Owner, Piano Studio, 1958-64, 1966-; Tchr, Highland Park Indep Sch Dist, 1964-66; Asst Prof of Piano & Music Lit, TX Christian Univ, 1975-81; Assoc Prof of Piano, Chm of Pedagogy Dept, Coor of Pedagogy & Prep Divs, Asst to Artist-in Residence, Lili Kraus, 1981-; Vis'g Prof in Piano Pedagogy, Brookhaven Col, 1978; Mu Phi Epsilon; Pi Kappa Lambda, Mortar Bd; Alpha Lambda Delta; Col Music Soc; Dallas Music Tchrs Assn; Ft Worth Music Tchrs Assn; Nat Music Tchrs Assn; Nat Piano Guild; Am Music S'ship Assn; Japan-Am Soc of Dallas-Ft Worth; Japanese-Am Wom's Cultural Exch Soc; r/Prot; hon/G B Dealey Awd for Yg Artists, 1st Prize, 1953; Elmer Scott Yg Artists Awd, 1st Prize, 1953; Fulbright Awd for Study Abroad, 1956-57; Appearances as Soloist w Dallas Symph Orch 1950 & 1953, Houston Symph Orch 1969; Dallas Civic-SMU Symph 1950-51-52-53, Ft

Worth Yth Orch, 1958; W/W of Am Wom.

EDWARDS, DOUGLAS PHILLIP oc/Admissions Director; b/Jan 12, 1943; h/229 Bailey Road, Rosemont, PA 19010; ba/Villanova, PA; m/Janet Gail; c/Phillip Ray, Laura Kay; p/Charley F Edwards, Martin, TN; M Virginia Tucker, Rosemont, IL; ed/BA, Pepperdine Univ, 1966; MA, Villanova Univ, 1980; pa/Tech Illustrator, Gen Electric Co, 1966-68; Dir of Admissions & Art Instr, NEn Christian Jr Col, 1968-; NEn Alumni Assn, Pres 1966-67; PA Assn of Col Admissions Cnslrs; Am Assn of Col Registrars & Admissions Ofcrs; r/Deacon, King of Prussia Ch of Christ, 1972-; hon/Gold Key, Scholastic Art Awd, 1956; Design W, LA Co Mus Show, Sculpture Selected to Be Showcased, 1965; Outstg Ser Awd, NEn Christian Jr Col, 1977; Spec Ser Awd, Camp Manatawny, 1976; W/W in E.

EDWARDS, RAY C oc/Chairman of the Board and President; b/Sep 1, 1913; h/396 Ski Trail, Kinnelon, NJ 07405; ba/Pompton Plains, NJ; m/Marjorie; c/David, Douglas, Diane, Ruth, Robert (dec), Helen; p/Ernest Alfred and Augusta Fee Edwards (dec); ed/BA, Univ of CA, 1935; pa/Engr, Carrier Corp, 1935-42; Physicist, Gen Lab, US Rubber Co, 1942-46; Accoustical Const, Fdr, Chm of Bd & Pres, Edwards Engrg Cor, 1947-; Lic'd Profl Engr in NY, NJ, VA, PA; Am Soc of Heating, Refrigeration & Air Conditioning Engrs; r/Prot; hon/Profl Pub; Theta Delta Chi; Holder of 25 Patents.

EELLS, GEORGE oc/Writer; b/Jan 20, 1922; h/514 North Rodeo Drive, Beverly Hills, CA 90210; p/Clark V and Martha Elizabeth Hardel Eells (dec); ed/Att'd, NWn Univ 1940-43, Columbia Univ 1945, Am Theatre Wing 1946; pa/Entertainment Editor, Parade Mag, 1945; Entertainment Editor 1948-60; Editor, Theatre Arts Mag 1962, Signature Mag 1963-67; This is Your Life TV Prog, 1971-72, 1983-84; Non-Fiction Course, Univ of So CA's Master of Profl Writing Prog, 1983; hon/Author of Pubs, The Life that Late He Led (Biog of Cole Porter which Won ASCAP Awd as One of 20 Outstg Non-Fiction Books, NY Times) 1967, Hedda & Louella (Dual Biog of Hopper & Parsons, & Basis for "Malice in Wonderland," CBS-TV, Starring Elizabeth Taylor & Jane Alexander) 1972, Reader's Digest Anthology of Unforgettable Characters 1968, Ginger, Loretta & Irene WHO? 1976, Merman (w Ethel Merman) 1978, High Times, Hard Times (Autobiog w Anita O'Day which Was Among NY Times Yr End Listing of Notable Books of the Yr) 1981, Mae West (a Biog w Stanley Musgrove), Robert Mitchum, a Biog 1984.

EFFEL, LAURA oc/Lawyer; b/May 9, 1945; h/111 Third Avenue, New York, NY 10003; ba/New York, NY; p/Louis Effel, Dallas, TX; Mrs Joseph D (Fay) Ray, Chandler, TX; ed/BA, Univ of CA-Berkeley, 1971; JD, Univ of MD, 1975; pa/Assoc, Burns, Jackson, Miller, Summit & Jacoby, 1975-78; Assoc, Pincus, Munzer, Bizar & D'Alessandro, 1978-80; Assoc Counsel, The Chase Manhattan Bk, NA, Legal Dept, Litigation Div, 1980-; ABA, Litigation Sect; Assn of the Bar of the City of NY; NY Wom's Bar Assn; hon/W/W in E.

EFRON, BRADLEY oc/Professor of Statistics and Biostatistics; b/May 24, 1938; h/625 Mayfield, Stanford, CA 94305; ba/Stanford, CA; c/Miles; ed/BS, CA Inst of Technol, 1960; MS 1962, PhD 1964, Stats, Stanford Univ; pa/Asst Prof, Dept of Stats 1966-67, Assoc Prof, Dept of Stats 1968-71, Prof, Dept of Stats 1972-, Prof of Commun, Fam & Preventive Med 1974-, Chm, Dept of Stats 1976-79, Chm of Math Scis Prog 1981-, Stanford Univ; Vis'g Lectr, Dept of Stats, Harvard Univ, 1967-68; Vis'g Scholar, Dept of Math, Imperial Col, London, 1971-72; Vis'g Prof, Dept of Stats, Univ of CA-Berkeley, 1979-80; Conslt, Rand Corp 1962-, Alza Corp 1971-, Jet Propulsion Lab 1971, LA Co Hosp 1966-71, Fed Trade Comm 1974-78, Am Col of Radiol 1976-; Royal Statl Soc, Fellow; Biometrics Soc; Fellow of the Univ, Stanford Univ, 1969-72; Assoc Editor 1968-69, Theory & Methods Editor 1969-72, Jour of the Am Statl Assn; Mem of the Coun, Inst of Math Stats, 1974-76; Exec Com, Assem of Math & Phy Scis, 1976-79; hon/Elected Fellow, Am Acad of Arts & Scis, 1983; Overseer, Harvard Dept of Stats, 1983-; MacArthur Prize Fellow, 1983; Zyskind Lectr, IA St Univ, 1982; Wald Lectr, Annual Meeting of the Inst of Math Stats, 1981; Rietz Lectr, Annual Meeting of Inst of Math Stats, 1977; Allan Craig Lectr on Stats, Univ of IA, 1976; Outstg Stat of the Yr, Chgo Chapt, Am Statl Assn, 1981; Ford Prize, Math Assn of Am, 1978; Fellow of the Inst of Math Stats; Fellow of the Am Statl Assn; Elected Mem of the Intl Stats Inst; Pubs, "Computer Intensive Methods in Stats" 1983, "Estimating the Error Rate of a Prediction Rule: Improvements on Cross-Validation" 1983, "A Leisurely Look at the Bootstrap, the Jackknife & Cross-Validation" 1983, "Maximum Likelihood & Decision Theory" 1982, "Transformation Theory: How Normal is a One Parameter Fam of Distbns?" 1982, "Computers & Statl Theory" 1981, "Nonparametric Standard Errors & Confidence Intervals" 1981; Num Other Pubs; W/W in Am.

EGERTON, JOHN R oc/Research Parasitologist; b/Dec 3, 1927; h/RD 2, Box 209, Neshanic Station, NJ 08853; ba/Rahway, NJ; m/Barbara J; c/Scott J, Craig L, Lynn A; p/Mr and Mrs Lawson Egerton, Sarasota, FL; ed/BS, Zool, CO A&M, 1951; MS, Zool 1951, PhD, Parasitology 1953, KS St Univ; mil/Med Dept, AUS, 1945-47; pa/Res Asst, KS St Univ, 1950-53; Instr 1953-54, Asst Prof 1954-55, Zool, OK A&M; Res Assoc 1955-66, Res Fellow 1966-70, Sr Res Fellow 1970-78, Sr Investigator 1978-, Merck Inst; Am Soc of Parasitologists, 1951-; World Assn for Advmt of Vet Parasitology, 1963-; Biometric Soc, 1955-; Mem, Standing Expert Com for Standardization of Anthelmintic Eval, WAAUP & USFDA/AHI; cp/Active in BSA, 1964-66; Nat Rifle Assn, NJ St Cert'd Hunter Safety, Ed Instr, 1970-; r/Prot; hon/Contbr to Profl Jours on Parasitology & Biometrics; Patentee in Field of Anthelmintic Composition & Utility; Sigma Xi, 1953; Phi Kappa Phi, 1952; Gamma Sigma Delta, 1951; Beta Beta Beta, 1950; Dir of World Rschrs; W/W in Technol Today; W/W E; Commun Ldrs & Noteworthy Ams; Men of

Achmt; Book of Hon; Am Men of Sci; DIB; Ldrs in Am Sci; W/W in Commerce & Indust.

EGGERT, FRANK MICHAEL oc/ Dental Educator, Immunology Researcher, Periodontist; b/Apr 4, 1945; h/11223-76 Avenue, Edmonton, Alberta T6G 0K2 Canada; ba/Alberta, Canada; m/Susan Louise; c/Frank Matthew Arthur; p/Frank Paul and Suse Eggert, Ontario, Canada; sp/C and Marjorie Denny, England; ed/DDS w hons 1969, MSc 1971, Dipl in Periodontics 1972, Univ of Toronto; PhD, Univ of Cambridge, 1978; pa/Res Fellow, Royal Col of Surgeons of Eng, 1976; Lectr, London Hosp Med Col Dental Sch, 1979; Assoc Prof, Stomatology, Fac of Dentistry, Univ of Alberta, 1981-83; Prof, Stomatology, Fac of Dentistry, Univ of Alberta, 1983-; Fellow, Royal Soc of Med; Royal Col of Dentists of Canada; Biochem Soc; Intl Assn for Dental Res; Brit Soc for Immunol; Royal Canadian Yacht Clb; r/Prot; hon/Profl Pubs; Estab'd Grant Alberta Heritage Foun for Med Res; Res F'ship Canadian Med Res Coun, 1969-74.

EGLITIS, IRMA oc/Professor and Doctor; b/Oct 13, 1907; h/123 East Lane Avenue, Columbus, OH 43201; ba/ Columbus, OH; m/John Arnold; p/Juris Georgs and Elizabete Liepinsh; ed/MD, maximum cum laude, Univ of Latvia, Fac of Med, 1931; Dipl, Latvian Bd of Dermatology & Venereal Diseases; Creat Prob Solving Inst, SUNY-Buffalo, Cert, 1968; pa/OH St Univ: Full Prof, Col of Med 1967-, Assoc Prof 1962-67, Asst Prof 1956-62, Instr 1952-56; Full Prof'ship, Col of Dentistry & Grad Sch, OH St Univ; Instr, Human Gross Anatomy, Ernst Moritz Arndt Univ, Fac of Med, Greifswald, Germany, 1944-45; Instr, Humam Gross Anatomy, Histology & Embryology, Univ of Latvia, Fac of Med, 1931-44; Other Former Positions; Am Med Wom's Assn: Nat Chm Resolutions Com 1972, Nat Constit & Bylaws Com 1970, Nat Mem of the Exec Bd & Nat Secy 1969, Nat Chm Med Opports & Pract Com 1968, Nat Chm of Med Ed & Pract Com 1967, Others; Am Assn Anatomists; Coun of Inst for Res in Vision; Columbus Med Wom's Assn: Pres 1961-63, 1968, VP 1959-60, Secy 1965-67, Secy-Treas 1958-59; Med Wom's Intl Assn; r/Ev-Luth; hon/Pubs, *Anatomy & Histology of the Eye & Orbit in the Domestic Animals* 1960, *The Rabbit in Eye Res* 1964; Recip, Cert of Merit & Pin from the AMA's "Fifty Yr Clb of Am Med" in Hon of 50 Yrs of Dedicated Ser to the Med Profession, 1982; Fellow, OH Acad Sci; Sigma Xi; OH St Univ: Pre-Clin Dist'd Tchg Awd (Med Students), Nom'd Pre-Clin Prof of Yr (Col of Med Students) 1975, Nom'd Outstg Tchg Awd, (Sr Med Class), Nom'd Pre-Clin Dist'd Tchg Awd, Med Class of 1974, Dist'd Ser Awd (Col of Dentistry), Awd from Col of Med; DIB; Commun Ldrs & Noteworthy Ams; Am Men & Wom in Sci; Ldrs in Am Sci; W/W: of Am Wom, of Am Ed, in MW, in US; The Am Registry; Intl Scholars Dir; Intl W/W in Commun Ser; World W/W: of Authors, of Wom, of Wom in Ed; Notable Ams; Quest W/W: Dist'd Citizens of N Am; Biogl Dir of Am Ed; Personalities of Am; Intl W/W in Ed; Men & Wom of Distn; Personalities of the W & MW; Dir of Dist'd Ams; DIB;

Dist'd & Outstg Personalities of W & MW; 5,000 Personalities of World; Commun Ldrs of the World; Latvju Enciklopedija; Foremost Wom of the 20th Cent; Intl Book of Hon.

EGLITIS, JOHN ARNOLD oc/Professor and Doctor of Medicine; b/Dec 16, 1902; h/123 East Lane Avenue, Columbus, OH 43201; ba/Columbus, OH; m/Irma Eglitis; p/Alesanders and Zelma Eglitis; ed/MD, maximum cum laude, Univ of Latvia Fac of Med, 1931; DMSc, PhD, Univ of Latvia Med, 1940; Dr Med Habil, Adv'd Grad Deg, 1942; Tropical Instn, Univ of Hamburg, Germany, 1947; Dipl, Creat Prob Solving Inst, SUNY-Buffalo, 1968; Cert, Bds of Oto-Rhino-Laryngology, Latvia, Germany, 1944; pa/Adv'd from Asst Instr to Instr, Lectr, Asst Prof (Pvt Docent), Assoc Prof (Docent) & Chm of Histology Inst, Univ of Latvia Fac of Med, Inst of Histology, 1927-44; Assoc Prof (Docent) of Histology, Ernst Moritz Arndt Univ Fac of Med, Greifswald, Germany, 1944-45; Assoc Prof (Docent) in Oto-Rhino-Laryngology, Christian Albrecht Univ of Kiel, Germany, 1945-46; Assoc Prof and Chm of Histology, Baltic Univ Fac of Med, Hamburg, Germany, 1946-49; Instr of Anatomy 1951-52, Asst Prof of Anatomy 1952-55, Assoc Prof of Anatomy 1955-60, Prof of Histology 1960-73, OH St Univ Col of Med; Prof of Histology, OH St Univ Col of Dentistry, 1967-73; Prof'ship in Grad Sch, Prof Emeritus 1973-, OH St Univ; Conslt, Brit Control Comm Med Ser, Germany; Spec for Ear-Nose-Throat (Oto-Rhino-Laryngology) Diseases, 1945-49; Med Pract, Germany, 1945-50; The Hon Sci Soc of Sigma Xi; Am Assn of Anatomists; OH Acad of Sci; Acad Student & Alumni Org Fraternitas Vesthardiana; hon/ Several Sci Pubs in Med Jours in US & Abroad in the Fields of Cardiovas, Glandular & Endocrine Divs; Man of the Yr, OH St Univ Col of Med, 1965; Golden Key & Cert, OH St Univ Col of Dentistry; Hon Dental Soc Omicron Kappa Upsilon, 1967; Nom'd for the Dist'd Tchg Awd, OH St Univ, 1970; Recip, Cert from the Col of Med, OH St Univ, for the Many Yrs of Devoted Ser to the Col of Med, His Students & the Fac, 1973; Recip, Dist'd Ser Awd (Plaque) from the Col of Dentistry, OH St Univ, in Sincere Apprec of the Dedication, Devotion & Many Contbns to Dental Ed, 1973; Recip, Recog & Apprec Cert Presented by Resolution of the Bd of Trustees, OH St Univ, for Loyal Ser to the Univ & the St of OH, 1973; Recip, Plaque from the Assn of the Grad Students of Anatomy, Col of Med, in Sincere Apprec for the Tchg & Inspiration to the Grad Students, 1973; First Prize from the Latvian St Culture Foun for Sci Res, DMSc Dissertation, 1940; F'ship, Fac of Med, Ernst Moritz Arndt Univ, Inst of Pathol; Postdoct F'ship, Univ of Strasbourg Fac of Med, Inst of Histology, France; Postdoct F'ship, Fac of Med, Inst of Histology & Embryology, Leopold Franzens Univ, Innsbruck, Austria; Recog Lttrs from Num OH St Univ Alumni, Indiv Students & Classes; Am Men & Wom in Sci; Ldrs in Am Sci; DIB, London; Notable Ams; W/W: in Am Ed, in MW; Personalities of the W & MW; Commun Ldrs of the World;

Commun Ldrs & Noteworthy Ams.

EHRENPREIS, SEYMOUR oc/Professor and Chairman, Department of Pharmacology; b/Jun 20, 1927; h/4339 Birchwood Avenue, Skokie, IL 60079; ba/North Chicago, IL; m/Bella Ruth; c/ Mark David, Eli Daniel, Ira Samuel; p/ William (dec) and Ethel Ehrenpreis, New York, NY; sp/Joseph Goodman, Chicago, IL; Adelle Goodman (dec); ed/BS, Col of City of NY, 1949; PhD, NY Univ, 1954; mil/USN, 1944-45; pa/Res Assoc, Univ of Pgh, 1953-55; Instr in Chem, Cornell Univ, 1955-57; Asst Prof of Biochem & Neurol, Columbia Univ, 1957-61; Assoc Prof of Pharm, Georgetown Univ, 1961-69; Assoc Prof, NY Med Col, 1968-71; Hd of Pharmacol, NY St Inst Neurochem & Drug Addiction, 1971-76; Prof & Chm of Pharm, Chgo Med Sch, 1976-; AAAS; AMA; Am Soc Biol Chemists; Am Soc of Pharm & Exper Therapeutics; Am Inst of Chems; NY Acad of Sci; Sigma Xi; Soc of Neuroscis; r/Hebrew; hon/Profl Pubs; Vis'g Prof of Pharm, Keio Univ, 1974; Meritorious Ser Awd, Col Univ Col Pharm Sci, 1976; Morris Parker Awd for Res, Chgo Med Sch, 1981; W/W in Frontiers of Sci & Technol; Am Men of Sci; Ldrs in Am Sci; Intl Scholar's Dir.

EHRLICH, BERNARD HERBERT oc/ Attorney; b/Apr 3, 1927; h/507 Bonifant Street, Silver Spring, MD 20910; ba/ Washington, DC; m/Edna Kraft; c/ Vivian Rose, Beverly Denise, Brenda Susan, Lisa Jean; p/Samuel Zachary and Elsie Klein Ehrlich, Silver Spring, MD; ed/AB 1946, LLB 1949, JD & MA 1950, George Wash Univ; Admitted to DC Bar, 1949; mil/USN, 1943-45; pa/Gen Counsel to Num Corps, Industs, 1949-; Mgr, Gen Counsel, Inst of Indust Launderers, Wash DC, 1949-; Counsel, Nat Home Study Coun, Nat Assn of Trade & Tech Schs, Nat Assn of Cosmetology Schs; ABA; Bar Assn of DC; Am Soc of Intl Law; Am Soc of Assn Execs; Soc of Am Travel Writers; Am Polit Sci Assn; cp/Am Hist Assn; hon/Author, Var Articles on Ed, Antitrust, Trade Regulation Probs in Innumerable Pubs; r/Jewish; hon/Recip, Ser Plaque, Am Inst of Launderers, 1966; Nat Assn of Trade & Tech Schs, 1967; Nat Home Study Coun, 1970; Phi Beta Kappa; Nu Beta Epsilon; Phi Delta Pi; W/W: in Am, in E, in Am Law, in Fin & Indust; DIB.

EHRLICH, GEORGE EDWARD oc/ Rheumatologist, Physician, Educator; b/ Jul 18, 1928; h/2223 Delancey Place, Philadelphia, PA 19102; ba/CIBA GEIGY, Summit, NJ 07901; m/Gail; c/ Charles Edward, Steven L Abrams, Rebecca Ann Abrams; p/Mrs Edward Ehrlich, New York, NY; ed/AB, cum laude, Harvard Univ, 1948; MB, MD, Chgo Med Sch, 1952; mil/USNR, Served to Rank of Cmdr; pa/Instr in Med, Cornell, 1959-64; Asst Prof, Assoc Prof, Prof, Med & Rehab Med, Temple Univ Sch of Med, 1964-80; Dir of Rheumatology, Albert Einstein Med Ctr & Moss Rehab Hosp, 1964-80; Prof of Med & Dir of Rheumatology, Hahnemann Univ Sch of Med, 1980-83; Adj Prof of Clin Med, NY Univ, 1983-; VP, Devel, Pharm Div, CIBA GEIGY, 1983-; Am Col of Phys; AMA; Am Rheumatism Assn; Am Col of Clin Pharm; Am Col of Rehab Med; 15 Other Med Orgs; cp/ Past Pres, Med Clb of Phila; Past Pres,

Arthritis Foun, En PA Chapt; Num Other Civic Orgs; hon/Pubs, 8 Med Books, incl'g, *Prognosis* (w J F Fries), *Rehab Mgmt of Rheumatic Conditions, Total Mgmt of the Arthritic Patient, Rheumatoid Arthritis;* Author, 200 Profl Articles; Philip Hench Awd, 1971; Dist'd Alumnus Awd, Chgo Med Sch, 1969; Alpha Omega Alpha Hon Med Soc; W/W: in Am, in the World, in the US.

EHRSAM, THEODORE GEORGE oc/Professor Emeritus of English; b/Dec 7, 1909; h/521 Piermont Avenue, River Vale, NJ 07675; m/Marcia; c/Jean E Sammons; p/Theodore and Wilhelmina Ehrsam (dec); sp/Mrs Betty Shapiro, Deer Park, NY; ed/BA 1931; MA 1932; PhD 1948; pa/Instr in Eng, Lehigh Univ, 1932-36; Instr, Hofstra Col, 1936-38; Staff, NY Univ, 1944-75; Prof Emeritus of Eng, NY Univ, 1975; Prof of Eng, Hudson Co Commun Col, 1975-; Mod Lang Assn; Alpha Kappa Psi Frat; Pres, Alpha Kappa Psi Foun; Lake Hopatcong Yacht Clb; Am Fdn of TV & Radio Artists; r/Prot; hon/Num Pubs; W/W in E; Dir of Am Scholars.

EICHE, JON JOSEPH oc/Personnel Manager; b/Jan 23, 1938; h/1081 North Wall Avenue, Cookeville, TN 38501; ba/Cookeville, TN; m/Evelyn Quintrell; c/Jon Guinn, Keith David; p/Mr and Mrs George O Eiche, Tampa, FL; sp/Mr and Mrs A G Quintrell; ed/BS, E TN St Univ, 1959; MA, IN Univ, 1966; Armed Forces Staff Col, 1975; Dept of St For Ser Inst, 1970; USA Inst for Adv'd Russian & E European Studies, 1968, Cert'd; pa/2nd Bn, 78th Field Artillery, 4th Armored Div, 1960-63; Asst S-2 XXIV Corps Artillery, US Forces in Rep of Vietnam, 1968-69; Instr, Intl Relats & Govt Dept, Def Info Sch, 1969-71; Asst Prof in Dept of Social Sci, US Mil Acad at W Point, 1971-74; 2nd Inf Div, Med Battalion Cmdr, Exec Ofcr Support Command, Opers Ofcr, Support Command, 1975-76; Prof of Mil Sci, TN Technol Univ, 1976-79; Pers Mgr, Porelon Inc, 1979-; Mem 1979-, Pres 1983, Am Soc for Pers Adm; cp/Am Legion, 1976-; Dean of Cnslrs, TN Am Legion Boys St, 1979; V Chm, TN Am Legion Boys St, 1980-81; Chm, TN Am Legion Boys St, 1981-82; Explorer Advr, BSA, 1980-81; Cookeville Mastersingers, 1979-82; Race Dir 1979, Pres 1980, Eagle Kountry Runners, 1979-; Nancy Ward Cherokee Foun, 1977-; Nat Rifle Assn, 1977; Asst Team Mgr, US Olympic Com, 1981; Omicron Delta Epsilon; Omicron Delta Kappa; Pres 1980-81, Bd of Dirs 1979-82, Mem, 1978-, Putnam Co Fam YMCA; Bd of Dirs 1980-83, Co Dr Co-Chm 1980, Co Dr Chm 1981, Pres 1982, Putnam Co U Way; Rotary Intl, 1976-; Vestry 1978-80, Sr Warden 1980, Key Layman 1980-83, Treas 1979-81, Lay Rdr 1979-, Chalice Bearer 1979-, St Michael's Epis Ch; Sigma Phi Epsilon; TN Epis Churchman, Mid TN VP; TN Tomorrow; St Cnslr, Hospice of Cookeville, 1981-82; Intl Foun of Employee Benefit Plans; TN Technol Univ Sch of Nsg Foun Trustee; r/Epis; hon/Pub'd Author; Bronze Star Medal, 1969; Meritorious Ser Med w OLC 1969, 1979; Air Medal, 1968; Joint Ser Commend Medal, 1971; Army Commend Medal, 1974; Meritorious Unit Commend w OLC 1968, 1969; Vietnam Ser Medal, 1968; Nat Def Ser Medal, 1959; Vietnam Cross of Gallantry w

Gold Palm, 1969; Rep of Vietnam Campaign Medal w 5 Stars 1968, 1969; Korea Ser Medal, 1976; W/W: Among Students in Am Cols & Univs, in S & SW; Personalities of S.

EIDSON, WILLIAM WHELAN oc/Professor of Physics; b/Jul 22, 1935; h/950 Conestoga Road, Bryn Mawr, PA 19010; ba/Philadelphia, PA; m/Janis Diane Fischer; c/William Benjamin, Duncan McBrayer, Christy Lorene; p/Mr and Mrs Alonzo D Eidson, Bryn Mawr, PA; ed/BS, Physics & Math, Tulane Univ, 1957; MS 1959, PhD 1961, IN Univ, Bloomington; pa/Tchg Asst 1957-59, NSF Pre-Doct Fellow 1959-61, Instr 1961-63, Asst Prof 1963-66, Assoc Prof 1966-67, IN Univ; Vis'g Prof, Univ of WA Seattle, Sum 1967; Chm & Prof, Univ of MO-St Louis, 1967-72; Vis'g Prof, KS St Univ Manhattan, Sum 1972, 1973; Hd & Prof, Drexel Univ, 1972-82; Vis'g Scist, Argonne Nat Lab, 1962-67; Vis'g Scist, Oak Ridge Nat Lab, 1970-75; Vis'g Scist, Legis Ofc of Res Liaison, Harrisburg, PA, 1983-84; Conslt, U Engrs; Conslt, Var Solar Energy Projs; Am Phy Soc, Mem of Nuclear Physics Subsect; Optical Soc of Am; Am Assn of Physics Tchrs; Sigma Xi; Sigma Pi Sigma; Phi Eta Sigma, Circle-K Clb; AAAS; IEEE; AAUP; NY Acad of Sci; Nat Sci Tchrs Assn; PA Acad of Scis; Inst of Applied Spectroscopy; Undergrad Physics Advr, IN Univ, 1961-67; Pres's Sci Adv Com, Physics Rep, IN Univ, 1962-67; Accrediting Assn HS Visits during 1969 (Clayton HS, Wm Cullen McBride HS); Prog Devel Conslt, Univ of AR-Little Rock, 1968, 1969; Elected to Bd of Dirs, Mbrship Chm, Phila Acad of Scis, Fall 1980; Hosted Sum Meeting of the Comm on Col Physics, Univ of MO-St Louis, 1969; Hosted MO Sect of AAPT, Univ of MO-St Louis; Elected Nat Councilor for the Soc of Physics Students, Representing St of PA, 1975-81; Elected Mem, Sci & Arts Com of the Franklin Inst, 1975-; Currently Chm, Michelson Medal Comm; Co-Sponsor of Conf "The Nat Energy Plan," AAAS, Sigma Xi & Franklin Inst, 1977; Co-Sponsored Conf on "The Energy Crises," 1975; Sigma Xi Lectr on Energy, 1979-80; Co-Sponsored Energy Conf, 1979; Sponsored Many Activs of the Soc of Physics Students, Sigma Pi Sigma & Other Sci Socs; Elected Mem of the Energy Ednl Advr Coun, Gtr DE Val, 1980-; Bd of Dirs, Inst for the Study of Civic Values, 1980-; Co-Chaired, Intl Nuclear Physics Wkshop, 1980; Elected Pres, Nat Coun for the Soc of Physics Students, 1981-83, Re-Elected 1983-85; Mem, Univ Corp for Atmospheric Res, 1978-81; hon/Author, Num Pubs; Hon Prof of Physics, Tianjin Univ, Tianjin China; Num Biogl Listings in Ed, Sci & Technol.

EILTS, HERMANN FREDERICK oc/University Professor of International Relations; b/Mar 23, 1922; h/67 Cleveland Road, Wellesley, MA 02181; ba/Boston, MA; m/Helen Brew; c/Conrad Marshall, Frederick Lowell; A and Meta D Eilts (dec); ed/BA, Ursinus Col, 1939-42; Att'd, Fletcher Sch of Law & Diplomacy, 1942; MA, w Distn, Sch of Adv'd Intl Studies of Johns Hopkins Univ, 1947; Arabic & Mid E Studies, Fgn Ser Inst, 1950; Mid E Studies, Univ of PA, 1951-52; Mid E Studies, Dropsie

Col, 1951-52; Dipl, w Distn, Nat War Col, 1961; Dipl, w Distn, Army War Col, 1972; mil/AUS 1942-46, 1st Lt, Mil Intell, N African & ETO; pa/Joined Fgn Ser, 1947; 3rd Secy, Consular & Adm Wk, Am Embassy, Tehran, Iran, 1947-48; 3rd Secy, Economic & Polit Wk, Am Embassy, Jidda, Saudi Arabia, 1948-50; Consul & Prin Ofcr, Am Consulate, Aden, Arabia, 1951-53; 2nd Secy, Chief of Polit Sect, Am Embassy, Baghdad, Iraq, 1954-56; Ofcr-in-Charge, Arabian Peninsula & Near En Reg Affairs, Dept of St, Wash DC, 1960-61; 1st Secy, Polit Ofcr of Mid E & Cyprus Affairs, Am Embassy, London, England, 1962-64; Cnslr & Dpty Chief of Mission, Am Embassy, Tripoli, Libya, 1964-65; US Ambassador to Saudi Arabia, Jidda, 1965-70; Diplomatic Advr, Army War Col, Carlisle Barracks, PA, 1970-73; US Ambassador to Egypt, Cairo, 1973-79; Prof of Intl Relats, Boston Univ (Current); Fellow, Royal Asiatic Soc; Fellow, Royal Soc for Asian Affairs; Mid E Inst; Am Fgn Ser Assn; Coun on Fgn Relats; Mid E Studies Assn of N Am; Wash Inst of Fgn Affairs; Bd of Trustees, Am Univ in Cairo; Adv Coun, Sch of Adv'd Intl Studies, Johns Hopkins Univ; Bd of Govs, Mid E Inst; Bd of Dirs, Faith & Hope; Brookings Instn, Steering Com, Proj on Energy & Nat Security 9 for US Dept of Energy; Bd of Dirs, Ursinus Col; Devel Adv Com, Mid E Res Inst, Univ of PA; cp/Fellow, Royal Geographic Soc; PA Hist Soc; Essex Inst; Fellow, Peabody Mus; r/Prot; hon/Pubs, "Ahmad bin Na'aman's Mission to the United States in 1840: The Voyage of al-Sultanah to NYC" 1942, "Sayyid Muhammed bin 'Agil of Dhufar: Malevolent or Maligned?" 1973; Dept of St Dist'd Hon Awd, 1979; Joseph C Wilson Awd, 1979; Dept of the Army Dist'd Civilian Ser Decoration, 1972; Arthur S Flemming Awd for Dist'd Govt Ser, 1953; LLD, Ursinus Col, 1959; LLD, Boston Univ, 1978; LLD, Dickinson Sch of Law, 1978; PHD, Cairo Univ, Egypt, 1979; LHD, Juniata Col, 1980; Ursinus Col Alumni of the Yr Awd, 1974; Johns Hopkins Univ Dist'd Alumnus Awd, 1980; Purple Heart; Bronze Star; Seven European/N African Campaign Stars; Men of Achmt; Commun Ldrs & Noteworthy Ams; The Blue Book; Intl W/W; W/W: in Am, in Govt, in the World, in Am Polit; Biographic Register.

EISELE, PATRICIA O'LEARY oc/Shopping Center Manager; b/Aug 31, 1935; h/2803 West 73rd Terrace, Prairie Village, KS 66208; ba/Leavenworth, KS; m/John G; c/Kathleen, Janice, Melissa, Patricia, John; p/George and Dorothy O'Leary (dec); ed/Att'd, St Mary of the Plains 1952-53, Sarachon Hooley Bus 1954-55; Current Student, Rockhurst Col; pa/Mktg Dir 1972-79, Mgr 1979-80, Ward Pkwy Ctr; Mktg Cnslr, John Knox Village, 1980-82; Gen Mgr, Leavenworth Plaza Shopping Ctr (Presently); Merchants Assn, 1977-80; Am Bus Wom; cp/Mem, Bd of Dirs, Arthritis Foun, 1980-; Bd of Dirs, Mid-Winter Art Fair, 1979-; Heart Assn; Easter Seals; Muscular Dystrophy; Ararat Shrine; BSA; C of C, Retail Coun, Tourism; Leavenworth Coun, St Mary's Col; hon/W/W of Am Wom.

EISNER, SISTER JANET oc/College President; b/Oct 10, 1940; ba/Boston,

MA; p/Mr and Mrs Eldon Eisner, Swampscott, MA; ed/AB, Emmanuel Col, 1963; MA, Boston Col, 1969; PhD, Univ of MI, 1975; Postdoct, Inst for Ed Mgmt; pa/Sec'dy Sch Tchr, Archdiocese of Boston, 1963-66; Dir of Admissions 1967-71, Dir of Emmanuel Col & City of Boston Pairings 1975-1978, Chp of Eng Dept 1977-78, Acting Pres 1978-79, Pres 1979-, Emmanuel Col; MA Bd of Regents of Higher Ed, 1980-; MA Bd of Reg Common Cols, 1978-81; Trustee, Trinity Col, 1979-; N Eng Enrollment Planning Coun, 1982; Adv Coun of Pres of Assn of Gov'g Bds, 1982-; hon/Rackham Pre-Doct F'ship; Rackham Prize F'ship; Ford Foun Awd; Tchg F'ships, Univ of MI, 1971-75.

EISON, JAMES ARTHUR oc/College Professor; b/Sep 13, 1950; h/114 Kingfisher Lane, Oak Ridge, TN 37830; ba/ Oak Ridge, TN; ed/BA cum laude, SUNY, 1972; PhD, Univ of TN, 1979; pa/Assoc Prof of Psych, Roane St Commun Col, 1982-; Res Assoc, Univ of TN, 1980-; Am Psychol Assn; Am Assn of Higher Ed; Am Ed Res Assn; SE Psychol Assn; hon/Profl Pubs; 1980 Tchg Awd for Commun Col Tchrs of Psychol, Am Psychol Assn.

EISSMANN, ROBERT FRED oc/ Plant Manager; b/Jan 17, 1924; h/266 Paterson Avenue, Little Falls, NJ 07424; ba/West Caldwell, NJ; m/June I Vreeland; c/Roy Norman; p/Fred A (dec) and Katherine E Eissmann, Wayne, NJ; ed/ Pratt Inst, 1942-43 & 1946; mil/AUS, 1943-46, Signal Corp; pa/Wireman, Wn Elect, 1946-49; Assem, Ind TV Co, 1949-51; Leadman, Bogue Elec, 1951-60, 1965-68; Wireman, Eng Asst Kearfott, 1960-65; Assem, Wireman, Hender Ind, 1968-72; Prodn Man 1972-80, Plant Mgr 1980-, MIPCO Inc; Elect Task Force MH5, Freight Container Standard Com ISO, 1982-83; cp/ Adm Bd, Little Falls U Meth Ch, 1946-; r/U Meth; hon/W/W in E.

EIZENSTAT, STUART E oc/Attorney and Lecturer; b/Jan 15, 1943; ba/ 1110 Vermont Avenue, Northwest, Suite 1050, Washington, DC 20005; ed/ BA, cum laude, Univ of NC, 1964; LLB, Harvard Law Sch, 1967; pa/Ptnr, Powell, Goldstein, Frazer & Murphy, 1981-; Adj Lectr, JFK Sch of Govt, Harvard Univ, 1981-; Guest Scholar, The Brookings Instn, 1981; Asst to the Pres for Domestic Affairs & Policy & Exec Dir of Domestic Policy Staff, The White House, 1977-81; Mem, Coun on Wage & Price Stability & ex-officio Mem of Economic Policy Grp, The White House, 1977-81; Dir, Policy Planning & Anal, Carter-Mondale Transition Planning Grp, 1976-77; Law Clk, Chief Judge of US Dist Ct (Judge Newell Edenfield), No Dist of GA, 1969-70; Res Dir, Pres Campaign of VP Hubert Humphrey; Res & Speechwriting, White House Staff, Pres Johnson, 1967-68; Gen Counsel's Ofc, Ofc of Ed, Dept of Hlth, Ed & Wel, Sum 1966; Intl Mgmt & Devel Inst, Wash Policy Coun; Am Judic Soc; ABA; DC Bar Assn; Wash Coun of Lwyrs; GA Bar Assn; cp/Prin Rep, Gov Carter Pres Campaign to Dem Party Platform Com, 1976, 1980; Issues & Policy Dir, Jimmy Carter Pres Campaign, 1976; Mem, St Dem Charter Comm, 1975-76; Issues Coor, Maynard Jackson Mayoral Campaign, 1974; Issues Coor, Gov Jimmy Carter Congl

Campaign Com, Dem Nat Com, 1973; Counsel to & Mem of Vice Pres Selection Com, Dem Nat Com, 1973; Issues Dir, Andrew Young Congl Campaign; Mem, St Dem Exec Com, St of GA, 1970-76; Mem & VP, Fulton Co Dem Party Exec Com, 1970-74; Issues Dir, Jimmy Carter Gubernatorial Campaign, 1970; Res Dir, Pres Campaign of VP Hubert Humphrey, 1968; Speechwriting & Res Asst, Staff of Postmaster Gen John Gronouski, Sum 1964; Congl Intern, Cong-man F Elliott Hagan, Sum 1963; hon/Pubs, "White House & Justice Dept after Watergate" 1982, "Andrew Young: The Path to Hist" 1973, "Accountants' Profl Liability: Expanding Exposure" 1972, "An Expanding Era of Civil Rts" 1971, "Defendant's Dilemma in Fed Employee Actions: Impleader of the US" 1971, "Mental Competency to Stand Trial" 1969, "Mutuality: Is This Doctrine Really Necessary?" 1968; Frequent Writer of Articles for The Wash Post & The NY Times; Spec Columnist, The Jerusalem Post; Awd for Outstg Ser to Sum Yth Prog, US Dept of Labor, 1980; Awd for Outstg Ser, Hebrew Aid Immigration Soc, 1980; Awd for Outstg Ser, Opports Industrialization Ctrs, 1970; Ldrs of Atlanta, Atlanta Mag, 1976; Yg Man of Yr Awd for Ldrship, Am Assn for Jewish Ed, 1973-74; W/W: in Am, in Am Lwyrs, in Am Jewry, in World Jewry, in Am Polit.

EL-AHRAF, AMER MOHAMED EL-MAHDY oc/Professor and Chairman of Health Science and Human Ecology; b/Jan 23, 1940; h/140 Pinehurst Court, San Bernardino, CA 92407; ba/ San Bernardino, CA; m/Lorraine; c/ Ranya Senea; p/Mohamed El-Mahdy El-Ahraf (dec); Senea Ibrahim Osman El-Ahraf, Zagazig, Egypt; sp/Fred and Mary Picciani, Redondo Beach, CA; ed/ DVM, Sch of Vet Med, Cairo Univ, 1962; MPH, Sch of Public Hlth, Univ of CA-LA, 1965; DrPH w distn, Univ of CA-LA, 1971; pa/Assoc in Tchg, Sch of Vet Med, Cairo Univ, 1962-63; Envir Cnslr, LA Hlth Dept, 1970-72; Assoc in Tchg in Public Hlth, Univ of CA, 1965; Asst Prof of Hlth, Univ of CA, 1965; Asst Prof of Social Ecol, Univ of CA, 1972-73; Prof & Chm, Dept of Hlth & Sci & Human Ecol, CA St Col, 1973-; Pres, Nat Envir Hlth Assn, 1980-81; Pres-Elect, Nat Envir Hlth Assn, 1979-80; 1st VP, Nat Envir Hlth Assn, 1978-79; Pres, CA Envir Hlth Assn, 1975-76; Bd of Dirs, So CA Public Hlth Asn, 1978; Am Public Hlth Assn; Others; r/Islam; hon/Num Profl Pubs; Pres Cit, Nat Envir Hlth Assn, 1977; Pres Cit, CA Envir Hlth Assn, 1972 & 1977; Delta Omega Public Hlth Honor Soc, 1971; W/W: Am, Hlth Care; Personalities in W & MW.

EL-BAZ, FAROUK oc/Executive; b/ Jan 1, 1938; ba/Itek Optical Systems, 10 Maguire Road, Lexington, MA 02173; m/Catherine Patricia O'Leary; c/Monira, Soraya, Karima, Fairouz; p/Mrs Zahia Hommouda, Cairo, Egypt; ed/ BSc, Chem & Geol, Ain Shams Univ, Cairo, 1958; MS, Geol, MO Sch of Mines & Metallurgy, 1961; PhD, Geol, Univ of MO-Rolla, 1964; pa/Demonstrator, Assiut Univ, Egypt, 1958-60; Lectr, Univ of Heidelberg, W Germany, 1964-65; Exploration Geologist, Pan Am-UAR Oil Co, Egypt, 1966; Supvr,

Lunar Exploration, Bellcomm, 1967-72; Dir, Ctr for Earth & Planetary Studies, Nat Air & Space Mus, Smithsonian Instn, 1973-82; Sci Advr, Pres Anwar Sadat of Egypt, 1978-81; VP, Sci & Technol, Itek Optical Sys, 1982-; AAAS; Am Mineralogical Assn; AIAA; Geol Soc of Am; Intl Astonom Union; Intl Assn of Sedimentologists; Planetary Soc; Royal Astronom Soc; Sigma Xi; Soc of Archaeological Scis; Explorers Clb; hon/ Pubs, "Say It in Arabic" 1968, "The Moon as Viewed by Lunar Orbiter" 1970, "Astronaut Observations from the Apollo-Soyuz Mission" 1977, "Apollo Over the Moon" 1978, "Apollo-Soyuz Test Project Earth Observations & Photo" 1979, "Egypt as Seen by Landsat" 1978, "Deserts & Arid Lands" 1984, "The Geol of Egypt" 1984; Cert of Merit in Ore Resvs & Rock Formation, US Bur of Mines, 1961; Medal for Exceptl Sci Achmt, NASA, 1971; Alumni Achmt Awd for Extraordinary Sci Accomplishments, Univ of MO, 1973; Cert of Spec Commend, Geol Soc of Am, 1973; Order of Merit, First Class, Arab Republic of Egypt, 1980.

ELBEIN, ALAN D oc/Professor of Biochemistry; b/Mar 20, 1933; h/6101 Sun Dial, San Antonio, TX 78238; ba/ San Antonio, TX; m/Elaine J; c/Steven, Bradley, Richard; p/Gersh Elbein (dec); ed/AB, Clark Univ, 1954; MS, Univ of AZ-Tucson, 1956; PhD, Purdue Univ, 1960; pa/Asst Res Biochem, Univ of CA-Berkeley, 1963; Asst Prof, Assoc Prof, Rice Univ, 1964-69; Prof of Biochem, Univ of TX Hlth Sci Ctr, 1969-; Am Soc of Biol Chems; Am Soc of Microbiol; AAAS; Am Soc of Plant Physiol; Am Acad of Microbiol; NIH; hon/Pubs, Over 100 Sci Papers, Over 15 Chapts in Sci Books; NIH Career Devel Awd, 1968-69; Edit Bd, Jour of Bacteriology, Plant Physiol; Arch Biochem Biophy Study Sect; Am Men of Sci; Personalities of the S.

ELFERS, ELKE ANNEMARIE oc/ Co-Owner and Manager of Shoe Store; b/Sep 8, 1944; h/14804 Wood Home Road, Centreville, VA 22020; ba/Burke, VA; p/Dr and Mrs W A Elfers; ed/BA, Barry Univ, 1968; MSLS, Cath Univ of Am, 1978; pa/Civilian Employmt, 1968; Co-Owner & Mgr, Stride Rite Chd's Footwear Ctr; cp/Orange Co Yg Republ's; r/Cath; hon/Profl Pubs; W/W in S & SW.

ELIAS, HANS GEORG oc/Consultant and Scientific Adviser; b/Mar 29, 1928; h/4009 Linden Drive, Midland, MI 48640; m/Maria Hanke; c/Peter C, Rainer M; p/Hermann Ludwig Georg and Elisabeth (dec) Elias, Hannover, Germany; ed/Dipl, Chem, Tech Univ of Hannover, 1954; Dr rer nat, Tech Univ of Munich, 1957; Habilitation, Swiss Fed Inst of Technol, Zurich, 1961; mil/ German Armed Forces, 1944-45; pa/Sci Asst, Tech Univ of Munich, 1956-59; Sci Hd Asst, Swiss Fed Inst of Technol, Zurich, 1960-63; Asst Prof, Swiss Fed Inst of Technol, 1963-71; Pres, MI Molecular Inst, 1971-83; Sci Conslt, The Dow Chem Co, 1983-84; Indep Conslt, 1985-; Am Chem Soc, Midland Chapt, Dir 1974-77; Am Chem Soc Polymer Nomenclature Comm, 1979-, Chmship 1980-82; r/Luth; hon/7 Authored, Edited or Co-Edited Books; Author, 178 Sci & Tech Pubs; 2 Patents; Editor &

Assoc Editor of 5 Sci Jours; Sigma Xi, Midland Chapt, Best Paper Awd, 1982; Am Men & Wom of Sci; W/W in Fin & Indust; Other Biogl Listings.

ELIASON, PHYLLIS MARIE oc/ Missionary; b/Dec 21, 1925; h/Box 20217, Main Facility, Guam 96921; ba/ Same; m/Albert Augustus (dec); c/ Phyllis Worthen (Mrs John), James, Nancy Wilkins (Mrs W D), Albert Augustus Jr; p/John Sylvester Underhill (dec); Catherine Males, Broderick, CA; ed/BA; MEd; pa/Instr Simpson Col Ext Sch; Tchr, Micronesia Bible Sch; Bookstore Mgr, 1978; Marriage Cnslr, 1980; AAUW; CEC; APGA: Bd of Dirs, Simpson Col, Guam; cp/VP, Guam Girl Scout Coun; Christian Wom's Clb; Guam Shell Clb; r/Prot; Dir Child Evang F'ship Micronesia; hon/Hon Mem, Huntsville, AL; Chi Omicron Gamma Col Hon Soc; W/W: in Commun Ser, in W; DIB.

ELIEZER, ISAAC oc/Associate Dean; b/Jan 19, 1934; ba/Oakland University, Rochester, MI 48063; m/Naomi; c/Eran, David, Ken; ed/MSc, magna cum laude 1956, PhD 1960, Hebrew Univ, Jerusalem; pa/Assoc Dean, Col of Arts & Scis & Prof of Chem, Oakland Univ, 1979-; Mgr of MHD & Energy Res & Adj Prof of Chem, MT St Univ, Bozeman, 1975-79; Sci Conslt & Editor; Intl Coun of Sci Unions; Intl Union of Pure & Applied Chem; Intl Union of Pure & Applied Physics; European Acad of Scis & Humanities; Royal Inst of Chem; Intl Studies Assn; AAAS; Sigma Xi; hon/90 Pubs in Profl Jours in the Areas of Sci & Ed.

ELISSALDE, GWENDOLYN SCHEUERMANN oc/Teacher, Researcher; Chief, Clinical Immunology Laboratory; b/Oct 7, 1939; h/1507 Medine, College Station, TX 77840; ba/ College Station, TX; m/Marcel Howell; c/Kitty Lynette, Daniel Paul, Nora Elena; p/Helen Friday Scheuermann, Beaverton, OR; sp/Marcel and Gertrude Elissalde, Beaumont, TX; ed/BS, SW TX St Univ, 1973; BS 1976, DVM 1977, PhD 1980, TX A&M Univ; mil/USN, 1958-59; pa/Electronics Tech Activation Anal Res Lab 1964, Lab Mech Radiation Biol 1964-66, Marine Geophysics Tech in Dept of Oceanography, Student Wkr 1975-77, Vet Clin Assoc 1977-80, Asst Prof in Col of Vet Med 1981-, TX A&M Univ; Am Vet Med Assn, 1977-83; Assn of Am Vet Med Cols, 1977-; Am Soc of Microbiol, 1978-81; Am Assn Vet Parasitologists, 1980-; AAAS, 1981-; r/ Unitarian; hon/Num Profl Pubs; Alpha Chi, TX Iota Chapt, 1972; BBB, Kappa Zeta Chapt, 1972; Charles Spurgeon Smith Awd in Biol, 1974; Phi Sigma, 1978; W/W in Am Wom.

ELIZABETH, PAMELA H oc/Assistant Professor of Psychology; b/May 31, 1942; h/580 Route 244, PO Box 252, Alfred Station, NY 14803; ba/Alfred, NY; c/Michael, Leanne, Donna Espindle; p/Henry and Carolyn Heaton, Foxboro, MA; ed/BS, Salem St Col, 1972; MA 1974, EdD 1979, Wn MI Univ; pa/Asst Prof of Psych, Alfred Univ, 1983-; Postdoct Res Fellow, Dept of Psychi & Behavioral Scis, SUNY-Stony Brook, 1980-83; Staff Psychol, Radford Univ Cnslg Ctr, 1978-80; Pre-Doct Intern, James Madison Univ Cnslg & Student Devel Ctr, 1977-78; Am Psychol Assn; Assn for Wom in Psych; Am Orthop-

sychi Assn; Intl Soc for the Study of Twins; Intl Soc for Human Ethology; AAAS; cp/NOW; hon/Pubs, "Comparison of a Psychoanalytic & a Client-Centered Grp Tng Model on Measures of Anxiety & Self-Actualization" in *Jour of Cnslg Psychol* 1983, "Childhood & Early Adolescent Conceptions of Sexuality" (a Review of *Chd's Sexual Thinking* by Goldman & Goldman) in *Contemp Psych* 1983, "Childhood Sex-Role Behaviors: Similarities & Differences in Twins" 1984; Co-Investigator, ADAMHA Small Grant "Genetic & Social Influences on Behavior Devel in Chd," 1982-83; NY St Hlth Res Coun, Postdoct Res Grant, 1982-83; Nat Res Ser Awd, NIMH (Instnl), 1980-82; Alcohol Tchg F'ship, MI St Dept of Public Hlth, 1974-75.

ELIZONDO, ELIZABETH PEARCE oc/Associate Professor of Education; b/ Jan 23, 1927; h/P141 Ft McIntosh, Laredo, TX 78040; ba/Laredo, TX; m/ Leonei; p/Dr Nicholas J and Fannie Dollar Pearce (dec); sp/Federico Elizondo, Zapata, TX; ed/BA, Mary Hardin Baylor, 1948; ME 1952, EdD 1971, Univ of Houston; pa/Elem Tchr, Houston TX, 1951; Elem Tchr, Pasadena TX, 1952-56, 1960-66; Life Sci Tchr, Webster TX, 1960-67; Instr, Univ of Houston, 1969-70; Assoc Prof of Ed, Laredo St Univ, 1971-; Assn of Supvn & Curric Devel; TX Assn of Gifted & Talented; TX Soc of Col Tchrs of Ed; Kappa Delta Pi; cp/Pres, Bd of Dirs 1981-82, Faith Acad; r/Bapt; hon/Profl Pub; NSF Acad Yr in Earth Sci, Univ of Houston, 1968-69; W/W in S & SW.

ELKINS, JAMES P oc/Physician; b/ Mar 20, 1924; h/2045 Lick Creek Drive, Indianapolis, IN 46203; ba/Indianapolis, IN; m/May R; c/James B, Paulette F Phillips, Patricia May Riggs; p/James H and Antonia Wohler Elkins (dec); sp/ Mrs Bruce D Reynolds, Norton, VA; ed/ MD, Univ of VA Mec Sch, 1947; mil/ AUS, 1949-54; pa/Pvt Med Pract, Ob-Gyn, 1954-73; Marion Co Dpty Coroner, 1965-74; Med Conslt, Disability Determination Div, IN Rehab Sers; Med Dir, Physcan Exams Inc; Ringside Phys, IN St Boxing Comm, Indpls Pal Clb & IN Golden Gloves; AMA; IN St Med Assn; Marion Co Med Soc; Am Col of Ob-Gyns; cp/Indpls Press Clb; Southport Masonic Lodge; Scottish Rite; Murat Shrine Temple; Nat Sojourners; Phi Chi; FOP; Police Leag of IN; '500' Fest Assocs; Life Mem, US Auto Clb; r/Presb; hon/Chief of Ob-Gyn, St Francis Hosp, Bch Grove IN, 1965-66; Hon Life Mem, Indpls Press Clb, 1983; W/W in MW.

ELLINGBOE, JAMES oc/Biochemist; h/63 Matawanakee Trail, Littleton, MA 01460; ba/Belmont, MA; m/Karin Ester Sofia Westlin; c/Randi Aina Sofia, Christopher Helge; p/Ellsworth and Helen Ellingboe, New Harbor, ME; ed/ AB, Chem, Oberlin Col, 1959; PhD, Biochem, Harvard Univ, 1966; pa/ Postdoct Fellow & Amanuens, Royal Caroline Inst, Stockholm, 1966-68; Asst Res Biochem, Sch of Med, Univ of CA-San Diego, 1968-70; Assoc in Psychi (Biochem) 1970-72, Prin Res Assoc in Psychi (Biochem) 1972-84, Assoc Prof of Psychi (Neurosci) 1984-, Harvard Med Sch; Chief, Drug Surveillance & Biochem Lab, Boston City Hosp, 1970-73; Chief, Biochem Lab, Alcohol

& Drug Abuse Res Ctr, McLean Hosp, 1973-; Am Chem Soc, 1960-; AAAS, 1965-; Fdn of Am Scists, 1975-; NY Acad of Scis, 1978-; Intern, Soc of Psychoneuroendocrinology, 1979-; Am Soc for Pharm & Exptl Therapeutics, 1981-; Soc for Neurosci, 1981-; Endocrine Soc, 1982-; Intl Soc for Biomed Res on Alcoholism, 1982-; hon/Author & Co-Author of Articles in Sci Books & Jours; Am Men & Wom of Sci; W/W: in E, in Frontier Sci & Technol, Among Writers.

ELLINGWOOD, BRUCE R oc/ Research Structural Engineer and Leader of Structural Engineering Group; b/Oct 11, 1944; h/879 Diamond Drive, Gaithersburg, MD 20878; ba/ Washington, DC; m/Lois D; c/Geoffrey D; p/Mrs Ronald F Huber, Woodstock, IL; ed/BS, Civil Engrg 1968, MS 1969, PhD, Civil Engrg 1972, Univ of IL-Urbana-Champaign; pa/Res Asst, Civil Engrg, Univ of IL, 1968-72; Res Engr, Nav Ship R & D Ctr, 1972-75; Res Structural Engr, Nat Bur of Standards, 1975-; Adj Prof of Civil Engrg, Johns Hopkins Univ, 1983-; ASCE, Chm of Com on Safety of Bldgs 1979-; Coms on Res, Structural Safety & Reliability, 1976-; Am Soc for Testing & Mats; Am Inst of Steel Constrn; Am Nat Standards Inst, Secy of Com on Design Loads 1977-; hon/Author, Over 50 Archival Pubs & Reports during 1971-84, in the Fields of Structural Reliability & Probability-Based Design, Structural Loads & Loading Criteria, Response of Structures to Fires, Fatigue & Fracture Reliability; Walter L Huber Prize, ASCE, 1980; Nat Capital Awd for Engrg Achmt, DC Joint Coun of Engr, Arch Socs, 1980; Silver Medal, US Dept of Commerce, 1980; Normal Medal, ASCE, 1983; St of the Art in Civil Engrg Prize, ASCE, 1983; W/W in Engrg.

ELLION, M EDMUND oc/Aerospace Executive; h/2152 Highland Oaks, Arcadia, CA 91006; ba/Los Angeles, CA; m/Dolores Dianne; c/Laurie Ann, Thomas Michael; p/Beatrice Elizabeth Patterson Ellion, Winthrop, MA; ed/BS, Tufts Univ & NEn Univ, 1944; MS, Harvard Univ, 1947; PhD, CA Inst of Technol, 1953; mil/USN 1944-46, Lt; pa/ Mgr, Technol Devel, Hughes Aircraft, 1964-; Pres, Dynamic Sci Corp, 1960-64; Exec Dir, Nat Engrg Sci Co, 1958-60; Engrg/Bus Conslt, 1953-58; Assoc Fellow, AIAA; Sr Mem, IEEE; r/ Prot; hon/Author & Co-Author, 34 Tech Pubs in Heat Transfer, Propulsion & Space Vehicle Technol; 12 Patents in Field of Space Vehicle Sys; Hyland Patent Awd, 1978; Caltech Inst Scholar, 1952; Am Men & Wom of Sci; W/W in W.

ELLIOT, JEFFREY M oc/Professor, Author; b/Jun 14, 1947; h/1419 Barliff Place, Durham, NC 27712; ba/Durham, NC; p/Gene and Harriet Elliot, Los Angeles, CA; ed/BA 1969, MA, Univ of So CA; Dr of Arts, Claremont Grad Sch; Cert in Grantsmanship, The Grantsmanship Ctr, 1980; pa/Tchg Asst & Res Asst, Univ of So CA, 1969-70; Instr of Polit Sci, Cerritos Col, 1970-72; Asst Prof of Hist & Polit Sci, Univ of AK-Anchorage Commun Col, 1972-74; Asst Dean of Acad Affairs & Asst Prof of Social Sci, Miami-Dade Commun Col, 1974-76; Asst Prof of Polit Sci, VA Wesleyan Col, 1978-79; Sr Curric Spec in Polit Sci, Ed Devel Ctr, 1979-81; Assoc Prof of Polit Sci, NC Ctl Univ, 1981-; Polit Sci Editor, The Borgo Press, 1979-; Contbg Editor, *The Bltn of the Sci Fiction Writers of Am*, 1983-; Contbg Editor, *Spectrum Mag*, 1982-83; Editor, *Contemp Authors' Guides*, 1982-; Nat Conslt, *Commun Col Frontiers*, 1975-; Contbg Editor, *Questar Mag*, 1979-81; Book Reviewer, Addison-Wesley Pub'g Com, 1981-; Contbg Editor, *Negro Hist Bltn*, 1978-79; Contbng Editor, *W Coast Writer's Conspiracy*, 1978-79; Assoc Editor, *Commun Col Social Science Qtrly*, 1972-76; Pres, Commun Col Social Sci Assn, 1974-75; Book Reviewer, Little Brown & Co, 1972-73; cp/Speechwriter, Res Asst, Campaign Strategist, US Sen Howard W Cannon, 1969-82; Chm of Bd, Crispus Attucks Theater for the Arts Foun, 1978-79; Election Commentator, WGH Radio, 1978; Chm, FL Com for Ed Stability, 1975; Commun Ser Adv Coun of Miami, 1975; Conslt, CA Clean Envir Act, 1970-72; Urban Affairs Advr, Mayor Samuel W Yorty of LA 1971-72; Radio Host, KPFK Radio, 1971-72; r/ Jewish; hon/Pub'd Author; Pi Sigma Mu; SPWAO Awd Finalist for Outstg Non-Fiction Achmt, 1981 & 1982; Balrog Awd Finalist, 1981 & 1982; Outstg Edr of FL Cit, 1976; Phi Delta Kappa, 1976; Dist'd Ser Through Commun Effort Awd, 1976; Outstg Edr Cit, 1973; Sem for Master Tchrs, 1973; Outstg Fac Advr Cert, 1972; Excel in Tchg Awd, 1971; Outstg Polit Sci Scholar Awd, 12970; Pi Sigma Alpha, 1967; Hon's Prog in Polit Sci, 1967; Fair Enterprise Medallion Awd, 1965; W/W: in World, in Am, in S, in W; Outstg Edrs of Am, Personalities S; Notable Ams of Bicent Era; DIB; Men of Achmt; Dir of Dist'd Ams; Contemp Authors; 5000 Personalities of World.

ELLIOTT, KENNETH M oc/Executive; b/Nov 8, 1921; h/93 West Shore Drive, Pennington, NJ 08534; m/Virginia Merrill; c/Linda, Karen; p/John B and Mary Adams Elliott (dec); ed/BSChE, Univ of TN; pa/Adv'd from Chem Engr to Grp Ldr in Devel Activs in Aviation Gasoline (Field Res Labs, Dallas, TX) 1942-46, Process Devel Activs & Applied Res Devel Activs (Res & Devel Labs, Paulsboro, NJ] 1946-64, Gen Mgr of Engrg 1964-67, VP of Engrg (Mobil Res & Devel Corp) 1967-, Mobil Oil Corp; Chem Engrg Consultor Com of Manhattan Col, 1976-; Bd of Dirs & Exec Com, NJ St Safety Coun, 1972-; Adv Bd to Mgmt Div, AIChE; Past Chm, Com on Refinery Equip, Am Petro Inst; hon/Author of Num Pubs, Primarily in Petro Refining; Am Petro Inst, Cert of Apprec, 1976; ASME Outstg Ldrship Awd, 1980; W/W: in Technol Today, in the Petro Indust, in Engrg; Men of Achmt.

ELLIOTT, MYRTLE EVELYN KEENER oc/Private Teacher; b/Apr 11, 1898; h/2709 Fourth Street, Bakersfield, CA 93304; ba/Same; m/Dr L Louis Elliott (dec); c/Winona Sample, James C Sample, Joan Hughes, Mary Ellen Agam; p/Mary Elizabeth and John William Keener (dec); ed/AB, Cornell Col, 1921; MA, Tchrs Col, Columbia Univ; Att'd OH St Univ; pa/Eng & Latin Tchr, Jackson Co HS, 1921-23; Hist & Latin Tchr, DeWitt Schs, 1923-25; Hd of Eng Dept & Dean of Girls, Kemmerer

WY, 1926-29; Dean of Girls & Eng, Pendleton OR, 1930-31; Girls' Advr, US Indian Ser, 1931-35; Latin & Eng Tchr, Cut Bank, 1944-46; Tchr of Educable Retarded Chd, Kern Co CA, 1946-68; Pvt Tchr, 1968-; Am Assn on Mental Deficiency Coun for Exceptl Chd; CA Tchrs Assn; Nat Tchrs Assn; CA Assn for Parents & Tchrs; Catholic Daughs; AAUW; IRA; Phi Beta Kappa; r/Rom Cath; hon/Pub'd Article; Honored by Kern Co Intl Rdg Assn, 1981; Alumnae Merit Awd, Cornell Col, 1977; W/W: in CA, of Am Wom.

ELLIS, GEORGE LELAND oc/Associate Research Scientist; b/Jan 14, 1928; h/3610 Northwest 42nd Terrace, Gainesville, FL 32605; ba/Gainesville, FL; m/Violeta; c/Alfredo, Marieta, Monica, George L Jr, Edward A; p/Herman and Ruby Ellis (dec); ed/BS 1950, MS 1958, NC St Univ; PhD, Univ of FL-Gainesville, 1968; mil/Sr Aircraft Electrician 1951-55, USAF; pa/Assoc Prof, Univ of FL-Gainesville, 1982-; Chief of Party Univ of FL INIAP Contract, Ecuador & Assoc Prof, Univ of FL-Gainesville, 1979-82; Mgr of Fam Farm & Res Conslt, Goldsboro, NC, 1978-79; Livestock Spec, World Bk/ INIA Agri Res Proj, Spain, IRI Res Inst, 1975-77; Chief of Party, NM St Univ/ USAID Contract, Paraguay & Assoc Prof, NM St Univ, 1973-75; Asst Chief of Party & Advr to Dean of the FAV, NM St Univ, 1971-72; Advr to the Dean of FAV & Dir of Nat Prog for Livestock Res & Ext, NM St Univ, 1968-71; PhD Cand, NIH F'ship, Univ of FL-Gainesville, 1964-68; Instr & Livestock Res Advr, USAID/NC St Univ Contract, Peru, NC St Univ, 1960-64; Instr, NC St Univ, 1957-60; MS Cand, Res Asst, NC St Univ, 1955-57; Tchr of Voc Agri, VA, 1950-51; Am Soc of Animal Sci; Latin Am Assn of Animal Prodn; Gamma Sigma Delta; Sigma Xi; hon/ Pubs, "Mineral Supplementation for Grazing Cattle in Tropical Regs" (in Press), "Nutritional Factors Affecting Mineral Status & Long-Term Carry-Over Effects in Sheep" 1984, "Reproductive Probs of Dairy Herds in Ecuador" 1983, "Eval of Mineral Supplements for Grazing Cattle in Tropical Areas"; Num Other Pubs; Hon Prof of the Nat Univ of Assuncion; Resolution #135/75 of the Superior Coun; Dist'd Collaborator Fac of Vet Sci, Asuncion, Paraguay, Resolution No 4175; Mem of Bd of Dirs, Am Sch of Asuncion of Asuncion Parents & Tchrs Assn of ASA, Pres & VP.

ELLSWORTH, FRANK L oc/College President; b/May 20, 1943; h/739 Harvard Avenue, Claremont, CA 91711; ba/ Claremont, CA; c/Kirstin Lynne; p/ Clayton and Frances Ellsworth, Wooster, OH; ed/AB, Liberal Arts, cum laude, Adelbert Col, Case Wn Resv Univ, 1965; EdM, Hist & Phil of Am Higher Ed, PA St Univ, 1967; MA, Lit, Columbia Univ in the City of NY, 1969; PhD, Hist of Ed, Univ of Chgo, 1976; PhD, Eng, Columbia Univ; pa/Prof of Polit Studies & Pres, Pitzer Col, 1979-; Instr, Col Div of the Social Scis, Univ of Chgo, 1975-79; Asst Dean, Univ of Chgo Law Sch, 1971-79; Prof of Lit, Dir of Spec Projs, Sarah Lawrence Col, 1970-71; Tchg Asst for Profs Maxine Greene & Louis Forsdale, Tchrs Col, Columbia Univ, 1967-70; Asst Dir of Law Devel

& Alumni Affairs, the Law Sch, Columbia Univ in the City of NY, 1968-70; Asst Dir of Devel, Tchrs Col, Columbia Univ in the City of NY, 1967-68; Asst Cnslr Coor, Dean of Students Staff, PA St Univ, 1966-67; Am Hist Assn; Coun for the Advmt of Sec'dy Ed; Hist of Ed Soc; Vis'g Com of the Bd of Overseers, Case Wn Resv Univ; Yg Pres' Org, YPO; Assn of Indep CA Cols & Univs; Bd of Fellows, The Claremont Univ Ctr; VP 1984-, Indep Cols of So CA Inc; SWn Univ Sch of Law; cp/Friends of the Huntington Lib; The Arts Clb of Chgo; LA World Affairs Coun; Town Hall of CA Assn; The Univ Clb of Claremont; The Univ Clb of LA; The Zamorano Clb of LA; hon/Pubs, "King's Col Goes A-Begging" 1970, *Student Activism in Am Higher Ed* 1971, *Law on the Midway: The Fdg of the Univ of Chgo Law Sch* 1977, "Am Legal Ed: Definition & Ingredients" 1978, Book Review of "The Am Law Sch & the Rise of Adm Govt" by Wm C Chase 1983; Edit Bd, *CA Lwyr*, 1984-; First Recip, Dist'd Yg Alumnus Awd, Wn Resv Col, Case Wn Resv Univ, 1981; Hon Chp, Salute to Minority Ed, The Golden St Minority Foun, 1980-; W/W in Am.

ELLSWORTH, LUCIUS F oc/Associate Vice Chancellor; b/Ju1 6, 1941; h/ Room 209, Collins Building, Florida Board of Regents, Tallahassee, FL 32301; ba/Tallahassee, FL; m/Linda V; ed/BA, Col of Wooster, 1963; MA 1966, PhD 1971, Univ of DE; pa/Assoc VChancellor, St Univ Sys; Dean, Col of Arts & Scis 1979-, Provost of Alpha Col 1976-79, Prof of Hist 1978, Univ of W FL; ACE Fellow, Univ of MN, 1975; Assoc Prof & Asst to Provost, Gamma Col 1974-75, Asst Prof of Hist & Asst to Provost 1971-74, Asst Prof of Hist 1969-71, Univ of W FL; Acting Coor, Hagley Grad Prog, Adj, Univ of DE & Eleutherian Mills-Hagley Foun, 1968-69; Vis'g Hons Prof, Villanova Univ, 1968; Res Hall Dir, Univ of DE, 1963-67; FL Hist Soc, Bd of Dirs 1979-, Pres-Elect 1984-; Deans of St Univ Sys Liberal Arts & Scis Cols, Chm 1980-81; Am Hist Assn; FL Endowment for the Humanities, 1983-, Exec Com 1984; cp/ Pensacola C of C 1980-, Action 76 Tourism & Hist Task Force, Chm 1972-75; hon/Pubs incl: *Pensacola: The Deep Water City*, 1982; *The Cultural Legacy of the Gulf Coast, 1870-1940*, 1976; *Traditionalism & Change: The NY Tanning Indust in the 19th Cent*, 1975; "NW FL's Forgotten People: The Creek Indians Since Removal" 1981, "House Rdg: How to Study Houses as Symbols of Society" 1980, "A Bicent Look at the US Tanner" 1976, Var Other Books & Articles; TV Progs, The Am Indust Revolution (Two 30 Minute Progs Produced for WSRE-TV) 1971, W FL's Forgotten People (One 1 Hour TV Documentary Produced for Public Broadcasting for AL, FL, NE, LA) 1981; Awd of Merit, Am Assn for St & Local Hist, 1984; Am Coun on Ed Fellow in Acad Adm, 1975-76; Rovensky Fellow in Bur Hist, Lincoln Ed Foun, 1967-68; Andelot F'ship, Univ of DE, 1965-67; Hagley F'ship, Univ of DE & Hagley Mus, 1963-65; Edwards Awd, Agri Hist Soc Awd; FL Endowment for Humanity Grant; Outstg Edrs in Am; Personalities of the S; Outstg Yg Men of Am; DIB; W/W in the S & SW; W/W in Am.

ELROD, DENNIS CAREY oc/Architect; b/Mar 30, 1953; h/1009 Oakmont Place, 8, Memphis, TN 38107; ba/Memphis, TN; p/Sybil R Elrod, Tullahoma, TN; ed/Att'd Motlow St Commun Col, 1972-74; BSET 1977, MSTE 1983, Memphis St Univ; MBA in Process; pa/Order Puller, Smotherman, Womack Wholesale Grocers, 1971-72; U Parcel Ser, 1972-78; Engrg Tech, Clark, Dietz & Assocs, Engrs, 1977-79; Intern Arch, Hall & Waller & Assocs, Archs, 1979-82; Intern Arch, Hnedak, Bobo, Gooch & Assocs, Archs/Interior Designers, 1982-; Col Civitan, 1972-74; Assoc'd Gen Contractors, 1975-77; Assn of Student Chapts/AIA, 1975-77; AIA, 1983-; Kappa Delta Pi; Phi Beta Pi; Architectural Licensure, Jun 1984; hon/Outstg Yg Men of Am.

ELROD, JULIA ANN oc/Resident in Pediatrics; b/Sep 29, 1956; h/10900 W 65 Terrace, Shawnee, KS 66203; ba/Kansas City, MO; m/Donald Kahl; c/Alison Marie; p/Glen and Beulah Elrod, Clinton, MO; sp/Ruth Kahl, Bella Vista, AR; ed/BA 1980, MD 1980, Univ of MO; pa/Resident in Pediatrics, Chd's Mercy Hosp, 1980-83; F'ship in Neonatology at Chd's Mercy Hosp, 1984-; Asst Prof, Univ of MO, 1980-; Fellow, Am Acad of Pediatrics; r/Meth; hon/Profl Pub.

ELROD, RACHEL ELAINE oc/Registered Nurse Instructor; b/Aug 9, 1937; h/770 Troy Court, Aurora, CO 80011; ba/Denver, CO; p/Dorothy Elrod, Lamar, MO; ed/Dipl in Nsg, MO Meth Hosp Sch of Nsg, 1955-58; BS 1963, MS 1964, Univ of CO; Num Other Sems & Classes; pa/OR & Med Univ Nurse, Menorrah Med Ctr, 1958-59; Med/Surg Nurse, Sparks Meml Hosp, 1959-60; Asst Col Nurse, Bethany Nazarene Col, 1959-61; Emer Rm Nurse, Hillcrest Hosp, 1960-61; Charge Nurse on Med Unit, Gen Rose Meml Hosp, 1961-62; Instr, Presb Med Ctr Sch of Nsg, 1964-66; Med/Surg Nsg Coor, Presb Med Ctr Sch of Nsg, 1966-68; Dir, Presb Med Ctr Sch of Nsg, 1968-70; Coor of Clin Experiences, Mercy Hosp, 1973; Ed Dir & Instr, Mercy Hosp Sch of Nsg, 1970-74; Instr in Nsg, Front Range Commun Col, 1974-; Am Nurses Assn, 1965-80; CO Nurses Assn, 1965-80; Involved Nurses for Polit Action in CO, 1975-80; Nat Leag for Nsg, 1966-70; CO Ed Assn; NEA; Sigma Theta Tau, Alpha Kappa Chapt; GASP; Arthritis Assn; r/Prot; hon/Pub'd Author; W/W in CO.

EMENER, WILLIAM G oc/Professor of Rehabilitation Counseling and Associate Dean; b/Jun 10, 1943; h/16404 Shagbark Place, Tampa, FL 33618; ba/Tampa, FL; m/Rae Dorothy; c/Karen Rae, Barbara Jean, Scott William; p/William and Rose Emener, Jackson, NJ; ed/BA, 1965; MA, 1968; PhD, 1971; pa/Resident Asst, Trenton St Col, 1964-65; Tchr of Sec'dy HS Eng, No Burlington Co Reg HS, 1965-66; Subst Tchr, All Grades, Bordenton Twp, 1966-67; Internship as Voc Guid Cnslr, E R Johnstone Tng & Res Ctr, 1967-68; Rehab Cnslr, E R Johnstone Tng & Res Ctr, 1968-69; Tchg Asst'ship, Univ of GA, Sum 1970; Instr'ship Practicum, Dept of Rehab Cnslng, Univ of GA, 1971; Asst Prof, Murray St Univ, 1971-74; Psychol, Cnslg, Pvt Pract, Murray, KY, 1972-74; Coor, FL St Univ, 1976-77; Res Conslt, FL Ofc of Voc Rehab, 1977; Asst Prof, FL St Univ, 1977-78; Dir, Univ of KY, 1978-80; Prof, Univ of S FL, 1980-; Assoc Dean, Univ of S FL, 1983-; APGA, 1971-; Assn for Cnslr Ed & Supvn, 1971-; So Assn for Cnslr Ed & Supvn, 1972-; Am Rehab Cnslg Assn, 1970-; Nat Rehab Assn, 1970-; Nat Rehab Cnslg Assn, 1970-; Nat Coun on Rehab Ed, 1971-; Nat Rehab Adm Assn, 1978-; Am Psychol Assn, 1975-, Div of Cnslg Psych 1976-, Div of Rehab Psych 1976-; FL Assn of Practicing Psychols, 1981-; NRCA Profl Devel Coun, Chp 1977-78; NRCA Sub-Coun, Mem 2 Yrs, Conf Progs 1974-76; ARCA Bd of Editors, 1975-; NCRE Bd of Editors, 1976-; NRCA Rep to Comm for Hlth Certifying Agencies, 1977-78; NRAA, VP 1981-82, Pres-Elect 1982-83, Chair of Profl Concerns Com 1982-83; NRAA, Pres 1983-84; NRA, Chair of Baker/Lorenz Spec Awds Com; Res Briefs Eval Com, Rehab Res Inst, Univ of FL, 1978-83; Edit Conslt, *Mgmt Control Project*, Univ of GA, 1979-; Edit Conslt, *REHAB BRIEFS*, 1981-83; Policy Bd, *Jour of Rehab Adm*, 1983-85; Guest Co-Editor, Spec Issue of *Jour of Rehab Adm* (in Press); Lic'd Psychol, KY, FL; Cert'd Rehab Cnslr; Cert'd Psychol; hon/Hon Mbrship, Rho Sigma Epsilon, Rehab Ed Hon Soc, 1979-; Pubs, "Impact of Govt Retrenchment on Professionalism: The Cases of Social Wk & Rehab" (in Press), "Grads' Views of Instrnl/Competency Areas in Rehab Cnslr Ed Progs" (in Press), "Client Feedback in Rehab Cnslr Eval: A Field-Based, Profl Devel Application" (in Press), "St Voc Rehab Agy Ldrship Behavior Styles" 1983, "A Philosophical Framework for Rehab: Implications for Clients, Cnslrs, & Agencies" 1983, "Corp Caring: EAP's Solve Personal Probs for Bus Benefits" 1983, *Rehab Adm & Supvn 1981, Selected Rehab Issues & Their Impact on People 1984, Employee Asst Progs: A Multidisciplinary Approach 1984*; Num Other Pubs; Cert of Apprec for Outstg Sers, FL Assn of Rehab Secys, 1977; Awd for an Outstg Contbn, Editor, *ARCA Newslttr*, 1975-78; Cert of Apprec for Outstg Sers & Contbns, SEn Reg Inst on Deafness, 1978; Cert of Apprec for Outstg Sers & Contbns, Nat Rehab Cnslg Assn, KY Rehab Cnslg Assn, 1979; Recip, Am Rehab Cnslg Assn 1980 Res Awd; Exemplary Ser Awd, Nat Rehab Cnslg Assn, 1982; The Advmt of Res in Rehab Adm Awd, Nat Rehab Adm Assn, 1982; Men of Achmt; Am Men & Wom of Sci; Outstg Yg Men of Am; W/W: in S, in S & SW, in Frontier Sci & Technol, Dir of Profls & Resources in Rehab; Personalities of Am.

EMERY, BETTY JO oc/Cosmetologist Exect; b/Oct 29, 1949; ba/Dana Point, CA; ed/Studied Psych & Cosmetology; pa/Chm of Pilgrim Trust Raising Fund, 1983; Treas, Pacific Ocean Foun for Orange Co Marine Inst; C of C, Dana Point, 5 Yrs; hon/Citizenship Awd, 1983; Resolution of Commend, Orange Co; W/W W; Personalities in Am.

EMETT, SHARON ELIZABETH oc/Teacher; h/700 3rd Avenue South, Great Falls, MT 59405; ba/Great Falls, MT; p/Truce W (dec) and Isabel Emett, Great Falls, MT; ed/BA, Univ of MT, 1960; Att'd, Univ of CO, 1974-75; Early Childhood Intl, Oxford, England, 1977; pa/Tchr, Gt Falls Public Schs, 1960-; Great Falls Ed Assn, Secy 1966-71, NCtl Dist Dir 1968-70; cp/Repub Pres Task Force; Repub Senatorial Clb; Sustaining Mem, Repub Nat Com; Local & Nat Repub Wom; Humane Soc of Cascade Co; r/Meth; hon/W/W of Am Wom.

EMIDY, LINDA ANN oc/Research Assistant; b/Jul 15, 1949; h/836 South Loomis Street, Chicago, IL 60607; ba/Chicago, IL; p/Raymond E (dec) and Mildred M Emidy, N Smithfield, RI; ed/BA, RI Col, 1971; MA, Ball St Univ, 1974; BSN 1977, MSN 1980, DNSc 1983, Rush Univ; pa/Tchr, US Peace Corps Vol, 1971-73; Staff Nurse, Univ of IL Med Ctr, 1977-79; Res Asst, Ruth-Presb St Luke's Med Ctr, 1982-; Nurse Practitioner, Grant Hosp, 1980; APHA; Biofeedback Soc of Am; IL Biofeedback Soc; Am Assn of Biofeedback Clin; Behavioral Med Soc; ANA; Wom in Hlthcare; Am Gerontological Soc; cp/Rush Alumni Assn; r/Rom Cath; hon/Sigma Theta Tau; Rush Local Hon Soc, 1977; Sigma Theta Tau Nat Nsg Hon Soc, 1978; Wom's Bd Scholar, 1980-83; Yg Commun Ldrs of Am.

ENDERS, THOMAS O oc/Assistant Secretary of State for Inter-American Affairs; b/Nov 28, 1931; ba/Department of State, Washington, DC 20520; m/Gaetana M; c/Claire, Alice, Domitilla Kennan, Thomas Ostrom; p/Mr and Mrs Ostrom Enders, Avon, CT; ed/BA in Hist and Ec, Yale Univ, 1953; Dr of Univ Deg in Colonial Hist, Univ of Paris, 1955; MA in Ec, Harvard Univ, 1957; pa/Entered Fgn Ser, 1958, First Serving in INR; Am Embassy Stockholm, 1960; Dept of St, EUR, Supvr Intl Economist, 1963-66; Spec Asst to Undersecy of St for Polit Affairs, 1966-68; Dpty Asst Secy for Intl Monetary Affairs, Dept of St, 1968; Dpty Chief of Mission, Am Embassy Belgrade, 1969; Dpty Chief of Mission 1970-73, Charge d'Affairs, Am Embassy Phnom Penh; Asst Secy of St for Ec/Bus Affairs, 1974-76; Am Ambassador to Canada, 1976-79; US Rep to European Communs, Brussels, 1979-81; Asst Secy of St for Inter-Am Affairs, 1981-; Var Civil & Profl Ofcs; hon/Arthur S Flemming Awd, 1970.

ENDLER, NORMAN SOLOMAN oc/Professor; b/May 2, 1931; h/52 Sawley Drive, Willowdale, Ontario M2K 2J5; ba/York University, Downsview, Ontario; m/Beatrice Kerdman Endler; c/Mark, Marla; p/Elie and Pearl Endler (dec); ed/BSc 1953, MSc 1954, McGill Univ; PhD, Univ of IL, 1958; pa/Psychol, PA St Univ, 1958-60; Lectr, Psych, York Univ, 1960-62; Asst Prof 1962-65, Assoc Prof 1965-68, Prof 1968-, York Univ; Conslt, Toronto E Gen Hosp, 1964-84; Mem, Adv Bd, Addiction Res Foun, 1977-83; Conslt, Clarke Inst, 1972-; Fellow, Am Psychol Assn; Fellow, Canadian Psychol Assn; hon/Pubs, "Holiday of Darkness" 1982, Co-Author, "Maturing in a Changing World" 1970, "Interactional Psych & Personality" 1976, "Contemp Issues in Developmental Psych" 1976, "Personality at the Crossroads: Current Issues in Interaction on Psychols, Personality & the Behavioral Disorders" 1984; Canadian Silver Jubilee Medal, 1978; Ontario Mtl Hlth Grantee, 1968-74; Canadian Coun Grantee; Social Sci & Humanities Res Coun Grantee, 1978-80; W/W in Frontier Sci & Technol.

ENDO, EDWIN YOSHIO oc/ Optometrist; b/Nov 30, 1953; h/1524 Pensacola Street, Honolulu, HI 96822; ba/Pearl City, HI; m/Amy; p/Mr and Mrs Rikio Endo, Puunene, HI; sp/Mr and Mrs Wally Arakawa, Waipahu, HI; ed/BS, Univ of HI; BS, So CA Col of Optom; OD, So Ca Col of Optom; Optometrist, Pvt Pract, 1980-; HI Optometric Assn; CA Optometric Assn; Am Optometric Assn; Optometric Ext Prog Foun; cp/Honolulu Japanese Jr C of C, Num Ofcs; Proj Concern; Save Your Vision Wk; YMCA Mbrship Dr Vol; George Ariyoshi for Gov of HI; Gryan G Chun for St Ho of Reps; r/ Christian; hon/Pub'd Author; Bronze Key Recip Awd, Honolulu Japanese Jr C of C, 1982; Recruiter Awd, Honolulu Japanese Jr C of C, 1982; Recruiter Awd, Honolulu Jaycettes, 1982; JC of the Qtr, Honolulu Japanese JCs, 1981; Com Chm of Qtr, Honolulu Japanese JCs, 1982; Exec Ofcr of Yr, 1982-83; W/W in W.

ENGEL, PETER ANDRAS oc/ Research Engineer; b/Jul 10, 1935; h/ 1004 Murray Hill Road, Binghamton, NY 13903; ba/Endicott, NY; c/Gregory Alexander, David Anthony; p/Geza Engel (dec); Herta Engel Koch (dec); ed/ Att'd, Budapest Tech Univ, 1953-56; BE, Vanderbilt Univ, 1958; MS, Lehigh Univ, 1960; PhD, Cornell Univ, 1968; pa/Designer, Nashville Bridge Co, 1957-58; Structural Analyst, Praeger-Kavanagh-Waterbury Engrs, 1959-62; Res Engr, The Boeing Co, 1962-65; Staff Engr 1968-71, Adv Engr 1971-83, Sr Engr 1983-, IBM; ASME, 1958-; hon/ Author of Book, *Impact Wear of Mats*, Elsevier, 1976; Over 50 Tech & Sci Articles Pub'd & Several Book Chapts Pub'd; A J Dyer Meml Prize, Vanderbilt Univ, 1958; Charles Russ Richards Meml Awd, ASME, 1983; W/W: in Technol, in Frontier Sci; Am Men & Wom of Sci.

ENGELHARDT, M VERONICE oc/ Educational Psychologist; b/Mar 29, 1912; h/304 East Linebaugh Avenue, Tampa, FL 33612; ba/Same; ed/BS in Ed 1937, MA 1938, PhD 1962, The Cath Univ of Am; pa/Elem & Sec'dy Sch Tchg & Adm; Col & Univ Instr, Assoc Prof of Ed, 1938-52; Diocesan & Commun Sch Supvr, Instr in Ed Psych, St Francis Normal Sch, 1952-57; Dean of Wom & Hd of Dept of Psych & Ed, Chaminade Col, 1957-60; Clin Instr at Child Ctr, Cath Univ; Supvr of Student Tchg, Cath Univ, 1957-60; Hd, Dept of Ed & Psych, Maria Regina Col; Fdr & Dir, Franciscal Lrng Ctr, Maria Regina Col, 1962-; Ofcs in the Rel Commun, Asst Mother Gen 1965-71, Chm of Pers Bd 1972-75, Chm of Communs Bd 1971-82, Editor of Commun Newslttr 1972-82; Am Psychol Assn; Am Ednl Res Assn; IRA; Nat Leag of Am Pen Wom, First VP & Editor of the Ctl NY Br 1981-83; hon/Authored the First 3 Books of the First Sci Textbooks Based on a Cath Phil of Ed, *God's World*, for Elem Grades; Co-Authored (w Sister M Eloise) a Book, "Songs About God's World"; Lectr & Spkr at Var Tchrs' Insts, Convs & Meetings in Dioceses in 11 Sts from Boston to KC, & as Far S as Mobile, AL; Guest Lectr, Franciscan Inst at St Bonaventure Univ, Sum 1983; Gave 2 Wkshops on the Myers-Briggs Type Indicator, 1984; Traveled Extensively in Europe, Vis'g Cols & Univs in 7 Countries, 1966; Att'd, Intl Biogl Conf in Amsterdam, Holland; Noted in Nat Soc of Poets, Poets' Hall of Fame of 1981; Personalities of Am.

ENGELMAN, MARGE ANN oc/ Director of Outreach; b/Oct 9, 1927; h/ 1164 Emilie Street, Green Bay, WI 54301; ba/Green Bay, WI; m/Dr Kenneth; c/Ann Kathleen, Barth Brian; p/ Reka Jeckel, Delavan, IL; ed/BA, Sociol, Wesleyan, 1949; MA, Rel Ed, NWn Univ, 1953; MS, Related Art & PhD, Ed & Aging, Univ of WI-Madison, 1977; pa/Instr, Univ of WI Ext 1963-65, Univ of WI, Fox Val, Menasha & Green Bay 1966-68; Asst to Asst Chancellor 1969-72, Dir Equal Opport 1974-79, Dir Outreach 1973-, Instr 1981-, Univ of WI-Green Bay; Trustee, Garrett Theol Sem, NWn Univ, 1975-; WI Humanities Com, 1976-79; St Adv Coun of Commun Ed, 1979-81; Am Coun of Ed; WI Planning Comm; Nat Identification of Wom in Higher Ed; Am Assn of Adult Ed, 1974-; Am Craftsmen Coun, Adult Ed Assn; WI; AAUE, Univ Leag; cp/Corp Bd of Bellin Hosp, 1978-; r/Meth; Univ Senate of the U Meth Ch, Comm on Theol Ed, 1980-; hon/Egas, 1948; Mortar Bd, 1949; Outstg Ser, 1949; Phi Kappa Phi, 1949; Recip, Elmer Winter Awd, WI Designer Craftsman Show, 1970; Phi Delta Kappa, 1980; Pubs, "The Response of Older Wom to a Creat Prob Solving Prog" 1981, "The Forgotten Fourth: Cooperating Fac Mems in Col TV Courses" 1977; *Contemp Design in Decorative Textiles in the Ch* 1965; "The Bishop Called" 1979, "The Cult of the Little Black Book" 1967, "Emotional Need & the Use of Symbols" 1959; W/ W of Am Wom.

ENK, GORDON A oc/Executive; b/ Jun 24, 1940; h/Box 144, Fox Creek Road, Medusa, NY 12120; ba/Medusa, NY; m/Elise W; c/Terrence A, Christopher C; p/Benedict and Irene Enk, Milwaukee, WI; ed/BA, Ripon Col, 1962; Master of Forestry, Yale Sch of Forestry & Envir Studies, 1967; Master of Phil 1970, PhD 1975, Yale Univ; mil/AUS, Signal Corps, Instructor 1962-65; pa/ Mkt Rschr, US Forest Ser, 1967; Resource Ec Analyst, Dept of Natural Resources, St of WA, 1969; Dir of Ec & Envir Studies, The Inst on Man & Sci, 1970-81; Pres, Gordon A Enk & Assocs Inc, 1981-; Pres, The Res & Decision Ctr Inc (Current); Mgr, Spec Projs Planning, Intl Paper Co, 1984-; AAAS; Am Ec Assn; Sigma Xi; Soc of Am Foresters; hon/Pubs, "Improving Impact Assessment: Increasing the Relevance & Utilization of Sci & Tech Info" 1984; "Res & Public Policy Needs for Victim Compensation Policy in the US" Aug 1982; "Assessing the Potential Hlth Consequences of Inhalable Combustion Particles from Coal-Fired Power Plants: An Integrated Agenda" Jun 1983; "An Assessment of the Sci Knowledge Base Related to the Compensation of Victims of Pollution-Induced Disease" Aug 1983; *Green Goals & Greenbacks: A Comparative Study of St-Level Envir Impact Statement Prog & Their Associated Costs* 1980, *Beyond NEPA Revisited: Directions in Envir Impact Review* 1980, *Value Issues in Technol Assessment: How to Understand & Deal w Them in a Decentralized Solar Energy Technol Assessment Prog* 1978; Var Other Pubs; Outstg Yg Men of Am; W/W in Frontier Sci & Technol.

ENLOE, I MARGARET oc/Vice President of Plumbing Corporation; b/Jan 21, 1936; h/Hacienda Heights, CA; ba/ So El Monte, CA; m/James Lee; c/ William Lee, Laurel Irene E Netz; p/ William Brown Van Fossen (dec); Irene McWilliams Bard, Pico Rivera, CA; sp/ Revis Lee and Hazel Ellen Scott Enloe (dec); pa/Clerk, So CA Gas Co, 1954; Ofc Mgr 1968, VP 1968-, Lee's Plumbing; cp/PTA, 10 Yrs; Little Leag & Pony Leag Aux, 5 Yrs; Bobby Sox Softball Mgr, 7 Yrs; Repub Woms Clb; Fin Dir, Local Bapt Ch; Treas, Local Election, 3 Terms; Commun Choir & Ch Choir; r/ Bapt; hon/W/W of Am Wom.

ENSOR, ALLISON RASH oc/Professor of English; b/Oct 3, 1935; h/3855 Sequoyah Avenue, Knoxville, TN 37919; ba/Knoxville, TN; m/Anne Lovell Ensor; c/Elizabeth Anne, Edward Mark; p/Allison R Ensor, Cookeville, TN; ed/BA, TN Tech, 1957; MA, Univ of TN, 1959; PhD, IN Univ, 1965; pa/ Asst Prof 1965-71, Assoc Prof 1971-80, Prof 1980-, Eng, Univ of TN-Knoxville; Mod Lang Assn; S Atl Mod Lang Assn; TN Philological Assn, Pres 1977-78; TN Col Eng Assn, Secy-Treas 1975-; Soc for the Study of So Lit; hon/Pubs, *Mark Twain & the Bible*, Univ of KY Press 1969, Norton Critical Edition of *A Connecticut Yankee in King Arthur's Court* by Mark Twain, W W Norton 1982; Author of Articles in Var Scholarly Jours; Dir of Am Scholars.

ENT, ELIZABETH oc/Attorney at Law; b/Aug 31, 1904; ba/730 Miller Street, San Jose, CA 95110; ed/BA, San Jose St Univ, 1926; Grad Student, Univ of CA, 1926-27; LLB, Univ of CA, Hastings Col of the Law, 1937; pa/Pvt Pract of Law; Trial Pract throughout CA; Appellate Pract the CA Ct of Appeals; Author of Var Articles for Profl Jours; Past Lectr in Interst & Intl Domestic Relats; Former Mag Feature Writer in the Field of Law for Laymen; Former Revising & Contbg Editor, Bancroft Whitney Co (St Codes, Law Digests, Legal Encys, Profl Textbooks) & Callaghan & Co (Profl Textbooks & Digests); ABA, Fam Relats Sect, Past Mem of Com on Support, Past Chm of Subcom on Enforcement of Interst Decrees 1960-61; Intl Fdn of Wom Lwyrs, Past Mem, Domestic Relats Com 1959; Nat Assn of Wom Lwyrs, Reg Dir 1959-63, Past Chm of Com on Fam Life & Child Wel 1956-61, Past Mem of Com on the Rts of the Mtlly Ill 1959-60, Past Del of the Ho of Dels 1957-59; St Bar of CA, Com on Conf Resolution 13-10 (Labor Law) 1975; Bar Assn of SF, Past Mem of the Bd of Editors 1953-57; Santa Clara Co Bar Assn, Edit Bd 1967-78, Legis Com 1974, Chm of Exec Bd of Juv Justice Sect 1974, Legal Panel, Disciplinary Review Bd for Jail Sys 1975-76, Exec Com of Correctional Reform & Crim Justice Com 1975-78, Inmates' Legal Ser Com 1978, Vol Atty of Commun Legal Sers Panel; Kappa Beta Pi Intl Legal Sorority, Past Dean of Alpha Eta Chapt, Past Dean of Mu Alumnae Chapt, Past Province Dean, Past Mem of the Intl Bd; Santa Clara Co Commun on the Status of Wom, Chp 1977-78, Chp of Legal & Ec Status Com 1974-77, 1978-80; Sheriff's Detention & Adv Bd, Chp 1979, Chp of Com on Site of Wom's Residential Ctr 1974,

Counsel 1975; Wom's Residential Ctr Adv Bd, Chp 1979-82, Mem 1974-79; Review Bds, Santa Clara 1974, Sonoma 1975; Supvrs Jail Task Force, Mem 1976-77; cp/Former Hostess, US Dept of St Prog for Fgn Visitors, 1953-56; Ad Hoc Com for Status of Wom Comm, Chp & Legis Advocate 1973-74; Outreach for Wom Inc, Co-Fdr & Counsel 1974-75, Fin Com 1975; BPW; LWV; Nat Assn of Christians & Jews; Santa Clara Co Human Relats Comm; Leag of Friends of the Comm on the Status of Wom, Co-Fdr & Counsel 1978-; Growth & Opport Inc, Bd 1982-, Counsel 1978-; Var Other Commun Activs; hon/Dist'd Wom Awds, Midpeninsula Girls' Clb, 1975, 1978; Ser Awd, Santa Clara Co Bar Assn, 1976; Leag of Friends of the Santa Clara Co Comm on the Status of Wom Spec Awd, Wom of Achmt, 1981; CA Black Wom's Coalition & Black Concerns Assn, Cert of Exemplary Polit Achmt, 1982; Elizabeth Ent Awd Created by Leag of Friends of Santa Clara Co Comm on the Status of Wom, 1983; Meridian BPW, Wom of Achmt Awd; Cambrian BPW, Wom of Achmt Awd.

EPP, MELVIN DAVID oc/Plant Geneticist and Tissue Culture Specialist; b/Jun 16, 1942; h/6740 Via San Blas, Pleasanton, CA 94566; ba/6560 Trinity Court, Dublin, CA 94568; m/Sylvia K Rieger; c/David S, J Terry; p/John Jr and Marie Harder Epp, Whitewater, KS; ed/BS, Wheaton Col, 1964; MS, Univ of CT, 1967; PhD, Cornell Univ, 1972; pa/Hort Trainee, Pan-Am Seed Co, 1964-65; Res Asst, Brookhaven Nat Lab, 1967; Res Assoc, Brookhaven Nat Lab, 1972-74; Sr Res Biologist, Monsanto Co, 1974-77; Res Supt (Plant Breeding), Philippine Packing Corp (Del Monte Corp), 1977-82; Mgr, Plant Propagation & Tissue Culture Res, Del Monte Corp, 1982-84; Prin Scist, ARCO Plant Cell Res Inst, 1984-; AAAS; Botanical Soc of Am; Genetics Soc of Am; Intl Assn for Plant Tissue Culture; CA Acad of Sci; hon/Pubs, "Application of Tissue Culture to Tropical Fruit Res," "Constancy of Chromosome Number of Cultured Haploid Datura," "Nuclear Gene-Induced Plastome Mutations in *Oenothera hookeri*," "The Homozygous Genetic Load in Mutagenized Pops of *Oenothera hookeri*"; Var Other Pubs; Author or Co-Author, Num Proprietary Res Documents of the Philippine Packing Corp; Grad Asst, Plant Sci Dept, Univ of CT, 1965-66; NIH Genetics Trainee, Cornell Univ, 1967-81; Damon Runyon Fellow, Brookhaven Nat Lab, 1972-74; W/W in Frontier Sci & Technol.

EPSTEEN, CASPER MORLEY oc/Plastic and Reconstructive Surgeon; b/May 6, 1902; h/5750 Kenwood Avenue, Chicago, IL 60637; c/Lynn, Robert; ed/BS 1923, MD 1925, Univ of IL; DDS, Loyola Univ, 1930; mil/AUS, 1942-46, Lt Col; pa/Instr in Anatomy, Univ of IL Col of Med, 1923; Instr of Pathol, Univ of IL Col of Med, 1924; Prof of Maxillofacial Surg, Cook Co Grad Sch of Med, 1947-59; Clin Prof of Surg, Chgo Med Sch, 1962-; Consltg Staff Meml Hosp of Springfield 1947-63, Jackson Pk Hosp & Med Ctr 1946-, Weiss Meml Hosp 1953-74, Ctl Commun Hosp 1964-, Chgo Meml Hosp

1932-48; Att'g Surg, Cook Co Hosp of Chgo 1947-59; Sr Att'g Surg, Michael Reese Hosp & Med Ctr; Pres, Chgo Med Soc, 1962-63; 2VP 1964, 1VP 1965, Ho of Dels 1947-75, IL St Med Soc; AMA; Pres 1963-64, Secy 1947-58, Am Soc of Maxillofacial Surgs; Am Burn Assn; Fellow, Am Col of Surgs; Fellow, Intl Col of Surgs; IL Soc for Med Res; Fellow, Ed & Sci Foun of IL St Med Soc; Intl Soc of Maxillofacial Surgs; Intl Assn of Maxillofacial Surgs; Pan Am Med Assn; Secy 1935, Pres 1936, S Chgo Br of Chgo Med Soc; Fdr & Orgr, *S-Side Med Assem*, 1938; Bd of Trustees, Intl Col of Surgs Hall of Fame, 1964-66 & 1979-; Adv Coun of Permanent Chm, Michael Reese Hosp, 10 Yrs; Delta Kappa Sigma; Phi Delta Epsilon; Alpha Omega; cp/Chgo Natural Hist Mus; Quadrangle Clb; Exec's Clb of Chgo; Nat Hist Soc; Art Inst of Chgo; Chgo Coun of For Affairs; Field Mus of Nat Hist; hon/Pub'd Author; Honorable Mention, Foun of Am Soc of Plastic & Reconstructive Surgs, 1952; Awd of Merit, Chgo Med Soc, 1963; Dist'd Awd, Am Soc of Maxillofacial Surgs, 1966; Ldrship Awd, Am Soc of Maxillofacial Surgs, 1960; Honor Awd, Michael Reese Hosp & Med Ctr, 1955; Honor Awd, Louis A Weiss Meml Hosp, 1960; Awd of Apprec, Chgo Med Soc, 1978; Special Achmt Awd, Am Soc of Maxillofacial Surgs, 1982; Guest of Hon, Intl Col of Surgs, 1971; Guest Editor, Am Jour of Surg, 1952; Num Hon & Awds for Sci Exhibits on Trauma of the Facial Bones & Pathol of the Facial Bones; W/W: in Am, in World; Intl Biographies; Nat Cyclopedia of Am; Am Men of Med; Outstg Ams; Nat Social Dir; Dist'd Ams.

EPSTEIN, DIANA oc/Artist, Writer Designer, Business Owner; b/Jun 17, 1936; h/143 East 62 Street, New York, NY 10021; ba/New York, NY; p/Samuel H Epstein, Elmwood Park, IL; ed/Univ of Chicago, 1954-57; Art Inst of Chgo; Chgo Inst of Fine Arts; pa/Lectr, Parsons Sch of Design; Appraiser, Antique Buttons; Writer, Articles on Antique Buttons in Mags & Jours; Designer of Fabrics & Clothing; Artist, Greeting Cards for CASPARI & Co; Owner, Tender Buttons, Rare & World Famous Button Shop; Nat Button Soc; r/Jewish; hon/Pub'd Author; W/W of Am Wom.

EPSTEIN, LOIS BARTH oc/Physician, Cancer Researcher, Professor of Pediatrics; b/Dec 29, 1933; h/19 Noche Vista Lane, Tiburon, CA 94920; ba/San Francisco, CA; m/Dr Charles J; c/David Alexander, Jonathan Akiba, Paul Michael, Joanna Marguerite; p/Benjamin (dec) and Mary Frances Perlmutter Barth; ed/AB, cum laude, Radcliffe Col, 1955; MD, Harvard Med Sch, 1959; pa/Resident in Pathol, Peter Bent Brigham Hosp, 1959-60; Intern in Med, N Eng Ctr Hosp, 1960-61; Fellow, Spec Fellow & Res Med Ofcr, NIAID & NIAMD, NIH, 1962-67; Asst & Assoc Res Phys, Cancer Res Inst, Univ of CA-SF, 1969-74; Assoc Dir, Cancer Res Inst, Univ of CA-SF, 1974-77; Prof of Pediatrics, Univ of CA-SF, 1980-; Assn of Am Phys, 1983-; Intl Soc for Interferon Res, 1983-; Wn Assn of Phys, 1981-; Am Soc for Clin Invest, 1977-; Am Assn of Immunologists, 1972-; Soc for Pediatric Res, 1977-; Am Assn for Cancer Res, 1977-; Am Soc of Hema-

tology, 1972-; Wn Soc for Clin Res, 1973-; Am Fdn for Clin Res, 1969-; Am Assn for Cancer Ed, 1975-; Assn for Wom in Sci, 1981-; Tissue Culture Assn, 1972-; Reticuloendothelial Soc, 1966-; The NY Acad of Scis, 1982-84; cp/Commonwlth Clb of CA, 1984-; Bd of Dirs 1979-, Chm of Endowment Com 1983-, Marin Symph Assn; Pres, Bd of Dirs, The Dance Assn, 1983-; Israel Tour Com, Bd of Jewish Ed, 1976-79; r/Jewish; hon/Author, Over 75 Pubs in Her Field of Res on Interferon & Tumor Immunol; Mem of Edit Bds of 6 Sci Jours; Mem, Nat Cancer Inst's Com on Cancer Ctr Support & Review, 1984-; Mem, Univ of CA's Cancer Res Coor'g Com, 1984-; Phi Beta Kappa, honoris causa, Radcliffe, 1980; W/W: of the World, in Frontier Sci & Technol, of Am Wom, in W, Dir of Profls & Resources in Cancer; Am Men & Wom of Sci; World W/W of Wom; Intl W/W of Contemp Achmt.

ERB, RICHARD LOUIS LUNDIN oc/Resort Community Hotel Executive; b/Dec 23, 1929; h/Grand Traverse Resort, Grand Traverse Village, MI 49610; ba/Same; m/Jean E; c/John Richard, Elizabeth Anne, James Easton, Richard Louis; p/Louis Henry and Miriam Lundin Erb (dec); ed/BA, Univ of CA-Berkeley; Postgrad, 1952; Student, SF Art Inst, 1956; mil/Served to Lt, Artillery, AUS, 1952-54; pa/Asst Gen Mgr, Grand Teton Lodge Co, 1954-62; Mgr, Colter Bay Village, Grand Teton Nat Pk 1962-64, Mauna Kea Bch Hotel 1964-66; VP, Gen Mgr, Caneel Bay Plantation Inc, 1966-75; Gen Mgr, Williamsburg Inn, 1975-78; Exec VP, Gen Mgr, Seabrook Isl Co, 1978-80; VP, Dir of Hotels, Sands Hotel & Casino Inc, 1980-81; VP, Gen Mgr, Disneyland Hotel & Inn-At-The Pk, 1981-82; Chief Operating Ofcr, Grand Traverse Resort Village, 1982-; Adv Bd, NWn MI Col, 1983; Chm Ednl Com of MI Lodging Assn; Dir, US 131 Area Devel Assn, 1983; VP 1969-71, Bd of Dirs 1968-76, Virgin Isls Montessori Sch; Bd of Dirs, Col of Virgin Isls, 1976-79; Mem of Adv Bd, Univ of So CA 1978-82, CA St Polytechnic Inst 1981-82, Orange Coast Commun Col 1981-82; VChm, Charleston Tourism Coun, 1979-81; Bd of Dirs, Anaheim Visitors & Conv Bur, 1981-82; Am Hotel & Motel Assn (Dir 1975-77, Trustee of Ednl Inst 1977-83, Exec Com 1978-83, Chm of Projs & Progs Com 1982-83), Caribbean (1st VP 1972-74, Dir 1970-76), Virgin Isls Hotel Assns (Pres, Chm of Bd 1971-76), Caribbean Travel Assn (Dir 1972-74), Intl (Dir 1971-73), SC (Dir 1978-82), VA, Williamsburg (Dir 1975-78), Atl City (VP 1981-82), CA Hotel Assns (Dir 1981-82), Atl City Casino Hotel Assn (Dir 1980-82), Nat Restaurant Assn; Beta Theta Pi; cp/Trident C of C; Tavern Clb; Golden Horseshoe Clb; German Clb; Rotary Clb of Traverse City, 1983; Gtr Bay Clb; Seabrook Isl; Kiawah Isl; Grand Traverse Resort; hon/Contbr, Articles to Trade Jours; Ser Merit Awd, 1976; Caribbean Assn Hon Life Mem, 1976; Extraordinary Ser Merit Awd, 1974; Virgin Isls Merit Awd, 1973; Am Hotel & Motel Assn Ser Awd, 1983; W/W: in E, in S, in Fin & Indust.

ERICKSON, ERNEST EUGENE oc/Professor of Engineering; b/Mar 29,

1919; h/1036 Pebble Beach Circle, Winter Springs, FL 32708; ba/Orlando, FL; m/Frances Thelma Tant; c/Marcelle Clark Guffey; p/Erick Henning Erickson (dec); ed/BEE 1949, MSE 1957, PhD 1961, Univ of FL; mil/USAAF, 1941-45; pa/Electronic Scist, USN Mine Def Lab, 1950-56; Res Engr, Sperry Microwave Tube Div, 1961-64; Assoc Prof, LA St Univ, 1964-69; Assoc Prof, Univ of Ctl FL, 1969-71; Prof of Engrg, Univ of Ctl FL, 1971-; Prof of Elect Engrg & Conslt, Univ of Malawi, 1984-85; IEEE, Orlando Sect, Secy 1977-78, VChm 1978-79, Chm 1979-80; IEEE Microwave Theory & Techniques Soc, Orlando Chapt, Secy 1971-72, VChm 1972-73, Chm 1973-74; IEEE Ed Soc; Am Soc for Engrg Ed; Eta Kappa Nu; Tau Beta Pi; hon/Contbr to Chapt 43 in Book, *Neuroelectric Research*; Author of Several Articles Pub'd in Profl Jours; Ctl FL Elect Engr of the Yr, IEEE Orlando Sect, 1982; W/W in S & SW.

ERICKSON, MILDRED BRINK-MEIER oc/Professor Emeritus and Assistant Dean Emeritus; b/Sep 8, 1913; h/511 Wildwood Drive, East Lansing, MI 48823; m/Dr Clifford E (dec); c/Dr W Bruce, Mrs Marilyn K Erickson-Esposito; p/Louis C and Anna G Brinkmeier (dec); ed/AA, Hannibal-LaGrange Col, 1932; BS, cum laude 1934, MA 1937, NWn Univ; PhD, MI St Univ, 1968; pa/Asst Dean of Lifelong Ed Progs 1975-, Asst Dean of Cont'g Ed at Univ Col 1972-75, Prof of Am Thought & Lang 1975-, Assoc Prof of Am Thought & Lang 1971-75, Coor for Cont'g Ed at Univ Col 1971-72, Cnslr at Univ Col 1968-75, Asst Prof of Am Thought & Lang 1968-71, Cnslr of Univ Col & Instr of Am Thought & Lang 1965-68, Asst Instr of Am Thought & Lang 1963-65, 1958-61, MI St Univ; APGA; Am Col Pers Assn; Acad Affairs Admrs; Am Assn for Higher Ed; NEA; Nat Univ Ext Assn, Chp of Div of Student Affairs; Soc for the Study of MWn Lit; Assn of Gen & Liberal Studies; MI Wom's Studies Assn; Comm on Mid-Life Careers of the Nat Voc Guid Assn; Adult Ed Assn, Co-Chp of Nat Conf Planning Comm 1977; Phi Mu, Alumnae Activs 1959-; AAUW, St Ed Com, Mem-at-Large 1981-; Equal Ptnrs in Ed, St Com 1982-; MI Ed Forum, 1981-; Higher Ed Adv Com for St Senator, 1980-; Bd Mem, F'ship in Support of Lifelong Ed, 1974-; MI St Univ Exec Com on Aging, 1974-; Phi Mu House Bd, 1980-84; Patroness, Sigma Alpha Iota, Music Hon; cp/MI Hlth Coun, 1981-84; Vol Action Ctr, Selection of Awardees; Chp, Com on Ec Security, MI White House Conf on Aging, 1980-81; Bd, MI Arthritis Foun, 1979-83; Zonta, Ser Clb & Var Coms 1975-; Neighborhood Assn, VP 1982-; YWCA, Diana Awds Com 1976, 1977, 1978, 1980; Vol Action Ctr, Judging Com Vols Recog Prog 1978, 1979, 1980; Lansing Wom's Bur, Bd Mem 1978-80; MI Dept of Civil Ser, Tng Plan Adv Task Force 1979, 1984; Lansing Sch Hlth Proj, Adv Bd, 1977, 1978; LWV, Citizens Adv Com, 1975-78; C of C, MI St Univ, Annual Resource Re-Assessment Dinner, 1968-78; Com on Aging, 1977; hon/Cited for Dedicated Ser to Lifelong Ed Progs, MI St Univ, 1980; Dist'd Wom of the Yr Awd, MI Assn of Professions, 1980; Awd for Outstg Ser, E Lansing Area Zonta Clb, 1981; Nat Bus-wom's

Assn, Laureate Chapt Awd, Bus-wom of the Yr, 1978; Maharishi Commun Awd, 1978; Cit of Excell, Gov of MI, 1978; Pres's Apprec for Ser Awd, Phi Kappa Phi, 1978; Phi Delta Kappa, Nat Scholastic Hon, 1977; Diana Awd, Ten Outstg Wom, YWCA, 1975; Cert of Recog, YWCA, 1975; Cert of Recog, MI Legis, 1975; Phi Kappa Phi, Nat Scholastic Hon, 1968-, MI St Univ Chapt Pres 1977, VP 1976, Secy 1975; Pi Lambda Theta, Nat Scholastic Hon, 1934-, NWn Univ Chapt Pres; S'ship Awds & Cits, NWn Univ, 1932-34; S'ship Awds, Hannibal-LaGrange Col, 1931-32; Valedictorian Awd, Hannibal HS, 1931; Pubs, *The Adult Female Human Being* 1975, 1978, 1980, *The Avalon Anthology* (Contbr) 1959, "Gen & Liberal Studies for the Non-Traditional Student" 1974-75, "Fund Helps Open U to 'Non-Trad'" 1974, "Lifelong Ed & Gen & Liberal Studies" 1974, "Opening the Door" 1974, Num Others; Dir of Am Scholars; DIB; The World W/W of Wom Biog; Personalities of the W & MW; Personalities of Am; W/W in MW.

ERICKSON, W BRUCE oc/Professor and Antitrust Economist; b/Mar 4, 1938; h/2849-35th Avenue South, Minneapolis, MN 55406; ba/Minneapolis, MN; p/Clifford E Erickson (dec); ed/BA 1959, MA in Ec 1960, PhD in Ec 1965, MI St Univ; pa/Staff Aid, Subcom on Antitrust, US Senate, 1960-62; Asst Prof of Ec, Bowling Green Univ, 1965-66; Asst Prof 1966-70, Assoc Prof 1970-75, Prof 1975-, Bus & Govt, Sch of Mgmt, Univ of MN; Chm, Dept of Mgmt, Univ of MN, 1976-80; Conslt to Attys Gen in Var Antitrust Cases; Conslt to Bus in Var Capacities; Mem of Var Bds; hon/Pubs, *An Intro to Contemp Bus* (3rd Edition 1981, 4th Edition 1985), *Small Bus in MN* (3rd Volume) 1979, *Bus & Govt Enterprise* (2nd Edition) 1981; Author of Var Articles in Profl Jours; Grad, magna cum laude; Var F'ships; W/W: in the World, in Am; Contemp Authors.

ERLENMEYER-KIMLING, L oc/Behavior Geneticist; ba/722 West 168 Street, New York, NY 10032; m/Carl F E Kimling; p/Floyd M and Dorothy Dirst (dec) Erlenmeyer; ed/BA 1957, PhD 1961, Columbia Univ; pa/Res Scist to Dir of Developmental Behavioral Studies, NY St Psychi Inst, 1961-; Instr to Prof, Columbia Univ Dept of Psychi, 1961-; Assoc Prof to Prof, Columbia Univ Dept of Human Genetics, 1974-; Vis'g Prof, New Sch for Social Res, Grad Psych Dept, 1972-; Fellow, Am Psychol Assn; Fellow, Am Psychopathological Assn; Soc for the Study of Social Biol, Bd of Dirs 1969-84, Secy 1972-75, Pres 1975-78; Am Soc of Human Genetics; Behavior Genetics Assn, Edit Bd of *Behavior Genetics* 1974-78; Edit Bd, *Jour of Preventive Psychi*, 1980-; Edit Bd, *Schizophrenia Bltn*, 1978-; hon/Author, Num Sci Articles & Books; BS, magna cum laude, Columbia Univ, 1957; Phi Beta Kappa, 1957; Sigma Xi, Columbia Univ, 1961; Columbia Univ S'ships, 1956-57, 1957-58; Travel Grants, 1963, 1966, 1978; NIH Peer Review Grp, 1976-80; Congl Comm on Huntington's Disease Wk Grp, 1976-77; Pres's Comm on Mtl Hlth Task Force, 1977-78; NIMH Peer Review Grp, 1981-85; W/W: in E, in Sci & Technol, in Frontier Sci & Technol; Commun Ldrs of the World.

ERTING, CAROL J oc/Assistant Professor of Linguistics, Research Scientist; b/Dec 1, 1948; h/5447 Chevy Chase Parkway, Northwest, Washington, DC 20015; ba/Washington, DC; m/Robert W Deller; c/Jonathan Erting Deller; p/Lilburn and Marilyn Erting, St Charles, MO; ed/BS, w Highest Distn, Communicative Disorders, Ed of the Deaf, NWn Univ, 1970; MA, Communicative Disorders, Ed of the Deaf, NWn Univ, 1972; Student, Sum Inst, Psycholinguistics & Total Communication, Lewis & Clark Col, 1972; Student, Univ of London Sch of Oriental & African Studies, 1976-77; PhD, Anthropology, The Am Univ, 1982; pa/Tchr, Spec Sch Dist of St Louis Co, 1970-71; Parent-Infant Edr, Atlanta Area Sch for the Deaf, 1972-74; Res Assoc, Linguistics Res Lab, Gallaudet Col, 1974-75; Res Scist, Res Inst, Gallaudet Col, 1977-; Tchg Experience: Taught Grad Level Course in Linguistics Dept 1983, Prof of Sems on Total Communication Sponsored by the Inter-Am Chd's Inst, UNESCO & Gallaudet Col 1982, Guest Lectr for Undergrad & Grad Courses in Sociol, Linguistics, Ed, Ednl Adm & Psych 1978-82, Adult Basic Ed Course Tutor (Gallaudet Col, Cont'g Ed Div) 1975, Sign Lang Classes at Dekalb Commun Col 1972-74, Parent-Infant Tchr at NWn Univ 1971-72, Sign Lang for Parents at NWn Univ 1971-72; Res Experience: Uruguayan Sign Lang Proj 1983-, *Deafness, Communication, & Social Identity: An Anthropological Anal of Interaction Among Parents, Tchrs, & Deaf Chd in a Pre-sch* 1977-, Clrm Interaction Proj (Deaf Presch) 1979-80, Mother-Child Interaction Proj 1977-80, Clrm Interaction Proj (Multicultural Pre-sch Clrm, Normally Hearing Chd) 1976, Fieldwk w Dr James Woodward at Gallaudet Col in Paris 1975, Res Assoc at Linguistics Res Lab (Gallaudet Col) 1974, Fieldwk in Collaboration w Dr James Woodward of Gallaudet Col in Sociolinguistics 1973-74; Am Anthropological Assn; The Assn for the Anthropological Study of Play; Am Ethnological Soc; Coun on Anthropology and Ed; Soc for Applied Anthropology; Soc for Latin Am Anthropology; Wash Assn of Profl Anthropologists; Anthropological Soc of Wash; Am Ed Res Assn SIG on Deafness; Conf of Am Instrs of the Deaf; Nat Assn of the Deaf; Conslt, PA Sch for the Deaf, 1983; Panel Mem for Gallaudet Nat Acad Sponsored Wkshop for Residents in Otolaryngology, 1983; hon/Pubs, "Attachment Behavior of Deaf Chd w Deaf Parents" 1983, "Deaf Chd & the Socialization Process" 1982, "Linguistic Socialization in the Context of Emergent Deaf Ethnicity" 1982, "An Anthropological Approach to the Study of the Communicative Competence of Deaf Chd" 1981; Num Other Pubs; Num Presentations; Outstg Grad Student, Anthropology Dept, The Am Univ, 1982; F'ship, Linguistic Soc of Am Sum Inst, Salzburg, Austria, 1979; Invited to Join Pi Gamma Mu, Nat Social Sci Hon Soc, 1975; NSF Grad F'ship, 3 Yrs, 1974; F'ship, The Am Univ, 1974; Chosen to Participate in the NAD-Sponsored Inst on Psycholinguistics & Total Communication, w Funding, 1972; F'ship, NWn Univ, 1971; Mortar Bd, Sr Wom's Hon, 1969-70; F'ship, NWn Univ, 1969; Jr Wom's Hon, 1968-

69; F'ship, St of IL, NWn Univ, 1968; Dean's List, NWn Univ, 1966-70.

ERTURK, ERDOGAN oc/Pathologist, Adjunct Professor of Oncology; b/ Sep 25, 1930; h/1 B University Houses, Madison, WI 53705; ba/Madison, WI; m/ Gulten Nevin Alp; c/Erdal, Nilgun Togay, Erol; p/Musa and Ayse (dec) Havran, Turkey; ed/DVM 1955, MS 1960, PhD in Pathol 1965, Univ of Ankara; Asst Prof 1965-72, Assoc Prof 1972-78, Prof 1978-80, Dept of Pathological Anatomy, Fac Vet Med, Univ of Ankara, Turkey; Adj Prof, Clin Sci Ctr, Dept of Human Oncology, Univ of WI Med Sch, 1978-; Am Assn Cancer Res, 1979-; AAAS, 1978-; Smithsonian Assn, 1979-; Sigma Xi, 1980-; NY Acad of Sci, 1981-; hon/Author, Over 180 Papers & Over 100 Abstracts in Referred Jours, Mostly Concerning Neoplastic Diseases, Oncology, Chem Carcinogenesis, Urinary Bladder, Renal, Breast, Intestinal Cancers & Hepatocarcinogenesis w Envir Pollutants; Vis'g Res F'ship from CENTO, Onderstepoort Res Inst, Pretoria, S Africa, 1962; Vis'g Proj Assoc, Div Clin Oncology, Univ of WI-Madison, 1962; Res F'ship from Turkish Sci Res Coun to Study the Effects of Envir Factors on Bladder Cancer.

ERVIN-CARR, C YVONNE oc/ Instructor, Consultant; b/Jun 10, 1946; h/4916 48th Avenue South, Seattle, WA 98118; ba/Seattle, WA; c/David Anthony Carr; p/Charles W (dec) and Christene R Ervin, Seattle, WA; ed/BA, Univ of WA, 1969; MEd, Univ of WA, 1971; pa/Tchr, Seattle Public Schs Dist #1, 1971-; PT Instr, Humanities Div, Seattle Ctl Commun Col, 1977-; PT Instr, Staff Tng & Devel Ofc, Univ of WA, 1979-; Conslt, ECS Effective Commun Skills, 1980-; Delta Kappa Gamma, Beta Chapt; Am Soc for Tng & Devel, Puget Sound Chapt; Wom's Profl & Managerial Netwk; Coun on Black Am Affairs; Nat Assn of Female Execs; Black Profl Edrs, Puget Sound Chapt; AAUW; NAACP: Nat Coun of Negro Wom; Urban Leag; cp/Univ of WA Alumni Assn; r/Bapt; hon/W/W of Am Wom.

ESLER, ANTHONY oc/Historian, Novelist; b/Feb 20, 1934; h/1523 Jamestown Road, Williamsburg, VA 23185; ba/Williamsburg, VA; m/Carol Clemeau; c/Kenneth Campbell, David Douglas; p/Mrs Helen Esler, Glen Ellyn, IL; ed/BA, Univ of AZ-Tucson, 1956; MA 1958, PhD 1961, Duke Univ; pa/ Col of William & Mary, 1962-, Prof of Hist 1972-; Vis'g Assoc Prof, NWn Univ, 1968-69; Am Hist Assn; World Hist Assn; Authors Guild; cp/Amnesty Intl; hon/Pubs, Hist: *The Generation Gap in Soc & Hist: A Select Bibliog* 1984, *Generations in Hist: An Intro to the Concept* 1982, *Generational Studies: A Basic Bibliog* 1979, *Bombs, Beards & Barricades: 150 Yrs of Yth in Revolt* 1971, *The Aspiring Mind of the Elizabethan Ygr Generation* 1966, Fiction: *Bastion* 1982, *Babylon* 1980, *The Freebooters* 1979, *Forbidden City* 1977, *Lord Libertine* 1976, *Hellbane* 1975, *Castlemayne* 1974; Phi Beta Kappa, 1955; Grad'd summa cum laude, Univ of AZ, 1956; Fulbright Postdoct Res F'ship, Univ of London, 1961-62; Am Coun of Learned Socs Res F'ship, 1969-70; W/W: in Am, in S; The Writers Dir; Dir of Am Fiction Writers; World W/W of Authors; Intl W/W of

Ed; Dir of Am Scholars.

ESPINAS, GLENDA ZAMUDIO oc/ Director of Finance; b/Oct 7, 1939; h/ 1414 Seventh Street, NW, #213, Washington, DC 20036; ba/Washington, DC; c/Glendalie E Fabia; p/Purita Amaranto Zamudio Espinas; ed/BBA, Univ of E, 1964; Att'd Albay Normal Col; pa/Secy, Contractor's Proj Dir, U Nats Devel Prog, 1968-70; Secy, Laguna Lake Devel Auth, 1970-71; Secy, Intl Rice Res Inst, 1971-74; Acct, Kramer Assoc, 1974-77; Dir & Bd Secy, Kramer Assoc Inc, 1975-77; Acct, Foun for Applied Res Inc, 1974-77; Acct, WA Bd of Rltrs, 1977-78; Dir of Fin, WA Bd of Rltrs, 1977-; Acct, WA Home Ownership Coun, 12979-; Acct, WA Rltrs Polit Action Com, 1978-82; DC Chapt, Am Soc of Wom Accts, Num Ofcs; Wash Chapt, Nat Assn of Accts; Vol, Nat Chd's Hosp Ctr; r/Rom Cath; hon/Most Outstg Betan Awd, Sigma Beta Lambda Sorority, 1964; Most Cooperative Betan Awd, Sigma Beta Lambda Sorority, 1963; W/ W of Am Wom.

ESPOSITO, LARRY WAYNE oc/ Planetary Scientist; b/April 15, 1951; h/ 1444 Snowmass Court, Boulder, CO 80303; ba/Boulder, CO; m/Diane Marie McKnight; c/Rhea Marie McKnight; p/ Mr and Mrs Albert Esposito, Schenectady, NY 12303; ed/BS, MIT, 1973; PhD, Univ of MA-Amherst, 1977; pa/Assoc Prof Dept of Astrophy, Planetary & Atmospheric Scis 1984-, Res Assoc Lab for Atmospheric & Space Physics 1977-, Univ Lectr 1979-84, Univ of CO-Boulder; Am Astronom Soc; Am Geophy Union; Intl Astronom Union; cp/Boulder Go Clb; hon/Writings Pub'd in: *Astrophy Jour, Astronom Jour, Icarus, Sci, Geophy Res Lttrs, Jour of Geophy Res*; Maj Reviews, Venus Clouds (Venus, *AZ Press* 1983), Saturn's Rings (Saturn, *AZ Press* 1984); W/W in Frontier Sci & Technol.

ESQUIVEL, AGERICO LIWAG oc/ Research Scientist; b/Jun 5, 1932; h/ 13912 Waterfall Way, Dallas, TX 75240; ba/Dallas, TX; m/Margo Ann; c/Cynthia Marie, Gregory Lawrence; p/Enrique F and Pacita R Liwag Esquivel (dec); ed/ AB 1955, MA 1956, Berchmans Col; PhD, St Louis Univ, 1963; pa/Res Scist, Res Inst for Adv Studies, 1963; Res Scist, Martin Co FL, 1964-65; Sr Res Engr, Boeing Co, 1966-71; Postdoct Fellow & Staff Res Assoc, Univ of So CA, 1971-73; Tech Staff, Hughes Aircraft Co, 1973-76; Tech Staff, TX Instruments, 1976-; Am Phy Soc; IEEE; Electrochem Soc; Am Soc of Metals; AIME; Am Crystallographic Soc; Sigma Xi; Pi Mu Epsilon; r/Cath; hon/Profl Pubs; Postdoct F'ship, Univ of So CA; NSF Res Assoc'ship, MIT; Am Men & Wom of Sci; W/W: in Technol Today, in S & SW; DIB.

ESSENBERG, MARGARET KOTTKE oc/Plant Biochemist; b/Apr 21, 1943; h/1601 North Denver Street, Stillwater, OK 74075; ba/Stillwater, OK; m/Richard Charles; c/Gavin Richard, Carla Jean; p/Frank J Kottke, Pullman, WA; ed/AB, Chem, Oberlin Col, 1965; PhD, Biochem, Brandeis Univ, 1971; pa/Res Assoc, Univ of Leicester, UK, 1971-73; Res Assoc 1973-74, Asst Prof 1974-81, Assoc Prof 1981-84, Prof 1984-, OK St Univ; Sigma Xi, 1965-; Treas of OK St Univ Chapt, 1978-80; Am Soc of Biol Chems, 1982-;

cp/Sierra Clb, 1967-, Mem of Exec Com of Stillwater Grp 1974-78; Chm, Stillwater Grp, 1977-78; hon/Pubs, "Single Cell Colonies of *Xanthomonas malvacearum* in Susceptible & Immune Cotton Leaves & the Local Resistant Response to Colonies in Immune Leaves" 1979, "Localized Bacteriostasis Indicated by Water Dispersal of Colonies of *Xanthomonas malvacearum* within Immune Cotton Leaves" 1979, "Identification & Effects on *Xanthomonas campestris* pv *malvacearum* of Two Phytoalexins from Leaves & Cotyledons of Resistant Cotton" 1982; Westinghouse Talent Search Top Forty, 1961; Nat Merit Scholar, 1961-65; AB from Oberlin Col, magna cum laude w High Hons in Chem, 1965; Awd for Dist'd Ser, OK Chapt of Sierra Clb, 1980; Am Men & Wom of Sci.

ESTES, JAMES RUSSELL oc/Professor and Curator; b/Aug 28, 1937; h/1906 Burnt Oak, Norman, OK 73071; ba/ Norman, OK; m/Nancy Elizabeth Arnold; c/Jennifer Lynn, Susan Elizabeth; p/Dow Worley and Bessie Estes (dec); ed/BS, Biol, MWn St Univ, 1959; PhD, Botany, OR St Univ, 1967; mil/ Capt, USAR, Field Artillery; pa/Asst Prof 1967-70, Assoc Prof 1970-82, Prof 1982-, Botany, Univ of OK-Norman; Curator of Bebb Herbarium, 1979-; Dir of OK Natural Heritage Prog, 1981-82; Am Soc of Plant Taxonomists, Secy 1980-83, Prog Chm 1980-83, Pres-Elect 1984-85; Botanical Soc of Am, Secy & Prog Chm for Systematics Sect 1982-83; SWn Assn of Naturalists, Bd of Govs 1979-82, Assoc Editor 1982-; hon/Co-Editor of *The Grasses & Grasslands of OK* (S R Noble Foun, 1976) & *Grasses & Grasslands: Systematics & Ecol* (Univ of OK Press, 1982); Contbr of Chapts to 5 Books; Author of Num Articles in Profl Jours; NSF Grantee, 1968-70, 1980, 1982-; NSF Fellow, 1965-67; Ortenburger Awd, 1975; Baldwin Awd, 1976; Danforth Assoc; W/W: in Frontier Sci, in S & SW.

ESTES, MARGARET TURNER oc/ Associate Vice President for Academic Affairs; b/Jul 1, 1924; h/503 Briarwick, Starkville, MS 39759; ba/MS St, MS; m/ John King (dec); c/John, Greg, David, Jennifer; p/William Jennings Bryant Turner (dec); ed/BA 1965; BA 1967, PhD 1972, Univ of KS; pa/Instr of ESL, Univ of KS, 1965-68; Instr of Sociol, Univ of KS, 1967-68; Asst Prof of Sociol, Haskell Indian Col, 1968-70; Asst Prof of Anthropology, Millersvle St Univ, 1971; Prof & Chair of Sociol, No AZ Univ, 1972-78; Assoc VP for Acad Affairs, MS St Univ, 1978-; Gov's Com on Wom, 1976; Gov's Task Force of Marriage & Fam, 1976-78; Orgr, Wom for Higher Ed; Orgr, MS Assn for Wom in Higher Ed; No AZ Fac Wom's Assn; MS FAc Wom's Assn; r/Congregationalist; hon/Pub'd Author; Fac Wom of Yr, 1973; Presented Honors Convocation Address, 1976; 2 Sociol S'ships in Her Name; W/W: of Intl Wom Edrs, in S & SW, of Am Wom.

ESTEVES-VALAZQUEZ, MABEL R oc/Product Regulations/Reliability Engineer; b/Mar 21, 1950; h/PO Box 3597, Aguadilla, PR 00605; ba/Aguadilla, PR; p/Rosaura Valaquez Del Rio, San Sebastian, PR; Esteban Figueroa Andujar, Jayuya, PR; ed/BSEE 1976, MSEE 1983, Univ of PR; Lic'd Profl Engr; pa/Physics Lab Instr, Univ of PR, 1975-76; Chm of Dept of Electronic Technol, Inst of Technol of PR, 1976-77; Design Engr, GTE Sylvania, 1977-79; Sr Design Engr, GTE Sylvania, Canovanas Plant, 1979-81; Mats/Reliability Engr 1981-82, Prod Regulations/Reliability Engr 1982-, Hewlett Packard; Co-fdr, Pres 1981-82, Soc of Wom Engrs, PR Sect; Bd of Dirs, Aguadilla Chap, Col of Engrs & Surveyors; Mem 1978-, 2nd Wom on Bd of Dirs 1979-82, Secy 1980-81, Org Com of 1979 Tech Cong on Energy Resources, AIEE; 1st Wom on Bd of Dirs 1979-80, Ed Com Chm, San Juan Chapt, CIAPR; Soc of Elect Engrs of PR; IEEE; IEEE Power Soc; IEEE Computer Soc; IEEE Reliability Soc; Am Soc for QC; Fdn of Bus & Profl Wom Clbs, PR, Hato Rey Clb; hon/Profl Pubs, TV & Radio Presentations; Holder of US Patent; Dist'd N Engr Awd, Soc of Wom Engrs, 1980; W/W in S & SW.

ETHERINGTON, EDWIN D oc/ Corporate Director; b/Dec 25, 1924; h/ 102 Bassett Creek Trail, Hobe Sound, FL 33455; ba/Same; m/Katherine C; c/ Edwin Jr, Kenneth, Robert; ed/Att'd, Wesleyan Univ, Yale Law Sch; mil/AUS, World War II; pa/Law Clk to the Hon Henry W Edgerton, US Ct of Appeals, DC, 1952-53; Atty, Wilmer & Broun, DC, & Milbank, Tweed, Hadley & McCloy, NYC, 1953-56; Asst Secy, Secy, VP, NY Stock Exch, 1956-61; Gen Ptnr, Pershing & Co, NYC, 1961-62; Pres, Am Stock Exch, NYC, 1962-66; Pres, Currently Pres Emeritus, Wesleyan Univ, 1967-70; Pres, Chm, Nat Ctr for Voluntary Action, DC, 1971-72; Chm, Nat Advtg Review Bd, NYC, 1973-74; Currently Corp Dir for Automatic Data Processing Inc, Saudi-US Trust, Technol Transitions Inc, US Trust Co of DE, US Trust Co of NY; Trustee, The Hammonasset Sch; Life Mem, Phi Beta Kappa Assn; cp/Intl Adv Coun, AZ Heart Inst; Chm, Hobe Sound Child Care Ctr; Hon Trustee, The Schumann Foun; Pilgrims of the US; Trustee, Martin Luther King Meml Ctr, GA; hon/Phi Beta Kappa, Hons, Distn, Creat Writing, Wesleyan Univ, 1952; Order of the Coif for Acad Excell, Yale Law Sch; Hon Degs: LHD at Am Intl Col; LLD at Amherst Col; LLD at Trinity Col; LLD at Wesleyan Univ.

ETTENSOHN, FRANCIS ROBERT oc/Associate Professor of Geology; b/ Feb 6, 1947; h/Route 5, Old Richmond Road, Lexington, KY 40511; ba/Lexington, KY; m/Beth Ann; p/Robert F and Aileen F Ettensohn, Cincinnati, OH; sp/ Richard N and Carole T Mosher, Cincinnati, OH; ed/BS w high hons 1969, MS 1970, Univ of Cinc; PhD, Univ of IL-Urbana-Champaign, 1975; mil/US Army Corps of Engrs, 1970; pa/Asst Prof of Geol 1975-81, Assoc Prof of Geol 1981-, Univ of KY; Conslt in Envir Geol, Black-shale Geol; Paleontological Soc; Pres SEn Sect, Paleontological Assn; Paleontological Res Inst; Intl Paleontological Assn; Geological Assn of Am; AAAS; KY Acad of Sci, Pres of Geol Sect, 1980; KY Geol Soc; Sigma Gamma Epsilon; cp/Asst Scoutmaster, BSA, 17 Yrs; r/Cath; hon/Profl Pubs; Phi Beta Kappa, 1969; Fenneman Fellow in Geol, Univ of Cinc, 1969-70; Univ of IL Fellow in Geol, 1971-74; Sigma Xi, 1974; Phi Kappa Phi, 1974; Fellow, Geol Soc of Am; Grantee, Geol Soc of Am; W/W: in S & SW; Am Men & Wom

of Sci.

EUBANKS, JOHN R oc/Safety Consultant; b/Sep 18, 1939; h/110 Fen Circle, Pearl, MS 39208; ba/Jackson, MS; m/JoAnn P; c/Tracey Jo; p/Rev John R Eubanks (dec); sp/Alma Pickett, Columbia, MS; ed/Att'd Univ of MS 1955-56, Univ of So CA 1960-61, Univ of GA Tech 1971; mil/USN, Lt; pa/ Safety Conslt, Universal Safety Inc, 1965-70; Safety Conslt, Capitol Safety, 1970-72; Mgr of Loss Control & Audit Dept, Zurich Ins Co, 1972-77; Safety-Claims Dir, Wellcraft Marine, 1977-78; Safety Dir, Burnup & Sims, 1978-80; Sr Loss Control Conslt, Kemper Ins, 1980-82; Safety Conslt, Comml Union Ins, 1982-; Am Soc of Safety Engrs, 1972-; cp/Masonic Lodge, 1966-; Rankin Co Rescue Ser; Vets of Safety, 1981-; Airplane Owners & Pilots Assn, 1977-; Miss Safety Coun, 1973-; r/So Bapt; hon/Profl Pubs; Good Samaritan Awd, Intl Safety Acad, 1976.

EUBANKS, MICHAEL ROY oc/Probation Investigative Officer; b/Jul 6, 1956; h/1039 William Street, Elizabeth, NJ 07201; ba/Elizabeth, NJ; p/Roy F Eubanks, East Orange, NJ; Doris M Eubanks, Elizabeth, NJ; ed/BA, Cheyney St Col, 1978; MDiv, The Regional Sem of the NE; AME Ch Min Tng Inst, 1980-82; pa/Claim Adjuster, The Hartford Ins Grp, 1978-79; Tchr, Roselle Bd of Ed, 1979-81; Probation Ofcr, Union Co Probation Dept, 1981-; cp/Alpha Phi Alpha; Salvation Army Adv Bd; Yth on the Move for Christ Mins; NAACP; Nat Urban Leag; Union Co Coun on Alcoholism; Cheyney St Col Alumni Assn; NJ Lyric Opera Co; NJ Coun of Arts; r/ AME; hon/W/W: Among Am HS Students, Among Am Cols & Univs; Outstg Yg Men of Am; Eagle Scout Cand; Lic'd Min, 1981; Ordained Min, 1984.

EVANS, CHARLES HAWES oc/ Medical Scientist; b/Apr 16, 1940; h/ 9233 Farnsworth Drive, Potomac, MD 20854; ba/Bethesda, MD; m/Nancy Engel; c/Heather Leigh; p/Charles Hawes (dec) and Jean Robinson Evans, South Orange, NJ; ed/BS, Union Col, 1962; MD 1969, PhD 1969, Univ of VA; Internship in Pediatrics, 1969-70; Resident in Pediatrics, 1970-71; mil/ USPHS, 1971-; pa/Res Assoc 1971-74, Sr Scist 1974-76, Chief of Tumor Biol Sect 1976-, Nat Cancer Inst; Assoc Editor, Jour of the Nat Cancer Inst, 1981-; Am Assn for Cancer Res; Am Assn of Immunologists; Intl Soc of Immunopharm; cp/Rotary Clb of Bethesda-Chevy Chase, Secy 1983-; Editor, The Azalean, Jour of the Azalea Soc of Am, 1983-; hon/Author, Over 60 Med Res Articles in Jours & Books, & Articles on Azaleas in Hort Jours; John S Horsley Meml Prize, Univ of VA, 1982; W/W: in E, in Frontier Sci & Technol; Am Men & Wom of Sci.

EVANS, EDGAR ERNEST oc/Associate College Professor (Retired); b/Jan 20, 1902; h/1433 Cleveland Avenue, Montgomery, AL 36108; m/Dr Zelia S Evans; ed/AB, Fisk Univ, 1930; MA, Univ of MI, 1948; mil/WW II, 1942-45; pa/Prin, Apopka Jr HS, 1931-34; Prin, Winter Garden, 1934-38; Prin, JR Lee HS, 1938-41; Prin, Siluria Jr HS, 1941-42; Prin, Waynesboro HS, 1945-48; Prof, AL St Univ, 1949-72; Prof, Tuskegee Inst, 1977; cp/Saint John AME Ch Sch Tchr, Trustee & Chm of

Fin Com for Ch Sch; Pres, Montgomery Dist LA Org AME .Ch; VP, AL Conf LA Org AME Ch & 2nd VP Pres LA Pres AME Ch St of AL; Phi Beta Sigma Chapt Chm of Publicity, Life Mem; Phi Delta Life Mem; Elk; 30th Deg Mason; Shaaban Temple 103 Potentate 1966-68, Dpty 1970-79; St Dir Phi Beta Sigma Frat 1955-71; Reg Dir of Bigger & Better Bus, 1973-75; Dir of Ed, So Pride Lodge, 1954-60; r/Meth; hon/St John AME Ch Man of Yr, 1977; Shaaban Temple 103 Plaque for Dist'd Ldrship to Shaaban Temple 1967-69; Phi Delta Kappa Frat Dist'd Ser for 29 Yrs; Am Soc for Study of Ed; W/W: in AL, in Am Ed, in Am, in Black Am; Intl Register of W/W; Personalities of S.

EVANS, ERNEST THOMAS oc/ High School Administrator; b/Jan 10, 1933; h/4025 Highland Park Drive, Columbia, SC 29204; ba/Columbia, SC; m/Lottie Gist; c/Reginald T, Tamara L, Michelle Y; p/Maria L Evans, Marion, SC; sp/Mr and Mrs Monroe Gist (dec); ed/BS, Johnson C Smith Univ, 1955; MEd, Univ of SC, 1973; mil/AUS, 1955-57, Cryptographer; pa/Math Tchr, Booker T Washington HS, 1958-68; Math Tchr, Hand Mid Sch, 1968-71; Asst Prin, Gibbes Mid Sch, 1971-81; Asst Prin, Eau Claire HS, 1981-; Mgr-Treas, Richland Tchr Fed Credit Union, 1967-; Civil Def Instr, Richland Co Sch Dist One, 1963-69; Phi Delta Kappa; Assn for Supvn & Curric Devel; SC Assn for Supvn & Curric Devel; SC Assn of Sch Admrs; Richland Co Assn Sch Admrs; Nat Assn Sec'dy Sch Prins; SC Assn Sec'dy Sch Prins; SC Assn Elem/Mid Sch Prins; NEA; SCEA; Richland Co Ed Assn; Richland One Tchrs Assn; SC Coun of Math Tchrs; cp/32nd Deg Mason; Shriner; Pres, Bradley Sch PTSA, 1980-81; Pres, Fairwold Mid Sch PTSA, 1982-83; r/ Meth; hon/SCEA Human Relats Awd Runnerup, 1980; Omicron Phi Chapt, Omega Man of Yr, 1981; Nat Treas, Johnson C Smith Univ Gen Alumni Assn, 1979-; NSF Grantee, 1960, 1961, 1962, & 1963; W/W in S & SW.

EVANS, FREDERICK E oc/Research Chemist; b/Nov 11, 1948; h/11340 Southridge Drive, Little Rock, AR 72212; ba/Jefferson, AR; m/Huey-Ing Tseng; p/Edward E Evans; ed/BS, Univ of MA, 1970; PhD, SUNY-Albany, 1974; pa/Chief, Spectroscopic Techniques Br, Nat Ctr for Toxicological Res, Food & Drug Adm, 1978-; Postgrad Res, Chem, Univ of CA-San Diego, 1975-78; Am Chem Soc; Am Assn for Cancer Res; Intl Soc of Magnetic Resonance; hon/Pubs, "Conformation & Dynamics of the C8-Substituted Deoxyguanosine 5'-Monophosphate Adduct of the Carcinogen 2-Acetylaminofluorene" 1984, "Evidence for a 2,3-Epoxide as an Intermediate in the Microsomal Metabolism of 6-Nitrobenzo(a)pyrene" 1983, "Conformation & Dynamics of 2-Amino- & 2-Acetylaminofluorene Nucleoside & Nucleotide Adducts" 1983, "Conformation of K-Region trans-Dihydrodiol Metabolites of Polycyclic Aromatic Hydrocarbons" 1983, "DNA Adducts Formed In Vitro & in Salmonella Typhimurium Upon Metabolic Reduction of the Envir Mutagen 1-Nitropyrene" 1983, "Conformation & Dynamics of Carcinogenic N-Substituted 2-

219

Aminofluorene Compounds Studied by Nuclear Magnetic Resonance Spectroscopy" 1983, Num Others; Food & Drug Adm Commendable Ser Awd, 1984; Am Men & Wom of Sci; W/W in S & SW.

EVANS, FREDERICK JOHN oc/Research Psychologist; h/36 Knickerbodker Drive, Belle Mead, NJ 08502; ba/Belle Mead, NJ; m/Barbara Joan Marcelo MD; c/Christopher Arthur, David Troy, Mark Frederick, Diana Joy; p/Frederick and Phyllis Evans, Bellambi, New South Wales, Australia; ed/BA in Psych 1959, PhD in Psych 1966, Univ of Sydney; mil/Capt, Australian Psych Corps, 1961-63; pa/Dir of Res, Carrier Foun, 1979-; Adj Prof, Rutgers Med Sch, 1980-; Adj Assoc Prof, Univ of PA, 1972-79; Assoc Prof, Univ of PA Med Sch, 1972-79; Sr Res Psychol, Inst of PA Hosp, 1964-69; Res Assoc, Harvard Med Sch, 1963-64; Soc for Clin & Exptl Hypnosis, Fellow, Pres 1981-83; Am Pain Soc, Fdg Mem, Bd of Dirs 1977-80; Am Psychol Assn, Fellow, Div 30 Pres 1978-79; Am Soc of Clin Hypnosis, Fellow; Intl Soc of Hypnosis, VChm, Coun of Reps 1983-85; hon/Pubs, "Effect of Therapeutic Instrns on Behavior & Physiol" (in Press), "Forensic Uses & Abuses of Hypnosis" 1983, "The Accessibility of Dissociated States: Hypnotizability, Control of Sleep & Absorption" (in Press), "The Placebo Response" (in Press), "Hypnosis" (in Press), "Sleep, Eating, & Weight Disorders" 1983, "Hypnosis & Sleep" 1982; Morton Prince Awd for Outstg Contbn to Psych, Soc for Clin & Exptl Hypnosis, 1974; Henry Guze Awd for Best Res Paper on Hypnosis, 1974, 1978; NE & Reg Rep, Proj Sleep; W/W: in Am, in World, in E; Am Men & Wom of Sci; Intl Dir of Dist'd Psychotherapists.

EVANS, H C JR (Deceased) oc/Former College President; b/Aug 18, 1927; ba/Formerly at Lees-McRae Col, Banner Elk, NC 28604; c/Mark Richard; ed/BA, cum laude, Carson Newman Col, 1950; MA in Student Pers Adm, Columbia Univ, 1951; EdD in Adm & Supvn, Univ of TN, 1958; Addit Grad Wk, Univ of CO & Lafayette Col; USAAC & USAFR, 25 Yrs of Ser; Lt Col, USAFR; Liaison Ofcr, Resv Ofcr Tng Corps & AF Acad; pa/Band Dir, Public Sch Music Tchr, Morristown City Schs, 1950-54; Guid Cnslr, Attendance Tchr, Morristown City Schs, 1954-55; Prin, Rose Elem Sch, Morristown, TN, City Schs, 1955-56; Assoc Prof of Psych-Ed, Carson-Newman Col, 1958-61; Placement Dir, Assoc Prof of Psych-Ed, Carson-Newman Col, 1962-63; Dir of Buck Hill Falls Sum Camp, 1961-67; Dir of Tchr Ed, Prof of Ed & Chm, Dept of Psych-Ed, Carson-Newman Col, 1963-67; Pres, Lees-McRae Col, 1967-84; Former Mbrships incl: Bd of Dirs, Indep Col Assn; Bd of Dirs, Ctr for Indep Cols & Univs; Pres, NC Assn of Jr Cols; Chm Num Col & Scout Fund Drives; Adv Com, NC Com on Intl Coop; Higher Ed Panel, Am Coun on Ed; Exec Com, NC Assn of Jr Cols; Treas, Exec Com, Indep Col Fund of NC; Adv Com for Higher Ed, Appalachian St Univ; Exec Com, Avery Co C of C; Exec Com, Appalachian Consortium; Ednl Com, NW Reg Ed Ctr; Life Mem, Phi Delta Kappa, Phi Delta Kappa Ed Hon Frats; Life Mem, NEA; Life Mem, TN PTA; Bd of Govs, Highland Univ;

Commun Adv Bd, Upward Bound/Spec Sers; Hon Mem, Phi Delta Kappa, Order of the Tower; Treas, Indep Col Fund of NC; IPA; cp/Kiwanis: Co-Fdr (Banner Elk Kiwanis Clb, Circle K of Carson-Newman, Circle K of Lees-McRae, Key Clb of Avery HS), 24 Yrs Mbrship & 16 Yrs Perfect Attendance, Past Prog Chm (Yth Activs, Circle K, Mbrship & Attendance, Voc Guid), Hon Mem of Circle K of Lees-McRae, CoChm of Carolinas Dist Mid-Winter Conf 1975, Adv of Key Clb of Avery HS 1978-84; Bd of Trustees for Carolinas Kiwanis Foun 1979-84; BSA: Chm of Area 1 (Daniel Boone Coun) 1975-76, Past Chm of Toe River Val Dist (Daniel Boone Coun), Mem of Exec Bd (Daniel Boone Coun), Scoutmaster for 30 Yrs, Explorer Advr for 20 Yrs, 40 Yrs in Active Scouting, Past Asst Dist Chm, Nat Jamboree Scoutmaster; Bd of Dirs, NC Student Theatre Guild Inc; Bd of Dirs, Avery Co C of C; Bd of Dirs, NC Nat Bk; Bd of Advrs, Newland Br of Watauga Savs & Ln; Am Legion; Masons; hon/Author Handbook for Student Tchg, Tom (a Musical Comedy), Crossroads (a Guide to E TN), The Devel & Use of Ednl Field Trips; TN Tchr of the Yr & Runner-Up for US Tchr of the Yr, 1957; Airman of the Yr as Outstg Resv Airman in the USAF (After Winning Airman of the Yr Awds for Wing, Div & Command), 1958; Yg Man of the Yr for Morristown, TN, & Runner-Up for TN's Yg Man of the Yr, 1955; Ambassador at Large, Morristown, TN, C of C; Col, Aide de Camp, Gov Buford Ellington's & Gov Frank Clement's Staffs, St of TN (Hon); Avery Co, NC, Man of the Yr, 1974; KY Col; W/W: in Am, in S & SW, in N Am, Among Authors & Jours, in TN, in Am Col & Univ Adm, in Am Ed; Quest's W/W Dist'd Citizens of N Am; Outstg Edrs of Am; Nat Register of Prominent Ams; Personalities of the S; Royal Blue Book; Commun Ldrs of Am; DIB; Am Men & Wom of Sci; Men of Achmt; Book of Hon.

EVANS, LENORE KNUTH oc/Artist, Watercolorist, Designer; b/Dec 4, 1920; h/PO Box 97, Mount Berry, GA 30149; ba/Mount Berry, GA; m/Thomas P; c/Paula Neuman, Christina, Bruce, Carol Russell; p/Paul and Esther Mitsch Knuth (dec); ed/Att'd, Chouinard Art Inst, 1940-41; BFA, w Hons, Univ of KS, 1942; pa/Artist, Draftsman, Hercules Inc, 1942-46; Artist, Draftsman, Planner, Tech Planning Assocs, 1947-48; Staff Artist, Designer, MI Technological Univ, 1967-80; Lectr, Instr, MI Technological Univ, 1970-80; Art Instr, Berry Acad & Berry Col, 1981-; Free-Lance Artist, Watercolorist & Designer; AAUW; Art Inst of Chgo; High Mus of Art; Metro Mus of Art; cp/Berry Wom's Clb; Commun Concert Assn; Rome Little Theatre; Rome Symph; Japan-Am Soc of GA; Artist of Wkly Sketches for Evening Democrat (Ft Madison, IA) 1964-67 & Daily Mining Gazette 1969-72; hon/Pubs, Books of Sketches, Our Town, Ft Madison, IA 1966 & Copper Country Sketchbook (Volume 1 1971, Volume 2 1972, Volume 3 1976); Num Purchase Awds & Show Prizes, 1962-; Drawings & Paintings in Pvt Collections Worldwide.

EVANS, MAUDE JEAN oc/Registered Nurse, Hypnotechnician; b/Sep

19, 1931; h/1837 South Kildare Avenue, Chicago, IL 60623; ba/Same; m/Albert; c/Cassandra, Mitchell, Dennis, Celia, Carl; p/Jesse and Mary Banks Gage (dec); ed/AA in Nsg, Malcolm X Col, 1970; BS, Col of St Francis, 1981; MS, Nat Col of Ed, 1983; LPN, Chgo Bd of Ed, 1958; Certs, Ethical Hypnosis Tng Ctr, Intl Guild of Hypnosis, Inst of Relaxation, Hypnosis & Behavior Modification (LA New Hosp), The Dacaran Inst of Applied Hypnosis; pa/Univ of IL Opthal Dept, 1982-; Univ of IL Pers Vis'g Nurse, 1979-82; Neuro Dept of Univ of IL, 1970-79; Hd Nurse, Rosewood Terrace Nsg Home, 1968; Univ of IL Hosp, 1960-67; Hinds VA Hosp, 1959-60; Profl Instr, Intl Guild of Hypnosis & the Dacaran Inst of Applied Hypnosis; Assn for Advmt of Ethical Hypnosis; Assn for Res & Enlightment; hon/Grad w Highest Hon, Col of St Francis, 1981; W/W of Am Wom.

EVANS-JONES, MARILYN BAILEY oc/State Legislator; b/Nov 19, 1928; h/321 Lynn Avenue, Melbourne, FL 32935; ba/Melbourne, FL; m/Edward E Jr; c/Hugh Jr, Cecile, Daniel, Mary Louise; p/Cecil C and Augusta Bailey, Jacksonville, FL; ed/BA, Duke Univ; FL Tchg Cert; FL Real Est Lic; pa/Brevard Subst Tchg, Ctl Jr HS & Melbourne HS; Real Est Salesperson, Evans-Butler Rlty Inc; FL Rep for AAUW, Nat Pilot Prog to Determine Needs of Sr Ams; Melbourne Br, AAUW, Legis Chm; Delta Delta Delta Alumnae Assn; cp/St Rep Serving 5th Term in the FL Ho of Reps, Dist 33 of Melbourne, Currently Serving on Rules & Calendar Com, Regulatory Reform, Ad Hoc Com on Chd & Yth; Elected 3 Times, Chm of the Brevard Co Legis Delegation; LWV; S Brevard Co Panhellenic; PEO; Melbourne Area C of C, 1st Wom Booster Mem 1971; Dist XII Mtl Hlth Bd Mem; Cousteau Soc; Concern Inc; FL Forestry Assn; Nat Repub Legis Assn; Repub St Com-wom; Former Mem: Am Legis Exec Coun, Nat Legis Task Force for Wom; FL Fdn of Repub Wom, Legis Com; Nat Fdn of Repub Wom: Bd of Dirs, Sr Am Proj Chm; Brevard Co Repub Exec Com; Srs Nutritional Aid Prog Adv Coun; Life Mem, Friends of Eau Gallie Lib; Other Civic & Polit Activs; r/U Meth: UMW Melbourne Dist Legis Del, Tallahassee & Wash DC; hon/Juv Guid Awd, Brevard Co PTA Coun; Hdstart Cert of Apprec for Vol Wk; Hon Life Mem, Wom's Soc of Christian Ser; Wom of Yr, Melbourne Area C of C, 1976; Good Govt Awd, Melbourne JCs; Nat Wom Legis of the Yr, Nom by Palm Bay Chapt, US JCs Aux; Cert of Apprec, Child Care Assn of Brevard Co Inc, 1983; Honoree for Accomplishments in the Mtl Hlth Field Dealing w Chd & Fams, The Parent Ed Resource Ctr Inc, 1983; Served as Secy of Legis Affairs, FL Conf of U Meth Wom; Selected Outstg Legis, Nat Repub St Legis Assn, 1984; Personalities of S; Notable Ams; W/W in Am Polits.

EVENSON, WILLIAM E oc/Professor of Physics; b/Oct 12, 1941; h/629 East 2875 North, Provo, UT 84602; ba/Provo, UT; m/Nancy Ann Woffinden; c/Brian K, Elizabeth, Joann, Andrew T, Bengte L; p/Raymond F and Berta W Evenson, St George, UT; ed/BS in Physics, Brigham Yg Univ, 1965; PhD in Theoretical Solid St Physics, IA St

Univ, 1968; pa/Res Assoc, Univ of PA, 1968-70; Asst Prof of Physics 1970-73, Assoc Prof of Physics 1973-79, Prof of Physics 1979-, Assoc Dir of Gen Ed 1980-81, Dir of Gen Ed 1981-82, Dean of Gen Ed 1982-84, Brigham Yg Univ; Vis'g Colleague in Botany, Univ of HI-Manoa, 1977-78; Am Phy Soc; Am Assn of Physics Tchrs; Sigma Xi; Phi Kappa Phi; Sigma Pi Sigma; UT Acad of Scis, Arts & Lttrs; Am Botanical Soc; HI Botanical Soc; HI Audubon Soc; Nat Audubon Soc; cp/Chm 1981-82, VChm 1979-81, UT Co Dem Party; UT St Dem Party Ctl Com, 1979-82; r/Ch of Jesus Christ of LDS: Bishop of Brigham Yg Univ 108th Ward 1971-74, High Coun of Brigham Yg Univ 1st Stake 1970-71, 1974-75, Mission to France 1961-63; hon/11 Pubs in Theoretical Solid St Physics (Magnetism, Melting, Diffusion) 1965-78 & 11 Pubs in Applications of Physics in Ecology (Plant Reproductive Allocation, Ecological Anal) 1978-84; Danforth Grad Fellow, 1965-68; NSF Cooperative Grad Fellow, 1965-66; Hon Woodrow Wilson Fellow, 1965-66; NSF Postdoct Fellow, 1968-69; Brigham Yg Univ Prof of the mo, Feb 1979; Outstg Yg Men of Am; W/W: in Frontier Sci & Technol, in Technol Today, in W; Am Men & Wom of Sci.

EVERS, BARBARA JO oc/Savings and Loan Executive; b/Jan 22, 1949; h/1650 8th Avenue, Apartment 103, San Diego, CA 92101; ba/San Diego, CA; p/Marvin (dec) and Dorothy Emerson, San Lorenzo, CA; ed/BS summa cum laude, Woodbury Univ; AA w hons & Cert in Real Est, Fullerton Col, 1979-80; Cert in Escrow, Cypress Col, 1982; Cert in Mortgage Bkg, 1979-80; pa/Ser Rep, Pacific Telephone Co, 1969-76; Loan Servicing Anal to Loan Adm Supvr, Coldwell Bkr Mgmt Corp, 1967-78; Mktg Ser Mgr & Document Control Mgr to Sys Devel Mgr, Standard Precision Inc, 1978-80; Proj Admr, Procedure Design & Pubs Mgr to Deposit Opers Adm Mgr, Home Fed Savs & Ln, 1980-; Opers Res Soc of Am; Wom in Mgmt; Nat Assn of Female Execs; Am Soc of Profl & Exec Wom; Proj Mgmt Inst; Inst of Mgmt Scis; Soc for Tech Communs; cp/San Diego Symph Assn; San Diego Repertory Theater; Canada Days & Home States Picnic; hon/Grand Cross of Color, Intl Order of the Rainbow for Girls, 1967; Curved Bar Awd, GSA; Nat Dean's List, 1979; Scholastic Letter w 4 Stars, Arroyo HS; CA St S'ship Fdn; Phi Gamma Kappa; Alpha Gamma Sigma Scholastic Honor Socs; Phi Gamma Kappa Key for Highest GPA in Bus Div, 1979; W/W of Am Wom.

EVERSMEYER, HAROLD EDWIN oc/Professor of Biological Sciences; b/Jul 7, 1927; h/820 North 19th, Murray,

KY 42071; m/Ruth J Stinson; c/Clair, Elaine, Kent, Denise; p/G F Eversmeyer, Manhattan, KS; ed/BS in Agri Ed 1951, PhD in Botany & Plant Pathol 1965, KS St Univ; mil/AUS, 1954-56; pa/Prof of Biol Scis, Murray St Univ, 1964-; NDEA Fellow, KS St Univ, 1960-64; Co Agri Ext Agt, Emporia, KS, 1956-60; cp/Kiwanis Clb, Pres 1969, 1983-84, Lt Gov 1970-71, 1971-72; hon/Dist'd Prof Awd, 1984; Men of Achmt; Am Men of Sci.

EWING, RICHARD EDWARD oc/Professor of Mathematics and Petroleum Engineering; b/Nov 24, 1946; h/1055 Granito, Laramie, WY 82070; ba/Laramie, WY; m/Rita Louise Williams; c/John Edward, Lawrence Alan, Bradley William; p/Olivia Clara Henrichson Ewing, Laramie, WY; ed/BA 1969, MA 1972, PhD 1974, Univ of TX-Austin; pa/Asst Prof, Oakland Univ, 1974-77; Asst Prof 1977-80, Assoc Prof 1980-81, OH St Univ; Vis'g Prof, Math Res Ctr, Univ of WI, 1978-79; Sr Res Mathematician, Mobil Oil Corp, 1980-83; Prof of Math & Petro Engrg, Univ of WY, 1983-; Dir, Ctr for Enhanced Oil Recovery, Univ of WY, 1984-; Am Math Soc, Editor Proc Symposia in Applied Math 1983-; Soc of Indust & Applied Math, Adv Coun 1981-82, Comm on Employmt Opports 1983; Soc for Petro Engrs; Intl Assn for Math & Computers in Simulation; Sigma Xi Soc; cp/BSA, Webelos Ldr 1981, Cubmaster 1982; r/Presb; hon/Author of 50 Jour Articles, 1975-84; Editor of Book & Two Spec Jour Issues on Math of Reservoir Simulation, 1983-84; Intl Lectr w About 40 Invited Intl Addresses; NSF Postdoct Fellow, Univ of Chgo, 1976-77; J E Warren Dist'd Prof of Energy & Envir, Univ of WY, 1984; Several Res Grants from NSF & Army Res Org; W/W: in W, in S, in SW, in MW, in Frontier Sci & Technol.

EYSTER, HENRY CLYDE oc/Retired College Professor; b/Jul 10, 1910; h/417 South Sage Avenue, Mobile, AL 36606; m/Dora May Trexler; c/Richard Alan; p/Roy Isaiah and Mary Susan Reed Eyster (dec); ed/AB, cum laude, 1932; MA, Botany, 1934; PhD, Botany, 1936; pa/Instr of Botany, NC St Univ, 1936-37; Asst Prof 1937-44, Assoc Prof of Botany 1944-46, Univ of SD; Res Plant Physiol, Kettering Res Lab, 1946-62; Assoc Prof 1946-50, Prof 1950-62, Antioch Col; Sr Res Biologist, Monsanto Res Corp, 1962-66; Prof of Biol 1966-80, Chm Nat Sci Div 1970-76, Mobile Col; Prof of Biol, Ret'd 1980-; AL Acad of Sci; Phycological Soc of Am; SD Acad of Sci, Editor of Proceedings of the SD Acad of Sci, 1940-46; OH Acad of Sci, VP Plant Sci Sect 1953-54; AAAS; Am Inst of Biol Scis; Botanical Soc of Am; Am Soc of Plant Physiol;

Genetics Soc of Am; cp/Lions Intl Clb, Pres of Yellow Sprgs, OH, Clb 1963-64, Other Ofcs Held; hon/Contbr, Chapts to Books & Articles to Num Sci Jours; Granted Tchg F'ship in Botany, Univ of IL, 1935-36; Invited to Gordon Water Pollution Conf, 1965; Cert of Merit for Dist'd Ser in Algal Nutrition Res, DIB, 1972; Tchr of the Yr, Black Awareness Soc, Mobile Col, 1979-80; Dist'd Prof, Mobile Col, 1976-80; Intl Algae Symp, Univ of L'ville, Participant 1962, Syracuse Univ Participant 1967; Intl Blue-Green Algae Symp, Madras Univ, India, Participant 1970; Intl Botanical Cong, Leningrad, Russia, Participant 1975, Univ of Sydney, Australia, Participant 1981; Am Men of Sci; Who Knows & What; Yg Men of Am; W/W: in AL, in Ecol; Outstg Edrs of Am; Personalities of W & MW; Personalities of S; Commun Ldrs of Am; DIB; Nat Register of Prominent Ams; 2,000 Men of Achmt; Intl W/W in Commun Ser; Men of Achmt; Am Men & Wom of Sci; Commun Ldrs & Noteworthy Ams.

EZELL, JAMES K oc/Life Insurance Consultant; b/Jul 21, 1924; h/1219 Shipwheel Lane, Gillette, WY 82716; m/Dorothy Cox; c/Janet Kay E Naramore, Sheryl Lynn E Gray; p/James William and Clara C Ezell (dec); sp/Walter C Cox, Jacksonville, TX; Maxine H Cox, Houston, TX; ed/BBA, Univ of Houston, 1953; Att'd SMU, LA St Univ; mil/USAAC, 1942-45; ETO, 5 Battle Stars; pa/Agt, Supt, Nat Life & Accident Ins Co, 1946-52; Agt, Mgr, C & I Life Ins Co, 1952-55; Agt, Mgr, Asst Tng Dir, Reg Mgr, VP & Agy Dir, Exec VP & Chief Agy Ofcr, Dir 1961-79, Fidelity Union Life Ins Co, 1955-82; Life Ins Conslt, 1982-; cp/Former Deacon, First Bapt Ch; Former Dir, TX Bible Soc; Former Dir, Sky Ranch; Former Dir, Trinity Christian Acad; Former Dir, Am Christian Col; r/Bapt; hon/Hall of Fame, Fidelity Union Life; W/W: in Am, in Fin & Indust, in World.

EZELLE, ROBERT E oc/Foreign Service Officer; b/Dec 5, 1927; h/102 Davis Drive, Weaverville, CA 96093; m/Lesly Marion; c/Robert L, Lesley Anne, John E, Paul S; p/Zonner Robert (dec); Nina L Smith, Weaverville, CA; ed/MS, Stanford Grad Sch of Bus, 1977; PhD, Univ of Vienna, Austria, 1960; mil/USAF, Overseas, 1949-52; pa/Vice Consul, Hong Kong, 1963-65; Consul, Bern, Switzerland, 1965-69; Consul, Naples, Italy, 1969-72; Consul, Bonn, Germany, 1972-75; Intl Relats Ofcr, St Dept, Wash DC, 1975-76; Dpty Consul Gen, London, England, 1977-80; Consul Gen, Tijuana, Mexico, 1980-84; Consul Gen, Paris, France, 1984-; hon/Dr HC, Nat Univ; W/W: in Am, in Govt, in W, in CA.

F

FAATZ, JEANNE oc/State Representative; b/Jul 30, 1941; h/2903 South Quitman Street, Denver, CO 80236; ba/Denver, CO; c/Kristin, Susan; p/C Keith and Elizabeth Ryan, Evansville, IN; ed/Att'd, IN Univ 1958-61; Bach Deg in Eng & Spch Ed, Univ of IL, 1962; Course in Data Processing, Univ of Denver; Att'd, Univ of No CO, Univ of CO Grad Sch of Communs; pa/CO St Rep, 1978-; Subst Tchr, Denver Public Schs (Current); Secy to CO Senate Majority Ldr, 1976-78; Exec Secy of Denver GOP Ctl Com, 1975-76; Eng and Spch Tchr, Cherry Creek Schs 1966-67 & Urbana Public Schs 1963-66; Staff to Dir, Student Tchg, Univ of IL, 1962-63; Sales Clk, J C Penney Co, 1957-61; cp/SW Denver Commun Mtl Hlth Adm Bd; SW Mtl Hlth Ctr Citizen's Adv Bd; Past Pres, Harvey Pk Improvement Assn; Fort Logan Mtl Hlth Ctr Citizen's Adv Bd; SW YMCA Bd of Mgrs; Past Pres, SW YWCA Adult Ed Clb; Represented GOP Wom at Nat Conf for Wom St Legis; CAWP, Eagleton Inst of Polit, Repub Com-wom, Mem of Yg Repubs of Denver; Bear Creek Repub Wom's Clb; Chm of Trans & Energy Com of Ho of Reps; Mem of Jud Com of Ho of Reps; hon/Named to Denver Post Gallery of Fame for Wk w Charities, Politics & Commun, 1978; Named as YWCA Outstg CO Wom Ldr; Recip, Pres's Awd for Exemplary Ser to Warren Village, 1982; Grad, magna cum laude, Univ of IL; W/W: of Am Wom, in Am Polit.

FACUSSE, ALBERT SHUCRY oc/Attorney at Law; b/Feb 10, 1921; h/6731 Manchester Street, New Orleans, LA 70126; ba/New Orleans, LA; m/May Bandak; c/Vivian Neuwirth, Denise Lentz; p/Nicholas and Maria Facussé (dec); sp/Issa Bandak, Chile; ed/LLB cum laude 1943, JD 1968, Loyola Univ; pa/Self-employed in Indust, Retailing, Wholesale, Merchandising, Export-Import, Bkg, Fin, & Public Relats, 1948-52; Self-employed in Mfg, Bkg, Retailing, Real Est, Govt, Gen Bus, Engrg, Med, and Sci, 1952-60; Attorney at Law, Pvt Pract, 1960-; LA St Bar Assn, 1957-; ABA, 1957-; Alpha Sigma Nu, Loyola Univ; IPA; r/Cath; hon/Considered by Govt Officials as Best Qualified Cand for Pres of US; W/W in Am; Intl W/W of Intellectuals; Men of Achievement.

FAIRBANKS, DOUGLAS JR oc/Entertainer; b/Dec 9, 1909; h/448 North Lake Way, Palm Beach, FL 33480; m/Mary Lee Epling; c/Daphne, Victoria, Melissa; p/Douglas Fairbanks Sr (dec); Mrs Jack Whiting (dec); ed/CA Polytechnic; Harvard Mil Sch; mil/USNR, 1941-52, Capt; pa/Films incl: *Stephen Steps Out, Little Caesar, Catherine the Gt, Gunda Din, Sinbad the Sailor, That Lady in Ermine*; Theater Wk incls: *My Fair Lady, Romeo & Juliet, Moonlight in Silver, Out on a Limb*; Radio Wk incls: *The Three Musketeers If I Were King, Tale of Two Cities, Everyman*; Recordings incl: "Beauty & the Beast & Other Fairy Stories," "Prince Valiant," " Three Musketeers"; Narrations for TV, Radio & Films incl: "The Life of Winston Churchill," "Career of Charlie Chaplin," "Hooray for Hollywood"; TV Appearances in "The Canterville Ghost," "Tom Jones," "The Crooked Hearts," Merv Griffin Talk Show, Dinah Shore's Talk Show; Pres, Doug-fair Corp, 1946-76; Pres, Fairtel Inc; Pres, Boltons Trading Corp; Pres, Westridge Inc; Assoc, Mus Mgmt Conslts; Chm, Douglas Fairbanks Ltd; Dir, Norlantic Recordings Ltd; Dir, Norlantic Devel Co Ltd; Dir, Cavalcade Films; Gov, Royal Shakespeare Theatre, 1952-; Shakespeare Theatre Trust, 1968-; Mem of Bd, Shakespeare's Globe Theatre Proj, UK, 1982; Bd Mem, NY Shakespeare's Globe Theatre Proj; cp/Coun on Fgn Relats, 1959-; Adv Coun, Denver Ctr for the Perf'g Arts, 1972-; Pilgrims Soc, 1951-; Intl Pres, Intl Cultural Ctr for Yth, 1964-; Edwina Mountbatten Trust, 1960-; Gov, Ditchley Foun, 1970-; Gov, Am Mus in Brit, 1965-; Pres, Brit-Am Alumni Assn, 1950-; VP, European-Atl Grp, 1955-; St John's Ambulance Brigade, Manchester & Salford Br, Pres 1958-; The Brook, NYC; The Knickerbocker, NYC; The Cent, NYC; The Metro, Wash DC; The Racquet, Chgo; The Myopia Hunt, Hamilton, MA; The Newport Rdg Rm, Newport, RI; White's, London; Buck's, London; The Garrick, London; The Naval & Mil, London; The Royal Automobile, London; Traveller's, Paris; Puffin's, Edinburgh; hon/Pub'd in *Collier's, Vanity Fair, Esquire, Liberty, The Saturday Evening Post, McCall's, Realities, Vogue, Time & Tide*; Reports, Jours for US Govt; Silver Star Medal, USA; Legion of Merit Medal w "V" Attachment, USA; Dist'd Ser Cross, UK; Chevalier of the Nat Order of the Legion d'Honneur Mil Div, France; Croix de Guerre w Palm, France; War Cross for Mil Valor, Italy; Knight Cmdr of the Most Excell Order of the Brit Empire, UK; Knight of Justice of the Most Venerable Order of the Hosp of St John of Jerusalem, UK; Ofcr of the Nat Order of the Legion d'Honneur Civil Div, France; Knight Grand Ofcr of the Royal Order of King George I, Greece; Knight Ofcr of the Order of Merit, Italy; Ofcr of the Order of the Star of Italian Solidarity, Italy; Cmdr of the Order of Orange-Nassau, Netherlands; Ofcr of the Order of the Crown, Belgium; Grand Ofcr of the Order of Merit, Chile; Ofcr of the Order of the So Cross, Brazil; Nat Medal, Republic of Korea; Spec Lttr of Commend, Chief of Nav Opers, USA, 1944, 1970; USNR Medal; Am Def Medal; Am Theatre Medal; European-African-Med E Campaign Medal; Victory Medal; US Jt Chiefs of Staff Badge; USN's Expert Pistol Shot Medal; Cmdr-in-Chief's Gold Medal of Merit, 1966; Cmdr's Cross of the Order of Merit, W Germany, 1982; City of Vienna's Medal, 1949; Pres Awd of Hon Citizenship of the Republic of Korea, 1955; Univ of Notre Dame Spec Awd for Contbn to Arts, 1971; Armed Forces Annual Recog Awd, 1972; Am Image Awd, Men's Fashion Assn of Am Inc, 1976; The New Sch Spec Awd for Intl Artistic Contbns, 1978; Intl Brotherhood Awd, Nat Conf of Christians & Jews, 1980; Gen William Booth Intl Awd, The Salvation Army, 1980; Hon LLD, Univ of Denver, 1974; Hon DFI, Westminster Col, 1966; Hon MA, St Cross Col, 1968; Vis'g Fellow, St Cross Col, 1969; Sr Churchill Fellow, Westminster Col, 1966; Hon Mem, Groupe Navale d'Assaut, 1950; Hon Mem, Battalion de Choc, 1950; Hon Mem, L'Assn des Anciens Combatants, 1950; Fellow, Boston Univ Libs, 1978.

FAIRCHILD, SHERMAN LEE oc/Manager of Systems and Programming; b/Mar 3, 1940; ba/West Haven, CT; m/Pamela N; c/Robin Lee, Todd Robert; p/George Sherman (dec) and Ruth L Fairchild, Sudbury, MA; sp/John M (dec) and Herta H Nicolson, Milford, CT; ed/BA, Columbia Pacific Univ, 1980; mil/USN, 1959-61; pa/Sys Anal, Sikorsky Aircraft, 1962-71; Sales Mgr, Wms Agy, 1971-75; Sr Programmer Anal, Yale Univ, 1975-76; Sr Programmer Anal, Peoples Bk, 1976-77; Mgr of Sys & Programming, Miles Pharms, 1977-; Nat Wholesaler Drug Assn; Prog Mgmt Inst; cp/U Way Fin Com, 1974; March of Dimes, 1974-75; JC Proj Bus; Mil Pharm CU Treas, 1978-80; Lafayette Lodge #141 AFAM; Jerusalem Chapt No 13 RAM; Jerusalem Coun No 16 R&SM; Hamilton Commandery No 5 KT; r/Epis; hon/Gov's Civic Ldrship Awd, 1974; CT Irregulars, 1974; W/W in Fin & Indust.

FAIREY, ROBERT LEE III oc/Environmental Manager; b/Apr 24, 1946; h/1101 Betsy Drive, Columbia, SC 29210; ba/Columbia, SC; p/R L and Nadeen W Fairey Jr, Rowesville, SC; ed/AA/LA, Spartanburg Meth Col, 1966; USEPA, Nat Tng Ctr; Tech Tng; QC, Process Control & Res & Dev, Monsanto Corp Textile Div, 1966-68; QC Process Control & Spec Projs, Greenwood Mills Inc Textile Dyeing & Finishing Plant, 1968-69; Field Monitoring Coor for Trident & Catawba Dist, SC Pollution Control Auth, 1969-70; Coor for Spec Projs in Water Quality Assessment, SC Pollution Control Auth, 1971-73; Asst Coor for Clean Lakes Prog & Envir Emer Response Team, SC Dept of Hlth & Envir Control, 1973-74; Oil & Hazardous Mat Spill Emer Coor, Tng Ofcr for Dist Spill Response Teams, SC Dept of Hlth & Envir Control, 1974-; Water & Pollution Control Assn of SC, 1970-; Nat Wildlife Fdn, 1969-; River Banks Zool Soc, 1973-; Sports Car Clb of Am, 1977-; SC Reg, SCCA, 1978-; Bd of Dirs, 1978-81; Properties Dir, 1980; License Dir, 1981-83; Progress Lodge 356 AFM, 1969-; DAU Cmdrs Clb; r/Prot; hon/Pub'd Author; TRI Cert of Envir Achmt, 1982.

FAIRWEATHER, GLADSTONE HENRY oc/Executive Director; b/Nov 30, 1935; h/1701 Primrose Drive, Nashville, TN 37212; ba/Nashville, TN; m/Evelyn; c/Violet; p/Arnold and Mariam Fairweather, Domica, West Indies; sp/William and Louise Blakney, Birmingham, AL; ed/BS, 1960; Masters in Guid Psych, 1964; Masters in Hlth Sers, 1970; pa/Dir of Ambulatory Sers, Meharry Med Col, 1974-79; Proj Dir, Greenburg Neighborhood Hlth Ctr, 1972-73; Paramed Conslt, NY City Hlth & Hosps, 1979; Coor, EYOA, Univ of So CA, 1966-70; Exec Dir, Matthew Walker Hlth Ctr, 1979-; Allied Hlth Assn; Nat Assn of Hlth Sers Execs; CA Assn of Cytotechnol; Am Hosp Assn; NY City Com of Hlth; Nat Com on Cytotechnol; Nat Assn of Neighborhood Hlth Ctrs; APHA; r/Pentecostal; hon/W/W in S & SW.

FAISON, DONNA GRAHAM oc/Teacher; b/Sep 20, 1950; h/Route 2, Box 745, Marion, VA 24354; ba/Marion, VA;

m/Vernon Gordon Jr; c/Olivia Dell, Vernon Gordon 'Tripp' III; p/V M and Claudia L Graham, Salisbury, NC; sp/ V G and Mary Dell Faison Sr, Salisbury, NC; BS, Appalachian St Univ, 1972; pa/Tchr, Corriher-Lipe Jr HS, 1972-76; Tchr, Marion Intermediate, 1976-; Gifted & Talented Tchr, Marion Intermediate, 1981-; NEA; VA Ed Assn; Smyth Co Ed Assn; Phi Delta Kappa, 1979-; ASCD, 1978-80; cp/Embroiders Guild of Smyth Co; Sunday Sch Tchr, 1981-; r/Meth; hon/W/W in S & SW.

FALCONE, LOUIS ALBERT oc/Musician, Composer, Industrial Design Consultant; b/Aug 21, 1951; h/1111 Cooperskill Road, Cherry Hill, NJ 08034; ba/Philadelphia, PA; m/Christina Marie; p/Albert Ernest and Emily Mary Falcone, Cherry Hill, NJ; ed/BS, Drexel Univ, 1974; pa/Interior Display, 1973-75; Estimator, Asst Prod Sup, Graphic Arts, 1976-80; Freelance Musician/Composer, 1976-; Deisgn Course Eval Forms; Nat Ital Am Foun; Am Ital Hist Assn; Am of Ital Descent; AMICI, Ital Studies Ctr, Univ of PA; r/Rom Cath; hon/Composed Song for Anniv of Birthday of Philip Mazzei, Fdg Father; HS Speech & Debate Soc; First Class, BSA.

FALKENBERG, CHARLENE CRUMPTON oc/Aviation Teacher, FAA Test Examiner; b/Feb 24, 1921; h/ 618 South Washington Street, Hobart, IN 46342; ba/Same; m/Walter Sigurd; p/Charlie and Helen Crumpton (dec); sp/Iver and Petra Falkenberg, (dec); ed/ Bus Degree, Massey Bus Col, 1940; Att'd IN Univ; pa/Adm Secy, Sch City of Gary, 1956-68; Adm Secy, Sch City of Hobart, 1968-80; VP, Pilot Ed, NW Aviation, 1980-83; Tchr, Pilot Ed, Cont'g Ed, Purdue Univ, 1972-82; Adult Ed, Pilot Aviation, Hobart Twp Schs, 1964-83; Hobart City Schs, 1982-; Merrillville Commun Schs, 1978-; Gary IN Ed Secs Assn, Pres 1966-68; Sigma Alpha Chi Sorority; Exptl Aircraft Assn; Aircraft Owners & Pilots Assn; Hobart Bus & Profl Wom; Gary Wom Clb; Intl Org of Wom Pilots; The Ninety-Nines; IN Dunes Chapt, North Ctl Sec, Intl Bd of Dirs, 1976; Dir, Secy, VP; hon/Pub'd Author; Powder Puff Derby Air Race; IN Fair Race; Illi-Nines Air Derby; 1st Place Achmt Awd, Chgo Area Chpt; Honored by EAA in 1980, 81, 82, 83; Accident Prev Cnslr, 1965; Winning Cnslr of Yr, 1976.

FALKINGHAM, HARRY HERBERT oc/Retired Marketing Executive; b/Nov 22, 1904; m/Mary Cecil Morris; p/ George Wendell and Jessie Stengel Falkingham (dec); ed/Grad, Normal Commun HS, 1924; Spec Tng, Profl Bus Mgmt, 1957; Spec Tng, Gen Acctg, 1945; mil/AUS, 1942-43, Overseas for 18 Months; pa/Salesman 1928-30, Dist Mgr 1930, Maytag Co; Salesman 1935-37, Sales Mgr 1937-39, Goodhousekeeping Shoppe; Dept Mgr, Bergner Dept Store, 1939-41; Salesman, Tom Smith Pontiac Co, 1941-42; Sales Ofc Mgr 1945, Dist Mgr 1946-50, En Sales Mgr 1950-52, Eureka-Williams Corp; Dist Mgr 1952-54, Mgr of Distbn Devel 1954-58, Gen Electric Co; Reg Mgr, Westinghouse Elect Corp, 1958-61; Pres, Gen Mgr, Climate Control Corp, 1961-70; Christian Sci Min, Armed Sers Pers, 1981-; Chm, Com

Devel Sheltered Living Facility, Christian Scists in KY; Pres, Live Wires, 1979; Mem, Nat Adv Bd, Am Security Coun, 1981; Current Columnist, *News Enterprise*; cp/Sustaining Mem, Republican Nat Com, 1981; Mem, US Senatorial Clb, 1981-82; Mem Repub Pres Task Force, 1981-82; Repub; r/Christian Scist; hon/Several Sales Awds; W/W of S & SW; Marquis W/W.

FALLACI, ORIANO oc/Writer, Journalist; b/Jun 29, 1930; h/c/o Rizzoli Publishers, 712 Fifth Avenue, New York, NY 10019; ba/Same; p/Edoardo Fallaci; Tosca Cantini (dec); ed/Liceo Classico 'Galileo Galilei', Univ of Med; pa/Spec Correspondent for *Europeo* Mag of Italy; Contbr: *NY Times Mag, Look Mag, Life Mag, The Washington Post, The Times of London, Der Stern, La Nouvel Observateur, Politika, Asahi Shinbun, Corricre della Sera*; War Correspondent in Vietnam, Pakistan, Mid E; hon/Pub'd Author; Laurea honoris causae in Lttrs, Columbia Col of Chgo, 1978; 'St Vincent Prize' for Journ; Bahcarella Prize.

FANSLER, KEVIN SPAIN oc/ Research Physicist; h/4044 Wilkinson Road, Havre de Grace, MD 21078; ba/ APG, MD; m/Sherry Rulana; c/Zoya, Kira; p/Alma Ruth Fansler, Weatherford, OK; ed/BS Physics 1960, MS Physics 1964, PhD Applied Sci 1974, Univ of DE; pa/Physicist, Nav Ordnance Lab, 1960-62; Physicist, AUS Chem Res Lab, 1965-67; Res Physicist, AUS Ballistics Res Lab (Current); AIAA, 1974-; AAAS, 1983-; cp/Harford Co Permanent Nom'g Caucus, 1977, 1979; hon/Author, Num Articles Concerning Fluid Flow about Projectiles in & Near Cannon, & Other Articles Concerning Projectiles in Gun Tubes & Electronic Pops in Nuclear Blast; Recip, Spec Act Awd, AUS, 1980; W/W in Frontier Sci & Technol.

FANTAUZZI, LAWRENCE ARNOLD oc/Executive; b/Oct 2, 1947; h/ 190 Heather Lane, Cortland, OH 44410; ba/Cortland, OH; m/Judith Ann Stull; c/Kelly, Wendy, Michael, Jason; p/ Lawrence and Wilma Fantauzzi, Yo, OH; ed/BS in Adm & Mgmt Sci 1970, MS Indust Adm 1970, Carnegie-Mellon Univ; pa/Ednl Res/Asst to Dean, Carnegie Mellon Univ; Corp Planning 1972-74, Asst Controller 1975, Mgr of Financial Anal & Planning 1976, Assocs Corp of N Am; Pres, Prime Info Sys Inc, 1977-; cp/Cortland JCs, Pres 1982, Secy 1981; TCSPR, Pres 1983, VP 1982, Treas 1981; St Fair Bd, Treas 1981, 1982, 1983; Rotary, 1978-79; C of C, 1979-81; Am Fdn of Astrologers, 1982-; hon/Hons Grad of Carnegie-Mellon Univ, 1970; W/W in Fin & Indust.

FARAGHER, THOMAS J oc/Board Chairman; b/May 20, 1941; h/13732 Hughes Lane, Dallas, TX 75240; ba/ Dallas, TX; m/Cristina; c/Robert; p/ Thomas Robert Faragher, Bermuda Dunes, CA; ed/BBA, Univ of WA, 1963; MBA, Stanford Grad Sch of Bus, 1975; mil/Lt Cmdr, Supply Corps, USN, 1963-65; pa/Credit Ofcr, Wells Fargo Bk, 1965-67; Stockbroker, Dean Witter & Co, 1967-70; Stockbroker, Reynolds Securities, 1970-73; VP, TX Commerce Bk-Houston, 1975-79; Chm of the Bd, TX Commerce Bd-Dallas, 1970-; Dir, TACA Inc; Dir, Ctl Bus Dist Assn; Dir, BBB of Metro Dallas; cp/Dir, Theatre Three; VP, Mem Bd of Trustees, Dallas/

Ft Worth Chapt, Leukemia Soc; Bd of Govs, Plaza Ath Clb, Plaza of the Ams; Dallas Rotary Clb; Former Mem, Mayor's Task Force on Downtown Historic Bldgs.

FARAH, BADIE NAIEM oc/University Professor and Consultant; b/Jan 15, 1946; h/37 Foxboro Drive, Rochester, MI 48063; ba/Ypsilanti, MI; p/Naim R and Afifi Farah (dec); ed/BS 1967, MA 1968, Damascus Univ; MS, Wayne St Univ, 1973; MSIE 1976, PhD 1977, OH St Univ; pa/Tchg Asst, Wayne St Univ, 1971-73; Res Assoc, OH St Univ, 1973-77; Sr Sys Anal, Gen Motors Co, 1977-78; Asst Prof, Oakland Univ, 1978-82; Asst Prof Info Sys & Ops Res, En MI Univ, 1982-; Advr to Bd of Dirs, S & G Grocer Co, 1979-81; Vis'g Gen Mgr, 1980-81; Sr Mem, AIIE; Assn for Computing Machinery; Opers Res Soc of Am; Inst of Mgmt Sci; MI Acad of Sci Arts & Lttrs; AAUP; Alpha Pi Mu; Exec Coun, ACM Detroit Metro Chapt, 1983; r/Syrian Orthodox; hon/Profl Pubs; W/W in Frontier Sci & Technol.

FARAH, FUAD SALIM oc/Professor of Medicine; b/Apr 5, 1929; h/113 Victoria Park Drive, Liverpool, NY 13088; ba/Syracuse, NY; m/ Mona-Haddad; c/Richard-Salim, Ronald-Samir, Joyce-Bahia, Ramsay-Sami; p/Salim and Nada Farah (dec); ed/ BA 1950, MD 1954, Am Univ of Beirut; pa/Intern 1954-55, Sr Asst Resident 1955-56, Resident 1956-57, Dept of Med, Am Univ Hosp; Fellow, Dept of Med, Div of Dermatol, Wash Univ Sch of Med & Barnes Hosp, 1957-59; Instr 1959-60, Asst Prof 1960-66, Dept of Med (Dermatol), Am Univ of Beirut; Diplomate, Am Bd of Dermatol Inc, 1965; Assoc Prof, Dept of Med (Dermatol), Am Univ of Beirut, 1966-74; Vis'g Lectr, Dept of Microbiol & Dept of Med (Dermatol), Wash Univ Sch of Med & Barnes Hosp, 1967-68; Dir, WHO Immunol Res & Tng Ctr, Beirut, 1972-76, 1976-; Prof of Med, Am Univ of Beirut, 1974; Vis'g Prof, Inst of Clin Immunol, Inselspital Bern, Univ of Bern, 1974-75; Prof of Med & Chief, Sect of Dermatol, SUNY Upstate Med Ctr, 1976-; The Med Alumni Assn of the Am Univ of Beirut, 1954; Lebanese Order of Phys, 1954; Lebanese Dermatologic Soc, Fdg Mem 1962, Pres 1970-72; Am Acad of Allergy, Corres'g Mem 1965; Intl Soc of Tropical Dermatol, 1966; The Soc of Investigative Dermatol, 1967; Am Assn of Immunologists, 1969; AAAS, 1969; Lebanese Assn for the Advmt of Sci, 1972; Sigma Xi Soc; Pres, Sigma Xi Clb of Am Univ of Beirut, 1971-72; Lebanese Assn of Public Hlth, 1972; The Reticuloendothelial Soc, 1972; Ctl NY Dermatological Soc, 1977; Assn of Profs of Dermatol Inc, 1976; hon/Knight of the Order of Cedars, Lebanon, 1958; Ofcr of the Order of Cedars, Lebanon, 1972; Pubs, "Basic Aspects of Immunol" (in Press), 1981, "Cutaneous Amebiasis" (in Press), 1982, "Cutaneous Leishmaniasis (Oriental Sore)" 1980, "Leishmaniasis in Clin Dermatol" 1978, "Leishmaniasis & Parasitic Diseases", 1984, "Hyperimmunoglobulin M Immunodeficiency (Dysgammaglobulinemia)" 1979, "Protozoal & Helminth Infections" 1979, 1985, "Behcet's Syndrome" 1979, Numerous Others.

FARAH, TAWFIC ELIAS oc/President, Middle East Research Group Inc; b/Aug 12, 1946; h/4379 N Seventh Street, Fresno, CA 93726; ba/Fresno, CA; m/Linda Maxwell; c/Omar Lee, Aliya Jane; p/Mrs Suhail Bathish, Cairo Egypt; sp/Mr Lee Maxwell, Fresno, CA; ed/BA 1971, MA 1971, CA St Univ-Fresno; PhD, Univ of NE, 1975; pa/Pres, Mid E Res Grp Inc,1979-; Assoc Prof of Polit Sci, Univ of CA-LA, Sums 1976, 1978, 1979-80; Asst Prof of Polit Sci & Dir of Polimetrics Lab, Kuwait Univ, 1975-78; Res Fellow, Ctr for Intl & Strategic Affairs, Univ of CA-LA, 1980-81; Sr Res Fellow, Mid E Res Grp Inc, 1975-79; Com Charged w Setting Admissions Policies at Kuwait Univ, 1978; Planning Com for the Grad Sch, Kuwait Univ, 1977; Prog Com, Conf on Info Sys in Kuwait, 1977; Editor, Jour of Arab Affairs; Intl Com for Social Sci Info & Documentation, 1978-; Manuscript Referee, Jour of the Social Sci, 1975-; Manuscript Referee, Jour of Gulf & Arabian Peninsula Studies, 1975-; Official Rep of Kuwait Univ Consortium for Polit & Social Res, Ann Arbor, MI, 1975-; r/Greek Orthodox; hon/Num Profl Pubs; Num Papers Presented at Confs; W/W in W.

FARLEY, BARBARA SUZANNE oc/ Attorney; b/Dec 13, 1949; h/Piedmont, CA; ba/San Francisco, CA; m/Arthur H Ferris; p/Mrs Barbara Ann Farley, Piedmont, CA; ed/BA, Mills Col, 1972; JD, Univ of CA, Hastings Col of the Law, 1976; Tchg Asst, Eng & Psych, Alameda Jr Col, 1971-72; pa/Paralegal, Pillsbury, Madison & Sutro, 1972-73; Law Clk to Justice Mathew O Tobriner, CA Supr Ct, 1975; Assoc, Pillsbury, Madison & Sutro, 1976-78; Assoc, Bronson, Bronson & McKinnon, 1978-80; Assoc, Goldstein & Phillips, 1980-84; Rosen Assoc, Wachtel & Gilbert, 1984-; Arbitrator, US Dist Ct for the No Dist of CA, 1981-; Judge Pro tem, SF Mun Ct, 1983-; CA Bar Assn; ABA, Served as Judge in Nat Moot Ct Competition Finals 1980; Am Trial Lwyrs Assn; SF Trial Lwyrs Assn; SF Lwyrs Com for Better Govt; hon/S'ship & Deans Hons, Mills Col, 1968-72; Mng Editor, Hastings Constitl Law Qtly, 1975-76; Edit S'ship, Hastings Col of the Law, 1975-76; W/W in Am Law.

FARLEY, OWEN ELI JR oc/Minister, History Instructor, Book Store Owner; b/Mar 3, 1935; h/2031 Morningside Drive, Pensacola, FL 32503; ba/Pensacola, FL; m/Clara Moonean; c/Owen Eli III, Deborah Vernice Maulding, Rebecca Mae; p/Owen E (dec) and Vernice T Farley, Florence, AL; sp/Mr and Mrs G G Mulligan, Florence, AL; ed/AB, Univ of N AL, 1956; MA, Univ of W FL, 1974; mil/USN-Active 1956-67, Resv 1967-78; pa/Electronic Warfare Ofcr, Air Traffic Control Ofcr, USN, 1956-67; Min, Ch of Christ of Canoe AL, 1966-80; Evening Registrar & Hist Instr, Pensacola Jr Col, 1967-; Min, Eastgate Ch of Christ, 1981-; Joint Owner, Farley's Old & Rare Books; Am Assn of Col Registrars & Adms Ofcrs, 1971-78; Sacrao & Facrao, 1971-78; Pensacola Hist Soc; Nat Hist Soc; Gulf Coast Hist; cp/Eagle Scout 1954, Explorer Advr 1954-56; Co-man 1966, Coun Explorer Activs Coor 1979, BSA; VP of Sigma Iota Chapt of Phi Alpha Theta, 1971; r/Ch of Christ; hon/ Pub'd Author; USN Air Medal, 1959;

Outstg Ath Ofcr, 1964, NAS Corpus Christi; Viet Nam Cross of Galantry, 1956; Num Navy Awds, 1959-67; Elder, Eastgate Ch of Christ, 1968-.

FARMAN, ALLAN GEORGE oc/ Director of Radiology; b/Jul 26, 1949; h/12517 Farmbrook Drive, Middletown, KY 40243; ba/Louisville, KY; m/Francoise Jeanne; c/Julie Melinda, Wendy Claire; p/Mr and Mrs G Farman, Birmingham, England; sp/M and Mme R Lemaire, Ivry-la-Bataille, France; ed/ BDS, Univ of B'ham, 1971; LDS, Royal Col of Surgs, 1972; PHD. Univ of Stellenbosch, 1977; EdS, Univ of L'ville, 1983; pa/Lectr in Oral Pathol, Univ of Witwatersrand & SAIMR, 1972-74; Assoc Prof of Oral Pathol, Univ of Stellenbosch, 1974-77; Assoc Prof of Oral Med, Univ of Wn Cape & Sr Spec in Radiol, Cape Provincial Adm; Hd of Oral Biol/Oral Pathol, Univ of Riyadh, Saudia Arabia, 1978-79; Assoc Prof, Sch of Dentistry & Grad Sch, Univ of L'ville, 1979-; Vis'g Prof, Univ of TX-San Antonio, 1981-; Intl Assn of Oral Pathols; Electron Microscope Soc of OH River Val; Radiological Soc of N Am; Am Acad of Dental Radiol; Intl Assn of Dento-Maxillofacial Radiol; Am Assn of Dental Schs; Am Acad of Oral Med; KY Consortium on Dental Aux Ed; Phi Kappa Phi; KY Natural Hist Soc; hon/ Num Profl Pubs; Leith Neumann Prize, 1970; Frank Stammers Prize, 1971; Philip Jennens Prize, 1971; Harry Crossley Awds, 1975-76; Royal Soc of S Africa, 1976; Grawemeyer Awd, 1983; W/W in Frontier Sci & Technol.

FARNER, DONALD S oc/Professor of Zoophysiology; b/May 2, 1915; h/ 4533 West Laurel Drive Northeast, Seattle, WA 98105; ba/Seattle, WA; m/ Dorothy C; c/Carla M, Donald C; p/John and Lillian S Farner (dec); ed/BS, Hamline Univ, 1937; MA 1939, PhD 1941, Univ of WI; mil/USNR, Ret'd; pa/ Instr in Zool, Univ of WI, 1941-43; Asst Prof of Zool, Univ of KS, 1946-47; Asst Prof of Zool, Univ of CO, 1947; Assoc Prof of Zoophysiol 1947-52, Prof of Zoophysiol 1952-65, Dean of the Grad Sch 1960-64, WA St Univ; Prof of Zoophysiol 1965-, Chm, Dept of Zool 1966-81, Univ of WA; AAAS; Am Chem Soc; Am Inst of Biol Scis; Am Ornithologists' Union; Am Physiological Soc; Am Soc of Zools; Cooper Ornithological Soc; Deutsche Ornithologische Gesellschaft; Intl Soc for Chronobiol; Ornitologiska Föreningen i Finland; Soc for Endocrinology; Soc for Systematic Zool; Wn Soc of Naturalists; hon/Author, Approximately 250 Articles, Reviews & Books, Mostly Concerning Var Aspects of Avian Biol & Physiol; Guggenheim Fellow, 1958; Sr US Scist, Alexander von Humboldt Stiftung, 1978; Hon DSc, Hamline Univ, 1962; Dist'd Alumnus, Hamline Univ, 1983; Brewster Medal, Am Ornithologists' Union, 1960; Am Men of Sci; W/W in Am; Intl W/W.

FARNSWORTH, SUSAN STEELE HIGGINS oc/Communication Consultant; h/Sep 8, 1949; h/Miami, FL; ba/ Miami, FL; m/Dan Collins; c/Christopher Sayers; p/Walter Sayers (dec); Marian Louise Higgins, Houston, TX; sp/Merton H and Mildred C Farmsworth, Miami, FL; ed/BJourn, 1971; pa/ Coor, McCann Erickson, 1971-72; Editor, The Gtr Houston Tchrs Jour, 1973; Sr Tax Editor, Edit Staff Supvr, Peat,

Marwick Mitchell & Co, 1974-77; Head, Farnsworth & Assoc, 1977-; Nat Assn of Female Execs; r/Epis; hon/Num Profl Pubs; Outstg Advtg Student Awd, Univ of TX, 1971; W/W of Am Wom.

FARQUHAR, BETTY MURPHY oc/ Artist, Poet; b/Jun 17, 1924; h/PO Box 127, Marion, TX 78124; ba/Same; m/ Winfred G; c/Frank, Michael, Cynthia; p/Hans Karl and Emma Edelmann Ritter (dec); ed/Cert'd Adm Asst, Germany, 1942; Secretarial Dipl, Nixon Clay Col, 1950; Student of Art, Mexican-Am Cultural Exch Ctr, San Antonio Art Inst & Under Pvt Tchrs in US & Mexico; pa/Secy, O Kaetzel, Triptis, Germany, 1943-44; Eng Tutor, 1945-46; Secy, Adjutant Gen's Dept, Austin, TX, 1950-52; Translator of Gothic Script for Instns & Indivs; San Antonio Artists Alliance; New Braunfels Art Leag; World Poetry Soc; TX Poetry Soc; TX Fine Arts Assn; Tagore Inst of Creat Writing; Fellow, Intl Acad of Poets; Am Acad of Poets; Accademia Leonardo Da Vinci, Rome; cp/Pres Task Force, Charter Mem 1982-83; German-Texan Heritage Soc; hon/Author, Over 90 Pubs in Anthologies & Mags; Num Paintings in Pvt Collections in US, Europe, Saudi Arabia & India; Pub'd in Gt Contemp Poems 1978, Today's Best Poems 1979, Gt Poems of the Wn World 1980, Our 20th Cent's Greatest Poems 1982, World Treasury of Gt Poems 1980, Today's Greatest Poems 1983, Our World's Best Loved Poems 1984, Album of Intl Poets 1981, Tracings of the Valiant Soul 1978, Visions of the Enchanted Spirit 1979, Dreams of the Heroic Muse 1982, Journeys of the Poet/Prophet 1983, Premier Poets Anthologies 1982, 1984; Appt as Poet Laureate Intl by Dr Stella Woodall, 1979; Elected Fellow of Intl Acad of Poets, 1981-; Hon Appt to Nat Bd of Advrs, Am Biogl Inst; Winner, New Worlds Poetry Contest, 1978, 1982; Prize for Patriotic Poetry, 1978; Poet Laureate of the mo, Accademia Leonardo Da Vinci, Dec 1981; Dipl of Hon of the Intl Gt Prize "The Glory," Rome, from Accademia Leonardo Da Vinci, 1982; Pres Medal of Merit, Pres Reagan, 1982; White House Hon Roll, 1982, 1983; 2 Awds of Merit, World of Poetry, Jan & May, 1984; Dipl of the Golden Palm, Accademia Leonardo Da Vinci, Rome, 1984; Poet Laureate Awd, CSSI & Awd of Recog, Rome, 1981; A Small Collection of Poetry on File at Univ of SF; Poems of Wisdom Contest Winner, 1978; Anthology Soc Winner, 1982; Personalities of the S; Commun Ldrs of Am; Dir of Dist'd Ams; DIB; Book of Hon; Intl Book of Hon; Intl W/W of Intells; W/W in Poetry; World W/W of Wom; Intl Register of Profiles; The Biogl Roll of Hon; Personalities of Am.

FARRELL, THOMAS G oc/Attorney; b/Aug 6, 1931; h/2329 West 231st Street, Torrance, CA 90501; ba/Los Angeles, CA; m/Suzanne Marion; c/ Colleen, Sean; p/Christine Litz, Evans City, PA; sp/Mr and Mrs Stanley Kellogg, Palm Desert, CA; ed/BA, Arts & Lttrs, PA St Univ, 1954; JD, SWn Univ Sch of Law, 1970; Att'd: Duquesne, George Wash Univ, Am Univs; mil/ USNR Ofcr in USN Judge Advocate Gen's Corps, Ret'd; pa/Atty Advr, Ofc of the Staff Judge Advocate, Space Div, LA AF Sta (Current); Adj Prof, Northrop Univ, 1984-85; Adj Prof, Woodbury Univ, 1974-79; Resident Counsel,

The Rand Corp, 1973-75; Asst Counsel, Def Logistics Agy, Def Contract Adm Sers Reg, LA, 1972; St Bar of CA; Irish Am Bar Assn; Nat Contract Mgmt Assn; Phi Alpha Delta; Chi Phi; cp/The Classical Assn; Am Legion; Toastmasters Intl; Downs Syndrome Cong; Assn of Retarded Chd; hon/Pres Downs Syndrome Parent Grp; hon/Pres Achmt Awd, Repub Nat Com, 1982; W/W: in Am Law, in W, in CA.

FARWELL, BYRON EDGAR oc/Author; b/Jun 20, 1921; h/PO Box 81, Hillsboro, VA 22132; ba/Same; m/Ruth; c/Byron, Joyce, Lesley; p/Ruth Saxby, Phoenix, AZ; mil/Capt, AUS, WW II & Korea; pa/Reg Dir, Gt Books Foun; Writer, Mgr of Public Relats on W Coast, Mgr of Commun Relats, Chrysler Corp; Dir of Public Relats, VP of Adm, Chrysler Intl, SA; Former Mayor of Hillsboro, VA; Royal Soc of Lit; Royal Geog Soc; hon/Author of Books, *The Man Who Presumed: A Biog of Henry M Stanley* 1957, *Burton: A Biog of Sir Richard Francis Burton* 1963, *Prisoners of the Mahdi* 1967, *Queen Victoria's Little Wars* 1972, *The Gt Anglo-Boer War* 1976, *For Queen & Country or Mr Kipling's Army* 1981, *The Gurkhas* 1984; Author of Articles, "Then the Gurkhas Came Ashore" 1982, "England's Beloved Gurkhas" 1982, "How the US Marines Captured the Falklands" 1982, "Stereotypes" 1982, "Gt Art, Rotten Message" 1982, "If the IRS Calls, Send Your Wife" 1982, "Why Not Bad-Mouth Bureaucrats?" 1982; Author of Num Other Articles; Author of Num Reviews; Creator of Chd's Book, *Let's Take a Trip*, 1954; Fellow, Royal Soc of Lit; Fellow, Royal Geog Soc; W/W in S; The Authors & Writers W/W.

FASSOULIS, SATIRIS GALAHAD oc/Communications Company Executive; b/Aug 19, 1922; h/20 Waterside Plaza, New York, NY 10010; ba/New York, NY; p/Peter George and Anastasia P Fassoulis (dec); ed/Att'd Syracuse Univ & CT St Col; mil/USAAF, 1941-45, First Lt; pa/VP 1945-49, Pres 1949-75, Commerce Intl Corp; Chm, Global Def Prods Inc & Global Communs Co, 1976-; Dir, Comml Exports Ltd & CIC Intl Ltd; Order of Ahepa; Am Def Preparedness Assn; US Congl Adv Bd; US Nav Inst; cp/NY C of C; NY Ath Clb; r/Epis; hon/Pres Cit, 1943; Air Medal w 3 OLC, 1943-45; Purple Heart, 1943; W/W in E.

FAULKNER, JAMES MURRY oc/Construction, Farmer, Writer; b/Jul 18, 1923; h/College Hill Road, Oxford, MS 38655; ba/Same; m/Nancy Watson; c/James Murry Jr, Thomas Wesley, Margaret Lucille; p/John Faulkner (dec); sp/Tom Watson (dec); ed/BA, Univ of MS, 1947; mil/USMC, Lt Col; Fighter Pilot in WW II & Korea; pa/Contractor-Engr; Writer and Lectr; r/Epis; hon/Pub'd Author; Dist'd Flying Cross; Air Medal.

FAVARO, MARY KAYE oc/Physician and Author; b/Sep 30, 1934; h/1866 Capri Drive, Charleston, SC 29407; ba/Charleston Heights, SC; m/B Philip; c/Justin Peter, Gina Sue; p/Harold and Genevieve Asperheim (dec); ed/BS Pharm, Univ of WI, 1956; MS Pharm, St Louis Col of Pharm, 1965; MD, Univ of WI, 1969; pa/Pvt Pract, Fam Pract & Pediatrics, 1974-; AMA; SC Med Assn; Fellow of Am Acad of Pediatrics; hon/Pubs, *The Pharmacologic Basis of Patient Care*,

W B Saunders, 4th Edition, 1981; *Pharm, An Introductory Text*, W B Saunders, 5th Edition, 1981; W/W in S & SW, of Am Wom; Personalities of the S; Intl W/W of Wom.

FAWCETT, MRS ROSCOE KENT (MARIE ANN FORMANEK) oc/Homemaker, Civic Leader, Philanthropist; b/Mar 6, 1914; h/North St & Hawkwood Lane, Greenwich, CT 06830; m/Roscoe Kent; c/Roscoe Kent Jr, Peter Formanek, Roger Knowlton II, Stephen Hart; p/Peter Paul and Mary Ann Stepanek Formanek (dec); ed/Hon PhD; Hamilton St Univ 1974, CO St Christian Col 1973; Att'd Harvard Univ Alumni Col, 1976, 1977, 1978, 1979, 1980, 1981, 1982, 1983, Rec'd 25 Certs; cp/Bd of Dirs: Merry Go Round for Aged, Merry Go Round Mews for Elderly, Greenwich Philharmonia, MS Soc, Cerebral Palsy, Nathaniel Witherell Aux; Greenwich Hosp; Grand Jury Duty, 1983-85; Supr Ct Jury Duty, 28 Wks, 1956-66; Weekend Vol Chm, 2 Yrs; Ser Cit, Var Coms, Woms Clb of Greenwich; Chm, Every Dr: ARC, Commun Chest, Mtl Hlth, Leukemia, Muscular Dystrophy; Wkr w Mtly Retarded Chd at Milbank Sch; Supr Ct Jury Duty, 24 Wks; Danced in Every Benefit in Mpls Since Age 15; Participating Mem, Huxley Inst for Biosocial Res; York Clb, NY; r/Cath; hon/Wom of Yr, Soroptimist Clb, 1967; Commun Ser Awd, U Cerebral Palsy Assn, Fairfield Co Inc, 1972; Marquis Biogl Lib Soc Adv Mem; Intl Biogl Assn; Ref Source Lib Human Resources, Am Bicent Res Inst; CT St Dept Hlth Cits, 1974, 1975; Hon Soc Am; Polit Sci Cert Awd, Harvard Univ, 1976; IPA; Intl W/W of Commun Ser Awd for Dist'd Ser To Commun; Gt Brit's Coronation Edition Royal Blue Book; 2,000 Wom of Achmt; W/W: in E, of Am Wom, of CT, of Am, of US; World W/W of Wom; Nat Social Dir; DIB; Nat Register of Prom Ams & Intl Notables; Marquis W/W; Intl Register of Profiles.

FEATHERSTONE, JOHN DOUGLAS B oc/Scientist, Department Chairman; b/Apr 26, 1944; h/2119 Clinton Avenue South, Rochester, NY 14618; ba/Rochester, NY; m/Patricia Helen; c/Mychelle Kathryn, Mark Simon; p/Alfred Douglas and Yvonne Featherstone, Wanganui, New Zealand; ed/BS Chem & Math, 1965; MS Phy Chem, 1975; PhD Chem, 1977; pa/QC Chem, Unilever, 1964-67; Tech Mgr, Chem Industs, 1967-72; Prodn Mgr, Quinoderm Pcom, 1972-74; Lectr, Pharm Chem & MRC Sr Res Fellow, 1977-80; Sr Res Assoc, Eastman Dental Ctr, 1980-84; Assoc Prof, Dental Res, 1981-84; Chm, Dept of Oral Biol, Eastman Dental Ctr, 1983-; Assoc, New Zealand Inst of Chem, 1967-77; Fellow, New Zealand Inst of Chem, 1978-; cp/Scout Ldr (Scout Assn of New Zealand) & Asst Nat Venturer Commr, 1963-71; New Zealand Outdoor Tng Adv Bd, 1978-80; New Zealand Search & Rescue Team; hon/Author, 51 Sci Articles & Book Chapts on Phy Chem & Dental Sci; Intl Assn for Dental Res Prizes: 1976 Colgate Travel Awd (New Zealand), 1976 Res Prize (Australia), Edward Hattan Awd 1977 (Copenhagen); Royal Soc of New Zealand Hamilton Awd, 1979; W/W in E.

FEDDERS, JOHN MICHAEL oc/

Division Director; b/Oct 21, 1941; h/4100 Massachusetts Avenue, Northwest, Apartment 306, Washington, DC 20016; ba/Washington, DC; c/Luke D, Mark A, Matthew C, John Michael (dec), Andrew M, Peter J; p/Mr and Mrs A H Fedders, Covington, KY; ed/BA, Jour, Marquette Univ, 1963; LLB, Cath Univ of Am, 1966; pa/Assoc, Firm of Cadwalader, Wickersham & Taft, NYC, 1966-71; Exec VP, Gulf Life Holding Co (Now Gulf U Corp), Dallas, 1971-73; Employed w Firm 1973-81, Ptnr 1975-81, Arnold & Porter, DC; Dir, Div of Enforcement, SEC, 1981-; ABA, Govt Rep, Coun Sect Litigation 1981-; Assn Bar, City of NY; DC Bar; Sigma Delta Chi; Phi Alpha Delta; cp/Repub; hon/Frequent Lectr & Writer on Topics Involving Corporate, Securities & Fin; Recip, Ser Awd, Marquette Univ, 1977; Achmt Awd, Cath Univ of Am Alumni Assn, 1982; Chm's Awd for Excell, SEC, 1982.

FEDERICO, PAT-ANTHONY oc/Research Psychologist; b/Mar 4, 1942; h/4493 Pescadero Avenue, San Diego, CA 92107; ba/San Diego, CA; m/Suzanne Marie Boudreau; p/Pasquale Federico (dec); Vincenna Caramanna (dec); ed/BA, cum laude, Univ of St Thomas, 1965; MS 1967, PhD 1969, Tulane Univ; mil/USAF 1969-72, Capt; pa/Res Psychol, AF Human Resources Lab, 1969-72; Honorarium Fac, Univ of CO Denver, 1969-71; Lectr, Dept of Psych, San Diego St Univ, 1972-73, 1977; Sr Res Psychol, Navy Pers Res & Devel Ctr, 1972-; Exec Dir, Human Factors Soc, San Diego Chapt, 1982-85; Pres, HFSSDC, 1981-82; Secy-Treas, HFSSDC, 1980-81; Adv Editor, *Jour Ednl Psychol*, 1984-; Mem, Intl Soc for Study of Indiv Differences; Am Ednl Res Assn; Cognitive Sci Soc; Psychonomic Soc; hon/Sr Author, *MIS & Orgnl Behavior*, 1980; Co-Editor, *Aptitude, Lrng, & Instrn: Volume 1, Cognitive Process Anal of Aptitude, Volume 2 & Cognitive Process Anal of Lrng & Prob Solving* 1980; Author, Over 70 Profl Pubs; Nat Def Act (Title IV) Pre-Doct Fellow, 1966-69; NSF Postdoct Pres Intern in Sci & Engrg, 1972-73; W/W: in W, in CA; Men of Achmt.

FEIGELSON, ERIC D oc/Astrophysicist; b/Apr 23, 1953; h/500 Toftrees Avenue, State College, PA 16803; ba/University Park, PA; p/Philip and Muriel Feigelson; ed/BA, Haverford Col, 1975; MS 1978, PhD 1980, Harvard Univ; pa/Staff Res Scist, MIT, 1980-82; Asst Prof, PA St Univ, 1982-; Am Astronom Soc, 1977-; Nat Radio Astronomy Observatory User's Com, 1984-; Fdn of Am Scists; Phi Beta Kappa; hon/Author, Num Articles in Profl Astrophy Jours & Symposia; X-ray & Radio Astronom Findings Appear in Var Textbooks & Mass Media Pubs; Pres Yg Investigator Awd, NSF, 1984-; NASA Grp Achmt Awd 1980, John Parker F'ship 1978; W/W in Sci Frontiers.

FEINMAN, JEFFREY PAUL oc/Executive; b/Nov 21, 1943; h/870 United Nations Plaza, New York, NY 10017; ba/200 Madison Avenue, New York, NY 10016; p/Dr Max L and Sylvia Feinman, New York, NY; ed/BS, NY Univ, 1965; MBA, Univ of RI, 1968; pa/Exec VP, Blair Corp, 1968-73; Pres, Ventura Assocs Inc, 1973-; cp/Dir, Goddard-Riverside Commun Ctr; r/Jewish; hon/

Pubs, *Catalog of Foods*, Doubleday 1971, *Catalog of Kits*, Morrow 1968, *Money Book of List*, Doubleday 1972.

FEINSOD, LAWRENCE S oc/Superintendent of Schools; b/Aug 3, 1946; h/1 Eliot Place, Short Hills, NJ 07078; ba/Madison, NJ; m/Sharon Rous; c/Rebecca Leigh, Bess Rous; p/Milton and Dorothy Feinsod, Maplewood, NJ; ed/BA in Spec Ed, 1968; MA in the Ed of the Emotionally Disturbed & Socially Maladjusted, 1970; Profl Dipl in Ednl Adm, 1973; EdD, 1980; pa/Tchr, McManus Jr HS, 1968-72; Asst HS Prin, Holmdel HS, 1972-75; Adm Prin 1975-76, Supt of Schs 1976-, Mt Arlington Public Sch Dist; Am Assn of Sch Adm; NJ Assn of Sch Adm; Rutgers Univ Alumni Assn; Fordham Univ Alumni Assn; NJ Sch Masters Clb; Kean Col Alumni Assn; Morris Co Admrs Assn; cp/Trustee, Mt Arlington Public Lib, 1975-84; Bd of Dirs, Occupl Ctr of Union Co/Union Co Rehab Inst, 1972-75; Doct Dissertation, "An Anal of the Devel of Orgnl Ideologies: The Behavioral Implications for the Public Sch Ldr (1980 US Copyright); hon/Hon'd by Mayor & Coun for Dedication to Chd of Mt Arlington, 1980; Pres, Sigma Theta Chi Alumni Assn, 1968-70; Phi Delta Kappa, Fordham Univ; Kappa Delta Pi, Fordham Univ, 1982; Devel'd Paperwk Control Model which Rec'd St & Nat Recog.

FEINSTEIN, JERALD LEE oc/Executive, Consultant; b/Jun 22, 1943; h/6826 Dean Drive, McLean, VA 22101; ba/Same; m/Dorothy Ellen; c/Andrew Morrison, Matthew Duane, Jennifer Squire; p/Seymore and Lenore Feinstein, Huntington, NY; ed/BS, Physics, Univ of OK, 1965; MS, Engrg, NJ Inst of Technol, 1970; pa/Sci Advr, AF; Sr Res Engr, Stanford Res Inst; Biotechnol Regulation, US Envir Protection Agy; Pres, Mgmt Analytic Support Inc; Indep Conslt, Software Devel; Mbrship Chm, IEEE, 1971-73; cp/Capital Area Bur of Rehab, Bd of Dirs 1980-; McLean Soccer Assn, Bd of Dirs 1978; hon/Author, "Artificial Intell Techniques for Intell Anal" & Many Classified Pubs on Anti-Ballistic Missile Def; Outstg Res Awd, Dept of Def.

FEIST, MARIAN JEAN MOCK oc/Retired Director of Nutrition; h/2331 Deblin Drive, Cincinnati, OH 45239; ba/Cincinnati, OH; m/Arthur W; p/Harlan Oscar and Bridget Matilda Hagan Mock (dec); ed/BS in Foods & Nutrition, cum laude, Seton Hill Col, 1942; Dietetic Internship, Good Samaritan Hosp, Cinc, 1942-43; Postgrad Courses in Sch of Ed, Foods & Nutrition, Univ of Cinc; Reg'd, Am Dietetic Assn, 1969-; pa/Dietitian in Adm, Therapeutic & Tchg, Allegheny Gen Hosp, 1943-48; Asst Adm Dietitian, Conemaugh Val Meml Hosp, 1948; Purchasing Dietitian, Asst Dir, Acting Dir, Dir of Nutrition Dept 1969-83, Good Samaritan Hosp; Gtr Cinc Assn, Treas (2 Terms), Adm Sect Chm (2 Terms), Legis & Consultation (2 Terms), Recruitment & Career Guid (2 Terms), Rep for the Sisters of Charity (2 Terms), Food Parade (1 Term), Chm of Computer Action Com (2 Terms), Pres-Elect (1 Term), Pres 1971-72, Pres's Adv Com (3 Terms), CoChm of Nat Nutrition Wk (1 Term), Participating Mem in Spkrs Bur & Conslt Ser; Pgh Dietetic Assn, Recording Secy (1 Term), Chm of Therapeutic Sect (1

Term); OH Dietetic Assn, Adm Sect Com (1 Term), CoChm of Exhibs Annual Conv 1976, Panel Participator Subject "Food Purchasing" at OH Dietetic Wkshop 1951, Lectr for Inst for Dietitians in Nsg Homes, Univ of Dayton 1967; Presided Over Session at OH Hosp Assn-Hosp Instnl & Ednl Food Ser Soc, 1971, 1982; Co-Authored Paper, "Food Freezers," 1956; Tchr for Day Care Cooks in Foods & Nutrition Purchasing & Menu Planning, for 3 Yrs; Paper Presented at Seminar, "Devel of a Computerized Food Ser Sys & the Dietitian" 1967; Lectr, Univ of Cinc Evening Col, "Menu Planning & Purchasing"; Lectr at Xavier Univ to Hosp Adm Students, "Planned Overs Not Left Overs," 1964; Am Dietetic Assn, Life Mem; Am Diabetic Assn; Cinc Restaurant Assn; OH Restaurant Assn; Nat Restaurant Assn; Nutrition Today Soc, Charter Mem; Am Soc for Hosp Food Ser Admrs; Soc for Advmt of Mgmt, Assoc Mem; Soc for Food Ser Sys; Am Dietetic Assn Pract Grp of Mems w Mgmt Responsibilities in Hlth Care Delivery Sys; IPA, 1980, 1981, 1982; r/Rom Cath; hon/Profl Pubs & Lectures; DAR, 1938; Sigma Kappa Pi, 1942; GSH Employee Awds, 1953, 1958, 1963, 1968, 1973, 1978, 1983; Recipe Submitted & Accepted for Cookbook, *Treasured Recipes*, 1982; W/W in Am Cols & Univs; The World W/W of Wom; Intl W/W of Intells; Personalities of the W & MW; Personalities of Am; DIB; Intl Book of Hon; 2,000 Notable Ams; Dic of Intl Contemp Achmt; Intl Book of Hon.

FELDBERG, MEYER oc/Dean and Professor of Business School; b/Mar 17, 1942; h/639 Pine Street, New Orleans, LA 70118; ba/New Orleans, LA; m/Barbara Erlick; c/Lewis, Ilana; ed/BA, Univ of Witwatersrand, 1962; MBA, Columbia Univ, 1965; PhD, Univ of Cape Town; pa/Dean & Prof of Mgmt, Univ of Cape Town, 1972-79; Assoc Dean & Dir of Exec Ed, NWn Univ, 1979-81; Dean & Prof of Mgmt, Tulane Univ, 1981-; Bd of Govs, Isidore Newman Sch; Reg Com, Inst of Intl Ed; cp/Intl House; Plimsoll Clb; hon/Pubs, "Interviews w Five Prominent Ams on US Investment in S Africa" 1978, "US Opposition to Am Bus Involvement in S Africa" 1976, "Bus Profits & Social Responsibility" 1975, Num Other Articles, *Orgnl Behaviour: Text & Cases* 1981, *Milton Friedman in S Africa* 1976, *Am Univs: Divestment of Stock in US Corporations w S African Affils* 1978; Num Papers, Lectures & Presentations; Univ Sportsman of the Yr, 1960; JCs Four Outstg Yg Men of the Yr Awd, 1972; Represented S Africa in Intl Swimming Competition, 1959; W/W: in Am, of the World; Intl W/W in Ed.

FELDER, DAVID C oc/Composer/Conductor/Professor; b/Nov 27, 1953; h/5993 East PCH, Number 8, Long Beach, CA 90840; ba/Long Bch, CA; p/Warren Jay and Nellie D Felder, Willoughby, OH; ed/BM, MMus, Miami Univ, 1975, 1977; PhD, Univ CA-San Diego, 1983; Cleve Inst Music; Yale Univ Sch Music; CA Arts; pa/Instr, Cleve Inst Music, 1978-79; Lectr, Cal St Univ, 1982-; BMI; cp/Composer's Forum; ASUC; Cleve Composer's Guild; Audio Engrg Soc; Col Music Soc; Am Music Ctr; hon/Author of Num

Pubs; NEA Composer's F'ships, 1978, 1981; OH Arts Coun Grant, 1978; Composer-in-Residence, Am Dance Fest, 1982; W/W Among Students in Am Univs.

FELDER, MONTA SUSAN McCLELLAND oc/Dentist, Dental School Assistant, Professor, Researcher; b/Nov 3, 1939; h/4521 St Mary Street, Metairie, LA 70006; ba/Kenner, LA; m/Ralph Francis; c/Loretta Lou, Christi Cherie, David Oather; p/Oather and Etta E McElrath McClelland (dec); ed/BS in Chem, magna cum laude, Ouachita Univ, 1962; DDS, LA St Univ Sch of Dentistry, 1976; pa/Secy, Little Rock Public Sch, 1957-58; Secy, Pk Hill Bapt Ch, 1958-59; Lab Wk for Gulf Oil Corp, Petrochems Div, 1963-66, 1966-67; Chem, Gulf S Res Inst, 1969-72; Student Rschr, LA St Univ Sch of Dentistry, 1975; Instr, Biomats Dept, LA St Univ Sch of Dentistry, 1976-81; Clin Asst Prof (gratis), Biomats Dept, LA St Univ Sch of Dentistry, 1981-; Pvt Pract in Dentistry, 1976-; NO Dental Assn Com Mem for Sci Activs, 1977, 1978; NO Dental Assn Del to LA Dental Assn, 1980; Hd, Local Arrangements Com, Am Assn of Wom Dentists Annual Meeting of the Am Dental Assn Conv, 1980; Secy-Treas 1981-82, 1982-83, Pres-Elect 1983-84, Pres 1984-85, LA St Univ Sch of Dentistry Alumni Org; hon/Pubs, "A Thermochem Invest of Cotton Flame Retardancy" 1970, "An Eval of Methylcellulose as a Vehicle for Topical Anesthetics" 1977, "Rubber Base Impression Mats: Stress-Relaxation Phenomena" 1976, "A Model Culture Sys w Human Gingival Fibroblasts for Evaluating the Cytotoxicity of Dental Mats"; Alpha Chi Nat Hon Soc; Nat Biol Hon Soc, Ouachita Univ; Nat Chem Hon Soc, Ouachita Univ; Iota Sigma Pi, Nat Hon Wom's Chem Soc; Student Rep of LA St Univ Sch of Dentistry to Annual Meeting of IADR in Miami Bch, 1976; Student Sr Res Awd, Local Chapt of AADR, LA St Univ Sch of Dentistry, 1976; Del for NO Dental Assn to LA Dental Assn, 1980, 1981, 1982; F'ship in Acad of Gen Dentistry, Boston, 1982; Personalities of Am.

FELDMAR, GABRIEL G oc/Assistant Chief of Staff, Editor, Adjunct Instructor; b/Apr 14, 1947; h/37 Eden Lane, Levittown, NY 11756; ba/Queens Village, NY; m/Suzanne; c/Monique; p/Tibor Feldmar, Forest Hills, NY; ed/BA, Queens Col, 1969; MA, Psych, Hunter Col, 1974; PhD, Psych, Hofstra Univ, 1983; pa/Asst Chief of Staff, NY St Ofc of Mtl Hlth & Chm of the Instnl Review Bd, Creedmoor Psychi Ctr, 1983-; Exec Coor of the Depts of Neuroscis & Spec Clin Studies 1980-82, Dir of Dept of Clin Res 1979-80, Asst Dir of the Dept of Res & Eval 1977-79, NY St Ofc of Mtl Hlth, Creedmoor Psychi Ctr; Clin & Res Psychometrist, Long Isl Jewish-Hillside Med Ctr, Hillside Psychi Div, 1974-77; NY St Assn for Retarded Chd, 1973-74; Clin & Res Neuropsychol 1980-, Clin Admr 1980-81, Bio-Behavioral Psychi, PC; Res Asst, NY St Inst for Basic Res in Mtl Retard, 1974-75; Res Asst, Riverside Res Inst, Columbia Univ, 1973-74; Clin Res Supvr in the MA Prog in Applied Psych, Adelphi Univ, 1982-; Instr, Dept of Med Ed, Creedmoor Psychi Ctr, 1977-; Instr of Clin Neuropsych, Long Isl

Jewish-Hillside Med Ctr, 1974-77; Adj Fac Mem in Psych Dept, Molloy Col, Rockville Ctr, 1982-; Adj Fac Mem in Psych Dept, NY Inst of Technol, 1982-; Adj Fac Mem in Psych Dept, St John's Univ, 1980-; Clin Adj Fac Mem in Psych Dept & Clin Res Internship Prog Supvr, C W Post Ctr of Long Isl Univ, 1980-; Adj Fac Mem in Psych Dept, St Francis Col, 1979; Exec Editor, "Symmetry," 1981-; Exec & Fdg Editor, The Jour of Urban Psychi, 1979-; Pres, Soc for Obsessive Compulsive Disorders, 1981-83; Am Psychol Assn; En Psychol Assn; Intl Neuropsychol Soc; r/Jewish; hon/Pubs, "Psychol Testing: A Hist Background" 1982, "Involuntary Commitment & the Role of Psychi" 1982, "Psychi & Neuropsychol Implications of Dose Reduction & Discontinuation of Antipsychotic Medication" 1981, "Prosopo-Affective Agnosia & Computerized Tomography Findings in Patients w Cerebral Disorder" 1980, Num Others; Num Presentations, Prog Evals & Res Studies; W/W in E.

FELTS, WILLIAM ROBERT JR oc/ Professor of Medicine; b/Apr 24, 1923; h/4827 North 27th Place, Arlington, VA 22207; ba/Washington, DC; c/William R III, Thomas W, Samuel C, Melissa J; ed/ BS, 1945; MD, 1946; mil/AUS; pa/Instr to Prof of Med, The George Wash Univ Sch of Med, 1956-; Am Soc of Internal Med, Bd of Trustees 1966-78, Pres 1976-77; Arthritis Foun, DC Chapt, Chair of Med Adv Com 1963-, VP 1983-; Control Data Corp, Mem of Profl Adv Bd 1976-83; DHHS, Nat Comm on Arthritis & Related Musculoskeletal Diseases 1975-76; Nat Arthritis Adv Bd, 1977-84; Nat Com on Vital & Hlth Stats, 1984-; Inst of Med of the Nat Acad of Scis, 1978-; Rheumatism Soc of DC, Pres 1963-64; Nat Capital Med Foun, Pres 1981-82; So Med Assn, Chm of Sect on Med 1980-81; Symp on Computer Applications in Med Care, Pres 1983-84; WHO, Temp Advr in Rheumatology, 1982, 1984; AMA, Chm CPT-4 Edit Adv Panel 1980-; Coun on Legis, 1981-, VChm 1984-; Mem of Exec Com 1983-; Am Rheumatism Assn; Others; hon/Num Pubs Concerning Internal Med, Rheumatology & Medl Socioec; W/W: in Am, in E, in Hlth Care, in VA, in World, in Frontier Sci & Technol, in S & SW, in World of Med, in Wash; Am Men of Sci; Commun Ldrs & Noteworthy Ams; Men of Achmt.

FENG, LILLIAN WAN-MING LEI oc/Assistant Administrator of Long Term Care Facility; b/May 5, 1923; h/ 2459-10th Avenue, Honolulu, HI 96816; ba/Honolulu, HI; m/Ping Tien; c/Paul CP, Howard CH, Lucy CH Feng Ho, May CM Feng Lee; p/Chin-Chang and Chen Shi Lei; sp/Fu-Jen Feng; ed/ BS 1978, MA 1979, Ctl MI Univ; Turner Nsg Sch of Hackket Med Ctr, 1946; pa/ Activ Coor Conslt, Asst Admr, Palolo, 1966-67; Hd Nurse, Am Nav Res, Taiwan Chinese Home, 1968-; Nsg Supvr & Instr 1952-66, Hd Nurse 1950-52, Taiwan TB Control Ctr; Hd Nurse & Instr, Am Presb Hosp, 1947-50; Asst Hd Nurse & Instr, Hackket Med Sch, 1946-47; Am Nurses Assn; HI Nurses Assn; cp/Nat Assn Activ Profls; Am Col Nsg Home Admrs; HI Pacific Gerontological Assn; Repub Pres Task Force; hon/Recog of 14 Yrs as Nsg Supvr at Taipet TB Control Ctr,

1965; W/W of Wom in Am.

FERBER, ROBERT R oc/Solar Research Project Manager; b/Jun 11, 1935; h/5314 Alta Canyada Road, La Canada, CA 91011; ba/Pasadena, CA; m/Eileen M; c/Robert Jr, Lynne; p/ Elizabeth Ferber, Alhambra, CA; ed/ BSEE, Univ of Pgh, 1958; MSEE 1966, PhD in Elect Engrg (Semiconductor Physics) 1967, Carnegie-Mellon Univ; pa/Mgr, Engrg Dept, WRS Motion Picture Lab, 1954-58; Res Engr, Westinghouse Res Labs, 1958-65; Mgr, Nuclear Effects Anal, Westinghouse Elect, 1967-71; Mgr, Adv'd Energy Sys Studies, Westinghouse AST, 1971-77; Mgr, Photovoltaic Mats & Collector R&D, PV Lead Ctr, Jet Propulsion Lab, 1977-; Dpty Tech Prog Chm, Ninth World Energy Conf, 1972-75; Sr Mem, IEEE; ISES; cp/Mem, Sch Bd, Franklin Reg Sch Dist, 1975-77; r/Luth; hon/ Author, Over 70 Tech Pubs in Energy & Nuclear Effects & Related Areas; Editor of 3 Book Sets; NDEA F'ship, 1966; Buhl Foun F'ship, 1965; W/W in CA; Am Men & Wom of Sci.

FERGUS, PATRICIA M oc/Retired Educator, Writer; b/Oct 26, 1918; h/510 Groveland Avenue, Minneapolis, MN 55403; p/Golden M and Mary A Fergus (dec); ed/BS 1939, MA 1941, PhD 1960, Univ of MN; pa/Assoc Dean of Col & Prof of Eng & Writing, Mt St Mary's Col, 1979-81; Dir, Writing Sems, Mack Truck Co, 1979-80; Asst Prof of Eng 1972-79, Dir of Writing Ctr 1975-77, Coor of Writing Conf 1975, Instr & Lectr in Eng 1964-72, Univ of MN; Adm Positions, US Govt, 1943-59; NCTE, Reg Judge 1974, 1976, 1977, St Coor of Awds in Writing Prog 1977-79; MN Coun Tchrs of Eng, Secy of Legis Com 1973-79, Chp of Careers & Job Opports Prog 1977-79, Spec Task Force on Tchr Licensure, St Dept of Ed Liaison Com 1978-79; Past Pres, Epsilon Chapt, Pi Lambda Theta; AAUW; AAUP; Reviewer for Pub'g Cos; Free-Lance Editor & Writer; Mgmt Team, Eitel Hosp Gift Shop; Bd of Dirs, 510 Groveland Assocs; r/St Olaf Cath Ch Choir, Mpls; hon/Author, Spelling Improvement, 4th Edition, McGraw-Hill Book Co, 1983; Articles, Reviews & Poetry in MN Eng Jour, Foun News, Downtown Cath Voice, Mountaineer Briefing, The Mpls Muse; Twin Cities Student Assem Awd for Outstg Contbns, 1975; Ednl Devel Grant, 1975; Horace T Morse-Amoco Foun Awd for Outstg Contbns to Undergrad Ed, 1976; Wm Randolph Hearst Grant at Mt St Mary's Col, 1980; W/W of Am Wom; World W/W of Wom; Personalities of E; DIB; Dir of Dist'd Ams; Others.

FERGUSON, ELIZABETH ADELE oc/Dance Educator, University Administrator, Choreographer; b/Jun 10, 1928; h/11628 Colmar Street, Dallas, TX 75218; ba/Dallas, TX; m/Joe Durwood; c/Susan Adele Zachary, Joann Elizabeth Browning; p/Fred Dillahunty and Nel Ryan Stewart; ed/BBA, N TX St Univ, 1949; MFA, So Meth Univ, 1967; pa/Assoc Chp Dance 1984-, Acting Chm of Dance 1982-84, Dir of Grad Dance 1979-82, Dir of Dance Preparatory 1969-78, Fac Position 1968-, Asst Prof 1972, Assoc Prof 1979, So Meth Univ; Am Dance Guild; Dance Hist Scholars; Coun of Dance Admrs; Cong on Res in Dance; Nat Assn of Schs of Dance, Ethics Com; AAUP; Dallas

Dance Coun, Bd Mem; Arts Magnet HS, Adv Bd Mem, 1984-; Profl Choreographer, 1964-; hon/Choreographer for So Meth Univ Dance Concerts, Theatre Three, Dallas Jr Leag; Co-Dir, Choreographer for Liberty Ranch!, Am Premier at So Meth Univ Bob Hope Theatre 1973, & Kennedy Ctr (Wash, DC) 1974; Outstg Prof Awd, 1977; Personalities of S; W/W of Am Wom.

FERNANDEZ, ERIC oc/Physician; h/ 18135 Northwest 66th Court, Miami, FL 33015; ba/Hialeah, FL; c/Katrina Lorenne, Candice Ann, Lorene Carin; p/Dr and Mrs A C Fernandez-Brito, Miami Lakes, FL; ed/BS, Univ of MD, 1965; MD, Univ of Salamanca, Spain, 1972; Internship & Residency, Univ of Miami Affil'd Hosps; pa/Clin Asst Prof of Med, Univ of Miami Sch of Med, 1978-; Chief of Med at Palm Sprgs Gen Hosp & Chief of Med at Palmetto Gen Hosp, 1981-; Police Surg, 1980-; Dade Co & FL Med Assns; Am Heart Assn; Am Soc of Internal Med; Am Col of Phys; ARC; Am Law Enforcement Ofcrs Assn; r/Christian; hon/Pub, "Acetaminophen Toxicity," in N Eng Jour of Med; AMA Phys Recog Awd, 1981; Var Running Awds; Grand Winner of Nat Asthma Ctr Bike-a-thon, 1980; W/ W: in S & SW, in the World of Intells, in FL; Personalities of the S; Dir of Dist'd Ams.

FERRARO, GERALDINE ANNE oc/ Member of Congress; b/Aug 26, 1935; h/22 Deepdene Road, Forest Hills, NY 11375; ba/Forest Hills, NY; m/John A Zaccaro; c/Donna, John Jr, Laura; p/ Antonetta Ferraro; ed/BA, Marymount Col, 1956; JD, Fordham Law Sch, 1960; pa/Pvt Pract in Law, 1962-72; Asst Dist Atty for Queens Co, 1974-78; Elected to US Ho of Reps, 1978-84; Tchr, NYC Public Sch Sys, 1956-60; Queens Co Bar Assn; Queens Co Wom's Bar Assn, Pres for Two Terms; Chair, 1984 Dem Platform Com; Cath Lwyrs Guild; Columbia Lwyrs Assn; r/Rom Cath; hon/Pubs, "Who Will Fight for the Worth of Wom's Wk" in Vital Speeches Nov 1982, Preface to A Wom's Guide to Credit by Elizabeth Block (Grosset & Dunlap) 1982; 1984, VP Cand, Dem Party; Nat Mother's Day Com, Mother of the Yr, 1982; DHL, Marymount Manhattan Col, 1982; W/W: of Am Wom, in Am Polits; World W/W of Wom.

FERREIRA, BEATRIZ VALADEZ oc/ Attorney; b/Jun 16, 1947; h/PO Box 374, Fairacres, NM 88033; ba/Las Cruces, NM; c/Juan Roberto Miguel; p/ Genovevo M Valadez, Roswell, NM; Priscilla Jimenez Cansino, Roswell, NM; ed/BA, Sociol, NM St Univ, 1970; MS, Ed, Univ of So CA, Heidelberg, W Germany, 1974; JD, Univ of NM, 1980; pa/Atty, Pvt Pract, Saenz, Gonzales & Ferreira Law Firm, 1982-84; Atty Advr, Dept of Trans, Wash DC, 1980-81; Legal Res Asst, Univ of NM Law Sch & Coor, Farmwkr Legal Rts Ctr, 1977-80; Coor, Adult Ed, NM St Univ, 1976-77; Ed Spec, Dept of Def, W Germany, 1971-76; Nat Assn of Def Lwyrs, 1983; Am Trial Lwyrs Assn, 1984; NM Trial Lwyrs Assn, 1983; ABA, 1983; Judic Soc, 1982; Delta Theta Phi Law Frat, 1977-80; Wom's Law Caucus; Nat Ldrship Inst; cp/Gov's Envir Adv Bd, 1984; Secy of St Voter's Task Force, 1983; Dona Ana Co Voter Ed Registration Proj, 1982; hon/Pub, "Liability w/ o Fault Under the Fed Water Pollution Control Act" in *Natural Resources Jour*, Jul 1979; Margaret Keiper Daily Clin Law Awd, 1979; Univ of NM Law Sch Clin Law Hon Awd, 1980; Client Cnslg Competition Regs, 1979; Outstg Yg Wom of Am.

FERREIRA, JO ANN J oc/Center Director; b/Dec 3, 1943; h/Rural Route 2, Box 110, Barrington Hills, IL 60010; ba/Chicago, IL; m/G Dodge; p/John W and June B Chanoux, El Paso, TX; ed/ BS, IN Mgmt 1965, MS, Quantitative Methods 1966, Postgrad 1972-74, Purdue Univ; pa/Present Dir, Computer Devel Ctr, U Airlines; Dir of Corporate Devel, Kearney Mgmt Consltg, 1975-83; Mgmt Conslt, Peat Marwick Mitchell & Co, 1974-75; Mgmt Conslt, Touche Ross & Co, 1970-72; Prior to Grad Sch, IBM; Assn for Corporate Growth, 1980-; Am Arbitrators Assn, 1983; hon/Author of Several Pubs in Misc Profl Jours; Cert'd Mgmt Conslt, 1980; Phi Kappa Alpha, Grad Acad Hon, 1969; W/W in Bus & Indust; W/W in MW.

FERRELL, REGINALD oc/Executive; h/5017 Dawnwood Court, Arlington, TX 76017; ba/Arlington, TX; m/Marianne; c/Falicia Elizabeth, Amberley Erryn; p/Fred (dec) and Frances Ferrell, Pt Neches, TX; ed/BS in Communs, Lamar Univ, 1966; pa/Radio-TV Personality & Announcer, 1961-66; Commls, Beaumont-Pt Arthur, TX, Floyd West & Co 1967, Wm S Merrel Co 1968-73; Sales & Sales Tng 1973-75, Field Manpower Devel Mgt, Am Optical; Mgr of Sales Tng & Devel, BASF Wyandotte Corp, 1975-80; Sr Conslt, PERCON, 1980-81; Current Pres, The Tng Sta Inc, Tng & Devel; Mgmt Conslt; Nat Soc of Sales Tng Execs; Am Soc of Tng & Devel; Nat Spkrs Assn; Am Soc of Profl Consits, 1975-82; hon/ Author, *Field Mgrs Guide to Successful Meetings* 1978, Meetings Mag *Shame Game & Shame Prog* 1982; W/W: in S & SW, of Tng & Devel.

FERRIGHETTO, JOHN oc/Engineering and Maintenance Manager; b/Apr, 22, 1930; h/110 McKenney Drive, Beaver, PA 15009; ba/Monaca, PA; m/ Ann (dec); c/John M, Lynn Ann; p/ Marino and Maria Ferrighetto, Colver, PA; ed/BS, Mineral Engrg, 1953; MS, Mineral Preparation Engrg, 1958; mil/ AUS, 1953-55; pa/Proj Engr, Wheeling Steel Corp, 1955-57; Proj Engr, St Joe Lead Co, 1959; Area Engr, St Joe Minerals Corp, 1960-80; Mgr, Engrg & Maintenance, St Joe Minerals Corp, 1980-; Nat Soc of Profl Engrs; hon/ Co-Author, "St Joe Reclaims Zinc w Heavy Media Separation" in *Mining Engrg*, Dec 1968; W/W in E.

FERRIS, THOMAS F oc/Professor and Chairman of Department of Medicine; b/Dec 27, 1930; h/1535 Hunter Drive, Wayzata, MN 55391; ba/Minneapolis, MN; m/Carol Connor; c/Richard, Deirdre, Thomas, Claudia; ed/AB, Georgetown Univ, 1952; MD, Yale Univ, 1956; mil/Capt (mc), AUS, 1957-59; pa/Prof & Chm, Dept of Med, Univ of MN Sch of Med; hon/Author, Approximately 100 Sci Articles on Hypertension & Renal Diseases.

FERRY, DIANE LOUISE oc/Associate Professor; b/Apr 24, 1947; ba/ Business Administration Department,

University of Delaware, Newark, DE 19716; p/Mr and Mrs W Glenn Ferry, Ligonier, PA; ed/BA, Gettysburg Col, 1969; MBA, Shippensburg St Col, 1974; PhD, Wharton Sch, Univ of PA, 1978; pa/Computer Sys Analyst, Dept of Army, 1970-74; Res Asst, Univ of PA, 1975-78; Instr, Temple Univ, 1977-78; Asst Prof, Univ of DE, 1979-; Am Psychol Assn, Indust & Orgnl Psych Div; Nat Acad of Mgmt; Am Mgmt Assn; Wilmington Wom in Bus; hon/ Pubs, *Measuring & Assessing Orgs*, w A H Van de Ven (John Wiley & Sons) 1980, "An Approach to Assessing & Mng Inter-Unit Interdependence," w J E McCann in *Acad of Mgmt Review* Jan 1979; Grad, cum laude, Gettysburg Col, 1969; Phi Beta Kappa, Gettysburg Col, 1969; Outstg Yg Wom of Am; W/W: of Am Wom, in E.

FESHARAKI, FEREIDUN oc/Project Director; b/Aug 27, 1947; h/566 Papalani Street, Kailua, HI 96734; ba/ Honolulu, HI; ed/BA, Ec, 1970; MA, Ec, 1971; PhD, Ec, Surrey Univ, England, 1974; pa/Fellow, Mid E Ctr, Harvard Univ; Prof of Ec, Nat Univ of Iran; Energy Advr to the Prime Min of Iran; Proj Dir, E-W Ctr, HI; Free-Lance Conslt to Govts in Mid E & Asia; Proj Dir, Petro Ec Studies; Edit Bd, *Jour of Energy Policy*; Intl Assn of Energy Economists; hon/Author, 4 Books, 4 Monographs & 30 Articles, incl'g, *OPEC, The Gulf & the World Petro Mkt* 1983, *OPEC & the World Refining Crisis* 1984, *Critical Energy Issues in Asia & the Pacific* 1982.

FESHBACH, SEYMOUR oc/ Research Psychologist; b/Jun 21, 1925; h/743 Hanley Avenue, Los Angeles, CA 90049; ba/Los Angeles, CA; m/Norma Deitch; c/Jonathan, Laura, Andrew; p/ Joseph and Fannie Katzman Feshbach (dec); ed/BA, City Col of NY, 1947; MS 1948, PhD 1951, Yale Univ; mil/1st Lt, Inf AUS, 1943-46; PTO; pa/Proj Dir, Army Attitude Assessmt Br, 1951-52; From Asst Prof to Assoc Prof, Univ of PA, 1952-63; Prof, Univ of CO, 1963-64; Prof, Univ of CA-LA, 1964-; Dir 1964-73, Fernald Sch, Chm of Dept, 1977-83; Conslt, CBS, Ednl TV, 1972; Vis'g Fellow, Wolfson Col, Oxford Univ, 1980-81; Wn Psychol Assn, Pres 1976-77; AAAS; Soc for Study of Social Issues; Soc for Res in Child Devel; Intl Soc for Res on Aggression, Presently Pres-Elect; Intl Soc for Study of Behavior Devel; ACLU; Phi Beta Kappa; Editor, *Aggression & Behavior Change: Biol & Social Processes*, 1979; Consltg Editor, *Aggressive Behavior*; r/Jewish; hon/Pubs, *TV & Aggression* 1970, *Psychol, An Intro* 1977, *Personality* 1983; Contbr, Chapt to Books & Articles to Profl Jours; Ward Medal, City Col of NY, 1947; Townsend Harris Medal; Dist'd Alumnus Awd, 1972; F'ship, Ward Foun Fund Advmt of Psychi; Dist'd Scist Awd, 1982; CA Psychol Assn; NIMH Grantee; NSF Grantee; Fellow, Am Psychol Assn; W/ W: in W, in CA.

FIELD, JULIA ALLEN oc/Environmental Planner, Futurist; b/Jan 5, 1937; h/3551 Main Highway, Miami, FL 33133; ba/Same; ed/BA, cum laude, Harvard Univ, 1960; Studied Landscape Arch, Harvard Grad Sch of Design, 1964-65; Att'd, Pius XII Grad Sch, Florence, Italy, 1961; PhD Prog, Walden Univ, Inst for Adv'd Studies, 1983-; pa/ Conceptual Planning Conslt, 1965-69;

Conslt, Comando Unificado del Sur, Colombia, 1981-; VP, Black Grove Inc, 1970-; Pres, AMAZONIA 2000, Colombia, 1972-; Pres, Acad of Arts & Scis of the Ams, 1979-; World Future Soc; UN Assn of the US; Planetary Citizens; Intl Assn for Hydrogen Energy; Am Farmland Trust; ACLU; Sociedad Colombiana de Ecologia; Participant (Prin Spkr) in Sems & Congs; hon/Pubs, Contbr to "Essays on Am Culture" 1961, Illustrated "Bodymarkings in SWn Asia" 1960, Edited "Game & Wildlife Presvs in the USSR" 1965, "A New Place for a Living City" 1968, Film "Man vs Nature" 1966, "Amazonia as a World Model" 1972, "Amazonia 2000" 1978, Poster Exhbn "Writing on the Wall" for "Cities in Context" 1968, 1972; DIB; W/W: in Technol Today, in S & SW, of Intells; Intl Book of Hon; Intl Register of Profiles; World W/W of Wom; Two Thousand Notable Ams; Five Thousand Personalities of the World; Personalities of Am; Men & Wom of Distn.

FIELD, SUSAN INGEBORG oc/Business Consultant, Budget Officer; b/ Nov 20, 1953; h/PO Box 9192, Providence, RI 02940; ba/Providence, RI; p/ Ellen Field, Providence, RI; ed/BA in Sociol 1976, BS in Biol 1976, MBA 1980, Providence Col; mil/1981-, 2nd Lt 1983-; pa/Bus Conslt, Self-Employed, 1981-; Budget Ofcr, RI ANG, 1984-; Res Biologist 1977-84, Adm Intern 1978-81, RI Hosp; Spec Lectr, Commun Col of RI, 1979-81; Dir, Nutri Sea Foods Inc, 1981-83; Assn of MBA Execs; Nat Assn of Female Execs; AAUW; cp/Repub Pres Task Force, 1982-; US Congl Adv Bd, St Advr 1982-; Toastmasters Intl, Pres; hon/Pub, "The Effects of Glucagon & Secretin on the Lower Esophageal Sphincter of the Cat" in *Gastroenterology*, 1979; Elk's Ldrship Awd, 1972; Valedictorian, St Francis Xavier Acad, 1972; W/ W: of Wom of the World, of Am Teenagers, of Am Wom.

FIELDS, CLYDE DOUGLAS oc/ Healthcare Administrator; b/Jun 6, 1932; h/3044 Golfview Drive, Greenwood, IN 46142; ba/Indianapolis, IN; m/ Barbara Marie Ott; c/Gayla Jean (dec), Douglas Jay, Angela Kay; p/Rev Arthur LaVerne and Mary Elizabeth Smith Fields, Connersville, IN; ed/BS, cum laude, Bus Adm, IN Ctl Univ, 1963; MBA, Butler Univ, 1968; mil/USN, 1952-56; pa/Crosley Div, Avco Mfg Co, 1950-51; Allison Div, Gen Motors Corp, 1951-64; Linde & Mats Sys Divs, Union Carbide Corp, 1964-69; Dir, Financial Affairs 1969-71, Asst Exec Dir 1972, Bartholomew Co Hosp; VP of Fin 1973-77, VP of Adm 1978-81, Sr VP 1981-82, Sr VP & Treas 1982-83, Meth Hosp of IN; Pres, Basic Am Hlthcare Mgmt Inc, 1983-; Assn for Sys Mgmt, 1965-77, Pres of S Ctl IN Chapt 1971-72; S Ctl IN Chapt, Nat Assn of Accts, 1970-72; IN Chapt, Hosp Financial Mgmt Assn, 1969-, Bd of Dirs 1973-74, Adv'd Mem Status 1974, F'ship 1983; Personal Mem, IN Hosp Assn, Coun on Fin 1973-79, Public Relats Adv Com 1977-83, Coun on Govt Relats 1980-83; Adv Grp Mem to Spectrum Res Inc, 1974-78; IN St Bd of Hlth Sect 1122 Financial Feasibility Com, Chm of Hosp Subcom 1977; Personal Mem, Am Hosp Assn, Task Force to Develop Interpreting Lang Regarding Operating

Margin Requirements, "Statement of Financial Requirements of Hlth Care Instns & Sers" 1978; IN Chapt, MW Pension Conf, 1979-81; Fac Mem, AMA Med Staff Ldrship Confs, 1979; Nom, Am Col of Hosp Admrs, 1980, Mem 1983; Adj Fac, Master of Hlth Care Adm Prog, IN Univ Sch of Med, 1979-82; Trustee, Bison Money Mkt Fund, an IN Bus Trust, 1982-; Secy-Treas, Alliance of Indpls Hosps, 1982-83; Treas, Wesley Med Care Corp, 1982-83; cp/Bd of Dirs & Chm, Ec Devel Com, Commun Action Prog of Bartholomew, Brown & Jackson Cos, 1972; Bd of Dirs & Treas, Bartholomew Co Chapt, IN Assn of Retarded Chd, 1971-72; S Indpls Kiwanis Clb, 1973-, Secy 1973-74, VP 1974-75, Pres-Elect 1975-76, Pres 1976-77; Bd of Dirs & Asst Treas, Meth Hosp Foun, 1973-82; IN Ctl Univ Bus Assn, 1973-84; Bd of Dirs, IN Ctl Univ Alumni Assn, 1975-84, Pres-Elect 1978-79, Pres 1979-80; Bd of Dirs, Perry Sr Citizens's Sers, 1977-80; Bd of Dirs, Wesley Manor Inc, (Formally NW IN Meth Home Inc), 1980-84; Bd of Trustees, IN Ctl Univ, 1981-; Chm, Hosp Div, Profl Unit, The U Way of Gtr Indpls, 1982, Chm, Profl Unit 1983, Chm Hlth/Med Cluster 1984; Asst Treas, Meth Hlth Foun, 1982-83; r/U Meth Ch, 1945-; Adm Bd, Coun on Mins & Fin Com, Chm of Staff-Parish Relats Com, Lay Del to the Annual Conf, Cert'd Lay Spkr, Ctr U Meth Ch; Bd of Dirs, Ecumenical Assem of Bartholomew Co Chs, 1970-72; Treas 1971; Ch Fdn of Gtr Indpls, 1974-81; Chm of Fin Com 1978-79, Bd of Dirs 1978-80; S IN Conf, IN Area, U Meth Ch, 1976-; Planning & Res Com 1980-83, Chm, Min Support Adv Com, 1984-; Chm of Com on Clergy Support 1980-83; Bd of Dirs, IN Coun of Chs, 1980-83, Bus & Fin Dept 1980-83; Devel Com, 1983-; hon/Gold Achmt Awd, Indpls Chapt of Assn for Sys Mgmt, 1969; ASM Merit Awd, S Ctl Indpls Chapt of Assn for Sys Mgmt, 1975; Wm G Follmer Merit Awd, IN Chapt of Hosp Fin Mgmt Assn, 1974; Robert H Reeves Awd, 1983, F'ship 1983; Recip, IN Dist's Dist'd Clb Pres Awd, Kiwanis Clb, 1976-77; W/W: in Fin & Indust, in MW, in the World; Personalities of the W & MW; Commun Ldrs of Am; Book of Hon; The Am Registry Series; Dir of Dist'd Ams; Personalities of Am; Two Thousand Notable Ams; Men of Achmt; Intl W/ W of Intells; DIB.

FIELDS, JERRY LEE oc/Geophysicist; b/Dec 18, 1943; h/1405 Glacier, Plano, TX 75023; ba/Dallas, TX; m/Mary; c/ Tracy, Katrina, Jennifer, Rebecca; p/ Granville and Raye Fields, Ladonia, TX; ed/Att'd, E TX St Univ, 1962-64; BA, Math, Univ of TX Arlington, 1975; pa/ Mobil Oil Corp, 1964-, Petro Geophysicist 1975-, Exploration Geophysicist 1978-, Assoc Geophysicist 1981-; Soc of Exploration Geophysicists; Dallas Geophy Soc; cp/Pk Forest Civic Assn, 1978-79; Dallas Folk Music Soc; Repub Men's Clb; Order of St Luke; hon/ Basketball S'ship, E TX St Univ, 1962; W/W in S & SW.

FIFIELD, CHERYL SCHNEIDER oc/ Teacher, Disc Jockey; b/Sep 10, 1955; m/Thomas Bradley; p/Mr and Mrs William Sadler, Carmel, NY; ed/BA in Communs & Ed, Univ of S FL, 1978; pa/Eng & Spch Tchr, LiveOak HS, 1982;

Eng Tchr, Jenerette Sr HS, 1980-82; Disc Jockey, WLBI, 1982; Disc Jockey/ Reporter, KANE, 1981-82; Disc Jockey/ Reporter, KNIR, 1980-81; Prodn, KDEA, 1981-82; Disc Jockey/Reporter, KANE, 1980; Tchr, Readak Ednl Sers, 1978-80; NCTE, 1977-82; Spch Communication Assn, 1977-82; hon/Alpha Epsilon Phi Outstg Sr Awd, 1978; Commun Ldrs of Am; W/W Among Students in Am Univs & Cols.

FILAR, DONALD A oc/Accountant and Business Owner; b/Mar 29, 1947; h/309 Tartan Green Court, Joppa, MD 21085; ba/Baltimore, MD; m/Karen Jean Robinette; p/Adam and Wanda Filar, Baltimore, MD; ed/Dipl in Acctg and Programming, Balto Inst, 1967; BS in Acctg, Balto Col of Commerce, 1969; pa/Acct, Wn Elect Co, 1969-; Owner, D A Filar & Co, Bkkpg & Tax Wk for Small Bus, 1977-; Essex Bus-men's Assn, 1978; IPA, 1981-84; cp/Treas, Pt Breeze Clb, 1975, 1976; Advr for Jr Achmt, 1975, 1976, 1977, 1979; Advr to Joseph Lee Rec Ctr, 1976-77; Vol for Infant Hearing Assessmt Prog, 1981-84; hon/Commun Ldrs of Am; Men of Achmt; Intl Book of Hon; 2,000 Notable Ams; W/W in E; Dir of Dist'd Ams.

FILNER, BARBARA oc/Science Policy Analyst and Writer; b/Nov 15, 1941; h/7008 Richard Drive, Bethesda, MD 20817; ba/Washington, DC; p/Samuel (dec) and Lily Filner, New York, NY; ed/BS, Biol, Queens Col, 1962; PhD, Biol, Brandeis Univ, 1967; pa/Dir, Div of Hlth Scis Policy, Inst of Med, Nat Acad of Sci, 1981-83; Sr Staff Ofcr, Div Hlth Promotion & Disease Preven, Inst of Med, Nat Acad of Sci, 1978-81; Asst Prof of Biol, Kalamazoo Col, 1977-78; Asst Prof of Biol, Columbia Univ, 1971-76; Public Hlth Ser Postdoct Fellow, Inst for Cancer Res, Phila, 1969-71; Res Assoc, AEC Plant Res Lab, MI St Univ, 1967-69; Assn for Wom in Sci, Pres-elect 1984, Newslttr Co-Editor 1975-; DC/Balto Assn for Wom in Sci, Exec Bd 1981-84; Fdn of Orgs for Profl Wom, Exec Bd 1982; NY Acad of Sci; AAAS; APHA; hon/Pubs, "The Phys' Role in a Changing Hlth Care Sys", 1983, "Infusion of New Fields into Med Ed", 1983, "Food Safety & Cancer" 1981, "Hlth Promotion for the Elderly; Reducing Functional Dependency" 1981, "Res Opports in Alcoholism" 1980, "Fed Support of Alcohol-Related Res" 1980, "Tchg Students to Read the Lit" 1979, "TMV Coat Protein Synthesis in vivo: Anal of the N-terminal Acetylation" 1974, "Some Aspects of Geotropism in Coleoptiles" 1970, "Changes in Enzymatic Activs in Etiolated Bean Seedling Leaves after Brief Illumination" 1968; Sigma Xi, 1975; German Hon Soc, 1961; Am Men & Wom of Sci.

FINCH, GAYLORD KIRKWOOD oc/Assistant Director of Research; b/ Nov 16, 1923; h/1412 Lakeside Drive, Kingsport, TN 37664; ba/Kingsport, TN; m/Barbara Schultz; c/Gaylord Kirkwood II, Pamela Sue Finch Dornsife, Christopher Robin, Robert Mitchell; ed/BS in Chem Engrg 1944, MS in Chem 1948, PhD in Organic Chem 1954, Univ of MI; mil/USN; pa/TN Eastman Co, Sr Chem & Chief Chem of Acid Div 1950-64, Supt of Acid Devel & Control Dept 1964-66, Asst Supt of Acid Div 1966-70, Asst Supt of Poly-

mers Div 1970-71, Asst Supt of Organic Chems Div 1971-72; Eastman Kodak Co, Dir of Chems (European Reg, Intl Photographic Div) 1972-74, Asst Gen Mgr of Chems (European Reg, Intl Photographic Div) 1974-75; TN Eastman Co, Staff Asst, Gen Mgmt & Staff 1975-76, Asst Dir of Res Labs; Eastman Chems Div, 1981-; Am Chem Soc, Local Sect Chm; Fellow of AIChE; cp/BSA, Var Com and Ldr Positions; Kiwanis, Local Sect Pres; Moose; Elks; PTA; UF Com; Am Legion; TN Eastman Hiking Clb; hon/Author of Several Patents, Papers & Pubs; Phi Lambda Upsilon, Chem Hon Soc; Tau Beta Pi, Chem Engrg Hon Soc; Sigma Xi, Sci Hon Soc; W/W in S & SW; Men of Achmt.

FINDLEY, BENJAMIN FLAVIOUS JR oc/Industrial Manager; b/Jan 1, 1947; h/402 San Gabriel Boulevard, Georgetown, TX 78626; ba/Austin, TX; m/ Karen Ann; c/Karolyn Annette, Susan Elizabeth; p/B F Findley Sr, Parkersburg, WV; ed/BS in Bus Adm 1968, MS in Indust Relats 1969, WV Univ; EdD in Bus Tchg, Univ of No CO, 1975; mil/ USAF 1969-85, Maj; pa/Tng Mgr, Abbott Labs, 1981-; Dir of Mgmt Devel Inst & Assoc Prof of Bus, SWn Univ, 1979-81; Asst Prof of Bus, SEn OK St Univ, 1976-79; Reg Pers Mgr, Pfizer Pharm Co, 1972-73; Pres, Findley Mgmt Consltg Co, 1976-85; Am Soc for Pers Adm, 1982-; Am Soc for Tng & Devel, 1981-; Acad of Mgmt, 1976-; Soc for Advmt of Mgmt, 1972-; Pres, Rotary Clb, Round Rock, TX, 1984; Delta Pi Epsilon, Bus Hon; r/Meth; hon/Author, *A Practical Guide to Job Application, Interviewing, & Resume Preparation* 1979, "The Job Satisfaction of Col Bus Tchrs: Factors & Inferences" in *Jour of Bus Ed* 1975, *Capital Devel Bond Sales* (TX Meth Foun) 1981; USAF Meritorious Ser Medal, 1984; Nat Def Trans Assn Awd, 1969; CO St Doct F'ship, 1974; W/W: in S & SW, in Am; Personalities of the S; Men of Achmt; W/W in Tng & Devel.

FINERTY, JOHN CHARLES oc/Vice Chancellor, Retired; b/Oct 20, 1914; h/ 1110 Bethlehem Street, Houston, TX 77018; m/Mildred King; c/Olivia (Mrs John Moore), Donna (Mrs James Gatewood); p/John L and Hulda Schulte Finerty (dec); ed/AB, Kalamazoo Col, 1937; MS, KS St Univ, 1939; PhD, Univ of WI, 1942; pa/Instr in Anatomy, Univ of MI, 1943-46; Asst Prof of Anatomy, Wash Univ, 1946-49; Prof & Hd of Anatomy, Asst Dean, Univ of TX-Galveston, 1949-56; Prof & Hd of Anatomy, Assoc Dean, Univ of Miami Sch of Med, 1956-66; Dean, Sch of Med 1966-71, Vice Chancellor 1971-84, Dean of Grad Studies 1974-84, LA St Univ Med Ctr; Am Assn of Anatomists, Prog Secy 1966-74, Pres 1975-76; TX Acad of Sci, Pres 1955-56; NO Hlth Planning Coun, Pres 1973; Endocrine Soc; Am Physiological Soc; cp/Rotary; r/Meth; hon/ Pub, Finerty & Cowdry *Textbook of Histology*, 1960; Author of Num Res Pubs in Cytophysiol, Radiation Res & Endocrinology; Rackham Fellow, Univ of MI, 1942-43; W/W: in the World, in Am.

FINK, MARTIN RONALD oc/Aeronautical Engineer; b/Apr 27, 1931; h/183 Woody Lane, Fairfield, CT 06430; ba/ Norwalk, CT; m/Jacqueline Fay Klein; c/Howard Jeffrey, Andrew Charles, Douglas Reuben; p/Mr and Mrs David Fink; ed/BS in Aeronaut Engrg 1952,

MS in Aeronaut Engrg 1953, MIT; pa/ Res Asst, MIT, 1952-53; Res Engr 1953-58, Supvr of Missile Aerodynamics 1959-63, Supvr of Aerodynamics 1964-67, Sr Consltg Engr (Aerodynamics) 1967-80, U Technols Res Ctr; Chief of Aerodynamics, Norden Sys, 1980-; AIAA, Assoc Fellow; Sigma Xi, Pres of Hartford Chapt 1980-81; Tau Beta Pi, Pres of Ctl CT Chapt 1972-73; Am Def Preparedness Assn; r/Reform Jewish; hon/Author of Num Pubs in Aeronaut Engrg Tech Jours; W/W: in E, in Technol Today, in Aviation & Aerospace, in Frontier Sci & Technol, of Contemp Achmt.

FINKELSTEIN, LEONARD B oc/ Superintendent of School District; b/ Dec 31, 1928; h/476 Susquehanna Road, Huntingdon Valley, PA 19006; ba/ Elkins Park, PA; m/Leila; c/Larry, Lisa, Lee, Lon; p/Yetta Finkelstein; ed/BS in Ed 1950, EdM 1950, EdD 1967, Temple Univ; mil/AUS, 1951-53; pa/Supt, Cheltenham Sch Dist, 1977-; Supt, Dist Six, Sch Dist of Phila, 1975-77; Dir of Alternative Progs, Sch Dist of Phila, 1972-75; Dir, Parkway Prog, Sch Dist of Phila, 1970-72; Elem & Sec'dy Sch Prin, Sci Tchr; Phi Delta Kappa; cp/Bd of Dirs, Cheltenham Art Ctr; Little Flyers Ice Hockey Org; Edrs Lodge; Energy Ed Adv Coun; r/Hebrew; hon/ Author, 20 Articles for Periods Related to Alternative Ed, Urban Ed, Gifted Ed; US Del to World Coun for Talented & Gifted; Outstg Ser Awd, Acad of Career Ed, Res for Better Schs; Edr of the Yr Awd, 59th St Bapt Ch; Chapel of the Four Chaplains Awd for Commun Ser.

FINKELSTEIN, RICHARD ALAN oc/Microbiologist; b/Mar 5, 1930; h/ 3207 Honeysuckle Drive, Columbia, MO 65201; ba/Columbia, MO; m/Mary Boesman; c/Sheri, Mark, Laurie, Sarina Nicole; p/Frank (dec) and Sylvia Lemkin Finkelstein, New York, NY; ed/BS, Univ of OK-Norman, 1950; MA 1952, PhD 1955, Univ of TX-Austin; mil/Maj, Med Ser Corps, USAR; Hon Discharge, USAR, 1966; pa/Tchg Fellow, Res Scist, Univ of TX-Austin, 1950-55; Fellow in Microbiol, Instr, Univ of TX SW Med Sch, Dallas, 1955-58; Chief of Bioassay Sect, Walter Reed Army Inst of Res, Wash DC, 1958-64; Dpty Chief, Chief of Dept of Bacteriology & Mycology, US Army Med Component, SEATO Med Res Lab, Bangkok, Thailand, 1964-67; Assoc Prof, Prof, Dept of Microbiol, Univ of TX SW Med Sch, 1967-79; Prof & Chm, Dept of Microbiol, Sch of Med, Univ of MO-Columbia, 1979-; Diplomate, Am Bd of Microbiol; Fellow, Am Acad of Microbiol; Fellow, Infectious Disease Soc of Am; Am Assn of Immunols; AAAS; Soc for Gen Microbiol; Pathol Soc of Gt Brit & Ireland; Am Soc for Microbiol, Pres of TX Br 1974-75; Chm, Div of Bacterial Infection & Pathogenesis, 1974-75; Div Councilor, Med Divs, Grp I, 1977-78; VChm, Chm, Annual Meeting Prog Com, 1976-82; hon/Author, Num Pubs in Sci Jours on Cholera, Enterotoxins, Gonorrhea, Role of Iron in Host Parasite Interactions; AUS Outstg Achmt Awd, AUS Sci Conf, 1964; Dept of the Army Outstg Perf Awd, 1965; Ciba-Geigy Lectr in Microbial Biochem, The Waksman Inst, Rutgers Univ, 1975; Vis'g Scist, Japanese Sci Coun, 1976; Recip, The Robert Koch Prize, Sci & Med,

Bonn, Germany, 1976; ASM Fdn Lectr, 1980-81; Divisional Lectr, Div B, ASM, 1981; Harden Lectr at the 20th Harden Conf, Wye Col, Kent, England, 1983; W/W in Am; World W/W in Sci; Am Men & Wom in Sci.

FINKL, CHARLES WILLIAM II oc/ Geologist; b/Sep 19, 1941; h/1808 Bay View Drive, Fort Lauderdale, FL 33305; ba/Boca Raton, FL; c/Jonathon William Frederick, Amanda Marie; p/Charles William and Marian L Hamilton Finkl, Evanston, IL; ed/BSc 1964, MSc 1966, OR St Univ; PhD, Univ of Wn Australia, 1971; pa/Instr, Natural Resources, OR St Univ, 1967; Demonstrator, Univ of Wn Australia, 1968; Staff Geochem for SE Asia, Intl Nickel Australia Pty Ltd, Perth, 1970-74; Chief Editor, Ency Earth Sci, NYC, 1974-; Dir of Inst Coastal Studies, Nova Univ, 1980-83; Current Prof, Dept Geol, FL Atl Univ; Pres, Resource Mgmt & Mineral Exploration Conslts Inc, 1974-83; Exec Dir, Capital Ed & Res Fdn, 1983-; Corres'g Mem, Intl Geog Union Comm on Geomorphological Survey & Mapping & Sub-Comm on Morphotectonics; Mem, Intl Geog Union Comm on River & Coastal Plains; Radio & TV Appearances; AAAS; Am Assn Petro Geologists; Am Geophy Union; Am Geog Soc; Am Quaternary Assn; Am Littoral Soc; Am Shore & Bch Preserv Assn; Assn So Agri Scists; Australian Soc Soil Sci; Australasian Inst Mining & Metallurgy; Brit Geomorphological Res Grp; Brit Soc Soil Sci; Canadian Geophy Union; Coastal Soc; Deutsche Bodenkundlichen Gesellschaft; Deutsche Geologische Vereininung; European Assn Earth Sci Editors; Estuarine & Brackish-Water Scis Assn; Fdn Am Scists; FL Acad Sci; FL Shore & Bch Presv Assn; Geol Assn Canada; Geol Soc Am; Geol Soc Australia; Geol Soc London; Geol Soc Miami; Geol Soc S Africa; Geologists Assn; Geosci Info Soc; Inst Australian Geographers; Intl Soil Sci Soc; Intl Union Geol Scis; Mineral Assn Canada; Nature Conservancy; Nat Pks & Conserv Assn; NY Acad Scis; Soil Sci Soc Am; Société de Belge de Pedologie; Soc Ec Paleontologists & Mineralogists; Soc Mining Engrs; Am Registry Cert Profls in Agronomy; Crops & Soils (Cert Profl Soil Scist); Am Scist Prof Geol (Cert Prof Geol Scist); Gamma Theta Upsilon; cp/Repub; r/Presb; hon/Contbr of Articles, Reviews to Profl Pubs & Newspapers; Author, Soil Classification, 1982; Vol Editor, Contbg Author, The Ency of Soil Sci, Part I: Physics, Chem, Biol, Fertility, & Technol, 1979; Series Editor, Van Nostrand Reinhold Soil Sci Series, 1983-; Vol Editor, Contbg Author, The Ency Applied Geol, 1984; Assoc Editor, Catastrophist Geol, 1978-83; Editor-in-Chief, Jour of Coastal Res, 1984-; Gamma Theta Upsilon, Nat Profl Geographic Frat, 1965; Order of the Orange Oar, OR St Univ, 1964; Nova Univ Spkrs Bur, 1982; W/W in S & SW.

FINKLE, BEVERLY ARTHUR oc/ Retired United States Army Colonel, Retired College Professor; b/Oct 11, 1915; h/Box 1120, Masquebec, Newfound Lake, Bridgewater, NH 03222; ba/Mount Lebanon, PA; m/Edith Kneeland; c/Ann Bard Pierce; p/Dr B A and Edna Whalen Finkle (dec); ed/AB 1938, MA 1946, Univ of NE; Postgrad, Boston

Univ, 1949-50; mil/AUS, 1941-45, 1948-49, 1950-68; pa/45th Inf Div, WW II 1942-45, Korea 1950-52; Assoc PMS, La Salle Col, 1952-55; 2nd Inf Div, AK, 1955-57; AUS Command & Gen Staff Col Fac, 1959-64; 1st Inf Div, 1961-62; HQs AUS Pacific, 1964-67; Robert Morris Col, Pgh, 1969-81; AAUP; Am Polit Sci Assn; Am Acad Polit & Soc Scis; Acad Polit Sci; NE PSA; PA PS & Public Adm Assn; IPA; cp/Nat Hist Soc; Calvin Coolidge Foun; World Affairs Coun; Am Security Coun; Truman Lib; Ctr Study Demo Insts; Ctr Study Presidency; Army-Navy Clb; Ret'd Ofcrs Assn; Resv Ofcrs Assn; VFW; 157 Inf Assn; MOWW; Am Legion; Elks Clb; r/Rom Cath; hon/Num Profl Pubs; W/ W in E; Outstg Edrs of Am; Intl W/W of Intells.

FINN, WILLIAM F oc/Physician; b/ Jul 23, 1915; h/3 Aspen Circle, Manhasset, NY 11030; ba/Manhasset, NY; m/Doris Henderson; c/Neil Charles, Sharon Ruth, David Stephen; ed/BA, summa cum laude, Holy Cross Col, 1936; MD, Cornell Univ Med Col, 1940; Intern, Albany Hosp, 1940-41; Intern 1941-42, 3rd Asst Resident 1942, 1st Asst Resident 1943, Resident 1944, Ob & Gyn, NY Hosp; mil/Comm'd 1st Lt 1943, Capt 1945-46; Active Duty, 1944-46; pa/Asst Att'g Ob/Gynecologist 1948-66, Assoc Att'g Ob/Gynecologist 1948-66, NY Hosp; Dir of Ob/Gyn 1952-59, Att'g in Ob/Gyn 1959-81, N Shore Univ Hosp; Assoc Att'g in Ob/ Gyn, St Francis Hosp, 1973-78; Courtesy Staff, Manhasset Med Ctr, 1959-70; Hon Ob/Gynecologist, N Shore Univ Hosp, 1981-; Conslt in Ob/ Gyn, Mercy Hosp, 1959-; Att'g Ob/ Gynecologist, St Francis Hosp, 1979-; J Whitridge Williams F'ship, Ob & Gyn, NY Hosp, 1946-47; Am Cancer Soc F'ship, Gyn, NY Hosp, 1950-51; Asst in Ob/Gyn 1942-43, Instr in Ob/Gyn 1944, Asst Prof of Ob/Gyn 1948-50, Assoc Prof of Clin Ob & Gyn 1950-66, Assoc Prof of Clin Ob & Gyn 1971-, Cornell Univ Med Col; Adj, Hlth Scis, C W Post Ctr; Diplomate, Am Bd Ob/Gyn, 1949, Recert'd 1979; Am Col of Surgs, 1950; Am Col of Ob/Gynecologists, 1951; Am Bd of Quality Assurance & Utilization Review; Lying-In Alumni Assn, 1943; NY Hosp Alumni, 1944; AMA, 1947; NY St Med Soc, 1947; NY Co Med Socs, 1949; Queens Gyn Soc (Past Pres), 1951; NY Obstetrical Soc, 1952; Nassau Co Med Soc, 1953; Nassau Obstetrical & Gynecological Soc (Past Pres), 1953; NY Acad of Sci, 1956; Am Fertility Soc, 1960; NY Gynecological Soc, 1960; Am Assn of Gynecological Laparoscopists, 1972; Am Assn of Colposcopists, 1973; Am Geriatrics Soc, 1974; Nassau Acad of Med, 1980; Chm, Maternal Wel Com; NY St Maternal & Child Wel Com; Nassau Co Med Soc; Chm, Abortion Review Com, Nassau Obstetrical & Gynecological Soc; cp/Foun of Thanatology, 1966, Presently Serving on Exec Com; Inst for Soc, Ethics & Life Scis, 1968; Soc for Life & Human Values, 1973; Am Philosophical Assn, 1973; Trustee, Village of Plandome Manor; r/ Comms on Min, Human Life & Hlth, Nat, Intl & Social Relats, Epis Diocese of Long Isl; Bd of Mgrs, Ch Charity Foun; hon/25 Yrs of Ser, N Shore Univ Hosp; 25 Yrs of Ser, NY Hosp; 25 Yrs of Ser, Dept of Ob & Gyn, N Shore

Univ Hosp; AMA Phys Recog Awd; Am Col of Ob & Gynecologists Current Med Ed Awd; Mercer Sch of Theol Dipl, 1963; Dist'd Ser Medal, Epis Diocese of Long Isl, 1983; Pubs, "Profls & Ethics" 1982, "Malignant Schwannoma Associated w Pregnancy," "Thanatological Aspects of Maternal Mortality" 1983, "Choosing a Place to Die" 1983, "The Functioning of an 'Ethics' Com in a Commun Hosp" 1982, "Gynecological Cancer: A Case Report" (in Press), "Pelvic Cancer's Impact on a Woman & Her Fam" (in Press), "The Dying Gynecological Patient" 1981, Num Others; Med Dir of NY; Dir of Med Spec; Am Col Ob, Gynecologists Dir; Am Fertility Soc Dir; Am Men of Sci; Am Men of Med; Commun Ldrs of Am; Wisdom; Nat Cyclopedia of Am Biog; DIB; Men of Achmt; Intl W/W Commun Ser; W/W: in E, in NY St, in US, in World; Am Heritage Res Assn; Intl Register of Profiles N Am Edition; Intl W/W of Intells; Notable Ams of Bicent Era; Am Biogl Inst; Fellow, Intl Biogl Assn; Third Book of Hon; Epis Lay Ldrship Dir; Academia Italia.

FINNIN, MARY J oc/Registered Nurse; ed/Dipl in Nsg, Ctl Islip Sch of Nsg, NY, 1956; BS in Nsg, Adelphi Univ Col of Nsg, 1958; MS in Nsg Ed, St John's Univ, 1960; Lic'd as Profl Nurse in FL, NY, MA; pa/Elected Dir, ANA Bd of Dirs, 1980-84; Elected to Bd of Trustees, Am Nurses Foun, 1982-84; Appt'd Chp, ANA Hall of Fame Com, 1982; Appt'd Mem, ANA Awds Com, 1981-82; Appt'd Mem, ANA Fin Com, 1982-84; Appt'd Chp, ANA Com on Coms, 1982-84; Nom'g Com, Nsg Archives, Mugar Lib, 1982-84; Mem, ANA, MA Nurses Assn, MA Nurses Assn Dist V, Sigma Theta Tau (Nat Hon Soc for Nsg), Nsg Archives Inc (Mugar Lib, MA); cp/MA Wom's Polit Caucus; Reg'd Lobbyist w MA House & Senate; hon/Acad of Distn Medallion, Adelphi Univ, 1979.

FIORENTINO, CARMINE oc/Lawyer; b/Sep 11, 1932; h/2164 Medfield Trail, Northeast, Atlanta, GA 30345; p/Pasquale, Lucy Coppola; ed/Studied Ct Reporting, Hunter Col, 1951; Studied Radio Announcing, Columbia Broadcasting Sch, 1952; LLB, Blackstone Sch of Law, 1954; LLB, John Marshall Law Sch, 1957; Studied Fiction & Non-Fiction Writing, Famous Writers Sch, 1962; pa/NY St Wkmen's Compensation Bd; NY St Dept of Labor, 1950-53; Acted as Ct Reporter-Hearing Stenographer for Gov Thomas E Dewey's Com of St Counsel & Attys, 1953; Served as Public Relats Secy, The Indust Home for the Blind, 1953-55; Served as Legal Stenographer, Rschr, Law Clk for Var Law Firms, 1955, 1957-59; Served as Secy for Import-Export Firm, 1956; Engaged in Pvt Law Pract, 1959-63; Atty-Advr, Trial Atty for US Dept of HUD & the Ofc of HUD Gen Counsel, as well as Legal Counsel for The Peachtree Fed Credit Union, 1963-74; Acting Dir, Elmira, NY Disaster Field Ofc, US Dept of HUD, 1973; Presently Engaged in Pvt Law Pract; Mem Bars, St of GA, DC; US Supr Ct; US Dist Ct, DC; US Second Circuit Ct of Appeals; US Dist Ct, No Dist of GA; US Fifth Circuit Ct of Appeals; GA Supr Ct; GA Ct of Appeals;

Pract'd US Ct of Claims; ABA; Fed Bar Assn; Atlanta Bar Assn; Decatur-DeKalb Bar Assn; Am Judic Soc; Old War Horse Lwyrs Clb; Assn of Trial Lwyrs; cp/Jr C of C; Toastmasters Intl; IPA; The Smithsonian Instn; Nat Hist Soc; Atlanta Hist Soc; AAAS; Am Mus of Natural Hist; Atlanta Botanical Gardens; Nat Audubon Soc; Sierra Clb; The Musical Heritage Soc; Gaslight Clb; Fdg Mem, Cent Clb, Repub Nat Com; Sustaining Mem, Repub Nat Com; Mem, Repub Pres Task Force; Columbian Repub Leag; hon/Author, Non-Fiction, Poetry; composer, Words & Music of Popular Songs & Hymns; Pub'd in *The Evening Star, The Nat Observer*; Hon Advr, Nat Bd of Advrs, Am Biogl Inst; Life Dynamics F'ship; Recommended for Policy-Making Position in Adm of Pres Dwight D Eisenhower, 1953; Recommended for White House Position in Adm of Pres Richard M Nixon, 1971; Assisted in Preparation of Banquets & Meetings for Pres Dwight D Eisenhower, Pres Richard M Nixon, Senator Irving Ives of NY, Senator Jacob Javits of NY, Gov Thomas E Dewey, Gov Nelson A Rockefeller, NY; Served as Pvt Tutor & as Monitor Appt'd by the GA St Bd of Bar Examrs Regarding the Testing of Law Sch Grads Who Sit for the GA St Bar Exam, 1959-61; Appearances on Netwk TV, Local TV & Radio Broadcasts; Appearances in Motion Pictures Narrated by Eva Le Gallienne & John C Daly; Acted as Public Relats Dir for Robert J Smithdas, 1st Deaf-Blind Person Ever to Earn a Master's Deg; Served on Atlanta Lwyr Ref Panel, 1959-63; Commend from Dir of US Dept of HUD, Elmira NY Disaster Field Ofc; Instructed Students in DC Public Sch Sys on US Constit, Bill of Rts; Served on Com Honoring Spec Asst to the Secy of St of the US; Personalities of S; Commun Ldrs & Noteworthy Ams; Notable Ams of 1978-79; W/W: in Am Law, in World, in S & SW; DIB; Men & Wom of Distn; Men of Achmt; Book of Hon; Intl W/W of Intells; Intl Register of Profiles; IPA Dir; Intl W/W in Commun Ser; The Am Cultural Arts Registry; The Am Bus Registry; The Anglo-Am W/W; The Dir of Dist'd Ams; Personalities of Am; Commun Ldrs of Am; 2,000 Notable Ams; Contemp Personalities; Personnages Contemporains; Zeitgenössische Personlichkeiten; Personaggi Contemporanei; 2,000 Dist'd Southerners; The Biogl Roll of Honor; Intl Roll of Hon; Others.

FIRK, FRANK WILLIAM KENNETH oc/Professor of Physics, University Administrator; b/Nov 2, 1930; h/100 High Street, New Haven, CT 06510; ba/New Haven, CT; m/Pamela Mary; c/John Richard, Peter Edward, Andrew Paul; p/Frank William and Ivy Grace Firk (dec); ed/BSc 1956, MSc 1965, PhD 1967, Univ of London; Hon MA, Yale Univ, 1977; mil/RAF, 1949-51; pa/Asst Exptl Ofcr 1952-56, Exptl Ofcr 1956-59, Sr Sci Ofcr 1959-62, Prin Sci Ofcr 1962-65, Aere, Harwell, England; Sr Res Assoc 1965-68, Assoc Prof of Physics 1968-77, Prof of Physics 1977-, Dir of Grad Studies 1970-73, Dir of Electron Acc Lab 1976-83, Chm of Dept of Physics 1980-83, Master of Trumbull Col 1982-, Yale Univ; Am Phy Soc, 1968-; Inst of Physics (London), 1958-;

Conslt for DOE/NSF & Univ of Chgo; hon/Author, Over 50 Articles in Profl Jours, 5 Review Articles in Books (1956-), Num Book Reviews; Undergrad Tchg Prize, Yale Univ, 1983; Am Men & Wom of Sci.

FISCHER, ROBBINS WARREN oc/Executive; b/Mar 31, 1919; h/5614 University Avenue, Cedar Falls, IA 50613; ba/Cedar Falls, IA; m/Jean Noreen Greenawalt; c/Barbara Jean, Martha Lou, Dorothy Ellen; p/Lewis Warren and Edith Robbins Fischer; ed/BA, Univ of CO, 1942; Postgrad, Univ of CO Sch of Law 1944-45, Rutgers Univ 1954; pa/Co-Owner, Operator, Fischer Farms, Turin, 1945-53; Sales Promotion Mgr, Paywav Feed Mills, KC, MO, 1953-55; Reg Sales Mgr, Bristol Myers Co, KC, MO, 1956-58; Campaign Dir, Burrell Inc, KC, MO, 1958-59; Asst to Pres, Soybean Coun Am, Waterloo, IA, 1960-63; Pres, Soypro Intl Inc 1963-, Soypro of IA 1973-, Intl Bus Assocs 1965-; VP, Continental Sova, Manning, IA, 1973-81; Chm of Bd, CEO, Burst Prods, Denison, IA, 1979-82; VChm, IA Farm Coun, 1950-53; Mem of Pres Kennedy's Task Force on Intl Trade in Agri Prods, 1962; Mem of Pres Reagan's Task Force, Intl Agri Devel, 1982-; Chm, Food & Agri Comm, Pres of Reagan's Task Force on Intl Pvt Enterprise, 1983-; Agribus Devel Coun, 1983-; Agri-Tech Comm Oilseeds & Prods, 1982-; Inst Food Technologists; Phi Beta Kappa; Delta Sigma Rho; Pi Gamma Mu; cp/Cedar Falls C of C (Dir); Monona Harrison Flood Control Assn, Pres 1951-54; Conglist; Rotary; Masons; Des Moines Clb; hon/W/W in the World.

FISCHER, ROGER RAYMOND oc/State Legislator; b/Jun 1, 1941; h/Overlook Drive, Washington, PA 15301; ba/Harrisburg, PA; m/Catherine Louise Trettel; c/Roger Raymond II, Steven Gregory; p/Raymond and Louise Fischer, Washington, PA; ed/BA, Math & Physics, Wash & Jefferson Col, 1963; Grad Wk in Nuclear Engrg, Carnegie Inst of Technol; mil/PA Air NG, Maj; pa/Res Engr, Jones & Laughlin Steel Res; cp/Mem, PA Ho of Reps 1966-, Mem Var Coms; Former Adv Mem, Wash Sch Bd; Bd of Dirs, City Mission; Boy Scout Merit Badge Cnslr; Elected Adv Mem of Wash Sch Bd, 1965-71; Chm of the House Ed Com; Former Minority Chm of the Vets Affairs Com; Mem, House Com Vets Affairs & Fisheries; Former Chm of the Basic Ed Subcom; Former Mem of the House Coms on Appropriations, Mil & Vets Affairs, Indust Devel, Profl Licensure, Public Utilities, Law & Order, & Conserv; Former Mem of the Jt St Govt Comms Task Forces on Vets Benefits to Investigate Prisons, Aid Black Lung Victims & Study Cost of Ed; Former Chm of the Police Subcom on the PA Crime Comm's Reg Planning Coun, 1970; Life Mem, Appalachian Trail Conf; Potomac Appalachian Trail Clb; Mem, PA Gov's Coun Phy Fitness & Sports; Keystone's Trails Assn; Life Mem, Warriors Trails Assn; PA Appalachian Trail Com; Wash Road Runners Clb; US Triathlon Fdn; Wash, Canonsburg Sportsmen's Clbs; Am Legion; Wash Lodge #164 F&AM; Other Civic Activs; r/Luth Ch of Am, Lay Asst; hon/Delta Epsilon, Math Hon; Lambda Chi

Alpha Frat; Ironman Triathlon, 1984; Dean's List, Wash & Jefferson Col; Physics Achmt Awd, Chem Rubber Co, 1961-62.

FISCHMAN, LEONARD LIPMAN oc/Economist; b/Jan 23, 1919; h/520 22nd Street, Northwest, Washington, DC 20037; ba/Washington, DC; m/Evelyn R; p/Murray M and Sadie G Fischman (dec); ed/AB, Ec, NY Univ, 1937; MA, Govt Ec, The Am Univ, 1939; mil/Served in Italy, AUS, 1941-46; pa/Asst Oper Hd, Pop & Housing Div, US Bur of the Census, 1940-41; Chief, Stats & Spec Studies Br, UNRRA Italy Mission, Rome, 1946-47; Economist, Ofc of Intl Trade, US Dept of Commerce, 1948-50; Economist, US Bur of Mines, 1950-53; Conslt, PR Ec Devel Adm, San Juan, 1953-58; Ec Conslt, Dir & Pres, Ec Assocs Inc, Wash DC, 1958-74; Sr Res Assoc, Fellow & Sr Fellow, Resources for the Future, 1973-79; Pres, Ec Assocs, 1980-; Am Ec Assn; Am Statl Assn; Fellow, AAAS; Nat Assn of Bus Economists; Soc for Intl Devel; Nat Economists Clb; Marine Technol Soc; Editor, *Minerals Yrbook*, 1950; hon/Pubs, *World Mineral Trends & US Supply Probs* (Resources for the Future) 1980, *Resources in Am's Future* w Hans H Landsberg & Joseph L Fisher (Johns Hopkins) 1963, Num Articles; Am Men & Wom of Sci; W/W in Fin & Indust; Contemp Authors.

FISHER, DOUGLAS ROY oc/Minister, Center Director; b/1919; h/1210 South Riverside Drive, New Smyrna Beach, FL 32069; ba/New Smyrna Beach, FL; m/Elizabeth Sutherland Young; c/Mary, Bonnie, Jean, Donna Lee; p/Frank Roy and Inez Campbell Fisher, Toronto, Ontario, Canada; ed/Att'd, Runnymede Col Inst 1935, Toronto Conservatory of Music 1936-37, No Bapt Sem 1938-39, Moody Bible Inst 1940-41; pa/Exec Dir, Chapel Mins, Indian River Lodge, Christian Conf & Retreat Ctr, 1972-; Min, Chgo Gospel Tabernacle, 1960-72; Min, Ch of the Open Door, Chgo, 1956-60; Min of Music, MW Bible Ch, 1944-55; Musical Dir, Chgoland Yth for Christ & Pioneer in Yth for Christ, 1940-; Radio Staff, WDLM, 1942-44; Ext Staff, Moody Bible Inst, 1940-42; Ext Staff, *Our Hope Mag*, NYC, 1940-42; Ordained to the Bapt Min, 1939; Organist, Pianist, Mem, Am Fdn of Musicians, 1937-; hon/Composer, Compiler, Arranger, Prodr of Sacred Music, Records, Tapes, incl'g *Song-a-Log*; Recording Artist, Singspiration Inc, Quality Sacred Recordings, Tru-Tone Records; Hon Doct Deg, 1970; W/W: in Chgo & IL, in the Ctl Sts, in MW.

FISHER, ELIZABETH CHRISTENSEN oc/Editor, Writer, Photographer; b/May 9, 1919; h/375 North 200 East, PO Box 396, Farmington, UT 84025; ba/Salt Lake City, UT; m/Etsil Robert (dec); c/Edward Robert, Ellen Fisher Trickler, Colleen Fisher Newey, Randall Etsil, Garth Newell (dec); p/Orsen Reuben and Anna Katherine Felix Christensen (dec); ed/Att'd, Univ of UT 1938-40, LDS Bus Col 1940-41; pa/Correspondent, *Deseret News*, 1951-60; Asst Editor, Photographer, *Wkly Reflex*, 1961-63; Asst Editor, *Br Clearings*, First Security Bks, 1962-64; Correspondent, *Salt Lake Tribune*, 1963-64; Photo-Journalist, *Magna Times*,

1963-64; Courthouse Reporter, *Davis Co Clipper*, 1961-64; Editor, *Wkly Reflex*, 1964-69; Free-Lance Photo-Journalist, Public Relats Exec, Editor, 1969-; Editor, *Utah Wom Speak*, 1979-; Nat Fdn of Press Wom, 1956-82; UT Press Wom, 1956-82, Pres 1958-60, 2nd VP 1965-66, 1st VP 1968-69, Recording Secy 1971-72, Histn 1972-82; UT Assn Indust Editors, 1961-63; IPA, 1982; Editor, Indust Brochures; Asst Editor, "My Farmington," 1975; Contbr of Articles & Features to Var Newspapers & Mags; cp/Davis Co Fair Bd, 1952-80; Davis Co Indust Comm, 1958-61; Public Info Bd, UT Div, Am Cancer Soc; Am Assn of Ret'd Persons, 1982-83; UT Assn of Wom, 1979-; Public Relats Mgr for Var Commun Progs, & UT Assn of Wom; hon/UT Wom of Achmt, UT Press Wom, 1981; 63 Press Awds; 2 Awds, UT Assn Indust Editors, 1961-63; 18 Awds, UT Press Assn; 4 Awds, Am Cancer Soc; 7 Awds, Nat Fdn of Press Wom; W/W: of Am Wom, in W.

FISHER, JONATHAN CORWIN oc/Consulting Engineer; b/Jun 8, 1920; h/4901 Tuckerman Street, Riverdale, MD 20737; ba/Hyattsville, MD; m/Virginia I; c/Robert Jon, Carol Gay, Janet Laurena; p/Robert William and Cora Laurena Skinner Fisher (dec); ed/AS, Green Mtn Jr Col, 1941; BS, Rensselaer Polytechnic Inst, 1943; Att'd, Univ of MD Grad Sch, 1946-52; pa/Gen Elect Co, 1944; Test Engr 1944-78, Sr Staff Engr 1964-78, Nav Surface Weapons Ctr; NKF Engrg Assn Inc, 1978-81; Proj Engr, Adv'd Technol & Res Inc, 1981-; Nat Soc of Profl Engrgs; cp/Am Def Preparedness Assn; The Wilderness Soc; The Am Forestry Assn; Nat Audubon Soc; hon/Pubs, NAVORD OD 45931 "Shock Hardening Shipboard Ordnance (Underwater Explosions)" Aug 1971, NOLTR-63-51 "Shock Tests of Weapon Stones Aboard the USS Thresher" (SS(N)593) Mar 1963; USN Meritorious Civilian Ser Awds, 1957, 1960; W/W in E.

FISHER, KENNETH LEE oc/Artist, Sculptor, Painter; b/Apr 28, 1944; h/1656 Southeast Clatsop, Portland, OR 97202; ba/Same; p/Mr and Mrs Henry John Fisher (dec); ed/MFA 1971, BFA 1969, BS 1968, Univ of OR-Eugene; mil/Army NG; pa/Self-Employed Artist, 1978-; Portland Art Assn, 1981-84; Ctr for Visual Arts, 1982-84; Cooperstown Art Assn, 1982-84, CA Cooperstown Art Assn, 1982-84; r/Monotheist; hon/Sculpture Reviews, *Corpus Christi Caller Times*, *Sun Mag*; First Place, 9th Annual Nat, J K Ralston Mus, Sidney MT, 1983; First Place, Hill Country Arts Foun 11th Nat, Ingram, TX, 1983; Cert of Recog, 10th Intl Dogwood Fest Art Exhbn, GA Tech Gallery, Atlanta, 1983; 1st Pl, Palm Bch Art Galleries, 3rd Intl Exhib, 1984; Hon Mention, Nat Art Apprec Soc "Around the World", 1984; Cert Recog, 11th Intl, GA Tech, 1984; Hon Awd, Art About Agri, OR St Univ, 1983; Hon Mention, Terrance Gallery Nat Juried Art Show, Columbia Greene Commun Col, 1982; First & Second Place, 8th Annual Nat, J K Ralston Mus, 1982; Cert of Recog, Black Forest Intl Painting & Sculpture Exhib, Black Forest Sch of Creat Art, 1982; M Grumbacher Bronze Medallion, Assoc'd Artists of Southport 2nd Annual Nat Exhib, Franklin Sq Gallery, 1982; First Place, 14th Nat Art

Show, Koshare Kiva, 1982; Top Awd, Joseph A Cain Meml Purchase Awd, 16th Annual Nat Drawing & Sculpture Exhib, Del Mar Col, 1982; Cert of Recog, 9th Intl Dogwood Art Exhib, GA Tech Gallery, 1982; First Place, Big Sky Biennial II, ID St Univ, 1982; Hon Men, 16th Nov Annual, Coos Art Mus, 1981; Num Exhbns throughout the USA; W/W: in W, in Am Art, in Art; Dic of Am Sculptors; Dir Dist Ams; Intl Dir of Exhib'g Artists.

FISHER, MILES MARK IV oc/Committee Clerk and Staff Director; b/Sep 25, 1932; ba/Washington, DC; p/Dr Miles Mark and Ada Virginia Foster Fisher (dec); ed/BA, Rel, VA Union Univ, 1954; Grad Study, Univ of Chgo, 1954-55; MDiv, VA Union Univ, Sch of Theol, 1959; MA, Ed (Guid & Cnslg), NC Ctl Univ, 1968; Dr of Min, Rel/Min, Howard Univ Div Sch, 1978; pa/Com Clk/Staff Dir/Secy, Com of the Whole, Coun of the DC, 1979-; Vis'g Asst Prof, Urban Mins, Div Sch, Howard Univ, 1978-80; Exec Secy, Nat Assn for Equal Opport in Higher Ed, 1969-78; Asst Prof of Ed & Cnslr, Norfolk St Univ, 1967-69; Social Studies Tchr, Whitted Jr HS, 1959-67; Conslt, Lawrence Johnson & Assocs, 1978-79; Spec Conslt for Pubs & Dissemination of Info, Inst for Sers to Ed, 1969-70; Conslt, Rec, Norfolk Model Cities Prog, 1967-69; Conslt, Norfolk City Schs & the Univ of VA Follow-Up Sem, 1968; Am Acad of Polit & Social Scis; Am Acad of Rel; Am Assn for Higher Ed; APGA; Am Soc of Ch Hist; DC Citizens for Better Public Ed Inc, Pres, Bd Mem; Howard Univ Alumni Assn; NC Ctl Univ Alumni Assn; Shaw Univ Div Sch, Bd of Trustees; VA Union Univ Alumni Assn; Num Past Profl Mbrships; cp/NAACP; Voice of Informed Commun Expression, Pres, Bd Mem; Num Past Civic Mbrships; hon/Pubs, "The Importance & Impact of Funding Sci Progs at Minority Instns" 1977, "The 1954 Supr Ct Desegregation Decision: Its Adverse Effects on Black Higher Ed" 1976, "The Pratt Decision" 1974, "Nat Assn for Equal Opport in Higher Ed: Crusader for The Black Col" 1970; Cert of Apprec, Nat Coun of Black Child Devel; DC Alumni Awd, VA Union Univ; W/W: in Am, in Black Am, in the World; Commun Ldrs & Noteworthy Ams; Contemp Notables; Ebony Success Lib; Intl Biog; Intl Inst of Commun Ser; Intl W/W in Commun Ser; Ldrs of Black Am; Men of Achmt.

FISHER, ROBERT ALAN oc/Laser Physicist, Consultant; b/Apr 19, 1943; h/Jacona Plaza, Route 5, Box 230, Santa Fe, NM 87501; ba/Los Alamos, NM; m/Andrea; c/Andrew L, Derek M; p/Leon and Phyllis Fisher, Atherton, CA; ed/AB w Hons in Physics 1965, MA in Physics 1967, PhD in Physics 1971, Univ of CA-Berkeley; pa/Lectr, Dept of Applied Scis, Univ of CA-Davis, 1972-74; Physicist, Lawrence Livermore Lab, 1971-74; Laser Physicist, Los Alamos Nat Lab, 1974-; Optical Soc of Am, Fellow; Am Phy Soc; IEEE, Sr Mem; VChm of 1981 Gordon Conf on Lasers & Nonlinear Optics; Prog Com of the 1981 Optical Soc of Am Meeting; Prog Com of the 1982 Intl Quantum Electronics Conf; Editor of Book, *Optical Phase Conjugation*, 1983; Guest Editor of a JOSA Spec Issue on Optical Phase

Conjugation, 1983; Presider of Optical Soc of Am Meeting Symp on Optical Phase Conjugation, 1981; AF ABCD Panel, 1982-84; Adv Com to the Provost, Univ of NM; Referee for Over 200 Manuscripts in Profl Jours; Reviewer of Proposals for Army Res Ofc, NSF, NRC, The Res Corp, USDOE Ofc of Basic Energy Scis; CoChm, 1983 Los Alamos Conf on Optical Phase Conjugation; Instr for Profl Growth Courses, Engrg Technol Inc, 1982-84; AF Red Team for Space-Based Laser Study, 1983-84; Assoc Editor, *Applied Optics*, 1984-86; Assoc Editor, *Optics Lttrs*, 1984-86; cp/ Santa Fe Opera; Coun for Intl Relats; Wheelwright Mus of Indian Ceremonial Art; Historic Santa Fe Foun; Mus of NM; Coach of 1984 Nat Champ Elem Sch Chess Team; hon/Author of Many Pubs in Nonlinear Optics & Phase Conjugation; Author of One Patent, "Optical Pulse Compression Technique"; Am Men & Wom of Sci; W/W: in Technol Today, in Frontier Sci & Technol, in Intl W/W Contemp Achmt; Men of Achmt; W/W Dir of Optical Scists & Engrs.

FISHGRAB, JIMMIE NELL oc/Learning Disabilities Teacher; b/Mar 14, 1946; h/Route 1, Box 238A, Indiahoma, OK 73552; ba/Lawton, OK; m/Ralph Merle; c/Jerry Wayne; Stepchd: Mark Allen, Melissa C, Merle Bonner; p/James Jackson and Mary Letha Ritter Smith, Keota, OK; ed/AS, Connors St Agri Col, 1966; BS, NEn St Univ, 1968; EdM, Ctl St Univ, 1975; pa/Bus Ed Tchr, Anderson Union High, 1968; Bus & Eng Tchr, Dulce Indep Sch Dist, 1968-70; Bus Instr, AR Sch of Bus, 1971-72; Eng Tchr, Olney Public Sch, 1972-74; Sch Psychometrist/Prescriptive Tchr, St Reg Ser Ctr 17, 1974-81; Lrng Disability Spec, Eisenhower High, 1981-; Assoc Mem, Am Psychol Assn; Nat Assn of Sch Psychols; CEC; NEA; OK Ed Assn; Public Ed Assn of Lawton; hon/W/W in S & SW.

FISK, JEAN A oc/Clinic Founder and Director; b/Jun 11, 1946; h/5046 South Ellis, Chicago, IL 60615; ba/Chicago, IL; p/Darwin Fisk (dec); Ardith Koepenick, Aberdeen, SD; ed/BS, Univ of WI-Oshkosh, 1972; MS, Ed, Univ of WI-Whitewater, 1974; Postgrad, Nat Col of Ed, No CO Univ; pa/Fdr & Dir, Chgo Clin for Child Devel, 1976-; Instr, Nat Col of Ed, 1974-77; LD Spec, Racine Co Spec Ed; LD Spec, NW Spec Ed Dist; Inser Dir & Conslt to Schs; CEC; Zonta; Assn for Chd w Lng Disabilities; Hyde Pk Bus-men's Assn; Exec Female Assn; hon/Pubs, *EMH-SLD???* 1972, *Handbook of Parents of Chd w Lrng Disabilities*; Title VI-D F'ship Grant, 1972; Outstg Elem Tchrs of Am; W/W of Am Wom.

FITCH, FRANK oc/Administrator, Consultant; b/Feb 13, 1943; h/200 Church, Number 207, San Francisco, CA 94114; ba/San Francisco, CA; p/ Frances Brooks, Evergreen, CO; ed/ Student of Psych, Univ of CO, 1960-64; pa/Dpty Dir, SF Pretrial Diversion Proj, 1976-; Exec Dir, Gay Commun of Concern, 1974-76; Bus/Computer Conslt, 1974-; Treas, SF Charter Comm, 1978-; cp/Treas, CA Dem Coun, 1981-; Treas, SF Aids Foun, 1983-; Treas, Castro St Fair Inc, 1981-; Del, Dem Mid-term Conv, 1978; Chair, Affirmative Action Adv Bd, SF Civil Ser, 1977-; Pres, Alice B Toklas Dem Clb,

1977-79; hon/Editor, "Ending Discrimination Agnst Lesbians & Gay Men," 1976; CA St Assem Resolution, 1979; SF Mayor's Awd of Merit, 1983; SF Bd of Supvrs Cert of Hon, 1983; W/W: in Am Polit, in W.

FITZGERALD, JAMES STERLING oc/Clinical Psychologist; b/Aug 1, 1944; ba/Decatur, GA; c/James Patrick; p/ Harold and Josephine Fitzgerald, Livingston, VA; ed/BA, 1974; EdM, 1975; EdS, 1977; MA, 1982; PhD Cand; mil/USAF, 1963-71; pa/Psychi Asst, Peachtree-Parkwood Mtl Hlth Hosp, 1974-76; Psychol, Ctl DeKalb Mtl Hlth Ctr, 1976-78; Pvt Pract, Atlanta, GA, 1978-; hon/ Author of Article in *Insight Mag*, Dec 1982; BA, summa cum laude, 1974; First Place, Psych Div, TN Acad of Sci, 1974; Rotary 4-Way Scholar, 1973-74; Hons Grantee, 1971-74; W/W: in Am Cols & Univs, in S & SW.

FITZGERALD, JANET ANNE oc/ College President; b/Sep 4, 1935; h/1000 Hempstead Avenue, Rockville Centre, NY 11570; ba/Same; p/Robert William and Lillian Shannon Fitzgerald (dec); ed/ BA in Math (magna cum laude) 1965, MA in Phil of Sci 1967, PhD in Phil 1971, St John's Univ; pa/Pres 1972-, Phil Prof 1969-, Molloy Col; Math Tchr, Bishop McDonnell HS, 1965-69; Tchr of Grades 5-8, St Thomas Apostle Sch, 1956-65; Tchr of Primary Grades, St Ignatius Sch, 1955-56; LI Reg Adv Coun on Higher Ed; r/Cath; hon/Pub, *Alfred Whitehead's Early Phil of Space & Time*, Univ Press of Am; Hon JD Deg, St John's Univ, 1982; Outstg Ldrship Ser to Higher Ed in NY, 1983; First Long Isl Wom Cited Achiever in Field of Ed, 110 Ctr for BPW, 1977; Cited as "Fall Gal," LI Sky Clb, 1980; Edr of the Yr, Assn of Tchrs of NY, 1980; Postdoct F'ship, NSF, "Inst on Hist, Sociol, Phil of Sci," Cath Univ of Am, 1971; Awd for Postdoct Wk, Carnegie Inst of Phil, Notre Dame Univ, 1971; NSF Tchg F'ship, 1965-67; Manhattan Col Grad S'ship, 1965; St John's Univ S'ship, 1965, S'ship for MA & PhD 1965-71; Gen Excell Awd, St John's Univ, 1965.

FITZGERALD, JEANNE TASHIAN oc/Writer and Editor; b/Apr 18, 1942; h/821 Hewett Drive, Ann Arbor, MI 48103; c/Alex, Alanna; p/Gerald and Elsie Fitzgerald, Hickory Hills, IL; ed/ EdB, Chgo St Univ; MA, Univ of Chgo; Postgrad Wk, Copenhagen Univ, Univ of MI; pa/Eng Tchr, Morgan Pk HS, 1964-68; Asst Editor, MI Acad of Sci, 1970-73; Editor, Dept of Surg, Univ of MI & Adm Editor, *The Annals of Thoracic Surg*, 1973-84; Free-Lance Writer, 1976-; Am Med Writers Assn, 1975-84, VP of MI Chapt 1984; Profl Wom in Communs, 1972-84; cp/MENSA, 1977-83; Commun Day Care Day Camp Parent Bd, 1983-84; hon/Pubs, "Endangered Land" 1978, "The Cycle of a Cent" 1977, "One Solution" 1979, "Left Brain? Right Brain? New Directions in Med Communs" 1978, "A Yoga Retreat" 1976, "Every Wom's Pharm" 1983; Fellow of the Am Med Writers Assn, 1982; Rapporteur & Editor; Symp on Molecular Anthropology; Wenner Gren Anthropological Foun; Burgwartenstein, Austria, 1976.

FITZGERALD, LAURINE ELISABETH oc/Dean of Graduate School; b/ Aug 24, 1930; h/3715 Pau Ko Tuk Lane, Oshkosh, WI 54901; ba/Oshkosh, WI;

p/Thomas F and Laurine I Fitzgerald (dec); ed/BS, Physiol 1952, MA, Cnslg 1953, NWn Univ; PhD, Cnslg Psych-Adm of Higher Ed, MI St Univ, 1959; pa/Residence Dir, Soc Prog Coor, Kendall Col, 1951-53; Instr, Psycho-Ednl Clin, NWn Univ, 1952-53; Dir of Developmental Rdg Lab, Hd Resident Dir, Instr of Eng, MI St Col, 1953-55; Area Dir of Residence Hall Complex, Instr of Ednl Psych, IN Univ, 1955-57; Tchg Grad Asst, Adm & Ednl Sers, MI St Univ, 1957-58; Cnslr of Student Cnslg Ser Ctr, Instr of Adm & Ednl Sers, MI St Univ, 1958-59; Assoc Dean of Students, Asst Prof of Psych & Ed, Univ of Denver, 1959-62; Asst Prof of Cnslg Psych, Staff Cnslr of Carnegie Foun Proj, Student Cnslg Bur, Univ of MN, 1962-63; Assoc Prof of Cnslg, Pers Sers & Ednl Psych, MI St Univ, 1963-68; Asst Dean of Students, MI St Univ, 1963-70; Prof of Adm & Higher Ed, MI St Univ, 1968-74; Assoc Dean of Students, Dir of Div of Ed & Res, MI St Univ, 1970-74; Dir, NE WI Cooperative Reg Grad Ctr, Univ of WI-Oshkosh, 1974-80; Dean of the Grad Sch, Prof of Cnslr Ed, Univ of WI-Oshkosh, 1974-; Coun of Grad Schs in the US, Task Force on Assessmt of Quality of Master's Deg Progs 1978, Steering Com of Wkshop for New Grad Deans 1975; MW Assn of Grad Schs, Exec Com 1978-, Chair of the Assn 1980-81, Pubs Com 1977-79; Am Col Pers Assn, Editor of *Jour of Col Student Pers* 1977-83, Assoc Editor of *Jour of Col Student Pers* 1965-77, Archivist 1982-, Exec Bd Mem 1968-70, Prog Chair of Annual Conv 1967-68, Secy 1965-67; APGA, Life Mem, Chair on Wom's Task Force 1982-83, Chair on Prog Com; Am Psychol Assn (Divs 15, 17, 35), 1960; Am Assn for Higher Ed, Rdr of Prog Proposals 1978, Mem of Fdg Mem of ASHE 1964; AAUA, Bd of Dirs 1979-82; Nat Assn for Wom Deans, Admrs & Cnslrs, Pres 1980-81, Pres-Elect 1979-80, VP 1972-74, KSP Trust Com 1979-82, Res, Ed, Prog, Pubs Coms; Nat Assn of Student Pers Admrs, Reader of Dissertation of the Yr Awd 1977-78; Nat Coun of Adm Wom in Ed, 1959-64, 1975-; AAUP, 1953-, Chapt Treas 1954-55; AAUW, 1952-; BPW Clb, 1962-, Pres 1980-81; cp/Black Wolf Twp Zoning Comm, 1982-; Lakelands Consortium in Support of the Arts Inc, 1982-; Girl Scout Coun Exec Bd, 1982-; Wom's Equity Action Leag, 1971-, Nat Adv Bd 1978-79, 1968-76, WI Convener 1975, Bd of Trustees & Fdr of Legal Def Fund 1972-74; Zonta Intl, 1960-76, Pres of Lansing Clb, Chair of Intl Status of Wom Com 1972-74; r/Congregational; hon/Pubs, *Col Student Pers: Rdgs & Bibliogs* 1970, *Cnslg Wom* 1978, *Thus, We Spoke: ACPA-NAWDAC, 1958-75* 1983; Co-Editor, Chapts in Texts, Monographs & Over 50 Articles Pub'd in Juried Profl Jours; Annuit Coeptis Dinner, Am Col Pers Assn, 1983; Pres Ser Awd, First Recip, Am Col Pers Assn, 1982; Mandala Awd, Col of Ed, Univ of WI-Oshkosh, 1980; Old Master's Prog, Profl Awd, Purdue Univ, 1979; Dist'd Ser Awd for Ldrship, Wom's Equity Action Leag, 1978; Selected as Participant, First ACE Nat Form for Identification of Wom Ldrs in Ed, 1977; Meml Ser Awd for Outstg Contbns to Wom & Ed, MI Assn for Wom Deans, Admrs & Cnslrs, 1977; Compatriot in Ed in

1976, Beta Theta Chapt of Kappa Delta Pi, 1976; Awd for Most Dist'd MI Wom in Ed, MI Fdn of BPW Clbs, 1973; Lena Lake Forrest F'ship Grant, Nat Fdn of BPW Clbs, 1966; Elin Wagner Foun Res F'ship, 1963; Evelyn Hosmer Awd for Outstg Fac Wom, Univ of Denver, 1962; W/W: in MW, of Am Wom; Contemp Authors; Intl W/W in Commun Ser; Commun Ldrs & Noteworthy Ams; World W/W of Wom.

FITZPATRICK, BLANCHE oc/Professor of Labor Economics; h/115 Bay State Road, Boston, MA 02215; ba/Boston, MA; p/Joseph Leo and Elizabeth Dorothy Bresnahan Fitzpatrick (dec); ed/BA, Tufts; MA, Stanford; PhD, Harvard, 1966; pa/Labor Relats, Raytheon; Price Economist, US Dept of Labor; Dir of Sales Anal, Polaroid; Asst Prof of Lesley Col; Asst Prof of CA St Univ-Fullerton; Prof of Labor Ec, Boston Univ, 1965-; Vis'g Prof, Goucher Col, 1980-82; MA Bd of Higher Ed, 1975-76; Trustee, Univ of Lowell, 1975-78; Adv Com, MD Bd of Higher Ed, 1980-82; cp/MA Gov's Comm on the Status of Wom, 1971-74; hon/Pubs, *Recurrent Unemploymt in Manchester* 1966, "Ecs of Aging" in *Understanding Aging* 1976, *Wom's Inferior Ed: An Economic Anal* 1976, "Ed & the MA Wom" in *Sex Bias in the Schs* 1977; Phi Beta Kappa; Intl W/W in Ed; W/W of Am Wom.

FLAHERTY, JOHN P oc/Justice of the Supreme Court of Pennsylvania; b/Nov 19, 1931; h/901 William Penn Court, Pittsburgh, PA 15221; ba/Pittsburgh, PA; c/John P III, Michael B, Kathleen, Thomas; p/J Paul Flaherty (dec); Mary G McLaughlin (dec); ed/BA in Phil, Duquesne Univ, 1953; JD, Univ of Pgh Sch of Law, 1958; mil/Lt, AUS, 1953-55; pa/Pvt Pract of Law, 1958-73; Mem of Fac, Carnegie-Mellon Univ, 1958-73; Judge, Ct of Common Pleas of Allegheny Co, 1973-; Pres, Judge Civil Div, 1978-; Justice of the Supr Ct of PA, 1979-; cp/PA Soc; Mil Hist Soc of Ireland; Irish Soc of Pgh; Friendly Sons of St Patrick; Irish-Am Cultural Inst; Gaelic Arts Soc; K Equity; Ancient Order of Hibernians; Am Legion; hon/Author of Many Pub'd Opinions & Articles; Named Man of Yr in Law & Govt, Gtr Pgh JCs, 1978; Distinguishing Alumnus 1977, Chm of Hon Exec Bd, PA Acad of Sci; W/W: in Am Law, in Am, in World; Others.

FLAHERTY, ROSE IZZO oc/Educator, K-6, District Reading Specialist; b/Feb 9, 1929; h/10 Orchard Street, Glen Head, NY 11545; ba/Manhasset, NY; m/Joseph A; p/P A (dec) and Mary N D'Andre Izzo; ed/BS, Ed, Potsdam St Tchrs Col, 1951; MS, Ed, St Lawrence Univ, 1954; Profl Dipl in Rdg Ed 1965, EdD in Rdg Ed 1974, Hofstra Univ; Cert'd in Common Br Subjects K-8; pa/Dist Rdg Spec, K-6, Manhasset Public Schs, 1980-; Diagnostic Rdg Spec, Manhasset, 1923-80; Hd Rdg Conslt, Manhasset Elem Sch (Est'd Primary Diagnostic Lrng Ctr), 1966-70; Clrm Tchr, Grades 3, 4, 5, 6, 1956-60; Clrm Tchr of Grades 2, 5, 8, 1951-56, & Supvr of Undergrads, SUTC Potsdam, Congdon Campus Sch; Taught Grad Courses at C W Post, LI Univ (Assoc Prof), Queens Col; Boces Grad Asst, Hofstra Univ; Rdg Clinician, Hofstra Univ; Nassau Rdg Coun, Pres, VP-Elect,

Prog Chp, VP, Treas, Mbrship Chp, Coor of Several Confs, Chp & Mem of Var Coms, Conf Spkr; NY St Rdg Assn, Current Pres, Secy, Coor of Several Confs & Insts on Var Coms; IRA, Comprehensive Mbrship, Conf Spkr, Wk'd on Coms; NEA, Life Mem; hon/Pubs, *About Rdg* 1968-70, "Boys' Difficulty Lrng to Read" in *Elem Ed* May 1966, "Perceptual Skills" (Olfactory & Gratatory) in *Instrs* Feb 1974; Cert of Apprec in Grateful Recog of Sustained Interest & Dedication on Behalf of NRC, 1980; Cand for Tchr of Rdg Awd, 1981; Cand for Rdg Edr Awd, 1982; IRA for Outstg Contbn to Rdg Coun Activs, 1982; W/W of Am Wom.

FLANAGAN, MAUREEN ANNE oc/Sales Manager; b/Oct 13, 1953; h/229 Rosewood Terrace, Linden, NJ 07036; ba/North Plainfield, NJ; p/Mrs Helen M Flanagan, Linden, NJ; ed/BA, Kean Col, 1975; pa/Sales Mgr, ASCO Intl Inc (Mfg Security Sys), 1983-; Prod Mgr, REA Intl Inc, 1977-82; cp/Ctl NJ Wom's Netwk Grp, 1980-; Union Co Wom's Polit Caucus, 1980-; Yg Dems of Union Co, 1980-; 9th Ward Dem Clb, 1980-; Plainfield Ski Clb, 1980-; Prog June 1980 Unsuccessful Cand for Freeholder, Union Co CoChp, 1981-82; hon/Dean's List, Kean Col, 1971-72; Nat Hon Soc, HS, 1970-71; W/W in Am Wom.

FLANAGAN, THOMAS JAMES oc/United States Navy Commander, Executive Officer; b/Dec 11, 1949; h/16 Heron Lane, Groton, CT 06340; ba/Groton, CT; m/Pamela Gwen Bearden; c/Shawn Thomas; p/Mr and Mrs Thomas V Flanagan, Mineola, NY; ed/BS, US Nav Acad, 1971; MS in Nuclear Engrg, MIT, 1972; Att'd, USN Nuclear Power Sch & Nuclear Prototype, 1972-73; mil/Active Duty, USN, 1967-; pa/Exec Ofcr, USS FL (SSBN 728), 1982-; Submarine Force Chem & Reactor Controls Ofcr, Staff Cmdr Submarine Force, US Atl Fleet, 1980-82; Engr Ofcr, USS L Mendel Rivers (SSN 686), 1977-80; Damage Control Asst, USS Memphis (SSN 691), 1976-77; Main Propulsion Asst, USS Whale (SSN 638); Am Security Coun, Nat Adv Bd; US Nav Inst; US Nav Acad Alumni Assn; Am Def Preparedness Assn; Nav Submarine Leag; hon/Pub, "Augmentation of Wet Natural Draft Cooling Tower Perf," Am Nuclear Soc at Annual Conf, 1973; Early Selected to Rank of Cmdr 3 Yrs Ahead of Classmates, 1st & Only Mem of Graduating Class of US Nav Acad to Be Selected; 1981 Norfolk Navy Decathalon Champ; Nat Hon Soc, 1962-63; W/W in S & SW.

FLECK, GEORGE MORRISON oc/Chemical Educator; b/May 13, 1934; h/Village Hill Road, Williamsburg, MA 01096-0301; ba/Northampton, MA; m/Margaret D Reynolds; c/Margaret Morrison, Louise Elizabeth; p/Ford and Deloris Fleck, Columbia City, IN; ed/BS, Yale, 1956; PhD, WI, 1961; pa/Instr, Univ of WI, Sum 1961; Asst Prof 1961-67, Assoc Prof 1967-76, Prof 1976-, Dept Chair 1968-71, 1983-, Smith Col; Sigma Xi; Am Chem Soc; Soc for Values in Higher Ed; Danforth Assocs; hon/Pubs, *Equilibria in Solution* 1966, *Chem Reaction Mechanisms* 1971, *Carboxylic Acid Equilibria* 1973, *Chem: Molecules That Matter* 1974, *Patterns of Symmetry* 1977, Num Articles in Sci Jours; Jack Merrilat Griffin Scholar,

1952-56; Wm H Danforth Fellow, 1956-61; E I duPont Nemours Fellow, 1960-61; Grants from NIH, NSF, US Ofc of Ed, Am Philosophical Soc.

FLEMING, MILO JOSEPH oc/Attorney-at-Law; b/Jan 4, 1911; h/120 W Jefferson Avenue, Watseka, IL 60970; ba/Watseka, IL; m/Lucy Anna; c/Elizabeth Fleming Weber; Stepchd: Michael Bartlett Russell, Jo Ann Russell Clemens; ed/AB 1933, LLB 1936, Univ of IL; John Marshall Law Sch; pa/Pvt Pract of Law, 1936-42, 1958-59; Pallissard & Fleming, Watseka, IL, 1942-46; Pallissard, Fleming & Oram, 1946-58; Fleming & McGrew, 1960-76; Fleming, McGrew & Boyer, 1977; Fleming & Boyer, 1977-80; Fleming, Boyer & Strough, 1980-82; Fleming & Strough, 1982-; Mun Atty; Developer, Belmont Acres; Asst Atty Gen, Iroquois Co, 1964-69; Pres, Belmont Water Co, 1976-81; Pres, Iroquois Co Devel Corp, 1961-68; cp/Grand Sr Warden of Grand Encampmnt of IL, IOOF, 1984-85; Grand Master, Grand Lodge of IL of the IOOF, 1964-65; Mem, Bd of Trustees of Odd Fellows Old Folks Home, Mattoon, IL, 1966-71; Mason, Shriner; r/Meth; hon/Num Pubs; Awd of Merit, Watseka C of C in Field of Indust Relats, 1983; Meritorious Ser Jewel, Grand Encampmnt of IL of the IOOF, 1980; Life Mem, Univ of IL Pres's Coun, 1979; Third Place (twice), USA, Competition for Baldwin Prize in Field of Mun Govt, 1932, 1933; DIB; World W/W; W/W: in Am Law, in Fin & Indust, in MW; 2,000 Notable Ams.

FLEMING, WILLIAM F oc/Management Consultant; b/Jan 23, 1951; h/2009 Royal Club Court, Arlington, TX 76017; ba/Dallas, TX; m/Katherine Margaret; c/Mary Margaret; p/Bill and Mary Fleming, Waxahachie, TX; ed/BBA, Mgmt & Mktg, Univ of TX-Arlington, 1974; pa/Reg Mgr, Phila Life, 1979-83; Asst Dir of Field Opers, Phila Life, 1977-79; Dir of Field Sers, Southland Life, 1974-77; Univ of TX-Arlington Alumni Assn, Bd of Dirs 1975-, Pres 1980; Arbitration Bd for Dallas-Ft Worth BBB; Camp Grad, Spruce, Dallas Assn of Life Underwriters; Dallas Est Planning Coun; Mem, Lancer's Clb; Bd Trustees, Phi Gamma Delta, Past Pres; cp/Vol, Jr Achmt; Easter Seals; Bd Dirs, Arlington YMCA; Mason, 32 Deg; hon/Univ of TX-Arlington Exec Clb; Past Pres of Univ of TX-Arlington Student Body; Past Bd Mem, TX Student Lobby; Order of Omega (Hon Frat); W/W in S & SW.

FLETCHER, JOHN EDWARD oc/Research Mathematician; b/Jun 12, 1937; h/4211 Norbeck Road, Rockville, MD 20853; ba/Bethesda, MD; m/Carol Ann Serra; c/Leah Reneé, Craig Alan; p/Mr and Mrs James C Fletcher, Zionville, NC; ed/BS in Aero Engrg 1959, MS in Applied Math 1961, NC St Univ; PhD in Math, Univ of MD, 1972; mil/Capt, USAF, 1961-63; pa/Res Assoc, NC St Univ, 1959-61; Adv'd Studies Div, Lockeed, GA, 1964-66; Lab of Applied Studies, NIH, 1966-72; Chief of Applied Math, LAS, DCRT, 1973-83; Acting Chief, LAS, DCRT, 1983-; Current Mem, Soc for Indust & Applied Math, Intl Soc on Oxygen Transport to Tissue; Past Mem, AAAS, NY Acad of Sci; Sigma Xi; Pi Mu Epsilon; Phi Kappa Phi; Tau Beta Pi; Pi Tau Sigma; hon/Num

Pubs in the Sci Lit; Phi Kappa Phi Scholastic Awd, 1956; Phi Tau Sigma VP, 1959; AIAA VP, 1959; Sr Aerospace Design Team Competition Winner, 1959; Outstg Ofcr Designation, USAF, GAFB, NY, 1963; Selected for AF Acad Instr Staff, 1964; Selected for Lockeed-GA Wk-Study Prog, 1964; Sustained High Perf Awd, 1968; Awd'd NIH In-Ser F'ship, 1969; Grp Chm, Life Scis Sessions, 1973 Sum Computer Simulation Conf, Montreal, Canada; Mem, Ad Hoc Com on Math Modeling; FWGPM, EPA Res Panel, 1973-77; DCRT Rep, Adv Com on Computer Usage to Dpty Dir for Sci, NIH, 1978-; Dir's Merit Awd, 1979; Personalities of the S; Men of Achmt; Am Men of Sci; W/W: in E, in Computers & Data Processing, in Am, in MD; DIB.

FLINT, LOU JEAN oc/State Administrator in Higher Education; b/Jul 11, 1934; h/450 East 100 South, Salt Lake City, UT 84111; c/Dirk Kershaw Brown, Kristi Susan B Felix, Flint Kershaw Brown; p/Ella D A McGlinch, Kaysville, UT; ed/EdS 1981, MEd 1974, Univ of UT-SLC; BS, Weber St Col, 1969; pa/Res Analyst & Prog Ofcr for the Ofc of the Commr of Higher Ed, 1981-; Ed Conslt for Ofc of Higher Ed & UT Sys Approach to Individualized Lrng (U-SAIL), TX, SC, FL, UT, 1979-81; Ed Spec, Dist I, Dept of Def, England, Scotland, Norway, Denmark, Holland, Belgium, 1977-79; Kgn Tchr, Muir Sch, Davis Dist, UT, 1968-77; St Prog VP, AAUW, 1983-85; St Wom's Chair, Delta Kappa Gamma, 1983-85; Chair, UT's Wom & Bus Conf, 1982-85; Am Coun on Ed, UT Planning Bd, 1982-; Adv Bd, Wom's Resource Ctr, UTC/ SLC, 1982-; Ednl Equity St Plan Com, Voc Ed, Title II, US Fed Govt, SLC, 1982-; hon/Pubs, "The Comprehensive Commun Col: Prob & Prospects" 1980, "Wom in Fac Positions in UT Sys of Higher Ed" 1981-, "Utah's Five Two-Yr Col Salary & Compensation Comparisons w Those of Peer Instns: A Basis for Equity Request" 1981; Awd of Apprec from Gov Matheson, 1983, 1984; Nat Identification Prog of ACE, 1982; Outstg Edr, London, England, 1979; Exemplary Tchr, UT St Bd of Ed, 1970-77; W/W in W.

FLOOD, FREDA PHOEBE oc/Television Executive; h/15 Pine Brook Road, Lincoln Park, NJ 07035; ba/Same; m/ Jimmy; p/Joseph Roberis, Surfside, FL; Rose (dec); ed/BA, Wm Paterson Col, 1976; AA, Co Col, 1973; pa/TV Exec & Opers Mgr, Channel 41-TV, Spanish Intl Netwk, 1962-; Astrological Conslt, Pres of Astrogreetings Inc, 1981-; Pres 1972, NJ Chapt, Nat Soc Geocosmic Res; Intl & Nat Assns of Female Execs; Am Wom Radio-TV; Columnist, The Lincoln Herald, 1980-82; cp/Toastmasters; hon/ Pub, "Solstices, Nodes & Eclipses-The Missing Links," 1974; Psi Chi Hon Soc, 1976; W/W of Am.

FLOWERS, KATHRYN oc/Writer; b/ Sep 23, 1939; h/PO Box 682, Tiburon, CA 94920; ba/Mill Valley, CA 94941; c/John Lakin, Dave Brandon, p/Gen Mgr, Priority Pub'g, 1980-; Fdg Ptnr, Bd Dir, Video Exper, 1980-; News Editor, Edit Writer, KCBS Radio SF, 1975-77; Anchor Reporter, Dir Opers, AMI News Bur, 1977-80; Contbg Ed, Nat Opinion Poll Mag, 1977; cp/Chwom & Commr, Tiburon Pks Comm,

1977-82; Commr Jt Belvedere Tiburon Comm, 1978-79; Tiburon Downtown Comte, 1981; Commr, San Anselmo Yth Soccer Assn, 1973; hon/Alpha Epsilon Rho, Nat Broadcasting Hon, 1961; Gamma Alpha Chi, Nat Woms Advtg Hon, 1961; W/W of Am Wom.

FLOYD, CHARLES E oc/Electrical Maintenance Engineer; b/Sep 10, 1953; h/Route 3, Blairsville, GA 30512; ba/ Murphy, NC; p/Mr and Mrs Willard C Floyd, Blairsville, GA; ed/BA, magna cum laude, Berry Col, 1975; Grad Student, N GA Col, 1976-78; pa/Elect Maintenance Engr, Clifton Precision Div of Litton, 1978-; Prof, Elect Installation & Maintenance, Tri Co Commun Col, 1980-; Chief Electrician, Stower's Elect Co, 1976-78; Electrician, Hughes Elect, 1975-76; Am Soc of Safety Engrs, 1978-; Lic'd Elect Contractor, NC, Unrestricted, 1977-; Lic'd Elect Contractor, GA, Unrestricted, 1978-; Lic'd Elect Contractor, TN, 1980-; cp/Aircraft Owners & Pilots Assn, 1979-; Masonic Lodge, 1982; Nat Rifle Assn, 1981-; hon/ Poetry Pub'd in Ramifications, 1973; W/ W: in Am Cols & Univs, in S & SW.

FLYNN, KEVIN FRANCIS oc/ Nuclear Chemist and Physicist; b/Oct 28, 1927; h/10057 South Longwood Drive, Chicago, IL 60643; ba/Argonne, IL; m/Norma Jean Williams; c/Karen M, Nancé J, James M, Mary T; p/Edward J and Anna M Flynn (dec); ed/BSChE 1950, MSChE 1952, IL Inst of Technol; mil/USN, 1945-47; pa/Nuclear Chem/ Physicist, Argonne Nat Lab, 1950-; Am Chem Soc; Am Nuclear Soc; Am Hlth Physics Soc; Sigma Xi; cp/Beverly Hills Human Relats Coun; Disabled Ams Rally for Equality; SW Com on Peaceful Equality; hon/Author, Approximately 100 Pubs in Var Tech Jours; 50 Oral Presentations Given at Var Tech Meetings; Phi Chi Psi Hon Sci Soc; Am Men of Sci.

FOARD, JAYNE McCOMMONS oc/ High School Counselor; b/Feb 22, 1929; h/PO Box 27, Chesapeake City, MD 21915; ba/North East, MD; m/Robert Taylor; c/Paula Foard Lutz, Robert Taylor Jr; p/Amor Perry (dec) and Ethel Jackson McCommons, Elkton, MD; ed/ BS in Ed, Salisbury St Col, 1950; EdM in Guid & Cnslg, Univ of DE, 1971; pa/ Elem Sch Tchr 1950-, Jr High Tchr of Eng 1959-68, Mid Sch Cnslr 1968-81, HS Cnslr 1981-, Cecil Co Bd of Ed in MD; Delta Kappa Gamma Soc Intl; NEA; APGA; cp/Wom's Col Clb, Pres 1974-75; OES, Worthy Matron 1963; Wom for Fed Restoration, Pres 1974-80; Chesapeake City Dist Civic Assn, Pres 1973-77; Elk Creek Presv Soc; Friends of Cecil Co Lib; Cecil Co Hist Soc; Took Lead in Movement to Restore Chesapeake City, MD, & to Est Its Historic Dist; hon/Wom of the Yr, Wom for Fed Restoration, Chesapeake City, MD, 1977.

FODOR, GABOR BELA oc/Centennial Professor of Chemistry; b/Dec 5, 1915; h/829 Augusta Avenue, Morgantown, WV 26505; ba/Morgantown, WV; p/Domokos Victor and Paula Maria Bayer Fodor; ed/Polytechnic Inst, Graz, Austria, 1934; PhD, Univ of Szeged, Hungary, 1937; DSc, Hungarian Acad of Sci, Budapest, 1952; pa/Univ Demonstrator, Lab Organic Chem, Szeged, Hungary, 1935-38; Res Chem, Chinoin Pharm, Ujpest, Hungary, 1938-45;

Assoc Prof of Chem 1945-49, Prof of Organic Chem 1949-57, Univ of Szeged, Hd, Lab Stereochem, Hungarian Acad of Sci, 1958-65; Prof, Laval Univ, Quebec, 1965-69; Cent Prof, WV Univ, 1969-; Am Chem Soc; Chem Soc of London; Swiss Chem Soc; Hungarian Acad of Scis; Canadian Inst of Chem; Proj Dir, Nat Foun for Cancer Res; hon/ Pubs, Organic Chem 1960, Organische Chemie 1966; Contbr of Num Articles to Profl Jours; Recip, Kossuth Medal, Hungary, 1950, 1954; Silver Medal, Univ of Helsinki, 1958; Fellow, Churchill Col, Cambridge, England, 1961; W/ W: in Am, in S & SW.

FOERSTER, DAVID WILLIAM oc/ Plastic Surgeon; b/Oct 6, 1933; h/1600 Coventry Park, Nichols Hills, OK 73120; ba/Oklahoma City, OK; m/ Barbara Jane; c/Scott Hervey, Steven Price, Lesia Jo Andres, Leslee Dawn Andres, Stanton William, Lara Jane; p/ Dr and Mrs Hervey A Foerster, Nichols Hills, OK; ed/BA, Yale Univ, 1954; MD, OK Univ, 1958; mil/AUS Med Corps, Active Resv, 6 Yrs; pa/Internship, Univ Hosp, OKC, 1958-59; Gen Surg Residency, Univ Hosps, OKC, 1959-62; Plastic Surg Residency, Barnes Hosp 1963-64, St Joseph Hosp 1964-65; Am Soc of Plastic & Reconstructive Surgs, 1967; Am Bd of Plastic Surg, 1967; Intl Soc of Aesthetic Plastic Surgs, 1976; Am Soc for Aesthetic Plastic Surg, 1974; Intl Soc of Clin Plastic Surgs, Fdg Pres 1975; OK Soc of Plastic Surgs, Pres 1969; Adm Editor, Aesthetic Plastic Surg Jour; hon/ Author of Num Sci Articles in Plastic Surg Jours; Inventor of Several Plastic Surg Devises & Instruments; Fellow, Am Col of Surg, 1979; Alpha Omega Alpha Hon Med Soc, 1957; W/W in S & SW.

FOGEL, HENRY oc/Executive Director of National Symphony Orchestra; b/Sep 23, 1942; h/8405 Carderock Drive, Bethesda, MD 20817; ba/Washington, DC; m/Frances Polner Fogel; c/ Karl Franz, Holly Dana; p/Julius and Dorothy (dec) Fogel, Miami Beach, FL; ed/Att'd, Syracuse Univ, 1960-63; pa/ VP & Prog Dir, WONO-FM, 1963-78; Orch Mgr, NY Philharm, 1978-81; Exec Dir, Nat Symph Orch, 1981-; Policy Com, Maj Orch Mgrs, 1982-; Bd of Dirs, Cultural Alliance, 1983-; Bd of Dirs, Syracuse Symph Orch, 1976-78; Record Reviewer, Ovation Mag 1981-, Fanfare 1980-, Jour ARSC 1981-; hon/Marquis W/W.

FOLEY, CHARLES BRADFORD oc/ College Music Professor; b/Jan 30, 1953; h/104 Westwood Drive, Greenville, NC 27834; ba/Greenville, NC; m/Diane Ellen Berger; p/Charles L and Barbara A Foley, Indianapolis, IN; ed/BA, Music Ed, magna cum laude, Ball St Univ, 1975; MM, Woodwind Perf 1977, DMA, Saxophone Perf 1983, Univ of MI, Ann Arbor; pa/Grad Tchg Asst, Univ of MI, 1975-77; Pt-time Instr of Woodwinds, Jordan Col of Music of Butler Univ, 1977; Instr of Woodwinds, Stephen F Austin St Univ, 1977-79; Asst Prof of Saxophone, E Carolina Univ, 1979-; Coor of Undergrad Studies in Music, E Carolina Univ, 1982-84; Acting Asst Dean, Sch of Music, E Carolina Univ, 1984-; Phi Mu Alpha Sinfonia Profl Music Frat; Pi Kappa Lambda Nat Music Hon Soc; Nat Hon Soc; Nat Forensic Leag; Music Tchrs Nat Assn; MENC;

NC Music Edrs Assn; Recording Released through Ednl Music Sers Inc, 1984; N Am Saxophone Alliance, Appt'd Reg Dir, 1982; Perf'd w Indpls Symphonic Band, the Longview (TX) Symph, the E TX Symph, the VA Symph; Served as Clinician & Adjudicator, NC & SC Bandmasters; hon/ Co-Authored, "A Comparison of Clarinet & Saxophone Concepts" in NC Music Ed, May 1983; IN Hoosier Scholar, 1971; Ball St, St S'ships, 1971-75; Grad of Ball St Hons Prog; Phi Mu Alpha S'ships, 1973-74; Univ of MI Sch of Music S'ships, 1975-77; Personalities of the S.

FOLLAIN-GRISELL, VERA SUE oc/ College Administration; b/Jul 6, 1950; h/1205 Prospect Avenue, Takoma Park, MD 20912; ba/Same; m/Didier Bernard; c/Noé René; p/Dr and Mrs Ted Lewis Grisell, Indianapolis, IN; ed/BA, Sociol & Psych, IN Univ, 1971; MA, Ednl Psych, Goddard Col, 1975; PhD Cand; pa/Currently in Pvt Pract; Cnslr, Prog Supvr, Cnslg & Placement Ctr, Gallaudet Col, 1978-82; Conslt, C S R Inc, 1981; Proj Mgr, Surrogate Parent Prog, Contemp Assocs, 1977-79; Deaf-Blind Coor, Public Schs of DC, 1977-78; Conslt, Millard Conklin Ctr for the Deaf-Blind, 1978; Rehab Cnslr w the Blind, Voc Rehab, St of MD, 1972-77; Conslt, Cnslg & Pers Sers, Grad Sch, Univ of MD-Col Pk, 1977; Conslt, Dept of Cnslg, Gallaudet Col, 1976; Conslt, Rockcreek Foun, 1973-75; Exec Dir, Presch for the Multihandicapped, 1970-71; Residential Dir, Foun for the Jr Blind, 1969; Cert'd Rehab Cnslr, Comm of Rehab Cnslr Cert; Cert'd Rehab Tchr of the Blind, Assn for Ed & Rehab of the Blind & Visually Impaired; Cert'd Braille Transcriber, Lib of Cong; Cert'd Tnr for Nat Inst on Drug Abuse; Assn for Ed & Rehab of the Blind & Visually Impaired; Am Deafness & Rehab Assn; APGA; G E Loeb Foun Inc, Bd of Dirs; Nat Rehab Cnslg Assn; Registry of Interpreters for the Deaf; Rho Chi Sigma, Rehab Cnslg Hon Soc, Xi Pres; r/Quaker; hon/Pubs, "Life-Career Devel Sers for Deaf Col Students" in Jour of Rehab of the Deaf Jul 1982, "Factors in the Design & Implementation of Substance Abuse Programming w the Deaf" in Deafness, Mtl Hlth & Substance Abuse Proceedings May 1981, "Labels: More Indep for Blind People" in Up Front Newspaper for the Disabled Winter 1982; W/W in E.

FONG, KENNETH WAYNE oc/Trust Investment Officer; b/Nov 5, 1955; h/ 2020 Silver Avenue, Las Vegas, NV 89102; p/Wing and Lilly Fong, Las Vegas, NV; ed/BS w High Distn in Bus Adm, Univ of NV-Las Vegas, 1978; MBA, SF St Univ, 1982; pa/Mgr, Retailing, Sears, Roebuck and Co, 1978-80; Tchg Asst, Sch of Bus, SF St Univ, 1981; Trust Investmt Ofcr, Val Bk of NV, 1982-; Am Inst of Bkg, 1982-; Am Bkrs Assn, 1982-; Assn of MBA Execs, 1980-; cp/Chinese Student Assn, Univ NV Las Vegas, Chm 1975, Treas 1976; VP of Sunrise Hosp Explorer Scouts, 1973-74; r/Elder, First Presb Ch, 1982-; Rep, Col Coun, Presb Ch in Chinatown, SF, 1976; hon/Phi Kappa Phi, Univ of NV-Las Vegas, 1977-78; Psi Chi, Univ of NV Las Vegas, 1977; Phi Lambda Alpha, Univ of NV-Las Vegas, 1975; Nat Student Exch Prog to Univ of

HI-Honolulu, 1976-77 (Univ of NV-Las Vegas Rep in Exch); Poetry, "Forgiveness" in Am Col Poetry Anthology 1976, "If Distorted" in Joyce Kilmer Meml Nat Poetry Contest 1981 & Rocky Mtn Poetry Qtrly; Nat Dean's List; W/W Among Students in Am Univs & Cols; Men of Achmt; Intl Yth in Achmt.

FONT, NYDIA E oc/Associate Professor of Music; b/Jul 21, 1927; h/553 Rosales Street, Santurce, PR 00909; ba/ Rio Piedras, PR; m/Arturo Vera (dec); c/Alfredo; p/Salvador Font (dec), Maria Luisa Chiesa-Font (dec); ed/Dipl in Piano 1949, Postgrad Dipl in Piano 1951, Juilliard Sch of Music; MMus, Univ of KS, 1968; Pvt Tchrs incl Yves Nat, Maurice Hewitt, Nadia Boulanger & Fernando Valenti; pa/Prof of Piano, Conservatorio Demusica de PR, 1960-67; Prof of Music 1960-, First Chm of Newly Formed Music Dept 1965-67, Chm of Dept of Music 1977-79, Carrilloneuse 1980-, Univ of PR; Ateneo Puertorriqueño, 1956-, Bd of Dirs 1961-63; Sociedad Musical de PR, 1973-, Activs Com 1975, VP 1977; Am Musicological Soc, 1974; Col Music Soc, 1976; AAUW, 1980; hon/Author of Several Articles on Schoenberg, Beethoven & 18th Cent Harpsichord Music, Pub'd by Cuadernos, Fac of Humanities Review, Univ of PR; Dipl as Outstg Wom in Music, Mayor of San Juan, PR; Intl W/W in Music; Musicians Dir; Diccionario de Personalidades Puertorriqueñas de Hoy.

FOOTE, EVELYN PATRICIA oc/ Military Police Group Commander; b/ May 19, 1930; h/1327 Arlene Court, Lilburn, GA 30247; ba/APO NY (Mannheim, Germany); p/Henry A and Evelyn W Foote (dec); ed/BA, Wake Forest Univ, 1953; MS, Shippensburg St Col, 1977; AUS Command & Gen Staff Col, 1972; AUS War Col, 1977; Exec Prog, Darden Grad Sch of Bus, Univ of VA, 1980; Student, St Dept Fgn Ser Inst, Germany, 1983; mil/AUS, Continuous Since Feb 1960; pa/Platoon Ldr, WAC Tng Bat, Ft McClellan, 1960-61; Recruiting Ofcr, 6th AUS Recruiting Dist, 1961-64; Co Cmdr, Ft Belvoir, 1964-66; Exec Ofcr, Public Affairs, AUS Vietnam, 1967; Exec Ofc, WAC Br, Ofc of Pers Opers, 1968-71; Progs Ofcr, ODCSPER-DA, 1972-74; Staff Ofcr, ODCSPER-FORSCOM, Ft McPherson, 1974-76; Cmdr, 2nd BT BN, Ft McClellan, 1977-79; Fac, AUS War Col, Carlisle Barracks, 1979-82; Cmdr, 42 MP Grp (Mannheim) APO NY, 1983-; AAUW; Nat Assn of Female Execs; Assn of AUS; WAC Vets Assn; Am Soc of Public Admrs; Inter-Univ Sem on the Armed Forces & Soc; cp/ NOW; hon/Contributed Articles to Var Profl Jours & Books, 1972, 1980, 1982; Sigma Phi Alpha & Phi Beta Kappa, 1953; Dist'd Mil Grad, Ofcr Basic Corps, 1960; Hon Grad, Ofcr Adv'd Corps, 1966; Mil Hons, Legion of Merit, Meritorious Ser Medal (2 OLCs), Army Commend Medal (1 OLC), Meritorious Unit Cit (USARV), Vietnam Cross of Gallantry, Gen Staff Identification Badge; W/W of Am Wom.

FORAN, KENNETH LAWRENCE oc/Director, Merit Systems Review and Studies; b/Aug 14, 1941; h/5001 Seminary Road, Alexandria, VA 22311; ba/ Washington, DC; p/Mr and Mrs Lawrence R Foran, Orange, VA; ed/AB,

Dartmouth Col, 1963; MPA, Harvard Univ, 1971; JD, Cornell Univ, 1970; Dipl, Cambridge Univ, 1972; mil/USMC Resv, Maj; pa/Law Clk, Hon Paul C Weick, US Ct of Appeals, 6th Circuit, 1972-73; Asst Prof of Law, T C Wims Sch of Law, Univ of Richmond, 1974-76; Prof of Law, Potomac Sch of Law, 1976-77; Cnsl, Subcom on the Constit, Com on the Jud, US Senate, 1977-78; Pvt Pract, 1979-82; Dir, Merit Sys Review & Studies, US Merit Sys Protection Bd, 1982-; cp/Alexandria Kiwanis Clb, Bd of Dirs 1980-82, Maj Emphasis Chm, Div 20, 1981-82; Alexandria Tourist Coun, 1982-; Geo Wash Birthday Celebration Com, Chm 1978-80; Legis Com, Alexandria C of C; Alexandria Perf'g Arts Coun, 1981-; Chm, Alexandria YMCA, 1981-; r/Epis; Vestry, Christ Ch; hon/Fed Bar Assn Commend, 1975; Evan-Lewis-Thomas Law Studentship Sidney Sussex Col; Littauer F'ship, Harvard Univ; Outstg Yg Men of Am; Personalities of the S; W/W in Am.

FORD, HAROLD EUGENE oc/United States Congressman; b/May 20, 1945; h/885 Twinkletown Cove, Memphis, TN 38116; ba/Washington, DC; m/ Dorothy Bowles; c/Harold Eugene Jr, Newton Jake, Sir Isaac; p/Newton J and Vera Ford, Memphis, TN; ed/BS; AA; pa/Current US Rep, 9th Dist, St of TN; Former US Rep, 8th Dist, St of TN; House Ways & Means Com, Select Com on Aging, King Subcom; cp/Mtl Hlth Bd; Shelby Co Commun Action Agy; Trustee, Rust Col; r/Bapt; hon/Majority Whip, TN St Legis, 87th Gen Assem; Fellow, Harvard Inst of Polit, Harvard Univ; Outstg Yg Man of Yr Awd, Memphis JCs, 1976.

FORD, JUDITH ANNE oc/Physical Educator, Former Miss America; b/Dec 26, 1949; h/1540 Whitney Boulevard, Belvidere, IL 61008; m/Edwin C Johnson; c/Bradley Edwin, Brian Ford; p/ Virgil and Marjorie Visser Ford, Belvidere, IL; ed/SWn LA Univ, 1967-68; BS, cum laude, Univ of IL, 1973; pa/Began Competition in Swimming & Diving at 8 Yrs of Age; Adv'd to Jr Olympics; US Gymnastics Team, 1965; Rep'd US in Intl Gymnaestrada, Vienna; Competed Natly & Intly on Trampoline, Won Num Medals & Trophies; Instr, Hd Life Guard, Belvidere Swim'g Pool, Sums 1963-68; Fair Queen: Boone Co 1966, IL St 1967; Miss IL, 1968; Miss Am 1969, Ext Travel; Ambassadress, Nat Bowling Coun, 3 Yrs; Pres's Coun on Phy Fitness & Sports; Nat AAU Com on Trampolining; Nat Jr Olympics Trampoline Com; Coaching Staff, Spec Olympics Inc; Num Appearances as Spkr, Model, Hostess, Judge, TV Talk Show Guest, Comml Actress, Dir & Asst in Gymnastic & Sports Clins, Others; Nat Spokesperson, Roses Inc, 1980-84 (Gives Demos on TV & to Var Orgs on Rose Arrangements & Rose Growing); Nat Spokesperson, Water Quality Assn, 1981- (Gives TV Demos on the Hardness of Water in Specific Areas & Radio & Newspaper Interviews on the Subject of Water Quality); hon/Featured on Mag Covers & in Num Feature Stories; Alpha Lambda Delta; Phi Kappa Phi; Nom for BSA Outstg Nat Yg Am Awd, 1971; Ofcl Chaperone for US Trampoline Team, 1972; Trophy for Outstg Contbn to Nat PE Progs, Am

Ftball & Basketball Conf, 1972; Cit Prot Foun of Gtr Chgo Bus Ldrs; Biogl Listings.

FORD, W ANTOINETTE oc/Assistant Administrator; b/Dec 14, 1941; h/2909 Park Drive Southeast, Washington, DC 20020; ba/Washington, DC; m/Melvin W; c/Regan; p/Rosemary Taylor, Philadelphia, PA; ed/Student of French, Laval Univ, Quebec, 1960; BS, Biol, Chestnut Hill Col, 1963; MS, Biol, The Am Univ, 1966; NSF Fellow, Stanford Univ, 1967; Oceanography Cert, US Dept of Navy, 1968; Inst of Polit Fellow, Harvard Univ, 1975; Mgmt Cert, Fed Exec Inst, 1976; pa/Mgr, Gen Motors Corp, 1978- (Pers: Human Resources Planning, Managerial Recruiting, Minority & Female Exec Devel; Mfg: Forward Planning for Mfg Opers in a Divisional Body & Assem Plant); Conslt, Govt Relats, Regulatory Anal, Pers Mgmt & Public Affairs, 1975-77 (Partial Client List: Dow Chem Co, Monsanto Corp, Dow Corning, So Railway Sys, Hanes Corp, Ogden Corp); Spec Asst to the Dir of the Ofc of Minority Bus Enterprise & Mktg Spec, Bur of Intl Commerce, Dept of Commerce, 1972-75; Oceanographer, Nat Oceanographic Data Ctr, Smithsonian Oceanographic Ctr, Bur of Comml Fisheries, 1964-71; Dpty Dir, Ofc of Fed Contract Compliance Progs, Dept of Labor, 1976-77; Pres Clemency Bd, 1975-76; White House Fellow, Asst to the Secy of Treas, 1971-72; cp/DC City Coun, 1973-75; hon/Outstg Ser Awd, Nat Hook-Up of Black Wom, 1979; Outstg Ser Awd, UN Assn, 1977; Am Coun of Yg Polit Ldrs, Rep to the Soviet Union 1974; Intl Peace Acad, US Del 1972; Most Successful Under-30 Wom, *New Woman*, 1971; Outstg Ser Awd, Smithsonian Instn, 1966; W/W in Black Am; Outstg Yg Wom of Am.

FORD, WALLACE L II oc/Executive Director and Chief Executive Officer; b/Jan 13, 1950; h/706 Riverside Drive, New York, NY 10031; ba/New York, NY; m/Rikki Elaine; p/Mr Wallace L Ford, Washington, DC; Mrs Carmen E Ford, Teaneck, NJ; ed/AB, Dartmouth Col, 1970; JD, Harvard Law Sch, 1973; pa/Exec Dir, CEO, St of NY Mortgage Agy, 1983-; Dpty Commr, NY St Dept of Commerce, Div of Minority Bus Devel, 1981-83; Exec VP, Gen Counsel, Amistad DOT Venture Capital Inc, 1979-81; Counsel to the Law Firm of Silvera, Brooks & Latimer, NY, 1979-81; Counsel to NY St Assem Com on Bkg (Assemblyman Herman D Farrell, Chm), 1979; Law Secy, NY St Supr Ct, First Jud Dist, 1975-79; Assoc, Golenbock & Barell, NY, 1973-75; Lics to Pract, NY St 1974, US Dist Ct (So), Dist of NY 1974, US Dist Ct (En), Dist of NY 1974; Am Arbitration Assn; Assn of the Bar of the City of NY; Dartmouth Col Alumni Assn of NYC, Former VP; Dartmouth Col Black Alumni Assn; Bd of Dirs, Edwin Gould Sers for Chd; Harlem Lwyrs Assn, Former Pres, Bd Mem; Feature Writer and Columnist, w Articles Appearing in *NY Law Jour, NY Voice, Amsterdam News, Essence*; Spchwriter for Congressman Charles B Rangel, NY St Senator Carl McCall, Mayor Richard Hatcher of IN, Earl Graves (Publisher of *Black Enterprise Mag*), David Dinkins (City Clk & Chm of the Coun of Black Elected Dems), O T Wells (Former Pres

of the Nat Bar Assn), Percy Sutton (Former Manhattan Borough Pres); Commentator, WNBC-TV 1978, WLIB-AM 1981-82; cp/Bd Mem, March of Dimes; hon/Pubs, "Don't Disrupt a Mechanism that Works" in *The NY Times Bus Sect* 1983, "Targeted Mortgage Bonds Revive Three Neighborhoods" in *The Bond Buyer* 1983; "One Hundred Ldrs of the Future," *Ebony Mag*, 1978; "Fifty Faces for the Future," *Time Mag*, 1979; "Legal Sers Awrd," *Caribbean Am Legal Inst*, 1981; Sr Fellow, Dartmouth Col.

FORD, WENDELL H oc/United States Senator; b/Sep 8, 1924; m/Jean Neel; c/Mrs Shirley Dexter, Steve; p/Senator and Mrs E M Ford (dec); ed/Att'd, Univ of KY; Hon Degs, Univ of KY, En St Univ, Morehead St Univ, Murray St Univ, Union Col, KY Wesleyan Col, Brescia Col; pa/US Senator, St of KY, 1974-; Chief Adm Asst, Former Gov Bert Combs, 1959; Elected to St Senate, Daviess & Hancock Cos, 1965; Elected Lt Gov, 1967; Elected KY's 49th Gov, 1971; Serves on Energy Subcoms, Energy Res & Devel, Energy Regulation, Water & Power; Commerce, Sci & Trans Com (Consumer, Communs & Sci, Technol & Space Subcoms); Ranking Minority Mem, Com on Rules & Adm; Dem Steering Com, Appt'd as Freshman 1975; Engineered the Election of Robert Strauss as Nat Dem Party Chm, 1973; Chm, Nat Dem Govs' Caucus, 1973, 1974; Chm, Dem Nat Campaign Com, 1976; Hd, Dem Senatorial Campaign Com, 1976-; cp/St Pres, KY JCs (Only Kentuckian to Be Elected Nat Pres of the JCs & Intl VP); KY March of Dimes; hon/One of Three Outstg Yg Men in KY, 1955; Recip, Am Cancer Assn's Layman Awd for Outstg Contbns in the Fight Agnst Cancer, 1958; March of Dimes "Ptnr in Progress" (the Org's Highest Indiv Awd of Apprec); Recip, BSA's Highest Ser Awd; Recip of the Highest Awd of Merit, Univ of L'ville & Wn KY Univ; First Kentuckian Ever to Be Elected to Consecutive Terms as Lt Gov, Gov & US Senator.

FOREHAND, MILDRED oc/Educator; b/Feb 1, 1931; h/2905 Haverford Road, Baltimore, MD 21216; m/Lloyd A; c/Gina, Lorisa, Dorita Virginia, Donnel; p/Ervin and Thelma McDaniels; ed/BS, NY Univ, 1953; MA, Univ of MD, 1969; Postgrad, Johns Hopkins Univ & NEn Univ; Tchr, Burke HS, 1954; Rec Dir, Balto Dept of Rec, 1956; Probation Ofcr, Supr Bench Balto, 1957; Dir of Ed, MD Chd's Ctr, 1959; Dir of Child Care, Balto Soc Sers, 1967; Eng Dept Hd 1969, Admr 1979, BCPS; MD Coun Tchrs of Eng Lang Arts, Jour Adv Bd; NCTE, Exec Com; Conf Sec'dy Sch Eng Dept Chps, Mbrship Chp 1981, Assoc Chp 1980, Chp 1982; hon/Pubs, *Annotated Bibliog on Spch Improvement* 1970, Articles in *Eng Jour* & "CSSEDC Qtrly," CSSEDC's *Notes for the Chp* 1982; Lambda Kappa Mu Sorority Meritorious Ser, 1967; Mt Holly Improvement Assn, Outstg Commun Ser, 1970; Balto City Fair, Spec Baltimorean 1973, Mayor & City Coun Apprec 1982, 1984; Intl Biog; W/W in MD.

FOREMAN, MARION BLANCHE PRESLEY oc/Elementary School Principal; b/Apr 15, 1925; h/101 Queens Circle, Ponoma City, FL 32405; ba/Ponoma City, FL; c/Linda Lou Foreman

Thomson, Leon Franklin; p/Mr and Mrs M F Presley (dec); ed/BA, 1967; MS, 1972; Spec Deg, 1979; Doct Deg in Ed, 1983; pa/Eng Tchr, Dupal Co, 1967-70; Cnslr, Nassau Co, 1970-72; Cnslr, St Johns Co, 1972-77; Cnslr, Bay Co, 1977-82; Prin, W Bay Elem Sch, Bay Co, 1982-; Reg Coor, Am Assn of Cnslr Edrs & Supvrs; Am Assn of Sch Admrs; cp/Pres, Goodwill Industs; Pres, Gulf Coast Broadcasting Mins Inc; VP, Bd of Trustees, Gulf Coast Sem; hon/Pub, *A Plan for Early Diagnostic/Prescriptive Lrng Progs*, FL St Univ, 1979; Hon Doct Deg, Gulf Coast Sem, 1982.

FOREST, HERMAN SILVA oc/Professor of Biology; b/Feb 18, 1921; h/19 Genesee Park Boulevard, Rochester, NY 14611; ba/Geneseo, NY; m/Grace Marie Wyman; c/Samuel, Benjamin; p/William H and Fannie S Silva (dec); ed/BA, Univ of TN, 1942; MS 1948, PhD 1951, MI St Univ; mil/Merch Marine, Nav Resv, 1942-44; Army, 1944-46, 1951-53; pa/Biol Instr, Col of Wm & Mary, 1953; Botany Instr, Univ of TN, 1954-55; Asst Prof, Univ of OK, 1955-58; Res Assoc, Univ of TN Res Ctr, 1958-60; Res Asst, Univ of OK Med Ctr, 1960-61; Res Assoc, Univ of Rochester, 1961-65; Prof, SUNY-Geneseo, 1965-; Prin Scist, Envir Resource Ctr at Geneseo, 1968-80; Mbrship in 14 Profl Orgs; Co-Fdr, Phycological Soc of Am & Intl Assn Vascular Aquatic Plant Biologists; Advr, NY St Depts of Hlth & Envir Conserv, 1965-74; Nat Lectr, Am Inst Biol Sci 1970, Sci Inst Public Info 1974; Chm, Intl Gr Lakes Res Conf, 1979; r/Jewish; hon/Pubs, *Handbook of Algae* 1954, *Jessie's Chd* 1959, *The Limnology of Conesus Lake in Lakes of NY St* 1978, 60 Reviewed Papers, 100 Tech Reports; Chief Editor, *Studies of Pollution Control in a Lakefront Commun, 1964-81*; W/W in E, in Am; Am Men & Wom of Sci.

FOREYT, JOHN P oc/Clinical Psychologist; b/Apr 6, 1943; h/7708 Nairn, Houston, TX 77074; ba/Houston, TX; p/John and Ann Foreyt, Manitowoc, WI; ed/BS, Univ of WI, 1965; MS 1967, PhD 1969, FL St Univ; pa/Asst Prof, FL St Univ, 1969-74; Asst Prof 1974-80, Assoc Prof 1980-, Baylor Col of Med; Fellow, Behavior Res & Therapy Soc, 1974-; Acad of Behavioral Med, 1979-; Am Psychol Assn, 1969-; hon/Author, Over 70 Articles on Psychol Res; Pub'd 7 Books; Hons Grad, Univ of WI, 1965; W/W in S; Am Men of Sci.

FORISHA-KOVACH, BARBARA ELLEN oc/College Dean and Management Consultant; b/Dec 28, 1941; h/38 Evans Drive, Cranbury, NJ 08512; ba/New Brunswick, NJ; m/Randy Louis Kovach; c/Deborah Duncan, Mark Kovach, Jennifer Kovach; p/Harry A and Margaret B Lusk, Tarzana, CA; ed/BA 1963, MA 1964, Stanford Univ; PhD, Univ of MD, 1973; pa/Asst Prof of Psych 1973-77, Assoc Prof of Psych 1977-83, Prof of Psych 1983-84, Chp, Dept of Behavioral Scis 1980-83, Univ of MI Dearborn; Pres, Human Sys Anal Inc, Ann Arbor, 1980-; Dean, Univ Col & Prof of Mgmt, Rutgers Univ, 1984-; Am Psychol Assn, 1977-; Am Mgmt Assn, 1984-; AAAS, 1983-; hon/Pubs, *Sex Roles & Personal Awareness* 1978, *Outsiders on the Inside: Wom & Orgs* 1981, *Power & Love: How to Wk for Success & Still Care for Others* 1982, *The Adolescent*

Experience: Devel in Context 1983; *Orgnl Sync: Making Your Job Wk for You* 1983, *The Flexible Org: A Unique New Sys for Mgmt Effectiveness & Success* 1984, Num Jour Articles; Phi Beta Kappa, 1963; Pi Lambda Theta, 1964; Daniel E Prescott Fellow, 1972-73; Susan B Anthony Awd, Univ of MI-Dearborn, 1981; Fac Recog Awd, Univ of MI-Ann Arbor, 1980; W/W in Frontiers of Sci & Technol; W/W in MW.

FORMAN, RUTH LOVE oc/Elementary School Teacher; b/Aug 20, 1938; h/3012 Wenonah Circle, Birmingham, AL 35211; m/Wilbert James; p/Willie James Pippen, Bess, AL; ed/BS, AL A&M Univ, Auburn Univ; pa/Elem Sch Tchr of Math, Rdg & Lang Arts, Grade 4, Jefferson Co Bd of Ed, 1962-; NEA; AEA; JCEA; AFT; Rdg Clb; Math Clb; ABIRA, Nat Bd of Advrs; hon/4-H Female Awd, 1972; 4th Grade Math Fair Co Winners for 5 Yrs; Awd for Outstg & Dedicated Ser, 1981.

FORMAN, W WAYNE oc/Sulphur Company Environmental Affairs Manager; b/Oct 30, 1944; h/4411 Copernicus Street, New Orleans, LA 70114; ba/ New Orleans, LA; m/Sharon K Schwarz; p/W H and Vera B Forman; ed/BS in Zool 1966, MS in Zool (Marine Biol) 1968, LA St Univ; Postgrad, PhD Prog, Tulane Univ; pa/Biol Aide, LA Dept of Wildlife & Fisheries, Grand Terre Marine Lab, 1966; Grad Tchg Asst, Dept of Zool, LA St Univ, 1966-68; Tchg Asst, Gulf Coast Res Lab, 1968; Biologist, Freeport Sulphur Co, Res & Devel Lab, 1968-79; Mgr of Envir Sers, Freeport Sulphur Co, 1979-; Am Fisheries Soc, Cert'd Fisheries Scist; Am Soc of Ichthyologists & Herpetologists; LA Acad of Scis; LA Envir Profls Assn, VP 1980, 1981, Cert'd LA Envir Profl; Water Pollution Control Fdn, Prog Com 1980, Asst Session Presider 1980; Nat Air Pollution Control Assn, Local Meeting Com 1982; LA Air Pollution Control Assn; LA Water Pollution Control Assn; LA Wildlife Biologist Assn, Pub Awd Com 1976, 1980; Gulf Sts Coun on Wildlife, Fisheries & Mosquito Control, Pres 1972; Gulf Estuarine Res Soc; Mem of the Reg Planning Comm, Gtr New Orleans, Adv Com on EPA "208" Progs (Water Quality); Am Inst of Fishery Res Biologists, Elected Mem; cp/Incl'd on List of "Louisiana Yth Orgs"as Biologist Who Can Aid in Conserv Projs, 1969; Fund Raiser, UF of NO, 1972; Advr, Jr Achmt of NO, 1972-73; Presented Num Talks on Marine Biol & Envir Matters to All Levels of Sch Grps & Civic Orgs, 1968-; hon/Pubs, "Notes on the Ecol of Six Species of Cyprinodontid Fishes from Grand Terre, LA" 1968, "An Inventory of the Biomass-An Ecological Approach to Envir Surveillance" 1970; Invited Spkr, LA Assn of Bus & Indust Hazardous Waste Sem, 1980; Pres, The LA Univs Marine Consortium Foun, 1981-; Invited Spkr, Soil Conserv Soc of Am, 1982; W/W in S & SW.

FORNIA, DOROTHY LOUISE oc/ University Administrator; b/Feb 14, 1918; h/6941 Driscoll Street, Long Beach, CA 90815; ba/Long Beach, CA; p/Margaret A Fornia, Long Beach, CA; ed/BS in Ed (Hlth & PE), MA in Hlth & PE 1944, OH St Univ; EdD,Phil, Adm, Univ of So CA, 1957; pa/Instr, Hlth & PE, OH Soldiers & Sailors Home,

1941-43; Grad Asst, Hlth & PE, OH St Univ, 1943-44; Prof, Hlth & PE, Wilmington Col, OH, OH Wesleyan Univ, Bowling Green St Univ, Univ of So CA; Prof & Dir of Grad Studies & Res, Sch of Applied Arts & Scis, CA St Univ Long Bch, 1956-; Dir of Gerontology Prog, CA St Univ Long Bch, 1976-; Num Speeches Made Pertaining to Gerontology & Grad Ed; Dir of Grad Studies & Res, Sch of Applied Arts & Scis, 1966-; Sch Adv Coun, 1966-82; Univ Res Coor, 1968-82; Chm, Univ Grad Coun, 1974-; Dir of Gerontology Prog, 1976-; Chm, Sch of Applied Arts & Scis Grad Coun, 1962-80; Adv Coun Human Devel, 1976-; cp/Bd of Dirs of Geriatric Hlth Care Sys, 1978-; Com Testimony & Witness for Congl Com on Aging, Rep Hannaford's Ofc, 1978; Dirs of Agy Progs on Aging, 1977; Ed Consortium on Gerontology, 1977; Planning Com Hlth Sems, St Mary's Hosp, 1978; Coun of Sponsors, Interfaith Action for Aging, 1979; Prog Com, CSUC Gerontology; hon/Pubs in *Gerontology Res Qtrly* 1979, *Jour of Hlth, Phy Ed, & Rec*; Fellow, Am Sch Hlth Assn, 1958; Delta Epsilon, 1959; Delta Psi Kappa, 1958; Phi Kappa Phi, 1958; Phi Lambda Theta, 1957; DIB; Ldrs in Ed; Personalities in W & MW; 2,000 Wom of Achmt; W/W: of Am Wom, in MW, in W; World W/W of Wom; Commun Ldrs of Am.

FOSS, LUKAS oc/Composer, Conductor, Pianist, Lecturer; b/Aug 15, 1922; m/Cornelia B; c/Christopher, Eliza; p/Martin and Hilde Schindler Foss (dec); ed/Studied Composition, Yale Univ Music Sch; Studied Piano & Conducting, Curtis Inst of Music; Studied Conducting, Berkshire Music Ctr at Tanglewood; Lycee Pasteur, Paris; pa/Music Dir/Conductor, The Milwaukee Symph, 1981-; Past Music Dir/Conductor, Bklyn Philharm; Vis'g Prof of Music, Manhattan Sch of Music, 1972-73; Music Advr/Conductor, Jerusalem Symph, 1972-75; Vis'g Prof of Music, Harvard, 1969-70; Dir/Conductor: Stravinsky Fest, NY Philharm 1965, Franco-Am Fest 1964; Other Former Positions; Guest Conductor, Maj Symph Orchs in US, Canada, Europe, Russia, Japan, Israel, Mexico & S Am; Guest Composer, Conductor & Lectr, Over 100 Am & Canadian Cols & Univs; Acad-Inst of Arts & Lttrs; hon/3 Hon Docts; 2 NY Music Critics' Awds; 9 Composition Awds, incl'g, Guggenheim F'ship, Prix de Rome Ditson Awd for Conductor Who Has Done Most for Am Music; NY St Coun on Arts Grant; NYC Awd for Spec Contbn to Arts; Num Printed Compositions; Pub'd Articles.

FOSTER, M CHRISTINE oc/Executive; b/Mar 19, 1943; h/2367 West Silver Lake Drive, Los Angeles, CA 90039; ba/ 3801 Barham Boulevard, Los Angeles, CA; m/Paul Hunter; p/Ernest A and Mary Foster, Los Angeles, CA; ed/BA, Immaculate Heart Col, 1967; MJ, Univ of CA-LA, 1968; pa/Dir of Devel & Res, Metromedia Prodrs Corp, 1968-71; Dir of Devel & Prodn Sers, The Wolper Org, 1971-76; Mgr of Film Progs, NBC TV Netwk, 1976-77; VPres of Movies & Mini-Series & VPres of Series, Columbia Pictures TV, 1977-81; VPres, Prog Devel, Grp W Prodns, 1981-; Wom in Film, Bd of Dirs, 1977-79; Archdiocesan Communs Comm, l1976-80; cp/Immaculate Heart HS, Bd of Trustees 1978-;

hon/Sigma Delta Chi Outstg Student, 1968; Kappa Tau Alpha Dist'd Student Awd, 1968; Archbishop Cantwell Awd for Gen Scholastic & Ser Excell, 1967; Kappa Gamma Phi Awd, 1967; Delta Epsilon Sigma Awd, 1967; Nat Acad of TV Arts & Scis "Emmy" Awd, 1971; W/ W: in Am, in W, of Am Wom, Among Cols & Univs; Outstg Yg Wom of Am.

FOSTER, RODNEY PATRICK oc/ Training Manager; b/Apr 30, 1951; ba/ 50 East North Temple, Salt Lake City, UT 84150; m/Lynell Porritt; c/Alisa Michelle, Paul Rodney, Melinda Joy, Emily Ruth; p/Cecil and Margaret Foster, St Regis, MT; ed/BA, cum laude, Brigham Yg Univ, 1974; Grad Wk in HRM, Univ of UT, 1977; pa/Adm Asst, First Presidency's Ofc, LDS Ch Ofcs, 1974-80; Mgr of Tng, Temple Dept, LDS Ch Ofcs, 1980-; Am Soc for Tng & Devel; Curric Writer for Intl LDS Ch Lesson Manuals; r/Mormon; hon/W/W: in Am, in W.

FOUNTAIN, ELEANOR MARGARET oc/Consulting and Training; b/ Oct 1, 1942; h/439 Deering Road, Northwest, Atlanta, GA 30309; ba/ Atlanta, GA; p/Leon Issac Fountain, Savannah, GA; Annie Stregles Fountain (dec); ed/SS in Secretarial Sci 1964, BBA w Minors in Psych & Jour 1964, GA So Col; MEd in Psychometry 1971, EdS in Psychometry 1974, PhD in Voc & Career Devel 1977, GA St Univ; pa/Fdr, Fountain Assocs, a Consltg & Tng Org, 1975-; Doct Res Asst to Dr Fred Otte, GA St Univ, 1975; Dir of the Eval & Ser Ctrs, A St Funded Ednl Prog, 1973-75; Instr & Dir of Testing, W GA Col, 1971-73; Info Ofcr for Public Relats, GA Dept of Ed, 1966-70; Instr, Greenleaf Bus Col, 1965-66; Pers Dir, Americana Res Inst, 1965; Am Soc of Tng Dirs; Am BPW Assn; Am Soc of Pers Admrs; Adm Mgmt Soc; cp/Displaced Homemakers; Gov's & Pres's Com on Employmt of the Handicapped; Gov's Prayer Breakfast; So Gov's Conf; Headstart; Judging for Yg Career Wom of the Yr Contest; Judge for Voc Opports Clbs of Am; hon/Dissertation, "Devel of Criterion-Referenced Test of EEO Knowledge" 1977.

FOUNTAIN, SHARON SLACK oc/ Personnel Educator, Management Consultant, Trainer, Administrator; b/Apr 21, 1947; h/15323 Valencia Street, Silver Spring, MD 20904; ba/Silver Spring, MD; m/Glen Harold; p/Richard Agnew Slack, Ft Lauderdale, FL; Nancy Witt Schubert, Spicewood, TX; ed/ Dental Assisting 1965-67, Psych 1970, Bus Adm 1976-78, Montgomery Col; Applied Behavioral Sci, Johns Hopkins Univ, 1982; Human Resource Devel, Am Univ, 1983-; pa/Mkt Res Asst, Resource Mgmt Corp, 1968-69; Spec Ed Asst, Pleasant View Sch, 1969-70; Secy, Univ of MD-Col Pk, 1970-72; Adm Asst, Hydronautics Inc, 1972-73; Org Mgr, Fashion Two-Twenty Cosmetics, 1972-74; Indust Security Admr, Technol Ser Corp, 1974-79; Sr Corporate Staff Mem, Life Dynamics Inc, 1979-80; Pres/Proprietor, Performance Devel Corp, 1980-; Free-Lance Writer; Pt-time Fac Mem, Westinghouse Sch of Applied Engrg Sci 1980-, Montgomery Col, Commun Sers Div 1981-, Howard Commun Col, Commun Ed Div 1979-; Nat Mem, Am Soc for Tng & Devel, 1979-; MD Chapt, Am Soc for Tng &

Devel, Bd of Dirs & Mbrship Chair 1980-82, Treas 1982-83, VP for Profl Devel 1983-; Nat Assn of Wom Bus Owners, 1979-82; Capital Chapt, Nat Assn of Wom Bus Owners, 1979-82; Wom Bus Owners of Rockville, MD, 1981-; cp/Repub Co Election Judge or Alt, 1976-; r/Prot; hon/Pub,"Dare to Be a Ten," 1982; MD Chapt, Am Soc for Tng & Devel, 2 Chapt Awds for Outstg Achmt & Contbns, 1981; Nat Am Soc for Tng & Devel, Reg II Awd for Outstg Achmt & Contbns in the Area of Mbrship Recruitment & Mgmt, 1981; W/W of Am Wom; Wom & Men on the Move.

FOWLER, CHARLES WINSOR oc/ Population Dynamicist; b/Apr 21, 1941; ba/Seattle, WA; m/Jean Forsyth; c/ Catherine Marie; p/Ervon and Merna D Fowler, Loup City, NE; ed/BA w Distn in Biol, Hastings Col, 1963; MS, Univ of WA, 1966; OTS, NSF F'ship to Study w Org for Tropical Studies, Sum 1966; PhD, Univ of WA Ctr for Quantitative Sci in Forestry, Fisheries, & Wildlife & Col of Fisheries, 1973; pa/Pop Dynamicist, Nat Marine Mammal Lab, Nat Marine Fisheries Ser, 1979-; Res Asst Prof, Dept of Wildlife Sci & Ecol Ctr Assoc, UT St Univ, 1977-79; Res Asst Prof, Dept of Wildlife Sci, UT St Univ, 1975-77; Postdoct Fellow, Dept of Wildlife Sci, Col of Natural Resources, UT St Univ, 1973-74; Predoct Res Assoc II 1970-72, Predoct Res Assoc I 1970, Univ of WA, Col of Fisheries; Computer Programming Conslt, Univ of WA, 1970; Tchg Asst for Course Entitled, "Application of Digital Computers to Probs in Aquatic Ecol," Univ of WA, 1969-70; Asst Prof of Biol, La Pontificia Universidad Javeriana, Bogota, Colombia, 1967-69; Lectr, San Jose St Col, 1966-67; Res Asst, Fisheries Res Inst, Univ of WA, 1963-66; Tchg Asst, Invertebrate Zool 1962, Tchg Asst, Gen Biol 1961, Hastings Col; Forestry Aid, US Forest Ser, 1960; Bus Mgr of Hastings Col Student Newspaper, 1960-62; Ecological Soc of Am; Nat Wildlife Fdn; Am Inst of Biol Scis; Sigma Xi; AAAS; r/Unitarian; hon/Pubs, "Selective Extinction & Speciation: Their Influence on the Structure & Functioning of Communities & Ecosystems" 1982, "Sperm Whale Pop & Anal" 1982, "En Tropical Pacific Ecosystem Modeling Study" 1981, "Density Dependence as Related to Life Hist Strategy" 1981, "An Overview of the Study of the Pop Dynamics of Large Mammals" 1981, "Comparative Pops Dynamics in Large Mammals" 1981, "Dynamics of Large Mammal Pops" 1981; HS Salutatorian, Loup City HS, 1959; Regents Recog S'ship,PTA S'ship, Univ of NE Regents S'ship, Hastings Col, 1959-63; Res Asst'ships, Univ of WA, 1963-66, 1969-73; Lewis Goldstein Meml S'ship, Univ of WA, Col of Fisheries, 1973; Co-Recip, Cong Meritorious Awd, Intl Cong on Applied Sys Res & Cybernetics, Acapulco, 1980; W/ W in W.

FOWLER, ELIZABETH MILTON oc/ Real Estate Executive; b/Jan 11, 1919; h/20101 Southwest 92nd Avenue, Miami, FL 33189; ba/Miami, FL; m/ Albert L Jr; c/Patricia Dawn Cecilia, Richard Gordon Sean; p/Arthur Wellington and Mattie Jean Hodges Milton (dec); ed/Studied Bus, Bowling Green

Bus Univ, 1938-39; mil/Spouse of Sr NCO, USAF, 25 Yrs; pa/Secy in Gov Cone's Mansion & Campaign Ofc for US Senator, 1939-40; Secy to Dir Wkmen's Compensation Comm, 1940-41; Secy to Supt Gibbs Ship Yard Repair Div, 1942-44; Secy to Elect Engrs, Reynolds, Smith & Hills, Archs & Engrs, 1946-49; Secy to Pres, Aichel Steel Corp, 1949-50; USAF Dep Sch, Ofc Asst, 1951; Fgn Ser Commun Relats Prog, "Oper Christmas," 1952; Admr, Ofc Mgr for Prin, VP, Am Dep Sch, Moron AFB, Spain, 1961-63; Owner-Mgr, "Elizabeth Properties," 1956-; Eglin AFB, 1970-71; Publicity Chm for FS, 1961-63, 1963-64, 1965-69; Nat Assn Female Execs, 1980-; cp/Chm, Ways & Means Com, Chattanooga HS, PTA, 1956-57; Asst Den Mother, Cub Scout Troop, 1970-71; USAF Fam Sers Vol Prog, Spain, Wash & FL, 1961-71; Dade City Crimewatch Org, 1980-; Am Security Coun Adv Bd, US Senatorial Clb & Nat Repub Congl Com, 1982-; Repub Pres Task Force, 1981-; Admr, Retiree Affairs Ofc, Homestead AFB, 1981-; r/Ch of Christ; hon/Recip, Fam Sers Tng Awd Pen, Gen Curtis LeMay, Strategic Air Command, Seville, Spain, 1961; USAF Tng FS Awd Pen, Tactical Air Command, McChord AFB, 1965; AF TIMES Recog Cert, Eglin AFB, 1968; 9 Yrs Ser Stripes FS Prog, 1961-71; Ser Bars for Up to 1500 Vol Hrs, 1971; Ser Apprec Awds as Den Mother for Scouts, 1969-70; 3 Lttrs, Meritorious Ser in Publicity from 3 Base Cmdrs, 1965-66; Several Certs of Apprec for Outstg Ser in Fam Sers Prog; Awd'd Am Flag from Pres Reagan's Repub Pres Task Force for Dedicated Ser, 1982; W/W of Am Wom.

FOWLER, FRANK E oc/Representative for Andrew Wyeth, Jamie Wyeth and Carolyn Wyeth; b/Jun 2, 1946; h/ 1213 Fort Stephenson Oval, Lookout Mountain, TN 37350; ba/Lookout Mountain, TN; m/Mary Elizabeth; c/ Christopher Andrew, Thomas Weston; p/Richard Calvin (dec) and Mamie Howell Fowler, Lookout Mountain, TN; ed/Grad, Baylor Sch for Boys, 1964; BBA, Univ of GA, 1969; pa/Art Dealer Representing Andrew Wyeth, Jamie Wyeth, Carolyn Wyeth & the Est of N C Wyeth; Adv Com for the Arts, John F Kennedy Ctr for the Perf'g Arts; Adv Bd, Univ GA Mus; Bd Dirs, Retirement Sers of Am; Dir, Commerce Union Bk, Chattanooga; Chm, Sustaining Fund, Baylor Sch, Chattanooga; cp/Nat Fin Com, Jimmy Carter Pres Campaign; Dir, The Chd's Home, Chattanooga; hon/Intl Soc of Appraisers; Appraiser's Assn of Am; Greek Horseman, Univ of GA; W/W of S & SW.

FOWLER, RUTH ANN oc/Homemaker, Home Economist, Motivational Speaker; b/Mar 31, 1938; h/1217 Roxmere Road, Tampa, FL 33629; ba/ Seffner, FL; m/Larry M; c/Tiana Kay, Carmen Suzette; p/Holland and Rhobenia Ringwald (dec) Benefiel, St Cloud, FL; ed/BS 1960, MS 1963, Purdue Univ; Adv'd Wk, Univ of So FL; pa/Tchr, Home Ec & Sci, Jr & Sr High, Brookston & Evansville, IN, & Ogden, UT, 1960-66; Instr, Asst Prof of Housing, Equip, Interior Design, UT St Univ & Ball St Univ, 1966-68; Ext Home Economist, Purdue Univ Cooperative Ext, New Castle, IN, 1968-75; Ext Home

Economist, Univ of FL Cooperative Ext, 1975-; FL St Pres, Assn Ext Home Ec Agts; Hostess, Wkly TV 30 Minute Prog, 6 Yrs Running on WEDU-TV 3; Wkly News Column, Sunday, Tampa Tribune, 4 Yrs; Nat Review, Innovative Prog, "Your Fam is Your #1 Bus," Master Homemaker Vol Prog; cp/PTA; Little Leag; Yg Life Coms; Ch Home Tour Com; Sunday Sch Tchr; r/Meth; hon/ALMA Awd, Am Home Appliance Mfrs, 1970; Nat Dist'd Ser Awd, Nat Assn Ext Home Ec Agts, 1980; Outstg Ednl Achmt Awds, Ldrship Devel, Human Relats, News Columns; Nat Winner, TV Feature, Nat Assn Ext Home Economists, 1983; Outstg Wom of Yr 1982, Beta Sigma Phi, Tampa City Coun.

FOWLER, SUSAN ANN oc/Head Operations Manager; b/Dec 30, 1954; h/1726 East 50th Street, Anderson, IN 46013; ba/Anderson, IN; p/Eugene and Margaret Fowler, New Castle, IN; ed/ BS in Mgmt & Fin, Ball St Univ, 1977; pa/Financial Advr to Mayor, City of Muncie, 1977-78; Hd Opers Mgr, RAX of IN Inc, Ft Wayne, 1978-; Nat Assn of Female Execs; Am Bus-wom's Assn; cp/Bd of Dirs, New Haven Fest Com; New Haven C of C; YWCA; UFW Aux; hon/Outstg Commun Involvement, New Haven C of C, 1980; W/W of Am Wom.

FOWLER, TED C oc/Executive; b/ May 1, 1936; h/4311 South Coltrane, Edmond, OK 73034; ba/Oklahoma City, OK; m/Sylvia Sue Sullivan; c/Julie Kay; p/Lloyd (dec) and Sally E Tomlinson Fowler, Memphis, TN; ed/BS, Geol, Univ of TX El Paso, 1958; pa/Geologist, Gr Wn Drilling Co, Midland, TX, 8 Yrs; Exploration Geologist, Gose Petro, Wichita Falls, TX, 2 Yrs; Chief Geologist/Div Mgr, Clarcan Petro Corp, 6 Yrs; Pres, Seneca Oil Co, 1974-; Am Assn Petro Landmen; OKC Landmen's Assn; OK Indep Petro Assn; OKC Geol Soc; cp/Active in 4-H & FFA Progs, OK Co; Edmond C of C; hon/W/W: in the Petro Indust, in Fin & Indust.

FOX, CARL BRANDON JR oc/Patent and Trademark Attorney; b/Feb 21, 1923; h/Route 6, Box 82A, Myrtle Beach, SC 29577; ba/Myrtle Beach, SC; m/Lucille Caroline Outlaw; c/Philip Frederick, Robert Outlaw; p/Carl B Fox (dec); ed/BS in Chem Engrg, Rice Univ, 1945; LLB, S TX Col of Law, 1955; pa/ Process Engr, Mathieson Chem Corp, 1946-53; Examr, US Patent Ofc, 1953-54; Patent Atty, Butler, Binion, Rice, Cook & Knapp, 1954-65; Self-Employed Patent Atty, Houston 1965-82, Myrtle Bch 1982-; Houston Bar Assn; Houston Patent Law Assn; St Bar of TX; Intell Property Sect, St Bar of TX; ABA; hon/Sr Chem Engrg Sem, Vanderbilt Univ, Nashville, 1980.

FOX, JOAN PHYLLIS oc/Principal Engineer and Executive; b/Jul 16, 1945; ba/1988 California Street, Berkeley, CA 94703; p/John A and Nonie L Fox, Rockledge, FL; ed/BS, Physics, Univ of FL, 1971; MS in Envir Engrg 1975, PhD in Envir Engrg 1980, Univ of CA-Berkeley; pa/Envir Conslt, Fox Consltg, 1981-; Prin Investigator & Dir, Coal & Oil Shale Progs, Lawrence Berkeley Lab, 1977-81; Invited Lectr, Dept of Conserv & Resource Studies, Univ of CA-Berkeley, 1980-; Proj Mgr, Oil Shale Prog, Univ of CA-Berkeley,

1976-77; Engr, Bechtel Inc, 1971-76; Res Asst, Lawrence Radiation Lab, 1971; Am Soc of Testing Mats, Subcom D 19.33 on Water Assoc'd w Synthetic Fuel Prodn; Water Pollution Control Fdn; AAAS; Public Lands Inst; Am Geophy Union; Am Chem Soc; Phi Beta Kappa; Sigma Pi Sigma; Nat Acad of Scis Com on Oil Shale; Oil Shale Mgmt Team; Oil Shale Envir Task Force & Exec Com; Paraho Oil Shale Data Eval Grp, Water Quality; Oil Shale Surrogate Standards Com; In-Situ Hydrology Task Force; Task Force on Oil Shale, St of CA; Fossil Energy Task Force; hon/ Pubs, "Eval of Control Technol for Modified In-Situ Oil Shale Retorts" 1983, "The Distbn of Mercury During In-Situ Oil Shale Retorting" 1984, "Hydrogeologic Consequences of Modified In-Situ Retorting Process, Piceance Creek Basin, CO" 1981, "The Partitioning of Maj, Minor, & Trace Elements during In-Situ Oil Shale Retorting", Num Others; BS w High Hons; W/W of Am Wom.

FOX, KENNETH oc/Physicist and Attorney; b/Aug 16, 1935; h/4513 Rising Lane, Bowie, MD 20715; ba/ Knoxville, TN; m/Christina Diana Sabin-Fox; c/Abram Jacob; p/Abraham and Jennie Fox; ed/BS, summa cum laude, Wayne St Univ, 1957; MS 1958, PhD 1962, Univ of MI; pa/Prof, Univ of TN-Knoxville, 1964-; US Nat Acad of Scis Sr Fellow, JPL/Caltech 1967-69, NASA/Goddard 1977-78; Am Astronom Soc; Am Phy Soc, Fellow; Intl Astronom Union; NY Acad of Scis; TN Acad of Sci, Explorers Clb, Fellow; ABA; TN Bar Assn; hon/Author of Nearly 100 Papers in Sci & Tech Jours, Chapts in Several Books; Co-Editor of NASA Wkshop Proceedings; Sigma Xi, 1956; Phi Beta Kappa, 1957; Sr Fulbright Scholar in France, 1975; Am Men & Wom of Sci; W/W in Technol Today.

FOX, LAURETTA EWING oc/ Retired Professor; b/Apr 25, 1910; h/ 1410 Southwest 35 Place, Gainesville, FL 32608; p/Leslie Evans and Mary Ellen McMaster Fox; ed/BS, magna cum laude, Westminster Col, 1931; MS 1932, PhD 1934, Univ of IL; Postdoct, Vanderbilt Univ Sch of Med, 1946; pa/Assoc Prof of Pharm, Univ of FL Col of Med, 1966-76; From Asst to Assoc Prof of Pharm, Univ of FL Col of Pharm, 1949-66; Assoc Prof of Chem, MS St Col for Wom, 1946-47; Hd, Dept Biol Scis, Cinc Col of Pharm, 1947-49; Arthur D Little Fellow & Asst Prof of Biochem, Vanderbilt Univ Sch of Med, 1945-46; Asst Assoc Prof of Biol, NWn St Col of LA, 1936-45; Hd of Sci Dept, Dodd Col, 1935-36; Hd of Biol Scis, Alderson-Broaddus Col, 1934-35; Am Inst of Chem; Fellow, AAAS; Am Med Soc; FL Acad of Sci; Am Pharm Assn; Sigma Xi; Phi Sigma; Sigma Delta Epsilon; Delta Kappa Gamma; hon/ Author of More Than 100 Sci Pubs Concerning Toxicities of Estrogens & Cholesteral Inhibitors & Toxic Constituents of FL Plants; PA St S'ship, 1927-31; Scholar & Fellow, Univ of IL, 1931-34; Book of Hon; 2,000 Wom of Achmt; Register of Profiles; Notable Am of the Bicent Era; Am Men & Wom of Sci.

FOX, ROBERT A oc/Executive; b/ Apr 25, 1937; h/PO Box 3575, San Francisco, CA 94119; ba/San Francisco,

CA; c/Lee Elizabeth, Christina Carolyn; ed/BA w High Hons, Colgate Univ, 1959; MBA, cum laude, Harvard Bus Sch, 1964; pa/Sales Mgr, Procter & Gamble, 1959-62; Gen Sales Mgr, T J Lipton, 1964-69; VP, Mktg, Canada Dry Corp, 1969-72; Pres & CEO, Canada Dry Intl, 1972-75; Exec VP, Hunt Wesson Food, 1975-78; Pres & CEO, RJ Reynolds Tobacco Intl, SA, 1978-80; Pres & CEO 1981-84, Chm & CEO 1985-, Del Monte Corp; Dir, Colgate Univ Alumni Corp; Dir, Aristek Communities Inc, Trustee Euro-Pacific Growth Fund, Standard Chem Inc, New Perspective Fund, Am Balanced Fund, Growth Fund of Am, Income Fund of Am; cp/Pres, SF C of C, 1984; Dir 1982-84; hon/W/W: in Am, in W, in Fin & Indust.

FOXX, ALAN J oc/Computer Graphics Director; b/Jun 7, 1959; h/28090 Tavistock Trail, Southfield, MI 48034; ba/Detroit, MI; p/Dr Harold C and Gloria Greenbert, Southfield, MI; ed/ BGS, Oakland Univ, 1982; pa/Computer Graphics Dir, Ctr for Creat Studies, Col of Art & Design, 1981-; Tchr, Computer Sci Courses, Grosse Pointe Acad; Tchr, Computer Graphics for Cont'g Ed Prog, Oakland Univ; Computer Graphics Conslt (WXYZ-TV, Channel 7); Orgr of Computer Camps for Chd, Grosse Pointe Acad & Oakland Univ 1981; Computer Programmer, Ins Concepts Inc, 1981; Writing Book on Computer Graphics & How it Relates to the Field of Art; IEEE, 1981-; ACM Soc, 1982-; hon/Author, "Colorful Circle & Circle Fill" in Creat Computing Mag, Jan 1983; En MI Univ Hon Roll, 1979.

FRAMIL, ARMANDO R oc/Hospital Representative; b/Aug 12, 1948; h/415 Southwest 28 Road, Miami, FL 33129; m/Maria; c/Carolynne, Carmen Victoria; p/Armando and Maria Framil, Key Biscayne, FL; ed/BA, FL Atl Univ, 1972; EdM, Univ of Miami-Coral Gables, 1977; pa/Hosp Rep, Merck, Sharp & Dohme, 1982-; From Yth Cnslr Supt, to Mgr, to Ec Planner, to Sr Bus Developer, City of Miami, 1977-82; From Yth Cnslr I, to Yth Cnslr II, to Grp Cnslr, FL St Dept Hlth & Rehab Sers, 1973-77; Metro Dade Yth Adv Bd Mem, 1978-84; FL St Juv Ofcrs Assn, 1974-84; cp/Spanish-Am Leag Agnst Discrimination, 1974-; hon/W/W in S & SW; Intl W/W of Contemp Achmt; Men of Achmt.

FRANCE, GARY ALLEN oc/Clinical Psychologist and Native American Artist; b/Dec 20, 1939; h/912 Belle Air, Edmond, OK 73034; ba/Edmond, OK; m/JoAnn Kovachevich; c/David; p/Mrs Thelma France, Albion, IL; ed/PhD, Clin Psych, OK St Univ, 1974; Clin Psych Intern, Gtr KC Mtl Hlth Foun & Med Sch, 1973-74; Child-Adolescent Psych Intern, Proviso Spec Ed Cooperative, 1970-71; pa/Zone Dir, Smoky Mtn Mtl Hlth Ctr, 1974-76; Dir, Edmond Guid Ctr, 1976-81; Adj Clin Psych Prof, OK St Univ, 1976-; Pvt Pract, Clin Psych, 1979-; Am Psychol Assn; OK Psychol Assn; Rep, Minority F'ship Prog, Am Psychol Assn, 1977-78; Reviewer, Minority Review Com, NIMH, 1980-82; Bd, Ethnic & Minority Affairs, Am Psychol Assn, 1980-; Present Exec Dir, Soc of Am Indian Psychols; hon/Author of Num Pub'd Articles in Psych, incl'g,

"Yellow Brick Road Revisited" in Jour of Consltg & Clin Psych; Paintings, "Shell Shaker" in Seminole Mus 1981, "Owl Transformation" in 5 Civilized Tribes Mus 1981; NDEA Fellow, 1968-69; Kappa Delta Pi, 1969; Pres Comm on Mtl Hlth, 1977; Heritage Awd, 1981, 5 Civilized Tribes Mus (Best Contbn to Tribal Art); First Native Am Awd'd PhD in Clin Psych in USA; W/W in S & SW; Men of Achmt.

FRANCIS, DEBBIE LOU oc/Finance Adjuster, Free Lance Model; Aug 16, 1954; ba/1263 Bandera Road, San Antonio, TX, 78228-4088; p/Robert Hugh Francis (dec); Fadra Sue Brown Francis, San Antonio, TX; ed/Att'd Sorbonne Univ, Paris, 1975-76; AA, San Antonio Col, 1979; BS, Univ of TX-San Antonio, 1984; Acctg Clk, SWn Bell Telephone Co, 1972-73; Agy Coor, St John's Studio, Honolulu, HI, 1973-74; Freelance Model, Europe & Scandinavia, 1974-77; Acctg Supvr, SWn Bell Telephone, 1977-78; Co-Owner, RH Francis Co, San Antonio, 1978; Freelance Model; Mem: Exec Secy 1982 & 1983, SW Div Dir 1984, Conv Com 1984, Allied Fin Adjusters Conf Inc; Time Fin Adjusters Inc; Intl Profl Adjusters Inc; Am Recovery Assn; Nat Fdn of Indep Bus; Mensa; cp/Bur of Missing Chd Inc, 1979-; Soc of Perf'g Arts; San Antonio Soc of Perf'g Arts, 1977-; r/Bapt; hon/ Ygest Person & 1st Wom Elected to an Exec Bd of Fin Adjusters; W/W: of Wom, of Intells, in Fin & Indust; DIB.

FRANCIS, JOHN ELBERT oc/Acting Dean; b/Mar 14, 1937; h/1406 Greenbriar. Drive, Norman, OK 73069; ba/ Norman, OK; m/Susan Ruth; c/John Carl, Steven Michael; p/Mr and Mrs John A Francis, Kingfisher, OK; ed/BS, Mech Engrg 1960, MS, Mech Engrg 1963, PhD, Engrg Scis 1965, Univ of OK; pa/Engr, Allis Chalmers Mfg Co, 1960; Asst Prof of Mech Engrg, Univ of MO-Rolla, 1964-66; Asst Prof, Assoc Prof, Prof, Aerospace & Mech Engrg 1966-, Asst Dean of Grad Col 1968-71, Assoc Dean of Col of Engrg 1981-, Univ of OK; AIAA; ASME; Am Soc of Engrg Edrs; Optical Soc of Am; NY Acad of Sci; Am Inst of Physics; Pi Tau Sigma; Sigma Xi; cp/Rotary; r/Rom Cath; hon/ Pubs, "Combined Radiative & Conductive Heat Transfer in a Planar Medium w a Flux Boundary Conduction Using Finite Elements" 1982, "Combined Conductive & Radiative Heat Transfer in an Absorbing, Emitting, & Scattering Cylindrical Medium" 1982, "A Finite Element Approach to Combined Conductive & Radiative Heat Transfer in a Planar Medium" 1982; SAE Ralph Teetor Awd, 1969; OSPE Wonders of Engrg Awd, 1974; W/W: in Engrg, in S & SW; Am Men & Wom of Sci.

FRANCIS, MARION DAVID oc/ Senior Research Scientist; b/May 9, 1923; h/10018 Winlake Drive, Cincinnati, OH 45231; ba/Cincinnati, OH; m/ Emily Liane; c/William Randall, Patricia Ann; p/George Henry Francis (dec); Marian Flanagan Francis, BC, Canada; ed/BA; MA; PhD; pa/Chem, Canadian Fishing Co, 1946; Lab Supvr, Univ of Brit Columbia, 1946-49; Res Assoc, Univ of IA, 1949-51; Chem 1952-76, Sr Scist 1976-, Procter & Gamble Co; OH Acad of Sci; Fellow, Am Inst Chems; Fellow, AAAS; Am Chem Soc, Tech Prog Chm of Ctl Reg Mktg 1983, Tech

Awds Chm 1981, 1982; Soc Nuclear Med; NY Acad Sci; Am Pharm Assn; Acad Sci; Am Soc Bone & Mineral Res; cp/Past Local Chm, Capt U Appeal; r/ Rom Cath; hon/Author of Sci Articles in Profl Jours & Book Chapters (88), Internal Confidential Tech Reports for Procter & Gamble (72), Patents (32); Phi Lambda Upsilon; Gamma Alpha; Chem of the Yr, Cinc Chapt ACS, 1977; Profl Accomplishment Awd in Indust, Tech & Sci Socs Coun of Cinc, 1979; Chosen Del for the China-US Sci Exch, Am Inst of Chems, 1984; Anglo Am Acad, Hon Fellow; W/W in Frontier Sci & Technol; DIB; Men of Achmt; Notable Am; Intl W/W in Commun Ser; Commun Ldrs & Noteworthy Ams; Men & Wom of Distn.

FRANCIS, RAYMOND LLEWELLYN III oc/Public School Teacher; b/Feb 1, 1955; h/307 North Main Street, Abbeville, SC 29620; ba/Abbeville, SC; p/Mr and Mrs Raymond L Francis Jr, Summerville, SC; ed/BA in Music Ed, Newberry Col, 1977; Currently Wkg on Master's Deg in Elem Ed, Armstrong St; pa/Hd Dir, Abbeville Co Band, 1981-; Dir, Hardeeville HS, 1978-81; Chief of Security, Newberry Col, 1976; Laborer, Holmquist Constn, Sums; Phi Mu Alpha; Nat Band Dirs Awds Review Bd; cp/Review Bd, BSA, 10 Yrs; Bd of Explorers, BSA; Order of Arrow; Christian Yth Grp Dir; r/Cath; hon/Tchr of the Yr, 1980; Tchr of the mo, 2 Times; Brotherhood, Order of Arrow, 1973; Phi Mu Alpha Warden; Merit of Commend for Bravery.

FRANK, GERALD W oc/Chief of Staff to United States Senator; ed/Att'd, Stanford Univ, Loyola Univ; BA, MA (w Hons), Cambridge Univ; Hon Dr of Bus Adm, Greenville Col; Hon JD, Pacific Univ; mil/Field Artillery, AUS 1943-46, ETO; pa/VP & Store Mgr, Meier & Frank Co, 1948-65; Spec Asst to US Senator Mark O Hatfield, 1966-72; Chief of Staff to US Senator Mark O Hatfield, 1973-; Pres, Frank Investmt Co; Dir, US Nat Bk of OR; Dir, Am Fed Savs & Ln Assn; Dir, Standard Ins Co; cp/Appt'd by VP Nelson Rockefeller to the Culver Comm on Reorg of the US Senate, 1975; Gen Chm, Mark Hatfield for US Senator Com, 1966, 1972, 1978; Chm & Mem 1957-73, Gov's Ec Devel Com, St of OR; Chm, OR Symph Soc, Ford Foun Matching Funds Campaign, 1967-71; Pres, Salem Area C of C, 1965-67; Mem, Bd & Former Pres, Marion-Polk Co U Good Neighbors; Trustee, OR Grad Ctr for Study & Res, 1963-69; Trustee, Willamette Univ; Chm, ZOOMSI Auction for the OR Mus of Sci & Indust & Portland Zoo, 1961; Gen Chm, Citizens' Conf, Leading to the All-Am City Awd for Salem, 1959; Mem, Bd & Coun Adv Com 1955-, Pres 1959-61, Cascade Area Coun, BSA; Dir, Jr Achmt-Columbia Empire Inc; Dir, Portland Rose Fest Assn; Hon Bd of Dirs, Sunshine Div, Portland Police Resvs; Adv Bd, Salvation Armt; St Vincent Hosp & Med Ctr Foun; Adv Bd, St Vincent Hosp & Med Ctr Bd of Dirs, Marion-Polk U Good Neighbors; Bd of Dirs, Willamette Coun Camp Fire; Bd of Overseers, OR Hlth Scis Univ; Bd of Dirs, Salem Public Lib Foun; hon/Winner, Awd for Exemplary Achmt in Ser to Yth, Jr Achmt of Portland, 1954; Portland, Vol of the Wk,

1955; Salem's Jr First Citizen, 1957; Salem First Citizen, 1964; Winner, US Jr C of C Dist'd Ser Awd as One of Three Outstg Yg Men of OR, 1957; Recip, OR Mus of Sci & Indust 1961 OMSI Awd for Contbn to the Growth of NW Sci Ed; Recip, Pacific NW Ser to Mankind Awd, Sertoma Intl, 1967; Named St of OR Outstg Salesman, 1961; Recip, Silver Beaver Awd, BSA, 1963; Recip, Ernest Thompson Seton Awd, Camp Fire, 1980; Recip, 1980-81 Dist'd Ser Awd, Wn OR St Col.

FRANK, SAM HAGER oc/College President; b/Jul 23, 1932; h/193 Longview Road, Staten Island, NY 10301; ba/ Staten Island, NY; m/Ellen Wilson Snow; c/Marian Elizabeth; p/Edward Lloyd Frank, Bradenton, FL; ed/BA 1953, MA 1957, FL St Univ; PhD, Univ of FL; mil/AUS; pa/Chm, Div of Social Scis, Tift Col, 1961-65; Dean, Col of Arts & Scis, Jacksonville Univ, 1967-78; Chancellor, LA St Univ-Alexandria, 1979-81; Pres, Wagner Col, 1981-; Pres, AAUP, 1963-64; cp/Campus Liaison Ofcr, Peace Corps, 1962-65; VP, Rotary, 1980-81; hon/Contbr to 2 Books on Mil Hist; Author of Num Articles, Many Book Reviews (in 11 Profl Jours) & Over 900 Hist Abstracts; Fulbright Lectr, India, 1965-66; Outstg Edr of Am, 1971, 1974; W/W in Am; Dir of Am Scholars.

FRANKLIN, CHARLES ELLSWORTH oc/Sociologist, Social Worker, Educator; b/Apr 1, 1947; h/2217 Elm Street, Denver, CO 80207; ba/Denver, CO; m/Cynthia Jean; c/Nathan Charles, Andrew Warner; p/William M and Alicelia H Franklin, Washington, DC; ed/BA, Psych & Sociol, Earlham Col, 1964; MSW, Univ of WA, 1973; PhD, Sociol, Univ of CO, 1981; pa/Ptnr, CO Discourse Conslts, 1981-; Pvt Pract, Psychotherapy, 1979-; Therapist IV, Bethesda Commun Mtl Hlth Ctr, 1973-; Assoc, Arvada Psychol & Fam Sers, 1981-; Honorarium Instr, Univ of CO-Denver, 1983; Resources Person, Loretto Hgts Col, 1982-; Adj Instr, Webster Col, 1982; Adj Field Fac, Univ of Denver, 1977-; Nat Assn of Social Wkrs, 1972-; Acad of Cert'd Social Wkrs, 1978-; Am Sociological Assn, 1982-; cp/Amigos de las Americas, 1974-75, Tng Asst; Am Friends Ser Com, 1966-71, Vol; r/Soc of Friends; hon/Pub, *Energy Resource Develt Socioeconomic Impacts & the Current Status of Impact Asst: An 11 St Review*, TOSCO Foun, Boulder, CO, 1978; Amigos de las Americas Ser Awds, 1974-78; WA St Dept of Social & Hlth Sers Traineeship, 1971-73; CO St Licensure, LSW II; Fluent in Spanish; W/W in W.

FRANKLIN, JOHN HOPE oc/James B Duke Professor of History; b/Jan 2, 1915; h/208 Pineview Road, Durham, NC 27707; ba/Durham, NC; m/Aurelia Whittington; c/John Whittington; p/ Buck Colbert and Mollie Parker Franklin (dec); ed/AB, Fisk Univ, 1935; MA 1936, PhD 1941, Harvard Univ; pa/Instr in Hist, Fisk Univ, 1936-37; Prof of Hist, St Augustine's Col, 1939-43; Prof of Hist, NC Col, 1943-47; Prof of Hist, Howard Univ, 1947-56; Chm, Dept of Hist, Bklyn Col, 1956-64; Prof of Am Hist 1964-82, Chm, Dept of Hist 1967-70, John Matthews Manly Dist'd Ser Prof 1969-82, Univ of Chgo; James B Duke Prof of Hist, Duke Univ, 1982-; Vis'g Prof, Harvard Univ, Univ of WI,

Cornell Univ, Salzburg Sem, Univ of HI, Univ of CA, Cambridge Univ; Chm of Bd, Fgn S'ship, 1966-69; Edward Austin Fellow, 1937-38; Rosenwald Fellow, 1937-39; Guggenheim Fellow, 1950-51, 1973-74; Pres's Fellow, Brown Univ, 1952-53; Sr Mellon Fellow, Nat Humanities Ctr, 1980-; Fulbright Prof, Australia, 1960; Jefferson Lectr in the Humanities, 1976; Bd of Dirs, Salzburg Sem, Mus Sci & Indust, 1968-80; Bd of Trustees, Fisk Univ, 1947; Ctr for Adv'd Study in the Behavioral Scis, 1976-82; Nat Humanities Ctr, 1982-; Nat Coun on the Humanities, 1976-78; IL Bell Telephone Co, 1972-80; Am Hist Assn, Pres 1978-79; So Hist Assn, Pres 1970-71; Org Am Hist, Pres 1974-75; Assn for Study of Negro Life & Hist; Am Studies Assn, Past Pres; Am Phil Soc; AAUP; Phi Beta Kappa, Senate 1966-, Pres 1973-76; Phi Alpha Theta; cp/Fellow, Am Acad of Arts & Scis; Bd of Mus of Sci & Indust, 1968-80; Chgo Public Lib, 1969-78; Orchestral Assn of Chgo, 1976-80; Pres Adv Bd on Ambassadorial Appts, 1977-81; US Adv Comm on Public Diplomacy, 1978-81; hon/ Pubs, *Free Negro in NC*, 1790-1860 1943, *From Slavery to Freedom: A History of Negro Ams* 1947, 1957, 1967, 1974, 1980, *The Militant S, 1800-1860* 1956, *Reconstruction After the Civil War* 1961, *The Emancipation Proclamation* 1963, *Land of the Free* 1965, *Illustrated Hist of Black Ams* 1970, 1973, *A Sn Odyssey: Travelers in the Antebellum N* 1976, *Racial Equality in Am* 1976; Mem, Edit Bd, *Am Scholar*, 1972-76; Holds Hon Degs from: Atlanta Univ, AZ St Univ, Bard Col, Boston Col, Bklyn Col, Brown Univ, Cambridge Univ, Carnegie-Mellon Univ, Cath Univ of Am, Columbia Univ, Dickinson Col, Dillard Univ, Drake Univ, Emory Univ, Fisk Univ, Govs' St Univ, Grand Val Col, Hamline Univ, Harvard Univ, Howard Univ, Univ of IL Chgo, IN St Univ, Kalamazoo Col, Lake Forest Col, Lincoln Col, Lincoln Univ, Long Isl Univ, Loyola Univ, Manhattan Col, Marquette Univ, Univ of MD, Univ of MA, Miami Univ, MI St Univ, Univ of MI, Morehouse Col, Morgan St Col, Col of New Rochelle, Univ of St of NY, Univ of NC-Chapel Hill, Univ of NC-Charlotte, NC Ctl Univ, No MI Univ, NWn Univ, Univ of Notre Dame, St Olaf's Col, Univ of PA, Princeton Univ, Rhode Isl Col, Ropon Col, Roosevelt Univ, Seattle Univ, Johnson Col, Smith Univ, Temple Univ, Univ of Toledo, Tougaloo Col, Trinity Col, Tulane Univ, Univ of Tulsa, Tuskegee Univ, Union Col, Univ of UT, VA St Col, Wash Univ, Wayne St Univ, Whittier Col, Wilmington Col, Yale Univ; W/ W: in the World, in Am; World Authors; Dic of Am Scholars.

FRAUENS, MARIE oc/Editor, Researcher, Technical Writer, Mil Ofcr; b/Jul 10, 1902; h/923 East Capitol, Washington, DC 20003; ba/Same; p/ Frank Henry and Amanda Stansch Frauens (dec); ed/AA; BJ; MA; Postgrad Studies; mil/USNR Ofcrs Sch; Hon Grad, Indust Col Armed Forces; USNR: Comm'd Lt (jg) 1943, Perm Rank Lt Cmdr 1949, Lt Cmdr (Ret'd) 1965; pa/ Liaison Ofcr, USN & US Armed Forces Inst; Tng Ofcr, Res & Devel in Fire Control Radar, USN Bur of Ordnance; Histn, Fire Control Radar, USN Bur Ordnance; Tng Ofcr, Nav Resv Tng

241

Pubs Proj; Tchr, Prin & Dir, All Extra-Curric Activs, Wardell (MO) HS; Math Editor, Row, Peterson & Co, Evanston, IL; Chief Editor, HS Prog, McGraw Hill Book Co, NYC; Tng Dir, John I Thompson & Co, Wash DC; Writer, Tactical Doctrine, Dept of Navy, Wash DC; Adm Ofcr, Ofc of Dir, Res & Engrg, Ofc Secy of Def; Rschr, MO St Hist Soc, Columbia; cp/YWCA, KC, MO; Cnslr, Italian Commun Settlement House, Chgo; Bd of Dirs, Nav Gun Factory Wel & Rec Assn; Active, Capitol Hill Restoration, DC; Swimming Instr, Pk Bd, KC, MO; r/Christian; hon/Pi Gamma Mu; Several Mil Medals; W/W: in E, of Am Wom, in Am, in World; World W/W of Wom; Intnl W/W Intells; Foremost Wom of Twentieth Cent.

FREAS, ANNIE BELLE HAMILTON oc/Businesswoman; b/Aug 9, 1904; h/3003 Natchez Trace, Nashville, TN 37215; m/Maurice Henry; p/James N and Emma B McLaughlin Hamilton; ed/Grad, Martin Col, 1923; pa/Co-Owner & Bkkpr, Husband's Nashville Gen Contracting Firm, 1958-; Secy & Gen Bkkpr, Freas & Houghland Gen Contractors Inc, 1963-; Secy-Treas, Freas Constrn Co Inc, 1967-; Former Bkkpr, Hd of Acctg Dept & Asst Comptroller, 1925-58; T L Herbert & Sons, W G Bush & Col, Sangravl Co, Nashville; Other Former Positions; Wom in Constrn: Charter Mem of Nashville Chapt, Dir 1961-63, VP 1963, 1964, Pres 1965, Reg #2 Dir 1966, Chm Chapt Activs, Bd Dirs Nat Assn 1966-, Chaired Coms; cp/Zonta Intl, Var Ofcs & Activs incl'g Histn, 1984-85; Nat Trust for Hist Presv; Ladies Hermitage Assn; Assn for Presv TN Antiquities; TN Botanical Gardens & Fine Arts Ctr; IPA; Cheekwood YWCA; r/Downtown Presb Ch, Nashville: Charter Mem, Pres Wom of Ch 1961-63, Life Mbrship, Pin & Cert for Outstg Wk; hon/Underwood Typewriter Co Medal, Martin Col; 1st Lady of the Day, WLAC Radio Sta; Wom in Constrn: Wom in Constrn of Yr 1965, Cert of Apprec for Wk as Chm of Career Day, Vanderbilt Univ; Dist'd Alumna Awd Recip, Martin Col, 1983; Other Certs of Apprec & Merit; W/W of Am Wom; DIB; The Royal Blue Book; 2,000 Wom of Achmt.

FREE, HELEN MAE oc/Professional Relations Consultant; b/Feb 20, 1923; h/3752 E Jackson Boulevard, Elkhart, IN 46516; m/Alfred H; m/Alfred H; c/6 Chd; p/James Murray, Clearwater, FL; Daisey Piper; ed/AB w Hons in Chem, Col of Wooster, 1944; MA in Mgmt, Hlth Care, Ctl MI Univ, 1978; pa/Instr, Mgmt, Cont'g Ed Dept, IN Univ-S Bend, 1977-; Miles Labs: Conslt of Ames Div 1982-, Dir of Clin Lab Reagents, Res Prods Div 1978-79, Dir of Mktg Ser 1979-82, Dir of Specialty Test Sys, Ames Co 1976-78, Ames Growth & Devel Sr New Prods Mgr Microbiol Test Sys 1974-76, New Prods Mgr 1969-74, Clin Test Systems or Chem Test Sys, Ames Tech Sers 1966-69, Ames Prod Devel Lab 1964-66, Others; Am Chem Soc: Bd Dirs, 1983-, St Joseph Val Secy, Chm, Councilor 1971-82, Div Biol Chem, Div Chem, Mktg & Ec, Others; Am Assn for Clin Chem, Bd Dirs, 1984-; Assn Clin Scists; Am Soc for Med Technol; Fellow: Am Inst Chems, AAAS; The Chems Clb (NYC); Iota Sigma Pi; Kappa Kappa Kappa; AAUW;

cp/UF; Elkhart Concert Clb; Bd of Dirs, Altrusa Clb, Elkhart Co; IN St Hlth Coor'g Coun; No IN Hlth Sys Coun; Bd of Dirs, YMCA; Other Civic Assns; r/1st Presb Ch: Elder 1974-, Chp, Stewardship Campaign 1974; hon/Profl Achmt Awd in Nuclear Med, Am Soc for Med Technol; Honoree at Hons Ldrship Luncheon #1, YWCA Elkhart Co; "Bellringer's Awd," Elkhart UF; Garvan Medal, Am Chem Soc, 1980; Dist'd Alumna, Col of Wooster, 1980; Silver Bowl, Professions, YWCA, 1981; St Joseph Val Sect, Am Chem Soc, 1981; Mosher Awd, 1983; Profl Pubs; Biogl Listings; Others.

FREEDMAN, DEBORAH ANN oc/Secondary Teacher; b/Mar 8, 1949; h/12518 Montecito, Seal Beach, CA 90740; ba/Garden Grove, CA; m/Anthony David; p/John A Knowlton, Bakersfield, CA; Patricia Knowlton, Long Beach, CA; ed/BA, Spanish, Univ of CA-Davis, 1971; MA, Ednl Adm, CA St Univ-Long Bch, 1981; Biling Cross-Cultural Tchg Credential, CA St Univ-Long Bch; pa/Garden Grove Unified Sch Dist 1972-, Tchr (Math, Jour, Spanish, ESL Math), Tchr on Spec Assignment as Asst Prin 1982, ESL Prog Coor, Mem of ESL & Math Curric Coms, Sch Improvement Site Coun, Fac Adv Com, Biling Adv Com, Budget & Funding Resources Com, Advr (Girls' Leag, Jour Clb, Math & Sci Clb), Supr (Saturday Sch, Newcomers' Clb, Student Prodr Prog); NCTM; CA Math Coun; Orange Co Math Assn; NEA; CA Tchrs Assn; Garden Grove Ed Assn; Am Assn of Tchrs of Spanish & Portuguese; Tchrs of ESL; Assn for Supvn & Curric Devel; Girls' Leag Advrs Assn, Newslttr Editor, Secy, Pres; AAUW; Cal Aggie Alumni Assn; CA St Univ-Long Bch Alumni Assn; cp/YWCA Sponsor; Docent, Rancho Los Alamitos; Treas, Bridgecreek Homeowners Assn; r/Cath; hon/Kappa Delta Pi; Phi Delta Kappa; Phi Kappa Phi; Pi Lambda Theta; Delta Kappa Gamma; W/W in W.

FREEMAN, ERNEST E oc/Tanner; b/Apr 13, 1935; h/RD #2, Box 102, Schuylkill Haven, PA 17972; ba/Reading, PA; m/Shirley A Brown; c/Scott Alan, David Alan; p/Harvey C and Cora S Bressler Freeman (dec); ed/Grad, Cressona HS, 1952; Cont'g Ed, Commonwlth of PA in Fire-Fighting; mil/Co B 38th Inf Regiment, 3rd Inf Div E-4; pa/Tanner (Hides), Garden St Tanning Inc & Subsidiaries w 30 Yrs Ser to Date; Former Fire Chief, Summit Sta Fire Co #1; Past Pres & Fire Chief; Current Asst Fire Chief; Past Financial Secy; AGWAY Inc; cp/Charter Mem, Wayne Twp Lions Clb, 10 Yrs Perfect Attendance Record, Past Pres, Attended 2 St Convs; r/U Ch of Christ, Pres for 10 Yrs.

FREEMAN, HAROLD F oc/Editor-in-Chief; b/Mar 1, 1918; h/912 Newcastle Avenue, Westchester, IL 60153; ba/Westchester, IL; m/Esther Lucille; c/Harold Philip; p/Harold F Freeman (dec); Leona Frances Powell (dec); ed/ThB; mil/85th Inf Div, 339 Inf Regiment, Co E (Italy), WW II; pa/Nat Exec Dir, Indep Fundamental Chs of Am, 1981-; Editor-in-Chief, Voice Mag, Ofcl Jour of Indep Fundamental Chs of Am, 1977-; Pastor: Vallejo Bible Ch, Vallejo, CA 1964-77, Salina Bible Ch, Salina, KS 1956-64, Grace Bapt Ch, St Louis, MO 1948-56; IFCA: Pres KS Reg,

Secy, VP, Pres No CA Reg, Nat Exec Com 1968-71, 1972-75, Rec'g Secy (Nat) 1968-71, 1972-75; Bd Mem, Bible Ch Crusade, Santa Rosa, CA, 1965-77; Adv Bd, Chinese Bible Evang, SF; Missionaries for Christ Intl, Bd Mem; Bd Mem, IL Bible Ch Mission; Adv Bd, Servicemen for Christ, Vallejo, CA; Others; r/Indep; hon/Hon DD 1983, LitD 1984; Contenders Awd, Am Coun Christian Chs; Combat Inf-man's Badge; 3 Battle Stars; W/W in Rel.

FREEMAN, JULIA DELORES oc/Third Grade Teacher; b/Jul 12, 1939; h/458 Ridgeway Court, Spring Valley, CA 92077; ba/San Diego; p/Neal C and Jewell Towns Freeman, Chattanooga, TN; ed/BS in Elem Ed, 1963; MA in Multicultural Ed, 1976; pa/Third Grade Tchr, San Diego Unified Sch Dist, 1971-; Tchr, KC, KS, Sch Sys, 1963-71; Phi Delta Kappa Sorority, Delta Upsilon Chapt in San Diego; San Diego Tchrs Assn; CA Tchrs Assn; San Diego Coun of Adm Wom in Ed; cp/Sundowners Toastmasters Clb, San Diego; r/Bapt; hon/W/W of Am Wom.

FREIMAN, ALLAN DENNIS oc/Data Processing Executive; b/Nov 22, 1944; h/20 Rawlings Drive, Melville, NY 11747; ba/Plainview, NY; m/Patricia Joyce; c/Lawrence, Barry, Adam; p/Seymour and Muriel Freiman, Westbury, NY; sp/Malvin and Marion Grene, Medford, NY; ed/BA, CUNY, 1967; pa/Programmer, Harcourt, Brace & World, 1962-66; Programmer Analyst, ITT Data Sers, 1966-68; Exec VP, Computer Ser Bur, 1968-75; Pres, Minicomputer Concepts Inc, 1975-; Micro Intnl Assn, 1982-84; Intl Database Mgmt Assn, 1983; Queens Col Alumni Assn, 1978-83; hon/W/W in Bus & Fin.

FREIREICH, EMIL J oc/Medical Doctor; b/Mar 16, 1927; h/810 Monte Cello, Houston, TX 77024; ba/Houston, TX; m/Haroldine Lee Cunningham; c/Debra Ann, David Alan, Lindsay Gail, Thomas Jon; p/David (dec) and Mary Klein Freireich, Miami, FL; ed/BS 1947, MD 1949, Univ IL Col Med; pa/Internship, Cook Co Hosp, 1949-50; Residency in Internal Med, Presb Hosp, 1950-53; Res Assoc, MA Meml Hosp, 1953-55; Investigator, Leukemia Ser, Nat Cancer Inst, 1955-65; Instr, Prof Med 1965-, Asst Hd, Dept Devel Therapeutics, Chief, Res Hematology 1965-72, Hd, Dept of Devel Therapeutics 1972-83, Chm, Dept of Hematology 1983-, Univ TX, MD Anderson Hosp & Tumor Inst; Ruth Harriet Ainsworth Prof of Devel Therapeutics, 1981-; Assn Am Phys; cp/Am Soc Clin Invest; Am Fdn Clin Res; Am Soc Clin Oncology; Am Soc Hematology; Intl Soc Hematology; Am Soc Clin Pharm & Therapeutics; Fellow, Am Col Phys; Am Med Assn; hon/Author of Num Pubs incl'g "Acute Leukemia: A Prototype of Disseminated Cancer", Cancer, 1984; Charles F Kettering Prize Gen Motors Cancer Res Foun, 1983; Hon Deg, DSc, 1982; Ruth Harriet Ainsworth Prof of Devel Therapeutics, 1980; W/W in Am.

FRENCH, BENJAMIN I JR oc/Public Relations Executive; b/Jan 6, 1924; h/241 Sunrise Hill Lane, Norwalk, CT 06851; ba/New York, NY; c/Gary B, Bradley M, Susan M; p/Benjamin I Sr and Blanche K French (dec); ed/BS, Jour, The PA St Col, 1948; mil/Psychol Res Ctr, USAAF, 1943-46; pa/Pres, The

French Connection; Exec VP, News Guide Assocs; VP, UPR Inc; Assoc'd Press Editor, 1948-55; RCA Public Affairs Dept 1955-84, Mgr of Consumer Prods Public Relats 1955-62, Mgr of Trade News 1962-68, Mgr of St & Local Govt Relats 1968-70, Dir of Consumer Affairs 1970-84; Soc of Consumer Affairs Profls in Bus, NY Metro Chapt, Pres 1979-81; Overseas Press Clb; Nat Press Clb; cp/NY Netherlands Clb; hon/Pubs, *Consumer Ser Manual*, Prentice Hall 1976, *Public Affairs Manual* 1970; SOCAP Consumer Affairs Profl of the Yr 1981, Outstg Achmt Awd 1976, Awd of Recog 1980; W/W: in the World, in Bus & Fin.

FRENCH, CHARLES STACY oc/Director Emeritus; b/Dec 13, 1907; h/11970 Rhus Ridge Road, Los Altos Hills, CA; ba/Stanford, CA; c/Charles Ephraim, Helena Stacy Halperin; p/Charles Ephraim and Helena Stacy French; ed/Att'd Loomis Sch & Harvard Univ; pa/Res Fellow, Biol, CA Inst of Tech, 1934-35; Guest Wkr, Kaiser Wilhelm Inst, Berlin-Dahlem, 1935-36; Austin Tchg Fellow, Biochem, Harvard Med Sch, 1936-38; Instr (Res), Chem, Univ of Chgo, 1938-41; Asst, Assoc Prof of Botany, Univ of MN, 1941-47; Dir, Dept of Plant Biol, Carnegie Inst, 1947-73, Dir Emeritus 1973-; Prof (By Courtesy) Biol, Stanford Univ; Chair, Wn Sect, Am Soc of Plant Physiols, 1954; Nat Acad of Scis; Am Acad of Arts & Scis; Deutsche Akad der Naturforscher Leopoldina; Soc Gen Physiols, Pres 1955-56; Botanical Soc of Am; cp/Harvard Clb of the Peninsula, Pres 1973-75; hon/Charles Ried Barnes Life Mbrship Awd, Am Soc of Plant Physiols, 1971; Awd of Merit, Botanical Soc of Am, 1973; Hon PhD, Göteborg, 1974; Pubs, Num Articles & Reviews in Tech Jours on Photosynthesis & the Spectroscopy & Functions of Plant Pigments; Annual Reports in Carnegie Inst of Wash Yr Book, 1948-; Intl W/W.

FRENCH, ELLA J oc/Medicaid Caseworker; b/Sep 25, 1929; h/3333 North Carrollton Avenue, Indianapolis, IN 46205; ba/Indianapolis, IN; m/Joe W (dec); c/Dr Michael W, Deborah French Keys, Vincent K, Gregory Mark; p/George and Lenton Martin Jackson (dec); ed/AB, Fisk Univ, 1950; Att'd, TN St Univ, Spec Ed, 1948-49; Att'd, AL A&M, 1950; pa/Tchr, Limestone Co Bd of Ed, 1950-54; Cnslr, Secy to Prin, Sr Class Sponsor, Trinity HS, 1954-62; Casewkr, Marion Co Dept of Public Wel, 1964-; Present Medicaid Casewkr, Marion Co Dept of Public Wel; cp/Den Mother, BSA, 1971-73; r/St Mark Ch of God in Christ; Missionary, 1962-; Lic'd Evangelist; Sunday Sch Tchr, Yth Dept Tchr, Dist Missionary, Buggs Temple Ch of God in Christ, 1973-82; Sponsor, Bible Study & Prayer Meeting Once a Wk; Sunday Sch Supt; hon/Cert of Apprec from BSA; Mother of the Yr Awd, BSA; IN N Yth Dept, Ch of God in Christ Sunday Sch Attendance Hon, 1980; Nat Coun of Negro Wom; Marquis W/W.

FRENCH, RUTH EVELYN oc/Retired Educator; b/May 5, 1905; h/2 Grove Street, Proctor, VT 05765; p/Charles and Grace Worden French (dec); ed/PhB 1927, MA 1941, Univ of VT; Adv'd Study, Smith, Temple Univ, Tchrs Col, Columbia, NWn Univ,

Rutgers Univ; pa/Atl City (NJ) HS: Eng Tchr 1946-58, Hd Eng Dept 1958-70, Dir Drama 1946-70; Spch & Drama Tchr, Northampton HS, MA, 1942-46; Other Former Positions; CoDir of 5 Pageants Held in Atl City Conv Hall; Tchr, Atl Commun Col, 1963-65; Past Pres, NJ Assn Tchrs of Eng; NJ St Div Delta Kappa Gamma; Atl City Br AAUW; Pres, Rutland Co Ret'd Tchr Assn, 1974-76; cp/Regent of Ann Story Chapt, NSDAR, 1980-83; Recording Secy, VT St DAR, 1983-; Pres, Proctor Hist Soc; Served as Stage Dir, Commun Concerts Series, Atl City; r/Union Ch of Proctor, Trustee 1974-78; hon/Pub'd Author, "XVII Cent Colonial James", 1983; Val Forge Freedom Awd, 1958; Ford S'ship; Intl Register of Profiles; World W/W of Wom; Book of Hon; Intl W/W of Intells; Commun Ldrs & Noteworthy Ams; DIB.

FRETT, MONICA V A oc/Special Education Teacher for Educationally Handicapped; b/Aug 28, 1952; h/Bergs Homes, Building 1, Apartment 1, St Thomas, US Virgin Islands 00802; ba/St Thomas, US Virgin Islands; c/Eaton A, Darrell A, Micah A; p/Freda M Blyden, St Thomas, US Virgin Islands; ed/AB, Early Childhood and Elem Ed, 1979; Cert in Social Sci, Mtl Hlth, 1981; Bach of Social Wk, 1983; pa/Spec Ed Tchr for Emotionally Disturbed Chd, Dept of Ed, US Virgin Isls, 1983-; Tchr Asst for Essex Co Col Day Care, 1979-80; Full-time Subst Tchr, Dept of Ed, US Virgin Isls, 1973-77; Internship in Mtl Hlth, 1980; Forum Coor for Sr Citizens, Assisting in Consultation & Ednl Tng Prog for Commun Agy Prog; hon/Awd of Merit from the Nat Dean's List, 1978-79; Dean's List from Essex Co Col 1978 & Salutatorian in the Mtl Hlth Prog 1981.

FREUND, E FRANCES oc/Histology Laboratory Supervisor; b/Oct 8, 1922; h/1315 Asbury Road, Richmond, VA 23229; ba/Richmond, VA; m/Frederic Reinert (dec); c/Frances, Daphne, Fern, Frederic; p/Walter R and Mabel W Loveland Ervin (dec); ed/BS, Wilson Tchrs Col, 1944; MS, Biol, Cath Univ, 1953; Cert in Mgmt Devel, VA Commonwealth Univ, 1975; Cert in Electron Microscopy, SUNY-New Paltz, 1977; Grad Studies Ed, George Wash Univ, 1944-48; Cert in Mgmt Devel, Am Mgmt Assn & VA Commonwlth Univ, 1982; Student, J Sargent Reynolds Commun Col, 1978; pa/Tech, Parasitology Lab, Zool Div, US Dept of Agri, 1945-48; Histology Tech, Pathol Dept, Georgetown Univ Med Sch, 1948-49; Clin Lab Tech, Kent & Queen Anne's Co Hosp, 1949-51; Histotechnologist, Surg Pathol Dept, Med Col of VA Hosp, 1951-; Supvr, Histology Lab, Surg Pathol Dept, Med Col of VA Hosp, 1970-; Am Soc for Med Technol, VChm of Histology Sect 1981-83; VA Soc for Med Technol, Rep to Sci Assem, Histology Sect 1977-78, Histology & Cytology Sects 1980-82; Richmond Soc of Med Technologists, Corres'g Secy 1977-78, Publicity Chm 1981-82; Nat Soc for Histotechnol, Charter Mem, By-Laws Com 1981-83, CEUs Com 1981-83, CoChp of Third Annual Reg II Sem 1981, Ho of Dels 1979-81; VA Soc of Histology Techs, VP 1982-84, By-Laws Com 1975, 1979-82, Bd of Dirs 1979-82, Chm of Fall Sem 1981; AL Soc

for Histotechnol; TN Soc for Histotechnol; AAAS; Assn for Wom in Sci; Am Soc of Clin Pathols, Affil VA Govtl Employees; Am Mgmt Assn; cp/Nat Geographic Soc; Am Mus of Natural Hist; Smithsonian Instn; Nat Trust for Historic Presv; YWCA; hon/Pub, "A Method of Staining *Trichomonas foetus* in Smears of Bovine Vaginal Secretions," Proceedings of the Helminthological Soc of Wash, DC, Jan 1949; Elected to Phi Beta Rho 1940, Kappa Delta Pi 1944, Phi Lambda Theta 1946, Helminthological Soc of Wash, DC 1948, Sigma Xi 1953, NY Acad of Scis 1979, Am Mgmt Assn 1982; Life Mem, ABIRA, 1981; Hon'd by Robert E Lee Coun, BSA Banquet, 1970; Ser Awd, 30 Yrs of Ser to Med Col of VA Hosp, 1982; W/W in S & SW; Intl Register of Profiles; Personalities of the S; World W/W of Wom; Book of Hon; 2,000 Dist'd Southerners; Biogl Roll of Hon.

FRICKE, RICHARD J oc/Attorney; b/Apr 17, 1945; h/94 Main Street, Ridgefield, CT 06877; ba/Ridgefield, CT; m/Carol; c/Laura, Ricky, Amanda; p/Richard I and Jeanne (dec) Fricke, Burlington, VT; ed/BA 1967, JD 1970, Connell Univ; pa/Assoc, Gregory & Adams, 1970-73; Ptnr, Crehan & Fricke, 1973-; Atty for Town of Ridgefield 1973-81; Am Bar Assn, 1970-; Norwalk Wilton Bar Assn, 1970-74; Danbury Bar Assn, 1973-; CT Bar Assn, 1970-; CT Bar Woms Rts Sect, 1978; cp/Bd of Dirs, Commun Kgn 1975-77, Commun Ctr 1981-; Ridgefield Lacrosse Leag, Pres and Fdr 1980-; Kiwanis, 1970-73, 1978, Secy of Wilton Br 1973; Bd of Dirs, Ridgefield Skating Clb; W/W: in E, in Am Law.

FRICON, TERRI M oc/Executive; b/Jul 19, 1945; ba/1048 South Ogden Drive, Los Angeles, CA 90019; p/Anthony and Josephine Fricon, Ripon, CA; ed/Att'd, San Jose St Univ, 1961; BMus, Univ of Miami, 1963; pa/VP, Ptnr, Wednesday's Child Prodns, 1967-72; Pres of Filmways Music Grp & Dir of Music Dept of Filmways TV, Filmways Pictures, 1973-81; Pres, Fricon Entertainment Co Inc, 1981-; Pres, CA Copyright Conf, 1980-81; Chp, Music Publishers' Forum, 1979-81; ASCAP Publishers Adv Com, 1979-; NAPAS; BMA; CMA; Nashville Songwriters Assn; NMPA; AIMP; hon/Pub'd Song, "I Can See it in Your Eyes"; Profession Achmt Awd, Soroptimist Clb, LA, 1977; Recip, Golden Staff Awd, Music & Arts Foun, 1975, 1976, 1977, 1978, 1979, 1980, 1981, 1982; W/W of Am Wom; World W/W of Wom; DIB.

FRIED, SAUL oc/Executive; b/Oct 24, 1916; h/1455 Parkside Drive, Vicksburg, MS 39180; ba/Vicksburg, MS; m/Marian W; c/Step-Child, Mrs David Hull; p/Mr and Mrs J M Fried; ed/Grad, Vicksburg HS, 1933; mil/USN, 1942-46; pa/Clk at Vicksburg C of C, 1933-36; Salesman, Feld Furniture Co, 1936-38; Salesman, Rice Furniture Co, 1938-42; Asst Mgr, Rice Furniture Co, 1946-52; Pres, Saul Fried Furniture Co, 1952-; Bd of Merchants, Nat Bk; Bd of MS Retail Furniture Dealers Assn & Past Pres; Past Bd Mem, Unifirst Savs & Ln Assn, 1970-80; cp/Chm, Adv Bd, Salvation Army; Bd Mem & Pres, Vicksburg C of C, 1966; Bd Mem, Vicksburg Hosp 1980-82, Vicksburg Country Clb 1966-72, BSA 1928-33; Kiwanis Clb

1952-, Past Bd Mem; r/Jewish; Bd Mem & Past Pres of Anshe Chesed Congreg & Pres of the Brotherhood; hon/Eagle Scout Awd, 1931; Retail Furniture Merch of the Yr, MS Furniture Travellers Assn, 1979; Kiwanis Clb 25 Yr Cert.

FRIEDL, RICK oc/Educator, Research Consultant; b/Aug 31, 1947; h/PO Box 3908, Chatsworth, CA 91313; ba/Same; m/Diane; c/Richard, Angela, Ryan; p/Raymond and Ione Friedl, Northridge, CA; ed/BA 1969, MA 1970, CA St Univ-Northridge; MA, Univ of CA-LA, 1976; BS, Univ of St of NY, 1979; PhD, Univ of Ctl CA, 1982; BSL, Glendale Univ Col of Law, 1984; pa/Dept Mgr, St Compensation Ins Fund, 1973-78; Instr, Univ of So CA, 1978-80; Admr, Beverly Hills City Col; Dir, CA St Univ-Northridge Alumni Assn, 1979; LA Trial Lwyrs Assn; Am Polit Sci Assn; hon/Pub, *The Political Economy of Cuban Dependency*, 1982; CA St Grad F'ship, 1970-72; W/W: in W, in World, in CA.

FRIEDMAN, DAVID MARTIN oc/Executive; b/Mar 30, 1947; h/One Tracey Drive, Lawrenceville, NJ 08648; ba/Princeton, NJ; m/Marcie; p/Mrs Florence Friedman, Brooklyn, NY; ed/MBA, Ec, George Wash Univ, 1978; MSEE, Columbia Univ, 1971; BEE, summa cum laude, City Col of NY, 1969; pa/Dir of Planning & Devel, RCA Netwk Sers, 1982-; Dir of Contract Progs 1978-82, Engr 1974-78, Gen Sers Adm; Sr Mem of Tech Staff, Computer Scis Corp, 1974; Engr, MCI Telecommuns, 1972-74; Mem of Tech Staff, Bell Labs, 1969-72; Assn of MBA Execs, 1978-; IEEE, 1967-74; Editor & Publisher, *TSP Reports*, Gen Sers Adm, 1978-82; hon/Author, "Effects of Competition on the Govts Communs Netwk: An Econometric Approach" 1975, "Economic Eval & Price Justification in Acquiring Sers from a Teleprocessing Sers Vendor" 1982, Others; NY Assn of Consltg Engrs S'ship, 1968; Blonder Tongue Foun Awd, 1968; Tau Beta Pi, 1967-69; Eta Kappa Nu, 1967-69; Admrs Awd for Excell, GSA, 1982; W/W in Bus & Fin.

FRIEDMAN, RONALD MARVIN oc/Scientific Adviser; b/Apr 26, 1930; h/3210 Arlington Avenue, Riverdale, NY 10463; c/Philip Max, Joelle Norma; p/Joseph (dec) and Helen Plotkin Friedman, Brooklyn, NY; ed/BS in Zool, Columbia Univ, 1960; MS Physiol 1967, PhD Cellular Biol 1976, NY Univ; pa/Dept of Biochem, Columbia Univ, 1975-76; Cancer Inst, Columbia Univ, 1977; Dept of Biochem, Yale Univ Sch of Med, 1977-78; Dept of Biochem Scis, Princeton Univ, 1978-79; Dept of Biochem, Inst of Basic Res, SI, 1979-81; NIH Fellow, Albert Einstein Col of Med, 1981-82; Current Sci Advr to Royal Arch Mason Res Foun Inc; Appt'd to Sloane Kettering Inst for Cancer Res; hon/Num Pubs in Field; Sigma Xi, NY Univ Chapt, 1976-; Am Soc for Cell Biologists, 1976; Harvey Soc, 1977-; NY Acad of Scis; W/W in E; Am Men & Wom of Sci; Dir of Dist'd Ams; Others.

FRIES, HERLUF BECK oc/Rancher, Investor; b/Apr 1, 1915; h/PO Box 2326, Oakhurst, CA 93644; m/Geraldine; c/Donna, Doug, Jean, Benta; p/Christian Fries; ed/HS Grad, 1932; pa/Farmer, Rancher, Oakhurst, CA, 1980-; Self-Employed Rancher Conslt for

Investors (All Categories), w Clients from Germany, Switzerland & Italy; St Pres, CA Yg Farmers, 1948; Fresno Co Farm Bur, Dir, Past VP; Past Pres, Raisin City Farm Bur; cp/Active in Raisin City Commun & Sch Activs; Served on Caruthers Fair Bd for Many Yrs; Repub; r/Luth; hon/Recip, CA St Farmer Deg, FFA, 1949; Hon St Farmer, 1950; Grand Marshall, Caruthers, 1979; W/W in W.

FRIIS, HELENE ELIZABETH ROGALSKI oc/Architect, Planner, Designer, Sculptress; b/Apr, 15, 1948; ba/West 1520 Third Avenue, Suite 301, Spokane, WA 99204; m/Terry Edwin; c/Angela Dominique; p/Kasimarz and Anastasia Rogalski; ed/BFA, Ft Wright Col of the Holy Names, 1966; BA in Ed 1968, Grad Studies in Interior Design & Fine Arts 1968, BS in Arch Studies 1971, BArch 1972, WA St Univ; pa/Instr of Fine Arts, Spokane Sch Dist, 1969; Assoc Arch, Designer/Planner, G F G & Assocs, 1972-74; Fdr, Owner, Principal, HEF Design, Archs & Planners, 1975-; Fdr, VP, 3D Devel Inc, 1982-; Dir of Mktg, HEF Design, Archs & Planners, 1975-; AIA; Coun Ednl Facilities Planners; Urban Land Inst; Nat Trust for Historic Presv; Spokane Bus Clb; r/Rom Cath; hon/One Wom Shows: Avant Guard Gallery 1965-66; Spokane Public Lib 1964; Univ of ID-Moscow 1968; Grp Shows: Avant Guard Gallery 1965, 1966, 1967; Waikiki Retreat 1967; Cheney Cowles Mus 1966; Permanent Collection: HEF Design, Archs & Planners & 3D Devel Inc; W/W of Am Wom.

FROHOCK, JO ANNE oc/Art Therapist and Psychotherapist; h/88 Bedford Street, New York, NY 10014; ba/New York, NY; c/John Robert; p/Joseph Steger and Virginia Annelle Clem Farrier (dec); ed/BA, Psych & Phil, NY Univ, 1975; Master of Profl Studies in Art Therapy & Creativity Devel, Art Therapy Res Scholar, Bklyn, NY, 1977; Assoc Mem, Inst for Expressive Anal; pa/Art Therapy Conslt, Coney Isl Hosp, 1978; Supvr, Activity Therapy, Adolescent Psychi, Metro Hosp Ctr, NYC, 1978-; Art Therapist/Psychotherapist in Pvt Pract, 1977-; Credentialized Profl Mem, Am Art Therapy Assn; APGA; hon/Author, "Music Therapy w an Adolescent Boy Who Jumped Seventeen Stories in an Attempt to Commit Suicide" 1983, "The Art Cure" 1982, "The Role of Activity Therapy on an Adolescent Inpatient Ser" 1981, "Reflections of the Electra Complex & Sibling Rivalry in the Kinetic Fam Drawings of Seven-Year-Old Identical Twin Girls" 1978; NY Univ, Univ Hons Scholar, Fdr's Day Awd; Pratt Inst, Recip of Grad Art Therapy Res S'ship, 1977; W/W in E.

FROMAN, FLORENCE ELAINE oc/Guidance Counselor; b/Aug 24, 1950; h/PO Box 1405, Oviedo, FL 32765; ba/Oviedo, FL; p/Mr and Mrs Archie J Tuten, Jacksonville, FL; ed/AA, 1969; BS, 1971; EdM, 1973; pa/Tchr of Emotionally Disturbed Chd, Robinswood Jr HS, 1972-74; Cnslr, Adult Ed, 1973-74; Emotional-Social Adjustment Tchr, Redbug Elem, 1974-75; Psychometrist, Acad Testing Conslts, 1974; Cnslr, Lawton Elem, 1975-; APGA; Am Sch Cnslrs Assn; FL Pers & Guid Assn; FL Sch Cnslrs Assn, Treas 1981-; Seminole

Co Elem Guid Cnslrs, Public Relats Chp 1979; hon/W/W in S & SW.

FROMHOLD, ALBERT THOMAS JR oc/Professor of Physics; b/Nov 25, 1935; h/2111 Robin Drive, Auburn, AL 36830; ba/Auburn, AL; m/Regina Giordano; c/Thomas William, Matthew Albert; p/Albert and Lillian Rutherford Fromhold (dec); ed/Bach of Engrg Physics 1957, Master of Nuclear Sci 1958; Auburn Univ; PhD in Engrg Physics, Cornell Univ, 1961; pa/Prof of Physics, Auburn Univ, 1965-; Res Scist, Sandia Lab, 1961-65; Vis'g Scist, Nat Bur of Standards 1969-70, IBM Yorktown 1975, 1976, Hokkaido Univ 1979, Oak Ridge Nat Lab 1980, 1981, NASA Huntsville 1983, 1984; Am Phy Soc (Nat); Am Assn of Physics Tchrs; Sigma Xi; Phi Kappa Phi; Past Mem, Electrochem Soc, AL Acad of Sci, SEn Sect of Am Phy Soc; cp/K of C, Grand Knight 1968-69; Toastmasters, Pres 1982-83; hon/Pubs, *Theory of Metal Oxidation, Volume I, Fundamentals* 1976, *Theory of Metal Oxidation, Volume II, Space Charge* 1980, *Anodic Behavior of Metals & Semiconductors, Oxides & Oxide Films, 1976, & Quantum Mechs for Applied Physics & Engrg* 1981; Jesse Beams Res Awd of the SEn Sect, Am Phy Soc, 1981; NSF Profl Devel Awd, 1980; Res F'ship, Japan Soc for the Promotion of Sci, 1979; NSF Postdoct Awds, Univ of FL Quantum Theory Inst, 1967; W/W: in S & SE, in Am, in SW, in Technol Today; Am Men & Wom of Sci; DIB; Men of Achmt; Personalities of the S.

FROMING, WILLIAM JOHN oc/Professor of Psychology; b/Jul 3, 1950; h/5907 Northwest 52nd Terrace, Gainesville, FL 32606; ba/Gainesville, FL; m/Karen Bronk; p/Mr and Mrs George Froming, Crivitz, WI; ed/BA, Univ of WI, 1972; PhD, Univ of TX-Austin, 1977; pa/Tchg Asst, Univ of TX, 1972-77; Res Assoc, Res & Devel Ctr for Tchr Ed, 1977; Asst Prof 1977-82, Assoc Prof 1982-, Dept of Psych, Univ of FL; Vis'g Assoc Prof, Univ of New Orleans Sum Prog, Innsbruck, Austria, 1983; Am Psychol Assn, Soc for Res in Child Devel; cp/Citizens Adv Bd for the Dept of Corrections (Co); hon/Pubs, *Statmaster* 1983, *Statmaster for Bus* 1984, *Behavioral Stats by Example* 1986; Num Articles in Profl Jours; WI Hon S'ship, 1968; NIMH, Fellow 1972-74; NSF Grantee, 1981-84; W/W: in S & SW, in Frontier Sci & Technol; Men of Achmt.

FROSCH, CAROL SNOW oc/Chair of Department of Education; b/Jul 23, 1947; ba/Department of Education, Oklahoma Baptist University, Shawnee, OK 74801; m/Steven P; p/Mr (dec) and Mrs Lester T Snow, Tonkawa, OK; ed/EdD, Univ of OK, 1980; ME, Ctl St Univ, 1974; BS, OK St Univ, 1969; Assoc, No OK Col, 1967; pa/Chair and Asst Prof of Ed, OK Bapt Univ, 1982-; Lectr, Ctl St Univ, 1982; Subst Tchr, Mid-Del Schs, 1973-80; Ofc Mgr, Ctl St Univ, 1969-72; Delta Kappa Gamma, Pres of Beta Omicron Chapt 1982-84; ASCD; OACTE; AACTE; NCATE; hon/Articles Pub'd in *OK Sch Bd Jour* Jan 1980 & May 1982, *Exec Edr* Jan 1982, *Ednl Ldrship* Feb 1982, & *NASSP Bltn* May 1981; Grad, summa cum laude (ME), 1974; Dean's Hon Rolls, Pres's Hon Rolls, 1965-80; Phi Kappa Phi, 1969; Beta Gamma Sigma, 1969; Phi Theta Kappa, 1966; W/W in S & SW; Outstg

Yg Wom of Am.

FROST, DIANNE BAILEY oc/Clinic Co-Founder and Co-Director; b/Sep 6, 1949; h/PO Box 3699, Augusta, GA 30904; ba/Augusta, GA; m/Dr K Bradley; p/O L (dec) and Frances G Bailey; ed/BS, magna cum laude 1972, EdM 1974, PhD 1976, Univ of GA; Postdoct Tng, Masters & Johnson Inst, 1980; pa/ Commun Psychol/Co-Dir of Marital/ Sexual Co-Therapy Ser, US Govt, W Germany, 1976-79; Co-Dir of Mtl Hlth & Alcohol Clin, Cordova Commun Hosp, 1980-81; Co-Fdr/Co-Dir, Frost Foun, Sex Therapy Clin, 1981-; Phi Kappa Phi, 1972; Phi Delta Kappa Hon Soc, 1974; Kappa Delta Pi Hon Soc, 1974; Am Psychol Assn, 1972; Sex Info & Ed Coun of US, 1977; Am Assn of Sex Edrs, Cnslrs & Therapists, 1978-; Cert'd Sex Therapist; hon/Pub'd in *Jour of Res & Devel in Ed* 1976, *Dissertation Abstracts Intl* 1976, *Med Bltn* 1976, 1979, *The Cordova Times* (Psychol Info Articles) 1980, 1981; AASECT Cert'd Sex Therapist, 1978; W/W: in S & SW, of Am Wom.

FROST, JANET OWENS oc/Assistant Professor of Anthropology; b/Mar 1, 1944; h/1104 Libra, Portales, NM 88130; ba/Portales, NM; m/Everett L; c/Noreen Karyn, Joyce Lida; p/Datus (dec) and Lida T Owens, Panguitch, UT; ed/AA, Col of So UT, 1964; BA, Anthropology, Univ of UT, 1966; MA, Anthropology 1969, PhD, Anthropology 1978, Univ of OR; pa/Grad Asst & Photog, Anthropology, Univ of UT, 1966-67; Grad Asst, Anthropology, Univ of OR, 1969-70; Asst Prof, En NM Univ, 1970-; Served as Adm Asst to VP of Acad Affairs & Tchr in Sum Sch, Univ of HI-Manoa, 1976; AAUW, Portales Br Pres 1978-80; Soc of Am Archaeol; Univ Wives & Wom, En NM Univ; Wn Social Sci Assn; NM Wom's Studies Conf; r/ LDS; hon/Pubs, "Study Guide to Accompany Hoebel: Anthropology: The Study of Man" 1972, "Summary Report of Archaeological Invest of Tutuila Isl, Am Samoa" 1976, "A Preliminary Definition of the Cultural Hist of Laucala Isl, Fiji" 1979; NSF Doct Dissertation Res Grant for Archaeological Settlement Pattern Study in Am Samoa, 1971-72, Univ of OR ($4,900); W/W of Am Wom; World W/W of Wom in Ed.

FROST, MARY KATHERINE oc/ Coordinator and Polysomnographer for Sleep Disorder Center; b/Nov 13, 1928; h/One Lafayette Plaisance, Suite 1617, Detroit, MI 48207; ba/Detroit, MI; p/ Philip and Elizabeth Eppert (dec); ed/ Cert in Acctg, Windsor Bus Col, 1946; Studied Voice, Toronto Conservatory of Music, 1946-47; Att'd, Am Inst of Bkg, 1954-57; AS, Wayne St Univ, 1967; pa/Bkkpr, Teller, Asst Acct, Toronto Dominion Bk, 1947-51; Comml Teller, Nat Bk of Detroit, 1951-54; Mgr, Customer Relats Ofcr, City Nat Bk, 1954-62; Psychobiol Res Supvr, Adm Asst, MI Dept of Mtl Hlth at Lafayette Clin, 1964-; Lectr, 1979-; Co-Fdr, Coor, Polysomnographer, Lafayette Clin Sleep Ctr, 1975-; Nat Assn of Female Execs, 1980-; Assn of Polysomnography Technologists, 1981-; MI Mtl Hlth Soc, 1983-; Mem, Fac, Wn MI Univ, MW Inst, 1984-; cp/Bd of Trustees, Leag of Cath Wom, 1974-; Bd of Dirs, Casa Maria Agy, 1974-81; Bd of Dirs, Casgrain Hall, 1974-; Bd of Dirs, Travelers Aid (Nat),

1973-; Pres, MI St Employees Assn, Chapt 73, 1977-81; Lafayette Clin Citizens Adv Coun, 1979-; VChm, St Assn Mtl Hlth Com, 1972-74; Reg Treas, MI St Employees Assn, Reg IX, 1970-72; Co-Fdr & Charter Mem, Windsor Light Opera Co 1948-, Treas 1948-51; The Ec Clb of Detroit, 1980-; The Five O'Clock Forum, Univ Clb of Detroit, 1978-; US Senatorial Clb, 1980-; Nat Repub Congl Com, 1980-; hon/Pubs, "The Effects of Acute Magnesium Deficiency on the Behavior of Rats" 1976, "Behavior of Rats as Affected by Acute Depletion & Repletion of Magnesium" 1977, "Effects of Postnatal Iron Deficiency on the Behavior of Rats" 1975, "Electroencephalographic Voltage & Frequency Patterns During Sleep in Humans" 1969, Several Others; Dist'd Employee Awd, Dept of Mtl Hlth, Lafayette Clin, 1981; W/W: of Am Wom, in Am, in World.

FRUHMANN, KAREN ANNE oc/ Laboratory Director; b/Aug 1, 1952; h/ 13 Seaview Drive, Bricktown, NJ; ba/ West Orange, NJ; p/Robert and Anna Mullin; ed/BA, Psych & Biol, magna cum laude, William Paterson Col, 1974; MT (ASCP), St Mary's Hosp, 1975; MS, Med Technol, summa cum laude, Fairleigh Dickinson Univ; Clin Lab Scist, Nat Cert Agy, 1978; PhD, SEn Univ; pa/Bench Technologist, & Hematology Sects, Raritan Val Hosp, Col Med & Dent, 1975-76; Chem Advr for Gen Diagnostic Prods, Biochem QC, Enzymology QC (Asst Supvr), Tech Writer Quality Assurance, Diagnostic Res, Chem Advr for Gen Diagnostic Prods, Warner Lambert Gen Diagnostics, 1976-78; Current Dir of Lab Sers, Kessler Inst for Rehab; Am Soc Clin Pathol; NY Acad of Sci; Am Soc Med Technol; NJ Soc Med Technol; Assn for Wom in Sci; r/ Presb; hon/Pubs, "A Hematologic View of T & B Lymphocytes" & "Interferons"; Alpha Mu Tau Hon S'ship, Hon Soc for Med Technol, 1977; W/W: of Am Wom, in E.

FRYM, JANET CAROLYN oc/Travel Executive; b/Oct 30, 1946; h/London, England; ba/London, England; p/Nancy D Brown, Mission Viejo, CA; ed/Att'd, Sonoma St Col 1964-65, Heards Bus Col 1965-66; pa/Travel Agt 1964-66, Mgr 1967-70, Sole Owner 1970-75, Grand World Travel; Travel Agt, Asst Mgr, Santa Rosa Travel, 196-67; Outside Sales Agt, Blue Marble Travel, 1976-77; Co-Owner, Enterprises Unltd, 1977-80; Mgr, Traveltime Inc, 1980-83; Opn Mgr, Bay Travel Inc, 1983-84; Adv Bd & Formation Bd, Marin Savs & Ln, 1974-; Mem, Nat Assn of Female Execs; Orange Co Sabre Clb (Airline Computer), Fdg Bd Mem, VP; hon/Pub, *Am Song Fest Anthology*, 1983; Sales Travel Achmt Awds, 1970-75; Hon Mention Awd, Am Song Fest, Lyric Competition, 1983; Inscribed Copy, Steve Miller Band's 1st Gold Album; W/W: in CA, in W.

FUENTES, MARTHA AYERS oc/ Playwright, Writer; b/Dec 21, 1923; h/ 102 Third Street, Belleair Beach, FL 33535; ba/Same; m/Manuel Solomon; p/ William Henry and Elizabeth Dye Ayers (dec); ed/BA, Eng, Univ of So FL, 1969; pa/Jewelry Sales Clk, Dept Store, Tampa, 1940-43; Clk Typist, Bkkpr, Wn Union, 1943-48; Writer, Playwright, 1953-; Instr at Writers' Wkshops; Dramatists Guild; Authors Guild;

Authors Leag of Am Inc; SEn Writers Assn; Soc of Chd's Book Writers; Am Theatre Assn; AAUW; r/Rom Cath; Mem of Many Rel Orgs; hon/"Two Characters in Search of an Agreement" (One-Act Play, Contemp Drama) 1970, "The Rebel" (TV Script for "Faith for Today") 1970, "Mama Don't Make Me Go to Col, My Head Hurts" (Play Produced by Univ of So FL) 1969; Contbr, Articles & Stories for Yg People to Nat Mags & Reg Pubs; Ione Lester Fiction Awd, Univ of So FL; George Sergel Drama Awd for "Go Stare at the Moon" (Full Length Play) 1969; Nat Playwrights Dir; Contemp Authors; DIB; Contemp Personalities; Others.

FUKS, JOACHIM ZBIGNIEW oc/ Physician, Assistant Professor of Medicine and Oncology; b/Mar 18, 1948; h/ 67 Studio Road, Stamford, CT 06903; m/Gail; c/Sara Esther; p/Herszlik (dec) and Bella Fuks, New York, NY; ed/HS Grad, Poland, 1965; Grad, Med Sch, Barcelona, Spain, 1975; mil/USPHS, Comm'd Ofcr; pa/Intern in Med, Mt Sinai Hosp Sers, 1975-76; Resident in Med, Mt Sinai Hosp Sers, 1976-78; NCI-Clin Assoc in Med Oncology, Balto Cancer Res Ctr, 1978-81; NCI-Sr Investigator, Balto Cancer Res Ctr, 1981-82; Staff Phys, Univ of MD Cancer Ctr, Univ of MD Hosp & Asst Prof of Oncology, Univ of MD Cancer Ctr, 1982-; Asst Prof of Med, Univ of MD Sch of Med & Staff Phys, Med Oncology Ser, VA Med Ctr, 1982-; Am Col of Phys; Am Soc of Clin Oncology; Am Fdn for Clin Res; NY Acad of Scis; AAAS; Reviewer, *Cancer Treatment Reports*, 1982-; Lic'd to Pract Med, NY 1975, MD 1980; hon/Pubs, "Infections in Patients w Non-Small Cell Lung Cancer" 1983, "Doxorubicin, Cyclophosphamide & Etoposide (ACE) by Bolus or Continuous Infusion for Small Cell Carcinoma of the Lung" 1983, "Combinatin Chemotherapy w Cisplatin (DDP) & Vindesine (VDS) for Non-Small Cell Lung Cancer" 1983, "Phase II Trials of 9, 10 Anthracenedicarboxaldehyde (ADC, NSC 336677) in Adv'd Non-Small Cell Lung Cancer" 1982, Num Others; Polish Student's Assn, Prize for the Best Res Paper, 1967; Polish Student's Sci Circle, Prize for the Best Res Wk, 1968; Marquis W/W.

FULLER, GARY R oc/Vocational Educator; b/Sep 16, 1940; h/3050 Riverwood Drive, Juneau, AK 99801; ba/ Juneau, AK; m/Nicole M Sipe; c/Trisha Leann, Krista Leann; p/Medford and Elsie Fuller, East Side, OR; ed/BS, Bus Adm 1962, EdM 1964, Linfield Col; EdD, OR St Univ, 1976; pa/HS Tchr, 1964-68; Bus Dept Chair, Dallas, OR, 1965-68; Asst Prog Supvr of Bus Ed, St Dept of Ed, Salem, OR, 1968-69; Prog Supvr, AK Dept of Ed, Juneau, 1969-72; Voc Coor, Univ of AK-Juneau, 1972-73; Grad Student, OR St Univ, 1973-76; Coor, Career Ed, AK Dept of Ed, Juneau, 1976-80; Prog Supvr, AK Dept of Ed, Juneau, 1980-82; Assoc Prof of Voc Tchr Ed, Univ of AK-Juneau, 1982-83; Prog Supvr, AK Dept of Ed, Juneau, 1982-; Am Voc Assn, Life Mem; AK St Voc Assn, Charter Mem, Pres 1982-83; Phi Delta Kappa, SE Chapt, Pres 1979; Gastineau Philatelic Soc, Pres 1974, 1977; Gastineau Aeromodier Soc, Pres 1978; Acad of Model Aeronautics, Assoc VP for AK; Am Soc for

Tng & Devel; Am Soc for Public Adm; Theme Editor, *Method Mag*, "Career Ed," 1984; hon/Pubs, "Voc Prog Eval" 1984, "The Need to Wk Together" 1982, "What You Do Is Important" 1981, "A Comparison of Philosophies of Experienced Tchrs of Voc Ed & Undergrad Voc Tchr Trainees" 1976, "RSVP Brings Relevance to Alaska" 1971, Others; W/ W in W.

FULLER, JOSEPH D III oc/Public Relations Director; b/Aug 30, 1947; h/ 1709 Archer Drive, Sherman, TX 75090; ba/Sherman, TX; m/Charlotte Ann Smith; c/Joseph Edward; p/Mr and Mrs J D Fuller Jr, McQueeney, TX; ed/ BA, Jour & Hist, cum laude, TX Christian Univ, 1969; MA, Jour & Hist 1971, PhD in Communication, Univ of TX-Austin; pa/Jour Instr & Pubs Advr, Seguin HS, 1970-71; Jour Instr & Daily Newspaper Advr, TX Christian Univ, 1971-76; Dir of Public Relats & Asst Prof of Communication Arts, Austin Col, 1976-; Pres, Lambda Chi Alpha Frat, TX Christian Univ Chapt, 1968; Pres, Soc of Profl Journalists, TX Christian Univ Chapt, 1969; Advr, SPJ at TX Christian Univ, 1971-76; NCCPA, River Press Clb, 1982; Coun for the Advmt & Support of Ed, 1976-82; ICUT Info Taskforce, 1976-82; cp/McQueeney Lions Clb, 1971; Sherman C of C, 1976-82; Chm, Sherman Conv & Visitors Bur, 1976-82; Denison C of C, 1976-82; Sherman Boys Clb, 1980-82; hon/Author, "Article in the Quill" 1973, Book Review & Articles in *Col Press Review*, *Roundtable*, *Jour Edr*; MN Star Awd, 1969; Ft Worth Press Awd, 1968; SPJ-SDX Mark of Excell Awd, 1975; NAIA Awd of Excell, 1980; W/ W in S & SW; DIB; Personalities of the S; Others.

FULLER, NANCY FAY oc/Pharmacy Librarian; b/Sep 23, 1945; h/Box 1511, Chickasaw Road, Oxford, MS 38655; p/ Joe B (dec) and Burris M Fuller, Oxford, MS; ed/MS in Lib Sci 1968, BA in Ed 1967, Univ of MS; AA, Wood Jr Col, 1965; pa/Pharm Lib, Univ of MS, 1976-; Hd Libn & Prof, St Tech Inst at Memphis, 1974-76; Asst Libn & Asst, Assoc Prof, St Tech Inst at Memphis, 1969-74; Periodicals Libn, George Peabody Col for Tchrs, 1968-69; Am Assn of Cols of Pharm, Sect of Libs/ Ednl Resources, Del to Ho of Dels 1981, 1982, Pres-Elect 1983-84; Am Lib Assn; SEn Lib Assn; MS Lib Assn; Fac Advr, Kappa Epsilon, Profl Pharm Frat; Served on 2 MS Lib Assn Coms; Served as Pres of Univ of MS Grad Sch of Lib & Info Sci Alumni Assn; cp/Pilot Clb of Oxford, 1980-, Advr of Compass Clb of the Univ of MS 1981-84, Bd of Dirs 1982-84, Dist Compass Area Ldr, LA/MS Dist 1983-84; r/N Oxford Bapt Ch; hon/Phi Theta Kappa, 1965-66; Kappa Delta Pi, Hon Ed Frat, 1968-; NDEA Grad Fellow, 1967-68; Outstg Yg Wom in Am; W/ W: in Lib & Info Sers, of Am Wom.

FULLER, THEODORE JR oc/Elementary Educator; b/Nov 4, 1937; h/7709 Claiborne, Houston, TX 77016; ba/ Houston, TX; p/Theodore (dec) and Bernice V Fuller, Hempstead, TX; ed/ BS 1959, EdM 1980, Prairie View A&M Univ; mil/AUS, 1961-63 (Vietnam 1962, Instr, Sig Corp 1961); pa/Voc Agri Tchr, Richards, TX, 1960; Elem Sch Tchr, Houston Indep Sch Dist, 1963-; NEA; NCTE; Assn Childhood Ed; Assn Supvn

& Curric Devel; IRA; Soc Chd's Book Writers; cp/Audubon Soc; Sierra Clb; Nature Conservancy; hon/Author of Feature Stories for *The Houston Forward Times*; Free-Lance Writer in Ednl & Feature Stories; Bd of Dirs, Houston Audubon Soc, 1973; W/W: in Pictorial Print Photo, PSA Jour, in S & SW.

FULLERTON, GREGORY LEE oc/ Attorney; b/Feb 18, 1950; h/436 South Audubon Drive, Albany, GA 31707; ba/ Albany, GA; m/Carol Hood; c/Christopher Todd, Elizabeth Rebecca; p/ Loren V and Lora M Fullerton, Albany, GA; ed/BA, Yale Univ, 1972; JD, Univ of VA, 1975; pa/Law Clk, Justice B Gunter, GA Supr Ct, 1975-76; Law Assoc, Alston, Miller & Gaines, Atlanta, 1976-78; Assoc, Watson, Spence, Lowe & Chambless, Albany, 1978-80; Ptnr, Watson, Spence, Lowe & Chambless, 1980-; Albany Est Planning Coun, Pres 1982-83, VP 1981-82; Ygr Lwyrs Sect, St Bar of GA, Bd 1980-84; St Bar of GA; ABA, Sects on Taxation & Real Property, Probate & Trust Law; cp/ Commun Concert Assn of Albany, GA, Pres 1981-83; Albany Symph Assn, First VP 1983-84, Dir 1979-; Albany Mus of Art, Pres 1983-85, First VP 1982-83, Second VP 1981-82; GA Citizens for the Arts, Dir 1981-83; Albany Area Arts Coun, 1981-83; Dougherty Co Kiwanis Clb, Dir 1981-82; Happy House Inc, Dir 1979-83; Dougherty Co Heart Assn, Dir 1979-83; hon/Pubs, "The Revenue Act of 1978-Death & Taxes Revisited" 1979, "Limits on Punishment & Entitlement to Rehabilitative Treatment of Institutionalized Juvs: *Nelson v Heyne*" 1974; Grad, magna cum laude, Yale Univ, 1972 (w Hons in Intensive Polit Sci); 1970 Patterson Prize for Best Col Thesis on Am Polit Sys "Reapportionment & Representation Theory: From the Polit Thicket into the Briar Patch," Edit Bd, *VA Law Review*, 1973-75; Ldrship Albany, 1984-85; 1984 Sertoma "Ldrship to Mankind" Awd; 1981 Dist Awd of Merit, Flint Dist, Chehaw Coun, BSA; W/W in S & SW.

FULLMER, HAROLD MILTON oc/ Biomedical Research Administrator; b/ Jul 9, 1918; h/3514 Bethune Drive, Birmingham, AL 35223; ba/Birmingham, AL; m/Marjorie Lucile; c/ Angela Sue Fullmer O'Connell, Pamela Rose Fullmer McLain; p/Rachel Eva Fullmer, North Liberty, IN; ed/BS 1942, DDS 1944, IN Univ; Doct Deg, Honoris Causa, Univ Athens, Athens Greece, 1981; mil/1st Lt & Capt, AUS, 1944-46; pa/Intern, Charity Hosp, 1946-47, Resident 1947-48, Vis'g Dental Surg 1948-53; Instr, Loyola Univ, 1948-49, Asst Prof 1949-50, Assoc Prof of Gen & Oral Pathol 1949-53; Conslt, Pathol, VA Hosps, 1950-53; Asst Dental Surg, Nat Inst Dental Res, NIH, 1953-54, Dental Surg 1954-56, Sr Dental Surg 1956-60, Dental Dir 1960-70, Chief Sect Histochem 1967-70, Chief Exptl Pathol Br 1969-70, Conslt to Dir 1971-72; Mem, Dental Caries Prog Adv Com, HEW, 1975-79, Chm 1976-79; Dir, Inst Dental Res, Prof of Pathol, Prof of Dentistry, Assoc Dean Sch of Dentistry, AL Med Ctr, 1970-, Sr Scist Cancer Res and Tng Prog, Sci Adv Com Diabetes Res & Tng Ctr, 1977-; Mem, Med Res Career Devel Com, VA, 1977-; Co-Editor, *Histopathologic Technic & Practical Histochem*; Conslt Editor, *Oral Surg,*

Oral Med, Oral Pathol, 1970; Editor, Fdr, *Jour of Oral Pathol*, 1972-; Assoc Editor, *Jour of Cutaneous Pathol*, 1973-; Edit Bd, *Tissue Reactions*, 1976-; Conslt Editor, "Gerondontology", 1981-; ADA, Conslt Coun Dental Res 1973-74; Intl Assn Dental Res, VP 1974-75, Pres 1976-77; Am Assn Dental Res, Pres 1976-77; Intl Assn Pathologists; Intl Assn Oral Pathologists, Co-Fdr 1976-, 1st Pres, Editor; Histochem Soc; Nat Soc Med Res, Dir 1977-79; Biol Stain Comm, Trustee 1977-; Comm'd Ofcrs Assn; cp/ Repub; Exch Clb, Pres 1952-53; r/Presb; hon/Over 100 Articles Pub'd in Sci Jours on Histochem Methods & Biochem of Connective Tissues; Recip, Isaac Schour Awd for Outstg Res & Tchg in Anatomical Scis, Intl Assn Dental Res, 1972; Fulbright Grantee, 1962; Dist'd Alumnus of Yr, IN Univ Sch of Dentistry, 1978; Dist'd Alumnus Awd, IN Univ, 1981; Fellow, Am Col Dentists, Am Acad Oral Pathol, AAAS (Chm Sect 1976-78, Secy Sect 1979-); W/W: in Am, in Sci from Antiquity to Present, in S & SW; in the World; Am Men & Wom of Sci; 2000 Notable Ams; Personalities of the S.

FUSILLO, LISA ANN oc/Assistant Professor; Dancer; Choreographer; Master Teacher; h/5532 Creekwood Drive, #2035, Fort Worth, TX 76109; ba/Fort Worth, TX; p/Matthew H (dec) and Alice E Fusillo, Temple Hills, MD; ed/DRBS, London, England, 1975; BS, George Wash Univ, 1976; MA 1978, PhD 1982, TX Wom's Univ; pa/Asst ₊Prof, TX Christian Univ, 1981-; Asst Prof (Adj), TX Wom's Univ, Sum 1981, Sprg 1981, Sum 1978, Grad Tchg Asst (Fall 1976, Fall 1977, Sprg 1978); Instr, Skidmore Col, 1978-81; Adj Fac, George Wash Univ, 1975-76; Free-Lance Master Tchr & Choreographer, TX, VA, MD, FL, DC, London, W Germany, Paris, SF, NY, 1973-; Royal Acad of Dancing; Imperial Soc of Tchrs of Dancing; Pavlova Soc; Dallas Dance Coun; Soc for Dance Res; Dance Hist Scholars; Nat Dance Assn (AAHPERD); AAUP; hon/Presented Paper to Nat Dance Assn, "The Ed of Creat Genius-Diaghilev's Influence on Leonide Massine," 1982; Contbr to the *Intl Dance Ency*, 1983; Book Review for Little, Brown & Co, 1983; Author, "A Hist & Pract of Balletic Mime" & "Leonide Massine: Choreographic Genius w a Collaborative Spirit"; Undergrad: Sigma Rho Delta (Dance Hon), Waytes Guild (Band Hon), Dean's List, Mortar Bd (Pres), Omicron Delta Kappa; Grad: Pi Lambda Theta (Ed Hon), Sigma Alpha Iota (Music), Outstg Grad 1981-82; 1st Am Awd'd the Royal Ballet Tchg Dipl; W/W: Among Students in Am Univs & Cols, of Am Wom; The Nat Col Register.

FUTTER, VICTOR oc/Executive; b/ Jan 22, 1919; h/17 Sunnyvale Road, Port Washington, NY 11050; ba/New York, NY; m/Joan; c/Jeffrey L, Ellen Victoria Shutkin, Deborah Gail; ed/BA, Columbia Col, 1939; JD, Columbia Univ of Law, 1942; mil/AUS, Maj Field Artillery; pa/Ptnr, Sills, Beck, Cunnis, Zuckerman, Rodin, Tischman, & Epstein, 1983-; Assoc, Sullivan & Cromwell, 1946-52; Mem of Legal Dept 1952-57, Asst Dir of Legal Dept 1957-68, Asst Gen Counsel 1968-76, Assoc Gen Counsel 1976-78, VP & Secy 1978-,

Allied Corp; Secy 1971-77, 1981-82, Mem of Bd of Dirs 1977-84, Mem of Ptnrship Com (AGNS) 1977-79, Allied Chem Nuclear Prods Inc; Secy, Allied Chem Foun, 1978-82; Am Law Inst, 1983-; Pres NY Reg 1983-84, Chm Nat Prog Com 1983-84, VP of NY Reg 1982-83, Treas of NY Reg 1981-82, Corporate Practs Com 1982-, Securities Law Com 1980-82, Ad Hoc Com on Proposed Fed Securities Code 1981-82, Chm of NY Reg Liaison Com 1980-82, Am Soc of Corporate Secretaries Inc, 1977-; Sect on Antitrust Law (Com on Sect &, Clayton) 1974-, Sect on Corp, Bkg & Bus Law, Sect on Intl Law 1976-, ABA; Com Intl Human Rts, 1983-; Com on Atomic Energy 1971-74, Com on Corporate Law 1965-68, Secy 1968, Com on St Legis 1948-50, Com on Nuclear Technol 1979-83; Assn of the Bar of the City of NY; Assn of Corporate Counsel of NJ, 1976-82; Intl Nuclear Law Assn, 1977-79; Com on Trade Regulation, Com on Legal Ed & Admission to the Bar 1982-, Corporate Counsel Sect 1981-, NY St Bar Assn; Stockholder Relats Soc of NY 1979-83; Spec Prof of Law 1976-78, Hofstra Law Sch; Pres 1972-74, Columbia Col Alumni Assn; cp/Trustee & Dpty Mayor, Village of Flower Hill, 1974-76; Bd of Dirs, NY Yg Dems, 1946-52; Chm of Bd of Dirs 1970-72, Columbia Col Fund; Alumni Senator, Three Terms, Columbia Univ Senate, 1969-75; CoChm of Fund Drive 1964, Bd of Dirs 1965-81, Port Wash Commun Chest; Pres 1968-70, Flower Hill Assn, 1966-70; Fdr & First Pres, Mt Holyoke Col Parents Assn 1979-80, Chm of Mt Holyoke Col Parents & Friends Com 1978-80; r/Hebrew; hon/Pubs, "The Case for Multinational Reprocessing Ctrs-Now" 1977, "Should the Proxy Statement Be Given a New Focus?" 1981, "Satisfying Corporate Accountability: The Roles of the Bd, the Corporate Sy, & the SEC Disclosure Rules" 1979, "Eval of Mun Bus Taxes" 1968, Others; Columbia Univ Alumni Medal for Dist'd Alumni Ser, 1970; Phi Beta Kappa, 1939; James Kent Scholar, 1942; W/W: in Am, in Am Law, in World.

FYE, PAUL McDONALD oc/Executive; b/Aug 6, 1912; h/Box 309, Woods Hole, MA 02543; ba/Woods Hole, MA; m/Ruth Elizabeth Heym; c/Kenneth Paul, Elizabeth Ruth; p/Orlando and Jennie Fye (dec); ed/BS, Albright Col, 1935; PhD, Columbia Univ, 1939; pa/ Asst Prof, Hofstra Col, 1939-41; Res Assoc, 1941-42; Res Supvr & Res Dir, Underwater Explosives Res Lab, 1942-47; Asst Prof of Chem, Univ of TN, 1947-48; Dept Chief & Chief of Explosives Res Dept 1948-56, Assoc Dir of Res 1956-58, Nav Ordnance Lab; Dir 1958-77, Pres 1961-, Woods Hole Oceanographic Instn; Trustee, St Cols of MA, 1966-67; MA Maritime Acad, 1981-; Bermuda Biol Sta for Res, 1960-; Univ Corp for Atmospheric Res, 1974-80; Bd of Dirs, Arthur D Little Inc 1969-85, Harbor Br Foun Inc 1975-81, Lord-Abbett Funds 1975-, Textron Inc 1969-85 (Exec Com 1971-85); Bd of Trustees, The Intl Fdn of Insts for Adv'd Study, VChm, Mbrship Com 1971-; Bd of Trustees, Law of the Sea Inst, Univ of HI, Exec Bd 1978-, Presiding Ofcr 1980-83; Mem of the Corp, Marine Biol Lab 1958-, The Charles Stark Draper Lab Inc 1974-; Am Acad of Arts & Scis; AAAS; Am Chem Soc; Am Geophy Union; Am Phy Soc; Am Soc of Limnology & Oceanography; Coun on Fgn Relats Inc; Marine Technol Soc, Pres 1968-69, Immediate Past Pres 1969-70, Hon Mem 1971-; US Nav Inst; USN Res & Devel Planning Coun; Pi Tau Beta; Sigma Xi; Phi Lambda Upsilon; Epsilon Chi; cp/Cosmos Clb, Wash DC; Univ Clb, NYC; hon/Author, Over 100 Articles on Oceanography & Photo Chem; USN Dist'd Public Ser Awd, 1977; Pres Cert of Merit, 1948; Hon Degs from Albright Col (DSc), Tufts Univ (DSc), SEn MA Univ (DSc), FL Inst of Technol (DSc), NEn Univ (LLD), Long Isl Univ (DSc); W/W in Am; Am Men & Wom of Sci.

G

GABBITA, KASI VISWANATH oc/ Assistant Research Engineer; b/Jul 26, 1943; h/1610 Preuss Road, #6, Los Angeles, CA 90035; m/Geetha; c/Somakiran, Siva Ranjani; p/Somasundaram (dec) and Varalakshmi, Machilipatnam, India; ed/BS, 1961; MS, 1963, PhD, 1972; pa/Jr Res Fellow, Sr Res Asst & Proj Asst, Indian Inst of Sci, Bangalore, India; Tech Dir, Ciers Res & Consultancy, Bangalore; Proj Assoc, Univ of WI-Milwaukee; Asst Res Engr, Univ of CA-LA; AAAS; Am Soc of Agronomy; Intl Humic Substances Soc; Soc of Envir Toxicology & Chem; Soc of Protozools; r/Hindu; hon/Author of Several Pubs in Leading Nat & Intl Sci Jours; Mem of Edit Bd of Sci Jours; Invited Author for Intl Profl Series; Reviewer for Sci Jours; Merit S'ship Grad, MS & PhD Progs, 1962-70; Commend, Bangalore Water Supply & Sewerage Bd, 1975; Cash Awd & Cit, AMCO Batteries 1976, Ramineni Romga Rao Transport Contractors 1977; W/W in W.

GABELMAN, JOHN W oc/Executive; b/May 18, 1921; h/23 Portland Court, Danville, CA 94526; ba/Same; m/Olive Alexander Thompson; c/Barbara Grace Gabelman Williams, Joan Lynn; p/ Charles Grover Sr and Cyprienna Turcotte Gabelman (dec); ed/Geol Engr 1943, Master of Geol Engrg 1948, DSc 1949, CO Sch of Mines; mil/USN, 1944-46; pa/Jr Engr, NJ Zinc Co, 1943-44, 1946; Instr, CO Sch of Mines, 1946-49; Geologist, CO Fuel & Iron Corp, 1949-51; Geologist, ASARCO, 1951-54; Dist Geologist, Latin Am Advr, Br Chief, US Atomic Energy Comm, 1954-75; Mgr, Exploration Res, UT Intl Inc, 1975-83; Ret'd, 1983; Current Pres, John W Gabelman & Assocs Inc; Fellow, Geol Soc of Am; Am Inst of Mining & Metall Engrs; Soc Ec Geologists; Am Assn Petro Geologists; Am Geophy Union; N CA Geol Soc; S African Geol Soc; Reg'd Prof, Engrg CO, NM (Inactive); Reg'd Geol, CA K of C; Beta Theta Pi Frat; Pres Clb, Hon Frat; hon/Author of 92 Profl Jour Pubs & Book, *Migration of Uranium & Thorium* 1977; Am Men of Sci; W/W: in CO, in Govt, in E, in MD, in W; Ldrs in Am Sci; Creat & Successful Personalities.

GABLEHOUSE, CHARLES JOHN oc/Aviation Editor, Airport Public Relations; b/Apr 16, 1928; h/82 Paulison Avenue, Passaic, NJ 07055; ba/New York, NY; m/Marge; c/Stephanie; ed/ Fordham Univ; Col of Wm & Mary; Hoffstra Col; pa/Assoc Editor, Bus/ Comml Aviation Mag, 1961-62; Tech Writer, Editor, Grumman Aircraft Engrg Corp, 1958-61; Aviation Editor & Airport Analyst, Port Auth of NY & NJ, 1962-; Staff Public Sers Rep, The Port Auth of NY & NJ Aviation Public Sers Div, Aviation Dept; AIAA; AHS; EAA; ASWA; ASCE; Soc for Tech Communs; Am Fdn of Tech Engrg; cp/ Hon Mem, Passaic Shakespeare Clb; hon/NY Chapt, Soc Tech Writers & Publishers Awd, 1963; Nat Awd for Book, *Helicopters & Autogiros*, Soc of Tech Writers & Publishers, 1970; *Helicopters & Autogiros*, Hailed by Critics in *Cinc Enquirer*, *Lib Jour*, *ALA Booklist*, *Wing, Flying* & *The Boston Globe*; Bronze Star, Korean War; Author, Num Profl Pubs; W/W: in E, in Aviation, in NJ.

GABLER, MEL oc/Annuitant, Executive; b/Apr 5, 1915; ba/Same; m/ Norma Elizabeth; c/James Melvin, Paul Richard, Don Allen (dec); p/Mr and Mrs O F Gabler (dec); ed/21 Yrs of Res, Review & Anal of Textbooks & Related Areas; mil/USAF, 4 Yrs; pa/Annuitant; Pres, Ednl Res Analysts; r/Bapt; hon/ Pub, *Textbooks on Trial*, Victor Books, 1976 (Selected by Book-of-the-Month Clb, 1977, Now in 4th Printing); Mel & Norma Gabler, Recognized Authorities in the Field of Textbook Content (Featured on *60 Minutes* & *World News Tonight*, Appeared on *Phil Donahue Show* & *Good Morning Am*, Subjects of Var News Articles); Mel & Norma Gabler Day, City of Longview, TX; Nat Del to White House Conf on Fams, 1980; TX Good Citizenship Medal, SAR, 1973; Top Awd of TX Freedom Forum, 1964; Cong of Freedom Awd, 10 Times; Lectr, Rice Univ, Brisbane Univ (Australia), Univ of TX; Stephen F Austin Univ, Phi Delta Kappa E TX Univ Chapt.

GABRIEL, BILLIE LUCILLE BURKLE oc/President Computer Industry; h/2888 Bayshore Drive, Newport Beach, CA 92663; p/Nick Angelo and Pearl Audry Burkle; ed/BS, Memphis St; Real Est Sales Lic, Lumbleau Real Est Sch; Many Units Toward MBA; pa/Bd Dirs, Mgr Fin, Adm, CA Data Processors, Data 100 Corp, 1971-75; Conslt, Computer Indust, 1976-79; VP, Gen Mgr, Isotronix Inc, 1980-81; Pres, Gabriel Computer Prods, 1981-83; Bd Mem, Pacific Data Sys, 1960-63; Bd Mem, ISI/Ling-Tempco-Vought, 1958-60; Fdr, Bd Dir, Bus & Profl Wom; 1958-60; cp/Fdr, Odyssean Yacht Clb, 1981-82; Fdr, Bd, Com for Ednl Excell, 1983-; Bd, VP, Braille Inst Aux OC, 1981-83; Fdr, Bus & Profl Wom, 1958-60; Mem, Am Mgmt Assn, 1973-74; Mem, Wn Electronic Mfrs Assn; Mem, Merch's & Mfrs, 1971-75; Campaign Wk, Repub Pty, 1976-82; hon/Proclamation, Mayor of Newport Bch, 1981; Commend, Balboa Dist/US Power Sqdrn, 1981; Cert Excell, Am Mgmt Assn, 1973; W/W in W.

GABRIEL, HERMAN WILLIAM oc/ Ecologist; b/Dec 21, 1933; h/PO Box 8929, Missoula, MT 59807; ba/Missoula, MT; p/Mrs Ruth G Hardy, Richmond, VA; ed/BS, VA Polytechnic Inst, 1956; Postgrad Wk, MI St Univ 1956, UT St Univ 1960-61; PhD, Univ of MT-Missoula, 1976; mil/AUS, 1956-58; pa/Forester, USDA Forest Ser, 1958-61; Forester, Teton Nat Forest, 1961-66; Forestry Ofcr, UN FAO, Quito, Ecuador, 1966-67; Tchg Assoc, Univ of MT Sch of Forestry, 1968-71; Chief of Envir Sect, US Army Corps of Engrs, AK Dist, 1971-74; Chief of Biol Resources Br, USDI Bur of Land Mgmt, AK St Ofc, 1975-78; Ldr, Spec Studies Grp, BLM, 1978-84; Conslt g Ecologist, Writer, Photog, 1985-; The Wildlife Soc; Soc of Am Foresters; Ecological Soc of Am; AK Acad of Engrg & Sci; AAAS; hon/Author of 20 Mag Articles & Sci Papers on Wildlife & Forestry; Dozens of Photos Printed in Many Nat Mags; Bur of Land Mgmt Spec Achmt Awd, 1980; W/W in W.

GADDES, RICHARD oc/General Director of Opera Company; b/May 23, 1942; ba/Opera Theatre of Saint Louis, PO Box 13148, #1 Kirthom Lane, Saint Louis, MO 63119; p/Thomas (dec) and Emilie Rickard Gaddes, Northumberland, England; ed/Grad, Trinity Col of Music, London, 1964; pa/Fdr, Wigmore Hall Lunchtime Concerts, 1965; Tchr, St Mary's Sch, London, 1962-63; Dir, Christopher Hunt/Richard Gaddes Artists Mgmt, London, 1965-66; Bookings Mgr, Artists' Intl Mgmt Ltd, London, 1967-69; Artistic Admr, The Santa Fe Opera, 1969-78; Gen Dir, Opera Theatre of St Louis, 1975-; Bd of Dirs, Wm Matheus Sullivan Foun, 1980-; Nat Opera Inst, Grants to Yg Am Singers 1978-; Nat Endowment for the Arts, Policy Panel 1982-; OPERA Am, Bd Mem 1979-82, Former VP; hon/Mu Phi Epsilon Recip, 1980; Rec'd 1st Annual MO Arts Awd, 1983; Hon Doct Musical Arts, St Louis Conservatory & Schs Arts, 1983; Nat Opera Inst Annual Awd; Hon DFA, Univ MO, 1984; Lamplighter Awd Recip, 1982; W/W in Am.

GAFFNEY, JAMES oc/Professor of Ethics; b/Feb 21, 1931; h/4420 Fontainebleau Drive, New Orleans, LA 70118, and 409 Napoleon Avenue, South Bend, IN 46617; ba/New Orleans, LA, & Notre Dame, IN; m/Kathleen McGovern; c/ Mary Elizabeth, Margaret Teresa; p/ James and Lucille Gaffney (dec); ed/BS, Sprg Hill, 1956; MA, Fordham, 1964; ThD, Gregorian, 1967; EdM, TX, 1970; pa/Prof of Ethics, Univ of Notre Dame, 1982-; Prof of Ethics 1979-, Assoc Prof 1976-79, Loyola Univ; Chm, Assoc Prof of Rel, IL Benedictine, 1973-76; Vis'g Lectr, Univ of Liberia, 1970-73; Assoc Prof of Phil, Univ Gonzaga, Florence, Italy, 1967-70; SCE; CTSA; CTS; AAR; Dante Soc; Soc of Christian Philosophers; Conf on Christianity & Lit; r/ Christian; hon/Author, *Moral Questions* 1973, *Focus on Doctrine* 1974, *Biblical Notes on the Lectionary* 1976, *Newness of Life* 1978, *Essays on Morality & Ethics* 1980, *Sin Reconsidered* 1983, & Many Jour Articles; Outstg Edrs of Am, 1975; Vis'g Lectureships in Bristol, Florence, Notre Dame, St Michael's; Intl W/W: in Ed, in Rel; Contemp Authors; Dir of Am Scholars.

GAFFORD, D DEAN oc/Family Physician; b/Oct 14, 1954; h/228 Valley Glen Drive, DeSoto, TX 75115; m/Carol Ann; c/Lindsay Diane; p/Mrs Madelon Gafford, Dallas, TX; ed/BS in Biol, Baylor Univ, 1977; DO, TX Col of Osteopathic Med, 1981; pa/Fam Phys, DeSoto Fam Med & Minor Emer Ctr; TMA; TOMA; AMA; AOA; AAO; ACGP; ACEP; cp/Baylor JCs, 1975-77, Pres 1976; DeSoto C of C, 1984; hon/ Intl Yth in Achmt.

GAGE, DOROTHY J oc/Accounting Technician; b/Jun 13, 1928; c/Chucky Seaman (dec), Chris, Terry (dec); p/ Seaman (dec) and Ruby Claborn, Los Gatos, CA; ed/HS Dipl, Santa Pauia, CA, 1946; pa/Acctg Tech, Nav Ship Weapon Sys Engrg Sta, 1969-82; Acctg Tech, Pacific Missile Range, 1967-69; Comptometer Operator, Carnation Co, 1958-66; Comptometer Operator, Golden St Dairy, 1948-57; Payroll Clk, Saticoy Lemon Assn, 1946-48; Charter Mem, BPW at NSWSWS, USNCBC, Pt Hueneme, 1969; cp/Charter Mem, Ventura Co Muscular Dystrophy Assn, 1955-, Ofcr, Bd Mem; Charter Mem, Hlth Agys of Ventura Co, 1965-80; Toastmistresses of Pt Mugu, 1968; hon/ Author of Book About Her Chd & Her Life w Muscular Dystrophy, Entitled

MD Lady (in Process); USA Congl Record for 25 Yrs as a Vol, 1980; CA Assem for 25 Yrs as a Vol, 1980; Recip, Commend from 6 Mayors of Ventura Co Cities, 1980; W/W of Am Wom.

GAGNE, PAMELA BASHORE oc/ Attorney; b/Oct 19, 1956; h/1121 Rodman Street, Philadelphia, PA 19147; ba/Philadelphia, PA; m/W Roderick; p/ Mr and Mrs Charles Eicker Bashore, Camp Hill, PA; ed/BA, cum laude, Vanderbilt Univ, 1977; Att'd, Georgetown Univ (Fgn Policy Div) 1975, Univ of San Diego & the Sorbonne Inst on Intl & Comparative Law 1978; JD, Dickinson Sch of Law, 1980; pa/Jud Clk to the Hon Gwilym A Price Jr, Superior Ct of PA, 1980-82; Assoc, Marshall, Dennehey, Warner, Coleman & Goggin, 1982-; ABA, 1980-, Com on Intl Law 1981-82; PA Bar Assn, 1980-; Phila Bar Assn, 1982-; Phi Alpha Delta, Legal Frat, 1978-, Treas of Mary Dashti Burr Chapt 1979-80; Dickinson Sch of Law Wom's Law Caucus, 1977-80, Treas 1978-79, VP 1979-80; Phi Alpha Theta, Hist Hon Soc, 1976; Chi Omega, Social & Civic Sorority, 1974-; Am Jurisp Awd for Excellent Achmt in the Area of Fed Pract, 1980; Dickinson Sch of Law Cert of Merit for Achmts in Advocacy, 1980; Intl Moot Ct Team Cert of Merit, 1980; Social Register.

GAINES, EDYTHE JONES oc/Commissioner; b/Sep 6, 1922; h/275 Kenyon Street, Hartford, CT 06105; ba/New Britain, CT; m/Albert D; c/Richard D, Mallory D; ed/AB, Hunter Col, 1944; MA, NY Univ, 1947; CAS 1966, EdD 1969, Harvard Univ; LLD, Montclair St, 1977; pa/Commr, St of CT Public Utilities Control Auth, 1979-; Conslt, Bd of Govs of the Gtr Hartford Consortium for Higher Ed, Univ of Hartford, Trinity Col, Hartford Col for Wom, St Thomas Sem, The Grad Ctr, St Joseph Col, 1978-79; Supt of Schs, Hartford, CT, 1975-78; Exec Dir, Ednl Planning & Support, NYC Public Schs, 1973-75; Dir, the Lng Cooperative, NYC, 1971-73; Commun Supt of Schs, Commun Sch Dist 12, NYC Public Schs, 1967-71; Prin, Joan of Arc Jr HS, NYC Public Schs, 1966-67; Asst Prin, Joan of Arc Jr HS, 1955-60; Core Curric Coor, Jr HS Div, NYC Public Schs, 1952-55; Tchr, Exptl Core Prog, Joan of Arc Jr HS, NYC, 1948-52; Tchr, Eng, Social Studies, Sci & Guid, Prospect Jr HS, NYC, 1945-48; cp/Bd of Trustees, Hartford Col for Wom; Bd of Trustees, Hartford Sem; Dir, CT Nat Bk & Hartford Nat Corp; Dir, Kaman Corp; Bd of Dirs, Hartford Stage Co; Bd of Dirs, CT Opera Assn; Corporator, Mt Sinai Hosp; Corporator, Hartford Hosp; Active Mem, St Francis Hosp; Bd of Dirs, Old St House; Chair, Comm on Min, Epis Diocese of CT; hon/Hall of Fame, Hunter Col, 1972; Wom of the Yr Awd, Bronx Div, NAACP; The Ecumenical Awd for Dedicated Ser to God & Commun, Bronx Coun of Chs, 1971; Montclair-N Essex YWCA Awd in Recog of Outstg Achmts in Ed, 1975; Wom of the Yr, Zeta Phi Beta Sorority, 1969; The Assn of Bronx Commun Orgs for Excell in the Field of Ed, 1973; U Negro Col Fund, Distn in Ednl Ser Awd, 1978; The African Am Hist Assn's Mary McLeod Bethune Awd, 1971; Nat Assn of Univ Wom, Queens, NY Br, in Recog of Dedication to Field of Ed; Cit

for Excell in Biling Ed, CT Biling Ed Assn, 1978; Conslt to Num Agys & Orgs as Well as Pres Kennedy, Johnson, Nixon, & Others; Assoc Conslt for the Nat Sch Bds Assn to Local Sch Bds in Their Superintendency Search Processes, 1977-; Cit, Excell in Govt, Ctl Asheville Optimist Clb, 1983; W/W: in E, of Am Wom, Among Black Ams.

GAINES, MARION LUCEINE oc/ College Professor, CPA; b/Sep 21, 1925; h/108 Greenway Drive, Greenwood, SC 29646; ba/Greenwood, SC; c/Thomas Clark Fitzgerald III, Tainis Marion Fitzgerald, Carolyn Sarah Fitzgerald; p/ Marion Little and Eloise Cave Gaines; ed/BS, Univ of NC, 1945; Att'd 1941-43, MBA 1964, Univ of SC; pa/Peat Marwick Mitchell, 1945-47; Darmody Todd CPA, 1947-48; J P Stevens, 1948-50; Ptnr, Fitzgerald & Co, 1950-63; Palmy Col, 1963-66; Midken's Tech, 1966-73; Winston Col, 1973-81; Landu Col, 1981-; cp/Zonta Intl, Former Treas; Nat Assn Accts, Former Dir & Treas; Am Inst CPA's; SC Assn CPA's; Piedmont Chapt CPA's; Bus & Profl Wom; r/Epis; hon/Phi Beta Kappa; Beta Gamma Sigma; Nom'd Yg Wom of Yr; W/W Among Am Wom; Personalities of S.

GAIPTMAN, SHARON ANN oc/ University Relations Director; b/Aug 30, 1948; h/PO Box 385, Juneau, AK 99801; ba/Juneau, AK; m/Peter K Freer; p/Irv and Ruth Gaiptman, Plainview, NY; ed/BA, SUNY-Brockport; MA, of AK-Juneau, 1982-; Sta Mgr & Prog Dir, KTOO-TV, 1978-81; Asst Dir, Programming, KETC-TV, 1974-78; AK Fundraising & Devel Coun; AAUA; Coun for the Advmt & Support of Ed; Nat Assn of Wom Deans, Admrs & Cnslrs; Nat Assn of Ednl Broadcasters, 1974-81; Nat Acad of TV Sers & Scis, 1976-78; Am Wom in Radio & TV, 1975-77; Ednl Chair, Bd of Dirs 1982-83, AAUW, 1982-; cp/Fdg Mem, Bd of Dirs 1983-, AK Aquarium Soc; Bd of Dirs 1984, AK Com, 1982-; Panel 1982, AK St Coun on the Arts; AK Visitors Assn, 1983-; VP 1982-83, 1983-84, Chair of *Gt Am Smokeout* 1981, Am Cancer Soc, Juneau-Douglas Unit, 1980-; Big Brothers/Big Sisters; Cent Hall Adv Bd, Cent Hall Dedication Com 1983, City & Borough of Juneau; Co-Chair, Decoration's Com, Inauguration '83; Bd of Dirs 1982-, Indep Public TV Inc; Bd Mem 1979-80, Juneau Arts & Humanities Coun, 1979-; Chair, Govt Affairs Com 1982-83, Juneau Ch of C; Juneau-Douglas Little Theatre, 1979-; Juneau Wom's Resource Ctr, 1980-; Chair, Growth & Devel Com 1983-84, Bd Mem 1981-82, 1982-83, Chair, Com of the Status of Wom & Human Rts 1981-82, 1982-83, Soroptomists Intl of Juneau, 1979-; SE AK Ath Assn, 1982-; hon/Nom'd, Juneau Outstg Bus Wom of the Yr, 1983; Outstg Yg Wom of Am.

GAITHER, BEVERLY JEAN oc/ Senior Credit Analyst; b/Feb 14, 1950; h/6020 Spanish Oak Road, Charlotte, NC 28212; ba/Charlotte, NC; p/Albert and Eddie Lou Gaither, Atlanta, GA; ed/ BS, Biol, Trinity Univ, 1974; pa/Lab Tech, City of Atlanta, 1975-77; Credit Analyst 1977-80, Sr Credit Analyst 1981-, CIT Corp; Assn of Wom in Bus; cp/Afro Am Cultural Soc; NAACP; World Fdn of Meth Wom; Nat Coun of Chs; Nat Bd of Christian Ed; r/Meth;

hon/Herbert Lehman Awd, 1968; Occupl Tng Prog Awd, 1969; Awd for Dedicated Ser, CME Ch, 1982; Personalities of S.

GAJEWSKI, WALTER MICHAEL oc/Manager, Radioactive Material Handling Engineer; b/Apr 4, 1923; h/3103 South Everett Place, Kennewick, WA 99337; ba/Richland, WA; m/Mary Maglieri; c/Lisa Marie King, Paul M, Stephen W; p/Mrs Mary Gajewski, Hartford, CT 09008; ed/BSEE 1949, MSE 1951, Univ of CT; mil/AUS Signal Corps, 1943-46; pa/Sect Mgr of Nav Nuclear Reactor Design 1950-60, Mgr of Prototype Reactor Tng Facility 1960-68, Asst Proj Mgr of Nuclear Aircraft Reactor Design 1968-70, Mgr of Engrg-LMFBR/FFTF Reactor Plants 1970-82, Mgr Hazardous Mat Handling Equip/Sys Design, Westinghouse Elect Corp; Profl Engr (Nuclear), CA; IEEE, 1950-84; ANS, 1949-84; ASME, 1955-80; Chm of Adv'd Reactors Com of NED/ASME, 1984-86; hon/Tau Beta Pi, 1949; Eta Kappa Nu, 1949; Sigma Pi Sigma, 1950.

GALASSO, GEORGE J oc/Scientist, Administrator; b/Jun 3, 1932; ba/ National Institutes of Health, Building 1, Room 111, Bethesda, MD 20205; m/ Joan Catherine Walsh; c/Catherine J, G John, George J; p/Giorgio and Lucia Surico Galasso (dec); ed/BS, Manhattan Col, 1954; PhD, Univ of NC, 1960; mil/ AUS, 1954-56; pa/Res Assoc 1960-62, Res Asst Prof 1962-64, Univ of NC; Assoc Prof, Univ of VA, 1964-68; Grants Assoc 1968-69, Antiviral Substances Prog Ofcr (NIAID) 1969-76, Chief of Infectious Diseases Br (NIAID) 1971-73, Chief of Devel & Applied Br (NIAID) 1973-83, Assoc Dir of Extramural Affairs 1983-, NIH; Am Acad Microbiol, Elected; Wash Acad of Sci, Elected; Infectious Disease Soc of Am, Elected; Am Soc Virology, Charter Mem; Am Soc for Microbiol; Inter-Am Soc for Chemotherapy, Charter Mem; AAAS; Sigma Xi; hon/Author, Over 70 Publ'd Sci Articles; Editor, *Antiviral Agts & Viral Diseases of Man* 1978, 1984, *The Biol of the Interferon Sys* 1981; Fdrs Ser Awd, Pkwood Commun, 1964; Scout Awds, 1971; Public Hlth Ser Superior Ser Awd, 1978; Am Bus Wom Boss of the Yr, 1978; Public Hlth Ser Spec Achmt Awd, 1981; Asst Secy for Hlth Awd Exceptl Achmt, 1983; Univ NC Dist'd Ser Awd; W/W: in E, in Sci.

GALEENER, FRANK LEE oc/Physicist; b/Jul 31, 1936; h/4035 Orme Street, Palo Alto, CA 94306; ba/Palo Alto, CA; m/Janet Louise Trask; c/Keith Lee, Matthew Lee; p/Daisy Elizabeth Lee Galeener, Norman, OK; ed/BS in Physics 1958, MS in Physics 1962, MIT; PhD in Physics, Purdue Univ, 1970; pa/ Physicist, MIT Lincoln Lab 1959-61, MIT Nat Magnet Lab 1961-64; Scist 1970-73, Mgr of Semiconductor Res 1973-77, Prin Scist 1977-, Xerox Palo Alto Res Ctr; Vis'g Scist, Univ of Oxford 1982, Univ of Cambridge 1983-84; Am Phy Soc; Am Ceramic Soc; Optical Soc of Am; Am Vacuum Soc; Sigma Xi; Sigma Pi Sigma; hon/Author, Over 70 Articles in Physics Res Jours; Co-Editor, *Structure & Excitations of Amorphous Solids* 1976, *The Physics of Mos Insulators* 1980; Woodrow Wilson Fellow, MIT, 1958; W/ W in W, in Am, in Frontier Sci & Technol.

PERSONALITIES OF AMERICA

GALL, ERIC P oc/Physician, Rheumatologist, Professor; b/May 24, 1940; h/830 North Sonoita Avenue, Tucson, AZ 85711; ba/Tucson, AZ; m/Katherine Theiss; c/Gretchen Theiss, Michael Edward; p/Edward (dec) and Phyllis Gall, Tucson, AZ; ed/AB in Zool 1962, MD 1966, Univ of PA; mil/AUS, 1968-70; pa/Internship, Univ of Cinc Med Ctr, 1966-67; Internal Med Residency, Univ of Cinc 1967-68, Univ of PA 1970-71; Rheumatology F'ship, Univ of PA, 1971-73; Asst Prof 1973-78, Assoc Prof 1978-83, Prof 1983-, Internal Med, Surg, Fam & Commun Med, Univ of AZ Col of Med; Chief of Rheumatology/ Allergy/Immunol, Univ of AZ, 1983-; Fellow, Am Col of Phys, Am Rheumatism Assn, Arthritis Hlth Professions Assn (Pres 1982-83), Arthritis Foun (Bd of Trustees 1980-, Ho of Dels 1981-, VChm 1982-83); Tucson Rheumatology Soc, Secy-Treas 1983-; hon/Pubs, "Hypersensitivity Reaction to Sulindac" 1983, "Arthritis Hlth Profls Fam Tree: Combined Care for Rheumatic Disease Patients" 1983, "The Med Mgmt of Cervical Arthritis" 1984, "Calcium Pyrophosphate-Deposition Disease", 1984, "The Exam of the Musculoskeletal Sys" 1983, "Professionalism Res & Directions-The AHPA in 1983: "Rheumatic Diseases-Rehab & Mgmt", 1984, Num Others; Alpha Epsilon Delta, Premed Hon Soc, 1960-62, Pres 1961-62; Alpha Omega Alpha, Univ of AZ, 1980; Bronze Star, AUS, 1970; Grad, cum laude in Zool, Univ of PA, 1962; W/W in W.

GALL, JOSEPH GRAFTON oc/ Research Biologist; b/Apr 14, 1928; h/ 107 Bellemore Road, Baltimore, MD 21210; ba/Baltimore, MD; m/Diane M Dwyer; c/Lawrence F, Barbara G; p/ John Christian and Elsie Rosenberger Gall (dec); ed/BS in Zool 1949, PhD in Zool 1952, Yale Univ; pa/From Instr to Prof of Zool, Univ of MN, 1952-63; Prof of Biol & Molecular Biophysics & Biochem, Yale Univ, 1963-83; Staff Mem, Dept of Embryology, Carnegie Instn of Wash, 1983-; Am Soc for Cell Biol, Pres 1967-68; Soc for Developmental Biol, Pres 1984-85; Genetics Soc of Am; AAAS; hon/Author, Num Sci Articles in Profl Jours; Am Acad of Arts & Scis, 1968; Nat Acad of Scis, 1972; E B Wilson Awd of the Am Soc for Cell Biol, 1983; Am Cancer Soc Res Prof of Developmental Genetics, 1984-.

GALLAGHER, ANNA HELEN oc/ Consultant; h/952 Agate Street, San Diego, CA 92109; ba/Same; m/John J; p/Filippo and Maria Antonia D'Amico Giordano (dec); ed/Dipl in Nsg, Phila Gen Hosp, 1939; BS 1950, MS 1951, EdD 1956, Univ of PA; Vis'g Scholar, Columbia Univ, 1963; mil/Nurse Fac Mem Tng Nurses for US Cadet Corps, 1942-45; pa/Dir, Dept of Nsg, ID St Univ, 1957-60; Fdr & 1st Chm, Dept of Nsg, NE LA St Univ, 1960-67; Fdr & 1st Chm, Dept of Nsg, SUNY-Brockport, 1967-71; 1st Dean & Fdr of the Col of Nsg, Lewis Univ, 1971-74; Chm, Undergrad Nsg Prog 1974-75, Fdr & 1st Chm, Dept of Cont'g Ed in Nsg 1975-76, Univ of MA Amherst; Hd, Dept of Nsg & Prof in Nsg, James Madison Univ, 1976-78; Conslt in the Field of Nsg Ed & Adm, 1978-; Will-Grundy-Kankakee Co Comprehensive Hlth Planning Coun & Hlth

Sers Manpower Coms, 1971-74; Ctl Shenandoah Hlth Adv Coun, Bd of Dirs 1977-78; ANA; AAUW; Pi Lambda Theta; Wn Reg Coun for St Leags for Nsg, Exec Com Mem 1958-60; Steering Com, Genesee Val Reg Planning for Nsg, 1968-71; hon/Author, Ednl Adm in Nsg, 1965; Co-Author, "A Phantasy (w Refs)" in Am Jour of Nsg 1970; Vis'g Scholar, Columbia Univ, 1963; Nurse Participant, Wom Power Conf, 1957; Dir, Planning Grant for Col of Nsg, Lewis Univ (Grantor: IL Comm on Higher Ed), 1971; Chm, Steering Com for Instnl Self-Eval, Lewis Univ, 1971-72; World W/W of Wom; W/W of Am Wom; Ldrs in Am Sci; Ldrs in Ed; Personalities of S; Commun Ldrs of Am; 2,000 Notable Ams.

GALLAGHER, JOHN J oc/Systems Ecologist, Consultant; b/Mar 30, 1914; h/952 Agate Street, San Diego, CA 92109; ba/Same; m/Anna Helen Giordano; p/Patrick and Catherine Dowling Gallagher (dec); ed/BA 1949, PhD 1955, Univ of PA; Postdoct Studies, Univ of TN-Knoxville, 1967-68; mil/USAF 1942-45; pa/Conslt, Phila Acad of Natural Scis, 1950-55; Res Assoc, Univ of PA 1955-56, ID St Univ 1957-60, NE LA St Univ 1960-67; Sr Res Assoc, SUNY-Brockport, 1968-71; Assoc Prof in Biol Scis 1971-74, Advr to Pres for Instnl Res 1971-74, Coor for Envir Devel 1971-74, Coor of Task Forces for Instnl Self-Eval 1971-73, Assoc Dean of Col of Nsg 1972-74, Co-Dir of Planning Grant for Col of Nsg 1971-72, Lewis Univ; Conslt, Ecol, 1974-; ID Acad of Scis, Fdg Com 1958-59, Constit Com 1958-60, Mbrship Com 1958-60; Mbrship Com, Am Microscopical Soc, 1959-60; AAAS; Sigma Xi; cp/ Will-Grundy-Kankakee Co Comprehensive Hlth Planning Coun, 1971-74; hon/Pubs, "Cyclomorphosis in the Rotifer Keratella cochlearis Gosse" 1957, "World List of Rofifer Wkrs" 1962; Co-Author, "A Phantasy (w Refs)" in Am Jour of Nsg, 1970; Author of Nine Other Pubs; Sigma Xi, Elected 1970; Meritorious Achmt Bronze Star, 1945; Psi Chi Superior Ser Awd, 1936; World W/W in Sci; DIB; Men of Achmt; Ldrs in Am Sci; Am Men & Wom of Sci; Commun Ldrs & Noteworthy Ams; Dir of Dist'd Ams; W/W: in W, in CA.

GALLANT, NANETTE oc/Telecommunications Consultant; b/Mar 14, 1956; h/3816 Fairway Circle, Las Vegas, NV 89108; ba/Same; p/Dr Richard and Kathryn Gallant, Las Vegas, NV; ed/ Cert in Surg Technol, UT Tech Col; BS, Mass Communs, Univ of UT; Post-Baccalaureate Studies in Nuclear Engrg & Math; mil/Cadet, HHC 162nd Support Grp, Univ of UT ROTC; pa/ Broadcast Conslt, NGP NV, 1984-; Chief of Res, Wn Spinal Clin, 1982-83; Consltg Engr to Pvt Phys, 1981-84; Remote Opers Engr, Skaggs Telecommuns Ser, 1981-83; Opers Engr, KUED-TV, 1978-80; Cert'd Surg Technologist/Cardiac Surg Spec, St Mark's Hosp, 1976-80; Assn of Surg Technologists, 1976-81, Pres 1977, Nat Rep 1978; Soc of Photo-Optical Instrumentation Engrs; Am Nuclear Soc; IEEE; SMPTE; SBE; AUSA; r/Rom Cath; hon/ Author of Multiple Articles for Intermtn Cath Newspaper 1982-83, & Articles Pub'd in UT Daily Chronicle Newspaper 1978-80; Nat Surg Technologist of the

Month, 1978; ROTC Ldrship Awd, 1984; Spurs Hon Soc, 1974; W/W in Frontier Sci & Technol.

GALLEGO-GARCÍA, JOSÉ MIGUEL oc/Chemist; b/Nov 5, 1955; h/ 1844 D Avenue, National City, CA 92050; ba/Baja CA, Mexico; p/Waldemar Gallego Muñoz and Josefina Garcia Baker; ed/Att'd, Preparatoria Federal Lazaro Cardenas, 1971-73; BS in Chem, Universidad Autonoma de Guadalajara, 1973-77; mil/Penthatlon Militar, Mexican Armed Forces; pa/ Oper Supvr of Water Plant of the St Water Comm in Tijuana, 1978-79; Res Chem at Quimica Organica de Mexico, 1979-81; VP, Chief Chem & Part-Owner of Laboratorios Industriales y Servicios Internacionales, 1981-; Contract w the Universidad Autonoma de Baja CA for Ser & Maintainance of Electronic Equip, 1982-; Tchr, Universidad Autonoma de Baja CA, 1981-84; Chem at Chem Energy of CA, 1984-; Pres, G C Sys, 1985-; Chem Soc of Mexico; Student Affiliate of Am Chem Soc, 1973-77; Pres & Fdr, Sociedad de Ciencias Experimentales, 1972-73; r/ Cath; hon/Pubs, "Programacion BASIC en Quimica," "Employmt Facts" 1981, "Psychol & the Programmable Calculator" 1980, "Molecular Parameters of Diatomic Molecules, a Prog for Programmable Calculators" 1981, Several Others; Spec Awd for Articles Contributed to TX Instruments Inc, 1979; Nom'd to Appear in W/W: in W, in Data Mgmt, 1983.

GALLETTI, PIERRE M oc/Scientific Researcher and Educational Administrator; b/Jun 11, 1927; h/36 Taber Avenue, Providence, RI 02906; ba/ Providence, RI; m/Sonia Aidan; c/Marc Henri; p/Henri R and Yvonne Galletti; ed/BA, Classics, St Maurice Col, Switzerland, 1945; MD 1951, PhD 1954, Univ of Lausanne, Switzerland; pa/VP of Biol & Med 1972-, Prof of Med Sci 1967-, Chm of Div of Biol & Med 1968-72, Brown Univ; Vis'g Prof of Physiol, Emory Univ, 1966-67; Eleanor Roosevelt Fellow of the Intl Union Agnst Cancer, Univ of Palermo, 1964-65; Assoc Prof of Physiol, Emory Univ, 1962-66; Am Soc for Artificial Internal Organs, Pres 1969-70, Prog Chm, Pub Com Chm, Secy-Treas; Biomed Engrg Soc; AAAS; IEEE; Am Col of Cardiol, Fellow; Am Physiological Soc; Am Heart Assn; Swiss Physiological & Pharmacological Soc; hon/Author of Heart-Lung Bypass 1962, Over 270 Jour Articles & Abstracts, Book Reviews, Chapts of Commentaries; Hon DSc Deg, Roger Wms Col, Bristol, RI, 1979; Hon Doct Deg, Univ of Nancy, France, 1982; W/W: in Sci, in Technol Today, in E.

GALLINGTON, ROGER WAYNE oc/Engineer; b/Dec 19, 1937; h/23913 6th Avenue South, Seattle, WA 98188; ba/Seattle, WA; m/A Louise Moreau; c/ Steven Craig, Elizabeth Lynn, Katherine Ann; p/Ralph O and Mary K Gallington, Tallahassee, FL; ed/BS in Mech Engrg 1960, MS in Mech Engrg 1961, PhD in Aeronaut & Astronautical Engrg 1969, Univ of IL; mil/USAF, 1961-81, Adv'd through Ranks to Lt Col in 1977; pa/Mech Engr, Missile Site Activation, USAF, 1961-64; Res Assoc, F J Seisler Res Lab, USAF Acad, 1967-71; Assoc Prof of Aeronautics, USAF Acad,

250

1971-75; Chief Advr, Vehicle Br, Nav Ship R&D Ctr, 1975-78; Aeronautics Lab Dir, USAF Acad, 1978-81; Sr Staff Engr, Martin Marietta Aerospace, 1981-83; Sr Scist, Sci Application Inc, 1983-; AIAA; Ground Test Tech Com, Rocky Mtn Sect VChm 1979-83, Instrument Soc of Am; r/Presb; hon/Contbr, Num Articles to Profl Jours on Physics & Aeronaut Engrg; Sigma Gamma Tau, Nat Hon for Aeronaut Engrg, 1967; Meritorious Ser Medals, 1971, 1975, 1981; AF Commend Medal, 1964; Navy Commend Medal, 1978; W/W in W.

GALLIVAN, LAURA LYN oc/ Chamber of Commerce Executive; b/ Oct 30, 1949; h/72645 Hedgehog Street, Palm Desert, CA 92260; ba/Palm Springs, CA; m/Patrick John; p/Edith M Gower, Palm Desert, CA; ed/Student of Spch, So IL Univ, 1967-69; pa/Exec VP, Palm Sprgs C of C, 1982-; Dir of Downtown Coun, St Paul Area C of C, 1979-82; Mktg Dir, Signal Hills Mall, 1977-79; Fund Raising Spec/Sales, Nasco Inc, 1975-77; Cosmetic Rep (Reg'd Cosmetologist, St of VA), Lord & Taylor, 1974-75; Cnslr/Sales Rep, Exec Staffing/Wn Temp Sers, 1972-74; Flight Attendant, NW Orient Airlines, 1969-72; Pt-time Instr, Inver Hills Commun Col, 1978-80; Pt-time Indep Beauty Conslt, Mary Kay Cosmetics, 1981-; Downtown Commun Devel Coun, Bd of Dirs; Carriage Hills Merchs Assn; Intl Coun of Shopping Ctrs; Am C of C Execs; Intl Downtown Execs Assn; cp/St Paul Winter Carnival Assn, Publicity & Public Relats Com; Lowertown Commun Coun; hon/Outstg Yg Wom of Am; W/W in MW; World W/W of Wom; Biogl Roll of Hon.

GALTON, HERBERT oc/University Professor; b/Oct 1, 1917; h/2807 Ousdahl Road, Lawrence, KS 66044; ba/ Lawrence, KS; ed/Schooling in Vienna, Austria; PhD in Russian Philology, Univ of London, England, 1951; pa/Sr Monitor, Monitoring Ser, The Brit Broadcasting Corp, 1939-56; Translator/ Editor, Fgn Broadcast Info Ser of the US St Dept (Br at Vienna), 1956-62; Prof of Slavic Langs, Univ of KS, 1962-; cp/Pres, B'nai B'rith Sunflower Lodge, 1983; r/Jewish; hon/Pubs, "Aorist und Aspekt im Slavischen" 1962, "The Main Functions of the Slavic Verbal Aspect" 1976, "Freedom from Illusions" 1984, 2nd Edition, Plus Num Articles in the Field of Slavic & Gen Linguistics; Exch Scholar, Bulgaria 1965, Czechoslovakia 1967-68, Yugoslavia 1970-71; Dic of Am Scholars; World W/W of Authors; DIB; W/W: in MW, in Intl Ed.

GALVAN, SABINO oc/Public Education Administrator; b/Oct 27, 1934; h/ 8215 Scarlet Oak Circle, Citrus Heights, CA 95610; ba/Carmichael, CA; m/Jo Ana K; c/Gregory P, Jeanette K, Stepchd: James, Peggy, Donna, Steve, Todd; p/Mr and Mrs Paul R Galvan, Little Field, TX; ed/BS, Sacramento St Col, 1967; AA, Sacramento Jr Col; mil/ USAF, 1954-58; pa/Dir of Acctg Sers 1980-, Asst Dir of Fin 1978-80, Sr Financial Analyst 1976-78, Chief Acct 1968-76, San Juan Unified Sch Dist; Adm Asst 1967-68, Acct 1965-67, Sacramento Co Ofc of Ed; Auditor-Appraiser, Sacramento Co Assessor's Ofc, 1963-64; Tax Examr, IRS, 1962-63; Auditor/Trainee, Dept of Fin, St of CA, 1962; St Chm Acctg R&D Com 1981-82,

Asst St Chm Acctg R&D Com 1978-79, 1979-80, St Ad Hoc Com 1978-79, 1979-80, St Bd of Dirs 1976-77, Pres of Sacramento Sect 1976-77, Pres-Elect of Sacramento Sect 1975-76, Secy of Sacramento Sect 1974-75, Bd of Dirs of Sacramento Sect 1972-73, 1977-78, CA Assn of Sch Bus Ofcls; Developmental Planning Com, San Juan Unified Sch Dist, 1977-78; Budget Com 1979-80, Bd of Dirs 1980-81, San Juan Admrs Assn; VP of Progs, Assn of CA Sch Admrs, Reg III, 1983-84; Pres 1982-83, Pres-Elect 1981-82, San Juan Admrs Assn; cp/Chm of Nom'g Com 1979, Bd of Dirs 1978-81, Chm of Planning Com 1979-80, Planning Com 1978-79, Pers Exec Com 1979-80, Pers Com 1978-79, Sch Employees Credit Union; Chm of Mbrship Com, Treas, BSA; U Way, Rep for Bus Sers Div, San Juan Unified Sch Dist; r/Bapt; hon/W/ W in W.

GAMBARO, ERNEST UMBERTO oc/Corporate Counsel; b/Jul 6, 1938; h/ 4221 Rousseau Lane, Palos Verdes, CA 90274; ba/El Segundo, CA; m/Winifred Sonya; p/Ralph and Teresa Gambaro; ed/BS in Aeronaut Engrg w Hons 1960, MS in Aeronaut Engrg w Hons 1961, Purdue Univ; Fulbright Scholar, Rome Univ, 1961-62; JD w Hons, Loyola Univ Law Sch, 1975; pa/Proj Engr of NASA/ DOD Gemini Experiments 1963-65, Mgr of Adv'd Plans (Manned Orbital Lab) 1966-69, Mgr of Sys Engrg 1969-75, Counsel 1975-80, The Aerospace Corp, 1962-80; Corporate Counsel & Asst Secy, Computer Scis Corp, 1980-; hon/Author of "Europe Alfresco" Newspaper Column & Num Profl Articles; USAF Commend for Contbns to US Manned Space Prog, 1969; Fulbright Scholar, 1961-62; Convair Awd for Grad Study, 1961; Pres's S'ship for Engrg Study, 1959-60; Hon Mayor & Outstg Yth of Niagara Falls, NY, 1956; W/W: in CA, in Am Law.

GAMBLE, KARL WILSON oc/Professor Emeritus; b/Feb 22, 1911; m/ Anne Shepko; ed/BS, CA St Col, 1933; EdM 1937, EdD 1950, Univ of Pgh; mil/ AUS, 1942-45; pa/Tchr, Nottingham Twp Schs, Wash Co, 1933-36; Prin, S Franklin Twp Sch, Wash Co, 1938-42; Cnslg Psychol, VA in Pgh, 1945; Dir of Duquesne Guid Ctr, Brownsville Guid Ctr, Wash Guid Ctr; Chief of Med Psych, Aspinwall Med Hosp, 1950; Dir of Vets' Guid Ctr, Univ of Pgh, 1951-60; Indust Psychol Conslt, Maynard Res Coun; Prof of Psych, CA St Col, 1961-76; APGA; Nat Soc of Ed; NEA; Am Col Pers & Guid Assn; Assn for Higher Ed; Am, PA & Pgh Psychol Assns; Am Charolaise Assn; Cert'd Elem Tchr, Elem Prin, Sec'dy Tchr, Sec'dy Prin & Supervising Prin, St of PA; hon/Recip, Battle Stars in Ctl Europe, Rhineland & Ardennes (The Battle of the Bulge); W/W E; DIB; 2,000 Men of Achmt; Intl W/W of Intells.

GAMBRELL, MILDRED KATHERINE oc/Retired Teacher; b/Mar 10, 1939; h/620 Cibilo Street, Lockhart, TX 78644; p/Mrs Nora Katherine Gambrell, Lockhart, TX; ed/BMus, Univ of TX, 1962; EdM, SW TX St Univ 1966; pa/ Elem Sch Music Tchr, Victoria Public Schs, 1962-64; Tchr, Dickinson Public Schs, 1964-75; Secy, Lockheed Electronics Corp, 1974-75; Pvt Piano Tchr; Alpha Delta Kappa Sorority, 1971-,

Recording Secy 1973; Beta Sigma Phi Sorority, Recording Secy 1972-, Treas 1973; AAUW, Recording Secy 1973; Bay Area Chorus, 1973; Ch Choir; Ch Organist, 1952-57; En Star Soc, Pianist 1973; PTA; TX St Tchrs Assn; cp/Vol, Hosp Aux, 1977; DAR; Magna Charta Dames Soc; Plantagenet Soc; Descendants of Mayflower Soc; r/Epis; Sigma Alpha Iota Hon Soc, Recording Secy 1960; Freshman Wom Music Awd, 1958; Pi Kappa Lambda Hon Soc, 1st Freshman Music Awd 1958; Hon Life Mbrship, PTA; Trophy, PTA; W/W: of Am Wom, in S & SW; World W/W of Wom; Intl W/W of Intells; Intl W/W in Commun Ser.

GAMBRELL, NORA KATHERINE oc/Retired Teacher; b/Apr 8, 1906; h/ 620 Cibilo Street, Lockhart, TX 78644; m/Sidney Spivey; c/Dr Thomas Ross, Mildred Katherine; ed/BS, SW TX St Univ, 1950; pa/Pres, Lockhart Clrm Tchrs Assn, 1956-, VP 1955, Treas 1954; VP, Delta Kappa Gamma Soc, 1960; cp/Vol, Hosp Aux, 1977; Pres, Meth Wom's Guild, 1950; Reporter, Ch Coun, 1977; Ch Choir, 60 Yrs; Secy, Lockhart TB Assn, 1954; Pres, Music Clb of Lockhart, 1973, VP 1974; Area Dir, Music Clb, 1976; Dir, Sr Citizens Soc of Lockhart, 1972; r/Epis; hon/Cit of Apprec, TB Assn, 1954; Ed S'ship Awd'd in Hon of Nora Gambrell, 1971; Life Mbrship Awd, Meth Wom's Guild, 1950; Cit of Apprec, Sr Citizens Soc of Lockhart, 1972; Intl W/W in Commun Ser; World W/W of Wom.

GAMBY, RAYMOND R oc/Dean of School of Business Administration, Consultant; h/702-B Heritage Village, Southbury, CT 06488; ba/Waterbury, CT; ed/BBA 1948, MBA 1952, CUNY; PhD (Benemeritus), Univ of Santo Tomas, 1954; Postdoct Studies, NY Univ, 1954-55; mil/Public Relats, AUS, 1943-46; Conslt to Pres, Post Col, Jan-June 1983; pa/Prof & Dean, Sch of Bus Adm, Post Col, 1981-83; Conslt to Pres, Prof & Dir of Instnl Res 1979-81, Acting VP 1979, Prof & Dean of Col of Bus Adm 1970-79, Detroit Inst of Technol; Prof & Dean, Inst of Adm, Ahmadu Bello Univ, 1968-70; Prof & Chm of Dept of Intl Bus Adm, Am Col of Switzerland, 1967-68; Assoc Prof, Haile Sellassie I Univ, 1962-67; Fdr & Mng Dir, Mut Fund Mgmt Share Co, 1965-67; Mgr, King Merritt & Co Ltd, 1959-62; Asst Dir, Christian Chd's Fund Inc, 1957-59; Reg'd Sales Rep, First Investors Corp, 1955-57; Pers Supt, Caltex Batangas Refinery, 1952-54; Sales Mgr & Acting Mill Supt, Marsman Devel Co, 1950-51; Pres & Gen Mgr, Belray Sales Enterprises Inc, 1948-51; Acad of Mgmt; Am Conf of Acad Deans; Am Ec Assn; N Eng Bus Ed Assn; The Assn for Instnl Res; The Nat Coun of Res Admrs; cp/Fdg Mem & Dir, Acctg Aid Soc of Detroit, 1973-81; Dir, Wom's Orch of Detroit, 1974-77; Hon Secy, Christian Chd's Fund, Hong Kong Com, 1957-59; Pres, Victoria Toastmasters, Hong Kong, 1958-60; hon/Pubs, Intl Tobacco Mktg 1970, The Impact of Fiscal Policies on the Devel of the Ethiopian Economy 1966, Industl Devel in Ethiopia 1964; Cert, Mgr of Sch Bd & Supvr of Schs, Dept of Ed, Hong Kong Govt, 1957-59; W/ W in E; Outstg Edrs of Am.

GANAPOL, BARRY DOUGLAS oc/ Professor and Consultant; b/May 15,

1944; h/4012 Calle Chica, Tucson, AZ 85711; ba/Tucson, AZ; m/Starr; c/Joshua; p/Manny and Mimi Ganapol (dec); ed/BS, Mech Engrg, Univ of CA-Berkeley, 1966; MS, Nuclear Engrg, Columbia Univ, 1967; PhD, Engrg Sci, Univ of CA-Berkeley, 1971; pa/Analyst, Swiss Fed Inst for Reactor Res, 1971-72; Engr, Ctr for Nuclear Studies, Scalay, France, 1972-74; Engr, Argonne Nat Lab, 1974-76; Prof, Univ of AZ, 1978-; Am Nuclear Soc; Soc for Indust & Applied Mathematicians; Am Math Soc; Sigma Xi; Gamma Beta Pi; hon/Author, Over 90 Articles in Tech Jours; Best Paper, Student Conf, 1970; Grad w Distn, Columbia Univ, 1967; AEC F'ship, 1969-71.

GANDHI, OM P oc/Professor of Electrical Engineering; b/Sep 23, 1934; h/3680 Apollo Drive, Salt Lake City, UT 84124; ba/Salt Lake City, UT; m/Santosh; c/Rajesh Timmy, Monica, Lena; p/Gopal Das and Devi Bai Gandhi (dec); ed/DSc 1961, MSE 1957, Univ of MI-Ann Arbor; Dipl of the Indian Inst of Sci, Bangalore, India, 1955; BS w Hons, Delhi Univ, India, 1952; pa/Prof of Elect Engrg 1973-, Assoc Prof 1967-73, Univ of UT-SLC; Dpty Dir 1965-67, Asst Dir 1962-65, Ctl Electronics Engrg Res Inst, Pilani, Rajasthan, India; Res Spec, Philco Corp, 1960-62; Fellow, IEEE; Chm, IEEE Com on Man & Radiation, 1980-82; Bd of Dirs, Bioelectromagnetics Soc, 1979-82; Chm, IEEE-Microwave Theory & Techniques Soc's Com on Microwave Biol Effects, 1979-83; Chm, 1982 Microwave Power Symp of the Intl Microwave Power Inst; Edit Bd, Jour *Bioelectromagnetics*; hon/Pubs, *Microwave Engrg & Applications* 1981, "Nonlinear Theory of Injected Beam Crossed Field Devices" in *Crossed Field Microwave Tubes* 1961; Author or Co-Author, Over 160 Jour Articles & Tech Conf Presentations; Elected Fellow of the IEEE, 1979; Dist'd Res Awd, Univ of UT, 1979-80; Recip of Spec Awd for Outstg Tech Achmt, IEEE UT Sect, 1975; Guest Editor, Proceedings of the IEEE Spec Issue on Biol Effects & Med Applications of Electromagnetic Energy, Jan 1980; Invited Spkr, Joint Plenary Session of the URSI & IEEE MTT-S & IEEE-AP Sympa, LA, Jun 1981; Keynote Spkr, 6th Annual Conf on Hyperthermia, Tokyo, Nov 1983; W/W: in Engrg, in W, in Technol Today; Dir of World Rschrs; Men of Achmt; Am Men & Wom of Sci; Intl W/W in Engrg; Commun Ldrs of Am.

GANDHI, SHIRISH MANILAL oc/Consulting Engineering Company Executive; b/Nov 17, 1931; h/2595 Chippewa Court, Walnut Creek, CA 94598; ba/Walnut Creek, CA; m/Jyoti S; c/Sunita, Rohini, Ranjana, Suschiel; p/Manilal Tricumlal and Savitri M Shah Gandhi (dec); ed/BE 1956, BE (Mech) 1957, Poona Univ; MSc (Engrg), London Univ, 1961; pa/Elect Engr, Ctl Electricity Generating Bd, London, 1962-67; Elect & Mech Engr, Westinghouse Elect Corp, 1967-70; Elect Engr, Bechtel Corp, 1970-73; Elect Engr, Kaiser Engrs, 1974-75; Conslt & Dir, Univ of CA-Berkeley, Lawrence Berkeley Lab, Lawrence Livermore Nat Lab, Hope Consltg Grp, Brit Petro, Morrison-Knudsen, 1975-84; Pres, SMG Consltg Engrs, 1975-; Royal Soc

Vis'g Scists Clb, 1959-63; Gen Secy-Treas, Assn of Indian Engrs, London, 1965-67; IEEE; Am Nuclear Soc, Legis Panel 1977-78; Instrument Soc of Am; Chem Engrg Prod Res Panel, 1982-83; AAAS; hon/Pubs, Res Report on Emer Facilities for Nuclear Power Plants 1981, "Digital Computer in Power" 1962, Several Reports on Devel of Medium Voltage Swichgear at Westinghouse Elect Corp, Reports on Mgmt & Technol of High Level Radioactive Waste, Res Papers on Fusion Power & Fast Breeder Reactor Design, Nova Laser Fusion Exptl Facility Constrn, & Other Topics; Govt of India Scholar, 1951-52; W/W: in Frontier Sci & Technol, in the World.

GANN, JILL PATRICIA oc/Resource Counselor; b/Jul 1, 1946; h/7 Cathedral Street, Annapolis, MD 21401; ba/Annapolis, MD; p/Joseph P and Laura Jean Kostyk, Annapolis, MD; ed/MBA, Ctl MI Uiv, 1980; EdM, Guid & Cnslg, Bowie St Col, 1978; MA, Am Studies, Univ of MD, 1974; BA, cum laude, Shepherd Col, 1969; pa/Present Cnslr, Resource, Anne Arundel Co Bd of Ed; Current Pt-time Assoc Prof, Anne Arundel Commun Col; Guid Chp, Corkran Jr High, 1980-83; Media Spec, Anne Arundel Co, 1970-78; Hd Tech Libn, Analytic Sers, Falls Ch, VA, 1968-70; APGA; Nat Voc Guid Assn; Am Sch Cnslrs Assn; MD Pers & Guid Assn, Secy 1982; MD St Nat Voc Guid, Wk Chp 1981-; Anne Arundel Co Chapt, MD Pers & Guid Assn, Secy 1980, Awds Chp 1982; Am Bus Wom; NEA; MD St Tchrs Assn; Tchrs Assn of Anne Arundel Co; Guid Adv Bd, Anne Arundel Co, 1982-; MD St Dept of Ed Guid Adv Bd; Adv Bd of Anne Arundel Commun Col; cp/World Futures Soc; r/Prot; hon/Pubs, "How Do You Like Your Eggs: A Visual & Occupl Guide to Understanding Type" 1982, "The Egg Hunt: Worker Preferences Based on Jungian Type" 1983, *Things to Think About When Establishing a Model Career Resource Ctr* 1983, "Fanciful Facts About the 1st Ofc" 1980, "Making the 1st Wk Fantastic" 1980, "Bibliotherapy" 1979; Outstg Guid Prog for Jr HS, Anne Arundel Co, 1982; Pres Cit, MD Pers & Guid Assn, 1982; Nat Dean's List; W/W: in E, Among Students in Am Cols & Univs.

GANN, LEWIS HENRY oc/Historian; b/Jan 28, 1924; h/562 Kendall, Apartment 32, Palo Alto, CA 94305; ba/Stanford, CA; c/Margarita, Thomas Michael; ed/MA, MLitt, PhD, Oxford Univ; mil/Royal Fusiliers (Brit Army), 1944-47; pa/Histn, Rhodes-Livingstone Inst (Now Inst for Social Res, Univ of Zambia), 1950-52; Asst Lectr, Univ of Manchester, England, 1952-54; Archivist & Editor, Nat Archives of Rhodesia, 1954-63; From Res Assoc to Sr Fellow, Hoover Instn, Stanford Univ; Fellow, Royal Hist Soc; Am Hist Assn; hon/Author, Co-Author & Co-Editor of 23 Pub'd Wks on the Hist of Africa, European Colonization & the Sociol of Imperialism; Stipendary Conslt, Historische Komission zu Berlin, 1975; Sr Res Assoc, St Anthony's Col, Oxford, 1980.

GANNON, RICHARD G oc/State Senator, Farmer, Rancher; b/Jul 29, 1950; h/Route 3, Box 60, Goodland, KS 67735; ba/Topeka, KS; m/Martha Ellen; c/Jessica Michelle; p/Bill and Geraldine

Gannon, Goodland, KS; ed/AA, Colby Commun Col, 1970; BS, Ed 1970-73, Grad Wk 1974-75, KS Univ; pa/VP, Rocking Chair Farms Inc, 1973-; St Senator, St of KS, 1976-; Corp Bd of the KS Univ Chapt of Acacia Frat, 1978-, Pres 1981-; Senate Minority Whip, KS Senate, 1985-88; Life Mem, KS Univ Alumni Assn, 1973-; cp/K of C, 1975-; BPOE, 1975-; 4-H Citizenship Ldr, 1980-; MWn Conf, Coun of St Govt, 1978-80; Nat Conf of St Legis, 1980-; Sherman Co Dems, 1975-, Chm 1975-76; 1st Congl Dist Dems, 1976-; hon/KS Vets of WW I, Cit for Meritorious Ser, 1978; Attended by Invitation, Atlantik Bruke Yg Ldrs Conf in Hamburg, W Germany; Outstg Yg Men in Am; Men of Achmt; Notable Ams; Personalities of the W & MW; W/W in Am Polits.

GANT, VICKIE LYNN oc/Public Relations Coordinator; b/Oct 20, 1956; h/3004 Stafford Street, Shreveport, LA 71107; ba/Grambling, LA; p/Jacob and Viola Gant, Shreveport, LA; ed/BA, Jour & Sociol, LA Tech Univ, 1977; MAT, Sociol 1980, Sec'dy Tchg Cert in Social Scis 1980, Grambling St Univ; pa/Correspondent, *Shreveport Times*, 1970-74; Grad Tchg Asst 1978-80, Public Relats Coor 1982-, Grambling St Univ; Theta Tau, Jour Frat, Secy 1976; LA Assn of Public Relats, 1983; cp/NAACP, 1978; hon/Author of Articles Pub'd in All St Newspapers & the *Jour of Higher Ed* 1983; Jour Awd, 1979; Public Relats Awd, 1980; Parish Commun Ser Awd, 1981; Student Ser Awd, 1978; Outstg Am HS Students; W/W.

GANTZ, NANCY JANE ROLLINS oc/Consultant in Nursing Services; b/Mar 7, 1949; h/2670 Northwest Eastway Court, Beaverton, OR 97006; ba/Same; m/Edwin W; c/Christopher James, Aimee Michelle; p/Troy G and Mary Emerson Rollins, Salishan, OR; ed/Dipl in Nsg, Good Samaritan Hosp & Med Ctr Sch of Nsg, 1973; pa/Good Samaritan Hosp, ICU, 1973-75; Dir of Nsg Sers, Roderick Enterprises, 1975-78; Dir of Nsg Sers, Holgate Ctr, 1978-80; Indep Nsg Conslt, 1980-84; Critical Care Unit Mgr, 1984-; Tuality Commun Hosp; Geriatric Nurses Assn; Good Samaritan Hosp & Med Ctr Sch of Nsg Alumni Assn; OR Heart Assn; AACN; ANA; AHA; cp/TVJA Sch Bd Mem, 1983-86; PTA, Pres 1983-84; hon/Fdr, The Geriatric Nurses Assn of OR, 1977; Nom for 1978 Nurse of the Yr, JGN; St Task Force, 1978-79; W/W: in Am Wom, in W.

GANUS, CLIFTON L JR oc/College President; b/Apr 7, 1922; h/208 South Cross, Searcy, AR 72143; ba/Searcy, AR; m/Louise Nicholas; c/Clifton L III, Deborah Duke, Charles Austin; p/Clifton and Martha Jewel Ganus (dec); ed/BA, Harding Col; MA, PhD, Tulane Univ; pa/Pres, Harding Col; Bd Mem: 1st Security Bk, Finest Foods; cp/Lions Clb; Bd Mem, C of C; r/Ch of Christ: Min, Elder; hon/7 Wash Medals for Address, Freedom Foun of Val Forge; Outstg Alumnus, Harding Col.

GAPEN, D KAYE oc/Director, General Library System; h/702 Seneca Place, Madison, WI 53711; ba/University, WI; p/Lester S Gapen, Seattle, WA; ed/MLS, Univ of WA Lib Sch, 1971; BA, Sociol, Univ of WA-Seattle, 1970; pa/Dir, Gen Lib Sys, Univ WI, 1984-; Dean of Libs & Prof, Univ of AL, 1981-84; Asst Dir for Tech Sers, IA St Univ, 1977-81; Instr & Hd of Quick Editing, OH St Univ, 1974-77; Instr & Asst Hd of Quick Editing, OH St Univ, 1972-74; Gen Cataloguer, Col of Wm & Mary, 1971-72; Beta Phi Mu; Alpha Lambda Delta; AAUP; Am Lib Assn; SEn Lib Assn; AL Lib Assn; hon/Pubs, "Cooperative Lib Resource Sharing Among Univs Supporting Grad Study in AL" 1982, "MARC Format Simplification" 1982, "Gen Specifications for an Authority-Driven On-Line Public Access Catalog" 1982, "Simplification of the MARC Format: Feasiblity, Benefits, Disadvantages, Consequences" 1981, Others.

GARBETT, ROSEMARY S oc/Business Owner; b/Jul 9, 1935; h/7810 High Star, Houston, TX 77036; m/Thomas M Garbett Jr (dec); c/Susan Garbett Kendrick, Thomas M III, Katherine A, Michael S; p/Rudolph George and Lorena Boenker Schneider (dec); ed/HS Grad; pa/Secy/Clk, 1956-59; Opers, Los Tios Mexican Restaurants, 1970-75; CEO, Los Tios Mexican Restaurants Inc, 1976-; Dir, BancTexas W, 1978-83; Dir of Westchase Corp, 1980-; Dir of TX Restaurant Assn & Houston Restaurant Assn, 1980-; Pres, Houston Restaurant Assn, 1982-83; cp/Dir & Exec Com Mem, Gtr Houston Conv & Visitors Coun, 1979-; Dir of Leukemia Soc, 1980-83; Dir of Houstonian, 1982-; Dir, Kidney Foun, 1980-82; Lifetime Mem, Houston Livestock & Rodeo Show; Charter Mem, Bob Smith Yacht Clb; Exec Com of Leukemia Soc; W/W Internation, Mem, Dir; Baylor Ten Com Mem, 1982-83; hon/Rosemary S Garbett Day in Houston, Jun 23, 1983; 1st Wom Pres of Houston Restaurant Assn in Its 41 Yr Hist; Outstg Restaurateur of Houston, 1980-81; World W/W of Wom; W/W: of Am Wom, of TX.

GARCIA OLIVERO, CARMEN SYLVIA oc/Executive, Professor of Social Research; h/San Julian 421, Urbanizacion Sagrado Corazon, Rio Piedras, PR 00926; p/Fernando Garcia Arana (dec); Martha Olivero Diaz, Rio Piedras, PR; ed/BS, MSW, Univof PR; Cert in Adv'd Curric in Casewk Pract, Cert in Marital Cnslg, PhD in Social Wk, Univ of PA; pa/Pres, Inst of Social Res Inc; Prof Social Res, Sch of Med, Univ of PR; Conslt to Asst Secretariat of Mtl Hlth, PR Dept of Hlth; Conslt to Asst Secretariat for Prev, PR Dept of Addiction Sers; hon/Intl W/W: in Ed, of Intells; Intl Register of Profiles; Enciclopedia Grandes Mujeres de PR; Dir of Distinguished Ams; Commun Ldrs of Am.

GARCIA, CHARLES ANTHONY oc/Optometrist; b/Dec 4, 1951; h/3334 Jenkins, San Antonio, TX 78247; ba/Universal City, TX; m/Teresa Lynn Garcia; c/Jason Nathaniel, Justin Paul, Jeremy Jon Charles; p/Mr and Mrs David Garcia, San Antonio, TX; ed/OD, 1977; BS, 1975; AS, 1972; pa/Pvt Pract of Optom, 1977-; Bexar Co Optometric Assn, 1977-; TX Optometric Assn, 1977-; Am Optometric Assn, 1977-; Coun on Sports Vision; Better Vision Inst; cp/Schertz-Cibolo Val Lions Clb; Gtr Randolph Area C of C, 1977-; hon/Outstg Yg Men of Am; W/W in S & SW.

GARCIA, F HENRY oc/Division Director; b/Mar 7, 1954; h/95000 Laur-

alan Drive, Austin, TX 78736; ba/Austin, TX; m/Catherine Anne; p/Mack Espinoza and Angelica Garcia, Austin, TX; ed/BA, Univ of TX, 1976; JD, Univ of TX Sch of Law, 1979; TX Real Est Brokers Lic, 1982; pa/Atty, Uniform Comml Code Div, Secy of St of TX, 1979-80; Dpty Dir, Uniform Comml Code & Notary Public Div, Secy of St of TX, 1980-84; Div Dir, Uniform Comml Code & Notary Public, TX Secy of St, 1980-; ABA, 1979-; TX Yg Lwyrs Assn, 1979-; Travis Co Bar Assn, 1979-; Nat Notary Assn, VP & St Dir, 1984-; Public Law Sect, Intell Property Right Sect; Corporate Bkg & Bus, Consumer Law Sects, 1980-; Comml Law Leag, 1980; cp/Gtr SW Optimist Clb, 1980; TX Local Recording Agt, Ins, 1984-; Mexican Am Dems, 1983; Voc Ofc Ed Com-man, 1981, 1983-84; hon/Pubs, "Texas Bus Opport Act" 1983, "Texas Notary Public Handbook" 1980, 1981, 1982.

GARCIA, GREGORIO MARTIN oc/School Psychologist; b/Dec 10, 1932; h/1293 Sherwood Drive, Vineland, NJ 08360; ba/Vineland, NJ; m/Felicia Guerra; c/Cristina, Paula, Javier; p/Ricardo Garcia (dec); ed/BA, Theol, magna cum laude, Ciudad-Rodrigo Sem Col, 1955; MA in Phil, cum laude, Cath Univ of Salamanca, 1958; Postgrad in Clin Psych, Univ of Madrid, 1964-67; Certs, Sch Psychol & Ednl Supvn, NJ St; pa/Prof of Phil, Ciudad-Rodrigo Sem Col, 1959-64; Cnslg Sers, Colegio Menesiano, Madrid, 1966-68; Panelist, Lectr, Madrid, 1964-69; Res & Planning Advr for Migrant Ednl Progs, Diocese of Buffalo, 1969-73; Coor, Spanish Cultural & Media Ctr, Atl Commun Col, 1974-78; Sch Psychol, Vineland Public Schs, 1978-; Dir, Biling Ednl Consltg, 1977-; NASP; ISPA; NJASP; AAMD; Assn for Supvn & Curric Devel; Contbr of Res in Field; hon/Bd of Trustees, Woodbine St Sch, 1977-83; Outstg Ednl Sers Awd, Atl Commun Col, 1978; Biling/Ednl Sers Awd, Atl Commun Col, 1975; W/W in E.

GARCIA, HENRY JR oc/Corporation Officer; b/May 30, 1949; h/1607 Opossum Circle, El Paso, TX 79927; ba/El Paso, TX; m/Carmen Ruth; c/Enrique Rene; p/Enrique and Rosenda Garcia, Fabens, TX; ed/Univ of TX-El Paso, 1977; pa/Ptnr, Isl Mercantile, 1967-; Owner, Henrys Printing, 1977-80; Editor, *The Luminario*, 1979-80; Chm of Bd, The El Paso Graphics Grp Inc, 1982-; Chm of Bd, Omarco Inc, 1983-; El Paso Red Cross Bd Dirs; Chm of Bd, Flying Fish Exclusive Charters Inc, 1983; Chm of Bd, Dockside of El Paso Inc, 1983; cp/El Paso JCs, 1980-; La Isla Renovation Com, Chm 1981-; Fabens JCs, Chm 1982, Pres 1981, VP 1980, Secy 1979; Intersts JCs, Treas 1971, VP 1972, Pres 1973; Asociacion de Mexicanos Americanos, VP 1972, Pres 1973; hon/Recog Awd, Juarez JCs, 1983; JC Senator #33306, 1982; George O Wilson Awd, TX JCs, 1982; Brigade Cmdr, TX JCs, 1982; Melvin B Evans Awds, TX JCs, 1981; Apprec Plaque from Juarez Camara Jr; Carlos Porras Awd, 1977; W/W: in S & SW, in Am Fin & Indust; Outstg Yg Men of Am.

GARCIA, KAY WELLING oc/Administrator; b/Oct 3, 1946; h/PO Box 4277, Bozeman, MT 59715; ba/Bozeman, MT; m/Norm D Kalbfleisch; c/Lani L; p/J H

Welling, Chadron, NE; Doris E Welling, Greeley, CO; ed/BS, Chem & Zool, MT St Univ, 1968; MT (ASCP), Med Technol Internship, 1969; pa/Dir, Ofc of Cont'g Ed for the Hlth Profl, MT St Univ, 1980-; Proj Dir, Lab Tng Proj, St Microbiol Lab Bur, 1979-80; Field Hlth Ofcr, Preven Hlth Bur, 1978-79; Spec Chem, Anaconda Reduction Wks, 1977-78; Med Technologist, Warm Sprgs St Hosp, 1974-76; Spec Chem, Anaconda Reduction Wks, 1974; Med Technologist Supvr, Powell Co Meml Hosp, 1972-74; Staff Med Technol, St Patrick's Hosp, 1971; Med Technologist Supvr, Clark Fork Val Hosp, 1971; Chief Med Technologist, Craig Rehab Hosp, 1970-71; Am Soc for Med Technol, 1972-; MT Soc for Med Technol, Secy 1975, Legis Com Chm 1975, 1976, Mbrship Chm 1979, Ed Com 1979, Ed Com Chm 1980, 1985; Secy 1981, 1982, Conv Planning Com 1985, Nom for Med Technol of Yr 1980; MT CAAMA Rep for ASCP, 1979, 1980, 1981; Am Soc for Clin Pathologists, Affil Mem 1969-; Am Soc for Hlthcare, Ed & Tng, Noms Com 1981; MT Soc for Hlthcare, Ed & Tng, Pres 1982-83, 1983-84; MT Public Hlth Assn, Noms Com 1981, Noms Com Chm 1982, Planning Com Chm 1983-84, Bd of Dirs 1985; CHEXchange; hon/W/W of Am Wom; Outstg Yg Ams; Outstg Yg Wom of Am; World W/W of Wom.

GARDIN, T HERSHEL oc/Administrator; b/Jul 21, 1947; h/Oak Park, MI; ba/Detroit, MI; m/Joy Beth Lewis; c/Naftali M, Dov E, Miriam S, Yehudis K; p/Abraham and Ruth Gardin, Oak Park, MI; ed/BA 1965, MA in Social Psych 1971, PhD in Public Hlth & Res 1983, Wayne St Univ; Columbia Pacific Univ; pa/Dir of Psychol Sers, Alexandrine House Inc, 1975-77; Social Analyst IV, Wayne Co Dept of Substance Abuse Sers, 1977-79; Res Assoc, Annis & Assocs, Bingham Farms, MI, 1979-81; Admr, Dept of Res, Statistical Anal & Reporting, Comprehensive Hlth Ser of Detroit (HMO), 1981-; Am Psychol Assn; APHA; Soc of Psychols in Addictive Behaviors; Soc for the Psychol Study of Social Issues; AAAS; r/Jewish; hon/Pubs, "Obstetrical Care in a Hlth Maintenance Org & a Pvt Fee-For-Ser Pract: A Comparative Anal" 1983, "The Impact of Rehabilitative Treatment for Alcoholism on Members' Subsequent Use of Inpatient Hospitalization" 1982, *The Closing of U Drug Abuse in Flint, MI: An Impact Eval* 1982, "The Use of Drugs in Metro Detroit" 1981, Others; Difco Awd Nom, APHA, 1983; Psi Chi Nat Hon Soc in Psych, 1970; W/W: in MW, in Frontier Sci & Technol.

GARDNER, E CLAUDE oc/College President; b/Jan 16, 1925; h/372 East Mill Street, Henderson, TN 38340; ba/Henderson, TN; m/Delorese Tatum; c/Phyllis Ann Hester, Rebecca Sue Cyr, Claudia Elaine Goodson, James David; ed/Jr Col Dipl, Freed-Hardeman Col, 1944; BS, Abilene Christian Univ, 1946; MA, SW TX St Univ, 1947; Addit Grad Study, George Peabody Col; pa/Chm, Dept of Ed & Psych 1949-56, Registrar 1950-68, Dean of Col 1956-69, VP 1969, Pres 1969-, Freed-Hardeman Col; Bd of Dirs, Chester St Bk; cp/Chester Co C of C; Public Ser Coun; TN Public Ser Com; hon/Editor, *Brigance's Sermons* 1951, *Van Dyke's Sermons* 1971; Author of

Articles Pub'd in the *Gospel Advocate*; Blue Key Hon Frat; Alpha Chi Hon Org; Alumnus of the Yr, Freed-Hardeman Col, 1972; Civitan Citizen of the Yr, 1976; Col, Gov's Staff, Gov Lamar Alexander.

GARDNER, HOWARD E oc/Psychologist, Writer; b/Jul 11, 1943; h/15 Lancaster, Cambridge, MA 02140; ba/ Cambridge, MA; m/Ellen Winner; c/ Kerith, Jay, Andrew; p/Mr and Mrs Ralph Gardner, Scranton, PA; ed/AB in Social Relats, Harvard Col, 1965; Rdg in Phil & Sociol, London Sch of Ec, 1965-66; PhD in Social Psych (Developmental Psych), Harvard Univ, 1971; Postdoct Fellow, Harvard Med Sch & Boston Univ Aphasia Res Ctr, 1971-72; pa/Sr Res Assoc, Harvard Grad Sch of Ed; Co-Dir, Harvard Proj Zero; Prof of Neurol, Boston Univ Sch of Med; Res Psychol, Boston Vets Adm Med Ctr; Acad of Aphasia, Gov'g Bd 1983-86; Am Ednl Res Assn, Arts & Ed Grp; Soc for Res in Child Devel; Intl Neuropsych Symp; En Psychol Assn; Authors' Guild; Cognitive Scis Soc; Intl Neuropsych Soc; Am Psychol Assn, Fellow of Divs 7 & 10; Merrill-Palmer Soc; hon/Pubs, *Frames of Mind: The Theory of Multiple Intelligences* 1983, *Art, Mind, & Brain: A Cognitive Approach to Creat* 1982, *Artful Scribbles: The Significance of Chd's Drawings* 1980, *Developmental Psych; An Intro*, 1982, Other Books; Author of 150 Articles in Scholarly Jours in the Areas of Developmental Psych, Neuropsych, Ed, Aesthetics & the Social Scis; Author of 57 Topical Articles, Intros & Book Reviews in Wide Circulation Pubs; Films, *Infancy, Lang, Cognition: Three Films on Child Devel* (Winner of Cine Golden Eagle, Chris Statuette, Am Film Fest Screening Awd), 1972; Phi Beta Kappa, Jr Yr, 1964; AB, summa cum laude, 1965; Frank Knox F'ship at London Sch of Ec, 1965-66; Num Grants from Var Instns, incl'g, Carnegie Corp, NSF, Sloan Foun; Claude Bernard Sci Jour Awd, 1975; MacArthur Prize F'ship, 1981-86.

GARDNER, JAY KENT oc/Executive; b/Mar 29, 1947; h/1118 West Sleepy Hollow, Peoria, IL 61615; ba/Peoria, IL; m/Constance Jane; c/Adam Jay, Joseph Paul, Anne Elizabeth, John Michael; p/ Lowell and Louise Gardner, Davenport, IA; ed/BA, Govs St Univ, 1983; AS, Data Processing, Scott Commun Col, 1969; pa/Sys Analyst, NCR Corp, 1968-70; Programmer/Sys Analyst, NW Bk & Trust, 1970-75; Opers Mgr, Financial Indust Sys, 1975-79; VP, Data Processing Microdata Corp, 1979-84; VP, Data Processing, MW Financial Corp, 1984-; VP; NCR Users Grp; cp/U Way; BSA, SME Chm 1983; Kiwanis; hon/W/ W: in Fin & Indust, in MW.

GARDNER, MARY BERTHA HOEFT CHADWICK oc/Retired Postmaster; b/Jun 13, 1914; ed/BS, UT St Univ, 1950; pa/Bkkpr, Model Dairy 1935-49, Weber Ctl Dairy 1949-51, Bishops Storehouse 1950-51; Tchr, Ogden, UT, 1950-51; Clk, Post Ofc, Honeyville, UT, 1956-72; Postmaster, 1972-81; Ed Newslttr, Nat Leag of Postmasters; AAUW; Pres, BPW Clb; Nat Assn Postmasters; Exec VP, Woms Career Support Ser; cp/Pres, Daughs of UT Pioneers; Pres, Honeyville Civic Clb; hon/Pubs, Recipe Book for UT St Dairy Wives 1961, Collection of Christmas

Ideas, Handwork 1965; Wom of the Yr, BPW Clb; Postmaster of the Yr, Nat Leag of Postmasters, UT, 1981; World W/W of Wom; W/W: of Am Wom, in W.

GARDNER, NORD ARLING oc/ Management Consultant; b/Aug 10, 1923; h/2995 Bonnie Lane, Pleasant Hill, CA 94523; ba/San Francisco, CA; m/ Thora Marie Stephen; c/Randall Nord, Scott Stephen, Craig Robert, Laurie Lee; p/Arling A and Ruth Lee Gardner; ed/BA, Univ of WY, 1945; MS, CA St Univ-Hayward, 1972; MPA, 1975; Postgrad, Univ of Chgo, Univ of MI, Univ of CA-Berkeley; mil/Comm'd 2nd Lt, AUS, 1942, Adv'd through Grades to Lt Col, 1964; Ret'd, 1966; pa/Pers Analyst, Univ Hosp, Univ of CA-San Diego, 1946-48; Coor, Manpower Devel, Univ of CA-Berkeley, 1968-75; Univ Tng Ofcr, SF St Univ, 1975-80, Pers Mgr 1976-80; Gen Mgr, CRDC Maintenance Tng Corp, SF; Pres, Dir, Sandor Assocs, Mgmt Conslts; Instr, Japanese, Psych, Supervisory Courses, 1977-78; Adv Coun, SF Commun Col Dist; Ret'd Ofcrs Assn; Am Soc Tng & Devel; No CA Indust Relats Coun; AAUA; Intl Pers Mgrs Assn; Col & Univ Pers Assn (W Coast Rep); IPA; cp/ Repub; Commonwlth of CA; hon/ Author, *To Gather Stones*, 1978; Decorated, Army Commend Medal; Commun Ldrs of Am; Men of Achmt; W/ W: in W, in CA; Intl W/W of Intells; Personalities of the W & MW; Biogl Roll of Hon; 2,000 Notable Ams; Intl Book of Hon; DIB.

GARDNER, VIRGINIA D oc/Former Extension Agent III, Home Economics Program Leader; h/PO Box 15353, St Petersburg, FL 33733; ed/BS, FL Agri & Mech Univ; EdM, NC St Univ; pa/ Negro Co Home Demo Agt, Girl's 4-H Clb Agt, US Dept of Agri-Fed Ext Ser, Univ FL-St Ext Ser, Jackson Co Bd Co Commrs; Negro Home Demo Agt, Girl's 4-H Clb Agt, US Dept Agri-Univ FL-Columbia Co Bd Co Commrs; Negro Co Home Demo Agt, 4-H Clb Agt for Boys/Girls, Asst Home Demo Agt, Asst Co Ext Home Ec Agt II, Ext Home Ec Agt III, Ext Agt III, Home Ec & Supervising Agt, US Dept Agri-Univ FL-Pinellas Co Bd Co Commrs; Ext Home Ec Dept, FL Cooperative Ext Ser, Univ FL, US Dept Agri, Sci & Ed Adm-Ext; Ext Agt III, Home Ec Prog Ldr for Ext Home Ec Dept, Pinellas Co, Largo, FL; FL St Assn of Negro Co & Home Demo Agts, Asst Secy, Fin Secy, Chm of Resolution, Chm Civic Com; FL St Assn of Negro Home Demo Agts, VP, Pres, Chm Public Relats; Nat Negro Home Demo Agts Assn, VP, Pres, Coun Com Chm; FL Home Ec Assn, Registration Com; FL Assn of Ext Home Ec Agts, 2nd VP, Chm Dist'd Ser Awd, Policy Improvement Com Chm Dist II Nom Com, Res & Studies Com, Chm Credentials Com; Alpha Delta Chapt, Epsilon Sigma Phi; Epsilon Sigma Phi, W Coast Home Ec Assn, Dist F, Chm Public Affairs Com; Am Home Ec Assn; cp/Jackson Co Hlth Com, Advr, Secy, Jackson Co Tng Sch PTA; Rec Com, Advr, Jackson Co; Upper Pinellas Coun on Human Relats, Bd of Dirs, Adv Com, Nom'g Com; March of Dimes Drive Chm; Social Ednl & Rec Clb, Secy; Bi-Racial Adv Com to Pinellas Co Sch Bd of Upper Pinellas Coun on Human

Relats, Elected Rep; Clearwater Neighbors Assn; Zeta Phi Beta, S'ship Com; Queen St Commun Assn, Pres; Negro Ldrship Inst, Grp Discussion Ldr, Upper Pinellas Chs & the FL Coun of Human Relats-Sum Proj Prog, Elected Rep; r/ Bapt; Yth Advr, Financial Planning, Mt Carmel Bapt Ch; Chm, Stewardship Ed Sect, Ch Stewardship Com, Mt Carmell Bapt Ch; Mem of Fin Com, Mt Carmel Bapt Ch; hon/Pub'd *Four Cultural Food Patterns of FL*; The Clearwater Hgts 4-H Clb Awd for Effective Ldrship; Agt of the Yr, FL St Assn of Negro Home Demo Agts & the Nat Negro Home Demo Agts Assn; Cert, Secy of Agri of the US Dept of Agri; Num Lttrs of Commend; World W/W of Wom.

GARDNER, WALTER HALE oc/ Professor Emeritus; b/Feb 24, 1917; h/ NE 1505 Upper Drive, Pullman, WA 99163; ba/Pullman, WA; m/Barbara Brown; c/Jeanne G Minert, Marolyn G Mortensen, Janet, Laurie G Boyce, Willard B; p/Willard and Rebecca Viola Hale Gardner (dec); ed/BS 1939, MS 1947, PhD 1950, UT St Univ; Att'd, Cornell, 1940-41; mil/USAF, 1941-46; Ret'd Resv, Lt Col; pa/Res Fellow, Ctl Sci Co, Chgo, 1939-40; Res Asst, Cornell Univ, 1940-41; Spec Instr, Math, UT St Univ, 1948-50; Asst Prof to Prof, WA St Univ, 1950-82; Concurrent Conslt, Intl Atomic Energy Agy, 1971-72; Prof Emeritus, WA St Univ, 1982-; Phi Kappa Phi; Sigma Xi; Wn Soc Soil Sci, Pres 1967; Am Soc Agronomy; Soil Sci Soc of Am, Editor-in-Chief of Jour 1966-69, Pres 1983; Exec Com 1980-, Pres 1985, Pac Div, AAAS; hon/ Pubs, *Soil Physics* 1972, *Hist Highlights of Am Soil Physics, 1776-1976*, & Num Sci Articles, Chapts in Books, Ency & Hist Pubs; Film, "Water Movement in Soil," 1960; Guggenheim Fellow, 1963-64; Fellow, Am Soc of Agronomy, 1966; Fellow, Soil Sci Soc of Am, 1976; Am Men & Wom of Sci; W/W in W.

GARFINKEL, PATRICIA GAIL oc/ Speechwriter, Poet; b/Feb 15, 1938; h/ 2031 Approach Lane, Reston, VA 22091; ba/Washington, DC; c/Jon Alan, Jef Adam; p/Rose and Wynn Walker, Flushing, NY; ed/BA in Hist & Polit Sci, NY Univ, 1959; Indep Tutoring in Poetry w Henry S Taylor, Am Univ, 1973-74; pa/Spchwriter for Cong-man Olin E Teague, Chm of Com on Sci & Technol, 1976-79; Spchwriter for Cong-man Don Fuqua, Chm of Com on Sci & Technol, 1979-; Writer's Ctr of Glen Echo, MD; Poets & Writers Inc; Acad of Am Poets; cp/Dem Wom of Capitol Hill; hon/Pubs, Book of Poems, *Ram's Horn* (Window Press), Over 25 Poems in Lit Mags & Jours, & Anthologies; Poetry-in-Public-Places Awd, NY St, 1977.

GARGANTA, NARCISO MERIOLES oc/Medical Librarian; b/Sep 18, 1932; h/4914 York Boulevard, Los Angeles, CA 90042; ba/Burbank, CA; p/ Francisco Legaspi and Leonore Merioles Garganta, Philippines; ed/Master's Deg-Lib & Info Sci, Pratt Inst, 1971; BSE, 1956; Pre-Med, 1959; pa/Dir, Med Lib, Burbank Commun Hosp, 1979-; Lib Asst, VA Med Ctr, 1978-79; Curric Devel Spec, RCA/MCDA, 1973-77; Med Libn, Milton Helpern Libn Legal Med, 1969-73; Serials Libn, Norris Med Lib, USC/LA Med Ctr, 1967-69; Dir, Tech Lib, United Drug/United Labs Inc,

1960-67; Display Coor, Philippine Ed Co Inc, 157-60; Mng Editor, *Intl Microform Jour of Legal Med*; Contbg Editor, *Vital Signs*; Med Lib Assn; Am Soc Info Sci; Med Lib Grp So CA & AZ; NY Geneal Soc; r/Rom Cath; hon/Acknowledged in *The Med Detectives* by Paulette Cooper, 1972; Mem, CA Local Bd 113; Marquis W/W in W; W/W in Lib & Info Sci; Biogl Dir Online Profls.

GARMHAUSEN, WINONA MARIE oc/Arts Administration Consultant; b/Jan 21, 1930; h/Route 9, Box 90K, Santa Fe, NM 87501; ba/Las Vegas, NM; m/Allen F; c/Jacqueline, Jeffrey, Jan, Jill; p/Frederick J Kunz (dec); Viola M Kunz, Ft Jennings, OH; ed/BS, OH No Univ, 1961; MFA, Bowling Green St Univ, 1964; PhD, Univ of NM, 1982; pa/Commun Relats Dir, C G Rein Gallery, Santa Fe, NM Legis Analyst Ed Comm, 1984; Prof, Conslt Arts Adm, NM Highlands Univ & Taos Public Schs, 1981-; Dir of Visual Arts Div, Col of Santa Fe, 1976; Cont'g Ed Com 1976-80, Grievance Com 1978-79, Wage & Salary Com 1977-79, Grants Com 1978-79, Ath Com 1979-80, Ad Hoc Com on Com Structure, Fac Coun 1979-80, Native Am Clb 1978-79, Art Clb Co-Sponsor 1978-80, Yrly Visual Arts Fac Shows; Appt'd 1st Arts Spec, NM St Dept of Ed, 1975-76, Chp Employee Devel & Troubled Employee Progs, Field Conslt 1974-75; Native Am Tutor, Jr High Lib Aide, Pojoaque, NM, 1972-74; Instr, OH St Univ, 1965-72, Advr to Campus Newspaper 1971-72, Chm Fine Arts Activs, Winter Quarter Symp 1970-71, CoChm Winter Qtr Symp 1969-70, Fine Arts Fest Coor 1967-69, Advr to Campus Yrbook 1966-67, Advr to Film Soc 1966-67, Advr to Black Student Union 1968-69; Chm of Art Dept, Tchr, Shawnee Local Schs, 1964-65; Asst Curator, Allen Co Mus, 1965-67; Tchr, Alger Local Schs, Alger, OH, 1961-62; Tchr, Lima Art Assn, 1959-69; Appt'd to OH Arts Coun, 1971; Appt'd to Gov's Coun on Employee Devel, 1974-76; Appt'd to Gov's Comm on Public Broadcasting, 1974-76, 1978-79; AAUP, Past VP, OH St Univ; Col Art Assn; Am Assn of Mus; Nat Art Ed Assn; NM Alliance for Arts Ed, Past Pres; Nat Art Ed Assn; hon/Author, Num Profl Pubs; Profl Articles on OH Courthouse Arch & Native Am Ed; Contbr to 6 Chapts in "Devel of OH's Cos & Their Historic Cthouses," Co Commrs of OH; Grants Funded; Humanities Grant through LEA 1976-78, Cont'g Grant through Spec Projs Art Ed Act 1976-78, Grant through Higher Ed Act, Col of Santa Fe for Outreach Wk, 1977-81; Num Biogl Listings.

GARMIRE, GORDON PAUL oc/Professor of Astronomy; b/Oct 3, 1937; h/RD #2, Box 256, Huntingdon, PA 16652; ba/University Park, PA; m/Audrey B; c/David, Rosemary, Chris, Marla, Lisa, Geoffrey; p/Paul and Ethel Garmire, Portland, OR; ed/AB, Harvard, 1959; PhD, MIT, 1962; pa/Staff 1962-64, Asst Prof of Physics 1964-67, Assoc Prof Physics 1967-68, MIT; Assoc Prof 1968-72, Prof 1972-81, Physics, CIT; Prof of Astronomy, PA St Univ, 1980-; Intl Astronom Union, 1971-; Am Astronom Soc, 1965-; Com-man, High Energy Astrophysics Div, Am Astronom Soc, 1973-75; VChm, High Energy Astrophysics Div, Am Astronom Soc,

1984, Chm 1985; hon/Pubs, "Observation of High Energy Cosmic Gamma Rays" in *Astrophy Jour* 1968, Plus 100 Articles in Sci Jours; Guggenheim F'ship, 1973-74; Fulbright F'ship, 1973-74; NASA Exceptl Sci Achmt Awd, 1978; Am Men of Sci.

GARNER, CHARLES WILLIAM oc/Educator, University Administrator; b/Apr 18, 1939; h/12 James Avenue, Kendall Park, NJ 08824; ba/New Brunswick, NJ; m/Karyl J Packer; c/Ronald Adam, Juliet Paige; p/Mr and Mrs Adam K Garner, State College, PA; ed/BS in Bus Ed (Acctg) 1965, EdM in Higher Ed Adm 1968, EdD in Voc Indust Ed 1974, PA St Univ; mil/USN, 1959-62, Airborne Sonar; pa/Chm 1982-, Tenured Assoc Prof 1981-, Grad Sch of Ed, Dept of Voc-Tech Ed, Rutgers Univ, The St Univ of NJ; Chm & Assoc Prof, Univ Col, Dept of Urban Ed, Rutgers Univ, The St Univ of NJ; Acting Vice Dean, Univ Col, Rutgers Univ, The St Univ of NJ; Univ Coor, Ft Knox Ctr & Asst Prof, Dept of Occupl & Career Ed, Univ of Louisville; Site Admr, March AFB & Asst Prof of Voc Ed Studies, So IL Univ; Adm Asst, Dept of Psych & Adj Prof, Dept of Voc Indust Ed, PA St Univ; Vis'g Grad Prof, Univ of NV-Las Vegas, 1983; AAUP; Am Voc Assn, Spec Needs & Bus Ed Divs; En Bus Ed Assn; Nat Assn of Voc Ed Spec Needs Pers; Nat Assn of Indust & Tech Tchr Edrs; NJ Assn of Voc Ed Spec Needs Pers, Pres 1981-82; Nat Bus Ed Assn; NJ Bus Ed Assn; NJ Voc Tchr Ed Assn; Voc Ed Assn of NJ; Recording Secy, Omicron Tau Theta, 1980-81; cp/BPOE, #1600, Exalted Ruler 1972-73; r/Sand Hills Presb Ch, Elder 1978-81; hon/Pubs, "Utilizing Lrng Ctrs in the Voc Shop" 1982, "Voc Progs & Curric Designed for the Disadvantaged" 1982, "Assessment 7 Intervention Strategies for the Disadvantaged" 1982, "Voc Ed" 1982, "Individualized Acad Improvement Progs for the Disadvantaged via an Assessment, Grp Specification, & Instrnl Plan" 1982, Num Others; Var Editorships; W/W in E.

GARNER, WILLIAM B oc/Boating Law Administrator; b/Feb 3, 1933; h/171 Kent Street, Montgomery, AL 36109; ba/Montgomery, AL; m/Sue Lane McCreless; c/William Torey; p/William F (dec) and Tivis Gray Garner, Gadsden, AL; ed/BS 1973, MPA 1976, Auburn Univ; mil/USN, 1952-56; pa/QC Inspector, Hayes Aircraft Corp, 1956-59; Republic Steel Corp, 1959-62; Dept of Conserv & Natural Resources Marine Police Div, Chief of Enforcement 1966-76, Dir of Marine Police Div 1976-; Adj Fac, Auburn Univ; Nat Boating Safety Adv Coun; Marine Engrg Coun, Underwriters Labs Inc; Pres, Nat Assn of Boating Law Admrs, 1983; Past Pres, SEn Boating Law Admrs Assn, 1976; St of AL Safety Coor'g Com; cp/Scouting Coor, Troop 406, Tukabatchee Coun, BSA, 1981; Masons; Frat Order of Police; hon/Author, Num Articles on Boating Law Adm & Law Enforcement for Profl Jours; Named St of AL Enforcement Ofcr of the Yr, AL Petro Coun, 1966; W/W in S & SW.

GARNES, MARLENE CAROL oc/Systems Analyst, US Navy; b/Oct 21, 1944; h/1850 Columbia Pike, Number 123, Arlington, VA 22204; ba/Washing-

ton, DC; c/Marlo Tracy; p/Mr and Mrs Johnie Garnes, Richmond, CA; mil/USNR; pa/Sr Sys Analyst, Wells Fargo Bk, 1982; Sr EDP Auditor, Crocker Bk, 1980-82; Analyst Programmer, Security Nat Bk, 1978-80; Mgmt Analyst, City of Atlanta, 1974-78; Computer Programmer, Alameda Co, 1973-74; Black Assn of Data Processing Profls, Secy 1981-82; hon/W/W: of Am Wom, in W.

GARRARD, JAMES FREDRICK oc/Senior Manager of Safety and Environmental Protection; b/Feb 26, 1938; ba/Pan American World Airways Inc, Aerospace Services Division, NSTL Facility Operations & Services, NSTL Station, MS 39529; m/Marolyn Ella Garrard; c/James Fredrick II, Janella Fae; ed/BS in Petro Geol, Lamar Univ, 1976; mil/Hon Discharge, AUS; pa/Sr Safty Supvr, E I DuPont De Nemous & Co Inc, 1962-77; Tech Safety Supvr, Pulman Kellogg, 1977-79; Loss Control Conslt, Factory Mut Engrg Sys, 1979; Dir of Fire, Safety & Loss Control, Wn Elect Co Inc, 1979-80; Sr Loss Control & Safety Conslt, AIG Conslts Inc, 1980; Asst Divisional Safety Mgr, Texaco Inc, 1980-81; Sr Mgr of Safety & Envir Protection, Pan Am World Sers, 1981-; Am Soc of Safety Engrs, Profl Mem; Am Chem Soc; AIChE, Cert #068697; Am Assn of Petro Geologists, Cert #W0269876; Nat Fire Protection Assn, Cert #A14566320000; Gulf Coast Soc of Safety Engrs; TX Acad of Sci; Soc of Fire Protection Engrs, Cert #4446; Am Indust Hygiene Assn, Deep S Sect; Gulf Coast Safety & Tng Grp; S Ctl LA Safety Coun; Nat L-P Gas Assn; TX Safety Assn; Safety Coun of Gtr Baton Rouge; Nat Safety Mgmt Soc, Cert #3629; ASSE, New Orleans Chapt; Gulf Coast Fed Safety Coun; ASSE, Houston Chapt; NSTL Safety Mgr Coun; Pan Am Mgmt Clb; Sys Safety Soc; Nat Safety Coun, Cert #14836175; MS Safety Coun; St Fire Acad, St of MS; hon/Patents Pending, Pullman Kellogg-World HQs, Factory Mut Engrg, AIG Conslts Inc; Pub, "Liquid Inclusions Within Quartz Crystals"; Holder of Fed Coast Guard Lic for the Safe Transfer of Hazardous Cargoes within US Inland Waterways; Cert'd Prod Safety Mgr, Sr Level, Cert #103; Cert'd Hazard Control Mgr, Master Level, Cert #1466; Secret Clearance, US Govt, 1981; Nat Safety Mgmt Soc; Nat VP of Opers for the St of MS; Outstg Yg Men of Am; Personalities of S; Intl Biog; W/W: in Am, in SW.

GARREN, MARY LOUISE oc/Gastroenterologist; b/Dec 24, 1948; h/PO Box 3738, Wilmington, DE 19807; ba/Elkton, MD; m/Lloyd R; c/Melissa Sue; p/Samuel R (dec) and Margaret Giordano, Buffalo, NY; ed/BA, Biol, SUNY-Buffalo, 1969; Att'd 1973, Internal Med 1976, Gastroenterology 1977, Med Col of PA; pa/Gastroenterologist in Pvt Pract; Med Staff, VP, Union Hosp, 1981-; Cecil Co Med Soc, 1977-; Cecil Co Disability Review Bd, 1981-; Am Soc of Gastrointestinal Endoscopists; Cecil Co Mtl Hlth & Hygiene Bd 1980-.

GARRETT, ROBERT DEAN oc/Insurance Company Executive; b/Apr 13, 1933; h/23 Oak Ridge Drive, Decatur, IL 62521; ba/Decatur, IL; m/Peggy Jean; c/Daniel Bryant, Evelyn, Brenda, Ronald; p/Roy Smith (dec) and Halene

Pickett Garrett; ed/Grad, Carmi, IL, Public Schs, 1950; mil/USAF, 1950-54; pa/US Post Ofc Dept, 1954-60; Supvr, Gen Telephone Co, 1961-67; VP 1977-, Fed Kemper Ins Co, 1970-; Pers Com, Nat Assn Indep Insurers, 1977-; Decatur Employee Assistance Coun, 1978-; Decatur Indust Relats Assn, 1977-; cp/Pres, Decatur Boys Clb, 1981-83; Coun of Commun Sers 1979-, Pres 1984; Decatur Geneal Soc, 1977-; Civil War Roundtable; hon/Boys Clb Bd Mem of the Yr, 1981; W/W: in MW, in Bus & Indust.

GARRETT, STEVEN HUGHES oc/Electrical Engineer; b/Jan 17, 1942; h/4321 Kuykendall Road, Matthews, NC 28105; ba/Charlotte, NC; m/Betty Jo; c/Brian Scott; p/Ira W and Dorthy F Garrett, Greensboro, NC; ed/BSEE, Univ of NC-Charlotte, 1972; Postgrad Wk, MBA, Queens Col, 1982; mil/USAF, 1964-68; pa/Plant Engrg, Deering-Milliken Co, Gaffney, SC, 1972-73; Plant Engrg, Deering-Milliken Co, Pendleton, SC, 1973-75; Plant Engrg, Westinghouse Elect Corp, 1975-; Pres, Bd of Dirs, Westinghouse Credit Assn, 1979-80; IEEE, 1968-; hon/Pub, "Industl Energy Conserv," Soc of Mfg Engrs, 1978; Westinghouse Patent Awds, 1979, 1981; US Patent in Ultrasonic Testing, 1980; W/W in SE.

GARRIS, KAREN ANN oc/Agricultural Commodity Grader, Equal Employment Opportunity Counselor; b/Sep 6, 1956; h/11125 South Van Ness Avenue, Inglewood, CA 90303; ba/Modesto, CA; p/Willie Franklyn and Helen Walker, Inglewood, CA; ed/SF St, 1974-76; BS, Tuskegee Inst, 1979; pa/Animal Caretaker, LA, 1970-74; Lib Asst, SF, 1974-77; Forestry Tech, Glendora, CA, 1977; Capine Res Asst, Tuskegee Inst, 1976-79; Forestry Tech, Hillsboro, GA, 1979; Agri Commodity Grader, Chico, CA, 1979-80; Agri Commodity Grader (Poultry), Modesto, CA, 1980-; EEO Cnslr; Nat Assn Female Execs; Org Profl Employees, Dept Agri; cp/The Spa; hon/Admrs Awd, Govt, 1983; W/W: in World, in E.

GARTRELL, CHARLES FREDERICK oc/Space Scientist, Engineer; b/Nov 4, 1951; h/10332 Ridgeline Drive, Gaithersburg, MD 20879; ba/McLean, VA; m/Vanessa Lynn; c/Charles Michael; p/Charles C Gartrell, Owings Mills, MD; ed/BA in Physics, Univ of MD, Balto Co, 1973; pa/Sys Analyst, RCA Am Communs, 1975-78; Task Mgr & Analyst, Computer Scis Corp, 1973-75; Current Space Scist/Engr, Gen Res Corp; AIAA; Optical Soc of Am; hon/Pubs, *Astrophysics Space Sys Critical Technol Needs* 1982, *Simultaneous Eccentricity & Drift Rate Control* 1981, *Time Optimized North-South Stationkeeping* 1983, *A Future Solar Orbital Transfer Vehicle Concept* 1983, *A View of Future Technol Needs for Space Trans,* 1984, *A Future Solar Orbital Transfer Vehicle Concept,* 1983; MD St Senatorial S'ship, 1972; AIAA Nat Capitol Sect, 1981 Yg Engr/Scist of the Yr Awd, Runner-Up; AIAA Nat Capitol Sect, 1982 Yg Engr/Scist of the Yr Awd, Finalist and Runner-Up; Guest Lectr on Future Satellite Communs Technol, George Wash Univ, 1982; W/W: in Aviation & Aerospace, in E.

GARY, BEVERLY A WILSON oc/Federal Official, Director of Personnel;

b/Oct 6, 1942; h/11506 Accolade Terrace, Clinton, MD 20735; ba/Washington, DC; m/James A; c/James A Jr; p/Dorothy J Wilson, Uniontown, PA; ed/Grad, Fed Exec Inst, 1983; EdM, Univ of MA-Amherst, 1983; Student, Bowie St Col, 1980-; pa/Dir of Pers 1974-, Dir of Employmt Br 1972-74, Position Classification Spec 1967-72, EEO Comm; Employee, Dept of Commerce, 1960-65; Intl Pers Mgmt Assn; Sr Exec Assn; Nat Assn of Female Execs; cp/Life Mbrship in NAACP; Wash Urban Leag; hon/Sr Exec Bonus, 1982; Outstg Perf Awds, 1965, 1970, 1976, 1977, 1979, 1981; W/W: in DC, of Am Wom.

GARZA, HECTOR oc/Assistant Graduate Dean; b/Apr 10, 1956; h/4820 Washtenaw Avenue, Ann Arbor, MI 48104; ba/Ypsilanti, MI; m/Irasema T; c/Jennifer Marie; p/Alejandro and Guadalupe C Garza, Donna, TX; ed/BGS 1979, MPH 1981, PhD 1985, Univ of MI; pa/Asst Grad Dean, En MI Univ, 1981-; Coor of Experiential Ed, Univ of MI, 1976-81; Am Assn for Higher Ed, Hispanic Caucus Chp 1983, CoChp 1982; Nat Assn for Chicano Studies; Nat Assn of Fgn Student Advrs; hon/Pubs, "El Grito de las Madres Dolorosas: A Film Review" 1984, "A List of Chicano/Latino Films & Their Distributors" 1984; 1980 Hispanic Col Grad of the Yr Awd, 1980.

GARZA, MARTIN HENRY oc/Health and Human Service Agency Administrator; b/Oct 21, 1940; h/1915 West Magnolia Avenue, San Antonio, TX; ba/San Antonio, TX; m/Evangelina Lopez; c/Martin Jr, Edward; p/Efrain C and Emma Vasquez Garza, San Antonio, TX; ed/MSW, Our Lady of the Lake Univ, Worden Sch of Social Sers, 1969; BA, St Mary's Univ, 1966; pa/Yth Sers Grp Wkr, House of Neighborly Ser, 1963-65; Proj Coor, San Antonio Neighborhood Yth Org, 1966-67; Manpower Devel Spec, US Dept of Labor, 1967; Chief of Social Sers & Commun Orgr, House of Neighborly Ser, 1969-71; Casewkr, 1971; Dir of Outpatient Sers 1972-76, Prog Dir 1976-79, Bexar Co Mtl Hlth Mtl Retard Ctr Drug Dependence Prog; Substance Abuse Prog Dir, Bexar Co Mtl Hlth Mtl Retard Ctr, 1979-; Drug Abuse Ctl Bd of Trustees, Secy-Treas 1976-79; Alamo Area Coun of Govt Reg Drug Abuse Adv Com, VChm 1977-78; Gov's St of TX Drug Abuse Adv Coun, 1979-; cp/Thomas Jefferson HS Band Booster, 1982-83; Woodlawn Hills Pop-Warner Ftball Assn, 1976-80; PTA, 1972-; hon/Grad Sch Thesis, "Food Intake Patterns of Low Income Families in San Antonio, TX," 1969; Opinion Survey Report, "Drug Dependence Prog Employee Satisfaction Study," 1970; Supvn Instrument, "Drug Dependence Prog Supvn by Objectives," 1974; Selected to All-Dist & All-City HS Ftball Team, 1959; Featured in Local Newspaper Article Entitled "Dedication Awarded," 1980; Nat Child Wel Grad Studies Stipend, 1967; Nat Student Def Undergrad Studies Loan, 1963; Dir of First Outpatient Drug Treatment Prog to Receive Accreditation by the Jt Comm on Hosp Accreditation, 1977; St of TX Lic'd Social Wkr, 1982-83; W/W in S & SW.

GASPER, JO ANN oc/United States Government Executive; b/Sep 25, 1946;

h/6243 Park Road, McLean, VA 22101; ba/Washington, DC; m/Louis Clement; c/Stephen Gregory, Monica Elizabeth, Jeanne Marie, Michelle Bernadette (dec); p/Joseph Siegleman and Jeanne Van Matre Shoaf; ed/BA 1967, MBA 1969, Univ of Dallas; pa/Adm Asst, Univ of Dallas, 1964-68; Asst Admr, Brit Convalescent Ctr, 1964-68; Pres, Medicare Ctrs Inc, 1968-69; Bus Mgr & Treas, Univ of Plano, 1969-72; Ins Agt for John Hancock Ins, 1972-73; Sys Analyst, 1973-75; Acctg & Bus Conslt, 1976-81; Editor & Publisher, *The Right Woman,* 1978-81; Editor & Publisher, *Fed Register,* 1980-81; Dpty Asst Secy for Social Sers Policy, Ofc of the Asst Secy for Planning & Eval, Dept of Hlth & Human Sers, 1981-; Exec Dir, White House Conf on Aging, Dept of Hlth & Human Sers, 1982-; Coun, Inter-Am Security, Bd of Dirs & Treas; White House Conf on Fams, Del; cp/Nat Fam Policy Adv Bd, Reagan/Bush Campaign; Franklin Area Citizens Neighborhood Watch; CoChm, St John's Refugee Resettlement Comm; hon/Author, "Future Directions of Long Term Care" in *Am Hlth Care Assn Jour* Jan 1983; Eagle Forum Awd, 1979; Wanderer Foun Awd, 1980; HHS Bronze Medal, 1982; Outstg Conservative Wom, 1980, 1981.

GASTON, EDWIN WILLMER JR oc/Educator; b/Feb 22, 1925; h/1305 North Street, Nacogdoches, TX 75961; ba/Nacogdoches, TX; m/Martha Middlebrook; c/J E F, Thomas M, W Kant; p/Mrs E W Gaston Sr, Nacogdoches, TX; ed/BS 1947, MA 1951, Stephen F Austin St Univ; PhD, TX Tech Univ, 1959; mil/Non-Comm'd Ofcr, USMC, Pacific Theater of War, 1942-46; pa/Mag & Newspaper Editing, Radio Broadcasting, Var TX & Reg Mags, Newspapers & Radio Stas, 1942-43, 1947-60; Dir of Pubs, From Asst to Assoc to Full Prof of Eng & Jour, 1950-53, 1955-64, 1965-, Stephen F Austin St Univ; Pt-time Instr, TX Tech Univ, 1953-55; Fulbright Lectr, Univ of Helsinki, Finland, 1964-65; Dean of the Grad Sch & Prof of Eng, Stephen F Austin St Univ, 1976-81; VP for Acad Affairs, Stephen F Austin St Univ, 1981-; Alpha Chi, Nat Pres 1967-79, Pres Emeritus 1979-, Nat S'ship Soc; Am Studies Assn; Mod Lang Assn; NCTE; SWn Am Lit Assn; S Ctl Mod Lang Assn; TX Folklore Soc, Treas 1970-, Past Pres; Wn Am Lit Assn; hon/Pubs, *The Early Novel of the SW* 1961, *A Manual of Style* 1961, *Conrad Richter* 1965, *Eugene Manlove Rhodes* 1967, Num Articles; Co-Editor, *SW Am Lit: A Bibliog* 1980; Nat Hon Soc, HS; Recip, Fulbright Lecturing Awd, Univ of Helsinki & Swedish Sch of Ec, Finland; Recip, Dist'd Prof Awd, SFASU; Recip, Dist'd Prof Awd, SFASU Alumni Assn.

GASTON, MARILYN HUGHES oc/Physician, Deputy Chief of Sickle Cell Branch; b/Jan 31, 1939; h/8612 Timber Hill, Potomac, MD 20854; ba/Bethesda, MD; m/Alonzo D; c/Amy Marie, Damon Allen; p/Myron and Dorothy (dec) Hughes, Cincinnati, OH; ed/AB, Miami Univ, 1960; MD, Univ of Cinc, 1964; pa/Dpty Chief, Sickle Cell Br, NIH; Dir, Cinc Comprehensive Sickle Cell Ctr; Assoc Prof of Pediatrics, Chd's Hosp; Am Acad of Pediatrics; Nat Med Assn; Links Inc; hon/Pubs, "The Cooperative Study of Sickle Cell Disease" 1982, "Treatment Aspects of Sickle Cell

Disease" 1981, "Concerning the Problem of Eval of Clin Severity in Sickle Cell Disease" 1981, "Comprehensive Sickle Cell Ctrs" 1977, "Decreased Opsonization for Streptococcus Pneumoniae in Sickle Cell Disease: Studies on Selected Complement Components & Immunoglobulins" 1977, Num Others; Pi Kappa Epsilon, 1964; Outstg Black Wom in Cinc, 1964; Optimist Wel Clb, 1974; City's Yg Ldr in Hlth, Cinc Post, 1974; Awd of Apprec, Jack & Jill Inc, 1975; Phyllis Wheatley Awd, St of OH, OH Black Wom's Ldrship Caucus, 1975; Temple Bible Col Hall of Fame, 1976; Wom of the Yr in Med, Harriet Tubman Black Wom's Dem Clb, 1976; Awd for Excell, Pgh Sickle Cell Soc, 1980; Commend Medal, Comm'd Corps, Public Hlth Ser, Dept of Hlth & Human Sers, 1981; W/W: of Black Ams, of Am Wom; Outstg Yg Wom in Am.

GAT, URI oc/Head of Nuclear Technology Development; b/Jun 28, 1936; h/238 Gum Hollow Road, Oak Ridge, TN 37830; ba/Oak Ridge, TN; m/Ruth Tasse; c/Irit, Erann; p/Werner Hagelberg (dec); Jenny Lore (dec); ed/BSc, Mech and Nuclear, IIT, Haifa, 1963; Dr Ing, Nuclear & Mats, RWTH, Aachen, Germany; mil/Israel AF, Capt, Jet Instr; pa/Res Assoc, Reactor Devel, KFA, Juelich, Germany, 1963-69; Asst Prof, Mech & Nuclear, Univ of KY, 1969-74; Mgr, Nuclear Res & Devel of Nuclear Reactors, Oak Ridge Nat Lab, 1974-; Am Nuclear Soc; US Metric Assn; ZPG; NPG; cp/ACLU; hon/Author, Var Pubs in Profl Jours; Patents; Wilhelm Borcherg Medaille, 1969; Sigma Xi; Var Biogl Listings.

GATES, GARY LOUIS oc/Consultant, Graduate Student; b/Sep 20, 1946; h/1161 Broadway, Apartment D, Alameda, CA 94501; ba/Same; m/Jane E; c/Micheal, Frisbe, Clancy, Tiger; p/Doris M Harriage, Alameda, CA; ed/AA, Col of Alameda, 1976; AS, Merritt Col, 1977; BA, Golden Gate Univ, 1979; MPA 1981, BS 1982, MS 1983, MA 1984, CA St Univ Hayward; mil/AUS Med Corp, 1964-65; pa/Sales; Elect Engrg; Food & Beverage Indust; Ed; Consltg in the Field of Juv Delinquency, Commun Relats, Media (Radio & TV); SF Press Clb; Media Alliance of SF; cp/Commonwlth of CA; K of C, 3rd & 4th Degs; Nat Pilot Org; Alameda Flying Clb; hon/Awd of Excell, Golden Gate Univ, 1978; Cert of Achmt, U Way, 1979; Oper Shore, Over 21 Awds (Awd of Excell 1980).

GATES, NINA MICHAEL oc/Mining Company Executive; b/Jun 25, 1935; ba/Ojai, CA; m/Oliver Perry (dec); c/Carl W Bailey, Michael P Bailey; p/Michael M and Annie T Evdokimo; ed/Att'd Public Schs, Nelson, Brit Columbia, Canada; pa/Wk Hist: Legal Secy, Securities Broker, Former Mem of Nat Assn of Securities Dealers; Presently Engaged in the Exploration & Devel of Mineral Lands, 1970-; Current Pres, The Atacami Corp; cp/US Senatorial Bus Adv Bd, Wash DC; hon/Recip, Justice W McDonald S'ship; W/W of Am Wom.

GATTIS, KATHLEEN oc/Retired Teacher; b/Oct 29, 1906; h/211 South High, Winchester, TN 37398; p/Mr and Mrs John Gattis (dec); ed/3 Yrs of Col Credits w Life Time Cert; pa/Currently a Tutor, since Retirement; Tchr of Rdg

& Spelling to the Handicapped, 1982; Tchr for 30 Yrs, Elem Grades; Supvr for Hat Corp of TN, 8½ Yrs; Cashier at Oak Ridge, TN, 2 Yrs during WW II; Nat Ret'd Tchrs Assn; Mid TN Ret'd Tchrs Assn; Franklin Co Ret'd Tchrs Assn; cp/XYZ'ers; r/Meth; hon/Author of Lttrs to the Editor in Co Paper & Two Poems.

GAVIN, VIDA R oc/Director of Special Services; b/Aug 12, 1941; h/141 Forest Street, PO Box B, Norwell, MA 02061; ba/Scituate, MA; m/Charles F; c/David A; p/Elena Strazdas, Centerville, MA; ed/BS 1968, EdM 1973, NEn Univ; Postgrad Wk, Emmanuel Col, Lesley Col, Cury Col; Doct Cand, NEn Univ, 1980-; pa/Dir of Spec Sers, Scituate, MA, 1981-; Dept Hd/Coor, Rdg & Spec Sers, Town of Dedham, MA, 1971-81; Eng Tchr, Town of Marshfield, MA, 1968-69; IRA; Assn of Supvn & Curric Devel; MA Assn of Chd w Lrng Disabilities; Delta Kappa Gamma; CEC; NE Coalition of Ed Ldrs Inc; hon/Outstg Sec'dy Edr of Am, 1974; Exemplary Jr High Resource Rm Prog, 1978; W/W in E.

GAY, ANNA BELLE GRAHAM oc/Housewife; h/844 Aldino-Stepney Road, Aberdeen, MD 21001; m/Herman P; c/Paul, Martha, Nancy, John; p/Waymon and Maggie Bailey Graham (dec); ed/BA, magna cum laude, Winthrop Col, 1942; pa/Mathematician, Aberdeen Proving Ground, 1942-45; Subst Tchr, 1963-75; 5 Yrs on Bd of Ed for Harford Co Public Schs, & 5 Yrs on Bd of Trustees for Harford Commun Col, Appt'd by Gov, 1970-75; cp/Pres, Harford Co Coun of PTA, 1967-68; Public Relats Chm for MD PTA, 1966-68; Pres, Aberdeen High PTA; IPA; r/Chm, Adm Bd, Grace U Meth Ch, 1978-79; Pres, Balto E Dist U Meth Wom, 1978-81; Pres, Grace U Meth Wom, 1976-78; hon/Hon Life Mem in MD PTA, Aberdeen Jr HS, 1966, Pres 1965-66; Hon Life Mem in Nat PTA, Harford Co Coun of PTA's, 1972, Pres 1966-68; Sustaining Missions Recog Pin, Grace U Meth Wom, 1981; Patron Mission Recog Pin, Balto E Dist U Meth Wom, 1981; Wom of Yr Mbrship Pin, Grace U Meth Wom, 1976; Meritorious Ser Awd, Ctl MD Heart, 1975; Public Relats Awd, Ctl MD Heart, 1974; Outstg Heart Vol, Ctl MD Heart, 1972; Outstg Ladies We Hold Dear, Hartford Col Homemakers' Coun; Personalities of S; World W/W of Wom; DIB; People Who Matter; Nom'd W/W in MD; W/W in Am Cols & Univs.

GAY, GRETCHEN M (REMER) oc/Hospital/Nursing Home Administrator, Business Owner; b/May 7, 1930; h/811 Layton Drive, Olathe, KS 66061; ba/Olathe, KS; c/Reginald Rondell, Jeffrey Louis; p/Donald M and Millie Jane (Mattox) Remer, Danville, AR; ed/AD Nsg, Johnson Co Commun Col, 1973; Studied Parapsych under Josqinn Cunanan (Philippines), 1978; pa/Student & Grad Nurse, Olathe Commun Hosp, 1972-73; Vets Hosp Night Supvr, Leavenworth, KS, 1973-77; Asst Dir of Nsg, Troost Ave Nsg Home, 1980-; Owner Conslltg Firm, Endless Horizons, 1982-; Co-Writer of Grant & Co-Fdr of First Level Six Tx., 197; Orgr of Nurse Advocate Tng Prog, Chgo, 1977; Holds Nsg Home Admrs Lic; Am Holistic

Nurses Assn; Metascience Foun; Soc for Improvement of Human Function; Assn for Res & Enlightenment; Martin Psychi Res Foun; Brain Mind; hon/Author Short Article in Pub of Mecca for Holistic Healing, 1980; W/W of Am Wom.

GAY, STEFFEN oc/Professor of Medicine, Director-WHO Center, Scientist, Physician; b/Mar 22, 1948; h/1100 Beacon Parkway, East V-102, Birmingham, AL 35209; ba/Birmingham, AL; m/Renate Erika (MD); c/Ann-Britt, Annietta; p/Peter (dec) and Ilse Gay, W Germany; ed/MD, Univ Med Sch, Leipzig, GDR, 1972; pa/Pre-Doct & Postdoct Fellow, Pathol, Univ of Leipzig, GDR; Resident in Internal Med, Poliklinik, Leipzig, GDR; Gen Practitioner, Bartenstein, FRG; Res Fellow, Max-Planck Inst Biochem, Munich, FDR, Sect Connective Tissue Res; Res Spec, Biochem, CMDJ Rutgers Med Sch, Piscataway, NJ; Vis'g Asst Prof of Pathol, Univ of AL-B'ham; NY Acad of Sci; Am Assn of Pathol; Am Rheumatism Assn; Deutsche Gesellschaft für Pathologie; Deutsche Gesellschaft für Rheumatologie; hon/Author, 147 Pubs (1 Book, 15 Chapts, 88 Orig Papers, 72 Abstracts), Book: Collagen & Physiol & Pathol of Connective Tissue 1978; Fdr, Editor-in-Chief "Collagen & Related Res"; Med Exam, summa cum laude, 1972; Alexander-Schmidt Prize for Thrombosis Res, 1975; Carol-Nachman Prize for Rheumatology, 1978; W/W: in Frontier Sci & Technol, in S; Am Men & Wom of Sci; 2,000 Notable Ams; Intl Book of Hon.

GAYLORD, THOMAS KEITH oc/Professor of Electrical Engineering; b/Sep 22, 1943; h/3180 Verdun Drive, Northwest, Atlanta, GA 30305; ba/Atlanta, GA; m/Janice L Smith; c/Grace M; p/Earl F Gaylord, Independence, MO; ed/BS in Physics 1965, MS in Elect Engrg 1967, Univ of MO-Rolla; PhD, Elect Engrg, Rice Univ, 1970; pa/Spec Tech Asst, Wn Elect Co, 1964-65; Postdoct Fellow, Rice Univ, 1970-72; Prof, GA Inst of Technol, 1972-; Sigma Pi Sigma; Tau Beta Pi; Kappa Mu Epsilon; Phi Kappa Phi; Sigma Xi; Eta Kappa Nu; AAAS; AAUP; AGIP; IEEE, Fellow; OSA, Fellow; SPIE; SPSE; hon/Author, Over 110 Tech Jour Papers in the Area of Optical Data Processing, Holographic Info Storage, Grating Diffraction, Electro-Optic Crystals, Semiconductor Mats & Instrumentation; Outstg Yg Engr of the Yr, GSPE, 1977; Curtis W McGraw Res Awd, ASEE, 1979; Outstg Tchr Awd, GA Tech, 1984; Cent Medal, IEEE, 1984; 3 Other Tchg Awds and 5 Other Res Awds; Num Biogl Listings.

GAYNOR, GENEVIEVE GOODEN oc/Counseling Specialist; b/Oct 2, 1945; h/4415 Roseneath Drive, Houston, TX 77021; ba/Houston, TX; m/Dr Michael Maurice; c/Michael Maurice, Marcus Gerard; p/Lonnie J Sr (dec) and Edith Gooden, Galveston, TX; ed/BS in Elem Ed, 1968; EdM in Cnslg & Guid, 1971; EdD, 1983; pa/Tchr, Houston Indep Sch Dist, 1968-78; Cnslr, Neighborhood Yth Corp, 1972; Univ Instr, TX So Univ, 1978; Ednl Instr, Aldine Indep Sch Dist, 1979-84; Voc Guid Ser Houston, 1984-; Wom of Achmt, Recording Secy, 1981-83; Jack & Jill of Am, Correspondence Secy, 1981-83; Squaws Inc,

Recording Secy, 1982-84; Pershing Mid Sch PTO, 1982-83; Inwood Sch PTA, 1979-; hon/Grad, cum laude, 1968; Outstg Yg Wom of Am; W/W in Am Cols & Univs.

GAYNOR, MICHAEL MAURICE oc/ Educator; b/Aug 13, 1943; h/4415 Roseneath Drive, Houston, TX 77021; ba/Houston, TX; m/Genevieve Gooden; c/Michael II, Marcus Gerard; p/Dorothy Walls Hatcher, Galena Park, TX; ed/ EdD, 1982; MA, 1972; EdM, 1970; BA, 1966; pa/Instructional Suprv, Houston Sch Dist, 1979-; TX Dept of Human Resources Suprv, 1975-79; Phi Delta Kappa; Assn for Supvn & Curric Devel; Assn for Individually Guided Ed; Assn Cnslg & Devel; CEC; TX Assn for Cont'g Adult Ed; hon/Author, "Effects of Acad Self-Concept on the Scholastic Perf of Urban Pupils"; Outstg Yg Edr, 1969; Outstg Yg Men of Am; W/W in S & SW.

GBEHO, JAMES VICTOR oc/Permanent Representative of Ghana to the United Nations; b/Jan 12, 1935; h/111 Overlook Road, New Rochelle, NY 10804; ba/New York, NY; m/Edith; c/ Eric, Anita, Kenneth; p/Philip Gbeho (dec); ed/Att'd, Achimota Sch, 1945-55; BA, Univ of Ghana, 1959; pa/Perm Rep to UN, 1980-; Perm Rep to European Ofc of UN, 1978-80; Dpty High Commr to UK, 1972-76; Posted to Peking, New Delhi, Lagos, Bonn; Chm, Preparatory Comm of UN Common Fund for Commodities, 1980-; Chm, UN Gen Assembly's First Com (Polit & Security), 1982; Chm, UN Disarmament Comm, 1984; Royal Commonwlth Soc; Interfuture; Mem of Intl Adv Coun; hon/Author, Africa's Call for Sanctions Agnst S Africa, 1982; Hugh & Mabel Smythe Intl Ser Cit, 1982.

GDOWSKI, SANDRA oc/Manager of Software Engineering Firm; b/Nov 3, 1953; h/24130 F Western Avenue, Harbor City, CA 90710; ba/Hawthorne, CA; p/Michael and Frances Gdowski, Harbor City; ed/BA, Math, Univ of CA-San Diego, 1975; Grad Studies in Elect Engrg, Univ of So CA, 1978-81; pa/Sci Programmer/Analyst, Technol Ser Corp, 1975-79; Software Design Engr, TRW-Def & Space Sys Grp, 1979-80; Mgr, Adv'd Sys Technol, The BDM Corp, 1980-; Armed Forces Communs & Electronics Assn; Am Mgmt Assn; Nat Assn of Female Execs; Am Soc of Profl & Exec Wom; hon/Pubs, "The Art of Multisensor Fusion & Correlation in a Tactical Surface Envir" 1982, "A Tech Approach to the Devel of a Target Acquisition Sys" 1982, "The Battlefield Exploitation & Target Acquisition (BETA) Sys & Its Applicability to ENSCE & JTFP" 1981, "The Total Aggregation Concept & Design in Multisensor Correlation in a Tactical Surface Envir" 1981, Others; CA St S'ships, 1971-73; Tech Pubs Awd, The BDM Corp, 1982; W/W of Am Wom.

GEAR, CHARLES WILLIAM oc/ Professor of Computer Science and Applied Mathematics; b/Feb 1, 1935; h/ 3302 Lakeshore Drive, Champaign, IL 61821; ba/Urbana, IL; m/Ann Lee Morgan; c/Kathlyn Jo, Christopher William; p/Charles James (dec) and Margaret Gear, Holmer Green, England; ed/PhD in Math 1960, MS in Math 1957, Univ of IL; MA in Math 1960, BA in Math 1956, Cambridge, England;

pa/Engr, IBM Brit Labs, Hursley, England, 1960-62; Prof, Univ of IL-Urbana-Champaign, 1962-; SIAM, Coun Mem, 1980-; ACM, Coun Mem, 1975-77; IEEE, Fellow 1984; AAAS, Fellow 1984; hon/Pubs, *Numerical Value Problems in Ordinary Differential Equations*, 1971; *Computer Org & Programming* (4th Edition) 1985, *Intro to Computers, Structured Programming & Applications* (in 9 Modules), Num Articles; Fulbright Fellow, 1956-60; Forsythe Meml Lectr Awd, 1979.

GEARREALD, CHERRI ELAINE oc/ Labor and Delivery Nurse; b/Mar 23, 1963; h/125 Sunset, Elk City, OK 73644; ba/Commun Hosp, Elk City, OK; m/ Mark Alan; c/Ranson Ty; p/Mr and Mrs Robert L Clem, Camargo, OK; ed/Grad, Leedey HS, 1981; Grad, Indian Meredian Sch of Practical Nsg, IMATVS, 1982; Lic'd LPN, 1982; pa/Nurses Aide at Vici Nsg Home, Sum 1980; OPN, Elk City Commun Hosp, 1982; OB 11-7 Charge Nurse, Cushing Reg Hosp, 1983; Student Mem, Nat LPN Assn, 1982; r/1st Christian Ch; SS Tchr, 1980-81; hon/Student Coun Mem, FHA Pres & Class Reporter (Wrote Articles for Sch Newspaper About Horse Shows, Nsg Sch & Fam Happenings) in HS; Miss LHS, 2nd Runner-up, 1980; OK St Champ in Girls Cutting in Rodeo, 1981; Selected for Ldrship Conf, KC, KS, 1980.

GEARY, BARBARA ANN oc/Concert and Recital Pianist; b/Jul 2, 1935; h/2545 South Birmingham Place, Tulsa, OK 74114; p/E F Geary, Tulsa, OK; ed/ BA in French, St Mary's Col, 1957; MM (Piano), IN Univ, 1961; Studied Piano Chiefly w Frederick Baldwin; Coached w Arthur Loesser & Vlado Perlemuter (Paris); pa/Former Piano Prof at OH Univ 1963-69, Univ of NC 1970; Am Liszt Soc; Debut, Wigmore Hall, London, UK, 1972; Perfs (Chiefly as Solo Recitalist) in US, Mexico, Wn Europe (England, Switzerland, Scotland, France, Spain, W Germany, Holland, Austria, Portugal, Greece); Soloist w Tulsa Philharm & OK Symph; hon/St Mary's Col Dean's List, 1954-57; Kappa Gamma Pi, Scholastic & Activity Hon, 1957; French Govt S'ship, 1970; Dir Dist'd Ams; Intl W/W in Music; Notable Ams of 1976-77; World W/W of Wom.

GEBO, EMMA JOKI oc/Assistant Professor and Chairman of Consumer Economics Department; b/Jan 1, 1945; h/2409 South Fairway, Pocatello, ID 83201; ba/Pocatello, ID; m/David Ray; c/Lorri Dawn, Paul Adrien, Robyn Jeanete; p/Vera and Waino Joki, Red Lodge, MT; ed/BS, Home Ec Ed, MT St Univ, 1966; MA, Ed, Univ of MT-Missoula, 1971; pa/Subst Tchr, ID & MT, 1967-75; Adult Edr, Pocatello, ID, 1975-76; Instr in Clothing & Textiles 1973, Instr in Clothing & Textiles & Voc Home Ec 1975-78, Asst Prof Home Ec 1978-80, Dept Chm & Voc Home Ec Tchr Edr 1980-, ID St Univ; Am Home Ec Assn, Nat By-Laws Com 1983-85, Mem 1967-; ID Home Ec Assn, Pres 1983-85; Am Voc Assn; ID Voc Assn; Nat FHA Tchrs Ed Task Force, 1978, 1981; Nat Assn Tchr Ed Voc Home Ec, Resource Sharing Com Chair 1984-85; Nat Coun Adm Home Ec; Phi Upsilon Omicron; Kappa Omicron Phi; FHA, Hon Mem & Asst St Advr; hon/Conducted Res Related to Competencies for

Voc Home Ec Tchrs, Surveys of Tchr Ed Progs & Mgmt Tool Usage by Univ Dept Chm in ID; Recognized by the ID Jaycettes as a Dist'd Yg Wom, 2nd Runner-up, 1982; Outstg Yg Wom of Am; W/W in W.

GeBORDE, LINDLEY EVAN oc/ Certified Financial Planner; b/Jan 18, 1943; h/2-883 Route 206, Chester, NJ 07930; ba/East Orange, NJ; c/Dion, Troy, Delise; p/Mrs Margaret Lewis, Georgetown, Guyana; ed/Chartered Financial Conslt; Chartered Life Underwriter; Cert'd Financial Planner; Chartered Financialist; pa/Sales Mgr, Rasmussen Assocs, 1969-72; Pres, Estate Ec Corp of Am, 1972-; Ec Devel Com, Wash Twp, NJ; cp/Morris Co, NJ, C of C; r/Hindu; hon/W/W in Fin & Indust; Men of Achmt.

GEE, E GORDON oc/University President; b/Feb 2, 1944; h/948 Riverview Drive, Morgantown, WV 26505; ba/Morgantown, WV; m/Elizabeth; c/ Rebekah; p/Mr and Mrs E A Gee, Salt Lake City, UT; ed/BA, Univ of UT, 1968; JD, Columbia Univ Sch of Law, 1971; EdD, Tchrs Col, Columbia Univ, 1972; pa/Law Clk, Chief Judge of US Tenth Circuit, 1972-73; Asst Dean, Univ of UT Law Sch, 1973-74; Jud Fellow, US Supr Ct, 1974-75; Assoc Dean & Prof of Law, Brigham Yg Univ, 1975-79; Dean, WV Univ Law Sch, 1979-81; Pres, WV Univ, 1981-; ABA; Chair, Rhodes S'ship Selection Com, WV; Am Law Inst; Adm Conf of the US; r/Mormon; hon/Pubs, *Ed Law & the Public Schs* 1978, *Law & Public Ed: Cases & Mats* 1980, *Violence, Values & Justice in the Schs* 1982, *Fair Employmt Practices & Procedures: Cases & Mats* 1982; Phi Delta Kappa; Phi Kappa Phi.

GEE, SISTER KATHERINE HOLLAND oc/College Professor; b/Aug 18, 1924; h/1000 Hempstead Avenue, Rockville Centre, NY 11570; ba/Rockville Centre, NY; ed/BA in Hist, St Joseph's Col, 1947; MA in Sociol, St John's Univ, 1971; EdD, Ednl Adm, Hofstra Univ, 1982; pa/Social Studies Tchr, Dominican Comml HS, 1951-68; Chp, Social Studies & Indep Study Ctr, St Agnes Cath HS, 1968-73; Chp, Sociol Dept, Molloy Col, 1973-80; Dir, Intl Peace & Justice Studies Inst, Molloy Col, 1981-; Am Sociological Assn; Assn Supvn & Curric Devel; Assn for Sociol of Rel; Am Ednl Res Assn; r/Rom Cath; hon/ Pubs, *An Exploratory Approach to an Invest of the Role of the Sec'dy Guid Cnslr in Two Pvt Girls' Schs in NY St*, *The Fam: Basic Sociological Concepts* 1980, "Whom Do We Serve?" 1967, "Sister Knows the Score" 1966, "Interracial Ed in Social Studies Classes" 1966; Phi Alpha Theta, 1983; Delta Epsilon Sigma, 1983; W/W in E; World W/W of Wom.

GEESLIN, WILLIAM FLEMING oc/ Executive; b/Jun 16, 1919; h/424 West Princess Anne Road, Norfolk, VA 23517; ba/Norfolk, VA; m/Mary Timmerman; c/William F Jr, John W, Christopher L; ed/BA in Jour, Mercer Univ; pa/FBI, 1942-47; Yg & Rubicam Advtg Agy, 1947-60; Manatee Co (FL) Devel Dir, 1961-63; VP, 1st Nat Bk of Bradenton (FL), 1963-64; Spec Rep & Asst VP, So Rwy Sys, 1967-82; VP of Public Relats, Norfolk So Corp, 1982-; Public Relats Soc of Am; RR Public Relats Assn; Am Mktg Assn.

GEHA, ALEXANDER SALIM oc/ Cardiothoracic Surgeon; b/Jun 18, 1936;

h/345 Ridge Road, Hamden, CT 06517; ba/New Haven, CT; m/Diane Redalen; c/Samia Marcelle, Rula Christine, Nada Alees; p/Salim M and Alice H Geha, Hamden, CT; ed/BS, summa cum laude 1955, MD, summa cum laude 1959, Am Univ of Beirut; MS, Surg & Physiol, Univ of MN, 1967; pa/Asst Prof of Thoracic & Cardiovas Surg, Univ of VT Col of Med, 1967-69; Asst Prof of Surg 1969-73, Assoc Prof of Surg 1973-75, WA Univ Sch of Med; Assoc Prof of Surg 1975-78, Prof of Surg 1978-, Assoc Chief, Sect of Cardiothoracic Surg 1978-82, Yale Univ Sch of Med; Chief, Sect of Cardiothoracic Surg, Yale Univ Sch of Med & Yale-New Haven Hosp Med Ctr, 1982-; Am Assn for Thoracic Surg; Am Col of Cardiol; Am Col of Chest Phys; Am Col of Surgs; Am Heart Assn; AMA; Am Physiological Soc; Am Surg Assn; Am Thoracic Soc; Assn for Acad Surg; Assn for Clin Cardiac Surgs; Ctl Surg Assn; CT Chapt, Am Col of Surgs; CT Soc of Am Bd of Surgs; CT Soc of Thoracic Surgs; Coun on Cardiovas Surg, Am Heart Assn; Intl Cardiovas Soc, N Am Chapt; Lebanese Order of Phys; N Eng Sts Chapt, Am Col of Chest Phys; N Eng Surg Soc; Pan Am Med Assn; St Louis Thoracic Surg Soc; Societa di Richerche in Chirurgia; Societe Internationale de Chirurgie; The Halsted Soc; The Soc of Thoracic Surgs; The Soc of Univ Surgs; The Soc for Vascular Surg; hon/Pubs, "Postoperative Care & Complications" (in Press), "Selection of Heart Valve" (in Press), "Noncardiogenic Pulmonary Edema Following Cardiopulmonary Bypass: An Anaphylactic Reaction to Fresh Frozen Plasma" 1984, "Complete Valve Replacement & Myocardial Revascularization" 1984, Num Other Articles; Alpha Omega Alpha, Am Univ of Beirut Chapt, 1958; Soc of Sigma Xi, 1967; Hon MS, Yale Univ, 1978; W/W: in Am, in E, in Frontier Sci & Technol.

GEHRELS, TOM oc/Professor; b/Feb 21, 1925; h/2235 East Hampton, Tucson, AZ 85719; ba/Tucson, AZ; m/Liedeke; c/Neil, George Ellery, Jo-Ann; ed/BS, 1951; PhD, 1956; mil/Spec Sers; pa/Res Assoc, IN Univ & McDonald Observatory, 1956-61; Assoc Prof, Inst for Atmospheric Physics & Lunar & Planetary Lab, Univ of AZ, 1961-67; Prof, Lunar & Planetary Lab, Univ of AZ, 1967-; V A Sarabhai Prof, Ahmedabad, 1978-79; Intl Astronom Union; Am Astronom Soc; hon/Editor, *Phy Studies of Minor Planets* 1971, *Planets, Stars & Nebulae Studied w Photopolarimetry* 1974, *Jupiter* 1976, *Protostars & Planets* 1978, *Asteroids* 1979, *Saturn*, 1984; Author, Over 100 Maj Sci Articles in Var Pubs; NASA Medal for Exceptl Sci Achmt, 1974; Var Biogl Listings.

GEIGER, HAROLD J III oc/Statistician; b/Feb 15, 1952; h/3555 Mendenhall Hoop, #116, Juneau, AL 99801; ba/Juneau, AL; p/Mr and Mrs W M Geiger, Portland, OR; ed/MS, OR St Univ, 1980; BS, So OR Col, 1977; pa/Biometrician, AK Dept of Fish & Game, 1982-; Math Stat, US Dept of Agri, 1980-82; Res Asst, OR St Univ, 1979-80; Am Fisheries Soc; Am Statistical Assn; AAAS; Exec Bd of Alaskan Chapt of Am Statistical Assn; cp/Big Brothers/Big Sisters.

GEISERT, WAYNE FREDERICK oc/College President and Economist; b/Dec

20, 1921; h/409 East College Street, Bridgewater, VA 22812; ba/Bridgewater, VA; m/Ellen Maurine Gish; c/Gregory Wayne, Bradley Kent, Todd Wilfred; p/Fred J and Martha Elizabeth Lauer Geisert; ed/AB in Ec, McPherson Col, 1944; PhD in Ec, NWn Univ, 1951; mil/USNR, Active Duty 1944-46; pa/Inst of Social Sci, Spch & Drama, Hamilton HS, 1946-48; Inst in Acctg & Ec at Kendall Col, 1948-50; Asst in Money & Bkg, NWn Univ, 1950-51; Assoc Prof to Prof of Ec, Dept Hd, Manchester Col, 1951-57; Dean, McPherson Col, 1957-64; Pres, Bridgewater Col, 1964-; Dir, First VA/Planters Bk of Bridgewater; Past Pres, Assn of VA Cols, 1971; Chm & Pres, Shenandoah Val Ednl TV Corp, 1979-84; Trustee, VA Foun for Indep Cols, 1971-; Pres, VA Foun for Indep Cols, 1976-78; Dir of the Coun of Indep Cols in VA; Treas 1982-83, VP 1983-84, Pres 1984-85, Coun of Indep Cols in VA; Conslt, Examr & Report Writer, N Ctl Assn of Cols & Sec'dy Schs, 1960-64; Conslt, Examr & Report Writer, So Assn of Cols & Schs, 1964-; cp/Rotary Intl; Pres, Harrisonburg-Rockingham Co C of C, 1980-81; Chm, U Way Effort, Harrisonburg-Rockingham Co, 1980; r/Ch of the Brethren, Served as Moderator 1973-74, Mem of Gen Bd 1977-82, Chm of Gen Sers Comm of the Gen Bd & Chm of the Pension Bd 1979-82; hon/Author, *Trans Costs in the Theory of Intl Trade* (NWn Univ), & Var Short Articles & Reports; Alumni Cit of Merit, McPherson Col, for Recognized Achmt, Ldrship & Ser, 1974; Cit of Ser, Harrisonburg-Rockingham C of C, 1981; Edr of the Yr Awd, Gtr Madison Inc, 1983; W/W: in Am, in Fin & Indust; in S & SW; Intl W/W in Commun Ser; W/W Hon Soc of Am; DIB.

GELFAND, JANICE ROHRS oc/Product Manager; b/Dec 6, 1951; h/2 Jonathan Road, Cherry Hill, NJ 08003; ba/Philadelphia, PA; m/Jeffrey Marc; c/Joshua Elliott; p/Mr and Mrs F Vernon Rohrs, Lutherville, MD; ed/BS w Hons in Chem, Univ of DE, 1973; Began MBA (Fin), Temple Univ, 1978; pa/Mktg Staff Asst 1973-74, Tech Sales Rep 1974-79, Asst Sales Mgr 1979-80, Prod Mgr of Mktg, Specialty Chems 1980-, Rohm & Haas; Chem Clb of Phila; Cooling Tower Inst; Chem Specialty Mfrs Assn; Am Mgmt Assn; hon/W/W of Am Wom.

GELINAS, WILLIAM PAUL oc/Association Executive; b/Aug 30, 1930; h/42 Woodridge Circle, West Hartford, CT 06107; ba/West Hartford, CT; m/Rita Ann Zielinski; p/William Joseph and Catherine Rae Gelinas; ed/BS in Bus Adm, Univ of Hartford, 1958; MA in Adm & Supvn, Ctl MI Univ, 1975; MPA 1976, DPA 1980, Nova Univ; mil/Served to Col, AUS, 1956-75; pa/Am Heritage Agy, 1954-, Chm of Bd 1980-; Exec Secy, Am Assn Profl Bridal Conslts, 1962-; Dir, Heritage Gen Contractors, Guaranty Bk & Trust Co; Am Soc Public Adm; Resv Ofcrs Assn; cp/Repub; Justice of Peace, W Hartford, 1960-66; Chm, Dist Com Mem Town Com, 1960-66; r/Rom Cath; hon/Parachutist Badge, 1951; Ranger Tab, 1951; Pathfinder Badge, 1952; Sr Parachutist Badge, 1952; Indust Col of Armed Forces, 1972; Command & Gen Staff Col, 1970; War Col, 1976; Army Achmt Med w OLC; Expert Inf-man Badge,

1952; Nat Def Ser Medal, 1952; Armed Forces Expeditionary Medal, 1952; Jumpmaster, 1952; Good Conduct, 1972; Army Resv Components Achmt Medal w Two OLCs, 1980; Armed Forces Resv Medal w Two Ten Yr Devices, 1980; Meritorious Ser Medal, 1980.

GENTILE, ANTHONY oc/Coal Mining Exec; b/Nov 1, 1920, Aquila, Italy; h/4 Normandy Drive, Wintersville, OH 43952; m/Nina A DiScipio; c/Robert H, Anita G Rice, Rita G Dutton, Thomas G; ed/Att'd Ygstown Univ (OH); mil/US Army, 1943-45, 1st Lt; USAR, Ret'd Capt; pa/Co-Owner, Pike Inn Restaurant, Bloomingdale, OH, 1946-52; Asst to Pres, Huberta Coal Co, 1952-55; Gen Mgr, Half Moon Coal Co, 1955-57; Gen Mgr 1957-59, Pres, Chm of Bd, OH River Collieries Co; VPres, Bannock Coal Co; Ptnr, Orchard Hill Devel Co; Ptnr, Rolling Acres Subdivs, Jefferson Co, OH; VPres, Martins Ferry Coal & Dock Co; Pres, Lafferty Trucking Co; VChm, Bd of Trustees, OH Val Hosp, Steubenville, OH; Dir, Mtn St Resources, SLC, UT; Past Pres, Bitner Mining Co, WV; Past Chm, N&G Constrn, Bloomingdale, OH; Past VPres, Twin-Seam Mining Co, Duke Coal Co, Classic Coal Co, WV; Past VPres, Sigel Trucking of Cadiz, OH; Former Bd Mem, Univ of Steubenville, St John's Med Ctr, Steubenville; Mem: Past Mem, US Small Bus Adm Bd of Advrs; Am Inst of Mining & Metal Engrs; Am Mining Cong; OH Acad of Sci; Chm, Mining & Reclamation Coun of Am; Spokesman, Coal Indust on Radio, TV, Newspapers & Trade Mags; hon/Traveled to 9 Countries in Europe w OH Gov James Rhodes on a Trade Mission; Hon'd w Exec Order of OH Commodore, 1965; Civic Ldr Awd, Weirtonion Lodge of Sons & Daughs of Italy, 1967; Citizen of Yr Awd, Wintersville, OH C of C, 1976; Hon DHL, Univ of Steubenville, 1977; Conserv & Reclamation Ser, Jeffersonian Lodge, Steubenville, 1979; W/W: in MW, in Commerce & Indust, in Fin & Indust; Royal Blue Book; Men of Achmt.

GENTRY, JESSE B oc/Criminal Investigator; b/Aug 9, 1942; h/Route #3, Box 124, Cameron, NC 28326; ba/Lillington, NC; m/Marsha Peggy; c/Janie, Jesse R, Joy, Tommy; p/Ethel Gentry, Sebring, FL; ed/Approx 13 Yrs of Ed; mil/AUS, Ret'd; pa/1st Sgt, AUS, 82nd Airborne Div, Ft Bragg, NC, 1958-78; Dpty Sheriff, Harnett Co Sheriffs Dept, 1978-80; Crim Investigator, Harnett Co Sheriffs Dept, 1980-; cp/Masonic Lodge, Schweinfort, Germany; Morelight Lodge #874.

GENTRY, MICHAEL LEE oc/Senior Research Consultant; b/Sep 20, 1942; h/1648 Crestwood Drive, Sierra Vista, AZ 85635; ba/Ft Huachuca, AZ; m/Lois Jean; c/Christopher Michael, Cynthia Lee; p/Mr and Mrs G P Gentry, Durant, OK; ed/BSEE, OK St Univ, 1964; MS, Nuclear Engrg, MIT, 1966; PhD, Univ of AZ, 1971; Att'd, US Army War Col, 1983; pa/Assoc Engr, Boeing Co, 1964-65; Engr, TX Instruments, 1966-67; Engr, CIA, 1971-73; Elect Engr, US Army, 1973-; Cochise Col P-T Instr, 1974-; Armed Forces Communs-Electronics Assn; cp/Chm, Sierra Vista Bd of Adjustments, 1977; Mem, Sierra

Vista Planning & Zoning Comm, 1978-79; hon/Author, Var Tech Papers & Articles, 1970-; W/W: in W, in Technol Today.

GEORGE, D KAY oc/Senior Account Executive; b/Sep 21, 1953; ba/PO Box 297, Brookline, MA 02146; m/Denis J Doyle; c/Scott P Doyle, Shawn B Doyle; ed/BA in Eng, cum laude, Univ of ME, 1975; pa/Sales Mgr, Dunfey Hotels Inc, 1971-80; Sr Account Exec, Time Inc, *Fortune Mag*, 1980-84; cp/Propets, Field Vol 1983; Mobilization for Animals, Fundraiser 1982-83; U Way, Chp (Eastland Hotel) 1974-75; hon/1984 Fortune Sales Achmt Awd; Sales Awd, Dunfey Hyannis Hotel.

GEORGE, JAMES Z oc/Research Physicist; b/Dec 29, 1922; h/15 Oakledge Road, Swampscott, MA 01907; ba/Melrose, MA; m/Winifred R; c/James K, Carolyn A; ed/BS, NEn Univ, 1948; Postgrad, Georgetown Univ, 1951-55; mil/USN; pa/Physicist, Nuclear Physics Radiation Lab, NIH, 1949-51; Physicist, US Med Res Inst, MA Spectrometry Lab, 1951-55; Sr Physicist, Molecularbeam Physics Lab, Nat Co, 1955-65; Res Physicist, Molecularbeams, JG Res & Technol, 1969-; Conslt, USNRL; Am Phy Soc, 1955-; NY Acad of Sci, 1984-; hon/Pubs, *Anal of Cesium Beam Resonator Devel 1984, Cesium Beam Resonator Anal & Eval 1984, Invest of the H/P 5062 Series CBR Electron Multiplier Decay Prob 1982, Devel of a Cesium Beam Clock for Satellite Application*, Others; Several Patents Awd'd; W/W: in Frontier Sci & Technol, in World; Men of Achmt.

GEORGE, JOHN HAROLD oc/Professor of Mathematics; b/Nov 29, 1935; h/63 Black Elk Road, Laramie, WY 82070; ba/Laramie, WY; m/Joanne M; c/Randal, Barbara, Thomas; p/A H George, Braydton, FL; ed/BS, Math, OH St Univ, 1957; MA in Math 1962, PhD in Math 1966, Univ of AL; pa/Sr Scist, NASA George C Marshall Space Flight Ctr, 1957-67; Prof of Math, Univ of WY, 1967-; Consltg, Exxon 1979-, DOE 1972-83, WRI 1983-; Soc of Indust & Applied Math, 1959-; Soc of Petro Engrs, 1982-; hon/Author of 50 Pubs in Control Theory, Chemically Reacting Sys, Statistical Modeling & Viscous Fingering in Oil Reservoirs; Alexander Von Humboldt Sr F'ship, 1973; Vis'g SIAM Lectr, 1975; W/W in W.

GERKING, SHELBY D oc/College Professor and Administrator; b/Dec 1, 1946; h/2526 Mount Shadow Lane, Laramie, WY 82070; ba/Laramie, WY; m/Janet L; c/Shelby Eun; p/Dr and Mrs S D Gerking, Tempe, AZ; ed/AB, Ec, IN Univ, 1968; MBA, Univ of WA, 1970; MA in Ec 1972, PhD in Ec 1975, IN Univ; pa/Asst Prof of Ec, AZ St Univ, 1977-78; Vis'g Asst Prof of Ec, IN Univ, 1977-78; Assoc Prof of Ec, Univ of WY, 1978-82; Prof of Ec 1982-, Dir of Inst for Policy Res 1980-84, Univ of WY; Reg Sci Assn, 1974-; N Am Core Grp, 1982-; Co-Editor, *Intl Reg Sci Review*, 1979-; Am Ec Assn, 1975-; hon/Pubs, "Tribute to William H Miernyk" 1983, "Compensating Differences & Interreg Wage Differentials" 1983, "Factor Rewards & the Intl Migration of Unskilled Labor: A Model w Capital Mobility" 1983, "The WY Economy: Hist Trends & Projections" 1982, Num Others; Henry M Oliver Prize in Ec, Awd'd by IN Univ,

1976; Finalist, PhD Dissertation Competition Sponsored by Reg Sci Assn & Ec Devel Adm, 1975; W/W in W.

GERNANT, ROBERT EVERETT oc/University Professor; b/Dec 3, 1941; h/10117 North Greenview Drive, Mequon, WI 53201; ba/Milwaukee, WI; m/Virginia Marie Kramer; c/Timothy R, Daniel E; p/Everett A Gernant, Geneseo, IL; ed/BS in Geol, Univ of IL-Urbana, 1963; MS in Geol 1965, PhD in Geol 1969, Univ of MI; Att'd Sum Sch, Univ of TX Inst of Marine Sci, 1965; pa/Shell Oil Co, 1963; Humble Oil & Refining Co, 1965; Prof of Geol, Univ of WI-Milwaukee, 1968-; Dir of Ctr for the Improvement of Instrn, Univ of WI-Milwaukee, 1983-; Sigma Xi, Pres of Milwaukee Chapt; Paleontological Soc; Phi Kappa Phi; cp/Water Planning Comm, City of Mequon, WI; Cub Scout Ldr; hon/Author, Sci Jour Articles & Monographs on Paleoecol & Evolutionary Patterns of Fossil Orgs, Also Articles on 19th Cent Photo of Wn US; Gulf Coast Assn Geol Soc's Best Paper Awd, 1967; Ermin Cowles Case Awd for Attainment in Sci Res, 1969; Personalities of the W & MW; W/W: in Frontier Sci & Technol, in W & MW; WI Men of Achmt.

GERSHBEIN, LEON LEE oc/Administrator; b/Dec 22, 1917; h/2836 Birchwood Avenue, Wilmette, IL; ba/Chicago, IL; m/Ruth; c/Joel Dan, Marcia Renee Rabinowitz, Carla Ann; p/Meyer and Ida Shutman Gershbein (dec); ed/BS in Chem 1938, MS in Chem 1939, Univ of Chgo; PhD in Chem, NWn Univ, 1944; mil/Chem Biol Res, NDRC (OSRD); pa/Dist'd Fellow & Res Assoc in Chem 1946, Asst Prof of Biochem 1947-53, Univ of IL Col of Med; Assoc Prof of Biochem, IL Inst Tech, 1953-57; Dir & Pres of NW Inst for Med Res, Dir of Labs of NW Hosp, Adj Prof of Biochem, IL Inst of Technol, 1957-; Am Chem Soc; IL St Acad of Sci; NY Acad of Sci; Soc Exptl Biol & Med; Am Oil Chems' Soc; Am Assn for Cancer Res; Am Fdn for Clin Res; Sigma Xi; Am Phy Soc; Am Assn Clin Chem; Soc Cosmetic Chem; Nat Acad of Clin Biochem; Soc for Applied Spectroscopy; Intl Soc for the Study of Xenobiotics; r/Jewish; hon/Author, Num Pubs in Biochem, Pharm & Oncology in Jours & Pubs of Learned or Profl Socs; Oscar Blumenthal Scholar, 1936-38; Pgh Glass Dist'd Fellow in Chem, 1942-44; Sigma Xi, 1940; Merit Awd, Chgo Chromatography Discussion Grp, 1978; Labcon Awd, 1983; Best Paper Awd, 1983 Annual Meeting, Am Oil Chem Soc; Am Men of Sci; W/W: in IL, in Frontier Sci & Technol; Marquis W/W; Dir of Profls & Res in Cancer.

GETTLE, JUDY ANN oc/Counseling Program Director; b/May 19, 1946; h/158 South Linwood Avenue, Pittsburgh, PA 15205; ba/Pittsburgh, PA; p/Warren and Julia Gettle (dec); ed/BA in Psych, Lebanon Val Col, 1968; EdM in Cnslr Ed, Slippery Rock St Col, 1973; Current Doct Cand in Cnslr Ed, Univ of Pgh; pa/Sci Tchr, N Allegheny Schs, 1968-74; Coor of Adolescent & Chd's Sers, No Communs MH/MR, 1974-80; Dir of Wom's Sers, YWCA of Gtr Pgh, 1980-; Pvt Pract, Mtl Hlth Cnslg, 1975-; AACD; Assn for Cnslr Edrs & Supvrs; Am Mtl Hlth Cnslrs; Presented Wkshop to Assn of Wom in Psych, Nat Conf, Mar 1980; hon/Henry Clay Frick Foun

S'ship, 1970; Cert'd Clin Mtl Hlth Cnslr, 1983; W/W: of Am Wom, in E.

GETTLEMAN, LAWRENCE oc/Dental Research Scientist, Prosthodontist; b/Jun 23, 1940; h/4601 Barnett Street, Metairie, LA 70006; ba/New Orleans, LA; m/Erica; c/Jacquelyn, Michael; p/Charles and Boots Gettleman (dec); ed/BA, Rutgers Univ, 1962; DMD, Harvard Univ Sch of Dental Med, 1966; MSD, St Louis Univ, 1969; mil/USPHS, 1968-70; pa/Phy Testing Lab Dir, Dental Hlth Ctr, USPHS, SF, 1968-70; Asst Prof, Prosthetic Dentistry, Harvard Sch of Dental Med, 1971-76; Assoc Prof & Dept Hd, Biomats, LA St Univ Sch of Dentistry, 1976-80; Sr Staff Assoc, Gulf S Res Inst, 1980-; Fellow, Acad of Dental Mats, Pres-Elect 1983-85; Boston & NO Socs, Am Assn for Dental Res, Pres 1976, 1980; Fellow, Acad of Gen Dentistry; Soc for Biomats; NO Dental Assn, Del; cp/Pontchartrain Shores Civic Assn, Pres 1984-85; Congreg Gates of Prayer, Treas 1982-84; NO Opera Clb, 1977-; Harvard Clb of LA, Schs Com; Public Radio Sta, WWNO, Adv Bd; Jaguar Clb, VP 1983; r/Jewish; hon/Pubs, "Maxillofacial Prosthetics Made from Thermoplastic Chlorinated Polyethylene", 1985, "Changes in Surface Roughness of Restorative Resins in a Bruxing Primate" 1984, "Self-Sanitizing Soft Denture Liners: Paradoxical Results" 1983, "Squamous Cell Carcinoma of the Tongue in a Yg Wom", 1984, "Acute Tissue Irritation of Polysulfide Rubber Impression Mats" 1983, Num Others; Eagle Scout, 1953; Nat Sci Fair, 4th Place, 1958; Milliken Awd, Harvard, 1966; Res Career Devel Awd, NIH, 1976; US Patent #4,432,730.

GETZ, ELIZABETH R oc/Career Consultant; b/Oct 20, 1943; h/2069 Bixler Circle, Decatur, GA 30032; ba/Atlanta, GA; p/Grace Weisheit Getz, Decatur, GA; ed/BFA, Music & Drama, Univ of KS, 1965; pa/Career Conslt, Robbins & Assocs, 1982-; Employee Relats Conslt, Meredith Radio Syndication Ser, 1981-; Communs Expert, WGST Newsradio 92, 1980-82; Commun Relats Dir, Ed Mgmt Corp, 1979-81; Self-Employed, TV, Radio, Concert & Recording Artist, 1965-78; Public Relats Soc of Am; GA Chapt Profl Devel Sect Chp, 1980-; Wom in Communs Inc, GA VP of Devel 1980-; hon/Co-Author, "Atlanta Guide to Street Running," 1978, & Articles for *On the Run Mag, Off Peachtree Mag*, 1978; Cert of Commend, Atlanta Police Dept, 1981; Cert of Apprec, Nat Com Arts for the Handicapped, 1980-81; Named on Commemorative Plaque, Hartsfield Atlanta Intl Airport, 1980; GA Emmy Nom, 1976; W/W in S & SW.

GEVINS, ALAN STUART oc/Brain Scientist; b/Feb 4, 1946; h/15 Napier Lane, San Francisco, CA 94133; ba/San Francisco, CA; p/Michael and Rose Gevins (dec); ed/BS, MIT, 1967; PhD (Cand), CA Inst Asian Studies, 1968-71; pa/Chief Scist & Pres, EEG Sys Lab Inc, 1981-; Dir, EEG Sys Lab, Univ of CA Sch of Med, 1971-81; Sr Sys Analyst, Berkeley Sci Labs, 1969-71; AAAS, Soc Biol Psychi; Am Epilepsy Soc; IEEE; Am EEG Soc; Soc Neurosci; Soc Psychophysiological Res; Neuropsych Soc; NY Acad Scis; hon/Sr Author, Over 50 Pubs in Sci Jours on Computer Anal of Human Brain Elect Activity & Human

Higher Cognitive Functions; Regents Prof, Univ of CA-Riverside, 1981; Grant Recip, NIH, Ofc of Nav Res, NSF; AF Ofc of Sci Res; Consltg Editor to Num Sci Jours.

GHAFFARI, AVIDEH BEHROUZ oc/Interior Designer, Decorator; b/Apr 17, 1943; h/425 East 58th Street, New York, NY 10022; ba/New York, NY; m/Abbas; c/Narsi, Borzou; p/Zabih and Homa; sp/Mahmoud and Zari; ed/BA, Art & Design Sch, Glasco, Scotland, 1966; Fdr & Pres, Polydecor Ltd, 1962-68; Pres, Pakab Co, 1963-75; Fdr & Pres, Avideco Co Inc, 1979-; Dir & Secy Treas, Matavi Inc, 1982-; Nat Assn Female Execs; Am Soc Interior Designers; Intl Soc Interior Designers; hon/Recip Awd of Merits, Imperial Govt of Iran, 1969; Marquis W/W of Am Wom.

GHETTI, BERNARDINO oc/Professor of Pathology and Psychiatry; b/Mar 28, 1941; h/1124 Frederick South Drive, Indianapolis, IN 46260; ba/Indianapolis, IN; m/Caterina; c/Chiara, Simone; p/Getulio Ghetti and Iris Mugnetti, Pisa, Italy; ed/Maturità, Liceo Classico, 1959; MD, Univ of Pisa, 1966; ca/Fellow, Psychi, Univ of Pisa, Italy, 1966-70; Fellow, Neuropathol 1970-73, Resident in Pathol 1973-75, Resident in Neuropathol 1975-76, Albert Einstein Col of Med; Asst Prof of Pathol 1976-78, Assoc Prof of Pathol & Psychi 1978-83, Prof of Pathol & Psychi 1983-, IN Univ Sch of Med; pa/Am Assn of Neuropathols; Soc for Neurosci; Assn for Res in Nervous & Mtl Disorders; Am Soc for Cell Biol; Sigma Xi; Pub'd Num Articles in Profl Jours, 1967-; hon/Silver Medal, Univ of Pisa for MD Deg, cum laude; W/W: in Frontier Sci & Technol, in World.

GHIL, MICHAEL oc/Research Scientist; b/Jun 10, 1944; h/110 Bleecker Street, New York, NY 10012; ba/New York, NY; m/Michèle R J Denizot-Ghil; c/Emmanuel Alexander; p/Louis and Ilona Cernat, Bat-Yam, Israel; ed/BSc (cum laude) 1966, MSc 1971, Technio, Israel Inst of Technol; MS 1973, PhD 1975, NY Univ; mil/Israeli Navy, 1967-71; pa/From Res Asst to Instr, Technio, Israel Inst of Technol, 1966-71; Asst/Assoc Res Scist, Courant Inst, NY Univ, 1971-75; Nat Acad Sci/NRC Res Assoc, NASA Goddard Inst Space Studies, 1975-76; Res Asst Prof of Math 1976-79, Res Assoc Prof of Atmospheric Sci 1979-82, Res Prof of Applied Math & Atmospheric Sci 1982-, Courant Inst; Fac Res Assoc, NASA Goddard Lab Atmospheric Sci, 1977-; Conslt, NOAA Nat Meteorological Ctr, Wash DC, 1982-; Am Meteorological Soc; Am Geophy Union; Am Math Soc; Soc of Indust & Applied Math; r/Jewish; hon/Editor, *Dynamic Meteorology: Data Assimilation Methods* 1981, *Turbulence & Predictability in Geophy Fluid Dynamics & Climate Dynamics* 1984; Author, *Topics in GFD & Climate Dynamics* 1985; Over 50 Res & Review Articles (1971-); Vis'g Prof, Intl Meteorological Inst (Stockholm, Sweden) 1978, Ecole Normale Supérieure (Paris) 1979, Istituto Fis Atmos (Rome) 1981, Intl Sch Physics ("E Fermi," Varenna, Italy) 1983; W/W in Frontier Sci & Technol.

GHOLSTON, HELEN ALBERTA oc/English Teacher; b/May 13, 1923; h/5322 Hilltop Drive, San Diego, CA 92114; ba/San Diego, CA; m/Andrew Jackson; c/Andrea, Juanita Smith, Corale Cobb, Wendy Holly, Michael, Andrew Jr; p/Albert and Helen McIlwain (dec); ed/AA, San Diego Commun Cols, 1973; BA in Eng w Distn 1976, MA in Ed 1980, San Diego Univ; pa/Microfilm Operator, San Diego City Civil Ser, 1957-58; Engaged in Real Est, 1961-70; Tutor, EEO Prog, San Diego Commun Cols, 1971-75; San Diego City Schs, 1977-; Eng Tchr 1979-, Dept Chm 1980-82, Abraham Lincoln Sr HS; Immediate Past Mem of Textbook Com, San Diego City Schs; NCTE; Assn Supvn & Curric Devel; Alumni Assn, San Diego St Univ; Am Bus Wom's Assn; cp/Browning Soc; Nat Coun of Negro Wom; hon/Author of Articles & Curric Mats, City Col, San Diego City Schs; Achmt Awd, Black Communs Ctr, San Diego St Univ, 1978, 1979; W/W of Am Wom.

GHOSH, DILIP KUMAR oc/Professor; b/Feb 6, 1947; h/206 Rabbit Run Drive, Cherry Hill, NJ 08003; ba/Philadelphia, PA; m/Shyamasri; c/Dipasri, Debasri; p/Sarat Chandra Ghosh (dec); Gouri Ghosh, Calcutta, India; sp/Satindra Nath and Usharani Dasgupta (dec); ed/BA, Ec; MA, Ec, 1973; PhD, Ec, 1976; pa/Assoc Prof Fin, Temple Univ, 1981-; Asst Prof Ec, Rutgers Univ, 1977-81; Asst Prof, OH St Univ & Denison Univ, 1975-77; Mem: Am Ec Assn; So Ec Assn; Royal Ec Soc; Asian Ec Assn; Australian Ec Assn; Smithsonian Instn; Bengali Cultural Soc; hon/Author of 4 Books: *Microec Anal; The Global Polits of Gold; Trade Distortions & Growth; Intl Trade & the Third World Ec Devel*; Contbr, Num Articles in Profl Jours; Recip, Quinlan Meml Medal; Ford Foun Grantee; Recip, Rutgers Univ Res Coun Grant; W/W in E.

GHYLIN, CLAIR oc/Attorney; b/Feb 10, 1929; h/3753 Bamboo Court, Concord, CA 94520; ba/Concord, CA; m/Helen; c/Craig, Chris, Clay; ed/LLB 1950, JD 1958, Univ of ND; mil/USAF, Capt; pa/Asst Atty Gen, ND, 1950-52; Pract of Law in Bismark, ND, 1955-56; Var Legal Positions w Standard Oil Co of CA in Rocky Mtn Sts & CA, 1956-; Pres, Am Assn of Petro Landmen, LA, 1970; Chm, Publichands, Wn Oil & Gas Assn, 1981-82; cp/Order of Coif, Blue Key Ser Frat; Bd of Dirs, ARC, Golden Gate Chapt, SF, 1980-82; r/Prot; Hon/W/W: in Am, in CA, in Am Law.

GIANNINI, A JAMES oc/Psychiatrist; b/Jun 11, 1947; h/2935 Whispering Pines, Canfield, OH 44915; ba/Youngstown, OH; m/Judith Ludvik; c/Juliette Nicole; p/Matthew and Grace Nistri Giannini, Younstown, OH; sp/Georgie and Virginia Ludvik, Fairfax, VA; ed/BS, Youngstown St Univ, 1970; MD, Univ of Pgh, 1974; Postdoct Cert in Psychi, Yale Univ, 1976; pa/Chief Res Asst, PA Gov's Justice Comm, 1974-75; Assoc Prof Psychi 1978-, Prog Dir 1980-, NE OH Med Col; VChm, Mahoning City Mtl Hlth Bd, 1982-; Assoc Prof Psychi, OH St Univ, 1983-; Mem: AMA, 1972-; Am Psychi Assn, 1975-; Acad Clin Psychi, 1976; Acad of Psychosomatic Med, 1970; Fellow, NJ Acad of Med, 1978-; Soc Neurosci, 1979-; Brit Brain Soc, 1979-; European Neurological Soc, 1979-; Fellow, Am Col Clin Pharm, 1983-; r/Rom Cath; hon/Author, *Psychi, Psychogenic & Psychosomatic Disorders*, 1979; *Neurologic, Neurogenic & Neuropsychi Disorders*, 1982; *Overdose & Detoxification Emers*, 1983; *Prins of Biol Psychi*, 1983; Over 46 Articles Pub'd in Profl Jours; Recip, Upjohn Awd, 1974; James Early Awd, Univ of Pgh, 1974; Yale Tchg Awd, 1976; Hon TN Squire, 1976; Fair Oaks Res Awd, 1979; Brit Med Assn Bronze Awd, 1982; W/W: in Frontier Sci & Technol, in MW, Among Intells, in Am Cols & Univs; Men of Sci; Men of Achmt.

GIBBONS, JOEL CLARKE oc/Economist; b/Apr 30, 1942; h/143 South Hawthorne Avenue, Elmhurst, IL 60126; ba/Chicago, IL; m/Crispina M; c/Eileen Hope, Marcus Aurelius; Hugh Montifolca; p/Francis J and Helen (dec) Gibbons; ed/BS w Hons, Georgetown Univ, 1964; PhD in Math, NWn Univ, 1970; MBA 1974, PhD in Bus 1979, Univ of Chgo; pa/Asst Prof of Math, Chgo St Univ, 1971-75; Lectr in Mgmt Sci 1975-76, Res Assoc 1978-79, Univ of Chgo; Asst Prof of Economics, IL Inst of Technol, 1976-82; 2nd VP & Res Analyst, Am Nat Bk, 1982; Am Economic Assn; Am Math Soc; Intl Assn of Energy Economists; hon/Pubs, "One-Dimensional Basic Sets in the Three-Sphere" 1972, "Finite Partitions of Spheres" 1982, "The Optimal Durability of Fixed Capital When Demand is Uncertain" 1983; Beta Gamma Sigma, 1975.

GIBBS, JACQUELINE oc/Entrepreneur; b/Mar 12, 1942; h/811 York, #109, Oakland, CA 94610; ba/Oakland, CA; p/George W and Isma Gibbs-Howard (dec); ed/BS Math & Sci, TN A&I St Univ, 1962; Study Tour of Europe & Brit Schs, Univ of CA-Santa Barbara, 1972; MA Adm & Supvn, CA St Univ-Hayward, 1973; 1st Yr Acctg Courses, LaSalle Ext Univ, 1977; Attends Average of 5 Annual Tax Sems, 1975-; pa/Proprietor & Operator, Gibbs' Bkkpg & Tax Ser, 1978-82 & 1984-; Co-Pres, Digital Acctg Inc, 1983-84; Completed & Passed, IRS Enrolled Agts Exam, 1978; Math Tchr, Peralta Col Dist, 1974-83; Tax Preparation, 1970-78; Tax Preparer, Tax Corp of Am, 1970-75; Tax Examr, IRS, 1967; Math Tchr, Berkeley Unified Sch Dist, 1967-81; Math Tchr, KC, KS Sch Dist, 1962-67; Mem: Nat Assn of Accts; Nat Assn of Enrolled Agts; Bay Area Wom Entrepreneurs; Consumer Affairs Tax Preparer Prog; Coalition of 100 Black Wom; Nat Assn of Tax Consultors; Nat Notary Assn; CA Assn of Enrolled Agts; Life Mem, St Orgr, Nat Coun of Negro Wom; Nat Assn of Female Execs; cp/Participant in Ldrship Lab, Bay Area Lrng Ctr, Oakland; Sponsor, W Campus Berkeley HS Girls' Clb; Co-Sponsor, Parents' Boosters Clb; Asst Dir, W Campus Berkeley HS Right-to-Read Prog, 1974; Chm, Berkeley Tchrs Assn Negotiating Com, 1974; r/Prot; hon/Outstg Sec'dy Tchr in Berkeley, 1974; Cert of Ldrship Devel, Cornell Univ, 1977; Sponsorship Awd, Pearl S Buck Foun, 1976; Outstg Sec'dy Edr of Am; W/W in W.

GIBBS, S JULIAN oc/Dental Radiologist, Radiology Professor; b/Apr 1, 1932; h/784 Greeley Drive, Nashville, TN 37205; ba/Vanderbilt Univ, Nashville, TN; m/Emily (Starnes); c/Phillip, Stephen, Julie; p/Inez M Gibbs, Sulligent, AL; sp/Lilla Starnes, Avondale

Ests, GA; ed/DDS, Emory Univ, 1956; PhD, Univ of Rochester, 1969; Cert'd, Am Bd of Oral & Maxillofacial Radiol, 1981; mil/USAF, Dental Corp, 1955-59, Capt; pa/Pvt Pract, Vernon, AL, 1959-63; Grad Student Fellow in Dental Res 1963-68, Asst Prof Radiol & Dental Res 1968-70, Univ of Rochester; Asst Prof Radiol & Dentistry 1970-76, Assoc Prof Radiol 1976-, Vanderbilt Univ; Mem: Am Col of Radiol; Pres 1979-80, Am Acad of Dental Radiol; VPres 1984-85, Am Bd of Oral & Maxillofacial Radiol; Am Dental Assn; Radiological Soc of Am; Assn of Univ Radiols; Hlth Physics Soc; Radiation Res Soc; Am Assn of Physicists in Med; Intl Assn for Dental Res; cp/BSA; r/U Meth; hon/Contbr to: The Phy Basis of Med Imaging, 1981; Dental Radiol, Principles & Interpretation, 1982; Digital Radiol, A Focus on Clin Utility, 1982; Author & Co-Author, Over 30 Papers in Sci Pubs; Over 50 Papers & Exhibs at Nat & Intl Meetings; Order of Arrow 1978, Wood Badge 1978, Scouters Tng Awd 1978, Dist Awd of Merit 1980, God & Ser 1983, BSA; W/W; W/W in SE.

GIBORI, GEULA oc/Associate Professor; b/Aug 8, 1945; h/8932 Pottawatami, Skokie, IL 60076; ba/Chicago, IL; m/Shimon; c/Gil, Ilan, Ron; p/Sabah Derzie, Tel-Aviv, Israel; ed/BS, Lebanese Univ, Beirut, 1967; MS, Sorbonne Univ, Paris, 1968; PhD, Tel-Aviv Univ, Israel, 1973; pa/Instr, Tel-Aviv Univ, 1972-73; Postdoct Fellow, Case Wn Resv Univ, 1973-75; Postdoct Fellow, Univ of MI-Ann Arbor, 1975-76; Asst Prof 1976-80, Assoc Prof 1980-, Univ of IL; Soc for the Study of Reprodn; Endocrine Soc; AAAS; Am Physiol Soc; Soc for Study of Fertility, England; r/Jewish; hon/Author, 8 Book Chapts, 40 Articles to Profl Jours, 37 Abstracts; Fulbright Grantee, 1973-74; CNRS Grantee, 1968-69.

GIBSON, CURTIS A oc/Life Support Systems Engineer; b/Nov 5, 1929; h/2806 Oxford Drive, Springfield, OH 45506; ba/Wright-Patterson AFB, OH; p/Frank Z and Helen W Cox Gibson (dec); ed/CHE, Univ of Cinc, 1952; PhD (Rel), DD (Hon), Universal Life Ch; pa/Life Support Sys Engr 1970-79, Aircraft Sys Engr 1979-, Mech Engr 1959-70, Chem Engr 1956-59, USAF; Chem Engr, Sylvania Elect Prods Co, 1952-54; Am Def Preparedness Assn; Intl Acad Profl Bus Execs; AF Assn; cp/BSA; r/Luth; hon/Am Biogl Inst; Intl Biogl Assn; Silver Beaver Awd, BSA; W/W: in MW, in World, in Aviation & Aerospace; Intl W/W of Intells; DIB; Men Achmt; Ernest Kay's Personal Hall of Fame, Commun Ldrs Am; 2,000 Notable Ams; ABI Bk of Yr; Am Registry.

GIBSON, ELIZABETH PAGE oc/Teacher; b/1947; m/Robert Kennedy Christopher; c/Robert Kennedy Christopher; p/Milby Jr and Elizabeth Page Gibson (dec); ed/Grad, Bennettville HS; Exec Secretarial Deg w Hons, Columbia Comml Sch; Grad, Col Transfer Prog, Greenville Tech Ed Col; pa/Tchr, Florence, SC, 4 Yrs; cp/Magna Charta Dames; Colonial Order of the Crown; r/Meth Ch; Plays Organ & Piano in 1st Meth Ch in Florence, SC.

GIBSON, G RUTH oc/University Professor, Vocational Special Needs Coordinator; b/Oct 13, 1927; h/1185 Winterberry Court, Lawrenceville, GA 30245; ba/Atlanta, GA; m/James Leslie; c/1st Capt David Priser, Joseph Priser, Anne Wilson, Micheal; ed/PhD, Ednl Ldrship in Voc Ed, GA St Univ, 1981; EdSp, Guid Cnslg, Univ of GA, 1972; EdM, Guid & Cnslg, W GA Col; BS, Sec'dy Ed, Manchester Col; 1949; pa/Asst Prof, Spec Needs Coor, Voc Dept, GA St Univ, 1975-; CVAE Coor for Disadvantaged Students, No Gwinnett HS, 1969-75; Prog Dir, YWCA, 1966-67, 1956-59; PE Tchr, Coach, Burlington (NJ) 1950-51, Manatee Co (FL) 1959-64, Coesse (IN) 1949-50; Cnslr, Kappa Delta Pi, GA St Univ, 1980-; Chp, Intl Convocation, Kappa Delta Pi, 1982-84; VP, NAVESNP/AVA, 1979-80; Ed Comm, GA Hosp & Travel Assn, 1981-85; Res & Devel Com, SN/AVA, 1982-84; Other Nat & Local Coms & Ofcs; Phi Kappa Phi; Life Mem, AVA; GVA; Life Mem, Kappa Delta Pi; Omicron Gamma; NAVESNP; GAVESNP; hon/Pubs, "Effect of CVAE & Wk Experience on Basic Employmt Skills & Wk Attitude of Disadvantaged HS Yth" 1981, "New Kid on Block, Yth Clb for Spec Needs Students" 1977, "Guide for Adm & Implementation of CVAE Prog in GA", 1983, "CVAE Coors' Manual" 1982, "Admrs' Guide for CVAE" & "Guide for Student Documentation" 1977-78; Editor, Spec Needs Jour; Edit Bd, NAVESNP Jour, 1980-84; Nat Dist'd Dissertation Awd, Kappa Delta Pi, 1982; VOCA Hon Life Mem, 1977; GA Voc Guid Tchr of Yr, 1975; W/W in S & SW; Wom Admrs in Voc Ed; Intl W/W.

GIBSON, LULU BARRY oc/Educator; b/1931; m/J P Dowd Jr; c/J P III, Elizabeth R; p/John Milby and Elizabeth Page (dec) Gibson; ed/Grad, Bennettsville HS; Att'd Winthrop Col, Two Yrs; Grad, St Andrews Univ; ME, Univ of SC; Presently Wkg on Doct, Univ of SC; cp/Hereditary Mem, Magna Charta Dames; Pres, SC CEC; Jr Charity Leag; r/Meth; hon/Called to Wash DC, by Pres Carter, Ford & Reagan to Discuss Plans in SC for Better Ednl Methods; W/W in Outstg Yg Am Wom; The Hereditary Register; Notable Ams of the Bicent.

GIBSON, THOMAS RICHARD oc/Plant Manager; b/1943; m/Susan Dianne Miller; ed/Att'd Mifford Col; pa/Plant Mgr of Allied Chems, 1973-; cp/Hereditary Mem, Most Noble Order of the Garter.

GIDDINGS, C BLAND oc/Nuclear Physician; b/Dec 28, 1915; h/1820 East Jensen Street, Mesa, AZ 85203; m/Elizabeth Ann Kiefer (dec); Dr Lucile Layton; c/Dr Luther Val, Thomas Crandall; p/Dr Luther E (dec) and Berneice Chipman Crandall Giddings, American Fork, UT; ed/Deg in Chem & Pre-Med/Cello Studies, Brigham Yg Univ, 1938; PhD in Biochem, MD, Univ of Cinc, 1940s; Intern, Seattle; Studies in Nuclear Med, Oak Ridge, TN, 1950; Bd Cert, Am Bd of Nuclear Med, 1973; Bd Cert in Pathol, 1955; mil/Served in the USAF, San Antonio, TX, 1953-55; pa/Nuclear Med Phys in Pvt Pract, Mesa, AZ, 1973-; Family Genealogist; Cellist; Former Faculty Mem of LA St Univ Med Sch, NO; Charter Mem, Soc of Nuclear Med; Fellow, Am Col of Nuclear Med; Pres, AZ Nuclear Med Phys; Fellow, Am Col of Pathols; Fellow, Am Col of Med Imaging; Dist'd Fellow, Am Col of Nuclear Med; cp/Fdg Mem, Pres 1967-68, Mesa Fine Arts Assn; Co-Fdr 1969, VP, AZ Cello Soc; Pres, Mesa Symp Orch (Formerly Sun Val Symph Orch), 1965-; hon/Artist of the Yr Awd, 1972; Awd of Apprec for 25 Yrs of Dedicated Ser, Mesa Symph Orch, 1982; W/W in W; Commun Ldrs & Noteworthy Ams.

GIDDINGS, J CALVIN oc/Professor of Chemistry; b/Sep 26, 1930; h/3978 Emigration Canyon, Salt Lake City, UT 84108; ba/Salt Lake City, UT; c/Steven B, Michael C; p/Luther W (dec) and Berneice Crandall Giddings, American Fork, UT; ed/BS, Brigham Yg Univ, 1952; PhD, Univ of UT, 1954; pa/Asst Prof 1957-59, Assoc Prof 1959-62, Res Prof 1962-66, Prof of Chem 1966-, Univ of UT-SLC; hon/Pubs incl, Chem, Man, & Envir Change, 1973, Plus Over 250 Others; Editor, Our Chem Envir 1972, Author, Dynamics of Chromatography 1965; ACS Awd in Chromatography & Electrophoresis, 1967; NE Lectureship Awd, Venable Lectr, NC, 1969; UT Awd, Local Sect of Am Chem Soc, 1970; Foster Lectures, SUNY-Buffalo, 1971; ROMCOE Awd, Outstg Envir Achmt in Ed, 1973; Fulbright Grant, Cayetano Heredia Univ, Lima, Peru, 1974; Tswett Medal in Chromatography, Dow-Bucknell Lectr, 1978; Stephen Dal Nogare Chromatography Awd, 1979; Univ of UT Dist'd Res Awd, 1979; Russian Sci Coun Chromatography Awd, 1979; ACS Awd in Analytical Chem, 1980; Phillips Lecture Series, Univ of Pgh, 1980; Banks Lecture (IA St), Kolthoff Lectures (Univ of MN), 1982.

GIDDINGS, LUTHER VAL oc/Evolutionary Geneticist; b/Apr 21, 1953; h/2011 McCausland, St Louis, MO 63143; ba/St Louis, MO; p/Crandal Bland Giddings, Mesa, AZ; ed/BS, Zool, Brigham Yg Univ, 1975; MS, Genetics 1977, PhD, Genetics 1980, Univ of HI; pa/Grad Res Asst in Genetics, Univ of HI, 1975-80; Postdoct Res Assoc in Biol 1980-83, Asst Prof of Biol (Acting) 1983-, Wash Univ; Soc for the Study of Evolution; Genetics Soc of Am; AAAS; Am Soc of Naturalists; Sierra Clb; Nature Conservancy; Arnold White Water Soc; hon/Author of Num Pubs in Profl Jours, 1974-; High Hons Grad, Hons Prog, Brigham Yg Univ, 1975; NIH Pre-doct Trainee in Genetics, 1975-78.

GIESSLER, EMILY SWEARINGEN oc/Senior Sales Director; b/Oct 19, 1940; h/422 North Third Street, Decatur, IN 46733; ba/Same; c/James Hugh Engle, Melinda Sue Engle; p/Milton and Lucile Swearingen, Decatur, IN; ed/BA, TX Christian Univ, 1962; MA, St Francis Col, 1966; pa/Dir, Ed & Ser, Am Cancer Soc, 1962-63; Tchr, N Adams Commun Schs, 1963-79; Self-Employed w Mary Kay Cosmetics, 1978-; Tri Kappa Sorority, Pres 1968-69; IPA; Nat Assn of Female Execs; r/1st U Meth Ch, Treas 1982-; hon/Miss Go-Give-Mary Kay Cosmetics, 1982; W/W of Am Wom.

GIESTING, WALTER EDWARD oc/Executive; b/Jul 16, 1918; h/10115 Parkwood Drive #2, Cupertino, CA 95014; ba/Same; m/Jeanne Fox; c/Walter E Jr, Judith R Graham; p/Walter E and Mae Brinkman Giesting (dec); ed/BS, Commerce, Xavier Univ, 1940; Att'd

Grad Sch of Bus, Univ of TX, 1971; mil/ AUS, Capt Ordnance 1942-46; pa/Var Mgmt Positions 1941-76, VP of Pacific Div 1966-71, NCR Corp; Pres, NCR de Baja CA, Mexico, 1966-76; Pres, Unitech Intl, 1976-; Sales & Mktg Execs Nat Assn of Accts; World Tech Assocs; Univ Clbs; cp/Rotary Intl; hon/Author, *Career Management for Today's Executive*, 1977; Bd of Dirs, Menlo Sys Inc, 1976-; Bd Dirs, Foothill Bk, 1983-; Past Pres, Los Altos Golf & Country Clb, 1979; W/W: in World, in Fin & Indust, in W; Intl Biogl Centre.

GIFFORD, CHARLES STEWART oc/University Educator; b/Jun 26, 1947; h/1006 Chimney Wood Lane, New Orleans, LA 70126; ba/New Orleans, LA; m/June West; p/Charles L and Dorothy A Gifford, Waukesha, WI; ed/ AA, Mt San Antonio Col, 1967; BA, Milton Col, 1970; EdM 1976, EdD 1976, Univ of GA; pa/Tchr at St Jerome Sch, 1970-72; Tchr/Coach, Athens Acad, 1972-74; Res Asst/Assoc, Univ of GA-Athens 1975-77; Asst Prof 1977-80, Dept Chm 1979-81, Assoc Prof 1980-, Acting Dean 1981-, Univ of NO; Assn for Supvn & Curric Devel, Mem & Presenter at 6 Nat Confs; IRA, Mem & Presenter at 2 World, 4 Intl & 6 Reg Confs; LA Assn for Supvn & Curric Devel, Mem & Conf Presenter; LA Rdg Assn, Coun Pres, 4 Conf Presentations; Presenter, Nat Sci Tchrs Assn Annual Conv, Nat Assn of Indep Schs Annual Conf, LA Phy Therapist Assn Annual Conf, So Assn of Cols & Schs Annual Conv, Am Assn of Sch Admrs Annual Conf, LA Med Technologists Annual Conf, LA Luth Schs Annual Conf, Nat Assn of Gifted Chd Annual Conv, NCTM Annual Conf; Nat Sch Bds Assn Conf; hon/Pubs, *Trends & Issues Affecting Curric* (Col Textbook), *Test-Taking Made Easier* (HS Textbook); Author, Over 25 Articles Pub'd in *The Am Sch Bd Jour*, *Phi Delta Kappan*, *The Kappa Delta Pi Record*, *Contemp Ed*, *Rdg Improvement*, *Rdg Horizons*; Phi Delta Kappa; Kappa Delta Pi; Featured on Radio & TV Interviews; Men Achmt; Outstg Yg Men of Am; W/W in S & SW; Personalities of S.

GILBERT, DANIEL LEE oc/Physiologist; b/Jul 2, 1925; h/10324 Dickens Avenue, Bethesda, MD 20814; ba/ Bethesda, MD; m/Claire; c/Raymond Louis; p/Mrs Louis Gilbert, Morristown, NJ; ed/AB, Drew Univ, 1948; MS, St Univ of IA, 1950; PhD, Univ of Rochester, 1955; mil/AUS, 1943-45; pa/ Instr, Univ of Rochester, 1955-59; Instr 1956-59, Asst Prof 1959-60, Albany Med Col; Asst Prof 1960-62, Assoc Prof 1962-63, Jefferson Med Col; Res Physiol 1962-, Hd of Sect on Cellular Biophysics 1963-71, Nat Inst Neurol & Communicative Diseases & Stroke, NIH; Fellow, AAAS; Am Chem Soc; Am Inst Biol Sci; Am Physiol Soc; Am Soc Pharm & Exptl Therapeutics; Biophy Soc; Corp of Marine Biol Lab; Intl Soc Study Origin of Life; NY Acad Sci; Soc Exptl Biol & Med; Soc Neurosci; Soc Gen Physiol; Undersea Med Soc; Sigma Xi; hon/Contbr of Articles to Profl Books & Jours; Editor of Book, *Oxygen & Living Processes*, 1981; Bowditch Lectr of the Am Physiol Soc, 1964; Purple Heart, AUS, 1945.

GILBERT, LYNN TENDLER oc/ Executive; b/Apr 26, 1938; h/11 Sigma Place, Riverdale, NY 10471; ba/New York, NY; c/Jay Austin, Jo Allison; p/ William D and Henrietta Glicksman Tendler (dec); ed/BA, Math, Univ of FL-Gainesville, 1959; Att'd Skidmore Col, 1955-56; pa/Pres, Co-Fdr, Gilbert Tweed Assoc Inc (Exec Search Firm), 1972-; Dunhill Pers, 1971-72, 1964-67; Pers Sers, 1962-64; Jobs Unltd, 1959-62; Nat Assn of Corp & Profl Recruiters, VP, Dir 1983-, Chair of NY Chapt 1982-, Mem 1981-; Intl Assn of Pers Wom, 1981-; cp/Spuyten Duyvil Inf, Trustee 1982-, Mem Adv Bd 1975-, Pres & Chp 1973-75; Treas 1971-73; Sigma Place/Palisade Ave Neighborhood Assn, Treas 1976-; Miami Bch Coun for the Arts, Treas 1961-63; Acorns Civic Theatre, Treas 1960-64; hon/Pub'd in AMA Handbook: *The Selection, Eval, Recruitment & Retention of Sales & Mktg Pers* 1983, *Bdrm Reports* 1981-82, *Ambassador Mag* 1977, Dow Jones-Irwin Mktg Handbook; W/W: of Am Wom, in E.

GILBERT, RICHARD GENE oc/ Research Plant Pathologist; b/Dec 3, 1935; h/623 East 3rd Street, Grandview, WA 98930; ba/Prosser, WA; c/Mark Dean, Jill Susanne Gilbert Matteson; p/ Martha Gilbert, Pueblo, CO; ed/BS Phy & Biol Scis 1961, MS Botany & Plant Pathol 1963, PhD Botany & Plant Pathol 1964, CO St Univ; mil/AUS, 1954-57; pa/Postdoctoral Position, Plant Pathol Dept, Univ of CA-Berkeley, 1964-65; Res Microbiologist (Beltsville, MD) 1965-70, Res Microbiologist (Phoenix, AZ) 1970-82, Res Plant Pathol (Prosser, WA) 1982-, USDA-ARS; Am Phytopathological Soc; Am Soc of Agronomy; Soil Sci Soc of Am; Phi Theta Kappa; Phi Kappa Phi; Sigma Xi; cp/Kiwanis; r/Unity; hon/Author, Num Res Pubs in Tech Jours; Recip, Unit Awd, USDA, 1973; NDEA Grad F'ship, 1961-64; Acad S'ship, Undergrad, 1959-61; W/W in W.

GILBERT, RUSSELL JAMES oc/ Senior Project Manager; b/Sep 18, 1952; h/6361 Rancho Mission Road #8, San Diego, CA 92108; ba/San Diego, CA; p/James and Veronica Gilbert, Port Washington, NY; ed/BS, Mgmt, St Johns Univ, 1974; MBA, Grad Studies, C W Post Col, 1975; JD, Wn St Univ Col of Law, 1980; pa/Sr Sys Analyst, Gen Dynamics, Electronics Div, 1977-; Sys Analyst, Leviton Mfg, 1976-77; Planning Control Analyst, Grumman Aerospace Corp, 1974-76; Nat Mgmt Assn, 1977-; Am Prodn Inventory Control Soc, 1979; Delta Theta Phi, Law Frat; Tau Kappa Epsilon, Intl Frat; hon/ Pubs, *Planning Mgmt Info Sys* 1981, *Mfg & Mat Control Systems for an Integrated Envir* 1978, Parts Labor Hist 1981, *Automated Data Collection Utilizing Bar Code Technol* 1984; Lions Clb Intl Awd, 1981; Gen Dynamics Cost Reduction Proposal ($168,000), 1978; W/W in Fin & Indust.

GILBERT, RUTH LOUISE LUYSTER oc/Manager of Tax Research and Planning; b/Dec 27, 1933; h/503 Gatehall Lane, Ballwin, MO 63011; ba/St Louis, MO; c/David Donald, Steven Craig; p/Alonzo Boyer and Eva Ella Mills Luyster (dec); ed/BS in Acctg, summa cum laude, Univ of MO-St Louis, 1972; CPA, MO; pa/Mgr of Tax Res & Planning, Mallinckrodt Inc, 1977-; Sr Tax Acct, Rubin, Brown, Gornstein & Co, 1975-77; Staff Tax Acct, Touche Ross & Co, 1973-75; Am Inst of CPAs; MO Soc of CPAs, St Louis Chapt Taxation Com 1976-77, Secy 1977-78, 1978-79, 1979-80, 1980-81, St Taxation Com 1980-81, 1981-82, Secy 1982-83, 1983-84, Editor of Column "Tax Talk" in Soc's Newspaper *the Asset* 1983-84, St Louis Chapt Cont'g Profl Ed Com 1976-77, 1977-78, Secy 1978-79, Chm 1979-80, St Cont'g Profl Ed Com 1979-80, 1980-81; Nat Assn of Accts, Asst Dir & Mem of Attendance Com 1975-76, 1976-77, Acquisition Com 1979-80, Relats Com 1979-80, 1980-81, Dir of Meetings Com 1981-82, Inst of Mgmt Acctg Com 1981-82, Spec Activs Com 1981-82, 1982-83, 1983-84, Dir of Cert of Mgmt Acctg Progs 1982-83, Meetings Com 1982-83, Dir of Socio-Ec Prog 1983-84; hon/Elected to Beta Gamma Sigma, VP 1972-73; Beta Alpha Psi, 1972; Univ Scholar, 1972; Psi Theta Kappa, 1971; W/W: of Am Wom, in Am Cols & Univs; World's W/W of Wom;

GILBERT, VIRGINIA oc/Assistant Professor of English, Writer, Photographer; b/Dec 19, 1946; h/3286 Fair Street, Lincoln, NE 68503; ba/Lincoln, NE; p/Blair and Florence Gilbert, Ingleside, IL; ed/BA in Eng, IA Wesleyan Col, 1969; MFA in Creat Writing-Poetry, Univ of IA, 1971; Further Study in Creat Writing, Univ of UT, 1974-75; pa/Asst Prof of Eng, Dir of the Creat Writing Prog & Rdg Series, AL A&M Univ, 1980-, (On Leave); ESL Instr, Col of Lake Co, IL, 1979-80; ESL Instr, Dept of Def Sub-Contracts, Iran, 1976-79; Tchg Fellow in Creat Writing, Univ of UT, 1974-75; Instr, Peace Corps, Korean Mid Sch Eng Prog, 1971-73; Sigma Tau Delta, Mem; Biennial Nat Conf 1984; Assoc'd Writing Progs; Poets & Writers Inc; Poetry Soc of Am, Past Mem of Intl Com; IPA; Intl Wom's Writing Guild, Poetry Wkshop Dir at Skidmore Col Conf, 1980; hon/Poems Pub'd in Many Lit Mags, incl'g, *So Poetry Review* & *NY Qtrly*; Outstg Yg Wom of 1980; Nat Endowment for the Arts Creat Writing F'ship, 1976; F'ship in Creat Writing, Univ of UT, 1974-75; 1st Place, Col Div, *Lyrical Iowa*, IA Poetry Assn, 1969; Harlan Awd, IA Wesleyan Col, 1966-69; Dir of Am Poets; Intl Authors & Writers W/W; W/ W of Am Wom; Dir of Dist'd Ams; Personalities of S; Num Others.

GIL del REAL, MARIA TERESA oc/ Health Researcher; b/Jan 5, 1941; h/76 Princeton, Avenue, Rocky Hill, NJ 08553; m/John R Romano; c/Christina Maria, John Alexander; p/Dr Antonio (dec) and Rosa Calvo Gil del Real, Princeton, NJ; ed/Assoc Deg, Bogota Bus Col, 1961; BA, summa cum laude, Rutgers Univ, 1979; Currently Att'g Columbia Univ for MPH Deg (Epidemiology); pa/Free-Lance Translator, Simultaneous Interpreter, 1977-79; Biling Editor, Princeton Intl Translations, 1979-80; Res Asst, The Robert Wood Johnson Foun, 1980-83; hon/Pub, *Potlatching & Face Maintenance Among the Kwakiutl of Brit Columbia*, 1980; Alpha Sigma Lambda Hon Soc; W/W of Am Wom.

GILL-THOMPSON, NORMA NOTTINGHAM oc/Executive, Private Consultant; b/Jun 26, 1920; h/4006 Townhouse Lane, Uniontown, OH 44683; ba/ Akron, OH; m/Edward G (dec), Herbert G Thompson; c/Marilyn A, Sally J Thompson, David E; p/Richard and

Esther (dec) Nottingham; ed/R B Turnbull Jr, MD, Sch of Enterostomal Therapy, Cleveland Clin Ednl Foun, 1958; B'ham Gen Hosp, B'ham, England, 1970; Dale Carnegie Course, 1974; Spanish Courses, 1979-82; Principles of Mgmt Engrg Agreement Ldrship Course, Cleveland Clin Foun, 1980; Intl Assn Enterostomal Therapy, Cert'd, 1981; pa/Dir & Fdr 1961-78, Asst 1974-78, R B Turnbull Jr, MD, Sch of Enterostomal Therapy, Coor of Enterostomal Therapy, Cleveland Clin Foun, 1978-81; Pres, Pvt Conslt, Worldwide Ostomy Ctr Inc; Conslt, Colon & Rectal Dept, Cleveland Clin Foun; Am Urology Assn, Allied Orig Mem 1972; U Ostomy Assn, Chm of 1st Conf 1962, Intl Assn for Enterostomal Therapy, One of Fdrs 1968; World Coun for Enterostomal Therapists, Fdr 1977, 1st Pres 1979-80; Lectr, Colo-Proctology Soc, Mar del Plata, Argentina, 1982; Lectr, Japan Colo-Proctologic Soc, Tokyo, 1982; Editor, *World Coun of Enterostomal Therapists Jour*, 1982-86; U Ostomy Assn; Intl Assn for Enterostomal Therapy; World Coun of Enterostomal Therapists; Intl Ostomy Assn, Profl Adv Bd 1980-83; Am Urological Assn, Allied; hon/Pubs, "Ostomy Care" 1982; Plus 250 Other Articles; World Coun of Enterostomal Therapists, Hon Mem, 1982; U Ostomy Assn, Hon Mem; Intl Assn for Enterostomal Therapy, Hon Mem; Norma N Gill Foun, Founded 1980, WCET; World W/W of Wom.

GILLESPIE, GEORGE HUBERT oc/ Physicist; b/Sep 9, 1945; h/364 Hillcrest Drive, Leucadia, CA 92024; ba/San Diego, CA; c/James S, Colin H, Ian G; p/Hubert W and Freida (dec) Gillespie; ed/BA in Elect Engrg & Physics 1968, MEE in Elect Engrg 1968, Rice Univ; MS in Physics 1969, PhD in Physics 1974, Univ of CA-San Diego; mil/ USAR, Capt 1967-75; pa/Engr, IBM, 1967; Res Asst, Los Alamos Sci Lab, 1968; Res Asst, Univ of CA-San Diego in La Jolla, CA, 1968-74; Staff Scist, Phy Dynamics Inc, 1975-; Assoc, La Jolla Inst, 1976-; Jour Referee, Phy Review A, 1981-; Am Phy Soc, 1975-; AAAS, 1979-; Bd of Trustees, Sky Mtn Life Sch Inc, 1983-; hon/Pubs, "Systematics of Electron-Stripping Cross Sects for Fast Hydrogenic Ions Penetrating Solids" 1984, "A Scaling Cross Sect for the Ionization of Atomic Hydrogen by Fast, Highly-Stripped Ions" 1982, "Excitation & Ionization Cross Sects for Fast Lithium Atoms & Ions Colliding w Atoms" 1982, "Born Cross Sections for Fast, Low-Charge-State Uranium Ions Colliding w Lithium Atoms & Ions" 1981, Num Others; Sigma Tau, 1967; W/W in Frontier Sci & Technol.

GILLETTE, ERIC ALLISON oc/ Senior Information Systems Specialist; b/May 4, 1935; h/PO Box 998-MB 424, El Segundo, CA 90245; ba/El Segundo, CA; c/Allison Ruth, Michelle Kristin; ed/BA, Alfred Univ, 1958; MBA, Syracuse Univ, 1960; pa/Sys Engr, Ford Motor, 1960-67; Sr Sys Conslt, Bell & Howell, 1967-68; Mgr of Comml Sys, C D Searle, 1968-73; Sys Conslt, Fed Resv Bk of Chgo, 1973-78; Sr Info Sys Spec, Computer Scis Corp, 1978-; Assoc Prof, Narper Col, 1968-72; Am Inst of Bkg, 1974-78; Assoc Prof, CA St Univ-Dominguez Hills, 1981-; APICS, Ed Dir; Assn for Sys Mgmt, Div Dir;

hon/Cert'd Data Processor, 1969; Cert'd Practioner Prodn & Inventory Mgmt, 1981; W/W in W.

GILLETTE, FRANKIE JACOBS oc/ Consultant; b/Apr 1, 1925; h/85 Cleary Court, #4, San Francisco, CA 94109; ba/ Same; m/Maxwell Claude; p/Frank and Natalie Taylor Jacobs (dec); ed/BS, Hampton Inst, 1946; MSW, Howard Univ, 1948; pa/Co-Owner, G & G Enterprises; Spec Prog Coor & Dist Chief, Com Sers Adm, Reg 9, 1968-81; Prog Coor, Staff Devel Progs, Univ of CA Ext, Berkeley, 1965-68; Nat Pres, Nat Assn Negro BPW Clbs Inc, 1983-; Bd of Dirs, Time Savs & Ln Assn, 1978-; cp/VChp, SF Handicapped Access Appeals Bd, 1982-; hon/Author, "The Organizer" 1978, "The Governor" 1979, Num NANBPWC Inc Articles & Reports ("It's Time" Newslttr); Alumnus of the Yr, Hampton Inst, 1966; Fed People Reach Out Awd, SF Fed Exec Bd, 1975; W/W in W, in CA.

GILLETTE-BALOG, DAWN L oc/ Motivational Therapist, Nutritionist; b/ May 5, 1940; h/595 Linda Vista Avenue, Pasadena, CA 91105; ba/Pasadena, CA; m/John F; c/Monica Marie, Teresa Alice; p/Edna Alice Gilpin, Lansing, MI; ed/BA, Immaculate Heart Col, 1974; MS, PhD, Donsbach Univ, 1981; Cert'd Biofeedback Therapist, 1983; pa/Prog Dir, Life Fitness Ctr, 1980-83; Prog Dir, Fdr, Lifestyle Dynamics, 1983-; Pasadena Commun Hosp Prog Dir, Nutritional Cnslr, Biofeedback Therapist, 1984-; Bd of Dirs, Immaculate Heart Col; CA Inst of Technol Assocs; cp/Pasadena C of C; hon/Appears in Book About Her Tng, *Power of Alpha Thinking, Miracle of the Mind*, by Jess Stearn; W/W in W.

GILLIAM, MARTHA ANN oc/ Research Microbiologist; b/Nov 15, 1940; h/9720 East Lorain Place, Tucson, AZ 85748; ba/Tucson, AZ; p/Hugh Edgar Jr and Mary Lola Davis Gilliam (dec); ed/BA, Bacteriology, Univ of TX-Austin; MS, Microbiol, Univ of WY, 1966; PhD, Microbiol, Univ of AZ, 1973; pa/Res Asst, Univ of TX, 1963-64; Radiochem, Wadley Res Inst, 1964-65; Res Microbiologist, USDA, 1969-; Acting Ctr Dir 1981-83, Res Ldr 1981-83, Carl Hayden Bee Res Ctr, USDA; Adj Asst Prof Microbiol & Immunol 1984-, Res Assoc 1973-, Univ of AZ; Soc for Invertebrate Pathol; AAAS; AZ-NV Acad of Sci; hon/Author of 75 Papers in Sci Jours & Book Chapts; US Dept Agri Cert of Merit, 1983; Sigma Xi, 1966; Gamma Sigma Delta, 1966; Hon Grad, Univ of WY, 1966; USDA Grantee, 1966-69; Apiculture Res Awd, Apiary Inspectors of Am, 1979; Linz S'ship Awd, 1959; Everts S'ship Awd, 1959; Dir of Dist'd Ams; Personalities of the W & MW; W/W: in W, in Commun Ser, of Am Wom; Intl Book of Hon.

GILLIS, STEVEN oc/Administrator, Scientist; b/Apr 25, 1953; h/3455 West Mercer Way, Mercer Island, WA 98040; ba/Seattle, WA; m/Anne E; c/Sarah Milne; p/Mr and Mrs Herbert Gillis, Chicago, IL; ed/PhD, Dartmouth Col, 1978; BA, Wms Col, 1975; pa/Tchg Fellow, Dartmouth Med Sch, 1975-78 Vis'g Scist, Sloan Kettering Inst, 1979; Asst Mem/Prof, Hutchinson Cancer Ctr, Univ of WA, 1980-82; Fdr, Dir of Res & Devel, Exec VP, Immunex Corp, 1981-; Sigma Xi, 1975; Phi Beta Kappa,

1975; NY Acad of Sci, 1982; AAAS, 1983; hon/Author, Over 100 Articles in Sci Jours, Books; Spec Fellow, Leukemia Soc of Am, 1978-82; Intl Immunopharm Prize, 1983; W/W in W, in Frontier Sci & Technol.

GILMAN, BENJAMIN ARTHUR oc/ United States Congressman; h/PO Box 358, Middletown, NY 10940; ba/Washington, DC; c/Jonathan, Harrison, David, Susan; p/Harry and Esther Gilman; ed/BS, Wharton Sch of Bus & Fin, Univ of PA, 1946; LLB, NY Law Sch, 1950; pa/Atty in Gen Pract of Law for 20 Yrs; Asst Atty Gen, NY St Dept of Law, 1953-55; Atty, NY St Comm on the Cts, 1955-57; Counsel to Assem-man Wilson VanDuzer's Com on Local Fin, St Legis, 1956-67; Elected for 3 Successive Terms to the NY St Assem (Served on Num Coms), 1967-72; Elected to US Ho of Reps, 1972; House Fgn Affairs Com; Congl Rep, UN Law of the Sea Conf; cp/Adv Com, NY St Yth Div's Start Ctr, 1962-67; PO & Civil Ser Com; House Task Force on Missing in Action; Select Com on Narcotics & Drug Abuse; Bd Chm, Middletown Little Leag; Past VP of Orange Co Mtl Hlth Assn; Orange Co Heart Assn; Hon VP, Hudson-DE Boy Scout Coun; hon/Dist'd Flying Cross; Air Medal w OLCs; Anatoly Shcaransky Humanitarian Awd, Rockland Co Com for Societ Jewry, 1979; Man of the Yr, Builders Assn of Hudson Val Inc, 1979; Dist'd Ser Awd, Adm Law Judges of the Dept of Hlth & Human Sers, 1980; Hon Warden, Fed Prison Sys, 1980; Patriot of the Yr, Dept of NY Resv Ofcrs Assn of US, 1981; Yeshiva Univ Dist'd Ser Awd, 1981; RAV TOV Intl Jewish Rescue Org, 1981 Humanitarian Awd, 1981; Pop Action Coun Legis of the Month Awd in Recog of Fostering Support to Solve World Pop Crisis, 1982; Hudson-DE Boy Scout Coun Dist'd Citizen Awd, 1983; Num Other Awds.

GILMAN, CAROL ANN oc/Systems Auditor; b/Nov 13, 1947; h/3663 Salem Drive, Lithonia, GA 30058; ba/Atlanta, GA; p/A W and Patricia V Gilman; ed/ BBA, GA St Univ, 1978; pa/Res Analyst, Fed Resv Bk of Atlanta, 1968-76; Internal Audit Mgr, Haverty Furniture Co Inc, 1978-82; Systems Auditor, J C Penney Co Inc, 1982-; Dir of Systems Auditing, John H Harland Co, 1983-; Inst of Internal Auditors; Reg AVP, Pres 1983-84, EDP Auditors Assn; AAUW; GA St Univ Alumni Soc; cp/Spkr on Auditing, Financial VP & Co-Fdr, Nat Action Archery Assn, 1978; DeKalb Co Militia Dists Comm; GA Wom's Polit Caucus; NOW; GA ERA; hon/GA Outdoor Archery Champion, 1977; GA Indoor Archery Champion, 1978; Order of Robin Hood, 1978; Recip of Maharishi Awd, Aths, 1977; Recip of Public Ser Awds, GA Wheelchair Ath Prog, 1977-78; W/W of Am Wom.

GILMAN, RICHARD CARLETON oc/College President; b/Jul 28, 1923; h/ 1852 Campus Road, Los Angeles, CA 90041; ba/Los Angeles, CA; m/Lucille Young (dec); c/Marsha, Bradley Morris, Brian Potter, Blair Tucker; p/George P B (dec) and Karen Elise Theller Gilman; ed/BA, Dartmouth Col, 1944; Spec F'ship, New Col, Univ of London, 1947-48; PhD, Boston Univ, 1952; mil/ USNR 1944-46, Lt (jg); pa/Pres of Col,

Prof of Phil, Occidental Col, 1965-; Dean of Col, Carleton Col, 1956-60; Exec Dir, Nat Coun on Rel in Higher Ed, 1956-60; Instr, Asst Prof, Assoc Prof, Phil, Colby Col, 1950-56; Tchg Fellow in Phil, Boston Univ, 1949-50; Tchg Fellow in Rel, Dartmouth Col, 1948-49; Bd of Dirs, Indep Cols of So CA, Pres 1983-84; Assn of Indep CA Cols & Univs; LA World Affairs Coun; Exec Ser Corps of So CA; Coun on Postsec'dy Accreditation, Pres Appt of the Assn of Am Cols; Newcomen Soc; Fellow, Soc for Values in Higher Ed; r/ Presb; hon/Author, "The Gen Metaphysics of Wm Ernest Hocking" (PhD Thesis) in *Festschrift* 1965, Var Articles in Higher Ed Mags & Jours; Borden Parker Bowne Fellow in Phil, Boston Univ, 1949-50; Hon Degs from Pomona Col (LLD 1966), Univ of So CA (LLD 1968), Col of ID (LLD 1968), Boston Univ (LLD 1969); Phi Beta Kappa, Alumni Mem 1980; W/W in Am, in W, in CA.

GILMARTIN, BARBARA J oc/Director of Rheological Research; b/Jan 30, 1952; h/19 Cambridge Street, Malverne, NY 11565; ba/Garden City, NY; m/Neil J; p/Mr and Mrs J Koechel; ed/BA, Physics 1974, MS, Physics 1976, PhD, Physics 1981, Adelphi Univ; pa/Res Asst 1976-79, Rheologist 1979-80, Dir of Rheological Res 1980-, Adelphi Res Ctr; Am Inst of Physics; Soc of Rheology; AIChE; hon/Num Pubs on Coal/Oil Mixtures; hon/Sigma Pi Sigma, Physics Hon Soc; Sigma Xi, Res Hon Soc; W/W in E.

GILSON, THOMAS QUINLEVAN oc/Labor Arbitrator, Professor; b/Jun 27, 1916; h/PH27A-2033 Nuuanu Avenue, Honolulu, HI 96817; ba/Honolulu, HI; m/Marie Jacques; c/Marie Ellen Pickel, Thomas Q Jr, William R; ed/AB, Ec, Princeton; MA, Pers & Guid, Columbia; PhD, Indust Mgmt, MIT; pa/Prof & Assoc Dean, Col of Bus Adm, Univ of HI, 1964-83; Prof & Chm, Mgmt Dept, Rutgers Univ, 1952-64; Res Assoc, Harvard & Instr, MIT, 1950-52; Nat Acad of Arbitrators; Am Soc for Public Adm, Pres of Honolulu Chapt 1979-80, 1981-82; Am Psychol Assn; Am Arbitration Assn; Am Soc for Pers Adm; hon/Pubs, *Fee Skills* 1962, Many Jour Articles 1944-83; Phi Beta Kappa, Princeton; Phi Delta Kappa, Columbia; W/W: in W, in Social Scis.

GIMBUTAS, MARIJA oc/Professor of European Archaeology; b/Jan 23, 1921; h/21434 Entrada Road, Topanga, CA 90290; ba/Los Angeles, CA; c/ Danute, Zivile, Rasa; ed/MA, Vilnius, 1942; PhD, Tubingen, 1946; pa/Prof of European Archaeol, Univ of CA-LA, 1963-; Curator of Old World Archaeol, Univ of CA-LA Mus of Cultural Hist, 1966; Archaeol Editor, *Jour of Indo-European Studies*; Am Inst of Archaeol; Am Anthropological Assn; Assn for the Advmt of Baltic Studies; Inst of Lithuanian Studies; hon/Pubs, *Die Balten* 1983, *The Goddesses & Gods of Old Europe, 6500-3500 BC* 1982, *Neolithic Macedonia 6500-5000 BC*, 1976, *The Prehist E Europe*, 1956, *The Balt*, 1963, *The Slavs*, 1971, *Bronze Age Cultures of Ctl & En Europe*, 1965, Others; *LA Times Wom of the Yr Awd*, 1968; *Fellow of Ctr for Adv'd Study in Behavioral Sci, Stamford, CA; Exch Prof w the USSR,

Acad of Scis, Wash, DC, 1968; Fulbright Fellow, 1981; Many Biogl Listings.

GINN, JOHN CHARLES oc/Newspaper Publisher, Communications Company Executive; b/Jan 1, 1937; h/Route 14, Box 57, Anderson, SC 29621; ba/ Anderson, SC; m/Diane Kelly; c/John Paul, Mark Charles, William Stanfield; p/Paul S Ginn, Anderson, SC; Bernice Louise Coomer (dec); ed/BJour, Univ of MO, 1959; MBA, Harvard Univ, 1972; mil/USAFR, 1959-61; pa/Reporter, Copy Editor, Chief of Copy Desk, *Charlotte Observer*, 1959-62; Editor, *Kingsport Times-News*, 1962-63; City Editor, *Charlotte News*, 1963-69; Dir of Corp Devel, *Des Moines Register & Tribune*, 1972-73; Editor & Publisher, *Jackson Sun*, 1973-74; Pres & Publisher, *Anderson Independent-Mail*, 1972-; VP, Harte-Hanks Communs Inc, 1978-; Pres, Cent Grp of Harte-Hanks Communs Inc, 1977-; Exec Com, SC Press Assn; SC Press Assn Foun Bd of Dirs; Chm, ASNE Res & Readership Com; Sigma Delta Chi, Soc of Profl Journalists; cp/ Pres, Pres-Elect, Bd of Dirs, Anderson Area C of C, 1977; Dir, So Newspaper Publishers Assn, 1980-; Pres, Anderson YMCA, 1975-76; Anderson Col Adv Coun; hon/R H Macy Retail Fellow, Harvard, 1972; Author of Best Edit of Yr, TN Press Assn, 1964, 1973, 1974; W/W in Am.

GINSBERG-FELLNER, FREDDA VITA oc/Pediatric Endocrinologist, Diabetologist; b/Apr 21, 1937; h/50 East 89th Street, New York, NY 10128; ba/ New York, NY; m/Michael J Fellner(MD); c/Jonathan Robert, Melinda Beth; p/Nathaniel and Bertha Ginsberg (dec); ed/AB in Chem, Cornell Univ, 1957; MD, NY Univ Sch of Med, 1961; pa/Pediatric Intern & Resident, Bx Mun Hosp Ctr, Albert Einstein Col of Med, 1961-62, 1963-64, 1965-66; Fellow in Pediatric Endocrinology & Metabolism, Albert Einstein Col of Med, 1962-63; 1964-65, 1966-67; Assoc in Pediatrics 1967-69, Asst Prof of Pediatrics 1969-75, Assoc Prof of Pediatrics 1975-81, Prof of Pediatrics 1981-, Mt Sinai Sch of Med; Dir of Div of Pediatric Endocrinology, Mt Sinai Hosp, 1977-; NY Diabetes Assn, Chm of Clin Soc 1980-81, VP 1983-; Chm, Camp NYDA for Diabetic Chd, 1977-; Am Diabetes Assn; Am Pediatric Soc; Soc for Pediatric Res; Endocrine Soc; Lawson Wilkins Pediatric Endocrine Soc; Am Acad of Pediatrics; NY Pediatric Soc; hon/ Author, Over 60 Articles & Chapts in Med Books & Jours on Childhood Diabetes, Endocrine Diseases & Childhood Obesity; Paul Lacy Awd, Nat Diabetes Res Interchange, Juv Diabetes Foun, 1982; Solomon Silver Awd in Clin Med, Mt Sinai Sch of Med, 1967; Grantee, NIH, Am Diabetes & NY Diabetes Assns, March of Dimes, Juv Diabetes Foun, Wm T Grant Foun; W/ W: in E, in Sci.

GINTAUTAS, JONAS oc/Physician, Neuroscientist; b/Oct 3, 1939; h/21226 73rd Street, Lubbock, TX 79412; ba/ Lubbock, TX; m/Kristina; c/Pasaka, Vadas; p/Mr and Mrs J Sinsinas, Lake Zurich, IL; ed/MD, Piragon Med Inst, Moscow, 1967; PhD, NWn Univ, 1975; pa/Phys, Cook Co Hosp, 1968-79; Clin Dir, Westchester Commun Clin, 1971-74; Assoc Prof of Psych, TX Tech Univ, 1975-77; Res Assoc, Physiol,

Assoc Prof & Dir of Res, TX Tech Univ Hlth Scis Ctr; Soc of Neurosci; AAAS; Intl Anesthesia Res Soc; r/Meth; hon/ Num Profl Pubs; Best Prof Awd, TX Tech Univ, 1977; W/W in S & SW.

GINTHER, CYNTHIA SUSAN oc/ Cable TV Marketing Consultant; b/Dec 31, 1953; h/2911 South Sidney Court, Denver, CO 80231; p/Howard G and Marie H Hansen Ginther, Laramie, WY; ed/AA, NW Col, 1972-74; BS, Univ WY, 1974-76; MBA Studies, CO St Univ, 1976-79; Mgr Advtg, Promotions, Public Relats, McDonald's Corp, 1975-77; Dir Advtg, Public Relats, CO St Univ, 1977-79; Corporate Mkt Mgr, Tele-Communs Inc, 1979-81; Mktg Conslt, Glennis Mkt, Conslts, 1981-; Nat Assn Female Execs; Wom in Cable; hon/Rec'd U Trans Union S'ship, 1974-76; Rec'd Jour S'ship, 1973; W/W: in Am Wom, in W.

GIOVINCO, GINA oc/Professor of Nursing; b/Jan 11, 1930; h/7727 Southwest 11th Avenue, Gainesville, FL 32607; ba/Gainesville, FL; c/Melinda, Michael, Craig; p/Ernest (dec) and Lucy; ed/PhD, Columbia Pacific Univ; EdD Cand, Temple Univ; MA, NY Univ; BSN, FL St Univ; mil/Commissioned Corps, USPHS, Lcdr; pa/Supvr, Ctl Sers & Emer Rm, 1959-61; Public Hlth Nsg, Kern Co Hlth Dept, 1961-62; Nurse Ofcr, USPHS, 1963-69; Instr, Pediatrics, Univ NM, Mtl Devel Ctr, 1969-70; Asst Prof Nsg 1970-74, Assoc Prof & Chm, 1974-75, Temple Univ; Assoc Prof & BSN Prog Dir, Hahnemann Col Allied Hlth, 1975-76; Nurse Dir & Admr, Home Hlth of Lehigh Val Inc, 1976-77; Assoc Prof & Chm, Col Misericardia, 1977-80; Nurse Dir, Sisters of Mercy Retirement Ctr & Convent, 1978-80; Assoc Prof Nsg, Univ So MS Grad Prog, 1980-82; Nat Leag Nsg; ANA; Commissioned Ofcrs Assn of USPHS; FL St Univ Alumni; NY Univ Alumni; AAUW; Am Assn Mtl Deficiency; APHA; PA Public Hlth Assn; PA Nurses' Assn; Royal Soc Hlth; Am Acad Polit & Social Sci; Bus & Profl Wom Inc; Altrusa Intl Phila; Guide of Our Lady of Sacred Heath Cath Nurses; Am Mgmt Assn; Soc Life Sci, Law, & Ethics, Hasting Ctr; Soc for Hlth & Human Values; PA Assn Aging; Assn Christian Therapist; MS Assn Wom Higher Ed; Assn Grad Fac in Commun Hlth/Public Hlth Nsg; Am Med Writers Assn; Intl Order of St Luke the Phys; r/Cath; hon/Num Pubs incl'g "Ethics & Its Application in Hlth Care", *Update on Ethics*, "Interpersonal", *Jour of Nsg Ethics*, 1978; Num Grants; Gov of NY Roster of Accomplished Profl Wom, 1966-68; NM Del to White House Conf on Chd, 1970-71; Citizen of Mo Nom'd by Mayor of Ambler, PA, 1972; Stipend from Hastings Ctr to Participate in Sem for Tchg Bio-ethics, 1976; Sigma Theta Tau, Gamma Lambda Chapt, 1980; Marquis W/W: of Wom, in S & SW; Personalities of S.

GIPSON, GARY STEVEN oc/Assistant Professor of Civil Engineering; b/ Jan 4, 1952; h/17735 Creek Hollow Road, Baton Rouge, LA 70816; ba/Baton Rouge, LA; m/Cheryl M; p/J L Gipson, Jackson, MS; ed/BS in Physics 1975, MS 1978, PhD in Engrg Sci 1982, LA St Univ; pa/Instr of Civil Engrg 1977-80, Res Assoc, Inst for Envir Studies 1980-82, Asst Prof of Civil Engrg 1982-, LA St Univ Baton Rouge; ASME; Soc of Engrg Sci; Am Phy Soc; Nat Soc of Profl Engrs; LA Engrg Soc; Am Acad of Mechs; hon/Pubs, "On the Transport of Gaseous Matter through Permeable Media between Cylindrical Cavities" 1981, "Properties of the Elect Field Distribn in the Field Ion Microscope as a Function of the Specimen Shank" 1980, "An Improved Empirical Formula for the Elect Field Near the Surface of Field Emitters" 1980; Sigma Xi Hon Res Soc, 1981; Mensa, Intl High IQ Soc, 1981; W/W in Frontier Sci & Technol.

GIRARDI, LAURENCE LEONARD oc/Design Firm President; b/Sep 23, 1953; ba/7529 Remmet Avenue, Canoga Park, CA 91303; p/Leonard and Annabella Girardi (dec); ed/AA, LA Pierce Col, 1975; pa/Art Dir, Wine World Mag, 1975-76; Art Dir, La Rose Graphics, 1976-77; Pres, Girardi Design, 1977-78; Pres, Grafica, 1978-; Free-Lance Design Conslt, Redken Labs Inc, 1980-; Design Conslt, Fiberwks Ctr for the Textile Arts, 1981-; Design Conslt, Jack Rutberg Fine Arts Inc, 1981-83; Alpha Gamma Sigma, Scholastic Hon Soc, 1974; Graphic Artists Guild, Nat & LA Chapts, 1981-; Nat Fdn Indep Bus, 1980-; Num Design Projs for Packaging, Trademarks & Illust; hon/Commun Recog Awd, LA Pierce Col, 1980; Screen Actors Guild, All Am Boy, Highest Hons, 1961; W/W: in W, in CA.

GIRAUDIER, ANTONIO oc/Writer, Painter, Musician; b/Sep 28, 1926; h/215 East 68th Street, New York, NY 10021; p/Antonio Geraudier Ginebra (dec); Mrs D Giraudier, Palm Beach, FL; ed/BLitt, Belen Jesuits, Havana 1944, Vedado Inst, Havana 1944; Grad, Univ of Havana Law Sch, 1949; Pvt Art Studies; pa/Singer & Pianist; 1-Man Exhibs: Smolin Gallery, NYC 1965, New Masters Gallery, NYC 1967, Avanti Galleries, NYC 1968, 1969, 1971, 1973, 1974, Palm Bch Towers 1969, Univ of Palm Bch 1970; 2-Man Exhbns: Welfleet Gallery, Cape Cod 1967, Welfleet Gallery, Palm Bch 1968, Avanti Galleries 1972; Num Grp Exhbns in US & Europe, 1964-; Rep'd Perm Collections: Fordham Univ, Lincoln Ctr, NY & Bronx, NY, Univ Palm Bch, Greenville Mus Art, Am Poets F'ship Soc, IL; Num Pvt Collections in US & Europe; Art Wk Reproduced in Over 41 Pubs in USA, Switzerland, Spain, Germany, Italy & France; Smithsonian Inst; Nat Trust Hist Presv; IL St Poetry Soc; Pres, Am Poets F'ship Soc; Portsmouth Arts Coun; Author, Num Books of Poetry, US, Cuba, Europe, 1957-; Has Written Over 2000 Poems-Prose; Contbr, Poetry to Compilations & Over 50 Anthologies; 260 Rdgs, USA & Abroad; Composer & Lyricist, 25 Songs; Words & Music; Over 500 Musical Gatherings; Own Musical Compositions; Books in Over 80 Libs; Owner, Over 6,000 of His Own Art Wks; hon/Premier Prix de Printemps, Paris, 1959; Hon Mention, Prairie Poet Collection, 1972; Hon Mention, Maj Poets Contest, 1972; Laureat Margerite d'Or, Paris, 1960; Danae Lit Designate, 1973; Cert of Merit: DIB, Men Achmt, Am Poets F'ship Soc, 1973; Hon Mem, L'Orientation Litteraire, Paris; Dipl & Medal, Intl Commun Ser; Dipl, Intl Biogl Assn; Life F'ship; Intl Biogl Assn, Intl W/W Commun Ser; 2 Certs of Awd in Envir

Contest & Maj Poets Contest, USA; Num Others; Writings in Over 100 Books, Grp of Indiv, Pub'd or Booked for Pub; NAm & World Edit Intl Register of Profiles; W/W: in E, in Am, in Chgo, in Am Art; Men of Achmt; Notable Ams of Bicent Era; Other Biogl Listings.

GIRSE, ROBERT D oc/Mathematics Professor; b/Nov 4, 1948; h/154 Ranch Drive, Pocatello, ID 83204; ba/Pocatello, ID; m/Linda R; c/Robert D II, Derek S; p/Russell C and Dorothy E Girse, Jennings, MO; sp/Thomas and Bernice Podorski, St Louis, MO; ed/BS 1972, MS 1974, So IL Univ; PhD, KS St Univ, 1979; pa/Math Prof, ID St Univ 1981-, No St Col, 1979-81; AMS; MAA; SIAM, Mem; Mem, Bd Dirs, Rocky Mtn Math Consortium, 1981-; Reviewer for Math Reviews, 1983-; Dist Commr, BSA, 1979-81; Camping Com, BSA, 1981-; hon/Pub'd in Profl Jours; Dist Awd of Merit, BSA, 1981; W/W in Frontier Sci & Technol.

GIRVIN, JOHN P oc/Neurosurgeon, Neurophysiologist; b/Feb 5, 1934; h/4 Linksgate Road, London, Ontario, N6G 2A7; ba/London, Ontario; m/Bettye; c/Douglas, Michael, Jane; ed/MD, Univ of Wn Ontario, 1958; PhD, McGill Univ, 1965; FRCS(C) Royal Col of Phys & Surgs of Canada, 1968; pa/Lectr, Physiol, McGill Univ, 1963-64; Asst Prof of Neurosurg & Physiol 1968-74, Assoc Prof 1974-84, Prof & Chm of Dept of Clin Neurol Scis 1984-, Univ of Wn Ontario; The Royal Col of Phys & Surgs; The Am Assn of Neurol Surgs; Neurosurg Forum; Canadian Neurosurg Soc; Res Soc of Neurol Surgs; The Am Epilepsy Assn; Dir & Pres Phys'Sers Inc Foun; Res Com, Ontario Mtl Hlth Foun; hon/Author, Num Physiol & Neurosurg Pubs; W/W.

GITTELSON, ABRAHAM JACOB oc/Educational Administrator; b/Oct 22, 1928; h/970 Northeast 172 Street, North Miami Beach, FL 33162; m/Shulamit; c/Ora, Moshe, Reva; p/William Libby; ed/BSS, City Col of NY, 1949; BRE, Yeshiva Univ 1950; MA, Hunter Col, 1953; pa/Assoc Dir, Ctl Agy for Jewish Ed, 1972-; Dir of Ed, Jewish Fdn of Gtr Ft Lauderdale, 1979-; Dir of Ed, Camp Ramah, Canada, 1968-72, 1975-76; Dir, SE Reg, U Synagogue, 1971-72; Dir of Ed, Beth Torah Congreg, 1958-71; Coun for Jewish Ed, VP 1977-79; Jewish Edrs Assem; Assn for Supvn & Curric Devel; Phi Delta Kappa; Nat Soc for Study of Ed; r/Jewish; cp/Rel Zionists of Am; hon/Author of Articles in Jewish Ednl Pubs; Co-Author, *Ten Lesson Plans on Jerusalem & Interdisciplinary Integration in the Jewish Sch*; Honoree, Combined Jewish Appeal, 1971; Annual Dinner, Ctl Agy for Jewish Ed, 1984.

GIZA, MARIE THERESA oc/Teacher; b/May 1, 1931; h/1723 Bank Street, Baltimore, MD 21231; ba/Baltimore, MD; p/Joseph F and Frances T Staniec Giza; ed/BA, Col of Notre Dame of MD, 1953; MA, Cert of Adv'd Study in Ed, The Johns Hopkins Univ, 1972; The Johns Hopkins Univ, 1982; pa/Elem Sch Tchr, Pvt Sch, 1953-56; HS Social Studies Tchr (9th-12th Grades), 1956-62; Elem Sch Tchr (Primary & Intermediate Grades), 1962-; Tchr of Polish Lang, Essex Commun Col,

1972-75; Instr, In-Ser Creat Writing Course for Tchrs, 1972-74; Treas, PTA, 1974-76; Ethnic Adv Com for Balto City Sch Tchrs, 1979-; cp/Secy, Polish Nat Alliance Grp 692, 1975-78; Delta Epsilon Sigma; Nat Scholastic Hon Soc; Eta Sigma Phi; r/Rom Cath; Pres, St Stanislaus Parish Coun, 1978-80; Former Pres, SE Area Coun, Balto Archdiocese; 1st Secy, Archdiocesan Pastoral Coun; hon/Contbr of Several Short Articles on Methods of Tchg, *Creat Tchr*, 1970-74; "What in the World is there in a Comic Book?" *MD Eng Jour*, 1984; Featured Tchr in 1984 issue of *Consumer Digest*; Recip, Elinor Parcoast Awd for Excell in Tchg Ec, 1978; Balto Polish Commun Awd, 1982; NDEA Fellow to Kutztown St Col, Lang Arts, 1956; Russian Scholar, Georgetown Univ, 1963-64; S'ships to Jagiellonian Univ (Krakow, Poland) 1974, Cath Univ (Lublin, Poland) 1976, Mikolaj Kopernik Univ (Torun, Poland) 1978, Univ of Oslo (Norway) 1973.

GLAD, JOAN BOURNE oc/Clinical Psychologist; b/Apr 24, 1918; h/1442 Irvine Boulevard, Number 130, Tustin, CA 92680; ba/Tustin, CA; m/Donald D (dec); c/Dawn JoAnne Glad Lundquist, Toni Ann Glad Saunders, Sue Ellen Glad Winmill, Roger B; p/Le Roy and Ethel G Rogers Bourne (dec); ed/BA, Univ of CA-LA, 1953; PhD, Univ of UT, 1965; pa/Dir, Child & Fam Guid Clin & Sch, Primary Chd's Hosp, SLC; Dir, Parent Ed, Chd's Hosp of Orange Co, CA; Admr, Fam Lrng & Devel Ctr, Santa Ana-Tustin Commun Hosp, Santa Ana, CA; Fdg Mem, Holistic Hlth Assn, 1979; Chm, Bd of Dirs, Fam Guid Ctr, Anaheim, 1981-82; r/LDS; hon/Pubs, "Keeping Your Own Identity" 1981, "Is Your God Big Enough?" 1955 (Winner Univ of CA-LA Essay for Rel in Life), "How to Teach Your Chd Tolerance & Coop" & *Rdg, Unltd* 1965; W/W: in W, of Am Wom; Intl W/W.

GLADYSZ, INZ ANTONI oc/Book Publisher, Writer, Politician; b/Dec 31, 1907; h/4566 Bermuda Street, Philadelphia, PA 19137; m/Maria; c/Krystyna, Janusz, Marta Bolt; p/Karol and Aniela Gladysz (dec); ed/Master's Deg, 1960; Doct Deg, 1962; pa/Book Publisher, Tarnow, Poland, 1932-67; Book Publisher, Writer, USA, 1967-; Pub'd, *Hasto Ogrodnicze-Rolnicze*, 1932; cp/Rep in Polish Govt, 1957; K for the Revival of Poland, Designated the Cross of a K, 1977; Mem, Orgr, Unions for Yth of Poland, 1927-39; Arrested by Gestapo & Detained in Concentration Camp of Gross Rosen, 1941-45; Cath Rep in Polish Govt, 1957-61; r/Cath; hon/Pub'd 37 Annals of Polish Calendars Entitled "Kalendarz Polski," 1936-; Author, "Polska Walczaca"; Pub'd 20 Periodicals of "Hasto Ogrodniczo-Rolnicze", 1932-64; Author of 14 Sci & 6 Polit Books, incl'g *Biografia Bylych Wiezniow Politycznych*, 1973, *Oboz Smierci*, 1972, *Wewnetrzna Inwazja Polski*, 1982.

GLASCOCK, MICHAEL DEAN oc/Senior Research Scientist; b/Jun 27, 1949; h/35 Vickie Drive, Columbia, MO 65202; ba/Columbia, MO; p/Malcolm D and Leta M Glascock, Hannibal, MO; ed/BS, Physics, Univ of MO-Rolla, 1971-; PhD, Nuclear Physics, IA St Univ, 1975; mil/1st Lt, USAR, 1975-79; pa/Res Assoc, Univ of MD, 1975-78; Sr

Res Scist, Univ of MO, 1979-; APS; ACS; ANS; Sigma Xi; Univ of MO Lib Com, 1981-84; VP, Sigma Pi Sigma, 1970-71; hon/Author of Many Articles in Profl Sci Jours; Dean's S'ship, 1967; Physics Dept S'ship, 1970; Phi Kappa Phi, 1971.

GLASER, MICHAEL SCHMIDT oc/ Professor of English; b/Mar 20, 1943; h/PO Box #1, St Mary's City, MD 20686; ba/St Mary's City, MD; m/ Kathleen Webbert; c/Brian Taylor, Joshua David, Daniel Caleb, Amira Dawn; p/Mr and Mrs M A Glaser, Glencoe, IL; ed/BA, Denison Univ, 1965; MA 1967, PhD 1971, Kent St Univ; mil/ Anti-War Poet; pa/Asst Prof 1970-74, Assoc Prof 1974-, Div of Arts & Lttrs (Acting Chair) 1979-81, Fest of Poets & Poetry (Co-Dir) 1974-, St Mary's Col of MD; Inst for Human Excell, 1973-, Chair 1976-80; St Mary's Co Arts Forum, Bd; cp/St Mary's Co Housing Auth Bd of Commrs, 1979-, Chair 1982-; St Mary's Co Wom's Ctr, Bd of Dirs 1978-; r/Jewish; hon/Author, Over 100 Poems & Stories Pub'd in a Variety of Mags, Jours & Newspapers Across the Country; Tchg F'ship, Kent St Univ, 1966-70; Hon Mention, Chester H Jones Poetry Competition, 1983; Personalities of the S; Outstg Yg Men of Am; Intl Biog of Poets & Writers.

GLASER, TED oc/National Account Manager, Industry Consultant; b/Aug 25, 1946; h/17401 South Oeonto, Tinley Park, IL 60477; ba/Rolling Meadows, IL; m/Carolyn; c/Colleen, Ted, Carrie; p/ Mrs Joanne M Glaser, Pales Heights, IL; ed/BS, Loyola Univ, 1972; mil/USMC, 1966-71; pa/Nat Acct Mgr, Indust Conslt, AT&T, 1981-; Acct Exec, Indust Conslt 1979-81, Acct Exec 1977-79, Communication Sys Rep 1975-77, IL Bell; Am Mgmt Assn; cp/K of C, Dist Dpty 1976-78; Tinley Pk Dist, 1978-79; r/Rom Cath; hon/Pub, AT&T, Profile of the Air Freight Fdg Indust, 1980-81; AT&T Nat Coun of Ldrs, 1981; IL Bell Pres Clb, 1981; AT&T Achievers Clb, 1980, 1981, 1982; W/W in Fin & Indust.

GLASGOW, NORMA FOREMAN oc/Commissioner of Higher Education; b/Nov 3, 1927; h/3 Country Club Drive, West Simsbury, CT 06092; ba/Hartford, CT; m/Keith W; c/Kim Alan Foreman; Kerry Joan Foreman Bellomy; p/Edd Terrell and Ruth Battles Holly, Hollis, OK; ed/BS in Ed, SWn OK St Col, 1947; MS in Ed, Univ of So CA, 1951; PhD in Communs, Univ of TX, 1971; pa/Proj Admr, Ednl Testing Ser, LA, 1947-50; Asst to Prodn Mgr, Pacific Press Inc, 1950-52; Ptnr, Farming & Cattle Oper, 1952-58; Instr, Public Schs in MI, OK & TX, 1958-64; Asst Dir, News Info Sers & Instr of Jour, W TX St Univ, 1964-67; Communs Spec, SW Ednl Devel Lab, 1967-70; Asst to the Commr, Coordinating Bd, TX Col & Univ Sys, 1971-77; Asst Commr for Sr Cols & Univs, TX Coor'g Bd, 1977-81; Commr of Higher Ed, St of CT, 1981-; Am Assn for Higher Ed; CT Ed Policy Sem, Adv Bd 1981-; CT St Bd of Ed, 1981-; CT St Coun on Ed for Employmt, 1981-; CT St Occupl Info Coor'g Com, 1981-; CT Student Loan Foun, Bd of Dirs 1981-; Coun on Postsec'dy Accreditation/St Higher Ed Exec Ofcrs Proj on Assessing Long Distance Lrng via Telecommuns Steering Com, 1982-; Ed Comm of the Sts, Commr 1981-,

Policies & Priorities Com 1983-; Gov's High Technol Coun, 1983-; Hartford Hosp, Corporator 1982-; St Higher Ed Exec Ofcrs Assn, 1981-, Exec Com 1982-, Ad Hoc Com on St Oversight, Accreditation & Lic'g 1982-, Task Force on the Study of Quality Standards & Accreditation 1982-, IEP Planning Bd 1982-85; Univ of CT Ednl Properties Inc, Bd of Dirs 1982-; hon/Study Dir & Editor, TX Higher Ed, 1968-80: A Report to the TX Legis, 1975; Editor, CB Report 1970-77, Coor'g Bd Annual Report 1970-77, Upper-Level Instns: A Report to the TX Legis 1972, The Critical Role of Org'd Res in TX Higher Ed 1972; Ida N Scharff S'ship, 1970-71; Emmett Walters Grad F'ship, 1968-69, 1969-70; Newspaper Fund Fellow, 1964; Sacred Heart Univ Ctr for Policy Issues for Ldrship in Higher Ed in CT, 1982; W/W of Am Wom.

GLASS, ANDREW JAMES oc/ Bureau Chief; b/Nov 30, 1935; h/2901 Brandywine Street, Northwest, Washington, DC 20008; ba/Washington, DC; m/Eleanor S; c/Samuel Sorrentino; p/ Mr and Mrs Martin A Glass, New York, NY; ba/BA, Yale Col, 1957; mil/USAR, 1958-64; pa/Financial Reporter 1959-62, Chief Congl Correspondent 1962-66, NY Herald Tribune; Nat Correspondent, Wash Post, 1966-68; Exec Asst, Senator Charles Percy (R-IL), 1968-70; Sr Editor, Nat Jour 1970-74, Cox Newspapers Wash Bur 1974- (Bur Chief 1977-); Nat Press Clb; Overseas Writers, Gridiron; Syndicated Columnist, NY Times News Ser, 1981-; cp/Fed City Clb.

GLAZER, BARBARA L oc/Psychotherapist; b/Mar 8, 1936; h/6310 Eastmont Court, Carmichael, CA 95608; ba/ Sacramento, CA; c/Deborah McCandlish, Leslie Friedman, Diane Friedman; p/Spencer and Isabelle Daniels, Hollywood, FL; ed/MS 1972, BA 1970, CA St Univ-Sacramento; pa/Psychotherapy & Cnslg, Adm, Supvn, Instrn, Org & Prog Devel, Staff Tng & Devel, Public Relats; Marriage, Fam & Child Therapy, The Consortium, Sacramento Pain Ctr, 1982-; Marriage, Fam & Child Therapy, Mtl Hlth Inst of Sacramento, Pain Ctr of Sacramento, 1978-82; Prog Dir, Client & Staff Sers, Commun Interaction Prog, 1975-82; Instr, Sacramento City Col, 1974-78; Cnslr, Dos Rios Chd's Ctr, N Sacramento Sch Dist, 1972-74; Am Assn of Cnslg & Guid; Am Mtl Hlth Cnslrs Assn; Org for Rehab Therapy; Jewish Bus & Profl Woms Netwk; cp/Crocker Art Mus Assoc; NOW; Nat Coun of Jewish Wom; Hadassah; hon/Wom of the Yr, Nat Coun of Jewish Wom, 1968; Pres, Juv Ser Coun, 1966-68; Communr Ser Awd, YWCA, 1983; Phi Kappa Phi, 1972; W/ W: in W, in CA.

GLENN, EVELYN NAKANO oc/ College Professor; b/Aug 20, 1940; h/ 85 Wendell Street, Cambridge, MA 02138; ba/Boston, MA; m/Gary A; c/ Sara, Patrick, Antonia; p/Makoto and Haru Nakano; ed/BA, Univ of CA-Berkeley, 1962; MA 1964, PhD, Harvard Univ; pa/Lectr, Harvard Univ Ext, 1971-73; Sr Rschr, Abt Assocs, 1970; Asst Prof, Boston Univ, 1972-84; Assoc Prof, FL St Univ, 1984-; Vis'g Asst Prof, Univ of HI, Manoa, 1983; MA Sociological Assn, Pres 1979-80; Sociologists for Wom in Soc, 1st VP 1974-76; Soc for the Study of Social

Probs, Chair of Edit and Pubs Com 1982-83; Am Sociological Assn, Com on the Status of Racial Minorities 1978-80; hon/Pubs, "Degraded & Deskilled: The Proletarianization of Clerical Wk" in Social Probs 1977, "Fam Strategies of Chinese Ams" in Jour of Marriage & Fam 1983, Other Articles in Social Probs, Ethnicity, Feminist Studies & Several Books.

GLENN, WILLIAM ALLEN oc/ Retired Educator and Newspaper Columnist; b/Mar 28, 1925; h/1319 Columbia Avenue, Gardendale, AL 35071; m/Ruth McClendon; c/Phyllis Glenn Kelly, Bryan C; p/Mrs Gertrude Glenn, Gardendale, AL; ed/AB in Sociol and Hist 1951, MA in Cnslg & Guid 1965, Univ of AL; Grad Wk, 1967, Am Univ; mil/USN, 1943-46; pa/Lic'd Min So Bapt Ch; Civilian Res Analyst, USAF, 1952-58; Sec'dy Dist Tchr & Prin, Morgan Co Schs, 1959-64; Cnslr, Prin & Fed Aids Supvr, Jefferson Co Schs, 1965-77; Ret'd, 1977; Hist Rschr & Newspaper Columnist, N Jefferson News, 1977-; Conslt, Cullman Co Mus, 1978-79; Alpha Kappa Delta; Phi Delta Kappa; Kappa Phi Kappa; AL Ed Assn; Nat Hist Soc; IPA; AL Textbook Revision Com, 1982; cp/Chaplain for AL Pres Inaugural Com, 1969; AL Com on Intergovtl Coop, 1972-76; Advr, Reagan-Bush Campaign Com, 1980; Repub Pres Task Force, 1981-85; hon/ Author of Biogs of Famed Ams for Radio Broadcast Freedoms Foun, 1967-69; Editor of Filmstrip Series for Schs, Hist of SC, 1968-69; Author of Rschr on Abraham Lincoln Fam Bible for Nat Pk Ser, 1976-85; Scholar, Shroud of Turin, 1978-83; Contbr of Articles to AL Sch Jour & AL Bapt, 1960-83; 3 Awds, Freedoms Foun at Val Forge, 1967, 1969, 1970; Gov's Cit, 1968; 2 Commends, Jefferson Co Bd of Ed, 1967-83; W/W in S & SW; Men of Achmt; Personalities of S; Commun Ldrs of Am; 2,000 Notable Ams.

GLENNER, GEORGE GEIGER oc/ Professor of Pathology, Research Pathologist; b/Sep 17, 1927; h/3108 Morning Way, La Jolla, CA 92093; ba/ La Jolla, CA; m/Joy Arlene; c/Sheldra, Jonathan, Amanda, Sarah; p/Francis R and Jennie Glenner (dec); ed/BA 1949, MD 1953, The Johns Hopkins Univ; mil/ USPHS, 1955-82; pa/Intern, Surg, Mt Sinai Hosp of NY 1953-54, Mallory Inst of Pathol at Boston City Hosp 1954-55; Asst Pathologist, Harvard Sch of Legal Med, 1955; Res Staff at Lab of Pathol & Histochem 1955-59, Chief of Sect on Histochem 1959-71, Chief of Sect on Molecular Pathol 1971-82, LEP, NIAMDD, NIH; Asst Pathol, Johns Hopkins Hosp, 1957-58; Att'g Phys, Univ of CA-San Diego Med Ctr, 1983-; Asst Pathol, Harvard Sch of Legal Med, 1955; Asst in Pathol, Johns Hopkins Univ Sch of Med, 1957-58; Guest Lectr in Histochem, Univ of KS Med Sch, 1960, 1961, 1964, 1965; Clin Assoc Prof of Pathol, Georgetown Univ Schs of Med & Dentistry, 1965-77; Vis'g Prof, Heller Inst, Tel-Hashomer Hosp, 1967; Chm, Dept of Med & Physiol, The Foun for Adv'd Ed in the Scis, NIH, 1968-80; Sr Vis'g Staff Pathol, Armed Forces Inst of Pathol, 1979-80; Prof Pathol 1980-82, Prof of Pathol 1982-, Univ of CA-San Diego Sch of Med; Fellow, Col of Am Pathols; Intl Acad of Pathol; Am Assn of Pathols; NY Acad of Sci; Am Assn

PERSONALITIES OF AMERICA

of Mil Surgs; Histochem Soc; San Diego Pathol Soc; Biol Stain Comm; Am Fdn for Clin Res; Am Soc of Biol Chems; hon/Pubs, *Tumors of the Extra-Adrenal Paraganglion Syst (Incl'g Chemoreceptors)* 1974, *Amyloid & Amyloidosis, 3rd Intl Symp* 1980, Over 150 Sci Articles; Phi Beta Kappa, 1949; USPHS Meritorious Ser Medal, 1971; German Nat Acad of Sci, 1973; World W/W in Sci; Am Meml of Sci.

GLOVER, JOHN ARMAND JR oc/ Media and Communications Consultant; b/Jun 27, 1952; h/1521 Haring Road, Metairie, LA 70001; ba/New Orleans, LA; m/Kathleen Deborah Brown; c/John A III; p/John A Glover (dec); ed/BAJ, LA St, 1974; EdM, Univ of NO, 1980; pa/Pres, John A Glover Cos; Edit Conslt, LA St Univ Sch of Dentistry; Editor, *The Daily Record*; Advtg Dir, *The Daily Record*; Prodn Mgr, Lehmberg & Lehmberg Advtg & Public Relats; Investigator, U Detective Agy; Phi Delta Kappa; Am Assn of Dental Schs; Am Assn of Dental Editors; Intl Assn of Bus Communicators; Coun for Basic Ed; Assn for Supvn & Curric Devel; cp/Nat Com, Kam's Fund for Hearing Res; r/Rom Cath; hon/Author, Chapt in Textbook *Hist of Dental Radiol* 1981, "A Comparison of Attitudes & Final Grades Among Freshman Dental Students" 1981, Prog Manual for Postdoct Pedodontic Res 1979; Kappa Delta Pi, Hon Ed, 1979; Phi Kappa Phi, 1980; Cand for Perm Diaconate, Rom Cath Ch; W/W in S & SW.

GLUCK, LARRY J oc/Art Educator, Artist, Writer; b/Apr 9, 1931; h/900 Rome Drive, Los Angeles, CA 90065; ba/Los Angeles, CA; m/Sheila Linda; c/ Peter Ross, Sarah Rebecca; p/Jane Gluck, Long Island, NY; ed/Cert of Illust, Pratt Inst; BA, Adelphi Col; mil/ Hon Discharge, AUS, Korean War; pa/ Instr of Art, Adelphi Col, 1955; Asst Art Dir, Sterling Advtg, NY, 1957; Adv Coor for Pres Art Show, 1964; Lectr on Art at Caneel Bay Plantation, 1964-67; Guest Lectr, Revitalization Conv in Detroit, 1978; Guest Lectr, New Civilization Conv, 1979; Fdr of Mission, Renaissance Fine Art Tng Ctrs, 1976; Fdr of "Dynamic Wkends of Drawing"; hon/Winner of Scholastic Art Awd for NYC, 1948; Winner of St Gaudens Medal of Art, 1948; Over 3,000 Paintings Painted for Admirers for Collections All Over the World, 1961-70; Full Page Spread on Gluck, NY *Herald Tribune*, Mar 1962; Paintings Shown on NBC *Today Show*, 1965; Appeared on Jack Douglas *Am Show*, 1966; Developed Style Known as "Alterism" in Oils, 1967; Pubs, *The Basic Line Drawing Course, The Basic Tone Drawing Course, The Basic Color Course, Beginning Oil Painting 7 Intermediate Painting*; Over 150 Taped Lectures on the Technol of Painting & Drawing; Over 200,000 Prints of Wk in Collections.

GOAD, DORIS JEAN HUFF oc/ Supervisor of Home Economics Education; b/Jun 15, 1939; h/2403 Romar Drive, Salem, VA 24153; ba/Roanoke, VA; m/Manford; p/Carson and Dollie (dec) Huff, Dugspur, VA; ed/BS, Radford Univ, 1962; MS, VA Polytechnic Inst & St Univ, 1973; pa/5th Grade Tchr, Cave Sprg Elem, 1962-66; Remedial Rdg Tchr, Cave Sprg Elem, 1966-67; Hd of Dept & Tchr of Consumer &

Homemaking Ed, Cave Sprg Intermediate Sch, 1967-72; Hd of Dept & Tchr of Consumer & Homemaking Ed, Hidden Val Intermediate, 1972-73; Supvr, Home Ec Ed, St Dept of Ed, Commonwlth of VA, Div of Voc Ed, 1973-; Nat Assn Voc Home Ec Tchrs, 1967-83; VA Voc Assn, 1967-83, VP 1973; VA Home Ec Tchrs' Assn, 1967-83, Pres-Elect 1972-73, Pres 1973-74; VA Home Ec Assn, 1968-83, Pres-Elect 1977-78, Pres 1978-79, Councilor 1979-80; Am Home Ec Assn, 1968-83; Delta Kappa Gamma, Pres of Beta Tau 1978-80; Phi Kappa Phi; Phi Delta Kappa; hon/Pubs, "Career Ed," Articles Pub'd in VVA Newslttr & VHEA Newslttr, Developed "Yg Homemakers of VA Handbook" 1980; Outstg Yg Edr, Cave Sprg JCs, 1970; Hon Mem, VA Assn, FHA, 1976; Outstg Cit Awd for Voc Ed, VVA, 1976; W/W in VA; Commun Ldrs in VA; Commun Ldrs in Am; WAVE, a Dir of Wom Admrs in Voc Ed; World W/W of Wom.

GODFREY, OLLIN oc/President; b/ Dec 10, 1930; h/PO Box 6314, Cincinnati, OH 45206; ba/Same; c/Ollin, Mark, David; ed/PhD, Univ of Nigeria; DLitt; mil/Navy;pa/Cnslr, Massive Neighborhood Devel Corp, E Harlem Commun Corp; VP, U Ldrship Corp; Pres, Prodr, Dir, Host "Minorities," WCYN, NYC; cp/Congl Clb, NRCC; IPA; Nat Repub Congl Com; Repub Perm Adv Bd; Repub Inner Circle; Dem Pres Assn; Repub/ Dem King Conv; Govtl Economical Control; Repub Nat Com; Repub Senatorial Com; hon/Pres Medal of Merit; W/W in W, in Fin & Indust.

GOETZ, ALEXANDER F H oc/ Senior Research Scientist and Program Manager; b/Oct 14, 1938; h/2494 Boulder Road, Altadena, CA 91501; ba/ Pasadena, CA; m/Rosa Cyrus-Goetz; p/ Alexander (dec) and Sylvia Scott Goetz; ed/BS in Physics 1961, MS in Geol 1962, PhD in Planetary Sci 1967, CA Inst of Technol; pa/MTS Bell Telephone Labs, 1967-70; Supvr, Solid Earth Applications Grp 1973-75, Mgr, Planetology & Oceanography Sect 1975-78, Jet Propulsion Lab; Sr (MTS), Proj Scist (Stereosat), 1978-80; Sr Res Scist & Prog Mgr, Imaging Spectrometry, Jet Propulsion Lab, 1980-; Vis'g Prof, Univ of CA-LA, 1983; Pres, Geoimages Inc, 1974-78; Assoc Editor, *Geophy Res Lttrs*, 1984-89; Edit Bd, *Ec Geol*; hon/Author, Over 70 Sci Articles; 3 Patents; Charles E Ives Awd, *Photo Sci & Engrg Jour*; 1982 Autometrics Awd, Am Soc Photogrammetry; 1982 Exceptl Sci Achmt Medal; 1982 NASA/DOI Wm T Pecora Awd; Am Men & Wom of Sci.

GOFF, MICHAEL EDWIN oc/Area Resource Manager; b/Dec 5, 1954; h/ PO Box 66, Kosciusko, MS 39090; ba/ Kosciusko, MS; m/Christine Rogers; p/ Maurice E and Chella D Goff, Leaf, MS; ed/BS, Forestry, MS St Univ, 1979; pa/ Dist Forester 1980-84, Tech Forester 1979-80, Weyerhaeuser Co; Home Builder, Smith Homes Inc, 1977-78; Exec Com, MS Soc of Am Foresters, 1984; Chm, Loblolly Chapt, Soc of Am Foresters, 1984; MS Forestry Assn, Tchrs Conserv Wkshop Com; Bd Dirs, MS Wildlife Fdn; cp/Bd Dirs, Kosciusko Lions Clb; Bd Dirs, Kosciusko C of C; Student, NY Inst of Photo; hon/Del, MS Ec Coun Ldrship MS Prog, 1983-84; Outstg Yg Men Am.

GOGUEN, JOSEPH AMADEE JR oc/ Computer Scientist; b/Jun 28, 1941; h/ 209 McKendry Drive, Menlo Park, CA 94025; ba/Menlo Park, CA; m/Kathleen Morrow; c/Heather, Healfdene, Alice; p/ Joseph and Helen Goguen, Pittsfield, MA; ed/BA, Harvard Univ, 1963; MA 1966, PhD 1968, Univ of CA-Berkeley; pa/Asst Prof, Univ of Chgo, 1968-73; Prof, Univ of CA-LA, 1974-81; Mng Dir, Structural Semantics, 1978-; Sr Computer Scist, SRI Intl, 1979-; Prin Mem, Ctr for the Study of Lang & Info, Stanford Univ, 1983-; IEEE; Assn for Computer Machinery; Am Math Soc; Math Assn of Am; Am Soc for Cybernetics; r/Buddhist; hon/Author, Over 90 Profl Pubs in Jours; Editor, *Theory & Pract of Software Engrg*, 1983; Sr Vis'g Fellow, Univ of Edinburgh, Scotland, 1974, 1978; IBM Fellow, T J Watson Res Ctr, 1972; W/W: in W, in Technol.

GOH, DAVID S oc/Professor; b/Jul 9, 1941; h/4 View Valley Drive, Carbondale, IL 62901; ba/So IL Univ, Carbondale, IL; m/Jane C; c/Alice, Nancy; p/Ying-hwa and Pei-shuh Goh; ed/PhD, Univ of WI Madison, 1973; MS, IL St Univ, 1969; pa/Psychol, Lincoln Devel Ctr, 1969-70; Asst Prof of Psychol, Univ of WI-La Crosse, 1973-75; Assoc Prof of Psychol, Ctl MI Univ, 1975-80; Prof & Dir of Sch Psych Prog, So IL Univ, 1980-; Am Psychol Assn; Nat Assn of Sch Psychols; Am Ednl Res Assn; Nat Coun of Measurement in Ed; Soc for Personality Assessment; Author of Many Book Chapts & Num Articles in Profl Jours; So IL Univ Fac Res Awd; hon/Chp of Invited Address & Paper Sessions, Am Psychol Assn Annual Conv, 1974-82; NASP Res Grant Awd, 1982; W/W: in Frontier Sci & Technol, in MW.

GOHAR, MOHAMED YOUSRY AHMED oc/Nuclear Engineer; b/Feb 3, 1947; ba/Argonne, IL; m/Iman Esmat O El-Dib; p/Ahmed Ahmed Gohar; Doria A Gharib; ed/BSc 1967, MS 1970, PhD 1974, Nuclear Engrg, Alexandria Univ, Egypt; pa/Asst Prof, Atomic Energy Establishment of Egypt, 1967-74; Res Assoc, Nuclear Engrg Dept, Univ of WI-Madison, 1974-77; Nuclear Engr, Argonne Nat Lab, 1977-; Am Nuclear Soc; Fusion Engrg Design Ctr, Oak Ridge Nat Lab; hon/Author, More Than 100 Sci Articles; Recip, Longevity Ser Awd, Argonne Nat Lab; W/W: in Frontier Sci & Technol, in World.

GOHIL, PRATAP oc/Physician and Surgeon; b/May 26, 1950; ba/405 Southway Boulevard, East, Kolcomo, IN 46902; ed/BA, 1975; MS, 1976; DPM, 1980; pa/Resident in Med & Surg of Foot, Cleveland Foot Clin, 1980-81; Pvt Pract, 1981-; Am Podiatry Assn, 1980; APHA, 1975; Assoc Mem, Am Col of Foot Surgs, 1982; Am Med Writers' Assn, 1980; r/Hindu; hon/Contbg Author to *Jour of Am Podiatry* Assn 1978-, *Jour of Foot Surg* 1980-, *Current Podiatry* 1980-; Am Col of Foot Surgs Awd, 1980; Assoc of Am Col of Foot Surgs, 1982; Fellow, Am Soc of Podiatric Dermatology, 1982; W/W in MW; Intl Authors' & Writers' W/W.

GOINES, BEVERLY TERRELL oc/ Manager of Technical and Marketing Communications; b/Dec 10, 1953; h/516 Whitestone, Memphis, TN 38109; ba/ Memphis, TN; m/James E; p/Mr and Mrs William F Terrell, Knoxville, TN;

ed/Master of Communs, OH St Univ, 1976; BS in Communs, Univ of TN, 1975; pa/Mgr of Tech & Mktg Communs, Humko Chem Div, Witco Chem Corp, 1983-; Edit Asst, Robert F Sharpe & Co, 1982-83; Public Relats Rep, 1st TN Bk, 1981-82; Rel Editor & Gen Assignment Reporter 1976-81, Reporter 1972-75, *Knoxville News-Sentinel*; Writer, Univ of TN Public Relats Dept, 1975; Soc of Profl Journalists, Sigma Delta Chi; Wom in Communs; Intl Assn of Bus Communs; AAUW; Delta Sigma Theta Sorority; Bd of Dirs, Univ of TN Nat Alumni Assn, Memphis Chapt; r/ AME; hon/Am Newspaper Publishers' Assn S'ship for Minority Students, 1972-75; Univ of TN-Knoxville Outstg Sr Wom, 1975; Kiplinger Fellow, OH St Univ, 1975-76; W/W of Am Wom.

GOINS, WILLIAM DORIS III oc/ Government Research Administrator; b/Apr 6, 1943; h/2506 Big Cedar Rd, Soddy, TN 35379; ba/Chattanooga, TN; m/Diane Johnston; c/William D IV, Clay Paul; p/William D Goins (dec); Lillian Palmer Maupin, Cleveland, TN; ed/BS in Nuclear Engrg 1966, MS in Metall Engrg 1969, Univ of TN; pa/Supvr, Welding Lab, Combustion Engrg, 1970-77; Prog Mgr, Nuclear Res, TVA, 1977-; Chm, Repair Welding Com, ASME Boiler & Pressure Vessel Code; Chm, Utilities Adv Com, Welding Res Coun; Secy, Metallurgy & Welding Com, Edison Elect Inst; Sys & Mats Com, EPRI; Tech Adv Com, Metal Properties Coun; r/Bapt; hon/Author, ASME Paper 84-PVP051 "Repair Requirement of Sect XI" 1984, & "Welding in Nuclear Engrg" (Deutscher Verband, Hamburg) 1979.

GOIZUETA, ROBERTO CRISPULO oc/Chairman of the Board and Chief Executive Officer; b/Nov 18, 1931; ba/PO Drawer 1734, Atlanta, GA 30301; m/Olga C de Goizueta; c/Olga Marie Rawls, Roberto S, Javier C; p/ Crispulo D and Aida Canera Goizueta; ed/BS, Yale Univ; pa/Am Film Inst; cp/ Variety Clbs Intl; Chm of Bd, CEO, The Coca-Cola Co; Bd of Dirs, Trust Co of GA; Bd of Dirs, Sonat Inc; Bd of Dirs, Ctl Atlanta Progress; Bd of Trustees, Emory Univ; Bd of Dirs, Ford Motor Co; Thr Bus Coun; Am Soc of Corp Execs; Bd of Govs, Lauder Inst; Atlanta Univ Ctr; Am Assem; The Bus Roundtable; Coun on Fgn Relats; US-USSR Trade Coun; Bd of Dirs, The Commerce Clb; cp/Mem, US C of C; Atlanta Arts Alliance; Bd of Govs, Boys Clbs of Am; U Way of Am; Mem, The Japan Soc; Mem, Capital City Clb; The Intl Clb of WA Inc; Hon Trustee, US-Asia Inst; r/ Cath; hon/Human Relats Awd, Inst of Human Relats of the Am Jewish Com, 1981; Crowley Alumnus Awd, Cheshire Acad, 1981.

GOLD, RAYMOND oc/Fellow Scientist, Nuclear Reactor Physicist; b/Oct 3, 1927; h/1982 Greenbrook Boulevard, Richland, WA 99352; ba/Richland, WA; m/Judith Reiner; c/Ilyse Karen Gold Ferraiuolo, Warren Glenn, Mark David, Garry Evan; p/Harry and Hilda Krauss Gold (dec); ed/BSc 1951, MSc 1954, NY Univ; PhD, IL Inst of Technol, 1958; mil/ USN, 1945-48, 1951-52; pa/Physicist, Columbia Univ, 1952-54; Grp Ldr, GE Co, 1954-55; Res Physicist, Armour Res Foun, 1955-58; Prof & Dept Chm, Lowell Univ, 1958-62; Sect Hd,

Argonne Nat Lab, 1962-72; Dir, Jt Ctr for Grad Study, 1972-75; Pres/Owner, RADS Inc, 1975-76; Fellow Scist, Westinghouse-Hanford, 1976-; AAUP; Am Nuclear Soc; Am Phy Soc; Am Soc for Engrg Ed; Exec Com, Physics Div, ASEE, 1965-66; Hlth Physics Soc; NY Acad of Scis; Sigma Xi, Pres of LTI Chapt 1961-62; Radiation Res Soc; Conslt, US Nav Radiol Def Lab 1959-60, Tech Opers Inc, Burlington, MA 1960-62, AVCO Corp, Wilmington, MA 1961-62, Martin Marietta Aerospace, Denver, CO 1974-75, Hanford Engrg Devel Lab 1974-76; Editor, *Reactor & Fuel Processing Technol*, 1965-68; r/Jewish; hon/ Num Profl Pubs; Patent-Holder; Outstg Paper Cit, Am Nuclear Soc, 1971; Bd of Dirs, NW Col & Univ Assn for Sci, 1973-74; W/W in W; Am Men & Wom of Sci; Who is Pub'g in Sci; W/W in Atoms; DIB.

GOLDBERG, ARTHUR ABBA oc/ Manager of Municipal Finance Department; b/Nov 25, 1940; h/83 Montgomery Street, Jersey City, NJ 07302; ba/ New York, NY; m/Jane E; c/Ari Matthew, Shoshona Eve, Benjamin Saul, Talia Akiva; p/Mr and Mrs Jack Geddy Goldberg, West End, NJ; ed/JD, Cornell Law Sch, 1965; BA w Hons, The Am Univ, 1962; pa/Exec VP, Mgr of Mun Fin & Dir, Matthews & Wright Inc, 1970-; Dpty Atty Gen, St of NJ, 1967-70; "Of Counsel," Law Ofcs of Jack Geddy Goldberg, 1967-; Adm Asst, Cong-man Michael A Feighan, 1966-67; Asst Prof of Law, Univ of CT, Sch of Law, 1965-67; Intern, Staff Mem, Senator Harrison A Williams Jr, 1962; Bar Admissions: NJ 1965, Fed Cts 1965, CT 1966, Supr Ct of US 1970; Nat Leased Housing Assn, Chm Emeritus; Housing & Devel Reporter, Adv Bd; Public Securities Assn, VChm, Fed Legis, Dist #1; Am, NJ and CT Bar Assns; Univ Clb; New Am Fed Credit Union, Pres; cp/Dir, Landamatics Corp; Ptnr, Shayna Enterprises; Dir, Bason Corp; Ptnr, Alfus Assn; Com for the Absorption of Soviet Emigrees, Chm; CASE Mus of Russian Contemp Art in Exile, Chm; CASE Commun Devel Corp, Pres; *The New Am*, Russian Lang Wkly Newspaper, Chm; Metro NY Coor'g Com for the Resettlement of Soviet Jewry, Chm; The New York Synagogue, Co-Pres 1970-78; Hebrew Free Loan of NJ, Treas 1976-; Pres, the Freedom Synagogue, 1982-; Yeshiva of Hudson Co, Dir 1976-; Boys Clb of Jersey City, Dir 1976-; Pres, Hudson Yeshiva Parents Grp, 1983-; hon/Pubs, "A Call to Action: St Sovereignty, Deregulation & the World of Mun Bonds" 1981, "Tax-Exempts in Jeopardy" 1980, "Tax-Exempt Financing of Housing: Why Must Wash Tamper with It?" 1979, "Developing Underwriting Techniques are Designed to Mkt & Safeguard Sect 8 Housing Bonds" 1978, Others; W/W: in E, in Fin & Indust, in Consltg, in Am Law; in Am Jewry, in World Jewry; Commun Ldrs of Am.

GOLDBERG, MICHAEL ELLIS oc/ Neuroscientist; b/Aug 10, 1941; h/5153 Tilden Street, Northwest, Washington, DC 20016; ba/Bethesda, MD; m/ Deborah B (MD); c/Joshua, Jonathan; p/ Samuel Goldberg (dec); ed/AB, magna cum laude, Harvard Col, 1963; MD, cum laude, Harvard Med Sch, 1968; mil/ USPHS, 1969-72; pa/Med House Ofcr

1968-69, Neurol House Ofcr 1972-75, Peter Bent Billgham Hosp; Staff Assoc, NIMH, 1969-72; Neurologist, AFFRI, 1975-78; Res Neurologist, NIH, 1978-81; Chief of Sect on Neuroophthalmologic Mechanisms, NEI, 1981-; Assoc Prof of Neurol, Georgetown Univ, 1981-; Soc for Neurosci; Am Neurol Assn; Am Acad of Neurol; Assn Res in Vision & Ophthal; Intl Neuropsychol Symp, Exec Com; hon/Author, Num Articles in Profl Jours; Phi Beta Kappa, 1963; Alpha Omega Alpha, 1968; S Weir Mitchell Prize of ANA, 1972; Mem, NSF Conslt Panel in Neurobiol; W/W in Frontier Sci.

GOLDBERG, MICHELE WYMAN oc/Training Consultant, Author; b/Aug 27, 1954; h/2813 Tremont Street, Philadelphia, PA 19136; ba/Same; m/ Alan Harvey; c/Jesse Wyman, Lee Michael; p/Joseph (dec) and Florence Wyman; ed/BA in Writing & Communication, PA St Univ, 1976; pa/Copywriter/Public Relats Asst, Tract Advtg, 1976-77; Admr/Instr, Phila Sch of Ofc Tng, 1978-81; Pres, Goldberg ETC (Communication Tng/Career Cnslg), 1981-; Bd of Dirs, VP of Human Sers 1982, VP of Communication 1983, Pres-Elect 1984, Phila Am Soc for Tng & Devel, 1982-; Nat Am Soc for Tng & Devel; Phila Orgl Devel Netwk; APGA; Am Voc Guid Assn; Intl Transactional Anal Assn; Nat Assn of Female Execs; hon/Pubs, *Effective Written Communication* & *Effective Communication Skills for Mgmt* 1982, *Writing for Results*, *Business Writing Basics*, 1984, *Telephone Communication Skills for Effective Customer Ser* 1983, "How to Turn Interviews into Job Offers" 1983, "Careers" (Wkly Column) 1981-82, "Sometimes" 1974, "The Jitterbug" 1973; W/W of Am Wom.

GOLDEN, TERESA VITAGLIANO oc/Manager; b/Jun 5, 1955; h/14 Sarah Lane, Hopewell Junction, NY 12533; ba/ Poughkeepsie, NY; m/George Patrick; c/ Helen Marie, George Christopher; p/ Vincent Jack and Audrey Fabini Vitagliano, Fairfield, CT; ed/MBA, Corporate Financial Mgmt, Pace Univ, 1979; BA in Ec & Bus, Col of Mt St Vincent, 1975; pa/Mgr, Graphics Mkt Support, 1984-; Adv Programming Planner 1983-84, Graphics Mkt Support Rep 1980-82, Sys Analyst 1979-82, IBM Corp; Financial Planning Sys Conslt, STSC, 1978-79; Accts Receivable Mgr, Itcl Corp, 1975-78; hon/W/W: of Am Wom, in Computer Graphics.

GOLDMAN, JOSEPH L oc/Scientist, Technical Director; b/Aug 25, 1932; ba/ International Center for the Solution of Environmental Problems, 3818 Graustark, Houston, TX 77006; c/Rachel Ann, Charles Israel, Michell Saundra; p/ Samuel Goldman (dec); Charna Malamud Greene (dec); ed/BS, TX A&M, 1958; MS 1960, PhD 1971, OK Univ; mil/USAF, 1951-55; pa/Tech Dir, ICSEP, 1976-; Assoc Dir of Res, Inst for Storm Res, 1966-75; Assoc Prof of Physics, Univ of St Thomas, 1967-75; Proj Supvr, Nesco, 1965-66; Res Meteorologist, Univ of Chgo, 1960-65; Res Scist, TX A&M Res Foun, 1958-60; Asst Meteorologist, Gulf Conslts, 1956-58; AAAS; Am Geophy Union; Am Meteorological Soc, Cert'd Conslt'g Meteorologist; Am Soc of Nav; Engrs Coun of Houston; Marine Technol Soc; Nat Coun of Indust Meteorologists; NY

Acad of Sci; Royal Meteorological Soc; hon/Author &/or Co-Author, Over 150 Papers, Chapts in *Urban Costs of Climate Modification* 1976 & *Wind Effects on Structures* 1976; Sigma Xi, 1962; Chi Epsilon Pi, 1969; W/W: in Am, in S; Personalities of S.

GOLDSBERRY, RONALD E oc/Executive; b/Sep 12, 1942; h/1205 Timberview Trail, Bloomfield Hills, MI; ba/ Madison Heights, MI; m/Betty; c/Renee, Ryan; ed/MBA in Fin and Mktg, Stanford Univ, 1973; PhD in Chem, MI St Univ, 1969; BS, summa cum laude, Chem, Ctl St Univ, 1964; mil/Completed 2 Yrs in AUS as Capt, 1971; pa/ Pres, Chief Operating Ofcr, Parker Chem Co, 1983–; VP & Fin Mgr, Occidental Chem Corp, Parker Surface Treatment Prods, 1981–83; VP, Bus Devel & Planning, Occidental Chem Corp, 1978–81; Dir, Corporate Planning Opers, Gulf Oil Corp, 1975–78; Mgmt Conslt, Boston Consltg Grp, 1973–75; Mktg Mgr, Hewlett Packard Co, 1972–73; Res Chem, NASA Ames Res Ctr, 1969–72; Asst Prof of Chem, Univ of CA-San Jose St, 1969–71; hon/ Several Papers Presented at Nat Chem Meetings & Pub'd in Sci Jours.

GOLDSMITH, HARRY LEONARD oc/Professor and Career Research Investigator; b/May 11, 1928; h/230 Wolseley Avenue, North, Montreal West, Quebec, Canada H4X 1W2; ba/ Montreal, Quebec, Canada; m/Valerie Phyllis Lefevre; c/Anne Catherine, Claire Louise; p/Louis and Sofie Goldsmith (dec); ed/BA w Hons 1950, BSc 1951, Balliol Col, Oxford Univ; PhD, McGill Univ, Montreal, 1961; pa/Asst Prof 1964–69, Assoc Prof 1969–72, Dept of Exptl Med, McGill Univ; Assoc Mem of Dept of Chem 1970–, Assoc Mem of Dept of Chem Engrg 1972–, Full Prof of Dept of Med, Div of Exptl Med 1972–, Dir of Div of Exptl Med, Dept of Med 1976–, McGill Univ; Investigator, McGill Univ Med Clin, Montreal Gen Hosp, 1964–; Scholar of the Med Res Coun of Canada, 1964–67; Career Res Investigator of the Med Res Coun of Canada, 1967–; Sigma Xi; Canadian Soc for Microcirculation; European Soc for Microcirculation; Am Physiological Soc; Canadian Soc for Clin Invest; Intl Soc of Biorheology; Soc of Rheology; Columbia Univ Sem on Biomats; Rheology Subcom, Intl Com on Haemostasis & Thrombosis; Edit Bd, *Microvascular Res*; cp/Montreal W Citizens Assn Exec, 1970–74; Co-Fdr of Local Newspaper, "The Informer," 1973; Cardinal Leger's Diocesan Ecumenical Comm, 1961–65; Editor of "Crosslight" Mag of the Newman Alumni of Canada, 1960–65; r/Cath; hon/Pubs, "Role of Cell-Wall Interactions in Thrombogenesis & Atherogenesis: A Microrheological Study" (in Press), "Platelet Aggregation in Poiseuille Flow" (in Press), "Radial Distbn of White Cells in Tube Flow" (in Press), "Leukocyte Margination in Blood Flow through Tubes" (in Press), Num Others; Newman Medal, Newman Alumni Socs of Canada, 1965.

GOLDSTEIN, LOIS T oc/Sculptor, Instructor, Art Dealer; b/Aug 29, 1933; h/9126 Southwest 130 Lane, Miami, FL 33176; ba/Miami, FL; m/James W Wallman; c/Jeffrey, Ellen, Daniel; p/Mrs E M Traub, Hallendale, FL; ed/Att'd, Univ

of IL Champaigne-Urbana 1951–52, Miami Dade Commun Col, Art Inst of Chgo 1948–50, Paris Am Acad 1977, 1981; pa/Instr, Clay Sculpture, Ceramic Leag of Miami, 1974–75; Instr, Clay Sculpture, Grove House, Coconut Grove, 1975–77; Self-Employed, Galerie Atelier, 1980–; Artist Equity Mem, 1974–83, Treas 1979; Equity Rep to Arts Coun of Cultural Affairs, 1979; WCA, 1977–83; Profl Artist Guild, 1977–81; Shows, Ocala Invitational Art Show (Juried) 1973, Coral Gables Art Show (Juried) 1973–74, Dadeland Art Show 1973–74, Grove House Annual Art Show 1977–78, Others; cp/Art Instr, Handicapped Chd, Dade Co Schs, 1965–67; Craft Dir, Boy Scouts Intl, SE Dist, 1965–67; Wkshops 1969–70, Art Dir & Editor of Bltn 1967–70, Nat Coun Jewish Wom.

GOLDSTEIN, SAMUEL J oc/Pediatric Psychologist; b/May 13, 1952; ba/ 3950 South 700 East, Suite 200, Salt Lake City, UT 84107; m/Janet; p/Nathan and Sarah Goldstein, Brooklyn, NY; ed/ PhD, Univ of UT, 1980; MA, Montclair St Col, 1976; BS, Polytechnic Inst of Brooklyn, 1973; Lic'd Psychol & Cert'd Sch Psychol, UT; pa/Clin Dir, Neurol, Lng & Behavior Ctr, 1982–; Sch Psychol, Jordan Resource Ctr, 1979–82; Clin Psych Resident, The Chd's Ctr, 1978–79; Am Psychol Assn; UT Sch Psych Assn; Media Psychol for KSTU-TV (Wkday Talk Show); hon/NY St Regents S'ship, 1979–83; W/W in W.

GOLDWIN, ROBERT A oc/Resident Scholar, Director of Constitutional Studies; b/Apr 16, 1922; h/1565 44th Street, Northwest, Washington, DC 20007; ba/Washington, DC; m/Daisy Lateiner; c/Nancy Goldwin Harvey, Jane Goldwin Bandler, Elizabeth, Seth; p/Alexander and Sed Goldwin (dec); ed/ BA, St John's Col, 1950; MA 1954, PhD 1963, Univ of Chgo; mil/US Cavalry 1942–46, Pvt to 1st Lt; pa/Adj Lectr in Public Policy, Harvard Univ, 1982–83; Resident Scholar & Dir of Constitl Studies, Am Enterprise Inst, 1976–; Spec Conslt to the Pres of US, 1974–76; Advr to Secy of Def, 1976; Spec Advr to the Ambassador, US Mission to NATO, Brussels, 1973–74; Dean & Charles Hammond Elliott Tutor, St John's Col, 1969–73; Conslt to the Under-Secy of Def, 1982–83; Adv Com, Law of the Sea, 1982–83; Bd of Fgn S'ship, 1977; Bd, Overseers Com to Vis Dept of Govt, Harvard Univ, 1975; Bd of Trustees, Woodrow Wilson Intl Ctr for Scholars, Smithsonian Instn, 1975–76; cp/Exec Bd, Wash Ctr of Am Jewish Com, 1983–84; r/Jewish; hon/Pubs, "Common Sense vs 'The Common Heritage'" 1983, "Locke & the Law of the Sea" 1981, "Rts vs Duties: No Contest" 1981, "Of Men & Angels: A Search for Morality in the Constit" 1977, Others; Editor, *How Capitalistic is the Constit* 1982, *How Democratic is the Constit* 1980; Medal for Dist'd Public Ser, Dept of Def, 1977; Profl Achmt Awd, Univ of Chgo Alumni Assn, 1977; Awd of Merit, St John's Col Alumni Assn, 1977; Fellow, Guggenheim Foun, 1966; Fellow, Fund for Adult Ed, 1959; Jour of Polit; Men of Achmt; Writers Dir.

GOLDYNE, MARC ELLIS oc/Dermatology Educator, Researcher; b/Oct 15, 1944; h/221 Marina Boulevard, San Francisco, CA 94123; ba/San Francisco,

CA; m/Gail Sokolow; c/Serena, Avram; p/Alfred Josef Goldyne MD (dec); ed/ AB, Univ of CA-Berkeley, 1966; MD, Univ of CA-SF; PhD, Univ of MN-Rochester, 1980; pa/Intern, French Hosp Med Ctr, 1970–71; Fellow in Dermatol, Mayo Clin, 1971–75; Res Fellow, Karolinska Inst, Stockholm, Sweden, 1975–78; Asst Prof 1978–84, Assoc Prof 1984–, Dermatol & Med, Univ of CA-SF; Hd, Dermatol Res, SF Gen Hosp, 1978–83; Am Fdn Clin Res; Soc Investigative Dermatol, Dir 1972–74; Wn Reg Soc Investigative Dermatol, Pres 1983–84; Fellow, Am Acad Dermatol; Soc Exptl Biol Med; Am Assn Immunologists; r/Jewish; hon/ Pubs, 30 Original Sci Invests 1971–84, 10 Sci Reviews 1975–84, Chapts in Lange's Textbooks of Basic & Clin Endocrinology & Basic & Clin Pharm 1982–83; Phi Beta Kappa, 1966; NIH Clin Investigator Awd, 1979–82; W/W in Frontier Sci & Technol.

GOLEN, RICHARD FRANK oc/ Computer Consultant; b/Dec 1, 1952; h/34 Greystone Avenue, North Dartmouth, MA 02747; ba/Same; m/Claire Jeanne; c/Ross Raymond, Erik Frank; p/ Frank Jr (dec) and Sophie Golen, North Dartmouth, MA; ed/BA, Mgmt, SEn MA Univ, 1974; MBA, Suffolk Univ, 1976; JD, Suffolk Law Sch, 1983; pa/ Asst Prof, SEn MA Univ, 1976–81; Vis'g Lectr, Suffolk Univ, 1982–83; Computer Ed Conslt, Ctr for Cont'g Ed, Bentley Col, 1982–; Sys Conslt, Golen Assocs, 1981–; Vis'g Lectr, SEn MA Univ, 1983–; Phi Delta Phi, 1982–; Delta Chi, 1971–; Sem, Tax Preparation on Microcomputers, Bentley Col, 1983; Admitted to MA Bar, 1985; cp/Porsche Clb Am, 1984; Boston Computer Soc, 1982; BMWCCA, 1979–; Mercedes-Benz Clb of Am, 1983–; hon/Dean's List, SEn MA Univ, 1972, 1973, 1974; Dean's List, Suffolk Univ, 1976; Dean's List, Suffolk Law Sch, 1982, 1983.

GOLFFING, FRANCIS oc/Journal Editor, Free-Lance Writer; b/Nov 20, 1910; h/272 Middle Hancock Road, Peterborough, NH 03458; m/Barbara; ed/Att'd, Univ of Berlin 1930, Univ of Goettingen 1931, Univ of Heidelberg 1932, Univ of Basel 1933–34; PhD, Univ of Basel, 1934; Postgrad Wk in Grenoble & Cambridge, England; mil/USAF, 1942–45; pa/Univ of UT, 1940–42; Bennington Col, 1948–68; Dean, Hawthorne Col, 1969; Dir of Humanities, Franklin Pierce Col, 1969–74; Dir, Kennedy Inst, Univ of Berlin, 1952–53; Prof of Comparative Lit, Univ of Tuebingen, 1956–57; Sr Fulbright Scholar, 1975–76; Wm Morris Soc, NY & Toronto; Victorian Studies Assn, Wash; Mod Lang Assn; Fulbright Assn; Common Cause; hon/Pubs, *Poems* 1952, *Nietzsche's Birth of Tragedy* 1954, *Selected Poems* 1962, *Collected Poems* 1981, *Likenesses* 1982, *The Jour of Pre-Raphaelite Studies* 1978; Ingram Merrill Awds for Poetry, 1968, 1969, 1971; Oscar William/Gene Derwood Awd for Poetry, 1982–83; W/ W in Am; Dic Am Scholars.

GOLINO, FRANK R oc/Career Diplomat; b/Oct 26, 1936; h/Via Marchesetti 25, Trieste, Italy 34142; ba/Trieste, Italy; m/Christina J Harrison; c/Fabrizio R, Louis R; p/Dominic F and Mary Dober Golino (dec); ed/AB, cum laude, Gannon Univ, 1957; MA, Fordham Univ, 1960; Cert, Bologna Ctr of Sch of Adv'd Intl Studies, 1959; pa/Prin Ofcr, Am Consulate, Trieste, 1981-; Consul, Am Consulate, Johannesburg, 1976-81; Second Secy, Am Embassy, Rome, 1974-76; Second Secy, Am Embassy, Valletta, Malta, 1972-76; Policy Planning Ofcr, Bur of African Affairs, Dept of St, 1970-72; Chm, Mid E-N Africa Area Studies, Fgn Ser Inst, Dept of St, 1968-70; Am Fgn Ser Assn; Am Polit Sci Assn; Intl Polit Sci Assn; Mid E Inst; Mid E Studies Assn; cp/ Rotary, Trieste; r/Rom Cath; hon/Mid E Editor, *Colliers Ency,* 1960-61; Contbr to Profl Jours; Superior Hon Awd, Dept of St, 1980; Italian Fgn Min F'ship, 1958; W/W in E.

GOLL, DARREL EUGENE oc/ Researcher; b/Apr 19, 1936; h/3940 East Alvernon Circle, Tucson, AZ 85718; ba/ Tucson, AZ; m/Rosalie Elaine; c/Laurene Elaine, Jeffrey Eugene, Kathleen Kay; p/Leon O (dec) and Maire E Goll, Garner, IA; ed/BS 1957, MS 1959, IA St Univ; PhD, Univ of WI, 1962; pa/Asst Prof, Depts of Animal Sci & Food Technol 1962-65, Assoc Prof, Depts of Animal Sci, Biochem & Biophysics, Food Technol 1965-70, IA St Univ; NIH Spec Fellow, Dept of Med, Univ of CA-LA, 1966-67; Am Chem Soc; AAAS; Am Soc of Biol Chems; Biophy Soc; Am Soc for Animal Sci; Inst of Food Technologists; Nutrition Today Soc; hon/Author, Approximately 150 Articles in Var Sci Jours, Chapts in Books & Review Articles; Samuel Cate Prescott Awd for Res by Scists Under 35, Inst of Food Technologists, 1970; Dist'd Meats Res Awd, Am Meat Sci Soc; W/W in W.

GONAS, JOHN S oc/Retired Judge; b/May 14, 1907; h/224 West Jefferson, South Bend, IN 46601; ba/South Bend, IN; c/John S Jr, Roy B; p/Samuel and Hazel Gonas (dec); ed/BS, Tri-St Col of Engrg, 1930; LLB, Blackstone Col of Law, 1930; LLM, Chgo Law Sch, 1933; pa/Assessor of Voters, Asst Prosecuting Atty, 1931; St Budget Com, 1940; J of P, 1935; St Rep, 1936-38; Senator, 1940-46; Senate Caucus Chm, 1943; Public Defender, 1945-46; Judge of Probate Juv Ct, 1949-58; Judge, Chief Justice, IN Appellate Ct, 1959; ABA; IN St Bar Assn; Appellate Sect of the ABA; Juv Ct Foun; World Assem of Judges; Engrg Soc; Phi Kappa Theta; cp/BPOE; IN Fraternal Cong, Past Pres 1951; Pres, Am Ethnic Foun Inc; r/Cath; hon/ Author, *The Chd & the Ct, How to Plane Your Estate, Delinquency: There is an Answer, 50 Yrs in Politics;* Co-Authored, *Trial Handbook for IN Lwyrs;* Named Hon Chief of the Chickasaw Nation of Indians, Gov of OK, 1959; Chieftan on the Staff of Sagamores of the Wabash, Gov of IN, 1961; KY Col, Gov of KY, 1959; OK Col, Gov of OK, 1962; AL Col, Gov of AL, 1964; Admiral of the Gt Navy of NE, Gov of NE, 1959; Del, Intl Conf of Juv Ct Judges, Brussels, Belgium, 1954; Participant, UN Conf on Crime & Delinquency, Geneva, Switzerland, 1955; Recip, Cert of Awd, Juv Ct Inst, 1956; Man of the Yr, S Bend Optimist Clb Awd; Alumni Dist'd Awd of Tri-St Univ, 1959; Cert of Apprec, USN; Men of Achmt.

GONZÁLEZ, CRISTINA oc/Assistant Professor of Spanish; b/Apr 9, 1951; h/3332 Peppermill Drive, West Lafayette, IN 47906; ba/West Lafayette, IN; m/Richard A Cohen; p/César Gon-

zález and Cristina Sánchez, Gijón, Spain; ed/PhD in Medieval Spanish Lit 1981, MA in Spanish Lit 1977, IN Univ-Bloomington; MA in Romance Philology, Univ of Oviedo, Spain, 1973; pa/Instr of Spanish 1981, Asst Prof of Spanish 1982-, Purdue Univ; Lectr in Spanish, Tufts Univ, 1980; Assoc Instr of Spanish, IN Univ, 1976-79; Instr of Spanish, Academia "Clarín," Oviedo, Spain, 1976; Tchr of Spanish, Instituto "Calderón de la Barca," Gijón, Spain, 1975; Other Previous Tchg Positions; Société Internationale Arthurienne; Medieval Acad of Am; Semiotic Soc of Am; Am Assn of Tchrs of Spanish & Portuguese; Mod Lang Assn of Am; MW Mod Lang Assn of Am; Hispanic Enlightenment Assn; Centro Español de Documentación y Estudios; Colegio Oficial de Doctores y Licenciados de Oviedo; hon/Pubs, *El Libro del Cavallero Zifar,* "Semiótica y Comunicación de Masas" 1982, Num Others; Res Grant, IN Univ Grad Sch, 1977; XL Sum Fac Grant, Purdue Univ, 1983; El Libro de Gijón; W/W of Am Wom.

GONZALEZ-LIMA, FRANCISCO oc/Neuroscientist; b/Dec 7, 1955; ba/ Ponce School of Medicine, PO Box 7004, Ponce, PR 00732; p/Dr Francisco and Jacinta Lima Gonzalez; ed/BS in Biol 1976, BA in Psych (cum laude) 1977, Tulane Univ; PhD in Anatomy 1980, Res Fellow in Neurophysiol 1981, Univ of PR Sch of Med; pa/Alexander-von-Humboldt Res Fellow in Neurosci, Inst for Zool, Tech Univ, Darmstadt, W Germany, 1982-83; Asst Prof 1980-83, Assoc Prof 1983-, Neuroanatomy, Dept of Anatomy, Ponce Sch of Med, 1980-; Soc for Neurosci; European Neurosci Assn; Nat Soc for Med Res; Nat Hon Soc in Psych; hon/Author, "Santiago Ramon y Cajal: Vida y Consejos de un Genio de la Ciencia" 1985, "Ascending Reticular Activating Systems: A 2-Deoxyglucose Anal" Brain Res, 1985, "Neural Substrates for Tone-Conditioned Bradycardia Demonstrated w 2-Deoxyglucose" Behav Brain Res, 1984, "Tolerance to the Behavioral Effects of Bromocriptine in Cats", *European Jour of Pharm,* 1984, Num Others; Hon Conslt, Radiol Dept, Med Ctr of PR, 1981-; Ad-Honorem Prof, Biol Dept, Cath Univ of PR; Invited Lectr, Colloquium of the Neuroethology Lab, Fac of Biol, Univ of Landes Hessen, 1982; Invited Lectr, Colloquium of the Max Planck Inst for Psychi, 1982; Invited Lectr, Colloquium of the Psych Dept, Univ of Konstanz, 1982; Invited Lectr, Colloquium of Behavioral Neurophysiol, Inst for Zool, St Univ of Groningen, 1982; Invited Lectr, Neurophysiol Colloquium, Max Planck Inst for Brain Res, 1983; W/W: in Frontier Sci & Technol, in the World; Am Men & Wom of Sci.

GONZALEZ-SANABRIA, OLGA D oc/Chemical Engineer; b/Apr 6, 1956; h/ 24510 J Clareshire Drive, North Olmsted, OH 44070; ba/Cleveland, OH; m/ Rafael Sanagria; c/Naomi Sanabria; p/ Meliton and Ana M Rivera Gonzalez, PR; ed/BS, Chem Engrg, Univ of PR, 1979; Currently Wkg on MS in Chem Engrg, Univ of Toledo; pa/Aerospace Engr 1979-81, Chem Engr 1981-, NASA Lewis Res Ctr; Electrochem Soc; AIChE; Tau Beta Pi; hon/Pubs, "Crosslinked Polyvinyl Alcohol Films as Alkaline

Battery Separators" 1983, "PVA Membranes as Alkaline Battery Separators" 1982; Incentive Awd, NASA Lewis Res Ctr; Contbr on Patent; W/W of Am Wom.

GONZÁLEZ VALES, LUIS E oc/ Executive Secretary; b/May 11, 1930; h/ B-12 San Patricio Meadows, Guaynabo, Puerto Rico; ba/Río Piedras, PR; m/ Hilda; c/Carmen I, Luis E Jr, Antonio S, María G, Rosa María, Gerardo, Rosario, Hildita; p/Ernesto González and Carmen Vales de González, Hato Rey, Puerto Rico; ed/BA in Hist, cum laude, Univ of PR, 1952; MA in Latin Am Hist, Courses toward PhD 1963-64, Columbia Univ; mil/Brigadier Gen, PRNG; pa/Exec Secy of Coun on Higher Ed 1967-, Exec Secy of Commonwlth Post Sec'dy Ed Comm 1974-, Asst Dean, Fac of Gen Studies 1965-67, Asst to the Dean of Gen Studies 1960-65, Asst to the Dir of Humanities, Fac of Gen Studies 1957-60, Univ of PR; Nat Hon Soc of Hist; Pres, Beta Delta Chapt of Phi Alpha Theta; Am Hist Assn; Acad of Polit Scis; Am Acad of Polit & Social Scis; Latin Am Studies Assn; PR Acad of Hist; Corres'g Mem, Real Academia de la Historia Madrid; Corres'g Mem, Academia de Geografía e Historia, Guatemala; NG Assn; Resv Ofcrs' Assn; Assn of AUS; Mil Order of the World Wars; hon/Premio Instituto de Literatura Puertorriqueña por la Obra Alejandro Ramírez y su Tiempo, 1978; Premio Colegio de Abogados de PR por la Obra Primera Diputación Provincial: Un Capítulo de Historia Institucional, 1976; Dic of Am Scholars; W/W in S & SW.

GOOCH-ZAMZOW, CLAUDIA E oc/Doll Artisan; b/Aug 2, 1936; ba/PO Box 4610, Santa Clara, CA 95054; m/ Dale; p/Rush; Lila (dec); ed/BA in Design, Shasta Col, 1956; BA in Costume Design, San Jose Univ, 1959; MA, CA Col Arts & Crafts, 1962; pa/Profl Doll Designer, 1965-; Curator, Bear Force Mus, 1982-; U Fdn of Doll Clbs; Intl Old Lacers; Embroiders Guild of Am; Peninsula Lace Maveriks, Fdr; Contemp Doll Artists Guild, Fdr; Lace Mus, Fdr; Doll Fashion Study Grp; Santa Clara Doll Collectors, Fdr; hon/ Textbook Reviewer, The Lace Mus; Author, 12 Articles in Trade & Collector Pubs; 21 Copyrights & 11 Trademarks for Proprietary Graphic & Doll Designs; Comm'd to Design 1st Teddy Bear for His Royal Highness Prince Wm of Wales, 1982; Master Doll Artisan, 1981; W/W: in W, in CA.

GOOD, SUSAN PAULINE oc/Executive; b/Aug 17, 1953; h/4860 North Woodrow, Number 119, Fresno, CA 96726; ba/Fresno, CA; p/Alfred Anton Good (dec); Elsbeth Bates, Fresno, CA; ed/AA, Jour, Reedley Col, 1973; BA, summa cum laude, Jour, CA St Univ-Fresno, 1975; pa/Reg Asst, Asst VP, Br Mgr 1982-, Br Promotions Mgr 1981-82, Ctl Savs & Ln; Dir of Advtg, 1st Savs, 1978-81; Acct Exec, Meeker Advtg, 1977-78; Acct Asst, Elvin Bell Public Relats, 1976-77; Past Pres, Fresno Advtg Fdn, 1983; CA St Univ-Fresno Alumni Assn, 1982; Inst of Financial Ed; 1st Lt Gov, Dist 14, Am Advtg Fdn; cp/Fresno City Co Comm on the Status of Wom, 1978; Current Chair, Fresno Co Dem Ctl Com; r/Rom Cath; hon/Silver Medal Awd, Am Advtg Fdn, 1982; Pt-time Prof, CA St

Univ-Fresno, 1982; Cert of Merit, Inst of Financial Ed, 1981; W/W: Among Am Wom, in CA.

GOODE, PHILIP R oc/Professor of Physics and Chairperson of Department; b/Jan 4, 1943; h/3027 North Sparkman Boulevard, Tucson, AZ 85716; ba/Newark, NJ; p/Philip Carl and Ruth Starr Gifford Goode, CA; ed/AB, Univ of CA-Berkeley, 1964; PhD, Rutgers Univ, 1969; pa/Res Assoc, Rutgers Univ 1969, Univ of Rochester 1969-71; Asst Prof, Rutgers Univ, 1971-77; Mem of Tech Staff, Bell Telephone Labs, 1977-80; Assoc Res Prof, Univ of AZ-Tucson, 1980-84; Prof & Chair, Physics Dept, NJ Inst of Technol, 1984-; Am Phy Soc; Am Astrophy Soc; Big C Soc, Berkeley; hon/ Author, Num Pub'd Articles in Profl Jours; W/W: in Frontier Sci & Technol, in World.

GOODHART, FERN S oc/Public Health Educator; b/Dec 31, 1955; h/885 Cherry Hill Road, Princeton, NJ 08540; ba/Trenton, NJ; m/Hanan M Isaacs; p/ Mr and Mrs Max Goodhart, Sunrise, FL; ed/MS in Public Hlth, Univ of MA Amherst, 1979; BS in Commun Hlth & PE, CUNY/Queens Col, 1976; Tchg Lic in Hlth & PE, K-12, NY, NJ, MA; pa/ Hlth Ed Conslt, Dental Hlth Prog 1984-, St Dept of Hlth Risk Reduction Prog 1983-84; Exec Dir, Gov's Coun on Phy Fitness, 1981-83; Hlth Ed Conslt, St Dept of Hlth Hypertension Prog, 1978-81; Intern, NYC Urban Corps 1975, NYC Pk and Rec Dept 1974; APHA, 1977-; NJ Public Hlth Assn, 1980-; Soc for Public Hlth Ed 1979-, Trustee 1983-85; Kappa Delta Pi, 1976-; Am Running & Fitness Assn, 1977-; Wom's Sports Foun, 1975-; Univ of MA Student Interview Panel, 1976-78; Univ of MA Grad Student Senator, 1977-78; Amherst Col 1st Aid Instr, 1976; S Hunterdon Hlth Coun, 1979-80; cp/ Lambertville Volleyball Clb, 1979-; Mercer Co Wom's Softball Leag, 1983-; Sierra Clb, 1984-; Lambertville Commun Players, 1980-82; Outdoor Clb of S Jersey, 1979-81; hon/Author of 12 Papers Presented to Profl Assns on Hlth Promotion, Hlth Ed, Fitness & Hypertension, 1977-84; Wm Madden Ser Awd, 1976; CUNY Peer Cnslg Tng Prog, 1974-76; Inst for Med in Sports, 1982-83; Police Comm's Conditioning Adv Bd, 1982-83; PE Majs Alliance Exec Bd, 1975-76; Field Hockey Varsity Co-Capt, 1974-76; Long Isl Press Ath Scholar, 1972; Intl W/W of Wom.

GOODIN, WILLIAM CHARLES oc/ Trade Publications Executive; b/Sep 18, 1917; h/11 Parkway Drive, Englewood, CO 80110; ba/Denver, CO; m/Emily Ellen Percefull; c/Sue Ellen Goodin Bach, Charles W; ed/BA in Ec, Univ of CO, 1941; Grad, W HS, Denver, 1936; mil/CIC AUS 1942-46, 1st Lt; pa/Chm of Bd 1979-, Chm of Bd & CEO 1979-83, Pres 1975-79, Owner (Through Merger in 1968, Petro Info Corp Became a Subsidiary of A C Nielsen Co) 1946-68, Petro Info Corp; Dir, Rocky Mtn Oil & Gas Assn; Interst Oil Compact Comm; Denver Landmen's Assn; Rocky Mtn Assn of Petro Geologists, Life Hon Mem; Soc of Petro Engrs of AIME; Am Assn of Petro Geologists; Rocky Mtn Petro Pioneers; Assn of Petro Writers; Indep Petro Assn of Mtn Sts; CO Oil & Gas Comm, Former Mem; Denver

Petro Clb, Life Hon Mem & Past Pres; 25 Yr Clb of Petro Indust; cp/Bd Mem, Bd of Univ of CO Foun Inc, 1983-; Bd Mem, Swedish Med Ctr Foun, 1979-; Cherry Hills Country Clb; Garden of God's Clb; Metro Clb; r/Presb; hon/ Betty McWhorter Awd, 1979; Denver Petro Clb Man of the Yr, 1963.

GOODMAN, JESS THOMPSON oc/ Manufacturing Executive; b/Jan 18, 1936; h/2725 Schifferdecker, Joplin, MO 64801; ba/Joplin, MO; m/Yvonne; c/Walter Raymond II; ed/AB, Polit Sci, Univ of MO, 1959; Postgrad, Pers Mgmt, George Wash Univ, 1968; MA, Nat Security Affairs, Nav Postgrad Sch, 1975; Postgrad, Strategy & Tactics, Nav War Col, 1976; PhD Cand, Intl Relats, Univ of HI, 1978; mil/Ofcr, USN, 1959-79; Lt Cmdr, USN, Ret'd; pa/ Quality Engr, Labarge Inc, Electronics Div, 1982-; Quality Assurance Mgr, Eagle-Picher Indust Inc, Electronics Div, Precision Prods Dept, 1980-82; Nav Sci Instr, Carl Junction, MO, Sch Dist, 1979-80; Sr Mem & Chm, Ozark Chapt 139, Soc of Mfg Engrs, 1984; Sr Mem & Chm-Elect, Joplin-Springfield Sect, Am Soc for QC, 1984; Pi Kappa Alpha Frat; cp/Joplin Assn for the Gifted; Joplin Boys Clb, Cent Clb; Joplin U Way; Life Mem, Univ MO Alumni Assn; Prog Chm, Joplin Kiwanis Clb, 1982; Masonic Frat; Shriners; Am Mensa Ltd; Many Others; r/Meth; hon/Pub, The Chinese Perception of the Spectrum of the Sino-Soviet Territorial Conflict, 1975; Univ of MO Curators Cert of Merit, 1958; Navy Commend Medal, 1969; 2 Navy Achmt Medals, 1970, 1973; W/W: in Aviation & Aerospace, in MW, in World, in Fin & Indust; Men of Achmt; DIB; Intl W/ W of Intells; Personalities of W & MW; Am Registry; Book of Hon; Intl Register of Profiles; Dir of Dist'd Ams; 2,000 Notable Ams; Biogl Roll of Hon; Commun Ldrs of Am.

GOODMAN, JULIUS oc/Nuclear Engineer, Theoretical Physicist; b/Jul 19, 1935; h/1630 Via Linda, Fullerton, CA 92633; ba/Norwalk, CA; m/Rachel; c/Marina; p/Isaac and Eugenia Guttman (dec); ed/MS in Theoretical Physics, St Univ, Odessa, USSR, 1958; PhD in Theoretical Physics, Inst Nuclear Physics, Tashkent, USSR, 1962; Hon Deg in Nuclear Physics, Inst of Technol, Odessa, USSR, 1965; pa/Sr Rschr, Inst Nuclear Physics, Tashkent, Acad Sci, USSR, 1958-63; Prof, Inst of Technol 1963-70, Polytech Univ 1970-76; Sr Engr, Bechtel Power Corp, 1980-; Am Nuclear Soc; Soc of Reliability Engrs; Publicity Chm 1983-84, LA Coun of Engrs & Scists; cp/Pres, Hatchiya Assn, CA 1982-; B'nai B'rith Lodge, Orange Coast; Toastmasters Clb; r/Judaism; hon/Author, About 150 Sci Articles in Profl Jours, Books, incl'g, Profl Ed 1975, Positron Diagnostics 1978; Patentee, Nuclear Reactor w UF-6; Marquis W/ W.

GOODSON, MAX REED (Deceased) oc/Former Professor Emeritus; b/Feb 5, 1911; h/Formerly of 715 South Los Topacios, Green Valley, AZ 85614; m/ Margaret Catharine; c/Nancy Kay Thomas, Charles Robert; p/Otis Richard and Eva Reed Goodson, Tuscola, IL; ed/BA 1933, MA 1936, EdM 1942, EdD 1949, Univ of IL; pa/Former Positions incl: Elem Tchr, Tuscola, IL, 1933; HS Sci Tchr, Mason City, IL,

1934; Prin, HS, Dana, IL, 1935; Sci Tchr & Coor, Student Tchg, Univ High, Univ of IL, 1936-43; IN Univ, 1944; Prin, Horace-Mann, Lincoln, NY, 1945-47; Assoc Dean of Ed & Prof, OH St Univ, 1948-57; Dean of Ed, Boston Univ, 1958-62; Editor-in-Chief, Ginn & Co, 1963-64; Prof of Ednl Policy Studies & Social Wk 1965-77, Dir of R & D Ctr 1965-67, Prof Emeritus 1977-84, Univ of WI-Madison; Fellow, Nat Tng Lab, 1949-60; Pres, NE Coun for Ec Ed, 1960; Pres, MW Reg Lab, 1967-68; Conslt, Madison Sch Sys, Dept of Public Ed, WI, 1970-77; cp/Former Activs incl: Chm, Unitarian Coun, 1970-75; Pres, Homeowners Assn, 1982; GV Forum, 1977-84; GV IL Clb Pres, 1983; r/ Unitarian-Universalist; hon/Pubs, Humanistic Considerations in Grad Ed & Res 1977, Human Foresight & Moral Re-Ed 1978, Desegregation & Re-Integration in Sch & Society 1981, Use of Human Sci in Resolving Public Issues 1981; Phi Delta Kappa, 1935; Kappa Phi Kappa, 1949; NY Acad of Sci, 1979; Human Relats Awd, Madison, WI, 1978; Dist'd Lectr, Univ of AZ, 1981; W/W: in Am, in World; Men of Achmt.

GOODSPEED, BARBARA oc/Artist; b/Sep 1, 1919; h/Holiday Point Road, Sherman CT 06784; ba/Same; p/George D and Bernice L Goodspeed; ed/Grad, Stoneleigh Col, 1939; Studied Art Ed, Clarence White Sch of Photo, NYC; Att'd, Famous Artists Sch; Took Art Classes, Frank Webb, Edgar A Whitney, Ray Loos; pa/Self-Employed Photog, 1940-52; Designer of Christmas Cards, 1952-71; China Restorer, 1971-78; Artist, Oils & Watercolors, 1960-; Pres & Bd, Kent Art Assn, 1970-83; Ofcr, Bd, Housatonic Art Leag, 1979-83; Grp & One-Man Shows, Sheffield, MA; Bd, Weantinogue Heritage (Land Trust), 1979-83; Am Artists Profl Leag, NYC; Hudson Val Art Assn; Nat Leag of Am Pen Wom, Wash, DC; Salmagundi Clb & Knickabocker Artists, NYC; Acad Artists; hon/Illustrated, "Forever Flowers" by R Metzler; Artist of the Yr Awd, Art Leag of Harlem Val, NY; Wom Artists II; World W/W of Wom; DIB.

GOODSTONE, GERALDINE H oc/ Health Marketing Executive, Consultant; ba/210 East 15th Street, New York, NY 10003; p/Mr Bertram Goodstone, Miami Shores, FL; Mrs Sylvia Goodstone, New York, NY; ed/MA, Hunter Col, 1971; Cert in Hlth Mktg, Wharton Sch, 1978; Hlth Study Prog, Sch of Labor & Indust Relats, Cornell, 1978; pa/Dir of Mktg, Hlth Examinetics Inc (Nationwide Hlth Testing Co), 1979-; Conslt, Fdr & Prin Ofcr, Corporate Hlth Planning Inc, 1978-; Dir of Corp Hlth Sers, Assoc Admr, Preven Med Inst, Strang Clin, 1972-78; Dir of Opers, Cine-Vox Prodns Inc, 1970-72; Dir, 34th St Midtown Assn, 1974-78; Acoustical Soc of Am, Mbrship Chair 1980; hon/Articles & Broadcasts, "Cost Effectiveness of Multiphasic Hlth Screening" 1977, "Voice of Am-Disease Preven" (WNYC-AM/FM) 1975-77; Pres, Zonta Clb of NY, 1981-82; Bd Mem, USO of Metro NY; W/W in Fin & Indust.

GOODYEAR, NELSON oc/Educator/Writer; b/Jan 12, 1912; h/15111 Bushard Avenue, Number 23, Westminster, CA 92683; ba/Same; m/Virginia B; c/Charles, Lydia, Katharine, Lawrence; ed/BA, Langs 1933, MA, Ed

Adm, 1950, Columbia Univ; PhD, CA Christian Univ, 1972; Public Adm, Yale, Syracuse; pa/Pvt Sch Tchr & Bus Mgr, 1934-39; Inspector, Def Industs & Met Analyst, 1939-45; Prof of Indust Mgmt, Univ of So CA, 1950-52; Tech Writer, 1950-72; VP & Dean, Christian Univ, 1972-83, Pres/Inactive Status 1984; Investor & Property Mgr, 1970-; AAUP; Inst of Human Engrg Scis; Psi Upsilon Frat; hon/Pubs, "Res Design & Planning for a Low Cost Microfilming & Projection Sys," 1940; USN Patent Applied for as Proj Engr Model Builder for Electro-Mech Resuscitator, 1944; Rotating Tool & Hardware Racks, 1947-52; Crash Proof Radio Rescue Transmitter, 1958; Illustrated Newspaper Feature Articles; Reports, Opers Maintenance & Tng Manuals on Planes, Guns, Tanks, Vessels, Submarines, Rockets, Space Vehicles; Currently Res Authoritative Biogl Data on Charles Goodyear & Other Goodyear Inventors; Sigma Iota Epsilon; Var Certs & Awds in Field; Men of Achmt.

GOOS, ROGER D oc/Mycologist; b/ Oct 29, 1924; h/4 Tanglewood Trail, Narragansett, RI 02882; ba/Kingston, RI; m/Mary Lee Engel; c/Marinda Lee Goos Cox, Suzanne; p/Gus and Georgianna Goos (dec); ed/BA 1950, MS in Botany 1955, PhD in Botany 1958, Univ of IA; mil/AUS, 1944-46, 1950-51; pa/ Mycologist, U Fruit Co, 1958-62; Scist, USPHS, NIH, 1962-64; Curator of Fungi, Am Type Culture Collection, 1964-68; Assoc Rschr & Vis'g Assoc Prof, Dept of Botany, Univ of HI, 1968-70; Assoc Prof & Prof of Botany, Univ of RI, 1970-; Chair, Dept of Botany, Univ of RI, 1971; Mycological Soc of Japan; Brit Mycological Soc; Mycological Soc of India; Mycological Soc of Am, Secy-Treas 1980-83, VP 1983-84, Pres Elect 1984-85, Pres 1985-86; Botanical Soc of Am; Am Phytopathological Soc; Am Soc Microbiol; AAAS; hon/Author of Approximately 60 Sci Articles in *Mycologia, Canadian Jour Botany*; W/W: in Am; in E; Am Men & Wom of Sci.

GORDON, CYRUS H oc/University Professor, Orientalist; b/Jun 29, 1908; h/130 Dean Road, Brookline, MA 02146; ba/New York, NY; m/Joan Kendall; c/Deborah Gordon Friedrich, Sarah Y Krakauer, Rachel Gordon Bernstein, Noah D, Dan K; p/Dr Benjamin Lee Gordon (dec); ed/AB 1927, MA 1928, PhD 1930, Univ of PA; mil/ WW II, AUS, 1942-46; Ret'd Col, USAF; pa/Instr of Hebrew & Assyrian, Univ of PA, 1930-31; Field Archeologist & Epigrapher as Fellow of the Am Schs of Oriental Res in Jerusalem & Baghdad, 1931-35; Tchg Fellow, Oriental Sem, Johns Hopkins Univ, 1935-38; Lectr in Bible & Ancient Hist, Smith Col, 1938-39, 1940-41; Inst for Adv'd Study, Princeton, 1939-40, 1941-42; Prof of Assyriology & Egyptology, Dropsie Univ, 1946-56; Prof of Mediterranean Studies, Brandeis Univ, 1956-73; Prof of Hebrew & Dir of the Ctr for Ebla Res, NY Univ, 1973-; r/Jewish; hon/ Author, *Ugaritic Textbook* 1967, *The Ancient Near E* 1965, *The Common Background of Greek & Hebrew Civilizations* 1965, *Poetic Legends & Myths from Ugarit* 1977, *Forgotten Scripts* 1982; Hon Fellow, Royal Asiatic Soc, 1975; Fellow, Am Acad of Arts & Scis, 1968; Fellow, Am Acad for

Jewish Res, 1980; W/W in Am; Others.

GORDON, DONALD A oc/Engineering Research Psychologist; b/Sep 16, 1918; h/8435 Brook Road, McLean, VA 22102; ba/Langly, VA; m/Grace Hartley; c/Caroline Camilla, Elizabeth Ruth, Alice Rena; p/John J and Camilla E Gordon (dec); ed/BA 1940, MA 1942, PhD 1946, Columbia Univ; pa/Lectr, Assoc Res Psychol, Univ of MI, 1955-59; Engrg Psychol, Bendix Sys Div, 1959-61; Human Factors Spec, Sperry Gyroscope Co, 1961-63; Engrg Res Psychol, Fed Hwy Adm, DOT, 1963-; Am Psychol Assn, 1947-; Human Factors Soc, 1979-; hon/Author of 55 Sci Articles Concerned w Probs of Human Engrg & Exptl Psych; Samuel M Burka Awd for Outstg Paper on Navigation or Space Guid, 1960; Ser Cit, US Ofc of Sci Res & Devel, Com on Med Res, 1945.

GORDON, LENORE oc/Infection Control Educator; b/Nov 23, 1931; h/ 215 Passaic Avenue, Passaic, NJ 07055; ba/Newark, NJ; p/Betty Gordon, Passaic, NJ; ed/BS, cum laude, Med Technol, Fairleigh Dickinson Univ, 1955; MA in Hlth Care Ed, Ctl MI Univ, 1977; pa/ Microbiologist, Babies Hosp, Columbia Univ, 1955-59; Microbiologist, Belinson Hosp, Petah Tikva, Israel, 1960-72; Hd Microbiol Sect, Barnert Meml Hosp, 1972-75; Instr, Infection Control, UMDWJ, 1977-; Am Soc Microbiol; Assn Practitioners in Infection Control; Am Soc Med Technol; Ctl MI Univ Alumni Assn; r/Jewish; hon/Pub, "Diversified Ednl Techniques in Infection Control" in *Infection Control & Urological Care*, 1983; W/W of Am Wom.

GORDON, PAMELA ANN oc/Pharmaceutical Sales Representative; b/Feb 17, 1953; h/104 Oriole Court, Royal Palm Beach, FL 33411; ba/Fort Lauderdale, FL; p/Norman A and Louise R Gordon, Royal Palm Beach, FL; ed/ Student, Barry Col, 1971-74; Cytotechnologist, Univ of Miami, 1975; BBA, FL Atl Univ, 1980; pa/Staff Cytotechnologist & Instr, Univ of Miami Med Sch, 1975-77; Chief Cytotechnologist, Diagnostic Lab, 1977-78; Pharm Sales Rep, Glaxo Inc, 1981-; Am Soc of Cytology; Am Soc of Clin Pathologists; FL Soc of Cytology; So Assn of Cytotechnologists; Delta Sigma Pi; Secy of Alumni Assn for Delta Sigma Pi, 1980-82; hon/Sales Achmt Awd, Glaxo Inc, for Fiscal Yr 1982; W/W of Am Wom.

GORDON, ROSE MARIA ELIZ oc/ Consultant, Counselor, Educator; b/ Aug 27, 1931; h/6955 Peggy Drive, Las Vegas, NV 89128; ba/Las Vegas, NV; m/Irv; c/Rocky, Maia, Heidi, Aaron; ed/ BS 1978, MS 1981, Univ NV-Las Vegas; pa/Adj Fac, Clark Co Commun Col, 1984; Grp Facilitator/Conslt, Indiv & Grp Cnslg, 1972-, PsychoL Pract; Conslt, Raleigh Hills Hosp, 1982-83; Cnslr/ Therapist, Lectr, Indiv & Grp Conslg, N Las Vegas Hosp, 1978-; Lectr, 1976-78; APGA; Nat Rehab Assn; ARCA; NV Rehab Assn; Am Fdn Tchrs; Nat Inst Mtl Hlth; Num Commun Ser Activs incl'g Commun Action Agnst Rape; Las Vegas Crisis Ctr, Cnslr Tng Sem; Musicians' Wives Clb; We Care Foun; hon/W/W in W; Personalities of W & MW.

GORE, LESLIE THOMAS JR oc/ Special Accounts Manager; b/Jun 7, 1948; h/7260 Northwest Court, Plan-

tation, FL 33317; ba/Ft Lauderdale, FL; m/Earline L; c/Aleshia Clark, Tawnya Clark, Christa Clark; p/Leslie T and Esther Gore, Edison, NJ; ed/BA, Tarkio Col, 1969; Elect Theory, NYC, 1971; Air Conditioning & Refrigeration, FL Tech, 1980; mil/USCG Resv; pa/Spec Accts Mgr, Robert J Fish & Co, 1982-; Salesman, Universal Brands, 1981-82; Salesman, So Wine & Spirits, 1980-81; Mgr, Wendy's, 1975-78; Owner, Mgr, Angry Squire Restaurant, 1970-74; cp/ Masons, 1969-; Former BSA Scoutmaster, 1967-71; DeMolay, 1961; hon/Eagle Scout, 1965; Order of the Arrow, 1963; God & Country Awd, 1964; Am Legion Good Citizenship, 1965.

GOREHAM, JACQUELINE SUE WILLIAMS oc/Educator; b/Jan 21, 1935; h/8805 West 80th Drive, Arvada, CO 80005; ba/Northglenn, CO; m/Donald James; c/Elizabeth Vanessa, Andrew Bentley; p/Logan A (dec) and Edith M Williams, Ridgefarm, IL; ed/BS in Home Ec, En IL Univ, 1957; Postgrad, CO St Univ, 1981-83; Att'd, Univ of No CO, 1973-80; pa/Asst Home Advr, Univ of IL Ext Ser, 1957-60; Free-Lance Home Economist in IL & CO, 1961-71; Tchr, Home Ec, York Jr High, 1972-76; Exec Dir, Dairy Coun of Gtr KC, MO, 1977-78; Tchr, Home Ec Dept Hd, Northglenn Jr High, 1979-; Communication Dir, CO Friendship Force; Am Home Ec Assn; CO Home Ec Assn (St Bd), Mbrship Chm 1981-82; St S'ship Chm 1984, Am Voc Assn; CO Ed Assn; AAUW; Delta Kappa Gamma; Kappa Omicron Phi; Sigma Sigma Sigma Alumni, VP 1983-84; cp/Charter Mem, Northglenn, CO, Arts & Humanities, VP 1973-76; r/Presb; hon/Co-Author, Quick Recipes Pamphlet, Univ of IL Ext, 1965; Tested Recipes for *Complete Fireplace Cookbook*, 1982; Represented US Treas, Savs Bonds Div, as Mrs US Savs Bonds, 1971-72; CO All-Am Fam Designate, 1971-72; Nat Correspondent Awd, Sigma Sigma Sigma Triangle Mag; W/W in W.

GORENSTEIN, PAUL oc/Astrophysicist; b/Aug 15, 1934; h/100 Memorial Drive, Cambridge, MA 02142; ba/ Cambridge, MA; p/Isidore and Bess Gorenstein, New York, NY; ed/Bach of Engrg Physics, Cornell Univ, 1957; PhD, Physics, MIT, 1962; pa/Fulbright Postdoct Fellow in Italy, 1963-65; Sr Scist, Am Sci & Engrg, 1965-73; Astrophysicist, Smithsonian Astrophy Observatory, 1973-; Am Phy Soc; Am Astronom Assn; AAAS; Intl Astronom Union; r/Jewish; hon/Editor, *Astronomy from Space* 1983, *Supernova Remnants & Their X-Ray Emission* 1983; Author, Num Pubs in Tech Jours; NASA Medal for Outstg Sci Achmt, 1973; NASA Certs of Recog (5), 1969-81; W/W in Am Sci.

GOREWITZ, RUBIN LEON oc/Certified Public Accountant; b/Jun 7, 1924; h/7 Danville Court, West Nyack, NY 10994; ba/New York, NY; m/Freide Heller; c/Heshi, Marian Esther, Shalom; ed/BBA, Col City of NY, 1951; mil/AUS, 1943-45; pa/Public Acct, J Scherago & Co, CPA's, NYC, 1942-48; Sr Public Acct, Leonard S Shair, CPAs, NYC, 1948-56; Controller, Herold Electronics Co, 1956-59; Pvt Pract, Public Acctg, Financial Concerns, NY St, 1959; VP, Dir, Robert Rauschenberg Inc; Conslt in New Bus Ventures; Fdr, Former Treas, Dir, Midsummer Inc, Experts in

Art & Technol; Am Inst CPAs; NY Soc CPAs; Nat Assn Cost Accts, Past Dir NYC Chapt; cp/The Real Univ of Sts; Abstract Ballet Contempo Inc; Fdr, Past Dir, Storytime Dance Theatre Inc; Inst for Chamber Music Inc; Traditional Jazz Band Co Inc; Foun for Vital Arts; Creat Dance Foun; Mod Dance Artists Inc; Seamus Murphy Dance Foun; Yuriko Dance Foun; Daniel Neagrin Dance Foun; Intermedia Foun; Fdr, Dir, Cunningham Dance Foun; Treas, Lightyrs Inc; Fdr, Financial Advr, Martha Graham Ctr; Chiemera Dance Foun; New World Wkshop; Dance Theatre Foun; Search Inc; Ctrs for Change; Chm of Bd, Dance Notation Bur; Bd of Dirs, Dance Theatre Wkshop; New Dance Grp Studio; Concert Artists Guild; Financial Advr, Perf Grp; Survival Arts Media; Open Theatre; Foun of Contemp Perf'g Arts; Music Drama Theatre; Cantors Assem of Am; Staff Acct Conslt, NY St Coun on Arts; Adv Dir, Mod Dance Foun; hon/Contbr of Articles to Art in Am Dance Mag.

GORIN, ROBERT MURRAY JR oc/Educator; b/Oct 29, 1948; h/51 Somerset Avenue, Garden City, Long Island, NY 11530; ba/Long Island, NY; p/Robert Murray and Vivian Schleider Gorin; ed/AB, MA 1970, Xavier Univ; MS in Ed, Hofstra Univ, 1974; MA, Fordham Univ, 1978; PhD, St Louis Univ, 1980; Att'd, St Louis Univ Sch of Law 1970-71, Inst of Moral Devel & Moral Ed (Harvard Univ) 1983; mil/AUS, 1968-69; pa/Social Studies Edr, Bellmore-Merrick Ctl HS Dist 1974-77, 1978-83, Rockville Centre Union Free Sch Dist 1977-78, Manhasset Public Schs 1983-; Curric Conslt, Bellmore-Merrick U Sec'dy Tchrs, 1982-83; Soc for Hist Ed; Am Hist Assn; Org of Am Histns; So Hist Assn; Acad of Polit Sci; Ctr for the Study of the Presidency; Long Isl Coun for the Social Studies; NY St Coun for the Social Studies; Nat Coun for the Social Studies, Ethics Adv Com 1982-87; Assn for Supvn & Curric Devel; Inst of Soc, Ethics & the Life Scis; Am Assn for St & Local Hist; Nat Trust for Historic Presv; Garden City Hist Soc; cp/Metro Opera Guild; Civil War Round Table of NY; r/Roman Catholic; hon/Taft Scholar, Robert A Taft Inst of Government, 1976; Phi Alpha Theta, Intl Hist Hon Soc; W/W in East; Long Island Leaders.

GOTTESMAN, STEPHEN T oc/Professor of Astronomy; b/Feb 23, 1939; h/2222 Northwest 27th Terrace, Gainesville, FL 32605; ba/Gainesville, FL; m/Celia Frances Docherty; c/Lorna Rachel, Ian Kenneth Jacob; p/Jacob F (dec) and Edna B Gottesman, Palm Bch, FL; sp/James S Docherty, Manchester, England; ed/BA, Colgate Univ, 1960; PhD, Victoria Univ Manchester, 1967; pa/Lectr, Univ Keele (England), 1968-69; Res Assoc, Nat Radio Astronom Obs, 1969-71; Res Fellow, CA Inst Tech, 1971; Asst Prof 1972-76, Assoc Prof 1976-81, Prof 1981-, Univ FL; Guest Prof, Onsala Space Obs, 1983; Vacation Conslt, Royal Obs Edinburgh, 1983; Conslt to Var Publishers; Proj Conslt, Nat Endowment for Humanities, 1976-77; Chm, IAU, 1979-; Mem, Nat Radio Astron Obs Useri Com, 1978-81, 1983-85; Intl Union Radio Sci; Royal Astronom Soc; Am Astronom Soc; hon/Author of Num Pubs; Phi Beta

Kappa; Fulbright Scholar; Leverhulme Fellow; W/W: in Frontier Sci & Technol, in S & SW; Am Men & Wom Sci.

GOTTLIEB, LEONARD S oc/Physician, Pathologist, Educator, Administrator; b/May 26, 1927; h/120 Willard Road, Brookline, MA 02146; ba/Boston, MA; m/Dorothy Apt; c/Julie Ann Texeira, William Apt, Andrew Richard; ed/AB cum laude, Bowdoin Col, 1946; MD, Tufts Univ Sch of Med, 1950; MPH, Harvard Univ, 1969; mil/Lt & Ltc MC, USNR; Asst Chief of Pathol, US Nav Hosp, 1955-57; pa/Dir, Mallory Inst of Pathol, Boston City Hosp, 1972-; Chief of Pathol, Univ Hosp, 1973-; Prof & Chm, Dept of Pathol, Boston Univ Sch of Med, 1980-; Am Soc for Exptl Pathol; Am Assn for the Study of Liver Diseases; Intl Acad of Pathol; Am Soc of Cell Biol; Am Gastroenterological Assn; New Eng Soc of Pathologists, Pres 1968-69; Am Soc of Clin Pathologists; Edit Bd, *Am Jour, Surg Pathol*; Am Inst of Nutrition; Col of Am Pathologists; hon/Author, Over One-Hundred Sci Articles on Human & Exptl Pathol of the Liver & Gastro-Intestinal Tract; James Bowdoin Scholar, 1945; Dir of the Mallory Inst of Pathol Foun, 1980-.

GOTTLIEB, SHELDON F oc/Dean of Graduate School and Director of Research; b/Dec 22, 1932; h/8213 Tahoe Drive, Mobile, AL 36609; ba/Mobile, AL; m/Eda; c/Stephen Eric, Pamela Lynn, Glenn Ira, William Scott; p/Elias and Dorothy Gottlieb (dec); ed/BA, Bklyn Col, 1953; MS, Univ of MA, 1956; PhD, Univ of TX Med Br, 1959; mil/AUS, 1954-56; pa/Dean of Grad Sch & Dir of Res, Univ of S AL, 1980-; Prof of Biol Scis 1972-80, Assoc Prof of Biol Scis 1968-72, IN Univ-Purdue Univ at Ft Wayne; Asst Prof of Physiol & Asst Prof of Anesthesiology, Jefferson Med Col, 1964-68; Res Physiol, Linde Div Union Carbide Corp, 1959-64; Aerospace Med Assn; AAAS; Am Inst of Biol Scis; Am Physiol Soc; Am Soc for Microbiol; Sigma Xi; Soc of Gen Physiols; Undersea Med Soc; Nat Coun of Univ Res Admrs; Coun of Grad Schs in the US; Conf of So Grad Schs; cp/Am Heart Assn, AL Affil-SW AL Reg, 1980-; Mobile C of C, Ed Com 1980-, Ec Devel Coun 1980-, Oil & Gas Com 1980-, Public & Govtl Affairs Coun 1980-; r/Jewish; hon/Pubs, "Formation of Decompression Bubbles in Bovine Serum & Synovial Fluid" 1982, "Two Midrashim & Evolution, an Ongoing Dialogue in Syncopation: Which One is Rel?" 1982 "An Anal of Advantages of a Single Adm at the IN Univ-Purdue Univ Fort Wayne Campus" 1971, "Anal of the Preliminary Draft of the Report of the Comm for Higher Ed as Pertains to Basic Res at the Fort Wayne Campus" 1972, "Modeling the Nervous Sys: Reaction Time & the Ctl Nervous Sys" 1977, "Pop Growth & the Logistic Curve" 1979, Num Others; Res Asst-'ship, Univ of MA, 1953-54; Res Asst-'ship 1956-57, Tchg F'ship 1957-59, Univ of TX Med Br; Ldrs of Am Sci; Outstg Edrs of Am; W/W: in MW, in S & SW, in Am.

GOULD, JANICE S CALDWELL oc/Investment Broker; b/Dec 20, 1942; h/1307 Detroit, Indianola, IA 50125; ba/Ankeny, IA; m/Troy Allen Taylor; c/Troy Bryan, Jonna Ryon; p/Gilbert R and Frances E Caldwell, West Newton,

IA; ed/BA, Univ of IA, 1967; pa/Subst Tchr, Las Vegas, 1973; Real Est Sales, Las Vegas, 1973-75; Stock Broker, Investmts, Dain Bosworth Inc, 1974-82; Stock Broker, Investmts, Edward D Jones & Co, 1982-; AAUW, St Legis Chm, Nat Conv Del 1975; Univ of IA Alumni Assn; Alpha Xi Delta Greek Sorority & Alumni Assn; cp/Zonta; La Sertoma; Citizens Ad Hoc Com, Law Sch for Univ of NV-Las Vegas (Pres, Secy, Orgr, Lobbyist, Adv Bd 1974-76); Clark Co Ctl Repub Com, (Precnt Capt, Histn, Bd of Dirs 1969-74), St Conv Del & Co Conv Del 1969-74, St Credential Com; Warren Co Repub Co Ctl Com & Precnt Capt 1979-82, Indianola Co Conv Del 1980, 1982, Dist & St Statutory Conv Del 1980, 1982; Originated 3 Co "Tri-TAG"; Tchr, Sec'dy Level, Sunday Sch; Mem, PEO (Charter Chapt Pres, St Conv Del & Chaplin); r/Prot; hon/W/W of Am Wom.

GOULD, MARY CATHERINE oc/Business Co-Owner; b/Oct 7, 1907; h/2404 Martin, Wichita Falls, TX 76308; ba/Same; p/Mr and Mrs Louis H Gould; ed/BS, So Meth Univ; Grad Wk, W TX St Univ; pa/Tchr of Primary Grades for 43 Yrs, Wichita Falls Indep Sch Dist; Salesman & Owner of Real Est Ofc, Louis H Gould Realty, 1944-; Helped Organize Local Tchrs Fed Credit Union; Local, St & Nat Orgs in Real Est & Ednl Orgs (Bd of Rltrs, NEA, TSTA, TRT); Life Mem, Cunningham PTA; Life Mem, Alpha Delta Pi Social Sorority; cp/St & Nat Repub Coms; Has Held Ofcs in Local Ednl, Social & Ch Orgs, incl'g Presidencies; DAR; Former SS Tchr; Heritage Soc; hon/Inclusion in Heritage Register of the USA; Made Life Mem, Cunningham PTA by Parents.

GOULD, STEPHEN JAY oc/Professor of Geology; b/Sep 10, 1941; h/29 Crescent Street, Cambridge, MA 02138; ba/Cambridge, MA; m/Deborah; c/Jesse, Ethan; ed/AB, Geol, Antioch Col, 1963; PhD, Columbia Univ, 1967; pa/Asst Prof of Geol 1967-71, Assoc Prof of Geol 1971-73, Prof of Geol & Alexander Agassiz Prof of Zool 1973-, Harvard Univ; NSF Fellow; Fellow of AAAS; Paleontological Soc; Soc of Systematic Zool; Soc for the Study of Evolution; Am Soc of Naturalists, Edit Bd of *Am Naturalist*, Pres 1979-80; Hist of Sci Soc; hon/Author, Approximately 145 Maj Articles, 1965-82; Pubs, *Ontogeny & Phylogeny* 1977, *Ever Since Darwin* 1977, *Hen's Teeth & Horse's Toes*, 1983, *The Panda's Thumb* 1980, *The Mismeasure of Man* 1981, Monthly Articles in *Natural Hist Mag* 1974-; Nat Mag Awd, 1980; Am Book Awd, Sci, 1981; Nat Book Critics Circle Awd for *The Mismeasure of Man*, 1982; Nat Assn Geol Tchrs, Neil Miner Awd, 1983; Silver Medal, Zool Soc Lond, 1984; Meritorious Ser Awd, Am Assn Systematics Collections, 1984; Medal of Excell, Columbia Univ, 1982; MacArthur Foun Prize F'ship, 1982-86.

GOULD, WESLEY LARSON oc/Professor of Political Science; b/May 15, 1917; h/693 Partington Avenue, Windsor, Ontario N9B 2N6; ba/Detroit, MI; m/Jean Sarah Barnard; c/Francis Barnard, Sarra Marie, Margaret Elizabeth Guldan; p/Francis Erie and Helen Marie Larson Gould (dec); ed/AB, Baldwin-Wallace Col, 1940; MA, OH St Univ, 1941; Postgrad Study, Univ of

CA-Berkeley, 1941-42; PhD, Harvard Univ, 1949; mil/US Army, PTO, 1942-45; pa/Instr, NEn Univ, 1946-49; Asst Prof 1949-58, Assoc Prof 1958-61, Prof 1961-67, Purdue Univ; Prof 1967-83, Prof Emeritus 1984-, Wayne St Univ; Vis'g Asst Prof, Boston Univ, Sum 1953; Conslt, Intl Law Study, US Nav War Col, Sum 1960; Vis'g Prof, NWn Univ, 1963-64; PhD Examr, Patna Univ, 1963-64; Fellow, Univ of Liverpool, 1974-75; Instr, Alumni Col, Baldwin-Wallace Col, 1984; Vis'g Scholar, Univ of Winnipeg, Sum 1979; Am Soc of Intl Law, Exec Coun 1959-62; Am, Intl & MW Polit Sci Assns; Intl Studies Assn, Exec Com, Intl Law Sect 1976-78; IN Acad of the Social Scis, Bd of Dirs 1958-60; Acad of Polit Sci; Am Soc for Public Adm; Soc for Gen Sys Res; Am Soc for Polit & Legal Phil; Law & Soc Assn; Assn for Canadian Studies in the US; AAUP; Pi Sigma Alpha; hon/ Pubs, *An Intro to Intl Law* 1957, *The Relation Between Intl Law & Mun Law in the Netherlands & in the US* 1961, *Law Books Recommended for Libs: Intl Law* (Annotated) 1968; *Intl Law & the Social Sci* 1970, *Social Sci Lit: A Bibliog for Intl Law* (Annotated) 1972, Contbns to Profl Books & Jours; Recip, Alumni Merit Awd, Baldwin-Wallace Col, 1984; Social Sci Res Coun Grant, 1957; Am Soc of Intl Law Grant, 1964; Purdue Univ Grants, 1957, 1959, 1961; Wayne St Univ Grant, 1970; Earhart Foun Grant, 1974; W/W: in Am, in World, in Am Law, in MW; Intl W/W of Intells; Contemp Authors; Men of Achmt; DIB; Intl Scholars Dir; Am Men & Wom of Sci: The Social & Behavioral Scis.

GOULDING, CHARLES EDWIN oc/ Consulting Professional Engineer; b/ Nov 23, 1916; h/2569 Volunteer Parkway, Bristol, TN 37620; m/Meta Isabell Hyslop; p/Charles and Eugenia Goulding (dec); ed/BS, Univ of Tampa, 1939; Postgrad Certs in Chem Engrg 1941, Civil Engrg 1941; MS 1944, PhD 1946, Univ of FL; Electronic Engr, Phila Wireless Inst, 1962; pa/Engr, US Phosphric Div, TN Corp, 1939-41; Instr, Univ of FL-Gainesville, 1941-46; Consltg Engr, Venezuelan Govt, Mins Public Wks, Caracas, 1946-49; Tech Dir, Consultec, Caracas, 1946-51; Tech Coor, Industs Fontura, Sao Paulo, Brazil, 1951-54; Chief Engr, Proj Dir, Bioquimica, Mexico City, 1954-57; Nuclear Tng Dir, NV Shipbldrs Corp, 1963-64; Instr, Chem, Temple Univ, 1964-65; Vis'g Lectr, Physics & Earth Sci, Univ of TN-Chattanooga, 1968-69; Sr Engr, E H Richardson Assocs, 1971-72; Prin Envir Engr, Nassaux-Hemsley, 1973-77; Chief Engr, Twin City Engrg Assocs, 1977-; Pres, T&M Machining Div, 1978-; Conslt, Chem Processes, 1957-68; Communication Engr, CD, Chambersburg, 1973-77; Res Dpty Sheriff, Sullivan Co, 1977-; Reg'd Profl Engr, DE, PA, MD, NJ, OH, KY, WV, VA, NC, SC, TN, LA, Venezuela; AIChE; Am Chem Soc; IEEE; Am Ordnance Assn; Nat Soc Profl Engrs; NY Acad Scis; US Congl Adv Bd; AAAS; Water Pollution Control Fdn; TN Soc Profl Engrs; Sigma Xi; Phi Sigma; cp/Repub Nat Com; Am Security Coun; Am Assn Ret'd Persons; Smithsonian Assocs; Kettlefoot Rod & Gun Clb; Moose; hon/Contbr, Articles to Tech Jours; Patentee (4); Hon Mayor,

Boy's Town, NE; Hon Grad Scholar, Univ of FL, 1944-46; Pres, Phi Sigma Nat Hon Biol Soc, 1946; Sigma Xi Hon Soc; Postdoct Hon Scholar, Univ of PA, 1962-63; Am Men of Sci; Bibliog of Scists & Engrs; Intl W/W of Biol Scists; W/W: in E, in World, in S & SW.

GOULDTHORPE, KENNETH ALFRED PERCIVAL oc/Editor and Publisher; b/Jan 7, 1928; h/3049 Northwest Esplanade Drive, Seattle, WA 98117; ba/Bellevue, WA; m/Judith Cutts; c/ Amanda Frances; p/Frances Elizabeth Gouldthorpe, Welling, Kent, England; ed/Att'd, Univ of London 1948-49, Bloomsbury Tech Inst 1949-50, Wash Univ 1951-53; Dipl, City & Guilds of London, 1949; mil/Royal Navy, Minesweepers, 1945-48; pa/Staff Photog 1951-55, Picture Editor 1955-57, *St Louis Post-Dispatch*; Nat & Fgn Correspondent, *Life* Mag, Time Inc, NYC, 1957-65; Reg Editor, Australia-New Zealand, 1966-68; Edit Dir, *Life*, Latin Am, 1969-70; Editor, *Signature* Mag, 1970-73; Mng Editor, *Penthouse* Mag, 1973-76; Publishing Conslt, 1976-79; Editor & Exec Publisher, *Adventure Travel* Mag, Seattle, 1979-80; Sr Ptnr, Pacific Pub'g Assocs, 1981-83; Editor & Publisher, *WA, the Evergreen St Mag*, 1984-, VP Evergreen Publishing Co; Nat Union of Journalists, UK, 1948-50; Am Newspaper Guild, 1951-55; MPA; NPPA; WPA; hon/Regular Contbr of Articles to Nat Mags, Books by Editors of *Life*; Recip, Awds of Excell, Nat Press Photogs Assn; AP & UP: Certs of Excell, Am Inst Graphic Arts, 1971, 1972, 1973; Spec Awds, NY Soc of Pubs Designers, 1980; Wn Pubs Assn Awds, Best Consumer Mag, Best Travel Mag, 1980; Nom, Pulitzer Prize for Coverage of Andrea Doria Disaster, 1956; Dir Intl Biog; W/W: in World, in E, in W, in Fin & Indust.

GOUNARIS, ANNE DEMETRA oc/ Professor of Chemistry and Field Biochemistry; b/Oct 27, 1924; h/Vassar College, Box 349, Poughkeepsie, NY 12601; ba/Poughkeepsie, NY; p/Demetrios and Kaliope Gounaris (dec); ed/RN Dipl, MA Gen Hosp, Sch of Nsg, 1946; AB, Boston Univ, 1955; PhD, Harvard Univ, 1960; pa/Res Assoc, Brookhaven Nat Lab, 1960-62; Res Assoc, Carlsberg Lab, Copenhagen, Denmark, 1962-64; Res Assoc, Rockefeller Univ, 1964-66; Prof, Vassar Col, 1966-; Vis'g Fellow in Med, MA Gen Hosp, 1978-83; Am Chem Soc; Am Soc of Biol Chems; Am Soc for the Advmt of Sci; NY Acad of Sci; AAUP; Sigma Xi, Nat Grp; Phi Beta Kappa, Nat Grp; hon/Author, Sci Res Pubs in Biochem Jours (Latest Pub in *Biochem Jour* 1982); Res Grant, NIH, USA, 1968-71, 1972-76; Collegium Dist'd Alumnae, Boston Univ, 1974; Ann Horton Res Fellow, Newham Col, Cambridge, England, 1980-81.

GOUSE, S WILLIAM JR oc/Executive; b/Dec 15, 1931; h/8410 Martingale Drive, McLean, VA 22102; ba/McLean, VA; m/Jacqueline Ann McLaughlin; c/ Linda Ellen, S William III; p/S William Sr (dec) and Charlotte Gouse, Utica, NY; ed/BS, MS, Mech Engrg 1954, DSc 1958, MIT; Reg'd Profl Engr, MA; mil/ Ballistic Res Lab, Aberdeen Proving Ground, MD, & Watertown Arsenal Lab, Watertown, MA, AUS Ordnance Corps, 1961-62; pa/Res Lab for Heat Transfer in Electronics 1954, 1955, Instr

in Mech Engrg 1956-57, Asst Prof 1958-65, Assoc Prof 1965-67, MIT; Instr of Physics, Lowell Inst, 1956-57; Sr Res Engr, Atomics Intl, 1960; Prof of Mech Engrg, Carnegie-Mellon Univ, 1967-69; Tech Asst, Ofc of Sci & Technol, Exec Ofc of the Pres of US, 1969-70; Assoc Dean of Carnegie Inst of Technol & the Sch of Urban & Public Affairs, 1971-73; Dir, Envir Studies Inst, Carnegie-Mellon Univ, 1971-73; Dir, Ofc of Res & Devel & Sci Advr to the Secy, US Dept of Interior, 1973-75; Acting Dir, Ofc of Coal Res, US Dept of Interior, 1974-75; Dpty Asst Admr for Fossil Energy, Energy Res & Devel Adm, 1975-77; Chief Scist, The MITRE Corp, 1977-79; VP 1979-80, VP & Gen Mgr 1980-83, Sr VP & Gen Mgr 1984-, Metrek Div, The MITRE Corp; Adj Prof of Engrg & Public Policy, Carnegie-Mellon Univ, 1980-; AIAA; AIChE; Am Soc for Engrg Ed; ASME; Am Soc of Heating, Refrigeration & Air Conditioning Engrs; Steam Automobile Clb of Am; AAUP; AAAS; Soc of Automotive Engrs; Solar Energy Soc; Intl Assn of Energy Economists; NY Acad of Sci; Wash Soc of Engrs; hon/ Pubs, "The Energy Security Act of 1980: How Did We Get There & What Might it Mean?" 1980, "The Future of Personal Trans" 1979, "Coal & Tar Sands" 1979, "Potential Resource Surprises" 1978, "Coal Use by Indust: Challenges & Opports" 1977, Num Others; Pi Tau Sigma, 1952; Tau Beta Pi, 1953; Sigma Xi, 1954; Visking Corp F'ship, 1954-55; Gen Elect Corp Edwin W Rice Jr F'ship, 1955-56; Soc of Automotive Engrs, Ralph R Teetor Fund Awd, 1965; Sir A L Mudslior Endowment Lectr in Technol, Al Alagappa Chettiar Col of Technol, Univ of Madras, 1969; Dist'd Lectr in Mech Engrg, PA St Univ, 1980; Fellow, ASME, 1981; Num Other Hons; Am Men of Sci; DIB; Intl W/W in Engrg; Men of Achmt; W/W: in Am, in Am Polits, in Ecol, in Frontier Sci & Technol, in Technol Today, in E, in S & SW.

GRABURN, NELSON HAYES HENRY oc/Professor of Anthropology; b/Nov 25, 1936; h/14 Wilson Circle, Berkeley, CA 94708; ba/Berkeley, CA; m/Katherine Kazuko Yaguchi; c/Eva Mariko, Cecily Atsuko Ring; p/Henry L K and Cecily M Graburn (dec); ed/ Att'd, King's Sch, Canterbury, 1950-55; BA, Clare Col, Cambridge, 1955-58; MA, McGill Univ, Montreal, 1958-60; PhD, Univ of Chgo, 1960-63; mil/Army Corps, Royal Artillery, Lance-Sgt; pa/ Res Asst, Anthropology, McGill Univ, 1958-59; Res Anthropologist, Govt of Canada, Sums 1959, 1960; Res Asst, Univ of Chgo, 1961-63; Res Assoc, NWn Univ, 1963-64; Asst Prof, Assoc Prof, Prof, Anthropology, Univ of CA Berkeley, 1964-; Res Assoc, Nat Mus of Ethnology, Osaka, 1979; Vis'g Rschr, Univ of Aix-Marseilles, 1980; Chair, Dept of Anthropology, Univ of CA-Berkeley, 1981-84; Fellow, Royal Anthropological Inst & Am Anthropological Assn; Assoc, Current Anthropology; Assoc Editor, *Annals of Tourism Res*; r/Ch of England; hon/Pubs, *Eskimos w/o Igloos* 1969, *Rdgs in Kinship & Social Structure* 1971, *Circumpolar Peoples* 1973, *Ethnic 7 Tourist Arts* 1976, *The Cultural Structure of Japanese Domestic Tourism* 1983, *The Anthropology of Tourism* 1983, Plus Num Articles; Exhibitioner, Cambridge,

1955; Lapitsky Fellow, McGill, 1958; Canada Coun Fellow, 1959; Univ Fellow, Chgo, 1960; NSF Grantee, 1967-69, 1979-80; Many Biogl Listings.

GRADISON, HEATHER J oc/Commissioner; b/Sep 6, 1952; ba/Interstate Commerce Commission, 12th and Constitution, Northwest, Washington, DC 20423; m/Willis D Jr; c/Maile Jo, Benjamin David; p/David Lowe Stirton and Dorothy Johanne Flatt Cox; ed/BA, Radford Univ, 1975; Att'd, George Wash Univ, 1976-78; pa/Sum Intern, Mgmt Trainee, Mkt Res Asst, Asst Rate Ofcr, & Rate Ofcr, So Rwy Sys, DC; Appt'd Commr 1982, VChm 1985, Interst Commerce Comm; Exec Level IV Pres Appointees Org; Repub Congl Wives Clb; Wom's Trans Sem; hon/W/ W in Am Law, in Am Polit.

GRAEFE, PETER ULRICH oc/Manufacturing Company Executive; b/Sep 27, 1942; h/30 Tudor Drive, Ocean Township, NJ 07712; ba/New Brunswick, NJ; m/Susan M; p/Heinrich (dec) and Hedwig Graefe, Waldkirch, West Germany; ed/MS in Chem Engrg, Univ of Essen, W Germany, 1968; pa/Mgr, Application Res, Polyurethanes, Desma, Bremen, W Germany, 1970-72; VP, Technol, IPRC Corp, 1972-76; Tech Dir, Fenner Am Ltd, 1976-79; Tech Dir, Polyurethanes, Albany Intl, 1979-83; Mgr, Rim & Plastic Fixtures Devel, Am Standard, 1983-; Polyurethane Mfg Assn; Soc of Plastic Engrs; cp/Goodspeed Operahouse Assn; hon/Six Patents in Field of Polyurethanes Processing & Chem; Paper, "PU Processing & Molding Techniques" at Polyurethane Mfg Assn, 1982; W/W in E.

GRAGASIN, JOSE VALLIENTE oc/ Retired Educator, Economist; b/Feb 28, 1900; h/104 South Collins, Baltimore, MD 21229; m/Socorro C Patricio; c/Jose Jr, Joscorro, Altagracia, Lilia, Raul, Evelyn, Digna, Walter; p/Laureano T Gragasin (dec); ed/AB 1922, BSc 1923, KC Univ; BD, Garret Theol Sem, 1926; PhD, Grad Sem of Social Sci, Chgo Law Sch, 1927; Hon DH, KC Univ; mil/Maj, Guerilla Force Underground Mil Ser; pa/Ed Conslt, U Brethren Mission Schs, 1928-33; Osias Cols, Tarlac, 1933-35; Agrarian Probs Rschr, Pres Manuel L Quezon, 1936-37; Economist, Adv, Dept of Agri, Philippine Commonwlth, 1938-47; Farmers Com Del, 1945-47; Economist, Philippine Farmers Fdn, 1948; Professorial Lectr at Grad Schs: The Nat Univ 1949-56, The Nat Def Col of the Philippines 1957-59, Feati Univ 1949-56, Univ Manila 1938-47, Univ of E 1947-65; Acting Dean, Grad Sch, Jose Rizal Col, 1956; VP, Acad Affairs/Concurrently Dean, Grad Sch, NEn Col, 1972-74; Hd Dept of Ec, 1948-49, Professorial Lectr, Univ of E, 1947-65; Pres, Philippine Agri Devel Co Inc, 1948-50; Echague Elect & Ice Plant Co, Inc, 1956-57; Other Positions: Fellow & VChancellor, Intl Acad Poets for SE Asia, 1984-; Eng Editor, Philippines, *Naimbag A Damag*, 1928-30; Poetry Soc of Am, 1983; Am Acad of Poets, 1980; The US Capitol Hist Soc, 1982; MD Hist Soc; MD St Poetry Soc; Am Ec Assn, 1954; Intl Acad Ldrship, 1969; Epsilon Tau Chi, 1923; Phi Beta Kappa, 1922; Philippine Ec Assn; Other Profl Orgs; cp/Intl Clb of MD; Philippine Am Assn Inc; Am Assn of Ret'd Persons; Other Civic Orgs; hon/Pubs, *The Attrib-*

utes to the Greatness of the Am People 1980, *What Makes the Filipinos A Great People*, 1983, *Philippine Agrarian Reform Code & Prog Under the New Soc*, 1972, *Philippine Economic Probs & Their Solutions*, 1949, Num Others, Num Poems Pub'd; Awd of Apprec in Recog of Dist'd Ser-Intl Understanding, Intl Clb of MD, 1980; Intl Awd of Hon & Distn for Outstg Edr-Economist-Ldr & Spiritu Crusader, Intl Acad Ldrship, 1970; Num Hons; Men Achmts; Intl W/W of Intells; Intl Biographical Ctr; Intl Dir Dist'd Ldrship; Personalities of Am Hall of Fame; Biogl Roll Hon; Ldrship Roll of Hon; "4000 Cream of Ilocandia", Ilocandia Yr Book I.

GRANT, DAWN MOORE oc/Nursing Service Director; b/Jun 17, 1941; ba/ San Marcos, TX; m/W E Jr; c/Denise Renee, Terry Alan; p/Oscar Allan and Elveree Alena Van Cleave Moore (dec); ed/Student of Nsg, LA St Univ, 1967-68; BSN, NWn St Univ, 1971; MSN, Univ of AL, 1972; pa/DON, Hays Meml Hosp, 1981-; Profl Ser Assoc, Mead Johnson Nutrition Div, 1980-81; Asst Dir of Nsg, Seton Med Ctr, 1979-80; Asst Prof, Univ of TX Sch of Nsg, 1978-79; Clin Spec, John Sealy Hosp, 1978; Asst Prof, TX Wom's Univ, 1973-78; Pediatric Instr, El Centro Col, 1978-80; Other Previous Positions; ANA; IN Nurses Assn; Coun of High Risk Perinatal Nurses; TX Nurses Assn; So Perinatal Assn; TX Perinatal Assn; Nat Perinatal Assn, Communication & Ed Com 1976-; cp/Am Heart Assn; Muscular Dystrophy Assn; March of Dimes; hon/Phi Kappa Phi; Student Nurse of the Yr, 1970-71; NSU's Nom for Nat Phi Kappa Phi F'ship, 1971; W/W Among Students in Am Univs & Cols.

GRANT, DONALD ANDREW oc/ Professor of Mechanical Engineering; b/ Jan 3, 1936; h/7 Fernwood Street, Orono, ME 04473; ba/Orono, ME; m/ June Farren; c/Judith Dawn, Jeffrey Donald; p/Morton A and Eunice H Grant, Deblois, ME; ed/BS in Mech Engrg 1956, MS in Mech Engrg 1963, Univ of ME; PhD in Mech Engrg & Applied Mechs, Univ of RI, 1969; pa/ Prof of Mech Engrg 1976-, Assoc Prof of Mech Engrg 1968-76, Asst Prof of Mech Engrg 1962-68, Univ of ME; Asst Prof of Mech Engrg, Inst of Mech Engrg, 1956-62; Conslt for Over 100 Industs, Sums & Acad Yrs; ASME; Tau Beta Pi; Sigma Xi; Pi Tau Sigma; Phi Kappa Phi; Reg'd Profl Engr; hon/ Author of Many Pubs in Profl Jours, incl'g, *Jour of Sound & Vibration, Jour of Applied Mechanics, Jour of Structural Mechanics, Intl Jour for Numerical Methods in Engrg*; Dist'd ME Prof, 1976; NSF Fac F'ship, 1968-69; DuPont Sum Awd; W/W: in E, in Frontier Scis & Technol, in Technol Today; Intl W/W in Engrg.

GRANT, DORIS JEAN oc/Junior High School Principal; b/Sep 1, 1932; h/ 1332 Kramer Drive, Carson, CA 90746; ba/Compton, CA; m/John C; c/Rita Renee, Cynthia Delise, Gregory, Darryl, Joyce Yvonne; p/George C and Annie Mae Brown (dec) Kelly, Hattisburg, MS; ed/BS, Eng, Alcorn St Univ, 1954; CA Tchg Credential, Univ of So CA, 1966; MA, Ednl Adm, CA St Univ-Long Bch, 1975; pa/Tchr 1967-73, Adm Asst 1973-75, Compton Sr High; Adm Asst 1975-76, Asst Prin (Continuation Sch and Teen Mother), Harriet

Tubman Sr High; Prin, Roosevelt Jr High, 1978-; Tchr, Compton Commun Col, Ext Prog 1970-75; Delta Sigma Theta Sorority, 1979; CA Tchrs Assn, 1967-82; Assn of CA Sch Admrs, 1981-83; PTA; cp/En Star, Queen Bee Chapt; r/AME; hon/Thesis, "Accountability-In Tchg Rdg," 1975; Dist'd Teacher Awd, 1973; W/W of Am Women.

GRANTHAM, JOSEPH MICHAEL JR oc/Executive; b/Aug 23, 1947; h/ Magnolia Road, Pinehurst, NC 28374; ba/Pinehurst, NC; c/Molly Meade, Joseph M III; p/J M Grantham, Smithfield, NC; ed/BS, Bus Mgmt, Real Est, E TN St Univ, 1969; Att'd, Oak Ridge Mil Acad; mil/IL NG, 1970-76; pa/VP & Mgr, Grand Hotel, Mackinac Isl, MI, 1970-78; Dir of Resort Opers & Gen Mgr, Pinehurst Hotel & Country Clb, NC, 1978-80; Chm of Bd & Pres, Indep Financial Investmts, 1980-, Carolina Hotels Incorporate, 1982-; Bd Dirs, Sandhills Area C of C; Bd of Dirs, MI Innkeepers Assn; MI C of C; cp/NC Hotel Assn; NC Travel Coun; Moore Co Shrine Clb; Masonic Lodge; Pinehurst Bus Guild; Chm & Bd of Dirs, No MI Conv & Visitors Br.

GRASSELLI, JEANETTE G oc/Director of Technology Support Department; b/Aug 4, 1928; h/150 Greentree Road, Chagrin Falls, OH 44022; ba/Cleveland, OH; m/Robert K; p/Nicholas W Gecsy and Veronica H Varga (dec); ed/BS, OH Univ, 1950; MS, Case Wn Resv Univ, 1958; pa/Dir Technol Support Dept 1983-, Dir of Analytical Scis Lab 1981-83, Mgr of Analytical Sers 1980-81, Coor of Analytical Sers 1978-80, Supvr of Molecular Spectroscopy 1972-78, Grp Ldr of Molecular Spectroscopy 1967-72, Proj Ldr of Molecular Spectroscopy 1955-67, Proj Assoc of Molecular Spectroscopy 1950-55, The Standard Oil Co, OH; Am Chem Soc, Cleveland & Nat; Am Soc of Testing Mats; Coblentz Soc; Fdn of Analytical Chem & Spectroscopy Socs; Jt Com on Atomic & Molecular Phy Data; Soc for Applied Spectroscopy, Cleveland Sect; Soc for Applied Spectroscopy, Nat; hon/Pubs, *Chem Applications of Raman Spectroscopy* 1981, *Atlas of Spectral Data & Phy Constants for Organic Compounds* 1975, "Infrared & NMR Spectroscopic Studies of the Thermal Degradation of Polyacrylonitrile", 1984, "The Routine Use of FT-IR & Raman Spectroscopy for Solving Non-routine Probs in an Indust Lab", 1984, "Computer-Assisted Quanititative Infrared Spectroscopy", 1984, Num Others; Phi Beta Kappa; Iota Sigma Pi, Pres, Fluorine Chapt; Mortar Bd, Pres, OH Univ Chapt; 11th Annual Chem Profession Awd, 1963; Cert of Merit Alumni Awd for Res in Chem, OH Univ, 1965; YWCA Cert of Achmt, 1977; Anachem Awd of Detroit Assn of Analytical Chems, 1978; DSc(Hon), OH Univ, 1978; YWCA Wom of the Yr, 1980; Williams-Wright Awd of Coblentz Soc, 1980; Soc for Applied Spectroscopy Dist'd Ser Awd, 1983; 2,000 Wom of Achmt in the World; W/ W: of Am Wom, in MW; Am Men & Wom of Sci; World W/W of Wom; Nat Register of Prominent Ams & Intl Notables; DIB.

GRASSLE, JOHN FREDERICK oc/ Senior Scientist; b/Jul 14, 1939; h/PO

276

Box 507, Woods Hole, MA 02543; ba/ Woods Hole, MA; m/Judith Payne; c/ John Thomas; p/Norah Grassle; ed/BS, Yale Univ, 1961; PhD, Duke Univ, 1967; pa/Asst Scist 1969-73, Assoc Scist 1973-83, Sr Scist 1983-, Woods Hole Oceanographic Instn; Tchg Asst 1961-63, Res Asst 1963-64, Duke Univ; Instr, Marine Ecol Course, Marine Biol Lab, 1972; Am Soc of Limnology & Oceanography; Am Soc of Naturalists; Am Geophy Union; Soc for the Study of Evolution; Sigma Xi; AAAS; Wn Soc of Naturalists; Australia Coral Reef Soc; hon/Pubs, "Recovery of a Polluted Estuarine System: A Mesocosm Experiment" 1984, "Intro to the Biol of Hydrothermal Vents" 1983, "The Biol of Hydrothermal Vents: A Short Summary of Recent Findings" 1982, "Replication in Controlled Marine Systems: Presenting the Evidence" 1982, Num Others; NSF Undergrad Awd, Yale Univ, 1959; NSF Predoct Awd, Duke Univ Marine Lab, 1964; NSF Oceanography Traineeship, Duke Univ Marine Lab, 1964-66; NSF Predoct F'ship, Duke Univ, 1965-66; Fulbright Postdoct Awd, 1967-69; W/W in Technol Today; Am Men & Wom of Sci.

GRATZ, ROBERT DAVID oc/Associate Vice President for Academic Affairs; b/Aug 6, 1944; h/Blanco Star Route Box CE-75, San Marcos, TX 78666; ba/San Marcos, TX; m/Judith Kay; c/Robert David Jr, Laura Gayle; p/ Robert O and Betty P Gratz, Port Arthur, TX; ed/PhD 1969, MA 1966, Bowling Green St Univ; BS, Lamar Univ, 1965; pa/Assoc VP for Acad Affairs 1981-, Prof 1984-, 1973-84, Assoc Prof of Spch Communication Dean of Applied Arts 1978-81, Acting Dean of Applied Arts 1977-78, Assoc Dean of the Grad Sch 1976-77, Sum 1975, Chm of the Dept of Spch & Drama 1973-77, Asst Prof of Spch 1969-73, SW TX St Univ; Instr of Spch, Univ of Toledo, 1967-69; Sum Sch Fac 1966, 1967, Tchg Fellow 1966-67, Res Asst & Pt-time Instr 1966, Grad Asst 1965-66, Bowling Green St Univ; Staff Announcer, KPNG Radio, 1963-65; Kappa Kappa Psi; Phi Mu Alpha Sinfonia; Pi Kappa Delta; Intl Communication Assn; World Future Soc; Spch Communication Assn; Am Assn for Higher Ed; AAUP; So Spch Communication Assn; TX Assn of Col Tchrs; TX Spch Communication Assn; cp/San Marcos Balcones Kiwanis Clb, 1971-; Hays Co Child Wel Bd, 1978-84; Crime Stoppers Inc, 1981; Urban Renewal Comm, 1977-79; Hays Co Crisis & Info Ctr Inc; r/Meth; hon/Pubs, *Orgl Communication & Higher Ed* 1981, "Technol & the Crisis of Self", 1984, "Public Ed Confronts the New Technols", 1984, "Problem-Solving Discussion Tn & T-Group Tn: An Exptl Comparison" 1970, Others; Dist'd Ser Awd, AF ROTC, 1981; W/W in S & SW; Personalities of the S; Dir of Am Scholars; Intl W/W in Ed; Outstg Yg Men of Am; Outstg Edrs of Am.

GRAVES, LARRY RICHARD oc/ Group Leader of Research and Development; b/May 5, 1942; h/11408 139th Street Court East, Puyallup, WA 98374; ba/Tacoma, WA; m/Sondra Lee; c/Kelly Ann; p/R W Graves, Tacoma, WA; ed/ BS, Chem, Univ of Puget Sound, 1965; mil/USAF, 1966; pa/Chem, Hooker

Chem Corp, 1965-66; Chem, Supervisingg Chem, Hercules Inc, 1966-73; Sr Chem, Grp Ldr, Pacific Resins & Chems, 1973-81; Grp Ldr, Prod Mgr, GA Pacific Corp, 1981-; GA-Pacific Resins FCU, Pres 1978, Treas, Mgr 1979-84; TAPPI, 1977; Am Chem Soc; cp/VP, Hercules Men's Clb, 1971-72, 1973; VP, Summit Yth Ctr, 1980-81; VP, Summit Yth Ctr Ath Assn,1979-80; Brookdale Golf & Country Clb; hon/ Recip, Awd of Recog, Summit Yth Ctr Ath Assn, 1980; Dist'd Scist Awd, GA-Pacific Corp, 1982.

GRAY, ELIZABETH DODSON oc/ Writer, Theologian; b/Jul 13, 1929; ba/ Bolton Institute, Four Linden Square, Wellesley, MA 02181; m/David Dodson; c/Lisa, Hunter; p/Fitzhugh James and Lillian Northam Dodson (dec); ed/BA, Smith Col, 1951; BD, Yale Div Sch, 1954; pa/Assoc, Bapt Min to Students, Harvard Sq, 1954-57; Ldrship Team, "Critical Choices for the Future," Sloan Sch, MIT, 1974-76; Co-Dir, Bolton Inst for a Sustainable Future, 1978-; Fdr & Dir, Roundtable Confs for Profl Wom, 1978-; Coor, Theol Opports Prog, Harvard Div Sch, 1978-; cp/US Assn for the Clb of Rome, 1977-, Co-VChair 1978-81; r/Epis; hon/Pubs, *Growth & Its Implications for the Future* 1974, *Chd of Joy: Raising Your Own Home-Grown Christians* 1975, *The Energy Oratorio* 1978, *Green Paradise Lost* 1979, *Patriarchy as a Conceptual Trap* 1981; Phi Beta Kappa, 1950; Sophia Smith Scholar, 1948, 1949, 1951; World W/W of Wom; DIB.

GRAY, EOIN WEDDERBURN oc/ Physicist; b/May 7, 1942; h/4905 General Hodges Northeast, Albuquerque, NM 87111; ba/Albuquerque, NM; c/Liam Charles, Michael Eoin; p/ Lt Col C R (dec) and Helen Gray, Newtownards, Northern Ireland; ed/ BSc w Hons 1964, PhD 1967, Queens Univ, Belfast, No Ireland; pa/Mem of Tech Staff, Sandia Nat Labs 1984-, Mts-Bell Telephone Labs 1969-84; Postdoct Res Fellow, Univ of Brit Columbia, 1967-69; Demonstrator, Physics Dept, Queens Univ, Belfast; Fellow, Inst of Physics, UK; Fellow, Am Phy Soc; Sr Mem, IEEE; Chem Inst of Canada; European Phy Soc; Former Assoc Editor, IEEE Transactions; r/ Anglican; hon/Author, Over 90 Pubs in Sci Jours; 1 Patent; Prize Paper Awd, Holm Conf on Elect Contacts, 1977; Am Men & Wom of Sci; W/W: in Frontier Sci & Technol, in Technol, in World.

GRAY, FREDERICK THOMAS oc/ Attorney; b/Oct 10, 1918; h/4701 Bermuda Hundred Road, Chester, VA 23831; ba/Chesterfield, VA; m/Evelyn Johnson; c/Frederick T Jr, Evelyn Gray Tucker; p/Franklin Pierce and Mary Gervase Pouder Gray (dec); ed/BA, Univ of Richmond, 1948; JD, T C Wms Sch of Law, Univ of Richmond, 1949; mil/ USAAC, Pacific; pa/Asst Atty Gen of VA, 1949-54; Atty, Wms, Mullen, Christian, Pollary & Gray, 1954-; Atty Gen of VA, 1961-62; Am Col of Trial Lwyrs; Instr, Univ of Richmond, 1980-82; Bd of Dirs, So Bk; Bd of Dirs, Pioneer Fed Savs & Ln Assn; cp/Mem of VA Gen Assem, Ho of Dels 1966-72, Senate of VA 1972-; VA Code Comm; VA Crime Comm; So Reg Ed Bd; VA Com on Constitl Govt; r/Meth; hon/Phi Beta Kappa, Univ of Richmond, 1950; Outstg Yg Man of Yr of Chesterfield Co,

1954; Am Col of Trial Lwyrs, 1974; DAR Medal of Hon, 1981; Gold Book of Outstg Virginians; W/W: in VA, in Am; Men of Achmt; Notable Ams.

GRAY, MARGARET EDNA oc/ Nurse Administrator; b/Jun 11, 1931; h/ 4112 Hyde Park Drive, Chester, VA 23831; ba/Petersburg, VA; p/Mr and Mrs W E Gray, Norfolk, VA; ed/Nsg Dipl, Norfolk Gen Hosp Sch of Nsg, 1952; BSN, Columbia Univ, Tchrs' Col, 1956; MSN, Univ of MD-Balto, 1966; EdD, VA Polytechnic Inst & St Univ, 1980; Asst Prof in Nsg Grad Prog 1980-, Adj Fac Mem for Outreach Grad Prog for One Yr (Pt-time), Univ of VA Sch of Nsg; Grad Res Asst for Sex Equity Proj, VA Polytechnic Inst & St Univ; Dir, VA Appalachian Tricol Nsg Prog & Assoc Prof of Nsg, 6 Yrs; Coor, Hlth Technol, VA Dept of Commun Cols, 3 Yrs; Ednl Dir, VA St Bd of Nsg, 4 Yrs; Med-Surg Nsg Instr & Coor, Riverside Hosp Sch of Nsg, 6 Yrs; Med-Surg Nsg Instr, Norfolk Gen Hosp Sch of Nsg, 2 Yrs; Staff Nurse, Hd Nurse, Asst Night Supvr, Norfolk Gen Hosp, 4 Yrs; VA Nurses Assn; hon/Pubs, "RN Completion Progs" 1982, "Interinstnl Nsg Progs: Solution or Prob?" 1982, "Devel of Hlth Technol Progs in the VA Commun Col Sys" 1971, "An Innovative Approach to Nsg Ed" 1973, Others; W/W of Am Wom.

GRAY, RUSSELL ORTON SR oc/ Consultant; b/Apr 26, 1920; h/242 Elm Street, Claremont, NH 03743; ba/ Claremont, NH; m/Mildred Rena; c/ Russell Orton Jr, Karl Irving; p/Karl and Christine Gray, Plymouth, NH; ed/ Grad, Plymouth HS, 1938; Att'd, Pgh Inst of Aeronautics, 1941; pa/Sheet Metal Wkr, Scott & Wms, 1941-43; Sheet Metal Wkr, Portsmouth Nav Ship Yard, 1943-45; Supvr of Sheet Metal Dept, Sweeney's Inc, 1946-56; Owner, Operator, Gray's Sheet Metal, 1956-83; Conslt, Gray's Sheet Metal; Mem, Small Bus Ser Bur Inc; cp/Past Asst Ldr, 4-H Clb; Past Treas, PTA; Mem, Claremont C of C, 1964-73; r/Epis; hon/W/W in E.

GRAY, THOMAS COLE oc/Firearms Dealer and Consultant; b/Jun 8, 1936; h/Route #1, Waco, GA 30182; ba/Waco, GA; m/Betty S; c/Lisa Sue; p/E W and Mary Elizabeth Gray (dec); ed/HS; mil/ Army Resv, 6 Yrs; pa/Lockheed Aircraft, 1955-59; Truck Driver, Skinner Co, 1959-61; Truck Driver, Atl Steel, 1961-65; Foreman, Atl Steel, 1965-81; Firearms Dealer, 1981-; cp/Tallapoosa JCs, 1960's; Mason, 1967; Shriner, 1971.

GREBENAU, MARK DAVID oc/ Researcher in Clinical Immunology; b/ Mar 26, 1951; h/46 Porter Road, West Orange, NJ 07052; ba/East Hanover, NJ; m/Ruth C; c/Maurice Jay, Julie Elena; p/Franz and Gisela Grebenau; ed/AA, BA 1972, Yeshiva Univ; MA 1976, MD 1978, PhD 1979, NY Univ; pa/Resident Phys, NY Hlth & Hosp Corp, 1978-81; Res Assoc, Assoc Phys, The Rockefeller Univ, 1981-83; Asst Dir of Clin Res, Sandoz Res Inst, 1983-; Am Assn of Immunologists; Am Col of Phys; AMA; Assn of Orthodox Jewish Scists; r/ Jewish; hon/Pubs, "Characterization of Cell Surface Proteins of Chicken Lymphoid Cells" 1981, "Antigen Induced Helper & Suppressor T Cells in Normal & Agammaglobulinemic Chickens" 1980, "Suppressor Cells in Transfer of

Agammaglobulinemia in the Chicken" 1980, "T Cell Tolerance in the Chicken" 1979, Others; Lita Annenberg Hazen F'ship Awd, 1980; W/W in Frontier Sci & Technol.

GREEN, FELICE JANETTE oc/Associate Professor of Education, Director of Reading Clinic; b/Jun 4, 1942; h/104 Oak Drive, Tuscumbia, AL 35674; ba/ Florence, AL; m/Alex C; c/Sheryl Denise, Alex Gershon; p/Mrs Janie T Donald, Tuscumbia, AL; ed/BS, TN St Univ, 1963; MA, Florence St Univ, 1972; EdD, Univ of AL, 1977; pa/Tchr, TN Val HS, 1964-66; Tchr, Moulton HS, 1966-67; Tchr, R E Thompson Elem Sch, 1967-68; Tchr, Blake Elem Sch, 1968-73; Fac, Univ of N AL, 1973-; Phi Delta Kappa; Kappa Delta Pi; Pres, Muscle Shoals Area Alumnae Chapt of Delta Sigma Theta Sorority Inc, 1981-; AL Rdg Assn; IRA; Pres, NW Coun of Intl Rdg Assn, 1984-; Assn for Supvn & Curric Devel; Res in Prog; Presenter at Profl Meetings; Conslt for Several Sch Sys; cp/Music Presv Soc Inc; r/Cath; hon/Edr of the Yr, NAACP, 1980; W/ W in S & SW.

GREEN, HARRY oc/Vice President of Scientific Liaison (Retired); b/Sep 7, 1917; h/5771 Fairway Park Ct, Boynton Beach, FL 33437; ba/Philadelphia, PA; m/Harriett; c/Ann Frankel, Jane; p/ Samuel and Mary Bogatin Green (dec); ed/AB in Chem 1938, MS in Chem 1939, PhD in Organic Chem 1942, Univ of PA; Harrison Fellow in Chem, Univ of PA, 1940-41; pa/Res Chem, Lion Oil Refining Co, 1941-44; Sr Res Organic Chem, Pennsalt Mfg Co, 1944-47; Res Assoc, Physiol Chem, Univ of PA, 1947-52; Chief, Biochem Res, Wills Eye Hosp, 1952-58; Asst Prof, Grad Sch of Med, Univ of PA, 1954-58; Sr Res Biochem, Smith Kline & French Labs, 1958-61; Grp Ldr 1961-64, Hd of Neurobiochem 1964-67, Dir of Biochem 1967-75, Dir of Sci Liaison 1975-80, VP of Sci Liaison & Technol 1980-81, VP of Sci Liaison 1981-, Smith Kline Beckman Corp; Am Soc Biol Chems; Am Soc Pharm & Exptl Therapy; Am Chem Soc; AAAS; Assn for Res of Nervous & Mtl Diseases; Intl Soc of Biochem Pharm; NY Acad of Sci; Sigma Xi; hon/ Pubs, 1942-73; Harrison Fellow in Chem, Univ of PA, 1940-41; W/W in E, in Frontier Sci & Technol; Am Men & Wom of Sci.

GREEN, JOHN JOSEPH (Deceased) oc/Retired Businessman; b/Nov 9, 1905; h/45 La Rose Avenue, Apartment 608, Weston, Ontario M9P 1A8; m/Winifred Maud Pascoe; c/Lorna, Janet; p/George Edward and Elizabeth Jarmey Green (dec); ed/BSc w Hons in Physics, ARCS 1928, DIC in Aeronautics 1929, Imperial Col of Sci & Technol, Royal Col of Sci; PhD, Aeronautics, London Univ, 1930; mil/Sqdrn Ldr, RCAF, 1943-45; pa/Jr Res Physicist, Nat Res Coun, Canada; Asst Res Engr 1930-43, Chief Res Engr 1943-45, RCAF Test & Devel Establishment; Chief Res Engr, Air Transport Bd, 1945-49; Def Res Bd, Chief of Div B & Sci Advr to the Chief of the Air Staff, RCAF, 1949-55; Def Res Mem, Canadian Jt Staff & Def Res Attaché, Canadian Embassy, DC, 1955-59; Chief Supt, Canadian Armament Res & Devel Establishment, 1959-63; Dir of Res 1963-68, Dir of Govt Relats 1968-70, Conslt 1970-72, Litton Sys Ltd; Bd of

Dirs, Leigh Instruments Ltd, 1970-79; hon/Author, Num Papers & Articles in Sci & Engrg Jours; Recip, MBE for Valuable Public Ser in the Field of Sci Res, 1943; Recip, King's Commend for Valuable Ser in the Air, 1945; Awd'd Hon Life Mbrship in Am Assn of Airport Execs in Recog of Extraordinary & Outstg Contbns to the Assn & Its Mems; Elected Fellow, Royal Aeronaut Soc, 1948; Elected Fellow, Inst of the Aeronaut Scis of USA (Now AIAA), 1950; Elected Fellow, Canadian Aeronaut Inst (Now Canadian Aeronautics & Space Inst), 1955; Awd'd Hon F'ship, CASI, 1971; Canadian W/W; W/W: in World Aviation, in Am, of Brit Engrs, in Brit Aviation; Am Men & Wom of Sci; World W/W in Sci; Nat Register of Prominent Ams & Intl Notables; Engrs of Distn; Men of Achmt; DIB.

GREEN, MI MI oc/Public Relations Director; b/Oct 3, 1947; h/15759 Romar, Granada Hills, CA 91344; ba/ Hollywood, CA; p/Jeffery and Ruthie Green, Waco, TX; ed/Deg in Psycho-Cybernetics, 1982; Dipl, 1965; Att'd, Prairie View A&M Col, 1967-69; pa/VP, Al Fann Theatrical Ensemble, 1981-; Public Relats Dir, 1977-; Dramatic Instr, 1973-; Lectr, Actress, Writer; Nat Assn for Female Execs; Pres, Millionaires Fann Clb; Chm of Charter Mbrship for Fann Inst for Higher Mind Devel; The Media Forum; Screen Actors Guild; Am Fdn of TV & Radio Arts; cp/Living Mins Intl; r/ Non-Denom; hon/LA Times Article, "Positive Thinking w Disco Beat," 1982; Outstg Ser Awd from LA Sch Bd, 1981; Hon Trustee to the Fann Inst for Higher Mind Devel; W/W of Am Wom.

GREEN, RUTH N CUMMINGS oc/ Elementary Teacher; b/Aug 25, 1928; h/ 506 West 31st Avenue, Bellevue, NE 68005; ba/Bellevue, NE; m/Robert C Jr (dec); c/Dana Green Schrad, Lisa Green Noon; p/Mr and Mrs W H Cummings (dec); ed/BS, Ed, Univ of Omaha (Now Univ of NE Omaha); 60 Hrs Beyond Deg; pa/Elem Tchr, Greenway Public Schs 1948-51, Hancock Co Schs 1951-54, Bellevue Public Schs 1962-83; Kappa Delta Pi; Alpha Delta Kappa; Bellevue Ed Assn; NE St Ed Assn; NEA; Metro Ednl Prog Agy; VP 1983-84, Pres 1984-85, Gtr NE Assn Tchrs of Sci; NE Acad Sci; cp/Audubon Soc of Omaha, Nat Audubon Soc; St Pres 1979-81, 1982-84, VP 1981-82, 1984-85, NE Ornithologists' Union; Inland Bird Banding Assn; NE Wildlife Fdn; r/Ch of Christ; hon/Writer, Monthly Nature Column for "Bird's Eye" (Review Pub of Audubon Soc of Omaha), Bi-Monthly Pub for NE Ornithologists' Union; Recip, 5 NSF S'ships, 1966-70; Audubon S'ship, 1975; W/W of Am Wom.

GREEN, VICTOR EUGENE JR oc/ University Professor and Agronomist; b/Sep 3, 1922; h/3915 Southwest Third Avenue, Gainesville, FL 32607; ba/ Gainesville, FL; m/Ada Ruth Hellert; c/ Judy Ellen Green Brewer, Philip Martin; p/Maj Victor E (dec) and Laura Mae Harris Green, Beauregard Parish, LA; sp/Carl W and Eva M Laatz Hellert (Dec); ed/BS 1947, MS 1948, LA St Univ; PhD, Purdue Univ, 1951; Att'd, AUS Command & Gen Staff Col, 1969; mil/WW II, 25th Inf Div, Gen MacArthur's HQs, Japan; Col, AUS Ret'd; pa/ LA Agri Exptl Sta, 1948-49; FL Agri

Exptl Sta, 1951-; Advr to Govt of Costa Rica 1965-68, Jamaica 1970-71, Panama 1973, Cape Verde 1978; UF Senate, Cmdr, USA 467 MID (Strategic), 1974-77, w-USAWC, Carlisle, PA; Soil and Crop Sci Soc of FL, Pres 1965; Resv Ofcrs Assn, Life Mem; Am Soc of Agronomy; Soil Sci Soc of Am; Crop Sci Soc of Am; Tropical Reg, Am Soc for Hort Sci; Asociacion Latinoamericana de Ciencias Agricolas; cp/Kiwanis Intl; r/Luth Ch, MO Synod; hon/ Author, Hundreds of Articles, Monographs, Bltns, Circulars, Res Reports, Sci & Tech, as Well as Popular Articles in Sci Jours, Mags & Newspapers Worldwide on Rice, Sorghum, Corn, Sugarcane, Millet, Aloe, Dioscorea, Sunflower; Diplomate, Min of Agri, Costa Rica, 1968; Honor al Merito, Programa Cooperativo para el Mejoramiento de Cultivos Alimenticios, Guatemala, 1980; W/W: in Frontier Sci & Technol, in S & SW.

GREENBAUM, SHEILA oc/Presiding Official of Merit Systems Protection Board; b/Mar 31, 1949; h/1539 Woodroyal West Drive, St Louis, MO 63017; ba/Kansas City, MO; m/Gary M Wasserman; p/Albert and Libbie Greenbaum, Havertown, PA; ed/BA, Case Wn Resv Univ, 1971; JD w Distn, Univ of MO KC, 1974; pa/Conslt, ACLU, Wn MO, 1974-75; Assoc, Law Ofc of Arthur A Benson, IL, 1974-76; Atty Advr, Dept of HEW, 1976-79; Chief Reg Civil Rts Atty, HEW 1979-80, Dept of Ed 1980-; 1st VP, ACLU, 1978-; Assn of Wom Lwyrs; Am, Fed, MO Bar Assns; Mayor's Adv Com on Human Relats; Treas, KC Chapt Fed Bar Assn; Nom'g Com, Yg Lwyrs Sect, KC Bar Assn; cp/ VChp, Jewish Commun Relats Bur Bd, 1979-; Wom's Polit Caucus; Former Bd Mem, St George's Halfway House; Task Force, Reduction of Teenage Pregnancy; r/Jewish; hon/Order of the Bench & Robe, 1974; Outstg Yg Wom of Am; W/W of Am Wom.

GREENBERG, FRANK JOSEPH SR oc/Nontraditional Experimental Educational Researcher, Lecturer, Writer, Administrator and Biblical Archaeologist; b/Jun 15, 1933; h/14 Lindsey Street, Dorchester, MA 02124-1399; ba/Same; m/Elizabeth Irene Bowser; c/Robin Elizabeth, Linda Ann, Diana Rose DiCicco, Frank Joseph Jr, Anita Louise McSorley, Daniel Jacob Harold; p/ Benjamin and Mary Cohen Greenberg; ed/BA, Sociol, Brentwood Col, 1958; BBA, Acctg, Canton Actual Bus Col, 1960; BD, Comparative Rel, Felix Adler Meml Univ, 1964; LLB, Constitl Law, Blackstone Sch of Law, 1967; EdM, Col & Adult Cnslg 1970, PhD, Indust Psych 1971, EdD, Col & Adult Cnslg 1971, Thomas A Edison Col; PhD, Biblical Archaeol, Athenaeum Ecumenical Div Inst, 1979; Var Dipls Rec'd; mil/Commodore, Navy Leag of the US; pa/Adj Prof, Bernadean Univ, 1982-; Adj Fac Mem, N Am Reg Col of World Univ, 1983-; Ext Indep Nontraditional Exptl Ednl Res & Devel, 1954-; Collegament/ Accademia Teatina per le Scienze, Pescara, Italy, 1979-; Self-Employed Tax & Security Acct, 1956-; Self-Employed Cnslg Psychol, Ednl Cnslr & Grp Psychotherapist, 1963-74; Staff Mem/Consultative Status in Biblical Archeol, Athenaeum Ecumenical Div Inst, 1979-; Chm/Adv Bd on

Profl, Ednl & Govt Matters, Hellenic Profl Assn of Am Intl, 1980-83; Exec Dir & Exec Secy, Hellenic Profl Assn of Am, 1982-83; Fdg Pres & Chm, Bd of Dirs, The Intl Col of Proctors & Preceptors Inc, 1982-; Lifetime Fellow, Alpha Psi Sigma Soc; Life Mem/Academician, Accademia Tiberina, Inst for Univ Cultural Activs & Further Studies; Lifetime Fellow, Am Acad of Behavioral Sci; Annual Mem, Am Assn for Higher Ed; Life Mem, Am Assn for the Advmt of Criminology; Lifetime Fellow, Am Assn of Criminology; Annual Mem, AAUA; Num Other Profl Mbrships; r/ Jewish; hon/Awd'd Dipl of Hon Proclaiming Outstg Acad Contbns, Theatine Acad of Scis, Pescara, Italy, 1979; Awd'd Cert of Inclusion in Recog of Dist'd Achmts, The Intl W/W of Intells, 1980; Awd'd Scroll of Hon Proclaiming Hon F'ship of the Anglo-Am Acad, Cambridge, England, 1980; Awd'd Cert of Hon in Recog of Having Demonstrated Outstg Achmts in Own Field of Endeavor, Marquis W/W in E, 1981; Num Other Hons; Book of Hon; Anglo-Am W/W; Commun Ldrs & Noteworthy Ams; DIB; Dir of Orgs & Pers in Ednl Mgmt; Dist'd Citizens of Am; Intl Authors & Writers W/W; Intl W/W: in Ed, of Intells; Men of Achmt; Num Other Biogl Listings.

GREENBERG, STANLEY ARTHUR oc/Company Executive; b/Aug 22, 1935; h/1713 Shenandoah Drive, Claremont, CA 91711; ba/Azusa, CA; m/Dale Lois; c/Lisa Leslie, Suzanne Francesca, David Phillip; p/Benjamin (dec) and Sara F Greenberg, Campbell, CA; ed/PhD in Chem & Physics 1960, MS in Chem 1958, Univ of AZ; AB in Chem, Cornell Univ, 1956; pa/Chief Engr 1984-, Mgr, Mech Engrg, Aerojet ElectroSys Co, 1982-84; Sr Spec, Tech Staff, Aerojet ElectroSys Co, 1981-82; Staff Scist, Lockheed Res Lab, 1960-81; AIAA; ASTM; ACS; Sigma Xi; Phi Lambda Upsilon, Pres of Phi Chapt 1960, Chm of Triennial Conv 1960; NASA Comm on Space Mats, 1978-80; cp/Cubmaster, CSA, 1978; AAU Track & Field Ofcl, 1972-77; Campbell Union HS Adv Bd, 1976-80; hon/Author, 50 Pubs in Area of Space Mats, Radiation Effects, Thermophysics, Spectroscopy, Photochem, Solar Energy, Electrochem; Petro Res Foun F'ship, 1958; NDEA Fellow, 1959-60; Cornell St S'ship, 1950-52; Lockheed Pub Awds (6), 1962-80; W/ W in W; Personalities of W & MW.

GREENBLATT, IRA JOSEPH oc/ Executive; b/Oct 5, 1932; h/400 East 54th Street, New York, NY 10022; ba/ New York, NY; c/David, Margo, Ellen; p/Louis Greenblatt (dec); Sarah Greenblatt Josephberg, Woodmere, NY; ed/AB, Cornell Univ, 1953; JD, NY Univ, 1957; mil/AUS, Financial Corps, 1954-56; pa/ Ptnr, Tenzer, Greenblatt, Fallon & Kaplan, NYC, 1956-80; Exec VP, HIG Corp, NYC, 1980-; Pres, TenGreen Energy Corp, 1980-; Pres, The Brandeis Sch, 1964-70; Trustee, Peninsula Cnslg Ctr, 1974-82; ABA; NY St Bar Assn; NY Co Bar Assn; NYC Bar Assn; hon/ W/W in E.

GREENE, JAMES H oc/Professor of Industrial Engineering; b/Mar 12, 1915; h/555 North 400 West, West Lafayette, IN 47906; ba/West Lafayette, IN; m/ Barbara; c/Timothy James, Robin Tower; p/Ralph and Inez Greene (dec);

ed/PhD in Engrg, MS in Engrg 1948, BSME 1947, Univ of IA; pa/Prof of Indust Engrg, Sch of Indust Engrg, Purdue Univ, 1948-; AIIE; Am Prodn & Inv Cont Soc; Am Soc of Engrg Ed; r/ Meth; hon/Pubs, Opers Mgmt 1984, Prodn & Inv Cont 1974, Prodn & Inv Cont Handbook, Am Prodn & Inv Cont 1970-84; Fulbright Awd, Tech Univ of Finland, 1960; Pres Awd, Am Prodn & Inv Cont Soc, 1970; Contemp Authors; W/W: Consltg, in Technol, in Engrg.

GREENE, KATHLEEN KING oc/ Manager; b/Jun 15, 1932; h/2367 Laurel Lane, Lake Park, FL 33410; ba/West Palm Beach, FL; c/Christopher T; p/ Vera H King, Lake Park, FL; ed/Att'd, Barry Col 1982, Babson Col 1974-76, MIT/Lowell 1967-68, Bryant & Stratton Col 1963, Palm Bch Jr Col 1950; pa/Mgr of EEO Progs 1981-, Exec Staff Asst 1980-81, Div Mgmt Conslt 1979-80, Proj Cost Engr 1978-79, Pratt & Whitney Aircraft; Mgr of Pers Relats 1977-78, Asst, Planning & Anal 1976-77, Div Admr 1966-76, Adm Secy 1965-66, The MITRE Corp; Exec Secy, Neelon Mgmt Co, 1962-65; Sta Mgr, Mackey Airlines, 1954-62; Am Mgmt Assn, 1978-82; Soc of Wom Engrs, 1982; FL Mgmt Assn, 1978-82; cp/Urban Leag of Palm Bch Co, Bd of Dirs 1981-82; Dist X Spec Olympics, Steering Com 1981-82; Commun Action Coun, Bd of Dirs 1982; HRS Vol Sers, 1981-82; Palm Bch Halfway House, Commun Relats Bd, 1981-82; FL A&M Univ Cluster, Chm of Equip Com 1981-82; AF Assn, 1981-82; hon/Num Spchs to Var Orgs; Wkshops for Am Mgmt Assn; FL A&M Univ Triple Ser Awd, 1982; Spec Olympics St Org Awd, 1982; US Treas Awd, Savs Bonds, 1976; Muscular Dystrophy Telethon Awd, 1981; W/W in S & SW; Palm Bch Register; Personalities of S.

GREENE, WILLIAM W oc/Clergy, Counselor; b/Aug 5, 1929; h/PO Box 18144, Ft Worth, TX 76118; ba/Same; c/Billie Dee, John W; p/William W and Mildred Pharr (dec); ed/BS 1961, MA 1962, EdD 1965, Univ of GA; Addit Studies, N TX St Univ, Univ of CA-SF; pa/Pastorates in Atmore (AL), Thomas (OK), Wharton (TX), Athens (GA), Santa Ana (CA), 1947-62; Prof of Sci & Music & Dir of Cnslg, SE Bible Col, 1962-67; Dean of Admissions & Cnslg, So CA Col, 1967-69; Prof & Chm of Dept of Psych & Cnslg, Bethany Col, 1969-75; Spec Lectr, Oxford Univ, London, England, Sum 1975; Pres, S Pacific Bible Col, Suva, Fiji, 1976-78; Dir of Devel, Far E Adv Sch of Theol, Manila, 1978-80; Pres & Cnslr, King's Kids Mins Inc, 1980-; NEA; APA; cp/ 1st Aid & EMT Instr, ARC; Rotary Intl; r/Assems of God; hon/Pubs, Intro to Psych 1973, Cultural Anthropology 1975; Phi Theta Kappa, 1959; Kappa Delta Pi, 1961; Phi Kappa Phi, 1964; Phi Delta Kappa, 1965; W/W: in W, in S & SW; Others.

GREENFIELD, IRWIN G oc/Unidel Professor of Material Science; b/Nov 30, 1929; h/605 North Country Club Drive, Newark, DE 19711; ba/Newark, DE; m/ Barbara; c/Richard, Hermine, Steven; p/ William and Sara Greenfield; ed/PhD in Metall Engrg 1962, MA in Metall Engrg 1954, Univ of PA; BA in Metallurgy, Temple Univ, 1951; pa/Unidel Prof Mat Sci, 1984-; Dean, Col of Engrg 1974-,

Acting Dean, Col of Engrg 1973-74, Prof, Dept of Mech & Aerospace Engrg 1963-, Univ of DE; Sr Res Metallurgist, Franklin Inst Lab for Res & Devel, 1953-63; Metallurgist, Nav Air Exptl Sta, 1951-53; Am Inst of Mining; Metall & Petro Engrg; Electron Microscope Soc of Am; Sigma Xi; Am Soc for Engrg Ed; AAAS; DE Assn of Profl Engrs; PE 5272; Nat Coun of Engrg Examrs; Am Soc of Metals; hon/Pubs, "Elastic-Plastic Anal of Indentation Damages in Copper, Part I: Wk Hardening & Residual Stress" 1983, "The Wear Mechanism Obtained in Copper by Repetitive Impacts" 1981-82, Wear Mechanism in Copper by Repetitive Impacts" 1981, "Surface Layer Hardening of Polycrystalline Copper by Multiple Impact" 1980, "A Study of Surface Layer Damage Due to Impingement Fatigue" 1979, Num Others.

GREENHOUSE, DENNIS E oc/Auditor of Accounts; h/9 South Catherine Street, Middletown, DE 19709; ba/ Dover, DE; m/Adelaide Elizabeth Donovan; p/Bernard and Sylvia Greenhouse, Wilmington, DE; ed/BA, Fairleigh Dickinson Univ, 1972; pa/Auditor of Accts, St of DE, 1983-; Sr Credit Rep, Intl Playtex Inc, 1981-83; Asst VP, Home Fed Savs, 1973-81; Nat Assn of St Auditors; NASACT, Mun Fin, Ofcrs Assn, Mid-Atl Intergovtl Audit Forum, Coun of St Gov Mason; cp/Past Master, Dem St Com; Bd Mem, New Castle Co Hd Start Inc; r/Jewish; hon/Ldrship Awd, Fairleigh Dickinson Univ, 1972; Outstg Yg Men of Am; W/W: in Fin & Indust, in World.

GREENSTEIN, TEDDY oc/Professor of Chemical Engineering; b/Mar 16, 1937; h/3000 Ocean Parkway, Brooklyn, NY 11235; ba/Newark, NJ; m/Judith Lefkowich; p/Sam (dec) and Serena Greenstein, Brooklyn, NY; ed/PhD in Chem Engrg 1967, MChE 1962, NY Univ; BChE, City Col of NY, 1960; pa/ Rating Engr, Davis Engrg, 1960; HS Math & Physics Tchr, 1963-64; Res Asst, Chem Engrg, NY Univ, 1964-67; Asst Prof of Chem Engrg 1967-78, Assoc Prof of Chem Engrg 1978-84, Prof of Chem Engrg 1984-, NJ Inst of Technol; AIChE; Am Soc for Microbiol; Am Soc for Engrg Ed; Soc of the Sigma Xi; Tau Beta Pi; Omega Chi Epsilon; Assn of Orthodox Jewish Scists; r/ Jewish; hon/11 Pubs in Low Reynolds Number Hydrodynamics; 2 Pubs in Biochem Engrg; Recip of Grants, NSF 1964, Inst Paper Chem 1965-67; Foun Adv Grad Study, Engrg, 1967-69; NY Univ Fdrs Day Awd, 1967; Tau Beta Pi Assn; W/W: in Technol Today, in Frontier Sci & Technol; Men of Achmt; Notable Ams; Am Men & Wom of Sci.

GREER, GAYLE LAVERNE oc/Franchising Executive; b/Mar 11, 1941; h/ 8130 South Tamarac Street, Englewood, CO 80112; ba/Englewood, CO; m/Alonzo Matthews; c/James Vandiver; p/Gloria Morgan, Tulsa, OK; ed/MSW 1971, BS 1965, Univ of Houston; pa/ Med Social Wk, Ben Turk Hosp, 1965-69; Dpty Dir, Houston Urban Leag, 1971-75; Exec Dir, Ft Wayne Urban Leag, 1975-78; Mgr of New Mkt Devel 1978-79, Dir of New Mkt Devel 1979-80, VP of Franchise Devel 1981-, Am TV & Communs Corp; Bd Mem 1982-, Wom & Bus Inc; Mem 1979-, Wom in Cable; Bd Mem, NE Area Hlth

Planning Com, 1976-78; 1st VP & Exec Dir, Coun of the Nat Urban Leag, 1977; Fdr & Mem, Denver's Urban Leag's Newcomer Con, 1980-; cp/Bd Mem 1982-, Safehouse, Shelter for Abused Wom & Chd; hon/Black Achievers in Indust Awd, 1982; Achmt Agnst the Odds Awd, Univ of Cinc, 1982; Mayor's Commend of Achmt, 1978; W/W in Black Am.

GREGORIADES, ANASTASIA oc/ Researcher in Virology, Educator; b/ May 5, 1940; h/21 Stuyvesant Oval, 7D, New York, NY 10009; ba/New York, NY; m/Demetrios T Stavropoulos; c/ Alexander Stavropoulos, Nicholas Stavropoulos; p/Diamantes (dec) and Olympia Gregoriades, New York, NY; ed/BA, Hunter Col, 1962; MA, CUNY, 1964; PhD, Cornell Univ Med Col of Basic Sci, 1968; pa/Assoc Prof of Microbiol, NY Col of Podiatric Med, 1983-; Assoc, Dept of Virology 1975-83, Asst, Dept of Virology 1972-75, Postdoct Fellow in Virology 1969-72, The Public Hlth Res Inst of NY; Am Soc for Microbiol; Harvey Soc; NY Acad of Scis; Assn for Wom in Sci; r/Greek Orthodox; hon/ Pubs in *Molecular Biol of Negative Strand Viruses* 1984, *Jour of Virology* 1984; Sloan Predoct F'ship, 1964-68; Sloan Fund F'ship towards MA Deg, 1962-64; W/ W in Sci.

GREGORY, CALVIN LUTHER oc/ Insurance Agent, Real Estate Agent, Clergyman; b/Jan 11, 1942; h/3307 Big Cloud Circle, Thousand Oaks, CA 91360; ba/Thousand Oaks, CA; m/Carla Deane Barnett Deaver; c/Debby Lynn, Trixy Sue, Harry Robert Deaver, Wesley Carl Deaver, Timothy Charles Deaver, Gregory David Deaver; p/Rev Jacob Gregory (dec); Ruth Cherchian Gregory Greulach, Los Angeles, CA; ed/ AA, LA City Col, 1962; BA, CA St Univ-LA, 1964; MDiv, Fuller Theol Sem, 1968; MRE, SWn Sem, 1969; PhD, Universal Life Ch, 1982; DD, Otay Mesa Col, 1982; mil/Aux Chaplain, Edwards AFB, CA; pa/Exec, Ins Agy Placement Ser, 1975-; Ins Agt, Allst Ins Co, 1973-75; Mgr, Prudential Ins Co, 1971-73; Polit Sci Tchr, Maranatha HS, 1970; Pastor, 1st Bapt Ch, Boron, CA; Hd Yth Min, Emanuel Presb Ch, LA; LA Apt Assn Mem, 1976; Ordained Min, Am Bapt Conv, 1970; CA Lics for Real Est, Life & Casualty Ins, 1971; Notary Public, St of CA, 1969; Mgr & Owner of 53 Apts, Hollywood & Inglewood, 1970-; Developer & Owner of Property in Wales, Gt Brit, Nova Scotia, Canada, NY, FL, TN, TX, MN, NM, NV, CA, WA, Brit Columbia, HI, Australia; r/Prot; hon/Pres's Cit; Whole Life Round Table Awd; Man of the Month (5 Months); Millionaire Awd, Prudential, 1972; Top 20 Salesman, SWn Co; W/W: in CA, in W.

GREITZER, EDWARD MARC oc/ Associate Professor; b/May 8, 1941; h/ 77 Woodridge Road, Wayland, MA 01778; ba/Cambridge, MA; m/Helen; c/ Mary Lee, Jennifer Elizabeth; ed/BA 1962, MS 1964, PhD 1970, Harvard; pa/ Res Engr, Pratt & Whitney Aircraft, 1969-70; Sr Res Engr, U Technols Res Ctr, 1976-77; Asst Prof 1977-79, Assoc Prof 1979-; Dept of Aeronautics & Astronautics, MIT; Conslt, 1977-; ASME; AIAA; Sigma Xi; Editor, *Handbook of Fluids & Fluids Engrg*; Assoc Editor, AIAA Jour; hon/Author, Approx 20

Pubs, Handbook Article; Several Invited Lectures; ASME Gas Turbine Power Awd, 1977, 1979; T Bernard Hall Awd, Inst Mech Engrg, 1976; ASME Freeman Scholar Awd, 1980; Am Men & Wom of Sci; W/W in Technol; Men of Achmt; Others.

GRENELL, ROBERT GORDON oc/ Professor of Psychiatry, Neuroscientist; b/Apr 3, 1916; h/204 East Highfield Road, Baltimore, MD 21218; ba/Baltimore, MD; m/Dena Schild; p/Max and Lee Gordon Grenell (dec); ed/BA, Col of City of NY, 1935; MSc, NY Univ, 1936; PhD, Univ of MN, 1943; mil/Govt Res in Aviation Med during WW II; pa/ Instr in Physiol, Yale Univ Sch of Med, 1943-45; Instr, Neuroanat, Yale Univ, 1945-47; Sr Fellow, NIH, E R Johnson Foun, Univ of PA, 1947-48; Sr Fellow, NIH, Dept of Biophysics, The Johns Hopkins Univ, 1948-50; Asst Prof 1950-52, Assoc Prof 1952-57, Prof 1957-, Inst of Psychi & Human Behavior, Univ of MD; Soc of Biol Psychi, Pres 1978; Am Physiol Soc; Assn for Res, Nervous & Mtl Disease; Soc for Neurosci; hon/Author, Approx 120 Articles in Sci Jours; Editor & Contbr to *Biol Founs of Psychi* 1976, *Psychi Founs of Med* 1978; Editor, *Jour of Neurosci Res*; Sigma Xi, 1943; Travel Awd, Am Physiol Soc, 1947; Fellow, AAAS; Nom for Baldwin Prize, AAAS, 1969; Nom for Gold Medal, Soc of Biol Psychi; W/W: in E, in Am, in World; Personalities of S.

GRESSAK, ANTHONY RAYMOND JR oc/Executive; b/Jan 22, 1947; h/17775 Nearbank Drive, Rowland Heights, CA 91748; ba/Los Angeles, CA; m/Catherine; c/Danielle Kristen Smith, Anthony Raymond III; p/Anthony R Sr (dec) and Anne T Gressak, Kailua, HI; ed/AA, UT St Univ, 1967; AUS OCS, 1968; mil/ AUS; pa/Exec VP, Silco Corp, 1982-84; Div VP, Food Sers, The Broadway, 1979-82; VP Mktg, Interstate Restaurant Supply, 1984-; Gen Mgr, Grand Canyon Nat Pk Lodges, Fred Harvey Inc, 1976-79; Food & Beverage Dir, Naples Bath & Tennis Clb & Big Sky MT, Aircoa, 1974-76; Resident Mgr, Royal Inns of Am, 1974; LA Chapt, Nat Restaurant Assn; cp/Life Mem, Order of DeMolay; Chaine des Rotisseurs-Maitre de Table, Les Escoffier Clb; Smithsonian Assn; Chef des Cuisine, LA Chapt; r/Cath; hon/Chevalier, Order of DeMolay, 1966; AUS, Silver Star & Bronze Star, 1970; Vietnamese Cross of Gallantry, Silver & Bronze Stars, 1970; Articles, *Cooking for Profit*, 1980; *Restaurant News*, 1980; W/W: in World, in Am; Personalities of Am.

GREW, ROBERT R oc/Lawyer; b/ Mar 25, 1931; h/8 East 96th Street, Apartment 4C66, New York, NY 10128; ba/New York, NY; m/Anne Gano Bailey; c/Christopher Adam; p/Edward Francis and Coletta Marie Grew (dec); ed/AB in Lttrs and Law 1953, JD 1955, Univ of MI; mil/USAF, 1955-57, 1st Lt, Judge Advocate, Gen Corps; pa/Law Clk for the Hon Robert W Sweet, Ofc of US Atty for So Dist of NY, Sum 1954; Carter, Ledyard & Milburn, 1957-; Intl, Am, NY St & NYC Bar Assns; MI St Bar Assn (Inactive); Lectr, Practicing Law Inst (Venture Capital Forum, Bks & the Securities Laws); Marquis W/W; W/W in Am Law; Intl W/W of Contemp Achmt.

GREY, JEAN S oc/Certified Public

Accountant; b/Jun 14, 1925; h/9 Spruce Lane, Syosset, NY 11791; ba/Lindenhurst, NY; m/Charles; c/Scott Martin, Shari Lynn; p/Edithe Sarette; ed/BBA, City Col of NY, 1950; pa/Public Acct w Kipnis & Karchmer, CPAs 1942-44, Clarence Rainess & Co, CPAs (Asst Hd of Tax Dept) 1944-54, 1960-65; Treas & Dir, Cee-Jay Extruders Inc, 1952-; Chapt Pres, Am Soc Wom Accts; Am Woms Soc CPAs; NY St Soc CPAs; Tax Inst, C W Post Col; BPW Clb; cp/Woms Hosp; Entert Corps; USCG Aux; Societe des Vignerons.

GREY, JERRY oc/Aerospace and Energy System Scientist; b/Oct 25, 1926; h/1 Lincoln Plaza, 25-0, New York, NY 10023; ba/Same; m/Florence Maier; c/Leslie Ann, Jacquelyn Eve; ed/ BME 1947, MS in Engrg Physics 1949, Cornell Univ; PhD, Aeronautics & Math, CA Inst of Technol, 1952; mil/ USN, 1944-46; pa/Instr, Cornell, 1947-49; Devel Engrg, Fairchild Engine Div, 1949-50; Hypersonic Aerodynamicist, Galcit, 1950-52; Sr Engr, Marquardt, 1951-52; Prof, Princeton, 1952-67; Pres, Greyrad Corp, 1959-71; ADM, AIAA, 1971-82; Pres, Calprobe Corp, 1972-81; Adj Prof, LIU, 1976-82; Dir, Applied Solar Energy Corp, 1979-; Publisher, *Aerospace Am*, 1982-; VP AIAA, 1966-71; Dir, Am Astronaut Soc, 1980-83; Pres, Intl Astronaut Fdn, 1984-; Fellow, Explorers Clb; IEEE; Am Nuclear Soc; NY Acad of Sci; AAAS; Sigma Xi; Phi Kappa Phi; Tau Beta Pi; Intl Solar Energy Soc; Dir, Scists Inst for Public Info, 1979-; r/Hebrew; hon/ Pubs, *Beachheads in Space* 1983, *Global Implications of Space Activs* 1982, *Intl Aerospace Review* 1982, *Space Tracking & Data Systems* 1981, *Aeronauts in China* 1981, "Enterprise", 1979, Num Other Books, 200 Articles; VP, Intl Acad of Astronautics, 1983-; W/W: in Am, in E, in World, in Energy, in Avaiation & Space.

GRIFFIN, JAMES C oc/Truck Driver; b/Oct 1, 1937; h/11463 Liggett Street, Norwalk, CA 90650; m/Rhea Lee; c/ Debra, Jamie, Virginia; p/Dewey Griffin, Corinth, MS; ed/HS Grad, 1956; pa/ Truck Driver, Milne Truck Lines Inc, 24 Yrs; cp/Past Ctl Com Chm for Polit Party; St Exec Com for Polit Party for Several Yrs; Norwalk C of C; Moose Clb; Elks Lodge; Norwalk Rod & Gun Clb; Nat Rifle Assn; Served on Dept of Motor Vehicles Public Adv Panel, 1976-80; Assem-man Buchr Yg's Adv Panel; r/Christian; hon/2 Million Miles Safe Driving Record; Recip, Safety Pins & Awds, Milne Trucklines, for Past 22 Yrs; Truck Driving Roadeos: 1st Place Heavy-Semi (St Roadeo) 1983, 1st Place Heavy-Semi (LA Area Roadeo) 1983, 7 Others; CA Trucking Assn Driver of the Mo, Jul 1981, Oct 1983; Trucker of Wk, KLAC Radio, 1974; Cand for Gov, St of CA, 1982; Cand for Senator, St of Ca, 1980; Cand for Cong, 33rd Congl Dist, 1974; Nom'd Citizen of the Yr, City of Norwalk, 1976, 1977, 1978, 1979, 1980; Elected 3rd 2-Yr Term for Chm of Norwalk Citizens Action Coun; Recip, Lttrs of Apprec for Help to Norwalk Sr Citizens Ctr.

GRIFFIN, ROBERT NORMAN oc/ Elementary School Principal; b/Mar 5, 1927; h/4314 Buckeystown Pike, Frederick, MD 21701; ba/Temple Hills, MD; m/Darlene Ness; c/Darrell Robert, Douglas Lee, Dana Jon, David Alan; p/

Edward (dec) and Edna Griffin, Baltimore, MD; ed/ThB, Walla Walla Col, 1950; EdM, Univ of MD, 1968; EdD, DePaul Univ, 1983; mil/AUS, 1945-46; pa/Tchr/Pastor, SDA Conf, ID & Balto, MD, 1950-52; Asst Pastor, Balto, MD, 1952-54; Dist Pastor, WV Conf, SDA, 1954-59; Tchr, Frederick Co, MD, Public Schs, 1959-62; Tchr, Prince George's Co, MD, Public Schs, 1962-65; Elem Prin, Prince George's Co, MD, Public Schs, 1965-; Pres, VP, Treas, Assn for Childhood Ed in Prince George's Co; Treas, Prince George's Co Prin's Assn, 1 Yr; Screening Com for Cands for Admr & Supvr Positions, 3 Yrs; Exec Bd Mem, Prin's Assn, 3 Yrs; Chm of Admrs' Cluster Grp; Conslt/Instr, Outdoor Ed Prog; r/SDA; hon/Commun Ldrs of S; W/W in E.

GRIFFIS, HUGH CLINTON III oc/Political and Legal Consultant; b/Sep 14, 1955; h/2364 Ridgeway Avenue, College Park, GA 30337; ba/East Point, GA; p/Hugh C Jr (dec) and Louise Coleman Griffis, College Park, GA; ed/Att'd, Woodward Acad, 1973; BA w High Hons in Hist & Polit Sci 1977, MA 1978, Emory Univ; pa/Staff, Ofc of Lt Gov of GA, 1978-79; Computer Opers, Trust Co Bk, 1979-80; Indep Polit & Legal Conslt, 1980-; Am Polit Sci Assn, 1978-; cp/Fulton Co Repub Com, 1980-; VChm, Atlanta Area Nat Eagle Scout Assn, 1977-; Var Positions, BSA, 1976-; So Hist Assn, 1978-; TN Squire Assn, 1975-; Orig Masters Soc, 1981-; ACLU, 1980-; r/Bapt; hon/Pub, *Ethnic Culture & 20th Cent GA Polits*, 1978; Pi Sigma Alpha & Phi Alpha Theta Hons, 1977-; Silver Nesa Wreath Awd, 1979; Scoutmaster's Key, 1978; W/W in S & W.

GRIFFITH, CAROLE LOTSTEIN oc/Communications Consultant; b/Sep 16, 1953; h/302 A Washington Valley Road, Basking Ridge, NJ 07920; m/William; p/Raymond Lotstein (dec); ed/BA, Fairleigh Dickinson Univ, 1975; pa/Tech Writer, Instrn Manuals, Singer Co, 1977-79; Supvr, Instrn Manuals-Worldwide, Singer Co, 1979-81; Methods Analyst/Writer, AT&T Mktg Grp; Communs Conslt, 1981-; Home Economists in Bus; cp/Navigator's Clb; r/Jewish; hon/Grad, cum laude, 1975; Mem of Phi Omega Epsilon Hon Soc; W/W: in Am Cols & Univs, in Am Women.

GRIFFITH, NINA CECELIA oc/Reading Specialist; b/May 1, 1942; h/1134 Valley Drive, Pasadena, MD 21122; ba/Pasadena, MD; p/Mr and Mrs Robert Griffith, Baltimore, MD; ed/BA, Univ of MD-Balto Co, 1971; BD, Theol Sem of the Reformed Epis Ch, 1971; EdM, Rdg, Univ of MD-Col Pk, 1976; Adv'd Grad Spec in Rdg, Univ of MD, 1982; pa/Dir of Christian Ed, Bishop Cummins Meml Ch, 1967-; Tchr, Sunset Elem, Pasadena, MD, 1971-73; Team Ldr 1973-75, Co-Team Ldr 1976-77, Rdg Resource Tchr 1977-, Anne Arundel Co Public Schs; IRA; St of MD Rdg Coun; Anne Arundel Co Rdg Coun; NEA; MD St Tchrs Assn; Tchrs Assn of Anne Arundel Co; Christian Edrs Assn; Wkshop Spkr, Anne Arundel Co Rdg Assn, Feb 1983; Spkr, St of MD Rdg Assn, Mar 1983; r/Reformed Epis; hon/Hon'd as a Tchr (One in a Million), Anne Arundel Co PTA; W/W in E.

GRIFFITH, WILLIAM HENRY oc/Manager of Product Safety; b/Dec 27,

1939; h/257 Gemini Drive, 2A, Somerville, NJ 08876; ba/Fairfield, NJ; m/Carole Lotstein; c/Ian Raymond, William Henry; p/Elizabeth Medinets, Lauderhill, FL; ed/BS, Rutgers, 1968; pa/Jr Engr, Diehl Mfg Co, 1957-63; Supvr, Drafting & Engrg Standards, The Singer Co, 1963-72; Mgr of Prod Safety, The Singer Co, 1972-; Intl Electrotech Comm, 1972-, Com Chm; Intl Standards Org, 1975-, Com Chm; Am Soc for Testing & Mats, 1977-; Bd of Cert'd Prod Safety Mgrs, 1979-; r/Jewish; hon/Pub, IEC Standard for Household Sewing Machines; Nat Hon Soc, 1957.

GRIM, PATRICK oc/Philosopher; b/Oct 29, 1950; h/115 Beach Street, Port Jefferson, NY 11777; ba/Stony Brook, NY; p/Elgas (dec) and Dorathy Grim, South Pasadena, CA; ed/AB in Phil 1970, AB in Anthropology 1970, Univ of CA-Santa Cruz; BPhil, Univ of St Andrews, Scotland, 1975; AM 1976, PhD 1976, Boston Univ; pa/Vis'g Asst Prof, SUNY-Stony Brook, 1976-77; Mellon Fac Fellow, Wash Univ, 1977-78; Asst Prof 1978-84, Assoc Prof 1984-, SUNY-Stony Brook; Am Philosophical Assn; Phil Sci Assn; Soc for the Philosophical Study of the Paranormal; Editor, *Phil of Sci & the Occult*, 1982; Co-Editor of Five Volumes of *The Philosopher's Annual*, 1978-83; Author, Var Articles in Scholarly Jours; Fulbright Fellow, 1970-71; Mellon Fac Fellow, 1977-78; W/W: in E, in Brit Ed; Men of Achmt.

GRIMARDI, JOSEPH ROCCO oc/Corporate Pilot; b/Aug 16, 1934; h/77 Cedar Hill Road, Newtown, CT 06470; ba/White Plains, NY; m/Mary Cannon; c/Susan Patricia, Maria Ellen, John Batiste; p/John B and Susan Grimardi, Chgo, IL; ed/HS Grad, 1952; USAF Aviation Mechanics, 1952-56; Airframe Powerplant, Teterboro Sch Aeronautics, 1957-58; Hortman Aviation, Pvt Comml Aviation Tng Enterprises, Inst Flight Safety Inc, ATP-Type Ratings, DA-20, G1159, NA265, 1961-68; mil/USAF, 1952-56; pa/Aircraft Mechanic, Flight Mechanic, USAF, 1952-1956; Mechanic, Sikorsky Aircraft, 1956-57; Teterboro Sch of Aeronauts, 1957-58; Mechanic, Intl Aviation, 1958-59; Flight Mechanic, US Industs, 1959-60; Flight Mechanic, US Steel, 1961-66; Pilot, Dow Jones Corp, 1966-68; Pilot, J E Seagrams Corp, 1968-73; Capt, View Top Corp, Div of Rapid Am Corp, 1973-; NBAA; WMAA; AOPA; cp/Little Leag (Past); Pop Warner Ftball; BSA & GSA; PTA; Var Cath Charitable Activs; r/Cath; hon/USAF, 2 Outstg Unit Awds, Good Conduct w 1 OLC; NBAA Million Mile Awd, 1971; W/W in Aviation & Aerospace.

GRINDEA, DANIEL oc/Executive, Economist; b/Feb 23, 1924; ba/Republic National Bank of New York, 452/5th Avenue, New York, NY 10018; m/Lidia; c/Sorin; p/Sami and Liza Grunberg (dec); ed/Master in Ec and Master in Law 1948, Inst of Ec Scis & Fac of Law, Bucharest, Romania; PhD in Ec, Inst of Fin & Planning, Leningrad, USSR, 1953; pa/Assoc Prof & Chm of Polit Economy Dept, Inst of Ec Studies, Bucharest, 1953-56; Assoc Prof, Acad of Social Scis, Bucharest, 1956-58; Assoc Prof, Univ of Bucharest, 1958-62; Assoc Prof 1962-69, Prof 1969-72, Agronomic Inst, Bucharest; Prof, Acad "Stefan

Gheorghiu" Bucharest, 1972-75; Pt-time Conslt, St Planning Com, Bucharest, 1953-56; Pt-time Conslt, Min of Fin, Bucharest, 1956-68; Intl Economist NY-USA 1976-78, Sr Intl Economist & Dept Hd of Intl Ec Unit 1978-79, VP & Sr Intl Economist 1979-84, Sr VP & Chief Economist 1984-, Repub Nat Bk of NY; Am Ec Assn & Nat Assn of Bus Economists, 1978-; Elected Mem, Intl Inst of Public Fin, Saarbrucken, W Germany, 1968; Elected Mem, Intl Assn for Res on Income & Wlth, New Haven, 1967; Elected Fdg Mem, Soc of Ec Scis, Bucharest, 1958; Sci Coun of the Ctl Statl Ofc, 1956; hon/Pubs, "The Nat Income in Socialist Repub Romania", 1967, "The Distbn of the Nat Income in Romania" 1974, "The Limits of Growth & the Human Alternative" 1972, "Critical View of the Romanian Price Sys" 1970, "Quelques Observations sur les Comparisons Internationales" 1968, Others; Sr Advr, US Congl Adv Bd, 1984; Corres'g Mem of the Acad of Social & Polit Scis, Bucarest, 1970; Awd'd 1st Prize, Min Ed for Studies on Nation Income, Bucharest, 1969; W/W: Fin & Indust, in World; Hambro Euromoney Dir; W/W in Fin & Indust.

GRITES, THOMAS J oc/Higher Education Administrator; b/Jun 24, 1944; h/1106 Spring Lane, Absecon, NJ 08201; ba/Pomona, NJ; m/Pamela Schell; c/Jeremy Schell, Emily Schell (dec), Lindsey Ruth; p/Felix Z and Mary Jane Grites, Danville, IL; ed/BS in Ed 1966, MS 1967, IL St Univ; PhD, Univ of MD, 1974; pa/Dir of Acad Advising, Stockton St Col, 1977-; Dir of Student Sers in Ed, Univ of MD-Col Pk, 1971-77; Dir of Housing, Univ of MD-Balto Co, 1970-71; Asst Dir of Housing, Univ of MD-Col Pk, 1969-70; Hd Resident Advr, En MI Univ, 1967-69; Nat Acad Advising Assn, Pres 1980-82; Am Col Pers Assn, Chair of Comm 1 1980-82; Phi Delta Kappa at Stockton, Res Rep 1981-84; Absecon Bd of Ed, 1982-85; Conslt to Over 40 Cols; hon/Pubs, *Acad Advising & Student Devel*, "A Skills Approach to Career Devel" 1983, "'Undecided' or Undecided: A Re-Exam" 1983, "The Clrm as an Instnl Resource: An Example in Computer-Assisted Advising" 1982, Num Others; Compatriot in Ed, Kappa Delta Pi, 1976; Plaque, Nat Acad Advising Assn, 1983; Alumni Achmt Awd, IL St Univ, 1983; W/W in E.

GROESBECK, LAURE ANNE ELISE de BRANGES de BOURCIA oc/Artist; b/Jan 31, 1936; h/3204 Leigh Road, Pompano Beach, FL 33062; ba/Pompano Beach, FL; c/Gretchen Atlee, Genevieve de Branges; p/Vicount Louis de Branges de Bourcia II, Heidelberg, West Germany; Diane McDonald de Branges de Bourcia, Pompano Beach, FL; ed/Att'd, Agnes Irwin Sch 1954, Phila Col of Art 1954-55; r/Epis; hon/Rehoboth Bch Art Leag Prize, 1944; Agnes Allen Art Prize, Agnes Irwin Sch, 1954; One-Man Shows, Agnes Irwin Sch 1973, Phila Cricket Clb 1973; W/W in S & SW; Personalities of S.

GROSS, KENNETH IRWIN oc/Professor, Mathematician, Administrator; b/Oct 14, 1938; h/1442 Whitman, Laramie, WY 82070; ba/Laramie, WY; m/Mary Lou; c/Laura Kathryn, Karen

Louise; p/Harry (dec) and June Gross, Chelsea, MA; ed/BA 1960, MA 1962, Brandeis Univ; PhD, Wash Univ, 1966; pa/Asst Prof, Tulane Univ 1966-68, Dartmouth Col 1966-73; Assoc Prof, Prof, Univ of NC, 1973-81; Prof, Hd of Math Dept, Univ of WY, 1981-; Am Math Soc; Math Assn of Am; Soc Indep App Math; AAUP; AAAS; NCTM; hon/Author, Num Res Articles in Profl Jours; Res Prof, Acad of Scis, Taiwan, 1979; Lester Ford Prize, MAA, 1979; Chauvenet Prize, MAA, 1981; Am Men of Sci.

GROSS, LOLA P oc/Education Program Specialist; b/Jun 15, 1934; h/934 East Manhatton Drive, Tempe, AZ 85282; ba/Phoenix, AZ; m/Douglas R; p/Robert and Mary DeLong, Three Rivers, MI; ed/BA 1957, MA 1962, Wn MI Univ; PhD, AZ St Univ, 1977; pa/Prog Mgr, St Coor for Gifted Progs, AZ Dept Ed; Fed Progs Admr, Hopi Public Schs; Asst Prof, Ball St Univ; Fac Assoc, AZ St Univ; Tchr, MI Schs; Pi Lambda Theta; AZ Sch Admrs; Assn Tchr Edrs; AZ Assn Tchr Edrs; Triple R Foun, Treas; AZ Assn Gifted & Talented; r/Prot; hon/Pubs; Participant in Convocation for Excell in Ed.

GROSS, RUTH TAUBENHAUS oc/Professor of Pediatrics, Director of General Pediatrics; b/Jun 24, 1920; h/601 Van Ness Avenue, San Francisco, CA 94102; ba/Palo Alto, CA; c/Gary E MD; p/Jacob and Esther Taubenhaus (dec); ed/BA, Barnard Col, 1941; MD, Columbia Univ Col of Phys & Surgs, 1944; pa/Intern, Pediatrics, Charity Hosp, 1944; Resident, Pediatrics, Tulane Univ, 1945; Resident, Pediatrics, Grasslands Hosp, 1946; Resident, Pediatrics, Babies Hosp, 1947-48; Instr, Radcliffe Infirm, 1949-50; Instr 1950-53, Asst Prof of Pediatrics 1953-56, Assoc Prof of Pediatrics 1956-60, Stanford Univ Sch of Med; Assoc Prof of Pediatrics 1960-64, Prof of Pediatrics 1964-66, Albert Einstein Col of Med; Chief of Pediatrics, Mt Zion Hosp & Med Ctr & Clin Prof of Pediatrics, Univ of CA-SF, 1966-73; Prof of Pediatrics 1973-, Assoc Dean of Student Affairs 1973-75, Dir of Div of Gen Pediatrics 1975-, Katharine Dexter & Stanley McCormick Prof of Pediatrics 1976-, Dir of Stanford Chd's Ambulatory Care Ctr at Chd's Hosp 1980-, Stanford Univ; Ambulatory Pediatric Assn; Am Acad of Pediatrics; Am Fdn for Clin Res; Am Pediatrics Soc; Inst of Med, Nat Acad of Scis; Intl Soc for Study of Behavioral Devel; Soc for Adolescent Med; Soc for Pediatric Res; Soc for Res in Child Devel; Wn Soc for Clin Res; Wn Soc for Pediatric Res; Co-Editor, *Developmental-Behavioral Pediatrics*, 1983; Phi Beta Kappa, 1940; Alpha Omega Alpha, 1944; Commonwlth F'ship for the Study of Human Genetics, Pavia, Italy, 1959-60; Henry J Kaiser Awd for Outstg & Innovative Contbns to Med Ed, 1976; Henry J Kaiser Sr Fellow, Ctr for Adv'd Study in the Behavioral Scis, 1980-81; Marquis W/W; Catalyst's Corporate Bd Resource; Am Men & Wom of Sci.

GROSSMAN, MICHAEL oc/Associate Professor of Genetics; b/Dec 21, 1940; h/2206 Valley Brook Drive, Champaign, IL 61821; ba/Urbana, IL; m/Margaret R; c/Aaron William, Daniel Benjamin; p/Benjamin (dec) and Alice

Grossman, Miami Beach, FL; ed/BS, City Col of NY, 1962; MS, VA Polytechnic Inst & St Univ, 1965; PhD, Purdue Univ, 1969; pa/Assoc Prof of Genetics 1974-, Asst Prof of Genetics 1969-74, Univ of IL; Res Geneticist (Animal), USDA, 1979-80; Vis'g Prof, Gadjah Mada Univ, Indonesia, 1974; Vis'g Prof, Instituto de Fitotechnia, Argentina, 1970; AAAS; AAUP; ADSA; ASAS; AGA, Coun Mem 1979-82; GSA; Biometric Soc; Gamma Sigma Delta; Phi Sigma; Sigma Xi; r/Jewish; hon/Author of Num Sci & Ednl Articles in Profl Jours; Danforth Fac Assoc, 1971; AMOCO Foun Instrnl Awd, 1972; Undergrad Instrnl Awd, Univ of IL, 1971, 1972; Am Men & Wom of Sci.

GRUBER, ROSALIND H oc/Counseling Psychologist; b/Feb 10, 1943; h/2150 Route 6A, West Barnstable, MA 02668; ba/Boston, MA; p/Lazarus and Beatrice England (dec); ed/BA, cum laude, SUNY-New Paltz, 1974; MA, Suffolk Univ, 1978; pa/Sch Registrar, Assn Help of Retarded Chd, 1970; Cnslr, Neighborhood Yth Corps, 1971-73; Liaison, Govt Subsidized Housing, 1975-77; Dir, Cnslr, Aradia Cnslg, 1978-; APGA; Humanistic Ed & Devel; Assn Wom in Psych; Lic'd Clin Soc Wkr; Nat Cert'd Cnslr; hon/W/W in E.

GRUNDY, GEORGE HENRY oc/Retired; b/Jan 8, 1912; h/164 Stone Avenue, Shafter, CA 93263; m/Lena Christine; c/Betty Louise Brown, Sharon Ruth Biloff, Sandra Gerene Bartlett; p/Cora Ann Findley Grundy, Quitaque, TX; ed/HS Grad; Cert of Completion of Studies in Spec Dists Mgmt, Univ of CA-Santa Barbara; mil/European Theatre, WW II, 4 Yrs; pa/Mechanic; Welder; Machinist; Packing Shed Foreman, Potato Indust; Farmer, 25 Yrs; Seed Potato Supvr, Gen Potato & Onion Distribrs Ltd, 10 Yrs; cp/Am Legion; VFW; Disabled Am Vets; Kiwanis Clb; Shafter Hist Soc; Shafter Improvement Coun; Shafter C of C; Shafter Potato & Cotton Fest; City Coun, 24 Yrs; CA Assn of Public Cemeteries; Leag of CA Cities; Spec Dists Assn of CA; Public Cemetery Dist #1 of Kern Co; Merit Awd for Outstg Civic Ldrship, 1960; Commun Ser, 1974; Public Ser, 1974; Citizen of the Yr, 1976; Outstg Ser, 1976; Cemeterian of the Yr, 1979; Outstg Contbn to Commun, 1983.

GRUNES, DAVID LEON oc/Agronomist; h/307 Salem Drive, Ithaca, NY 14850; ba/Ithaca, NY; m/Willa Freeman; c/Lee Alan, Mitchell Ray, Rima Louise; ed/BS in Agri, Rutgers Univ, 1944; PhD, Soil Sci, Univ of CA-Berkeley, 1951; mil/AUS, Inf, 1944-45; pa/Res Soil Scist, Agri Res Ser, USDA, 1950-; Tech Asst Expert, Intl Atomic Energy, UN, 1963-64; Am Soc of Agronomy; Chm, Div S-4, Soil Fertility & Plant Nutrition; Soil Sci Soc of Am; AAAS; Intl Soc of Soil Sci; Coun for Agri Sci & Technol; Sigma Xi; hon/87 Pub'd Tech Articles; Co-Editor of One Book; Recip, USDA Awd for Res, 1959, 1982; Fellow, AAAS, ASA, SSSA; Var Biogl Listings.

GRYCNER, EDWARD oc/Manufacturing Company Executive; b/May 1, 1924; h/796 North Via Miraleste, Palm Springs, CA 92262; ba/Palm Springs, CA; m/Iris Lila Kehr; c/Henry, Richard, Gregory, Pamela, Nancy, April,

Michelle; p/Robert and Victoria Von Grutzner; ed/MBA, Sch of Ec, London Univ, 1949; BS in Fgn Trade, Sch of Fgn Trade, 1949; pa/Export Traffic Mgr, George Wehry Co, 1951-55; Export Controller, US Borax Corp, 1956-66; Mgr, Intl Opers, Ingersoll Rand, 1966-67; Dir, Intl Opers, Revell Inc, 1967-70; Pres, Grycner Toys Intl, 1970-; Grycner Leisure Grp, & Grycner Moped Corp, 1970-; Chm of Bd, Pres, Grycner Moped Corp, 1977-; Lectr, Fgn Trade St Univs, CA, 1978-; Fgn Trade Assn, So CA; Am Sporting Goods Assn; cp/LA C of C; Palm Sprgs C of C; Am Hobby Assn; LA Intl Clb; hon/Recip, Cert, Am Soc Intl Execs, 1967; Contbr, Num Articles on Intl Trade to Mags.

GRYCZ, ANNE CUNNINGHAM oc/Executive; b/Apr 7, 1944; h/1142 Guinda Street, Palo Alto, CA 94301; ba/Palo Alto, CA; c/Michal Jozef, Anastasia Christina; p/Albert W (dec) and Elizabeth G Cunningham, Las Vegas, NV; ed/BA 1965, Sec'dy Tchg Credential (CA) 1966, Univ of SF; MA Cand in Human Values, Grad Theol Union, Univ of CA-Berkeley; pa/Tchr of Spanish, Santa Clara U Sch Dist, 1966-67; Exec Dir, Ecumenical Tchrs' Faire, 1970-80; Secy/Asst to Pres 1976-80, VP 1981-, Behaviordyne Inc; Conslt for Parents of Handicapped Chd, 1968-; Bd of Dirs, Palo Alto Adolescent Sers Corp, 1982-; Bd of Dirs, Peninsula Exec Grp, 1983; Bd of Dirs, Nat Jesuit Hon Soc, 1968-76; AAUW, 1980-; Corp Planners Assn, 1981-; r/Rom Cath; hon/Co-Author, *The Guide Pak*, 1978; Var Articles, *The Migrant Echo*, 1970-76; W/W: in W, of Am Wom, Among Students in Am Univs.

GUBBINS, KEITH EDMUND oc/Thomas R Briggs Professor of Engineering, Professor of Chemical Engineering; b/Jan 27, 1937; h/523 Highland Road, Ithaca, NY 14850; ba/Ithaca, NY; m/Pauline Payne; c/Vanessa Clare, Nicholas Peter; p/Joyce Gubbins, Comberton, Cambridge, UK; ed/BSc in Chem (1st Class Hons), Queen Mary Col, Univ of London, 1958; PhD in Chem Engrg, King's Col, Univ of London, 1962; pa/Vis'g Lectr, Univ of London, 1960-62; Postdoct Fellow 1962-64, Asst Prof 1964-68, Assoc Prof 1968-72, Prof 1972-76, Univ of FL; Endowed Chair, T R Briggs Prof'ship in Chem Engrg, Cornell Univ, 1976-; Eppley Foun Fellow, Chem Engrg Dept, Imperial Col, London, 1971-72; Vis'g Conslt, Theoretical Physics Div, UK Atomic Energy Auth, 1971; Vis'g Prof, Physics Dept, Univ of Guelph, 1971, 1972, 1973, 1976; Vis'g Prof of Physics, Univ of Kent, 1975; Vis'g Prof of Chem, Univ of Oxford, 1980-81; Vis'g Prof of Chem Engrg, Univ of CA-Berkeley, 1982; Edit Bd, Molecular Physics; Am Assn of Chem Engrs; Prog Com (Thermodynamics & Mass Transfer), AIChE, 1974-81; Nat Acad of Scis Com to Study Formation of NRCC (Nat Resource Ctr for Computing in Chem), 1976-77; hon/Pubs, "Molecular Theory of Fluid w Gaussian Overlap Potentials" 1983, "Fluid Phase Equilibria: Experiment, Computer Simulation & Theory" 1983, "The Effect of Nonaxial Quadrupole Forces on Liquid Properties" 1983, "The Impact of Lionel Staveley's Res on the Theory of Liquid Mixtures" 1983, "Thermodynamics & Structure of

Dense Fluid Mixtures of Hard Dumbells" 1983, Num Others; Eppley Foun F'ship, Imperial Col, 1970-71; Sigma Tau, Tau Beta Pi Awd for Excell in Undergrad Tchg, 1968, 1974; Outstg Ser Awd for Res, Univ of FL, 1975; Annual Awd of Canadian Soc of Chem Engrg for Best Paper, 1973; Nat Acad of Scis, Com on Nat Resource Ctr for Computing in Chem, 1976-77; Reilly Lectr, Notre Dame Univ, 1978; Invited Lectr 1975-, Danish Chem Soc 1975, Gordon Res Conf on Liquids 1975, 5th Oaxtepec Meeting on Statl Mechs 1976, 1st Intl Conf on Fluid Phase Equilibria 1977, Others; Am Men of Sci; W/W in Technol Today; Intl W/W in Engrg.

GUDEHUS, DONALD HENRY oc/ Astrophysicist; b/Sep 13, 1939; h/1031 Barton Drive, #109, Ann Arbor, MI 48105; ba/Ann Arbor, MI; p/Herman Andrew Gudehus (dec); Katherine Pauline Hirner, Whiting, NJ; ed/BS in Physics, MIT, 1961; AM in Physics, Columbia Univ, 1963; MA in Astronomy 1967, PhD in Astronomy 1971, Univ of CA-LA; pa/Engr/Scist, McDonnell-Douglas Aerophysics Lab, 1964-67; Postdoct Scholar, Astronomy Dept, Univ of CA LA, 1971-75; Asst Prof, Physics Dept, LA City Col, 1974-81; Asst Res Scist, Dept of Physics, Univ of MI-Ann Arbor, 1981-; Am Astronom Soc; Lorquin Entomological Soc; hon/Author of Many Sci Articles for Profl Jours; Composer, Music for Film, "Water in the Wilderness" 1973, "Suite of Dances" 1973, Many Piano Pieces; NASA Predoct Traineeship, 1967-70; W/W in Frontier Sci & Technol.

GUERNSEY, NANCY PATRICIA oc/Product Support Engineer; b/Oct 12, 1955; h/14 Third Street, Ronkonkoma, Long Island, NY 11779; ba/Long Island, NY; p/Orville Wendell and Dorothy Maccia Guernsey, Irvington-on-Hudson, NY; ed/BEME, Manhattan Col, 1977; MS, Nuclear Engrg (in Progress), PINY; pa/Asst Engr, Weight Opt & Tech Devel 1977-79, Sys Integration 1979-83, Grumman Aerospace; Govt Support Sys Div, Configuration Mgmt, Reliability, Maintainability & Human Factors, Harris Corp, 1983-; AIAA, 1976; SWE, 1973; ANS, 1976; PIA, 1974; AOPA, 1975; NAFI, 1980; Pvt Pilot, Aircraft, Single Engine, Land; Free-Lance Writer; cp/Nat Rifle Assn, 1979; Sperry Flying Clb, 1981, Secy; 99's/Intl Org of Wom Pilots, 1981, NY-NJ Sect News Reporter & Air Age Ed Chm, Long Isl Early Fliers; Grumman Rod & Gun Clb; r/Epis; Lic'd Lay Rdr/Chalice Admr, Epis Ch; hon/Pub, "Bewildered Beginner," in AOPA Pilot Mag, Sep 1980; W/W: in HS, in Col, in Aviation & Aerospace.

GUERRA, MIRTHA oc/Certified Public Accountant; b/Mar 11, 1946; ba/ 1000 Brickell Avenue, Suite 500, Miami FL 33133; p/Dr Jose R and Mirtha (dec) Guerra, Tampa, FL; ed/BBA, Univ of Miami, 1972; MSM in Taxation, FL Intl Univ, 1981; pa/Mgr in Charge of Tax Dept, Alexander Grant & Co, 1982-; Mgr, Ernst R Whinney, 1972-82; Pres, Latin BPW Clb; Past Pres, Miami Chapt, Am Soc of Wom Accts; Am Inst of CPAs; FIA Inst of CPAs; Lectr, World Trade Inst; cp/Bd Mem, Gtr Miami U; Bd Mem, SALAD; Bd Mem, Friends of Cuban Mus.

GUICE, M W T h/2913 21st Street, Gulfport, MS 39501.

GUINIER, EWART oc/Professor Emeritus; b/May 17, 1910; h/29 Robinson Street, Cambridge, MA 02138; m/ Eugenia Paprin; c/Clothilde Yvonne, Lani, Sary, Marie; p/Howard Manoah Guinier (dec); Marie Beresford (dec); ed/ BS, cum laude; MA; JD; mil/AUS 1942-66; pa/Prof Emeritus, Afro-Am Studies, Harvard Univ; Life Mem, Nat Bd, Assn for Study of Afro-Am Life & Hist; Org of Am Hist; Alpha Phi Alpha; cp/Life Mem, NAACP; hon/Author of Enumerable Articles, 1938-; Hon MA, Harvard Univ, 1970; Several Other Hon Degs; Carter G Woodson Awd; W/W in World; Others.

GUINN, HENRY ALAN oc/Restaurant Consultant, Business Manager; b/ Mar 22, 1952; h/3411 Weston Place, Palo Cedro, CA 96073; m/Carla Denise; c/Daniel Joseph Highfill, Elizabeth Lorraine; p/Henry V and Alsace-Lorraine Jones Guinn, Bristol, TN; ed/ BS in Hist, TN Tech Univ, 1975; Grad Wk in Ednl Psych, 1976; mil/ROTC (Army), 1970-72; pa/Unit Mgr, Pizza Hut, 1974-76; Area Gen Mgr, Pizza Hut Inc, 1976-77; Field Ser Rep 1977-78, Nat Mgr of Equip Sales 1978-79, Franchise Ser Inc; Franchise Opers Rep 1979-80, Dir of Franchise Devel (Canada) 1981, Pepsico Food Ser Intl; Gen Mgr, PM Foods Ltd, 1981-82; Franchise Area Dir, Wendy's Intl Inc, 1982-84; Pres, AVM Conslts Ltd, 1982-83; Sr Ptnr, Tri-Am Consltg Ltd, 1983-84; VP & Dir of Opers, NW TAG Enterprises, Inc, 1984-; Omicron Delta Kappa; cp/Am Radio Relay Leag; Canadian Radio Relay Leag; Woodrow Wilson Ctr for Scholars; r/ Meth; hon/Past VP, Wichita Amateur Radio Clb, 1977; Past Pres, Wichita Amateur Radio Clb, 1978; Public Ser Awds, Am Radio Relay Leag, 1969-73; W/W in W.

GUNNING, LAURIE FROYDIS oc/ Private Vocational Counselor and Consultant; b/Mar 11, 1950; h/6891 South Yukon Way, Littleton, CO 80123; ba/ Littleton, CO; m/William C Jr; c/William C III, Bryn Taira; p/E F Marsek, Littleton, CO; Fröydis Lenore Deupree, Davis, CA; ed/BA, Sociol, CA St Univ-Northridge, 1972; MEd in Adult Cnslg w Hons, Univ of MO-St Louis, 1980; pa/Pvt Pract, Voc Cnslr/Consult, 1983-; Mgr of Ed Div, Mincomp Corp, 1980-82; Voc Rehab Cnslr, Voc Cnslg & Rehab Sers, St Louis, MO, 1979-80; Ofc Coor & Advr, Univ W/O Walls, Loretto Hgts Col, 1974-77; Nat Voc Guid Assn; CO Assn of Cnslg & Devel; CO Voc Guid Assn, Public Relats Rep; Rocky Mtn Career Planning Assn, Treas; hon/Co-Authored Slide/Tape Presentation, "Grp Interpretation of the Strong-Campbell Interest Inventory," 1981; Authored, "Mincomp Manual for the Strong-Campbell Interest Inventory Interpretive Report," 1981; Recog Awd, Univ of Denver's Adm Sers Dept, 1980; W/W in W.

GUNTER, BENJAMIN DEAN oc/ University Professor and Department Chairman; b/Feb 8, 1935; h/918 Baldwin Road, Richmond, VA 23229; ba/Richmond, VA; m/Carolyn Harshbarger; c/ Elizabeth Heath Gunter Daly, Charles Robert; p/Ray Robert and Gladys Martin Gunter, Collinsville, VA; ed/BA, Bridgewater Col, 1956; BFA, Richmond

Profl Inst, 1963; EdM, Univ of VA, 1963; mil/Adj Gen Ofc, AUS, 1958-59; pa/ Public Sch Tchr, 1956-57; Buyer, M W & Co, 1957-58; Interior Designer, Schewels, 1963-65; Asst Prof, Dept of Interior Design 1965-69, Prof & Chm of Dept of Interior Design 1969-, VA Commonwlth Univ; Ednl Conslt; Interior Design Edrs Coun Inc, Reg Chm 1969-71, Corres Secy 1971-73, Pres 1973-75, 1975-77, Bd of Dirs 1969-81, Chm of Bd 1977-81; Foun for Interior Design Ed Res, Nat Accreditation Com 1973-79, Guid Com 1979-82, Bd of Visitors 1982-; Intl Design Ed Foun, Bd of Dirs 1977-81, Chm of Bd 1979-81; ASID, 1963-; IBD, 1980-; IES, 1973-; Adv Com, Nat Ctr for a Barrier Free Design, 1982-; r/Presb; hon/Design Wk Pub'd in *Interior Design Mag* 1983, *Richmond News Ldr* 1968, 1975; W/W in S.

GUNTER, DANIEL LEE oc/Optometrist in Private Practice; b/Sep 26, 1950; h/405-5 Sheoah Boulevard, Winter Springs, FL 32708; ba/Winter Springs, FL; m/Charlotte Ann; c/Jacqueline Michelle; p/Ralph D and Ruby W Gunter, Orlando, FL; ed/Att'd, Stetson Univ, 1968-70; BS in Ec, Wake Forest Univ, 1972; BS in Visual Sci 1974, OD 1976, IL Col of Optom; mil/AUS 1976-82, Comm'd 2nd Lt 1972, Adv'd through Ranks to Capt; pa/Engr, Walt Disney World RR, 1970-74; Credit Analyzer, Playboy, Chgo, 1974-76; Staff Optometrist, Hlth Clin, BAD Kreuznach, W Germany, 1976-79; Chief, Eye Clin, Ft Stewart, GA, 1979-81; Pvt Pract, Optom, 1982-; Am Optometric Assn, 1972-; Optometric Ext Prog, 1972-; FL Optometric Assn, 1976-; Col of Optometrists in Vision Devel, 1980-; cp/VP, Montgomery Co Explorer Scouts, 1968; Sailing Conslt, Chgo Sea Explorer Scouts, 1974-76; Pershing Rifles, 1968-72, VP 1972; Scabbard & Blade, 1970-72, Pres 1972; Winter Sprgs Sertoma, 1982; r/Meth; hon/Pubs, "Lyden Johnson-The Grt Society" 1968, "Orlando-Unemploymt & Under Employmt" 1972, "Pupilio-irometer-A Measuring Device" 1976; ROTC Scholar, Wake Forest Univ, 1970; Dean's List, Wake Forest Univ, 1970-72; Prof of Mil Sci Awd, 1972; Awd'd Patent for Invention, Chgo, 1976; Decorated, Army Commend Medal, 1980; W/W in S; Personalities of S; Men of Achmt.

GUNTER, JOHN BROWN oc/Real Estate Developer; b/May 22, 1919; h/ 2215 Crabtree Lane, Johnstown, PA 15901; m/Dorothy Mulhollen; c/Jerrol; p/John B and Mary Barr Gunter (dec); ed/Att'd, Val Forge Mil Acad Jr Col, 1939; BS, Bus & Mgmt, Univ of MD, 1941; mil/Adv'd through Ranks to Lt Col, AUS, 1941-46; pa/Exec Dir, Johnstown UF, 1946-48; Trainee & Store Mgr, Sears Roebuck, 1948-52; Adm Asst, Controller, Asst Treas, Secy, Corporate VP, Pres, Dept Store Div, 1952-78; Pres & Dir of Winston Corp 1978-84, VP & Dir of Johnstown Tribune Publishing Co 1980-84, Secy & Dir of Intl Refractories Inc 1981-84, Trustee of Johnstown Savs Bk, Instr of Mgmt at Univ of Pgh-Johnstown, 1978-; Ret'd Dir, Nat Retail Merchs Assn; Ret'd Dir, PA Retailers Assn; Phi Delta Theta; cp/Mensa; Past Pres, Gtr Johnstown C of C; Past Pres, Gtr Johnstown U Way; Masonic; r/Prot; hon/Decorated, Order of Brit Empire, WW II; W/W: in Am, in Fin & Indust.

GUPTA, SURENDRA PRATAP ocl Research Supervisor; b/Dec 29, 1946; h/ 4348 East 86th Street, Tulsa, OK 74137; ba/Tulsa, OK; m/Meera; c/Ajay, Amit; p/Mr and Mrs B P Gupta, Jaipur, India; ed/BSc 1968, MS 1970, PhD 1972, Chem Engrg; pa/Res Supvr 1984-, Res Assoc 1981-84, Staff Res Engr 1978-81, Sr Res Engr 1973-78, Amoco Prodn Co; Postdoct Fellow, Purdue Univ, 1973; AIChE; Am Chem Soc; Soc of Petro Engrs; Editor, Soc of Petro Engrs, 1978-80; r/Hindu; hon/Papers, "Micellar Fluid/Polymer Phase Effects in Micellar Flooding", 1982, "Dispersive Mixing Effects on the Sloss Field Micellar Sys" 1981, "Compositional Effect on Displacement Mechanisms of the Micellar Fluid Injected in the Sloss Field Test" 1980, "Effect of Fractional Flow Hysteresis on Recovery of Tertiary Oil" 1978, Others; Grad'd w Hons & Awd'd Gold Medal, BSc; Awd'd Nat Merit S'ship, 1963-68; W/W in S & SW.

GUPTA, VIJAY KUMAR ocl/Associate Professor of Chemistry; b/Apr 27, 1941; h/1447 New Way Drive, Xenia, OH; ba/Wilberforce, OH; m/Surjit M; c/Sonia, Angela, Ashish; p/Rattan Lal Gupta, Xenia, OH; Sharda Devi (dec); ed/BS w Hons in Chem 1961, MS w Hons in Chem 1962, PhD in Chem 1969, Panjab Univ, Chandigarh, India; pa/ Assoc Prof of Chem, Ctl St Univ, 1969-; USAF-SCEEE Res Fellow, Sums 1984, 1981; Chem, LLNL, Sum 1980; NSF Indust Res Fellow, Sum 1979; Am Chem Soc; Assn of Energy Engrs; The Electrochem Soc; AAUP; cp/India Clb of Metro Dayton, Public Relats Chm 1975; Hindu Commun Org, Mem of Constit Com 1981; r/Hindu; hon/Author, Several Res & Ednl Articles in the Field of Thermodynamics & Energy Conversion Technols, incl'g: "Likelihood of a Solar Society" 1984, "Waste Utilization to Conserve Energy" 1983, "Prospects of Hydrogen as an Energy Carrier for the Future" 1983, "Cogeneration-An Energy Conserv & Cost Savs Approach" 1983, "High Energy Density Non-Aqueous Battery Sys" 1983, "Electrochem Studies of Calcium & Calcium-Lithium Alloys in Thionyl Chloride Electrolyte Sys" 1983, Num Others; Hon'd by Phy Org Class (1975-76) as Tchr, Advr & Friend; Awd'd Several Res F'ships; Am Men & Wom of Phy Scis; W/W in Frontier Sci & Technol.

GUSKEY, THOMAS R ocl/Professor; b/Feb 15, 1950; h/3505 Adoric Court, Lexington, KY 40502; ba/Lexington, KY; m/Jeanette T; c/Jennifer M, Michael T; p/Mr and Mrs Robert C Guskey, Yardley, PA; ed/PhD, Univ of Chgo, 1979; EdM, Boston Col, 1975; BA, Thiel Col, 1972; pa/Assoc Prof, Univ of KY, 1978-; Dir, Bur of Res & Devel, Chgo Public Schs, 1976-78; Eval Conslt, City Cols of Chgo, 1975-76; Res Asst, Boston Col, 1974-75; Tchr, St Andrew Sch, 1972-74; Am Ednl Res Assn; Am Ednl Assn; Nat Coun on Measurement in Ed; Nat Soc for the Study of Ed; Soc for Res in Child Devel; hon/Author of *Implementing Mastery Lng*, 1985, Articles Pub'd in *Am Ednl Res Jour*, 1984, *Res in Higher Ed*, 1984, *Jour of Ednl Res* 1982, *Commun & Jr Col Jour* 1982, *The Prin* 1982, *Contemp Ednl Psych* 1982, *Jour*

of *Tchr Ed* 1981, *Applied Psychol Measurement* 1981, & 15 Others; Outstg Achmt Awd in Res, Univ KY, 1980, 1981, 1982, 1983, 1985; W/W in S & SW; Outstg Yg Men of Am; DIB; Outstg Col Aths in Am.

GUTEKUNST, RICHARD RALPH ocl/Dean of College of Health Related Professions; b/Jan 20, 1926; h/3705 Northwest 25th Avenue, Gainesville, FL 32605; ba/Gainesville, FL; m/Anna Fetterman; c/Mary Jane Ellickson, Richard M, Jo Anne Loughery; ed/BS, Bacteriology, Phila Col of Pharm & Sci, 1951; MS in Bacteriology 1957, PhD in Virology 1958, Cornell Univ; mil/ USNR, 1943-46; USN, 1951-68; Ret'd Cmdr, 1968; pa/Dean, Col of Hlth Related Professions & Prof of Med Technol & Microbiol, Univ of FL-Gainesville, 1980-; Dean, Col of Allied Hlth Professions 1975-80, Prof of Microbiol, Immunol & Prof of Pathol 1974-80, Assoc Prof of Microbiol, Immunol & Prof of Pathol 1968-74, The Hahnemann Med Col & Hosp; Chief of Virology Div, Nav Med Field Res Lab, Camp Lejeune, 1964-68; Naval Med Res Inst, Nat Naval Med Ctr, 1963-64; Asst Chief, Virology Div, Naval Med Res Unit (NAMRU) #3, Cairo, Egypt, 1960-63; Asst for Tech Coordination, NAMRU #4, 1958-60; Am Soc of Allied Hlth Professions, Pres 1982-84; Am Soc of Microbiol; AAAS; NY Acad of Sci; APHA; Fellow, Am Acad for Microbiol; Assn for Practitioners of Infection Control; Bd of Dirs, Phila Col of Pharm & Sci Alumni Assn, 1975-78; cp/Supvr, Lower Gwynedd Twp, 1973-80; r/Ch Coun, St Peter's Luth Ch, 1972-77, Pres 1974-77; Examining Com, SEn PA Synod, Luth Ch in Am, 1976-80, Chm 1978-80; Ch Coun, Univ Luth Ch, 1982-; hon/Author, 41 Profl Articles in Var Refereed Jours; Navy Commend Medal for Med Res, 1968; Outstg Edr in Am, 1975; Lindback Awd for Excell in Tchg, 1975; Fac Achmt Awd, Col of Allied Hlth Professions, Hahnemann Med Col & Hosp, 1980; Am Men of Sci; W/W: in Hlth Care, in Am.

GUTHKE, KARL SIEGFRIED ocl Professor of German; b/Feb 17, 1933; h/Hillside Road, Lincoln, MA 01773; ba/ Cambridge, MA; m/Dagmar von Nostitz; c/Carl Ricklef; p/Karl and Helene (dec) Guthke; ed/MA, Univ of TX, 1953; PhD, Univ of Göttingen, 1956; pa/From Instr to Prof of German Lit, Univ of CA-Berkeley, 1956-65; Prof of German, Univ of Toronto, 1965-68; Prof of German, Harvard Univ, 1968-; Am Philosophical Soc, Grant-in-Aid, 1961-62; Vis'g Prof, Univ of CO 1963, Univ of MA 1967; Mod Lang Assn; Am Lessing Soc, Pres 1971-72; Acad Lit Studies; Lessing-Akad; Schiller-Ges; hon/Pubs, *Erkundungen: Essais zur Literatur von Milton bis Traven* 1983, *Der Mythos der Neuzeit: Das Thema der Mehrheit der Welten in Literatur und Philosophie von der Kopernikanischen Wende bis zur Sci Fiction* 1982, *Haller im Halblicht: Vier Studien* 1981, *Das Abenteuer der Literatur: Studien zum literarischen Leben des deutschsprachigen Länder von der Aufklärung bis zum Exil* 1981, Other Books; Walter C Cabot Prize, Harvard, 1977; Guggenheim Fellow, 1965; Nat Endowment for the Humanities Fellow, 1979; Am Coun Learned Soc Fellow, 1972-73; W/W: in World, in Am.

GUTIERREZ, FERNANDO JOSE ocl Counseling Psychologist; b/Mar 1, 1951; h/500 King Drive, #1008, Daly City, CA 94015; ba/Santa Clara, CA; p/ Alberto Rodolfo Gutierrez, Boston, MA; ed/EdD, Boston Univ, 1981; MS in Ed, Purdue Univ, 1974; BA, MI St Univ, 1973; pa/Cnslg Psychol, Univ of Santa Clara, 1981-; Cnslg Psychol, SF St Univ, 1980-81; Psych Intern, Solomon Carter Fuller Mtl Hlth Ctr, 1979-80; Psych Intern, Tri-City Mtl Hlth Ctr, 1977-78; Cnslr, Univ of WI Stevens Point, 1975-77; Am Psychol Assn, 1982-; Assn of Cnslg & Devel, 1974-; Wn Reg Coor, Profl Staff Devel; Nat Assn of Minority Students & Edrs in Higher Ed, 1982-84; cp/Pres, Assn of Hispanic Orientation, Rec and the Arts, 1979-80; Chd's Com, Adv Coun to Commr Mtl Hlth, Commonwlth of MA, 1980; hon/Pubs, "Bicultural Personality Develt: A Process Model," *Advances in Bilingual Ed Res* (in Press), "Wkg w Minority Cnslr Ed Students" 1982, "Don't Sell Out Student Pers" 1974; Pi Lambda Theta, Nat Ed Hon, 1978-; Kappa Delta Pi, Nat Ed Hon, 1974-; HEW Fellow, 1978; W/W: in Frontier Sci & Technol-Psych Div, in Am, in W.

GUTIERREZ, SALLY GROVER ocl Managing Associate; b/Jul 16, 1948; h/ 965 Calle Miramar, Redondo Beach, CA 90277; ba/Manhattan Beach, CA; m/ Thomas Andrew; p/Mrs N Tuckett Gover, Redondo Beach, CA; ed/MPA, 1983; BA, Psych, 1971; pa/Mng Assoc, Cabrera Assocs, 1982-; Policy Analyst, The White House, 1982; Asst Dean, Univ of So CA, Sch of Public Adm, 1980-82; Dir, Civic Ctr Campus, Univ of So CA, 1977-80; Assoc Dir, Ofc of Prog Devel, Univ of So CA, 1975-77; Dir, Area Ctr Progs, Univ of So CA, 1973-75; Pres, LA Chapt, Am Soc for Public Adm, 1983; Chair, Nat Com for Wom, ASPA, 1978, 1979; Nat Coun Mem, ASPA, 1982; Fdr & Chair, CA Wom & Govt, 1975; Bd of Dirs, Mun Mgmt Assts (MMASC), 1977; cp/VP, Santa Monica, YWCA, Bd of Dirs 1982, 1983; LA Jr C of C Govt Affairs Com, 1982; r/Epis; hon/Pubs, "Mentoring" in *Public Mgmt Wom*, "Internships" in MMASC Career Handbook; TELACU Wom of the Yr, 1977; Henry Reining Awd, LA Metro Chapt of ASPA, 1976, 1977; Thomas Bradley Affirmative Action Awd, 1980; Cert of Commemoration, LA Co, 1977; Outstg Yg Wom of Am; Personalities of W; Intl Personalities.

GUTMAN, GEORGE ANDRE ocl Molecular Geneticist; b/Sep 15, 1945; h/ 3080 Tyler Way, Costa Mesa, CA 92626; ba/Irvine, CA; m/Janis Lynn Schonauer; c/Pierre Daniel, Marie Elizabeth; p/Peter Max and Frances Friedl Gutman, New York, NY; ed/AB, Columbia Col, 1966; PhD, Stanford Univ, 1973; pa/Postdoct Fellow, Stanford Univ, 1973-74; Postdoct Fellow, Walter & Eliza Hall Inst, Melbourne, 1974-77; Asst Prof 1977-82, Assoc Prof 1982-, Univ of CA-Irvine; hon/Pubs, "A Standard Nomenclature for Rat Immunoglobulin Allotypes" 1983, "Rat Kappa Chains: Evolution of Proteins & Genes" 1983, "Natural Cytotoxicity in Rats: Strain Distribn & Genetics" 1982, "Recent Gene Duplications in the Rat Kappa J-Segment Cluster" 1982, "Rat Kappa Chain J-Segment Genes: Two

Recent Gene Duplication Events Separate Rat & Mouse" 1982, Num Others; Fulbright/Hays Scholar, 1966-67; Arthritis Foun Fellow, 1974-77; Res Career Devel Awd, 1978-83; W/W in Frontier Sci & Technol.

GUY, EDWARD LEE oc/Real Estate Investor; b/Oct 28, 1937; h/7546 Armand Circle, Tampa, FL 33614; c/Stacy Lee; p/Lee Livingston Guy (dec); ed/BA, Catawba Col, 1969; mil/AUS, 1960-62; pa/Pres, Super Chek Sys Inc, 1977-; Pres & Gen Mgr, Multi-Chek Sys Inc, 1972-77; Owner, Inventory Ser Co, 1970-72; Adm Asst, Conslts Ser Co Inc, 1969-70; cp/Am Mensa Ltd; Tampa Bay Mensa; The Intl Legion of Intell; r/Bapt; hon/Recip, F M Knetsche Awd, 1967; Notable Am Awd, 1984; W/W in Fin & Indust; Personalities of S; 2,000 Notable Ams; Biogl Roll of Hon.

GUYTON, SUZANNE oc/Chiropractor; b/Jun 7, 1947; h/146 Spyglass Hill Road, San Jose, CA 95128; ba/San Jose, CA; p/Robert E and Eleanor Nixon, Kenward, CA; ed/BS, 1973; DC, Palmer Col of Chiro, 1977; pa/Chiropractor in Pvt Pract, 1977-; Am Chiro Assn; CA Chiro Assn; Nat Assn for Female Execs; Parker Sch for Profl Success; r/Presb; hon/Grad, summa cum laude, Palmer Col of Chiro; Cert of Merit, Palmer Col of Chiro Clin, 1977; Pi Tau Delta, Intl

Chiro Hon Soc, 1977; Diplomate, Nat Bd of Chiro Examrs, 1978; World W/ W of Wom; Biographical Roll of Hon; Life F'ship, ABIRA; W/W in W.

GUZIK, RUDOLPH P oc/Manager of Advanced Research; b/Sep 26, 1939; h/5751 North Richmond, Chicago, IL 60659; ba/Chicago, IL; c/Sharon Keri, Audrey Lynn, Lauren Briana; p/Patricia Ann Guzik, Frankfort, IL; ed/Student, Mech Engrg (IIT) 1956-58, Chinese Mandarin-USAF (Yale) 1959, Mech Engrg (IIT) 1960-61; BS, Physics & Math, IIT, 1970; MS, Applied Physics, NEn IL Univ, 1975; pa/Mgr of Adv'd Res, Rockwell Intl; Proj Mgr & Sr Engrg Physicist, Bell & Howell Corp, 1978-81; Conslt, Engrg Physics, Imaging Technol Conslts, 1974-78; Assoc Editor, Physicist & Proj Ldr, Apeco Corp, 1967-73; SPSE; SID; SPIE; OSA; APS; ESA; TAPPI; WFS; AAAS; cp/Mensa; hon/Pubs, *The Grt Divide* (Pending) 1983, "Sci & Art" 1976, "Image Transform Systems" 1976, "Three-Phase Aspects of Creativity" 1976, Others; Editor & Contbg Artist, *CHIME*, Mensa of IL, 1969; Editor, *Proceedings of Imaging in the 70's Forecasting Symp*, SPSE, 1971; SPSE Nat Ser Awd, 1975; Chgo Area Student Sci Conf Judge, 1973-; Vis'g Artist Lectr, Sch of the Art Inst, 1976; Pres,

Bell & Howell Engrs Clb, 1979; Invited Spkr, ESA Conf, 1981; VP, Engrg, SPSE, 1981-82; Dir, Raymond David S'ship Fund, 1982; Maj Role in Chgo Music Theatre Prodn, Dec 1982; W/W in MW; Personalities of Am; Men of Achmt; Roll of Hon.

GYOR, HARRIET S oc/Director of Phobia Clinic, Author, Publicist; b/Dec 25, 1942; ba/Westminster, CA; c/Julie Ann, William Jon; p/William A and Joyce D Gardner, Fountain Valley, CA; ed/Att'd, Compton Jr Col 1960-61, Univ of CA-Berkeley 1961-62, Rio Hondo 1963-65, CA Col of Hypnosis 1983; pa/Sign Lang Tchg Asst, Jersey Elem Sch, 1971-74; Dir of Phobia Clin (TERRAP-Orange Co), 1976-; Owner, PGI Publishing Co, 1980-; Hypnotist, Hypnotherapist, 1983-; Assisting Coor, 8 Hour CE Sems for RNs & Pharms, Golden W Col, 1979, 1981; Phobia Soc of Am; Am Booksellers Assn, 1982; So CA Book Publicists, 1983; cp/Social Readjustment Vol, Norwalk St Hosp, 1965-67; r/Rel Sci; hon/Pubs, *Living in Hell: An Agoraphobic Experience* 1980, 1982, *ACT: Anxiety Control Techniques* 1983; Cert'd as Ldr/ Tchr of TERRAP Progs for Those w Multiple Phobias, 1977; Interviewed, TV, Radio & Newspapers, 1977-; W/W in Am Wom.

H

HAACKE, EWART MARK oc/ Research Scientist; b/Jan 24, 1951; h/ 2312 Glendon Road, University Heights, OH 44118; ba/Highland Heights, OH; m/Linda Theresa Clarke; c/Bryon Clarke; p/Ewart and Helena Haacke, Islington, Ontario, Canada; ed/ PhD, Theoretical High Energy Physics 1978, MSc, Theoretical High Energy Physics 1975, BSc, Math & Physics 1973, Univ of Toronto; pa/Res Assoc/ Instr, Case Wn Resv Univ, 1978-84; Res Geophysicist, Gulf Res & Devel Co, 1981-83; Sr Res Scist, Picker Intl, 1983-; Am Phy Soc; Soc of Indust & Applied Math; cp/Ontario Geneal Soc; Wn Resv Hist Soc; Berks Co Hist Soc; r/Anglican/ Cath; hon/Pubs, "Demo of a Flexible Fast Scan Technique Radiology" (E M Hacke et al) 1984, "A Discussion of Periodic Motion & Flow in NMR Imaging" Assn of Univ Radiologist Meeting 1984, "Parameter Estimation in Linear Functions Relat'ships in *Am Jour of Physiol* 1983, "Multiple Scattering in One Dimension II" 1981, "Multiple Scattering in One Dimension I" 1981, "Toward an Understanding of the Electroprodn R Ratio" 1980, "From Charge-Conjugation Asymmetries to the Trilinear Gluon Coupling" 1980, "Scaling Violations & the Proton-Neutron Mass Difference" 1979, Num Others; E F Burton F'ship, 1977; Ontario Grad S'ship, 1976, 1975; E C Stevens F'ship, 1974; Victoria Col F'ship, 1970; Ontario Scholar, 1969; RCI Math Awd, 1969; Ontario Senior Math Contest, 1969; Ontario Junior Math Contest, 1967; W/W in Frontier Science & Technology.

HABECKER, EUGENE B oc/College President; b/Jun 17, 1946; h/901 Ray Street, Huntington, IN 46750; ba/ Huntington, IN; m/Marylou Napolitano; c/David Eugene, Matthew Joseph, Marybeth; p/Mr (dec) and Mrs Walter E Habecker, Palmyra, PA; ed/BA, Taylor Univ, 1968; MA, Ball St Univ, 1969; JD, Temple Univ, 1974; PhD, Univ of MI, 1981; pa/Asst Dean & Financial Aid Dir, En Col, 1970-74; Asst Prof of Polit Sci & Dean of Students, George Fox Col, 1974-78; Exec VP 1979-81, Pres 1981-, Huntington Col; Bd, Assoc'd Cols of IN; Bd, Indep Cols of IN Inc; Exec Com, IN Conf on Higher Ed; Bd, Christian Col Coalition; cp/Rotary; Ec Devel Com, C of C; r/Dir of Ed, Ch of the U Brethren in Christ Denomination; Prot; hon/ Pubs, *Affirmative Action in the Indep Col* 1977, More Than a Dozen Articles in Jours, incl'g, *Improving Col & Univ Tchg, Jour of Col & Univ Law, Christian Scholars Review, CUPA Jour;* Grad, cum laude, Taylor Univ, 1968; W/W: in W, in MW, in Am; Dir of Am Scholars; Intl W/W in Ed.

HACKENBRACHT, PHILLIP DOUGLAS oc/Farmer; b/Mar 2, 1950; h/ 51300 CR116, Fresno, OH 43824; ba/ Coshocton, OH; ed/BS in Agronomy, OH St Univ, 1968-72; pa/Lawn Spec & Power Crew Chief, Scotts Lawn Care Ser, 1973, 1974; Area Supvr, Perf-a-Lawn Corp, 1975, 1976; Agronomist, Na-Churs Plant Food Co, 1976-78; Farmer, 1978-; Coshocton Co Farm Bur, Bd of Dirs 1981-85; Coshocton Co Ext Ser Adv Bd, 1982-85; Am Soc of Agronomy, 1971-; cp/Lions Clb

Intl, 1st VP 1982-83; r/U Ch of Christ; hon/W/W in MW.

HACKLANDER, EFFIE HEWITT oc/ Assistant Dean of College of Human Ecology; b/Oct 10, 1940; h/4211 Ann Fitz Hugh Drive, Annandale, VA 22003; ba/College Park, MD; m/Duane; c/ Jeffrey, Alan, Craig; p/Mr and Mrs Kenneth Hewitt, Walnut Grove, MN; ed/PhD 1973, MA 1968, MI St Univ; BS, Univ of MN, 1966; pa/Asst Dean 1982-, Asst Provost 1979-80, Div of Human & Commun Resources, Univ of MD; Asst Prof, Dept of Textiles & Consumer Ec 1973-, Lectr 1971-73, Univ of MD; MD Home Ec Assn, Chair of Res Com; Manuscript Reviewer, Am Home Ec Assn & Assn for Consumer Res; hon/Pubs, "Motivating Factors in the Mktplace" 1982, "Consumption & Use of the Winged Bean by Sri Lankan Villagers" 1982, "Fam. Decision-Making- A Discussion" 1979, "A Cost-Effectiveness Study Comparing Three Forms of Food" 1978, Others; Agusta L Searles Acad S'ship, 1958; W/W: in Ed, of Am Wom; World W/W of Wom; Dir of Dist'd Ams.

HACKNEY, HOWARD SMITH oc/ Farmer, County Executive Director; b/ May 20, 1910; h/2003 Inwood Road, Wilmington, OH 45127; ba/Wilmington, OH; m/Lucille; c/Albert M, Roderick Allen, Katherine Ann Becker; p/ Volcah M and Gusta Anna Smith Hackney (dec); ed/BS, cum laude, Wilmington Col; pa/Co Ext Dir, ASCS; NASCOE; St & Nat Dir, Duroc Swine & Southdown Sheep Assns; Wilmington Col Agri Adv Com; Mem Bd of Trustees, Wilmington Col; r/Quaker; hon/Inducted into the OH St Fair Hall of Fame; NASCOE Pres's Awd; Chi Beta Phi Sci Awd; OH St & MW Area NASCOE Awd for Ser to Agri; Num Awds for Livestock; Clinton Co Agri Soc Awd; W/W in Rel; Personalities of Am; Personalities of S; Personalities of W & MW; Commun Ldrs & Noteworthy Ams; Book of Hon; Notable Ams; Intl W/W: in Commun Ser, of Intells; DIB; Intl Register of Profiles; Men of Achmt; Men & Wom of Distn.

HADDEN, JOHN WINTHROP oc/ Academic and Research Physician; b/ Oct 23, 1939; h/824 South Orleans, Tampa, FL 33606; ba/Tampa, FL; m/Elba Mas; c/Paul Jennings, John Winthrop II; p/David R Hadden MD, Spring Valley, CA; Joanna J Hadden, Cold Spring Harbor, NY; ed/BA, Yale, 1961; MD, Columbia P&S, 1965; Cert of Med Residency, Roosevelt Hosp, 1969; pa/ Dir, Lab of Immunopharm, Meml Sloan-Kettering Cancer Ctr, 1973-82; Dir, Prog of Immunopharm, Prof of Med & Med Microbiol & Immunol, Univ of S FL Med Ctr, 1982-; Intl Soc of Immunopharm, VP 1982-; Bch Place Condo Motel Assn, Pres 1983-84; 150 E Tenants Corp, Pres 1979-81; Interleukin II Inc, Sci Adv Bd 1983-; hon/ 160 Sci Papers & Textbook Chapts; 42 Sci Abstracts; 5 Textbooks Edited; 3 Patents; Angier Res Prize, 1961; Kellogg Res Prize, 1967, 1968, 1969; Est'd Investigator, Am Heart Assn, 1972-77; W/W: in Frontier Sci & Technol, in E; NY Soc Register.

HADLEY, LUCILE FISHER oc/ Retired Teacher, Historian; b/Oct 8, 1915; h/1133 Lebanon Road, Clarksville, OH 45113; m/Herbert Miller; c/

Mary Ellen Krisher, Harriett Hillman, Christine Snyder, Anna Jean Dempsey, Herbert Jonathan; p/Howard D and Clistie Carey Fisher (dec); ed/Tchrs Dipl, Wilmington Col, 1936; Addit Wk, Miami Univ, En KY Univ; pa/Tchr, New Vienna, OH, Sch, 1936-38; Tchr, Little Miami Sch Sys, 1959-75; Trustee & Genealogist, Clinton Co Hist Soc, 1970-83; Wilmington Col Trustee, 1976-82; OH Ed Assn; Clinton Co Ret'd Tchrs Assn, 1975; cp/Elder, Springfield Friends Meeting, 1960-; Clk-Treas, Springfield Cemetery Assn, 1972-84; George Clinton Chapt, DAR, 1975; r/ Quaker; hon/*Quaker Country Cooking Cookbook,* 1955; Com Chm, *Quaker Hist Collections Springfield Friends Meeting,* 1809-59 (1st Edition), 1809-81 (2nd Edition) 1982; *Cemetary Records of Clinton County, OH, 1798-1978;* Warren Co Del, OH Ed Assn, 1964; Named to 1st Fams in OH, OH Geneal Soc, 1979; Home Named to Nat Register of Historic Places, 1978.

HADZIJA, BOZENA WESLEY oc/ University Associate Professor; b/Jan 5, 1928; h/408 Highview Drive, Chapel Hill, NC 27514; ba/Chapel Hill, NC 27514; c/Renata Smith, Branka Agg; ed/ BSc, 1949; MSc, 1951; PhD, 1960; pa/ Lectr, Univ of CT-Storrs, 1961-64; Sr Lectr, Univ of Ghana, W Africa, 1964-71; Assoc Prof, Sch of Pharm, Univ of NC, 1971-; Am Pharm Assn; Am Assn Cols of Pharm; r/Rom Cath; hon/Author, 25 Sci Papers in Profl & Sci Jours; Tanner Awd for Excell in Tchg, 1975; Best Instr Awd, Sch of Pharm, 1979, 1982; Order of the Walkyries; Mem of Rho Chi; Sigma Si; Phi Delta Sigma; Kappa Epsilon; W/W in S & SW.

HAGAN, PAUL WANDEL oc/Priest; b/Nov 18, 1930; h/1301 South Ruston, Evansville, IN 47714; ed/BMus Ed, Univ of Evansville, IN; MS, IN St Univ; Studied w Marcel Dupre, Jean Langlais, Andre Marchal, Rolande Falcinelli, Marie-Claire Alain, Anton Heller, Flor Peeters; pa/Priest, Music Tchr, Organist, Evansville, IN; St Paul's Parish, Marion, IN; Music Tchr, IN Univ Reg Campus, Ft Wayne, IN; Organist, St Joseph Ch, Ft Wayne, IN; Organ Concerts in France, Germany, Netherlands, Scotland, Sweden, India, USA; Mem: AGO; Phi Mus Alpha; hon/Compositions incl: "Life of Christ in Sound," "Sketches of Paris Chs," "3 Petite Elegies," "Psalm Chorale Preludes," 8 Volumes; Nom'd for Hon DMus, Univ of Evansville, 1972; Comm'd by Univ of St Andrews to Compose a Scottish Suite for Organ; Num Others.

HAGGARD, FORREST DELOSS oc/ Administrative Pastor; b/Apr 21, 1925; h/6816 West 78th Terrace, Overland Park, KS 66204; ba/Overland Park, KS; m/Eleanor V Evans; c/Warren Arthur, James Arthur, William Dean, Katherine Ann; p/Arthur M and Grace Hadley Haggard (dec); ed/AB, Phillips Univ, 1948; MDiv 1953, DD 1967, MA 1960, Univ of MO; pa/Adm Pastor, Overland Pk Christian Ch, 1953-; Pres, KC Area Mins, 1959; Pres, KS Mins Assn, 1960; Chm, Intl Conv Christian Ch, 1966; Chm, Grad Coun Sem Christian Ch, 1970; Pres, Nat Evangelistic Assn, 1972; Pres, World Conv Chs of Christ, 1975-80; cp/Pres, Jo Co Mtl Hlth Assn, 1960-62; Pres, Bd of Dirs, KS Masonic

Home, 1974-75; Bd of Dirs, KS Masonic Foun, 1971-78; Grand Master, Masons in KS, 1974-75; Grand Chaplain, Royal Arch Intl, 1975-78; Grand Chaplain, Supreme Coun Order Demolay, 1980-81; r/Christian; hon/Author, *Clergy & the Craft*, Articles to Many Rel Fraternal Mags, incl'g, *The Disciples*, *World Call*; Contbr to Books, *This We Believe, Power for Today, Preaching on the Old Testament*; Editor, *Hist of KS Masonry*; 33rd Deg Freemasonry, 1965; Spec Reg of Grand Lodge of St of Israel, 1968; Fellow, Philalethes Soc, 1978; Hon Grand Master Saskathchewan, 1976; Hon'd Citizen, City of Overland Pk, 1983; Hon Legion of Hon, Order of Demolay; Order of Arrow, BSA; W/W in Am; Men & Wom of Distn; Men of Distn; W/W in World.

HAHN, JANE ELZA oc/Elementary Teacher, Teacher Consultant; b/Oct 1, 1945; h/10775 Runningbrook Drive, St Louis, MO 63137; ba/St Louis, MO; m/William C; p/Mrs Elza Kratovil, St Louis, MO; ed/BS, Ed, SE MO St Univ, 1967; EdM, Univ of MO-St Louis, 1971; pa/Primary Tchr, Riverview Gardens Sch Dist, 1967-; Lang Arts & Math Conslt, Local Sch Dists, 1973-; Pt-time Tchr, Webster Col, 1979-81; Dir, Title I Rdg Prog, Riverview Gardens, 1972; MO St Tchrs Assn; r/Rom Cath; hon/Pubs, *Compounds, Contractions, & Crocodile Tears* 1982, *Plurals, Possessives, & Peppermint Sticks* 1982, *The Monster Res Book* 1980, *Caldecott Capers: Activs to Ten Caldecott Medal Winners* 1980, *Exploring Lit: Gamevelope I* 1980, Others; World W/W of Wom; Outstg Yg Wom of Am.

HAIRE, CAROL DIANE oc/University Professor, Speech-Language Pathologist, Educational Diagnostician, Consultant; b/Jun 24, 1949; h/4810 Stonehedge Road, Abilene, TX 79606; ba/Abilene, TX; p/Lloyd F and M Vera Smith Haire, Muleshoe, TX; ed/BA 1970, EdD 1976, TX Tech Univ; MA, N TX St Univ, 1971; Cert, Clin Competence in Spch Pathol, ASHA; TX Ed Agy Certn; pa/Spch Pathol, Cooke Co Public Schs, 1972; Spch Pathol, Muleshoe Public Schs, 1973-74; Instr, Col of Ed, TX Tech Univ, 1974-76; Prof/Clin Supvr, Communicative Disorders Ctr, Howard Payne Univ, 1976-77; Dir, Spch-Lang Pathol & Audiology, Prof, Hardin-Simmons Univ, 1977-; Pvt Pract, 1972-; Spch-Lang Pathol Conslt, Outreach Home Hlth Sers of MW TX, 1983-; Spch-Lang Pathol Conslt, Eastland Manor Home Hlth Sers, 1983-; Spch-Lang Pathol Conslt, Upjohn HlthCare Sers, 1981-83; Spch-Lang Pathol Conslt, Mesquite Villa & Big Sky Ranch Intermediate Care Facilities for the Mtly Retarded, 1981-; Conslt, Spch-Lang Pathol, W Ctl TX Home Hlth Agy, 1980-83; Am Soc of Allied Hlth Professions; Am Spch-Lang-Hearing Assn; TX Spch-Lang-Hearing Assn; Big Country Spch & Hearing Assn, Pres 1979-80; Phi Delta Kappa; CEC; Div for Chd w Communication Disorders; Nat Student Spch-Lang-Hearing Assn, Hon Mem, Sponsor of Hardin-Simmons Univ Chapt; Hardin-Simmons Univ Gen Fac & Fac Assem Ofcr, Secy 1980-81; Lic'd to Pract Spch-Lang Pathol, St of TX; r/Bapt; hon/Author, "Effects of an Inservice Ed Model for Supportive Pers on Factors Regarding Exceptl Chd" 1976, "Spch, Lang &

Hearing Therapy Mats" 1975; Num Papers Presented; Phi Kappa Phi, 1976; Outstg Yg Wom of Abilene, Abilene, TX, JC Wom, 1983; W/W in S & SW; Personalities of S; World W/W of Wom; Dir of Dist'd Ams; Intl W/W of Intells; Book of Hon; Personalities of Am; Commun Ldrs of Am; 2,000 Notable Ams; 5,000 Personalities of World; Intl Book of Hon; DIB; Commun Ldrs of World.

HAIRSTON, JAMES JOSEPH JR oc/System Safety Engineer; b/Sep 30, 1937; h/16122 White Star, Houston, TX 77062; ba/Houston, TX; m/Carole K; c/James J III, Christopher M, Leak K; p/Mrs Elsie E Hairston, Jay, FL; ed/MS, Sys Safety, Univ of So CA, 1977; BS, Math, Jacksonville Univ, 1962; mil/USAF, 1954-57, 1962-78; Ret'd; pa/Sys Safety Engr, Boeing Aerospace Co, 1978-; Merrell Stevens Shipyard, 1957-62; Am Soc of Safety Engrs; Sys Safety Soc; r/Bapt; hon/Pub, "Nuclear Safety Analysts Computer Prog," SW Symp of Reliability Engrs, Albuquerque, NM, 1981; 40 Medals, incl'g, 9 Air Medals; Marquis W/W; Personalities of S.

HAISCH, BERNHARD MICHAEL oc/Astrophysicist; b/Aug 23, 1949; h/847 San Ramon, Moss Beach, CA 94038; ba/Palo Alto, CA; m/Pamela S Eakins; c/Katherine Stuart, Christopher Taylor; p/Gertrud Haisch, Indianapolis, IN; ed/PhD in Astrophysics 1975, MS 1973, Univ of WI-Madison; BS, Astrophysics, IN Univ, 1971; Att'd, St Meinrad Col, 1967-68; pa/Staff Scist, Space Scis Lab 1982-, Res Scist, Electro-Optics Lab 1979-82, Lockheed Palo Alto Res Lab; Res Assoc, JILA, Univ of CO Boulder, 1975-77, 1978-79; Vis'g Scist, Univ of Utrecht, The Netherlands, 1977-78; Fellow, Royal Astronom Soc; Am Astronom Soc; Intl Astronom Union; Astronom Soc of the Pacific; Phi Beta Kappa; Phi Kappa Phi; Sigma Xi; hon/Author of Num Articles in *Astrophy Jour, Astronomy & Astrophysics, Jour of the Astronautical Scis, Am Jour of Physics, Sky & Telescope, Solar Physics,* Pubs of Astronomical Soc of the Pacific, Var Symp Proceedings; WI Alumni Res Foun Fellow, Univ of WI-Madison, 1971-72; Am Men & Wom of Sci; W/W in Frontier Sci & Technol.

HALARIS, ANTONY S oc/Director of Computing Center; b/Mar 5, 1939; h/8 Mildred Parkway, New Rochelle, NY; ba/New Rochelle, NY; m/Niobe; c/Elpi, Spyros, Dinitris; ed/BA in Math 1965, MS in Indust Engrg & Opers Res 1968, NY Univ; Currently Pursuing PhD in Computer Sci/Indust Engrg, PINY; pa/Dir of Computing Ctr 1968-, Asst Dir of Computing Ctr 1966-68, Chm of Computer & Info Scis Dept 1973-81, Assoc Prof of Computer & Info Scis 1966-, Iona Col; AIIE; Assn for Computer Machinery; Am Statl Assn; Assn for Sys Mgmt; AAUP; Data Processing Mgmt Assn.

HALBREICH, URIEL oc/Psychiatrist; b/Nov 23, 1943; h/2166 Broadway, New York, NY 10024; ba/Bronx, NY; m/Tatiana; c/Jasmin; p/Ziporah Halbreich, Jerusalem, Israel; ed/MD, 1969; mil/Israeli Army & Navy 1969-78, Cmdr; pa/VChief Med Ofcr, Israeli Navy, 1970-72; Var Positions from Resident to Temporary Chief Phys, Dept of Psychi, Hebrew Univ, Hadassah Med

Sch, 1972-78; Chief Psychi, Israeli Navy Reserves, 1976-78; Res Psychi, Columbia Univ, 1978-80; Dir, Div of Behavioral Endocrinology 1981-82, Dir, Div of Biol Psychi 1982-84, Albert Einstein Col of Med; Am Col of Neuropsychi Pharm; Am Psychi Assn; Endocrine Soc; Soc of Biol Psychi; Intl Soc of Psychoneuroendocrinology; r/Jewish; hon/Author, 31 Profl Articles & 1 Book, *Transient Psychosis* 1984; Ben Gurion Awd, 1976; Govt Awd, 1978; Nat Res Ser Awd, NIH, 1978-80; W/W: in World, in Frontier Sci & Technol.

HALFERTY, DIANE HARRIET oc/Entrepreneur, Lecturer, Writer; b/Feb 22, 1937; h/18036 49th Place, Northeast, Seattle, WA 9815; m/Guy P III; c/Geoffrey David, Denise Diane, Keary Douglas, Courtney Caryn; p/Ben and Lavina E Simmons Rosen (dec); ed/Att'd, Univ of Miami, 1954-56; BS, Willamette Univ, 1958; Tech Assoc of Law, Edmonds Commun Col & Univ of WA, 1976; pa/Med Secy, Drs Ahem, Crosby, Elgin, Lindall, Michelle, Morton & Skub, 1957; Mgr, C P Keeler Co, Asst Bldr's Hardware & Supply Co, 1958; Purchasing Dir, Pacific Plastics Co, 1959; Pres, Creativity Unltd Inc, 1966-73; Pres, Gt Pacific Devel Co Inc, 1976-83; Assn of Mobile Home Pk Owners, VP 1980, Chair, Polit Action Com, Pres 1981-82; cp/Race Chair, NW Reg Sports Car Clb of Am, 1958; Red Cross Instr, 450 Hr Vol, 1959; Little Sch of Seattle Toy Fair Co Chair, 1966; Exec Bds, Lake Forest Pk Sch, Kellogg Jr HS, 1978; AAU Stroke and Turn Judge, LWV, 1978-; NOW; King Co Juv Ct Guardian Prog, 1981-; King Co Housing Task Force, Chair, King Co Ordinance Adv Com 1979-81, Land Use Res Coun 1975; Chair, Shoreline SD Human Rights, PTSA Coun; Co-Chair, Consumers Agnst GM, 1983; hon/Winner, Carl Gregg Dohney Meml Oratorical Contest, Willamette Univ, 1956; Guest Lectr, Univ of CA-Berkeley, 1983; Outstg Citizen Awd, 1977; World W/W of Wom; W/W of Am Wom; Personalities of Am.

HALIGAS, WILLIAM JAMES oc/Executive Manager; b/May 2, 1926; h/7340 Independence Street, Arvada, CO 80002; ba/Denver, CO; m/Betty Ann; c/Terrie Ideker, Lorie Price, Larry; p/Kenneth and Laura Haligas (dec); ed/Grad, Elgin HS; mil/USN Battleship, 1943-46; pa/Fdr and Owner, Dry Wall Supply Inc (6 Sales Location in CO w Mfg Facilities of Paint & Joint Compounds); Past Owner, Wn Gypsum Co, Santa Fe, NM; cp/Masons, Consistory, Shrine; r/Prot.

HALL, ANITA A oc/Elementary Teacher, Speed Reading Coordinator; b/Jul 29, 1945; h/Route 3, Shamrock, TX 79079; ba/Shamrock, TX; m/Raymond; p/Mr and Mrs Wallace Smith, Altas, OK; ed/BS (cum laude) 1966, ME 1968, SWn OK Univ; Biling Cert, TX Ed Agy, 1979; pa/Tchr in OK for 5 Yrs; Tchr in TX for 10 Yrs; cp/VP, Thalian, 1970; Secy 1975, Pres 1978, Local TSTA; Human Resource Chp, Area TSTA; Sunday Sch Tchr; r/Bapt; hon/SW OK Career Girl of the Yr, 1970.

HALL, BLAINE H oc/Humanities Librarian; b/Dec 12, 1932; h/230 East 1910 South, Orem, UT 84058; ba/Provo, UT; m/Carol; c/Suzanne, Cheryl, Derek; p/James O and Effie Hill Hall (dec); ed/BS in Eng 1960, MA in Am Lit 1965, MLS 1971, Brigham Yg Univ; mil/AUS, 1953-54; pa/Eng Tchr, Davis Co, UT, Schs; Instr, Eng, Brigham Yg Univ; Sr Libn, Humanities Lib, Harold B Lee Lib, Brigham Yg Univ; ALA; ACRL; MPLA; ULA; Freedom to Read Foun; Chd's Lit Assn of UT; Editor, *Utah Libs* 1972-78, *MPLA Newslttr* 1978-83; Pres, UT Lib Assn, 1980-81; Mtn Plains Lib Assn Exec Bd, 1978-83; Chm, UT Adv Com on Lib & Info Sers, 1983-; r/LDS; hon/Pubs, *Using the Lib: The Card Catalog* 1971, *Collection Assessment Manual* 1982; Author, Num Reviews & Articles for Profl Jours; Phi Kappa Phi, 1960; H W Wilson/ALA Lib Period Awd, 1977; W/W in Lib & Info Sers.

HALL, DAVID SR oc/Clergyman, Consultant, Advisor; b/Dec 22, 1938; h/1338 K Street, Southeast, Washington DC 20003; ba/Washington, DC; m/Rosemary A L; c/Endora, Jerome, La'Teju M, Altoria N; p/Lottie E Hall, Washington, DC; ed/PhD, 1979, DD, 1978; BS, 1967; MDiv, 1964; BA, 1960; mil/AUS, USAR, DC NG; Ret'd; pa/Dir, Christian Concern for Commun Action, 1970-; Pastor, Grady's Chapel Rock Bapt Ch, 1976-; cp/Dir of Public Relats, NAACP, 1978; Reg Dir, SCLC, 1976; Chaplain, NBWPLC, 1977; Coor, LCEPA, 1974-76; Organizer, MBA, DC, BP, 1969; Elected Commr, Adv Neighborhood Comm, ANC-GBIO, 1984; r/Bapt; hon/Cert of Apprec, 1962, 1966, 1977; W/W in E.

HALL, JAMES WILLIAM oc/College President; b/Oct 14, 1937; h/173 Phila Street, Saratoga Springs, NY 12866; ba/Saratoga Springs, NY; m/Wilma; c/Laura, Janet, Carol; ed/PhD 1967, MA 1964, Univ of PA; MSM, Union Theol Sem, 1961; BMus, Bucknell Univ, 1959; pa/Pres, Empire St Col, SUNY, 1971-; Acting Pres, St Univ Col at Old Westbury, 1981-82; Asst VChancellor, SUNY, Ctl Adm, 1966-71; Asst Prof, SUNY-at Albany, 1966-71; Instr in Music, Cedar Crest Col, 1961-66; Mem of Many Adv Coms; AAHE; AASCU; ACE; AHA; r/Prot; hon/Pubs, *Forging the Am Character* 1971, *In Opposition to Core Curric* 1982, Many Articles; Danforth Grad F'ship, 1959-67.

HALL, LaVERNE CORINE-WILLIAMS oc/Paper Doll Publisher; b/Jan 26, 1938; h/PO Box 1212, Bellevue, WA 98009; ba/Bellevue, WA; m/Ellsworth C; c/George Floydale Foster III, LaWayne Charles Foster, Mahji B'Vance; p/Mr and Mrs Lucius C Williams, Portland, OR; ed/BS in Bus Adm, Portland St Univ, 1973; Sec'dy Tchg Cert, 1973; pa/Retail Mgmt, J C Penney; Affirmative Action Ofcr, Lake Wash Sch Dist; Jr HS Tchr, Lake Wash Sch Dist; Pres/Gen Mgr, VELB Assocs (Creators, Designers, Publishers & Mkters of Ethnic Paper Dolls); Iota Phi Lambda Sorority, Current VP; cp/Bellevue Civil Ser Comm, Appt'd by City Mgr 1974, Chp (2 Terms), VChp (2 Terms), Current Commr; Bd Mem, Totem Girl Scout Coun, 6 Yrs; Com of Mgmt, E Cherry YWCA, 7 Yrs; Seattle Sect, Nat Coun of Negro Wom, Pres for 4 Yrs, Current Chp of the Annual Tribute to Black Hist; Intl Toastmistress Clbs, Pres, VP, Secy, Treas, Coun Del; Former Bd Mem for Wom's Progs, Bellevue Commun Col; r/Bapt; hon/Pub, "My Little Mahji"; Created "Bridg

ing Generations," 28 Piece Collection of Photographic & Visual Art Renderings; Created the Ethnic Toy & Ednl Fair; Asst Prodr & Prog Coor, Career Conversations; Created Seattle Sect, NCNW Annual Tribute to Black Hist; Coor, 1984 Blacks in Govt, Dr Martin Luther King Jr Commemoration Activs; KIXI Citizen of the Day, 1980; Totem Girl Scout Very Spec Person Awd, 1981; Commun Ser, 1980; Seattle Sect, NCNW "Bridging Generations," 1983; City of Bellevue, Commun Ser Awd, 1983, 1984; KOMO-TV, "Profiles in Black," 1984.

HALL, PEARL REGINA oc/Account Executive; b/Apr 18, 1954; h/PO Box 341, Montgomery, AL 36101; ba/Montgomery, AL; c/Dana; p/Harry and Virginia Hall, Montgomery, AL; ed/BA, Huntingdon Col, 1976; pa/News, Public Affairs, WXVI, 1976; Acct Exec, Public Affairs Dir, WQIM, 1978-79; Acct Exec, WXVI-Radio, 1980; Alonet 1981, Sales Dir 1982, WZTN; Acct Exec, WXVI, 1983-; Advtg Clb; IPA-Lowell Howard; r/Bapt; hon/Hon Mention Hector Awd, Troy St Univ, 1979; W/W; Outstg Ams; W/W in Am; Personalities of S; World W/W of Wom.

HALL, SARAH oc/Domestic; b/Sep 30, 1928; h/2535 Horne Drive, Charlotte, NC 28206; ba/Charlotte, NC; ed/Grad, W Charlotte HS; cp/Domciliary Home Commun Adv Com; hon/Am Biog, Nat Bd of Advrs; Cert of Recog, Christian Wom Retreat, Pauling, NY, 1972; 25 Yrs Ser, St James U Ch of God, 1949-72; Most Outstg Wom of Yr, Yth Dept, 1978; Awds for Apprec, 1978, 1979, 1981, 1982; Personalities of S; 2,000 Notable Ams; W/W; Biogl Roll of Hon.

HALLER, CHARLES E oc/Executive; b/Sep 5, 1924; h/134 Summit Terrace, Kinnelon, NJ 07405; ba/New York, NY; m/Eleanor M; c/Carolyn Gierisch, Debra Lee Geoffrey, Charles, Mark; p/William C Haller, Bridgeport, CT; ed/BSEE, Rensselaer Polytechnic Inst, 1948; mil/USN, 1943-46; pa/Proj Engr, Wn Union Telegraph Co, 1948-56; Devel Engr 1956-59, Assoc Lab Dir 1959-61, ITT Fed Labs, ITT; VP & Dir of Plant & Engrg, ITT World Communs, ITT, 1961-67; VP & Dir of Engrg 1967-69, Pres 1969-74, ITT Def Communs Div, ITT; Dir of Intl Opers, ITT Aerospace, Electronics, Components & Energy Grp, Brussels, ITT, 1974-79; Grp Dir, Intl Opers, ITT Telecommuns & Electronics Grp, NA, ITT, 1979-83; Pres, ITT Asia Pacific Inc, ITT, 1983-; IEEE, Fellow 1970; Nat Security Indust Assn; Electronics Indust Assn; Aerospace Indust Assn; AFCEA, Dir 1970-75; r/Christian; hon/Pub, *Communs Switching Sys*, 1963; Marquis W/W.

HALLET, JEAN-PIERRE oc/Explorer, Sociologist, Naturalist, Author, Producer, Lecturer; b/Aug 4, 1927; h/PO Box 277, Malibu, CA 90265; c/Marc, Bernard; p/Andre Hallet (dec); Berthe Hallet, Brussels, Belgium; ed/Att'd, Univ of Brussels 1945-46, Sorbonne 1947-48; Studied, Agronomy, Sociol; mil/Belgian Resistance 1942-43, Army 1944-45; pa/Fdr, Pres, The Pygmy Fund, 1974; Owner, Jean-Pierre Gallery (African Arts), Malibu, 1975-; Prodr, 2 Ednl Films for *Ency Britannica*, 1975; Prodr, Dir, Feature Documentary, *Pygmies*,

1973; Org'd, Jean-Pierre Hallet's Spec Safaris (Leads Each Sum), 1969-; Lectr, Var Orgs in US & Fgn Countries, 1961-; Num Other Profl Activs; hon/Writer, Over 30 Nat Mag Stories & Narrator of TV Specs, 1963-; Author, *Congo Kitabu* (translated in 19 Langs, *Rdr's Digest Book Clb Selection, Alt Selection, Book-of-the-Month Clb*), 1966; *Animal Kitabu*, 1967; *Pygmy Kitabu*, 1973; Featured in "The Abe Lincoln of the Congo," *Sepia* Mag, 1965, as 1 of 20 *Men of Courage* w John F Kennedy & Capt J Lovelle, 1972, *Great Survival Adventures* 1973, *Guideposts* Cover Story 1977; Humanitarian of Decade, ACF, 1977; Hon Citizenship, Several Sts & Cities; Fellow Mem, World-wide Acad Scholars; Mayor's Commend (for Saving Pygmies from Extinction), LA; K of Mark Twain; Hon Mem, Honolulu Adventurers' Clb; Recip, Best Book Awd, ALA; Most Outstg Spkr of Yr, LA Adventurers' Clb, 1965; Pioneered the 1st Large-Scale Intro in Ctl Africa of the High-Protein Winged Bean, Potentially Saving Millions of Hungry & Starving People, 1982-; Num Other Awds & Certs of Merit & Apprec; 2,000 Men of Achmt; Other Biogl Listings.

HALLFORD, DENNIS MURRAY oc/Professor of Animal Science; b/Feb 11, 1948; h/1135 Calle del Encanto, Las Cruces, NM 88005; ba/Las Cruces, NM; m/Marilyn Williams; c/Amy Denise; p/Tommy and Tiny Hallford, Abilene, TX; ed/BS, Gen Agri, Tarleton St Univ, 1970; MS in Animal Sci 1973, PhD in Reproductive Physiol 1975, OK St Univ; pa/Instr of Animal Sci, Tarleton St Univ, 1970-71; Grad Asst, OK St Univ, 1971-75; Asst Prof 1975-79, Assoc Prof 1979-84, Prof 1984-, Animal Sci, NM St Univ; Am Soc of Animal Sci; Grad Paper Competition Judge, 1982-85; Wn Sect, Am Soc of Animal Sci; Sigma Xi; Alpha Zeta; Alpha Chi; Gamma Sigma Delta; Theriogenology; r/Meth; hon/Pubs, "Influence of Dietary Sewage Solids on Fleece Characteristics and Weight Responses of Fine-Wool Ewes" 1983, "Growth Response of Peruvian Criollo Goats Consuming Varying Levels of Acacia macracantha, Leucaena leucocephala & Corn Stalks" (in Press), "Serum Profiles of Beef Steers in Different Prodn Situations" 1983, "Effectiveness of Antelope Pass Structures in Restriction of Livestock" 1983, Serum Profiles in Fine Wool Sheep" 1982, Num Others; 1st Place, Grad Student Paper Competition, So Sect, Am Soc of Animal Sci, 1974; Cardinal Key's Outstg Tchr at NM St Univ, 1977; Outstg Tchr in Col of Agri & Home Ec, NM St Univ, 1980; Outstg Grad Tchr/Advr, Col of Agri & Home Ec, NM St Univ, 1983; W/W in W; Am Men & Wom of Sci.

HALLOCK, VIRGINIA LEE oc/Seminar Consultant, Writer, Lecturer; b/Feb 3; h/840 Ree Del Court, Northeast, Salem, OR 97301; m/Robert J Koetz; c/William L, Col David B; ed/BA, Eng & Ed, Univ of OR, 1960; Grad Wk in Cnslg, Psych, TV Tchg; Cert'd Graphoanalyst, 1966; Var Courses, Willamette Univ, Wn Bapt Col; pa/Instr 1957-75, Hd of Acad Dept 1962-75, Merritt Davis Col of Bus; Self-Employed as Conslt, Sems for Govt, Bus & Indust, 1975-; Public Spkr at Convs, Confs; Pers Selection through Handwriting Anal, Behavior Modification;

Feature Story Writer, *OR Jour, Bend Bltn,* 1942-57; Capital Area Media Public Relats Org, 1981-83; Active Bus Promoters, 1980-83; OR Press Wom, 1978-82; Capital Area Media & Public Relats Assn, 1981-83; cp/Salem Toastmaster, 1973-80, Secy 1975; Salem Area C of C, 1975-83, Chm of Social Ed Coun 1980; OR Consumer Adv Bd, 1979-82, Conv Bur 1980-83; r/Epis; hon/Pubs, *Bus Communication-The Tri-Ask Technique* 1973, *Charm & Charisma* 1974, "Ed by Choice" 1983, Hundreds of Feature Stories in *OR Jour* 1948-57; OR Graphoanalyst of the Yr, 1972; Graph Nat Awd Excell of Perform, 1972; Toastmaster of the Yr, 1975; Dist'd Ser Awd, Grapho, 1975; W/W of Am Wom; Dir of Handwriting Analysts.

HALPERT, CLAIRE D oc/Executive; c/Wendy Claire; p/Frank X and Clara A Dostal (dec); ed/BFA, NY Univ, Parsons Sch of Design, 1966; Postgrad Studies, Sch of Visual Arts, NYC; pa/Art Dir, R H Macy & Co, 1966-68; Art Dir, Ufferman, Shoemaker & Domenech, Advtg, Puerto Nuevo, PR, 1968-69; Advtg Conslt, Wash DC, 1972-75; Edr & Pres, Halpert & Assocs, Advtg, 1975-; Am Advtg Fdn; The Advtg Clb of Wash DC; The Eastport Bus Assn; hon/Bus Review of Wash, *The Gaithersburg Gazette*; Bi-line in *The Sentinel Newspapers* 1977, *N VA People Mag* 1978; Hon Chm, Publicity Com for the 1981 Addy Awds, DC; W/W in E.

HALSEY, JAMES ALBERT oc/Music Industry Impresario, Booking Agent, Personal Manager, Festival Producer; b/Oct 7, 1930; m/Minisa Crumbo; c/Sherman, Gina; p/Ed and Carrie Messick Halsey; ed/Grad, Indepedence HS, 1948; Grad, Independence Jr Col, 1950; mil/AUS, 1954-56; pa/The Jim Halsey Co Inc (Clients incl Roy Clark, Lynn Anderson, Razzy Bailey, Jimmy Dean, Freddy Fender, Merle Haggard, Nitty-Gritty Dirt Band, Oak Ridge Boys, Roy Orbison, Tammy Wynette, & Many Others); Churchill Records & Video Ltd; Norwood Advtg Co; VP, Gen Artists Corp, 2 Yrs; Bd of Dirs, Country Music Assn, Acad of Country Music, Mercantile Bk & Trust, Citizen's Nat Bk; Pres, Intl Fdn of Fest Orgs; cp/Bd of Dirs, Thomas Gilcrease Mus Assn; Bd of Trustees, Philbrook Art Ctr; hon/FIDOF Oscar, Intl Fdn of Fest Orgs, 1982; Hubert Long Awd, Mervy Conn, 1982; Cit, Golden Orpheus Fest, Sunny Bch, Bulgaria, 1982; Dist'd Kansan, *Topeka Capital-Jour* Edit Bd, 1980; Outstg Artistic Achmt, Booking, *Cashbox Mag*, 1980; Ambassador of Country Music, SESAC, 1978; Jim Reeves Meml Awd, Acad of Country Music, 1977; Booked 1st Country Artist in Las Vegas; Took 1st Country Music Concert Package to Soviet Union; Num Other Accomplishments; W/W: in Am, in MW, in Fin & Indust.

HAMBLETT, HOWARD ARTHUR oc/Millwork Manufacturing; b/Oct 4, 1923; h/PO Box 1100, Derry, NH 03038; ba/Same; m/Lucille; c/Mark Russell, Paul Arthur; p/Arthur Eugene Hamblett (dec); ed/Adv'd Bus Deg, Univ of NH, 1948; mil/USAF, 1942-45; pa/Owner, Mgr, Pres, Dir, Howard Enterprises 1950-, Ventures Intl 1970-80; Pres, Hamblett Assocs, Hamco Corp; Pres, Hamblett Co; DAV, So NH Bldrs Assn; cp/Pres, Bd of Dirs, NH

Right-to-Wk Assn, FOE; Derry C of C; Repub Sr Clb; r/Bapt; hon/Contbr, Articles to Profl Jours; Purple Heart, 1944; Man of the Yr, Intl Lumbermans, 1951, 1967; W/W in E.

HAMBRIGHT, RICKY RAY oc/Student; b/Jun 26, 1961; h/Route 8, Box 690, Gaffney, SC 29340; p/Joe Dean and Carolyn Hambright, Gaffney, SC 29340; ed/Dipl, Blacksburg HS, 1979; AA, Spartanburg Meth Col, 1981; BS, Greensboro Col, 1983; Mem, Student Nat Ed Assn, 1983; r/Bapt; hon/Best Offensive Lineman, Best Blocker, All-Conf, Ftball; MVP, Baseball, 1983; Dean's List.

HAMED, AWATEF A oc/Professor; b/Jun 17, 1944; h/5925 Kenwood Road, Cincinatti, OH 45243; ba/Cincinatti, OH; m/M Fathy Hussein; p/Abdel El-Ghany Hamed, Cairo, Egypt; sp/Ehsan A Sabry (dec); Ed/Dipl Eng, 1965; MSc, 1969; PhD, 1972; pa/Prof 1980-, Assoc Prof 1976-79, Asst Prof 1973-76, Grad Res Asst 1968-72, Dept of Aerospace Engrg & Applied Mechanics, Univ of Cinc; Aerodynamic Engr, 1965-67; Aircraft Estab, Helwan, Egypt; Mem: Sigma Xi; Assoc Fellow, Coun Mem, Session Orgr, AIAA; VChm Ed Com of Gas Turbine Div, Symp Orgr, ASME; Amelia Earhart Com Chm Dist V, Zonta Intl; hon/Num Articles Pub'd in Symp Proceedings & Num Tech Reports; NASA Awd for Creat Tech Innovation, 1983; Best Paper Awd, AIAA, AFIT, 1981 & 1975; Amelia Earhart Fellow, 1967-68, 1969-70 & 1970-71; W/W: in Aviation & Aerospace, in Technol Today; Am Men & Wom of Sci; Outstg Yg Wom of Am; Others.

HAMER, MYRON C oc/Executive; b/Jan 19, 1932; h/Box 336, RR 1, Yarmouth, ME 04096; ba/Portland, ME; m/Meredith Rollins; c/Davidson H, Eric B, Andrew K, Bruce R; ed/AB, cum laude, Amherst Col, 1953; MBA, Harvard Bus Sch, 1957; mil/USMC 1953-55, 1st Lt; pa/Pres, Ventrex Lab Inc, 1978-; Fin Mgr (Europe) 1975-78, Med Prod Controller 1973-75, VP of Mfg (Steuben Div) 1967-73, Other Mgmt Jobs 1957-67, Corning Glass Wks; Bd Mem, Ventrex Labs Inc, 1979-; cp/Treas, ME Opera Assn, 1979-82; U Way, SE Steuben Co, Pres 1973, Bd Mem 1968-74.

HAMILTON, DORIS SIMMONS oc/Retired Educator; b/Apr 23, 1914; h/Route 3, Box 255, Laurel, MS 39440; m/Grady Burke (dec); p/Oscar D and Era Magee Simmons (dec); ed/BS 1937, MA 1954, Univ of So MS; pa/Civilian Employee, USAAC, 1944-45; Tchr, Voc Home Ec, Moselle 1937-40, Brandon 1940-41, Hattiesburg 1941-42, Jones Co Schs 1945-54, Laurel City Schs 1954-71; Supervisory Tchr, Univ of So MS, 1941-42, 1947-71; Jones Co Tchrs Assn, Pres 1953-54; MS Home Ec Assn, Treas 1964; Delta Kappa Gamma Soc, Zeta St Pres 1965-67; BPW Clb; Laurel Clrm Tchr; Laurel Ed Assn, Pres; Pres, MS Voc Home Ec Tchrs, 1968-70; MS Voc Assn, 1970-71; MS Ret'd Tchrs, 1982-83; cp/MS 4-H Adult Ldrs Coun, Pres 1952-53; Altrusa Clb, Pres, Laurel 1957-58, 1970-73; Red Cross Bd & Tchr, 1946-; MS Chgo Clb, 1983-84; Farm Bur, Bd & Wom's Chair; Coun of Aging, Chair, Adv Com 1982; SS Tchr; hon/Articles in Newslttrs as St Pres; 4-H Ldrship Awd, 1953; MS 4-H Alumni

Recog Awd, 1954; Named Wom of Achmt, BPW Clb, 1975; Diana Awd, 1978; Zeta St Delta Kappa Gamma Outstg Sers Awd, 1979; W/W: in Am Ed, of Am Wom, in S & SW, in US; Commun Ldrs of Am; DIB.

HAMILTON, FRANCES V oc/Co-Owner of Business; b/Jun 30, 1938; h/Route 1, Box 222, West Paducah, KY 42086; ba/Same; m/B A; c/Sandra Strauss, Curtis, Eddie, Donna; p/Mrs Birdie Reeves, Paducah, KY; ed/Grad, Lincoln HS; Student of Secretarial Sci, Paducah Commun Col, 1967; pa/Receptionist, Pennwalt Chems, 1967-69; Dept Hd Secy, Union Carbide Corp, 1969-77; Field Rep, Cong-man Carroll Hubbard, 1977-81; Co-Owner, Automotive Ser Inc, 1969-; Pres, Duchess Chapt, Am Bus Woms' Assn, 1975; Pres, Paducah, KY, Lake Chapt, Profl Secys Intl, 1978; cp/C of C Bd Mem, 1979-82; Wn KY Easter Seal Bd of Dirs, 1977-83; Dem Exec Com, 1978-83; Purchase Area Devel Dist, 1982-83; r/Ch of Christ; hon/Wom of Yr, Am Bus Woms' Assn, Duchess Chapt, 1972; Secy of the Yr, Paducah, KY, Lake Chapt, Profl Secys Intl, 1981; KY Col, 1977; Duchess of Paducah, 1973; McCracken Co Fiscal Ct Awd, 1981; Personalities of S.

HAMILTON, LAURA ANN oc/Retail; b/Nov 16, 1939; h/1611 Trailridge Drive, Arlington, TX 76012; ba/Ft Worth, TX; p/Mr and Mrs H W Hamilton Sr, Arabi, GA; ed/Att'd, Valdosta St Col, 1957-58; BS in Social Wel, FL St Univ, 1961; Grad Study in Ed, Univ of GA-Athens, 1961-62; MSW, FL St Univ, 1965; pa/Conslt for Social Wk Projs, Title I, Elem & Sec'dy Ed Act, Pupil Pers Div, GA Dept of Ed, 1966-68; Conslt for Title III, Elem & Sec'dy Ed Act Projs, Div of Planning, Res & Eval, GA St Dept of Ed, 1968-71; Conslt, Prog Evals & Audits, Robert Davis Assocs Inc, 1971-72; Chief, Div of Planning, Eval, Monitoring & Anal, SC Dept of Social Sers, 1973-76; Reg Dir for Social Sers, Regs 01 & 02, TX Dept of Public Wel, 1976-77; Ptnr, Kaye Fleming Boutique & Bridal Corner, 1978-; Instr, Human Resource Ctr, Univ of TX-Arlington, 1977-79; Acad of Cert'd Social Wkrs; Am Public Wel Assn, Nat Social Sers Com & CoChp of Subcom on Financing 1977-78; Am Soc for Public Adm, Prog Chp for SC Chapt 1975-76; Nat Assn of Social Wkrs; cp/Helped Establish Rape Crisis Coalition in Columbia, SC; hon/W/W: in Am Wom, in S & SW.

HAMILTON, RHODA LILLIAN ROSEN oc/Educator, Guidance Counselor, Administrator; b/May 8, 1915; h/255 East Waldo Street, Groveland, FL 32736; ba/Kadena Air Base, Okinawa, Japan; c/Perry Douglas, John Richard; p/Reinhold August and Olga Peterson Rosen (dec); ed/Grad, Moser Col, 1933; BS, Ed, Univ of WI, 1953; MAT, Rollins Col, 1967; mil/Civilian DAC, TUSLOG, Istanbul, Turkey, 1960-65; pa/Secy to Pres, Ansul Chem, 1934-36; Profl Pers Cnslr, The Med Bur, Chgo, 1954-56; Adm Asst, Ernst C Schmidt Esquire, 1956-58; Assoc Prof, OH St Univ, 1958-60; Guid Cnslr, Groveland HS, 1965-68; Guid Cnslr, Dodds (PACAF), 1968-; Phi Delta Gamma; NEA; OEA; r/Epis; hon/Pub, *Poetry of the Mid E*, 1967; Nat Awd of Commun Achmt, 1947; W/W of Am Wom; Personalities of S; DIB.

HAMILTON-KEMP, THOMAS ROGERS oc/Professor; b/May 13, 1942; h/868 Laurel Hill Road, Lexington, KY 40504; ba/Lexington, KY; m/Lois Groce; p/Thomas Rogers and Catharine Rose Hamilton Kemp, Lebanon, KY; ed/AA, St Catharine Col, 1962; BA 1964, PhD in Organic Chem 1970, Univ of KY; pa/ Asst Prof 1970-75, Assoc Prof 1975-, Univ of KY; Am Chem Soc; Am Soc for Horticultural Sci; Sigma Xi; Tissue Culture Assn; AAUP; hon/Author, Articles in Sci Jours.

HAMM, GEORGE ARDEIL oc/Educator, Hypnotherapist; b/Aug 13, 1934; h/1864 South Bearden Court, Oxnard, CA 93033; ba/Oxnard, CA; m/Marilyn Kay Nichols; c/Robert Barry, Charles Ardeil II, Patricia Ann; p/Charles Ardeil and Vada Lillian Sharrah Hamm (dec); ed/RH, Hypnotherapy, Hypnotism Tng Inst, LA, 1983; MS, Cnslg 1981, MA, Ed Adm 1979, CA Luth Col; MA, Music 1961, BS, Music 1958, AZ St Col; Dipl, Inst of Rel; mil/USMC, Korea, 1953-55; pa/Music Tchr, Needles Public Schs, 1958-61; Music Tchr/Dept Chair 1961-79, Career Ed Tchr/Cnslr 1979-82, Psych Tchr 1982-, Hueneme HS; Sport Psych Conslt in Pvt Pract; Am Assn for Cnslg & Devel; Assn of Mormon Cnslrs & Psychotherapists; AFT; N Am Soc for Psych of Sport & Phy Activity; Am Coun of Hypnotist Examrs; CA Hypnotist Examrs Coun; r/Mormon; hon/Paper Presented, Nat Coaching Conf, St Louis, 1977; Author, 30 Articles Pub'd in a Variety of Nat & Intl Jours Devoted to Judo; Phi Delta Kappa; Kappa Delta Pi; Phi Mu Alpha; Design & Implementation of Sport Psych Model for Am Judo, Olympic Tng Ctr, CO; Judo, 5th Deg Black Belt; Sr Coach; US Judo Assn & US Judo Inc; W/W in W.

HAMMARSTEN, JAMES FRANCIS oc/Physician, Professor; b/Mar 25, 1920; h/2754 Argentina Lane, Boise, ID 83704; ba/Boise, ID; m/Dorothea Marie Jung; c/Linnea Louise Hammarsten Ingold, James Eric, Richard Anders; p/ Francis Ragnar and Julia Linnea Hammarsten (dec); ed/BS 1943, MB 1944, MD 1945, Univ of MN; mil/AUS, 1943-47; USAF, 1953; Current Col, USAR; pa/Asst Prof, Univ of MN, 1949-53; From Asst Prof to Prof, Univ of OK, 1953-62; Prof, Univ of MN, 1962-66; Prof & Hd of Dept of Med, Univ of OK, 1966-78; Prof of Med, Univ of WA, 1978-; Dist'd Prof, Boise St Univ, 1982-; Am Col of Phys; Am Thoracic Soc, Pres 1969-70; Ctl Soc for Clin Res, Pres 1970; Am Lung Assn; Bd of Dirs 1968-80, 1984-; cp/Rotary, Boise; ID Archeological Soc, Bd 1981-; r/Luth; hon/Author, Over 100 Articles in Med Jours, Chapts in 5 Books; Co-Editor, *Med Care of the Surg Patient*, 1977; Hon Fellow, Am Col of Chest Phys, 1971; Hammarsten Lectureship, Univ of OK, 1979; Hammarsten Pulmonary Conf, 1978; Dist'd ID Citizen, 1980; W/W: in Am, in W.

HAMMER, LILLIAN oc/Poet; h/15 Elmwood Street, Albany, NY 12203; m/ Jack; c/Ruth, Helen; pa/Intl Acad of Poets; Hon Mem, UPLI, Philippines; Anniversario di Merito Dipl Accademia Leonardo da Vinci, 1980; Hon VP & Hon Rep, CSSI, Italy, 1974-75; hon/Ocarina World Poetry, Madras, India; Pancontinental Premier Poets; World Poetry

Soc Intercontinental; SAP Fellows Mag; Laurel Leaves, U Poets Laureate Intl; Outstg Contemp Poetry; Intl Poetry Centre; Book of Hon; Dic of Bicent Era; World W/W of Wom.

HAMMOND, J PARKS oc/Architect; b/Jun 14, 1947; h/1126D East 60th Street, Tulsa, OK 74105; ba/Tulsa, OK; p/Mr and Mrs N G Hammond, El Dorado, AR; ed/BA, Arch, 1971; BArch, 1978; Master of Landscape Arch, 1980; mil/USN, 1970-76; pa/Landscape Arch Designer, Earth Design Assocs, 1979; Landscape Arch/Arch, Bozeman Assocs, 1980; Landscape Arch/Arch, HTB Inc, 1981-84; Arch/Landscape Arch, McCone Ptnrs Inc, 1984-; AIA, Assoc 1976; Am Soc of Landscape Archs, 1978, Ed Sem Chm 1982; cp/JCs, 1981; Pres, Exch Clb, 1984; hon/Co-Author, *Rural Residential Devel*; USN Achmt Medal, 1974; Nat Merit Scholar, 1965; Thomas Jefferson Meml Soc Scholar, 1978, 1979; W/W in SW.

HAMMOND, MARK STEVEN oc/ Health Care Executive; b/Sep 10, 1956; h/2640 Angell Avenue, San Diego, CA 92113; ba/San Diego, CA; p/Clyde N and Gloria G Hammond; ed/Master in Bus Mgmt, Univ of Redlands, 1983; BA in Indust Psych, San Diego St Univ, 1980; pa/VP of Opers, Indust Med Corp, 1982-; Hosp Admr, Longer Life Foun, 1980-82; Am Mgmt Assn; r/Meth; hon/ Grad Thesis, "Med Pract Mgmt through the Design & Devel of Standardized Policies & Procedures," 1983; Grad, Top 10% in Class; Lic'd Hlth Care Admr at 23 Yrs Old; W/W in W.

HAMPTON-KAUFFMAN, MARGARET FRANCES oc/Corporate Planning and Venture Consultant; b/May 12, 1947; h/1065 West Paces Ferry Road, Northwest, Atlanta, GA 30327; ba/ Gainesville, FL; m/Kenneth L Kauffman; p/Mr and Mrs William Wade Hampton III, Gainesville, FL; ed/MBA w Concentration in Fin, Columbia Univ Grad Sch of Bus, 1974; BA, summa cum laude, French, FL St Univ; pa/Sr VP, Corporate Planning, Bk S Corp, 1981-; VP, Corporate Fin & Planning, The Nat Bk of GA, 1976-81; Asst VP & Bkg Indust Spec, Mfrs Hanover Trust Co, 1975-76; Financial Analyst, Fed Resv Bd of Govs, 1974-75; Bd of Dirs, Accent Enterprises Inc 1979-, Atlanta Profl Wom's Dir 1981-, GA Exec Wom's Netwk (Secy 1982-83); Wom's Commerce Clb, 1981-; Planning Execs Inst, 1978-; Am Inst of Bkg, 1976-; cp/1st VP 1982-84, Treas 1981-82, Bd of Trustees 1980-85, GA Chapt, Leukemia Soc of Am; Atlanta Wom's Forum, 1980-; Adv Bd, Atlanta Symph, 1985; High Technol Task Force, Atlanta C of C, 1982-83; r/Epis; hon/Alcoa Foun Fellow, 1973; FL St Univ Hall of Fame, 1969; Phi Beta Kappa; Mortar Bd; Beta Gamma Sigma; Garnet Key; FL St Univ, Homecoming Ct 1968, Mil Ball Queen 1968; Nat Col Queen Finalist, 1968; An Outstg Yg Wom in Am, 1978; W/W: in World, in Fin & Indust, of Am Wom, in S & SW, Among Students in Am Cols & Univs; Intl W/W of Intells; 2,000 Notable Ams.

HAMRA, SAM F JR oc/Attorney, Owner of Restaurants; b/Jan 21, 1932; h/3937 St Andrews Drive, Springfield, MO 65804; ba/Springfield, MO; m/June S; c/Sam F III, Karen Escine, Michael Kenneth, Jacqueline Kay; p/Mrs Victoria Hamra, Steele, MO; ed/BS, Univ of

MO Bus Sch, 1954; LLB, Univ of MO Law Sch, 1959; mil/Lt, AUS Field Artillery, 1954-56; pa/Assoc, Law Firm of Miller, Fairman, Sanford, Carr & Lowther, 1959-65; Presently in Law Pract, Sam F Hamra Jr, Atty & Cnslr; Chm of Bd & Pres, Wendy's of SW MO Inc & Wendy's of MO Inc; Bd of Dirs, Landmark Bankshares Corp; VChm of Bd of Dirs, Landmark Bk of Springfield; Chm of Bd of Dirs, Landmark Bk, Glenstone, Springfield; cp/VP/Pres 1984-85, Fdn of Syrian Lebanese-Am Clbs; Charter Pres, Rotary Clb, 1967-68; Pres, JCs, 1963-64; Bd of Dirs, Springfield C of C, 1971-77; Masons; Scottish Rite; Shrine; MO Univ Alumni Assn Aths Com, 1981-; Trustee, Jefferson Clb, Univ of MO, 1980-; VP, Cedars Clb of the Ozarks, 1981; Bd of Dirs, MO Inst for Justice Inc, 1980; St of MO, Gov's Labor & Employmt Com, 1980; CoChm, Heart Fund Dance Ticket Sales, 1981; Corporate Chm, Cerebral Palsy Telethon; Del, Dem Nat Conv, 1972, 1980; Num Other Civic & Political Activs; r/Epis; hon/Springfield's Outstg Yg Man of the Yr, 1966; MO's Outstg Yg Man of the Yr, 1967; W/W: in MW, in Am Law, in Fin & Indust, in Am Polit, in World; W/W Hon Soc of Am; Commun Ldrs & Noteworthy Ams; DIB; Personalities of Am; Men of Achmt.

HANDELMANN, GAIL E oc/Scientist; b/Mar 13, 1954; h/25 Eastmoor Drive, Silver Spring, MD 20901; ba/ Bethesda, MD; m/Thomas L O'Donohue; p/Raymond C and Marjorie A Handelmann, Ramsey, NJ; ed/BA, PA St Univ, 1976; PhD, Johns Hopkins Univ, 1981; pa/Staff Fellow, NIH, 1981-; Soc for Neurosci; Intl Soc for Developmental Neurobiol; AAAS; hon/Author of 25 Articles Pub'd in Sci Jours; NSF Predoct F'ship, 1978; NIGMS PRAT Fellow, 1982; World W/W of Wom.

HANDLEY, HERBERT M oc/Professor of Research Design; b/Jul 7, 1934; h/Box 3123, Mississippi State, MS 39762; ba/Mississippi State, MS; ed/BS, Univ of N AL, 1955; EdM 1962; EdD 1966, Univ of GA; pa/Sci Tchr, Fairview HS; Sci Tchr 1958-61, Sci Coor & Tchr of Gifted 1962-64, Glynn Acad; GA Gov's Hons Prog, 1964, 1966; Gainesville Jr Col, 1966-68; Assoc Prof 1968-71, Sr Rschr & Prof of Curric & Instrn 1972-82, Dist'd Prof 1983, MS St Univ; Phi Kappa Phi; Phi Delta Kappa; Kappa Delta Pi; Am Ednl Res Assn; Nat Assn for Res in Sci Tchg; Dir, Mid-S Ednl Res Assn, 1979-82; r/Epis; hon/ Author of Res Articles in *Jour of Res in Sci Tchg*, *Jour of Voc Ed*, *Jour of Negro Ed*, *Jour of Res & Devel*, *Elem Eng*, *Jour of Voc Behavior*; MS St Univ Alumni Awd for Tchg & Res, 1978; Dist'd Prof of Curric & Instn, 1982; PDK Dist'd Ser Awd, 1982; Personalities of S; W/W in Intl Ed.

HANEY, MARY BELL oc/Civil Engineer; b/Nov 10, 1946; h/318 Amistad Boulevard, Universal City, TX 78148; ba/San Antonio, TX; m/Donald Lee; c/ James, Donald; p/James and Suzanna Trout; ed/PhD Cand, Univ of TX, 1979-; MS in Envir Sys Engrg 1968, BSCE 1967, Clemson Univ; pa/Vis'g Lectr & Adj Prof, Univ of NM, 1970-72; VP, Engrg, Ruben Rodriguez Land Devel Inc, 1970-74; Asst Proj Mgr 1976-78, Proj Engr 1978-, Pape-Dawson Consltg Engrs Inc; Reg'd Profl Engr, TX; Nat Soc Profl Engrs; TX Soc Profl Engrs,

Dir 1980, Treas 1981, Secy 1982, Spkrs Bur 1979-; Soc Wom Engrs; Assn Wom in Sci; Nat Assn Female Execs; Am Statl Assn; ASCE; San Antonio Coun Engrg Ed; Tau Beta Pi; Phi Kappa Phi; Sigma Tau Epsilon; cp/Properties Com, GSA; Water Pollution Control Fdn; Planetary Soc; NOW; YWCA; Universal City Lib Bd; r/Meth; Prot Wom of Chapel, Pres of Clb 1975-76; hon/Contbr, Articles to Profl Pubs; Outstg Yg Engr of Yr Awd, Bexar Chapt 1982, & TX St Yg Engr of the Yr 1982, TX Soc of Profl Engrs; Wom's Badge, Tau Beta Pi, 1965; Outstg Yg Wom in Am; W/W of Am Wom.

HANLEY, KEVIN JOSEPH oc/ Orthodontist, Dental Educator; b/Oct 25, 1952; h/7 Cornfield Road, Simsbury, CT 06070; ba/West Hartford, CT; m/ Carmella Marie Rosetti; p/Richard J and Mary C Hanley, Utica, NY; ed/BA, Psych, SUNY-Buffalo, 1974; DDS, SUNY-Buffalo Sch of Dentistry, 1978; Cert of Proficiency, Orthodontics, Univ of CT Sch of Dental Med; pa/Asst Prof in Residence 1980-83, Asst Clin Prof 1983-, Univ of CT Hlth Ctr, Dept of Orthodontics; Orthodontist, Pedo-dontic-Orthodontic Assocs, 1983-; Am Assn of Orthodontists; NEn Soc of Orthodontists; CT St Soc of Orthod-ontists; Am Dental Assn; CT St Dental Assn; Hartford Dental Soc; Omicron Kappa Upsilon Hon Dental Frat, Lambda Lambda Chapt; r/Rom Cath; hon/Pubs, *Mod Edgewise Mechanics-Segmented Arch Technique*, "Bioelect Per-turbations of Bone-Res Directions & Clin Applications" 1984; Election to Omicron Kappa Upsilon Hon Dental Frat, Lambda Lambda Chapt, 1978; W/ W in Frontier Sci & Technol.

HANLEY, MARY B oc/Business Owner; b/Mar 23, 1951; h/1806 Higdon Avenue, #3, Mount View, CA 94041; ba/Palo Alto, CA; m/Edward N Apodaca; p/George Walter and Helen F Hanley, San Mateo, CA; ed/Att'd, Foothill Col 1976-79, De Anza Col 1978-79, Col of San Mateo 1970-72, AZ St Univ 1969-70; pa/Owner & Fdr, Hanley Secretarial Sers, 1979-; Ward Secy, Secy to Chief of Otolaryngology, Secy to Chief of Psych, VA Med Ctr, 1971-79; Secy, Wn Reg HQs of Household Fin, 1970-71; Fdr, Mem, Treas 1980-83, Mbrship Chm 1979-, Peninsula Bus Sers Assn; r/Cath; hon/W/W in W.

HANNS, CHRISTIAN ALEX-ANDER oc/Vocational and Educational Personnel Consultant; b/Sep 12, 1948; h/312 Jefferson Avenue, Linden, NJ 07036; ba/Trenton, NJ; p/Christian J Hanns, Parlin, NJ; ed/Dipl, Career Acad of Broadcasting, 1966; Dipl, Def Info Sch, 1967; BA, MA 1973, Kean Col of NJ; ABD, Rutgers Univ, 1980; pa/Dir of Tng & Testing Gerotoga Industs (Present); Conslt, NJ Dept of Hlth (Present); Dir, Cnslg, J E Runnells Hosp, 1978; Dir, Cnslg/Curric, Ednl Resource Inst, 1974; Dir, Cnslg/Testing, Union Col, 1976; Secy, Bd of Dirs, Assn of Commun Ed; Secy, Bd of Trustees, Union Co Psychi Clin; Chair, Cnslg, Assn for Adult Ed; cp/Chm, Bd of Dirs, Clara Barton Aux; Chair, Ways & Means, ARC, Bd of Dirs; Fund Drive, Walk-a-Thon, March of Dimes; Chm, Human Sers, Salvation Army; Bd of Dirs, Krippled Kiddies, BPOE; r/Chm Pastor, Parish Relats, U Meth Ch; Bd of Dirs, Metro Ecumenical Min; hon/

Pubs, *Wkbook on Job Preparedness*, *Wkbook on Consumer Issues*, *Wkbook on Legal Issues*, *Making Money While Unemployed*, *Job Readiness Cnslg Manual*; Editor, *Employmt Spec Newslttr*, Union County Registry for Human Sers; NJ Dept of Ed, Pioneering Flexible Testing & Cnslg, 1974; Vol of the Yr, City of Linden, 1980; Commun Edr of the Yr, 1983; W/W: in E, Intl of Intells.

HANSEN, ELLENMAE CURTIS oc/ Nursing Educator; b/Jun 12, 1920; h/ 10564 Avenida Magnifica, San Diego, CA 92131; ba/Vista, CA; m/Peter Christian; c/Judith Ellen; p/James Oliver (dec) and Bertha Belle Curtis, Orange, CA; ed/Dipl, Akron City Hosp Sch of Nsg, 1942; BS 1970, MA 1972, AZ St Univ; mil/USN Nurse Corps, WWII; pa/ Adv Com, Voc Nurse Prog, Mira Costa Col, 1981; Dir, Nsg Progs, Palo Vista Col of Nsg, 1978-; Asst Dir, Psychi Tech Prog, Hillcrest Col, 1978; Staff Nurse, Villa View Commun Hosp, 1977-78; Fac, Mesa Commun Col, 1975-76; Fac, En AZ Col, 1974-75; Bd of Dirs, CA Voc Nurse Edrs; CA Assn of Hlth Career Edrs; CA Leag for Nsg; Nat Leag for Nsg; Alumni Assn, Akron City Hosp & AZ St Univ; CA Assn of Post-Sec'dy Schs; Nat Assn of Hlth Career Schs; So CA Assn of Voc Nurse Edrs; ARC; Adv Com, Voc Nurse Prog, Mira Costa Col & Beverly Manor Home Hlth Care Agy; Navy Leag of the US; r/Epis; hon/Mem Consortium, Golden W Col, Module Writer for Psychi Tech Prog, 1978; Authored Curric & Modules, Voc Nurse Prog, Palo Vista Col of Nsg, 1979; Pi Lambda Theta, Beta Kappa, AZ St Univ, 1972; BS w Distn, AZ St Univ, 1970; W/W: in CA, of Am Wom, Among Contemp Nurses.

HANSEN, GEORGE oc/United States Congressman; b/Sep 14, 1930; m/ Connie; c/Steve, Jim, Pat, Bill, Joanne; ed/Bach Deg w Hons in Hist & Russian; Grad Wk in Ed; Grad, Acctg & Mgmt, Bus Col; mil/USAF; Nav Resv Ofcr; pa/ Tchr, HS Sci, Math & Social Studies; Elected to Cong, 1964, 1966, 1974, 1976, 1978, 1980; Dpty Under Secy, Dept of Agri; Nat Dir, St & Co Opers, Agri Stabilization & Conserv Ser; Dpty VP, Commun Credit Corp; House Repub Policy Com; Sr Mem, Coms on Bkg, Fin & Urban Affairs & Agri; Vets' Affairs Com; House Repub Policy Com; Rank-ing Repub, Domestic Monetary Affairs Subcom; Hd, Nat STOP OSHA Cam-paign; Orgr, Am Security Coun Task Force on Caribbean & Ctl Am Security & Repub Congl Govt Exec Agy Review Task Force; Dpty VP, Commodity Credit Corp; hon/Author, Book Expos-ing Abusive Tactics of the IRS; Recip, Num Achmt Awds & Hons; Num Biogl Listings.

HANSEN (ASHTON), KATE PEGGY oc/Editor, Professor, Speech Consultant; b/Sep 11, 1948; h/5046 Ducos Place, San Diego, CA 92124; ba/ San Diego, CA; p/Lester Leopold, Boca Raton, FL; Louise Monroe, Hartwood, VA; ed/BS in Spch Communication 1970, MA in Platform Arts 1972, Bob Jones Univ; MA in Spch Communica-tion, San Diego St Univ, 1979; pa/Instr, Bob Jones Univ, 1970-72; Asst Prof, Christian Heritage Col, 1972-76; Prof, San Diego City Col, 1976-83; Editor, *Where* Mag, 3M, 1980-83; Spch Conslt, Marine Corps, San Diego Gas & Elect

& Pacific Telephone; Wn Spch Assn, 1985; Communicating Arts Grp, 1982; r/Prot; hon/Pubs, "Take Home Pictures" in *Where* Mag 1982, "Coping w Student Criticism" in *Guide* 1977 & *Emily* 1972; W/W: of Am Wom, Among Cols & Univs.

HANSEN, STANLEY SEVERIN oc/ Astronomer, Computer and Aerospace Scientist; b/Sep 16, 1945; h/420 South Catalina Avenue, #208, Redondo Beach, CA 90277; ba/El Segundo, CA; p/ Stanley S Sr and Gertrude Hansen (dec); ed/BS, Physics, Univ of MO-Rolla; MS 1972, PhD 1980, Astronomy and Phys-ics, Univ of MA-Amherst; pa/Rschr, Oak Ridge Assoc'd Univs, 1966; Sys Devel Staff, IBM, 1967-70; Fac, Mt Holyoke Col, 1971-73; Astronomer, Onsala Space Observatory, 1973; Fac, Univ of MA-Amherst, 1974; Astrono-mer, Nat Radio Astronomy Observa-tory, 1974-81; Mem of the Tech Staff, The Aerospace Corp, 1982-; Am Astro-nom Soc; Tau Beta Pi Engrg Hon Frat; cp/Advr, Aerospace Corp's Explorer Scout Post; hon/Pubs, "VLBI Maps of the Water Vapor Masers Towards Orion A from 1972-1978" 1984, "The Magnetic Fields in the Kleinmann-Low Nebula as Derived from Hydroxyl Maser Radiation" 1982, "VLBI Obser-vations of the V=1 and V=2 SiO Masers in W Hydra & VX Sagittarius" 1980, "VLBI Observations of the SiO Maser in Orion" 1979, Others; W/W: in Frontier Sci & Technol, in Technol Today, in World, in W.

HANSON, BRADFORD CHARLES oc/Research Geologist; b/Jun 1, 1945; ba/Baton Rouge, LA; p/Claude A and Lucille M Hanson, Gulfport, MS; ed/BS, Geol, Univ of MD, 1970; MS, Geol, Univ of AR, 1973; Postgrad Studies, Geol, Univ of KS; pa/Sr Res Geologist, LA Geol Survey, 1980-; Consltg Geologist, US Soil Inc, 1979; Asst Prof, Wn MI Univ, 1978-79; Asst Prof, W TX St Univ, 1977-78; Sr Res Scist, Univ of KS Ctr for Res, 1972-77; Sigma Xi; Am Assn of Petro Geologists; Baton Rouge Geol Soc, Charter Mem; TX Geol Soc; Nat Water Well Assn; Sigma Gamma Epsilon, VP of Alpha Psi Chapt 1971, Pres of Alpha Chapt 1973; Guest Lectr, Area HS; cp/JCs; r/Prot; hon/Pubs, "Ground Water in Louisiana-An Eval of Current Water Resources by Specific Aquifer" 1981, "Geologic & Hydrologic Probs Associated w Siting of Hazardous Waste Facilities in Coastal Plain Envirs w Empasis on So Louisiana" 1981, "Procedure for Evaluating the Geologic Integrity of Existing Hazardous Waste Sites in Louisiana" 1981, "Experiments on the Radar Backscatter of Snow" 1977, Others; W/W in S & SW; Per-sonalities of S.

HARALSON, MABLE KATHLEEN oc/Executive Assistant; b/May 8, 1935; h/PO Box 515, Abbeville, SC 29620; ba/ Columbia, SC; p/Ralph Q (dec) and Minnie Murphy Haralson, Greenwood, SC; ed/BS, Univ of SC, 1974; MPH, Univ of TN, 1976; pa/Adm Asst 1968-74, Hlth Edr 1974, SC Dept of Hlth & Envir Control; Dist Dir of Hlth Ed, Appalachia I Hlth Dist, 1976-79; Exec Asst, SC Water Resources Comm, 1979-; Bd of Dirs, Envir Ed Assn of SC, 1983-84; So Hlth Assn, Chm of Hlth Ed Sect 1981; SC Public Hlth Assn; cp/ Gov's Beautification & Commun

Improvement, Adv Bd Mem; r/Bapt; hon/Pubs, "Hlth Ed Delivered the Goods" 1981, "Our Water, It's Too Valuable to Waste" 1982; Dist'd Ser Awd, So Hlth Assn, Hlth Ed Sect, 1981; USPH Traineeship, 1976; W/W in S & SW; Dir of Dist'd Ams; Personalities of S; Intl Biogl Dir; Others.

HARBAY, EDWARD WILLIAM oc/ Nuclear Operations; b/May 16, 1937; h/ 22271 Derby Road, Woodhaven, MI 48183; ba/Detroit Edison, Enrico Fermi 2 Nuclear Power Plant, 6400 N Dixie Hwy, Newport, MI 48166; m/Marian M Belavic; c/Katherine Mary, Julie Ann, Marla Jean; p/Edward F and Helen M Virostek Harbay (dec); ed/BS, Math 1961, Grad Courses in Chem Engrg 1962-63, Univ of Pgh; pa/Rocket Devel Engr, Hercules Inc, Allegany Ballistics Lab, 1961-66; Reactor Core Contract Admr, Westinghouse Elect Corp, Bettis Atomic Power Lab, 1966-74; Engr, Daniel Intl, 1974-75; Asst Dist Mgr, Cyclops Corp, 1975-77; Purchasing Agt, Daniel Intl, 1977-78; Buyer, Contract Admr, Nuclear Engr, Detroit Edison, 1978-; Nat Soc of Profl Engrs; Am Nuclear Soc; r/Rom Cath; hon/W/W: in Frontier Sci & Technol, in World.

HARCOURT, ROBERT NEFF oc/ Educational Administrator, Journalist; b/Oct 19, 1932; h/720 Acequia Madre, #7, Santa Fe, NM 87501; ba/Santa Fe, NM; p/Stanton Hinde and Mary Neff Harcourt, Westfield, NJ; ed/BA, Gettysburg Col, 1958; MA, Columbia Univ, 1961; Selected Grad Courses at 5 Other Univs; mil/AUS 1954-56, Pers & Public Relats Spec, Germany; pa/Social Case Wkr, NJ St Bd of Child Wel, 1958-61; Asst Registrar at Hofstra Univ, Asst to the Evening Dean of Students at CCNY, 1961-62; Housing Staff, Univ of Denver, 1962-64; Admr, Inst of Am Indian Arts, 1965-; Phi Delta Kappa Intl, Exec Bd, Local Chapt; Am Assn for Cnslg & Devel; Assn for Specs in Grp Wk, Charter Mem; Adult Student Pers Assn, Charter Mem; Santa Fe Coun on Intl Relats; Alpha Tau Omega; Alpha Phi Omega; Mem, Safari Clb Intl; cp/ SAR; Adv'd Sr Master, Exec Bd of Local Unit, Am Contact Bridge Leag; r/Prot; hon/Pubs, "Cyclic Regeneration" (Presented to Intl Conf on Gen Semantics in Denver) 1968, Var Newspaper Articles; Post Masters F'ship, Univ of Denver, 1962-64; Hon OKIE, OK Gov Dewey Bartlett, 1970; Col Aide-de-Camp, NM Gov David Cargo, 1970; Participant, IAIA Fac Exhib, Kennedy Ctr, Wash DC, 1973; Tchr Ldr, Eisenhower Student Ambassador Prog, 1979; Art Judge, Mesa Verde NP Navajo Exhib, 1983; W/W in SW.

HARDAWAY, EVELYN RENÉE oc/ Data Processing Manager; b/Dec 19, 1948; h/5118 15th Avenue, Columbus, GA 31904-5744; p/Mrs Vesta M Hardaway, Columbus, GA; ed/Att'd, Johnson C Smith Univ 1967-68, Am Inst of Bkg 1969-70; pa/Auditing Clk, First Nat Bk of Columbus, 1969-72; Ofc Mgr, CAGLE Inc, 1972-74; Acct Exec, Flair Pers Ser, 1974-76; Mgr, Tech Advr, Am Mgmt Sers, 1976-80; Data Processing Mgr, Katy Commun Hosp, Life Mark Corp, 1981-; Nat Assn of Female Execs, 1978-; cp/Former Big Sister of Houston, 1979; r/Bapt; hon/Recip, Opers Excell Awd, Houston Dist, Am Mgmt Soc, 1979; Cert, Mgmt, Orientation

Wkshop, Life Mark, 1981; Cert, Mgmt Devel Wkshop, Life Mark, 1982; W/W Am Wom.

HARDEMAN, CAROLE HALL oc/ Administrator; b/Mar 24, 1945; h/1709 Northeast 58th, Oklahoma City, OK 73111; ba/Norman, OK; c/Paula Suzette; ed/BA, Fisk Univ; MA, PhD, Univ of OK; Addit Studies, Univ of CA LA; pa/Chair of Fine Arts Dept, NE HS, OKC Public Sch Sys; Vocal Music Instr, Choral Dir, 1968-75; Black Hist Instr, Oscar Rose Jr Col, 1975; Prog Devel Spec, SW Ctr, Univ of OK, 1975-77; SW Ctr: Proj Dir of Math, Curric Devel Proj for US Ofc of Ed 1977-79, Proj Dir, Inst for Ednl Equity in Math & Sci Clrms for US Dept of Ed (Title IV) 1979, Proj Dir for Sci Curric Devel, US Dept of Ed (Wom's Ednl Equity Act) 1979-82, Dir of SW Ctr for Human Relats Studies 1982-; Adm Ofcr, Univ of OK & Adj Prof of Human Relats & Ed, Grad Col, 1980-; OK Assn of Black Pers in Higher Ed, 1977-; Alpha Kappa Alpha; Nat Assn of Wom in Math; ASCD; AASA; Am Ednl Res Assn; Nat Univ Cont'g Ed Assn; Nat Alliance of Black Sch Edrs, Chair of Policy Devel Comm, Mem of Exec Bd; Univ Adm Ofcrs Coun; cp/ Urban Leag; YMCA; YWCA; Links Inc; OKC Chapt, Jack & Jill of Am; r/Bapt; hon/Pubs, *Mathco: A Prog to Enhance Yg Wom's Understanding to Interdisciplinary Uses of Math in Career Choices* 1982, *Math: Who Needs It?* 1981, *Coping w Col: The Quality of Life for Minority Students in Higher Ed Instns in OK* 1977, *Sounds of Sci: A Multicultural, Multidisciplinary Sci Curric for Mid Sch Students* 1982, "Issues That Impact on Black Students in White Cols & Univs" 1982; Tchr of Yr, 1968, 1975; Recip, Superior 1st Place Trophies for Var Choirs & Ensembles at Dist & St Music Fests & Contests, 1970-75; Glee Clb Rated Best in St, 1974; Invited by Govt of Nassau, Bahamas, to Perf 5 Concerts, 1973; Viking Singers Rec'd More Invitations Than Any Other HS Choir in OK; Resolution, OK St Legis for Outstg Musicianship & Perf in City, St, Nat & World; Orgr, Fdr, Viking Singers (Winners of Sweepstakes Trophy, Tri-St Music Fest, Phillips Univ, 1975); Nom, NUCEA Awd for Creativity, Univ of OK; Earned Perfect GPA in Doct Studies, 1975-79; Hon'd as Fam of the Yr, 1980; First Black & First Female to Assume Ldrship of SW Ctr for Human Relats Studies, Univ of OK; Personalities of S; W/W in S & SW.

HARDIN, JOYCE FAYE oc/Professor of Education; b/Jan 26, 1936; h/5230 87th Street, Lubbock, TX 79424; ba/ Lubbock, TX; m/Daniel C; c/Mara Gwen Ashley, Danna Faye Willis, Terra Dee; p/Ralph and Viola Smith (both dec), Albuquerque, NM; ed/BS, Abilene Christian Univ, 1953; ME, En NM Univ, 1963; EdS 1970, EdD 1978, OK St Univ; pa/Public Sch Tchr, CA 1957-58, Seoul, Korea 1970-74, Abilene, TX 1975-76; Missionary to Korea, 1958-75; Prof of Elem Ed, Korea Christian Col 1963-74, Abilene Christian Univ 1974-75, Lubbock Christian Col 1976-; Phi Kappa Phi Hon Frat; Delta Kappa Gamma, Pres 1980-82; Assn for Supvn & Curric Devel; Phi Delta Kappa, Secy 1981-82, VP 1982-84, Pres 1984-85; NEA; TX St Tchrs Assn; W TX Assn for Supvn & Curric Devel; TX Soc of Col Tchrs of Ed; TX Assn for the Improvement of

Rdg; r/Ch of Christ; hon/Author, Var Chapts in Books; Many Contbns to Monthly Pubs in Korea & US; F W Mattox Dist'd Tchr Awd, 1980; Danforth Assoc, 1981-86; Hilda Maehling F'ship, 1983-84; Neil S Bryan Christian Ed Awd, 1985; Personalities of S.

HARDING, EDWARD LLOYD oc/ Credit Manager; b/Feb 22, 1953; h/615 Bank Street, Washington, NC 27889; ba/Washington, NC; ed/BS, Hlth & PE, Atl Christian Col, 1976; pa/Pres, H E Harding & Son Inc, 1976-77; Party Chief, Rodman & Waters Land Surveying & Civil Engrg, 1977-81; Credit Mgr, Lowe's of NC, DBA Lowe's of Wash, 1982-; Beaufort Co Alumni Assn, Atl Christian Col, 1983, VP & Pres-Elect; cp/Wash JCs, 1977-82, Bd of Dirs 1978-79, Secy 1980-81; Beaufort Co Fundraising Chm, NC Heart Assn, 1977; r/Epis; hon/Wash JCs: Pres Awd of Hon 1977, Speak Up Awd 1977-81, Spoke Awd 1977, Spark Plug Awd 1978-80, Key Man Awd 1979, Proj Chm Awd 1980; W/W: in S & SW, in Fin & Indust; Outstg Yg Men in Am.

HARDISON, O B JR oc/Administrator; b/Oct 22, 1928; ba/Department of English, Georgetown University, Washington, DC 20007; m/Marifrances Fitzgibbon; c/Charity, Sarah, Laura Agnes, Osborne, Matthew; ed/BA 1949, MA 1950, Univ of NC; PhD, Univ of WI, 1956; pa/Tchg Asst, Univ of WI, 1950-53; Instr of Eng, Univ of TN, 1954-56; Instr of Eng, Princeton Univ, 1956-57; From Asst Prof to Prof of Eng 1957-67, Prof of Eng & Comparative Lit 1967-69, Univ of NC; Dir, Folger Shakespeare Lib, 1969-84; Prof, Georgetown Univ, 1984-; Phi Beta Kappa, 1949; Chm 1965, Co-Chm 1966, SEn Inst of Medieval & Renaissance Studies; Mod Lang Assn (Exec Coun), 1968-71; Renaissance Soc of Am (Exec Coun), 1969-70, 1985-; Trustee, Univ of Detroit, 1970-79; Chm, Indep Res Lib Assn, 1973-74; Chm, Nat Humanities Alliance, 1984-; Bd of Dirs, Am Assn for Higher Ed, 1980-; Edit Bd, *Milton Studies* 1967-, *Eng Lit Renaissance* 1969-, Jour of Medieval & Renaissance Studies 1970-; Num Formal Lectures Given; hon/Pubs, *Entering the Maze: Change & Identity in Mod Culture* 1982, *Pro Musica Antiqua* 1977, *Toward Freedom & Dignity: The Humanities & the Idea of Humanity* 1972, "The Poetry of Nothing" 1984, "The Meaning of Meaning" 1983, "Shakespeare's Political World" 1981, "Logic vs the Slovenly World of Shakespearean Comedy" 1980, "Shakespeare on Film: The Developing Canon" 1979, Num Others; Fulbright Fellow, 1953-54; Folger Lib Fellow, 1958; Guggenheim Fellow, 1963-64; *Time* Mag Cover, Dist'd Tchrs in the US, 1966; Recip, Haskins Medal, Medieval Acad of Am, 1967; Nickolas Salgo Awd for Dist'd Tchg, 1968; Hon DLitt, Rollins Col, 1969; Fellow, Am Antiquarian Soc, 1972-; Hon DLitt, 1974; Cavaliere Ufficiale della Republica Italiana, Decoration of the Govt of Italy, 1974; Order of the Brit Empire, 1983; W/W Adv Bd, 1975-; Man of the Yr, *The Washingtonian* Awd, 1977; Hon DHL, York Col, 1977; Hon DHL, Georgetown Univ, 1977; Hon DLitt, Amherst Col, 1980; John F Kennedy Meml Vis'g Fellow, New Zealand, 1980.

HARDY, CAMILLE oc/Assistant to

Dean of Fine and Applied Arts; b/Oct 14, 1944; h/813 West University Avenue, Champaign, IL 61820; ba/Champaign, IL; c/Miranda Camille; p/James (dec) and Mary Combs, Mt Airy, NC; ed/BA, Duke Univ, 1965; MA, Univ of NC, 1968; PhD, Univ of MI, 1971; pa/Asst to Dean of Fine & Applied Arts, Univ of IL, 1979–; Guest Scholar in Dance, Cornell Univ, 1982; Period Dance Spec, Univ of TX-Austin, 1978–79; Prof of Dance Hist, Univ of IL, 1973–78; Dance Histn, Nat Acad of Arts, 1973-78, 1982-; Bd of Dirs, Soc of Dance Hist Scholars, 1982–85; Bd of Dirs, Dance Critics Assn, 1980-83; Choreography Panel, Nat Endowment for the Arts, 1983–86; Multi Arts Panel 1980-83, Dance Panel 1979-80, IL Arts Coun; Prog Advr in Dance, NEA, 1979-83; hon/Author, Dance Reviews & Articles Which Appear in *Dance Mag*, *Ballet News*, *Ballet Review*, *Dance Chronicle*, *Dance Res Jour*, *Arabesque*, *Am Arts*; NEA Grant for Black Arts Fest, E Carolina Univ, 1972; Tchr Ranked as Excellent by Her Students, Univ of IL, 1978; Grant for the Improvement of Undergrad Tchg, Univ of TX-Austin, 1979; W/W of Am Wom.

HARDY, CAROLE MORGAN oc/Criminal Justice Consulting, Marketing; b/Jul 26, 1946; h/1033 Rockcrest Drive, Marietta, GA 30062; ba/Atlanta, GA; m/Joseph Carl; p/Sophia Hasty, Madison Heights, MI; ed/BA, Wayne St Univ, 1969; MA, Metro Col Inst, London, England, 1973; Postgrad, Oxford Univ, 1977; Dir of Ed, Detroit House of Corrections, 1969-72; Adm Aide to Councilwoman Erma Henderson, Detroit Common Coun, 1972-73; Conslt/Progs Advr, Wayne Co Sheriff's Dept, 1971-72; Dept of Polit Sci Instr, Detroit Inst of Technol, 1974; Dir, Rape Crisis Ctr, 1974-77; Conslt, Wn Interst Comm for Higher Ed, 1977-78; Conslt, Nat Inst of Corrections, 1977–; Assoc/Proj Dir, Tng Assocs, 1979-81; Dir, Justice Mgmt Enterprises, 1980-83; Public Adm Instr, Golden St Univ, 1981-83; Crim Justice Instr, Canada Col, 1982; Mktg Dir/Conslt, Justice Sys Inc, 1983–; Alliance for Am Innovation; Am Jail Assn; Am Corrections Assn; Nat Assn of Female Execs; Soc for Mktg Profl Sers; Grad Assn of Polit Scists, Chp 1972; cp/NOW; San Jose, CA, C of C; hon/Pubs, "Service Delivery Models: A Summary of Examples" 1982, "Developing Mtl Hlth Sers for Local Jails" 1981, "Ethical & Legal Barriers to Effective Public Policy Res" 1978, "Ser Delivery Models" 1978, Others; Pi Sigma Alpha Hons Frat, 1972; CO's Outstg Yg Wom; W/W of Am Wom; Outstg Yg Wom in Am.

HARDY, DOUGLAS KIRKMAN oc/Fine Dining & Catering, Real Estate Development; b/Jul 16, 1945; h/816 East 930 North, Pleasant Grove, UT 84062; ba/Provo, UT; c/Heather Lynne, Holly Ann, Troy Brandon, Whitney Marquette, Cameron Paige; p/H H & Lynne K Hardy, Orem, UT; ed/BS, Sch of Bus Mgmt, Brigham Yg Univ, 1970; mil/US Army, 19th Spec Forces, (Airborne) (Medic); pa/Real Est Salesman, Tarracor Inc, SLC, 1971; Mgr of 3 Fast Food Opers, Clyde H Davis & Assocs, SF, 1972; Salesman in Wholesale Meats, Vergo Meats, Lehi, UT, 1973; Owner & Operator, DeVon Chop House,

Orem, UT, 1973-75; Owner & Operator, R Spencer Hines Restaurant, Provo, UT, 1975–; Mem: Am Culinary Fdn; Beehive St Chefs Assn; Provo & SLC, C of C; Lic'd Rltr, UT Bd of Rltrs; UT Heritage Foun; UT St Hist Soc; at Brigham Yg Univ: Charter Mem 1963, Nat Alumni Pres, Sigma Epsilon Frat; r/LDS; Recip, UT Heritage Foun Bicentl Merit Awd, 1983; Assoc'd Students of Brigham Yg Univ Dist'd Ser Awd, 1983; Dir of Prominent Men & Wom of Provo; W/W in Am Restaurants.

HARDY, MARIE PAULA oc/Head of Education Department; b/Feb 24, 1926; h/Saint Mary College, Leavenworth, KS 66048; ba/Same; p/Judge and Mrs Russell C Hardy (dec); ed/BS, BA 1962, St Mary Col; MA, Univ of NE, 1969; PhD, Univ of IL, 1972; Univ of Newcastle-Upon-Tyne; Univ of Baroda, India; pa/Tchr; Hd, Sec'dy Eng Dept, Billings Ctl HS; Acting Chp, Ed Dept 1972-74, Assoc Prof 1978-81, Chp of Ed Dept 1978–, Prof of Ed 1981–, St Mary Col; Curric Bds, KS, MO, CA, IL, MT, NE; Demonstrator, Spkr, Ednl Convs; Del, NO Invitational Conf, 1968; Ofcr, Billings Br of IRA; Charter Mem, Intl Rocky Mtn Rdg Specs; Drama Comm, York Intl Conf, York, England, 1971; Conslt, Wkshop of NCTE, Las Vegas, 1971; Conslt, Spkr, Nat Coun on Lang Arts in the Elem Sch, 1972; Conslt, NWn Univ Spch Dept, 1972; Drama Wkshop, KS St Col of Pgh, 1972; Conslt, Gtr Cleveland Schs Wkshop, 1973; Wkshop, Sec'dy Eng Tchrs & Grad Students, So IL Univ, 1974; Others; Editor, *Artstrek '82*; Instrnl Rep, KS Assn of Higher Ed, 1973-77; Consortium Chm, Coop Urban Tchr Ed, 1973-74; KS Conf on Eng Ed, VP 1973-74, Pres 1975-79; KS Assn of Cols for Tchr Ed, Secy 1973-74, Exec Com 1974-75, Treas 1975-76, Instrnl Rep 1977-78, VP 1980-81; NEA; Assn of Tchr Edrs; Am Assn of Cols for Tchr Ed; NCTE; AAUW; IRA; Spec Interest Grp Netwk on Adolescent Lit; Nat Assn of Elem Sch Prins; Nat Assn of Sec'dy Sch Prins; Assn of Supvn & Curric Devel; Assn of Indep Liberal Arts Cols for Tchrs; KS Assn of Tchrs of Eng; KS Assn of Cols for Tchr Ed, Pres 1983-84; KS Assn of Higher Ed; KS Assn of Gifted, Talented & Creat; AACTE Ldrship Conf, Sum 1983 & 1984; ICET Conf, 1983; r/Cath; hon/Num Profl Pubs; NDEA Grant for Study, Univ of NE; Tuition S'ships, Univ of NE; Triple T F'ship, Univ of IL; Scholar-in-Residence, Univ of Newcastle-Upon-Tyne, England; Delta Epsilon Sigma; Phi Alpha Theta; Outstg Edr in Am, 1975; Sum Gac Sem, Univ of Baroda, India, 1976; Dir of Dist'd Ams; W/W: in World, in MW.

HARDY, RALPH W F oc/Science Administrator; b/Jul 27, 1934; h/Box 364, Unionville, PA 19375; ba/Wilmington, DE; m/Jacqueline M; c/Steven F R, Christopher F J, Barbara J, Ralph W B, Jonathan D T; p/Wilbur B and Elsie M Hardy (dec); ed/BSA, Univ of Toronto, 1956; MS 1958, PhD 1960, Univ of WI; pa/Asst Prof, Univ of Guelph, 1960-63; Res Biochem 1963-67, Res Supvr 1967-74, Assoc Dir 1974-79, Dir of Life Scis 1979-84, DuPont; Pres, Biotechnica Intl Inc, 1984–; Prof Life Scis, Cornell Univ, 1984–; Treas, Bd of Trustees, Am

Soc Plant Physiologists, 1973-76; Secy, Exec Com, Am Chem Soc, Div of Biol Chem, 1978-81; Exec Com, Nat Res Coun, Bd on Agri, 1983-85; Mem, Nat Res Coun, Com on Life Sci & Bd on Basic Biol, 1984-87; Intl Coun of Sci Union's Com on Genetic Experimentation, 1981–; Several Edit Bds; r/Epis; hon/Pubs, *Nitrogen Fixation in Bacteria & Higher Plants* 1975, *A Treatise on Dimitrogen Fixation* 1977-79; Gov Gen's Silver Medal, 1956; WI Alumni Res Foun Fellow, 1956-58; DuPont Fellow, 1959; Am Chem Soc, DE Awd, 1969; W/W Frontier Sci & Technol; Am Men & Wom in Sci.

HARGROVE, GARY THOMAS oc/Lieutenant Paramedic; b/Jan 29, 1955; h/2320-23rd Avenue, Gulfport, MS 39501; ba/Gulfport, MS; m/Susan M; c/Danielle Leigh; p/Mr and Mrs H T Hargrove, Gulfport, MS; sp/Mr and Mrs C C Rogers, Gulfport, MS; pa/Lt Paramedic, Gulfport Fire Dept, 1975–; Paramedic, Mobile Medic Ambulance Ser, 1975–; Dispatcher, Gulfport Police Dept, 1975; r/Bapt; hon/MS Gulf Coast Emer Med Ser Dist Excell Awd, 1981; Harrison Co Bd of Supvrs Dist'd Ser Awd, 1980; City of Biloxi Commend Awd, 1983; MS Glf Coast Emer Ser Dist Cert of Merit, 1982; VFW Outstg Fireman Awd, 1979; Outstg Yg Man of Am Awd, 1982; Exch Clb Outstg Fireman of Yr Awd, 1983; JCs Outstg Yg Fireman of Yr Awd, 1983.

HARGROVE, JERRY EDWARD JR oc/Roman Catholic Priest; b/Dec 11, 1949; h/920-11th Street, Northeast, Washington, DC 20002; ba/Same; ed/MS, Loyola Col, 1982; Theol Studies, The Cath Univ of Am, 1972-76; BA, Univ of AR; mil/Chaplain (Capt), DC Army NG; pa/Assoc Pastor, Holy Name Cath Ch, 1983–; Chaplain, Elizabeth Seton HS, 1984–; Assoc Pastor, St Peter's Ch, 1979-83; Assoc Pastor, Nativity Ch, 1976-79; Tchr, Cnslr, Chaplain, St Cecilia Acad, 1974-78; Phi Mu Alpha Sinfonia; Alpha Phi Alpha; Nat Acad of Cert'd Clin Mtl Hlth Cnslrs; Mil Chaplains Assn, VPres; Am Assn for Cnslg & Devel; cp/NAACP, Life Mem; K of C; K of St John; r/Rom Cath; hon/W/W in E.

HARITUN, ROSALIE ANN oc/Professor of Music Education, Clarinetist; b/May 30, 1938; h/206 North Oak Street, Apartment 8, Greenville, NC 27834; ba/Greenville, NC; p/Mr and Mrs George Haritun, Great Bend, PA; ed/BME, Baldwin-Wallace Conservatory of Music, 1960; MS in Music Ed, Univ of IL Champaign-Urbana, 1961; Profl Dipl 1966, EdD 1968, Postdoct Study 1971, Tchrs Col, Columbia Univ; pa/Assoc Prof of Music Ed, Sch of Music, E Carolina Univ, 1972–; Music Instr, Title I Music Prog, NYC Bd of Ed, 1971-72; Music Ed Instr, Sch of Music, Temple Univ, 1968-71; Doct Tchg Fellow, Tchrs Col, Columbia Univ, 1966-68; Elem Instrumental Music Tchr, 1961-63; Clarinetist/Saxophonist, Greenville City Wind Orch, Greenville Pks & Rec Dept, 1975-82; Prin Clarinetist, "S Elizabeth City Opera Co, The Albermarle Players, 1981; Clarinetist, Sigma Alpha Iota Alumni Woodwind Quintet, 1970-71; Prin Clarinetist, Tchrs Col Symph Orch, Columbia Univ, 1967-68; Prin Clarinetist, Long Isl Opera Wkshop Orch, 1963-65; Choir

Dir, Adult Choir, Landmark Bapt Ch, 1975-; Pi Kappa Lambda, Pres of Beta Zeta Chapt, Sch of Music, E Carolina Univ 1977-79, 1979-81, 1981-83; Sigma Alpha Iota, Fac Advr of Beta Psi Chapt, Sch of Music, E Carolina Univ 1978-; Pres Beta Alpha Chapt 1984-86, Exec Bd Mem & Chm of World F'ship Com 1980-83, Delta Kappa Gamma; Secy/Treas Mid-Atl Chapt 1985-86, Chm of Music Ed Div 1981-83, Col Music Soc; r/Bapt; hon/Pubs, "Daily Tchg Routines: Red-Tape or Reality?" (in Press), "Basic Tchg Skills for Beginning Music Tchrs" 1977, "TV for Developing Tchg Skills" 1975, "A Sequential Approach to Behavior Objectives in Music Ed" 1974; W/W: of Am Wom, in S & SW, in Am, of Intells, of Musicians; Personalities of S; World W/W of Wom; Men & Wom of Distn; DIB.

HARMON, ALISON GENINE JONES oc/Learning Disabilities Specialist; b/Jan 18, 1953; h/1374 Northfield Drive, Mineral Ridge, OH 44440; m/Robert Foster Sr; c/Robert Foster Jr; p/Samuel (dec) and Katherine P Jones, Youngstown, OH; ed/BS in Ed, Bowling Green St Univ, 1975; EdM, Kent St Univ, 1979; Elem Adm Cert (Principalship), 1980; Cert, Univ of Ghana, Africa, 1973; pa/Tchr, Youngstown Bd of Ed, 1975-80; Elem Prin 1980-81, Lng Disabilities Resource Tchr 1981-, Girard City Schs; Nat Exec Bd Mem & MW Reg Dir, Delta Sigma Theta Sorority Inc, Local Pres 1973, 1978, Reg Rep 1974-76, Reg Nom'g Com Chp 1980, Exec Dir of Search Com 1983, Conv Planning Com 1982-83; Cath Col Wom, Mbrship Chm 1982-83; CISV, Adult Del to Norway 1979; Girard Ed Assn, Negotiating Team Mem 1984; Ballet Wn Res, Bd Mem 1983-84; Phi Delta Kappa, 1981-84; cp/Youngstown Chapt, NAACP, GRAC Com Ward Capt; Dpty Coor, Mahoning Co Jesse Jackson for Pres Campaign, 1984; Chd's Intl Sum Villages, Adult Del Representing USA to Norway 1979; Jr Clb Advr, Nat Meeting Planning Com & Bd Mem 1979-82; r/Cath; St Mary's Ch CCD, Instr & Choir Mem 1980-83; F'ship Study at the Univ of Ghana, 1973; Mortar Bd, 1974; Pres's Dist'd Ser Awd, 1975; W/W in Am Cols & Univs; Outstg Yg Wom in Am.

HARMON, KATHLEEN MARY oc/Systems Analyst; b/Mar 11, 1934; h/83 Calle Vadito, Northwest, Albuquerque, NM 87120; ba/Albuquerque, NM; c/Sandra, Victoria Jeanne, Mary Dale, Walter, William; p/Bernard F Grall; ed/LLM, Antioch Sch of Law, 1983; Bach of Univ Studies 1978, Assoc in Human Sers 1973, Univ of NM; pa/Computer Programmer 1971-75, 1980-, St Prog Admr 1975-80, Employmt Security Dept; ABWA; cp/Pres Com on Employmt of Handicapped, Gov's Com on Concerns of HCP, 1976-; Mensa; Civitan; Toastmasters; Bd Mem, Lovelace Med Ctr; Consumer Coun, Public Ser Co & Mtn Bell Telephone; NM Adv Coun on Voc Tech Ed; r/Rom Cath; hon/ABWA Wom of the Yr, 1977; Profl Handicapped Wom of the Yr, SW Dist, Pilot Clbs, 1980 & 1985; W/W of Am Wom.

HARNAD, STEVAN ROBERT oc/Research Psychobiologist; b/Jun 2, 1945; h/57 Princeton Avenue, Princeton, NJ 08540; ba/Princeton, NJ; p/Steven

Hesslein (dec) and Susan Harnad, Montreal, Canada; ed/BA w Hons in Psych 1967, MA in Psych 1969, McGill; MA in Psych, Princeton, 1971; pa/Res Psychol, NJ Bur of Res in Neurol & Psychi, 1971-73; Res Psychophysiologist 1973-75, Res Conslt 1979-83, Dept of Psychi, Rutgers Med Sch; Current Res Psychobiologist, Princeton; Editor & Fdr, *The Behavioral & Brain Scis*, Cambridge Univ Press, 1976-83; Exec Com 1977-83, Prog Chm 1981, Soc for Phil & Psych; Pubs Com, Intl Neuropsychol Soc, 1982; hon/Pubs, *Origins & Evolution of Lang & Spch* 1976, *Lateralization in the Nervous Sys* 1977, *Categorical Perception* (Forthcoming); *Peer Commentary on Peer Review* 1983, Many Articles; Canada Coun Fellow, 1969-71; Quebec Postgrad Fellow, 1969.

HARNISCH, DELWYN LYNN oc/Professor; b/Dec 15, 1949; h/507 Shurts Street, Urbana, IL 61801; ba/Champaign, IL; m/Patricia Lee; c/Harlan Fritz, Heather Lynn, Heidi Christine; p/Fritz Harnisch, Scribner, NE; ed/BS, Ed, Concordia Tchrs Col, 1971; EdM 1977, PhD 1981, Univ of IL-Urbana-Champaign; pa/Math & Sci Tchr, Dept Chm, Hong Kong Intl Sch, 1971-75; Univ of IL: Res Asst 1975-79, Res Assoc 1979-80, Asst Prof, Dept of Ednl Psych 1981-, Chp, Ofc of Ednl Testing, Res & Ser; Am Ednl Res Assn, 1975-, Asst Prog Chair 1977; Adult Ed of USA, 1975-; Nat Coun on Measurement in Ed, 1975-; Izaak Walton Leag; r/Luth; hon/Pubs, *Rdg & Lit: Am Achmt in Intl Perspective* 1981, *An Intro to Computer Applications in Stats*, 1984; "A Comparison of Appropriateness Indices" 1983, "Item Response Patterns: Applications for Ednl Practice" 1983, "Wom & Math: A Cross Nat Perspective" 1984, "The Validity of the Title I Eval & Reporting Sys" 1982, Num Others; Res to Post Awd, Adult Ed Assn of the USA, 1981; NSF Fellow, 1971.

HARPEL, THOMAS R oc/Naval Officer; b/Sep 28; p/Richard Pearl and Mary Katherine Gross Harpel; ed/Student, City Col, Sandusky, OH; mil/Joined USN, 1965, Adv'd through Grades to Chief Petty Ofcr, 1973; Assigned to Vietnam, 1966-73; pa/Alcohol & Drug Abuse Cnslr, Career Cnslr, Ldrship/Mgmt Instr, USS Ranger, 1976-; Fleet Res Assn; cp/US, Milpitas (St Dir), Jr C of C; Am Legion; Repub; hon/Decorated, Air Medal w OLC, Others; W/W in W.

HARPER, DAVID MICHAEL oc/Architect; b/Atlanta, Feb 9, 1953; ba/Miami, FL; p/Cleveland B and Mary Ruth Harper, Forest Park, GA; ed/BArch, Univ of Miami, 1974; Grad, Inst for Arch & Urban Studies, Mus of Mod Art, NYC, 1974; pa/Designer, Peter Vanderklaauw Archs, Miami, 1974-75; Supvr of Arch Design, Burger King Corp, Miami, 1975-77; Asst to Pres, Dir of Bus Devel, Ferendino, Grafton, Spillis, Candela Archs, Coral Gables, 1977-79; Pres & Chm of Bd, Harper & Buzinec Archs/Engrs Inc, Miami, 1979-; Reg'd Arch, St of FL; AIA, 1977-, Bd of Dirs 1980-83; S Fl Chapt AIA Bd of Dirs, 1981-84; Vis'g Lectr, FL St Univ Grad Sch of Bus, 1982; Soc Mktg Profl Sers, 1978-; Omicron Delta Kappa, Lambda Chi Alpha; cp/Trustee, Gtr Miami C of C, 1984-; Gov's Clb of FL, 1982-; hon/Prin Wks incl Over 100 Projs

in FL from Pensacola to Key West: Schs, Justice Facilities, Mil Projs, Ofc & Comml Bldgs, Mult-fam Housing & Hosps; Overseas Projs in: PR, Mid-E & Guantanamo Bay, Cuba; Recip, Alpha Rho Chi Medal in Arch, Univ of Miami, 1975; Randolph Wedding Design Awd, 1974; Featured in & Named one of 41 to watch in 1981, *Miami Mag*; Featured in May 1984 "Achiever" Sect of *FL Trend Mag*; First Prize, Design, Competition for HQs Bldg for the FL Reg AIA, Tallahassee, 1982; Nat AIA/ACA Cit of Design Excell for 100 Man Commun Correctional Ctr, Jacksonville, FL, 1984; Nat AIA/ACA Cit of Design Excell for 1000 Bed Pre-Trail Stockade Facility, Miami, 1984; Selected by AIA among 20 Firms in US Achieving Excell in the Art & Bus of Arch, 1984.

HARPER, JOAN oc/Assistant Vice-President and Cashier; b/Mar 5, 1937; h/2035-10th Northwest, Ardmore, OK 73401; ba/Ardmore, OK; m/Bob; c/Kelly Rae, Robert Christian; p/Joe and Raeburn Volino, Ardmore, OK; ed/Dipl, Dickson HS, 1955; Dipl in Bkg, The Sch for Bk Adm, Univ of WI, 1983; pa/Secy, Gulf Oil Co, 1955-56; Secy, El Paso Nat Gas Prods Co, 1956-58; Secy, Frankfort Oil Co, 1958-61; Bk Teller, Nat Bk of Verden, 1962-64; Bk Teller, Lincoln Bk & Trust Co, 1964-65; Asst VPres & Cashier, Exch Nat Bk & Trust Co, 1966-; Bk Adm Inst, So OK Chapt, Secy 1981-83, Pres 1983-84; Am Inst of Bkg, Chickasaw Study Grp, Murray St Col, VP 1982-83; cp/Cancer & Heart Funds; Lung Assn; U Way; OES; r/Adm Bd Mem, First U Meth Ch, 1982-; hon/Valedictorian of Grad'g Class, 1955; Recip, Am Bkrs Assn Pres Cit, Exch Nat Bk, Ardmore, OK, 1984.

HARPER, NANCY LEA oc/Associate Dean of Liberal Arts; b/Feb 27, 1947; h/10 Glendale Court, Iowa City, IA; ba/Iowa City, IA; p/Joe and Willa Brown, Kansas Ness City, KS; ed/BA, Eng & Spch, Emporia St Univ, 1969; MA, Eng Composition & Lit, Univ of No IA, 1970; PhD, Communication Theory & Rhetoric, Univ of IA, 1973; pa/Asst Prof of Communication, Rutgers Univ, 1973-76; Asst Prof of Jour & Mass Communication, Hd of Mass Communication 1976-78, Asst Dean of Liberal Arts 1978-82, Assoc Dean of Liberal Arts 1982-, Assoc Prof of Communication 1979-, Univ of IA; Intl Communication Assn, 1973-; Spch Communication Assn, 1972-; AAUP, 1973-, Mem of Nom'g Com 1978, Chair of Task Force on Essentials of Ed 1980, Referee for Var Conv Progs & Jours; Rep to US Dept of Ed, 1982; Assn for Commun Adm; hon/Pubs, *The Clusters Source Book: Balancing Career Preparation & Liberal Learning* 1981, *Human Communication Theory: The Hist of a Paradigm* 1981, "Promoting the Dept to Outside Agencies: What Do Communication Majs Know & What Can They Do?" 1982, "The Spch Communication Assn Campaign for the Essentials: A Preliminary Report" 1980, Num Others; Univ of IA Grants, 1973, 1977, 1982; NW Area Foun Grant for Proj on Liberal Arts & Employmt, 1979-81; NEH Grant, 1980; Outstg Yg Wom of Am; W/W of Am Wom; World W/W of Wom.

HARRELL, PAULA DENISE oc/Instructor of Piano; b/Oct 10, 1954; h/123-C Village Lane, Greensboro, NC

27409; ba/Greensboro, NC; p/Mr and Mrs John D Harrell Jr, Durham, NC; ed/BA, Music, NC Ctl Univ, 1976; MM, Ch Music, OH St Univ, 1978; pa/Instr in Piano/Organ, NC A&T St Univ, 1983–; Music Instr, Fairmont City Sch Sys, 1979-83; Organist, First Bapt Ch, Fairmont, 1979-81; Pvt Piano Studio, Fairmont, 1979-83; Asst Choral Dir, NC Gov's Sch-E, Sums 1980-81; Organist/ Pianist, White Rock Bapt Ch, 1971-76; Secy, Duke Univ Med Sch, 1978-79; Organist, Parkview U Meth Ch, 1976-78; NC Music Edrs Assn; Music Edrs Nat Conf, NEA, 1979–; PTA Exec Coun, 1980-82; hon/Durham Wom's Clb Piano Composition Winner, 1972; Am Legion Girls St Rep, 1971; Madge Hargraves Fam and Ch Ser Awd, 1972; Hillside High Hon Grad, 1972; Delta Sigma Theta S'ship, 1972; Alpha Kappa Mu Hon Soc, 1975-77; Black Enterprise Mag, Top 100 Black Col Students, 1975-76; NC Ctl Univ Ruth Edwards S'ship to Outstg Sr Music Maj, 1975-76; Choir Accompanist Awd, 1976; Student Govt Assn Awd, 1976; Univ Hons Prog, 1972-76; Campus Echo Student of the Month, 1976; Tau Gamma Delta Community Ser Awd, 1976; Fairmont Jr Wom's Clb, Hon for Achmt in Ed, 1981; Fairmont Elem Tchr of the Yr, 1981-82; Outstg Yg Wom of Am.

HARRIES, KARSTEN oc/Professor of Philosophy; b/Jan 25, 1937; h/16 Morris Street, Hamden, CT 06517; ba/ New Haven, CT; m/Elizabeth Wanning; c/Lisa, Peter, Martin; p/Wolfgang (dec) and Ilse Harries, Orlando, FL; ed/BA 1958, PhD 1962, Yale Univ; pa/Instr, Yale Univ, 1961-63; Asst Prof, Univ of TX-Austin, 1963-65; Asst Prof 1965-66, Assoc Prof 1966-70, Prof 1970–, Chm of Dept of Phil 1973-78, Yale Univ; Lectr, Univ of Bonn, Germany, Winter Semesters 1965 & 1968; AAUP; Am Philosophical Assn; Soc for Phenomenology & Existential Phil; Am Soc for Aesthetics; hon/Pubs, The Meaning of Modern Art 1968, The Bavarian Rococo Church: Between Faith & Aestheticism 1983, Over 50 Articles & Reviews; Guggenheim F'ship, 1971-72.

HARRINGTON, FRANCES T oc/ Assistant Professor; b/Aug 27, 1946; h/ 102 Ivy Lane, Petersburg, VA 23805; ba/Petersburg, VA; c/Franz; p/Mr and Mrs David Taylor Sr, Lillington, NC; ed/BS 1968, EdM 1971, NC Ctl Univ; Grad Study, Univ of SC Columbia; PhD, So IL Univ, 1983; pa/Current Asst Prof, VA St Univ; Grad Asst of Spec Ed Dept & Res & Tchr Asst/Doct Rep to Fac 1983, Grad Asst & Spec Ed Tchr Asst 1982, Instr of Dept of Spec Ed 1982, Grad Asst of Spec Ed Res & Tchr Asst 1981, So IL Univ; Asst Prof, Spec Ed, SC St Col, 1976-81; Prin Investigator, 1890's Res, "An Invest of Communication in Rural Chd," SC St Col, 1978; Instr, Claflin Col, 1976; Instr, SC St Col, 1973-76; Cnslr, NC Dept of Voc Rehab, 1972-73; Other Previous Positions; CEC; NEA; Phi Delta Kappa; r/Bapt; hon/Res & Pubs, "Race, Presence of IQ Info, Tchr Behavior Rating Info, Perceived Disability & Profl Role Title of the Rater in the Placement of Behavior Disordered Students" 1983, "The Effects of Psychotic Parents Upon Fam Relat'ships: A Review" 1981, "Developing Quantitative & Qualitative Arithmetic Concepts in Educable Retarded

Yth" 1970; Grad F'ship, NC Ctl Univ, 1969; Outstg Wom of Am; Outstg Edrs of Am.

HARRINGTON, SANDRA MAY oc/ Teacher; b/Sep 21, 1948; h/1224 Palmetto Road, Box 5, Eustis, FL 32726; ba/Mt Dora, FL; p/James Jerome and Julia Harrington, Eustis, FL; ed/AA, Niagara Co Commun Col, 1968; BS, St Univ Col at Buffalo, 1970; MS, Nova Univ, 1979; pa/Tchr, Trainable Mtlly Handicapped 1971-78, Tchr, Educable Mtlly Handicapped 1978-81, Okeechobee Co; Dean of Students, Okeechobee HS, 1981-82; Dean of Students, Okeechobee Jr HS, 1982-83; Tchr, Varying Exceptionalities, Mt Dojra HLS, 1983–; FL Assn Sch Admrs, 1981-83; Assn for Supvn & Curric Devel, 1980–; CEC, 1971–, VP of Tri-Co Sect 1972-73, Pres of Okeechobee Sect 1973-74; PTSA, 1981-83; Spec Olympics Game Com, 1982-83; BPW Clb of Mt Dora, FL, 1983–; hon/Tchg Idea in Another 100 Winning Ideas, 1979; Entricy Herald Achmt Awd, 1968; Student Govt Awd, 1968; FL Dept of Ed Grantee, 1976; Cert of Apprec, Okeechobee Cub Scouts, 1977; Winner of the FL Lrng Resource Sys Alpha Contest, 1979; Perfect Grade Point Average at Nova Univ; W/W of Am Wom.

HARRIS, DIANNE oc/Staff Development Specialist, Equal Employment Opportunity Coordinator; b/Jan 21, 1953; h/914 Delachaise Street, New Orleans, LA 70115; ba/New Orleans, LA; m/Ellsworth Jr; c/Deanna Andrienne, Erroll Joseph; p/Mr and Mrs Sandy McFarland, New Orleans, LA; ed/ BS in Nsg, 1975; Lic'd and Cert'd Nsg Home Admr, 1982; pa/RN Appt, VA Hosp, 1975; Grad Nurse, Flint Goodridge Hosp, 1976; Adm Asst, Ray Newman & Assocs, 1980; Staff Devel Spec, 1980–; EEO Coor, EEO; Am Soc for Tng and Devel; Nat Assn for Female Execs Inc; cp/Gospel Music Wkshop, Med Ser Dept, James Cleveland Foun; Elks; BPOE of W; Yg Wom of Distn Temple #1291, Treas, Preceptor; Am Foun for Negro Affairs of NO, LA; Mayor's Sum YH Employmt Prog; r/ Bapt; hon/W/W in S & SW.

HARRIS, GEORGIA JACOBS oc/ Antiques Shop Owner, Antiques Show Promoter; b/Feb 8, 1920; h/PO Box 187, Columbus, TX 78934; ba/Same; m/ Volum Lawrence (dec); c/Patricia Georgia, Martha Ann, Janice Marie, Kathryn Jane; p/Lee Thomas and Lillie Deliah Walker Jacobs (dec); ed/Self-Educated; pa/Opened Antiques Shop, Schulenburg, TX, 1945; 38 Yrs in Antique Bus, Columbus, TX, 1950–; Charity Antiques Shows: Columbus (TX) Charity Show 1964, Chappell Hill (TX) Heritage Show, La Grange (TX) Charity Show, Gonzales (TX) C of C Show, San Marcos (TX) Heritage Show, Sharpstown Mall Show, Brenham (TX) Hist Soc Show; r/Bapt; hon/W/W: of Am Bus Wom, in S & SW, of Am Wom.

HARRIS, LEE KELLY oc/Banker; b/ Jun 22, 1935; h/27581 Tres Vistas, Mission Viejo, CA 92692; ba/Santa Ana, CA; m/Ruby Lee; c/Lee K Jr, Bradford W; p/Mrs Gwen A Harris, Columbus, NE; ed/MS in Mgmt, US Naval Postgrad Sch, 1966; BS in Bus Adm, Univ of NE, 1956; mil/USN, 1956-58, 1961-68 (Nav Aviator Designated 1961); Ret'd Capt; pa/Exec VPres, Wesbay Capital Corp,

1984–; Sr VP & Br Admr, Westlands Bk, 1982-84; VP & Reg Credit Admr, Am City Bk, 1980-82; VP, U CA Bk, 1969-80; Pres, Bk of Monroe, 1968-69; Life Mem, Sigma Chi Frat, Prior Active Chapt Consul; Assn of Naval Aviators; Naval Resv Assn; Univ Ath Clb; r/Prot; hon/W/W: in Fin & Indust, in World, in Orange Co, in Aviation & Aerospace, of Intells; Men of Achmt.

HARRIS, LOUISE oc/Researcher, Writer; h/395 Angell Street, Providence, RI 02906; ba/Providence, RI; p/ Samuel P and Faustine M Borden Harris (dec); ed/AB, Brown Univ; Pvt Organ Study; pa/Rschr, Curator, C A Stephens Col; Tchr, Recitalist of Organ & Piano, 1928-42; Music Career, 1930-50; Genealogy 1956-61, Rschr 1961–; Life Mem, Am Guild of Organists; Smithsonian Assocs; Res Wk of "Youth Companion"; cp/Am Heritage Soc; Nat Trust for Hist Presv; Nat Wildlife; Hist Socs: Nat, E Providence; Wkg for Better Flag Laws & Correcting Author of Pledge of Allegiance for 1976, Writing Stories on Authorship of Pledge for Pub; Wn RI Civic Hist Soc; Brown Alumnae; 1st Fdr, Med Sch at Brown Univ; Elected to Corp of RI Hosp; Vol Wkr w Chd; r/Prot; Ch Organist; hon/ Life Fellow: Intercont Biogl Assn, Intl Inst for Commun Sers; Life Patron, Intl Biogl Assn; Lib of Human Resources of Am Bicent Res Inst; Charter Mem, Chancellor's Coun, 1982; Pub'd Author, Num Books & Compiled Books of C A Stephens, Collection Brown Univ; Num Dipls, Certs of Merit, Medals, Plaques, Var England Dics & Hon Socs; Book of Hon; Commun Ldrs & Noteworthy Ams.

HARRIS, PAULETTE PROCTOR oc/ Faculty Member of School of Education; b/Oct 5, 1949; h/3033 Park Avenue, Augusta, GA 30909; ba/Augusta, GA; m/Kenneth Lamar Harris; p/Paul Eugene (dec) and Ilma Hankinson Proctor, Augusta, GA; ed/BA in Elem Ed & French 1971, EdM in Elem Ed & Gifted Ed 1974, Augusta Col; DEd, Univ of SC, 1983; pa/Tchr, Remedial Rdg Instr, Instrnl Lead Tchr, Ednl Diagnostician, Richmond Co Bd of Ed, 1971-78; Fac, Sch of Ed, Augusta Col, 1978–; Rho Chapt, Delta Kappa Gamma, Corres'g Secy 1980–; Phi Delta Kappa, CSRA Chapt Res Ofcr 1981-82; IRA, CSRA Chapt Mbrship Chm 1982-83; NCTE; AAUW; GA IRA; r/Prot; hon/Author of Articles Pub'd in Eric, 1980–; Tchr of the Yr, Houghton Elem, 1974; Dean's List, Augusta Col, 1967-71; W/W in S & SW.

HARRIS, WILLIAM H oc/College President; b/Jul 22, 1944; h/1238 Beman Street, Augusta, GA 30904; ba/ Augusta, GA; m/Wanda F; c/Cynthia Maria, William James; p/Mrs Sallie Harris, Fitzgerald, GA; ed/BA, Paine Col, 1966; MA 1967, PhD 1973, IN Univ; pa/Instr of Hist, Paine Col, 1967-69; Assoc Instr of Hist 1969-71, Lectr in Hist 1972-73, Asst Prof of Hist 1973-77, Acting Affirmative Action Ofcr 1977-78, Assoc Prof of Hist 1977-81, Dir of CIC Minorities F'ships Prog 1977-82, Assoc Dean of Grad Sch 1979-82, Prof of Hist 1982, IN Univ; Current Col Pres, Paine Col; Org of Am Histns, 1980-82; Assn of Grad Schs, 1980–; UNCF's Strengthening the Humanities Prog, 1980–; Exec Coun, Assn for Study of Afro-Am Life & Hist,

1980-; cp/CoChm, Bloomington Proj Commitment, 1972-; Bloomington Bd of Public Safety, 1975-78; r/Christian Meth Epis; hon/Pubs, *Keeping the Faith: A Philip Randolph, Milton P Webster, & the Brotherhood of Sleeping Car Porters, 1925-37* 1977, *The Harder We Run: Black Workers Since the Civil War* 1982; So F'ships Fund Fellow, 1970-71; Fulbright Fellow, 1978-79; ACLS Fellow, 1979-80.

HARRIS-NOEL, ANN GRAETSCH oc/College Professor, Private Consultant; h/535 East Judson Avenue, Youngstown, OH 44502; ba/Youngstown, OH; m/C Dale Noel; c/Laurie Ann Harris, Kelli Beth Harris; p/Albert and Hattie Graetsch (dec); ed/BS in Geol, Kent St Univ, 1956; MS in Geol, Miami Univ, 1959; Addit Wk, Argonne Nat Lab, VPI, OH St Univ, NM St Univ; pa/ Res Engr, Ferro Corp 1958, US Geol Survey 1959; Col Prof, Youngstown St Univ, 1961-; Consltg, 1977-; OH Acad of Sci, Fellow; Sigma Xi; N Am Thermal Anal Soc, Charter Mem; Am Inst of Profl Geologists; Nat Assn of Geol Tchrs; No OH Geol Soc; Geol Soc of Am; Mem, Phi Kappa Phi; r/Meth; hon/ Pubs, *Geol of Nat Pks* 1975, 1977, 1983, "The Amazonites of CO" 1979; Wom of the Yr, YWCA, 1978; Dist'd Prof- 'ship, Youngstown St Univ, 1978; Jefferson Awd, 1981; Public Ser Wom's Repub Clb, 1983; Appt'd to Adv Comm on Energy, by Gov Celeste of OH, 1984-87; W/W of Am Wom.

HARRISON, CYNTHIA GANT oc/ Teacher; b/Dec 27, 1954; h/3004 Stafford Street, Shreveport, LA 71107; ba/ Shreveport, LA; m/Willie Jr; p/Mr and Mrs Jacob Gant, Shreveport, LA; ed/BA in Eng & Social Studies, cum laude, LA Tech Univ, 1976; EdM in Adm & Supvn, So Univ, 1981; Postgrad Studies, LA St Univ, 1981-; pa/Tchr of Eng & Social Studies 1976-, Softball Coach, Asst Track Coach & Dir of Green Oaks Dance Troupe & Highsteppers 1977-81, Green Oaks Flag Corps 1977-82, Green Oaks HS; Asst Rec Dir, Caddo Commun Action Agy, 1979-80; 1st Female Police Aux Ofcr, Shreveport Civil Def, 1980; PTA; NEA; LA Edrs Assn; Caddo Ed Assn; Caddo Coun of Tchrs of Eng; Sigma Tau Delta, Eng Frat; Zeta Phi Beta Sorority Inc; cp/Cooper Road Civic Clb; Citizen Study Com, City-Parish Govts; r/Bapt; hon/Caddo Rookie Tchr Nom, 1976; Tchr of Distn, 1977-78; Edr of the Yr, 1978-79; Outstg LA Edr, 1981; W/W Among Am Wom.

HARRISON, HANNAH JANE oc/ Coloratura Soprano, Pianist, Rancher, Movie Extra; h/5201 Franklin Road, Nashville, TN 37220; p/Orval and Lena McKenzie Harrison, Parma, MO; ed/BS in Ed, SE MO St Univ, 1973; EdM, Music Ed, Univ of MO, 1975; Grad Studies, IN Univ 1976-77; Att'd, George Peabody Col for Tchrs of Vanderbilt Univ 1978-80, Memphis St Univ 1978, Vanderbilt Univ 1979; Pupil of Voice, Virginia Pyle (MO), Roger Havranek (IN), Richard Paige (TN), Louis Nicholas (TN); Pupil of Master Voice, Eileen Farrell, The Met, IN; Pupil of Voice, David Blackburn, NY & TN; Pupil of Piano, Richard Morris, OH, Col Conservatory of Cinc; pa/Tchr, New Madrid Co Enlarged Sch Dist; Tchr, w The Branton Agy, 1984; Coloratura Soprano, The Nashville Symp & The Nashville Opera Guild, Opera, *Madame*

Butterfly (Puccini), 1981; Soprano Soloist for Var Chs; Coloratura Soprano, St George's Epis Ch; Appeared in Movies, *Country Gold*, *Living Proof*, *What Comes Around*; Appeared on TV, "Boone," "You Can Be a Star," "Symph Sunday" Benefit; Pianist, Ch, Weddings, Profs' Tea, Benefit Fashion Show, Accompanist for Soloists; The Metro Opera Guild, 1977-85; Alpha Delta Pi Alumni Clb; Alpha Delta Pi, VP, Chaplain, Efficiency Chm; Univ Players; Student Nat Ed Assn; MO St Tchrs Assn; Assn for Childhood Ed; Student Senate; MENC; Assn of Wom Students; Nashville Symph Chorus, 1980-84; Dist Choir; Quad-St Chorus; Bicent Choir; Collegium Musicum; Coloratura Soprano, Vine St Christian Ch Choir, First U Meth Ch Choir; Nashville Symph Chamber Chorus, 1980-82; (Robert Shaw) Fest Chorus; cp/Capitol Clb of TN, 1985; Yg Repubs, 1980-85; Gov's Com, 1982; r/Meth; hon/Hon TN Col; Curator's Awd; Regent's S'ship; Salutatorian; APAKAW, Hon Soc; S'ship Awd; Recog on OH Psychol Test; Descendant of Thomas Jefferson, 3rd Pres of the US.

HARRISON, JOSEPH oc/Attorney, University Teacher, Writer; b/Sep 26, 1956; h/Apartment 148, 2020 Continental, Tallahassee, FL; ba/Same; p/ Howard and Lillian Harrison; ed/Dr of Jurisp, Vanderbilt Univ Sch of Law, 1982; MS, Criminology, FL St Univ, 1978; BA, St Univ of NY, 1976; pa/Med/ Legal Rschr, Tallahassee, FL, 1984-; Instr, FL St Univ, 1977-78; Res Assoc, Tel Aviv Univ Law Fac, 1975-76; ABA; Acad of Crim Justice Scis; cp/Assn for Humanist Sociol; Greenpeace; World Wildlife Fdn; Omega Inst for Holistic Studies; hon/Pubs, "New Evidence in Psychopharm as it Relates to Critical Criminology" 1982, "Endorphins & Legal Issues" 1981, "White-Collar & High-Level & Corporate Criminality" 1981, "Illegal Drug Use by Israeli Yth" 1975.

HARRISON, YVONNE E oc/Director, Research and Development; b/Apr 29, 1939; h/17 Clearview Road, East Brunswick, NJ 08816; ba/Hoffmann-La Roche Inc, Nutley, NJ 07110; m/Dr Melvin C Johnson; p/Herman Hugo and Georgia Mae Hall Harrison (dec); ed/BS in Zool, Howard Univ, 1959; MA in Pharm 1970, PhD in Pharm 1972, Howard Univ Col of Med; pa/Dir, Res & Devel Coordination 1984-, Dir, Pharm Res & Devel Coordination 1983-84, Asst Dir, Dept of Pharm Res & Devel 1980-83, Asst Dir, Dept of Exptl Therapeutics 1974-80, Biol Res Coor, Dept of Biol Res, 1972-74, Hoffmann-La Roche Inc; Res Assoc, Dept of Pharm, Howard Univ Col of Med, 1970-72; Res Asst, Wellcome Res Labs, Burroughs Wellcome Co, 1964-69; AAAS; Am Mgmt Assn; Am Men & Wom of Sci; Am Pharm Assn Acad of Pharm Scis; Am Physiol Soc; Am Soc for Pharm & Exptl Therapeutics; Assn for Wom in Sci; Consumer Hlth Info & Resource Ctr, NYC, Bd of Dirs 1981-; Fdn of Am Scists; Fdn of Am Socs for Exptl Biol; Intl Soc of Ecotoxicology & Envir Safety; NY Acad of Scis; Sigma Xi; Soc of Res Admrs; r/Epis; hon/Pubs, "Stimulatory Effect of Charcoal Broiled Hamburgers on the Hydroxylation of 3, 4-Benzpyrene by

Enzymes in Rat Liver & Placenta" 1971, "An Exptl Model in Dogs for Studying Interaction of Drugs w Bishydroxycoumarin" 1969, "Stimulatory Effects of Cigarette Smoking on the Hydroxylation of 3,4-Benzpyrene & the N-Demethylation of 3-Methyl-4-Mono-Methylaminozao-Benzene by Enzymes in Human Placenta" 1969, Others; YMCA of NY Black Achiever in Indust, 1974; YWCA Twin Tribute to Wom in Indust, 1975; Nat Assn for Equal Opport in Higher Ed Dist'd Alumni Awd, 1983; Am Men & Wom of Sci; W/W: in E, of Am Wom, in Frontier Sci & Technol.

HART, B SAM oc/Minister of the Gospel; b/Apr 8, 1931; h/6701 Cresheim Road, Philadelphia, PA 19119; ba/ Philadelphia, PA; m/Joyce E; c/Sharon R, D Anthony, Robert S, Randall G, Patrice D; p/Mr and Mrs Arthur I Hart (dec); ed/Master's Equivalence, 1966; Hon DDiv, 1968; pa/Dir, Fdr, "Grand Old Gospel Hour," 1962-; Tchr, Phila Public Schs, 1958-68; Fdr, Pres, Grand Old Gospel F'ship Inc, 1961-; Fdr, Pres, Radio Sta WYIS, Hart Broadcasting Co Inc, 1976-; Calvary Gospel Chapel, Fdr & Pastor 1960-73; Camp Skymount, Dir 1970-77; Germantown Christian Assem Inc, Fdr & Pastor 1973-81; Montgomery Co Bible F'ship, Fdr & Pastor 1981-; r/Indep; hon/Pub, *Real Soul Food*, Daily Bible Study Guide, 1977-; Nat Rel Broadcasters, Awd of Merit, 1976; Christian F'ship Ctr, 1972; Phila Col of Bible, 1981; Mayor of Phila, 1981.

HART, LOIS BORLAND oc/Public Speaker, Author, Publisher; b/May 15, 1941; h/PO Box 320, 119 Longs Peak Drive, Lyons, CO 80540; ba/Same; m/ Arnold L; c/Christopher, Richard; p/ Leslie and Laura Randolph Borland, Edgewater, FL; ed/EdD, Univ of MA Amherst, 1974; MS, Syracuse Univ, 1972; BS, Univ of Rochester, 1966; pa/ Pres, Ldrship Dynamics, 1980-; Tnr, Mtn Sts Employers Coun, 1979-80; Pres, Orgl Ldrship Inc, 1977-80; Field Sers Coor, Univ of MI Ann Arbor, 1975-77; Am Soc of Tng & Devel; AAUW; cp/Toastmasters Intl; NOW; Redstone Mus in Lyons, CO, Bd Mem; hon/Pubs: *The Computer Quest Series*, 1985; *Saying Hello: Getting Your Grp Started* 1983; *Saying Goodbye: Ending a Grp Experience* 1983; *The Sexes at Wk* 1983, *Moving Up! Wom & Ldrship* 1981, *Lrng from Conflict* 1980, *Conf & Wkshop Planners' Manual* 1979; Am Field Ser, Ams' Abroad Prog to Greece, 1958; W/W in W, of Am Wom.

HART, MARGIE RUTH oc/Publisher; b/Oct 28, 1943; h/36832 Colby Avenue, Barstow, CA 92311; ba/Barstow, CA; m/Len; c/Chipman D, Sandra L, Karen J, Richard W, Leonard P, Carl S; p/Lonnie and Carrie Sellers, Cheraw, SC; ed/Att'd, Greenville Tech 1964-65, Barstow Jr Col 1983; pa/Asst Mgr, D & L Assocs, 1977-78; Br Mgr, Caroline Emmons Jewelry Co, 1978-79; Microwave Sales Spec, Whirlpool Corp, 1979; Sales Rep, Cleaves Ofc Prods, 1979; Asst Mgr, Publisher, *The Am Patriot Mag*, 1982; Cand for St Assem, 61st Dist, CA, 1984; Subst Tchr, Pickens Jr High, 1975-79; cp/Chwom, 1st Supervisorial Dist of San Bernardino Co, CA, for the Am Indep Party, 1983-; PTA, 1978; Congl Dist Coor, Freedom Coun; Concerned Wom for Am; Moral Majority;

r/Indep Bapt; hon/Regular Column, "Margie's Corner" in *The American Patriot Magazine*; Good Establishment Cert, Picken, SC, 1977; Certs of Apprec, PTA, 1978; Second Amendment Foun, 1982; W/W in W.

HART, PATRICIA JOYCE STONE oc/Director of Middle Grades; b/Mar 28, 1929; h/Route 3, Box 102, Vale, NC 28168; ba/Newton, NC; m/Paul Marshall; c/Richard Edward, Sandra Kay, Susan Gay; p/William E and Edna I'Dell Stone (dec); ed/BA, Carson-Newman Col, 1953; MA 1974, EdS 1975, Appalachian St Univ; ArtsD, Univ of Ctl AZ, 1978; pa/6th Grade Tchr, Centerville Elem Sch, 1957-59; 7th & 8th Grade Tchr, San Rafael Jr High, 1959-61; Spec Ed Tchr, Salem Elem Sch, 1961-62; Tchr, Edneyville Elem Sch, 1964-66; Tchr, Drama, Eng, Rdg, Davie Co HS, 1966-76; Rdg Coor, Catawba Co Schs, 1976-81; Mid Grades Dir, Catawba Co Schs, 1981-; Delta Kappa Gamma; Phi Delta Kappa; NC Assn of Suprvs & Admrs; Nat Mid Sch Leag; Assn of Supvn & Curric Devel; NC IRA, Rec'g Secy 1979-81, VP-Elect 1981-82, VP 1982-83, Pres 1984; r/Meth; hon/Davie Co Tchr of the Yr, 1974; Davie Co Terry Sanford Awd Nom, 1975; W/W in S & SW; Personalities of S.

HART, WILLIAM BRANTLEY oc/Executive; b/Nov 19, 1935; h/1246 Nancy Lee Way, Decatur, GA 30035; ba/Atlanta, GA; m/Salena Watson Clark; c/William Jr; p/Francis M (dec) and Frances H Hart, Anderson, SC; ed/LLM 1972, LLB 1969, Atlanta Law Sch; BS in Bus Adm, Presb Col, 1957; Deg, LA St Univ Sch of Bkg, 1966; Grad, Adv'd Mgmt Course, Am Mgmt Assn, 1970; Grad Cert, Comml Bkg, Am Inst of Bkg, 1961; mil/Capt, AUS Armor; pa/Current Grp VP & Dir of Spec Compensation, Var Other Positions 1957-, First Nat Bk of Atlanta; Pres, Presb Col Alumni Assn, 1971, Bd of Dirs 1970-72; Presb Col Bd of Visitors, 1975-77, Bd of Trustees 1978-, Pres Search Com 1978-79, Chm of Hon Degs Comm 1982-83; cp/Trustee, Thornwell Home for Chd, 1978-; r/Elder, Presb Ch; Atlanta Presb Coun, 1972-76, 1981-, Chm of Div of Adm 1975, 1982-83, Chm of Coun 1976; hon/Alumni Ser Awd, 1972; W/W in S & SE; Personalities of S; Atlanta Neighbor of the Month.

HARTLAGE, LAWRENCE C oc/Professor of Neurology; b/May 11, 1934; h/Shenandoah Stables, Evans, GA 30809; ba/Augusta, GA; m/Patricia L; p/Cliften P and Mary L Hartlage, Coguina Key, FL; ed/BSc, OH St Univ, 1959; MA 1962, PhD 1967, Univ of Louisville; mil/AUS, 1956-58; pa/Asst Prof of Neurol, IN Univ Med Ctr, 1970-72; Prof, Med Col of GA, 1972-; Nat Assoc of Neuropsychols, Pres 1978-80; hon/Author, *Mtl Devel Eval of the Pediatric Patient* 1973, Num Profl Pubs; Fellow, Am Psychol Assn, 1976; W/W in Am; World W/W.

HARTMAN, MAURICE GEORGE oc/Systems Engineer; b/Dec 15, 1940; h/2709 Bayberry Way, Fullerton, CA 92633; ba/Fullerton, CA; m/Theona Catherine Popp; c/Joy Charlene, Douglas Alan; p/Mrs V M Hartman, Ft Wayne, IN; ed/BS, Engrg Math, Purdue Univ, 1964; MS, Engrg Math, Univ of Tulsa, 1966; Postgrad Studies, Jt Ctr for Grad Studies, WA/OR, 1976-77; pa/

Engrg Analyst, Universal Oil Prods Co, 1966-73; Sr Engr, Westinghouse, 1973-75; Sr Engr, Exxon Nuclear Co, 1975-77; Sr Res Scist, Battelle Pacific NW Labs, 1977-78; Engrg Tech Staff, Aerospace Corp, 1978-82; Sys Engr, Hughes Aircraft Co, 1982-; Mem: VChm, Anaheim CBMC; Fdr & Chm, Crusade for Life Inc of N Orange Co; Fdr & Past Pres, Aerospace Corp Employees Assn, Making a Difference Clb; Bd Mem, Hughes Employees Assn Bible Clb; AIAA; INMM; ANS; AMS; SIAM; MAA; r/Christian; hon/Contbr, Articles to Profl Jours; Kappa Kappa Psi, Nat Hon Music Frat, 1962; Kappa Mu Epsilon, Nat Hon for Math, 1966; W/W: in W, in MW.

HARTMAN, NANCY LEE oc/Physician; b/Jul 29, 1951; h/PO Box 98, Roslyn, NY 11576; p/Mr and Mrs Richard L Hartman, Lockhaven, PA; ed/MD, The Am Univ of the Caribbean, 1981; MS, Med Biol, C W Post Ctr, LI Univ, 1977; BA, Biol, Lycoming Col, 1974; AA, Med Technol, Harcum Jr Col, 1971; pa/First Yr Resident; MD; Microbiologist; Med Biologist; Med Technologist; Microbiol Lab, N Shore Hosp, 1981-82; Paramedic, Porta Medic, 1981-82; Lab Supvr, CLI Labs Inc, 1981-82; Pt-time Wk in Hematology Lab, Nat Hlth Labs Inc, 1982; Started, Org'd & Supervised Microbiol Dept, N Shore Labs Inc, 1976-78; Mbrships: Am Soc for Microbiol, 1976; Am Soc of Clin Pathols, 1974; Intl Platform Assn; NY Acad of Scis; hon/Recip, Allied Hlth Professions Traineeship Grant, 1975-77; W/W: of Am Wom, in Am; World W/W of Wom; Intl W/W of Intells; Foremost Wom of Twentieth Cent; 5000 Personalities of the World; Dir of Dist'd Ams.

HARTMANN, BRUCE oc/Research Physicist; b/Jun 30, 1938; h/10614 Dunkirk Drive, Silver Spring, MD 20902; ba/Silver Spring, MD; m/Judith; c/Eric, Lisa, Kevin; p/Mrs Helen Hartmann, Dickeys Mt, PA; ed/BA, Physics, cum laude, Cath Univ, 1960; MS, Physics, Univ of MD, 1966; PhD, Physics, Am Univ, 1971; pa/Res Physicist, Nav Ordnance Lab, 1960-75; Hd, Polymer Physics Grp, Nav Surface Weapons Ctr, 1975-; Am Phy Soc; Soc of Rheology; Acoustical Soc of Am; Phi Beta Kappa; hon/Author, Num Pubs in Profl Jours, incl'g, *Jour of Chem Physics*, *Jour of Applied Physics*, *Jour Acoustical Society of Am*, *Jour of Applied Polymer Sci*, Others; Merit Pay Perf Awd, 1981; Sustained Superior Perf Awd, 1982; Am Men & Wom of Sci; W/W: in E, in Frontier Sci & Technol.

HARTNETT, VIVIAN C CHASE oc/Homemaker; b/Jul 8, 1918; h/225 Hillard Avenue, Warwick, RI 02886; m/Joseph Arthur; c/Muriel Harriet Hartnett Wright, James Arthur; p/Horatio Thaddeus Sr and Flora B Leonard Chase (dec); ed/HS Grad; One Yr Step-Up Course; Night Ednl Class, 1969-70; Christian Ed Classes, 14 Yrs; mil/US Cadet Nurse Corps; pa/Child Care, 60 Yrs; Pres Wkr, Lew Mfg Co, 1938-43; Def Plant Wiring Liberty Ships Panels, Hamel & Dahl, 1943; Student Nurse, US Cadet Corps, 1945; Ofc Secy, Greenwood Commun Ch, Presb, 1961-69; cp/Franklin Mint Collectors Soc, Charter Mem; Smithsonian Instn, Assoc Mem for 10 Yrs; Nat Soc DAR,

Jr Mbrship, Lineage Res 1974-77, 1983-86, Constit Wk Com 1974-77, US of Am Bicent 1974-77, Registrar 1978-84, Recording Secy, Vice Regent, Regent 1965-68, 1974-77; RI St Soc, DAR, St Chm of CAR, St Libn 1968-71; St Chm of Yorktown Bicent Com 1980-83, St Vice Regent 1977-80, St Regent 1980-83, Hon St Regent 1983-, St Lineage Res Com 1983-86; RI Regent's Clb, 1965-; Nat Soc, DAR, Mem of the Bd of Mgmt 1980-83; Skyscrapers Inc, Histn 1977-78; RI Hist Soc; Quidnessett Country Clb, Charter Mem; r/Presb; hon/Author, Pres's Message in the Ch Paper, "Fishermen's News" 1970-71, and St Regent's Message in "The RI DAR News" 1980-83; Editor, "The RI DAR News," 1977-80; DAR Good Citizenship Medal, 1937; Cert of Awd, RI Med Ctr; Cit, RI Ho of Reps in Recog of the Yr of the French, 1781-1981; The Hereditary Register of the USA; DIB.

HARTSELL, ROBERT ALTON PARKER JR oc/Instructor in Social Work; b/Jun 12, 1942; h/2610 Crane Drive, Salisbury, NC 28144; ba/Salisbury, NC; m/Duane Mae Thompson; c/Robert Thompson, Benjamin Parker, Boger Alton; p/R Parker Sr (dec) and Annie Livengood Hartsell, Kannapolis, NC; ed/AB, Sociol, High Point Col, 1964; MSW, Grp Wk, Univ of NC Chapel Hill, 1969; pa/Instr in Social Wk, Catawba Col, 1980-; Guest Lectr, Pfeiffer Col 1982, Livingstone Col 1978-80, Catawba Col 1977; Dir of Partial Hospitalization Sers, Tri Co Mtl Hlth Ctr, 1975-79; Dir of Lincoln Co Mtl Hlth Ctr, Gaston-Lincoln Mtl Hlth Area 1974; Social Wkr, Piedmont Area Mtl Hlth Ctr, 1972-74; Cnslr, NC Dept of Voc Rehab, Charlotte Ofc, 1971; Supvr of Fam & Chd's Sers, Cabarrus Co Dept of Social Sers, 1969-71; Med Social Wkr, Cabarrus Co Dept of Social Sers, 1964-67; Social Wkr, Murdoch Ctr, Butner, NC, & Chapel Hill City Schs, 1969; Dial Help, Phone Cnslg, 1979-, Bd of Dirs, Pres of Dial Help Bd 1980-82; Nat Assn of Social Wkrs, 1967-; Acad of Cert'd Social Wkrs, 1971-; NC Coun on Social Wk Ed, 1980-; cp/Rowan Co Human Ser Coun, 1980-82; Rowan Co, NC, 2000 Com, 1982-83; Granite Quarry Elem Sch PTA, 1976-; r/First U Meth Ch; hon/Elected to Fac Senate, Catawba Col, 1983-86; Intl W/W Commun Ser; DIB; Personalities of S.

HARVELL, DURWARD GRADY oc/Headmaster of Academy; b/Aug 27, 1941; h/Route 3, Box 429-A, Greensboro, AL 36744; ba/Greensboro, AL; m/Estelle Margaret Amstutz; c/Laura Allison; p/Manly Curtis (dec) and Reba Atwood Ezzell Harvell, Wallace, NC; ed/BA, Wn KY Univ, 1969; EdM, Univ of MS, 1973; EdS, Univ of AL, 1982; mil/AUS 1960-63, Pers Spec, SP5 E-5; 1166 MP Co (NG) 1982-, Asst Opers Sgt SGT E-5; pa/Headmaster, So Acad, 1982-; Dir of Spec Ed 1975-81, Tchr 1974-75, Pender Co Schs; Tchr, Prince Wm Co Schs, 1971-74; Tchr, Newport News City Schs, 1970-71; Phi Delta Kappa, 1981-; Am Assn of Sch Adm, 1981-; Kappa Delta Pi, 1981-; Nat Assn of Sec'dy Sch Prins, 1982-; CEC, 1975-82; cp/Lions Clb, 1978-80; r/Epis; hon/W/W in S & SW; Personalities of S.

HARVIE, MARION ELINORE oc/

Retired Administrator, Counselor, Educator; b/May 15, 1926; h/Southwind at Whispering Pines, Georgetown, FL 32039; ed/BS, St Univ of NY; Cert'd Alcoholism Cnslr, NY St; Grad Study, Adelphi Univ; Specialized Tng, S Oaks Foun; Freeport Alcoholism Foun; Hofstra Univ; Green Mtn Col, 1944-47; pa/ Dir, Employee Assistance Prog & Alcohol & Substance Abuse Ctr, Village of Freeport, 1972-85; Exec Secy, Var Corps, incl'g, MCA Artists Ltd, Baldwin Piano Co Artist Div, Sperry Rand, KLM Royal Dutch Airlines, 1947-71; Nat Alcoholism Cnslrs Assn; NY Fdn of Alcoholism Cnslrs; Mtl Hlth Assn; Exec Bd, ALMACA; cp/Secy, Human Rts Comm, 1972-78; Exec Bd, Yth Sers Coun, 1976-79; Adv Bd, Freeport Yth Outreach Proj, 1976-85; Commun Adv Bd, Freeport Hosp Ctr for Alcoholism, 1977-85; Stabilization & Affirmative Housing Task Force, 1976-85; Atl SW Civic Assn, 1963-85; Bd of Dirs, Hi-Hellow Child Care Ctr, 1980-85; Exec Bd, Assn of Labor & Mgmt Admrs & Conslts on Alcoholism, 1977-85; r/ Christian; hon/Contbr, Column in Wkly Local Newspaper, *The Leader*, "The Choice is Yours," 1978-85; Wom of the Yr Awd for Contbns to the Field of Alcoholism, NY St Alliance of Wom & Alcohol Abuse, 1981; Recip, NY St Cit for Having Devel'd Commun Awareness Campaign, "It's OK Not to Drink," 1981; W/W: in Am Wom, in E.

HASAN, S ZAFAR oc/Professor and Dean of College of Social Work; b/Jul 5, 1930; h/735 Brook Hill Drive, Lexington, KY 40502; ba/Lexington, KY; m/ Nuzhat Ara; c/Shirin, Simin, Akbar, Jafar; p/Alia (dec) and Saiyid Akhtar Hasan, Lucknow, India; ed/BA w Hons 1948, MS, LLB 1949, Dip SS 1950, Univ of Lucknow, India; MSSW 1955, Dr of Social Wel 1958, Columbia Univ; pa/Res Asst 1950-51, Lectr in Social Wk 1951-57, Rdr in Social Wk 1957-65, Prof 1965-71, Univ of Lucknow; Prof of Social Wk 1971-, Dean, Col of Social Wk 1979-, Univ of KY; Com on Nat Legis & Adm Policy, Task Force on Coun Structure, Coun on Social Wk Ed; Adv Coun, Multidisciplinary Ctr on Gerontology & Human Devel Prog Adv Bd, Univ of KY; Coun of Social Wk Ed; Indian Assn of Tnd Social Wkrs; r/Islam; hon/Pubs, 4 Books, Several Res Reports, Over 30 Papers & Articles (Mainly in the Areas of Social Policy, Social Adm, Social Security, Social Wk Ed & Res); UN Social Wel S'ship, 1954-56; Outstg Edrs of Am Awd, 1973; Invited as Rose Morgan Vis'g Prof, Univ of KS, 1974; Indian Jour of Social Res; Outstg Edrs of Am; Educationists in India; Reference Asia.

HASAN, SYED MOHAMMAD oc/ Chemist, Chemical Engineer, Company President; b/Jan 1, 1931; h/9852 Vicksburg, Huntington Beach, CA 92646; ba/ Huntington, Bch, CA; m/Rahida Khatoon Azim; c/Farhat, Khalid, Rafat, Nusrat, Saeeda, Tario; p/Summa Khatoon, Huntington Bch, CA; Siddiq Hasan (dec); sp/A Azaim and Aitia Khatoon, Pakistan; ed/BSc, Univ of Karachi, Pakistan; Chem & Chem Engrg Courses, Univ of So CA & Univ of CA-LA, 1964-66; MS Prog Mgmt Sci, West Coast Univ, 1974; pa/Sci Tchr (Chem Physics) Marie Colaco Eng

Sec'dy Sch, Karachi, Pakistan, 1957-60; Chem, Chief Chm, Globe Elect Co, Gardena, CA, 1962-68; Sr Mfrg Engr, Burroughs Corp, Pasadena, CA, k1968-69; Sr Chem Process Engr, Lockheed Elect Co, LA, CA, 1969-75; Tech Dir/Owner, Super Chem Enterprises, LA, 1975-80; Pres, H & R Chems Incorp, Super Chem Enterprises, LA, 1980-; Mem: CA Circuit Assn; Consltg Chem Assn; Am Mgmt Assn; r/Islam; hon/W/W in W.

HASENOEHRL, DANIEL NORBERT FRANCIS oc/Benedictine Monk-Priest, Chaplain; b/Jul 12, 1929; h/PO Box 19113, Portland, OR 97219; ba/Wilsonville, OR; p/N F and Anna Meyer Feucht Hasenoehrl (dec); ed/ Att'd, Univ of Portland, 1947-49; BA, Mt Angel Sem, 1951; Ordained Priest, 1960; MEd, Univ of Portland, 1958; Grad Study, Univ of OR, Mt Angel Sem, Gonzaga Univ, Rutgers Univ, Mus Art Sch; OR St Sys of Higher Ed; mil/AUS, 1952-54, NATO (SHAPE) Paris, France, 1953-54; pa/Cnslr/Tchr, Mt Angel Preparatory, 1960-64; Prof, Acad Dean, Registrar, Acting Pres, Mt Angel Sem, 1964-72; Asst Pastor, Our Lady of Sorrows Parish, 1972-75; Chaplain, Marylhurst Col, 1975-81; Chaplain, Dammasch St Hosp, 1975-; Nat Assn of Cath Chaplains, 1976-; Am Assn for Cnslg & Devel (AACD), 1962-; Many Hort Assns & Hand Weavers Guilds; Benedictine Monk, Mt Angel Abbey, 1956-; r/Rom Cath.

HASSETT, CAROL ALICE oc/Psychologist; b/Apr 19, 1947; h/105 Franklin Avenue, Malverne, NY 11565; ba/ 236 Mineola Boulevard, Mineola, NY 11501; m/John J; c/John J Jr; p/Mr and Mrs Joseph Lusardi, Bradenton, FL; ed/ BS, St John's Univ, 1968; EdM 1974, PhD in Psych 1981, Hofstra Univ; pa/ Tchr, Day Elem Sch, 1968-69; Adj Asst Prof, Hofstra Univ, 1980-81; Psychol, Nassau Co Dept of Drug & Alcohol Addiction (Outpt Unit), 1981-84; Pvt Pract, 1984-; Am Psychol Assn; NY St Psychol Assn; Nassau Co Psychol Assn; Mtl Hlth Assn; Nat Register of Hlth Ser Providers; Cert'd Adv'd Emer Med Tech; Pre-Hosp Critical Care Tech; cp/ Bd of Govs, Kings Co Cadet Corps, 1966-72; Bd of Dirs, Malverne Vol Ambulance Corps, 1976-; r/Rom Cath; hon/Pubs in *Jour of Psychi Treatment & Eval* 1981, 1983, *Alcoholism Clin & Exptl Res* 1983.

HASTINGS, CHARLOTTE SHEILA oc/Visual Artist and Writer; b/Aug 12, 1944; h/27 Norwood Avenue, Staten Island, NY 10304; ba/Same; ed/BA, Goddard Col, 1980; Att'd, Univ of MN for 3 Yrs, Mpls Sch of Art for 2 Yrs; pa/Art Tchr, Clb Med, Haiti, 1983; Pub'd Fiction Writer, New Am Lib, 1983; Copy Writer, Berkeley Books, 1982; Rdr, Simon & Schuster, 1982; Dir, The Staten Isl Arts Wkshop, 1980-81; Tchr, Creat Drawing, Curtis HS, 1981; VChp, Ingham Co Arts Comm, 1979; Exec Dir, E Lansing Arts Wkshop, 1978-79; Publicity Coor, Grants Writer, E Lansing Arts Wkshop, 1977-78; Editor, Lancer Books Inc, 1975-77; Free-Lance Editor, Proofreader, Copywriter, Random House, Ballentine Books, Dell Books, Bantam, 1973-74; Editor, *The Speculum*, 1970-73; Romance Writer, New Am Lib; Exhbns, "Planer Surfaces," 22 Wooster Gallery 1983, Grp

Show, Mus of Contemp Art 1982, "Strictly Abstract," 22 Wooster Gallery 1982, Num Others; Num Collections; hon/Pubs, *Welcome Intruder* 1982, *Love Has No Pride* 1983; Arts Fest Participant, Clb Med, Dominican Republic, 1983; Arts Fest Participant, Clb Med, Haiti, 1982; Residence Grant, VA Ctr for the Creat Arts, 1981; Residence Grant, H Garver Miller S'ship for Abatement of Fees, Ossabaw Isl Proj, 1977; Residence Grant, Helen Wurlitzer Foun, 1976; Marcia Enbody S'ship, Univ of MN, 1962.

HATAJACK, FRANK J oc/Commercial Diver, Welder; b/Jul 1, 1945; h/78 Schill Avenue, Kenner, LA 70062; ba/ Belle Chasse, LA; m/Susan N Gray; p/ Helen L Hatajack, Ronkonkoma, NY; ed/BS, Geol Engrg, MI Technological Univ, 1968; Comml Diver, Divers Inst of Technol, 1972; mil/USN 1968-72, E-5 Aviation Elect Tech; pa/Jr Asst Exploration Geologist, Consolidated Mining Co of Canada, 1966; Comml Diver/ Welder, Taylor Diving & Salvage Co, 1973-; Soc of Mining Engrs; Soc of Exploration Geophysicists; Inst of Diving; Mineralogical Soc of Am; Am Radio Relay Leag; Sigma Rho, VP 1967; r/SDA; hon/Eagle Scout, BSA, 1960; Commend, USN, 1971; W/W S and SW; Personalities of S.

HATCH, ORRIN GRANT oc/United States Senator, Attorney; b/Mar 22, 1934; ba/135 Russell Senate Office Building, Washington, DC 20510; m/ Elaine Hansen; c/Brent, Marcia, Scott, Kimberly, Alysa, Jesse; p/Jesse and Helen Kamm Hatch, Midvale, UT; ed/ BS in Hist and Phil, Brigham Yg Univ, 1959; JD, Univ of Pgh Law Sch, 1962; pa/Ptnr, Law Firm of Thomson, Rhodes & Grigsby, 1962-69; Sr Ptnr, Law Firm of Hatch & Plumb, 1969-76; US Senator, 1976-; Salt Lake Co Bar Assn; ABA; PA Bar Assn; Chm, Labor & Human Resources Com & the Constit Subcom of Jud Com; Mem: the Budget Com, the Select Com on Intell, & the Gov'g Bd of Ofc of Technol Assessment; cp/ AFL-CIO; Bd of Dirs, Ballet W; Hon Nat Ski Patroller; Help Eliminate Litter & Pollution (HELP) Assn; r/Mormon; hon/ Pubs: Author, *The Value of Life*; *The Equal Rts Amendment: Myths & Realities*; Articles incl: "Strategy to Help Democracy Thrive" in *Wash Times*; "The Equal Rts Amendment Ext: A Critical Anal" in *Harvard Jour of Law & Public Policy*; "Should the Capitol Vote in Congress? A Critical Anal of the DC Representation Amendment" in *Fordham Urban Law Jour*; Others; Recip, Over 75 Awds in First Term in Recog of Outstg Achmts in Many Different Areas of Legis & Public Ser, incl'g, Mr Free Enterprise.

HAUSEY, WILLIE R oc/Government Relations Coordinator; b/Jan 26, 1933; h/6133 Tremain, Citrus Heights, CA 96910; ba/Sacramento, CA; m/Kathy; c/ Frond, Rodney; p/Joseph Burnell and Eva Matthews (dec); ed/BS in Ed, 1978; AA in Ed, 1953; mil/AUS, Aide to Gen Hawse, Spec Sers; pa/Pres, Hausey and Assocs, Legis Advocates, 1983-; Govt Relats Coor, Watts Hlth Foun, 1983-; Legis Advocate, SCCO, 1983-; Chief Dpty Dir, CA Social Sers, 1981-82; Adm Coor, Senator Rodda, 1969-80; cp/ Sacramento Co Affirmative Action Com; VChair, Citrus Hgts Planning Coun; VChair, Sacramento C of C

Crime Preven; Mem of Task Force, Congressman John Conyers' Crim Justice Brian Trust Com; Sacramento Co Grand Jury; Com Chair, Am River Hosp; Bd, Sacramento Co Wel Adv Comm; Pres, Sacramento Co Dem Ctl Com; 5th Assem, Dist Dem Com; Trustee, NAACP; r/Allen Chapt, AME Ch; hon/CA St Legis; Sacramento Co Bd of Supvrs; NAACP; Urban Leag; Sacramento Sch Dist; Golden Empire Coun; Eskaton Am River Hosp; SAEOC: Wel Comm.

HAUSMANN, WERNER KARL oc/Pharmaceutical Company Executive; b/Mar 9, 1921; ba/5000 Post Road, Dublin, OH 43017; m/Helen Margaret; c/Gregory; p/Carl and Johanna Hausmann (dec); ed/Att'd, Swiss Fed Inst of Technol; MS in Chem Engrg, 1945; DSc, 1947; mil/Served to First Lt, Swiss Army, 1941-46; pa/Res Assoc, Rockefeller Inst for Med Res, 1949-57; Res Grp Ldr, Lederle Labs, 1957-66; Assoc Dir, QC, Ayerst Labs, 1966-71; Dir, QC, Stuart Pharms, 1971-74; Dir, Quality Assurance, Analytical Res & Devel, Adria Labs, 1974-; Fellow, NY Acad of Scis; AAAS; AIC; Chem Soc of London; The Royal Soc of Chem; ASQC, Chm of Columbus Sect, Cert'd Quality Engr; Chem Soc of London; APhA; APhS; ACS; ASM; Am Soc Biol Chem; Parenteral Drug Assn; Fdn Intl Pharmaceutique; cp/IPA; Toastmasters Intl; Pres, Ednl TV Assn, 1970-71; r/Presb; hon/Pubs, "Doxorubicin Hydrochloride-Aluminum Interaction" 1983, "Vendor Quality Assurance in the Drug Industry" 1976, "Analytical Method for Streptothricin-Type Antibiotics: Structure of Antibiotic LL-BL136" 1972, "New Streptothricin-Type Antibiotics," Others; Res Fellow, Univ of London, 1947-48; Awd'd Fellow Status in 6 Profl Socs; W/W: in MW, in Fin & Indust, in Frontier Sci & Technol, in World, in Am; Intl W/W of Intells.

HAUSSERMANN, JOHN WILLIAM JR oc/Classical Music Composer; b/Aug 21, 1909; h/Highland Towers, Apartment 2000, 1071 Celestial Street, Cincinnati, OH 45202; ba/Same; c/John W III, Blanchard Selby; p/John William and Jessie Edith Moonlight Hausermann (dec); ed/CO Col; Hon DMus, Cinc Conservatory of Music, 1939; pa/Bd of Dirs, Westchester Conservatory of Music, 1944; Trustee, Cinc Col Conservatory of Music; Life Mem, NAACC, 1959; Lifetime Fellow, Intl Inst of Arts & Lttrs; The Bohemians Musicians Clb of NYC; Bd Mem, Am Music S'ship Assn, 1981; Hon Mem, Phi Mu Alpha Sinfonia, Eta-Omicron Chapt; Fdr, Contemp Concert Series, Cinc, 1934-41; Composed "Preludes Symponiques for Piano" 1932-33, "Seven Chorals on Orig Themes for Organ" 1933, "The After Christmas Suite for Orch" 1934, "Symph No 1" 1937-38, "#1 & #2 Sonata in One Movement for Organ Solo" 1939, Num Others; r/Christian Scist; hon/Hon Mem, Alumni Bd of Govs, Col Conservatory of Music, Cinc Conservatory of Music, 1957; Dist'd Alumni Awd, 1981; Music Featured in Num Mus and Libs; Biogl Ency of the World; Nat Ency of Am Biog; W/W E; DIB; Baker's Dic of Music; Grove's Dic of Music; Guide to the Pianist's Repertoire.

HAVASI, GEORGE oc/Anesthesiologist; b/Nov 23, 1941; ba/Amarillo, TX; m/Ilona; p/Mrs Anna Hengsperger, Welland, Ontario, Canada; ed/MD, cum laude, Budapesti Orvostudomanyi Egyetem, Budapest, Hungary, 1966; pa/Assoc Anesth, Mississauga Gen Hosp, 1976-77; Assoc Anesth, Regina Gen Hosp, 1978; Asst Anesth, Lectr, Toronto Gen Hosp & Univ of Toronto, 1978; Asst Prof of Anesthesiology, TX Tech Univ, 1979-; Anesth, High Plains Bapt Hosp; AMA; TX Med Assn; TX Soc of Anesth; Canadian Anesthetists' Soc; Am Soc of Anesths; Am Soc of Cardiovas Anesths; Wn Pharm Soc; Intl Anesthesia Res Soc; Am Soc of Reg Anesths; r/Rom Cath; hon/Author, Many Sci Articles in Profl Pubs, incl'g, *Canadian Anesthetists' Society Jour, Critical Care Med*, Others; Certs, Intl Anesthesia Res Soc 1980, NY St Soc of Anesths 1981; W/W in S & SW.

HAVEMEYER, JOHN F III oc/Real Estate Appraiser, Consultant; b/May 26, 1939; ba/Appraisal Research Incorporated, 315 South Franklin Street, Syracuse, NY 13202; m/Nancy K; c/Christopher, Debrah, Holly, Steven, Christine, Edmund; p/Mrs Elizabeth R Havemeyer, Doylestown, PA; ed/BS, Allegheny Col, 1962; MBA, DBA, Pacific Wn Univ; pa/Pres, Appraisal Res Inc; MAI Mem, Am Inst of Real Est Appraisers; Sr Real Property Appraiser, Soc of Real Est Appraisers, Nat Instr of Pres Chapt 148, 1978-80; r/Meth; hon/W/W in Real Est.

HAVEN, SHARON OWEN oc/Field Editor, Writer; b/Feb 9, 1943; h/3136 Falcon Street, San Diego, CA 92103; ba/Same; m/Clayton; c/Matthew, Amy; ed/BA, Intl Relats, Pomona Col, 1965; MA, Polit Sci, Columbia Univ, 1966; pa/San Diego Field Editor for *Wom's Day, Better Homes & Gardens, Metro Home, Decorating & Crafts Ideas*, 1980-; Habitat Editor, *San Diego Home & Garden*, 1980-; Free-Lance Articles & Edit for, *Good Ideas, Home Mag, Fam Circle, McCall's, San Diego Mag, Goodlife Mag, 1,001 Home Ideas*; Author, *Room to Grow: Making Your Child's Bedroom an Exciting World*, 1979; Free-Lance Designer, Wk Featured in Num Periods, 1973-81; Co-Editor, *Zero Pop Growth Monthly Jour*, 1972; Staff Writer, Ctr for the Study of Dem Instns, 1966-67; Dir, Ulrey Home for Boys, 1972; Instr, Polit Sci, Westmont Col, 1967-69; Am Soc of Interior Designers, Press Mem; AIA, Press Affil; cp/San Diego Zool Soc; SOHO; San Diego Hist Soc; San Diego Symph Soc; Mus of Man; YMCA; hon/Thesis Hons, 1965; Phi Beta Kappa, 1965; magna cum laude, 1965; Cordell Hull Awd in Intl Relats, 1965; Woodrow Wilson Fellow, Columbia Univ, 1965-66; W/W in W.

HAWKE, BERNARD RAY oc/Planetary Scientist; b/Oct 22, 1946; ba/PGD-HIG, University of Hawaii, Honolulu, HI 96822; p/Arvil A Hawke (dec); Elizabeth E Skees, Upton, KY; ed/BS in Geol 1970, MS in Geol 1976, Univ of KY; MS in Geol Scis 1977, PhD in Geol Scis 1978, Brown Univ; mil/AUS 1970-72, Airborne, Inf, Vietnam; pa/Field Geologist, USGS, 1967-68; Res Asst, Univ of KY Chem Dept, 1973-74; Res Asst, Brown Univ Geol Dept, 1974-78; Asst Astronomer, Inst for Astronomy, Univ of HI, 1978-79; Assoc Prof, Planetary Geoscis Div, HI Inst of

Geophysics, Univ of HI, 1980-; Dir, NASA Pacific Reg Planetary Data Ctr, Univ of HI, 1982-; Alpha Tau Omega Social Frat, 1967-70; Sigma Gamma Epsilon, Hon Earth Sci Soc, 1967-74; Sigma Xi, Res Soc, 1978-; Geochem Soc; Meteoritical Soc; Am Geophy Union; cp/Elizabethtown JCs, 1969-70; r/Cath; hon/Author of Over 100 Planetary Sci Articles for Profl Jours; Prin Investigator for Num NASA Res Grants, 1979-; Num Undergrad S'ships; Univ of KY Deans List, Num Times; W/W: in Am, in W.

HAWKINS, JEFFREY LYNN oc/Planning Director; b/Feb 26, 1950; h/5303 Middle Warren Road, Pine Bluff, AR 71603; ba/Pine Bluff, AR; m/Christine Jean Ellis; c/Joseph Andrew, Carrie Lynn; p/Richard Hawkins, Pendleton, IN; Jean Tanner, Wing, AL; ed/AA, Bethany Luth Col, 1970; BS in Urban Studies, Mankato, MN, 1972; pa/Trans Planner, IN St Hwy Comm, 1972-74; Trans Planning Dir, SE AR Reg Planning Comm, 1974-76; Exec Dir, SE AR Reg Planning Comm, 1976-; Secy, AR Assn of Devel Orgs, 1982; Am Planning Assn; Dir, Pine Bluff Railroad Demo Proj, 1978-; Dir, Pine Bluff City Planning, 1982-; Dir, Pine Bluff Area Trans Study, 1974-; cp/Gov's CDBE Com; St Adv Com on the Census, 1981-; AR Rural Clean Water Com, 1980-; Dir, Jefferson Co Flood Hazard Preven, 1979-; r/Luth; hon/Essay Pub'd, *Am Poetry Press*, 1968; Outstg Col Aths of Am; Personalities of S; W/W in S & SW.

HAY, DENNIS WAYNE oc/College Music Instructor; b/Jul 22, 1954; h/1137 West Hearn, Blytheville, AR 72315; ba/Blytheville, AR; m/Molly; c/Emily; p/Mrs Betty Tarpley, Blytheville, AR; ed/BME w Distn, AR St Univ, 1977; MM, Piano Perf, N TX St Univ, 1983; pa/Organist, Choirmaster, 1st Presb Ch, 1975-76; Organist, 1st Bapt Ch, 1976-77, 1979-; Pvt Piano Instr, 1970-; Piano & Organ Instr, MS Co Commun Col, 1981-; AR Music Tchrs Nat Assn, Bd 1979-; Phi Mu Alpha, 1973-77, Treas; Nat Guild of Piano Tchrs, 1979-; Phi Eta Sigma, 1974; Orpheus Music Clb, VP; r/Bapt; hon/Hons Awd for Student w the Highest GPA, Music Dept; W/W in Am Cols & Univs.

HAY, ELIZABETH KERR oc/Assistant Professor of Medical and Surgical Nursing; b/Apr 11, 1943; h/3808 Harding Place, Nashville, TN 37215; ba/Nashville, TN; p/Alexander and Elizabeth Hay, Murfreesboro, TN; ed/AB, Randolph-Macon Wom's Col, 1965; BS, Columbia Univ, 1967; RN, Columbia Presb Med Ctr, 1967; MSN, Vanderbilt Univ, 1976; pa/Orthopaedic Staff Nurse, Presb Hosp, 1967-69; Nsg Supvr, Instr, Firestone Hosp, 1969; Hd Nurse, Supvr, Rogosin Kidney Disease Treatment Ctr, NY Hosp, Cornell Med Ctr, 1970-74; Staff Nurse, Hemodialysis, Nashville VA Hosp, 1974-75; Clin Spec of Adult Neurosurg and Orthopaedics, Instr of Med & Surg Nsg 1976-79, Asst Prof of Med & Surg Nsg 1979-, Vanderbilt Univ; ANA, Chair of Div on Med & Surg Nsg Pract, Nat Assn of Orthopaedic Nurses Jt Com to Devel Standards of Orthopaedic Nsg Pract 1982-85; Nat Assn of Orthopaedic Nurses, CoChm 1980-81, Pres 1981-82, Past Pres 1982-83; Orthopaedic Nurses Assn, 1978-80, Pres-Elect of Mid TN

Chapt 1978-79, Pres of Mid TN Chapt 1979-80; Sigma Theta Tau, Treas of Iota Chapt 1982-84, Num Other Positions; TN Nurses' Assn; hon/Pubs, "External Fixation: Option for Fractures"1981,"A Tchg Plan for External Fixation" 1981; Shirley Titus Awd for Excell in Undergrad Tchg, Vanderbilt Univ Sch of Nsg, 1981; Ellen Greg Ingalls Awd for Excell in Classroom Tchg, Vanderbilt Univ, 1982; Excell in Clin Instrn Awd, Vanderbilt Univ Sch of Nsg, 1982; Outstg Yg Wom of Am; W/W of Am Wom; World W/W of Wom.

HAYES, JACK oc/Associate Professor of Preventive Medicine, Consultant in Tropical Disease; b/Apr 28, 1937; h/ 2801 19th Lubbock, TX 79410; ba/ Lubbock, TX; m/Janice E Vaughn; c/Jodi, Jarrod, Tamblyn, Tiffany, Kevin; p/ Barbara Hayes Caldwell, Lewisville, TX; ed/BS, 1960; MS, 1962; PhD, 1973; mil/ AUS, Germany, 1955-57; pa/Chm, Natural Sci, S En IL Col, 1962; Res Assoc, Ctr for Zoonoses Res, Univ of IL, 1964-68; Instr, Sch of Public Hlth, Univ of TX, 1968-73; Assoc Prof, Preventive Med, Hlth Sci Ctr, TX Tech Sch of Med, 1973-; Am Soc of Tropical Med & Hygiene, 1968-; Wildlife Disease Assn, 1968; Am Mosquito Control Assn, 1966; Ciencia E Cultura, Brazilian, 1976; r/Presb; hon/Beta Beta Beta, 1962; Kappa Delta Phi, 1963; Phi Delta Kappa, 1962.

HAYFLICK, LEONARD oc/Professor, Director of Center for Gerontological Studies; b/May 20, 1928; h/7711 Southwest 103rd Avenue, Gainesville, FL 32608; ba/Gainesville, FL; m/Ruth; c/Joel, Deborah, Susan, Rachel, Anne; p/Mrs Edna Hayflick, Philadelphia, PA; ed/BA 1951, MS 1953, PhD 1956, Univ of PA; mil/AUS; pa/Prof of Zool, Dir of Ctr for Gerontological Studies, Univ of FL, 1981-; Sr Scist, Chd's Hosp Med Ctr, 1976-81; Prof of Med Microbiol, Stanford Univ Sch of Med, 1968-76; Pres, Gerontological Soc of Am, 1982-83; VP, Tissue Culture Assn, 1974-76; Bd of Councillors, Soc for Exptl Biol & Med, 1984-86; hon/Pubs, "The Serial Cultivation of Human Diploid Cell Strains" 1961, "Growth of a Mycoplasma Causing Human Primary Atypical Pneumonia" 1962; Brookdale Prize, Gerontological Soc of Am, 1980; Am Fdn for Aging Res Ldrship Awd, 1983; 30th Karl August Forster Lectureship, Acad of Sci & Lit, Mainz, Germany, 1983; W/W: in Am, in W; Am Men & Wom of Sci.

HAYMOND, PAULA J oc/Assistant Director of Residential Treatment; b/ Sep 29, 1949; h/10555 Turtlewood Court, #2710, Houston, TX 77072; ba/ Houston, TX; p/Dr and Mrs George M Haymond, Warsaw, IN; ed/EdD, Cnslg/ Cnslr Ed, IN Univ, 1982; MS, Ed/Sch Psychometry 1973, BA, Psych 1971, Butler Univ; pa/Asst Dir of Residential Treatment, Bayou Place, 60 Bed Chd's Psychi Hosp/Residential Treatment Facility; Div Hd, Human Sys Devel, Lund Consltg Inc, 1981-82; Behavioral Clinician, Diagnostic Unit, IN Girls Sch, 1978-80; Behavioral Clinician & Affirmative Action Expeditor, Diagnostic Unit 1977-78, Behavioral Clinician of Psych Dept 1973-77, IN Boys Sch; Delta Delta Delta; Kappa Kappa Kappa Philanthropic Sorority; IN St Employees Assn, Chapter Pres 1974-75, Del Assem

Rep 1974, 1975; IN St Employees Fed Credit Union, Orgl Com 1976, Charter Secy 1976; IN Correctional Assn, 1973-78; Am Correctional Assn, Profl Mem, 1976-77; cp/Bloomington, IN, LWV, 1979-80; Rudi Foun, 1979-81; Bloomington Coalition, 1980; Human Factors Soc, 1981-82; NOW, Spring Br, TX, 1982-83; LWV, 1982-83; hon/Pub, "A New Look at an Old Team: A Correlational Study of the Rorschach and MMPI w Adolescent Female Delinqs," 1982; W/W in Am Wom.

HAYNES, MACK W JR oc/Coordinator; b/Mar 29, 1948; h/11523 Ensbrook, Houston, TX 77099; ba/Houston, TX; m/Gretchen H; p/M W Haynes Sr, Opelousas, LA; ed/BS, 1973; Postgrad, 1974-75; pa/Sys/Netwk Coor 1983-, Sys Mgr 1982-83, IEPS Sys, Tenneco Oil Co; Programmer, Exxon Prodn Res Co, 1975-82; IEEE; IEEE Computer Soc; Dec User's Grp; ACM; SEG; CSH; hon/W/ W: in Sci & Technol, in W & SW, in Finance & Industry, in Computergraphics; Intl W/W of Contemp Achmt.

HAYNES, RUTH ELAINE oc/Certified Public Accountant, Administrator; b/Sep 21, 1943; h/6405 Willow Springs, Arlington, TX 76017; ba/Ft Worth, TX; c/Jim Michael, Christine Elaine; p/Jack E and Viola E Gelvin, Perryton, TX; ed/ AA, Del Mar Col, 1973; BBA, TX A&I, 1976; MBA, Corpus Christi St Univ, 1977; pa/Adj Instr, Tarrant Co Jr Col, 1980-83 & 1985-; St of TX Comptroller of Public Accts, 1976-; Auditor, Corpus Christi Audit Ofc, 1976-78; Sr Tax Acct, Ft Worth Audit Ofc, 1976-83; Supvr, Chgo Audit Ofc, 1983-84; Supvr, Ft Worth Audit Ofc, 1984-; Cost Acct, Leonard Constrn Co, 1975-76; AAUW; Corpus Christi St Univ Alumni; Phi Theta Kappa Alumni; Pres, Del Mar Bus Clb, 1975-76; cp/Mensa; Former GSA Ldr, 6 Yrs; APO; BSA Sponsor; APO Sponsor at TCJC, 1982-83; r/Luth; hon/All 3 Degs, summa cum laude; Hall of Fame, Del Mar Col, 1976; Phi Theta Kappa, 1976; W/W: of Am Jr Cols, in Fin & Indust.

HAYS, MARGUERITE JOHNSTON oc/Director of University Relations; b/ Dec 2, 1931; h/327 West Prentiss Avenue, Greenville, SC; ba/Greenville, SC; m/Thomas F; c/John Thomas, Christopher Scott; p/John E and Ruth Marguerite Jones Johnston; ed/Att'd, Agnes Scott Col 1950-51, Univ of PA 1954; BA, Furman Univ, 1954; pa/Copy Writer, Oper Dir, WFBC-TV, 1956-61; Editor & Public Info Spec, Liberty Life Ins Co, 1961-63; Editor of The Furman Mag 1963-, Pubs Editor 1965-73, Dir of Communs 1973-80, Dir of Pubs 1980-82, Dir of Univ Relats 1982-, Furman Univ; Past Mem, Am Wom in Radio & TV, Am Assn of Indust Editors, Am Alumni Coun, Am Col Public Relats Assn, Public Relats Soc of Am; Current Mem, Coun for the Advmt & Support of Ed, Past Mem of Bd of Dirs (CASE Dist III), Chm of Media Awds Col (CASE Dist III); cp/Greenville C of C; hon/Edited & Pub'd Articles in The Furman Mag, 1963-; Awds for Pubs, Coun for the Advmt & Support of Ed 1981, 1979, 1977, 1976, Am Alumni Coun 1974, 1971, 1969, 1968, Nat Sch Public Relats Assn 1981, 1980, Bapt Public Relats Assn 1972, Advtg Fdn of Greenville (3 Awds) 1981, (4 Awds)

1983, (1 Awd) 1984.

HAYWARD, RICHARD LEE oc/Loss Prevention Engineer; b/Sep 3, 1933; h/ 1750 Lombardy Drive, Boulder, CO 80302; ba/Boulder, CO; m/Beth; c/ Donna, Tom, Carol; p/Mrs Charles Scott Hayward, Boulder, CO; ed/Elect Engrg, CO Univ, 1956; mil/USN, Electrician; pa/Maintenance Foreman to Assoc Engr 1958-81, Safety Engr 1981-83, Loss Preven Engr 1983-, Syntex Chems; cp/Scouting; Vol Wk, Boulder Co; Nat Fire Protection Assn; r/Meth; hon/Boulder Co Vol Awd, 1983; Scouting Awd, 1981-82; Ch Wk Awds, 1980; W/W in W.

HAYWOOD, BRUCE oc/College President; b/Sep 30, 1925; h/605 North Sixth Street, Monmouth, IL 61462; ba/ Monmouth, IL; m/Gretchen; c/Margaret, Elizabeth; p/Joseph (dec) and Eva L Haywood, Yorkshire, England; ed/BA 1950, MA 1951, McGill Univ; PhD, Harvard Univ, 1956; mil/Brit Intell, 1943-47; pa/Instr, Harvard Univ, 1951-54; Prof, Dean, Provost, Kenyon Col, 1954-80; Pres, Monmouth Col, 1980-; Am Assn of Tchrs of German, 1955-; Dir, Assoc'd Cols of the MW, 1980-; Conslt, Nat Endowment for the Humanities, 1972-; cp/Rotary, 1980-; r/ Presb; hon/Pubs, Novalis: The Veil of Imagery 1959, Many Articles on Higher Ed, Lit & Romanticism; DHL, Kenyon Col, 1980; W/W in Am.

HAZLITT, HENRY oc/American Editor and Author; b/Nov 28, 1894; h/65 Drum Hill Road, Wilton, CT 06897; m/ Frances S Kanes; ed/Col, City of NY; pa/Mem, Staff of Wall Street Jour, 1913-16; Financial Staff, NY Evening Post, 1916-18; Wrote Monthly Financial Lttr, Mechs & Metals Nat Bk, NY, 1919-20; Financial Editor, NY Evening Mail, 1921-23; Edit Writer, NY Herald 1923-24, The Sun 1924-25; Lit Editor, The Sun, 1925-29; Lit Editor, The Nat, 1930-33; Editor, Am Mercury, 1933-34; Edit Staff, NY Times, 1934-46; Edit Bd, The Am Scholar, 1941-44; Assoc, Newswk Mag, Writer of Column, "Business Tides," 1946-66; Syndicated Columnist, LA Times Syndicate, 1966-69; Co-Fdr, Co-Editor w John Chamberlain 1950-52, Editor-in-Chief 1953, The Freeman; hon/Pubs, The Wisdom of the Stoics 1984, From Bretton Woods to World Inflation 1984, The Inflation Crisis, & How to Resolve It 1978, The Conquest of Poverty 1973, Num Others; Hon LittD, Grove City Col, 1958; Hon LLD, Bethany Col, 1961; Hon SScD, Universidad Francisco Marroquin, Guatemala, 1976.

HEAD, CATHERINE HELEN oc/ Teacher; b/Dec 18, 1946; h/1048 South Crescent Heights Boulevard, Los Angeles, CA 90035; ba/Los Angeles, CA; c/Tiffani Patrice, Amir Michelle; p/ Reeves B Jefferson, Silver Spring, MD; Dorothy A Johnson, Uniontown, PA; ed/BA, Howard Univ, 1969; EdM, Univ of So CA, 1972; pa/Tchr, LAUSD, 1970-; LA Alliance of Black Sch Edrs, 1982-83, Pres 1983-84; LA Task Force, Assault on Illiteracy, 1983-84, VP; Black Ldrship Coalition on Ed; cp/So Christian Ldrship Conf; NAACP; r/Prot; hon/ Awd, Coun of Black Edrs (Apprec for Participation in Prog, Educating the Black Child).

HEALER, ALPHALETA oc/Retired Educator; b/Mar 30, 1916; h/3303-45, Lubbock, TX 79413; m/Thomas Leo; c/

Charles Leo, David Kennon; ed/BA, Abilene Christian Univ, 1935; MA, TX Technological Univ, 1955; CCC, 1968; pa/Tchr, Hale Ctr, TX, 1935-37; Tchr, Sudan, TX, 1937-38; Tchr, Lubbock, TX, 1953-60; Spch Pathology, Pvt Schs, 1960-76; Conducts Num Wkshops on Tongue Thrust, 1970-; Guest Lectr, TX Technological Univ; ASHA; TX Spch & Hearing Assn; S Plains Spch & Hearing Assn; NEA; St Tchrs Assn; CEC; Kappa Kappa Iota, Alpha Conclave; cp/Knife & Fork Clb; Lubbock Wom's Clb; Past Pres, Progressive Study Clb; Lubbock Garden Clb; r/Ch of Christ; hon/Pubs, *Tongue Thrust, Diagnosis & Correction* 1971, 1973, *Spch & Lang Improvement* 1973; Valedictorian, 1931; Conslt & Guest Spkr, Wkshops, TX Spch & Hearing Assn, 1972, 1973; Conslt, Wkshops for Schs, Dental Assn, Ednl Sers; Personalities of S; DIB; 2,000 Wom of Achmt; World W/W of Wom; W/W Biogl Record-Child Devel Profls; Commun Ldrs & Noteworthy Ams; Commun Ldrs of Am; Men & Wom of Distn.

HEARD, FRED W oc/Director of Department of Commerce; b/Sep 9, 1940; h/1239 High Street, Southeast, Salem, OR 97302; ba/Salem, OR; m/ Adair; c/Frederick, Robin, Heather; p/ Darrell Heard, Klamath Falls, OR; ed/ BA in Gen Studies 1963, MA in Polit Sci 1968, So OR St Col; pa/Appt'd Dir of OR St Dept of Commerce, 1983-; OR Ho of Reps, 1968-70; Asst Prof, OR Inst of Technol, 1970-82; Elected Senate Pres, 1981-83; Elected Senate Majority Ldr, 1975, 1977, 1979; Mem, Ways & Means Com, 10 Yrs; Klamath Falls Tchrs Assn, Past Pres; OR St Employees Assn; cp/St CoChm, Carter for Pres Campaign, 1976-80; Klamath Co U Good Neighbors Bd of Dirs; Dem Precnt Com-man, 1965-83; Klamath Co Mus Bd; Klamath Falls Kiwanis Clb; r/Epis; hon/Invited to Meet Pope John Paul II on His Visit to the US, 1979; Liberty Awd, SDA Ch; Awds from VFW & Am Legion; W/W: in Govt, in Am Polit, in NW, in Am Communs; DIB.

HEARD, ROSE MARIE oc/Executive; b/Nov 30, 1930; h/423 South Holt Avenue, #202, Los Angeles, CA 90048; ba/Los Angeles, CA; p/Mary Bradshaw, Saginaw, MI; ed/BA in Bus Adm 1981, MBA 1981, Doct in Bus Adm 1983, Univ of Beverly Hills; mil/USAF, 1948-52 (WAFs); pa/From Clerical Positions to Asst VP of Trust Adm, Union Bk Trust Dept, 1957-76; From Asst Dir of Pension Trust Dept to Asst VP of Pension Trust Adm, IRA/KEOGH/SEP & Investmt Annuity Prods, Beverly Hills Savs Pension Trust Dept, 1976-; Adj Mem, Beverly Hills Bar Assn; cp/ NAACP; Past Matron, Secy, Star of Judea Chapt #82, OES, CA Jurisd; Past Most Ancient Matron, Present Most Ancient Matron, Daughs of Zion Ct #17, CA Jurisd, Heroines of Jericho; r/ Meth, CME; hon/Grad Cert, Am Inst of Bkg in Trust, 1963; W/W in W.

HEARTH, DONALD PAYNE oc/ Research Center Director; b/Aug 13, 1928; h/204 Graves Circle, Newport News, VA 23602; ba/Hampton, VA; m/ Joan Smith; c/Susan H McDaniel, Douglas P, Anne H, Janet H; p/Alvin G Hearth, St Petersburg, FL; ed/BS in Mech Engrg, NEn Univ, 1951; Hon DSc, George Wash Univ, 1978; Hon EngD, NEn Univ, 1982; Postgrad Wk, Univ of

CA-LA, Univ of So CA; Grad, Fed Exec Inst; pa/Dir, NASA, Langley Res Ctr, 1975-; Dpty Dir, NASA's Goddard Space Flight Ctr, 1970-75; Dir of Planetary Progs 1967-70, Mgr of Adv'd Progs, Lunar & Planetary Progs 1962-67, NASA HQs; Former Dept Mgr, Marquardt Corp; Former Aeronaut Rschr, NASA's Lewis Flight Propulsion Lab; AIAA, Fellow, Com for Intl Activs; Am Astronautical Soc, Fellow; Nat Space Clb, Bd of Govs; Appt'd by Gov Robb, Bd of Dirs for VA's Ctr for Innovative Technol; Indust Adv Com, Univ of VA; Dir-at-Large for Nat Coun, Mem of Corp, NEn Univ; Adj Prof, George Wash Univ, Bd of Dirs, Public Broadcasting Sta WHRO; Bd of Dirs, U V A Bk; r/Unitarian; hon/Pubs, "Society's View Toward Sci & Technol" 1978, "Hypersonic Technol-Approach to an Expanded Prog for Astronautics & Aeronautics" 1976, "Outlook for Space, a Synopsis Report to the NASA Admr" 1976, "A Forecast of Space Technol, 1980-2000" 1976, Num Others; NASA Exceptl Ser Medal, 1969; NASA Exec Perf Awd, 1975; NASA's Highest Awd, Dist'd Ser Medal, 1975; NASA Equal Opport Medal, 1981; Awd'd Rank of Meritorious Exec, Pres Carter, 1980; Awd'd Rank of Dist'd Exec, Pres Reagan, 1981.

HEATH, BRENT EDWARD oc/Social Studies and Journalism Educator; b/Aug 24, 1953; h/1232 West 15th Street, Upland, CA 91786; ba/Ontario, CA; m/ Carol Mae; c/Justin Bryant; p/Victor E and Dawn I Heath, Tustin, CA; ed/AA, Social Scis, Highline Commun Col, 1973; BA, Hist & Ed, Seattle Pacific Univ, 1975; Postgrad Wk in Polit Sci, San Jose St Univ, 1977; MA, Sec'dy Ed, CA St Univ Northridge, 1981; pa/Social Studies/Eng Tchr, Christian Ctr Schs, 1975-77; Social Studies/Eng Tchr, Los Primeros Sch, Pleasant Val Sch Dist 1977-79; Social Studies/TV Prodn Tchr, Cabrillo Jr High, Ventura Unified Sch Dist, 1979-80; Social Studies/GATE Social Studies/Jour/Eng Tchr, De Anza Jr High, Ontario-Montclair Sch Dist, 1980-; Nat Coun for the Social Studies, 1975-; CA Coun for the Social Studies, 1977-; So CA Social Sci Assn, 1977-; Baldy-Vista Social Studies Coun Pubs Editor, 1983-; Assn for Supvn & Curric Devel, 1982-; The So CA Jour Ed Assn, 1981-; Inland Jour Ed Assn, 1981-; r/ Prot; hon/Pubs, *Energizing the World Hist Prog w Practical Curric Units* 1984, "The Novel in the Social Studies Clrm: A Curric Approach" 1982; Dean's Hon Roll, Seattle Pacific Univ, 1974, 1975; Awd'd Plaque, Whitman Jr High, for Outstg Cadet Tchg, 1975; Granted Study F'ship, Taft Inst for Govt, 1977; Awd'd Plaques for Outstg Jour Tchg, De Anza Jr High, 1981, 1983; Social Studies Dept Chp, De Anza Jr High, 1983-; Conf Presenter, CA Coun for the Social Studies, 1983, 1984; W/W in W.

HEATH, HUNTER III oc/Medical Scientist, Educator, Physician; b/Jun 8, 1942; h/1739 Walden Lane, Southwest, Rochester, MN 55902; ba/Rochester, MN; m/Glenna A Witt; c/Ethan Ford; p/Hunter Jr (dec) and Velma M Heath, Lubbock, TX; ed/BA, Chem, TX Technological Col, 1964; MD, Wash Univ Sch of Med, 1968; Internship 1968-69, Residency in Med 1969-70, Univ of WI Hosps; F'ship in Endocrinology &

Metabolism, Walter Reed Gen Hosp, Walter Reed Army Inst of Res, 1970-72; Res F'ship in Mineral Metabolism, Mayo Grad Sch of Med, 1974-76; mil/Capt, USAR, 1970-72; Major, USAR, 1972-74; pa/Hd, Endocrine Res Unit, Mayo Clin & Mayo Foun, 1984-; Prof of Med, Mayo Med Sch, 1984-; Conslt in Endocrinology & Internal Med, Endocrine Res Unit, Mayo Clin & Mayo Foun, 1976-; Assoc Prof of Med 1980-84, Asst Prof of Med 1976-80, Mayo Med Sch; Chief, Endocrinology Sect, Dept of Med, Lttrman Army Med Ctr, Presidio of SF, CA, 1972-74; Clin Instr, Dept of Med & Dept of Ambulatory and Commun Med, Univ of CA SF Med Ctr, 1973-74; Am Col of Phys, Fellow; Am Fdn for Clin Res; Am Soc for Bone & Mineral Res; Am Soc for Clin Invest; Ctl Soc for Clin Res; Endocrine Soc; hon/Pubs, "Therapeutic Decision-Making in Asymptomatic Hypercalcemia & Primary Hyperparathyroidism" 1984, "Impaired Vitamin D Metabolism w Aging in Wom: Possible Role in Pathogenesis of Senile Osteoporosis" 1984, "Tests of Parathyroid Function: Utility & Limitations" 1984, "The Parathyroid Glands in Familial Benign Hypercalcemia/Hypocalciuric Hypercalcemia" 1984, Num Others; Edit Bd, *Jour of Clin Endocrinology & Metabolism*, 1980-83; Publs Com, Endocrine Soc, 1983-; Edit Bd, *Am Jour of Physiol*, 1982-; Prog Chm, 1982 Meeting, Am Soc for Bone & Mineral Res; Chm, Ed Com, Am Soc for Bone & Mineral Res, 1982-85; W/W in Frontier Sci & Technol.

HEATHERLY, JAMES P oc/Business Systems Manager; b/Feb 10, 1949; h/ 16527 Craig Drive, Oak Forest, IL 60452; ba/Chicago, IL; m/Nona Jean Mangrum; c/James Patrick Jr, Wendy Melissa; p/William A (dec) and Annamae Heatherly, Chicago, IL; ed/BA in Eng 1977, MBA in Mktg 1980, De Paul Univ; pa/Acct Exec, IL Bell, 1969-79; Conslt, The Omni Grp, 1979-80; Conslt, Robert Donahue & Assocs, 1980-81; Dir of Telecommuns, Carson Pirie Scott & Co, 1981-83; Current Bus Sys Mgr, Montgomery Ward; Current Prof, Mktg & Telecommuns, De Paul Univ; Am Mgmt Assn; Am Mktg Assn; Intl Communs Assn; Chgo Indust Communs Assn; cp/ Oak Forest Baseball Assn; Marist HS Fathers' Clb; r/Rom Cath; hon/Author, Var Articles for Auerbach Publishers Inc, Var Articles for Indust (Telecommuns) Periods; Ednl Awd, Am Mktg Assn, Chgo Chapt, 1982; Ser Awd, Oak Forest Baseball Assn, 1983; W/W: in Fin & Indust, in MW.

HEBERLEIN, GARRETT THOMAS oc/Biologist, Dean of Graduate School; b/Apr 11, 1939; h/1111 Bourgogne, Bowling Green, OH 43402; ba/Bowling Green, OH; m/Donna Lee Frohm; c/ Wendy Ann, Edward Garrett; p/Edward Garrett and Ruth Andrus Heberlein; ed/ AB, OH Wesleyan Univ, 1961; MS 1963, PhD (NIH Fellow) 1966, NWn Univ; Postdoct, Univ of Gent, Netherlands, 1966-67; pa/Asst Prof & Assoc Prof of Biol 1967-73, Chair of Biol Scis Dept 1970-73, NY Univ; Assoc Prof, Chair, Dept of Biol Scis, Univ of MO-St Louis, 1973-76; Prof & Chair, Dept of Biol Scis 1976-80, Dean of Grad Col & Vice Provost for Res 1976-80, Bowling Green Univ; Beta Beta Beta, Biol Hon;

301

Sigma Xi, Sci Hon; NY Acad of Scis; AAAS; Am Soc for Microbiol; Am Inst of Biol Scis; Am Soc of Plant Physiols; Nat Sci Tchrs Assn; Nat Assn of Biol Tchrs; AAUA; OH Acad of Sci; Plant Growth Regulator Wkg Grp; Nat Coun of Univ Res Admrs; Phi Gamma Delta Social Frat, 1957-; cp/Fund Raising Coms, LWV, Am Cancer Soc, U Way; Kiwanis Intl, 1978-; Junto, 1979-, Pres 1982-83; r/Elder, First Presb Ch, 1979-; hon/"Approaches to Increasing Res Productivity" 1983, "Current Grad Ed Issues in the USA" 1983, "Res Adm: Philosophies, Objectives, & Challenges in the USA" 1983, "Grad Ed in OH: Critical Issues & Priorities for the 1980's" 1981, Num Others; NY Univ Sigma Xi Yg Scist Awd for Dist'd Res, 1970; Grants, Am Cancer Soc 1967-69, Arts & Sci Fund 1967-70, NIH 1963-, Jane Coffin Child Meml Fund for Med Res 1966-72, FDA 1976-77, NSF 1976-82; W/W: in Am, in MO Ed, in MW, in Frontier Sci & Technol; Outstg Edrs of Am; Am Men & Wom of Sci; Notable Ams; Personalities of W & MW; Men of Achmt; Dir of Dist'd Ams; 2,000 Notable Ams.

HEBERT, MAURICE GIRARD oc/ Teacher, Coordinator; b/Dec 30, 1921; h/88 Forest Drive, RFD 9, Bedford, NH 03102; ba/Manchester, NH; m/ Georgette T; c/Susan Carol Hébert Speath, Russell Albert, Raymond Richard; p/Albert W and Marie Anne Brown Hébert (dec); ed/BS, BA 1955, MA 1957, Boston Col; Postgrad, LI Univ 1970-71, Keene St Col 1976-77, NH Col 1977-78; EdM, Univ of NH; mil/USAF, 1942-45, ETO; pa/Tool Designer, Gen Elect, 1941-54; Sales Engr, MPB Inc, 1955-61; Sales Mgr, Hartford Precision Prods, 1961-63; VP, Mktg, Logan Electronics, 1963-65; Mkt Rschr, Stonybrook, NY, 1965-70; Assoc Prof, Mktg, NH Vac/Tech Col, 1971-73; Tchr, Coor, Ctl HS, 1973-; Advr, Distributive Ed Clbs Am; Advr, Manchester Yth Entrepreneure; Bd Dirs, Bus Ed, NH Col; NH Profl Standards Bd, NH Bd of Ed; Recruiter, Boston Col; Pres, NH Voc Assn, 1979; Pres, NH DETCA, 1978, 1983; Am Voc Assn, VChm, N Eng Mbrship 1979, Pres Ctl 1978; Chm, NH Distributive Ed Curric Consortium; Nat Assn Dist Ed Tchrs; Chm, Dist Ed Dept, Ctl High; Manchester Ed Assn; NEA; Am Ec Assn; Am Mgmt Assn; cp/ Secy-Treas, Bedford Kiwanis; r/Cath; hon/Pubs, "The Best Season" 1954, "A Monograph of the Ball Bearing Ind" 1957; Tchr of the Yr, Mkt & Dist Ed, 1982; W/W in E.

HEBERT, RAYMOND E JR oc/Executive; b/Jun 23, 1937; h/1296 San Ysidro Drive, Beverly Hills, CA 90210; ba/ Beverly Hills, CA; m/Karen Liner; c/ Shelly Lin, Stac Allan; p/R E Hebert Sr, Huntington Beach, CA; ed/BS, Univ of CA LA, 1959; MBA, CA, 1963; mil/ USN, Lt, 1959-61; pa/Brand Mgr, Armour & Co, 1961-64; Mkt Dir, Norton Simon, 1964-67; Exec VP, AMR Inc, 1967-71; Pres, MCI Inc, 1971-77; Pres, Knapp Communication Corp (*Arch Digest, Bon Appetit, Geo Mag*), 1978-82; Current Pres, Hebert & Assocs Inc; Yg Pres Org; cp/Pres, Jr Chamber; Boy Scouts Nat Com; Jonathan Clb, LA; Union Leag Clb of NY; r/Cath.

HECKER, RICHARD oc/Utility Executive; b/Nov 25, 1930; h/2281 Southw-

est 81 Avenue, Miami, FL 33155; ba/ Miami, FL; m/Sheila Davis; c/Mark Robert, Philip Davis; p/Harry (dec) and Gertrude Hecker, Miami Beach, FL; ed/ BBA, Univ of Miami, 1958; MBA, Nova Univ, 1976; Public Utility Mgmt Course, GA Tech, 1976; pa/Supvr of Transmissions-Distn 1969, Supvr of Labor Relats 1971, Mgr of Wkrs' Compensation 1976-, Mgr of Safety (Acting) 1977, FL Power & Light Co; Pres, LU 359, Intl Brotherhood of Elect Wkrs, 1966; VP, Self-Insurers of FL Inc, 1982-83; Adv Rules Com for Self-Insurers, FL Dept of Labor, 1982-83; Acad of Trial Lwyrs Safety Awds Com, 1982-83; Soc of Law & Med; So Assn of Wkrs' Compensation Admrs; Intl Assn of Indust Accidents Bds & Commrs; cp/Pres, USO-Homestead, 1979-; hon/W/W in S & SW.

HECKER, RICHARD JACOB oc/ Research Scientist in Plant Genetics; b/ Mar 26, 1928; h/1100 Morgan Street, Ft Collins, CO 80524; ba/Ft Collins, CO; m/Diane M; c/Carol J, John D, Ann M, Douglas R; ed/BS in Agronomy, MT St Univ, 1958; PhD in Plant Genetics, CO St Univ, 1964; mil/AUS, 1952-54; pa/ Res Ldr & Geneticist 1972-, Geneticist 1964-72, USDA; Am Soc of Agronomy; Am Soc of Crop Sci, Chm of Variety Registration 1980-; Am Soc of Sugar Beet Technologists, Dir 1978-80; Wn Soc of Crop Sci; Sigma Xi; Gamma Sigma Delta, Chapt Pres 1969; r/Cath; hon/Author, 87 Sci Articles & Reports Pub'd in 12 Sci Jours, Proceedings & Books, 1964-84; Meritorious Ser Awd, Am Soc of Sugar Beet Technologists, 1980; Superior Ser Awd, USDA, 1968; Cert of Merit, Agri Res Ser; Am Men & Wom of Sci; W/W in W.

HEDSTROM, JOSEPH CHARLES oc/Senior Operations Research Analyst; b/Sep 21, 1952; h/1805 Roswell Road, Apartment 33A, Marietta, GA 30062; ba/Marietta, GA; p/Mr and Mrs R A Hedstrom, Dothan, AL; ed/BS in Indust Engrg, Univ of AL, 1975; MS in Indust Engrg, GA Tech, 1976; pa/Indust Engr, Ford Motor Co, 1977-78; Opers Res Analyst 1978-80, Sr Opers Res Analyst 1980-, Lockheed-GA Co; Tau Beta Pi, 1974-; IIE, 1974-; Alpha Pi Mu, 1975-; Univ of AL Nat Alumni Assn, 1975-; GA Tech Alumni Assn, 1977-; ORSA, 1978-; Nat Mgmt Assn, 1978-; Univ of AL Capstone Engrg Soc, 1981-; AIAA, 1982-; r/Cath; hon/AIIE, Univ of AL IE Awd, 1975; Univ of AL Edgar Boyd Kay S'ship Awd, 1973, 1974; Outstg Yg Men of Am; W/W in Frontier Sci & Technol.

HEDTKE, DELPHINE L oc/Educator, Consultant, Costume Designer, Author, Lecturer; b/May 25, 1932; h/ 1661 Western Avenue, North, Saint Paul, MN 55117; ba/Saint Paul, MN; ed/ BA, Gustavus Adolphus Col, 1953; Postgrad, Univ of CA-LA, NY Univ; MA w Hons 1968, PhD 1977, Univ of MN; pa/Current Asst Voc Prog Dir & Home Ec Conslt, Rosenville Area Schs #623; Admr, Second & Post Second Home Ec, MN & CA Public Schs; Univ Fashion & Apparel Tchr, Coor & Col Ed Tchr, Haute Couture & Theatre Costume Designer; Am & MN Voc Assns; Am & MN Home Ec Assns; AAUW; Metro Adm Wom in Ed; Nat & MN Ednl Assns; MN Assn of Voc Admrs; Nat Supvrs of Home Ec; Nat Assn of Female Execs; hon/Illustrator, Chd's Music Book, *Tiny

Tunes for Tiny Tots; Author, *Apparel/ Fashion Dimensions, a Multidisciplinary Approach*, Articles in Profl Jours in Field, AV Mats for 3M Ednl Div; World W/ W of Wom; Ldrs of Am Elem & Sec'dy Ed; W/W: in MW, of Am Wom; Adm Wom of Am; Intl W/W of Intells.

HEFFERNAN, PETER JOHN oc/ Hospital Administrator; b/Feb 19, 1945; h/352 Mayflower Circle, Hanover, MA 02339; ba/Waltham, MA; m/Rosemary M; c/Peter John, Matthew Paul; p/ Kenneth and Vivian LaCourse Heffernan, Bristol, CT; ed/BA, Providence Col, 1967; MBA, George Wash Univ, 1971; mil/MA Army NG, 1969-75; pa/Adm Resident 1970-71, Asst Dir 1971-74, VP for Adm & Gen Sers 1974-78, Exec VP & Chief Operating Ofcr 1978-, Waltham Hosp; Fellow, Am Col of Hosp Admrs, 1983; Bd of Dirs, Hosp Sers of N Eng, 1980-; Bd of Dirs, Charles River Profl Standards Review Org, 1983-; Instrnl Conf Coun, N Eng Hosp Assem Inc, 1976; Hlth Care Mgmt Assn of MA, 1970-; cp/Bd of Dirs, Waltham Boys Clb, 1977-; Waltham Lions Clb, 1970-; r/ Cath; hon/USPHS Traineeship, 1969-70; McDonald's Hamburger Corp Col S'ship, 1963; W/W in E.

HEGNEY, SUSAN K oc/College Instructor of Communication; b/Aug 12, 1952; h/6 Ridgeway, Goshen, NY 10924; ba/Middletown, NY; Stone Ridge, NY; p/Edward and Margaret Hegney, Goshen, NY; ed/MS in Spch, 1975; BS, 1974; AA, 1972; pa/Instr, Ulster Co Commun Col, Sprg (Full-time) 1983, Fall (Pt-time) 1982; Adj Instr, Orange Co Commun Col, Sums & Pt-time, 1975-; Instr (Full-time), Jr Col of Albany, 1977-81; NYS Spch Communication Assn, Exec Coun 1979-; cp/ARC Instr of First Aid & CPR, 1982-; Nat Ski Patrol Sys Inc, 1970-; r/ Rom Cath; hon/"Wom of Ireland" Lyric Theatre, Irish Lit By & About Irish Wom, 1979-; Pub, *Today's Greatest Poems*, 1983; Alpha Psi Omega, Oneonta St Univ, 1974; World W/W of Wom.

HEGWOOD, RANDOLPH C oc/ Administrator; b/Jul 25, 1949; h/18 Labette Court, Little Rock, AR 72205; ba/Little Rock, AR; m/Peritha Taylor; c/Ashley Nika, Karisa Carmelle, Mark Anthony, Delicia Antionette; p/Garland and Hattie Hegwood, Camden, AR; ed/ Cert of Tng, Twin Cities OIC, 1973; BA, cum laude, Univ of AR-Pine Bluff 1976; Grad Wk Toward MA, WA St Univ, 1976-77; mil/AUS, Vietnam, 1970-72; pa/Prog Supvr, NYC Prog, Camden, AR, 1973; Spec Asst to Student Union Dir, Univ of AR-Pine Bluff, 1976; Tchg Asst, WA St Univ, 1976-77; Asst Dir of Pub Div, AR Sect of St Ofc, 1977-78; Cnslr, OIC, 1978-79; CDBG Dir 1979-80, Tng Dir 1980-83, Exec Dir 1983, Little Rock OIC; AR Selective Sers Bd, 1981-83; UAPB Alumni Assn, 1976-83; Nu Gamma Alpha, 1972-83; Assn of Social & Behavioral Scists, 1974-78; Bd of Dirs, Nat Assn of Students in St Cols & Univs, 1976-78; Alpha Kappa Mu Nat Hons Soc, 1975-76; cp/Assoc Mem, Oper Push, 1980-83; Big Brothers of Pulaski Co, 1977-81; r/AME; hon/Pubs, "Music Styles as an Example of African Culture Survivals in the New World" 1976, "Contbns of Blacks to AR's Devel" 1978; VP, Univ of AR-Pine Bluff Student Govt, 1975; Pres, Univ of AR-Pine Bluff

Student Govt, 1976; Outstg Ldrship Awd, 1976; Panelist for the Nat Citizens Participation Coun's Reg VI Annual Conf, 1981; Outstg & Dedicated Sers Awd, 1980; Collaborator for Urban Leag's Nat Endowment for the Humanities "Cultural & Historical Awareness through Multi-Media Project," 1979-80; Dpty Registrar for Pulaski Co, 1979-80; Panelist for KWSU-TV Sponsored Afro-Am Perspective, "Roots: Myths of Reality"; Conducted Sem on Police Brutality, 1976; Co-Fdr of Commun Based Recycling Prog, 1975; Conslt, Formation of Student Coalition of Black Cols & Univs, 1974; Conslt, Formation of the Nat Assn of Students in St Cols & Univs, 1974; W/W in Am Cols & Univs.

HEILIG, MARGARET CRAMER oc/ Director of College Health Service; b/ Jan 17, 1914; h/605 Mason Avenue, Drexel Hill, PA 19026; ba/Media, PA; m/David; c/Judith Heilig Johnson, Bonnie Heilig Mueller, Barbara Heilig Leone; p/William Stuart and Margaret Snader Cramer (dec); ed/BA, Wilson Col, 1935; MSW, Univ of PA, 1940; AAS, Nsg, DE Co Commun Col, 1970; pa/Dir of Col Hlth Ser 1976-, Col Nurse 1971-76, DE Co Commun Col; Infirm Dir 1978-, Camp Nurse 1970-78, Hlth Asst/Camp Nurse 1970-78, Paradise Farm Camps; Maternal-Infant Care, 1970-71; Crozer Chester Med Ctr, 1970; Upper Darby Adult Sch, 1958-68; Chd's Bur of Phila, 1940-42; House of Indust Settlement House, 1937-39; Chd's Bur, 1935-37; Am Col Pers Assn; Am Col Hlth Assn; Am Nsg Assn; PA Nsg Assn; APGA; SEn PA Col Hlth Nurses Assn, Pers 1983-85; Home & Sch Assn, VP, Prog Chm 1961-64; cp/ Millbourne Fire Co Wom's Aux, Pres 1945-47; Mother's Grp, Drexel Hill Jr HS, Pres 1960-61; Girl Scout Troop Ldr; Upper Darby Rec Bd, 1956-58; Upper Darby Adult Sch Bd, 1956-68; LWV; Brandywine Conservancy; Tyler Arboretum; r/Soc of Friends; hon/ Editor, *Life Lines* 1973-, *What to Do If* 1975, *Hlth Awareness*, *ACHA Jour* 1977, *Otitis Externa-A Two Year Study to Follow-Up* 1979, *Homesick & at Camp.*

HEILMAN, EARL BRUCE oc/University President; b/Jul 16, 1926; h/7000 River Road, Richmond, VA 23229; ba/ Richmond, VA; m/Betty June Dobbins; c/Bobbie Lynn Hudgins, Terry H Sylvester, Nancy H Davis, Sandra June, Timothy Bruce; p/Earl B and Nellie S Heilman, Port Royal, KY; ed/AA, Campbellsville Jr Col, 1948; BS 1950, MA 1951, PhD 1961, Peabody Col; Hon LLD, Wake Forest Univ & KY Wesleyan Univ; HHD, Campbell Univ; mil/Marine Corps, 1943-47; pa/Pres, Univ of Richmond, 1971-; Pres, Meredith Col, 1966-71; Adm VP, Prof of Ednl Adm, Peabody Col, 1963-66; VP & Dean, KY So Col, 1961-63; Coor of Higher Ed, St of TN, 1960-61; Controller & Bursar, George Peabody, 1957-60; Treas, Georgetown Col, 1954-57; Treas, Housing Proj, City of L'ville, 1954-57; Bus Mgr, KY Wesleyan Col, 1952-54; Asst Prof of Acctg, KY Wesleyan Col, 1952-54; Instr of Acctg, Belmont Col, 1951-52; Auditor, Albert Maloney & Co, CPAs; Instr of Bus Ed, George Peabody Col, 1950-51; Tchr, Bkkpg, Nashville City Schs, 1950; Field Conslt for Var Orgs; Pres, So Assn of Cols for Wom, Coun

of Indep Cols in VA, VA Foun for Indep Cols; Bd of Trustees, So Assn of Cols & Schs, Com on Cols; Bd of Dirs, Ctl Fidelity Bk, NA, Fidelity Bkrs Life Ins Co, A H Robins Co Inc; Phi Beta Kappa; Omicron Delta Kappa; Beta Gamma Sigma; Pi Omega Pi; Kappa Phi Kappa; Lambda Chi Alpha; Kappa Delta Pi; cp/ Richmond Rotary Clb; Downtown Clb; Dir, Metro Richmond C of C, Richmond Public Lib; r/Bapt; hon/W/W: in World, in Am, in Am Ed, in S & SW, in Col & Univ Adm; Ldrs in Ed; The Blue Book; Ldrs of the Eng Speaking World; Personalities of S.

HEINRICH, ADEL VERNA oc/Professor; b/Jul 20, 1926; h/Highland Avenue, Waterville, ME 04901; ed/BA, Flora Stone Mather Col, Case-Wn Resv Univ; MSM, Union Theol Sem; AMusD, Univ of WI-Madison; pa/Prof Mus, Colby Col, Waterville, ME, 1964-; Sum Fac Mem, Colby Ch Music Inst, 1964-; Asst Orch Conductor, Colby Commun Symph Orch, 1964-74; Colby Humanities Travel Grant (Europe), 1978-79; Mellon Grant to Devel Course on Shakespeare & Music, 1978-79; Colby Humanities Grant for Res (Harvard 1979-80, Brit Mus, Fitzwm Mus, Libs at Oxford & Cambridge, Gt Brit, 1982); Others; Am Musicological Soc; Intl Leag of Wom Composers; Am Guild Organists; cp/Num Indiv & Grp Recitals & Indiv Compositions Perf'd; hon/9 Complete Perfs of Bach's "Die Kunst Der Fuge"; Perf'd as Guest Organist Under Margaret Hillis in NYC; Perf'd in Severns Hall, Cleveland, Portland Symph Hall, Others; Orig Compositions: Hour Prog w Vesper Concert Series, 1977; 3 Wks for Spectra 1, Sponsored by NEA & Westbrook Col, 1979; 2nd Prog for Spectra 1, St Joseph's Ch, Portland, ME, 1979; Shakespearean Text Prog, Colby Wom's Grp, Colby Col, 1979; Featured Performer, Spectra 2, Univ of ME-Orono, 1982; Recital, 1st Nat Cong on Wom in Music, NY Univ, 1981; One of 27 Wom Selected for Recital of AWC at Univ of MI Sch of Music, 1st Conf on Wom in Music; Contemp Am Composers; ME Composers & Their Works; Contemp Concert Music by Wom: A Dir of Composers & Theirs Works; W/W: of Am Wom, in E, in Music & Musicians' Dir; Other Biogl Listings.

HEINZE, RUTH-INGE oc/Research Associate; b/Nov 4, 1919; h/2321 Russell #3A, Berkeley, CA 94705; ba/ Berkeley, CA; ed/Asian Studies 1974, Asian Studies 1971, Anthropology 1969, Univ of CA Berkeley; Gr Latinum 1967, Eng/German, Italian, Spanish 1952, Interpreter Col, Berlin; pa/Nat Dir of Indep Scholars of Asia 1981-, Dir of Asian Folklore Studies Grp 1977-, Res Assoc of Ctr for S & SE Asian Studies 1973-, Univ of CA-Berkeley; Res Fellow, Inst of SE Asian Studies, Singapore, 1978-79; Staff Res Asst, Human Devel Prog, SF, 1975; Lectr, Mills Col, Oakland, 1974; Lectr, Chiang Mai Univ, Thailand, 1972; Res Fellow, Nat Mus, Bangkok, Thailand, 1972; Prodr and Writer of Monthly Ednl Radio Prog, SFB, Berlin, Germany, 1962-63; Assn for Asian Studies, 1968-; Intl Assn for the Study of Traditional Asian Med, 1981-; Exec Secy, Fulbright Alumni Assn, No CA Br, 1982-; r/Luth; hon/ Pubs, *Tham Khwan, a Socio-Psychological*

Study of a Thai Custom 1982, *The Role of the Sangha in Modern Thailand* 1977, *The Biog of Ahjan Man* 1977, Over 100 Essays in Profl Jours; Fulbright-Hays Res Grant, 1978-79; Outstg Citizen of German Descent, 1980.

HEITMAN, BETTY GREEN oc/ Co-Chairman of Republican National Commitee; b/Nov 27, 1929; h/655 Waverly Drive, Baton Rouge, LA 70806; ba/Washington, DC; m/Dr Henry S; c/ Donna, Thomas, Perry, Paul; p/George Anderson (dec) and Inell Cooper Green, Prescott, AR; ed/BS, TX Wom's Univ; pa/Adm Dietician, Hotel Dieu Hosp 1950-51, Clarkson Meml Hosp 1951-52; Pediatric Dietician, Charity Hosp, 1952-53; cp/Pres, LA Repub Wom, 1967-71; Treas, Nat Fdn of Repub Wom, 1971-76, First VP 1976-78, Pres 1978-80; Co-Chm, Repub Nat Com, 1980-; r/Epis; hon/Dist'd Alumna Awd, TX Wom's Univ; Named Hon TX Citizen by Gov Wm Clements; W/W: in Am, of Am Wom, in World.

HELD, JOE ROGER oc/Director of Research Services Division; b/Jun 23, 1931; h/16305 Grande Vista Drive, Rockville, MD 20855; ba/Bethesda, MD; m/Carolyn F; c/Lisa Held Doseff, Robert Joseph, Leslie Held Clark, Teresa Held Hamilton; p/Edward and Carmen Held, Woodland Hills, CA; ed/AA, Pasadena City Col, 1950; BS 1953, DVM 1955, Univ of CA Davis; MPH, Tulane Univ, 1959; mil/Comm'd Ofcr, USPHS, 1955-; pa/Asst Surgeon Gen, Rear Admiral, USPHS, 1978; Grant Admr, Primate Ctrs, Animal Resources Br, NIH, 1962-64; Res Parasitologist, Nat Inst of Allergy and Infectious Diseases, 1964-67; Epidemiologist, Pan Am Hlth Org, Buenos Aires, 1967-69; Chief of Vet Resources Br 1969-72, Div Dir 1972-, Div of Res Sers, NIH; Conslt, World Hlth Org; Sci Authority Endangered Species, Dept of Interior; Biol Res Review Com, Nat Bur Standards, 1976; Engrg Tech Commun Adv Com, Montgomery Col, 1976; AAAS; Am & DC (Pres 1975) Vet Med Assns; Conf of Public Hlth Vets, Secy-Treas 1960-62; USPHS Comm'd Ofcrs Assn, Bd of Dirs 1973-; Am Assn for Lab Animal Sci; Nat Capital Assn of Lab Animal Sci, Pres 1972-73; Am Soc of Tropical Med & Hygiene; Foun for Adv'd Ed in the Scis; Assn of Mil Surgs of the US, Exec Bd 1976, 1982; hon/Author, 51 Pubs in Var Sci Jours; Meritorious Ser Medal, USPHS, 1972; Dist'd Ser Medal, USPHS, 1982; Outstg Alumna Awd, Sch of Public Hlth & Tropical Med, Tulane Univ, 1977; Alumni Achmt Awd, Sch of Vet Med, Univ of CA Davis, 1982; K F Meyer Gold-Headed Cane Awd, Am Vet Epidemiological Soc, 1982; Am Men & Wom of Sci; W/W: in Govt, in E, in Am, in Hlth Care.

HELENIUS, MIRIAM (ELIZABETH NELSON) oc/Retired Soprano Singer; b/Apr 6, 1902; h/55 Old Washington Street, Pembroke, MA 02359; ba/Same; c/Robert Anders Park, Herbert Warner Park, Cynthia Park, Charles Frances Park, Neale Christopher Park; p/Mr and Mrs Antero Wilhelm Helenius (dec); ed/ Student of Voice, Piano, Theory, New England Conservatory, 1918-1921; Student of Voice, Royal Conservatory in Sweden 1922, Finland 1928; pa/ Performed in Num Operettas in Boston, Scotia (NY), Chgo; Sang in Finnish for

Finnish Grps, Quincy, Pembroke and NY; Sang in Finland Pavilion, World's Fair, 1939; Ch Soloist and Organist, Summit (NJ), Bernardsville, 1940's; Assisting Musical Therapist, Greystone (NJ), 1950's; Ch Soloist, Duxbury (MA), 1960-75; Directed Num Theatrical Prodns for Public Presentation at Local Schs and Commun Ctrs; cp/PTA, Pres at Somerville 1937; Org'd Wom's Forum of Wash Val, 1941; r/Christian Scist; hon/Recordings, *Music of Finland* 1955, *Folksongs of Finland* 1955; Selected Finnish Soprano Soloist for The World's Fair, Finnish Pavilion, 1939; Finnish-Am Blue Book, The Finnish Imprint.

HELGANZ, BEVERLY BUZHARDT oc/Staff Personnel Manager; b/Jun 7, 1941; h/PO Box 1825, Jacksonville, FL 32201; ba/Jacksonville, FL; m/Charles F Jr (dec); p/Mr M O Buzhardt, Jacksonville, FL; Mrs Jeanne M Crabb, Whittier, CA; ed/AA 1962, BA 1974, Jacksonville Univ; pa/Bus Ofc Supvr 1959, Tng Supvr 1966-76, Employee Relats Supvr 1977-78, Staff Supvr of Equal Employmt Opport 1978-79, Asst Mgr of Bldg Opers 1979-80, Assoc Mgr of Real Est 1980, Staff Mgr of Pers 1980, So Bell T&T; Jacksonville Alumnae Panhellenic Assn, Chaplain, Recording & Corres'g Secys, VP, Pres 1981-82, Chm of Past Pres's Adv Coun 1982-83; Zeta Tau Alpha, Pres 1969-70, 1971-72, 1976-77, Dist Pres 1979-81, Secy 1974-75, 1982-83; Beta Sigma Phi, Pres 1964-65, 1967-68; ABWA, Treas 1968-69, Pres 1969-70; Jacksonville Alumni Assn; Telephone Pioneers of Am, Mbrship Chm 1979-80; cp/Pilot Intl; r/Meth; hon/Beta Sigma Phi, Girl of the Yr Awd, 1965; ABWA, Merit Awd 1967, Wom of the Yr Awd 1969; Zeta Tau Alpha, Alumnae Cert of Merit 1975, Hon Ring 1976; Outstg Yg Wom of Am; W/W: of Am Wom, in S & SW, in Fin & Indust; World W/W of Wom; Personalities of S; Personalities of Am.

HELGEMOE, JANET MARILYN oc/ Registered Dietitian; b/Dec 25, 1931; h/ 3 Woodland Circle, Bow, NH 03301; m/ Raymond A; c/Scott A, Eric W, Greg P; p/Wallace (dec) and Emily Galeucia, Pelham, NH; ed/BS in Dietetics 1953, EdM in Cnslg 1982, Univ of NH Durham; Dietetic Internship, Scripps Metabolic Clin, 1954; pa/Adm Dietitian, Scripps Metabolic Clin 1954-55, Lawrence Gen Hosp 1955-56; Clin Dietitian, Fac Adult Ed, Tacoma (WA) 1969-71, Portsmouth (NH) 1972-73, Durham (NH) 1973-74, Concord (NH) 1975-; Dir of Consumer Info, NE Egg Mktg Assn, 1974-75; Columnist, *Portsmouth Herald,* 1972-73; Conslt Dietitian to Long Term Care Facilities, 1976-; Pvt Pract, Cnslg Dietitian Assoc, 1978-; Instr in Nutrition, Merrimack Val Col, 1981-; NH Dietetic Assn, Pres 1976, Editor 1974-76, Bylaws 1980, Public Relats 1975-76; Conslt Dietitians in Hlth Care Facilities Area 7 Coor, 1980-82; NH Conslt Dietitians in Hlth Care Facilities Fdr & Chm, 1978-80; Am Dietetics Assn; Am Home Ed Assn; APGA; hon/ Pubs, *Galusha-Galeucia Fam of Early N Eng* 1968, Conslt Dietitians in Hlth Care Facilities Newslttr (6:1, 6:1, 6:3); Portsmouth Navy Wife of Yr, 1971; W/W in E.

HELGEMOE, RAYMOND ALBIN oc/Professor; b/Mar 30, 1929; h/3 Woodland Circle, Bow, NH 03301; ba/

Durham, NH; m/Janet; c/Scott, Eric, Greg; p/Albin and Hazel Pekkarinen Helgemoe (dec); ed/BS, Univ of MN, 1951; MBA, Pacific Luth Univ, 1972; PhD (ABD), Univ of NH, 1974; mil/ Cmdr, USN, 1951-74; Ret'd; pa/ Warden, NH St Prison, 1974-78; Prof, Univ of NH, 1979-; NHTROA, Pres 1983; Am Correctional Assn, 1971-; Am Criminology Assn, 1974-; Am Sociological Assn, 1977-; NE Assn Crim Justice Edrs, Pres-Elect 1984; cp/Daniel Webster Coun, BSA, Coun Commr 1979-83, VP 1983-; Bow Men's Clb, 1974-; Masonic Order, 1972-; Concord Country Clb, 1974-; r/Prot; hon/Legion of Merit, 1968; Jt Sers Commend, 1971; Scouter of Yr, Minuteman Coun (MA) 1966, Mt Rainier Coun (WA) 1970; Dist'd Awd of Merit, Daniel Webster Coun, 1978; Silver Beaver Awd, 1978; Vol Assistance, 1971.

HELLMANN, ROBERT ALVIN oc/ Environmental Consultant; b/Jul 7, 1927; h/301 Ellis Drive, Brockport, NY 14420; ba/Brockport, NY; c/Robert Walter, Jonathan Frederick; p/Walter C and Julia Cameron Hellmann; ed/BS 1954, MS 1957, Cornell Univ; EdD, Columbia Univ, 1966; mil/AUS, 1945-46; pa/Instr in Natural Sci & Lectr in Botany, Am Mus of Natural Hist, NY, 1956-61; Instr, Tchrs for E Africa Proj, Tchrs Col of Columbia Univ & Makerere Univ Col, Kampala, Uganda, 1961-62; Assoc Prof, Biol Scis, SUNY-Brockport, 1963-83; Member-at-Large, Monroe Co Envir Mgmt Coun, 1972-; Reg 8 Forest Pract Bd, 1975-; r/Congregationalist; hon/ Author, Num Articles on Conserv & Envir Mgmt for Popular & Profl Jours; Phi Delta Kappa, 1955; Kappa Delta Pi, 1961; W/W: in Sci & Technol.

HELMS, WINSTON CRAIG oc/Professional Engineer; b/Jul 3, 1951; h/3048 Sigmund Circle, Columbia, SC 29204; ba/Fort Jackson, SC; m/Kathryn; c/ Winston Craig Jr; p/Mr and Mrs P W Helms, Columbia, SC; ed/BS in Civil Engrg 1976, ME in Civil Engrg 1980, Univ of SC; mil/USN 1971-73, Opers Spec; pa/Staff Engr, SC Dept of Hlth & Envir Control, 1977-80; Res Asst, Instr, Univ of SC, 1980; Civil Engr, Chief Contract Admr, Directorate of Engrg & Housing, 1981-; Nat Soc of Profl Engrs; SC Soc of Profl Engrs; Am Water Wks Assn; Water Pollution Control Fdn; Am Soc of Sanitary Engrs; Water Pollution Control Assn of SC; Reg'd Profl Engr, SC; cp/SC St Constable; r/Bapt; hon/Var Res Studies; Omicron Delta Kappa; Pi Mu Epsilon; Chi Epsilon; Outstg Yg Men of Am; W/ W in S & SW; Personalities of S.

HELVERING, JIMMY LELAND oc/ Head Counterman; b/Jan 19, 1943; h/ 207 Melody Lane, Henderson, TN 38340; ba/Jackson, TN; m/Linda Dorrene Ray; c/Jack Warren; p/James and Ethel Helvering, Bradford, AR; ed/ Grad, Bradford HS, 1960; Att'd, Hardin Col, 1961; mil/4F; pa/Counterman, Bonwood Auto Parts, 1973-75; Mgr, O&A Auto Parts, 1975-82; Hd Counterman, Hassell's Auto Parts, 1982-83; cp/W TN Heart Assn, Chm of CPR Com 1981-, CPR Instr 1976-, Instr Tnr in CPR 1979-, ECC Com 1981-, Bd of Dirs 1980-; Jackson-Madison Co Red Cross, CPR Instr 1976-, Multimedia First Aid Instr 1976-, Instr Tnr in CPR and

MMFA 1983, First Aid Com 1981-; Chester Co Red Cross, 1978-, Chm 1982-, Dir of 8th Dist 1981-; Chester Co Rescue Squad, 1975-, 2nd Lt 1983, Chaplain 1979; Woodmen of the World, Pres 1970-77, 1981-; r/Ch of Christ; hon/Mr Woodman Awd, Man of Yr, 1974, 1978; First Aid Prog Awd, ARC, 1976-77; Cert of Merit, Madison Co JCs, 1978; Outstg Vol for Safety Sers, Madison Co Red Cross, 1978-79; Outstg Sers Awd, Am Heart Assn, 1979; CPR Instr of Yr, Am Heart Assn, 1980; Chester Co Rescue Squad's Man of Yr, 1982; Outstg Sers Awd, Madison Co Red Cross, 1982.

HELVERING, LINDA DORRENE RAY oc/Secretary; b/Jan 3, 1945; h/207 Melody Lane, Henderson, TN 38340; ba/Jackson, TN; m/Jimmy Leland; c/Jack Warren; p/John A and Myra Ray, Henderson, TN; ed/Grad, Chester Co HS, 1963; Att'd, W TN Bus Col, 1963-64; pa/Pt-time Secy 1963-64, Secy 1964-76, Atty Lloyd Tatum; Secy, Ct of Crim Appeals, Judge Lloyd Tatum, 1976-; cp/Chester Co Cancer Soc, Chm of Annual Talk-A-Thon 1979-, Pres 1981, 1982; Chester Co Heart Assn, Co Chm 1980, 1981, 1982, 1983-; Jackson-Madison Co Red Cross, CPR Instr 1978-, Multimedia Instr 1978-, First Aid Com 1981-; Chester Co Red Cross, 1978-; Woodmen of the World, Secy 1981-; PTA, W Chester Elem PTA Pres 1977-78, 1978-79, Chester Co Coun of PTAs Pres 1979-80, 1980-81; Chester Co Jr High Pres 1981-82, 1982-83; r/Meth; hon/Wom of Woodcraft Awd, Wom of Yr, 1974, 1978; Cert of Apprec for Saving a Life, Am Heart Assn, 1979; Outstg Ser Awd, Am Heart Assn, 1980; Outstg Ser Awd, Am Cancer Soc, 1980; Over the Top Awd as Chm of Chester Co Heart Assn, Am Heart Assn, 1981; Outstg Ser in the Cause of Cancer Control, Chester Co Cancer Soc, 1981; Outstg Vol Ser Awd, Madison Co Red Cross, 1982; Being All Heart Awd, Am Heart Assn, 1982; Dist'd Ser Awd, Am Heart Assn, 1983.

HEMBY, DOROTHY JEAN oc/College Counselor, Administrator; b/Aug 21; h/PO Box 11, East Orange, NJ 07019; ba/Paterson, NJ; p/Mr Samuel Hemby, Greenville, NC; Mrs Queenie Evans, Greenville, NC; ed/MA, Student Pers, 1977; BA, Sociol & Ed, 1975; AA, Sociol, 1973; pa/Col Cnslr, Passaic Co Col, 1978-; Col Cnslr, Kean Col of NJ, 1976-77; Pt-time Tchr, Newark Bd of Ed, 1973-76; NJ Assn Black Edrs, 1980-; NJ Ednl Opports Fund Profl Assn Inc, 1977-; Black Wom in Higher Ed, 1979-; APGA, 1977-; Am Cnslg Pers Assn, 1977-; Behavioral Social Sci, 1975-; Commun Col Cnslrs Assn, 1975; cp/700 Clb, PTL Clb, 1975-; r/Prot; hon/Grad, cum laude, 1973; Grad, summa cum laude, 1977; NJ Pers Assn S'ship, 1976; Cnslrs Awd for Dedicated Ser; W/W: Among Wom, in E, Among Black Ams; Commun Ldrs of Am.

HEMINGWAY, BETH ROWLETT oc/Author and Lecturer; b/May 6, 1913; h/1604 Derek Lane, Richmond, VA 23229; ba/Same; m/Harold; c/Ruth Hemingway Mitman, Martha Scott; p/ Mr and Mrs Robert Archer Rowlett (dec); ed/Att'd, Col Sch, 1926-30; BMus, Hollins Col, 1934; pa/Self-Employed, Author of 5 Books, Lectured in 18 Sts, Spent Month on Lecture Tour of

Australia 1966, Taught at Garden Clb of GA's Symp (Univ of GA) 1976, Demonstrated Flower Arranging in England during Queen's Silver Jubilee 1977; Demonstrated Flower Arranging on TV, 1961-69; Pres, Clay Sprg Garden Clb, 1953-55; Writer for *Richmond-Lifestyle Mag*, 1976-79; Nat Leag of Am Pen Wom, 1979-; VA Writers Clb, 1979-; Richmond Hort Assn, 1962-; VA Fdn of Garden Clbs, 1960-; Richmond Coun of Garden Clbs, Past Chm, 1960-; Barton Garden Clb, Pres 1959-61, 1974; cp/Vol, Hermitage Meth Home, 1977-79; r/U Meth; hon/Pubs, *A Second Treasury of Christmas Decorations* 1961, *Flower Arrangement with Antiques* 1965, *Christmas Decorations Say Welcome* 1972, *Antiques Accented by Flowers* 1975, *Beth Hemingway's No Kin to Ernest* 1980, Monthly Column for *Richmond Times-Dispatch*; Nat Coun of St Garden Clb's Cert of Merit, 1972; Life Mbrship in VA Fdn of Garden Clbs & Richmond Coun of Garden Clbs, 1967; W/W: of Am Wom, in S & SW; VA Lives, The Old Dominion W/W.

HIBBS, WILLIAM ERNEST oc/Clergyman; b/Sep 28, 1950; h/2059 North Woodstock Street, Apartment 305, Arlington, VA 22207; ba/Washington, DC; p/William Edward, Camden, NJ; Ruby Adelle, Fort Worth, TX; ed/BBA, George Wash Univ, 1970; MTh, Univ of St Thomas, Houston, 1976; Ordained Priest, Rom Cath Ch, 1976; pa/Pres, Interfaith Coun on Human Rts, 1978-; Secy-Treas, Parker Supply Co Inc; VP, Mandinka Village Projs Inc, 1978-; Chm, Co-Exec Dir, Washington Based Nat Ecumenical Coalition Inc, 1976-; NEC's NGO Del to the UN ECOSOC; UNHCR; Am Soc Assn Execs; cp/Bd Dirs, Balto Theatre Fest; Bd Dirs, Balto Performing Arts Wkshop Assn; Bd of Dirs, U Images Inc; IPA; r/Cath; hon/Contbr, Articles to Profl Pubs, Nat & Intl Newspapers & Jours; Reverend Wm E Hibbs Day, Sep 28, 1980, in Wash; Lttrs of Commend from Former VP Walter Mondale & House Spkr Thomas O'Neil; NEC's Man of the Yr Awd, 1981-82; W/W in E.

HICKERSON, JERRY HOWARD oc/Director of Continuing Education and Summer School; b/May 19, 1941; h/6100 Meadowdale Drive, Winston-Salem, NC 27105; ba/Winston-Salem, NC; m/Karen VanSickle; c/Heather, Darren, Brian, Shannon; p/Howard and Nellie Hickerson, Hohenwald, TN; ed/BS in Ed 1963, MA 1968, PhD 1975, Kent St Univ; pa/Tchr of Eng, Asst Coach, Ath Dir, Aurora HS, 1966-67, 1963-67; Asst Prof of Eng, Sprg Arbor Col, 1968-69; Asst Prof of Ed, Univ Sch, 1969-72; Asst Prof of Eng, Kent St, 1972-74; Assoc Prof of Ed 1974-76, Dir of Devel Res 1976-77, Tuskegee Inst; Asst to Dean, New Col, Univ of AL Tuscaloosa, 1977-80; Dir, Div of Cont'g Ed, Winston-Salem St Univ, 1980-; AL Assn for Childhood Ed, VP 1975-76; Nat Assn for Core Curric, Bd of Dirs 1978-80; Phi Delta Kappa; Assn for Supvn & Curric Devel; NC Adult Ed Assn; NC Assn of Col & Univ Sum Session Dirs; Tuscaloosa Commun Players, VP 1979-80; cp/GSA, Bd of Dirs 1979-80; Forsyth Co U Way Venture Grant Steering Com; Forsyth Co Yth Planning & Tng Coun; r/Presb; hon/Pubs, "Core in a Univ HS" 1982, "Model

for Advisement in an Individualized Undergrad Col," "Issues in Sec'dy Humanities" 1978, "Drama as Springboard to Successful Student Writing" 1974, "Black Studies in a White, Mid-Class Sch" 1970, Others; Phi Epsilon Kappa Profl Frat, Campus Pres at Kent St 1962-63; Public Ser Awd, Summit Co Wel Soc (w Wife); W/W in S & SW; Personalities of S.

HICKINGBOTHAM, BARBARA A oc/Administrator; b/Dec 7, 1937; h/17 Windsor Court, Little Rock, AR 72212; c/Herren Curtis, Frank Todd; ed/Att'd, Quachita Univ 1955, AR A&M 1956, Grad Ctr (Little Rock) 1964, NY Sch of Interior Design 1965, Martin McDaniel Sch of Real Est 1977, Univ of AR Ext Ctr 1979, Louis A Allen Assn Inc Profl Mgrs Sem and Wkshop 1981; pa/Pvt Tutoring, 1959-65; Interior Decorating on Consignment, 1965-68; Nat Investors Life, 1968-70; Owner, A Q Restaurants Inc, 1970-74; Public Relats Dir, Secy of St, 1974-77; Ct Clk, Mun Ct, 1979; Exec Dir, Nat Soc to Prevent Blindness, 1979; Dir of Single Parent Dept, Campus Crusade for Christ, 1981-; cp/Jr Dept Clb, Prog Com, Pleasant Val Country Clb; Publicity Com, Fund Raiser, AR Heart Assn; Fund Raiser, March of Dimes; Yg Dems By-Laws Com; Altrusa Intl Bd Mem; r/Immanuel Bapt Ch; hon/W/W: of Am Wom, in Am.

HICKS, DONALD ALBERT oc/Associate Professor of Sociology and Political Economy; b/Mar 31, 1947; h/3110 Kristin Court, Garland, TX 75042; ba/Richardson, TX; m/Tanya Lea Collins; p/Jane M Hicks, South Bend, IN; ed/PhD, Univ of NC Chapel Hill, 1976; BA, IN Univ, 1969; mil/USN 1971-75, Lt; pa/Assoc Prof of Sociol & Polit Economy, Univ of TX-Dallas, 1979-; Sr Urban Policy Staff, Pres's Comm for a Nat Agenda for the Eighties, EOP, 1980-81; Asst Dean for Grad Studies & Res 1976-78, Asst Prof of Sociol & Polit Economy 1975-79, Univ of TX-Dallas; Assn for Public Policy Anal & Mgmt; Reg Sci Assn; r/Luth; hon/Pubs, *Transition to the 21st Cent: Prospects & Policies for Ec & Urban-Reg Transformation* 1983, *Urban Am in the Eighties: Perspectives & Prospects* 1981; Fellow, Lincoln Inst of Land Policy, 1982-83; Fellow, Gerontological Soc, 1977-78; Phi Beta Kappa, 1969; W/W in S & SW; Personalities of S; Who's Where Among Writers; Men of Achmt.

HIGGINS, PAUL JOSEPH oc/Molecular Biologist, Cancer Researcher; b/Jul 30, 1946; h/1858 Byrd Drive, East Meadow, NY 11554; ba/New York, NY; m/Denise Laura Cote; c/Jennifer Ann, Stephen Paul, Craig Evan, Erik James, Sean Patrick; p/Vincent John (dec) and Lucille Higgins, New York, NY; ed/BS, Iona Col, 1968; MS, Long Isl Univ, 1973; PhD, NY Univ, 1976; pa/Res Assoc 1976-79, Assoc 1979-, Meml Sloan-Kettering Cancer Ctr; Asst Prof, Cell Biol & Genetics, Cornell Univ, 1980-; Harvey Soc; NY Acad of Scis; Am Assn for Cancer Res; Am Soc for Cell Biol; Am Soc for Microbiol; r/Rom Cath; hon/Author, Over 100 Sci Papers; Recip, Yg Investigator Awd, Nat Cancer Inst, 1980-83; W/W in Frontier Sci & Technol.

HIGGINSON, THOMAS J oc/Professor of Management, Millwright; b/May 18, 1940; ba/SEn MA Univ, North

Dartmouth, MA 02747; m/Anna Margaret Gardner; c/Matthew, Christopher, Thomas Samuel; p/Thomas J and Susan H Higginson (dec); ed/BS 1962, MBA 1963, EdD 1979, Boston Univ; pa/Prof of Mgmt, SEn MA Univ, Div of Cont'g Studies; Conslt, Var Firms; Constrn, in Field; Nat & NE Bus Ed Assns; Nat Assn for Career Ed; Am Fdn of Tchrs; cp/K of C; Lions; Elks; MA Lobsterman's Assn; r/Cath; hon/Pub, "A Study of the Job Opports for Bus Adm, Grads in the Contract Constrn Indust" 1979; Eagle Scout, Order of the Arrow, Ad Altare Dei, BSA; W/W in Fin & Indust.

HILL, JERRY MATTHEWS oc/Associate Professor of Education; b/Aug 28, 1940; h/504 Pepperdine, Edmond, OK 73034; ba/Edmond, OK; c/Jaree Lynn; p/Mr and Mrs Hayter Matthews, Groves, TX; ed/BS, Elem Ed, Lamar Univ, 1961; EdM, Elem Ed, Stephen F Austin St Univ, 1963; EdD, Elem Ed, Rdg McNeese St Univ, 1973; pa/Grade 4 Tchr, Pt Arthur Indep Schs, 1961-62; Grade 4, Springdale, AR, Schs, Fall 1962; Grade 4, Pasadena, TX, Schs, Sprg 1963; Grade 6, Title I Rdg, Advet Night Sch, Pt Arthur Indep Schs, 1965-72; Assoc Prof of Ed, Ctl St Univ, 1974-; Higher Ed Rdg Coun; Edmond Rdg Coun; OKC Rdg Coun; Wn Hgts Rdg Coun; OK Rdg Coun, St Parliamentn; IRA; Assn for Supvn & Curric Devel, Nat Bd Mem; OK Assn for Supvn & Curric Devel, St Pres; Delta Kappa Gamma, Chapt First VP; Phi Delta Kappa, Chapt Exec Bd; Delta Theta Chi; TX St Tchrs Assn, Life Mem; cp/DAR; r/Meth; hon/CSU Outstg Fac Wom, 1976; CSU Charter Mem, Mortar Bd, 1978.

HILL, LEMMUEL L oc/Technical Director; b/Mar 17, 1933; h/12307 Keel Turn, Bowie, MD 20715; ba/Dahlgren, VA; m/Suzanne Kennedy; c/Doug, Lee, Barry, Ann; p/Mamie L Hill; ed/BS, Physics, Rensselaer Polytechnic Inst, 1959; PhD, Physics (Nuclear Theory), Cath Univ of Am, 1967; mil/USN, 1950-55; pa/Hd of Nuclear Physics Br 1968, Hd of Physics Res Div 1973, Asst to Hd of Underwater Weapons Dept 1974, Sci Advr to Cmdr of Nav Surface Force (Atl) 1975, Hd of Radiation Physics Div 1976, Hd of Res & Technol Dept 1977, Hd of Weapons Sys Dept 1979, Tech Dir of Ofc of Nav Technol, Nav Mat Command 1980, Tech Dir 1983-, Nav Surface Weapons Ctr; hon/Pres Awd for Meritorious Exec Ser, 1982; Navy Superior Civilian Ser Awd, 1983.

HILL, MARCELLA WASHINGTON oc/Assistant Professor of Mathematics; b/Sep 5, 1927; h/1502 Gallatin Place, Northeast, Washington, DC 20017; ba/Washington, DC; m/Wendell T Jr; c/Wendell T III, Philip E; p/Dr and Mrs P C Washington, Los Angeles, CA; ed/BS, Chem and Math, magna cum laude, Jarvis Col, 1946; MS, Ed and Eng, Drake Univ, 1949; Student of Communs, Wayne St Univ, 1975-77; PhD, Ed, Pacific Wn Univ, 1981; GradCert, Adult Tng Spec, Georgetown Univ, 1982; pa/Math Tchr, St Louis Public Schs, 1950-52; Math Tchr, LA Public Schs, 1954-60; Math Tchr, Yorba Linda Public Schs, 1965-70; Instr, Math Ed, Chapman Col, 1968-70; Math Tchr, Detroit Public Schs, 1970-77; Math Tchr, DC

Public Schs, 1978-79; Math Prof, Univ of DC, 1979-; Treas, Secy, Pharm Guild Aux, 1956-60, 1974-78; Delta Sigma Theta Sorority; Assn of Howard Univ Wom; AAUW; NEA; NCTM; Other Orgl Mbrships; cp/Toastmasters Intl; Ch Wom U; Nat Coun of Negro Wom; r/Prot; hon/Pub, *Math in Action*, 1970; 4 Yr Col Scholar, 1943; Chem Awd, 1946; Music Awd, 1946; Personal Cit, Wayne St Fac Wives, 1973; Personal Cit, Wom Coun of Concerns, 1974; Toastmasters Intl, 1st, 2nd, 3rd Place Trophies, 1977; Disneyland Ser Awd.

HILL, ORVILLE F oc/Consultant; b/ Jan 6, 1919; h/1510 Southeast 127th Avenue, Vancouver, WA 98684; ba/ Same; m/Alta Lee Meeker; c/Diane Louise, James Michael, Barbara Jean; p/ Edgar M Hill (dec); ed/PhD in Chem 1948, MS in Chem 1941, Univ of IL; BS, Chem, Millikin Univ, 1940; pa/ Conslt, Nuclear Fuel Cycle; Staff Scist, Battelle-NW, 1977-84; Prin Chem Engr, Atl Richfield (Hanford Co) 1967-77, Isochem Inc 1965-67, Gen Elect Co 1964-65; Mgr, Tech Grps, Gen Elect Co, 1948-64; Am Chem Soc, 1942-, Chm of Richland Sect 1949-50, Councilor 1954-81; Am Nuclear Soc; AIChE; AAAS, Fellow; Alpha Chi Sigma; r/Epis; hon/Author, Num Pubs & Papers; Hon DSc, Millikin Univ, 1963; Awd for Recog of Outstg Ser, Richland Sect, Am Chem Soc; Sigma Xi; Phi Lambda Phi; Am Men of Sci; W/W: in W, in Technol Today.

HILL, PAMELA oc/Television News Executive Producer and Vice President; b/Aug 18, 1938; h/169 East 80th Street, New York, NY 10021; ba/New York, NY; m/Thomas G Wicker; c/Christopher, Cameron Wicker, Grey Wicker, Kayce Freed, Lisa Freed; p/Mr and Mrs Paul Abel, Muncie, IN; ed/BA, Bennington Col; Jr Yr Abroad, Univ of Glasgow, Scotland; Grad Study, Universidad Autonoma de Mexico; pa/Fgn Affairs Analyst, Rockefeller Pres Campaign, 1961-65; Res, Dir of Res, Assoc Prodr, Dir of White Paper Series, Prodr of Edwin Newman's "Comment," NBC News, 1970-73; Current TV News Exec Prodr & VP, ABC News; Dir's Guild of Am; Writers Guild of Am E; Trustee, Bennington Col; hon/Pub, *US Fgn Policy, 1945-65*, 1966; Photos Pub'd in Var Mags & Books; Var Emmy Awds; NY St Broadcasting Awd, 1979; Overseas Press Clb Awd, 1982; Matrix Awd, 1980; YWCA Salute to Wom Achievers, 1982; Num Other Awds; W/W: of Am Wom, in Am.

HILL, SARA L oc/Architect; b/May 25, 1951; h/721 Louisa Street, New Orleans, LA 70117; ba/Same; p/Lawrence and Mary Allanson (dec) Hill, Verona, NJ; ed/BArch, cum laude, Tulane Univ, 1974; BFA, magna cum laude, Newcomb Col, 1974; pa/Chief Arch Designer, Mathes, Bergman & Assocs Inc, Archs, 1974-76; Arch Designer, J B Blitch & Assocs, Archs, 1976-77; Arch Conslt, F Monroe Labouisse Jr, Arch, 1977-79; Staff Arch, Vieux Carre Comm, 1979-80; Ptnr/Gen Contractor, V C Bldrs, Gen Contractors, 1982-; Owner, The Hill Co, Archs, 1982-; Arch Conslt, Riley Assocs, Archs, 1982-; AIA; Constrn Specifications Inst; Bd of Dirs, Tulane Univ Alumni Assn, 1977-82; Nat Trust for Hist Preserv; Soc of Arch Histns; LA

Contractors Assn; r/Meth; hon/Pubs, "New Orleans Home Care Handbook" 1978, "Louisiana House Types" 1971, "The Arts of Time & Space" 1973, "Gt Louisiana Recipes" 1971; AIA Medal & Cert for Highest Scholastic Average in Class, Sch of Arch, Tulane Univ; 1974; Class of 1914 Prize in Art for Best Portfolio of Drawings from Animals, Sch of Art, Newcomb Col, 1974; Nat Semi-Finalist for Thomas J Watson F'ship in Amount of $7,000 for Worldwide Travel & Study, Newcomb Col, 1974; Blue Ribbon Awd, Annual Juried Show, Sch of Art, Newcomb Col, 1973; Num Other Hons; W/W of Am Wom.

HILL, WALTER ANDREW oc/Associate Professor of Soil Science; b/Aug 9, 1946; h/PO Box 71, Tuskegee Institute, AL 36088; ba/Tuskegee Inst, AL; c/Shaka W T; p/H Soloman and Tessie Paisley Hill, Kansas City, KS; ed/BA, Lake Forest Col, 1968; MAT, Univ of Chgo, 1970; MS, Univ of AZ, 1973; PhD, Univ of IL, 1977; pa/Undergrad Res Asst, Lake Forest Col, 1967-68; Chem Tchr, Chgo Bd of Ed, 1969-71; Grad Res Asst 1971-73, Irrigation & Fertility Spec 1973-74, Univ of AZ; Grad Res and Tchg Asst, Univ of IL, 1974-77; Asst Prof 1978-80, Assoc Prof 1980-, Dept of Agri Scis, Tuskegee Inst; Proctor, Hons Prog, Tuskegee Inst, 1983-84; VChm, USDA Reg Com S-187, 1983-84; Am Soc Agronomy; Soil Sci Soc of Am; Am Soc Hort Sci; Intl Soc Trop Root Crops; Intl Soil Sci Soc; NY Acad of Sci; r/AME; hon/Author, Chapts in Books, Num Jour Articles; UNCF Dist'd Scholar Awd, 1984; Plucknett Outstg Res Paper Awd, 1983; Outstg Yg Man in Am Awd, 1983; Dist'd Ser Awd, Carver Plant and Soil Sci Clb; Carver Res Ass; Danforth Assoc; Sigma Xi; Gamma Sigma Delta; Iron Key Awd, Lake Forest Col.

HILLE, RITA KATHRYN oc/Owner and Broker of Realty Company; b/Oct 26, 1933; ba/RKH Realty, 133 Main Street, Los Altos, CA, 1979-; c/Lani, Sheila, Julia, Lisa; p/Clarence Henry and Delma Lurella Wetzel Gordon; ed/BS, Bus Mgmt, San Jose St, 1974; AA, Social Sers, San Jose City Col, 1972; Sales Lic 1975, Broker Lic 1977, Anthony Sch; Grad, Rltrs Inst, 1978; mil/Hosp Corpsman 3rd Class, USN, 1951-53; pa/Sales Assoc, Bell Rltrs Inc, 1975-77; Owner, RKH Rlty, 1977-; Loan Broker, Refin Cnslrs Inc, 1982-; Pvt Pilot, 1976; Nat Assn of Rltrs, 1975-; San Jose & Los Altos Real Est Bds, 1975-; Palo Alto Real Est Bd, 1979-; Sunny Vale Real Est Bd, 1980-; Menlo Pk Real Est Bd; cp/LWV, 1974-; Los Altos Equal Opport Com, 1978-79; Chm, MLS Prog Com, 1979-; Repub; r/Presb; Sunday Sch Tchr; hon/ Originated the *Creekside Chronicle*, a Tract Newspaper in San Jose, 1969; Mem of Million $ Clb, 1977; W/W in Real Est in Am.

HILLIARD, ANNIE P oc/Business Manager, Business Teacher; b/Dec 24, 1944; h/5372 Phelps Luck Drive, Columbia, MD 21045; ba/Washington, DC; m/ Ronald E Hilliard; p/Jessie Melvin and Mary Lawson Toler, Roxboro, NC; sp/ Mary Jackson Hilliard, Phila, PA; ed/BS, Elizabeth City St Univ, 1967; MA, Trinity Col, 11971; MS, The Johns Hopkins Univ, 1978; pa/Sec'dy Tchr, DC Schs, 1968-; Bus Instr, IRS, 1978; Mem: Nat Bus Ed Assn, 1970-;

En Bus Ed Assn, 1971; Nat Assn Female Execs; Zeta Phi Beta Sorority Inc, MD St Dir, 1980-82; Phi Delta Kappa Intl, 1982; Nat Geographic Soc; r/Prot; hon/ Cert of Awd of Outstg Ser, DECA & Spingarn, 1979; Cert of Apprec for Vol Commun Ser, WACADA Inc, 1983; Career Ed Awd, 1975; Cer tof Awd, ATSSL, 1976; W/W of Am Wom.

HIMLER, MARSHA SUE oc/Associate Administrative Analyst; b/Mar 26, 1943; h/688 Gorge Road, Middleburgh, NY 12122; ba/Albany, NY; p/John Milton and Ruth Burks Himler, St Petersburg, FL; ed/BS, Bus Mktg, IN Univ, 1964; Postgrad Wk, Cornell Sch of Indust & Labor Relats; Student of Cnslg & Guid, Syracuse Univ; mil/ LCDR, USNR, 1973-; pa/Assoc Adm Analyst 1982-, Career Info Sys Conslt 1980-82, Sys Analyst 1978-80, Mgmt Info Sys Spec 1977-78, Employmt Cnslr 1970-77, Employmt Interviewer 1966-70, NYS Dept of Labor; Owner, Stonecroft Farm, 1976-; Owner, Himler Data Sers, 1970-74; Intl Pers in Employmt Security; Nat Assn of Female Execs; cp/Mensa; Am Driving Soc, Judge, Nat Mbrship Com; Welsh Pony Soc of Am, Life Mem; NEn Welsh Pony Assn, Dir 1968-, Secy; Repub Pres Task Force, Charter Mem; NY Repub St Com; r/Epis; hon/Quill & Scroll, 1960; NMSQT, Hon Mention, 1959; NYS, DAR Essay Awd, 1959; W/W: of Am Wom, in Fin & Indust.

HINES, MARY EMMA oc/Teacher, Businessperson; b/Jul 5, 1934; h/16032; Indian Creek, Cerritos, CA 90701; ba/ South Gate, CA; m/Theadore; c/Emma Corenia, Herbert Lee, Harold Louis, Joel Lynn, Janee Latricia; p/Walter and Emma Mae Harvey, Bolton, MS; ed/BS, Jackson St Univ; Life Credentials for the St of CA, Univ of CA LA; MA, Lavern Univ; pa/Tchr, Hinds Co, St of MS, 1958-64; Dept Chp of Eng Dept, Gompers Jr High, 1977-83; Tchr, LA City Schs, 1966-; Validation Com, Dept Chp, Coor of Other Activs, LA City Schs; U Tchrs of LA; NEA; Nat Coun of Tchrs; r/Pres of Mission, Gtr True Love Dist Assn, 1981-; Sunday Sch and Bible Tchr, Yth Pres, New Covenant Missionary Bapt Ch; hon/Cert of Merit by Author Study Clb; Trophy, Best Tchr, 1973; Cert of Merit by Title I of Gompers Jr High; Cert of Apprec, New Covenant Missionary Baptist Ch.

HINES-BATTLE, ETHEL BEATRICE oc/Clinical Specialist and Coordinator of Nursing Research; b/Dec 4, 1933; h/303 Eventide Drive, Murfreesboro, TN 37130; ba/Murfreesboro, TN; p/J Edward Jr and Willie S Hines, Alexandria, LA; ed/BSN, Dillard Univ, 1955; MSN, Vanderbilt Univ, 1970; pa/ Coor of Nsg Res 1973-, Equal Employmt Opport Cnslr 1973-81, Clin Spec (Neuro-Psychi) 1970-, Supvr (Neuro-Psychi) 1966-69, Staff Nurse (Neuro-Psychi) 1962-66, VA Med Ctr; Instr, Psychi Nsg (Jt Appt), Vanderbilt Univ, 1973-; Nurse Profl Standards Bd, VA Med Ctr, 1966-; Courtesies Com, Vanderbilt Univ, 1975-; Quality Assurance Com 1978-, Patient Ed Com 1980-, Therapy Spec 1967-, VA Med Ctr; r/Gordon Meml Meth Ch; hon/ Pubs, "Efficacy of Small Group Process w Intractable Neuro-Psychi Patients" 1973, "Eval of a Dietary Regimen for Chronic Constipation: Report of a Pilot

Study" 1980, "Self Medication Among Psychi Patients & Adherence After Discharge" 1982, Others; Grad, cum laude; Alpha Kappa Mu Hon Soc; Commend for Nsg Res, Dpty Asst Chief Med Dir for Nsg Progs, VA Ctl Ofc, Wash DC, 1982; Personalities of S; Book of Hon; DIB; Intl Register of Profiles; World W/W of Wom.

HINNEN, DEBORAH A oc/Diabetes Nurse Specialist; b/Jan 13, 1953; h/ Route 1, Box 135B, Augusta, KS 67010; ba/Wichita, KS; m/Richard L; c/Amanda Sue, Bryan L; p/Garland and Mildred Bare, Douglas, KS; ed/BSN 1975, MSN 1978, Wichita St Univ; pa/Staff Nurse, Wesley Hosp, 1975; Nsg Fac, Butler Co Commun Col, 1975-77; Diabetes Nurse Edr 1976-, Pediatric Fac 1976-, Univ of KS Sch of Med; Am Diabetes Assn; ANA; Am Assn of Diabetes Edrs; Pvt Pilot Lic, Single Engine, 1974-; Adv'd Reg'd Nurse Practitioner, 1981; r/Prot; hon/Var Pubs; Student Govt Pres, 1973; Delta Psi Omega, Nat Dramatic Frat, 1973; Grad, cum laude, Wichita St Univ, 1975.

HINRICHS, JAMES EDWARD oc/ Periodontal Clinical Research; b/Sep 17, 1949; h/1635 Chatham Avenue, Arden Hills, MN 55112; ba/Minneapolis, MN; m/Linda Kathleen Mason; c/Scott Jeffery, David James; p/Edward J and Helen C Hinrichs, Wahoo, NE; ed/BS, Univ of NE, 1971; DDS 1975, MS 1979, Univ of NE Col of Dentistry; pa/Gen Pract Resident, Wood VA Hosp, 1975-76; Clin Instr, Creighton Sch of Dentistry, 1976-77; Clin Instr, Univ of NE Col of Dentistry, 1977-79; Asst Prof, Univ of MN Sch of Dentistry, 1980-; Pvt Practitioner, Bloomington, MN, 1980-; Am Acad of Periodontology, 1977-; Am Dental Assn, 1973-; Bloomington Dental Study Clb, 1980-, Pres 1981-82; Am Dental Soc of Anesthesiology, 1980-, St Pres 1983-84; Intl Assn Dental Res, 1982-; MN Dental Assn, 1980-; Mpls Dist Dental Soc, 1980-; r/Cath; hon/Author, Var Jour Articles in Field; Dean's Hon List, 1973, 1974, 1975; Scholarly Achmt Awd, Intl Col of Denists, 1975; First Place Univ of NE Med Ctr Res Forum, 1979; Omicron Kappa Upsilon, 1985; W/W in Frontier Sci & Technol.

HINZE, WILLIE L oc/Chemist, Educator, Consultant; b/Jan 17, 1949; h/ 2200 Faculty Drive, Apartment #1-H, Winston-Salem, NC 27106; ba/ Winston-Salem, NC; m/Wen-wen Chu; p/Willie L H Hinze, Houston, TX; Alma Tresseler Hinze, Tomball, TX; ed/AA, Blinn Col, 1969; BS 1970, MA 1972, Sam Houston St Univ; PhD, TX A&M Univ, 1974; pa/Lectr in Chem, NIH Postdoct Fellow, TX A&M Univ, 1974-75; Instr in Chem, Blinn Col, 1974-75; Asst Prof of Chem 1975-80, Assoc Prof of Chem 1980-84, Prof of Chem 1984-, Wake Forest Univ; Am Chem Soc; Am Inst of Chems; Sigma Xi; Assn of Ofcl Analytical Chems; Royal Soc of Chem, London; Soc for Applied Spectroscopy; NC Acad of Sci; hon/Author, Num Pubs in Field; Phi Beta Kappa, 1969; Valedictorian, Blinn Col, 1969; Grad, summa cum laude, Chem, 1970; Phi Lambda Upsilon, 1974; Num Grants; W/W: in World; in Frontier Sci & Technol, in S & SW; Am Men & Wom of Sci.

HIPSCHER, JEROME JAY oc/Stu-

dent; h/17850 Northeast 6th Avenue, North Miami Beach, FL 33162; ba/ North Miami, FL; m/Joan Miller; c/ Joseph Wolfe, Marla Hipscher Wolfe, Phillip, Hara Amy, Stephanie Ann Wolfe; ed/Jr Acct Cert, Col Inst, 1952; AA, Queensborough Commun Col, 1977; BA, Polit Sci, FL Intl Univ, 1981; mil/AUS, Korean War; pa/US Postal Ser, 1959-76; Aide to St Senator John Santucci, 1972; Exec Dir, Jamaica Bay Coun, 1972-77; Internship, US Senator Richard Stone, 1981; Internship, Dade Co Commr Barry Schriber, 1981; Internship, Citizen Dispute Settlement Ctr (Mediator), 1981; Polit Sci Assn, 1980-; ASPA, 1982-; cp/N Miami Bch Beautification Com (Mayoral), 1982-; Student Govt Senate & Budget Coms, 1980-; Box Ofc, Ruth Foreman Theatre, 1981-; Queens Coun on the Arts, 1980; r/ Jewish; hon/Student Govt Certs of Apprec, 1980-; Pres Recog Awd, 1978; US EPA Spec Merit Awd, 1976; Queens Borough Pres Apprec Awd, 1974; W/ W in S & SE.

HIRAHARA, PATRICIA DIANE oc/ Television Producer, Marketing and Media Consultant, Commercial Photographer, Announcer; b/May 10, 1955; ba/PO Box 4581, Anaheim, CA 92803; p/Frank and Mary Hirahara, Anaheim, CA; ed/BA, CA St Univ-Fullerton, 1977; AA, Cypress Col, 1975; pa/Mktg, Public Relats Mgr, Pressaid Ctr, 1982-; Mktg Conslt, Disneyland, 1982; Mktg Conslt, Sonywks, 1982; Publicist, Nippo Mktg & Advtg's Hon Chm, Yuriko Saisho's So CA Tour, 1982; Publicist, Tokyo Metro Gov Shunichi Suzuki's So CA Visit, 1981; VP, Asst Gen Mgr, Asian Intl Broadcasting Corp, 1980-81; Creator, Prodr, Host, "IMAGES," 1980; Public Affairs Dir, U TV Broadcasting, 1977-80; Editor, TV Mate Mag, 1979-80; Co-Owner, Hirahara Photo, 1977-; Reporter, Orange Co Columnist, Photog, Kashu Mainichi CA Daily News, 1974-77; cp/Anaheim Sister Cities Com, Public Relats Rep, TV Prodr, Interpreter 1982-; Heart Mtn Reunion, Public Relats Conslt 1982; Little Tokyo Lions Clb, "News Lines" Bltn Editor 1982-; Announcer, Disneyland, Hollywood Pk, Lotus Fest, Orange Food Fair, Ventura Co Fair, 1978-; Japanese Am Citizens Leag; hon/Guest Columnist, TV Fan Mag, 1977; Spec Thank You, Disneyland, 1982; Finalist, Chef Kiku Cooking Contest, 1979; Perm Mem, Alpha Gamma Sigma, 1975; Suburban Optimist Ser Awd, 1975; Orange Co Nisei Queen, 1974; Seventeen Mag Nat Yth Adv Coun S'ship Awd Winner, 1973; Personalities of W & MW.

HIRES, CLARA S oc/Scientific Researcher; h/152 Glen Avenue, Milburn, NJ 07041; p/Charles E and Clara K Smith Hires (dec); ed/BA, Cornell Univ, 1928; Att'd, Tchrs Col, Columbia Univ, Rutgers Univ, Montclair Tchrs Col, Univ of PA; pa/Tchr of Sci, Edgewood Sch 1920-25, Buxton Country Day Sch 1929-32, Shore Road Acad 1932-34; Owner, Mistaire Labs, 1929-; AAAS; NY Acad of Sci; Am Fern Soc; NJ Acad of Sci; Botanical Soc of Am; Paleontological Soc; Am Geol Inst; Torrey Botanical Clb; NY Botanical Garden; NY Microscopical Soc; Am & NY Hort Socs; Intl Soc of Stereology; LA Intl Fern Soc; Brit Pteridological Soc; Intl Biogl Assn; Sigma Delta Epsilon,

Kappa Chapt; Am Mus of Natural Hist; AAUW; cp/Vol, Trustee on Mgmt Bd, Overlook Hosp, 1938-42; Maplewood Garden Clb; Summit Nature Clb; Summit Col Clb; Wellesley & Cornell Clbs; LWV; WY Assn; hon/Author, Spores, Ferns, Microscopic Illusions Analyzed, 1965, 1978; Contbr, Articles to Profl Jours; Keynote Spkr, Stereology Proceedings of 2nd Intl Cong, 1967; Awds, Orchid & Hort Socs, 1935; Am Men of Sci; Ldrs in Am Sci; W/W: of Am Wom, in E, in Am; World W/W of Wom; 2,000 Wom of Achmt; DIB; Intl Authors & Writers W/W; Intl W/W of Intells; Intl Book of Hon.

HIRT, JANET ROSE oc/Educator; b/ Mar 14, 1942; h/766 North Main Street, Meadville, PA 16335; ba/Springfield, PA; p/Ira George and Gladys Gertrude McLaren Hirt (dec); ed/AB, En Col, 1964; MA, Allegheny Col, 1969; MA, Villanova Univ, 1973; MS, Drexel Univ, 1977; Postgrad, Oxford Univ, 1970; Att'd, Sussex Univ, 1972; pa/Copy Editor, Am Bapt Bd of Pubs, 1964; Tchr of HS Eng 1964-73, 1976-, Cnslr 1973-75, Springfield Sch Dist; Am Lib Assn; Mod Lang Assn; NCTE, Life Mem; NEA; PA St Ed Assn; Springfield Ed Assn; AAUW; Eng Spkg Union; cp/ Buten Mus of Wedgwood, Life Mem; Wedgwood Collectors Soc, Charter Mem; r/Prot; hon/World W/W of Wom; W/W of Am Wom; DIB.

HITT, HERBERT DAN oc/United Methodist Clergyman; b/Feb 5, 1935; h/ 601 West Barron, Everman, TX 76140; ba/Everman, TX; m/Hazel Sims; c/ LaWanda Ann Hitt Downs, Michael Dan, Janyce Kay Hitt Christenberry; p/ James Cleveland and Emily Louisa Alday Hitt (dec); ed/BA, Baylor Univ, 1958; Postgrad Wk, Brite Div Sch, TX Ctl Univ, 1960; Specialized Tng, Perkins Sch of Theol, So Meth Univ, 1957; pa/ Pastorates: Oak Br 1950-51, Bardwell 1951-52, Meirs Settlement 1952-53, Aquilla 1953-54, Rosenthal-Mooreville 1954-57, Waco-Wesley 1957-58, Loving & Jean 1958-59, St Paul-Breckenridge 1959-62, Ft Worth-Wesley 1962-63, Salem-Graham 1963-64, Bangs 1964-66, Waco-Hillcrest & Bosqueville 1966-68, Ft Worth-Asbury 1968-72, Ft Worth-St Paul 1972-75, Cleburne-St Paul 1975-77, Saginaw 1977-81, Everman 1981- (All in TX); cp/Past Pres, Saginaw Lions Clb; Chm, Div Alcohol Probs & Gen Wel; Past Treas, Ctl TX Co Bd Christian Social Concerns; Former Mem, Kiwanis Clb, Optimist Clb; Lion, 1964-; r/U Meth; hon/Recip, Pres Awd, Lions Intl, in Recog of Exceptl Ldrship and Devoted Ser, 1982; Lion of the Yr Awd, Saginaw Lions Clb, 1982; W/W: in TX Today, in Meth Ch; Personalities of S; DIB; Commun Ldrs & Noteworthy Ams.

HOADLEY, WALTER E oc/Senior Research Fellow; b/Aug 16, 1916; ba/ Bank of America Center, Room 4970, PO Box 37000 (Department #9996), San Francisco, CA 94137; m/Virginia Alm; c/Richard A, Jean Hoadley Price; p/ Walter Evans and Marie Howland Preece Hoadley (dec); ed/AB 1938, MA 1940, PhD 1946, Univ of CA-Berkeley; Hon DCS, Franklin & Marshall, 1963; LLD, Golden Gate Univ, 1968; Hon Dipl, El Instituto Technologico Autonomo de Mexico, 1974; LLD, Univ of the Pacific, 1979; pa/Exec VP & Chief

Economist, Bk of Am NT&SA, 1966-81; Sr Res Fellow, Hoover Instn, Stanford Univ, 1981-; Dir, Armstrong World Industs 1962-, Lucky Stores Inc 1981-, Robert A McNeil Corp 1982-, PLM Inc 1982-, Pacific Gas Transmission 1983-, Soule Steel 1982-; Var Past Positions; Am Statl Assn; Conf of Bus Economists; Intl Mgmt & Devel Inst, Dir & Mem of Exec Com 1980-; US Coun for Intl Bus, Chm of Com on Intl Monetary Affairs 1980-; cp/Intl C of C, VP of Comm on Intl Monetary Relats 1980-; Conserv Foun, Trustee 1974-; r/Meth; hon/Columnist, *Dun's Bus Month*; Author, Num Articles on Forecasting, Global Fin & Other Ec Subjects in Var Pubs; Ec Commentator, KRON-TV, SF; Phi Beta Kappa, 1937; Fellow, Am Statl Assn, 1955; Fellow; Nat Assn of Bus Economists, 1968; Fellow, Intl Acad of Mgmt, 1981; Berkeley Fellow, Univ of CA, 1979; W/W: in Am, in CA, in Fin & Indust, in World, in W; Commun Ldrs & Noteworthy Ams; Intl Yrbook & Statesmen's W/W; Intl W/W of Intells.

HOANG, DUC VAN oc/Clinical Professor of Pathology; b/Feb 17, 1926; h/3630 Barry Avenue, Los Angeles, CA 90066; ba/Los Angeles, CA; m/ Mau-Ngo T Vu; c/Hoang Diem Nga, Hoang Quy Luat, Hoang Thanh Tung, Hoang-Vu Duc-An; p/Tham Thi Nguyen, Davis, CA; ed/MD, Univ of Hanoi Sch of Med, Vietnam, 1953; mil/ Army of the Repub of Vietnam, 1952-63; pa/Clin Prof of Pathol, Univ of So CA, 1978-; Dean, Univ of Minh Duc Sch of Med, 1970-71; Dean, The ARVN Mil Med Sch, 1959-63; Univ of So CA Alumni Assn; Univ of So CA Salerni Collegium; Fondation du Prix Mondial de la Paix; Am Com for Integrating En and Wn Med; cp/Vo Vi Assn of Am; r/Cath; hon/Pubs, *Towards an Integrated Humanization of Med* 1957, *The Man Who Weighs the Soul* 1959, *En Med-A New Direction?* 1970, Var Short Stories; Translator, *Pestis, Intro to the Wk of Albert Camus*, Vietnamese Translation of *La Peste*; Editor, *The E*; PhD (DrHC) in Oriental Med, 1983.

HOARE, PAUL MICHAEL oc/ Founder and Director; h/161 Bunker Hill Street, Boston, MA 02129; ba/ Same; m/Ann Schlosberg; c/"America" Maryann K Schlosberg Hoare; p/James J Hoare (dec); Mary T Walsh-Hoare; ed/ AB, Eng and Phil, Boston Col, 1965; Grad Ed Courses for Sec'dy Eng Tchrs Cert, Boston Univ, Boston St; pa/Editor, Ledger Pub, 1 Yr; Contract Tchr, City of Boston, 1966-69; Free-Lance Writer & Conslt; Fdr & Dir, Space Stas World Peace Plan Inst 1983, Am Space Action Netwk 1975, Space Sci Film Foun 1981; Space Sci & World Peace Programming Conslt, Res & Devel; Intl Inst; UN Assn; Theosophical Soc; cp/Boston Visual Artists Union; Boston Film Video Foun; Bus Execs Agnst Nuclear War; Union of Concerned Scists; High Tech Profls for Peace; r/Am Cath; hon/Co-Editor, *Where's the Music Coming From?*; 3rd Yr Col, 1st Semester Dean's List.

HOBSON, J ALLAN oc/Psychiatrist; b/Jun 3, 1933; h/138 High Street, Brookline, MA 02146; ba/Boston, MA; m/Joan Merle Harlowe; c/Ian, Christopher, Julia; p/John and Anne Hobson, New London, NH; ed/BA, Wesleyan Univ, 1955; MD, Harvard Med Sch,

1959; mil/Lt, USPHS, 1960-; pa/Dir, Lab of Neurophysiol, MA Mtl Hlth Ctr, 1967-; Asst Prof of Psychi 1969-74, Assoc Prof of Psychi 1974-78, Prof of Psychi 1978-, Harvard Med Sch; Consltg Psychi, Beth Israel Hosp, 1982-; Var Past Mbrships; hon/Author, *The Brainstem Core, Neuronal Activity in Sleep*, 108 Articles; B Rush Gold Medal for Best Sci Exhib, Am Psychi Assn, 1978; Other Hons; W/W in E; Men of Achmt.

HOCHBERG, FREDERICK GEORGE oc/Solar Engineer; b/Jul 4, 1913; h/6760 Hillpark Drive, Los Angeles, CA 90068; ba/Burbank, CA; c/ Frederick George, Ann; p/Frederick Joseph and Lottie A LeGendre Hochberg (dec); ed/BA, Univ of CA LA, 1937; mil/Ensign, USNR, 1944-46 (WWII); pa/ VP & Gen Mgr, Solar Engrg Co Inc, 1977-; VP, Vicalton SA, Mexico, 1976-; Mgmt Conslt, Fred J Hochberg Co, 1974-; VP & Gen Mgr, Mo Hickory Corp, 1972-74; VP, Treas, Dir of Bus Affairs, Wm L Pereira Assocs, Planners, Archs, Engrs, 1967-72; Other Former Positions; Soc CA Accts; Am Arbitration Assn Panel; Other Profl Activs; cp/ Mensa; LA C of C; Secy, Avalon City Planning Com, 1956-58; VChm, Town Hall W; Dir & Pres, LA Child Guid Clin; Former Chm, Friends of Avalon Foun; Former Mayor, City of Avalon; Others; hon/Man of Yr, Catalina Isl, 1956; Pub'd Author; W/W: in W, in Fin & Indust, in World; in CA; DIB; 2,000 Men of Achmt; Blue Book.

HOCKENBERRY, RONALD KENT oc/Teacher, Concert Pianist; b/May 15, 1933; h/105 Runnymede Avenue, Wayne, PA 19087; ba/Wayne, PA; m/ Jeanne Carney; c/Thomas Lloyd, David Neal, Carl Nevin; p/Nevin E and Elva Jones Hockenberry, Stuart, FL; ed/BS, cum laude, W Chester Univ, 1955; Att'd, PA St Univ, 1962; Musical Studies, New Sch of Music; Studies in London, Paris & Amsterdam; mil/USN, Lt; pa/Tchr, Newtown Square 1955-62, Huntington (NY) 1962-64, Swarthmore 1964-68, Radner 1968-84, New Sch of Music 1962-68, Wilmington Music Sch, PA St Univ 1956-62; Conductor, Phila, 1960-84; Concert Pianist, European Tours, 1978-83; Journalist, Travel Articles; PSEA; RTEA, Pres 1982; SEA, Pres 1962-64; MENC; NEA; Phi Delta Kappa; r/Unitarian; hon/Composer, 7 Musicals for Chd; Author, Profl Articles, Travel Articles for Suburban Pubs; Theodore Presser Awd, 1955; Hon Ldr, Cub Scout Pack #6, Cookstown, Co Tyrone, No Ireland.

HODGES, DEWEY HARPER oc/ Research Scientist; b/May 18, 1948; h/ 3255 Trebol Lane, San Jose, CA 95148; ba/Moffett Field, CA; m/Margaret Elin Jones; c/Timothy, Jonathan, David, Philip; p/Plummer M and Etha M Harper Hodges; ed/BS w High Hons in Aerospace Engrg, Univ of TN-Knoxville, 1969; MS 1970, PhD 1973, Aeronaut & Astronautical Engrg, Stanford Univ; mil/Served to Capt, AUS, 1973-77; pa/Res Scist 1970-, Theoretical Grp Ldr of Rotorcraft Dynamics Div 1980-, AUS Aeromechs Lab, NASA Ames Res Ctr; Lectr, Dept of Aeronautics & Astronautics, Stanford Univ; Prof of Theol, No CA Bible Col; Assoc Fellow, Assoc Editor of Jour 1981-83, AIAA; Creation Res Soc; Am Helicopter Soc; Tau Beta Pi; Pi Tau Sigma; cp/

Acacia Clb; r/Elder, Christian Commun Ch; hon/Contbr, Num Articles to Tech Jours; Recip, NASA Tech Utilization Awd, 1975; Tech Brief Awd, 1976; Dept of Army Commend Medal, 1977, Ofcl Commend, 1978; AUS Res & Devel Achmt Awd, 1979; Dept of Army Ofcl Commend, 1983.

HOEFS, PAUL THEODORE II oc/ Rancher; b/Nov 30, 1926; h/Box 727, Wood Lake, NE 69221; m/Patricia Anderson; c/Paul, Sheri, Mary, Jan, Boni, John, Patrice, Jim, Mark; p/Paul A and Margaret Mary Roberts Hoefs; ed/Student, Public Schs, Prairie Duchien, WI; pa/Rancher, Wood Lake, NE, 1944-; Former Aerobatic & Spray Pilot; Nat Cattle Assn, Dir 1979; NE Stock Growers Assn, Past VChm of Brand & Theft, Past Chm of Public Lands, Pres 1981-82; Aircraft Owners and Pilots Assn; SD Stock Growers Assn; Sandhills Cattle Assn; Farm Bur Clb; cp/Former Vol Fireman; Past Pres, Sch Dist 7, Sch Dist 95; Past Pres, Cherry Co Hosp Bd, Cherry Co Hosp Foun; Past Bd of Dirs, Gtr NE Hlth Sys Agy; Past Trustee, Sacred Heart Ch.

HOELLER, MARY LOUISE oc/Nurse Educator, Director of Department of Surgical Nursing; b/Dec 5, 1928; h/PO 21976, Shreveport, LA 71120; ba/ Shreveport, LA; p/Grace A Hoeller, San Antonio, TX; ed/Nsg Dipl, St Joseph Sch of Nsg, 1951; Postgrad Course in OR Adm, 1953; BS, Nsg Ed, De Paul Univ, 1954; Master in Nsg, LA St Univ, 1977; pa/Asst Prof of Surg/Perioperative Nsg & Dir of Dept of Surg Nsg, LA St Univ Med Sch; Dir, Surg, Technol Prog, Charity Hosp of LA, 1978-80; Instr, Dipl Prog, Nashville, TN, 1965-75; Other Previous Positions; r/Cath; hon/Pubs, *Curric Guide for Surg Technol Progs* 1982, "Surgical Intervention" 1971, 1974, *Surg Technol: Basis for Clin Practice* 1974, *The OR Technician* 1965, 1968, Others; Nat Hon Soc for Nsg, Sigma Theta Tau; W/W in Frontier Sci & Technol.

HOERBER, JOHN LEONARD VI oc/ International Marketing Manager; b/ Mar 31, 1951; h/708 Glen Eagle Court, Danville, CA 94583; ba/San Leandro, CA; m/Jean Marie; c/John Leonard VII; p/John L Hoerber V, Miami Shores, FL; ed/MBA, Intl Mktg, Pepperdine Univ, 1978; BS, Marine Trans, US Merchant Marine Acad, 1973; mil/USN, 3 Yrs; Current Lt, USNR; pa/Intl Mktg Mgr, RDI Inc, 1982-; Sales Mgr, Tracor Inc, 1979-82; Prod Mgr, Magnavox, 1977-79; Mkt Devel Rep, Sperry, 1973-77; Radio Tech Comm for Maritime Ser on Spec Com 65 (Collision Avoidance) & Spec Com 78 (Fed Radionavigation Plan); Nat Marine Electronics Assn; Reg VP, USMMA Alumni Assn; cp/Ofcr's Clb, Kings Pt; Ldrship Contbr, Kings Pt Fund; r/Cath; hon/ Author, 38 Articles Pub'd in Intl Marine Jours & Mags; Chaired & Presented Papers at Several Marine Tech Confs, incl'g, RTCM, NMEA, Expo Pesca, and Pvt Sems; MBA Thesis, Top 1 Percent of Those Submitted, 1978; Grad'd w Hons, USMMA, 1973; W/W in SW; Personalities of S.

HOFER, VIRGINIA EVA HOLLY oc/ Kindergarten Teacher and Special Needs Coordinator; b/Jul 10, 1928; h/ 205 Wisconsin Avenue Northwest, Huron, SD 27350; ba/Huron, SD; m/ Kenneth Eugene (dec); p/Rufus Holly and Louisa Holly Patrick (dec); ed/BS, Evangel Col, 1961; MA, Univ of MN, 1969; pa/Pvt Piano Instr, Huron, SD, 1946-53; Secy, A S Avery, 1947; Clk, Ritchey's Music Store, 1947-52; Tchr, 2nd and 3rd Grade, Huron Indep Sch Dist, 1953-60; Subst Tchr, Huron Indep Sch Dist & St Martin's Ch Sch, 1980-82; Tchr, 2nd & K-6 Spec Lng & Behavioral Probs, St Paul Indep Sch Dist, 1961-77; Curric Spec, SD Vital Info for Ed & Wk & Career Competency Proj, 1978-79; Conslt 1978, 1979-80, Adm Asst 1981, SD Vital Info for Ed and Wk; Kgn Tchr, James Val Christian Sch, 1982-83; Spec Needs Coor, Chd Deserve Equity Proj, Rural Alternatives Inst, 1982-83; Adj Instr, Huron Col Cont'g Ed, 1982; SD Ed Assn, 1953-60, 1978-79; Huron Ed Assn, 1953-60, 1978-79; NEA, 1953-70; Assn for Childhood Ed, 1953-60; MN Ed Assn, 1961-77; City of St Paul Ed Assn, 1972-77; Am Fdn of Tchrs, 1975-77; Am Voc Assn, 1979-80; SD Voc Assn, 1979-80; Pheasant Chapt, SD Pers & Guid Assn, 1978-79; Assn for Christian Ednl Internation, 1982-83; r/ Assem of God; hon/Compiler/Developer, Decoder-Finn 360 for SLBP 1973-74, Huron Career Ed Plan & 4 Activity Books 1978; Developer, 6 Career Info Tchg Units, SD View, 1980; W/W: Biogl Record-Child Devel Profls, in Am Wom, in MW.

HOFFMAN, EDWARD FENNO III oc/Sculptor; b/Oct 20, 1916; h/353 Oak Terrace, Wayne, PA 19087; ba/Same; m/ Nadine Kalpaschnikoff; c/Susan R Johns, David F, Cynthia L Carosso; p/ Edward F and Elizabeth R Hoffman; ed/ Student, PA Acad of Fine Arts, 1946-50; mil/WW II, 5 Yrs; pa/Asst to Paul Manship, 1951; Sculptor in Residence, Henry Clews Meml Art Foun, La Napoule, France, 1952-55; Sculptor in His Own Studio, 1955-; Solo Exhbns, Galerie Internationale (NYC) 1977, Grand Ctl Art Galleries (NYC) 1970, Woodmere Art Gallery (Phila) 1966, Art Assn of Newport (RI) 1965, Others; Permanent Collections, Phila Mus of Art, PA Acad of the Fine Arts, Garden of the Col of Phys & Surgs, St Mathews Rom Cath Ch, Nat Acad of Design, Portland Mus of Art, NC Mus of Art, Brookgreen Gardens, Num Others; Nat Sculpture Soc, 1st VP 1973-76; Nat Acad of Design, Academician; Allied Artists of Am; Am Artists Profl Leag; Artists Equity; r/Epis; hon/Thomas R Proctor Prize, Nat Acad of Design, 1982; Coun of Am Artists Socs Prize, Am Artists Profl Leag, 1981; Hexter Prize, Nat Sculpture Soc, 1979; Speyer Prize, Nat Acad of Design; Silver Medal, Nat Sculpture Soc, 1973; Watrous Gold Medal, Nat Acad of Design, 1972; Gold Medal of Hon, Am Artists Profl Leag, 1972; Anna Hyatt Huntington Awd, Am Artists Profl Leag, 1970; Medals & Coins, 102nd Issue, The Soc of Medalists 1981, Baldwin-Wallace Col Medal 1976, Huebner Gold Medal, The Am Col (Bryn Mawr) 1975, Stokes Medal, Planned Parenthood 1975, Others; Num Other Hons; W/W: in Am Art, in E; Intl W/W Art & Antiques; Am Artists of Renown.

HOFFMAN, LEAH JANE oc/ Speech-Language Pathologist in Private Practice; b/Jun 10, 1953; h/1305 Wychwood Road, Charleston, WV 25314; m/ Randall James; c/Matthew Ross; p/Matt

(dec) and Betty J Fisher, Charleston, WV; ed/BS 1974, MS 1975, Postgrad in Ed Adm 1976-79, WV Univ; pa/ Spch-Lang Pathologist, WV Indust Sch for Boys, 1974-75; Spch-Lang Pathol & St Conslt, WV Hd Start Progs, 1976; Coor for Spch-Lang Pathols, Kanawha Co Schs in WV, 1976-79; Dir of Exceptl Chd Progs, Boone Co Schs in WV, 1979-82; Owner & Dir, Spch & Lang Therapy Clin, 1982-; Adj Instr, WV Col of Grad Studies Inst; WV Spch & Hearing Assn; ASHA; CEC, St & Nat; Netwk, A Wom's Org; cp/Windsor Forest Garden Clb; Wom's Clb; r/Cath; hon/Recip, Grant Awd, WV Indust Sch for Boys, 1974-75; W/W in S & SW; Personalities of S.

HOGAN, FANNIE BURRELL oc/ Librarian, Head of Bibliographic Instruction; b/Apr 6, 1923; h/1981 Valley Ridge Drive, Southwest, Atlanta, GA 30331; ba/Atlanta, GA; c/Erica W Jones, Maria Monique Whipple; p/Mr and Mrs Alexander Burrell Sr (dec); ed/BA, Eng, Dillard Univ, 1945; MSLS, Atlanta Univ, 1950; MA, Eng, Atlanta Univ, 1978; pa/Eng Tchr, Gilbert Acad, 1945-49; Hd Libn, Claflin Col, 1950-54; Hd Libn & Dir of Lib Orientation 1954-82, Tchr of Med Record Adm, Libnship Course & Tchr of Chd's Lit 1956-69, Clark Col; Current Libn & Hd of Bibliographic Instrn, Atlanta Univ Ctr, Robert W Woodruff Lib; Am Lib Assn; Metro Lib Assn; Phi Delta Kappa; Col & Res Libs; Atlanta Univ Ctr Consortium Chapt, Phi Delta Kappa; r/ U Meth; hon/Author of Poem, "All Ages Can Learn" in Phylon Mag, 1981; All Expense Paid Study Tour to Poland, Clark Col, 1973; W/W in S & SW; DIB.

HOHU, MARGARET KUULEI oc/ Gerontology Consultant, Educator, Nurse; b/Feb 21, 1924; h/28041 Camel Heights Circle, PO Box 159, Evergreen, CO; p/Edmund K and Fannie Werner (dec) Hohu, Volcano, HI; ed/AA, Nsg, Univ of Houston, 1947; RN, Jefferson Davis Hosp Sch of Nsg, 1947; Cert'd Reg'd Nurse Anesthetist, Baylor Univ Med Ctr Sch of Nurse Anesthetists, 1953; BS, Allied Hlth, CO Wom's Col, 1975; MA, Gerontology 1977, EdD, Gerontology & Ed 1979, Univ of No CO; pa/Inser Edr/Staff Devel Conslt, Nsg Homes, 1982-; Intravenous Therapist, Swedish Med Ctr, 1982-; Voc Edr, 1980-; Gerontology Conslt & Lectr, 1978-; Adj Prof in Gerontology, Greeley & Denver, 1979-; Nurse Anesthetist, Anesthesia Assocs of Greeley, 1975-78; Staff Nurse Anesthetist & Instr, Fitzsimons Army Med Ctr, 1970-75; Num Previous Positions; CO Assn of Nurse Anesthetists; SD Assn of Nurse Anesthetists; Wn Gerontological Soc; Gov's White House Conf on Aging; Mt Evans Hospice, 1980-; APGA Aging Proj; Doct Voc Ed Assn; Denver Free Univ, Evergreen Br; Nat Assn of Female Execs; Nat Coun on Aging; CO Gerontological Soc; AAUP; Kappa Delta Pi, Ed Hon Soc; cp/ Greeley Meals on Wheels Bd of Dirs; r/Bapt; hon/Pubs, Pre-Retirement & Retirement Ed Prog: A Ldrship Tng Manual 1979, Tomorrow is Mine 1979, Many Gerontology Articles for Profl Jours & Newspapers; Gov's CO Doct Awd Nom, 1979; W/W Am Wom; W/W in W.

HOLBROOK, BOYD LYNN oc/Data Processing Manager; b/Dec 24, 1947; h/ 1470 Cahoon Street, Ogden, UT 84401;

ba/Syracuse, UT; m/Margaret V; c/ Arlene Rowe, Kenneth Webster, Sherry Lynn Holbrook, Christie Sue Holbrook, Russell Webster, Karyn Webster; p/ Walter H and Connie J Holbrook, Plain City, UT; sp/Richard and Olive Vandenberg (dec); ed/BS, Webster St Col, 1975; mil/US Army; pa/Computer Sys Engr, TRW, 1979-81; Sr Sys Analyst, EIS, 1978-79; Sr Programmer/Analyst, WMC, 1974-78; Mem: Pres 1980-82, Secy/Treas 1983-84, WRC; Pres, USRC, 1983-84; Wn Dir, FRC, 1984; Silver Star, 1969; Purple Heart, 1969; Vietnamese Gallantry Cross, 1969; Air Medal, 1969; W/W in W.

HOLDEN, FREDERICK THOMPSON oc/Petroleum Geology; b/Jun 23, 1915; h/1601 Medkiff Road, #214, Midland, TX 79701; ba/Midland, TX; p/ Fred B Holden (dec); ed/AB, Denison Univ, 1937; Postgrad, KS Univ, 1938; PhD, Univ of Chgo, 1941; pa/Geologist, Carter Oil Co, 1941-46; Dist Geologist, Jackson, MS, 1946-52; Staff Geologist, Tulsa, OK, 1952-54; Sr Geologist, Shreveport & OKC, OK, 1954-60; Sr Geologist 1960-67, Sr Profl Geologist 1967-71, Humble Oil & Refining Co; Exploration Geologist 1971-73, Sr Exploration Geologist 1973-75, Geol Scist 1975-78, Sr Geol Scist 1978-, Exxon Co, USA; Fellow, Geol Soc of Am; Am Assn of Petro Geologists; Am Inst of Profl Geologists, OK Sect Secy-Treas 1967-68; Shreveport Geol Soc; MS Geol Soc, VP 1951-52; W TX Geol Soc; OKC Geol Soc; r/Presb; hon/ Author, Num Articles in Geol Jours, 1942-62; Hon DSc, Denison Univ, 1980; W/W: in S & SW, in Technol Today; Am Men & Wom of Sci.

HOLIDAY, MARTHA JEAN oc/ Fashion Show Stylist, Publicist, Author; b/Jan 20, 1926; h/119 East 83rd Street, New York, NY 1008; ba/Same; m/ William McNally; p/Nester L and Mary Alice (Hutch) Lessick (dec); sp/Louis J and Margaret (Doolan) McNally (dec); ed/BA, CA St Tchrs Col, 1948; Att'd NY Univ Sch of Retailing, 1948-49; pa/ w Slenderlia, NYC, 1952-56; Asst Fashion Promotion Dir, Simplicity Patterns Co, 1957-; Prodr of Fashion Shows, Biltmore Hotel, NYC, 1957-59; Others; Freelance Fashion Show Dir & Stylist; Fashion Columnist; Mem: Intl Platform Assn; Fashion Grp Intl; Am Wom in Radio & TV; Nat Bus Diners; r/Metaphysics; hon/"Holiday on Fashion"; Other Pubs; Meritorious Awds, 1962-; Fund Raising for Fashion Show, 1962; Others; W/W: in E, of Am Wom; Intl W/W of Wom

HOLLAND, DIANNE DAVIS oc/ Cytotechnologist; b/Dec 25, 1953; h/5 Parkway Commons, Shreveport, LA 71104; ba/Shreveport, LA; p/Chester Clarance and Eloise Ebarb Davis, Shreveport, LA; ed/Att'd, NE LA Univ, 1971-73; BS, Biol, Univ of S AL, 1975; Cert, Univ of S AL Sch of Cytotechnol, 1977; pa/Cytotechnologist, Phys & Surgs Hosp 1977-, Willis-Knighton Meml Hosp 1981- (Pt-time), VA Hosp 1982 (Pt-time); Am Soc of Cytology; Am Soc of Clin Pathols; So Assn of Cytologists; LA Soc of Cytology; r/Cath; hon/ Pub, "The Cytodiagnosis of Lung Cancer: Comparison Between Sputa, Bronchial Brushings & Bronchial Washings" in The Scanner, 1978; W/W of Am Wom.

HOLLINGER, PAULA COLODNY oc/Member of the Maryland House of Delegates; b/Dec 30, 1940; h/3708 Lanamer Road, Randallstown, MD 21133; ba/Annapolis, MD; m/Paul; c/ Ilene, Marcy, David; p/Samuel (dec) and Ethel Colodny, Silver Springs, MD; ed/ RN, Mt Sinai Hosp Sch of Nsg; pa/Public Hlth Sch Nurse for Balto Co Dept of Hlth, 1973-78; Resident Camp Nurse, 1974-77; Myasthenia Gravis Spec, Acute Stroke Unit, Univ of MD Hosp, 1971-73; Clin Instr, Psychi Nsg, Tuskegee Inst, 1969-70; cp/MD Ho of Dels (Assigned to Envir Matters Com), 1978-; Nat Conf of St Legis, 1983; Chair, Legis Com, Wom's Legis Caucus, 1983; LPN Task Force, 1983; Gov's Task Force on Violence & Extremism, 1983; Other Past Mbrships; r/Jewish; hon/ Recip, Murry Guggenheim Awd for Excell in Nsg; Mem, Nat Order of Wom Legis, MD Assn of Elected Wom; W/ W: in Am Polit, in E, in Am, of Am Wom; Notable Ams; Personalities of Am; Personalities of S; Dir of Dist'd Ams.

HOLLOMON, J HERBERT oc/Director of Center for Technology and Policy; b/Mar 12, 1919; h/121 Carlton Street, Brookline, MA 02146; ba/Boston, MA; m/Nancy Gade; c/Jonathan Bradford, James Martin, Duncan Twiford, Mrs Elizabeth Wheeler Vrugtman, Peter Richter; p/John Herbert and Pearl Twiford Hollomon (dec); ed/BS in Physics 1940, DSc in Metallurgy 1946, MIT; pa/Current Dir of Ctr for Technol & Policy, Boston MA; Dir of Ctr for Policy Alternatives 1972-83, Prof of Engrg 1973-, Japan Steel Indust Prof 1975-, Vis'g Prof of Engrg 1972-73, Conslt to the Pres & Provost 1970-72, MIT; Pres 1968-70, Pres-Designate 1967-68, Prof at Salzburg Sem in Am Studies 1969, Univ of OK; Num Previous Positions; Am Soc for Metals, 1942-, Fellow; Metall Soc of Am Inst of Mines, Metall and Petro Engrs, 1944-; AAAS, 1948-; Am Phy Soc, 1948-, Fellow; Soc for the Hist of Technol, 1960-; Nat Acad of Engrg, 1964-, Fdg Mem; Am Inst of Chems, 1969-, Fellow; cp/Harvard Clb; Cosmos Clb; hon/Pubs, "Mgmt & the Labor of Love" 1983, "Mng, w Heart" 1982, "Productivity, Who is Responsible for Improving It?" 1982, Num Others; Sigma Xi, 1940-; Am Acad of Arts & Scis, 1959-, Fellow; Royal Swedish Acad of Engrg Scis, 1974-, Fgn Mem; Hon Degs, DSc, Carnegie Mellon Univ 1967, DSc, NWn Univ 1967, EngD, MI Technological Univ 1969, EngD, Rensselaer Polytechnic Inst 1966, LLD, Univ of Akron 1968, EngD, Worcester Polytechnic Inst 1964; Num Other Hons; W/W: in Am, in E, in Engrg; Intl Yrbook & Statesmen's W/ W.

HOLLOWAY, ERNEST LEON oc/ University President; b/Sep 12, 1930; h/ PO Box 666, Langston, OK 73050; ba/ Langston, OK; m/Lula Mae "Peggy" (dec); c/Ernest Jr, Reginald, Norman; p/ J M Holloway, Boley, OK; ed/BS, 1952; MS, 1955; PhD, 1970; pa/Prin, Boley HS, 1953-62; Registrar, Dean of Student Affairs, VP for Adm, Interim Pres, Pres, Langston Univ, 1963-; Nat Assn for Equal Opport in Ed; Alpha Phi Alpha Frat Inc; cp/Lions Clb Inst, Secy; r/Epis.

HOLLOWAY HENDRIX, RUBY FAYE oc/Retired Teacher; h/2629 Lake Park Drive, Box 243, La Marque, TX

77568; m/Allen; c/Clarence Billy Brown Jr, Robert Lee Brown, Alice Marie Lewis Graham, Patricia Ann Lewis Glynn, Michael Vincent Thomas; p/Frederick D and Ethel Lougenia Steen Holloway (dec); ed/BS, Paul Quinn Col, 1949; EdM, Univ of TX Austin, 1953; pa/Prin, Tchr, Bell Co Supt, Pecan Sch, 1941-42; Prin, Tchr, Williamson Co Supt, Circleville Sch, 1942-49; 2nd Grade Tchr, La Marque Indep Sch Dist, 1949-51; Tchr of Exceptl Chd, Galveston Indep Sch Dist, 1951-81; Ret'd, 1981; Departmental Secy, Tchrs St Assn of TX, 1966-67; Pres, Galveston Clrm Tchrs Assn, 1976-77; Pres, Galveston Ed Assn, 1978-79; Current Pres, Galveston Ret'd Tchrs Assn; Life Mem, TX St Tchrs Assn; cp/Wom's Hosp Aid Soc; Present Mem, Galveston Co Hist Comm; r/ AME; Fdr w Husband, Primm Chapel AME Ch, 1957; hon/Cert of Awd for Profl Excell, Alpha Tau Zeta Chapt of Zeta Phi Beta Sorority, 1979; Grad Hon Student, Univ of TX, 1953; Recip, Vol Ser Awds, Univ of TX Med Br, 1979, 1980, 1981, 1982; W/W in Am.

HOLMAN, STERLING WILLIAM oc/Human Services Administrator; b/ Apr 30, 1936; h/745 East Lewis Street, Pocatello, ID 83201; ba/Fort Hall, ID; m/Leila Helena; c/Marie, Michelle, Mark, Omar, Victor; p/Sterling and Ruth Case (dec); ed/PhD in Psych, Univ of CA, 1977; mil/USN, 1956-60; pa/ Human Sers Admr, Ft Hall Indian Reservation, 1978-; Dir, Turk St Ctr, SF, 1975-78; Conslt, Pvt Pract, SF, 1972-75; Prog Dir, Mendocino St Hosp, 1967-72; Conslt, Roche Labs, 1960-66; Pres, ID Soc of Indiv Psych; Reg VP, ID Mtl Hlth Assn; Pres, ID Assn Cnslg & Devel, 1982-83; Chm, ID Bd of Alcohol/Drug Cnslr Cert, 1983; ID Psychol Assn; Am Orthopsychi Assn; N Am Soc of Adlerian Psych; Am Assn of Cnslg & Devel; Fellow, Intl Coun of Am Univ; hon/Author, Num Profl Articles; Dist'd Ser Awd, Commun Sers Adm, 1978; Shoshone-Bannock Cup for Outstg Sers, Shoshone-Bannock Tribes, 1980; Pres Top Ten Awd, Roche Labs, 1963; W/W in W.

HOLMES, THELMA ILA SLOWE oc/ Elementary Teacher; b/Dec 10, 1927; h/ 1611 North West 32nd Street, Miami, FL 33142; ba/North Miami Beach, FL; p/Claude and Rosetta Safronia Jones Slowe (dec); ed/BS, FL A&M Univ, 1964; MS, 1976; Ed Spec, 1980; pa/Tchr, Floral Hgts Elem, 1964; Tchr, Holmes Elem Sch, 1964-69; Elem Tchr, Greynolds Pk Elem, Dade Co Public Sch Sys, 1969-; Subst Tchr, Dade Co Public Sch Sys, 1957-63; Dade Co PTA, 1957-; VP, U Tchrs of Dade, 1980-; FL Ed Assn, 1964-; Am Fdn of Tchrs, 1974-; Assn Supvn & Curric Devel; FL Assn of Supvn & Curric Devel; Nat Coalition of Labor Union Wom; Coalition of Labor Union Wom; Tchr Ed Coun; Assn of Tchr Ed; FL Assn of Tchr Ed; S FL Labor Coun; A Phillip Randolph Inst; Phi Delta Frat, 1978-; Maynard R Bemis Soc; Nat Assn for Female Execs Inc; Nova Univ Alumni Assn; FL A&M Univ Alumni Assn; cp/NAACP; YMCA, Carver Br; So Christian Ldrship Conf; ARC, Sch Dirve; Dem Party; r/Liberty City Ch of Christ; Adult Sunday Sch Tchr, 1979-; hon/Cert of Apprec, Metro Dade Co, 1978; Human Relats Awd, CTA, 1973; Cert of Awd of Merit for Tchg, Grey-

nolds Pk Elem, 1980-81; Dist'd Ser Awd, U Tchrs of Dade, 1977-78; Vol Ser & Dedication, 1978-79; "Tiger-Cope" Legis Awds, 1977-78, 1979-80; US Dept of Labor Mgmt Sers Adm Cert, 1979; W/W in S & SW.

HOLOWAY, THEODORE RODNEY oc/Electrical Engineer; b/Oct 11, 1949; h/506 Reavis Street, PO Box 1111, Tullahoma, TN 37388; ba/Tullahoma, TN; p/Clayton F and Irene S Holoway, Knoxville, TN; ed/BS in Elect Engrg, cum laude, Univ of TN, 1972; Postgrad Wk, Univ of TN 1979-81, Mid TN St Univ 1981-82; pa/Elect Maintenance Engr, Scottish Inns of Am, 1973-77; Electrical Engineer, Developing Computer-Aided Design & Mfg Sys (CAD/CAM), Sverdrup Tech/ARO Inc, 1977-80; Proj Engr, Indust Computer Automation, Control Sys, Color Graphics & Ergonomic Design, Sverdrup Tech, 1980-; IEEE; APA; Registration Chm, Mid TN Soc of Profl Engrs; cp/ Toastmasters; Masons; Shriners; Mission Pilot-Civil Air Patrol; r/Meth; hon/ Author, Tech Reports, Computer Automation; Tau Beta Pi, Engrg; Eta Kappa Nu, Elect Engrg; Gamma Beta Phi, S'ship; Recip, Yg Engr of the Yr Awd, Mid TN Soc of Profl Engrs, 1981; Personalities of S; W/W in S & SW; Men of Achmt.

HOLSTE, THOMAS J oc/Professor of Art; b/Jan 12, 1943; h/Star Route Box 796, Orange, CA 92667; ba/Fullerton, CA; p/Richard E and Ethelyn P (dec) Holste, Downey, CA; ed/BA 1967, MA 1968, CA St Univ-Fullerton; MFA, Claremont Grad Sch, 1970; pa/Prof of Art, CA St Univ Fullerton, 1971-; Exhbns, Solomon R Guggenheim Mus (NYC), Mus of Mod Art (NYC), LA Co Mus of Art, Newport Harbor Art Mus (CA), La Jolla Mus of Contemp Art (CA), Ft Worth Art Mus (TX), Num Others; Collections, Solomon R Guggenheim Mus, Chase Manhatten Bk (NYC), ITT (NYC), Patrick Lannon Foun (FL), Others; hon/W/W in Am Art.

HOLTKAMP, DORSEY EMIL oc/ Medical Research Scientist; b/May 28, 1919; h/Cincinnati; ba/Merrell Dow Pharmaceuticals Incorporated, 2110 East Galbraith Road, Cincinnati, OH 45215; m/Marianne Church Johnson (dec); Marie P Bahm Roberts (dec); c/ Kurt Lee, Stepsons: Charles Timothy Roberts, Michael John Roberts; p/Emil H and Caroline M Holtkamp; ed/AB 1945, MS 1949, PhD 1951, Univ of CO; pa/Grp Dir, Med Res Dept, Merrell Dow Pharms Inc, Subsidiary of Dow Chem Co, 1981-; Grp Dir, Endocrine Clin Res, Med Res Dept, Merrell Nat Labs, Div of Richardson-Merrell Inc, 1970-81; Hd, Dept of Endocrinology, Wm S Merrell Co, Div of Richardson-Merrell Inc, 1958-70; Endocrine-Metabolic Grp Ldr, Biochem Sect, Res & Devel Div, Smith, Kline & French Labs, 1957-58; Other Former Positions; Fellow, AAAS, Am Inst Chems; Am Assn for Lab Animal Sci; Am Chem Soc; Am Inst Biol Scis; Affil Mem, AMA; Am Soc for Pharm & Exptl Therapeutics; Am Soc Zools; Soc for Exptl Biol & Med; Assoc Mem, Cinc Acad of Med; Other Profl Socs; hon/W/W World; W/W: in Fin & Indust, in MW, in E; 2,000 Men of Achmt; Wisdom Ency (Wisdom Hall of Fame); Nat Register of Prom Ams & Intl Notables; DIB; Other Biogl Listings.

HOLTWICK, PHILIP BARRETT oc/ Real Estate Broker; b/Oct 15, 1921; h/ 10108 Branwood Lane, Dallas, TX 75243; ba/Dallas, TX; m/Sarah Estelle Fleming; p/Charles Jansen and Mary M Barrett Holtwick; ed/BBA, GA St Univ, 1958; MBA, George Wash Univ; 1968; mil/AUS, 1940-75; Adv'd through Grades to Col; Exec Ofcr, Frankfurt Army Med Ctr, 1972-74; Surg's Ofc, Mil Dist Wash, 1974-75; pa/Asst Dir, Catawba Hosp, 1976-79; Real Est Broker, Dallas, 1979-; Asst Prof, Baylor Univ Grad Sch, 1968-71; Chm, Bd of Dirs, Frankfurt Clb Sys, 1973-74; Am Col Hosp Admrs; hon/Decorated, Legion of Merit, Iron Cross (Fed Republic of Germany).

HOLZBOG, THOMAS JERALD oc/ Architect, Planner, Teacher; b/Oct 25, 1933; h/1301 Warnall Avenue, Los Angeles, CA 90024; ba/Los Angeles, CA; m/Wendy A Wilson; c/Jessica, Arabella; p/Walter and Dorothy (dec) Holzbog; ed/BA, Yale Univ, 1960; MArch, Harvard Univ, 1968; mil/AUS, Honorably Discharged, Capt; pa/Assoc Arch Successively, Paul Rudolph (New Haven), Candilis Woods (Paris), Sir Leslie Martin (Cambridge, England), Sir Denys Lasdun (London), I M Pei (NYC), 1960-67; Pres, Holzbog & Matloob Assocs, Archs and Planners, LA and Boston, 1967-; Mem of Fac, Pratt Inst, Columbia Univ, RI Sch of Design, Harvard Univ, Tufts Univ, CA Polytechnic Univ; Past Mem, Mayor's Task Force for Urban Design, NYC; Chm, Lexington Design Adv Com; Hist Dists Comm; Bd of Dirs, Interfaith Housing; AIA, Arch Ed Com, LA Chapt; Am Soc Landscape Archs; Am Inst Cert Planners; Nat Inst Arch Ed; Arch Assn, London; hon/Contbr, Articles to Profl Jours; Exhibited Wk in Num Exhbns; Recip, Num Arch Design Awds; Fulbright Fellow; W/W.

HOOD, BURREL SAMUEL III oc/ University Professor; b/Dec 14, 1943; h/411 Myrtle Street, Starkville, MS 39759; ba/Mississippi State, MS; m/ Billie Lane Williams; c/Kelli Elizabeth; p/Chief B S and Rosemary Juel Hood, Starkville, MS; ed/BS; MMusEd; EdD; mil/AUS; Army NG, Adm Pers Spec; pa/ Prof of Music Ed, MS St; MENC; MS Music Edrs Assn, Pres; Assn Childhood Ed Intl; MS Alliance for Arts Ed; MENC Res Soc; Music Conslt; Music Adjudicator; Phi Delta Kappa; Phi Kappa Phi; Phi Mu Alpha Sinfonia; cp/Masonic Lodge, Past Master; Knight Templar; Hamasa Shrine Temple; Starkville Shrine Clb; Former JC; r/1st Bapt Ch, Starkville; Deacon, Chm Music Com, Chm Music Bldg Com, Bldg Steering Com, Budget Com, Sanctuary Choir, Instrumental Music Coor; hon/Intl W/ W Commun Ser; DIB; Intl W/W Music; Commun Ldrs and Noteworthy Ams; Book of Hon; Personalities of S; Men of Achmt.

HOOK, RALPH CLIFFORD JR oc/ College Professor and Consultant; b/ May 2, 1923; h/311 Ohua Avenue, Apartment 11D, Honolulu, HI 96815; ba/Honolulu, HI; m/Joyce F; c/R Clifford II, John G; p/Mrs Ruby S Hook, Lee's Summit, MO; ed/BA 1947, MA 1948, Univ of MO; PhD, Univ of TX, 1954; mil/Active Duty, 1941-44; Ret'd Col, AUS; pa/Prof and Chm of Mktg Dept 1983-, Prof 1974-83, Dean 1968-74,

Univ of HI; Dist'd Prof, NE LA Univ, 1979; Prof of Mktg 1960-68, Dir of Bur of Bus Sers & Exec Devel Progs 1958-67, AZ St Univ; Lectr, Univ of TX, 1951-52; Asst Prof, TX A&M Univ, 1948-51; Intl Coun for Small Bus, Pres 1963; Sr VP 1982-83, Dir 1983-84; Am Mktg Assn, Dir of Honolulu Chapt 1983-84; HI World Trade Assn, Pres 1973-74; Reg Small Bus Adm Adv Coun, Chm 1981-; r/Meth; hon/Pubs, *Mktg Ser* 1983, Over 100 Books, Monographs & Articles in Profl & Bus Jours; Named to Fac Hall of Fame, AZ St Univ, 1977; Recip, Alumni Cit of Merit, Univ of MO, 1969; Dist'd Ser Awd, Nat Def Trans Assn, 1977; Legion of Merit, AUS, 1977; W/W: in Am, in World; Ldrs of HI.

HOOVER, HERBERT ALFRED oc/ Professor of Education; b/Oct 28, 1928; h/Box 133, College of the Virgin Islands, St Thomas, Virgin Islands 00802; ba/ St Thomas, Virgin Islands; m/Geraldine R; c/Conrad R, Terry C; p/Ernest J and Annie J Hoover (dec); ed/BA, Bus Ed, St Augustine's Col, 1954; EdM, St Louis Univ, 1960; PhD, Sch Adm & Supvn, So IL Univ, 1966; pa/Prof of Ed 1969-, Dir of Student Tchg 1969-74, Chm of Tchr Ed Div 1971-74, 1979-82, Chm of Grad Studies Coun 1973-76, Col of the Virgin Isls; Assoc Prof of Ed 1966-69, Chm of Dept of Ed 1967-69, Morgan St Col; Instr & Resident Cnslr, So IL Univ, 1964-66; Elem Sch Tchr, E St Louis, IL, 1957-63; Bus Ed Tchr, McIver HS, 1954; Phi Delta Kappa; Assn for Supvn & Curric Devel; Virgin Isls Voc Ed Bd, 1982-84; r/Epis; hon/Pubs, *Student Tchg at the Col of the Virgin Isls* 1972, "Observations & Recommendations Concerning Public Ed in the USs Virgin Isls" 1976; Co-Capt, St Augustine's Col Ftball Team, 1952; W/W Among Am Col & Univ Students; Student Ldrs; Ldrs in Ed; Commun Ldrs & Noteworthy Ams.

HOOVER, LARRY ALLAN oc/Marketing Executive; b/Jun 13, 1940; h/801 Croydon Street, Sterling, VA 22170; ba/ McLean, VA; m/Frances Mango; c/ William Christopher; p/Robert Paul and Ruby Kyles Hoover, Charlotte, NC; ed/ MS, Mgmt of Technol, Am Univ, 1979; BS, Exptl Stats, NC St Univ, 1965; AA, Elect Engrg, Charlotte Col, 1961; pa/ Analyst/Programmer, The Lane Co, 1965-67; Mem of Tech Staff, Computer Scis Corp, 1967-79; Proj Mgr, Synergistic Cybernetics Inc, 1969-74; Prog Mgr, Boeing Computer Sers, 1974-80; Dir of Sys Studies, CRC Sys Inc, 1980-81; Dpty Dir of Adv'd Progs, Planning Res Corp, 1982-; Assn for Sci, Technol & Innovation, 1978-, Mbrship Chm; Am Mgmt Assn, 1974-; World Futures Soc, 1979-; Am Ec Assn, 1976-79; Wash Acad of Scis, 1981-, Policy Planning Com; AAAS, 1977-79; r/Epis; hon/Pubs, *Audit Package for Spec Nuclear Mats* 1968, "SAS as an Interactive Info Mgmt Sys" 1981; Pi Alpha Alpha Nat Hons Soc, VP 1981-82; Hon Phy Sci & Applied Math Sci Coun, NC St Univ, 1964-65; W/W in S & SW; Personalities of S; Commun Ldrs of Am.

HOOVESTOL, RICHARD ARTHUR oc/Civil Engineer; b/Apr 18, 1928; h/4026 Craig Drive, Duluth, GA 30136; ba/Decatur, GA; m/Rachel Ann Rundle; c/Brent, David E, Jon, Steven; p/Hazel E Hoovestol, Almont, ND; ed/ PhB 1953, BS in Civil Engrg 1952, Univ of ND; pa/Prin Civil Engr, Spec Projs

Engr, DeKalb Co, 1974-82; Design Engr, Havens & Emerson, Consltg Engrs, 1973; NSPE; GSPE; ASCE; Surveying & Mapping Soc of GA, Atlanta Chapt, VP; r/Prot; hon/Author, 2 Pubs on Bridges; GSPE, DeKalb Chapt, Secy of the Yr, 1979-80; Engr of the Yr in Govt, Atlanta Metro Area, 1978; Engr of the Yr in Govt, St of GA, GSPE, 1981-82; Sigma Tau, Nat Scholastic Hon Soc; W/W: in S & SW, in Engrg, in Technol Today.

HOPKINS, BARBARA oc/Public Relations Executive; b/Sep 26, 1948; h/1115 25th Street, #C, Santa Monica, CA 90403; ba/Los Angeles, CA; m/Philip Joseph; p/Philip Rising and Caroline Dickason Peters, Los Angeles, CA; ed/ AA, Santa Monica Col, 1971; BS, Botany, San Diego St Univ, 1976; pa/ Pres, Humbird Hopkins Inc, 1980-; Ptnr, Signet Properties, 1973-; Campaign Conslt, Repub Congl & Assem Cands, 1978-79; Reg Publicist, YWCA, 1977; Editor, *Aztec Engr*, 1976; Tech Editor, C Brewer & Co, 1975; ASCE; IEEE; Soc of Automotive Engrs, Reg Publicity Hd; Intl Assn of Bus Communicators; Am Soc of Mag Photogs, Reg Publicist; Sales & Mktg Execs Assn; Comml & Indust Properties Assn, Fdg Mem; cp/Mayor's Coun on Libs, LA; hon/Pubs, *The Layman's Guide to Raising Cane-An Agri Guide to the Hawaiian Sugar Indust* 1976, *The Student's Survival Guide* 1977, 1978; Awd of Apprec, Kiwanis Clb, 1977; W/ W Among Students in Am Univs & Cols.

HORADAM, VICTOR WILLIAM oc/ Medical Oncologist, Hematologist; b/ May 20, 1950; h/12856 Noel #2098, Dallas, TX 75230; ba/Dallas, TX; m/ Terry Lynn Baxter MD; p/Gilbert and Lillian Horadam, Victoria, TX; ed/BA, Univ of TX-Austin; MD, SWn Med Sch, 1976; pa/Internship 1976-77, Residency in Med 1977-79, F'ship in Infectious Diseases 1979-80, St Paul Hosp; F'ship, Hematology/Oncology, Univ of TX Hlth Sci Ctr, 1980-82; Am Col of Phys, 1976-; r/Luth; hon/Pubs, "In Vitro Activity of N-Formimidoyl Thienamycin, a Crystalline Derivative of Thienamycin" 1980, "Pharmacokinetics of Amantadine Hydrochloride in Subjects with Normal and Impaired Renal Function" 1981, "Mycobacterium Fortuitum Infection After Total Hip Replacement" 1982, Others; Diplomat, Am Bd of Internal Med, 1980; Res Fellow, Am Cancer Soc, 1981-82; W/W in S & SW.

HORAN, EILEEN FRANCES oc/ English Department Chairperson and Teacher; b/Mar 20, 1944; h/Apartment 10, 350 Esplanade, Pacifica, CA 94044; ba/Burlingame, CA; p/Mr and Mrs Cornelius Patrick Horan, North Providence, RI; ed/BA, Eng/Ed, Salve Regina Col, 1966; MA, Theatre Ed/Rehabilitative Drama, Emerson Col, 1972; pa/ Eng Dept Chp, Adv'd Placement Coor, Mercy HS, 1980-; Eng Dept Instr, Advr of Mercy Players, Mercy HS, Middletown, CT, 1977-80; Creator & Coor of Touring Theatre Arts Prog (Creat Dance, Drama, Puppetry), Pilot Prog for Sisters of Mercy Mid Sch, 1976-77; Eng Dept Instr, Dir of Xavier Players, Fdr of Xavier Players Chd's Theatre Div, St Xavier Acad, 1967-76; 7th & 8th Grade Instr, Advr of Student Coun, St John Bapt, 1966-67; CA Assn of Tchrs of Eng,

1981-82; N Eng Coun of Creat Arts Therapies, 1977-; NCTE, 1967-; Ednl Theatre Assn of RI, 1967-77, Bd Mem 1972-73, Publicity/Prog Chm; r/Cath; hon/Pub, "From Loneliness to Holiness" 1977; RI Drama Fest, N Eng Drama Fest, First Place Awds on Both Levels, 1968-72; Tchr of the Yr, Mercy HS, 1981-82.

HORGER, EDGAR OLIN III oc/ Physician and Educator; b/May 30, 1937; h/712 Angus Court, Mount Pleasant, SC 29464; ba/Charleston, SC; m/Polly Collins; c/Edgar Olin IV, David Collins, Patricia Bowen; p/Dr and Mrs E O Horger Jr (dec); ed/BS, Furman Univ, 1959; MD, Med Col of SC, 1962; mil/Capt, USAR, Ret'd; pa/Prof of Ob & Gyn 1976-, Prof of Radiol 1978-, Dir of Maternal-Fetal Med 1973-, Assoc Prof of Ob & Gyn 1971-76, Asst Prof of Ob & Gyn 1969-71, Med Univ of SC; Asst Prof of Ob & Gyn, Univ of Pgh, 1968-69; Other Previous Positions; AMA; SC Med Soc; Charleston Co Med Soc; Am Col of Obs & Gynecologists; S Atl Assn of Obs & Gynecologists, Exec Bd 1982-; Other Profl Mbrships; r/Epis; hon/Pubs, More Than 60 Articles in Med Jours & 8 Chapts in Textbooks; Alpha Omega Alpha, 1961; Cert, Am Bd of Ob & Gyn 1970, Div of Maternal-Fetal Med 1974; Personalities of S; 2,000 Men of Achmt; 2,000 Dist'd Southerners; W/W: in SC, in S & SW, in Am.

HORMANN, MARILYN SOPHIE oc/Reflective Strategic Thinker and Planner; b/Mar 12, 1936; h/12550 Lake Avenue, Suite 1001, Lakewood, OH 44107; p/William August and Clara Marie Heckmann Hormann; ed/BS, Valparaiso Univ, 1958; AM, John Carroll Univ, 1965; Postgrad, Univ of MI 1973, Hebrew Univ in Jerusalem 1982; pa/Tchr, Cnslr, Cleveland Luth HS Assn, 1958-62; Cnslr, Cleveland Public Schs, 1962-75; Dir, Career Planning & Placement 1977-80, Coor of Orgl Devel 1980-81, Coor of Strategic Planning 1982-, Dir of Equity Career Ed 1975-76, Maple Hgts City Schs; Pres, Career Life Planning Sers Inc, 1977-; Cleveland Ed Assn, Pres 1978-; NEA, Life Mem; APGA; Am Mgmt Assn; Assn for Supvn & Curric Devel; Phi Delta Kappa; r/Epis; Luth Metro Min, Charter Trustee 1968; Presb Ch, Ordained Elder 1978; hon/ Book Reviewer; Contbr, Articles to Profl Jours; Conf Presenter; Conslt in Field; Co-Author, *Maple Hgts Equity Career Ed Curric Guide*, 1976; Freedoms Foun Val Forge Tchrs Medal, 1965; Mott Fellow, 1972-73; Gen Elect Foun Guid Fellow, 1967, 1982; Martha Holden Jennings Foun Tchr Ldrship Awd, 1968, 1969, 1970; W/W: of Am Wom, in Fin & Indust; Outstg Yg Wom of Am; DIB.

HORN, KAREN N oc/Executive; b/ Sep 21, 1943; h/504 Saddleback Lane, Gates Mills, OH 44040; ba/Cleveland, OH; m/John T; c/Hartley John; p/Aloys and Novella Nicholson, Carmel Valley, CA; ed/BA, Math, Pomona Col, 1965; PhD, Ec, Johns Hopkins Univ, 1969; pa/ Economist, Bd of Govs of the Fed Resv Sys, 1969-71; VP, Economist, 1st Nat Bk of Boston, 1971-78; Treas, Bell of PA, 1978-82; Pres, Fed Resv Bk of Cleveland, 1982-; Trustee, Case Wn Resv Univ, 1983; Bus Adv Coun; Grad Sch of Indust Adm, Carnegie-Mellon

Univ, 1983; Corp Vis'g Com, Dept of Ec, MIT, 1982-83; Yg Pres Org, 1983; cp/Gtr Cleveland Roundtable, 1983; Cleveland Tomorrow, 1982-83; 50 Clb of Cleveland, 1982-83; hon/W/W.

HORN, J R MARION oc/Executive; b/Aug 9, 1942; ba/PO Box 22184, Lexington, KY 40522; m/Elaine B; c/ Stuart M, Sonya E, Starr Douglas; p/ Marion and Glady B Horn, Inez, KY; ed/BS, Campbellsville Col; Att'd, NY Inst of Fin; mil/USNR, 1964-66; pa/Acct Exec, W E Hutton, 1970; VP of Devel, Instr, Campbellsville Col, 1973-74; Pres, Horn Coal & Coke, 1974-79; Pres, Pellot Coal Export Co, 1979-81; Chm of Bd, Marion's Picassos Inc, 1980-; Pres, US Mortgage & Trusts, 1980-; VP, Fin, Video Communication Inc, 1982-; Owner, Editor, Publisher, *Martin Co Mercury Newspaper*, 1978-80; cp/Masonic Lodge; Scottish Rite; 32nd Deg Mason, Lexington Consistory #1; Lake Cumberland Hlth Com, 1975, Dir; KY St Dept Voc Ed, 1975; Citizens Task Force; r/So Bapt; hon/All Area Baseball; All Dist & All Reg Basketball; KY Col, 1967; Eisenhower Awd, 1967; W/W in Fin & Indust; Personalities of S.

HORNSBY, J RUSSELL oc/Lawyer; b/Jul 3, 1924; h/480 South Lake Sybelia Drive, Maitland, FL 32751; ba/Orlando, FL; m/Peggy; c/Lawrence H, James Russell, Kevin L, Tonya L, David Brandon, Richard Earl; p/Benjamin Franklin and Lillie Weiss Hornsby (dec); ed/Col of Law, Ctl Col of KY; LLB, John B Stetson Univ, 1950; mil/USMC; pa/ Law Ofcs of J Russell Hornsby, 1950-; Am, FL, & Orange Co Bar Assns; Acad of FL Trial Lwyrs; Intl Acad of Law and Scis; cp/Loyal Order of Moose, Gov 1955; Legion of the Moose; Am Legion; C of C; Rolling Hills Country Clb; r/ Epis; hon/Awd, Outstg Commun Ser for 1978, Orlando, FL.

HOROSZEWSKI, KATHLEEN HAGERTY oc/Segment Manager; b/ Mar 5, 1942; h/2 Overbrook Road, Randolph, NJ 07869; ba/Basking Ridge, NJ; m/Roman Donald; c/Meredith Hagerty, Roman III; p/George E (dec) and Brigid Hagerty, Randolph, NJ; ed/BA 1969, MBA 1970, Univ of Cambridge; pa/Current Segment Mgr (Aerospace) Staff (Mkt Mgmt) 1981-83, AT&T; Acct Exec 1977-81 Tech Acct Exec, Sys Mgr, Sales Mgr 1977, SWn Bell; Dir of Adm, Elmer Fox, CPA, 1977; Audit Dept, Arthur Young, 1973-77; DPMA, 1977-81; Am Assn of Sys Mgrs, 1979-80; AIAA, 1983; cp/NOW, 1977-; hon/Author, Many Internal Bell Sys Pubs; MBA w Hons, 1970; W/W of Am Wom.

HORSWELL-CHAMBERS, MARGARET oc/Retired Engineer; b/Jan 19, 1916; h/Box 1263, La Marque, TX 77568; ba/La Marque, TX; m/W F Chambers (dec); c/W F Chambers; p/ Alfred and Margaret Maloney Horswell (dec); ed/BA, Fine Arts & Humanities, Col of the Mainland; Grad Wk, Sumie Painting, Mineral & Fossil Identification, Bus Mgmt; pa/Corps of Engrs, 1962-72; Am Oil Co, 1954-62; MM Kellogg, 1942; Scomet Engrg, 1936-42; Time Mgmt Conslt, 1936-; Tchr, Drafting & Tech Illusts, Engrg Col Co-op Students; Owner, Gen Drafting Ser, Patent Drafting Tech Illusts, 1934-; Owner, Bluebonnet Lapidary Art Studio, 1972-; Sculpture, Paintings, Orig

Design, Lost Wax Cast Jewelry, Genn Carvings, Originally Designed Jewelry in Silver & Gold & Gem Stones; Phi Sigma Alpha; Phi Theta Kappa; cp/Desk & Derrick Clb, VP; Order of St Luke (Ret'd); Daughs of the King; Wom of St Michaels; AARP; Mainland Choral; St Michaels Choir; Galveston Co Gem & Mineral Soc; Fdr, Jr & Yth Ch Choirs; hon/Tech Drawings & Illusts for Tech Jours & Congl Documents; Articles & Poems for *The Courier*; Phi Sigma Alpha, Sweetheart 1976-77, Wom of the Yr 1977-78; Fdg Mem, Phi Sigma Alpha; Cert of Apprec, Corps of Engrs, 1980; Cert of Apprec, Dale Carnegie Courses, 1979; Cert, St Michaels Epis Ch, 1979-80; Personalities of S; Dir of Dist'd Ams; Intl W/W of Wom; Book of Hon.

HORTON, CARRELL PETERSON oc/College Professor; b/Nov 28, 1928; h/2410 Buchanan Street, Nashville, TN 37208; ba/Nashville, TN; c/Richard Preston; p/Mr and Mrs P S Peterson, Jacksonville, FL; ed/BA, Fisk Univ, 1949; MA, Cornell Univ, 1950; PhD, Univ of Chgo, 1972; pa/Instr & Res Assoc in Sociol, Fisk Univ, 1950-55; Statl Analyst, Proj Admr and Coor of Pediatric Res, Dept of Pediatrics, Meharry Med Col, 1955-66; Instr 1966-67, Asst Prof 1967-71, Assoc Prof 1971-76, Prof of Psych 1976-, Chm of Psych and Dir of Div of Social Scis 1976-, Fisk Univ; Bd of Dirs, Rochelle Tng & Habilitation Ctr, 1975-; Bd of Dirs, Nashville Wesley Foun, 1977-; Periodic Reviewer, NSF, Nat Res Coun, Dept of Ed, 1979-; Bd of Dirs, Belmont Samaritan Pastoral Cnslg Ctr, 1983-; r/U Meth; hon/ Author, Var Articles in Profl Jours, 1958-76; Grad, summa cum laude, Fisk Univ, 1949; Grad Asst'ship, Cornell Univ, 1950; NSF Sum Fac F'ship, 1967; Ford Foun Fac F'ship, 1969-70; IBM Fac F'ship, 1971; W/W: in S & SW, of Am Wom; DIB; Personalities of S.

HORTON, JOHN FOWLER oc/Real Estate Sales; b/Mar 28, 1950; h/8215 Ash Valley, Spring, TX 77379; ba/ Houston, TX; m/Mary Elaine; c/Robert Fowler, Christine Michelle; p/M Ramsey Horton (dec); Norma Crume, Greenville, SC; ed/BBA, Baylor Univ, 1973; pa/Real Est Sales, GA Pacific Corp 1973-77, LA Pacific 1979-80, US Home Corp 1980-; Houston Lumbermans Assn, GA Pacific; Nat Home Bldrs Assn, US Home; r/Christian; hon/Sales Contest Winner, GA Pacific, 1975, 1976, 1977, 1978, 1979; US Home Sales Perf Winner, 1980, 1981, 1982, 1983; Top 15 Percent in Sales Nationwide, 1980, 1981, 1982, 1983.

HORTON, RONALD L oc/Director of Music; b/Apr 8, 1948; h/PO Box 953, Chatham, VA 24531; ed/BA, Music Ed, Marshall, 1970; MA, Horn Perf, Radford, 1976; PhD, Music, Columbia Pacific, 1983; pa/Dir of Music, Hargrave Mil Acad, 1976-; Band Dir, Altavista HS, 1974-76; Dir of Music, Clifton Forge Schs, 1973-74; Band Dir, Tazewell HS, 1970-73; Cont'g Ed Instr, Danville Commun Col, 1983; Interim Band Master, 90th Army Band (Vang), 1978; Adj Instr, SW VA Commun Col, 1973; First Horn, Roanoke Symph Orch, Chamber Arts Trio, Greensboro Chamber Orch, MD Ballet Co, Lynchburg Fine Arts Orch, Huntington Commun Symph; Chm, VA Dept of Ed Accreditation Com, 1983; Chm, All-VA

Band Auditions (Horn), 1982; Judge, Alexandria Music Fest, 1981; Chm, Lions of VA Parade, 1980; Cnslr, VA Music Camp, 1979; Col Music Soc; Phi Mu Alpha Sinfonia; Nat Band Assn; Intl Horn Soc; Music Edrs Nat Conf; VA Music Ed Assn; Col Band Dirs Nat Assn; Christian Instrumental Dirs Assn; VA Band and Orch Dirs Assn; hon/Fdr, SEn Mil Schs Band Fest, 1977; Fdr, Hargrave Musical Vesper Series, 1976; Intl W/W in Music; W/W in S.

HORTON, THOMAS CLIFFORD SR oc/Farmer, Rancher, General Contractor, Water Cooperative Executive; b/Jan 23, 1916; h/NSR Box 150, Edgewood, NM 87015; m/Rita Shook; c/Rita-Loy Horton Thomas, Sharron Horton Geilenfeldt, Thomas Clifford Jr; p/Claude C (dec) and Ethel Madole Horton; ed/Grad, Menaul Sch of U Presb Ch, USA, 1936; pa/Farmer, Rancher, Santa Fe & Bernalillo Cos, 1936-; Charter Mem & First Secy, Edgewood Soil Conserv Dist, 1942-43; Adv Com, Santa Fe Co Long Range Planning Prog, 1948-49; Farm Instr, Edgewood Dist St Col, 1947-49; Orgr, No One-Half, Estancia Val for REA Comm, 1949-50; Public Relats Ofcr, Ctl NM Elect Cooperative, 1950-52; Sub-Contractor, Road Constrn, Allison-Haney, 1953-54; NWn Engrs, Denver Col 1953-54, Floyd Hake 1953-54; Gen Contractor, NM, 1954-; Bldg Supvr, Bd of Nat Missions, U Presb Ch, USA, NM, AZ, UT, TX, AK, 1954-71; Asst to Dir of Bd Properties Div 1961-71, Fdr & Pres of Entranosa Water Corp 1974-81 (Corp Changed to Entranosa Water Cooperative Assn 1981), Comptroller of Entranosa Water Cooperative 1981-; Santa Fe Co Road Adv Com, 1983; Menaul Sch Alumni Assn; cp/Dem; Masonic Order; Estancia 33 AF&AM, 1945-; Rotary Intl.

HORWITZ, RONALD M oc/Dean of School of Economics and Management; b/Jun 25, 1938; h/26060 Radclift Place, Oak Park, MI 48237; ba/Rochester, MI; m/Carol; c/Steven, Michael, David, Robert; p/Harry and Annette Horwitz; ed/PhD, Financial Adm, MI St Univ, 1964; MBA 1960, BS 1959, Wayne St Univ; CPA, MI, 1960; pa/Staff Acct, Nida & Bokolor, CPAs, 1956-60; Grad Fellow 1960-61, Asst Prof 1962-63, Wayne St Univ; Asst Prof, Assoc Prof, Chair of Dept of Acctg & Fin, Univ of Detroit, 1963-79; Hlth Care Spec, Arthur Young & Co, 1974-75; Dean, Sch of Ec & Mgmt, Prof of Mgmt, Oakland Univ, 1979-; MI Assn of CPAs; Am Inst of CPAs; Financial Mgmt Assn; Am Acctg Assn; Acctg Aid Soc of Metro Detroit, Fdr & Dir; En MI Chapt, Hlthcare Financial Mgmt Assn; cp/ Providence Hosp, Adv Bd of Trustees, VChm, Chair, Fin Com; Gtr Detroit Area Hlthcare Coun, Trustee, Adv Panel; hon/Author, Var Pubs; MI Accountancy Foun Grant, 1962; Am Bkrs Assn, Stonier Fellow, 1962-63; Ford Foun Fin Res Grant, 1965; Life Master, Am Contract Bridge Leag.

HOSBACH, HOWARD DANIEL oc/ Executive; b/Mar 9, 1931; h/104 Green Way, Allendale, NJ 07401; ba/New York, NY; m/Eugenia Elizabeth Paracka; c/Susan Hosbach Murray, Cynthia Hosbach Miezeiewski, Beth Ann, Alyssa; p/Howard D and Marjorie V Hoffer Hosbach; ed/BS 1953, MBA

1967, Fairleigh Dickinson Univ; mil/ AUS, 1953-55; pa/Advtg Mgr 1958-62, Dir of Mktg 1962-66, Gen Mgr, Dealer & Lib Sales 1966-69, McGraw-Hill Book Co; Grp VP 1970-73, Exec VP 1973-80, Pres & CEO 1981-, Standard & Poor's Corp; Dir 1970-, Chm, Standard & Poor's Compustat Ser Inc; Dir, Standard & Poor's Securities Inc, Standard & Poor's Intl; VChm, Fairleigh Dickinson Univ Devel Coun, 1981-; Trustee, Peirce Jr Col, 1981-; r/Rom Cath; hon/ Marquis W/W; Poor's Register.

HOSKINS, CHARLES ROSS oc/ Executive; b/Jun 26, 1941; h/4964 Prince Edward Road, Jacksonville, FL 32210; ba/Jacksonville, FL; m/Jo; c/Ashley A, Charles R Jr; p/Mrs C R Hoskins, Ewing, VA; ed/BS, Univ of TN, 1963; Prog for Mgmt Devel, Harvard Bus Sch, 1971; mil/Army Security Agy, 1966-72; pa/ Exec VP, Citizens & So Nat Bk, 1963-78; Exec VP, BancOhio Nat Bk, 1978-83; Pres, FL Nat Bk, 1983-; Bd of Trustees, Franklin Univ, Ctr for Sci and Indust; Bd of Dirs, Nat Alliance of Bus-men; cp/Bd of Trustees, Columbus USA Assn, Columbus C of C; Chm, Devel Com of Gtr Columbus; r/Epis; hon/ Outstg Yg People of Atlanta, 1974; Ldrship Atlanta, 1976; W/W in Am; Personalities of S.

HOUCK, ALAN P oc/Certified Public Accountant; b/Jun 29, 1947; h/2125 Kimberly Circle, Eugene, OR 97405; ba/ Eugene, OR; m/Kathleen Ruth; c/Eric A, Mark A, Brian C; p/Albert and Pauline Houck, Portland, OR; ed/BA in Math, Seattle Pacific Univ, 1969; MA in Math 1971, BBA in Acctg 1973, Cleveland St Univ; pa/Tchr of Math, Cleveland Public Schs, 1969-72; Staff Acct, Brubaker, Helfrich & Taylor, 1972-74; Staff Acct 1974-79, Ptnr 1979-, Minihan, Kernutt, Stokes & Co; Treas, Emerald Exec Assn, 1978-; Treas, Eugene Christian Sch, 1975-; Treas, Polit Cands (Var Times); cp/Kiwanis; r/ Bapt; hon/W/W in W.

HOUSE, PAULINE oc/Assistant Superintendent of Elementary Education; b/Jul 17, 1928; h/Route 2, Box 688, Bono, AR 72416; ba/Jonesboro, AR; m/ Monroe; c/Paul Monroe, Dennis Keith, Charlotte Marie; p/Barney and Myrtle Nutt, Fordyce, AR; ed/BSE, 1961; MSE, 1965; pa/Customer Ser Ofcr, Sears, 1946; Acctg, 1950-60; Elem Tchr 1963, Elem Prin 1972, Asst Supt, Instrn 1975, Asst Supt, Pers 1976, Asst Supt, Elem Ed 1977-82, Jonesboro Public Schs; Jonesboro Clrm Tchr Assn, VP 1967-68; Alpha Beta Chapt, Alpha Delta Kappa, Pres 1966; Phi Delta Kappa, Secy 1980-81; AR Coun of Elem Ed, 1973-76; Editor, "District Report," Qtrly Supplement to Local Newspaper, 1978-82; cp/ Altrusa, VP 1979-80; YMCA, Bd 1976; U Way, Bd 1980; Civic Improvement, City Beautiful Proj, 1977-78; Suspected Child Abuse & Neglect Bd, 1982; Bd of Govs, Craighead Meml Hosp, 1978-80; r/Christian; hon/W/W in S & SW; Personalities of S; Outstg Tchrs of Am.

HOUSER, THOMAS LEONARD oc/ Interior Designer; b/Aug 17, 1948; h/ 624 Georgetown Drive, Nashville, TN 37205; ba/Nashville, TN; m/Sarah Nichols; c/Nathan Thomas, Benjamin Luke, Joel Andrew; p/Stanley Jacob and Florence Antoinette (dec) Houser; ed/ BA, Music, Maryville Col, 1970; MS, Interior Design, Univ of TN, 1976; mil/

AUS, 1970-73; pa/Interior Designer, Earl Swensson Assocs, 1976-78; Interior Design Team Ldr, Gresham & Smith, 1979; Dir of Interiors, Earl Swensson Assocs, 1979-; Inst of Bus Designers; Am Soc of Interior Designers; r/Elder, Presb Ch in the US, 1979; hon/Personalities of S; W/W in S & SW; Men of Achmt.

HOUSLANGER, NEAL PETER oc/ Podiatrist; b/Apr 20, 1949; ba/310 Willis Avenue, Mineola, NY 11501; m/Bonnie Jean; c/Lisa Marie, Stacey Lynn, Karen Anne; p/William Benson and Rhoda Grace Houslanger, Franklin Square, NY; ed/BA, St Univ of NY Stony Brook, 1971; DPM, NY Col of Podiatric Med, 1976; Fellow, Acad of Ambulatory Foot Surgs, 1981; pa/Pvt Pract; Staff, Long Isl Jewish Hosp & Med Ctr; Am Podiatry Assn; Podiatry Soc of the St of NY; Nassau Co Podiatry Soc, Sci Chm; Am Col of Sports Med; cp/Kiwanis Clb of Mineola, 1979-; L I Chapt, March of Dimes Birth Defect Foun, Bd of Dirs 1981-; hon/Dipl, Nat Bd of Podiatric Examrs, 1976; Podiatrist of the Yr, Nassau Co, 1981; W/W in E; Biogl Dir of Am Podiatry Assn.

HOWARD, HARRIETTE ELLA PIERCE oc/Assistant Professor of Molecular Biology; b/Dec 23, 1954; h/ 3935 Rosehill Road, #3206, Fayetteville, NC 28301; ba/Fayetteville, NC; p/ Lowry P and Agnes Marie Howard, Texarkana, AR; ed/BA in Biol, Fisk Univ, 1975; MA 1978, PhD 1981, Biol, Atlanta Univ; pa/Res Asst, Atlanta Univ, 1976-81; Lab Instr, Spelman Col, 1979-81; Asst Prof of Molecular Biol, Fayetteville St Univ, 1981-; Am Soc of Cell Biol; Beta Kappa Chi; cp/OES; r/ Bapt; hon/Pub, "Reassociation Kinetics of *Colinus virginianus*," Biomed Support Res Symp, 1983; Selected as Future Yg Ldr, *Ebony* Mag, 1983; Atlanta Univ Hon Soc; Recip, $149,000/3 Yr Res Grant, NIH; Outstg Yg Wom in Am, 1982.

HOWARD, JOHN WILFRED oc/ Commercial Artist; b/Aug 20, 1924; h/ RR #2, Corinth, KY 41010; ba/Same; m/ Leona Belle Thompson; c/Bonnie Darlene, Connie Marie, Sharon Kaye, Terresa Lynn, Sandra Lee; p/John David and Veral Kemper Howard, Corinth, KY; ed/8th Grammer; Col Credits in Art; mil/Army Inf, 1945-47; pa/ Self-Employed Farmer, 1940-45; Life & Hlth Ins Agt, 1972-79; Comml Artist, Wk Displayed in *Artists USA*, Intly Distributed Art Book; Assoc Artist, Creat World Inc; r/Bapt; hon/Competed w Artists All Over the US and Canada, Won Pres's Top Awd, 1981; Other Awds; W/W in S & SW; W/W; Personalities of S.

HOWARD, KARAN ANICA oc/Executive; b/Dec 23, 1939; h/6432 Brownlee Drive, Nashville, TN 37204; ba/Nashville, TN; m/Samuel H; c/Anica Lynne, Samuel H II; p/Charles C and Wilmenta M (dec) Wilson, Ottawa, KS; ed/BS, Bus Ed, Emporia St Univ, 1963; Basic Cert, Am Inst of Bkg, 1977; pa/Exec VP, Phoenix of Nashville Inc & WMAK-FM, Phoenix of Hendersonville Inc, 1980-; Bkg Ofcr, Third Nat Bk, 1974-80; Bd of Dirs, CABLE (A Wom's Netwkg Org for Bus & Profl Wom); cp/Nat Prog Dir, Jack & Jill of Am, 1983-; Bd of Dirs, Florence Crittenton Home & Sers, 1976-81; Bd of Dirs, Cumberland Val Girl Scout Coun, 1978-81; r/Bapt; hon/

Keynote Spkr, Phi Gamma Nu Fdrs Banquet, 1977; World W/W of Wom; Outstg Yg Wom of Am.

HOWARD MARY FRANCES oc/ Director of Special Services and Assistant Dean for Student Services; b/Mar 14, 1954; h/1716 D Avenue, Northeast A3, Cedar Rapids, IA 52402; ba/Cedar Rapids, IA; p/John and Frances Howard, Alton, IL; ed/BA 1976, MA 1977, Univ of IA; pa/Dir of Spec Sers & Asst Dean for Student Sers, Coe Col, 1978-; Asst Dir of Developmental Ed, Univ of WI-Oshkosh, 1978; Grad Asst for Spec Support Sers 1976-77, Info Spec, Campus Info Ctr 1973-76, Orientation Advr 1973-76, Univ of IA; Mid-Am Assn of Ednl Opport Prog Pers, IA Chapt; Assn of Black Wom in Higher Ed; IA Student Pers Assn; Delta Sigma Theta Sorority Inc; Nat Assn of Remedial & Developmental Studies in Postsec'dy Ed; cp/ Cedar Rapids Civil Rts Comm; r/AME; hon/Dedication & Ser Awd, Pre-Col Prog, 1978; Alpha Awds for Outstg Grad Student, 1977; Gwendolyn Brooks Awd for Scholastic Achmt & Campus Activs, 1976; Other Hons; W/W of Am Wom; Outstg Yg Wom of Am.

HOWARD, WILLIAM REED oc/ Executive; b/May 26, 1922; h/2868 Fairmont Road, Winston-Salem, NC 27106; ba/Winston-Salem, NC; m/ Lusadel Moore (dec); c/Thomas Morton, David Patrick, William Reed Jr; p/Albert Thompkins and Antha Jane Taylor Howard (dec); ed/LLB, George Wash Univ Law Sch, 1956; AB, George Wash Univ, 1952; mil/USAAC, 1942-43, 1943-46; pa/Sr VP 1978, Exec VP 1980, Pres & COO 1981, Pres & CEO 1983-, Piedmont Airlines; VP, Sr VP, En Airlines (Miami), 1971-78; Staff VP (Legal), En Airlines (NY), 1967-71; Wachovia Bk & Trust Co, Dir; cp/ Winston-Salem C of C, Dir 1980-83; U Way of Forsyth Co, Dir 1979-82; ARC, Pres 1974-76; hon/W/W: in Am, Fin & Indust, of World Ldrs in Govt & Indust.

HOWELL, JOHN McDADE oc/University Administrator; b/Jan 28, 1922; h/605 East Fifth Street, Greenville, NC 27834; ba/Greenville, NC; m/Gladys David; c/David Noble, Joseph Lee; p/ John William; ed/BA 1948, MA 1949, Univ of AL; PhD, Duke Univ, 1954; mil/ USAAF, 1942-45; pa/Chancellor 1982-, Vice Chancellor 1973-79, Dean of Grad Sch 1969-73, Dean of Arts & Scis 1966-69, Chair, Dept of Polit Sci 1963-66, Prof of Polit Sci 1961-, E Carolina Univ; Am Polit Sci Assn; Am Soc of Intl Law; So Polit Sci Assn; Intl Studies Assn, Nat & Reg; r/Prot; hon/ Author, Num Pubs in Field; Phi Beta Kappa; W/W: in Am, in Am Cols & Univ Admrs, in World, in S & SW; Am Men of Sci.

HOYER, STENY HAMILTON oc/ Congressman; b/Jun 14, 1939; h/6621 Lacona Street, Berkshire, MD 20747; ba/Washington, DC; m/Judith Elaine Pickett; c/Susan Buchanan, Stefany Cleveland, Anne Hamilton; p/Steen and Jean Hoyer (dec); ed/BS, Univ of MD-Col Pk, 1963; JD, Georgetown Univ Law Ctr, 1966; pa/Exec Asst, US Senator Daniel Brewster, 1962-66; Gen Pract of Law, Haislip & Yewell, 1966-69; Gen Pract of Law, Hoyer, Fannon & Johnston, 1969-81; MD St Senator, 1966-79; Pres, MD Senate, 1975-79; Cong-man, Fifth Dist of MD, 1981-; Phi

Sigma Alpha; Delta Theta Phi; Sigma Chi Frat; Bd of Trustees, Univ of MD Alumni Assn; Am & MD Bar Assns; Am Trial Lwyrs Assn; Am Judic Soc; cp/Bd of Trustees, Balto Mus of Art; Balto Coun of Fgn Relats; Profl Adv Coun, Mtl Hlth Assn of Prince George's Co; Ducks Unltd; Crescent City JCs; Hon Mem, Dist Hgts Vol Fire Dept; r/Bapt; hon/Outstg Grad'g Male Student, Univ of MD, 1963; St Ofcl of the Yr, MD Mun Leag, 1971; Outstg Yg Dem, MD Yg Dems, 1975; Dist'd Alumnus Awd, Univ of MD, 1976; Legis of the Yr, MD St Attys Assn, 1977; Man of the Yr, Wash Psychi Soc, 1983.

HRUSKA, ELIAS NICOLAS oc/ Financial Planner; b/Jul 7, 1943; h/139 Salice Way, Campbell, CA 95008; ba/ San Jose, CA; m/Maria; c/Sonia K, Shala M, Karin M; p/Silvia Warren, Redwood City, CA; ed/MA 1968, BA 1966, w Hons, Univ of CA-Berkeley; pa/Owner, Elittruska & Assocs, 1982-; VP 1982-, Pres 1980-82, VP of Ins 1978-80, Acct Exec 1976-78, Apex Financial Corp; Intl Assn of Financial Planners; IPA; r/Cath; hon/Publisher of Monthly Newslttr, *Investmt Briefs*; Author of Poetry Book, *This Side of Other Things*; Tchg F'ship, 1966-70; Tower & Flame Hon Soc, 1963; Grad & Upper Div Hon Soc, 1966; Deptl Cit for Outstg Achmt, 1968.

HSU, BENEDICT SHIUNG oc/Correspondent; b/May 1, 1933; h/11205 Schuylkill Road, Rockville, MD 20852; ba/Same; m/Lena; c/John Y, Peter Y; p/ Leh-Chu Chen, Tainan, Taiwan; ed/ BA, Chung-Hsin Univ, 1958; MS, Georgetown Univ, 1971; mil/Chinese Army, 1953-54; Interpreter, USAF, 1955-56; pa/Reporter, *Hsin-Shen Daily*, Taipei, 1954-57; Reporter, *China Daily News*, Taipei, 1957-60; Reporter, *China Times*, Taipei, 1960-67; Correspondent, *Kao-Hsiung Hsin-Wen-Poa*, Kaohsiling, 1967-75; Correspondent, *Newsdom Wkly*, Hong Kong, 1968-; US Correspondent, *Taiwan Daily News*, Taichung, 1981-; hon/Author, *Little League Baseball in China* 1969, *Chi-Cheng, The Fastest Wom in the World* 1970, *The Fight for China's Representation* 1971, *The World as I See It* 1975, *China, Alive in the Bitter Sea* 1982; Asia Foun Grantee, 1964; Best Reporting Awd, World-Wide Overseas Chinese Assn, 1972.

HSU, CHING-YU oc/State Advisor for US Congressional Advisory Board; b/Dec 25, 1898; h/21-20 21st Street, Long Island City, NY 11105; ba/Long Island City, NY; m/Anna Yuen-chi Ting; c/Stephen, Yu-kuan, Victor, Yin-po, Yin-sho, Margaret; p/F Shi-kan Hsu and M Shu-yi Li (both dec), Hunan, China; ed/Grad, Hunan Col of Law, 1921; Postgrad Res, Oxford Univ, England, 1922-25; mil/Cmdr of Peace-keeping Army in Hunan, WW II, 1938-44; pa/ Prof of Phil, Kwan Hwa Univ, Shanghai, 1925-27; Dpty Dir, Editing & Translation Bur, Nationalist Govt, 1928-30; Dir, Assn for Sci Studies in Nanking, 1928-30; Prof Phil, Hunan Univ, 1930-32; Acting Chm, Nat Com for Planning, 1932-34; Chm, Intl Sci Soc, Shanghai, 1926-28; Commr, Interior of Ctl Polit Coun, 1936-39; Hd of Acad Lecture Corps & Ldr of Inspection Grp of New Life Movement, 1937; Escaped Communist Persecution & Arrived in Hong Kong, 1950; Phil Prof, Chun Chi

Col & Res Fellow, Inst of Oriental Studies, Univ of Hong Kong, 1953-58; Prof of Chinese Hist, Bapt Col at Kowloon; Immigrated to US in 1958; Became Naturalized Citizen of US, 1964; Fdr, China Rebuilding Fdn, 1964; Mem Adv Bd, Am Nat Security Coun, 1974-; St Advr, US Congl Adv Bd, Currently; cp/Sustaining Mem, Nat Repub Com, 1975-; hon/Author of Num Books incl'g: *Phil of Love*, 1921, Changsha; *Phil of Confucious*, 1925, London; *Phil of the Beautiful, Contemp Polit Thought of the W, Critique on Marxism*, 1928, Shanghai; *Co-wealthism & the New Age*, 1975, New York; *On Chinese Culture*; *The Prob of China*, Hong Kong; Recip, Medal of Merit, Presented by Pres Reagan, 1981; W/W: in Am, in World, in US.

HSUEH, CHUN-TU oc/Professor of Government and Politics; b/Dec 12, 1922; h/2011 Gatewood Place, Silver Spring, MD 20903; ba/College Park, MD; m/Cordelia Te-hua Huang; ed/ MA, PhD, Columbia Univ; LLB, Chaoyang Univ Col of Law, China; Cert, China Sch of Jour, Hong Kong; External Student, Eng Lit, Raffles Col, Singapore; Current Prof of Polit, Univ of MD; Chm of Wash & SE Reg Sem on China, 1974-; Chm of Exec Com of the Asian Polit Scists Grp in USA, 1975-; Vis'g Com, Dept of Intl Relats, Lehigh Univ, 1979-; Bd of Dirs, *The Asia Mail*, 1978-; Chm, Com on Scholars of Asian Descent, Assn for Asian Studies, 1981-; Exch Vis'g Scholar, Peking Univ, 1983; Instr, Harvard Univ 1979, Columbia Univ 1969, Hist Dept of Univ of Hong Kong 1962-64; Vis'g Prof & Acting Dir, E Asian Polit Res Unit, Free Univ of Berlin, 1970; Other Previous Positions; hon/Pubs, *The Chinese Red Army, The Dynamics of Chinese Politics, Selected Writings of a Decade* 1964, Others; W/W: in Am, in World.

HU, JOHN CHIH-AN oc/Specialist Engineer in the Aerospace Industry; b/ Jul 12, 1922; h/16212 122nd Avenue, Southeast, Renton, WA 98055; ba/ Seattle, WA; m/Betty Siao-Yung; c/ Arthur, Benjamin, Carl, David, Eileen, Franklin, George; p/Chi-Ching and Chao-Hsian (Tsen) Hu (dec); ed/BS, Nat Ctl Univ, 1946; MS, Univ of So CA, 1957; pa/Spec Engr, The Boeing Co, 1966-; Res Chem, Prods Res & Chem Co, 1962-66; Res Chem, Chem Seal Corp of Am, 1961-62; Res Assoc, Chem Dept, Univ of So CA, 1957-61; Dir, Res Dept, Plant #1, Taiwan Fertilizer Mfg Co, 1947-54; Am Chem Soc; Chinese Am Chem Soc; Chinese Chem Soc; hon/ Author of Many Profl Papers in Maj Jours; Contbg Author, 2 Books; Lectr of Profl Symposia; UN Lectr/Conslt in China; Phi Lambda Upsilon; Cert'd Profl Chem, Approved by Nat Cert Com; Boeing Awds for Patents & Pubs; Patentee, Chromatopyrography; W/W in W.

HU, SHAU-CHUNG oc/International Trading; b/Nov 1, 1941; h/973, 44th Street, Apartment 1A, Brooklyn, NY 11219; ba/New York, NY; m/Margaret; c/Zong-guang; p/Po-han (dec) and Ti-fei Wu Hu; ed/BA, Tamkang Univ, Taiwan; ABD, IA St Univ; pa/Sr VP, Chinese Native Prods Ltd, 1976-; Sr VP, Pearl River Chinese Prods Emporium, 1978-; Dir, Pearl River Chinese Food Mfg Co, 1982-; Nat Coun of US-China Trade, 1976-; cp/Sino-Am C of C, VChm

1981-; Nat Com on US-China Relats Inc, 1976-; hon/Author, "Friend of Taipei City Council, Republic of China," w the Compliments of Spkr Clement C P Chang; W/W in Fin & Indust.

HUBBARD, MARGARET ELEA-NOR oc/Public Affairs and News Director; b/Nov 8, 1931; h/52 Park View Avenue, Warwick, RI 02888; ba/Warwick, RI; m/Lincoln W; c/Cameron Munsie, Harriet Katherine; p/Perci L C and Harriet E Wilson Munsie (dec); ed/Att'd, RI Sch of Broadcasting 1978, Barbara's Modeling & Finishing Sch 1976, 1977, Providence Col (Public Spkg 1976, Jour 1978), Johnson & Wales Bus Sch 1953; 3rd Class Engrs Lic, Fed Communs Comm; pa/Appeared on Many TV & Radio Talk Shows; Creator, "Thoughts to Live By" for WLNE, "Mediations" for WJAR, RI St Coun of Chs & RI Assn of Evang Chs; RI Press Clb; RI Advtg Clb; cp/Publicity Chm, Providence Chapt, Harmony Inc, 1968-70; Public Relats Dir, First Presb Ch, 1969-; Ruth Rebekah Lodge, Past Noble Grand; r/Deaconess, First Presb Ch, 1969; RI Assn of Evang Chs; Child Evang F'ship Bd; hon/W/W of Am Wom; Personalities of Am; Dir of Dist'd Ams; Commun Ldrs of Am; World W/W of Wom.

HUBBARD, SARAH C oc/Teacher; b/Jan 16, 1935; h/2702 Yale Avenue, San Angelo, TX 76904; ba/San Angelo, TX; p/Mr and Mrs C W Hubbard (dec); ed/BS 1957, EdM 1963, MS Col; pa/Tchr, Natchez-Adam Co Public Schs 1958-65, San Angelo Indep Sch Dist 1965-; NEA, 1965-; Nat Coun for the Social Studies, 1964-81; TX Coun for the Social Studies, 1965-; San Angelo Coun for Social Studies, 1965-; TX St Tchrs Assn, 1965-; TX Clrm Tchrs Assn, 1965-81; r/Bapt; hon/San Angelo HS Tchr of the Yr, 1971; Freedoms Foun Tchrs Medal, 1971; Ldrs of Am Sec'dy Ed, 1972.

HUCK, LARRY R oc/Executive; b/Aug 10, 1942; h/14203 Northeast 10th Place, Bellevue, WA 98007; ba/Bellevue, WA; m/Linda K; c/Kimberlie, Brandon V, Larry R II; p/Frank J (dec) and Helen B Huck, Everett, WA; ed/Att'd, Edmonds Commun Col, Seattle Commun Col, WA Tech Inst; mil/USMC, 1959-64; pa/Salesman 1964-65, Crew Chief 1965-66, Edgerton Realty Salesman 1966-69, Kirby Co Sales Mgr 1969-70, Kirby Co; Salesman, Sanico Chem Co, 1969-71; Salesman, Synkoloid Co, 1971-75; Tech Sales Rep, Ethyl Corp, Visqueen Div, 1975-77; Wn Sales Mgr, B&K Films Inc, 1977-; Pres, NW Mgrs' Assn Inc, 1977-; Nat Sales Mgr, Gazelle Inc, 1979-81; Nat Coun Salesmen Org Inc; Mfrs Agts Nat Assn; Am Home Mfg Assn; Hardware Affiliated Reps Inc; Door & Hardware Inst; cp/VP, Bellevue Nat Little Leag; Coor, CYO Basketball; r/Cath; hon/W/W in W.

HUCKSTADT, ALICIA ANNETTA oc/Nurse Educator; b/Dec 30, 1949; ba/Box 41, Wichita State University, Wichita, KS 67208; m/Loren D; p/Allen and Emma Cole, Lakin, KS; ed/AB, Garden City Commun Jr Col, 1973; BSN 1975, MN 1978, Wichita St Univ; PhD, KS St Univ, 1981; pa/Asst Prof 1981-, Coor for Cont'g Ed 1981-82, Instr 1976-81, Proj Coor & Instr of Alcohol Ed & Tng 1975-76, Wichita St Univ; Surg-Intensive Care Nurse, St

Francis Reg Med Ctr, 1975-76; Lectr & Conslt on Alcoholism, 1975-; Pres, Epsilon Gamma Chapt, Sigma Theta Tau, 1982-; Fac Conslt, Eligibility Chp, Epsilon Gamma Chapt, 1980-82; Bd of Dirs, KS St Nurses Assn, Dist VI, 1983-; ANA, 1975-; AAUP, 1982-; r/Cath; hon/Pubs, "Work/Study-A Bridge to Practice" 1981, "The Gerontological Knowledge Level of Nurses" 1983; Phi Kappa Phi, 1974; Sigma Theta Tau, 1979, Grad w Deptl Hons, magna cum laude, Wichita St Univ, 1975; W/W of Am Wom.

HUDSON, MICHAEL PATRICK oc/Aerospace Engineer; b/Jan 3, 1957; h/18515 Egret Bay Boulevard, #709, Houston, TX 77058; ba/Houston, TX; p/Delbert and Doris Hudson, Girard, KS; ed/BSAE, Wichita St Univ, 1979; pa/Aerospace Engr, McDonnell Douglas Tech Sers Co, 1980-; Engrg Asst, Cessna Aircraft Co, 1979; AIAA; Sigma Pi Sigma; hon/W/W: in Aerospace Engrs, in Frontier Sci & Technol.

HUEBNER, RICHARD ALLEN oc/Executive Director; b/Jul 31, 1950; h/2700 Leeds Lane, Charlottesville, VA 22901; ba/Charlottesville, VA; m/Marsha Lawrence; c/Angela Carol, Holly Anne; p/Otto LeRoy Huebner (dec); ed/BBA, Pers Mgmt and Adm Mgmt, Univ of WI-Madison, 1972; pa/Mgr, Lakeshore Stores, and Proj Asst, Univ of WI-Madison, 1972-73; Chapt Conslt 1973-74, Tng Dir 1974-76, Exec Dir 1976-, Kappa Sigma Frat; Asst Editor, *The Caduceus*, Kappa Sigma, 1976-; Admr, Kappa Sigma Meml Foun, 1980-; Frat Execs Assn, 1976-, Pubs Com Chm 1981-; Am Soc of Assn Execs, 1976-; Assn of Frat Advrs, 1976-; Univ of WI Alumni Assn, 1978-; cp/Greencroft Clb, 1976-; Charlottesville-Albemarle JCs, 1977-; VA JCs, 1977-; ARC, 1978-, CPR Instr 1978-; Vol Action Ctr, 1981-, Bd of Dirs 1981-, VChm 1982-; Blue Ridge Mtn Rotary Clb, 1983-, Com Chm 1983-; Camp VA JC, 1983-, Bd of Dirs 1983-; U Way, Thomas Jefferson Area, 1984-, Bd of Dirs 1984-; r/St Mark Luth Ch, 1977-, Usher 1979-, Asst Financial Secy 1980-, Liturgical Asst 1982-; hon/Lt Col Comm, St of GA, 1983; Dist Dir of the Month, VA JCs, 1983-84; Top Growth Awds, VA JCs, 1983-84; Dist Dir of the Quarter, Skyline Reg JCs, 1983-84; Num Others Hons; Intl Book of Hon; 2,000 Dist'd Southerners; Commun Ldrs of the World; Biogl Roll of Hon; 5,000 Personalities of the World; Am Registry Series; Num Other Biogl Listings.

HUEBSCH, TONY LOUIS oc/Communications Dir; b/May 12, 1929; h/359 Pleasant Drive, Southeast, Cedar Rapids, IA 52403; ba/Cedar Rapids, IA; m/Suzanne; c/Scott, Rebecca Newmeister, Katy Hanson; p/Mrs Mae Huebsch, McGregor, IA; ed/BA 1951, MBA 1972, Univ of IA; mil/USAF, 1951-53; pa/Edit Staff, *Omaha World-Herald*, 1953-54; Editor, Indust Pubs, Collins Radio Co, 1954-60; Advtg Mgr, TX Div, 1960-61; Advtg Mgr, Collins Avionics Divs, 1961-79; Dir, Communs, Avionics Grp, Rockwell Intl, 1979-; Aviation/Space Writers Assn; Am Advtg Fdn; Cedar Rapids Mgmt Clb; US Power Sqdrns; Collins Credit Union; cp/Bd of Dirs, Cedar Rapids Symph; Past Mem Bd of Dirs, Cedar Rapids Commun Theater;

Optimists Intl; r/Past Bd of Deacons, Trustees, Presb Ch.

HUGHES, JAYNE K oc/Executive; b/Dec 16, 1948; h/3028 Chamblee Tucker Road, Chamblee, GA 30341; ba/Atlanta, GA; m/Kenneth L; c/Shea; p/Mr and Mrs W L Haight, Winter Park, FL; ed/AA, Seminole Jr Col, 1969; BS, Math, Ctl FL Univ, 1971; Grad Prog, Actuarial Sci, GA St Univ; Var Mgmt, Ins, DP Classes; pa/Underwriting Clk 1972, Underwriting Asst 1973, Asst Underwriter 1975, Aviation Underwriter 1977, Data Processing Mgr 1979, Info Resource Advr to the CEO 1982-, Present Asst VP, SEn Aviation Underwriters Inc; Pvt Pilot w Instrument Rating; Atlanta Assn of Ins Wom; Data Processing Mgmt Assn; Aircraft Owners and Pilots Assn; hon/Pubs, "ERA-Pro" 1978, "The Red Baron-My Kind of Fun" 1981 (Both in *Atlanta Ins Wom*); hon/W/W in S & SW.

HUGHES, SAMUEL THOMAS JR oc/Assistant Dean of Graduate Program in Nursing; b/Dec 30, 1938; h/7031 Westlake Avenue, Dallas, TX 75214; ba/Arlington, TX; p/Samuel T and Lula I Hughes, Neodesha, KS; ed/Dipl in Nsg, 1959; BSN, St Mary of the Plains Col, 1963; MSNEd, IN Univ, 1965; EdD, N TX St Univ, 1976; mil/Capt, USAF Nurse Corp, 1967-69; Present Lt Col, USAFR, USAF Med Ctr, Keesler; pa/Current Asst Dean of Grad Prog in Nsg, Univ of TX-Arlington Sch of Nsg; Dean & Prof, MS Col Sch of Nsg, 1980-81; Assoc Prof, Univ of TX-Arlington Sch of Nsg; Assoc Prof, Baylor Univ, 1973-79; Chm, Dept of Nsg, MWn St Univ, 1968-73; Instr, Butler Co Commun Jr Col, 1965-67; Instr, Wesley Sch of Nsg, 1963-64; Staff Nurse, Trinity Hosp, 1960-63; Asst Dir of Nsg Ser, Wm Newton Meml Hosp, 1959-60; ANA; TX Nurses Assn, VP of Dist #3 1983-85; Nat Leag for Nsg; TX Leag for Nsg; Gerontological Soc; Resv Ofcrs Assn of USA; Sigma Theta Tau, Alpha Chapt, Life Mem; Phi Delta Kappa, Dallas Chapt; r/Prot; hon/Pubs, "Tchg Nsg Home Pers to Be Helpers" 1978, "A Quantitative Determination of Prog Impact: A Proposal" 1980, "Personal Assessment of Health Status: A Plan for Action" 1977, "The Effect of Massed Versus Spaced Clin Practice in Learning Ob & Psychi Content in a Sch of Nsg" 1980; Ser Awd, TX Nurses' Assn, 1975; 2nd Runner-Up, Fac of the Yr, Baylor Univ Sch of Nsg, 1975; Outstg Med Mobilization Augmentee for USAF Nurse Corp, 1979; Res Awd, Univ of TX-Arlington Sch of Nsg, 1982; Outstg Edrs of Am.

HUGHES, WILLIAM J oc/Member of the United States House of Representatives; b/Oct 17, 1932; h/1019 Wesley Road, Ocean City, NJ 08226; ba/Washington, DC; m/Nancy L; c/Nancy Lynn, Barbara Ann, Tama Beth, William J Jr; p/William W Hughes (dec); ed/AB, Rutgers Univ, 1955; JD, Rutgers Univ Law Sch, 1958; pa/Mem of Cong, 1975-; Gen Law Pract, 1959; First Asst Prosecutor, 1960-70; cp/Ocean City Hist Soc; Ocean City C of C; r/Epis; hon/Recog, Nat Exch Clb for Outstg Ser to Exch Mvt & Presentation of Big E Awd; Meritorious Ser Awd, NJ Shore Bldrs Assn; Book of Golden Deeds, Exch Clb of Ocean City; Dist'd Ser Awd, NJ Coast Guard Aux; W/W: in E, in Am Polits; Contemp Ams.

HUGINE, ANDREW JR oc/Assistant Vice President for Academic Affairs; b/Jun 21, 1949; h/PO Box 1958, Orangeburg, SC 29117; ba/Orangeburg, SC; m/Abbiegail H; c/Andrew III, Akilah Latrelle; p/Mr and Mrs Andrew Hugine Sr, Green Pond, SC; ed/PhD, Higher Ed, MI St Univ, 1977; EdM, Math Ed 1975, BS, Math 1971, SC St Col; pa/Asst VP for Acad Affairs 1980-, Asst/Dir for Instnl Self-Study 1978-80, SC St Col; Asst Prof, Instnl Res, MI St Univ, 1977-78; Dir of UYA 1973-75, Dir of Spec Sers Prog 1972-73, SC St Col; Assn of Instnl Res; Am Assn of Higher Ed; Epsilon Omega Chapt of Omega Psi Phi Frat, Basileus; SC St Employees Assn; Phi Delta Kappa; Alpha Kappa Mu Hon Soc; cp/Orangeburg Co U Way, Bd Mem; Edisto Masonic Lodge, Sr Warden; r/Meth; ho/Pubs, *From Phil to Practice: A Fac Salary Model 1980, The Relat'hip Between Selected Departmental Variables & Publication Productivity 1977;* Personalities of S; W/W Among Students.

HULEN, MARJORIE JANE oc/Research Administrator, Management Accountant; b/Sep 23, 1921; h/2311 El Paseo, Alhambra, CA 91803; ba/Los Angeles, CA; m/Ray R; c/Lynn R; p/Perry E Kellogg (dec); Garnett Doty Kellogg (dec); ed/Att'd, E LA Jr Col, Pasadena City Col; pa/From Clk-Typist to Exec Secy, A O Smith Corp, 1948-60; Exec Secy, Sterling Elect Motors, 1960-61; Res Secy, Pasadena Foun for Med Res, 1961-65; Exec Secy 1965-70, Ofc Mgr 1970-74, Bus Mgr 1974-79, Exec Dir 1979-, Profl Staff Assn, Univ of So CA; Profl Secy Internat, Pres 1969-71; Assn of Accts, Bd of Dirs 1976-; Soc of Res Admrs, Pres of So CA Chapt 1982-83; Am Soc of Assn Execs; Nat Assn for Female Execs; r/Prot; hon/Nat Public Relats Awd, Nat Assn of Accts, 1979; W/W: of Am Wom, in W, in CA Bus; World W/W of Wom.

HULL, CONSTANCE MAE oc/School District Administrator; b/Nov 29, 1928; h/42899 Green River Drive, Sweet Home, OR 97386; ba/Sweet Home, OR; m/Howard Donald; p/Lysle Latourelle and Lillian Henriett Gilman (dec); ed/Att'd, Macalester Col 1946-47, Miss Wood's Kgn-Primary Tng Sch 1947-49, Univ of OR-Eugene 1968; BS, Elem Ed, OR St Univ, 1966; MS, Ed Media, OR Col of Ed, 1976; Basic Supvr's Credentials, OR Col of Ed, 1978; pa/Kgn Tchr, Albert Lea, MN, 1949-50; 1st Grade & Kgn Tchg, St Paul, MN, 1950-57; 1st/2nd Combination Tchr, Missoula, MT, 1958; 3rd Grade Tchr, Sweet Home, OR, 1961-65; Sch Libn, Sweet Home, OR, 1965-78; Instrnl Mats Ctr Dir/Lib Supvr (Dist Admr Position), Sweet Home, OR, 1978-; Confederation of OR Sch Admrs; NW Wom in Ednl Adm; Am Assn of Sch Admrs; Assn for Supvn & Curric Devel; OR Assn of Sch Supvrs; Am Lib Assn; OR Lib Assn; OR Ednl Media Assn; Dist OR Ednl Media Assn; Assn of Ednl Commun & Technol; NW Coun for Computer Ed; Delta Kappa Gamma Intl; Nat Fdn of BPW; AAUW; cp/OES; Order of Rainbow for Girls; r/Presb; hon/Author, Media, Curric & Computer Activity Guidebooks for Dist,

Articles on Lib/Media Mgmt & Sers in Profl Pubs; Aspiring Author of Chd's Stories (Dog & Indian Legends); W/W: in W, of Am Wom.

HULSEY, RUTH LENORA oc/Manager of Employment Development Department; b/Nov 28, 1921; h/1246 East Shamrock Avenue, San Bernardino, CA 92410; ba/Fontana, CA; m/William A; c/William A, Steven G, Alicia L; ed/Att'd, Pasadena Jr Col 1938-40, San Bernardino Val Col 1963-65; pa/St of CA Employmt Devel Dept, 1960-, Supvr of San Bernardino Field Ofc 1969-75, Supvr of So Reg Ofc in Riverside 1975-78, Employmt Prog Mgr & Asst Mgr of Ontario Field Ofc 1979-80, Mgr of Fontana Field Ofc 1980-; Dir, CA St Employees Credit Union, 1972-75; Employer Adv Coun, 1978-; Intl Assn of Pers Employmt Security; CA St Employees Assn; cp/Bloomington C of C; Fontana C of C; Rialto C of C; San Bernardino C of C; Urban Leag, 1965-, Ed Com 1965; Arrowhead Allied Arts Coun, 1966-72; Social Lites Inc, 1963-, Pres 1964-66, 1980-81, Bd of Dirs 1980-, Recording Secy 1981-; r/Meth; hon/Outstg Wom of Rialto, 1982; W/W of Am Wom.

HUMBERGER, FRANK EDWARD oc/Counseling Psychologist; b/July 10, 1914; h/Box 100 Star Route, Eastsound, WA 98245; ba/Same; m/Jackeline A; c/Sallie M, Edward McDowell, Janet Gayle; p/Frank L Humberger (dec); sp/James Armstrong (dec); ed/BS Case Inst Technol, 1935; BD, SF Theol Sem, 1959; ThD, Pacific Sch of Rel, 1967; pa/Sales, Republic Steel Corp, 1935-40; Engr, Powell Valve, 1940-45; Owner & Mgr, Tech Metal Processing, 1945-59; Pastor, 1st U Presb Ch, Turlock, CA, 1960-68; Pastor, Stinson Bch, 1958-60; Assoc Prof, SF St Univ, 1967-70; Lectr, Univ of Pacific, 1970-72; Dir, Lafayette Ctr Conslg Ed, 1968-78; Pres, CA Hlth Grp, 1974-78; Chm, Gov's Worker Task Force, UPUSA, 1965-68; Dir Col of Communs & Relats, SF St Univ, Fellow, Am Assn Past Cnslrs; Clin Mem, (Cert'd Supvr) Am Assn of Marriage & Fam Therapists; cp/Blue Key; Tau Beta Pi; St Francis Yacht Clb; Bellevue Ath Clb; Orcas Tennis Clb; Orcas Yacht Clb; r/Presb; hon/Author, *Developing Effective Cnslg Styles, 1979; Outplacement & Inplacement Cnslg,* 1984; Var Articles Pub'd in Profl Jours; Highest Hons, SF Theol Sem, 1959; Pres, Student Body, SF Theol Sem, 1959; Pres, San Juan Human Sers Assn, 1983; Pres, Phi Kappa Psi, 1935; W/W: in Rel, in W.

HUMPHREY, ALBERT S oc/Executive; b/Jun 2, 1926; h/4030 Charlotte Street, Kansas City, MO 64110; ba/London, England; m/Myriam 'de Baere; c/Albert S III, Virginia Potter, Johnathan Benton Cantwell, Heidi, Roosje Willems, Jonas Willems; p/Albert S Jr (dec) and Margaret Elizabeth Benton Humphrey, Kansas City, MO; ed/BSc, Chem Engrg, Univ of IL, 1946; MSc, Chem Engrg, MIT, 1948; MBA, Fin, Harvard Sch of Bus Adm; mil/LCDR, USNR; pa/Staff Engr, E Coast Tech Ser Div, Esso Standard Oil Co, 1949; Chief of Chem & Protective Grp Chief, Chem Ofcr, AUS Chem Corp, 1952; Asst to Pres, Penberthy Instrument Co, 1955; Chief of Prod Planning, Boeing Airplane Co, 1956; Mgr, Value Anal, Small Aircraft Engine Div, GE, 1960; Mgr,

R&D Planning, P R Mallory & Co Inc, 1961; Hd of MAFIA, Gen Dynamics Inc, 1963; Dir, Intl Exec Sem in Bus Planning, Stanford Res Inst, 1964; Chm, Bus Planning & Devel, 1969-; Conslt to Num Companies, incl'g, Lear Siegler Inc, Ottawa Silica Sand, J C Carter, Gen Dynamics Centrifugal Prods, Continental Coffee Co, Faultless Starch Co; Dir, Treasured Prods Inc, Triade Inc, Galley W Inc, Aqua Media Inc, Delta Control Inc, Integrated Graphics Inc, Coffenco Intl, Petras Petrochemische Anwendungssysteme GmbH, Tower Lysprodukter a/s, Tower Lamps Ltd; AIChE; Sci Res Soc of Am; Sigma Xi; Tau Beta Phi; r/Ch of England; hon/Author, Var Pubs; Grad, High Hons, Univ of IL, 1946; DIB; Ldrs of Eng Spkg World; Royal Blue Book; W/W: of Am Ed & Sci, in W, in CA, in Engrg, in World; Nat Register of Prom Ams; Personalities of W & MW; Men of Achmt; Brit Inst of Dirs; Brit Inst of Mktg.

HUMPHREY, THOMAS WARD oc/Librarian; b/Oct 20, 1948; h/152 Crescent Drive, Clovis, NM 88101; ba/Clovis, NM; m/Billie Powell Staton; c/Sybil Rene, Laura Nicole; p/James W and Violet Rene Ward Humphrey, Hartford, KY; ed/BA, Elem Ed, KY Wesleyan Col, 1970; MLS, Peabody Col of Vanderbilt Univ, 1972; Addit Wk, Wn KY Univ; pa/Lib Asst, Asst 'Prof of Lib Sci, KY Wesleyan Col, 1970-79; Lib Dir, Ctl WY Col, 1979-83; Dir of Lib & Lng Resources, En NM Univ, 1983-; Am Lib Assn; KY Hist Soc; Nat Grigsby Fam Assn, 1980-; W Ctl KY Fam Res Assn, 1979-; Var Previous Mbrships; r/U Meth; hon/Author, Var Pubs; W/W in W.

HUMPHREYS, LOIS HAGY oc/Business Owner and Manager; b/Sep 25, 1931; h/Route 1, Box 545, Abingdon, VA 24210; ba/Abingdon, VA; m/Paul E; c/Richard E, Jill H; p/Howard B Hagy (dec); Deltia H Shupe, Abingdon, VA; ed/Att'd, Am Floral Arts Sch, 1969; VA Rltrs Lic, 1976; pa/Dental Asst, Dr Harry Loving and Dr A C Bucharan Jr, 1949-54; Maxine's Ladies Fashions, 1955-66; Bkkpr, Gentry Furniture, 1967; Audio Visual Coor, Abingdon Elem Sch, 1968-69; Owner & Mgr, Humphreys Flowers & Gifts, 1970-; Rltr, Johnson Real Est & Auction; Blue Ridge Profl Floral Assn, 1971-, Pres 1978-80, Treas 1973-78; cp/PTA, 1960, Treas 1962-67, Pres 1968-70, Dist Dir 1971; Wash Co C of C, 1970-; Johnston Meml Hosp Aux; r/Abingdon U Meth Wom; U Meth Ch, 1944-82; hon/PTA Life Mbrship, VA; W/W in S & SW.

HUMPHRIES, FREDERICK S oc/University President; b/Dec 26, 1935; h/2904 John A Merritt Boulevard, Nashville, TN 37203; ba/Nashville, TN; m/Antoinette; c/Robin Tanya, Frederick Jr, Laurence; p/Mr (dec) and Mrs Thornton Humphries, Apalachicola, FL; ed/PhD, Phy Chem, Univ of Pgh, 1964; BS, Chem, FL A&M Univ, 1957; mil/Ofcr, AUS Security Agy, 1957-59; pa/Pres, TN St Univ, 1974; VP, Inst for Sers to Ed, 1970-74; Dir of Thirteen-Col Curric Prog 1968-74; Dir of Three-Univs Grad Prog (Humanities) 1970-74, Dir of Two-Univs Grad Prog in Sci 1973-74, Dir of Interdisciplinary Prog 1973-74, Dir of Knoxville Col Study of Sci Capability of the Black Col 1972-74, Dir of Innovative Instnl Res Consortium 1972-73, ISE; Other Previous Positions;

Am Assn of Higher Ed; AAAS; AAUP; Am Chem Soc; Nat Assn for St Univs & Land Grant Cols; NAFEO; Nat Assn for Equal Opport in Higher Ed; r/Cath; hon/Author, Num Pubs; Nat Urban Leag Fellow, 1966; Grad Res Fellow, Univ of Pgh, 1960-64; Grad Tchg Asst, Univ of Pgh, 1959-60; Num Other Hons.

HUNDERUP, RENÉ A oc/Pharmaceutical Company Executive; b/Nov 28, 1944; h/25 Wagon Trailway, Willowdale, Ontario, Canada M2J 4V4; ba/ Same; p/Peter and Ruby Hunderup, Virum, Denmark; ed/Dipl in Commerce, Copenhagen, 1966; MBA, Copenhagen Sch of Ec & Bus Adm, 1974; pa/Comml Apprentice, E Asiatic Co, Copenhagen, 1963-66; Export and Shipping Mgr, Denison Deri Ltd, UK, 1966-68; Shipping Mgr, Danish Hardwood, Copenhagen, 1968-69; Asst Export Mgr, Novo Industri A/S, Copenhagen, 1969-71; Asst Export Mgr, Danochemo A/S, Copenhagen, 1971-73; Export Mgr, Marsing & Co, Copenhagen, 1973-74; Sales Mgr, Toronto, 1974-78; Canadian Mktg Dir, ACIC Ltd, Toronto, 1978-; Pres, ScanCorp Mgmt Ltd, Toronto, 1978-; Pres, ScanCorp Holdings Inc, Toronto, 1980-; Assn Danish Civil Ec; Scandinavian Canadian Bus Assn, Dir 1980-82, VP 1982-; Canadian Drug Mfrs Assn, Secy 1983-; cp/Intl Balut Fdn, Canada, Gen Secy-Treas 1980-; Canadian Assoc'd Royal Danish Whist Clb, Fdg Mem 1975; Royal Danish Yacht Clb; r/Prot; hon/W/W: in Commonwlth, in World.

HUNT, BERNICE oc/Author, Psychotherapist; b/Jun 15, 1920; h/8 Ledgewood Commons, Millwood, NY 10546; ba/Same; m/Morton; c/Eugene Kohn, Judith Wolman, Barbara Adler; p/Joseph and Sara Herstein; ed/MS, LIU, 1983; MA, St Univ of NY Empire; Att'd, Univ of WI; pa/Pvt Pract; Free-Lance Writer; Editor-in-Chief, Dandelion Press, 1978-81; Adj Prof, Southampton Col, LIU, 1976-78; Guest Lectr, Notre Dame Univ, TX A&M, Univ of IA, Others; Authors Guild; Am Assn of Journalists & Authors; Am Mtl Hlth Assn; Gerontological Soc; hon/Author, More Than 60 Books, incl'g, Intimate Partners, 1979; Author, Articles in Popular Mags; W/W: in E, of Am Wom; World W/W of Wom; Contemp Authors.

HUNT, ELIZABETH HOPE oc/Psychologist in Private Practice, Author, Researcher, Lecturer, Civic Activist; b/ Oct 14, 1943; h/2650 Cresta De Rata, Eugene, OR 97403; ba/Eugene, OR; m/ John Volney Allcott MD; c/Hunt Allcott, Elizabeth Allcott; p/Emory S and I Elizabeth Burkette Hunt, Chapel Hill, NC; ed/AB, Sweet Briar Col, 1965; MSW, Univ of PA, 1971; PhD, Univ of OR-Eugene, 1980; pa/Civil Rights Spec, Dept of HEW, 1971-74; Doct Fellow 1974-77, Res Asst 1978-79, Univ of OR-Eugene; Psychol in Pvt Pract, 1980-; Co-Chp, Spkrs' Bur, Phys for Social Responsibility, 1982; Am Psychol Assn; OR Psychol Assn; Lane Co Psychols' Assn; cp/Peace Corps Vol, Santiago, Chile, 1967-69; Bd Mem, Lane Co Relief Nursery for Abused Chd, 1982-; r/Prot; hon/Pubs, "Indep & Dependence in Mildly Retarded Adolescents" 1981, "A Behavioral Exploration of Dependent & Independent Mildly Retarded Adolescents & Their Mothers" 1983; Doct

Fellow, Rehab Res & Tng Ctr, Univ of OR, 1974-77; Netwk of Profl Wom, 1983; W/W: of Am Wom, in W.

HUNT, GERTRUDE LOYOLA oc/ Executive; b/Feb 16, 1925; h/6 Rolling Acres Drive, Cumberland, RI 02864; ba/ Pawtucket, RI; p/John F and Gertrude Daley Hunt (dec); ed/RI Public Sch Sys; pa/Acct 1943-48, Exec Secy 1948-56, Secy of Retirement Bd 1951-64, Royal Elect Co Inc; Adm Asst 1956-61, Asst Secy 1961-64, ITT Royal Elect Corp; Asst Secy, ITT Wire & Cable Div, 1964-69; Bd of Dirs 1963-72, Asst Treas 1963-65, VP 1965-69, Chm, Bd of Dirs & Pres 1969-72, Hon Mem, Bd of Dirs 1972-, ITT Royal Fed Credit Union; Asst Secy, ITT Caribbean Indust Prods 1967-80, ITT Royal Elect Div 1969-; Pres, N Eng Reg Chapt, Royal Elect Div; cp/ITT Qtr Cent Clb, 1978-82; Perpetual Com for Implementation & Cont'd Devel; Lib for Capt G Harold Hunt Elem Sch.

HUNT, JAMES EDWARD oc/Professional Civil Engineer; b/Jun 19, 1947; h/8519 Baumgarten Drive, Dallas, TX 75228; ba/Dallas, TX; m/Kathy Jo Krehbiel; c/Joseph James; p/Elmer Hal and Juanita Mildred Tibey (dec) Hunt, Lone Oak, TX; ed/BS in Civil Engrg, Univ of OK; pa/Engr Asst II, Survey Party Chief 1970, Engr Asst III Supervising Bridge Constrn 1972, Assoc Res Engr Supervising Road & Bridge Constrn 1974, Resident Engr Supervising Hwy Constrn Projs Totaling $61 Million 1978, Sr Resident Engr Supervising Hwy Constrn Projs 1982-, TX St Dept of Hwys & Public Trans; Bd of Dirs, Dist 18 THD Employees Credit Union, Treas 1977-79, VChm 1979-; Nat Soc of Profl Engrs, 1974-; TX Soc of Profl Engrs, 1974-; Univ of OK Alumni Assn, Life Mem; TX Public Employee Assn, 1970-; cp/Univ of OK Clb of Dallas, 1974-; r/Rom Cath; hon/ Hons Class, Jesuit Col Prep, Dallas; Deans Hon Roll, Univ of OK; Reg'd Profl Engr, TX #36893; W/W in S & SW; Personalities of S.

HUNTER, DUNCAN LEE oc/United States Representative; b/May 31, 1948; h/1020 C Street, #3, Coronado, CA 92118; ba/Washington, DC; m/Lynne L; c/Duncan D, R Samuel; p/Mr and Mrs Robert O Hunter, La Jolla, CA; ed/JD, 1976; mil/AUS, 1969-71; pa/Atty in Own Pract, 1976-80; US Rep, 1981-; cp/ Repub Class of 1980, Pres 1983-; Asst Reg Minority Whip, 1983-; Navy Leag; Several Cs of C; r/Bapt; hon/Pubs, "Views on Defense of Cheap Hawk" 1982, "Thoughts on the Mid-E" 1983; Watchdog of the Treas, NFIB, 1982-83.

HUNTER, GORDON COBLE oc/ Banker; b/Jul 29, 1894; h/115 Academy Street, Roxboro, NC 27573; ba/Roxboro, NC; m/Ethel Gray Wilson; c/ Rebecca Vance (Mrs V Paul Vittur), Rachel Gray (Mrs George J Cushwa); p/Samuel G and Lalah Vance Coble Hunter; ed/Student, Univ of NC, 1915-17; Grad, Am Inst of Bkg, 1927; mil/From Pvt to 2nd Lt, Inf, AUS, 1917-19; pa/Am Exch Nat Bk, 1919-31; Bk Examr, FDIC, 1933; Exec VP 1933-57, Pres 1957-, Chm of Bd 1960-, Peoples Bk; Chm of Bd Emeritus, First Nat Bk; Dir, Morris Telephone Co, Reinforced Plastic Container Corp, Roxboro Devel Corp; Am Bkrs Assn, Nat Res Coun 1955-57, Exec Com

1946-49, Reg VP 1958-60, NC Legis Com 1960-62; NC Bkrs Assn, Pres 1945-46; cp/Roxboro C of C. 1st Pres 1935; Treas, Bd of Commrs, Town of Roxboro, 1934-60; Person Co Chm, ARC, 1937-38; Polio Fund, 1938-; USO Drive, 1943-44; NC Chm, Nat Foun 4-H Clb, 1955-57; Orgr, Bd of Dirs, Person Co Meml Hosp; NC Bd of Conserv & Devel; Vol Chm, War Bond Sales for 10 Cos, 1942-45; Am Legion, Past Cmdr, Lester Blackwell Post; Order of Long Leaf Pine; Rotarian, Past Pres; r/ Meth, Steward; hon/Citizen of the Yr, 1956; Recip, Cert of Apprec for Ldrship in War Savs Bonds Sales from Secy of Treas; Dist'd Ser Awd, US Treas; Outstg Ser Recog, Roxboro Exch Clb; Cit for 25 Yrs Ser, March of Dimes; Fellow, IPA; Tar Heel of Wk, News & Observer, 1957; Admiral, NC Navy, 1961.

HUNTER, JEFFREY CHARLES oc/ Project Manager; b/Oct 19, 1938; h/923 N San Antonio, Pomona, CA 91767; ba/ Azusa, CA; p/Theodore Lee and Dorothea Wilson Hunter; ed/BS 1962, MS 1964, San Diego St Univ; MAM, Univ of Redlands, 1979; pa/Sr Chem, Paper and Mats, Avery Label Div Res, 1966-71; Mats Lab Supvr of Res Dept 1971-76, Prod Devel Spec of Resale Div 1976-79, Proj Mgr of Consumer Div 1979-, Consumer and Ofc Prods Grp, Avery Intl Am Chem Soc; Tech Assn of the Pulp & Paper Indust; Assn of MBA Execs; Coun of Reprographics Execs; cp/Ontario-Pkway Kiwanis; Kiwanis Intl, Secy 1980, 1981, 1982; Mt San Antonio Circle K Advr; r/Epis; hon/ Co-Author of Articles in Field; Grad, Bus Inst, Univ of Redlands, 1980-; Fac Mem in Bus & Sci, Col of Profl Studies, Univ of SF, 1981-; St Chm of Curric Design Com, Col of Profl Studies, 1982, 1983, 1984; W/W: in CA, in W; Men of Achmt.

HUNTER, MILDRED CECILIA oc/ Social Worker; b/Dec 6, 1947; h/1649 E 50th Street, Chicago, IL 60615; ba/ Chicago, IL; p/Mr and Mrs Cecil Th Hunter, Pensacola, FL; ed/BA, Fisk Univ, 1969; MSW, WA Univ, 1971; MPH, Univ of IL, 1976; pa/Prog Mgr, IL Fam Planning Coun, 1978-83; Field Instr, Univ of Chgo Sch of Social Ser, 1981-83; Outside Lectr, Malcolm X Col, 1982; Hlth/Social Sers Conslt, Kirschner Assocs, 1976-; Prog Dir, Cook Co Hosp, 1974-75; Casewkr, IL Chd's Home & Aid Soc; cp/APHA; Black Caucus of Hlth Wkrs of APHA (MW Reg Chp), 1979-; Chgo Bd of Ed's Sch Hlth Adv Com; March of Dimes 1983 Salute to Babies Banquet Com; US 1st Congl Dist of IL Hlth Task Force; Alpha Kappa Alpha Sorority; Fisk Univ Alumni Assn, Metro Chgo Area Clb; Alumni Assn Bd of Dirs VPres, Univ of IL Sch of Public Hlth; Cert'd IL Social Wkr; r/Cath; hon/Editor of Conf Proceedings, Cnslg Adolescents in a Fam Planning Clin; Lambda Chapt, Delta Omega Hon Soc; Outstg Wom of Am; W/W of Am Wom; Personalities of W & MW.

HUNTER, W DEAN oc/School Teacher; b/Sep 24, 1931; h/9818 Dekoven Drive, Southwest, Tacoma, WA 98499; ba/Tacoma, WA; m/Cynthia C; c/Jane J, David C, Anne K; ed/BA, Sociol, 1956; MA, Cnslg & Guid, 1974; EdD, Ednl Ldrship, 1984; mil/USMC, 6 Yrs;

USAF, 20 Yrs; pa/Command Pilot, Dpty Cmdr and Base Cmdr, USAF; Dir of Devel, Knapp Bus Col; Salesmgr, Lakewood Rlty Co; Pres, NW Col of Goldsmithing; Sec'dy Voc Tchr, Clover Pk Sch Dist; Sigma Chi Frat; Phi Delta Kappa; NCAA Coaches Assn; cp/Eagle Scout, BSA; Master Mason; 32nd Deg Mason; Scottish Rites; Shriner; Naja Temple; Order of Daedalians; Clover Pk Kiwanis Clb; Pierce Co Vol Dpty Sheriff; r/Prot; hon/Hon Grad, Indust Col of the Armed Forces; Grad (MA), magna cum laude, Ball St Univ; Most Outstg DO Tchr, WA St, 1980; Most Outstg Chapt Advr, Sigma Chi Frat, 1980; One of the Highest Decorated Ofcrs, USAF, 1967; W/W in US.

HURD, WALTER LEROY JR oc/ Corporate Director of Product Assurance; b/Jul 8, 1919; h/18120-82 Oxnard Street, Tarzana, CA 91356; ba/Burbank, CA; m/Ann Vivian Cornell; c/ David, Caroline, Drew, Bruce, Kevin; p/Walter Leroy and Mary Daisy Gibbon Hurd (dec); ed/BA, Morningside Col, 1940; MA, San Jose St Univ, 1977; mil/ Lt Col, USAAF, 1941-46; USAFR, 1946-49, Ret'd 1979; pa/Current Corp Dir of Prod Assurance, Lockheed Corp; Dir of Prod Assurance 1966-67, Rel & Quality Engrg Mgr 1958-65, Lockheed Missiles & Space Co; Quality Control Mgr, Nat Seal Div, Fed Mogul, 1954-58; Other Previous Positions; Am Soc for Quality Control; European Org for QC; Nat and CA Socs of Profl Engrg; AIAA, Assoc Fellow; r/Prot; hon/Author, Var Pubs; Recip, Initial Plaque Awd, San Fernando Val Sect, Am Soc for Quality Control, 1983; Recip, Engrg 1979 Merit Awd, San Fernando Val Engrs' Coun; Elected Hon Mem, Philippine Soc for QC 1969, Australian Org for QC 1969, New Zealand Org for Quality Assurance 1978; Other Hons; W/W: in World, in Am, in W, in Fin & Indust, in Engrg; Engrs of Distn.

HURDLE, BESS oc/Community Specialist; b/May 17, 1945; h/1338 Levis Street, Northeast, Washington, DC 20002; ba/Same; c/James William III, Obai; p/Mrs Bessie Walker, Reading, PA; ed/Att'd, Reading Area Commun Col, 1975-78; pa/Exec Dir of Wel Rights, 1978-81; cp/Com Mem, PA St Food & Nutrition, 1978-81; Coor, Black Wom in Polit Action, 1979; Intl Readers Assn of DC; Coor, Vol Clearing House; Nat St Law for Adult Ed; Help Put the Conv of Nat Wom of Color Together; Active in Wider Opports for Wom; Bd Mem, My Sister Place, DC, MD, PA; hon/ Ebony Fashion Show, Sep 16, 1981; IPA; W/W of Wom in Am.

HURLEY, ANN MARIE oc/Receiver of Taxes; b/Jul 13, 1925; h/2 Coe Place, Huntington, NY 11746; ba/Huntington, NY; m/John D Jr; c/Rev John E, Patty Ann Hurley McGovern; p/Timothy Charles and Mary Frances Lacey O'Neill; ed/Att'd, Drakes Bus Sch, Cornell Univ Sem for Tax Receivers; Student, Pvt Bkkpg Supervisory Course at Guaranty Trust Co; pa/Bkkpg Supvr, Guaranty Trust Co 1942-47, Continental Bk & Trust Co 1947-48, NY Trust 1948-49; Hd Bkkpr, Prin Clk, Dept Receiver of Taxes 1960-67, Receiver of Taxes 1967-, Town of Huntington; Pres, NYS Receivers and Collectors Assn, 1982; Pres, Suffolk Co Receivers, 1969-83; cp/Blue Ribbon Com to Revise

Suffolk Co Tax Act; NYS Commun Affairs Adv Bd; Resolution Com of the NYS Assn of Towns; Past Pres, Heatherwood Civic Assn; r/Rom Cath; Elected Mem, Parish Coun, St Elizabeths Ch; hon/First & Only Female Grand Marshal of Huntington St Patrick's Day Parade, 1976; Wom of the Yr, Nassau & Suffolk BPW Clbs, 1982-83; W/W of Am Wom.

HURST, JAMES C oc/Associate Vice President for Academic Affairs, Chief Student Affairs Officer, Professor of Psychology; b/Jun 19, 1935; h/1070 Hidalgo Drive, Laramie, WY 82070; m/ Joan Rees; c/Kathy, Jeff, Brad, Jennifer; p/Leo C and Ione Salt Hurst, Ogden, UT; r/AS, Weber St Col, 1959; BS w High Hons, Univ of UT, 1961; PhD, Brigham Yg Univ, 1966; Internship, Cnslg Psych, Duke Univ, 1965-66; mil/ AUS, 1953-55, Korea 1954-55; pa/Assoc VP for Acad Affairs, Chief Student Affairs Ofcr, Prof of Psych, Mem of Grad Fac, Univ of WY; Dean of Students & Asst VP for Student Affairs, Prof of Cnslg Psych, Mem of Grad Fac, Univ of TX-Austin, 1976-81; Dir of Univ Cnslg Ctr, Assoc Prof of Psych, Mem of Grad Fac, CO St Univ, 1970-76; Other Previous Positions; Am Psychol Assn, Div 17, Cnslg Psych, Fellow; WY Psychol Assn; Rocky Mtn Psychol Assn; Am Assn for Cnslg & Devel; Am Col Pers Assn; Nat Assn of Student Pers Admrs; Phi Kappa Phi Hon Soc; Soc of Sigma Xi; hon/Author, Pub'd Books and Articles, incl'g, *Dimensions of Intervention for Student Devel* 1980, *Nine Outreach Progs* 1974, "The Psychotherapist & One-Way Intimacy" 1982; Designated Mem, Am Col Pers Assn Sr Scholar Prog, 1983; Contbn to Knowledge Awd, Am Col Pers Assn, 1982; Ombudsman Outreach Awd, Univ of TX, 1981; Hon Mem, Phi Eta Sigma, Univ of TX, 1981; Num Other Hons; W/W in W.

HURWITZ, T ALAN oc/Associate Dean; b/Sep 17, 1942; h/100 Holley Brook Drive, Penfield, NY 14526; ba/ Rochester, NY; m/Vicki; c/Bernard R, Stephanie Vera; p/Harold and Juliette Hurwitz, Kansas City, MO; ed/Att'd, Morningside Col 1961-63, Rochester Inst of Technol 1972-76; BSEE, Wash Univ, 1965; MSEE, St Louis Univ, 1970; EdD, Univ of Rochester, 1980; pa/Assoc Electronics Engr 1965-67, Sr Computer Programmer 1967-70, McDonnell-Douglas Corp; Ednl Spec 1970-73, Chp of Support Sers 1973-79, Nat Tech Inst for the Deaf; Assoc Dean, Rochester Inst of Technol, 1979-; Nat Assn of the Deaf, Pres 1982-84, Bd Mem 1977-86; Empire St Assn of the Deaf, Pres 1975-79, Bd Mem 1974-81; Alexander Graham Bell Assn; Conv of Am Instrs for the Deaf; Conf of Ednl Admrs of Schs for the Deaf; Am Assn of Higher Ed; r/Jewish; hon/Pubs, "Real-Time Graphic Display for Deaf Students" 1982, "Reflections: Past, Present & Future Outlook" 1982, "Future of the Deaf Commun" 1981, Num Others; Rotary Awd, 1958; Jour S'ship Awd, 1961; CIDAA Meritorious Awd, 1971; Thomas F Fox Awd, 1979; CIDAA Dist'd Alumnus Awd, 1981; W/W in E; Outstg Men of Am.

HUSEMANN, ROBERT WILLIAM oc/Chief Engineer; b/May 24, 1931; h/ 12802 Teaberry Road, Silver Spring, MD 20906; ba/Washington, DC; m/J

Eileen R; p/Edgar W (dec) and Ruth D Husemann, Crystal River, FL; ed/BA in Math, BSME, Balparaiso Univ, 1954; Student of Bus Adm, Am Univ, 1957-64; mil/AUS, Counterintell Corps, 1954-56; pa/Sales-Engr, Honeywell Inc (Comml Div), 1956-57; Sales-Engr, Barber-Colman Co, 1957-64; Sales-Engr, Honeywell Inc (Indust Div), 1964-67; Designer-Estimator, C V Carlson Co, 1967-75; Chief Engr, Ctl Heating Plant, Gen Sers Adm, 1975-81; Asst Chief Engr 1981-83, Chief Engr 1983-, US Capitol Power Plant, Arch of the Capitol; ASHRAE, 1968; Am Inst of Plant Engrs, 1979; r/Christian & Missionary Alliance; hon/W/W in E.

HUSEYIN, KONCAY oc/Professor and Chairman; b/Jul 10, 1936; h/569 Glascow Street, Kitchener, Ontario N2M 2N6; ba/Waterloo, Ontario; m/ Tuncay; c/Neyzar, Zahal, Hulya; p/S Vicdan (dec) and Salih Huseyin, Nicosia, Cyprus; ed/MSc, Technological Univ of Istanbul, 1960; PhD 1968, DSc in Engrg 1979, London Univ; pa/Structural Engr, Tumpane Co, Ankara, Turkey, 1960-65; Asst Prof, Engrg Scis, METU, Ankara, 1968-72; Assoc Prof, Sys Design 1972-75, Prof 1975-, Chm 1978-, Univ of Waterloo; Vis'g Prof, Darmstadt Technische Hochschule, 1978, 1983; Am Acad of Mechs; APEO; GAMM; Others; hon/Author of 2 Res Monographs on Stability Theory 1975, 1978, Many Res Papers in Jours & Conf Proceedings; Co-Author & Co-Editor, 2 Books, 1976, 1977; S'ship, Min of Ed, Turkey, 1954-60; NATO F'ship, 1965-67; NRC Postdoct F'ship, 1969; Alexander von Humboldt Foun F'ship, 1977, 1983; Am Men & Wom of Sci; Intl W/W in Ed.

HUTCHCROFT, JOHN CARTER oc/ Conductor; b/Apr 30, 1941; h/1221 Laing Street, Delray Beach, FL 33444; ba/Boca Raton, FL; m/Cynthia Ruth; c/ Stephen Ward, Brian Lee, Wendy Susan, Julie Diane; p/Clyde and Margaret Grey (dec) Hutchcroft, Pine Beach, NJ; ed/BS in Music Ed, Lebanon Val Col, 1964; MM in Brass Perf and Conducting, Ithaca Col, 1965; PhD in Music Theory, FL St Univ, 1983; Further Conducting Study, Univ of No CO; pa/Dir of Music, Franklin Acad & Prattsburg Ctl Schs, 1965-68; Conductor, Instr of Music, Okaloosa-Walton Jr Col, 1968-75; Fdr, Conductor, Okaloosa-Walton Co Commun Symph, 1972-75; Conductor, Asst Prof of Music, Cumberland Col, 1975-78; Conductor, Music Dir, Lexington Music Theatre Inc, 1977-78; Asst Conductor, FL St Univ Symph & Opera Theatre, 1978-79; Fdr, Conductor, Chamber Orch of the Cumberlands, 1979-80; Conductor, Assoc Prof of Music Theory, Cumberland Col, 1979-80; Resident Conductor, FL Atl Univ, 1980-; Prin Trombonist, Palm Bch Opera, Gtr Palm Bch Symph, Palm Bch Ballet, 1980-; Phi Mu Alpha Sinfonia Frat of Am; Am Symph Orch Leag; KY Music Edrs Assn; MENC; FL Music Edrs Assn; FL Bandmasters Assn; FL Orch Assn; Col Band Dirs Nat Assn; hon/Pubs, *A Manual for Brass Players* 1974, Many Articles in Profl Jours on Conducting & Rehearsal Techniques; Orchestral Editor, *Skills for Musicianship, Volume I*; Outstg Dir, Stagecrafters Commun Theatre, 1975; Guest Spkr, KY Music

Edrs Assn Conv, 1980; Orpheus Awd for Outstg Contbns to Music of Am, 1976; Guest Conductor, Chgo Civic Orch, Palm Bch Symph, Ctl KY Yth Symph, Univ of Miami Symph, Others; Var Other Hons.

HUTCHINGS, HAROLD MICHELL oc/College Administrator; b/Jan 31, 1942; h/46 Strawberry Lane, RFD #1, Southbridge, MA 01550; ba/Worcester, MA; c/Timothy, Margot, Zachary; p/ Mrs Margie Hutchings, Elmira, NY; ed/ EdD 1980, EdM 1976, Univ of MA; BA, Mansfield St Col, 1965; pa/Chm of Div of Hlth and Human Sers, Quinsigamond Commun Col, 1981-; Asst Prof of Spec Ed, Keene St Col, 1979-; Dir of Mtl Retard Sers, MA Dept of Mtl Hlth, 1976-79; Asst Supt for Emotional & Social Devel, Adolescent Day Treatment Prog, Northampton Child & Fam Ser Ctr, 1975-76; Proj Coor, Wk Opport Ctr, W Springfield Public Schs, 1972-75; Supvr of the Follow Through Prog, Elmira City Sch Dist, 1969-71; Other Previous Positions; MA Assn for Chd w Lng Disabilities; MA Assn for Retarded Citizens; Assn for Retarded Citizens, Hampshire Co Br Pres; MA Mtl Hlth Assn; CEC; N Eng Assn of Human Sers; hon/Pubs/Position Papers, *Mtl Hlth, Substance Abuse, Mental Retardation Components* 1977, *Commun Programming/Ednl Concerns for Mtlly Retarded Adults* 1980.

HUTCHINS, JEANNE BAHN oc/ Councilwoman; b/Mar 12, 1922; h/75 Indian Spring Lane, Rochester, NY 14618; ba/Rochester, NY; m/Frank M; c/Katharine H Welling, Virginia H Valkenburgh, Patricia H Murphy, Constance H Mills; p/Carl E and Marie Hall Bahn, Pittsford, NY; ed/BA, Wells Col, 1943; MPA, SUNY, 1980; pa/Bacteriologist/Chem, Univ of Rochester/Strong Meml Hosp, Manhatten Proj, Atomic

Energy, 1943-45; Lib Asst, Ft Benning, GA 1946-47, Dartmouth Col Lib 1947-48; Town Bd Legis, Town of Brighton, 1976-; Trustee, Monroe Savs Bk 1978-, Wells Col 1977-, Ctr for Govtl Res 1979-; cp/U Way of Gtr Rochester, 1974-; Bd of Dirs, St Ann's Home, 1982-; Monroe Co Human Resources Coun, 1975-; Pres, Rochester Female Charitable Soc, 1983-; Wom's Bd of Dirs, Highland Hosp; Bd of Dirs, Rochester Area Foun; Wom's Coun, Rochester Inst of Technol, 1970-; LWV, 1977-; Brighton C of C, 1976-; Susan B Anthony Clb, 1976-; Brighton Repub Clb, 1976-; Mid-Town Tennis Clb, 1975-; Rochester Dist Golf Assn, 1970-; Wn NY Wom's Golf Assn, 1972-; St Communities Aid Assn; r/Vestry Wom 1977-83, Treas 1983-, St Paul's Epis Ch; hon/Pub, "Long-Term Hlth Care," 1980; Forman Flair Awd for Commun Ser, 1978; Grant Garvey Awd, Am Soc for Public Adm, 1980; Fam Ser of Rochester Awd, 1983; W/W of Am Wom.

HUTCHINSON, JANICE GERTRUDE oc/Pediatrician, Assistant Director of Health Education; b/Sep 22, 1947; h/3217 South Calumet, Chicago, IL 60616; ba/Chicago, IL; p/M Dorothy Howell Hutchinson (dec); ed/BA, Stanford Univ, 1969; MD, Univ of Cinc, 1973; MPH, Univ of IL, 1980; pa/Att'g Pract & Adm, USPHS, 1978-82; Asst Dir of Hlth Ed, AMA, 1982-; Am Acad of Pediatrics; Admissions Com & Fac Advr, Rush Med Col, 1978-80; cp/Chgo Area Wom's Sports Org, Bd Mem; Hyde Pk Wom's Lit Clb; hon/Pediatric Columnist, *The Black Fam Mag*, "Ask Dr Jan," 1980-; Ten Outstg Yg People, Chgo JCs, 1976; Kizzy Achmt Awd, 1977; W/W of Am Wom.

HUTSON, JANET KERN oc/ Teacher; b/Nov 27, 1924; h/215 South Sixth Street, Denton, MD 21629; ba/ Ridgely, MD; m/Wallace E; c/W Edward Jr, Janet Hutson Magaha; p/Clarence J and Mildred R Kern (dec); ed/Master's Equivalency, Univ of MD, 1977; Tchr of Voc Cosmetology; pa/Self-Employed, Owner-Mgr, Janet's Beauty Shoppe, Denton & Goldsboro, MD, 1942-74; Tchr in Voc Ed, 1966-; Past St Pres 1980-81, MD St BPW Clbs Inc; Congl Com, MD St Tchrs' Assn; cp/Vice Mayor of Denton, 1983; r/Prot; hon/ Wom of the Yr, St BPW Clbs, 1980; W/ W in E.

HUZURBAZAR, VASANT SHANKAR oc/Professor of Statistics; b/Sep 15, 1919; h/3755 East Buchtel Boulevard, #206, Denver, CO 80210; ba/ Denver, CO; m/Prabha; c/Snehalata, Aparna; p/Shankar Abaji Huzurbazar (dec); ed/BA w Hons, Bombay Univ, 1940; MA, Banaras Hindu Univ, 1942; PhD, Cambridge Univ, 1949; pa/Sampling Expert, Govt of Bombay, 1950-52; Sr Prof, Hd of Dept of Math & Stats, Univ of Poona, 1953-76; Fulbright Vis'g Prof, IA St Univ, 1962-64; Vis'g Prof, Univ of Manitoba, 1976-79; Prof of Stats, Col of Bus Adm, Univ of Denver, 1979-; Fellow, Royal Statistical Soc, London; Cambridge Philosophical Soc; Am Statistical Assn; Intl Statistical Inst; Indian Nat Sci Acad; Pres, Indian Statistical Assn, 1972-79; Pres, Stats Sect, Indian Sci Cong Assn, 1966-67; r/ Hindu; hon/Pubs, *Sufficient Statistics* 1976, 3 Other Books & 35 Res Papers in Var Statistical & Math Jours; Chancellor's Gold Medal, Banaras Hindu Univ, 1942; Adams Prize for Outstg Res in Math, Cambridge Univ, 1959-60; Padma Bhushan Awd, Pres of India, 1974; Nat Lectr, Univ Grants Com of India, 1975-76; W/W: in World, in W.

I

IGO, JOHN N JR oc/Professor of English, Drama Critic; b/May 29, 1927; h/12505 Woller Road, San Antonio, TX 78249; ba/San Antonio, TX; p/Mr and Mrs John Igo, San Antonio, TX; ed/BA in Eng & Chem 1948, MA in Eng & Psych 1952, Trinity Univ; pa/Acquisitions Libn, Eng Fac, Trinity Univ, 1952-53; Eng Fac, San Antonio Col, 1953-; SCMLA; SCCEA; TCTE; CCTE; TX Folklore Soc; SW Am Lit Assn; Bexar Lib Assn; Friends of San Antonio Public Lib, VP; Spch Arts Assn, VP; r/Rom Cath; hon/Pubs, *Alien* 1977, *Day of Elegies* 1973, *Golgotha* 1971, Others; Nat Lit Awd, Nat Soc of Arts & Lttrs, 1954; Poetry Soc of TX Pub Awd, 1977; Piper Foun Prof of Yr, 1975; Archbishop's Medal, 1978; Personalities of S; W/W in SW; Intl Authors & Writers W/W.

IMBRECHT, CHARLES RICHARD oc/Chairman of California Energy Commission; b/Feb 4, 1949; h/4230 Euclid Avenue, Sacramento, CA 95822; ba/Sacramento, CA; m/Alida; p/Earl Richard and Hazel Berg Imbrecht, Ventura, CA; ed/BA, Occidental Col; JD, Loyola Univ; pa/Chm, CA Energy Comm, 1983-; Assemblyman, CA St Assem, 1976-82; Former Atty Advr, Interst Commerce Comm; Ventura Bar Assn; ABA; cp/Ventura Downtown Lions Clb; JCs; Ventura and Oxnard Cs of C; Ventura Co Repub Ctl Com; hon/Sigma Alpha Epsilon; 2 Cits of Outstg Perf, Fed Govt; Former Ritcher Nat Study Fellow; Former Argo Public Affairs Fellow.

IMHOFF, MYRTLE MARY ANN oc/Retired; b/Oct 7, 1910; h/54 Rockview, Turtle Rock Vista Apartments, Irvine, CA 92715; p/Clyde C and Laura E Imhoff (dec); ed/BA, Ed & Music, Harris Tchrs Col; MA, Psych, St Louis Univ; PhD, Ed and Psych, Wash Univ; pa/Retired Prof of Ed, Sch of Ed, CA St Univ-LA; Prof of Ed, Sch of Ed, CA St Univ-Fullerton, 1960-68; UNESCO Curric Expert & Advr to the Min of Ed, Thailand, 1959-60; Spec, Early Elem Ed, US Ofc of Ed, 1958; Lectr in Ed 1952-53, Doct Study 1950-52, Wash Univ; Other Previous Positions; Am Psychol Assn; CA Psychol Assn; Kappa Delta Pi; Am Orthopsychi Assn; Num Past Mbrships; hon/Author, Num Pubs; World W/W of Wom; La Societe Internationale de W/W; 2,000 Wom of Achmt; Outstg Edrs of Am; Nat Register of Prom Ams and Intl Notables; DIB; W/W of Am Wom, in Am Ed; Num Other Biogl Listings.

INGELS, MARTY oc/Entertainer and Business Executive; b/Mar 9, 1936; h/7560 Hollywood Boulevard, Hollywood, CA 90046; m/Shirley Jones; c/David, Shaun, Patrick, Ryan (All Stepchd); p/Jacob (dec) and Minnie Ingerman; pa/Comedian; Ingels Inc (Acquires Celebrity Talent for Var Projs & Clients throughout the World), 1977-; cp/Nat Chm, Leukemia Foun; Bds of Dirs, 9 Commun Orgs; Initiator, Nat Action for Sanity Again; hon/Recip, 4 Hon Degs.

INGLE, PAULINE STEPHANIA oc/Assistant Director of Nursing; b/Jun 1, 1918; h/127 Main Street, Sevierville, TN 37862; ba/Sevierville, TN; m/Dr Ronald J (dec); c/Le Anne Ingle Dougherty, Elizabeth K Ingle Bach; p/Dr and Mrs Charles Henry Hoffman (dec); ed/RN, Knoxville Gen Hosp; Postgrad Course, Vanderbilt Univ & Univ of Cinc; pa/Staff Nurse, Hosps in KY & OH, 1939-40; Supvr, Gibson Hosp, 1940-45; Public Hlth Nurse, Sevier Co, TN Hlth Dept, 1946; Staff Nurse, Sevier Co Med Ctr, 1965-79; Asst Dir of Nurses, Sevier Co Hlth Care Ctr, 1979-; Hlth Chm, Sevier Elem Sch; TN Nurse Assn; Beta Sigma Phi; cp/PTA, Pres; Sevier Co Lib Bd, 1952-53; Sevierville Garden Clb, 1947; Vol Ednl Chm for 7 Cos, Am Cancer Soc; Vol Meml Chm, Am Cancer Soc, 20 Yrs; r/Presb; hon/3 Dist'd Awds, Am Cancer Soc, 1967, 1972, 1983; W/W of Am Wom.

INGRAM, ARBUTUS BOYD oc/Assistant to Chairman; b/Mar 29, 1930; h/7823 Alpine Road, Northwest, Roanoke, VA 24019; ba/Roanoke, VA; m/Alexander Fountin; p/Ted Lee and Gladys Spencer (dec) Boyd, Ferrum, VA; ed/Att'd, Ferrum Jr Col 1947, Cornett Bus Sch 1948; pa/Secy to VP, Clover Creamery Co, 1948-50; Secy to Pres 1950-75, VP & Asst to Pres 1976, Current Asst to Chm of Bd, Double Envelope Corp; Past Mem, Roanoke Chapt, BPW Clb (Secy and Recording Secy); Roanoke Chapt, Profl Secy Intl; cp/Past Chm, Homes Trust Com, Civic Affairs Com; Past Bd Mem, Parliment-arian of Alpine Garden Clb; Past Pers, Secy, N Roanoke Civic Leag; Jefferson Clb, Roanoke; r/Vestry Mem, St James Epis Ch; hon/Voted Outstg Mem of 1982, Profl Secys Intl, Roanoke Chapt; W/W in VA Communs, in S & SW; 2,000 Notable Ams.

INGRAM, JOHN RANDOLPH II oc/Attorney at Law; b/Jul 2, 1957; h/1385 North 6th Street, Albemarle, NC 28001; ba/Albemarle, NC; m/Kimberly Doby; c/Lauren Elizabeth; p/Mr and Mrs John R Ingram, Cary, NC; ed/BA, Polit Sci, E Carolina Univ, 1979; JD, Campbell Univ Sch of Law, 1983; pa/Treas & Conslt, The Commr's Coun, 1979-83; Atty, Brown, Brown & Brown, Attys at Law, 1983-; NC St Bar, 1983; NC St Bar Assn, 1983; Stanley Co Bar, 1983; Kappa Alpha Order Alumni Assn, 1979; Am Bar Assn Yg Lwyrs Div, 1983; r/Bapt; hon/Dean's List, E Carolina Univ; Pi Sigma Alpha, Hon Polit Sci Frat, 1978; Phi Alpha Theta, Hon Hist Frat, 1979; Br Bkg & Trust Estate Planning Awd, 1983; Most Outstg Third Yr Student at Campbell Univ Law Sch, 1983.

INGRAM, KEITH TALBERT oc/Agronomist; b/Aug 18, 1953; h/94-100-225 Anania Drive, Mililani Town, HI 96789; ba/Aiea, HI; m/Christine R; p/Billy G and Suzanne G Ingram, Camarillo, CA; ed/AB in Psych 1974, MS in Plant Sci 1976, Univ of CA-Riverside; PhD, Agronomy, Univ of FL-Gainesville, 1980; Tchg Asst, Plant Sci Dept, Univ of CA-Riverside, 1975-76; Res Asst, Agronomy Dept 1976-80, Asst Scist, Agri Engrg Dept 1980-81, Univ of FL; Assoc Agronomist, Crop Sci Dept, Hawaiian Sugar Planters' Assn, 1981-; Am Soc Agronomy; Crop Sci Soc of Am; Soil Sci Soc of Am; Hawaiian Sugar Technol, Agri Prog Chair 1984; Am Soc Plant Physiol; Soil & Crop Sci Soc of FL; cp/Toastmasters, Clb Pres 1982; St Sci & Engrg Fair, Judge 1982, 1983, 1984; St Forensic & Spch Clb, Judge 1982, 1983; hon/Authored or Co-Authored More Than 8 Sci Pubs; Phi Beta Kappa, 1974; Gamma Sigma Delta, 1979; Phi Kappa Phi, 1980; Fred Hall Agronomic Res Awd, 1981; W/W in W.

INGRAM, RICHARD EUGENE oc/Business Owner; b/Apr 21, 1953; h/127 Roberta Street, Narrows, VA 24124; ba/Same; p/Ray E (dec) and Mildred Pritchard Ingram, Narrows, VA; ed/BA, Psych, VA Polytechnic Inst and St Univ, 1975; MA in Psych 1980, Adv'd Grad Cert in Sch Psych 1981, James Madison Univ; Current Doct Student, Instrnl Sys Technol, IN Univ; pa/Team Ldr, Lynchburg Tng Sch, 1975-77; Programmer/Rschr, Army Res Inst, 1979, 1980; Sch Psychol, Charlestown, WV, 1980-82; Owner, Microlearn Computer Prods, 1981-; Nat Assn of Sch Psychols; hon/Pubs, *Making Money w Your Microcomputer* 1982, Var Articles; BA, w Hons & Distn; Fed Sum Intern, 1979, 1980; Current Univ F'ship, IN Univ; W/W in S & SW; Men of Achmt; Personalities of S.

INGRAM, ROBERT BRUCE oc/Lawyer; b/Jul 19, 1940; ba/4340 Redwood Highway, Suite 352, San Rafael, CA 94903; m/Judith Jennings; c/Stephanie, Ashley, Robert; p/Earl John and Francis F Ingram, Des Moines, IA; ed/BA, Drake Univ, 1962; JD, Wm & Mary Law Sch, 1970; mil/Capt, USAF, 1964-68; pa/Assoc Atty, Belli & Choulos, 1970-78; Law Ofcs of Robert B Ingram, 1978-; ABA; Assn of Trial Lwyrs of Am; CA Trial Lwyrs Assn; SF Trial Lwyrs Assn, Dir 1977; cp/Chm of Bd, VP, Treas, Am Heart Assn, Marin Co Chapt; Elks Clb; r/Presb; hon/Pubs, *The Consequences of an Improper Award* 1970, Others; Current Decisions Editor, *Wm & Mary Law Review*; Chief Justice, Law Sch Hon Ct, 1969, 1970; Pres, George Wythe Chapt, Phi Alpha Delta Legal Frat, 1969; W/W: of Am Law, in CA.

IODICE, RUTH GENEVIEVE WORK oc/Poet, Writer, Educator, Homemaker; b/August 16, 1925; h/22 Avon Road, Kensington, CA 94707; ba/Same; m/Cosimo Leo; c/John Kay; p/John Mason (dec) and Irene Christine Marie Heinlin Work, Evansville, IN; ed/BA, IN St Univ, 1948; Grad Wk in Eng, Univ of Chgo 1951-54, Univ of CA 1963-65; pa/Eng & Lang Arts Tchr, Benton Harbor (MI) 1949-50, Evansville (IN) 1950-53, Zion (IL) 1953-57, Waukegan (IL) 1960-63, Kenosha (WI) Adult Sch 1954-55; Self-Employed as Tutor, Editor, Writer, Handcrafted Toy Maker, 1963-81; Employed to Teach Eng to Ofc Skills Students of Local ROP, 1981-; Past Pres, Zion Ed Assn; AAUW; Editor-in-Chief, *CA St Poetry Qtrly*, 1976; Fdg Editor, *Blue Unicorn*; cp/Dir, Berkeley YWCA Bd, 8 Yrs; Berkeley's Excell in Yth Com; PTA; U Way; r/Served as Secy to the Adm Bd, Coun on Mins, Trinity U Meth Ch; hon/Poetry Soc of Am; Poets & Writers of Am; Nat Fdn of St Poetry Socs; Recip, Many Poetry Prizes on Local, St & Nat Levels; IN St Univ, Alpha Phi Gamma Nat Jour Hon, Kappa Delta Pi Ed Hon, Mortar Bd, Dean's List; DIB; Intl Authors & Writers W/W; World W/W of Wom; Intl W/W in Poetry; Personalities of W & MW.

IRVIN, JAMES W oc/Construction; b/Nov 14, 1938; h/10236 Second Avenue, Inglewood, CA 90303; ba/Los Angeles, CA; m/Loystene L; c/Raynaldo, Gary, Kevin, Brian, Keisha; p/Charlie and Willie Mae Reed, Los Angeles, CA; ed/Grad, Booker T Wash HS; mil/USMC; pa/Pres, Irvin & Assocs Intl; cp/Monroe PTA, Pres 1974; Morningside HS PTA, Pres 1975; Morning-side HS Dad's Clb, Pres 1977-78; Inglewood Unified Sch Dist Facility Com, 1979-83; City of Inglewood, CA, Commr of Constrn Appeals Bd; r/Christian; Temple of Believers Commun Ch, Usher Bd, Pres 1980; hon/PTA Hon Ser Awd, 1976; Dad's Clb Ldrship, 1977-79; Carpenters Apprenticeship, 1971.

IRWIN, DIANNE E oc/Director of Learning Assistance Center; b/Jul 22, 1946; h/918 West Edgemont Drive, San Bernardino, CA; p/Mr and Mrs Jacque Shaw, Barstow, CA; ed/BA, Psych, CA St Col, San Bernardino, 1972; MA, Psych, CA St Univ-Fullerton, 1974; PhD, Human Behavior & Ldrship, US Intl Univ, 1979; pa/Dir, Lng Assistance Ctr, CA St, 1974-; Psychometrist, CA St Col, San Bernardino, 1974-78; Lectr, CA St Col, Fullerton, 1973; Lectr, Val Col, 1973; CA St Dept of Ed Legal Compliance Com, 1979-82; Am Psychol Assn, 1979-; Am Col Pers Assn, 1978-83; Wn Col Lng Ctr and Rdg Assn, 1977-; hon/Pubs, "Impact of Voice Input on Student Vocab Bldg" 1983, "Peer Writing Tutor Tng Prog" 1982, "Fill-in-Ograms as a Lrng Strategy" 1982, "Dealing w Non-Tenure Situation Stress" 1981, Others; W/W in W.

IRWIN, PAT oc/Chief Justice of the Oklahoma Supreme Court; b/Jun 12, 1921; h/1325 Andover Court, Oklahoma City, OK 73120; ba/Oklahoma City, OK; m/Margaret Boggs; c/Margaret Ann, William J; p/Mr and Mrs Marvin Irwin (dec); ed/LLB, OK Univ, 1949; mil/USMCR, Discharged Capt 1946; pa/Dewey Co Atty, 1949-50; OK St Senate, 1951-54; Secy-Commr of St Land Ofc, 1954-58; Justice, OK Supr Ct, 1959-.

ISSACS, GREGORY SULLIVAN oc/Manager of Marketing Communications; b/Jan 18, 1947; h/2098 Mound Street, Los Angeles, CA 90068; ba/Glendale, CA; p/Robert and Imogene Isaacs, Davidson, NC; ed/BA, Univ of Miami; MM, IN Univ; pa/Instr of Music, Simpson Col, 1971-73; US Postal Ser, NE Reg, 1974-76; Pacesetter Sys 1976-79, Mgr of Mktg Communs 1979-, ITT; Conductor and Musical Dir, SE LA Symph, W Coast Opera Assn; r/Meth; hon/W/W in CA.

ISAACSON, EILEEN B oc/Manager of Staff and Organizational Development; h/7 Riley Road, Morganville, NJ 07751; ba/Trenton, NJ; c/Sharlene, Charles; p/Eleanor Prescott, NYC; ed/EdD, Rutgers Univ, 1982; MS, Brooklyn Col, 1964; pa/Dir, Tng Devel & Orgl

Devel, Technol Transfer, 1982-; Supvr of Tng & Devel, Tng & Ed Ctr, 1977-82; Dir of Staff Tng & Devel, Marlboro Proj, 1974-77; Adv Bd Mem, T A Edison Col, 1982-83; ASTD, 1982-83; OD Netwk, 1982-83; Soc for Perf & Instrn, 1982-83; cp/Monmouth City Bd Drug Abuse Ser, 1976-79; Marlboro Twp Mayor's Coun, 1973-76; St Tng Support Prog Coor, 1982-83; r/Cath; hon/Author, "Job Satisfaction, Self Actualization & Ednl Attitude in Relat'ship to Acad Achmt," Mgmt, Supvn & Ldrship Articles; Kappa Delta Pi, 1983; Phi Delta Kappa, 1983; Commun Ser Awds, Monmouth City Bd Drug Sers 1979, Marlboro Twp 1976.

ISACOFF, MARK oc/Psychological Consultant; b/Mar 2, 1953; ba/Kings County Hospital Center, J Building, Brooklyn, NY 11203; m/Mindy Schwartzman; c/Adam; p/David and Hannah Isacoff, Brooklyn, NY; ed/BA in Psych 1975, MSEd in Sch Psych 1977, PD (Adv'd Cert in Sch Psych) 1977, Brooklyn Col; Adv'd Tng Prog, Clin Bio-Feedback, Inst for Psychosomatic Res, 1982; pa/Dir of Treatment, Div of Child & Adolescent Psychi, Kings Co Hosp/Downst Med Ctr, 1982-; Clin Instr in Psychi, Downst Med Ctr, 1980-; Psychol, Kings Co Hosp Ctr, 1980-; Staff Psychol, Howard Beach Child Guid & Fam Cnslg Ctr, 1979-; Adj Lectr, Dept of Psych, Bklyn Col, 1979-81; Adj Lectr, Sch of Ed (Grad Studies), Bklyn Col, 1979-80; Conslt Psychol, Bd of Ed, City of NY, 1978-80; Psychol Cnslr, Bklyn Col of the CUNY, 1978-79; Adj Asst Prof, Dept of Psychol, Queens Col of the CUNY, 1978-79; Conslt Psychol, Bd of Ed, City of NY, 1977; Brooklyn Col Alumni Assn, 1974-, Bd of Dirs; Assn of Sch Psychols of Bklyn Col, 1976-77, Pres; Bklyn Psychol Assn, 1980-, Bd of Dirs; Am Psychol Assn, 1978-, Assoc Mem; Am Orthopsychi Assn, 1979-; Nat Assn of Sch Psychols, 1978-; hon/Pub, "Depression: Symptoms versus Diagnosis in 10,412 Hospitalized Chd & Adolescents, 1957-1977," 1981; W/W in E.

ISACOFF, STUART M oc/Editor, Writer, Composer, Pianist; b/May 20, 1949; h/230 Slocum Way, Ft Lee, NJ 07024; ba/Katonah, NY; p/David and Hannah Isacoff, Brooklyn, NY; ed/BA in Phil 1971, MA in Music Composition 1974, Bklyn Col; pa/Free-Lance Editor, Music Conslt, Pianist, Composer, Writer, 1972-75; Music Dir, Dance Prog, Bklyn Col Perf'g Arts Camp, 1975; Fac Mem, Jazz Studies Prog, Wm Paterson Col, 1976-79; Ednl Conslt, Oxford Univ Press, 1978-80; Creator & Editor of

Keyboard Classics Mag, Dir of Shacor Inc; Free-Lance Author & Composer, 1980-; hon/Pubs, *Do-It-Yourself Handbook for Keyboard Playing* 1982, *Twelve Jazz Preludes* 1981, *Tchg Piano* 1981, *Jazz Master: Thelonious Monk* 1979, Num Others; Res Grant (Rockefeller), Inst for Studies in Am Music, Bklyn Col.

ISHAM, QUENTIN DELBERT JR oc/State Senator, Independent Insurance Agent; b/Apr 30, 1944; h/3232 West Devils Lake Road, Lincoln City, OR 97367; ba/Lincoln City, OR; m/Paulette; c/Shane Gordon, Shaun Lane, Shannon; p/Quentin D and Leah S Isham, Aumsville, OR; ed/BS, Weber Col, 1967; MA, CO St Univ, 1969; mil/AUS, 1st Lt; pa/Tchr, Siuslaw HS, 1962-64; St Senator, 1977-; Agt & Ptnr, John Danforth, Isham & Sprague, 1977-; Nat Conf of St Legis; Exec Com, Wn Conf of Coun of St Govts; Nat Fdn of Indep Bus; cp/Lincoln City & W Val C of C; OR Coast Assn; N Lincoln Lions Clb; Lincoln City Rotary; OR St Dem Ctl Com, 1974-84.

IVY, MARGARET oc/Teacher, Lecturer; b/Sep 17, 1915; h/235 Top Hill, San Antonio, TX 78209; m/J L; c/Joe Lee, Marvin Olin; p/Edward Ottmers (dec); ed/BS, San Marcos, 1940; EdM 1956, MA, PhD 1976, Trinity Univ; pa/Tchr, Edgewood 1945-56, NE Indep Sch Dist 1956-71, St Mary's Univ 1971-80; Bobbin Lace Tchr, SW Craft Ctr, 1980-; TX Supvrs & Prins, 1956-71; cp/Cub Scouts, 1973-79; Symph Orch, San Marcos, 1929-37; So Music Camp, Cnslr 1939-41; hon/Author, Articles for Profl Jours, Curric Guides in Elem Rdg, Social Studies & Math; Phi Delta Kappa, 1936; Delta Kappa Gamma, Secy 1937.

IZATT, REED McNEIL oc/Professor of Chemistry; b/Oct 10, 1926; h/3624 North Little Rock Drive, Provo, UT 84604; ba/Provo, UT; m/Helen Marie Felix; c/Susan, Linda, Neil, Ted, Steven, Anne Marie; ed/BS, UT St Univ, 1951; PhD, PA St Univ, 1956; pa/Postdoct Position, Carnegie Mellon Univ, 1954-56; Prof of Chem, Brigham Yg Univ, 1956-; Vis'g Prof, Univ of UT-SLC, 1972; Vis'g Prof, Univ of CA-San Diego, 1977; Am Chem Soc; AAAS; The Chem Soc, London; Sigma Xi, Pres of Brigham Yg Chapt 1980-82; UT Acad of Scis, Arts & Lttrs; r/LDS Ch; hon/210 Pubs; Annual Sigma Xi Lectr, Brigham Yg Univ, 1966; Karl G Maeser Res & Creat Arts Awd, Brigham Yg Univ, 1967; NIH Career Devel Awd, 1967-72; Annual Fac Lecture, Brigham Yg Univ, 1970; UT Awd, Am Chem Soc, 1971; Brigham Yg Tchr of Month, 1974; Huffman Awd, Calorimetry Conf, 1983.

J

JACINTO, GEORGE A oc/Program Director, Educator; b/Dec 21, 1949; h/PO Box 15002, Orlando, FL 32858; ba/Orlando, FL; p/George P and Isabelle A Joseph Jacinto, San Juan Bautista, CA; ed/EdM, Col of ID, 1982; BS, CA St Univ-Fresno, 1974; AA, Monterey Peninsula Col; pa/Dir of Rel Ed & Yth Mins, Ch of St Andrew, 1983–; Cnslr, Grant Writer, Salvation Army Alcohol Rehab Ctr, 1982; Diocesan Yth Dir, Cath Diocese of Boise, 1980-83; Dir of Yth Min, St James Congreg, 1977-80; Yth Min, Ch of St Michael, 1976-77; Pastoral Asst, Ch of St Peter, 1975; Other Previous Positions; Am Assn for Cnslg & Devel; Assn for Rel & Value Issues in Cnslg; Assn for Humanistic Ed & Devel; Public Offender Cnslr Assn; Yth Mins Netwk; World Future Soc; Assn for Transpersonal Psych; r/Rom Cath; hon/W/W in W.

JACKSON, DENNIS LEE oc/Veterinarian; b/Sep 3, 1932; h/PO Box 688, Hope Mills, NC 28348; ba/Fayetteville, NC; m/Helen Young; c/Dennis Lee Jr, Elsha Jackson Cromer, Helen Lee, Jessica; ed/Pre-Vet, NC St Col, 1958; DVM, Sch of Vet Med, Univ of GA, 1962; mil/USAF; pa/Vet; Small Animal Acad of NC, Past Pres; Bd of Vet Med, NC, Secy-Treas 1974-84 (2.5 Yr Terms); cp/Exch Clb of Gtr Fayetteville, Charter Mem & Past Pres; Mason; Shriner; r/Meth.

JACKSON, HERMOINE PRESTINE oc/Psychologist; b/Mar 11, 1945; h/1 Norwalk Avenue, Buffalo, NY 14216; ba/West Seneca, NY; p/Herman P Sr (dec) and Ella B Jackson, Wilmington, DE; ed/BA, French, 1967; MA, Psych, 1979; pa/Tchr, Phila Public Schs, 1968-74; Instr, Ctl MI Univ, 1979-81; 1981–; AAMD; APA; PAWNY; r/Bapt; hon/Pubs, "Manual of Assessment Instrument for the MR/DD Pop" 1978, "Increasing Verbal Output Among Institnlized Retarded Adults" 1979; Outstg Instr, Ctl MI Univ, 1981; W/W in E.

JACKSON, LORRAINE MORLOCK oc/Research Scientist; b/Mar 11, 1939; h/911 Ashton Road, Cornwell Heights, PA 19020; ba/London, Ontario, Canada; m/Douglas N; c/Douglas N III, Lorraine Diana Sophia, Charles Theodore VI; p/Jacob (dec) and Sophie Morlock, Cornwell Heights, PA; ed/BSc, Bloomsburg St Col, 1960; EdM 1961, PhD 1983, PA St Univ; pa/Postdoct Fellow, Psych, Univ of Wn Ontario, 1983–; Res Scholar, Univ of IA, 1983; Psychometrist, Middlesex Co Bd of Ed, 1978; Res Asst, Psych, Univ of Wn Ontario, 1976-77; Pres, Ontario Assn of Chd w Lng Disabilities, 1976-77; Other Previous Positions; Pres, Ontario Assn for Chd w Lng Disabilities, 1976; Editor, London French Sch Newslttr, 1970; cp/Ednl VP, Toastmasters, London, 1982; hon/Pubs, "Linear Structural Equation Anal of Technical & Nontechnical Career Paths of Engrs" 1983, "Psychographics for Social Policy Decisions: Wel Asst" 1979, "A Feasibility Study to Examine the Effectiveness of an Interface Between Student Guid Info Ser (SGIS) & Jackson Voc Interest Survey (JVIS)" 1976, Others; Hon Soc of Phi Kappa Phi, 1980; Hon Soc of Pi Lambda Theta, 1983; PhD

Thesis Nom'd for 1983 Edwin B Newman Grad Awd for Excell in Res Est'd by APA & Psi Chi, 1983; Social Scis & Humanities Res Coun of Canada Postdoct Res F'ship, 1983; W/W: in E, of Am Wom.

JACKSON, RICHARD P oc/Associate Professor of English; b/Nov 17, 1946; h/3413 Alta Vista Drive, Chattanooga, TN 37411; ba/Chattanooga, TN; m/Margaret; c/Amy; ed/PhD, Yale Univ, 1976; MA, Middlebury Col, 1972; BA, Merrimack Col, 1969; pa/Eng Tchr, Drury HS, 1969-73; Col Tchr, Asst Prof, Assoc Prof, Univ of TN-Chattanooga, 1976–; SAMLA; MLA; CCLM; AWP; r/Cath; hon/Pubs, Part of the Story 1983, Acts of Mind 1983, Essays in Num Jours; Editor, The Poetry Miscellany, 1971–; Robert Frost Fellow, Bread Loaf Writers' Conf, 1983; NEH F'ship, 1978; NEA Grants, 1977, 1978, 1980, 1981, 1982, 1983; Contemp Authors; Dir of Am Poets & Fiction Writers.

JACKSON, WILLIAM MORGAN oc/Graduate Professor of Laser Chemistry; b/Sep 24, 1936; h/5300 MacArthur Boulevard, Washington, DC 20016; ba/Washington, DC; m/Lydia B; c/Eric, Cheryl; p/Mr William Jackson (dec); Mrs W L Russell, Mobile, AL; ed/BS, Morehouse Col, 1956; PhD, Cath Univ of Am, 1961; pa/Grad Prof of Laser Chem 1982–, Prof of Physics and Astronomy 1982–, Prof of Chem 1974–, Howard Univ; Study F'ship, German Acad Exch Ser, Astrophysics Inst, Univ of Erlangen, 1981; Adj Res Prof, Howard Univ, 1974; Sr Chem, Goddard Space Flight Ctr, NASA, 1970-74; Vis'g Assoc Prof, Univ of Pgh, Dept of Physics, 1969-70; Others; Am Chem Soc; Am Phy Soc; AAAS; Soc of Sigma Xi; Optical Soc of Am; Nat Org of Black Chem & Chem Engrg; Phi Beta Kappa; hon/Pubs, "Laser Measurements of the Effects of Vibrational Energy on the Reactions of CN" 1984, "Vacuum UV Laser Induced Scission of Simian Virus 40 DNA" 1984, Num Others.

JACKSON-BEECK, MARILYN oc/Health Economist; b/Feb 12, 1951; h/4005 West 48th Street, Edina, MN 55424; ba/St Paul, MN; m/David A Beeck; c/Emily A Beeck; p/Archie A Jackson (dec); ed/PhD, Univ of PA, 1979; MA 1974, BA 1972, Univ of WI; pa/Hlth Economist, Dept of Hlth Ec, Blue Cross & Blue Shield, 1980–; Asst Prof, Res Assoc, Cleveland St Univ, 1978-80; Res Scholar, Univ of PA, 1975-78; MN Coalition on Hlth Care Costs, 1981–; MW Assn for Public Opinion Res; Intl Communication Assn; cp/Mpls-St Paul Citizens Leag, 1980–; r/Epis; hon/Author, Num Articles in Profl Jours, Book Chapts, Book Reviews; Phi Beta Kappa, 1972; Phi Kappa Phi, 1971; Univ of PA Fellow, 1975-78; Vilas Fellow, Univ of WI, 1972-74; Willard G Bleyer Res Fellow, Univ of WI, 1974; World W/W of Wom; Outstg Yg Wom of Am.

JACKS, GLORIA MARGARET oc/Community Program Developer; b/Jul 28, 1924; h/4401 Saratoga Place, Northeast, #1, Olympia, WA 98506; ba/Olympia, WA; c/David Van de Mark, Cassadra Van de Mark Lown, William N Van de Mark, Kathryn Van de Mark Binkley, Lois Jacobs McKee, Alice Jacobs Baxter, Mildred Jacobs Baxter, George H Jr; p/Merle H Price, Seattle, WA; ed/

AA, Wn WA Univ, 1972; pa/Checker, Chroma-Crystalike Photofinishing Co, 1957-63; Commun Cnslr, MORE Inc, 1966-67; Br Mgr, Rural Ec Opport, 1967-68; Acting Dir, Asst to Dir, REO, 1968-70; Social Ser Asst, Commun Affairs Asst, Commun Affairs Conslt, WA St Ofc of Ec Opport, 1970-73; Commun Affairs Conslt, Commun Prog Developer, Planning & Commun Affairs Agy, 1973–; hon/W/W of Am Wom.

JACOBS, JOY ANN oc/Painter, Professional Artist; b/Oct 6, 1938; h/3052 Woodbury Road, Shaker Heights, OH 44120; ba/New York, NY; c/Nicholas Anthony, Andrea; p/David and Sara Rosenblum (dec); ed/BA, Cleveland Inst of Art, 1967; pa/Am Greeting Card Designer, 1954-59; Artist in the Schs, Cleveland Area Arts Coun, 1976-84; Lectr, Abstract Art, 1976-84; Prog Dir for Art to Inmates, Justice Ctr, 1979-80; Art Conslt, Ronald McDonald House, 1980; Aesthetic Awareness Instr, Cleveland St Univ, 1981-84; Gallery Dir, Am Shakespeare Fest, 1983; Exhibiting Artist, 1974-84; Art Conslt for Fundraising Benefits, 1980-84; Cleveland Mus of Art, 1960-84; Cleveland Mus of Art Jr Coun, 1980-84; Print Clb, Cleveland Mus of Art, 1980-84; Bd Mem, Cleveland Ctr for Contemp Art, 1983-84; Chm, Artists Adv Bd, Cleveland Ctr for Contemp Art, 1983-84; Cleveland Soc for Contemp Art, 1979-84; Cleveland Inst of Art Alumni Soc, 1979-84; Bd Mem, Highland View Art Therapy Studio, 1979-82; New Org for Visual Arts, 1978-84; Spaces, Alternative Gallery, 1982-84; Indiv Exhbns, Columbus Mus of Art 1983, Gund Gallery 1982, New Gallery of Contemp Art 1981, 1978, Others; Grp Exhbns, Contemp Ctr of Art 1982, New Gallery of Contemp Art 1981, Lake Erie Col 1980, Artreach 1979, Others; Collections, Cleveland Foun, Mt Sinai Hosp, Ctl Nat Bk, Num Others; Var Pvt Collections; hon/Am Jewish Com, Cleveland Wom of Achmt, Nat Archives, Oral Tapes, 1983; F'ship Grant, OH Arts Coun, 1979; Listed Among Am Artists in Annual "Art in Am," 1982-83.

JACOBS, LAURENCE WILE oc/Professor of Marketing; b/May 26, 1939; h/1474 Kamole Street, Honolulu, HI 96821; ba/Honolulu, HI; m/Susan S; c/Andrew W, Julie B; p/Arthur and Josephine Jacobs (dec); ed/BS, Univ of PA, 1961; MBA 1963, PhD 1966, OH St Univ; pa/Asst, Assoc, Full Prof, Univ of HI, 1966–; Res Asst, Mktg Sci Inst, 1965-66; Grad Asst, OH St Univ, 1961-65; Am Mktg Assn; Sales & Mktg Execs; hon/Pubs, Advtg & Promotion for Retailing: Text & Cases 1972, TIMSIM-A Computerized Mgmt Game for Travel Indust Mgmt 1968; Outstg Edrs of Am, Nat Spkrs Bus of Am Mktg Assn, 1975; W/W in W; Am Men & Wom of Sci.

JACOBSEN, PARLEY PARKER oc/Accountant; b/Jul 21, 1924; h/2144 Highland Drive, #150, Salt Lake City, UT 84106; ba/Salt Lake City, UT; m/Malia Luengthada; c/Karen Ann, Steven Craig, Kelli, Kathleen Alice, Kimberli; p/Andrew and Anna Sorenson Jacobsen; ed/Student, Univ of WI 1942-43, Henager's Bus Col 1946-47; Student of Acctg, Univ of UT, 1947-53; mil/USNR, 1942-46; USAR, 1951, 1953; pa/Staff Acct, Ernst & Ernst, CPAs, 1952-54;

Owner, Secy-Treas, Abajo Petro Co (Also Kmco Oil Co), 1957-59; Ptnr, Hansen, Jacobsen & Barnett, CPAs, SLC, & Predecessor Firm, 1954-; Ptnr, H & J Investmt Co, Real Est, SLC, 1963-77; VP, Fin 1964-, Corporate Conslt 1977-, VP, Legal & Auditing 1980-, Harman Mgmt Corp; Treas, Dir, Harman Assocs Cos; Estates Inc; Treas, 225 Harman Affiliated Cos; CPA; CIA; CISA; CM; Am Inst CPAs; UT Soc CPAs, Com on Auditing Processes 1955-56; Nat Restaurant Assn; Data Processing Mgmt Assn; Inst CPM; Inst Internal Auditors; EDP Auditors Assn, Dir 1980-81, 1983-84; VFW Clb; Nat Mgmt Assn; Am Mgmt Assn; cp/Salt Lake C of C; hon/W/W: in W, in Fin & Indust, in World.

JACOBSON, FELIX I oc/Chemical Engineer, Scientist; b/Apr 15, 1940; h/ 14 Lafayette Avenue, Westwood, NJ 07675; ba/Paramus, NJ; m/Alla T; p/ Ioshua F Jacobson (dec); ed/PhD in Polymer Chem, Inst of Petrochem Synthesis, Acad of Scis, USSR, Moscow, 1971; MS in Chem Tech Engrg, Moscow Chem-Technological Inst, 1963; pa/Grp Ldr, Res Dept Hd, Moscow Oil Refining Plant, Polypropylene Sci Lab, Moscow, 1963-77; Prin Chem, Grp Ldr, Sr Engrg Assoc, Dart & Kraft Inc, Res & Devel Ctr, 1979-; Am Chem Soc, 1979; r/ Jewish; hon/Author, Over 50 Pubs; Patentee in Field; Contbr, Articles to Profl Jours; Contbr, Papers at USSR Nat Conf, 1970, 1972; W/W in E.

JACOBSON, GLORIA NADINE oc/ University Administrator; b/Jul 12, 1930; h/415 Ridgeview, Iowa City, IA 52240; ba/Iowa City, IA; m/Richard T Sr; c/Richard T (Skip) Jr, Douglas L, William A; p/Christian Frederick and Amanda M Larson (dec); ed/BBA, Univ of IA, 1974; pa/Secy 1950-51, 1952-55, Secy to the Dean, Col of Nsg 1955-56, Exec Secy to the Dean, Col of Pharm 1962-71, Adm Asst 1971-75, Adm Assoc 1975-81, Asst to the Dean, Col of Pharm 1981-, Univ of IA; Phi Gamma Nu, Profl Bus; Kappa Epsilon, Profl Pharm; r/ Luth; hon/W/W; of Am Wom; World W/ W of Wom.

JACOBSON, KAY C oc/Counselor, Psychologist; b/Aug 16, 1944; h/3967 North 450 West, Provo, UT 84604; ba/ Provo, UT; m/S Russ; c/Kristi, Sterling Kim, Kevin Russell; p/Lorimer S and Phyllis T Christensen, Provo, UT; ed/ BS, UT St Univ, 1966; MA, Brigham Yg Univ, 1968; pa/Coor of Cnslr/ Psychols, Provo Sch Dist, 1980-; Tchr, Brigham Yg Univ, 1976-; Cnslr/Psychol, Provo Sch Dist, 1968-; NEA; UEA; PEA; NASP; UASP; Secy-Treas; Delta Kappa Gamma Soc Intl; cp/JC Wives, Secy 1976; r/LDS; hon/W/W in W.

JAE oc/Sculptress; b/Jan 9, 1947; h/ 48 West 73rd Street, New York City, NY 1023; ba/New York City, NY; p/ Benjamin and Shirley Shareff, Brooklyn, NY; ed/BA, Pace Univ, 1964; Att'd, Inst del Arte, Pietiasanta, 1970-72; Pvt Tutelage Under Bruno Lucchesi (NYC), Manola (Spain), Jacques Upschitz (Italy), Moustakis (Greece); pa/32 Exhbns in 6 Countries & 2 Maj Mus Exhbns (in a 12 Yr Time Period); Artists Equity; Salmagundi Clb; Intl Assn of Art; Artists Leag of Brooklyn; hon/W/W: of Am Wom, in NYC; World W/W of Wom; Dir of Dist'd Ams; Intl Wom Artists Archives.

JAEGER, PAUL JOSEPH oc/Dentist; b/Jan 15; h/900 East 9th Avenue, Anchorage, AK 99501; ba/Anchorage, AK; m/Maria; c/Dr Sharon, Ronald Alan, Donna Michelle, Brenda Kay, Kathy Jo, Mary Denise, Michele Therese; ed/DMD, Wash Univ; F'ship, Royal Soc of Hlth; F'ship, Am Endodontic Soc; mil/1944-54; cp/St Cmdr, VFW; Life Mem & Trustee, Disabled Am Vets; r/ Rom Cath; hon/Best Secy Awd, Xi Psi Phi Frat; Strang Awd in Orthodontics, 1959.

JAEGER, SHARON ANN oc/Fulbright Professor, Poet, Publisher, Translator; b/Jan 15, 1945; h/PO Box 100014 DT, Anchorage, AK 99510; ba/Lisboa, Portugal; p/Dr Paul and Catherine S Jaeger; ed/BA, summa cum laude, Univ of Dayton, 1966; MA in Eng, Boston Col, 1971; DA in Eng, SUNY-Albany, 1982; pa/Fulbright Lectr, Portugal, 1983-84; Editor, Intertext, 1982-; Co-Editor, Sachem Press, 1980-; Pt-time Instr, Writing Wkshop, SUNY-Albany, 1979-80; Pt-time Instr, Writing Ctr, Rensselaer Polytechnic Inst, 1978-79; Fac Secy & Records Spec, Sch of Nsg, Univ of AK-Anchorage, 1978; Free-Lance Editor, Univ of PA Press, SUNY Press, Pvt Clients, 1980-; Pres, CLAS, Univ of PA, 1982-83; Coor, Jawbone Rdg Series, 1981-82; Poetry Soc of Am; Acad of Am Poets; Am Lit Translators Assn; Am Comparative Lit Assn; MLA; NEMLA; ISHR; IAPL; Am Studies Assn; SCE; STS; Phila Writers Org; Poetry Soc of AK; hon/Author, Articles in Dic of Am Book Publishing, Poems in Num Mags & Anthologies, Book Reviews, Cassette Tapes; Fulbright Lectureship, Portugal, 1983-84; Res F'ship, Univ of PA, 1982-83; Pres F'ship, St Univ of NY at Albany, 1979-82; Alpha Sigma Tau Hon Key, 1966; Austrian Govt S'ship for German Study, Sum 1966; Chaminade Awd for Excell, 1966; Poetry Awds & Grad Asst'ships; DIB; World W/W of Wom; Foremost Wom of the 20th Century; Outstg Yg Wom of Am; Intl Authors & Writers W/W; 2,000 Notable Ams.

JAFFE, SYLVIA SARAH oc/Collector of Art, Medical Technologist; b/May 16, 1917; h/1913 South Quincy Street, Arlington, VA 22204; ba/Same; m/ David; p/Sam and Rose Turner (dec); ed/BS in Med Technol, Univ of WI, 1940; pa/Med Technologist, Watts Hosp Lab, 1940-45; Res Hematology Technologist in Leukemia, Sloan Kettering Meml Hosp Lab, 1946-47; Chief Med Technologist in Hematology, Arlington Hosp Lab, 1948-55; Chief Technologist in Diagnostic Hematology, Georgetown Univ Hosp, 1959-70; Art Collector, 1970-; Am Soc Med Technologists; Affil Mem, Am Soc of Clin Pathols; Am Wom in Sci; r/Jewish; hon/Contbr, Sci Papers Based on Orig Res in Hematology to Profl Socs; W/W of Am Wom; Am Soc of Clin Pathols Yrbook.

JAHNIGEN, GEORGE AZIO oc/ Project Manager; b/Oct 8, 1941; h/117 Caragana Court, Sterling, VA 22170; ba/Washington, DC; m/Josette Christiane; c/Monica Nicole; p/Ester Bisci, Miami, FL; ed/BS, Indust Engrg, Univ of FL, 1967; MEA, George Wash Univ, 1971; mil/AUS; pa/Proj Mgr & Supervisory Analyst, US Gen Acctg Ofc, 1973-83; Supervisory Indust Engr, Nat Bur of Standards, 1971-73; Indust Engr,

Dept of the Navy & VA, 1967-71; Gen Engr, Chrysler Corp, 1963-65; AIIE, 1967-, Corres'g Secy, Chm of Hons & Awds, Profl Devel; Nat Soc for Profl Engrs; Wash Opers Res Coun; r/Luth; hon/Author, "A Cost-Effectiveness Approach to Systems Selection in a Vets Adm Hosp" 1971, "Optimal Design of a Heating & Ventilating Sys" 1969; Multiple Certs of Merit & Outstg Perf, 1983, 1982, 1980, 1976; Dean's List, Univ of FL.

JAIN, ANANT VIR oc/Analytical Chemist in Toxicology; b/Mar 15, 1940; h/220 Spalding Circle, Athens, GA 30602; ba/Athens, GA; m/Gagan; c/ Anuraag, Ritu Gagan; p/Mr and Mrs (dec) R D Jain, Meerut, India; ed/PhD, Purdue Univ, 1972; MSc 1962, BSc 1959, Meerut Col (Agra Univ); pa/Hd, Toxicology Sect 1982-, Assoc Analytical Toxicologist 1981-82, Analytical Chem 1974-81, Athens Diagnostic Lab, Univ of GA; Res Assoc 1972-74, Chem Analyst 1966-72, Res Asst 1964-66, Purdue Univ; Lectr in Chem, DAV Col, India; Am Chem Soc; Soc of Toxicology; Assn of Ofcl Analytical Chems; Fac Advr, India Students Assn, Univ of GA Students Union, 1980; DAV Col, 1963; Secy for Social, Cultural & Entertainment Affairs, Meerut Col Students Union, 1961; r/Jain; hon/Author, More Than 20 Sci Pubs in the Area of Analytical Chem, Analytical Toxicology & Toxicology; First Place in MSc Exam (2 Gold Medals), Meerut Col, 1962; First Place Cert, Am Oil Chems Soc, for the Determination of Aflatoxins in Corn Meal; Am Men & Wom of Sci; W/W in S & SW.

JAMBOR, ANTON EDWARD oc/ Business Owner and Manager; b/Jul 5, 1931; h/3200 36th Avenue, Northeast, Minneapolis, MN 55418; ba/Moundsview, MN; m/Dolores M; c/Susan, Robert, Karen; p/Theodore and Mary Jambor (dec); mil/Navy; pa/Tool & Die Maker, 1951-71; Orch Ldr, 1951-71; TV Show, 1964-68; Coliseum Ballroom Ptnr, 1970-72; Owner/Mgr, Belrae Ballroom, 1971-; Pres, Nat Ballroom & Entertainment Operators, 1981, 1982; Pres, MN Ballroom Operators Assn, 1977, 1978, 1979; cp/4th Deg, K of C; Eagles; Polish Am Clb; Riflesmens Assn; MN Deer Hunters Assn; r/Cath; hon/ Originator & Fdr, Nat Mag of the Nat Ballroom & Entertainment Opers Assn; Commend of Excell Awd, Broadcast Music Inc, for Outstg Ballroom Operator & Contbn to Enjoyment of Music, 1981.

JAMES, DAVID (AKA BOWLER CLARK) oc/Media Consultant; b/Mar 28, 1938; h/911 East 100 North, Provo, UT 84601; ba/Provo, UT; c/Darci, Dena, Shavri; mil/AUS; p/Radio Prog Dir, KEYY, Provo; Night Clb Mgr, UT; Entertainment Dir, Las Vegas; Radio Prog Dir, SLC; ABC Radio Netwk, LA; Radio Sta Mgr, ID; Disk Jockey, UT, CO, NY, AZ, WA, ID, CA; Nat Assn of Broadcasters; cp/March of Dimes; Arthritis Foun; Dem Dist Chm; r/LDS; hon/Gold Mike Awd; News Reporting Awd, Assoc'd Press; Ser Awds, March of Dimes, VFW, UT Alcohol Foun, Voice of Democracy, Arthritis Foun, Girl Scouts, Muscular Dystrophy; W/W in Radio; Prom Men & Wom of UT.

JAMES, FORREST DON oc/University President; b/Sep 14, 1927; h/10

Highwood Circle, Avon, CT 06001; ba/ New Britain, CT; m/Gerti Hauser-James; c/Kevin Scott, Kurt Dee; p/Mr and Mrs Forest James, Oklahoma City, OK; ed/AB, cum laude, OKC Univ, 1951; STB Deg, Boston Univ Sch of Theol, 1954; mil/USN, 1946-47; pa/Pres, Ctl CT St Univ, 1968-; Acting Pres 1967-68, VP for Acad Affairs 1965-67, Univ of RI; Acting Dean, Asst Dean, Dir of Intl Studies, Instr, Asst Prof, Assoc Prof, Miami Univ, 1958-65; Intl Assn of Univ Pres, Former Chm of N Am Coun, Exec Com; Am Assn of St Cols & Univs; N Eng Bd of Higher Ed; Phi Mu Alpha Sinfonia; Phi Delta Kappa; Trustee, New Britain Bk & Trust Co; Corporator, Am Savs Bk of New Britain; Lambda Chi Alpha Frat; cp/Dir & Corporator, New Britain Gen Hosp; Trustee, Klingberg Fam Ctr; Hon Mem, Rotary Clb of New Britain; r/ Prot; hon/Co-Author, Handbook of Col & University Adm; LLD, Kyung Hee Univ, 1978; Doct in Bus Adm, Kyung Hee Univ, 1981; Lucinda Bidwell Beebe F'ship, Boston Univ Grad Sch; Rotary Foun F'ship, Univ of Zurich; Dist'd Ser Alumni Awd, OKC Univ, 1970; LLD, Briarwood Col, 1983; W/W: in E, in Am, in Am Ed.

JAMES, SHIRLEY BARBER oc/College Counselor; b/Sep 5, 1946; h/4761 Sylvan Drive, Savannah, GA 31405; ba/ Savannah, GA; m/Robert Earl; c/Robert II, Anne Camille, Rachelle Elizabeth; p/ Mr and Mrs Eli B Barber, Georgetown, SC; ed/EdM, Guid & Cnslg, Harvard Grad Sch of Ed, 1970; BA, Psych, Eng & Sec'dy Ed, Spelman Col, 1968; pa/ Intern, Dept of Child Wel, NYC, 1967; Bus Rep, N Eng T&T, 1968-69; Cnslr, Savannah St Col, 1971-; Delta Sigma Theta Sorority, 1977; Spelman Alumnae Assn, 1970; APGA, 1975; Nat Orientation Dirs Assn, 1978; cp/Jr Leag of Savannah (AJL), 1981; Jack & Jill of Am Inc, VP 1975; Bd of Dirs, SAFE Shelter, Hodge Day Care Ctr, Parent & Child Devel Sers, YWCA, Voluntary Action Ctr, 1972-; Hlth Sers Com, U Way, 1982; r/AME; hon/Editor & Co-Publisher, The Savannah Tribune, a Wkly Newspaper; W/W Among Students in Am Univs & Cols; Outstg Yg Wom in Am.

JANKOWSKI, JANET MARIE oc/ Speech and Language Pathologist; b/ Nov 5, 1949; h/1425 Bedford Street, Stamford, CT 06905; ba/Stamford, CT; m/John Paul Chmielowiec; p/Chester Jankowski (dec); Sophie Modzelewski, Worcester, MA; ed/BA, French, Anna Maria Col, 1971; MS, Spch, Emerson Col, 1974; pa/ French Tchr, St Mary's HS, 1974; Spch Pathol, Stamford Public Schs, 1974-; Alpha Mu Gamma Nat Fgn Lang Hon Soc; ASHA; cp/Vol Spch Pathol, Mercy Ctr, 1974; r/Christian; hon/W/W of Am Wom; World W/W of Wom.

JANOWITZ, TAMA oc/Writer; b/ Apr 12, 1957; h/463 West Street, #707A, New York, NY 10014; p/Phyllis Janowitz, Ithaca, NY; ed/MFA in Fiction (Pending), Columbia Univ; MFA Wk, Yale Univ Sch of Drama; MA, Fiction, Holling Col, 1979; BA, Barnard Col, 1977; pa/Mem, Assoc'd Writing Prog; hon/Pubs, Am Dad 1981, Short Fiction in Paris Review, The MS Review (3 Times), The Agni Review & The Pawn Review,

Non-Fiction in Mademoiselle; S'ship, MFA Prog, Columbia, 1983; Nat Endowment for the Arts Awd in Fiction, 1982; Fellow, Fine Arts Wk Ctr in Province-town, 1981; S'ship, Yale Sch of Drama, 1981; Guest Editor, Mademoiselle, 1977; W/W of Am Wom.

JANVEJA, MARIA ANNETTE oc/ Nursing Home Administrator; b/Apr 4, 1951; h/3681 Christyway, Saginaw, MI 48603; ba/Chesaning, MI; m/Subhash C; ed/Assocs Deg, 1971; BA w Hons, MI St Univ, 1973; Postgrad Wk, Univ of MI, 1978-80; Lic'd Nsg Home Admr, 1974-; pa/Hostess, Cashier, Managerial Positions, Theresa's Restaurant (Fam Bus), 1962-74; Admr 1974-, Activity Dir, Social Dir & Asst Admr 1974-75, Chesaning Rest Home Inc; Phi Beta Kappa, 1970-71; Am Col of Nsg Home Admrs, 1975-80; Corres'g Secy, NE Reg, Hlth Care Assn of MI, 1976-80; r/Cath; hon/W/W of Am Wom.

JARAMILLO, MARI-LUCI oc/Associate Dean of College of Education; b/ Jun 19, 1928; h/2301 Artesanos Court, Northwest, Albuquerque, NM 87108; ba/Albuquerque, NM; m/J Heriberto; ed/PhD, Curric and Instrn, Univ of NM, 1970; MA 1959, BA 1955, Ed, NM Highlands Univ; pa/Assoc Dean, Col of Ed 1982-, Spec Asst to the Pres 1981-82, Univ of NM; Dpty Asst, Secy for Inter-Am Affairs, Dept of St, Wash, DC, 1980-81; Am Ambassador, Tegu-cigalpa, Honduras (Nom'd by Pres Carter), 1977-80; Col of Ed, Univ of NM, 1965-77; Coun of Am Ambassa-dors; Hispanus Adv Com, Wash DC; Nat Comm on Sec'dy Sch for Hispanics; Math Com, Chd's TV Wkshop, NYC; Task Force on Approved Progs for the Profl Standards Comm; r/Cath; hon/ Pubs, "Poverty, Ethnicity, Ed, & Me" 1982, "Cultural Pluralism: Implications for Curric" 1977; Gold Medal Awd, Nat Hispanic Univ, SF, 1982; Order of the Gt Silver Cross, Order of Franciso Morazan, Tegucigalpa, Honduras, 1980; Biog incl'd in Spanish Speaking Heroes, 1973; World W/W of Wom; W/W: in Am, of Am Wom.

JARNAGIN, MADALINE SCH-RECK BRETZ oc/Retired Free-Lance Writer; b/Dec 19; h/Polecat Creek, Summerdale, AL 36580; m/Roy C; p/ John R and Jennie Mae Weibly Schreck (dec); ed/Att'd, PA St Univ, Univ of Pgh; pa/Tchr, Schs in PA (Col Twp, Waring-ton Twp, Aliquippa, Sewickley), 1933-74; TV Wk; Radio Wk; Writer for Several Newspapers; BPW; Pres, Sew-ickley Tchrs Assn, 1955-58, Secy; Delta Kappa Gamma; The Pensters Clb; cp/ Social Chm, Area II & Allegheny Co; Chm, Nat Def; Prog Chm of Vice Regent, DAR, 1975, 1982; Press Chm, Wom's Clb of Sewickley; Centre Co & Sewickley Hist Assns; AL Pres Garden Clb; r/Meth; hon/Author, Many Arti-cles Over Many Yrs; Articles in Centre Co Heritage; Helped w Mat for Book, Col Twp Before & After 1875; Cited by AUS for Bonds Sold during WW II, 1000 Mile Clb, U Airlines, 1963; Wom of Yr, BPW, 1975; Wom in PA Public, 1974; Many More Hons; Wom in Public Ofc; DIB.

JARNAGIN, ROY CHESTER oc/ Publisher; b/Jan 31, 1913; h/Polecat Creek, Summerdale, AL 36580; m/ Madaline Schreck Bretz; c/Elizabeth Sue Jarnagin Morgan, Roy Chester III, Carol

Ann; ed/BS, MS St Univ, 1935; mil/Lt (jg), USN, 1942-45; pa/Mng Editor, Morning Star, 1946-47; Reporter, UPI, 1948-49; Mng Editor, Turrentine Pub'g Co, 1950-52; Mng Editor, Sorrow Pub'g Co, 1952-55; Edit Rschr, Atlanta Jour, 1956-58; Editor, Penguin Books, 1959; Fdr/Pres, So Pub'g Co, 1959-73; Nat Writers Clb, 1980-; The Pensters Clb, 1980-; cp/SAR, 1981-; r/Unitarian-Universalist; hon/Pubs, UFOs: The Extrauniversal Connection 1977, Christianity & the Narrow Way 1982, Feature Stories, Edits & Columns in Var Newspapers & Mags While Wkg as a Journalist Over a Period of 30 Yrs.

JARRETT, JOYCE CRISCOE oc/ Manager; b/Oct 13, 1938; h/2416 Lawn-dale Drive, Greensboro, NC 27408; ba/ Greensboro, NC; m/Ralph R; c/Patti Jessup Finney; p/Langester C and Louise Joyce Criscoe, Greensboro, NC; ed/ Assoc Deg in Bus Adm, Guilford Col; pa/Mgr of The Lorillard Informer & Com-mun Media Relats, Lorillard Tobacco Co, 1965-; Celanese Corp (Tech Pubs), 1963-65; Booth & Osteen, Attys, 1959-63; Intl Assn of Bus Communi-cators, Nat, Dist III, NC/Piedmont Chapt; Carolinas Assn of Bus Commun-icators; Mem of The Bd, Wom's Profl Forum; Public Relats Soc of Am; cp/U Way, Chm 1983-84; r/Bapt; hon/Mgr & Editor, The Lorillard Informer, Employees Mag Which is Distributed to 5,500 Employees in NC, KY (Louisville & Lexington), PA, NY, VA; Outstg Bus Wom in Greensboro, 1982; Del to Gov's Conf on Ldrship Devel for Wom, 1982; First-Place Awd, Communicator Com-petition for Writing Employee-Oriented Feature, Intl Assn of Bus Communica-tors, 1982; Acad Achmt in The Col of Tobacco Knowledge, 1981; Other Hons; W/W of Am Wom; Personalities of S; 5,000 Personalities of World; World W/ W of Wom.

JASTREM, JOHN F oc/Certified Public Accountant, Audit Manager; b/ May 28, 1955; h/631 First Street, Hermusa Beach, CA 90254; ba/Los Angeles, CA; p/Mr and Mrs Frank Jastrem, Plains, PA; ed/BS, Acctg, cum laude, Wilkes Col, 1977; pa/Audit Mgr, Arthur Andersen & Co, 1977-; Ingersall Cand, Internship, Internal Audit, 1976; Current Pt-time Instr, El Camino Col; Nat Assn of Accts, Pres of LA So Bay Chapt 1983-84; Am Mgmt Assn; cp/LA Jr C of C; LA Ath Clb; r/Cath; hon/ W/W: in Fin & Indust, in W.

JAUHAR, PREM P oc/Research Direc-tor, Consultant; b/Sep 15, 1939; h/230 West Campus View Drive, Riverside, CA 92507; ba/Riverside, CA; m/Raj; c/ Rajiv, Sandeep, Suneeta; p/Ram Lal and Maya Jauhar; ed/BS, 1957; MS, 1959; PhD, 1965; pa/Assoc Prof Genetics, Indian Agri Res Inst, New Delhi, 1963-72; Mem Postgrad Fac, 1965-72; Sr Sci Ofcr, Welsh Plant Breeding Sta, Aberystwyth, Univ of Wales, 1972-75; Res Assoc, Univ of KY, Lexington, 1976-78; Res Cytogeneticist, Univ of CA-Riverside, 1978-81; Cytogeneticist, City of Hope Nat Med Ctr, Duarte, CA, 1981; Res Dir, US Agri Labs, Riverside, CA, 1982-; Genetics Soc of Am; Am Genetic Assn; Crop Sci Soc of Am; Tissue Culture Assn of Am; Linnean Soc of London; cp/Area Capt, Am Heart Assn, 1981-; VP, Riverside Rel Temple; hon/Author Cytogenetics & Breeding of Pearl

Milet & Related Species, 1981; Contbr Articles to Profl Jours, 4 Chapts in Books; Genetics Soc of Am Awd to Attend & Present 2 Papers at XIV Intl Cong of Genetics, Moscow, USSR, 1978; Chancellor's Medal; Golden Jubilee Gold Medal; Irwin Gold Medal; Harcourt Butler Medal, 1955-59; Guest Lctr at Several European Labs; W/W: in Frontier Sci & Technol, in W, in Am; Am Men & Wom of Sci.

JAUNZEMS, IMANTS oc/International Entrepreneur; b/Oct 18, 1931; h/ 2825A, Waialae Avenue, Honolulu, HI 96826; ba/Honolulu, HI; p/Elza Jaunzems, Tacoma, WA; ed/Grad, Univ of HI Honolulu; Att'd, Lewis Restaurant Mgmt Sch, UN Interpreters Sch; mil/ AUS, 1950-56, 1957-58; pa/IRO Translator-Interpreter, 1948-49; 66th CIC Reg 12 Interrogator, Interpreter, Translator, 1949-50; Investigator, WA St Lig Control Bd, 1960-61; Owner, Tiki Clb, 1961-62; Mgr, Winthrop Hotel; cp/ VFW, 1951-; DAV, 1960-; NRCC; US Congl Adv Bd; ASC Nat Adv Bd; RNC, Sustaining Mem 1980-; r/Luth; hon/ Author, Articles on Fgn Affairs; Num Mil Awds, incl'g, Purple Heart, Korean Pres Cit, Silver Star.

JAVITS, JACOB K oc/Former United States Senator, Lawyer; b/May 18, 1904; ba/375 Park Avenue, New York, NY 10152; m/Marian Ann Borris; c/Joy D, Joshua M, Carla; p/Morris and Ida Littman Javits; ed/LLB, NY Univ, 1926; 37 Hon Degs; mil/Comm'd Maj, AUS, 1942; Asst to Chief of Opers in CWS; Served in US ETO and PTO, 1942-45; Discharged as Lt Col; Col, Chem Warfare, NYNG, AUS; pa/Trial Lwyr; Mem of Firm, Javits, Trubin, Sillcocks & Edelman, 1958-71; Mem 80th-83rd Congs, 21 NY Dist; Atty Gen, NY, 1955-57; US Senator from NY, 1957-81; Counsel, Firm of Trubin, Sillcocks, Edelman & Knapp, 1981-; Adj Prof, Polit Sci, SUNY-Stony Brook, 1982-; Lectr on Ec & Polit Subjects; cp/Chm, N Atl Assem Polit Com, Com of Nine, Parliamentn's Com for Less Developed Nats; US Del, 25th Anniv, UN Gen Assem, 1970; Nat Comm Marijuana & Drug Abuse, 1971-73; Am Legion; VFW; Jewish War Vets; City Ath Clb; Harmonie; hon/Author, *A Proposal to Amend the Anti-Trust Laws* 1939, *Discrimination USA* 1960, *Order of Battle, a Repub's Call to Reason* 1964, *Who Makes War* 1973, *Javits: The Autobiog of a Public Man* 1981, Series of Articles on Polit Phil for Repub Party 1946; Decorated, Legion of Merit, Commend Ribbon.

JEFFORDS, DAVID NORMAN oc/ Public School Administrator; b/May 20, 1925; h/162 Barton, Marion, AR 72364; ba/Marion, AR; m/Roselin Eloise Lomenick; c/Jeffrey, Christopher; p/Mrs Jetta M Jeffords, West Memphis, AR; ed/ BGS, Rollins Col, 1962; MSE, Memphis St Univ, 1969; EdS, AR St Univ, 1973; mil/USAF, Combat and Flying Ofcr, 25 Yrs; Ret'd Capt; pa/Social Sci Clrm Tchr, Crawfordville, AR, 1970-71; HS Prin, Weiner, AR, 1971-74; HS Prin, Wynne, AR, 1974-76; Mid Sch Prin, Marion, AR, 1976-; Asst Supt, Marion, AR; Alpha Tau Omega Frat, Scribe; NEA Mtl Hlth Ctr Bd; AR Assn Supts; NASSP; ASCD; Marion Ed Assn, Past Pres; cp/VFW, Up through Cmdr; Am Legion; Kiwanis; Lion's Clb, Past Pres, Dist Gov; r/Meth; hon/Columnist, Mil

Newspaper, France, 1955-57; Editor & Feature Writer, Marion Sch Dist Pub for Parents, 1982-84; Air Medal (Twice), 1945; Dist'd Flying Cross, 1945; Phi Beta Kappa, 1962; 1st Mil Mem to Grad "Operation Bootstrap," Orlando AFB, 1962; W/W in S & SW.

JEFFREY, MARGIE SUE oc/ICC Transportation Law and Brokerage; b/ Jun 19, 1935; h/9505 Elm Lane, Crystal Lake, IL 60014; ba/Marengo, IL; m/ Joseph W; c/Danny R Market, Tony A Market, Lee Ann Market; p/Madeth E and James Andrew Baughn (dec); ed/ Att'd, McHenry Co Col 1977-79, Col of Adv'd Traffic 1977, Col of Transport Law 1977; pa/Gen Exempt Carrier Opers Mgr, Mkt Produce Trucking, 1959-70; VP, Farm Ser & Supplies Inc, ICC Regulated Contract & Common Carrier Trucking Opers, 1970-; Pres, MLB Mktg, Trans Brokerage, 1980-; Am Soc of Traffic & Trans; Nat Assn of ICC Practitioners; Chgo Reg Chapt, AIICP; Delta Nu Alpha Trans Frat Inc; Traffic Clbs Intl; Trans Res Forum of Chgo; Wom's Traffic Clb of Evansville, IN; Nat Com for Motor Fleet Supvr Tng; Am Trucking Assn; cp/C of C; r/ Prot; hon/W/W of Am Wom.

JEFFRIES, CHARLES COLE JR oc/ Director of Administrative and Civil Law, Special Assistant for Congressional Liaison; b/Oct 4, 1948; h/4507 Mohican Trail, Valrico, FL 33594; ba/ Tampa, FL; m/Cheryl Fahl; c/Courtney Dawn; p/Col C C Jeffries, San Antonio, TX; Mrs Lawson D Hornor, West Helena, AR; ed/BS in Bus Adm 1970, JD 1973, Univ of AR; LLM, Intl Law, summa cum laude, George Wash Univ, 1979; mil/Lt Cmdr, USN Judge Advocate Gen's Corps, 1973-; pa/Dir, Adm & Civil Law Div & Spec Asst to the Cmdr-in-Chief for Congl Liaison, Ofc of the Legal Advr, HQs, US Ctl Command, MacDill AFB; Legis Counsel & Congl Liaison, Ofc of Legis Affairs, 1979-83; Summary Ct-Martial Ofcr & Command Judge Advocate, NAVSTA Anacostia, Nat Law Ctr, George Wash Univ, 1978-79; Counsel, Phy Eval Bd, Nat Nav Med Ctr, 1978; Other Previous Positions; Student Bar Assn; Phi Alpha Delta Law Frat; ABA; Kappa Sigma Frat; Navy Fed Credit Union; Fed Bar Assn; AR Bar Assn; TX St Soc; AR St Soc; Senate Staff Clb; Congl Staff Clb; cp/ Army-Navy Clb; Nat Lwyrs Clb; Tampa Yacht & Country Clb; hon/Author, Var Articles; Meritorious Ser Medal; Nat Def Ser Medal; Sea Ser Medal; Expert Pistol Marksmanship Medal; W/W: in Am Law, Among Students in Am Cols & Univs; Nat Lwyrs Register; Nat Student Register.

JELINEK, JAMES JOHN oc/Emeritus Professor of Education; b/Apr 7, 1915; h/228 East Concorda Drive, Tempe, AZ 85282; ba/Tempe, AZ; m/Elizabeth Louise; c/Lawrence James; p/James John and Rose Jelinek (dec); ed/BS, Univ of IL, 1937; MA, NWn Univ, 1940; PhD, IN Univ, 1951; mil/Lt, USNR; pa/Editor, Civil Ser News of IL, 1937-38; Tchr, Kewanee, IL, HS, 1938-41; Asst Prof in Jour, Univ of Detroit, 1941-45; Assoc Prof of Social Scis, Univ of MO-Rolla, 1945-53; Prof of Ed 1953-77, Emeritus Prof of Ed 1977-, AZ St Univ; Res Dir, The J L Hudson Co, 1941-43; Assn for Supvn & Curric Devel, Bd of Dirs,

Editor, Reg Pres, 1938-; Far Wn Phil of Ed Soc, Editor, Pres, 1965-; Am Ednl Res Assn, 1937-; Am Philosophical Assn, 1945-; Am Ednl Studies Assn, 1953-; AAUP, 1941-; John Dewey Soc, Factotum & Exec Com, 1945-; NEA, St Rep, 1938-; Other Mbrships; hon/Pubs, *Commitment: Alternative Approaches to the Tchg of Responsibility in Sch & Society* 1982, *Discipline: The Prob of Violence in Sch & Society* 1981, Num Others; All Writings incl'd in Archives of the Hoover Instn on War, Revolution & Peace; Awds in Intl Salons for Photographic Art; Am Men of Sci; Dir of Am Philosophers; Intl Biog; Num Other Biogl Listings.

JENAWAY, WILLIAM F oc/Fire Protection Engineer; b/Aug 7, 1951; h/563 General Armstrong Road, King of Prussia, PA 19406; ba/Philadelphia, PA; m/Karen Elizabeth Young; p/William F (dec) and Rosaline Jenaway, Millsboro, PA; ed/MA, Communication, CA St Col, 1978; BSBA, Waynesburg Col, 1973; AS, Fire Protection, Commun Col of Allegheny Co, 1974; Grad Studies, Fairleigh-Dickinson Univ, 1976-77; Dipl, Law Tng for Exec Ldrship, LaSalle Univ, 1977; Cert'd Hazard Control Mgr, 1981; Cert'd Safety Profl (to Be Assigned), Cert'd Defensive Driving Instr, 1980; Cert'd Fire Tng Instr, PA, 1974; Cert'd Fire Protection Spec, 1983; pa/Dir, Fire Protection Tech Sers for INA Loss Control Sers Inc, a CIGNA Grp Co, 1981-; Reg Loss Control Mgr, Loss Control Engrg Dept, Kemper Ins Grp, 1977-81; Fire Protection Conslt, Loss Preven Diagnostics Inc, 1975-77; Fire Ser Experience, 1969-; Soc of Fire Protection Engrs, 1980; Intl Assn of Fire Chiefs, 1978; Intl Soc of Fire Ser Instrs, 1977; Nat Fire Protection Assn, 1973; Am Soc of Safety Engrs, 1978; SWn PA Fire Chief's Assn, 1973; Am Ins Assn's Fire Protection Com, 1982-; r/Rom Cath; hon/Pubs, "Vols Attack River Rescue Probs" 1975, "Tng Level for Class Set w Help of Questionaire" 1975, "Put Ldrship in Your Bldg's Fire Control Prog" 1976, "Impressing the Need for Fire Protecion on Bus Operators" 1977, Num Others; W/W in E.

JENKINS, FRANK GARLAND oc/ School Administrator; b/Jun 2, 1947; h/ 6509 Red Top Road, Chillum, MD 20783; ba/Alexandria, VA; p/Leroy Hamilton Jenkins (dec); ed/BS, Math & Bus, DC Tchrs Col, 1970; MA, Cnslg Psych, Fed City Col, 1973; Currently Wkg towards EdD, Adm & Curric, George Wash Univ; pa/Math Tchr 1970-76, Prog Facilitator & Math Conslt 1976-77, Guid Cnslr 1977-80, Math Dept Chm 1974-75, DC Public Schs; Adm Aide 1980-81, Guid Dir 1981-82, Asst Prin 1982-, Fairfax Co Public Schs; VA Ed Assn; NCTM; Assn Supvn & Curric Devel; Am Assn Sch Admrs; APGA; Phi Delta Kappa; Kappa Alpha Psi; r/Cath; hon/W/W in E.

JENKINS, HAL EPHRAIM oc/Assistant Professor of Education; b/Aug 6, 1949; h/3 Beckley, Shawnee, OK 74801; ba/Shawnee, OK; m/Judy Shaw; c/Hall Jefferson, Molly Elizabeth; p/Mr (dec) and Mrs H E Jenkins, Sallis, MS; ed/ AA, 1969; BSE, 1971; EdM, 1974; EdS, 1975; EdD, 1978; mil/CPT, OK NG, 11 Yrs; pa/Asst Prof of Ed, OK Bapt Univ, 1982-; Hist Instr, Kosciusko, MS, Public Schs, 1979-81; Res & Curric Spec 1978, Grad Res Asst 1977, MS St Univ; Drug

Ed Coor 1974-76, Instr & Asst Prin 1972-74, Kosciusko, MS, Public Schs; NEA, 1972-; AERA, 1978-80; Phi Delta Kappa, 1974-; AAUP, 1982; APGA; r/ So Bapt; hon/Pubs, "The Relat'ship of Beginning Tchrs' Scores on the NTE & Other Selected Variables to Their Competency in Tchng" 1978, "Voc Ed Funding Structures in the US" 1980, "Needs Assessment for Voc Ed in MS" 1980; W/W in Am Jr Cols.

JENKINS, LLOYD GARY oc/Senior Account Executive, Executive Recruiter; b/Jun 23, 1941; h/38 Museum Way, San Francisco, CA 94114; ba/San Francisco, CA; p/Mrs Georgia Jenkins Burton, Trenton, NJ; ed/BS, Polit Sci, Rutgers Univ, 1963; pa/Sr Acct Exec, Ldrship Inc, 1984-; Exec Recruiter or Conslt, Lloyd G Jenkins & Assocs 1983-84, Gary Nelson & Assocs 1982-83, Allied Recruiters Inc 1980-82, Cadillac Assocs 1976-80; cp/Bd of Dirs, Pride Foun, 1980-84; CA & SF Arts & Ath Inc, 1982-; Exec Com, Chm, Pers Com, Dir, Outreach; hon/W/W in W.

JENKINS, WILLIAM PRESSLEY oc/ Optometrist; b/Jul 29, 1944; h/PO Box 250,' Walhalla, SC 29691; ba/Walhalla, SC; m/Linda Faye Moore; p/Mr and Mrs Jenkins, Kings Mtn, NC; ed/Grad, Kings Mtn HS, 1962; BA, Ctl Wesleyan Col, 1966; OD, So Col of Optom, 1971; pa/ Ptnr, Drs Bell, Watson & Jenkins, PA, 1972-; Assoc'd w Dr Spitz, 1971-72; Appalachian Optometric Assn; SC Optometric Assn; Am Optometric Assn; Fellow, Am Acad of Optom, 1979; Phi Theta Upsilon Frat; Adj Fac Mem, So Col of Optom; cp/Lions Clb; Bd of Adm, Local Wesleyan Ch.

JENKINS, YVONNE MARIE oc/ Psychologist; b/Jan 8, 1952; h/860 Harrison Avenue, Apartment 812, Boston, MA 02118; ba/Boston, MA; p/ Mr and Mrs Robert L Jenkins, Tulsa, OK; ed/BS, Psych, Ctl St Univ, 1969; EdM, Cnslr Ed, Boston Univ; PhD, Cnslg Psych, Boston Col; pa/Psychol, NEn Univ Cnslg and Testing Ctr, 1981-; Psychol, Fuller Mtl Hlth Ctr, 1980-81; Voc Rehab Cnslr, MA Rehab Comm, 1974-77; Social Wkr, Drew Comprehensive Hlth Ctr, 1972; Social Wkr, Retarded Chd's Prog, 1970-72; VP, Gtr Boston Assn of Black Psychols, 1982-83; Am Psychol Assn, Prog Com for Div of Psychotherapy; APGA; Alpha Kappa Alpha Sorority; Frantz Fanon Collective of Boston; r/AME; hon/Pub, "Dissonant Expectations: Professional Competence versus Personal Incompetence," 1982; W/W of Am Cols & Univs.

JENKS, SARAH I oc/Administrative Nurse; b/May 5, 1913; h/17700-88 Avalon Boulevard, Carson, CA 90746; ba/Irvine, CA; c/Dean F Thompson; p/ Mrs Mary Cuckie, Carson, CA; ed/RN, St Joseph Mercy Sch of Nsg, 1934; Student, Univ of CA LA, Ext, 1959-70; Att'd, W Coast Univ, 1974-78; COHN-Bd Cert'd in Occupl Hlth Nsg, 1973; Nurse Practitioner, Univ of CA-LA, 1973-74; Preceptorship, Martin Luther King Hosp; pa/Staff Nurse 1936-37, Hd Nurse 1937-38, Supvr 1938-40, CA Hosp; Indust Nurse, May Co, 1940-43; Ofc Nurse, Burbank (CA) 1944-45, Ft Dodge (IA) 1946-47; Ofc Mgr, Ingelwood Med Clin, 1957-58; Occupl Hlth Nurse, Hawthorne, CA, 1958-73; Supervising Nurse, Occupl Hlth Ser, LA Co, 1972-75; Chief Occupl Nurse, US Nav Reg Med Ctr, 1975-81; Adm Nurse, Occupl Hlth Ctr, Univ of CA-Irvine, 1981-; Nsg Chm, ARC, 1964-70; ANA, 1936-79; Chm, Occupl Nurse Forum-Am Nurses, 1968-72; CA St Nurses Assn, Dist Pres, Centinela Val 1963-65; Chm of OccuplHlth Nurse Sect & Chm of Intersectional Coun, CA St Nurses Assn, 1965-67; Am Occupl Hlth Nurses Assn, 1972-; r/Presb; hon/ Recip, Schering Nurse Awd, CA, 1979; W/W of Am Wom.

JENNINGS, BRUCE MARTIN III oc/ Manager; b/Aug 25, 1947; h/7434 Northwest 106th, Oklahoma City, OK 73132; ba/Oklahoma City, OK; m/ Jennifer L; c/Beau R, Tate A, Erica L; p/Bruce M Jennings Jr, Sheridan, WY; ed/BS 1970, MA 1974, TX A&I Univ; mil/USN, Electronics, 1969-75; pa/Sum Employee, Mobil Oil, 1965-66; Div Chem, Halliburton Sers, 1974-79; Mgr, R&D, Nat Cementers, 1979-80; Mgr, US Opers, Am Fraemaster, 1980-81; Sta Mgr, Co and UT, Nat Cementers, 1981-83; Tech Sales, Nat Chems, 1983-; API; SPE of AIME; NACE; cp/Nat Rifle Assn; r/Presb; hon/Pubs, "A Study of the Host-Vector Relat'ship in an Animal Pop of S TX" 1974, "Resistance of Warm-Blooded Animals to Snake Venoms" 1975; BSA, Eagle Scout w 2 Palms, 1963; Brotherhood Order of the Arrow, 1964; W/W: in Am, in Fin & Indust.

JENNINGS, COLEMAN ALONZO oc/Chairman of Department of Drama; b/Nov 21, 1933; h/2109 Schulle Avenue, Austin, TX 78703; ba/Austin, TX; m/ Lola H Jennings; c/Coleman Charles, Adrienne Elise; p/Vaudra Roderick and Elsie Fox Jennings, Taylor, TX; ed/BFA 1958, MFA 1961, Univ of TX-Austin; EdD, NY Univ, 1974; mil/AUS, Ground Control Operator, USA & Europe, 1953-55; pa/Chm, Dept of Drama, Univ of TX-Austin; Pres, Chd's Theatre Assn of Am, 1975-77; Theatre Panel, TX Comm on the Arts & Humanities; TX Alliance for Arts Ed; cp/Fdr & Dir, Sum Theatre Proj, Austin Pks & Rec Dept & Dept of Drama, 1965-; US Comm for UNESCO, Representing Am Theatre Assn, 1969-75; hon/Pubs, Six Plays for Chd by Aurand Harris, The Hon Urashima Taro, Creat Drama in the Elem Sch, Lrng Ptnrs: Rdng & Creat Dramatics, Plays Chd Love: A Treasury of Contemp & Classic Plays for Chd 1981; Spec Cit from Mayor of Austin for Contbns of the Touring Prodn of Yankee Doo, 1976; W/W in S & SW.

JENSEN, HELEN oc/Business Owner and Manager; b/Jun 30, 1919; h/19029 56th Lane, Northeast, Seattle, WA 98155; ba/Seattle, WA; m/Ernest; c/ Ernest Zane, Ronald Lee; ed/HS Grad; pa/Gen Mgr, Wn Opera Co, 1962-64; Bus Mgr 1968-69, Conslt 1969-70, Portland Opera Co; Owner, Mgr, Agt to Musical Artists, Helen Jensen Artists Mgmt, 1970-; CoChm, Seattle Commun Concert Assn, 1957-62; Secy, Seattle Symph Orch Fam Concerts, 1959-61; Hostess, Radio Prog, 1959-61; Fdr and Dir 1956-84, Pres 1965-66, Seattle Opera Guild; Fdr & Dir, Seattle Opera Assn, 1964-83; Preview Artists Coor, Seattle Opera, 1981-84; First VP, Music & Art Foun, 1982-84; Pres, Seattle Civic Opera, 1981-84; Pres, Northshore Perf'g Arts, 1981-82; hon/ Pub, "Opera for All," 1982; Cert for Achmts, Wom in the Arts, 1973; Cert as Fdr of the Seattle Opera Assn, 1974; Cit, Northgate Forum Celebrity Lecture Series, 1980; Awd of Distn, Seattle Opera Guild, 1983; W/W of Am Wom; Dir of Dist'd Ams.

JENSEN, VIOLA VAN oc/Writer; b/ Jun 2, 1927; h/1825 Sandra Lane, Grand Prairie, TX 75052; m/Donnell Christian; c/Vickie Lee Black, Ronald Lynn; p/Roy Edgar and Viola Lillian Lewis (dec); ed/ HS Grad; pa/Wk'd as Saleslady, John Rudin & Co, 1969-83; cp/Co-Fdr w Husband, Wake Up Am, Assn Dedicated to Informing the Public Concerning Drug & Narcotic Abuse, 1970-78; Pres, Wom's Bapt Missionary Assn, LA; Nat Pres 1963-65, St Yth Promoter 1965-70, Bapt Missionary Assn of Am; r/Bapt; hon/Co-Author, Yes, I've Been High, 1971; Author, Blessed is the Wom; Staff Writer, Focus; Wom of Yr, John Rudin Co, 1969.

JETT, JOYCE LENORA oc/Manufacturer's Representative; b/Oct 10, 1935; h/11614 Southlake Drive, Houston, TX 77077; ba/Same; c/Melody Lynn, Kirby Alan, John David; p/David Milford (dec) and Ruth Leota Sadler, Johnson City, TN; ed/Illuminating Engrg Soc, 1966; Lighting Ctr, 1968; TX Hotel & Motel Sch, 1976; pa/Sales, M&M Lighting, 1961-65; Mgr, BASCO, 1965-70; Pres, J J Lighting Co, 1970-72; Dir of Sales & Columnist, Houston Mag, 1972-73; Dir of Sales, Med Ctr, Holiday Inn, 1974-77; Rep, Bill Teiber Agy, 1978-; cp/Houston Hispanic C of C, Dir 1978-79; hon/DAR Citizenship Awd, 1951; Recip, Awd, Houston Fire Dept, 1976; Lttr of Apprec, Nat Easter Seal Soc, 1976; Lttr of Apprec, Muscular Dystrophy Assn, 1976; Cert of Recog, El Consulado de Mexico, 1976; Cert of Apprec, City of Houston, 1978; Key to City, 1979; Letter of Recog and Awd, Cruz Roja Mexicana, 1978; TX Nat Theatre's Awd, 1980; Cert of Apprec, Shriners Hosp for Crippled & Burned Chd, 1981; Hon Fire Marshal, City of Houston, 1981; W/W of Am Wom.

JEWELL, HELEN S oc/Director of Private Pre-School; b/Sep 10, 1920; h/ 13180 Saint Andrews Drive, Seal Beach, CA 90740; ba/Santa Monica, CA; m/ Stanley S Sims; c/H Richard, Janis I; p/ William Ralph and Ethel Peters Stevens (dec); ed/Assoc Deg, Primary Ed, Drake Univ, 1941; BSE in Elem Ed 1972, MSE in Early Childhood Ed 1975, Wn IL Univ; Postgrad Wk, Univ of WI, So IL Univ, Univ of MO, Nat Col of Ed; pa/Tchg, Van Meter (Kgn & 1st), Akron (1st), Cedar (1st & 2nd), Harding Sch (5th); Subst, K-8, All Subjects, for 12 Yrs; Coor, Instr, Early Childhood Ed Dept, Carl Sandburg Col; Lead Tchr, Campus Lab Sch, CA St Univ-LA; Monmouth Ed Assn, St Rep 1974; AAUW, Ed Chm 1973; So CA Assn of Ed for Yg Chd, Exec Bd, Ways & Means Chair 1983-84; cp/Girl Scouts, Shabonne Coun, Exec Bd of Dirs 1962-71; r/Ed Com, Faith Presb Ch, 1973; hon/Kappa Delta, Drake Univ, 1940; Phi Kappa Phi, Wn IL Univ, 1975; W/W: in MW, in W; Men & Wom of Distn.

JILANI, ATIQ A oc/Manufacturing Company Executive; b/Feb 1, 1948; h/ PO Box 3212, Oak Brook, IL 60521; m/ Khalida; c/Hussain Shaheed, Ibrahim; p/ Siddig Ahmed and Nasima Jilani; ed/BE, NED Engrg Col, Karachi Univ, 1969; MS, Tuskegee Inst, 1971; Cert of Mgmt, Wharton Sch of Mgmt, Univ of PA,

1982; Att'd, NWn Univ 1980, Purdue Univ 1978; pa/VP, GM & Chief Operating Ofcr, Borg-Erickson Corp, 1980-; Mgr of Engrg, Chgo Marine Containers, Div of Sea Containers, 1978-80; Prod Engr, Borg-Warner Corp, 1974-78; Design Engr, Lummus Indust, 1971-73; ASME; Nat Soc Profl Engrs; ASAE; Am Mgmt Assn; Am Soc Agri Engrs; Charter Mem, Assn of Energy Engrs; Am Inst of Plant Engrs; Soc of Mfg Engrs; r/Muslim; hon/Contbr, Articles to Profl Jours; Holder, 11 US & Intl Patents; Reg'd Profl Engr, IL; Cert'd Mfg Engr, MI; Cert'd Plant Engr, OH; AEC Traineeship, 1970-71; W/W: in MW, in Technol Today, in Fin & Indust; Men of Achmt.

JILEK, ANITA GAIL oc/General Manager of Marketing Services Agency; b/Sep 20, 1951; h/425 West Belmont Avenue, Chicago, IL 60657; ba/Chicago, IL; p/Mr and Mrs Rupert Jilek, Western Springs, IL; ed/BS 1973, MA 1974, Univ of IL; pa/Sales Rep, R O Stensland, 1974-75; Retail Sales Mgr, Zenith Radio Corp, 1975-76; Spec Projs Div Mgr, House of Vision Optical Inc, 1976-80; Dist Mgr, 20th Cent Fox, 1980-81; Gen Mgr, Feldman Assocs, 1981-; Advtg & Design Sers Ltd, Bd of Dirs 1981-; AAUW, 1982-; Nat Assn of Female Execs, 1980-; cp/Cook Co Blood Bk, 1977-; hon/Univ of IL Dist'd Grad; W/W: Among Am HS Students, of Am Wom.

JOE, HOWARD TONG oc/Senior Chemist Supervisor; b/Apr 10, 1937; h/911 Edgebrook Drive, Baytown, TX 77521; ba/Baytown, TX; m/Catherine Wong; c/John Christopher, Ann Christine; p/Mr and Mrs S C Joe, Midland, TX; ed/BS 1960, MS 1970, Univ of CA; PhD, Univ of Houston, 1975; pa/Chief Chem, Petro Analytical Lab, 1972; Sr Res Analyst, NASA, Johnson Space Ctr, 1975-76; Sr Chem Supvr, Mobay Chem Corp, 1976-; Am Chem Soc; cp/Dem Party; r/Bapt; hon/Author, 2 Pub'd Articles, 1964, 1978; Nat S'ship for MS Deg, Univ of CA, 1968-69; W/W in S & SW; Personalities of S.

JOHN, JOSEPH oc/Executive; b/Mar 14, 1938; h/1401 Crestview Drive, San Carlos, CA 94070; ba/Mountain View, CA; m/Urmila; c/Melind; p/Thomas and Kunjamma John; ed/BSc, Madras Christian Col, 1958; MS, Univ of Madras, 1960; PhD, FL St Univ, 1968; MBA, Pepperdine Univ, 1980; pa/Sci Ofcr, Jr Res Ofcr, Atomic Energy Establishment, Bombay, 1959-64; Sr Scist, Staff Scist, Gulf Gen Atomic Co, 1968-72; Prog Mgr, Tech Application Dept, Gulf Radiation Tech Co, 1972-73; VP 1977-83, Mgr of Nuclear Sys Div 1976-83, IRT Corp, 1973-83; VP 1983-, Gen Mgr of Energy & Envir Div 1983-, Pres and Dir 1983-, Acurex Waste Technols Inc; Am Phy Soc; Am Nuclear Soc; Am Soc Nondestructive Testing; ASTM; Am Mgmt Assn; Soc Advmt Mgmt; San Diego Bd of Rltrs; CA Assn Rltrs; Nat Assn Rltrs; Am Def Preparedness Assn; cp/Assn AUS; Rotary Clb Intl; r/Christian; hon/Author, Over 100 Tech Pubs in Sci Jours, Tech Books & Reports; Recip, Cooke Meml Prize 1953, Hensman Meml Awd 1950, Sanders Meml Prize 1951, Bicknell Meml Prize 1952; IAEA Fellow, 1964-66; AEC Fellow, 1958-59; FL St Univ Grad Fellow, 1966-67; W/W: in W, in Fin &

Indust, in Commun Ser, in CA Bus & Fin, in World; Am Men & Wom of Sci; Personalities of W & MW.

JOHNEN, ELIZABETH THERESA oc/Assistant Director of Developmental Education; b/Jul 20, 1953; h/1430 McCoy Avenue, Northeast, Salem, OR 97303; ba/Salem, OR; m/Robert Allan; p/Russell and Florence Mastrota, Espyville, PA; ed/MS in Ed, Elmira Col, 1980; Rdg Spec Cert, Elmira Col, 1980; BS in Ed of Exceptl Chd, PA St Univ, 1975; pa/Asst Dir of Devel Ed, Chemeketa Commun Col, 1983-; Adult Ed Instr & Prog Coor, Boise St Univ, 1983; Conslt, EDL/Arista Pub'g Co, 1983-; Test Item Writer, Am Col Testing Prog, 1983-; Adult Ed Instr & Rdg Spec, Blue Mtn Commun Col, 1981-83; Resource Rm Tchr, Tooele Co Sch Dist, 1980-81; Spec Ed Tchr, Williamson HS, 1977-79; Spec Ed Tchr, Cresson St Sch & Hosp, 1975-76; CEC, Chapt Secy 1973-; IRA, 1980-; OR Rdg Assn, 1983-; OR Developmental Studies Org, 1981-; Wn Col Rdg & Lng Assn, Basic Rdg Spec Interest Grp Chp 1982-; Assn for Supvn & Curric Devel, 1983; Nat Assn for Remedial/Developmental Studies in Postsec'dy Ed, 1983-; NW Adult Ed Assn, 1983-; Pi Lambda Theta, Profl Wom in Ed, 1974-; Phi Kappa Phi, 1974-; cp/NOW, Chapt Secy 1982-; Assn for Retarded Citizens, 1975-; Army Commun Ser, Com on the Handicapped, Chp 1980-81; r/Rom Cath; hon/Pub, *Challenging Adults to Read Effectively, a Guide for Tchrs & Tutors*, 1982; Army Commun Ser Awd, 1981; Lonnie Williams Meml S'ship, 1975; Assn for Retarded Citizens S'ship, 1975; W/W in W; Outstg Yg Wom of Am.

JOHNS, L JEAN oc/Director of School of Nursing; b/Aug 8, 1929; h/212 North Foote Avenue, Colorado Springs, CO 80909; ba/Colorado Springs, CO; m/Daniel E; c/Michael David, Cynthia Jo; p/Harold E (dec) and F Evelyn Janke O'Blenes, Sun City, AZ; ed/Dipl, NE Meth Sch of Nsg, 1952; BS, NE Wesleyan Univ, 1952; MS, Univ of CO, 1975; pa/Dir 1975-, Instr 1968-75, Beth-El Sch of Nsg, Meml Hosp; Instr, Penrose Hosp Sch of Practical Nsg, 1963-69; Instr, Seton Sch of Nsg, Penrose Hosp, 1960-62; Staff Nurse, Lincoln Gen Hosp 1952-55, Vets Hosp 1957-59, Bryan Meml Hosp 1956-57; Pres, CO Nurses Dist #3 1976; Bd Mem, Hlth Assn 1980-, Pikes Peak Commun Col Sch of Nsg Adv 1976-, So CO Univ Sch of Nsg Adv Bd 1978-; ANA; CNA; NAACOG; Sigma Theta Tau; Alpha Gamma Delta; NLN Bd of Review, 1979-83; cp/Pres, Help Line Bd 1977-78, PEO Pres 1974-75; r/Prot; hon/Contbg Author, *Ob Nsg*, 1980.

JOHNSON, ALICE LORETTA oc/Speech Pathologist; h/14809 Channel Lane, Santa Monica, CA 90402; ba/Same; p/Axel and Carrie Nelson Johnson (dec); ed/BA, No MI Col; MA and EdD, Columbia Univ; Postgrad, Univ of Paris & McGill Univ; pa/Tchr, Saginaw, MI, Schs; French Tchr, Saginaw HS; Cryptographer, US War Dept, Wash, DC; Eng Instr, Panzer Col; Audiologist, Spch Clinician, St Luke's Hosp; Asst Prof Eng, Wagner Col, NY; Assoc Prof, St Col, E Stroudsburg; Tchr, Lang & Hearing Impaired, NYC Bd of Ed; Pvt Pract, Spch Pathol, NYC & Santa Monica, CA; AAUP; ASHA; AAUW;

Sigma Tau Delta; cp/LWV; r/Swedish Luth; hon/Author, "Supportive Instruction for Hearing Impaired Students," 1968; Intl W/W of Contemp Achmt; W/W: in W, in CA.

JOHNSON, BENJAMIN LEIBOLD oc/Education Specialist, Training Analyst; b/Nov 23, 1950; h/5515 Cache Road, #L-6, Lawton, OK 73505; ba/Ft Sill, OK; p/Murrell Faxton and Chlora Pauline Naylor Johnson, Raytown, MO; ed/BA in Polit Sci & Geog 1971, BS in Ed (Social Studies) 1974, MS in Ed (Social Studies) 1976, Ctl MO St Univ; mil/USN, 1976-79; pa/Subst Tchr, Raytown & Independence, MO, Public Schs, 1974-76; Wayne Regan Inc, Rltrs, 1976; Tchr, Chm of Social Studies, Eng & French Depts, Breckenridge, MO, Public Schs, 1979-80; Career Intern, Ed Spec, Ft Sill, OK, 1980-82; Ed Spec, Tng Analyst, Directorate of Tng Developments, 1982-; Pt-Time Master Jeweler, Classique Creations Inc, 1982-; Assn of Am Geographers; Nat Coun for the Social Studies; Am Acad of Polit & Social Scis; Nat Space Inst; NCTE; Am Cong on Surveying & Mapping; Nav Enlisted Resv Assn; Assn of Supvn & Curric Devel; cp/Acad of Sci Fiction, Fantasy & Horror Films; Nat Rifle Assn; N Am Darting Assn; Am Sq Dance Soc; Masons; Scottish Rite; Order of DeMolay; hon/BSA, God & Country, 1964; BSA, KC Area Coun, Micosay, 1965; BSA, Eagle Scout, 1965; BSA, Explorer Scout, 1966; Gamma Theta Upsilon, 1971; W/W in S & SW; Personalities of S.

JOHNSON, BETTYE STOKES oc/Retired Secondary Special Education Supervisor; b/Apr 6, 1935; h/4808 Avondale Circle, Colorado Springs, CO 80917; m/Weston O; c/Dennette Marie, Jocelyn Genene; p/Mr and Mrs J L Stokes (dec); ed/BA, MA in Spec Ed, Stanislaus St Col; Att'd, Savannah St Col, Howard Univ, Ithaca Univ; Grad Hours in Spec Ed Voc Ed, Univ of No CO; pa/Sec'dy Spec Ed Supvr, Sch Dist #11, CO Sprgs, 1975 to Retirement; Choreographer for Several Sch Plays & Advr to Minority Students, Coronado HS; Tchr & Diagnostician, Coronado HS, 1970; Other Previous Positions; Curric Planning & Prog Devel, CO Sprgs Spec Ed, Pre-Voc Prog, Career Voc Eval Ctr, Wk Experience & Study Prog, 1975-83; r/Epis; hon/Awd'd Cert, CO Sprgs Alumnae Chapt, Delta Sigma Theta Sorority Inc, for Meritorious Ser, 1984; Awd'd Plaque, CO St Voc Dept, for Support, Dedication & Loyalty to Voc Ed in CO, 1983; Awd'd Plaque, Staff of Sch Dist #11, for Ldrship & Supvn of Sec'dy Spec Ed Progs, 1983; Num Other Hons.

JOHNSON, CARL HAROLD oc/Clinical Psychologist; b/Sep 5, 1943; h/11527 Stillbrook Road, Richmond, VA 23236; ba/Richmond, VA; m/Anne Eckert; c/Lindgren Hale, Carl Heath; p/Carl Harold MD (dec) and Nancy McCurdy Keith Johnson, Gettysburg, PA; ed/BA, Dickinson Col, 1965; MA, Loyola Col, 1973; PhD, Univ of GA, 1975; pa/Parole/Probation Agt, MD Div of Parole & Probation, 1969-73; Staff Psychol, McGuire VA Hosp, 1975-; Pvt Pract of Clin Psych, 1980-; Am Psychol Assn; SE Area Psychol Assn; VA Psychol Assn; Richmond Area Psychol Assn, Past Pres; Nat Register of Hlth

Ser Providers in Psych; Asst Clin Prof, Dept of Clin Psych, VA Commonwlth Univ; Clin Instr, Dept of Psychi, Med Col of VA; r/Epis; hon/Pubs, "Role-Reversed Systematic Desensitization in the Treatment of a Writing Phobia" 1982, "Use of a Feeding Procedure in the Treatment of A Stress-Related Anxiety Disorder" 1982, "Thought-Stopping & Anger Induction in the Treatment of Hallucinations & Obsessional Ruminations" (to Be Pub'd), "Relaxation Therapy for Somatoform Disorders" 1981, Others; Diplomate in Clin Psych, Am Bd of Profl Psych, 1981; W/W in S; Personalities of S.

JOHNSON, CAROL HANCOCK oc/ Assistant Staff Manager; b/Mar 21, 1947; c/Heather Lynn; p/Ophelia B Hancock, Athens, GA; ed/BA, Radford Univ, 1969; Presently Studying for MBA, Brenau Col; pa/Ser Rep, OH Bell Telephone, 1969-72; Ser Rep, S Ctl Bell, 1972-77; Ser Rep (Marietta, GA) 1977-78, Asst Mgr, RSC (Decatur, GA) 1978-82, Asst Staff Mgr (Atlanta, GA) 1983-, So Bell Telephone; cp/Vol, Am Cancer Soc 1979, Heart Fund 1980; r/ Epis; hon/W/W of Am Wom.

JOHNSON, CHARLES FOREMAN oc/Architect, Graphic Designer, Teacher, Architectural Photographer, Systems Engineer, Consultant; b/May 28, 1929; m/Beverly Jean Hinnendale; c/Kevin, David; p/Charles E and E Lucile Casner Johnson; ed/Student, Union Jr Col, 1947-48; BArch, Univ of So CA, 1958; Postgrad Studies in Sys Engrg, Univ of CA-LA, 1959-60; pa/Apprentice Prog for Arch Students, 1980-; Free-Lance Arch Photog, 1971-; Conslt, Stereo, Video Sys Planning & Equip Review, 1960-; Charles F Johnson, Prin, Pvt Pract in Arch, Interiors, Color & Graphic Design, LA 1953-68, Santa Fe (NM) 1968-; Conslt, NM Reg Med Prog, NM St Dept of Hosps & Instns, NM St Planning Ofc, 1968-70; Dir of Opers & Facility Planning, TRW Sys, Sys Engrg & Integration Div, 1964-68; Other Previous Positions; Creative Wks in Arch, Civic, Photo, Writing; Delta Sigma Phi; Pres 1974, Santa Fe Coalition for the Arts; cp/El Gancho Tennis Clb; hon/Pioneered Video in Bus Communication & Mgmt, *Bus Wk Mag*, 1967; W/ W in W; Men of Achmt; Biogl Roll of Hon; Personalities of W & MW; 2,000 Notable Ams; Intl W/W of Intells; Biogl Roll of Hon; Intl W/W of Contemp Achmt; Commun Ldrs of World.

JOHNSON, CLARENCE JR oc/ Assistant Professor of Horticulture; b/ Nov 5, 1946; h/B-2, 801 Orange Street, Fort Valley, GA 31030; ba/Fort Valley, GA; m/Linda D; p/Clarence and Cora Johnson, Chicago, IL; ed/BS, Gen Agri, Alcorn St Univ, 1968; MS, Agronomy Soils & Plant Physiol, MS St Univ, 1973; PhD, Plant Physiol & Plant Breeding, Cornell Univ, 1977; mil/1969-71; pa/ Asst Prof, Plant Sci, Prairie View Univ, 1977-78; Asst Prof, Plant Sci, TN St Univ, 1978-80; Asst Prof, Hort, Ft Val St Col, 1981-; Intl Soc for Hort Sci; Am Soc for Hort Sci; Am Soc of Agronomy; So Assn of Agri Scists; Sweet Potato Collaborators Wk Grp; Alpha Kappa Mu Hon Soc; r/Bapt; hon/Pubs, "Soil Preparation for the Home Garden," "Use of Mulch in the Home Garden," "Fall Gardening in Mid GA," "Almost Any-

thing Grows"; W/W in S & SW; Personalities of S.

JOHNSON, DOROTHY PURNELL oc/Elementary School Teacher; b/Aug 23, 1930; h/829 Ormond Street, Macon, GA 31204; ba/Macon, GA; m/Frank; c/ Cheryl Teresa; p/James Thomas Purnell, Macon, GA; p/Willie Mae Purnell, Macon, GA; ed/BS, Savannah St Col, 1953; MA, NY Univ, 1959; Cert in Supvn, Univ of GA, 1977; pa/Ward Clk, Med Ctr of GA, 1952-53; Tchr, Primary Grades, Monroe Co, 1953-55; Primary Tchr, Bibb Co Public Sch Sys, 1955-; Zeta Phi Beta Sorority, 1951-; GAE; BAE; NEA, 1953-; cp/GA Coalition of Black Wom, 1980-; NAACP, 1959-; Voter Leag of Bibb Co, 1980-; Ebony Socialites, 1971-; Unionville Improvement Assn, 1974-; r/Bethel Christian Meth; Sunday Sch Tchr, 1959-; Missionary Soc, 1959-; Gospel Choir, 1961-; hon/Matilda Hartley's Tchr of the Yr, 1975-76; Recip, McKibben Lane Awd for Excell in Tchg, Bibb Co, 1981; Hon Appt to the Nat Bd of Advrs, Am Biogl Inst, 1982; Outstg Elem Tchrs of Am; W/W of Am Wom; Personalities of S; Dir of Dist'd Ams.

JOHNSON, FAITH E oc/Coordinator of Afro-American Affairs; b/Jan 7, 1951; h/4505 College View Drive, Dayton, OH 45427; ba/Dayton, OH; c/Christopher Harris; p/Cleo M Johnson, Dayton, OH; ed/Currently Pursuing Ed Spec Deg in Adm; MS, Cnslr Ed, Univ of Dayton, 1977; BA, Communication Arts, OH St Univ, 1974; pa/Coor of Afro-Am Affairs, Univ of Dayton, 1981-; Moderator, Black Achmt, WONE, WTUE Radio, 1981-; Columnist, *Dayton Black Press*, 1981-; Adm Ofcr, Darke Co Common Pleas Ct, 1980; Cnslr, Montgomery Co Ct of Domestic Relats, 1977-80; Adj Instr, Univ of Dayton Crim Justice Dept, 1979-80; Am Wom in Radio & TV, Mbrship Chp 1982; Black Wom in Higher Ed, 1982-; APGA, 1982-; Nat Coun Black Studies, 1982-; Phi Delta Kappa; Miami Val Psychol Assn; cp/Budget Coor, W Area YWCA Com, 1981-; Vol Probation Wkr, Montgomery Co Juv Ct Apathy Prog, 1975-80; r/Meth; hon/Kizzy Awd Recip for Acad & Profl Accomplishments & Commun Ser, 1981.

JOHNSON, GWENAVERE A oc/ Artist; h/2054 Booksin Avenue, San Jose, CA 95125; ba/San Jose, CA; m/J Wendell; c/John Forrest; ed/Att'd, Mpls Sch of Art, 1930; BA, Art Ed, Univ of MN, 1937; MA, Art, San Jose St Univ, 1957; pa/Asst'ship, Art, Univ of MN, 1936-37; Art Tchr, Hillbrook Sch, 1947-52; Art Tchr & Supvr, Santa Clara Public Schs, 1952-55; Art Tchr & Chm of Dept, Woodrow Wilson Jr High, 1955-70; Art Tchr, Abraham Lincoln HS, 1970-75; San Jose Art Leag; Los Gatos Art Assn; Santa Clara Art Assn; Soc of Wn Artists, SF; Delta Phi Delta; Nat Leag of Am Penwom; Artists' Equity Assn; hon/Master of Painting, Honoris Causa, 1982; Dipl of Merit, Univ of Arts, Italy, 1982; Gold Medal for Artistic Merit, Intl Parliament, USA, 1983; Golden Centaur Awd, Accademia Italia, 1983; Dipl of Nations Prize, Accademia Italia; Accademia delle Nasione, Centro Studie Ricerche delle Nazione; W/W in W; Intl Dic of Contemp Artists; Contemp Personalities; Artists USA.

JOHNSON, JAMES TERENCE oc/ College President; b/Oct 25, 1942; h/ 2108 Smiling Hill Boulevard, Edmond, OK 73034; ba/Oklahoma City, OK; m/ Martha; c/Jennifer, Jill, Tiffanie; p/Mr and Mrs Clifford Johnson, Springfield, MO; ed/BA, OK Christian Col, 1964; JD, So Meth Univ, 1967; pa/Staff Legal Counsel 1968-72, VP 1972-73, Exec VP 1973-74, Pres 1974-, OK Christian Col; Coun of Indep Cols, Bd of Dirs; OK Indep Col Foun, Bd of Dirs; OK Bar Assn, Law Schs Com; cp/OK City Rotary Clb; Freedoms Foun at Val Forge, Bd of Dirs; Ldrship, OKC; r/Ch of Christ; Hon LLD, Pepperdine Univ, 1980; W/W in Am.

JOHNSON, JORENE KATHRYN oc/ Administrator; b/Jan 6, 1931; h/5200 Race Road, Cincinnati, OH 45239; ba/ Cincinnati, OH; m/Roland E; c/Lorin I, Melissa K A; p/Adam and Kathryn Freitag (dec); ed/MPA, Univ of Cinc, 1975; BFA, Pratt Inst, 1952; pa/Furniture Designer, Jacques Bodart Inc, 1952-54; Interior Decorator, Albert Paruin & Co 1955-57, Maria Bergson Assocs 1957-61; Ofc Mgr, Res Asst 1973-74, Res Mgr 1974-75, The Cinc Inst; Exec Dir, Friends of Cinc Pks, 1975-77; Commun Coor, Col Hill Forum, 1977-; Zoning Secy, Inspector, Green Twp Zoning Bd, 1982-; cp/ Mayor's Energy Task Force, 1982-83; Planning Bd, Cinc Commun Chest, 1982-; Prog for Cinc Action; VP, LWV of Cinc Area, 1971-73; Dir of Publicity 1969-; Envir Chm, Wom's City Clb, 1974; Co-Convenor, City Mgr's COPE Task Force on Pks, Rec & Open Space, 1972; Other Mbrships; r/Unitarian; hon/Editor, *Proceedings of Criminal Justice Conf*, 1971; Editor, Co-Author, *NW Local Sch Dist, Know Your Schs*, 1970; Pub'd Article in *The Futurist*, 1969; W/W of Am Wom.

JOHNSON, KEITH H oc/Acting Chairman and Associate Professor of Department of Finance; b/Nov 23, 1940; h/3408 Farmington Road, Lexington, KY 40502; ba/Lexington, KY; m/B'Ann M; c/Jeffrey; p/Ada O Johnson, Kewanee, IL; ed/BS 1963, MS 1965, PhD 1970, Univ of IL; pa/Res Assoc, Univ of IL, 1968-69; Asst Prof 1969-75, Assoc Prof 1975-, Acting Chm 1982-83, Dept of Fin, Univ of KY; Am Fin Assn; So Fin Assn; En Fin Assn; Am Ec Assn; Financial Mgmt Assn; Financial Execs Inst; Lexington Fin Assn; r/U Meth; hon/Authored Over 40 Articles & Papers; W/W in S & SW; Personalities of S.

JOHNSON, KENNETH LEROY SR oc/Retired Regular Air Force Officer, Realtor, Program Manager Executive; b/Jan 24, 1922; h/3020 South Sheridan, Wichita, KS 67217; m/Tran Thi Phuong; c/Jeffrey John, Candy Ann, James John; p/ Kenneth LeRoy Jr, Terri Ann, Jeff J; p/ Stanley C and Nell L Lundberg Johnson; ed/Student, KS St Col 1940-42, Univ of So CA 1956-57; BS, Univ of Omaha, 1959; mil/Comm'd, USAF, 1942; Adv'd through Grades to Col, 1960; Flew Combat Missions, WWII (25), Korea (67), Vietnam (86); Ret'd, 1969; pa/ Contract Mgr & Mgr, Air Dept Pacific Archs & Engrs Co, Vietnam, 1970-75; Prog Mgr, Bell Helicopter Intl, Tehran, Iran, 1977-79; ERA Rltr Assoc, 1980-81; Nat Assn Security Dealers; Nat Assn of Rltrs; cp/Repub; Mason; hon/Decorated, Dist'd Flying Cross w One OLC, Bronze Star, Purple Heart, Air Medal w 77 OLCs, Plus 24 Other Campaign Medals.

JOHNSON, LORETTA IRENE oc/ Country Music Promotion, Publicity and News; b/Nov 29, 1941; h/PO Box 177, Wild Horse, CO 80862; ba/Wild Horse, CO; p/Mack Johnson, Wild Horse, CO; Audrey Johnson, Lamar, CO; pa/Self-Employed, Co-Owner of Own Bus, Tri-Son Inc (Loretta Lynn Intl Fan Clb, Intl Fan Clb Org, Tri-Son Promotions & News); Free-Lance Writer, Columns Appear Monthly in *Music City News, Country Song Round-Up, Country Music Round-Up*; Country Music Assn Inc; Acad of Country Music; r/Unaffiliated Prot; hon/Contbr of Articles to *Little Nashville Express, CMI, Country Music People, Kountry Korral*; KY Col, Named by Gov Louie B Nunn, 1971; Aide-de-Camp, Gov's Staff of St of LA, 1974; CO Country Music Hall of Famer, 1980; Certs of Apprec & Plaques from Var Orgs; World W/W of Wom.

JOHNSON, LOUDILLA MAXINE oc/Country Music Promotions and Publicity; b/Sep 16; h/PO Box 177, Wild Horse, CO 80862; ba/Same; p/Stanley Mack Johnson; Audrey I Johnson; ed/ Grad, Kit Carson HS, 1956; pa/ Self-Employed, Co-Owner of Own Bus, Tri-Son Inc (Loretta Lynn Intl Fan Clb, Intl Fan Clb Org, Tri-Son Promotions & News); Free-Lance Writer, Columns Appear in *Music City News, Country Song Round-Up, Country Music Round-Up*; Country Music Assn Inc; Acad of Country Music; Broadcast Music Inc; hon/ Contbg Writer, *Little Nashville Express, CMI, Country Music People, Kountry Korral*; Writer of 2 Pub'd & Recorded Songs; KY Col, Named by Gov Louie B Nunn of KY, 1971; Aide-de-Camp, Gov's Staff of St of LA, 1974; CO Country Music Hall of Fame, 1980; Certs of Apprec & Plaques from Var Orgs; World W/W of Wom.

JOHNSON, MABLE BUTLER oc/ English Teacher; b/Feb 21, 1944; h/425 Chappell Road, Northwest, Apartment A-2, Atlanta, GA 30318; ba/Atlanta, GA; p/Mrs Gladys Butler, Gainesville, GA; ed/BA, Paine Col, 1964; MA, Atlanta Univ, 1972; EdS, GA St Univ, 1978; pa/Eng Tchr, Treutlen Co Tng Sch 1964-65, Gainesville Bd of Ed 1965-70, Atlanta Bd of Ed 1970-; Pt-time Eng Tchr, Mercer Univ, Upward Bound Prog, 1980; Secy, Phi Delta Kappa, 1982-83; Secy, Phi Delta Kappa, 1983-84; Atlanta Assn of Edrs; NCTE; Atlanta Coun of Tchrs of Eng; GA Coun of Tchrs of Eng; Assn for Supvn & Curric Devel; cp/LWV; NAACP; hon/Tchr of Yr, J E Brown High, 1982; Star Tchr, J E Brown High, 1980, 1976; Local Am Legion Awd, for Outstg Ser to Oration & Boys' St; Nat Dean's List, 1983.

JOHNSON, MARNETTE MOLES oc/Systems Engineering; b/Nov 18, 1939; h/7740 South Wellington Street, Littleton, CO 80122; ba/Denver, CO; m/Orval E; c/Bryan S; p/James J Moles, Kearney, NE; Evelyn A Moles, Madison, NE; ed/BA in Math, MacMurray Col, 1961; Postgrad, Univ of MI 1970, 1973, Univ of KY 1978, Def Intell Sch 1978; Wkg on MBA, Wn Univ; pa/Computer Programmer, Dayton AF Depot, 1961-64; Mathematician, Nav Electron-

ics Lab, 1964-73; Computer Spec, Nav Ocean Sys Ctr, 1973-79; Sr Sys Analyst, Exec Engr, CALSPAN Field Sers Inc, 1980-81; Computer Sys Spec, Sys Devel Corp, 1981-82; Staff Engr, Martin Marietta, Denver Aerospace, 1982-; Assn of Computer Machinery; Computer Soc of IEEE; Digital Equip Corp Users Soc; Assn of Sys Mgmt; Amway Distbrs Assn; cp/Toastmasters Intl; r/ Pentecostal Assemblies of God; hon/ Author, Several Programmed Instrn Manuals for Govt Pubs; Freshman Hons Convocation, Univ of NE, 1958; Dean's List, 1960; Upper 10 Percent of Col Grad'g Class, 1961; 1st Female Profl Exch from NELC (NOSC) to NISC (NAVINTCOM), 1978; W/W of Am Wom.

JOHNSON, MELVIN C oc/Manager of Toxicology; b/Aug 29, 1933; h/17 Clearview Road, East Brunswick NJ 08816; ba/Princeton, NJ; m/Yvonne; c/ Marion, Denise, Eric; p/Robert (dec) and Bessie Edmonds Johnson, Newark, NJ; ed/BS in Biol, Rutgers Univ, 1962; MS in Pharm, McGill Univ, 1968; PhD in Pharm, Howard Univ, 1972; mil/USN 1953-57, Hon Discharge; pa/Toxicologist, Am Cyanamid Co, 1977-; Toxicologist, Hercules Inc, 1972-77; Pharmacologist (Scist) 1968-70, Pharmacologist (Asst Scist) 1962-66, Warner-Lambert Res Inst; Soc of Toxicology; Am Acad of Clin Toxicology; NY Acad of Sci; AAAS; Am Inst of Biol Sci; Mid-Atl Chapt, Soc of Toxicology; Teratology Soc; r/Cath; hon/Author, Several Pubs in Field; F'ship, Warner-Lambert Res Inst, 1966-69; W/W in E; Men & Wom of Sci.

JOHNSON, MIGNON BOLDEN oc/ Retired; b/Feb 12, 1916; h/2015 South Fillmore Street, Arlington, VA 22204; m/Ernest E; ed/AB, VA St Col, 1936; Master's Deg, Guid & Cnslg, NY Univ, 1951; Addit Grad Studies, Howard Univ, Cath Univ, George Wash Univ, Am Univ; pa/Tchr, Elem & Sec'dy, VA, 1936-44; Attendance Ofcr, Wash DC Public Schs, 1944-51; Tchr, Cnslr, Prin, DC Jr High Schs, 1951-73; Conslt, Cnslr, Arlington Career Ctr, 1974-80; cp/En Area Asst Dir 1972-77, En Area Dir 1979-83, The Links Inc; Civil Ser Commr, 1977-81; Mbrship Ret'd, NASSP, DCASSP; r/Meth; hon/Awds, Omega Wives 1959, Links 1981, Randall Jr Ath Dept 1972.

JOHNSON, R BRUCE oc/Chemical Executive; b/Apr 8, 1928; h/2009 Dilloway, Midland, MI 48640; ba/Midland, MI; m/Margery Howe; c/Wynn, Carol, Stephen, Herrick; p/Rogers B and Dorothy Aiken Johnson, Midland, MI; ed/BA 1949, MBA 1955, Harvard Univ; mil/USAF 1951-53, 1st Lt; pa/Sales Tng 1955-57, Field Salesman (Pgh, PA) 1957-61, Plastics Sales Mgr (Dow Europe) 1961-65, Bus Mgr (Styrenic Polymers) 1965-70, Corporate Prod Dir (Specialty Prods) 1970-76, VP of Supply, Distbn & Planning 1976-80, Grp VP of Supply, Distbn, Planning & Fin 1980-, Dow Chem Co; cp/Midland Commun Tennis Ctr, Pres 1975-77, Mem of Operating Bd 1973-, Treas 1977-80; r/ Prot.

JOHNSON, RICHARD DAMERAU oc/Chief of Biosystems Division; b/Oct 28, 1934; h/11564 Arroyo Oaks, Los Altos, CA 94022; ba/Moffett Field, CA; m/Catherine C; c/Gregory N, Eric C,

Karen D, Laurana W; p/Earl G Johnson, New Canaan, CT; ed/AB, Oberlin Col, 1956; MS 1960, PhD 1962, Carnegie Mellon Univ; SM, MIT, 1982; Chief of Biosys Div 1976-, Chief of Life Scis Flight Experiments Ofc 1973-76, Asst Div Chief of Planetary Biol Div 1972-73, Tech Asst for Viking Biol 1970-72, Res Scist of Exobiol Div 1963-70, NASA Ames Res Ctr; Lectr, Stanford Univ, 1974-83; Conslt in Biotechnol, Separation Scis Inc, 1983; Other Previous Positions; AIAA; ACS; AAAS; hon/ Pubs, "Life Scis Experiments on the Space Shuttle" 1983, "An Anal of Bus Opports in Biomed Res & Clin Med: Two-Dimensional Gel Electrophoresis" 1982, Others; Sustained Superior Perf Awd, 1969; Grp Achmt Awds, 1975, 1977, 1978, 1981; NASA Exceptl Ser Medal, 1977; Alfred P Sloan Fellow, 1981-82; Appt'd to Fed Sr Exec Ser, 1979; Am Men & Wom of Sci; W/W: in W, in Technol Today, in Frontier Sci & Technol, in Am; Commun Ldrs of Am; Dir of Dist'd Ams.

JOHNSON, ROBERT LESLIE oc/ Business Owner and Manager; b/Jun 23, 1916; h/7210 Home Avenue, PO Box 391, Harbert, MI 49115; ba/Harbert, MI; m/Irene Louise Turiansky; c/ Rebecca S; Stepchd: Edward S Czekaj, Paul A Czekaj; p/Arthur E Johnson, Harbert, MI; Gertrude M Zeiger Johnson (dec); ed/BS, Chem Engrg, MI St Univ, 1939; mil/AUS 1941-46; Maj, Army Resv; Active Resv 1950-65, Field Artillery; pa/Chem Engr, SoCA Gas Co, 1946-47; Chem Engr 1947-54, Supvr of Chem Div Res & Testing Lab 1954-76, Dept Supvr of Engrg & Res Lab 1976-81, Ret'd 1981, Consumers Power Co; Owner, Mgr, Color Aids Co, 1959-; Reg'd Profl Engr, St of MI; NACE, Cert'd Corrosion Spec; ASTM, Subcom Secy 1967-80; Resv Ofcrs Assn, Exec Coun (MI) 1960-; Cong of Interallied Ofcrs of Resv, Comm IV 1975-82; EEI Chem Com, 1954-78, Chair of Analytical Sect; ASM, 1965-75; MI St Univ Engrg Alumni Assn; German Am Nat Cong; VASA Order of Am; cp/Repub Party; r/Bapt; hon/W/W: in MI, in MW, in S & SW.

JOHNSON, ROSEMARY oc/Art Teacher; b/Sep 22, 1932; h/1350 East Colonial Drive, Salisbury, NC 28144; ba/Salisbury, NC; c/Rosemary Taylor Blount, Glenn Charles Taylor Jr, Donna Taylor Thomas, James Foster Taylor, Jennifer Anne Taylor; p/James Henry and Rosalie Webb Johnson (dec); ed/ Att'd, Gulf Pk Jr Col 1950, 1951, Univ of AL 1952; BA, AL Tchrs Col, 1953; Grad Sch, Univ of NC-Greensboro, 1977; pa/Clrm Tchr, B'ham City Schs 1954, Rowan Co Schs 1957; Art Spec, Salisbury, Rowan, Davie Co, 1972-; Early Childhood Art Ed Prof, Catawba Col; Nat Art Tchrs; NC Art Tchrs; NC Mus of Art; Nat Art Edrs; Presently Wkg on Sequential Art Prog for Elem Clrm Tchrs; cp/GSA, Past Brownie Scout Ldr; Rowan Christian Min, Girls Aux Ldr; r/Bapt; hon/Murals in Rowan Co Schs, Granite Quarry & Mt Ulla Schs; Hon Cadet, Col ROTC, Univ of AL, 1953; Campus Favorite, 1951; World W/W of Wom.

JOHNSON, VELMA KAY oc/Country Music Promotions and Publicity; b/ Jun 26, 1944; h/PO Box 177, Wild Horse, CO 80862; ba/Same; p/Mack S Johnson;

Audrey Irene Johnson; ed/Grad, Kit Carson HS, 1962; pa/Self-Employed, Co-Owner of Own Bus, Tri-Son Inc (Loretta Lynn Intl Fan Clb, Intl Fan Clb Org, Tri-Son Promotions & News); Free-Lance Writer, Columns Appear in *Country Song Round-Up, Country Music Round-Up;* Country Music Assn Inc; Acad of Country Music; r/Prot; hon/ Contbr, Articles to *CMI, Country Music People, Kountry Korral;* KY Col, Named by Gov Louie B Nunn of KY, 1971; Aide-de-Camp, Gov's Staff of St of LA, 1974; CO Country Music Hall of Fame, 1980; Certs of Apprec & Plaques from Var Other Orgs; World W/W of Wom.

JOHNSON, WILLIAM GEORGE oc/ Professor of Economics, Senior Research Associate; b/Dec 20, 1934; h/ 28 Cross Road, Dewitt, NY 13224; ba/ Syracuse, NY; m/Saundra; c/Laura, Andrea, Todd, Lauren; p/William P (dec) and Jeanne Camus Johnson; ed/BS, Univ of PA, 1956; MA in Ec, Temple Univ, 1968; PhD in Ec, Rutgers Univ, 1971; Postgrad, Ctr for Law and Ec, 1978; mil/ Ens/Lt (jg), USS Marias (AO-57), US Sixth Fleet, 1956-58; pa/Asst Comptroller, Graphic Arts Dept, E I DuPont de Nemours & Co Inc, 1963, 1966; Ec Analyst, SKF Industs Inc, 1966-67; Res Asst, Bur Ec Res 1967-69, Assoc Dir, Disability & Hlth Ec Sect 1970-72, Adj Asst Prof of Hlth Ec 1971-79, Asst Prof of Ec 1971-73, Rutgers Univ; Asst Prof of Ec 1973-75, Assoc Prof 1975-80, Prof of Ec 1980-, Sr Res Assoc of Hlth Studies Prog 1980-, Maxwell Sch, Syracuse Univ; Prof of Adm Med 1977-, Dir of Hlth Studies Prog 1974-80, SUNY, Syracuse; Am Ec Assn; Indust Relats Res Assn; cp/Adirondack Mtn; hon/Contbg Author, *Public Policy Toward Disability*, 1976; Contbr, Articles on Hlth Ec to Profl Jours.

JOHNSON, WILLIAM LARRY oc/ Chairman of Department of Mathematics; b/Jan 19, 1943; h/Route 2, Box 517, Big Sandy, TX; ba/Big Sandy, TX; m/ Dr Annabel Marie; p/Henry W Johnson, Nocona, TX; ed/BS in Ed, N TX St Univ, 1967; EdM, TX Christian Univ, 1976; EdD, TX Tech Univ, 1980; AA, Ambassador Col, 1983; pa/Wichita Falls ISD, 1967-69; Arlington ISD, 1969-74; Hawkins ISD, 1974-77; Proj Dir 1979-80, Secy-Treas 1980-81, Pedamorphosis Inc; Stat, TX Tech Univ, 1979-81; Chmn of Dept of Math, Ambassador Col, 1981-; Hawkins Clrm Tchrs Assn; Am Ednl Res Assn; Nat Soc Study Ed; Phi Delta Kappa; SWn Ednl Res Assn; r/ Worldwide Ch of God; hon/Pubs, "Response Alternatives in Likert Scaling" 1984, "Ldrship Tng Needs for Prins: A TX Study" 1983, Others; Alpha Chi, 1964; Omicron Delta Kappa, 1979; Phi Kappa Phi, 1981; Helen DeVitt Jones Ldrship F'ship, TX Tech Univ, 1978-79; W/W: Among Students in Am Univs & Cols, in W.

JOHNSON, WILLIAM McCRAY oc/ Plant Pathologist; b/Mar 17, 1950; h/ Route 5, Box 139, Stillwater, OK 74074; ba/Langston, OK; p/McCray and Clara Johnson, Pittsville, VA; ed/BS w Hons, Biol Sci, Univ of MD, 1972; BS in Botany 1976, PhD in Plant Pathol 1976, OK St Univ; pa/Asst Prof 1976-78, Assoc Prof 1979-80, Prof 1981-, Langston Univ; Alpha Kappa Mu Hon Soc; Beta Kappa Chi Sci Soc; Sigma Xi Sci Soc; Am Phytopathological Soc; r/U Meth; hon/

Author of Several Pubs in Nat Referred Sci Jours; Sigma Xi Grad Res Awd, OK St Univ Chapt, 1976; FFA Am Farmer Deg, 1971; W/W in Am Cols & Univs; Am Men & Wom of Sci.

JOHNSON-COUSIN, DANIELLE PAULETTE oc/University Educator; b/ Nov 7, 1943; h/1027 Draughon Avenue, Nashville, TN 37204; ba/Nashville, TN; m/Harry M; c/Eliza Suzanne Johnson; p/Edouard Henri (dec) and Suzanne Louise Maurer Cousin, Geneva, Switzerland; ed/Certificat de Maturité, cum laude, Col de Genève, 1962; BA, Univ of AK, 1966; MA, Purdue Univ, 1968; PhD, Univ of IL-Urbana, 1977; Postgrad Wk, Oxford Univ, NWn Univ, Univ of Münich; pa/Vis'g Lectr, Univ of IL, 1976-77; Asst Prof of French, Amherst Col, 1979-82; Asst Prof of French, Andrew W Mellon Fellow, Vanderbilt Univ, 1982-; Other Vis'g Positions in Switzerland & USA: Mod Lang Assn; SAMLA; Assn Suisse de Litt Comp et Gen; Soc des Etudes Staëliennes, Paris; AAUP; AAUW; Soc Suisse des Ecrivains; Soc Genevoise des Ecrivains; Hist Soc PA; Soc des Etudes Romantiques; AATF; ACLA; ICLA; r/Prot; hon/ Contbr of Articles to Profl Jours; Hon Fellow, Inst Adv'd Studies in the Humanities, Univ of Edinburgh, Scotland; Univ of MA Oxford S'ship, 1968; Univ of IL Sum Fellow in Comp Lit, 1971; Univ of IL Fellow in Comp Lit, 1972-73; Répertoire des Ecrivains Suisses; Nat Fac Dir; W/W of Am Wom; Intl Dir of 18th Cent Studies.

JOHNSTON, MARJORIE D oc/Profession Services Analyst; b/Sep 19, 1943; h/5709 West 71 Circle, Arvada, CO 80003; ba/Boulder, CO; c/Stephen Ray, Deborah Diane; p/Earl L Whipple, McKinleyville, CA; Ruth J Purcell, Honolulu, HI; ed/Cert, Computer Programming, La Salle Univ, 1973; pa/ Profession Sers Analyst, Control Data Corp, 1982-; Sr Analyst, Programmer, Kaiser Foun, 1982; Contract Programmer, Computer Asst Inc, 1981-82; Sr Analyst, Programmer, Los Alamos Nat Lab, 1972-81; Theta Rho, Pres 1960; cp/En Star, Worthy Matron 1977, 1978; Rebekah's; r/Christian; hon/W/W in W.

JOHONG, JOONDU oc/Executive; b/ Dec 14, 1926; h/191 Valley Road, Riveredge, NJ 07661; ba/New York, NY; m/Uyeon Ju; c/Seung-A, Lasan; p/ Jongwon and Somak Johong (dec); ed/ Student, Pusan Nat Fisheries Col; pa/ Sales Mgr, Barclays & Co, Seoul, 1950-55; Dir, Korea Trade Ctrs, LA, CA, Bangkok, London, Brussels, 1962-79; Ec Advr to Govt of Ghana, 1978; Current Resident VP in USA & Exec Dir, Korea Trade Promotion Ctr; Current VP & Bd Mem, Korea Promotion Corp; Korea Trade Res Assn; Mkt Res Assn of Britain; cp/NY Rotary Clb; hon/Author, Many Export Promotion Articles; Indust Suktap Medal from Korean Govt, 1979; Lectr & Spkr at Domestic & Intl Trad Sems.

JONASSEN, GAYLORD D oc/Chief Executive Officer, Chairman of Board; b/Oct 13, 1932; h/9 Wood Lane, Smithtown, NY 11787; ba/Hauppauge, NY; m/Shirley A; c/Glenn, Brenda; p/Alma Stelter Jonassen, Bradenton, FL; ed/BS, Mech Engrg, AZ St Univ, 1960; mil/ USN, 1950-54; pa/Fdr, Pres, Chm of Bd, Intl Protein Industs Inc, 1973-; Exec VP,

Tech Dir, Opers & Mktg, Telecommuns Industs Inc, 1970-73; Div Mgr, Aircraft Instrumentation, Atl Sci Corp, 1968-70; Prod Mgr, Reg Sales Mgr, Kinemotive Corp, 1967-68; Contracts Admr, New Prods Mgr, Sales Promotion Mgr, Deutch Relays Inc, 1965-67; Devel Engr, Mgmt Trainee, Wn Elect Co Inc, 1960-65; Tech Troubleshooter, Prodn Devel Engr, Machine Designer, Motorola Semiconductor, 1955-60; cp/Spec Bd of Arbitration, 1982-; Ch Deacon Bd, 1972-; Exec Com, Kings Col Parents Assn, 1981-; Tennis & Suffolk Co Softball Leag; r/Bapt; hon/Hon Grad, US Naval Tng Ctr, 1951; Baseball S'ship, AZ St Univ, 1955-59; Am Soc for Testing Mats Fellow, 1958; Dist'd Achmt Awd, Col of Sci & Engrg, AZ St Univ, 1982; W/W in E.

JONES, BARCLAY GEORGE oc/ Professor of Nuclear and Mechanical Engineering, Associate Chairman of Nuclear Engineering; b/May 6, 1931; h/ 310 East Holmes Street, Urbana, IL 61801; ba/Urbana, IL; m/Rebekah Imogene Scolnick; c/Deborah May, Allison Lynn, Catherine Leigh; ed/ BEng, Mech Engrg, Univ of Saskatchewan, 1954; MS 1960, PhD 1966, Nuclear Engrg, Univ of IL; mil/RCAF; pa/Atomic Energy of Canada Ltd, 1954; Eng Elect, Rugby, England, 1955; AERE, Harwell, England, 1955-57; Canadair, Montreal, 1957-58; Westinghouse Atomic Power, 1958; Univ of IL-Urbana, 1958-60, 1963-; Argonne Nat Lab, 1960, 1976; TRW Sys, 1965; Aero Acoustics, Tech Com; AIAA; Univ Wide, Engrg Col and Dept Coms; cp/Champaign Co Mtl Hlth Bd, 1983-; r/Presb; hon/Author, Over 60 Pub'd Articles & 50 Reports; Athlone F'ship, 1954-56; Haliburton Awd, 1982-83; Grad Col Fellow, 1960-63; W/ W in MW.

JONES, CALVIN PAUL oc/Historian, Educator, Consultant; b/June 13, 1934; h/RFD #2, Waddy, KY 40076; ba/Same; m/Stella Mae Wigginton; c/James Edwin, Leticia Gay, Melissa Ann; p/ Russell Emrick and Mary Agnes Livingston Jones (dec); ed/BA 1955, PhD 1966, Hist, Univ of KY-Lexington; MA, Ednl Adm, En KY Univ, 1959; pa/Histn & Conslt, Commonwlth Activs Inc, 1983-; Vis'g Lectr in Hist, Univ of KY-Lexington, 1983-84; Casewk Spec, KY Cabinet for Human Resources, Dept for Social Ins, 1983; Subst Tchr, Anderson Co Schs, 1982-; Title I Tchr, Grades 1-4, Acad Sch, KY St Reformatory, 1982; Sr Histn, KY Heritage Comm, 1976-81; Adj Lectr in Hist, Morehead St Univ, 1972-75; Prof of Hist 1972-75, Dir of Instnl Res & Prof of Hist 1971-72, Hd of Dept of Hist & Polit Sci, Prof of Hist & Polit Sci 1970-71, Pikeville Col; Dean of Col & Prof of Hist, Salem Col, 1968-70; Other Previous Positions; Mbrship in Var Profl Hist Assns; AAUP, 1964-68, Chapt Pres at Pikeville Col 1965-66; Mbrship in Var Profl Ednl Assns; Victorian Soc, 1978-81; r/Presb/Bapt; hon/Pubs, "The Images of Simon Bolivar as Reflected in Ten Lding Brit Periods, 1816-1830" 1984, "Book About Pikeville Col Tchrs Reveals Dr Geza Nagy Story Who Fled From Soviets in Hungary to US" 1983, Others; Title V-E F'ship, Higher Ed Act of 1965; Nat Def Ed Act F'ship, Inst in Adv'd Ec, Univ of NE-Lincoln, 1967; Haggin Grad

F'ship in Hist, Univ of KY, 1963-64; Other Hons; Dir of Am Scholars; Ldrs in Ed; Personalities of S; Men of Achmt; DIB.

JONES, CLARA PADILLA oc/Secretary of State; b/Sep 2, 1942; h/228 Crestview Drive, Southwest, Albuquerque, NM 87105; ba/Santa Fe, NM; m/Ronald A; c/Mary Clara Davis, Suzanna; p/Julian Sr (dec) and Suzanna Padilla; ed/Student, El Camino Col, Albuquerque Career Inst; pa/Buyer, Mdsg Mgr, Bullocks Dept Stores, 1959-68; Cosmetics Buyer, Dillards Dept Stores, 1968-78; Rltr, Julian Padilla & Assocs, 1978-; NM Secy of St, 1983-86; Org of BPW; SW Bkrs, Bd of Dirs; Nat Assn of Secys of St; Albuquerque Career Inst, Pres, Bd of Dirs; cp/Zonta; Las Amigas de Nuevo Mejico, Fdr & Pres; NM Dem Party, Mem of St Rules Com; Bernalillo Co Val Dem Wom, Past Pres; Bernalillo Co Dem Party, Past VChair; Am GI Forum, Bd of Dirs, NM Kidney Foun, Bd of Dirs; r/Cath; hon/Spirit of Excell, Albuquerque Hispano C of C; Dist'd Past Pres Awd, Bernalillo Co Val Dem Wom; Ser Above Self-Espanola, NM Rotary Clb; St Bus Awd, NM Highlands Univ; Cert of Merit, Am GI Forum; W/W: in Am, in W, in Am Polits; World W/W Wom; Personalities of W & MW.

JONES, CLARICE RHODES oc/Teacher; b/Dec 31, 1925; h/7818 South Harvard Boulevard, Los Angeles, CA 90047; ba/Inglewood, CA; c/Iverne Clarice; p/Charles Benton and Fannie Lillian Bailey Rhodes (dec); ed/BA, TX So Univ, 1949; MS in Ed, Univ of So CA, 1969; pa/Dancer, Carmen Jones 1943-44, Katherine Dunham 1945-46; Rec Dir, Dance Spec, City of LA, 1955-62; Tchr, Spec Ed, Public Sch, Duarte, CA, 1963-69; Tchr, 4th Grade, Public Sch, 1970-; Delta Sigma Theta, 1950-; Chi Kappa Rho, 1961-68; CA Tchrs Assn; NEA; PTA; Sch Adv Coun, 1970-, Chp; cp/Inst of Rel Sci, 1970-; Nat Coun of Negro Wom, 1965-; YWCA; NAACP; Urban Leag; r/Sci of Mind; hon/Pubs, "Folk Dancing" 1968, "Dancing Motivate" 1969, "Project Invest" 1978, "Consolidate Application" 1978, 1979, 1980, 1981, 1982; Tchr of Yr, 1982-83.

JONES, DIANNE CHRISTINE oc/Associate Professor; b/Dec 13, 1951; h/Route #3, Kettle Moraine Drive, Whitewater, WI 53190; ba/Whitewater, WI; p/Earl and Barbara Jones, Lancaster, OH; ed/BS, En KY Univ, 1974; MS, Wn IL Univ, 1975; EdD, WV Univ, 1979; pa/Univ of WI-Whitewater, 1979-; Res Asst, WV Univ, 1978-79; F'ship, Tchg Asst, Univ of WI-Madison, 1977-78; Instr, Basketball Coach, Univ of WI-Whitewater, 1975-77; Tchg Asst, Wn IL Univ, 1974-75; Am Alliance of Hlth, PE, Rec & Dance; MW Assn of Hlth, PE, Rec & Dance; West Assn of PE for Wom; Nat Assn of PE for Higher Ed; Nat Wom's Ath Caucus; Nat Wom's Basketball Coaches Assn; N Am Soc for the Sociol of Sport; N Am Soc of the Psychol of Sport & Phy Activity; Assn of Univ of WI Fac; WI Assn of Hlth, PE & Rec; Delta Psi Kappa; Eta Sigma Gamma; Kappa Delta Pi; hon/Pubs, "Why Are Students Dropping Out of HS Aths" 1983, "Anxiety & Its Effect on Ath Perf" (in Preparation), "Developing a Player to Player Denial Defense"

1983, "Sideline Fast Break" 1983, Others; Blanche M Trilling F'ship, Dept of PE, Univ of WI-Madison, 1977; WI Wom's Intercol Ath Conf Basketball Coach of the Yr, 1981; W/W: Among Yg Wom in Am, in Am Cols & Univs; Outstg Col Aths in Am.

JONES, GERRE LULE oc/Marketing Consultant, Author; b/Jun 22, 1926; h/2123 Tunlaw Road, Northwest, Washington, DC 20007; ba/Washington, DC; m/Charlotte M Reinhold; c/Beverly Anne Jones Putnam, Wendy S MD; p/Eugene R (dec) and Carolyn R Newell Jones, Bethesda, MD; ed/BJourn 1948, Postgrad 1953-54, Univ of MO; mil/USAAF, 1944-45; Ret'd Maj, USAFR; pa/Sr VP, Barlow Assocs Inc, 1977-78; Editor, Publisher, *Profl Mktg Report*, 1976-; Pres, Gerre Jones Assocs Inc, 1976-; Exec VP, Gaio Assocs Ltd, 1972-76; Mktg Conslt, Ellerbe Archs, 1972; Dir of Mktg and Communs, Vincent G Kling Ptnrship, 1969-71; Other Previous Positions; Intl Radio & TV Soc; Nat Assn of Sci Writers; Public Relats Soc of Am; Intl Assn of Chiefs of Police; Sigma Delta Chi; Alpha Delta Sigma; Overseas Press Clb; KC Press Clb; Army & Navy Clb; r/Prot; hon/Pubs, *How to Mkt Profl Design Sers* 1973, *How to Prepare Profl Design Brochures* 1976, *Public Relats for the Design Profl* 1979, *How to Mkt Profl Design Sers* 1982; Made Hon Mem, AIA, 1979; W/W: in E, in World, in Fin & Indust.

JONES, GRANT oc/State Senator; b/Nov 11, 1922; h/1509 Woodridge, Abilene, TX 79605; ba/Abilene, TX; m/Anne Smith; c/Morgan Andrew, Janet Elizabeth Jones Pliego; p/Morgan and Jessie Kenan Wilder Jones (dec); ed/BBA, So Meth Univ, 1947; MBA, Wharton Sch of Fin, Univ of PA, 1948; Passed St Bar & Lic'd to Pract Law, 1974; Hon Doct Deg, Abilene Christian Univ, 1981; mil/WW II, Pilot in Troup Carrier Command; pa/Ins Agt; TX Ho of Reps, 1964-72; TX St Senate, 1972-; Chartered Property & Casualty Underwriter, Chm of Casualty Com of TX Assn of Ins Agts, Bd of Dirs; Pres, TX Assn of Ins Agts; Chm, Senate Fin Com; Ad Valorem Tax Study Com; Com to Study Bd of Pardons & Paroles; Com on Financial Instns; Curric Study Com; St Audit Com; Legis Budget Bd; TX 2000 Comm; Other Mbrships; r/Meth.

JONES, HELEN COOK oc/Writer; b/Jan 17, 1917; h/1519 Oxford Street, Apartment I, Berkeley, CA 94709; ba/Same; m/Hardin (dec); c/Carolyn Jones Kenter, Hardin, Nancy Jones Snowden, Mark; ed/BA, Univ of CA-LA, 1938; Grad Study, Univ of CA Berkeley 1938, Univ of So CA 1939; pa/Tchr of Home Ec, Hollywood HS 1939-42, Pleasant Hill Intermediate Sch 1953-54; Writer, 1954-; cp/Univ of CA Fac Wives Fgn Student Com, 1970-80; Bd of Dirs, Am Coun on Drug Ed, 1978-; Adv Bd, Parents Who Care, 1981-; Contbg Editors Bd, Coms of Correspondence, 1982-; Chm, Marijuana & Hlth, 1979-; Bd of Dirs, Berkeley City Clb, 1984-; r/Prot; hon/Pubs, *A Guide to Berkeley & the Bay Area* 1958, 1965, *The Low Fat, Low Cholesterol Diet* 1951, 1971, 1984, *Sensual Drugs: Deprivation & Rehab of the Mind* 1977, *Exec Hlth* 1984, *The Marijuana Question & Sci's Search for an Answer* (in Press); Elected to Omicron Nu, 1938; Contemp Authors; DIB; World W/W

Wom; W/W of Am Wom.

JONES, JACK DELLIS oc/Executive; b/Mar 3, 1925; ba/Getty Refining and Marketing Company, PO Box 1650, Tulsa, OK 74102; m/Sarah Katherine Kramer; c/Margaret K, Elizabeth Jones Blaylock, Susan L; p/Henry Clifford and Dora Dean Dellis Jones (dec); ed/BS, US Nav Acad, 1947; JD, Univ of Tulsa, 1955; mil/USN, 1947-50, 1951-53; pa/Engr, Sunray Oil Co, 1953-55; Atty 1956-64, Div Atty 1964-65, VP 1966-74, Pres of En Opers 1974-77, Grp VP 1980-, Getty Oil Co; Pres, Getty Refining & Mktg Co, 1977-; Dir, First Nat Bk & Trust Co of Tulsa, 1977-; Univ of Tulsa, 1981-; AR Basin Devel Assn, 1978-; Am Petro Inst, 1980; cp/Trustee, Hillcrest Med Ctr, 1977-; Adv Bd, Tulsa Salvation Army, 1977-; Dir, Tulsa Opera, 1977-; Tulsa Area U Way, 1982-; Metro Tulsa C of C, 1977-; r/Epis; hon/W/W: in Fin & Indust, in World of Oil & Gas, in W, in Am; Standard & Poor's Register.

JONES, LEON oc/University Professor; b/Dec 26, 1936; h/3104 Castleigh Road, Silver Spring, MD 20904; ba/Washington, DC; m/Bobbie Jean; c/Stephanie Ruth, Gloria Jean; p/Lander Corbin (dec) and Una Bell Jones, Crawfordsville, AR; ed/JD, Cath Univ of Am, 1981; Ednl Doct Deg, Univ of MA-Amherst, 1971; BS, Univ of AR-Pine Bluff, 1963; mil/USN, 1958-62; pa/Math Stat, Army Procurement & Supply Agy, 1963-64; Time-Study Engr, Intl Harvester Co, 1966-68; Lectr, Sch of Ed, Univ of MA-Amherst, 1970-71; Coor, Res & Eval, Acting Assoc Dean, Col of Human Lng & Devel, Govs St Univ, 1971-72; Asst to VP for Acad Affairs (Res & Devel) 1972-73, Full-time Fac Mem 1973-, Dir of Ctr for Ednl Res & Devel 1974-76, Sch of Ed, Howard Univ; Spec Res Asst, Dpty Majority Whip, 97th Cong, US Ho of Reps, 1982-; Fac Sponsor, Howard Univ Baha'i Clb, 1975-; Exec Ofcr, PTA, Galway Sch, 1975-; Eval Res Soc, 1980-; IPA; Nat Lwyrs Guild; Nat Conf of Black Lwyrs, 1981-; Am Inst of Parliamentns, 1982-; cp/NAACP, 1973-; r/Bahai Faith; hon/Pubs, "Ednl Eval: Ser of Menace" 1981, *From Brown to Boston: Desegregation in Ed, 1954-1974* 1979, "Sch Desegregation in Retrospect & Prospect" 1978, "Brown Revisited: From Topeka KS, to Boston MA" 1976, "Desegregation in Ed Since 1954" 1974, "A Methodological Approach to Eval" 1974, "Outsider Aids in Eval" 1969; Ford Foun Awd for Sch Desegregation Res, 1975-76; Howard Univ Grant for Sch Desegregation Res, 1973-75; Fellow, Nat Ldrship Tng Inst, US Ofc of Ed, 1969-71; Intl W/W in Intells; Contemp Authors; Men of Achmt.

JONES, LINDA MAY oc/Tour Guide and Tour Guide Trainer; b/Nov 9, 1937; h/12857 Highway 119, Golden, CO 80403; ba/Denver, CO; m/Verl; c/Chris Dale Conard, Carin Dené Conard, Curtis Dean Conard; p/Forrest Edward Carlson (dec); Edith Fulton, Harper, KS; ed/Att'd, Univ of KS, Wichita St Univ, Univ of Denver, Univ of CO; pa/Wrangler, Skyland Camp, 1954-56; Tour Guide, Queen City Tours, 1976-; Mgr, Tour Guide Sers, Queen City Tours, 1979-; Lead Guide, CO Guide Co, 1983-; Hist Denver, 1972-; Molly Brown House Day Chm, 1974-79; VP,

Molly Brown House Adv Coun, 1977-78; Life Mem, Univ of KS Alumni Assn; cp/DAR, St Ofcs; Mensa; Intertel; r/Meth; hon/Pub, *Mile High Denver, a Guide to the Queen City*, 1981; Phi Alpha Theta, 1957; Outstg Jr Mem, DAR for CO, 1970; Outstg Jr Mem, Wn Div, DAR, 1970; W/W: Among Am Wom, in W; World W/W of Wom; Intl W/W of Wom; Outstg Yg Wom of Am.

JONES, MARGARET B oc/Early Childhood Education; h/10232 2nd Avenue, Inglewood, CA 90303.

JONES, PATRICIA oc/Second Grade Teacher; b/May 29, 1953; h/2254 Hannaford Avenue, Norwood, OH 45212; ba/Norwood, OH; p/John Hoyt and Eva Mae Perry Jones (dec); ed/BS, magna cum laude, Elem & Early Childhood Ed, Cumberland Col, 1975; EdM, Lng Disabilities & Emotionally Disturbed Chd, Xavier Univ, 1975; pa/Phy Handicapped Tchr, Yealey Elem Sch, Boone Co Sch Sys, 1975-76; Second Grade Tchr, Sharpsburg Primary Sch, Norwood Public Sch Sys, 1976-; NEA, 1973-; OH Ed Assn, 1976-; Norwood Tchr Assn, 1976-; PTA, 1975-; cp/Wom's Missionary Union, 1971-; Cinc Zoo, 1982-; cp/Home Bible Study, 1979-; New Bethel Bapt Ch, 1966-; Ch Choir, 1969-; Ch Ensemble, 1982-; Mission Friends Ldr, 1983; Vacation Bible Sch Dir, 1975-79, 1982, 1983; r/So Bapt; hon/Norwood Bd of Ed Cont'g Contract, 1979; Mtl Hlth Assn Reach Out Awd, 1976; Outstg Yg Wom of Am; W/W of Am Wom.

JONES, PEGGY LaVERNE oc/Health Administrator; b/Dec 25, 1939; h/1325 Plymouth Way, Sparks, NV 89431; ba/Reno, NV; c/Matt, Erin, Todd; p/James and Hazel Menghini, Verdi, NV; ed/Student of Public Relats & Bus Adm, Univ of Tampa 1959-61, Orange Coast Col 1963-64, Cerritos Jr Col 1967-69; pa/Free-Lance Public Relats, 1964-74; Clin Coor, Planned Parenthood of No NV, 1975-76; Exec Dir, MS Soc of No NV, 1976-79; Supvr, Washoe Co Med Soc, 1979-80; Dept Hd, St Mary's Hosp, 1980-82; Dir, Heart Inst of No NV, a Div of St Mary's Hosp, 1982-; Am Hosp Assn; ABWA; Am Mgmt Assn; Am Soc of Dirs in Vols; Reno Wom in Advtg; Nat Assn of Female Execs; cp/Cardiac Task Force, St Mary's Hosp; CPR Com, Am Heart Assn; Advr to Med Explorer Scout Post #211 for St Mary's Hosp; Homemaker Upjohn, Bd Mem; Com to Aid Abused Wom & Chd, Bd Mem; 4H Resource Ldr; hon/W/W in W.

JONES, RICHARD ALLEN oc/Executive, Reading Coordinator; b/Aug 16, 1931; h/Eagleview Farm Cottage Road, South Dayton, NY 14138; m/Ruth Kelley; c/Jonathan, Suzanne, Stephen, Gregory; p/Paul A (dec) and Nettie Shearer Jones, Tarentum, PA; ed/BA, Roberts Wesleyan Col, 1953; BD, Asbury Sem, 1957; MA, Univ of Buffalo, 1971; MS, Fredonia St Univ, 1971; Adv'd Studies, Alfred Univ, Syracuse Univ, Pgh-Xenia Sem, Univ of Buffalo, Jamestown Col; pa/Tchr, Lower Burrell, PA, 1957; Min, Salamanca, NY, 1957-59; Min, Belfast, NY, 1959-61; Min, S Dayton, NY, 1961-66; Tchr, Rushford, NY, 1960-61; Tchr, Gowanda, NY, 1961-62; Rdg Coor, Pine Val Schs, 1962-; Pres, Eagleview Enterprises, 1980-; Operator, Arabian Horse Farm, Eagleview Farm, 1972-; IRA,

1967-; NY Rdg Assn, 1967-, Bd of Dirs 1968-69; Fdg Pres, Chautauqua Co Rdg Assn, 1968-70, Mem 1968-; NY St U Tchrs, 1962-; Pine Val Tchrs Assn, 1962-, Pres 1967-70, Negotiator 1967-70; Am Horse Shows Assn, 1971-; Intl Arabian Horse Assn, 1971-; Arabian Horse Assn of NY, 1975-, Bd of Dirs 1977-80; Intl Dressage Assn, 1976-; Wn NY Dressage Assn, 1976-; cp/Conservative Party Com-man, 1979-; r/Genesee Conf Free Meth Ch, 1957-80; Orchard Pk Presb Ch, 1981-; hon/W/W: of Outstg Yg Men, in Rel, in Ed, of Civic Ldrs, in Fin & Indust.

JONES, ROBERT LEWIS oc/Management Consultant; b/Aug 12, 1924; h/2027 East Rice Drive, Tempe, AZ 85283; ba/Tempe, AZ; m/Nita; c/Stacey; p/Mrs Howard Lowman, Childress, TX; ed/BA w Distn, Univ of AZ, 1949; MAE 1970, PhD 1975, AZ St Univ; mil/USN, Capt; pa/Radio/TV Announcer, Writer, Dir, 1949-56; Copywriter, Tng Spec, Mgr (Employee Devel, Org Devel, Manpower Resources, Exec Devel), AZ Public Ser Co, 1956-75; Prof/Dir, Ctr for Bus Studies, Grand Canyon Col, 1975-82; Dir of Consltg Sers, VP, The Thoren Grp, 1982-; Am Soc for Tng & Devel; Phoenix Pers Mgmt Assn; cp/Toastmasters; r/Prot; hon/Co-Author, *Gen Bus*, 1976; Author of Var Articles; Nat's Outstg Tnr, ASTD, 1981; Nat Torch Awd, ASTD, for Indiv Contbn, 1979; US Small Bus Adm, 1977; US Dept of Labor, 1972; City of Phoenix Mayor's Awd, 1972; Phoenix C of C, 1971; AZ Dept of Ed, 1968; W/W: in W, in Consltg; Dir of Dist'd Ams; Men of Achmt; 2,000 Notable Ams; Intl Book of Hon; Commun Ldrs of World.

JONES, ROBERT O oc/Professor Emeritus of Psychiatry, Psychiatrist in Private Practice; b/Mar 31, 1914; h/6504 Jubilee Road, Halifax, Nova Scotia B3H 2H4; ba/Halifax, Nova Scotia; m/Mary Allen; c/David R, Louisa E Jones-Dupont; ed/BSc 1933, MDCM 1937, Dalhousie Univ; Postgrad Study, Maudsley Hosp, London, England, 1938-39; Henry Phipps Psychi Clin, Johns Hopkins Univ, 1939-41; pa/Assoc Prof of Med (Psychi) 1941-48, Prof & Hd of Dept of Psychi 1948-75, Prof Emeritus of Psychi 1976-, Dalhousie Univ; Vis'g Prof, Royal Free Hosp, London, England, 1975-76; Halifax Med Soc; Nova Scotia Med Soc; Canadian Med Assn, 1965, 1966; Charter Pres, Canadian Psychi Assn, 1951; Life Fellow, Am Psychi Assn; Emeritus Charter Fellow, Am Col of Psychi; hon/Pubs, "Ed of Mtl Hlth Wkrs in Canada in Post War Yrs" 1982, "The Insanity Def: Riel to Hinckley" 1982; Others; Hon EngD, Nova Scotia Tech Univ, 1970; Fellow, Royal Col of Psychi of Gt Brit, 1982; Canadian Med Assn Medal of Ser, 1982; Canadian Cent Medal, 1967; Queens Jubilee Medal, 1978; Ofcr of Canada, 1981; W/W in Canada; Debrett's Guide to the Canadian Estab.

JONES, ROLAND LEO oc/Performer and Teacher of Violin and Viola; b/Dec 16, 1920; h/3004 South Kearney, Denver, CO 80222; m/Carol Anne Day; ed/BMus, Univ of MI; 5 Yrs Study in NYC, Columbia Univ & Pvtly; 3 Yrs w Nat Orch Assn Tng Orch; Sums at Interlochen Music Camp, Meadowmount Music Sch & Tanglewood Music Sch; pa/Soloist w Ann Arbor Civic

Symph, 1951, 1953; Violinist, Denver Symph Orch 1960-74, Jackson Hole, WY, Fine Arts Fest 1964-65; Tours throughout USA & Canada; Fdr & 1st Violinist, Highland Chamber Players, 1978-79; Fdr & 1st Violinist, Highland String Quartet, 1978-; Recordings w Orch, "Hilena" by Alberto Ginastera, & "Concerto No 2" by Chopin; CO MTA; MTNA; Musicians Soc of Denver Inc; cp/Denver Art Mus; hon/Recip, S'ships to Interlochen Nat Music Camp & Tanglewood Music Sch.

JONES, ROSALIE MAY (DAYS-TAR) oc/Dancer, Choreographer, Teacher; b/Nov 1, 1941; ba/Stapleton Building, 104 North Broadway, Suite 319-320, Billings, MT 59101; p/Mr (dec) and Mrs W O Jones, Cut Bank, MT; ed/Postgrad Study w Jose Limon, Julliard Sch, 1969; MS in Dance, Univ of UT SLC, 1968; BFA in Music, Ft Wright Col, 1964; WI Mime Co Apprentice, 1973; Postgrad Study, Phila Dance Acad, 1968; Study w Hanya Holm, CO Col, 1962; pa/Solo Concert, Daystar: An Am Indian Wom Dances, 1982-; Fdr & Artistic Dir, Daystar: An Am Indian Theatre, 1980-82; Instr, Native Am Studies, En MT Col, 1983-84; Asst Supvr, Dept of Public Instrn, 1979-80; Video Prodn Conslt, Univ of MN, 1977-78; Lectr in Theatre Arts 1975-77, Artist-in-Residence 1977-78, Mt Senario Col; Other Previous Positions; Com on Res in Dance, 1978; Theatre Intl, Bd of Dirs 1975-78; Wn St Reg Theatre, 1976-78; WI Arts Bd, Adv Panel 1974-77; WI Mime Co Assoc, 1974-; WI Wom in the Arts, 1975-77; r/Cath; hon/Writer & Prodr, Film/Video Prodns, *Am Indian Music & Dance* 1977, *With Drum & Song*; WI Indian Dance 1974, Others; Solo Appearances, Kennedy Ctr for the Perf'g Arts 1982, Native Am Ctr for the Living Arts 1981, 1984, Heard Mus 1981, Buffalo Bill Hist Mus 1981, Many Others; Var Film Appearances.

JONES, RUTH ELIZABETH oc/Program Administrator; b/Oct 5, 1943; h/4226 Redstone Drive, San Antonio, TX 78219; ba/San Antonio, TX; m/Thaddies Jr (dec); c/Thaddies III; p/Benjamin Bowman and Elizabeth Angeline Jones (dec); ed/BA, TX So Univ, 1967; pa/Juv Probation Ofcr 1975-80, Commun Assistance Prog Coor 1980-82, Juv Probation Comm Coor 1982, Current Prog Admr, Bexar Co Juv Probation Dept; Delta Sigma Theta Inc, 1975-; TX Probation Assn, 1978-; TX Corrections Assn, 1981-; cp/Bd of Dirs, YWCA, 1974-80, VP; U Way, 1977-81; Vol Coun, San Antonio St Hosp, 1973-75; Ec Opport Devel Corp, 1975-77; Ella Austin Commun Ctr, 1974-83, Pres 1978-82; Dem Wom of Bexar Co, 1971-, Pres 1974; Planning Comm, City of San Antonio, 1978-; TX St Dem Exec Com, 1978-; Top Ladies of Distn, 1982-; r/Rom Cath; hon/Outstg Commun Ser Cit, City of San Antonio, 1980; Dist'd Public Ser Cit, TX Ho of Reps, 1973; Outstg Contbns towards Good Govt Cit, TX St Senate, 1975; Comm'd Yellow Rose of TX by Gov of TX, 1978; Ser Awd, Ella Austin Commun Ctr, 1982; Num Certs of Apprec from Var Orgs; W/W: of Am Wom, in Am Polit; World W/W of Wom.

JONES, VIRGIL CARRINGTON oc/Professional Writer; b/Jun 7, 1906; h/15000 Lee Highway, Centreville, VA

22020; m/Geneva Carolyn Peyton; c/ Virgil Carrington Jr, Judith Watkins; p/ Alonzo Lewis and Virginia Terrell Graves Jones (dec); ed/Att'd, VA Polytechnic Inst, 1924-26; BA in Jour, magna cum laude, Wash & Lee Univ, 1930; pa/City Editor, *The Huntsville Times*, 1931-37; Reporter, *The Times-Dispatch*, 1937-41; Reporter, *The Evening Star*, 1941-43; Reporter, *The Wall Street Jour*, 1943-45; Mgr, Wash Public Relats Ofc, The Curtis Pub'g Co, 1945-51; Free-Lance Writer, 1961-63; Adm Asst, Congressman Wm M Tuck of VA, 1963-69; Profl Writer, NASA, 1967 to Retirement; r/Christian; hon/Pubs, *Log of Apollo 11* 1969, *Roosevelt's Rough Riders* 1971, *Birth of Liberty* 1964, Others; Sigma Delta Chi S'ship Awd, 1929; DC Civil War Round Table Gold Medal Awd for Meritorious Writing, 1957; 2,000 Notable Ams; Men & Wom of Distn; Book of Hon; Men of Achmt; Intl Register of Profiles.

JONES, YVONNE JOHNSON oc/ Curriculum Supervisor, Educational Administrator; b/Aug 23, 1947; h/429 Parnell Place, Philadelphia, PA 19144; ba/Philadelphia, PA; m/Eric E; c/Jeffrey B; p/James and Dorothy Watson, Philadelphia, PA; ed/BS, Cheyney St Col, 1969; MA, Norfolk St Col, 1977; EdM, Antioch Univ, 1978; Current Doct Cand, Urban Ed, Temple Univ; pa/ Opports Industrialization Ctr, 1969-70; Tchr, Simon Gratz HS, 1970-75; Tchr, Tnr, Affective Ed Prog, 1975-79; Vis'g Prof, Childcare, Temple Univ, 1978-82; Curric Supvr, Phila Sch Dist, 1979-; Edrs Roundtable; Black Wom's Ed Assn; Nat Assn of Female Execs; Sigma Gamma Rho Sorority; Phila Assn of Sch Admrs; Assn of Supvrs & Curric Developers; Nat Black Child Devel Inst; r/Bapt; hon/Co-Author, *Parent's Guide to Helping Chd Cope* 1978, *Edr's Manual on Discipline, K-12* 1980; Richard Humphrey Scholar, 1966-68; Sigma Gamma Rho Campus Sorority, 1967; Inter-Greek Coun Commun Ser Awd, 1981; NSF Fellow, 1971; Outstg Yg Wom in Am, 1982; W/W: in Am Cols & Univs, in E.

JONES-WILSON, FAUSTINE CLARISSE oc/Professor of Education, Editor; b/Dec 3, 1927; h/908 Dryden Court, Silver Spring, MD 20901; ba/Washington, DC; m/Edwin L Wilson Sr; c/ Yvonne Dianne Jones, Brian Vincent Jones; p/Mrs Perrine C Patterson, Oakland, CA; ed/AB, AR Agri, Mech & Normal Col, 1948; AM 1951, EdD 1967, Univ of IL-Urbana; pa/Howard Univ: Editor of *Jour of Negro Ed*, Dir of Bur of Ednl Res, Prof of Ed, Grad Prof 1978-, Chm of Founs Dept, Prof of Ed, Grad Prof 1976-78, Other Positions; Assoc Prof, Adult Ed Dept, Fed City Col, 1970-71; Asst Prof, Dept of Ed, Howard Univ, 1969-70; Asst Prof, Col of Ed, Univ of IL-Chgo Circle, 1967-69; Other Previous Positions; Am Ednl Studies Assn; Am Ednl Res Assn; John Dewey Soc; Soc of Profs of Ed; Wash Wom's Forum; Metro Wash Assn for Adult & Cont'g Ed; S Atl Phil of Ed Soc; cp/ NAACP; r/Meth; hon/Pubs, *The Changing Mood in Am: Eroding Commitment?* 1977, *A Traditional Model of Ednl Excell: Dunbar HS of Little Rock, AR* 1981, Num Articles; Runner-Up Prof of the Yr, Sch of Ed, 1982; NOBUCS, Cert of Recog & Apprec for Outstg Perf & Participation in Black Col Wk, 1981; Cert from Univ

Without Walls, for Dist'd Ser, 1980; Num Other Hons; W/W: of Am Wom, Among Black Ams; Contbns of Black Wom to Am; Contemp Authors.

JORDA-MONTESCLAROS, MILAGROS BAGARES oc/Pediatric Physician; b/Jul 28; h/2003 Alta Vista Drive, Columbus, GA 31907; ba/Ft Benning, GA; m/Rodolfo F Montesclaros; c/ Giovanni, Myra Jean; p/Paulino L Jorda (dec); Arcadia R Bagares (dec); ed/AA, Pre-Med, w High Hons, Divine Word Univ, 1956; MD, Univ of Santo Tomas, 1961; pa/Rotating Intern, Mary Immaculate Hosp, 1963-64; Pediatric Res, Baroness Erlanger Hosp-Chd's Hosp, 1966-68; Pediatric Pathol & Clin Pathol Res, Nymed Col & Metro Hosp, 1968-69, 1974-76; Anatomical Pathol Res, Carney Hosp, 1972-74; Pediatric Staff Phys, Martin Army Commun Hosp, 1976-; Fellow, Am Acad of Pediatrics, 1982-; VP, Phil Am Med Assn of GA, 1983-84; Assn of Fed Phys, 1980-; r/Rom Cath; Alto, St Anne's Cath Ch Choir, 1979-; hon/AMA Phys's Recog Awd, 1979-82, 1982-85; Diplomate, Am Bd of Pediatrics, 1981; Bd Edigible, Anatomic & Clin Pathol; World W/W of Wom; Marquis W/W; Dir of Med Specs.

JORDAN, MICHELLE DENISE oc/ Attorney at Law; b/Oct 29, 1954; h/8014 South Perry Avenue, Chicago, IL 60620; ba/Chicago, IL; p/John and Margaret Jordan, Chicago, IL; ed/JD, Univ of MI, 1977; BA, Polit Sci, magna cum laude, Loyola Univ, 1974; pa/Asst St's Atty in St's Atty's Ofc, 1977-82; Pvt Pract, 1982-; Chgo Bar Assn, Cook Co Bar Assn, IL St Bar Assn, 1977-; Profl Wom's Aux of Provident Hosp, 1980-81; Alpha Sigma Nu, Nat Jesuit Hon Soc, 1974-; Pi Sigma Alpha, Nat Acad Hon Soc in Polit Sci, 1974-; cp/Leag of Black Wom, 1978-80; Oper Push, 1971-; Oper Breadbasket, 1968-71; hon/Oper Push's Wom's Day Awd, 1978; Outstg Yg Wom of Am; W/W Among Black Ams.

JORDAN, R BRUCE oc/Retired State of California Hospital Administrator, Part-time Professor; b/Mar 10, 1912; h/ 110-41 Street, Apartment 705, Oakland, CA 94611; m/Dorothy Caig; p/ Albert Raymond and Aimee Best Jordan (dec); ed/BA, Public Adm, Sacramento St Univ, 1952; MBA, Pers & Labor Relats, Stanford Univ Grad Sch of Bus, 1959; Lic'd Public Acct, St of CA; St of CA Standard Tchg Credential, 1960; mil/AUS, S Pacific, 1943-46; pa/Acct, Auditor 1947-48, Mgmt Analyst 1948-52, Chief Analyst 1952-59, St Bd of Equalization, St Dept Employmt; Chief Mgmt Analyst, HQs Ofc, St Dept Mtl Hygiene, 1959-63; Bus Admr, Atascadero St Hosp 1963-68, Patton St Hosp 1968-70; Mgmt Conslt, Hosps in Victoria, Brit Columbia, Canada, 1970-; Instr, Sacto City Col, 1951-62; Conslt, Govt of Iran, & Fac, Univ of Tehran, 1956; Instr, Univ of CA-Davis 1963, Cuesta Col 1967-68, Monterey Peninsula Col; Profl Lectr, Golden Gate Univ, Monterey Campus; Chm, Grievance Review Bd, Monterey Peninsula Unified Sch Dist; Monterey Co Ombudsman Prog, 1976-; cp/Fdr, Adv Bd Mem, Monterey Co Sr Hearing Ctr, 1977-; Treas, Experience Inc, 1973-; Bd of Dirs, Monterey Co Sr Aide Prog; Adv Bd, Alliance on Aging; Fdr, Pres, Concerned Sr Citizens; Monterey Peninsula Clb,

1974-77; Adv Grp, Monterey Sr Day Care Ctr, 1977-78; Able Toastmaster, Toastmasters Prog; r/Prot; hon/Pubs, *Mgmt Anal in Hlth Sers* 1980, *Supvn-Effective Mgmt-The Making of a Productive Wk Force* 1982; Recip, Bronze Achmt Awd, Mtl Hosp Ser, 1963; W/W: in W, in CA.

JOWERS, SANDRA THOMAS oc/ Moving and Storage Company Executive; b/Oct 4, 1950; h/3408 Lakeside Drive, Rockwall, TX 75087; ba/Dallas, TX; m/Joseph Jacob; p/Carl Dexter and Anita Lorraine Garver Thomas; ed/BS in Sociol, BS in Bus Adm, E TX St Univ, 1972; pa/Ofc Mgr 1972-74, Pres 1974-, Thomas Van & Storage Inc; BPW Clbs, Conv Del, Yg Careerist Chm 1980; SW Warehouse & Transfer Assn, Dir 1979-, VP 1981; Dallas Movers Assn, Dir 1974-, Pres 1979; Alpha Chi; r/Meth; hon/Named as Outstg Yg Wom of Am, 1981; W/W in Fin & Indust.

JOYCE, JOSEPH JAMES oc/Assistant General Counsel; b/Sep 28, 1943; h/16 Woodchuck Court, Norwalk, CT 06854; ba/Purchase, NY; m/Suzanne S Sheridan; c/Joseph, Michael, Peter, Kevin; p/Edward R and Mary E Jordan Joyce, Chicago, IL; ed/BS, Xavier Univ, 1965; JD, Loyola Law Sch, 1968; Admitted to Bar, St of IL, 1968; pa/Mem, Firm of Hill, Sherman, Meroni, Gross & Simpson, 1968-72; Atty 1972-74, Trademark Counsel 1974-77, Asst Gen Counsel 1977-, PepsiCo Inc; Com Chmship, US Trademark Assn; ABA; IL Bar Assn; Other Mbrships; r/Cath; hon/Pubs, "How to Select & Protect a Trademark" 1977, "Devels Affecting Trademark Use & Licensing" 1977; W/W in E.

JUDD, DAVID EDWARD oc/University Instructor, Marriage and Family Therapist; b/Apr 24, 1930; h/9825 Docena Drive, Gaithersburg, MD 20879; ba/Same; c/Peter S, Erika A Chandran; p/Bertha E Judd, Philadelphia, PA; ed/BA, Temple Univ, 1953; MA, Am Univ, 1959; PhD, Univ of MD, 1974; mil/Capt, AUS, 1953-55; pa/Tchr 1955-61, Admr & Pupil Pers Wkr 1962-84, Montgomery Co Public Schs; Current Instr, Univ of VA; Clin Mem, Am Assn of Marriage & Fam Therapists; Fellow, Am Orthopsychi Assn; Fellow, Intl Assn of Pupil Pers Wkrs; Cert'd Sex Cnslr, Am Assn of Sex Edrs, Cnslrs & Therapists; r/Mennonite; hon/ Editor, *Jour of the Intl Assn of Pupil Personnel Wkrs*; W/W in E.

JUMALON, MARILYN LILA oc/ Executive and Administrator; b/Nov 27, 1943; h/Box 61A St Peters Church Road, Waldorf, MD 20601; ba/Clinton, MD; c/Ernesto V II, Christopher T; ed/ AA, Mgmt, Charles Co Commun Col, 1979; pa/Supvr of Loan Dept 1968-73, Br Mgr of Clinton Ofc & Sr Bkg Ofcr 1973-81, 23mm Deposits Adm Supvr & 2nd VP of 10 Br Ofcs 1981-, Equitable Bk; Nat Assn of Bk Wom Inc, 1974-, Secy 1975-76, VChm 1976-77, Chm 1977-78, Ed and Tng Chm 1979-82; BPW Clbs Inc, 1976-, Treas 1980-81, Pres-Elect 1981-82, Pres 1982-83; Prince George Co Bd of Trade, 1976-, Treas 1982-83; r/Prot; hon/Pub, "Finances-Fair Credit Rules & the Wom," 1981; *Wall Street Jour* Awd, Upon Grad from Charles Co Commun Col, 1979.

JUNG, GARY BRUCE oc/Executive; b/Nov 23, 1939; h/425 Ena Road, Apartment 1001B, Honolulu, HI 96815;

ba/Honolulu, HI; m/Leslie E Reile; p/Col and Mrs Gordon C Jung, Charleston, WV; ed/Att'd, CO St Col 1957-59, George Wash Univ 1967, Univ of HI 1973-74; mil/AUS, 1960-62; pa/Sales Mgr, Collier Corp, 1962-66; Computer Programmer, Fed Govt, 1966-68; Pers Dir, Control Data Corp, 1968-70; Owner, Kono Kai Enterprises, 1970-77; Owner and Pres, Diversified Financial Planning Inc, 1977-82; Pres and CEO, E A Buck Planning Sers Inc, 1982-; Nat Assn of Underwater Instrs, 1970-79; Innerspace Pacifica, Exec Dir 1975-77; Intl Assn for Financial Planning, 1980-, VP of HI Chapt 1981-82, Pres 1982-83, 1983-84; cp/Mayor's Water Safety Com, 1976; HI Coun of Dive Clbs, Pres 1977; HI C of C; r/Prot; hon/Financial Planning: The Future is Now" 1983; Outstg Mem of the Yr, Intl Assn for Financial Planning, HI Chapt, 1982-83; W/W in W.

JUNG, LYNNETTE CLAIR oc/Chief of Mental Health Clinic; b/Aug 7, 1940; h/505 2nd Avenue, North, Glasgow, MT 59230; ba/San Francisco, CA; p/ Joseph L Jung (dec); Mr and Mrs Herb Friedl, Glasgow, MT; ed/BA, Col of St Catherine, 1961; MSW, Univ of UT Sch of Social Wk, 1965; Post-Master's, 2 Yr Prog in Grp Psychotherapy, Psychi Inst, 1977; mil/Active Duty (Maj), AF, 1974-; pa/Chief, Mtl Hlth Clin, USAF Hosp, Osan AB, Korea, 1982-; Dir, Human Devel Prog, Lowry AFB & Dir of Sexual Dysfunction Clin, Fitzsimons Army Med Ctr, 1979-82; Psychi Social Wkr, Malcolm Grow USAF Hosp, Andrews AFB, 1974-79; Team Chief, Monterey Co Soc Sers, 1973-74; Conslt, Child Wel & Staff Devel, CO Dept Social Sers, 1968-73; Psychi Soc Wk, CA Dept of Mtl Hygiene, 1965-68; BPW; Nat Assn of Social Wkrs; Acad of Cert'd Social Wkrs; Am Grp Psychotherapy Assn; Am Orthopsychi Assn; Am Chd's Soc; Soc of AF Social Wkrs; r/Cath; hon/Pub, "Diagnostic Divorce, Co-Ldr Impotence" in *Jour of Grp Studies*, 1976-77; Valedictorian, Glasgow HS, 1957; BA w Hons; Pi Gamma Mu, Nat Social Sci Hon; AF Commend Medal; Meritorious Ser Medal; W/W of Am Wom; World's W/W of Wom.

JUST, FAYE JORDAN oc/Business Co-Owner; b/Jun 6, 1925; h/Oxnard, CA; ba/2790 Sherwin Avenue, #10, Ventura, CA 93003; m/Virgil Louis; c/ Babetta, Sandra, Audrey; p/Neadham Guice (dec) and Ethel Doude Jordan, Woodland Hills, CA; ed/Engrg Student at Var Times, Univ of CA-LA & Univ of So CA, 1943-63; AA in Mech Engrg, Pierce Col, 1965; BSBA (Opers Res) & Math, Univ of CA-Northridge, 1969; pa/Loftswom, Flying Wing, Northrope Aircraft, 1943-45; Rockwell Intl, 1947-70, Sr Res Engr, Rocket Engines; Co-Owner, Just Marine Engrg Conslts, 1972-77; Co-Owner, Just Enterprises (Antique Restoration Bus), 1977-; r/ Prot; hon/Author, Many Classified Documents for the Aerospace & Assoc'd Mil Orgs; W/W of Am Wom.

JUST, VIRGIL LOUIS oc/Antique Conservator and Restorer; b/Mar 27, 1925; h/3850 Harbor Boulevard, Oxnard, CA 93030; ba/Ventura, CA; m/ Faye Jordan; c/Adrienne, Wesley, Brian, Kevin, Randy; p/Louis and Anna Just (dec); ed/BSME, 1949; mil/WWII Pilot, Navy; pa/Rocket Engines Test Engr (Prog Mgmt), Rocket Engines Sys Engrg Mgr, Rocket Engines & Water Jet Engines, Rockwell Intl, 1949-77; Co-Owner, Just Enterprises, Restoration & Conserv of Antiques, 1977-; cp/ Topanga Water Sys; Topanga C of C, Var Ofcs; Active in Topanga Affairs, 1950-71; r/Prot; hon/Author, Num Articles on Sailing, Tech Data for Rockwell Intl.

PERSONALITIES OF AMERICA

K

KADABA, PANKAJA KOOVELI oc/ Research Associate; b/May 15, 1928; h/ 3411 Brookhaven Drive, Lexington, KY 40502; ba/Lexington; m/Prasad; c/Lini; p/Subramani and Mangalamma (dec); ed/BS, MS, PhD, Univ Delhi; pa/Univ KY, Col Pharm, Res Assoc 1968-80, Asst Prof 1980-83, Assoc Prof 1983-; Assoc Prof Chem, Morehead St Univ, 1965-66; Christian Brothers Col, 1966-68; Res Assoc, Brown Univ, 1957-60; Guest Scholar, Univ KY, 1954-55; Fulbright Fellow, Univ WI, 1953-54; Am Chem Soc; Intl Soc Heterocyclic Chem; Res Organic Chem: 1, 2, 3-Triazolines, Chem Reaction Mechanisms & Synthesis of Heterocycles, 1, 3-Cycloaddition Reactions, Role of Protic & Dipolar Aprotic Solvents; cp/ Lexington Art Leag; r/Hindu; hon/NIH Grant Drug Devel, 1982-85; Chp, Ninth Intl Cong Heterocyclic Chem, 1983; Sigma Xi Res Hon; Fulbright-Smith Mundt Fellow, 1953-54; Visit'g Scist Univ Ljubjana, Yugoslavia; Holds Several Patents; Author Num Res Pubs Profl Jours; Am Men & Wom Sci; Personalities of S; DIB; World W/W Wom; Intl W/W in Ed; W/W: of Wom in Ed, in Tech Today.

KAFKA, MARIAN STERN oc/Physiologist, Neuroscientist; b/Mar 30, 1927; h/7834 Aberdeen Road, Bethesda, MD 20014; ba/Bethesda; m/John S; c/David Egon, Paul Henry, Alexander Charles; p/Adele L Stern, Richmond, VA; ed/BA 1948, PhD 1952; pa/Physiol, Biol Psychi Br, NIMH, 1974-; Physiol, Hypertension-Endocrine Br, Nat Heart Lung Inst, 1968-74; Hlth Sers Postdoct Fellow, Endocrinology Br, Nat Heart & Lung Inst, 1965-68; Res Asst, Dept Int Med, Yale Univ Sch Med, 1954-57; Res Asst, IL Neuropsychi Inst, Univ IL Sch Med, 1953-54; Res Asst, Dept Physiol Chem, Emory Univ Sch Med, 1952-53; Am Physiol Soc; Endocrine Soc; Biophy Soc; Soc Neurosci; AAAS; Am Physiol Soc, Cent Com, Public Info Com; Public Info Com, FASEB; Pres, NIMH-NINCDS Assem Scists; NIMH, Sci Dir Conf Com, Clin Res Review Com; hon/Mod Lang S'ship, Tchrs Fgn Langs Richmond (VA) Public Sch Sys, 1944; Phi Beta Kappa, 1948; Marie J Mergler F'ship Physiol, Univ Chgo, 1950; Sigma Xi, Univ Chgo, 1952; Author Num Papers Sci Jours, Book Chapts; W/W: in E, of Am Wom, of Wom, in Technol Today; Biogl Lib Soc; Intl Scholars Dir; Two Thousand Wom of Achmt; Personalities of S; DIB; World W/W in Commun Ser; Am Men & Wom Sci.

KAHLENBERG, MARY HUNT oc/ Dealer in Antique and Ethnographic Textiles; h/1424 North Ogden Drive, LA, CA 90046; ba/Same; m/Rob Coffland; ed/Grad Study: Art Inst Chgo 1965-66, Master Sch Craft Berlin 1964-65, Berlin Acad Fine Arts 1963-64, Austrian Acad Applied Arts Vienna 1962-63; Undergrad Study: BA Art Hist, Boston Univ, 1961-62; Scandinavian Sem Denmark 1960-61, Simmons Col Boston 1958-60; pa/Pres, Textile Arts Inc, 1978-; Curator, LA Co Mus Art, 1968-78; Vis'g Lectr, CA St Univ-Fullerton, 1977; Vis'g Lectr, Univ CA-LA, 1975; Asst Curator, Textile Mus, Wash DC, 1967-68; Conserva-

tionist, Textile Conserv Centre London, 1966-67; Instr, Textile Design, Univ of TN, 1965; hon/IBM Fellow, Aspen Design Conf, 1981; Author *Walk in Beauty: The Navajo & Their Blankets* 1977, *A Book About Grass: Its Beauty & Uses* 1982; Author Num Catalogs; W/W: of Am Wom, in Am Art, in W; Contemp Authors; World W/W of Wom; Personalities Am.

KAHN, LISA oc/Professor; b/Jul 15, 1924; h/4106 Merrick, Houston, TX 77025; ba/Houston; m/Herbert Finkelstein; c/Peter Kahn, Beatrice Villarroel; ed/PhD, Univ Heidelberg (Germany), 1953; pa/TX So Univ, Pt-time Asst Prof to Prof; AATG; WAGS; SGAS; SCOLT; SCMLA; MLA; German Texan Heritage Soc; Intl PEN, London; r/Jewish; hon/Pubs, *In Her Mother's Tongue* 1983, *David am Komputer* 1982, *Utahs Geheimnisse* 1981, Num Others; Smith-Mundt S'ship, 1951-52; Res Awd, TX Intl Consortium, 1976; Pub Grant, Inst Fgn Relats, Stuttgart, 1978; NEH Grant Ethnic Langs, 1981; Alexander von Humboldt Stipend, 1982-83; Pub Grant, Inter Nations, 1983.

KAHN, SANFORD RICHARD oc/ Associate Professor; b/Jul 24, 1940; h/ 3413 Osage Avenue, Cincinnati, OH 45205; ba/Cinc; p/Harry Jack and Jean Passman Kahn, Cinc; ed/BBA 1962, MBA 1963, PhD 1967, Univ Cinc; pa/ Univ Cinc, Assoc Prof Acctg 1971-, Dept Chp Bus & Commerce Dept 1969-72, Asst Prof Acctg 1968-71, Instr Acct 1966-68, Grad Tchg Asst 1965-66; Auditor, Frat Purchasing Bd Univ Cinc, 1979-82; Alumni Mem: Alpha Kappa Psi, Beta Alpha Psi; Fac Advr, 504 Clb; Yavneh Day Sch, Bd Mem 1975-83, VP Pers 1981-82; Fac Rep Ctr Bd, Univ Cinc, 1978-83; hon/Pubs, "The Accts Guide to Computer Sys," "Duties & Liabilities of Public Accts,""Acctg & Fed Regulation," *Choice Mag*, Num Others; Presented Num Lectures & Spchs.

KAINER, JAMES EDWARD oc/Pharmacy Manager; b/Jul 13, 1949; h/2827 Glenn Lakes, Missouri City, TX 77459; ba/Houston, TX; m/Rami Jean; c/Matthew Kainer, Paige Renfro; p/Mr and Mrs Edward Kainer, Victoria, TX; ed/ AA, Victoria Col, 1969; BS Pharm, Univ Houston, 1972; pa/Pharm Mgr, Sav-On Drugs Katy Fwy, 1978-; Staff Pharm, Sav-On Drugs Westheimer, 1976-78; Hd Pharm, St Joseph's Triangle Pharm, 1972-76; cp/Life Mem, Houston Livestock Show & Rodeo Assn; Univ Houston Cougar Clb; Taxi Squad & Couger Cagers; TN Squire; r/Rom Cath; hon/ Sav-On Drugs, Reg Pharm Mgr Yr 1981, Pharm Mgr Yr 1982.

KAISER, CHARLES FREDERICK oc/ Associate Professor; b/Dec 30, 1942; h/ 1416 Birthright Street, Charleston, SC 29407; ba/Charleston; m/Judy; c/ Edward, Michael; p/Alexander and Etta Kaiser (dec); ed/BS Psych 1964, MA Psych 1967, City Col CUNY; PhD Psych, Univ Houston, 1972; pa/Col Charleston, Assoc Prof Psych 1977-, Asst Prof Psych 1972-77; Adj Asst Prof, Dept Phy Med & Rehab, Med Univ SC, 1981-; Pres, Charleston Psychol Assn, 1979; Treas, SC Psychol Assn, 1979-81; Biofeedback Soc SC, Co-Fdr, Pres 1981-; Mbrship Com, Biofeedback Soc Am, 1983-84; Am Psychol Assn; SEn Psychol Assn; cp/Former Bd Mem, SC Lung Assn; Charleston Mtl Hlth Assn;

r/Jewish; hon/Pubs, of a Short Form of the Multiscore Depression Inventory," *Jour Cnsltg & Clin Psych* 1983, "Differences Between Gifted Adolescents & Their Peers on a Measure of Self-Actualization," *Resources in Ed* 1981, Num Others; W/W: in S & SW, in Biobehavioral Scis.

KAISER, PHILIP MAYER oc/Political Consultant; b/Jul 12, 1913; h/2101 Connecticut Avenue Northwest, Washington, DC 20008; m/Hannah Greeley; c/Robert Greeley, David Elmore, Charles Roger; p/Morris Baird Kaiser (dec); ed/BA, Univ WI, 1935; BA, MA, Oxford Univ, 1939; pa/Ret'd Ambassador, Austria 1980-81, Hungary 1977-80; Mem Bd, Guiness Mahon, 1975-77; Chm & Mng Dir, *Ency Britannica* Intl, London, 1969-75; Min, Am Embassy London, 1964-69; Ambassador, Senegal & Mauretania, 1961-64; Prof Intl Labor Relats, Am Univ, 1959-61; Spec Asst, Gov NY, 1955-58; Labor Advr, Comm for Free Europe, 1953-54; Asst Secy of Labor Intl Affairs, 1949-53; Dir, Ofc Labor Affairs, Dept Labor, 1947-49; Exec Asst to Asst Secy of Labor, 1946-47; Bd of Ec Warfare, 1942-46; Economist, Bd Govs Fed Resv Sys, 1939-42; Bd Dirs, Am Pitchley, F D R Foun; Bd Govs, Weizmann Ins; Mem Coun Fgn Relats; r/Jewish; hon/Pubs, *Hist Makers: Woodrow Wilson* 1973, *Gt Ideas Today: Old Prob & New In Intl Relats* 1976; Phi Beta Kappa, 1935; Rhodes Scholar, 1935; W/W: in Am, in World; Intl W/ W.

KALMAN, GABOR J oc/Research Professor; b/Dec 12, 1929; h/357 Clinton Road, Brookline, MA 02146; ba/ Chestnut Hill, MA; m/Suzana; c/A Ron, Katalin; p/Geza Kalman, Budapest, Hungary; Ilona Kalman (dec); ed/Dipl EE 1952, DSc 1961; pa/Res Prof Physics, Boston Col, 1970-; Exch Prof, 1976; Vis'g Prof Physics, Brandeis Univ, 1966-70; Dir, Res Ctr, Nat de la Recherche Sci, France, 1965-67; Prof Assoc, Univ Paris, 1961-65; Lectr, Technion, Israel Inst Technol, 1957-61; Res Scist, Ctl Res Inst Physics, Budapest, 1952-56; Dir, Adv'd Study Inst, NATO, 1966, 1977; Expert AF Cambridge Res Labs, 1966-67; Harvard Univ, Assoc Ctr Astrophysics 1973-77, Vis'g Scist 1974; Vis'g Fellow, Jt Inst Lab Astrophysics, Univ CO, 1965-66; Res Dir, Intl Ctr Theoretical Physics, Trieste, 1981; Vis'g Scist, Obs of Paris, Meudon, France, 1973-74; Groupe de Recherches Ionospheriques, Orleans, France 1974, Oxford Univ 1975; Fellow, NY Acad Scis; r/Jewish; hon/Pubs, "Nonlinear Effects in Plasmas" 1957, "Stongly Coupled Plasmas" 1978, Num Articles, Contbns to Sci Jours; Am Men & Wom Sci; W/W: in E, in Frontier Sci & Technol; Men Achmt; Intl W/W of Intells; Commun Ldrs & Noteworthy Ams; Intl Book of Honor; Five Thousand Personalities of the World; DIB.

KAMIENIECKI, SHELDON oc/Professor; b/Jan 29, 1952; h/Westminster, CA; ba/Department of Political Science, University of Southern California, Los Angeles, CA 90089-0044; m/Elizabeth Sanasarian; p/Joseph and Rachel Kamieniecki, Brooklyn, NY; ed/BA 1974, MA 1976, PhD 1978, Dept Polit Sci, SUNY-Buffalo; pa/Univ So CA, Asst Prof 1981-, Dir Social Sci Data Lab 1981-, Grad Advr 1982-83; CA St

335

Col-San Bernardino, Asst Prof 1978-81, Coor Paralegal Studies Prog 1979-82, Fac Conslt & Instr Computer Ctr 1979-81; SUNY-Buffalo, Instr 1977-78, Tchg Asst 1976-77, Co-Proj Dir 1978, Proj Dir 1977-78; Col Rep, Col Social Sci Res & Instrnl Counc, 1978-81; Col Rep, Inter-Univ Consortium for Polit & Social Res, 1978-; Am Polit Sci Assn; MW Polit Sci Assn; Policy Studies Org; Wn Polit Sci Assn; Exec Bd, So CA Fdn Scists; hon/BA magna cum laude; Pubs, "Open & Closed Sys of Decision Making: The Case of Toxic Waste Mgmt," *Public Adm Review* 1984, "Are Social Class Measures Interchangeable?" *Polit Behavior* 1984, "Congruence Between Public Opinion & Congl Actions in Energy Issues, 1973-1974," *Energy Sys & Policy* 1983, Num Others; Num Profl Papers, Conf Participation, Book Reviews, Consultations, Res Presentations; NY St Regent's S'ship, 1970-74; SUNY-Buffalo, Albert Ziegele S'ship 1973-74, Grad Res Asst'ship Dept Polit Sci 1974-76, Grad Res Asst'ship Survey Res Ctr 1975; SUNY-Buffalo Envir Studies Ctr, Rockefeller Foun F'ship 1976, 1977, 1978, Ford Foun F'ship 1976-77, Argonne Nat Lab Grant 1978; Haynes Foun Fac F'ship, Univ So CA, 1982.

KAMINE, CHARLES S oc/Attorney at Law; b/Nov 4, 1952; h/8450 Arborcrest Drive, Cincinnati, OH 45236; ba/Cincinnati; m/Darlene M; c/Elida B; p/Martin and Mildred Kamine, Denver, CO; ed/BA, Brandeis Univ, 1973; JD, Univ Denver Col Law, 1975; pa/Asst Atty Gen, St OH, 1982-; Atty at Law, 1978-; Assoc, Beckman, Lavercombe, Fox & Weil, 1976-77; Cinc Bar Assn, 1976-; Chm, Yg Lwyrs Sect, 1981-82; Chm, Real Property Law Com, 1982-; Mem Exec Com, 1981-82; OH St Bar Assn, 1976-; ABA, 1977-; Bd Mem, Am Judic Soc; cp/Bd Mem, Comprehensive Commun Child Care; Bd Mem, Courtyard Lrng Ctr; hon/BA cum laude; Pubs, "Copyright Law- Copyright of Fraudulent Mats," *Denver Law Jour 1974*, "A Guide for the Lwyr Who'd Just About Rather Die Than Probate," *Cinc Bar Assn Report 1981, Probate Law 1979-82;* Nathan Burke Awd, Univ Denver, 1975.

KAN, HENRY oc/Engineering Supervisor; b/Oct 10, 1921; h/1666 34th Avenue, San Francisco, CA 34122; ba/SF; m/Linda; c/John, Grace; p/S Y Kan and W H Li (dec); ed/BS Mech Engrg, Nat Sun Yat-Sen Univ (China), 1945; ME Mech Engrg, City Col NY, 1967; MBA, Golden Gate Univ, 1976; pa/Bechtel Petro Inc, Proj Engr, Engrg Supvr Petro & Nuclear Projs, 1969-; Adm Mgr, Foremost Dairies Taiwan Ltd 1967-69; Taiwan Sugar Corporaton, Supt Steam Powerplant, Dist Chief Engr, Asst to VP; ASME; Mem Adv Bd, Am Security Coun; cp/Treas, Bechtel Toastmaster Clb; Mem Repub Congl & Senatorial Coms; r/Elder, Golden Gate Reformed Ch; hon/Profl Engr; Contbg Editor, Tech Handbook Taiwan Sugar Industs; Cit Excellent Perf, Min Economic Affairs, ROC, 1956; Men Achmt; W/W in W; DIB.

KANARKOWSKI, EDWARD JOSEPH oc/Corporate Communications Executive; b/May 5, 1947; h/132 Yellowbank Road, Toms River, NJ 08753; ba/Roseland, NJ; m/Carol Ann Miller; c/Edward, Kelly Ann, Paul,

Karen, Kevin; p/Mr and Mrs Joseph Kanarkowski, Highlands, NJ; ed/BA, St Peter's Col, 1969; mil/AUS, 1969-73, Capt; Currently Maj, ANG; pa/Automatic Data Processing Inc, Dir Corporate Communs 1983-, Mgr Corporate Communs 1978-83, Staff Writer 1977-78; Assignment Writer, *Daily & Sunday Register*, 1975-77; Corporate Communs Conslt, 1973-75; cp/Life Mem, Third US Inf Marne Div Assn; Assoc Mem, NJ Mil Acad; Mem, NYC Chapt, IABC; Mem, NG Assn US; r/Rom Cath; hon/Pubs, Over 300 Articles *Daily & Sunday Register*, 1975-77; "Massiah vs US- The Warren Court's Showdown W Our Right to Counsel" 1969; Army Commend Medals, 1971, 1972 & 1973; AUS Expeditionary Force Medal, 1971-72; IABC Achmt Medal, 1979; W/W: in Fin & Indust, in E; Men of Achmt.

KANE, RICHARD oc/Corporate President; b/Sep 5, 1928; h/5 Kenneth Court, Kings Point, NY 11024; ba/New York, NY; m/Racquel; c/Brandi, Cindi; ed/Univ MO; City Col NY; mil/AUS, 1951-53, Psychol Warfare; pa/Pres, Marden-Kane Promotion Co Inc, 1958-; S J Reiner Co, 1955-58; Rodale Mfg Co, 1953-55; WNEW NY, 1948-50; PMAA; NIPSE; MCEI; cp/Friars Clb; hon/Var Pubs Promotional Field; W/W: in E, in Am.

KANE, WILLIAM EVERETT oc/Merchant Banker, Financial Strategist, International Attorney; b/Aug 12, 1943; h/63 La Rancheria, Carmel Valley, CA 93924; ba/LA, CA; c/William Everett, Katherine Elizabeth; p/Hon Coty Everett Kane, Lake Blackshear, GA; ed/BA, Princeton Univ, 1966; BS, Woodrow Wilson Sch Intl Affairs, 1966; LLB, JD, Yale Law Sch, 1970; Cert, Fac Law Univ Madrid, 1964; Univ So CA-LA, Postgrad Studies Genetic Engrg 1978, Computer Scis 1975-78; mil/Baylor Mil Sch, 3rd Army; pa/CEO, Cal Fed Syndications, 1982; Pres & Chm Bd, K & K Properties Inc, 1975-82; Pres & Chm Bd, Kane & Kelly Assocs Inc, 1975-; Sr Ptnr, Kane & Keilly 1975-79; Dir & Chief Overseas Div, First Nat Fin Corporation, 1973-75; Fdr & Gen Mgr, Continental IL Ltd, 1971-73; Legal Counsel Asia, Citicorp Leasing Intl, 1971-72; Assoc, Graham & James, 1970-71; Assoc, Cavelier, Venegas, & Esquerra, 1966-67; Fac Instr, Nat Univ Colombia, 1966-67; Staff Conslt, Inst Def Anal, 1964-66; Proj Dir Latin Am, Proj Camelot US Govt, 1965; CA St Bar Assn, 1971; ABA, 1971; Intl Bar Assn, 1975; Am Soc Profl Strategists, Mem 1965-, Pres Four Yrs; cp/Colonial Clb; Princeton Clb; Pacheco Clb; hon/Pubs, *Civil Strife in Latin Am* 1972; Bd Editors, *Yale Law Jour*, 1968-70; Editor, *Burning Water* 1965-66; Bus Mgr, *Nassau Lit Mag*, 1965-66; Columnist, *Daily Princetonian*, 1965-66; Var Monographs & Articles in Fields of Ec & Strategic Scis; W/W; Am Authors; Intl Bkrs Guide.

KANEKO, RYOJI LLOYD oc/Instructional Technologist; b/Apr 11, 1951; h/906 Torrance Boulevard, #5, Redondo Beach, CA 90277; ba/El Segundo, CA; p/Hayao and Yoshiko Kaneko, Monterey Park, CA; ed/BA Eng/Creative Writing, CA St Univ-Long Bch, 1974; Profl Designation Tng & Human Res, Univ CA-LA, 1984; pa/Tng Admr, Hughes Aircraft Co- EDSG, 1980-; Supvr/Tng Instr, Teledyne- Geotronics,

1975-80; Music/Marching Instr, Third Generation Drum & Bugle Corps, 1973-75; Am Soc Tng & Devel, Mem, Editor *LA Interchange Newslttr* 1982-; cp/Intl Assn Quality Cirs, 1983-; All-Am Judges Assn, 1973-; Wn Sts Judges Assn, 1983-; Freelance Correspondent, *Drum Corps News*, 1973-; *Prospector Yrbook* 1972; r/Var Depts First Christian Ch; hon/Outstg Contbn Awd, ASTD-LA, 1983 & 1984; Ath Lttr in Rowing, CA St Univ-Long Bch, 1974; Golden Press Card Awd, 1972; W/W in W.

KANET, ROGER EDWARD oc/Professor and Head of Department of Political Science; b/Sep 1, 1936; h/1007 South Victor Street, Champaign, IL 61821; ba/Urbana, IL; m/Joan Alice Edwards; c/Suzanne Elise Zelle, Laurie Alice Kanet; p/Robert G Kanet, Cinc, OH; ed/PhB, Berchmanskolleg, Pullach-bei-Muenchen, Germany, 1960; AB, Xavier Univ, 1961; MA, Lehigh Univ, 1963; AM 1965, PhD 1966, Princeton Univ; pa/Univ IL, Prof Polit Sci 1978-, Hd Dept Polit Sci 1984-, Assoc Prof Polit Sci 1973-78; Jt Sr Fellow, Columbia Univ Res Inst Communist Affairs & Russian Inst, 1972-73; Univ KS, Asst Prof Polit Sci 1966-69, Assoc Prof 1969-73; Am Assoc Advmt Slavic Studies; APSA; Intl Com Soviet & E European Studies; Intl Studies Assn; Intl Polit Sci Assn; MW Polit Sci Assn; MW Slavic Conf; hon/Editor & Author Num Pubs; Univ IL, Campus Awd Excellence Undergrad Tchg 1981, Polit Sci Awd Excellence Undergrad Tchg 1984; Men & Wom Distn; DIB; W/W: of Am, in MW, in World; Am Men & Wom Sci; Contemp Authors; Commun Ldrs & Noteworthy Ams; Personalities of W & MW; Men Achmt; Biogl Roll Hon.

KANG, MANJIT SINGH oc/Geneticist, Plant Breeder; b/Mar 3, 1948; h/1221 Bacom Point Road, Pahokee, Florida 33476; ba/Belle Glade, FL; m/Georgia Anna Crocker; p/Gurdit S and Parminder K Kang, Ludhiana, India; ed/BA Agri, 1968; MS Plant Genetics, 1971; MA Botany, 1977; PhD. Crop Sci Genetics & Plant Breeding, 1977; pa/Asst Prof Plant Genetics, Univ FL Agri Res & Ed Ctr, 1981-; Res Assoc Agronomy, Univ MO-Columbia, 1980; Cargill Inc, Res Sta Mgr 1979, Sr Plant Breeder Hybrid Corn Res Sta 1977-78; Res Assoc, Ctr Biol Natural Sys WA Univ, 1977; Grad Res Asst, Agronomy Dept Univ MO-Columbia, 1977; So IL Univ-Carbondale, Preceptor Plant & Soil Sci 1972-74, Res Asst 1971-72; Tchg Asst Biol Sci, So IL Univ-Edwardsville, 1969-71; AAAS; Am Soc Agronomy; Crop Sci Soc Am; Am Genetic Assn; Am Soc Sugar Cane Technols; Sigma Xi; Gamma Sigma Delta; hon/Several Pubs in Field of Plant Genetics & Breeding Var Sci & Profl Jours; BS Honors; India Coun Agri Res Merit S'ship, 1964-68; Preceptorship, 1972-74; W/W in S & SW; Personalities of the S.

KANIA, RICHARD ROMAN EDWARD oc/Assistant Professor of Justice Administration; b/Mar 9, 1947; h/PO Box 18824, Greensboro, NC 27419; ba/Greensboro; m/Lynne Catherine Mercier; c/Stephanie Anne; p/Joseph F and Hedwig B Majewska Kania, Delray Bch, FL; ed/BA, FL St Univ, 1968; MA 1974, PhD 1982, Univ VA; mil/

AUS, 1968-72; USAR, Major; pa/Asst Prof, Guilford Col, 1982-; Edr, Univ NC-Charlotte, 1980-82; Sr Public Safety Planner, Jefferson Planning Dist, 1976-79; Police Ofcr, Charlottesville, VA, 1974-76; Acad Crim Justice Scis; Am Acad Polit & Social Scis; Am Anthropological Soc; Am Soc for Ethnology; Am Sociological Assn; Assn for Polit & Legal Anthropology; Soc Applied Anthropology; r/Rom Cath; hon/Num Pubs on Applied Anthropology, Sociol, & Crim Justice; BA Hons; Grad Student Writing Prize, So Anthropological Soc, 1980; Res Fellow, Ofc NC Gov, 1980-81; W/W in S & SW.

KANTROWITZ, ADRIAN oc/Heart Surgeon; b/Oct 4, 1918; h/70 Gallogly Road, Pontiac, MI 48055; ba/Detroit, MI; m/Jean Rosensaft; c/Niki, Lisa, Allen; p/Rose and Bernard A Kantrowitz (dec); ed/BA, NY Univ, 1940; MD, St Univ NY Med Sch, 1943; Internship, Jewish Hosp Bklyn NY, 1944; mil/AUS, 1944-46, Major Med Corps; pa/Sinai Hosp Detroit, Chief Sect Cardiovas Surg 1978-83, Chm Dept Cardiovas Thoracic Surg 1973-78, Chm Dept Surg 1970-73; Maimonides Med Ctr, Dir Surg Sers 1964-70, Att'd Surg 1955-70, Dir Cardiovas Surg 1955-64; Consltg Surg, Good Samaritan Hosp, 1954-55; Asst Vis'g Surg, Flower, Metro, Bird S Coler, Morrisania Hosps, 1952-55; Asst Resident Surg, Mt Sinai Hosp NY, 1947; Montefiore Hosp NY, Adj Surg 1951-55, Asst Res Surg Pathol, Chief Res Surg, 1948-50; Prof Surg, Wayne St Univ Sch Med 1970, SUNY 1955-70; Adj Prof Physics, Oakland Univ Col Arts Scis, 1976-; Instr Surg, NY Med Col, 1952-55; Tchg Felow Physiol, Wn Res Univ Sch Med, 1951-52; Num Edit Appts Profl Jours, Res Appts, Profl Accreditations; Acad Surg Detroit; AAUP; Am Col Cardiol; Am Col Chest Phys; Am Col Surgs; Am Heart Assn; AMA; Am Physiol Soc; Num Others; hon/Cleveland Awd, 1981; Hon Mem, La Sociedad Dominicana de Cardiologia, 1980; Mordecai Ben David Awd, Yeshiva Univ, 1978; Pres Cabinet Awd, Univ Detroit, 1972; Num Others; Holds Five Patents; Nearly 200 Profl Pubs; Nearly 100 Abstracts Pub'd; Over 20 Chapts in Books; Profl Exhibs, Films; Dir Med Spec; W/W: in Am, in E, in Am Ed, in Artificial Organ Res; Ldrs Am Sci; Am Men of Med; DIB; Current Biog; Nat Register Prom Ams & Intl Notables.

KAO, RACE LI-CHAN oc/University Educator; b/Dec 1, 1943; h/812 Haverton Drive, St Louis, MO 63141; ba/St Louis; m/Lidia Wei Liu; c/Elizabeth C, Grace W; p/Yu-Ho and Tsing Tsou Kao, Taipei, ROC; ed/BS, Nat Taiwan Univ, 1965; MS 1971, PhD 1972, Univ IL; mil/ROTC of ROC, Second Lt; pa/Asst Prof Dept Surg, Wash Univ, 1982-; Univ TX Med Br, Asst Prof Dept Surg, Physiol & Biophysics 1977-82, Dir Cardiothoracic Res 1977-82; Asst Prof, Dept Physiol, Hershey Med Ctr; Am Physiol Soc; Am Heart Assn; Intl Soc Heart Res; Nat Soc Med Res; NY Acad Sci; AAAS; cp/Nutrition Today Soc; Pres, Univ TX Chinese Assn, 1981; r/Christian; hon/Over 40 Pubs, Articles in Fields of Myocardial Metabolism Under Ischemia, Anoxia, & Hypertrophy, Protection of Ischemic Myocardium, Regulation of Isolated Cardiomyocyte

Metabolism; Sch'ship Nat Taiwan Univ, 1962-65; Liaopei S'ship, 1961-65; Fellow, Am Heart Assn, 1975; W/W in S & SW.

KAPLAN, ALAN M oc/Professor and Department Chairman, Microbiology and Immunology; b/Dec 10, 1940; h/3434 Brandon Drive, Lexington, KY 40502; ba/Lexington, KY; m/Eva; c/Ali Michelle; p/Albert J Kaplan (dec); Esther Kaplan, Miami, FL; ed/BS, Tufts Univ, 1963; PhD, Purdue Univ, 1969; Postdoct Fellow, Univ Toronto, 1969-72; pa/Prof & Chm Dept Microbiol & Immunol, Univ KY Col Med, 1982-; Res Dir, Cancer Ctr, 1980-82; Med Col VA/VA Commonwlth Univ, Dpty Chm Dept Microbio 1981-82, Prof 1979-82, Assoc Prof 1975-74, Asst Prof Depts Surg Microbiol 1972-75; NY Acad Sci; Am Soc Microbiol; Am Assn Immunol; Am Assn Cancer Res; Am Assn Microbiol; Chm, Intl Soc Immuno Pharm; Sigma Xi; AAAS; Reticuloendothelial Soc; Soc Exptl Biol & Med; r/Jewish; hon/Pubs, Over 100 Articles Profl Jours, Over 100 Abstracts Presented at Reg, Nat & Intl Meetings; Outstg Med Col VA Grad Fac Mem Awd, 1978; Postdoct F'ship Med Res Coun CA, 1969-72; Am Men of Sci; W/W in S & SW.

KAPLAN, JOSEPH M oc/Safety Council Association Administrator; b/May 29, 1914; h/8871 Saint Ives Drive, Los Angeles, CA 90069; ba/LA; m/Henrietta; c/Paul Dana, Drew Allan; ed/BA, Univ CA-LA; Grad, Bur Street Traffic Res Harvard Grad Sch Traffic Engrg, 1938; mil/AUS, WW II; pa/Gtr LA Chapt Nat Safety Counc, Assoc 1939-, Pres 1979-; Past Dir, So CA War Manpower Conserv Prog; Nat Chm, Conf St & Local Safety Orgs; Am Soc Safety Engrs; Inst Traffic Engrs; Nat Assn Exposition Mgrs, So CA Indust Safety Soc; CA Assn Safety Couns; Pres, Vets Safety Intl, 1976; cp/Bd Dirs, March of Dimes; Rotary; Bd Councilors, Inst Safety Sys Mgmt, Univ So CA; hon/Conslt, White House Conf on Traffic Safety; Am Soc Assn Execs, Chartered Assn Exec, Key Awd 1974; First Cert'd Hazard Control Mgr, Master Level, Intl Hazard Control Mgr Cert Bd, 1983; Annual Awd Hon, Assn Safety Couns, 1973; Assn Exec Yr, So CA Soc Assn Execs, 1979; W/W in Am; Commun Ldrs & Noteworthy Ams.

KAPLAN, PETER L oc/Psychologist; b/Jan 24, 1949; h/1417 Beech Court, Ft Collins, CO 80521; ba/Ft Collins, CO; m/Helen; c/Ben, Joshua; p/Marvelle and Seymour Kaplan, Miami, FL; ed/AA 1968, BS 1970, Univ of FL; MA, FL Atl Univ, 1973; PhD, CO St Univ, 1977; pa/Vis'g Asst Prof, Univ of Brit Columbia, 1977-78; Vis'g Asst Prof, CO St Univ, 1978-83; Staff Psychol, Larimer City Mtl Hlth Ctr, 1980-82; Pvt Pract, 1980-84; AAAS; Am Psychol Assn; Sigma Xi; r/Jewish; hon/Postdoct Fellow, Nat Inst of Neurol, Communicative Diseases & Stroke, 1978-80; W/W in W.

KAPLAN, RICHARD ALAN oc/Defense and Strategic Affairs Specialist; b/Mar 20, 1951; h/4500 South Four Mile Run Drive, Apartment 823, Arlington, VA 22204; p/Murray M (dec) and Beatrice R Kaplan; ed/AA, Canada Col, 1973; BA 1975, BA 1976, MA 1981, San Francisco St Univ; Att'd, Univ of London King's Col, 1978-80; Grad, Indust Col of the Armed Forces 1976,

Nat Def Univ 1984; ISODARCO, Univ of Rome, 1980; mil/USA, 1968; pa/Mng Editor, *Jour of Contemp Revolutions*, 1974-76; Mng Editor, *New Labor Review*, 1976-78; Rschr, Dept of War Studies, Univ of London King's Col, 1978-80; Def & Strategic Affairs Spec, 1980-; Intl Inst for Strategic Studies; Royal U Sers Inst for Def Studies; Fgn Assoc, Royal Inst of Intl Affairs; Assoc, Intl Inst of Humanitarian Law, US Strategic Inst; US Naval Inst; AF Assn; Assn of the USA; Life Mem, Am Def Preparedness Assn; Nat Adv Bd, Am Security Coun, 1978-; US Cong Adv Bd, 1982-; Brit Atl Com, 1978-; Am Soc of Intl Law; Am Fgn Law Assn; Intl Inst of Air & Space Law; Am Br, Intl Law Assn (Appt'd to Com on Armed Conflict of the Am Br of the Intl Law Assn 1982, & to the Com on Intl Terrorism 1983); Appt'd Nat Def Exec Reservist by Fed Emer Mgmt Agy, 1983; Appt'd to Appeal Bd of Selective Ser Sys; hon/Author, *An Interdisciplinary Study of the Intl Law of Armed Conflict*, 1981; Phi Alpha Theta; Delta Tau Kappa; Pi Sigma Alpha; Fellow, Royal Geog Soc; Fellow, Inter-Univ Sem on Armed Forces & Soc, Univ of Chgo; 2 Certs for Outstg Achmt, US Congl Adv Bd; Cert of Apprec, 5th Spec Forces Grp, AUS, 1982; 2 Certs of Apprec, Fed Emer Mgmt Agy, 1983; Jane's W/W: Aviation & Aerospace, in W.

KAPLAN, STEVEN SAMUEL oc/Lawyer, Director of Legal Services; b/May 20, 1944; h/44 Joseph Place, Wayne, NJ 07470; ba/Little Falls, NJ; m/Anita Safran; c/Staci Michelle, Jennifer Robyn; p/Irving Kaplan, Ft Lee, NJ; Rose Kaplan, Wayne, NJ; ed/BA, NY Univ, 1966; JD, IN Univ Sch of Law, 1969; pa/Asst Passaic Co Prosecutor, 1969-74; Contract Atty, NJ Ofc of Public Defenders, 1974-76; Pvt Practitioner, 1974-; Dir of Legal Sers, Local 464 Prepaid Legal Ser Benefit Fund, 1976-; NJ St Bar Assn, 1970-; ABA, 1969-; Passaic Co Bar Assn, 1970-80; Am Prepaid Legal Ser Inst, Charter Mem 1974-; Nat Resource Com for Consumers of Legal Sers, 1975-; cp/Chm, W Paterson Bd of Adjustment, NJ, 1969-70; r/Jewish; hon/W/W in E.

KAPPA, MARGARET McCAFFREY oc/Director of Housekeeping; b/May 14, 1921; h/The Greenbrier, White Sulphur Springs, WV 24986; ba/Same; c/Nicholas Joseph, Christopher Francis; ed/Ext Courses, Univ of MN 1944, 1945, NY Univ 1947; BS, Hotel Mgmt, Cornell Univ, 1944; Dale Carnegie Course, 1978; pa/Asst to Exec Housekeeper, Kahlen Hotel, 1944; Exec Housekeeper, St Paul Hotel, 1944-47; Exec Housekeeper, Plaza Hotel, 1947-51; Exec Housekeeper & Pers Mgr, Anderson House, 1951-52; Resident Mgr, Housekeeper, Pers Dir, Athearn Hotel, 1952-58; Asst Mgr in Charge of Housekeeping 1958-76, Dir of Housekeeping 1976-84, The Greenbrier; Consltg Tchr of Housekeeping, Soviet Union 1968, Hannover (W Germany) & Singapore 1973, The Bahamas 1975, Aruba 1980, Other Places; Pres, NY Chapt, Nat Exec Housekeepers Assn, 1950-51; Pres, Cornell Soc of Hotelmen, 1981 (First Wom Pres Since 1925); Charter Mem, Greenbrier Co Quota Clb Intl; cp/VP, St Charles Borromeo Parish Assn, 1982-83; White Sulphur Sprgs Woms Clb; Assoc Mem, C of C;

White Sulphur Sprgs Beautification Com, City Coun; r/Cath; hon/Pubs, "Latest Housekeeping Techniques" 1970, "Happy Looks for Instnl Interiors" 1974, "Developing a Successful Relat-'ship w Your Interior Designer" 1974, "Org-Housekeeping is the Heart of It" 1982; Hon Life Mem, NY Hotel & Restaurant Soc; Dipl of Hon, Nat Soc Culinaire Philanthropique, 1961; W/W of Am Wom; World W/W of Wom; Personalities of S; Dir of Dist'd Ams.

KARDON, JANET oc/Institute Director; ba/University of Pennsylvania, 34th and Walnut Streets, Philadelphia, PA 19104; m/Robert; c/Nina, Leroy, Ross; p/Mrs Shirley Stolker Frieberg; ed/BS, Ed, Temple Univ; MA, Art Hist, Univ of PA; pa/Lectr, Gwynedd Mercy Col, 1967; Lectr 1968-75, Dir of Exhbns 1975-78, Phila Col of Art; Dir, Inst of Contemp Art, Univ of PA, 1978-; US Commr, Venice Biennale, 1980; Conslt Panelist, Nat Endowment for the Arts, 1975-; Visual Arts Panel Mem 1978-, Spec Projs Panel Mem 1978-, PA Coun on the Arts; Am Assn of Art Mus Dirs, 1980-; Panel Mem, Mus Sem, Balto Mus of Art 1981-; hon/Author, Var Pubs; Helena Rubenstein F'ship in Mus Studies, Whitney Mus of Am Art, 1975; Res Grant for Feasibility Study for Nat Documentation Ctr, Nat Endowment for the Arts, 1978.

KARPEN, MARIAN JOAN oc/Financial Executive; b/Jun 16, 1944; p/Cass John (dec) and Mary Jay Karpen; ed/AB, Vassar Col, 1966; Postgrad, Sorbonne, Paris; MBA Prog, NY Univ Grad Sch of Bus, 1974-77; pa/Sr VP & Prin 1977-, Nat Mgr of the Retail Mun Bond Dept, Pvt Investors Sers Grp 1977-79, A G Becker Paribas; VP & Mun Bond Coor, Faulkner Dawkins & Sullivan, 1976-77; Acct Exec, Oppenheimer & Co 1975-76; Blyth Eastman Dillon 1973-75; Nationally Syndicated Newspaper Columnist & Photojournalist, Queen Features Syndicate, 1971-73; Fashion Editor, *Boston Herald Traveler*, 1969-71; Lectr & TV Commentator, 1969-71; Paris Fashion Editor, *WWD*, Fairchild Pubs, 1968-69; TV & Radio Commentator, Capital Cities Netwk, 1968-69; Other Previous Positions: Edit Bd, "Retirement Planning Strategist," Newsletter Mgmt Corp; Reg'd Rep w NYSE & NASD; Pres's Clb, A G Becker Paribas; Wom's Ec Roundtable; Am Soc of Profl Exec Wom; Eng Spkg Union; cp/Skating Clbs of NY & Boston; Vassar Clb of NY; Friend Vol of Whitney Mus of Am Art; hon/Author, Num Articles & Photos in Newspapers & Mags World-Wide, 1966-; Lectures/Sems on Investmts, 1978-; Var Jour Awds & Achmts; Cit Winner, FL Met World Sailfish Tour, 1983; W/W: in World, in Fin & Indust, in E, of Am Wom; World W/W of Wom; Commun Ldrs of Am; DIB; Contemp Personalities; Personalities of Am.

KARPICKE, JOHN ARTHUR oc/Systems Engineer; h/1152 Ivy Lane, Indianapolis, IN 46220; ba/Indianapolis, IN; m/Susan G; c/Jeffrey Denyes; p/Mr and Mrs Herbert A Karpicke, Sebring, FL; ed/BS, MI St Univ, 1972; PhD, IN Univ, 1976; mil/USN, Vietnam Vet; pa/Postdoct Fellow, Psychobiol Res Grp, FL St Univ, 1976-77; Asst Prof, Valparaiso Univ, 1977-81; Mem Tech Staff, Bell Labs, 1981-83; Sys Engr, AT&T Con-

sumer Prods, Consumer Prods Labs, 1983-; AAAS; Am Voice Input/Output Soc; NY Acad of Scis; hon/Author Articles in Jours incl'g *Jour of Exptl Analysis of Behavior, Animal Lrng & Behavior, Jour of Exptl Psychobiol: Animal Behavior Processes, The Psychol Record*, 1973-80; Bell Labs & AT&T Articles, 1981-84; Gen Psychol Intro Wkbooks, 1979, 1982; NIH Fellow, 1976; NIMH Grantee, 1979; Hon Mem, Delta Theta Phi Law Frat, 1978; W/W in Frontier Sci & Technol.

KARRAS, CIRIPOMPA DONNA oc/Dental Hygienist; b/Aug 1, 1951; h/3673 South Lewiston Street, Aurora, CO 80013; ba/Aurora, CO; m/Donald George; p/George and Eleanor Nyles Ciripompa, Wheeling, WV; ed/AB/BS, Dental Hygiene, W Liberty St, 1973; MA, Commun Hlth, WV Univ, 1978; Cert'd EMT, Univ of SD, 1980; Instr of CPR; pa/Dental Hygienist, Dr Guiliani, 1973-78; Asst Prof/Assoc Chair, Dept of Dental Hygiene, Univ of SD, 1979-82; Migrant Hlth Prog, 1982; Dental Hygienist, Dr N Engel, Dr J Green, 1982-; WV Dental Hygiene Cont'g Ed, Chair 1976-79, Pres-Elect 1979; Am Dental Hygiene Assn, 1973-; SD Dental Hygiene, 1979-82, Newslttr Editor; Clay Co Ambulance Dept; EMT Assn; Nat EMT Assn; SD EMT Assn; Univ Senate, 1980-82; Am Assn of Dental Schs; Col Dental Hygiene Assn, Del to St Conv; r/Greek Orthodox; hon/Outstg Ser Awd, Clay Co Ambulance Dept, 1982; W/W of Am Wom.

KARWOSKI, RICHARD CHARLES oc/Professor of Art, Practicing Painter and Printmaker; b/Oct 3, 1938; h/28 East 4 Street, New York, NY 10003; ba/Brooklyn, NY; ed/BFA, Pratt Inst, 1961; MA, Columbia Univ, 1963; pa/Prof of Art, NYC Tech Col of CUNY, 1969-; Art Admr & Designer, Simon & Schuster Book Co, 1968-69; Art Editor, *Fam Circle* Mag, 1966-67; Bd of Dirs, NY Artists Equity Assn Inc, 1982-; Adv Bd, HS of Art & Design, 1977-; Chm, Alumni Assn, Art & Design HS, 1977-; Gallery Dir, Grace Gallery, NYC Tech Col, 1970-81; Nat Arts Clb; Art Wk in Pvt & Public Collections throughout the US, incl'g, The Newark Mus, OK Art Ctr, TN Fine Art Ctr, The Wichita Mus, The Heckscher Mus, Guild Hall Mus, Butler Inst of Am Art, Detroit Art Inst, Everhart Mus, AR Fine Art Ctr, The Helen Foresman Spencer Mus of Art, The Everson Mus; r/Cath; hon/Watercolor Page in *Am Artist* Mag, 1979; Review, *The NY Times*, 1980; Purchase Awd, Prints, USA, 1982; Commencement Spkr, Art & Design HS, Avery Fisher Hall, 1979; W/W: in Am Art, in E.

KAST, GLORIA E oc/International Library Consultant; h/4600 Robertson Avenue, Sacramento, CA 95821; ba/Same; m/Clifton I; c/Carrie M Harmon, Gloria E Bale; p/Louis R Meder (dec); Carrie E Kolb (dec); ed/BA, Webster Col; MA in Lib Sci, St Louis Univ; pa/Col Libn, Grant Tech Col, Am River Col; Chief Area Libn, McClellan AFB; Adm Libn, Am Univ, Cairo, Egypt; Prof of Lib Sci, Universidad de Antioquia, Medellin, Colombia; Res & Devel Sci Info Ofcr, Winban, En Caribbean; Sr Lectr, Fulbright Scholar, Bogota, Colombia; hon/AAUW; Smith-Munot Awd; Fulbright Res Grant; Fulbright Scholar

& Lectr; Rockefeller Grantee.

KASTL, JOHN D oc/Optometrist; b/Apr 8, 1951; h/PO Box 810, Mannford, OK 74044; ba/Same; m/Barbara Darlene Simpson; c/Jill Lynn; p/Franklin Leon Kastl Sr, Tulsa, OK; Launis Pamelia Kastl (dec); ed/BS, NEn OK St Univ, 1973; OD, Univ of Houston, 1977; Postgrad Wk, Tulsa Univ, 1973; Cert in Respiratory Therapy, Univ of Chgo, 1974; pa/Respiratory Therapist, St John's Hosp 1969, St Francis Hosp 1973, St Luke's Hosp 1976, TX Chd's Hosp 1976, TX Heart Inst 1976; Pvt Pract of Optom, 1978-; EMT, Mannford Ambulance Sers; CPR Instr for Am Heart Assn; Am & OK Optometric Assns; cp/Pres, Mannford Bd of Ed; Pres, Creek Co Sch Admrs Assn; Bd of Dirs, Golden Age Sr Citizen Housing Auth; Bd of Trustees, Mannford Public Lib; Mannford C of C; Mannford Lions Clb; Mannford Round-Up Clb; r/Meth; hon/Nat Student Register; W/W: on Am Col & Univ Campuses, in S & SW; Personalities of S.

KASWER, BARBARA ANNE oc/Registered Nurse; b/Dec 22, 1939; h/50 Maryanne Lane, Stamford, CT 06905; ba/Stamford, CT; p/Stanley J and Irene E Kaswer, Stamford, CT; ed/Nsg Dipl, 1960; CCRN, 1982; Currently Enrolled in BSN Prog; pa/Staff Nurse, Med/Surg, 1960-65; Sr Charge Nurse, ICU/CCU, 1965-71; Hd Nurse, ICU/CCU, 1971-81; Staff Devel Fac-Instr, 1981-; Am Assn Critical Care Nurses, 1971-; Cath Nurses Assn; Am Cancer Soc, 1982-; r/Cath; hon/Editor, Hosp Staff Newspaper, "Info-Mat," 1981-.

KASZNIAK, ALFRED WAYNE oc/Clinical Neuropsychologist, Associate Professor; b/Jun 2, 1949; h/7630 North Chapalla Place, Tucson, AZ 85704; ba/Tucson, AZ; m/Mary Ellen Beaurain; c/Jesse B, Elizabeth B; p/Ann Kaszniak, Niles, IL; ed/BS 1970, MA 1973, PhD in Clin Psych 1976, Univ of IL-Chgo; Internship, Clin Neuropsych, Rush Med Col & Hosps, 1973-74; pa/Instr 1974-76, Asst Prof of Psych 1976-79, Rush Med Col; Asst Prof of Psychi (Neuropsych) 1979-82, Assoc Prof of Psychi (Neuropsych) 1982-, Univ of AZ-Tucson; Chm, Patient Sers, Bd of Trustees, So AZ Chapt, Nat MS Soc, 1980-82; Med & Sci Adv Bd, Nat Alzheimer's Disease & Related Disorders Assn, 1981-; Bd of Dirs, Tucson Chapt, Alzheimer's Disease Assn, 1982-; AZ Hd Injury Foun; hon/Author of Articles in *Annals of Neurol* 1978, *New Eng Jour of Med* 1979, *Cortex* 1979, 1980, 1981, 1982, *Neurol* 1979, 1981, *Neurosurg* 1981, *AZ Med* 1982, *Jour of Clin Neuropsych* 1983, Several Others; Res F'ship, Gerontological Soc of Am, 1980; Dist'd Contbn Awd for Dissertation Res, Div 20, Am Psychol Assn, 1978; W/W: in W, in Biobehavioral Scis; DIB.

KATSH, ABRAHAM I oc/University President Emeritus, Professor Emeritus; b/Aug 10, 1908; h/45 East 89th Street, New York, NY 10028; m/Estelle Wachtell; m/Maskell Ethan, Salem Michael, Rochelle Senna; ed/BS 1931, MA 1932, Dr of Jurisp 1936, NY Univ; Grad S'ship Student, Islamic Inst of Princeton Univ, 1941; PhD, Dropsie Col for Hebrew & Cognate Lng, 1944; Hon Dr of Hebrew Lttrs, Hebrew Union Col-Jewish Inst of Rel, 1964; Other Hon Degs: DD, Spertus Col 1970, DD, Univ of Dubuque 1971, LLD, Lebanon Val Col 1971, LLD, Dropsie Univ 1976, DHL, Villanova Univ 1977; pa/Lectr, Prof of Hebrew Culture & Ed, Prof of Hebrew & Near En Studies, Dist'd Prof of Res, Dir of Inst of Hebrew Studies, Current Prof Emeritus, NY Univ; Pres, Dist'd Res Prof, Current Pres Emeritus, Dropsie Univ; hon/Author, *Biblical Heritage of Am Democracy* 1977, *Kaplan Diary* 1973, Others; Recip of Num Grants; Charles Kramer Res Fellow, Inst for Jewish Policy Planning & Res, Synagogue Coun of Am; Mordecai Ben David Dist'd Awd, Yeshiva Univ; Avodah Awd, Jewish Tchrs Assn, NY; Nat Bd of Lic Awd for 2 Decades of Chmship; Num Other Hons.

KATZ, J LAWRENCE oc/Chairman of Department of Biomedical Engineering; b/Dec 18, 1927; h/838 Maxwell Drive, Schenectady, NY 12309; ba/ Troy, NY; m/Gertrude Seidman; c/ Robyn Laurie, Andrea Lee, Talbot Michael; p/Frank and Rose Katz; ed/BA 1950, MS 1951, PhD 1957, Physics, Polytechnic Inst of Bklyn; mil/Electronic Tech's Mate 2nd Class, Navy, 1946-48; pa/Chm of Dept of Biomed Engrg 1983-, Prof of Biophysics & Biomed Engrg 1972-, Rensselaer Polytechnic Inst; Prof of Surg, Albany Med Col, 1977-; Vis'g Prof of Biomechs, Chengdu Univ of Sci & Technol, 1982; Vis'g Prof of Biophysics & Biomed Engrg, Instituto de Fisica e Quimica de Sao Carlos, Universidade de Sao Paulo, 1978; E Leon Watkins Vis's Prof, Wichita St Univ, 1978; Vis'g Biophysicist, Dept of Orthopaedics Res, Chd's Hosp, 1978-80; Vis'g Lectr on Orthopaedics, Harvard Univ Sch of Med, 1978-80; Dir, Ctr for Biomed Engrg, Rensselaer Polytechnic Inst, 1974-82; Other Previous Positions; Nat Res Coun's Res Assoc'ship Panel on Life Scis, 1982-; US Nat Jt Com on Biomechs, 1983-; Edit Adv Bd, *Jour of Mats Sci*, 1979-; Am Soc of Mech Engrs; Assn for the Advmt of Med Instrumentation; Other Mbrships; cp/Prog Adv Bd, Albany CP Ctr for the Disabled, 1982-; hon/Author, Num Pubs; Sigma Xi; Sigma Pi Sigma; NSF Foun Sci Fac Fellow; Guggenheim Fellow, 1978; Patent Awd'd; Other Hons.

KATZ, SUSAN A oc/Poet, Teacher; b/Dec 3, 1939; h/12 Timothy Court, Monsey, New York, NY 10952; m/ Donald I MD; c/David Lawrence, Elizabeth Cheryl; p/Edward M and Selma Stark Arons (dec); ed/BFA, OH Univ, 1961; pa/Former Ins Agt, Med Secy; Full-time Writer/Tchr of Poetry; Appt'd, Poets in the Schs Inc Prog Rdg Panel; Invited Participant, Rockland Commun Coun Vis'g Writers Series, 1978-79; Invited to Read Poems at Libs & Cols; Conducted Poetry Wkshops for Finkelstein Meml Lib, Sprg Val Sr Citizen Writing Prog, The Alms House Poets of Rockland Co, Wellsprg Poetry, & Other Indep Adult & Yg-Adult Writing Grps; Active in NY St Poets in the Schs Inc Prog; Former Tchr, Mktg Poetry Course, Rockland Commun Col; Poems Have Appeared in the Following Pubs: *Manhattan Poetry Review* 1983, 1984, *Home Planet News* 1983, *Song: The Music of Free Verse* 1981, *Smackwarm: A Lit Review* 1982, *Maelstrom Review* 1981, *Urthkin* 1979, 1980, Num Others; Poems Have Appeared in the Following Anthologies: *Lyrical Treasures-Classic & Modern* 1983,

Loss of Chd Anthology 1984, *The Mother's Death Anthology* 1984; hon/Walt Whitman Awd Finalist for Book-Length Poetry Collection, *A Falling From Grace*, 1980; White Mtn Press Poetry Awd, 1981; Henry V Larom Awd, 1976; Elected to Poetry Soc of Am; Fellow, Intl Acad of Poets, 1981; Mushroom Poetry Awd, 1982; Other Hons; Dir of Am Poets; Intl W/W in Poetry; World W/W of Wom; Intl Register of Profiles.

KATZMAN, HAROLD oc/Teacher, Salesman; b/Jul 26, 1954; h/1504 West Rosewood Court, Ontario, CA 91762; ba/Ontario, CA; p/Mr and Mrs Jack Katzman, Ontario, CA; ed/BS, Geol, CA Polytechnic Univ, 1977; pa/Tchr, Chaffey Jt Union HS Dist, 1978-; Sales Assoc, Broadway Dept Store, 1982-; Lectr 1978-79, Tchr/Lab Asst 1973-77, Earth Sci Dept, CA Polytechnic Univ; VP, CA Polytechnic Univ Alumni Assn, 1981-83, Bd Mem, 1978-; cp/Pomona Val Coin Clb, VP 1976, Pres 1977, Secy 1976-77, 1983; Upland Coin Clb, VP 1979, Pres 1982-83; Bear Gulch Rock Clb, VP 1981-82; Numismatic Assn of So CA, Recording Secy 1982-83; CA St Numismatic Assn, Local Publicity Chm 1982; San Bernardino Co Coin Clb; Redlands Coin Clb; Covina Coin Clb; W End Opera Assn; r/Jewish; hon/ Mem of CA Polytechnic Univ Nat Model UN Team That Won Best Del Awd, 1977; Recip, First Place Awds for Numismatic Exhibs at Numismatic Assn of So CA Conv, 1983; Recip, Assoc'd Students Inc Senator of the Yr Awd, 1975-76; Outstg Grad'g Sr, Earth Sci Dept, CA Polytechnic Univ, 1977; Student Govt Ldr of the Yr, 1979; W/ W Among Students in Am Univs & Cols; Outstg Yg Men in Am.

KAUFMAN, FRANK ALBERT oc/ United States District Judge; b/Mar 4, 1916; h/Brooklandville, MD; ba/United States Courthouse, Baltimore, MD 21201; m/Clementine Alice Lazaron; c/ Frank Albert, Peggy Ann; p/Nathan Hess and Hilda Hecht Kaufman; ed/AB, summa cum laude, Dartmouth, 1937; LLB, magna cum laude, Harvard Univ, 1940; pa/Atty, Ofcs of Gen Counsel Treas, Lend Lease Adm & FEA, 1941-42, 1945; Lend Lease Rep, Turkey, 1942-43; Bur Chief, Psychol Warfare, AFHQ & SHAEF, 1943-45; Assoc, Firm of Frank, Skeen & Oppenheimer, 1945-47; Ptnr, Firm of Frank, Bernstein, Conaway, Kaufman & Goldman, 1948-66; US Dist Judge, MD, 1966; Lectr, Univ of Balto 1948-62, Univ of MD 1953-54; Chm, Gov of MD's Comm to Study Sentencing Crim Cases, 1962-66; Goucher Col, 1957-; Am, MD, Balto & Fed Bar Assns, 1945-; Bd of Govs, ABA, 1982-; Phi Beta Kappa, 1937-; Num Past Mbrships; cp/ Rule Day, Wranglers, Law Roundtable.

KAVELIN, JOHN HOWARD oc/ Show Designer; b/Jan 7, 1944; h/4321 Los Feliz Boulevard, #303, Los Angeles, CA 90027; ba/Glendale, CA; p/Mr H Borrah Kavelin, Haifa, Israel; ed/MFA, Brandeis Univ, 1970; BFA, Carnegie Tech, 1965; mil/AUS, Spec Sers/Entertainment, 1966-67; pa/Art Dir for TV Shows, incl'g, *Close Ties & Richard Pryor Burn Fund Telethon*; Asst Art Dir for TV Shows, incl'g, *Bob Newhart Special II, Sanford*; Designer, "The Wild Ride of Mr Toad," Fantasyland '83, Walt Disney Prodns; Chm of the Bd, Light Yrs Intl,

1980-83; Co-Host, *The Spiritual Revolution*, a 26 Wk Series on the Baha'i Faith; r/Baha'i Faith; Chm, Spiritual Assem of the Baha'is of LA, 1982-; hon/ Drama-logue Awd, Set Design for *Close Ties*, LA Public Theatre, 1982; W/W/in W.

KAYE, LORI oc/Lecturer, Author, International Consultant, Actress; b/ Jun 19, 1941; ba/Molori Publications, 11684 Ventura Boulevard, Suite 134, Studio City, CA 91604; p/Eldin Bert and Katherine Angeline Varkulas Onsgard; ed/Att'd, Univ of NM 1958-60, Detroit Inst of Art 1956-57; pa/Pres, Molori Pubs, 1979-; Pres, KLM Advtg, 1979-; Intl Conslt, Nat Dir of Admission, A&T Inst of Travel & Tourism, 1982-83; Intl Conslt, Acad Pacific, 1981; Intl Conslt, Glendale Col of Bus & Paramed, 1980; Sch Dir, Caroline Leonetti Ltd, 1975-79; Owner-Pres, Lori Kaye Cosmetics, 1965-73; Sales Dir 1964-70, VP, Owner, Dir & Reg Dir 1962-73, Spch & Drama Instr 1960-73, John Robert Powers; Actress, Warner Brothers Studio, 1960-64; Radio & TV Commls, 1960-83; Other Previous Positions; Nat Assn of Female Execs, 1981-83; Screen Actors Guild, 1960-; Am Fdn of Radio & TV Artists, 1961-; cp/Nat Geographic Soc, 1956-82; hon/Author, Num Pub'd Wks in Self Devel, Sales, Mgmt.

KAZEK, GREGORY JOSEPH oc/ Engineering Project Manager; b/Oct 26, 1947; h/14 Oakledge Road, Swampscott, MA 01907; ba/Salem, MA; m/ Deanne Joan; c/Gregory Joseph Jr, Geoffrey Stanley, Rachel E; p/Stanley Kazek, Wickliffe, OH; ed/BS in Physics, Case Inst of Technol, 1968; MS, Physics, John Carroll Univ, 1971; PhD in Elect Engrg, Case Wn Resv Univ, 1974; mil/ USMCR; pa/Engr, Sr Engr, Res Physicist, Gen Elect Co, 1969-79; Sr Proj Engr, Reliance Elect Co, 1979-83; Current R&D Engrg Proj Mgr, GTE Prods Corp; Am Phy Soc; IEEE; Illuminating Engrg Soc; hon/Contbr, Num Articles to Profl & Tech Jours; Patentee, Radiation Dominated Gaseous Conductors as Lighting Sources & Circuit Components; IR100 Awd, 1971; W/W: in Frontier Sci & Technol, in World.

KAZOR, WALTER ROBERT oc/ Engineering Manager; b/Apr 16, 1922; h/1120 88th Avenue, North, St Petersburg, FL 33702; ba/Tampa, FL; m/Gloria Rosalind Roma; c/Steven, Christopher, Kathleen; p/Steven S (dec) and Josephine Kazor, Avonmore, PA; ed/BS, Mech Engrg, PA St Univ, 1943; MS in Mech Engrg 1953, MLttrs 1957, Univ of Pgh; mil/Lt, USN, 1944-46; pa/Res Engr, Gulf Oil Corp, 1946-57; Mfg Engr 1957-63, Mgr of Quality Assurance 1963-71, Reliability Engrg Mgr 1971-77, Mgr of Quality Assurance, Breeder Reactor Proj 1977-81, Engrg Mgr of Mfg Nuclear Ser Facility 1981-, Westinghouse Elect Corp; ASME; ASQC; cp/BSA, Bd of Dirs 1958-63; Pres, Lions Clbs, 1960-61, 1977-78; Pres, Ath Clbs of Rancho HS, 1965-66, 1970-71; r/Cath; hon/Author, Recent Tech Papers in Applied Stats 1982, and Non-Destructive Testing 1981; Patent in Robotics, 1976; Mil, Philippine Liberation Medal, 1945; W/W in S & SE.

KEATON, LORAS oc/Social Studies Teacher; h/223 Chestnut Street, Southwest, Atlanta, GA 30314; ba/ Canton, OH; p/Mrs Delores Miller,

Canton, OH; ed/BS, 1974; MA, 1980; pa/Tchr, Canton City Schs Bd of Ed, 1974–; Leila Green Edrs Coun, Parliamentn 1981-82; Canton Profl Ednl Assn, 1974-82; NEA, 1974-82; OH Ed Assn, 1974-82; ECOEA, 1974-82; r/Prot; hon/Canton Commun Ser Awds, 1980, 1981.

KEATON, MOLLIE M oc/Social Studies Teacher; h/50 Chestnut Southwest, Atlanta, GA 30314; ba/Canton, OH; p/Mrs Delores Miller, Canton, OH; ed/BS, 1974; MA, 1980; pa/Tchr, Canton City Bd of Ed, 1974–; Canton Profl Ednl Assn, 1974-82; NEA, 1974-82; OH Ed Assn, 1974-82; ECOEA, 1974-82; Leila Green Ed Coun, VP 1981-82; r/Prot; hon/Tchr of Month, Canton City Schs, 1981; Canton Commun Ser Awds, 1980, 1981.

KEEHN, NEIL FRANCIS oc/Executive; b/Oct 24, 1948; h/2603 Third Street, Santa Monica, CA 90405; ba/Santa Monica, CA; p/Russell E and Mary L Keehn, Phoenix, AZ; ed/BS 1970, MSEE 1970, AZ St Univ; pa/Mem of Tech Staff, Technol Ser Corp, 1972-74; Mem of Tech Staff, Hughes Aircraft, 1974-77; Assoc Prog Mgr, TRW Inc, 1977-79; Mgr, Adv'd Concepts, Mil Space Sys Div, Sci Applications Inc, 1979-80; Pres, Strategic Sys Scis, 1980–; IEEE, VChm of Aerospace Def Panel 1972-76, Chm 1976-79; VChm of Tech Prog at Winter Conv 1974; AIAA; US Strategic Inst; Intl Inst of Strategic Studies; r/Cath; hon/Author, "Impact & Utilization of Space Force Structures in a Protracted Strategic Conflict: A Net Assessment" 1980, Num White Papers on Adv'd Concepts for Space/Missile Force Structure Planning & Devel; Outstg Ser Cit, 1974 IEEE Winter Conv; Outstg Ser Cit, IEEE Aerospace and Electronic Sys Grp, 1977; W/W: in W, in Frontier Sci & Technol, in Aviation & Aerospace, in World; Personalities of W & MW.

KEEN, MARY L oc/Real Estate and Property Management; b/Jan 8, 1937; h/4220 Cranbrook Drive, Powell, TN 37849; ba/Oak Ridge, TN; m/Hampton C; c/Michael, Mark; p/Roger Pope, Colquitt, GA; ed/Real Est Courses, Att'd, Univ of TN; pa/Re-examination Clk, Knoxville Devel Corp, 1971-76; Receptionist and Secy, Bull Run Oil Co, 1976-77; Mgr, Properties, M&M Properties, 1977-80; Loan Correspondent, Am Midland Inc, 1980-81; Shearson/Am Express, 1981-82; Real Est & Property Mgmt, Chris Power Inc, Cent 21, 1983–; Am Bus Wom of Cumberland Belle, VP 1979; Zeta Nu; Beta Sigma Phi, Recording Secy, VP 1981-82; r/Bapt; hon/W/W in S & SE; World W/W of Wom.

KEENAN, MARY STEWART oc/Hotelier, Executive; b/Jan 19, 1931; h/PO Box 2766, Yountville, CA 94599; ba/Yountville, CA; m/Robert Millard; c/Deborah Jean, Valerie Lynn, Robert Stuart, Ralph Edward; p/Richard Alexander Stewart (dec); Lulua Dell Stewart Gillespie, Napa, CA; ed/Att'd, Pacific Union Col Acad, Univ of OR, Napa Col; pa/Pres, Burgundy House Antiques, Burgundy House Hotel, Burgundy House Inc, Bordeaux House Hotel, Property of Calistoga Cellars; Am Hotel & Motel Assn; Am Motel Assn; cp/Napa C of C, Wom's Div; hon/Coverage in Over 75 World Newpapers, Books &

Mags, incl'g, *Glamour, Bon Appetit, Classic Country Inns of Am, The Anchorage Times, Golf, Travel & Leisure, The Times* (London), *House & Garden;* TV Coverage; Upper Napa Val Assn Awd of Merit for Restoration; W/W: in CA, of Am Wom.

KEENE, RUTH FRANCES oc/Supply Systems Analyst; b/Oct 7, 1948; h/4916 West Pinchot Avenue, Phoenix, AZ 85031; ba/APO, NY; p/Seymour and Sally Keene, Phoenix, AZ; ed/BS in Math, AZ St Univ, 1970; MS, Mgmt Sci, Fairleigh Dickinson Univ, 1978; pa/Inventory Mgmt Spec, AUS Electronics Command, 1970-74; Inventory Mgmt Spec, AUS Communs & Electronics Mat Readiness Command, 1974-79; Chief, Inventory Mgmt Div, Crane Army Ammunition Activity, 1979-80; Supply Sys Analyst, HQs, 60th Ordnance Grp, Zweibruecken, W Germany, 1980–; Assn for Computing Machinery, 1966–; Federally Employed Wom, 1974–; Soc of Logistics Engrs, 1976–; AAAS, 1979–; Nat Assn for Female Execs, 1979–; AAUW, 1979–; Soc of Profl & Exec Wom, 1980–; Am Soc for Public Adm, 1981–; Assn of Info Sys Profls, 1981–; cp/NOW, 1978–; r/Jewish; hon/Outstg Perf Awd, AUS Electronics Command, 1973; Letter of Apprec, AUS Communs & Electronics Mat Readiness Command, 1978; Lttr of Commend, Crane Army Ammunition Activity, 1980; W/W: of Am Wom, in W, of Am Wom; Dir of Dist'd Ams; Book of Hon.

KELLERMANN, KENNETH IRWIN oc/Astrophysicist; b/Jul 1, 1937; h/Box 2, Green Bank, WV 24944; ba/Green Bank, WV; m/Henny; p/Alexander Kellermann (dec); ed/SB, MIT, 1959; PhD, CA Inst of Technol, 1963; pa/Asst Scist 1965-67, Assoc Scist 1967-69, Scist 1969-78, Sr Scist 1978–, Asst Dir 1977, Nat Radio Astronom Observatory; Dir, Max Plank Inst Radio Astronomy, 1978-80; Res Assoc 1969, Fairchild Fellow 1981, CA Inst of Technol; Intl Astronom Union, Chm Radio Astronomy 1983-84; Intl Union Radio Sci, Chm of Radio Astronomy 1976-78; r/Jewish; hon/Editor, *Galactic & Extragalactic Radio Astronomy, VLBI & Compact Radio Sources;* NSF Fellow, 1966; Warner Prize, AAAS, 1971; Nat Acad of Sci Gould Prize, 1973; Am Acad of Arts & Scis Rumford Prize, 1970; W/W.

KELLOGG, BRUCE MICHAEL oc/Real Estate Investor; b/Jan 3, 1947; h/PO Box 18966, San Jose, CA 95158; ba/San Jose, CA; m/Diane Linda; c/Jeremy, Catherine, Michael, Elizabeth; p/Harlan and Hilma Kellogg, North Plainfield, NJ; ed/BSEE, Rutgers Col, 1969; MBA, Golden Gate Univ, 1976; pa/Real Est Investor, San Jose, CA, 1973–; Securities Investor, Wilmington, NC, 1970-73; pa/Tri-Co Apt Assn, 1976–; CA Apt Assn, 1976–; Nat Apt Assn, 1976–; Nat Multihousing Coun, 1982–; San Jose Bd of Rltrs, 1982–; CA Assn of Rltrs, 1982–; Nat Assn of Rltrs, 1982–; r/Cath; hon/Pub, "Computer Comparison of Systems for Commodity Trading" in *Commodity Jour Mag,* Jul 1972, Jan 1973, Mar 1973; W/W: in CA, in W.

KELLY, JAMES FRANCIS JR oc/Training and Development Manager; b/Nov 18, 1930; h/3403 Kennelworth Lane, Bonita, CA 92002; ba/San Diego, CA; m/Charlane Agnes Hughes; c/Terrence Porterfield, Robina Erin, Carisa Ann; p/Mrs James F Kelly, New

Haven, CT; ed/BS in Ed, So CT St Univ, 1952; MS in Mgmt, US Nav Postgrad Sch, 1966; Prog for Mgmt Devel, Harvard Univ Grad Sch of Bus, 1971; mil/USN 1952-83, Comm'd Ensign 1953, Adv'd through Grades to Capt 1973, Commanded 3 Ships (Pacific Fleet) 1969-80, Asst Chief of Staff, Commanded Nav Surface Force (US Pacific Fleet) 1978-80, Cmdg Ofcr of Navy Pers Res & Devel Ctr 1980-83, Ret'd Capt 1983; pa/Joined Gt Am Fed Savs Bk; Harvard Bus Sch Alumni Assn; US Nav Inst; US Navy Leag; Am Soc for Tng & Devel; Bd of Dirs, Gtr San Diego Indust-Ed Coun; Free-Lance Writer; cp/Harvard Clb of San Diego; Lions Clb of San Diego; Westwood Country Clb; r/Rom Cath; hon/Contbr of Articles to Profl Jours; Regular Columnist for *Navy Times,* 1978–; Essayist, 1984 *Nav Review;* Author of the Yr, US Nav Inst Proceedings, 1979; 2 Awds of Legion of Merit, 1973, 1983; Bronze Star, 1970; Navy Commend Medal, 1968; W/W in W.

KELLY, JEAN NEWTON oc/Executive; b/Jun 13, 1938; h/314 Minnesota Street, Lantana, FL 33462; ba/West Palm Beach, FL; m/Kevin E; c/Greg, Geof, Stefanie; p/Dorothy B McCormick, Lantana, FL; ed/BS, Univ of RI, 1960; pa/Copywriter, WMTW, 1967-69; Prodn Asst, WEAT, 1969-71; Copywriter 1971-73, Creat Dir 1973–, VP 1977–, Wm F Haselmire Advtg; AAAF, Bd of Dirs; Advtg Clb of the Palm Bchs, 1982, Past Pres; r/Prot; hon/W/W: in Am Univs & Cols, in S & SW.

KELLY, MARGARET McLAURIN RICAUD oc/Registered Genealogist, Retired Teacher, Writer; h/402 Fayetteville Avenue, Bennettsville, SC 29512; p/Robert Barry and Lulu M Croslaud Ricaud (dec); ed/BA, Winthrop Col; Postgrad Wk, Duke Univ, Univ of SC, Univ of NC, Univ of FL, Univ of Miami; pa/Author, *Jack & the Flying Saucer,* Other Chd's Stories; Author, *The Ricaud Fam, Hist of Marlboro Co, SC* 1979; Poetry Has Appeared in *New Voices;* Writer, Features & News, SC Newspaper; Nat Soc Poets; Cert'd Genealogist, Wash DC; Nat Geneal Soc; cp/Bethea Assn of the US; Secy, Worland Assn, 1959; Mayflower Soc; SC Hist Soc; Nat Geographic Soc; Col Dames XVII Cent; Nat Argument Soc; Pres, U Daughs of the Confederacy, 1983-84; Others; r/Meth; hon/Rec'd Humanitarian Awd for Poetry; Wk incl'd in *The Charleston Poetric Review, New Voices of Am Poetry,* Others; Dir SC Writers; W/W: of Am Wom, in S & SW; Writer's Dic; World W/W of Wom.

KELLY, NANCY MONROE oc/Medical Technologist; b/May 9, 1932; h/100 Walnut Circle, Bristol, TN 37620; ba/Bristol, TN; c/David Monroe, Kevin Lee, Shannon Elizabeth; p/Mrs Clayton Lee Monroe, High Point, NC; ed/BS, Wake Forest Univ, 1954; MT, Bowman Gray Sch of Med, 1954; MA (Spec in Instrnl Communs), E TN St Univ; pa/City Hosp, Winston-Salem, NC, 1954-56; Res Technologist, Bowman Gray, 1956-57, 1960-63; Med Technologist (Hematologist), Bristol Meml Hosp, 1976–; Upper E TN Soc of Med Technologists, Secy 1980-81, Pres 1981-83; cp/TN St Legis Adv Bd, Com & Subcom; PTA, Exec Bds, Pres; Band Boosters, Exec Bds; Jr Leag, Exec Bd, 6 Yrs; r/Prot; Ch Altar Com; hon/BMT,

Recog St Level-ASMT; Beta Beta Beta; Gamma Sigma Epsilon; Phi Delta Kappa; W/W of Am Wom.

KELLY, PATRICIA JEAN oc/Director of Publications; b/Dec 27, 1946; h/ 3415 Wyandot, Denver, CO 80211; ba/ Denver, CO; m/John Anthony Mukauetz; p/Edward and Helen Kelly, St Louis, MO; ed/BA, Webster Col, 1969; Att'd, Univ of MO & Wash Univ 1967, Univ of CO 1976; pa/Designer/ Writer, Cemrel Inc, Pub'd by Viking Press & Lincoln Ctr, 1969-73; Photog/ Designer/Tchr, Gulf Isls Nat Seashore, 1973-74; Dir of Pubs, Metro St Col, 1975-; Co-Fdr, Pinon Press, 1979-82; Denver Art Dirs Clb, 1976-84; Denver Advtg Fdn, 1976-84; Wom in Communication, 1980-84; Soc of Chd Book Writers, 1980-84; Univ of Col Designers Assn, 1979-84; Higher Ed Soc of the Rockies, 1978-84; hon/Pubs, *Thriving* 1980, *Grass Roots Adm* 1980, Num Books & Filmstrips Pub'd by Viking Press & Lincoln Ctr, 1969-73; St Louis Art Dir Creativity Awd, 1975; NPS Creativity Awd, 1975; NY Art Dirs Creativity Awd, 1976; Simpson Idea Lib, 1980; Outstg Yg Wom of Am, 1981; NSEO Design Awd, 1983; Soc of Bus Communicators Awd, 1983; W/W.

KELM, CAROL HELENA RANEY oc/ Museum Curator and Free-Lance Indexer; b/Aug 28, 1929; h/432 North Elmwood Avenue, Oak Park, IL 60302; ba/Oak Park, IL; m/Raymond Louis, p/ Carl Delano and Ellen Minnesota Keyes Raney (dec); ed/Att'd, Reed Col, 1947, 1948; BA, Hist, WA St Col, 1952; BLS, Univ of CA-Berkeley, 1953; pa/Cataloguer, Univ of CA-Davis Lib, 1953-56; Subject Cataloguer, Serials Div Hd, Yale Univ Lib, 1956-65; Asst Catalogue Libn, Jt Bk/Fund Lib IMF, 1965-66; Chief, Catalogue Dept, Smithsonian Instn Lib, 1966-69; Resources & Tech Sers Div Exec Secy, Am Lib Assn, 1969-77; Curator, Hist Soc of Oak Pk & River Forest, 1981-; Am Lib Assn; Ch & Synagogue Lib Assn; Am Soc of Indexers; Phi Beta Kappa; Phi Kappa Phi; Phi Alpha Theta; cp/Unity Temple Restoration Foun, Secy 1979-81; r/Prot; hon/ W/W of Am Wom.

KELTNER, VICKI F oc/Executive; ed/ BFA, Radio/TV Prodn/Mass Communs, So Meth Univ; Spec Studies, Lit Inst, London, England; pa/Pres, Small Bus Pubs, 1978-; Assoc, Mktg Sers Mgmt Co, 1975-78; Mgmt Asst, Public Relats Ofcr, Small Bus Adm, 1975-; Pres of Lynn Advtg & Public Relats Co, The Fairfield Co, 1971-72; Other Previous Positions.

KENDALL, DAVID P oc/Engineering Supervisor; b/Oct 11, 1929; h/RD 1, Box 198K, Troy, NY 12180; ba/Watervliet, NY; m/Barbara Smith; c/Walter A, William L, Wayne D, Wendy M; p/ Walter Albert and Sylvia Phelps Kendall (dec); ed/BME 1957, MS 1962, Applied Mechs, Rensselaer Polytechnic Inst; mil/ AUS, 1953-55; pa/Process Devel Engr, Component & Mat Test Engr & Mats Res Engr, AUS, Watervliet Arsenal, 1956-77; Chief, Mats Engrg Sect, Armament R&D Ctr, 1977-84; SESA, Local Sect Chm, 1968; ASTM; ASME, Mem of Spec Wkg Grp on High Pressure Vessels 1981-; r/Ctr Brunswick Meth Ch, Fin Chm 1978-84; hon/Author, Book Chapt in *Mech Behavior of Mats Under Pressure* 1970, Over 30 Papers in Profl

Jours on High Pressure Mech Behavior of Mats, Fracture Mechs; 2 Patents; Army R&D Achmt Awd, 1962, 1977; Siple Awd, 1977; Inventor of the Yr, En NY, 1976.

KENDRICK, JEFFREY GLENN oc/ Director of Development; b/Oct 25, 1946; h/Route 6, Box 302, Morristown, TN 37814; ba/Jefferson City, TN; m/ Barbara; c/Heather, Valerie; p/Mr and Mrs J T Kendrick, Hernando, MS; ed/ BS, Pers Mgmt, MS St Univ, 1973; mil/ AF, 1967-70; Army, 1973-80; pa/Dir of Devel 1983-, Asst Dir of Devel 1980-83, Asst Prof of Hist 1978-80, Carson-Newman Col; Co Cmdr 1977-78, Comptroller 1976, Army, Okinawa, Japan; Bapt Public Relats Assn, 1981; Coun for Advmt & Support of Ed, 1981; r/Bapt; Gideons, 1982-; hon/Outstg Yg Man of Am, 1981; Mil: Meritorious Ser Medal, Army Commend Medal, Vietnam Ser Medal, Nat Def Medal, Vietnam Campaign Medal.

KENEDY, DAVID GERARD oc/ Comptroller; b/Jun 14, 1946; h/546 Manatuck Boulevard, Brightwaters, NY 11718; b/New York, NY; m/Mary Ann; c/David Bradley, Julie Ann; p/Arthur R Kenedy, Bay Shore, NY; ed/BS, Acctg, Univ of Steubenville, 1969; Assoc Deg in Bus Adm, St Gregory's Col, 1967; pa/Comptroller, Law Firm of Jackson, Lewis, Schnitzler & Krupman, 1980-; Treas & Comptroller 1975-80, Acct 1975-77, Am Intl Grp Inc; VP & Treas, Mark Kenedy Inc, 1973-75; Jr Acct, Am Fidelity Fire Ins Co, 1971-73; Staff Acct, Muldowney & Co, 1968-71; ABA, Legal Adm Sect; Assn of Legal Admrs, Nat & NY Chapt; r/Rom Cath; hon/W/W in Fin & Indust.

KENNADY, JAN W oc/Homemaker and Volunteer; b/Feb 4, 1937; h/206 Elmwood, New Braunfels, TX; m/Don S MD; c/Lisa Chism, Rocky Lockwood, Vance Lockwood; p/Mrs Margaret Westmoreland, Kingsville, TX; ed/ Student of Bus, 1959; pa/Adm Asst, St John the Divine, 1964-80; cp/Pres, TX Acad of Fam Phys, 1984; Pres, Comal Med Aux, 1982-83; Pres, Mid TX Symph Guild, 1982-83; Pres, Book Review Clb, 1982-83; Pres, Comal Garden Clb, 1984-86; VP, Repub Wom, 1983-85; Pres, Commun Ser Ctr, 1984-85; VP, Humane Soc, 1983-84; VP, Circle Arts Theatre, 1983-84; Num Other Coms & Bds; r/Presb.

KENNEDY, DUNCAN TILLY oc/ Neuroscience, Medical Education; b/ May 13, 1930; h/1428 West Gilbert, Muncie, IN 47303; ba/Muncie, IN; m/ Emma Lou Hanna; c/John Robert, Hanna Lou Elizabeth, Elsbeth Love; ed/ BS, Phy Therapy, Columbia Univ, 1955; AM, Phy Therapy/Anatomy, Stanford Univ, 1964; PhD, Anatomy/Physiol, Wayne St Univ, 1966; Post PhD, Neurophysiol, Univ of WI, 1970-72; pa/ Assoc Prof of Anatomy, Dept of Physiol & Hlth Sci 1978-, Asst Dir of Muncie Ctr for Med Ed of the IN Univ Sch of Med 1980-, Ball St Univ; Adj Asst Prof of Anatomy 1983, Adj Asst Prof of Anatomy 1977-83, IN Univ Sch of Med; Num Previous Positions; AAAS, 1966-; Detroit Physiol Soc, 1966-; MW Anatomists Assn, 1968-; Soc for Neurosci, 1970-; AAUP, 1974-; Soc of Sigma Xi, 1975-; Am Assn of Anatomists, 1976-; Sigma Zeta, Xi Chapt, 1976-; IN Acad of Sci, 1976-; hon/Pubs, "Auditory

Nerve Fiber Responses to Wide Band Noise & Tone Combinations" 1978, "Intracellular Anal of Antidromically & Synaptically Activated Nucleus Reticularis Tegmenti Pontis Neurons" 1974, Others; Var Grants Awd'd; Fac Res Awd, Wayne St Univ, 1974; NIH Spec Res F'ship, 1970-72; Soc of Sigma Xi Student Res Awd, 1966; NIH Predoct F'ship, 1962-66; Nat Foun for Infantile Paralysis Phy Therapy Tchg F'ship, 1960-62; Am Men & Wom of Sci; W/ W: in Frontier Sci & Technol, in MW.

KENNEDY, GAY L oc/Executive Director of Senior Services Agency; b/ May 23, 1931; h/6020 North Flora, Fresno, CA 93710; ba/Fresno, CA; c/ Steven H Gall, Kenneth J Gall (dec); p/ Howard R and Harriet E Kennedy, Fresno, CA; ed/BS, Acctg, CA St Univ-Fresno, 1981; pa/Self-Employed, Gay L Kennedy, Bkkpg Ser, 1965-78; Dir, Displaced Homemakers, 1981-83; Dir, Sr Aides, 1983-; Exec Dir, Older Ams Orgs of Fresno & Madera Cos; VP, Displaced Homemakers Netwk; Older Wom's Leag; Fresno Career Wom; Nat Coun Sr Citizens; cp/Mayor's Appt to Citizens Adv Com; Soroptomist Intl; LWV; NOW; Nat Wom's Polit Caucus; Human Sers Coalition; Past Pres, Wom's C of C; Former Troop Ldr, GSA; Former Bd of Dirs, ARC; Past Pres, C of C; r/Cath; hon/IRS Enrolled Agt; W/ W in W.

KENNELLY, BARBARA B oc/Congresswoman; b/Jul 10, 1936; ba/Abraham A Ribicoff Federal Building, 450 Main Street, Hartford, CT 06103; m/ James J; c/Eleanor Bride, Barbara Leary, Louise Moran, John Bailey; p/John M and Barbara Leary Bailey; ed/BA, Ec, Trinity Col; Cert, Harvard Bus Sch; Master's Deg in Govt, Trinity Col, 1981; Hon Doct, Sacred Heart Univ; pa/ Elected, US Rep from CT's First Dist, Jan 1982; Secy of St, CT, 1979-82; Bd of Trustees, Trinity Col, Hartford Col for Wom; cp/Hartford Ct of Common Coun, 1975-79; Chaired, Hartford City Coun's Ed, Public Safety & Zoning Com & Spec Com to Investigate the Hartford Coliseum Roof Failure; Past Pres, 2 Large Social Ser Agys; VChw, Hartford Comm on Aging, 1971-75; Dir, Hartford Arch Conservancy, 1979-82; Chm, CT Elected Ofcls for Soviet Jewry, 1981; Mem: House Ways & Means Com, Subcoms on Select Revenue Measures & Public Asst & Unemploymt Compensation, Steering Com of NE-MW Congl Coalition, Exec Com of Congl Caucus for Wom's Issues, Exec Bd of Congl Arts Caucus; Dir, Hartford's Riverfront Recapture Inc; r/Cath.

KENTERA, CHRIS WILLIAM oc/ University Press Executive; b/Aug 20, 1925; h/721 Cricklewood Drive, State College, PA 16801; ba/University Park, PA; m/Carla Della Roach; c/Gregory Owen, Marc Alan; p/Chris W Sr and Clara B Kentera; ed/BA 1950, BS 1950, Univ of MO; mil/US Inf, ETO, 1944-45; pa/From Field Rep & Manuscripts Rep to Col Dept Editor to Sr Editor, Prentice-Hall Inc, 1950-64; Edit Dir, The Free Press, 1964-65; Exec Editor, Addison Wesley Pub'g Co, 1965-67; Dir, NY Univ Press, 1967-73; Dir, PA St Univ Press, 1973-; Dir, Am Univ Pubs Grp Ltd, London; Dir, PA St Univ Press Ltd, London; Pub'g Conslt; Adv Coun, The Papers of Martin Van Buren; Am

Assn of Univ Presses; Am Polit Sci Assn; Am Ec Assn; Col Art Assn; Mod Lang Assn; Beta Gamma Sigma; cp/Bd of Dirs, The US Gymnastic Safety Assn; Toftrees Country Clb; hon/W/W: in World, in Am, in E; Dir of AAUP; Lit Mkt Place; IPA.

KEPNER, RITA oc/Sculptor; b/Nov 15, 1944; h/Box 2035, Seattle, WA 98111-2035; m/John Matthiesen; c/Stewart Matthiesen; p/Peter (dec) and Helena T Kramnicz, Renton, LA; ed/Student, Elmire Col, Yale Art Lib, Univ of WA; BA, Harpur Col, SUNY-Binghamton, 1966; pa/Exhbns: Warsaw (Poland) 1981, Intl Sculptors Symp (Hungary) 1977, Poland 1976, 1977), Seattle Art Mus 1976, Portland Art Mus 1976, Manawata Art Gallery (New Zealand) 1977, Others; Public Collections: Warsaw Nat Mus, City of Seattle, City of Znin (Poland), City of Zalaegerszeg (Hungary), King Co Arts Comm, Others; hon/Position of Cultural Liaison between Poland & USA, 1975-; Bronze Medal, Zalaegerszeg, Hungary, 1976; Jury's Choice, Hajnowka, Poland, 1976; Elected Mem, Italian Acad of Art, 1981; Dipl of Merit, Univ of Art, Terme, Italy, 1982; Travel Grants for Artistic Res for Kosciuszko Foun, 1975-81; Position of Artist in Residence, City of Seattle, 1975, 1978; W/W: in Am Art, of Am Wom; Am Artists of Renown; Men & Wom of Distn.

KER, ANN STEELE oc/Composer, Music Educator, Church Musician; b/Nov 10, 1937; h/1607 North Springhill Road, Warsaw, IN 46580; ba/Huntington, IN; c/Kelly Lynne, Karen Elizabeth, Kristin Ann; p/Mrs George A (Winifred F) Steele, Warsaw, IN; ed/Att'd, DePauw Univ 1955-57, Butler Univ 1957-58; BME, IN Univ, 1974; MA to Be Completed, Univ of Notre Dame, 1983; pa/Organist, First Presb Ch, 1969-79; Dir of Music, Ctl Christian Ch, 1979-80; Dir of Music, Redeemer Luth Ch, 1980-; Fac, Huntington Col, 1975-; Lakeland Commun Concert Assn, Concert Critic & Bd Mem 1975-83; Leag of Wom Composers; Am Guild of Organists, Bd Mem 1978-81; Am Choral Dirs Assn; Nat Guild of Piano Tchrs; Wom in Music; r/Luth; hon/Pubs, "Hear This!" 1973, "Three Men on Camelback" 1982, "Triptych" 1980, "One Glorious God" 1983, "For Me, O Lord, We Sing" 1983; W/W in Am Music-Classical; Intl W/W in Music; World W/W of Wom.

KEROHER, RUTH F oc/Retired Educator; b/Dec 2, 1907; h/7640 Nall Avenue, Prairie Village, KS 66208; m/William Clyde; p/Elmer J and Anna G Fults; ed/BA Elem Ed & Eng Lit, 1947; Cert'd Spec in Rdg, 1970; Life Tchg Cert Elem Ed, 1927; pa/Elem Tchr, Shawnee Mission Sch Dist, Johnson Co, KS, 1927-75; Spec Rdg Tchr, 1970-75; VP, Shawnee Mission Hist Soc, 1977-78; Br Pres, AAUW, 1979-81; Pres, Shawnee Mission Le Sertoma Ser Clb, 1981-82; Bd of Dirs, Johnson Co Christmas Bur Assn, 1977-84; hon/Author, A Hist of Johnson Co Christmas Bur, 1983; Named Gift of $500.00 to Nat AAUW Grad F'ship Prog.

KERR, NANCY KAROLYN oc/Pastor, Coordinator PEACE; b/Jul 10, 1934; h/407 Warner Street, Cincinnati, OH 45219; ba/Same; c/Richard Charles Williams, Donna Louise Williams; p/Rev Owen W Kerr (dec); Rev Iris I Kerr, Memphis, MO; ed/AA Sociol, Boston Univ, 1953; BA Sch Theol, Univ Bridgeport CT, 1955; BA Psych, Hofstra Univ, 1968; Adv'd Studies Psych, Adelph Univ Inst Adv'd Psychol Studies (Clin Psych), 1968-72; PhD Cand, NY Med Col, 1972-72; pa/Pastor, Cinc Mennonite F'ship, 1981-; Coor, PEACE, 1981-; Asst Prof, Messiah Col 1978-80, NE MO St Univ 1980-82; Devel Disabilities Cnslr, Mennonite Mtl Hlth Inc, 1975-78; Coor Home Sers, City & Co Denver, 1974-75; Psychol, Devel Eval Ctr, 1973; Res Cnslt, NY Med Col, 1972-73; Teen Prog Dir, YWCA Waterbury CT, 1966-67; Meth Ch 1955-72, Yth Min, Chd's Wk Secy, Camp Prog Dir, Bd Ed, Songbook Com, Bd Christian Concerns, Sexism Task Force; Am Psych Assn, Mem 1971-, Div Child Psych, Devel Psych, Mtl Retard; Soc Study Psych/Social Issues, 1975-; Am Assn Mtl Deficiency, 1972-; cp/Charter Bd Mem, Waterbury CT Planned Parenthood, 1965-67; Bd Mem, MW Chd's Home, 1973-74; Bd Mem, Boulder CO ARC, 1974-78; Bd Mem, Ctr for Peace Ed, 1981-; r/Mennonite; hon/Author Several Chapts in Books, Several Booklets; Hist Awd in DAR, 1951; Dean's List, Boston Univ 1951-52, Univ Bridgeport; Spanish Awd, Psych Hons, Unv Boston, 1966; Fellow, NY Med Col, 1968-71; W/W: in Am, of Am Wom.

KESSLER, DORIS HENRIETTA oc/Administrative Team Chief; Major, United States Army; b/Sep 19, 1935; h/370 C Park Avenue, Highland Park, IL 60035; ba/Fisheridan, IL; p/Mr and Mrs F A Molinari, W Mifflin, PA; ed/BS, PA St Univ, 1957; Grad Studies, Univ of Pgh & Am Univ; mil/Maj, AUS; pa/Tchr, Duquesne HS, 1958-68; Co Cmdr, Ft Jackson, SC, 1973-74; ADP Ofcr, Computer Sys, Ft Belvoir, VA, 1976-79; Proj Ofcr, HQs Dept of Army, Wom in the Army Study, 1977-78; Chief, Cmd & Control Software, Pacific Cmd, Camp Smith, AZ, 1979-82; Chief Adm Tm, Ft Sheridan Readiness Grp, 1982-; cp/Nat Assn of Female Execs; Mil Dist of Wash Ofcrs Clb; Metro Mus of Art; Metro Opera Assn; hon/Author Articles in Army Mag 1980, Resv Ofcrs Mag 1980; Com-wom, Allegheny Country, Pgh, PA, 1963-67; Meritorious Ser Medal; Army Commend Medal (2 times); W of Am Wom.

KESSLER, JEAN S oc/Executive Secretary; b/Oct 20, 1954; h/Piscataway, NJ; ba/Two Corporate Place South, Piscataway, NJ 08854; p/John S and Henrietta Margueritte Kessler, East Brunswick, NJ; ed/Exec Secy Dipl, Taylor Bus Inst, 1973; Att'd NY Christian Inst, 1973-75; AA Secretarial Sci, Middlesex Co Col, 1981; Student, Rutgers Univ, 1981-; Cert Profl Secy, 1980; pa/Carter-Wallace Inc, Secy to Dir 1977-78, Exec Secy to Corporate VP 1978-80; Continental Ins, Exec Secy to VP 1981, Exec Secy to Sr VP 1981-; Profl Secys Intl, New Brunswick Chapt Chm Civic Com 1980-81, Chm Secy Yr Com 1981-82, Mem Nom'g Com 1981, Mem Audit Com 1982, Mem Ways & Means Com 1981-82; Nat Assn Female Execs; Nat Christian Secys Assn; cp/Am Mensa Ltd; r/Christian; hon/Secretarial Student Yr Awd, Taylor Bus Inst, 1973; Dean's List, Highest Typing Speed, Tied for Highest Steno Speed, Secy Yr, Profl Secys Intl New Brunswick Chapt, 1982; Nom'd Secy Yr, Profl Secys Intl NJ Div, 1982; W/W of Am Wom.

KETCHAM, ALLEN FRANCIS oc/Business Research Consultant; b/Dec 6, 1945; h/2005 Merriman, Corpus Christi, TX 78412; ba/Corpus Christi; m/Gale; c/Damian, Thane; p/Allen and Frances Ketcham, Kalamazoo, MI; ed/BS, IN Univ, 1973; MEd 1975, PhD 1982, Univ AZ; MBA, Corpus Christi St Univ, 1983; mil/USAR, 1963-68; pa/Dir, Ketchem & Assocs Inc, 1981-; Dir, Modal Analytics Co, 1977-81; Vis'g Asst Prof, Texas A & I Univ; Assoc Fac Memb, Pima Col; Am Mktg Assn; Comparative & Intl Ed Soc; SW Mktg Assn; r/Epis; hon/Pubs, "An Empirical Anal of Suicide in Nueces Co, TX," Coastal Bend Med 1981, "Comments on the Nueces Co Elderly," Coastal Bend Med 1980; Others; Contbg Author, Hoover Inst on War, Revolution & Peace; W/W in Fin & Indust.

KETTLEWELL, NEIL M oc/Neuroscience Educator and Sculptor; b/May 27, 1938; h/172 Fairway Drive, Missoula, MT 59803; ba/Missoula; m/Toni Ann; c/Brant Regnar; p/George and Barbara Kettlewell, Akron, OH; ed/BA, Kent St, 1962; MA 1965, PhD 1969, Univ MI; mil/USAR, 1958-66; pa/Univ MT, Assoc Prof Psych 1976-, Asst Prof 1970-75, Lectr 1969-70; Pres, Superior Land Devel Co Inc, 1973-; Gen Mgr, Sunrise Art, 1980-; Pres, CareWest, 1982-; Univ MI, Programmer 1963-69, Sys Analyst 1967-69; Neurosci Soc; Intl Brain Res Org; NY Acad Scis; Intl Sculpture Soc; r/Epis; hon/Contbr Num Articles Sci Jours, 1968-; Phi Eta Sigma; Psi Chi; Pi Mu Epsilon; Kent St Biol Hon; Pres Scholar, Univ MI; Am Men & Wom of Sci; W/W in Frontier Sci & Technol; Contemp Wn Artists.

KEYSERLING, MARY DUBLIN oc/Consulting Economist; b/May 25, 1910; h/2610 Upton Street, Northwest, Washington, DC 20008; ba/Same; m/Leon H; p/Dr and Mrs L I Dublin (dec); ed/BA, Barnard Col, 1930; Student, London Schof Ec, 1931-32; Completed All Course Requirements & Exams for PhD in Ec Except Thesis Pub, Columbia Univ Grad Sch, 1933; pa/Staff Mem, Com on Costs of Med Care, 1930; Legis Asst, St Charities Aid Assn, 1931; Tchr of Ec, Sarah Lawrence Col, 1933-38; Exec Dir, Nat Consumers Leag, 1938-40; Coor, Hearings Ho of Reps Com on Nat Def Migration, 1941; Chief, Res & Stats Div, Ofc of Civilian Def, Asst to Mrs Eleanor Roosevelt, 1942; Economist, Fgn Ec Adm, 1943; Chief, Liberated Areas Div, Fgn Ec Adm, 1944-45; Chief, Spec Progs Div, Ofc of Intl Trade, US Dept of Commerce, 1946-49; Dir, Intl Ec Anal Div, US Dept of Commerce, 1950-53; Assoc Dir, Conf on Ec Progress, 1953-63; Dir, Wom's Bur, US Dept of Labor, 1964-69; Ec Conslt, Lectr, Writer, 1969-; hon/Author, 3 Books and 400 Articles; Phi Beta Kappa, 1930; LLD, Bryant Col, 1965; LHD, Wom's Med Col, 1968; Medal of Distn, Barnard Col, 1980; W/W: in Am, in E, of Am Wom; World W/W of Wom; Intl W/W in Commun Ser.

KHALIL, TAREK M oc/Professor; b/Jun 12, 1941; h/4225 San Amaro Drive, Coral Gables, FL 33134; ba/Coral Gables, FL; m/Abla; c/Basil, Ronnie; p/

Mr and Mrs M Khalil; ed/BME, 1964; MSIE, 1968; PhD, 1969; pa/Prof of Indust Engrg, Prof of Biomed Engrg, Prof of Public Hlth, Prof Neuro Surg; Dir, Envir Hlth & Safety Prog; Chm, Grad Fac of Sch of Engrg & Arch, 1978-80; Assoc Prof Indust Engrg, 1974-77; Asst Prof Indust & Sys Engrg, Dir Human Perf Lab, Univ of FL, 1969-74; VP Reg IV, Bd of Trustees 1982-, AIIE; Past Pres Miami Chapt 1976, Dir Miami Chapt 1977, AIIE; cp/ Com for Total Employmt of Handicapped SF; Coor, Proj HOPE Biomed Engrg Prog, Egypt; Sigma Xi; Alpha Pi Mu; hon/IIE Fellow Awd, 1982; Outstg IE, Miami Chapt, 1982; Ergonomics Div Awd AIIE; Human Factors Soc Tak A Kraft Awd, 1986; W/W: in S & SW, in Engrg; Am Men & Wom of Sci.

KHAN, WINSTON oc/Professor of Material and Physical Sciences; b/Mar 12, 1934; h/Calle Uroyan, AD4, Mayaguez, Puerto Rico 00709; ba/Mayaguez, Puerto Rico; m/Joan Acklima Aziz; c/ Alima, Selina, Shereeza, Winston Jr, Alim; p/Amanath and Saffeeran, Port-of-Spain, Trinidad; ed/BSc 1956, MSc 1958, London; Dipl in Mat Physics 1961, PhD 1964, Birmingham, England; pa/Lectr & Chm, Mat, Univ of W Indies, Trinidad, 1964-69; Asst Prof & Dir, Mat, Univ of PR-Cayey, 1970-74; Prof of Physics, Univ of PR-Mayaguez, 1974-; Assn Mat Modelling; Am Mat Assn; SIAM; Am Phy Soc; AAAS; Mat Phy Soc, London; Mat Soc Trinidad; Assn Wave Phenomena; Soc of Com Scholars to UK; Smithsonian; cp/Postal Commemorative Soc; hon/Author, "Turbulence Phenomena" 1972, Several Tech Articles & Papers; Pentagon Grant, "Theoretical & Exptl Interfacial Turbulence," 1982-85; Attended & Presented Petition for a "Pay Differential" for Tchrs & Profs of Mat & Sci at Coun of Higher Ed Meeting, 1983; Acting in Adv Capacity to Nat Sci Bd on Pre-Col Ed, Sci & Technol, 1982-; Hon Awd, Frontiers in Sci & Technol, 1982; Presented Paper on "Turbulence Phenomena" at Intl Conf, Math Modelling, 1981; Representations for the Incorporation of Courses in "Physics of Fluids" at Adv'd Levels, 1979; Hon Man of Achmt Awd, 1978; Num Other Hons.

KHARE, BISHUN N oc/Research in Astrochemistry; b/Jun 27, 1933; h/39 Highgate Circle, Ithaca, NY 14850; ba/ Ithaca, NY; m/Jyoti R; c/Reena, Archana; p/Dwarka Nath Srivastava and Ram Pyari, Varanasi, Uttar Pradesh, India; ed/BSc in Physics, Chem & Math 1953, MSc in Physics w Specialization in Spectroscopy 1955, Banaras Hindu Univ; PhD, Physics, Syracuse Univ, 1961; pa/Current Sr Res Physicist, Lab for Planetary Studies, Ctr for Radiophysics & Space Res; Assoc, Harvard Univ, 1966-68; Physicist, Smithsonian Astrophy Observatory, 1966-68; Assoc Res Scist, Ontario Res Foun, 1964-66; Postdoct Res Assoc, SUNY-Stony Brook, 1962-64; Postdoct Res Assoc, Univ of Toronto, 1961-62; Grad Res Asst, Syracuse Univ, 1956-61; Am Phy Soc; AAAS; Am Astronom Soc; Am Chem Soc; Intl Astronom Union; Intl Soc for the Study of the Origin of Life; Life Mem, Astronom Soc of India; Div of Planetary Sci, AAS; Div of Chem Physics, APS; Sigma Xi, Planetary Soc; hon/Pubs, "Metabolism of Tholins by

Microorganisms: Implications for Spacecraft Contamination" (in Press), "Reflection Spectra of Model Titan Atmospheres & Aerosols" (in Press), Num Others; Am Men & Wom of Sci; W/W: in Am, in E, in Technol Today, in Frontier Sci & Technol; Leading Conslts in Technol.

KHASNAVIS, PRATYUSH KUMAR oc/College Professor; b/Jun 15, 1942; h/ 9531 Sophora Drive, Dallas, TX 75249; ba/Dallas, TX; m/Concepcion Guadalupe Harper-Tinajero; p/Dr and Mrs N C Khasnavis (dec); ed/BA 1960, MA 1962, EdB 1963, EdM 1964, Banaras Hindu Univ; EdD, Baylor Univ, 1969; pa/Univ Coor & Col Prof, Bishop Col, 1969-; Proj Dir, "Steps Toward Excell in Tchr Ed," 1970-71; Dir, Tchr Ctr, 1972-73; Instr, Peace Corps Tng Ctr, Univ of MO-Columbia, 1966; Instr of Ed, K B Deg Col, Mirzapur, Uttar Pradesh, India; Chm, Tchr Ed Coun, Bishop Col, 1981-83; Mem of Preser Coun, Dallas Indep Sch Dist, 1975-; hon/Pubs, *Tchg of Social Studies in India* 1983, "Improving Indo-Am Relats" 1982, "Human Relats in the Public Sch Setting" 1982, "Ed for Intl Understanding" 1980, Others; Merit Recip, Inst of Intl Ed, 1968-69; Dean's Hon List, Baylor Univ, 1967; Merit Recip, Banaras Hindu Univ, 1962-64; Men of Achmt; W/W in S & SW; DIB.

KHOURY, SARKIS JOSEPH oc/ Professor of Finance and International Finance; b/Aug 10, 1946; h/15415 Old Bedford Trail, Mishawaka, IN 46545; ba/Notre Dame, IN; m/Joyce; c/Mona, Leila, Natalie; p/Joseph Sarkis Khoury, Ehmej, Lebanon; ed/PhD in Intl Fin, Wharton Grad Div, Univ of PA, 1978; MBA, Boston Univ Sch of Mgmt, 1971; BS in Acctg, SEn MA Univ, 1970; Assoc Deg in Indust Acctg, Centre Belge, Beirut, 1966; pa/Current Mem of Fac of Fin & Bus Ec, Univ of Notre Dame; Asst Prof of Fin & Coor of Grad Prog in Bus, Bucknell Univ, 1977-80; Adj Asst Prof of Fin, Drexel Univ, 1976-77; Instr of Acctg, SEn MA Univ, 1973; Instr of Acctg, Boston Univ, 1971; Acct Exec, Paine, Webber, Jackson & Curtis, 1972-73; Gen Cashier, Newport Hotel, 1969; Cashier, Fed Resv Bk of Lebanon, 1965-66; Am Fin Assn; Wn Ec Assn; Acad of Intl Bus; Financial Mgmt Assn; hon/Pubs, *Speculative Mkts* 1983, *Investmt Mgmt: Theory & Practe* 1983, *Int Fin-A Focused Anal* 1983, *Math Methods in Fin & Ecs* 1981, Num Articles; Beta Gamma Sigma Soc; Awd'd Assoc Deg of Distn; Earned BS Deg w High Distn; Awd'd MBA w Hons; Tchg Asst'ship at Boston Univ; $2,200 Grants from the Wharton Sch; Winner of First Prize in 1979 Nat Dissertation Competition, Sponsored by Acad of Intl Bus; Winner of Paul Fenlon Tchg Awd, Given to Best Tchr in Col of Bus, Univ of Notre Dame, 1981, 1982; W/W in Fin & Indust.

KICIMAN, M O oc/Supervisor of Advanced Structural Methods; b/Jul 24, 1932; h/1520 East Second Street, #104, Long Beach, CA 90802; ba/Los Angeles, CA; m/Ayla; c/Nafo; ed/BS, Robert Col, 1953; MS, Univ of TX, 1959; PhD, Univ of CA-LA, 1964; pa/Sr Structural Res Engr, N Am Aviation, 1960-66; Prof, Pres of the Univ, Mid E Tech Univ, 1966-82; Current Supvr, Adv'd Structural Methods, Rockwell Intl; Am Soc of Engrg Ed; hon/Author, Several

Articles of Optimization Procedures, *Intro to Probability & Stats* 1974.

KICLITER, ERNEST EARL JR oc/ Professor of Anatomy; b/Jun 19, 1945; h/Avenue Wilson, 1367, Apartment 203, Condado, Santurce, Puerto Rico 00907; ba/San Juan, Puerto Rico; m/ Veronica; p/Ernest Earl (dec) and Betty W Kicliter; ed/BA in Psych, Univ of FL, 1968; PhD in Anatomy, SUNY, Upst Med Ctr, 1973; pa/Asst Prof of Physiol & Neuroanatomy, Univ of IL, 1974-77; Assoc Prof of Anatomy 1977-84, Prof of Anatomy 1984-, Univ of PR; Am Assn of Anatomists; AAAS; Assn for Res in Vision & Ophthal; Soc for Neurosci, PR Chapt, Secy-Treas 1978-79, Pres 1979-80; cp/Cajal Clb; J B Johnston Clb; hon/Author, Var Pubs; Ford Foun Fellow, 1967-68; NIH Fellow, 1968-74; Elected Mem, Sigma Xi, 1975; Elected Fellow, AAAS, 1983; Am Men & Wom of Sci; W/W: in S & SW, in Frontier Sci & Technol.

KIDD, MARINA von LINSOWE oc/ Senior Systems Consultant; b/Jul 21, 1952; h/8016 Hartwick Way, Sacramento, CA 95828; ba/Sacramento, CA; m/Russell William; c/Kira Christina von Linsowe; p/Carl Victor (dec) and Dorothy Mae von Linsowe, San Jose, CA; ed/Student, Portland Commun Col 1975, Portland St Univ 1976, Am River Col 1982-; pa/Sr Sys Conslt, Burroughs Corp, 1983-; Data Processing Mgr, Re-Search Exec Recruiters, 1983; Data Processing Mgr, J&W Sci Inc, 1981-83; Data Processing Mgr, Portland Fish Co, 1979-81; Computer Operator, Harsh Investmt Co, 1978-79; Sacramento Wom's Netwk, Spec Events Com; Nat Assn Profl Saleswom; cp/Mensa; Am River Orch, Concertmistress; San Jose Yth Symph, 1970-71; Portland Jr Symph, 1971; San Mateo Symph, 1971-73; r/Luth; hon/Bk of Am Music Awd, 1970; W/W in CA, in W.

KIDWELL, ALBERT LAWS oc/Petroleum and Economic Geologist; b/Jan 1, 1919; h/14403 Carolcrest, Houston, TX 77079; m/Marian Raukin; c/William Albert, Betty Jo Evans, Patricia Alice Lown, Thomas Paul; p/Albert Lewis and Josephine Laws Kidwell (dec); ed/BS, Mining Engrg, MO Sch of Mines, 1940; MS, Geol, Wash Univ, 1942; PhD, Geol, Univ of Chgo, 1949; pa/Geologist, MO Geol Survey, 1944-47; Res Geologist, Carter Oil Co Prodn Res Lab, 1950-65; Sr Res Assoc, Exxon Prodn Res Co, 1965-84; Tulsa Geol Soc, Pres 1964-65; Am Assn of Petro Geologists; Geol Soc of Am; Am Mineralogical Soc; Soc of Ec Geologists; Am Inst of Profl Geologists; r/Meth; hon/Author, Num Pubs on Mineralogy, Ec Geol & Petro Geol; Atomic Energy Comm F'ship, 1948-49; Am Men of Sci; W/W in Frontier Sci & Technol.

KIDWELL, MICHELE ANN FALIK oc/Art Historian; b/Jun 1, 1944; h/495 West End Avenue, New York, NY 10024; c/Nord Eugene; p/Abe and Rena Falik, Long Island, NY; ed/Student, Woodmere Acad, Wheaton Col, Hunter Col; pa/Fac, Art Hist Courses, Sr Col, New Sch & Cont'g Ed, NY Univ; Art Lectures for Pvt &/or Charitable Orgs, incl'g, Metro Mus of Art, UN, Cooper-Hewitt Mus, Cols and Libs; Bd Mem, UJA Art Auction Com; Col Art Assn; Visual Arts Panelist, "Arts in Transition: Creat Responses,"

Co-Sponsored by the Congl Arts Caucus, US Conf of Mayors & the Humanities Inst, Bklyn Col, 1982; hon/Pub'd in *Arts* Mag 1982, 1983, *Wisdoms Child* 1977, 1978, *The Art Jour* 1975, 1976; Ednua Kunc F'ship for Grad Studies, Hunter Col, 1975; Radio Interview w Ruth Klebener Over Columbia Univ Sta, 1983; Wom Wkg Home.

KIEFER, WILLIAM LEE oc/Computer Marketing Executive; b/Aug 19, 1946; h/1656 Grape, St Louis, MO 63147; m/Joyce Ann Cwiklowski; c/Jason Lee, William Andrew; p/Nellie Emma Lindsey Veselsky; ed/AA w Hons, St Louis Jr Col Dist; BS, Univ of MO-St Louis; mil/USMC, SSGT (E-6), Vietnam Ser; pa/Microdata Corp, A McDonnell Douglas Subsidiary; GAF Corp; Dem Dir of Elections, City of St Louis; Past Pres, Univ of MO-St Louis Bus Alumni; Bd Mem, Univ of MO Alumni Assn; Alumni Alliance of Univ of MO; Data Processing Mgmt Assn; cp/Past Pres, N Pk Neighborhood Assn; St Louis Ambassadors; Former Dem Com-man, City of St Louis; r/Cath; hon/NPNA Newslttr Editor; MO Senate Awd, 1977; W/W: in Bus & Fin, in MW, in World.

KIEHNE, ANNA M oc/Systems Procedure Analyst; b/Dec 15, 1947; h/2445 East Del Mar, Pasadena, CA 91107; ba/Los Angeles, CA; p/Alvina and Anna M Kiehne, Preston, MN; ed/BA, Bus Adm, 1969; Postgrad, CA St Univ LA 1974-78, Univ of CO-Denver 1980; pa/Sys Analyst, Home Savs of Am, 1983-; Acct, ECA/Intercomp, 1981-83; Acctg Supvr, Majestic Investmt, 1979-81; Tour Guide, Denver, 1979-82; Nat Assn of Accts; cp/Nat Wom's Polit Caucus, Election Judge 1980-82, Del in Primary Co & St Caucuses 1980, 1982; r/Luth; hon/Cert, Flexible Budgeting & Perf Reporting, 1982; W/W in W.

KILLEA, LUCY oc/Deputy Mayor, Assemblywoman; b/Jul 31, 1922; h/3248 Brant Street, San Diego, CA 92103; ba/San Diego, CA; m/John F; c/Jay, Paul; p/Nelson Lytle and Zeline Pettus (dec); ed/PhD in Latin Am Hist, Univ of CA-San Diego, 1975; MA in Hist, Univ of San Diego, 1966; BA, Incarnate Word Col; pa/Sworn in as Assemblywom, 79th Dist, 1982; Councilwom, 8th Dist, City of San Diego, 1978-82; Exec VP, Fronteras de las Californias, 1977-78; cp/LWV; Friends of Lib, Univ of CA-San Diego; Neighborhood House; Latin Am Arts Com, Fine Arts Soc of San Diego; Comm of the Californias Envir Com, 1979-; r/Cath; hon/Pubs, "The Polit Hist of a Mexican Pueblo: San Diego, 1925-1845" 1966, "Fronteras 1976: A View of the Border from Mexico" 1976, "True Origins of Spanish Colonial Ofcls & Missionaries" 1976-77; Wom of the Yr, San Diego Irish Cong, 1981; Nom for Mbrship on Univ of CA Bd of Regents, 1981; Alumna of Distn, Incarnate Word Col, 1981; Honoree at Leukemia Soc Annual "Good Guys" Banquet, 1980; Num Other Hons.

KILLIAN, GRANT ARAM oc/Clinical Psychologist; b/Nov 3, 1949; h/2202 Cypress Bend Drive, #805, Pompano Beach, FL 33069; ba/Coral Springs, FL; p/Leo and Ann Killian, Delray Beach, FL; ed/PhD 1981, MA 1975, Univ of Chgo; BA, New Col, 1972; pa/Asst Prof, Sch of Profl Psych, Nova Univ, 1982-; Clin Psychol, Pvt Pract, 1982-; Am

Psychol Assn; FL Psychol Assn; Nat Register of Hlth Ser Providers in Psych; hon/Pubs, "The Effects of Psychotropic Drugs on Cognitive Functioning in Schizophrenia & Depression"(in Press), "The Practitioner's Dilemma: Depression or Early Dementia" 1983, "Depression versus Early Dementia: A Brief Clin Checklist" 1983, "Intro & Theories of Affective Disorders" 1981, Others; Acad Awds, Tabor Acad, 1966-67; Noyes Foun Awd, Univ of Chgo, 1974-76; Nat Res Ser Awd, Univ of Chgo, 1977-78; Noyes Foun Awd, Univ of Chgo, 1977-78; NIMH, St Elizabeth's Hosp, 1981-82; W/W in Frontier Sci & Technol.

KILLIAN, HULDA DARLYNE ATKINSON oc/Art Resource Teacher; b/Oct 9, 1928; h/PO #92188, Atlanta, GA 30314; ba/Atlanta, GA; m/William Herty Jr; c/William Herty III, Michael Anthony, Darnita Ruth; p/Joseph Donahue Sr (dec) and Gladys Lenore Peyton Atkinson, Atlanta, GA; ed/BA, Spelman Col, 1948; Former Student, Atlanta Univ, Atlanta Col of Art; EdM (Art Ed) 1968, EdS 1978, Univ of GA-Athens; Further Study, Univ of GA; pa/Tchr, Atlanta Public Schs, 1956; Art Resource Tchr, Atlanta Public Schs, Area II, 1977-; GA Assn of Mid Sch Prins; AAE; GAE; NEA; Nat Art Ed Assn, For Over 18 Yrs; Black Artists of Atlanta; Univ of GA Alumni Assn; Nat Alumnae Assn of Spelman Col; cp/Charter Mem, African-Am Fam Hist Assn, Bd Mem 1981-82; World Future Soc, 1973-; GA World Future Soc; High Mus; r/Cath; hon/Presenter at the Ed Sect of the World Future Soc, "Take a Giant Step into the Future, a Visual Art Approach to Future Studies," 1978; Presenter at Second Genesa Conf, Mt Gilead, NC, "Genesa in Art for the Adolescent," 1982; Developed Art Curric for the Pilot Mid Sch for the St of GA, 1967-68; Developed & Taught a Pilot Future Studies Class at Sammye E Coan Med Sch, 1977; W/W in S & SW; Spelman Col Dir.

KILPATRICK, CAROLYN CHEEKS oc/State Representative; b/Jun 25, 1945; h/7445 LaSalle Boulevard, Detroit, MI 48206; ba/Lansing, MI; c/Kwame, Ayanna; p/Marvel Cheeks, Detroit, MI; ed/MS, Ed Adm, Univ of MI; BS, Wn MI Univ; AS, Ferris St Col; pa/Tchr, Detroit Public Schs; St Rep, Elected 1978; Nat Conf of Black St Legis; Nat Order of Wom Legis; cp/Nat Org of 100 Black Wom; House Appropriations Com Mem; Majority Whip, Ho of Reps; Chp, MI Legis Black Caucus; r/Pan African Orthodox; hon/Anthony Wayne Awd for Ldrship; Dist'd Legis Awd, Univ of MI; W/W: in Black Am, in Am Polit.

KIM, KYO SOOL oc/Program Manager; b/Sep 10, 1942; h/9236 Quick Fox, Columbia, MD 21045; ba/Washington, DC; m/H Choo; c/Dennis, Paul; p/Sung Yul and Jung Ja Kim (dec); ed/BS, Seoul Nat Univ, 1968; PhD in Physics, Brown Univ, 1974; mil/Korean Army, 1963-65; pa/Instr, Seoul Nat Univ, Col of Engrg, 1968; Res Asst, Dept of Physics, Brown Univ, 1970-74; Grp Mgr, U Engrg & Constrn Inc, 1974-79; Prog Mgr, US Nuclear Regulatory Comm, 1979-; Am Nuclear Soc, Tech Prog Com Mem; Mats Res Soc, Steering Com Mem; Korean Nuclear Soc; hon/Author, 15 Articles & Monographs on Subjects of

Mats Sci & Nuclear Engrg; Innotech Res F'ship, 1970-74; NRC High Quality Perf Awd, 1981; Invited Lectr, Korean Atomic Energy Res Inst, 1978, 1982; Invited Lectr, Taiwan Atomic Energy Coun, 1983.

KIMELBERG, HAROLD KEITH oc/Research Professor of Neurosurgery, Professor of Anatomy, Associate Professor of Biochemistry; b/Dec 5, 1941; h/11 Candlewood Lane, Delmar, NY 12054; ba/Albany, NY; m/Pamela; c/David, Michael; p/Maurice (dec) and Sarah Kimelberg, London, England; ed/BS w Hons in Zool, Univ of London, King's Col, 1963; Att'd 1963-65, PhD in Biochem 1968, SUNY-Buffalo; pa/Postdoct Fellow, Johnson Res Foun, Univ of PA, 1968-69; NIH Postdoct Fellow, Dept of Exptl Pathol 1969-70, Asst Res Prof, Dept of Biochem 1970-74, Roswell Pk Meml Inst; Res Assoc Prof of Neurosurg & Biochem, Albany Med Col of Union Univ, 1974-80; Res Prof of Neurosurg, Assoc Prof of Biochem, Prof of Anatomy, Adj Assoc Prof of Biol, SUNY-Albany, 1980-; Biophy Soc; Sigma Xi; Am Soc for Neurochem; Am Soc of Biol Chems; Soc for Neurosci; hon/Author, 24 Review Articles & Invited Chapts, 52 Jour Papers, 27 Pub'd Abstracts of Presented Communs; W/W: in Frontier Sci & Technol, in E.

KINDRED, ARTHUR LEE oc/Administrative Manager; b/May 5, 1946; h/174-15 Linden Boulevard, Addisleigh Park, NY 11433; ba/New York, NY; m/Mabel T Crosby; c/Arthur Lennon, Kristen Elizabeth; p/Andrew and Estell Rias, Buffalo, NY; ed/BA, 1974; MBA, 1981; pa/Jr Underwriter 1967-69, Human Resource Spec 1969-75, Coun Dpty Dir 1975-77, Planner 1977-79, Adm Mgr 1979-, City of NY; cp/U Dem Clb, 1971-; Reed's Boys Clb, 1978; Queens Co Dem Org, 1970-; r/Bapt; Allen Ch, 1976-; hon/NYC HS Spkr VIP.

KING, J B oc/United States Army Administrative Sergeant; b/Jul 24, 1944; h/Route 1, Box 884, Forsyth, GA 31029; ba/APO, NY; m/Ethel; c/George Bernard, Zelda Darlene; p/Reason and Lillie Mae King, Forsyth, GA; ed/Att'd, Univ of MD 1979, 1980, Ctl TX Col 1980, 1981; BBA, SWn Univ, 1982; mil/1963-; pa/AUS: PFC (E3) 1964, Spec 4th Class (E4) 1965, Sgt (E5) 1966, Staff Sgt (E6) 1968, Sgt First Class (E7) 1977, Stenographer 1966-67, Inf Platoon Sgt (Vietnam) 1968-69, Adm Instr 1969-71, Adm Sgt (Vietnam) 1971-73, Instr, Adm Sch 1973-75, PSNCO 1976-77, Adm NCO (Germany) 1977-; cp/Masons: Worshipful Master 1978-79, High Priest 1981-82, Eminent Cmdr 1981-82, Asst Dpty Grand Master 1981-, Pres of Past Master's Coun 1980-, Spec Dpty Grand High Priest 1983-, Grand Inspector Gen (33 Deg) 1981-; Num Civic & Social Activs in Mannheim Mil Commun; r/Bapt; hon/Grand Inspector Gen, 33 Deg, Highest Deg of Masonary, 1981; Spec Dpty Grand High Priest, Royal Arch Masonary, 1983.

KING, JOHN DOUGLAS oc/Systems Scientist, University Teacher; b/Jun 1, 1934; h/10287 Grayfox Drive, San Diego, CA 92131; ba/San Diego, CA; m/Shirley Anne; c/Douglas, Lynn Angela, Linda, Alan, Pamela, Gary; p/Mrs Mary C King, Atlanta, GA; ed/Dr of Bus Adm, 1980; Master of Aerospace Opers Mgmt, 1969; BS, 1951; mil/ USN 1956-77, Ofcr; pa/Opers Analyst, DAVLYN Enterprises, 1977; Mgmt Analyst, Northrop Sers Inc, 1977-78; Mem of Tech Staff, INTERCON Corp, 1978-79; Mem of Tech Staff, PE Sys Inc, 1979-83; Sys Scist, Computer Scis Corp, 1983-; Am Mgmt Assn; Nat Mgmt Assn; USIU/CWU Alumni Bd of Dirs, 1981-; cp/Assn of Old Crows; Ret'd Ofcrs Assn; Scripps Ranch Commun Theatre, Bd of Dirs 1979-80, 1983-; r/ Ch of England; hon/Lowry Meml S'ship, 1952; Navy Commend Medal, 1972; W/ W in W.

KING, JOHN ETHELBERT oc/Professor and Chair of Department of Higher Education; b/Jul 29, 1913; h/ 1707 Colonial Drive, Carbondale, IL 62901; ba/Carbondale, IL; m/Glennie Beanland; c/Rebecca Ferris King Wright, Wynetka Ann King Reynolds; p/John Ethelbert and Iosa Wynetka Koontz (dec); ed/PhD in Rural Ed, Cornell Univ, 1941; MS in Ednl Adm, Univ of AR, 1937; BA in Latin & Eng, N TX St Univ, 1932; mil/Comm'd Ser, USN Deck Ofcr, Discharge as Lt SG; pa/Prof & Chm of Dept of Higher Ed 1970-, Prof & Chm of Dept of Ednl Adm & Founs 1968-70, Vis'g Prof of Dept of Ednl Adm & Founs & Dept of Higher Ed 1967-68, So IL Univ-Carbondale; Pres & Prof of Higher Ed, Univ of WY-Laramie, 1966-67; Pres & Prof, Emporia St Univ, 1953-66; Provost & Prof, Univ of MN-Duluth, 1951-53; Other Previous Positions; Kappa Delta Pi; Phi Delta Kappa; Phi Kappa Phi; Am Assn of Higher Ed; Am Assn of Cols for Tchr Ed; NEA; Intl Coun on Ed for Tchg; Lambda Chi Alpha, 1936-; Nat Dept of Rural Ed, 1943-; r/Presb; hon/ Pubs, *Money, Marbles, & Chalk: Student Financial Support in Higher Ed* 1975, *Wk & the Col Student* 1976, Others; Hon Degs, No MI Univ 1966, Col of the Ozarks 1965; Dist'd Alumnus Cit Awd, N TX St Univ, 1965; Kansan of the Yr, 1954; Blue Key; Sphinx Clb; Dist'd Alumnus, Univ of AR, 1983; W/W in World.

KING, MARCIA GYGLI oc/Artist; b/ Jun 4, 1931; h/626 Evans Avenue, San Antonio, TX 78209; ba/New York, NY; c/Rollin White Jr, Edward Prescott; p/ Robert Prescott and Ruth Farr Gygli, Chagrin Falls, OH; ed/BA, Smith Col, 1953; MFA, Univ of TX, 1981; pa/One Wom Shows in TX, WA & Gtr NY Area; Visual Arts Critic, Express-News Pub'g Co, 1976-77; Fdr, Dir, Docent Prog, McNay Art Mus, 1964-65; Lectr, Univ of TX Div of Cont'g Ed, 1976; Docent, Nat Gallery of Art, 1956-60; Intl Wom's Yr, Houston, TX, Panel on Status of Wom in Art in the SW, 1977; One of Five Artists Chosen for Ofcl "Bicent Tribute Show," Instituto Mexicano de Inter Cambio Cultural, 1975; r/Epis; hon/Honoree, Outstg Wom in San Antonio, Wom's Polit Caucus, 1979; Painting on Front of Invitation to Wom in "San Antonio Art," Univ of TX Hlth & Sci Ctr, 1976; First Purchase Prize, Delta Annual, AR Art Ctr, 1974; Best of Show 1971, First Purchase Prize 1972, TX Watercolor Show; Five Other Maj Reg Awds; Num Others Hons; W/ W in Am Art.

KING, MARY F STALLINGS oc/ Internal Revenue Agent; b/Jan 18, 1951; ba/325 Chestnut Street, Philadelphia,

PA 19106; m/Gregory Sr; c/Sterling Philip, Gregory Jr; p/Harold Sr (dec) and Marie B W Stallings, Norfolk, VA; ed/ BS, Acctg, 1973; pa/Internal Revenue Agt, IRS, 1973-; VA St Col Acctg Clb, 1970-73; cp/GSA, Ldr 1979-80, Cookie Chp 1978-80; r/Philippian Bapt Ch, 1977-, Trustee 1979-, Christian Ed Dept (Present), Yth Forum 1980-, Sunday Sch Tchr 1979-, Income Tax Returns Preparation 1978-; Vacation Bible Sch, Tchr 1981; pa/VA St Col Dean's List, 1972-73; IRS Commend Lttrs, 1976-82; Outstg Yg Wom of Am.

KING, VEREDA JOHNSON oc/ Assistant Professor of Economics; b/ Dec 6, 1952; h/703 Reid Street, Apartment 1, Greensboro, NC 27406; ba/ Greensboro, NC; m/David Alvin; p/Mr and Mrs Charlie G Gore, Elizabethtown, NC; ed/BA, Ec, Johnson C Smith Univ, 1974; MBA, NC Ctl Univ, 1979; Doct Cand, Ec, Duke Univ; pa/Sys Programmer, Am Mortgage Ins Co, 1976-77; Sys Analyst, NC Ctl Univ, 1977-80; Asst Prof, Bennett Col, 1980-; Alpha Kappa Alpha Sorority, 1972-; Am Ec Assn; cp/YWCA, 1981-; r/Bapt; hon/ Pub, "Resource Requirement Predictions Model-A Case Study for NC Ctl Univ," 1977; BA, cum laude, Johnson C Smith Univ, 1974; Deptl Awd, Duke Univ, 1982-83; Prudential Programming S'ship, 1973; Sigma Rho Sigma, 1973.

KINGHAN, GENE PAUL oc/Science Teacher, Chairman; b/Jul 3, 1935; h/Box 791, Southold, NY 11971; ba/Shelter Island, NY; m/Anita V; c/Anita J Czartosieski, Veronica A Grattan, Mark E, Kevin M, John E; p/John and Ruby Grenis (dec); ed/BS, Wilmington Col, 1959; MS, Miami Univ, 1961; Addit Grad Credit, NM St Univ, Long Isl Univ, Hofstra Univ; mil/AUS, 1957-59; pa/ Army Ed Ctr, 1958-59; Northmont HS, 1959-61; Wyeth Labs & Abbott Labs, 1961-63; Sci Tchr & Chm, Shelter Isl HS, 1963-; NY St Marine Ed Assn, 1975-, Pres 1975-79, VP 1977-79; Nat Marine Ed Assn, 1977-; Nat Biol Tchrs Assn, 1967-; Suffolk Co & NY St Sci Tchrs Assns, 1964-; AAAS; NY Acad of Sci; cp/BSA Merit Badge Coun; r/ Rom Cath; hon/Author, 2nd Sourcebook for Sci Supvrs, Sci Fairs, 1976; Lab & Field Experiences, Ocean Sci Lab, 1973; Editor, *Ll Sci Cong Booklet*, 1978-82; Contbr to Profl Pubs; Outstg Sci-Math Tchr, Suffolk Co Soc of Profl Engrs, 1981; Outstg Sci Tchr, Suffolk Co Sci Tchrs Assn, 1979; Outstg Biol Tchr of the Yr, NY St, NABT, 1980, Finalists 1976-77; Nom, Pres Cit for Excell in Sci, NY St, 1983; W/W in E.

KINNAN, JOSEPH EDWARD oc/ United States Air Force Colonel; b/Sep 13, 1938; h/1441 Pampas Place, Montgomery, AL 36117; ba/Maxwell AFB, AL; m/Sandra Adel DeLuca; c/Christopher, Catherine, Mary Elizabeth, Monica, Rachel, Molly; p/Mr and Mrs J P Kinan, Avon Park, FL; ed/BS, Geod, Univ of FL, 1961; MS, Geodetic Sci, OH St Univ, 1968; EdM, Ednl Psych, Wayne St Univ, 1975; mil/USAF Active Duty; pa/USAF: Dpty Missile Crew Cmdr 1962-65, Squadron Cmdr 1965-66, Gravity Survey Dept Chief 1968-70, Airlift Clearance Auth in Turkey 1973-75, Chief of Cartography, Def Mapping Sch 1975-78, Air Univ Chief of Res 1979-; Asst Prof of Aerospace

Studies, Univ of FL, 1970-73; Am Geophy Union, 1967-70; Am Soc of Photogrammetrists, 1966-78; APGA, 1978-80; cp/St Vincent, DePaul, 1963-68; Christian Fam Movement, 1966-68; St Augustine Parish Coun, 1970-73; Charismatic Renewal, 1970-; r/Rom Cath; hon/Pubs, "Black Awareness Wk" 1973, "The Def Mapping Sch" 1978; AF Commend Medal, 1973; Meritorious Ser Medal, 1975; Def Meritorious Medal, 1978; Vol of Yr, Montgomery, AL, 1981.

KINNEY, SHIRLEY LaVONNE PHELPS oc/Conveyances Clerk; b/Mar 6, 1926; h/5000 Marmon Street, Casper, WY 82604; c/James P Williams Jr, John Walter Williams III, Deanna Lynne Christian, Richard Earle Holmes; p/ Nellie M Phelps, Casper, WY; ed/RN; AAS, Casper Col, 1974; Reg'd Cosmetologist, Hoosier St Beauty Col, 1955; pa/Cosmetologist, Owner & Operator, Cinderella Beauty Salon, Casper; Reg'd Staff Nurse, Natrona Co Meml Hosp, 1974-75; Devel'd & Dir'd Recreational Therapy Prog, Natrona Co Meml Hosp, 1975-76; Clk Typist, USGS, 1980-; Current Conveyances Clk, BLM; Past Mem, Nat Cosmetologist Assn; Nat Nurses Assn; cp/Toastmistress; Mt View Org for Chd; Past Pres, Home Demo Assn; Past Pres, PTA; Den Mother, Cub Scouts; Pres, Concerned Citizens of Mt View, 1977-78; VISTA Vol for Nsg Home Reform, 1979-80; hon/Author, "Portraits on China"; Nom for Dem House, 1978; Nom for Nat Winthrop Rockefeller Awd, 1980; Personalities of W & MW; Dir of Dist'd Ams; Intl W/W of Intells; W/W in W; World W/W of Wom.

KINRA, VIKRAM KUMAR oc/Associate Professor of Aerospace Engineering; b/Apr 3, 1946; h/812A Navarro Drive, College Station, TX 77840; ba/ College Station, TX; m/Anita; c/ Anushka Guriya; p/Chaudhary Gurmukh Chand (dec) and Gianvati Kinra, Rohtan, India; ed/PhD, 1975; MS, 1968; BTech, 1967; pa/Asst Prof of Mech Engrg, Univ of CO-Boulder, 1975-82; Assoc Prof of Aerospace Engrg, TX A&M Univ, 1982-; Soc for Exptl Stress Anal, 1974-; Composites Com 1983-; Am Soc for Engrg Ed, 1977-; Am Soc of Mechs, 1976-; ASME, 1979-, Com on Composite Mats of Applied Mechs Div 1983-; Pi Tau Sigma, 1980; Sigma Xi, 1981; Soc of Automotive Engrg, 1982; Soc of Engrg Sci, 1983; hon/Author, 25 Tech Articles in *Wave Propagation, Ultrasonics, Fracture Mechs, Composite Mats, Nondestructive Testing*; New Engrg Edr, Dean's Nom to the Sum Annual Meeting of the Am Soc for Engrg Ed, 1977; Dow Outstg Yg Fac Awd, Am Soc for Engrg Ed, 1980; Ralph R Teetor Ednl Awd, Soc of Automotive Engrs, 1982.

KINSELLA, FRANCES GERTRUDE MOYLAN oc/Manager of Rental Properties; b/Jul 1, 1915; h/42 Tenth, Chillicothe, MO 64601; m/Joseph Lawrence; c/Joseph Raymond, Frances Ann Kinsella Hayes, Lawrence Anthony, Kathryn Apollonia Kinsella Reece; p/ Charles Henry and Apollonia Martin Moylan (dec); ed/Att'd, NW MO St Tchrs Col & NE MO St Tchrs Col; pa/ Tchr, Livingston Co Schs, 1933-36, 1946-50; Tchr, Eng, USAF, Chillicothe Bus Col, 1950-51; Bkkpr & Home Designer, 1951-54, 1963-70; City Clk,

City of Chillicothe, 1959-63; Yth Spec, MO St Tng Sch for Girls, 1970-79; Current Mgr, Kinsella Rental Properties; cp/Publicity, Chillicothe Fine Arts Coun, 1967; Pres, Livingston Co Hlth Assn, 1957-59; Nat Leag of Am Pen Wom, Br Pres 1950-54; BPW Clb, Radio Chm; Hedrick Med Ctr Aux, Life; Pres, Livingston Co Dem Wom, 1950-54, 1960-64; r/Cath; hon/Contbr of Poetry, Essays & Reports to Newspapers, 1940's & 1950's; Inaugural Invitation to Johnson & Humphrey Inauguration, 1965.

KIRBY, J AUBREY oc/Architect, Solar Specialist; b/Jan 31, 1932; h/460 Archer Road, Winston-Salem, NC 27106; ba/Winston-Salem, NC; m/Nancy Ellen Ridge; c/Rick, Mark, Ann, Beth; p/James Claudous and Mary Helen Rhyne Kirby (dec); ed/BArch, OK St Univ, 1958; pa/Pres, J Aubrey Kirby Assocs Inc, 1964-; AIA, NC Chapt, Winston-Salem Sect, Pres 1963, Dir 1964, 1965; NC Solar Energy Assn; cp/Kiwanis Clb, Dir 1982, 1983; U Way, 1963-65; r/Meth; hon/Author, Articles in Local Press; Gov's Energy Achmt Awd, 1981; Alumnus of the Yr, High Point Col Forsyth Alumni, 1981-82; Randolph E Dumont Design Awd, 1975; W/W S & SW; Personalities of S.

KIRK (LAUVE), "MISS HELEN" E oc/Retired Medical Assistant, Supertwin Statistician; b/Nov 9, 1915; h/PO Box 254, Galveston, TX 77553-0254; ba/Same; c/Jane Lauve Skinner (Mrs Ronal Skinner); p/Lorena M and Albert E Kirk (dec); ed/Spec Ed, Med Asst'g & Med Secretarial Sers; Cont'g Ed, Study Multiple Births; pa/Conslt & Advr to Parents Multiple Births; Med Secy, H K Davis (Psychi), 1963-82; Med Asst, O T Kirksey MD (Surg), 1959-62; Med Asst, P B Kamin MD (Pediatrician), 1950-59; Asst Med Tech, Eleven Phys, 1938-42; Intl Soc Twin Studies; Nat Mothers of Twins Clbs; Intl Twins Assn; Past Pres, TX Med Assts Assn, 1964-65; Tri-level Med Asst Assn; cp/Bd Mem, Sister City Prog; r/Prot; hon/Author Num Newspaper Articles; Contbr Worldwide Sources for Multiple Birth Stats; Conslt, Ctr for Multiple Birth, Authors; Fdg Mem, Intl Soc for Twin Studies, 1974; Helen Kirk Supertwin Registry, 1980-; Bd Dirs, Ctr for Study Multiple Births, 1981; TX Med Asst Yr, 1969; Hon Mem, Five Mothers of Twins Clbs; World W/W of Wom.

KIRKPATRICK, KAY DONNA oc/Manager Restaurant and Lounge; b/Jul 31, 1937; h/3480 Adah Avenue N E, Albany, OR 97321; ba/Albany; m/Donald Eugene; p/William H and Mabel N Luehr, Tucson, AZ; ed/Grad, Cedar Falls HS, 1955; pa/H & W Inc, Tom Tom Restaurant, Mgr 1980-, Asst Mgr 1972-80; Ofc Mgr/Secy, Key Adjustment, Las Vegas, 1960-63; Legal Secy, Morton Galane, 1959-60; Ofc Mgr, B & J Realty, 1955-56; Real Est Investmt; Landscaping; Interior Decorating.

KIRSCHBAUM, JOEL BRUCE oc/Molecular Geneticist; b/Aug 29, 1945; h/424 Staten Avenue, Oakland, CA 94610; a/Richmond, CA; m/Felicity Russell; p/Howard William Kirschbaum (dec); Willie Jensen Kirschbaum, Los Altos, CA; ed/BA Chem, Pomona Col, 1967; MA 1972, PhD Molecular Biol, Harvard Univ; pa/Supvr Molecular Biol, Stauffer Chem Co, 1981-; Instr Neuropathol, Harvard Med Sch, 1977-81;

Res Assoc Neurosci, Chd's Hosp Med Ctr, 1977-81; Charge de recherche, Dept Molecular Biol, Univ Geneva, 1975-77; Course Instr, EMBO Adv'd Lab Course Molecular Genetics, Univ Geneva, 1976; Asst Instr, Cold Sprg Harbor Sum Course Bacterial Genetics, 1971; Tchg Fellow, Harvard Univ, 1969; AAAS, 1978-; Am Numismatic Assn, 1983-; hon/Pubs, "Potential Implications of Genetic Engrg and Other Biotechnols to Insect Control," Annual Review Entomol 1985, "A Mutation in the Gene for the β' Subunit of Escherichia Coli RNA Polymerase Which Specifically Affects Transcription of the rpoBC Operon," Jour Molecular Biol 1978, Num Others; James A Lyman Prize Chem, Phi Beta Kappa, Pomona Col, 1967; Woodrow Wilson Fellow, Harvard Univ, 1967-68; Helen Hay Whitney Postdoc Fellow, 1973-75; Fellow, Med Foun Boston, 1977-79; Prin Investigator, Am Cancer Soc, 1979-81; Am Men & Wom Sci; W/W in W.

KIRSCHNER, RONALD ALLEN oc/Plastic Surgeon; b/Jan 18, 1942; ba/Suite IL-17, Two Bala Place, Bala Cynwyd, PA 19004; m/Olivia Barbara; c/Andrew Scot, Julie Renee; p/Hy and Eleanor Kirschner, Del Ray Bch, FL; ed/BA, Univ Col NY Univ, 1962; DO 1966, MS 1972, Phila Col Osteopathic Med; Cert'd Facial Plastic Surg, 1974; Cert'd Otorhinolaryngology, 1974; mil/Med Corps, USNR, Med Sch Liason Ofcr; pa/Att'd Phys, Hosp Phila Col Osteopathic Med, Suburban Gen Hosp; Chm, ENT & Plastic Surg Depts, Suburban Gen Hosp; Conslt, Hosp Phila Col Osteopathic Med, Bur Voc Rehab, Immunodiagnostics Lab 1978-81, Allergy Mgmt Sys Inc, Lazer Corporation 1982; Chief Med Advr Courtlandt Grp, 1979-; Edit Conslt, AOA Jour, 1977-; Med Editor, Med Portfolio; Edit Referee, JAOA, 1980-; Editor-in-Chief, Probe, 1984; Preceptor, Hd & Neck & Plastic Surg, Xanar Laser Div Johnson & Johnson, 1982; Phil Col Osteopathic Med, Asst Prof 1972-74, Assoc Prof 1974-76, Clin Assoc Prof 1976-; OCOO; AOA; Phila Co Osteopathic Assn; AAO; Nat LOG, VP 1979, Pres Elect 1980; Assoc Fellow, Phil Acad Facial Plastic Surg; Fellow, SENTAC; Fellow, Phila Laryngologic Soc; Fellow, Pan Am Allergy Assn; Intl Assn Logopedics & Phoniatrics; Pres, Survivors Clb PCOM, 1981-82; MWn Biolaser Inst; Pres, Inst Applied Laser Surg, 1982; Fellow, Am Acad Otolaryngology Hd & Neck Surg Inc; Fellow, Am Soc Laser Med & Surg, 1982; Assoc Fellow, Acad Facial, Plastic, & Reconstructive Surg, 1983; Fellow, Pan Am Otolaryngology Soc, 1983; cp/Freemason, Grand Lodge PA, Columbia Lodge #91; Variety Clb, Tent 13; NY Univ Clb; Alumni Assn, NY Univ, Phila Col Osteopathic Med; r/Jewish; hon/Pubs, "Psychologic Aspects of Amplification," Hearing Aid Jour 1982, "Vascular Isl Pedicle Flap for Reconstruction Nasal Defects," Am Jour Otolaryngology 1980, Num Others; Video-Tape Presentations; Sems; Lectures; F'ships; Ednl Presentations; Devel Instruments; Lindbach Foun Awd Dist'd Tchg, 1973; Legion Hon, Chapel Four Chaplains, 1982; Dist'd Ser, Caduceus Chapt LOG, 1982; W/W in E.

KIRWAN-TAYLOR, PETER ROBIN oc/Vice Chairman, Danville Resources

Inc; b/Jan 18, 1930; h/40 East 80th Street, New York, NY 10021; ba/NYC; m/Nancy; c/Antonia, Charles, Laura, Helene, John; p/John Kirwan-Taylor, Vaud, Switzerland; ed/Grad, Winchester Col England 1943-48, Trinity Col Cambridge 1949-50; mil/Rifle Brigade & 21st SAS (Artists) TA; pa/VP, Danville Resources Inc, 1981-; Maxwell Cummings & Sons Holdings Ltd, 1976-81; English Property Corporation, 1970-76; Hill Samuel & Co Ltd, 1960-70; Peat Marwick Mitchell, 1950-60; r/Ch of England; hon/W/W: in Canada, in World; Dir Dirs; Men Achmt; DIB.

KIRWIN, W CHANDLER oc/Associate Professor; b/May 31, 1941; h/Hog Hill Farm, Rural Route #3, Rockwood, Ontario, Canada; ba/Guelph, Ontario, Canada; m/Ann Marvell; c/Elizabeth Brayton, Meghan Dickinson; ed/BA Art Hist, Princeton Univ, 1965; MA 1968, PhD 1972, Stanford Univ; pa/Assoc Prof Dept Fine Art, Univ Guelph, 1981-; Lectr Dept Art, Smith Col, 1980; Asst Prof Dept Fine Arts, Amherst Col, 1972-79; Lectr, Col Art Assn 1978, Brampton Lectures Columbia Univ 1980, Warburg Inst 1980, Convegno Internazionale Berniniano 1981; r/Epis; hon/Pubs, Sculpture in St Peter's Rome: From the Age of Michelangelo to the Age of Canova 1984, "Bernini's Decoro: Some Preliminary Observatins on the Baldachin & on His Tombs in St Peter's," Studies in Iconography 1982, Num Others; Book Reviews; Italian Govt Grant, 1966-67; Samuel H Kress Foun F'ship, 1969-71 & 1980; Amherst Col Fac Grant, 1973-79; Univ Guelph New Fac Grant, 1981.

KISSINGER, WALTER B oc/Company Executive; b/Jun 21, 1924; h/Lower Drive, Huntington Bay, NY 11743; ba/Melville, NY; m/Eugenie Van Drooge; c/William, Thomas, Dana Marie, John; p/Paula Kissinger, NYC; ed/BA, Princeton, 1951; MBA, Harvard, 1953; mil/AUS, Capt, 1943-46; pa/Allen Grp, Chm, CEO, Pres, 1969-; Jervis Corporation, Exec VP, Chm, Dir, 1964-68; Asst to Pres, Jerrold Corporation, 1963-64; Harman-Kardon, VP, Gen Mgr; Glass-tite Industs, Exec VP, Dir, 1960-62; Pres, Adv'd Vacuum Prods, 1957-62; Asst to VP Fgn Opers, Gen Tire & Rubber Co, 1953-56; Mem Adv Bd, Mfrs Hanover Trust Co; Mem Adv Coun, Hist Dept, Princeton Univ; Dir, Nat Counc US-China Trade; hon/W/W in Am; Standard & Poor's Reg Corps, Dirs & Execs.

KITADA, SHINICHI oc/Research Biochemist; b/Dec 9, 1948; h/478 Landfair Avenue, Apartment 5, Los Angeles, CA 90024; ba/LA; p/Dr and Mrs Koichi Kitada, Osaka, Japan; ed/MD, Kyoto Univ, 1973; MS 1977, PhD 1979, Univ CA-LA; pa/Intern, Kyoto Univ Hosp, 1973-74; Resident Phys, Chest Disease Res Inst, Kyoto Univ, 1974-75; Res Scholar, Lab of Biomed & Envir Sci, Univ CA-LA, 1979-; Am Oil Chem Soc; NY Acad Sci; AAAS; Smithsonian Inst Assocs; Sigma Xi; hon/Japan Soc Promotion Sci Fellow, 1975-76; Edna Lievre Fellow, Am Cancer Soc, 1981-82; Author Num Articles; W/W in W.

KITCHEN, EMILY K oc/Data Processing; b/May 4, 1933; h/4419 Old Fox Trail, Midlothian, VA 23113; ba/Richmond, VA; m/William E; p/Mrs Karl E Kraemer, Norfolk, VA; ed/BA,

Randolph-Macon Wom's Col, 1955; pa/ Jr Engrg Asst, VA Elect & Power Co, Rate Res, 1955-57; Math, Chem & Physics Instr, Essex Co HS, 1958-60; Math Aide, Computer Programmer, Nav Anal, 1960-63; Computer Programmer, Task Ldr, Nat Resource Eval Ctr, 1963-66; Sr Programmer, Nat Radio Astronomy Observatory, 1966-68; Coor, Tech Sers, R&D, A H Robins Co, 1968-; COMMON, an IBM User's Grp, Pres 1978-80, Bd of Dirs 1975-; DECUS, Digital Users Grp, Symp Com 1981-; r/Presb; hon/Vis'g Instr, Computer Sci, Randolph-Macon Col, 1973-75; Outstg Yg Wom of Am.

KITTO, KATHLEEN LEONE oc/ Instructor in Department of Metallurgy and Mineral Process Engineering; b/Oct 7, 1956; h/643 South Main Street, Butte, MT 59701; ba/Butte, MT; p/H Stanley and Elizabeth M Kitto, Butte, MT; ed/MS in Metall Engrg 1981, BS w High Hons in Metall Engrg 1978, AS in Engrg 1976, MT Col of Mineral Sci & Technol; pa/Adj Instr, Dept of Metallurgy & Mineral Process Engrg 1981-, Res Engr 1978-81, MT Col of Mineral Sci & Technol; Student Metall Engr, Hanna Mining Co, 1977; Am Soc for Metals, 1976-; Am Ceramics Soc, Refractories Div 1978-; Metall Soc of Am Inst of Mining, Metall and Petro Engrs, 1981-; cp/Human Resource Coun, Com Mem 1978-81; HS Sci Fair, 1977-; r/Rom Cath; hon/Pubs, "Operability & Mats Perf of a Regenerative Heat Exchanger during 1000+ Hours of Oper" 1981, "Thermomech Properties of MHD Refractory Mats" 1981, "Effect of Thermal Cycling on the Creep of Two Spinel Refractories" 1981, "Effects of Thermal-Stress Cycling on a Fusion-Cast Spinel Refractory" 1980, Others; Num One in 1978 Grad'g Class, MT Col of Mining Sci & Technol; Newmont Scholar, 1974-78; Anaconda Sci Sch, 1972-74; Westinghouse Talent Search Top 200, 1974; Mu Beta Pi, 1977, 1978; Alpha Sigma Mu; W/W of Am Wom.

KITZMILLER, ANN LOEHNERT oc/ Director of Promotions; b/Jan 22, 1931; h/5026 Wintersong Lane, Westerville, OH 43081; ba/Columbus, OH; c/Beth Ann Kitzmiller Sparks (Mrs Robert Elwood), Joseph Scott; p/Frank and Elizabeth Brightman Loehnert (dec); ed/ BS in Elem Ed, OH St Univ, 1953; Att'd, Denison Univ, 1949-50; pa/Elem Tchr, Columbus Public Schs, 1953-55; Subst Tchr, Jefferson Local Sch Dist, 1960-68; Gtr Columbus Conv & Visitors Bur, 1979-81; Dir of Promotions, Aladdin Shrine Temple, 1981-; Bd of Trustees, Columbus Area Tourism Coun, 1983-; Chm, Fed Dist So Appeal Bd Selective Ser Sys, 1983-; Kappa Alpha Theta, Columbus Alumnae Chapt Pres 1958-60; cp/OH Soc DAR, St Nat Def Chm, St Recording Secy, St Vice Regent, St Regent; Nat NSDAR Resolutions Com, 9 Yrs; NSDAR Spkrs Staff; Area Rep, Nat VChm, NSDAR Nat Def Com; r/Presb; hon/Pub'd in *Conservative Digest, Kappa Alpha Theta Mag, Ohio DAR News, Nat Society DAR Mag*; Hon St Regent, OH Soc DAR, 1983; Nat Eagle Awd, Eagle Forum; SAR Good Citizenship Medal; World W/W of Wom; Hereditary Register of the USA; Intl Register of Profiles; Intl W/W of Intells.

KLASSEN, KATHRYN ANNE oc/

Editor; b/Mar 16, 1934; h/42 Treaty Road, Drexel Hill, PA 19026; ba/Philadelphia, PA; m/Francis W News; c/ Teresa Christine, Jean Ann, Eric Paul, Rachel Sue; p/Henry J Goering, Moundridge, KS; ed/Att'd, Bethel Col; BA w Hons, Roosevelt Univ, 1968; MA, IN Univ, 1971; pa/Mng Editor, *Holiday* Mag, Curtis Pub'g Co, 1974-77; Editor, *Going Places*, Chilton Co, 1977-79; Acquisitions Editor, *Realites* Mag, Intermed Communs, 1979-81; Mng Editor, *Sprg*, Rodale Press, 1981-82; Adj Assoc Prof, Temple Univ, 1983-; hon/Author, *Gt Escapes: An Exec's Guide to Fine Resorts*, Chilton Book Co, 1980; Cert of Merit, Short Story Contest for Col Sophomores, *The Atl Monthly*; First Place F'ship Awd in Short Story, IN Univ Writer's Conf; Golden Bassett Awd for Edit Excell, The Fashion Bur, NY; First Place, Best Editing of Contributed Mat, Chilton Edit Awd; World W/W of Wom; W/ W in Am.

KLEIN, MARTIN oc/Executive; b/ Apr 5, 1941; h/Klein Drive, Salem, NH 03079; ba/Salem, NH; m/Diane Marie Parenteau; c/Allen Jameson, Robin; ed/ BSEE, MIT, 1962; pa/Prog Mgr, Sonar Sys, EG&G Intl, 1962-67; Pres, Klein Assoc Inc, 1968-; Lectr, Sonar, Ocean Exploration, Loch Ness & Other Fields of Interest at Tech Soc Meetings, Univs & Grade Schs, as well as Local Bus & Civic Orgs; IEEE; Acoustical Soc of Am; Brit Acoustical Soc; Soc for Hist Archaeol; Instrument Soc of Am; Hydrographic Soc, UK; Oceanic Soc; Acad of Applied Sci; US Nav Inst; Inst of Navigation; Boston Computer Soc; Num Other Mbrships; hon/Pubs, "High Resolution Sea Bed Mapping" 1984, "A Modular Sonar Sys for Seabed Mapping" 1982, Num Others; Elected Fellow, Marine Technol Soc & Explorers Clb; Small Bus-man of the Yr, St of NH, 1983; Pres's "E" Export Awd, 1983.

KLEMKE, JUDITH ANN oc/Mortgage Banking Executive; b/Jul 22, 1950; h/18 West 206 Lathrop Lane, Villa Park, IL 60181; ba/Lisle, IL; m/Keith Michael Kurzeja; p/John S Klemke, Brookfield, IL; ed/BS, Univ of IL Champaign, 1972; pa/VP, First Fam Mortgage Corp, 1980-; Sr VP, First Financial Savs & Ln, 1976-82; Asst VP, Ben Franklin Savs & Ln, 1973-76; Mortgage Bkrs Assn; Nat Assn of Female Execs; Am Soc of Profl & Exec Wom; AAUW; Univ of IL Alumni Assn, Life Mem; Alpha Gamma Delta; r/Luth; hon/W/W in Am Wom.

KLEMM, WILLIAM R oc/Professor, Brain Research Scientist; b/Jul 24, 1934; h/Route 3, Box 473, Bryan, TX 77802; ba/College Station, TX; m/Doris M; c/ Laura, Mark; p/Mr and Mrs L W Klemm, San Antonio, TX; ed/DVM, Auburn Univ, 1958; PhD, Univ of Notre Dame, 1963; mil/Col, USAFR, HQ Aerospace Med Div; pa/From Asst Prof to Assoc Prof, IA St Univ, 1963-66; From Assoc Prof to Prof, Dept of Biol & Dept of Vet Anatomy, TX A&M Univ, 1966; USAF Resv Assignments: Liaison Ofcr (AF Acad), Res Scist (Sch of Aerospace Med), Planning Analyst & Dir for Devel Planning (Aerospace Med Div); Soc for Neurosci, 1972-; Am Physiol Soc, 1965-; Sigma Xi, 1963-; r/Presb; hon/Author, 200+ Sci Jour Articles, Books: *Animal Electroencephalorgraphy* 1969, *Sci, the Brain & Our Future* 1972, *Applied Elects for Vet Med & Animal Physiol* 1976, *Discovery*

Processes in Mod Biol 1977; Dist'd Achmt Awd in Res, TX A&M Univ, 1979; Edit Bds, *Commun Behavioral Biol, Psychopharmacol, Jour of Electrphy Techniques*; W/W: in Frontier Sci & Technol, in S & SW; Am's Names & Faces; Intl W/W in Ed; Contemp Authors; Men of Achmt.

KLIMESZ, HENRY ROMAN oc/ Economics Professor; b/Jun 26, 1926; h/ 63 Lodges Lane, Bala Cynwyd, PA 19004; p/Jan Siegmund and Louise Klimesz; ed/BS, Sch of Maritime Commerce, Univ of Gdansk, 1950; BA 1952, MEcon 1957, Ctl Sch of Planning & Stats, Warsaw, Poland; MBA Temple Univ, 1965; MA, Univ of PA, 1975; pa/ Intl Trade Spec, Varimex Ltd, Warsaw, 1950-54; Mkt Analyst, Editor, Polish Chamber of Fgn Trade, 1954-58; Export Sales Mgr, Tiona Petro Co, 1961-66; Assoc Prof of Ec, Atl Commun Col, 1967-80; Res Assoc, Warsaw Univ, 1980-82; Associate Prof of Ec & Bus, Westminster Col, 1982-83; Am Ec Assn; Acad of Intl Bus; Polish Inst of Arts & Scis; Rencontres Creatives Internationales; r/Rom Cath; hon/Co-Author, *Statl Abstracts for Fgn Trade Execs* 1957, *Poland's Trade through the Black Sea in XVIII Cent* 1970; Editor, *Rynki Zagraniczne*, 1957-58; Author, Num Articles & Monographs in Polish Ec Periods, 1955-58; Senatorial Scholar, 1965-67; Meritorious Ser Awd for Contbns to Ed, 1977; Hist of XVIII Cent Art; W/W in E; Dir of Mems, Polish Inst of Arts & Scis; Am Ec Assn.

KLINE, EDWARD SAMUEL oc/Biochemist; b/Jun 26, 1924; h/4011 Hanover Avenue, Richmond, VA 23221; ba/ Richmond, VA; m/Bernice G; c/Andrew P, Matthew T; p/Morris and Bessie Kline (dec); ed/BA, Microbiol, Univ of PA, 1948; MS 1955, PhD 1961, Biochem, George Wash Univ; pa/Bacteriologist, Walter Reed Inst of Res, 1954-57; Biochem, Armed Forces Inst of Pathol, 1957-61; Postdoct Fellow, IN Univ, 1961-63; Asst Prof 1963-68, Assoc Prof 1968-, Med Col of VA; AAAS; Sigma Xi; VA Acad of Scis; cp/ Nature Conservancy; Nutrition Today Soc; r/Jewish; hon/Contbr of Orig Res to Biochem & Biol Jours; US Patent #2,937,787, 1960; Merit Awd, US Govt, 1960; W/W: in Am, in S, in Frontier Sci & Technol.

KLINKE, PATRICIA GARDNER oc/ Leader and Volunteer in Civic, Cultural and Philanthropic Organizations; Fund Raiser; b/Nov 19, 1929; h/5567 Sycamore Grove, Memphis, TN 38119; c/ Kathryn Ann, Jeffrey Patton; p/Dr Milo Fay Gardner (dec); Hilda Christine Patton (dec); ed/Att'd Univ of TN 1947-49, Harvard Alumni Col 1979-83; BS, Memphis St Univ, 1951; cp/VP, Bd of Dirs, Le Bonheur Chd's Med Ctr, 1982-; Pres, Hosp Aux, 1982-83; Hosp Fund Drive Chm, 1976; Bd of Dirs, The Intl Grp of Memphis, 1966-70; Wom's Com of Fifty, Memphis Orchestral Soc, 1983; Life Mem, Assn for the Presv of TN Antiquities, 1964; Friends of Dixon Gallery, 1979-; Memphis Symph Leag, 1969-; Pres, Brookhaven Garden Clb, 1960; Pres, Oak Grove Garden Clb, 1967; The Josephine Circle Inc, 1979-; r/Presb; hon/Hosp Fund-Raising Awd, 1971-81; Wom's Com of Fifty, Memphis Orchestral Soc, 1983.

KLOEPFER, MARGUERITE FONNESBECK oc/Free-Lance Writer and

Novelist; b/Nov 13, 1916; h/306 East Hawthorne Street, Ontario, CA 91764; ba/Same; m/Lynn W; c/William Leon, Kenneth Lynn, Kathryn K, Robert Alan; p/Leon and Jean Brown Fonnesbeck (dec); ed/BS, UT St Univ, 1937; pa/Free-Lance Writer throughout Lifetime; Author, Bentley 1979, But Where is Love 1980, The Heart & the Scarab 1981, Singles Survival 1979, Short Stories for Seventeen, Wom's Day, Teen Digest; Reprinted in Anthologies, Nineteen from Seventeen & Widening Views; Travel & Other Articles for Ontario Daily Report & Star Free Press; cp/Lwyrs Wives of CA, St Pres 1974-75; Lwyrs Wives of San Bernardino Co, Pres 1957-58; Nat Charity Leag Inc, Nat Pres 1968-70; Nat Charity Leag, Foothill Chapt, Pres 1965-67; Univ of So CA Inter-Frat Mothers Clbs Coun, Pres 1971-72; Univ of So CA Town and Gown; Freedoms Foun, LA Ball Co Chm 1972; hon/Contemp Authors; Intl Authors & Writers W/W; World W/W of Wom; Love's Leading Ladies; Lib Jour.

KLORFEIN, FRUEMA oc/Real Estate Saleswoman; b/Mar 7, 1931; h/North Woods Road, Palm Beach, FL 33480; m/Elliot H MD; c/Stephen Richard, Tamara Joy, Jonathan Scott; p/Harry and Thelma Aborn Nannis (dec); ed/BS, Simmons Col, 1952; Postgrad Wk, Tulane Univ 1953-55, Harvard Univ 1953; pa/Jr Exec, Wm Filene & Sons Co, 1952-53; Elem Sch Tchr, Jefferson Parish (LA) 1953-54, New Orleans (LA) 1954-55, Miami (FL) 1955-56; HS Tchr, US Armed Forces Sch, Kitzingen, W Germany, 1957-58; Elem Sch Tchr, Miami, FL, 1958-59; Real Est Saleswom 1970-84, Broker Saleswoman 1984-, Robert E List Co; Bkkpr, Klorfein & Wanuck, MD, PA, 1969-; cp/Hadassah, Pres 1967-69; Angel of Mercy Com, 1963-82; Bd, FL Reg Hadassah, 1966-71; VP, B'nai B'rith, 1963; Bd, LWV, 1971; Bd of Dirs, Wom's Aux to Palm Bch Co Med Soc, 1964-65; Bd, Jewish Fdn, 1967-69; Bd of Wom's Div 1979-81; hon/Hadassah Pres Awd, 1969; Ser Awd, 1966; Awd of Merit, U Jewish Appeal, 1975; W/W in S & SW.

KLOTZ, KENNETH A oc/Data Processing Executive; b/Apr 8, 1945; h/Route 3, Box 3166, Bulverde, TX 78163; ba/San Antonio, TX; m/Rose Marie; c/Nicole Denise, Jason Kyle, Jamie Dihann; p/Mr and Mrs Ambrose Klotz, Savage, MN; ed/BS in Math 1967, BS in Phy Sci 1967, Winona St Univ; MBA, Adm Mgmt, N TX St Univ, 1978; mil/Army 1968-70, E-5; pa/Programmer, Univac, 1967; Programmer, USAA Ins Co, 1968-70; Data Processing Ofcr, Repub Nat Bk of Dallas, 1970-78; Mgr, Corp Sys Div, Tesoro Petro Corp, 1978-; Assn for Sys Mgmt, San Antonio Chapt, Secy 1979, Pres 1980; cp/Boy Scouts; Bulverde Ath Assn, Bd Mem, Commr of Baseball Prog; r/Cath; hon/W/W in S & SW.

KLUG, MARILYN J oc/General Contractor and Real Estate Investor; b/Mar 18, 1936; h/2853 West 100th Avenue, Anchorage, AK 99502; ba/Same; m/Douglas; c/Bryce Karl, Bruce Allan, Brenda Lee Pearce; p/Walter Henry Otte (dec); Mrs Ressa Beagley, Great Bend, KS; ed/Grad, Gt Bend HS; Att'd, Ft Hays, St Col, for 2 Yrs; pa/Wk'd for Corps of Engrs, Ft Riley, KS, for

5 Yrs; Hd Secy, Airport Div, FFA, for 6 Yrs; Real Est Investor, for Past 16 Yrs; Owner: Motel, 3 Condominiums in FL, 5 Condominiums at Alyeska Ski Resort, 29 Rentals; Gen Contractor & Real Est Agt; AK Visitors Assn, for Past 3 Yrs; Netwkg AK, Bus Wom Org; ABWA, Anchorage Chapt; r/Meth; hon/Lifetime Mbrship in PTA; Govt Awds while Wkg for Govt; 4-H Awds while Mem for 8 Yrs.

KLYBER, CHUCK oc/Association Principle Executive Officer; b/Aug 19, 1937; ba/Springfield, IL; m/Sondra; c/Kevin, Korby, Karla, Kimberley; p/Marie Bianco, Rock Island, IL; ed/BS, OH Christian Col, 1964; LLB, LaSalle Univ, 1969; CAE, Am Soc of Assn Execs, 1980; mil/USN; pa/Profl & Trade Assns; Labor Ldr; Am Soc of Assn Execs; IL Soc of Assn Execs; Author, The Magnificent Money Machine, Inner Confrontations; cp/Past Fdg Pres, Millan JCs; r/Cath; hon/St of IL Senate Resolution, 1967; IL Ho of Reps Resolution, 1976, 1981; Outstg Local JC Pres, IL JCs, 1967; Top 10 Awd of Hon, ASPE, 1977; Dist'd Ser Awd, Milan JCs; Gienssenbier Meml Awd, 1967; Outstg Perf Awd, HI JCs, 1969; CAE Awd of Hon, Am Soc of Assn Execs, 1980.

KNAPHEIDE, LILLIAN ANNE WIESNER oc/Math Teacher; b/May 19, 1952; h/PO Box 548, Waller, TX 77484; ba/Waller, TX; m/William M; c/Christy Anne, Donna Anne; p/Frederick C and Mary A Wiesner, Waller, TX; ed/BS in Elem Ed, Univ of Houston, 1976; Grad Wk in Prog, Prairie View A&M Univ; Grad Wk, TX A&M Univ, 1978; pa/Title I Math Tchr, Waller Indep Sch Dist, 1978-; Assn of TX Profl Edrs; Waller Co Assn of TX Profl Edrs, Pres 1982-83; Assn of Compensatory Edrs of TX; Assn for Supvn & Curric Devel; r/Meth; hon/W/W in S & SW; Personalities of S.

KNIC KREHM, GLEN ALLEN oc/Management Consultant; b/Mar 27, 1948; h/12 Melville Avenue, Dorchester, MA 02124; ba/Cambridge, MA; m/Pamela; p/Allen F and Evelyn (dec) Knic Krehm, Pasadena, CA; ed/BA, magna cum laude, Occidental Col, 1971; BS 1971, MBA 1973, Columbia Univ; pa/Pres, Bay Resource Corp, 1983-; Mgr 1977-83, Conslt 1973-77, Boston Conslttg Grp; Pres, Our Mkt Supermkt Inc, 1980-81; Analyst, Exxon, 1971-72; cp/Nat Trust for Hist Presv; Soc for Presv of New Eng Antiquities; Codman Sq & Fields Corner Commun Devel Corps; hon/Phi Beta Kappa; Tau Beta Pi, Engrg; Sigma Pi Sigma, Physics; Pi Mu Epsilon & Kappa Mu Epsilon, Math; Beta Gamma Sigma; Walter D Smith Meml Awd (First in Class at Columbia Univ), 1973; Samuel Bronfman F'ship (Merit F'ship), 1972; Roswell C McCrea Prize, 1972; W/W in Fin & Indust.

KNIGHT, GEORGINE MARIE oc/Medical Technologist; b/Feb 22, 1954; h/458 Monument Avenue, Wyoming, PA 18644; ba/Kingston, PA; p/George and Eleanor Knight, Wyoming, PA; ed/BS in Med Technol, Wilkes Col, 1977; pa/Med Technologist, Asst Crew Chief (Chem), Nesbitt Meml Hosp, 1977-; Am Soc of Clin Pathols (Affil, Reg'd Med Technologist), 1977-; Pianist; Organist; Yg Musicians Soc of Wilkes-Barre & Scranton, 1969-73; Nat Hon Soc, 1971, 1972; r/Rom Cath; hon/Pianist & Winner of 1971 Wilkes-Barre Philharm

Talent Competition; Superior Ratings in Auditions Sponsored by Nat Guild of Piano Tchrs, incl'g, the Col Freshman Dipl in Perf, 1969-73; W/W of Am Wom.

KNIGHT, LYNDA FRANCES oc/Assistant Attorney General; b/Mar 3, 1948; h/3808 Governors Drive, Apartment C-119, Montgomery, AL 36111; ba/Montgomery, AL; p/Alice R Knight, Clayton, AL; ed/BA, Hist, Huntingdon Col, 1970; LLB, Jones Law Inst, 1974; pa/Libn, Montgomery Co Law Lib, 1971-74; Legal Res Aide to Atty Gen, St of AL, 1974-76; Asst Atty Gen, St of AL, 1976-; AAUW, 1971-72;; BPW, 1972-77; cp/Montgomery Adult Christian Singles, 1978-82, Corres'g Secy 1979-80, 1982; r/Christian-Assem of God.

KNIGHT, MAX oc/Editor, Author, Translator; b/Jun 8, 1909; h/760 Grizzly Peak Boulevard, Berkeley, CA 94708; ba/Same; m/Charlotte; c/Anthony, Martin; ed/LLD, 1933; pa/Prin Editor, Univ of CA Press, 1950-76; Pubs: Christian Morgenstern's Galgenlieder 1963-81, Johann Nestroy: Three Comedies 1966, Hans Kelsen's Pure Theory of Law 1967, Return to the Alps 1970, Otto Maenchen's The World of the Huns 1973, "Schweyk" in Bertot Brecht, Collected Plays 1975, A Confidential Matter: Richard Strauss/Stefan/Zweig 1977, The Orig Blue Danube Cookbook 1979, "A Florentine Chansonnier" in Monuments of Renaissance Music 1983.

KNIGHT, PHYLLIS PRICE oc/Designer of Apparel Accessories, Marketing and Management Consultant; b/Mar 4, 1939; h/505 North Lake Shore Drive, Chicago, IL 60611; ba/Same; c/Larry Lee, Donna Carol; p/Amos Anderson and Flora Jane Seals (dec) Price, Kingsport, TN; ed/Grad w Hons, Morristown HS, 1957; pa/Pres, PK Creations, 1982-; Dir of Mktg, Sales Mgr, Huntington Industs Inc, 1981; VP of Mktg & Opers, Sch Calendar Co Inc, 1972-81; Co-Buyer, Indust, Wallace Hardware Co Inc, 1965-72; Nat Assn of Female Execs; ABWA, Chm of Prog Com 1981; Wom in Sales, Chm of Ways & Means 1983; Wom in Mgmt; Nat Assn of Wom Bus Owners; cp/C of C, Chm of Public Relats Com 1980-81; Nat Soc Fundraising Execs; Netwk for Yth Sers, Chm of Fin Com 1983; Com of 200, Nom; hon/Spec Recog, Co Sida Awd; Delta Flying Col Awd; W/W of Am Wom; Personalities of W & MW.

KNOWLES, RICHARD JAMES ROBERT oc/Medical Physicist; b/Aug 2, 1943; h/4 East 28th Street, #718, New York, NY 10016; ba/New York, NY; m/Stephanie R Closter; c/Guenevere Regina; p/Richard E (dec) and Pauline H Knowles, Topeka, KS; ed/HBS, St Louis Univ, 1965; MS, Cornell Univ, 1969; PhD, Polytechnic Inst of NY, 1979; pa/Sr Med Physicist, NY Hosp-Cornell Med Ctr, 1982-; Dir, Radiation Physics Lab, Downst Med Ctr, 1981-82; Chief Med Physicist, Long Isl Col Hosp, 1977-81; Am Phy Soc; Am Assn of Physicists in Med; Hlth Physics Soc; Soc of Nuclear Med; Soc of Photo-Optical Instrumentation Engrs; NY Acad of Scis; Radiol & Med Physics Soc of NY; hon/Author, 30+ Tech Pubs, incl'g, "NMR: The New Frontier in Diagnostic Radiol" 1984, "Computer Assisted Imaging in Radiol" 1984; Sigma Xi Sci Res Soc, 1979; Pi Mu Epsilon Math Frat, 1964; Alpha Sigma Nu S'ship

Frat, 1964; W/W in Frontier Sci & Technol.

KNOX, GRACE oc/Western Artist, Art Instructor, Judge; b/Sep 21, 1930; h/Box 284, Carlsbad, NM 88220; m/Robert Lee; c/Jeffery Warren, Harold Lee; p/James Warrner and Martha Jane Landess; ed/Grad, W High, 1948; Att'd, NEn CO Col; Pvt Art Instrn w Wm Barry Schimmell, 1969; Self-Ed; pa/Art Show Judge of Nat & Reg Shows, Rodeo Parade Judge, Instr at Wkshops, 1970-; First One-Person Show, 1969; Invitational Shows in Prescott (AZ), Santa Anna (CA), Post, Herford & Pecos (TX); Shows, Nebraskaland Days, Galleria Del Sol, Wn Heritage, First Avenue Galleries, McAdoo Galleries, Cowgirl Hall of Fame, Beef Empire Days, Wn Bk of El Paso, Wn Art Celebration, Tucson Collects the W, Peppertree Ranch Show, Num Others; Judge at Lea Co Fair, Eunice Area Show, Carlsbad Rodeo Parade, Carlsbad Christmas Light Parade, Roswell Fine Art Leag Nat Show, October Affair; Roswell Fine Art Leag, 1982; VP, U Coun of Artists, 1984; hon/Wk Appears in *NM Sketch Book*, *Scholastic Mag*, *The Paint Horse Jour*, *Heritage of an Outlaw*, *How to Feed a Starving Artist Cookbook*, Num Others; Hon Life Artist Mem, Mtn Oyster Clb, 1974; Commun Ser Awd, 1958; Hon Mem, Carlsbad Area Art Assn, 1958; Hon Mem, Roswell Fine Art Leag, 1982.

KNOX, HAROLD L oc/Executive; b/Apr 21, 1918; h/21531 Thorofare Drive, Grosse Ile, MI 48138; ba/Monroe, MI; m/Mary; c/Dr Michael D, Christopher A, Harold Eric; p/William W and Elsie Knox (dec); ed/BSME, 1943; mil/USAAF, 1944-46; pa/Chm, Bd of Dirs & Pres, Detroit Stoker Sistemas Energeticos Ltda, Brazil, 1982-; Chm, Bd of Dirs & Pres, Capital Conveyor Co, 1980-; VP, U Indust Corp, 1977-; Chm, Bd of Dirs, MW Metall Lab Inc, 1974-; Pres 1974-, Bd of Dirs 1970-, Exec VP 1970-74, Asst Chief Engr 1957-70, Asst Supt of Ser & Constrn 1951-57, Detroit Stoker Co; Tech, Gt Lakes Steel Corp, 1937-41; ASME, 1962-; Air Pollution Control Assn, 1964-; Instr, US Power Sqdrn, 1972-; Bd of Dirs, Am Boiler Mfrs Assn, 1975-; cp/Coun for Ed, 1958; Chm, Needs Com for the Grosse Ile, MI, Sch Sys, 1964; r/Presb.

KNOX, TRUDY oc/Psychologist; b/Aug 11, 1926; h/168 Wildwood Drive, Granville, OH 43023; ba/Granville, OH; ed/BS, NWn Univ, 1948; MA, Univ of FL, 1951; EdD, Univ of AR, 1973; pa/Psychol, St of OH, 1951-62; Pvt Pract as Clin Psychol, Grp Psychotherapist, Mgmt Conslt, 1962-; Co-Fdr, Columbus Metro Clb, 1976; Fdr, Charter Pres, OH Spkrs Forum, 1979; Nat Spkrs Assn, 1977; Am Psychol Assn; Am Grp Psychotherapy Assn; APA Divs of Consltg Psych & Orgl Indust Psych; hon/Co-Author, *So Bus Review*, 1976; Author, *OH St Univ Bltn of Bus & Economic Res* 1977, Book Reviews for *Jour of Contemp Psych & Intl Jour of Grp Psychotherapy* 1978; W/W: of Am Wom, of Intl Ed, in MW.

KNUDSON, GREGORY BLAIR oc/Bacterial Geneticist; b/Aug 9, 1946; h/8123 Old Hagerstown Road, Middletown, MD 21769; ba/Fort Detrick, MD; m/Kathryn H M; c/Todd C, Kimberley; ed/BA 1969, MA 1971, CA St Univ-Fullerton; PhD, Univ of

CA-Riverside, 1977; mil/Lt, AUS Chem Corp, 1970-73; Capt, AUS Med Ser Corp, 1978-81; pa/Bacterial Geneticist, GS-12, AUS Med Res Inst of Infectious Diseases, 1981-; Genetic Soc of Am; Am Soc for Microbiol; AAAS; NY Acad of Sci; r/Meth; hon/Pubs, "A Plasmid in *Legionella pneumophila*" 1980, "Plasmid Isolation in *Legionella pneumophila* & Legionella-Like Organisms" 1981, "The Role of Inducible DNA Repair in W-Reactivation & Related Phenomena" 1983; Nat Def Ser Medal; Armed Forces Ser Medal; Armed Forces Resv Medal.

KOBAYASHI, ALBERT SATOSHI oc/Professor of Mechanical Engineering; b/Dec 9, 1924; h/14019 Bagley Avenue, North, Seattle, WA 98133; ba/Seattle, WA; m/Elisabeth Midori; c/Dori Kobayashi Ogami, Tina, Laura; ed/BS, Univ of Tokyo, 1947; MSME, Univ of WA, 1952; PhD, IL Inst of Technol, 1958; pa/Tool Engr, Konishiroku Photo Indust, 1947-50; Design Engr, IL Tool Wks, 1953-55; Res Engr, Armour Res Foun of IL Inst of Technol, 1955-58; Col Fac Conslt, The Boeing Co, 1958-76; Asst Prof 1958-61, Assoc Prof 1961-65, Prof 1965-, Univ of WA; Conslt, Math Scis NW, 1962-; ASME, Fellow; Soc for Exptl Stress Anal, Fellow; Sigma Xi; Soc of Engrg Scis; Tau Beta Pi; r/Presb; hon/Author, 220 Papers in Exptl Stress Anal, Structural Anal, Biomechs & Fracture Mechs; F G Tatnall Awd 1973, B J Lazan Awd 1981, R E Peterson Awd 1983, Wm Murray Medal 1983, Soc for Exptl Stress Anal.

KOCHANOWSKY, BORIS J oc/Professor Emeritus of Mineral Engineering Management; b/1905; ed/Diplom Ingenieur in Mine Surveying 1927, Diplom Ingenieur in Mining Engineering 1929, Bergakademie, Freiberg, Germany; Grad Study, Univs at Jena, Kothen, Clausthal Tech (Zurich, Switzerland); Dr Ingenieur Deg, Univ of Clausthal, 1955; pa/Res Assoc, Bergbauverein, Essen, Germany, & Bergakademie, Freiberg, 1930-33; Appt'd Asst to the Pres & Mgr of Opers, Devel & Res 1933, Current Conslt for the Co, Rheinische Kalksteinwerke GmbH (Subsidiary of German U Steel Corp); Appt'd Prof of Miing Engrg & Ec, Univ of Cuyo, San Juan & Mendoza, 1948; Appt'd to Fac of PA St Univ, 1953; Est'd & Became Chm of Mineral Engrg Mgmt Prog, PA St Univ, 1968; Prof Emeritus of Mineral Engrg Mgmt, PA St Univ; Conslt to Mining & Equip Firms in USA & Abroad; Am Inst of Mining Engrg; Am Soc for Engrg Ed; hon/Co-Author, 3 Textbooks on Open-Pit Mining; Author, 66 Papers in 14 Am & 16 Fgn Jours, Over the Past 2 Decades; Am Men of Sci; Ldrs in Am Sci; W/W in E; Nat Register of Prominent Ams; DIB; Intl W/W of Intells; Intl Register of Profiles.

KOCHARD, BEVERLY J oc/College Administrator; b/Oct 25, 1951; h/717 Hawthorne Road, Bethlehem, PA 18018; ba/Bethlehem, PA; m/Dale A; p/Mr and Mrs John H Gaston, Bridgewater, NJ; ed/BS, Eng, Moravian Col, 1973; EdM, Ednl Adm, Lehigh Univ, 1978; pa/Reporter & Copy Editor, *The Express*, 1973; Dir, McShea Ctr, Allentown Col, 1973-80; Asst Dean of Students, Moravian Col, 1980-; Bd of Dirs, BB/BS of Northampton Co, 1981-83; PCPA; NASPA; ACU-I;

PASPA; cp/Bethlehem C of C Profl Wom's Com, 1981-; Chair, Campus U Way Campaign, 1981; hon/W/W: of Am Wom, Among Students in Am Univs & Cols; Outstg Yg Wom of Am.

KOCHIS, BRENDA LOUISE oc/Clinical Laboratory Section Supervisor; b/Sep 17, 1946; h/West 44-26th Avenue, Spokane, WA 99203; ba/Spokane, WA; p/Stephen and Maryana Kochis, Wilder, ID; ed/BA, Univ of ID, 1970; MA, Ctl MI Univ, 1984; CLS & MT, St Luke's Sch of Med Technol, 1971; CLSp (H), NCAMLP & ASCP, 1979; pa/Staff Med Technologist, St Luke's Meml Hosp, 1971-81; Conslt in Lab Sers, Grand Coulee Hosp 1978-81, Med-eze Care Ctr 1983-84; Clin Lab Sect Supvr, St Luke's Hosp, 1981-; WSSMT, Treas 1975-79, Pres-Elect 1980-81, Pres 1981-82, Bd Mem 1982-, Chm of Student Del Com 1982-83, Fin Com 1980-81, *Lab Oratory* Editor 1978-84; ASMT, Reg IX Coun 1980-84, Pres Coun 1980-82, Del to House 1980, 1981, 1983, 1984; ASMT E&R Fund Inc, Trustee 1980-, Chm 1984-85, AV Chair 1982-84, Exec Com 1983-; r/Cath; hon/Author, Articles in Each Issue of *Lab Oratory*, 1978-84; WSSMT Mem of the Yr, 1979; Pubs Awd, 1980, 1981; WSSMT Cert of Merit, 1983, 1984; WSSMT Pres Awd, 1984; ASMT Pres Cert of Apprec, 1982, 1983, 1984; Omicron Sigma, 1979, 1980, 1981, 1982, 1983, 1984; ASMT Bd Cert of Apprec, 1984.

KOCSIS, THERESA JULIA oc/Volunteer, Retired Art and Religion Teacher; b/May 22, 1907; h/200 Pennington Avenue, Apartment 422, Passaic, NJ; ba/Passaic, NJ; p/Julius Kocsis (dec); Teresia Gyuris Kocsis Baldoyin (dec); ed/BS in Ed, Fordham Univ, 1955; Methods & Tchr Courses, St John Col; Equivalent MA; Att'd, NY Univ, Pace Col, Hunter Col, Bklyn Col, NYC Commun Col; Art Tng in OH, 16 Yrs; pa/Prin, Immaculate Conception Elem; Secy to Labor Relats Mgr, Ebasco Sers, Intl Engrg Co, 1957-59; Art Instr, NYC Bd of Ed, 1964-72; Sr Art Tchr, NYC Sch, for 5 Yrs; Secy, Art Edrs of the City of NY, 1965-71; Libn & Receptionist, Art Ctr, Hot Sprgs, AR, 1980; Poets' Roundtable of Hot Sprgs; cp/Bd of Dirs, Commun Players in Hot Sprgs; Charter Mem, Spa Writers Clb; r/Cath; hon/Author, 2 Books of Poems: *Everything Reminds Me of You* 1970, *To Love Means to Hurt a Lot*; Pub'd in *Ext, an Anthology of Mod Poetry* 1968, *Poetry Parade* 1969, *Poets of AR* 1981, *Hot Sprgs Roundtable Anthology*; Papers, "How Tchg of Ethics Could Eliminate Crime" & "What Constitutes a Valid Work of Art"; Named Poet Laureate of the Month, Leonardo da Vinci Intl Acad, Rome, Sep 1981; Second Prize in Nat Rel Poster Contest, "Feed the Hungry"; Bronze Medal, Alliance Francaise; Hon Mention, NYC Coliseum at Intl Art Show; Cambridge Book of Poetry.

KOCZWARA, CHRISTINE JOY oc/Associate Professor of Art and Art Education; b/May 19, 1945; h/775 Fisk Road, Cookeville, TN 38501; ba/Cookeville, TN; p/John Joseph and Sophie Ann Koczwara, Cookeville, TN; ed/BFA, Ringling Sch of Art, 1967; MA, Wm Paterson Col of NJ, 1972; Grad Study, Wn MI Univ, 1979; pa/Assoc Prof of Art & Art Ed, TN Technological Univ; Exhbns: Nat Gallery of Art, US Nav

Acad Mus, TN Technological Univ, Univ of TN-Knoxville, Am Artists Profl Leag Grand Nat, Knickerbocker Arts, Salmagundi Clb, Nat Arts Clb, Nat Acad, Drew Univ, Num Others; AAUP, 1972-; TN Ed Assn, 1972-; NEA, 1972-; TN Art Ed Assn, 1972-; Phi Delta Kappa, 1977-; Salmagundi Clb, 1973-; Navy Art Coop & Liaison Com, 1967-; USMC Combat Artist, 1967-; USMC Combat Correspondent's Assn, 1979-; Am Artists Profl Leag, 1964-; TN Art Leag, 1972-; Num Other Mbrships; r/ Epis; hon/Outstg Fac Awd, TN Technological Univ, 1982; Outstg Wom in Am; Outstg Yg Wom of Am; DIB; Others.

KOELLE, GEORGE BRAMPTON oc/ Distinguished Professor of Pharmacology; b/Oct 8, 1918; h/205 College Avenue, Swarthmore, PA 19081; ba/ Philadelphia, PA; m/Winifred Angenent MD; c/Peter Brampton, William Angenent, Jonathan Stuart; p/Frederick C and Emily M Brampton Koelle (dec); ed/BSc, Phila Col of Pharm & Sci, 1939; Hon DSc, 1965; PhD, Univ of PA, 1946; MD, Johns Hopkins Univ, 1950; Hon MD, Univ of Zurich, 1972; mil/AUS 1942-46, From Pvt to 1st Lt; pa/Asst Prof of Pharm, Columbia Univ, Col of P&S, 1950-52; Prof of Pharm 1952-65, Dean 1957-59, Grad Sch of Med, Univ of PA; Chm, Dept of Pharm 1959-81, Dist'd Prof 1981-, Sch of Med, Univ of PA; Am Soc Pharm & Exptl Therapeutics, Pres 1965; Intl Union of Pharm, Secy Gen 1966-69, VP 1969-72; AAAS, VP 1972; Gtr Phila Comm for Med-Pharm Sci, Chm 1976-; cp/Sons of the Copper Beeches, 1954-; r/Luth; hon/Author, 170 Pubs on Pharm of Anticholinesterase Agts, Histochem of Cholinesterases, Electron Microscopy, Neurotrophic Factor; Abel Prize, 1950; Guggenheim F'ship, 1963; Nat Acad of Sci, 1972; Univ of Turku Meml Medal, 1972; Intl W/W; W/W: in World, in World of Sci, in Am.

KOELZER, WILLIAM oc/Marketing Consultant; b/May 25, 1942; h/620 9th Street, Huntington Beach, CA 92648; ba/Santa Ana, CA; m/Kathi; c/Jacqui, Shelley; p/Charles and Lois Koetzer, Portland, MI; ed/BA in Jour, San Jose St Univ, 1968; AA in Jour, Orange Coast Col, 1965; mil/USN, 1961-63; pa/Editor, Mich-Out-of-Doors 1968, Otsego Co Herald Times 1969; VP, Cochrane Chase Livingstone Co Inc, 1969-75; Pres, Gold Rush Advtg, 1977-78; VP, Basso & Assocs, 1979-80; Pres, Koelzer & Assocs, 1980-83; Co-Owner & Exec VP, Travel Reps Inc; Public Relats Soc of Am, Accredited Mem & Mem of Cnslrs Sect 1974-; cp/Wn Sts Promotional Mgr, The Hunger Proj, 1982; Bd of Dirs, Orange Co Holiday Proj, 1981; hon/ Author, Scuba Diving: How to Get Started, 1976; Co-Author, Mktg Prob Solver, 1977; Top Mktg Awd, PRSA LA Chapt, 1975; Orange Co PRSA Chapt, 2 Best Category Awds, 1982; W/W in W.

KOHNERT, JILL ILENE oc/Stockbroker; b/Jun 18, 1950; h/6908 Moonmont, Austin, TX 78745; ba/Austin, TX; p/Creighton and June Kohnert, Houston, TX; ed/Att'd, So Meth Univ 1968-69, Univ of TX 1970; BA in Spanish, Univ of Houston, 1972; pa/ Exec Secy/Asst Acct, Real Est and Arch Firms, 1972-74, 1975; Pers, Houston Mus of Fine Arts, 1975-77; Exec Asst

to Exec Dir, St Bar of TX, 1978-81; Exec Dir and Gen Mgr, TX Lwyrs' Ins Exch, 1981-83; Exec Asst, TX Commerce Bk, 1983; Stockbroker, Rotan Mosle Investmts Sers Inc; Austin Bus Forum; Exec Wom Intl; Nat Assn of Female Execs; Am Inst of Bkg; cp/Pilot Clb Intl; PEO Sisterhood; Zachary Scott Theatre Guild; Laguna Gloria Art Guild; hon/ Sprg Arts Fest Finalist, Houston Mus of Fine Arts, 1968; W/W of Am Wom.

KOLB, CHARLES EUGENE oc/Physical Chemist, Research Director; b/May 21, 1945; h/51 Woodmere Drive, Sudbury, MA 01776; ba/Billerica, MA; m/ Susan Foote; c/Craig Eugene, Mary Colette; p/Charles E and Doris M Kolb, LaVale, MD; ed/SB, Chem Physics, MIT, 1967; MA 1968, PhD 1971, Phy Chem, Princeton Univ; pa/Sr Res Scist 1971-75, Prin Res Scist 1975-, Dir of Ctr for Chem & Envir Physics 1977-79, Tech Dir of Applied Scis Div 1979-80, VP & Dir of Applied Scis Div 1980-84, VP & Dir of Res 1984-, Aerodyne Res Inc; MIT Corporate Vis'g Com for Student Affairs, 1981-; Adv Bd, MIT Reg Laser Ctr, 1981-; Am Chem Soc; Am Phy Soc; Optical Soc of Am; Combustion Inst; AAAS; Union of Concerned Scists; r/Meth; hon/Author, Over 40 Profl Jour Articles & Book Chapts; Res Assoc in Atmospheric Chem, Harvard Univ, 1976-; Res Affil, MIT Spectroscopy Lab, 1981-; W/W in Frontier Sci & Technol; Am Men & Wom of Sci.

KONDRACKA, ELIZABETH TERESA oc/Physician; b/Apr 15, 1945; h/1903 Redwood Avenue, Melbourne Beach, FL 32951; ba/Lewisville, TX; m/ Alex; c/Anthony Joseph; p/Antoni and Anna Cwiek; ed/MD, Univ of Warsaw, Poland, 1970; pa/Resident in Fam Pract, TX Tech Univ & Anniston (AL), 1977-80; Med Practice, Fam Practice, Lewisville, TX, 1980-; AMA; AAFP; TX Med Assn; Denton Co Med Assn; World Med Assn; hon/Diplomate, Am Bd of Fam Prac; Fellow, Am Acad Fam Pract; W/W of Am Wom.

KONRAD, MICHAEL WARREN oc/ Scientist; b/Dec 20, 1936; h/1676 Arbutus Drive, Walnut Creek, CA 94595; ba/ Emeryville, CA; m/Wanda Devlaminck; c/Michele, Hans, Robin; p/Adm and Mrs E G Konrad; ed/BS, Physics, CA Inst of Technol, 1958; PhD, Biophysics, Univ of CA-Berkeley, 1964; mil/USNR; pa/ Asst Prof, Chem, Univ of CA-LA, 1966-75; Assoc Staff Scist, Molecular Biol, Univ of CA-Berkeley, 1975-80; Sr Scist, Cetus Corp, 1980-; AAAS; Am Soc of Biol Chems; hon/Pub, Biosynthesis of Human Proinsulin, 1981; Woodrow Wilson Fellow, 1958-59.

KOPECKO, DENNIS JON oc/Senior Research Microbiologist; b/Jan 14, 1947; h/4601 Flower Valley Drive, Rockville, MD 20853; ba/Washington, DC; m/ Patricia Guerry-Kopecko; c/Jennifer Kristen; p/Norbert R and Dorothy E Kopecko, Richmond, VA; ed/BS, Biol, VA Mil Inst, 1968; PhD, Microbiol, Va Commonwlth Univ, 1972; Postdoct Study, Stanford Univ Sch of Med, 1972-76; mil/AUS 1976-79, CPT, MSC; pa/Res Scist 1976-79, Sr Res Microbiologist, Dept of Def 1979-, Walter Reed Army Inst of Res; Pt-time Consltg Res Scist, Genetic Res Corp, 1981-82; Am Soc Microbiol, 1968-; Genetics Soc of Am, 1980-84; Soc of Sigma Xi, 1971-;

Fed Exec & Profl Assn, 1979-; DC Br of Am Soc Microbiol, Mem-at-Large 1979-; Mid-Atl Reg Extrachromosomal Genetic Elements Grp, 1976-; r/Rom Cath; hon/Pubs, "Devel of a DNA Hybridization Diagnostic Detection Sys for Salmonella typhi" 1984, "Constrn of a Fused Plasmid Specifying Shigella flexneri 2a Antigens & Its Transfer to the Salmonella typhi Ty21a Oral Vaccine Strain" 1984, Num Others; Alpha Sigma Chi Frat for Ldrship, 1972; Editor & Reviewer for Maj Jours & One Book Series; Hon Grad, AUS MSC Ofcr Basic Sch, 1976; Num F'ships, incl'g, Bk of Am-Giannini Med Res Foun F'ship 1973-75, C F Aaron F'ship (Stanford Univ) 1972-73; Hons for Acad Excell & Ldrship, Alpha Sigma Chi Frat, 1971-72; Other Hons; W/W: in Sci, in E, in Frontier Sci & Technol.

KOPP, NANCY K oc/Delegate of the Maryland General Assembly; b/Dec 7, 1943; h/6301 Dahlonega Road, Bethesda, MD 20816; ba/Annapolis, MD; m/Robert E; c/Emily, Robert; p/ Lester and Barbara Kornblith, Bethesda, MD; ed/BA, Wellesley Col, 1965; MA, Univ of Chgo, 1968; pa/Instr of Polit Sci, Univ of IL Chgo, 1968-69; Staff, Spec Subcom on Ed, Ho of Reps, 1970-71; Legis Asst, Montgomery Co Del, MD Gen Assem; Am Polit Sci Assn; AAUW; cp/LWV; Common Cause; r/ Jewish; hon/Nat Def Fellow, Charles Merriam Scholar, Univ of Chgo, 1968; Wellesley Col Scholar, 1965; MD AAUW Outstg Ser Awd, 1979; Outstg Yg Wom of MD; W/W: of Am Wom, in Am Polits; World W/W of Wom.

KOPP, STEVEN HOWELL oc/Assistant Commissioner; b/Sep 28, 1945; h/ 1519 Brent Drive, Knoxville, TN 37923; ba/Knoxville, TN; m/Katherine Harris; c/Lisa Michelle; p/John B and LaNelle R Kopp, Andersonville, TN; ed/BA, Wittenberg Univ, 1968; JD, Nashville YMCA Night Law Sch; mil/USN, 1968-72; pa/Asst Commr, TN Dept of Conserv, 1982-; Chief of Legal Sers, Dept of Conserv, Div of Surface Mining & Reclamation, 1981-82; Atty, Pvt Pract, 1980-81; Exec Dir, TN Energy Auth (St Energy Ofc); TN & ABA; Am Soc for Public Adm; Legal Counsel for RID of Oak Ridge-Anderson Co Inc; cp/ Atomic City Kiwanis Clb; Oak Ridge Rowing Assn; Asst Scoutmaster; E TN Chapt of Seventh Step Foun Inc; r/ Presb; hon/Top 10 Percent of Law Sch Grad'g Class, 1978; Am Jurisp Awd for S'ship in Constitl Law, 1976; W/W in S & SW.

KORAN, DENNIS HOWARD oc/ Editor; b/May 21, 1947; h/5428 Hermitage Avenue, North Hollywood, CA 91607; ba/Los Angeles, CA; m/Roslynn Cohen; c/Michael; p/Dr Aaron Baer and Shirley Mildred Kassan Koran; ed/BA, Univ of CA-Berkeley, 1970; Student, Univ of Leeds (England) 1966-67, Loyola Law Sch 1982-; pa/Co-Fdr & Co-Editor, Cloud Marauder Books, 1967-71; Fdr, Editor, Panjandrum Books (Panjandrum Poetry Jour), 1971-; Coor'g Coun of Lit Mags, 1971-; Poets & Writers Inc, 1975-; Lovers of the Stinking Rose, 1973-; cp/Dem; VISTA Vol, Served as Govt Conslt Wkg w Seminole Indians in OK, 1970-71; Pres, Temple Yth Grp, 1964; r/Jewish; hon/ Pubs, VACANCIES: Poems 1969-75 1975, Num Poems in Lit Mags, incl'g, "Beatitudes," "Amphora," "Poetry Now," "SF Phoenix," "Fuse," & "Skywriting"; Book in Prog, *Before the Dawn: A Chronicle of the Sixties*; Ephebian Soc, 1964; Grants for Pub'g from Coor'g Coun of Lit Mags 1971, 1973, 1975, 1978, Nat Endowment for the Arts Lit Prog 1974, 1976, 1978, 1980-81; W/W: in CA, in Intl Poetry.

KORETZ, JANE FAITH oc/Associate Professor of Biology; b/Aug 12, 1947; h/102 25th Street, Troy, NY 12180; ba/Troy, NY; p/Norman J and Natalie C Koretz, Teaneck, NY; ed/BA w High Hons, Swarthmore Col, 1969; PhD, Dept of Biophysics, Univ of Chgo, 1974; pa/MDA Postdoct Fellow, MRC Cell Biophysics Unit, London, England, 1974-76; Res Affil, Dept of Physiol, CMDNJ, 1976-77; Asst Prof 1977-83, Assoc Prof 1983-, Biol Dept, Rensselaer Polytechnic Inst; Biophy Soc, 1978-; Assn Res Vision & Ophthaly, 1978-; Am Soc Biol Chems, 1983-; IEEE Computer Soc, 1980-; Assn for Wom in Sci, 1980-; AAUP; hon/Author, Var Articles, Abstracts, Book Chapts in Sci Jours & Invited Papers at Symposia, 1972-; Sigma Xi; Recip of Grants from NIH, NSF, MDA, 1978-; Outstg Yg Wom of Am; W/W in E.

KORI, SHASHIDHAR H oc/Neuro-Oncologist; b/Jun 18, 1949; h/2268 Stillman Road, Cleveland, OH 44118; ba/Cleveland, OH; m/Shylaja; c/Ajay; ed/MD, Kasturba Med Col, Mangalore, India, 1970; pa/Chief of Neurol Ser 1983-, Neurologist 1980, VA Med Ctr; Dir of Post-Herpetic & Oncological Pain Clin 1980-, Chief of Neuro-Oncology 1980-, Assoc Neurologist 1980-, Univ Hosps; Asst Prof in Neurol, Case Wn Resv Univ Sch of Med, 1980-; Cancer Pain Res F'ship, Meml Sloan Kettering Cancer Ctr, 1978-80; Immunobiol Postdoct F'ship, Sloan Kettering Inst for Cancer Res, 1979-80; F'ship in Neuro-Immunol 1979-80, F'ship in Neuro-Oncology 1978-80, Meml Sloan Kettering Cancer Ctr; AMA; Am Acad of Neurol; Intl Assn for the Study of Pain; Am Pain Soc; En Pain Assn; Am Soc of Internal Med; Neuroscis Assn; Am Soc for Neurological Invests; Soc for Neuroscis; hon/Pubs, "Brachial Plexus Lesion in Cancer Patients: Clin Findings in 100 Cases" 1981, "Familial Plasminogen Activator Deficiency a Cause of Cerebrovascular Thrombosis" 1979, Others; Distn in Pathol in Forensic Med, 1969; Best Outgoing & Most Deserving Student of Med Sch, 1970; Nat Res Ser Awd of Public Hlth Serv, NIH, 1979-80; Am Men & Wom of Sci; W/W in Frontiers of Sci & Technol; Intl Alumni Dir of MSKCC.

KORMES, JOHN WINSTON oc/Attorney-at-Law; b/May 4, 1935; h/1070 Edison Avenue, Philadelphia, PA 19116; ba/Philadelphia, PA; m/Frances Wisniewski; c/Mark Vincent; p/Mark and Joanna Kormes, Fort Lauderdale, FL; ed/BA, Univ of MI, 1955; JD, Univ of MI Law Sch, 1959; mil/USAF, 1956-57, Airman Second Class; pa/Atty, Pvt Pract of Law, 1961-; Asst Dist Atty, City of Phila, 1973; Phila Bar Assn, 1961-; Plaintiff's Trial Lwyrs Assn, 1963-; Am Arbitration Assn, 1967-; NY St Assn of Trial Lwyrs, 1966; Am Trial Lwyrs Assn, 1965-; Am Bar Assn, 1981-; Fed Bar Assn, 1965-; cp/Re-Elect

the Pres Com, 1972; Rizzo for Mayor Com, 1971, 1975; City of Phila Lic & Inspection Review Bd, 1972-73; Asst City Solicitor, City of Phila, 1974-80; Lion's Clb, 1960-; Masons, 1963-; Am Legion, 1973-; Shrine, 1968-; Lehigh Consistory, 1968-; K of Pythias, 1964-; Vol, Red Cross Flood Relief Prog; Police Ath Leag; BSA, Troop Com Ldr; ARC; Phila Flag Day Assn; K of Khorassan; r/Prot; hon/Pub, Song, "I'm So Lonesome," 1952; Delta Sigma Rho, 1955-; Mensa, 1975-; Intertel, 1976-; Lwyrs in Mensa, 1979-; NY Intercol Legis Assem Awd, 1954; RI Model Cong Awd, 1954; W/W: in E, in Am Law, of Intells; Men of Achmt.

KOSKINEN, JOHN A oc/Executive; b/Jun 30, 1939; h/1846 Redwood Terrace, Northwest, Washington, DC 20012; ba/Washington, DC; m/Patricia Salz; c/Cheryl Ann, Jeffrey Alan; p/Mr and Mrs Yrjo Koskinen; ed/LLB, Yale Law Sch, 1964; BA, Duke Univ, 1961; Att'd, Cambridge Univ, 1964-65; pa/Pres & CEO 1979-, Pres & COO 1977-79, VP 1973-77, Victor Palmieri & Co Inc; Adm Asst to Senator Abraham Ribicoff of CT, 1969-73; Legis Asst to Mayor John Lindsay of NYC, 1968-69; Other Previous Positions; VP, Bd of Dirs, Nat Captioning Inst, 1979-; St Bars of CA & CT; Real Est Broker, CA, PA, DC, NC, NJ, NY; Duke Univ Gen Alumni Assn, 1977-; Duke Univ Bd of Visitors, Inst of Policy Scis & Public Affairs, 1981-; hon/Phi Beta Kappa, 1960; Grad, magna cum laude, 1961; Order of Coif, 1964; Grad, cum laude, 1964; W/W: in Fin & Indust, in Wash, in Real Est in Am, in World.

KOSS, GRACE JOHNSEN oc/Business Executive, Columnist; b/May 13, 1919; h/R4, Sunset Shores, Luxemburg, WI 54217; ba/Green Bay, WI; m/J Don Sr; c/Joseph, John, James; p/A H (dec) and Mary Holub Johnsen, Green Bay, WI; ed/Att'd, Drake Univ, 1937-39; pa/Taught Spch in Diocesan Elem Schs, Green Bay, 1940-43; Tchr, Pvt Spch Studios, Green Bay, 1940-50; Staff Writer 1965-69, Editor of Lay Org Page 1975-, *The Spirit*; Pres, Cheese Hut Inc; Nat Fed of Press Wom, Reg Dir 1976-80; Nat Press Clb; Am Coun for Better Broadcasts, Past VP of WI Coun; Bd of Dirs, WI Reg Writers; WI Acad of Sci, Arts & Lttrs; Kappa Kappa Gamma; Zeta Phi Eta; cp/Nat Coun of Cath Wom, Provincial Pub Rel; Coun of Cath Wom, Pres; Green Bay Deanery, Pres; Green Bay Cath Woms Clb, Pres; Cabrini Lib, Fdr, Pres; MacDowell Clb, Pres; LWV of Green Bay, Public Relats & Bltn Editor; Brown Co Commun Coun, Secy 1953-59; Brown Co Commun Relats & Social Devel Comm; Brown Co Comm on Aging; r/Cath; hon/Topical Columnist, Wkly Diocesan Newspapers, 17 Yrs; Over 50 St & Nat Writing Awds; Cits from Am Coun for Better Broadcasts; Music Fdn of Am; W/W: of Am Wom, in W & MW.

KOSTAKOPOULOS, HARALAMBOS SERGIOS oc/Senior Economist; b/Oct 28, 1950; h/590 Fort Washington Avenue, New York, NY 10033; ba/New York, NY; p/Sergios and Maria Kostakopoulos, Levadia, Greece; ed/PhD 1979, MPhil 1979, MA 1976, Columbia Univ; BA, Pace Univ, 1973; pa/Res Asst, Fin Adm, City of NY, 1973-74; Asst Prof, SUNY-Oswego, 1978-79; Asst

Prof, CUNY, Hunter Col, 1979-80; Sr Economist, Merrill Lynch, 1980-; Am Ec Assn; Econometrica; r/Greek Orthodox.

KOTAY, MILES oc/Public Relations Manager; b/Dec 20, 1949; h/1515 East 20th Street, Tulsa, OK 74120; m/Vicki; c/Kerriann; p/Victor (dec) and Catherine Kotay; ed/BS, Jour, KS St Univ, 1971; Col Prep Dipl, Ctl Dauphin E HS, 1967; pa/Editor, *Hebron Jour-Register*, 1971-72; Info Asst 1973-75, Info Supvr 1975-76, Advtg Supvr 1976-78, Public Relats Mgr 1978-, SW Bell Telephone Co; Tulsa Press Clb; IABC; PRSA; cp/Bd of Dirs, OK Spec Olympics; Jr Achmt of Gtr Tulsa; Tulsa Rugby Clb; r/Serbian Orthodox; hon/Emmy for TV Ad Featuring Decorator Telephones, 1977; Rookie of the Yr, Tulsa Gridiron, 1978; Wm Werd Ellis Awd, 1982; W/W in S & SW; Men of Achmt.

KOTHARI, HARSHED VASANJI oc/Pipe Stress Engineer; b/Nov 2, 1950; h/1003 Arbor, Cherrywood Apartments, Clementon, NJ 08021; ba/Cherry Hill, NJ; m/Bharti Harshed; c/Jay Harshed; p/Vansanji Vallabhji and Vijyalaxmi V Kothari (dec); ed/BEng, Mech Engrg, Univ of Bombay, India, 1974; MSME, Univ of MO-Rolla, 1976; Postgrad Wk, 1976-77; Res Asst, NSF Grantee, 1975; Tchg Asst, Univ of MO-Rolla, 1976-77; pa/Proj Engr, Sundstrand Aviation Co, 1977-78; Proj Design Engr, MTE Hydraulics Inc, 1978-81; Pipe Stress Engr, Stone & Webster Engrg Co, 1981-; ASME; Sigma Xi; Phi Kappa Phi; cp/Pres, India Cultural Assn of Gtr Rockford, 1977-78; Bd of Dirs, India Cultural Assn of Gtr Rockford, 1978-79; VP, Rockford Table-Tennis Clb, 1979-80; r/Hindu; hon/Pubs, "Optimum Design of Helical Springs" 1980, "Effect of Band or Line Shape on Rad Transfer in a Non-Gray 2-D Medium" 1977; Dean's S'ship, Univ of MO-Rolla, 1975; W/W in E.

KOUTROTSIOS, DIANE T oc/Artist and Designer; b/Mar 31, 1945; h/4138 South Artesian, Chicago, IL 60632; ba/Same; m/Demetrios; c/Angela; p/George Bajoriunas (dec); Julia Bajoriunas; ed/Att'd Chgo City Col, 1968; Ray Vogue Sch of Design, 1969; Am Acad Art, Chgo; Graphic Arts Deg, 1978; pa/Prodn Artist, H&R Studio, Chgo, IL, 1978-80; Pvt Art Tchr, 1978-81; Pres, Diane's Studio, Inc, 1981-84; Mem, Balzekas Mus of Baltic Arts & Culture, 1981; VP, Pres, Spectrum Art Guild, 1980-84; Art Fair Judge, Evanton Art Fair, 1980; Judge, Albany Pk Art Fair, Chicago, IL, 1978; Chm, Beverly Hills Art Fair, 1978; Judge, Andersonville, Chgo, 1979; Pvt Piano Tchr, 1984; hon/Exhibits: Aborigine Art, Culture & Hist, Brighton Pk Lib, 1983; Gold, Silver, Bronze Medals for Portrait Work, 1978-81; Silver Medal for Graphic Art, Hild Lib, Chgo, IL, 1977; Baltic Artists Dir; Universal Art Promotions Dir.

KOVALIC, JOAN M oc/Attorney; b/Dec 27, 1948; h/3519 West Place, Northwest, Washington, DC 20007; ba/Washington, DC; m/Keith E Bernard; p/Margaret D Kovalic, Pittsburgh, PA; ed/BA in Social Relats 1970, MS in Public Adm 1972, Carnegie-Mellon Univ; JD, George Wash Univ Law Sch, 1979; pa/Counsel, Regulation/Legis Issues, Envir, Water Quality/Resources; Dpty Dir, Ofc of Water Prog Opers, Envir Protection Agy, 1980-82; Asst

Counsel for Water & Envir, Com on Public Wks & Trans, US Ho of Reps, 1973-80; Manpower Prog, Policy & Budget Analyst, Ofc of the Asst Secy for Policy, Eval & Res, US Dept of Labor, 1972-73; Water Resources Prog, Policy & Legis Analyst, Com on Envir Public Wks, US Senate, 1971; PA Bar, 1979; DC Bar, 1980; US Dist Ct & US Ct of Appeals for DC, 1980; ABA; PA Bar Assn; Phi Alpha Delta Legal Frat; DC Bar Assn; Water Pollution Control Fdn; Fed Water Quality Assn; Am Public Wks Assn; Wom's Ec Roundtable; Pres, Sch of Urban & Public Affairs Alumni Assn, Carnegie-Mellon Univ, 1980-82; hon/ Pubs, "Funding to Meet Am's Water Needs" 1982, "Changing Directions in Water Mgmt" 1982, Others; Outstg Perf Rating, Sr Exec Ser, US Envir Protection Agy, 1982; Gold Medal Awd for Exceptl Ser, US Envir Protection Agy, 1982; Superior Perf Awd, Ofc of the Secy, US Dept of Labor, 1973; Other Hons; W/W of Am Wom.

KRAMER, EMMANUEL MARTIN oc/Archaeologist, Teacher; b/Mar 18, 1928; h/503 Laverock Road, Glenside, PA 19038; ba/Elkins Park, PA; m/Judith Levine; c/Henry, Gary, Benjamin; p/ William and Sonja Kramer, Elkins Park, PA; ed/BS in Ed 1950, MS in Ed 1952, Temple Univ; Grad Studies in Archaeol, Nat Univ of Mexico, Univ of London, Paris, 1952-63; pa/Tchg Position, Phila Sch Dist, 1950-56; Tchr 1956-, Hist Dept Chm 1976-79, Cheltenham HS; Tchg Positions, Harvard Univ 1972, Phila Col of Art 1966; Current Adj Prof, Beaver Col; Cheltenham Twp Hist Comm, 1974-79; NEA; Archaeol Inst of Am; Soc for Hist Archaeol; hon/Author, *Observations on Aspects of Rel Arch in Wn Europe*, "The Archaeol of Local Hist" 1979, "Treasures in the Trash" 1980, "The Glass Bottle Container" 1981, "Archaeol on the Wm Penn House Site" 1982; Var Local Commun Awds for Lectures; Two $25,000 Grants from Wm Penn Foun, 1981, 1982; W/W in E.

KRAMER, SISTER MARY ALBERT oc/Professor of Nursing Education; b/ Jul 26, 1914; h/342 Oakland Avenue, Pittsburgh, PA 15213; ba/Pittsburgh, PA; p/Albert and Mary Kramer (dec); ed/PhD 1962, MSNE 1948, Cath Univ of Am; BSN, Univ of Dayton, 1941; Dipl, St Joseph's Hosp Sch of Nsg, 1938; pa/Prof 1980-, Assoc Prof 1971-80, Dir of Grad Prog in Nsg Adm/Nsg Ed 1977-79, Univ of Pgh Sch of Nsg; Chp of Dept of Ed & Psych 1966-71, Dir of Student Sers 1965-66, Chaminade Univ; Dir of Admissions & Records, Maria Regina Col, 1962-65; Dir of Nsg, St Elizabeth Hosp, 1956-60; Dir of Nsg, St Francis Hosp, 1940-56; Hd Nurse Asst, OR Supvr, Night Adm Supvr, St Joseph Hosp Hlth Ctr, 1938-40; Advr, Univ of Pgh Students for Life, 1980-; Secy, Univ Senate, 1982-; Secy, Univ Senate Coun, 1982-; Univ Fac Exec Com, 1982-; Curric Com of Grad Tchg Fac, 1979-; PA Nurses Assn; ANA; PA Leag for Nsg; Nat Leag for Nsg; Coun for Grad Ed for Adm in Nsg; Coun on Nsg Res of PA Nurses Assn; Profl Adv Bd of People Concerned for the Unborn Child; cp/Pennsylvanians for Human Life, 1977-; r/Rom Cath; hon/Pubs, "A Nsg Objectives Bk-Fantasy or Good Sense?" 1974, "Weighting & Distribut-

ing Course Grades" 1974, Others; Nat Leag for Nsg F'ship for Doct Study; Recog in US Congl Record; Ser Awd, Univ of Pgh Sch of Nsg; Other Hons; Outstg Tchrs of Am; Men & Wom of HI; W/W: in World Med, Among Contemp Nurses; World W/W of Wom; .

KRAMER, SUSAN ALICE oc/Executive; b/Oct 23, 1950; h/1027 Hilts Avenue, Los Angeles, CA 90024; ba/Los Angeles, CA; p/Mr and Mrs Raphael Kramer, Los Angeles, CA; ed/BA summa cum laude, Univ of CA LA Sch of Fine Arts, 1971; EdM w Hons, Univ of CA-LA Grad Sch of Ed, 1972; pa/ Supvg Tchr, LA Unified Sch Dist, 1971-75; Prof, CA St Univ Dominguez Hills, Dept of Ed, 1974-75; Hd, Prod Devel, Walt Disney Telecommuns & Non-Theatrical Co, 1976-79; Pres & Owner, Walker/Kramer & Assocs Inc & Cinefilm Communs Assocs, CFCA Inc, 1980-; Wom in Bus (Publicity Com) 1982, 1983; IFPA, Film & Video Communicators (Film Awd Judge), 1981-; hon/Pub Credits for Juv Lit & Instrnl Curricula (Macmillan, Ency Britannica, Houghton Mifflin); Phi Beta Kappa, 1971; Pi Lambda Theta Hon Sorority for Wom in Ed, 1972; Alpha Lambda Delta Hon Sorority for Superior Scholastic Achmt, 1969; W/W of Am Wom.

KRAUS, ANNA JOSEPHINE oc/ Medical Record Administrator; b/Apr 11, 1927; h/114 Linsdale Drive, Butler, PA 16001; ba/Butler, PA; p/Alexander B (dec) and Bernadine L Kraus, Brookville, PA; ed/BA in Med Record Adm, 1958; AA in Reg'd Nsg, 1969; MPH in Med Record Adm, Univ of CA-LA, 1972; MS in Tchr Preparation in Allied Hlth Professions, SUNY-Buffalo, 1973; pa/Med Record Asst and Dir, Var Hosps in CA & PA; Med Record Conslt in Var Hosps in CA, PA & WV, 1959-69, 1970-74; Asst Dir, Med Record Adm Prog, York Col/Hosp, 1974-75; Short-term Med Record Conslt for WHO, Princess Margaret Hosp, 1975, 1976; Dir of Med Record Adm Prog, Alderson-Broaddus Col, 1976-81; Chief of Med Info Sect, VA Med Ctr, 1981-; Treas & Pres, CA Med Record Assn, 1966, 1968; Chm, Var Coms in Med Record Assn in CA, PA & WV; Pres, WV Med Record Assn, 1980-82; Secy, Student Nurses Assn, 1968-69; AAUW, Pres-Elect 1981; AHA; ANA; WV Nurses Assn; Intl Mgmt Coun; cp/Bd of Dirs, Ctl WV Cath Commun Sers; r/Cath; hon/Ldrship & Ser, Student Nurses Assn, 1969; W/W: in Allied Hlth, in S & SW, of Am Wom.

KREMENLIEV, BORIS A oc/Composer; b/May 23, 1911; h/10507 Troon Avenue, Los Angeles, CA 90064; m/Elva Florence; c/Gregor, Elana; ed/BMus 1935, MMus 1937, DePaul Univ; PhD, Eastman Sch of Music, Univ of Rochester, 1942; mil/AUS, Psychol Warfare, ETO, 1943-45; pa/Music Dir, S German Netwk, 1945-46; Music Critic, *Melos*, Germany; Prof of Music (Composition & Ethnomusicology), Univ of CA-LA, 1947-78; Compositions: *Three Sketches* for Alto Saxophone 1983, *The Chd* for Coloratura, Piano & Mandoline 1983, *Elegy* (Sydney Symph Orch) 1982, *Crucifixion* (Melbourne Symph Orch) 1981, *KOAN No 77* for Contralto & Chamber Ensemble 1979, *Sonata for String Bass & Piano* 1972, *Suite for Harpsichord* 1970, *Balkan Rhapsody*, Num Other

Compositions; ASCAP; Soc for Ethnomusicology, First VP 1942-47, Pres (So CA) 1941-71; Film Composers Assn of the US; Am Fdn of Musicians; hon/Pubs, *Bulgarian-Macedonian Folk Music* 1952, "Mnogoglasie: A Compositional Concept in Rural Bulgaria" 1983, "Multidisciplinary Approach to Ethnomusicology" 1982, Num Others; Am Philosophical Soc Penrose Awd, 1955; Ford Foun Grant, Field Trip to the Balkans, 1962; ASCAP Awd for Dist'd Contbn to Am Music, 1968, 1969, 1970, 1971, 1972, 1973; F'ship, Inst of Creat Arts, to Compose Opera *The Bridge*, Libretto by Elva Kremenliev, 1966-67; Bulgarian Acad of Scis, 1978; W/W: in Am, in World; Grove's Dic of Music & Musicians; Die Muzik in Geschichte und Gengenwart; Dic of Am Scholars; Others.

KREMSER, JANET GORDON oc/ Nursing Instructor; b/May 17, 1941; h/ 7810 Sandpiper Drive, New Orleans, LA 70128; ba/Metairie, LA; m/Robert H; c/David Gordon; p/Lennox A and H Jacquelin Gordon, Baldwin, NY; ed/BS in Ed, SUNY-Plattsburg, 1963; MPS, C W Post Ctr of Long Isl Univ, 1975; pa/ Nsg Instr, LPNs, Jefferson Parish Voc Tech Sch, 1982-; Asst Dir of Nsg for Inser, Tulane Med Ctr, 1978-79; Asst Dir of Nsg for Ed, Temple Univ Hosp, 1976-77; Nsg Instr, SUNY-Stony Brook, 1974-75; Asst Dir of Nsg, Lydia E Hall Hosp, 1973-74; Nsg Instr, Voc Ed and Ext Bd 1972-74; Queens Hosp Ctr Sch of Nsg 1968-72; Sch Nurse-Tchr, 1963-68; r/Presb; hon/ Pubs, "Circ 0 Elect Beds" 1976, "IV Therapy" 1978; W/W of Am Wom; World W/W of Wom.

KRENKEL, MARGARET ELLEN A oc/Retired; b/Apr 24, 1913; h/619 East Erie Drive, Tempe, AZ 85282; m/John Henry; p/Thomas Marlin III and Effie Margaret Aistrope (dec); ed/Att'd, Creston Jr Col 1931-32, Capitol City Comml Col 1935-37; Stenographer Cert, AZ St Univ, 1952-53; pa/Bkkpr, Secy, IA Wesleyan Col, 1937-39; Ck Typist, Valparaiso Univ, 1944-45; Secy to Pres, NM Wn Univ, 1945; Secy to Liberal Arts Dean 1946, Asst Recorder 1947-50, Recorder 1950-52, Secy, Registrar's Ofc 1952-57, Credentials Secy 1957-71, Credentials Supvr 1971-75, Ret'd 1975, AZ St Univ; Am Assn of Ret'd Persons, 1960-83; Theta Kappa Sorority, 1943; cp/Secy-Treas, Histn; Corres'g Secy, Guard; VP, Pres, Del to Conv, PEO Sisterhood, 1931-81; AZ St Fac Wives, 1947-83; Scrap Book Chair Auditor, VP & Pres, Tempe Wom's Clb, 1975-79; r/Presb; Active in First U Meth Ch & First U Presb Ch, 1949-81; hon/ Salutatorian, 1931; 20 Yr Ser Awd, AZ St Univ, 1967; 25 Yr Ser Awd, AZ St Univ, 1972; Cert of Apprec, AZ St Univ, 1975; 50 Yr Mem Awd, PEO Sisterhood, 1981; World W/W of Wom; DIB.

KREPPS, ETHEL CONSTANCE oc/ Attorney; b/Oct 31, 1937; h/3326 South 93rd East Avenue, Tulsa, OK 74145; ba/ Tulsa, OK; m/George Sr; c/George Jr, Edward Howard Moore; p/Mrs Pearl Moore Goomda, Oklahoma City, OK; ed/RN, St John's Med Ctr, 1971; BS, Univ of Tulsa, 1974; JD, Univ of Tulsa Col of Law, 1979; pa/Atty, Pvt Pract, 1979-; Atty, Native Am Coalition of Tulsa Inc (for Indian Child Wel Act), 1981-; ABA; OK Bar Assn; Fed Bar

Assn; Tulsa Co Bar Assn; OK Assn of Wom Lwyrs; Phi Alpha Delta; Assn of Am Indian Alaskan Native Nurses; Tulsa Wom Lwyrs Assn; Am Assn of Nurse Attys; cp/N Am Indian Wom's Assn; OK Fdn of Indian Wom; OHOYO; Commun Ser Coun; r/Bapt; hon/Pubs, "A Strong Med Wind" 1979, OK Memoires" 1981; Trial Lwyr's Assn, ABA, Nat Essay Awd, 1978; Intl W/W of Contemp Achmt; Personalities of S; Personalities of Am; Dir of Dist'd Ams; W/W in Fin & Indust; World W/W of Wom.

KRIMIGIS, STAMATIOS MIKE oc/ Physicist, Researcher, Consultant; b/ Sep 10, 1938; h/613 Cobblestone Court, Silver Spring, MD 20904; ba/Laurel, MD; c/Michael Stamatios, John Geras; p/Michael and Angeliki Tsetseris Krimigis (dec); ed/BS, Univ of MN Mpls, 1961; MS 1963, PhD 1965, Univ of IA-Iowa City; pa/Res Assoc & Asst Prof of Physics, Univ of IA-Iowa City, 1965-68; Supvr of Space Physics Sect 1968-74, Supvr of Space Physics & Instrument Grp 1974-81, Chief Scist of Space Dept 1980-, Applied Physics Lab, Johns Hopkins Univ; Prin Investigator on Var NASA Spacecraft, NASA HQs, 1966-; Conslt, NASA HQs, 1971-; Space Sci Bd, Nat Acad of Scis, 1983-; Chm, Com on Solar & Space Physics, SSB, NAS, 1983-; hon/Author, Var Pubs; Fellow, Am Geophy Union, 1980; NASA Exceptl Sci Achmt Medal, 1981; Fellow, Am Phy Soc, 1984.

KRIMSKY, JEFFREY STEPHEN oc/ Learning Disabilities Specialist, Hypnotherapist, Psychotherapist; b/Jun 7, 1948; h/161-32 Jewel Avenue, Flushing, NY 11365; ba/Flushing, NY; m/Joyce Helen Steinfeld; c/Daniel Jarrett; p/Mr and Mrs Jack Krimsky, Valley Stream, NY; ed/EdD, St John's Univ, 1982; CAS, Hofstra Univ, 1976; MS 1973, BS 1971, C W Post Col; Cert'd Hypnotherapist, 1976; Cert'd Clin Psychotherapist, 1983; pa/Spec Ed Tchr Coor & LD Spec, Bd of Ed, NYC, 1972-; Spec Ed Prog Supvr, St John's Univ, 1974-80; Spec Ed Curric Devel & Staff Supvr, Mind Power Dynamics, Ednl Sers of NY, 1977-82; Adj Prof, Spec Ed Dept, St John's Univ, Maimonides Col & McGill Univ, 1978-81; Pvt Pract, Hypnotherapy, Psychotherapy, 1976-; Writer of Nat Pubs, Spec Ed Curric Guides, Grant Writing & Devel of Resource Mats; Lectr for Nat Assn on Lng Styles; Assn for Supvn & Curric Devel; Phi Delta Kappa; CEC; Edrs for World Peace; Nat Assn on Lng Styles; Assn for Chd w Lng Disabilities; St John's Univ Alumni Assn; AIH; AIPB; cp/Exec Bd, K of Pythias, 1983; Exec Bd, Dem Clb, 1982-; r/Jewish; hon/Pubs, *The Miracle Success Report* 1977, *Lrng Styles Theory* 1981, *Smokers Die Yg* 1983; Outstg Dissertation Awd Finalist, ASCD, 1982; NY St Merit S'ship, Biol Awd, Microbiol Awd, Dean's List, Music S'ship; W/W in E.

KRISHEN, ALOK oc/Research Statistician; b/Mar 14, 1952; h/821 North Howard Avenue, Elmhurst, IL 60126; ba/Morton Grove, IL; m/Trieu; c/ Calvin; p/Viapak (dec) and Nirmal Krishen, Luphiana, India; ed/BSc w Hons 1971, MSc w Hons 1973, Ctr for Adv'd Studies, Panjab Univ, India; MS, Stats, FL St Univ, 1976; Wkg towards Deg in Chem Engrg, IL Inst of Technol; pa/Stat, FL Dept of Envir Regulation,

1976-78; Stat, Searle Pharms, 1978-79; Stat 1979, Statl Coor 1981, Sr Stat 1982, Res Stat 1983, Travenol Labs; Am Statl Assn, 1976-; Biometrics Soc, 1980-; r/ Hindu; hon/Pub, "A Water Quality Index," Proceedings of 11th Intl Conf on Computer Sci & Stats, 1979; W/W in MW.

KRISHEN, KUMAR oc/Coordinator of Research and Technology Programs; b/Jun 22, 1939; h/4127 Long Grove, Seabrook, TX 77586; ba/Houston, TX; m/Vijay Lakshmi; c/Lovely, Sweetie, Anjala Selena; p/Sri Kanth and Dhanwati Bhat (dec); ed/PhD in Elect Engrg 1969, MS in Elect Engrg 1966, KS St Univ; MTech 1964, BTech 1962, Radio Physics/Electronics, Calcutta Univ, 1964; BA, Jammu & Kashmir Univ, 1959; pa/Current Coor of Res & Technol Progs, Mgr of Adv'd Microwave Progs 1976-82, NASA/Johnson Space Ctr; Staff Scist, Lockheed Elects Co, 1969-76; Asst Prof, KS St Univ, 1968-69; IEEE, Sr Mem; AIAA; Sigma Xi; Eta Kappa Nu; Phi Kappa Phi; r/ Hindu; hon/Author, One Chapt in Book, More Than 22 Pubs; Highest Merit, Shalimar HS, 1954; Highest Merit, J&K Univ, 1959; Gold Medal, Silver Medal, Calcutta Univ, 1964, 1963; Outsg Perf, Lockheed, 1974; Outstg Perf, NASA, 1979; Am Men & Wom of Sci; W/W: in Technol Today, in S & SW.

KRISHNA, NEPALLI RAMA oc/ Scientist; b/Nov 20, 1945; ba/Birmingham, AL; p/Nepalli Gopala Krishna and Jayaprada Murthy, India; ed/BS 1965, MS 1966, Andhra Univ, Waltair, India; PhD, Indian Inst of Technol, Kanpur, India, 1972; Postdoct Fellow, GA Tech, 1972-74; Res Assoc, Univ of Alberta, Canada, 1974-76; pa/Assoc Scist, Cancer Ctr 1976-, Asst Prof of Biochem 1979-, Dir of NMR Core Facility, Cancer Ctr 1984-, Univ of AL B'ham; Am Phy Soc; Biophy Soc; Smithsonian; hon/Pub'd Num Res Articles in Var Refereed Intl Jours; Indian Atomic Energy Nat Merit S'ship, 1965; Metcalfe Gold Medal Recip, Andhra Univ, 1966; Recip of Rao Meml Awd, Andhra Univ, 1966; Leukemia Soc of Am Scholar, 1982-87; W/W in Frontier Sci & Technol.

KRISHNAN, PALANIAPPA oc/ Assistant Professor, Research Agricultural Engineer; b/Apr 25, 1953; h/3930 Northwest Witham Hill Drive, #23C, Corvallis, OR 97330; ba/Corvallis, OR; m/Chitra; c/Prashanth; p/L Krishnan, Madras, India; P L Lakshmi, Madras, India; ed/BTech w hons, Indian Inst of Technol, 1975; MS, Univ of HI, 1976; PhD, Univ of IL, 1979; pa/Asst Prof, Res Agri Engr, Agri Engrg Dept, OR St Univ; Am Soc Agri Engrs; Nat Soc Profl Engrs; OR Soc Profl Engrs; Sigma Xi; Gamma Sigma Delta; Alpha Epsilon; VChm, Spec Crops Processing Com of the Am Soc Agri Engrs; Chm, EPP & FE Tech Div, ASAE-PNW; Fac Advr, India Students Assn, 1981-82; Pres, India Students Assn, Univ of IL, 1977; Pres, Agri Engrg Soc, Indian Inst Technol, 1973-74; hon/Author Num Tech Articles in Sci Jours; A C Pandya Trophy for Best All-Rounder, 1973-74; Hunter Fellow, Univ of IL, 1977-78; W/ W: in W, in Frontier Sci & Technol.

KRISHNAN, PARAMESWARA oc/ Professor of Sociology; b/Nov 20, 1936;

h/3217 104 A Street, Edmonton, Canada T6J 4A1; ba/Edmonton, Canada; m/ Leela; ed/MS, 1958; MA, 1970; PhD, 1971; pa/Stat, Govt of Rajas Than, 1958-62; Lectr, Univ of Rajas Than, 1962-67; Grad Student, Cornell, 1967-71; Asst Prof 1971-75, Assoc Prof 1975-78, Prof 1978-, Univ of Alberta; Canadian Pop Soc Coun, 1974-76; Fdr & Editor, *Canadian Studies in Pop*, 1974-82; Dir, Pop Res Lab, Univ of Alberta, 1972-75; r/Hinduism; hon/Pubs, "Math Models of Sociol" 1977, "Fam & Demography" 1976; Vis'g Prof, Cambridge Univ, 1976; Prof Visitante, El Colegio de Mexico, 1982-83; Biog of Edrs.

KRISTOFER, DAISY R oc/Director of Dietetic Services; b/Jan 20, 1925; h/ 600 Garden Lane, Bristol, TN 24201; ba/Johnson City, TN; m/Andrew; c/ Andrea, Jacqueline, Andrew II, Margaret; p/Harry B and Edith Martin (dec); ed/BA, Univ of KS, 1951; MS, St Univ of IA, 1953; pa/Elem & Sec'dy Sch Tchr, KS; Student, Chief Dietitian at Bristol Meml Hosp, 1952, 1953; Therapeutic Dietitian, Meml Hosp in Johnson City, & Prof of Sci at Sullins Col, 1956-76; Former Consit, Dietitian & Tchr of Nutrition to E TN St Nsg Students; Clin Dietetics, Meml Hosp, to Dir of Dietetic Sers, New Hosp; Am Dietetic Assn; VA Dietetic Assn; Cities Dietetic Assn; Clin Nutrition Soc of GA Bapt; Cities Reg Diabetes Assn; Nutrition Today Soc; BPW; Bd of Trustees, Sullins Col; r/ Meth; hon/Victor B Colby Outstg Edr Awd, 1976; W/W in S & SW; Outstg Edrs of Am.

KRONSTADT, NANCY ALICE oc/ Survey Administrator; b/Dec 8, 1951; h/5109 Crossfield Court, #11, Rockville, MD 20852; ba/Bethesda, MD; p/Nat Kronstadt, Rockville, MD; ed/EdM in Col Cnslg & Student Pers Adm, Univ of DE, 1975; BA in Sociol, Univ of MD, 1973; pa/Survey Admr, Price Waterhouse, 1980-; Asst Dir of Residential Life 1978-80, Area Coor 1975-78, Ithaca Col; Asst Complex Coor 1974-75, Hall Dir 1973-74, Univ of DE; cp/Exec Mgr, "Holiday Project," a Proj Set Up to Promote Commun Involvement in Bringing Christmas/Hanukah into Nsg Homes, Hosps, Orphanages; hon/W/W in E.

KROTHAPALLI, RADHA KRISHNA oc/Clinical Assistant Professor; b/May 4, 1951; h/2746 Baldwin Brook Drive, Montgomery, AL 36116; ba/Montgomery, AL; m/Shirley Marie Hunt; p/Lakshmi Narasamma Krothapalli, Amarthalur, A-P, India; ed/MD, 1974; pa/Resident in Internal Med, Montgomery Internal Med Prog, 1977-80; Fellow in Nephrology, Baylor Col of Med, 1980-83; Clin Asst Prof, Univ of AL B'ham, 1983-; Am Col of Phys; Am Fdn for Clin Res; Am Soc of Nephrology; Intl Soc of Nephrology; Nat Kidney Foun; AMA; Am Soc of Artificial Internal Organs; hon/Author, Var Pub'd Articles; Nat Merit S'ship, Govt of India, 1967-73; S Dakshina-Murthy's Prize in Social & Preven Med, 1973; Nat Kidney Foun F'ship, 1982-83; W/W in Frontier Sci & Technol.

KRSUL, THEODORE RICHARD oc/ Health Services Administrator; b/Apr 21, 1941; h/710 Bradford Court, Fort Walton Beach, FL 32548; ba/Eglin AFB, FL; m/Carol L; c/Joseph T, Linda B; p/

353

Theodore T and Emily C Krsul, Pittsburgh, PA; ed/Assoc in Bus, Univ of MD, 1974; Bach in Bus, Kent St Univ, 1975; Master in Pers Mgmt, Ctl MI Univ, 1977; mil/USAF 1959-, Capt; pa/Admr, Med Clin, USAF, 1982-; Dir, Med Pers 1981-82, Dir, Med Resource Mgmt 1980-81, USAF Sqdrn Cmdr 1978-79, Exec Ofcr of Space Shuttle Ofc 1978-79, Patrick AFB; Aide-de-Camp to Cmdr, Def Elect Supply Ctr, 1976-77; USAF Enlisted Ser, 1959-75; Am Mgmt Assn, 1978-; FL Hosp Assn, 1979-; Inst of Cert'd Profl Mgrs, 1982; Nom, Am Col of Hosp Admrs, 1982; Life Mem, AF Sgt's Assn, 1981-; r/Cath; hon/Author, Tng Manual, *Radio Fingerprinting Techniques*, 1970; Decorated Bronze Star, 1971; AF Outstg Exec Ofcr, 1977; Patrick AFB Outstg Ofcr of the Yr, 1978-80; Outstg Yg Men of Am; W/W in S.

KRUDOP, JAMES DEAS oc/College Administrator; b/Jan 18, 1947; h/1213 First Avenue, BW, Andalusia, AL 36420; ba/Andalusia, AL; m/Hollace Moore; c/Ashley Frances, Hadyn Lorraine; p/Bellaire and Sara Frances Krudop, Andalusia, AL; ed/BS, Auburn Univ, 1969; MA 1973, PhD 1975, Univ of AL; pa/Dean of Student Affairs, Pt-time Spch Instr, Lurleen B Wallace St Jr Col, 1978-; Dir of Sch Relats 1974-78, Pt-time Spch Instr 1975, B'ham-So Col; Grad Adm Asst to the Assoc Dean of Intl Projs 1973-74, Asst Dir for the Systematic Desensitization of Spch Anxieties Exptl Prog in the Spch Dept 1974, Univ of AL; Other Previous Positions; AL Jr & Commun Col Assn, 1982-; AL Jr & Commun Col Deans of Students Assn; AL Col Pers Assn; AL Assn of Student Financial Aid Admrs; So Assn of Student Financial Aid Admrs; AL Assn of Col Registrars & Admissions Ofcrs; Coun of AL Admissions Ofcrs; AL Col Public Relats Assn; AAUA; Spch Commun Assn of Am; cp/Andalusia Rotary Clb, World Champ-'ship Domino Com 1978-; r/Bapt; hon/Plaque of Apprec for Friendship, Professionalism, Ldrship & Dedication, AL Assn of Commun & Jr Cols Deans of Students, 1982; Cert of Apprec for Outstg Ser, AL Jr & Commun Col Assn, 1980; Perf Awd, AL Pers & Guid Assn, 1980; Outstg Yg Man of Am, 1978, 1981; Recog as Outstg New Mem, AL Col Pers Assn, 1979-80; Other Hons.

KRUEGER, ARTUR W oc/Independent Management Consultant; b/Jan 16, 1940; h/4923 Imogene Drive, Houston, TX 77096; ba/Houston, TX; m/Jodi A Bowman; p/Werner G and Charlotte Klein Krueger (dec); ed/MSc, Columbia Univ Grad Sch of Bus, 1978; Betriebswirt (Grad), Wirtschafts-Akademie, Bremen, Germany, 1968; pa/Prin/Ptnr, Am European Consltg Co, 1979-; Gen Mgr/Mktg Mgr, Rosental Grp (Germany), in Fgn Subsidiaries in USA, Scandinavia, Spain, 1970-79; Am Mgmt Assn; Columbia Bus Assocs; Intl Bus Coun; cp/C of C of the US; German Am C of C; Houston C of C; hon/W/W in Fin & Indust.

KRULFELD, RUTH MARILYN oc/Professor of Anthropology; b/Apr 15, 1931; h/4012 North Woodstock Street, Arlington, VA 22207; ba/Washington, DC; m/Jacob Mendel; c/Michael David; p/Leon and Frances Rosenberg Pulwers (dec); ed/PhD, Yale Univ, 1974; BA, cum

laude, Brandeis Univ, 1955; Other Study, Harvard Sum Sch, Am Univ, LA St Univ; pa/Prof of Anthropology 1976-, Assoc Prof 1973-76, Asst Prof 1964-72, George Wash Univ; Instr, Am Univ; Res in Anthropology, Indonesia 1960-62, Singapore 1950-52, Jamaica 1967, Costa Rica, Nicaragua & Panama 1968; Res Cont'g, Caribbean & Wash DC; Am Anthropological Assn; Anthropologycal Assn of Wash; r/Jewish; hon/Pubs, "The Sasak" (in Press), "Sasak Attitudes toward Polygyny & the Changing Position of Wom in Sasak Peasant Villages" (in Press), Others; Currier S'ship, Yale Univ, 1958; Foun for Study of Man Grantee, 1954; Ford Foun Fellow, 1960-62; Am Coun of Learned Socs & Social Sci Res Coun Grantee, 1963; George Wash Univ Fac Res Grant; W/W of Am Wom; Intl W/W of Wom.

KRUMINS, ANITA oc/Chairman of Business and Technical Communication Department; b/Nov 15, 1946; h/70 London Street, Toronto, Ontario M6G 1N3; ba/Toronto, Ontario; m/George Swede; c/Jerry, Andy; p/Gotthard and Ida Krumins, Wittenberg, WI; ed/BA, summa cum laude 1973, MA 1974, York Univ; pa/Instr 1975-81, Chm of Bus & Tech Communication Dept 1981-, Ryerson Polytech Inst; Canadian Soc of Chd's Authors, Illustrators & Performers; Am Bus Communication Assn; hon/Author of Chd's Books, *Quillby, the Porcupine Who Lost His Quills* 1980, *Who's Going to Clean Up the Mess?* 1981, *Mr Wurtzle & the Halloween Bunny* 1982; York S'ship, 1974; Canada Coun Doct F'ship, 1974; W/W in the Commonwlth.

KRYSTUFEK, ZDENEK oc/Professor of Political Science and Jurisprudence; b/May 11, 1920; h/805 29 Street, Boulder, CO 80303; ba/Boulder, CO; p/Max (dec) and Karla Krystufek, Prague, Czechoslovakia; ed/JUDr, Prague, 1948; PhD in Theory of St and Law, Prague, 1963; Diplóme d'Etudes Superieures Européennes, 1965; JSM, Stanford, 1971; Sr Res Fellow 1967-, Czechoslovak Acad of Scis, 1954-68; Adj Fac Mem, Charles Univ Sch of Law, 1958-68; Prof of Polit Sci & Jurisp, Univ of CO-Boulder, 1973-; Vis'g Appts, Univ of Vienna 1968, Centre National de la Recherche Scientifique 1969, Hoover Inst 1969-70; Am Assn for Phil of Law & Social Phil; Am Soc for Legal Hist; Intl Sociological Assn; Am Polit Sci Assn; Czechoslovak Soc of Arts & Sci, USA; hon/Pubs, *The Soviet Regime in Czechoslovakia* 1981, *Hist Founs of Legal Positivism* 1967, Articles & Co-Authored Books in the Fields of Polit Theory & Jurisp; F'ships: L'Institut Universitaire 1963-65, Columbia Univ Sum Prog in Am Law 1967, Stanford Univ Sch of Law 1970-71, Coif 1975; Univ of CO Prize for the Best Scholarly Article, 1976; Intl W/W: in Ed, in Am Law, in W; Commun Ldrs of the World; Dir of Am Scholars.

KUBILUS, NORBERT JOHN oc/Corporate Officer; b/Oct 6, 1948; h/PO Box D402, Landing, NJ 07850; ba/Princeton, NJ; m/Margaret B; c/Jessica; p/Vity and Ursula Kubilus, Cedar Grove, NJ; ed/ScB, Seton Hall Univ, 1970; MS, Rensselaer Polytechnic Inst, 1972; CDP, Inst for Cert of Computer Profl, 1979; pa/Res Assoc, Rensselaer Polytechnic Inst, 1971-72; Sys Prog 1972-74, Sys Anal 1974-76, Mgr of

Quality Assurance 1976-78, Mgr of Corporate Support Sers 1978-79, Mgr of Data Mgmt Software Devel 1979-80, Asst VP 1980-, RAPIDATA Inc; Adj Fac, NJIT, 1976-; Div VP, Nat Data Corp, 1981-83; VP, Ednl Testing Ser, 1983-; Assn for Computing Machinery, Nat Lectr 1976-80; Digital Equip Computer Users Soc, US Exec Bd 1977-80; Data Processing Mgmt Assn; N Am Soc for Corporate Planning; Inst for Cert of Computer Profls, Ambassador 1980-; r/Rom Cath; hon/Author, Articles & Papers, 3 Courses Pub'd by Ed for Mgmt; Sigma Pi Sigma, 1968; Upsilon Pi Epsilon, 1978; NSF Traineeship, 1970-71; W/W: in E, in Fin & Indust.

KUFTINEC, MLADEN M oc/Professor and Chairman of Department of Orthodontics; b/Apr 18; h/5706 Apache Road, Louisville, KY 40207; ba/Louisville, KY; m/Ljiljana; c/Sandra Tatjana; p/Matija Kuftinec, Louisville, KY; ed/Doct in Med Stom, Univ of Sarajevo, Yugoslavia, 1965; Cert in Orthodontics, Harvard Sch of Dental Med, 1968; DSc, MIT, 1971; DMD, Harvard Sch of Dental Med, 1972; pa/Prof & Chm, Dir of Grad Prog in Orthodontics, Grad Sch Fac, Univ of L'ville Sch of Dentistry, 1976-; Steering Com, Reg Team for Treatment of Craniofacial Anomalies, 1977-; Conslt, Nat Bd of Dental Examrs, 1977-; Reviewer, *Jour of Dental Res* 1979-, *Am Jour of Orthodontics*; Intl Assn for Dental Res; Am Assn for Dental Res; Nutrition Today Soc; Am Assn of Orthodontists; So Soc of Orthodontists; VA Orthodontic Soc; KY Orthodontic Soc; r/Cath; hon/Author, Over 30 Papers, Chapts & Abstracts; Spec Res Awd, Nis, Yugoslavia, 1963; Edward Hatton Res Awd, Intl Assn Dental Res, SF, 1968; Sigma Xi, 1971; Omicron Kappa Upsilon, 1976.

KUIPER, JAMES ALAN oc/Professor of Art; b/May 20, 1945; h/865 F Yak Road, Fairbanks, AK 99701; ba/Fairbanks, AK; c/Joshua James, Seth Alan, Jesse Lee; p/Alke and Betty Lane Kuiper, South Holland, IL; ed/MFA, Painting, MI St Univ, 1976; BA, Eng, Calvin Col, 1968; pa/Vis'g Prof of Art, Univ of AK-Fairbanks, 1983-84; Asst Prof of Art 1980-83, Instr of Art 1977-80, Calvin Col; Adj Drawing Instr, Grand Val St Cols, 1974-77; Art Instr, Grand Rapids Christian HS, 1973-77; Other Previous Positions; Visual Arts Adv Panel, AK St Coun on the Arts, 1984; Vis'g Artist, TX Christian Univ, 1982; Phi Kappa Phi, Nat Hon Soc, MI St Chapt, 1976-; One Person Exhbns: Gallery One 1984, Univ of AK-Fairbanks 1984, Ctl MI Univ 1983, TX Christian Univ 1982, Battle Creek Art Mus 1982, Grand Val St Cols 1981, Gov's Residence 1981, Grand Rapids Art Mus 1981, Lockerbie Gallery 1981, Num Others; Num Grp Exhbns.

KUKLA, EDWARD RICHARD oc/Rare Books Librarian; b/Jan 31, 1941; h/Northwest 225 Timothy Street, Apartment 2, Pullman, WA 99163; ba/Pullman, WA; p/Mrs Frank J (Clara-Belle) Kukla, Mikado, MI; ed/AB, cum laude, Wayne St Univ, 1962; AM 1963, AMLS 1973, Univ of MI; pa/Rare Books Libn, WA St Univ, 1979-; Asst Libn for Rare Books & Manuscripts, Greenfield Village & Henry Ford Mus, 1974-78; Media Mobile Libn, St Lib of MI, 1972; Asst Instr, MI St Univ, 1970-72; Assn of Col & Res Libs; Am Lib Assn; Pacific NW Lib Assn; WA Lib Assn; Bibliogl Soc of Am; Book Clb of WA; Beta Phi Mu & Phi Beta Kappa, Local & Nat Chapts; Univ of MI Sch of Lib Sci Alumni Assn, Life Mem; cp/Pullman Stamp Clb, Pres 1980-; hon/Pubs, *The Scholar & the Future of the Res Lib Revisited* 1973, *The Struggle & the Glory: A Spec Bicent Exhbn* 1976; Mbrship in MI Jr Acad of Sci, Arts & Lttrs, 1958; C Allan Harlan S'ship, 1958; Phi Beta Kappa, 1962; Sigma Delta Pi, 1973; Beta Phi Mu, 1973; W/W in W.

KULAKOW, ALLAN MARVIN oc/Director of African Programs; b/Aug 9, 1932; h/8816 Hidden Hill Lane, Potomac, MD 20854; ba/Washington, DC 20037; m/Naomi Katz; c/Adam Edward, Seth Andrew; p/Samuel and Evelyn Kulakow (dec); ed/BA, Univ of WI, 1953; Fulbright Scholar, Univ of Toulouse, Univ of Paris, 1953-54; MA & ABD, Harvard Univ, 1958; Att'd, Univ of So CA, 1975-76; PhD, Am Univ, 1983; pa/Dir, African Progs, Acad for Ednl Devel, 1976-; Pres, Kulakow Assocs, 1972-76; The Kettering Foun, 1972-73; Asst Dir of Public Affairs, US Envir Protection Agy, 1970-72; Corp for Public Broadcasting, 1969-70; Dir of Lang Tng, US Peace Corps, 1963-69; Fgn Ser Inst, Dept of St, 1958-63; hon/Pubs, *Beyond Open Access* 1972, Num Studies in Aspects of Intl Devel & Communs 1976-; Phi Beta Kappa, 1953; Fulbright Scholar, 1953-54; Grad'd w Hons, Univ of WI, 1953; Num Ser Awds, Univ of WI, 1950-53; W/W in E.

KULLBERG, GARY W oc/Executive; b/Dec 15, 1941; h/50 East 89th Street, New York, NY 10028; ba/New York, NY; m/Audrey E; c/Eric A; p/Walter and Neva Kullberg, White Plains, NY; ed/BS, Univ of RI, 1963; mil/ROTC, Dist'd Mil Student; pa/Controller, WCD Inc, 1963-66; VP, Mgmt Supvr, Ogilvy & Mather, 1966-77; Sr VP, Acct Dir, Wells, Rich, Greene, 1977-83; Pres & Co-Fdr, Fredericks Kullberg Amato Pisacane (Advtg Agy), 1983-; cp/NY Ath Clb, 1977-; r/Prot; hon/Author, Num Articles in Advtg & Mktg Trade Press; Scabbard & Blade, 1963; W/W: in Advtg, in E.

KUROSKY, ALEXANDER oc/Professor; b/Sep 12, 1938; h/6605 Golfcrest, Galveston, TX 77551; ba/Galveston, TX; m/Anna Kinik; c/Lisa Kathryn, Tanya Kristine, Stephanie Ann; p/Peter and Stella Gemper Kurosky (dec); ed/BSc, Univ of Brit Columbia, 1965; MSc 1969, PhD 1972, Univ of Toronto; pa/Res Tech, Canada Dept of Agri, 1959-64; Res & Devel Chem, Canadian Breweries Ltd, 1965-67; Asst Prof 1975-78, Assoc Prof 1978-82, Prof 1982-, Univ of TX Med Br; Am Soc Biol Chems; Am Chem Soc; Canadian Biochem Soc; AAAS; Sigma Xi; Soc of Human Genetics; r/Rom Cath; hon/Author, Approximately 90 Articles in Sci Jours; Dist'd Tchg Awd, Grad Sch of Biomed Scis, Univ of TX Med Br; Province of Ontario Grad F'ship, 1968-71; W/W: in Am, in S & SW, in Frontier Sci & Technol; Intl W/W of Contemp Achmt; 2,000 Notable Ams.

KURTZ, ARTHUR DIGBY oc/Composer, Pianist, Teacher; b/May 7, 1929; h/685 Oakwood Avenue, Webster Groves, MO 63119; ba/Dellwood, MO; p/Mrs Margaret Digby Kurtz, Webster

Grove, MO; ed/MA, St Louis Inst of Music, 1958; Studied w Nadia Boulanger, 1959-61; Studied at the Sorbonne, 1961-63; mil/Army, 1951-53; pa/Tchr, Pvtly & at Univ Level; Am Music Ctr, 1971-; Am Soc of Univ Composers, 1982-; r/Christian; hon/Pvt Pubs, *OP XIII, Three Piano Preludes* 1964, *OP XXI, Three Concert Pieces for Trumpet & Piano* 1968, *OP XXIX, Concerto for Piano & Orch* 1972, *OP XXXII, Five Little Concertos,* Many More; Winner, Nadia Boulanger Competition; Unaccompanied Flute Solo Lit of the 20th Cent; W/W in Am Music: Classical; Intl W/W in Music; 125 Ans de Musique pour Saxophone.

KURTZ, MAX oc/Consulting Engineer, Lecturer, Writer; b/Mar 25, 1920; h/33-47 91st Street, Flushing, NY 11372; ba/Same; m/Ruth Ingraham; p/Samuel and Ida Malkin Kurtz (dec); ed/BBA, City Col of NY, 1940; Civil Engrg, Army Spec Tng Prog; mil/AUS, 1943-45; pa/Kurtz Steel Constrn Corp, 1946-56; Consltg Engr, 1956-; Kings Co Chapt, Nat Soc of Profl Engrs; Editor, "Kings Co Profl Engr," 1967-72; r/Jewish; hon/Author of Num Pubs, incl'g, *Handbook of Engrg Ec* 1984, *Engrg Ec for Profl Engrs' Exams* 1984, *Structural Engrg for Profl Engrs' Exams* 1978, *Comprehensive Structural Design Guide* 1968; Hon Awd, Kings Co Chapt of Nat Soc of Profl Engrs; W/W: in Engrg, in E, in Technol Today; Dir of Dist'd Ams; Men of Achmt; Intl W/W Engr; Intl W/W of Intells; Intl Register of Profiles.

KURTZ, THEODORE STEPHEN oc/Psychoanalyst; b/Apr 25, 1944; h/PO Box 529, Cold Spring Harbor, NY 11724; ba/Same; m/Mariba J; p/Maxwell and Evelyn Kurtz, Flushing, NY; ed/AB, Psych, Boston Univ, 1964; MA, Psych, NY Univ, 1965; Tng in Psychoanalysis, NY Soc of Freudian Psychols, 1968-74; pa/Indep Pract, Psychoanalytic Psychotherapy, 1966-; Conslt to Indust in Staff Devel, 1970-; Asst Prof, C W Post Col of Long Isl Univ, 1974-81; Prin, Luther E Woodward Sch for Emotionally Disturbed Chd, 1970-74; Fellow, Am Orthopsychi Assn; Clin Mem, Am Assn for Marriage & Fam Therapy; Clin Mem, Acad of Psychols in Marital, Sex & Fam Therapy; Nassau Co Psychol Assn; Am Acad of Psychotherapists; Am Grp Psychotherapy Assn; Am Soc for Tng & Devel; Am Psychol Assn; r/Jewish; hon/Pubs, "What's a Nice Broker Like You Doing on a Plateau Like This" 1982, "Sunday is a Day of Paradox" 1980, "Burn-Out" 1980, "Being Married & Being Lonely" 1981, "Cocaine & Quaaludes" 1982, "Regressive Phenomena Among Graduating Univ Students" 1976, "A Consideration of Emotional Disturbance in Boys" 1970; W/W: in E, in Am Jewry; Dic of Intl Biog; Men of Achmt.

KUSHNIRSKY, FYODOR I oc/Assistant Professor of Economics; b/Jul 19, 1936; h/1811 Hoffnagle Street, Philadelphia, PA 19152; ba/Philadelphia, PA; m/Svetlana Naroditsky; c/Eugene, Ilya; p/Iosif (dec) and Ffida Kushnirsky, Israel; ed/MS in Ec, Polytechnic Inst, Lvov, 1960; MS in Math, Univ of Kiev, 1967; PhD in Ec, Nat Economy Inst, Moscow, 1968; pa/Hd of a Sect, Dir of Econometric Projs, Sci Res Inst of Planning & Norms of Gosplan USSR, Kiev, 1965-78; Adj Assoc Prof, Asst Prof of Ec, Temple Univ, 1980-; Am Ec Assn;

Assn for Comparative Ec Studies; En Ec Assn; hon/Pubs, *Modeling Economic Growth in the Republic* 1974, *Soviet Economic Planning, 1965-80* 1982; Grantee, Nat Coun for Soviet & E European Res, 1980-82; W/W in E.

KUSINITZ, MARC oc/Correspondent; b/Aug 8, 1948; h/340 East 34th Street, New York, NY 10016; ba/Lake Success, NY; m/Anna Louise; c/David Nathan; p/Mr and Mrs Samuel A Kusinitz, Newport, RI; ed/BA, NY Univ, 1971; MS, Univ of RI, 1974; PhD, NY Univ, 1980; pa/Res Scist, NY Univ Med Ctr, 1979; Res Scist, NJ Col of Med & Dentistry, 1980; Asst Editor 1980-82, Assoc Editor 1982-83, *Scholastic Sci World Mag*; Correspondent, *NY St Jour of Med,* 1983-; Nat Assn of Sci Writers; NY Acad of Scis; AAAS; Var Free-Lance Writing & Editing.

KUSSEROW, RICHARD PHILLIP oc/Inspector General of Health and Human Services; b/Dec 9, 1940; h/Route 602, Casanova, VA 22017; ba/Washington, DC; m/Mary Stunkard; c/Carrie Elizabeth; p/R B and Eve Kusserow, Pocono Valinda, CA; ed/BS in Polit Sci 1963, MA 1964, CA St Univ LA; Addit Postgrad Wk, So Meth Univ, John Marshall Sch; mil/USMC 1965-67, Capt; pa/Case Ofcr, CIA, 1967-68; Lectr, CA St Univ-LA; Spec Agt Supvr, FBI, 1969-81; Inspector Gen, Dept of Hlth & Sers, 1981-; Assn of Fed Investigators; Nat Wel Fraud Assn; Intl Assn of Chiefs of Police; Am Soc for Indust Security; r/Presb; hon/W/W in World.

KUTINA, JAN oc/Research Professor; b/Jul 23, 1924; h/4201 Massachusetts Avenue, Northwest, Washington, DC 20016; ba/Washington, DC; m/Irena Kutinova; c/Irene, Jan; p/Jan and Amalie Tauberova Kutina; ed/PhMr 1948, RNDr 1949, CSc (PhD Equivalent) 1956, Docent 1954, Charles Univ, Prague; pa/Assoc Prof of Geochem, Charles Univ, 1954-68; Vis'g Prof of Ec Geol, Lehigh Univ, 1968, 1969; Consltg Geologist, Bethlehem Steel Corp, 1974, 1975; Conslt, UN, NY, w Missions to Latin Am & Africa, 1970-74; Consltg Geologist, W A Bowes Inc, 1976-; Vis'g Res Scist, Geol Survey of Canada, 1969, 1970; Sr Res Scist 1977-79, Res Prof 1980-, Am Univ; Chief of Lab of Global Tectonics & Metallogeny, Am Univ; Chief Editor, *Global Tectonics & Metallogeny;* r/Rom Cath; hon/Pubs, 94 Titles, 1 Book; Secy Gen of the Intl Assn on the Genesis of Ore Deposits, 1964-69; Clube de Mineralogia, Brazil, Hon Mem; W/W in Frontier Sci & Technol.

KUYATT, CHRIS E oc/Physicist, Director of Radiation Research Center; b/Nov 30, 1930; h/2904 Hardy Avenue, Wheaton, MD 20902; ba/Washington, DC; m/Patricia L; c/Chris S, Brian, Alan, Bruce; p/Chris A and Rosalie L Kuyatt (dec); ed/PhD in Physics 1960, MS in Physics 1953, BS in Physics & Math 1952, Univ of NE; pa/Res Assoc, Dept of Physics, Univ of NE, 1959-60; Physicist, Electron Physics Sect 1960-69, Chief of Electron & Optical Physics Sect 1970-73, Chief of Surface & Electron Physics Sect 1973-78, Chief of Radiation Physics Div 1978-79, Dir of Ctr for Radiation Res 1979-, Nat Bur of Standards; Am Physical Soc, Fellow; AAAS; Philosophical Soc of Wash; Sigma Xi, Mbrship Com 1982-; cp/Concertmaster, Rockville Mun Concert Band, 1972-;

hon/Author, Over 80 Tech Pubs, 2 Review Articles (on Electron Optics, Electron Scattering, Exptl Atomic Physics); Elected to Phi Beta Kappa & Sigma Xi, 1952; US Dept of Commerce Silver Medal, 1964; Am Men & Wom of Sci; W/W: in Technol Today, in Am.

KUYKENDALL, PATRICIA A oc/ Executive Director of Surgical Operating and Acute Care Support Services; b/Mar 27, 1935; h/15442 Edenvale, Friendswood, TX 77546; ba/Galveston, TX; m/James K; p/Theresa Ensley, Kewanee, IL; ed/Dipl in Nsg, St Anthony's Hosp Sch of Nsg, 1960; BS in Nsg, Incarnate Word Col, 1961; MS in Nsg Med-Surg Supvn, St Louis Univ, 1965; pa/Exec Dir & Dir of Nsg for Surg Operating & Acute Care Support Sers 1981-, Dir of Nsg, Inpatient Sers for Surg Operating Suite, Recovery Rm, IC Units & Sterile Processing Dept 1980-81, Univ of TX Med Br, John Sealy Hosp; Assoc Fac Asst, Univ of TX Med Br Sch of Nsg, 1978-; Asst Dir of Nsg in Charge of Surg Operating Suite, Univ of TX Med Br, John Sealy Hosp, 1977-80; Instr, Tech-Voc Prog, Col of the Mainland, 1976; Num Other Previous Positions; ANA; Nat Leag for Nsg; TX Nurses Assn; Sigma Theta Tau, Beta Beta Chapt; AORN; hon/Selected to Participate in Johnson & Johnson Wharton Fellows Prog in Mgmt for Nurses, 1983; W/W of Am Wom.

KYRALA, GEORGE A oc/Physicist; b/Apr 20, 1946; h/382 Catherine, Los Alamos, NM 87544; ba/Los Alamos, NM; m/Trish Mylet; c/Michaelene, Kamal; p/Amine and Moura Khayrallah; ed/BS, Am Univ of Beirut, 1967; MPhil 1969, PhD 1974, Yale Univ; pa/Res Asst, Yale Univ, 1969-74; Postdoct Res Fellow & Lectr, JILA, Univ of CO, 1974-76; Res Fellow, Physics Dept & Optical Sci Ctr, Univ of AZ, 1976-78; Staff Mem, Los Alamos Nat Lab, Univ of CA, 1978-; Am Phy Soc; Arab Phy Soc; r/Greek Orthodox; hon/Author, More Than 25 Articles Concerning Lasers, Optics, Atomic Physics, Laser Fusion & High Speed Photo; Michael Chiha Prize, 1964; Rockefeller Fellow, 1967; Gibbs Fellow, 1967, 1968; Am Men & Wom of Sci; W/W: in Sci & Technol, in Laser & Quantum Electronics.

L

La CASSE, JANET W oc/Travel Consultant; b/Oct 7, 1927; h/Box 116, Fort Montgomery, NY 10922; ba/West Point, NY; m/Paul Leon; p/Arthur M and Marion Harvey (dec); ed/Assoc Deg, Burdett Col, 1947; pa/Asst Credit Mgr, Gilchrist's Dept Store, 1947; Exec Secy to Bus Mgr Aths 1948-63, Adm Asst to Ath Dir 1963-73, Dir of Spec Activs 1973-79, US Mil Acad, Army Ath Assn; Asst to Pres, NY St Beer Wholesalers, 1979-82; Travel Conslt, Newburgh Travel, 1982-; Col Ath Bus Mgrs Assn, Publicity Com 1972-74, Awds Com 1975-76, Secy-Treas 1977-83; cp/Pres, Gilbert Stuart Gym Clb; Vice Regent, DAR, W Point Chapt, 1979-83; r/Prot; hon/Featured in Army-Vanderbilt Ftball Prog, 1974; Commend from Supt of US Mil Acad for Handling Pres & VIP Needs at Army-Navy Ftball Games, 1975; Num Commends for Org'g & Supvg Protocol Events at US Mil Acad & Donor Progs for Army Ath Assn; Janet La Casse Day at Army-VMI Ftball Game, 1981; World W/W of Wom.

LACEY, WILBERT oc/University Psychiatrist; b/Dec 1, 1936; h/3601 Tyrol Drive, Landover, MD 20785; ba/Washington, DC; m/Bernardine; c/Amando, Elthon, Jacinta, Sherri; p/Mrs Katie Johnson, Washington, DC; ed/BS 1959, MD 1968, Howard Univ; mil/1st Lt, AUS Inf, Ft Ord, CA, 1960-62; pa/Univ Psychi, Howard Univ, 1972-; Asst Prof, Howard Univ Col of Med; Nat Med Assn; Am Inst of Hypnosis; Am Psychi Assn; Am Col Hlth Assn; DC Med Soc; Kappa Alpha Psi; r/Rom Cath; hon/Consultation Ser to Col Students, NMA Jour, Nov 1972; W/W: in Black Am, in Am, in E, in MD.

LACIVITA, MICHAEL JOHN oc/Corporate Safety and Security Director; b/Jun 26, 1924; h/3220 Eldora Drive, Youngstown, OH 44511; ba/Youngstown, OH; m/Margaret Mary Savoia; c/Linda Marie Krieger, Sandra Marie Vicarel; ed/BS in Bus Adm, Youngstown St Univ, 1951; mil/USN, 1943-46; pa/QC Mgr 1965-67, Prodn Supt 1967-71, Republic Rubber Div, Aeroquip Corp; QC Mgr, Cylinder Div 1971-75, Corporate Safety Dir 1975-79, Corporate Safety & Security Dir 1979-, Comml Shearing Inc; Am Soc of Safety Engrs, 1976-; Am Soc for QC, Youngstown Sect, Chm 1974; Forging Indust Assn, Nat Safety & Hlth Com 1980-83; Mahoning Co Safety Campaign Com, Chm 1977-83; r/Cath; hon/Pub'd in Nat Safety News Mag 1978, Navy Lifeline Mag 1981, Profl Safety Mag 1983, OH Monitor Mag 1978, Industl Safety & Hygiene News 1983; Recip, Kodak Intl Newspaper Snapshot Awds, 1951, 1958, 1960, 1961, 1969, 1975; W/W in MW.

LACKEY, DAVID MOORE oc/Vice President and Manager of Security Sales; b/Apr 29, 1947; h/Route 4, Box 4152, Chico, CA 95926; ba/Chico, CA; c/Mark T, Jeffrey S, Jake F, Mollee Moore; p/Jack Jr and Helen T Lackey, Tahoe City, CA; ed/BA, Bus & Ec, Pacific Univ, 1968; pa/Asst Mgr, Sales, First CA Co, 1968; Sales, Blyth & Co; Ptnr, VP, Mgr of Chico Ofc, Dir, Hammerbeck & Co; cp/Rotary Clb; C of C; Chico Yth Soccer; r/Epis; hon/Articles in OR Jour & NY Times, 1975, 1976; W/W: in Am, in Fin & Indust.

LACKEY, RICK D oc/Technical Sales Consultant; b/Jul 14, 1951; h/10233 Topeka Drive, Charlotte, NC 28212; ba/Seattle, WA; m/Josie E; c/Cameron Marie, Melanie Brooke; p/Escar and Betty Lackey, Statesville, NC; ed/AS, Brookes Inst of Technol, 1971; BS, Rochester Inst of Technol, 1973; Cert, Zerox Consltg Schs; pa/Sales Conslt, Pako Corp, Mpls, MN, 1975-80; Tech Sales Conslt, CX (Sys) Corp, Seattle, WA, 1980-; Soc of Photo Finishing Engrs; PMA; PP of A; NCPPA; NWFPPA; PPSCA; cp/Ancient Free & Accepted Masons; hon/Author, NC A Public Arts Experience, Photographic Illustrator, 3rd Cent Artist, 1974.

LACOSTE, PAUL oc/University President; b/Apr 24, 1923; h/356 Woodlea Avenue, Montreal, Quebec H3P 1R5; ba/Montreal, Quebec; m/Louise Marcil; c/Helene, Anne-Marie, Paul-Andre; p/Manoir Fleury, Montreal; ed/BA 1943, MA 1944, LPh 1946, LLL 1960, Universite de Montreal; F'ship, Univ of Chgo, 1946-47; Doct, Universite de Paris, 1948; pa/Prof of Phil 1946-, Prof of Law 1961-68, Vice-Rector 1966-68, Exec Vice-Rector 1968-75, Rector 1975-, Universite de Montreal; Called to Bar, Quebec, 1960; Pvt Pract, 1964-66; Quebec Ed Coun, 1964-68; Royal Comm on Bilingualism & Biculturalism, 1965-71; Quebec Univs Coun, 1969-77; Bd of Dirs, Ecole polytechnique, Institut de recherches cliniques, Ecole des hautes etudes commerciales; Conf of Rectors & Prins of Quebec Univs, Pres 1977-79; Assn of Univs & Cols of Canada, Pres 1978-79; Association des universites partiellement ou entierement de langue française, Pres 1978-81; Montreal Bar Assn; cp/Montreal Mus of Fine Arts; r/Cath; hon/Pubs, Justice et paix scolaire 1962, A Place of Liberty 1964, Le Canada au seuil du siecle de l'abondance 1969, Principes de gestion universitaire 1970, Education permanente et potentiel universitaire 1977; Hon LLD, McGill Univ 1975, Univ of Toronto 1978; Ofcr of the Order of Canada, 1977; DIB; Dir of Am Scholars; W/W: in Am, in E, in Canada, in World, in Commonwealth, of Authors; W/W Intl; Debrett's Illustrated Guide to the Canadian Estab.

LAFFERTY, JUDY ANN oc/Psychologist, Psychotherapist, Analyst; b/Jul 19, 1939; h/2339 North Catalina Street, Los Angeles, CA 90027; ba/Los Angeles, CA; p/Mrs A R Lafferty, Sioux City, IA; ed/BA, Univ of Albuquerque, 1969; MS, CA St Univ, 1971; PhD, CA Grad Inst, 1975; Postgrad, Univ of So CA, 1978-80; Lic Cnslr, CA Andrus Vols, Gerontology Ctr, Univ of So CA, 1978-; pa/Analyst, Disability Eval Bur 1971-81, Opers Assessment 1981-83, QC Bur 1983-, CA St Dept of Social Sers; Tchr & Bd Mem, Interagy Coun of Aging; Am Psychol Assn; Am Gerontological Soc; Am Rehab Cnslr Assn; CA Psychol Assn; LA Co Psychol Assn; cp/Cath Archdiocese of LA, 1981-; Home Visitors Prog, Cath Wel Bur, 1981-; Dem; r/Rom Cath; hon/Pub, "Devel of New Psychol Profile-Post Traumatic Stress Disorder" 1975; Lectr, CA St Psychol Assn Convs, 1979-83; USPHS Trainee, 1970-71; Reg White House Conf on Aging, 1982; W/W: in W, in Am Wom, of Profls & Resources in Rehab, in CA; Personalities of W & MW.

LAFFOON, KAREN LOU oc/Teacher of Reading; b/Jan 9, 1941; h/3426 Belle Isle Drive, San Diego, CA 92105; ba/National City, CA; p/Ruby Lewis Laffoon; Mary E Laffoon, El Cajon, CA; ed/BA 1964, Master's Deg in Ed 1980, San Diego St Univ; Credentials in Ed: Gen Jr High 1964, Gen Sec'dy 1964, Spec Sec'dy 1964, Spec Cred for Severly Emotionally Disturbed-Severly Lng Disabled 1979; pa/Salesperson, Sears-Roebuck, 1959-64; Subst Tchr, San Diego City Schs, 1965-67; Tchr, Nat City Jr HS, 1967-; Sigma Alpha Iota, Profl Music Frat, 1963-65; SEA; CTA; NTA; cp/Multi-Cultural Faire Chp, 1968, 1969; r/Chula Vista Ch of God; Ch Soloist, First Congregational Ch, 1967-72; hon/Pub, Hist of Nat City in Wkbook, 1980 (Study Guide & 350 Slides); Sword of Hon, Sigma Alpha Iota, 1964; Plaque in Apprec, Nat City Jr HS Students, for Ser to Them, 1979-80; W/W: in W, Among San Diego Wom.

La FLEUR, JAMES KEMBLE oc/Executive; b/Apr 23, 1930; h/4337 Talofa Avenue, Toluca Lake, CA 91602; ba/San Diego, CA; m/Helene; c/Kathleen, Michele, Juliet; ed/BS, CA Inst of Technol, 1952; MBA, Pepperdine Univ, 1980; mil/NG; pa/Design Engr, Boeing Airplane Co, 1952; Devel Engr, Air Res, Garrett Corp, 1952-56; Pres, Dynamic Res Inc, 1957-59; Pres, Chm, The La Fleur Corp, 1960-65; Pres, Chm of the Bd, Indust Cryogenics Inc, 1966-71; Pres, CEO, Chm of the Bd, GTI Corp, 1975-; ASME, Chm of Nuclear Cycles 1973-75; cp/Soaring Soc; Duquesne Clb; Renaissance Clb; Univ Clb; NYYC; Lakeside Golf Clb; Caltech Assocs 7 Alumni Clb; r/Prot; hon/Patentee, Turbomachinery & Close Cycle Gas Turbine, Cryogenic Equip; Several Papers for ASME & Gas Turbine Div, Different Articles in Mgmt (NYU, INC, Bdroom); Author, Res & Devel Ptnrship, a Financial Breakthrough for Inventors & Small Businesses; Outstg Yg Men of Am; Am Men of Sci; W/W: in Technol, in Sci, in W, in Am.

LAHMAN, WARREN EMANUEL oc/Mechanic, Salesman; b/Sep 5, 1925; h/Route #3, Box 2, Dayton, VA 22821; ba/Same; m/Crystal Irene; c/Bertie Lou; p/Paul and Minnie Lahman (dec); ed/Att'd, Rockingham Co, VA, Public Schs, 1932-40; Aircraft & Engine Factory Course, Consolidated Vultee Corp, 1963; Dale Carnegie Course, 1963; mil/USAAF, 1944-46; cp/Lions Clb, 1960-; Pres of Own Clb, 1970-71; Served in Dist 24-C Cabinet as Zone Chm, 1971-72; Dist Chm, Sight 1972-73, Safety 1973-74, Care 1974-75; Dpty Dist Gov, 1977-78; Corvair Clb of Am, Collector; r/Prot.

LAINGEN, LOWELL BRUCE oc/Foreign Service Officer; b/Aug 6, 1922; h/Quarters 15, Fort Lesley J McNair, Washington, DC 20024; ba/Washington, DC; m/Penelope Babcock; c/William, Charles, James; p/Palmer K and Mabel Laingen (dec); ed/BA, St Olaf Col, 1947; MA, Univ of MN, 1949; mil/USN, 1943-46; pa/Entered Fgn Ser, 1949; Appt'd Consular Ofcr in Hamburg, 1951-53; Ec Ofcr in Tehran, 1953-54; Acting Prin Ofcr at Meshed, 1954-55; Ec Ofcr, Tehran, 1955-56; Dpty, then Ofcr-in-Charge, Greek Affairs, Dept of St, 1956-50; Assigned as Polit Ofcr, Karachi, 1960; Ofcr-in-Charge of Pakistan/Afghanistan Affairs, 1964-67; Dpty Chief of Mission in Kabul; Country Dir for Pakistan & Afghanistan, 1971-73; Country Dir for India, Nepal, Sri Lanka & the Maldive Isls, 1973; Acting Dpty Asst Secy of St for Near E & S Asian Affairs, 1973-75; Appt'd Dpty Asst Secy for European Affairs, 1975;·Ambassador to Malta, 1977-79; Hd, Am Del at CSCE Conf on the Mediterranean in Malta, 1979; Charge d'Affaires for the Embassy in Tehran, 1979; VP of Nat Def Univ, 1981-; r/Epis; hon/Recip, St's Meritorious Hon Awd, 1967; Dist'd Alumnus Awd, St Olaf Col, 1975; Dept of St's Awd for Valor, 1981.

LAINO, JOSEPH FRANCIS II oc/ Director of Career and Co-operative Education; b/May 4, 1953; h/135 Magnolia Terrace, Springfield, MA 01108; ba/Agawam, MA; p/Louis J (dec) and Victoria S Laino, Springfield, MA; ed/ MA, Human Resource Devel, Am Intl Col, 1981; EdM, Commun Ed, Springfield Col, 1978; BA w Hons in Hist, Am Intl Col, 1975; AA, Gen Studies & Automotive Tech, Springfield Tech Commun Col, 1975; pa/Career Cnslr & Job Developer, CETA Prog, City of Springfield, 1975-76; Grad Asst, Dept of Tchr Ed, Springfield Col, 1976-77; Dir of Career Ctr, Career Cnslr, Palmer, MA, Public Schs, 1978; Dir of Career & Co-operative Ed, Agawam Public Schs, 1979-; AAUA, 1979; AAUP, 1976; Am Indust Arts Assn, 1980; Am Intl Col Alumni Assn, VP 1982-83; APGA, 1979; Assn for Humanistic Ed, 1979; Am Sch Cnslrs Assn, 1979; Nat Employmt Cnslrs Assn, 1979; Am Pub Wel Assn, 1976; Assn of Sch, Col & Univ Staffing, 1983; Assn for Humanistic Psych, 1980; Assn for Supvn & Curric Devel, 1980; Am Voc Assn, 1979; Life Mem; Cooperative Ed Assn, 1979; Coun for Voc Ed, 1980; Coun for Basic Ed, 1978; MA Commun Ed Assn, 1978; MA Sch Cnslrs Assn, 1981; MA Tchrs Assn, 1977; MA Voc Guid Assn, 1979; Nat Assn for Indust Ed Coop, 1979; Nat Commun Ed Assn, 1979, Life Mem; NY Acad of Scis, 1982; Am Mus of Natural Hist, 1977; ARC, 1978; r/Rom Cath; hon/Pub, *Developing a Commun Based Career Ed Prog Specifically Designed & Geared for Grades 5-12*; Dean's List, Springfield Tech Commun Col, 1973; Dean's List, Am Intl Col, 1974, 1975; Grad Asst'ship, Springfield Col, 1976; Outstg Yg Man of Am, 1982; W/W in E; Outstg Yg Men of Am.

LAKSHMANAN, VAIKUNTAM IYER oc/Manager of Mineral Processing and Hydrometallurgy Groups; b/Oct 7, 1940; h/3921 Selkirk Place, Mississauga, Ontario L5L 3L5; ba/Mississauga, Ontario; m/Sarada; p/Tharuvai Vaikuntam Iyer and Rukmini Ammal (dec); ed/BSc, 1961; MSc, 1963; PhD, 1968; pa/Res Asst, Inst of Sci, Bombay, India, 1964-67; Chief Chem, H&R Johnson, Ltd, Bombay, 1967-68; Res Fellow 1969-72, Lectr 1972-75, B'ham Univ; Fellow, CANMET, Canada, 1975-76; Assoc Scist, Noranda Res, 1976-77; Res Scist, Eldorado Nuclear Ltd, 1977-81; Mgr, Hydrometallurgy & Engrg Scis Grps, Ontario Res Foun, 1982-; Pt-time Prof, Chem Engrg, McMaster Univ, 1982-; Chm, Canadian Uranium Prodrs Metall Com, 1982-83; Secy, Hydromet Sect, Canadian Inst of Mining & Metal-

lurgy Com, 1982-83; Royal Inst of Chem, UK; Soc of Chem Engrg; Inst of Mining & Metallurgy; hon/Author, Nearly 40 Tech Pubs & Contributed Chapts in Books, 1967-83; Recip, Chem & Metall Awds, Res Instns, India, UK; Mem, Canada Inst of Mining & Metallurgy, Inst Mining & Metallurgy, UK.

LALOMIA, SAMUEL JR oc/Civil and Structural Engineer; b/Jan 31, 1947; h/ 311 South Thompson, Jackson, MI 49203; ba/Jackson, MI; m/Alberta L; c/ Christopher P, Brent S; p/Samuel Lalomia Sr, Buffalo, NY; ed/Bach of Civil Engrg, Univ of Detroit, 1969; pa/ Design Engr 1969-75, Supvg Civil/ Structural Engr 1975-81, Proj Mgr 1981-84, Consltg Engr 1984-, Gilbert/ Commonwlth Assocs Inc; Nat Soc of Profl Engrs; MI Soc of Profl Engrs, Chm of Yg Engrs Com, VP of Jackson Chapt 1984; r/Cath; hon/Yg Engr of the Yr, MI Soc of Profl Engrs, 1983.

LAMBERT, MARIE M oc/Judge of the Surrogates Court; b/Nov 18, 1920; h/737 Park Avenue, New York, NY 10021; ba/New York, NY; m/Grady L; c/Gregory Lee; p/Nicola and Lucia Macri (dec); ed/BA, Brooklyn Col, 1941; JD, NY Univ Law Sch, 1944; pa/Chadbourne, Hunt, Jaeckle & Brown, 1944-46; Carroad & Carroad, 1946-49; Pvt Pract, 1949-74; Ptnr, Katz, Shandell, Katz & Erasmous, 1974-77; Judge of Surrogate's Ct, NY Co, 1978-; Ext Trial Wk in All Cts, St, Fed & Civil Field; Surrogate of NY Co; Arbitrator in Am Arbitration Assn; Pre-trial Master in Civil Ct of City of NY; Exec Com, Surrogate's Ct Assn; VP, NY Assn of Wom Judges; Nat Assn of Wom Judges; Bd of Dirs, Am Justinian Soc of Jurists; Lectr & Mem, Nat Probate Coun; Am Judges Assn; NY St Trial Lwyrs Assn, Bd of Dirs 1955-; cp/Charter Mem, Bd of Dirs, Italian Execs of Am Inc; Adv Coun, Spec Social Sers Inc; Pres, Jr Wom's Leag; Secy, Sr Citizens' Assn; Num Other Civic Activs; hon/Hon'd by AMITA as Wom Who Contributed Most to Field of Law of USA, 1975; Hon'd by Fdn of Italian-Am Orgs for Public Ofc for Contbns to Polit Process; Columbian Lwyrs Rapallo Awd; Law Day Awd; Bklyn Wom's Bar Helen Wolfsohn Awd; Wom of Achmt, NY Univ Alumni Clb.

LAMBOU, MADELINE C GOMILA oc/Artist, Writer, Retired Research Scientist; b/Jul 29, 1908; h/5105 Arts Street, New Orleans, LA 70122; ba/ Same; m/Paul O; c/Richard Paul; p/John G and Christina Marti Gomila (dec); ed/ BA, Newcomb Col, Tulane Univ, 1928; MS, Tulane Univ, 1929; pa/Mgmt Conslt 1982-83, Secy-Treas 1974-82, Respiratory Therapeutics Inc; Ret'd 1974, EEO Cnslr 1973-74, Res Scist 1968-74, Res Analyst 1960-68, Chem 1945-60, Jr Chem 1943-45, Asst Sci Aide 1942-43, So Utility Res & Devel Div, USDA; Asst City Chem, NO, LA, 1929-42; Am Chem Soc, 1929-; Fellow, Inst of Chems; Sigma Xi; Charter Mem, Past Pres, NO Br, Res Soc of Am; Gulf Coast Sect, Inst of Food Technologists, Secy-Treas 1968-69, Secy 1970-71, Pres 1972-73; Org of Profl Employees, USDA, Pres 1973; Nat Leag of Am Pen Wom, Crescent City Br, 1951-, Br Pres 1956-58, Treas 1966-68, VP 1970-72, LA St Pres 1972-74, Nat Articles Contest Chm 1958, Nat Ballad Contest

Chm 1971-72, Nat Meml Poetry Contest Chm 1982-86; Bd of Dirs, Deep S Writers' & Artists' Conf Inc, 1964-75, Nat Lit Contest Chm 1962, 1969, 1970, Pres 1966-68, Treas 1974-75; Fed Bus Assn of NO Area; Nat Assn of Ret'd Fed Employees; Am Assn of Ret'd Persons; Nat Fdn of St Poetry Socs; LA St Poetry Soc, Nat Poetry Day Contest Chm 1982, Mem of NO Chapt; Am Poetry Leag, AZ Chapt; cp/NO Mus of Art; Metro Mus of Art; Smithsonian Assocs; Former BSA Den Mother, 2 Yrs; r/Cath; hon/Contbr, More Than 55 Articles, Chapts in Books & Patents on Foods & Agri Chem to Profl Jours & Pubrs of Books; Contbr of Articles & Poems to Lit Pubs; Elected to Tulane Univ Chapt of Sigma Xi, 1947; Elected Fellow, Am Inst of Chems; Recip, Ser Awd, Deep S Writers' & Artists' Conf, 1966; Nat Pres's Cit, Nat Leag of Am Pen Wom, 1974; Recip, Cert of Apprec, USDA, 1974; World W/W Wom; W/W of Am Wom.

LAMBROSE, G DOUGLAS oc/Financial Planner, Accountant, Developer; b/ Aug 10, 1946; h/28 Glenn, Irvine, CA 92714; ba/Newport Beach, CA; m/ Susan D; c/Joshua, Jessica; p/C Gustave and Anne A (dec) Lambrose, Miami Beach, FL; ed/BS, Bkg, Fin & Acctg, NY Univ, 1970; Enrolled Agt Authorized to Pract Before the IRS, 1979; NASD Securities Lic, 1970; CA Real Est Licencee, 1979; pa/Financial Planner, Acct, Developer, for Over 12 Yrs; Pres, Financial Sers & Devel Co; Intl Assn of Financial Planners; Am Ec Coun; VP, Fin Soc at NY Univ, 1968-69; cp/Univ Ath Clb; Chm of Adv Bd, Clb Camelot; Newport Bayview Yacht Clb, 1980-82; r/Christian; hon/Co-Editor & Contbr to "Enterprise," NY Univ Pub; Presently Writing Book for Profls on Financial Planning; Dean's List, 1965-69; Phi Alpha Kappa Hon Soc, NY Univ, 1969-70; W/W: in CA, in Fin & Indust; Personalities of W & MW.

LAMME, DENNIS WAYNE oc/Executive; b/Mar 19, 1955; h/3829 Logan Avenue, Loveland, CO 80537; ba/ Windsor, CO; m/Cindy Kay Wright; c/ Kelly Marie, Jacob Fremont, Kristen Kay; p/John Robert and Earlene Marie Trump Lamme, Maryville, MO; ed/BS in Radio/TV/Film/Spch, NW MO St Univ, 1976; pa/Acct Exec, KKJO, 1976-77; Gen Mgr, KVMT-FM, 1977-78; Sta Mgr, KYEZ-FM, 1978; Acct Exec, WRMN, 1978-79; VP & Gen Sales Mgr for Brewer Broadcasting (KUAD-FM & KSGR-AM in Windsor, CO, & KKBG-FM in Hilo, HI), 1979-; Alpha Epsilon Rho; Am Advtg Fdn; Am Mgmt Assn; Am Film Inst Assn; Mktg, Advtg & Communs Assn; cp/Chm, Bd of Dirs, Thompson Val Presch, 1982-84; r/Presb; hon/Hons Assem, NW MO St Univ, 1975; Eagle Scout Awd; W/W in W.

LAMOUTTE, SYLVIA M oc/Executive Director; b/Nov 29, 1935; h/267 San Jorge Street, Apartment 12-C, Santurce, Puerto Rico 00912; ed/Master's Deg w Hons 1960, Bach's Deg w Hons 1958, New Eng Conservatory of Music; pa/Exec Dir, Corp of the PR Symph Orch, 1981-; Pvt Music Tchr in PR, 1960-80; Panelist & Music Critic on "Mirador Puertorriqueño," TV Prog; Author & Publisher of 25 Music Books, 1964-80; Public Jr HS; Piano Tchr, New

Eng Conservatory of Music, 1959-60; Perfs in PR, MA, Dominican Republic; Am Musicological Soc, New Eng Chapt; Nat Guild of Piano Tchrs, Fac Mem; Am Music S'ship Assn; Univ Soc; Other Mbrships; hon/Walter W Naumburg S'ship, 1959-60; Pro Arte Musical Medal; Nat Bd of Advrs, Am Biogl Inst, 1982; Hon Mem, Pi Kappa Lambda; Intl W/W in Music.

LAMPE, JUNE IRENE oc/Co-Owner of Gallery, Teacher, Restoration Artist; b/Nov 5, 1915; h/6169 Paris Avenue, New Orleans, LA 70122; ba/New Orleans, LA; m/Frederick F; c/Deborah Cheryl (Mrs Michael Herrera), Barbara Layon (Mrs David Bishop); p/Mr and Mrs John W Bowen (dec); ed/HS Grad, 1933; 25 Yrs Tng, Pvt Tchrs Restoration Art; pa/Reporter, *Nat Beauty Mag*, 1960-65; Tchr, Means Fine Arts, 1963-68; Tchr, Restoration Artist, Lampe Gallery; Appraiser of Art; NO Mus of Art; Profl Picture Framers Assn; Intl Soc of Appraisers; cp/Com of 21; r/Epis; hon/Currently Writing a Book, *New Glazes for Today's Old Masters*; St Fair, Huron, SD, 1949-51; Outstg Commun Art Awd, 1977; Noel Goldblatt, Signature Series Collection, 1981; Noel Goldblatt on Wom of the Decade, People of the Cent; World W/W of Intells; World W/W of Wom; Intl Register of Profiles; Am Artists of Renown.

LAMPKIN, GLADYS E oc/Professional Beautician; b/Sep 9, 1912; h/4709 North Everest, Oklahoma City, OK 73111; ba/Same; m/Lloyd L (dec); c/O Loretta Walker; p/Addie and Thomas Bell; ed/Att'd OK City Public Schs; Grad, Profl Bus Sch, Chgo; BS, Nat Beauty Culturist Leag of Cosmotology, Wash DC; pa/Mgr of Local Shop, 10 Yrs; Owner/Mgr, Lampkin's Beauty Fashions, 1962-; Holder, Demonstrator License; Charter Mem, OK Beauty Culturist Leag, 1946; Theta Nu Sigma Sorority of Nat Beauty Culturist Leag Inc; cp/Bd Mem, OK Hist Soc; OK Air Space Mus Onmiplex; Nat Assn of Mature Persons; hon/Has her own Pvt-Ext Collection of Hist Beauty Culture Artifacts & has done Showings for OK Hist Soc & Var Orgs upon Request; 1949-50 St of OK's Most Outstg Hair Stylist & Color Artist; Pres, St Beauty Culturist Leag; Cert of REcog, Fdn of Colored Wom's Clb; OK Black Heritage Commun of OK Hist Soc; Pres Emeritus, St Beauty Culturist Leag Inc, Dean Eta Chapt; Affil'd w Musical Drama "Freedom Child"; Presented Local TV Talk Show for Contbns to Field of Cosmotology; Presented as Cover Feature & Story of Nat Beauty Mag "Many Ways to Beauty."

LANCASTER, BARBARA JEANETTE oc/Professor and Chairman of MSN Degree Program; b/Nov 3, 1944; h/3916 River View Drive, Birmingham, AL 35243; ba/Birmingham, AL; m/l Wade; c/Melinda Leigh, Jennifer Denise; p/James H Miller, Fort Worth, TX; ed/BSN, Univ of TN, 1966; MSN, Case Wn Resv Univ, 1969; PhD, Univ of OK, 1977; pa/Staff Nurse, Clin Res Ctr, Univ of TN, 1966; Staff Nurse, Mt Sinai Hosp of Cleveland, 1967-68; Nurse Clinician, Univ Hosps of Cleveland, 1969-70; Clin Instr, Case Wn Resv Univ, 1969-70; Instr 1970-73, Asst Prof 1973-74, Assoc Prof 1974-77, TX Christian Univ; Assoc Prof 1977-81, Prof

1981-, Univ of AL Sch of Nsg; ANA; Nat Leag for Nsg; APHA; Assn of Grad Fac in Commun Hlth/Public Hlth Nsg; AL Acad of Sci; r/Bapt; hon/Pubs, *Commun Hlth Nsg Processes & Practs for Promoting Hlth* (in Press), *Concepts of Adv'd Nsg Pract: The Nurse as a Change Agt* 1981, "Identificaiton of Risk Factors for Teen-age Smoking & Eval of a Biofeedback Intervention" (in Press), Num Others; Outstg Media Awd, Reg 2, Sigma Theta Tau for Book, 1982; Book of the Yr Awd, *Am Jour of Nsg*, 1981; Excell in Writing Awd, ANA, TX Nurses Assn, 1976; Outstg Clin Paper, OH Nurses Assn, 1969; W/W of Am Wom; Intl W/W in Ed.

LANE, BRUCE STUART oc/Attorney; b/May 15, 1932; h/3711 Thornapple Street, Chevy Chase, MD 20815; ba/Washington, DC; m/Ann Elizabeth; c/Sue Ellen, Charles M, Richard I; p/Stanley S and Frances M Lane, University Heights, OH; ed/Student, Boston Univ, 1948-49; AB 1952, JD 1955, Harvard Univ; mil/Maj, USAR-JAGC, Hon Discharge; pa/Assoc, Squire, Sanders & Dempsey, 1955-59; Sr Trial Atty, Tax Div, Dept of Justice, 1959-61; Tax Atty, Dinsmore, Shohl, Barrett, Coates & Deupree, 1961-65; Secy, Asst Gen Counsel, Corporate & Tax Matters, Communs Satellite Corp, 1965-69; VP, Gen Counsel, Corp Nat Housing Ptnrships, 1969-70; Pres, Lane & Edson, PC, 1970-; ABA; Am Law Inst; Am Col Real Est Lwyrs, Bd of Govs; Anglo-Am Real Property Inst; Phi Beta Kappa; cp/ Incorporator, Dir, Past Pres, DC Inst of Mtl Hygiene; Past Chm, Citizens Com Sect 5, Chevy Chase; Former Mem, Montgomery Co Hist Presv Com; hon/Co-Editor-in-Chief, *Housing & Devel Reporter*; Pubs, "Tax Refund Litigation" 1964, "Limited Ptnrships: Legal & Bus Aspects" 1981, Num Others on Tax, Ptnrship & Real Est Law; W/W in Am Law.

LANE, GARY oc/Law Professor and Government Affairs Consultant; b/Jan 2, 1946; h/8313A South Yorktown, Tulsa, OK 74137; ba/Tulsa, OK; p/J Roger Lane, Jamaica, NY; ed/BA, City Univ of NY, 1966; JD, Univ of San Diego, 1969; LLM, George Wash Univ, 1970; MA, Univ of So CA, 1972; LLM, NY Univ, 1974; Grad Studies, Harvard Law Sch 1976, Univ of So CA Bus Sch 1981; pa/Assoc Prof of Law, O W Coburn Sch of Law, Oral Roberts Univ, 1983-; Prof of Bus Adm, Pepperdine Univ Grad Sch of Bus & Mgmt, 1982-83; Assoc, Overton, Lyman & Prince, Attys, 1983; Corporate Atty, Luth Hosp Soc of So CA, Pacific Hlth Resources, Law Ofcs of Peter C Rank, 1982; Gen Counsel & Exec Asst to the Pres, Maj Properties, Real Est, 1981; Pvt Pract in LA & Wash DC, 1977-78; Other Previous Positions; Num Bar Mbrships; Conslt on Constitl Law to Congl Com Staffs of Both Houses; Advocate for Corps, Trade Assns, Pvt Indivs, Before Congl & St Legis Coms, Fed Agys & Pvt Orgs; hon/Author, Several Pub'd Scholarly Articles & Commentaries; Spec Cert of Ser, US Ho of Reps, 1972; Dist'd Citizen Ser Awd, San Diego Bd of Ed, 1969; Other Hons; W/W: in W, in Fin & Indust, in CA, in World; Intl Bus-men's W/W.

LANE, LARRY QUENTIN oc/Community College President; b/Nov 22,

1934; h/1211 Greenwood Trail, Northwest, Cleveland, TN 37311; ba/Cleveland, TN; m/Evelyn S; c/Darlene; p/Berdie D Lane (dec); ed/BS, Mid TN St Univ, 1954; MA, George Peabody Col for Tchrs, 1959; EdD, Univ of TN, 1973; mil/AUS, Med Lab Spec 1957-58; pa/Pres 1978-, Dean of Acad Affairs 1973-78, Dir of Res 1971-73, Dir of Cont'g Ed 1971, Cleveland St Commun Col; Exec Dir, Chattanooga Model Cities Prog, 1969-71; Dir of Staff Pers Sers, Chattanooga Public Schs, 1967-69; Other Previous Positions; NEA; TN Ed Assn; E TN Ed Assn; Cleveland St Commun Col Ed Assn; hon/Dist'd Alumnus Awd, Mid TN St Univ, 1979; Rotarian of the Yr, Cleveland Rotary Clb, 1981-82; Personalities of S; Outstg Edrs of Am; W/W: in Am Ed, in Am Univs & Cols; DIB.

LANE, ROGER L oc/College Teacher and Researcher in Zoology; b/Jul 4, 1945; h/2706 Burlingham Drive, Ashtabula, OH 44004; ba/Ashtabula, OH; m/Paulette Hruban; c/Leigh Stanlie, Brooke Christine, Taylor Catherine; p/Andy (dec) and Flora Lane, Ransom Canyon, TX; ed/BS 1968, MS 1971, PhD 1974, Univ of NE; mil/AUS, 1968-70; pa/Vis'g Lectr in Biol, John F Kennedy Col, 1973-75; Asst Prof of Biol Scis 1975-80, Assoc Prof of Biol Scis 1980-, Kent St Univ, Ashtabula Campus; AAAS; Am Microscopical Soc; Am Malacological Union; Am Soc of Zools; Crustacean Soc, Charter Mem; Nat Assn of Biol Tchrs; OH Acad of Sci; cp/ Ashtabula Co Animal Protective Leag, VP 1979-; r/Cath; hon/Pubs, "A Developmental Invest of the Reproductive Systems of *Armadillidium vulgare* (Latreille) & *Porcellionides pruinosus* (Brandt) (Isopoda)" 1977, "Histochem of the Reproductive Systems of *Armadillidium vulgare* (Latreille) & *Porcellionides pruinosus* (Brandt) (Isopoda)" 1980; NDEA Grad F'ship, Univ of NE, 1970-73; Kent St Univ Reg Campuses Tchg Devel Awd, 1980; Kent St Univ Reg Campus Fac Profl Devel Awd, 1983; W/W in Frontier Sci & Technol.

LANG, ANTON oc/Plant Scientist; b/ Jan 18, 1913; h/1538 Cahill Drive, East Lansing, MI 48823; ba/Michigan State University, East Lansing, MI 48824; m/Lydia Kamendrowsky; c/Peter, Michael, Irene Kleiman; p/George and Vera Davidov Lang (dec); ed/Dr Nat Sci (PhD Equivalent), Univ of Berlin, 1939; pa/Sci Asst, Kaiser Wilhelm Inst of Biol, Berlin, 1939-49; Res Assoc, Dept of Genetics, McGill Univ, 1949; Res Fellow, Sr Res Fellow, Div of Biol, CA Inst of Technol, 1950-52; Asst & Assoc Prof, Dept of Botany, Univ of CA-LA, 1952-59; Prof of Biol in Charge of Earhart-Campbell Plant Res Lab, CA Inst of Technol, 1959-65; Dir, MI St Univ Atomic Energy Comm (Later US Dept of Energy) Plant Res Lab & Prof of Botany, 1965-78; Prof 1978-83, Current Prof Emeritus, MI St Univ; Vis'g Prof, Univ of CA-Riverside, 1984; AAAS, Fellow; Am Soc of Plant Physiols, Pres 1970-71; Soc for Developmental Biol, Pres 1968; German Botanical Soc, Hon Mem 1982; Nat Acad of Scis, Adv Com on USSR & En Europe 1964-67, 1977-78; Org'g Com, XI Intl Botanical Cong, Seattle, 1969; NSF, Adv Com for Biol & Med, 1968-71; Nat Acad Scis, Nat Res Coun, Com on the Effects of Herbicides in Vietnam, Chm 1971-74; Pres's Com on the Nat Medal of Sci, 1976-79; Author, Over 100 Profl Papers, Reviews, Chapts; Co-Mng Editor, *Planta* Intl Jour of Plant Biol, 1967-; Bd of Advrs, *Gt Soviet Encyclopedia*, 1976-82; cp/Bd of Trustees, Argonne Univs Assn, 1965-71; hon/Sr Postdoct F'ship, NSF, 1958; Leopoldina German Acad of Naturalists, Elected 1965; Nat Acad of Scis, Elected 1967; Am Acad of Arts & Scis, Elected 1968; Sr Scist Awd, Sigma Xi, MI St Univ Chapt, 1969; Hon VP, XII Intl Botanical Cong, Leningrad, 1975; Dist'd Fac Awd, MI St Univ, 1976; Charles Reid Barnes Life Mbrship Awd & Stephen Hales Prize, Am Soc of Plant Physiols, 1976; Cert of Merit, Botanical Soc of Am, 1979; Hon LLD, Univ of Glasgow, 1981.

LANG, CONRAD MARVIN oc/Professor of Chemistry; b/Jul 1, 1939; h/3015 Cherry Street, Stevens Point, WI 54481; ba/Stevens Point, WI; m/Louise June Swanson; c/Kevin Alan, Kurtis Erik, Kenneth Marvin; p/A Conrad and Myrtle O Lang, Stevens Point, WI; ed/BS, Chem & Math, Elmhurst Col, 1961; MS, Chem, Univ of WI-Madison, 1964; PhD, Phy Chem, Univ of WY-Laramie, 1970; pa/Prof of Chem 1979-, Assoc Prof 1970-79, Asst Prof 1966-70, Instr 1964-66, Univ of WI-Stevens Point; W B King Vis'g Prof of Chem, IA St Univ, 1976-77; Am Chem Soc, Councilor from Ctl WI Sect 1973-, Chm of Local Sect Activs Com 1978, 1979, 1980, Chm of Com on Noms & Elections 1983-; r/Evang Free Ch of Am, Gt Lakes Dist Bd Mem; hon/Author, Many Articles & Texts Pub'd in Sci & Tech Jours; Nat Def Ed Act, Title II Fellow 1967-70; Ctl WI Sect, Am Chem Soc Awds, Outstg Ser Awd 1979, Outstg Contbn to Chem 1983; W/W in MW; Am Men & Wom of Sci.

LANG, DOE oc/Communication Specialist, Author, Actress, Educator; h/610 West End Avenue, New York, NY 10024; ba/New York, NY; c/Andrea Ilona, Brian Simpson; p/Samuel Nathaniel and Florence Edith Caplow (dec); ed/BA, Bennington Col; Postgrad (Fulbright Fellow), Univ of Perugia, Italy 1951, Acad of St Cecilia, Rome 1951-52; Postgrad, Juilliard Sch of Music 1961-63, New Sch for Social Res 1975-76; pa/Profl Actress in Broadway Shows, incl'g, *West Side Story, Mame*, Num Off-Broadway Shows, Num TV Commls, Voice-Overs, Dubbing of Fgn Films; Appeared Daily on Day-Time TV as Karen Adams in *As the World Turns*, for 7 Yrs; Also Appeared in *The Edge of Night & Another World*; Mem of Fac, New Sch for Social Res; Lectr; TV & Radio Interviews & Appearances; Assn Human Psych; Assn Transpersonal Psych; DeToqueville Soc; Am Psychol Assn; Screen Actors Guild; AFTRA; Actor Equity Assn; Assn Wom Bus Owners, Dir 1978-79; cp/Fdr, Dir & Mistress of Ceremonies of Peoples Party to Save the NY Public Lib & Perf'g Arts Lib, 1972; Fdr & Dir, Symph Space Cultural Ctr, NYC; Mem, Music Com, Cathedral of St John the Divine; hon/Author, *The Charisma Book: What It Is & How to Get It* 1980, *The Secret of Charisma* 1982; Contbr of Articles to Mags; Subject of Num Articles; Dist'd Achmt, W/W: in Am Edrs, of Am Wom.

LANGGUTH, DAVID LAWRENCE
oc/Decorating Consultant; b/Dec 25, 1948; h/2400 2nd Avenue, Altoone, PA 16602; ba/Altoona, PA; m/Phyllis M (Callahan); c/Matthew; p/Mr & Mrs V H Langguth, Altoona, PA; ed/Att'd St Francis Col, 1967; Ringling Bros Sch of Art, 1971; pa/Decorating Conslt, SCM Div of Glidden Durkee, 1966-76; S&W Indust Sales Dept Hd, 1976-78; Interior Designer Coor, Ethan Allen Carriage House, 1978-; Am Soc of Interior Designers, 1978-; Nat Bd of Tech Assistance for Barrier Free Design; Freelance Interior Design Conslt to Var Newspapers; cp/Charter Mem, Hollidaysbury Ambuc's; hon/Guest Lctr, Mt Aloysis Jr Col & IN Univ of PA; Journeyman Plumber's Lic, City of Altoona, 1983; W/W in E.

LANGSAM, WALTER CONSUELO
oc/University President Emeritus; b/Jan 2, 1906; h/1071 Celestial Street, Cincinnati, OH 45202; ba/Cincinnati, OH; m/Julia Elizabeth; c/Walter Eaton, Geoffrey Hardinge; ed/BA, City Col of NY, 1925; MA 1926, PhD 1930, Columbia Univ; pa/Instr of Hist 1927-35, Asst Prof of Hist 1935-38, Columbia Univ; Prof of Hist, Union Col, 1938-45; Pres, Wagner Col, 1945-52; Pres, Gettysburg Col, 1952-55; Pres 1955-71, Pres Emeritus & Dist'd Ser Prof 1971-, Univ of Cinc; Trustee, Endicott Col, 1949-; Trustee, Univ of Cinc Foun, 1978-; Trustee, Cinc Inst of Fine Arts, 1955-; Cinc Hist Soc, Trustee Emeritus 1982-; hon/Pubs, *Cent Hist of the Comml Clb of Cinc, 1880-1980* 1981, *Cinc in Color* 1978, *The World & Warren's Cartoons* 1977, *The Common Mkt: Probs & Prospects* 1974, Num Others; 12 Hon Docts; DAR Americanism Medal, 1975; Silver Beaver Awd, BSA, 1973; Good Neighbor Awd, Isaac M Wise Temple, 1972; Num Other Hons; Intl W/W; W/W: in Am, in World; DIB; Intl Authors & Writers W/W; Intl W/W in Commun Ser; Commun Ldrs of Am; Dir of Am Scholars; Others.

LANIER, ROGER A oc/University Administrator; b/Nov 13, 1950; h/1714 Barclay Drive, Richardson, TX 75081; ba/Dallas, TX; m/Jere Rhea Ensey; c/Stacie Rhea, Robert Brett; p/Burt and Velma Lanier, Oklahoma City, OK; ed/PhD 1977, MS 1974, Univ of OK Hlth Sci Ctr; BA, OKC Univ, 1973; pa/Assoc Dean & Assoc Prof, Univ of TX Hlth Sci Ctr, 1980-; Asst Dean & Assoc Prof, Univ of TX Med Br, 1977-80; Asst Prof of Psych, S OKC Jr Col, 1976-77; Eval Spec, Univ of OK Hlth Sci Ctr, 1974-76; Am Soc of Allied Hlth Professions, Bd of Dirs 1981-, CIM Dir 1982-, Fin Com 1981-, Noms Com 1980-, JAH Edit Bd 1980-; TX Soc of Allied Hlth Professions, Bd of Dirs 1979-, Num Past Positions; Am Ednl Res Assn; APHA; Eval Netwk; SW Ednl Res Assn; r/Bapt; hon/Pubs, "Fac Eval Practices Among Occupl Therapy Chairpersons: A Comparative Study" 1982, "Student Selection for a Specialist in Blood Bank Technol Prog: The Predictive Validity of Var Admissions & Prog Measures" (Pending), "Profl Perf of Phys Assts: A Comparison of Phys Asst & Phys Ratings" 1982, "Legal Guidelines for Evaluating & Dismissing Med Students" 1981, Num Others; Cert of Apprec, Am Occupl Therapy Foun, 1982; Gavel Awd, TX Soc of Allied Hlth Professions, 1982; Cert of Merit, Am Soc of Allied Hlth Professions, 1981;

Gov's Appointee, Long Range Planning Task Force for the St of OK, 1977; Fellow, Scholar-Ldrship Enrichment Prog, Univ of OK, 1975-77; Grad, cum laude, OKC Univ, 1973; Psi Chi, 1972; Blue Key, 1972; Outstg Yg Men of Am.

LANNES, WILLIAM JOSEPH III oc/Electrical Engineer; b/Oct 12, 1937; ba/142 Delaronde Street, New Orleans, LA 70174; m/Patricia Anne; c/David, Kenneth, Jennifer; p/Mr and Mrs W J Lannes Jr, New Orleans, LA; ed/BSEE, Tulane Univ, 1959; MSEE, US Nav Postgrad Sch, 1966; mil/USMC 1959-70, Lt through Maj; pa/Assoc Engr 1970, Utility Engr 1971, Sys Engr 1976, Engrg Supvr 1977, Present Mgr of Substa Engrg, LA Power & Light Co; Pt-time Engrg Instr, Univ of NO, 1979-80; IEEE, Chm of NO Sect 1981-82; Dir, 5th Dist Savs & Ln; Dir, New Life, NO Area; VChm, Univ of NO Engrg Adv Coun; Indust Advr, Elect Power Res Inst; Com-man, Edison Elect Inst & SEn Elect Exch; Power Engrg Soc; cp/U Way, 1975, 1976, 1981; Com-man for BSA, 1972-76; r/Cath; hon/Pubs, "Cost-Effectiveness Anal of Substa Arrangement" 1982, "The GIS Option at 500 KV" 1980, "Little Orphan Ontos"; Bronze Star w Combat "V," 1970; Cross of Gallantry, RSVN, 1970; Cert of Merit from Mayor of NO, 1964; Outstg Ser Awd, NO, IEEE, 1976; Soc of Sigma Xi, 1966; Eta Kappa Nu, 1973; Reg'd Profl Engr, LA; W/W in S & SW.

LANT, JEFFREY LADD oc/Management Consultant; b/Feb 16, 1947; h/50 Follen Street, Suite 507, Cambridge, MA 02138; ba/Same; ed/BA, summa cum laude, Univ of CA-Santa Barbara, 1969; MA 1970, PhD 1975, Harvard Univ; Cert of Adv'd Grad Studies, Higher Ed Adm, NEn Univ, 1976; pa/Coor of Student Sers, Boston Col Evening Col, 1976-78; Asst to the Pres, Radcliffe Col, Harvard Univ, 1978-79; Pres, Treas, Dir, Jeffrey Lant Assocs Inc, 1979-; r/Prot; hon/Pubs, *The Unabashed Self Promoter's Guide: What Every Man, Wom, Child & Org in Am Needs to Know About Getting Ahead by Exploiting the Media* 1983, *The Consult's Kit: Establishing & Operating Your Successful Consultg Bus* 1981, 1983, *Devel Today: A Guide for Non-Profit Orgs* 1980, 1983; Editor, *Our Harvard: Reflections on Col Life by Twenty-Two Dist'd Grads* 1982, *Insubstantial Pageant: Ceremony & Confusion at Queen Victoria's Ct* 1979, 1980; Author, Over 400 Articles Pub'd Worldwide; Ofcl Cit, City of Cambridge, MA, 1983; Ofcl Cit, Gov of MA, 1982, 1978; Ofcl Cit, Boston City Coun, 1978; Ofcl Cit, MA Ho of Reps, 1977; Woodrow Wilson Fellow, 1969; Harvard Prize Fellow, 1969-75; Harvard Col Master's Awd, 1975; Sir Henry Jones Prize, Moral Phil, Univ of St Andrews, 1968; W/W: in E, in Fin & Indust, in Consltg; Men & Wom of Distn; 5,000 Commun Ldrs; Contemp Authors.

LANTHIER, PATRICIA ANN oc/Principal of Private School in Hospital; b/Jul 21, 1950; h/Box 4494, Princeton, FL 33032; ba/Miami, FL; p/Louis Arthur (dec) and Patricia Hurley Lanthier, Spartanburg, SC; ed/BS, Elem Ed/Spec Ed; MS, Sch Adm & Supvn; pa/Tchr, Saxon Ed Ctr, Spartanburg Sch Dist #6, 1972-74; Tchr 1974-76, Asst Dir of Ed 1976-80, Psych & Ednl Diagnostic Spec 1980-82, Dir of Ed 1982-, Grant Ctr Hosp; CEC; Assn for Supvn & Curric

Devel; Broader Opports for the Lng Disabled; r/Rom Cath; hon/Spkr, Tchr Ed Div, CEC Annual Conf, 1982; W/W in S & SW.

LANTZ, RUTH COX oc/Teacher, Writer, Artist; b/Jan 11, 1914; h/1040 Springdale Road, Northeast, Atlanta, GA 30306; m/J Edward; c/Thomas Edward, John Harvey, Alma Esther; p/Harvey Warren and Daisy Frisbie Cox (dec); ed/AB, Emory Univ, 1934; MA, Univ of MI, 1942; Spec Studies at Yale Art Sch & Pratt Inst; pa/Instr of Spch, Vanderbilt Univ, 1946-52; Spch Tchr, St Mary's Acad, 1952; Instr, Christian Ed, Interdenom Theol Ctr, 1960-69; cp/U Ch Wom of GA, Chm of Publicity 1955-56, Mbrships 1956, Public Relats 1961, VP; Camp Fire Girls, Atlanta Coun, Dist Camping Chm 1956-58, Pres 1958-60, Prog Chm 1961-64, Reg Exec Com 1961-66, Secy 1962-66, Nat Coun 1966-68; F'ship of Reconciliation, Nashville Pres 1950-51, Nat Coun 1950-55; r/U Meth; hon/Co-Author, *Plays for Happier Homes* 1957, *Bible Characters in Action* 1955; Author of Num Poems, Articles, Plays, U Meth Lesson Mats; Editor, *The Shepherdess*, 1950-58; Several Prizes for Poems, Articles, The Atlanta Writers Clb; W/W: of Am Wom, in S & SW; Intl W/W of Poetry.

LANZKRON, ROLF W oc/Manager of Engineering; b/Sep 12, 1929; h/35 Gardner Road, Brookline, MA 02146; ba/Sudbury, MA; m/Amy Virginia Yarri; c/Lisa, Sophie, Paul; ed/CPA, Israel, 1948; BSEE, Milwaukee Sch of Engrg, 1953; Doct Deg in Math & Elect Engrg 1956, Master's Deg in Elect Engrg 1955, Univ of WI; pa/Dpty Dir of Air Traffic Control Directorate, Dir of Graphics Sys Bus Area, Asst Graphics Mgr, Prog Mgr of Wash Post Ray Edit, Prog Mgr of TPN-19, Prog Mgr of Computer Display Channel, Raytheon, 1968-; Div Chief, Apollo Prog, NASA, 1962-68; Br Chief, Sys Integration, Martin Co, 1960-67; IEEE; Am Rocket Soc; Am Math Assn; AIAA; Air Traffic Control Assn; Inst of Radio Engrg; Am Mgmt Assn; r/Jewish; hon/Author of Var Profl Pubs; Scholastic Hons, Dean's List; Sigma Xi; W/W: in E, in Aviation, in Fin; Men of Sci Yearly; 2,000 Men of Achmt; DIB.

La-PIERRE, PHILIPE STEPHEN oc/Director of Research and Development; b/Oct 16, 1938; ba/485 Madison Avenue, New York, NY 10022; m/Margaret Mary; c/Stephen Philip, Linda Mary; p/Valantine and Veronica La-Pierre, San Juan, Trinidad; ed/BSc, London, 1961; Fellow of Cable TV Engrs, England, 1976; Sr Mem, Cable TV Engrs, USA, 1980; MRSTE, England, 1975; MSERT, England, 1974; CEng, England, 1978; pa/Sr Electronics Engr, Rediffusion England, 1950-76; Intl Sys Mgr, Speywood Electronics, Wembley Engrg, 1976-79; Dir of R&D Carib Electronics, FL, 1979-80; Dir of R&D Inflight Motion Pictures, 1980-; r/Ch of England; hon/Soc of Cable TV Engrs, 1981; AEA, 1982; Royal TV Soc, 1976; W/W in Fin & Indust.

La PORTE, WILLIAM BRUCE oc/Chief Administrator of School District; b/Jul 13, 1925; h/882 Elkridge, Brea, CA 92621; ba/Whittier, CA; m/Virginia Andrew; c/Dean Bruce, Diane La Porte Lanois, Dan Andrew; p/William Ralph and Lura Adams La Porte (dec); ed/BA,

1953; MS, 1965; mil/USAAC; pa/Chief Admr, Tri-Cities Reg Occuptl Prog Dist, 1974- (Secy to the Bd of Mgmt); Conslt, SE LA Co Reg Occupl Prog Dist, 1982; Conslt, St Dept of Ed, 1976-77; Chm 1975, 1976, Mem 1974, CA St Voc Ed Sch Dist Review Team; Pt-time Prof, CA St Univ-LA, 1973, 1975-77; Coor, Career Ed, Whittier Union HS Dist, 1967-74; Pt-time Instr, Rio Hondo Col, 1963-64; Curric Coor 1960-63, Indust Arts Dept Chm 1959-61, 1963-67, Instr 1959-67, Pioneer HS; Other Previous Positions; Alpha Phi Omega; Am Indust Arts Assn; Am Voc Assn; Assn of CA Sch Admrs, Charter Mem; CA Assn of Reg Occupl Ctrs & Progs; CA Assn of Voc Ed; CA Assn of Wk Experience Edrs; CA Coun of Indust Arts Supvrs; CA Indust Ed Assn; Epsilon Pi Tau; Local Admrs of Voc Ed & Practical Arts; LA Co Indust Ed Assn; Phi Delta Kappa; Num Past Ofcs Held in Profl Orgs; cp/E Whittier Lions; Pico Rivera C of C & Legis Com; Santa Fe Springs C of C/Indust Leag; Whittier Area C of C & Ed Com; r/La Habra Meth Ch, 1955-; hon/Pubs, "A Sch Involving Project" 1958, "Auto Safety Check" 1957, Num Articles for Assns' Newslttrs; Hon Plymouth Trouble Shooter, Chrysler Corp, 1978; W/W: in W, in CA, in Am Ed.

LAPUCK, JACK LESTER oc/Executive; b/Aug 28, 1924; h/8 Lovett Road, Newton, MA 02159; ba/Watertown, MA; m/Ruth G; c/Dr Robert, Susan, Debra Saunders; p/Bernard and Ray Lapuck, Boston, MA; ed/BS, 1946; MS, 1949; ScD, 1960; mil/Army, 1946-47; pa/Tchg Fellow, Univ of MA, 1947-49; Montgomery Co Hlth Dept, 1950; Chem, Food & Drug Res Labs, 1950; Lab Dir, VP, Waltham Labs, 1951-66; Pres, Lapuck Labs Inc (Consltg & Testing Lab), 1966-; Past Chm, NE Sect, Analytical Chem Grp, Am Chem Soc, 1965; Chm, Ednl Com, MA Assn of Sanitarians, 1962; Instr, MA Dept of Ed, 1955-68; Instr, Boston St, 1968-70; Pres, MA Coun of Indep Testing Labs, 1983; Abstractor, Am Chem Soc, 10 Yrs; cp/Treas & Asst Scoutmaster, BSA, 2 Yrs; Pres, Temple Emanuel Brotherhood, 1975; r/Jewish; hon/Pub, "Effect of Surface Active Agents on Bacterial Decomposition," 1949; MA Mangold Nom, 1965; Am Men of Sci; W/W: in E, in Fin & Indust.

LARGMAN, KENNETH oc/Chairman and Chief Executive Officer of World Security Council; b/Apr 7, 1949; ba/World Security Council, World Trade Center, San Francisco, CA 94111; c/Jezra; p/Franklin (dec) and Roselynd Largman; ed/Student, SUNY, 1969-70; pa/Indep Strategic Analyst, 1970-79; Chm, CEO, World Security Coun, 1980-; AF Assn; Am Astronautical Soc; AIAA; World Affairs Coun; Commonwlth Clb; hon/Pubs, *Space Peacekeeping* 1978, *Preventing Nuclear Conflict: An Intl Beam Weaponry Agreement* 1979, *Space Weaponry: Effects on the Intl Balance of Power & the Prev of Nuclear War* 1981, *Threats, Vulnerabilities & Safeguards of Coordinated US/Societ Space Def Systems* 1983; Co-Author, *Preventing Nuclear War: Coor'g US & Soviet Space Def to Protect Agnst Nuclear Attack*, 1982; W/W: in Frontier Sci & Technol.

LARSEN, KENNETH M oc/Editor, Publisher, Consultant; b/Jun 5, 1946; h/

PO Box 569, Albion, CA 95410; ba/Mendocino, CA; p/Frank and Klara Larsen, Ignacio, CA; ed/BA, Antioch Col, 1968; Cand Phil, Univ of CA-Davis, 1975; pa/Foreman, SF Voc Rehab Wkshop, 1967-71; Grad Student, Lectr, Rschr, Sociol, Univ of CA-Davis, 1971-77; Assoc Pres, Hooper Billstein & Assocs, Arts Mgmt Conslts, 1977-79; Dir, Rural Arts Sers, 1980-; CA Confdn of the Arts, Chair of Commun Arts Task Force 1982-83; Alliance for Cultural Democracy, Co-Chair of Pubs 1983-84; hon/Pubs, "Crime Fighting or Arts Devel?" in *Connections*, 1984; Alfred P Sloan Scholar, 1967; Regents Fellow, 1976.

LARSEN, R PAUL oc/Vice Ptesident of University Extension; b/Dec 1, 1926; h/1175 Cedar Heights, Logan, UT 84321; ba/Logan, UT; m/Lorna Anderson; c/Nanette K, Peggy Rinehart, Mark B, Cynthia K Bennett; p/Ariel and Vera Larsen (dec); ed/BS, UT St Univ, 1950; MS, KS St Univ, 1951; PhD, MI St Univ, 1955; mil/US Merch Marine, 1945-46; Lt, AUS, 1951-53; pa/From Asst Prof to Prof of Hort, MI St Univ, 1955-68; Supt, Tree Fruit Res Ctr, WA St Univ, 1968-82; VP, Univ Ext, UT St Univ, 1982-; Bd Mem & Exec Com, Ctl WA Bk, 1975-83; Pres, Am Soc for Hort Sci, 1975-76; cp/Pres, Wenatchee, WA, Rotary, 1975-76; Chm, Commun Devel Coun, 1973-76; VP, Boy Scouts Coun, 1980-82; r/LDS; hon/Author, Over 200 Profl Pubs, Book Chapt, Ext Bltns; Columnist, *Am Fruit Grower Mag*, 1957-82; Outstg Ext Spec, MI St Univ, 1967; Fellow, Am Soc for Hort Sci, 1971; Dist'd Ser Awds: Intl Cherry Res Symp, MI St Hort Soc, WA Fruit Ind; Am Men of Sci; W/W in W.

LARSON, JANE WARREN oc/Ceramic Artist; b/Jun 2, 1922; h/6514 Bradley Boulevard, Bethesda, MD 20817; m/Clarence E; c/Lawrence E, Lance S; p/Dr and Mrs Stafford L Warren (dec); ed/BA in Eng, cum laude, Univ of Rochester, 1943; MFA, Ceramics, Antioch Univ, 1982; pa/Tech Editor, Tech Libn, Dept Admr, TN Eastman Corp, Union Carbide Corp & RAND Corp, 1943-57; Artist's Equity; Kiln Clb of Wash DC; cp/Indep Agy Wives, Pres 1972-73; Achmt Rewards for Col Scists Inc; r/Metro Ch, Wash DC, VP 1979; Presb; hon/Pub'd in *Ceramics Monthly* Jun 1968, Jun 1970, Oct 1970, May 1972, *Craft Horizons* Jun 1973, Feb 1975; Phi Beta Kappa, 1943; Juror's Mention for Excell, Invitational Sh Show, 1973; Other Awds at Reg & Nat Shows; W/W: of Am Wom, of Am Artists.

LASH, HENRY J oc/Professor of English Education; b/Jul 7, 1920; h/Route 2, Box 44, Montevallo, AL 35115; ba/Montevallo, AL; m/Mrs Mary O; c/David, James, Laura Ann; p/Stephen P Lash (dec); ed/EdD 1970, MA 1958, Univ of AL; BA, Eng, Brown Univ, 1949; mil/USAAF, 1942-45; USAF, 1950-52; pa/Info Spec, US Govt, 1954; Clrm Tchr, Mobile (AL) Co, 1955-68; Prof of Eng Ed, Univ of Montevallo, 1970-; Phi Delta Kappa, 1958-68; Kappa Phi Kappa, 1974-; NEA, 1972-; NCTE, 1972-; Nat Coun for the Social Studies, 1974-; Exec Secy, AL Coun for the Social Studies, 1978-; r/Cath; hon/Author, Article in *The Profl Edr*, Book Review in *AL Assn of Sec'dy Sch Prins Bltn*.

LATZ, DOROTHY L oc/Professor,

Writer; b/Dec 9, 1930; h/PO Box 265, New Rochelle, NY 10802; p/Joseph G (dec) and Dorothy S Latz; ed/Doct, Comparative Lit, Univ of Paris (Sorbonne), 1969; MA, Eng, Fordham Univ, 1962; Lic, French, Univ of Grenoble, France, 1971; BA, Eng, Col of New Rochelle; Doct Cand, Theol, Univ of Strasbourg, 1983; pa/Humanities Div Chm 1975-76, Mod Langs Dept Chm 1975-78, Assoc Prof of Humanities 1975-78, Adj Prof of Eng 1979-83, Var Cols in Metro NY Area; Translator, Abaris Books, NYC 1983-, St Paul Press 1980; Fdr, Past Pres, & Past Pres of Bd of Dirs, Alliance Francaise of Rockland Co, 1975-79; Mem, Lectr, Session Orgr, "Sixteenth Cent Studies Conf," 1981-; Mem & Lectr, Mod Lang Assn, Christianity & Lit Conf, Intl Medieval Theatre Soc; Poetry Soc of Am; r/Cath; hon/Pubs, "On Medieval Theatre" 1981, Translation of P R Regamey's *Renewal in the Spirit* 1980, Poetry in *Poesie USA* & *Christianity & Lit* 1981, 1982; Elected Mem, Columbia Univ Sems on the Renaissance, 1982; Elected Mem, Poetry Soc of Am, 1982; Intl W/W in Poetry; Intl W/W of Authors; World W/W of Wom.

LAUDENSLAGER, WANDA LEE oc/ District Coordinator of Speech, Language and Hearing; Real Estate Broker; General Building Contractor; b/Jul 22, 1929; h/37733 Logan Drive, Fremont, CA 94536; ba/Newark, CA; m/Leonard; c/Leonard II, Dawn Marie; p/Victor Vierra Silveira (dec); Florence Silveira, San Leandro, CA; ed/AA, Col of San Mateo, 1960; BA 1962, MA 1965, San Jose St Univ; Cert'd in Standard Supvn 1971, Tchg 1962, Spch, Lang & Hearing Pathol 1962, Standard Designated Sers 1971; CA Lic'd Audiometrist, 1966; Real Est Broker, 1978; Gen Bldg Contractor, 1979; Nat Certn of Clin Competence in Spch Pathol, Am Spch, Lang & Hearing Assn, 1963; Lic'd by CA St Bd of Med Examrs for Pvt Therapy as Spch Pathol, 1974; pa/Spch Pathol, Newark Unified Sch Dist, 1962-65; Dist Coor, Spch, Lang & Hearing Dept, 1965-; Self-Employed Real Est Broker & Gen Bldg Contractor; Am Spch, Lang & Hearing Assn; Assn of CA Sch Admrs; Newark Schs Admrs Assn, Treas; Sch Admrs Spec Sers; Nat Assn of Rltrs; CA Assn of Rltrs; So Alameda Co Bd of Rltrs; hon/Phi Kappa Phi; Alpha Gamma Sigma; Pi Lambda Theta; Kappa Delta Pi; Cong of Parents & Tchrs Life Mbrship; Crown Zellerback Foun; San Jose St Univ Dept of Ed Hons, 1962; Life Patron, ABIRA; Life Fellow, IBA; DIB; W/W: in W, in CA; World W/W of Wom; Intl W/W of Intells; Book of Hon; Dir Dist'd Ams; Commun Ldrs of the World; 5,000 Personalities of the World; Men & Wom of Distn; Biogl Roll of Hon; Intl W/W of Contemp Achmt.

LAUER, JAMES LOTHAR oc/ Research Professor of Mechanical Engineering; b/Aug 2, 1920; h/7 North East Lane, Ballston Lake, NY 12019; ba/ Troy, NY; m/Stefanie Blank; c/Michael S, Ruth; p/Dr Max Lauer (dec); ed/AB 1942, MA 1948, Temple Univ; PhD, Univ of PA, 1948; Postdoct Fellow, Univ of CA-San Diego, 1964-65; pa/Res Chem 1944-52, Res Scist 1953-64, Sr Res Scist 1965-77, Sun Oil Co; Res Prof of Mech Engrg, Rensselaer Polytechnic Inst, 1978-; Asst Prof of Physics, Univ

of PA, 1948-52; Adj Prof of Chem, Univ of DE, 1952-60; Pres, DE Val Sect, Soc of Applied Spectroscopy, 1977; Am Chem Soc; Am Phy Soc; Optical Soc of Am; Spectroscopy Soc of Canada; cp/ Penn Wynne, PA, Civic Assn, 1960-77; Country Knolls Civic Assn, 1978-; r/ Jewish; hon/Author, *Infrared Fourier Transform Spectroscopy-Chemical Applications* 1978, About 120 Pubs in Tech Jours Relating to Molecular Spectroscopy, Combustion & Electrostatics; Originator of 30 Patents; Coblentz Soc Lectr of 1978; Gordon Res Conf Spkr, 1982; Grantee of AF Ofc of Sci Res, 1974-; NASA-Lewis Res Lab, 1974-; Ofc of Nav Res, 1979-81; Commun Ldrs of Am; W/W in Am; Am Men & Wom of Sci.

LAUREANO-COLÓN, JUAN A oc/ Clergyman, Founder and Executive Director; b/Dec 11, 1946; h/Urb Jard de San Lorenzo, 2nd Street, A-15, San Lorenzo, PR 00754; ba/San Lorenzo, PR; m/Ana Lydia; c/Jose A, Milagros G, Enid, Yojaira I, Viviana J, Nancy; p/Juan and Dolores Laureano-Colon, San Lorenzo, PR; ed/AA, KC Commun Col, 1977; BS, KS Newman Col, 1979; Master of Theol, Intl Bible Inst & Sem, 1980; mil/Army 1964-80, Vietnam; pa/ Exec Dir & Fdr, The Christian Homes & Ctrs of PR & Latin Am; Ordained to Min by Bapt Ch, 1979; Biblical Geol Soc; cp/Smithsonian Instn; JCs; Lions Clb; Latin Studies; r/So Bapt; hon/ Decorated w Silver Star, Bronze Star, Air Medal, Army Commend Medal, Vietnam Ser, Vietnam Campaign, Vietnamese Galantry Cross; W/W in S & SW.

LAVENDER, EULA MAE TAYLOR oc/Artist, Handcrafter; b/Apr 14, 1923; h/1930 Highway 9, Black Mountain, NC; m/1st H W Morris; 2nd Howard H Lavender; c/William Randolph Morris, Gerald Lee Morris, H Taylor Morris (dec), David Andrew Morris (dec); p/ John Randolph and Ida Marlowe Taylor (dec); pa/Former Positions: Seamstress & Tailor, Electronic Wkr at Kearfott & C P Clare, Farmer, Tile Setter, Dept Store Clk, House Painter, Furniture Designer, Census Enumerator, Blue Prints; Master Craftswom in Afghans, Capes, Bedspreads, Baby Sets, Doll Clothes, Hot Pads, Doilies, Tablecloths, Handmade Christmas Ornaments, Bells, Baskets, Boots, Stockings, Wreaths, Lapel Pins, Skates, Santas, Snowflakes, Quilts & Pillows; Artist, Oil Paintings of Sea Scapes, Landscapes, Still Life & Rock Crafts; Opened Shop in Her Home, Handcrafts by Lavender, 1979; Exhibited throughout St of NC, Richmond (VA), OH & SC; Crafts in USA, Japan, Germany, Quebec, Ontario, Nova Scotia, Prince Edward Island, Yukon Territory, Saskatchewan, Manitoba, Alberta, Brit Columbia, New Brunswick, Mexico, Brazil, Taiwan, Egypt, Republic of China, England, Denmark, Switzerland, Khartoum, Sudan, Kenya, S Africa, Australia; hon/ Prizes & Awds for Afghans; Featured on "Carolina Camera," Human Interest Prog on WBTV, Charlotte, NC; Personalites of S; Intl Book of Hon; Commun Ldrs of Am; Dir of Dist'd Ams; 2,000 Notable Ams; World W/W of Wom; Biogl Roll of Hon; Intl Book of Hon; Intl W/W of Intells; 5,000 Personalities of World; Commun Ldrs of World;

Personalities of Am; Intl Register of Profiles.

LAVORGNA, GREGORY J oc/Patent Attorney; b/Apr 30, 1950; h/113 Earlington Road, Havertown, PA 19083; ba/Philadelphia, PA; m/Christine J; c/Stephanie N, Cynthia F; p/Emanuel (dec) and Mafalda Gentile Lavorgna; ed/ BSEE 1972, MSEE 1975, Drexel Univ; JD, cum laude, Temple Univ Sch of Law, 1981; pa/Patent Atty, Seidel, Gonda & Goldhammer, PC, 1981-; Electronics Engr, Gen Elect Co, 1975-79; Electronics Engr, RCA Corp, 1972-75; ABA; PA & Phila Bar Assns; Assn of Trial Lwyrs of Am; Phila Patent Law Assn; Justinian Soc; r/Moderator & Trustee, First Bapt Ch of Phila; hon/Editor-in-Chief 1971-72, Assoc Editor 1970-71, *Drexel Tech Jour*; Phi Eta Sigma, 1967; Eta Kappa Nu, 1971; Tau Beta Pi, 1972; Milton C Sharp Meml Awd, Barrister's Awd, Temple Univ Sch of Law, 1981; W/W Among Students in Am Univs & Cols.

LAWER, BETSY oc/Executive; b/Jul 27, 1949; ba/PO Box 720, Anchorage, AK 99510; m/David A; c/Sarah Anne; p/D H and Betty Cuddy, Anchorage, AK; ed/BA in Ec, Duke Univ, 1971; Credit toward Master's Deg in Mktg, CA St Univ Sacramento; pa/VP in Charge of the Mktg Div, Dir, First Nat Bk of Anchorage; First Nat Bk of Anchorage Employees Clb; Bd Mem, AK Coun on Ec Ed, Past Treas; Advtg Fdn of AK; Public Relats Soc of Am; Press Clb; Am Inst of Bkg; cp/Anchorage Woms Clb; Anchorage Symph Opera Woms Leag; AK St C of C; Bd Mem & Treas, Providence Hlth Care Foun; AK St Trooper's Safety Bear Prog; Bd Mem, Neighborhood Watch; hon/Selected as Outstg Yg Wom, 1982; W/W in W.

LAWRENCE, DAVID ANTHONY oc/Educator; b/Aug 1, 1951; h/768 North Grand Avenue, Orange, CA 92667; ba/Orange, CA; p/Cecil and Bernadine Lawrence, Orange, CA; ed/ AA in Arch, Orange Coast Col, 1971; BA in Indust Arts Ed, CA St Univ-Long Bch, 1973; MA in Secy Ed/Sch Adm, Univ of SF, 1978; pa/Indust Arts Instr 1976-, Dist Dept Chm of Indust Arts 1979-, Orange Unified Sch Dist; Practical Arts Dept Chm, Villa Pk HS, 1978-; St Chm of Indust Arts Div, Am Voc Assn, 1980-; Arch/Engrg Prof, Rancho Santiago Commun Col Dist, 1976-; Epsilon Pi Tau, Profl Frat of Indust Arts Edrs, Long Bch Chapt; r/Rom Cath; hon/Author, Lttrs to Indust Arts Div Mems in CA for Am Voc Assn, 1980, 1981, 1982, 1983; Pres's List, CA St Univ-Long Bch, 1973; Dean's List, CA St Univ-Long Bch, 1971-74; S'ship, Epsilon Pi Tau Frat; W/W: in Am Edrs, in Am.

LAWRENCE, GEORGE H oc/Trade Association President; b/Nov 1, 1925; h/8707 Eaglebrook Court, Alexandria, VA 22308; ba/Arlington, VA; m/Shirley Jo Thompson; c/Michael, Linda, George Jr, Amy Jo; p/Chester and Pearl Lawrence (dec); ed/BS in Indust Engrg, OK St Univ, 1949; LLB, S TX Col of Law, 1957; mil/USMC, 1943-46; pa/Petro Engr, Humble Oil & Refining Co, 1949-59; Atty, then Asst Mgr, Natural Gas Div, Humble Oil Co, 1959-63; Indep Legal Pract & Petro Consltg, Houston, 1963-64; Natural Gas Coor, Am Petro Inst, 1964-68; Mgr, then Dir, VP, Exec

VP 1968-76, Pres 1976-, Am Gas Assn; Am Bar Assn; Soc of Petro Engrs; Nat Soc of Profl Engrs; VA Soc of Profl Engrs; Am Soc of Assn Execs; TX Bar Assn; Dir, Nat Energy Foun; Dir, Coun Energy Studies; cp/Kiwanis; Dir, Ctr for Urban Envir Studies; Trustee, Ford Theatre Foun; r/Meth; hon/Author, Monographs & Reports in Field; Recip, Awd, Ctr for Urban Envir Studies, 1979; Dist'd Ser Awd, Natural Energy Resources Org, 1980; OK St Univ Hall of Fame Inductee, 1983; W/W: in World, in Am, in S & SW, in Fin & Indust.

LAWRENCE, MARGIE TURNER oc/ Resource Specialist; b/Feb 15, 1950; h/ 1916 West 76th Street, Los Angeles, CA 90047; ba/Lakewood, CA; m/Dwayne Lawson; c/Brian; p/Mr and Mrs Ira Turner, Memphis, TN; ed/MA, CA St Univ-LA, 1979; BA, Loyola Marymount Univ, 1974; pa/Resource Spec 1980-, Tchr to Ednlly Handicapped Chd 1978-80, Long Bch Unified Sch Dist; Tchr, Compton Unified Sch Dist, 1977-78; Tchr, Normandic Christian Sch, 1974-77; Assoc'd Wom for Pepperdine, Former Treas for Dist #6; Nat Cong of Parents & Tchrs; hon/Julia Ann Singer Presch Awd for Outstg Contbns to Chd, 1978.

LAWRENCE, ROBERT MacLAREN oc/Marketing Professor, Consultant; b/ Oct 5, 1946; h/2511 Briarwood Lane, Marlborough, MA 01752; ba/Lawrenceville, NJ; p/Robert and Georgiana Lawrence (dec); ed/PhD 1980, Adv'd Profl Cert 1974, MBA 1973, NY Univ; BBA, Hofstra Univ, 1972; Undergrad Wk, Columbia Univ; pa/Prof of Mktg, Rider Col, 1979-; Asst Prof, Bus Adm, Monmouth Col, 1976-79; Pvt Conslt, 1975-; Prod Mgr, Doubleday & Co, 1973-75; Conslt, US Dept of Labor, 1970-73; Am Mktg Assn; Acad of Mgmt; Assn of MBA Execs; Am Mgmt Assn; Direct Mktg Assn, Ed Div; cp/ Canterbury Clb; Urban Corps, 1970; r/ Epis; Advr, NJ Epis Diocese; hon/ Author, Num Articles on Mktg Strategy, Direct Mktg & Technol in Profl Jours & Practitioner Pubs; George F Baker Scholar, 1970-74; Doct Fellow, 1978-79; W/W in E; Outstg Yg Ams.

LAWSON, A E oc/Commissioner; b/ Jun 23, 1929; h/6024 Walhonding Road, Bethesda, MD 20816; ba/Washington, DC; m/Louise W; c/Barbara S, Karl A, Erica L, Diana E; ed/BA, Univ of Pgh, 1954; LLB, Harvard Law Sch, 1957; mil/ AUS, 1951-53; pa/Commr, Fed Mine Safety & Hlth Review Comm, 1978-; Atty, U Steelwkrs of Am, 1966-78; Atty, Columbia Gas Sys, 1962-66; Atty, Fogarty & Schreiber, 1957-62; Adj Instr, Carnegie Mellon Univ, 1977; Trustee, Univ of Pgh, 1969-; cp/VChm, Mt Lebanon Dem Party, 1976-78; r/Unitarian Universalist.

LAWSON, ELESA STEVES oc/Pianist, Educator; b/Dec 17, 1933; h/5053 Arroway Avenue, Covina, CA 91724; ba/Covina, CA; c/Steven, Michael, Cheryl; p/Richard Avery and Pauline, Riverside, CA; ed/BMus w Distn, Univ of Redlands, 1955; MA in Ednl Adm, Azusa Pacific Univ, 1981; pa/Public Sch Tchr, 1962-; Tchr, Mem of Cnslg Team and Curric Team, Badillo Sch, 1968-; Proprietor, Lawson Piano Studio, 1955-; Music Dir, Covina Sum Theater, 1969-79; NEA-CTA; Music Tchrs Assn of CA (Dir of San Gabriel Val Chapt),

1965-; Charter Oak Edrs Assn, 1962-; PTA, Local Treas; cp/BSA, Woms Aux Chm 1965-75; r/Presb; hon/Pubs, "Help for Tchrs of ESL Students" 1981, "Sch Closure Plan for Charter Oak Unified School District" 1978; PTA Hon Ser, 1969; PTA Cont'g Ser Awd, 1980; Mortar Bd VP of Chapt, 1954; Mensa, 1980; Pi Kappa Lambda, 1955; Sigma Alpha Iota, 1952; W/W of Am Wom.

LAWSON, JAMES EDWARD JR oc/ Geophysicist; b/Dec 27, 1938; h/Stonebluff Route 2, Box 85C, Haskell, OK 74436; ba/Leonard, OK; m/Carole June; c/Adrianna Vashti; p/James Edward and Edwina Amalia Lawson (dec); ed/BA 1965, BS 1965, MS 1968, PhD 1972, Univ of Tulsa; pa/Geophysicist, Univ of OK Earth Scis Observatory, 1970-78; Chief Geophysicist, OK Geophy Observatory, 1978-; Adj Prof of Geophysics, Univ of OK, 1980-; Sigma Xi, Life; Seismological Soc of Am, Life; Am Geophy Union, Life; AIPAC; Sigma Pi Sigma; cp/Intl Soc of Blood Transfusion; Am Assn of Blood Bks; ARC, OK Reg, Former Bd Mem; r/Prot; hon/Author, Var Pubs; Ontario Scholar, 1960; Cited in 1972 by Mrs R Nixon for Outstg & Dedicated Vol Wk to the Commun & Nat; Tulsa Red Cross Cent Hall of Fame, 1981; W/W in Frontier Sci & Technol.

LAYNE, JOHN FRANCIS oc/Accountant; b/Mar 25, 1928; h/731 Bongart Road, Winter Park, FL 32792; ba/ Orlando, FL; m/Esther A Ornberg; c/ Loretta E, John W, Mark L; p/Lawrence E and Blanche E Tetzlaff Layne (dec); ed/AA, Valencia Jr Col, 1971; BSBA, Univ of Ctl FL, 1972; mil/USAF 1948-70, CWO-4 (Ret'd); pa/USAF: Adv'd through Grades from Pvt 1948 to CWO-4 1964, Intercept Dir 1957, 1958, Weapons Controller & Missileman through 1961, Test Controller in Air Proving Ground Ctr 1962-65, Standardization Eval Controller (Okinawa & Vietnam) 1966-70; Acct 1971-73, Controller 1974-77, Elect Specialty Inc; Financial Field Rep, Tupperware, Div of Dart, 1978-; Ofcr, FL Accts Assn, 1975-76; Nat Assn of Accts; Nat Assn of Public Accts; Nat Assn of Enrolled Agts; cp/VP, Ctl FL Assn of Sq Dancers, 1977-78, Pres 1978-79; Chm, FL St Sq & Round Dance Conv, 1978; Ofcr, FL Fdn of Sq Dancers, 1978-82, Pres 1982-83; r/Prot; hon/Author, Monthly Articles to *Sq Dance* Mag, "Bow & Swing," 1982-83; Decorated, Bronze Star 1970, Vietnamese Hon Medal 1970; Cits, Boy Scouts Far E Coun 1968, Am Sq Dance Soc 1982-83; W/W in Fin & Indust.

LAZARUS, HAROLD oc/Professor, Management Consultant, Lecturer; b/ Jan 16, 1927; h/225 Wellington Road, Garden City, NY 11530; ba/Hempstead, NY; m/Dr Carol Nunes; c/Mark Leander, Eric Lewis; p/Anna Fritz Lazarus, Brooklyn, NY; ed/PhD 1963, MS 1952, Columbia Univ Grad Sch of Bus; BA, Col of Arts & Scis, NY Univ, 1949; mil/USN, 1945-46; pa/Prof of Mgmt, NY Univ Grad Sch of Bus Adm, 1963-73; Dean, Sch of Bus, Hofstra Univ, 1973-80; Res Dir, AT&T Manpower Lab, 1970-71; Adj Prof, Columbia Univ Grad Sch of Bus & Tchrs Col, 1969-70; Prof of Mgmt, Hofstra Univ, 1980-; Lectr, Harvard Univ, Cornell Univ; Pres, Phi Beta Kappa Alumni; Past Pres, En Acad of Mgmt; Past Pres, Mid

Atl Assn of Cols of Bus Adm; Dir: Diplomat Electronics Corp, Ideal Toy Corp, Bond Clothing Stores, Superior Surg Mfg Corp, NY Sch of Psychi, Continental Plastics Corp, Ideal Intl Inc, Interst Molding & Hobbing Co, Crown Rec Inc, Rust Warehousing Corp, Alabe Prods Inc; VP, Soc for Admt of Mgmt; hon/Pubs, *People-Oriented Computer Systems* 1983, *Progress of Mgmt* 1977, *Human Values in Mgmt* 1968, *Am Bus Dic* 1957, 45 Articles on Mgmt, *Manage Yourself, Useful Answers to Important Questions* 1984; Sr Edit Advr, *Ency of Mgmt*, 1982; Bronfman F'ship, 1960-62; Columbia F'ship, 1949-50; Ford Motor Co F'ship; Metro Life Ins Co F'ship; War Ser S'ship; Awd for Tchg Excell, NY Univ; Phi Beta Kappa; Beta Gamma Sigma; Beta Alpha Psi; Mu Gamma Tau; W/W in E.

LAZO, JOHN STEPHEN oc/Scientist, Educator; b/Dec 15, 1948; h/262 Stonehedge Lane, Guilford, CT 06437; ba/New Haven, CT; m/Jacqui Lynne Fiske; c/Jacquelyn Kristina Fiske; p/John and Mildred Lazo; ed/AB, Chem, Johns Hopkins Univ, 1971; PhD, Pharm, Univ of MI, 1976; pa/Assoc Prof 1983-, Asst Prof 1978-83, Dept of Pharm & Sect of Developmental Therapeutics, Yale Univ Sch of Med; Postdoct Fellow, Dept of Pharm, Yale Univ Sch of Med, 1976-78; USPHS-NIH Predoct Res Trainee, Dept of Pharm, Univ of MI, 1971-76; Other Previous Positions; Am Soc for Pharm & Exptl Therapeutics; AAAS; Tissue Culture Assn; Am Assn for Cancer Res; NY Acad of Scis; hon/ Pubs, Pulmonary Endothelial Dysfunction in the Presence or Absence of Interstitial Injury Induced by Intratracheal Injection of Bleomycin to Rabbits" 1983, "Prolonged Reduction in Serum Angiotensin Converting Enzyme Activity After Treatment of Rabbits w Bleomycin" 1983, Num Others; Assoc Editor, *Pharm & Therapeutics*, 1984-; US Pharmacopeial Conv Expert Adv Panel on Hematologic & Neoplastic Disease, 1984-; NIH Postdoct F'ship, 1978; Am Cancer Soc Postdoct F'ship, 1977; Phi Lambda Upsilon, 1971; Johns Hopkins Univ Tuition S'ship, 1971.

LEAFGREN, FRED oc/Assistant Chancellor of Student Life; b/Jul 27, 1931; h/3734 Oak Moraine Court, Stevens Point, WI 54481; ba/Stevens Point, WI; m/Thomasina; c/Deanna Lynn; p/George (dec) and Elsie Leafgren, Champaign, IL; ed/BS, 1954; BS, Cnslg & Guid, 1959; PhD, Cnslg & Psych, 1969; mil/Lt, Adjutant Gen Corp, 1956-58; pa/Dean of Men, Slippery Rock St Col, 1962-65; Dir of Housing 1965-72, Assoc Dean of Students 1972-75, Exec Dir of Student Life 1975-79, Current Asst Chancellor of Student Life, Univ of WI-Stevens Pt; Am Col Pers Assn, Comm Directorate; Pres, Reg Assn of Col & Univ Housing Ofcrs, Mem of Neurolinguistic Programming; Assn of Psychol Type, Intl Transactional Anal Assn Inc; Phi Delta Kappa; Delta Phi; Treas of Hlthy Am; Adv Coun of Wellness Ctr, Fox Val; Bd of Dirs, Wellness Resources, Atlanta, GA; Bd Mem, Stevens Pt Area Wellness Comm; Bd of Dirs, Nat Wellness Org; r/Presb; hon/Pubs, "Strategies for Coor'g All Student Life Sers to Enhance Wellness Opports" 1983, "Occupl Wellness for Profls" 1983, Others.

LEARNARD, JAMES MICHAEL oc/

Insurance Agent; b/Jun 13, 1947; h/ Route 1, Box 117, Green Street, Graniteville, SC 29829; ba/Aiken, SC; c/ Sean Patrick; p/James F Learnard, North Augusta, SC; ed/AA, FL Jr Col, 1966; r/Rom Cath; hon/Album Released, "Songs of Love," Fall 1982; 45 RPM Record Released, Fall 1982; Personalities of S; 2,000 Notable Ams; Biogl Roll of Hon.

LEASURE, BETTY JEAN oc/Homemaker; b/Jul 11, 1925; h/5522 Kappel Street, New Martinsville, WV 26155; m/ John Franklin; p/Francis Marion & Susan Olive Blake Cross (dec); ed/ Christian Ser Tng, Ch of the Nazarene, 6 Yrs; Student of Sociol, W Liberty St Col, 1970; Student of Creat Writing, WV No Commun Col, 1979; CEU, WV Univ, 1981; pa/Former Glass Tchr; Poetry Writer (Over 72 Poems); Pianist; Singer; World of Poetry; *Author/Poet Mag*; Titular Mem, Centro Studi e Schambi Internazionali Accademia Leonardo da Vinci; Gtr Nat Soc of Pub'd Poets Inc; Writings: Essay in *So Agriculturist*, 3 Poems in *Spirit of the Free* 1944, 1 Poem in *Pageant of Poetry* 1943, 1 Poem in *Best-Loved Contemp Poems* 1979, Summer Theme 1979, Christmas Theme 1979, St Patrick's Day 1980; r/Nazarene; hon/ Cert of Bible Memorization Awd, 1961; Consecrated Ser Awd, 1969; Christian Ser Tng: Reg'd Tchr 1960, Qualified Tchr 1961, 3rd Cert of Progress 1963, Cert'd Tchr 1963; CST Tng Awd, 1963; Sunday Sch Adm: Reg'd in SS Adm 1964, Qualified in SS Adm 1965, Cert'd in SS Adm 1966; Churchmanship Dipl, 1960; Ch Sch Wkr's Dipl, 1961; Harvest Times Campaign Cert, 1978; Recip, Diploma di Benemerenza, Roma, Italia; Awd, Accademia Leonardo da Vinci, Centro Studi e Schambi XXX Internazionali Culturale, 1980; Tchr of the Month Awd, Ch of the Nazarene, 1982; Commun Ldrs of Am Awd, 1979-80; W/ W in Poetry; Poet's Hall of Fame Book; Intl W/W of Intells.

LEAVITT, KATHLEEN JACOBS oc/ Early Childhood Educator; b/Feb 25, 1953; h/467 22nd Avenue, San Mateo, CA 94403; ba/1225 Greenwood Street, San Carlos, CA 94070; m/Richard Edward; c/Julia Kathleen; p/Malcolm and Jean Chesley Jacobs, Millbrae, CA; ed/AA, Col of San Mateo, 1973; Att'd, Univ of HI, 1974; BA, Humboldt St Univ, 1976; MA, Sonoma St Univ, 1977; pa/Pres of the Bd & Adm Dir, Kindercourt Inc, 1978-; Coor & Dir, Parent Power Inc, 1980-; Col Instr, W Val Col, Fam Life Sci Dept, 1977-; Cambrian Sch Dist, 1980-, Coor & Dir of Student Success Proj 1982-; Dir for Tot Time Prog, City of Rohnert Pk-Presch, 1976-77; Dir of Lng Action & Adopt-a-Grandparent Prog, Humboldt St Univ, 1975-76; Elem & Presch Tchr, Moore Avenue Sch, 1974-75; Tchr for Biling Chd, Merry-go-Round Presch & Day Care, 1973-74; Hd Tchr, Highlands Acad & Presch, 1972-73; Tchrs Asst, Hd Start Prog, Lawrence Day Care Ctr, 1970-72; Tutor & Tchrs Asst, Turnbull Sch, 1968-70; Asst Tchr, St Catherines Sch, 1966-68; Pvt Nursery Sch Assn; Profl Assn of Childhood Edrs; CA Assn of Early Childhood Ed; Nat Assn for the Ed of Yg Chd; r/Cath; hon/Author, *Parent Power Newslttrs* 1983, *Focus-Involvement-A Handbook for Adults as Tchrs in Presch Progs* 1977; Humboldt St

Univ Dean's List, 1974-76; Sonoma St Univ Dean's List, 1977; W/W of Am Wom.

LEAVOY, KENNETH LINDSAY oc/ Executive; b/May 19, 1953; h/1556 Grand Boulevard, North Vancouver, British Columbia V7L 3X8; ba/Same; p/ Ernest (dec) and Jean Leavoy, North Vancouver, British Columbia; ed/BA, Bus Adm, Principia Col, 1975; pa/ Divisional Mgr 1975-79, Corporate Buyer 1979-80, Simpsons-Sears; Operating Engr 1980-83, Ofc Mgr 1982-, VP 1983-, Leavoy Excavating Ltd; cp/Brit Columbia Camping & Rec Guild for Christian Scists; r/First Ch of Christian Scists, Boston, MA; hon/Provincial Champs, Lacrosse, 1969; MVP Provincial HS All-Star Basketball Game, 1971; Canadian Nat Basketball Team Trials, 1972; All IL-IN Col Soccer Conf, 1st Team Selection & Scoring Champ, 1974; Provincial Finalist, Seagram Mixed Curling Champ'ships, 1979; Bronze Medal, Canadian Sr Men's Fastball Champ'hips, 1980; Pres, Jr HS; Men's Org Pres, Principia Col, 1974-75.

LEAVOY, NORMAN PHILIP oc/ Executive; b/May 7, 1950; h/1556 Grand Boulevard, North Vancouver, British Columbia, Canada V7L 3X8; ba/Same; p/William Ernest L (dec) and Jean Daugherty Leavoy, North Vancouver, British Columbia; ed/BA w Hons, Principia Col, 1972; pa/Adm Ofcr, Toronto-Dominion Bk, Pacific Div, 1972-73; Operator 1973-, Ofc Mgr 1977-82, Mgr 1983, Leavoy Excavation Ltd; r/Christian Scist; Lay Minister, Christian Sci Ch, 1976-79, 1982-83; hon/W/W: in Fin & Indust, in World.

LEBO, ROGER V oc/Associate Research Biochemist, Institute Associate; b/Mar 1, 1948; h/588 Miramar Avenue, San Francisco, CA 94112; ba/ San Francisco, CA; m/Susan Southard; c/2 Boys; p/Stanley and Irene Lebo, Tower City, PA; ed/PhD, Duke Univ, 1974; BS, PA St Univ, 1970; AS, Chaffey Col, 1968; pa/Assoc Res Biochem, Dept of Med, Univ of CA-SF, 1983-; Assoc 1980-, Dir of Cell Sorting Facility 1980-81, Res Assoc 1978-80, Howard Hughes Med Inst, Univ of CA-SF; Asst Res Biochem, Dept of Med, Univ of CA-SF; Other Previous Positions; Am Soc of Human Genetics, 1978-; Soc for Analytical Cytology, 1980-; Am Genetic Assn, 1981-; Am Fdn for Clin Res, 1982-; hon/Pubs, "High-Resolution Chromosome Sorting & DNA Spot-Blot Anal Localize McArdle's Syndrome to Chromosome 11" 1984, "Separation & Analysis of Human Chromosomes by Combined Velocity Sedimentation & Flow Sorting Applying Single & Dual Laser Flow Cytometry" 1984, "Chiasma Within & Between the Human Insulin & Beta-Globin Gene Loci" 1983, Num Others; NIH Trainee, GM 28078, Univ Prog in Genetics, 1970-74; Interdeptl Res Awd, Duke Univ, 1974; W/W in Frontier Sci & Technol.

LEBRON, LUIS A oc/Consultant on Immigation and Business Law; b/Jun 12, 1927; h/1130 White Plains Road, Bronx, NY 10472; ba/Bronx, NY; m/Ida; c/ Sonia, Luis A Jr; p/Marcos (dec) and Maria Lebron, New York, NY; ed/Dipl, Crim Justice, Spadea Criminology Sch, 1948; BS 1954, LLB 1957, NY Univ; mil/ USN, 1944-46; pa/Field Investigator w NYC Law Dept, 1952-60; Agt, US Intell

Ser, 1960-64; Admitted to NY Bar, 1964; Pvt Pract as Conslt on Immigration & Bus Law, 1964-; Conslt, Treas Dept of PR, 1964-65; Nat Assn of Conslts; r/Cath; hon/Author, *The Govt & You* 1974, *Bus, the Backbone of Am* 1975, *Illegal Alien* 1977; Com-man of Yr, Yg PR Dems, 1954; Purple Heart, 1945; First Native PR Appt'd to NYC Law Dept.

LECHTMAN, PAMELA JOY oc/ Travel Editor; b/Apr 29, 1943; h/668 Camino Rojo, Thousand Oaks, CA 91360; ba/Woodland Hills, CA; m/Allen L; c/Arthur Thomas, Anthony Grant; ed/BS, Univ of MN, 1965; Cert'd Travel Cnslr, Inst of Cert'd Travel Agts, 1979; pa/Art Tchr, St Paul Indep Sch Dist, 1966-67; Tchr, Alameda, CA, Unified Sch Dist, 1967-68; Travel Agt, 1975-79; Free-Lance Travel Writer, 1979-82; Travel Editor, *Shape Mag*, 1982-; Instr, Tourism, Ventura Commun Col, 1977-80; AAUW, Thousand Oaks Br; Prodr, "Update," KVEN Radio, 1974-78; hon/Author, "You're on the Air," Articles in *News Chronicle*; Delta Phi Delta, Nat Hon Art Frat, 1963-65; Named Grant Fellow, AAUW, 1976.

LEDBETTER, SANDRA GALE SHUMARD oc/Administrative Assistant to the Governor; b/Oct 18, 1948; h/7 Foxhunt Trail, Little Rock, AR 92207; ba/Little Rock, AR; m/Joel Y Jr; c/ Elizabeth Talbot, Ann Sahy, Mildred Myonne Mitzi; p/Mr and Mrs Frank N Shumaro Jr, Little Rock, AR; ed/BA, Univ of AR-Little Rock, 1971; pa/Tchr, Pulaski Co Spec Sch Dist 1970-72, Miss Selma's Sch 1972-74, Pulaski Acad 1975-82; Scheduling & Appt Secy, Gov Bill Clinton of AR, 1982-; cp/Alumnae Pres, Delta Zeta Sorority, 1976-79; Bd of Dirs, Big Bros of Pulaski Co, 1978-79; Bd of Dirs 1981-82, Mem 1978-, Jr Leag of Little Rock; Exec Com 1976-, St Dem Com 1976-, Pulaski Co Dem Com; Del Dem Nat Conv, 1980 (Floor Whip); St Treas, Kennedy for Pres Bd, 1979-80; Co-Chm, Jefferson Jackson Day, 1980; St Platform Com, 1980; Co-Chm, St Adv Com, 1981; Riverfest Vol Chm, 1981; AR Art Ctr Hostess Com, 1975-77; Curric Com, Pulaski Acad, 1976-78; Carti Vol, 1978-80; Close-up Ar Bd, 1981-; hon/W/W: in Am Politics, of Am Wom.

LEDERER, DEBRA YUHAS oc/Educational Administrator; b/Aug 23, 1950; h/41 Beverly Road, Oradell, NJ 07649; ba/Saddle River, NJ; c/Jeremy Bryant, Jessica Lynne; p/Lt Col John Yuhas, San Antonio, TX; Mrs Marjorie Mae Stuart, Orlando, FL; ed/PhD, Univ of MD, 1980; MEd, Towson St Univ, 1976; BA, Univ of MD, 1974; pa/Asst Prin, Saddle River Bd of Ed, 1982-; Adj Prof, Kean Col, 1980-; Adj Grad Prof, Fairleigh Dickinson Univ, 1981-; Asst Prin, River Dell Jr HS, 1980-82; Grad Asst, Rdg Ctr 1978-79, Fac Lectr, Asst Prof 1979-80, Res Asst, Clin Supvr, Supvr of Undergrad Students 1979, Univ of MD-Col Pk; Eng Tchr 1974-76, Lang Arts Tchr for the Gifted & Talented Progs 1976-78, Howard Co, MD; IRA; NJ Rdg Assn; r/Am Bapt; hon/Pubs, "The Relat'ship Between the Theoretical & Empirical Res of the Specific Comprehension Strategy & the Directed Rdg Thinking Activity" 1982, "Implications of Schema Theory & the Tchg of Critical Rdg Skills to Gifted Elem

Students" 1982; Phi Kappa Phi; W/W in E.

LEDESMA, ADANIVIA MARRERO oc/Retired Teacher; b/Nov 18, 1912; h/PO Box 327, Utuado, PR 00761; m/Nicolas de Jesus; c/Ivan de Jesus; p/Ramon B Marrero (dec); ed/BEd; BA; Postgrad Studies; Dramatic Arts Studies; mil/Appt'd Chief Registrar, Selective Ser, Utuado, PR, 1940; pa/Elem Sch Tchr, 1933-37; HS Tchr, Drama & Lang, 1940-68; Jury Commr, 1969; Supvr of Cultural Activs in NEn Ctl Reg of PR; Voc Guid Tchr, 1974-76; Public Relats Ofcl, 1976; Pres, Wom's Bus & Profl Org, 1968; Dir, Tchrs' Cooperative, 1974; cp/Pres, Anti-TB Assn, 1969; Pres, Cultural Ctr, 1969; r/Cath; hon/Pub, "La Borincana" (Poem), Dramatized & Presented on TV; Pub, "La Cascada del Jobo Otuarina" (Legend); Author, Poems & Dept of Ed Books; Patron's Feast Dedicated in Her Hon by Mun Gov, 1972; Hon'd by Am Legion, Lions Clb, Tchrs' Assn, Others.

LEE, CHIN-TIAN oc/University Professor; b/Jun 22, 1940; h/156 Beng-bing Street, Y-Papao Estates, Dededo, Guam 96912; ba/UOG Station, Guam; m/Shu-Teh; c/Corinna, Frances; p/Pou-Tong; Wu-Me (dec); ed/BS 1964, MS 1967, Nat Taiwan Univ; MS 1969, PhD 1971, Univ of WI; mil/Chinese AF ROTC, 1964-65; pa/Grad Res Asst, Nat Taiwan Univ, 1965-67; Grad Res Asst 1967-71, Biologist 1971-74, Univ of WI; Asst Prof 1974-80, Assoc Prof 1980-, Univ of Guam; Am Soc of Hort Sci, 1974-; Am Soc of Agronomy, 1979-; Am Soc of Hort Sci in Tropical Regs, 1976-; r/Christian; hon/Author, 12 Res Papers (Guam Agri Exptl Sta) 1974-83, 4 Res Papers (Hort Scis) 1979, 1981, 1983, 2 Res Papers (*Agronomy Jour*) 1972, 1971; Guam Legis Resolution 141 to Recognize His Contbns to Agri, 1982; USDA Tropical Agri Res Grantee, 1981-85; Travel Awd to Attend Intl Symp on Winged Bean, 1981; Travel Awd to Attend Intl Symp on Sweet Potato, 1981; L F Chao Fellow, 1965-66; Yth Anti-Communist Fellow, 1963-64; W/W in W.

LEE, CHONG WON oc/Executive; b/Jan 15, 1926; h/22 Heritage Drive, Lexington, MA 02173; ba/Lexington, MA; m/Kim; c/Eugene, Arnold; p/Choo Yong Lee (dec); ed/BSEE, City Col of NY, 1950; MSEE, Syracuse Univ, 1963; pa/Res Engr, Gen Elect Electronics Lab, 1960-69; Engrg Mgr, Raytheon, SMDO, 1969-74; Pres, Lee Labs Inc, 1974-; IEEE; r/Meth; hon/Pubs, "Varactor S-Band Direct Phase Modular" 1966, "High Power Negative Resistance Amplifier" 1972; US Patents: "Microwave Frequency Amplifier Constructed Upon a Single Substrate" 1972, "High Frequency, Multi-Throw Switch Employing Hybrid Couplers & Reflection Type Phase Shifter" 1976; Managerial Awd, Gen Elect Co, 1968.

LEE, DAVID FREDERICK III oc/Bank Executive; b/Feb 5, 1954; h/184 Country Club Drive, San Francisco, CA 94132; ba/San Francisco, CA; p/Hon Frank Francis and Theresa Hui Lee, San Francisco, CA; ed/MBA in Fin & Mgmt 1981, BS in Intl Bus 1976, Univ of SF; St Ignatius Col Preparatory, 1972; pa/VP, The Hibernia Bk, 1983-; Exec VP, Ellision Enterprises USA Inc, 1980-83; Asst VP, Am Pacific St Bk, 1980;

Corporate Bkg Ofcr, U CA Bk, 1978-80; Asst to Pres, Ellision Enterprises, 1975-78; Dir: Topgear Design Centre Ltd (Hong Kong), Timetrade Co Ltd (Hong Kong), CYK Pty Ltd (Australia), Hummingbird Ltd (Thailand & Hong Kong), Ellision Enterprises Ltd (Hong Kong); Conslt to Posner & Ferrera; Commonwlth Clb of CA; World Affairs Coun of CA; World Trade Assn; Univ of SF Alumni Assn; cp/CA Repub Party; r/Rom Cath; hon/Pubs, *The Future of Multinat Corporations* 1977, *Between Two Worlds-Mexico: OPEC & the Trilateral World* 1981; Beta Gamma Sigma, Life Mem 1976; W/W in Fin & Indust; Personalities of W & MW; Intl Bus-men W/W.

LEE, HARRY WILLIAM oc/Education and Research; b/Sep 26, 1938; h/1017 North Almon, Moscow, ID 83843; ba/Moscow, ID; m/Evelyn L; c/Larissa Dawn, Brenda Carol; p/Robert E (dec) and Laura R Lee, Moscow, ID; ed/BSCE 1972, MSCE 1977, PhD in Agri Ed 1983, Univ of ID; mil/AUS, 1961-63; pa/Asst Co Planner, Latah Co, 1972-73; N ID Reg Dir, Bur of St Planning, 1973-79; Agri Engrg Dept Res Assoc 1979-80, Asst Prof of Forest Engrg 1980-84, Univ of ID; Am Soc of Agri Engrs, 1980-84; Campus Planning Com, 1981-84; cp/Palouse Audubon Soc, 1980-84, Publicity & Newslttr; hon/Author, Latah Co Flood Plain Anal 1973, Flood Ins Brochure 1976, "Infiltration into Frozen Soil Using Simulated Rainfall" 1983; Outstg Civil Engrg Student, ASCE, 1972; W/W in Frontier Sci & Technol.

LEE, KAREN ANNE oc/Tax Accountant; b/Jun 12, 1955; h/111 South Main Street, Newton, NH 03858; ba/Hampton, NH; c/Nicholas D; p/Harold W and Betty J Ferrer, Shoreview, MN; ed/MST, Bentley Col, 1984; BS in Bus Adm, magna cum laude, Merrimack Col, 1977; pa/Tax Acct, The Signal Cos, 1981-; Revenue Agt, IRS, 1977-81; Tax Conslt, Self-Employed Pt-time, 1981-; AICPA; NH Soc of CPAs; BPW Clb; Nat Assn of Female Execs; r/Epis; hon/Achmt Awd, MA Soc of CPAs, 1979; CPA, NH, 1980; W/W in E.

LEE, KWANG-SUN oc/Associate Professor and Director of Neonatology; b/Aug 30, 1941; h/5510 South Kimbark, Chicago, IL 60637; ba/Chicago, IL; m/On-sook; c/Jennifer, Iris; ed/MD, Seoul Nat Univ, 1965; F'ship in Neonatology, Albert Einstein Col of Med, 1971-73; pa/Instr of Pediatrics 1973-74, Asst Prof of Pediatrics 1974-78, Assoc Prof of Pediatrics 1978-80, Albert Einstein Col of Med; Assoc Prof & Dir of Neonatology, Univ of Chgo, 1980-; Soc for Pediatric Res; Am Acad of Pediatrics; APHA; IL Perinatal Assn; cp/Adv Com, March of Dimes, Chgo Metro Chapt; hon/Pubs, "Effect of Milk Feeding & Starvation on Intestinal Bilirubiin Absorption in the Rat" 1983, "Recent Trends in Neonatal Mortality: The Canadian Experience" 1982, Num Others; Clin Investigator Awd, Nat Inst of Arthritis Metabolism & Digestive Diseases, 1976-79; Irma Hirschl Career Scist Awd, 1978-80; DIB.

LEE, MICHAEL DAVID oc/Television and Motion Picture Producer; b/Dec 30, 1950; h/4347 Pacheco Street, San Francisco, CA 94116; ba/San Francisco, CA; p/John and Ruth Wong, Oakland, CA; ed/MBA, Golden Gate Univ, 1983; BA, SF St Univ, 1972; AA,

Merrit Jr Col, 1971; pa/Current Host/Prodr, KVCR-TV; Pres, Media Inc, SF & Beverly Hills, 1978-; Pres, ON-AIR Auctions Inc, 1980-; Gen Mgr, Pacifica Commun TV Inc, 1982; Prodr for ABC TV, 1975-78; Screen Actors Guild; Am Fdn of TV & Radio Artists; cp/Commonwlth Clb of CA; Am Mensa Soc; hon/W/W: in W, in CA.

LEE, SIN HANG oc/Pathologist; b/Nov 17, 1932; h/1450 Chapel Street, New Haven, CT 06511; m/Kee Hung Hau; c/Emil, Karen; p/Yat-sun Lee (dec); ed/MD, Wuhan Med Col, People's Republic of China, 1956; pa/Asst Lectr in Bacteriology, Sichuan Med Col, Chengdu, China, 1956-61; Demonstrator in Pathol, Univ of Hong Kong, 1961-63; Rotating Intern, S Balto Gen Hosp, 1963-64; Resident 1964-66, Instr in Pathol 1966-67, Cornell-NY Hosp; Pathol Fellow, Meml Hosp for Cancer, 1967-68; Asst Prof of Pathol, McGill Univ, 1968-71; Assoc Prof of Pathol 1971-73, Assoc Clin Prof of Pathol 1973-, Yale Univ; Att'g Pathol, Hosp of St Raphael, 1973-; Royal Col of Phys & Surgs of Canada; AAAS; Intl Acad of Pathol; Am Assn of Pathols; Pathological Soc of Gt Brit & Ireland; NY Acad of Scis; hon/Pubs, "Histochem Estrogen Receptor Assay" 1981, "The Histochem of Estrogen Receptors" 1981, "Sex-Steroid Hormone Receptors in Mammary Carcinoma" 1981, "Estrogen & Progesterone Receptors in Breast Cancer-A New Approach to Measure" 1980, "Hydrophilic Macromolecules of Steroid Derivatives for the Detection of Cancer Cell Receptors" 1980, Num Others; Patentee in Field of Res; Diplomate, Am Bd of Pathol, 1966; Cert'd Spec in Gen Pathol, Canada, 1966; FRCP, Canada, 1967.

LEEDOM, E PAUL oc/Bank Officer; b/Jun 11, 1925; h/243 Garden Place, West Hempstead, NY 11552; ba/Brooklyn, NY; m/Mildred E; c/Paula A McCabe, George E; p/Eldridge and Beatrice Leedom (dec); ed/BS, Gen Phy Scis, Univ of MD, 1951; MBA, Adelphi Univ, 1967; mil/USN, 1943-46; AUS 1951-52, Signal Corps, Capt; pa/VP, Anchor Savs Bk, 1974-; Pres, Digimatics Inc, 1968-74; Var Mgmt Positions, Ambac Industs Inc, 1957-68; Civilian Tech Conslt, Aberdeen Proving Ground, MD, 1953-57; Delta Mu Delta; cp/Men's Com, Boy Scout Troop; Dist Capt, U Commun Fund; Treas, LI U Campus Min; Life Mem, Repub Nat Com; Treas, Ch-in-the-Garden; r/Bapt; hon/Corridor of Dist'd Alumni, Sch of Bus, Adelphi Univ; W/W in Fin & Indust.

LEESON, JANET CAROLINE oc/Artist, Executive; b/May 23, 1933; h/6713 West 163rd Place, Tinley Park, IL 60477; ba/Same; m/Raymond Harry; c/Warren Scott, Debra Delores, Barry Raymond; p/Harold Arnold and Sylvia Aino Makikangas Tollefson (dec); ed/HS Grad, Ewen, MI, 1951; Att'd, Prairie St Col, 1971-76; Leadertech Sem Tng, 1975; Wilton Master Cake Decorating, 1973; Many Wkshops & Sems; pa/Mgr, Peak Ser Cleaners, 1959-60; Co-Owner, Hd of Fgn Trade Dept, Ra-Ja-Lee TV, Ofc & Adm, 1962-68; Bkkpr, Cake Demonstrator, Tchr of Cake Decorating, Wilton Enterprises, 1970-75; Ofc Mgr, Pat Capenter Assocs, & Cake Decorating Tech, Penney, 1974-75; Pres, Leeson's Party Cakes Inc, 1975-;

Retail Bakers Assn, 1982; ABWA, Genesis Charter Chapt, 1981–; cp/ Public Relats & Hospitality Chm, Bremen Twp Repub Org, 1981-82; hon/ Specialty Cakes & Articles About Them Appear in Nav Pub 1980-81, US Robert A Owens Article, *Founthill Castle* (Victorian Soc Pub); Yearly Top Hons in Art, 1938–; 1st Place in Portraits, Charcoal & Pencil, 1959-60; 1st Place, Sewing, 3rd Place, Child's Outfit, 1954-60; 1st Place, CARBA Conv, 1978, 1980; W/W of Am Wom.

LEFEBVRE d'ARGENCÉ, RENE-YVON MARIE MARC oc/Director and Chief Curator of Art Museum; b/Aug 21, 1928; h/16 Midhill Drive, Mill Valley, CA 94941; ba/San Francisco, CA; m/Ritva Anneli Pelanne; c/Chantal, Yann, Luc; p/Marc Lefebvre d'Argencé (dec); Andrée Thierry (dec); ed/Collège St Aspais, Fountainebleau; Lycée Albert Sarraut, Hanoi; Licencié-è-Lettres, Ecole Libre des Sciences Politiques, 1952; Pembroke Col, Cambridge Univ; Chinese 1950, Japanese 1951, Finnish 1952, Breveté de l'Ecole Nationale des Langues Orientales Vivantes; mil/ Served w Free French Forces, WW II; pa/Dir & Chief Curator, Asian Art Mus of SF, 1969–; Dir, Avery Brundage Collection, 1965-68; Curator, Asiatic Collections, M H de Young Meml Mus, SF, 1964; Prof of Art Hist, Univ of CA-Berkeley, 1962-65; Other Previous Positions; Inst of Sino-Am Studies, 1981–; VP, Chinese-Am Biling Sch, 1981–; Trustee, Beaudry Foun, 1977–; cp/SF-Shanghai Sister City Com, 1980–; SF-Seoul Sister City Com, 1980–; SF-Osaka Sister City Com, 1980–; Adv Coun of the Marin Cultural Ctr, 1981–; r/Rom Cath; hon/Pubs, *5,000 Years of Korean Art* 1979, *Asian Art: Museum & Univ Collections in the SF Bay Area* 1978, *Bronze Vessels of Ancient China in the Avery Brundage Collection* 1977, Others; Chevalier de la Légion d'Honneur, France, 1983; Ofcr of Culture Merit Order, Korea, 1981; Other Hons; W/W: in France, in Am, in Am Art, in W; Writers Dir; Dic of Nat Biog; Intl W/W of Commun Ser; Contemp Authors; Others.

LeFEVRE, CAROL BAUMANN oc/ Associate Professor of Psychology; b/ Nov 26, 1924; h/1376 East 58th Street, Chicago, IL 60637; ba/Chicago, IL; m/ Perry Deyo; c/Susan LeFevre Hook, Judith Ann, Peter Gerret; p/Bernhard Robert and Eunice Leone Hoyt Heston Baumann (dec); ed/AA, Stephens Col, 1944; MA 1948, MS 1965, PhD 1971, Univ of Chgo; pa/Tchr, Chgo Theol Sem Nursery Sch 1962-63, Univ of Chgo Lab Sch 1965-66; Asst Prof of Psych 1970-74, Assoc Prof 1974–, Acting Chm of Dept of Psych 1970-71, Chm of Dept of Psych 1971-77, Asst Dir of Inst of Fam Studies 1973-82, Dir of Inst of Fam Studies 1982–, St Xavier Col; Intern in Clin Psych w Adlerian Pvt Practitioners, Chgo, 1973-75; Pvt Pract, Clin Psych, 1975–; Reg'd Psychol, IL; IL Psychol Assn; Am Psychol Assn; Gerontological Soc; N Am Soc of Adlerian Psych; AAUP; Phi Beta Kappa; cp/NOW; r/U Ch of Christ; Univ Ch; hon/Res & Articles on Returing Wom Grad Students' Changing Self-Conceptions, Wom's Roles, Inner City Chd's Perceptions of Sch; Co-Editor, *Aging & the Human Spirit: A Rdr in Rel & Gerontology*; W/W of Am Wom; World W/W of Wom;

Intl W/W in Ed.

LE FONTAINE, JOSEPH RAYMOND oc/Publisher, Writer; b/Apr 6, 1927; ba/PO Box 872, Vashon Island, WA 98070; c/Stephen, Bruce, David, Suzanne Le Fontaine Conley; p/Joseph Romeo and Charlotte Henrietta Bertrand Le Fontaine; ed/BSME, Rochester Inst of Technol, 1949; mil/AUS, 1944-46; pa/Design Engr, Nat Engrg Co 1950-52, Houston Fearless Corp 1952-54; Chief Engr, Koehler Aircraft Prods Co 1955-58, Skyvalve Inc 1959-65; Dir of Res & Devel, Snap Tite Inc, 1965-67; Dir of Res & Devel, Scoville Fluid Prods, 1967-69; Nat Sales Mgr, Wn Precipitation Co, 1969-72; Rare Book Dealer, LA & NYC, 1972-76; Writer, Publisher, Vashon Isl, WA, 1976–; Author, *A Directory of Buyers: Old Books & Paper Americana* 1978, *Turning Paper to Gold: The Paper Miners Manual* 1982, *The Investors Guide to Rare Books* 1978, *You Can Write Yourself a Fortune* 1979, *Intl Book Collectors Dir* 1983; Editor, Publisher, *The InvestArt Almanac* 1975-77, *Graphic Arts Collector* 1975-76, *Info Marketers Newslttr* 1978-79; Tchr, Writing Sems; Com of Small Mag Editors & Publishers; Nat Writers Clb; cp/Repub; r/Epis.

LEHMANN, ARNOLD O oc/Retired College Professor; b/Apr 14, 1914; h/ Route 4, Box 271, Watertown, WI 53094; ba/Watertown, WI; m/Esther; c/ Philipp, Richard, Edwin; ed/BA, 1936; BMus, 1938; MA, Music, 1938; PhD, 1966; mil/AUS Signal Intell; pa/Univ of WI Bands, 1937-39; Colfax, WI, Sch Sys, 1940-42; Concordia Col & Univ of IN Ext, 1946-50; Cleveland Luth HS, 1950-62; NWn Col, 1962-80; Ret'd 1980; Col Band Dirs Nat Assn; Am Musicological Soc; Phi Mu Alpha Sinfonia; Watertown Commun Concerts Assn; r/Luth; hon/Author, Var Pubs; AAL Fac F'ship, 1966, 1967; Intl W/W in Music.

LEIBOVICI, DOROTHEA L oc/Physician; b/May 10, 1936; p/Ketty Leibovici, State of Israel; ed/Col Grad, Classical Ed, Romania, 1953; MD, Med Sch, Bucharest, Romania, 1959; Postgrad Tng in Internal Med & Nephrology, USA, 1982; pa/Phys, Romania, 1959-69; Phys, Israel, 1970-74; Internal Med, Lebanon Hosp Ctr 1976-77, Meth Hosp 1977-78, VA Hosp 1979, Chgo Med Sch 1979-80; Nephrology Fellow, NY Med Col, 1981-82; AMA, 1977–; Am Col of Phys (Assoc), 1978–; Am Soc of Internal Med (Assoc), 1978–; NY Acad of Scis, 1981–; Lic'd to Pract Med in NY, ME, IL; r/Jewish; hon/Awds for Lit Compositions in Romania; Phys Recog Awd, 1983-86; W/W of Am Wom.

LEIGH, EMILY A oc/Bank Executive; b/Apr 12, 1926; h/2505 Teresa Court, Turlock, CA 95380; ba/Hilmar, CA; m/ Keith B; c/Daniel, Larry, Maryann; p/ Mr and Mrs Sarafin Moraie, Turlock, CA; ed/Bk of Am Ed Sch, SF; AIB, Modesto Jr Col; pa/Began as Bkkpr, Bk of Newman, 1943-50; Mgr of Hilman Ofc, Bk of Am, 1956-77; VP, Mgr, Golden Val Bk, 1977–; CIA Financial Corp, Dir; cp/C of C, Past Pres; Soroptimist, VP; r/Rom Cath; hon/Basketball Mother of the Yr, 1965; 1st Wom Bkr into Lending Position, Bk of Am, 1972; W/W in W.

LEIGH, JAMES HENRY oc/Marketing Educator; b/Feb 6, 1952; h/2809 Hillside Drive, Bryan, TX 77801; ba/

College Station, TX; m/Jane Ellen Hudson; c/James Daniel; p/John Marshall Leigh (dec); Ethel Elizabeth Eppright Leigh Davis, Austin, TX; ed/ BBA w Hons 1974, MBA 1976, Univ of TX-Austin; PhD in Bus Adm, Univ of MI-Ann Arbor, 1981; pa/Adm Asst to the Pres, Univ of TX-Austin, 1974-76; Res Assoc, Univ of MI, 1977-79; Asst Prof of Mktg, En MI Univ, 1980-81; Asst Prof of Mktg, TX A&M Univ, 1981–; Am Mktg Assn; Am Inst for Decision Scis; Assn for Consumer Res; Am Acad of Advtg; Inst of Mgmt Scis, Acacia; hon/Co-Fdr & Co-Editor, *Current Issues & Res in Advtg*, 1978, 1979, 1980, 1981, 1982, 1983; Author, "A Review of Situational Influence Paradigms & Res" 1981, "On Interaction Classification" 1980, Several Papers Given at Profl Confs; Am Mktg Assn Doct Consortium Fellow, 1978; Gen Elect Fellow, 1976-77; C E Griffin S'ship Recip, 1976; Beta Gamma Sigma, 1976; Phi Eta Sigma, 1971; W/W in S & SW.

LEISURE, PETER KEETON oc/Trial Attorney; b/Mar 21, 1929; h/One East End Avenue, New York, NY 10021; ba/ New York, NY; m/Kathleen Blair; c/ Mary Blair, Kathleen Keeton; p/George S (dec) and Lucille P Leisure; ed/BA, Yale Univ, 1952; LLB, Univ of VA, 1958; mil/ Served as Lt, USAR, 1953-55; pa/Assoc, Firm of Breed, Abbott & Morgan, 1958-61; Asst US Atty, So Dist of NY, 1962-66; Ptnr, Firm of Curtis, Mallet-Prevost, Colt & Mosle, 1967-78; Ptnr, Firm of Whitman & Ranson, 1978–; Bd of Dirs, Yth Consultation Sers, 1971-78; VP, Fed Bar Coun, 1973-78; Am Law Inst; Lectr, Practising Law Inst, 1968-70; ABA; St & City Bar Assns; Contbr of Articles to Legal Jours; cp/Bd of Dirs, Retarded Infants Sers, 1968-78, Pres 1971-75; Bd of Dirs, Commun Coun of Gtr NY, 1972-79; Trustee, Ch Clb of NY, 1973-81; r/Epis; hon/Fellow, Am Col of Trial Lwyrs; Fellow, Am Bar Foun, 1976–; W/W: in Am, in World, in Am Law; Dir of Directors.

LEMIRE, DAVID STEPHEN oc/ School Counselor; b/May 23, 1949; h/ Box 2326, Evanston, WY 82930; ba/ Evanston, WY; ed/BA in Psych/Sociol 1972, MEd in Social Sci 1974, Linfield Col; EdS in Cnslg Psych, ID St Univ, 1979; PhD Cand, Univ of WY-Laramie; pa/Sch Cnslr, Goshen Co Sch Dist 1978-81, Aspen Sch Dist 1981-82, Uinta Co Sch Dist 1982–; Admissions Cnslr in Student Sers, ID St Univ Sch of Voc-Tech Ed, 1976-78; Tng Cnslr, New Day Prods Inc, 1975-76; Student Cnslr, Yamhill-Carlton HS, 1974; WY Pers & Guid Assn; CO Pers & Guid Assn; Assn for Cnslr Ed & Supvn; Assn of Col Pers Admrs; APGA; Wn Col Rdg Assn; hon/ Pubs, "The Sch Cnslr as Consult in the Rural or Small Sch" (in Press), "The Rural Sch Tchr & the Cnslr-Consult" (in Press), "The Cnslr as Consult: The Application of Adlerian Consultg Methods in Schs" (in Press), "The Encouragement Coun" 1982, Num Others.

LEMOINE, HELEN LOUISE oc/Director of Nursing; b/Feb 20, 1929; h/PO Box 115, Cottonport, LA 71327; ba/ Plaucheville, LA; m/Albert L; c/Annette Escude, Michael Escude, Donna Escude McInnis; p/Chester R Riddels, Valley View, TX; ed/HS Grad, Tioga, TX, 1948;

Grad, Parkland Hosp Sch of Nsg, 1951; pa/Staff Nurse, Wichita Falls Clin & Hosp 1952, McConnell & Dupree Clin & Hosp 1955-65, Bayou Vista Manor Nsg Home 1965-66; Dir of Nsg, Avoyells Manor Nsg Home, 1966-; LA Hlth Care Assn Dirs of Nsg in Action; Past Mem, St Bd for LA Hlth Care Assn Dirs of Nsg in Action, Reg Rep for Reg IV; cp/Past Mem, Am Legion Aux; Ladies Alter Soc; Padro Pio Ct, Cath Daughs; Nurses' Book Clb; r/St Mary's Assumption, Choir; Cath; hon/W/W of Am Wom.

LEONARD, ANGELA MICHELE oc/Researcher, Librarian; b/Jun 26, 1954; h/1604 Jackson Street, Nashville, TN 37208; ba/Nashville, TN; p/Dr and Mrs Walter J Leonard, Nashville, TN; ed/AB, cum laude, Harvard/Radcliffe Cols, 1976; MLS, Vanderbilt/Peabody Univ, 1982; GSAS, Harvard Univ, 1978-80; GSA, Howard Univ, 1977-78; Mod Archives Inst, 1983; pa/Rschr, Fisk Univ, 1981-; Instr, Eng, Nashville St Tech Inst, 1980-81; Instr, Eng, Trevecca Nazarene Col, 1979; Conslt, Seigenthaler Assocs, 1979-; Subst Tchr, Boston Public Sch Dept, 1977; Coder, Radcliffe Col, 1976-77; Rschr, Harvard Univ, 1976; Student Asst, Harvard-Fogg Arts Lib, 1975; Student Asst, Harvard-Widener Lib, 1974-75; Student Asst, Newton S HS Lib, 1971-72; Alpha Kappa Alpha Sorority; Am Lib Assn; Black Caucus of the Am Lib Assn; Am Assn of St & Local Hist; AAUW; cp/NAACP; Nashville Urban Leag; r/Cath; hon/Pubs, "Fisk Profile: Carroll Moton Leevy" 1982, "Themes in the Black Am Experience: Ten Black Classics of the Harlem Renaissance" 1981, "Fisk Profile: Constance Baker Motley" 1981, "One Fisk Fam: The McCrees" 1980, "A Maceo Walker: Living a Life of Example" 1980; hon/Beta Phi Mu Intl Lib Sci Hon Soc, 1982-; F'ships: Harvard GSAS 1978-80, Vanderbilt/Peabody 1981-82; Outstg Yg Wom of Am; W/W in S & SW.

LEONARD, RICHARD JAMES oc/Safety Engineer; b/Aug 12, 1942; h/9266 Northwest 13th Place, Coral Springs, FL 33065; ba/Boca Raton, FL; m/Mary Jo Kelsay; c/Mark, James, Kathleen, Dawn; p/Donald and Betty Leonard, San Jose, CA; ed/Grad, Samuel Ayer HS, 1961; Num Spec Courses Taken; mil/AUS, 1961-64; pa/Stenographer/Ct Reporter, AUS, 1961-64; Security Ofcr, Fireman, Ambulance Attendant 1965-67, Safety Engr for Mfg Plant Devel Lab 1967-75, Safety Dir for Santa Teresa Lab 1975-79, IBM San Jose; Safety Engr, IBM Rochester, 1979-80; Safety Staff Asst for Safety and Indust Hygiene, IBM Boca Raton, 1980-; Corporate Audit Team Mem for Inspection of IBM San Jose Plant; Am Soc of Safety Engrs; Nat Safety Mgmt Soc; Vets of Safety; Nat Safety Coun; Intl Soc of Fire Ser Instrs; cp/Shelter Mgmt, Civil Def, 1967-74; Key Man Devel Instr/Defensive Driving Instr, Santa Clara Co Nat Safety Coun, 1972-74; Repub; r/Christian; hon/Profl Consltg Cert, Intl Loss Control Inst; Reg'd Profl Safety Engr, St Bd of Registration, Dept of Consumer Affairs, Sacramento, CA; Awd of Hon Cit for Best Safety Record in Santa Clara Co, 1976; Awd of Merit Plaque, Nat Safety Coun, 1976; W/W: in S &

SW, in Fin & Indust; Personalities of S; .

LEONTIEF, WASSILY W oc/Director and Professor; b/Aug 5, 1906; h/37 Washington Square East, New York, NY 10011; ba/New York, NY; m/Estelle Marks; c/Svetlana Leontief Alpers; p/Wassily Leontief (dec); ed/MA, Univ of Leningrad, 1925; PhD, Univ of Berlin, 1928; pa/Dir, Inst for Ec Anal 1978-, Prof 1975-, NY Univ; Henry Lee Chair of Polit Economy 1953-75, Prof of Ec 1946-53, Assoc Prof 1939-46, Asst Prof 1933-39, Instr 1932-33, Harvard Univ; Dir, Harvard Ec Res Proj 1948-72, Chp, Soc of Fellow 1965-75, Harvard Univ; Conslt, UN Devel Programme, 1980-; Pt-time Gen Conslt, Ofc of Technol Assessment, 1980-; Bd of Trustees, NC Sch of Sci and Math, 1978-86; Num Past Profl Mbrships; hon/Pubs, *Military Spending: Facts and Figures, Worldwide Implications and Future Outlook* 1983, *The Production and Consumption of Non-Fuel Minerals to the Year 2030 Analyzed within an Input-Output Framework of the US and World Economy* 1983, Num Others; Alfred Nobel Meml Prize in Ec, 1973.

LERNER, MAX oc/Author, Columnist, Professor; b/Dec 20, 1902; h/25 East End Avenue, New York, NY 10028; ba/New York, NY; m/Edna Albers; c/Constance, Pamela (dec), Joanna, Michael, Stephen, Adam; p/Benjamin and Bessie Podel Lerner (dec); ed/AB, Yale Univ, 1923; Student of Law, 1923-24; AM, Wash Univ, 1925; PhD, Robert Brookings Grad Sch of Ec and Govt, 1927; pa/Asst Editor, Mng Editor, *Encyclopedia of Social Sciences*, 1927-32; Social Sci Fac, Sarah Lawrence Col, 1923-35; Chm, Fac, Wellesley Sum Inst, 1933-35; Dir, Consumers' Div, Nat Emer Coun, 1934; Lectr, Govt, Harvard Univ, 1935-36; Editor, *The Nation*, 1936-38; Prof, Polit Sci, Williams Col, 1938-43; Vis'g Prof, Govt, Sum Sch, Harvard Univ, 1939-41; Edit Dir, PM, 1943-48; Columnist, *New York Star*, 1948-49; World-Wide Syndicated Columnist, *New York Post* and *Los Angeles Times* Syndication, 1949-; Prof, Am Civilization 1949-73, Dean of Grad Sch 1954-56, Current Prof Emeritus, Brandeis Univ; Dist'd Prof of Human Behavior, Grad Sch of Human Behavior, US Intl Univ, 1974-; Welch Prof, Am Studies, Notre Dame, 1982-; Am Civil Liberties Union, Nat Com; Hudson Inst, Public Mem; Assn of Humanistic Psych; hon/Pubs, *Ted and the Kennedy Legend* 1980, *Values in Education* 1976, Num Others; Selected, Brandeis Univ 1982, Albion Col, Wilberforce Univ, New Sch for Social Res, Williams Col; W/W World; Jewish Year Book; Intl Yr Book and Statemen's W/W; W/W; W/W Am.

LESLIE, LYNN R oc/Independent Consulting Engineer; b/Apr 18, 1920; h/909 North Gale Avenue, East Wenatchee, WA 98801; ba/Seattle, WA; m/Imeloa Ford; c/Brent K, Jay B, Mary I, Susan L Guinn; p/Mr and Mrs L H Leslie, Ellensburg, WA; ed/BA, Chem, Whitman Col, 1950; BS, Public Hlth, Univ of WA Seattle, 1954; mil/USAAF, 1942-45; pa/Public Hlth Dept 1952-56, Engr Dept 1956-67, City of Seattle; Reg Maintenance Engr, WA St Pks, 1967-69; Indep Conslrg Engr, 1969-; Am Soc of Profl Draftsmen; Nat Pres 1965; APHA, 1955; 30 Yr Mem of Grange; cp/Toastmaster Area Pres, 1947; Am Heart

Assn; r/Prot; hon/Phi Sigma Soc, Univ of WA, 1954; Silver Star Cert of Nat Grange, 1975; W/W Fin and Indust; Intl Bus-men's W/W.

LESLIE, WILLIAM METHVEN oc/Public Affairs Executive; b/Aug 22, 1935; ba/Chevron USA, 1201 South Beach Boulevard, La Habra, CA 90631; m/Josephine Ann Canterbury; c/William Methven III, Eric Parker, Ryan Shannon; Stepchd: Stephen Canterbury, Stanley Howard; p/William Methven and Marion Ellen Tibbs Leslie; ed/Student, Occidental Col, 1954-56; BA in Ec, SF St Univ, 1961; MBA, Golden Gate Univ, 1974; Postgrad, 1978-; mil/AUS, 1956-58; pa/Employee 1969-76, Public Affairs Mgr of Wn Opers 1976, Standard Oil Co; Public Affairs Mgr, Chevron USA, 1977-; Pres-Elect, So CA Consortium Indust Ed Couns, 1983-84; cp/Repub; Bd of Dirs, CA Lyric Grand Opera, 1983; Life Mem, Jr Chamber Intl Senators; LA Co Yth for Vol Action, Commun Liaison Com; Chaffey Col; LA Mayor Bradley Consensus 2000 Subcom Air Pollution, Envir Concerns and Water Resources; Past Pres, Industrial Div, SF Rec and Pk Dept, 1974-76; Other Civic Mbrships; r/Bapt; hon/Recip, Outstg Dist Gov in St, CA JCs, 1969; Outstg Public Relats Prog in US, Nat Arbor Day Foun, 1973; Hon'd by CA Legis Resolution 24, Jt Rules Com, 1983; Hon'd by CA Legis Resolution 14, Assem Rules Com, 1983; Num Other Hons; W/W W.

LESTER, VIRGINIA LAUDANO oc/College President; b/Jan 5, 1931; h/240 Kable Street, Staunton, VA 24401; ba/Staunton, VA; c/Pamela, Valerie; p/Emily Downs Laudano, Holland, PA; ed/BA, PA St Univ, 1952; MEd, Temple Univ, 1955; PhD, Union Grad Sch, 1972; ACE Pres's Inst, 1976; GWU Inst on Ed Ldrship, Wash Policy Sem, 1980; AUS War Col Nat Security Sem, 1981; pa/Current Pres, Mary Baldwin Col; Acting Dean, St-Wide Progs, Empire St Col, 1976; Vis'g Fac Fellow, Harvard Univ Grad Sch of Ed; Sr Assoc Dean and Assoc Prof, St-Wide Progs, Empire St Col, SUNY, 1975-76; Conslrg Core Fac, Union Grad Sch, 1975-82; Assoc Dean and Assoc Prof, St-Wide Progs, Empire St Col, SUNY, 1973-75; Adm Internship, Goddard Col, 1971; Asst to Pres and Dir of Ed Res 1968-72, Dir of Ed Res 1967-68, Skidmore Col; Other Previous Positions; Am Assn of Higher Ed; Am Acad of Polit and Social Scis; Am Coun on Ed; Coun on Postsec'dy Accreditation; r/Soc of Friends; hon/Pubs, "Non-Classroom Route to a Degree: Empire State College" 1973, "Doing as Being, or Vice Versa" 1974, "Women's Studies at Empire State College" 1975, Others; Dist'd HS Alumni Awd; Freshman Sch of Ed Awd; Chimes; Pi Lambda Theta; Pi Gamma Mu; W/W Am; Personalities of S; DIB; Commun Ldrs of Am; Num Other Biogl Listings.

LESTER, W BERNARD oc/Executive Director; b/Jan 9, 1939; h/1420 Miller Lane, Lakeland, FL 33801; ba/Lakeland, FL; m/Elaine Purnell; c/Mark Alan; p/Mr William D Lester, Havana, FL; ed/BS in Agri 1961, MS in Agri Ec 1962, Univ of FL; PhD in Agri Ec, TX A&M Univ, 1965; mil/AUS, 1956; pa/Exec Dir 1979-, Dpty Exec Dir 1976-78, Ec Res Dir in Ec Res Dept 1969-76, FL Dept of Citrus; Res Economist, Ec Res Dept, FL Citrus Comm, Univ of FL, 1967-68; Other Previous Positions; Criteria Selection Com, Nat Alpha Gamma Rho HQs Proj; Am Mktg Assn; So Agri Ec Assn; r/Meth; hon/Author, Num Ec Res Reports Primarily Regarding FL Citrus, But Also Incl'g Analyses for Var Other Agri Commodities; Prom People in FL Govt; W/W S and SW; W/W Fin and Indust.

LESTREL, PETE E oc/Research Anthropologist; b/Feb 19, 1938; h/7327 De Celis Place, Van Nuys, CA 91406; ba/Sepulveda, CA; m/Dagmar C; c/ Nicole, Valerie; p/Dr and Mrs Hans Lestrel (dec); ed/AB 1964, MA 1966, PhD 1975, Univ of CA LA; mil/USAR, 1957-64; pa/Engr, N Am Aviation, 1962-65; Instr, Santa Monica City Col, 1967-73; Asst Prof of Anthropology, Case Wn Resv Univ, 1973-75; Asst Prof 1977-80, Assoc Prof 1981-, Univ of CA LA Sch of Dentistry; Res Anthropologist, VA Med Ctr, 1976-; Edit Bd, *Human Biology Journal*, 1980-83; Fellow, Human Biol Coun; Am Assn of Physical Anthropologists; Am Assn of Dental Res; Intl Assn of Dental Res; hon/Pubs in Var Jours, incl'g, *Science* 1970, *Yearbook of Physical Anthropology* 1974, *Growth, Journal of Dental Research* 1978, *Human Biology* 1982; Author, Var Book Chapts; W/W Frontier Sci and Technol.

LEUNG, HUNG-KEN oc/Artist; b/May 14, 1933; h/316 East-14 Street, Oakland, CA 94606; ba/San Francisco, CA; m/Chan Yim Yung; c/Thomas, Simon, Richard, Stephen; p/Leung Tuen and Wong Lai Tee (dec); ed/Self-Taught Artist; pa/Developed Painting Style, 1952-65; Tchr (Selected as Lifetime Consltg Mem), En Artist Sch, 1966-69; Founded H Leung's Art Gallery, Hong Kong, 1967-76; Founded H Leung's Art Gallery, Oakland, CA, 1981; Founded Galleria Fine Art & Graphics Co, SF, 1984; Hong Kong Arts Com Mem; Asia Soc of Arts; VP, Soc of Arts, N Am; Oakland Art Assn; Asia Art Mus Soc of SF; Sustaining Mem, Paul Harris Intl; Marine Art Assn; Intl Art Exhbns: Kon's Fine Art 1963-67, Blue Boy Art Gallery and Kavlaine Intl Arts 1969-70, Stephen Lowe Art Gallery 1973, Asia Soc of Arts 1977, 18th Asia Mod Art Exhbn 1982, 19th Asia Mod Art Exhbn 1983, Plumas Co Mus 1983, Alta Bates Show 1983, C E Smith Mus 1984; Publication in Over 25 Color Graphics Wk Exhbns Over the World, 1963-67; Paintings Chosen for Fine Art Calendar, Brit Am Tobacco Co, 1971; Pub'd Posters; 7 Ltd Edition Graphics; Recip, Cert of Merit, Asia Soc of Arts, 1977; Awd of Merit, Oakland Art Assn, Alta Bates Show, 1982; Gold Medal Awd as Paul Harris Fellow, Rotary Foun of Rotary Intl, 1982; Recip, Dir's Cit, Coordination Coun for N Am Affairs Ofc in SF, 1984; DIB.

LEVERENCE, WILLIAM oc/Architectural Designer; b/May 3, 1947; h/5945 Avery Street, Orlando, FL 32808; ba/Same; m/Lora Ruth Mosier; c/Merry Joe, Heather Leanne, Sarah Ruth; p/William and Eleanor Gloria Perna Leverence, Markham, IL; ed/Student, Wn IL Univ, 1965-67; BS in Envir Design, Univ of OK, 1976; mil/USMC, 1970-73; pa/Proj Mgr, Robert A Harris, Arch, 1981-; Pres, Aerographics Design Grp, 1976-; Ptnr, The Team Approach,

1976; Hd Draftsman, Planning Dept, City of Norman, 1974-76; Theta Xi, 1966; Sooner Aviation, 1976; r/Luth; hon/Leatherneck Awd, 1970; Stick & Rudder Awd, 1976; Merit Awd, Prodrs Coun of OK, 1977; 1st Hon Awd for Overall Design Excell, Passive Residential Design Competition of the FL Solar Energy Ctr, 1980; W/W S and SW.

LEVI, HENRY THOMAS oc/Manager; b/May 5, 1941; h/1651-A 33rd Street, Southwest, Allentown, PA 18103; ba/King of Prussia, PA; m/Cathy Ann Ellsworth; p/Henry Louis and Elinor Stigora Levi, Nanticoke, PA; ed/BS, Franklin Pierce Col, 1966; GJ, Canadian Jeweller Inst, 1976; Dipl, Gemological Assn of Great Brit, 1977; Gemological Inst of Am, 1977; mil/6 Yrs in Control Grp, AUS; pa/Owner, Levi Jeweller, 1974-77; Mgr, Mussel Man Jeweller, 1976-79; Mgr, Phila Diamond Exch, 1980-; Gemological Assn of Great Brit; Canadian Gemological Assn; Australian Gemological Assn; Gemological Mineral Soc, Zimbabwe; Jewellers of Am; IPA; r/Jewish; hon/Pub'd in *Lapidary Journal* 1977, *Canadian Gemologist* 1977, *Jewellry World* 1977; Awd for Outstg Sales Perf, McCrory Corp, 1966; 1st in Diamond Sales Contest, 1979; W/W Am; Book of Hon; DIB.

LEVIN, A LEO oc/Center Director; b/Jan 9, 1919; ba/1520 H Street, Northwest, Washington, DC 20005; m/Doris; c/Allan D, Jay M; p/Issachar and Minerva Shapiro Levin (dec); ed/BA, Yeshiva Col, 1939; JD, Univ of PA, 1942; Univ Fellow, Columbia, 1946-47; Fellow, Ctr for Adv'd Study in the Behavioral Scis, 1959-60; mil/USAF, 1942-46; pa/Instr and Asst Prof of Law, Univ of IA, 1947-49; Asst Prof, Assoc Prof, Prof, Law, Univ of PA, 1949-69, 1970-; Vice Provost, Univ of PA, 1965-68; Exec Dir, Comm on Revision of the Fed Ct Appellate Sys, 1973-75; Dir, Fed Jud Ctr, 1977-; Bd of Trustees, Bar Ilan Univ, 1967-; Nat Inst of Corrections Adv Bd; cp/Hon Pres, Jewish Pub Soc of Am; r/Jewish Orthodox; hon/Author, Var Pubs; Hon LLD, Yeshiva Univ, 1960; Hon LLD, NY Law Sch, 1980; Dist'd Ser Awd, Univ of PA Law Sch Alumni, 1974; Mordecai Ben David Awd, Yeshiva Univ, 1967; Delivered: White Lectures, LA Univ 1970, Jeffords Lecture, NY Law Sch 1980; W/W Am Law; Intl W/W Contemp Achmt; DIB.

LEVINE, GEOFFREY oc/Nuclear Pharmacist, Research Scientist, Educator; b/Sep 2, 1942; h/6360 Monitor Street, Pittsburgh, PA 15217; m/Jill Robin; c/Julie, Karen, Lisa; p/Eli Levine, Landover, MD; Florence Pollack (dec); ed/BS in Pharm 1965, MS in Radiol Hlth 1967, Temple Univ; PhD in Envir Hlth Engrg, NWn Univ, 1978; pa/Assoc Prof of Radiol, Univ of Pgh Sch of Med, Dept of Radiol, Div of Nuclear Med, 1972-; Clin Asst Prof, Pharmaceutics, Univ of Pgh Sch of Pharm, Dept of Pharmaceutics, 1972-; Radiopharm Instr, Presb-Univ Hosp Sch of Nuclear Med Technol, 1974-79; Coor, MS Prog in Radiopharm, Univ of Pgh Sch of Pharm, 1972-; Radioisotope Com, Univ of Pgh, 1973-; Com Mem, Radiopharm Adv Com to Hlth Ctr Ctl Radiopharm, 1973-; Dir, Radiopharm Sers, Univ of Pgh Hlth Ctr, 1971-; Nuclear Pharm, Presb-Univ Hosp, 1972-; Var Previous Positions; Am Assn of Radiopharm

Scists; Soc of Nuclear Med; Rho Chi; Hlth Physics Soc; Sigma Xi; Hlth Physics Soc of Wn PA; Am Pharm Assn; Nat Soc of Nuclear Med; AAAS; Am Soc of Hosp Pharms; Acad of Pharmaceutical Pract, Sect on Nuclear Pharm; PA Col of Nuclear Med and Nuclear Physics; Radiation Res Com, Montefiore Hosp, 1978-; Pharm Staff Appt, Montefiore Hosp, 1975-; Radiopharm, Presb-Univ Hosp, 1972-; r/Jewish; hon/Num Profl Pubs and Presentations; Plaque from Am Pharm Assn Acad of Pharm Pract, in Recog of Outstg Ser to Nuclear Pharm Sect, 1977-78; Fdrs Awd, APhA, Acad of Pharm Pract, Sect on Nuclear Pharm, 1981; W/W E; Dir of World Rschrs.

LeVINE, MYRON LOUIS oc/Optometrist; b/Nov 21, 1930; h/10587 Holman Avenue, Los Angeles, CA 90024; ba/Los Angeles, CA; m/Nancy Lou; c/Jeffrey, Bradley, Steven; p/Mr (dec) and Mrs Jack LeVine, Los Angeles, CA; ed/BS 1953, OD 1954, Pacific Univ; pa/Pvt Pract, W LA, 1954-60; Grp Pract, 1960-81; Ptnrship Pract, 1982-; LA Co Optometric Assn; Am Optometric Assn, Charter Mem, Contact Lens Sect and Multidisciplinary Pract Sect; cp/Mason; B'nai B'rith, Pres 1961-62; r/Jewish; hon/Author, Profl Articles in Var Jours, 1955-83; LA Co Optometric Ser Awd of Merit; Dist #4 Chain Maker Awd; Past Pres Ser Awd, B'nai B'rith; W/W W.

LEVINSKAS, GEORGE JOSEPH oc/Director of Environmental Assessment and Toxicology; b/Jul 8, 1924; h/526 Fairways Circle, Creve Coeur, MO 63141; ba/St Louis, MO; m/Ruth Irene Hublitz; c/Robert John, Nancy Jane, Edward Joseph; p/Joseph and Frances Eurkunas Levinskas (dec); ed/AB, Chem, Wesleyan Univ, 1949; PhD, Pharm, Univ of Rochester, 1953; mil/AUS, 1943-46; pa/Res Assoc, Atomic Energy Proj, Univ of Rochester, 1952; Res Assoc, Lectr, Asst Prof, Indust Toxicology, Grad Sch of Public Hlth, Univ of Pgh, 1953-58; Res Pharmacologist, Chief Indust Toxicologist, Dir of Envir Mtl Hlth Lab, Am Cyanamid Co, 1958-71; Mgr, then Dir, Envir Assessment and Toxicology, Monsanto Co, 1971-; Am Chem Soc; Am Indust Hygiene Assn; Am Soc Pharm and Exptl Therapeutics; Soc of Toxicology, Charter Mem; Envir Mutagen Soc, Charter Mem; AAAS; NY Acad Scis; r/Rom Cath; hon/Author, Tech Articles on Pharm and Toxicology of Indust and Agri Chems and Food Additives, Chem of Bone Mineral; Diplomate, Am Bd of Toxicology, Acad of Toxicological Scis; NRC Predoct Fellow, 1949-52; Graham Prize for Excell in Natural Sci, Wesleyan Univ, 1949; Phi Beta Kappa; Soc of the Sigma Xi; W/W Am; W/W Technol Today; W/W Frontier Sci and Technol; Am Men and Wom of Sci; Ldrs in Am Sci; Biogl Dir of Occupl Hlth and Safety Specs.

LEVITIN, LEV B oc/Professor; b/Sep 25, 1935; h/1069 Beacon Street, Apartment 9, Brookline, MA 02146; ba/Boston, MA; m/Julia Shmukler; c/Boris; p/Ber Levitin (dec); Tsetsilia Gushansky (dec); ed/MSc, summa cum laude, Moscow Univ, 1960; PhD, USSR Acad of Scis, 1969; pa/Sr Res Scist, Inst for Info Transmission Probs, Moscow, USSR Acad of Sci, 1961-73; Sr Lectr,

Tel-Aviv Univ, 1974-80; Vis'g Scist, Heinrich-Hertz Inst, Berlin, 1980; Vis'g Prof, Bielefeld Univ, W Germany, 1980-81; Vis'g Scist, Inst für Optoelectronic, Oberpfaffenhofen, W Germany, 1981; Vis'g Prof, Syracuse Univ, 1981-82; Prof, Boston Univ, 1982-; Popov Sci and Engrg Soc, 1962-73; IEEE, 1976-, Sr Mem 1983-; Israel Statistical Assn, 1978-80; AMS, SIAM, AAUP, 1981-; ACM, 1982-; AAAS, ASEE, 1983-; cp/Bd Mem, Antitotalitarian Soc, 1981-; Amnesty Intl, 1983-; Resistance Intl, 1984-; hon/Author, 45 Sci Pubs, 9 Items in Encys, About 20 Reviews; Sci Editor of 2 Books in Russian; Translations of 3 Books.

LEVI, DAVID HOWARD oc/Astronomical Observer; b/May 22, 1948; h/Route 7, Box 414, Tucson, AZ 85747; ba/Same; p/Nathaniel and Edith Levy; ed/BA, Acadia Univ, 1972; MA, Eng, Queen's Univ, 1979; pa/Astronomy Writer, 1971-; Observing Asst, Planetary Sci Inst, 1982-; Instr for Sch Grps 1980-82, Floor Mgr 1981-82, Flandrau Planetarium; Active Pvt Observation Prog Involving More Than 6,500 Recorded Observing Sessions, 1959-; Astronomy Instr at Var Chd's Camps, 1966-70, 1976-81; Coor and Tchr, Ednl Activs of the Kingston Ctr, Royal Astronom Soc of Canada, 1978-80; Observer and Contbr, Am Assn of Variable Star Observers, 1964-; Co-Orgr, AAVSO Sprg Meeting, 1981; RASC, Nat Hist Com 1980-, Nat Awds Com 1980-, VP of Kingston Ctr 1980-; Pres, Tucson Amateur Astronomy Assn, 1980-83; Chm, Astronom Leag 1985 Nat Conv; Recorder, Meteor Sect, Assn of Lunar and Planetary Observers, 1983-; Authorized Biographer for Bart J Bok, 1982-; hon/Pubs, *A Vigil for Variables: A Beginner's Guide to Observing Variable Stars* 1984, *A Children's Universe: A Guide for Teaching Astronomy for Teachers and Parents* 1984, "The New ALPO Meteor Section" 1983, "Telescopes and Children" 1983, Num Others; Messier Cert, Hon Cit, Astronom Leag, 1983; Messier Cert, RASC, 1981; Merit Awd, RASC, Victoria Gen Assem, 1981; Pi Lambda Theta, 1980; Ednl Refractor Telescope: Third Prize at Stellafane Competition 1979, Merit Awd at Riverside Telescope Makers Conf 1980, Merit Awd at TX Star Party 1983; Dean's List, Acadia Univ, 1971; Chant Medal, RASC, 1980; Outstg Yg Men of Am; W/W W.

LEVI, DEBORAH L oc/Center Director; b/Aug 5, 1949; h/21131 Northeast 22 Court, North Miami Beach, FL 33180; ba/Hollywood, FL; m/Elliot MD; c/Jonathan, Emily; ed/BA w Hons in Spec Ed, Univ of IL Chgo, 1971; MA w Hons in Rdg and Lang Devel, Wash Univ, 1973; EdD, Nova Univ, 1979; pa/Hd Tchr, Lng Disability Prog, BISOLE, 1971-72; Tchr, Ballwin, MO, 1972-74; Nat Rdg and Lng Conslt, *Encyclopedia Brittanica*, 1971-75; Vice Prin, Lng Disabilities Spec, Hillel Commun Day Sch, 1974-75; Ednl Diagnostician and Remediation Spec, Pvt Pract, 1975-79; Dir, Devel Resource Ctr, 1979-; CEC; Assn for Chd w Lng Disabilities; FL Assn of Indep Spec Ed Facilities; Orton Soc; Fdr, St Orton Soc and St Bd of Dirs, 1982; r/Jewish; hon/Author of Textbook, *Alternatives Publishers-A Learning Center Approach to Learning*; W/W

Am; Outstg Personalities of S; Brit Psychol Bulletin.

LEVY, EUGENE HOWARD oc/Professor of Planetary Sciences, Head of Planetary Sciences Department, Director of Lunar and Planetary Lab; b/May 6, 1944; h/5442 East Burns Street, Tucson, AZ 85711; ba/Tucson, AZ; m/Margaret Rader; c/Roger Philip, Jonathan Saul, Benjamin Howard; p/Isaac P (dec) and Anita H Levy; ed/AB in Physics, w High Hons, Rutgers Univ, 1966; PhD in Physics, Univ of Chgo, 1971; pa/Postdoct Fellow, Physics and Astronomy, Univ of MD, 1971-73; Asst Prof, Physics and Astrophysics, Bartol Res Foun, 1973-75; Asst Prof, Assoc Prof, Prof 1975-, Dept Hd and Lab Dir 1983-, Univ of AZ; APS; AAS; AGU; IAU; Phi Beta Kappa; Sigma Xi; Num Nat and Intl Adv Panels, Bds, for Space Sci Progs and Policies; hon/Author, Num Articles in Profl Jours; NASA Predoct Fellow, 1966-69; Postdoct Fellow, Ctr for Theoretical Physics, 1971-73; NASA Dist'd Public Ser Medal, 1983.

LEVY, MAURICE SASSON oc/University Professor, Executive; b/May 3, 1936; h/Belsize 15, Hampstead, Quebec H3X 3J7; ba/Montreal, Quebec; m/Josiane Lipfeld; c/Laurence Deborah, Michael Sasson; p/Mrs Esther Tarrab Levy, Paris; ed/Master of Electronic Engrg, Univ of Paris, 1960; MBA, 1962; Doct in Mgmt Scis, Sorbonne, Paris, 1981; pa/Sales Promotion and Mktg Mgr, Jeumont-Schneider, Paris, 1963-69; Mktg and New Bus Devel Mgr, LMT, ITT, Paris, 1969-74; Exec, ITT Europe, Brussels, Belgium, 1974-80; Dir, Intl Div CIT-Alcatel, Paris, 1980-81; Pres and CEO, MLS, 1981-; Current Prof, Univ of Quebec; Mem of the Bd, Patrimoine Historique et Artistique de la France, 1968-; hon/Pubs, "Strategies des Produits" 1969, *Les Strategies d'Innovation de l'Entreprise* 1969, *Strategie des Prix de Vente* 1974, "Marketing Audit" 1982.

LEWIS, CECELIA MAE oc/Retired Janitor; b/Oct 3, 1917; h/927 Roosevelt Street, Bemidji, MN 56601; c/Linda Sharon; p/Theodore Southal and Elisabeth Raabe Broden (dec); ed/Dipl, Bemidji HS, 1936; Att'd, Bemidji St Col 1948; Att'd Wkshops, Bemidji Area Voc Tech 1968-71, AFSCME Labor Ed 1966-67; Att'd, George Meany Ctr 1971, 1975, 1979, Anoka-Ramsey Commun Col 1979-80; pa/Custodial Wkr I, Bemidji St Col, 1947-49, 1957-67; Custodial Wkr II 1967-72, Sr Janitor 1972-80, Ret'd 1980, Bemidji St Univ; MN St Employees Union; Bemidji Ctl Labor Body, AFL-CIO, Secy 1974-83, Editor 1981-83, Chair of Polit Fund 1981-83; cp/LWV, 1st VP 1982, Intl Relats Dir 1980-83; Bi-Co Commun Action Prog Inc, Exec Bd-Labor Rep, Pvt Sector, 1980-83; hon/Plaque and Cert, World W/W Wom, 1982; Plaque, Intl W/W Intells, 1982; W/W Am Polit; Intl Register of Profiles.

LEWIS, CHARLES B oc/Dean, Educator and Missionary; b/Sep 20, 1913; h/908 North Union, PO Box 53, Natchez, MS 39120; ba/Natchez, MS; p/Irvin J and Lizzie Lewis; ed/AB, Leland Col, 1944; BD 1947, ThM 1948, ABT Sem; Cand for DMin, Missionary Bapt St; pa/Edr-Missionary; Dean of Rel, Dean of Chapel, Col Pastor, Natchez

Col; MS Phil Assn; Assn of Bapt Profs of Rel; Nat Assn of Adult Edrs; cp/Natchez Bus and Civic Leag; r/Bapt; hon/W/W Ed; W/W Rel; W/W; W/W Black Am.

LEWIS, DAVID EDWIN oc/Trust Banking Officer; b/Aug 16, 1945; h/PO Box 3023, Reno, NV 89505; ba/Reno, NV; m/Bonne Ann; p/Edwin N and Marie Lucy (dec) Lewis, Las Vegas, NV; ed/Hons Grad, Pacific Coast Bkg Sch, Seattle, 1982; Assoc in Applied Sci in Law Enforcement 1977, Assoc in Applied Sci in Money and Bkg 1976, Wn NV Commun Col; Am Inst of Bkg Certs, 1975; BS, Bus Adm, Instnl Mgmt, Univ of NV Reno, 1968; mil/AUS, US and Europe, 1968-70; pa/Trust Ofcr in $30 Million Trust Dept, Pioneer Citizens Bk of NV-Reno, 1976-; Loan Ofcr 1975-76, Asst Cashier/Opers Ofcr 1974-75, 1970-74, Pioneer Citizens Bk of NV-Reno; Chief Clk, Army Basic Tng Unit, AUS Gen's Staff, Germany, 1968-70; Am Inst of Bkg; Estate Planning Coun, 1980-; NV Bkrs Assn; cp/Reno Host Lions, 1975-; YMCA, 1978-; r/Cath; hon/W/W W.

LEWIS, MARY BERNS oc/Lead Engineer of Robotics and Artificial Intelligence; b/Jun 21, 1951; h/6359 South Clifton, Derby, KS 67037; ba/Wichita, KS; m/Richard; p/Marie Corcoran Berns, Western Springs, IL; ed/MS, Physics, Univ of Chgo, 1978; BS w Highest Hons, Math, Univ of IL Chgo, 1974; pa/Engr 1978-, Lead Engr 1981-, Boeing Mil Airplane Co; Tchg Asst, Univ of Chgo, 1976, 1977; Tchg Asst, Univ of IL, 1975; Sr Mem, Robotics Intl; Am Assn for Artificial Intell; Life Mem, Phi Kappa Phi Hon Soc, 1974-; hon/Pubs, "Artificial Intelligence in Computer Aided Manufacturing" 1982, "Artificial Intelligence in Electronics" 1983; Art Wks incl'd in *Artists USA*, 1982; Highest Distn in Math, Univ of IL, 1974; Book of Acad Hons, Univ of IL, 1975; W/W Am Wom.

LEWIS, THEODORE GYLE oc/Computer Scientist; b/Dec 2, 1941; h/4400 Sulphur Springs Road, Corvallis, OR 97330; ba/Same; m/Madeline E Rubin; c/Leslie Paige Williams, Todd Elliott; p/Gyle H and Lois M Lewis (dec); ed/BS in Math, OR St Univ, 1966; MS, PhD, Computer Sci, WA St Univ, 1971; pa/Boeing Co, 1966; Sylvania Electronic Def Sys, 1968; Univ of AZ, 1967; WA St Univ, 1968-71; Univ of MO Rolla, 1971-73; Univ of SW LA Lafayette, 1973-76; OR St Univ, 1977-; Assn Computing Machinery; IEEE Computer Soc; Assoc Editor, *Computer Magazine*, 1980-81; VChm, SIGMICRO, Assn Computing Machinery; hon/Pubs, *Using the Osborne-1 Computer* 1983, *Using the IBM Personal Computer* 1983, *Microbook: Data Management for the Apple* 1982, *Software Engineering: Analysis and Verification* 1982, Num Others; Intl W/W Ed.

LI, SHU-TIEN oc/Professor Emeritus; b/Feb 10, 1900; p/Wan Kwei and Shu Chang Li; ed/BSCE, summa cum laude, Nat Peiyang Univ, 1923; PhD in Trans, Structural and Hydraulic Engrg, Cornell Univ, 1926; pa/Prof Emeritus 1970-, Prof of Civil Engr and Exec Dir of Interdisciplinary Grad Coun for Geotechnol, SD Schs of Mines and Technol; Chief Tech Wrtr, Palmer and Baker Engrs Inc, 1955-61; Vis'g Prof of Civil Engrg, Rutgers Univ, 1953-54;

Consltg Engr, SE China, Taiwan, NY, 1949-55; Dean of Engrg and Dean of Sci, Nat Feiyang Univ, 1946-49; Pres, Nat Peiyang Siking Inst, 1944-46; Num Other Previous Positions; Consltg Engr, AL, SD, WY, CO, NV, CA, 1955-; Fdr, Chm, Pres, Li Instn of Sci and Technol and Its Grad Sch, World Open Univ, 1972-; hon/Authored and Pub'd 16 Books and 800 Papers and Articles in 17 Countries; Recip, First Class Hydraulic Medal 1935, Victory Decoration 1946, Republic of China; Coun Mem, Nat Acad of Peiping, 1948; Phi Tau Phi; Phi Kappa Phi; Sigma Xi.

LiBASSI, PATRICIA C oc/Writer; h/4990 Pine Ledge Drive West, Clarence, NY 14031; ba/Buffalo, NY; m/Paul Joseph; c/Michael, Mark, David, J Douglas, Patricia A, Suzanne Marie; p/David (dec) and Mary; ed/RN, St Joseph's Nsg Sch, 1949; SB, IN Cont'd Ed, IN Univ; Att'd, Univ of Buffalo, St Univ of NY Buffalo; Var Writing Courses; pa/Delivery-Labor Supvr, St Joseph Hosp, 1949; Staff Nurse 1951-52, Night Supvr 1950, Wm Coleman Hosp for Wom; Staff Nurse, Emer Room, Fifth Ave Hosp, 1950; Staff Nurse, Ft Heavenworth Army Hosp, 1954; Staff Nurse, Buffalo Gen Hosp 1956, Chd's Hosp 1958; Pvt Duty, St Joseph Intercommun Hosp, 1968; cp/Notre Dame Alumni Wives, 1957; Call for Action, 1976-; Co-Dir, Dir, Reg Dir of NE, Mem of Nat Bd of Dirs, Call for Action Inc, NYC; Am Film Inst; Nat Writers Clb; r/Rom Cath; hon/Author, Several Articles; "Slice of Life" in *Buffalo Evening News*; Monthly Column, Youngstown Yacht Clb, 1978-; W/W Am Wom.

LIBERATORE, MATTHEW JOHN oc/Assistant Professor of Management, Consultant; b/Jun 23, 1950; h/271 Woodlake Drive, Holland, PA 18966; ba/Villanova, PA; m/Mary Jane Cunningham; c/Kathryn, Michelle; p/Mr and Mrs Matthew A Liberatore, Philadelphia, PA; ed/BA, cum laude, w Distn in Math, Univ of PA, 1972; MS 1973, PhD 1976, Opers Res, Univ of PA; pa/Asst Prof of Mgmt, Villanova Univ, 1983-; Asst Prof of Mgmt, Temple Univ, 1980-83; Mgr, R & D Planning and Eval, 1978-80; Mgr of Opers Res, FMC Corp, 1976-78; Opers Res Analyst, RCA Corp, 1974-76; Mgmt Res Analyst, Mgmt and Behavioral Sci Ctr, Univ of PA, 1972-74; Phila Chapt, Opers Res Soc of Am/The Inst of Mgmt Scis, Pres-Elect, VP 1981-82, Pres 1982-83, Past Pres 1983-84; Am Inst of Decision Scis; Opers Res Soc of Am; Inst of Mgmt Scis; Acad of Mgmt; Am Prodn and Inventory Control Soc; r/Cath; hon/Pubs, "A Dynamic Production Planning and Scheduling Algorithm for Two Products Processed on One Line" (in Press), "Synthesizing R & D Planning and Business Strategy: Some Preliminary Findings" 1983, "RDE Multiproject Planning and Control: A Discussion of Issues for Developing a Decision Support System" 1983, "The Practice of Management Science in R & D Project Management" 1983, Num Others; Mayor's Scholar to Univ of PA, 1968; Invited Spkr, Phila TIMS/ORSA, 1979; Pub'd Paper Selected as "Paper of the Year for 1983," *R & D Management*.

LICH, GLEN ERNST oc/Professor of English and German; b/Nov 5, 1948; h/Westland Place, 718 Jackson Road,

Kerrville, TX 78028; ba/Kerrville, TX; m/Lera Patrick Tyler; c/James Ernst Lich-Tyler, Stephen Woolfley Lich-Tyler, Elizabeth Erin Lich-Tyler; p/Mr and Mrs Ernst Perry Lich, Comfort, TX; ed/Dipl, Univ of Vienna, Austria, 1970; BA, SWn Univ, 1971; MA, Univ of TX, 1976; MA, SW TX St Univ; mil/Direct Comm, 1st Lt, 1975; Present Rank, Capt, Mil Intell, TX Army NG; pa/Instr in Eng, SW TX St Univ, 1975-79; Instr in Eng, Univ of NO, 1979-80; Asst Prof of Eng and German, Schreiner Col; Mod Lang Assn; Am Studies Assn; Am Assn of Tchrs of German; NCTE; TX Folklore Soc; NG Assns of US and TX; Pi Kappa Alpha; hon/Pubs, "J Frank Dobie, Writer and Folklorist" 1981, "Julia Mood Peterkin, Writer" 1981, "Animal Metaphors and Verbal Abuse: A Study of Social Relations and Values Among German-Speaking Farmers on Cypress Creek, Kerr County, Texas" 1982, "Tom Outland: A Central Problem" (in Prodn), *The German Texans* 1981, Others; Volume Editor, *German Culture in Texas: A Free Earth, Essays from the 1978 Southwest Symposium*, 1980; Asst Editor, *Retrospect and Retrieval: The German Element in Review, Essays on Cultural Preservation*, 1981; Nat Endowment for the Humanities Grant, 1978; Num Profl Consultantships, 1977-83; TX Book Awd, 1981; German-Am S'ship Awd, 1982; Dir of Am Scholars; W/W S and SW.

LIEBERMAN, S BERNARD oc/Temple Administrator; b/Oct 23, 1924; h/3939 North Murray #506, Shorewood, WI 53211; ba/Milwaukee, WI; m/Ilaine; c/Dr Cheryl Anne, Ellyn Sue; p/William and Edyth Lieberman (dec); ed/HS Grad, 1942; Att'd, John Tarleton Col; mil/US Inf 1943-45, T/5 Corporal; cp/Clk Typist, US Govt, 1942-43; Mgr, Baicker's Wallpaper and Paint, 1945-46; Ptnrship, Weberman's Printery, 1956-64; Dir, Yth Activs, Jewish Commun Ctr, 1964-65; Exec Dir, Temple Israel, 1965-76; Exec Dir, Temple Emanu-el, 1976-78; Temple Admr, Congregation Emanu-el B'ne Jeshurun, 1978-; Exec Com, Nat Assn of Temple Admrs, 1965; Am Cemetery Assn, 1967-; Am Soc for Tng and Devel, 1979-; Am Mgmt Assn, 1976-; cp/Postal Customers' Coun of Dayton and Miami Val, 1972; Pres, Nanticoke Lions Clb, 1963-64; Dist 14-H Public Relats Ofcr, 1966; VFW; Jewish War Vets; UF, Public Relats Com, Steering Com of Gtr Nanticoke Area; Salvation Army, Bd Mem; ARC, Bd Mem; U Jewish Appeal, Div Chm, Public Relats-Spec Presentations, Awds Chm; r/Jewish; hon/Pubs, "Penetrating Public Relations" 1968, "How to Develop New Sources of Income" 1970, "Telling the Story of Public Relations-A Look at What We're Printing" 1976, "In Time of Sorrow" 1974; Recip, Freedom's Foun Medal, Val Forge.

LIEBERMAN, STEPHEN JACOB oc/Orientalist, College Teacher; b/Mar 21, 1943; h/7400 Haverford Avenue, Apartment E-309, Philadelphia, PA 19151; ba/Philadelphia, PA; p/Martin J and Selma L Lieberman, Alhambra, CA; ed/Att'd, Columbia Col of Columbia Univ 1960-61, Sem Col of Jewish Theol Sem 1960-61, Hebrew Univ of Jerusalem 1963-64; AB, Univ of MN, 1963; PhD, Harvard Univ, 1972; pa/Asst Prof

1971-73, Assoc Prof 1973, NY Univ; Res Spec, Sumerian Dic Proj, Univ Mus of Univ of PA, 1976-79; Vis'g Fellow, Princeton Univ, 1979-81; Res Assoc, Univ Mus of Univ of PA, 1981-; Assoc Prof of Assyriology and Semitic Linguistics, Dropsie Col, 1982-; Am Hist Assn; Am Oriental Soc; Am Schs of Oriental Res; Archaeol Inst of Am; Assn for Jewish Studies; Brit Inst of Archaeol at Ankara; Brit Sch of Archaeol in Iraq; E Coast Assyriological Colloquium; Fondation Assyriologique Georges Dossin; Linguistic Soc of Am; N Am Conf on Afro-Asiatic Langs; Soc of Biblical Lit; cp/Amnesty Intl; ACLU; r/Jewish; hon/Pubs, "The Years of Damiqilishu, King of Isin" 1983, "Of Clay Pebbles, Hollow Clay Balls and Writing: A Sumerian View" 1984, Others; Fellow in Mesopotamian Civilization, Baghdad Ctr Com of the Am Schs of Oriental Res, 1970-71; Fellow, Nat Endowment for the Humanities, 1975-76; Fellow, J S Guggenheim Foun, 1979-80; Inaugural Fellow, Foun for Mesopotamian Studies, 1980-82; W/W E.

LIEBMANN, SEYMOUR W oc/Construction Consultant; b/Nov 1, 1928; h/3260 Rilman Drive, Northwest, Atlanta, GA 30327; ba/Atlanta, GA; m/Hinda Adam; c/Peter Adam, David W; p/I Liebmann, Spring Valley, NY; Etta Waltzer Liebmann (dec); ed/BSME, Clarkson Col of Technol, 1948; Grad, AUS Engr Sch; US Army Cmd & Gen Staff Col, 1966; Indust Col of the Armed Forces, 1963; US Army War Col, 1971; mil/Ret'd Col, Corps of Engrs; AUS, 1948-52; USAR; pa/Area Engr, Constrn Div, E I DuPont DeNemours, Inc, 1952-54; Constrn Planner, Lummus Co, 1954-56; Prin Mech Engr, Perini Corp, 1956-62; VP, Boston Based Contractors, 1962-66; Dir & VP 1967-74, Pres 1974-79, A R Abrams, Inc, Atlanta, GA; Pres, Liebmann Assocs, Inc, 1979-; Reg'd Profl Engr; Fellow, Dir, Prog Chm, VP, Pres Atlanta Post 1983, Soc of Am Mil Engrs; Soc of 1st Infantry Div, Res Ofcrs Assn of US; Assn of the US Army; Engrs Clb of Boston; Am Arbitration Assn, Panel of Construction Arbitration, 1979-; Life Mem, US Army War Col Foun; Life Mem, US Army War Col Alumni Assn; cp/Zoning Chairman, City of Atlanta Neighborhood Planning Unit, 1983-; Nat Adv Bd, Am Security Coun; Nat Unday Com; Mem 1968-, VP 1978, Mem Exec Com 1975-79, USO Coun; Asst Scoutmaster & Explorer Post Advr, Mem of Troop Com, Troop #298, Northside Meth Ch, 1980-; Alumni Adv Com, Alumni Bd of Govs, Clarkson Col; 32 Deg Mason; Shriner; Appalachian Trail Clb; Atlanta C of C, 1983-; hon/Soc of Am Mil Engrs Nat Awd of Merit, 1982, 1983; Nat USO Awd of Recog, 1979; Elected as Adult Mem to Scouting Order of the Arrow, 1983; Clarkson Col Alumni Assn Golden Knight Awd for Dist'd Ser, 1983; Elected to Old Guard of Gate City Guard, Atlanta, 1979; Cert of Achmt, Dept of Army, 1978; Legion of Merit, Meritorious Ser Medal, 1978; Listed in Nat Forensic Ctr 1983 & 1984 *Forensic Sers Dir*; W/W: S & SW, Fin & Indust; Men of Achmt.

LIGHTFEATHER, MELODY (TOOMA-QUAT) oc/Artist, Educator; b/Nov 18, 1951; ba/Same; m/James Gallegos-Lightfeather; p/Waqiui, Jemez

Pueblo; ed/BA in Ed and Art, cum laude, Glenville St Col, 1981; Comm'd Artist for Largest Comm in 20th Century, Intl Regency Hotel, 1982; Artist-in-Schs, 1982; Resident Artist in Schs, Gilmer Co, WV; Lectr; Indian Arts and Crafts Assn, 1982; Intl Fine Arts Guild, 1982; NM Watercolor Soc, 1981, 1982; Kappa Delta Pi Hon Ed Soc, 1980, 1981, 1982; hon/Dean's Hon List Awardee, 1979, 1980, 1981; Publicity in Art Awd, 1980; Kappa Delta Pi, Pres 1980-81; Bd of Regents S'ship Awd, 1978-81; Blue Ribbon Art Awd, NM St Fair, 1982; CO Art Fair Awd, 1982; Beulah Art Fest, 1982.

LIKINS, WILLIAM HENRY oc/College Vice President for Development; b/Feb 7, 1931; h/1062 Oram Drive, Adrian, MI 49221; ba/Adrian, MI; m/Martha Ann Grant; c/Jeanne Marie, William Henry Jr, David Scott; p/Mr and Mrs William H Likins, Louisville, KY; ed/PhD, Peabody Col, Vanderbilt Univ, 1979; ThD, Boston Univ, 1961; MDiv, Emory Univ, 1954; AB, Asbury Col, 1948; Att'd, Harvard Univ; pa/VP, Adrian Col, 1979-; Doct Cand, 1977-79; Exec Dir, Comm on Higher Ed, 1976-77; Bd of Higher Ed, U Meth Ch, 1967-76; Min, Fisk Meml Meth Ch, 1962-67; Men, Covenant Meth Ch, 1956-62; cp/Pres, Goodwill-LARC, 1982-; r/U Meth; hon/Author, More Than 125 Pubs w Distribution in Excess of 30 Million Copies in Profl Pubs, Newspapers and Addresses; Orme M Miller Fellow, Emory Univ, 1956; W/W MW; Personalities of S.

LILHOLT, HAROLD CARL oc/Corporate Financial Executive; b/Sep 9, 1930; h/158 Fairview Avenue, Oneida, NY 13421; ba/Oneida, NY; m/Clare Jeanette Willey; c/Patricia Ann Hobbs, Paul Andrew, David Allen; p/Harold Luther and Margaret Lilholt, Niagara Falls, NY; ed/BS, Syracuse Univ, 1955; MBA, Kent St, 1961; Postgrad Wk, Harvard Grad Sch of Bus Adm; Corporate Financial Mgmt, 1980; mil/AUS, 1948-51; pa/Financial Dir, European Opers, B F Goodrich Co, 1955-68; Exec VP and Chief Financial Ofcr, Oneida Ltd, 1968-; Bd Mem, Leavers Mfg Co, Camden Wire Co, Oneida Mexicana, Rena Ware Dist, Oneida Ltd Corp, Lincoln Bk; Lincoln Bk Intl Adv Bd; cp/Bd Mem, Am Sch and Am Prot Ch; Co-Fdr, Am Baseball Foun of Holland; Bd Mem, Am C of C; Oneida City Hosp, Bd of Govs 1975-82; Ctl NY Hlth Sys Agy, 1979-81; NY St Trustee, 4H Foun, 1980-81; Syracuse Univ Ath Fund Raising, 1972-82; Musical Box Soc Intl, 1981-82; r/Prot; hon/W/W Am; W/W World.

LIN, EYIH oc/Clinical Chemist; b/Jan 8, 1941; h/1903 Beechwood Court, Florence, AL 35630; ba/Sheffield, AL; m/Susan Tu; c/Thomas, Connie; p/Ai-Lai and Seh Huang Lin, Taiwan; ed/PhD, Univ of MO KC, 1972; pa/Asst Dir of Clin Lab, Helen Keller Meml Hosp, 1972-; MLT Prog Coor, Wallace St Commun Col, 1981-; MLT Prog Coor, NE MS Jr Col, 1975-; Clin Instr, Univ of AL B'ham, 1973-76; Am Assn for Clin Chem; Am Chem Soc; Soc for Applied Spectroscopy; AAAS; Nat Acad of Clin Biochem; Nat Registry in Clin Chem; Am Bd of Bioanal; hon/Author, Several Pubs in Profl Jours; Four Ser

Awds, Helen Keller Meml Hosp, 1981, 1980, 1979, 1978; W/W S and SW; Personalities of S; DIB.

LIN, PEI-JAN PAUL oc/Associate Professor, Diagnostic Radiological Physicist; b/Aug 25, 1946; h/30 West 002 Danbury Drive, Warrenville, IL 60555; ba/Chicago, IL; m/Keiko M; c/Rika, Rina; p/Mr and Mrs Jintoku Hayashi, Tokyo, Japan; ed/BS in Physics, Rikkyo Univ, 1969; MSc in Physics, DePaul Univ, 1973; PhD in Sci, Univ of Tsukuba, 1981; pa/Instr 1973, Assoc 1976, Asst Prof 1978, Assoc Prof 1982, Dept of Radiol, NWn Univ Med Sch; Affiliated Profl Staff, NWn Meml Hosp, 1975; Diagnostic X-ray Imaging Com of Am Assn of Physicists in Med, 1980-; Chm, Task Grp of AAPM Com, 1983-; Pres-Elect, MW Chapt, AAPM, 1983-; Dir, AAPM Sum Sch, 1984; r/Buddhism; hon/Author, More Than 30 Pubs in Field of Diagnostic Imaging Radiation Safety and Quality Assurance and Perf Testing of Imaging Equip.

LIN, SHIH-CHIA CHEN oc/Scientist, Researcher; b/Nov 3, 1917; h/7345 Pebble Beach Drive, El Cerrito, CA 94530; ba/San Francisco, CA; m/Teh Ping; c/Florence Jean, Henry John; p/Tse-kung Chen (dec); ed/BS in Chem, Ctl Univ, 1940; MS in Oceanography, Scripps Instn, 1951; PhD in Biochem, Univ of CA Berkeley, 1954; pa/Jr Res Pharmacologist 1960-61, Asst Res Pharmacologist 1961-67, 1973-, Univ of CA SF; Biochem Pharmacologist, SRI Intl, 1967-68; Am Soc for Pharm and Exptl Therapeutics; Intl Soc for the Study of Zenobiotics; Wn Pharmacological Soc; Sigma Xi; Iota Sigma Pi; hon/Author, Var Articles in Profl Jours; W/W Frontier Sci and Technol.

LIN, WUU-LONG oc/Economist, Development Planning; b/Apr 28, 1939; h/61 Old Knollwood Road, White Plains, NY 10607; ba/New York, NY; m/Ai-Ai Anna Kuo; c/Pansy, Joel; p/Yeu-chung Lin, Taiwan; Lu-Jing Lu (dec); ed/PhD, Stanford Univ, 1972; MS, KS St Univ, 1968; BS, Nat Taiwan Univ, 1965; mil/Lt, Chinese Army; pa/Economist, UN, 1978-; Econometrician, Food and Agri Org, Rome, 1974-77; Res Assoc, Vis'g Scholar, Stanford Univ, 1972-75; Consltg Econometrician, FMC Intl, 1973-74; Vis'g Economist, Chinese-Am Jt Comm on Rural Reconstruction, Taipei, 1971; Res, Harvard Univ, 1970; Res Assoc, KS St Univ, 1968; Am Ec Assn; Lifetime Mem, Stanford Univ Alumni Assn; Pres, Student Assn of Col of Agri, Nat Taiwan Univ, 1962; Chm, Com of Nat Movement Toward Self-Realization, Nat Taiwan Univ, 1962; hon/Author or Co-Author, Book Review in Journal of Policy Modelling 1982, Articles in Econometrica 1978, American Journal of Agricultural Economics 1976, ADC Teaching Forum 1975, Var Others; F'ship, Stanford Univ, 1968-72; Grantee, NSF, 1971-72; Chinese Statistical Assn First Awd, 1962; Phi Kappa Phi, 1968; W/W E.

LIND, NANCY A oc/Elementary Teacher; b/Nov 6, 1956; ba/1111 Lawerence Avenue, Lake Forest, IL 60045; p/Mr and Mrs S C Lind, Sheboygan, WI; ed/MAE, No MI Univ, 1981; BSE, Univ of WI Whitewater, 1977; pa/3rd Grade Tchr, Lake Forest Public Schs, 1983-; 1st Grade Tchr, St Mary's Sch, 1978-83; Rdg Tchr, Upward Bound Prog, No MI

Univ, 1981-; IRA; NCTE; NEA; cp/Commun Chorale; r/Cath; hon/Silver Scroll, 1977; Grad, summa cum laude; Dean's List, 7 Semesters; W/W Among HS and College Students; Intl Yth in Achmt; Outstg Yg Wom in Am.

LINDLEY, JANE ANN oc/Government Administrator; b/Oct 2, 1942; h/2435 Mary Place, Fort Washington, MD 20744; ba/Washington, DC; p/Gerald Davis Lindley, Rochester, IN; Mary Jane Lindley, Fort Washington, MD; ed/BA, Butler Univ, 1964; MLS, Univ of MD, 1973; pa/Lib Reference and Acquisitions Spec 1964-71, Reference Libn/Bibliographer 1971-76, Congl Res Admr, Congl Res Ser 1976-82, Public Affairs Spec, Congl Res Ser 1982-, Lib of Cong; Conslt, Battelle Meml Inst, 1970-; Nat Assn of Female Execs; Spec Libs Assn; Wom in Info Processing; Beta Phi Mu; Kappa Kappa Gamma; r/Bapt; hon/Outstg Univ Student, 1964; Lib of Congress Intern, 1975; Recip, Cultural Spec Grants, US Info Agy, 1981, 1982; W/W Am Wom; W/W Wash; Congl Staff Dir.

LINDLEY, JUDITH MORLAND-CONROW oc/Executive; b/Mar 25, 1948; h/PO Box 97, North Palm Springs, CA 92258; ba/Same; m/Jimmy McCoy; c/Pamela Irene Ames, Jimmy Joseph-Howard; p/Mrs Hazel Caesar, San Diego, CA; ed/HS, La Canada High; pa/Owner/Operator, Tri-Color Cattery, 1973; Pres/Fdr, Calico Cat Registry Intl, 1978; Operator, Animal Helpline, 1979; r/Mormon; hon/Pubs, Calico Cat Registry Handbook 1978, Articles in Cat World 1981, Cat Fancy 1982; W/W Am Wom; W/W W.

LINDO, BENICE ZINNET oc/Educational Consultant, Public Speaker; b/Oct 21, 1937; ba/Box 5090, Beverly Hills, CA 90210; m/Jess Samuels (dec); c/Lisa Rachel; p/Louis and Dora Stackel Richman; ed/BA, cum laude, Ed, Bklyn Col, 1959; MA w Hons in Rdg, CA St Univ LA, 1971; Postgrad, Univ of CA Riverside, 1973-75; PhD in Psych, US Intl Univ, 1977; Cert'd Tchr, NY, CT, CA, Israel; pa/Var Tchg Positions, 1959-64; Miller-Unruh Rdg Spec, Lawndale Unified Schs, 1967-69; Instr, Eng, Rdg, Tel Aviv, 1969-70; Miller-Unruh Rdg Spec, Compton Unified Schs, 1970-74; Instr, Rdg Lab, Compton Jr Col, 1971-74; Instr, Ed, Pepperdine Univ, 1972-78; Instr, Dept of Humanities, Univ of CA LA, 1974-; Dean of Financial Planning and Mgmt, So Sts Univ, 1982-; Tng and Devel Tnr, Assertive Discipline Courses, Ednl TV, Canter & Assocs, 1978-81, CA St Univ Fullerton 1978-79, Univ of La Verne 1979-81, Univ of HI 1980-; Instr, Dept of Arts Mgmt Tng, Bus Hlth and Indust Corps, Univ of CA LA, 1980-; Instr, Nationwide Presentations Assertiveness Tng, Schaffer Pubs Inc, 1982-; Prog Coor, Dept of Humanities, Lng Resources Ctr, Ext Div, Univ of CA LA, 1974-76; Reg Dir, CA Commun Cols Tutorial Assn, 1977-78; Adm Dir, Lng Resources Ctr, 1976-78; Pres, Chm of Bd, Lindo Ednl Corp, 1978-; Ednl Conslt; Bd of 'Advrs, Cert Planners of Am; Nat Assn Female Execs; Rdg Specs of CA; cp/Millionaire's; r/Sci of Mind Ch Clb; hon/Author, Instant Phonics Kit 1971, Black Ghetto Dialect Textbook 1972, Instant Record Keeper for Individualized Reading 1973, Instant Contracts for Prescriptive Teaching 1973, The Assertive Parent Kit 1981; Host, Impact Radio Show, 1976; W/W W.

LING, ROBERT F oc/Professor of Statistics, Consultant; b/Apr 21, 1939; h/102 Brookwood Drive, Clemson, SC 29631; ba/Clemson, SC; m/Sue; ed/MA, Math, Univ of TN, 1963; MPhil 1968, PhD in Stats 1971, Yale Univ; pa/Prof, Dept of Math Sci, Clemson Univ, 1977-; Vis'g Prof, Owen Grad Sch of Mgmt, Vanderbilt Univ, 1982; Vis'g Prof, Grad Sch of Bus, Univ of Chgo, 1983; Am Statistical Assn, Assoc Editor of Jour 1977-; Classification Soc, Edit Bd of Jour 1983-; Intl Assn for Statistical Computing; hon/Pubs, Exploring Statistics with IDA 1979, IDA: A User's Guide to the Interactive Data Analysis and Forecasting System 1982, Conversational Statistics with IDA 1982, Res Articles in Var Profl Jours; Mensa; Fellow, Am Statistical Assn; Am Men of Achmt; W/W Technol Today; Am Men and Wom of Sci; W/W Frontier Sci and Technol; W/W World.

LINKSZ, JULIA FRAKNOI oc/ Research Regarding Mental Health Status of a Non-Psychiatric Patient Population; b/Feb 12, 1915; h/35 East 84th Street, New York, NY 10028; ba/ New York, NY; m/Arthur; p/Isidor and Ethel Friedlander (dec); ed/Dipl, Univ of Budapest, 1938; PhD, summa cum laude, Univ of Szeged, Hungary, 1945; Postdoct Fellow, Menninger Foun, 1958-60; pa/Res Regarding Mtl Hlth Status of a Non-Psychi Patient Population, 1978-; Clin Psychol, TN Dept of Mtl Hlth and Mtl Retard, 1976-78; Proj Mgr, Personalized Progs for Sentenced Offenders, Dade Co Dept of Rehab, 1975-76; Assoc, then Asst Prof, Dept of Psychi, Med Sch, Univ of PA, 1960-75; Sr Psychol, then Dir, Psychol Tng, Inst of Phy Med and Rehab, NY Univ Med Ctr, 1962-65; Other Previous Positions; Fellow, PA Psychol Assn; Am Psychol Assn; Am Grp Psychotherapy Assn; En Psychol Assn; TN Psychol Assn; Phila Soc of Clin Psychols; NY Soc of Clin Psychols; World Mtl Hlth Assn; Menningen Sch of Psychi Alumni Assn; Archivist, Histn of Semmelweis Sci Soc; hon/Pubs, "Emotional and Cognitive Aspects of Schizophrenia" 1977, "Intensive Short-term Treatment with Limited Goals for Hospitalized Psychiatric Patients" 1977; W/W Am Wom.

LINNEN, EVELYN J oc/Bank Manager; b/Nov 15, 1944; h/13569 Antares, Littleton, CO 80124; ba/Denver, CO; c/Christopher; p/Charles and Evelyn Knell, Lakewood, CO; ed/Att'd En MT St Col; pa/Ofc Mgr, Fidelity Fin Co, Billings, MT, 1963-73; Collections Supvr, J C Penney Co, Denver, CO, 1973-74; Pre-Legal Supvr, GEFCO, Denver, CO, 1974-77; Corporate Ofcr & VP, U Bk of Littleton, Litleton, CO, 1977-83; cp/Zonta Intl, 1984-.

LIOU, KUO-NAN oc/Professor of Atmospheric Sciences; b/Nov 16, 1943; h/3401 South Monte Verde Drive, Salt Lake City, UT 84109; ba/Salt Lake City, UT; m/Agnes L Y; c/Julia C C; ed/BS, Taiwan Univ, 1965; MS 1968, PhD 1970, NY Univ; pa/Res Assoc, Goddard Inst for Space Studies, 1970-72; Asst Prof, Univ of WA Seattle, 1972-74; Assoc Prof 1975-80, Prof 1980-, Dir of Grad Studies 1981-84, Univ of UT SLC; Radiation Energy Com, Am Meteoro-

logical Soc, 1977-85, Chm 1982-83; CoChm, AMS Fifth Conf on Atmospheric Radiation, 1983; Panel of ISCCP, Climate Res Com, Nat Acad of Scis, 1984-87; hon/Author, An Introduction to Atmospheric Radiation 1980, "Recent Progress in Atmospheric Radiation" 1984, "A Two-Dimensional Radiation-Turbulence Climate Model: Sensitivity to Cirrus Radiative Properties" 1984, "A Numerical Experiment on the Interactions of Radiation, Clouds and Dynamic Processes in a General Circulation Model" 1984, Num Others; Fdrs Day Awd, NY Univ, 1971; Gardner Fellow Awd, Univ of UT, 1978; Fellow, Optical Soc of Am, 1983.

LIPKIN, BERNICE SACKS oc/ Science Administrator; b/Dec 21, 1927; h/1331 Belhaven Road, Bethesda, MD 20817; ba/Bethesda, MD; m/Lewis; c/ Joel, Libbe; ed/BS, NEn Univ, 1949; MA, Boston Univ, 1950; PhD, Columbia Univ, 1961; pa/US Govt, 1963-; NIH, 1972-; Sigma Xi; IEEE; APA; Sigbio; r/ Jewish; hon/Pubs, Picture Processing and Psychopicturics 1970, Num Articles in Image Processing, Picture Processing and Text Manipulation Programming Stratigies; Sigma Xi, 1961; Epilepsy Soc Postdoct F'ship, 1961-62.

LIPSCOMB, JOHN ROBERT oc/ College Administrator; b/Apr 26, 1922; h/Box 435, Mount Berry, GA 30149; ba/ Mt Berry, GA; m/Lenore Wyatt; c/ Daniel Wyatt, Patricia Ann, Roberd Edward; p/Oscar C and Ella Cornelison Lipscomb (dec); ed/Att'd Berry Col, Butler Univ; BS, Univ of MD; MS, The George Wash Univ; USA Cmd & Gen Staff Col; mil/Lt Col, USA; pa/Career Ofcr, USA, 1945-65; VP for Resources, Berry Col, 1965-; Higher Ed Assn; Coun for Advmt & Support of Ed; Assn of USA; AF Assn; cp/Friends of Free China; Rotary; Am Heart Assn; hon/ Author, "A Living Legend," Hist of Berry Col; Legion of Merit; Jt Sers Commend Medal; Army Commend Medal; S'ship Medallion, Univ of MD; Intl W/W Contemp Achmt.

LIPSITT, LEWIS PAEFF oc/Professor, Research Scientist; b/Jun 28, 1929; h/63 Boylston Avenue, Providence, RI 02906; ba/Providence, RI; m/Edna Duchin; c/Mark S, Ann D; p/Joseph and Anna Paeff Lipsitt (dec); ed/BA, Univ of Chgo, 1950; MS, Univ of MA, 1952; PhD, Univ of IA, 1957; mil/USAF, 1952-54; pa/Instr of Psych 1957-58, Asst Prof of Psych 1961-66, Prof of Psych 1966-, Dir of Child Study Ctr 1967-, Prof of Med Sci 1974-, Brown Univ; Pres, Div 7, Am Psychol Assn, 1980-81; Chair, Com on Res Support, APA, 1982-83; Mbrship Secy, Intl Soc for the Study of Behavioural Devel, 1981-83; Mem at Large, Sect J, AAAS, 1982-; hon/USPHS Spec Res Fellow, London, 1966, 1972-73; Guggenheim Fellow, London, 1972-73; Fellow, Ctr for Adv'd Study in the Behavioural Scis, 1979-80; W/W World; W/W E; W/W Frontier Sci and Technol; Men of Achmt.

LIPSY, JACK HOWARD oc/Publisher; b/Jun 27, 1917; h/1139 Woodbrook Drive, Largo, FL 33540; ba/Largo, FL; m/Helen Macko; c/Barbara Jean Tokarske, Bette Jane Lipsy-Stephens; p/ Jack and Florence Lipsy (dec); ed/BS 1939, MA 1951, Postgrad 1953, NJ St Col; Postgrad, Rutgers Univ 1954, 1966,

Univ of S FL 1966; mil/Served to Lt Cmdr, USNR, 1942-45; pa/Host, Radio Show, The Sentinel Listens, 1981-; Publisher, Largo Sentinel, 1974-; Dir, Placement, Res and Testing, Nat Aviation Acad, St Petersburg-Clearwater, 1967-68; Dir, Hd Start Child Devel and Fam Sers of Pinellas Co, 1966-67; Ednl Conslt and Reg Pers and Sales Mgr, Field Enterprises Ednl Corp, 1958-66; Adm Prin, Deal Schs, 1957-58; Other Former Positions; FL Press Assn; Nat Notary Assn; cp/Repub Exec Com; Lions; Rotary; Masons; r/Epis; hon/ Contbr, Articles to Profl Jours; Purple Heart; Navy Cross.

LIROFF, MARILYN oc/Attorney; b/ Jun 11, 1945; h/7361 Northwest 35th Court, Lauderhill, FL 33319; ba/Fort Lauderdale, FL; m/Kenneth Paul; c/Erica Ruth, Johanna Beth; p/Jack and Esther Pardo, Lauderhill, FL; ed/BA, St Univ of NY Buffalo, 1967; MA in Hist, Queens Col of NY, 1973; JD, summa cum laude, Nova Law Ctr, 1979; pa/ Tchr, Hist, Lindenberg HS, 1967-69; Tchr, Hist, Ctl HS, 1969-71; Adj Prof, Nova Law Ctr, 1982; Assoc Atty, Weaver, Weaver & Lardin, 1979-; B'nai B'rith Justice Unit; hon/Pubs, "Prevailing Defendant's Right to Recover Attorney Fees in an Action under Title VII of the Civil Rights Act of 1964: Christianburg, Garment Co vs Equal Employment Opportunity Commission," 1979; Law Review; Dean's List; Wentworth Foun Awd; CJS Awd for Significant Legal S'ship.

LISTER, IRVIN C oc/Chiropractor, Lecturer; b/Oct 18, 1933; m/Dorothy Elizabeth Clevenger; c/Elizabeth Ann, David Canon, Linda Dianne; ed/Att'd, Univ of Tuscaloosa 1951-52, Del Mar Col 1953-54, Tulane Univ 1954-55, Wm & Mary Col 1955-57; DC, Logan Col of Chiro, 1961; Postgrad, LA St Univ, 1974; mil/Served in USN Hosp Corps, 1952-56; pa/Pvt Pract in LA, 1961-; Lic'd in FL, LA; Delivered Lecture, X-ray Interpretation, Chiro Assn of LA, 1971; Lectr on Chiro throughout SW LA, 1975-76; Chiro Assn of LA, Pres 1964-65, Pres of Dist III 1961-63, Bd of Dirs 1963-64, 1965-66, Chair of Spkr's Bur 1966-70; Intl Chiropractors Assn; Am Chiro Assn; Parker Chiro Res Foun; cp/Lafayette Lions Clb; hon/Lion of the Yr, 1961.

LISZAK, MARY REGINA oc/Assistant to Chancellor and Affirmative Action Director; b/Jun 22, 1956; h/Box 357, Auke Bay, AK 99821; ba/Juneau, AK; m/Randall William Ackley; c/Holly Elizabeth, Randall, Linda, Katherine; p/ Joseph Michael and Rose Marie, Avon Lake, OH; ed/AA, 1976; BS, Biol, 1979; pa/Asst to the Chancellor/Affirmative Action Dir, Univ of AK Juneau, 1981-; Am Assn for Affirmative Action, AK Chapt, Bd of Dirs 1982-; U Students of Univ of AK Juneau, Pres 1980-81, Rep 1979-80; AK Statewide Student Assn, Bd of Dirs 1980-81; cp/Soroptimist, 1982-; Long Range Planning in the Arts Com, 1978-; r/Rom Cath; hon/ Outstg Chem Student, 1976; Outstg Dancer, CAPHER, 1978; Outstg Yg Wom of Am.

LIT, JOHN oc/University Professor and Department Chairman; b/Aug 31, 1937; h/139 Briarcliffe Crescent, Waterloo, Ontario N2L 5T6; ba/Waterloo, Ontario; m/Chi-Mui; c/Wilson Moses,

Eugene Stephen; p/Po-Woo, Hong Kong; Kit-Wai (dec); ed/BSc 1958, DipEd 1961, Hong Kong Univ; DSc, magna cum laude, Universite Laval, 1969; pa/Prof and Chm of Physics 1980-, Assoc Prof 1977-80, Wilfrid Laurier Univ; Adj Prof 1980-, Adj Assoc Prof 1977-80, Univ of Waterloo; Assoc Prof 1975-77, Asst Prof, Universite Laval; Canadian Assn of Physicists, Chm, Div of Optics 1977-78; Optical Soc of Am, R W Wood Prize Com 1978; *Canadian Journal of Physics*, Guest Editor 1979, 1980, 1982; *Journal of the Optical Society of America*, Assoc Editor 1974-79; r/Anglican; hon/Author, Over 100 Articles on Optics; Am Men and Wom of Sci; W/W E.

LITTELL, NORMAN MATHER oc/ Retired Lawyer; b/Sep 8, 1899; h/855 Mason Avenue, Deale, MD 20751; m/ Katherine Maher (dec); c/Katherine M, Norman Mather; p/Joseph and Clara Munger Littell (dec); ed/AB, Wabash Col, 1921; MA, Christ Ch Col, Oxford Univ, England, 1924; Postgrad, Harvard Univ Law Sch, 1925; LLB, Univ of WA Law Sch, 1939; SATC, Wabash Col, 1920-21; pa/Fgn Correspondent, Phila Pub Ledger, Leag of Nations, Geneva, 1923; Admitted to WA St Bar, 1929; Assoc, US Supr Ct, 1933; Law Firm, Bogle, Bogle & Gates, 1929-34; Spec Asst US Atty Gen and Asst Solicitor, Dept of Interior, Representing Adm Petro Code and Pacific Coast Petro Agy in NW Sts, 1934-35; Ptnr, Law Firm of Evans, McLaren & Littell, 1936-39; Asst Atty Gen, US, in Charge Public Lands Div, 1939-44; Gen Corporate and Intl Law Pract, Wash, 1944-; Gen Counsel, Claims Atty, Navajo Tribe Indians, 1947-67; Am, Intl, Fed, Inter-Am, MD, DC Bar Assns; Am Soc Intl Law; Beta Theta Pi; cp/Intl C of C; Oxford Soc, Wash; Orgr, Exec Secy, Nat Com Against Nazi Persecution of Minorities, 1941-44; Orgr, 1st Pres, Am Yth Hostels; Testified Before Congl Coms in Aid of Fgn Investments, 1948-51; Appt'd Mem, Congl Adv Com, 1980; hon/Author, *Trails of the Sea*, 1982; Contbr, Articles, Papers on Fgn Investmt Law to Profl Jours; W/W World.

LITTLE, ELBERT LUTHER JR oc/ Botanist, Dendrologist; b/Oct 15, 1907; h/924 20th Street, South, Arlington, VA 22202; ba/Washington, DC; m/ Ruby Rema Rice; c/Gordon Rice, Melvin Weaver, Alice Conner; p/Elbert Luther and Josephine Conner Little (dec); ed/ BA 1927, BS 1932, Univ of OK; MS 1929, PhD 1929, Univ of Chgo; pa/Asst Prof of Biol, SWn OK St Univ, 1930-33; Asst to Assoc Forest Ecologist, Forest Ser, USDA, 1934-41; Dendrologist 1942-67, Chief Dendrologist 1967-76, Forest Ser, Wash, DC; Collaborator 1965-76, Res Assoc 1976-, US Natural Mus of Hist, Smithsonian Instn; Fellow, Soc of Am Foresters; Wash Acad of Scis; OK Acad of Sci; AAAS; Explorers Clb; Botanical Soc of Am; Am Soc of Plant Taxonomists; Am Inst of Biol Scis, Governing Bd, 1956-60; Intl Soc for Plant Taxonomy; Sociedad Botanica de Mexico; hon/Pubs, *Checklist of United States Trees* 1979, *Atlas of United States Trees* 1971-81, *Audubon Society Field Guide to North American Trees, Eastern Region and Western Region* 1980, *Forest Trees of Oklahoma* 1981, *Important Forest Trees of the*

United States 1978, Articles; Superior Ser Awd, USDA, 1960; Dist'd Ser Awd, 1973; Dist'd Ser Awd, Am Forestry Assn, 1981; Profl Achmt Awd, Univ of Chgo, 1982; W/W Am; W/W World.

LITTLE, FLORENCE HERBERT oc/ Teacher; b/Jul 7, 1911; h/St James Place, 333 Lee Drive, Apartment 327, Baton Rouge, LA 70808; m/Alfred Lamond (dec); c/Alan Rush, Barbara Joan L Votaw; p/Charles Arthur and Bertha Schlachter Herbert (dec); ed/BA, MI St Univ, 1932; MSE, Drake Univ, 1962; Grad Study, Wn St Col, Denver Univ; pa/Accompanist 1931-35, Undergrad Tchr 1932, MI St Univ; Pvt Piano and Voice Lessons, 1932-55; Subst Tchr, 1933-35; Tchr, Bridgeport 1956, Holt 1945-46, Hanover 1949-50, Pittsford 1950-53, Des Moines 1953-73; Pvt Tutor and Subst Tchr, St Charles and St John the Bapt Parishes, 1980-; Kappa Kappa Iota, Pres 1969-70, 1979-81, Treas, St VP 1975-76, 1980-81; Mu Phi Epsilon, Corresponding Secy; ABWA, Treas 1977-78; NEA, Life Mem; ISEA; DMEA; AAUW; cp/Baton Rouge Recorder Soc; Capitol City CB Clb; Baton Rouge Orchid Soc; River Parish Fam CB Clb, Corresponding Secy 1979, 1980, VP 1982; St John Civil Def Unit; Friends of the Cabildo; Smithsonian Instn; Jefferson Orchid Soc; AARP; r/ Presb; hon/Nat Hon Soc; NSF Grant, 1963-64; Personalities of W and MW; Notable Ams; Commun Ldrs and Noteworthy Ams; Book of Hon; Am Registry Series; Personalities of S; World W/W Wom; DIB; Intl W/W Commun Ser; Men and Wom of Distn; Anglo-Am Academs; Intl W/W Intells.

LITTLE, SANDRA LYNN oc/Educator; b/Jul 30, 1941; h/RD 3, Box 418C, Shippensburg, PA 17257; ba/University Park, PA; m/Larry J; c/Caroline A; p/ Chester Leon Kelso; Yvonne Evelyn Bergeman, Cashmere, WI; ed/BA, Univ of LaVerne, 1963; MS, IN Univ, 1964; PhD, PA St Univ, 1984; pa/Asst Dir of Rec, Oak Pk Rec Dept, 1966-70; Supt of Rec, Elk Grove Pk Dist, 1970-71; Rec Supvr, Presch Dir, Johnson Co Pk and Rec Dist, 1972-73; Rec Coor, Pk Ridge Pk Dist, 1973-75; Instr, Triton Col, 1974; Instr, Rec and Pks, PA St Univ, 1975-; Rec and Pk Commr, Borough of Shippensburg, 1978-79; cp/Civic Symph, Oak Pk-River Forest, Bd of Dirs, Secy 1964-71; Oak Pk Village Day Care Ctr, Bd of Dirs 1967-68; LWV, KC, VP 1971-73; Ctl PA Fest of the Arts, Eval Chair 1981-83; hon/Pub, "Cooperative Goal Structuring," 1982; Reviewer for Num Texts in Rec and Pks; Hons Grad in PE, Univ of LaVerne, 1963; Commun Sers Awd, So IL Univ, 1967; W/W Am Cols and Univs; W/W Am Wom.

LIU, YUNG Y oc/Engineer and Manager; b/Mar 20, 1950; h/2043 Sunnydale, Woodridge, IL 60517; m/Teresa; c/ Sharon H Y, Alvin H L; p/Kan C and Mon W Chou; ed/BS, Nat Tsing-Hua Univ, 1971; MS 1976, ScD 1978, MIT; mil/AF, Republic of China, 1971-73; pa/ Prin Investigator of Liquid Metal Fast Breeder Reactor Pin Performance 1978-, Prin Investigator of Solid Breeder Mech Properties 1982-, Mgr of Solid Breeder Tritium Recovery 1983-, Mgr of Solid Breeder Perf/Lifetime Eval and Spec Mats 1983, ANL; Staff Engr, Entropy Ltd, 1977-78; Am Nuclear Soc;

Am Soc of Metals; Am Ceramics Soc; Fusion Power Assocs; Editor-in-Chief, *Free Chinese Monthly*, 1973-75; r/Bapt; hon/More Than 30 Contributed and Invited Papers in Profl Jours.

LIVINGSTON, JAY oc/Composer, Lyricist; h/ASCAP, One Lincoln Plaza, New York, NY 10023; m/Lynne; c/ Travilyn, Lara; p/Maurice and Rose Livingston (dec); ed/Pvt Piano and Harmony Lessons, Pgh; BA, Univ of PA, 1937; Univ of CA LA Ext Courses in Orchestration and Film Scoring; mil/ AUS, WWII; pa/Exclusive Contract, Paramount Pictures, 1945-53; Non-Exclusive Contract, Paramount, 1953-55; Free-Lance, All Maj Studios, incl'g, Paramount, Warners, 20th Century-Fox, Disney, Independents; ASCAP; Am Guild of Authors and Composers; Dramatists Guild, Motion Picture Acad; TV Acad; Record Acad; Composers and Lyricists Guild; Indiv Popular Songs Pub'd, Plus Songs for Over 100 Motion Pictures ("To Each His Own," "Golden Earrings," "Silver Bells," "Bonanza," "Mister Ed," "Buttons and Bows," "Mona Lisa," "Que Sera Sera," "Tammy," "Dear Heart,"), 1938-; Acad Awd Oscars for "Buttons and Bows" 1947, "Mona Lisa" 1951, "Que Sera Sera" 1956; Oscar Nominations for "Almost in Your Arms" from *Houseboat*, "Dear Heart," "Tammy"; Songwriters Hall of Fame, 1973; W/W Am; W/W World; W/W Theatre.

LIVINGSTON, RICHARD EUGENE JR oc/United States Government Executive; b/Aug 11, 1930; h/14717 Braddock Road, Centreville, VA 22020; ba/ Washington, DC; c/Leslie Diane, Richard Eugene III; p/Esther Virginia Gabbert Livingston, Lake Mary, FL; ed/ US Civil Aeronautics Sch of Air Traffic Control, 1958; MS in Bus Adm, George Wash Univ, 1969; Grad Wk, Col of the Armed Forces, 1969; BS in Ed, PA St Univ, 1953; mil/AUS Aviation, 1953-57; Army NG, 1957-66; USAR, 1967-; pa/ Chm, FAA, Rotorcraft Task Force, 1981-; FAA/NTSB Prog Mgr, 1979-81; US Dept of Trans Rep, Am Embassy, Bonn, W Germany; Dir, FAA Exec Secretariat, 1976-77; Chief, Air Traffic Div, FAA New England Reg, 1971-76; Air Traffic Control and Mgr, 1957-71; Assn for the Indust Col of the Armed Forces, Life Mem; PA St Univ Alumni Assn, Life Mem; Resv Ofcrs Assn of the US, Life Mem; Nat Aviation Clb, Life Mem; Am Army Aviation Assn, 1982-; Am Helicopter Soc, 1982-; AIAA, 1982-; Helicopter Assn Intl, 1981-; Intl Soc of Air Safety Investigators, 1981-; Bd of Dirs, PA St Alumni Clb of Gtr Metro Wash Area, 1980-81; r/Epis; hon/ Outstg Fed Employee Awd, 1981-82, 1980-81, 1970-71, 1969-70; US Govt Spec Achmt Awd for Formulation of FAA Nat Rotorcraft Master Plan, 1983; W/W E.

LIVINGSTON, SALLY DUKE oc/ Resources Consultant to Organizations and Entrepreneurs; b/Oct 23, 1932; h/ 866 Cortez, Foster City, CA 94404; ba/ Same; c/Michael, Barbara, David, Margaret Anne Gannon; p/Frances Montgomery Duke, Wichita, KS; ed/BA, Urban Studies/Commun Ldrship, SF St Univ, 1975; Certs: Graphics Facilitation and Process Consltg, Sibbet & Assocs and Interaction Assocs, 1979-81; pa/ Fdr/Prin, MAINSTREAM Planning

Assocs, 1975-; Staff Assoc, CORO Foun, 1975; Intern, Kramer Blum & Assocs of SF, 1974-75; Chair/Reg Dir, Call for Action Inc, 1969-73; Wom Entrepreneurs of Bay Area, Ed Dir 1979-80, Pres 1982, Chair for Long Range Planning 1983; Adv Bd, *Business Woman Magazine*, 1983; Bd of Dirs, Secy, ACTIVATE, 1981-; Bay Area Orgl Devel Netwk, 1980-; r/Prot; hon/Soroptomist Awd, Wom Helping Wom, 1983; Excell Ldrship, Wom Entrepreneurs, 1983; Wom's Caucus and Chapt Awd, Golden Gate Chapt, Am Soc for Tng and Devel, 1976, 1981; W/W CA; W/W W.

LIZUT, NONA M oc/Administrator of Health Services Division; b/Aug 8; h/1408 Santa Rosa Drive, Santa Fe, NM 87501; ba/Santa Fe, NM; m/William J; c/Charles P Price III; p/Charley and Alba Moore (dec); ed/HS Grad, Tucumcari, NM, 1941; Student of Bus Adm, NM St Univ, 1941-42; pa/Secy 1942-44, Envir Div 1941-68, NM St Hlth Dept; Adm Secy 1968-74, Adm Asst to Dpty Dir 1974-78, NM Hlth and Social Sers Dept; Adm Asst to Dpty Secy 1978-82, Admr of Hlth Sers Div 1982-, NM Hlth and Envir Dept; NM Water Pollution Control Assn, Adm Ofcr 1946-71, Hon Lifetime Mem; NM Public Hlth Assn, Secy-Treas 1962-68, Pres-Elect 1969; Nat Secys Assn, 1955-72; Capitol City BPW, VP, Prog Chm; cp/Santa Fe C of C, Woms Div, 1977-; NM Round Dance Assn, Past Pres, Newsletter Editor; r/Presb; hon/W/W Am Wom; W/W W.

LLAURADO, JOSEP G oc/Nuclear Medicine Physician, Scientist, Educator; b/Feb 6, 1927; ba/Veterans Administration Hospital-115, Loma Linda, CA 92357; m/Deirdre Mooney; c/Thadd, Oleg, Montserrat, Raymund, Wilfred, Mireya; ed/BS, BA, Balmes Inst, Barcelona, 1944; MD 1950, PhD in Pharm 1960, Univ of Barcelona Sch of Med; MS, Biomed Engrg, Drexel Univ; pa/Res Asst, Royal Postgrad Sch of Med at Hammersmith Hosp, London, 1952-54; Asst Prof, Univ of Otago Sch of Med, Dunedin, New Zealand, 1954-57; Fellow, M D Anderson Hosp and Tumor Inst, 1957-58; Fellow, Univ of UT Col of Med, SLC, 1958-59; Sr Endocrinologist, Pfizer Med Res Labs, 1959-61; Assoc Prof, Univ of PA Sch of Med, 1963-67; Prof, Marquette Univ and Med Col of WI, 1967-82; Clin Dir, Nuclear Med Ser, VA Med Ctr, 1977-82; Chief, Nuclear Med Ser, VA Hosp, 1983-; Prof, Dept of Radiation Scis, Loma Linda Univ Sch of Med, 1983-; Fellow, Am Col Nutrition; Soc of Nuclear Med, Computer and Acad Couns; Sr Mem, IEEE; Fdg Mem, Soc Math Biol; Charter Mem, Biomed Engrg Soc; Endocrine Soc; Am Physiological Soc; Am Soc for Pharm and Exptl Therapeutics; Royal Soc of Hlth; Other Profl Mbrships; hon/Author, More Than 250 Pubs in Sci Jours; Rockefeller Foun Vis'g Prof, Universidad del Valle, Colombia, 1958; USA Rep to Symp on Dynamic Studies w Radioisotopes in Clin Med and Res, Intl Atomic Energy Agy, Rotterdam 1970, Knoxville 1974; IEEE Milwaukee Sect Meml Awd for Dedication to Biomed Engrg, 1975; Commend Cert, BSA, 1980; W/W Frontier Sci and Technol; Dir Med Specs; W/W Technol Today; World W/W Sci; Am Men of Sci.

LLOYD, DENISE ELAINE oc/Mental Health Counselor; b/Jan 22, 1959; h/704 Cowgirl, #4, Chillicothe, MO 64601; ba/Trenta, MO; p/James H Lloyd, Kansas City, MO; ed/BA in Psych, Lincoln Univ, 1980; MS in Cnslg, Ctl MO St Univ, 1981; pa/Juv Attention Ctr Residential Cnslr, 1979-80; KC Pks and Rec Ldr, Juv Ct Ser, 1980, 1981; Back-Up Yth Wkr 1981-82, Mtl Hlth Cnslr 1982-, Ctl MO Mtl Hlth Ctr; Div Fam Sers Permanancy Placement Team; BPW; Nat Assn of Female Execs; Alpha Kappa Alpha Sorority Inc; r/Bapt; hon/Dist'd Am Awd; Outstg Scholastic Achmt; Am Outstg Names and Faces; W/W Among Am Cols and Univs.

LO, ALLEN KWOK-WAH oc/Executive; b/Sep 2, 1937; h/5022 Hidden Branches Drive, Dunwoody, GA 30338; ba/Atlanta, GA; m/Amy; c/David; p/Lo Kwong Man and Lee Bo Chun; ed/Indust Engr, Hong Kong Tech Col; pa/Indust Designer, NCR Hong Kong, 1959-64; Asst Mgr, 3D Indust Ltd, Hong Kong, 1964-67; Dir of Res and Devel, Ashahi Ltd, Tokyo, 1967-70; VChm, Nimslo Corp, and Pres, Nimslo Res, 1971-; cp/Pres, Chinese Am Inst, Atlanta; hon/More Than 100 Patents in the Field of 35mm 3-D Photographic Sys; Winner, One of the Ten Outstg Engrg Achmt Awds in the US for Nimslo 3-D Photographic Sys, Nat Soc of Profl Engrs, 1983; W/W World; W/W Fin and Indust.

LOCKETT, VERNON EARL oc/Social Worker; b/Oct 27, 1944; h/4126 Woodmont, Houston, TX 77045; ba/Houston, TX; m/Bettie; c/Roderick, Jerry; p/Mr and Mrs Henry Postiell, Houston, TX; ed/BA, Rec and Sociol, So Univ, 1968; Master of Social Wk, Univ of Houston, 1973; pa/Asst Chief of Spec Progs 1978-, Casewkr III 1976-78, Mtl Hlth, Mtl Retard Auth of Harris Co; Dir of Sum Yth Prog, Neighborhood Centers-Day Care, 1974-76; cp/Past Pres of Brentwood Dolphins, Little Leag Football Org, 1974-78; Bd Mem, TX Alliance of Info and Referral Sers, 1982; r/Cath; hon/Co-Author of Article, "Introducing Black and Chicano Content into Social Work Curriculum: A Recommendation" in *Social Work Education Reporter*, 1972.

LOGAN, BARBARA G oc/Pharmacist; b/Dec 20, 1941; h/1203 Bay Street, Beaufort, SC 29902; ba/Beaufort, SC; m/William Thomas; c/Richard E Akers Jr, Matthew G Akers, Elizabeth, Mary Frances, Barbara A; p/Mr and Mrs Malcolm Goodwin, Beaufort, SC; ed/BS in Pharm, Univ of NC, 1964; MS in Biol, Univ of SC, 1978; pa/Pharm, Duke Univ Hosp, 1965; Pharm, Eckerds, 1966-70; Pharm, Beaufort, Jasper Comprehensive Hlth (Dir of Pharm), 1971; Current Pharm, Aimar's Pharm; Profl Spkr, Pharmacology, to Med Grps; cp/Bd of Dirs, Beaufort Beautification; hon/Author, Articles Pub'd in *Palmetta Pharmacist Magazine*, 1982; Pharm Senate Awd, Univ of NC, 1964; SC Wom Pharm of the Yr, 1982.

LONG, GERALDINE E oc/Professor of Nursing; b/Jul 9, 1951; h/14034 Southwest 106 Terr, Miami, FL 33186; ba/Coral Gables, FL; c/Lawrence John; p/William S Kerridge and Geraldine A Talcott, Miami, FL; ed/BSN 1973, MSN 1980, Univ of Miami; PhD, Univ of FL, 1983; pa/RN, Mercy Hosp, 1973-77; Childbirth Edr, PACE, 1975-78; Instr 1977-80, Asst Prof 1981-83, Undergrad Curric Coor 1983-84, Univ of Miami; ANA; NLN; Phi Kappa Phi; Sigma Theta Tau; Kappa Kelta Pi; Phi Delta Kappa; ANF; r/Cath; hon/Donaldson Awd, 1973; Preferred Prof, 1980; W/W Am Wom.

LONG, LEONARD MICHAEL oc/Engineering Consultant; b/Jul 6, 1955; h/3030 Congress Boulevard, #69, Baton Rouge, LA 70808; ba/Baton Rouge, LA; p/William Anthony Jr and Joyce Eiserloh Long, Metairie, LA; ed/BS in Mech Engrg 1977, MS in Mech Engrg 1979, LA St Univ; pa/Proj/Maintenance Engr, Vulcan Mats Co, 1979-80; Proj Engr, Beard Engrg Inc, 1980-; ASME, Chm of Baton Rouge Sect; cp/Condominium Assn, Bd of Dirs, Treas; r/Rom Cath; hon/Contbr, Articles to Transactions of the ASME; W/W Frontier Sci and Technol; W/W World.

LONG, RICHARD L JR oc/Engineering Educator, Researcher; b/Jun 5, 1947; ba/Department of Chemical Engineering, New Mexico State University, Box 3805, Las Cruces, NM 88003; ed/BA in Chem Engrg, 1969; PhD in Chem Engrg, 1973; mil/1st Lt EN, USAR, Cmdr 377th Engrg, 440th Cmd, 1976-78; pa/Res Engr, E I DuPont, 1974-78; Prof, Lamar Univ, 1978-81; Prof, NM St Univ, 1981-; Indep Conslt, 1978-; AIChE, Chm of Rio Grande Sect, 1984; r/Meth; hon/Pubs, *A Guide to Writing and Problem Solving for Chemical Engineers* 1983, *Application of Interfacial Mechanics in Liquid/Liquid Mixing* 1983, "On Phenomenological Mechanochemical Continuum Models of Muscle" 1981; Phi Lambda Upsilon; Omega Chi Epsilon; Sigma Xi Res Awd, 1973; W/W Technol Today; W/W Engrg; W/W W.

LOPEZ, SARA I oc/Project Engineer; b/May 1, 1951; h/1731 Vincente Road, Concord, CA 94519; ba/San Francisco, CA; m/David Mata; c/Ricky; ed/BS, Indust and Chem Engrg, Universidad Centroamericana, 1975; MBA, Univ of SF, 1983; pa/Proj Engr, Bechtel Petro Inc, 1980-; Indust Engr, Shaklee Corp, 1979-80; Indust Conslt, Ctl Bk of Nicaragua, Managua, 1978; Prodn and Quality Control Mgr, Jaboneria Prego, SA, Granada, Nicaragua, 1977-78; Mixing and Baking Supt, Nabisco Cristal, Managua, 1976-77; Plant Engr, Polimeros Centramericanos, SA, Managua, 1975-76; Am Inst of Indust Engrs, 1979-; CA Alumni Assn, 1981; Assn of MBA Execs Inc, 1983; Am Chem Soc, 1981; cp/St Stephen's Wom's Guild, 1981; Rosicrucian Order, 1982; r/Cath; hon/Best HS Grad, 1969.

LOPEZ-GILSTRAP, MICHELLE ANN oc/Public Relations Director; b/Oct 19, 1951; h/1655 Vassar, Houston, TX 77006; ba/Houston, TX; m/Jose G Lopez; ed/BA, Jour, Ctl St Univ, 1973; pa/Public Relats Dir, Twelve Oaks Hosp, 1981-; Public Relats Coor, Jordan Assocs, 1980-81; Editor, OK Bkrs Assn, 1978-80; Editor, Am Fidelity Assurance, 1974-75; BPW, 1978-81; Pres of Town Clb Chapt 1979-81, Pres-Elect 1978-79; Intl Assn of Bus Communicators, 1978-; Treas 1978-79; OK Chapt, Public Relats Soc of Am, 1980-; Houston Area Hlth Public Relats Soc, 1981-; TX Public Relats Soc, 1981-; TX Hosp Public Relats and Mktg Soc, 1981-; Am Soc for Hosp Public Relats, 1982; r/Cath;

hon/OK Bkrs Assn Pres's Awd, 1980; Tech Communication Awd, Soc for Tech Communication, Houston Chapt, 1983; Yg Career Wom, Town Clb Chapt, BPW; Dist 10 Yg Career Wom, OK BPW; W/W S and SW; Personalities of S; World W/W Wom; Outstg Yg Wom of Am.

LORBEER, VIRGINIA L oc/Business Education Teacher and Student Activities Director; b/May 31, 1941; h/13965 East Oxford Place, Aurora, CO 80014; ba/Denver, CO; p/Earl C Lorbeer, Hays, KS; Alice L Schlemeyer Lorbeer (dec); ed/BS in Bus Ed and Eng, 1963; MA in Sec'dy Sch Adm, 1973; Postgrad Wk, 1976; pa/Bus Ed and Student Activs, Cheerleader, Pep Clb and Hon Cadet Sponsor, Manual HS, 1964-81; Bus Ed Tchr, Student Activs Dir, Student Coun Sponsor, Montbello HS, 1981-; Opport Sch (Night Sch), 1964-; Passenger Relats Agt, TWA, 1976-; Pt-time Model; Nat Cheerleader Assn; CO Bus Ed Assn; CO Ed Assn; r/Meth; hon/Pubs, "Building School Spirit" and *Let's Cheer*; Outstg Pep Clb and Cheerleader Sponsor, Rocky Mtn News; W/W Am; Personalities of W and MW; W/W Am Wom; DIB.

LORD, JACK oc/Actor, Director, Producer, Artist; b/Dec 30, 1930; ba/ Hawaii Five-0 Studios, Honolulu, HI 96816; m/Marie; p/William Lawrence and E Josephine O'Brien Ryan; ed/BS in Fine Arts, NY Univ, 1954; pa/Exhibs: Corcoran Gallery, Nat Acad Design, Whitney Mus, Bklyn Mus, Lib of Cong, Bibliotheque Nationale, Paris; Representation in Perm Collection, Metro Mus of Art; Appearances on Broadway in *Traveling Lady, Cat on a Hot Tin Roof*; Motion Picture Perfs: *Court Martial of Billy Michell, Williamsburg-The Story of a Patriot, Tip on a Dead Jockey, God's Little Acre, Man of the West, Hangman, True Story of Lynn Stuart, Walk Like a Dragon, Doctor No*; Leading Roles in TV Prodns: *Omnibus, Playhouse 90, Goodyear Playhouse, Studio One, US Steel*; TV Film Appearances: *Have Gun Will Travel, Untouchables, Naked City, Rawhide, Bonanza, Americans, Route 66, Gunsmoke, Stagecoach West, Dr Kildare, Greatest Show on Earth, Star Stoney Burke Series*; TV Appearances on *Combat, Chrysler Theater, 12 O'Clock High, Loner, Laredo*, Others; Star of *Hawaii, Five-O*; Creator, TV Shows, *Tramp Ship, Yankee Trader, McAdoo, The Hunter Series*; Writer of Original Screenplay, *Melissa*, 1968; Pres, Lord and Lady Enterprises Inc, 1968-; hon/Recip, St Gauden's Artist Awd 1948, Fame Awd 1963; Named to Cowboy Hall of Fame, 1963; Theatre World Awd, *Traveling Lady*, 1959.

LORD, WINSTON oc/President of Council on Foreign Relations; b/Aug 14, 1937; h/740 Park Avenue, New York, NY 10021; ba/New York, NY; m/Bette Bao; c/Elizabeth Pillsbury, Winston Bao; p/Oswald Bates and Mary Pillsbury (dec) Lord, Hobe Sound, FL; ed/BA, magna cum laude, Yale Univ, 1959; MA w Hons, Fletcher Sch of Law and Diplomacy, 1960; mil/Served w AUS, 1961; pa/Ofc of Congl Relats 1962, Ofc of Polit-Mil Affairs 1962-64, Ofc of Intl Trade 1964-67, Mem of Negotiating Team and Spec Asst to Chm of US Del to the Kennedy Round of Tariff Negotiations (Geneva) 1965-67, Dept of St; Intl Security Affairs, Policy Planning Staff 1967-69, Mem of Staff of Nat Security Coun, White House 1969-73, Spec Asst to Asst to the Pres for Nat Security Affairs 1970-73, Dir of Policy Planning Staff, Dept of St 1973-77, Pres of Coun on Fgn Relats 1977-, Dept of Def; Bd of Dirs: Atl Coun of the US, Ctr for Inter-Am Relats, Coun on Fgn Relats, Intl Rescue Com, Americas Soc; Bd of Govs: Atl Inst for Intl Affairs; Bd of Advrs: Fletcher Sch of Law and Diplomacy, Am Ditchley Foun; Asia Soc; Trilateral Comm; hon/Pub, "Our Careening Foreign Policy" in *Newsweek*, 1983; Dept of St Dist'd Hon Awd to Policy Planning Staff, 1977; LLD, Williams Col, 1979; W/W Am; W/W E; DIB; Intl Book of Hon; Intl W/W Intells; Profl Assn Execs.

LORET de MOLA, MARIA M oc/ Director of Marketing Information and Support; b/Sep 12, 1945; h/380 Prospect Avenue, Hackensack, NJ 07601; ba/ Secaucus, NJ; p/Melchor and Angela Loret de Mola, Miami, FL; ed/BS in Math 1966, MS in Math 1969, Fairleigh Dickinson Univ; pa/Proj Engr, Bendix Corp, 1966-69; Sys Analyst, ITT Data Sers, 1969-70; Tech Rep 1970-75, Tech Mgr 1975, En Reg Support Mgr 1975-78, Gen Elect Info Sers Co; Mgr, Sys Anal and Support, ITT World Communs, 1978-81; Dir of Mktg Info and Support, ITT US Transmission Sys, 1981-; Nat Assn of Female Execs; Intl Org of Wom in Telecommuns; IPA; hon/ Gen Elect Outstg Tech Rep, 1974; W/ W Am Wom; Men and Wom of Distn; W/W E.

LOS, CORNELIS ALBERTUS oc/ Econometrician; b/Dec 14, 1951; h/530 Riverside Drive, Apartment 3-B, New York, NY 10027; ba/New York, NY; m/ Diana Nikkolos; c/Francesca Rose Eloise; p/Klaas Los, Alkmaar, The Netherlands; ed/Candidatus, cum laude (Fellow) 1974, Doctorandus 1976, Univ of Groningen; Res Student, London Sch of Ec, Sch of Slavonic and E European Studies, 1975-76; Dipl, Inst Social Studies, The Hague, 1977; MPhil 1980, PhD 1983, Columbia Univ; pa/Tchg Asst 1978-80, Instr 1980-81, Columbia Univ; Adj Lectr, Hunter Col, 1980; Adj Lectr, CCNY, 1980; Economist, Fed Res Bk of NYC, 1981-; The Econometric Soc; Am Statistical Assn; Am Ec Assn; IEEE; AAAS; NY Acad of Scis; TSA&F Soc; UN Assn; r/Greek Orthodox; hon/ Author of Profl Res Papers and Reports, Book: *Econometrics of Models with Evolutionary Parameter Structures*; Fulbright Hays Travel Grantee, 1977; Lady van Renswoude of the Hague Foun, 4 Awds, 1974-75; Others.

LOTSPEICH, CAROL SAWYER oc/ Botanical and Ecological Consultant; b/ Dec 25, 1936; h/1130 Palmer Avenue, Winter Park, FL 32789; ba/Winter Park, FL; m/Lowell L; c/Lorelei, Lee, Karl; p/ Tom and Jackie Sawyer, San Miguel de Allende, Mexico; ed/BA, Univ of FL, 1959; Postgrad Studies, Univ of Ctl FL, Univ of FL, 1978; pa/Envir Conslt, Bio-Engrg Sers, 1976-78; Pres, Lotspeich and Assocs Inc; Fdr and Dir, FL Native Plant Soc, 1981-; FL Acad of Scis; Ecol Soc of Am; Soc for Range Mgmt; Tree Ring Soc; Assn of SE Biologists; hon/Contbr, *Progress in Wetlands Utilization and Management*, 1981; Orlando's Outstg Wom in Professions, 1982; Appt'd to the Orange Co Pks Adv Bd, 1981.

LOUGHLIN, MARY ANNE E oc/ Television Producer, Show Host; b/Jul 30, 1956; h/195 Triumph Drive, Northwest, Atlanta, GA; p/Dr and Mrs John F Loughlin, St Petersburg, FL; ed/BS, Mass Communs, FL St Univ, 1977; pa/ Prodr/Show Host, WTBS-TV, 1981-; News Prodr/Anchor, WECA-TV, 1977-81; Reporter, WFSU-FM, 1976; Am Wom in Radio and TV; Wom in Communs; Wom in Cable; r/Rom Cath; hon/Wom of Achmt, Atlanta Chapt of AWRT, 1982; Wom at Wk Broadcast Awds, Nat Comm on Wkg Wom, 3rd Place, 1982; 2 GA Emmy Awd Noms, 1982; W/W S and SW; Personalities of S.

LOVE, JIMMY DWANE oc/Chemist; b/Feb 2, 1946; h/PO Box 225, Honesdale, PA 18431; ba/Honesdale, PA; m/ Kathryn Janiece Head; c/Jeffrey Mark, John Kevin; p/Dwane and Loveta Love, Tulia, TX; ed/BS 1969, MS in Chem 1976, Stephen F Austin St Univ; pa/Mgr of Quality Control, Planning and Shipping 1982-, Mgr of Tech Sers 1978-81, Lab Mgr 1969-77, Moore Bus Forms; Owner of Love's Car Wash, 1978-; Am Chem Soc, 1983; cp/TAPPI, 1975-78; Dorflinger-Suydam Wildlife Sanctuary, 1983; r/Deacon, N St Ch of Christ, 1978-81; hon/W/W S and SW.

LOVE, MILDRED L oc/Vice President of Program Operations; b/Oct 25, 1941; h/25 West, 132nd Street, New York, NY 10037; ba/New York, NY; p/ Willie B and Irene B Love, Zwolle, LA; ed/BS, So Univ, 1963; Att'd, Univ of Pgh, 1968-69; pa/VP for Prog Opers, Nat Urban Leag Inc; Nat Assn of Black Social Wkrs; So Univ Alumni Assn; Nat Assn for Public Hlth Admrs; Delta Sigma Theta Inc; NY St Coun on Fam Planning; cp/NAACP; Nat Yth Advocacy Coalition CBO Wk Grp; Nat Comm on Unemployment Compensation; Bd of Mgrs, Harlem Br, YMCA; First VP, Nat Yth Employment Coalition; Bd of Public Affairs Coun; Coun on Ec Ed; Commun Adv Bd, NY Hosp; Social Action Com, N Manhattan Br, Delta Sigma Theta Soc; r/Gtr Cannan Bapt Ch; hon/Ford Foun F'ship; Recip, Num Hons and Commun Ser Awds; W/W Am Cols and Univs; W/W Among Black Ams.

LOVELADY, DAVID E oc/Commanding Ofcr; b/Feb 1, 1944; h/4106 Kipling Street, Virginia Beach, VA 23452; ba/New York, NY; m/Marilyn T Homer; p/Mr and Mrs H L Lovelady, Birmingham, AL; ed/BS, US Naval Acad, 1966; US Naval Test Pilot Sch, 1972; mil/USN, 1966-; US Naval Acad, 1962-66; pa/Br Ofcr, Weps Tng Ofcr, VF-213, 1968-71; 214 Combat Missions in Vietnam; Test Pilot, Naval Air Test Ctr, 1972-74; Safety Ofcr, Maintenance Ofcr, Opers Ofcr, VF-24, 1975-78; Hd, F-14 Flight Test, Pacific Missile Test Ctr, 197-80; Exec Ofcr 1981-82, Cmdg Ofcr 1982-, VF-143; Soc of Exptl Test Pilots, 1974-; Tailhook Assn, 1976-; Ret'd Ofcrs Assn, 1978-; Naval Inst, 1982-; US Naval Acad Alumni Assn, 1966-; r/Bapt; hon/12 Air Medals; 2 Navy Commend Medals; Navy Achmt Medal; Vietnamese Air Cross of Gallantry; Var Campaign and Ser Medals; Hon Grad, Aviation Safety Ofcrs Sch, 1975; Interviewed for Astronaut, 1980; Outstg Yg Men of Am; W/W S and SW.

LOW, JOHN HENRY oc/International Banker; b/Apr 5, 1954; h/64 East 86th Street, New York, NY 10028; ba/New York, NY; p/Mr and Mrs Henry J Low, New York, NY; ed/BSE, Elect Engrg and Computer Sci, Princeton Univ, 1976; Att'd, St Paul's Sch 1968-72, St Bernard's Sch 1960-68; pa/Mellon Bk, 1976-, Mgmt Trainee/Credit Analyst 1976-78; Credit Analyst, Frankfurt, W Germany, 1978-80; Intl Rep 1980, Asst Intl Ofcr 1980-81, Intl Ofcr 1981-82, Asst VP 1982-, Correspondent Bkg; Formerly w Morgan Guaranty Trust Co of NY, Sums 1971, 1973, 1974, 1975; AIAA; Aircraft Owners and Pilots Assn; Former Mem, Bd of Dirs, Princeton Alumni Assn of Wn PA, 1978-80; cp/Princeton Clb of NY; Univ Clb, NY; Harvard-Yale-Princeton Clb of Pgh; Univ Clb, Pgh; W/W E; W/W Aviation and Aerospace.

LOW, WALTER CHENEY oc/University Professor and Scientist; b/May 11, 1950; h/4565 Broadway, Indianapolis, IN 46205; ba/Indianapolis, IN; m/Margaret Mary; p/George C and Linda Q Low, Arroyo Grande, CA; ed/BS, Univ of CA Santa Barbara, 1972; MS 1974, PhD 1979, Univ of MI; pa/Res Fellow, Cambridge Univ, 1979-80; Res Fellow, Univ of VT Col of Med, 1980-83; Asst Prof, IN Univ Sch of Med, 1983-; AAAS; Soc for Neuroscis; Sigma Xi; Eta Kappa Nu; NY Acad of Scis; Phi Sigma Kappa; CA Scholastic Fdn; hon/Pubs, "Differences in Transmission through the Dorsal Column Nuclei in Spontaneously Hypertensive and Wistar-Kyoto Rats" 1983, "Independence of Blood Pressure and Locomotor Activity in Adult Hypertensive and Normotensive Rats" 1983, "Embryonic Septal Transplants Across a Major Histocompatibility Barrier: Survival and Specificity of Innervation" 1983, "Field Potential Evidence for Extrasynaptic Alterations in the Hippocampal CA1 Pyramidal Cell Population during Paired Pulse Potentiation" 1983, Num Others; NIH Res Ser Awd, 1979-80, 1981-83; AGAN Res Fellow, Am Heart Assn, 1980-81; NSF/NATO Postdoct F'ship, 1979-80; NIH Predoct F'ship, 1975-78; Univ of CA Hons Grad, 1972; CA St Scholar, 1968-72; Univ of CA Alumni Scholar, 1968-69; CA Scholastic Fdn Life Mem, 1968; Univ of CA Hons at Entrance, 1968; Am Men and Wom of Sci; W/W Frontier Sci and Technol.

LOWENGRUB, MORTON oc/Dean of Research and Graduate Development, Professor of Mathematics; b/Mar 31, 1935; h/1319 East First Street, Bloomington, IN 47401; ba/Bloomington, IN; m/Carol; c/John, Wendy, Paul; ed/BA, NY Univ, 1956; MS, CA Inst of Technol, 1958; PhD, Duke Univ, 1961; pa/Dean of Res and Grad Devel 1982-, Dir of Grad Studies 1970-72, Chm of Math Dept 1977-80, Assoc Prof to Prof 1967-, IN Univ; Asst Prof, Wesleyan Univ, 1963-67; Asst Prof, NC St Univ, 1961-63; Instr, Duke Univ, 1960-61; Edit Com, *Mathematics Reviews*, 1981-; Elected Mem, Coun of the Am Math Soc, 1981-; hon/Pubs, *Calculus with Analytic Geometry* 1976, *Classical Applied Mathematics* 1975, Others; Leverhulme Foun Res F'ship, Univ of Glasgow, 1962-63; NSF Postdoct F'ship, 1966-67; Sr Res F'ship, Sci Res Coun of Great Brit, 1974-75.

LOZOWSKI, MARY oc/Cytologist; ba/Nassau Hospital, Department of Pathology, 259 First Street, Mineola, NY 11501; p/William and Mary Charlotte Kapustka Lozowski; ed/BS, Fordham Univ, 1976; CT, Meml Sloan-Kettering Cancer Ctr, 1975; Postgrad, Hofstra Univ, 1978-; pa/Cytotechnologist, JFK Meml Hosp and Med Ctr, 1976-77; Cytology Supvr/Lectr, Pathol Dept, Nassau Hosp, 1978-; Metro Chapt, Kosciuszko Foun, Corresponding Secy 1982-84; Intl Acad of Cytology; Am Soc of Clin Pathologists; Am Soc of Cytology; Gtr NY Assn of Cytotechnologists; AAAS; hon/Pubs, "Metastatic Malignant Fibrous Histiocytoma in Lung Examined by Fine Needle Aspirate" 1980, "The Combined Use of Cytology and Colposcopy in Enhancing Diagnostic Accuracy in Preclinical Lesions of Uterine Cervix" 1982; W/W Am Wom.

LUBINSKI, ROSEMARY B oc/Associate Professor; b/Dec 5, 1946; h/30 Parkwood Drive, Amherst, NY 14226; ba/Amherst, NY; p/Leo Lubinski, Amherst, NY; ed/BA, Bloomsburg St Col, 1968; MA 1969, EdD 1976, Columbia Univ; pa/Spch Therapist, Scranton Public Schs, 1969-71; Instr, Marywood Col, 1970-71; Coor of Sch Progs, Columbia Univ, 1971-75; Instr, NY Univ, 195; Spch Pathologist, Jewish Hosp, 1972-75; Prof, St Univ of NY Buffalo, 1975-; ASHA; NY St Spch and Hearing Assn; Netwk in Aging; Spch and Hearing Assn of W NY; r/Rom Cath; hon/Pubs, "The Elderly Aphasic in the Nursing Home: Three Clinical Issues" 1983, "Language and Aging: An Environmental Approach to Intervention" 1981, Others; Ofc of Ed F'ship, 1968-69, 1971-75; Var Grants from St Univ of NY Buffalo; W/W Am Wom.

LUCAS, AUBREY KEITH oc/University President; b/Jul 12, 1934; m/Ella F Genn; c/Frances, Carol, Alan, Mark; p/Keith C (dec) and Audell Robertson Lucas; Hons 1955, MA 1956, Univ of So MS; PhD, FL St Univ, 1966; pa/Pres, Univ of So MS, 1975-; Pres, Delta St Univ, 1971-75; Dean of Grad Sch, Coor of Res and Prof of Higher Ed 1970-71, Registrar and Assoc Prof of Edni Adm 1963-70, Univ of So MS; Other Previous Positions; Bd of Dirs, Am Coun on Ed, 1984-; Bd of Dirs, Am Assn of St Cols and Univs, 1983-85; Comm on Nat Devel in Postsec'dy Ed; Omicron Delta Kappa; Phi Kappa Phi; Pi Kappa Pi; Pi Gamma Mu; Pi Tau Chi; Kappa Delta Pi; Phi Delta Kappa; Red Red Rose; Newcomen Soc of N Am; Kappa Pi; Pi Kappa Delta; MS Arts Comm, Chm; Phi Theta Kappa Hon Mem, Mem Nat Bd of Dirs 1980-; cp/Kiwanis Clb; Hattiesburg C of C; U Way; r/Parkway Hgts U Meth Ch; hon/Pub, *The Mississippi Legislature and Mississippi Public Higher Education: 1890-1960*; W/W Am; W/W S and SW; W/W Am Cols and Univs; DIB; Ldrs in Ed.

LUCAS, JOHN EDWARD oc/Director of Public Relations; b/Sep 22, 1953; ba/535 Pacific Avenue, San Francisco, CA 94133; m/Christine A; p/Mr and Mrs Joseph S Lucas, Miami, FL; ed/AA, Santa Monica Col, 1975; BA, Univ of CA Berkeley, 1977; pa/Staff Reporter, *Daily Californian*, 1976; Staff Reporter, *Novato Advance*, 1977-78; Exec Asst Ofcr, Bldg Indust Assn of No CA, 1978-79;

Public Relats Writer 1979-81, Edit Sers Mgr, David W Evans Inc; Dir of Public Relats, Evans Communs; Public Relats Soc of Am, SF Chapt, 1980-, Mbrship Chp 1983, Profl Devel Chp 1984; Bay Area Communs Coun; Intl Assn of Bus Communicators, 1979-; cp/Bay Area Yg Blues, 1982-; r/Rom Cath; hon/Writer, More Than 70 Feature Articles in Profl Trade Pubs on Behalf of Num Agy Clients; Accredited by PRSA as a Profl Public Relats Practitioner, 1984; Recip, Achmt of Merit Awd for Feature Writing from PRSA, No CA Chapts, 1982; W/W W; O'Dwyer's Dir of Public Relats Execs.

LUCKY, ROBERT W oc/Executive Director; b/Jan 9, 1936; h/238 Kemp Avenue, Fair Haven, NJ 07701; ba/Holmdel, NJ; m/Joan Jackson; c/David, Karen; p/Mr and Mrs Clyde A Lucky, Pittsburgh, PA; ed/BS in Elect Engrg 1957, MS 1959, PhD 1961, Purdue Univ; pa/Mem of Tech Staff 1961, Supvr of Signal Theory Grp 1964, Hd of Data Theory Dept 1965, Dir of Electronic Sys Res Lab 1977, Exec Dir of Communs Res Div 1981, AT&T Bell Labs; IEEE, Pres of Communs Soc 1977-79, VP 1977-79, Exec VP 1981; USAF Sci Adv Bd, 1978-, VChm 1983-; r/Meth; hon/Pubs, *Principles of Data Transmission* 1968, *Computer Communications* 1974; Outstg Yg Engr, 1967; Dist'd Alumnus, Purdue Univ, 1969; Armstrong Awd, IEEE, 1974; W/W Am.

LUM, ROBERT SING GHUN oc/Airport Architect; b/Aug 19, 1947; h/801 East Leslie Drive, San Gabriel, CA 91775; ba/New York, NY; m/Jasmine Ouyang; p/Mr and Mrs Edward Lum, Mission Viejo, CA; ed/Master of Urban and Reg Planning 1976, BArch 1972, VA Polytechnic Inst and St Univ; pa/Airport Arch, ICAO-UNDP, 1982-; Arch Rep, Trinidad and Tobago Horse Race Track Complex Proj, Froehlich & Kow, FAIA, 1980-82; Proj Arch, Froehlich & Kow, FAIA, 1979-80; Chief Arch, Lagos, Nigeria, Kola Bankole & Assocs, 1976-79; AIA; Royal Inst of Brit Archs; Nigerian Inst of Archs; Am Planning Assn; Smithsonian Inst; Constrn Specification Inst; r/Ch of Jesus Christ of LDS; hon/2nd Place, Univ Chess Tournament, 1970; Nat Student Register, 1969, 1970, 1971; Men of Achmt; W/W Commonwealth; Intl Register of Profiles; DIB; W/W Intells.

LUND, ANDERS EDWARD oc/Administrator; b/Sep 26, 1928; h/1108 College Avenue, Houghton, MI 49931; ba/Houghton, MI; ed/Mech Engrg, USN, 1946-49; BS, Sch of Forestry, CO St Univ, 1955; MF 1956, DF 1964, Sch of Forestry, Duke Univ; pa/Dir, Inst of Wood Res, MI Technological Univ, 1974-; Conslt, Forest Prods Cos, US Govt, St Govts, 1973-; Hd, TX Forest Prods Lab, 1967-73; Prof, TX A&M Univ; AWPA New Preservatives Eval; ASTM Metrication; RTA Res and Devel; ASTM Com on Wood; ASTM Com on Structural Adhesives; AWPA Site Selection; hon/Author, Over 18 Pubs in the Field of Wood Sci and Preservatives, 1962-83; Holder of Over 30 US Patents w Num Fgn Counterparts; Elected Fellow, Inst of Wood Sci, England; W/W Am.

LUND, SISTER CANDIDA oc/College Chancellor; h/7900 West Division Street, River Forest, IL 60305; ba/Same;

p/Fred S Lund (dec); Katharine Murray Lund Heck (dec); ed/BA, Ec and Polit Sci, Rosary Col; MA in Polit Sci, Cath Univ of Am; PhD in Polit Sci, Univ of Chgo; pa/Pres 1964-81, Chancellor 1981-, Rosary Col; Bd of Dirs, The Thomas More Assn, 1975-; Bd of Trustees, Clarke Col, 1981-; Coun Mem, IL Humanities Coun, 1982-; Bd of Trustees, Carnegie Foun for Advmt of Tchg, 1970-78; Bd of Dirs, Am Coun on Ed, 1977-81; cp/Commr, IL Comm on the Status of Wom, 1977-; r/Rom Cath; hon/Pubs, *Coming of Age* 1982, *Nunsuch* 1984, Others; Dist'd Citizen Awd, Prot Foun of Gtr Chgo, 1980; Profl Achmt Awd, Univ of Chgo Alumni Assn, 1974; Fellow, Royal Soc of Arts, London; Hon Docts: DLitt, Lincoln Col 1968, LLD, John Marshall Law Sch 1979, DHL, Marymount Manhattan Col 1979.

LUNDEEN, ROBERT WEST oc/Chairman of the Board; b/Jun 25, 1921; ba/2030 Dow Center, Midland, MI 48640; m/Betty Charles Anderson; c/ John Walter, Peter Bruce, Nancy Patricia; p/Arthur Robert and Margaret Florence West; ed/BS, Chem Engrg, OR St Univ, 1942; Student of Meteorology, Univ of Chgo, 1943; mil/AUS, 1942-46; pa/Res and Devel Engr 1946, Bus Anal and Proj Planning 1956-66, The Dow Chem Co; Pres, Dow Chem Pacific, 1966-78; Pres, Dow Latin Am, 1978; Exec VP 1978-82, Current Chm of the Bd, The Dow Chem Co; Trustee, Com for Ec Devel; Adv Coun, Japan-US Ec Relats; Vis'g Com, Univ of MI Grad Sch of Bus; Adv Com, Dept of Chem Engrg, Univ of CA Berkeley; Trustee, OR St Univ Foun; Dir, The Dow Chem Co; Dir, Dowell Schlumberger; Dir, Chem Bk and Trust Co; r/Prot; hon/Var Pubs; Bronze Star Medal, USAF, 1945; Order of Indust Ser Merit, Repub of Korea, 1977; W/W Am; Intl W/W; Standard and Poor's Register.

LUNDQUIST, CARL H oc/College President; b/Nov 16, 1916; h/1900 Asbury Street, St Paul, MN 55113; ba/ St Paul, MN; m/Nancy Mae Zimmerman; c/Carole Spickelmier, Eugene, Jill Anderson, Susan; p/Henry and Esther Gustafson Lundquist (dec); ed/BA, Sioux Falls Col, 1939; BD, Bethel Theol Sem, 1943; ThM, En Bapt Theol Sem, 1946; DD 1957, ThD 1960, No Bapt Theol Sem; pa/Ordained to Min, 1944; Pastor, Elim Bapt Ch, 1943-53; Pres, Bethel Col and Sem, 1954-82; Pres, Christian Col Consortium, 1982-; F'ship of Evang Sem Pres, Chm; Nat Assn of Evangelicals Bd of Adm; World Bapt Cong of Urban Evang and Missions; cp/ Am for Jesus Nat Planning Com; Bapt Hosp Fund; Bapt World Alliance; Other Mbrships; hon/W/W.

LUNN, JOSEPH KENNETH oc/Insurance Executive; b/Apr 16, 1946; h/326 Hawthorn Road, Baltimore, MD 21210; ba/Baltimore, MD; p/Joseph and Evelyn Lunn, Chicago, IL; ed/Chartered Property and Casualty Underwriter, 1983; MA, Clin Psych, Roosevelt Univ, 1982; BA, N Pk Col, 1969; pa/Spec Proj Mgr, Alexander & Alexander Inc, 1983-; Interface Support Mgr 1982-83, Interface Analyst 1981-82, Personal Underwriting Spec 1976-81, Kemper Grp; Other Previous Positions; hon/One of Chgo's Ten Outstg Yg Citizens, 1980; Beautiful People Awd, Chgo Urban

Leag, 1980; Commun Ser Awd, STEP Inc, 1979; Dist'd Ser Awd, Chgo JCs, 1975; Vol of the Yr, Mtl Hlth Assn of Gtr Chgo, 1974; Personalities of W and MW; W/W Fin and Indust; W/W MW; W/W Ins; 2,000 Notable Ams.

LUPASH, LAWRENCE O oc/Senior Analyst, Staff Scientist; b/May 29, 1942; h/1401 South Harbor Boulevard, Apartment 3P, La Habra, CA 90631; ba/ Huntington Beach, CA; m/Corina C; p/ Ovidiu N and Stefania Maria Lupas, Bucharest, Romania; ed/MS 1965, PhD 1972, Polytechnic Inst of Bucharest; pa/ Proj Engr 1965-68, Sr Engr 1971-72, Inst for Automation, Bucharest; Rschr, Romanian Acad of Scis, Bucharest, 1968-71; Asst Prof, Polytechnic Inst of Bucharest, 1966-68, 1971-72; Sr Rschr/ Lectr, Univ of Bucharest, 1972-79; Vis'g Lectr, Univ of Tirana, Albania; Sr Analyst/Scist, Intermetrics Inc; IEEE; Soc of Indust and Applied Math; ACM; Am Philatelic Soc; r/Greek Orthodox; hon/Author, Num Articles to Profile Pubs (More Than 50); Co-Author of Book, *Numerical Techniques in System Theory*, 1974; Recip, Repub Awd, Polytechnic Inst of Bucharest, 1962; Romanian Acad of Scis Grantee, 1968; Case Wn Resv Univ Grantee, 1969.

LUPULESCU, AUREL PETER oc/ Associate Professor; b/Jan 1, 1923; h/ 21480 Mahon, Southfield, MI 48075; ba/ Detroit, MI; p/Peter Vichentie and Maria Ann Dragan Lupulescu (dec); ed/ BS, cum laude, Liceum, Rome, 1942; MD, magna cum laude, Sch of Med, Bucharest, 1950; MS, Endocrinology, Univ of Bucharest, Fac of Sci, 1965; Fed Lic, Med and Surg, 1971; PhD, Biol, Univ of Windsor, Canada, 1976; pa/ Chief, Lab Investigations, Inst of Endocrinology, Bucharest, 1950-67; Res Assoc, St Univ of NY Downst Med Ctr, 1968-69; Asst Prof 1969-72, Assoc Prof 1973-, Med, Sch of Med, Wayne St Univ; Vis'g Scist, Inst Med Pathol, Rome, 1967; Consltg Phys, VA Hosp; NY Acad Scis; AMA; AAAS; FASEB; Am Soc Cell Biol; Soc Exptl Biol and Med; Electronic Micro Soc Am; Soc Invest Derm; Am Assn of Pathologists; MI St Med Soc; Wayne Med Soc; r/Greek Orthodox; hon/Author of 264 Sci Papers Pub'd in Different Jours in USA and Elsewhere, 4 Chapts in Books, 5 Books (*Steroid Hormones* 1958, *Ultrastructure of Thyroid Gland* 1968, *Hormones and Carcinogenesis* 1983); AMA Phys's Recog Awd, 1983-86; W/W Sci and Technol; W/W World.

LYLES, CHARLES HARPER oc/Executive Secretary; b/Jun 24, 1913; h/Route 7, Box 277A, Ocean Springs, MS 39564; ba/Same; m/Clairece Harp; p/Mr and Mrs Charles G Lyles, Ruston, LA; ed/ BS, LA Polytechnic Inst, 1938; mil/7th Armored Div, ETO, 1942-45; pa/Field Stat, Bur of Fisheries, Dept of Interior, 1938-52; Liaison Ofcr, Intl Comm for the NW Atl Fisheries, 1952-55; Supvr, Stats, SA and Gulf, 1955-60; Chief, Stats, BCF, 1960-70; Chief, Stats, Gulf Coast Res Lab, 1972-74; Dir, MS Marine Conserv Comm, 1974-77; Dir, Gulf Sts Marine Fisheries Comm, 1977-83; Fishery Stats of the US, 1963-67; The Mackerel Fishery; The Squid Fishery; r/Bapt; hon/Outstg Perf, BCF, 1959; Meritorious Ser, 1969.

LYLES, DONALD R oc/Columnist, Seminar Leader, Lecturer, Free-Lance

Writer, Resumé Writer, Editor; b/Apr 11, 1946; h/PO Box 3689, Los Angeles, CA 90078; ba/Brea, CA; p/Roy and Elzie Freeman Lyles, Palestine, TX; ed/ Student, Creat Writing and Jour, El Camino Col, LA SW Col, CA St Univ LA; Student, Arch Drafting, Prairie View Univ, 1965-67; mil/Served in Vietnam, AUS, 1968-69; pa/Ent Columnist/Free-Lance Celebrity Interviewer, Good Publications, 1971-81; Free-Lance Mag Writer, 1970-; Columnist, *The National Afro-American*, 1970; Columnist, *The Houston Informer* and *Texas Freeman*, 1971; Columnist, *The Frontier News*, 1972-74; Life Mem, Clover Intl Poetry Assn; Fdg Ofcr, Am Acad of Authors; cp/Publicity Dir, Essie McSwine's Unique Shades of Brown Modeling Clb; r/ Bapt; hon/Columns, Articles and Poems Have Been Pub'd in Over 100 Pubs in US, Canada and Overseas; Cert of Achmt, Am Poets F'ship Soc, 1974; Intl W/W Poetry; Men of Achmt; W/W Intl Acad of Poets.

LYNCH, SISTER FRANCIS XAVIER oc/Director of Development; b/Oct 21, 1918; h/1750 Quarry Road, Yardley, PA 19067; ba/Same; p/Mr George F Lynch (dec); ed/RN, A Barton Hepburn Hosp, 1936; BS in Nsg Ed, Cath Univ, 1942; MS in Adm/Biol Scis, Cath Univ, 1948; PhD, honoris causa, Humane Lttrs, Long Isl Univ, 1967; pa/Hosp Nsg, 1936-37; Entered Grey Nuns of the Sacred Heart, 1937; Hd, Biol Dept 1944, Dean, Sch of Nsg 1951-61, Pres 1962-69, D'Youville Col; Dir of Devel, Grey Nuns Motherhouse Congreg, 1971-; AAUW, 1955-; Acad of Polit Sci, 1964-; Nat Cath Devel Conf, 1971-; Bd of Dirs, A Barton Hepburn Hosp, 1976-; r/Cath; hon/DHL, Long Isl Univ, 1967.

LYNCH, HAROLYN MOODY oc/ Teacher of Emotionally Handicapped; b/ Jul 12, 1945; h/1750-14 Sedgwick Avenue, Bronx, NY 10453; ba/NY, NY; m/Wilbert; c/Krystal Jeane; p/Coralee Moody, NY, NY; ed/BS Elem Ed, Morgan St Col; MA Ed Equiv, Hunter Col, 1971; pa/Tchr of Emotionally Handicapped, NY City Bd of Ed, 1967-; Tchr of Adult Ed, Riker's Isl Wom Inmates, 1972-74; Tchr of Eng as 2nd Lang, Dominican Adults, 1975-76; Tchr of Kindergarten Arts & Crafts, 1968-75; U Fdn of Tchrs, 1967-; Tchr Cnslr, Proj 2nd Choice, Columbia Tchr's Col, 1972-74; hon/Dean's List, OR ST Col, 1967.

LYNCH, MARGARET MAHONEY oc/Business Executive, Investor, Realty Owner; b/Sep 8, 1920; h/501 Forest Avenue, Palo Alto, CA 94301; ba/San Francisco, CA; m/Joseph David; c/ Timothy Jeremiah, Suzanne Marie; p/ Jeremiah J and Susan McKean Mahoney, San Francisco, CA; ed/Dipl, 1940; Student of Real Estate and Fin, Univ of CA SF; Student of Mgmt, Lone Mtn Col; pa/Clk, Mahoney Rlty Co, 1950; Gen Ptnr, Owner, Mahoney Estate Co, 1961; Pres and Owner, Mahoney Rlty Co, 1970; Prin and Owner 1977, Dir 1978, Mahoney Estate Co; Owner, Mahoney Corp; CA Roundtable; Bus Coun; CA Hotel and Motel Assn; Chp, Fgn Ec and Fin Com; CA Bkrs Assn; Am Real Est Exch Assn; cp/Bay Area Coun; World Affairs Coun; Dir, Nat Gallery of Art; Trustee, SF Opera Assn; Dir, U Negro Col Fund; Trustee, Andrew Mellon Foun; Trustee, SF Mus of Art; Trustee, Metro Opera Assn of NY; Trustee, US Wild Life Persv Fund; Chw, Boys Town of Italy Social Com; Chp, World Affairs Coun; Fgn Relats Com; SF Downtown Assn; Trustee, Nat Endowment for Humanities; St Francis Yacht Clb; Palo Alto Hills Country Clb; Commonwealth Clb; Comml Clb; Hibernia Bkrs Clb; Palo Alto Woms Clb; CA Woms Clb; SF Woms Clb; Poinciana Clb; Pebble Bch Golf and Sailing Clb; Castilleja Woms Clb; hon/Mayor's Social Hostess for Queen Elizabeth's Civic Reception, 1983; W/W Am Wom; W/W Am; W/W World; W/W Fin and Indust.

LYONS, JAMES E oc/Chief Executive Officer; b/Oct 21, 1928; h/1824 East Lake Cannon Drive, Lakeland, FL 33880; ba/Winter Haven, FL; m/Ollie; c/Eddie, Katherine; p/Janie Louise Lyons, Camden, SC; ed/BS 1958, MBA 1961, The Nat Col; PhD, Clayton Univ, 1972; mil/USAF; pa/Chm, Chief Exec, Ctl Supply Corp, 1963-67; Chm, Chief Exec, Leasetran Corp, 1967-; Dealer, Owner, Tropical Pontiac, 1961-63; FL Coun of 100, 1970-; Air Coun, AF Assn, 1979-; Dir, Fed Resv Bk, 1971-78; cp/ Chm, Alliance w the Republic of Colombia, SA, 1970-73; r/Bapt; hon/DSc, FL Inst of Technol, 1978; DHL, Hawthorne Col, 1982; DSc, SWn Univ, 1982; Champion of Higher Ed, Chief Awd, 1976; W/W Fin and Indust; Personalities of S; Cambridge Intl Bus-man's W/W.

LYONS, JOHN MATTHEW oc/Telecommunications Executive; b/Nov 5, 1948; h/305 East 86th Street, New York, NY 10028; ba/New York, NY; p/Matthew Joseph (dec) and Anna Lyons; ed/ BSEE 1970, MSEE 1976, Roosevelt Univ; PhD in Communs, Loyola Univ, 1979; BSE 1981, MBA 1982, Century Univ; mil/USAF, 1967-70; pa/Engr/ Prodr, WRFM, 1965-69; Sr Facilities Planning and Proj Engr, WWRL/Sonde-

rling Broadcasting Co, 1969-76; WWRL and WRVR/Riverside Broadcasting Co, 1976-78; Asst Chief Engr, WOR, 1978-80; Chief Engr, WRKS-FM/RKO Gen Inc, 1980-; Fdr/Owner, Short Lines Co, 1980; Fellow, Soc of Broadcast Engrs, 1977, Dir 1974-78; Cert'd Sr Broadcast Engr, 1977; IEEE; Intl Radio and TV Soc; ASCAP; BMI; Am Mgmt Assn; AES; Radio Adv Com, Mus of Broadcasting; cp/Pres, Vets Hosp Radio and TV Guild, Nat Org, 1982-, Bd of Dirs 1978-; r/Cath; hon/Num Pubs; Fellow, Soc of Broadcast Engrs, 1977; Cert'd Sr Broadcast Engr, 1977; Finalist, Intl Radio and TV Fest, 1982; Exec Prodr, WOR Radio 60th Anniversary; W/W E.

LYONS, JOHN WINSHIP oc/Director of National Engineering Laboratory; b/Nov 5, 1930; h/7430 Woodville Road, Mt Airy, MD 21771; ba/Washington, DC; m/Grace; c/Margaret, Mary Ann, John Louis; p/Louis Martin and Margaret Wade Lyons (dec); ed/AB in Chem, Harvard, 1952; AM in Physics and Chem 1963, PhD in Physics and Chem 1964, Wash Univ; mil/Army; pa/Dir, NEL 1978-, Dir, IAT 1977-78, Dir CFR, IAT 1973-77, Nat Bur of Standards; R&D Positions, Monsanto Co, 1955-73; Adv Com on Engrg, NSF; Adv Coun, Col of Engrg, Univ of MD; Bd of Dirs, NFPA, 1978-84; Chm, St Louis Sect, Am Chem Soc; Fellow, AAAS, Wash Acad of Sci; Am Chem Soc; Sigma Xi; cp/CoChm, Bidwood #19 Block Ptnrship; r/Pres, Parish Coun, St Peter's Ch, 1982; hon/Author, 3 Books, 6 Book Chapts, 30 Articles, 54 Invited Lectures, Dealing w Rheology, Phosphorus Chem, Polyelectrolytes, Fire Retardants, Fire Res; Gold Medal, Dept of Commerce, 1977; Pres's Mgmt Improvement Awd, 1978; Dist'd Exec Rank Awd from Pres Reagan, 1981; W/W Am; W/

W Frontier Sci and Technol; DIB; W/ W E.

LYTLE, MICHAEL ALLEN oc/Assistant to the Chancellor; b/Oct 22, 1946; h/1806 Langford, College Station, TX 77840; ba/College Station, TX; p/LTC (Ret'd) Milton Earl and Geraldine Faye Young Lytle, Rose Hill, KS; ed/AB, IN Univ, 1973; Cert of Adv'd Grad Study, Sam Houston St Univ, 1977; MEd, TX A&M Univ, 1978; Doct Study, TX A&M Univ; mil/1st Lt, AUS, Vietnam, 1970-72; Maj, USAR; pa/Subst HS Tchr, Butler Co, KS, 1969; Instr, Crim Justice, Cleveland St Commun Col, 1974-77; Adj Instr, Crim Justice, Univ of TN Chattanooga, 1974-76; Tchg Asst 1977-80, Intern, Adm Asst, Ofc of the Vice Chancellor for Legal Affairs 1980, Staff Assoc, Ofc of the Chancellor 1980-81, Asst to the Chancellor 1981-, TX A&M Univ; Acad of Crim Justice Scis; Am Soc for Higher Ed; Am Judic Soc; Am Soc for Public Adm; Fellow, Inter-Univ Sem on Armed Forces and Soc; Policy Studies Org; Resv Ofcr Assn; Am Def Preparedness Assn; cp/ Bryan-Col Sta C of C; TX Com for Employer Support of the Guard and Resv, Exec Dir; Army and Navy Clb; r/Epis; hon/Pubs, "Legal Factors Related to Access to Campuses of Public Colleges and Universities," "A Conceptual Typology of the Role of the University Attorney," "Legislation, Litigation, and the Administration of Higher Education," "Another View of the Academic Cornucopia: Off-Duty Education and the Officer Corps" 1979, Others; Bronze Star Medal; Army Commend Medal w Second OLC; Staff Ser Hon Medal First Class, Vietnam; Phi Delta Kappa; W/W S and SW; Personalities of S.

M

MACDONALD, KENNETH DAN-IAL oc/Appliance Distribution Company Executive; b/Aug 18, 1936; h/873 Chestnut Street, Waban, MA 02168; ba/Cambridge, MA; m/Louise Patnod; c/Scott, Allison, Gregory; p/Danial Archibald and Elizabeth (Macleod) Macdonald; ed/Student, Boston Univ, 1958-59; pa/Purchasing Agt 1958-60, Sales Mgr 1960-71, VP 1971-, MGMS Assocs, Cambridge, MA; Exec VP, Maytag Boston Ser Ctr, Cambridge, 1979-; Nat Chm Com, Appliance Parts Distbrs Assn; Rental Housing Assn; Mfrs Adv Coun to HUD; cp/Repub Party; Pres, Waban Weblos BSA, 1974; Waban Little Leag Baseball, 1975; Treas, Boston Yg Life, 1981; Treas, Newton Yacht Clb, 1982; Pres, Clan Donald Fam Sydney, Nova Scotia, 1970-82; Chief Clk, Wash Mil Dist, 1956-58; Windsor Clb, Waban, MA; Newton Yacht Clb, Newton, MA; r/Presb; hon/Contbr Articles to Var Trade Jours; Outstg Achmt Awd Trainee Counterman, 1977.

MacDONALD, MILA JOY oc/Realtor; b/Jun 22, 1933; h/4101 South Tropico Drive, La Mesa, CA 92041; ba/Same; m/Rodney Ian; c/Carlos Ramirez, Meredith Joy, Kimberly Lynne; p/Meredith Williams (dec) and Mildred Madden Powell.

MACE, SHARON ELIZABETH oc/Physician; b/Oct 30, 1949; h/8243 Merrie Lane, Chesterland, OH 44026; ba/Cleveland, OH; p/James H Mace Sr, Whitesboro, NY; Leona H Mace (dec); ed/BS, Syracuse Univ, 1971; MD, Upstate Med Ctr, St Univ NY, 1975; pa/Dir Ed & Prehosp Care, Att'g Phys & Fac Mem, Dept Emer Med & Emer Med Residency Prog, Mt Sinai Med Ctr, 1980-; Helicopter Flight Phys, Cleveland Metro Gen Hosp, 1982-; Res Assoc, Dept Investigative Med, Mt Sinai Med Ctr, 1979-1980; Cardiol Fellow 1977-79, Pediatric Intership & Residency 1975-77, Case Wn Resv Univ Hosps; Nat Chapt, OH Chapt, Ed & Mbrship Coms, Am Col Emer Phys; Nat Chapt, Instr Adv'd Trauma Life Support & Adv'd Cardiac Life Support, Soc Tchrs Emer Med; r/Congregationalist; hon/Num Pubs in Med Jours incl'g (w others) "Echocardiographic Abnormalities in Infants of Diabetic Mothers" Jour of Pediatrics 1979, "The Trisomy 9 Syndrome" Jour of Pediatrics 1978, "Hypertensive Encephalopathy. A Cause of Neonatal Seizures" Am Jour Diseases Chd 1983, "Neural Control of Heart Rate" Pediatric Res 1983; Acad Appt, Case Wn Resv Univ, Sch of Med in Depts of Med & Pediatrics, Div Emer Med, 1982; W/W Am.

MacINTYRE, WILLIAM JAMES oc/Physicist; b/Nov 26, 1920; h/3108 Huntington Road, Shaker Heights, OH 44122; ba/Cleveland, OH; m/Patricia N; c/Kathleen S, Steven J; p/Helen Hoyt MacIntyre, Harrisburg, PA; ed/BS 1943, MA 1947, Wn Resv Univ; MS 1948, PhD 1950, Yale Univ; mil/AUS, 1943-46; Active Duty, Europe, 1943-46; pa/Physicist, Cleveland Clin Foun, 1972-; Sr Instr 1952 to Prof 1971-73, Sch of Med, Wn Resv Univ; Dir, 2nd Reg Tng Course Med Applications Radioisotopes, Cairo, Egypt, 1961; Conslt, FDA, Bur Radiological Hlth, 1976-; Pres, Soc Nuclear Med, 1976-77; Chm, Fed'd Coun Nuclear Med Orgs, 1978-81; Chm, Report Com on Scanning, Inst Comm Radiological Units & Measurements, 1966-75; Chm, Sci Com 18B, Nat Coun Radiation Protection, 1972-; hon/Author, 185 Articles in Sci Press, 31 Book Chapts, 2 Books; Phi Beta Kappa, 1942; Sigma Xi, 1948; W/W: Sci, Frontier Sci & Technol, MW; Am Men of Sci.

MACIUSZKO, JERZY J (GEORGE) oc/Professor & Library Director (retired); b/Jul 15, 1913; h/133 Sunset Drive, Berea, OH 44017; ba/Berea, OH; m/Kathleen Lynn; c/Christina Aleksandra; p/Bonifacy and Aleksandra Maciuszko (dec); sp/Thomas and Stephanie Mart, Rocky River, OH; ed/MA, Univ Warsaw, Poland, 1936; MS, Wn Resv Univ, 1953; PhD, Case Wn Resv Univ, 1962; mil/AUS, 1945-46, Liason Ofcr; pa/Tchr, Warsaw Model Sec'dy Sch, 1936-37 & 1938-39; Insp, under Brit Min Ed Polish Sec'dy Schs in England, 1946-51; Tchr, Alliance Col, 1951-52; Asst Hd, Fgn Lit Dept, Cleveland Public Lib, 1953-63; Hd, John G. White Dept, Cleveland Public Lib, 1963-69; Lectr, Polish Lang & Lit, Case Wn Resv Univ, 1964-69; Chm, Dept Slavic Studies, Alliance Col, 1969-73; Chm, Alliance Col Yr Abroad Com, Dir Alliance Col Yr Abroad Prog, Jagellonian Univ, 1969-74; Chm, Div Slavic & Mod Langs, Alliance Col, 1973-74; Prof & Lib Dir 1974-78, Prof Emeritus 1978-, Baldwin-Wallace Col; Chm, Am Lib Assn, Slavic Subsection, Div Col Res Libs, 1968-69; Am Assn Admt Slavic Studies; Chapt Pres, Am Assn Tchrs of Slavic & E European Langs, 1965-66; Charter Mem, Assn Admt Polish Studies, Assn Polish Writers Exile; Assn Polish Univ Profs & Lectrs Abroad; Polish Inst Arts Scis Am; The Kosciuszko Foun; Polish Am Hist Assn; Pres, Cleveland Public Lib Staff Assn, 1964-65; Pres, Case Wn Resv Univ Lib Sch Alumni Assn, 1970-71; Mod Lang Assn; r/Luth; hon/Author, Contest Winning Short Story, Book Intros, Books incl'g The Polish Short Story in English 1968, Book Chapts; Contbr to Profl Periods in England; Short Story Translator; Contbr Ency of World Lit in 20th Century; The Kosciuszko Foun Doct Dissertation Awd, NY, 1967; The Hilbert T Ficken Awd, Baldwin-Wallace Col, Berea, OH, 1973.

MACK, DIANA TRIMBLE oc/Manager Interior Department; b/Apr 24, 1953; h/1117 South Owyhee Street, Boise, ID 83705; ba/Boise, ID; m/John Frederick; p/Shelley Dell Trimble and Iris Joaquine, Boise, ID; sp/Jane Phare Fraser Mack, Boise, ID; ed/BA, Univ of ID; pa/Lombard-Conrad Archs, 1983-; Conslt, Hewlett Packard, 1982-83; Trimble and Assocs, 1977-82; Showroom One, 1976-77; Sales & Mktg Execs; Exec Women Intl; cp/Kappa Kappa Gamma; Crane Creek Country Clb; Lady Fitness.

MACKEY, THOMAS STEPHEN oc/Registered Professional Metallurgical Engineer; b/July 14, 1930; h/1210 Sunset Lane, Texas City, TX 77590; ba/Texas City, TX; m/Catherine; c/Thomas, Karen, Doris, Susan, Kathy, Michael & Ellen; p/Thomas Patrick Mackey (dec); Delia Mackey; ed/BS, Manhattan Col; MS, Columbia Univ; PhD, Rice Univ; Dr Jurisp, South TX Sch of Law; pa/Pres, Key Metals & Minerals Engrg Corporation; Sr Metall, Jacobs Engrg; Engr,. Wah Chang Corporation; Gen Mgr, TX City Tin Smelter; Tech Advr, Associated Metals & Minerals; Fellow Instn Mining & Metallurgy, England; Fellow Am Inst Chemists; Am Inst Profl Geologists; Chm, Com on Lead-Zinc-Tin, Chm, World Symp Lead-Zinc-Tin, Am Inst Mining, Metall & Petro Engrs; Am Soc Testing Mats; Nat Soc Profl Engrs; Nat Def Exec Resv; TX Soc Profl Engrs; Am Soc Metals; Geochemical Soc Am; Australasian Inst Mining & Metallurgy; Bd Mem, The Metall Soc, AIME; Intl Bar Assn; hon/Author Num Profl Pubs incl'g "Review of Recent Developments in Tin—1982" Jour of Metals 1983, "Alteration and Recovery of Ilmenite & Rutile" Australian Mining 1972; Outstg Engr, TX Soc Profl Engrs; W/W Engrg.

MacKINNEY, ARTHUR C oc/Vice Chancellor for Academic Affairs & Professor of Psychology; b/October 16, 1928; h/1532 Yarmouth Point Drive, Chesterfield, MO 63017; ba/Saint Louis, MO; m/Lois; c/Gordon L, Nada L; p/Arthur Clinton (dec); Doris Long MacKinney; ed/BA, William Jewell Col, 1951; MA 1953, PhD 1955, Univ MN; mil/AUS, 1946-47, 1951; pa/Vice Chancellor Acad Affairs, Univ MO, 1976-; Dean Grad Studies Res, Prof Psych & Mgmt, Wright St Univ, 1971-76; Dean Col Sci & Soc, Prof Psych, Univ WI-Parkside, 1970-71; Asst Prof, Assoc Prof, Prof Psych, Prof Indust Relats, IA St Univ, 1967-70; Div Indust Psych, Mem Ed Com 1961-71, Chm Ed Com 1962-63 & 1967-70, Chm Doct Guidelines Subcom 1964-65, Chm Master's Guidelines Subcom 1966-67, Editor The Indust Organl Psychol 1972-76, Mem Exec Com 1976-79, Chm Profl Affairs Com 1980-81, Chm Planning Com 1979-80, Pres 1981-82, Chm Comm Accreditation 1969-70, Secy-Treas, Coun Chm Grad Depts Psych 1969-71, Am Psychol Assn; Pres 1966-67, Mem-at-large Exec Coun 1964-68, Mem Bd Examrs 1968-70, IA Psychol Assn; Pres 1966, Secy-Treas 1962, Ctl IA Psychol Assn; Mem Exec Bd 1971-73, Chm Public Info Com 1971-73, OH Psychol Assn; Mem Exec Com 1971-76, Pres-Elect 1973-75, Pres 1975-76, Editor The Miami Valley Psychologist 1972-76, Miami Val Psychol Assn; Secy 1981-82, Pres 1983-84, MO Psychol Assn; hon/Author Num Pubs incl'g "Talking down: realistic or not." Management Review 1953, "Race and Sex Differences in Student Retention at an Urban University" College and University 1982; Fellow, Am Psychol Assn, 1970; Cit for Achmt, William Jewell Col/Cattell Res Design Awd; Div Indust-Orgnl Psych, Am Psychol Assn; W/W: Am, MW; Men of Achievement.

MacMULLIN, ROBERT BURNS oc/Consulting Chemical Engineer, Writer; b/Sep 18, 1898; h/5137 Woodland Drive, Lewiston, NY 14092; ba/Niagara Falls, NY; m/Olive Bethea (Kunkel); c/Bethea Jeanne, Hyypia, Constance Anne, Aust, Robert Bruce; p/Robert B MacMullin and Margaret Isabel (Stockman) (dec); sp/Karl Friedrich Kunkel and Eliza Anne (Tracy) (dec); ed/Bowdoin Col; SB, MIT, 1920; mil/CWS, Cpl, 1st Gas Regiment, WW I; pa/Hydrographer, US Coast & Geodetic Survey, 1916; Shift Suprv, Deepwater Dye Wks, E I DuPont de Nemours, 1917-18; Supt, Transatlantic

Chem Co, 1919; Res Chem, Mgr Dev, Mathieson Alkali Wks Inc (Olin Corporation) 1920-1945; Conslt, Tech Coor, TIIC & FIAT Opers Germany, US FEA & Dept Commerce, 1945-46; Founder, Prin Ptnr 1946-71, Assoc Emeritus 1972-, R B Mac Mullin; Chp, Am Chem Soc; Secy 1930, Emeritus 1970, WNY; Chp, Am Inst Chem Engrs; Secy 1939-40, Fellow, 1972, WNY; Fellow, Am Inst Chem, 1971; Hon, Assoc Conslt, Chem & Chem Engrs, 1972; Life, NY St Soc Prof Engrs, 1972; Am Assoc Adv'd Sci; Emeritus, Am Inst Min & Met Engrs, TMS, 1971; Emeritus, Electrochemic Soc, 1971; Chp, Ind Elect Div, 1949; Pres, 1st Gas Reg't Assoc, 1971; Editor Gas Attack, 1972-82; Chp, Air Pollution Control Bd, Niagara Falls, 1956; cp/Pres, Niagara Frontier Coun, BSA, 1958, 1959; PSI Upsilon Frat; r/ Prot; hon/Author, Contbr many textbooks incl'g *With E of the First Gas* 1919, *Odyssey of a Chemical Engineer* 1983; ACS, Schoelkopf Medal, 1958; Soc Chem Ind, Perkin Medal, 1972; Electrochem Soc, Electrochem Engr Medal, 1976; AIChE, Pract Awd, 1982; AIChE, Fdrs Awd, 1983; Japan Soda Ind Cit, 1979; BSA, Silver Beaver, 1961; Am Men of Sci; W/ W: Am, Engrg.

MacRORIE, CAROL A oc/Distribution Manager; b/Feb 14, 1946; h/1749 East Mountain Road, Westfield, MA 01085; ba/Westfield, MA; c/Frank Gulla (Adopted); p/Harold D MacRorie (dec); Irene MacRorie, Little Falls, NY; ed/ Att'd Northeastern Univ, 1973-76; Holyoke Commun Col, 1977-; pa/ Inventory Control Clk, Salada Foods Inc, 1964-69; Distbn Supvr, Addison-Wesley Publishing Co, 1969-73; Distbn Mgr, Digital Equip Corporation, 1973-; Am Mgmt Assn; Nat Assn Female Execs; Intl Mat Mgmt Soc; Am Prodn & Inventory Control Soc; Nat Org Wom; Delta Nu Alpha; r/Cath; W/W Am Wom.

MADDEN, SARA LEE oc/Teacher/ Department Chairperson; b/Mar 24, 1928; h/3503 Harpers Ferry Drive, Stockton, CA 95209; ba/Stockton, CA; m/Donald Madden (dec); c/Robert Dewey Houk; p/Delbert Dewey and Arva Allene Clark Imel; sp/John E Madden and Ann Capitanich (dec); ed/ BS, Univ of Wichita, 1964; pa/Secy, Ofc Vets Affairs, 1949-50; Secy, Engrg Dept, KS St Univ, 1951-52; Exec Secy, Transport Co TX, 1958-61; Tchr, Wichita HS, 1964-; Tchr, Franklin HS, 1964-; Dept Chp, Adult Ed, SS J Delta Commum Col, 1965-82; Nat Bus Ed Assn; Wn Bus Ed Assn; CA Bus Ed Assn; Am Voc Assn; CA Assn Voc Ed; Stockton Tchr's Assn; Am Assn Univ Wom; Kappa Delta Pi; Delta Kappa Gamma, 1st Exec VP Zeta Chapter; cp/ En Star; r/Presb; hon/Outstg Bus Ed Student of Year, (Nat Bus Ed Assn), 1983; W/W W.

MADEJ, SUE BATTAGLIA oc/Clinical Director; b/Feb 20, 1942; h/1115 Granite Drive, Bethlehem, PA 18017; ba/Bethlehem, PA; m/Joseph John Madej; c/Deborah Sue, Deirdre Leigh, Jeanne Marie; p/Dominic T Battaglia (dec) and Ilva Battaglia Hughes, Reedville, VA; sp/Helen Madej Smith, Severna Pk, MD; ed/BA, Univ MD, 1963; AA, Harford Commum Col, 1975; MS, Univ St Joseph, 1983; pa/Fgn Lang Tchr, Balto City Dept Ed, 1963-64; Staff

RN, Franklin Sq Hosp, 1975-76; Staff RN-ER GBMC, 1976; Staff RN (ICU & ER), Cardiac Stress Lab, Clin Instr, Muhlenberg Med Ctr, 1976-81; Hd Nurse ECU, St Luke's Hosp, 1981-83; Clin Nsg Dir, Muhlenberg Med Ctr, 1983-; Nurse Rep, Proctor & Gamble, 1980-; Area Coor, Hlth Care Resources, 1981; EDNA, 1975-83; ANA, 1975-77; NAMP, 1983; NGS, 1983; CCNA, 1980-81; cp/Welcome Wagon, 1975-79; St Francis Guild, 1978-; MNA, 1976-77; CCD Instr, 1973; G S Am, 1968-81; r/ Rom Cath; hon/Dean's List, W/W E.

MADLAING, ART GABOT oc/Real Estate Broker, Notary Public; b/Aug 18, 1947; h/730 Madrid Street, San Francisco, CA 94112; ba/Daly City, CA; m/ Virginia B Jimenez; c/Darlene Vi, Wynema Joy; p/Emilie B Madlaing and Elena S Gabot, Pangasinan, Philippine; sp/Anastacio A Jimenez (dec) and Rufina Barte, Pangasinan, Philippines; ed/Att'd Univ Philippines, 1967; Writer's Course, Cert, Overseas Missionary F'ship, 1972; Philippine Bible Col, 1973; CA Sch Real Est, Chamberlin Real Est Schs, 1978 & 1980; pa/Co Forester, Taggat Industs Inc, 1967; Forest Sta Warden, Timber Mgmt Ofcr, Asst Reg Info Ofcr, Bur Forrestry, 1968-75; Commum Editor, Forum Philippines, 1976; Account Exec, Putnam Financial Sers, 1976-78; Real Assoc, 1979; VP, Intl Rltrs Corporation, 1980; Pres, Equity Intl Real Est Inc, 1981; Owner-Broker, Am Bkrs Rlty, 1982; Real Est Columnist, "Philippine News", 1981-; Mem, Nat Notary Assn, 1979-; Mem, SF Bd Rltrs, 1979-; Mem, CA Assn Rltrs, Nat Assn Rltrs, 1979-; Life Mem, Zeta Beta Rho Hon Frat, 1966-; Mem, U Pangasinanes Am, 1980-; Editor & Press Relats Ofcr, Daly City JCs, 1979-80; Secy, Baguie-Californians No CA; Bd Dir, Binalonians No CA, 1979-; cp/Mem, FASAE Toastmasters Intl, 1982; r/Ch of Christ; hon/Author "RP-German Forestry Tng Ctr" *Focus Philippines* 1975, "Binalonan-A Town to Watch" *Gulf Express* 1975, "A Plea for Christian Unity" 1974; Entrance Scholar 1964, Col Scholar 1967, Bur Forestry Scholar 1964-67, Univ Philippines; Most Outstg Ofcr, Baguie-Californians, 1981; Outstg Editor, Daly City JCs, 1979 & 1980; Num Biographical Listings incl'g W/W: W Am CA.

MAGALLANES, RAYMOND DONAL SR oc/Real Estate Investments and Sales; b/Dec 11, 1925; h/641 Forrest Avenue, Biloxi, MS 39530; ba/Biloxi, MS; m/Bonnie Diaz; c/Raymond Donal, Jill Patrice, Terrie Ann; p/Clemente Magallanes (dec) and Dorothy Mitts; sp/ George Joseph Diaz (dec) and Thelma Diaz, Biloxi, MS; ed/BS, Tulane Univ, 1952; MS, Univ So MS, 1981; mil/USA, Ret'd Maj, 1944-46, 1952-67, 1970-73; pa/Self Employed, 1968-70; Public HS Tchr, 1973-77 and 1979-82; St Pres, MS Am Fdn Tchrs, AFL/CIO 1977-79; Real Est Investmts & Sales, 1982-; Am Soc Civil Engrs, 1949-50; Resv Ofcrs Assn, 1952-70; Assn US Army, 1956-64; Assn Army Aviation, 1954-68; Num Commum Orgs; r/Rom Cath; hon/Author Num Pubs; Recip Num Awds incl'g Nat Endowment Humanities Grant; Bronze Star Medal; 3 Commend Medals; 3 Air Medals; 2 Meritorious Unit Cit.

MAGNESS, ROBYN CHERI oc/ Paralegal; b/May 9, 1951; h/5702 North

19th Drive, Phoenix, AZ 85015; ba/ Glendale, AZ; p/Phoenix,AZ; ed/AA, Phoenix Col, 1971; BS 1973, MA 1974, No AZ Univ; pa/Tchr, Flagstaff Public Schs, 1973-76; Instr Yavapai Commum Col, 1975; Dir, Carefree Daycare Ctr, 1975-76; Paralegal, Ofc Mgr, Commum Legal Sers, 1977-; Mem Bd Dirs 1982-, Co-Pres 1984-, Little Candle Commums; cp/Asst Treas, Soroptimist Intl Kachinas, 1982-; Mem, Glendale C of C, 1983-; r/Cath; hon/Dean's List 1970-71, Hon Bd 1971, Phoenix Col; S'ship for Expt Intl Living to Italy; Phi Kappa Phi NAU, 1973; Sigma Delta Pi (Spanish Hon), 1973; W/W W.

MAHAN, NANCY ELLEN oc/Paralegal (Certified Legal Assistant); b/Nov 27, 1938; h/14907 Berry Road, Accokeek, MD 20607; ba/Marlboro, MD; p/ Gerald E Mahan and Ethel G (dec); ed/ Att'd Univ MD, 1980; pa/Real Est Secy, O'Malley, Miles, Farrington, & McCarthy, 1983-; Paralegal, Pullum & Saylor PA, 1982-83; Paralegal, Michaelson & Simmons PA, 1980-82; Paralegal, Beatty & McNamee, 1956-80; Secy, Wachtel, Wiener & Schlezinger, 1962-66; Mem, Nat Assn Female Execs Inc; Mem, Am Soc Notaries; Mem, Nat Capital Area Paralegal Assn; cp/Mem, Peninsula Ath Leag; Cnslr Yth Grp; r/ Meth; hon/W/W Am Wom.

MAHESH, VIRENDRA B oc/Regents Professor, Robert B Greenblatt Professor, Chairman Department of Endocrinology; b/Apr 25, 1932; h/2911 Sussex Road, Augusta, GA 30909; m/Sushila Kumari Mahesh; c/Anita Mahesh Schwarz, Vinit Kumar; ed/BS, Patna Univ, 1951; MS, Delhi Univ, 1953; PhD, Delhi Univ, 1955; D Phil, Oxford Univ, 1958; pa/Res Fellow, Univ Delhi, 1953-56; Assam Oil Co Fellow, Oxford Univ, 1956-58; Traveling Fellow Welcome Foun, Universitat Basel, 1958; James Hudson Brown Meml Fellow, Yale Univ Sch Med, 1958-1959; Asst Res Prof 1959-63, Assoc Res Prof 1963-66, Prof Endocrinology 1966-70, Regents Prof Endocrinology 1970-, Dir Ctr Pop Studies 1971-, Chm Dept Endocrinology 1972-, Med Col GA; Robert B Greenblatt Prof, 1979-; Am Assn Lab Animal Sci; Am Assn Univ Profs; Am Fertility Soc; Biochemical Soc (England); Chem Soc; Endocrine Soc; Sigma Xi; Intl Soc Neuroendocrinology; NY Acad Sci; Soc Biol Chem; Soc Gynecologic Invest; Soc Study Reproduction; Pres, Intl Soc Reproductive Med, 1980-82; hon/Rubin Awd, Am Soc, 1963; Billings Silver Medal, 1965; Best Tchr Awd, Sch Med, 1972; Outstg Fac Awd, Sch Grad Studies, 1981.

MAHONEY, JAMES J oc/Historical Society Administrator; b/Nov 6, 1946; h/Route 1, Mineral Springs Road, Highland Mills, NY 10930-9801; ba/ Yonkers, NY; p/Frank J Mahoney and Virginia (Bartlett), Sloatsburg, NY; ed/ BA, St Josephs Sem, 1970; MLS, Pratt Inst, 1975; MA, Manhattan Col, 1978; pa/Assoc Libn, St Joseph's Sem, 1971-79; Exec VP, The Scholars Windmill Ltd, 1979-80; Ptnr, Liberty Rock Book Shoppe, 1974; Indep Cnslt, Publishing & Book Trade, 1980; Exec Dir, US Cath Hist Soc, 1974; r/Rom Cath; hon/Author of "An Overview of Recent Cath Hist Projs in US" *US Cath Histn* 1983; Books Reviews "Over the Line" *The Arts Magazette* 1983-84.

MAIBENCO, HELEN CRAIG oc/ Professor; b/June 9, 1917; h/1324 South Main Street, Wheaton, IL 60187; ba/ Chicago, IL; m/Nicholas P Maibenco DDS (dec); c/Douglas Craig, Thomas Allen; p/Benjamin C Craig and Mary (Brown) (dec); sp/Paul and Julia Maibenco (dec); ed/BS, Wheaton Col, 1948; MS, De Paul Univ, 1952; PhD, Univ IL Med Ctr, 1956; pa/Asst Prof, Assoc Prof, Prof, Univ IL Col Med Chicago, 1956-; Prof, Rush Med Col, 1973-; Var Positions in, Am Assn Anatomists; AAAS; Am Soc Zool; The Endocrine Soc; cp/Sigma Xi; Univ IL Alumni Assn; De Paul Univ Alumni Assn; Wheaton Col Alumni Assn; hon/Sigma Xi, 1960; Wheaton Col Scholastic Hon Soc, 1955; Num Listings incl'g W/W Frontier Sci & Technol; DIB; AM Men & Wom Sci.

MAIL, PATRICIA DAVISON oc/ Public Health Educator; b/Dec 10, 1940; h/2500 South 370th Street, Federal Way, WA 98003; ba/Seattle, WA; p/ George Allen and Constance Mail, Tucson, AZ; ed/BS, AZ, 1963; MSPE, Smith Col, 1965; MPH, Yale Univ, 1967; MA, AZ, 1970; Alcoholism Cert, Seattle Univ, 1974; USPHS, Commissioned Corps; pa/Instr, Greenfields Sch, 1967-68; Public Hlth Edr, USPHS/IHS, 1970-79; Public Hlth Ed Chief, Portland Area IHS, 1979-83; Instr, Seattle Univ, 1974-78; Chp 1981, Sect Coun 1982-84, Public Hlth Ed Sect APHA; Editor, Pacific NW SOPHE, 1974-83; Mem, AAAS, Am Sch Hlth Assn; Soc Med Anthropology; Soc Public Hlth Ed; r/ Epis; hon/Num Pubs incl'g *Annals Am Acad Polit & Social Sci* 1978, *Behavior Sci Res* 1977; PHS Trainership, 1965-67; NDEA F'ship, 1968-70; PHS Commend Medal, 1982; W/W Am Wom.

MAINOR, RAYFER EARLE oc/Creative Writer; b/March 25, 1955; h/Post Office Box 967, Stillwater, OK 74076; ba/Oklahoma City, OK; p/Henry and Rosetta Mainor, Waco, TX; ed/BA, Paul Quinn Col, 1978; MA, Prairie View A & M Univ, 1980; EdD, OK St Univ; pa/ Student Devel Spec, OKC Commun Col; Personal Social Devel Instr, Langston Univ; Res Assoc, OK St Univ; Univ Redland; U Poet Laureates Intl; Intl Poetry Soc; World Poetry Soc; Intl Black Writer's Conf; Centro Studi E Scambi Internazionali; OK Hist Soc; LA Mun Arts Dept; hon/Author *Poems* I, *Tribute to Blackness*, *The Life and Times of Sister Mercie Menefee*; U Poet Laureat Awd; Cambridge England's Intl W/W Bronze Medal Poetry; Silver Medallion; Golden Plaque; Num Cit incl'g Pres Kennedy, Johnson, Nixon, Ford, Carter, and Regan; Num Listings Men Achievement; W/W Poetry; Intl Register Profiles.

MAITZEN, DOLORES ANN oc/ Educator; b/Nov 2, 1952; h/3702 East Dahlia Drive, Phoenix, AZ 85032; ba/ Tempe, AZ; m/Robert H Jr; p/Joseph and Angeline Svacik, Phoenix, AZ; sp/ Mr and Mrs Robert H Maitzen Sr; ed/ BS, IL St Univ, 1973; MS, Chgo St Univ, 1976; pa/Tchr, Josephinum HS 1973-75, Queen of Peace HS 1976-79; Coor Home Ec Related Occups & Tchr Home Ec, N HS, Phoenix Union Dist, 1979-81; Asst Prof, Asst St Univ, 1981-; Mem, AZ Assn Voc Home Ec Edrs, St Mbrship Chm, 1981-; NEA; Assn Supvn Curric Devel; AZ Ed Assn; Am Voc Assn; AZ Voc Assn, Secy 1983-84, Bd Dirs, Exec

Bd; Am Home Ec Assn; AZ Home Ec Assn; cp/IL St Univ Alumni Assn; Adv Coun Nat Restaurant Assn; AZ St Univ Wom's Fac Assn; Alpha Gamma Delta; Yg Ladies St Joseph Ch; hon/Prof'l Recog Awd, 1982, 1983, 1984; Elem Sec'dy Adult Ed Awd, 1982; W/W W.

MAKI, HOPE MARIE oc/Artist, Art Teacher; b/Jan 14, 1938; h/3985 Langley Avenue, Pensacola, FL 32504; ba/Same; c/Richard Clarence McCall, James William McCall, Claudia Marie McCall; p/ William Edward Duncan and Myrle Marie Howard, Saint Joseph, MO; ed/ Att'd Art Instrn Inc, 1958; Comml Art Sch; pa/Tchr, Pensacola Jr Col, 1980-84; Pollak Trng Ctr, 1984-84; Okaloosa Walton Jr Col; Hope Marie Art Sch & Gallery, 1969-79; AK Leag Artists; Arts & Design Soc; Pensacola Artists Inc; cp/ Nat Mus Wom Arts; r/Bapt; hon/Illust for Creat-A-Books Inc, 1982-84; Elgin AF Paper "Eagle"; Num Recog incl'g Norman Rockwell, Charles Schultz, Liberace; USO; Awds Am Cancer Soc; DIB; World W/W Wom; Intl W/W Intells; Intl Register Profiles; Foremost Wom of the 20th Cent; Intl Book of Hon; W/W & Why of Successful FL Wom; Personalities of S; Intl Dir of Dist'd Ldrship; Others.

MAKK, AMERICO IMRE oc/Painter (fine arts); b/Aug 24, 1927; h/1515 Laukahi Street, Honolulu, HI 96821; ba/ Same; m/Eva; c/A B; p/Pal Makk and Katalin Samoday; ed/Saint Benedictin Gimn; Hungarian Nat Acad Fine Arts; pa/Prof Fine Arts, Academia de Belas Artes; Professoro de Belas Artes de Associacao Paulista de Belas Artes; Ofcl Artist Brazilian Govt; VP, Am Hungarian Art Assn; CoChm, Cerebral Palsey/ Carnegie Intl Ctr Exhbn; CoChm, HI Heart Assn Art Heart Exhbn; Am Profl Art Leag; Fifty Am Artists Assn; Associacao Paulistas de Belas Artes; Associacao Dos Professionais de Imprensa; Intl Art Exch; Metro Mus Art; Arpad Acad; Accademia Italia delle Arti; cp/Two/Ten Assn; Nat Geog Soc; hon/Num Pubs Nat & Intl incl'g *Am Review Art & Sci*, *Diario las Americas*, *Cue Mag*, *The Miami Herald*, *Aloha Mag*, *Gazeta do Noticias*, *Diario Cãricca*; Num Awds incl'g Centenarium Prize, 1948; Intl Art Exch Dirs, 1967; Gold Medals, Arpad Acad, 1981, 1983; White House Oval Ofc Recog, 1984; Intl W/W Art.

MAKK, EVA oc/Fine Artist; b/ December 1, 1933; h/1515 Laukahi Street, Honolulu, HI 96821; ba/Same; m/Americo Imre Makk; c/A B; p/Bert Holusa and Julia Ribenyl, Hungary; ed/ Acad Fine Arts, Paris; Acad Fine Arts, Rome; pa/Prof Fine Arts, Academia de Belas Artes; Professora de Belas Artes de Associacao Paulista de Belas Artes; Ofcl Artist Brazilian Govt; Dir, Am Hungarian Art Assn; Dir, World Fedn Hungarian Artists; CoChm, Cerebral Palsey/Carneigie Intl Ctr Exhbn; CoChm, HI Heart Assn Art for Heart Exhbn; Am Profl Art Leag; Fifty Am Artists Assn; Associacao Paulistas de Belas Artes; Associacao Dos Professionais de Imprensa; Intl Art Exch; Metro Mus Art; Arpad Acad; Accademia Italia delle Arti; cp/Nat Geog Soc; hon/Num Pubs Nat & Intl incl'g *Am Review Art & Sci*, *Diario las Americas*, *Park Ave Social Review*, *El Paso Herald Post*, *Revista Contemporanea*; Num Awds incl'g Silver Medal,

1953; Acad First Prize, 1958; Gold Medal World First Prize Painting, 1979; Gold Medals, Arpad Acad, 1981, 1983; Portrait Pres & Mrs Ronald Reagan, 1984; White House Oval Ofc Reception, 1984; US Senate Exhbn, 1984.

MAKRIS, ANDREAS oc/Composer; b/Mar 7, 1930; h/11204 Oak Leaf Drive, Silver Spring, MD 20901; ba/Washington, DC; m/Margaret Lubbe; c/Christos, Myron; ed/Nat Conservatory Salonica, 1950; Exch Student Prog, Philips Univ, 1950; KC Conservatory/Mannes Col Music, 1956; Aspen Music Fest, Fontainbleau Sch; pa/Composer in Residence, Nat Symph Orch, 1979-; Adv to Maestro Rostropovich, 1979; Mem, ASCAP, 1958; r/Greek Orthodox; hon/Prin wks incl "Scherzo for Violins" 1966, "Aegean Fest" 1967, "Fanfare Alexander" 1980; Recip Cit Greek Govt, 1980; Grantee, Nat Endowment Arts, 1967; Martha Baird Rockefeller Fund, 1970; Damrosh Foun, 1958; Awd, ASCAP, 1980.

MALER, ROGER oc/Advertising Executive; b/Mar 12, 1937; h/Post Office Box 435, Mount Arlington, NJ 07856; ba/Arlington, NJ; m/Wendy Friedman; c/Janine, Roger, Kyra, Paige; p/Lugero Roger and Rose Malerba; ed/ BA, Bklyn Col, 1959; NYC Commun Col, 1961-62; mil/NG, USAF; pa/Advtg & Promotion Supvr, Warner-Lambert Co, 1969-72; Creat Dir, Victor & Richards Inc, 1968-69; Pres, CEO, Thompson Maler Inc, 1972-77; Maler, Miller & Brown, 1977-79; Roger Maler Inc & Dimedco, 1979-; VP, Mt Arlington Bd Ed, 1973-78; Mayor, City of Mt Arlington, 1979-; Mem, Bus Profl Advtg Assn; Cert, Bus Communicator, 1962; Biomed Mktg Assn; Pharm Advtg Clb; NJ Sch Bds Assn; NJ Mayors Assn; Fdr, Pres, Landlord Mayors Assn; NJ Conf Mayors; hon/W/W E.

MALLATT, MARK EDWARD oc/ Dentist, Educator; b/July 6, 1950; h/ 1753 Esther Court, Plainfield, IN 46168; ba/Indianapolis, IN; m/Kathleen Ann (Quill); p/Russell C and Marjorie Mallatt, Crown Point, IN; sp/Thomas E and Rosemarie Quill, Indianapolis, IN; ed/ BS, IN Univ, 1972; DDS, IN Univ Sch Dentistry, 1975; pa/Clin Res Assoc, 1975-77; Instr Preventive Dentistry, 1977-78; Asst Prof Preventive Dentistry, 1978-; Assoc Dir Clin Res, Oral Hlth Res Inst, IN Univ, 1978-; Am Assn Dental Res; Am Assn Dental Schs; Am Dental Assn; IN Dental Assn; Indianapolis Dist Dental Soc; Intl Assn Dental Res; cp/Psi Omega Nat Dental Frat; VP, IN Sect Am Assn Dental Res, 1982; Pres, IN Sect Am Assn Dental Res, 1983; hon/Num Pubs incl'g *Jour Periodontal Res*, *Jour Oral Therapeutics & Pharm*, *Jour Oral Med*, *Oral Pathol & Oral Surg*; Am Psi Omega Nat Achmt Awd, 1974; W/ W Frontier Sci & Technol.

MALLEY, CHARLES EDWARD oc/ Manager; b/Jan 19, 1954; h/89-51 202 Street, Hollis, NY 11423; ba/New York, NY; p/Max and Sylvia Malley, Hollis, NY; ed/BS Physics, BS Math, St Univ NY, 1976; MBA, Adelphi Univ, 1980; Doct Profl Studies, Pace Univ; pa/Mem Programming Staff, Am T & T, 1977-79; Staff Asst, Budgets & Force, NY Telephone Co, 1979-80; Staff Spec Investmt Studies, 1980-82; Staff Mgr, Investmt Studies, 1982; Mgr, Bell Indep Relats, Am T & T, 1982; Dr Profl

Studies Student Assn; Intl Platform Assn; cp/Delta Mu Delta; hon/Physics 1976, MBA 1980 Hons; F'ship, Univ PA, 1976; W/W Fin Indust.

MALLON, THOMAS FRANCIS JR oc/Foreign Exchange Broker; b/Jan 2, 1944; h/22 Bagatelle Road, Dix Hills, NY 11746; ba/New York City, NY; m/Elizabeth Ann Kiely; c/Eileen Elizabeth, Erin Cristin; p/Thomas Francis and Rose Marie (McDonnell) Mallon; ed/M, BBA, Manhattan Col, 1966; Att'd Hofstra Univ, 1966-71; pa/Acctg Clk, Exxon, 1965-66; Fgn Exch Clk, Dealer, Brown Brothers, Harriman & Co, 1966-69; Chief Fgn Exch Dealer, Banca Nazionale del Lavora, 1969-70; Asst Cashier, Fgn Exch Dealer, Security Pacific Intl Bk, 1970-71; Owner, Pres, Thomas F Mallon Assocs, 1971-72; Pres, Dir, Kirkland Whitaker & Mallon, 1972-75; Secy-Treas, Dir, Mallon & Dorney Co Ltd, 1975-80; Mallon & Dorney Co (Can) Ltd, 1979-80; Lectr, Am Inst Bkg; Mem, Fgn Exch Brokers Clb; cp/Strathmore Civic Assn; Intl Platform Assn; Intl Biographical Assn; r/Rom Cath; hon/Contbg Author "The Roche Currency Survey" 1978-80; Guest Spkr MIBS Prog, Univ SC, 1978; Num Listings incl'g W/W: World, Fin & Indust, E, Germany, W & MW.

MALOFF, JON M oc/Insurance Agent and Consultant; b/August 29, 1941; h/Marmot Circle, Jamesville, NY 13078; ba/Fayetteville, NY; c/Scott C, Seth A; p/William Maloff, Syracuse, NY; ed/BA, Syracuse Univ, 1963; CPCU, 1973; pa/Comml Casualty Underwriter, Aetna Casualty & Surety Co, 1963-66; Ptnr, Ins Agt, Shimberg & Gerber Inc, 1966-76; VP, Alexander & Alexander Inc, 1976-81; Ins Agt, Miller Agy, 1981-; cp/Bds Dirs Jewish Home Ctl NY Inc, Syracuse Jewish Fdn, Jewish Commum Ctr Syracuse Inc; Past Pres, Jewish Fam Ser Bur; VP, Syracuse Jewish Fdn & Jewish Commum Ctr Syracuse; Secy, Lafayette Country Club; U Way Ctl NY Inc; Sterling Com, Human Sers Coun, Jewish.

MALONEY, MOIYA JANE oc/Counseling Psychologist; b/June 28, 1938; h/Route 2, May Road, Potsdam, NY 13676; ba/Same; p/Justin C Maloney, Spokane, WA; ed/BS, Marylhurst Col, 1963; Att'd Ft Wright Col, 1968; EdM, St Lawrence Univ, 1981; EdD, Intl Graduate Sch, 1983; pa/Tch, 1960-69; Cnslr Mtl Hlth Clin, 1971-75, 1976-; Acting Dir Mtl Hlth Clin, 1975; Cnslt, Geriatric Day Care Ctr, 1976-; Psychi Social Wkr & Cnslr, NY Dept Mtl Hygiene, 1976-; Am Pers & Cnslg Assn; Am Mtl Hlth Cnslrs Assn; NY St Mtl Hlth Cnslrs Assn; NY St Cnslrs Assn; No NY Zone Cnslrs Assn; Am Psychol Assn; World Cong Profl Hypnotists; cp/Potsdam-Canton Hosp Guild; LWV; Bd Dirs, Pres, Citizens Against Violent Acts, St Lawrence Co; r/Rom Cath; hon/Author "A Study of Transition Former Nuns from Rel to Secular Life"; Nationally Cert'd Cnslr, 1983.

MALZ, GRACE CHARLENE oc/Personnel Administrator/Business Executive; h/109 Pleasant View Drive, Post Office Box 175, Seville, OH 44273; ba/Westfield Center, OH; m/Sam; c/John, Michael, Stephen; p/Chester and Ethel (Young) Chaney, Seville, OH; ed/BSIM, Univ Akron, 1964; Post graduate Wk; Num Sems; pa/Long Distance Operator,

Star Telephone, 1945-47; Supvr, No OH Telephone, 1947-48; Secy, Wn & So Life, Wadsworth & Cleveland, 1948-50; Reporter, Seville Chronicle, 1945-49; Policy Typist, OH Farmers, 1953-58; Secy to VP Pers, 1958-63; Pers Asst, 1963-72; Pers Admr, Westfield Co, 1972-; VP, Pleasant Hill Mgmt, 1969-; VP, GraceLane Inc, 1978-; Secy, Country Manor Sq, 1978-; cp/Past Matron 1973, Treas 1974-84, OES; Co Fdr 1975, Adv Bd 1975-79, Past Mother Adv 1976-78, May-Swagler Assem-Order Rainbow Girls; Co Fdr, VP, Bus Wom's Investmt Clb, 1981-83; White Shrine, Seville ME C; Trustee, Seville Bd Public Affairs, 1979-82; Mem, Seville Planning Zoning Comm, 1979-80; Chm, World's Largest Yard Sale, 1981; Co Fdr, Prog Chair 1982, Gen Chm 1983, Capt Bates Fest; Pres, Seville C of C, 1983; Mem, Chapt Pres 1976-77, Nat Com 1976-78, Reg Publicity Pro Com, Am Soc Pers Adm; Akron Area Merit Awd Chair, 1976-; JVS 1974-81, Cloverleaf HS 1979-81, Wayne Col 1978-81, Adv Bd; Wayne Co JVS Adult Ed Bd, 1980-82; hon/Num Profl & Civic Articles, Pamphlets, Brochures; Cum Laude, Akron Univ; Runner-up Outstg Bus Wom-Medina Co, 1980-81; W/W Am Wom.

MANALIS, M S oc/Research Physicist, Educator; b/October 16, 1939; h/390 Merida Drive, Santa Barbara, CA 93111; ba/Santa Barbara, CA; m/Marilyn Jean; c/Jeremy, Scott, Andrew; p/Barney Manalis (dec) and Kathryn; sp/Douglas and Lottie White; ed/BA, CA St Univ, 1961; MS, Univ NH, 1964; PhD, Univ CA, 1970; pa/Physics Instr, Colby Col, 1963-64; Scist, Jet Propulsion Lab, CA Inst Technol, 1965; Res Scist, Univ CO, 1966; Physicist, Nat Bur Standards, 1967; Scist, The Te Co, 1970-72; Lectr, Dept Physics, Univ CA, 1975; Res Physicist, Quantum Inst, Univ CA, 1972-79; Res Physicist, Adj Lctr, Envir Studies, Univ CA, 1975-; Am Inst Physicists; Am Assn Physics Tchrs; cp/Energy Consltg Santa Barbara Co Bd Supvrs; Friends of the Earth; Sigma Xi; r/Deism; hon/Num Pubs incl'g "Nonthermal Saha Equation and the Physics of a Cool Dense Helium Plasma" 1971, *Preliminary Wind Siting Study of Anacapa Island* 1980; Num Grants incl'g Gen Motors Fellow, 1967-68; UC Sea Grant A-032 "Power Generator Inertailly Coupled to Seawaves" 1977-78; Equip Purchase Wind Assessmt, Hearst Corporation, 1982-; W/W Frontier Sci Technol.

MANDRELL, BARBARA ANN oc/Professional Singer and Musician; b/Dec 25; h/Gallatin, TN; ba/Nashville, TN; m/Ken Dudney; c/Matthew, Jaime; p/Irby and Mary Mandrell; pa/Performer, Standel Amplifiers, 1960; Num TV Perfs incl'g, "Town Hall Party", "Five Star Jubilee", "Barbara Mandrell & the Mandrell Sisters", "Hee Haw"; Num Concert Tours incl'g with Johnny Cash Show, the Mandrells, to Mil Commums Overseas; Recording Artist, CBS Records, ABC Records, MCA Records; Num Affil incl'g Grand Ole Opry; Am Fdn Musicians; Am Fdn TV & Radio Actors; Acad Country Music; Sr VP, Country Music Assn; Nat Acad Recording Arts & Sci; Screen Actors Guild; OES; r/Hendersonville Chapel; hon/Num Music Awds incl'g Female

Vocalist Year, Country Music Assn, 1979 & 1981; Outstg Artistic Achmt, Cashbox, 1979; Entertainer of Year, Country Music Assn, 1980 & 1981; Favorite All-Around Female Entertainer, People's Choice Awds, 1982; Musician of Year, Music City News Awds, 1981 & 1982; Favorite Variety Star, US Mag, 1982; Commum Ser Awd, Nat Wom Execs, 1979.

MANDULA, BARBARA B oc/Senior Staff Officer; b/Dec 19, 1941; h/500 23rd Street Northwest, Washington, DC 20037; ba/Washington, DC; m/Jeffrey; p/Isaac (dec) and Mollie Blumenstein, Bronx, NY; ed/BS, City Col, 1962; PhD, Brandeis Univ, 1969; pa/Num Res Assoc Positions incl'g City of Hope Med Ctr 1968-69, Princeton Univ 1969-70, Univ So CA Med Sch 1971-73, MA Gen Hosp 1974-76, Nat Acad Sci 1978-; Contbg Editor, Assn Wom Sci, 1978-; hon/Pubs in *Biochemical Pharm*; AAAS Mass Media Fellow, 1977.

MANGAN, M JENE oc/Director, Instructional Services; b/Feb 9, 1929; h/1303 North Paradise Court, Anaheim, CA 92806; ba/Anaheim, CA; p/Fred (Dec) and Helen Fumelle Van Boxtel, Clintonville, WI; ed/BS, WI St Univ, 1949; MS, Univ WI, 1958; pa/Tchr WI 1949-60, CA 1960-61; Tchr 1961-65, Cnslr 1965-68, Asst Prin 1968-79, Sr HS Prin 1979-80, Anaheim Union HS Dist; Dir, Inst Sers, 1980-; Exec Bd, So Counties Wom Ednl Mgmt, 1983; Assn CA Sch Adm; Assn Supvr & Curric Devel; CA Assn Gifted; PTA; Am Assn Univ Wom; Anaheim Sec'dy Sch Adm Assn; r/Rom Cath; hon/Pi Lambda Theta, 1958; W/W W.

MANGRUM, CLAUDE THOMAS JR oc/Corrections Administrator; b/Dec 10, 1930; h/2332 Arrow Head Avenue, San Bernardino, CA 92405; ba/San Bernardino, CA; m/Elaine Marie (Carter); c/Dianna Lynn, Lisa Michele, Robert Anthony; p/C T and Lillian Mangrum, Danville, VA; sp/Churchill and Julia Carter; San Bernardino, CA; ed/ThB, Malone College, 1952; BA, Youngstown Univ, 1956; MA, Kent State Univ, 1958; MPA, Univ So CA, 1972; pa/Min, Friends Ch, 1952-59; Probation Ofcr, Supvr, Dir, Asst Chief Probation Ofcr, San Bernardino Co Probation Dept, 1962-; Pres, CA Probation Parole & Correctional Assn, 1977-78; Treas, Wn Correctional Assn, 1981-82; Secy, Am Probation & Parole Assn, 1981-83; cp/Panel Chair, Arrowhead U Way, 1980-; Pres, Fam Ser Agy, 1977-79; Pres, Exch Clb, 1980-81; r/Friends; hon/Author *Profl Practitioner in Probation*, Num Articles in Var Profl Jour; Pepperdine Awd Corrections, 1980; Haye Awd, Writing in Corrections, 1981; Spec Awd, Chief Probation Ofcr CA, 1983; W/W W; Men of Achmt; Personalities W/MW.

MANHOLD, JOHN H oc/Pathologist, Author, Sculptor; b/Aug 20, 1929; h/352 Shunpike Road, Chatham Township, NJ, 07928; ba/Newark, NJ; m/Enriqueta Andino; ed/BA, 1941; DMD, 1944; MA, 1956; mil/1944-46, 1950-55; pa/Instr, Pathol, Tufts Univ Col Med & Dental, 1947-50; Asst Prof, Chm, Dept Pathol & Oral Pathol, Washington Univ, 1954-56; Assoc Prof 1958, Prof & Chm 1959-, NJ Col Med & Dental; Pres, Acad Psychosomatic Med, 1977; AAAS; Am Psychol Assn; Instrnl Assn

PERSONALITIES OF AMERICA

Dental Res; Am Soc Clin Pathol; cp/
Sigma Xi; r/Prot; hon/Num pubs incl'g
Introductory Psychosomatic Dentistry 1956,
Outline Pathol 1960, *Clin Oral Diag* 1965,
Practical Dental Mgmt: Patients & Pract
1984; Fellow, Acad Psychosomatic Med,
Am Col Dental, Intl Col Dentistry; Pres
Awd, Alumni of Univ Med & Dental
NJ; Awd of Achmt, Balto Col Phys &
Surg; Num Sculpture Awds; W/W: Sci,
E, Am Art.

MANICHE, BARBARA LANE oc/
Owner & Manager; b/Jul 18, 1942; h/
4817 Brookdale Ave, Oakland, CA
94619; ba/Oakland, CA; c/Stephanie
Alise; p/Oliver C and Valerie Lane,
Oakland, CA; ed/AA 1979, BA Golden
Gate Univ; Cert, Heald Col Bus, 1972;
Att'd St Mary's Col, 1981; Owner &
Mgr, Maniche's Clerical Sers; Del
Monte Corporation, 1966-81; Payroll &
Pers Clk, 1966-69; Indust Relats Clk,
1969-72; Secy Public Affairs, Envir
Protection, Indust Engrg, 1972-74;
Payroll Tax Acctg, 1974-81; Cand,
Peralta Col Bd, 1972; Dir Ed LWV, 1980;
Mem, Nat Assn Female Execs; Mem,
Nat Notary Assn; Notary Comm,
1982-87; cp/Mem, Oakland C of C; hon/
Author of *Fat Cats with Fabricated Brains*;
Cert Recog, 1976; W/W W.

MANIERI, MICHAEL JOSEPH oc/
Industrial Hygienist, Safety Profes-
sional; b/Dec 16, 1951; h/100 Glen Eyrie
Avenue, San Jose, CA 95125; ba/Santa
Clara, CA; p/Michael and Lucille
Manieri, Massapequa, NY; ed/BS, NY
Inst Technol, 1973; MS, Wayne St Univ
Sch Med, 1976; pa/Corporate Indust
Hygienist/Safety Spec, Applied Mats
Inc, 1984-; Mgr Corp Safety & Indust
Hygiene, Avantek Inc, 1981-83; Dept
Occup Safety Hlth, 1980-81; Assoc
Indust Hygienist, Employee Benefits Ins
Co, 1977-80; Corporate Indust Hygie-
nist, SRI Intl, 1976-77; Mem, Am Indust
Hygiene Assn,1976-; Am Soc Safety
Engrs; Ctl Coast Cos Safety Coun,
1976-; Bay Area Electronics Safety
Group, 1980-; Penninsula Indust Bus
Assn, 1981-; Com Mem, NC Sect AM
Indust Hygiene Assn Symp, 1982-83;
Participator, Mediterranean Fruit Fly
Occupl Hlt Study, 1981; Mem, Semi-
conductor Indust Assn, 1981; Am
Electronics Assn, 1981; Soc Biomedical
Sci, NY Tech, 1969-73; Mem, US Ski
Assn, 1980; cp/Tau Epsilon Phi Frat,
1970-73; Hon/Author of "Hygienic
Guide Scenes" *Am Indust Hygiene Assn*
1976-77; W/W W.

MANLEY, AUDREY FORBES oc/
Physician; b/Mar 25, 1934; h/2807-18th
Street Northwest, Washington, DC
20009; ba/Rockville, MD; ed/AB, Spel-
man Col, 1955; MD, Meharry Med Col,
1959; Intern, St Mary Mercy Hosp,
1960; mil/US Public Hlth Ser, Capt; pa/
Staff Pediatrician, Chgo Bd of Hlth,
1963-66; Pvt Pract, Chgo, IL, 1963-66;
Assoc in Pediatrics, N Lawndale Neigh-
borhood Hlth Ctr; Asst Prof, The Chgo
Med Sch; Instr in Pediatrics, Asst Med
Dir, Woodlawn Chd Hlth Ctr, 1967-69;
Univ of Chgo, 1967-69; Asst Dir for
Ambulatory Pediatrics, Mt Zion Hosp and Med Ctr,
Pediatrics, Mt Zion Hosp and Med Ctr,
1969-70; Med Conslt, Spelman Col,
1970-71; Med Dir, Fam Planning Prog
and Chm, Hlth Careers Adv Com,
Spelman Col, 1972-76; Orgr/Prog
Conslt, Fam Planning Prog and Inst for
Col Pers in Fam Planning, 1972-76; Med

Dir, Grady Meml Hosp Fam Planning
Clin, Chief of Med Sers, Emory Univ
Fam Planning Prog, 1972-76; Med Dir,
Bur of Commun Hlth Ser, DHEW,
1976-77; Med Dir, Bur of Commun Hlth
Sers, Sickle Cell Disease; Comm'd Ofcr,
USPHS Capt 06 Med Dir Chief, Genetic
Diseases Ser Br Ofc for Maternal and
Child Hlth Bur of Commun Hlth Sers,
1978-; Clin Instr in Pediatrics, Cook Co
Sch of Nsg, 1961-63; Lectr, Pediatrics
and Child Care, The Chgo Med Sch,
1965-67; Clin Instr in Pediatrics, Mid-
way Tech Allied Hlth Tng Prog for
Para-Meds, 1966-69; Instr in Pediatrics,
Pritzker Sch of Med, 1967-69; Clin Asst
Prof, Univ of CA Med Sch, David Geffen
Pediatrics, 1969-70; Asst Prof, Emory
Univ/Grady Meml Hosp, 1972-76;
Pediatric Care Conslt, Cook Co Hosp
Nurseries, 1963-65; Participating Phys,
Hdstart/EPSDT, 1965-69; Co-Chm,
Coun for BioMed Careers, Annual Hlth
Careers Conf, 1966-67; Exec Com,
Treas, Bd of Dirs, Coun for BioMed
Careers, 1966-69; Adv Coun, Barat Col
"Upward Bound" Prog, 1966-69; Adv
Coun, Hdstart, Chgo Com on Urban
Opport, 1966-69; Com for Recruitment
of Minority Students, Univ of Chgo
Med Sch, 1968-69; Conslt, Gov Com on
Hunger and Malnutrition in IL, 1969;
Med Conslt, Am Aacad of Pediatrics,
1969; Grp Ldr, Med Tm, "Operation
Crossroads Africa", 1963; Mem,
Soviet-Am Clin Pediatric Conf, 1968;
European Ed Exc Prog, 1970; Med and
Public Hlth Progs Site Visits, 1971-72;
Med Conslt, 1973-76; Spelman Col
Alumnae Assn, 1955; Meharry Alumni
Assn, 1959; Am Acad of Pediatrics,
1967; Nat Med Assn, 1968; Am Public
Hlth Assn, 1972; AAUW, 1972; Nat
Acad of Sci, Inst of Med, 1976; AAAS,
1978; Operation Crossroads Africa
Alumni Assn, 1981; cp/Hlth Manpower
Task Force, Atlanta Regl Comm,
1971-74; Chm, Ser Com, Atlanta Area
Fam Planning Coun, 1971-74; Grants
Review Com, Nat Inst of Hlth; 1972-75;
Bd of Dirs, Ser Com, Easter Seal Soc,
1972-75; Bd of Dirs, Atlanta Univ Ctr,
1974-76; Bd of Dirs, Atlanta Southside
Comprehensive Neighborhood Hlth
Ctr, 1974-76; Liaison Com for Hlth and
Social Sers Planning, 1974-76; Commr,
Atlanta Regl Com, 1974-76; Visiting Fac
Com, Harvard Univ and Radcliffe Col,
1974-81; hon/Spelman Col, 1951-55;
Zeta Phi Beta S'ship, 1951; Jesse Smith
Noyes Foun, 1955-59; Wom of the Yr,
Zeta Phi Beta, 1962; Chgo Com on
Urban Opport, Commun Ser Cert,
1966; Bd of Trustees, Spelman Col,
1966-70; Elected, Fellow, Am Acad of
Pediatrics, 1967; VP, Cook Co Chd's
Hosp, 1973; Inst of Med, Nat Acad of
Sci, 1976; Outstg Ldrship Awd, AAUW,
1976; Atlanta Regl Comm Public Ser
Awd, 1974-76; Clark Col Wom
Resource Ctr; Commun Ser Awd, 1977;
Mary McLeod Bethune Achmt in Govt
Awd of the Nat Coun of Negro Wom;
Nat Assn of Sickle Cell Screening and
Ed Clins, Awds of Apprecs; Student Nat
Med Assn, 1980; Spelman Col, Awds
of Apprec, Hlth Careers and Fam
Planning, 1976; Author of Num Pubs,
W/W: Am Wom, Black Ams; Personal-
ities of the S; Outstg Yg Wom of Am.

MANN, EDWARD COLEMAN oc/
Associate Professor Engineering Technology; b/Sep 4, 1947; h/6512 Saginaw

Road, Memphis, TN 38134; ba/Mem-
phis, TN; c/Douglas; p/Mr and Mrs J
Edward Mann, Leechburg, PA; ed/BA,
Thiel College, 1969; EdM 1971, EdD
1976, PA St Univ; pa/Assoc Prof Engrg
Technol 1983-, Asst Prof 1979-83,
Memphis St Univ; Proj Dir 1981-, Inst
Dir 1983-, Inst Asst Dir 1981, 1982, TN
Dept Ed; Dept Chm, Asst Prof 1978-79,
Proj Dir 1978-79, Asst Prof 1976-79,
Dept Hd Ed Ser, Asst Prof 1975-76,
Adm Intern 1973-74, St Tech Inst
Memphis; Res Asst 1974-75, Grad Asst
1970-71, 1972-73, PA St Univ; Career
Ed Cnslr, Ctl Westmoreland Co Schs,
1971-72; Social Casewkr, Dept Public
Asst, 1969-70; Num Cnslg Positions
incl'g St Tech Inst, Shelby Co Penal
Farm, PA St Univ; Num Cnsltg Posi-
tions incl'g TN Electronics Inc, Memphis
Urban Leag, Fayette Co Schs; Prog Chm
Nat Clin, Am Tech Ed Assn, 1977; Prog
Chm Tech 1978-80, Policy Chm
1980-83, Ed Div, Am Voc Assn; Pres,
TN Voc Assn, 1982-83; Prog Chm, TN
Tech Ed Coun, 1976; Am Pers & Guid
Assn; Nat Voc Guid Assn; TN Pers &
Guid Assn; Mem Co-Chp 1977-78, Chm
1978-79, TN Voc Guid Assn; Am Voc
Ed Res Assn; Nat Assn Indust & Tech
Tchr Edrs; Mem Policy Com, Nat Assn
Instnl Ldrs Tech Edrs, 1979-81; Nat
Employmt & Tng Assn; TN Employmt
& Tng Assn; hon/Num Pubs incl'g *TN
Tchr-Coors Handbook* 1980, "Eval of the
Conf", *The Fourth Annual PA Conf
Post-Sec'dy Occupl Ed* 1973, "Tech Ed Div,
1978 AVA Conv Highlights", *Sch Shop*
1978; Phi Delta Kappa; Iota Alpha Delta;
TN St Chm for Career Guid Wk, 1976;
Outstg Yg Men Am; W/W S & SW;
Outstg Ser Awd, Tech Ed Div, Am Voc
Assn, 1981.

MANNIX, L BERNICE oc/Assistant
Vice President; b/Jun 23, 1922; h/708
Milwaukee Avenue, Deer Lodge, MT
59722; ba/Deer Lodge, MT; m/William
T J Mannix (dec); c/Katherine M
Mccaffery, Mary B Cooper, Margaret
V Biggerstaff, Teresa M Mannix; p/Jens
M and Lena (Markelson) Hansen Sr
(Dec); sp/Fred and Kate (VanGundy)
Mannix (dec); ed/BA, Univ MT, 1944;
pa/Teller, Deer Lodge Bk & Trust,
1944-45; Bkkpr, Mannix Feed, 1948-63;
Bkkpr, Barmont Sales, 1966-67; Acctg
Dept 1967-69, Installment Loan Sec
1969-76, Asst Cashier 1976-78, Asst VP
1978-, Real Est Loan Ofcr, Trust Ofcr,
Escrow Ofcr, Deer Lodge Bk & Trust;
cp/Ldr, 4-H, Deer Lodge, 1961-71; Secy,
Coun 1965-68, Pres 1969-71, Powell
4-H Coun; Pres 1981-83, VP 1978-80,
Secy 1974-77, Powell Co Mus & Arts;
Mother FHA 1965-66, St Chapt 1965;
Chm, Rocky Mt Grp 1977, St Mem Chm
1983, Nat Assn Bk Wom; Last Spike
Cent Com, 1983-83; Alderperson, City
Deer Lodge, 1984; Commun Chorus;
Ch Choir; Am Legion Aux; Secy
1957-58, Pres 1959, Wom Clb; Treas,
Hosp Aux, 1984-; Sons & Daughs
Norway; r/Cath; hon/Powell Guards,
1937; Thespians, 1939; Scholastic Lttr,
1939; Nat Hon Soc, 1939; DAR Good
Citizenship, 1940; Grand Cross Colors
Rainbow, 1941; Spurs, 1941; W/W: W,
Am Wom.

MANNO, BRUNO VICTOR oc/
Director of Research and In-Serivce
Programs; b/May 2, 1947; h/3246 Grace
Street Northwest, Washington, DC
20007; ba/Washington, DC; p/Vincenzo

383

and Antoinette Manno, Cleveland, OH; ed/BA 1970, MA 1972, Univ Dayton; PhD, Boston Col, 1975; pa/Asst Prof, Dir Ofc Moral & Rel Ed, Univ Dayton, 1975-78; Vis'g Prof, Cath Tchrs Col, 1978; Vis'g Res Assoc Nat Opinion Res Ctr, Univ Chgo, 1978-79; Vis'g Fellow Div Sch; Dir Res, Data Bk & In-Ser Progs, Nat Cath Ed Assn, 1979-; Bd Dirs, Univ Dayton, 1982-; Mem, Col Theol Soc; Assn Profs & Res Rel Ed; Nat Cath Ednl Assn; Cath Theol Soc Am; Rel Ed Assn; Am Acad Rel; cp/ Polanyi Soc; Phi Sigma Tau; r/Rom Cath; hon/Author *How to Ser Students with Fed Ed Prog Benefits* 1980; Co-Editor, *The Earth is the Lord's*: Essays in Stewardship, 1978; Contrb Num Articles & Reviews to Rel & Scholarly Jours.

MANOUKIAN, NOEL E oc/State Supreme Court Chief Justice; b/Jan 1, 1938; m/Louise Marie; c/Jacqueline Marie, Joseph Edwin; p/Hagop (Dec) and Rose Manoukian, Reno, NV; ed/BA, Univ Pacific, 1961; LLB & JD, Univ Santa Clara, 1964; pa/Dept DA, Douglas Co, NV, 1965-67; Chief Justice, Supr Ct of NV, 1983-84; Chm Bd & Pres, NV Dist Judges Assn, 1975-77; Mem 1977, Chm 1983-84, NV Jud Ed Coun; CoChm, Com Cts Rules Civil Procedure, 1980-82; CoChm, NV St Bar Appellate Advocacy Handbook Com; Bd Dirs, Am Judic Soc; St Bar Com on Jud; St Bd Pardons; Chm, Conf Chief Justices Arbitration Com, 1983-; CoChm, NV St Bar-Judiciary Alt Dispute Resolution Study Com, 1983-84; Mem, NV St Bar Com on Judiciary, 1983-; Att'd Num Sems incl'g SW Jud Conf 1975-, Nat Jud Col 1975-, Am Bar Assn Appellate Judges Sem 1979-; Num Articles Pub incl'g "Vigilance to Preserve Law is Def Agst Another Holocaust" *The Jewish Reporter* 1978, "Take a Load Off Justice" Reno Gazette-Jour, 1983; Num Lectrs incl'g NV Judges Assn Sems, Wn NV Peace Ofcrs Assn; Num Orgs & Activs incl'g Hon Life Mem, St Chm Public Ed, Past Chm Bd & Past Chm Exec Com, Past V Chm Bd Dirs, Mem, Am Cancer Soc, 1946-; NV St Pers Adv Comm, 1971-73; Juv Justice & Juv Delinquency Preven Adv Com; Mem, No NV Child Abuse & Trauma Adv Com, 1975-77; cp/Past Pres 1969-70, Mem, Tahoe-Douglas C of C; NV Area Coun, BSA, Exec Com, 1977-; Nat Pony Express Assn, 1983-; hon/W/ W Students Am Univs & Cols; Edwin J Owens Lwyr of Year Awd, Univ Santa Clara Law Sch; SAR/DAR Good Citizen's Medal.

MANRIQUE, LUIS A oc/Senior Research Associate; b/Dec 26, 1948; h/ 1290-D Maunakea Street Number 349, Honolulu, HI 96817; ba/Ithaca, NY; m/ Haunani; p/Prospero and Thelma Manrique, Huancayo, Peru; sp/Reginald and Elaine Nash, Honolulu, HI; ed/BS, 1970; MS, 1973; PhD, 1982; pa/Agronomist, Intl Potato Ctr, 1975-77; Res Assoc 1979-82, Asst Res 1983, Univ HI; Sr Res Assoc, Cornell Univ, 1984; Am Soc Agronomy, 1977-; Soil Sci Soc Am, 1977-; Intl Soc Tropical Root Crops, 1980-; Intl Soil Sci Soc, 1982-; Potato Assn Am, 1983-; hon/Num Pubs in SSSAJ, Am Potato J, & Univ HI Agric; Sigma Gamma Delta.

MANSUR, LOUIS K oc/Materials Scientist; b/Apr 18, 1944; h/105 Timbercrest Drive, Clinton, TN 37716; ba/

Oak Ridge, TN; m/Helen Ruth; c/ Kendra, Joanna, Warren; p/Adelea Mansur, Lowell, MA; sp/Thomas A Hotz, Fort Smith, AK; ed/BS, Lowell Technol Inst, 1966; MENG, Cornell Univ; PhD, Cornell Univ; pa/Reactor Engr, US Atomic Energy Comm, 1966-67; Reactor Physicist, USAEC, 1968-70; Res Sci 1974-82, Grp Ldr 1983-, Oak Ridge Nat Lab; Chm 1981-82, Mem 1976-, Am Soc Metals; Am Soc Advmt Sci, 1974-; Am Nuclear Soc, 1968-; Metall Soc Am, 1976-; cp/ Sigma Xi; hon/Num Pubs; Fellow Am Nuclear Soc; Dept Energy Mats Sci Awd; Univ S'ship; Hons Grad.

MANUEL, VIVIAN oc/Executive; b/ May 6, 1941; h/785 Park Avenue, New York, NY 10021; ba/New York, NY; p/ George T Manuel, Long Island, NY; ed/ BA, Wells Col, 1963; MS, Univ WY, 1965; pa/Conslt 1978-80, Dir Corporate Affairs 1976-78, Std Brands; Corporate Rep, Bus/Fin, Corporate Public Info 1972-76, Account Supvr 1968-72, GE; Mgmt Analyst, Navy Dept, 1966-68; Bd of NYWICI; Wom Execs in PR; Wom Ec Roundtable; Wo Bus Owners; Am Mgmt Assn; Am Soc Profl & Exec Wom; hon/GE Mgmt Awd, 1972; Sustained Superior Perf Awd, Dept of Navy, 1967; W/W Am Wom.

MANUSO, JAMES S J oc/Corporate Consultant; b/Nov 9, 1948; h/50 East Tenth Street, New York, NY 10003; ba/ Same; m/Susan Alexander; p/John D and Eleanor S Manuso; ed/BA, Washington Sq Col, NYU, 1970; MA, New Sch Social Res, 1972; PhD, 1978; MA, Columbia Bus Sch, 1983; Cert Mgmt, Harvard Bus Sch, 1981; pa/Asst VP & Dir Prog, Planning & Devel 1980, Chief Psychol 1974-80; Equitable Life Assurance Soc US; Cnslt, Am Hlth Foun, 1980-; Mgr, Equip Control Dept, Am Export Isbrandtsen Lines, 1966-67; Num Adv Positions incl'g Advr, Washington Bus Grp Hlth, 1978; Nat Inst Drug Abuse, 1978; Chm, Fed Drug Abuse Preven Wk, 1973, 1974; Rehab Cnslr, NY St Ofc Drug Abuse Sers, 1970-72; Sr Cnslt, McGraw-Hill Prodns, 1978; Adv, ABC Pictures Intl, 1979; Instr, New Sch Social Res, 1976-; Clin Supvr, New Sch Soc Res, 1977-; Clin Supvr, Col Univ, 1978-; Cnslt, Acad Review, 1979; Past Pres, NY Biofeedback Soc, 1981-82; CoFdr, Secy & Treas, Am Inst Stress, 1979-; Mem of Var Assns incl'g Am Psychi Assn, Am Psychol Assn, Mensana Clin; r/Epis; hon/New Sch Scholar, 1973-78; Mem Ec, Psychol & Washington Sq Col Coat of Arms Hon Soc, 1970; Rampart Col Scholar, Dept Ec, 1968; NY Univ Hons Prog Student, 1967-70; W/W: E, Frontier Sci & Technol, Biomed Sci.

MANYAM, BALA oc/Associate Professor of Neurology and Pharmacology; b/Oct 15, 1942; ba/Springfield, IL 62708; c/Shaila; p/Kolar Venksteser (dec) and Swarnam Venktesier, Bangalore, India; ed/BS, MB, Bangalore Univ, 1967; Residency, Thomas Jefferson Univ, 1975; F'ship 1976; Diplomate Am Bd Psychi & Neurol, 1983; pa/Instr, Dept Neurol 1975-80, Asst Prof, Dept Neurol 1980-83, Assoc Prof, Dept Neurol 1983-, Asst Prof, Dept Pharm 1981-83, Assoc Prof, Dept Pharm 1983-, Jefferson Med Col Thomas Jefferson Univ; Staff Neurol 1975-80, Dir, Mvt Disorders Clinc 1977-, Asst Chief,

Neurol Ser, 1982-, VA Med Ctr; Mem, World Fed Neurol, 1977-; Mem, Sect Neuropharmacology, Am Acad Neurol, 1981-82; Chm 1980-81 & Mem 1978-82, Res & Dev Com, Chm, Lab Eval Com 1980-81, Mem, Lib Adv Com 1980-83, Mem, Resident Review Co 1981-, Mem, Hosp Ed Com 1982-, Mem, Med Records Com 1982-, VA Med Ctr; Am Acad Neurol, 1975-; Am Soc Pharmacology & Expt Therapeutics, 1981-; Sigma Xi, 1975-; Phila Neurol Soc, 1976-; Emeritus Mem, Am Soc Neurol Invest; r/Hindu; hon/Num Pubs incl'g "Amantadine in Essential Tremor" 1981, "Isoniazid Induced Reduction Serum Cholesterol" 1983; Govt Mysore S'ship, 1965-67; Grad with Distn in Med, Bangalore Univ, 1967; Spec Perf Awd, VA, 1977, 1983; W/W Frontier Sci & Technol.

MAO, CHI CHIANG oc/Physician and Scientific Researcher; b/Aug 7, 1942; h/12108 Stone West, Houston, TX 77035; ba/Houston, TX; m/Shelly G; c/Hua-Ching, Dillon, and Noreen; p/ Sung-Nien Mo and Chin Y Mo, Taipei, Taiwan; ed/BS, 1965; PhD, 1971; MD, 1981; mil/Army; pa/Phys, Baylor Col Med, Afil Hosps, 1983-; Phys, Univ TX Med Sch Houston, Afil Hosps, 1981-83; Phys, Tidelands Gen Hosp, Harris Co Psych Hosp Houston, 1983-; Res Sci, Univ Tx Med Sch Houston, 1978-79; Res Sci, Nat Inst Mtl Hlth, 1972-74, 1975-77; Vis'g Prof, Nat Taiwan Normal Univ, China Med Col, 1974-75; hon/ Num Pubs; Trustee, Inst Chinese Culture, Houston, TX, 1981-86.

MAPPES, CARL RICHARD oc/ Resources Manager and Interpreter; b/ Feb 17, 1935; h/Star Route 5, Box 223, Kimberling City, MO 65686; ba/Same; c/Tanya Lizette Mappes; p/Theodore Roosevelt Mappes, Kimberling City, MO; Elsie Day Mappes (dec); ed/BA, Univ of MT, 1965; PhD, Univ of CA, Univ of Wash, NWn Univ, Mount Holyoke Col, Univ of MA, Univ of NC, 1979; mil/USN, 7th Fleet, 1953-61; pa/ Public Relats Rep, Assn Am Railroads, 1953-54; Design Engr, Kendrick and Redinger, 1954-55; Design Engr, Counts and Lawrence, 1955-56; Design Engr, Wm Singleton Co, 1958-59; Sci Res, ARCON, 1956, Greenland Expedition; Customer Ser Rep, En Airlines, 1960-61; Resources Mgr; US Forest Ser USDA 1966; MT Nat Park Ser, USDI, 1966, WY & AZ; Info Spec, 1967-68, MT & NM; Photographer, US Dept of Agri, Ofc of Info, 1969; Resources Mgr, Nat Park Ser, USDI, 1969, FL; Info Spec, NM, NY, MO, 1969-80; Social Sci, US Dept of Commer, 1980, MO; Resources Mgr, 1980-81; Interpreter, Nat Park Ser, USDI, AZ, 1981-82; Journalist, Larimer Pubs & PBS & NBC, 1983; Am Geographical Soc; Am Ornithologists Union; Am Soc of Ichthyologists and Herpetologists; Am Soc of Limnology and Oceanography, Inc; Am Soc of Mammalogists; Arctic Inst of N Am; British Ecol Soc; British Ornithologists Union; Ecol Soc of Am; Freshwater Biol Assn; Marine Biol Assn of the U Kingdom; Royal Geographical Soc; Royal Photog Soc of Great Britain; Soc of Photogs in Communs; hon/Author of Approx 13,600 Pubs Worldwide Continuously Since 1947; 1st Pl Awds, Metro Civic Arch and Engr Designs, Wash, DC, 1955, 1956, 1959;

Public Spkg in MD, 1958, AZ 1966; Feature Writing in MO, 1971; Feature Writer and Syndicate Dir of Photogs; Feature Writer and Syndicate Dir of Writers; Intl Authors and Writers W/ W; DIB; Intl W/W of Intells; Mem of Achmt; Personalities of the W & MW; W/W: in Am, in the MW, in Am Art.

MARASHIO, PAUL WILLIAM oc/ Educator; b/May 30, 1941; h/141 Bluff Street, Salem, NH 03079; ba/Salem, NH; m/Nancy Feeny; p/Peter (dec) and Catherine Marashio, Medford, MA; sp/ James and Lillian Feeney, Claremont, NH; ed/BEd, Keene St Col, 1963; MA, UNHCAS Wesleyan Univ, 1968; pa/Hist Tchr, Somersworth Sch Distric, 1963-66; Hist Dept Hd, Salem HS, 1966-69; Supvr Curric 1969-70, Prin 1970-77, Woodbury Sch; Curric Coor 1977; cp/Indian Hist Soc; Phi Delta Kappa; NH Hist Soc; Salem Hist Soc; Hist District Comm; Salem Hist Mus; r/Cath; hon/Author of Num Hist & Ednl Articles; SHS Tchr of Year, 1970; Fellow, AZ St Univ; Fellow, Exeter Writing Proj, NWP; Fellow, Nat Humanities Sems, Dartmouth; Ed Awd, NH Coun for Better Schs; W/W in Am E.

MARAVIGNA, MARIA oc/Artist and Sculptor; h/19 Middlesex Street, Winchester, MA 01890; ba/Same; ed/ Boston Univ Art Sch, 1932-33; Mus Fine Arts Sch, 1933-34; Pvt Studies w Var Experts in Field, 1930-36; pa/Artist & Sculptor-Mushrooms, 1936-; Portraits & Paintings, All Media; Num Solo Shows; Owner, Giftshop & Art Gallery, 1941-50; Sculpture, Ceramic Mushroom Sculptures (Used by Lectrs in Botany Classes); Over 200 Invitational or Self-Sponsored Exhibs over US, Libs, Art Galleries, Art & Garden Ctrs; Mycol Confs; Bks; TV Progs; Clbs; Invitational 3-Yr Travelling Exhib, Boston Public Lib & 27 Brs; Spec Exhibs incl'g MA Audubon Soc, 1965; Newport Art Assn, 1966; NY Bot Gdn, 1967; Boston Univ, 1968-75; SF, Acad Arts & Scis, 1970; Springfield Mus Sci, 1971; Mus Sci, 1977; Thousands of Sculptures Carried by Art Galls; Art Ctrs; Mus; Frequent Lectr in Field; Spec Commns & Perm Exhibs incl'g WM A Springer Meml Collection, 1970; Kingwood Ctr, Mansfield, OH; Mem Exhib, New Caanan Art Ctr, 1972; NY Bot Gdn, 1978; Intensive Prog, Toxic Mushrooms, Requested by AMA & Am Col Emer Phys, 1980 Spec Comm Large Perm Poisonous Exhib, Centro Gen De Intoxicaoiones, Hosp De El Valle, Venezuela, 1969; 1975, Pubs Feature Stories & Mushroom Portraits, Wild Mushrooms; MA Hort Mag Mbrships incl'g Hon Life, Boston Mycol Club; Copley Soc Boston; N Am Mycol Assn; Am Mycol Soc; NY Botan Gdn; MA Audubon & Hort Socs; hon/Am Mus Nat Hist Hons incl'g Yankee Superlatives—Full Page, Only Person to Hand-Sculpture Thousands of Bot Accurate Ceramic Mushroom Sculptures, Reps of over 3000 Different Natural Species, 1977.

MARCHI, GARY MICHAEL oc/ Futurist, Creative Business-Market Development Consultant; b/Feb 25, 1953; h/Post Office Box 40296, San Francisco, CA 94110; ba/Same; ed/Intl Corporate Bus Sch, Aervoe/Dynamin Corporate Bus Sch, 1972-74; pa/Bus & Mkt Advr, Owner Spirit of the Future Unltd, 1974-; Creat Media Advr, Owner

Media Network Sys Div, 1979-; Bus & Mkt Devel Conslt, Fund Raising Advr, Fund Raising Sers Div, CA Corporation, 1972-73; sp/Fdr, Creat Dir Spirit of the Future Creative Inst, 1976-; Co-Fdr, VP, Venture Devel Assn, 1981-; hon/ Creator-Prodr of "Future Consumer", Wkly Radio-TV Documentary Series, 1979-; Created the" Future-Logic Sys & Creat Sys Devel for Applied Creat Thinking, Lrng & Planning"; Applied Res Manual "Reestablishing the US Constit, Bill of Rights" & "Clearly Defining the Free Enterprise Sys", Author of "Cnslts Contracts Kit" 1983; W/W W.

MARCHI, LORRAINE JUNE oc/ Executive Director; b/Jun 5, 1923; h/305 East 24 Street, New York, NY 10010; ba/Same; m/Robert L Marchi; c/Jeffrey Gene, Debra, Beth Marchi; ed/Att'd Stanford Univ, 1941-42; Univ CA Berkeley, 1942-43; pa/Fdr, Com to Aid Visually Handicapped Chd, 1954; Fdr, Pres, Aid to Visually Handicapped, 1957; Exec Dir, Nat Aid to Visually Handicapped, 1959-; Secy 1955-66, Pres 1966-69, Conf CA Exceptl & Rehab Needs; Bd Chm, Langley Porter Neuropsychiatric Inst, 1960-72; hon/ Humanitarian Ser Cert, Van Nuys CA C of C, 1965; Spec Ser Awd, LA Co Soc of Ophthalmology, 1971; Hon Awd, Am Acad of Ophthalmology & Otolaryngology, 1978; Cert Apprec, Am Acad of Ophthalmology, 1978; Wom of Yr, SF Section, Nat Coun Jewish Wom, 1957; One of Ten Dist'd Wom in SF, 1959; Worlds W/W Wom; W/W Am Wom; DIB.

MARIEL oc/Professional Photographer, Business Owner; b/Aug 5, 1938; h/Post Office Box 814825, Dallas, TX 75381; ba/Same; c/Scott Craig Goodwin, William Cullen Coombes, Anna Maria Coombes, Joel Howard Coombes, p/William N Turner, Palos Verdes, CA and Mary Lincoln, Yarnell, AZ; pa/Owner, Lazarus Enterprises, 1981-; Owner, Pres, CEO, AZ Custom Iron Inc, AZ Custom Steel, AZ Custom Mfg Inc, Eagle Erectors Inc, WCS Constrn Inc, 1967-81; Am Subcontractors Assn; Nat Assn Female Execs; Am Soc Profl & Exec Wom; Nat Assn Wom Bus Owners; Intl Platform Assn; Nat Assn for Self-Employed; Intl Photo Soc; cp/All Ofcs Held in AZ Steel Fabricators Assn, 1975-80; AZ Field Erectors Assn; Mensa; Intertel; r/RLDS; hon/Featured in Nationwide Ad by Employers Ins Wausau, 1980; Only Wom to Hold AZ Steel Erection Lics, 1980; Num Listings incl'g Bk of Hon; Dir Dist'd Ams; Personalities Am; Intl Register Profiles; Intl W/W Intells; Men & Wom Distn; World W/W Wom; W/W: Am Wom, Fin & Indust, W, World.

MARINER, WILLIAM MARTIN oc/ Doctor of Chiropractic; b/Jan 2, 1949; h/428-B A Street, Encinitas, CA 92024; ba/Del Mar, CA; c/Joshua Kassel, Morgen Kassel; p/William Joseph and Ellen Scott Mariner, Pittsford, NY; ed/ Doct of Chiro; BS, LA Col of Chiro; AA, Phoenix Col; pa/Dir, Pacific Hearing Arts Ctr, 1980-; Asst Dean, LA Col Chiro, 1977-80; Adm Conslt, Fac Mem, CA Acupuncture Col, 1978-80; Dir, GRD Hearing Arts Ctr, 1975-77; Phy Therapist, ARE Clin, 1975-76; Mgr, Gurn's Grainery, 1974-75; Intl Col of Applied Kinesiology; Am Chiro Assn;

Coun on Nutrition; CA Chiro Assn; Holistic Dental Assn; Assn for Humanistic Psychol; British Homeopathic Assn; Am Acad Holistic Chiro; hon/ Nums Articles of Intl Col of Applied Kinesiology; Summa Cum Laude Grad, LACC, 1980; Deans List, 1976-80; Delta Sigma, 1980; W/W: Students in Am Univ & Cols, CA, Personalities in Am.

MARKEY, MICHAEL L oc/Executive; b/Jun 6, 1943; h/48 Tappan Lane, Orinda, CA 94563; ba/Orinda, CA; m/ Irene Torngren; c/Michael Arnold, Victoria Ingrid; p/Arnold Leo (dec) and Wanda L Markey, Denair, CA; sp/ George (dec) and Bette Torngren; ed/ BS, San Jose St Univ, 1966; MBA, Univ Santa Clara, 1967; CFP, 1976; mil/ USAFR; pa/Fdr, Mng Ptr, Orinda Financial Grp, 1973-; VP, First Orinda Corporation, 1971-73; Ptnrship, Markey/Coit Investmts, 1969-; Sr Internal Auditor, Foremost-McKesson Inc, 1968-70; NASD Reg'd Prin w Fin Planners Equity Corporation; Reg'd Investmt Advr; Past VP of Ed of, Bd Dirs, E Bay Chapt, Intl Assn Fin Planners; Inst Cert'd Fin Planners; CA Real Est Broker; CoChm of 1980 Gtr Bay Area Fin Planning Conf; Chm Real Est Outlook Progs, 1980-81; Prog Chm of 1984 Fin Planning Conf Bay Area; Adv Bd, "Financial Planning Digest"; hon/Articles in "Fin Planner Mag".

MARKMAN, RONALD HAL oc/ Artist, Craftsman; b/Jan 14, 1944; h/80 Old East Road, Melville, NY 11747; ba/ Same; m/Carmella Francese; c/Jacob Abraham, Oliver Emanuel; p/Mac and Priscilla Markman, Huntington, NY; sp/ Daisy Rhodes, Luray, VA; ed/BFA, Sch of Visual Arts, 1964; mil/Conscientious Objector; pa/Free-Lance Artist, Painter, Glass Craftsman; Exhibns include: A Touch of Glass (Atlanta, GA) 1979, Neiman-Marcus Glass Show (Atlanta, GA) 1979, Glassmasters Guild (NY, NY) 1979, Contemp Art Glass (NY, NY) 1980, Hammerquist Gallery (NY, NY) 1980, D&R Renwick Souvenir Show of the Nat Collection of Fine Arts at the Smithsonian Instn (Washington, DC) 1982; Long Island Glass Carvers; Huntington Twp Art Leag; East End Art Leag; cp/Lower Eastside Rock Musicians Assn; Cosmic Drifters; hon/Pubs include "Glass" for *Glass Studio* Mag and "Animal Images" for Renwick Gallery Pub; Fragile Arts Finalist, Renwick Gallery Souvenir Show, 1980; New York State Artisans Awd, 1982; So Tier Arts Assn Awd, 1982; Nom'd to W/W Am Art.

MARKS, DAVID R oc/International Private Investigator; b/Dec 3, 1941; h/ 2575 Southeast 9th Street, Pompano Beach, FL 33062; ba/Pompano Beach, FL; p/William and Louisa W Marks (dec); ed/Rec'd Certs & Trng in Pvt Invest; Investigative Theory & Pract; Pvt Security; Crim Justice; Narcotics Invest; Arson Invest; Police Supvn & Mgmt; Crime Preven; Marksmanship w Mod Handguns; Crime Scene Search & Phy Evidence; Org'd Crime;' mil/USMC, 1959-63, Fire Team Ldr w USMC Spec Forces; pa/World Assn Detectives Inc; C of C USA; C of C Pompano Bch; r/Cath; hon/Nums Hons & Awds incl'g Commend from Mayor Pompano Bch, FL; Nat Comm Profl Law Enforcement Standards; Cert Achmt in Crim Invest; Am Police Ser; Am Fdn Police

Merit Awd; Good Samaritan Awds; Nat Police Mus & Hall of Fame; FL Assn Pvt Investigators Inc; Detective of Yr Awd of Merit; Intl Acad Criminology; Good Guys Clb Am Cert.

MARKS, JOHN D oc/Songwriter and Publisher; b/Nov 10, 1909; h/117 West 11th Street, New York, New York, NY 10011; ba/ New York, NY; c/Michael, Laura, David; p/Louis and Sadie Marks (dec); ed/BA, Colgate Univ, 1931; Att'd Columbia Univ; Studied in Paris; mil/AUS, Capt; pa/Composer of Num Songs incl'g "Rudolph the Red-Nosed Reindeer", "I Heard the Bells on Christmas Day", "Rockin' Around the Christmas Tree", "A Holly Jolly Christmas", "Everything I've Always "Anyone Can Move A Mountain"; Composer of Scores for TV Specs incl'g "Rudolph the Red-Nosed Reindeer", "Rudolph's Shiny New Year", "Rudolph & Frosty", "The Tiny Tree", & "The Ballad of Smokey the Bear"; Composer of TV Commls incl'g GE; Adv Com, Past Bd Dirs, ASCAP; Org'd, St Nicholas Music, 1949; Num TV Appearances incl'g "Mike Douglas", "Today", "Ed Sullivan", "Merv Griffin"; Participated on USO Songwriters Unit, 1963; Judge, Stephen Foster Meml Singing Contest, 1964; hon/W/W: Am, World; Bd Trustees, Chm Pres Clb, Colgate Univ; Rec'd Dist'd Alumni Awd, 1979; Bd Govs, Marshal Chess Clb; Bd Govs, Nat Acad TV Arts & Scis; Mem NARAS & CMA; Bronze Star Medal; Four Battle Stars.

MARRA, ROSEMARY AGLI oc/ Bookkeeper; b/Apr 11, 1947; h/350 Earle Street, Central Islip, NY 11722; ba/ Hauppauge, NY; c/Roger Paul, Sherry Marie; p/Armando J Marra, Dallas, TX and Edna Urbanovicwz, FL; ed/AAS, Suffolk Commun Col; pa/Bkkpr, Polymer Plastics Corporation, 1981-83; A W Sperry Instruments, Inc, 1983-; cp/Ctl Islip Yth Soccer Clb, By-Laws Com & Acctg Positions, 1983-84; BSA Pack 518; CINY Brightside Civic Assn; 3rd Prct Com Coun; hon/Personalities of Am; W/W in Am Wom.

MARSH, SHIRLEY M oc/State Senator; b/Jun 22, 1925; h/2701 South 34th Street, Lincoln, NE 68506; ba/Lincoln, NE; m/Frank Marsh; c/Sherry Marsh Tupper, Stephen, Dory, Corwin, Mitchell, Melissa; p/Dwight McVicker, Lincoln, NE; sp/Frank Marsh (dec); ed/ BA 1972, MBA 1978, Univ NE; pa/ Placement Asst, Univ NE, 1966-70; Casewk Practicum, Lancaster Co Welfare Dept, 1971-72; Vis'g Prof, NE Wesleyan Univ, 1978; Vis'g Prof, Doane Col, 1980; St Legis, 1972-; Past Chair, Wom Netwk-Nat Conf St Legis,1982-83; Nat Order Wom Legis, Pres 1978; Adv Com Am Col Ob & Gyn, 1980-; Exec Com, Nat Conf St Legis, 1982-84; Nat Fed Bus & Profl Wom; hon/Author *A Standard of Need for St of NE Relating to Aid to Dependent Chd*, Univ NE, 1978; NE Chapt Am Acad Pediatrics & NE Pediatric Soc Ser to Chd Awd, 1983; Univ NE Col Med Cent Awd for Dist'd Ser to Child Hlth, 1981; Cert Apprec, NE Wom Hwy Safety, 1981; Wom in Public Ofc; Marquis W/W; Dir Dist'd Ams.

MARSHALL, CHRISTOPHER WALKER oc/Winery Marketing Executive; b/Apr 1, 1950; h/20 Pleasant Street, Franklin, MA 02038; ba/ Franklin, MA; m/Diane F; p/Howard W and Gladys Marshall, Wellesley, MA; sp/ Anne Frankel, Grassy Key, FL; ed/BA, Lake Forest Col, 1972; Univ Madrid/ Instituto Internacional, 1970, 1971; Post Grad, Harvard Univ, 1973; pa/Store Mgr, Berenson's Wines & Spirits, 1972-75; En US Sales Mgr, G C Sumner Assocs, 1975-79; US Mktg Dir, C W Marshall Co, 1979-; Intl Food & Wine Soc; Les Amis du Vin; K of the Vine; Rioja Exporters Assn; hon/Author of *The Spanish Ec Miracle 1959-1969* 1972; Co-Author of *Prospects in the Mid E* 1973; W/W Fin & Indust.

MARSHALL, JEANIE oc/Human Resource Development Consultant; h/ 15 Ashley Drive, Ballston Lake, NY 12019; m/Donald W Marshall; p/Dr Wilfred and Mary Combellack, Southbury, CT; sp/Thomas and Gladys Marshall, Lockport, NY; ed/BA, Boston Univ, 1966; MS, Am Univ, 1982; pa/ Pres, Marshall House, Inc, 1981-; Human Relats Tnr, St Univ NY Albany, 1979-81; Owner, Marshall House Craft Design, 1971-81; Admr, Tchrs Ins & Annuity Assn, 1968-71; Assn Humanistic Psychi, 1981-; Am Soc Tng & Devel; Schnectady Br Pres, Am Assn Univ Wom, 1972-; Assn Psychol Type; cp/ Profl Devel Recog Admr, Assn Creat Change, 1983-; Newslttr Editor, Hudson Mohawk Tng & Devel Soc; hon/ Num Pubs incl'g Tnr Types "Strategies for Enhancing Tng Skills" 1983, "Handling Difficult Behaviors at Meetings" 1982, "Enhancing Skills in Supvn" 1981; Num Tng Modules, 1980-; W/W Am Wom.

MARSHALL, PATRICIA A oc/Assistant Director of Appraisal; b/Dec 21, 1941; h/523 Maywood, Houston, TX 77053; ba/Houston, TX; c/Robin Christine, Sherry Lynn; p/Warren V and Charlene McCarley Stafford, Dallas, TX; ed/BS 1972, MEd 1976, Univ Houston; Post Grad, Houston Bapt, 1981-; pa/Secy, TX A & M Engrg Expt Sta, 1961-62; Nurse Aide, St Josephs Hosp, 1962-63; Dr Asst, Secy, 1964-69; Tchr 1973-76, Ednl Diagnostician 1976-81, Asst Dir Appraisal 1981-, Sprg Br Indep Sch Dist; Tchr Adult Cont'g Ed, 1980-; Tutor Grade Sch & Junior HS Chd; Prog Chm, Houston-Met Diagnostician Conf, 1982; Coun Exceptl Chd; TX Ednl Diagnostician Assn; TX St Tchrs Assn (Lifetime Mem); NEA; Assn Chd Lrng Disabilities; Sprg Br Ed Assn; Assn Retarded Chd; TX Elem Prins & Supvrs Assn; cp/Exec Female Civic Org & Clbs incl'g Country Playhouse; Past Worthy Adv, Order of the Rainbow for Girls, 1958; Lead Tchr, Early Chd Dept, St Paul's Meth Ch, 1968-70; hon/Lifetime Mem, Phi Kappa Phi Hon Soc, 1977; W/W Am Wom; Bd Reg'd Ednl Diagnostician, 1981-83; Outstg Ser Awd, Country Playhouse; Devel Individualized Kgn Math Curric, Sp Br Indep Sch Dist, 1973.

MARSHALL, SUSAN THOMPSON oc/Manager Microcomputer Systems; b/Oct 28, 1952; h/15 Armour Road, Mahwah, NJ 07430; ba/New York, NY; m/Tad A Marshall; c/Lindsey Anne and Abigail Ekman; p/William and Helen Ekman, Ridgewood, NJ; sp/J Howard and Penelope Marshall, Irvington, NY; ed/BA, St Lawrence Univ, 1974; pa/ Mgr, Micro Sys 1982-, VP, IMS/ Adserve 1981-82, Mgr, Graphics 1980-81, VP, Gen Mgr, Telmar Bus Sys, 1977-80, Interactive Mkt Sys, Telmar Grp Inc; Mem 1981, Secy 1982-83-, VP 1983-84, Bd Dirs, Ad Data Processing Assn; r/Luth; hon/Dean's List, 1970-74; Maggie Holmes Directing Awd, 1974; W/W E, Intl W/W Intells.

MARTAN, JOSEPH RUDOLF oc/ Attorney/Insurance Company Executive; b/Mar 28, 1949; h/4056 Gilbert Avenue, Western Springs, IL 60558; ba/ Schaumburg, IL; p/Joseph J and Margarete Martan, Western Springs, IL; ed/ BA, Univ IL, 1971; JD, IL Inst Technol, 1977; mil/USAR, 2 Lt 1971, Capt 1978, Active Duty 1972-74, 1974-83; pa/ Assoc, Law Ofcs Vincent C Lopez, 1978-80; Litigation Counsel, Goldblatt Brothers Inc, 1980-81; Br Counsel, IL Am Fam Ins Grp, 1981-; Assn AUS; Resv Ofcrs Assn; Assn Trial Lwyrs Am; IL St Bar Assn; Chgo Bar Assn; Mem, Civil Prac Com, 1983-84; Du Page Co Bar Assn; cp/Pres, 1979-81, W Suburban Com Band Inc, 1975-; Bohemian Lwyrs Assn Chgo; Metro Opera Guild; hon/Pi Sigma Alpha, Polit Sci Hon Soc, 1971; John W Davis Cup Appellate Advocacy, 1976; Army Commend Medal, 1980; W/W Fin & Indust.

MARTELLI, LAUREN LOUISE oc/ Executive; b/Feb 28, 1946; h/1045 Grant Avenue, Pelham Manor, NY 10803; m/ Marco; c/Kira, Vanessa, Marco; p/ Louise Thombs, Bronx, NY; sp/John and Desdemona Martelli, Croton Falls, NY; ed/BS, Iona Col; Katherine Gibbs Secretarial Sch, 1964; Barbizon 1963; pa/Adm Asst, BASF Wyandotte; Adm Asst, Freiden/Cooper, Sales Mgr, Universal Play Sys Inc; Ofc Mgr, Marco Martelli Assocs; VP, Universal Play Sys; VP, Marco Martelli Assocs, Inc; Chm, Comml Mbrship, NYSRPA, 1982-83; NRPA, 1980-; NYASPHA, 1980; cp/ Vestry Bd Mem, 1983, Christ the Redeemer; Lic Lay Rdr, Epis Ch, 1980, 1972-81; Manor Clb; Nom Chm, 1979-81, 1974-81; Cardboard Co, 1974-77; Eastchester Commun Theatre; r/Epis; hon/Author of Num Pubs incl'g Editor, "Voice Jour" NYSRPS; Pres Cit, 1983, NYSRPS.

MARTIN, BOYD ARCHER oc/Institute Director; b/Mar 3, 1911; h/1314 Walenta Drive, Moscow, ID 83843; ba/ Moscow, ID; c/William Archer and Michael Archer; ed/BA, Univ ID, 1936; MA & PhD, Stanford Univ; pa/Hd, Dept Social Sci 1947-55, Asst Dean 1949-55, Dean 1955-70, Col Ltrs & Scis, Dir, Bur Public Res, 1959-73, Dir, Inst Human Behavior, 1973-, Univ ID; Tchg Asst 1936-38, Acting Instr 1939-40, Vis'g Prof 1946, 1952, Stanford Univ; Instr 1938-39, 1940-43, Asst Prof 1943-44, 1944-47, Prof 1947-70, Borah Dist'd Prof Emeritus 1973, Univ ID; Vis'g Prof 1962-63, Affil w Ctr Study Higher Ed 1962-63, Univ CA Berkeley; Chm, Adv Coun Higher Ed ID, 1947-66; Am Assn Univ Profs; Exec Coun, Am Polit Sci Assn, 1952-53; Am Soc Public Adm; Affil w Ctr Study Higher Ed, 1963-64; Constitutional Revision Comm ID, 1965-70; Fgn Policy Assn; Pres, Pacific NW Polit Sci Assn; Chm 1965-66, Steering Com NW Conf Higher Ed, 1962-67; Pres, Wn Pol Sci Assn, 1950; cp/Chm, Borah Foun, 1947-55; Conslt to ID Mun Leag; Gov's ID Cent Comm; Chm, Gt Plains UNESCO Conf, 1947-66; ID Comm Humanities & Arts; Pres, Kiwanis, 1947-; Legis Com, Moscow C of C, 1970-78; N ID C of C; r/ Prot; hon/Author Num Pubs incl'g *The Direct Primary in ID* 1947, "Why Suffrage Discrimination?" *Am Scholar* 1945, "The 1972 Nat Polit Convs" *The Daily Idahonian* 1972; Num Awds & Cits incl'g ID Statesman Dist'd Citizen Awd, 1971; Univ ID Alumni Hall of Fame, 1976; AM Men & Wom Sci; Commun Ldrs & Noteworthy Ams; Ldrs in Ed; Nat Register Prom Ams; W/W: Am, Am Col & Univ Adm, Am Ed, ID, W, World.

MARTIN, CHIPPA oc/Counseling Psychologist; b/Sep 6, 1942; h/2150 Route 6A, West Barnstable, MA 02668; ba/Boston, MA; c/Tara and Beth; p/ Murray Riback, Flushing, NY, Rose Kaplan (dec); ed/BA, Queens Col, 1964; MA, Goddard Col, 1978; pa/Tchr, Manhasset NY HS, 1974-65; Tchr & Humanities Advr, Millbrook NY HS, 1972-74; Certifier, Cambridge MA Govt Housing, 1975-77; Dir & Cnslr, Aradia Cnslg Boston, 1978-; VP, Leag Preserv Hudson Val, 1972-; Lic Social Wkr MA Nat Cert'd Cnslr; Mem, Am Pers & Guid Assn; Assn Spec Grp Wk; Assn Wom Psych; hon/St Gaudens Medal for Drawing, Metro Mus Art, 1960; W/W E.

MARTIN, CLARENCE WILLIAM oc/Executive, General Manager; b/Jan 31, 1930; h/Route 2, Box 152, Friona, TX 79035; ba/Friona, TX; m/Martha Wynona (Carter); c/Martha Ann, Larry, Mike, Greg, Keith, Kathy; p/Calvin William Martin, Friona, TX, and Lela Blanche (Baxter) (dec); pa/Rancher, 1946-83; Farwell Feed Lot, 1958-63; Pres & Gen Hi Plains Feedyard, 1967-83; VP & Dir, W Friona Grain, 1963-83; VP & Dir, Tri-Co Elevator, 1969-83; VP & Dir, Friona Fertilizer Inc, 1976-83; Chm, Agri & Ranching Com, 1978-83; Mem & Past Dir, TX Cattle Feeders Assn; Mem, TX SEn Cattle Raisers; Mem, Nat Cattleman's Assn; cp/Dir 1968-70, Mem 1968-84, Friona C of C; Mem, Dir, W TX C of C, 1972-83; r/Ch of Christ; hon/Awd, Livestock Mag Denver, 1979; W/W S & SE, World; Fin & Indust.

MARTIN, GARY RUNNING BEAR oc/Psychologist; b/Nov 29, 1949; h/Post Office Box 41, Flint Station, Fall River, MA 02723; ba/Taunton, MA; c/Chuanastar Cloud; ed/AA, Bristol Commun Col, 1976; BA, SEn MA Univ, 1978; MA, RI Col, 1980; pa/Dir, Mohawk Relief Fund, 1973-76; Dir, Am Indian Soc, 1976-81; Cnslr, Upward Bound, 1977-78; Prog Coor, People Inc, 1978-80; Voc Coor, Crystal Sps Sch, 1979-80; Psychol, Paul A Dever St Sch, 1980; Am Assn Mtl Deficiency; Am Pers & Guid Assn; Assn Cnslr Ed & Supvn; Am Indian Soc; hon/"Cognitive Functioning Inventory", in Process of Standardization; Dean's List, SEn MA Univ, 1978; W/W E.

MARTIN, JOHN L oc/Legislator, Educator, Business; b/Jun 5, 1941; h/ Post Office Box 250, Eagle Lake, ME 04739; ba/Augusta, ME; p/Frank and Edwidge Martin; ed/BA, 1963; pa/Instr, Univ ME Ft Kent, 1972-; Instr, Ft Kent Commun HS, 1964-72; St Legis, 1965-; Minority Ldr, 1971-74; Spkr House, 1975-; Pres 1979-82, Mem, Bd Dirs 1976-, St Legis Ldrs Foun; Chm, New Eng Caucus St Legis, 1981-82; r/Rom Cath.

MARTIN, MARY AGNES oc/Legis-

lator; h/34 Pegasus Drive, Groton, CT 06340; ba/Hartford, CT; m/Howard (dec); c/John Thomas, Howard Wright, Kathleen Helen Martin Pollard; p/John Kukon, Groton, CT; pa/Groton Rep Town Meeting, 1964-68; Minority Ldr; Groton Bd Selecmen, 1969-71; Groton Town Coun, 1973-74; St House Reps, 1971-72; St Senate, 1975-; Asst Majority Ldr, 1981; Asst Majority Ldr Human Sers, 1983; cp/Groton Dem Town Com, 1966; Groton Fdn Dem Woms Clb, 1964; r/Cath.

MARTIN, MONA HELEN oc/Supervisor of Research and Records; b/Jun 24, 1951; h/263 Grand Street, Hornell, NY 14843; ba/Alfred, NY; m/Thomas J; c/ James H and Tina M; p/Clayton A Teator II (dec) and Ramona L Teator, Hornell, NY; sp/James H Martin (dec) and Helen Q Martin, Hornell, NY; ed/ Att'g Alfred Univ; pa/Records Clk 1974-75, 1976-78, Supvr Records 1975-76, Assoc Devel Res 1978-79, Supvr Res & Records 1979-, Alfred Univ; cp/Vol, Civil Def Disaster Preparedness Steuben Co; Bd Dirs, Alfred/ Allegany Ednl Employees Fed Credit Union; r/Cath; hon/W/W E.

MARTIN, THOMAS BROOKS oc/ Executive; b/Jun 23, 1935; h/51 Stoney Brook Road, Montville, NJ 07045; ba/ Boonton, NJ; c/Kevin, Stephen, Timothy, Brian, Kathleen; p/Paul and Eleanor Martin, South Bend, IN; ed/BS, Univ Notre Dame, 1957; MS 1960, PhD 1970, Univ PA; pa/Pres, RFL Indust Inc, 1983-; Chm & Pres, Threshold Technol Inc, 1970-83; r/Cath; hon/Nums Papers & Books; 20 Patents; W/W: Electronics, Fin & Indust.

MARTIN, WANDA oc/Assistant Cashier, Training Director; b/Oct 10, 1931; h/145 West Lee Street, Sulphur, LA 70663; ba/Lake Charles, LA; m/John Richard; c/John Michael, Kathy Ann, Keith Alan; sp/Fred E Jackson and Lula Belle (Dickens) (dec); ed/Mathieu Bus Col, 1948-49; Univ SEn LA, 1981; pa/ Bkkpr, Calcasieu Marine Nat Bk, 1949-51; Asst Cashier, Tng Dir, Proof & Transit Supvr, Lakeside Nat Bk, 1965-83; Chm, Nat Assn Bk Wom 1983-84; Secy, Quota Clb, 1983-84; Am Bus Wom Assn; r/Pentecostal; hon/W/ W Am Wom.

MARTIN, WILLIAM COLLIER oc/ Health Care Administrator; b/Aug 16, 1926; h/3225 Pursell Drive, Pensacola, FL 32506; ba/Pensacola, FL; m/Alice Nickle; c/Mary Anne, Patricia Jean, William Collier Jr, Nancy Lee; p/William Henry Martin (dec); sp/Edgar Ralph Nickle, Henderson, NC and Alice Williams Nickle, Pensacola, FL; ed/Att't Univ GA 1943-44, 1946-49, BS 1950; Postgrad, 1950-52, Charlotte Meml Hosp; Univ OK, 1969; AUS Command & Gen Staff Col, 1971; US Civil Def Staff Col, 1972; mil/USN, 1944-52; AUS, 1959-77; pa/Adm Intern/Resident, Charlotte Mem Hosp, 1950-52; Admr, Rockmont-Aragon Hosp, 1952-54; Asst Admr/Admr, St Agnes Hosp, 1954-56; Admr, Florence-Darlington TB Sanatorium, 1956-58; Adjutant/ Med Co Cmdr, AUS Hosp, 1959-61; Cmdr/Adm Ofcr, AUS Med Ser Detachment, 1961-64; Cmdr, 5th Evacuation Hosp, 1964-65; Adjutant/Exec Ofcr, 55th Med Grp, 1965-67; Cmdr, 47th Gen Hosp, Fitzsimons Gen Hosp, 1967-68; Dir for Security, AUS Med

Ctr, Ryukyu Isls, 1968-71; Med Opers Ofcr, HQs VII US Corps, 1971-73; Chief, Tng, Exercises, Readiness, AUS Med Command, 1973-74; Dir for Security, Fitzsimons Army Med Ctr, 1974-77; Exec Dir, Thomas Rehab Hosp, 1977-78; Dir 1979-, Pres 1979-81, Secy 1982-, Public Hlth Trust Escambia Co; Exec Dir, Hospice NW FL, 1982-; Num Orgs incl'g GA Hosp Assn, 1952-54; Reg Secy, NC Hosp Assn, 1954-56; AAMSUS, 1968-; Nat Rehab Assn, 1977-78; ASTD, 1977-; NC Assn Hosp Devel, 1977-78; cp/Chapt Secy, Chapt Chaplain, Phi Delta Theta Soc Frat, 1943-; VFW, 1957-; York Rite, 1970-; Scottish Rite, 1967-; r/Meth; hon/ Author "Hospice-A Developing New Direction Hlth Care" *The Exec*; Num Articles; Num Mil Awds; White House Com Disaster Planning, 1975-77; Pres Com Employmt Handicapped, 1977-78; Cert'd Lay Spkr, U Meth Ch, 1980; NC Gov Adv Com Rehab Ctrs, 1977-78; W/ W: S & SE, Fin & Indust; Pers S; Men Accomplishment; Two Thousand Notable Ams; Intl W/W Intells; Dir Dist'd Ams.

MARTINA, CARMEN ANTHONY oc/Podiatric Medicine and Surgery; b/ Sep 21, 1941; h/13 Dunhill Drive, Voorhees, NJ 08043; ba/Haddon Heights, NJ; ed/BA, Rutgers Univ, 1964; DPM, PA Col Podiatric Med, 1971; Residency, St Luke's & Chd's Med Ctr, 1971-73; mil/AUS, 1965-71, Automatic Rifleman; pa/Corpsman, St Luke's, Chd's Med Ctr, 1969-71; Instr, Gloucester Commun Col, 1972; Conslt Podiatrist 1972-73, Clin Instr Dept Surg 1973-74, Co-Chief Surg, Assoc Prof Podiatry Surg 1974, PA Col Podiatric Med; Chm Dept Podiatric Med & Surg, Phila Med Ctrs Inc, 1974-75; Surg, Podiatrist, Pvt Pract, 1973-; James C Giuffre Med Ctr, Phila, & W Jersey Hosp Sys, Camden, NJ, Hosp Affil; Am Podiatry Assn; NJ Podiatry Assn; Am Diabetes Assn; Am Public Hlth Assn; Diplomate, Nat Bd Podiatry; Diplomate, Am Bd Podiatric Orthos; Bd Eligible, Am Bd Podiatric Surg; Fellow, Am Col Foot Orthos; Fellow, Am Soc Podiatric Med; Fellow, Assn Hosp Podiatrists; Assoc Mem, Am Acad Podiatric Sports Med; Mem, Am Col Sports Med; Mem, Am Col Podopediatrics; Assoc Mem, Intl Soc Profl Hypnosis; CoChm, Dept Podiatric Surg, Broad St Hosp, 1974-76; Mem House of Dels, NJ Podiatry Soc, So Div, 1978, 1979, 1980, 1981, 1983; NJ St Capt, Am Col Sports Med, 1981; Adv Bd, Hlth Careers Acad Inc, US Olympic Skating Team, Achilles Orthotic Lab Inc, Vascular Lab Inc, Podiatry Conslt; cp/Am Legion; Sons Italy; Goebel Collector's Clb; Zool Soc Phila; hon/Num Awds & Certs incl'g PA Podiatry Students Awd Merit & Ser, 1970, 1971; Am Col Foot Roentgenologists Awd, 1971; PA Heart Assn, 1971; Am Acad Human Sers Awd, 1974-75; Am Soc Podiatric Med, 1982; W/W E; W/W NJ, US Public Relats Ser, 1974-75.

MARTINEAU, FRANCIS EDWARD oc/Editor and Publisher, Association Executive; b/Jan 15, 1921; h/7204 Clarendon Road, Bethesda, MD 20814; ba/Same; m/Dorothy M (Clanfield); c/ Jane E Mandeville, Jill M Wettrich, Gail k Parker, Paul F; p/Edward F and Yvonne M (Langlois) Martineau (dec); sp/Ronald (dec) and Mrs Ronald A

Clanfield, Toronto, Canada; ed/Att'd Air Univ; Indust Col Armed Forces; Pilot, RCAF, 1941-44; Pilot, USAAC, 1944-48; Pilot, Opers Ofcr, Intell Staff Ofcr, Cmdr in USAF, Air NG, AF Resv, 1949-75; Reporter, Attleboro MA Sun, Pawtucket RI Times, Woonsocket RI Call, 1938-46; Pres, Frank Martineau, INC, Advtg/Public Relats, 1946-66; Exec Dir, Aircraft Owners & Pilots Assn Foun, 1967-69; Dir Public Relats, Air Line Pilots Assn, 1969-71; Gen Mgr, Nat Assn Cos, 1972; Pres, Martineau Corporation, 1973-; Editor, Publisher, Assn Trends Wkly News Mag; Exec Dir, Am Leag Lobbyists; Mem, Am Soc Assn Execs; Public Relats Soc Am; Aviation/Space Writers Assn; AF Assn; Ret'd Ofcrs Assn; NG Assn; World Future Soc; Nat Assn Execs Clb; cp/Pres, Woonsocket Citizens Leag; VP, Woonsocket City Coun; Rep Congl Cand, 1958; Gov Aide, St Chief Safety Ed, 1959-60; BSA; Silver Beaver; Pres, Lt Gov, Kiwanis Intl; r/Rom Cath; hon/Num Pub'd Articles; W/W: Indust & Fin, E, World, Assn Mgmt.

MARTINEZ, HECTOR RAPHAEL (Doctor of Devastation) oc/Engraver, Television Producer, Business Executive; b/Aug 28, 1949; h/444 Hudson, New York, NY 10014; ba/NY, NY; c/Cindy, Laurie-Lee; p/Ralph and Florida Martinez, NY, NY; ed/Courses in Comml Art; Tng in Sports; pa/Dir, Am Shotokan, Kodokan; DoJo, USA, Performances in Cable TV; Etcher/Engraver, Greenspan/Kushland; VP, Leacock Communs; Co-Prodr, Cable TV Show "Singles Connection & Cable Mag"; Chm, Martial Arts United into 1 Org, 1975; hon/Subject of Several Mag Articles on Martial Arts; Wk in Engraving Appears in Num Mags & Prods; NY St Karate Champ, 1974-; Holder of Record for Breaking 14-1" Bds w 1 Blow of his Hd; 5th Deg Black Belt; Many Biogl Listings.

MARTINEZ, MARIA ELENA oc/Administrator; b/Jan 9, 1948; h/9719 Planter Street, Pico Rivera, CA 90660; ba/Monterey Park, CA; c/Andre Eric; p/Henry C and Maria Elena Martinez, Pico Rivera, CA; ed/AA, 1968; BA, 1970; MS, 1976; Doct Student; pa/Prog Asst, GLACAA, 1972-73; Tchr/Supvr, 1973-75; Conslt, Lng Tree, 1975-79; Commun Col Instr, 1975-76; Staff Trnr, Charles Drew Post Grad, 1975-77; Dir, Aliso Pico Ctr, U Way, 1978-79; Coor, Ofc Commun Sers, 1979-82; Coor, Pres Ofc, 1982-; Mem, LA Commun Col Dist Admrs Assn, 1979-; Mem, Commun Col Commun Sers Assn, 1979-; Chp 1975-76, Ways & Means, First VP, Metro Chapt, 1974-75, So CA Assn Ed Yg Chd; Mem, E LA Col Alumni Assn, 1975-; cp/CoChp, Bus/Ed Com, C of C, 1982-; Mem, Plaza de la Raza, 1980; Mem, Latin Am Profl Wom Assn, 1979; VChp, Assoc Leag Mexican Am Adult Developmentally Disabled Prog, 1977-81; r/Cath; hon/Ser Awd, YMCA, 1983; Fellow, Hispanic Ldrship USC, 1981; Outstg Yg Wom Am, 1980; Ser Commun Awd, LA DA, 1975; Outstg Col Ser, 1965; Asn Student Wom Orgs.

MARTZ, MIRIAM COBB oc/Owner, Data Processing Service; b/Dec 5, 1938; h/170 Crestwood Court, Alpharetta, GA 30201; ba/Alpharetta, Ga; c/Julie Marie; p/Mrs Robert Cobb, La Grange, GA; ed/Att'd Marsh Bus Col, 1959; pa/

Supvr-Computer Opers, Equifax, 1959-70; Mgr-Data Processing, Crum & Forster, 1974-81; Pres, Owner, Accuracy Plus Inc, 1981-; Nat Assn Female Execs; Intl Word Processing Assn; Alpharetta Bus Assn; r/Unity; hon/W/W Am Wom.

MARVEL, JOHN A oc/President Emeritus; b/Mar 13, 1922; h/1345 Old Pecos Trail, Sante Fe, NM 87501; ba/Same; m/Frances J; c/Merrill Ann Martin, John Alan, Marvin Kim; p/Mr and Mrs F H Marvel, Liberal, KS; sp/Mr and Mrs C M Smith, Manchester, OK; ed/BS, NWn St Univ, 1946; MEd 1952, EdD 1955 Univ OK; mil/AUS, 1943-46; pa/Prin, Tchr, Coach, Hazelton Public Schs, 1946-52; Prin, Eugene Field Sch, 1952-53; P/T Instr, Univ OK, 1953-55; Prin, Univ Lab Sch 1955-58, Dir, Adult Ed & Commun Sers 1958-62, Dean & Prof Ed 1962-66, Univ WY; Pres, Adams St Col, 1966-77; Pres, Consortium St Cols Col, 1977-82; Dist'd Vis'g Fellow, Univ New Eng, Australia, 1983-; cp/Phi Delta Kappa, Kappa Delta Pi, Phi Theta Phi; Rotary Intl; Masonic Lodge; Sigma Tau Gamma; U Meth Ch; Bd Dir, IL Sch Theol; Bd Fellows, Gallaudett Col; Prof for World Peace; r/Prot; hon/Num Articles incl'g "NV Public Schs-A Further Look", "Eval Am Overseas Schs"; Pres, Am Assn Col & Univ; Secy, Am Coun Ed; Ldr, Eval Team to Peoples Republic China; Hon Docts from Univ No CO and Adams St Col; Outstg Alumnus, NWn St Col; Sigma Tau Gamma Frat; Recip, Danforth Fellow; Cit from CO Legis; W/W: Am, Am Ed, World, Deans & Pres.

MARVELLE, JOHN DAVID oc/Educator; b/Nov 22, 1950; h/8 Kingsley Road, Norton, MA 02766; ba/Same; m/Elise Manning; c/Jared Manning; p/John and Hazel Gladys (Brown), Mansfield, MA; sp/John and Marie (Trotter), Clearwater, FL; ed/BA 1972, MEd 1976, Bridgewater St Col; Post Grad, Univ MA, 1979-; pa/Tchr, Mansfield Public Schs, 1972-76; Dir, Proj IMPACT, 1976-80, Dir, Proj LIFE, 1980-83, Ednl Conslt, 1978-, Norton, MA; Instr, MA Bay Commun Col, 1980; Pres, Attleboro Area Bd MA Dept Social Sers, 1981-; Mem, Stwide Adv Coun, MA Ofc Chd, 1973-75; r/Cath; hon/Editor, "The Edupac Presch Prog" 1980, "The Edupac Kgn Prog" 1983, CoAuthor, *Parents: You Are Tchrs*; Recip, MA Validation Awd as Dir Proj IMPACT, 1978; Dist'd Edr Awd, Charles F Kettering Foun; Phi Delta Kappa; W/W E.

MASINO, JOAN ELIZABETH GRAYSON oc/Elementary Counselor; b/Oct 18, 1946; h/3309 Nancy Ellen Way, Owings, Mills, MD 21117; ba/Laurel, MD; m/Bernard Wilson; c/Kristen Grayson; p/Harry and Elizabeth Grayson, College Park, MD; sp/Bernard L (dec) and Marian L Masino, Laurel, MD; ed/BS 1968, MEd 1977, PhD 1985, Univ MD; pa/Elem Tchr 1968-78, Elem Cnslr 1978-, Prince George's Co Bd Ed; Pres, Timber/Valley Assn Inc, 1981-83; Pres 1982-84, VP 1980-82, MD Sch Cnslrs Assn; Exec Bd & Licensure Com, MD Pers & Guid Assn; Am Sch Cnslrs Assn; Am Pers & Guid Assn; NEA; Legis Com, MD St Tchrs Assn; Legis Chair, Prince George's Co Edrs Assn, 1979-81; Phi Kappa Phi Hon Soc; ESAA Citizens Adv Com, 1976-80; r/Rom Cath; hon/

Phi Kappa Phi; W/W E.

MASSETTI, CECILIA A oc/Psychologist, Consultant; b/May 24, 1954; h/8256 Road 26, Madera, CA 93637; ba/Madera, CA; p/Fred and Evelyn Massetti, Madera, CA; ed/BS, St Mary's Col, 1976; MA, Univ CA, 1977; MA, Univ SF; pa/Cnslr, Intern Psychol, Woodland Jt Unified Sch Dist, 1977-79; Intern Psychol, Sacramento Med Ctr, 1978-79; Psychol, Conslt, Coor Staff Devel, Tnr Human Devel Tng Inst, Madera Co Dept Ed, 1979-; Assn Am Univ Wom; Assn CA Sch Admrs; Assn Supvn & Curric Devel; CA Assn Sch Psychol; cp/St Joachin's Parish Coun, 1982-86; Madera Hist Soc; r/Rom Cath; hon/Magna Cum Laude Grad, St Mary's Col; Cum Laude, St Mary's Col; W/W: W, Col & Univ Students.

MASSEY, DEBORAH SIMS oc/Business Owner; b/Mar 5, 1952; h/4698 North Springs Road, Kennesaw, GA 30144; ba/Marietta, GA; m/Robert; c/Adam Foster and Jennifer Patricia Pauline; p/Mr and Mrs Frank F Sims, Dunwoody, GA; sp/Mr and Mrs Max M Missry (dec); ed/Att'd Kennesaw Col, 1974, 1975, 1976; pa/Housewife, Music Tchr, CoFdr "Creations Etc", 1974-81; Ch Yth Dir, Choir Dir, Heritage Presby, 1980-83; Mem, Cobb Co C of C, 1983; r/Presby; hon/First to Coin Term "Silk Florist".

MASSIER, PAUL F oc/Manager of Research and Technology; b/Jul 22, 1923; h/1060 North First Avenue, Arcadia, CA 91006; ba/Pasadena, CA; m/Dorothy H; c/Marilyn Massier Schwegler and Paulette Massier Holden; p/John and Kate Massier (dec); sp/Andrew (dec) and Anna Hedlund, Arcadia, CA; ed/BS, Univ CO, 1948; MS, MIT, 1949; mil/AUS, 1943-46; pa/Pan Am Refining Corporation, 1947-48; Design Engr, Maytag Co, 1949-51; Res Engr, Boeing Co, 1951-55; Res Engr 1955-58, Grp Supvr 1958-81, Proj Mgr Res Sect 1981-, Jet Propulsion Lab; Assoc Fellow, Am Inst Aeronautics; Mem, Tech Coms, Nuclear Propulsion, Aeroacoustics; cp/Sigma Xi; Trustee, Arcadia Cong Ch; Orgr, Chm Num Conf Sessions; r/Prot; hon/Auth of Over 100 Reports incl'g "Cycle Anal—Type F-5 Airborne Gas Turbine Power Unit", 1952, "Model 502 Second Stage Turbine Test (0.80 Chord Blade)", 1951; Hons Grad, Univ CO; Apollo Achmt Awd, NASA, 1969; Basic Noise Res Awd, NASA, 1981; Outstg Ser Awd, PTA, 1970; W/W: Frontier Sci & Technol, Aviation, W, Engrg & Sci So CA; DIB; Personalities W & MW; Biographical Roll Honor.

MASTERYANNI, JANITH KAY oc/Home Economist and County Extension Director; b/Aug 10, 1935; h/2701 Poinciana Court, Punta Gorda, FL 33950; ba/Punta Gorda, FL; p/Kathryn Masteryanni, Indianapolis, IN; ed/BS, Butler Univ, 1960; MS, Purdue Univ, 1968; pa/Co Ext Dir, Charlotte Co Cooperative Ext Ser, 1979-; Ext Agt, Home Ec Prog Ldr, Miami, FL, 1974-79; IN Cooperative Ext Ser, 1960-74; Wk w Yth Grps in Home Ec, 4-H Clb Wk, Commun Devel & Marine Sci; Mem, Am Home Ec Assn; Mem, Nat Assn Ext Home Economists; Mem, FL Home Ec Assn; 1st VP, 2nd VP, Public Relats Com Chm, FL Assn Ext Home Ec Agts; Prog Chm, 1981-82, ABWA; cp/Epsilon Sigma Phi,

Ext Hon Frat; Altrusa Inl; Charlotte Co C of C; Secy 1980-81, Dir 1981-82, Pres 1982-83, Zonta Intl Punta Gorda-Port Charlotte; hon/CoAuthor *Evaluating the Impact of Public Expositions on Energy Conserv* 1981; W/W Am Wom, Personalities of S.

MASTRIA, ERNEST D oc/Clinical Psychologist; b/Dec 6, 1947; h/146 Berkshire Road, Hasbrouck Heights, NJ 07604; ba/Jersey City, NJ; p/Ernest and Rose Mastria, Hasbrouck Heights, NJ; ed/BA 1969, MS 1971 En WA St Univ; Psy D, Rutgers Univ, 1977; pa/Staff Psychol, Holley Ctr, 1972-75; Dir Chd's Sers, Christ Hosp, 1975-78; Conslt, YWCA Grp Home Boys & Girls, 1976-; Pvt Pract, 1980-; Mem, Am Psychi Assn; Mem, NJ Psychi Assn; Mem, Hudson Co Mtl Hlth Bd, 1980-82; r/Rom Cath; hon/Author of "Treatment Child Abuse by Behavioral Intervention, A Case Report" *Child Welfare*, 1974; W/W E.

MASZKIEWICZ, RUTH CONLOQUE oc/Nurse Educator; b/Jul 24, 1928; h/216 East Patty Lane, Monroeville, PA 15146; ba/Pittsburgh, PA; m/Steve (dec); c/Stephen, Valli, Daniel, Mark, Suzanne, Amy; p/Sylvester and Alvina Conloque; sp/John and Josephine Maszkiewicz; ed/Nsg Dipl, 1950; BS Nsg Ed, 1954; EdM, 1969; PhD, 1977; pa/ Assoc Prof Nsg, Grad Prog Dir-Med Surg Nsg 1978-, Asst Prof, Pulmonary Nsg Spec, Grad Prog, Med-Surg Nsg 1975-77, Asst Prof Cardiovas Nsg Undergrad Prog 1972-74, Univ Pgh; Chm, Critically Ill Patient, Presbyterian-Univ Hosp, 1967-72; ANA; Am Assn Critical Care Nurses, Gtr Pgh Chapt, 1974-; cp/Braddock Gen Hosp Student Org, Pres, Secy, Treas, 1947-50; Braddock Gen Hosp Alumnae Assn, 1950-; Alpha Tau Delta Nsg Soc, Secy, Treas, 1952-; Duquesne Univ Alumni Assn, 1954-; PA Nurses Assn, Dist 6, Chp, Comm on Nsg, 1950-; Sigma Theta Tau, Eta Chapt, Pres, Pres Elect, Cnslr, 1974-; The Carroll F Reynolds Hist Soc, 1978-; Intl Hist Nsg Soc, 1981-; Coun Nurse Rschrs, 1982-; Nat Leag Nsg, 1982-83; r/Rom Cath; hon/Ldrship in Nsg Awd, 1981; Sigma Theta Tau, Nat Hon Soc Nsg; W/W Am Wom.

MATEKER, EMIL JOSEPH JR oc/ Executive; b/Apr 25, 1931; h/419 Hickory Post Lane, Houston, TX 77079; ba/ Houston, TX; m/Lolita A Winter; c/ Mark Steven, Anne Marie, John David; p/Emil J Mateker, Camdenton, MO; ed/ BS 1956, MSR 1959, PhD 1964, St Louis Univ; mil/AUS, 1951-54, Comm'd 2nd Lt; pa/Pres 1964-, VP 1974-, Aero Ser Div, VP 1970-74, R & D, Mgr 1969-70, Geophy Res, Wn Geophy Co; Pres, Litton Resources Sys, 1977; Pres, Westrex, 1974-77; Conslt, 1962-70; Assoc Prof Geophysics, WA Univ, 1963-65; Instr Geophysics, St Louis Univ, 1960-63; Geophysicist, Standard Oil Co CA, 1957-60; Soc Exploration Geophysicists, 1955; Am Geophy Union, 1955; Seismological Soc Am, 1955; AAAS, 1963; Geophy Soc Houston, 1969; European Assn Exploration Geophysicists, 1970; cp/Sigma Xi; r/ Rom Cath; hon/Author of Num Pubs incl'g *Generation of Seismic Waves, Seismic Vibrations, Reg Tectonics*; Intl Book Hon; W/W: Technol, Houston, Frontier Sci & Technol; Personalities S; Am Biographical Inst; Am Men & Wom Sci; Intl W/

W Intells; Standard & Poor's Register.

MATHENY, TOM HARRELL oc/ Attorney; h/Post Office Box 221, Hammond, LA 70404; ba/Hammond, LA; p/ Whitman and Lorene Harrell; ed/BA, SEn LA Univ, 1954; JD, Tulane Univ, 1957; pa/LA Bar, 1957; Ptnr, Pittman & Matheny, 1957; LA St Jr C of C, 1964; Am Bar Assn Com on Probate; LA Bar Assn Chm, Com on Legal Aid, Com on Prison Reform; 21st Jud Dist Bar, Secy-Treas, VP 1967-68, 1971; Comml Law Leag of Am Com on Ethics; LA Alumni Coun Pres, 1963-65; Acad Rel & Mtl Hlth; Intl Platform Assn; LA Assn Claimants Compensation Attys; SEn LA Col Alumni Assn, Dir, Pres 1961-62, Bd Spec Fund, 1959-62, Dir Tangipahoa Chapt; Tulane Alumni Assn; UN Assn Am Trial Lwyrs Assn; Am Jud Soc; Law-Sci Inst; World Peace Through Law Acad Com on Conciliation; Am Acad of Polit & Social Sci; Am Acad of Law & Sci; Law Sci Inst; Hammond Assn of Commerce, Dir 1960-65; Phi Delta Phi; Phi Delta; Phi Alpha Delta; cp/Pres, Jud Coun, U Meth Ch, 1976-80; Pres, Nat Assn of Conf Lay Ldrs U Meth C; Conf Lay Ldr, LA Annual Conf U Meth Ch, 1966-; Bd of Trustees, Scarritt Col; Hon Secy, US Com for the Audenshaw Foun; Del, World Meth Conf in London, 1966, Denver 1971, Dublin 1976; Del to Gen Conf, U Meth Ch, 1968, 1970, 1972; VP, Edwards & Assocs, S Brick Supply, Inc; Gen Coun First Guaranty Bk; Fac, SEn LA Univ, Holy Cross Col of NO; Chm, Advmt Com Hammond BSA, 1960-64; Dist Coun, 1957-66; Exec Bd, Istrouma Area Coun, 1966-; Campaign Mgr, Dem C & for Gov of LA, 1959-60, 1963-64; Bd of Dirs, Tangipahoa Parish Assn for Retard Citizens, 1957-67; Hammond U Givers Fund, 1957-68; LA Coun of Chs; LA Interch Conf; Trustee, Centenary Col; Hon Trustee, John F Kennedy Col; Chm of Bd, Wesley Foun; r/Meth; hon/Layman of the Yr, LA Annual Conf of the U Meth Ch, 1966, 1973; Crackpot Clb of Great Brit; Outstg Man of LA JCs, 1964; Dist'd Ser Awd for 1960, 1964; Hammond Jr C of C; Layman of the Yr for LA, Kiwanis Intl, 1972; Hon Doct of Laws, Centenary Col of LA & Depauw Univ; Dist'd Alumnus Awd, 1981, SEn LA Univ; W/ W: Ed, Bus, S & SW, Meth, the World, Am Law, Fin & Indust; DIB; Outstg Yg Men of Am; Personalities of the S; Outstg Civic Ldrs of Am; Royal Blue Book; Commun Ldrs of Am, Men Achmt; 5000 Personalities World.

MATHEWS, GRANT JAMES oc/ Nuclear Astrophysicist; b/Oct 14, 1950; h/5950 Cypress Point Drive, Livermore, CA 94550; ba/Livermore, CA; m/Christine R; p/Kenneth and Agnes Mathews, Saginaw, MI; ed/BS, MI St Univ, 1972; PhD, Univ MD, 1977; pa/Res Assoc, Univ CA, Lawrence Berkeley Lab, 1977-79; Res Fellow, CA Inst Tech, 1979-81; Physicist, Univ CA, Lawrence Livermore Nat Lab, 1981-; Am Phys Soc, Nuclear Physics Div, Astrophysics Div; Am Astronom Soc; r/Foursquare; hon/Num Pubs; Sigma Xi; Res Excell Awd, 1978.

MATHEWS-ROTH, MICHELINE MARY oc/Principal Research Associate in Medicine; b/Jul 26, 1934; h/192 Commonwealth Avenue, Boston, MA 02116; ba/Boston, MA; m/Robert Steele Roth, PhD; c/John; p/John F Mathews

(dec) and Micheline Van Smith; sp/ Clyde C and Gertrude Roth; ed/BS, Col St Elizabeth, 1956; MD, NY Univ Sch Med, 1961; pa/Predoct F'ships, NY Univ Sch Med 1957, Harvard Univ 1958-59; Internship, Pathol, Boston City Hosp, 1962-63; Res F'ships, NY Univ 1961, Univ CA Berkeley 1961-62, Harvard Med Sch 1962-64, Channing Lab, Boston City Hosp 1963-64, Dept Biol, Harvard Univ 1964-65; Acad Appts, Res Assoc, Bacteriology & Immunol, 1965-69, Assoc, Bacteriology & Immunol, 1969-71, Assoc, Microbiol & Molecular Genetics, 1971-74, Prin Res Assoc, Med, 1974, Harvard Med Sch; Hosp Appts, Asst Phys, 1973-74, Boston City Hosp, Jr Assoc Med, 1977-82, Peter Bent Brigham Hosp, Assoc Phys 1982-, Brigham & Wom Hosp; Asst Lab Instr, 1966, 1978, Lab Instr, 1979, 1981, Harvard Med Sch; US Nat Com Photobiol, 1976; Com Envir Hlt & Safety, Harvard Med Sch, 1976; Safety Com 1974-77, JCAH Core Com 1974-77, Dir Safety, Channing Lab 1974-77, Boston City Hosp; Dir Safety, Channing Lab 1977-, Infection Control Com 1978-79, Peter Bent Brigham Hosp; Assoc Editor, 1974; Mem, Am Soc Microbiol 1958, Am Soc Photobiol 1972, Am Fdn Clin Res 1974, Sigma Xi 1976, Am Soc Clin Invest 1977; hon/Beta Beta Beta, Nat Biol Hon Soc, 1954; Magna Cum Laude, BS, 1956; Kappa Gamma Pi, Wom Scholastic Hon Soc, 1956; Hon Bacteriology, MD, 1961; Borden Awd Med Res, 1961; Num Articles & W/W Listings.

MATSESHE, JOHN WANYAMA oc/ Practice Gastroenterology, Assistant Clinical Professor; b/Jun 5, 1941; h/621 Nordic Court, Libertyville, IL 60048; ba/ Libertyville, IL; m/Rebecca Zezenge; c/ Lily, Carolyn, Lynn, Andrew; p/James Matseshe (dec) and Anyachi Nyikuli, Kenya; ed/BA, Adams St Col, 1966; MB, CHB, MD, Makerere Univ, 1969; pa/ Conslt, Mayo Clinic, 1977-78; Asst Prof, Mayo Med Sch, 1978; Consltg Gastroenterologist, Condell Hosp, St Therese Hosp, VA Hosp, 1979-; Mem, AMA, Am Col Phys, Am Gastroenterological Assn; Bd Mem, Am Cancer Soc, Lake Co Chapt; Sigma Xi; r/friend; hon/Num Articles; Recip Mayo Foun F'ship, 1976; Recip Nat Inst Hlth F'ship, 1977; Intl Biographical Cntr; W/W: MW, Med Spec.

MATSUDA, FUJIO oc/University President; b/Oct 18, 1924; h/2234 Kamehameha Avenue, Honolulu, HI 96822; ba/Honolulu, HI; m/Amy; c/ Bailey, Thomas, Sherry, Joan, Ann, Richard; ed/BS, Rose Polytechnic Inst, 1949; ScD, MIT, 1952; mil/AUS, 1943-45; pa/Pres 1974-, VP Bus Affairs 1973-74, Dir Engrg Expt Sta, 1962-63, Chm Dept Civil Engrg, 1960-63, Prof Engrg 1962-64, 1974-, Assoc Prof Engrg 1957-58, 1959-62, Asst Prof Engrg 1955-57, Univ HI; Res Asst Prof Civil Engrg, Univ IL, 1954-55; Res Engr 1952-54, Res Asst 1950-52, MIT; Dir, Dept Trans, St HI, 1963-73; Pres, Shimazu, Matsuda, Shimbukuro & Assocs, 1960-63; Consltg Structural Engr, 1958-60; Park & Yee Ltd, 1956-58; Hydraulic Engr, USGS, 1949; Dir, C Brewer & Co Ltd & C Brewer HI Ltd, 1973-; Gov, Honolulu Symph Soc, 1974-; Dir, Hawaiian Elect Co, 1975-; Dir, Hawaiian Elect Industs, 1981-; Dir,

UAL Inc & United Airlines, 1975-; Trustee, Japan-Am Soc Honolulu, 1976-; Dir (ex officio), Res Corporation Univ HI, 1974-; Mem, Jud Coun HI, 1975-85; Mem (ex officio), Stadium Auth, 1974-; Bd Govs (ex officio), E-W Ctr, 1975-; Trustee (ex officio), Univ HI Foun, 1974; Bd Govs, Plaza Clb, 1979-; Dir, HI Inst Electronics Res, 1979-; Dir, Mauna Kea Properties (UAL Inc Subsidiary), 1981-; Bd Visitors, The Parsons Corporation, 1979-; Adv Bd, Duty Free Shoppers Ltd, 1982-; Am Soc Civil Engrs; Nat Soc Profl Engrs; Social Sci Assn Honolulu; HI Jt Coun Ec Ed; US Army Civilian Adv Grp; Exec Com 1977-84, VP 1979-80, Pres 1980-82, Wn Col Assn; Army Sci Bd, 1978-80; Exec Com, Trans Res Bd, Nat Res Coun, 1982-; cp/(Hon Mem) Rotary Clb; The 200 Clb; hon/Rose Polytechnic Inst Hon Alumnus Awd, 1971; HI Engr Yr, 1972; Airport Opers Coun Intl Dist'd Ser Awd, 1973; US Dept Trans Awd for Exceptl Public Ser, 1973; Nat Acad Engrg, 1974; Univ HI Dist'd Alumnus Awd, 1974; Rose-Hulman Inst Tech Hon D Engrg, 1975; Life Mem, Pacific Coast Assn Port Auths; Tau Beta Pi; Sigma Xi; Hon Mem, Chi Epsilon; Hon Mem, Beta Gamma Sigma; W/W: Am, Engrg, World, W, Persons & Orgs HI; Men & Wom HI; Am Men & Sci; Engrs Jt Coun; Ldrs Ed; Ldrs HI; Men Achmt.

MATTEI, JANET AKYUZ oc/Astronomer, Executive Director; b/Jan 2, 1943; h/8 Cedar Road, Littleton, MA 01460; ba/Cambridge, MA; m/Michael Mattei; p/Bella and Baruh Akyuz, Izmir, Turkey; sp/Michael and Georgina Mattei, New Haven, CT; ed/BA, Brandeis Univ, 1965; MA, Ege Univ, 1970; MS, Univ VA, 1972; PhD, Ege Univ, 1982; pa/Tchr, Am Col Inst, 1967-69; Res Asst, Maria Mitchell Observatory, 1969; Tchg Asst, Ege Univ, 1969-70; Tchg Asst, Hayden Planetarium, 1971; Dir Asst 1972-73, Dir, 1973-; Am Assn Variable Star Observers (AAVSO); hon/Num Articles Pub'd; Recip Wien Intl S'ship, Brandeis Univ, 1962-65; Prin Investigator Grants Made to AAVSO by NSF; NASA, Res Foun, 1979-82, 1980, 1981; W/W: Am Wom, Frontier Sci & Technol, Technol Today; World W/W Wom; Am Men & Wom Sci.

MATTHEWS, ALONZO RUSSELL oc/Manager, Equal Opportunity Affairs; b/Apr 27, 1943; h/8130 South Tamarac Street, Englewood, CO 80112; ba/Denver, CO; m/Gayle L Greer; c/Laura R, Alonza R, Audra, James V Greer; p/Walker and Laura Matthews, Grenada, MS; sp/Gloria Morgan, Tulsa, OK; ed/BS, Rusty Col, 1965; MS, Univ MO, 1972; pa/Mgr, Equal Opport Affairs, Anaconda Minerals Co, 1979-; Corporate Recruiter 1978-79, Fin Security Analyst 1977-78, Ctl Soya Co Inc; Exec Dir, Battle Creek Urban Leag, 1974-77; Prog Admr, Urban Leag KC, MO, 1968-73; Tchr, KC,MO, 1967-68; Tchr, Cleveland, MS, 1965-67; Yg Profls Unltd, 1969-72; Equal Opport Forum; Am Mgmt Assn, 1969-82; Am Soc Pers Admrs; cp/Omega Psi Phi Frat; Ft Wayne IN, Legal Action Com, 1974-79; Com VP, Urban Leag Metro Denver, 1979-82; S Pkwy U Meth Ch; NAACP; Mile Hi U Way Prog Adv Com; Denver Employmt & Tng Pvt Indust Coun; r/U Meth; hon/Model Cities Awd, 1970; Com Ser Awd, 1975; Ford

Foun F'ship, 1971; Urban Leag Com Ser Awd, 1980; Ctr Yth & Com Sers Inc Ser Awd, 1981; St CO Public Ser Inst Awd, 1979; Nat Urban Leag BEEP Awd, 1982; Employmt Concilio of Hispanic.

MATTHEWS, BARBARA ANN oc/Account Executive; b/Oct 16, 1951; h/16211 Downey Avenue, Number 2, Paramount, CA 90723; ba/LA, CA; p/Mr and Mrs William N Matthews, SC; ed/BA 1973, MBA 1976, Univ SC; pa/Public Relats Dir, U Way, Columbia, 1973-75; SC Med Assn, 1975-76; Mng Pi Sigma Epsilon NYC, 1976-78; Account Exec, Pacific Telephone LA, 1979-82; Am Bell LA, 1983-; cp/Mem, LA Trans Clb; Nat Alumni VP 1982-83, 1983-84, Wn Div Alumni Dir 1981-82, Wn Reg Alumni Dir 1980-81, Pi Sigma Epsilon; hon/Mng Editor, SC Med Assn Jour, 1975-76; Editor & Publisher "Dotted Lines" 1976-78; W/W: Students, in CA, Among Wom Am.

MATTHEWS, WILLIAM S oc/Farmer; b/Apr 27, 1935; h/Route 1, Box 151-A, Turkey, NC 28393; ba/Same; c/Helen Rose, William S Jr, David Lewis; p/David and Maxine Matthews, Turkey, NC; ed/Assoc Deg, Sampson Tech Col, 1952; mil/AUS, 1956-58; pa/Constrn Engr, 1960-75; Self-Employed Farmer, 1958-; VChm 1971-75, Chm 1975-83, Dem Precnt; Sampson Co Planning & Devel, 1977-83.

MAUE-DICKSON, WILMA oc/Manager, Department of Educational Services; b/Apr 15, 1943; h/8330 Southwest 138 Terrace, Miami, FL 33158; ba/Miami, FL; m/David Ross Dickson, PhD; c/Eric Paul; p/Donald Maste (dec) and Mildred C Maue, Orland Pk, IL; ed/BA, Univ Rockford Col, 1964; MA, NWn Univ, 1968; PhD, Univ Pgh, 1970; Att'd Univ Exeter, 1962-63; Vol, US Peace Corps, 1964-66; Clin Asst, Tchg & Res Asst, Instr, NWn Univ, 1966-68; Instr, Anatomy & Physiol, Carlow Col, 1970-72; Dir Res, Mercy Hosp, 1969-74; Adj Asst Prof, Spch & Theatre Arts, Asst Prof, Anatomy 1974-75, Assoc Dir, Cleft Palate Ctr, 1970-75, Univ Psg; VP, Bicom Co, 1968-78; Dir, Craniofacial Res, Mailman Ctr Child Devel 1976-79, Assoc Prof Surg & Pediatrics 1976-79, Adj Assoc Prof Surg 1980-, Univ Miami Sch Med; Assoc Mgr 1980-82, Mgr 1982-, Ednl Sers, Cordis Corporation; Am Assn Phonetic Scis, 1972; Am Acad Advmt Sci, 1973-75; Craniofacial Biol Grp, 1975-79; Am Assn Anatomists, 1975-79; Assn Res Otolaryngology, 1974-79; Am Cleft Palate Ednl Foun, 1975-79; Am Cleft Palate Assn, 1975-79; Am Spch & Hearing Assn, 1968-79; Miami Assn Communication Spec, 1978-79; Soc Craniofacial Genetics, 1976-79; hon/Num Lectures, Sems, Shortcourses, Sci Exhibs, Sci Papers; Nums Hons & Awds incl'g Lttr Commend from Ethiopian Min of Ed for Sers, 1966; Lttr Commend from Lyndon B Johnson for Outstg Ser as Overseas Vol, 1966; Student Senate Lttr of Commend for Outstg Contbns, 1968; Am Spch & Hearing Assn Awd, 1970; Outstg Yg Wom PA, 1971; Phi Beta Kappa, Eta IL, Rockford Col, 1976; Am Men & Wom Sci, 1976; Sigma Xi, 1978; World W/W Wom, 1980; Charter Mem, Phi Beta Kappa, Delta Chapt FL, 1983.

MAURER, LUCILLE oc/State Legislator; b/Nov 21, 1922; h/1023 Forest Glen Road, Silver Spring, MD 20901;

ba/Annapolis, MD; m/Ely Maurer; c/Stephen Bennett, Russell Alexander, Edward Nestor; p/Joseph J Darvin and Evelyn L (dec); sp/William and Fannie Maurer (dec); a/Att'd Univ NC—Greensboro, 1938-40; BA, Univ NC—Chapel Hill, 1942; MA, Yale Univ, 1945; pa/Economist, US Tariff Comm, 1942-43; Ec & Mkt Res for Pvt Firms, 1957-60; Conslt, Nat Ctr Ednl Stats, 1969-70; Montgomery Co Bd Ed, 1960-68; Bd Trustees, Montgomery Commun Col, 1960-68; MD Constitutional Conv, 1967-68; Ho of Dels, 1969-; Intergovtl Adv Coun, US Dept Ed, Pres Appt, 1980-82; Carnegie Foun Advmt Tchg, Nat Governance Panel, 1980-; Adv Com for Ed, LWV, 1979-81; Ed Adv Com Block Grants, 1981; St Employmt & Tng Coun, 1979-; Comm Funding Public Ed, 1977-78; Structure & Governance Ed (Rosenberg Comm), 1973-75; Task Force on Sch Fin (Lee Task Force) 1972; cp/LWV Montgomery Co, Bd Mem, 1950; Am Assn Univ Wom; NOW; Montgomery Co Hist Soc; Montgomery Co Mtl Hlth Assn; Jewish Social Ser Agy; Bd Dirs, Jewish Coun for Aging, 1978-82; r/Jewish; hon/Ann London Scott Meml Awd, MD NOW, 1981; Nat Ldrship Awd, Inst Ednl Ldrship, 1981; Am Assn Univ MD, 1978, 1980; Montgomery Co Ed Assn, "Hornbook Awd", 1972; Delta Kappa Gamma (Hon Mem); W/W: Am Wom, World Jewry, Govt, Am Polit; Commun Ldrs & Noteworthy Ams; Intl W/W Commun Ser; Personalities S; World W/W Wom.

MAVRICH, DOROTHY L oc/Music Teacher; b/May 12, 1920; h/1300 West Acres Road, Joliet, IL 60435; p/Louis (dec) and Amelia Mavrich; ed/Att'd Joliet Metro Bus Col, 1941; Joliet Conservatory of Music, 1942; Piano Tchr Cert; pa/Receptionist, Joliet Conservatory Music, 1939-42; Tchr, Joliet Conservatory Music, 1942-74; Piano Tchr, 1974-; Secy 1977-78, Dir 1977-80, Joliet Ballet Soc Inc; Joliet Public Lib Bd, 1977-80; Pres, Rialto Sq Arts Assn, 1975-; Secy/Treas, Will Co Metro Exposition & Auditorium, 1978-; hon/Author of Thinking, Why Not, A Journey Through Music Land; Congressman's Medal of Merit Awd, 1980; IL St Hist Soc Awd, 1981; Hon Zontian Awd from Zonta Clb of Joliet for Commun & Preserv Wk, 1982.

MAXWELL, CHARLES ALAN oc/Franchise; b/Jul 13, 1955; h/110 Marion Drive, Broussard, LA 70518; ba/Same; m/Carol Lynne (Cole); c/April Lynn, David Wayne, Larisa Ann; p/Arlie Wayne Maxwell, Broussard, LA, and Glenna Faye Malcolm, Stratford, TX; sp/Mr and Mrs David Cole, Amarillo, TX; ed/AAS, Amarillo Col, 1975; BS, Univ Hous, 1977; pa/Opers Mgr, Target Stores, 1975-79; Pres, Fast Food Mgmt, 1979-82; Owner, Mod Mgmt Sys, 1982-; Phila Area Franchise, Popeyes Fried Chicken, 1982-; Nat Restaurant Assn; TX Restaurant Assn; Am Mgmt Assn; Pres Assn of Am Mgmt Assn; hon/Outstg Yg Men Am, W/W Am Fin & Indust.

MAY, AVIVA (RABINOWITZ) oc/Educator; h/1239 Asbury Avenue, Evanston, IL 60202; ba/Same; m/Stanley Lee May; c/Rochelle (Chelley) Mosoff, Alan Noah, Risa May McPherson, Ellanna Malka; p/Rabbi Samuel and

Paula (Gordon) Rabinowitz (dec), Israel; sp/Anna Meyers May, Hollandale, FL; ed/BA, NEn IL Univ, 1979; AA, Oakton Commun Col, 1978; pa/Tchr, Pianist, 1948-; Music Dir, McCormick Hlth Ctr, Cove Sch, 1978-79; Adj Prof, Lectr, Spertus Col Judaica, NEn IL Univ, Jewish Commun Ctrs Chgo, 1980-; Cont'g Ed, Mini-U, NEn IL Univ, 1978-80; Folksinger, Guitarist, 1962-; Music Composer; Creator, Tchg Method " Psychol Musical Method", 1972-; Fdr, Charter Mem 1974, Secy 1974-76, N Shore Music Tchrs Assn; Mem, IL St Music Tchrs Assn; Am Col Musicians; Sherwood Sch Music; IL St Assn Lrng Disabilities; cp/YIVO Inst Jewish Res; Nat Yiddish Book Exch; Chgo Jewish Hist Soc; Friends Holocaust Survivors; hon/Tchr of First Adult B'nai Mitzva in Chgo, 1973; W/W Am Wom; Chgo Jewish Source Book; Conf Jewish Wom Dir; Num Articles Pub'd; Reported in Am Music Tchr Mag, 1979; Yiddish as Second Lang, Nat Assn Temple Admrs, 1980; Piano Reviews in IL St Music Tchrs Assn Newslttr, 1983; Performed & Composed Music in Documentaries, 1968, 1979; Yiddish Expertise Used in Ofc Spec Invest, Washington, DC.

MAY, EVELYN YEOMANS EBBS oc/ Secondary English Teacher (Retired); b/ Sep 17, 1919; h/630 East 36th Street, Savannah, GA 31401; c/Marion M, Reginald F; p/John H Ebbs Sr (dec) and Alice A Ebbs, Savannah, GA; ed/BA, Spelman Col, 1942; MA, Columbia Univ; pa/Sec'dy HS Eng Tchr, Savannah-Chatham Co Bd Ed, 1943-82; NEA, GA Assn Edrs, Chatham Co Assn Edrs, 1945-82; Prog Chm, 1965-69, Parent-Tchrs-Students Assn, 1943-82; Ed Advr, Student Action for GA, 1977-82; cp/NAACP, 1943-; Sustaining Mem, Assn Study Afro-Am Life & Hist Inc, 1978-; Pres, Savannah Chapt, 1975-81, Nat Alumnae Assn, Spelman Col, 1943-; Prince Hall of En Stars, 1943-45; Order Clk, 1975-76, Sheba Num 70, Intl F & M, Mason of OES, 1974-76; Corres Secy, 1980-81, Alumnae Chapt Delta Sigma Theta Sorority, 1977-; Orgr, Alice F Roberts Four Leaf Clover, Socio-Civic Clb, 1973; Chi Xalers Social Club, 1965-; r/Bapt; hon/ Tchr of Yr, 1960; Tchr Yr Adult Ed, 1981; Achmt Awd, 1981; Cert Apprec, PTA, 1981; Cert Apprec, Pres Ed Comm, Second Bapt Ch.

MAY, JANIS SUSAN oc/Writer; b/ Aug 16, 1946; h/10453 Foxton, Station C, Dallas, TX 75238; ba/Same; p/Donald W (dec) and Aletha B May, Dallas, TX; ed/Att'd Trinity Univ & SMU; Pvt Studies in Voice & Langs; pa/Writer, 1970-; Casting Dir, Peggy Taylor Talent Inc, 1971-80; Singer, 1965-78; Collateral Teller, ILD Dept, Nat Bk Commerce, 1968-70; Account Exec, Don May Advtg, 1962-68; Bus & Profl Wom Clb, Mexican-Am Chapt; Cosmos Review Class; Yg Wom Arts; hon/ Author of Where Shadows Linger & The Avenging Maid, Num Short Stories, Articles, Radio Commls, Indust Films, etc; Intl Biographical Ctr Pub.

MAYER, CHARLES HENRY oc/Parts Manager, Heavy Duty Truck; b/Jul 18, 1927; h/3473 Springbrook, Kalamazoo, MI 49004; ba/Kalamazoo, MI; c/ Kathryn Marie; p/John W (dec) and Marietta Mayer, Rapid City, SD; ed/

Corres Courses in Law; Dun & Bradstreet in Financial Statements; Dale Carnegie Courses; Nat Safety Coun Courses; mil/USN, 1945-47; Secy/ Treas, C & R Transfer Co, 1972-75; Secy/Treas, Dakota Heavy Hauling Inc, 1972-75; Terminal Mgr, Johnstons Fuel Liners, 1974-75; Ptnrship in Oil Field Welding & Trucking, Anchor Enterprises, 1975-76; Parts Mgr, Daleidens Inc, 1977-; cp/Life Mem, VFW; Cmdr Post 54, Battle Creek, MI, 1977-79, Adjutant for Third Dist, Dept MI, 1978-79; Am Legion; Bd Dirs 1977-, Pres 1981-83, TB & Emphysema Assn; Bd Mem on Sub Com on Human Studies Representing Vet Orgs, Battle Creek Med Ctr; r/Presb; hon/One of Pioneers of Child Custody for Men, 1960-63, One of First Fathers to Gain Child Custody in 1963.

MAYER, LAWRENCE STEPHEN oc/ Professor and Statistical Consultant; b/ Nov 14, 1946; h/4123 North 57th Street, Phoenix, AZ 85018; ba/Tempe, AZ; p/Mrs Andrew G Mayer, Scottsdale, AZ; ed/BA 1967, MS 1968, PhD 1971, OH St Univ; Att'd AZ St Univ, 1964-65; pa/Assoc Prof, Stats, Princeton Univ, 1973-79; Dir, Anal Ctr, Wharton Sch, Univ PA, 1979-82; Vis's Prof, Stats, Stanford Univ, 1982-83; cp/ Resv Game Ranger, AZ Game & Fish Dept; Cert'd & Sworn St Police Ofcr, 1983-; hon/Num Pubs in Res Jours in Stats, Biostats, & Public Policy; Phi Beta Kappa, 1967; Hon Grad Psych, 1967; W/ W.

MAYER, SYDNEY LOUIS oc/Publisher; b/Aug 2, 1937; h/46 Lowndes Square, London SW1, England; also 32 Sherwood Avenue, Greenwich, CT 06830; ba/London, England and Greenwich, CT; m/Charlotte Wilhelmina Bouter; c/Patrick Michael (dec); p/ Sydney Louis and Elizabeth Madeleine (Sandorf); ed/BA 1962, MA 1962, Univ MI; MA, 1965, Yale Univ; pa/Dir, Univ MD in UK, 1972-73, Lectr, Hist, Univ MD, 1966-76; Vis'g Asst Prof, Intl Relats, Univ So CA, 1969-81; Dir, Bison Books, London, 1974-; Fellow Royal Geog Soc; Mem, Inst Hist Res Clbs: Yale (NYC); Yale, Savage (London); Univ MI, Fairfield Co, (Conn); Pres's Univ MI; hon/Author Books incl'g The World of SE Asia, 1967; MacArthur, 1970; MacArthur in Japan, 1973, Wars of the 20th Century, 1975, The Two World Wars, 1977; W/W.

MAYE-WILSON, PATRICIA ANN oc/Special Needs Teacher; b/Dec .2, 1945; h/85 Camden Street, Number 323, Boston, MA 02118; ba/Same; c/ Amani Brent Wilson, Dino Lavon Maye, Willie Thomas Maye; p/Mrs Mary Lee Maye, Roxbury, MA; ed/BS, 1974, Boston St Col; MEd, 1978, Boston Univ; pa/Spec Needs Tchr, Boston Public Schs, 1975-; ABCD, Compliance Monitor; cp/Pres, Black Alumni Assn Inc, Boston St Col, 1974-; r/Prot; hon/ Author of Poetry, Boston St Col, Fine Arts Mag, 1971-74; W/W Among Students Am Univs & Cols.

MAYFIELD, MICHAEL WADE oc/ Student; b/Oct 9, 1962; h/1929 Honore Avenue, North Chicago, IL 60064; ba/ North Chicago, IL; p/Hugh and Larcine Mayfield, N Chgo, IL; ed/Wn IL Univ; cp/Quill & Scroll, 1981; hon/Col Hons: 1st Pl Floor Decorating Contest, Wn IL Univ, 1982; HS Hon: Num 1 Rating Comic Strip "Silly Sally" Nat Scholastic

Press Assn, 1979, 1981; 1st Pl IL St Anti-Smoking Poster Contest, IL Lung Assn, 1979-81; 1st Pl Book Marker Contest, N Chgo Public Lib, 1979; 2nd Pl Arthritis Foun Poster Contest, 1980; 1st Pl Hire the Handicapped Poster Contest, DAV, 1980; 2nd Pl ACT-SO Olympics Art Category, NAACP, 1980; 4th Pl Hire the Handicapped Poster Contest, DAV, 1981; 2nd Pl Book Cover Contest, IL Jr Acad Sci, 1981; Mgr of the Yr, 3rd Runner-Up Wrestling USA Mag 1980; Mgr of Yr, 1st Runner-Up Wrestling USA Mag 1981; Winner 1 Freshman Num & Ten Varsity Lttrs, N Chgo Commun HS, 1977-81; Mgr Awd for 4 Yrs Ser, N Chgo Commun HS, 1981; Art Exhibs: Neal Jr HS Art Showing Dist 64, 1973 & 1975; Lake Co Art Exhibs, Waukegan Belvidere Mall, 1976; 1st Pl Parking Sticker Contest, Wn IL Univ; Black Heritage Art Exhib, N Chgo Br NAACP, 1980; Am Heritage Art Showing, N Chgo Public Lib, 1980; Intl Yth in Achmt; Commun Ldrs of Am; W/W Among AM HS Students; Yg Personalities Am; Dir Dist'd Ams.

MAYHEW, HARRY C oc/Associate Professor of Education; b/Jan 8, 1940; h/Route 5, Box 244, Forest Hills, Morehead, KY 40351; ba/Morehead, KY; m/Ann; c/Cara; p/John Burton (dec) and Eva Mayhew, Washington, DC; ed/ BA, MA, MHE, Morehead St Univ; EdD, Ball St Univ, 1970; pa/Instr, Jour 1962, Instr, Eng 1963-67, Doct Study 1968-70, Asst Prof, Ed, Assoc Prof, Ed, 1970-, Adm Positions, Dir, Microtchg, Morehead St Univ; KY Assn Cont'g Ed; KY Assn Tchr Edrs; cp/Phi Delta Kappa; Phi Kappa Phi; Bd Dirs, First Christian Ch Morehead, 1970-; Pres 1984, VP 1982, 1983, Rowan Co, KY Hist Soc; r/Christian Ch, Disciples Christ; hon/ Auth of Num Pubs incl'g "Capturing Sci on Videotape" Sci & Chd, 1982, "Related Res Class Size", Resources in Ed, 1984; Recog Awd, Past Dir Alumni Relats, Morehead St Univ, 1975; Recog Awd, Optimist Clb Morehead, 1979, 1980; Hon Deg, Dr Writing for Pub, Phi Delta Kappa Ednl Foun & IN Univ Se Ed, 1984; Outstg Yg Men Am; Personalities: S & E; W/W S & SW.

MAYNARD, ROBERT C oc/Editor and Publisher; b/Jun 17, 1937; h/1015 Sunnyhills Road, Oakland, CA 94610; ba/Oakland, CA; m/Nancy Hicks; c/Dori J, David H, Alex C; p/Samuel Christopher and Robertine Isola (Greaves) Maynard (dec); sp/Al Hall and Eve Keller, NY, NY; ed/Nieman Fellow, Harvard Univ, 1966; pa/Reporter, Afro-Am News, 1956; Reporter, York Gazette & Daily, 1961-67; Reporter, Washington Post, 1967-72; Assoc Editor/Ombudsman, 1972-74; Edit Writer, 1974-77; Editor & Publisher, Oakland (CA) Tribune, 1979-; Former Chm, Inst Jour Ed; Mem, Assem Behavioral Scis Nat Acad Sci, 1979-; Mem, Mexican-Am Legal Def & Ednl Fund, 1978-; Mem, Comm Public Understanding about Law of Am Bar Assn, 1979-; Bd Dirs, Bay Area Coun; Mem, Marcus Foster Ednl Inst; Nat Bd Dirs, Media & Soc Sems; Mem, Wn Reg Adv Bd Am Press Inst; Bd Dirs, Am Soc Newspapers Editors; Mem, Nat News Coun; Mem, Govt Affairs Com, Coun Fgn Affairs, Am Newspaper Pubs Assn; Mem, Commonwealth Clb CA; Mem, Edit Bd CA

Lwyr; Bd Dirs, Col Preparatory Sc; Bd Dirs, Oakland C of C; Chm, YMCA Capital Devel Com; hon/W/W: in World, Am, SW, among Black Ams, W.

MAYO, JOHN S oc/Executive Vice President; b/Feb 26, 1930; h/83 May Drive, Chatham, NJ 07928; ba/Murray Hill, NJ; m/Lucille; c/Mark Dodgson, David Thomas, Nancy Ann, Lynn Marie; ed/BS 1952, MS 1953, PhD 1955, NC St Univ; pa/Mem, Tech Staff, Computer Res 1955-58, Supvr, Tl Carrier Sys 1958-60, Dept Hd, PCM Terminal Dept 1960-67, Dir, Ocean Sys Lab 1967-71, Exec Dir, Ocean Sys Div 1971-73, Exec Dir, Toll Electronic Switching Div, 1973-75, VP, Electronics Technol, 1975-79, Exec VP, Network Sys 1979-, Bell Labs; Mem, Adv Panel Ofc Technol Assessmt, 1982-84; Mem, Gov's Task Force, Com Sci & Technol, 1982-83; Mem, Am Assn Engrg Socs, Com on Engrg Utilization, 1983-; Mem, Bd Dirs, Nat Engrg Consortium, 1974-76; Conf Chm & Coms, Intl Solid-St Circuits Conf, 1961-69; hon/ Nums Articles & Pubs; IEEE Fellow, 1967; Nat Acad Engrg, Mem, 1979; Alexander Graham Bell Medal, 1978; Outstg Engrg Alumnus, NCSU, 1977; W/W E, Am; Intl W/W Engrg.

MAZZA, TERILYN McGOVERN oc/ Executive of Communication Services; b/Apr 25, 1952; h/1085 Warburton Avenue, Yonkers, NY 10701; ba/NY, NY; m/Mario G; p/Edward Joseph and Mary Ryan McGovern, Albany, NY; sp/ Anthony and Mario Mazza, Ithaca, NY; ed/BA, Marymount Col, 1974; Att'd Royal Acad Dramatic Art London, 1972-73; Univ London Westfell Col, 1972-73; MA, St Univ NY Albany, 1976; pa/Exec Communication Sers 1983-, Publisher, Promotion Mgr 1981-83, Am Bus Press; Promotion, Res Mgr, Hearst Newspapers, 1979-81; Public Relats Dir, Lake George Opera Fest, 1978-79; Co Mgr, Cohoes Music Hall, 1976-78; Bd Dirs, Ad Club, NY Tri-City Chapt, 1980; Bd Dirs, Troy Cromatics, 1979-81; Bd Dirs, Eng Spkg Union, 1976-81; Mem, Ad Wom NY; Wom Direct Response, Am Wom Radio & TV; Overseas Press Clb; Am Newspapers Publishers Assn; r/Rom Cath; hon/Intl Newspaper Promotion Assn Yrbook, 1982; Monthly Column Editor; W/W Indust & Fin.

MAZZAROPPI, LORETTA LUCRE-ZIA oc/Professor, Business Management; b/Jan 2; h/14 Winfield Drive, Little Silver, NJ 07739; ba/Madison, NJ; p/Thomas V (dec) and Jennie M Mazzaroppi, Red Bank, NJ; ed/BS, Monmouth Col, 1968; MBA, St Univ NY Albany, 1969; PhD, LA St Univ, 1976; pa/Prof 1976-, Vis'g Assoc Prof 1973-74, Fairleigh Dickinson Univ; Grad Tchg Fellow, LA St Univ, 1974-76; Assoc Prof, Coor Bus Studies, Career Progs, Clinton Commun Col, St Univ NY, 1969-73; AAUW; Nat Assn Female Execs; Am Bus Communication Assn; Orgnl Behavior Tchg Soc; r/Rom Cath; hon/Beta Gamma Sigma; Nat Scholastic Hon Soc Bus/Mgmt Students; Lamda Sigma Tau; Monmouth Col Hon Soc; W/W Fin & Indust.

McADOO, PHYLLIS IMOGENE oc/ Elementary School Supervisor; b/Feb 4, 1932; h/3825 Winding Way, Cincinnati, OH 45229; ba/Cincinnati, OH; m/ Robert E; c/Marcia LaVerne, Teressa

Annette; p/Thomas L and Minnie Watson Gaston, Sheffield, AL; sp/ Argen and Minnie Eatman McAdoo; ed/ BS, Univ Cin, 1955; MEd, Xavier Univ, 1959; Post Grad Hrs, Miami Univ, Oxford, OH; pa/Tchr, 1955-64; Elem Asst Prin, 1964-67; Supvr, 1967; Nom'g Com 1974-75, Treas 1975-76, Cinc Assn Admrs & Supvrs; Ctl Ofc Profl Coun; Ctl Ofc Employees Assn; OH Assn Elem & Sch Prins; Cinc Coun Edrs; Publicity Chm, 1963, Cinc Tchrs Assn; cp/Ed Com, 1967, N Avondale Neighborhood Assn; Chm, 1972-83, Kathryn Jo Guise Trust Fund; Nom Com, 1972, Delta Kappa Gamma Soc; Dean Pledges, 1954, Alpha Kappa Alpha Sorority; VP, 1972, Cinc Chapt Jack & Jill Am; Newslttr Editor, 1971-73, Buckeye Explorers Chapt Nat Campers & Hikers; r/Prot; hon/Dean's List, Univ Cinc, 1955; Ser Awd; Cinc Public Schs, 1972; Outstg Edrs Am; W/W Am Ed.

McALLISTER, PATRICIA FAITH oc/Law Clerk; b/May 14, 1958; h/2809 Barr Avenue, North Las Vegas, NV 89030; ba/Las Vegas, NV; p/Garland Edward (dec) and Nancy B McAllister, Las Vegas, NV; ed/BA 1980, JD 1983, OH No Univ; pa/Legal Intern, Bellefontaine Legal Aid; Probation Asst, Clark Co Juv Ct Sers; Law Clk, Eighth Jud Dist Ct; cp/Phi Alpha Delta Legal Frat; Pres, Alpha Xi Delta Alumnae Frat; Assoc Mem, Wom Legal Assn; r/Meth.

McANENY, EILEEN SUSAN oc/ Attorney, Corporate Law Department; b/May 31, 1952; h/826 Lombard Street, Philadelphia, PA 19147; ba/Philadelphia, PA; m/Michael D Gallagher, Esquire; p/ William and Mary McAneny, Narberth, PA; sp/Frank Gallagher, Browns Mills, NJ; ed/BA, Rosemont Col, 1974; JD, Villanova Univ, 1977; pa/Atty, SmithKline Beckman Corporation, 1981-; Assoc, German, Gallagher & Murtagh, 1980-81; Assoc, La Brum & Doak, 1977-80; Law Clk, Marshall, Dennehey, Warner, Coleman & Goggin, 1976-77; Law Clerk, Wertheimer & Kane, 1975-76; Tort & Ins Pract, Prods, Gen Liability & Consumer Law Com, Litigation, & Yg Lwyrs Div, Am Bar Assn; PA Bar Assn; Phila Bar Assn; Prod Liability & Employee Compensation Sect, Nat Assn Mfrs; Lectr, PA Pharm Assn Annnual Meeting, 1979; Freshman Moot Ct Team; r/Rom Cath; hon/ Author of "The Name Game-Reversed" Facts of Live, *Savvy* 1981, "All in a Day's Wk" *Reader's Digest* 1982; Appellate Ct Advocacy Hons Prog (Moot Ct Competition); Rosemont Col S'ships; Dean's List, Rosemont Col; Spec Acad Hons Prog, Rosemont Col; Delta Epsilon Sigma Nat Hon Soc; Kistler Hon Soc; Danforth F'ship Nom; W/W Am Law, among Wom World, Am Cols & Univs.

McBEE, JOE DAVID oc/Library Professional, Head of Serials and Binding; b/Aug 22, 1947; h/Post Office Box 127, Oklahoma Avenue, Sewanee, TN 37375; ba/Sewanee, TN; p/Ernest Howard and Elizabeth Lucille McBee (dec), Sewanee, TN; ed/BA, FL St Christian Univ, 1971; Post Grad Lib Sci, Middle TN St Univ, 1975; Post Grad Ed Adm, TN St Univ, 1981-; pa/Circulation Asst 1967-72, Serials & Binding Dept Hd 1972-, Jessie Ball duPont Lib, Univ of the S; Road Commr, 1st Dist Franklin Co, 1974; Secy 1978-82, Chm 1982-, Franklin Co Hwy Comm; Franklin Co

Democratic Exec Comm, 1980-; Precnt Chm, Democratic Party Sewanee, TN, 1974-; cp/Mem, Bd Dirs, Sewanee Commun Action, 1978-; Pres 1982, Mem Bd Dirs, Sewanee Yth Ctr, 1981-; Mem 1975-, Pres 1979-80, Mem Bd Dirs 1977-81, Sewanee Civic Assn; Mem, Bd Dirs 1975-, Mem 1975-, Secy 1975-82, Sewanee Commun Meml Assn; Mem, EQB, Sewanee, 1979-80; Mem, Bd Dirs 1980-81, Mem, 1980-, Mem, Commun Relats Communs Com 1980-81, Chm Mem Retention Com 1981, Chm Banquet Com 1981, Franklin Co C of C; Mem, Adult Ed Com, Franklin Co, 1981-; Sewanee Meml Cross Restoration Com; Sewanee Public Sch Renovation Com; Mem, TN Lib Assn; Mem, Mid-St Lib Assn; Franklin Co Hist Soc; Employees Com of Univ S, 1977-80; Am Soc Indexers; Sewanee Commun Coun; Sewanee Bus Dist Improvement Com, 1981-; Aid, Senator Ernest Crouch Ofc, 1981-; r/Grace F'ship Ch, Trustee 1974-, Mem 1968-; Secy/Treas 1968-; Chm Bd Trustees 1976-; hon/Author of *Winchester-Herald Chronicle Obituaries Name Index*, Honored w Senate Jt Resolution, 1982; W/W S & SW.

McCABE, DONALD LEE oc/Physician, General and Psychiatric; b/Nov 5, 1925; h/3221 Greenwood Avenue, Sacramento, CA 95812; ba/Sacramento, CA; m/Jean; c/Geoffrey, Timothy, Eleanor, Traill, Karyn, Derek; ed/Att'd Haverford Sch, Ursinus Col, Haverford Col, Phila Col Osteopathic Med, DO, 1950, Phila Mtl Hlth Clin, Psychoanalytic Studies Inst, 1956-62; mil/USNR, Pre-Med, 1944-45; pa/Phys, 1951-68; Psychi Phys, Harrisburg St Hosp, 1969-73; Psychi, DE Val Mtl Hlth Foun, 1973-74; Grp Pract, Sacramento, 1974-82; Gen Pract & Psychi, 1983-; Am Osteopathic Assn, 1951-83; Phys & Surgs CA, 1974-83; Am Col Gen Practitioners Osteopathic Med & Surg, 1965-83; Acad Psychosomatic Med, 1970-83; Am Col Neuropsychiatry, 1965-83; Acad Orthomolecular Psychi, 1975-83; hon/Num Articles Pub'd incl'g "Why People Smoke", JOPSC, "Orthomolecular Res", JOPSC, 1976; Fellow, Am Col Gen Pract Osteopathic Med & Surg; Fellow, Am Public Hlth Assn, 1969; Fellow, Acad Psychosomatic Med; Fellow, Intl Biographic Assn; Personalities in W; W/W: W, CA; Men of Achmt; Academie du Lausanne.

McCAIN, MILDRED LYNN oc/Real Estate Broker, Part Owner and Executive; b/Jan 22, 1945; h/Post Office Box 722, Newport, NC 28570; ba/Newport, NC; m/Ernest L; c/Dana Lynn and Dawn Leigh; p/Charles C Edwards Sr (Grandfather), Atlantic, NC; sp/Lucy McCain, Newport, NC; ed/Miller Motte Bus Col, 1963-64; Att'd Carteret Tech Col & Univ NC, 1970-81; c/Credit Clk, 1964-65; Secy, 1965- 66; Sr Credit Clk, 1966-69; Cosmetic Conslt, 1969-; Bk Teller, 1973-75; Ofc Mgr 1975-80, Sales Mgr 1980-83, Real Est Broker 1975-, Part Owner, 1983, Murdoch Properties Inc; Pres 1980, VP 1979, Secy/Treas 1978, By-Laws Chm 1982, Fin Chm 1983, City-Carteret Co Bd Rltrs; External Affairs Com 1980, Make Am Better Sub-Com 1980, Secy, External Affairs Com 1981, Dir 1980, 1981, 1982, 1983, 1984, Commun Devel Chm 1983, 1984, NC Assn Rltrs; Sub-Com, Commun Revitalization 1982, Make Am Better

Com 1983, 1984, Small Bd Forum 1983, Nat Assn Rltrs; Fin Chm 1983, Parade of Homes Chm 1983, Secy 1984, Carteret Co Home Bldrs; NC Home Bldrs; Nat Assn Home Bldrs; Nat Assn Real Est Appraisers; Wom Coun Rltrs; cp/Carteret Co C of C; Adv Coun at Newport Elem Sch; r/Prot, Parkview Bapt Ch; hon/Morehead City-Carteret Co Bd Rltrs, Rltr of Yr, 1980; NC Assn Rltrs, Reg Ser Awd, 1981, 1982; W/W Real Est in Am; NC Gov's Awd, Order of Long Leaf Pine, 1982; C of C Cert of Recog, 1983; Carteret Co Home Bldrs Cert of Recog, 1983; Carteret Co Home Bldrs, Assoc of Yr, 1983.

McCALL, EDWARD H oc/Scientific Processing Consultant; b/Dec 11, 1938; h/4710 Debra Lane, Shoreview, MN 55112; ba/St Paul, MN; m/Judith I; c/Scott Edward, Cathy Ann, Douglas James, p/Ephriam Forrest (dec) and Mariada H McCall, Oxford MS; sp/Emil J and Irma Bohn, Mason City, IA; ed/BS, IA St Univ, 1960; MS 1970, PhD 1979, Univ MN; pa/Jr Engr, Panhandle En Pipeline Co, 1958; Chem Engrg Rschr 1960-63, Programmer 1963-68, 3- M Co; Programmer, Proj Mgr 1968-79, Rschr, Sci Conslt 1979-, Sperry Univac; Adj Asst Prof, Univ MN, 1979-84; Opers Res Soc; Math Programming Soc; Soc Indust & Applied Math; ACM; IEEE Computer Soc; cp/Asst Scoutmaster, Indianhead Coun BSA, 1974-80; Ftball Coach, Moundsview Jr Ftball Leag, 1979-80; hon/Author of Num Articles on Math Programming; W/W Frontier Sci & Tech.

McCALLA, MARY ELLEN oc/Artist, Educator; b/Jun 15, 1944; h/264 Scenic Ridge Road, Kalispell, MT 59901; ba/Same; p/Martin Joseph and Carolyn (Butin) Travers, Kalispell, MT; ed/Att'd Univ OK, 1962-63; BS, Memphis St Univ, 1966; pa/Art, Vocal Music Tchr, Memphis Public Sch Sys, 1967-75; Artist, 1976-; One Wom Show, Four Pheasants, Kalispell, MT, 1979; Grp Shows, Ligoa Duncan Arts, 1977, Four Pheasants, Kalispell, MT, 1979; Exhibited w Ligoa Duncan Arts, NYC, 1977, 1978; Raymond Duncan Galleries, Paris, France, 1978; Memphis NEA; TN Ed Assn; Memphis Ed Assn; W TN Ed Assn; Treas, 1967-69, W TN Vocal Music Ed Assn; MENC; Asst Secy Inservice Tng, 1973-74, Memphis Art Ed Assn; MT Choral Dirs Assn; Intl Soc ·Artists; Les Surindependants; Intl Fine Arts Guild; cp/Alpha Gamma Delta; Mu Phi Epsilon; hon/Recip Prix de Paris, Ligoa Duncan Arts, 1977; Salon des Surindependants, Les Surindependants, Paris, 1977; W/W in W.

McCARTHY, JOHN FRANCIS JR oc/Corporate Executive; b/Aug 28, 1925; h/19171 Via del Caballo, Yorba Linda, CA 92686; ba/Anaheim, CA; m/Camille D; c/Margaret, Megan, Jaime M, Nicole E, John F; p/John Sr (dec) and Margaret Josephine McCarthy, West Roxbury, MA; sp/John F Martinez, Stanton, CA, and Vera Overholtzer, Garden Grove, CA; ed/BS 1950, MS 1951, MIT; PhD, CA Inst Technol, 1962; mil/USAAF, 1944-46; pa/Corporate VP, Gen Mgr, Northrop Corporation, Electro-Mech Div; Dir, ENSCO, Inc; Dir, The MacNeal-Schwendler Corporation, Bd Chm, Technol Exch Ctr; Ctr Dir, NASA Lewis Res Ctr, 1978-82; Prof, Dept

Aeronautics & Astronautics 1971-78, Prof & Dir, Ctr Space Res 1974-78, MIT; Conslt Indust, 1971-78; VP, LA Div/Space Div, Rockwell Intl Corporation, 1961-71; Opers Analyst, HQ Strategic Air Command, 1955-59; Proj Mgr, Aeroelastic & Structures Res Lab, MIT, 1951-55; Supvr, Trans World Airlines, 1946-47; Fellow, Former Dir, Am Inst Aeronautics & Astronautics; Fellow, Am Astronautical Soc; Fellow, Royal Aeronaut Soc; Conslt, Ofc Under Secy Def Res & Engrg, Dept Def; Mem, Coun-at-Large, Former Mem, Pres Coun, Am Mgmt Assns; US Mem, Prog Com, Intl Coun of Aeronaut Scis; Mem, Adv Bd, Dept Mech Engrg, Aeronaut Engrg & Mech, Rensselaer Polytechnic Inst, Former Mem, USAF Sci Adv Bd; Former Mem, Bd Govs, Nat Space Clb; Former Mem, Bd Trustees, Cleveland Nat Air Show; Former Chm, Aeronaut Sys Div Adv Grp, AF Sys Command; Former, Mem, Jt Strategic Target Planning Staff Sci Adv Grp, Jt Chiefs Staff; Former Chm, Cleveland Fed Exec Bd; cp/Mem, Sigma Gamma Tau, Nat Hon Aeronaut Soc; Mem, Res Soc Am; Mem, Sigma Xi; Mem, Cosmos Clb; Mem, Assn Old Crows; Mem-at-Large, Am Mgmt Assn; Former Mem, the 50 Clb Cleveland, r/Unitarian; hon/Auth of Num Pubs incl'g "The Case for the B-1 Bomber", *Intl Security* 1976, "Reducing Oil Dependence", *Astronautics & Aeronautics* 1980; Mem, Nat Acad Engrg, 1981; Dist'd Ser Medal, NASA, 1982; Decoration for Exceptl Civilian Ser, USAF, 1978; Prof Emeritus, MIT, 1982; Devel Apollo Command & Ser Modules for N Am Aviation; Awd USAF Meritorious Civilian Ser Awd for wk on C-5 Transport Aircraft, 1973; Wk Done in First Supersonic Flutter Model Testing at MIT; Apollo Achmt Awd, NASA, 1969; Patent, Impact Landing Sys, 1969; W/W: A, E, MW, Technol Today, Engrg; Jane's W/W Aviation & Aerospace; Am Men & Wom Sci; Intl Biographical Ctr; DIB; Men & Wom Distn; Men of Achmt; Intl W/W Engrg; Commun Ldrs & Noteworthy Ams; Book of Honor.

McCARTHY, JOSEPH A oc/Operations Manager, Petroleum and Construction Management; b/Sep 21, 1945; h/405 North Meadow Drive; Ogdensburg, NY 13669; ba/Ogdensburg, NY; m/Elaine Premo; c/Kelly Rae, Scott Patrick, Daniel Joseph, Michael Edward; p/Ruth F McCarthy, Ogdensburg, NY; sp/Dorothy Premo, Ogdensburg, NY; ed/BA, St Bonaventure Univ, 1967; mil/AUS Field Aux, Commissioned Second Lt, 1967-69; pa/Mgr Opers 1981-, Loss Control Coor 1979-81, Retail Mktg Mgr 1977-79, Augsbury Corporation; Proj Supvr, Algonquin Constrn Co, 1971-76; Field Engr, Pers Admr, Turner Constrn Co, 1967-70; Am Mgmt Assn; Am Petro Inst; Nat Safety Coun; Am Soc Safety Engrs; Empire St Petro Assn; Soc Indep Gasoline Marketers Am; cp/BPO Elks; r/Rom Cath; hon/Guest Spkr, Sigma Annual Conv, 1981; Two-Time "Eagle Awd" Winner Outstg Achmt, 1980, 1981; Guest Spkr, Soc Indep Gasoline Marketers Am; Marquis, W/W E; Num Mil Awds incl'g Bronze Star, Army Commend Medal.

McCARTHY, RHODA A oc/Assistant Director Nurses Forensic Unit; b/Apr 6, 1928; h/1506 4th Avenue, Northeast, Jamestown, ND 58401; ba/

Jamestown, ND; m/James L; c/Kathryn Palmquist, Margaret Griffin, Shirley Membrila, John, Patrick; p/Roy (dec) and Emma Hall, Woodworth, ND; sp/Jack and Fern McCarthy (dec), Pingree, ND; ed/BCS, BS; pa/Staff Nurse, Jamestown, ND; Dir Nurses, Trinity Hosp; Staff Nurse, Hibbing, MN; Staff Nurse, Waukegan, IL; Clin Nurse, Asst Dir Nurses, State Hosp; Asst Dir, Forensic Unit; Past Chapt Pres, Current St Pres, ND Public Employees Assn; Lobbyist, ND; Mem, ANA; cp/Charter Mem, Past Pres, Eagles Aux; VFW Aux; Toastmasters Intl; r/Cath; hon/Employee of Yr, St Hosp, 1978; W/W Univs & Cols & W/W Am Wom.

McCARTHY, ROBERT JOHN oc/Lawyer; b/Dec 31, 1946; h/354 Santa Clara Avenue, San Francisco, CA 94127; ba/San Francisco, CA; m/Suzanne B; c/Brendan, Matthew, Ryan, Margaret & Robert Jr; p/John and Dorothy McCarthy, San Pedro, CA; sp/John and Georgia Bazzino, Santa Rosa, CA; BA, Univ Santa Clara, 1969; JD, Univ Chgo, 1972; pa/Assoc Atty, Cooley, Godward, Castro, Huddleson & Tatum, 1972-74; Assoc Atty, Broad, Khourie & Schulz, 1974-76; Chief Dept DA, City of SF, 1976-80; Ptnr, McCarthy & Schwartz, 1980-; Mem, CA Bar Assn, 1972-; cp/Exec VP, SF Housing & Devel Corporation, Mem, Olympic Clb, SF; Bd Dirs, SF Big Brothers, 1981-; Cabinet Mem 1981-, Gen Counsel 1983-, Democratic Party; VP St Brendans Sch, Mem Bd Dirs SF Renaissance, 1983-; r/Cath; hon/Fellow, Dept HUD; Ctr for Urban Studies Univ Chgo, 1971, 1972; Llewelyn Cup; Outstg Advocate Univ Chgo, 1970, 1971; Osgood & Hall, Outstg Advocate, 1971; Pres Scholar, Univ Santa Clara, 1965, 1969.

McCAUGHRIN, SCOTT JAMES oc/Systems Programmer; b/Jun 7, 1943; h/401 1/2 East Michigan Avenue, Urbana, IL 61801; ba/Urbana, IL; m/Wendy Bordoff; p/Walter Scott McCaughrin (dec), Dunedin, FL; sp/Jack Bordoff, Windsor, Ontario; ed/BS 1974, MS 1977, Wayne St Univ; MS, Univ IL, 1982; mil/AUS, 1965-67, Platoon Sgt; pa/Underwriter, Reliance Ins, 1969; Supt Clk, Chevrolet Gear & Axle, 1970-72; Sys Programmer 1977-79, Instr Dept Math 1979-82, Univ IL; Assn Computing Mach; Math Assn Am; cp/Cousteau Soc; r/Presb; hon/Chi Gamma Iota Scholastic Hon Soc.

McCAUGHRIN, WENDY BORDOFF oc/Educational Consultant, Learning Abilities Program; b/Nov 23, 1944; h/401 1/2 East Michigan Avenue, Urbana, IL 61801; ba/Urbana, IL; m/Scott James; p/Jack and Tillie Starker Bordoff (dec), Windsor, Ontario; sp/Dr and Mrs Walter McCaughrin (dec), Grosse Pointe, MI; ed/BA, Wayne St Univ, 1967; BA, Univ Windsor, 1971; MA, Merrill Palmer Inst, 1977; MS, Univ IL, 1981; PhD Prog; pa/Guid Cnslr, Instr, McGregor Sec'dy Sch, 1967-70; Rdg Therapist Instr, W F Herman Sec'dy Sch, 1971-77; Ed Conslt, Mercy Hosp, 1981-; ASHA; Intl Rdg Assn; Orton Soc (Dyslexia); cp/Cousteau Soc; r/Jewish; hon/Kappa Delta Pi Hon Soc, 1983; Res F'ship, 1978-80; Spch & Hearing Dept, Univ IL Pub Rdg, Writing Tests.

McCLELLAN, ROGER ORVILLE oc/Executive; b/Jan 5, 1937; h/1111 Cuatro

Cerros, Southeast, Albuquerque, NM 87123; ba/Albuquerque, NM; m/Kathleen; c/Eric John, Elizabeth Christine, Katherine Ruth; p/Gladys Lavern McClellan, Richland, WA; sp/Billie Dunagen, Tenino, WA; ed/MMgmt, Robert O Anderson Grad Sch Mgmt, 1980; DVM, WA St Univ, 1960; pa/Pres & Dir, Inhalation Toxicology Res Inst, Lovelace Biomedical & Envir Res Inst, 1976-; VP & Dir Res Adm 1973-76, Asst Dir Res 1966-73, Lovelace Foun Med Ed & Res; Scist, Med Res Br 1965-66, Sr Scist, Biol Dept 1965, US Atomic Energy Comm; Sr Scist 1963-64, Biol Scist 1959-62, Jr Scist 1957-58, Hanford Labs, GE Co; Res Asst, WA St Univ, 1957-60; Adj Prof, Univ AK Med Sch, 1970-; Clin Assoc, Univ NM Sch Med, 1971-; Adj Prof, Univ NM, 1973-83; Adj Prof, WA St Univ, 1980-; Num Appts incl'g Conslt, NIH, 1968-71; Mem, Adv Bd Vet Specialties, AVMA, 1973-76; Mem, Hlth & Envir Res Adv Com, Dept Energy, 1984-; Num Affils incl'g Prog Com 1970-73, Chm 1972, Hlth Physics Soc; Fellow, AAAS; Am Vet Med Assn; Bd Dirs, NM Zool Soc, 1970-72; WA St Vet Med Assn; Soc Exptl Biol & Med; cp/Sigma Xi; Phi Kappa Phi; Phi Zeta; Alpha Psi; r/Luth; hon/Num Sci Pubs; Elda E Anderson Awd, Hlth Physics Soc, 1974; Am Men & Wom Sci; W/W World; W/W Sci.

McCLELLAND, KENNETH CHARLES oc/Patient Services Manager; b/ Dec 9, 1953; h/11104 North Blackwelder, Oklahoma City, OK 73120; ba/ Oklahoma City, OK; m/Susan Patricia Latham; c/Matthew Charles; p/Leroy C McClelland, Lake Mary, FL; sp/H H Latham, Oklahoma City, OK; ed/BS, OKC Univ, 1976; BS, OK Bapt Univ, 1978; pa/Asst Min Music & Yth, First Bapt Ch, 1975; Admitting Supvr 1975-77, Patient Sers Mgr 1977-, Deaconess Hosp; Adv'd Mem, Hosp Financial Mgmt Assn; cp/Mem, OK Soc Hosp Social Wk Dirs; Moderator, Britton Bapt Ch, 1982; r/So Bapt; hon/ S'ship, OKC Univ, 1972-76; Deans, Pres Hon Roll, OK Bapt Univ, 1977-78; W/ W Am S & SW Edition.

McCLELLAND, MARY ALICE oc/ Foreign Service Office (Retired); b/Jul 6, 1924; h/5300 Holmes Run Parkway, Number 1518, Alexandria, VA 22304; ba/Washington, DC; p/Roswell D (dec) and Eva Blinn McClelland, Brownwood, TX; ed/Ba, Univ TX El Paso, 1944; pa/ Mexico 1944-50, Paraguay 1951-53, Austria 1954-56, Australia 1956-57, Israel 1957-58, Greece 1959-61, Korea 1961-65, Washington, DC 1965-68, 1978-83, Viet Nam 1968-72, Thailand 1972-75, Korea 1975-78, Dept of St; Am Fgn Ser Assn; cp/Delta Delta Delta Sorority; Smithsonian Inst Assocs; r/ Prot; hon/Viet Nam Civilian Ser Awd, 1969-70; W/W Am Wom.

McCLINTOCK, EVA KARIN oc/ Corporate Vice President; b/Mar 23, 1938; h/5183 Melbourne Drive, Cypress, CA 90630; ba/Sante Fe Springs, CA; m/Ronald James; c/Kurt, James, Scott; p/Franz Slawinski and Lydia Petrat (dec); sp/John H McClintock, Ventura, CA; ed/Grad, Bus Sch, W Germany, 1953-57; pa/Avon Prods, 1966-76; Divisional Sales Mgr, Luzier Cosmetics, 1976-77; Dir Sales, Training Pola USA Inc, 1977-79; Dir Mktg, VP Sales, Corporate VP, 1981-, Concept

Now Cosmetics; Mem, 1972, ABWA; cp/We Can Wom Netwk; Den Mother, CSA, 1966-68; r/Luth; hon/Avon, Mgmt Excell Awd, 1968; Avon 1972 Circle of Excell, 1975 Circle of Excell Awd; W/W Am Wom.

McCLUNG, SISTER ROSE ANNELLE oc/Dean, School of Business and Public Administration; b/Dec 16, 1925; h/411 Southwest 24th Street, San Antonio, TX 78285; ba/Same; p/Mr and Mrs Guy L McClung (dec); ed/BS, Our Lady Lake Univ, 1946; MA, Cath Univ Am, 1965; pa/Tchr, Bus, St Francis Xavier HS, 1948-49; Providence Ctl HS, 1949-56; Providence HS, 1956-62; Chm, Dept Bus Adm 1962-74, Div Bus Studies 1974-80, Sch Bus & Public Adm 1980-, Our Lady Lake Col; AAUP; Am Acctg Assn; Am Economic Assn; Nat Assn Female Execs; Data Processing Mgmt Assn; Univ Aviation Assn; Soc Logistics Engrs; World Future Soc; NBEA; Nat Assn Bus Tchr Ed; Am Soc Tng & Devel; Am Soc Pers Adm; r/Cath; hon/Cert Apprec, Soc Logistics Engrs, 1976; Outstg Alumna Profession Awd, Our Lady Lake Univ, 1979; VChm, TX Bus Ed Assn, 1979; Outstg Edrs Am; W/W: Fin & Indust, World, Am Wom; Dir Dist'd Ams; Two Thousand Dist'd Southerners.

McCOIN, JOHN MACK oc/Social Worker; b/Jan 21, 1931; h/310-B Kiawa Street, Leavenworth, KS 66048; ba/ Battle Creek, MI; p/Robert Avery and Ollie Osborne McCoin (dec); ed/AA, Wingate Jr Col, 1954-55; BS, Appalachian St Tchrs Col, 1955-57; MSSW, Richmond Profl Inst, 1961-62; PhD, Univ MN, 1973-77; Att'd Univ NC, 1959-60; NY Univ, 1969; Postgrad Ctr Mtl Hlth, 1970; Acad Hlth Scis, AUS, 1975-78; Univ Chgo, 1978; mil/Served in USAR, USMC; pa/Social Wkr, VA Med Ctr, 1981-; Assoc Prof, Grand Val St Cols, 1979-81; Asst Prof, Univ WI, 1977-79; Social Wkr, FDR VA, 1975-77, 1968-73; Sr Psychi Social Wkr, Cornell Univ Med Ctr, 1966-68; Psychi Social Wkr, Toledo Mtl Hygiene Clin, 1964-66; Child Welfare Case Wkr, Wake Co Welfare Dept, 1963-64; Clin Social Wkr, Dorothea Dix St Hosp, 1962-63; Social Ser Wkr, John Umstead St Hosp, 1960-61; Social Ser Wkr, Broughton St Hosp, 1958-59; HS Tchr, Brevard Co Bd Ed, 1956-57; Aircraft Repairman, USMC Air Sta, 1948-52; Adj Prof, Kellog Commun Col, 1981-; Asst Chief, Social Wk Ser, Conslt, Reynolds Army Commun Hosp, 1981-; Social Wkr, Conslt, Hawley Army Med Ctr, 1980-; Logistics Ofcr 1975-77, Social Wkr 1972-73, 344th Gen Hosp, USAR; Chief Social Wkr, 5501st Gen Hosp, USAR, 1973-75; Asst Chief Staff Pers, 5540th Support Command, USAR, 1979-; Social Wk Conslt, 44th Gen Hosp, USAR, 1978-79; Chm, Psychi Aftercare Com, Westchester Co Commun Mtl Hlth Bd, 1971-73; Outreach Mtl Hlth Wkr, Mtl Hlth Assn Westchester Co, 1968-73; Acad Cert'd Social Wkrs; Am Soc Public Adm; Cert'd Social Wkr, MI, 15920; Cert'd Social Wkr, NY, 4845; Coun Social Wk Ed; Nat Assn Social Wkrs; Register Clin Social Wkrs; Resv Ofcrs Assn US; r/Bapt; hon/Author of "Adult Foster Homes: Their Mgrs & Residents"; Outstg Perf Awd, FDR VA Hosp, 1971; Ed Grant, Nat Inst Mtl Hlth, 1974; Ed Grant, Univ WI, 1978;

Superior Perf Awd, VA Med Ctr, Battle Creek, MI, 1982; Am Biographical Res Assn Mem, 1981-83; Biographical Roll Hon; Book Hon; Commun Ldrs Am, World; DIB; Dir Dist'd Ams; Five Thousand Personalities World; Intl Book Hon; Intl Biographical Assn, Mem, 1981-83; Men & Wom Distn; Intl W/ W Intells; W/W MW.

McCOLLOUGH, MICHAEL LEON oc/Associate Instructor; b/Nov 3, 1953; h/988 Eigenmann Hall, Bloomington, IN 47406; ba/Bloomington, IN; p/Stribling Mancell and Vivian Hazel McCollough, Cherokee, NC; ed/BS 1975, MS 1981, Auburn Univ; PhD Cand, IN Univ; pa/ Lab Instr 1974-75, Grad Instr 1975-77, Lab Tech 1977-78, Auburn Univ; Assoc Instr, IN Univ, 1978-; Am Astronom Soc; Royal Astronom Soc; Astronom Soc Pacific; Am Phy Soc; Optical Soc Am; Am Assn Physics Tchrs; Soc Physics Students; r/Bapt; hon/Author of Articles; Sigma Pi Sigma; Assoc Mem, Sigma Xi; W/W Frontier Sci & Tech.

McCOMBS, HARRIET GWENDOLYN oc/Assistant Professor Yale University; b/Nov 9, 1954; h/111 Park Street, Apartment 14-P, New Haven, CT 06511; ba/New Haven, CT; p/ William & Harriet McCombs, Columbia, SC; ed/BS, Univ SC, 1974; MA 1976, PhD 1978; Univ NE; pa/US Ho of Reps Congl Intern, 1976; Am Psychol Assn, 1976-; Sigma Xi; Sigma Gamma Rho, 1974-; r/AME; hon/Author of Num Pubs; Ygst PhD Grad at Univ NE, Age 23; Am Psychol Assn Minority F'ship; W/W Frontier Sci & Technol.

McCORMICK, JAMES MICHAEL oc/Consultant; b/Dec 12, 1947; h/7 Bon Mar Road, Pelham Manor, NY 10803; ba/New Rochelle, NY; m/Marsha E; p/ James J McCormick, Annandale, VA; sp/ Edward and Liddy Durham; ed/The Hill Sch, 1965; BS (w Distn) 1969, Master's Deg 1970, Cornell Univ; pa/Bell Telephone Labs, 1970-73; Dir of Adv'd Sys & Mkt Planning, McKinsey & Co, NY Stock Exch/SIAC, 1973-75; Engagement Mgr, McKinsey & Co, 1975-77; VP, Dir NY Ofc, ROI Consltg, 1977-80; Pres, 1st Manhattan Consltg Grp, 1980-, Pres, 1st Manhattan Telecommuns Consltg, 1980-; cp/Larchmont Yacht Clb; Lawrence Bch Clb; hon/W/ W E.

McCOY, JANICE M oc/Vice President Nursing Services; b/Oct 11, 1945; h/749 Wonderview Drive, Dunlap, IL 61525; ba/Peoria, IL; m/David L; c/ Marsha Lynn, Mark David; p/C Clark (dec) and M Maxine Kaiser, Peoria, IL; sp/David O (dec) and Viola A McCoy, Peoria, IL; ed/RN Dipl, St Lukes Meth Hosp Sch Nsg, 1966; BS, Col St Francis, 1983; pa/Ofc Nurse, Cedar Rapids, IA, 1966-67; Staff Nurse, Univ IA Hosp, 1969-70; Staff Nurse, St Lukes Meth Hosp, 1971; Staff Nurse, Mendota Commun Hosp, 1971-74; Staff Nurse, St Francis Med Ctr, 1975-78; Patient Care Coor 1978-80, VP, Nsg Sers 1980-, Proctor Commun Hosp; Nurses Assn Am Col Ob & Gynecologists; Am Soc Nurse Admrs; IL Soc Nurse Admrs; Nat Leag Nsg; IL Leag Nsg; Nat Assn Female Execs; Profl Adv Com, 1981-, Vis'g Nurses Assn; cp/Adv, Proctor Med Explorer Scouts, 1981-; CoChm, Christmas Tree Lane (Ch Bazaar), 1976-77; CoChm, Vietnamese Refugee Fam Relocation Proj, 1975; Pres, Newcomers

Clb, Mendotta, IL, 1973; Host Fam, Am Field Ser, 1982-83; r/Meth; hon/Cert, Nurses Assn Am Col Ob & Gynecologists, 1980; Cert in Adv'd Fetal Monitoring, 1978; W/W Am Wom.

McCRARY, ROBERT WAYNE oc/Political and Advertising Consultant; b/Aug 28, 1946; h/910-B Glastonbury Circle, Jackson, MS 39211; ba/Jackson, MS; m/Mable Lawson; c/Robert Wayne Jr; p/Helen McIlhenny, Nashville, TN; sp/Mr and Mrs James Lawson, Church Hill, TN; ed/BA, WV St Col, 1978; mil/USCG, Hon Discharge 1965; pa/Pres, M & M Prodns, 1971-78; Broadcast Prodn Dir, Walker & Assocs, 1978-81; Creat Dir, Maris, West & Baker, Inc, 1981-; Bd Dirs, MS Epilepsy Foun, 1981-; Bd Dirs, Memphis Epilepsy Foun, 1979-81; cp/KY Col; Hon (Aide-de-Camp)Lt Col, AL; Bd Dirs, Jackson Zoo; Personal Image Conslts, 1980-82; Am Film Inst; TN Org Prodr Suppliers; r/Prot; hon/Num Pubs; MS Gov's Coun Tourism; MS Gov's Coun 84 World's Fair; W/W: Ad, SE, 1980/81; 2 First Pl Awds, 1979 Houston Intl Film Fest; FCC Awd, Best TV Documentary/Writer 1969; First, Second, Third Pl Awds, 1978 Miami Intl Film Fest; Num Local & Reg Awds for Excell Ad, Writing, Film Prodn.

McCREDIE, KENNETH BLAIR oc/Physician; b/Jul 2, 1935; h/7655 South Braeswood, Number 63, Houston, TX 77071; ba/Houston, TX; m/Maria Isabel Delgado; c/Wendy Jane, Anna Margaret, Jennifer Mary; p/Gordon Blair and Margaret J McCredie (ded), Christchurch, New Zealand; sp/Francisco and Carmencita Delgado, Manila, Philippines; ed/Canterbury Univ, 1953-54; Otago Univ Med Sch, MB, ChB, 1954-60; Mem 1966, Fellow 1973, Royal Australasian Col Phys; Fellow, Philippine Col Phys, 1979; mil/Royal New Zealand Army Med Corps, Capt; pa/Intern 1961-62, Resident 1962-65, Napier Hosp; Resident 1965-66, Sr Fellow 1966-69, Prince Henry Hosp; Proj Investigator 1969-70, Asst Internist 1970-73, Assoc Internist 1973-76, Chief Leukemia Ser 1973, Internist 1974, Prof Med 1978, Prof Dept Dental Oncology 1979, Dept Dept Hd & Chief 1981, Univ TX Sys Cancer Ctr MD Anderson Hosp & Tumor Inst; Asst Prof 1973-74, Assoc Prof 1974, Univ TX Med Sch; Assoc Prof, Univ TX Hlth Sci Ctr, 1977; Royal Soc Med; Royal Australasian Col Phys; Hematology Soc Australia; Am Fdn Clin Res; Am Soc Hematology; Intl Assn Comparative Res Leukemia & Related Diseases; NY Acad Sci; Am Assn Cancer Res; Am Col Phys; AMA; Am Soc Clin Oncology; Intl Soc Exptl Hematology; Wkg Grp Leukocyte Procurement Nat Cancer Inst; Edit Bd, Exptl Hematology; TX Med Assn; Harris Co Med Soc; SW Cancer Chemotherapy Study Grp; VP, Med & Sci Affairs; Chm, Med & Sci Adv Com, Leukemia Soc Am Inc; VP, Leukemia Soc Am, TX Gulf Coast Chapt; hon/Sir James Wattie Vis'g Prof, 1980; Outstg Ser Mankind, 1981, Leukemia Soc Am Tx Gulf Coast Chapt; Dr John J Kenney Awd, Leukemia Soc Am Inc, Num Pubs.

McCRORY, JANET CLAIRE oc/Diplomat, Foreign Service Officer; b/Mar 18, 1928; h/1311 Nebraska Street, Mound City, MO 64470; ba/New York; p/Florence M McCrory, Mound City,

MO; ed/BA, Univ NE, 1949; pa/Fgn Ser, 1962-; Budget Ofcr in Follow Embassies: Djakarta, Indonesia; Tel Aviv, Israel; Buenos Aires, Argentina; Bucharest, Romania; Beijing, PRC; Vienna, Austria; Santo Domingo, Dominican Republic; Jidda, Saudi Arabia; Dept Army Civilian in Hague, Netherlands & Washington, DC, 1951-62; AAUW; Am Fgn Ser Assn; W/W Am Wom.

McCUE, JUDITH CLAIRE oc/Mental Health Counselor/Human Resources Consultant; b/Sep 9, 1946; h/336 Barefoot Drive, California, MD 20619; ba/Lexington Park, MD; m/John James McCue Jr; p/Cecil and Hazel Brown, Birmingham, AL; sp/John J Sr (dec) and Virginia McCue, San Jose, CA; ed/BS, Univ AL, 1968; MA, Bowie St Col, 1978; pa/Edr, St Mary's Co Public Schs, MD, 1971-78; Mtl Hlth Cnslr, Calvert Co Public Schs, MD, 1971-83; Assoc Therapist, Frank Gunzburg, PhD, PA, Lexington Park, MD, 1981-; Pt-Time Fac, Charles Co Commun Col, 1981-83; Br Pres, AAUW, 1976-78; Appt, St Mary's Co Coun Chd & Yth, 1982; MD St Coalition Against Rape & Sexual Assault, 1981; Task Force Coor, Sexual Assault Crisis Unit for St Mary's Co, 1980-; Assoc Mem, Am Psychol Assn, 1983; Mem, APGA; Am Mtl Hlth Cnslrs Assn; hon/Nat Deans List, 1978; W/W E.

McCURDY, JOHN GRIBBEL JR oc/Broadcaster; b/Jul 6, 1949; h/5309 Briley Place, Bethesda, MD 20816; ba/Washington, DC; p/John G McCurdy, Philadelphia, PA, and Ann Snyder Costello (dec), Ithaca, NY; pa/Announcer, Newsman, Radio Sta WELM, 1971-72; Newsman, Westinghouse Broadcasting Co (KYW-TV), 1973-80; Mgr, Electronic Jour NBC, 1980-82; Asst Dir, ENG/Newsfilm ABC News, 1982-; Mem, Soc Motion Picture & TV Engrs; cp/Mem, Phila Cricket Clb; Mem, Pen & Pencil Clb; hon/Miami Legion Hon Awd Heroism, Miami, FL, 1977; W/W: Fin & Indust, World.

McDANIEL, GENEVIEVE (BELL) oc/Educator (Retired); b/Oct 14, 1915; h/Route 2, Box 22, Hurricane, WV 25526; m/Edgar N McDaniel (dec); c/Joseph S & Rebecca M Thompson; p/Romie Clair (dec) and Ida Russell Bell, Hurricane, WV; ed/BA 1960; MA 1964; Post Grad Hours; pa/Tchr, Beverly Hills Jr HS, 1959-64; Supervising Tchr Eng, Ona Jr HS, 1964-68; Pt-Time Instr, Marshall Univ; Assoc Prof, Glenville St Col, 1968-76; Mem, AAUW, 1959; Secy, AAUW Am Lit Study Grp, 1961-64; Charter Mem, AAUW Glenville St Col, 1968; Treas, WV Col Eng Tchrs, 1972-74; VP 1962-64, Pres 1964-67, WV Coun Tchrs Eng; Orgr, Pres Cabell Co WV Tch Eng; Dept Chm Eng, Beverly Hills Jr HS, 1963-64; cp/Pres, Altizer Elem Sch, 1946; Ways & Means Chm, Gallaher Elem Sch, 1948-51; Num Positions in Beverly Hills Wom Clb, 1948-58; Grp Ldr, CampFire Girls, 1949-59; Orgr PTA, Beverly Hills Jr HS, 1955; Pres, Delta Kappa Gamma, Delta Zeta Chapt, 1974-76; Charter Mem 1977, Treas 1978-80, Pres 1980-82, Dir 1982-, Kanawha Val Geneal Soc; Est'd KVGS Geneal Lib; Est'd WV Pioneer Ancestor Ceremony, 1980; VP, WV Hist Soc, 1980-83; Mem, Upper Vamdalia Hist Putnam Co; Mem 1976, Editor 1983, St Albans Hist Soc; VP, Ret'd

Tchrs Putnam Co, 1981-83; Mem, DAR, 1981; r/Presb; hon/Editor of Num Pubs; DAR Citizenship Medal, 1931, 1934; Mem, Delta Kappa Gamma, 1965-63; Kappa Delta Pi, 1957-83; Personalities of S; W/W Am W; Notable Ams of Bicent.

McDANIEL, MARJORIE WYVONNE CLAPP oc/High School Librarian and Real Estate Broker; b/Aug 25, 1933; h/413 Panhandle Street, Canadian, TX 79014; ba/Canadian, TX; m/Charles Raymond; c/Shannon Kaye, Sharron Leigh, Shawn Michael; p/Earl Hamilton and Willie Juanita Martin Clapp, Sulphur Springs, TX; sp/Charlie and Dixie McDaniel, Borger, TX; ed/BA, TX Technol Univ, 1954; Masters, E TX St Univ, 1973; pa/Phillips Petro Co, 1955-58; Natural Gas Pipeline Co Am, 1959-62; Instr, Frank Phillips Univ, 1955-58; HS Media Dir, Canadian Indep Sch Dist, 1971-83; cp/Chapt Pres 1973-80, Treas 1975-78, 1981-83, Daughs Republic TX; Chapt Pres, Colonial Dames XVII Century, 1981-83; DAR; Chapt Pres, Chd Am Revolution, 1978-82; Chm, DAR Good Citizen Awd, 1971-79, 1982-83; Organizing Pres, Nu Phi Mu, 1955-56; Beta Sigma Phi, 1957-58; Phi Delta Kappa, 1980-82; r/Bapt; hon/W/W Am Wom.

McDONALD, ALLAN JAMES oc/Engineering Administrator; b/Jul 9, 1937; h/4050 North 900 West, Pleasant View, UT 84404; ba/Brigham City, UT; m/Linda Rae Zuchetto; c/Gregory Allan, Lisa Marie; Lora Lynn, Meghan Rae; p/Mr and Mrs John William McDonald Sr (dec), Bozeman, MT; sp/Mr and Mrs Remy Zuchetto (dec), Allen Park, MI; ed/BS, MT St Univ, 1959; MS, Univ UT, 1967; Engr, Wasatch Div 1959-67; Proj Engr, Solid Rocket Motor Progs 1967-74, Mgr, Devel Proj Dept 1974-76, Mgr, Propellant Devel Dept 1976-79, Mgr, Proj Engrg Div 1979-, Morton Thiokol Inc; Mem, AF Tech Propulsion Panel, 1982-; Judge Sci Fair Com, Weber St Col, 1978-; Bd Dirs 1976-, Trustee 1981-, Pres 1976-79, St Joseph HS; Coach, Little Leag Ftball, 1972-75; Coach, Little Leag Baseball; Pres, 1971-72, 1972-74, CCD Prog, St James Cath Ch, 1976-79; r/Cath; hon/Num Pubs; Outstg Engr UT, AIAA, 1971; En MT Col Scholar, 1955-57; MT St Univ Scholar, 1958-59; Assoc, Fellow, Past Chm, UT Sect, AIAA; Mem 1979-83, Pres 1984-86, Solid Rocket Tech Com; Tau Beta Pi, Phi Kappa Phi; Sigma Chi; Life Mem Republican; cp/4th Deg K of C; Elks; Ogden Ath; Patentee Solid Rocket; Pyrotechnic Sys; W/W E.

McDONALD, SAMMANTHA L M oc/Customer Service Supervisor; b/Nov 18, 1949; h/13530 Longfellow Lane, San Diego, CA 92129; ba/4901 Morena Boulevard, Suite 210, San Diego, CA 92117; m/Jerry Boone; c/Nicole Charise; p/Louis G and Ethelyn G Nichols, West Sedona, AZ; ed/AB, Art, San Diego Mesa Col, 1978; BBA in Pers Mgmt 1980, MBA in Indust Relats 1983, Nat Univ; pa/Customer Info Rep 1970-80, Customer Info Analyst 1980-81, Customer Ser Supvr 1981-, San Diego Gas & Elect; Career Wom's Assn, 1980-82; Nat Univ Alumni Assn; Guest Spkr, Wom's Studies Classes, Nat Univ; SDG&E Energy Spkr Corps, 1980-; cp/Citizens Adv Com, San Diego City Schs; VP 1974, Pres 1975; Dimensions,

PERSONALITIES OF AMERICA

1982-83; Gtr San Diego C of C Mbrship Drive, 1982; Mbrship Chair 1984, Pres 1985, Bd of Dirs 1984-86, Mira Mesa Scripps Ranch C of C; hon/Wom of the Month, San Diego Mesa Col, 1970; Dean's Hon Roll; Grad, cum laude, Nat Univ, 1980; Sch Citizens Adv Com Ser Awd, 1975; W/W: in Am Jr Cols, Among San Diego Wom, of Am Wom, in Fin & Indust, in CA.

McDONALD, SYLVIA CORNELIA oc/Teacher (Retired); b/Jul 10, 1921; h/4400 Lindell, Apartment 17-L, St Louis, MO 63108; m/Bruce (dec); p/James Elmer and Mary Darline (Wilhoit) Williams (dec); sp/Jack and Daisy McDonald (dec); ed/Att'd Stowe Jr Col, 1939-41; BS, Lincoln Univ, 1944; MEd, St Louis Univ, 1960; Post Grad 1971-73; So IL Univ, 1971; Purdue Univ, 1966; pa/Tchr, Lincoln Elem Sch, 1944-58; Remedial Rdg Tchr, Collinsville Com Unit 10, 1958-65; Tchr, Collinsville Bd Ed, 1965-81; Mem, Nat Ret'd Tchrs Assn, 1976-83; cp/Ldr, Girl Scouts, 1950-51; Mem, Phy Improvement Com, Mbrship Com, Housing Com, YWCA, 1981-83; Delta Sigma Theta Sorority, 1942-83; Am Woodmen; r/Bapt; hon/W W Am Wom.

McDONNELL, EDWARD LAURENCE oc/Real Estate Development, Company Executive; b/May 13, 1912; h/3440 Winchell Lane, Post Office Box 20256, Billings, MT 59104; m/Evelyn Marie Cutz; c/Thomas C, Victoria M, Virginia D; p/George Edward and Clara Lucinda (Woodward); ed/Att'd Gonzaga Univ, 1934; pa/Mgr, MT Mustard Seed Co, 1935-39; Ptnr, McDonnell Seed Co, 1940-47; Owner, Mgr, E L McDonnell & Co, 1947-60; Pres, Trans-World Seeds Ltd, 1960-66; Orgr, Owner, Mgr, Argo Supply, 1966-77; Ptnr, McBorg Properties, 1978-80; GEL Properties, 1980-; Orgr, 1st Pres, Pacific NW Pea Growers & Dealers Assn, 1949-53; cp/K of C; r/Rom Cath; hon/Author of Articles; Devel, Comml Fertilizer Applicator Equip; W/W W.

McDOWELL, LEE RUSSELL oc/Professor, Animal Nutrition; b/Apr 11, 1941; h/13 Southwest 15-B, Archer, FL 32618; ba/Gainesville, FL; m/Lorraine Marie Worden; c/Suzannah Lee, Joanna Marie, Teresa April; p/Russell Gale (dec) and Ida May Lee McDowell, Newark, NY; sp/Charles A and Dorothy R Worden, Tybee Island, GA; ed/AAS, Alfred Agri & Tech, 1961; BS 1964, MS 1965, Univ GA; PhD, WA St Univ, 1971; pa/Livestock Farm, 1965; Peace Corps, 1965-67; Asst Prof 1971-77, Assoc Prof 1977-83, Prof 1982-, Dept Animal Sci, Univ FL; Am Dairy Assn; Am Soc Animal Sci; Am Inst Nutrition; Am Forage & Grassland Coun; Coun Agri Sci & Tech; Asociacion Latinoamericana de Produccion Animal; r/Meth; hon/Author of Num Pubs incl'g *Latin Am Tables of Feed* 1974; NY St Farmer Awd, 1959; Top 5% Class, Univ GA, 1963; Alpha Zeta, 1970; Gamma Sigma, 1974; Gustav Bohstead Awd, Nat Mineral Res Awd Animal Sci, 1984; W/W: S & SE, Frontier Sci & Tech.

McELWAIN, JUANITA MURIEL oc/Assistant Professor, Director of Music Therapy; b/Jan 17, 1928; h/2010 West Beech Street, Portales, NM 88130; ba/Portales, NM; m/Ogla D; c/Thomas George; p/George Myron (dec) and Muriel Stilwell, Portales, NM; sp/

Jennings Bryon (dec) and Evelyn McElwain, Elkins, WV; ed/BME 1958, MME 1959, MMus 1974, PhD 1978, FL St Univ; pa/Music Tchr, Jennings FL, 1961-62; Tchr, Piano & Organ, Monterey Bay Acad, 1962-67; Tchr, Piano & Organ, Antillian Union Col, 1967-69; Music Therapist, Sunland Tng Ctr, 1979-80; Asst Prof, Dir Music Therapy, En NM Univ, 1980-; Profl Adv Com, Com Sers, 1981-; Campfire Coun, Bd Dirs, 1982-; Assem Dels, Nat Assn Music Therapists Inc, 1982-; r/SDA; hon/Author of *The Effect of Spontaneous & Analytical Listening on Evoked Cortical Activity in Left & Right Hemispheres of Musicians & Nonmusicians* 1979; Pi Kappa Lambda; W/W Am Wom.

McENCROE, PAUL ROGER oc/Restaurant Owner and Operator; b/Dec 4, 1922; h/1551 Larimer Street, Denver, CO 80202; ba/Golden, CO; m/Joanna Marie (Zipprich); c/John J, P Andrew, Linda C Lindsay, Anne M Pressman; p/John J and Irene McEncroe; sp/Ray W (dec) and Mildred L Zipprich, Denver, CO; ed/BS, NWn Univ, 1947; Post Grad, Univ Denver, 1964; mil/USAAF, 1943-45, Navigator; pa/Burroughs Corporation, 1968-69; VP CO/WY Restaurant Assn, 1983-84; Past Pres, CO Food Indust Gourmet Soc; cp/Jefferson Co CO Sch Bd, 1969-77; Adv Bd, St Anthony Hosp "Flight for Life" 1973-78; Bd Mem, Lookout Mtn Fire Protection Dist, 1978-82; CO Tourism Bd, 1983-; Instr, CO St Bd Commun Cols; Conduct Sems, CO Mtn Col Sys; hon/Lakewood CO Sentinel Newspaper "Man of Yr", 1977; Dist'g Ser Awd, CO/WY Restaurant Assn, 1981; Restaurants & Instns Mag, "Dining Dynasties Am".

McFADDEN, VELMA DREWERY oc/Social Worker; b/Nov 27, 1933; h/1408 Willow Avenue, Bellevue, NE 68005; m/Edward Sr; c/Patricia Ann, Edward Jr, Karen, Denese, Kenneth Michael; p/Bennie and Ada Drewery, Haddock, GA; sp/Florence McFadden, Darlington, SC; ed/BA, Bellevue Col, 1972; MA, CA Christian Univ, 1975; MSW, Univ NE, 1982-83; mil/USAF, 1951-54; pa/Dir Base Nsg, Sembach AFB, 1970; ABWA; VP, 1980-81, Nat Assn Black Social Wkrs; cp/Social Wkr, Douglas Co Social Sers, 1972; Exec Dir, Bryant Ctr Commun House, Omaha, 1975; Owner/Mgr, Ms Baut Give Ltd, 1979; Area Dir, Big Brother Big Sister of the Midlands; NAACP; Urban Leag NE; Alpha Kappa Alpha Sorority Inc; Reg Secy/Treas, 1981-83, Jack & Jill Am Inc; r/Prot; hon/W/W Am Wom; Citizen Wk, 1973.

McFANN, MARGUERITE VIRGINIA oc/Real Estate Broker; b/Nov 8, 1926; h/1450 Boyden Avenue, Lancaster, CA 93534; ba/Lancaster, CA; m/Virgil Lewis; c/Wayne, Judith, Linda K (dec); p/Ernest Harold French and Leila Ellen Bishop Roberts; sp/Demetrius McFann (dec); ed/Att'd Miami Jacobs Bus Col; Dayton Univ; Antelope Val Col; Univ CA LA; pa/Owner/Dir, Teen Screen Modeling Agy, 1961-65; Secy, NASA, Edwards AFB, 1957-61; Real Est Broker, 1971-83; Mem, Exec Female Assn; Republican Wom Clb; Wom Clb; Quartz Hill; Christian Wom Clb, Rebecca; Royal Neighbors Am; Mem Bd of Trade; r/Prot; hon/W/W Am Wom.

McFARLAND, MARTHA ANN oc/Associate Professor Education; b/Aug 6,

1940; ba/Lynchburg, VA; ed/BA, NWn St, 1967; MEd, Univ MS, 1971; PhD, FL St Univ, 1979; pa/Caddo Parish Sch Bd, 1967-70; W Shreveport Acad, 1970; Natchitoches Acad, 1971; Reg Dir, Early Chd Ed Reg VI, Ednl Ser, 1971-73; Instr, Dir Kgn Berry Col, 1973-78; Assoc Prof, Liberty Bapt Col, 1979-; Conductor Num Wkshops; Assn Chd Ed Instr; VA Assn Chd End; Leon Co Assn Chd Under Six; Piedmont Area EC Assn; So Assn Chd Under Six; VA Assn Chd Under Six; VP Infants, 1972-73, WV Assn Chd Ed; Phi Delta Kappa; Intl Platform Assn; r/Bapt; hon/Contbr Artticles to Profl Jours; Personalities S; Personalities Am; W/W: S & SW, World Wom, World Intells.

McGAHAN, CAROLYN STREET oc/Team Teacher of Dyslexic Individuals; h/306 South Clark Lane, Paris, TX 75460; ba/Same; m/F E McGahan; c/Dave Sue Broadway, Ava Joyce Wolters; ed/MS, N TX St Univ, 1954; pa/CoDir Clin Tchg, NET Ed Sers Co Inc; hon/Author of Num Pubs.

McGAHAN, F E oc/Team Teacher of Dyslexic Individuals; h/306 South Clark Lane, Paris, TX 75460; ba/Same; m/Carolyn Street; c/Dave Sue Broadway, Ava Joyce Wolters; ed/BS, N TX St Univ, 1935; MS 1939, Post Grad, Univ TX-Austin; Univ MI; pa/Clrm Tchr, Lewisville, TX, 1927-35; Supt Schs, Cunningham, TX, 1935-54; Asst Supt Schs, Dir Spec Sers to Chd, 1954-66; CoDir Clin Tchg, NET Ed Sers Co Inc, 1966-82; Vis'g Lectr, Univ Houston, 1957-66; Pres, Lamar Co Soc Mtl Hlth, 1938; 1st VP, Nat Coun Fam Life; Life mem, CEC; PTA; TCEC; NEA; Nat Pers & Guid Assn; TX Soc, Lrng Disabled Indivs; Mem, Gov's Com, ST Prog Lrng Disabled; Phi Delta Kappa; Kiwanis Clb; Knife & Fork Clb; Shriner, Dallas TX; hon/Author of Num Pubs; Am Legion Awd; Commun-Sch Centered War Effort, 1943; W/W: Am Ed, Ed in S & SW; Sch-Commun Integrated Efforts, 1943; Cit, Early Chd Ed, Early Detection, 1960; Parent Ed in Programming the Spec Child, 1961; Commun Org Ed Spec Child (Kiwanis) 1964; Cit, 55 Yrs Dedication & Commitment to Equal Ed Opports, 1982.

McGEE, JANET M oc/Real Estate Sales; b/Jun 11, 1958; h/1907 Woodlands Drive, Smyrna, GA 30080; ba/Atlanta, GA; p/John P and Louise F McGee, Portsmouth, NH; ed/BS 1981, AS 1980, AA 1979, Colby Sawyer Col; Hlth Record Adm Prog, USPHS, 1981; pa/QC Mgr, Corporate Hlth Corporation, 1983-84; Claims Spec, Blue Cross/Blue Shield, 1982-83; Fin Cnslr, CHAMPUS Hlth Benefits Advr, Wyman Pk Hlth Sys, 1981-82; Reg'd Record Admr, Am Med Record Assn; r/Cath; hon/Pres S'ship, 1977; Nat Deans List, 1978, 79, 80; Alpha Chi; Pres, 1979-80, VP/Secy 1978-79, Phi Theta Kappa Hon Soc; Secy, Student Govt, 1979-80; Yg Commun Ldrs Am; Intl Yth Achmt.

McGEE, SEARS oc/Justice, Supreme Court of Texas; b/Sep 29, 1917; h/5325 Western Hills Drive, Austin, TX 78731; ba/Austin, TX; m/Mary Beth; c/James Sears, Mary Gray Neilson, Claire Logan Holmes, Alice Gray Ruckman, George Sears, Erwin Smith; p/James Butler and Alice Sears McGee (dec); sp/Ladye M Peterson, Austin, TX; ed/Att'd Rice Univ, 1934-36; LLB, Univ TX, 1940; mil/

USN, 1943-46; pa/Admitted to Bar, 1940; Judge Co Ct, 1948-54; Judge 151st Dist Ct, 1954-55; Pvt Pract, 1955-58; Judge 55th Dist Ct, 1958-69; Justice, Supr Ct TX, 1969-; Instr, Civil Law Procedure, Univ Hous Col Law, 1950-52; Secy/Treas, Houston Jr Bar, 1947; Mem, TX Bar; cp/Past Mem, Houston Commun Coun; Past Mem, Bd Dir Ctl Br YMCA; Past Pres, Houston Coun Deaf Chd; Houston Rose Soc; Phi Delta Theta; r/Epis; hon/Served, Nat Awds Jury for Freedoms Foun, Val Forge, PA, 1971; Cert Merit Awd, Appellate Judges Conf, Am Bar.

McGHEE, GEORGE RUFUS JR oc/ Associate Professor Geology & Ecology; b/Sep 25, 1951; h/23 Courtlandt Street, New Brunswick, NJ 08901; ba/New Brunswick, NJ; m/Marae Wilcox Paschall; p/George Rufus (dec) and Mary London Cobb; sp/Hal Beasley (dec) and Deva M Paschall; ed/BS, NC St Univ, 1973; MS, Univ NC-Chapel Hill, 1975; PhD, Univ Rochester, 1978; pa/Hydrologic Field Asst, US Geol Survey, 1972-73; Geprufte Wissenschaftliche Hilfskraft, Univ Tubingen, 1977; Asst Prof 1978-83, Assoc Prof 1983-, Rutgers Univ; Vis'g Scist, Field Mus Natural Hist, 1981; Res Assoc, Am Mus Natural Hist, 1982; Gastdozent, Univ Tubingen, 1982, 1984; Intl Palaeontological Assn; Paleontological Soc; Die Palontologische Gesellschaft; Palaeontological Assn (Brit); Soc Systematic Zool; Geol Soc Am; Soc Economic Paleontologists & Mineralogists; Paleontological Res Inst; AAAS; r/Quaker; hon/Author of Num Sci Articles; Tchg Fellow, Univ NC-Chapel Hill, 1975; Fellow, Dept Geol Sci, Univ Rochester, 1975-78; W/W Frontier Sci & Technol; Am Men & Wom Sci.

McGINTY, (OMA) VALJEAN oc/ Corporate Marketing Director; b/May 6, 1931; h/280 South Avenida Caballeros, Palm Springs, CA 92263; ba/Palm Springs, CA; c/Michael Guy McGinty; ed/PhD Cand, Profl Sch Humanistic Studies; pa/Conslt, Med Weight Clin, 1974-78; Dir Sales, Le Baron Hotel, 1970-74; VP Fin, Holiday Inns, 1967-70; Ofc Mgr/Conslt, Pacific View Constrn Co, 1957-67; Owner, Valjean's Variety, 1954-56; Owner, Allure Salon, 1955-57; Devel, Constrn Proj (Preliminary), 1978-80; Cnslr, Hypnotherapist, Practitioner, Masseuse Therapist, 1980-; Min-Elect, 1983-; Real Est Licenseel, 1983; Lectr, 1983-; Pres, Wom Constrn, 1965-67; VP, Sales & Mktg Exec, 1972-74; 1978-80; VP 1976-78, Bd Dir 1983, Sci Mind; Visitors' Task Force, City Palm Sprgs, 1983; Mayor Com Bond Issue, 1983; P R Symph W, 1983; Pres Clb, C of C, 1983; Hotel Sales Mgmt Assn, 1970-74, 1982-; r/Rel Sci; hon/Author of Num Newslttrs; P R "Sales & Mktg Exec", 1972, 1974; Deans List, Alameda Col, 1977; March of Dimes, 1982; Swift Airline, 1982; Little Leag, 1965; W/W Sales.

McGRAIL, JEAN KATHRYN oc/ Artist; b/May 1, 1947; h/669 Columbia Avenue, Elgin, IL 60120; ba/Same; p/ Robert and Mary McGrail, Elgin, IL; ed/ BS, Univ WI, 1970; MFA, Cranbrook Acad Art, 1972; Att'd Chgo Art Inst; Num Lectrs, Wkshops; pa/Included in Num Invitational & Juried Exhbns in Mus, Galleries, Cols & Other Public Instns; NY Gallery Affil, 1980-82; Chgo

Artist Coalition; hon/W/W World Wom; Intl Register Profiles; Am Artists Renown.

McGRATH, SAREPTA ROYAN oc/ Executive/Sales; b/May 28, 1957; h/ 5404 94, Lubbock, TX 79424; ba/ Lubbock, TX; p/William R (dec) and Royetta McGrath, OKC, OK; ed/TX Tech Univ; pa/Adm Secy, Univ TX Hlth Sci Ctr, 1977-79; Tech Sales Rep 1979-81, Pres/Sales 1981-, Cardiovas Sys Inc; ABWA; Nat Assn Female Execs; cp/World Wildlife Fund; Nat Audubon Soc; r/Epis; hon/Outstg Sales Achmt Awd, 1982; W/W Am Wom.

McGREGOR, DOUGLAS HUGH oc/ Physician, Pathologist; b/Aug 28, 1939; h/9400 Lee Boulevard, Leawood, KS 66206; ba/KC, MO; m/Mizuki Kitani; c/ Michelle Sakuya, David Kenji; p/Harleigh Heath and Joyce Ellen McGregor (dec); sp/Asao Kitani, Fumino Kitani and Kikari, Yamaguchi, Japan; ed/Univ Edinburgh, 1961-62; BA 1961, MD 1966, Duke Univ; Intern, Resident II, Chief Resident, Dept Pathol, Univ CA LA Med Ctr, 1966-68; Chief Resident, Dept Pathol, Queens Med Ctr, Honolulu, HI; mil/USPHS, Surg, Lt Cmdr, Atomic Bomb Casualty Comm, 1968-71; pa/Staff Psychol 1973-, Dir Anatomic Pathol 1975-, KC VA Med Ctr; Asst Prof 1973-77, Assoc Prof 1977-82, Prof 1982-, Dept Pathol & Oncology, Univ KS Med Ctr; Intl Acad Pathol, 1976-; Am Assn Pathologists (Fdn Exptl Biol & Med) 1976-; Col Am Pathologists (Fellow) 1976; Soc Exptl Biol & Med, 1977-; Am Soc Clin Pathologists (Fellow) 1972-; AAAS 1977-; NY Acad Sci, 1977-; Secy/Treas, 1982-83, Pres 1983-84, KC Soc Pathologists; AAUA, 1982-; hon/Num Pubs; NC 1966, CA 1968, Med Licensure; NIH Grant Reviewer, 1978-; Profl Jour Manuscript & Book Reviewer, 1977-; Recip Res Grants, NIH, 1980-81, Merek, Sharp & Dohme, 1980-; W/W: KS, MO, MW, Frontier Sci & Technol, World.

McGREGOR, GEORGE LOYD oc/ Consulting Engineer; b/May 25, 1905; h/1955 East Chevy Chase Drive, Brea, CA 92621; ba/Brea, CA; m/Ida Mary (Klein); c/Maurice Paul, Lavonne, William, Janis Russo; p/William G and Callie Laplant McGregor (dec); sp/Ralph B and Cora Looker Klein (dec); ed/Coast Artillery Radio & Radar Sch, 1941; Army Ser Schs, 1943; CAA (FAA) Aeronaut Ctr (Corres), 1946-48; Capitol Radio Engrg Inst, 1948-54; Teletype Corporation Sch, 1949; Engr-in-Tng, USC, 1958; Electronics Course, 1967; mil/AUS, 1941-45, T/Sgt; USAF, IN Air NG, 1946-53, Chief Warrant; pa/Tchr, St NE, 1921-37; Asst Chief Engr, Radio Stas KGNF, KGFW, 1937-40; Audio Engr, Goodall Elect, 1940-41; Facilities Maintenance Tech, CAA, (FAA), 1945-53; Design Engr, ITT-Farnsworth, 1953-56; Components Engr 1956-60, Components Engr 1962-63, Ground Sys Grp 1963-67, Hughes Aircraft Co; Standards Engr, Nortronics, 1960-61; Standards Engr, Hoffman Electronics, 1961-62; Components Engr, ITT Gilfillan, 1967-68; Avionics Radio Ser & Parts Man, Golden West Skyways, 1968-70; Asst Ranger 1970-74, Asst Cub Master, Cub Master, Asst Scout Master, Scout Master, Unit Commr, Area Commr, OA

Advr 1959-84, BSA; Plant Engr, Sprg Crest Co, 1974-84; Commun Ofcr, Sqdrn Cmdr, Grp Commandant Cadets, IN & CA Civil Air Patrol, Rank Maj, 1946-62; Standards Engrg Soc, 1956-68; IEEE, 1956-68; cp/Loyal Order Moose, 1952-58; Am Legion, 1961-68; K o C, 1957-84; DAV, Lifetime Mem; r/Cath; hon/Author of Num Manuals; Citizen of Wk, KNX Radio, LA, CA, 1982; Num BSA Awds.

McGUIRE, MARGARET JEANNE oc/Marketing Manager; b/Oct 15, 1950; h/614 Crescent Avenue, Sunnyvale, CA 94087; ba/Mountain View, Ca; c/Shelly Anne; p/Edward and Dolores Schuberger, Pittsburg, KS; ed/BS, Pgh St Univ, 1971; pa/Mktg Mgr, Pulnix Am Inc, 1982-; Bd Dir, Seeker Security Sys, 1980-; Mktg Mgr, Homesearch Div, Executrans Inc, 1977-79; Dir Corporate Sers, Eugene Brown Co, 1975-77; Asst VP, Br Mgr, Amortibane Investmt Co, 1973-75; Loan Processor, Reg Investmt Co, 1971-73; Ptnr, Conslltg Firm, 1979-82; Am Soc Indust Security, 1982-; Nat Assn Female Execs, 1982-; Pres, Bd Dirs 1980, Secy, Bd Dirs 1978, Homeowners Assn; Career Adv Bd, Mademoiselle Mag, 1980; hon/Deans List; DAR Good Citizen 1967; W/W Am Wom.

McGURN, BARRETT oc/Writer, Lecturer; b/Aug 6, 1914; h/5229 Duvall Drive, Westmoreland Hills, MD 20816; ba/Same; m/Janice Ann McLaughlin; c/ William Barrett III, Elizabeth Hehn, Andrew, Lachie, Martin Barrett, Mark Barrett; p/William Barrett and Alice Schneider McGurn (dec); sp/William F and Gertrude Fitzmaurice McLaughlin (dec); ed/BA, Fordham Univ, 1935; DLitt, 1958; mil/AUS, 1942-45, S/Sgt; pa/Reporter 1936-66, Bur Chief, Rome 1946-52, 1955-62, Paris 1952-55, Moscow 1957, NY Herald Tribune; Soldier War Correspondent, Yank, the Army Wkly, 1942-45; US Embassy Press Attache, 1966-68; US Embassy Cnslr Press Affairs, 1968-69; Press Spokesman, US Supr Ct, 1973-82; VP 1951-52, Pres 1961, 1962, Stampa Estera, Assn Fgn Correspondents Italy; Pres, Overseas Press Clb Am, 1963-65; Kenwood Clb, Wash; Cosmos Clb, Wash; Nat Press Clb, Wash; Citizens Org, VP, 1984; r/Rom Cath; hon/Author of *Decade In Europe* 1958, *A Reporter Looks at the Vatican* 1962; Decorated, Knight-Ofcr, Italian Nat Order Merit, 1962; Vietnam Psychol Warfare Medal, 1st Class, 1969; St Dept Meritorious Awd, 1972; LI Univ Best Fgn Correspondent Awd, 1956; Silurians Jour Awd, 1966; W/W: Am, World, Blue Book, Current Biography, E; Cath W/W; Writers W/W.

McILHANY, STERLING FISHER oc/ Executive, Writer, Lecturer, Artist; b/ Apr 12, 1930; h/6376 Yucca Street, Los Angeles, CA 90028; ba/Same; p/William Wallace and Julia Fisher McIlhany (dec); ed/BFA, Univ TX, 1953; Att'd Univ CA LA, 1953-56; Accademia delle Belle Arti, 1958; St Univ NY, 1961, 1963; pa/Tchg Asst, Univ CA LA, 1953-56; Sr Editor, Reinhold Book Corporation, 1961-69; Instr, Sch Visual Arts, 1966-69; Radio Show Host, "Books & the Artist", WRVR NY, 1961-63; Art Supvr, Honolulu Art Acad, 1955; Pres, Art Horizons Inc, 1960-81; Sr Editor, Litton Ednl Publishing, 1968-70; Sr Editor, Am

Artist Mag, 1969-71; Editor, Med Meetings Mag, 1979-80; Pres, Fdr, IFOTA Inc, 1981-; Nat Soc Lit & the Arts; cp/Commun Ser Chm, St Luke's Fields Outreach, NYC, 1979-; St Advr, US Congl Adv Bd; The Smithsonian Assocs; Am Mus Natural Hist; Fellow, Exec Bd, Free Theatre; r/Rom Cath; hon/Author of *Banners & Hangings* 1966, *Art as Design: Design as Art* 1970, *Wood Inlay* 1973; Author of Num Articles & Screen Scripts; Students Intl Travel Assn, 1952; Rotary Intl F'ship, Accademia delle Belle Arti, Rome, Italy, 1957-58; Fellow, Human Resource US, Wash, DC, 1976; Fellow, Christ Col Cambridge; The So CA Motion Picture Coun Bronze Halo Awd as Actor, Dir, Humanitarian, 1983; Intl Biographical Ctr; W/W: Am, World, Fin & Indust, Intells; Burkes Peerage; Two Thousand Notable Ams; Commun Ldrs Am; Dir Dist'd Ams; 5000 Personalities of World.

McINTOSH, TRACY KAHL oc/ Assistant Professor, Medical Research; b/May 8, 1953; h/29 Lakeville Place, Jamaica Rains, MA 02130; ba/Boston, MA; m/Dr Cynthia Trumpp; p/Mrs Roe McIntosh, Westport, CT; sp/Mr and Mrs T Trumpp; ed/BA, Williams Col, 1975; PhD, Rutgers Univ; pa/NIH Post Doct Res Fellow 1980-82, Asst Prof 1982-, Dir Trauma Res Ctr 1983, BU Med Ctr; Vis'g Prof, Univ Sao Paulo; Chief, Sect Hd Injury, Neural Injury Res Ctr, Univ CA SF, 1984-; AAAS, Mem 1979-; NY Acad Sci, Mem 1981-; Soc of Psychoneuroendocrinology, Mem 1978-; cp/Friends of Elderly-Vol Boston, 1983; Sigma Xi, Mem 1975-; The Shock Soc, 1984-; r/Unitarian; hon/Author of Num Articles & Books; Nat Merit Scholar, 1971; Phi Beta Kappa, 1975; Am Heart Assn Achmt Awd, 1983; W/ W Frontier Sci & Technol.

McIVER, ERCELL BURTON oc/ Elementary Principal; b/Dec 26, 1932; h/215 Piedmont Avenue, Northeast, Suite 702, Atlanta, GA 30308; ba/ Atlanta, GA; c/Mrs Parada Ellene Rocquemore, Ms Cecelya Arlene Taylor; p/William Jones (dec) and Carmen Ercell Williams Burton, Atlanta, GA; ed/ BS 1961; MA 1964; MEd 1971; EdS 1982; pa/Tchr, Marietta City Schs, 1961; Tchr, Atlanta Public Schs, 1961-75; Asst Prin, Pitts Elem, 1975-77; Prin, Chattahoochee Elem, 1977-79; Prin, Bethune Elem, 1979-; Assn Supvn & Curric Devel; Atlanta Assn Sch Prins; Nat AESP; GA AESP; cp/Fulton Co Grand Jurors Assn; Delta Sigma Theta Sorority; NCNW; r/Epis; hon/PTA, Recog Awds; W/W S & SW.

McKEE, JOHN CAROTHERS oc/ Management Sciences, Industrial Psychology; b/Apr 25, 1912; ba/Stanton, Ca; ed/BA 1935, MA 1937, Univ So CA; PhD, Univ Tulane, 1947; Indust Mgmt Conslt, 1938-66; Exec Advr Fin Mgmt 1966-68, Dir, Fiscal Mgmt 1968-70, McDonnell Douglas; Dir, McKee, Wright-Laverne Col Mgt Ctr, 1970-; Dir, Cavalier Fencing Schs, 1935-72; VP, Santa Monica Hlth Spot-Shoes Inc, 1949-56; Pres, Valumetrics Inc, 1964-68; Dir, Advion Corporation, 1969-70; Pres, Mentroa Corporation, 1971-72; VP, Consearch Corporation, 1971-72; Ptnr, McKee Wright Mgmt Conslt; AAAS; Pres, 1951-55, Am Stat Assn; Nat Mgmt Assn; Inst Mgmt Sci;

Intl Assn Chiefs Police; hon/Author of Num Pubs.

McKEEN, CHESTER M JR oc/Executive; b/Mar 18, 1923; h/2310 Woodsong Trail, Arlington, TX 76016; ba/ Fort Worth, TX; m/Alma Virginia; c/ David R, Karin G Stockwell, Thomas K; p/Chester M and Nettie A Fox McKeen (dec); sp/Virgil S and Alma Brooking Pierce (dec); ed/BS 1962, MBA 1962, Univ MD; Army Command & Gen Staff Col, 1958; Indust Col Armed Forces, 1966; mil/AUS, 1942-77, Maj Gen; pa/Dir, Logistics Div, Bell Helicopter Intl, 1977-79; VP, Procurement, 1979-82, VP, Materiel, 1982-, Bell Helicopter Textron Inc; SW Reg VP, Am Def Preparedness Assn, 1974-; Pres, VP Mbrship, Ft Worth Chapt, Assn AUS, 1975-; Am Helicopter Soc, 1978-; Am Mgmt Assn, 1981-; r/Prot; hon/Author of Num Pubs; AUS Legion Merit, 1969, 1972, 1977; Dist'd Ser Medal, 1977; W/ W: MW, Am, World, S & SW; DIB; Jane's W/W Aviation & Aerospace; Men Achmt.

McKENZIE, FLORETTA DUKES oc/ Superintendent of Public Schools; b/ Aug 19, 1935; h/1231 Emerson Street, Northeast, Washington, DC 20017; ba/ Washington, DC; m/Dona; c/Kevin, Dona; p/Ruth Dukes, Washington, DC; ed/BS, DC Tchrs Col, 1956; MA, Howard Univ, 1957; EdD Cand, 1965, 1979-80, George Washington Univ; PhD, Am Univ, 1952-62; pa/Supt, DC Public Schs, 1981-; Ed Conslt, PSI Inc, Ford Foun, 1981; US Ed Dept, 1979-81; Dept Asst Secy, Ofc Sch Improvement, 1980-81; US Del UNESCO; Task Force Ldr, US Ed Dept Transition Team, 1980; Dept Commr, Bur Sch Improvement, 1979-80; Dept Supt Schs, Montgomery Co Public Schs, 1978-79; Asst St Dept Supt Schs, MD, 1977-78; Area Asst Supt, Montgomery Co Public Schs, 1974-77; Dept Supt, Ednl Progs & Sers, DC Public Schs 1973-74; Acting Supt, DC Public Schs, 1973; Spec Asst, Supt Adm Sch Units & Ednl Progs, 1972-73; Acting Dept Supt Instrn, 1972; Exec Asst to Supt Schs, 1971-72; Wash, DC Bd Ed, Asst to Asst Supt in Charge Sec'dy Schs, 1969-71; Dir, Opport Proj Ed Now, Talent Search Agy, HEW, Wash, DC, 1967-69; Tchr, Cnslr, Roosevelt HS 1965-67, Tchr, Kelly Miller Jr HS 1960-65, Wash, DC Bd Ed; Tchr, Balto, MD Bd Ed, 1957-60; OH Univ 1980, Col Entrance Exam Bd Proj ACESS 1970-71, 1973, Study Comm, Howard Univ 1974, Nat Acad Sch Execs, AASA 1974-78, Conslt; Num Spkg Engagements; Adv Com, Wash Ofc Col Entrance Exam Bd; Ednl Prods Info Exch; Pres Appt Jud Review Com; Am Assn Sch Admrs; Ofc Ed, Basic Skills Task Force; AASA, Adv Bd, Ford Foun, Wom Supts Proj; cp/Mem, Urban Leag; Yg Wom Ser Leag; Purity Bapt Ch; Nat Conf Christians & Jews; r/Bapt; hon/ Cash Awd, US Ofc Ed, 1980; Outstg Ser Awd, Montgomery Co NAACP, 1979; First Wom to Serve w US Ofc Ed as Dept Commr; Commend Outstg Perf, DC Bd Ed, 1973; Mayor's Dist'd Public Ser Awd, 1973; Kelly Miller Home & Sch Assn, Dist'd Alumnae Awd; Hon Life Mbrship, MD Cong Parents Tchrs Inc; Outstg Ser Awd, Montgomery Co Bd Ed, 1979; W/W Am Cols & Univs; Gamma Theta Upsilon, Nat Geographic Hon Soc; Phi Alpha

Theta, Nat Hist Hon Soc.

McKENZIE, VICTOR MICHAEL oc/ Teaching Fellow Harvard University; b/ Oct 22, 1947; h/869 East Fayette Street, Syracuse, NY 13210; ba/Cambridge, MA; m/Francine; c/Michelle, Rhonda, Michael II, Rochelle, Krystian; p/Charles and Ellen McKenzie, Brooklyn, NY; sp/Oscar and Lucy Belle, Brooklyn, NY; ed/AA, NY Tech Col, 1975; BA, Queens Col, 1977; MSc, Syracuse Univ, 1979; Postmasters Cert Advanced Study, 1980, Harvard Univ; PhD, Syracuse Univ, 1983; MEd, Harvard Univ, 1984; mil/AUS, 1971-73; pa/Res Analyst, Envir Protection Agy, 1977-79; Rschr, Tng, Devl, Res Inc, 1979-80; Lectr, Syracuse Univ, 1980-82; Conslt, Hutchings Psychi Ctr, 1982-83; Tchg Fellow, Harvard Univ, 1983-84; AAAS; NY Acad Sci; APGA; Am Psychol Assn; r/ Cath; hon/Author of Article; Syracuse Univ Tchg Asst'ship, 1982; Syracuse Univ Grad F'ship, 1982-83; W/W Fin & Indust.

McKINNEY, BETTY JO oc/Publisher; b/Jul 16, 1941; h/1901 South Garfield Avenue, Loveland, CO 80537; ba/Loveland, CO; m/George W; p/Lee and Virginia Underwood, Loveland, CO; sp/Alfred and Evelyn McKinney, Freeman, MO; ed/Att'd Tarkio Col, 1961-63; CO St Univ, 1966-69; pa/Asst Dir, Public Info, Tarkio Col, 1963-65; Pub Spec, Univ Communs Dept, CO St Univ, 1966-81; Pres, Publisher, Alpine Pubs Inc, 1976-; Mem, Rocky Mtn Publishers Assn; Com Small Mags & Publishers; cp/Am Shetland Sheepdog Clb; Am Kennel Clb; Nat Writers Clb; Wom Bus Owners Assn; WESA; r/Prot; hon/Author of *Sheltie Talk* 1976, *Beardie Basics* 1978; W/W Am Wom; Personalities W.

McKINNEY, GEORGE W JR oc/ Bankers Professor; b/May 27, 1922; ba/ Charlottesville, Va; m/Lucille Christian; c/George W III, Mary M Schweitzer, Ruth M Gerbe; p/George W and Charlotte A McKinney; sp/Neil and Lida Martin Christian; ed/BA, Berea Col, 1942; MA 1948, PhD 1949, Univ VA; Grad, Stonier Grad Sch Banking, Rutgers Univ, 1948; mil/AUS, 1942-46, Capt; pa/Fin Economist, Dept Mgr, Asst VP, Richmond Fed Resv Bk, 1948-60; Asst VP & Economist, VP & Economist, Sr VP & Mgr, Investmt Adm Div, Sr VP & Mgr, Economic Res & Planning Div, Sr VP & Chm, Economic Adv Com, Irving Trust Co, 1960-82; VA Bkrs Prof, Bk Mgmt, Univ VA, 1982-; Fellow, Pres 1965-66, Nat Assn Bus Economists; Exec Coun 1968-72, Gov'g Coun 1972-73, Exec Com 1980-81, Am Bkrs Assn; r/Prot; hon/Author of "Fed Taxing & Spending in VA" 1950, "The Fed Resv Discount Window" 1960; Fellow, Nat Assn Bus Economists, 1967; Dist'd Alumnus Awd, Berea Col, 1974; William F Butler Awd, Excell in Bus Ec, NY Assn Bus Economists, 1983; W/W: Am, Bkg, E; Worlds W/W Commerce & Indust; Contemp Authors.

McKUEN, ROD oc/Author, Composer, Performer; b/Apr 29, 1933; h/ Post Office Box G, Beverly Hills, CA 90213; ba/Same; c/Jean Marc, Marie-France; pa/Composer, Lyricist of Num Songs incl'g "Jean", "A Boy Named Charlie Brown", "Love's Been Good to Me"; Num Collaboration incl'g w Jacques Brel, Henry Mancini, John

Williams, Johnny Cash, Petula Clark, Noel Coward; Composer Classical Wks incl'g "Concerto Four Harpsichords", "Symph Num 1"; Commissioned Classical Wks incl'g "Symph Num 3" for Menninger Foun 50th Anniv; Composer Film & TV Scores incl'g "Joanna" 1968, "The Prime of Miss Jean Brodie" 1969, "A Boy Named Charlie Brown" 1970; "The Bch" 1984; Performer Num Songs; Record Prodr Num Personalities incl'g Frank Sinatra, Kingston Trio, Claudette Colbert, Royal Philharm Orch, Nat Symph; Author Num Wks incl'g "And Autumn Came" 1954, "Lonesome Cities" 1968, "Hand in Hand" 1977, "Suspension Bridge" 1984; Pres Num Cos incl'g Rod McKuen Enterprises, Cheval Books, Stanyan Records, Discus Records, New Gramaphone Soc; VP, Tamarack Books; Dir, Animal Concern Foun; Exec Pres, Am Guild Variety Artists (AGVA); Bd Dirs, Am Ballet Theatre; Bd Dirs, Ballet Petrov; Bd Dirs, Am Dance Ensemble; Mem Num Assns incl'g ASCAP; AFTRA; SAG; Actors Equity; Trustee, Univ NE; Trustee, Freedoms Foun; hon/ Recip Grand Prix du Disc, Paris, 1966, 1974, 1975, 1982; Golden Globe Awd, 1969; Motion Picture Daily Awd, 1969; Grammy Awd, Best Spoken Word Album, "Lonesome Cities" 1969; Emmy Awd, "Say Goodbye" 1970; Menninger Foun Awd, 1974; Freedoms Foun Medal Hon, 1975; Entertainer Yr Awd, 1975; Horatio Alger Awd, 1975; Num Awds & Cits.

McLAMB, MICHAEL STUART oc/ Controller; b/Feb 4, 1951; h/Route 5, Box 55, Dunn, NC 28334; ba/Dunn, NC; m/Beverly Gaile Tyndall; c/Neil Stuart; p/Mr and Mrs William L McLamb, Salemburg, NC; sp/Mr and Mrs D C Tyndall, Dunn, NC; ed/BBA, Campbell Col, 1973; CPA, 1978; pa/Dynamic Enterprises Inc, 1973-74; Sr Acct, Oscar N Harris, CPA, 1974-78; Controller 1978-, Dir 1980-, Dyneteria Inc; Dir 1982-, VP 1974-82, Nat Estates Inc; Sec/ Treas, Mayfair Leasing Inc, 1981-; NC Assn CPA; Am Inst CPA; Mem 1973-, Secy/Treas 1974-75, JCs, Dunn, NC; r/ Free Will Bapt, Bd Deacons, 1976-80, Chm, Deacon Bd, 1980, Asst SS Tchr, 1975-79, VP, SS Class, Pres, SS Class, 1981; hon/W/W: Among Student Am Univs & Cols, S & SW.

McLAUGHLIN, WILLIE oc/Teacher of Agriculture; b/Aug 2, 1927; h/214 North Bethune Street, Greenwood, SC 29646; ba/Greenwood, SC; m/Flora Louise Graves; c/Ronald, Bruce, Gerlean; ed/BS 1956, MS 1965, SC St Col; Att'd Clemson Univ; mil/Served in HI, Korea, 1946-51; pa/Tchr, Brewer HS, Greenwood HS, Greenwood Voc Ctr, 1956-; Mem, SC & NEA; SC Agri Tchrs Assn; Am Voc Assn; Mem, SCEA Del Assem, Past Pres, Greenwood Co Ed Assn; cp/Past Post Cmdr, Am Legion Post 224, Greenwood, Past Post Adjutant, Past Bus Mgr, Mem Post Exec Com, Past St Vice Cmdr, Past Dist 15 Cmdr, Former Mem, Credentials Com, Go Getters Com, Am Legion; Past VP, SC St Col Alumni Assn; Past Advmt Chm, BSA; Past Secy, Greenwood Mus; r/U Meth, Ch Sch Supt, Trinity U Meth Ch; hon/Am Legion Outstg Ser Awd, 1962, 1966; Dist'd Ser Awd & 20 Yr Ser to Agri Ed in SC, 1976; Personalities S.

McLEOD, MARILYNN HAYES oc/ Reading Supervisor, Farmer; b/Jan 2, 1924; h/Post Office Box 38, Clio, SC 29525; ba/Bennettsville, SC; m/Charles Edward; c/Cary Franklin, Mary Marilynn; p/Cary V and Benna P Hayes (dec); sp/Mary Ruth Allen McLeod, Clio, SC; ed/BA, Furman Univ, 1946; EdM, Univ SC, 1952; pa/Clrm Tchr, Hamer-Kentyre Sch, 1944-45; Clrm Tchr, Bennettsville City Schs, 1946-59; Clrm Tchr, Clio Elem, 1960-63; Asst Prof, St Andrews Col, 1964-67; Instr, Univ SC, 1970; ETV Instr, Univ SC, 1971; Rdg Tchr, Bennettsville HS, 1975; Title I Coor, Dir Instrn, Sum Sch Dir Elem & Sec'dy Title I Progs, Sum Sch Dir Kgn-Primary Progs, Conslt Spec Proj to Write Curric Guides, Psychol Testing, Sch-Nurse Prog, Tchr-Tng Progs, Curric Supvr, Rdg Supvr & Math Supvr Chapt I Progs, Marlboro Co Sch Dist, 1967-; Served Num Profl Assns & Coms incl'g Nat Rdg Assn; St Intl Rdg Assn; Pee Dee Intl Rdg Assn; NEA, Life Mem; SC Ed Assn; Marlboro Co Ed Assn; cp/Marlboro Co Assn Retarded Chd; Marlboro Co Mtl Hlth Assn; Marlboro Arts Coun; Marlborough Hist Soc; Dillon Co Farm Bur; Clio Fed'd Wom Clb; CSA, Den Mother; r/Meth, Num Positions incl'g SS Tchr, Study Course Tchr, Ch Organist; hon/Delta Kappa Gamma S'ship Awd; Grant to Attend Gesell Inst Child Devel; Hon Mem, St Andrews Col NC Student Tchrs Assn; Art Awds, Florence Mus Art; Carolina Ed Assn Awd, 1983; Commun Ldrs & Noteworthy Ams; DIB; Intl W/W Commun Ser; W/W: S & SW, Child Devel Profls.

McLEOD, NANCY JANE oc/City Administrator, Planning Coordinator; b/Jun 19, 1946; h/3753 East Bloomfield Road, Phoenix, AZ 85032; ba/Phoenix, Az; p/Kenneth Leroy McLeod, Mesa, AZ and Velma Jane Muchmore (dec); ed/BA 1967, MBA 1970, Univ AZ; Att'g AZ St Univ, Doct Public Adm Prog, 1981-; pa/Planning Coor 1974-, Adm Asst & Acting Chief Prog Planner 1973-74, Adm Aide 1972-74, Human Resources Dept, City of Phoenix; Pres 1980-81, 1981-82, 1st VP 1978-79, 1979-80, 2nd VP 1977-78, BPW Clb; Dist V BPW, Auditor, 1983; Am Mgmt Assn; ASPA; Am Planning Assn; cp/AZ Hist Soc; Ctl AZ Mus; Adm VP, 1981, Pk Ctl Toastmasters; r/Prot; hon/Wom Yr 1982-83, Outstg Mem 1980-81, Yg Career Wom Yr 1974, BPW Clb Phoenix; W/W Am Wom.

McLEOD, PEDEN B oc/Attorney, S C Senate; b/Sep 3, 1940; h/512 Hampton Street, Walterboro, SC 29488; ba/ Walterboro, SC; m/Mary Waite Hamrick; c/Mary Carlisle, Peden Brown Jr, Rhoda Lane, John Reaves; p/Mr and Mrs Walton J McLeod Jr, Walterboro, SC; sp/Mrs W C Hamrick, Gaffney, SC; ed/ BA, Wofford Col, 1962; JD, Univ SC, 1967; mil/USAR, 1962-72, Capt; pa/ Mem, SC Ho of Reps, 1972-79; Am, SC Bar Assn; Secy, Colleton Co Bar Assn; Ho of Dels; Dir, First Nat Bk; cp/JCs; Elks; Moose; Masons; Cancer-Soc; Mtl Hlth Assn; Lions; Shriners; City Coun, 1970-72; Am Legion, 1971-72; Dist Chm, BSA, 1967-71; r/Meth; hon/W/W Am Cols & Univs; Outstg Yg Men Am; JCs Dist'd Ser Awd, 1972; Colleton Co Friend Ed Awd, 1976-77, 1980; Am Acad Fam Phys Apprec Awd, 1978; USC

Apprec Awd, 1980; Wofford Yg Alumnus Yr Awd, 1980.

McLUCAS, JOHN LUTHER oc/Corporate Official; b/Aug 22, 1920; h/309 North Lee Street, Alexandria, VA 22314; ba/Washington, DC; m/Harriet Dewey; c/Pamela McLucas Byers, Roderick K, Susan, John C; p/John Luther and Viola Conley McLucas (dec); ed/BS, Davidson Col, 1941; MS, Tulane Univ, 1943; Doct, PA St Univ, 1950; mil/USN, World War II; pa/VP, Tech Dir, Haller, Raymond & Brown Inc, 1950-57; Pres, HRB-Singer Inc, 1958-62; Dept Dir Res & Engrg, DOD, 1962-64; Asst Secy Gen Sci Affairs, NATO, Paris, 1964-66; Pres, CEO, Mitre Corporation, 1966-69; Under Secy, AF, 1969-73; Secy AF, 1973-75; Admr FAA, 1957-77; Pres, COMSAT Gen Corporation; Pres, COMSAT World Sys Div; Exec VP & Chief Strategic Ofcr Communs Satellite Corporation, Wash, DC, 1977-; Fellow, Pres, AIAA; Fellow, IEEE; Mem, Nat Acad Engrg; VChm Bd, World Trap Foun; Mem, Bd Dirs, C-COR Electronics Inc; Chm Bd, Arthur C Clarke Foun of US; Mem, Bd Wash Trustees Fed City Coun; Opers Res Soc Am; NY Acad Sci; AAAS; Chief Execs Forum; Sigma Xi, Sigma Pi Sigma; Mem, Bd Trustees, Intl Economic Studies Inst; Mem, Cosmos Clb; AF Assn; Am Astronautical Soc; RTCA; AF Sci Adv Bd; r/Presb; Dist'd Public Ser Awd, 1964, 1973, 1975 DOD, Wash, DC; Hon, Dr Sci, Davidson Col, 1974; Hon, Dr Aerospace Mgmt, Embry-Riddle Aeronaut Univ, 1975; Dist'd Ser Medal, NASA, 1975; Exceptl Civilian Ser Awd, Dept AF, 1975; Dist'd Alumnus Awd, Tulane Univ, 1976; Secy's Awd, Outstg Achmt, Dept Trans, 1977; Dist'd Alumnus Awd, Penn St Univ, 1977; Dist'd Ser Awd, Aero Clb, 1977; AIAA Reed Aeronautics Awd, 1982; Num Patents.

McMANUS, REV MICHAEL FRANKLIN oc/Minister of Youth and Senior Citizens; b/Jan 30, 1942; h/434 Granville Drive, Winston-Salem, NC 27101; ba/Winston-Salem, NC; m/ Mona Faye Willis; c/Mark Franklin; p/ Mrs Louise Claxon McManus, New Boston, OH; sp/Mrs Lena Willis, Portsmouth, OH; ed/Att'd Bob Jones Univ, 1960-61; BRE, Piedmont Bible Col, 1963-68; Cert'd Instr Evang Tchr Tng Assn; Ordained Bapt Min, 1978; pa/Min Yth & Ed, Fayetteville St Bapt Ch, 1967-72; Temple Hgts Bapt Ch, 1973-74; Assoc Pastor Yth & Ed, West Hill Bapt Ch, 1974-78; Yth & Visitation Pastor, Salem Bapt Ch, 1978-; cp/Mem, Christian Camping Intl; Dir, Salem Bapt Ch Charter Positive Action Christ; 2nd VP, Alumni Assn Piedmont Bible col, 1979-81; r/Bapt; hon/Personalities S.

McMORRIS, F ARTHUR oc/ Research Scientist; b/Sep 17, 1944; h/ 4333 Larchwood Avenue, Philadelphia, PA 19104; ba/Philadelphia, PA; p/Mr and Mrs W A McMorris, Deerfield Beach, FL; ed/BA, Brown Univ, 1966; PhD, Yale Univ, 1972; pa/Asst Prof, Wistar Inst, 1974-; AAAS; Am Soc Cell Biol; Am Soc Neurochemistry; Am Soc Human Genetics; Soc Devel Biol; Soc Neurosci; cp/Mem Bd Dir & Exec VP, 1976-, Spruce Hill Commun Assn; r/ Prot; hon/Hon, Brown Univ, 1966; Sigma Xi; NIH Postdoct F'ship, 1972-74; Am Men & Wom Sci; W/W: E, Frontier Sci & Technol.

McMULLIN, MARY JO oc/ Nurse-Assistant Director of Nursing; b/ Jul 8, 1933; h/Route 2, Lamonte, MO 65337; ba/Sedalia, MO; m/Jesse Francis; c/James, Thomas, Rose Mary, Jane; p/ Robert and Rose Welliver (dec); sp/ Matthew (dec) and Eunice McMullin, Sedalia, MO; ed/Dipl Nsg, St Mary's Hosp, 1954; Donnelly Col, 1951-52; CCU Nsg, St Fair Commun Col, 1970; Stoma Nsg Jewish Hosp, 1976; pa/Staff Nurse, St Mary Hosp; 1954-55; Staff Nurse 1955-58, Hd Nurse 1958-70, Asst Dir Nsg 1970-, Bothwell Hosp; Nurse, Stoma, 1976-; MO Nsg Assn; 10th Dist Nsg Assn; VP, 1982-83, Am Nsg Assn; Adv Com Ext, Profl Nsg Assn Bothwell Hosp; cp/4-H Club Ldr, 1955-; Pettis Co Ext Coun, 1981-; r/Cath; hon/Ext Ldrs Hon Roll, Univ MO, 1982; MO St Fair, Farm Fam Awd, 1978; W/W Am Wom.

McMURRAY, KAY oc/Director, Federal Mediation and Conciliation Service; b/Mar 18, 1918; h/4932 Sentinel Drive, Bethesda, MD 20816; ba/Washington, DC; m/Robert Jean Rankin; c/Kathleen Wanger, Julia Lynn, Mollie; p/John and Clara Louise Dahlquist McMurray (dec); ed/BA 1940, MBA 1948, Stanford Univ; pa/Capt 1940-49, Conslt Govt Affairs 1971-72, U Air Lines Inc; Asst to Pres, Inland Empire Ins Co, 1949-53; Exec Admr, Airline Pilots Assn Intl, 1953-71; Mem 1972-73, 1974-76, Chm 1973-74, 1976-77, Nat Mediation Bd; Conslt & Arbitrator, Bethesda, MD, 1977-83; Dir, Fed Mediation & Conciliation Ser, 1982-; Bd Dirs, Jt Action Commun Ser Inc, 1974-82; r/Epis; hon/ Arbitration Awds; W/W: Am Polit, Am, Fin & Indust.

McMURRIN, TRUDY ANN oc/Director, Southern Methodist University Press; b/May 28, 1944; ba/Dallas, TX; m/Dr Mick McAllister; c/Natalie Roberta Howard, Jeoffrey McAllister; p/ Sterling and Natalie McMurrin, Salt Lake City; ed/BA, Univ UT, 1981; Editor 1967-74, Asst Dir 1974-80, Editor-in-Chief 1980-, Univ UT Press; Conslt, Lectr for Pvt Grps, 1967-; Art Dir, Co-Designer Awd Winning Books, 1972-; Mem, Coalition to Save Our Sch Libs, 1981-; Mem, Adv Bd, Chd's Mus UT, 1979-81; Mem, Com Rowland Hall-St Mark's Sch Cent Symp Quality Pre-Col Ed, 1980-81; Nat Endowment Humanities Fellow; Am Assn St & Local Hist Fellow, 1977; Inst Am W, Fellow, 1981, 1982; Mem, Assn UT Pubs, Pres 1978; Assn Am Univs Presses; Wn Univ Presses; Soc Scholarly Pub; Wn Book Pubs Assn; Wn Lit Assn; UTT Lib Assn; Medieval Acad Am; cp/UT St Hist Soc; UT Opera Assn; UT Cinema Coun; W/ W: Am Wom, W.

McNAIR, NIMROD JR oc/Businessman, Consultant, Speaker; h/4090 North Lake Creek Cove, Tucker, GA 30084; ed/BS, MS.

McNEAL, LYLE GLEN oc/Professor; b/May 16, 1942; h/85 Quarter Circle Drive, Nibley, UT 84321; ba/Logan, UT; m/Nancy Wickie; c/Susannah R, Jenny L, Ian B, Ilene L; p/Mr and Mrs Darrell G McNeal, Torrance, CA; ed/BS Animal Husbandry, CA St Polytech Univ, 1964; MA Animal Breeding, Univ of NV, 1966; PhD Reproductive Physiol, UT St Univ, 1978; pa/Co Agri Ext Agt, Univ of NV, Douglas Co, 1966-69; Prof Animal Sci, CA St Polytech Univ, San Luis Obispo, CA, 1969-79; Prof Animal

Sci, Emphasis Sheep & Wool, UT St Univ, Logan, 1979-; Nat Wool Growers Assn, 1965-; Chm, Nat Ram Sale Com; Am Soc of Animal Sci, 1964-; UT Wool Growers Assn, 1979-; Boy Scouts of Am, 1950-; Coun Agri & Sci Technol, 1984-; Am Soc of Testing Materials, 1984; hon/Author, *Wool Eval & Judging Manual*, 1982; *Sheep Producers Handbook for American Suffolk Sheep Soc*, 1982; Dist'd Tchr Awd, CA Polytech St Univ, 1972-73; Prof of Yr, Col of Agri, UT St Univ, 1982-83; Hon Lifetime Mem, Am Polypay Sheep Assn, 1981; Best All-Around Agri Instr, 1977-78; Hon Lifetime Mem, Boots & Spurs Clb, CA Polytech St Univ, 1973; W/W Frontier Sci & Technol.

McNEESE, LEONARD EUGENE oc/ Fossil Energy Program Director; b/May 11, 1935; h/103 Morgan Road, Oak Ridge, TN 37830; ba/Oak Ridge, TN; m/Mildred Gurene Allen; c/Gregory Eugene, Sharon Nanette, Michael Alan; p/Leonard and Rosemary Hall McNeese, Amherst, TX; sp/Horace J and Mary I Crump Allen, Decatur, TX; ed/BS, TX Tech Univ, 1957; MS, Univ TN, 1962; pa/Res Grp Ldr, Oak Ridge Nat Lab, 1957-69; Sect Hd, Chem Tech Div, 1969-74; Dir, Molten-Salt Reactor Prog, 1974-76; Assc Dir, Chem Tech Div, 1976; Dir, Fossil Energy Prog, 1976-; Mem, AIChE; Am Nuclear Soc; Exec Com 1980-83, Secy/Treas 1983-84, Vice Chm/Chm 1984-86, Alt Energy Tech & Sys Div; ASME; r/Meth; hon/Num Pubs.

McNULTY, IRENE MAY oc/Retired; b/Aug 3, 1911; h/247 Riverside Drive, Binghamton, NY 13905; p/Martin and Nora McNulty; ed/BS 1936, MA 1940, NY Univ; pa/Elem Tchr, 1932-37, Binghamton City Sch Dist; Jr HS Social Studies Tchr, 1937-43; Jr HS Guid Cnslr, 1943-52; Sr HS Guid Cnslr, 1952-58; Dir Acad Studies, 1958-71; Dir Sec'dy Ed, 1971-79; Dir Curric, 1979-82; Life Mem, NEA; ASCD; NYSASCD; Life Mem, AAUW; pa/Zonta Clb Intl; CDA; hon/Broome Co Status Wom Coun Wom of Yr Awd; Pres Bd Mgrs Binghamton Gen Hosp; W/W: Am Ed, Sec'dy Ed, E.

McNULTY, JANE VICKERS oc/Reading Specialist; b/Nov 5, 1926; h/1541 Westchester Avenue, Winter Park, FL 32789; ba/Orlando, FL; m/Frank M; p/ Lewis (dec) and Emma McEachern Vickers, Douglas, Ga; ed/BS, Univ GA, 1947; MA, Rollins Col, 1965; pa/Glynn Co Schs 1947-49, 1954-60, Daytona Bch FL 1949-50, Trion GA Public Schs 1950-51, Douglas GA Public Schs 1951-52, Muscogee Co Schs 1952-54, Elem Tchr; Rdg Tchr, Orange Co FL, 1961-76, 1981-; Curric Resource Tchr, 1976-81; Rdg Tchr; Pres, FL Rdg Assn, 1982-83; Adv, Orange Co Rdg Assn, 1981-83; Tchr Tnr, Orange Co, 1975-76; Conslt, Right to Read, 1977; Mem, FL Rdg Assn; Intl Rdg Assn; cp/ Histn, Alpha Delta Kappa, 1971-72; Alpha Delta Kappa; r/Anglican; hon/ Outstg Elem Edr Am, Outstg Person Rdg Orange Co FL, 1979, 1980; W/W S & SW.

McPHERSON, KAREN MICHEL oc/ Independent Radio Producer, Photographer; b/Sep 1, 1946; h/24 Fifth Avenue, Number 622, New York City, NY 10011; ba/Fairbanks, AK; m/Roger Blair; p/Martin M and Ellen S Michel,

Los Angeles, CA; sp/Blair and Madge McPherson, Menlo Park, CA; ed/BA, SF St Col; EdM, Univ AK; pa/Indep Radio Prodr, Exec Dir, Inst AK Native Arts; Prodr/Reporter, AK Public Radio Netwk; Prodr/Dir/Writer, Dena Aka Video Ctr; Dir, Nulato Biling/Bicultural Prog; Dir, AK Native Oral Lit Proj; Art Tchr, Barrow Sch; Bd Mem, Fairbanks Chapt, NOW; Bd Mem, Chm, Visual Arts Com, AK Assn Arts; r/Jewish; hon/ Solo & Grp Photo Exhibs; Radio Progs; Outstg Yg Wom Am; Grants for Radio Prodn from AK St Coun on Arts, Nat Endowment Arts & Nat Public Radio; Awds from Wom in Radio & TV, Sigma Delta Chi, AK Press Clb.

McQUILKIN, JOHN ROBERTSON oc/College President; b/Sep 7, 1927; h/ Post Office Box 3122, Columbia, SC 29230; ba/Same; m/Muriel Webendorfer; c/Robert, David, Virginia, Amy, Kent; p/Robert Crawford and Marguerite McQuilkin (dec); ed/BA, Columbia Bible Col, 1947; MDiv, Fuller Theol Sem, 1950; pa/Tchr, Columbia Bible Col, 1950-52; Hdmaster, Ben Lippen Sch, 1952-56; Missionary to Japan, 1956-68; Acting Pres, Japan Christian Col, 1962-63; Tchr, Japan Bible Sem, 1962-64; Evang Theol Soc; Am Bible Soc; Am Soc Missiology; F'ship, Evang Sem Pres; r/Bapt; hon/Num Pubs incl'g "How Biblical is the Ch Growth Mvt" 1974, "Crucial Dimension in World Evangelization", "Indep" 1977; Hon Doct, Wheaton Col.

McREYNOLDS, MARY McCULLOH oc/Teacher; b/Feb 18, 1930; h/15 Plaza Olas Atlas, Albuquerque, NM 87109; ba/Albuquerque, NM; m/Col Zachariah A (dec); c/Gregg C, Barbara McReynolds Dent, Zach A; p/Judge and Mrs C C McCulloh, Farmington, NM; sp/Mr and Mrs O B McReynolds (dec); ed/BA 1951, MA 1972, Univ NM; Doct Cand, Univ NM; pa/Secy, USAF, Intell, Germany, 1953-54; Tchr, Annondale, VA, 1962-65; Tchr, AHS, 1968-84; Social Studies Curric, 1973-75; Univ NM Tchg Asst, 1975-76; cp/Kappa Kappa Gamma; Phi Kappa Phi; Phi Kappa Delta; ASCD; NMCSS; NCSS; Fundraiser, Univ NM, 1977-83; AFT; ATF; Fdn Rep, AHS; Bd Dirs, UNM Gtr Fund; Ldr, GSA; Sponsor, Black Student Union, 1979-82; Campaign Mgr St Senate, 1976; Dem Del to St, 1984; r/ Epis; hon/Phi Kappa Phi, Pi Alpha Theta, 1951; Phi Delta Kappa; W/W W.

MEADOW-ORLANS, KATHRYN P oc/Research Sociologist; b/Jun 12, 1929; h/2848 Northampton Street, Northwest, Washington, DC 20015; ba/Washington, DC; m/Harold Orlans; c/Lynn, Robert; p/Orien A (dec) and M Wilma Pendleton; ed/BA, Denison Univ, 1951; MS, Univ Chgo, 1953; PhD, Univ CA, 1967; pa/Sr Res Scist 1981-, Dir, Child Devel Res Unit 1979-81, Dir Res, Kendall Demo Elem Sch 1976-81, Dean, Kendall Demo Sch 1979-80, Gallaudet Col; Lect, Adj Prof, Univ CA-SF, Res Dir, Mtl Hlth Sers Deaf, Langley Porter Neuropsychi Inst, 1968-76; Prog Com 1979-83, Edit Bd 1983-, Soc Res Child Devel; Am Annals Deaf, Edit Bd, Conf Am Instrs Deaf, 1981; DC Sociological Soc; Am Sociological Soc; hon/Author of "Sound & Sign, Chd Deafness & Mtl Hlth" 1972, "Deafness & Child Devel" 1980; APA Media Awd, 1973; Cal St Univ Northridge, Daniel T Cloud Awd,

Outstg Contbns Deafness, Intl W/W Wom, Am Men & Wom Sci, W/W E, Contemp Authors.

MEDAVOY, MIKE oc/Executive Vice President, Orion Pictures; b/Jan 21, 1941; h/1451 North Amalfi Drive, Pacific Palisades, CA 90272; ba/Los Angeles, CA; m/Marcia; c/Brian, Michael, Melissa; p/Mike and Dora Medavoy, LA, CA; sp/Henry and Roz Rogers, LA, CA; ed/BS, Univ CA-LA, 1963; mil/USAR; pa/Mailrm, Casting Dir, Universal Studios, 1963; Theatrical Agt Trainee, Bill Robinson, 1964; VP, 1966, GAC/MCA, VP, IFA, 1971, Motion Picture Dept; Sr VP Charge Prodn, U Artists, 1974; Exec VP, Orion Pictures Corporation, 1978; Pres, Filmex; Bd Trustees, Univ CA-LA Foun; Com Mem, Com Cure Cancer Through Immunization, Univ CA-LA; Steering Com, Royce 270, Univ CA-LA; Vis'g Com, Dept Public Relats, Boston Mus Fine Arts; CoChm, Olympic Sports Fdn Com; CoChm, Music Ctr Unified Fund Campaign; Bd Govs, Sundance Inst; Bd Dirs, CA Mus Sci & Indust; r/Jewish; hon/Hon Grad, Univ CA-LA.

MEDINA, ELBA IRIS oc/Management Consultant, Certified Public Accountant; b/May 2, 1953; h/N-1 20th Street, Magnolia Gardens, Bayamon, Puerto Rico 00619; ba/San Juan, PR; p/Julio Medina and Maria Luisa Mendez, PR; ed/BBA, Acctg & Computer Sci, 1975; pa/Staff to Sr, Price Waterhouse & Co, 1975-79; Sr to Mgr, Peat Marwick Mitchell & Co, 1979-; Nat Assn Accts; Am Mgmt Assn; Am Inst CPA; Colegio de Contadores Publicos Asociados de Puerto Rico; r/Cath; Conducted Var Sems; W/W S & SW.

MEDVED, DENISE L oc/Vice President, Creative Director; b/May 21, 1952; h/88 Davenport Ridge Road, Stamford, CT 06903; ba/Stamford, CT; p/Martin and Doris William Medved, Heiskell, TN; ed/BS, Univ TN, 1974; Att'd Wesleyan Col; Post Grad Univ TN; pa/Promotion Coor 1974-75, Ednl Spkr 1980-, Copy Supvr, Direct Mail Mktg Agy; Direct Mktg Agy, 1975-76, Assoc Creat Dir 1976-78, Creat Dir 1978-, VP 1981; Actress; Freelance Writer Maj NY Firms, 1978-82; Com Mem, NY Wom in Communs; Greenwich Dem Wom, Ofcr; Mem, Nat Assn Female Execs; Wom Communs; Assn Bus & Profl Wom; cp/Phi Kappa Phi; River Hills Ski Clb, Ofcr; Delta Delta Delta; Active in Dem Party/Cand Campaigns; Bapt Clbs; Dem Wom; r/Prot; hon/Ygst VP & First Wom VP, Direct Mktg Agy Inc; Fdr & Creator of Nat Pub "Businesswoman", 1976-; Formerly on Pres White House Com on Yth Guid; W/W Am Wom; Outstg Wom Communs by AAUW; 5000 Personalities World; W/W Bus & Indust; Prom Wom Ad.

MEEHAN, JAMES WILLIAM JR oc/Prof and Chairman, Department of Economics; b/Mar 4, 1941; h/12 Cherry Hill Drive, Waterville, ME 04901; ba/Waterville, ME; m/Joan Hansen; c/Kara Anne, Shana Anne, Jason William and Kathrine Marie Meehan, Trenton, NJ; ed/BA, St Vincent Col, 1962; PhD, Boston Col, 1967; pa/Economist, Antitrust Div, Dept of Justice 1966-67; Asst Prof, NWn Univ, 1967-72; Economic Advr to Commr, FTC, 1970-71; Asst to Dir, Bur Ec, FTC, 1971-73; Asst Prof 1973-, Assoc Prof 1977-82, Prof 1982-,

Chm Social Sci Div 1981-, Chm Dept Ec 1982-, Colby Col; Am Ec Assn; So Ec Assn; r/Cath; hon/Author of Num Pubs incl'g "Jt Venture Entry in Perspective", *The Antitrust Bultn* 1970; Recip Num Grants; Vis'g Scholar, Harvard Law Sch, 1980; W/W E.

MEEKINS, JOHN FRED oc/Astrophysicist; b/Oct 4, 1937; h/5624 Ravenel Lane, Springfield, VA 22151; ba/Washington, DC; m/C Ann Turner; c/David George and Brian John; p/Donald Meekins, Roslyndale, MA, and Signe (dec); sp/George and Alberta Turner, Brunswick, ME; ed/BA, Bowdoin Col, 1959; PhD, Cath Univ Am, 1973; pa/Res Physicist 1959-79, Astrophysicist 1979, Naval Res Lab; Mem, Am Astronom Soc; cp/Sigma Xi; Asst Scoutmaster, BSA, 1980-82; hon/Num Articles Pub'd; Am Men & Wom Sci; W/W: Technol Today, Frontier Sci & Technol.

MEFFERD, M G oc/State Oil and Gas Supervisor and Interim Director, Department of Conservation, State of California; b/Sep 28, 1931; h/4746 Papaya Drive, Fair Oaks, CA 95628; ba/Sacramento, CA; m/Marjorie Rose; c/Tim Lee, Richard Douglas, Patrick Charles, Scott Alan; ed/BA, Univ IA, 1957; Grad/Voc Studies at Univ CA-LA, Univ So CA, Golden West Jr Col, St CA Mgmt Devel Inst; mil/AUS Engrs, 1952-54; pa/Oil & Gas Engr 1959-73, Energy Ofcr 1973, St Fuel Allocation Ofcr 1973-75, Acting Chief & Chief Dept, St Oil & Gas Supvr 1975-76, St Oil & Gas Supvr, Chief of CA Div Oil & Gas 1976-, St of CA; Interim Dir, CA Dept Conserv, 1983-; CA Reg'd Geologist Num 1005; Am Assn Petro Geologists, Pacific Sect; Soc Petro Engrs AIME; Am Petro Inst; Sacramento Petro Assn; Geothermal Resources Coun; Comstock Clb; hon/Author of Num Pubs; Vice Chm, Interstate Oil Compact Comm; W/W: Sacramento, W, World Oil & Gas; DIB.

MEGARGEE, EDWIN INGLEE oc/Psychologist; b/Feb 27, 1937; h/3348 East Lakeshore Drive, Tallahassee, FL 32312; m/Sara Jill Mercer; c/Elyn Jean, Edwin I Jr, Christopher John, Stephen Andrew, Heather Lynn Dunham; p/S Edwin and Jean Inglee Megargee; sp/Dr James W Mercer, Quincy, FL; ed/BA, Amherst Col, 1958; PhD, Univ CA, 1964; pa/Asst Prof, Univ TX, 1964-67; Assoc Prof 1967-70, Prof 1970-, FL St Univ; Fellow, Am Psych Assn; Pres, 1973-75, Am Assn Correctional Psychol; VP, 1984-85, Intl Differential Treatment Assn; Cosmos Clb; hon/Author of Num Pubs; Phi Beta Kappa, Sigma Xi, Delta Sigma Rho, 1958; Contemp Authors; W/W S & SW.

MEHAFFEY, COY REEVES oc/Financial Executive; b/Feb 7, 1927; h/Route 1, Box 90, Arden, NC 28704; ba/Enka, NC; m/Clara Gasperson; p/Rufus Rutledge and Mary Estelle Morgan (dec); sp/George C (dec) and Mada L Gasperson, Raleigh, NC; ed/BS, Wn Carolina Univ, 1965; mil/AUS, 1945-47; pa/Engrg Aide 1948-56, Supvr Property Acctg 1957-61, Adm Asst to Chief Plant Engr 1961-62, Cost Supvr Engrg 1962-71, Dept Mgr Res Gen Sers 1971-, Am Enka Co; Soc Res Admrs; cp/Lions Clb; r/Bapt; hon/W/W S & SW.

MEHOS, NANCY ASIMO oc/Educator; b/Sep 28, 1946; h/121 Georgetown Road, Weston, CT 06883; ba/Weston,

CT; p/George and Demetria Mehos, Weston, CT; ed/BA, Nat Col Ed, 1968; MA, Wn CT St Col, 1977; pa/Tchr, Eugene Field Elem Sch, 1968-70; Tchr, James Fennimore Cooper Jr HS, 1970-72; Tchr 1972-, Team Ldr 1974-, Weston Middle Sch; Financial Com 1981, Exec Bd 1981-82, Wn Mid Sch Parent Tchr Org; Assn Supvn & Curric Devel; CT Ed Assn; NEA; Wn Tchrs Assn; cp/Writer for Mid Link Newslttr, 1981-82; Phi Delta Kappa; r/Greek Orthodox; hon/Recip 2nd Place Awd, Buffalo Grove Outstg Yg Edr, 1971; W/W E.

MEHRMANN, CRAIGANN oc/Registered Nurse, Clinical Coordinator; b/Jan 6, 1953; h/426 West Granada Avenue, Hershey, PA 17033; ba/Harrisburg, PA; p/C Craig and Martha Mehrmann, Hershey, PA; ed/BS, Bloomsburg St Col, 1974; AA, Harrisburg Area Commun Col, 1979; Att'g PA St Univ; pa/Subst Tchr, 1974-77, Middletown Area & Ctl Dauphin Sch Dists; Nsg Asst 1978, Staff Nurse 1979-80, MS Hershey Med Ctr; Staff Nurse, Holy Spirit Hosp, 1979; Staff Nurse, Clin Edr, Clin Coor, Hillcrest Clin & Cnslg Ser, 1980-; Vol, ARC; Vol Spkr's Bur, Am Cancer Soc; Dist Treas, 1982-84, PA Nurses Assn; ANA; Nurses Assn Am Col Ob & Gyn, Hershey/Harrisburg Area Chapt, Coor, 1982-; Kipona Chapt, Recording Secy, ABWA, 1982-83; r/Meth; hon/ARC Nurse, 1981; W/W Am Wom.

MEHTA, JAWAHAR L oc/University Cardiologist; b/Aug 10, 1946; h/6604 Northwest 18th Avenue, Gainesville, FL 32601; ba/Gainesville, FL; m/Paulette; c/Asha; p/Mohan L and Iswar D Mehta, Bhiwani, Haryana, India; ed/BS 1962, MD 1967, Panjab Univ; pa/Assoc Med 1980-, Asst Prof 1976-80, Univ FL; Instr Med, Univ MN, 1975-76; Instr Med, St Univ NY, 1973-75; Fellow, Am Col Phys; Am Col Cardiology; AHA-Coun Circulation, Coun Clin Cardiology; r/Hindu; hon/Num Pubs; Mem, Edit Bd Num Med Jours; Guest Spkr Num Nat & Intl Sci Meetings; W/W S & SW.

MEHTA, RAGU NANDAN oc/Physician, Health Care Specialist; b/Aug 22, 1917; h/65 Park Street, Caribou, ME 04736; ba/Same; m/Krishna Rosalie; c/Pravina K, Suneela R, Krishn Alexander, Rani J J; ed/BA, Med Col, Govt's Bd Indiaan Med, Lucknow, 1944; DMRD, Queen's Univ, 1962; MEd, Univ MD, 1957; CHA, Hlth Hosp Adm, Univ Saskatchewan, 1965; Cert Mgmt Alcoholism, Laurentian Univ, 1974; pa/Gen Med Pract, 1950's; Jr, Sr Asst, Chief Resident Radiologist, Balto City Hosp, 1956-60; Sr Resident Radiologist, Gen Hosp, Queen's Univ, 1960-62; Chief Radiologist, Grand Falls Hosp, 1962-; Acting Admr, Miramichi Rehab Ctr for Mtlly Retarded, Min Social Wel, 1973; Dir, Alcoholic Clin, 1974-75; r/Vedic, Indo-Aryan Brahmanic; hon/Author of Num Pubs; Invited Spkr Num Insts & Hosps; Men Achmt; Indust Resource Dir; Spkrs & Lectrs Dir.

MEHTA, RAJENDRA G oc/Cancer Research; b/Aug 31, 1947; h/16537 South 76th Avenue, Tinley Park, IL 60477; ba/Chicago, IL; m/Raksha P Buch; c/Sonkulp R; p/Mr and Mrs G H Mehta, Dabhoi, Gujarat, India; sp/Mr and Mrs P B Buch, Gandhinagar, Gujarat, India; ed/BS 1966, MS 1968,

PERSONALITIES OF AMERICA

Gujarat Univ; PhD, 1974, Univ NE; Post Doct, F'ships, Univ Rochester, 1974-76, Univ Louisville Sch Med, 1976-77; pa/ Assoc Biochem 1977-78, Res Sci 1978-79, Sr Biochem 1977-, Lab Pathophysiol, Life Sci Div, IIT Res Inst; Am Assn Cancer Res; Intl Soc Breast Cancer Res; Endocrine Soc; r/Hindu; hon/ Author of Num Pubs; Res Grants from Nat Cancer Inst; Intl Travel Grant from NSF; Outstg New Citizen Yr Awd, 1982-83, Citizenship Coun; Marqui's W/W.

MEHTA, SHAHROKH M oc/Manager, Finance and Administration; b/ Nov 20, 1939; h/107 Rosewell Meadow, Dewitt, NY 13214; ba/Syracuse, NY; m/ Gool S Khambatta; c/Kershaw, Parastu; ed/Bach Commerce, Univ Karachi, 1961; Assoc Mem, Inst Chartered Accts, 1963; pa/Area Admr, Reading & Bates Offshore Drilling Co, 1963-71; Grp Financial Mgr, Pars Toshiba Indust Co, 1971-76; Mgr, Contract Adm & Financial Control, Carrier Intl Corporation, 1983; Controller Financial & Adm, Carrier Thermo Frig Corporation, 1976-79; Asst to VP Fin 1980-81, Mgr Fin & Adm Indust Refrigeration Div 1982, Carrier Intl Corporation; Assoc Mem, Brit Inst Mgmt, 1974; r/Zorastrian (Parsee); hon/W/W Fin & Indust.

MEIER, WILBUR L JR oc/Dean, College of Engineering; b/Jan 3, 1939; h/596 Shadow Lane, State College, PA 16801; ba/University Park, PA; m/Judy Lee Longbotham; c/Melynn, Marla, Melissa; p/Wilbur L Meier and Ruby (dec); sp/Mr and Mrs J T Longbotham, Lufkin, TX; ed/BS 1962, MS 1964, PhD 1967, Univ TX; pa/Planning Engr, TX Water Devel Bd, 1962-66; Res Engr, Univ TX Austin, 1966-67; Asst Prof 1967-68, Assoc Prof 1968-70, Prof 1970-73, Asst Hd Dept Indust Engrg 1972-73, TX A & M Univ; Prof & Hd, Sch Indust Engrg, Purdue Univ, 1974-81; Dean, Col of Engrg, PA St Univ, 1981-; VP Chapt Opers 1981-83, VP Reg VIII 1978-81, Opers Res Div Reg Chm 1971-73, Prog Chm 1973-74, Dir 1975-76, Engrg Economy Div Pub Chm & Newslttr Editor 1972-73, Ctl IN Chapt Num 35 VP 1975-76, Pres 1976-77, Reg VIII Reg Chm, Ednl, & Profl Devel, AIIE; TX Soc Profl Engrs, Chapt Dir Travis Chapt 1964, IN Soc Profl Engrs, Chapt Dir, Potter, Chapt 1976-77, Nat Soc Profl Engrs; Asst Prog Chm, TX A & M Univ Chapt 1970-71, Pres, TX A & M Univ Chapt 1971-72, Newslttr Editor, Indust Engrg Div 1975-76, Secy, Indust Engrg Div 1977-78, Chm, Indust Engrg Div 1978-83, Am Soc Engrg Ed; Mem, Engrg Accreditation Comm, Soc Mfg Engrs; Secy/Treas Austin Br 1965-66, Mem, Res Com, Tech Coun Water Resources Planning & Mgmt 1972-74, Chm Res Com, Water Resources Planning & Mgmt Div 1974-75, ASCE; Fac Advr, Opers Res Soc Am, 1969-71; VP, Inst Mgmt Sci, 1971-72; VP, Univs Coun Water Resources, 1972-74; Mem, Am Assn Engrg Soc; Editor, Marcel Dekker Pub Co; Chm, Nat E-CAM; Mem, Engrg Legis Task Force Nat Assn St Univs & Land-Grant Cols; Conslt, Ofc Technol Assessmt, 1982-; Conslt, Computer Graphics Intl Inc; Conslt, TX Gov's Ofc; Conslt, Water Resources Engrs Inc; Conslt, Envir for Tomorrow Inc; Conslt, Kaiser Engrs Inc; r/Bapt; hon/

Author of Num Pubs; Outstg Yg Engr, 1966, TX Soc Profl Engrs; Tau Beta Pi, Alpha Pi Mu, Phi Kappa Phi, Chi Epsilon, Sigma Xi, Hon Soc; W/W: Am, MW, S & SW, Engrg, Technol Today, World; Am Men & Wom Sci; DIB; Intl W/W Engrg; Men Achmt.

MEIJER, PAUL HERMAN ERNST oc/Professor of Physics, Physicist; b/ Nov 14, 1921; h/1438 Geranium Street, Northwest, Washington, DC 20064; ba/ Washington, DC; m/Marianne S; c/ Onko (dec), Miriam, Daniel, Mark & Corinne; p/Herm W (dec) and Elisabet A A Meijer-Kossman, Wassenaar, Netherlands; sp/Egon and Olga Schwarz (dec); ed/Bach, Technol Univ Delft, 1942; Doct, Univ Leyden, 1951; pa/Leyden 1952-53; Case Inst Technol 1953-54; Duke Univ 1954-55; Univ DE 1955-56; Cath Univ Am 1956-; Nat Bur Standards 1960-; Am Phy Soc; European Phy Soc; Phy Soc Netherlands; Intl Assn Math Physicists; Sigma Xi; Fdn Am Sci; AAUP; hon/Author of Num Pubs; Guggenheim Fellow, 1956; Fulbright F'ship, 1953; Sr Fulbright Scholar, 1978; Vis'g Prof Univ Paris; W/W; Am Men Sci.

MELDON, GERI MICHELLE oc/ Jewelry Designer; b/Feb 4, 1944; h/Suite 316-1187 Coast Village Road Number 1, Montecito, CA 93108; ba/Montecito, CA; p/Paul and Rhoda Meldon (dec); ed/ Stephens Col 1962-63; Parsons Sch Design 1963-64; Cleveland Inst Art 1964-68; Dipl Silversmithing 1968; Gemological Inst Am 1968-69; Grad Gemologist Residence Dipl 1969; CA Lifetime Tchg Credentials Adult Ed, Univ CA-LA 1972; CA St Univ, BA, 1974; pa/Instr Jewelry & Design, LA Dept Rec & Pks, 1970-76; Retail Sales, May Co Fine Jewelry 1974-75, Tiffany & Co 1975-77, Slavick's Jewelers 1977; Instr Jewelry Retailing & Am Gem Soc Course Selling & Merchandising at Gemological Inst Am, 1977-78; Free-Lance Jewelry Designer, 1970-; CA Jewelers Assn; Nat Assn Jewelry Appraisers; Mfg Jewelers & Silversmiths Am; r/Ch Rel Sci, Secy Ch Guild & Newslttr Art Editor, Ventura Co Ch Rel Sci, 1980-84; hon/Recip 2nd Pl Awd 1980, 1st Pl, 2nd Pl, Most Orig, 1981, 1st Pl & Best in Show, 1982, Oxnard CA Cake Decorating Competition; W/ W: Jewelry Indust, CA, Am Wom.

MELENDEZ, PEDRO SEGUNDO oc/ Teacher and Student; b/Aug 6, 1950; h/ 4835 Moorhead Avenue, Boulder, CO 80303; ba/Boulder, CO; m/Teresinha Pereira; c/Pedro Alberto; p/Alberto and Ema Paez de Melendez, Chile; sp/ Pindaro de Paula Pereira (dec) and Albertina, Brazil; ed/BA 1980, MA 1982, Univ CO; pa/Tchg Asst, Dept Spanish & Portuguese, Univ CO, 1980-82; Editor, 1982; Pres, Sigma Selta Pi, 1981-82, Univ CO; hon/Author of Num Pubs incl'g "La Revolucion Mexicana Bajo el Punto de Vista de Los de Abajo", *Vida Universitaria*, 1978, "Relacoes Diplomaticas entre os Estados Unidos e a Uniao Sovietica", *Revista do Ateneu Angrense de Letras, 1982*, "Noche", *International Poetry*.

MELLICHAMP, JOSEPHINE WEAVER oc/Writer/Historian; b/Sep 30, 1923; h/1124 Reeder Circle, Northeast, Atlanta, GA 30306; ba/Huntsville, AL, Atlanta, GA; m/Stiles A Sr; c/Stiles A Jr, Joseph Capers III; p/James

Thomas Hampton Weaver and Bonnie Clyde Bauguess Weaver (dec); sp/Joseph Capers Sr and Annie Pearce Mellichamp (dec); ed/BA, Emory & Henry Col, 1943; Att'd Grad Sch, Emory Univ, 1950-51; pa/HS Eng Tchr, Lansing & Jefferson HS, 1943-50; Edit Asst, Emory Univ, 1951-53; Free Lance Writer, 1953-75; Libn 1957-79, Asst Hd Libn, Atlanta Constit; Price Comparer, Macy's, 1944; Clerical Wkr, E I du Pont de Nemours, 1944; Annual Assoc Mem, Am Biographical Inst; Annual Assoc & Nat Advr, ABIRA; Annual Fellow, Intl Biogrpahical Assn; Patron, Mem, Dixie Coun Authors & Journalists Inc; Donor, Sponsor, DCAJ's Annual Josephine Mellichamp Jour Awd, 1979-; Mem, IPA; Nat Leag Am Pen Wom Inc; SEn Writers Assn Inc; Atlanta Writers Clb; cp/Atlanta Hist Soc; Village Writers Grp Inc; Friends of Emory Univ Libs; Smithsonian Assoc; r/Meth; hon/Author of *Senators from GA*, 1976, *GA Heritage*; GA Author Yr, 1976; Emory & Henry Sigma Mu S'ship Awd, 1941; Mem 1974, Bd Vice Chm 1976, Atlanta Jour-Constit Employee's One-Pledge Plan Bd Trustees U Way; Contemp Authors; Intl Authors & Writers W/W; World W/W Wom; Intl W/W Intells; Intl Register Profiles; DIB; 2000 Notable Ams; 5000 Personalities World; Intl Book Hon.

MELVILLE, THOMAS ROBERT oc/ University Lecturer, Consultant; b/Dec 5, 1930; h/830 East 24th Street, Houston, TX 77009; ba/Houston, TX; m/ Margarita Bradford Furber; c/Margarita I and Thomas A; p/Arthur G and Isabelle M Melville, Newton, MA; sp/Andrew (dec) and Dolores Bradford, El Paso, TX; ed/BA 1952, MRE 1957, Univ St NY; MA 1973, PhD 1976, Am Univ; pa/ Missionary, Fgn Mission Soc Am, 1957-67; Grad Studies Res, Am Univ, 1968-73; Prof, Cath Univ Chile, 1973-75; Lectr, Univ Houston, 1976-; cp/VP, Rio Grande Assoc, 1979-; Fellow, Am Anthropological Assn, 1977-; Mem, Latin Am Anthropological Soc, 1977-; Mem, Soc Applied Anthropology, 1977-; r/Rom Cath; hon/Author of Num Articles & Pubs incl'g *Whose Heaven, Whose Earth?* 1971; Am Univ Grad Student F'ship, 1969-73; Rabinowitz Foun Res S'ship, 1973-75; Nat Inst Mtl Hlth Doct F'ship, 1976-77.

MELVIN, PETER JOSEPH oc/ Mathematical Astronomer, Aerospace Engineer; b/Mar 12, 1944; h/10772 19th Avenue Southwest, Seattle, WA 98146; ba/Tukwila, WA; m/Alice Sue; c/Robert Dennis, Chloe Ann; p/William L Melvin, Seattle, WA, and Virginia Smith, Seattle, WA; m/Max and Ruby Turner, Champaign, IL; ed/BA, Wn Wash St Col, 1965; MS 1966, PhD 1970, Univ IL; pa/ NASA Trainee, Univ IL, 1966-68; Res Asst 1968-70, Instr Phy Sci 1970-72, Asst Prof 1972-77, Vis'g Res Assoc, Applied Math Div, Nat Bur Standards, 1977; Sr Engr, Martin Marietta Denver Aerospace, 1977-80; Staff Engr 1980-83, Sr Spec Engr, Boeing Computer Sers, Engrg Technol Applications Div, 1983-; Mem, AIAA; hon/Author of Num Pubs; W/W: MW, W.

MENAKER, LEWIS oc/Associate Dean; b/Apr 15, 1942; h/1132 14th Street South, Birmingham, AL 35205; ba/Birmingham, AL; p/David and Sophie Menaker, Norwich, CT 06360; ed/DMD, Tufts Univ, 1964; Dsc, MIT,

402

1971; mil/USAF, 1965-69; pa/Asst Prof, Investigator 1971-73, Assoc Prof, Scist 1973-77, Asst Dean Adm Affairs 1975, Prof Dentistry 1977, Sr Scist 1977, Chm Depts Oral Biol, Commun & Prev Dentistry 1983, Assoc Dean Acad Affairs 1981, Univ AL; Am Dental Assn; AAAS; Am Soc Prev Dentistry; Intl Assn Dental Res; AL Soc Prev Dentistry; Royal Soc Promotion Hlth, Nutrition Today Soc; AL Dental Assn; B'ham Dist Dental Soc; Am Assn Dental Schs; r/Jewish; hon/Author of Num Pubs incl'g *Biologic Basis Wound Healing*, 1975, *Biologic Basis Dental Caries* 1984; Univ CT, Tuition S'ship, 1959, 1960; Tufts Univ Sch Dental Med, Jr & Sr S'ships; Robert R Andrews Res Soc; Sr Hon Progs Tufts Univ; MIT-NIDR Post Doct F'ship 1967-71; Sigma Xi; First Pl, Am Dental Assn-Johnson & Johnson Preventive Dentistry Awd, 1975; Omicron Delta Kappa, UAB Circle, Nat Ldrship Hon Soc; Cert Apprec, VA, 1982; Fellow Am Col Dentists, 1984; W/W: Hlth, S & SW, Frontier Sci & Technol; Personalities S.

MENDELS, JOSEPH oc/Physician/ Psychiatrist; b/Oct 29, 1937; h/37 Greenhill Lane, Philadelphia, PA 19151; ba/Philadelphia, PA; m/Ora; c/Gilla Avril, Charles Alan, David Ralph; p/ Max and Lily Mendels, Mowbry Cape, S Africa; sp/Dr & Mrs Wilfred Kark; ed/MB, ChB Univ Cape Town, 1954; MD, 1960; pa/Res Fellow, Univ NC Sch Med, 1965-67; Prof, Univ PA Sch Med & VA Hosp; Chief Depression Res Prog; Dir, Psychopharm Prog, 1967-80; Pres, Med Dir, Therapeutics Inc & Phila Med Inst, 1981; Fellow, Am Col Neuropsychopharm; Fdg Mem, Royal Col Psychi; r/Jewish; hon/Author of *Concepts Depression* 1970, *Biol Psychi* 1973; Lester N Hofheimer Awd Dist'd Res, Am Psychi Assn, 1976; W/W: US, World, Frontier Sci & Technol.

MENDELSON, SOL oc/Scientist/ Educator; b/Oct 10, 1926; h/446 West 25th Street, New York, NY 10001; p/ David C and Frieda Cohen Mendelson; ed/BS cum laude, CCNY; MS 1957, PhD 1961, Columbia Univ; pa/Current Res in Phy Behavior Crystalline Mats & Scholarly Endeavors; Made Significant Discoveries in Mech Behavior of Solids, Epitaxial Growth of Semiconductor Films & Theory of Mechs for Diffusionless Phase Transformations; Prof Physics & Engrg, Baruch Col CCNY; Sr Scist, Bendex Res Labs (Southfield, MI) 1967-68; Other Positions; Am Phy Soc; Am Soc Metals; Metall Soc AIME; Mats Res Soc; NY Acad Scis; Am Assn Physics Tchrs; AAAS; Fdn Am Scist; hon/ Contbr Num Articles Profl Jours; Sigma Xi; Tau Beta Pi; Pi Tau Sigma; Biol Listings.

MENDEZ, ANA G h/573 Abolicion Street, Hato Rey, PR 00912; m/Jose Mendez Rivera; c/Dora, Grecia, Jose F; p/Francisco Gonzalez Monge, Mayaguez, PR and Ana Confresi Sanchez, Cabo Rojo, PR; ed/BS, Univ PR, 1940; MA, NY Univ, 1948; HHD, Cath Univ PR, 1975; pa/CoFdr, Dir, PR HS Commerce, 1941-52; Pres Bd, PR Jr Col, 1952-; Lecturing Prof, Univ PR, Bus Dept, Sch Bus Adm; Fdr PR Elem Sch, 1950; Cord Adm Dean 1949-51, Pres 1952-69, PR Jr Col Foun, 1969-70; Pres 1970-74, Spec Advr Bd Dirs 1974-, Ana G Mendez Ednl Foun; Pres, Edit Turabo Inc, 1975; Tchrs Assn PR, 1949-;

NEA, 1950-; Am Assn Jr Cols Comm Admissions, 1957-59; AAUW, 1957-; Academia de Artes y Ciencias de PR, 1965; Assn Cols & Univs PR, Pres, 1969-70; S'ship Fund, Grand Union PR, Chm, 1969-; Assn Commun & Jr Cols, Mem Bd Dirs, 1972-75; Num Coms incl'g Gov's Com Employmt of Physically Handicapped, Chm, 1961-75; St Comm Higher Ed, 1964; Consejo Consultivo de Instruccion Vocacional, Chm, 1973; Small Bus Adv Bd PR, Mem, 1964, 1976; PR St Fdn BPW Clb, Pres, 1957-59; Intl Conf Rehab Social Com, Mem, 1959; Ednl Com Preven Accidents PR, Chm, 1962-64; Coun Preven Accidents, Pres, 1964-74; ARC, PR Chapt Pres, 1963-65; Mem 1974, Campaign Chm 1975, Chm Bd Govs 1976, U Fund PR; White House Conf Chd & Yth Com Social Wel, 1960; hon/Author of Num Pubs; Delta Pi Epsilon, 1948; Phi Theta Kappa, Hon Mem, 1961; Num TV & Public Appearances; Citizen of Yr, Dept Ed PR, 1959; Cit Semi-Finalist, Lane Bryant Awd, 1960; Hon by PR Fdn BPW Clb, 1964; Medal Merit, Am Legion Dept PR, 1970; Top Mgmt Awd, Sales & Mktg Execs Assn, 1972; Proclaimed One of Outstg Wom Intl Yr, 1975; Pontificial Medal, 1975.

MENDIK, BERNARD H oc/Real Estate Developer; b/May 24, 1929; h/ 207 East 71st Street, New York, NY 10021; ba/New York, NY; m/Susan; c/ Laurie, Kevin, Todd; p/Michael and Yetta Mendik, New York, NY; sp/Alex (dec) and Jean Batkin, New York, NY; ed/BBA 1955, LLB 1958, CCNY; Mem, NY Bar, 1958-; mil/AUS, 1950-53; pa/ Ptnr, Silverstein & Mendik, 1957-78; Owner, Mendik Co, 1978-; Gov, Real Est Bd NY, 1981-; Mem, Bds Rlty Foun NY; Rlty Advr Bd Labor Relats; Trustee Citizens Budget Com Inc; Mem, Bd Trustee Montafiore Med Ctr & Moshula Preserv Com; Past Pres, Mem, Bd Jewish Guild Blind & Guild's Nsg Home; NYU Adj Assoc Prof; r/Hebrew; hon/NY Law Sch Review, 1955-58; NYU Awd Tchg Excell, 1981.

MERCE, ANNE MARIE oc/Reinsurance Underwriter; b/Nov 5, 1947; h/ 189 Princeton Arms North, Cranbury, NJ 08512; ba/Princeton, NJ; p/Russel Merce, Guernsey, OH, and Leona Mae Berry Merce, Cranbury, NJ; ed/BMus Ed, Westminster Choir Col, 1972; pa/ Tchr & Ednl Conslt, Nat Keyboard Arts Assocs, 1972-73; Homeowners Ins Underwriter, Walter B Howe Inc, 1973-74; Adm Asst to Pres 1974-79, Asst VP 1980-, E D Sayer Inc; Mem, Nat Assn Female Execs Inc; Mem, APIW Inc; Mem, Am Soc Profl & Exec Wom; r/Bapt; hon/Recorded Album, "Amazing Grace", 1983; Dean's List, 1972; Music Edrs Assn Gold Cert w Hons, 1960; W/ W am Wom.

MERRILL, MAURICE HITCH-COCK oc/Lawyer, Arbitrator; b/Oct 3, 1897; h/800 Elm Avenue, Norman, OK 73069; ba/Norman, OK; m/Orpha Anita Roberts (dec); c/Jean Merrill Barnes; p/ George and Mary Hitchcock Merrill (dec); sp/James Lafayette Roberts (dec); ed/BA 1919, LLB 1922, Univ OK; SJD, Harvard Univ, 1925; mil/AUS, 1918; pa/ Student Asst 1918-19, Instr 1919-22, Prof 1936-68, Res Prof 1952-68, Acting Dean 1945-46, Univ OK; Lwyr, 1922-26; Assoc Prof, Univ ID, 1925-26; Asst Prof 1926-28, Prof 1928-36, Univ

NE; Atty, Univ OK Res Inst, 1951-72; Grand Counsel, Bar Assn, 1971-; Supr Ct OK, 1965-68; Pres, 1964-65, Cleveland Bar Assn; Natl Acad Arbitrators, 1962-; OK Bar Assn, 1922-; Am Bar Assn, 1946-; r/Meth Epis; hon/Author of Num Pubs; Dist'd Ser Cit, Univ So OK, 1968; Pres Awd, OK Bar Assn, 1972; Upton W Summers Awd, 1964; Order Humane Lttrs, OK Christian Col, 1974; W/W: Am, Am, World; Ency Am Scholars.

MERRIWEATHER, MARIE ANTI-ONETTE oc/Graphic Artist, Illustrator; b/Mar 2, 1955; h/3001 South King Drive, Suite 203, Chicago, IL 60616; ba/ Same; p/Richard and Florence Merriweather, Chgo, IL; ed/Att'd No IL Univ; BFA, Chgo St Univ, 1977; pa/Graphic Artist, Teddy Bear Graphics, Pres 1983-; Edit Cartoonist, Chgo Daily Defender, 1981-83; Graphic Artist, No IL Univ, 1976-77; Advtg Asst, Tatham-Laird & Kupner Adv, 1978-80; Dir, Bear Care Sum Art Prog; Assn Am Edit Cartoonists; Art Inst Chgo; cp/ Chgo Coun Fgn Relats; Teddy Bear Clb; Sigma Gamma Rho Sorority, VP; r/ Cath; hon/Author of Num Articles; TV Appearances; Kizzy Image & Achmt Awd, 1982; Chgo Maj Sports Assn, 1981, 1982.

MERTA, PAUL JAMES oc/Cartoonist; h/4831 Myrtle Avenue, Sacramento, CA 95841; ba/Sacramento, CA & Hilo, HI; p/Stanley F Merta, Sacramento, CA, and Mary Ana Merta (dec); ed/AA, Bakersfield Jr Col, 1962; BS, San Jose St Col, 1962; mil/AF, 1962-; pa/ Cartoonist, Nat Mags, 1959-; Civilian Electronics Engr, AF/Missiles San Bernardino, ALC, CA, 1962-65; Electronics Countermeasures Engr; Acquisition Prog Mgr, Airlogistics Command, Sacramento, CA, 1965; TV Film Animator; Owner, Merge Films, 1965-; Owner, The Photo Poster Fac, 1971-; Owner, Restaurant "La Rosa Blanca", Sacramento, 1980-; Polit Cartoonist, CA Jour, 1958-59; Sacramento U, 1979; Sacramento Legal Jour, 1979-; Ardvark Mag, 1979; Host/Prodr, "Gasp Theatre", ChL 40, Sacramento, 1980-; Bldr, Rentals HI, 1980-; hon/W/W W.

MESKELL, UNA oc/Mental Health Nurse Specialist, Educator; b/Mar 9, 1947; h/3235 Grand Concourse, Bronx, NY 10468; ba/Bronx, NY; p/Mr and Mrs Stephen Meskell, Queens, NY; ed/MS, Hunter Col, 1981; BA, Marymount Manhattan Col, 1976; St Clare's Hosp Sch Nsg, 1968; pa/Staff Nurse 1968-69, Hd Nurse Psychotherapeutic Nsg 1969-72, Evening Nurse Supvr 1972-76, Nsg Supvr Days Psychi 1976-80, Bronx Mun Hosp Ctr; Mtl Hlth Nurse Spec, Hebrew Hosp Chronic Sick 1980-; Clin Instr, Med Aid Tng Ctr, 1982-; Conslt 1980-; Lectr 1978-; Mem, Commun Bd Bronx Mun Hosp Ctr, 1979-80; Grievance Chwom Bronx Mun Hosp Ctr Unit, NY St Nurses Assn, 1975-80; Nat Leag Nsg, Marymount Manhattan Col Alumni Assn; St Clare's Hosp Nsg Sch Alumni Assn; Hunter Col Alumni Assn; AAUW; r/Rom Cath; hon/Hon Grad, 1976; W/W Am Wom.

MESSNER, JOSEPH A oc/Child Wel Executive; b/Mar 1, 1924; h/Rapidsview 7, Gloucester, Ontario K1G 3N3; ba/ Ottawa, Ontario; m/Linda; c/Patricia M, William D, Peter U; ed/Gymnasium, Matura, 1942; Akademisch Geprufter

Ubersetzer, 1948; Diplom Dolmetscher, 1949; Philosophicum, 1949; mil/ 1942-46; pa/Investigator, USDP Screening Mission, Austria, 1949; Sect Hd, Intl Refugee Org, Austria, 1951; Lectr, US Info Ctr, Austria, 1952; Social Wkr, Cath Wel Bur, Ontario, 1952-54; Exec Dir, Cath Chd's Aid Soc, Ontario, 1954-65; Spec Lectr, McMaster Univ, Ontario, 1954-65; Exec Dir, Chd's Aid Soc, Ottawa/Carleton, 1965-; Nat Exec Dir, Friends of SOS-Chd's Villages, Canada, 1969-; Bid Dirs, CAS; Treas, Bd Dir, SOS; Bd Dirs, OACAS; r/Rom Cath; hon/Author of "Day Care-Right or Remedy", *Canadian Wel*, "SOS—Chd's Village, A Viable Alternative", *SOS-Messenger*; Ontario Sports Awds; W/ W: E, Sports; Canadian W/W.

MESZAROS, PEGGY JEAN SISK oc/ Professor and Associate Dean; b/Apr 3, 1938; h/1111 Woodcrest Drive, Stillwater, OK 74074; ba/Stillwater, OK; m/Alexander Louis; c/Lisa, Elizabeth, Louis; p/Mr and Mrs Eugene L Sisk, Hopkinsville, KY; sp/Mr and Mrs Alex Meszaros, Bethlehem, PA; ed/BS, Austin Peay St Univ, 1963; MS, Univ KY, 1972; PhD, Univ MD, 1977; pa/Assoc Dean, Prof, OK St Univ, 1979-; St Supvr Home Ec, MD St Dept Ed, 1977-79; Dept Chp Home Ec, Assoc Prof, Hood Col, 1973-77; Home Ec Tchr, Omaha, NE, 1972-73; Home Ec Tchr, Hopkinsville, KY, 1963-67; Num Res Activs incl'g Full Grad Fac Status, Hood Col, 1977, OK St Univ, 1979-; Devel Attitude Scale for Advrs of Student Orgs, 1978; Devel, Conducted Eval Plan for So Reg Home Ec Wkshop Communication, 1981; Num Consltg & Public Ser incl'g NC Ext Home Ec Prog Review, 1982; St Team Eval Home Ec Dept, Union Col, 1975; Assn Admrs Home Ec Long Range Planning Com, 1981-; Bd Dirs 1980-82, VP St Affil 1979-82, Chm Ad Hoc Code Ethics Com 1978-, Fin Com 1982-83, Am Home Ec Assn; VP 1982-83, Chm Home Ec Defined Com 1981-, OK Home Assn; Pres, MD Home Ec Assn, 1978-79; Br Coor, Fam & Wk Proj, 1981-, AAUW; Chm, 1981-82, So Reg Admrs Home Ec; Bd Dirs, FHA, 1976-80; Planning Com, 1981-82, Wkshop Emerging Admrs Home Ec; Am Coun Consumer Interests; World Future Soc; Nat Assn Wom Deans, Admrs, Cnslrs; AAHE; cp/Conslt Bd Dirs, Stillwater Arts & Humanities Coun, 1982; Tourism Com, Stillwater C of C, 1981-; Info Ofcr, Lahoma Newcomers, 1981-81; r/Epis, St Andrews Epis Ch, Christian Ed Com, 1981-83, Vestry, 1983-86; hon/Author of Num Pubs incl'g "Ldrship Devel: A Basic Issue Home Economists" *IL Tchr Contemp Roles* 1980, "Lttr to St Pres" *AHEA Action* 1981; EPDA Fellow, 1976-77; Outstg Edrs Am, 1975; Kappa Delta Pi; Kappa Omicron Phi; Phi Delta Kappa; Phi Upsilon Omicron; W/W Am Wom; Selected "Most Likely to Succeed As Admr", Admrs Agri, Forestry & Home Ec, KS St Univ, 1980.

METCALF, ROGER DALE SR oc/ Dentist; b/Jul 24, 1950; h/5608 Trails Edge Drive, Arlington, TX 76017; ba/ Arlington, TX; m/Linda Susan Cervenka; c/Roger Dale Jr, Kellie Anne; p/ Frank Metcalf, Ft Worth, TX, and Pauline (dec); sp/Robert and Lucille Cervenka, Waco, TX; ed/BS 1973, DDS 1977, Baylor Univ; pa/Pvt Dental Pract,

1977-; VP, Arlington Univ, Am Cancer Soc, 1982; Am Dental Assn; TX Dental Assn; Ft Worth Dist Dental Soc, 1977; Acad Gen Dentistry, 1979; Delta Upsilon Frat, 1970; r/Bapt; hon/Author of "Nix Lost Pix" *Mod Photo* 1982, "More on Dentistry & Healing" *Jour Am Dental Assn* 1976; Am Dental Soc Anesthesiology Graduation Awd, 1977; MENSA, 1980; Alpha Epsilon Delta, 1972; Beta Beta Beta, 1972; W/W S & SW, Dallas.

METZ, MARY S oc/College President; b/May 7, 1937; h/President's House, Mills College, Oakland, CA 94613; ba/Oakland, CA; m/F Eugene; c/ Mary Eugena; ed/BA summa cum laude, Furman Univ, 1958; PhD magna cum laude, LA St Univ, 1966; pa/Prof 1976-81, Provost, Dean Acad Affairs 1976-81, Hood Col; Assoc Prof French 1972-76, Tenured 1972, Asst Prof 1966-67, 1968-72, Instr 1965-66, Asst to Chancellor 1975-76, Spec Asst Chancellor & Am Coun Ed Fellow Acad Adm 1974-75, Dir Elem & Intermediate Progs 1966-74, LA St Univ; Vis'g Asst Prof French, 1967-68, Univ CA Berkeley; Govt Relats Adv Coun, Nat Assn Indep Cols & Univ, 1982-85; Edit Bd, 1982-85, "Liberal Ed"; VP, Wn Col Assn, 1982-84; Exec Com, 1982, Assn Indep CA Cols & Univs; Bus-Higher Ed Forum, Am Coun Ed, 1981-; Del Assem, 1976-78, Mod Lang Assn; S Ctl Mod Lang Assn, 1966-76; AAUW, 1972-76; Zonta, 1976-80; Delta Kappa Gamma, 1975-80; AAUP, 1966-; Phi Kappa Phi, 1966-; Exec Com, LA Conf Cols & Univs, 1975; cp/Nat Bd Nat Ednl Film Fest, 1983; Citizens' Com Selection of Supt Schs, 1981; Frederick Preserv Advrs, 1976-81; Commun Commons, 1978-81; Gov's Task Force Wom & Credit, LA, 1975-76; Adv Bd Baton Rouge Mtl Hlth Vol Prog, 1970-74; Num Col & Univ Com Ser; hon/Num Pubs incl'g *Reflets du Monde Francais* 1971, 1978, Le Francais a Vivre 1972, 1978; Phi Beta Kappa, 1980; Dist'd Alumni Awd, 1977; Am Coun Ed Fellow Acad Adm, 1974-75; Outstg Edrs Am, 1972; Fulbright F'ship to France, 1962-63; S'ship Cup, 1958; Intl W/W Ed; World W/W Wom in Ed; Personalities S; DIB; World W/W Wom; Contemp Authors; Outstg Edrs Am; W/W Am Cols & Univs.

MEYER, CALVIN FLOYD oc/Principal; b/Sep 17, 1943; h/212 Greenfield Road, Columbia, SC 29206; ba/Columbia, SC; m/Shirley Ann Meadows; c/ Larry Calvin, Christopher Patrick, Janet Renee; p/Mrs Sue Meyer, Columbia, SC; sp/Mrs Ethel Meadows, Lake Wales, FL; ed/BA 1965; MRE 1968; MA 1973; PhD 1971; EdD 1979; pa/Prin 1981-, Asst Prin 1978-81, Admin Asst 1976-78, Tchr 6th Grade 1975-76, Richland Sch Dist 2; Adj Prof, Univ SC, 1980; Tchr 4th-5th Grade, Polk Co FL, 1973-75; Tchr 5th, Jefferson Co KY, 1977-73; Min Ed, Val View Bapt, Louisville, KY, 1972-72; Tchr, Creston HS, 1968-70; Tchr, Remount Bapt Sch, 1965-66; Pastor, Oakview Bapt Ch, 1968-70; Pastor, Bethel Bapt Ch, 1974-75; NAASP; ASCD; Sec'dy Curric Chm; SCASA, Pub Com; SCASCD, Per Recog Com; Gideons PTA, 1978-82; Nat Mid Sch Assn; Palmetto Tchrs Assn; SCEA; NEA 1976-80; r/So Bapt; hon/ Author of Num Articles incl'g "Back to Basics: Making Dick & Jane Read" *The*

Palmetto Schmaster 1981; Cum Laude, Carson Newman Bapt Col, 1965; Phi Alpha Theta, 1965; Nom'd Outstg Am Citizen, 1975; Nom'd SC Honoree, 1980; Outstg Sch Admr, SC Assn Sch Admrs, 1982; W/W: KY, S & SW.

MEYER, DANA JO oc/Director of Sales; b/Dec 12, 1949; h/Post Office Box 691, Solana Beach, CA 92075; ba/La Jolla, CA; m/Robert Brandt; p/Dr and Mrs William Dickson, Houston, TX; sp/ Mr and Mrs George Meyer, St Louis, MO; ed/Univ TX; pa/Dir Sales, La Jolla Village Inn, 1978-; Reg Sales Mgr, Holiday Inns, 1972; ABWA, 1983-84; Bd Meeting Planners Assn, 1983; cp/Bd Dirs, Country Friends, 1980; r/Luth; hon/Miss Houston 1972; Miss TX 1972; Mrs Am 1st Runner-up 1978; W/W: So Wom, CA, W.

MEYER, PAUL JAMES oc/Business Executive; b/May 21, 1928; ba/Waco, TX; m/Jane Gurley; c/James Jr, Larry, Bill, Janna, Leslie; p/August Carl and Isabel Rutherford Meyer (dec); mil/ AUS, Paratroopers, 1946-48; pa/Ins Sales, 1948-57; Sales Exec, Word Inc, 1958-59; Fdr, Success Motivation Inst Inc, 1960-; Am Mgmt Assn; Am Franchise Assn; Nat Spkrs Bur; cp/Mem, Waco C of C; Dir, U Negro Col Fund; BSA; Dir, Baylor-Waco Foun; Devel Coun, Waco Hillcrest Meml Hosp; Dir, Vanguard Sch; Co-Owner, Lakewood Tennis & Country Clb; Bd Mem, Waco Boys' Clb; Bd Mem, Waco Boys' Clb Foun; Bd Mem, Retina Foun SW; Bd Mem, Haggai Inst Adv'd Ldrship, Singapore; Mem, Nat Repub Fin Com, 1964; r/Bapt; hon/Author of Num Pubs incl'g "Dynamics Personal Motivation", "How to Become Financially Indep"; Nat Sales Ldrship Awd, Houston Sales Execs Clb; 1977 Man/Boy Awd, Waco Boys' Clb; Achmt Awd, Success Clb Great Brit; Americanism Awd, Houston JCs; Hon VP, Sales Execs Clb S Africa; Hon Dr Aviation Ed Deg, Embry-Riddle Aeronaut Univ; Hon Dr Humane Lttrs Deg, Ft Lauderdale Univ; Spec Cit, Haggai Inst Adv'd Ldrship, Singapore; Freedoms Foun Awd, 1983; DIB; Notable Ams; Notable Personalities Am; Personalities S; Am Registry Series; Commun Ldrs & Noteworthy Ams; Men Achmt; Intl W/W Commun Ser; W/W: S & SW, Am.

MEYER, PHYLLIS BARBARA oc/ Travel Agency Owner/Executive; b/Sep 12, 1942; h/3409 Leawood Drive, Omaha, NE 68123; ba/Bellevue, NE; c/ Michael B; p/Mr and Mrs H W Bland, Union Springs, AL; ed/AA, Gulf Park Col, 1962; Univ NE, 1973; pa/Mgr, Eielson AFB Aero Clb, 1969-71; Sales Mgr, NE Clothing, 1973-75; Exec VP, TV Travel Inc, 1975-82; Pres, Travel ETC Inc, 1979-82; Pres/Owner, TV Travel Bellevue Inc, 1982-; Nat Assoc Female Execs; Am Soc Travel Agts; cp/ C of C, VP, 1982-84; Dir, Inst Career Advmt Needs Inc, 1982-83; YWCA, Fin 1980; ALTRUSA; r/Prot; hon/Outstg Chm, 1981-82; Bd Dirs, A Growing Concern Inc; Conslt, Royal Tours Travel; W/W Am Wom.

MEYER, WALTER oc/Director Syracuse University Institute for Energy Research; b/Jan 19, 1932; h/17 Horseshoe Lane, Chittenango, NY 13037; ba/ Syracuse, NY; m/Jacqueline; c/Kim, Holt, Eric, Leah, Suzannah; p/Walter and Ruth Killoran Meyer (dec); ed/

BSChE 1956, Masters Chem Engrg 1957, Syracuse Univ; PhD, OR St Univ, 1964; NSF, Sci Fac Fellow, OR St Univ & MIT, 1962-63; pa/Dir, Inst Energy Res, Niagara Mohawk Energy Prof, Syracuse Univ, 1982-; Prof, Chm Nuclear Engrg 1972-82, CoChm, Fdr Energy Sys & Resources Prog 1974-82, Univ MO; Mem, Bd Dirs, Am Nuclear Soc, 1981-84; Chm, Public Info Com, 1974-79; Chm. Nuclear Engrg Div, AIChE, 1979-80; Am Chem Soc; Touring Lectr, 1976-80, 1982; r/Presb; hon/ Author of Num Articles; Named 1st Niagara Mohawk Energy Prof, Syracuse Univ, 1982; Robert Lee Tatum, Prof Engrg, Univ MO, 1976-82; W/W: US, MW.

MEYERS, CAROL L oc/Archaeology of Religion; b/Nov 26, 1942; h/3202 Waterbury Drive, Durham, NC 27707; ba/Durham, NC; m/Eric M; c/Julie Kaete, Dina Elisa; p/Dr Harry and Irene Lyons, Kingston, PA; sp/Shirlee Meyers, Norwich, CT; ed/BA, Wellesley, 1964; MA 1966, PhD 1975, Brandeis Univ; pa/Asst Prof Dept Rel 1977-, Instr Ctr Cont'g Ed 1978-79, Vis'g Lectr 1976-77, Duke Univ; Conslt, WNET-TV, 1981-82; Conslt, Nat Geographic Soc, 1980; Vis'g Asst Prof 1979, Pt-time Lectr 1976-77, Lectr 1975, Univ NC—Chapel Hill; Conslt, Near En Pictorial Archives, 1975-76; Instr, Acad Jewish Studies Without Walls, 1974-78; Lectr, Hebrew Union Col Sum Sem, 1973-74; Lectr 1974, Assoc Dir 1978-, Core Staff, Field Archaeologist 1974, 1975, 1977, 1978, Meiron Excavation Proj; Lectr 1971, 1972, Area Supvr 1970-71, Jt Expedition Khirbet Shema; Tchg Asst, Boston Area Sem Intl Students, 1965-67; Edit Asst 1964-65, Asst Registrar 1963, Ashdod Excavation Proj; Field Supvr 1972, Area Supvr 1971, Jt Expedition Meiron; Area Supvr, Jt Expedition Tell Gezer, 1964-67; Vol, Masada Excavations, 1964-65; Vol, Tell Arad Excavations, 1964; Student Staff, Univ Chgo Excavations Beit Yerah, 1963; Student Staff, Harvard Peabody Mus Expedition Hell Gap, 1962; Trustee 1976-78, Com Archaeological Policy 1976-81, Com Pubs 1977-, F'ship Com 1979-, Am Schs Oriental Res; VP, NC Chapt Archaeological Inst Am, 1976; Am Del, Intl Conf Christians & Jews, 1976; Convener, Symp Archaeol Trade E Mediterranean, 1979; Edit Com, Dissertation Series Am Sch Oriental Res, 1978; Acad Com, World Jewish Cong Heritage Comm, 1978-; Corporate Rep Duke Univ Am Schs Oriental Res, 1980-; CoChp 1981, Steering Com 1982-, Sem Sociol of Monarchy, Soc Biblical Lit; Edit Com, Biblical Archaeologist, 1982-; VP, Albright Inst Archaeological Res, 1982-; Am Acad Rel; Assoc Jewish Studies; British Sch Archaeol Jerusalem; Cath Biblical Assoc; Israel Exploration Soc; Palestine Exploration Soc; Society Values Higher Ed; r/Jewish; hon/Author of Num Pubs incl'g "Jachin & Boax in Rel & Polit Perspective", Cath Biblical Qtrly 1983, "Jerusalem, Palestine, & the Jewish World: 200 BC to AD 200", 1983; Wellesley Col Scholar, 1962-64; Grant 1966, F'ship 1967-69, Brandeis Univ; Meml Foun Jewish Culture F'ship, 1968-69; Thayer Fellow, Albright Inst Archaeological Res, 1975-76; Undergrad Tchg Coun, Duke Univ, Grant, 1978-79; Cooperative Prog Judaic Stu-

dies, Pubs Grant, 1981; Res Coun Pubs Grant 1981, Res Coun Fac Sum F'ship 1981, Duke Univ; Nat Endowment Humanities, Indep Study & Res F'ship, 1982-83; Vis'g Scholar, Oxford Ctr Postgrad Hebrew Studies, 1982-83; Vis'g Fellow, Queen Elizabeth House, Oxford Univ, 1982-83; 5000 Personalities World; W/W: Am Wom, Wom World.

MEYERS, LARRY oc/Psychotherapist; b/Apr 5, 1933; h/1404 North Tustin Avenue, N-3, Santa Ana, CA 92701; ba/ Santa Ana, CA; m/Flora; c/Brian, Nathan, Debra, Dan; p/Kallman and Bettie Meyers (dec); sp/Samuel and Esther Heitzer (dec); ed/PhD Psych, 1983; PhD Human Behavior 1970; MA Hist, 1965; MA Rel Ed, 1956; BA Polit Sci/Sociol, 1954; pa/CA Psychological Ser Ctr; Jewish Ed; Univ CA-SD, SWn CC, Univ AL, Univ Bridgeport, Coastline CC, Pt-time Col Tchg, 1970-; Am Psychological Assn; Soc Clin & Exptl Hypnosis; APGA; Nat Assn Temple Edrs; r/Jewish; hon/Author of Nums Pubs incl'g Tchg Jewish Rel Sch, 1967; Four Curric Awds Jewish Ed Creat Contbn; DIB; W/W: W, World Jewry, S.

MEYERS, PATRICIA A oc/Manager of Newspaper; b/Oct 20, 1932; h/Route 2, Post Office Box 218, Forreston, IL 61030; ba/Forreston, IL; m/Richard D; c/Joey, Stuart, William, Robert; p/Elmer (dec) and Marie Brockmeier, Forreston, IL; sp/Harry Meyers, Forreston, IL, and Mary Duke, Polo, IL; ed/Att'd No IL Univ, 1950-51; pa/Acct, Micro Switch, 1951-57; Ofc Asst 1974-89, Mgr 1980-, Forreston Jour; r/Meth; hon/Former Yth F'Ship Ldr; W/W Am Wom.

MEYSTEDT, LUCILLE E oc/Hospital Night Supervisor; b/Nov 21, 1923; h/ Route 4, Box 259, Rusk, TX 75785; p/ Harry E and Mary Ethel Collins Scheper (dec); ed/Grad, Nsg Sch St Marys Sch Nsg, 1946; pa/Gen Duty Nsg, St Francis Hosp, 1947-49; Dir Nsg, Cape Osteopathic Hosp, 1949-51; Pvt Duty Nsg, 1952-55; Mgr Plumbing Co, 1951-62; Staff Nurse, SW MO Hosp, 1962-66; Night Supvr, Poplar Bluff Hosp, 1966-68; Dir, Nsg Mineral Area Osteopathic Hosp, 1968-70; Night Supvr, Rusk Meml Hosp, 1970-74, 1981-; Night Supvr, Newburn Meml Hosp, 1974-76; Night Supvr, Rusk St Hosp, 1976-; Nsg Advr, Fairview Nsg Home, 1958-64; Mem, 8th Dist Nsg Assn, 1950-; Mem, MO Nsg Assn, 1950-; Mem, Nat Nurses Assn, 1950-; cp/Pres, Secy/Treas, Obedience Chm, Show Chm, SW MO Kennel Clb, 1955-70; St Louis Pekingese Clb; Nat Pekingese Clb; Am Legion Aux, 1958-68; Pres Legion Aux, 1959-60; Chm, Nat Dog Wk, 1959-66; Chm, Nat Dog Wk Cherokee Co, 1970-74; Bi-Wkly TV Prog on Animal Care, 1962-66; Mem 1971-, Bd Mem 1971-72, Longview Kennel Clb; Assoc Mem, Italian Greyhound Clb, 1973; Mexican Kennel Clb, 1969-76; Am Kennel Clb Judge, 1970-; Mexican Kennel Clb Judge, 1972-; hon/Author of Num Articles; Recip Awd Outstg Wk Dog World, 1961; Personalities S; W/ W World.

MICHAEL, COLETTE VERGER oc/ Professor of French; b/May 3, 1937; h/ 5 Moraine Terrace, Dekalb, IL 60115; ba/Dekalb, IL; c/Barbara Joan, Peggy Ann, Monique Janine, Alan Marc, David Lawrence, Gerard Alexander; p/Ray-

mond Verger, Marseille; ed/BA Phil, MA Romance Lang, Univ WA; MA Hist Sci, PhD French, Univ WI, 1973; pa/ Lectr, Univ WI; Prof, Shimer Col; Prof French, No IL Univ, 1977-; Am Assn Tchrs French; cp/Am Philosophical Assn; African Lit Assn; 18th Century Studies Assn; hon/Author of Num Pubs incl'g Choderlos de Laclos: The Man, His Wks, & His Critics 1982; Ford F'Ship 1970-73; NEH F'Ship 1977.

MICHAEL, SHIRLEY PARISI oc/ President and Owner, Construction Corporation; b/Jan 2, 1941; h/192 Woodland Avenue, Summit, NJ 07901; ba/Union, NJ; m/Don; c/Renee, Don Jr, Edwin G Pastrof; p/John and Margaret Parisi, Garwood, NJ; ed/HS Grad; pa/ Comptroller, Crane & Co, 1959-71; Comptroller & Owner, Doorway to World Travel, 1971-74; Pres, Owner, Deerpath Constrn, 1974-; Pres, Owner, Rockwell Newman Co, 1978-; r/Cath; hon/W/W Bus & Fin in Am.

MICHAELS, HOWARD BRIAN oc/ Medical Physicist (Cancer Research and Treatment); b/May 29, 1949; h/51 Kentland Crescent, Willowdale, Ontario, Canada M2M 2X7; ba/Ontario, Canada; m/Lois S; ed/BA 1971, MS 1973, PhD 1976, Univ Toronto; pa/Asst Prof Radiol 1982-, Asst Prof Med Biophysics 1982-, Hd Div Clin Physics 1981-, Tutor 1974-75, Lab Demonstrator Physics Dept 1971-74, Univ Toronto; Chief Physicist, Toronto-Bayview Clin, 1981-; Asst Prof 1979-81, Res Fellow Radiation Therapy 1976-79, Harvard Univ; Asst Radiation Biophysicist 1978-81, Res Fellow 1976-78, MA Gen Hosp; Postdoct Fellow 1976, Sum Res Student 1969, 1970, Ontario Cancer Inst; Am Assn Physicists Med, 1977-; Assn Profl Engrs Province Ontario, 1976-; Canadian Assn Physicists: Div Med & Biol Physics, 1977-; Radiation Res Soc, 1973-; NE Soc Radiation Oncology, 1980-81; Engrg Inst Canada, 1967-71; hon/ Author of Num Pubs incl'g "On the Reaction of Hydrated Electrons w Oxygen", Radiation Physics & Chem 1977; Elected to Fac Coun, Univ Toronto Fac Applied Sci & Engrg, 1969-71; Del Cong Canadian Engrg Students, 1970; Second Mile Engr Awd, Univ Toronto, 1971; Hon Designation Conferred w Bach's Deg, 1971; 5th Intl Cong Radiation Res Travel Awd, 1974; Radiation Res Soc Travel Awd, 1976; Radiation Res Soc Yg Scist Awd, 1978; 6th Intl Cong Radiation Res Travel Awd, 1979; 7th Intl Cong Radiation Res Travel Awd, 1983; W/W Frontier Sci & Technol.

MICHEL, RICHARD CHRIS oc/ Research Economist; b/Dec 25, 1945; h/ 2103 1/2 S Street Northwest, Washington, DC 20008; ba/Washington, DC; p/ James P (dec) and Dina Noun Michel, Rochester, NY; ed/BA, Syracuse Univ, 1967; MPA, Wharton Grad Div, Univ PA, 1975; pa/Sr Economist, Ofc Secy Hlth, Ed, Wel, 1975, 1977-79; Assoc Analyst, Congl Budget Ofc, 1975-76; Sr Res Assoc, Urban Inst, 1976-77, 1979-; Am Economic Assn; Wn Economic Assn; cp/Wharton Clb Wash; Syracuse Clb Wash; r/Greek Orthodox; hon/W/W E.

MICHEL, WERNER oc/Executive Vice-President Television; b/Mar 5; h/ 1001 Casiano Road, Bel Air, CA 90049; ba/Los Angeles, CA; m/Rosemary; ed/ Univ Berlin; Univ Paris, PhD 1933; pa/

Radio Writer; Dir, Co-Author Two Broadway Revues, 1938, 1940; Dir, French Feature Films; Dir, Broadcast Div, Voice of Am, 1942-46; Prod, Dir 1946-48, Asst Prog Dir 1948-50, CBS; Dir, Kenyon & Eckhart TV Dept, 1950-52; Prod, DuMont TV Netwk, 1952-55; Dir, Electronicam TV-Film Prod, 1955-56; Prod, Benton & Bowles, Proctor & Gamble, 1956-57; VP & Dir, TV-Radio Dept, Reach, McClinton Advtg Inc, 1957-62; Conslt, TV Programming & Comml Prod, N W Ayer & Son Inc; VP, Dir, TV Dept, SSC & B Advtg, 1963; Prog Exec, ABC-TV Hollywood, 1975; Dir, Dramatic Progs, 1976; Sr VP, Creat Affairs, MGM-TV, 1977, 1980; Exec VP, Wrather Entertainment Intl, 1979; Guber-Peters/ Centerpoint Prods, 1983; r/Jewish.

MICHIELS, R VIC JR oc/Architect; b/Mar 18, 1938; h/1476 Indian Forest Trail, Stone Mountain, GA 30083; ba/ Norcross, GA; m/Bettye; c/R Vic III, Shahn, Channing; p/Campti, LA; sp/ Baton Rouge, LA; ed/BS 1963; BArch 1966; mil/AUS; pa/Locatell Inc 1968; Toombs, Amisano & Wells 1968; Saggus, Vaught, Spiker & Howell 1970; AIA; GA Assn Arch, Bd Dirs, 1976; cp/ Kiwanis Intl, Chapt Pres, 1981; GA Conservancy; Nat'l Hist Trust; r/Bapt; hon/AIA-Atlanta Chapt, Ser to Chapt, 1977; AIA Nat Conv, 1975, Spec Awd; W/W S & SW; Intl Biographe.

MICKELSEN, OLAF oc/Educator, Researcher, Human Nutrition, Retired; b/Jul 29, 1912; h/Route 1, Lula, GA 30554; ba/East Lansing, MI; m/Clarice Lewerenz; c/Elizabeth M Kurczynski, Margaret M Funk; p/Frederick and Marie Mickelsen (dec), Perth Amboy, NJ; sp/Roy Blass and Helene Krause Lewerenz (dec), Tomahawk, WI; ed/BS, 1935, Rutgers Univ; MS 1937, PhD 1939, Univ WI; pa/Chem, Univ Hosps 1939, Assoc Prof 1948, Univ MN; Chief Chem, USPHS, 1948; Chief Lab Biochem & Nutrition, NIAMD, NIH, USPHS, 1951; Prof, MI St Univ, 1962-79; Vis'g Prof, Tehran, Inst Nutrition Sci & Food Tech, 1977-79; Dist'd Vis'g Prof, Univ DE, 1979-81; Num Profl Contbns & Sers incl'g Edit Bd, Jour Agri & Food Chem, 1954-56; Mem, Sci Adv Com, Am Inst Baking, 1972-75; Am Bd Nutrition; 1963-66, Pres 1973-74, Fellow 1983, Am Inst Nutrition; Brit Nutrition Soc; Am Chem Soc; Am Soc Biol Chem; Soc Exptl Biol & Med; cp/ MSU Chapt Secy, 1967-69, Sigma Xi; Phi Kappa Phi; r/Prot; hon/Author of Num Pubs; Phi Beta Kappa; Omicron Nu; Sigma Xi Sr Res Awd, 1973; Dist'd Fac Awd, MSU, 1974; Hon Mem, Water Conditioning Assn Intl; Emmett J Culligan Awd, World Water Soc, 1972; W/W Am; Am Men Sci; Ldrs Am Sci; Nat Fac Dir; World W/W Sci.

MIDDLETON, ANTHONY WAYNE JR oc/Physician; b/May 6, 1939; h/2798 Chancellor Place, Salt Lake City, UT 84108; ba/Salt Lake City, UT; m/Carol Samuelson; c/A Wayne III, Suzanne Kathryn Ann, Jane; p/Dr and Mrs A W Middleton, Salt Lake City, UT; sp/Dr and Mrs Cecil Samuelson, Salt Lake City, UT; ed/BS, Univ of UT, 1963; MD, Cornell Univ Med Col, 1966; Internship, Univ of UT Hosps, 1966-67; Gen Surg Residency, NY Hosp, 1967-68; Urology Residency, MA Gen Hosp, 1970-73; mil/ USAF, Capt, 1968-70; pa/Staff Mem,

Primary Chd's Med Ctr, LDS Hosp, Holy Cross Hosp, Univ of UT Hosp; Asst Clin Prof, Dept of Surg, Div of Urology, Univ of UT, 1977-; Clin Fac, Dept of Fam & Commun Med, Univ of UT, 1978-; Beta Theta Pi Pres, 1961; AMA; UT St Med Soc; Treas, 1975-77, Salt Lake City Med Soc; Pres, 1975-76, UT St Urological Assn; Treas, Salt Lake City Surg Soc, 1977-78; Bd of Govs, UT St Med Ins Assn, 1979-; Chm, Holy Cross Hosp, Div of Urology, 1980-82; Chm, Salt Lake Co Med Soc Hosp Liason Com, 1981-82; Chm, UT Med Polit Action Com, 1981-; r/LDS; hon/ Author of Num Pubs; Phi Eta Sigma, 1959; Skull & Bones, 1963; Phi Beta Kappa, 1963; Alpha Omega Alpha, Cornell Univ, 1965; 1st Prize, Pres Essay Contest, NE Sect, Am Urologic Assn, 1973; Staff Pres, Prim Chd's Med Ctr 1982-83; Pres, SLC Med Soc, 1983-84; Personalities of W & MW; Dir of Dist'd Ams; ABI; Book of Hon; Men of Achmt; W/W; Dir of Med Specs in the W.

MIDDLETON, PAULETTE BAUER oc/Scientist, Research in Air Quality; b/ Dec 8, 1946; h/1345 Elder, Boulder, CO 80302; ba/Boulder, CO; m/John William; c/Maren Katherine; p/Paul and Grace Bauer, Beeville, TX; sp/David and Helen Middleton, Wapato, WA; ed/BA 1968, MA 1971, PhD 1973, Univ TX-Austin; pa/Post Doct Fellow 1975, Scist 1979-, Vis'g Scist 1977, Mem 1975-, Nat Ctr Atmospheric Res; Res Assoc, 1976-77, St Univ NY-Albany, Atmospheric Res Ctr; Res Asst, Instr, Res Assoc, Dept Chem & Chem Engrg, Univ TX-Austin, 1964-75; Air Pollution Control Assn; AAAS, 1975-; r/Cath; hon/Author of Num Pubs; Iota Sigma Pi, 1968; Pi Lambda Theta, 1968; W/W: Am Wom, Am Technol; Am Men & Wom Sci.

MIELE, ANTHONY W oc/Director, Alabama Public Library Service; b/Feb 12, 1926; h/431 Eufaula Court, Montgomery, AL 36117; ba/Montgomery, AL; m/Ruth; c/John Robert, Elizabeth Ann, Anthony W Jr, Terri Ann; p/Louise Troyano, Poughkeepsie, NY; sp/Helen Cassidy, Evergreen Park, IL; ed/BS, Marquette Univ, 1951; MLS, Univ Pgh, 1966; mil/USN; pa/AL Public Lib Ser, 1975-; Asst Dir, IL St Lib, 1970-75; Pt-time Tchg, Thornton Jr Col, 1969-70; Asst Dir, Oak Pk Public Lib, 1968-70; Dir, Elmwood Pk Public Lib, 1967-68; Ptnr, Mgr Restaurant, 1960-66; Vice Chm, Public Printer's Adv Coun Govt Depository Libs, 1973-76; Chm, AL Govt Documents Round Table, 1974-75; Assoc Editor, Govt Pubs Review, 1973-; Secy/Chief Ofcrs St Lib Agys; Am Lib Assn; r/Cath; hon/Author of Num Pubs; Mem Lib Hon Soc, Beta Phi Mu; John Cotton Dana Awd, 1981; W/W: Am, S & SW.

MIGDALOF, BRUCE HOWARD oc/ Xenobiologist; b/Jul 19, 1941; h/156 Richardson Road, Robbinsville, NJ 08691; ba/New Brunswick, NJ; m/Joan; c/Barrie Ruth, Amanda, Shari-Lynne, Jonathan; p/Samuel and Jessica Migdalof, North Miami Beach, FL; sp/Fannie Selman, Spring Valley, NY; ed/BA, Cornel Univ, 1962; MS, Purdue Univ, 1965; PhD, Univ Pgh, 1969; pa/Sr Scist, Sanoz Pharm, 1969-72; Sr Scist 1972-75; Grp Ldr, Drug Dispositon, McNeil Pharm, 1975-77; Dept Dir, Dept Drug Metabolism, E R Squibb & Sons

Inc, 1977-; AAAS; Am Chém Soc; Am Soc Pharm; Exptl Therapeutics; A Ph A Acad Pharm Sci; NY Acad Sci; Chm, Drug Metabolism Discussion, 1976-78; CoFdr 1980, Cnslr 1981-, Intl Soc Study Xenobiotics; r/Jewish; hon/Author of Num Pubs; Sigma Xi, 1961; Phi lambda Upsilon, 1961; Men Achmt; W/W: E, Frontier Sci & Technol.

MIGL, DONALD RAYMOND oc/ Optometrist-Primary Vision Care; b/ Sep 18, 1947; h/2600 Pinecrest Drive, Nacogdoches, TX 75961; ba/Nacogdoches, TX; m/Karen Sue Coale; c/ Christopher Brian; p/Ervin L and Adele M Boenisch Migl, Pearland, TX; sp/ Robert T and Louise Coale, Selma, AL; ed/BS 1970, BS 1978, OD 1980, Univ Houston; Post Grad, Univ AL, B'ham Med Ctr, 1974-76; pa/Optometrist, Drs Stockwell & Migl, 1981-; Pharm, Westbury Hosp Pharm, 1976-81; Lab Instr, Univ Houston Pharm, 1980; Shades Mtn Pharm, 1974-76; Ben Taub Hosp, 1970-81; Meml Hosp Houston, 1969-70; St Luke's & TX Chd's Hosp, 1967-69; Am Pharm Assn; TX Pharm Assn; Am Soc Hosp Pharm; Am Optometric Assn; TX Optometric Assn; Piney Woods Optometric Assn; Am Col Optometric Phys; cp/Rotary Intl; C of C; US JCs; r/Epis; hon/Cert Recog, Am Pharm Assn, 1970, TX Optometric Assn, 1979; Gold Key (Optometric) & Omicron Delta Kappa (Univ) Hon Ldrship Soc; First Person to Grad from Two Univ Houston Ctl Campus Hlth Professions; Rotary Intl, 1982; Interdisciplinary Hlth Teams, 1977; W/W S & SW.

MILAM, MARY GRATTAN oc/Sociologist, Linguist, Writer; b/May 10, 1930; h/6222 Malcolm Drive, Dallas, TX 75214; ba/Same; c/Melinda Sue, David Leake Jr, Barnaby Walker; p/Francis Patrick Grattan (dec) and Catherine Lyons Grattan Byrnes, Kansas City, KS; ed/BA 1969, MA 1971, N TX St Univ; PhD, 1977, TX Wom Univ; pa/Tchg Asst, N TX St Univ, 1969-70; Tchg Asst, Laredo St Univ, 1974-75; Cnslg, 1977-79; Res Sociolinguistics, England & India, 1980-82; cp/Alpha Kappa Delta, 1969; GSA, 1960-70; Day Camp Dir, 1965-66; Den Mother & Ldr Tnr, CSA, 1962-64; r/Cath; hon/Author of Num Pubs; GSA Troop Ldr Awd; Hon Grad, 1969; GSW Awd, 1966; Den Mother Awd, 1964; W/W S & SW.

MILES, D HOWARD oc/Professor of Chemistry; b/Jan 4, 1943; h/608 Hospital Road, Starkville, MS 39759; ba/MS St, MS; m/Leara Farris; c/Kristin Grace, David Howard; p/Delbert and Grace Miles, Tarrant, AL; sp/Ethel Farris, Terrant, AL; pa/NIH Post Doct Fellow, Stanford Univ, 1969-70; Fac Mem 1970-, Asst Prof 1970-76, Assoc Prof 1978, MS St Univ; Prog Ofcr, NSF, 1979; Chm MS Sect 1976-77, Chm Elect MS Sect 1975-76, Awds Chm MS Sect 1977-78, Am Chem Soc; Am Chem Soc Congl Sci Cnslr to Senators James Eastland & Thad Cochran; Presider, Nat Am Chem Soc Meeting New Orleans, 1977; Presider, 24th SEn Reg Meeting, Am Chem Soc; Dir, MS Acad Sci; Phytochem Soc N Am; Am Pharm Assn; Am Soc Pharmacognosy, Mem Nom'g Com; Conslt MS Hazard Assessmt Proj Pesticides Undergoing Registration Standard Review; Reviewer Manuscripts Jour Am Chem Soc, Jour Organic Chem, Jour Nat Prods, Jour Pharm Sci;

Referee for Proposals Submitted to Petro Res Fund, NSF, NIH; Mem Num Univ & Public Ser Coms incl'g Chm Fac & Staff Subcom Creat Arts Complex Drive, Mem Ethics Com Fac Coun, MS St Univ, Past Pres, VP, Am Cancer Soc, Oktibbeha Co; Commr Fin Starkville Area Yth Basketball Assn, C of C, Optimist Clb, Starkville; r/Meth; hon/ Author of Num Pubs incl'g "Solubility Studies of the Fe (III)-di-sec-Butyl Phenylphosphonate Complex" *Jour AL Acad Sci* 1965; Post Doct F'ship, NASA, 1965-67; NIH Predoct F'ship, 1967-69; NIH Postdoct F'ship, 1969-70; Theta Chi Delta; Theta Sigma Lamda; Sigma Xi; MSU Sigma Xi Awd, 1973; Outstg Yg Edrs Am; Am Men & Wom Sci; MS St Univ 1977 Alumni Awd Excell Tchg & Res; Starkville, MS JCs Outstg Yg Col Prof Awd 1977; Outstg Yg Men Am; Outstg Chem Awd, MS Sect Am Chem Soc, 1979.

MILETICH, IVO oc/Professor, Department Head; b/Apr 18, 1936; h/ 618 Exchange Avenue, Calumet City, IL 60409; ba/Chicago, IL; m/Mira Sara; c/George Edward, Marina; ed/BA, Acad Ed Split, 1960; Univ Zagreb, 1959-61; MA, Univ Skopje, 1966; Cert, Eng Lang Inst, 1969; Grad Sch Lib Sci Russia Univ, 1971; pa/Tchr, Prof, 1959-65, Yugoslavia; Asst to Bibliographer Lang & Lit, Univ Chgo, 1967-71; Bibliographer & Instr, Old Dominion Univ, 1971-74; Tchr, Ctl YMCA Col, 1969-71, 1974-; Asst Prof, Dept Hd, Chgo St Univ, 1974-; Tchr, Berlitz Sch, 1980-; Translator; CoChm, Chgo Acad Lib Coun; Am Translators Assn; YMCA Fac, Co-Ed; VA Profl Librarianship Assn; Am Fdn Tchrs; AAUP; Am Assn Advmt Slavic Studies; hon/Author of Num Pubs; Beta Phi Mu; Intl Lib Sci Soc, Univ Pgh; VA Profl Librarianship Cert; W/ W MW; Intl W/W Intells; YMCA Recog Achmt Cert.

MILLARD, AMOS DANIEL oc/Dean of Admissions/Registrar; b/Aug 24, 1923; h/5047 114th Northeast, Kirkland, WA 98033; ba/Kirkland, WA; m/ Lorna Mae; c/Daniel Paul, Donald Wesley, David Lawrence, Dean Mark; p/Mr and Mrs Amos D Millard, Prairie, WA; ed/BA, NW Col, 1945-49; MA, Chgo Grad Sch Theol, 1955-58; pa/ Registrar, Fac 1949-, Dean Admissions 1949-, NW Col; NW Col Alumni Assn, 1949-; Am Assn Col Registrars/Admissions Ofcrs, 1954-; Pacific Coast Assn Col Registrars/Admissions Ofcrs, 1955-; WA Coun HS-Col Relats, 1975-; cp/Spiritual Life Comm, NW Dist Coun, Assemblies of God, 1974-; r/Assem God; hon/Author of Num Pubs; NW Col Hon Soc, 1949; Delta Epsilon Chi Hon Soc, 1958; Alumnus Yr Awd, NW Col Alumni Assn, 1972.

MILLER, DEANE GUYNES oc/ Owner, Beauty, Cosmetic Business; b/ Jan 12, 1927; h/1 Silent Crest, El Paso, TX 79902; ba/El Paso, TX; m/Richard G; c/Jay Michael, Marcia Miller Butchofsky; p/Margaret and James T Guynes (dec); sp/Grace and Jake Miller (dec); ed/BBA; pa/Owner, Pres, The Velvet Door Inc; Chm Bd, Wom C of C, 1969; cp/Pres, YWCA, 1966; VP, Sun Bowl Assn, 1970; Bd, El Paso Symph Assn, 1970-73; Bd, El Paso Mus Art, 1973-84; Assoc Dir, Pan Am Round Table, 1983-85; Chm, El Paso Intl Airport Bd, 1983-85; r/Epis; hon/Outstg

Wom Field Civic Endeavor, El Paso Herald Post.

MILLER, GEORGE J oc/ Paleontologist-Lecturer; b/Nov 15, 1921; h/State Road 762, Julian, CA 92036; ba/El Centro, CA; m/Patricia Klar; ed/BS, CA St Univ, 1967; MS, ID St Univ, 1975; mil/USN, 1942-45; pa/ Res Assoc, LA Co Mus, 1965-; Asst Curator, Vertebrate Paleontology, ID St Univ Mus, 1967-68; Coor, Rancho La Brea Proj, 1969-72; Curator, Paleontology, Imperial Val Col Mus, 1972-; Soc Vertebrate Paleontology; The Paleontological soc; Sigma Xi; hon/Author of Num Pubs; Men Achmt; W/W W, Dist'd Ams.

MILLER, JACK BURION II oc/Electrician; b/Oct 19, 1955; h/113 Myers Street, Cumberland, KY 40823; ba/ Same; c/Amy Nicole; p/Ruth Helton Miller, Cumberland, KY; ed/Att'd RETS Electronic Inst, Assoc Deg; pa/Parker Funeral Home, Cumberland, KY; Repairman, US Steel Mining, Lynch, KY; Switchman, Continental Telephon Co, Cumberland, KY; J M Elect Wiring & Repair; Cumberland Vol Fire Dept; KY Col; Pres 1983-84, Bd Dirs, Corporate Bd, Cumberland Rotary Clb; r/ Bapt; hon/Outstg Rotarian Wk.

MILLER, JAN DEAN oc/Professor of Metallurgy; b/Apr 7, 1942; h/1886 Atkin Avenue, Salt Lake City, UT 84106; ba/ Salt Lake City, UT; m/Patricia Ann; c/ Pamela Ann, Jeanette Marie, Virginia Christine; p/Mary Virginia Miller, St College, PA; sp/Mr and Mrs Roy Rossman, Pennsylvania Furnace, PA; ed/BS, PA St Univ, 1964; MS 1966, PhD 1969, CO Sch Mines; pa/Res Engr, Anaconda Co, 1966; Asst Prof 1968-71, Assoc Prof 1972-77, Prof Metallurgy 1978-, Univ UT; Res Engr, Lawrence Livermore Lab, 1972; Soc Mining Engrs; Prog Chm 1982-83, Bd Dirs 1980-83, Past Chm Mineral Processing Div 1982, AIME; Sigma Xi, Am Sci Affil; hon/Author of Num Pubs; Dist'd Extractive Metallurgy Prof, CO Sch Mines Cent Celebration, 1974; Marcus A Grossman Awd for "Surface Deposit Effects in Kinetics of Copper Cementation by Iron", 1974; Eleventh Recip Van Diest Gold Medal, Periodically Awarded to Outstg Alumni CO Sch Mines in Mineral Indust, 1977; Mellow Met Prof, Univ UT, Outstg Tchr, 1978, 1982; W/W: Technol Today, Engrg; Men Achmt.

MILLER, JANETTE HEARN oc/Coordinator of Media Services; b/Nov 29, 1947; h/1900 Whitebark Street, North, Augusta, SC 29841; ba/Augusta, GA; m/Carey B; c/Kevin, Jason; p/Mr Francis Hearn, Eatonton, GA; sp/Mr and Mrs Paul Miller, Augusta, SC; ed/BSN, Med Col GA; Att'g Grad Sch, Univ SC; pa/ Coor Media Ser, Univ Hosp, 1976-; Charge Nurse, Self Mem Hosp, 1976; Nurse Recruiter, Nurse Instr Hosp Ed, Univ Hosp, 1972-74; Med, Maximum Care, Eugene Meml Hosp, 1971-72; Clin Spec, Talmadge Hosp, 1971; Chm, 1978-80, Augusta Area Com Hlth Info Resources; Hlth Ed Media Assn; Am Soc Tng Devel; Intl TV Assn; r/Meth; hon/ Author of "Reconstrn Mother Child Relationship in Regressed Catatonic Schizophrenic" 1968, "Open Heart Surg" 1978; GRAACY Awds TV PSA's on Prenatal Class, Smoking, 1980; Hon Mention, NAACOG, Expectancy, 1979; Outstg Yg Wom SC, 1980; Outstg Yg

Wom Am; W/W.

MILLER, JIM WAYNE oc/Professor; b/Oct 21, 1936; h/Eastland Drive, Bowling Green, KY 42101; ba/Bowling Green, KY; m/Mary Ellen Yates; c/ James Yates, Fred Smith, Ruth Ratcliff; p/Mr and Mrs James Woodrow Miller, Leicester, NC; ed/BA, Berea Col, 1958; PhD, Vanderbilt Univ, 1965; pa/Instr, Ft Knox Dependent Schs, 1958-60; NDEA Fellow, Vanderbilt Univ, 1960-63; Asst Prof, Wn KY Univ, 1963-67; Assoc Prof 1967-70, Prof 1970-, Vis'g Prof, Berea Col Appalachian Studies Prog, 1973-; Poet-in-Residence, Ctr Col KY, 1984; Pres, KY Humanities Coun Inc, 1973-74; Pres, Appalachian Studies Conf, 1982-83; r/Meth; hon/Author of *Copperhead Cane* 1964, *The More Things Change The More They Stay the Same* 1971; *Alice Lloyd Awd, Appalachian Poetry, Alice Lloyd Col, 1967; Sigma Tau Delta, Hon Eng Awd, Wn KY Univ, 1969; Wn KY Univ Fac Awd Creativity, 1976; Wn KY Univ Fac Awd Public Ser, 1982; Hon Doct Lttrs, Berea Col, 1981; Dist'd Alumnus Awd, Berea Col, 1983; Fellow, Corporation Yaddo, 1983; Contemp Authors; Critical Survey Short Fiction, 1981; Dir Am Poets & Writers.

MILLER, JOAN MARY oc/Associate Professor Humanities; b/Sep 10, 1941; h/1418 Pearce Park, Erie, PA 16502; ba/ Erie, PA; p/Roy W and Hedwig J Sakowicz Miller, Pittsburgh, PA; ed/BA, Carlow Col, 1963; PhL, Institut Catholique de Paris, 1967; Grad, Rel Studies 1969, Postgrad 1968-70, 1973-78; Univ Louvain; Ecole Pratique des Hautes Etudes, 1969-70; pa/Tchr, St Elizabeth HS, 1962-64; Pensionnat des Ursulines, 1968-70; Assoc Prof, Villa Maria Col, 1970-73, 1978-; Coor Freshman Yr Studies Prog, 1972-73; Translator, Rschr, Prospective, Brussels, 1974-78; Translator, Ctr Socio-Rel Res, Louvain, 1973-77; Lctr, Univ MD, 1975; AAUP; Am Cath Phil Assn, Secy/Treas NWNY Reg, 1971-73; Am Phil Assn; Am Translators Assn; Intl Phenomenological Soc; Intl Platform Assn; Ground Zero; LWV; Soc Phil & Psychol; Soc Wom Phil; r/Rom Cath; hon/Author of "French Structuralism: A Multidisciplinary Bibliog" 1981; S'ship, Carlow Col, 1959-63; Asst'ship, OH Univ, 1963; Delta Epsilon Sigma, 1963; World W/ W Wom; W/W: Am Wom, E; Communy Ldrs Am; Contemp Authors; DIB; Dir Am Scholars.

MILLER, KENNETH M oc/Electronics Industry Executive; b/Nov 20, 1921; h/16904 George Washington Drive, Rockville, MD 20853; ba/Rockville, MD; m/Sally B; c/Barbara A Reed, Nancy J Hathaway, Kenneth M Jr, Roger A; ed/ IL Inst Technol, 1941; Univ CA-LA, 1961; pa/Pres, CEO, Dir, Penril Corporation, 1973-; Pres, Dir, Wilcox Elect; Inc, VP, Worldwide Wilcox Elect; VP & Gen Mgr, Computer Indust Inc; Pres & Dir, Infonics, Inc; VP, Gen Mgr, Lear Jet Corporation; Gen Mgr, Fdr Metrics Div, Gen Mgr Am Indust Sewing Machine Div, Singer Co; VP & Gen Mgr, Instrument Div, Schlumberger; VP & Gen Mgr, Motorola Aviation Elect, Inc; Gen Mgr Comml Avionic Div, Lear Inc; Sr Mem, IEEE; Sr Mem, Instrument Soc Am; Life Mem, Am Radio Relay Leag; Life Mem, Qtr Century Wireless Assn; Life Clb, Radio

Clb Am; AF Assn; Aircraft Elect Assn Aircraft Owners & Pilots Assn; Am Def Preparedness Assn; AIAA; Am Soc Non-Destructive Testing; Armed Forces Communs & Elect Assn; Soc Automotive Engrs; cp/Assn Old Crows; Pres, Bridgeport CT C of C; Trustee Pk City Hosp Bridgeport, CT; Mem, Bd Assocs Univ Bridgeport; Mem, Bridgeport Reg Planning Assn; r/Cath; hon/Am Men Wom Sci; DIB; Ldrs Am Sci; Ldrs Elect; Ldg Men USA; Men Achmt; Royal Blue Book; W/W: CA, E, Fin & Indust.

MILLER, LYNNE CATHY oc/Parasitologist; b/Dec 25, 1951; h/823 Lightstreet Road, Bloomsburg, PA 17815; ba/Bloomsburg, PA; m/Gary Franklin Clark; p/Albert and Lorraine Shirley Sweet Miller, Boston, MA; ed/BS, Univ RI, 1974; MS, Univ TX, 1977; PhD, NM St Univ, 1980; pa/Clin Pharm Intern, 1974-75; Postdoct Fellow Med Entomol, NM St Univ, 1980-81; Prof 1981-, Pre-Pharm Advr 1981-, Dir Internships 1982-, Coor Hons Prog 1981-, Pre-Med Advr 1981-, Bloomsburg Univ; AAAS; PA Acad Sci; Mem, Rocky Mtn Conf Parasitologists; cp/Fellow Sigma Xi; Phi Kappa Phi; Beta Beta Beta; Rho Chi, Chapt Fac Advr 1984; Mem, Univ-Wide Sabbatical Com; Mem, Univ-Wide Fac Hlth & Wel Com; Fac Advr, Univ Biol Clb, 1981-; Active Sponsor, Ronald McDonald House, 1981-; r/Jewish; hon/Author of Num Pubs; Commonwealth PA Fac Res Grant, 1981, 1982, 1983, 1984; Giardiasis Nat Expert, 1984; Hons Grad, Univ RI, 1974; Reg'd Pharm.

MILLER, SAMUEL CLIFFORD oc/Museum Director; b/May 6, 1930; h/375 Mount Prospect Avenue, Newark, NJ 07104; ba/Newark, NJ; m/Rosetta Averill; p/Loren and Blanche Baron Miller (dec); sp/Mary Averill Stanton; ed/BA, Stanford Univ, 1951; Postgrad, NY Univ, Inst Fine Arts, 1962-64; mil/AUS, 1951-53; pa/Asst Dir, Albright-Knox Art Gallery, 1964-67; Asst Dir 1967, Dir 1968-, Newark Mus; Trustee, Newark Mus; Trustee, Westminster Choir Col Bd; Port Auth NY & NJ Art Com; NJ Adv Com Channel 13; Assoc Art Mus Dirs; Am Assn Mus; NE Mus Conf; Mus Coun NJ; r/Rom Cath; hon/Outstg Citizen NJ Awd, Advtg Clb NJ, 1980; Nat Conf of Christians & Jews, 1982, Brotherhood Awd; Hon Deg Doct Lttrs, Rutgers Univ, 1983; Hon Doct Fine Arts, Seton Hall Univ, 1976; W/W: Am, E, World, Am Art; Men Achmt; DIB.

MILLER, SANFORD ARTHUR oc/Director, Bureau of Foods, FDA; b/May 12, 1931; h/4928 Sentinel Drive, Bethesda, MD 20016; ba/Washington, DC; m/Judith; c/Wallis Jo, Debra Lauren; p/Howard (dec) and Lillian Kenter Epstein, NY, NY; sp/Benjamin and Charlotte Cohen, Boston, MA; ed/BS, City Col NY, 1952; MS 1956, PhD 1957, Rutgers Univ; mil/Army Med Corps, 1953-54; Corporal, Asst to Chief Toxicologist; pa/Jr Chem 1951, Chem 1952, Army Chem Ctr MD; Asst to Chief Toxicologist, Army Med Ctr Wash, 1953-54; Tchg Asst, Rutgers Univ, 1955-57; Res Assoc 1957-59, Asst Prof Nutritional Biochem 1959-65, Assoc Prof Nutritional Biochem 1965-70, MIT; Prof Nutritional Biochem; Dir, Tng Prog Oral Sci, 1970-; Vis'g Lectr Nutrition, Tufts Univ Sch Dental Med, Boston Univ Sch Med, Harvard Univ Sch Med, 1963-; Dir, Bur

Foods, FDA, 1978-; Chm Com Biochem Nutrition 1967-69, Mem Nat Prog Com 1967-72, Chm Fellows Com 1977-78, Am Inst Nutrition; Nat Cnslr 1966-69, Secy NE Sect 1968-69, Vice Chm NE Sect 1969-70, Chm NE Sect 1970-71, Nat Chm Com Nutrition Ed 1969-72, Inst Food Technologists; Meetings Com, Fdn Am Soc Exptl Biol; Vice Chm 1972, Chm 1973, Gordon Res Conf; Prog Com, Wn Hemisphere Nutrition Cong, 1977; Am Chem Soc; AAAS; Sigma Xi; NY Acad Sci; Animal Care Panel; Hon Fellow, Mark L Morris Animal Care Panel; Soc Teratology; Perinatal Res Soc; Am Inst Dental Res; Soc Pediatric Res; r/Jewish; hon/Author of Num Pubs; Outstg Tchr Yr Awd, MIT, 1975; 1981 Conrad A Elvehjem Awd, Am Inst Nutrition; Public Hlth Ser Awd, 1982; Braverman Meml Lectr, Technion-Israel Inst Technol, 1982; Samuel W Johnson Meml Lectr, CT Agri Expt Sta, 1982; Dept Hlth & Human Ser Dist'd Ser Awd, 1983; Am Men & Wom Sci; W/W: Am, E, Wash DC, Frontier Sci & Technol; Fdn Am Soc Exptl Biol.

MILLER, THERESA ANN oc/Police Officer, Patrol Division; b/Sep 6, 1949; h/313 Pine Drive, Ocean Springs, MS 39564; ba/Ocean Springs, MS; p/Shiron W Sr (dec) and Mary Alice Miller, Ocean Springs, MS; ed/BS, Univ So MS, 1971; pa/Lab Tech/Secy, Gulf Coast Res Lab, 1971-79; Pre-Placement Interview/Housing Advr, Fed Emer Mgmt Agy, 1979-80; Dispatcher 1981-82, Patrolman 1982-, Ocean Sprgs PD; MS Law Enforcement Ofcrs Assn, 1981-; Ocean Sprgs Police Ofcrs Assn, 1981-; cp/Phi Kappa Phi Hon Frat, 1970-; r/Rom Cath; hon/Phi Theta Kappa, 1968; Outstg Student, MS Law Enforcement ofcrs Tng Acad, 1983; W/W Am Jr Cols.

MILLER, TRUDI C oc/Program Director, National Science Foundation; b/Feb 4, 1941; h/2229 39th Place, Northwest, Washington, DC 20007; ba/Washington, DC; p/Paul Miller, Phoenicia, NY; ed/BA, Cornell Univ, 1962; PhD, Univ NC-Chapel Hill, 1969; pa/Fac, St Univ NY, 1967-72; Prog Dir, NSF, 1972-; APSA; ASPA; Inst Mgmt Sci; Opers Res Soc Am; Am Inst Decision Sci; hon/Author of Num Pubs; Pi Sigma Alpha Awd, Best Paper 1980 Annual Meeting APSA; W/W Am Wom.

MILLMAN, PETER MacKENZIE oc/Astronomer; b/Aug 10, 1906; h/4 Windsor Avenue, Ottawa, Ontario K1S 0W4; ba/Ottawa, Ontario; m/Margaret Bowness Gray; c/Barry Mackenzie; Cynthia Gray Millman Floyd; ed/BA, Univ Toronto, 1929; MA 1931, PhD 1932, Harvard Univ; mil/RCAF, 1941-46, Active Ser; pa/Astronomer, Lectr, David Dunlap Observatory, Univ Toronto, 1933-45; Chief Stellar Physics Div, Dominion Observatory, 1946-55; Hd Upper Atmosphere Res, Nat Res Coun Canada, 1955-71; Guest Scist, NRCC, 1971-; Pres, Meteoritical Soc, 1962-66; Nat Pres, Royal Astronom Soc Canada, 1960-62; cp/Cnslr, Smithsonian Inst, 1966-72; Bd Dirs, Yth Sci Foun Canada, 1966-71; VP Financial, Ottawa Music Fest Assn, 1962-67; r/Anglican; hon/Author of Num Pubs incl'g *This Universe of Space* 1961; *Meteorite Res* 1969; J Lawrence Smith Medal, Nat Acad Sci, 1954; Gold Medal, Phys Sci, Chechoslovak Acad Sci, 1980; Cent Medal

Canada, 1967; Queen's Silver Jubilee Medal, 1977; Fellow Royal Soc Canada, 1959-; W/W: Am, World, from Antiquity to Present; Canadian W/W; Am Men & Wom Sci.

MILLS, JESSE COBB oc/Librarian; b/Feb 13, 1921; h/2001 Emoriland Boulevard, Knoxville, TN 37917; ba/Knoxville, TN; ed/BS, Harvard, 1942; MS, Univ TN, 1949; MLS, Rutgers, 1960; Att'd Univ PA, 1951-54; pa/William Iselin & Co Inc, 1946-51; Instr, Univ TN, 1946-51; Grad Instr 1951-54, Libn 1954-66, Univ PA; Libn, Univ TN, 1966-69; Chief Libn, TN Val Auth, 1969-; Chm, St Adv Coun Libs; cp/Pres, E TN Hist Soc, 1972-76; Bd, Knoxville Kiwanis Clb; VP, Phila Chapt, Soc Architectural Histns, 1965-66; r/Meth; hon/Author of Num Articles; Libn Yr TN, 1981; W/W Am.

MILLS, JON LESTER oc/Attorney, State Representative; b/Jul 24, 1947; h/6117 Southwest 11th Place, Number A, Gainesville, FL 32607; ba/Gainesville, FL; pa/Marguerite Mills, Coral Gables, FL; ed/BA, Stetson Univ, 1969; JD, Univ FL, 1972; mil/USAR, 1969-72, First Lt; pa/Mem, Ho of Reps, St of FL, 1978-; Ptnr, McGalliard, Mills & deMontmollin, Attys-at-Law, 1981-; Dir, Ctr Govtl Responsibility 1973-81, Dir, Res Impoundment Proj 1972-73, Adj Assoc Prof Law, Holland Law Ctr, Univ FL; First Lt, AUS, 1972; Aide to Judge, Second Dist Ct Appeals, 1972; Investigator, Clk, Miami Public Defender's Ofc, 1970; Num Legis & Adm Experiences; FL & Am Bar Assn; Phi Delta Phi Legal Frat; FL Assn Adolescent Devel; Am Assn Retarded Persons; Univ FL Dept Envir Engrg Sci Vis'g Com; cp/FL Bar Constit Revision Com, 1976-77; Chm, 1976-77, Gainesville Citizens Adv Bd Com Devel; FL Cancer Control & Res Adv Bd; r/Meth; hon/Author of Num Pubs; Outstg Yg Men Am, 1976; Outstg Mem FL Ho of Reps Awd, 1979; Univ FL Yg Dem Hubert H Humphrey Awd, 1979-80; Disabled Citizens Action Legis Awd, 1980; FL Coun Handicapped Orgs Outstg Ser Awd, 1980; Allen Morris Awd, Most Outstg First-Term Mem of House, Runner-up in 1979-80.

MILLS, JUDITH LANELLE oc/Government Administrator; b/Sep 12, 1949; h/3880 South Oak, Kennewick, WA 99337; ba/Kennewick, WA; p/Thomas F and Esther L Walsh, Kennewick, WA; ed/Columbia Basin Col, 1974-75 Police Sci, 1967-68 Bus Mgmt; pa/Dir, Emer Dispatch Ctr, 1977-; Dispatcher, City of Richland, 1972-76; Dept Sheriff, Franklin Co Sheriff's Ofc, 1976; Nat Exec Com, Assn Public Safety Comm Ofc, 1981-; Pres, WA Chapter APCO, 1982-83; Chm, WA St Dispatcher Cert Prog; Chm, WA St Assn Communication Dirs, 1982; Communication Dir, Benton-Franklin Fixed Nuclear Facility, 1982; Instr, WA ST Tng Comm; r/Bapt; hon/W/W: Am, W.

MILLS, LOLA MARIE oc/Division Five Director, Baptist Memorial Geriatric Hospital; b/Oct 26, 1931; h/2024 North Harrison, San Angelo, TX 76901; ba/San Angelo, TX; m/Brady O; c/Martha Ellen Carlisle, Glenda Jayne Bradley; p/Mr and Mrs A B Horn, San Angelo, TX; sp/Mr and Mrs J G Mills (dec), Bronte, TX; ed/Bronte Hosp Sch Nsg, 1958-59; pa/Staff LVN, Bronte Hosp, 1952-67; Charge Nurse, Div Dir

Bapt Meml Geriatric Hosp, 1967-84; Appt'd to TX Bd Voc Nurse Examrs, 1982-; 2nd VP 1976, Secy 1975-76, 1972-73, Mem 1960-84, LVNA TX; Mem Com, Nat Assn Practical Nurse Ed & Ser, 1978-79, Mem 1961-84; cp/ San Angelo Toastmistress Clb, 1970-74; Secy/Treas, San Angelo Chapt Credit Unions, 1970-74; Camp Nurse, Paisano Bapt Encampment; Secy/Dir, Shannon Fed Credit Union, 1982-84; March of Dimes; ARC Vol; r/Bapt; hon/Hons Grad, Bronte Hosp Sch Nsg, 1959; Secy/ Treas TX Bd Voc Nurse Examrs, 1983-84.

MILLS, SHERRY R oc/Executive Director, Colorado Arts for the Handicapped; b/Apr 3, 1940; h/2220 Glenwood Circle, Colorado Springs, CO 80909; ba/Colorado Springs, CO; m/ Ronald K; c/Tracy R, Darren K; p/Ray and Lorena Gregory, Woodland Park, CO; sp/Mabel Mills, Neodesha, KS; ed/ BME, Univ CO, 1962; MA 1979, Admr's Cert 1981, UCCS; pa/Harrison Sch Dist II Clrm, 1962-65; Music Tchr, 1965-66; Sum Music Tchr, CO Sprg Dist II, 1958-68; Spec Ed Music Spec, 1976-81; Coor & Exec Dir, CO Arts Handicapped, 1981-; Pvt Music Tchr, 1962-78; Music Tchr, Rocky Mtn Rehab Ctr, 1971-76; MENC; CEC; Am Assn Mtl Deficiency; Foun Exceptl Chd; r/Presb; hon/Author of Num Pubs; Title IV-C Grants, 1980, 1981, 1982; Foun Exceptl Chd Grant, 1981; Num Grants & Awds; W/W W.

MILLSPAUGH, MEREDITH PLANT oc/Dir, Evergreen House Foundation of Johns Hopkins University; b/Jan 6, 1929; h/203 Ridgewood Road, Baltimore, MD 21210; ba/Baltimore, MD; m/Martin Laurence Sr; c/Mrs J Howison Schroeder, Martin Laurence III, Mrs J Porter Durham, Thomas Edwin Davenport; p/Mrs Graeme D Plant, Macon, GA; sp/Martin Laurence and Elisabeth Park Millspaugh (dec); ed/Att'd St Mary's Jr Col, 1949; Wesleyan Conservatory Fine Arts, 1951; pa/Dir Evergreen House Foun, Johns Hopkins Univ, 1981-; Owner, Mgr, VIP Tours Balto, VIP Projs Unltd, 1969-82; Dir, Downtown Discovery Tour Prog, City of Balto, 1967-75; cp/Comm Hist & Architectural Preserv, 1978-; Bd Trustees, Peale Mus, 1973-80; Bd Dirs, Edgar Allen Poe Soc, 1974-; Bd Dirs, Soc Preserv MD Antiquities, 1962-65; r/ Epis; hon/W/W.

MILTON, LEROY JR oc/Law Enforcement Officer; b/Aug 29, 1945; h/5951 Kissing Oak, San Antonio, TX 78247; ba/Lackland AFB, TX; m/Diane Hunt; c/Stephanie, Pamela, Yolanda, Dede; p/ Leroy Milton Sr, Beaufort, NC; sp/R T Hunt, Kilgore, TX; ed/AA, Rollins Col, 1976; BS, Rollins Col, 1978; MA, 1982, Adm Jus & Human Relats, Webster Col; mil/USAF, Capt; pa/Non-Commissioned Ofcr in Charge, Aeromedical Ser, Patrick AFB, 1974-78; Shift Cmdr, Police, Dover AFB, 1978-80; Dept Cmdr, Lackland AFB, 1980-; DE Chief Police, 1978-80; FOP, 1979-81; Police Marksman Assn, 1981-; r/Epis; hon/ Viet Nam Combat Vet, 11 Air Medals; Dist'd Flying Cross.

MIMS, LAMBERT CARTER oc/Commissioner of Public Works; b/Apr 29, 1930; h/3008 Bryant Road, Mobile, AL 36605; ba/Mobile, AL; m/Reecie Phillips; c/Dale, Danny; p/Mrs Jeff Mims Sr, Uriah, AL; sp/Mrs W V Phillips, Mon-

roeville, AL; ed/HS Grad, Uriah, AL; pa/ Elected Public Wks Cmmr, Mobile, AL, 1965, Reelected, 1981; Mayor, Mobile, AL; Retail & Wholesale Bus, 1958-65; cp/AL Leag Municipalities; Nat Leag Cities; US Conf Mayors; Mil Affairs Com, Mobile Area C of C; Past Pres, Mobile Co Mun Assn; Dir, VP 1978-79, Pres 1979-80, Am Public Wks Assn; Kiwanis Clb; Former Mem, Mobile JCs; r/Bapt, Riverside Bapt Ch; hon/Author of For Christ & Country 1969; Mobile's Most Outstg Yg Man 1965; Prin Spkr Gov's Inaugural Breakfast, 1967, 1971.

MIN, KYUNG—WHAN oc/Pathologist; h/5109 Aspen Drive, West Des Moines, IA 50265; ba/Des Moines, IA; m/Young Jin; c/Kwanhong Christopher, Wonhong David; ed/MD, Seoul Nat Univ, 1962; pa/Pathol, Mercy Hosp Med Ctr, Assoc Prof, Creighton Univ, 1978-; Asst Prof, Baylor Col Med, 1971-78; Fellow, Am Col Phys; Col Am Pathol; Am Soc Clin Pathol; Am Assn Pathol; Intl Acad Pathol; Electron Microscopy Soc Am; AAAS; r/So Bapt; hon/Author of Num Pubs incl'g "Peculiar Cytoplasmic Inclusions in a Case of Glioblastoma Multiforme" Ultrastruct Pathol 1981, "Transformed Lymphocytes Versus Histiocytes" Amer J Clin Pathol 1984; W/ W Frontiers Sci & Technol.

MINER, JOHN BURNHAM oc/University Professor; b/Jul 20, 1926; h/651 Peachtree Battle Avenue Northwest, Atlanta, GA 30327; ba/Atlanta, GA; m/ Barbara W; c/Barbara Long, John T, Cynthia Wieczorek, Frances, Jennifer; ed/BA 1950, PhD 1955, Princeton Univ; MA, Clark Univ, 1952; mil/AUS, 1944-46, European Theater; Res Assoc, Columbia Univ, 1956-57; Mgr Psychol Ser, Atlantic Refining Co, 1957-60; Prof, Univ OR, 1960-68; Prof, Dept Chm, Univ MD, 1968-73; Res Prof, Doct Prog Chm, GA St Univ, 1973-; Fellow, Acad Mgmt, Jour Editor, 1973-75; Fellow, Am Psychol Assn; Indust Relats Res Assn; Fellow, Soc Personality Assessmt; Am Soc Pers Adm; r/Prot; hon/Author of Num Pubs incl'g The Mgmt of Ineffective Perf 1963, Theories of Orgnl Behavior 1980; Dist'd Prof Awd, GA St Univ, 1976; James A Hamilton Hosp Admr's Book Awd, 1979; Contemp Authors; W/W.

MINER, MICHAEL ALAN oc/Insurance Salesman; b/Mar 7, 1952; h/Post Office Box 1378, Aiken, SC 29802-1378; ba/Aiken, SC; p/H Clay and E Kate Miner, Aiken, SC; ed/BS, Univ SC; pa/Asst Mgr, Barclay Am Financial Ser, 1973-75; Agt, Life Ins Co GA, 1975-83; Agt, United Ins Co Am, 1983-84; Life Underwriters, 1976-84; r/ Bapt; hon/Nat Sales Achmt Awds, 1978, 1982; Ldg Ordinary, 1980, 1981, 1982; Pres Clb Conv Qualifier, 1984.

MINIX, NANCY ALICE HOLDER oc/Teacher; b/Jun 30, 1949; h/900 Convington Avenue, Bowling Green, KY 42101; ba/Alvaton, KY; m/Dennis Orville, c/Christopher Dennis; p/John and Marie Holder, Scottsville, KY; sp/ Orville and Vivian Minix, Rock Field, KY; ed/BS 1971, MS 1972, Wn KY Univ; EdD, Vanderbilt Univ, 1981; pa/Jr HS Math Tchr, Warren Co Bd Ed, 1972-82; Corres'g Secy, 197274, IRA; NEA, 1972-; KY Ed Assn, 1972-; Third Dist Ed Assn, 1972-; Warren Co Ed Assn, 1972-; NCTM, 1976-78; Assn Supvn & Curric Devel, 1978-80; cp/Gamma

Sigma Sigma Nat Ser Sorority, 1970-; r/Meth; hon/Pubs; Outstg Tchg Awd, Social Studies, 1981; Gamma Sigma Sigma, Outstg Ser Awd, 1971-; Pres Scholar, 1971; Dean's List, 1971; IRA Pres Awd Outstg Contbn, 1975; W/W S & SW.

MINNIEAR, DIANE R NAS-WORTHY oc/Advertising Executive; b/ Feb 24, 1941; h/4116 Ransom Street, Long Beach, CA 90804; ba/Los Angeles, CA; p/Cmdr Robert W and Esther Beckenstein Nasworthy, USN Ret'd; ed/ Att'd Long Bch City Col, Pacific Christian Col, MN Bible Col, CA St Univ-Long Bch; pa/Sales Exec, GTE Dir Corporation; Advtg Exec; Mgr, Nat Yellow Pages, Budget Rent-a-Car Corporation; Dir, Nat Yellow Pages Adv, Transamerica Mktg Sers; hon/GTE Yellow Pages All Star, 1975; W/W W.

MINOR, MICHAEL oc/Attorney; b/ Apr 21, 1946; h/Post Office Drawer 500, Kaufman, TX 75142; ba/Terrell, TX; m/ Susan Raney; p/Lillian Minor, Bowie, TX; sp/Mr and Mrs B J Lennon, Houston, TX; ed/BA, TX Christian; JD, S TX Col Law, 1976; pa/Dir Public Affairs, TX Dem Party, 1970; Asst Co Atty, Hale Co, TX, 1978-79; Asst Crim DA, Kaufman Co, TX, 1979-81; Pvt Pract Law, 1982-; Am Bar Assn; St Bar TX; TX Co & DA Assn; Kaufman Co Bar Assn; cp/Kaufman Co Lib Bd; r/Rom Cath; hon/W/W Am Law; Personalities S.

MINTON, NORMAN ALTON oc/ Research Nematologist; b/Oct 12, 1924; h/2210 Murray Avenue, Tifton, GA 31794; ba/Tifton, GA; m/Doris; c/ Cathy; ed/BS 1950, MS 1951, PhD 1960, Auburn Univ; mil/AUS, Tech Sgt; pa/ Res Nematologist, US Dept Agri Tifton, GA, 1964-; Res Nematologist, US Dept Agri Auburn, AL, 1955-64; Horticulturist, Berry Col, 1953-55; Asst Co Agri Agt, AL Agri Ext Ser, 1951-53; Soc Nematologists; Am Phytopathol Soc; GA Assn Plant Pathol; Soc Nematologists; Admissions & Credentials Com 1976-77, Treas 1977-79, Pres Elect 1979-80, Pres 1980-81, Tifton Sigma Xi Clb; Gamma Sigma Delta; "Nematropica" Assoc Editor, 1977-; r/Meth; hon/ Author of Num Pubs; GA Soybean Assn Res Awd, 1978; Jt Recip Soc Nematologists Best Economic Paper Awd, 1981; Rec'd 3 Overseas Ser Bars; European, African, Mid En Theatre Campaign Ribbon w Two Bronze Stars; Asiatic-Pacific Theatre Ribbon; Philippine Liberation Ribbon; Victory Ribbon; Army Occup Medal, Japan; Good Conduct Medal.

MINTZ, RONALD E "BARON" oc/ Artist; b/Jan 21, 1926; h/14510 Southeast 167th Street, Renton, WA 98055; ba/Same; m/Mildred Tilson; c/Richard, Robert; ed/Att'd Duke Univ, Univ NC-Chapel Hill, George Wash Univ, Jackson St Univ, Air Univ, BA, MS, PhD; Studied in Munich-Garmisch-Oberammergau; mil/USAF, Col; pa/ One Man Art Show, 1955; Art Exhbns, Restorative Painting Conserv, Pvt Instrn, Wash DC, 1956-; Est'd Macropaedia Conserv, 1974; Creator"Chromoformism" Abstract Art Form Technique; hon/Legion Merit; Meritorious Ser Medal; W/W: Am Art, W, Aviation & Aerospace; IPDA Dir; AIC Dir; IIC Dir; AFIO Dir.

MINTZER, DAVID oc/Vice President

for Research and Dean of Science; b/ May 4, 1926; h/736 Central Street, Evanston, IL 60201; ba/Evanston, IL; m/ Justine; c/Elizabeth Amy Porray, Robert Andrew; p/Herman and Anna Katz Mintzer (dec); sp/Emanuel I and Rose Scharf Klein (dec); ed/BS 1945, PhD 1949, MIT; pa/Asst Prof, Brown Univ, 1949-55; Assoc Prof, Yale Univ, 1955-62; Prof Mech Engrg & Astronautical Sci 1962-, Prof Astrophysics 1968-, Assoc Dean 1970-73, Acting Dean, Tech Inst 1971-72, VP Res, Dean Sci 1973-, NWn Univ; Nat Acad Sci, NRC, 1963-73; Bd Trustees 1975-, Chm 1980-81, EDUCOM; Bd Trustees, Adler Planetarium, 1976-; Fellow, Am Phys Soc; Acoustical Soc Am; ASME; Sigma Xi; cp/Tau Beta Pi; Pi Tau Sigma; hon/ Author of Num Pubs; Am Men & Wom Sci; Men Achmt; W/W: Am, Technol Today.

MIRAND, EDWIN ALBERT oc/Associate Institute Director; b/Jul 18, 1926; h/925 Delaware Avenue, Buffalo, NY 14209; ba/Buffalo, NY; p/Thomas P and Lucy P Mirand (dec); ed/BA 1947, MA 1949, Univ Buffalo; PhD, 1951, Syracuse Univ; DSc, Niagara Univ, 1970; DSc, D'Youville Col, 1974; pa/Assoc Dir 1967-, Hd Dept Ed 1967-, Roswell Pk Meml Inst, 1951-; Hd, W Seneca Labs, 1961-81; Hd Dept Biol Resources, 1973-84; Hd Dept Viral Oncology, 1970-73; Dir, Cancer Res, 1968-73; Dean, RPMI Grad Div 1967-; Res Prof, Grad Sch 1955-, St Univ NY-Buffalo; Am Assoc Cancer Res; Radiation Res Soc; NY Acad Sci, Life Mem & Fellow; Am Soc Zool; Soc Exp Biol & Med; r/ Cath; hon/Author of Num Pubs; Recip Billings Silver Medal AMA, 1963; Awd Sci Res, Mammalian Tumor Viruses, Med Soc St NY, 1963; Cit Awd Sci, Col Arts & Sci, St Univ NY, 1964; Secy/ Treas, AACI, 1967-; Pres, Intl Soc Gnotobiol, 1983-84; Secy/Gen of 13 Intl Cancer Cong.

MIRANDA, FRANK JOSEPH oc/ Dental Educator, Dental Practitioner; b/ Jun 30, 1946; h/6645 Whitehall Drive, Oklahoma City, OK 73132; ba/Oklahoma City, OK; m/Joan E Antes; c/Cory Michael, Erin Christine; p/Joseph F and Vivian M Lewis Miranda (dec); sp/ Harold and Fay Antes, Syracuse, NE; ed/Univ CA-LA, 1964-67; DDS, Univ CA-LA, 1971; MEd 1976, MBA 1979, Ctl St Univ; pa/Pvt Prac Dentistry, Lynwood Chd's Foun, 1971-72; Clin Instr, Univ CA-LA Sch Dentistry, 1971-74; Assoc Dentist, Proj ACORDE, USPHS, Dept HEW, 1972-74; Asst Prof Operative Dentistry 1974-80, Assoc Prof Operative Dentistry 1980-, Pvt Pract Dentistry 1974-, Univ OK Col Dentistry; Consltg Odontologist, Ofc Chief Med Examr, St of OK, 1974-80; Adj Fac, Cert'd Dental Assisting Prog, Rose St Col, 1980-; Mem, Am Dental Assn, 1974-; Mem, OK Dental Assn, 1974-; Mem, Acad Operative Dentistry, 1975-; Mem 1975-, Pvt Sect Operative Dentistry 1981-82, Chair-Elect 1982-83, Chm 1983-84, Am Assn Dental Schs; Mem 1975-, Pres OK Chapt 1980-82, Am Assn Dental Res; Mem, Intl Assn Dental Res, 1975-; Mem, IADR Dental Mats Grp, 1982-; Mem, Acad Intl Dental Studies, 1982-; Mem, Am Col Dentists, 1983-; cp/Dir 1982-, Treas 1983-84, Secy 1984-, OK Hlth

Sers Fed Credit Union, Bd Dirs; Mem 1978-84, Vice-Chm 1983-84, Affirmative Action Coun, OK Hlth Sci Ctr; Vol Fac, 1982-, Free Dental Clin; OK Hispanic Assn Higher Ed, 1981-; Nat Secy, 1974-, Coun Operative Dentistry Edrs; Mem, Exam Review Com 1981-84, Chm, Operative Subcom 1982-84, Ctl Reg Dental Testing Ser; Panelist, Hispanics in Hlth Professions, Unity Prog, KTVY Channel 4, OKC; Assoc Editor, 1983-; Jour OK Dental Assn; Edit Adv, 1983-; Dental Student Jour; hon/Author of Num Pubs; UCLA Regents Scholar, 1964-68; Omicron Kappa Upsilon, 1971; Kappa Delta Pi, 1975; Summa Cum Laude, Ctl St Univ, 1976, 1978; Selected Tchg Standout, 1977; Best Clin Tchr Awd, 1978; Outstg Clrm Instr Awd, 1980; Fellow, Acad Gen Dentistry, 1980; Best Clrm Tchr, 1981; Fellow, Acad Dentistry Intl, 1981; Fellow, Acad Intl Dental Studies, 1982; Best Clin Instr Awd, 1983; Fellow, Am Col Dentists, 1983; W/W Frontier Sci & Technol, 1984.

MITCHELL, JO BENNETT oc/Educational Administrator; b/Jan 14, 1928; ba/Seattle, WA; m/Robert C; c/Drake Curtis, John Douglas, Mari Cecilia; p/ Hilary J and Inez Drake Bennett (dec); sp/Mabel Higgins Mitchell, Cloudcroft, NM; ed/BA, 1949, NM St Univ; MA, 1981, Pacific Oaks Col; pa/Day Care Tchr, 1949-50; Nursery Sch Tchr, 1950-51; Tchr, Campus Pre Sch, NM St Univ, 1961-65; Tchg Assoc, Hebeler Lab Sch, CTL WA Univ, 1970-82; Dir, AK-NW Ext Ctr, SF Theol Sem, 1982-; NOW; Nat Assn Ed Yg Chd; Assn Chd Ed Intl; WA Assn Edrs Per Early Chd Progs, St VP 1980; cp/Phi Delta Kappa; Later Yrs Hist Com; Assoc Presb Ch Edrs; Soc Adv Cont'g Ed Clergy; Org Modiale pour Ed Prescholiare; Westminster Foun, 1979-82; Bd Mem, United Min Higher Ed, 1977-82; AAUW; AAUP; rel/U Presb Ch, Mem, Elder; hon/Presentor at Nat Conf Nat Assn Ed Yg Chd, 1978, 1982; W/W Am Wom.

MITCHELL, MARTHA RAYE oc/ Litton Microwave Consultant, Wedding Consultant and Caterer; b/Apr 10, 1938; h/Route 3, Box 85, Winfield, AL 35594; ba/Same; m/Joe Wayne; c/ Deborah Cheryl Mitchell Ingle, Vicki Rene Mitchell Potts, Michael Wayne; p/ Willis Michael (dec) and Christine McKay, Winfield, AL; ed/HS Grad; Bus Deg 1956; pa/Wimberingly Thomas Ofc, 1956; McKay & Mitchell Store, 1957-80; R P McDavid Co Inc, Litton Microwave Conslt, 1982-; Winfield Adult Ed Tchr, 1982; Microwave Cooking Classes, 1982; Owner & Operator, Martha's Reception Ser, 1981-; cp/ Cadette Co-Ldr, 1972-73; GSA, Co-Ldr, 1970-71; r/Free Will Bapt; Author of Microwave Cook Book, 1982; Cert Superior Achmt Vocal Study, 1982-83.

MITCHELL, MICHAEL EUGENE oc/ Executive, Senior Staff Engineer at Hughes Aircraft Company; b/Jun 29, 1930; h/147 South Kingsley Street, Anaheim, CA 92806; ba/Fullerton, CA; m/Joan B (dec); c/Michael T, Donald G, Nicole M; p/Otto E and Helen E Mitchell (dec); sp/Donald and Margaret Beard, Chicago, IL; ed/BSEE & BS Engrg Math, 1953, Univ MI; Grad Courses, Univ OK, 1962-64; mil/USNR, 1948-59; pa/Mem, Tech Staff, Bell Telephone Labs, 1953-57; R & D Proj Engr, Consltg Engr

Mil Communs, GE Adv'd Devel Coun, 1957-75; Sr Staff Engr, Hughes Aircraft Co, 1975-; AAAS, 1972-79; Treas Univ MI Br 1952-53, Prof Grp Info Theory 1962-, Chm Syracuse Chapt 1974-75, Computer Soc 1964-, IEEE Communs Soc 1965-, IEEE; Math Soc Am, 1963-73; cp/Kappa Alpha Psi, 1949-, Treas Univ MI Chapt 1952-53; r/Prot; hon/Author of Num Pubs; Jr C of C S'ship, 1948; Kalamazoo Citizens Grant, 1949; Kappa Rho Sigma; Univ MI Hon; Eta Kappa Nu, 1952; Tau Beta Pi, 1952; Phi Kappa Phi, 1953; Sigma Xi, 1953; AIEE-IRE Annual Awd, Univ MI, 1953; RESA, 1960, 1970; DIB; W/W: Fin & Indust, E, Ed, US.

MITCHELL, PATRICIA ANN oc/ University Teaching; b/Sep 17, 1946; h/ 894 Bolton Circle, Benicia, CA 94510; ba/San Francisco, CA; m/Larry W; c/ Candyce; p/Mr and Mrs James G Turner, Brandywine, MD; sp/Mr and Mrs Thomas Mitchell, Bowling Green, KY; ed/BS, Morgan St Col, 1968; MS, So IL Univ, 1970; PhD, Cath Univ Am, 1978; pa/Asst Prof, Univ SF, 1977-; Rdg Spec 1970-77, 1st Grade Tchr 1968-70, P G Co Public Schs; IRA; Am Ed Res Assn; Nat Assn Female Execs; AAUP; r/Meth; hon/Author of "A Feminist Approach to Wom's Col", 1983; Outstg Yg Wom Am; W/W W.

MITCHELL, RUSSELL HARRY oc/ Dermatologist; b/Oct 19, 1925; h/Route 2, Box 99, Leesburg, VA 22075; ba/ Leesburg, VA; m/Judith Lawes; c/Kathy Ellen, Gregory Alan, Jill Elaine, Crystal Anne; p/William John and Anna Lillian Mitchell (dec); sp/Jack and Crystal Lawes Douvarjo (dec); ed/St Ambrose Col, 1944-45; Notre Dame Univ, NROTC, 1945-46; BS, BA, Univ MN, 1947-51; Univ PA, 1968-69; Internship, Gorgas Hosp, Canal Zone, 1951-52; Residency, Naval Hosp, Phila, 1967-68, 1968-70; mil/USN, 1943-45, 1953-81, Adv'd Through Grades to Capt, 1st Marine Div 1965-66, Panama 1952-64, Post War Civil Ser; pa/Asst Chief, Gorgas Hosp, 1955-64; Chief Med & Surg Wards, AZ St Hosp, 1965; Cmdg Ofcr 1st Med Bn & Asst Div Surg, 1st Marine Div, 1965-67; Residency Tng Naval Hosp, Phila & Univ PA, 1967-70; Chief Dermatol 1970-73, Chief, Out-Patient Ser 1972-73, Pensacola Naval Hosp; Staff Dermatol, Nat Naval Med Ctr, 1973-; Lectr Dermatol, 1970-73; Asst Prof, Georgetown Univ Med Sch, 1975-; Conslt Dermatol, Prince William Hosp, 1974-; Staff, Loudoun Meml Hosp, 1978-; Fellow, Am Acad Dermatol; Fellow, Am Col Phys; Am Med Assn; Assoc Mil Surgs; Assoc Mil Dermatol; Naval Inst; Soc Am Archaeol; Phi Chi Med Frat; Diplomate, Am Bd Dermatol; Fellow, Explorers Clb; Diplomate, Pan Am Med Assn; Assoc Mem, Marine's Meml Clb; Loudoun Co Med Soc; Dermatol Foun; Mem, Royal Col Phys; Mem, L S B Leakey Foun; Mem, Am Archaeol Inst; r/Prot; hon/ Author of Num Pubs incl'g "A Possible Gold Pectoral" Am Antiquity 1964; "Sarcoidosis w Cutaneous Lesions Localized to the Dorsum of Feet" Archives Dermatol 1979, Co-Author; Caballero Orden de Vasco Nunez de Balboa, Republic Panama, 1952; Decorated Bronze Star w Combat V; Vietnam Gallantry Cross w Palm & Clasp.

MITCHELL, ULYSS STANFORD oc/

Minister, Sociologist, World Affairs; b/ Jul 2, 1902; h/33 Linda Avenue, Number 2111, Oakland, CA 94611; m/Viola Elizabeth; c/Robert Lewis, Marcia Ann Cousins, Ellen May Ogden; p/Robert and May Mitchell (dec); ed/BA, MA, THB, BD, ThD; m/ROTC; pa/Assoc Min, White Temple Sandiago, 1928-32, Atherton Bapt LA 1932-34; City Temple, Sioux Falls SD, Dir Adult & Social Ed; No Bapt Conv, 1934-39; Pastor First Bapt Ch, Berkeley CA, 1939-43; Exec Dir, Nat Conf of Christians & Jews, 1943-7; Exec, Ch World Ser, 1947-49; Pres, Foun Humanity, 1959-80; Intl Res & Travel to Est World Univ for UN; US Coun Ch; Am Fdn Scist; cp/World Federalists; Commonwealth Clb CA; Kiwanis; Ch Min Coun; Del 1945 Fdg UN; r/Prot; hon/Author of "Objective Christian Ed", "The Manchurian Situation", "Asian Studies"; World Forensics, UN Assn; Men Achmt; W/W World; W/ W Am; Rel Readers Am.

MITRA, SHOUMYA SUCHI oc/ Student; b/Apr 26, 1960; h/742 South 101st East Avenue, Apartment 20, Tulsa, OK 74128; p/Anil Kumar Mitra, Chittagong, Bangladesh; ed/HS Grad; Att'd Chittagong Govt Col 1978; pa/ Pres, Intl Student Assn, Rogers St Col; r/Hindu; hon/LEEPOP Awds, Rogers St Col Foun.

MITTELSTAEDT, JOAN NAOMI oc/Educator, Business Owner; b/Feb 9, 1950; h/304 Quarry Lane, Neenah, WI 54956; ba/Same; c/Robert John; p/H Arthur and Naomi Steiner, Chilton, WI; ed/BS 1972, MS 1978, Univ WI-Stevens Point; pa/Edr, Menasha Public Schs, 1972-; Bus Owner, Fox Val Bus Conslts, 1978-; NCTE, 1973; WI Coun Tchrs Eng, 1973; Secy, Am Fdn Tchrs, Local 1166, 1974-76; WI Reg Writers, 1976; Assn Supvn & Curric Devel, 1983; Delta Zeta, 1969; Delta Kappa Gamma, 1977; Worldwide Diamond Assn, 1979; cp/ Public Spkr Free Enterprise, Entrepreneurship, Assertiveness, 1978-; Netwk Dir, Nat Assn Female Execs, 1981-; Repub Pres Task Force, Charter Mem, 1982-; r/Epis; hon/Amway Gold Direct Distbr, 1979; W/W Am Wom; Outstg Yg Wom Am.

MIXSON, ELIZABETH W oc/ Resource Teacher Learning Disability and Emotional Handicapped; b/Sep 7, 1926; h/Route 2, Box 185, DeLand, FL 32720; ba/DeLand, FL; m/James K; p/ Rosa L White, Tallahassee, FL; sp/Marie S Mixson; ed/BS, FL St, 1951; MEd, Stetson Univ, 1974; pa/Williston FL 1948-55, Charleston SC 1956-61, Enterprise Elem 1961-65, Woodward Ave Elem 1966-, Tchr; CEP; NEA; Volusia Ed Assn; FL Tchg Profession; Volusia Co Assn Chd w Lrng Disability; AAUW; cp/Delta Kappa Gamma; r/Bapt; hon/W/ W: Am Wom, Child Devel Profls.

MODLIN, HOWARD S oc/Attorney; b/Apr 10, 1931; h/1120 Park Avenue, New York, NY 10028; ba/NY, NY; m/ Margot S; c/James, Laura, Peter; p/ Martin and Rose Modlin (dec); ed/BA, Union Col, 1952; JD, Columbia Law Sch, 1955; pa/Assoc 1956-61, Ptnr 1961-76, Mng Ptnr 1976-, Weisman, Celler, Spett, Modlin & Wertheimer, & Predecessors; Secy/Dir, Amadac Indust Inc, Century Glove Inc, Fedders Corporation & Gen DataComm Indust Inc; Dir Am Book-Stratford Press Inc, Trans-Lux Corp; Am Bar Assn; Assn

Bar City NY & DC Bar Assn; cp/Vice Chm Bd Dirs, Daugh Jacob Geriatric Ctr; Bd Dirs, Univ Settlement House; hon/W/W Fin & Indust.

MOELLER, BEVERLEY BOWEN oc/ Agricultural Company Executive; b/Oct 12, 1925; h/1590 Forest Villa Lane, McLean, VA 22101; ba/Brazil; m/Roger David; c/Roger Bowen, Wendell, Claire M Rygg, Barbara Bowen, Thomas David; p/G Walter Bowen (dec); sp/ Grace A Moeller, Pasadena, CA; ed/BA, Whittier Col, 1956; MA 1965, PhD 1968, Univ CA-LA; pa/Writer, Val News & Greensheet, 1961-64; Val Col 1968-69, Univ CA-LA 1970, Petroleos Brasileiros 1972-73, Tchr; Pres, Nova Pioneira Agroindustrial, LTDA, Belem & Paragominas, Para, Brazil, 1982-; cp/ Ventura Co Grand Jury, 1965; Treas, Ventura Co Commun Action Com, 1965-66; CA Reg Water Control Commun, 1970-71; Dir, Associacao Cultural Brasil-Estados Unidos, 1972-73; IEEE Dir Northernva, 1978-81; Inter-Am Soc; Intl Soc Tropical Foresters; hon/ Author of Num Pubs; Ventura Co Commend Commun Ser, 1966; IEEE Commend, 1982, 1983; Dean's List Cornell Univ 1944, Whittier Col, 1956; W/W Am Wom.

MOELLER, DADE W oc/College Professor; b/Feb 27, 1927; h/27 Wildwood Drive, Bedford, MA 01730; ba/ Boston, MA; m/Betty R; c/Garland R, Mark B, William Kehne, Matthew P, Elisabeth Anne; p/Mrs Robert Moeller, Malabar, FL; ed/BS, MS, GA Inst Technol, 1948; PhD, NC St Univ, 1957; mil/USN, 1944-46; USPHS, 1948-66; Chief Radiological Hlth Tng, Taft Sanitary Engrg Ctr, 1957-61; Ofc Charge, NEn Radiological Hlth Lab, 1961-66; Harvard Univ, 1966-; Pres, 1971-72, Hlth Physics Soc; Am Nuclear Soc; APHA; Am Conf Govtl Indust Hygienists; r/Presb; hon/Author of Num Pubs incl'g "Standard Radioassay Technics--A Status Report", Hlth Lab Sci, 1967, Co-Author of "Criteria for Dose Limits to the Public", Am Jour Radiol, 1983; AM, Hon, Harvard Univ, 1969; Recip Dist'd Achmt Awd, Hlth Physics Soc, 1982; Cert Apprec, US Nuclear Regulatory Comm, 1976; W/W: Engrg, Am; Am Men Sci.

MOESER, ELLIOTT LYLE oc/Superintendent of Schools; b/Nov 9, 1946; h/ Route 4, Box 14, Blackfoot, ID 83221; ba/Blackfoot, ID; m/Susan Joan; c/ Aaron Paul, Matthew Edward, Adam Elias; p/Lyle and Marion Moeser, Butte des Morts, WI; sp/Paul and Ruth Rhodes, Lakewood, CO; ed/BS, Midland Luth Col, 1969; MA, Univ WI-River Falls, 1972; Spec Cert, Univ WI-Milwaukee, 1977; PhD Prog, Univ MN; pa/Social Studies Tchr, Milwaukee Jr HS, 1969-72; Asst Prin, S Milwaukee Jr HS, 1972-74; Prin, Webster Stanley Mid Sch, 1974-77; Supt, Somerset WI, 1977-80; Supt, Blackfoot ID, 1980-; Mem Legis Com 1980-, Chm Legis Com 1983, ID Assn Sch Admrs; cp/Bd Dirs, 1982-, Blackfoot Kiwanis Clb; Blackfoot Rotary Clb; Bd Dirs, 1982-, Gtr Blackfoot Area C of C; Bd Dirs 1981-83, Pres 1982-83, Friends Channel 10; r/Luth; hon/Author of Num Pubs; W/W: WI, Among Students Am Univs; Outstg Yg Men Am.

MOFFAT, JOHN WILLIAM oc/Professor of Physics; b/May 5, 1932; h/293

Crawford Street, Toronto, Ontario M6J 2V7; ba/Toronto, Ontario; m/Patricia Ohlendorf; c/Sandra, Tina; p/Esther Winther Moffat, Copenhagen, Denmark; ed/PhD, Trinity Col, Cambridge Univ, 1958; pa/Sr Res Fellow, Imperial Col, 1957-58; Scist, Res Inst Adv'd Studies, 1958-60; Prin Scist, 1961-64; Scist 1960-61; Assoc Prof 1964-67, Prof 1967-, Dept Physics, Univ Toronto; Dept Sci & Indust Res Fellow, 1958-60; NSERC Can Grantee, 1965; Fellow Cambridge Phil Soc; r/Prot; hon/Author of Num Pubs; W/W: World, Am, Frontier Sci & Technol.

MOFFIC, HILLARD STEVEN oc/ Psychiatrist; b/May 5, 1946; h/5239 Loch Lomond, Houston, TX 77096; ba/ Houston, TX; m/Lynn Rusti; c/Stacia, Evan; p/Sam and Misha Moffic, Chicago, IL; sp/Ervin and Harriett Hansher, Milwaukee, WI; ed/MD, Yale Univ, 1971; Residency Psychi, Univ Chgo, 1975; mil/AUS, 1975-77, Maj; pa/Clin Dir, Calhoun-Cleburne Mtl Hlth Ctr, 1975-77; Clin Dir, West End Mtl Hlth Clin, 1977-; Assoc Prof Psychi, Baylor Col Med, 1982; Num Orgs incl'g Conslt, Drug & Alcohol Progs, AUS, 1975-77; Conslt, Jewish Fam Ser, 1977-78; Com Mbrship, Am Assn Social Psychi, 1981-; r/Jewish; hon/Author of Num Pubs; Outstg Tchr, Baylor Col Med, 1981; W/ W S & SW.

MOHAN, BRIJ oc/Professor and Dean; b/Aug 9, 1939; h/1573 Leycester Drive, Baton Rouge, LA 70808; ba/ Baton Rouge, LA; m/Prem Sharma; c/ Anupama Sharma, Apoorva Sharma; p/ Dr Ram P Sharma and Shree D Sharma, Mursan, UD, India; sp/B P Sharma and Anand D Sharma, Guna, MP, India; ed/ BA 1958, MSW 1960, Agra Univ; PhD, Lucknow Univ, 1964; pa/Prof, Dean, LA St Univ, 1976-; Acad Spec, Univ WI 1975-76; Lectr 1963-75, Res Scholar 1960-63, Lucknow Univ; Mem, Nat Assn Social Wkrs, 1975-; Mem, Coun on Social Wk, 1976-; Life Mem, Indian Assn Tnd Social Wkrs; Intl Assn Schs of Social Wk; r/Hindu; hon/Author of "Social Psychi in India", 1973, "India's Social Probs", 1968; W/W: Among Writers, S & SW, Louisiana, Indo-Am; Profl Social Wkr's Dir.

MOHAN, C oc/Research Computer Scientist; b/Jun 3, 1955; h/309 Tradewinds Drive #10, San Jose, CA 95123; ba/San Jose, CA; m/Kalpana; p/K and Radha Chandrasekaran; ed/BTech Chem Engrg, Indian Inst of Technol, 1977; PhD Computer Sci, Univ TX-Austin, 1981; pa/Res Staff Mem, IBM San Jose Res Labs, 1981-; Res/Tchg Asst, Univ TX-Austin, 1977-81; Vis'g Scist, Hahn-Meitner-Institut (Berlin), 1980; Vis'g Scist, Institut Nat de Recherche en Informatique et en Automatique (France), 1979; Secy 1975-76, Pres 1976-77, Computer Clb, IIT; IEEE Computer Soc & Assn for Computing Machinery & Bay Area Tamil Assn; hon/Author Num Articles on Database & Distributed Sys, Oper'g Sys & Networking in Jours & Conf Proceedings; hon/Nat Merit S'ship in India, 1971-77; S'ship, French Govt's Centre Intl des Etudiants et Stagiares, 1979; Phi Kappa Phi; IBM Pre-Doct F'ship, 1981; W/W Frontier Sci & Technol.

MOLANO, CELIA oc/Clinical Laboratory Director; b/Oct 9, 1938; h/357 Lerida, Urb Valencia, Rio Piedras, PR

00923; ba/Rio Piedras, PR; c/Otilda I Pinilla; p/Felipe Molano (dec) and Isabel Cardenas, Rio Piedras, PR; ed/BS, Panama Univ, 1957; Post Grad, Spec Anal, Panama Univ, 1959-61; Virology Anal, Gorgas Hosp; Masters, Univ PR, 1976; Advance Microbiol, Med Sci Sch, Univ PR, 1982; pa/Med Technol, Gorgas Meml Lab, 1957-62; Asst Parasitology Prof 1960-61, Asst Microbiol Prof 1960-62, Panama Univ; Asst Microbiol Prof, Spec Anal Med Technol Sch, 1961-62; Microbiologist, FDA, 1961-62; Lab Dir, Pavia Hosp, Santurce PR, 1962-68; Lab Dir, Soto Lab, Caguas PR, 1963-68; Owner & Lab Dir, Dispensarios de Salud Lab, 1967-75; Owner & Lab Dir, San Martin Hosp, 1968-; Asst Admr 1975-80-, Pers Dir 1977-83, San Martin Hosp; Pres, Lab Sers Grp, 1980-; Dir, Celia Molano & Assocs, 1980-; Bd Dirs, Student Del 1976, Voter 1977, Secy 1978-79, Elect Pres 1979-80, Pres 1980-81, Past Pres 1981-82, PR Hosp Admrs; PR Hosp Assn; Hosp Financial Mgmt; Am Soc Clin Pathologists; Am Soc Med Technologists; PR Col Med Technologist; PR Profls Assn; Bd Dirs, PR Cancer Leag, 1970; Bd Dirs, Trustee 1970-, Secy & Voter, Num Coms, I Gonzalez Martinez Oncological Hosp; Fdr, Mem, Med Technologist Assn Panama, 1968; Bd Dirs, Voter 1980, Elect Pres 1981, Pres 1982, PR Labs Owners Assn; r/Cath; hon/Nums Sems & Pubs; Best Student Master Hlth Ser Adm, Julio A Perez Awd, 1976; Pres Awd, PR Hosp Adm, 1976, 1977, 1978; Recog "Hd Start" Prog, 1976; Recog from Pres PR Hosp Adm, 1980, 1982; Recog Hosp Financial Mgmt Assn PR, 1981; Recog PR Cancer Leag, 1980, 1982.

MOLLENKAMP, JANE COHN oc/Public Relations Account Supervisor; b/Feb 16, 1946; h/24 Standish Avenue, Northwest, Atlanta, GA 30309; ba/Atlanta, GA; c/Carrick Gray, Jennifer V; p/Milton and Jean Cohn, West Point, GA; ed/BA, Newcomb Col Tulane Univ, 1968; Att'd Harvard Univ 1966, GA St Univ 1969-71, 1983-84; pa/Public Relats Account Supvr, Wemmers Communs; Dir 1982-84, Commun Relats Conslt 1980-82, Midtown YWCA; Legis Aid, City Coun Mem, E Valentine, 1979-81; Polit Campaign Mgr, 1978-81; Atlanta Chapt, Am Mktg Assn; cp/Bus Asst Com, Sem Coor, Mem, Midtown Bus Assn; Civic Assn, V Chm; Gubernatorial Campaign Steering Com; Tulane Alumnae Com; Atlanta Presv Ctr; LWV; r/Jewish; hon/Num Pubs; Mayoral Awd, Dist'd Commun Ser, 1979.

MONACO, ANTHONY P oc/Professor Surgery, Harvard Medical School; b/Mar 12, 1932; h/25 Farlow Road, Newton, MA 02158; ba/Boston, MA; m/Mary Louise; c/A Peter, Mark Churchill, Christopher Donato, Lisa Oudens; p/Donato (dec) and Rose Monaco, Philadelphia, PA; sp/John and Louise Oudens, Manchester, NH; ed/BA, Univ PA, 1952; MD, Harvard Med Sch, 1956; pa/Sci Dir, Cancer Res Inst, 1980-; Chief Div Organ Transplantation, NE Deaconess Hosp, 1975-; Prof Surg, Harvard Med Sch, 1977-; Trustee, NE Organ Bk, 1970-; Bd Dirs, Kidney Foun MA, 1978-81; Mem, Harvard Med Sch Alumni Coun, 1979-81; Chm, NE Organ Bk, 1981-; r/Cath; hon/Author

of "Biol of Tissue Transplantation", "Transplantation Proceedings" 1981; Phi Beta Kappa, Univ PA, 1951; Nat Scholar, Harvard Med Sch, 1952-56; Alpha Omega Alpha, 1955; Henry Asbury Christian Awd, 1956; Lederle Med Fac Awd, 1968; W/W: E, Am, Frontier Sci & Technol.

MONAGHAN, MARY PATRICIA oc/Writer and Teacher; b/Feb 15, 1946; h/7.2 Mile Farmers Loop, SR, Box 30141-H, Fairbanks, AK 99701; ba/Fairbanks, AK; m/Roland E Wulbert; p/Edward J and Mary Monaghan, Anchorage, AK; sp/Morris and Anna Wulbert (dec); ed/BA 1967, MA 1971, Univ MN; MFA, Univ AK, 1981; pa/Editor, Univ AK, 1969-71; Public Relats Dir, Walker Art Ctr, 1973; Editor, MN Public Radio, 1974-75; Aide, AK St Legis, 1976; Wom's Editor, Daily News Miner, 1976-77; Instr, Tanana Val Commun Col, 1978-; Fairbanks Arts Assn, Lit Chm, 1982; NOW, Fairbanks Chapt, Correspondent, 1983; Fireweed Press, Pres, 1982; Authors' Guild, 1982-; Fairbanks Wom Writers' Salon, 1980-; Phi Kappa Phi, 1980-; r/Quakers; hon/Author of Book of Goddesses & Heroines, 1981, 1982, Winterburning, 1984; Indi Artists' F'ship, AK St Coun Arts, 1980; Arts Travel Awd, 1979; St Fiction Awd, 1979; W/W Am Wom.

MONDAL, KALYAN oc/Elec and Comp Engineer; b/Aug 17, 1951; h/1803 Latta Street, Allentown, PA 18104; ba/Allentown, PA; m/Chitralekha; c/Indrani; p/Dwijendra N (dec) and Bijali Mondal, Calcutta, India; ed/BSc 1969, B Tech 1972, M Tech 1974, Univ Calcutta; PhD, Univ CA, 1978; pa/Res Asst, Univ CA-Davis, 1975-77; Res Asst, Univ CA-Santa Barbara, 1977-78; Lectr, Univ CA-Santa Barbara, 1978-79; Asst Prof, Lehigh Univ, 1980-81; Mem Tech Staff, AT & T Bell Labs, 1982-; IEEE, 1976-; ACM, 1980-; Sigma Xi, 1978-; Eta Kappa Nu, 1978-; Secy, India Assn, Davis, CA, 1975-76; r/Hinduism; hon/Author of Num Articles; Gold Medal, Univ Calcutta, 1972, 1974; Res Grant, 1981; W/W Frontier Sci & Technol.

MONDOUX, ROBERT WAYNE oc/Psychotherapist; b/Sep 11, 1949; h/68 Sedgwick Street, Jamaica Plain, MA 02130; b/Boston, MA; p/Gerard Bertrand and Iola Marie Barthelemy Mondoux; ed/BA, Plymouth St Col, 1971; MEd, Boston St Col, 1976; Postgrad, Suffolk Univ; pa/Psychi Aide, NH Hosp, 1971-72; Mtl Hlth Wkr, Augusta Mtl Hlth Inst, 1972-73; Mgr, Cnslr N Cottage Prog Alcoholics, 1973-78; Psychol Tech Outpatient Clin, Psychol Ser, 1974-77; Cnslr 1977-80, Ld Cnslr 1981-82, Hlth Sci Spec 1982-, Drug Dependence Treatment Ctr; Dir, Sedgwick St Commun Residence Alcoholics, 1978-; Grp Psychotherapy Cons Drug & Alcohol Units, Tufts NE Med Ctr, 1981-82; Clin Supvr, Cons St Jude House, 1981-; Psychotherapist, Cnslg Assocs, 1982-; Mem, APGA; Nat Assn Mtl Hlth Wkrs; Am Rehab Cnslg Assn; Assn Spec Grp Wk; Assn Cnslr Ed & Supvn; Intl Halfway House Assn; MA Coalition Substance Abuse Providers; N Atl Reg Cnslr Supvn Assn; hon/W/W E.

MONROE, FREDERICK LEROY oc/Manager, Chemical Control; b/Oct 13, 1942; h/315 Bridle Trail, Indian Trail,

NC 28079-9650; ba/Matthews, NC; c/Sara; p/H S Monroe and M R Monroe, Redmond, OR; ed/BS, OR St Univ, 1964; MS, WA St Univ, 1974; mil/USAF, Ret'd Maj; pa/Air Pollution Control Ofcr, 1968-69; Air Pollution Res, 1969-74; Envir Engr, Ore-Ida Foods, 1974, 1977; Conslt, 1977-78; Wastewater Applications Engrg, 1978-79; Chem Control Mgr, 1980-; Air Pollution Control Assn; Water Pollution Control Fdn; Am Chem Soc; cp/Kiwanis; r/Unity; hon/Author of "Air Emissions of Plywood Veneer Dryers", 1971; Cert'd Waste Water Treatment Operator.

MONTAGNE, JOHN oc/Professor Emeritus of Geology; b/Apr 17, 1920; h/17Hodgman Canyon, Bozeman, MT 59715; ba/Bozeman, MT; m/Phoebe M Corthell; c/Clifford, Mathew H; p/Henry (dec) and Ella S de la Montagne, Bozeman, MT; sp/Mr and Mrs Morris E Corthell, Laramie, WY; ed/BA, Dartmouth Col, 1942; MA 1951, PhD 1955, Univ WY; mil/AUS, Mtn Inf, 10th Mtn Div, Pvt-Capt, 1942-46, Medit Theatre, 1945; pa/Sci Tchr, Prin, Jackson HS, 1946-48; Ranger, Grand Teton Nat Pk, 1948-49; Asst to Dir Admissions, Dartmouth Col, 1949-50; Instr, Asst Prof, CO Sch Mines, 1953-57; Asst Prof, Prof 1957-83, Prof Emeritus 1983-, MT St Univ; Cert, Profl Geologist, Am Assoc Profl Geologist; Secy, Rocky Mtn Sect 1960-68, Chm 1982, Fellow Geol Soc Am; Mem, Quaternary Assoc; Treas, 1966-73, Am Assoc Petrol Geol, Intl Glaciological Soc Am; cp/Chm, Intl Snow Sci Wkshop, 1982; Bd Dirs, Pres 1973-74, Bridger Bowl Ski Area Inc; Mem Bd Dir, Pres 1960-, Yellowstone Lib & Mus Assoc; Fdg Mem, Pres 1965, MT Wilderness Assn; Pres 1967, Dist Gov 1979, Rotary Clb Bozeman; r/Prot; hon/Num Articles & Pubs; Phi Kappa Phi; MT St Univ Alumni Assn; W/W W; Am Men & Wom Sci.

MONTGOMERY, OLIVE WOLFE SCHMAUSS oc/Educator, Executive; h/185 Perry Avenue, Silvermine, CT 06850; ba/Same; m/Carl John Schmauss; c/Joan Kratzer, Mary-Ann Montgomery, Lee Donnelley, John Cavanagh, Daniel Montgomery; p/M Goode and Katharine Slayback Wolfe (dec); ed/Oxford Sch, 1928; Hartford Sch Music; Smith Col, 1932; Piano Student of Aurelio Giorni, Rome & NYC & Bruce Simmonds, Yale Sch Music; pa/VP, Randall Advtg Agy, 1942; Radio Writer of Serials, Drama; Fdr, Pres, Montgomery Agy, 1947-; NYC Concert Pianist, 1927-42; Actress, Stage & Screen; Treas, CT St Assn, Past Pres, Treas, Greenwich Br, Nat Leag Am Penwom; Fdr, Shakespeare Theatre, Stratford CT; Fdr, Lincoln Ctr for Perf'g Arts, NYC; Fdr, Norwalk Symph Orch, Norwalk, CT; Bd Dirs, New Haven Symph Orch, 1932-42; Bd Dirs, Neighborhood Music Sch, 1930-42; Mem, DAR, Drum Hill Chapt; Mem, Smith Col Clb; Mem, Eng Spkg Union; Mem, Jr Leag Am; r/Congregational Ch; hon/Intl W/W Wom; W/W: E, Am Wom; 5000 Personalities World.

MONTGOMERY, RICHARD MATTERN oc/Retired Air Force Officer, Company Director; b/Dec 15, 1911; h/Post Office Box 93, Longboat Key, FL 33548; c/Nancy, Richard M Jr,

Thomas C; p/Charles W Sr and Eva Mattern Montgomery; ed/BS, US Mil Acad, 1933; Student Flying Tng Ctr (San Antonio, TX), 1933-34; AC Tech Tng Sch, 1937-38; Air War Col, 1946-47; mil/AUS, 2nd LT, 1933, USAAC, 1934; Adv'd through Grades to Lt/Gen, 1962; Chief Insp, Test Pilot Panama Air Depot, (France Field, CZ), 1935-37; Assigned Chanute Field (IL), 1937-38; Flying Instr, Flight & Stage Cmdr, Randolf Field (TX), 1938-42; Dir, Flying Tng, Army Air Field, (Enid, OK), 1942; Cmdr, Army Air Field, (Indep, KS), 1943; Chief Indiv Tng Div Ofc Asst, Chief Air Staff Tng (Pentagon, Wash, DC), 1943-44; Cmdr, 383d Bomb Wing, 1944-45; Mem, Jt Strategic Plans & Opers Grp HQs, Far E Command (Tokyo, Japan), 1947-48; Cmdr, 51st Jet Fighter Wing, Naha AFB (Okinawa), 1948-49; Dep Cmdr, 97th Bomb Wing, Biggs AFB (El Paso, TX), 1949-51; Dep Chief Staff HQS, Strategic Air Command (Omaha, NE), 1951-52, Chief of Staff, 1952-56; Dept Cmdr 2nd AF, Barksdale AFB (Shreveport, LA), 1956-58; Cmdr 3rd Air Div, (Strategic Air Command), Guam, Mariannas Isls, 1958-59; Asst V-Chief Staff, HQs, USAF (Wash, DC), 1959-62; V-Cmdr-in-Chief, USAF, Europe, 1962-66; Ret'd 1966; pa/Dir, Gen Sers Life Ins Co (Wash), 1968-82; Freedoms Foun Valley Forge (PA); Exec VP Devel 1967-68, Reg VP 1968-76, Coun Trustees 1976-; cp/Former Commr, Town of Longboat Key; Order of Daedalions; AF Assn; Repub Party; 32° Mason; Shriner; Scottish Rite; r/United Meth; hon/ Decorated DSM w Oak Leaf Cluster, Army & AF; Legion of Merit w Oak Leaf Cluster; Army Commend Metal w 2 Oak Leaf Clusters; Silver Beaver, Silver Antelope Awd, BSA; Gold Medal Humanitarian Awd, Penn St Univ.

MONTHAN, DORIS BORN oc/ Author/Editor; b/May 26, 1924; h/Post Office Box 1698, Flagstaff, AZ 86002; ba/Flagstaff, AZ; m/Guy; c/William Edgar; p/Edgar J and Linda Vogt Born (dec); sp/Jessie Rae Monthan, Tucson, AZ; ed/Univ AZ, 1943-44; NY Univ, 1948-49; Columbia Univ, 1950-51; No AZ Univ, 1976-82; pa/Wom's Editor, Tucson Daily Citizen, 1944-45; Sect Editor, Wom's Wear Daily, 1945-46; Assoc Editor, Simplicity Mag, 1949-51; Advtg Mgr, Crown Sleep Shops, 1953-67; Editor, Northland Press, 1970-72; Editor, Mus No AZ, Mus Notes, 1972-75; cp/Flagstaff Fest Arts, Bd Dirs, 1971-82; Asst Leag Flagstaff, 1983-; Kappa Kappa Gamma, Alumnae Clb No AZ, 1970-; Panelist, AZ Comm Arts, 1983-; r/Epis, Vestry, Epis Ch Epiphany, 1983; hon/Author of *Art & Indian Individualists* 1975, *Nacimientos* 1979; Border Reg Lib Assn Awd, 1975; Rounce & Coffin Clb Awd, Best Wn Books, 1975; Achmt Awd, Kappa Kappa Gamma Frat, 1984; W/W: Am Art, Am Wom, W; World W/W Wom; Dir Dist'd Am.

MOODY, FORREST BANKSTON oc/Consultant Forester; b/Jan 29, 1930; h/1821 Wildwood, Orange, TX 77630; m/Frances Roberts; c/Alan B, Robert W, Kenneth W, John C; p/Forrest B and Rhoda L Moody (dec); sp/Seanee and Sallie E Roberts; ed/AA, Jones Jr Col, 1949; BSF 1951, MSF 1953, Univ FL; pa/Mgmt, Marcolin Brothers, 1958;

Res, TX Forest Ser, 1962; Mgmt, Gen Box Co, 1967-78; Nat Assn Rltrs; TX Bd Rltrs; Forester Prods Res Soc; Soc Am Foresters; cp/Orange Shrine Clb, 2nd VP; Little Cypress Lions Clb, 3rd VP; r/Bapt; hon/Alpha Zeta, Zi Sigma Pi, 1950; W/W: S, S & SW.

MOODY, WILLIS ELVIS JR oc/ Professor, Ceramic Engineering, Attorney; b/Mar 30, 1924; h/4545 Northside Parkway, Apartment 13-K, Atlanta, GA 30339; ba/Atlanta, GA; c/Susan E, Michael T, Peggy A, Willis E III, William S; p/Willis E and Inez McDade Moody (dec); ed/BS 1948, MS 1949, PhD 1956, NC St Univ; JD, Woodrow Wilson Col Law, 1979; mil/USAAC, 1943-46; pa/ Ceramic Engr, Spark Plug Div, Elect Auto-Lite Co, 1949-50; Ceramic Engr, Lab Corp, 1950-51; Instr, Ceramic Engr & Metallurgy, NC St Univ, 1951-56; Prof Ceramic Engr, GA Inst Tech, 1956-; Pres 1980, Nat Inst Ceramic Engr; Trustee 1965-68, Am Ceramic Soc; Gov 1979-81, Am Assoc Engr Soc; Pres 1963, Ceramic Ed Coun; Chm Mats Div 1971, Am Soc Engr Ed; St Bar GA; Am Bar Assn; r/Meth; hon/Author of Num Articles; W/W: Am, W, Engrg, S & SW.

MOORE, DALTON JR oc/Consultant Engineer and Geologist; b/Mar 25, 1918; h/4065 Waldemar Drive, Abilene, TX 79605; ba/Same; p/Dalton (dec) and Anne Yonge Moore, TX; ed/Tarleton St Univ, 1938; TX A&M Univ, 1942; Civil Def Col, Surrey, UK, 1944; US Command & Gen Staff Col, 1945; Army War Col, 1945; mil/AUS, 1940-52, Perm Rank Maj; pa/Chief Reservoir Engr, Chgo Corporation, 1947-49; Mgr, Burdell Oil Co, 1950-52; Mgr, Wimberly Field Unit, 1953-56; Pres, Dalton Moore Engr Co, 1956-82; Consltg Profl Engr & Geologist, 1956-82, Profl Engr Num 08704; Am Inst Mining, Metall & Petrol Engrs, 1940-82; Am Arbitration Assn; Intl Platform Assn; Am Assn Ret'd Persons; Abilene Geol Soc; r/Epis; hon/ Author of Num Pubs; Num War Medals & Cits, WW II; W/W: Chgo IL, Intells.

MOORE, DAN TYLER oc/Board Chairman of International Platform, Writer, Speaker; b/Feb 1, 1908; h/2264 Berkshire Road, Cleveland Heights, OH 44106; ba/Same; m/Elizabeth Oakes, c/ Dan Tyler III, Luvie Moore Owens, Harriet Moore Ballard, Elizabeth Moore Thornton; p/Dan Tyler and Luvian Butler Moore (dec); sp/Herbert King and Harriet Walker Oakes (dec); ed/BS, Yale Univ, 1931; mil/Maj Paratroops, World War II, Chief of Counter Intell, OSS in Mid E; pa/Dir Gen, Bd Chm, Intl Platform Assn, 1964-; Cabinet Ofcr 1934-38, Chief Div Securities, 1938-42; Reg Adm, Security Exch Comm; Reg Dir, Ofc Civilian Def, 5th Core Area, World War II; Am Cancer Soc; Muscular Dystrophy; Distaff Foun; cp/Mus Nat Hist; r/Epis; hon/Author of *The Terrible Game* 1957, *Cloak & Cipher* 1962; Num Hons & Biographical Listings.

MOORE, JOHN ROBERT oc/Manager, Owner Accounting Tax Practice; b/Jul 15, 1947; ba/Charlotte, NC; m/ Geni; c/John J, Michele Nicole; p/Mr and Mrs John N Moore, Kings Mountain, NC; ed/BA, Belmont Abbey Col, 1970; pa/Owner, J Robert Moore & Assoc, 1981-; Cash Controls Mgr 1980-81, Asst Acctg Mgr 1979-80, Auditor 1979, Barclays Am Corporation, 1979-81; Sr

Financial, Acct Corporate Acctg, ARA Sers Inc, 1976-78; Sr Financial, Acct Corporate Acctg, Fidelcor Inc, 1974-76; Audit Staff, Sr Asst Acct, Deloitte Haskins & Sells, 1970-71; Audit Analyst, Blue Cross/Blue Shield, 1972; Assoc Dir, Mem Attendance, 1980-81, Charlotte Gold Chapt, Nat Assn Accts; Dir, S'hip Com, 1980-81, Charlotte Chapt, Fdg Treas Phila Chapt, 1973-74, Fdg VP Charlotte Chapt, 1972, Nat Assn Black Accts; cp/Phila Chapt, Commun Accts, Vol Sers, 1978-79; Belmont Abbey Col Alumni Assn; NC Ctl Univ Alumni Assn; Arts & Sci Coun Dept Ldr-Barclays Am Corporation, 1979-81; United Way Dept Ldr-Barclays Am Corporation, 1979-80; r/Meth; hon/ 1st Recip, Dr Martin Luther King Jr Full Tuition S'ship; W/W Am Cols & Univs.

MOORE, NELWYN BARNARD oc/ Professor of Child and Family; b/Apr 14, 1930; h/809 Belvin, San Marcos, TX 78666; ba/San Marcos, TX; m/Jerry Lloyd; c/Jerry Lloyd Jr, Amy Jo; p/ Clarence G (dec) and Lenora C Barnard, Tuleta, TX; sp/Bruce D Moore (dec); ed/ BS 1951, MEd 1963, SW TX St Univ; PhD, Univ TX-Austin, 1973; pa/Tchr Sec'dy Homemaking, Tivy HS, 1951-54; Dir, Lab Nursery Sch, Dept Home Ec 1963, 1964, Asst Instr to Prof 1963-83, SW TX St Univ; Am Home Ec Assn; Nat Assn Ed Yg Chd; TX Assn Ed Yg Chd; So Assn Chd Under Six; Am Assn Marriage & Fam Therapist; Nat Coun Admrs Home Ec; Intl Fdn Home Ec; Ch Child Dev/Fam Relats Sect & Bd, 1978-80; TX Home Ec Assn; Pres Elect, Pres, SW TX St Univ Chapt, 1981-83, TX Assn Col Tchrs; V-Chm, Ed Sect, 1982-84, Nat Coun Fam Relats; Pres Elect, Pres & Bd, 1979-81, TX Coun Fam Relats; Nat Assn Hon Soc, 1982; Pres Elect, Pres & Bd, 1982-86, Phi Upsilon Omcron; Bd, V-Chm, 1976-80, Phi Upsilon Omicron Ednl Fdn; Groves' Marriage & Fam Relats; Phi Kappa Phi; Omicron Nu; Delta Kappa Gamma; cp/ Chm Hays Co Com Aging, 1971-73; Chm Bd, Christian Perf'g Arts Ctr Yg People; Pres, VP BD, TX Assn Perf'g Arts, 1977-79; Hays Co Wel Bd, 1979-82; Trustee, First Bapt Ch, San Marcos, 1981-83; r/Bapt; hon/Author of Num Pubs incl'g "Fam Relats/Child Devel Survey", *AHEA Action*, 1980; Kappa Lambda Kappa, Outstg Tchr Awd, 1969; Prof Lecuter Series Lectr, SW TX St Univ, 1975; Outstg Edrs Am, 1975; W/W: Child Devel, S & SW.

MOORE, PHYLLIS C oc/Library Director; b/Jan 31, 1927; h/5625 Greenridge Road, Castro Valley, CA 94546; ba/Alameda, CA; m/R Scott; c/Alan, Jeanne, Philip; p/John O and Gladys J T Clark, Binghamton, NY; sp/Perry and Alice (dec); ed/BA, Hartwick Col, 1949; MA 1951, MS 1954, Syracuse Univ; DLitt, CO St Univ; PhD, Univ WI; pa/ Libn, Free Lib Phila, 1954-57; US Govt, Spec Sers, Europe, 1957-62; Sr Libn, Yonkers Public Lib, 1962-67; Lib Dir, Hastings-on-Hudson Public Lib, 1967-68; Conslt, AV Ser, Westchester Co Lib Sys, 1968-72; Dir, Falls Church Public Lib, 1972-77; Dir Libs, City of Alameda, 1978-; CoChm, Cooperative Resources 1962, Exec Coun 1975-79, Am Lib Assn; Chm, 1978-79, Bay Area Lib & Info Sys; AAUW; cp/Exec Dir, 1980-, Mask & Lute; Adv Bd, Defenders of Wildlife; Philharm Soc; Publicity Chm

1982, Exec Bd 1983, Mozart Fest; hon/ Author of Num Pubs incl'g "Command Perf" 1961, "Mission Accomplished" 1962; Elliott Howell Reed Meml Awd, 1949; NY Col Drama Fest, Best Actress, 1949; Arts & Lttrs Awd, Univ MD, 1968; Libn of Yr, VA Lib Assn, 1973; 7 USAREUR Awds; W/W: W, Am Wom; Intl W/W Commun Ser; World W/W; Notable Am; DIB.

MOORE, RICHARD ALAN oc/Public Relations Official, National Guard Officer; b/May 15, 1945; h/RFD 2, Box 810, Augusta, ME 04330; ba/Augusta, ME; m/Kisuk Kim; c/Kimberly Anne, Heidi Sue; p/Albert Read Jr Moore (dec) and Barbara Hersey Moore LaForge; ed/ BA, Univ ND, 1969; MA, Univ ME, 1970; US Army Command & Gen Staff Col, 1980; mil/AUS, 1964-67, ME ANG, 1972-; pa/Dir Pub Info, 1974-, ME Dept Public Safety; St Public Affairs Ofcr, 1976-; HQs, ME ANG, Direct Comm-1972, Current Rank: Lt Col; News Media Spec & Staff Asst, 1971-74, ME Dept Human Sers; Prog Dir, 1970-71, WNWY-FM, Norway, ME; Sta ME, 1966-67, Am Forces Korea Netwk, Tongduchon Radio Affil; Mem, Public Relats Soc Am; Charter Mem, ME Public Relats Coun; ME Press Assn; ME Assn Broadcasters; Soc Profl Jours; NG Assn US; Salvation Army Adv Bd, Augusta Corps; Gov's Public Info Adv Com; cp/Rotary Intl; Sigma Delta Chi; r/Bapt; hon/Phi Beta Kappa, 1969; Outstg Grad Jour, 1969; Pi Sigma Alpha, 1970; APR, Accredited in Public Relats, Public Relats Soc Am, 1978; W/ W E.

MOORHEAD, JAMES ROBERT oc/ Manager of Safety; b/Oct 1, 1950; h/ 2 Nitawood Drive, Little Rock, AR 72206; ba/Little Rock, AR; p/Robert G and Margaret Moorhead, Indianapolis, IN; ed/BS 1973, MBA 1983, IN St Univ; pa/Mgr Safety, 1974-76, Rebsamen Inst; Safety Engr, 1973-74, H B Zachary Co; Safety Engr, Stone & Webster Engrg Co; Am Soc Safety Engrs; Nat Safety Coun; Nat Safety Mgmt Soc; hon/Author of Num Articles; Cert; Assn Risk Mgmt; W/W S & SW.

MOORMAN, WILLIAM JACOB oc/ Regional Manager, Agronomic Services; b/Jan 15, 1923; h/810 Fallwood, Columbus, MS 39701; ba/Columbus, MS; m/Mildred; c/David Morris, Margaret Jane; p/Elmer Orville and Abbie L Mood; sp/Clifford C (dec) and Edna Hahn Morris, Minneapolis, KS; ed/Univ KS, 1942-43; KS St Univ, 1946-47; mil/ AUS, 1942-46; Operator, Moorman Feed & Seed Co Inc, 1947-61; Northrop King Co, 1961-; Territory Sales Mgr, 1961-64; Reg Sales Mgr, 1965-68; Sales Div Prom Mgr, 1968-73; Dist Sales Mgr, 1973-74; Div Sales Prom Mgr, 1974-82; Reg Mgr Agronomic, 1982; Nat Agri Mktg Assn; Dallas TX Ag Clb, 1973; cp/Nickersonks Lions Clb, 1948-61; OES, 1948-51; r/Meth; hon/Author of Num Pubs; Sunbelt Dairyman; So Beef Prodr; Delta Report, Progressive Farmer; W/W S & SW.

MORAHAN, DANIEL MICHAEL oc/ Industrial Engineer; b/Aug 15, 1940; h/ 4005 74th Place, Landover Hills, MD 20784; ba/Same; p/Mrs John J Morahan; ed/AA, 1963; BBA, George Wash Univ, 1965; Computer Lrng Ctr; pa/Owner, M-METRA Enterprises Ltd, 1973-82; Manpower Economist, US Army Chief

Staff, 1968-74; Indust Economist, US Dept Labor, Bur Labor Stats, 1965-68; Lib Tech, US Lib Cong, 1959-65; Nat Ctr Commun Crime Preven, 1982-83; Mem, Jt Pres/Congl Steering Com, 1982-84; MD St Rep to Congl Adv Bd; Am Security Coun, 1982-83; Am Def Preparedness Assn, 1969-82; Assoc Mem, US Naval Inst, US Naval Acad, 1982-83; hon/Lttrs Commend, AUS Chief Staff, 1974; Ofc Chief Chaplain, 1971; Insp Gen, 1971; Burke's Peerage; Intl W/W Intells.

MORALES DOMINGUEZ, ARTURO MARCIANO oc/Consulting Engineer Mining Field; b/Jan 27, 1915; h/San Buenaventura 437, Mexico, DF 14620; ba/Mexico, DF; m/Elvira Peinado Anchondo; c/Virginia, Leticia, Patricia; p/Carlos A Morales, Ambrosia Dominguez (dec); sp/Atanasio Peinado, Maria Anchondo (dec); ed/BS, Univ TX, 1939; BS, 1944, MIT; pa/Miner (mucker), Groundhog Mine, ASARCO, 1939; Mine Supt, Minas de Rayon, 1940-41; Mine Mgr, San Rafael y Anexas, 1941-42; Student & Grad Asst Mineral Dressing, MIT, 1942-44; Opers Engr, Pan Am World Airways, 1944; Maintenance Mgr, Mexicana de Aviacion, 1950-52; Pres, Can-Mex, S A Mining Co, 1950-52; Fdr, Bufete de Ingenieros, 1951-; Mexico Sect Am Inst Mining Engrs, 1974; Asociacion de Ingenieros de Minas Metalurgistas y Geologos de Mexico, 1950; cp/MIT Clb Mexico, 1950; MIT Alumni; UTEP Alumni; Junta de Colonos Clb de Golf Mexico, 1971; Churubusco Country Clb; Club de Golf Mexico; Contbg Mem, Orquesta Camara de la Ciudad de Mexico; Univ Clb; Consejo Nacional de Tecnologia y Ciencia, 1972; Fundacion Mexicana para el Desarrollo Rural, Contbg Mem; r/ Cath; hon/Author of Num Pubs; Best Tech Paper, Asoc Ing Min y Geo de Mex, 1971; Dist'd Mem Awd, Soc Mining Engrs of AIME, 1980; W/W W; Men of Achmt; Intl W/W Intells.

MORAN, EDGAR M oc/Physician, Chief, Hematology-Oncology; b/Apr 28, 1928; h/885 Palo Verde Avenue, Long Beach, CA 90815; ba/Long Beach, CA; m/Huguette M; c/Daniel, Andre; p/ Leon and Catty Moran; sp/Gerard and Anne Leger Moncton, Canada; ed/MD, Univ Bucharest, 1952; mil/Navy, 1956-58; pa/Prof Med, Univ CA-Irvine, 1978-; Dir, Dept Med Oncology, City Hope Med Ctr, 1976-78; Assoc Prof Med, Univ Chgo, Pritzker Sch Med, 1975-76; Am Soc Clin Oncology; Am Assn Cancer Res; Am Soc Hematology; Am Fdn Clin Res; Intl Soc Hematology; Intl Soc Chemotherapy; hon/Author of Num Pubs; Outstg New Citizen Yr Awd, 1976; Searle Awd, 13th Intl Cong Chemotherapy, 1983.

MORAN, MARLENE JUNE oc/Food Service Manager; b/Mar 17, 1939; h/34 Walnut Avenue, Bethlehem, WV 26003; ba/Bridgeport, OH; m/Fred U; c/Roy L and Fred Jr; p/Helen Yordan, Wheeling, WV; ed/Univ FL Corres, 1975; Food Ser Supvr Cert, NIFI, 1977; Cert Apllied Foodser Sanitation; pa/Dietary Aide 1967-71, Secy 1971-75, Food Ser Supvr 1967-71, OVMC; Food Ser Mgr, 1975-82, Peterson Hosp; Heartland Lansing, FSM, 1982-; Pres 1976-77, 1979-80, Pres-Elect 1982-83, Editor Bultn 1977-, WV Hosp Inst Ednl Food Ser Soc; r/Meth; hon/WV Ambassador

Public Ser Among All People, 1982; Laughlin Awd, 1957; Save Awd, 1981; Cash Saving Fair Idea, 1982; W/W: Wom, S & SW.

MORELLI, JOYCE ANDERS NELSON oc/Registered Nurse; b/Oct 5, 1942; h/1795 Upper Chelsea Reach, VA Beach, VA 23454; ba/VA Beach, VA; m/ Armand Joseph Morelli; c/William W Nelson III, Paige Marie Nelson; p/Ruby Frances Ragland, Rockville, MD; sp/Mr and Mrs Armando John Morelli, Richmond, VA; ed/Dipl, Johnston Willis Hosp Sch Nsg, 1964; Cert'd Am Bd Quality Assurance & Utilization Review, 1978; Cert, Stress Mgmt FL Hlth Inst, 1980; Cert'd ARC Nurse, 1965; pa/Evening Supvr, Johnston-Willis Hosp, 1965-68; Pt-time Evening Supvr, Forest Hill Manor, 1969; Aetna Claims Review, 1977-78; Pt-time Evening Supvr, Staff Nurse, Retreat for the Sick, 1973-74; Pt-time Night Supvr 1970-71, Supvr Utilization Reviews 1978-79, Tucker Pavillion Staff Psychi 1975-77, Chippenham Hosp; Dir, Home Hlth Care & Profl Ser, UpJohn Hlth Ctr, 1979-81; Evening Supvr Adolescent Closed Unit 1981-82, Pt-time Primary Nurse Adolescent Closed Unit 1982-, TPI; ANA; UNA; ARC; cp/Num Commun Activs incl'g Johnston-Willis Hosp Alumnae, 1964-83; So Civic Org Bd Mem 1969-76; r/Presb; hon/Author of Num Newslttrs & Articles; W/W: Am Wom, W; Personalities S.

MORGAN, ANNE YOCUM oc/Clinical Director Chem Dep Unit; b/Jan 7, 1933; h/1554 Kings Road, Harvey, LA 70058; ba/New Orleans, LA; c/William D, James Sherman; p/E J and B Johnson Yocum; ed/BA, 1975; MSW, 1977; pa/ Outpatient Therapist, S AR Reg Hlth Ctr, 1977-79; Dir Fam Therapy 1980-82, Clin Dir CDU 1982-83, Dir CDU 1983-, FEH Hosp, CDU; Nat Assn Social Wkrs; NO Pvt Practicioners; Acad Cert'd Social Wkrs, 1979; Bd Cert'd Social Wkrs, LA, 1980; r/Meth; hon/Phi Kappa Phi, 1975; W/W Am Wom.

MORGAN, GARY oc/Assistant Professor of Journalism; b/Nov 5, 1943; h/ Box 5012, Greeley, CO 80631; ba/ Denver, CO; c/Stephen, David; p/ Howard and Loyola Morgan; ed/AB, NM Highlands Univ, 1966; MA, CO St Univ, 1968; PhD (in progress), Univ of No CO; pa/Asst Prof of Jour, Metro St Col, 1977-; Asst Dir, Info Ser, Univ of No CO, 1968-77; Info Dir, Mtn/Plains Intercol Ath Assn, 1968-71, 1974-76; Grad Tchg Asst, Eng Dept, CO St Univ, 1966-68; Part-time Asst Sports Info Dir, CO St Univ; Announcer, KZIX Radio, Ft Collins, CO, Sports Info Dir, NM Highlands Univ, 1964-66; Part-time Reporter, *Daily Optic*, Las Vegas, NM, 1963-66; Sports Editor, *Star-News*, Nat City, CA, 1960-61; So CA Prep Sports Editor, Los Angeles *Examiner*, 1959-61; Pres, Nat Col Baseball Writers Assn, 1976; CO Press Assn; Eng-Spkg Union; hon/Author, *3 Ft Rails* 1972, *Sugar Tramp* 1975, *Rails Around the Loop* 1976, *Otto Perry's Rio Grande* 1979, *There Was So Much Laughter* (poems) 1984, *Silver Plume: Rush to Riches* 1984; Num Articles & Poems; Commun Ser Awd, Denver Comm for Commun Relats, 1978; S'ship for Study in England, Eng-Spkg Union, 1983.

MORGAN, GARY LEE oc/Youth Pastor; b/Jun 30, 1956; h/140 Greenwood, Hereford, TX 79045; ba/Hereford, TX; m/Ronda Yvonne; c/Joshua Lee; p/Rev and Mrs Gerald L Morgan, West Milton, OH; sp/Rev and Mrs Ronald Barber, Warren, OH; ed/Mt Vernon Nazarene Col, 1979; pa/Ch Nazarene, Monroe, OH, Ch Nazarene, Franklin, OH, Ch Nazarene, Hereford, TX, Min Yth & Mus; Ofcr, Ctl OH Dist Nazarene Yth Intl Coun, 1979-80; Ofcr, SWn OH Dist, Nazarene Yth Intl Coun, 1983-84; r/Prot; hon/All OH Yth Choir, 1972.

MORGAN, GILBERT EDWARD oc/Controller-Treasurer; b/Oct 29, 1931; h/7635 Southwest 99th Court, Miami, FL 33173; ba/Miami, FL; m/Shirley A; c/Anita L Whittemore, Gilbert E II, Patricia L; p/Frank H and Anne S Morgan, Ispwich, MA; sp/Bruce and Jessie Jordan, Borden, IN; ed/Dipl, US Armed Forces Inst; BBA, Univ Miami, 1962; mil/USAF, 1954; pa/Controller/Treas, Williamson Cadillac Grp, Multi Corporations, 1967-; Ofc Mgr, Deel Motors Inc, 1963-67; Sales Agt, Nat Airlines, 1956-63; Mem, Secy, 1980-81, Nat Assn Accts; cp/Repub Nat Com; Masonic Order 32nd Deg; Mahi Shrine; Nat Senatorial Com; Nat Congl Com; Kiwanis; r/Luth; hon/Pres Task Force, 1982; Delta Sigma Pi, Lifetime Mem; W/W Fin & Indust.

MORGAN, MARCIA CHILDS oc/Teacher; b/Feb 21, 1913; h/1681 Huntington Turnpike, Trumbull, CT 06611; ba/Shelton, CT; m/Edward Carroll; c/Marsha Morgan Fish, Edward Childs, Kingsley David, Sarah Morgan Orifice, Margaret Morgan Blanda; p/Edward Delano and Marcia Tribon Childs, Brooklyn, NY; sp/Edward Miles and Minnie Jaynes Morgan, Northfield, MA; ed/BA, Moravian Col, 1936; MS, So CT St Univ, 1972; pa/Bridgeport Post, 1950-61; Wilcoxson Sch, Stratford, CT, 1962-63; Unquiooa Sch, Fairfield, CT, 1965-68; Huntington Sch, Shelton, CT, 1970-82; Shelton Intermediate, 1982-83; CT Ret'd Tchrs Assn; Nat Ret'd Tchrs Assn; Shelton Fdn Tchrs; cp/Trumbull Zoning Comm, 1953-58; Trumbull Civil Ser Comm, 1959-61; Dir, Fairfield Co Ext Ser, 1968-82; Life Mem, Trumbull Hist Soc; Life Mem, Moravian Col Alumni Assn; Mem, SCSU Alumni Assn; Nat Audubon Soc; r/Epis; hon/Trumbull Exch Clb, 1957; W/W Am Wom.

MORGAN-McROY, AGNES DeJOYCE oc/Executive Director, Industry Cluster Program; b/Oct 21, 1951; h/1572 Jacks Drive, Tallahassee, FL 32301; ba/Tallahassee, FL; m/Dr Warren W Morgan; p/Fletcher McRoy and Agnes C Young, Cocoa, FL; sp/Woodrow and Vivian Morgan, New York, NY; ed/AA, Brevard Commun Col, 1971; BSW, Tuskeegee Inst, 1973; MA, FL St Univ, 1983; MBA Prog, FL A & M Univ; pa/Exec Dir, FAMU/Indust Cluster Prog, 1979-; Proj Coor, FL Drug Abuse Trust, 1976-77; Adm Asst, Ofc Gov, Legal Affairs, 1975-76; Supvr/Therapist, Brevard Co Mtl Hlth Ctr, 1973-75; Instr, Brevard Commun Col, 1974-75; Pres, Silver Dome Chapt, 1980-81, ABWA; Mem, NCNW, 1980; cp/Delta Sigma Theta Sorority Inc, 1983; Tallahassee Urban Leag, Bd Dirs, 1983; Secy/Treas, 1979, Tallahassee Tuskegee Alumni Clb; Bd Dir, FAMU Booster Inc, 1979-81; Mem, FL A & M

Univ Alumni; Mem, NAACP; Mem, Commun Adv Bd, FL A & M Univ, Dept Jour, 1981; Mem, Nat Hookup Black Wom Inc; Mem, FL Ec Clb; r/Meth; Bethel AME Ch; hon/Wom Yr, ABWA, 1981; Miss Army ROTC, Tuskegee Inst, 1972-73; Koch Thesis Awd, 1972; Outstg Tchrs Awd, 1975; W/W: Am, Am Wom; Outstg Yg Wom Am.

MORGANOFF, ABRAHAM DAVID oc/Neurologist; b/Jun 28, 1949; h/21 Mountain Avenue, Warren, NJ 07060; ba/Plainfield, NJ; m/Fern Barbara; c/Jessica Hope, Gregory Neil; p/Harry and Gloria Morganoff; sp/Nathan and Grace Roth, Old Bridge, NJ; ed/BS, City Col NY, 1971; MD, Anatomy Med Col Guadelejara, 1975; Resident Med 1977, Residency Neurol 1977-80, NJ Med Col; pa/Pvt Pract Neurol, 1980-; Clin Instr Neurol, Dept Fam Pract, Rutgers Med Sch; Att'g Neurol Dept Med, Muhlerberg Hosp; Conslt Neurol; Am Epilepsy Soc; Am Acad Neurol; AMA; NY Acad Sci; NJ Med Soc; Somerset Co Med Soc; Plainfield Area Med Assn, Treas; Neurol Assn NJ; Stroke Com, Am Heart Assn; Mtn Jewish Commun Ctr, Treas 1981-83; hon/W/W E; Phys Recog Awd, 1976-83.

MORIYAMA, RAYMOND oc/Architect-Planner; b/Oct 11, 1929; h/32 Davenport Road, Toronto, Canada M5R 1H3; m/Sachi; c/Mark Michi, Murina Lei, Midori, Jason Jun, Adrian Keiju; p/John and Nobuko Moriyama; sp/Tameji (dec) and Tsuruko Miyauchi; ed/BArch, Univ Toronto; MArch, McGill Univ; pa/Sr Ptnr, Moriyama & Teshima Planners Ltd, 1958-; Design Tutor, Univ Toronto, 1961-63; cp/Chm, Mid Canada Conf Task Force Envir & Ecological Factors, 1969-70; Mem, Coun, Ontario Col Art, 1972-73; Dir, Canadian Guild Crafts, 1973-75; Chm Bd, Ecological Res Ltd, 1970-; Pres, Grp One Ltd; Benefactor Mem, Art Gal Ontario, Royal Ontario Mus, Canadian Opera Guild; Bd Mem, MTV, Toronto, 1979-; hon/LLD, Brock Univ, 1973; LLD, NY Univ, 1979; F'ship Ryerson Polytech, 1980; DEng, Univ Nova Scotia, 1980; LLD, Trent Univ, 1981; Contemp Arch; MacMillan Ency Archs; Canadian W/W; W/W Am.

MORIZUMI, S J oc/Senior Staff Scientist; b/Nov 13, 1923; h/29339 Stadia Hill Lane, Rancho Palos Verdes, CA 90274; ba/El Segundo, CA; m/H Morizumi; c/Michael N; p/M Morizumi, San Francisco, CA; ed/BS, Univ CA-Berkeley, 1955; MS, CA Inst Technol, 1957; Phd, Univ CA-LA, 1970; mil/USAF, AUS, CCD; pa/Aerodynamicist, Douglas Aircraft Co, 1955-60; Sr Scist Space Technol Lab/TRW, 1960-81; Dir, HRT/Textron, 1981-82; Sr Scist, Hughes Aircraft Co, 1982-; Sigma Xi; AIAA; hon/Author of Num Pubs; Tau Beta Pi; Pi Mu Epsilon; Gustav A Aicher S'ship; Lecturships Space Sci.

MOROSO, MICHAEL JOSEPH oc/Aerospace Engineer; b/Jan 26, 1923; h/964 Lansing Lane, Costa Mesa, CA 92626; ba/Long Beach, CA 90846; m/Jody Mary; c/Barbara, Michael Jr, Robert, Philip; p/John and Antonietta Moroso (dec); sp/Faye and Mary Scripter (dec); ed/BSME, Univ WI, 1952; Naval Aviator 1945; mil/USN, 1943-47; pa/Customer Engr, Douglas Aircraft Co, 1979-; Sr Engr, Northrop Corp, 1976-79; Engr/Scist Spec, McDonnell

Douglas Astronautics Co, 1970-76; McDonnell Douglas Vandenburg Launch Ctr, 1965-70; Assoc Fellow, AIAA, 1956-; Naval Reserve, 1948-64; ANA, 1983-; cp/BSA, Advmt Com; Little Leag Baseball Mgr & Coach; Adjutant, Fin Ofc, Am Legion; Douglas Mgmt Clb; St John's Men's Clb; r/Cath; hon/Author of Num Pubs; Assoc Fellow, AIAA, 1982; Naval Aviator, 1945; Hon, Bausch & Lomb Sci Awd, 1941; W/W: Aviation & Aerospace, W.

MORRELL, JAMES F oc/Vice President-Corporate Planning; b/Jul 9, 1931; h/213 Thornton Circle South, Camillus, NY 13031; ba/Syracuse, NY; m/Mary Anne Boessneck; c/James C, Lisa A, Diane M; ed/BBA, LeMoyne Col, 1952; CPA, 1959, NY; mil/USAF, 1952-54; pa/Price Waterhouse & Co, 1954-62, Methods; Methods Analyst 1962-63, Supvr Res & Stats 1963-64, Staff Asst 1964-65, Adm Asst 1965-67, Asst Controller 1967-71, Controller 1971-73, VP Corporate Planning 1973-, Niagara Mohawk Power Corporation; Nat Assn Bus Economists; NY Assn Bus Economists; Planning Execs Inst; N Am Soc Corporation Planners; Am Inst CPAs; Edison Elect Inst; Am Gas Assn; NY St Soc CPAs; Strategic & Long Range Planning Soc; r/Rom Cath; hon/W/W.

MORRIS, ALVIN L oc/Meteorologist; b/Jun 7, 1920; h/15759 Sunshine Canyon, Boulder, CO 80302; ba/Boulder, CO; m/Nadean Davidson, c/Andrew N, Nancy L, Mildred M, Ann Elaine, Jane C; p/Roy E and Eva E Morris (dec); sp/Jesse M and Esther Whipple Davidson (dec); ed/BS, Univ Chgo, 1942; MS, US Navy Postgrad Sch, 1953; mil/USN, Ens to Lt, 1942-46, Lt to Capt, 1950-62; pa/Ofcr, USN, 1942-46; Meteorologist, Pacific Gas & Elect Co, 1947-50; Ofcr, USN, 1950-58; Dir Res, USN Weather Res Facility, 1958-62; Sci Admr, Nat Ctr Atmospheric Res, 1963-75; Pres, Ambient Anal Inc, 1976-83; Chm, Com Atmospheric Measurements, Am Meteorological Soc, 1979-81; Chm, Meteorology Com, Am Soc Testing & Mats, 1973-77; Am Geophy Union; r/Prot; hon/Author of Num Pubs incl'g "Handbook Sci Ballooning", 1975, "Air Quality & Atmospheric Ozone", 1977; US Weather Bur, Civil Aeronautics Adm F'ship to Univ Chgo, 1941; Cert'd Consltg Meteorologist, Am Meteorological Soc; Ldrs in Am Sci; 2000 Men Achmt; DIB; Men Achmt; W/W: W, Fin & Indust; Intl Book Honor.

MORRIS, EDWARD KNOX JR oc/University Educator, Behavioral Scientist; b/May 4, 1948; h/2112 Vermont Street, Lawrence, KS 66044; ba/Lawrence, KS; p/Mr and Mrs Edward K Morris, Gladwyne, PA; ed/BS, Denison Univ, 1970; MA 1974, PhD 1976, Univ IL; pa/Asst Prof, Dept Human Devel, 1975-81, Assoc Prof 1981-, Courtesy Asst & Assoc Prof Psychol, Univ KS; AAAS; Div 25 Public Info Ofcr, Am Psychol Assn; Am Soc Criminology; Assn Behavior Anal; Assn Advmt Behavior Therapy; Nat Coun Crime & Delinquency; Soc Res Child Devel; hon/Author of Num Pubs; Psi Chi, 1969-70; Hon Grad, 1970; Outstg Yg Men Am; W/W Biobehavioral Sci.

MORRIS, ERNEST oc/Vaquero Artist and Cowboy; b/Dec 13, 1927; h/

300 Vaquero Road, Templeton, CA 93465; ba/Same; m/Blanche; c/Ralph, Linda; p/Donald Arthur Morris and Jessie Ann Eliza Simmons (dec); sp/Joseph and Mary Grudzinski (dec); mil/USN, 1946-47, 1950-54; r/Prot; pa/Cowboy & Horse Breaking, Frank Williams (Kern & Monterey Co), Ed Smith, Carrisa Ranch (S L O Co), 1943-46, 1948-50, 1955-56; Ranching, Horse Breaking, Rawhide Wkr, Artist, Bronze Sculptor, 1957-84; cp/Pres, Paso Robles & Atascadero Art Clbs Inc, 1963-66; Life Mem, VFW, 1965-; r/Prot; hon/Author of "Rawhide Wkr" 1958, "Reinsman of W" 1970, "From Dude to Cowman" 1970, "Cow People" 1977, "Ja'quima to Freno" 1977; Famous Artist Schs, 1964; LA Times "On the Move", 1966; "Cowboy in Art", 1968; Aqui-Santa Maria Times, 1981-82; Conf of CA, Hist Soc; W/W CA.

MORRIS, LaRONA J oc/Administrative Assistant; b/Nov 16, 1942; h/1610 North 45 Street, East St Louis, IL 62204; ba/Belleville, IL; m/Oreido S; c/Bryant K, Ricci D, Crystal R; p/Norma L Walls, Belleville, IL; sp/Simie and Jewel Morris, E St Louis, IL; ed/BS 1974, MS 1979, SIU-Edwardsville; pa/Mil Airlift Command, Scott AFB, 1960-72; Public Relats Dir, Mayor-E St Louis, 1972-74; Dpty City Clk, City E St Louis, 1974-75; Adm Asst, E St Louis City Coun, 1975-79; Adm Asst, St Clair Co Reg Supt Schs, 1979-; IL Assn Wom Sch Admrs; PH Delta Kappa Profl Frat; IL Basic Skills Adv Com; St Clair Co Most Difficult Child Com; Sch Dist 189 Curric Com; E St Louis Spec Ed Adv Com; E St Louis Minimum Competency Skills, Testing Com; Nat Notary Assn; Notaries Assn IL Inc; cp/IL Yg Authors & Conf/Reg Coor; Very Spec Arts Fest Com; St Clair Co Tchrs Inst Planning Com; IL Comm Minority Wom; E St Louis Polit Wom Inc; IL Black Caucus Local Elected Ofcls; NOW; Bd Dirs, St Clair Co Big Brothers/Big Sisters; Sigma Gamma Rho Sorority Inc; Bd Dirs, YWCA St Clair Co; Metro-E Lioness Clb; OES; St Clair Co Urban Leag; NAACP; Phi Delta Kappa Profl Frat; IL Assn Wom Sch Admrs; r/Pentecostal; hon/Author of Num Pubs; Most Outstg Civilian Awd, Scott AFB, 1971; Rec'd Congl Invitation White House Tour, 1975; Rec'd Invitation Pres White House Forum Inflation, 1975-78; Commun Ldr, So IL Assn Clb Wom; Wom Power; Outstg Ldrs & Noteworthy Ams; Outstg Yg Wom Am; 1982-83 Edition Commun Ldrs Am; Biographical Roll Hon.

MORRIS, MARGARET WHISTLE oc/Director of Student Financial Aid; b/Feb 3, 1938; h/126 Harbor View Lane, Largo, FL 33540; ba/St Petersburg, FL; p/Mrs Stella C Whistle, Blytheville, AR 72315; ed/BS, Univ AR, 1959; MA, Wake Forest Univ, 1969; pa/Dir Financial Aid, Eckerd Col, 1980-; Financial Aid Spec II, Hillsborough Commun Col, 1971-80; Instr, St Petersburg Jr Col, 1969-71; Tchr, Memphis Public Schs, 1959-61; Treas 1982-84, St Conf Chm 1982, St Conf Co-Chm 1981, Cert Com 1981-84, FL Assn Student Financial Aid Admr; 1973-, So Assn Student Financial Aid Admrs; 1977-, Fine Arts Soc FL Gulf Art Ctr; 1974-77, BPW Clb; hon/Author of "The Completion Wn NC Railroad: Polits Concealment" *NC Hist Review* 1975; 1979 Cert Financial Aid Adm;

Personalities S.

MORRIS, ROBERT HOWARD oc/Mechanical and Nuclear Engineering Consultant; b/Sep 27, 1950; h/Post Office Box 672, Avila Beach, CA 93424; ba/Avila Beach, CA; m/Diana H; p/Warren L and Margaret C Morris, Roanoke, VA; sp/Charles W and Eustine S Humphreys, Harriaman, TN; BS, Univ HI, 1974; MS, Univ WI, 1976; pa/Devel Assoc III, Oak Ridge Nat Lab, 1976-80; Sr Engr, Burns & Roe Inc, 1980-83; Sr Engr, Nutech Engrs, 1983-84; Pres, RHM Engrg, 1984-; Reg'd Profl Engr; Mem, Am Soc Mech Engrs; hon/Author of Num Pubs; W/W: Frontier Sci & Tech, Amg Students Am Col & Univ.

MORRISON, JAMES LEWIS oc/School Principal, Consultant; b/Jul 21, 1941; h/Box 70, Brockville, Ontario K6V 5V1; c/Scott, Michelle; p/Mary Lou Morrison, Brockville, Ontario; ed/BA, Queen's Univ, 1972; EdM, Univ Ottawa, 1978; mil/Royal Canadian Naval Air; pa/Royal Canadian Navy, 1958-61; Sch Prin, Spragge Ontario, 1964; Sch Prin, Greenville Bd Ed, 1967-81; Exec Dir, Rideauwood Inst, 1981-82; Dir, TRIAD Consltg, 1980-83; Chm, Intl Coun Alcohol & Other Addicts, 1978; Chm, Prin Profl Devel Com, 1978-80; Chm, Dist Hlth Coun Com, 1979-82; Chm, Coun Addictions Ed Com, 1980-81; Presenter, Tourist Devel Sems, 1981-83; r/United Ch Canada; hon/Author of Num Pubs; W/W: Sci & Indust, World.

MORRISON, LURA GENE oc/Coordinator, Instructor Reading and Writing Lab; b/Apr 19, 1947; h/108 Kimberly Circle Number 213, El Dorado, AR 71730; ba/El Dorado, AR; p/Thomas Henry Morrison, McAllen, TX, and Violet T Morrison, Ft Worth, TX; ed/BA, Houston St Univ, 1969; EdM 1975, PhD 1978, E TX St Univ; pa/Tchr, San Benito TX, 1970; Tchr, HS Eng, Harlingen TX, 1970-73; Asst Instr, E TX St Univ, 1974-78; Coor, Migrant Prog, Kaufman TX, 1978-79; HS Eng Tchr, Plano TX, 1979-80; Coor, Instr Devel Studies Rdg & Writing Lab, 1980-; IRA; Phi Delta Kappa; Kappa Delta Pi; Sigma Tau Delta; hon/Outstg Yg Edr Yr; W/W S & SW.

MORRISON, MINION KC oc/Professor; b/Sep 24, 1946; h/118 Ferris Avenue, Syracuse, NY 13210; ba/Syracuse, NY; m/Johnetta B Wade; c/Iyabo Abena; p/Elvestra Morrison, Jackson, MS; sp/Lula Wade, Louisville, MS; ed/BA 1968, MA 1979, PhD 1977; pa/Assoc Prof & Chm, Syracuse Univ, 1978, 1983; Asst Prof, Hobart Col, 1977; Asst Prof, Tougaloo Col, 1974; APSA; African Studies Assn; Nat Conf Black Polit Scist; Intl Polit Sci Assn; African Polit Sci Assn; cp/Transafrica; NAACP; r/Prot; hon/Author of "Ethnicity & Polit Integration" 1983, "Housing the Urban Poor in Africa" 1982; Outstg Yg Men Am; Res Grant, Nat Endowment Humanities; Res Grant, Ford Foun; Res, NSF; Tchr of Yr, Tougaloo Col; Fellow, Ford Foun Mid E & Africa Field Res; Fellow, So F'ships Fund; Fellow, Univ WI; W/W: Am Cols & Univs, E.

MORROCCO, JOHN THOMAS oc/Director Sales and Marketing; b/Jan 1, 1949; h/220 LaCava Road, Bristol, CT 06010; ba/Manchester, NH; m/Donna S; c/Marcie, Jason; p/Alfred F and Esther

L Morrocco, Bristol, CT; sp/Anthony and Jennie V Sileo, Bristol, CT; ed/BS, Quinnipiac Col, 1971; MBA, Univ New Haven, 1973; pa/Mkt Mgr, Amphenol N Am, 1977-79; Galite Div, Galileo Electro Optics Co, 1979-81; Dir Sales & Mkt, Phab Corp, 1981-; Am Mktg Assn; Optical Soc Am; cp/Chm, Bristol Zoning Bd Appeals, 1978-; Elks; r/Cath.

MORROW, CAROL L oc/Associate General Counsel and Assistant Secretary; b/May 7, 1943; h/719 President, San Antonio, TX 78216; ba/San Antonio, TX; m/Gary; c/Quinn Alexander, William Erwin; p/Mr and Mrs E C Kline, San Antonio, TX; sp/Mr and Mrs Barney Morrow, New Braunfels, TX; ed/BA, SW TX St Univ, 1966; JD, S TX Col Law, 1977; Life Ofc Mgmt Assoc Courses; pa/Asst Gen Counsel, Asst Secy, GPM Life Ins Co, 1977-; Am, TX, & San Antonio Bar Assn; Assn Life Ins Counsel; Am Corp Counsel Assn; Estate Planners Coun; LWV; cp/Polit Action Com; Civic Clb; r/Presb; hon/GPM Fed Credit Union Bd Dirs, 1978-; W/W: Am Law, SW, World, Wom.

MORTELL, BONNIE PATRICIA oc/International Exchange Administrator, Educator; b/Jun 29, 1945; h/13920 93rd Avenue Northeast, Kirkland, WA 98034; c/William Robert; p/William H and Loretta E Lennox, Seattle, WA; ed/BA, Seattle Univ, 1970; Postgrad Wk, 1970-; pa/Tchr, Lake Wash HS, 1970-; Chp, Fgn Lang Dept, Lake Wash HS, 1975-; Gtr Seattle Area Rep 1972-77, Asst Dir 1977-78, Intl Prog Dir 1978-, Iberoamerican Cultural Exch Prog; Pres, Intl Exch Netwk WA ST, 1983-; WA Assn Fgn Lang Tchrs; Nat Assn Tchrs Spanish & Portuguese; Kappa Gamma Pi; r/Cath; hon/W/W W.

MORTON, RANDALL EUGENE oc/Senior R & D Engineer, Specializing in Fiber Optics; b/May 4, 1950; h/10320 181st Northeast, Redmond, WA 98052; ba/Lynnwood, WA; m/Lori Kay; c/Nicole Ashley; p/Eugene R and Kathryn H Morton, Seattle, WA; sp/Edward and A Mary Turner, Kent, WA; ed/BS 1972, MS 1974, PhD 1979, Univ Wash; pa/Elect Estimator, Rainier Elect Co, 1969-71; Tchg Asst, Univ WA, 1973-77; Exec Conslt, Holloran & Assocs, 1977; Corporate Conslt, AGA Conslts, 1981-82; Sr Mfg Systems Analyst 1982, Sr Engr R & D 1983-; ELDEC Corporation; Est'd Innovative Concepts, 1984-; Chm 1982, Pres 1982-84, Am Nuclear Soc, Puget Sound Sect; Mem, IEEE; Mem, Soc Automotive Engrs Standards Com; Mem, SAE Aerospace Avionics & Integration Standards Com; cp/Seattle Canoe Clb, Pres 1973-74; r/Prot; hon/Author of Num Pubs; Num Ath Awds; W/W: Among Am HS Srs, Frontier Sci & Technol, World.

MOSBACH, MARIE THERESA SCHAEFER oc/Humanities Teacher, Consultant; b/Jul 27, 1928; h/422 Salmon Brook Street, Granby, CT 06035; ba/Windsor, CT; m/Michael Mosbach; c/Maureen Copolof, T Brendan Mahan; p/Loretta Schaefer, Fairfield, CT; ed/BA, Albertus Magnus Col, 1950; MA 1968, PhD 1978, Univ CT; pa/Tchr, Elem & Sec'dy Schs, 1950-54; Tchr, Sec'dy Schs, 1962-64; Tchr, Sec'dy Schs, 1966-83; Supvr, Eng Dept, 1969-74; Instr, Univ CT, 1970-73; Instr, New Sch Social Res, 1982-83; Conslt, Intensive Jour Prog, Dialogue House,

1981-83; Ednl Rschr, 1978-83; Windsor Ed Assn; CT Ed Assn; NEA; Assn Supvn & Curric Devel; NCTE; World Future Soc; Nat Netwk Tchrs & Jour Users; r/Cath; hon/W/W E.

MOSCOSO, CARLOS GUILLERMO oc/Consultant Tropical Agricultural Sciences; b/Mar 31, 1921; h/Post Office Box 1746, Plant City, FL 33566; b/Same; m/Julia Caroline McHenry; c/Caroline Frances Moscoso Billoch, Francisco Moscoso McHenry; p/Guillermo H and Carmen Vera de Moscoso (dec); sp/Roland and Nina Gaskins McHenry (dec); ed/BS, Univ SWn LA, 1948; MS, LA St Univ, 1951; Postgrad Studies, PhD, 1951-53, LA St Univ; DSc, Sussex Col Technol, 1977; Grad US Army Intell Sch, 1964; mil/NG PR, 1936-39; ROTC Cadet Corps, 1942-44; AUS, 1945-46; USAR, Commissioned 1st Lt, Adv'd Through Grades to Lt Col, 1953-81; pa/Asst Horticulturist 1958, Assoc Horticulturist 1959, Horticulturist & Hd Seed Farms Div 1960-65, Horticulturist In Charge Specialized Seed Prog 1965-69, Asst Dir in Charge of all Agri Res Sub-Sta 1969-76, Agri Expt Sta, Univ PR; Advr & Conslt, Agri Comm, Ho of Reps, 1969-74; Conslt, World Book Ency; Landscape Conslt, Antilles Command, Ft Brooke PR, 1960; Num Res Accomplishments; Latin Am Coun; VFW; Res Ofcrs Assn; Assn US Army; Am Assn Ret'd Persons; AAAS; Botanical Soc Am; Asociacion de Agricultores de PR; Colegio de Agronomes de PR; Horticultural Soc; Am Soc Agri Sci; cp/Am Legion; Ofcrs Clb PR NG; USCG Clb; r/Cath; hon/Author of Num Pubs incl'g "La Chironja: Una Nueva Fruta Citrica Puertorriquena" 1976; Sigma Xi; Phi Kappa Phi; Gamma Sigma Delta; Asst'ship, F'ship, LA St Univ; Mil Awds & Recogs; Num Awds Agri Expt Sta, Univ PR; Num Awds Univ PR; W/W: S & SW, Am.

MOSELEY, JAMES FRANCIS oc/Attorney; b/Dec 6, 1936; h/7780 Holly Ridge Road, Jacksonville, FL 32216; ba/Jacksonville, FL; m/Anne M, James F Jr, John M; p/Mrs J O Moseley, Jacksonville, FL; sp/Mr and Mrs C McGehee; ed/BA, The Citadel, 1958; LLB, Univ FL Col Law, 1961; mil/USAR, Capt, 1961-63; pa/Ptnr, Toole, Taylor, Moseley & Joyner; Pres, Jacksonville Bar Assn; Exec Com, Maritime Law Assn US, 1978-81; cp/Chm, Bd Trustees, Jacksonville Lib Sys, 1982-83; Pres, United Way Jacksonville, 1980; r/Bapt; hon/Nums Articles on Maritime & Admiralty Law.

MOSELEY, LAURICE CULP oc/Business President and Founder; b/Feb 15, 1927; h/2543 Wildwood Drive, Montgomery, AL 36111; ba/Montgomery, AL; m/Ernest B Moseley Jr; c/Randall D Culp, Robert C Culp; p/John C Foshee and Alma Roma Hand (dec); sp/Ernest B Sr and Ida Moseley, Montgomery, AL; ed/Air Univ Ext Inst; pa/Acct, Secy, Auditor, US Gov't, 1949-59; Owner, Culp Piano & Organ Co Inc, 1955; Electronic Organ Ser, 1976-; Owner, Crown Gems Intl, 1971-; Owner, Bd Dirs, Dimensions, 1980-; Ptnr, Moseley Piano & Organ Ctr, 1958-; Nat Assn Music Merchants, 1959-83; cp/Montgomery C of C, 1962-80; Soroptimist, So Montgomery, 1971-77; Kimball Dealer Adv Com,

1983-84; r/Bapt; hon/Author of "Six Lessons Towards Keyboard Mastery" 1978; hon/Dealer Achmt Awds, 1962-, Kimball Piano & Organ Mfrs; W/W Am Wom.

MOWERY, BOB LEE oc/Director of University Libraries; b/Jun 22, 1920; h/259 North Broadmoor Boulevard, Springfield, OH 45504; m/Peggy S; c/Margaret Paul, Mary McLean; Robert Kerr; John Franklin; p/Kerr Lee and Ella Holman Mowery (dec); sp/John Milton and Annie Rhyne Setzer (dec); ed/BA, Catawba Col, 1941; BLS, MA Univ Chgo, 1946, 1951; mil/AUS, 1941-46, Maj; pa/Catalog Libn, Dickinson Col, 1947-51; Libn, Murray St, 1951-53; Hd Libn, McNeese St, 1953-58; Hd Libn, Stetson Univ, 1958-64; Dir Univ Lib, Wittenberg Univ, 1964-; Am Lib/OH Lib Assn; cp/Rotary; Univ Clb; Yg Mens' Lit Clb; r/Luth; hon/Author of Num Pubs; Pres, Arthur Machen Soc, 1965-80; Dir/Treas, OH Col Lib Ctr, 1967-71; Dir, OHIO NET, 1978-; Nat Def Fgn Lang Fellow, 1967; Social Sci Res Coun Fellow, 1968; W/W: Am, World.

MOYA, AURY oc/Director; b/Mar 17, 1934; h/Siena 307, College Park, Rio Piedras, PR 00921; ba/San Juan, PR; m/Julio Damiani; c/Frank Xavier, Robert Michael, Cristina Damiani; p/Eduviges and Anastacia Rodriguez, PR; ed/BD; Postgrad Wk; pa/Sch Tchr, 1956-; Encharged Tchr, Rural Sch Yoga Career; Intl Affairs, 1975; Recog as Key Figure, 1982; Fdr, Centro de Karma Yoga; Fdr, Orden Morada; r/Cath; hon/Author of Num Articles; Num Acknowledgements.

MOYER, ROBERT WITHROW oc/Retired Educator; b/Nov 17, 1917; h/311 East Vine Street, Wilmington, OH 45177; m/Juanita; c/Robert, Vivienne; p/Elsie and Hazel Moyer (dec); sp/Roy and Lillie Purcell (dec); ed/BS, OH Univ, 1939; MA, OH St Univ, 1948; mil/AUS, 1941-46, Ret'd Lt Col; pa/Tchr, 1940-41, Madison Mills Bd Ed; Tchr Eng & Spch, Elem Prin, Bloomingburg Bd Ed, 1946-49; Supt Schs, Jackson Local Sch, 1949-56; Supt Schs, Kingston, 1956-58; Supvr, Clinton Co Sec'dy Schs;, 1958-62; Wilmington HS Prin, Wilmington City Bd Ed, 1962-67; Asst Supt Schs, Montgomery Co Bd Ed, 1967-76; Mayor, Wilmington City, 1976-83; OH Ed Assn; Clinton Co Ret'd Tchrs Assn; Ret'd Ofcrs Assn; cp/Rotary Hon Mem; BPOE; r/Prot; hon/Former Pres, OH Mayor's Assn; W/W MW.

MPELKAS, CHRISTOS CHARLES oc/Plant Physiologist, Manager Horticultural, Lighting Technology; b/Apr 16, 1920; h/12 Mansfield Street, Lynn, MA 01904; ba/Danvers, MA; m/Angeline; c/Charles, John, William, Katherine; p/Charles and Katherine Mpelkas (dec); sp/John and Bessie Vlahakis (dec); ed/Assoc Deg, Agri & Tech Inst, 1942; BS, Univ MA, 1949; MS, Univ CT, 1950; USAF, 1943-46; pa/Mgr, Horticultural Lighting Technol 1977, Plant Physiol, Sr Applications Engr 1961-77, GTE Sylvania Lighting Prods; Res Devel Spec, Univ MA, Coop Ext Ser, 1971-77; Illuminating Engrg Soc; Am Soc Horticultural Engrs; Am Soc Photobiol; MA Conserv Comm; r/Greek Orthodox; hon/Author of Num Pubs; W/W E; Am Men Sci; Commun Ldrs Am.

MUELLER, HERBERT JOSEPH oc/

Research Associate; b/Feb 17, 1941; h/3533 West Lakefield Drive, Milwaukee, WI 53215; ba/Chicago, IL; p/Herbert L and Ann S Mueller (dec); ed/BS, Marquette Univ, 1964; MS 1966, PhD 1969, NWn Univ; pa/Nat Inst Dental Res Predoct Trainee, NWn Univ, 1964-69; Asst Prof & Chm, Dept Dental Mat, Loyola Univ, 1968-71; Res Assoc, Am Dental Assn, 1980-; Am Soc Metals; Intl Assn Dental Res; Soc Biomats; r/Cath; hon/Author of Num Pubs; Pi Tau Sigma; Tau Beta Pi; Scholastic Hons Mats Sci; Sigma Xi; Acad Dental Mats.

MULANI, ASHOK S oc/Systems Analyst; b/Sep 1, 1950; h/160 Overlook Avenue, Apartment 6 L1, Hackensack, NJ 07601; ba/New York, NY; m/Mrs I S Mulani, Bombay, India; ed/Bach Technol, Indian Univ Technol, 1972; MS, Univ WI, 1975; pa/Sr Proj Dir, Modest Indust, 1976-78; Chief Sys Analyst, Micro Computer People Ltd, 1978-79; Pres, Nitash Inc, 1980-; Computer Soc India; Edit Advr, Computer Soc, Hong Kong, 1976-77; r/Hindu; hon/Recip Indian Inst Technol, Gold Medals, 1970, 1971; W/W E.

MULLEN, PATRICIA DOLAN oc/University Professor and Behavioral Scientist; b/Nov 19, 1944; h/3772 Ingold Street, Houston, TX 77005; ba/Houston, TX; m/Lawrence R; c/Katharine Grace; p/Pat and Dorothy Dolan, LaCanada, CA; sp/Nina Mullen, Salinas, CA; ed/BA 1966, MLS 1970, MPH 1971, PhD 1975, Univ CA-Berkeley; Postdoct Fellow, Johns Hopkins Univ, 1979; pa/Asst Prof, Univ Ca-Berkeley, 1974-75; Asst Prof, Univ Wash, 1975-77; Assoc Dir, Hlth Ed Dept, Grp Hlth Cooperative Puget Sound, 1976-79; Sr Policy & Res Fellow, Dept Hlth & Human Sers, 1979-82; Assoc Dir, Ctr for Hlth Promotion Res & Devel, Assoc Prof, Sch Public Hlth, Univ TX Hlth Sci Ctr; VP, Soc Public Hlth Ed; Gov'g Coun & Action Bd, Am Public Hlth Assn; Am Anthropological Assn; Am Sociological Assn; Intl Union Hlth Ed; hon/Author of Num Articles; Res F'ship, Dept Hlth & Human Ser, 1981-82; NIH, Cardiovascular Res F'ships, 1978-79; Hlth Policy Prog Fellow, 1974; USPHS, F'ship, 1970-75; Outstg Yg Wom Am; W/W Hlth Care; World's W/W Wom.

MULLER, WILLIAM oc/Educational Administrator; b/May 26, 1940; h/110 Cumberland Place, Lawrence, NY 11559; m/Lois; c/Gregory, Debbie, Pamela; p/Fred (dec) and Helen Mueller; sp/Alex and Brinnie Levine, Flushing, NY; BS 1961, MA 1963, NY Univ; 6th Yr Cert, Queens Col, 1966; PhD, Fordham Univ, 1975; mil/USCG; pa/Wantagh Sr HS 1961, Wantaugh Jr HS 1962-66, Tchr; Adm Intern Discipline 1966, Adm Intern Supvn 1967, Dept Students; Inst Asst, Summer Inst Sch Admrs on Contemp Status of Acad Subjects, Queens Col, 1966; Lead Tchr, Mulligan Jr HS, 1970; Mem, Adj Fac, Fordham Univ, 1971; Asst Prin, E Northport Jr HS, 1972; Prin, E Northport Jr HS, 1983; Nat Assn Sec'dy Sch Prins; Sch Admrs Assn NY State; Treas, Northport Assn Sch Admrs; r/Jewish; hon/Author of Num Pubs; Phi Delta Kappa; Kappa Phi Kappa; W/W E.

MULLING, EMORY WADE oc/Human Resource Executive; b/Jun 30, 1947; h/3093 Rockaway Road, Atlanta, GA 30067; ba/Marietta, GA; m/

Kathryn; c/Allison; p/Juanita C Mulling, Meeter, GA; sp/Mr and Mrs Bernard Jackson, Atlanta, GA; ed/BA, GA So Col, 1969; mil/AUS, Mil Intell; pa/Asst Pers Mgr 1972, Pers Mgr 1973, Genuine Parts Co (NAPA); Pers Admr 1976, Div Pers Mgr 1978, Corporate Human Resources Planning Mgr 1989-, Gold Kist Inc; VP Pers, 1981, RTC Trans; Div Human Resource Mgr, 1983, Taco Bell; Am Soc Pers Admrs, VP 1982, 1983; cp/Kiwanis Clb Peachtree, Atlanta, Secy 1982, Bd Dirs 1978-79; Atlanta C of C, Pres Com, 1975; Fdr & Coor, St-Wide GA Nsg Home Pageant, 1976-; r/Meth, Briarcliff United Meth Ch, Adm Bd 1982-83, VP Men's Clb 1982; hon/ Outstg Yg Men Am; Pres Cup, 1976, Kiwanis; Dist'd Human Resources Profl Awd, 1983, Am Soc Pers Admrs; Apprec Awd, 1982, GA Hlth Care Assn; Reso-lution Commend, GA Gen Assem, 1964.

MULLINS, JAMES B oc/Vice Presi-dent, Claims, CNA Insurance; b/Jun 19, 1934; h/5 Buckingham Drive, Prest-bury, Aurora, IL 60504; ba/Chgo, IL; m/ Joann; c/Kiann, Kala-Joy; p/Mrs Frank M Mullins Sr, Sellersburg, IN; sp/Mr E D Barnett, Dallas, TX; ed/Att'd Howard Payne Col, 1952-53; Kilgore Jr Col, 1953-54; BA, N TX St Univ, 1956; Postgrad Wk, So Meth Univ Law Sch, 1959-60; pa/Adjuster 1956-58, Supvr 1958-60, Dist Claim Mgr 1961-67, Div Claim Mgr 1967-69, Reg Claim Mgr 1970--76, Zone Claim Mgr 1976-77, Allstate Ins; VP, CNA Ins Co, 1977-; cp/Campaign Coor, United Fund, 1956-57; Mem, Repub Nat Comm, 1979-80; Mem, Claim Mgmt Coun; VP, Pres, Lt Gov, Dir, 1958-62, Civitan Intl; r/Prot; hon/Author of Num Pubs; hon/ Outstg Dist Mgr of S, 1965; Best Reg in E, 1975; W/W: World, Fin & Indust, MW; Personalities W & MW; Men Achm.

MUMMERT, THOMAS ALLEN oc/ Manufacturing Company Executive; b/ Dec 24, 1946; h/1448 Palmetto Avenue, Toledo, OH 43606; ba/Toledo, OH; m/ Icia Linda Sheurer; c/Sherry Lynn, Robert Thomms, Michael Allen; p/ James Mummert, Sarasota FL, Betty T Comer, Toledo OH; sp/Mr and Mrs Glenn S Sheurer, Toledo, OH; ed/ Toledo Univ, 1965-66; mil/USNR, 1965-71, Active Duty, 1968-69; pa/Pres, Mummert Elect & Mfg Co Inc, 1969-70; Res Engr, Am Lincoln Corp, 1970-73; Test Engr, Dura Div, Dura Corpora-tion, 1973-74; Res Dept Hd, Jobst Inst Inc, 1974-; Assn Advmt Med Instru-mentation; Nat Mgmt Assn; Am Soc Engrg Ed; Am Soc QC; AAAS; OH Acad Sci; NY Acad Sci; Laser Inst Am; Biol Engrg Soc; r/Bapt; hon/Num Patents incl'g "Sequential Dual Window Oper-ating Mechanism" 1974, "Therapeutic Appliance Flexing Jts" 1980; W/W: MW, Fin & Indust, Frontier Sci & Technol, Technol Today; Personalities Am; Personalities W & MW; Intl Book Hon; Men Achmt; Intl W/W Intells; DIB; Intl Register Profiles.

MUNSCHY, DOROTHY G oc/Manu-facturer Footwear; h/1512 Locust Ravine, Bakersfield, CA 93306; ba/ Bakersfield, CA; m/Roy Charles; c/ Charleyne Dianne Branson, Michelle Marie O'Neal; p/Manuel A (dec) and Mary Silva Lopes; ed/Bakersfield Com-mun Col; pa/Co-Owner, Val Wide Sal Ctr, 1966-78; Real Est Sales, 1967-77;

Pres, Chm Bd, Etta-Kit Enterprises Inc, 1976-82; Owner, Dir, Big Foot Specialty Footwear, 1982-; Intl Mktg, 1982-; Res & Anal, 1976-; hon/Domestic & Fgn Patents, 1972-.

MUNSON, NORMA FRANCES oc/ Biologist, Nutritionist Researcher; b/ Sep 22, 1923; ba/Same; p/Glen E (dec) and Frances Wilson Munson, Baudette, MN; ed/BA, Concordia Col, 1943-46; Univ MN, 1949-59; Masters' Biol, Univ MO, 1954-55; Univ IN, 1957; Doct, PA St Univ, 1957-62; Lake Forest, 1972-78; Wn MI Univ, 1965; pa/Aitkin HS, 1946-48; Detroit Lakes HS, 1948-54; Libertyville HS, 1955-79; AAAS; LHS EA; IEA; NEA; cp/IL Audubon Coun; IL Envir Coun; NABT; Lake Co Audubon Soc; r/Pres, Ruling Elder; hon/ Author of Num Pubs; Chgo Heart F'ship; Nat Sci Fellow; Delta Kappa Gamma; C of C Achmt Awd; Ldrs Am Sci; W/W Am Wom.

MURAYAMA, MAKIO oc/Research Biochemist; b/Aug 10, 1912; h/5010 Benton Avenue, Bethesda, MD 20814; ba/Bethesda, MD; c/Gibbs Soga, Alice Myra; p/Hakuyo Murayama and Namiye Miyasaka (dec); ed/BA 1938, MA 1940, PhD 1953; pa/Res Biochem, Chd's Hosp MI, 1943-48; Res Biochem, Harper Hosp, 1950-54; Res Fellow Chem, CA Inst Technol, 1954-58; Spec Res Fellow, NIH-Cavendish Lab, 1958; Res Biochem, NIH-Bethesda MD, 1958-; r/Zen Budhist; hon/Author of *Sickle Cell Hemoglobin: Molecule to Man* 1973; CRC Critical Reviews in Biochem, 1973; Martin Luther King Jr Med Achmt Awd, 1972; W/W: World, Am; DIB.

MURPHY, ELISABETH ANNE oc/ Teacher of the Hearing Impaired; b/Dec 23, 1950; h/1104 West White, Marion, IL 62959; ba/Marion, IL; m/Donald E; c/Megan Elisabeth, Matthew Edward; p/ Paul and Mary Kathryn Hoga, Elgin, IL; sp/Bill and Eva Murphy, Marion, IL; ed/ BA, MacMurray Col, 1973; pa/Tchr, Williamson Co Spec Ed Coop, 1973-; Sign Lang Instr, So IL Univ, 1978-; Sign Lang Instr, John A Logan Col, 1975-79; NEA; IEA; MEA; IL Tchrs of Hearing Impaired; Telecommuns for Deaf Inc; Telecommunicators of Ctl IL; Secy, 1977-79, Little Egypt Assn of Deaf; r/ Cath; hon/Coun on Ed Deaf Inc, Profl Cert, 1977; W/W Am Wom.

MURPHY, LEE V oc/Risk Manage-ment Consultant; b/Feb 15, 1923; h/ 7956 Keene Road, Derby, NY 14047; ba/ Buffalo, NY; m/Marjorie Kelly; c/ Patricia Lee, Timothy S, Michael T and Paul Kelly; p/Leo Thomas (dec) and Eda Schulze Murphy, Buffalo, NY; sp/ Charles B and Hattie Davis Kelly (dec); ed/ME, NC St Col, 1942-46; mil/ USAAF, A & E M, 1943-46; pa/ Morrison-Knutsen, Ragner-Benson, J Ichley Co, Bethlehem Steel Erection, Stone & Webster Engrg, Oper Engr; Steel Mills, First Atomic Engine Facility, Power Plant, Constrn; Moving of Bridges & Bldgs, 1948-62; All Lines Safety Engr, Employers Liability Assu-rance Co, 1962-68; All Lines Engr, Br L P Mgr, Asst Reg Mgr 1968-79, Nuclear Shop Supvr 1968-79, Employers-C U Assurance Co; Instr, St Univ NY-Buffalo & Erie Commun Col; Dir Safety Sers, S C C Buffalo, 1979-80; Cert'd, Hazard Control Mgr, 1977-83; NIA Buffalo Light Rail Rapid Transit

Proj, 1980-; CHCM; Past Pres, 1971, Assn Ins Engrs; Am Soc Safety Engrs; cp/Ldr, Supervisory Tng Course & Driver Tng Course; 4-H Safety Tng Instr; Erie Co Civil Def, Dir Town of Evans, 1959-63; BSA, Troop Cub Mas-ter, 1964-69; CoFdr & 1st Pres, 1956-62, Evans Aux Police Clb; Nat Bd Boiler & Pressure Vessel Insp, 1963-83; hon/W/ W E; CHCM Dir; Intl Inst Safety & Hlth.

MURPHY, LEWIS C oc/Mayor, City of Tucson, AZ; b/Nov 2, 1933; h/3134 Via Palos Verdes, Tucson, AZ 85716; ba/Tucson, AZ; m/Carol C; c/Grey, Timothy, Elizabeth; p/Waldo and Eliza-beth Murphy, Tucson, AZ; ed/BS 1955, LLB 1961, Univ AZ; mil/USAF, 1955-58, Pilot; pa/Pvt Law Pract, 1961-67, 1975-; Trust Ofcr, So AZ Bk, 1967-69; City Atty 1970-71, Mayor 1971-, City of Tucson; US Conf Mayors Bd Trustees; Nat Leag Cities; AZ & Pima Co Bar Assn; AZ Acad; cp/Exec Com Mem, Leag AZ Cities & Towns; VP, Ctl AZ Proj Assn Bd Dirs; Davis-Monthan AFB Civilian Ad-Com; Tucson C of C Jobs Devel Com; r/Prot.

MURRAINE, ELLEN W oc/Assistant Director, Personnel Office; b/Jul 24, 1945; h/Post Office Box 2298, St Thomas, VI 00801; ba/St Thomas, VI; m/Franklin; c/Lawrence T, Stephen T; p/Theodore Boschulte (dec) and Ann Boschulte Solberg, St Thomas, VI; ed/ BA, Col St Elizabeth, 1967; MA, Col of VI, 1980; pa/Pers Tech 1967-70, Chief Pers Tech 1970-76, Asst Dir 1976-, Govt of the VI; Pt-time Prof, Col of VI, 1980-; cp/Corres Secy, 1979, Hibiscus Soc; Hlth Manpower Task Force, 1980; Rebel Boy Ath Clb; Parent Com, BSA Troop 156; Confrat Christian Doctrine, Tchr, 1980; r/Rom Cath; h/Author of "Listing Positions in Exec Br-Govt of the VI", 1980; Accredited Pers Mgr, 1983; W/W S & SW.

MURRAY, JANET PATRICIA oc/ Principal; b/Apr 1, 1946; h/808 Challen Circle, Mobile AL 36608; ba/Mobile, AL; p/Mr and Mrs James G Murray, Mobile, AL; ed/AA, Sacred Heart Col, 1966; BS 1968, MA 1973, Univ S AL; Additional Hours in Adm, Univ S AL, 1979-80; pa/ Tchr 1968-73, Tchr/Asst Prin 1973-80, Prin 1980-, St Ignatius Sch; NCTM; NCEA; ACLD; ASCD; PDK; cp/Hospi-tality Chm, Mobile Name-of-Site Meet-ing of NCTM, 1977; Num Ch & Social Sys Coms; r/Cath; hon/Diocesan Math Conslt, 1972-76; Dean's List; Outstg Clrm Tchr, 1977; W/W S & SW.

MURZYN, JANICE COLLEEN oc/ Administrative Director, Nuclear Med-icine; b/Jul 27, 1948; h/3630 North Sandia Drive, Peoria, IL 61604; ba/ Peoria, IL; m/Thomas E; p/Mr and Mrs Marvin E Mulally, Peoria, IL; sp/Mr and Mrs Edward W Murzyn, Hammond, IN; ed/Meth Hosp Ctl IL Sch Radiologic Technol, 1968; Nuclear Med Inst, 1973; pa/Staff Nuclear Med Technologist 1971-74, Chief Nuclear Med Technol-ogist 1974-79, Adm Dir Nuclear Med, 1979-, Meth Med Ctr IL; Soc Nuclear Med; Ctl IL Assocs & Tech Affils; Am Hosp Radiol Admrs; Soc Radiologic Technologists; r/Meth; hon/W/W Am Wom.

MUSE, WILLIAM JOSEPH oc/Archi-tect, Planner; b/Feb 25, 1943; h/17607 Junegrass Place, Parker, CO 80134; ba/ Dever, CO and Miami, FL; m/Deborah Jean Hirt; c/Stacy Allen, Darren Joseph,

Valerie Danielle; p/Fred and Catheren Kinder Muse, St Tampa, FL; sp/Doris Biggs Hirt (dec) and John Hirt, Tampa, FL; ed/BA, Univ S FL, 1964; Hillsborough Commun Col, 1967; Univ Miami, 1979; Grad Studies, George Wash Univ, 1979; pa/Pres, The Muse Org, 1977; Muse Interior Design, 1979; Planning Conslt, 1974; Hosp Planning Conslt, 1976; AIA, Am Inst Planners; AAAM; AHA; So FL Planning Coun; cp/Dade Co Rapid Transit Auth; SW Miami Civitan; S Miami Rotary; S Dade C of C; Denver C of C; Denver Civitan; BSA, Exec Coun Com; r/Bapt; hon/Pubs; W/ W in S & SW.

MUSGRAVE, GARY EUGENE oc/ Lead Project Engineer; b/Nov 26, 1947; h/15811 Roxton Ridge, Webster, TX 77598; ba/Houston, TX; m/Barbara Shames; c/David Westley; p/George and Evelyn Musgrave, Hixon, TN; sp/Irving and Ruth Pincus, Silver Spring, MD; ed/ BS 1969, MS 1976, PhD 1979, Auburn Univ; pa/Asst Prof, Univ GA, 1978-79; NIH Postdoct Fellow, 1979-80; Res Physiol, VA Hosp, 1980-82; Asst Prof, Engrg Proj Dir, Med Col VA, 1982-84; Lead Engr, Space Adaptation Res Proj, GE (MATSCO); Am Soc Clin Pharmacol & Therapeutics; Am Fdn Clin Res; AAAS; Am Soc Pharmacol & Exptl Therapeutics; cp/Lions Clb, Dir, 1984; r/Cath; hon/Author of Num Pubs; ETA Kappa Nu; Sigma Xi; Rho Chi; NIH Fellow; W/W Frontier Sci & Technol.

MUSIC, EDWARD C oc/Company Executive; b/May 12, 1924; h/341 S Lake Drive, Prestonsburg, KY 41653; m/ Thelma Keith; c/Peggy M Carter, Judy M Shaw; p/Sam K and Nora Davis Music; pa/Purchased & Operated, C H Smith Motor Co (Prestonsburg), 1949-53; Org'd B & D Motor Co, & Music-Colvin Motor Co, 1956; Car Dealer for Edsel 1957, Chevrolet 1958, & Buick 1959; Pres, Archer-Music Enterprises, Music-Carter-Hughes Chevrolet Inc, Music Motor Co Inc, C & M Leasing Co Inc, Mtn Pkwy Chair Lift Inc, Jesse James Enterprises Inc & Music Enterprises Inc; 1983 Buick Dealer-Rep to Cinc OH Zone; cp/Chm, Prestonsburg Indust Foun; Prestonsburg Indust Coun (Chm of BD Dirs); VChm, Highland Reg Med Ctr; Bd of Prestonsburg Kiwanis Clb, 1982-83; LIfe Mem, Kiwanis Intl, Prestonsburg KY; Appt'd by Gov Julian Carroll of KY to Tourism Com for KY; hon/Outstg Citizen Awd, Prestonsburg C of C; W/ W KY; Personalities of S; Book of Hon.

MUSTAFA, S JAMAL oc/Professor of Pharmacology; b/Jul 10, 1946; h/103 Club Pines Drive, Greenville, NC 27834; ba/Greenville, NC; m/Yasmeen; c/Zishan, Farhan, Adnan; p/S M Mustafa (dec) and Ahmad Jehan Zucknow, India; sp/M A Khan (dec) and Hajra Begum Moradabad, India; ed/BS, MS, PhD, Lucknow Univ, 1969; NIH Postdoct Trainee, Univ VA, 1971-74; pa/ Asst Prof 1974-77, Assoc Prof 1977-80, Univ S AL; Assoc Prof 1980-83, Prof 1983-, E Carolina Univ; Am Soc Pharmacol & Exptl Therapeutics; Am Physiological Soc; Soc Exptl Biol Med; Intl Soc Heart Res; AAAS; NY Acad Sci; Am Heart Assn; Islamic Med Assn; Sigma Xi; Muslim Students Assm; r/Islam; hon/Author of Num Pubs; NIH Trainee, 1971-74; Invited Guest Spkr; NIH Grant Recip, 1976-; Vis'g Scist Coun Sci

& Indust Res, 1984; W/W: in Frontier Sci & Technol, in Am.

MUTH, ERIC PETER oc/Licensed Optician; b/Jul 25, 1940; h/25 Park Land Place, Milford, CT 06460; ba/Milford, CT; m/Rachel Hubbard; c/Eric Van, Karl George, Ellen Anna; p/Erich Walter Muth (dec) and Anna Byrnes, Stamford, CT; sp/Mr and Mrs G Hubbard, Milford, CT; ed/BA, Charter Oak Col, 1978; Master's & PhD, Columbia Pacific Univ, 1983; mil/AUS, 1957-59, CT ANG, 1960-69; pa/Pres, Park Lane Opticians Inc; Treas, Conrad Kasack Opticians Inc; Secy, Plaza Opticians; Bd Trustees, CT Visual Hlth Ctr, 1982; Conslt, Optical Indust, OSHA Eyewear & New Prod Devel; Reg Mbrship Chm, Nat Acad Opticianry; Pres 1974, CT Opticians Assn; Pres 1980, CT Guild of Opticians; Mem, Nat Coun Sports Vision; Intl Eye Fdn; British Guild Opticians; Assn Dispensing Opticians England; Opticians Assn CT & Am; CT Contact Lens Soc; cp/Scoutmaster; Chm, Law & Safety Com, Milford C of C; Milford Rotary Clb; Conslt, Nat Acad Ophthal Fdn Mus & Smithsonian Mus; hon/Author of Num Pubs incl'g "Mgmt Opticianry" 1983; Optician of Yr, 1975, CT Opticians Assn; Optician of Yr, 1981, CT Guild of Rx Opticians; W/W in E.

MYERS, BERNICE oc/Licensed Practical Nurse, Alcoholism and Drugs; b/ Mar 14, 1947; h/2050 Liberty, Ogden, UT 84401; ba/Ogden, UT; p/Benjamin Myers and Goldie Roskelley, Ogden, UT; ed/LPN, Weber St, 1971; Weber Co Mtl Hlth Casewk Cert, 1982; pa/Supply Tech, Dec Hosp, 1965-68; Charge Nurse, Golden Manor Nsg Home, 1972; Charge Nurse, Detox Unit, St Benedicts Hosp, 1973; Charge Nurse, Parkview Nsg Home, 1974; Charge Nurse, Weber Co Alcohol Detox Unit, 1975; Weber Co Jail, 1983; cp/CPR Nurse; Mem Organizing Bd, Weber Co Fire Dept Aux; Instr, CPR Heimlich Maneuver; r/Mormon; hon/Univ UT Sch Alcoholism & Drugs, 1977; Cert Merit, 1977, 81; Newspaper Article; W/W of Am Wom.

MYERS, LUEBURDA JAMISON oc/ Educator and Coach; b/Apr 6, 1935; h/ 333 Holcomb Drive, Shreveport, LA 71103; ba/Shreveport, LA; m/Kenneth; c/Rhett J, Kenneth S; p/Joseph Sr (dec) and Luebirda F Jamison, Napoleonville, LA; sp/Jesse (dec) and Janie L Myers, Shreveport, LA; ed/BS, Grambling Col, 1957; MA, NWn St Univ, 1968; Additional Hours at NWn & LA Tech Univ, 1971; pa/PE, Girls' Basketball Coach, Tennis Coach, Civics Tchr, Caddo Parish Sch, 1957-; Gen Prog Chm 1983-84, Retirement Prog Chm 1981-83, Caddo Assn Edrs; LA Ed Assn Resolution, 1981; Budget Com 1983, Tenure Com 1982, LA Assn Edrs; Fdr, Coor, Tchr, Pan-Hellenic Coun, Shreveport Wkly Tutorial Prog, 1981; LA Conf United Meth Wom Secy Prog Resources, 1983-85; Caddo Profl Improvement Prog Com, 1982-85; r/United Meth; hon/Sec'dy Outstg Social Studies Tchr of Month; Fdr, Phys Culture Clbs Inc, 1983; Fdr, Pub "Giant Bultn" Newslttr; Outstg LA Edrs; Outstg Sec'dy Edrs of Am.

MYERS, MARY L oc/Spiritual Leader; b/3427 Denson Place, Charlotte, NC 28215; ba/Same; ed/Att'd Num Cols & Univs; Rec'd DD; pa/

Participated in Rel Confs; Intl Prayer Ldr; Assisted in Tng Conf, Nat Org ABWA; Began Newspaper "My Lady's News"; Est'd Spiritual Study Ctr, Spiritual Univ; hon/Author; Num Certs & Recogs.

MYERS, MELVIN LEWIS oc/Teacher of Handicapped Students; b/Oct 3, 1936; h/5427 Alba, Houston, TX; ba/Houston, TX; c/Kerry Y, Melvin L Jr; ed/BS, Prarie View A & M Univ, 1959; MEd, Univ AZ, 1971; MS, Monmouth Col, 1983; mil/1959-79, Lt Col; pa/Tchr Handicapped Students 1979-; Supvn & Curric Devel, CEC; NEA; TX St Tchrs Assn; cp/NAACP; Ret'd Ofcrs Assn DAV; r/ Prot; hon/Bronze Star, Meritorious Ser Medal, Republic Vietnam Gallentry Cross; W/W in E.

MYHRA, DAVID OLAF oc/ Free-Lance Consultant in Energy Site Planning; b/Mar 3, 1939; h/1566 Mullet Lane, Naples, FL 33962; ba/Same; m/ Julie Marie; c/Cynthia Lee, Diana Marie; p/Olaf and Elizabeth Myhra, Wahpeton, ND; sp/George and Lenore Sercl, Sioux Falls, SD; ed/BS, No St Col, 1962; MA 1973, PhD 1978, Princeton Univ; MS, ND St Univ, 1965; mil/USMC, 1962-64; pa/Economist, Space Div, GE Co, 1965-72; Sr Scist, Power Sys Grp, Westinghouse Elect Corp, 1972-77; Pres, Myhra Assocs Inc, 1977; Lectr in Planning, George Wash Univ, 1977-82; Am Planning Assn; AF Hist Foun; r/ Rom Cath; hon/Author of Num Pubs incl'g "Energy Plant Sites" 1980; Rockefeller Foun Fellow, 1977-78; W/W in Fin & Indust.

MYKYTA, MARY ANN oc/Commercial Testing and Inspection Laboratory Executive; b/Aug 5, 1937; h/5912 Colwyn Drive, Harrisburg, PA 17109; ba/ Harrisburg, PA; m/Lubomya; c/Maria Lydia; Natalie Vera; John; Laryssa Ann; p/Roland Walls (dec) and Anna E King, Seaford, DE; sp/Wasyl Mykyta and Julia Powch (dec), Seaford, DE; ed/Meml Hosp Sch Nsg, 1958; Am Soc Notaries; pa/Med-Surg Charge Nurse, Meml Hosp, 1958-60; Ptnr, VP, Sales Mgr, DE Val Indust X-Ray Co, 1960-65; Rltr Assoc, Gordon Weinberg Real Est, 1968-72; Ptnr, VP, Rental Properties Gen Mgr, Commonwealth Trading & Mortgage Corporation, 1970-72; Sales Rep 1972-74, Sales Dir 1974-75, VP/ Gen Mgr 1975, VP/Dir Real Est Opers & Investmts 1976, Astrotech Inc; Assoc Dir, VP, Allentown Testing Lab, 1983-; Nat Assn Female Execs; Am Mgmt Assn; Assn Notaries; cp/Nat Hosp Alumni Assn; Sanford Alumni Assn; Cert'd Testing Labs Inc, Bd Dirs; Notary Public; r/Byzantine Cath; hon/Author of Num Pubs; Am Soc Notaries Cert of Commend; W/W of Am Wom.

MYSLINSKI, NORBERT R oc/Neuroscientist; b/Apr 14, 1947; h/108 Rock Rimmon Road, Reistertown, MD 21136; ba/Baltimore, MD; p/Bernard and Amelia Myslinski, Depew, NY; ed/ BS, Canisius Col, 1969; PhD, Univ of IL, 1973; mil/AUS, 1977, Capt; pa/Res Assoc, Tufts Univ, 1973-75; Asst Prof 1975-80, Assoc Prof 1980-, Univ of MD; Res Fellow, Bristol Univ, 1984-85; Am Soc Pharm & Exptl Therapeutics; Brit Brain Res Assoc; European Brain & Behavior Soc; NY Acad Sci; Soc Neurosci; Sigma Xi; MD Soc Med Res; AAUP; AAAS; Am Assn Dental Schs;

Diving Dentists Soc; Fdn Am Scists; Intl Assn Dental Res; MD Soc Med Res; Intl Union Pharm; Neurosci Grp Intl Assn Dental Res; Num Coms; r/Rom Cath;

hon/Author of Num Pubs; Mem Bd Dirs, MD Soc Med Res; Univ of MD Instrnl Media Achmt Awds; USPH Traineeship Awd; Dist'd Grad Awd; Col

Richardson Hon Soc; Col Pres Cit Acad Achmt; NY St S'ship; Recip Num Res Grants; W/W in Sci & Technol.

N

NACHLINGER, OLA THROYS oc/ Math Teacher; b/Oct 28, 1933; h/212 North Ermen Lane, Osceola, AR 72370; ba/Osceola, AR; m/Bobby Joe; c/Ron Jolan, Ola TaLyna, Lorie Lea, Angela Sue, Barbara Jill; p/O T and Jewel Barton, Osceola, AR; ed/BA, TX Technological Col, 1961; Postgrad, Univ of AR, 1979; pa/Tel Operator, SW Bell, 1950-51; Clk, Snyder, TX; VA, Lubbock, 1953-59; Social Security Adm, Lubbock; Tchr, Hist Dept, Lubbock HS, 1963; Libn & Math Tchr, Osceola, AR, Sys, 1969-; Chm, Title 1 Prog, 1979; Chm, Band Parents Org, 1980, 1981; NCTM; Supvn & Curric Devel Assn; NE AR Coun Tchrs of Math, Secy & Treas 1981, 1982-83; AR Coun Tchrs of Math; BPW Clb; cp/Ldr, Girl Scouts, 1973-76; Dist Commun Ldr, Cub Scouts, 1975-81; Den Mother Ldr, 1969-79; Chm, Dist Scouting Pow Wow, 1977-79; r/Ch of Christ; hon/Dist Awd of Merit for BSA, 1973; Tchr of Yr, Osceola, 1979, 1981; Nom for Citizen of the Yr, 1978; Silver Fawn, BSA, 1976; W/W in S & SW; W/W.

NADIN, MIHAI oc/Professor, Director; b/Feb 2, 1938; h/50 Fosdyke Street, Providence, RI 02906; m/Elvira; c/Ari, Esther, Elisabeth; p/Ana Catap, Brasov, Romania; ed/Prof Dr Phil Habil, Univ of Munich, 1980; PhD 1972, MA 1968, Univ of Bucharest; MS, Polytechnic Inst of Bucharest, 1960; pa/Prof, RI Sch of Design, 1982-; Dir, Inst for Visual Communication & Semiotics, 1983-; Lectr, 1978-; Vis'g Prof, Wm A Kern Inst Prof'ship in Communication, Rochester Inst of Technol, 1983-84; Adj Prof, Ctr for Res in Semiotics, Brown Univ, 1981-83; Num Other Previous Positions; NY Acad of Scis; Assn for Computing Machinery; Semiotic Soc of Am; Intl Assn for Semiotic Studies; Am Soc for Aesthetics; hon/Pubs, *Sign & Value* 1981, "Can Field Theory Be Applied to Communication Theory," "The Semiotic Processes of the Formation & Expression of Ideas" 1983, Others; W/W in Frontier Sci & Technol.

NAGORSKI, ZYGMUNT oc/Vice President of Institute; b/Sep 27, 1912; h/91 Central Park West, New York, NY; ba/New York, NY; m/Marie A; c/Maria T, Andrew Z, Teresa A; p/Marie and Zygmunt Nagorski (dec); ed/LLD, Univ of Cracow; mil/Polish Army under Brit Command, 1940-47; pa/Editor, Fgn News Ser, 1950-56; Fgn Ser Ofcr, USA, 1956-66; Spec Asst to the Pres, Fgn Policy Assn, 1966-68; Dir, Progs Coun on Fgn Relats, 1969-78; VP, The Lehrman Inst, 1979-81; Current VP, Aspen Inst for Humanistic Studies; Am Polit Sci Assn; cp/Mid-Atl Clb of NY; r/Rom Cath; hon/Pubs, "Psych of East-West Trade" & Num Articles for NY *Times, Christian Sci Monitor, Wall Street Jour* & Others; Meritorious Ser Awd, US Govt, 1965; Ofcr Cross, German Fed Republic; Leopold II Ofcrs Cross, Belgium; W/ W in E; Famous Writers.

NAHAI, FOAD oc/Plastic Surgeon; b/ Sep 23, 1943; h/3200 Nancy Creek Road, Northeast, Atlanta, GA 30327; ba/Atlanta, GA; m/Shahnaz; c/Fariba, Farzad; ed/Premed Col and Med Sch, Univ of Bristol, England; Internship, U Bristol Hosps; Gen Surg, Johns Hopkins Hosp; Resident in Plastic Surg, Emory

Univ Affil'd Hosps; pa/Asst Prof of Surg, Emory Univ Affil'd Hosps, 1980-; Am Bd of Surg Diplomate; Am Bd of Plastic Surg Diplomate; Fellow, Am Col of Surgs; AMA; BMA; ASPRS; hon/ Pubs, *Clin Atlas of Muscle & Musculocutaneous Flaps* 1979, *Clin Applications for Muscles & Musculocutaneous Flaps* 1982; Russell Cooper Prize, 1968; Gold Medal Paper Presentation, Bristol, England, 1976; Outstg Resident Awd, 1977; Third Annual Resident Competition Awd, 1977; Best Paper Awd, 1980; James Barrett Brown Awd, 1982; W/W: in Am, in SE.

NAKACHE, MARGARET ANN oc/ Artist, Watercolorist; b/Dec 17, 1932; h/1448 Woodacre Drive, McLean, VA 22101; ba/Same; m/Fernand Robert; c/ Catherine Alice, Patricia Eileen; p/Mr and Mrs J C Lynch, West Hyannisport, MA; ed/BFA, RI Sch of Design, 1954; French Cert, Ecole National Superior des Beaux-Arts, Paris, 1956; pa/Artist, Universal Films, NY, 1956-57; Artist (Designed Cadette Handbook), Girl Scouts of USA HQs, 1959-61; Current Pres, Mgmt of Am Netwk for Artists, KACHE Ltd; Artists Equity, 1978-80; Nat Leag of Am Penwom, 1979-83, Art Chm 1982; cp/Wom's Clb of McLean, 1979-83, Art Chm 1982-83; r/Cath; hon/Jurist, Series of Six Reg Exhibs, "Nature Appreciation through Visual Art"; 2nd Place, Cape Cod Art Assn, 1956; 2nd Place, McLean Art Clb, 1979; 1st Place, Vienna WC's, 1980; London Awd, VA Mus of Fine Art, 1982; W/ W: in Am Art, of Am Wom.

NAKANISHI, ALAN T oc/Optometrist; b/Nov 2, 1948; m/Rea; c/Chanel, Tiana; p/Joe Nakanishi, San Francisco, CA; ed/AA 1969, BS in Physiological Optics w Hons 1971, OD w Hons 1973, Univ of CA; pa/Am Optometric Assn, 1972-; CA Optometric Assn, 1972-; Bay Area Optometric Coun, 1972-, Sem Chm 1978-, Pract Asst Com 1979-, PAC Chm 1980-, Bd of Dirs 1979-; Alameda Contra Costa Cos Optometric Soc, 1972-, Dir 1978-, Pres-Elect 1983-; Nat Eye Res Foun, 1972-; Intl Orthokeratology Sect, 1973-; Univ of CA Alumni Assn, 1973-; Grad Students' Hon Soc, 1971-; Am Optometric Foun, 1973-; Nat Assn for Profls, 1973-; Better Vision Inst, 1973-; BBB, 1974-; CA Public Vision Leag, 1976-; Intl Contact Lens Clin, 1981-; Coun of Sports Vision, 1979-; Kenneth B Stoddaru Soc, 1979-; Fdn of Am Scists, 1980-; cp/Blue Key Exch, Arbitration Bd 1979-; Bus Exch, 1980-; Tradewinds, 1981-; Walnut Creek C of C, 1973-; Sight Conserv Chm 1978-; Japanese Am Citizens Leag, 1975-; Lions Eye Foun, Bd of Advrs 1980-; Repub; Soc of Am Magicians, 1977-; Pacific Coast Assn of Magicians, 1979-; Pantera Intl, 1978-; Pantera Owners Clb of Am, 1978-; Royal Hawaiian Adventure Clb, 1977-; Rosicrusian Soc, 1979-; M H de Young Mus Soc, 1978-; Nirvana Foun, 1978-; Am Nat Red Cross, 1978-, Instr of First Aid & CPR 1979-; Mt Diablo Aquarium Soc, 1979-; Am Jogging Assn, Steeplechaser 1979-; Am Juggling Assn, 1980-; SF Underwater Photographic Soc, 1981-; Concord Sch of Karate, 1978-, Asst Instr 1981-, Bulletin Editor 1982-; Kajukembo Assn of Am, 1981-; r/Prot; hon/CA Optometric Assn Spkr's Awd, 1981, 1982; Am Optometric Assn Recog

Awd, 1980, 1981, 1982, 1983; ACCCOS Yg Optometrist of the Yr, 1979; Dean's Coun, Univ of CA-Berkeley, 1979; Other Hons; W/W: in W, in Professions, in CA.

NAMDARI, BAHRAM oc/General and Vascular Surgeon, Surgical Treatment of Obesity; b/Oct 26, 1939; ba/ Great Lakes Medical and Surgical Center, 2315 North Lake Drive, Milwaukee, WI 53211 (E Ofc), 6000 South 27th Street, Milwaukee, WI 53221 (S Ofc); m/Kathleen Wilmore; c/3 Chd; p/ Rostam and Sarvar Bondarian Namdari; ed/MD, Fac of Med, Univ of Tehran, 1966; pa/Resident in Surg, St John's Mercy Med Ctr, St Louis, 1969-73; F'ship in Cardiovas Surg w Dr Michael DeBakey, Baylor Col of Med, 1974; Gen & Vascular Surg, Surg Treatment of Obesity, Great Lakes Med and Surg Ctr, SC; Active Staff Mem, St Mary's Hosp, Milwaukee, 1976-; Med Soc of Milwaukee Co; St Med Soc of WI; WI Surg Soc; Milwaukee Acad of Surg; AMA; Fellow, Am Col of Surgs; Michael DeBakey Intl Cardiovas Soc; Affil, Royal Soc of Med; hon/Author, "Untoward Effects: Vagotomy of Drainage Procedures," 1973; Awd from Physics Dept, Fac of Med, Univ of Tehran, for Invention of Ophthalmologic Device; Awd for Best Thesis in Med Sch, 1966; Awd Presented during St John's Mercy Med Ctr Cent for Pub'd Res on New Method of Pylorplasty; Cert'd by Am Bd of Surg; Grant for Res and Creation of 2nd Invention; 2 Patents Rec'd, 1984, Other Patents Pending; W/W in MW; Dir of Med Specs; Personalities of W & MW; Men of Achmt; Book of Hon; Intl W/ W of Intells.

NANCE, BEVERLY McKINLEY oc/ Adult Distributive Education Teacher and Coordinator; b/Jul 5, 1953; h/1510 London Drive, Murray, KY 42071; ba/ Benton, KY; m/John Ned III; p/William Wayne and Gloria McKinley, Belleville, IL; ed/MA in Voc Ed; MA in Ed; BS in Distributive Ed, 1975; pa/Adult Distributive Ed Instr, Marshall Co Voc Ctr, 1978-; CBVE St Coor, KY Dept of Voc Ed, 1977-78; Sec'dy Distributive Ed Instr, Murray Voc Ctr, 1975-77; Murray St Univ Alumni Assn, 1975-81; Nat Bus Ed Assn, 1975-83; Nat Assn of DE Tchrs, 1975-83; KY Assn of DE Tchrs, 1975-83; Am Voc Assn, 1975-83; KY Voc Assn, 1975-83; First Dist Ednl Assn, Pres 1982-83; Rep at Both St & Nat Level DECA Confs, 1975-78; Pi Omega Pi, Gamma Upsilon Chapt, 1973; cp/ Packard Automobile Clb, 1980; Bradford Exch, 1980-; Franklin Mint Collector's Soc, 1980; Twin Lakes Antique Automobile Clb of Am, Reg Chapt, 1978-, Life Mem; r/Meth; hon/Pubs, *A Handbook for DECA Sponsors* 1980, *Retailing Curric Units* 1979, *DE Curr Units* 1977; BPW Org Mem, 1981; Delta Pi Epsilon, 1980-82; Distributive Ed Hall of Fame, 1980; Outstg Distributive Ed Tchr of the Yr for Reg I, 1977; CBVE Innovative Prog Improvement Demonstration Site at Murray Voc Sch, 1976-77; Nat Bus Edrs Assn Awd, 1975; Dean's List Student, Murray St Univ, 1975; Am's Outstg Yg Wom.

NANCE, FRANK L oc/Mortgage and Lease Broker, Real Estate Developer; b/ Jul 17, 1924; h/4034 East 24th Place, Tulsa, OK 74114; ba/Tulsa, OK; m/ Mary Lou; c/David, Dace, Dianne

Marrs, Philip Hood; p/Alvah L and Effie Alice Willis Nance (dec); ed/Student, Cornell Univ, 1945; BS, Murray St Univ, 1948; mil/Served w USMCR, 1942-45; Am Legion, Cmdr 1950; pa/ Pres, F L Nance & Assocs, Consltg, Investmts, 1952-; Pres, SpeedSpace Inc, Aero-Bilt Portable Bldg Co, Ser Bldg, Sys; VP Prefabrication Inc, 1974-; VP, Habitat Devel Inc; Industrialized Bldg Conslt; Am Mgmt Assn; Am Soc Profl Conslts; Constrn Specifications Inst.

NAPLES, JOHN DANIEL oc/Physician, Gynecologic Surgeon; b/Aug 23, 1934; h/58 Dan Trog Drive, Buffalo, NY 14221; ba/Buffalo, NY; m/Jeanne; c/ Maria, Christopher, Jill; p/Dr John D Naples Sr (dec); ed/BA, Canisius Col, 1955; MD, Georgetown Univ Sch of Med, 1959; mil/USN, Lt Cmdr 1966-68; pa/Internship, Buffalo Gen Hosp, 1959-60; Resident, Ob & Gyn, SUNY-Buffalo, 1960-64; Pvt Med Pract, Buffalo, 1964-66, 1968-; Bd of Regents, Canisius Col; AMA; NY St Med Soc; Erie Co Med Soc, Exec Com; Am Col Ob & Gyn; Am Col of Surg; Am Fertility Soc; Intl Fertility Assn; r/Cath; hon/ Author, Num Books, Chapts & Articles in Var Med Jours; Beta Beta Beta, 1954; Alpha Sigma Nu, 1955; Assn of Profs of Gyn & Ob, 1981; W/W in E; Personalities of E.

NARDE, NORMA GREEN oc/ Free-Lance Journalist, Poet, Partner in Husband's Business, Homemaker; b/ Nov 27, 1939; h/1 Pleasant Street, Corning, NY 14830; ba/Same; m/Joseph S; c/Kenneth, Theresa, Carmen, Joseph M; p/Kenneth Raymond (dec) and Florence Crandall Greene, Corning, NY; ed/Grad, Corning Northside HS, 1957; Inst of Chd's Lit; Nat Writers Clb Practical Writing Course; pa/Qtrly Newslttr, *Norma's Notions*, Nat Poets & Writers of Fiction & Non-Fiction, 1979-; Monthly, *A Page From Norma's Jour*, 1980-; Chief of Pub'g, U Amateur Press, 1980-83; Manuscript Mgr, U Amateur Press Assn of Am, 1980-83; cp/Corning Painted Post Area Humane Soc, Secy 1979-82; hon/Fiction Laureate, U Amateur Press, 1981; Writer of the Yr Awd, Artist of the Yr Awd, for Inky Trails Pubs, 1982; Inky Trails Civic Awd, 1982; Dir of Dist'd Ams.

NARVAEZ, AMALIA L PTASZEK oc/Educator, Guidance Counselor; b/Jan 28, 1948; h/86 Division Avenue, Spring Valley, NY 10977; ba/Bronx, NY; c/ Gloria Lee; p/Avraham B Ptaszek, Bronx, NY; ed/BA, 1970; MA, 1973; MS, 1983; Adv'd Cert, Adm and Supvn (in Progress); pa/Tchr, Theodore Roosevelt HS; Secy, Sigma Delta Pi Soc, CCNY, 1968; Pres, Cnslg Students Assn, H H Lehman Col, 1980-81, 1981-82; APGA; hon/W/W.

NASH, ROYSTON H oc/Conductor, Music Director; b/Jul 23, 1933; h/87 Hinckley Circle, Osterville, MA 02655; ba/Osterville, MA; m/Joyce G; c/Adrian W, Kelvin H; p/Sydney Nash (dec); Ellen Hulbert (dec); ed/Royal Acad of Music, London, 1951-55; Exeter Col, Oxford; BMus, Southampton Univ; Licentiate, Royal Acad of Music, 1954; ARCM, 1955; Cert of Merit, Conducting, 1955; ARAM, 1975; mil/Capt, Royal Marines; pa/Trumpet, BBC Orch, 1956; Free-Lance Conducting & Var Engagements as Conductor & Player; BBC Studio Strings & Concert Orch,

1966-70; Music Dir & Prin Conductor, D'Oyly Carte Opera Co, London, 1970-79; Conductor & Music Dir, Cape Cod, Cape Ann & Sinfonie-by-the-Sea Orchs; Pres, Manchester, England, Gilbert & Sullivan Soc, 1980-; r/Meth; hon/Recordings: Eight Sets of Recordings w the D'Oyly Carte Opera Co & the Royal Philharm Orch (Feature of the Recordings is the Inclusion of Previously Unrecorded Orch Music of Sir Arthur Sullivan); W/W in E.

NASH-MORGAN, LEONORA ELIZABETH oc/Physician, Surgeon; b/Aug 13, 1910; h/3700 14th Street, Moline, IL 61265; ba/Moline, IL; m/John Dickinson Morgan; c/John Dickinson Jr, Leonora Elizabeth, Harlan Kellogg, Elizabeth Emily Hillenstedt; p/George Harlan and Edna Snell Nash (dec); ed/ BA 1932, MA 1933, Mt Holyoke Col; F'ship for Study & Res, Harvard Univ Med Sch, 1934; MD, Univ of MI, 1938; Internship & Residency, Univ Hosp of Ann Arbor; pa/Phys, Surg, Univ of No IA, 1940; Pvt Pract, Moline & Erie, IL, 1941-42, Moline, IL, 1952-; AMA; IL St Med Soc; Fellow, Am Acad of Fam Phys; IL Acad of Fam Phys; Rock Isl Co Med Soc; Luth Hosp; Oak Glen Nsg Home, Med Adv Staff & Chm of Utilization Review; Alpha Epsilon Iota; cp/Ctr for the Study of the Presidency, Nat Adv Coun; Harvard Clb of Chgo; Intl Soc for Adv'd Ed; r/Christ Epis Ch; St Boniface Epis Ch; hon/Res: "The Permeability of Capillaries," "The Effect of Increased Oxygen Pressures on Animals Infested with Tetanus"; US Patent for a Specialized Humidifier; W/W of Am Wom; World W/W Wom.

NASSAR, OSCAR oc/Executive; b/ Jan 19, 1947; h/Ingenieros 261, Monterrey, NL Mexico; ba/Monterrey, NL Mexico; c/Oscar; p/Jacobo Nassar; Maria Massu; ed/Electro-Mech Engr, ITESM, 1965-70; Automatic Control Master, ITESM, 1970-71; mil/1965-66; pa/Gen Elect Trainee, USA and Mexico, 1971-73; Gen Mgr, CIFE, 1973-75; Gen Dir, Consultoria Indust Electrica, SA, 1975-77; Pres, Compania Indust Electrica, SA, 1977-82; Pres, Ciesa; Fac Inst Tech y de Estudios Superiores de Monterrey; Assn Mech and Elect Engrs, Monterrey; r/Cath; hon/Pub, *Mathematical Model of a Turbina*, 1970; Patent Phase Failure Relay, 1977; W/W World; Men of Achmt; W/W Intells.

NASSER, ADEL oc/Senior Research Geophysicist; b/Apr 1, 1947; h/6550 Hillcroft, #349, Houston, TX 77081; ba/ Houston, TX; m/Vicki Paski; p/Salah and Samiha Khalil, Alexandria, Egypt; ed/BS in Physics, Alexandria Univ, 1970; MS in Physics 1974, MS in Geophysics 1976, Purdue Univ; pa/ Geophysicist, Wn Geophy Co, 1977; Geophysicist 1979, Sr Res Geophysicist 1981, Exxon Prodn Res Co; Soc of Exploration Geophysicists, Assoc Mem 1976; r/Moslem; hon/Author, Research Proprietary Co Reports (Tech and Res Application); Co-Author, Geophysics Book, Given in Conjunction w Tchg Exxon Schs Worldwide; Compensation Awd, Exxon, 1980; S'ships, Alexandria Univ, 1967-70; Tchg and Res Asst'ships, Purdue Univ, 1972-76; W/W S and SW.

NATCHER, WILLIAM H oc/United States Representative, Member of Congress; b/Sep 11, 1909; h/638 East Main Street, Bowling Green, KY 42101;

ba/Washington, DC; m/Virginia Reardon; c/Celeste Natcher Jirles, Louise Natcher Murphy; p/Mr and Mrs J M Natcher (dec); ed/AB, Wn KY Univ; LLB, OH St Univ, 1933; mil/USN, 1942-46; pa/Fed Conciliation Commr, 1926-37; Co Atty of Warren Co for 3 4-Yr Terms; Elected Commonwealth Atty, 1951-53; Elected to US Cong, 1953; cp/Kiwanis Clb; Odd Fellows; Am Legion; r/Bapt; hon/Awds in Ed, Hlth and Agri.

NAUGHTON, JODIE-KAY MARIE oc/Staging Coordinator for ABI Material; b/Sep 9, 1951; h/8032 North 45th Street, Brown Deer, WI 53223; ba/ Milwaukee, WI; m/Robert Anthony Memmel Jr; p/Joseph Martin and Evelyn Marie Milne Naughton, Chicago, IL; ed/ Assoc Deg, Bus Adm, Wright City, 1979; BA, Bus, Lakeland Col, 1983; EST Tng, 1979; Communication Wkshop, 1979, 1981; pa/Hawthorn-Mfg Location, 1969-74; Acctg/Pricing, Rolling Mows Ctl Reg HQs, 1974-79; VP, Wright Newman Ctr, 1977, JA Advr 1974, 1975; cp/Bd of Dirs: Crewe Clb, Wewaukean Clb, Concerned Consumers Leag; Asst to MW Reg Coor, Hunger Proj; Creator, Wecowacko Clown Troupe; Pres, Future Pioneers 1979; Participant, MW Consumer Cong, 1982; Participant, Holiday Hosp Proj, 1979, 1980, 1981; Delegate Aid, Democratic Conv, 1968; r/Cath.

NAUGLE, MARGARET VANCE oc/ Director of Community Relations; b/ Nov 17, 1946; h/PO Box 1152, 202 Court Street, West Point, MS 39701; ba/Columbus, MS; m/Andrew Kincannon III; c/Laura Natalie Pickens; p/James O'Neil (dec) and Allie Laura Stevens Vance, West Point, MS; ed/BS, Bus and Combined Scis, MS Univ for Wom, 1970; MEd, Adult and Voc Ed, MS St Univ, 1977; EdD, Ednl Ldrship, MS St Univ, 1980; pa/Dir of Commun Relats, Golden Triangle Reg Med Ctr, 1982-; Adj Prof, Univ of AL, 1980-; Tech Writer and Tng Spec, Weyerhaeuser Columbus Proj, 1979-82; Dir of Adult Ed, MS Band of Choctaw Indians, 1976-79; Tech Advr, Fermodyl Labs Inc, 1975-76; Tchr, Pickens Co Schs, 1974-75; Tchr, Hendry Co Schs, 1973-74; Tchr, Lowndes Co Schs, 1970-73; Admissions Ofcr, MS St Col for Wom, 1969-70; Other Previous Positions; Am Soc for Hosp Public Relats; Nat Assn for Hosp Devel; Public Relats Assn of MS; MS Hosp Assn; Golden Triangle Advtg Fdn; Nat Assn for Public Cont'g and Adult Ed; Adult Ed Assn for the USA; Assn for Supvn and Curric Devel; Am Soc for Tng and Devel; cp/Soroptimist Intl of Columbus; Toastmasters Intl Possum Town Toastmasters, Charter Mem 1981, Secy-Treas 1982; Concerned Citizens of Clay Co; Columbus-Lowndes C of C; Career Wom's Guild; hon/Pubs, "A Comparison of the EDL Learning 100 Program and the Workbook Method of Teaching Reading to Choctaw Adults" 1980, "Adult Education Annual Report" 1975, 1976, 1977, 1978, 1979, "Capsule Communique" 1982, "Choctaw Adult Education Program-A Request for Funding to the Department of the Interior, Bureau of Indian Affairs" 1976, 1977, 1978, 1979, Others; Outstg Adult Edr, 1979; W/W S and SW; World W/ W Wom.

PERSONALITIES OF AMERICA

NAVE, MICHAEL ERNEST oc/Lecturer Specializing in Occupational Safety; b/Jul 7, 1952; h/485 East Bullard, Fresno, CA 93710; ba/Fresno, CA; p/ Ernest and Theresa M Nave, Fresno, CA; ed/MS in Hlth Sci, CA St Univ Fresno, 1978; BA in Polit Sci, 1975; pa/Lectr, Dept of Hlth Sci, CA St Univ Fresno, 1983-; Indep Safety Conslt, 1980-83; Safety Conslt, Wise Ins Agts, 1978-80; Loss Control Conslt, EBI Co, 1977-78; CA Agri Coor'g Com, 1980-; Ctl Val Coun of Safety Supvrs; Am Soc of Safety Engrs, Student Chapt Coor 1983, Mem 1979-; cp/First Aid and CPR Instr, ARC; r/Cath; hon/Phi Kappa Phi Hon Soc, 1983; MS w Distn, 1978; Guest Spkr, Golden W Safety Cong, Nat Safety Coun, 1980, 1981, 1982; W/W W.

NEAL, ELAINE MARIE oc/Consultant on Administrative Systems; b/May 24, 1943; h/172 Chestnut Street, S-1, Waltham, MA 02154; ba/Same; p/ Thomas Scott and Marjorie A Neal, Woburn, MA; ed/BS, Ed, Bridgewater St Col, 1965; Grad, Dale Carnegie Course in Public Spkg, 1979; pa/Conslt on Adm Sys and Mgmt Devel, Realization Mgmt (Own Bus), 1979-; Mgr of Credit and Collection, Ofc Sers and Intl Customer Ser for USCI Div 1973-79, and Mgr of Credit and Collection of Customer Ser and EDP for MacBick Div 1967-73, C R Bard Inc; cp/ Johannes Kelpius Lodge, Master 1981-82, Dpty Master 1980-81; AMORC, Rosicrucian Subordinate Body; Spkr for SBA of Concord, 1979-80; Conslt for SCORE of Manchester, 1979-80; Guest Spkr, Nashua Rotary Clb, Newcomers of Nashua, Parents without Partners, Boston Col; Chm of Ed for Intl Mgmt Assn in Nashua, 1980; r/Universal in Belief; hon/Book in Process on Cosmic Attunement; Grad w Hon, Woburn Sr HS, 1965; Recip, First Rotary Camp S'ship Ever Awd'd to Girl Scout in Woburn, 1957; Recip, Plaque for Outstg Ldrship in Org'g the Rosicrucian Booth at 1981 Boston Lifestyles Show.

NEALE, AUDREY A oc/Coordinator of Home School Visitation and Chemical Abuse Program; b/Sep 1, 1933; h/ 332 Ventura Drive, Youngstown OH 44505; ba/Youngstown, OH; m/Luther C; c/Randy C, Wayne C, Dennis C; p/ Harry C (dec) and Alice H Bowser, Worthington, PA; ed/BS in Ed, 1955; MS in Ed, Guid and Cnslg, 1971; MS in Ed, Sch Adm, 1983; pa/Tchr, Liberty HS 1955-57, Hubbard HS 1958-60, Youngstown Schs 1961-68; Home Sch Visitor, Youngstown Schs, 1968-79; Coor of Home Sch Visitation, Youngstown Schs, 1978-83; Chem Abuse Prog, Youngstown Schs 1983, Youngstown St Univ 1976-79; Coor of Home Sch Visitation and Chem Abuse Prog, Youngstown Public Schs; Youngstown Fdn of Tchrs, Secy 1965-67; Youngstown Sch Admrs, 1979-83; Delta Kappa Gamma, 1975-83; Youngstown Area U Way, Planning Coun, 1983; r/ Bapt; hon/Dist'd Ser Awd, Reg Coun on Alcoholism, 1983.

NEARY, JOSEPH T oc/Biochemist, Neurobiologist; b/Oct 14, 1943; h/54 Shore Street, Falmouth, MA 02540; ba/ Woods Hole, MA; m/Judith A; c/Robert, Suzanne; p/Joseph F (dec) and Mary C Neary, Carbondale, PA; ed/BS, cum laude, Univ of Scranton, 1965; PhD, Univ of Pgh, 1969; pa/USPHS-NIH Postdoct Fellow, Univ of IL, 1969-71; Assoc in Biochem, Asst in Med, MA Gen Hosp and Harvard Med Sch, 1971-78; Staff Scist and MBL Investigator, Marine Biological Lab, 1978-; AAAS; Soc for Neurosci; Am Chem Soc; r/ Cath; hon/Author, 26 Pubs in Profl Jours, incl'g, *Science, Nature, Journal of Biological Chemistry*.

NEASE, HOWARD C oc/Business Owner/Executive; b/Feb 9, 1934; h/4551 Cars Kaddon, Toledo, OH 43615; ba/ Toledo, OH; m/Johnie Lois; c/Rick, Randy, Gregory, Debra, Jeffery; p/ Francis H. Nease (dec); Lena B Nease, Dodge City, KS; sp/Mrs Joe Miller, Nowata, OK; ed/MDH, Univ of Metaphisic; Att'd Bkr Univ; pa/Sales Dir, Mutual of Omaha, 1954-74; Pres, Personal Dynamics, Inc, 1974-; Pres, Global Labs Inc, 1979-; Pres, Briteway Prods, 1978-; Pres, Prod Devel Inst, 1976-; Pres, Neaco Mktg Sys; cp/C of C; Advr, St of OH, Nurse Tng, 1980-82; Better Bus Bur; hon/Author Sev Tng Manuals for Van Bus, 1974-; Many Newspaper Articles for Personal Dynamics Newspaper; Spkr at Convs, Sales Meetings, Other Gatherings; Inventor, Wind Jennie, Auqo Airo Mist Sys; Fdr, Personal Dynamics, Inc, 1974; W/W: Bus & Fin.

NECHAMKIN, HOWARD oc/Professor of Chemistry; b/Aug 18, 1918; h/325 Glenn Avenue, Lawrenceville, NJ 08648; ba/Trenton, NJ; m/Murielle; c/ Emily, David Alan Katz; p/Mrs Celia Nechamkin, Brooklyn, NY; ed/BA, Brooklyn Col, 1939; MS, Polytechnic Inst of Brooklyn, 1949; EdD, Sci, NY Univ, 1961; pa/Bur of Standards, R H Macy & Co, 1939-42; Chief Chem, Hazeltine Electronics Corp, 1942-45; Assoc Prof, Pratt Inst, 1945-61; Prof of Chem, Trenton St Col, 1961-; Phi Lambda Upsilon; Am Inst of Chems, Fellow; AAUP; ACS; hon/Author, 52 Articles on Chem, 6 Books on Chem; Phi Kappa Phi; Outstg Edrs of Am; W/ W E; W/W Ed; W/W Engrg; Am Men of Sci.

NEE, SISTER M COLEMAN oc/ College President; b/Nov 14, 1917; h/ Marywood College, Scranton, PA 18509; ba/Same; p/Coleman and Nora Hopkins Nee (dec); ed/BA, 1939; MA, 1941; MS, Math, 1959; Doct Study, Univ of Notre Dame, 1951-59; pa/Sec'dy Tchr, Scranton Schs 1939-41, Marywood Sem 1944-55; Col Tchr 1959-68, Dir of Pers-IHM Rel Cong, Pres 1970-, Marywood Col; PA Col and Univ, Exec Com 1978-81; Com for Indep Cols and Univs; Nat Cath Ed Assn; cp/Dir, C of C, Scranton, Secy 1983-84; Adv Bd, YWCA, Scranton; Jr Leag of Scranton; r/Rom Cath; hon/NSF Fellow, 1957-59; W/W; W/W Rel.

NEIDELL, NORMAN SAMPSON oc/ Co-Founder and Executive; b/Mar 11, 1939; h/10354 Taylorcrest, Houston, TX 77079; ba/Houston, TX; m/Elizabeth Joy Reay; c/Shani Elizabeth Reay, Helen Penelope Celia, Richard Alexander Reay, Nicholas Hamilton Troy, Victoria Allison Calandra; p/Harry and Eva Neidell, Long Island, NY; ed/PhD, Geodesy and Geophysics, Cambridge Univ, 1964; Postgrad Dipl, Imperial Col, 1961; BA, NY Univ, 1959; pa/Res Geophysicist, Gulf Res and Devel Co, 1964-68; Asst Dir of Res, Tech Asst to Pres, Seiscom-Delta Inc, 1968-71; Adj Prof of Geophysics, Univ of Houston, 1971-; Fdr, Conslt, N S Neidell & Assocs, 1971-; Co-Fdr, Conslt, Dir, GeoQuest Intl Inc, 1973-80; Co-Fdr, Exec VP, Dir, Zenith Exploration Co Inc, 1977-; Soc Exploration Geophysics; Am Assn Petro Geol; Geophysical Soc of Houston; Houston Geol Soc; European Assn Exploration Geophysics; Marine Tech Soc; Soc Photo Optical Instr Engrs; IEEE; Am Inst of Profl Geologists; Assn of Petro Conslts, Pres 1982; r/Jewish; hon/Author of Book, *Stratigraphic Modeling and Interpretation-Geophysical Principles and Techniques*, Var Pubs; Phi Beta Kappa; Grad, cum laude, NY Univ, 1959; Woods Hole Oceanographic Inst F'ship, 1960, 1961; NSF F'ships, 1962-64; Soc of Exploration Geophysics Best Presentation Awd, 1973; W/W S and SW; W/ W Technol Today.

NEILL, ROBERT H oc/Director of Nuclear Waste Repository Evaluation Group; b/Feb 9, 1930; h/1056 Governor Dempsey Drive, Santa Fe, NM 87501; ba/Santa Fe, NM; m/Townley B; c/Helen Rosemary; p/William J (dec) and Rosemary A Neill, Lyndhorst, NJ; ed/ME, Mech Engrg, Stevens Inst of Technol, 1951; MS, Radiological Hlth, Harvard Univ Sch of Public Hlth, 1962; mil/ Comm'd Corps, USPHS; pa/Engr, Foster Wheeler Corp, 1951-56; Var Positions, Bur of Radiological Hlth, USPHS, 1956-78; Dir, Envir Eval Grp, NM Hlth and Envir Dept, 1978-; Chair, Radiological Hlth Sect, APHA, 1984; Hlth Physics Soc; Bd of Trustees, Santa Fe Preparatory Sch; Nat Acad of Scis Uranium Mill Tailings Panel; hon/ Author, Var Papers and Pubs in Radiological Hlth Field; Public Hlth Ser Meritorious Ser Medal, 1972; US Advr, World Hlth Org, 1982, 1984; W/W W.

NEIMAN, ROBERT LeROY oc/Management Consultant, Executive Recruiter; b/Feb 9, 1930; h/9401 North Natchez, Morton Grove, IL 60053; ba/ Chicago, IL; m/Barbara Milkes (dec); c/ Debra Bea; p/Maurice (dec) and Shirley Neiman, Chicago, IL; ed/BS w Hons in Communs 1951, MA in Social and Behavioral Sci 1952, Univ of IL; mil/ USAF, 1st Lt 1951-53; pa/Asst to Pres, Utility Plastic Packaging Co, 1953-54; From Dept Mgr to VP, Castls & Assocs, 1954-73; VP 1973-77, Sr VP 1977-, Mendheim Co; Sr Mem, Soc of Mfg Engrs; APGA; Am Mgmt Assn; Nat Assn of Corporate and Profl Recruiters; cp/Chm, Barbara Neiman Meml Foun of Am Cancer Soc, 1983-; Chm, M K Neiman Meml Foun of Am Cancer Soc, 1972-75; Skokie Val Kiwanis, Prog Chm; AF Assn; hon/ Author, Articles in Field; Sigma Delta Chi; Sigma Delta Pi Hons; W/W MW; W/W Fin and Indust.

NEITZEL, SARAH CAIN oc/Associate Professor of History; b/Dec 25, 1943; h/1800 West Kuhn, Apartment A, Edinburg, TX 78539; ba/Edinburg, TX; p/Robert (dec) and Gwendolyn Neitzel, Marksville, LA; ed/BA, Millsaps Col, 1965; MA, Univ of SWn LA, 1969; PhD, TX Tech Univ, 1974; pa/Instr in Hist, Univ of SWn LA, 1969-70; Asst Prof of Hist, Val City St Col, 1975-76; Asst Prof of Hist 1974-75, 1976-82, Assoc

423

Prof of Hist 1982-, Pan Am Univ; Am Hist Assn; So Hist Assn; Wn Assn for German Studies; Conf Grp on German Polit; Phi Alpha Theta, Intl Hist Hon; r/Epis; hon/Pubs, *Why Hitler?* 1971, "The Evolution of August Bebel's Social-Political Credo, 1861-1871" 1979, "The Salzburg Catholic *Gesellenverein*: An Alternative to Socialism" 1982; Deutscher Akademischer Austauschdienst (DAAD) Fellow, 1972-73; Am Philosophical Soc Fellow, 1978; Pan Am Univ Res Grant, 1980; W/W S and SW.

NELL, VARNEY REED oc/Society President; b/May 3, 1925; h/3126 Juniper Lane, Falls Church, VA 22044; ba/Washington, DC; m/Rose M; c/ Edward L, Catharine G, April Jane, Stephen Voorhees; p/Clyde Smith and Grace May Reed Nell; ed/BA, Univ of WA, 1949; Indust Col of Armed Forces, 1972; Grad Study, Am Univ, 1961-62; Nat Inst on Genealogical Res, 1981; mil/ AUS, Inf and Mil Govt for Bavaria; USAF, Intell 1950-78, Lt Col, Regular; cp/Nat Genealogical Soc, Life Mem, Pres 1982-86, 1st VP 1980-82; Chm, Genealogical Hall of Fame Com, 1981-86; Columbia Hist Soc; OH Genealogical Soc; OH, Genealogical Soc; Fairfax Co, VA, Genealogical Soc; Montgomery Co, MD, Dist Soc; W-Ctl KY Fam Res Assn; Arlington Co, VA, Genealogical Clb; Harry S Truman Lodge #649, F&AM; Scottish Rite, 32 Deg; Kena Temple, Masmic Shrine; Nat Inst on Genealogical Res Alumni Assn; Annebe Jans and Everardus Bogardus Descendants Assn; r/First Christian Ch; hon/Editor, "Entitled" by Richard B Dickenson, NGS Spec Pub #47; Nat Genealogical Soc Dist'd Ser Awd, 1981; Mil Hons: Combat Inf Badge, Bronze Star Medal w OLC, USAF Meritorious Ser Medal w 2 OLCs, Jt Sers Commend Medal, USAF Commend Medal w 2 OLCs, USAF Outstg Unit Awd w OLC and Combat Valor Device, AUS Good Conduct Medal, Am Campaign Medal, European-African-Mid En Campaign Medal w 2 Battle Stars, WWII Victory Medal, Army of Occupation Medal, Nat Def Ser Medal w OLC, Vietnam Campaign Medal w 4 Battle Stars, USAF Longevity Ser Awd w 1 Silver and 1 Bronze OLC, Republic of Vietnam Campaign Medal w Device, Vietnamese Cross of Gallantry w Palm; W/W Geneal and Heraldry.

NELSON, ALAN JAN oc/President of the American Guild of Variety Artists; b/Sep 18, 1944; h/6356 Ventura Canyon, Van Nuys, CA 91401; ba/New York, NY; p/Arthur and Laura Nelson, North Hollywood, CA; ed/AA, LA Val City Col; BS, Val St Col; MS, CA St Col LA; pa/Fund Raiser, U Way Inc, 1970; Assoc Exec Dir, Oak Hill Lng Sers, 1971; Commun Sers Dir, City of S El Monte, 1972-73; VP, Eu Gray Lighting Co, 1975; Exec Dir, Search Consortium, 1977; Nat VP 1979, Pres 1980-, Am Guild of Variety Artists; VP, Assoc'd Actors and Artists of Am (AFL-CIO), 1980-; 4th VP of Theatre Auth, 1980-; Col in the Assoc'd Spec Invest and Police Intl Inc; Pres, AJN Halleluyah Inc, 1981-82; Pres, L&N Prodns, 1975-82; r/Christian Jew; hon/Writer, Wkly Show Biz Column for *Back Stage* Newspaper; Co-Writer of Screenplays, *Barney Moses, Merlin, Chrisanta*; Cit from Senator

Skevin, St of NJ, for the Advmt of Bldg a Stronger Future for Live Entertainment, 1981; Golden Mask Awd for Outstg Achmt in the Entertainment Indust, 1982; Outstg Ser Plaque from AGUA, 1981; W/W World; W/W Am.

NELSON, IRIS D oc/Guidance and Rehabilitation Counselor; b/Jul 5, 1937; h/235 West 102 Street, New York, NY 10025; ba/Bronx, NY; p/Simon (dec) and Bertha Rapkine Nelson, Livingston Manor, NY; ed/BA, Zool, Barnard Col of Columbia Univ, 1959; MA in Developmental Psych 1964, EdM in Psychol Cnslg and Rehab 1980, Tchrs Col of Columbia Univ; pa/Res Asst to Chm Zool Dept, Columbia Univ, 1959-64; Tchr, Activity Therapist, Psychi Treatment Ctr, 1964-67; Tchr, NYC Public Schs, 1967-80; Elem and Jr HS Guid Cnslr, Jr High Tchr, Spec Ed, NYC Bd of Ed, 1970-77; Assoc Chp, Com on the Handicapped, Div of Spec Ed and Pupil Pers Sers, 1977-78; Cnslr, Yth Employmt and Tng Prog, 1978-81; Cnslr, Bronx Ctr for Career and Occupl Sers, 1982-; Wom's Am ORT, Edrs Chapt; APGA; Am Rehab Cnslrs Assn; Nat Voc Guid Assn; NY St Cnslg Assn; NY St Rehab Cnslrs Assn; NY St Mtl Hlth Cnslrs Assn; NYC Pers and Guid Assn; Jt Coun for Mtl Hlth Sers Inc, Bd Mem; AAUW; Nat Rehab Assn; Nat Rehab Cnslg Assn; Metro NY NRA Chapt, Bd Mem; Assn of NY St Edrs of the Emotionally Disturbed; cp/ ACLU; Annual Commun Sponsor, W Side Commun Conf; Jewish Labor Com, Edrs Chapt; r/Jewish; hon/Contbr, Articles to Profl Pubs; Rho Chi Sigma Rehab Cnslg and Sers Hon Soc, Life Mem; Kappa Delta Pi Hons Soc in Ed, Alumna Mem; W/W E.

NELSON, MACK C oc/College Professor; b/Nov 14, 1947; h/Route 3, Box 146-A1C, Fort Valley, GA 31030; ba/ Fort Valley, GA; m/Addie M; c/Cheryl G, Cynara T; p/Viola N Powe, Oakland, CA; ed/BS, Alcorn St Univ, 1970; MS, Tuskegee Inst, 1974; PhD, Univ of IL, 1977; mil/AUS, 1970-72; pa/Asst Co Supvr (USDA), Farmers Home Adm, 1970-77; Asst Prof of Agri Ec, Prairie View A&M Univ, 1977-78; Asst Prof of Agri Ec, Ft Val St Col, 1978-; r/Prot; hon/Pubs, "Economics Impact of Soil Erosion Control" 1979, "An Economic Analysis of Soil Erosion Control in a Watershed Representing Corn Belt Conditions" 1979, "Emerging Research Issues Directed at Small Low-Income, Limited Resource Farmers" 1978; Grad, cum laude, Alcorn St Univ; Gamma Sigma Delta, Hon Soc for Agri; Chi Gamma Iota; Personalities of S.

NELSON, MARY JEAN oc/Executive; b/Mar 5, 1914; h/37 Willow Lane, Lindenhurst, NY 11757; ba/Lindenhurst, NY; c/Judith Ramsauer, Robert; ed/HS Grad, 1930; Student, NY St Agri Inst, 1963; pa/Sales; Buyer, Edelman Brothers; Hellman's Bay Shore; Pres, M J Nelson Rlty, 1967; LI Bd of Rltrs; cp/ Active in Girl Scouting, Heart Clin and Foun; hon/Dist'd Ser Awd, S Shore Suffolk Chapt of LI Bd of Rltrs, 1976-78.

NELSON, R DOUGLAS oc/Environmental Engineering Firm Executive; b/ Apr 15, 1935; h/2109 Neuse Cliff Drive, New Bern, NC 28560; ba/New Bern, NC; m/Jean H; c/Raymond D Jr, Susan R; ed/MS, Envir Engrg, MI Tech Univ, 1965; BS, Natural Resources Mgmt, NC

St Univ, 1958; mil/AUS, 1958-60; pa/ Pres, R Douglas Nelson & Assocs, 1982-; Envir Mgr, Texasgulf Chems Inc, 1979-82; St of NC Dir, Ofc of Coastal Mgmt, 1974-79; Pres, Devel Technol Inc, 1971-74; Engrg and Res Mgr, Thiohol Chem Corp, 1968-71; Fishery Engr, US Fish and Wildlife Ser, 1963-68; Bd of Trustees, Craven Commun Col; Curric Adv Com, Martin Co Commun Col; Am Chem Soc; Soc of Envir Sci; Pollution Control Fdn; Am Planning Assn; cp/Craven Co Com of 100; C of C; Neuse Coun, BSA, 4 Yrs; r/Bapt; hon/ Pubs, "Agency Roles and Authorization in Industrial Development" 1979, "Toward Cost/Benefit Analysis of Land Resource Planning" 1973, Others; Profl Engr, 1972; Cert'd Fisheries Biologist, 1965; Cert'd Planner, APA, 1972; W/W Sci.

NEMITOFF, ARTHUR PAUL oc/ Rabbi; b/Jul 29, 1954; h/6442 Old Chatham Lane, Houston, TX 77035; ba/ Missouri City, TX; p/William Nemitoff (dec); Henrietta Dalke, Miami, FL; ed/ BA, Wash Univ, 1977; MAHL 1980, Rabbinic Ordination 1981, Hebrew Union Col, Jewish Inst of Rel; pa/Rabbi, Congreg Beth El, 1983-; Asst Rabbi, Congreg Beth Israel, 1981-83; Student Rabbi, Meir Chayim Temple, 1980-81; Student Rabbi, Temple Sinai, 1979-80; Student Rabbi, Temple Beth Sholom, 1977-79; Bd Mem, B'nai B'rith Hillel Foun, 1983-; Ctl Conf of Am Rabbis, 1981-; SW Assn of Reform Rabbis, 1981-; Kallah of TX Rabbis, 1981-; Gtr Houston Rabbinical Assn, 1981-; Coalition for Alternatives in Jewish Ed, 1982-; Com on Singles, SW Reg of Union of Am Hebrew Congreg, 1981-; Tri-Cities Ministerial Alliance, 1983-; cp/M D Anderson Clergy Com on Cancer Care, 1981-; r/Jewish; hon/Pubs, *A Basic Judaism Reader* 1982, "Aunt Rose 2" (Poetry) 1982, "The Unbinding of Issac" (Poetry) 1984; Recip, Cora Kahn Prize for Sermon Delivery and Oratory, HUC-JIR, 1981; Outstg Yg Men of Am.

NESBIT, DORIS PARSONS oc/Educational Specialist in Adult Education; b/Sep 16, 1932; h/3301 Southwest 98 Avenue, Miami, FL 33165; ba/Miami, FL; c/Suzan Shae, D Byron, Shelton P; p/Dorette (dec) and Thelma Mangum Parsons, Coral Gables, FL; ed/BS in Ed, Queens Col, 1954; MS, Adm and Supvn, K-12, Univ of Miami Coral Gables, 1973; Doct, Voc, Technological and Occupl Ed, Nova (in Progress); pa/Tchr, Lakeview Elem 1954-57, Pulaski HS 1957-59, Retarded Teenagers, Asheville City Schs 1960-61, Dade Co Public Schs 1962-; Dept Chair 1969-70, Curric Spec 1970-71, Palmetto Jr High; Dept Chair 1971-77, Adult Basic Ed, Ed Spec 1977-78, Ed Spec, Adult Prog Sers 1978-82, Rockway Jr High; Pres, Around the Corner Sub/Deli Inc, 1981-82; Nat Assn of Core Curric, Bd of Dirs 1965-83, VP 1969, Pres 1970; ASCD; NACPE; Delta Kappa Gamma Soc Intl, Chapt Pres; Beta Sigma Phi, Pres, Charlotte, NC, Pulaski, VA; Mtl Hlth Assn of Dade Co; cp/St Indian Proj Chair; Urban Leag Guild, Miami, Parliamentarian 1977-79; r/Bapt; hon/ Pubs, Staff Devel Modules for Tchg Adults-FAU Proj, Lng Activs Packages-Four in Communs: Career-Electronics & Four in Home Ec, Co World Cultural Guide and ITV Daily

Lessons, LAPs Cash Register (Consumer Ed), Substance Abuse 1979-*New Directions for Continuing Education: Attracting Instructors of Adults*, "Supervision and Monitoring"; ACLU F'ship, Columbia Univ, 1965; Taft Inst F'ship, UNCC, 1968; Beta Sigma Phi Girl of the Yr, 1959; BSA Boy Power, 1969; Delta Kappa Gamma, Mu St S'ship, 1973, 1977; W/W S & SW.

NeSMITH, VERA C oc/Free-Lance Administrative Secretary; b/Oct 24, 1917; h/1912 Weber Street, Orlando, FL 32803; m/J Vernon (dec); c/Patricia E Messer; Stepchd: John S, James E; p/ Ernest H and Edith E Cox (dec); pa/Instr/ Secy, Orlando Secretarial Sch, 1937-38; Exec Secy, Voc Rehab, 1938-76; Adm Secy, Dept of Hlth and Rehab Sers, 1976-80; Ret'd, 1980; Free-Lance Secretarial Wk, Wk for Kelly Sers; Am Assn of Med Assts; FL St Soc, AAMA; Orange Co Chapt, AAMA, Life Mem; cp/Intl Biogl Assn; Life Fellow, Am Biogl Inst; John Young Planetarium and Mus; Am Assn of Ret'd Persons; Nat Bd of Advrs, Am Biogl Inst; r/Broadway U Meth Ch, 1932-; hon/Outstg Mem Awd, Orange Co Chapt, AAMA, 1982; Cert of Merit, Dept of Hlth and Rehab Ser, 1980; Outstg Ser Awd for FL St Soc Conv, AAMA, 1980; Lifetime Mbrship Awd, Orange Co Chapt, AAMA, 1979; Engraved Silver Bowl for 40 Yrs Outstg Ser, Voc Rehab, Dept of Hlth and Rehab Sers, 1978; Num Other Hons; W/W Am Wom; Am Social Registry; W/W Am Wom in S and SW; World W/W Wom; Commun Ldrs and Noteworthy Ams; Dir of Dist'd Ams; Num Others Biogl Listings.

NESS, JAN oc/Artist; b/Aug 25, 1944; h/51 Hitching Post Road, Bozeman, MT 59715; ba/Same; m/James M; c/Teresa, Marc, Quinn; p/Robert and Gladys Larsen, Billings, MT; ed/Self-Taught; pa/Self-Employed Artist; Am Artists of the Rockies Assn; r/Luth; hon/Wk Featured in *Montana Prospector Magazine*, 1982; Artist and Wk Featured in Book, *Contemporary Western Artist* by Peggy and Harold Samuels; Artist Featured in Cookbook, *How to Feed a Starving Artist*, Compiled by Miriam Wolf; Featured in *People of the Century* by Noel Goldblatt.

NETI, SUDHAKAR oc/Associate Professor of Mechanical Engineering; b/ Sep 27, 1947; h/3524 Moravian Court, Bethlehem, PA 18017; ba/Bethlehem, PA; m/Kathy Louise; c/Leela Parvathi; p/Chiranjeeva Rao and Meenakshi Neti, Madras, India; ed/PhD 1977, MS 1970, Mech Engrg, Univ of KY; BE, Mech Engrg, Osmania Univ, 1968; pa/Assoc Prof of Mech Engrg and Mech 1983-, Asst Prof of Mech Engrg and Mech 1978-83, Lehigh Univ; NASA-ASEE Sum Fac Fellow, NASA-Ames Res Ctr, 1978; Res Asst, Univ of KY, 1970-77; Tech Conslt to Many Cos, incl'g, Leeds & Northrup, Babcock & Wilcox, GPU, PA Power & Light Co, Buckeye Pipe Co; ASME, Prog Dir 1982-; Sigma Xi; FEMA Fall Out Shelter Analyst; ASME Rep for EWJPC, 1981-82; cp/Am Cancer Soc Vol, 1980-; U Way Campaign Solicitor, 1981-82; Lehigh Univ Table Tennis Advr, 1981-; hon/Pubs, "Raman Scattering in Two-Phase Flows with Applications to Temperature Measurements" 1983, "Combined Hydrodynamic and Thermal Development in a Square Duct" 1983, "Computation of Laminar

Heat Transfer in Rotating Rectangular Ducts" 1983, "Forced Convective Nonequilibrium Post-CHF Heat Transfer Experiments in a Vertical Tube" 1983, Num Others; Awd'd Res Grants and Contracts by NSF, Nuclear Regulatory Comm, Elect Power Res Inst; Patent Pending on Laser Velocimeters; W/W E.

NEUFVILLE, PIERRE de oc/International Stock Broker; b/Sep 15, 1924 h/ 4 East 74th Street, New York, NY 10021; ba/New York, NY; m/Jeanne; c/ Olivier; ed/BA, Sorbonne, 1946; mil/ Free French, 1942-45; pa/Asst/VP, La Cruz Linares Spain, 1947-50; Coca Cola Intl, Paris, 1950-54; Mgr, Sales Promotion, France Press, Paris, 1954-56; Mgr, Hayden Stone, 1954-64; Resident Ptnr, Bache France, 1964-73; Intl Stock Broker, Lehman Bros Inc; NY Acad of Scis; cp/Advr to the CoChm, US Congl Adv Bd; r/Taoist; hon/Medaille Militaire, Croix de Guerre (3); W/W Fin; W/W World.

NEUMAYER, ROBERT CHARLES oc/Aerospace Engineering Manager; b/ May 14, 1937; h/8104 South Spruce Court, Englewood, CO 80112; ba/ Wakefield, MA; c/Deborah Ann, John Robert; p/Charles A Neumayer, Carroll, IA; ed/Master of Engrg Adm, Univ of UT, 1973; MS, Chem Engrg, Univ of WA, 1969; BS, Chem Engrg, IA St Univ, 1959; mil/USAF, 1960-80; pa/Devel Engrg, Union Carbide Chems Co, 1959-60; USAF: Comm'd as 2nd Lt 1959, Adv'd to Lt Col 1976, Ret'd 1980, Served as Pilot, Instr Pilot, Flying Safety Ofcr, Engr, Engrg Mgr, Staff Ofcr, Tech Dir; Mgr, Test and Eval, Martin Marietta Aerospace, 1980-; cp/Elks, 1972-; r/Cath; hon/Tau Beta Pi, 1958; Phi Kappa Phi, 1959; Phi Lambda Upsilon, 1959; Mil Decorations: AF Commend Medal 1973, AF Meritorious Ser Medal 1980, Air Medal 1969, Vietnam Ser Medal 1967, Republic of Vietnam Campaign Medal 1967, Republic of Vietnam Gallantry Medal w Palm 1967; W/W E.

NEVLING, HARRY REED oc/Personnel Director of Hospital; b/Sep 15, 1946; h/1432 Brookfield Drive, Longmont, CO 80501; ba/Longmont, CO; m/ Joanne Carol Meyer; c/Terry John; ed/ So Sch of Agri, 1960-64; Intermediate Speed Radio Operators Course 1966, Radio Teletype Operators Course 1966, Warrant Ofcr Rotary Wing Aviators Course 1968, Engr Ofcr's Basic Course 1972, AUS; AA, Bus, Rochester Commun Col, 1973; BA, Bus Adm and Ec, Winona St Univ, 1974; mil/Enlisted E1-E5, Radio Operator-Combat Duty 1965-68, Warrant and Chief Warrant Ofcr, Helicopter Pilot 1968-70, Comm'd First Lt and Capt, Corps of Engrs-Supply, Batallion Adjutant 1970-72, AUS; Capt, Corps of Engrs, USAR, 1972; pa/Plastics, IBM Corp, 1973; VP, Lic'd Broker, DAVID Rlty Corp, 1976; Pers Dir, Longmont U Hosp, 1977-; Conslt for Bus, Commun Col of Denver, NM Campus, 1983.

NEW, O THEODORE oc/Podiatric Physician and Surgeon; b/May 2, 1935; h/2112 Trellis Place, Richardson, TX 75081; ba/Dallas, TX; m/Dianne; ed/ DSc, Hahnemann Meml Inst of Hlth Scis, 1981; BEd 1983, BA 1958, Univ of Miami; Dr of Podiatric Med, OH Col of Podiatric Med, 1964; pa/Pvt Pract of Podiatric Med and Surg, 1964-; Am

Podiatry Assn; TX Podiatry Assn; Dallas Co Podiatry Assn; Acad of Ambulatory Foot Surg; Am Soc of Podiatric Angiology; Am Med Writers Assn; Inter-Am Cong of Phys and Surgs; cp/Dallas Hist Soc; hon/Pubs, "Ambulatory Foot Surgery," "The Dew on the Rose," "Pain and Neurology"; Pres, Am Soc of Podiatric Med, 1982, 1983; Pres and Fdr, Am Assn of Plastic and Reconstructive Foot Surg; Pres, Am Soc of Podiatric Angiology, 1981, 1982, 1983.

NEWBERT, C LEONARD oc/Minister; b/Jan 1, 1926; h/744 Hathaway Road, New Bedford, MA 02740; ba/New Bedford, MA; m/Beverly E; c/David L, Jane Elizabeth Avila; p/Cecil and Flora Orff Newbert (dec); ed/AB, cum laude, 1951; BD, cum laude, 1954; PhD, 1983; mil/Cmdr, USNR, 25 Yrs (Ret'd); pa/ Pastor, First Presb 1952-54, Ch of the Nazarene 1954-82, Chs in Millinocket, ME 1954-64, Waltham, MA 1964-68, Framingham, MA 1968-73, New Bedford, MA 1973-; Appt'd Chaplain of Historic Seamen's Bethel of *Moby Dick* Fame, 1979; Mil Chaplains' Assn of Am, Pres of New England Chapt 1973-74; cp/New Bedford Port Soc; Chaplain, The Mil Order of World Wars; r/Prot; hon/Author, Many Articles in Both Rel and Secular Books, incl'g, "A Few Entries from the Chaplain's Log" 1980, "So Your Getting Married" 1982; Naval Hosp Cert of Ser, 1974; Am Legion Cit for Meritorious Ser, 1981.

NEWKIRK, GORDON ALLEN JR oc/ Astrophysicist; b/Jun 12, 1928; h/3797 Wonderland Hill, Boulder, CO 80302; ba/Boulder, CO; m/Nancy; c/Sally, Linda, Jennifer; ed/AB, Harvard Univ, 1950; MA 1952, PhD 1953, Univ of MI; mil/AUS, 1953-55; pa/Sr Scist, High Altitude Observatory, 1973-; Assoc Dir, Nat Ctr for Atmospheric Res, 1979; Dir 1968-79, Acting Dir 1968, High Altitude Observatory, Nat Ctr for Atmospheric Res; Prof Adjoint of Dept of Physics and Astrophysics 1965-73, Prof Adjoint of Dept of Astro-Geophysics 1961-65, Univ of CO; Other Previous Positions; Intl Astronom Union; Sigma Xi; Am Astronom Soc; AAAS; Res Soc of Am; Com V Union Radio Scientifique Internationale; Am Geophy Union; Intl Astronautical Soc; hon/Author, Num Pubs in Var Profl Jours; Boulder Scist Awd, 1965; Hon Mention, NCAR Publication Prize, 1967; NCAR Technol Awd, 1973; W/W World; W/W Am; W/ W W; W/W Technol.

NEWLIN, JANINE JORDAN oc/ Interior Designer, Kitchen and Bath Design Consultant; m/George C; c/ Jennifer Anne Williams, Pamela Nan Williams, Ian Clifford Williams; Nicholas C C; p/F Bertram and Barbara Jordan, NY; ed/BA, Chatham Col, 1955; Att'd, Chatham Col 1951-53, Columbia Univ 1953-54; Student of Frank Reilly 1949, Henry Koerner 1951-52, Pompeo DeSantis 1953-54, Amy Jones 1964, Anthony Toney 1964-65; pa/Kitchen and Bath Conslt/Interior Designer, 1975-; Interior Designer, 1965-74; Fdr and Pres, Intl Edit Arts, 1957-64; Ptnr, Schwinn-Jordan, 1956-59; Copy Chief's Asst, J Walter Thompson, 1955-56; Child and Jr Fashion and Illustrator's Model, Cover Girl, 1935-58; Intl Soc of Interior Designers; Soc of Cert'd Kitchen Designers; Profl Affil, AIA, Westchester Mid Hudson Chapt; Westchester Assn of Wom Bus Owners; cp/ Repub; r/Soc of Friends; hon/Featured in *Woman's Day Remodeling Magazine* 1983, *Kitchen and Bath Design News* Mag 1984, and Num Other Pubs; W/W Am Wom.

NEWMAN, MICHELE MARIE oc/ Graphic Artist, Drafting Specialist; b/ Dec 15, 1954; h/4249 Freeport Way, Denver, CO 80239; ba/Denver, CO; p/ Eric Carl Newman Jr (dec); Roy and Harriet Ann Wilder Scafe, Denver, CO; ed/BS, Geography, AZ St Univ, 1977; pa/Map Drafter 1977-79, Exploration Drafter 1979, Lead Geologic Drafter 1980, Exploration Drafting Spec Tech 1982-, ARCO; Exploration Drafter, Amerada Hess, 1979; Pres and Treas, Petromerican Cartographics Inc, 1983-; Am Inst Design and Drafting, CO Secy 1980-81; Rocky Mtn Energy Drafters, Dir 1983-84; Am Soc Photogrammetry; Am Cartographics Assn; Assn Am Geographers; AAUW; ABWA; Mem of Indust Adv Coun, Denver Inst of Technol; cp/Girl Scouts USA; Assn of Desk and Derrick Clbs, Spec Projs Rep, Mile High Spkrs Bus Chm; ARCO Civic Action Prog; r/Meth; hon/Poem Pub'd in *Our Twentieth Century's Greatest Poems*, 1982; Deg of Excell, Nat Forensics Leag, 1973; Dean's Hon Roll, 1977; W/W Among Students in Am Univs & Cols; W/W in W.

NEWMAN, RAY GENE oc/Medical Center Administrator; b/Aug 23, 1941; h/1506 Millbrook Drive, Arlington, TX 76012; ba/Dallas, TX; m/Andrea Dawn Thacker; c/Melissa Dawn, Rachel Andrea, Betsy Jill; p/Clifton A (dec) and Ruby J Goodwin Newman, Ada, OK; ed/ MBA, CA St Univ Long Bch, 1971; BS, E Ctl St Univ, 1963; PhD Cand, Adm, Univ of TX Arlington; mil/USN, Lt 1963-68; pa/Chief Operating Ofcr 1982-, Chief Financial Ofcr 1979-82, Dallas Co Hosp Dist; Grp Controller and Financial Dir, Hosp Affiliates Intl Inc, 1975-79; Corporate Controller, UMEDCO Inc, 1974-75; Controller, Hawthorne Commun Hosp, 1972-74; Other Previous Positions; Nat Assn of Public Hosps, Secy, Exec Com 1982-; Chm, Adv Com, Medicare Grp Appeal, Dallas-Ft Worth Hosp Coun; Am Col of Hosp Admrs, Dallas Chapt, Prog Com 1982-; Dallas-Ft Worth Hosp Coun, Audit and Fin Com 1982-; Am Inst of CPAs, 1976-; TX Soc of CPAs, 1976-; Am Col of Hosp Admrs, 1978-; Am Hosp Assn, 1980-; TX Hosp Assn, 1980-; Hosp Financial Mgmt Assn, 1971-; CPA, TX, 1976; Fellow, Hosp Financial Mgmt Assn, 1976; cp/Rotary Intl, Brookhollow Clb, 1982-; r/Fielder Road Bapt Ch, Adult Tchr 1979-, Deacon 1972-; hon/Pubs, "Success Factors in the Implementation of a Comprehensive Hospital Information System" 1981, Others.

NEWSOM, DAVID D oc/Associate Dean of School of Foreign Service; b/ Jan 6, 1918; h/3308 Woodley Road, Northwest, Washington, DC 20008; ba/ Washington, DC; m/Jean C; c/John, Daniel, Nancy, Catherine, David K; p/ Fred Stoddard Newsom (dec); ed/AB, Univ of CA, 1938; MS, Jour, Columbia Univ, 1940; LLD (Hon), Univ of the Pacific, 1978; mil/USN, 1942-46; pa/ Reporter, *San Francisco Chronicle*, 1940-42; Publisher, *Walnut Creek Courier-Journal*, 1946-47; US Fgn Ser w Postings in

Karachi, Oslo, Baghdad, London; Ambassador to Libya, 1965-69; Asst Secy of St for African Affairs, 1969-73; Ambassador to Indonesia 1974-77, to Philippines 1977-78; Undersecy of St for Polit Affairs, 1978-81; Assoc Dean, Sch of Fgn Ser, Georgetown Univ; Coun on Fgn Relats; Adv Com, Coun on Rel and Intl Affairs; Asian Agenda Com, Asia Soc; r/Prot; Rockefeller Public Ser Awd, 1973; Dept of St Dist'd Hon Awd, 1980; W/W Am.

NEWTON, EILEEN ELIZABETH oc/ Artist and Author; b/Sep 14, 1951; h/ PO Box 306, Belmont, MA 02178; ba/ Same; m/Chas D; c/ElanDesiree, Amber Elizabeth; p/Muriel Bernier Morey, Belmont, MA; ed/Colby-Sawyer Col; Boston Univ, 1969-70; Cert'd Archaeological Illustrator, 1983; pa/Artist and Quiltmaker, 1965-; Edit Conslt, MIT, 1982-; Bd of Dirs, KIXE-TV, 1979-80; Assoc Dir, The Show Inc, 1982; cp/ Mem, Num Artistic, Cultural, Historical and Genealogical Socs; Rec Commr, City of Willows, CA, 1979-80; Mensa, 1976-; hon/Pubs, "StainedGlass is Easy" 1977, "Fresh Designs" 1983, "Sea Breezes" 1983; W/W E.

NEZU, ARTHUR MAGUTH oc/Clinical Administrator, Professor; b/Nov 24, 1952; h/452 Churchill Road, Teaneck, NJ 07666; ba/Hackensack, NJ; m/Christine Maguth; c/Frank, Alice, Linda; p/ Tetsuo and Mary Nezu, Jamaica, NY; ed/BA in Psych 1974, MA in Clin Psych 1976, PhD in Clin Psych 1979, St Univ of NY Stony Brook; pa/Prin Investigator, Social Prob Solving Therapy for Depression Grant Proj 1983-, Clin Asst Prof, Dept of Psych 1982-, Maj Advr, Inst for Ldrship Studies 1980-, Prin Investigator of Social Prob Solving and Depression Grant Proj 1980-81, Assoc Dir of Natural Setting Therapeutic Mgmt Grant Proj 1980-, Asst Dir/Coor of Tng, Div of Psychol Sers 1978-, Fairleigh Dickinson Univ; Clin Asst Prof, Dept of Commun Dentistry, Fairleigh Dickinson Univ Sch of Dentistry, 1981-; Adj Fac, Dept of Psych, Ramapo Col of NJ, 1980; Other Previous Positions; Am Psychol Assn; Phi Beta Kappa Assn of NY; En Psychol Assn; Assn for the Advmt of Behavior Therapy; Soc of Behavioral Med; Am Assn of Dental Schs; hon/Pubs, "Cost Containment in Dentistry and Its Impact on the Distribution of Services" 1983, "Social Problem Solving in Adults" 1982, "Effects of Problem Definition and Formulation on Decision Making in the Social Problem Solving Process" 1981, Others; NY St Regents S'ships, 1970-74; Undergrad Psych Awd, 1974; Phi Beta Kappa, 1974; Res/ Tchg F'ships, 1974-77; Fairleigh Dickinson Univ Bd of Trustee's Hon, 1982; W/W E.

NICHOLLS, GORDON H oc/Substance Abuse Counselor; b/Sep 2, 1935; h/5726 Northwest 86th Terrace, Tamarac, FL 33321; ed/BS in Ed and Psych, 1961; MS in Cnslg Psych 1965, UT St Univ; Vis'g Student in Cnslg Psych, Cornell Univ, 1963-64; Doct Study, Univ of Miami, 1971; Doct Dissertation in Progress, FL Atl Univ; mil/AUS, Pers Clk 1956-58; pa/Substance Abuse Cnslr, Coral Ridge Psychi Hosp, 1983-; Probation Aide, Dept of Corrections, 1978-83; Unit Treatment and Rehab Spec, S FL St Hosp, 1977-78;

Coor of Vets' Affairs, Ft Lauderdale Col, 1976; Misc Jobs, 1971-76; Cnslr, Mira Loma Rehab Ctr, 1969-70; Cnslr, No MI Univ, 1967-69; Cnslr, Newark Col of Engrg, 1966-67; Cnslr, RI Col, and Pt-time Psychi Aide in Mtl Hosp, 1964-66; Grad Asst, Cornell Univ, 1963-64; Grad Asst in Ednl Psych, UT St Univ, 1962-63; Phi Delta Kappa; Psi Chi; APGA; Am Psychol Assn; hon/ Pubs, "Counseling and/or Discipline" 1968, *Get Better Grades-A College Study Guide Designed for Group Discussions* 1968, *The Programed Text as an Aid to Teaching Spelling in Junior High School* 1965; W/W S and SW.

NICHOLSON, ROSEMARY THOMAS oc/District Manager; b/Feb 10, 1941; h/1131 Southeast 34th Street, Cape Coral, FL 33904; ba/Fort Myers, FL; c/Keith Wade, Sheila Kay, Glenn; p/Roosevelt Ted and Mary Adeline Burt Thomas (dec); ed/Grad w Hons, Meridian HS, 1958; Att'd, GA St Univ 1976-77, Edison Commun Col 1981; pa/ Dist Mgr 1980-, Asst Dist Mgr 1979-80, Supvr of Reg Commr's Inquiries Staff 1978-79, Asst Dist Mgr 1975-78, Social Security; Staff Asst, Reg Ofc Sys, 1974; Opers Supvr 1973, Claims Rep 1969-72, 1972-73, Ser Rep 1966-69, Clearance Ser Clk 1965, Claims Devel Clk 1965, Social Security; ABWA, VP of Cape Coral Caloosa Chapt 1981-82, Pres of FL Gold Chapt 1979, Pres of Southside Charter Chapt 1977, Other Past Offices Held; VP, SW Chapt of FL Assn of Hlth and Social Sers, 1981-83; Nat Assn of Female Execs; Am Soc of Profl and Exec Wom; Atlanta Reg Mgmt Assn; cp/Bd of Dirs, Commun Coordinating Coun of Lee Co, 1982-83; Corresponding Secy, Zonta Intl, Ft Myers Clb Netwk, Ft Myers Chapt; r/Fin Com, First Bapt Ch, 1982-85; hon/Instr in Nuts and Bolts of Pers Mgmt for New Supvrs, 1975-82; Southside Charter Chapt, ABWA, Wom of the Yr, 1978; Var HHS Awds (Superior Perf, High Quality Increase); W/W Am Wom.

NICHOLSON, THEODORE ROOSEVELT oc/Communications Consultant, Public Speaker; b/Apr 14, 1947; h/6511 Ross Street, Philadelphia, PA 19119; ba/Schenectady, NY; c/Tasheea Thedora, Thema Ariel, Dennis Sinclair; ed/MBA, Mgmt/Mktg, La Salle Col, 1984; Mktg Courses, Wharton Sch, 1977; Legal Tng, Dickinson Sch of Law, 1969-70; Legal Tng, Univ of Cinc Law Sch, 1969; BA, Polit Sci, Ec, Lincoln Univ, 1969; mil/Ofcr w Tng in Mil Intell, Civil Affairs and Logistics, USAR; pa/ Nat Acct Exec, Gen Elec Corp, 1982-; Bus Conslt, Proj Design Ofcr and In-and-Out Trader, Self-Employed, 1978-82; Pres and Chief Operating Ofcr, Bus Sers Co Inc, 1975-78; VP of Sales, Fifth Dimensions Inc, 1974-75; Bus Opers Mgr, Bell of PA, 1973-74; Other Previous Positions; Am Mgmt Assn; Soc for the Advmt of Mgmt; Nat Alliance of Bus-men; IPA; Intl Investmt Conf; US Resv Ofcrs Assn; cp/JCs; Dist Exec/Fund Raiser, BSA; Dir, Houston Drug Preven Prog; Block Capt, Ross Street Neighbors; Fund Raiser, U Way; hon/Dist'd Ser Awd and Century Awd, BSA; Humanitarian Ser Awd, AUS; Featured in *Black Enterprise Magazine*, 1976; W/W E; Men of Achmt; W/W Indust and Fin; Dir of Dist'd Ams; Biogl Roll of Hon; Personalities of Am; Men and Wom of Distn.

NICKEL, HERMAN W oc/United States Ambassador to South Africa; b/Oct 23, 1928; h/4448 Hawthorne Street, Northwest, Washington, DC 20016; ba/Washington, DC; m/Phyllis Fritchey; c/Clayton Alexander; p/Walter and Wilhelmine Nickel (dec); ed/Abitur, Arndt-Gymnasium, Berlin, 1946; BA, Union Col, 1951; JD, Syracuse Univ Col of Law, 1956; pa/US High Comm, 1951-53; Hd, Res Unit, Fgn Policy Assn, 1956-58; Journalist w Time Inc, 1958-81; Correspondent in Wash, Johannesburg and Bonn, Bur Chief in Bonn, Tokyo and London, 1977-81; Bd of Editors, Fortune, 1982; US Ambassador to S Africa; Assoc, The Lehrman Inst, 1981-; r/Luth; hon/Regular Contbr to Time, Life, Fortune, for 23 Yrs; W/W; Intl W/W.

NICOLAE, GHEORGHE oc/Research Manager; b/Oct 2, 1943; h/3709 West Leland, Chicago, IL 60625; ba/Chicago, IL; m/Mariana L; c/Bogdan O, Iulia C; p/Gheorghe Nicolae, Chicago, IL; ed/PhD in Chem, 1974; MS in Chem, 1966; pa/Prof Assoc, Univ of Bucharest, Romania, 1967-79; Res Chem, Wallace A Erickson & Co, 1980-81; Res Mgr, Confi-Dental Prods Co, 1981-; Assn Finishing Processes of Soc Mfg Engrs, 1982-83; Intl Assn Dental Res, 1983; Am Assn Dental Res, 1983; Am Chem Soc, 1983-84; r/Orthodox; hon/Author of Pubs Concerning Heterocycling Compounds, Monomers, Adhesives, Photocuring Sys, Photopolymerization, Organometallic Compounds, Dyes for Lasers, Sensitizers, Analytical Chemistry, Depolluting Agent for Marine Oil.

NIDOSITKO, JAMES MICHAEL oc/Guidance Counselor; b/Sep 9, 1941; h/54 Lakeview Avenue, Falmouth, MA 02540; ba/Falmouth, MA; m/Joanne Dzioba; c/Rebecca Stella, James Jr; p/John (dec) and Evelyn Costa Nidositko, Teaticket, MA; ed/BS in Ed 1964, MS in Ed 1967, Bridgewater St Col; Postgrad Wk, Worcester St Col 1975, MA Maritime Acad 1973-76; pa/Tchr, The Falmouth Intermediate Sch, 1964-71; Guid Cnslr, Title III, Adult Basic Ed Prog, Falmouth, 1968-71; Guid Cnslr, Falmouth Intermediate Sch 1971-73, Lawrence Sch 1973-; The Cape and Isls Guid Assn, VP; MA Sch Cnslrs Assn, Trustee; NEA; APGA; MA Tchrs Assn; Falmouth Edrs Assn; cp/Histn, The Falmouth Militia, 1975-; Co of Mil Histns; Mil Figures Collectors of Am; r/Rom Cath; Eucharistic Min, St Patrick's Ch, 1979-; hon/Apprec Awd, Falmouth Edrs Assn, 1979; TV Appearance for MA Sch Cnslrs Wk, 1977; W/W E.

NIEKAMP, DOROTHY RINEHART oc/Librarian; b/Aug 4, 1932; h/5435 East Young Road, Bloomington, IN 47401; ba/Bloomington, IN; m/Walter E; p/George Stewart (dec) and Alma Westholt Rinehart, Tulsa, OK; ed/BME, Univ of Tulsa, 1954; MLS, IN Univ, 1966; Pvt Pilot, 1967; Comml Pilot, 1973; pa/Tchr, Natrona Co Schs; Assoc Libn, Cataloging Dept, IN Univ Lib, 1966-; Ninety-Nines Inc; Intl Org of Wom Pilots; Am Lib Assn, Resources and Tech Sers Div; Am Aviation Hist Soc; Libn for the Ninety-Nines; r/Unitarian; hon/1st Amelia Earhart Res Scholar, Ninety-Nines Inc, 1978.

NIELSEN, VERNON JAMES oc/Businessman; b/Feb 28, 1949; h/63 Lancaster Cres, St Albert, Alberta, Canada T8N 2N9; ba/Edmonton, Alberta, Canada; m/Wilma J; c/Candice, Gregory, Jennifer; p/Hilda Nielsen, Westbank, British Columbia; ed/Bach of Commerce, 1971; pa/Sales, Occidental Life Ins Co, 1971-72; Dist Mgr, Gen Food Ltd, 1972-75; Sales Mgr, Pres, Barry Brokerage Ltd, 1975-78; Chm of Bd, Nelcor Holdings Ltd, 1979-; Canadian Food Brokers Assn, Exec Coun 1981; Nat Food Brokers Assn, Reg Rep 1982; r/St Stevens U Ch, Elder and Bd of Dirs 1975; hon/W/W Fin and Indust.

NIEMI, ALBERT W Jr oc/Director of Research and Acting Dean of College of Business; b/Aug 30, 1942; h/190 Rolling Wood Drive, Athens, GA 30605; ba/Athens, GA; m/Maria Di Sano; c/Albert William III, Edward Charles; p/Albert W Niemi, Easton, MA; ed/AB, Stonehill Col, 1964; MA 1965, PhD 1969, Univ of CT; pa/Asst Prof of Ec 1968-71, Assoc Prof of Ec 1971-75, Assoc Dean of Col of Bus Adm 1976-78, Chm of Dept of Ec 1981-82, Prof of Ec and Dir of Res 1975-, Acting Dean of Col of Bus Adm 1982-, Univ of GA; Am Ec Assn; Ec Hist Assn; So Ec Assn; Wn Ec Assn; So Reg Sci Assn; Assn of Univ Bus and Ec Res, Secy-Treas; SE Ec Anal Conf; Bus Hist Conf; r/Cath; hon/Pubs, Understanding Economics 1978, US Economic History 1975, 1980, Others; Beta Gamma Sigma; Phi Kappa Phi; Delta Epsilon Sigma; W/W S and SE; Intl W/W Ed; Men of Achmt; W/W Am; W/W World.

NIIZUMA, MINORU oc/Sculptor, Adjunct Professor; b/Sep 29, 1930; h/463 West Street, New York, NY 10014; ba/New York, NY; m/Yuko; c/Ta Andre, Ko Christopher; p/Takeshi and Fumiko Niizuma, Nagoya-Shi, Aichi-Ken, Japan; ed/BFA, Nat Tokyo Univ of Arts, 1955; pa/Tchr, Brooklyn Mus of Art Sch, 1964-70; Adj Prof, Columbia Univ, 1972-; Sculptors Guild; Stone Sculpture Soc of NY, Fdr; NY Artists Equity Assn; One-Man Shows: Mekler Gallery 1983, Rosenberg Fine Arts Gallery 1982, Contemp Sculpture Ctr 1979, Seibu Mus of Art 1976, Others; Grp Shows: Am Acad and Inst of Arts and Lttrs, Pgh Intl Carnegie Inst, Whitney Mus of Am Art, Nat Mus of Mod Art, Mus of Mod Art; Perm Collections: Mus of Mod Art, Nat Mus of Mod Art, Albright Knox Art Gallery, Rockefeller Univ, Hirshhorn Mus and Sculpture Garden, Guggenheim Mus; hon/W/W Am; W/W E; Men and Wom of Distn.

NIKOLAI, ROBERT JOSEPH oc/Associate Dean of the Graduate School, Professor of Biomechanics in Orthodontics; b/Apr 6, 1937; h/7134 Stanford Avenue, University City, MO 63130; ba/St Louis, MO; m/Susan E Shannon; c/Catherine, Teresa, Margaret, David, Philip; p/Joseph L and Martha H Nikolai, Sun City, AZ; ed/Pre-Engrg, IL Benedictine Col, 1955-57; BS in Mech Engrg 1959, MS 1961, PhD 1964, Theoretical and Applied Mechs, Univ of IL Urbana-Champaign; pa/Assoc Dean of the Grad Sch 1972-, Prof of Biomechs in Orthodontics 1976-, St Louis Univ; Affil Prof of Civil Engrg, Wash Univ, 1980-; Conslt to Orthoband Co Inc, 1975-; Reg'd Profl Engr, MO; Am Acad of Mechs; Sigma Xi; Intl and Am Assns of Dental Res; Orthodontic Ed and Res Foun; r/Rom Cath; r/Pubs, Bioengineering Analysis of Orthodontic Mechanics 1984, and Num Res Articles; Edit Conslt, Journal of Biomechanics, 1982-; Manuscript Reviewer for American Journal of Orthodontics, 1981-; NIDR Res Grant, 1984; Sabbatical Leave Grant, Univ of CT Hlth Ctr, 1981; Am Men and Wom of Sci.

NILAVER, GAJANAN oc/Doctor of Medicine; b/Aug 30, 1946; h/790 Holly Street, New Milford, NJ 07646; ba/New York, NY; p/Shanker and Nalini S Nilaver; ed/MB and BS, Univ of Madras, India, 1968; Resident in Neurol, 1972-75; NIH Nat Res Ser Postdoct Fellow, Neuroendocrinology, Columbia Univ, 1975-79; Res Assoc and Asst Neurologist 1979-81, Asst Prof of Neurol and Asst Att'g Neurologist 1982-, Columbia Univ; AMA; Soc for Neurosci; Am Acad of Neurol; AAAS; NY Soc of Electronmicroscopists; NY Acad of Scis; r/Hindu; hon/Pubs, "The Development of Motilin-Like Immunoreactivity in the Rat Cerebellum and Pituitary as Determined by Radioimmunoassay" 1984, "Colonization of the Developing Murine Nervous System and Subsequent Phenotypic Expression by the Precursors of Peptidergic Neurons" 1984, "VIP Containing Neurons" 1984, "Morphology and Synaptology of VIP-Immunoreactive Neurons in the Central Nucleus of the Rat Amygdala" 1984, Num Others; Recip, NIH Nat Indiv Res Awd, 1975-79; W/W Frontier Sci and Technol.

NILES, FREDERICK ADOLPH oc/Executive; b/Sep 12, 1918; h/1125 Long Valley Road, Glenview, IL 60025; ba/Chicago, IL; m/Marye Evelyn Yates; c/Stephanie, Deborah, Victoria, Regina, Frederick; p/Frederick William and Louise Niles (dec); ed/BA, Univ of WI, 1941; mil/Served to Capt, AUS, WWII; pa/Orgr, Film Div, Kling Enterprises, 1948-55; Fdr 1955, Pres, Fred A Niles Communs Ctrs Inc, Visuals, Communs, Mktg; Bd of Dirs, World Bus Coun, 1975-, Pres 1980-81; Dir, Means Corp; Chgo Pres's Org, Pres 1976; Nat Acad TV and Radio Arts and Scis; AFTRA; Screen Actors Guild; Intl Film Prodrs Assn; Soc Motion Picture and TV Engrs; Chief Execs Forum; Screen Dirs Guild; Actors Equity; Bd of Dirs, Chgo Film Fest; cp/Bd of Dirs, Jr Achmt and Salvation Army; Friars; Variety; r/Prot; hon/Recip, Emmy Awd, 1959; Spec Awd, Jr Achmt, 1977; Spec Awd, US Indust Film Coun, 1980; Gold Hugo Awd, Chgo Intl Film Fest, 1980; Man of the Yr, City of Hope, 1974; W/W Am.

NIMBERG, GERALD oc/Financial Consultant; b/Jun 29, 1943; h/408 Queen Anne Road, Cherry Hill, NJ 08003; ba/Maelton, NJ; m/Ann Ruth; c/Jeffrey Martin, Stephanie Sharon; p/Mr and Mrs Theodore Nimberg, Boston, MA; ed/BS in Math, Worcester Polytechnic Inst, 1966; MBA in Fin, Wharton Sch of Fin, 1970; CFP Cert in Financial Planning (Pending), Col of Financial Planning; pa/Current Sr Ptnr, Investmt Cnslg Firm of Smith, Nimberg & Hirsh; Current Dir of Planning for Decision Data Computer Corp; Financial Conslt, Self-Employed, 1980-82; Financial Planning Inst; Nat Microfilm Assn, 1970-74; cp/Cherry Hill Twp Repub Com; r/Jewish; hon/Pub'd Articles in The Small Business Association Journal, 1968; MA St

S'ship; Dean's List, Worcester Polytechnic Inst, Wharton Sch; W/WE; Commun Ldrs of the World.

NINE-CURT, CARMEN JUDITH oc/Professor of English as a Second Language; b/Oct 29, 1922; h/616 Estuario Street, Caparra Heights, PR 00920; ba/Rio Piedras, PR; p/Mr José Nine; Mrs Ana R Curt de Nine; ed/BA, St Joseph's Col, 1943; MA 1944, EdD 1966, Columbia Univ; pa/Instr, Assoc Prof, Prof, ESL, Univ of PR, 1946-; Dir, Dept of Basic Eng, Fac of Gen Studies 1968-74, Coor of TESOL, Sch of Ed 1975-, Univ of PR; Bd of Trustees, Inter-Am Univ, 1975-; Dir, Eng Dept, Fac Gen Studies, Univ of Puerto Rico, 1968-75; Only Wom Mem, Bd of Trustees, Inter-Am Univ, 1975-; Coor, TESOL, Grad Dept, Sch of Ed, Univ of Puerto Rico, 1981-; cp/Girl Scouts of PR, San Juan, 1946-62; Pres, SJ Ldrs; r/Cath; hon/Pubs, "Understanding Verbal and Non-Verbal Communication as They Apply to Learning/Teaching Problems in the Language Arts" 1981, "Teacher-Student Interaction in the Hispanic/Anglo Classroom" 1981, "The Education of the Puerto Rican Child and the Hemispheres of the Brain" 1980, Others; Dr Honoris Causa in Human Lttrs, LaSalle Col, 1983; Dist'd Rschr Awd in Communication, Spch and Com, 1983.

NISBETT, EDWARD GEORGE oc/Staff Metallurgist; b/Feb 24, 1929; h/1262 Conewango Avenue, Warren, PA 16365; ba/Irvine, PA; m/Barbara; c/Simon, Andrew; p/James and Edith Nisbett (dec); ed/BSc w Hons 1952, ARTC 1952, Metallurgy, Glasgow Univ; Reg'd Profl Engr, PA, 1969; mil/RAF; pa/Asst Wks Metallurgist, Bristol Aero Engines, 1952-53; Wks Metallurgist, Eng Elect Co, 1953-58; Chief Metallurgist, Nat Vulcan Engrg Ins Co, 1958-67; Staff Metallurgist, Nat Forge Co, 1967-; ASM, Past Chapt Chm; Metals Soc; ASME, Chm of S Grp on Castings, Forgings and Bolting of SC 11; ASTM, Chm of Subcom on Forgings of Com on Steel; r/Rom Cath; hon/Author, Num Metall Papers for Tech Jours; Contbr, ASM; Fellow, Instn of Metallurgists, 1967; Fellow, Am Soc for Metals, 1979.

NISHIUWATOKO, TETSU oc/Chief Representative; b/Sep 20, 1941; h/3 Horizon Road, Fort Lee, NJ 07024; ba/New York, NY; m/Kazuko; c/Tsutomu, Mitsuru; p/Jukichi and Hanae Nishiuwatoko; ed/BA, Takushoku Univ, 1964; Intl Inst for Studies and Tng, Trade Univ, 1971-72; pa/Staff of Intl Div, Kajima Corp, 1964-68; Kajima Corp Rep in Okinawa, 1971-73; Chief Rep, Kajima Corp, NY Rep Ofc, 1973-; Mem of the Bd, Kajima Devel Corp; Real Est Bd of NY Inc; Am Mgmt Assn; Japan Ec Inst; cp/Pres, PTA; Japanese Sch of NY, 1979-80; Japanese C of C of NY Inc; Marco Polo Clb; Nippon Clb Inc; Rotary Clb of NY; r/Buddhist; hon/W/W: in World, in Fin & Indust.

NIXON, DORIS MILLER oc/Director of Educational Services; b/May 27, 1925; h/4001 Grove Avenue, Richmond, VA 23221; ba/Richmond, VA; m/Edward Winslow (dec); c/Ned Winslow, Maureen Miller; p/Ellis Norman and Bessie Howell Miller (dec); ed/Spec Courses, Col of the Albemarle, 1969; Grad, Perquimans HS, 1942; Reg'd Bridal Conslt, Nat Bridal Ser, 1965; pa/

Bridal Conslt and Buyer 1955-79, Treas 1973-79, Louis Selig Jewelers; Dir of Ednl Sers for the Nat Bridal Ser, 1976-; VP, Jewelry Gift Div, Nat Bridal Sers, 1979-; cp/Active in Parent Tchrs Org as Pres; Pres, Perquimans Co Hist Restoration Soc, 1977; Cabin Ldr, Am Yth Foun, 1965-70; Active as 4-H Clb Ldr and Mem, NC 4-H Devel Foun; r/Pres; hon/Co-Author, "Your Wedding and How to Enjoy It," "Make Room for the Groom"; Feature Writer on "Table Tops and Business" in *Modern Jeweler Magazine*, 1977-82; Tabletop Editor for *Gifts and Decorative Accessories* Mag, 1977-; Feature Writer Mthly on "Bridal Business" in *Southern Jeweler Magazine*, 1983-; W/W Jewelry Indust.

NOBLE, CLYDE EVERETT oc/Experimental Psychologist, Professor; b/Jun 7, 1922; h/766 Riverhill Drive, Athens, GA 30606; ba/Athens, GA; m/Janet Lauderdale; c/Susan, David William, Robert Edward, Steven Clarke; p/Clyde E Noble Sr (dec); Grace Onstott Noble, Brookhaven, MS; ed/BA, MS, Tulane Univ; PhD, Univ of IA; mil/USAF, WWII, Korean War; Ret'd Col, USAFR; pa/Instr, Tulane Univ, 1949; Asst Prof, LA St Univ, 1953-57; Assoc Prof to Prof, Univ of MT, 1957-64; Prof, Univ of GA, 1964-; Vis'g Prof, Univ of WI 1969, St Univ of NY 1971, Harvard Univ 1973; Pres, So Soc Phil and Psych, 1975-76; Edit Bd, *Journal of Motor Behavior, Mankind Quarterly, Perceptual and Motor Skills*; Phi Beta Kappa; Sigma Xi; Fellow, Psychonomic Soc; cp/Fdr and Bd Chm, Classic City Band; Fdr and Ldr, The Confederate Brass; cp/SAR; Mil Order of World Wars; r/Presb; hon/Hartman Medal; McDonald Awds; Mensa; Fellow, AAAS; Jefferson Davis Medal; Sinfonia Hon Life Mem; Named by Inst Sci Info as Author of *Citation Classic*; Author or Co-Author of 4 Books and 130 Articles; Am Men and Wom of Sci; Ldrs in Am Sci; W/W; Hereditary Register of the USA.

NOBLE, JAMES VAN PETTEN oc/Lawyer; Assistant Attorney General; b/Apr 4, 1922; h/615 East Barcelona Road, Santa Fe, NM 87501; ba/Santa Fe, NM; m/Sara Jane Crail; c/James Van Petten Jr, Sara Ann, Charles Fulton; p/Merrill Emmett and Martha Van Petten Noble (dec); sp/Catherine Crail, La Crosse, WI; ed/Att'd Univ NM 1940-43; LLB 1949, JD 1968, Univ CO; mil/USAAF 1943-45, 2/Lt; AUS 1942-43; pa/Spec Asst Atty Gen, St Hwy Dept, NM, 1970-; Chief Counsel & Dir Merc Investmt Corp, 1970-; St of NM: Asst Atty Gen 1968-70, 1963-68; Atty, Las Vegas 1958-60; Other Former Positions; Dir, Las Vegas Portland Cement Co; Mem Com Rules for Crim Procedures & Instrns NM Supr Ct; NM Bar Coms Real Property, Land Titles; Am, NM, San Miguel Co Bar Assns; cp/Exec Com, Bd Dirs NM Soc Crippled Chd; Mayor's Santa Fe Action Airport Com; Bd Dirs Las Vegas Commun TV Inc, Las Vegas Devel Corp; Jr C of C; hon/Author (w Ben S Galland), "Re-statement of the Laws of Corps"; Biogl Listings.

NOHE, B L'ESSOR oc/Executive; b/Dec 1, 1943; h/200 Springs Road, Bedford, MA 01730; ba/Concord, MA; m/Richard E; c/Louis William; p/Thomas Wayman Hill; Roberta Steffen Moore; ed/BA, De Paul Univ, 1976; MPH, Mgmt and Adm, Sch of Public Hlth, Univ of

IL; pa/Pres, Qual Corp Assocs Inc, 1979-; Quality Assurance Advr 1980-, Adm Ofcr to the Assoc Chief of Staff for Res and Devel 1980-, Prog Analyst 1980, W Roxbury VA Med Ctr; Instr in Quality Assurance, Sch of Public Hlth, Univ of IL at the Med Ctr, 1979; Other Previous Positions; Am Acad of Med Admrs; Indep Conslts of Am; Am Sociological Assn; Inter-Am Soc; APHA; IL Public Hlth Assn; Am Acad of Hlth Admrs; AAAS; Acad of Polit Sci; Pi Gamma Mu; Nat Hist Soc; Hastings Ctr; Smithsonian Inst; Milbank Meml Fund; De Paul Univ Alumni Assn, 1977-; Univ of IL at the Med Ctr, Sch of Public Hlth Alumni Assn, 1978-; hon/Pi Gamma Mu, Nat Social Sci Hon Soc, 1976; Outstg Perf Awd, VA, 1972; Nom, Wom of the Yr, VA, 1979; Personalities of E; 2,000 Notable Ams; Commun Ldrs of Am; Dir of Dist'd Ams; Men of Achmt; Intl Book of Hon; Intl Register of Profiles; Biogl Roll of Hon; Intl W/W Intells; Registry of Am Achmt; World W/W Wom; 5,000 Personalities of World.

NOLAN, ROBERT WILLIAM SR oc/Executive; b/Jul 13, 1943; h/14584 Whittington Court, Chesterfield, MD 63017; ba/St Louis, MO; m/Lou Ann; c/Christine Ann, Robert N Jr, Patrick Alvin, Angela L; p/Vincent J Nolan (dec); ed/BS in Commerce, St Louis Univ, 1964; CPA, 1966; pa/Pres, SCS/Compute Inc, 1981-; Chm of Bd, Indep Tax Corp, 1980-; Pres, Systematic Computer Sys Inc, 1972-79; VP, Programmed Tax Sys Inc, 1971-72; Am Inst of CPAs and MO Soc of CPAs, 1967-; Bd Mem, Linda Vista Montessori Sch, 1981-82; cp/Bd Mem, W Co Soccer Leag, 1980-; Soccer Chm, Linda Vista Sch, 1980-83; r/Cath; hon/W/W Fin; W/W MW.

NOLDEN, EUGENE NAKONECHNY oc/Free-Lance Architectural Designer; b/Jun 22, 1914; h/PO Box 966, Hunter, NY 12442; ba/Hunter, NY; m/Stanislava; c/Victor; p/Ilarion Nakonechny (dec); Lubow Slizewsky (dec); ed/Grad, Art Sch in Kiev, Ukraine, 1930; Arch Fac Grad, Ukrainian St Art Inst in Kiev, 1939; St Exam Dipl, Arch and Artist; pa/Dipl Arch, 1940-49; Chief Arch Designer, Ray R Gauger & Co, 1950-58; Arch Designer, Frederic P Wiedersum & Co, 1958-59; Arch Designer, Parsons, Brinckerhof, Quade & Douglas, Engrs, 1959-63; Arch Designer, Shreve, Lamb & Harmon Profl Corp, 1963-74; Assoc, Ray R Gauger Co, Archs and Engrs, 1950-58; Elected Corresponding Mem, Ukrainian Acad of Arts and Scis, 1962; Smithsonian Nat Assocs; r/Greek Orthodox; hon/Author of Many Essays Concerning Contemp Art, Arch; 1st Prize Awd, Arch Competition for Design of Ukrainian Cath Ch in Munich, Germany, 1948; Other Hons; Men of Achmt.

NONG oc/Artist; b/Oct 10, 1930; h/999 Green Street, San Francisco, CA 94133; ba/San Francisco, CA; ed/LLB; mil/AUS; USAF; pa/One-Man Exhbns: Korean Cultural Ser 1983, 1982, Choon Chu Gallery 1982, Hartman Rare Art 1981, Tongin Art Gallery 1978, Nat Mus of Mod Art 1975, SF Zool Garden 1975, Others; Grp Exhbns: Korean Cultural Ser 1982, Galeria de Arte Misrachi 1979, Galerie Hexagramme 1975, SF Mus of Art 1972, Oakland Art Mus 1971, Others; Perm Collections:

Santa Barbara Mus of Art, E B Crocker Art Gallery, GA Mus of Art, Govt of the Repub of China Nat Mus of Hist, Others; Commr, Asian Art Comm, City and Co of SF; cp/Chm, SF-Seoul Sister City Com; hon/Pub, *Nong Questions*, 1983; Lttrs of Apprec, Republic of Korea; Cert of Dist'd Achmt, St of CA; Proclamation, City and Co of SF; Intl W/W in Art and Antiques; Men of Achmt; DIB; Intl W/W Intells; Personalities of W and MW; Num Other Biogl Listings.

NOODLEMAN, JEFFREY SCOTT oc/Nuclear Physician, Radiologist; b/ May 24, 1953; h/1323 South Carmelina Avenue, #103, Los Angeles, CA 90025; ba/Los Angeles, CA; p/Mr and Mrs Ben Noodleman, Arcadia, CA; ed/BA in Chem 1975, BS in Biol Scis 1975, MA in Chem 1976, Univ of CA Irvine; MD, Loyola Stritch Sch of Med, 1979; pa/ Pathol Resident, Univ of CA Irvine, 1979-80; Med Resident, LA Co, Univ of So CA Med Ctr, 1980-81; Radiol/ Nuclear Med Resident, VA W LA, 1981-; Radiological Soc of N Am; Am Col of Radiol; hon/Pub, "Strongyloides Appendicitis," 1981; Phi Beta Kappa, 1975; BA, summa cum laude, 1975; BS, summa cum laude, 1975; Hons Extraordinary in Chem, 1973; Nat Merit Letter of Commend, 1970; W/W CA.

NORBACK, CRAIG THOMAS oc/ Author, Book Producer; b/Nov 14, 1943; h/1013 Hughes Drive, Hamilton Square, NJ 08690; ba/Princeton, NJ; m/ Dr Judith; p/Howard George Norback; Maybelle Veronica Montaigne Riccaby Cossé; ed/BS, Wash Univ, 1967; pa/ Author, 1972-75; Pres, Book Producing Firm of Norback & Co Inc, 1976-; hon/ Pubs, *500 Questions New Parents Ask* 1982, *ABC Complete Book of Sports Facts* 1981, *ABC Monday Night Football 1980-81* 1980, *The Allergy Encyclopedia* 1981, *America Wants to Know* 1983, *The American Express Business Almanac* 1984, Num Others; Appeared on *Merv Griffin Show*, 1983; W/W in E.

NORDBY, EUGENE JORGEN oc/ Orthopaedic Surgeon; b/Apr 30, 1918; h/6234 South Highlands, Madison, WI 53705; ba/Madison, WI; m/Olive Marie Jensen; c/John Jorgen; p/Herman Preus Nordby (dec); ed/AB, Luther Col, 1939; MD, Univ of WI Med Sch, 1943; mil/ AUS 1944-46, Capt, Med Corps; pa/ Orthopaedic Surg, Madison Gen Hosp, 1947-; Pres, Bone and Jt Surg Assn, 1968-; Madison Gen Chief of Staff, 1957-63, Bd of Dirs 1957-76; WI Phys Ser Div, 1958-, Chm 1978-; Dane Co Med Soc, Pres 1957-58; St Med Soc, WI, Councilor 1961-76, Chm 1968-76, Treas 1976-; Assn Bone and Jt Surgs, Treas 1968-72, Pres 1973-74; Am Acad Orthopaedic Surg, Chm of Bd of Councilors 1973-74, Bd of Dirs 1972-74; Clin Orthopaedic Soc; Intl Soc for Study of Lumbar Spine; Phi Chi Med Frat, 1940-; cp/Pres of Bd, Norwegian Am Mus, 1968-; r/Luth; Pres, Bethel Ch Coun, 1957-58; hon/Assoc Editor, Clin Orthopaedic and Related Res; Sigma Sigma Hon Med Frat, 1940; Eagle Scout, 1934; Dist'd Ser Awd, Luther Col, 1964; Coun Awd, St Med Soc of WI, 1976; Knight 1st Class, Royal Norwegian Order of St Olav, 1974; W/W Fin and Indust; W/ W MW; W/W World; Personalities of W and MW.

NORMAN, WALLACE oc/Executive; b/Feb 5, 1926; h/Box 208, Houston, MS

38851; ba/Houston, MS; m/Maurene Collums; c/Wallace Jr, Karen Jean, Emily June, Lauren Beth, John Crocker; p/ Leland Fleming (dec) and Alma Lucile Brown Norman, Houston, MS; ed/ Student, E Ctl Jr Col 1942, Univ of MS 1946, Millsaps Col 1946; BS, OK City Univ, 1948; mil/Served w USNR, WWII; pa/Owner, Mgr, Wallace Norman Ins Agy, 1949-; Norman Oil Co, 1956-; Pres, Nat Leasing Co, 1969-; Pres, US Plastics, 1969-; Pres, Calhoun Nat Co, 1974-; Pres, Norman Trucking Co, 1975-; Pres, Plastics of Am, 1982-; Exch Clb; MS Ec Coun; MS Assn of Ins Agts, 1949-; MS Mfg Assn; Am Waterworks Assn; cp/Chm, Running Bear Dist, BSA, 1971-73; DAV; VFW; Am Legion; Gideons Intl; r/Meth; hon/W/W S and SW; 2,000 Notable Ams; Dir of Dist'd Ams.

NORFLEET, MORRIS L oc/University President; b/Dec 15, 1930; h/328 University Boulevard, Morehead, KY 40351; ba/Morehead, KY; m/Loistene; c/Douglas; p/Mr and Mrs Hewey Norfleet, Nancy, KY; ed/PhD in Ed 1962, MS in Ed 1957, Purdue Univ; BS, Univ of KY, 1952; pa/Pres 1977-, Acting Interim Pres 1976, VP for Res and Devel 1968-76, Prof of Ed and Dir of Res and Prog Devel 1965-68, Assoc Prof of Ed and Dir of Student Tchg 1962-65, Morehead St Univ; Instr of Ed, Purdue Univ, 1960-62; Other Previous Positions; Am Assn for Tchr Ed; Am Assn for Higher Ed; Am Coun on Ed; Am Ednl Res Assn; Coun for Advmt and Support of Ed; Nat Col and Univ Res Admrs; Soc for Col and Univ Planning; Phi Kappa Phi; Phi Delta Kappa; cp/ Lions; Kiwanis; Rowan Co Planning Com; Optimist Clb; Others Civic Mbrships; hon/Phi Delta Kappa, Outstg Contbns to Ed, 1976; KY Dept for Human Resources, Contbns to Yth Residential Prog, 1974; Morehead Optimist Clb, Contbns to Yth, 1975; Outstg Edrs of Am; Nat Dir of Admrs in Higher Ed; Phi Delta Kappa Nat Dir of Rschrs; Outstg Personalities of S.

NORRIS, PATRICIA KILMER oc/ Public Relations Executive; b/Feb 7, 1933; h/4121 Kennicott Lane, Glenview, IL 60025; ba/Same; m/James Alexander; c/Melissa Polk, Benjamin White II; p/Hugh (dec) and Patricia Polk Kilmer, New Rochelle, NY; ed/Grad, Rye Co Day Sch, 1951; Student, Sweet Briar Col 1951-52, Westchester Comml Sch 1953-54; pa/Asst Beauty Editor, *Glamour* Mag, 1954-55; Sr Exec Secy, McCann-Erickson Inc, 1955-59; Secy to Pres and Ofc Mgr, Thomson-Leeds Inc, 1959-62; Dir, Public Relats, Glenview Pk Dist, 1975-78; Free-Lance Writer, Public Relats, 1978-; cp/Recording Secy, Glenview Aux, 1968-70, Pres 1970-72; VP, Pres' Coun of All Auxs, Skokie Val Hosp, 1972-73, Pres 1973-74; A Fdg Mem and Recording Secy, Save the Grove Com, 1973-75; Citizens Adv Com for the Grove, 1975-76; Glenview Bicent Comm, 1976; Active Mem, Northfield Twp Repub Wom's Clb, 1974-, Publicity Chm 1977-79; 10th Dist Repub Wom's Clb, 1974-; Publicity Com-man, Glenbrook So HS Instrumental Leag 1978-79, Area Hist Soc Coachhouse/Lib 1978-79; Pres, The Grove Heritage Assn, 1979-83; r/Epis; hon/Author, Several Articles, *Glenview Times* 1978, *Illinois Wildlife* 1974; Editor,

"Rustlings from the Grove," 1980-81; Annual Report, Grove Heritage Assn Inc, 1979-80, 1980-81; Cert of Merit from the Village of Glenview, 1977.

NORTON, ALAN PAUL oc/Executive Management Consultant; b/Feb 22, 1943; h/59 Huntford Road, Northeast, Calgary, Alberta T2K 3Y8; m/Lynda Diane Dunbar; c/Alana Lea; p/Chester Paul and Betty Luxford Norton; ed/Cert in Bus Adm (Fin), So Alta Inst, Tech, 1971; pa/Collection Supvr, Calgary Gen Credit Ltd, 1964-66; Area Fin Mgr, Massey-Ferguson Industs Ltd, 1966-67; Retail Credit Analyst, Gulf Oil Canada Ltd, 1968-70; Crew Tng Ofcr, Universal Ambulance Ser Ltd, 1970; Fin Correspondent, Allis-Chalmers Credit Corp, 1970-71; Instrnl Admr, St John Ambulance, 1972-73; Div Credit Mgr, Neonex Shelter Ltd, 1973-77; Credit Mgr, Westburne Divs Engrg and Plumbing Supplies Ltd 1978-79, Alta Elect Supply Ltd 1978-79; Gen Mgr, The Marsh Grp of Cos, 1979-; Wn Reg Credit Mgr, Gough Elect Ltd, 1979-80; VP, Fin, Eastlake Devel Corp Ltd, 1980-81; Pres, Alan P Norton & Assocs, 1981-; Chm, Area Adv Com, Creditel of Canada Ltd, 1978-81; Notary Public, Calgary, 1976-; Alumni Mem, Delta Sigma Rho and Phi Kappa Sigma; cp/Coalition for Life; Alliance for Life; Calgary Pro-Life Assn, Dir, VP; Right to Life; r/Mormon; hon/ Contbg Author to Several Articles on Financial Mgmt, Receivables Control, Ed, and Life Issues; Decorated, Order of St John; Recip, Provincial Shield, Alta Provincial Coun of St John Ambulance, 1971; Priory Vote of Thanks of St John Ambulance, Gov Gen, Canada, 1974.

NORTON, FRANK TRACY oc/Tennis Company Executive, Tennis Professional; b/Jan 20, 1936; h/126 Madrone Avenue, San Francisco, CA 94127; ba/ Arnold, CA; m/Loretta Yvonne; c/Lynn Dora, Lisa Marie, Lori Ann; p/Tracy Murray and Loretta Gladys Buchel Norton (dec); ed/Grad, Elect Engrg, Intl Correspondence Schs, 1957; Mod Bus Prog, Alexander Hamilton Inst, 1967; Am Law and Procedure, LaSalle Ext Univ, 1970; Microprocessors and Microcomputers, Nat Radio Inst, 1980; pa/ Elect Design Engr, Pacific Gas & Elect Co, 1954-; Pres and Chm of Bd, Tennis Outings Inc, 1976-; Exec Dir, Clb Tennis, 1978-; Tennis Profl, Sequoia Woods Country Clb, 1976; Tennis Profl, Meadowmont Village Swim and Racquet Clb, 1974-80; Cert'd w Profl Tennis Registry, 1977-; Assoc Mem, US Profl Tennis Assn, 1979-; Profl Stringers Assn, 1978-; Bd of Dirs, Indust Div, SF Rec and Pks Dept, 1972-78, VP 1977-78; hon/Author, Var Pub'd Articles; Men of Achmt; Intl W/W Intells; W/W Fin and Indust; Am Registry Series.

NOSSAMAN, HAROLD WARREN oc/Deputy Regional Administrator; b/ Aug 25, 1932; h/7009 Cottonwood, Shawnee, KS 66216; ba/Kansas City, MO; m/Mary Lou; c/Gary, Debra; p/ Bernard and Ethel Nossaman, Isabel, KS; ed/BBA, Wichita St Univ, 1962; mil/ USAF, 1951-55; pa/Loan Ofcr, Amortibanc Investmt Co, Wichita, 1963-65; Asst VP, Amortibanc, Liberal, 1965-66; Loan Ofcr, SBA, Wichita, 1966-74; Reg Loan Spec 1974-80, Acting Asst Reg Admr, Mgmt 1980-81, Asst Reg Admr for Fin and Investmts 1981-83, Dpty

Reg Admr, Reg VII 1983-, SBA; MO Bkrs Assn; Credit Com, Fed Credit Union; Wichita St Alumni Assn; cp/Masonic Lodge; Scottish Rite; Shrine; Am Legion; Elks; r/Meth; hon/SBA Spec Achmt Awd, 1976; MW Bkg Inst Awd, 1977; Ldrship Sys Awd, 1975, 1977; SBA Silver Metal Nom for Meritorious Ser, 1982; Exceptl/Outstg Perf Ratings, 1977, 1978, 1979, 1981, 1982, 1983; W/W Fin and Indust.

NOVAK, DARIA I oc/Department of State Employee; b/Feb 1, 1957; h/863 Golden Arrow Street, Great Falls, VA 22066; ba/Washington, DC; ed/BA, Univ of WY, 1978; Student, Georgetown Univ, 1976; Cert, Inst for Comparative Polit and Ec Sys; Cert in Chinese Lang, Taiwan Nat Normal Univ, 1980; Presently in MA Prog, George Wash Univ; pa/Dept of St, Ofc of Chinese Affairs, 1979-; Ofc of Chinese Affairs, Ec Sect, 1980; Ofc of Reg, Mil and Theatre Forces, Bur of Intell and Res, 1979; Ofc of Thailand, Indonesia, Malaysia, Burma and Singapore Affairs, Bur of E Asian and Pacific Affairs; Assn for Asian Studies; Asia Soc; Soc for Med Anthropology; IPA; r/Rom Cath; hon/Pub, *China's Rise to World Power*, 1983; Meritorious Hon Awd 1982, Awd for Excell 1980, Dept of St; Wolcott Fellow, George Wash Univ, 1982; Edison Fellow to Georgetown Univ, 1976; W/W Am Polit; W/W S; Notable Commun Ldrs; Nat Dean's List.

NUÑEZ, JOSEPHINE O oc/Administrative Assistant; b/Oct 29, 1932; h/325 Madison, San Antonio, TX 78204; ba/San Antonio, TX; m/Ruben R; c/Peter, Michael Anthony, Mary Elizabeth Muzuca; p/Joe and Juanita Orozco, San Antonio, TX; Grad, San Fernando Cathedral HS, 1950; St Mary's Univ Cont'g Ed for Real Est, 1969; Dyer Sch of Real Est, 1969; Student, Our Lady of the Lake Univ of San Antonio; Adm Asst to Dr Daniel E Jennings, Dean of the Worden Sch of Social Ser, Our Lady of the Lake Univ, 1971-; Secy to Brother Victor A Naegele, St Mary's Univ, 1968-71; Secy to Msgr Erwin Juraschek, Cath Chancery Ofc, 1965-68; Secy to Raymond Shafer, Teamsters Local 657, 1962-65; Other Former Positions; cp/Cath Divorcees; Dem Wom of Bexar Co; Our Lady of Pillar Christian Renewal Ctr; Cursillista; Parent-Tchrs Clb; Other Civic Org Mbrships; hon/W/W Am Wom.

NWUKE, EJI I oc/Manufacturing Company Executive, Biochemist; b/Apr 5, 1950; ba/3028 Abilene Street, Aurora, CO 80011; c/Enyinnah Jonas Olisaemeka; p/Chief J H E Nwuke and Roseannah Nwukes Court Okomoko, Nigeria; ed/GCE, Univ of London, 1971; WASC, Okrika Grammar Sch; Student, Stella Manis Col; BS, Metro St Col; PhD Student (Spec), UCHSC; mil/Bienfran Army, 1967-70; pa/Accts Exec, Mersten Mfrs 1974-77, TX Refinery Corp 1978; Pres, Owner, Nwuke Enterprises, Aurora, Frankfurt (Germany), Nigeria; hon/Pubs in *Nature* Mag 1977, *Orthopaedic Research Society* 1977, *Journal of International Neuromuscular Disease* 1977; Pres, Nigerian Student Union; W/W Fin and Indust; W/W World.

O

OATEY, JENNIFER SUE oc/Recreational Sports Administrator; b/Aug 30, 1949; h/333 Oak Grove, #308, Minneapolis, MN 55403; ba/Minneapolis, MN; p/Elwyn and Phyllis Larson, Brainerd, MN; ed/PhD in Ed, Univ of MN, 1981; MA in Tchg 1973, BS 1971, NM St Univ; pa/Asst Intramural Dir, NM St Univ, 1973-74; Campus Ctr Coor, Brainerd Commun Col, 1974-75; Intramural Supvr, Stephen F Austin St Univ, 1975-76; Asst Recreational Sports Dir, Univ of MI, 1976-77; Assoc Dir of Rec Sports, Univ of MN, 1977-; MN St Dir for Nat Intramural Rec Sports Assn, 1977-81; *NIRSA Jour* Edit Bd, 1981-; MN Coun on Hlth Promotion and Wellness; Treas of Adv Bd, Univ YWCA, 1982-83; NIRSA; CIRA; cp/Sons of Norway; r/Luth; hon/Author, Num Articles Pub'd in *NIRSA Journal* and Annual Conf Proceedings; Poetry Pub'd by Blue Mtn Arts Inc as Notecards and in Anthologies; Phi Theta Kappa, 1968; Bach's Deg w Hons, 1971; Outstg Yg Wom in Am; W/W Am Wom.

OBLOW, JOYCE LOCKWOOD oc/Retail Sales Specialist; b/May 30, 1941; h/1283 Kaeleku Street, Honolulu, HI 96825; ba/Honolulu, HI; m/Allen B; c/Scott James Kalani, Mark Richard Kainoa; p/William S and Ruth N Lockwood, Tampa, FL; ed/AA, Green Mtn Col, 1961; pa/Advtg and Mktg Dir, Ala Moana Shopping Ctr, 1981-83; Retail Sales Spec, KITV, 1983-; Has Own Radio Show, KGU, 1984-; Sales and Mktg Execs; HI Advtg Fdn; Am Mktg Assn; Intl Coun of Shopping Ctrs; cp/Honolulu Surfing Assn; r/Prot; hon/W/W W.

O'BRIEN, KATHLEEN ANN oc/Alderman; b/Mar 19, 1945; h/2204 Seabury, Minneapolis, MN 55406; ba/Minneapolis, MN; m/Jeffrey Harrison Loesch; p/Philip E and Dorothy R O'Brien, Minneapolis, MN; ed/PhD Cand, Hist, Univ of MN; MA, Hist, Marquette Univ, 1969; BA, Hist, Col of St Catherine, 1967; pa/Dir, Wom's Hist Ctr, 1980-81; Res Assoc, MN Hist Soc, 1973-80; Instr, Univ of MN, 1978-79; Alderman, Mpls City Coun; Wom Histns of the MW, VP 1976-78; Upper MW Ethnic Studies Assn, Sec-Treas 1977-79; Nat Trust for Hist Preserv; cp/Dem Farmer Labor Party St Ctl Com, 1978-81; Legis Dist Chair, 1978-81; r/Rom Cath; hon/Pubs, *The Immigrant Experience: A Minnesota Curriculum Resource Unit* 1979, *A Social History of Women: Curriculum Materials* 1982, *Historic Resources in Minnesota* 1979; Pi Gamma Mu, Social Sci Hon Soc, 1967; Phi Alpha Theta, Hist Hon Soc, 1969; W/W MW; W/W US Polit.

O'BRIEN, KELLY J oc/Lawyer; b/Dec 22, 1937; ba/16027 Ventura Boulevard, 4th Floor, Encino, CA 91436; c/Cindylou Browning, William Daniel; p/Walter Daniel and LaVerne Inez Lang Hardin; ed/JD, Woodland Univ-Mid Val Col of Law; USD, Intl Law, Oxford Univ; Intl Law, The Hague, 1979; pa/Law Ofcs of Kelly O'Brien, 1980-; Previous Law Clk, Beverly Hills City Atty; US Ct of Appeals Ninth Circuit, 1981; Atty at Law by Supr Ct of the St of CA, 1980; US Fed Ct, 1980; Staff Atty, Wom's Legal Clin; Staff Atty, Haven Hills Battered Wom's Ctr; Am Bar Assn; CA

St Bar Assn; LA Co Bar Assn; Assn of Trial Lwyrs of Am; LA Wom Lwyrs Assn; CA Trial Lwyrs Assn; LA Trial Lwyrs Assn; CA Wom Lwyrs Assn; San Fernando Val Wom Lwyrs Assn; Irish Am Bar Assn of CA; cp/Dem Party St Del, 1979; Dem Circle, 1982, 1983; Coro Foun Alumni Assn, 1979-83; Sherman Oaks Dem Clb; r/Meth; hon/Atty Gen's Staff, St of TX, 1953; Atty Gen Girls St, St of TX, 1953; Student Bar Pres, Law Sch, 1977-78; CA St Student Bar Assn Pres, 1977-78; Resolution by CA St Senate, 1978 (by Hon Allan Robbins); Resolution by CA St Assem, 1978 (by Hon Tom Bane); Achmt Awds: Edmund G Brown Jr 1978, The White House (Pres Carter) 1978, US Senate (S I Hayakawa) 1978; Law Student of the Yr, YWCA, 1978; Coro Foun Wom's Polit Affairs, 1979, 1980; Life Mem and Staff Atty, Wom's Legal Clin, 1980-83; Achmt Awd, CA Senator Alan Sieroty, 1978; W/W W; W/W CA.

O'BRIEN, LAWRENCE FRANCIS oc/Commissioner of National Basketball Association; b/Jul 7, 1917; h/8600 United Nations Plaza, New York, NY 10017; ba/New York, NY; m/Elva Brassard; c/Lawrence F III; p/Lawrence Francis and Myra Theresa Sweeney O'Brien (dec); ed/LLB, NEn Univ, 1942; Num Hon Degs; mil/AUS, WWII; pa/Commr, Nat Basketball Assn, 1975-; Pres, O'Brien Assocs, Mgmt, Consltg, 1969, 1973-75; Pres, McDonnell & Co Inc, Investmt Bkrs, 1969; Temporary and Perm Chm, Dem Nat Conv and Chm, McGovern Pres Campaign, 1972; Other Previous Positions; hon/Author, *The O'Brien Manual* 1969, *No Final Victories* 1974; Recip, Israel Prime Minister's Medal for Dist'd Ser to Dem and Freedom, 1978; Brotherhood Awd Honoring LFOB for Dist'd Ser in the Field of Human Relats, Nat Conf of Christians and Jews, 1977; Other Hons.

O'BRIEN, PAMELA RENEE oc/Chief Administrative Assistant; b/Apr 4, 1950; h/2605 South Indiana Avenue, Chicago, IL 60616; ba/Chicago, IL; p/Maj Augustus Jr and Gerraldine Miller O'Brien, Clearwater, FL; ed/MA, NEn IL Univ, 1983; AB, Univ of IL, 1975; Certs: John Marshall Law Sch 1978, Howard Univ Sch of Bus and Public Adm 1980; mil/USAR, Sgt (Comm as 1st Lt Pending); pa/Chief Adm Asst, St Rep Larry S Bullock, 23rd Legis Dist, 1982-; Mktg Rep, E/W Oil Sers, 1980-81; Proprietor, Gifts of Love, Imports, 1980; Exec Asst, Gtr Roseland Commun Org, 1980; Financial Planner, Prudential Life Ins Co/A Gibbs & Assocs, 1978-80; Social Wkr/Coor, Near S Parent Child Ctr, 1977-78; Other Previous Positions; cp/Toastmasters Intl, 1979, 1980; Yg Dems, Pres/Treas 1973-75, 1973-82; Black Wom Ltd, Pres/Fdr, Social/Civic Org; Debs Ser Leag, YWCA; Links Intl; hon/Hon'd as Raising Most Funds for Lions Intl, Debs Ser Leag, YWCA, 1967, 1968; Featured in *Essence Magazine*, 1975; W/W Am.

O'BRIEN, WILLIAM FRANCIS oc/Clinical Psychologist; b/Aug 9, 1948; h/143 Moline Drive, Newport News, VA 23606; ba/Hampton, VA; m/Julia Crimmings; c/Erin Elizabeth; p/George E and Mary M (dec) O'Brien; Westfield, MA; ed/PhD 1975, MA 1972, Psych, OH St Univ; BA, Sociol, LeMoyne Col, 1970; pa/Staff Psychol, VA Med Ctr, Battle

Creek, MI, 1975-79; Coor, Alcohol Rehab Unit 1979-, Asst Chief, Psych Ser 1982-, VA Med Ctr; Asst Adj Prof, En VA Med Sch; Asst Adj Prof, St Leo Col, Langley AFB, VA; r/Rom Cath; hon/Pubs, "Self-Concept, Self-Acceptance and Vocational Maturity" 1973, "Concurrent Validity of Holland's Theory for Non-Degree Black Working Men" 1976; Awd for Spec Act of Ser, VA, 1982; W/W S and SE.

OCAMPO, AURORA NAZARENO oc/Registered Professional Nurse; b/Oct 23, 1941; h/264 Sharpe Avenue, Staten Island, NY 10302; ba/Brooklyn, NY; m/Manuel (dec); p/Tomas V Nazareno, Staten Island, NY; ed/GN, Philippines Gen Hosp, Univ of the Philippines, 1963; BSN, Philippines Wom's Univ, 1965; Pediatric Nurse Assn, Cornell Univ, NY Hosp, 1973; MA, NY Univ, 1979; mil/USANC, Capt (Resv); pa/Critical Care Nurse, VA Med Ctr, 1980-; Pediatric Nurse Assn, 1973-80; Public Hlth Nurse, 1969-73; Exch Visitor Nurse, 1966-67; APHA, Mbrship Advocate 1982-; ANA; NY St Nurses Assn, Dist 13; Nat Assn of Pediatric Nurses; cp/Philippino-Am Civic and Cultural Commun of Staten Isl, Secy 1980-; r/Cath; hon/World W/W Wom.

O'CONNELL, ROBERTA WHITE oc/International President; b/Jul 12, 1922; h/25824 Sugar Pine Drive, Pioneer, CA 95666; ba/Same; m/Jerry F; c/Maureen O'Connell-Carter, Sharon L Helldorfer; p/Emery H (dec) and M Elizabeth White, Pioneer, CA; ed/BA in Mus, San Jose St Univ, 1945; pa/Pvt Tchr of Piano, 1953-66; Choir Dir, First Meth Ch, 1955-58; Dist Dir 1964-66, Exec Secy-Treas 1968-83, Intl Pres 1983-, Mu Phi Epsilon; San Jose Alumni Chapt, Mu Phi Epsilon; Pres 1955-57; cp/Peninsular Wom's Chorus, Pres 1954; Couples Clb, First Meth Ch, Chair Couple 1958; GSA, Troop Ldr 1957-59, Sum Camp Dir 1960; Vacation Bible Sch, First Meth Ch, Dir 1954; r/Prot; hon/Contemp Notables; World W/W Wom; W/W Am Wom; Intl W/W Commun Ser; DIB; Notable Ams of 1967-77; Commun Ldrs and Noteworthy Ams; W/W W; W/W Mu Phi Epsilon.

O'CONNOR, BARBARA HENRIETTA oc/Canine Beautician; b/Aug 19, 1936; h/0558 Pass Road, Gulfport, MS 39501; ba/Gulfport, MS; m/Frank Earl; c/Sandra Evelyn; p/Lottie Annie Brannan, London, England; ed/Grad, Avondale Pk Girls Sch, 1953; Monkspark Inst of Animal Husbandry, Show Grooming and Kennel Mgmt, 1955-57; pa/Brit Broadcasting Corp; Bkrs Trust Co of London; Eng Spkg Union; Instr of Dog Grooming for 15 Yrs; Show Dog Handling Instr, 1971-72; Owner and Operator, Canine Country Clb; Life-time Mem, Nat Dog Groomers Assn of Am; r/Bapt; hon/Pet News Writer for *The Owl Newspaper*, 1969; Introduced the Apricot Toy Poodle Puckshill and Greatcoats Line to the MS Coast in 1968, and the Brit Bedlington Terrier (Finishing 5 Champions).

O'DONNELL, WALTER GREGORY oc/Professor of Management Emeritus; b/Feb 3, 1903; h/PO Box 182, Ashfield, MA 01330; ba/Amherst, MA; m/Angelina; c/Charles, Roger, Kathleen, Arleen; p/Walter T and Margaret O'Donnell; ed/BA, Eng and Social Sci, Wn Resv Univ,

1932; LLB, Cleveland-John Marshall Law Sch, 1930; MA, Ednl Phil and Ec, Wn Resv Univ, 1944; PhD, Ec and Phil, Columbia Univ, 1959; pa/Prof of Mgmt, Emeritus, Univ of MA; Vis'g Prof of Mgmt, St Univ of NY Plattsburg, 1982; Dist'd Vis'g Prof of Mgmt, Bowling Green St Univ, 1978-81; Prof of Bus Adm in Residence, Univ of CT, 1977-78; Dist'd Vis'g Prof of Mgmt, Bowling Green St Univ, 1975-76 (Return Engagement), 1974-75; Prof of Mgmt, Univ of MA, 1956-73; Vis'g Prof, Instituto Tecnologico y de Estudios Superiores, 1972; Vis'g Prof, Univ of Madrid, 1963; Vis'g Prof of Mgmt, Univ of NM, 1967-68; Assoc Prof of Indust Relats, Univ of Pgh, 1951-52; Instr, Dept of Ec, Columbia Univ, 1948-51; Assoc Prof of Ec, FL St Univ, 1947-48; Instr, Ec, OH St Univ, 1943-47; Assoc Prof of Ec and Polit Sci, John Carrol 1937-43; Assoc Prof, Notre Dame Col, 1935-37; Cleveland Public HS, 1930-35; Dist'd Vis'g Prof of Mgmt, Georgetown Univ, 1973-74; Dist'd Vis'g Prof of Mgmt, Loyola Col, 1973; Vis'g Prof, Brooklyn Polytechnic Inst, 1968-70; Vis'g Prof and Ednl Conslt, Univ of Puerto Rico, 1961; Vis'g Assoc Prof of Mgmt, Rutgers Univ, 1954-56; Vis'g Lectr, OH Wesleyan Univ, 1946; Other Previous Positions; Appt'd to Long-Range Planning Com, Inst of Mgmt Scis, 1974-; Fdr, Orgr, Exec Secy, Col of Mgmt Phil, Inst of Mgmt Scis, 1960-; AAAS, 1950-; Acad of Mgmt, 1960-; hon/Pubs, "Bridging the Private and Public Sectors of Economic Development" 1972, "Management Development in the Private and Public Sectors of Industrializing Nations: Similarities and Differences" 1969, Num Others; Awd'd 10 Res, Ednl and Travel Grants in Past 10 Yrs; Beta Gamma Sigma; W/W Ed; Ldrs in Sci; Am Men of Sci; W/W Commerce and Indust; W/W Mgmt Consltg; W/W E; DIB; Num Others.

OHLSON, VIRGINIA M oc/Assistant Dean and Director of Office of International Studies; h/5254 North Spaulding Avenue, Chicago, IL 60625; ba/Chicago, IL; p/Otto and Hulda Ohlson (dec); ed/AA, Liberal Arts, N Pk Col, 1933; Dipl, Nsg, Swedish Covenant Hosp Sch of Nsg, 1937; BS, Biol Scis 1946, MA w Hons in Nsg Ed 1955, PhD in Ed 1969, Univ of Chgo; pa/Asst Dean of Intl Studies 1981-, Coor of Intl Prog Planning 1980-81, Prof of Dept of Public Hlth Nsg 1970-, Col of Nsg, Univ of IL; Prof of Dept of Preven Med and Commun Hlth, Col of Med, Univ of IL, 1970-; Prof of Grad Col, Hlth Scis Ctr, Univ of IL, 1970-; Hlth Ser Adm, Sch of Public Hlth, Univ of IL, 1971-; Hd of Dept of Public Hlth Nsg 1970-80, Acting Dean 1971-72, Assoc Prof and Chm of Dept of Public Hlth Nsg 1963-70, Col of Nsg, Univ of IL; Asst Prof, Grad and Undergrad Instrn in Public Hlth Nsg, Univ of Chgo Dept of Nsg Ed; Nsg Conslt, Rockefeller Foun, 1952-54; Other Previous Positions; r/Prot; hon/Pubs, "Nursing in America-Opportunities, Challenges and Conflicts" 1982, "Japanese Nursing Association: Memories and Expectations" 1982, Others; Hon VP, APHA, 1982; Japanese Min of Hlth and Wel Awd, 1982; First Intl Hon Mbrship Awd, 1982; Num Other Hons.
OHMAN, RICHARD MICHAEL oc/

Assistant Professor of Art; b/May 8, 1946; h/PO Box 20183, Cincinnati, OH 45220; ba/Chillicothe, OH; ed/BA, Mercyhurst Col, 1972; MFA, OH Univ, 1975; mil/AUS; pa/Instr, Asst Prof, Freshman and Sophomore Studio Arts, Art Dept, OH Univ, 10+ Yrs; Free-Lance Artist; Paintings, Drawings and Photographs Have Been Exhib'd in 60+ Juried Reg, Nat and Intl Exhbns, incl'g, Intl Photo Soc, 35th and 41st Annual Exhbn of Contemp Art, 39th Mid-Yr at Butler Inst, Am Painters in Paris; hon/Artwks Have Been Reproduced in Art Instrnl Texts, Exhib Catalogues in Conjunction w Exhbns, Newspaper Articles/Reviews of Grp and One-Man Exhbns, Artist Directories, Slide Libs; Artwks Have Rec'd Awds at Juried Exhbns, incl'g, Annual Exhib at Intl Photo Soc, 1981; Yassinnoff Meml Awd for Drawing, 1977; Awd for Paintings at Lithopolis Fine Arts Fest, 1978; Hon Mention for Painting at Erie Arts Coun Sum Fest, 1973; Recip, S'ships and Grants, incl'g, Indiv Artist Grant, OH Arts Coun; Authored Orgl Grants from OH Arts Coun for the Brotherhood Creat Arts Clb and the Visual Arts Ctr; W/W Am Art; Artists/USA; Artist's File/St of OH; Cinc Art Survey; Intl Artists Dir.

OHRENSTEIN, ROMAN A oc/Professor of Economics, Educator, Rabbi; b/Jun 12, 1920; h/28-74 208 Street, Bayside, NY 11360; ba/Garden City, NY; m/Ruth Silberstein; c/Gena Ann, Ilana Rose; p/Joseph Barukh and Gena Feifkopf (dec); ed/MA in Ed 1948, PhD, cum laude, Ed 1949, Postgrad in Med 1949-51, Univ of Munich, Ludhig Maximilian Univ; MHL, The Jewish Theol Sem of Am, 1955; Ordained Rabbi, JTS of Am, 1955; Postgrad, Ec, Columbia Univ, 1963-64; pa/Rabbi, Auburn, NY 1955-57, Pittsfield, MA 1957-60, Atlanta, GA 1960-62, NYC 1962-66; Prof of Ec 1964-, Chm of Ec Dept 1976-78, 1982-, Jewish Chaplain on Campus 1970-, Nassau Col, St Univ of NY Garden City; Orgr and Session Chm, Third World Cong of Social Ec, CA St Univ Fresno, 1983; Chaplain, Nassau Co Civil Preparedness, 1965-; Prof of Ed, Am Col in Jerusalem, 1968-73; Other Previous Positions; Coun of Orgrs, UJA, 1978-; Rabbinical Assem; NY Bd of Rabbis; Am Ec Assn; Hist of Ec Soc; Learned Soc; NY Acad of Scis; hon/Author, *Inventories during Business Fluctuations* 1973, *Inventory Control as an Economic Shock Absorber* 1975, Others; St Univ of NY Fellow, 1968, 1970; Dist'd Ser to Ec Sci, IBC; Commun Ldrs and Noteworthy Ams Awd, Am Biogl Inst; W/W E; W/W Am Jewry; Men of Achmt; Men and Wom of Distn.

O'KEEFFE, JOHN J JR oc/Executive; b/Dec 21, 1941; h/11 Dante Street, Larchmont, NY 10538; ba/New York, NY; m/Valerie Moore; c/Anna Gould, John Moore; p/John J and Mary Snee O'Keeffe (dec); ed/BA, Fairfield Univ, 1965; JD, George Wash Univ Law Sch, 1968; pa/Atty, Pan Am World Airways, 1968-72; Atty, Trans World Airlines, 1972-77; Corporate Secy and Asst Gen Counsel, Trans World Airlines Inc 1977-83, Trans World Corp 1978-83; VP, Gen Counsel and Corporate Secy, Trans World Corp, 1983-; NY St Bar Assn, 1968-; cp/Larchmont Yacht Clb, 1980-; r/Cath; hon/W/W Am.
OLDENDORPH, JAMES EDWARD

oc/Advertising Executive; b/Jul 25, 1945; h/1680 West 22nd Street, San Pedro, CA 90732; ba/Santa Monica, CA; c/James Edward Jr, Jessica Sara; p/Mrs Edward Oldendorph; ed/BA, Univ of MO Columbia, 1967; pa/Reg Advtg Mgr 1968-70, NY Mktg Mgr 1970-71, LA Mktg Mgr 1971-73, Seven Up Co; Dir of Mktg, Seven Up Bottling Cos of So CA, 1973-78; Mktg Mgr, Plus Products, 1978-79; VP, Acct Sers, Seideman & Moisecce, 1979-83; VP, Acct Supvr, Louis & Salol Advtg, 1983-; Am Mktg Assn; Sales and Mktg Execs Clb of LA; Univ of MO Alumni Assn; Sigma Alpha Epsilon; r/Cath; hon/Marsy Awd, 1982; Effie Awd, 1983; Sandi Awd, 1983; W/W W.

OLDHAM, HOWARD T oc/Printer, Businessman; b/Dec 25, 1943; h/5016 Briar Grove, Liberty, TX 77575; ba/Liberty, TX; m/Stephana Stelly; c/Dawn Alexis, Stephen Wesley; p/Dr Andrew Wesley Oldham, Greensboro, NC; mil/USMCR, 1961-69; pa/Palmer Paper Co, 1970-72; Mgr, Fannin Bus Forms, 1972-74; Pres, Gulf Coast Graphics, 1974-75; Owner, Patton Printing Co (Now Oldham Printing Co), 1975-; Pres, Houston Litho Clb, 1975; Printing Industs of the Gulf Coast, 1972-; VP, Graphic Communs Coun, 1974; cp/Adv Coun, San Jacintoo Col, 1975; TX Gov's Comm on Human Resourses, 1975; Del, TX Dem Conv, 1972; Pres, Liberty Co Heart Assn, 1981-82, 1982-83; Liberty Dayton Area C of C, 1976-; Rotary Clb of Liberty, 1976-; Publicity Dir and Bd of Dirs, Trinity Val Exposition, 1978; r/Meth; Bd of Dirs, First U Meth Ch, 1979-81; hon/Houston Litho Clb Man of the Yr Awd, 1972; Ednl Progs Awd, 1973; W/W S and SW.

OLIPHANT, V SUSIE F oc/Assistant to Supervising Director of Science; b/Sep 3, 1938; h/910 Luray Place, Hyattsville, MD 20783; ba/Washington, DC; m/John H; c/Kendall Benet, Johahn Bentley; p/Leon and Fannie Francis, Skippers, VA; ed/BS, Zool and Chem, Howard Univ, 1958; MS, Sci Ed and Supvn, Univ of VA, 1974; Currently Pursuing PhD, Adm Policy, Univ of MD; Completing Course Wk, MEd, Gifted Ed, Howard Univ, 1980-; pa/Asst to Supervising Dir of Sci 1982-, Resource Tchr of Gifted/Talented Ed Prog 1979-82, Peer Asst Tchr of Reg I 1978-79, DC Public Schs; Tchr, Ballou HS of Sci and Math, 1975-78; Jr High Sci Tchr, DC Public Schs, 1963-75; Electron Microscope Tech, NIH, 1962-63; Nat Sci Tchrs Assn; Am Ed Res Assn; CEC; Nat Assn for Gifted Chd; Assn for Supvn and Curric Devel; Bd of Dirs, METCON Inc; Phi Delta Kappa; Minority/Disadvantaged Gifted Com of TAG, 1982, 1983; VP for Mbrship, Phi Delta Kappa, Howard Univ, 1983; r/AME; hon/Pubs, *A Mathematics Resource Guide in Gifted Education, Identification of Academically/Creative Gifted/Talented Students in the District of Columbia Public Schools*; NSF F'ship, Univ of VA, 1973-74; USDE Ofc of the Gifted and Talented F'ship, Howard Univ, 1979-80; Internship, Ofc of the Gifted and Talented, USDE, 1980; Kappa Delta Phi, Nat Hon Soc in Ed; W/W E.

OLIVE, LINDSAY S oc/University Distinguished Professor Emeritus; b/Apr 30, 1917; h/PO Box 391, Highlands, NC 28741; ba/Highlands, NC; m/Anna

Jean; p/Lindsay S and Sada W Olive (dec); ed/AB 1938, MA 1940, PhD 1942, Dept of Botany, Univ of NC Chapel Hill; pa/Instr of Botany, Univ of NC Chapel Hill, 1942-44; Mycologist, USDA, 1944-45; Asst Prof of Botany, Univ of GA, 1945-46; Assoc Prof of Botany, LA St Univ, 1946-49; Assoc Prof and Prof of Botany, Columbia Univ, 1949-67; Prof 1968-69, Univ Dist'd Prof of Botany 1969-82, Univ of NC Chapel Hill; hon/Author, 150 Articles, Chapts of Several Books, Book: *The Mycetoans* 1975; Sigma Xi, 1942; Phi Beta Kappa, 1942; AAAS Fellow, 1945; Guggenheim Fellow, 1956; Pres, Mycological Soc of Am, 1966; Hon Mem, Brit Mycological Soc, 1975; Mycological Soc of Am Dist'd Awd, 1982.

OLIVEIRA, SOLANGE RIBEIRO oc/ University Associate; b/Oct 19, 1929; m/ Leopoldo Correa Moura; c/Antonio de Oliveira Sette Camara, Ana Flavia Moura; p/Antonio da Costa Oliveira (dec); ed/BA in Lttrs, Fed Univ of Minas Gerais, Brazil; PhD in Lttrs, Fac of Lttrs, Fed Univ of Minas Gerais, Brazil; Fulbright Awd for Lecturing and Res in Comparative Lit, Univ of NC Chapel Hill; pa/Lectr in Eng, Fed Univ of Minas Gerais, 1960-80; Lectr in Ed, Fac of Ed, Fed Univ of Minas Gerais, 1960-67; Fulbright Rschr, Univ of NC Chapel Hill, 1980-82; Assoc Rschr, Brit Coun S'ship, London Inst of Ed, 1982-83; Hd of Dept of Germanic Lttrs, Fed Univ of Minas Gerais, 1976-80; Rep of Eng Area, Bd of Grad Studies of Fac of Lttrs, Fed Univ of Minas Gerais, 1978-80; LASA; MLA; r/Christian; hon/Pubs, *A Trip to the Moon* 1976, *The Blue Earth* 1978, *A Tour of Brazil* 1980, *A Barata e a Crisalida: O Romance de Clarice* (Forthcoming).

OLIVER, CURTIS LARRY oc/Assistant Principal; b/Jul 23, 1948; h/100 Crosscreek Drive, Grapevine, TX 76051; ba/Grapevine, TX; m/Linda Ethridge; c/Letisha; p/Curtis H and Daisy Bridges (dec) Oliver, Grapevine, TX; ed/BS in Ed, N TX St Univ, 1970; MEd, TX Christian Univ, 1981; pa/Tchr 1970-82, Chm of Math Dept 1979-82, Grapevine-Colleyville Indep Sch Dist; Asst Prin, Grapevine Mid Sch, 1982-; Pt-time Instr, Tarrant Co Jr Col, 1981-82; TX Assn Sec'dy Sch Prins, 1982-; Assn for Supvn and Curric Devel, 1981-; Assn TX Profl Edrs; cp/ Grapevine City Coun, 1975-; Grapevine Kiwanis Clb, 1979-, VP 1980-81; Grapevine Golf Assn, 1979-; N TX Coun of Govts, 1975-; Chm of City Utility Com, 1978; Chm, City Facility Com, 1980-; r/Bapt; hon/Tchr of Yr, GHS, 1980-81; Outstg Yg Men of Am; W/W S and SW.

OLIVER, FREDERICK HASTINGS oc/Marketing Executive; b/Aug 28, 1932; h/427 Northwest 181 Street, Seattle, WA 98177; ba/Bellevue, WA; m/ Sandra Mary; c/Maria B, Jeannette R, Jonathan Frederick; p/Donald Hastings Oliver, East Quogue, NY; ed/HS; mil/ US Coast Guard; pa/In Maj Power Plant Constrn in Fgn Countries Holding Managerial Positions and Over-All Proj Mgmt, for 20 Yrs; Pres, The JMJ Mktg Corp, 1983-.

OLIVER, LEAH JOYNES oc/Psychiatric Social Worker; b/May 23, 1934; h/ 17 Rich Street, Mattapan, MA 02126; ba/Boston, MA; c/Mrs Dorothy Scott J Brown, Washington, DC; ed/BA, cum laude, VA Union Univ, 1956; MA w

Hons, Simmons Sch of Social Wk, 1969; Postmasters Cert in Mtl Hlth Ed, Boston Univ Sch of Social Wk, 1973; pa/Conslt, St James Ednl Ctr, 1969; Social Wk Therapist, Parents' and Chd's Sers, 1971; Adj Prof in Fam Relats, Simmons Col, 1972-74; Adj Prof in Communication, Lesley Col, 1978-81; Lectr, Child Abuse, European Med Command, Berchtesgarden, Germany, 1978; Nat Assn of Social Wkrs; cp/ Former Mem, Bd of Dirs, YWCA; Hill House Teen Ctr; r/Bapt; hon/Pubs, "Peramiters and Indicies of Inadequate Nurturance" 1977, "Manpower Training for Effective Case Management in the Field of Child Abuse" 1978; Dist'd Bostonian, Boston Bicent Com, 1980; Dir of Clin Social Wkrs, Nat Assn of Social Wk.

OLIVER, LINDA ETHRIDGE oc/ Bank Executive; b/Feb 19, 1949; h/100 Crosscreek Drive, Grapevine, TX 76051; ba/Grapevine, TX; m/Curtis L; c/Letisha; p/Ferris and Opal Ethridge, Colleyville, TX; ed/Am Inst of Bkg; pa/ Bkkpg 1967-70, Supvr of Bkkpg 1970-74, Asst Cashier and Loan Secy 1974-79, Asst VP and Loan Ofcr 1979-80, VP, Security Ofcr, Real Est Ofcr 1981-, 1st Nat Bk of Grapevine; cp/Grapevine C of C, Bd of Dirs 1982-83; Wom's Div of C of C, Pres 1982-83, Exec Bd 1981-83; Am Cancer Soc, Treas 1981-82; Grapevine Commun Chorus, Charter Mem, Fin Com 1982-83; r/Bapt; hon/Outstg Yg Wom of Am.

OLIVER, WILLIAM DONALD oc/ Orthodontist; b/Dec 14; h/467 Washington Road, Barrington, RI 02806; ba/ Barrington, RI; m/Deborah Williams; c/ Brandon Williams Ball, Ryan Williams Ball, Heather Elizabeth; p/Dr and Mrs A W Oliver, Naples, FL; ed/BSc, Physics, 1964; DDS, 1968; MSD, 1970; mil/AF; pa/Olympic Ski Team, 1960; Pres, Orthodontic Enterprises Intl, 1973-78; Intl Offshore Racing, Regale, 1973-79; Alfa Romeo Touring Team, 1970-74; Am Dental Assn; RI Dental Assn; Canadian Dental Assn; European Orthodontic Soc; Am Assn of Orthodontists; Canadian Assn of Orthodontists; cp/ Fdn Intl d'Automobile; Royal Ocean Racing Clb; Rotary; r/Prot; hon/Pubs in *Journal of Clinical Orthodontics* 1970, *American Journal of Orthodontics* 1970, *Rhode Island Dental Journal* 1978; Carter Meml Awd, 1964; M T Dohan Prize, 1966; W/ W.

OLM, KENNETH W oc/Professor of Business Administration; b/Feb 5, 1924; h/2706 Macken, Austin, TX 78703; ba/ Austin, TX; m/Surrenden Hill; c/Fred J, Robert L, Ken W Jr; p/Erwin L and Edith Hinkel Olm (dec); ed/Lawrence Univ; BA, Pomona Col, 1947; MA, Univ of NM, 1949; PhD, Univ of TX, 1958; mil/ USAAF, 1943; pa/Prof of Mgmt 1984-, Assoc Prof of Mgmt 1960-83, Asst Prof of Mgmt 1955-60, Univ of TX Austin; Vis'g Prof of Mgmt, Univ of NM, 1966-67; Acad of Mgmt; SW Mgmt Assn, Pres 1966-67; Am Inst of Indust Engrs; Am Fin Assn; cp/Rotary Clb of Austin; r/Epis; hon/Pub, *Management Decisions and Organizational Policy* 1966, 1971, 1977, 1981; Ford Foun Fac F'ship, Harvard Univ Grad Sch of Bus, 1960; W/W W; W/W Ed.

OLMO, JAIME ALBERTO oc/Medical Doctor; h/920 Josefa Gil de la

Madrid, Rio Piedras, Puerto Rico 00924; m/Joaquina Rivas; c/Jaime A, Carlos A, Rosa I, Javier A; Ruth de Lourdes (dec); p/Juan and Emilia González Olmo; ed/ MD, Santiago de Compostela Univ, Spain, 1956; BS, Univ of Puerto Rico, 1950; pa/Med Dir, 1977-; Fam Pract, Pt-time; Mem of Staff: Drs Hosp, Hosp San Carlos, Auxilio Mutuo, Tchrs Hosp, San Martin Hosp; Asociación Médica de Puerto Rico; AMA; Assn of Phys and Surgs; Am Bd of Utilization Review Phys; Am Acad of Med Dirs; Fellow, Intl Assn of Phys and Surgs; Fellow, Royal Acad of Med; Fellow, Am Acad and Fam Phys; cp/BSA; hon/Corpus Christi Knights; Awd from Spanish Govt, "Officer-Méito Civil"; Medals from Boy Scouts, Exch Clbs.

OLSEN, MARGARET ANN oc/Executive; b/Jul 22, 1944; ba/3489 West 72nd Avenue, Suite 100, Westminster, CO 80030; p/Carl Johan and Ruth Vera Olsen, Chicago, IL; ed/Dipl in Nsg, Swedish Covenant Hosp Sch of Nsg, N Pk Col, 1962-65; Student, Univ of IL, 1965-66; BS, No IL Univ, 1966-68; Intl Transactional Anal Assn, 1972-74, Clin Mbrship 1974; pa/Nsg Asst, Swedish Covenant Hosp, 1962-65; Charge Nurse, Mercy Hosp, 1965-66; Asst Charge Nurse, Luth Gen Hosp, 1966-68; Hd Specialty Nurse, Ft Logan Mtl Hlth Ctr, 1968-74; Conslt, Adams Co Mtl Hlth Ctr, 1973-74; VP, Financial Dir, Instr, Rocky Mtn Transactional Anal Inst Inc, 1974-75; Conslt, Rimel Assocs in Psychi, PC, 1974-75; Therapist, Profl Cnslg Assocs, 1974-77; Instr, Profl Tng Ctr, 1975-77; Therapist, Denver Mtl Hlth Grp, 1977-80; Mgr, VP, Pres, Westminster Coin & Jewelry Ltd, Westminster Coin Ctr, 1974-; Bd of Govs, Adelphi Univ Inst of Numismatic and Philatelic Studies; Intl Soc of Appraisers, Assn of Personal Property Appraisers; ANA; CO Nurses Assn; IL Nurses Assn; Swedish Covenant Hosp Sch of Nsg Alumni Assn; No IL Univ Alumni Assn; Intl Transactional Anal Assn; Financial Dir, Rocky Mtn Transactional Anal Assn; Am Numismatic Assn; Nat Assn Coin and Precious Metals Dealers; Facts Trading Info Sys; Nat Assn of Female Execs; CO Coin Dealers Assn; CO-WY Numismatic Assn; CO Ednl Numismatic Assn; Soc of Paper Money Collectors; Intl Org of Wooden Money Collectors; Bk Token Soc; Check Collectors Round Table; BPW; Wom Bus Owners Assn; hon/W/ W Am Wom.

OLSEN, MARTHA BROWN oc/Commissioner; b/Jun 6, 1947; h/5025 Hillsboro Road, 7H, Nashville, TN 37215; ba/Nashville, TN; m/Robert J; p/Raymond and Mary Elizabeth Brown, Cookeville, TN; ed/BS, TN Tech Univ, 1970; Dipl in Ed, Univ of Wn Australia, 1971; TN St Univ Grad Sch of Ed, 1977-78; Grad Prog in Public Adm, Univ of TN, 1978; Exec Mgmt Prog in St and Local Govt, Harvard Univ Kennedy Sch of Govt, 1979; pa/Admissions Cnslr, TN Tech Univ; Asst Dir of Admissions and Records, Univ of TN; Dir of Devel and Alumni Relats, Univ of TN; Exec Asst to Chancellor, Univ of TN; Asst Commr of Revenue Opers, TN Dept of Revenue; TN Tech Ed Foun, Chm 1981-82; AAUW; cp/Nashville Bar Aux, TN Tech Fund Raising Com; r/Vine St Christian; hon/TN Outstg Yg Wom,

1979; Intl Yth in Achmt Awd, 1981; Mortar Bd, Wom's Hon Soc; Phi Kappa Phi; W/W Among Students in Cols and Univs; W/W Am Wom.

OLSON, DONNA RAE oc/Medical Technologist, Educational Technologist; b/Oct 20, 1947; h/6001 Landon Lane, Bethesda, MD 20817; ba/Bethesda, MD; p/Mr and Mrs Roy W Olson, Bethesda, MD; ed/AB in Biol 1964, BS in Med Technol 1966, MA in Ednl Technol 1973, Cath Univ of Am; MA in Hlth Care Mgmt and Supvn, Ctl MI Univ, 1981; pa/Clin Chem Technol Supvr 1965-69, Tchg Coor, Sch of Med Technol 1969-72, Wash Hosp Ctr; Clin Chem Technologist, NIH, 1972-; Affil Mem, Am Soc of Clin Pathologists; Am Soc of Med Technologists; Am Mgmt Assn; Clin Lab Mgmt Assn; Tchg Coor, DC Soc of Med Technologists, 1979-81; r/Cath; hon/Profl Acknowledgement of Cont'd Ed, Am Soc for Med Technol, 1976, 1977; Superior Wk Perf Awd, US Dept HEW-Public Hlth Ser, 1977; Superior Perf Awd, Computer Cadre, US Dept HEW-NIH, 1978; Employee Suggestion Cash Awd, US Dept HEW-NIH, 1978; Med Technol Cert, Am Soc of Clin Pathologists, 1965-; Cert, Clin Lab Scist, Nat Cert Agy for Clin Lab Scists, 1980-; W/W Am Wom.

OLSON, MARIAN L oc/Chief of Planning and Environmental Compliance Branch; b/Oct 15, 1933; h/1519 Southeast Madison, Bartlesville, OK 74003; ba/Bartlesville, OK; p/Sherwood (dec) and Katherine Lahman, Tulsa, OK; ed/AA, Liberal Arts, Wm Woods Jr Col, 1953; Polit Sci 1954, MA in Elem Ed 1962, Univ of CO; EdD, Higher Ed Adm, Univ of Tulsa, 1969; pa/Chief of Planning and Envir Compliance Br, US Dept of Energy, Bartlesville Energy Technol Ctr, 1979-; Prog Analyst 1977-79, Tech Asst for Planning and Budget, Div of Coal Conversion and Utilization 1976-77, Staff Asst, CCU 1975-76, US Dept of Energy, Wash, DC; Prog Assoc in Res Adm, MT St Univ, 1970-75; Other Previous Positions; Kappa Delta Pi; Phi Alpha Theta; Gamma Epsilon Alpha; Am Assn for Budget and Prog Anal; Wom in Energy, St Bd of Dirs; hon/Pubs, "Utilities in the Transportation Fuel Business? Why Not?" 1982, "Unconventional Sources of Natural Gas: Laws, Regulations, and Development" 1980, "Development of Coadbed Methane as an Energy Source" 1979, "What's Holding Up Coalbed Methane Development?" 1978, "Institutional Constraints to the Development of Coadbed Methane" 1978; Ldrs in Ed; W/W Am Wom; DIB; W/W Govt.

OMAN, LAFEL EARL oc/Attorney-at-Law, District Judge Pro-Tem; b/May 7, 1912; h/510 Camino Pinones, Santa Fe, NM 87501; ba/Santa Fe, NM; m/Arlie Giles; c/Sharon O Beck, Phyllis O Bowman, Conrad Lafel, Kester Lafel; p/Earl A and Mabel Larsen Oman (dec); ed/LLB, 1936; JD, Univ of UT Col of Law; mil/USN 1943-46, Lt; pa/Law Pract, SLC and Helper, UT, 1937-39; Law Pract, Las Cruces, NM, 1948-66; Denver, CO, US Civil Ser Comm, Investigator and Field Examr, 1940-43, 1946; Albuquerque, NM, Vets Adm Ofc of Chief Atty, 1946-48; ABA; NM Bar Assn; UT Bar Assn; Dona Ana Co Bar Assn, Pres 1952-53; First Jud Dist Bar Assn; SWn Legal Foun Local

Rep, Law-Sci Acad; Def Res Inst; Am Trial Lwyrs Assn; Phi Alpha Delta; Inst of Jud Adm; Sect of Jud Adm, ABA; Appellate Judges Conf; Nat Legal Aid and Defender Assn; Am Judic Soc, Bd of Dirs 1970-74; Cont'd Legal Ed of NM Inc, Bd of Dirs; Am Law Inst; Conf of Chief Justice; Asst City Atty, Las Cruces, 1958-59; City Atty, T or C, 1959-61; NM Bd of Bar Examrs, 1964-66; NM Jud Standards Comm, 1968-70, 1971-72; NM Jud Coun, 1972-76; NM Ct of Appeals, 1966-70; NM Supr Ct, 1971-; Chief Justice, NM Supr Ct, 1976-77; cp/Rotary Clb of Las Cruces, 1948-66, Pres 1952-53; Rotary Clb of Santa Fe, 1966-, Dir 1973-74, VP 1975-76, Pres 1976-77; NM Hist Soc; Hist Soc of Santa Fe; Santa Fe Opera Guild; Vis'g Nurse Ser of Santa Fe Inc, Bd of Dirs 1980-, Pres 1983-; hon/Jud Ser Awd, Judge of the Yr, St Bar of NM, 1974; Herbert Harley Awd, Am Judic Soc, 1974; Outstg Ser Awd, St Bar of NM, 1974; Credential in Recog and Apprec of Active Ser on Supr Ct of NM, Jud Conf of NM, 1976; Meml, Legis of St of NM, 1977; Testimonial of Gratitude and Respect, NM Jud Coun, 1977; Symbol of Apprec, All Law Clks and Secy of NM Ct of Appeals, NM Supr Ct, 1977; Cert of Apprec, Colleagues on NM Supr Ct, for Contbns Made, 1977; W/W World; W/W Am; W/W W; W/W Am Law.

O'NEILL, CATHERINE ANN oc/Free-Lance Writer; b/Dec 25, 1950; h/3014 Dent Place, Northwest, Washington, DC 20007; ba/Washington, DC; m/Michael Glennon; p/Edward and Lois O'Neill, Canfee, Tuosist via Killarney, Ireland; ed/The Sidwell Friends Sch, 1968; BA, Eng, Middlebury Col, 1972; MA, Eng, Georgetown Univ, 1977; pa/Tchr, Nat Cathedral Sch for Girls, 1972-76; Asst to the Lit Editor, *The New Republic*, 1976-77; Asst Editor, *Books & Arts*, The Chronicle of Higher Ed, 1977-78; Writer, Spec Pubs Div, The Nat Geographic Soc, 1979-82; Reporter, *USA Today*, 1982-83; Writer, Nat Geographic Soc, 1983-; Wash Writers Pub'g House, Edit Bd; r/Epis; hon/Pubs, *The Daffodil Farmer* 1979, Num Articles; Grad, cum laude, Middlebury Col, 1972; Fellow, VA Ctr for the Creat Arts, 1981; Fellow, Alfred Univ Sum Place, 1983.

O'NEILL-BARBER, KATHLEEN MARIE oc/Resource Room Coordinator; b/Oct 5, 1954; h/16 Walnut Street, Montvale, NJ 07645; ba/Garfield, NJ; m/Dr James Joseph Barber; p/John and Anne O'Neill, Smithtown, NY; ed/AA, Liberal Arts, Suffolk Co Commun Col, 1972; BA, Stony Brook Univ, 1975; MS, Spec Ed, C W Post Univ, 1977; Doct Cand, Human Devel and Orgl Studies, Boston Univ, 1979-83; pa/Resource Room Coor, Garfild Public Schs, 1982-83; Spec Needs, Jr HS, Chelsea Public Schs, 1981-82; Alcoholic and Psychi Cnslr, New England Meml Hosp, 1980-81; Resource Room Title I, Quincy Public Schs, 1980-81; Spec Ed, Mid Country Schs, 1977-79; Admitting Ofcr, Smithtown Gen Hosp, 1972-77; Cnslr, Assn for Help of Retarded Chd, 1972; r/Cath; hon/Pi Lambda Theta S'ship, Alpha Gamma Chapt, 1980-81; Intl Exch, Employmt Prog to England, UN Plaza, 1980; Indiv Travel/Study Prog: England and France, La Verne Univ, 1979; Scholastic Travel S'ship,

Ireland Coun for Intl Ednl Exch, 1978; U Comml Travelers of Am, S'ship for Grad Studies, 1977; W/W Am Cols.

ONGLINGSWAN, WILLIAM T oc/Physician; b/Apr 8, 1946; h/PO Box 222, Willimantic, CT 06226; ba/Windham, CT; m/Rebecca; c/Aaron John, Alastair Joseph; p/Francisco and Angela Tiu Ongkingyee, Manila, Philippines; ed/BA, Manila Ctl Univ, Far En Univ, 1954; MD, cum laude, Manila Ctl Univ Col of Med, 1961; mil/CT Air NG, 1978-, Lt Col 103rd Clin Cmdr 1978-79; pa/Intern, N Gen Hosp, 1960-61; Resident Phys, San Lazaro Hosp, 1961-62; Phys in Med/Surg, Marian Gen Hosp, 1962-64; Intern, Grace Gen Hosp, 1964-65; Resident, St Boniface Gen Hosp, 1965-66; Resident, St John Gen Hosp, 1966-67; Victoria Gen Hosp and Pathol Inst, 1967-69; Assoc Dir, Kings City Labs, 1970-73; Med Ofcr, Fall River Union Gen Hosp, 1969-70; Pvt Med Pract, 1961-; AF Ofcr, Med Flight Surg, 1978-; Epsilon Delta Chi, Fellow; St Police Surg, 1979-; Willimantic Police Surg, 1978-; Dir of Hlth, City; Alternate Dir, Town of Windham, 1979-; FAA Med Examr, 1979-; Am Fam Phys, Fellow; Mil Surgs Assn, Fellow; Civil Aviation Med Assn, Fellow; USAF Flight Surgs, Fellow; Alliance of USAF Flight Surgs, Fellow; cp/K of C, 3rd and 4th Deg; Kiwanis Clb, Pres for 2 Terms; Elks Clb; Nat Security Coun; Repub Pres Task Force; r/Cath; hon/HS Hon; Col High Hon; CT Air Guard Unit Cit; Willimantic Police Dept Ser Medal; Martial Arts Medals; Soccer Medal, Trophies.

ONLEY, NONA S oc/Executive; b/Jun 20, 1949; h/28129 Peacock Ridge Drive, Rancho Palos Verdes, CA 90274; ba/Salt Lake City, UT; p/Kenneth and Elaine Peters, Rockford, IL; ed/Grad, Stillman Val HS, 1967; pa/Sales, Filter Dynamics Inc, 1974-76; Wn Reg Mgr, Armor All Prods, 1977-80; VP, Espree Prods, 1980-; Netwk Dir, Nat Assn of Female Execs; Mem, Automotive Parts and Accessories Assn, Specialty Equip Mfrs Assn; hon/W/W Am Wom.

OPALA, MARIAN P oc/Supreme Court Justice; b/Jan 20, 1921; h/5709 Northwest 64th, Oklahoma City, OK 73132; ba/Oklahoma City, OK; c/Joseph Anthony; ed/BS in Ec, OK City Univ, 1957; JD, OK City Univ Sch of Law, 1953; LLM, NY Univ Col of Law, 1968; LLD, OK City Univ, 1981; pa/Adj Prof, Univ of Tulsa Col of Law, 1982-; Justice, Supr Ct of OK, 1978-; Judge, Wkrs' Compensation Ct, 1978; Presiding Judge, St Indust Ct, 1977-78; Adj Prof, Univ of OK Col of Law, 1969-; Adm Dir, Cts of OK, 1968-77; Legal Asst to Justice McInerney, OK Supr Ct, 1967-68; Prof of Law, OK City Univ Sch of Law, 1965-69; Pvt Pract in OKC, 1965-67; Other Previous Positions; Phi Delta Phi Legal Frat; Am Soc for Legal Hist; NY Univ Inst of Jud Adm; OK Heritage Assn; Fellow, Am Bar Foun; Coun on Juv Delinquency, Exec Com 1970-; hon/Order of the Coif; Val Forge Hon Cert, Freedoms Foun at Val Forge, 1980; OCU Dist'd Alumni Awd, 1979; Am Soc for Public Adm's Awd for Public Admr for Month of Dec, 1978; OK Bar Assn's Law and Citizenship Ed Spec Com, 197-78; Other Hons; W/W.

OPIE, KATHLEEN oc/Teacher of Language Arts and Social Studies; b/Jan

13, 1944; h/14331 West Virginia Drive, Lakewood, CO 80228; ba/Lakewood, CO; m/William G; c/Sandy; p/Alfred and Anna Iacobucci, Denver, CO; ed/BA, Elem Ed and Bus Ed, CO St Col, 1966; MA, Elem Sch Adm, Univ of No CO, 1971; pa/Jefferson Co Public Schs: Green Mtn 1966-67, Belmar 1967-70, Eiber 1971-74, Irwin 1975-83, Eiber 1983-; NEA; Pi Lambda Theta, Pres 1981-83, Treas 1976-78; Delta Kappa Gamma; CO Assn for Supvn and Curric Devel; CO Coun for Social Studies; Nat Coun for the Social Studies; CO Language Arts Soc; Treas, CO Coun for the Social Studies, 1983; Registration Chp, Rocky Mtn Reg Social Studies Conf, 1983; r/Cath; hon/Chp and Curric Writer for 5th Grade Jefferson Co Public Schs Social Studies Tchrs' Guide, 1981-82; Writer for Career Ed Guide, Jefferson Co Schs, 1978; Appt'd by Gov of CO to St's Profl Practices Comm, 1974; Presenter at NE Reg Social Studies Conf, 1982; Presenter at Rocky Mtn Reg Social Studies Conf, 1982; W/ W W.

OPLER, LEWIS ALAN oc/Director of Psychopharmacology Unit; b/Apr 16, 1948; h/106 New England Drive, Stamford, CT 06903; ba/Bronx, NY; m/Annette Arcario; c/Mark Gregory, Daniel Joseph, Michelle Suzanne, Douglas Jonathan; p/Charlotte Sagoff, Acton, MA; ed/BA, magna cum laude, Biochem Scis, Harvard Univ, 1969; PhD in Pharm 1976, MD 1976, Albert Einstein Col of Med; pa/Asst Prof of Psychi, Albert Einstein Col of Med, 1979-; Dir of Psychopharm Unit, Bronx Psychi Ctr, Albert Einstein Col of Med; Psychi, Bronx Psychi Ctr, 1979-; Am Psychi Assn, 1980-; cp/Harvard Clb of Fairfield Co, 1980-; r/Jewish; hon/Author, Articles in Basic Sci and Clin Psychi Jours (for Example, "Tardive Dyskinesia and Institutional Practice: Current Issues and Guidelines" in *Hospital and Community Psychiatry*, 1980).

O'QUINN, MILTON L oc/Information Systems Executive; b/Apr 19, 1944; h/4822 Valleyview South, West Bloomfield, MI 48033; ba/Birmingham, MI; m/Kathleen Amelia Jamerson; c/Kathleen Louise, Lynn, Milt, John, Lisa; p/John William and Cleodia Dawkins O'Quinn, Chicago, IL; ed/BA, Tillotson Col, 1967; Student, Univ of Chgo Grad Sch of Bus 1968-72, Loyola Univ Grad Sch of Indust Relats 1973-74; mil/USNR, 1962-68; pa/Sales Rep, Lever Bros, 1967; Acct Mgr, Procter & Gamble Toiletries Div, 1968-71; Acct Mgr, Sys Spec 1971-74, 6500 Prod Spec 1975-76, Sales Mgr 1976-78, Br Mgr of Sales 1978-80, Reg Sales Opers Mgr 1980-81, Reg Mgr of Sales Progs 1981-82, Reg Sales Mgr 1982-, Xerox Corp; Regional Sales Mgr 1982-, Regional Sales Mgr Sys Mktg Div 1983-84, Electronic Laser Printers, Arlington Heights, IL; Regional Mgr, Agt, Dealer, Mktg, Birmingham, MI, 1985; Kappa Alpha Psi Frat; Bd of Dirs, Marcy-Newberry Assocs; cp/Fdr, O'Quinn Royal Gladiators Drum and Bugle Corps; Past VP, W-Side Assn for Commun Action; BSA, comm of BSA #3365, Former Scoutmaster 4 Yrs; Century Clb; Lions Clb Intl, Southfiled Br; r/Prot; hon/BSA, Eagle Scout, 1958; All City Basketball, Chgo, 1962; Sales Rep of the Yr, Proctor & Gamble, 1969; Sales Mgr of the Yr,

Xerox, 1977; W/W MW; W/W Am; W/ W World; W/W Fin and Indust; W/W Commun Ldrs.

ORLANS, F BARBARA oc/Executive Director; b/Jan 14, 1928; h/7106 Laverock Lane, Bethesda, MD 20817; ba/Washington, DC; m/Herbert Morton; c/Andrew, Nicholas; p/Christopher and Flora Hughes (dec); ed/PhD in Physiol 1956, MSc in Physiol 1954, London Univ, England; BSc in Physiol and Anatomy, B'ham Univ, England, 1949; pa/Exec Dir, Scists Ctr for Animal Wel; Sci Ofcr, Cardiac Diseases Br 1979-, Exec Secy of Nat Heart, Lung and Blood Adv Coun 1977-79, Hlth Scist Admr, Review Br 1975-77, Nat Heart, Lung and Blood Inst, NIH; Grants Assocs Prog, Div of Res Grants, NIH, 1974-75; Sr Staff Scist, Population Info Prog, Biol Scis Communication Proj, George Wash Univ Med Ctr, 1973-74; Other Previous Positions; Am Soc for Pharm and Exptl Therapeutics; Am Heart Assn; Nat Sci Tchrs Assn; Nat Assn of Biol Tchrs; hon/Pubs, *Animal Care: From Protozoa to Small Mammals* 1977, "Animal Welfare" 1980, Num Others; Res Fellow, Asthma Res Coun of Great Brit, 1954-56; Riker Fellow, 1959-60; Blue Pencil Awd, Nat Assn of Govt Communicators, 1980; Am Men and Wom Sci; World W/W Wom; W/W Technol; W/W Frontier Sci and Technol.

ORPHAN, BECKY STAIKOS oc/Educational Administrator; b/Feb 23, 1931; h/6600 North Ridge, Chicago, IL 60626; ba/Chicago, IL; p/Pelagia Staikos, Chicago, IL; ed/BS 1957, MS 1963, Chgo Tchrs Col; Ednl Spec Deg, FL St Univ, 1979; pa/Instr, Chgo St Univ, 1974-77; Conslt, NEn Univ Desegregation Sem, 1982-; Sch Prin, L A Budlong Sch, 1971-; Prin, Mason Primary and Child Parent Ctr, 1969-71; Chgo Public Sch Tchr, Mayer Sch 1961-69, Knickerbocker Sch 1957-61; Sum Coor, Lakeview HS 1964-65, Senn HS 1967, 1968; Chp, IL St Biling Adv Coun, 1982-83; IL St Biling Adv Coun, 1977-; Pres, Aux One of Chgo Prins' Assn, 1974-79; VP, Hellenic Coun on Ed, 1974-75; AHEPA, 1963-; Ednl Adv Com of Gov Thompson's Task Force on Chd, 1982; Biling Adv Com, Chgo Bd of Ed, 1982-; r/Greek Orthodox; hon/Co-Authored Previous Chgo Bd of Ed Language Arts Curric and Sci Curric; Authored First Greek Biling Fed Proposal and St of IL Proposal; Grad F'ship Awds, Fed, Sums of 1977, 1978, 1979; Outstg Ser Awd, Budlong Sch, Greek Biling Coun, 1975; W/W Am Wom; W/ W World's Wom; W/W MW; Commun Ldrs in Am; Book of Hon; Dist'd Ams; Men and Wom of Distn.

ORSER, ROYAL E oc/High School Principal; b/Apr 7, 1938; h/1917 View Drive, Elko, NV 89801; ba/Elko, NV; m/Diane A; p/Rolf Orser Sr, Las Vegas, NV; ed/BS, Bemidji St Univ, 1962; MA, Univ of the Pacific, 1967; mil/6 Months Active Duty; 5½ Yr Active Resv; pa/Prin, Carlin Combined Sch, 1984-; Prin 1978-83, Vice Prin 1973-78, Elko Jr Sr HS; Prin, Northside Elem, 1972-73; Prin, Wells Combined Schs, 1968-72; Tchr, Elko HS, 1962-68; cp/Rotary, 1972-82; Chm, Elko Co Repub Party, 1979-80; Mem and Chm, NV St Coun on the Arts, 1979-83, Pres, Wells C of C, 1971; r/Meth; hon/Pub, Excell in Ed for US Dept of Ed, 1984; Hon St Farmer,

Hon Life Mem, Future Homemakers HS; Hon'd as One of 77 in US for Excell in Ed, 1983; Outstg Edrs of Am.

ORSZULAK, RICHARD STEWART oc/Chief Accountant; b/Oct 4, 1957; h/PO Box 1795, Pittsburg, KS 66762; ba/Pittsburg, KS; m/Tammy; p/John and Cleo Orszulak, Girard, KS; ed/BSBA, Pittsburg St Univ, 1979; Postgrad Wk in Acctg, Pittsburg St Univ, 1980; pa/Acct, Biron Inc 1981-82, DFW Petro Inc 1982-83; Owner, Mgmt and Financial Sers, 1983-; Chief Acct and Asst to the Pres, Hagman's Inc, 1983-; Am Ec Assn; Nat Assn of Accts; Am Fin Assn; Financial Mgmt Assn; En KS Oil and Gas Assn; Am Football Coaches Assn; Pittsburg St Univ Alumni Assn; Girard HS Alumni Assn; Crawford Co Farm Bur; Prodrs' Coop Assn; cp/F'ship of Christian Athletes; r/Bapt; Girard Bible Ch; hon/W/W MW; Outstg Yg Men of Am; Personalities of W and MW; Biogl Roll of Hon; Men of Achmt; Intl Book of Hon; 2,000 Notable Ams; Commun Ldrs of World; Intl W/W Intells; W/W Fin and Indust; Dir of Dist'd Ams.

OSBORN, TERRELL JAN oc/Assistant Professor of Management; b/Oct 19, 1941; h/1826 Meadowbrook Road, Prescott, AZ 86301; ba/Prescott, AZ; m/Elizabeth Lynn Stafford; c/Kristin Nicole; p/Ralph Osborn, Tucson, AZ; LouVelma Pearl Osborn (dec); ed/Dr of Bus Adm, US Intl Univ, 1980; MBA, Univ of UT, 1977; BA, Chem, Univ of KS, 1963; mil/AF Ofcr, 1963-83; Ret'd, 1983; pa/F-4 Phantom Fighter Pilot and Instr Pilot in US and Combat, USAF, 1965-75; Dir of Safety, Luke AFB, 1975-78; Chief, Aircraft Accident Final Eval Br, HQs, USAF, 1978-83; Asst Prof of Mgmt, Embry-Riddle Aeronautical Univ, 1983-; Am Soc of Safety Engrs; Soc of Air Safety Investigators; Intl Coun for Small Bus; Acad of Mgmt; cp/Morning Kiwanis Clb of Redlands, Pres 1982-83; Mile-Hi Kiwanis Clb of Prescott; hon/Author, 10 Articles in AF Safety and Mgmt Jours during the Yrs 1979-83; Dist'd Flying Cross, 1967; AF Chief of Staff Indiv Safety Awd, 1977; Election to Beta Gamma Sigma, Nat Bus and Mgmt Hon, 1977; Outstg Yg Men of Am; W/W W; W/W CA.

OSBORNE, MICHAEL J oc/Minister; b/Mar 31, 1952; h/Route 5, Box 207, Troutville, VA 24175; ba/Troutville, VA; m/Susan Hudson; c/Shay Michael; p/Ralph (dec) and Ruth M Osborne, South Boston, VA; ed/BS, Averett Col, 1977; MDiv, SEn Bapt Theol Sem, 1983; pa/Min, Mt Zion Bapt Ch 1980-81, Calvary Bapt Ch 1981-83, Troutville Bapt Ch 1983-; VP, Fin, Soc for Advmt of Mgmt, Averett Chapt, 1977; Assn Christian Marriage Enrichment; cp/VP, Halifax JCs, 1979; Chaplain, Halifax JCs, 1980; Bapt Chd's Home Rep, Beulah Assn, 1982-83; Var Yth Orgs; Coach, Yth Football, Baseball, Basketball, Soccer; F'ship of Christian Athletes; VP, Univ of Richmond Chapt, FCA; r/Bapt; hon/Nat Hon Soc, 1970.

OSBORNE, WALTER WYATT oc/Consultant, Author; b/Oct 31, 1925; h/4209 Saltwater Boulevard, Tampa, FL 33615; ba/Same; m/Flora Drewry Bethell; c/Walter Wyatt Jr, Bethell Anne, Alease Drewry, Anders Wright Osborne Gonzalez; p/Garnett Elmer Osborne, Hampton, VA; Maggie Elvira Anderson Osborne (dec); ed/BS in

Agronomy 1951, MS in Plant Pathol and Physiol 1958, VPI & SU; PhD, Plant Pathol and Nematology, Rutgers Univ, 1962; mil/AUS, 2½ Yrs; pa/Prof (Ret'd) of Plant Pathol, VPI & SU; Prior Dir, Field Res and Ext Activs on the Control of Diseases of Tobacco, Soybean and Peanuts in VA; Sigma Xi; Soc of Nematologists; European Soc of Nematologists; Org of Tropical Nematologists; Am Phytopathological Soc; Potomac Div, Am Phytopathological Soc; So Div, Am Phytopathological Soc; Am Soc of Agronomy; VA Acad of Sci; VA Pesticide Assn; VA Plant Protection Conf Orgl Chm; AAAS; r/Meth-Epis; hon/Pubs, "Effect of Temperature on Development and Reproduction of *Globodera solanacearum*" 1982, "Influence of *Meloidogyne incognita* on the Content of Amino Acids and Nicotine in Tobacco Grown Under Gnotobiotic Conditions" 1975, "Relationships between the Population Density of *Meloidogyne incognita* and Growth of Tobacco" 1975, "Peanut Pod Rot Disease Control" 1973, Num Others; Ldrship Awd, So Soybean Disease Wkrs, 1980; Recip, Awd of Excell, So Soybean Disease Wkrs' Coun, 1974; Nat CoChm of Soc of Nematologists/Am Standards for Testing and Mats Com, 1973; Man of the Yr in Agri, Colombia, S Am, 1972; Num Other Hons; Intl W/W Ed.

O'SHAUGHNESSY, MARIE MARGUERITTE MORTON oc/Early Elementary Educator; b/Mar 21, 1924; h/4695 Forest Drive, Watkins Lake, Pontiac, MI 48054; ba/Pontiac, MI; m/Alvin Carl; c/Doris Sharon June, Laura Kathryn June, Alice Dawn June Addison, George Widman Morton June, Stephen Charles June, Jennifer Ellen June; Stepchd: Laurel O'Shaughnessy Likens, Roxanne O'Shaughnessy, Kathleen Hammergren; p/Charles Stuart (dec) and Marie P Morton, Birdsboro, PA; ed/BA, summa cum laude, Olivet Col, 1946; Postgrad, Wayne St Univ, 1957-58; Postgrad in Ed, Oakland Univ, 1968-70; MA in Guid and Cnslg, Oakland Univ, 1975; Student, Mary Grove Col, 1978; pa/St of MI Social Wkr, MI Social Sers in Pontiac, 1966-68; Tchr, 2nd and 3rd Grades, Four Towns Elem Sch in Waterford, 1970-; Student Govt Sponsor, Four Towns Sch, 1975-; Cnslr, Substance Abuse, RAP Ctr, 1975; NEA; MI Ed Assn; Waterford Ed Assn; APGA; Am Sch Cnslrs Assn; MI Elem Sch Guid Assn; AAUW, 1952-66; cp/NOW; GSA, Com Chair for 2 Yrs, Asst Ldr for 2 Yrs, Ldr for 10 Yrs for Jr, Cadette and Sr Trail Blazer Troops of Cass Lake; r/Soc of Friends; hon/W/W MW; World W/W Wom; Intl Book of Hon.

OSIGWEH, CHIMEZIE A B oc/University Professor; b/Nov 11, 1955; h/PO Box 932, Kirksville, MO 63501; ba/Kirksville, MO; m/Brenda Jean; c/Chinelo Amarachi-Genevieve Nkiruka, Chinenye Nkechinyere-Vivian Nneka; p/Mr and Mrs Joseph A A Osigweh, Owerri, Nigeria; ed/PhD 1982, MLHR 1981, MA 1980, OH St Univ; BSc w Hons, magna cum laude, E TN St Univ, 1978; pa/Asst Prof of Bus Adm, NE MO St Univ, 1982-; Res Assoc, Mershon Ctr for Res, 1982, 1979; Instr of Intl Relats 1981, Grad Tchg Assoc of Polit Sci 1981, OH St Univ; Acad of Mgmt; Acad of Intl Bus; Am Inst for Decision Scis; Assn of Vol Action Scholars; Behavioral Scis

Conf; Case Res Assn; MW Bus Adm Assn; r/Christianity; hon/Pubs, *Improving Problem-Solving Participation* 1983, *Petals of Fire* 1984, *Professional Management* (Forthcoming), *Pyramids of Shame: The Poems of George Aton* (Forthcoming), Many Learned Articles in the Areas of Indust Relats, Prob-Solving, Mgmt, Ec and Intl Bus; OH St Univ Nom for Morris Abrams Awd in Intl Relats, 1982; Dean's Lists, 1976-78; W/W Among Students in Am Univs and Cols; Intl Yth in Achmt.

OSSINK, NANCY LEE oc/Executive; b/Mar 30, 1944; h/926 Keith Avenue, Anniston, AL 36201; ba/Anniston, AL; c/Tammy Sue, Vicki Marie; p/John and Doris Lenting, Muskegon, MI; ed/Grad, Muskegon HS, 1962; Completed Wom's Gen Course in Orthotics and Prosthetics, 1980; Completed Orthotics Class, 1981; Completed Mastectomy Class, 1981; pa/Owner, Pres, Anniston Hlth and Sickroom Supplies, 1976-; Opened, Piedmont/Anniston Hlth and Sickroom Supplies, 1982-; Asst Admr 1973-78, Ofc Mgr 1972-73, Anniston Rehab Ctr; Nat Assn of Retail Druggists, 1981; Am Surg Trade Assn, 1981; Nat Cert in Fitting of Orthotics and Prosthetics; Appt'd by Blue Cross Blue Shield, Orthotics and Prosthetics Advr, 1981; Durable Med Equip Adv Bd for St of AL, 1981-; NE AL Reg Med Ctr Home Hlth Care Adv Bd, 1980-; r/Assem of God; hon/Nom'd from Calhoun Co for Outstg Yg Bus Wom of Am, 1973; W/W S and SW.

OSTAR, ALLAN WILLIAM oc/Higher Education Association President; b/Sep 4, 1924; h/6322 Walhonding Road, Bethesda, MD 20016; ba/Washington, DC; m/Roberta Hutchison; c/Karen, Rebecca, John; p/William and Rose Mirmow Ostar (dec); ed/BA in Psych, PA St Univ, 1948; Awd'd, 13 Hon Degs from Cols and Univs throughout US; mil/Combat Infantryman in Europe w 42nd Rainbow Div, WWII; pa/Pres 1979-, Exec Dir 1965-79, Am Assn of St Cols and Univs; Dir, Jt Ofc of Instnl Res, Nat Assn of St Univs and Land-Grant Cols, 1959-65; Other Previous Positions; Higher Ed Adv Com of Ed Comm of the Sts; Secretariat of the Am Coun on Ed; Pres, Am Energy Wk; Adv Coun, Univ of MD Inst for Res in Higher and Adult Ed; r/Unitarian; hon/Author, Num Articles; Among the 44 Most Influential Ldrs in Am Higher Ed, *Change Magazine*; Among First Grp of Edrs to Be Invited to People's Repub of China, 1975; Cent Achmt Awd, Univ of So CO, 1979; Alumni Fellow, PA St Univ, 1975; Recip, World Peace through Ed Medal, Intl Assn of Univ Pres, 1975.

OSTBY, ROSE MARY oc/Personnel and Administrative Business Consultant; b/Jan 26, 1932; h/1832 Northwest Douglas Place, Corvallis, OR 97330; ba/Corvallis, OR; m/Kenneth A; c/Jeffrey, Kyle, Kevin; ed/BA, Bus Adm, Am Home Study Inst, 1957; Student, Julliard Sch of Music 1950-51, Hunter Col 1951-52; pa/Self-Employed: Co-Owner, Pacific Rug & Furniture 1973-82, Pers and Adm Bus Conslt 1973-, Rose M Ostby Secretarial Typing Ser and Word Processor 1974-79, Temporaries Unltd 1974-78, Rose M Ostby Bkkpg Ser 1973-75, Wise Pers Agy 1973-79; Employmt Cnslr, Action Pers Agy, 1971-72; Employmt Cnslr, Snelling &

Snelling Employmt Agy, 1970-71; Other Previous Positions; hon/Nom'd OR Bus Ldr of the Yr-Golden Pioneer Awd, 1979; Nom'd for First Citizen Awd, 1979; Nom'd for First Citizen Awd and One of Three Finalists, 1978; Progress and Prosperity Awd, 1978; Pres's Awd, C of C, 1978; George Awd, C of C, 1976; W/W Am Wom.

OSTROM, BARBARA DIANE oc/Interior Designer, Business Owner; b/Nov 28, 1942; h/28 Hopper Farm Road, Upper Saddle River, NJ 07458; ba/Same; m/Roy Daniel; c/Meredith Joy, Roy Daniel III; p/Mr and Mrs Robert Mead, Bergenfield, NJ; ed/BFA, NY Univ, 1964; MS, Interior Design, Pratt Inst, 1967; Cert, Traphagen Sch of Fashion; Cert, NY Sch of Interior Design; pa/Owner, Barbara Ostrom Assocs Inc, 1973-; Home Fashion Coor, Bloomingdales, 1971-73; Dir of Design, CNI, 1970-71; Dir of Design, Katzman Assocs Inc, 1964-70; Am Soc of Interior Designers, Secy, Bd of Dirs; AIA; cp/Altrusa, Bd of Dirs; r/Christian; hon/Pub'd in *House Beautiful, House and Garden, McCalls, Family Circle, NY Times, Interior Design, Interiors*; Columnist, *The Town Journal*; W/W E; W/W Am Wom; Commun Ldrs of Am; Men and Wom of Distn.

OSWALD, ERNEST JOHN oc/Food Service Employee; b/Jan 20, 1943; h/128 Laguna Street, San Francisco, CA 94102; ba/Fremont, CA; p/Mr and Mrs Ernest Oswald, Bronx, NY; ed/BA, Eng Lit, Fordham Univ, 1973; AAS, Retail Bus Mgmt, Bronx Commun Col, 1967; pa/Poetry Editor, *Heirs Mag*, 1973-81; r/Epis; hon/Poetry Pub'd in Approx 50 Lit Mags in US and Europe; Small Press Book Reviewer (Free-Lance) w Appearances in Several Small Press Reviewers; Intl W/W Poetry; Poets and Writers.

OSWALD, ROY oc/Owner and Manager of Rental Property; b/Jul 20, 1944; h/1136 Lombard Drive, Montgomery, AL 36109; ba/Same; p/Johnnie E and Ruby C Oswald, Montgomery, AL; ed/BS in Bus Adm, Troy St Univ, 1969; Dipl in Graphic Arts, John Patterson Tech Col; mil/AUS, Vietnam, 1969-71; pa/Salesman, Oswald's Bus Machines, 1971; Sanitarian, Montgomery Co Hlth Dept, 1971-72; Buyer, St of AL Mtl Hlth Dept; Salesman, OTASCO, 1973; Social Wkr, Autauga Co DPS, 1973-76; Self-Employed, Owner and Mgr of Rental Property; Acad of Am Poets; Intl Acad of Poets; Am Poets F'ship Soc; POETS; Wn World Haiku Soc; Soc of Christian Poets; hon/4 Poetry Books Pub'd, *After the Storm-The Rainbow* 1977, *Venture Inward* 1978, *Fruitful Thoughts* 1981, *Inner Echoes*; Am Biogl Inst; Intl Biogl Assn; Recip, Many Prizes, Awds, Certs, in Var Recognitions for Poetry, 1977-; Intl Authors W/W; Men of Achmt; Personalities of S; Dir of Dist'd Ams; 2,000 Notable Ams; Intl Book of Hon; DIB.

OTA, MARLENE MAE oc/Cytotechnologist; b/Nov 4, 1948; h/1285 Blazewood, Riverside, CA 92507; ba/Loma Linda, CA; m/Koichi Robert; p/Chi and Aiko Omori, Moses Lake, WI; ed/Cert in Cytology, Univ of WA, 1971; BS in Bus Adm, Univ of Redlands, 1981; pa/Cytotechnologist, Wn Clin Lab 1972-74, N Area Cytology Lab (Pt-time) 1972-74, St Bernardino Hosp (Pt-time) 1974-76, Parkview Hosp, 1980-; Prog

Dir, Sch of Cytotechnol and Supt of Cytotechnol Dept 1975-, Instr, Sch of Cytology 1975-, Instr, Pathol Residents 1975-, Loma Linda U Med Ctr; Am Soc Clin Pathologists; Assoc Mem, Am Soc Cytology; Am Soc Cytotechnol; CA Assn Cytology; hon/W/W Am Wom.

OTTAWAY, LOIS MARIE oc/Manager of Media Relations; b/Oct 9, 1931; h/201 North President, #3A, Wheaton, IL 60187; ba/Wheaton, IL; p/Mr Albert H Ottaway, Viola, KS; ed/BS, Tech Jour, KS St Univ, 1953; MA, Jour, Univ of IA, 1962; Spec Studies, Wheaton Col; pa/Mgr of Media Relats, World Relief, 1982-; Mgr of News Ser 1965-81, Advr, Student Publications 1959-65, Asst to Dir, News Ser 1958-59, Wheaton Col; Asst Dir, Sports Info, KS St Univ, 1953-57; Programmed Activs for Correctional Ed Inst, 1971-; Suburban Press Clb, Bd of Dirs 1982-; r/Prot; hon/ Author, Num Articles in Rel Periodicals; Vol of Yr, PACE, 1972; Sr Ldr Designation (One of 30), KS St Univ; Phi Kappa Phi; Mortar Bd Hon Socs; W/W Rel; W/W MW; Intl W/W Commun Ser; DIB.

OTTO, ELEANOR oc/Free-Lance Writer, Musician; h/400 West 43 Street, 27-T, New York, NY 10036; ba/New York, NY; c/Mrs Eva-Lee Baird; ed/BA, Univ of Rochester; Grad Studies, Columbia Univ; Music Studies, Juilliard Sch of Music, Manhattan Sch of Music; Pvt Vocal and Ballet Lessons; Grad Sch Courses in Ed, City Col; pa/Taught Adults for NY City Bd of Ed; Sang 2 Seasons in Chautauqua Opera Co; Has Performed in Num Operatic Presentations; Beggar Lady in *La Boheme*, Metro Opera, Lincoln Ctr, 1981-83; Has Lectured, Sung and Danced at Num Events Sponsored by NY Poetry Forum, NY Shelley Soc and at Christmas (1982); Read Poetry and Sang, Poe Cottage; Pub'd 3 Book of Poetry; Pub'd Art Song, "Forsythia"; ASCAP; Am Guild of Musical Artists; Eng-Spkg Union; Mark Twain Assn; NY Poetry Forum, 2nd VP; Authors and Artists of Am, Nat Recording Secy, Bd; The Shelley Soc of NY; NY City Chapt, CAAA; hon/2 Certs of Merit, Bronx Hist Soc; Certs of Merit, Centro Studi e Scambi Internazionali, Rome, Italy; Num Poetry Prizes; Cultural Doct, World Univ.

OTTO, KLAUS oc/Scientist; b/Sep 18, 1929; h/35173 West Six Mile Road, Livonia, MI 48152; ba/Dearborn, MI; m/ Christa Thomsen; c/Ina N, Peter N; p/ Theodor M W A Otto, Germany; ed/ Vordiplom 1954, Dipl 1957, Dr Rer Nat 1960, Univ of Hamburg, W Germany; pa/Res Asst, Univ of Hamburg, 1959-60; Postdoct Fellow, Argonne Nat Lab, 1960-62; Sr Res Scist, Ford Motor Co, 1962-73; Prin Res Sci Assn, 1973-81; Staff Scist, 1981; Am Chem Soc; AAAS; Sigma Xi; Res Soc of N Am, Secy-Treas 1969-81; MI Catalysis Soc, Secy Treas 1978-79, VP 1979-80, Pres 1980-81; NY Acad of Sci, Deutsche Bunsengesellschaft; r/Agnostic; hon/ Author of Num Pubs; Am Men and Wom in Sci; W/W MW; W/W Technol Today; W/W Intells; Men of Achmt; Who is Doing What in Sci and Technol.

OVERBY, GEORGE ROBERT oc/ Chancellor of Administration, President of the Board of Directors; b/Jul 21, 1923; h/5927 Windhover Drive, Orlando, FL 32805; ed/BA, FL St Univ; EdM and Specialist in Ed, Univ of FL; PhD, FL St Univ; pa/Chancellor of Freedom Univ, The Univ Without Walls; hon/Life Patron: Am Biogl Inst Res Assn, Intl Biogl Assn; Life Fellow: Intercontinental Biogl Assn, Intl Inst in Commun Ser; Life Mem: US Naval Aviation Mus, Kappa Delta Pi; Phi Delta Kappa; Am Assn of Higher Ed, NEA of the USA; Am Registry Series; Intl W/ W Intells; Prominent Life Underwriters of Am; Intl Register of Profiles; Book of Hon; W/W World; W/W Am; Commun Ldrs and Noteworthy Ams; Num Other Biogl Listings.

OVERHOLT, MILES HARVARD oc/ Television Consultant; b/Sep 30, 1921; h/8320 Frederick Place, Edmonds, WA 98020; ba/Seattle, WA; m/Jessie Foster; c/Miles Harvard, Keith Foster; p/Miles Harvard and Alma Overholt (dec); ed/ AB, Harvard Col, 1943; mil/USMCR; pa/Mktg Analyst, Dun & Bradstreet, 1947-48; Collection Mgr, Standard Oil of CA, 1948-53; Br Mgr, RCA Ser Co, 1953-63; Opers Mgr, Classified Aerospace Proj, RCA, 1963; Pres, CPS Inc, 1964-67; Mem, Pres's Exec Com, Gen Time Corp, 1970-78; Gen Mgr, Dir, Ser, Talley Industs, 1967-78; VP, Gen Mgr, NW Entertainment Netwk Inc, 1979-81; Cable Conslt, 1981-; Assn Home Appliance Mfrs; Nat Assn Microwave Distribution Ser Cos; cp/Harvard Clb; hon/Decorated, Bronze Star, Purple Heart (Two); W/W W.

OVSAK, SHELLEY JEAN oc/Ticket Agent, Ground Hostess; b/Apr 14, 1951; h/219 East 89 Street, New York, NY 10028; ba/Camp Springs, MD; p/Jan and Elinor Ovsak, New York, NY; ed/St Vincent Ferrer HS, 1969; Grace Downs Model and Air Career Col, 1969-70; AA in Home Ec, Pensacola Jr Col, 1974; BS in Hlth, PE and Rec 1976, MS in Hlth Ed 1977, Univ of W FL; MA in Hlth Care Adm, Ctl MI Univ, 1981; Currently Wkg on PhD in Hlth Care Adm, CA Wn Univ; mil/USN, 1970-73; USAF, 1979-; pa/Ticket Agt, Air Passenger Spec, Ground Hostess, USAF, 1982-; Alpha Delta Pi Nat Sorority; Delta Chi Omega Local Sorority; Phi Epsilon Kappa PE Hon; Chi Gamma Iota Vets Scholastic Hon; Sigma Iota Epsilon Profl Mgmt Frat; r/Rom Cath; hon/Greek Wom of the Yr; S'ship of the Yr Awd; Nat Alpha Delta Pi S'ship Awd of Excell; World W/W Wom; W/W Am Wom; Intl Yth in Achmt; Commun Ldrs of Am; Intl Register of Profiles; W/W Among Students in Am Cols and Univs; g/PhD.

OWEN, GARY DALE oc/Marketing Consultant, Food and General Merchandise Broker; b/Oct 3, 1936; h/8116 South Logan Drive, Littleton, CO 80122; ba/Littleton, CO; m/Beverly Jean Bretzing; c/Scott D, Kim D, Kurt D, Kristin D, Michael D; p/J H Garfield (dec) and Zoe V Owen, Boise, ID; ed/ Student, Boise Jr Col, ID St Col, 1963; BA, Mktg, Cornell, 1978; mil/USAR, 1954-63; pa/Non-Food Merchandiser, Mtn Sts Wholesale, 1961-68; Retail Grocer Owner, 1961-68; Non-Food Operator, Ryan Wholesale, 1973-75; Non-Food Merchandiser, Nat Tea Co, 1976-77; Buyer/Merchandiser, Assoc'd Grocers of CO, 1978; Founded, Gary Owen Mktg Ltd 1978, Mktg Mgmt Inc 1978; Current Pres, CO Food Brokers Assn; Denver Area Mfrs Reps Assn; Am Soc of Notaries; Nat Food Brokers Assn;

Nat Assn for Self-Employed; cp/Elks; Lions; Past Pres, JCs; Nat Rifle Assn; Appt'd to Govs Dept of Agri 7 Person Adv Bd for "Always Buy Colorado Committee"; Denver C of C; Asst Dist Commr, BSA; r/LDS; hon/Monthly Columnist for *Rocky Mountain Food Dealers Association Magazine*; Num Articles on Merchandising for Nat Trade Jours; Sales Blazer of the Yr, *Non-Food Merchandising Magazine*, 1971; Broker of the Yr, Goody Hair Care, 1978; Indust Exec of the Yr, Rocky Mtn Food Dealers, 1980; W/W W.

OWEN, STEVEN EARL oc/Resource Teacher, Curriculum Consultant; b/Jul 29, 1947; h/PO Box 504, Merced, CA 95341; ba/Merced, CA; m/Janet Gail Smith; c/Richard Earl, Shawn Marie; p/ Leland Earl (dec); Lucille Varda Owen, Atascadero, CA; ed/BA, 1969; CA Credentials, 1970; MA, 1984; pa/ Merced City Sch Dist Tchr; MCSD Resource Tchr; Curric Conslt; Instr, Fresno Pacific Col; CA Tchrs Assn; NEA; CA Math Coun, Ctl Sect Affil Rep; Nat Assn of Biol Tchrs; Nat Sci Tchrs Assn; Fdr and Chm, Merced Co Math Coun; cp/Merced Breakfast Kiwanis; r/Bapt; hon/Pubs, "From Head to Toe" 1982, "The Whole Body Book I" 1983, "Essentials of a Short Story" 1982, "Elements of Fiction" 1982, "Key to Balancing Equations" 1978, 1981, "Animal Springs," "The Mountain Men," "California Here We Come"; W/ W W.

OWENS, DANNIE KEITH oc/Assistant to the Pastor, Student Director of Training; b/Dec 10, 1961; h/36 Madison Avenue, PO Box 1278, Madison, NJ 07940; ba/Newark, NJ; m/Darcell Denise Watson-Owens; p/Marsden M and Ruby L Owens, Scotch Plains, NJ; ed/BA, Polit Sci and Phil, Wm Paterson Col, 1983; MDiv Cand, Drew Univ; pa/ Dormitory Dir, Stevens Inst of Technol, 1983; Subst Tchr, Scotch Plains Public Schs Sys, 1983-; Pastoral Asst, St Matthew's U Meth Ch, 1981-83; Data Entry Clk, Am Telephone and Telegraph, 1981; Yth on the Move for Christ Ministries; Black Ministerial Caucus, Drew Univ; Inter-Varsity Christian F'ship; cp/NAACP; r/Bapt; hon/ Authored Many Articles in Wm Paterson Christian Newsletter Jour; Dorm Dir's Awd, Stevens Tech, 1983; Var Ath Awds, Inter-Scholastic and Inter-Col; Org'd and Directed Bible/F'ship Ministries, Wm Paterson Col, 1981-83.

OWENS, GREGORY GEORGE oc/ Director of Service Programs; b/Nov 4, 1954; h/101 Summit Avenue, Mount Vernon, NY 10552; ba/Mount Vernon, NY; m/Diana Valdes; p/Dr and Mrs Alfonzo B Owens, Mount Vernon, NY; ed/BA in Sociol, Rider Col, 1976; MSW, Crim/Juv Justice, Univ of PA, 1978; pa/ Casewkr, Chd's Village, 1978-79; Dir of Mt Vernon Ctr 1979-80, Dir of Ser Progs 1980-, Westchester Urban Leag Inc; Exec Com, Westchester Chapt of Assn of Black Social Wkrs, 1982-; cp/ NAACP, 1983; Westchester Urban Leag, 1983; Chm, Coalition for Equal Representation, 1982-; Commun Action Grp Adv Bd, 1980-; Chm, Housing and Neighborhood Devel Inst, 1983; r/Meth; hon/Outstg Yg Man of Am Awd, 1980, 1982.

OWENS, PATRICK FRANCIS JR oc/ Educator; b/Feb 25, 1935; h/5341 Santa

Anita Avenue, Temple City, CA 91780; ba/Los Angeles, CA; m/Donna Lee Hunt; c/Kirk; p/Patrick F and Alice A Owens; ed/Air Frame and Power Plant Lic, Northrop Inst of Technol, 1959; Voc Tchg Credential, Univ of CA LA, 1972; mil/AUS; pa/Mechanic, Haglan Aircraft Motors, 1959-60; Distributor, Triumph Motorcycles, 1960-71; Race Mechanic, 1960-66; Ser Sch Instr, 1966-68; Ser Mgr, 1968-71; Instr of Motorcycle Repair, LA Trade-Tech Col, 1971-; CA Voc Assn, Secy 1979-; Life Mem, Am Motorcyclist Assn (Active in Raising Funds); Dist 37, Road Rider Assn Legal Def Fund, 1983-; Am Voc Assn, 1978-; cp/San Gabriel Val Taxpayers Assn, 1975-78; Com to Get Proposition 13 on CA St Ballot, 1976-78; Triumph Intl Owners Clb; Big Brothers of Gtr LA; r/Rom Cath; hon/Author of *Motorcycle Mechanics Workbook*, 1972, 1973; Editor, Var Motorcycle Mechanics Books; Writer, Num Articles for Motorcycle Mags, Newspapers and Newslttrs; Cert of Achmt, LA Trade-Tech, 1981; Est'd Outstg Student Awd to Biannually Recognize Grads of Motorcycle Repair and Indust Tng, LA Trade-Tech; W/W W.

OZMON, KENNETH LAWRENCE oc/University President; b/Sep 4, 1931; h/5895 Gorsebrook Avenue, Halifax, Nova Scotia B3H 1G3; ba/Halifax, Nova Scotia; m/Elizabeth Ann Morrison; c/Angela Francene, Kendi Elizabeth; p/Mr and Mrs Howard A Ozmon, Portsmouth, VA; ed/BA, St Bernard Col, 1955; MA, Cath Univ of Am, 1963; PhD, Univ of ME, 1968; pa/Pres, St Mary's Univ, 1979; Dean of Arts 1972-78, Chm of Dept of Psych 1969-72, Assoc Prof 1969-78, Univ of Prince Edward Isl; Asst Prof, CA St Univ Chico, 1968-69; Lectr, St Joseph's Tchrs Col, 1964-65; cp/Bd of Dirs, U Way of Halifax/Dartmouth, 1980-82; Provincial Bd of Dirs, Canadian Assn for Mentally Retarded, 1980-82; Nat Coun, Canadian Human Rights Foun, 1976; Selection Com, J H Moore Awds for Excell, 1983; r/Rom Cath; hon/Author of Num Articles in Psychol Jours; Trustee S'ship, Univ of ME, 1965-67; NDEA F'ship, Univ of ME, 1967-68; Canadian W/W; Intl W/W Ed.

P

PACE, SHIRLEY LOVON oc/President of Education-Child Care Centers; b/Oct 7, 1983; h/PO Box 638, Houston, TX 77001; ba/Houston, TX; m/Roy; c/ Julia, Sheretta; p/Lillie Mae Brown, Midway, TX; ed/SWn Univ, 1970; pa/ Pres, La Rochelle Acad Inc 1970-, La Rochelle Commun Devel Inc 1980-; Wkg Wom of Am; Home Ec Cooperative Ed, Chm 1980-; Nat Female Exec; cp/ C of C, Meadows Garden, Pres 1980-; r/Ch of Christ; hon/Home Ec Cooperative Ed Most Outstg Employer, 1970-80; W/W Houston; W/W Am Wom.

PAGE, DREW ERNEST oc/Retired from Music Profession; b/Jan 5, 1905; h/1412 Cottonwood Place, Las Vegas, NV 89104; ba/Same; m/Margaret Fay; c/Margie Drew Page McCann, Netta Fay Page Carver; p/Ben Richer and Lillian Hendricks Page (dec); ed/HS Dipl, 1924; Att'd, Sum Session, A&M Col, OK, 1923; Pvt Tutoring, Chgo, 1937-38; Att'd, Phoenix Conservatory of Music, 1924-25; mil/OK Nat Guards; pa/Clarinet, Max Montgomery w Carnival, 1924-25; Saxophone-Clarinet, Johnny McFall 1926, Ted Fiorito 1927, McFall 1928, Jack Crawford 1929-30; Radio Staff Bands and Theaters, Dallas, 1931-34; Paul Ash, Bob Crosby, NBC Radio Staff, Chgo, 1934-38; Harry James, 1939-40; Ben Pollack, LA, 1941; Johnny "Scat" Davis, 1942; Horace Heidt, Phil Harris, Radio Staff of Jack Benny Show, Wingy Manone, Red Nichols, 1943-45; Freddy Martin, 1945-47; Jack Fina, 1948; Free-Lance, 1949; Will Osborne, 1950; Billy Roe Trio, 1951-57; Charlie Ventura, Lounge Grps and Show Bands, Las Vegas, 1958-63; Freddie Masters, En Sts, Greenland, Jamaica, Puerto Rico, and Cuba, 1965-68; Gil Bowers, Hello Dolly, 1968; Cabaret, 1969; Jack Morgan, Russ Morgan Orch, Las Vegas, 1970-76; Bill Rand, Las Vegas, 1977-82; ACCAP, 1981; Las Vegas Press Clb, 1982; AARP, 1976; E Ctl Univ Alumni Assn, OK, 1982; Writers Clb, Las Vegas, 1981; r/ Prot; hon/Pubs, Drew's Blues: A Sideman's Life with the Big Bands 1979, Articles for Las Vegas Musician's Desert Aria Newsletter 1983-84; ASCAP Awd for Drew's Blues, 1980; Album of the Wk, TV, LA, 1956; Book and Recordings in Perm Archives of Celebrated Oklahomans, 1983.

PAGEL, DEBORAH JOANNE oc/ Health Physicist; b/Apr 25,1955; h/4035 Washington, Westmont, IL 60559; ba/ Morris, IL; m/Richard Arlin; p/Mr and Mrs Raymond F Heppeler, Clarendon Hills, IL; ed/BS in Biol, Elmhurst Col, 1981; pa/Hlth Physicist, Commonwealth Edison/Dresden Nuclear Power Sta, 1981-; Argonne Nat Res Lab, 1977-81; MW Chapt, Hlth Physics Soc; Nat Am Nuclear Soc; ANLEARS, 1980; Chgo Chapt, Am Nuclear Soc; Wom's Link, 1979; Assn for Wom in Sci; r/Rom Cath; hon/Pubs, "The Effectiveness of the Heavy-Ion Radiation Criterion as an Index of Accelerator Radiation Levels," 1978; Phi Kappa Phi, Nat Hon Soc, 1979-; Alpha Chi Nat Hon Soc, 1975; Num 1 Grad in Col, Class of 1981; W/ W Frontier Sci and Technol.

PALMER, ARNOLD DANIEL oc/ Professional Golfer; b/Sep 10, 1929; h/

PO Box 52, Youngstown, PA 15696; ba/ Same; m/Winifred Walzer; c/Margaret Anne Reintgen (Mrs Douglas), Amy Lyn Saunders (Mrs Robert Leroy III); p/Milfred J Palmer (dec); Doris L Palmer (dec); mil/USCG; pa/Pres, Arnold Palmer Enterprises; Bd of Dirs, ProGrp Inc; Pres, Arnold Palmer Cadillac; Pres and Owner, Latrobe CC; Pres and Pt-Owner, Bay Hill Clb and Lodge; Bus Assoc, Ironwood CC; Bd of Dirs, Latrobe Area Hosp; Other Profl Positions; Profl Golfers Assn of Am; Laurel Val Golf Clb; Rolling Rock Clb; Duquesne Clb; Oakmont CC; Others; r/Presb; hon/PGA Tour Victories incl: Bob Hope Desert Classic 1973, 1971, 1968, Citrus Invitational 1971, Westchester Team Champ 1971, PGA Nat Team Champ 1970, Heritage Classic and Danny Thomas Diplomat Classic 1969, Kemper Open 1968, Thunderbird Classic, Am Golf Classic, Tucson Open and LA Open 1967, Num Others; Hon LLD, Wake Forest Univ; Hon HHD, Thiel Col; PGA Player of Yr, 1960, 1962; Charter Inductee, World Golf Hall of Fame; Inductee, Am Golf Hall of Fame; Bob Jones Awd, US Golf Assn; Wm D Richardson and Charles Bartlett Awds, Golf Writers Assn of Am; Gold Tee Awd, Metro NY Golf Writers Assn; Man of Silver Era, Golf Digest; Mem, US Ryder Cup Team, 1961, 1963, 1965, 1967, 1971, 1973 (Capt 1963-75); Arthur J Rooney Awd, Cath Yth Assn; Sportsman of Yr, Sports Illustrated, 1960; Author, 5 Golf Books; Others.

PALMER, EDWARD LEO oc/Professor of Social Psychology; b/Aug 11, 1938; h/Route 1, Box 1792, Pine Road, Davidson, NC 28036; ba/Davidson, NC; m/Dr Ruth Ann; c/Edward Lee, Jennifer Lynn; p/R Leon and Eva Brandenburg Palmer, Hagerstown, MD; ed/BA, Gettysburg Col, 1960; BD, Luth Theol Sem, 1964; MS in Clin Psych 1967, PhD in Social Psych 1970, OH Univ; mil/USAR; pa/Tchg Fellow, OH Univ, 1966-67; Asst Prof, W MD Col, 1968-70; Asst Prof 1970-77, Assoc Prof 1977-, Davidson Col; Guest Rschr, Ctr for Res in Chd's TV, Harvard Univ, 1977; Intl Communication Assn, Div 3, Mass Communication; Am Psychol Assn, Div 8, Personality and Social; SEn Psychol Assn, Mbrship Com; So Assn for Public Opinion Res; Soc of SEn Social Psychols; Adv Bd, WDAV Public Radio Sta; hon/ Pubs, Children and the Faces of Television: Teaching, Violence, Selling 1980, "Children's Understanding of Nutritional Information Presented in Breakfast Cereal Commercials" 1981; Invited Contbr, Wiley Encyclopedia of Psychology, 1982; NC Gov's Com Res Grant, 1971; Phi Beta Kappa, 1960; DIB; Men of Achmt; Contemp Authors; W/W S and SW.

PALMER, ROSEYLEE KATHRYN oc/Chairman of Fine Arts Division; b/ Sep 27, 1923; h/1409 Marigold, Borger, TX 79007; ba/Borger, TX; m/Everett S Jr; c/Jerry Everett; p/J M and Arizona Steen (dec); ed/Student, Odessa Col, AA, Frank Phillips Col; BS in Art Ed, MA, Postgrad Study, W TX St Univ; Postgrad Study, N TX St Univ; Pvt Study; pa/Asst Cashier, First Nat Bk; Free-Lance Comml Artist; Free-Lance Fine Artist; Chm, Fine Arts Div, Frank Phillips Col; Amarillo Art Alliance; Amarillo Art Ctr; TX Fine Arts Assn;

TX Jr Col Tchrs Assn; Artists Studio Inc; Intl Soc of Artists; SWn Watercolor Soc; Cowgirl Hall of Fame; Magic Plains Arts Coun; Maj Exhbns: W TX St Univ, Odessa Col, Frank Phillips Col, TX St Capitol, Nat Cowgirl Hall of Fame, Carson Co Square House Mus, Lake Meredity Aquatic and Wildlife Mus, Layland Mus, Others; Maj Collectors: Sutphen Pit Bar-B-Q Restaurants, Layland Mus, Colie Donaldson, Alexander Office Supply, Num Others; cp/ NM Wildlife Fdn; Nat Wildlife Fdn; hon/ Pub, A Study of Synthetic Paints and Painting Methods; Local, St and Nat Art Exhib Awds; Awds for Commun Ser; Awd of Excell in Fine Arts, Artist Studio Inc, 1978; Nom for TX Panhandle Dist'd Wom Awd, 1976, 1978, 1980, 1981; W/ W TX; Blue Book of TX Panhandle; Am Artists of Renown; World W/W Wom; Personalities of S.

PALTROWITZ, CAROLYN FRIEDMAN oc/Corporate Marketing Manager; b/Dec 5, 1950; h/401 East 80th Street, New York, NY 10021; ba/New York, NY; m/Michael; p/Ben and Pauline Friedman (dec); ed/Student, Mktg Courses, Hunter Col, 1971; Grad, Columbus HS, 1968; pa/Secy to Dir of Sales 1968-70, Asst to Various Product Mgrs (Var Divs) 1970-71, Asst to Mktg Mgr, Salon Div 1971-72, Revlon Inc; Corporate Mktg Mgr, Faberge Inc, 1972-; Cosmetic Career Wom; Fragrance Foun; The Fashion Grp; hon/ Featured in Mass Retailing Merchandiser 1974, Ambiance Magazine 1978, Madison Avenue Magazine 1975; Var Merit Awds, HS; W/W Am Wom.

PAMBOOKIAN, HAGOP SARKIS oc/Educational Psychologist, University Professor; b/Dec 18, 1932; h/PO Box 2113, Elizabeth City, NC 27909; ba/ Elizabeth City, NC; p/Sarkis (dec) and Tamom Karageuzian Pambookian, Beirut, Lebanon; ed/Dipl in Pedagogy, Melkonian Ednl Inst, 1953; BA in Psych, Am Univ of Beirut, 1957; MA in Ednl Psych, Columbia Univ Tchrs Col, 1963; PhD in Ednl Psych, Univ of MI, 1972; pa/Assoc Prof of Psych, Elizabeth City St Univ, 1980-; Sr Fulbright Lectr, Yerevan St Univ, 1978-79; Asst Prof of Ednl Psych, Marquette Univ, 1974-78; Res Assoc, Ctr for Res on Lng and Tchg, Univ of MI, 1974; Other Previous Positions; Univ of MI Alumni Assn; Am Psychol Assn; Intl Coun of Psychols; Nat Assn for Armenian Studies and Res; Nat Assn for the Ed of Yg Chd; Phi Delta Kappa; Soc for Cross-Cultural Res; SEn Psychol Assn; hon/Pubs, "Teachers and Teaching in the Soviet Union" 1982, "The Impact of Family on Child's Personality in American Studies" 1980, Others; Oliver Max Gardner Awd Nom, Elizabeth City St Univ, 1982; Fulbright F'ship, Lectureship, USSR, 1978; Cit for Dist'd Career and Commun Ser, Bd of Supvrs, Milwaukee Co, 1978; Bd of Govs, IPA, 1976; Other Hons; W/W E; Men of Achmt; DIB; Commun Ldrs of Am; W/W MW; Other Biogl Listings.

PAN, HUO-PING oc/Research Chemist; b/Feb 13, 1921; h/5295 South Jellison Street, Littleton, CO 80123; ba/Denver, CO; m/Chiou-Wen Sha; c/Peno; p/ Bai-ming and Won-ching Chen Pan (dec); ed/BS in Chem, Nat SW Assoc'd Univ, China, 1946; PhD, Food Sci, Univ of IL, 1954; pa/Staff Mem, Div of Indust Res 1954-55, Staff Mem, Div of Sponsored Res 1955-57, Res Assoc 1957-58, MIT; Asst Biochem, Agri Experiment Sta 1958-63, Asst Res Prof, Dept of Chem Engrg 1963-64, Univ of FL; Res Biochem, Patuxent Wildlife Res Ctr 1964-74, Res Chem, Patuxent Wildlife Res Ctr 1974-77, Res Chem, Denver Wildlife Res Ctr 1977-, US Fish and Wildlife Ser, US Dept of the Interior; AAUP, 1959-64; Am Chem Soc; Am Inst of Biol Sci; Am Soc for the Advmt of Sci; Intl Soc for the Study of Xenobiotics, Charter Mem; Sigma Xi; Phi Tau Sigma; hon/Pubs, "A Trap for Condensed Water from Laboratory Compressed Air Outlet" 1983, "Alkyl Chain Length and Acute Oral Toxicity of p-aminophenones" 1983, *Bulletin of Environmental Contamination and Toxicology* 1983, "Analytical Techniques for Fluorescent Chemicals Used as Systemic or External Wildlife Markers" 1981, Num Others; Suggestion Awd, US Fish and Wildlife Ser, 1971; Awd for Outstg Pub, Denver Wildlife Res Ctr, 1981; Spec Achmt Awd, US Fish and Wildlife Ser, 1981; Ldrs in Am Sci; Am Men and Wom of Sci; W/W Technol Today; W/W W.

PAOLINI, SHIRLEY J oc/University Dean, Associate Professor; h/1242 St Gotthard Avenue, Anchorage, AK 99504; ba/Anchorage, SK; m/Mauri; c/Kenneth, Marco, Angela, Laura; p/Mrs Ann Smith, Anchorage, AK; ed/PhD, Univ of CA-Irvine; MA, CA St Univ Fullerton; Swiss Govt Fellow, Univ of Lausanne; BA, magna cum laude, Mt St Mary's Col; pa/Dean of Univ Affairs, Assoc Prof of Humanities, AK Pacific Univ, 1979-; Art Reach Dir, Anchorage Arts Coun, 1978-79; Dir of Planning, Chaminade Univ, 1975-78; Asst Prof, Asst Spec, Univ of HI Manoa, 1973-75; Asst Dir of Ed, Nat Sys Corp, CA, 1971-73; Ednl Conslt, 1973-; World Affairs Coun; Mod Lang Assn; Am Comparative Lit Assn; Philological Assn of the Pacific Coast; Coun for the Advmt of Experiential Lng; r/Rom Cath; hon/Pub, *Confessions of Sin and Love in the Middle Ages*, 1982; Editor, HI Open Prog Manual and Texts; Author, Profl Articles and Poems; French Govt Consulate Awd, 1954; *Atlantic Monthly* Poetry Prize, 1953; W/W Among Am Wom.

PAPARELLA, JULIA BOLAND oc/Associate Professor of Nursing; b/Jul 12, 1921; h/1607 County Line Road, Villanova, PA 19085; ba/Villanova, PA; m/Dr Benedict A; c/Dr Thomas E; p/Mr and Mrs James Boland (dec); ed/BSN, Ed 1954, MS, Ed 1956, Univ of PA; MS, Lib Sci, Villanova Univ, 1975; mil/Army Nurse, Corps Resv, WWII, USA and Europe; pa/Val Forge Army Hosp, 1943; 5th Gen Hosp (Harvard Univ Unit), England and France, 1943-46; USAR, 338th Med Grp HQs, Chief Nurse, Rank: Col; From Instr to Assoc Prof of Nsg, Col of Nsg, Villanova Univ, 1955-; ANA; Nat Leag for Nsg; Critical Care Nurses Assn; Assn of Mil Surgs of US; Resv Ofcrs Assn; Am Lib Assn; ASCLA, Com Mem, Bd Mem, Exec Com; Secy of Fam Ser of Montgomery Co, 1982-83; Alumni Class Rep, Univ of PA, 1956-; r/Rom Cath; hon/African/European Theater of Oper Medal and 4 Battle Stars.

PAPAS, PAUL N II oc/Executive; b/Feb 15, 1951; h/PO Box 253, Dedham, MA 02026-0253; m/Brenda; c/Erica M, Paul N III, Margaret M; p/Nicholas M and Bessie Papas; ed/BS, Crim Justice, Thomas Jefferson Col of Law; mil/USAR, Ofcr; pa/Owner, Centre Assocs, Real Est, 1970-; Fdr and Owner: Paul N Papas II Ins Agy 1974, Bay St Appraisers and Investigators 1974, Concept Leasing 1976, Capital Investmt Adv Sers 1975, Capital Return Co 1975, Unltd Concept Ads 1975, Paul N Papas II Photo 1978, Athens Am Bk 1983; Justice of the Peace, 1972-; Alpha and Omega Legal Res, 1983; Nat Assn of Fire Investigators; cp/Fdr and Dir, Christians for Justice, 1984; r/Trustees Ch of the Annunciation; Greek Orthodox; Chm, Dedham Repub Town Com, 1973-76; Dedham Charter Comm, 1976; Town Rep, 1972-82; Ex-POW; hon/Repub of Yr, 1972-73; W/W E.

PAPAYANOPOULOS, LEE oc/Professor and Researcher; b/May 1, 1939; h/31 Burnett Terrace, West Orange, NJ 07052; ba/Newark, NJ; p/John (dec) and Elli Papayanopoulos; ed/Doct, Engrg and Opers Res, Columbia Univ; Master's, NY Univ, 1966; Bach of Engrg Physics, Cornell, 1964; pa/Sys Engr 1964-67, Rschr 1967-73, IBM; Grad Sch Prof, Rutgers Univ, 1973-; Math Programming Soc; Inst of Mgmt Scis; AAUP; Delta Phi; Conslt to Govtl Agys, Cts and Many Corps in US and Abroad; hon/Author, Num Articles in Profl Jours, Book: *Democratic Representation and Apportionment: Quantitative Methods, Measures and Criteria* 1973; Cornell Univ S'ship, 1959-64; Fulbright S'ship, 1959-62; ACM Nat Lectr, 1971-72; Ofcl Reapportionment Expert, NY St, 1967-.

PAQUET, JEAN-GUY oc/University Rector; b/Jan 5, 1938; h/1517, rue Commerciale, Saint-Romuald d'Etchemin, Quebec G6W 1Z6; ba/Quebec; p/Laurent W and Louisianne Coulombe Paquet (dec); ed/BSc in Engrg Physics, Universite LLaval, 1959; MSc in Aeronautics, Ecole nationale superieure de l'aeronautique de Paris, 1960; DSc in Elect Engrg, Universite Laval, 1963; pa/Lectr, Elect Engrg Dept 1961-62, Asst Prof, Elect Engrg Dept 1962-67, Hd of Elect Engrg Dept 1967-69, Assoc Prof, Elect Engrg Dept 1969-71, Vice-Dean (Res), Fac of Sci 1969-72, Prof of Elect Engrg 1971-, Vice-Rector (Acad) 1972-77, Rector 1977-, Universite Laval; Spec Asst to VP (Sci), Nat Res Coun of Canada, Ottawa, 1971-72; Order of Engrs of the Province of Quebec; Association canadienne française pour l'avancement des sciences; Assn of Sci Engrg and Technol Commun of Canada; IEEE; Am Soc for Engrg Ed; Soc of Res Admrs; Canadian Assn of Univ Res Admrs; AAAS; Innovation Mgmt Inst of Canada; Coun of Univs of the Province of Quebec, 1973-77; NY Acad of Sci, 1980-; Am Mgmt Assn, 1980-; Inst of Public Adm of Canada, 1980-; Num Other Profl Mbrships; r/Rom Cath; hon/Author, 2 Books and More Than 50 Pubs in Sci Jours on Control Sys Engrg, Many Papers on Res, Devel and Sci Policy; Fellow, Royal Soc of Canada, 1978; Fellow, AAAS, 1981; Hon Deg, DSc, McGill Univ, 1982; Hon JD, York Univ, 1983.

PARADISE, MICHAEL EMMANUEL oc/University Chancellor; b/Mar 26, 1928; ba/11120 Glacier Highway, Juneau, AK 99801; m/Ann Ramos; c/Maria, George, Andrew; ed/BSc, Morningside Col, 1955; Master's 1958, DrEdD 1962, Univ of No CO; pa/Chancellor, Univ of AK Juneau, 1979-; Pres of Ctl Tech Commun Col, 1970-73; Pres of NEn NE Col, 1968-72; Staff Mem, Chadron St Col, 1962-68; AAAS; Am Assn of Commun and Jr Cols; Am Assn of Higher Ed; Am Assn of St Cols and Univs; Am Mgmt Assn; Am Voc Assn; Assn for Study of Higher Ed; hon/Pub'd Articles on Adm Pressures, Non-Traditional Ed and Govt Affairs in *Trustee Quarterly*, *The CUPA Journal*, *Community and Junior College Frontiers*, and Others; Mil Citations; Cits of Apprec from Students; Commends from Fac, Chadron St Col Fac Senate, No NE Col Fac Senate, Ctl Tech Comm Col Fac Senate Assn; W/W World; W/W Am; W/W MW; W/W W; W/W US; W/W Am Polit; W/W Am Ed; W/W NE; Col Adm; Am Men and Wom of Sci; 2,000 Notable Ams; Commun Ldrs and Noteworthy Ams; Num Other Biogl Listings.

PARARAS-CARAYANNIS, GEORGE oc/Director of Center; b/Nov 8, 1936; h/PO Box 8523, Honolulu, HI 96815; ba/Honolulu, HI; c/George, Nicole; ed/BS in Chem and Math, Roosevelt Univ, 1959; MS in Chem 1963, MS in Oceanography 1959, Univ of HI; PhD in Marine Scis, Univ of DE, 1975; pa/Dir, Intl Tsunami Info Ctr, UNESCO-IOC, 1974-; Oceanographer, U S Coastal Engrg Res Ctr, 1972-74; Oceanographer, AUS Corps of Engrs, NY, 1971-72; Dir, Mermex, SA, 1970-71; Dir, World Data Ctr, A-Tsunami, 1967-70; Res Geophysicist, HI Inst of Geophysics, Univ of HI, 1963-67; Am Geophy Union; Marine Technol Soc; Am Soc of Oceanography; Intl Union of Geodesy and Geophysics; Pacific Sci Assn; Am Nuclear Soc; Tsunami Soc; r/Greek Orthodox; hon/Author, More Than 60 Sci and Tech Articles, Monographs and Reports; Several Govtl Recogs and Awds; W/W W; W/W Technol; W/W Oceanography.

PARQUE, RICHARD ANTHONY oc/Writer, Consultant, Educator; b/Aug 10, 1935; h/PO Box 52, Downey, CA 90241; ba/Same; m/Lan Thi; c/Kenneth Richard, James Vo, Phat; p/Joe and Helen Parque; ed/BA in Sci 1958, MA in Ed 1966, CA St Tchg Credential (Life Dipl) 1961, CA St Univ LA; mil/USMC; pa/Sci Tchr, Yucaipa HS, 1961-66; Ed Advr/Conslt, CA St Univ Sys, 1966-68; Sci/Math Tchr, Univ of the W Indies, 1968; Profl Devel Admr, Ed and Tng, McDonnell Douglas Astronautics Co, 1968-71; Pres, Parque Consltg Assocs, 1971-76; Adj Fac Mem, Univ of CA Irvine, 1972-73; Corporate Dir of Ed and Tng, Ralph M Parsons Co, 1976-78; Pres, Parque Consltg Assocs, and Novelist/Poet/Author, 1978-; Aerospace Tech Writer, 1978-; Adj Fac Mem, CA St Univ LA, 1980, and Univ of CA LA, 1982; CA Tchrs Assn, 1961-73; Nat Sci Tchrs Assn, 1961-73; Nat Mgmt Assn, 1968-71; Am Soc for Tng and Devel, 1968-84; Orgl Devel Netwk, 1973; The Conslt Netwk, 1983-84; cp/Nat Audubon Soc, 1978-84; Intl Trumpet Guild, 1978-84; Repub; r/Christian; hon/Pubs, *Sweet Vietnam* 1984, Num Articles in *Employee Relations Bulletin*, *School Science and Mathematics*, *Manage*, *Supervision*, *Soldier of Fortune*, *New Breed* and Other Nat Mags; Pub'd in Poetry Anthologies, incl'g, *PS*, *The Universe Sings*,

PS, God Loves You, The Poet, Vietnam: An Anthology of Voices, Others; NASA Sci Tchg Awd of Merit, 1966; Studebaker-Rockne Trophy, San Bernardino Col, 1955; All-En Conf, 1955; All-San Gabriel Val Leag, 1952-53; Ath of the Yr, Bell Gardens HS, 1953; W/ W CA; W/W W.

PARHAM, DAVID RENE oc/Computer Programming Consultant; b/Mar 24, 1951; h/1320 Sunset, Iowa Park, TX 76367; ba/Iowa Park, TX; m/Ella Denise Wright; c/Cory David, Heather Denise; p/Albert C and Alyne J Parham, Munday, TX; ed/Deg in Exec Automation, Draughon's Bus Col, 1971; Att'd, MWn St Univ, 1972-76; pa/Computer Programmer, then Data Processing Mgr, Wichita Gen Hosp, 1971-80; Proprietor, David Parham and Assocs (Providers of Software Support for IBM Computers), 1980-; Data Processing Mgmt Assn, Chapt VP 1979; cp/Repub; r/Bapt.

PARK, OK-CHOON oc/University Professor and Corporation Researcher; b/Dec 30, 1944; h/3098 Evelyn Street, Roseville, MN 55113; ba/Albany, NY; m/Young-Soon; c/Michael Hun, Christine Jin; p/Dal-Moon and Eon-Yeon Y Park, Korea; ed/PhD 1978, MA 1976, Univ of MN; pa/Asst Prof, SUNY-Albany, 1981-; Sr Rschr, Control Data Corp, 1979-; Res Fellow, Hlth Ser Ctr, Univ of MN, 1978-79; Am Psychol Assn; Am Ednl Res Assn; Paper Reviewer, Assn for Ednl Communication and Technol; Assn for Devel of Computer-Based Instrn; hon/Pub'd Articles Appear in *Review of Educational Research, Journal of Educational Psychology, American Educational Research Journal;* Recip, 2 Res Grants from the St Univ of NY Res Founs; W/W E; W/W MW; W/W Sci and Technol.

PARK, ROY H JR oc/Advertising Media Executive; b/Jul 23, 1938; h/53 Highgate Circle, Ithaca, NY 14850; ba/ Ithaca, NY; m/Tetlow Parham; c/Elizabeth P, Roy H III; p/Roy H and Dorothy Dent Park, Ithaca, NY; ed/BA in Jour, Univ of NC Chapel Hill, 1961; MBA in Mktg, Cornell Univ, 1963; pa/Sr Acct Exec, Rev Bd Exec, J Walter Thompson Co, 1963-70; VP, Mktg and Acct Mgmt, Kincaid Advtg Agy, 1970-72; VP, Park Outdoor Advtg, 1971-75; VP, Advtg and Promotion, Park Broadcasting Inc, 1976-81; Mng Dir, Agri Res Advtg Agy, 1976-81; VP and Gen Mgr, Park Outdoor Advtg, 1981-; cp/Exec Com, Tompkins Co Repub Fin Com, 1983; Chm, Ithaca Assem Cotillion, 1979-81; CoChm, Fin Com, MacNeil for Assem, 1978, 1982; Fin Com, Spec Chd's Ctr Inc, 1979; Bd of Dirs, Tompkins Co Coun of the Arts, 1976; Publicity Dir and Bd Chm, Jr Olympics, 1975; Public Relats Dir, Tompkins Co Conf and Tourist Coun, 1976; Chm, Public Relats Com, U Way of Tompkins Co, 1973-74; Tompkins Co C of C, Var Past Positions; r/Presb; hon/Author, Articles in *Seventeen, American Way, The Rural New Yorker, The News and Observer* (Raleigh, NC), *The Chapel Hill Weekly, The Raleigh Times, Durham Morning Herald;* W/W Advtg; W/ W E.

PARKER, BOBBY DOUGLAS oc/ Vocal Music Teacher, Professional Photographer; b/Feb 12, 1935; h/8119 Webster, Arvada, CO 80003; ba/ Arvada, CO; m/Nelda Arlene; c/Steven Douglas, Gregory Allan, Kirby Lynn; p/

Luther Joseph and Inez Beatrice (dec) Parker, Wellington, KS; ed/Vocal Music Maj, KS St Univ, 1953-56; Bach of Music Ed 1960, Master of Music Ed 1964, Wichita St Univ; Specs Deg in Sch Adm, Univ of CO Boulder, 1975; Profl Photo Deg, Mod Sch of Photo, 1981; Profl Photo Deg, NY Inst of Photo, 1983; mil/AF NG 1956-60, Staff Sgt, Pers Specs; pa/Owner, Universal Creations, Photo Studio, 1979-; Choir Dir, Edgewater U Meth Ch, 1983-; Guest Relats Dept, Coors Brewery, 1976-82; Choir Dir, S Broadway Christian Ch, 1973-75; Vocal Music Dir, Hackberry Elem Sch, Jefferson Co Public Schs, 1974-; Vocal Music Dir, Wheat Ridge HS, Jefferson Co Public Schs, 1973-74; Announcer of News, Sports, Music and Salesman, KLEY Radio, 1966-73; Choir Dir, Sumner Co Commun Chorus, 1966-73; Choir Dir, Wettington U Meth Ch, 1966-73; Other Previous Positions; Phi Mu Alpha, 1959-84; Phi Delta Kappa, 1975-80; Am Choral Dirs of Am, 1966-80; Music Edrs Nat Coun, 1960-; KS Music Edrs Assn, 1960-73; CO Music Edrs Assn, 1973-; KS Edrs Assn, 1960-73; CO Edrs Assn, 1973-; NEA, 1960-; Inst of Cert'd Photogs, 1979-81; Photographic Soc of Am, Divs of Slides, Nature, Color and Black/White Pictures, 1979-; Am Photographic Soc, 1979; Profl Photogs of Am, 1979-; Rocky Mtn Profl Photogs of Am, 1979-; Wedding Photographers Intl, 1979-; cp/ Masonic Lodge #150, 1956-; Scottish Rite Mason, 1969-; El Jebel Shrine, 1974-; Nat Rifle Assn of Am, 1975-78; Assoc Mem, US Golf Assn, 1975-80; Nat Model Railroading Assn, 1978-81; Var Other Past Civic Mbrships; r/So Bapt; hon/Radio Telephone 3rd Class Operators Permit, Fed Communs Comm, 1966-; Pres Sports Awd in Skiing, 1975; Awds of Merit, Wedding Photogs Intl; Cert of Merit, Profl Photogs of Am, W Coast Sch of Photo, 1981; Cert of Merit, Profl Photogs of Am, Hon Mention on Bay City Print, 1980; Cert of Merit, Profl Photogs of Am, Bay City and Val of Stone Prints, 1980; Cert of Merit, Am Foun for Photographic Art Ltd, 1980; Cert of Awd, Best Wn Motels Inc, 1980; Awd of Spec Commend, NY Inst of Photog, 1983; Other Hons; W/W.

PARKER, LUCY T oc/Psychologist, Clinical Director, Senior Consultant; b/ Jan 21, 1933; ba/Suite 108, 25 Boylston Street, Chestnut Hill, MA 02167; m/Dr Robert Alan; c/Karen Sue, Janet Lee Goldman, Geoffrey Samuel, Ann; p/Dr Joseph and Maria Thimann (dec); ed/ EdD, Boston Univ, 1974; PhD, Heed Univ, 1973; EdM 1965, BS 1958, Boston Univ; pa/Clin Dir and Sr Staff Psychol, Chestnut Hill Psychotherapy Assocs, 1970-; Sr Conslt, The Parker Assocs, 1977-; Sr Conslt, MA Tchrs Assn, 1974-78; Sr Cnslg Psychol, Leslie B Cutler Child Guid Clin, 1967-70; Consltg Psychol, Walker Home for Chd, 1968-72; Sch Adjustment Cnslr, Needham Public Schs, 1964-67; Other Previous Positions; Am Assn of Marriage and Fam Therapy, CoChp of Reg Screening Bd 1981; MA Assn of Marriage and Fam Therapy, Reg Bd 1981-82; Am Assn of Sex Edrs, Cnslrs and Therapists; Am Psychol Assn; Am Grp Psychotherpay Assn; hon/Pubs, "The Management of Behavior in a

Pediatric Clinical Setting" 1974, "Behavior: The Neglected Aspect of Eye Safety" 1973, Others; Diplomate, Intl Assn of Profl Cnslg and Psychotherapy, 1983; Diplomate, Am Bd of Behavioral Med, 1982; Fellow, Am Acad of Sci, Am Acad of Optom, Intl Coun of Sex Ed and Parenthood, Intl Biogl Assn; W/W Am Wom; Intl Book of Hon; Others.

PARKER, ROBIN ZACHARY oc/ Architect, Business Executive; b/Mar 28, 1946; h/10965 Southwest 95 Street, Miami, FL 33176; ba/Miami, FL; m/ Lydia Leach; c/Britt Zachary, Melahn Lyle; p/Alfred Browning Parker; Martha Gifford; ed/Arch, Univ of FL, 1966-69; Urban Planning, Univ of Toronto, 1969-71; Arch Engrg, Univ of Miami, 1972-75; pa/Dir, Alfred Browning Parker, Archs, 1974-; Pvt Pract, Arch, Miami, 1975-; Investmt Conslt, Terra Investmt Corp, Honduras, 1978-; Founding Dir, Solar Reactor Engines Inc, 1981-; VP, Solar Reactor Corp, 1979-81; Corporate Mem, AIA; cp/Intl Explorers Soc; r/Congregational; hon/ Pubs, "Indigenous Architecture" in *Designer's Quarterly* 1982, FL S Chapt, AIA Jour 1981; Exquisite Arch Awd, Long Art Mus; W/W S and SW.

PARKER, WALTER LEWIS oc/Private International Consultant; b/Mar 31, 1942; ba/5CC GP (AFCC), Robins AFB, GA 31098; m/Eileen Frances Green; c/Kevin Walter, Eric William, Laura Eileen; p/William J and Josie M Hensley Parker, Akron, OH; ed/Student, Univ of Philippines, 1967-68; Voc/ Tech Cert, Univ of MD, 1975; BS in Psych, Univ of So MS, 1976; MA in Cnslg Psych, Ball St Univ, 1981; mil/ USAF, 1962-83; pa/Electronics Tech, 1962-66; Electronics Supvr, 1966-68; Public Relats Supvr for Communs Support Element, US Strike Command, 1968-71; Electronics Supvr, Engrg, 1971-75; Quality Control Supvr, 1975-76; AF Recruiter, 1976-78; Classified Duty w USAF Security Ser, 1978-79; Communs Supvr, 1979-82; Maintenance Control Supvr, Robins AFB, 1982-83; Prof, City Col, 1981-82; Conslt, Athens, 1979-82; Am Psychol Assn; APGA; Am Col Pers Assn; Nat Employmt Cnslrs Assn; Nat Voc Guid Assn; Public Offender Cnslrs Assn; Aircraft Owners and Pilots Assn; AF Sgts Assn, Life; Univ of So MS Alumni Assn, Life; Ball St Univ Alumni Assn; cp/Masons, Life; r/Prot; hon/AF Commend Medal; Dean's List, Univ of MD, 1974-75; Dean's List, Univ of So MS, 1975-76; W/W World.

PARKIN, JEFFREY ROBERT oc/ Legal and Technical Consultant; b/Jun 20, 1950; h/Mauwee Brook Way, Kent, CT 06757; ba/Same; m/Ann Clark; c/ Todd Jeffrey, Melissa Ann; p/George R and Lillian S Parkin, Swansea, MA; ed/ BS, Mech Engrg, Cornell Univ, 1972; MSME, Univ of TX, 1973; JD, Wn New England Col, 1979; pa/Sr Nuclear Engr, Combustion Engrg Inc, 1975-80; Atty and Engrg Mgr, Kero-Sun Inc, 1980-83; Pres, Jeffrey R Parkin & Assocs, Tech and Legal Conslts, 1983-; r/Prot; hon/ W/W in Aviation and Aerospace.

PARKS, RICHARD D oc/University Professor, Producer, Author; b/Aug 29, 1938; h/55 South 6th Street, San Jose, CA 95112; ba/San Jose, CA; p/Charles and Josephine Marie Parks, Orleans, NE; ed/BA, cum laude, San Jose St Univ,

1962; MA, Univ of WA, 1964; PhD (ABD), Stanford Univ, 1971; pa/Profl Actor, 1943-; Instr, Univ of WA, 1963; Instr, San Jose St Univ, 1964; Instr, Stanford Univ, 1966-67; Asst Prof, San Jose St Univ, 1968-71; Assoc Prof, Univ of WA, 1971-72; Assoc Prof 1972-, Dir of Theatre 1974-78, Coor of Music Theatre 1981-, San Jose St Univ; Prodr, Nat Broadcasting Co, 1977-; Actors Symp of Hollywood, Exec Dir 1980-; CA Ednl Theatre Assn, Exec Secy-Treas 1978-80; Am Theatre Assn; Dramatist Guild and Authors Leag of Am; IPA; AAUP; Am Film Inst; r/Epis; hon/Pubs, *Overcome Stage Fright* (Book) 1979, *Wild West Women* (Play) 1980, *Ken Kesey's Further Inquiry* (Play Adaptation) 1980, *Early American Theatre* (Tchg Supplement) 1981, *The Facts of Life* (Play Adaptation) 1982, *Career Preparation for TV-Film Actor* (Handbook) 1983; Best Actor Awds, HS, Col, Univ; S'ships and F'ships, San Jose St Univ, Univ of WA, Stanford; Reg I Best Directing Awd, Am Col Theatre Fest, 1976; Best Prodr Awd, Nat Broadcasting Co, Creat Sers Dept, Each Yr Since 1977; W/W W; Dir of Am Scholars; W/W CA; DIB; Dir of Theatre Histns; Personalities of W and MW.

PARMERLEE-GREINER, GLORIA ROSALIE oc/Educator, Coordinator of Teen Parenting Program; b/Sep 4, 1940; h/1755 Foothills Drive, South, Golden, CO 80401; ba/Boulder, CO; m/Floyd Dale; c/Tannya Lynn Lane, Scott Gale Lane; p/Milton and Gladys Deason, Gilbert, AZ; ed/BA w Hons, Univ of So CO, 1968; MA, Univ of CO, 1973; Postgrad, CO St Univ, Univ of No CO, Univ of CO, CO Sch of Mines; pa/Sci and Home Ec Tchr 1969-80, Tchr/Coor of Teen Parenting Prog 1980-, Boulder Val Public Schs; CO Ednl Assn; Boulder Val Schs Ednl Assn; NEA; Am Home Ec Assn; CO Home Ec Assn; Am Voc Assn; CO Voc Assn; Phi Beta Kappa; Delta Kappa Gamma; cp/Boulder Mother House Bd; YWCA Boulder Teen Ctr Bd; Past Mem, GSA, BSA, 4-H Clbs; r/Presb; hon/Author, Articles to Profl Jours and Popular Mags; BA w Hons, Univ of So CO, 1968; Mbrship in Phi Beta Kappa and Delta Kappa Gamma; W/W W.

PARR, GRANT V S oc/Cardiothoracic Surgeon; b/Dec 30, 1942; h/300 Quarry Lane, Haverford, PA 19041; ba/Philadelphia, PA; m/Helen Frye; c/Kathleen Gage, Helen Johnston; p/Ferdinand and Helene V S Parr, Morristown, NJ; ed/AB w Hons, Wesleyan Univ, 1965; MD, Cornell Univ Med Col, 1969; Internship, Univ Hosps of Cleveland, 1969-70; Residency: Univ Hosps of Cleveland 1970-71, Dept of Surg, Univ of Al Hosps and Clins 1971-74, Chief Resident of Dept of Surg, Univ of AL Hosps and Clins 1974-75, Cardiovas and Thoracic Dept of Surg, Univ of AL Hosps and Clins 1975-77; pa/Asst Prof, Dept of Surg, Div of Cardiovas and Thoracic Surg, Milton S Hershey Med Ctr, PA St Univ, 1978-82; Clin Assoc Prof of Surg, Presb-Univ of PA Med Ctr; Fellow: Am Col of Surgs, Am Col of Cardiology, Am Col of Chest Phys; Am Assn for Thoracic Surg; Soc of Thoracic Surgs; Intl Cardiovas Soc; Assn for Acad Surg; PA Assn for Thoracic Surg; Soc of Critical Care Med; DE Co Med Soc, 1982; Phila Co Med Soc, 1982; PA Med Soc, 1978; AMA,

1978; Am Heart Assn, Fellow, Coun on Cardiovas Surg 1982; Assn for the Advmt of Med Instrumentation; Am Soc for Artificial Internal Organs Inc; hon/Pubs, "Clinical Effectiveness of Mechanical Ventricular Bypass in Treating Postoperative Heart Failure" 1983, "Coarctation in Taussig-Bing Malformation of the Heart: Surgical Significance" (in Press), "Successfull Management of Right Ventricular Failure with the Ventricular Assist Pump Following Aortic Valve Replacement and Coronary Artery Bypass Grafting"(in Press), "A Data Management System for Perfusion Technology" (in Press), Num Others; Hons in Physics, Wesleyan Univ, 1965; Sigma Xi, Sci Hon Soc, 1965; NIH Acad Tng Grant, 1972-73; Elected Best Tchr, Presb-Univ of PA Med Ctr, 1983; Outstg Yg Men of Am; W/W E; W/W Am; Intl W/W Intells.

PARR, JERRY STUDSTILL oc/Assistant Director; b/Sep 16, 1930; h/13640 Glenhurst Road, Gaithersburg, MD 20878; ba/Washington, DC; m/Carolyn Miller; c/Kimberly Susan, Jennifer Lynn, Patricia Audrey; p/Oliver and Patricia Studstill Parr (dec); ed/BA, Vanderbilt Univ, 1962; mil/USAF, 1950-54; pa/US Secret Ser: Spec Agt 1962-68, Supervisory Protective Assignments, w VPs Humphrey, Agnew and Ford, Directed Security for Fgn Hds of St, incl'g, Queen Elizabeth, Emperor Hirohito, King Hussein, Abba Eban, King Juan Carlos, Chancellor Willie Brandt, Pres Tito 1969-78, Spec Agt in Charge, Vice Pres Protective Div (Mondale) 1978-79, Spec Agt in Charge, Pres Protective Div (Pres Carter and Reagan) 1979-82, Asst Dir, Protective Res 1982-; Intl Assn Chiefs of Police; Am Soc for Indust Security; Sr Execs Assn; r/Bd of Dirs, Heritage Christian Ch; hon/Commends, US Ho of Reps 1981, US Senate 1981, St of MD 1981; Legion of Hon Awd, NYC Police Dept, 1981; Valor Awd, US Secret Ser, 1981; Exceptl Ser Awd, US Treas, 1981; *Parade Magazine*/IACP Awd, 1981; Spec Achmt for Heroism, Assn of Fed Investigators, 1981; Nom, Pres Rank Awd, 1982, 1983; W/W E; W/W MD; Men of Achmt; Dir of Dist'd Ams; Commun Ldrs of World.

PARRISH, JOHN WESLEY JR oc/University Professor; b/Mar 5, 1941; h/1929 Prairie, Emporia, KS 66801; ba/Emporia, KS; m/Paula Schmanke; c/Corinne Danelle, Wesley Allen; p/John W Sr (dec); Mrs Dorothy I Prine, Massillon, OH; ed/BS, Denison Univ, 1963; MA 1970, PhD 1974, Bowling Green St Univ; mil/USN, Served to Lt, 1964-67; pa/Sci Tchr, Northside Jr HS, 1967; Vis'g Instr, Dept of Biol, Kenyon Col, 1973; NIH Postdoct Fellow, Zool Dept, Univ of TX Austin, 1974-76; Asst Prof of Biol 1976, Assoc Prof 1982-, Emporia St Univ; Am Ornithologists' Union; Ornithological Soc; KS Acad Sci; KS Ornithological Soc, Life Mem; Soc for the Study of Reproduction; Kanza Audubon Soc, VP 1977, Pres 1978-80, Bd 1980-; r/Prot; hon/Co-Author, 2 Lab Manuals, 8 Articles in Profl Jours, 15 Abstracts in Profl Jours (All Dealing w Comparative Animal Physiol); Soc Sigma Xi, 1974; NSF Predoct Fellow, Bowling Green St Univ, 1969-73; Res Grantee, ESU Res Com, 1977, 1979, 1980, 1981, 1982, 1983, 1984; Student Awd, Am Ornithologists' Union, 1971;

W/W Frontier Sci and Technol.

PARRISH-HARRA, CAROL WILLIAMS oc/Minister, Lecturer, Author; b/Jan 21, 1935; h/PO Box 1274, Tahlequah, OK 74465; ba/Tahlequah, OK; m/Charles Clayton Harra; p/Clarence Elmer Williams (dec); Corinne Parrott Neff, Leesburg, FL; ed/Grad, Orlando HS, 1951; Ordination through Spiritual Ctr of St Petersburg, 1971; pa/Accts Control Mgr, Caladesi Nat Bk, 1963-66; Capital Formation Cnslr, Anal Coor, 1966-71; Assoc Min, Temple of the Living God, 1971-75; Pres, FL Humanistic Inst, 1974-75; Dir, Villa Serena Spiritual Commun, 1976-81; Pres, Light of Christ Commun Ch, 1981-; Trustee, Nat Bd, Nat Coun Commun Chs, 1981; ABWA; Spiritual Frontiers F'ship; Nat Conf of Christians and Jews; Ctr of Man, FL Univ Sys, 1972-76; cp/NOW; Wkshop Ldr, Pres's Coun on Status of Wom in Am, 1974; r/Christian; hon/Pubs, *New Age Handbook on Death and Dying* 1982, *Messengers of Hope* 1983, Articles to *Spiritual Frontiers Journal* 1979-80, 1980-81; 12 Tape Cassettes Entitled, "Adventures in Awareness Series I, II and III"; 6 Tape Cassettes on "Healing, Meditation, and New Age Christianity"; 4 Tape Cassette Series Entitled, "Coming to the Sunrise"; W/W Am Wom; W/W S and SW; World W/W Wom.

PARROTT, ROBERT B oc/Executive; b/Feb 1, 1913; h/10333 Vermilyea Pass, Fort Wayne, IN 46804; ba/Fort Wayne, IN; m/Paula V; c/Michael V, Christopher R, Stephen C; p/Alfred H Parrott (dec); ed/BS, ND St Univ; Hon PhD, Hon LLD, 1960; mil/US Inf, 1940-43; pa/VP, Cargill Inc, 1935-56; Exec VP 1956-78, Bd of Dirs 1957-78, Ctl Soya Co Inc; Pres, Robert B Parrott Inc, 1978-; Bd of Dirs, Chgo Bd of Trade, 1972-76; Nat Grain and Feed Assn, 1970-78; Advr to Commun Futures Trading Comm, 1975-78; Bd of Dirs, Varied Industs Inc; Bd of Dirs, Early and Daniel Co, 1978-81; Bd of Dirs, Gen Grain Co, 1978-81; Bd of Dirs, Tidewater Grain Co, 1978-81; cp/Parkview Hosp, 1974-78; r/Epis; hon/Papers Pub'd by IN Univ Grad Sch of Bus; Frequent Lectures at Harvard's Grad Sch of Bus; Congl Appearances; Hon LLD, ND St Univ, 1960.

PARSON, ERWIN RANDOLPH I oc/Regional Manager for Readjustment Counseling Veterans Centers; b/Jun 5, 1943; h/316 Pemaco Lane, Uniondale, NY 11553; ba/Montrose, NY; m/Jane Marie Begert; c/Marlena Marie, Erwin Randolph II; p/Fenney T and Myrtle I Parson, Cambria Heights, NY; ed/BS in Career Psych, Univ of MA, 1972; MA in Clin Psych, Adelphi Univ, 1975; PhD in Clin Psych, Inst of Adv'd Psychol Studies, Adelphi Univ, 1977; Cert in Psychoanal and Psychotherapy; mil/Army, Medic in Vietnam, 1965-67; pa/Mtl Retardation Fellow, NY Med Col, 1973-75; Staff Psychotherapist and Psychodiagnostician, Brooklyn Ctr for Psychotherapy, 1975-77; Grad Clin Asst, Psychol Ser Ctr, Adelphi Univ, 1976; Intern Clin Psychol, Rusk Inst (Inst of Rehab Med), NY Univ, Bellevue Med Ctr, 1976; Asst Clin Prof of Psych, Inst of Adv'd Psychol Studies, Adelphi Univ, 1977; Consltg Psychol to Proj Headstart; Clin Coor, Treatment Team I, and Dir of Crisis Mgmt Team, Queens Chd's Psychi Ctr, 1977-79; Pvt Pract,

1978-; Dir, Inst for Psychol Diagnostic Testing and Guid, Supvr of Psychotherpay and Testing, Long Isl Consultation Ctr, 1977-; Sr Psychol, Dir of Vietnam Vets Clin Prog, and Consultation and Ed Conslt, Queens Hosp Commun Mtl Hlth Ctr, 1979-81; Nat Conslt to Oper Outreach Prog, VA Ctl Ofc and Reg Med Ednl Ctr, 1980-82; Nat Fac, Oper Outreach, VA Ctl Ofc, 1979-; Reg Mgr, NEn Vietnam Vets Outreach Ctrs, 1981-; Num Radio and TV Appearances and Newspaper Interviews, 1979-; Frequent Lectr and Conslt on Psychol Trauma/Survivor Psych; Staff Psychotherapist, Postdoct Psychotherapy Ctr, Adelphi Univ, 1978-; Contbr, Articles to Profl Jours in Psych and Psychi; NY Vietnam Vets Meml Comm; Am Psychol Assn; Soc of Clin Psychols; Adelphi Soc for Psychoanal and Psychotherapy; Other Profl Mbrships; r/Prot; hon/Pubs, "The Case for Utilizing the Community Mental Health Center as Site for Psychotherapy with Vietnam Veterans" 1981, "Vietnam Veterans and Posttraumatic Stress Disorder" 1982, "On Health and Disorder in Vietnam Veterans: An Invited Commentary" 1982, "The Reparation of the Self: Clinical and Theoretical Dimensions in the Treatment of Vietnam Combat Veterans" 1983, Others; Freedom Foun Awd, 1967; Dr Martin Luther King Jr Awd, NY Soc of Clin Psychols, 1982; NEn Reg Team Ldrs Hon Awd, Oper Outreach, VA, 1983; Lic'd Clin Psychol, NY St; Body Bldr/Ath Awd, Ctl Queens YMCA, 1961; Record of Facinating People; Long Isl Consultation Ctr/Long Isl Inst of Mtl Hlth; W/W E.

PARSONS, PATRICIA ANN oc/K-12 Media Specialist; b/Jan 17, 1951; h/624 North Main, Box 654, Evart, MI 49631; m/J Mark; c/Caleb Joseph; p/Donald R and K Lucille Wakeman Hudson, Byron, MI; ed/BA, Sprg Arbor Col, 1973; Student, Univ of MI, 1974-75; MA, Ctl MI Univ, 1983; pa/Rdg Tchr 1974, Elem Grades Libn 1975-81, Grade Sch Edr 1982, K-12 Media Spec 1982-, Evart Public Schs; MI Ed Assn; Evart Ed Assn; NEA; Evart BPW; MI Cheerleading Coaches Assn, Bd of Dirs 1978-80, VP 1980-81, 1982-83, St Championship Com 1979-; Lectr at MCCA Clins, 1979, 1981, 1982; MI Assn for Media in Ed; r/Free Meth; hon/Author, Articles in MCCA Newsletter, 1980, 1981, 1982; Alpha Sigma Kappa Acad Hon, Sprg Arbor Col, 1973; Coach of MCCA St Runner-Up Cheerleading Team, 1983; W/W Am Wom; World W/W Wom.

PARTIN, WINFRED oc/Minister, Author; b/Oct 19, 1946; h/414 Oak Street, Morristown, TN 37814; ba/Morristown, TN; m/Lucille; c/Patsy Gail, Pamela Kaye, Paul Timothy; p/Orville and Mary Partin, Clairfield, TN; ed/Student, Buford Ellington Voc Sch, Am Sch; pa/Ordained Min, 1966-; Pastor, Nevisdale Bapt Ch 1968-74, Warren Bapt Ch 1974-76, Anthras Bapt Ch 1977-79, King's Settlement Bapt Ch 1981-; Free-Lance Writer, 1964-; Campbell Co Bapt Assn, 1978-; cp/Nat Rifle Assn, 1971-75; Smithsonian Assoc, 1973-; r/So Bapt; hon/Articles Pub'd in *Harper's Weekly* 1973, *Message* 1982, *Stamp World* 1982, *Pulpit Helps* 1977-; Poetry Pub'd in *Sunshine*, 1982.

PARTRIDGE, WILLIAM FRANKLIN JR oc/Attorney at Law; b/Jul 16, 1945; h/2029 Harrington Street, Newberry, SC 29108; ba/Newberry, SC; m/Ilene S; c/Allison Langford, William F III; p/William F Partridge Sr, Newberry, SC; ed/BS, Hist, The Citadel, 1967; JD, Univ of SC Law, 1970; mil/Maj, USAFR; pa/Ptnr in Law Firm of Pope and Hudgens, PA, 1974-; SC Bar, Public Issue Com 1982-83; Newberry Bar, Pres 1982-83; Assn of Citadel Men; cp/Lions Clb; Palmetto Clb; Country Clb of Newberry; Cotillion Clb; r/Meth; hon/One of Five Original Appointees by the SC Supr Ct on Fam Selection Adv Bd of the Fam and Matrimonial Lwyrs for Specialization in SC; W/W Am Law; W/W S.

PASCHAL, ANNE BALES oc/Mathematics Teacher; b/Oct 10, 1929; h/801 West Avenue, D, San Angelo, TX 76901; ba/San Angelo, TX; m/Bill; c/Douglas, Susan, Paul; p/Wirt Bales (dec); Louise Fletcher, Winters, TX; ed/BS 1970, MEd 1983, Angelo St Univ; pa/Math Tchr, 1970-; Pres of Bd of Dirs 1979-80, Concho Ed FCU; NCTM; Kappa Delta Pi; Delta Kappa Gamma; Pi Mu Epsilon; Sigma Tau Delta; Alpha Chi; Pi Delta Kappa; TSTA; NEA; Local Treas 1978-79, TSTA and CTA; Wkshop Presenter; r/Prot; Acad Excell Awds, 1968, 1969; Ldrship and Achmt Awds, 1969, 1970; Tchr of the Yr, 1978; W/W Am Wom; Personalities of S; W/W Am Col and Univs.

PASCHAL, JAMES ALPHONSO oc/Higher Education Planner; b/Aug 11, 1931; h/117 Chinquapin Circle, Columbia, SC 29210; ba/Columbia, SC; m/Mimia L; c/Maret Elvara; p/Bouie and Mary Paschal (dec); ed/BA, Xavier Univ; MS, Ft Val St Col; EdD, Univ of SC; mil/AUS Inf, 1951-53; pa/Coor of Facilities (Higher Ed); Dir of Student Affairs; Dir of Cnslg; Dir of Student Pers Sers; Sch Social Wkr; Libn and Classroom Tchr; Alpha Phi Alpha Frat; APGA; SC Pers and Guid Assn; SC Col Pers Assn; cp/Downtown Optimist Clb; r/Cath; hon/Author, "Effects of Perceptual Learning Experiences on Group IQ Test Scores of High School Failures" 1963, "Effects of Activity Group Counseling and Tutoring on Changing Reading Ability, Grade Point Averages and Attitude of Deficient Veteran Students" 1977.

PASCHALL, AMY KING oc/Public Relations Specialist; b/Feb 9, 1951; h/3803-E North Decatur Road, Decatur, GA 30032; ba/Atlanta, GA; p/Eliza K Paschall, Atlanta, GA; ed/BA in Communs, Grinnell Col, 1973; Num Staff Tng Courses Offered by GA Dept of Labor; Currently Wkg for BS in Data Technol, DeKalb Commun Col; pa/Public Relats and Info Spec, GA Dept of Labor, 1973-; Conslt to Gov's Ofc, Deaf and Hearing-Impaired Citizens, 1979-; Conslt to Planning and Human Sys Inc, 1979; Wom in Communs Inc, 1972-; Intl Assn of Pers in Employmt Security, 1973-, Chm of Publicity Com 1982-83, 1980-81, 1979-80; Editor of GA IAPES Newsletter, 1975-; cp/Gov's Coun on the Deaf, 1979-; Metro Atlanta Task Com on the Handicapped, 1978-; r/Christian Sci; hon/Outstg Handicapped Profl Wom of the Yr, Decatur Pilot Clb, 1982; Best Intl Chapt Pub, IAPES, 1981, 1982; St Rep, Intl IAPES

Publicity Com, 1980-81, 1982-83; Outstg Yg Wom of Am; W/W Am Wom.

PASSALACQUA, CARLOS M oc/Engineer, Writer; b/Jun 11, 1912; h/2205 General Patton Street, Santurce, PR 00913; m/Ana J de Passalacqua; c/Ana Josefa, Sylvia P de Garcia, Carmen Inés P de Blondet; p/Antonio Passalacqua (dec); ed/BS, Civil Engrg, 1934; pa/Hydroelect Wks, Housing, Highways, Factories and Other Ec Devel, 1935-53; Mem and Chief of Staff, PR Planning Bd, 1946-51; Pres, PR Indust Devel Co, 1953-61; Pres, Casals Fest Org; Fdr and Sr Ptnr, Passalacqua & Cia, Ec, Planning, Arch, Engrg and Fin; Life Mem, ASCE; Mem and Pres for a Yr, Coun of Higher Ed, Univ of PR, 1973-79; Mem, Governing Bd, Lesley Col, 1969-75; Advr to Caribbean Comm of the Govts of the US, Great Brit, France and The Netherlands, 1950-57; r/Cath; hon/Author, *Poetry and Philosophy* 1972, *Noche, fuente* (Poetry) 1976, *El llanto de la nada* (Poetry) 1977; Author of a Number of Tech Papers on Social & Ec Planning & Indust Devel; HHD, honoris causae, Conservatory of Music of PR, 1974.

PASTERNAC, ANDRÉ oc/Physician; b/Jul 22, 1937; h/3465 Redpath Street, Montreal, Quebec, Canada H3G 2G8; ba/Montreal; p/Jacques and Regine Pasternac, Toulouse, France; ed/Math Supérieurs, Lycée Henri IV, Paris, 1955-56; PCB, MCL, 1957; MD, Univ of Toulouse, France, 1963; BA, Polit Sci, Toulouse, 1963; Cert, Biochem, Toulouse, 1964; Res Scholar (Fulbright), Harvard Med Sch, 1968-71; mil/Desgeneltes Hosp, Lyon, France; pa/Fellow, Cardiology, Peter Bent Brigham Hosp, 1968-69; Fellow in Cardiology, Chd's Hosp Med Ctr, 1969-71; Fellow, Cardiology, Univ of Toronto, 1971-72; Asst Prof of Med, Montreal Heart Inst and Univ of Montreal, 1972-77; Vis'g Assoc Prof of Med, McGill Univ, 1975-76; Assoc Prof of Med, Montreal Heart Inst and Univ of Montreal, 1978-; Fellow, Am Col of Cardiology, 1975; Am Heart Assn, Coun on Clin Cardiology 1976; Canadian Cardiovas Soc, 1974; French Cardiac Soc, 1973; Am Fdn for Clin Res, 1973; Intl Study Grp for Heart Res, 1973; NY Acad of Sci, 1980; Am Soc of Law and Med, 1981; r/Cath; hon/Author, Var Articles in Profl Jours; W/W E; Canadian W/W.

PASTREICH, PETER oc/Symphony Executive Director; b/1938; m/Dr Ingrid Eggers; c/Anna, Milena; Emanuel, Michael; ed/BA, magna cum laude, Yale Univ, 1959; pa/Exec Dir, SF Symph, 1978-; Exec Dir, St Louis Symph Orch, 12 Yrs; Bus Mgr, KS City Philharm; Mgr, Nashville Symph and Greenwich Village Symph; Asst Mgr, Denver Symph and Balto Symph; Fdr, Com for Symph Orchs and the Arts, MO; Exec Com, Am Symph Orch Leag; VP, Exec Com, CA Confdn of the Arts; Bd Mem, Stern Grove Fest; Recommendation Bd, Avery Fisher Artist Prog, Yale Univ Coun's Com on Music; hon/Contbr, Articles to Newspapers; Dist'd Alumnus Awd, Yale Univ Band, 1977.

PATAKY, MARIE ANN oc/Certified Public Accountant; h/Box 1442, Palmer Square, Princeton, NJ 08540; ba/Same; p/Elizabeth Pataky, Pittsburgh, PA; ed/BS in Bus Adm, Robert Morris Col, 1974; AS in Data Processing, Commun Col of Allegheny Co, 1970; pa/Auditor,

Peat Marwick, Mitchell & Co, 1974-76; Tax Acct, F L Roterman & Assocs, 1976-77; Acctg Conslt, Career & Life Planning Inst, 1977-78; Tax Acct, Westinghouse Elect, 1978-80; Internal Auditor, Johnson & Johnson, 1980-81; Tax Supvr, The Interpublic Grp of Cos Inc, 1981-; Financial Conslt, Dir, Contrarian Investmt Inst, 1981-; CPA, PA, 1976; Robert Morris Scholar, 1972-74; Am Inst of CPAs; PA Inst of CPAs; Nat Assn of Accts; Am Wom's Soc of CPAs; Inst of Cert's Financial Planners; Intl Cert'd Financial Planners; cp/Treas, Chd's Hosp Fund, 1979-80; hon/W/W Am Wom.

PATE, LARRY EUGENE oc/University Professor; b/Jan 27, 1945; h/3217 Saddlehorn Drive, Lawrence, KS 66044; ba/Lawrence, KS; m/Kathryn Anne Clyde; c/Benjamin David, Anna Kathryn, Lesley Elizabeth; p/Leslie Edgar Pate (dec); Mildred Georgia M Pate, Alta Loma, CA; ed/BA, summa cum laude 1971, MS 1973, Univ of CA Irvine; PhD, Univ of IL Urbana-Champaign; mil/Capt, Armor Br, AUS, 1965-70; pa/Assoc Prof 1981-, Asst Prof 1978-81, Univ of KS; Vis'g Assoc Prof, Univ of So CA, 1981, 1982; Vis'g Asst Prof, Univ of WI Madison, 1977-78; Vis'g Asst Prof, Univ of NE Lincoln, 1975-77; Res/Tchg Asst, Univ of IL Urbana-Champaign, 1973-75; Engr Schedules Analyst, McDonnell Douglas Astronautics, 1972-73; Res Asst, Public Policy Res Org, Univ of CA Irvine, 1972-73; Acad of Mgmt, Prog Com 1979-82; AAAS; Am Inst for Decision Scis, Prog Com 1979-83; Am Psychol Assn; Brit Psychol Soc; Intl Assn of Applied Psych; cp/YMCA Soccer Coach, KC, 1981-82; hon/Author, 20 Articles, 28 Papers Presented at Reg, Nat and Intl Meetings of Profl Socs; Articles Pub'd in *Journal of Social Psychology, Journal of Management, Academy of Management Review, Group and Organization Studies, Journal of Psychology,* and Others; Hons Scholar, Sch of Bus, Univ of KS, 1981-83; Am Men and Wom of Sci; DIB; Men of Achmt; Intl W/W Intells; W/W MW; Outstg Yg Men of Am; W/W Frontier Sci & Technol.

PATEL, DILIP NARAYANBHAI oc/Chemical Engineer; b/Sep 17, 1951; h/16 Windsor Garden, 5-A Woodside Avenue, Danbury, CT 06810; ba/Danbury, CT; m/Sumitra; c/Chirag; p/Narayanbhai J, India; Savitaben N Patel (dec); sp/Bahechardas H (dec); Ichchhaben B Patel, India; ed/BS Chem Engrg, Gujarat Univ, India, 1973; MS Chem Engrg, IL Inst of Technol, Chicago, 1975; Postgrad, Inst of Gas Technol, Chicago, 1976-77; pa/Res Assoc, Fuel Cell Engrg Dept, Inst of Gas Technol, Chicago, 1975-76; Sr Proj Engr, Fuel Cell R&D Dept, Energy Res Corp, Danbury, CT, 1977-79; Prog Mgr, Fuel Cell R&D Dept, Energy Res Corp, 1979-; Am Inst of Chem Engrs; Chem Engrg Prod Res Panel; India Assn of Gtr Danbury, Exec Com, 1980; hon/Author Sev Tech Papers & Reports on Fuel Cells, 1977-83; Presented Paper "Predictive Testing for Fuel Cells" at Electrochem Soc Meeting in Denver, 1981; Presented Paper "Assessmt of Phosphoric Acid and Triflouromethane Sulfonic Acid Fuel Cells for Vehicular

Powerplants" at Intersoc Energy Conversion Engrg Conf, Los Angeles, 1982; F'ship, Inst of Gas Technol, 1976-77; Govt of India Nat Merit S'ship, 1968-73; Ranked 2nd in Univ during 1st 3 Yrs of BSChE; W/W E.

PATTEN, JACQUELINE LaVETTA oc/Cover Designer, Art Director, Photographic Consultant; b/Jan 6, 1948; h/1239 Ward Avenue, Bronx, NY 10472; ba/Same; c/LaCheun LaVette, LaSarah Renata; p/Bernard and Sarah Patten, Bronx, NY; ed/BS in Psych, Sociol, Photo 1980, MS in Ed 1982, Hunter Col; pa/Photographic Asst to Max Waldman, Theatre and Dance, 1977-80; Art Dir and Photographic Conslt, *Journal of African Civilizations,* 1981-; Free-Lance Photog, Specializing in Hand-Painted Photographs, 1970-; Photographic Soc of Am; r/Unitarian; hon/Featured in *Black Photographers Annual* 1980, *Journal of African Civilizations* 1981; Exhib'd in Mus of the City of NY, 1979; 7th Annual Lincoln Ctr Photography Awd, 1980; *Mademoiselle's* 14th Annual Photography Competition, First Prize, 1980; W/W E.

PATTEN, RONALD JAMES oc/College Dean; b/Jul 17, 1935; h/39 Storrs Heights Road, Storrs, CT 06268; ba/Storrs, CT; m/Shirley Ann Bierman; c/Christine Marie, Cheryl Ann, Charlene Denise; p/Rudolph (dec); Mrs Cecelia Pataconi, Gaastra, MI; ed/BA 1957, MA 1959, MI St Univ; PhD, Univ of AL, 1963; mil/AUS, Field Artillery, Capt 1958; pa/Dean, Sch of Adm, Univ of CT, 1974-; Dir of Res, Financial Acctg Standards Bd, 1973-74; Hd of Dept of Acctg, VA Polytechnic Inst and St Univ, 1966-73; Vis'g Prof, Univ of TX Austin, 1972; Vis'g Prof, Univ of MN, 1969; Vis'g Prof, Grad Sch of Profl Acctg, NEn Univ, 1967; Prof 1967-73, Assoc Prof 1965-67, VA Polytechnic Inst and St Univ; Asst Prof, Univ of CO, 1963-65; Other Previous Positions; Beta Gamma Sigma; Beta Alpha Psi; Delta Sigma Pi; Phi Kappa Phi; Am Acctg Assn; Scabbard and Blade; Am Inst of CPAs; Nat Assn of Accts; CT Soc of CPAs; r/Luth; hon/Pubs, "Data Center Opens" 1980, "Management Information Systems in the Business School-A Suggested Approach" 1978, "Material Costs" 1978, "Information Systems in the MBA Curriculum" 1978, Num Others; CPA Cert, 1964; Nat Quartermaster Awd, Nat Quartermaster Assn, 1956; Outstg Edrs in Am; W/W Am; Am Men and Wom of Sci; Men of Achmt.

PATTERSON, E TERRY oc/Free-Lance Artist, Teacher; b/Jul 25, 1921; h/407 Edward, Box 2338, Big Spring, TX; ba/Elgin, TX; m/R Pat; c/James R, Joanna; p/Mr and Mrs James E Terry (dec); ed/Att'd, Howard Payne Univ, TX Tech, Howard Col; 8 Yrs of Pvt Art Instrn; pa/44 One-Wom Shows, incl'g, Grand Ctl Gallery, Lagunis Gloria Art Mus, Wom's Federated Clb, W TX Mus, S Plains Col, Mus in Canyon and Lubbock (TX), Elizabeth Ney Mus, Mus of Art; Has Exhib'd More Than 500 Grp Exhbns in NY, Fed German Republic and Many Other Locations; Collections: Franklin Mint Co, Smithsonian, TX Bd of Rltrs Mus, Cosden Oil Co, Howard Co Ct House, Howard Col, Others; Fdr, First Reg Chapt, TX Fine Arts Assn, and The Big Spring Art Assn; hon/Recip, Over 500 Intl, Nat and St Awds; 16 TX Fine Arts Cits; US RBM,

NY; Wom of Outstg Achmt in the Arts, World W/W of Wom; DIB; W/W Am; W/W Am Art; Notable Ams; Personalities of US; Men and Wom of Distn.

PATTERSON, FAE oc/Educator, Band Director; b/Oct 31, 1947; h/98 South 350 East, Clearfield, UT 84015; ba/Ogden, UT; p/J Alex and Fern A Patterson (dec); ed/BS, Weber St Col, 1969; MS, UT St Univ, 1973; mil/Currently Serving, USAFR; pa/Music and PE Tchr, Lyman Sch Dist #6, 1969-70; Music Tchr, W Side Sch Dist, 1970-75; Ogden City Sch Dist, 1975-; NEA; UEA; Local Tchrs Orgs; UT Music Edrs; Reg Rep, UMEA, 1977-79; r/LDS.

PATTERSON, PEGGY JEAN oc/Owner of Realty Company, Broker; b/Nov 10, 1940; h/Route 1, Box 76, Otto, NC 28763; ba/Franklin, NC; m/Morris; c/Aletha Darlene, Kenneth Douglas; p/Jay B and Aletha Moore, Otto, NC; ed/Att'd, Franklin HS, SWn Tech Col; pa/Secy, John Phelan Real Est, 1973-74; Broker, Jones Real Est, 1974-75; Owner, Broker, Pres, Patterson Rlty Inc, 1977-; BBB; NC Assn of Rltrs, St Dir 1980-82; Franklin Bd of Rltrs, Pres 1981, Secy 1979, Dir 1979-82; Nat Assn of Female Execs; Local Merchants Assn; BPW Clb, Secy 1982-83; cp/Franklin C of C, Dir 1980; r/Bapt; hon/Recip, Mbrship Awd, Franklin Area C of C, 1980; Beautification Awd, Franklin Garden Clb, 1980; Rltr of Yr, 1982; W/W Am Wom.

PATTERSON, PEGGY LOU oc/Provost Marshal of the United States Army; b/Jun 21, 1944; h/GEB 4217 Apartment K, 6660 Zweibrucken, West Germany; ba/APO NY; c/Kiila Michelle; p/Walter and Cinderella Patterson, Weleetka, OK; ed/BA, Crim Justice, Golden Gate Univ, 1979; Mil Police Advance Course, 1978; Counterterrorism Course, 1982; Race Relats, 1973; Creat Prob Solving, 1973; Wk Simplification, 1974; Correctional Adm, 1978; Security Mgmt Course, 1978; mil/AUS, 1965-; pa/Basic Tng, Ft McClellan, 1965; Adv'd Indiv Tng, Ft Leonardwood, 1965; Pers Spec/Pers Sgt, Ft Knox, 1965-69; Adm Non-Comm'd Ofcr, Vietnam, 1969-70; Pers Sgt, Aeromed Res Lab, Ft Rucker, 1970; Ofcr Cand, Ft McClellan, 1971; Cmdr, HHC, USAPERSCEN, and Cmdr, Wom's Army Corps Co, Oakland Army Base, 1973; Adjutant, AUS Pers Ctr, Oakland Army Base, 1974; Logistics Ofcr (S-4), Ft Lewis, 1976; Cmdr, 9th Inf Div Mil Police Co, Ft Lewis, 1976-77; Asst Prof of Mil Sci, LA St Univ, 1979-82; Provost Marshal, US Mil Commun Activity, Zweibrucker, W Germany, 1982-; Assn of the AUS, 1978-; Info Ofcr Supervising and Editing the *US Army Personnel Center Times,* 1973-74; r/Bapt; hon/All Star Basketball Team, 1966, 1967, 1968; Meritorious Ser Medal, 1982; Army Commend Medal, 1969, 1971, 1974, 1977; Good Conduct Medal, 3 Awds; Bronze Star Medal, 1971; Vietnam Ser Medal, 1971; Vietnam Campaign Medal, 1971; Nat Def Ser Medal, 1971; W/W Am Wom.

PATTERSON, VIOLET ALFORD oc/Teacher and Coordinator; b/Jan 23, 1927; h/3626 North New Haven Avenue, Tulsa, OK 74115; ba/Tulsa, OK; m/Lee Virgil Sr; c/Emily V, Gwynell Elaine, Lee Virgil Jr, James; ed/BS, Langston Univ, 1950; MS, OK St Univ, 1967; Further Study, OK St Univ, OK

Univ, NEn St Univ; pa/Chief Clk, Boley St Sch for Boys, 1950-63; Pers Clk, N Am Rockwell, 1963-65; Cooperative Ofc Ed Tchr/Coor 1965-, Bus Dept Chp 1976-, Tulsa Public Schs; OK Bus Ed Assn, Treas, Secy, VP and Newsletter Editor; Voc Bus and Ofc Ed, Pres, VP, Secy, Treas, 1965-; Adm Mgmt Soc, Newsletter Editor, Mem of Bd, 1970-; TCTA Del, 1982-83; VP, LUAA Alumni; AVA; NEA; OEA; CEBOE; OWPA; NBEA; OVA; LUAA; cp/ YWCA; r/Mem of Fac of St and Nat Bapt Tng Union; Dir of Christian Ed, Morning Star Bapt Ch, 1975-; hon/Outstg Voc Bus Tchr of OK, 1982; Del and Presenter, Am Voc Assn, 1977, 1978, 1979; OBEA Presenter, 1979; Selected to Participate in OK Extern Prog, 1976; Alpha Kappa Alpha Sorority, Pres, VP, Secy, Treas, Chair of Many Coms, 1964-80; Delta Pi Epsilon.

PATTI, JOSEPH HARRY oc/ Teacher, Adjunct Professor; b/Dec 2, 1942; h/616 Olive Street, Hinesville, GA 31313; ba/Hinesville, GA; m/Ruth Riner; c/Jami Marie, Teri Dawn; p/ Joseph J Patti, Hinesville, GA; Frances M Patti, Hinesville, GA; ed/BS, Biol, GA So Col, 1970; MS, Entomology 1973, PhD, Entomology 1978, Clemson Univ; mil/AUS, 1965-66; pa/Biol Tchr, Bradwell Inst, 1982-; Entomologist, AUS Corps of Engrs, Envir Resources Br, 1978-; Adj Prof of Biol, St Leo Col Resident Ctr, 1977-; HS Chem and Biol Tchr, Hd of Sci Dept, Bradwell Inst, 1975-78; Grad Res and Tchg Asst, Clemson Univ, 1971-75; Other Previous Positions; Entomological Soc of Am; GA Entomological Soc; SC Entomological Soc; Sigma Xi; Am Registry of Profl Entomologists; AAAS; Am Inst of Biol Scis; Am Coun on Sci and Hlth; r/Meth; hon/Pubs, "Mosquito Distribution Records within the Richard B Russell Dam and Lake Area" 1982, "Trunk Diameter and Vertical Growth of Loblolly Pine, *Pinus taeda* L, in Relation to Populations of *Cinara* spp and *Essigella pini* Wilson" 1982, Others; Tchr of the Yr (Runner-Up), Bradwell Inst, 1976-77; W/W S and SW.

PATTISHALL, CHARLENE H oc/ Videoconferencing Manager; b/Apr 2, 1946; ba/Chrysler Corporation, PO Box 857, Detroit, MI 48288; p/Charles L and Gladys H Pattishall, Tampa, FL; ed/ Master of Ednl Communs Media (TV) 1974, Bach of Visual Arts (Photo) 1973, GA St Univ; pa/Media Mgr, Chrysler Corp, 1983-; Hd of Media Ctr, Kennesaw Col, 1977-83; Hd of Prodn, Valencia Commun Col, 1977; Intl TV Assn, Dir of Mbrship; Capital City BPW Clb; cp/Cobb Co C of C, Communs Bd; Atlanta Wom's Netwk, Dir; r/TV Com, Peachtree Christian Ch; hon/Pubs, "Teleconferencing: Just Give Me the Basics," "Cable Television-The Missing Link," "Media Management in Higher Education," "A Profile of Educational Media Facilities in Higher Education within the State of Georgia," "Kennesaw College: Developing a Media Center"; Mortar Bd, 1974; ITVA Ldrship, 1981-82, 1982-83; Outstg Yg Wom of Am.

PATTON, DENNIS DAVID oc/Professor of Radiology and Nuclear Medicine; b/Aug 4, 1930; h/6502 Pontatoc Road, Tucson, AZ 85718; ba/Tucson, AZ; m/Pamela Ruth; c/James Patrick,

William Christopher; p/Norma R Gotzian, Camarillo, CA; ed/BA, Physics, Univ of CA Berkeley, 1953; MD, Univ of CA LA, 1959; pa/Assoc Prof of Radiol, Univ of CA Irvine, 1968-70; Assoc Prof of Radiol, Vanderbilt Univ, 1970-75; Prof of Radiol, Univ of AZ, 1975-; AMA; AZ Med Assn; Pima Co Med Soc; Soc of Nuclear Med; Am Col of Radiol, Fellow; Am Col of Nuclear Phys, Fellow; Am Col of Nuclear Med, Fellow; Assn Univ Radiologists; Radiological Soc of N Am; Soc for Med Decision Making; cp/Brentwood Optimist Clb, 1958-65; Org'd and Operated Boy Scout Troup for Handicapped; r/Meth; hon/Author, 54 Articles, 23 Abstracts, 8 Book Chapts, 3 Books, 1 Syllabus/Slide, 6 Book Reviews; Top Man Awd, Santa Monica, CA, 1961; Dist'd Fellow, Am Col of Nuclear Med; W/W W; W/W AZ; Am Bd of Med Specialties; W/W Frontier Sci and Technol; Am Men and Wom of Sci.

PAULICK, MARIHELEN HREES oc/ Supervisor of Training Centers; b/Apr 29, 1943; h/73 Western Avenue, #6, Trenton, NJ 08618; ba/Trenton, NJ; p/ John Paulick (dec); Maria Hrees Marcy, Ventnor, NJ; ed/MA, Guid and Cnslg, Rider Col, 1970; BS, Ed and Social Scis, Univ of Pgh, 1964; pa/Secy, Univ of Pgh, 1964; Secy, WFPG-AM-FM, 1965; Instr, Atl City Voc Sch, 1965; Trenton Manpower Skills Ctr, 1965-67; Mercer City Commun Col, 1967-72; Instr, Clerical Tng 1967-73, Supvr 1973-76, Reg Mgr 1976-, Civil Ser Tng Ctr, NJ Dept Civil Ser; NJ Bus Ed Assn; Am Voc Assn; Am Soc Tng and Devel; Intl Pers Mgmt Assn; Profl Pers Assn; Nat Bus Ed Assn; Voc Ed Assn, NJ; Phi Delta Kappa; NJ Real Est Lic; cp/US Figure Skating Assn; Fleetwood Soc; Boehm Porcelain Guild; Franklin Mint; hon/Am Legion, 1956; Hon Employee Awd, St of NJ, 1969; NJ Senatorial S'ship, 1961-64; W/W E.

PAULK, LORAINE h/Post Office Box 921, Goodlettsville, TN 37072.

PAULUS, NORMA JEAN oc/Secretary of State; b/Mar 13, 1933; h/3090 Pigeon Hollow Road South, Salem, OR 97302; ba/Salem, OR; m/William G; c/ Elizabeth, William; ed/LLB, Willamette Law Sch, 1962; pa/Secy to Harney Co Dist Atty, 1950-53; Legal Secy, Salem, 1953-55; Secy to Chief Justice, OR Supr Ct, 1955-61; Self-Employed Appellate Lwyr, 1962-76; Counsel, Firm of Paulus & Callaghan, 1973-76; Mem, OR Ho of Reps, 1971-76; Secy of St, OR, 1977-; Dir, Nat Soc of St Legis, 1971-72; Nat Order of Wom Legis, 1973-76; OR St Bar Assn; Marion Co Bar Assn; BPW Clb; cp/Zonta Intl; Wom's Polit Caucus, Willamette Univ; Bd of Trustees, Dir, Benedictine Foun; hon/Recip, Golden Torch Awd, BPW, 1971; Dist'd Ser Awd, City of Salem, 1971; Named to "Women of the Future" by *Ladies Home Journal*, 1979; Abigail Scott Duniway Award, Wom in Communs, 1979; Wom of the Yr Awd, OR Wom Lwyrs, 1982; W/W Am Wom; Dir of Dist'd Ams; W/W Am; W/W W; W/W Am Polit.

PAYNE, SUSAN F oc/Museum Executive; b/Feb 17, 1941; h/Evergreen Farm, Washington, CT 06793; ba/ Washington, CT; m/John H III; c/John H IV, Sarah Shadle; p/Mr and Mrs F P Frantz, Phoenix, NY; ed/BS, Simmons Col; pa/Pres, CEO 1983-, Exec VP 1982, Dir of Devel 1981, Dir of Ed 1977, Am

Indian Archaeological Inst; Chm, Town of Wash's Historic Dist Comm, 1976-81; hon/W/W Am Wom.

PEACOCK, LaRITA WILLIAMS oc/ Computer Systems Development Manager; b/Mar 24, 1954; h/899 Clopper Road, #T2, Gaithersburg, MD 20878; ba/Washington, DC; m/Hubert Leonard Jr; p/Charles Eugene Williams Sr, Madisonville, KY; Clara Smith Williams, Madisonville, KY; ed/BA, Princeton Univ, 1973; MBA, Stanford Univ, 1975; pa/Sys Analyst, Exxon, 1976-79; Mgr of Sys Devel 1983-, Sys Analyst 1980-83, Roy Rogers Div, Marriott Corp; Nat Assn of Female Execs; AAUW; r/Bapt; hon/W/W Am Wom.

PEALER, SARAH ANN oc/Registered Dietitian; b/Feb 7, 1921; h/313 Terrace Drive East, Clearwater, FL 33515; ba/Clearwater, FL; m/Daniel Edward; p/Gerald Darland (dec) and Kathleen M deBord Tanner, Coral Gables, FL; ed/Student, Brenan Col, 1939-40; BS in Home Ec, Univ of AL, 1944; Postgrad, Univ of AL, Univ of S FL, St Petersburg Jr Col; pa/Foods Instr, Dade Co Bd of Public Instrn, 1945-46; Dist Home Economist, Frigidaire Distributor, 1948-56; Home Ser Dir, Orlando Utilities Comm, 1960-64; Dir of Home Ec, Tupperware Intl HQs, 1964-54; Dir of Home Ec, FL Dept Natural Resources, 1966-67; Clin Dietitian 1968-77, Mgr of Dietary Dept 1977-80, Clin Dietitian, Renal Empasis 1980-, Morton F Plant Hosp; Am Dietetic Assn; FL Dietetic Assn; Gulf Ctl Dist, FL Dietetic Assn; Nutrition Today Soc; Alpha Gamma Delta; cp/Past Pres, Pilot Clb of Clearwater, 1973-74; hon/Author, Wkly Column, "Currently Cooking," *Orlando Sentinel*, for Orlando Utilities Comm, 1960-64; W/W S and SW.

PEARLMAN, NANCY SUE oc/Environmentalist, Broadcaster; b/Apr 17, 1948; h/1783 South Wooster Street, Los Angeles, CA 90035; ba/Los Angeles, CA; p/Carl and Agnes Pearlman, Santa Ana, CA; ed/MA, Urban Studies and Planning, Antioch Univ/W, 1979; BA, cum laude, Anthropology, Univ of CA LA, 1971; Var Tchg Credentials; pa/ Pres, Multi-City Sers, Communication/ Broadcasting ConsIts; VP, Eco-View, Geneological Res and Pub'g; Environmentalist; Conservationist; Preservationist; Lectr; Spkr; Tchr; Writer; Media and Communs Consit; Admr; Athlete; Traveler; Exec Dir and Fdr, Ecol Ctr of So CA, 1972-; Radio Show Host/Commentator, KMGG's "Environmental Directions"; CoChp, Griffith Pk Adv Com; CA Wilderness Coalition's Adv Com; CA Desert Alliance's Adv Com; Ofcr, Citizens for Mojave Nat Pk; Rep, Nat Citizens Coalition on Waste, Antioch Alumni; Co Sanitation Dists of LA Co's Solid Waste Envir Citizens Adv Com; Mem of Num Envir, Profl, Ednl and Social Cause Orgs; Bd of Dirs, Desert Protective Coun; Advr, Universal Pantheist Soc; hon/Pubs, *Ecological Action Checklist*; Guest Appearances on Radio and TV Talk Shows in LA and Orange Co Areas, 1969-; Holder of Over 100 Trophies, Medals and Ribbons in Equestrian, Running, Swimming and Triathlon Events; Other Hons; W/W Am Wom; World W/W Wom; Intl W/ W Commun Ser; Commun Ldrs and Noteworthy Ams.

PEARLMAN, SHELDON oc/Executive; b/Jan 24, 1938; h/25 Quails Trail, Stamford, CT 06903; ba/Ridgefield, CT; m/Rhoda; c/Joseph, Susan, Karen; p/ Joseph and Lena Grossberg Pearlman (dec); ed/BEE, NY Univ, 1959; MSEE, Univ of So CA, 1962; pa/Engr, Airborne Instruments Lab, 1959-60; Engr, Northrup Corp, 1960-62; Sr Sys Engr, Corporate Sys Ctr, U Aircraft, 1962-68; Instr, Univ of CT, 1964-66; Sr Computer Communs Engr, Data Prods, 1968-71; Fdr, Exec VP, Computrol-Kidde, 1971-; r/Bd of Dirs, Congreg Beth Israel, 1966-68; Bd of Dirs, Congreg Agudath Sholom, 1976-79; hon/Inventions: Core Rope Memory Matrix 1966, 2 Megabaud Coherent FSK Modem 1976, Megalink Local Area Netwk 1979; W/W E.

PEARSON, NORMAN oc/Land Consultant and Policy Planner; b/Oct 24, 1928; ba/PO Box 5362, Station A, London, Ontario N6A 4L6; m/Gerda Maria Josefine Riedl; p/Joseph and Mary Pearson (dec); ed/PhD in Land Ec, Intl Inst for Adv'd Studies, 1979; MBA, Pacific Wn Univ, 1980; BA w Hons in Town and Country Planning, Univ of Durham, UK, 1951; pa/Pres, Chm of Bd of Govs 1983-, Adj Prof, Sch of Bus 1980-, Pacific Wn Univ; Pres, Norman Pearson Planning Assocs Ltd, 1976-; Profl Consltg Pract as Planner, 1962-; Adj Prof, Intl Inst for Adv'd Studies, 1980-82; Prof of Polit Sci, Univ of Wn Ontario, 1972-77; Assoc Prof of Geography, Chm and Dir of Ctr for Resources Devel, Univ of Guelph, 1967-72; Asst Prof, Geography and Planning, Univ of Waterloo, 1963-67; Dir of Planning for Burlington and Suburban Area Planning Bd, and Commr of Planning for Town of Burlington, 1959-62; Dir of Planning, Hamilton-Wentworth Planning Area Bd, 1956-59; Planning Analyst, City of Toronto Planning Bd, 1955-56; Other Previous Positions; Fellow, Royal Town Planning Inst, UK; Intl Soc of City and Reg Planners, 1972; Canadian Inst of Planners; Am Inst of Planners, 1973; Ontario Land Economist, 1963; Real Est Profl Appraiser; Am Inst of Cert'd Planners, 1978; Canadian Assn of Cert'd Planning Techs, 1979; hon/ Co-Author or Co-Editor of 4 Books; Author, 68 Articles in Refereed Acad and Profl Jours or Chapts in Books, 171 Articles in Non-Refereed Jours, Reports and Conf Papers or Abstracts, 46 Newpaper Articles or Book Reviews; Life Fellow, Royal Ec Soc; Life Fellow, Intercontinental Biogl Assn; Life Mem, US Com for Monetary Res and Ed; Life Fellow, Am Geographical Soc, 1976; Life Fellow, Atl Ec Assn, 1978; Intl Frat of Lambda Alpha, 1969; Fdr Mem, Brit Sociological Assn, 1953; Fellow, Intl Inst for Adv'd Studies, 1980; Pres's Prize (Bronze Medal), Royal Town Planning Inst, UK, 1957; DIB; Am Men and Wom of Sci; W/W MW; Men of Achmt; Intl W/W Commun Ser; Other Listings.

PECK, PAULINE C oc/Senior Editor; b/Sep 30, 1927; h/825 Randolph Road, Middletown, CT 06457; ba/Middletown, CT; m/David Tebbutt; c/Kathleen R Ross, Lt William L Ross, Sharon M Ross; p/Elmer V H and Eileen M Fay Brooks, Sandwich, MA; ed/BS in Ed, Boston St Col, 1947; Grad Studies, NEn Univ, Ctl CT St Col, 1959-63; pa/Elem Sch Tchr, Boston, 1947-49; Social Wkr, Boston, 1949; Elem Sch Tchr, MA, ME, 1953-55; Mgr/Bkkpr, Armour & Co, 1955-58; Elem Sch Tchr, Lynnfield and Gloucester, MA, 1958-61; Editor 1961-72, Sr Editor 1972-, Xerox Ed Pubs (Wkly Reader); Career Advr, Wesleyan Univ, 1976-; IRA; Wom in Communs Inc; Nat Soc of Poets; CT Rdg Assn; Hartford IRA; Nat Assn for the Ed of Yg Chd; r/Deist; hon/Pubs, *Liberty B Mouse Comes to America* 1977, *Liberty B Mouse Goes to a Party* 1978, *The Ghastly Green Ghost* 1979, *Buddy Bear and the Big Scare* 1980, *Buddy's No-Cook Cookbook* 1980, *Buddy's ABC Coloring Book* 1980, *The Day Buddy Bear Ran Away* 1981, Others; Alumnus of the Yr, Boston St Col, 1970; Recip, Ed Press Awds, Ed Pres Assn of Am, 1968, 1969, 1977, 1982, 1983; Spkr at Third World Cong on Rdg, Singapore, 1978; Spkr at 2nd Australian Rdg Conf, 1978; Spkr at Many Nat Rdg Confs, 1979-; W/W Am Wom; W/W; Pub'd Poets of Am.

PEDDIE, EDWARD C oc/Executive; b/Jun 7, 1941; ba/PO Box 749, Gainesville, FL 32602; m/Patricia; c/Carmel, Brian; ed/Bach Deg, FL St Univ; Master of Hosp Adm, Univ of MN; mil/AUS, 3 Yrs; pa/Pres, CEO, Santa Fe Hlthcare Sys Inc, 1982-; Pres, Alachua Gen Hosp Inc, 1976-; Var Mgmt Positions, Tallahasse Meml Hosp, Bapt Hosp in Memphis, Bapt Hosp in Pensacola, Mackfee Army Hosp, White Sands Past Dir, FL Hosp Assn; Past Pres, Assn of Vol Hosps of FL; Bd of Dirs, Vol Hosps of FL; Bd Mem, Hlth Activs Mgmt Prog Inc; Am Col of Hosp Admrs; Nat Coun of Commun Hosps; Univ of MN Alumni Assn; cp/C of C; Tip-Off Clb; Quarterback Clb; Served on Bd of Dirs, Civitan Reg Blood Ctr and U Way; Blue Cross Blue Shield; Kiwanis Clb; Gainesville Golf and Country Clb; hon/Pubs, *The Development of a Scale to Determine the Need for Social Accomodations in Pediatric Units,* "Reorganizing the South Vietnam Medical Services".

PELLICER, JAMES O oc/Professor of Spanish American Literature; b/Jan 13, 1927; h/22 Schrade Road, Briarcliff Manor, NY 10510; ba/New York, NY; m/Norma Isabel Juárez de Pellicer; c/ Jennifer Gabrielle, James Scott; p/Jaime Pellicer (dec); ed/PhD, NY Univ, 1972; MA, Adams St Col, 1967; Licenciado en Filosofía, Instituto San José, La Plata, Argentina, 1950; pa/Prof of Spanish Am Lit 1972-, Chm of Spanish Curric Com 1981-, Hunter Col, City Univ of NY; Prof of Spanish, King's Col, 1968-71; Prof of Latin and Spanish, Adams St Col, CO Univ, 1967; Am Assn of Tchrs of Spanish and Portuguese; Latin Am Studies Assn; Iberoamerican Writers and Poets Guild, NY; r/Bapt; hon/Pubs, *Guide for Teaching Spanish to Native Speakers* 1975, 1976, "Bilingualism in the US: Present Significance and Future Course" 1975, Num Others; Fdrs Day Awd, NY Univ, 1973.

PELOSI, PHILIP ANTHONY oc/ Assistant Superintendent of Schools; b/ Nov 9, 1949; h/35 Butler Street, Waterbury, CT 06704; ba/Watertown, CT; p/ Mr and Mrs Felix J Pelosi, Waterbury, CT; ed/BA, magna cum laude, Math, Assumption Col, 1971; MA in Math 1972, PhD in Sec'dy Ed 1978, Univ of CT; Postgrad, Wesleyan Univ 1975, Univ of CT 1979; pa/Tchr, Math, Watertown High, 1972-77; Metric Coor for Watertown, 1978-79; Curric Writer for Lng Disabilities, Univ of CT, 1976-78; Grad Asst, Dept of Ednl Psych 1977-78, Adj Prof of Math 1979, Wn CT St Univ; Adj Prof of Math, Post Col, 1980-83; Math Tchr, Watertown, 1978-83; Asst Supt of Schs, 1983-; NCTM; Assn Tchrs of Math in New England; Assn Tchrs of Math in CT; Assn for Supvn and Curric Devel; cp/ Bd of Dirs, Miss CT S'ship Pageant Inc, 1982-83, Chm of Judges 1981; r/Rom Cath; hon/Pubs, "In Search of Computational Errors" 1983, "Mathematics and the Slow Learner, K-6" 1981, "Mathematics and the Handicapped, K-12" 1981, "Relax with Metrics" 1980, Others; Phi Delta Kappa; Nat Math Hon Soc, VP 1971; Kappa Mu Epsilon; W/ W E.

PEÑA, MODESTA CELEDONIA oc/ Gifted Education Resource Teacher; b/ Mar 3, 1929; h/PO Box 353, San Diego, TX 78384; ba/Alice, TX; p/Encarnacion E and Teófila G Peña (dec); ed/BA 1950, MA 1953, TX St Col for Wom (Now TX Wom's Univ); Cert, Supvn 1979, Cert, Prin 1961, Cert, Supt 1981, TX A&I Univ; pa/Tchr of Eng, San Diego HS, 1950-76; Asst Supt for Curric and Instrn, San Diego Indep Sch Dist, 1976-80; Tchr of Eng, Bee Co Col, 1975-76; Gifted Ed Resource Tchr, Wm Adams Jr High, 1980-; San Diego PTA, VP 1961; TX St Tchrs Assn, Recording Secy 1952-53, 1963-64, First VP 1957-58, 1966-67, Pres 1961; NCTE; TX Coun of Tchrs of Eng; Delta Kappa Gamma; Chapt Recording Secy 1972-74, First VP 1974-76, Pres 1976-78, Mem of St S'ship Com 1979-81; Phi Delta Kappa, Chapt Treas 1978-79; r/St Francis de Paula Cath Ch Choir (Alto, Alternate Accompanist), 1952-58, 1968-70; hon/Salutatorian, San Diego HS, 1946; Newspaper Fund Inc F'ship, Univ of TX, 1964; Outstg Sec'dy Edr, 1974; W/W S and SW.

PENZIAS, ARNO ALLAN oc/ Research Executive, Astrophysicist; b/ Apr 26, 1933; h/419 South 5th Avenue, Highland Park, NJ 08904; ba/Murray Hill, NJ; m/Anne Barras; c/David Simon, Mindy Gail, Laurie Ruth; p/Karl and Justine Penzias, West Palm Beach, FL; ed/BS, City Col of NY, 1954; MA 1958, PhD 1962, Columbia Univ; Var Hon Degs; mil/AUS Signal Corps, 1954-56; pa/Mem of Tech Staff 1961-72, Hd of Radio Physics Res 1972-76, Dir of Radio Res Lab 1976-79, Exec Dir of Res, Communs Scis 1979-81, VP of Res 1981-, Bell Labs; Lectr 1967-72, Vis'g Prof 1972-, Princeton Univ; Res Assoc, Harvard Col Observatory, 1968-80; St Univ of NY, 1974-; Vis'g Com, CA Inst of Tech, 1977-79; Max Planck Fachbeirat, 1978-80, Chm 1980-; NSF, Astronomy Adv Com 1977-79, Indep Panel on Sci and Technol 1982-; Nat Acad of Scis, 1975-; Intl Astronom Union, 1970-; Com of Concerned Scists, VChm 1976-; Am Acad of Arts and Scis, 1974-; Am Phy Soc, 1959-; Am Astronom Soc, 1970-; r/Jewish; hon/Author, Approximately 100 Articles, Dealing Primarily with Sci Subjects; Nobel Prize for Physics, 1978; Herschel Medal of Royal Astronom Soc, 1977; Henry Draper Medal of Nat Acad of Scis, 1977; Am Men and Wom of Sci; W/W Am; W/W World; W/W E; W/W Frontier Sci and

Technol; Men of Achmt.

PERATE, HANNAH MARY oc/Educator; b/Oct 3, 1946; h/PO Box 224, Wrightwood, CA 92397; ba/Wrightwood, CA; p/Frank Leo and Hannah Mary Perate, Winter Park, FL; ed/BA, Russell Col, 1969; MA, CA St Col, 1981; Standard Tchr Credential, 1974; Rdg Spec Credential, 1981; pa/Tchr, St Athanasius Sch 1968, Holy Name Sch 1969-72, Our Lady of Angels Sch 1972-75, St Pius X Sch 1975-78, Sacred Heart Sch 1978-79, Wrightwood Elem Sch 1979-; Eucharistic Min for Schs, 1972-78; IRA; Assn Supvn and Curric Devel; CA Alumni Assn; Nat Cath Ednl Assn, 1978-79; CA PTA, 1979-; Intl Soc of Artists, 1978-79; cp/Charter Mem, Repub Pres Task Force; Nat Right to Life Com; Nat Rifleman's Assn; Cath Yth Org Ath Dept, 1976-81; Spiritual Dir, Mother's Clb, Holy Name Sch, 1969-70; r/Rom Cath; hon/Pubs, "Haiku" 1982, "Yearning" 1982, "Green Dreams" 1981, "Water" 1979, "The Transforming Power of a Yellow Rose" 1981 "A Long Day in October" 1982; Phi Kappa Phi, 1980; Basketball and Softball Coach of the Yr, 1975-76; W/WW.

PERCELL, LLOYD EDGAR oc/Exeutive, Owner of Various Corporations; b/Feb 27, 1931; h/3259 Liahona Way, Las Vegas, NV 89121; ba/Las Vegas, NV; m/Pamela Jo Hershey; c/Richard, David, Bradley, Lisa Marie; p/Selvin John Percell, Portsmouth, OH; Florence Bell Jones Percell, Dayton, OH; ed/Student, Glendale City Col 1953-54, LA City Col 1955, Univ of CA LA 1955-56 (Bus Adm and Indust Engrg Majs); mil/USMC, NCO, 1950-52; pa/Chief Operating Ofcr, Exec Cos, 1974-; Dir, Investor, Chief Exec to Corps Engaged in Fields of Aviation, TV, Motion Pictures, Oil/Gas, Pipelines, Wind Power Energy, Recreational Vehicles, Trucking, Publishing, Printing and Art; Chief Operating Ofcr, Carco Cos, 1966-73; Chief Operating Ofcr, Aerospace Assocs Inc, 1963-65; Gen Mgr of Comml Sales, Lear Corp, 1957-62; Wn Reg Sales 1956-57, Field Sales Engr 1955-56, Indust Engr 1954-55, Prodn Engr 1953-54, Collins Radio Co (Now Rockwell Corp); OH Oil and Gas Assn; Nat Bus Aircraft Assn; Helicopter Assocs Intl; Aircraft Fin Assn; Nat Assn of TV Prog Execs; Assn of Local and Transport Airlines; Am Soc of Tool Engrs; Wn Electronics Mfrs Assn; Aeronautics Soc; Mortgage Bkrs Assn; cp/Repub Nat Party; Am Power Boat Assn of Detroit; Pacific Offshore Powerboat Racing Assn of Van Nuys; Boat Owners Assn of US; hon/Authored and Pub'd, "What You Need to Know About the Oil/Gas Business," "What You Need to Know About Owning a Recreational Vehicle," "What You Need to Know About Owning an Aircraft," "What You Need to Know About the Art Industry," Others; Exec Prodr of TV Shows, "Fun & Fitness," "Miss Phoebe's Garden," "Cosmic Frontiers," "Las Vegas Alive," "The Joan Rivers Special"; Var Mil Decorations; W/W W; W/W Fin and Indust; W/W Am.

PERDIUE, ROBERT L oc/Podiatrist; b/Apr 10, 1945; h/14102 Broken Tree, San Antonio, TX 78229; ba/San Antonio, TX; m/Mary Jane Leslie; c/Rand LaMar, Andrew Leslie; p/Raymond Lee Perdiue, Muncie, IN; Marie Ermal LaMar Perdiue (dec); ed/BA, Physiol, So IL Univ, 1967; MS, Biol, Incarnate Word Col, 1971; DPM, Podiatry, IL Col of Podiatric Med, 1975; mil/AUS, 1967-70, 1975-77; pa/Chief, Podiatry Ser 1975-77, Dir of Podiatric Ed 1977, US Reynolds Army Hosp; Clin Instr, Dept of Podiatric Med, CA Col of Podiatric Med, 1978; Clin Asst Prof, Dept of Fam Pract, Univ of TX Hlth Sci Ctr, Podiatry Residency Prog, 1978-; Bd of Dirs, Alamo Gen Hosp, 1979; Am Assn of Hosp Podiatrists; Am Bd of Podiatric Surg, Diplomate; Am Soc of Podiatric Dermatologists, Fellow; Am Soc of Podiatric Med, Fellow; Am Podiatry Assn; Beta Sigma Gamma Nat Hlth Sci Hon Frat; Nat Bd of Podiatric Examrs, Diplomate; TX Podiatry Assn; cp/Scottish Rite and Shrine; r/Presb; hon/Pubs, "Osteoid Osteoma of Talus: A Case Report" 1980, "Solitary Neurofibroma of the Foot: A Case Report" 1980, "Macrodactyly: A Rare Malformation Review of Literature and Case Report" 1979, Others; W/W SW.

PEREIRA, TERESINHA ALVES oc/Writer, Professor of Literature; b/Nov 1, 1934; ba/Department of Spanish and Portuguese, Univ of Colorado, Boulder, CO 80309; m/Pedro Meléndez; c/Luzia Martins, Emilia Martins, Pedro Alberto Meléndez; p/Pindaro de Paula (dec) and Maria Albertina Alves Pereira, Brazil; ed/Tchr Cert, Instituto de Educacão, Brazil, 1952; PhD in Spanish, Univ of NM, 1972; pa/Instr of Portuguese, Tulane Univ, 1962-68; Lectr of Portuguese, Stanford Univ, Sum 1968; Vis'g Asst Prof of Portuguese, Georgetown Univ, 1973-74; Prof of Lit, Univ of CO, 1975-; World Poetry Soc; Intl Poetry Soc; Am Poetry Soc; Canadian Soc of Poets; Canadian Playwrights Assn; União Brasileira de Torvadores/Ateneu Angrense de Letras, Brazil; Academia de Letras do Piaui, Brazil; Academia de Felgueiras, Portugal; Sociedad Argentina de Letras; Associación de Escritores Mexicanos, Mexico; hon/Pubs, *Anti-Poem for Christmas and Other Non-Christmas Poems* 1972, *Line of a Broken Alphabet, While Springtime Sleeps* 1973, *Alien* 1974; Books Have Been Pub'd in Brazil, Portugal, Mexico, Colombia, and Have Been Translated into Swedish, Japanese, Hebrew, Italian, French and Many Other Langs; Awd'd, Brazilian Nat Prize for Playwright, 1972; Poet of the Yr, Canadian Soc of Poets, 1977; Prize for Lit from União Brasileira de Escritores, Brazil; Dir of Am Scholars; Yr Book in Mod Lang Studies; Dir of Am Poets; Intl W/W Poetry.

PEREZ-PERAZA, JORGE A oc/Research in Cosmic Ray Physics and Solar Physics; b/Jul 23, 1944; ba/Instituto de Geofísica, UNAM, 04510-CU, México 20, DF; m/Maria del Carmen Rivera R; c/David Didier, Esther Cecilia, Jorge Daniel; p/Carlos Pérez Rivero; ed/BSc, Escuela Suprerior de Física y Matemáticas del Instituto Politécnico Nacional, 1968; MSc 1970, PhD 1972, Faculté de Sciences de la Université de Paris; mil/Mexican Army, 1965; pa/Prof of Physics, Instituto Politécnico Nacional, 1966-68; Asst of Res, Laboratoire de Physique Cosmique du CNRS Verriere le Buisson, France, 1971-72; Titular Rschr in Solar Physics and Cosmic Ray Physics, Instituto de Astro-

nomía 1973-81, Titular Rschr in Solar Physics, Cosmic Ray Physics and Space Physics, Instituto de Geofísica 1981-, Prof of Plasma Physics, Fac of Scis 1973-, UNAM; Advr of Planetarium of the IPN, 1976-79; Am Geophy Union; Intl Astronom Union; Am Astronom Soc; Astronom Soc of the Pacific; Indian Astronom Soc; Indian Phy Soc; Instituto Panamericano de Geografía e Historia; Com for Space Res; Academia de la Investigacíon Científica; r/Cath; hon/Grantee: Instituto Nacional de la Investigación Científica 1968-69, COFAA and CONACYT 1970-73, French Govt 1968-73, TATA Inst of Fundamental Res, Bombay 1980, Acad of Scis of Moscow 1983; W/W Frontier Sci and Technol.

PERKINS, DEBORAH J oc/Management Executive; b/Aug 25, 1950; h/3495 Balboa, Reno, NV 89503; ba/Reno, NV; p/Janet McAllister, W Frankfort, IL; ed/BS Bus, So IL Univ, 1972; BA Med Record Adm, Hillcrest Med Ctr, Tulsa, OK, 1973; pa/Dept Hd, Med Records, Meml Hosp, Belleville, IL, 1973-74; Dept Hd, Med Records, Franklin Hosp, Benton, IL, 1974-77; ICD-9-CM Coor, Am Med Record Assn, Chicago, IL, 1977-79; Dept Hd, Med Records, St Mary's Hosp, Reno, NV, 1979-81; Dir of Support Sers, St Mary's Hosp, 1981-; Am Med Record Assn, Mem 1983-, IL Del to Annual Meeting in Las Vegas of House of Dels 1977, Del to House of Dels in Chicago (IL) 1980, Del to House of Dels in San Antonio (TX), Del to House of Dels Los Angeles (CA) 1982, Del to House of Dels Boston (MA); IL Med Record Assn, Exec Bd 1976, Nom'g Com 1977, Others; Chicago & Vicinity Med Record Assn, 1978; Pres, NV Med Record Assn, 1982-84; cp/Condo Bd of Dirs, The Knolls, Reno, NV, 1981-82, 1982-83; hon/Author, "Incentive Pay for Med Transcriptionists," *The Echo*, IL Med Record Assn, 1974; Treas, IL Med Record Assn; Elected Pres-elect, NV Med Record Assn; Elected to Am Med Record Assn Nom'g Com; Mem Am Med Record Assn Subcoun on Bylaws & Resolutions, 1982-84; "Alpha Gam Girl" Alpha Gamma Delta Sorority, So IL Univ, Carbondale, IL, 1972; Pi Omega Pi, Nat Hon Bus Frat, So IL Univ, 1972.

PERKINS, ESTHER R oc/Literary Agent, Writer; b/May 10, 1927; h/PO Box 48, Childs, MD 21916; ba/Childs, MD; p/C Roberts and Esther Terrell Perkins (dec); ed/Att'd, W Chester St Tchrs Col, 1945-47; Spec Courses, Univ of DE, 1965-69; pa/Acctg Clk, E I DuPont De Nemours, 1947-65; Records Spec, Univ of DE, 1966-77; Ptnr, The Holly Press, 1975-82; Self-Employed, Owner, Esther R Perkins Lit Agy, 1978-; Am Soc of Profl and Exec Wom, 1981-; Nat Writers Clb; cp/Bd Mem, Cecil Co Arts Coun, 1982-; DAR; r/Meth; hon/Pubs, *Backroading through Cecil County* 1977, *Things I Wish I'd Said to You* 1978; W/W Am Wom.

PERKINS, GLENN R oc/Executive; b/Nov 3, 1947; h/241 Woodland Road, Storrs, CT 06268; ba/Storrs, CT; m/Linda S Swalm; c/Dain E; p/Milo O and Rosamond T Perkins, York, ME; ed/BS in Elect Engrg, NEn Univ, 1972; AS, Elect Engrg Technol, Wentworth Inst, 1969; pa/Assoc Test Engr, Newport News Shipbldg & Drydock Co, 1972-73; Devel Engr 1973-78, Prin Devel Engr

1978-79, Supvr, Inser Inspection Grp 1979-81, Combustion Engrg; Pres, NDE Engrg Conslts Inc, 1981-; ASNT; ANS; cp/BSA, Cubmaster 1982-84; hon/Pub, "Preplanning and Performance of Nuclear Plant ISI Outages," 1981; W/ W Frontier Sci and Technol.

PERKINS, JAYNE MARGUERITE oc/Executive; b/Mar 12, 1913; h/121 Boren Avenue, North, Seattle, WA 98109; ba/Seattle, WA; m/Clinton R (dec); p/Mr and Mrs Walter E Reynolds (dec); ed/Att'd, Wash Univ 1930-33, Univ of CA Berkeley 1939-40; pa/Acct, E I DuPont; Self-Employed, 1941-; Owner of Apts and Comml Properties; Secy-Treas, Blair House; Treas, Magnolia Bayshore; Treas, Perkins Mgmt Co; Pres, Chm of Bd, NW Home Furnishings Mart Inc; Bd of Trustees, Seattle Downtown Devel Assn, 1976 (Still Active); Bldg Owners and Mgrs, 1967 (Still Active); Apt Owners and Operators, Bd of Trustees 1966; First Hill Improvement Clb, Pres and Past Chm of Bd, 1967-80; Nat Home Fashions Leag, 1972-, Past Nat Treas; cp/Seattle C of C; r/Prot; hon/Hon Guest, Matirix Table, Seattle Wom in Communs, 1974-; Hon Mayor of First Hill, 1974; W/W Fin and Indust; W/W W; 2,000 Wom of Achmt; Nat Register of Prom Ams; DIB.

PERKINS, ROBERT GREEN oc/Teacher, Instructor; b/Dec 3, 1926; h/Route 6, Linda Circle, Box 501, Elizabethton, TN 37643; ba/Elizabethton, TN; m/Christine H; c/Helen Jane Sams; ed/Wkshops; Sum Courses; Night Classes; Correspondence Courses; Att'd, Steed Col 1957, Tri-City Tech Inst 1971, E TN St Univ 1980; Ednl Background in Engrg, Indust Arts and Voc Ed; mil/Navy, 2 Yrs; pa/Chem Div 1944, Res and Devel, Engrg, Supvr Over Elect Dept in Polyester Plant, Supvr Over Elect Dept at Viscose Plant, Beaunit Corp; Electricity and Electronics Instr, Elizabethton St Area Voc-Tech Sch, 1979-; AVA, Carter Co Rep 1980, 1981, 1982, 1983; TVA; TEA; cp/Dashiell Masonic Lodge #238; Tiger Val PTA, Pres for the Sch Yrs 1955, 1956, 1957, 1958; Tiger Val Citizen's Clb, Secy 1958, 1959; Carter Co Grand Jury, Foreman 1960's; r/Prot; hon/Contbr, Articles About Voc Ed, "Training of the Handicapped," "The Advantages of Vocational Education," "The Needs of Industry," "Programs Offered at the Elizabethton Area School," "Job Interviewing Techniques," and "Vocational-Technical School Help in Developing Skill and Trade," in *The Elizabethton Star*; Has Written and Presented Talks to Sr Classes at Elizabethton and Happy Val HS on "The Importance of Continuing Your Education".

PERKINS, ROBERT JAMES oc/Instructor; b/Jul 12, 1952; h/130 Marcella Street, Roxbury, MA 02119; ba/Boston, MA; p/Ms Hattie Andrew Perkins, Prichard, AL; ed/MA in Spec Ed, Univ of MA 1983; MEd, Boston St Col, 1980; BA in Sec'dy Ed, Hist and Eng, Stillman Col, 1975; EdD Cand, Univ of MA Amherst; pa/Ednl Spec, Roxbury Multi-Ser Ctr, 1981-; Conslt, Ed Support Ser, ASWALA House, Roxbury, MA, Br, YWCA, 1979-81; Instr, Madison Pk HS, 1980-; Tchr, Cnslr, McKinley Sch, 1977-80; Boston Tchr Union, Sch Union Activist, Pres

and Rep 1977-80; Black Edr Alliance, 1977-; Kappa Alpha Psi Frat; cp/NAACP; r/Presb; hon/Author, Articles in *Black Enterprise Magazine* 1981, *Boston Globe* Newspaper 1979-80, *Bay State Banner*; Outstg Social Studies Instr, 1977-78; Outstg Achmt Awd, Kappa Alpha Psi Frat.

PERKINS, WILLIAM MAX oc/Marketing Administrator; b/Feb 3, 1947; h/2413 Maple Leaf Drive, Jacksonville, FL 32211; ba/Jacksonville, FL; c/Christopher Michael; p/John F and Glenna E Perkins, Evansville, IN; ed/BS in Mktg, IN St Univ, 1974; mil/USAF, 1966-70; pa/Mktg Admr 1979-, Internal Auditor 1976-79, Opers Mgr (Rock Isl, IL) 1974-76, Mgmt Trainee (Danville, IL) 1974, Ryder Truck Lines Inc; cp/Coach, Jacksonville Yth Baseball, 1976-79; Tchr/Conslt, Proj Bus Div of Jr Achmt, 1981-; r/Cath; hon/Grad w Hons, cum laude, IN St Univ, 1974; W/W S and SW.

PERLOVSKY, LEONID I oc/Geophysicist; b/Nov 11, 1948; h/8837 Dunlap, Houston, TX 77074; ba/Houston, TX; m/Olga J; c/Ilya, Boris; p/Isaac E Perlovsky; Riva B Bormashenko; ed/MS in Physics, summa cum laude, Novosibirsk Univ, 1971; PhD in Theoretical Physics, Jt Inst for Nuclear Res, Dubna, 1975; pa/Asst Prof of Applied Math 1975-77, Assoc Prof 1977-78, Siberia Civil Engrg Inst; Res Prof of Psychi, NY Univ, 1979-80; Sr Res Physicist 1980-81, Res Spec 1981-83, Sr Res Spec 1983-, Exxon Prodn Res Co; Conslt w Siberia Agri Inst 1975-78, Software Devel Inc 1979-80; Soc for Exploration Geophysicists; Soc for Profl Well Log Analysts; Soc for Indust and Applied Math; hon/Contbr, Articles to Profl Jours; W/W Frontier Sci and Technol; W/W World.

PEROVICH, JOHN oc/University President; b/Feb 9, 1924; h/1901 Roma, Northeast, Albuquerque, NM 87106; ba/Albuquerque, NM; m/June; c/Robert, Jane; ed/BBA 1948, MBA 1949, Univ of NM; mil/2nd Lt, USAAC, 1943-45; pa/Purchasing Agt 1950-51, Acting Comptroller 1951-52, Comptroller 1953-67, VP for Bus and Fin 1967-82, Pres 1982-, Univ of NM; Commr, Wn Interst Comm for Higher Ed; Bd of Dirs, Univ of NM Foun; Nat Assn of St Univs and Land-Grant Cols; cp/Bd of Dirs, Albuquerque C of C, 1982-; Kiwanis; Bd of Dirs, NM Med Foun; r/Prot.

PERROT, WILLIAM ALBERT JR oc/English Teacher; b/Sep 15, 1953; h/PO Box 105, Middleton, Nova Scotia B0S 1P0; ba/Auburn, Nova Scotia; p/William Albert Perrot, Wake Forest, NC; Virginia Pace Doyle, Petersburg, VA; ed/BMus (Ed), Westminster Choir Col, 1975; pa/Tchr, W Kings Dist HS, Kings Co Dist Sch Bd, 1975-; Bd of Dirs, Nova Scotia Choral Fdn, 1976-, Pres 1981-83; cp/Fdg Conductor, Kings Chorale (Commun Choir), 1982; r/Meth.

PERRY, CARRIE SAXON oc/State Legislator; h/203 Ridgefield Street, Hartford, CT 06112; ba/Hartford, CT; c/James McKinley III; p/Ms Mabel Saxon; ed/Howard Univ; pa/Exec Dir, Amistad House Inc; Rep, CT Gen Assem (Serving 2nd Term); cp/Dem; Gov's Statewide Hlth Coor'g Coun; Bds of Dirs, Gtr Hartford Process Inc; Planned Parenthood; Africare; Upward Bound; Urban Leag of Gtr Hartford; Gtr

Hartford Black Dem Clb; Capitol Reg Mtl Hlth Adv Com; hon/WKND's and CT Mutual's Ldr of the Mth Awd; Gtr Hartford YWCA's Wom of the Yr Awd; Black People's Union, Univ of Hartford, Outstg Commun Sers Awd; Cert of Merit for Dist'd Achmt; Ancient and Accepted Scottish Rite of Freemasonry Cert of Merit; CT Minority Bus Assn's Salute; W Mid Sch Cert Awd for Black Hist Month; World W/W Wom.

PERRY, JACQUELINE CHERYL oc/Lead Equal Opportunity Specialist; b/Aug 29, 1947; ba/General Services Administration, 18 & F Streets, Washington, DC 20405; p/James E Perry, New York, NY; Jessie M Perry, Bronx, NY; ed/BA, City Univ of NY, 1970; MS, Mgmt of Human Resources, Univ of UT, 1976; Dipl, Dept of the Army, 1981; mil/USAR, 1976-81; pa/Mgmt Trainee 1970-71, Inventory Mgmt Spec 1971-72, Equal Opport Spec 1972-78, Supervisory Equal Opport Spec 1978, Reg EEO Ofcr 1979, Gen Sers Adm, NYC; Equal Opport Spec 1979-83, Lead Equal Opport Spec 1983-, Gen Sers Adm Ctl Ofc; Supervisory Equal Opport Spec, US Dept of Labor, Ofc of Fed Contract Compliance Progs, 1978-79; Am Soc for Public Adm; Conf of Minority Public Admrs; APGA; Federally Employed Wom Inc, Reg Coor 1975; Fed Mgrs Assn; cp/Nat Coun of Negro Wom Inc; NSF Grantee, 1969; W/W E; W/W Am Wom; World W/W Wom.

PERRY, JAMES LAWRENCE JR oc/Social Services Administrator; b/Sep 27, 1946; h/232 Highland Drive, Hueytown, AL 35023; ba/Birmingham, AL; m/Sandra Jo Norman; c/Rebecca Lane, Gwendolyn Lonelle, James Lawrence III; p/J Lawrence Perry Sr, Hertford, NC; Maggie Ethel Lane Perry (dec); ed/BA, NC Wesleyan Col, 1968; Att'd, B'ham Sch of Law, 1973-74; Cert in Credit Union Mgmt, Univ of AL B'ham, 1977; MPA, Univ of AL B'ham, 1983; pa/Social Ins Claims Rep, Social Security Adm, Field Opers, 1968-69; Social Ins Claims Examr, Social Security Adm, SEn Prog Ser Ctr, Ctl Opers, 1969-74; Social Ins Spec 1974-76, Asst Process Module Mgr 1976-79, Chief Auditor 1979-80, Process Mgr 1980-, Social Security Adm; Am Soc for Public Adm, 1980-; SEPSC Mgmt Assn; Am Mgmt Assn; Legis Del, Social Security Employees Credit Union, 1978-, Chm of Credit Com 1978-81, 1982-; St Adv Coun, AL Dept of Pensions and Security, 1981-; Ednl Awareness Com, St Adv Coun, AL Dept of Pensions and Security, 1982-; cp/Big Brothers, 1974-; Advocacy Chm, AL Friends of Adoption, 1980-, Dir 1980-; Participant, White House Conf on Volunteerism, 1982; r/VChm, Coun on Mins, First U Meth Ch, 1980-82, Lay Spkr 1980-; hon/Directed Nat Task Force to Rewrite Social Security Adm Audit Procedures, 1980; Awd for Outstg Contbn to Rel Life of Wesleyan Campus, 1968; Spec Achmt Awd, Social Security Adm, 1973, 1980; 2 Lttrs of Commend, Social Security Adm, 1981; Commrs Cit, Social Security Adm, 1975; Cert of Merit, Fed Ser Campaign for Nat Hlth Agys, 1976; W/W S and SW.

PERRY, MARION J H oc/Poet, Professor; b/Jun 2, 1943; h/123 Park Place, East Aurora, NY 14052; ba/Orchard Park, NY; m/Franklyn A H; c/Judith A

H, Scott H H; p/Armin and Adah Helz, Delafield, WI; ed/BA in Eng and Phil, 1964; MA in 20th Century Lit, 1966; MFA in Poetry, 1969; MA, Rdg Spec, 1979; pa/Prof: W Liberty St Col 1966-68, Albright Col 1968-70, SUNYAB/EOC 1970-74, Pt-time at Erie Commun Col, Medaille Col and Empire St Col 1975-80, Erie Commun Col 1980-; Poets and Writers; Poetry Soc of Am; hon/Pubs, *Icarus* 1980, *The Mirror's Image* 1981, *Establishing Intimacy* 1982; Winner in All Nations Poetry Contest, 1980, 1981; Intl W/W.

PERRY, RUBY MILLER oc/Student; b/Apr 13, 1935; h/3646 Wilmont Avenue, Roanoke, VA 24017; c/Gordon, Steven, Janice, Melissa; ed/GED, AA Deg Med Secretarial Sci, 1984; AA Med Adm Asst; pa/Student; Treas, Future Secy Assn, 1982-83; Secy, Med Clb, 1982-83; Typist for Col Instrs; Spec Ser Tutor, 1981-83; hon/Dean's List, 1982-83; Nat Dean's List, 1983-84; Ser Awd Nat Bus Col, 1983; Awd for 3.8 Grade Pt Average, 1983.

PERRY-OVERALL, EMMA NANCY oc/Postal Employment Development Training Technician; b/Dec 15, 1937; h/1123 Appianway Street, Little Rock, AR 72204; ba/Little Rock, AR; c/Michael Andre, Reginald Louis; p/Dr Levi Steven Overall (dec); Mrs Mildred Smith Overall, Little Rock, AR; ed/BA in Bus Ed, Philander Smith Col, 1975; Att'd, Univ of AR Grad Sch, Mgmt/Supvn Cont'g Ed Div, 1980-81; pa/Acctg Clk, Gen Ofc, Acting Housing Mgr, Little Rock Housing Auth, 1962-65; Distn Clk, Career, Job Instr, Mail Processing Unit, Little Rock Postal Ser, 1966-69; Multi-Position Letter Sorter Machine Operator, Acting MPLSM Operator Tnr, Mail Processing Unit, 1969-73; PEDC Tng Tech, Employee and Labor Relats Unit, 1973-; 204B Detailed Acting Supvr, Customer Sers and Collections and Delivery Units, 1980; 204B Acting MPLSM Supvr, Mail Processing Unit, 1983-; Little Rock Postal Ser EEO Adv Com, Publicity Mgr 1981-82, Chp 1982-; Nat Assn of Female Execs, 1980-; Delta Sigma Theta Sorority Inc, 1975-; Nat Tchrs and AR Tchrs Assns, Supportive Mem 1981; AAUW, 1983-; cp/Adv Bd, Urban Leag of AR, Chp 1983-; AR for the Arts, Supporting Mem 1981-; r/African Meth; hon/Recip, Quality Step Increase Awd, PEDC Tng Tech, Little Rock Postal Ser, 1974; W/W Am Wom.

PERSON, DONALD AMES oc/Pediatric Rheumatologist; b/Jul 17, 1938; h/3022 Winslow, Houston, TX 77025; ba/Houston, TX; m/Blanche Audrey Durand; c/Donald Ames Jr, David Wesley; p/Ingwald Halder Person (dec); Elma K Person, Fargo, ND; ed/BS, Med, Univ of ND, 1961; MD, Univ of MN, 1963; mil/LTC, Med Corps, AUS; pa/Rotating Intern, Mpls/Hennipin Co Gen Hosp, 1963-64; Resident in Neurosurg 1967, Fellow in Microbiol 1968-70, Mayo Clin; Instr to Asst Prof of Virology and Epidemilogy & Internal Med 1971-77, Resident in Pediatrics 1978-80, Asst Prof of Pediatrics 1980-, Baylor Col of Med; Am Acad of Pediatrics, Sect of Rheumatology; AAAS; Am Fdn for Clin Res; AMA; Am Rheumatism Assn; Am Soc for Microbiol; Am Soc of Tropical Med and Hygiene; Arthritis Foun, Am Juv Arthritis Org;

Arthritis Foun, TX Gulf Coast Chapt (Bd of Dirs and Med Adv Bd); Assn of Mil Surgs of the US; Assn of the AUS; Harris Co Med Soc; Houston Acad of Med; Houston Pediatric Soc; Intl Org of Mycoplasmologists; Intl Pediatric Rheumatology Clb; NY Acad of Scis; ND Acad of Sci; Pediatric Rheumatology Collaborative Study Grp; Soc for Exptl Biol and Med; Soc for Pediatric Res; So Soc for Pediatric Res; SW Sci Forum; TX Med Assn; TX Pediatric Soc; TX Rheumatism Assn, Councillor 1983-84; Tissue Culture Assn, Gulf Coast Chapt; US Fdn of Culture Collections; r/Luth; hon/Author, More Than 80 Pub'd Abstracts and Sci Articles in the Med Lit, Book: *Juvenile Rheumatoid Arthritis*; Postdoct Fellow of Arthritis Foun, 1973-75; Sr Investigator, Arthritis Foun, 1975-77; W/W S and SW; W/W Frontier Sci and Technol; Personalities of S; Men of Achmt.

PETERS, DIANE PECK oc/Artist, Designer; b/May 14, 1940; h/531 Chamberlain Street, Corpus Christi, TX 78404; ba/Same; m/George; c/George III, Louise Irene, Marie Diane, Wilfred John; p/Mr and Mrs Wilfred J Peck, Corpus Christi, TX; ed/Student, Univ of OK, LA Tech Univ, Del Mar Col; pa/Designer in Stained Glass, Olszewski Stained Glass Studio, 1969-73; Operator of Art Studio, 1973-; SWn Watercolor Soc; Wn Fdn Watercolor Soc; KY Watercolor Soc; LA Watercolor Soc; AL Watercolor Soc; Watercolor Soc of S TX; Assoc Mem: Allied Artists of Am, Am Watercolor Soc, Audubon Artists; r/Cath; hon/Featured in *Corpus Christi Caller Times* Feb 1979, *Corpus Christi Times* Jun 1979, Dec 1979; Exhib'd in KY Watercolor Soc 2nd Annual Exhbn, Owensboro Mus of Fine Arts 1979, Allied Artists of Am 65th Annual Exhbn, Nat Acad Galleries 1979; Merchants Watercolor Awd, OK 3rd Annual Nat Open Exhbn, 1977; John Herweck $200 Awd, TX Watercolor Soc Exhb, 1977; W/W Am Art; W/W SW; W/W Am Wom; World W/W Wom.

PETERS, WILLIAM JOHN oc/Realtor Associate; b/Mar 19, 1932; h/328 East St John Street, Lake City, FL 32055; ba/Lake City, FL; c/James Ervin, Jennifer Leigh; p/Ervin Elmer and Lena Braun Peters (dec); ed/BS in Forestry 1958, MS 1965, Univ of MN; mil/USAF, 1951-54; pa/Res Asst, Inst of Paper Chem, 1956; Res Asst, Sch of Forestry, Univ of MN St Paul, 1957-58; Interim Asst, Sch of Forestry, Univ of FL Gainesville, 1960-64; Biol Lab Tech 1965-74, Res Forester 1974-82, US Forest Ser, SEn Forest Experiment Sta; Rltr-Assoc, Sun Country Rlty, 1982-; Soc Am Foresters; Forest Prod Res Soc; Am Botanical Assn; Nature Conservancy; cp/Columbia Co Envir Coun, Pres 1978, Dir 1976-78; Four Rivers Audubon Soc, Pres 1978-80, Dir 1980-; Lake City Optimist Clb, Pres 1971-73; Lions; r/Our Redeemer Luth Ch, Pres 1977-78; hon/Author, Num Pub'd Articles in Field of Forestry; Patentee in Field of Forestry; I-R 100 Awd for US Forest Ser, 1974; Phi Eta Sigma, Univ of WI, 1950; Xi Sigma Pi, Univ of MN, 1957; Outstg Chapt Pres of Yr, FL Audubon Soc, 1980; W/W S and SW.

PETERSEN, NEIL FREDERICK oc/Geologist; b/Mar 28, 1943; h/21315 Park Bluff, Katy, TX 77450; ba/Houston, TX; p/Frederick Peter and Alma Margaret Eller Petersen, Mineola, NY; ed/BA, Hofstra Univ, 1964; MS, Univ of PA, 1967; pa/Geochem, Shell Oil Co, 1967-73; Res Spec 1973-75, Tech Spec for Resource Devel and Exploration 1975-77, Proj Mgr of Resource Technol 1977-79, Kerr McGee Corp; Grp Supvr, Exploration Geochem, Superior Oil, 1979-; Geochem Soc; Geol Soc Am; Am Assn Petro Geologists; Am Chem Soc; r/Luth; hon/Pubs: Co-Authored, "Models for Comparison of Anomalous Vitrinite Reflectance Values with Maturation Indices from the Los Angeles Basin, California" 1983, "Genetic, Transformation, and Level of Organic Metamorphic Characteristics of Alaska North Slope Oils and Source Rocks" 1983, Authored, "Regional Petroleum Geochemical Assessment of Israel" 1980; W/W S and SW.

PETERSEN, NORMAN WILLIAM oc/Director of Programs, Comptroller; b/Aug 26, 1933; h/1143 Greenway Road, Alexandria, VA 22308; ba/Alexandria, VA; m/Ann Nevin; c/Richard N, Robert W, Anita, David A; p/Jens Edlef (dec) and Marie Petersen, Lake Forest, IL; ed/Student, Purdue Univ, 1952; BS in Elect Engrg, Univ of NM, 1956; MS in Electronics Engrg w Distn, Naval Postgrad Sch, 1962; mil/USN, 1952-, Comm'd Ensign 1952, Adv'd through Grades to Capt 1976; pa/Shops Engr, Naval Sta, Key W, 1956-59; Mil Pers Dir, Bur Yards and Docks, 1956-60; Public Wks Ofcr, Fleet-Anti-Air-Warfare Tng Ctr, Damn Neck, VA, 1962-64; Engrg Coordination Ofcr, Sowest Navfaceng Com, San Diego, 1964-66; Exec Ofcr, Amphibious Constrn Bat One, 1966-67; Force Civil Engr, Com Navair Pac, 1967-70; Public Wks Ofcr, Nas Mir Amar, 1970-73; Exec Ofcr, Navy Public Wks Ctr, Great Lakes, 1973-75; Commanding Ofcr, Navy Civil Engrg Res Lab, 1975-78; Commanding Ofcr, Navy Public Wks Ctr, SF Bay, 1978-80; Current Dir of Progs and Comptroller, Navy Facilities Engrg Command; Soc Am Mil Engrs; Am Public Wks Assn; IEEE; Am Soc Mil Comptrollers; Navy Leag; Sigma Xi; Lamba Chi Alpha, Pres, VP 1954-56; cp/Bd of Dirs, U Way, 1975-78; Am Philatelic Soc; Germany Philatelic Soc; Mexico Elmhurst Philatelic Soc; r/Prot; hon/Meritorious Ser Medal (Twice); Navy Commend Medal; Navy Unit Cit; Meritorious Unit Commend; Vietnam Armed Forces Merit Citation-Gallantry Cross; Vietnam Merit Cit, Civil Action-1st Class; W/W in S and SW; W/W in CA.

PETERSEN, WILLIAM BERT oc/Optometric Physician; b/Apr 3, 1940; h/PO Box 2139, Tuba City, AZ 86045; ba/Tuba City, AZ; p/Mr and Mrs E W Petersen, Dillon, MT; ed/Att'd, Wn MT Col, 1958-61; BS 1963, OD 1964, Grad Studies in Physiological Optics 1964-65, Pacific Univ; Spec Studies, Creighton Univ, 1968; Grad Studies in Psych, Peabody Col, 1975-77; mil/From 2nd Lt to Maj, USAF, 1965-80; From Lt Cmdr to Capt 1980-, USPHS; pa/Clin Instr, Pacific Univ, 1964-65; Adj Prof, So CA Col of Optom, 1980-; Adj Prof, So Col of Optom, 1980-83; Adj Prof, So Col of Optometric Med, 1983; Chief, Optom, Navajo Area Indian Hlth Ser, USPHS, NAIHS HQs, 1980-; Dpty Dir

449

of Eye Clin 1980-81, Dir 1981-, Tuba City IHS Hosp; Var Assignments w USAF; Am Optometric Assn, 1965; Omega Epsilon Phi; Am Acad of Optom, Fellow 1977; Armed Forces Optometric Soc; Am Col of Optometric Phys, Fellow 1981; Liaison Ofcr to All US Mil Optometric Ofcrs, Am Col of Optometric Phys; Bd of Dirs, Am Col of Optometric Phys, 1982; Comm'd Ofcrs Assn, USPHS; Assn of Mil Surgs of the US; Comm'd Ofcrs Optometric Assn, USPHS, 1981; Exec Secy, Comm'd Ofcrs Optometric Soc, 1981-; Navajo Area Comm'd Ofcrs Assn, USPHS, 1980; cp/Mus of No AZ; Phoenix Art Mus; MT St Hist Soc; So Arts Foun; Smithsonian Instn; Cowboy Hall of Fame; Lions Clb Intl; Animal Protection Inst of Am; Keep Am Beautiful Foun; Thomas Gilcrease Mus Assn; hon/Hon Dr of Ocular Sci, So Col of Optom, 1983; Meritorious Ser Medal w 1 OLC; AF Commend Medal; Small Arms Expert Marksmanship Ribbon; Armed Force Longevity Ser Awd Ribbon w 2 OLCs; Nat Def Ser Medal; Vietnam Ser Medal w 4 Bronze Ser Stars; Air Medal w OLC; AF Outstg Unit Awd w 1 Silver OLC and 4 Bronze OLCs and Valor Device; Republic of Vietnam Gallantry Cross w Palm; Republic of Vietnam Campaign Medal; Assn of Mil Surgs of the US Medal; Intl Biographic Assn, Fellow 1976; W/W Intells; W/W W; Intl Register of Profiles; Men of Achmt; Intl Biogl Yrbook; DIB; Dir of Dist'd Ams; Blue Book of Optometrists; W/W Am; Personalities of World.

PETERSON, DORIS LORRAINE COX oc/Counselor; b/Apr 30, 1924; h/122½ Marstellar Street, West Lafayette, IN 47906; ba/West Lafayette, IN; c/R Erik, Kendall Cox, G Bradford; p/Henry Alfred and Flora Belle Smith Cox (dec); ed/BS, magna cum laude, Syracuse Univ; MS, Cornell Univ; PhD Cand, Purdue Univ; pa/Geosci Cnslr, Purdue Univ, 1978-; Sem Prof and St Proj Coor, E MI Univ, 1976-78; Sr Advr, Culver Mil Acad, 1974-76; Grad Wkshop Dir, Marywood Col; Ext Home Economist, Rutgers Univ, 1972-74; Other Previous Positions; Secy 1964-70, En Reg Conf of Col Nutrition Tchrs; AAUW, 1980; Nat Assn of Wom Deans, Admrs and Cnslrs, 1980; NJ Del to Nat Home Ec Conv, 1974; Curric Showcase Presenter, 1978; NJ Home Ec Ext Assn Bd, 1972; r/Meth; hon/Pubs, *Competency-Based Consumer Education in Home Economics, Field Testing and Revision of CBCE in Home Economics*, Others; Highest Syracuse U Ath Awd for Wom, 1946; Dey Bros Awd, 1946; Phi Delta Kappa, 1981; Kappa Delta Pi, 1982; Eta Pi Upsilon, Mortar Bd 1946; Omicron Nu, 1946; Outstg Chi Omega Awd, 1945; W/W Am Wom; W/W Am Cols.

PETERSON, EDWIN CUTHBERT oc/Counselor, Educational Administrator, Adult Educator; b/Feb 11, 1936; h/PO Box 592, Honolulu, HI 96809; ba/Hickam AFB, HI; p/Edwin B Peterson, Sault Sainte Marie, MI; Gladys M Cuthbert (dec); ed/Dipl, Indust Col of the Armed Forces, Nat Def Univ, 1979; EdD in Adm and Supvn 1974-77, Cert in Urban Affairs and Public Adm 1971-72, Univ of So CA; Cert of Adv'd Grad Study, Guid and Cnslg, Univ of MA, 1967; MA, Ednl Adm, No MI Univ, 1965; MS, Guid and Cnslg, Univ of WI, 1963; BS in Hlth, PE and Rec, No MI Univ, 1958; pa/Chief, Ed Div, HQ Pacific Air Forces, Hickam AF Base, 1972-; Chief of Ed Br, HQ Aerospace Def Command, Ent AF Base, 1967-72; Chief of Ed Br, HQ Eighth AF (SAC), Westover AF Base, 1965-67; Ed Sers Ofcr, 410th Bombardment Wing (H)(SAC), K I Sawyer AF Base, 1963-65; Ednl Advr, 327th Figher Wing (ADC), Truax Field, 1961-62; Ednl Advr, 507th Fighter Wing (ADC), Kuncheloe AF Base, 1958-60; Nat Cert'd Cnslr, 1983-88; VP for Progs, Adult Ed Assn of the USA, 1978-79; Nat Forum on Lng and the Am Future, 1978-79; St of HI Del, Adult Ed Assn of the USA, 1975-77; CoChm, First Commun Col of the AF, 1977-78; Am Assn for Adult and Cont'd Ed, 1965-; Am Assn for Cnslg and Devel, 1967-; HI Pers and Guid Assn, 1976-; hon/Meritorious Civilian Ser Medal, Dept of AF, 1983; Nom'd, 1983 Nat Public Ser Awd; Outstg Perf or Sustained Superior Perf Awds, 1983, 1982, 1980, 1977, 1971, 1970, 1966, 1964; Dist'd Alumni Awd, No MI Univ, 1981; Meritorious Ser Awd, Adult Ed Assn of the USA, 1979; Outstg Ser Awd, Commun Col of the AF, 1979; Career Ed Awd, Ed for Public Mgmt, US Civil Ser Comm, 1971; Var Strategic Air Command Awds; W/W W.

PETERSON, ERNEST A oc/Associate Professor; b/Jun 16, 1931; h/13165 Southwest 11th Lane Circle, Miami, FL 33184; ba/Miami, FL; c/Jason, Leslie; p/Ernest Andrew (dec) and Mildred Peterson, Woefeboro, NH; ed/BA, Rutgers Univ, 1959; MA 1961, PhD 1962, Princeton Univ; mil/S/Sgt, USAF, 1951-55; pa/Pres, Noise Anal Conslts Inc, 1970-; Assoc Prof, Univ of Miami Dept of Psych, 1969-; Fac, Univ of Miami Sch of Med Biomed Engrg Dept, 1969-; Asst Assoc Prof, and Chief, Univ of Miami Sch of Med Dept of Otolaryngology, Div of Auditory Res, 1964-; Dir, Univ of Miami Sch of Med Evoked Auditory Response Lab, 1974-78; Fac Mem, Dade Co Student Ldrship Devel Prog, 1980-; Fac Mem, Univ of Miami Sch of Med, Biomed Engrg Prog, 1969-; Fac Participant, Dade Co Lab Res Prog, 1967-; Practica in Res Techniques, Resident, Med Student Lectures, Univ of Miami Sch of Med Dept of Otolaryngology, Div of Auditory Res, 1964-; Fac Participant, Univ of Miami Biol Hons Prog, 1967-69; Other Previous Positions; AAAS; AAUP; Am Psychol Assn; Acoustical Soc of Am, Planning Com; Sigma Xi; Soc for Neuroscis; Univ of Miami Soc for Life Scis; Assoc Mem, Nat Assn Noise Control Ofcls; Am Auditory Soc; Centurian Clb, 1978-79; Fellow, Inst for the Study of Aging, Univ of Miami; FL Br, Am Assn of Lab Animal Sci; NY Acad of Scis; hon/Pubs, "Noise Raises Blood Pressure without Impairing Auditory Sensitivity" 1981, "Noise and Laboratory Animals" 1980, "Noise and Cardiovascular Function in Rhesus Monkeys: II" 1980, "Continuing Studies of Noise and Cardiovascular Function" 1978; T F Vale Prize for S'ship; Phi Beta Kappa, Jr Yr; Dean's List, 8 Semesters; Sigma Xi, Jr Yr; Hon German, Lit and Psych Socs; Henry Rutgers Scholar; Woodrow Wilson Nat Fellow; NIH Predoct Fellow; NSF Predoct Fellow (Declined); NIH, Nat Inst of Neurological Diseases and Blindness, Postdoct F'ship, Sensory Psych; NIH Career Devel Awd; Am Men of Sci; W/W S and SW; DIB; W/W Frontier Sci and Technol; W/W Among Students in Am Univs and Cols.

PETERSON, FRANK D oc/Consultant; b/Sep 1, 1899; h/101 South Hanover Avenue, Lexington, KY 40502; ba/Lexington, KY; m/Jewell Callison; c/George Alden (dec); p/John Artiberry and Lou V Peterson (dec); ed/AB, Centre Col, 1924; Spec Wk, Univ of Chgo, 1932; Spec Wk, Bowling Green Bus Col, 1924; Spec Wk, Univ of KY, 1935; LLD, honoris causa, Georgetown Univ, 1953; pa/Dir, Secy, Bellaire Enterprises, Gen Ptnrship, 1977-82; Dir, Secy, Saylor's Corp, 1976-80; Dir, Secy, Lexington Fire Protection Corp, 1975-82; Dir of Am Fam Sec Ins Inc, 1962-82; Pres, Treas, Dir, Town & Country Rlty Co Inc, Gen Tire Ser Inc; Mbrship, Spindletop Res Inc, 1960; Pres, 7 Kings Inc, Franchise Sys, Jiffy Franchise Sys, 1967-71; Treas, Secy, R L Sanders Co Inc, 1968-78; Secy, Treas, Dir, Royce E Blevins Co Inc, 1963-72; Secy, Treas, Dir, SEn Sts Securities Inc, 1963-64; VP, Bus Adm 1955-63, Fdr of Col, Bus Mgmt 1953, Univ of KY; Other Previous Positions; So Assn Col and Univ Bus Ofcrs; Phi Delta Kappa; Omicron Delta Kappa; Beta Gamma Sigma; Kappa Sigma; cp/Mason; Kiwanian; Lexington Country Clb, 1942-82; Civil War Round Table; Chamberlain Lit Soc; Thoroughbred Clb of Am; Life Mbrship, Pres Clb, Georgetown Col; hon/Author, Uniform Financial Accounting Sys for Cos, Cities and Grade Schs Dists for KY 1933, Articles; Dist'd Ser Awd, Kiwanis, 1977; Recip, Cert of Apprec, So Assn Cols and Univ Bus Ofcrs 1956; Cert of Aprec, Campbellsville, KY, Col 1953, City of Louisville 1937, Taylor Co, KY 1958; Dist'd Ser Awd, Univ of KY, 1974; Dist'd Alumni Centre Col Awd, 1980; Named KY Col, 1938, 1942-; W/W Ed in KY; W/W S; W/W Am; W/W World.

PETERSON, JAMES ROBERT oc/Executive; b/Oct 28, 1927; h/1816 Eastwood Avenue, Janesville, WI 53545; ba/Janesville, WI; m/Betty Windham; c/Richard James MD, Lynn Ann Anderson, Susan Kathryn, John Windham; p/Clyde and Pearl N Deliere Peterson (dec); ed/BS in Mktg, cum laude, Univ of IL, 1952; Exec Prog, Stanford Univ, 1967; mil/Lt, USN, 1945-50; pa/Brand Mgr, Grocery Prods 1952-76, Brand Supvr, Flour 1953-57, Dir of Mktg 1957-61, VP of Mktg 1961-66, VP, Gen Mgr of Grocery Prods 1966-68, Grp VP, Consumer Cos 1968-71, Pres and Dir 1973-76, Pillsbury; Exec VP, Dir, R J Reynolds Industs, 1976-82; Pres, CEO and Dir, The Parker Pen Co, 1982-; Dir: Avon Prods Inc, The Dun & Bradstreet Corp, Waste Mgmt Inc, Bancwis Corp; Bd of Regents, St Olaf Col, 1973-; Competitive WI, 1982-; r/Luth; hon/Bronze Table Awd, 1952; Beta Gamma Sigma, Dir's Table.

PETERSON, JOHN BURL oc/Administrator; b/May 26, 1919; h/1954 Melrose Street, Madison, WI 53704; ba/Madison, WI; m/Velma La Vada; c/Karl H, Kurt B; p/John B Peterson (dec); Fern L Peterson, Monett, MO; ed/BS 1947, MS 1948, Univ of MO; mil/USAF 1941-46, Capt; pa/Asst Co Agri Agt w Univ of MO, 1948; Asst Prof, Animal

450

Husbandry w Cornell Univ, 1948-50; Dist Ext Dairyman, Univ of TN, 1950-53; Ext Rep w Am Breeders Ser, 1953-64; Distn Mgr, Am Breeders, 1964-; Univ of MO Dairy Clb; Am Dairy Sci Assn; Alpha Zeta; Dairy Shrine Clb; r/Luth; hon/Author of Num Pubs; Personalities of W and MW; W/W NY Agri; W/W MW; W/W Fin and Indust.

PETERSON, MARGARET MARY oc/Radiation Therapy Dosimetrist and Consultant; b/Jul 25, 1948; h/645 Topaz Street, Redwood City, CA 94061; ba/San Pablo, CA; p/Andrew J and Margaret Peterson, Roselle Park, NJ; ed/BBA, 1982; AA, Bus Adm, 1981; RTT in Radiation Therapy Technol, 1970; RT in Radiologic Technol, 1968; pa/Chief Technologist, Brookside Hosp, 1983-; Relief Technologist throughout No CA, 1982; Clin Conslt for ATC med Technol Inc, 1981-82; Mgr of Radiation Therapy, Peninsula Hosp and Med Ctr, 1976-81; Chief Tecnologist, So Bay Hosp, 1973-76; Am Assn of Med Physicists; CA Soc of Radiologic Technologists; AAMD; NCSRTT; ACR Com on Radiation Therapy Technol; ASRT; ARRT; r/Cath; hon/Outstg Student in Radiation Therapy Class, 1969-70; W/W Am Wom; W/W CA.

PETRY, HENRY DAVID oc/Physician and Surgeon; b/Sep 16, 1941; h/PO Box 7, Sunrise Beach, MO 65079; ba/Laurie, MO; m/Betsy Anne; c/Paul David, Beth Anne; p/Oscar H and Evelyn Petry, Rocky Mount, MO; ed/Student, Lincoln Univ, 1959-63; Dr of Osteopathy, Kirksville Col of Osteopathic Med, 1967; Internship, C E Still Osteopathic Hosp, 1967-68; pa/Asst Chief Med Ofcr, MO St Penitentiary for Men, 1968-69; Staff Secy, Charles Still Hosp, 1969-70; Pres, Strait and Petry Inc, 1972-82; Vice Chief of Staff 1977-79, Chief of Staff 1979-81, Lake of the Ozarks Gen Hosp; Am Osteopathic Assn, 1968-83; MO Assn of Osteopathic Phys and Surgs, 1968-83; Med-Legal Mem, MAOPS, 1977, 1978, 1979, 1982, 1983; MAOPS Rep to MO St Bur of Narcotics and Dangerous Drugs, 1974-75; cp/Boy Scouts, Eagle Scout, Wood Badge and Vigil Mem, Order of the Arrow; r/Choir Dir, Ozark Chapel Meth Ch; hon/Order of Merit, Lake Dist of BSA; Vigil Mem, Order of the Arrow.

PETRY, THOMAS MERTON oc/Civil Engineering College Professor, Professional Engineer; b/Sep 25, 1944; h/1402 Apache Street, Arlington, TX 76012; ba/Arlington, TX; m/Susan Marie Nolte; c/Karol Lynne, Kimberly Dawn, Benjamin Thomas; p/Oscar and Evelyn Petry, Rocky Mount, MO; ed/BS in Civil Engrg, Univ of MO Rolla, 1967; MSCE, Univ of MO Columbia, 1968; PhD, Civil Engrg, OK St Univ, 1974; mil/USAR Comm 1967, Active Duty 1969-71, Discharged as Capt 1972; pa/Civil Engr, IL Highway Dept, 1967; Installation Foreman, SWn Bell Telephone Co, 1968-69; Asst Instr, Civil Engrg, OK St Univ, 1973-74; Field Engr, Parcher-Holibarton-Heiliger, Geotech Conslts, 1974; Asst Prof 1974-80, Assoc Prof 1980-, Univ of TX Arlington; ASCE; ASEE; NSPE and TSPE; ASTM and ASTM Com D-18; Intl Soc for Soil Mechs and Foun Engrg; Coms on Chem Stabilization of Soil and Rock and Lime and Lime-Flyash Stabilization of the Transportation Res Bd, Chm of the Com on Chem Stabilization of Soil and Rock; r/U Meth; hon/Pubs, "Significance of Sample Preparation Upon Soil Plasticity," "Relationship Between Shrinkage Properties and Plastic Index," "Design of Laterally Loaded Reinforced Concrete Piers Using Soil-Structure Interaction," "Geotechnical Engineering Considerations for Design of Slabs on Active Clay Soils," Others; Chi Epsilon Hon Frat; Nat Soc of Scabbard & Blade; Tau Beta Pi Hon Frat; Sigma Xi; Sci Res Soc; ASCE Cert of Apprec, 1980; ASCE Awd for Outstg Ser, 1981; W/W Among Students in Am Cols and Univs; W/W S and SW; Outstg Yg Men of Am.

PETTIJOHN, JOYCE LORRAINE oc/Pharmacist; b/Jan 7, 1955; h/PO Box 3111, Bellevue, WA 98009; ba/Kirkland, WA; p/Elzo Irving and Verona Muriel McKittrick Pettijohn, Portland, OR; ed/BS in Pharm, w Hons, OR St Univ, 1978; Postgrad Study in Bus, Univ of Puget Sound, 1980-81; pa/Staff Pharm 1979-80, Sr Staff Pharm 1981-, Evergreen Pharm Sers; Bd of Dirs, Hlth Prods Inc; Am and WA Pharmaceutical Assns; Lic'd Pharm in WA, CA, OR; cp/Wom's Netwk of Seattle.

PETTY, SHARON E oc/Controller; b/Nov 13, 1943; h/4725 South Pearl Street, Las Vegas, NV 89121; ba/Las Vegas, NV; m/Douglas; c/Scott, Eric; p/E B Jardon, Sedona, AZ; Darleen Georges, Las Vegas, NV; ed/Att'd, Univ of NV Las Vegas, 1973; Rec'd Designation of Cert'd Hospitality Acct Exec, 1983; pa/Controller, Maxim Hotel and Casino, 1980-; Chief Acct, Asst Controller, Controller, Aladdin Hotel and Casino, 1973-80; Corp Acct, KRUG-Thomas Ptnrship, 1964-73; Bd Mem, Stwide Credit Union, 1983-84; Pres, Las Vegas Chapt, Intl Assn of Hospitality Accts, 1980; cp/2nd Amendment Foun; Pres of Parents Com, Troop 143, BSA, 1983-84; S'ship Donor, Univ of NV Las Vegas; r/Treas, Christ Epis Ch, 1983, 1984; Chrysler Leasing Sys Acctg Hon Awd, 1970, 1971, 1972; Intl Assn of Hospitality Accts 1st Place Mbrship Awd, 1980-81; W/W W.

PEVEAR, ROBERTA CHARLOTTE oc/State Representative; b/Jul 4, 1930; h/Drinkwater Road, Hampton Falls, NH 03844; ba/Same; m/Edward Gordon; p/Frank Albert Gibson (dec); Thirza Estelle Hickford, Brentwood, NH; ed/Grad, Comml Studies, Gould Acad, 1947; pa/Legal and Exec Secy, Johnson & Johnson, 1959-66; Exec Secy, Adm Asst, Sears, Roebuck & Co, 1967-70, 1971-77; NH St Rep, 1979-80, 1981-82, 1983-84; Clk of Envir and Agri Standing Com, 1983-84; Exec Bd and Co Home Com, Rockingham Co Legis Del; Chm, Ins Subcom for Exec Bd; Notary Public; Justice of Peace; Nat and NH Order of Wom Legis; IPA; cp/Nat Soc DAR; VFW Aux; Am Legion Aux; Gen Fdn of Wom's Clbs; Hampton Monday Clb; Hampton Falls Fire Dept Aux; Hampton Falls Friends of Lib; Concerned Citizens of Hampton Falls; r/Prot; hon/Hampton Falls Grange Commun Citizen Awd, 1982; 5-Yr Ser Awd, Rockingham Co Planning Comm, 1983; W/W Polit; W/W Am Wom; World W/W Intells; World W/W Wom; W/W E; Intl Register of Profiles; DIB.

PEVERLEY, LUCILLE CARLEENE oc/Instructor; b/Jan 18, 1934; h/972 Harwood Street, San Diego, CA 92154; m/William E; c/Mark D, Rebecca Owens, Timothy E, Elizabeth Huckabone; p/James Madison and Dorothy Elizabeth Harbin, San Diego, CA; ed/Student, Univ of Redlands, 1969, 1970; BA, San Diego St Univ, 1979; pa/Tchr, Elem Sch, Ctl Elem Sch, 1962-66; Cafeteria Mgr, 1963-77; Instr, Chula Vista Rec Dept, 1971-75; Instr, Home Ec, Sweetwater Adult Sch, Montgomery Adult Sch, SWn Jr Col, 1974-; Sweetwater Tchrs Assn; San Diego Food Ser Assn; CA Sch Employees Assn; Ctl PTA, Hon Life Mem; r/Bapt; hon/Author, Let's Have a Party, 1979; W/W W.

PEYSER, JOAN oc/Editor, Writer on Music; b/Jun 12, 1931; h/19 Charlton Street, New York, NY 10014; ba/New York, NY; c/Karen Edna, Anthony C, Monica Lu; ed/Student, Smith Col, 1947-49; BA, Barnard Col, 1951; MA, Fac of Phil, Concentration on Music, Columbia Univ, 1956; pa/Editor, The Musical Quarterly; Writer on Music; Am Musicological Soc; Music Critics Assn; cp/Andiron Clb; hon/Pubs, The New Music: The Sense Behind the Sound 1970, Boulez: Composer, Conductor Enigma 1976, Twentieth Century Music: The Sense Behind the Sound, 50 Articles in New York Times; ASCAP Awd for Excell in Writing on Music, 1967, 1970, 1982; Baker's Biogl Dic.

PFAFF, LUCIE oc/Assistant Professor of Marketing and Economics; b/Sep 17, 1929; h/518 Morse Avenue, Ridgefield, NJ 07657; ba/Riverdale, NY; m/Hans (dec); c/Harry Hans; p/Heinrich and Lucie Baral, Waiblingen, Germany; ed/BA, Pace Univ, 1968; MA 1970, PhD 1972, German, NY Univ; MA in Ed 1980, MBA in Intl Bus 1981, Fairleigh Dickinson Univ; pa/Instr, German, NY Univ, 1971-73; Lectr, German, Fairleigh Dickinson Univ, 1973-76; Asst Prof, Montclair St Col, 1976;l Acad Recorder, Fairleigh Dickinso Univ, 1977-80; Lectr, Ec, Rockland Commun Col, 1980-82; Asst Prof, Ec and Mktg, Col of Mt St Vincent, 1982-; Am Assn Tchrs of German, Treas of NJ Chapt; Mod Lang Assn; Faust Soc; Contbg Mem, Faust-Blätter; cp/Deborah Hosp Foun; hon/Pubs, The Devil in T Mann's Doktor Faustus and P Valery's Mon Faust, Articles in Profl Jours on Lit Topics and Tchg Methods, Intl Trade; BA, magna cum laude, Pace Univ; Hon Soc, Acad Excell Awd, 1968; NY Univ: S'ships 1969-71, Fdr's Day Awd 1973; W/W World of Wom.

PHELPS, DANIEL HUBBARD oc/Doctor of Podiatric Medicine; b/Apr 20, 1944; h/504 West Shaw, Tyler, TX 75701; ba/Tyler, TX; m/Linda Kay; c/Rex, Ron, Robert, Shelly, Tammy; p/Hubbard and Harriet Phelps, Whitehouse, TX; ed/AA, Tyler Jr Col, 1964; BS, Stephen F Austin Univ, 1966; DPM, IL Col Podiatric Med, 1975; Resident, Univ of TX Med Sch, 1976; pa/Sect Mgr, Hotel Monopol Wargerooge, W Germany, 1965; Div Rep, Amoco Prodn Co, 1966-71; Computer Instr, Tyler Jr Col, 1968; Podiatrist, Nan Travis Clin, 1976-79; Pvt Pract, 1979-; Del, Am Podiatry Students Assn, 1971; Staff, Rusk Meml Hosp, Nan Travis Meml Hosp, Med Ctr, Commun Hosp; cp/Dir, Jacksonville JCs, 1977; 1st VP, E TX Yg Dems, 1970; Kiwanis Clb Mem, 5 Yrs;

r/Bapt; hon/Diplomate, Nat Bd of Podiatry Examrs; Durlacher Hon Soc, Podiatry, 1975; W/W S and SW.

PHILIPPAKOS, TASSOS N oc/ Senior Analyst; b/Oct 25, 1947; h/1744 66th Street, Brooklyn, NY 11204; ba/ New York, NY; p/Nickolaos Philippakos, Athens, Greece; ed/MBA in Fin, 1978; BA in Ec, 1971; mil/Greek Army, 1972-74; pa/Sr Analyst, Moody's Investors, 1982-; Investmt Analyst, Metro Life, 1980-82; Indust Analyst, Merrill Lynch, 1974-79; Pres, Hellenic Am Bkrs Assn; Elect Equip Anal of NY; Aerospace Analysts of NY; NY Soc of Securities Analysts; cp/Hellenic Univ Clb; r/Greek Orthodox; hon/W/W Aviation and Aerospace.

PHILLIS, ARLENE MARIE oc/ Home Economics Teacher; b/May 14, 1936; h/1933 Oakwood Drive, Ft Collins, CO 80521; ba/Ft Collins, CO; c/ Kirk Rolfs, Scott Rolfs; p/Mr and Mrs Herb Watts, Manhattan, KS; ed/BS, 1959; Voc Cert, 1967; pa/Home Ec Tchr, Alexander HS 1959-61, Blevins Jr High 1968-, Lincoln Jr High 1967-68; Poudre Ed Assn, 1967-; CO Ed Assn, 1967-; NEA, Life Mem; Poudre R-1 Home Ec Tchrs, Pres 1970-72, 1977; Am Voc Assn, 1983; CO Assn Voc Ed Tchrs, 1983; Am Home Ec Assn, 1965-70; Alpha Delta Kappa, 1977-; r/Bapt; hon/ Co-Author, "Keys to the Core" 1982, Poudre R-1 Sch Dist Jr High Curric Guide 1983; W/W W.

PHILLIPS, CLEO J oc/Social Studies Teacher; b/Sep 10, 1941; h/8309 Northeast 33rd Street, Spencer, OK 73084; ba/Spencer, OK; m/Mary Louise Henderson; c/Czerny Deushai, Meidra Juliaette; p/Sim and Julia Phillips (dec); ed/MEd 1984, BA 1980, Ctl St Univ; Cert of Completion, Law Enforcement Tng Ed, 1979; Cert of Graduation, Preston Road Sch of Preaching, 1971; Cert of Completion, Nat Profl Truck Driver Tng, 1967; Cert of Completion, Universal Equip Tng Sch, 1961; pa/ Social Studies Tchr, Grade 7, Mid Sch; Campus Police, Ctl St Univ, 1979-80; Campus Police, OK Christian Col, 1974-79; Security Ofcr, Peterson Security Ser, 1972-74; Ch Min, Chs of Christ, 1971-77; r/Ch of Christ; Serves as a Deacon in Charge of Worship Ser in Local Ch Congreg.

PHILLIPS, COLLIS NIMROD oc/ Chief of Office of Policy Analysis and Information; b/Mar 20, 1945; h/3829 El Camino Place, Alexandria, VA 22309; ba/Washington, DC; p/Mrs Madie Phillips, Tabb, VA; ed/BA, Ec, Lincoln Univ, 1967; Post-Baccalaureate, Dept of Ec, Oberlin Col, 1968; MA, Ec 1975, PhD, Ec 1977, Syracuse Univ; Sr Exec Course, Fed Exec Inst, 1983; mil/Active Duty, 1968-71; Presently Maj, USAF; pa/ Chief, Ofc of Policy Anal and Info, Wom's Bur, US Dept of Labor, 1983-; Intl Economist, Bur of Intl Labor Affairs, US Dept of Labor, 1977-83; Instr, Ec Dept, George Mason Univ, 1979; Labor Economist, Ofc of Policy Eval and Res, US Dept of Labor, 1975-77; Res Fellow, Brookings Instn, 1974-75; Am Ec Assn; Resv Ofcrs Assn; cp/US Tang Soo Do Karate Fdn; r/Bapt; hon/Pubs, "Descriptive Analysis of the Data Used in Longitudinal Manpower Study," "Economic Dislocation: Causes, Consequences and Responses," "An Essay in Economic Thought: The Ricard-

ian and Heckecler-Oblinian Doctrines of Foreign Trade"; Army Accomation Medal, 1983; US Dept of Labor Awd for Perf While on Ofcl Duty at OECD in Paris, 1979; Res F'ship, The Brookings Inst, 1974; NDEA Title 10 F'ship, Syracuse Univ, 1971.

PHILLIPS, MICHAEL LYNN oc/ Contract Manufacturing Manager; b/ Jun 18, 1952; h/2024 North Memorial Parkway, A-S, Huntsville, AL 35810; ba/Huntsville, AL; p/M L and Margaret Phillips, Erwin, TN; ed/BS in Mech Engrg 1976, MBA 1978, TN Tech Univ; mil/ROTC, 1970-71; pa/Night Clk, Clinchfield YMCA, 1970; Machine Operator, Crystal Ice, Coal and Laundry, 1970; Engrg, Union Carbide Corp, 1971-72, 1973-74; Salesman, SWn Co, 1975; Report and Instrn Manual Writer, Citizens Bk, 197-78; Team Mgr and Tng Mgr 1979-80, Team Mgr 1980, Contract Mfg Mgr 1980-, Procter & Gamble; ASME; NSPE; Order of Engrs; AMBA/TN Tech Univ Alumni Assn; Theta Tau, 1972-; cp/Huntsville C of C; Yg Repubs, 1982-; r/Prot; hon/ Tau Beta Pi, 1972-; Pi Tau Sigma, 1972-; Kappa Mu Epsilon, 1972; Phi Kappa Phi, 1973; Omicron Delta Kappa, 1975; NSF Undergrad Res, 1972; SWn Co Gold Awd, 1975; SWn Superstar, 1974; Top-Twenty Sales Awd, SWn, 1974; Citizens Bk and Col of Bus Adm S'ships, 197, 1978; Acad Wreath, ROTC, 1970; Marksman, ROTC, 1970; Jerome Barnum Ldrship Tng, 1972; W/W Among Students in Am Univs and Cols; Outstg Yg Men of Am; W/W S and SW; Outstg Yg Men of Am.

PHILLIPS, ROSEMARY WOOLEY oc/Business Owner, Executive Director; b/Dec 7, 1946; h/Box 370, Nome, AK 99762; ba/Wasilla, AK; m/C J; p/Haywood and Helen Wooley, Montevallo, AL; ed/BS, Univ of Montevallo; MS, NM St Univ; pa/Cnslr, Public Hlth, 1966, 1967; Vista Vol, Elim, AK, 1968; Cnslr, Beltz Dorm, 1970-73; Retail Bus Owner, 1972-; Fish Broker and Exec Dir, Iditarod Trail Com; Adv Bd Mem, AK Airlines and AK Nat Bk, Iditarod Bd of Dirs 1976-80; Nome Bar Owners, Past Pres; cp/Chm, Month of Iditarod, 1973-82; Nome City Coun, 1978-82; Bd of Dirs, AK Visitors Assn; Bd, Nome C of C, Pres 1979-81; Nome Kennel Clb, Bd 1975-; Pres, AK Coastal Zone Mgmt Bd; Pioneers of AK, Igloo #1; hon/Nome Bus Owner Awd, 1981; Outstg Ser Awd, 1980; Runner-Up, Alaskan of the Yr, 1982; Outstg Yg Wom of Am; W/ W W.

PHUTELA, RAMESH CHANDER oc/ Research Associate; b/Dec 23, 1951; h/ 2732 Benvenue Avenue, #1, Berkeley, CA 94705; ba/Berkeley, CA; p/Mr and Mrs Mulkh Raj Phutela, Fazilka, India; ed/PhD, Univ of Hull, 1978; MS, Punjab Agri Univ, 1975; BS, Panjab Univ, 1972; pa/Postdoct Fellow, Univ of Otago, 1978-79; Res Assoc, Univ of Chgo, 1979-81; Res Assoc, Lawrence Berkeley Lab, Univ of CA Berkeley, 1981-; Am Chem Soc; N Am Thermal Anal Soc; hon/Author, 20 Pub'd Res Papers in Field of Thermodynamics; Univ of Hull Res Studentship, 1975-77; Men of Achmt; Intl W/W Intells; DIB.

PIASECKI, FRANK NICHOLAS oc/ Executive; b/Oct 24, 1919; h/Tunbridge Road, Haverford, PA 19041; ba/Sharon Hill, PA; m/Vivian O'Gara Weyer-

haeuser; c/Lynn, Nicole, Frederick, Frank, Michael, John, Gregory; p/ Nikodem and Emilia Lotocki Piasecki (dec); ed/Student, Mech Engrg, Towne Sch, Univ of PA; BS in Aeronautical Engrg, Guggenheim Sch of Aeronautics, NY Univ; pa/Reg'd Profl Engr, Aircraft Designer, Platt-LePage Aircraft Corp, 1940-41; Aerodynamicist, Edward G Budd Mfg Co, 1941-43; Founded, PV-Engrg Forum (Res Grp), 1940; Pres and Chm of Bd, Piasecki Helicopter Corp, 1946; Pres and Chm of Bd, Piasecki Aircraft Corp, 1955; AIAA, Fellow; Hon Fellow and Past Pres, Am Helicopter Soc; Soc of Automotive Engrs; Soc of Exptl Test Pilots; Am Soc of Profl Engrs; Soc of Mil Engrs; Assn of AUS; Navy Leag of US; Am Def Preparedness Assn; hon/Has Delivered Over 35 Papers and Lectures; PENJERDEL Aviation Awd, 1983; ASME Spirit of St Louis Awd, 1983; Philip H Ward (Franklin Inst) Gold Medal, 1979; Leonardo da Vinci Awd, Navy Helicopter, 1974; Dir of Dist'd Ams; W/W Engrg; W/W Am; Jane's W/ W Aviation and Aerospace.

PICKERING, GEORGE WILEY oc/ Owner and Director of Camps; b/Feb 4, 1927; h/Camp Rockmont, Black Mountain, NC 28711; ba/Black Mountain, NC; m/Janie W; c/George W II, Jennifer Jane; p/E Spurgeon and Mattie Dent Pickering (dec); ed/BS in Ed, MS Col, 1952; mil/USAF; pa/Dir/Fdr, Camp Rockmont, 1956-; Owner/Dir, Camp Merri-Mac, 1966-78; Fdr/Dir, Camp Hollymont, 1983; Camp Ridgecrest for Boys; Bapt Sunday Sch Bd of the So Bapt Conv, 1947-55; SEn Sect, Am Camping Assn, VP 1964; Trustee, Mars Hill Col, 1967-83; Bd of Advrs, Sanford Preparatory Sch, DE; Bd of Advrs, So Highland Handicraft Guild; Blue Ridge Broadcasting Corp, Exec Bd and Bd of Dirs, Secy 1972-; cp/C of C; r/Bapt.

PIEDRA, JORGE de la oc/Orthopedic Surgeon; b/Feb 11, 1923; ba/Parkview Professional Building, Morrison Drive, Princeton, WV 24740; m/June; c/Ana Maria, Jorge A, James M; ed/Pre-Med, Facultad de Ciencias, Univ of San Marcos, Lima, Peru, 1941-42; Med Ed at Med Sch, Univ of San Marcos, 1943-50; Internship, Army Hosp, Lima, 1951-52; MD, 1952; Rotating Internship, Augustana Hosp, 1952-53; mil/ Peruvian Army Med Corps, 1951-52; pa/Residency in Orthopedic Surg, St Francis Hosp 1953-54, Charlotte Meml Hosp 1954-57; Acting Chief, Orthopedic Dept, Social Security Adm Hosp, Lima, 1958-59; Att'g Orthopedic Surg, Mullens Hosp, 1960-66; Pvt Pract, Orthopedic Surg, 1966-; Affiliated to Princeton Commun Hosp; AMA; WV St Med Assn; Mercer Co Med Assn; Am Fracture Assn; So Med Soc; Latin Am Soc of Orthopedic Surg; Orthopedic Res and Ed Foun; Intl Col of Surg; Peruvian Acad of Surg; Peruvian Am Med Soc; Bd of Dirs, Princeton Commun Hosp; Mem, Several Coms of Princeton Commun Hosp Med Staff; AMA Recog Awds, 1969, 1972-74, 1977, 1981; Certs of Med Lic'g Bd of WV, 1963, and St Med Bd of OH 1963; F'ship in Orthopedic Surg, Intl Col of Surgs, 1977; W/ W S and SW.

PIEPER, GEORGE FRANCIS oc/ Aerospace Center Administrator; b/Jan 1, 1926; h/3155 Rolling Road, Edgewater, MD 21037; ba/Greenbelt, MD; m/Barbara Ferguson; c/Pamela, Lynell Pieper Smillie; p/George F and Katherine Cross Pieper (dec); ed/BA, Wms Col, 1946; MS in Engrg, Cornell Univ, 1949; PhD, Yale Univ, 1952; pa/Staff Mem, Radiation Lab, MIT, 1944-45; Instr, Asst Prof, Physics, Yale Univ, 1952-60; Hd, Exptl Satellites Proj, Applied Physics Lab, Johns Hopkins Univ, 1960-64; Dpty Asst Dir for Adv'd Res 1964-65, Dir of Scis 1965-83, Asst Ctr Dir for Policy, Planning and Devel 1983-84, Assoc Ctr Dir Dir 1984-, NASA/ Goddard Space Flight Ctr; Fellow: Am Phy Soc, AIAA; Am Astronom Soc; Am Geophy Union; AAAS; Cosmos Clb, 1965-69; hon/Contbr, Articles in *Physical Review*, *Journal of Geophysical Research*, and Others; NASA Medal for Exceptl Sci Achmt, 1979; NASA Medal for Outstg Ldrship, 1977; W/W E; W/W Frontier Sci and Technol.

PIERATT, JOHN DAVID oc/Staff Process Engineer; b/Feb 14, 1941; h/13 River Ridge Road, Pisgah Forest, NC 27868; ba/Pisgah Forest, NC; m/Nancy Elizabeth; c/Jennifer Lynn, Suzanne Marie, Cynthia Elaine, Cheryl Lee, Gina Marie; p/Ernest Pieratt, Brookville, OH; Lillian T Pieratt, Dayton, OH; sp/Mary and Royal Ranney, Naples, FL; ed/Att'd DeVry Inst of Technol, Chicago, 1974-76; Var Ednl Sems; pa/Var Postions from 1959 to 1963; Printing Apprentice, Pressman, St Regis Flexible Pkg, Middletown, OH, 1963-67; Wkg Foreman, Wheeler-Van Label, Grand Rapids, MI, 1967-68; Printing Pressman, St Regis Flexible Pkg, 1968-75; Wkg Foreman, Miami-Valley Paper, 1975-77; Plant Supvr, Universal Pkg, Centralia, IL, 1977-79; Print Supvr, Wheeler-Van Label, Grand Rapids, MI, 1979-81; Staff Process Engr, Olin Corp, Pisgah Forest, NC, 1981-; Gravure Tech Assn, 1979-; Graphic Arts Tech Foun, Mem 1979-, Field S'ship Interviewer 1980; Am Soc of Tech Writers; hon/W/ W S & SW.

PIERCE, HELENE J oc/Social Editor; h/7319 Yinger, Dearborn, MI 48126; ba/ Detroit, MI; m/Frank J; c/Robert, Diane Kadrovach, Suzanne Lawrence, Janice Holda, John; ed/Student, WI Acad of Arts, Univ of MI, Henry Ford Commun Col; pa/Columnist, Editor, *Dearborn Independent*, *Dearborn Press*, *Dearborn Times Herald*; Social Editor, *Detroit Polish Daily News*, English Edition, 5 Yrs; cp/Mayor John O'Reilly Adv Bd, Telecommunication Com; Dearborn Citizens Traffic Safety Secy, 17 Yrs; Edison Inst; Detroit Polish Fest Bd of Dirs; Daughs of Isabella; VFW; Ladies Aux; Am Cancer Soc; US Capitol Hist Soc; Dearborn Symph; Commun Arts Coun; Commun Hlth Coun; Dearborn Hist Soc; Orchard Lake Ladies Aux; r/Cath; hon/Dearborn Wom of the Yr; St Anne Awd; Ed Crowe Awd; Ernie Pyle Awd; Vol of Yr Awd; Outstg Citizen of the Yr; U Foun Awd; Bd of Ed Awd; St of MI Tributes; Pioneer Clb Awd; Univ of MI Cert of Recog; Traveled w Pope John Paul II, 1979; Commun Ldrs and Noteworthy Ams; Notable Am of the Bicent Era; World W/W Wom.

PILLOW, WALTER LESTER oc/Logging Contractor; b/Aug 28, 1946; h/ Route 2, Box 342A, Gladys, VA 24554; ba/Same; m/Mary Garrett; c/Valentina Marie; p/Earl B Sr (dec) and Dorothy

D Pillow, Gladys, VA; ed/GED Dipl, 1968; mil/Navy, 2nd Class Petty Ofcr, 4 Yrs; Navy Resv, 1966-75; pa/Millwright, Maintenance Dept, Lynchburg Foundry, 1970-73; Logging Contractor, 1973-; r/Bapt; hon/Hon Discharge, USN, 1975; VA Forestry Loggers Merit Awd, 1983.

PINE, CHARLES JOSEPH oc/ Licensed Psychologist, Director of Behavioral Health Services; b/Jul 13, 1951; h/365 West Grove, Rialto, CA 92376; ba/Banning, CA; m/Mary Day-Pine; c/Charles Andrew, Joseph Scott; p/Charles and LaVern Pine, Rialto, CA; ed/AB, Univ of Redlands, 1973; MA, CA St Univ LA, 1975; PhD, Univ of WA, 1979; Postdoct, Univ of CA LA, 1980-81; pa/Psych Tech, Seattle Indian Hlth Bd, USPHS Hosp, 1977-78; Psych Intern, VA Outpatient Clin, 1978-79; Instr and Asst Prof, OK St Univ, 1979-80; Asst Prof, Psych, Native Am Studies and Wom Studies Prog, WA St Univ, 1981-82; Dir, Behavioral Hlth Sers, Riverside-San Bernardino Co Indian Hlth Inc, 1982-; Am Psychol Assn; Nat Indian Cnslrs Assn; Soc of Indian Psychols, Pres 1981-83; Wn Psychol Assn; AAAS; CA St Psychol Assn; Fellow, Menninger Foun; Sigma Alpha Epsilon Nat Frat; Edit Conslt, *White Cloud Journal*; hon/Pubs, "American Indian Mental Health Research Issues" (In Press), "Suicide in American Indian and Alaska Native Tradition" 1981, "Obese and Non-Obese American Indian and Caucasian Performance on the Mini-Mult MMPI and I-E Scale" 1983, "Education and Training of American Indian Clinical-Community Psychologists" (in Press), "Field-Dependence Factors in American Indian and Caucasian Obesity" (in Press); Univ of WA Inst of Indian Studies Grantee, 1975-76; Univ of CA LA Inst of Am Cultures Grantee, 1981-82; W/W in CA; W/W in W.

PINE, FRANK L oc/Executive; b/Nov 5, 1917; h/2004 Vista Caudal, Newport Beach, CA 91660; ba/Santa Ana, CA; m/Martha Marchak; c/Dixie, Shelley, Douglas; p/Roy Edward and Ruth Willie McGuire Pine (dec); ed/Grad, Chino HS, 1936; Att'd, Univ of CA LA, 1940, 1941; mil/Lt, USN, Ret'd 1955; pa/Lockheed Aircraft, 1940, 1942; Naval Aviator Cadet through Lt, USN, 1942-55; Prod Test Pilot, Pacific Airmotive, 1956-58; Fire Tanker Pilot/Owner, So CA, 1958-59; Pilot, Paul Mantz Air Sers, 1959-61; Gen Mgr and VP of Opers, Tallmantz Aviation Inc, 1961-78; Pres, Tallmantz Aviation, 1978-; Aero Clb of So CA; Quiet Birdmen; Screen Actors Guild; Assn of Naval Aviation; Soc of Exptl Test Pilots, Corporate Div; Explorers Clb; Exptl Aircraft Assn; Aircraft Owners and Pilots Assn; Seaplane Pilots Assn; cp/Balboa Bay Clb; Mesa Verde Country Clb; r/Christian; hon/Victory Medal and Pacific Campaign Medal; W/ W Aviation; W/W So CA.

PINE, MARTHA M oc/Executive; b/ May 2, 1931; h/2004 Vista Caudal, Newport Beach, CA 92660; ba/Santa Ana, CA; m/Frank L; p/Michael (dec) and Mary Hosko Marchak, Newport Beach, CA; ed/Grad, Minooka HS, 1949; Att'd, Scranton Bus Sch 1949-50, IBM Bus Sch 1951, Long Bch Col 1953, 1954; pa/Asst to Paul Mantz of Mantz Air Sers, 1955; VP and Treas, Tallmantz

Aviation Inc, 1965-; Soc of Exptl Test Pilots; Screen Actors Guild; Aero Clb of So CA; Whirlygirls; cp/Orange Co Music Ctr, Sound of Music Chapt; Newport Harbor Guild; Repub Wom of Newport Bch; Newport Harbor Art Mus; Balboa Bay Clb; Mesa Verde Country Clb; r/Cath; hon/W/W Aviation; W/W CA.

PINKSTON, GERRY CAMILLA oc/ Assistant Professor; b/Apr 16, 1948; h/ 2012 Rolling Creek, Edmond, OK 73034; ba/Edmond, OK; p/Mr and Mrs Don Pinkston, Chickasha, OK; ed/BS in Ed (HPER), OK St Univ, 1971; MEd (HPER), Ctl St Univ, 1975; EdD in Higher Ed and Ath Adm, OK St Univ, 1982; pa/Softball Coach and Asst Prof, Ctl St Univ, 1975-; Phy Therapy Aide, St Anthony Hosp, 1972-75; Tchr of PE and Hist, Chickasha Jr High, and Sr High Girls Tennis Coach, Chickasha, 1971-72; AAHPERD; SPAHPERD; OAHPERD; Assn for Intercol Aths for Wom, St Pres and Pres-Elect 1978-81; SWAIAW Exec Bd, 1980-81; F'ship Christian Aths Fac Sponsor, 1975-; Edmond Tennis Assn; NAIA; cp/ARC; r/Wesley Foun Bd, Meth Ch; hon/Phi Kappa Phi, 1982; Kappa Delta Pi, 1981; Phi Epsilon Kappa, 1981; Delta Kappa Gamma, 1980; Delta Psi Kappa, 1976; CSU Softball Team Placed 9th in 1980 and 8th in 1982, Nationally (One Pitcher Was an All-Am 1982); Outstg Yg Wom of Am.

PIRKLE, ESTUS W oc/Pastor, Evangelist, Christian Film Producer; b/Mar 12, 1930; h/PO Box 80, Myrtle, MS 38650; m/Annie Catherine; c/Letha Dianne, Gregory, Don; p/Grover Washington Pirkle (dec); ed/Norman Jr Col, 1949; BA, Mercer Univ, 1951; BD, Master of Rel Ed 1956, Master of Theol 1958, SWn Bapt Sem; DDiv, Covington Theol Sem, 1982; pa/Pastor, Evangelist; Author of Christian Books; Prodr, 60-Minute Color 16mm Film Full-Length Motion Pictures, "If Footmen Tire You, What Will Horses Do?" 1972, "The Burning Hell" 1974, "The Believer's Heaven" 1977; Preacher, 40 Revivals, Confs, Camp Meetings, Each Yr; r/Over 2,000,000 Have Professed Faith in Jesus Christ at the Showing of His Films; hon/Pubs, *Preachers in Space* 1969, *If Footmen Tire You Out, What Will Horses Do?* 1969, *Book of Sermon Outlines* 1973, *Who Will Build Your House?* 1978; "The Burning Hell" Has Been Translated into Spanish and Portuguese and Has Been Distributed All Over the World; Valedictorian, Norman Jr Col, 1949; Grad, cum laude, Mercer Univ, 1957.

PIRSCH, CAROL McBRIDE oc/State Senator, Supervisor of Community Relations; b/Dec 27, 1936; h/4223 Aurora Drive, Omaha, NE 68134; ba/ Omaha, NE; m/Allen I; c/Penni Elizabeth, Pamela Elaine, Patrice Eileen, Phyllis Erika, Peter Allen, Perry Andrew; p/Mrs Lyle E McBride; ed/ Grad, Ctl HS, 1954; pa/Justice of the Peace, 1962-66; Data Processing, Omaha Public Schs, 1966-68; Wage Practices, Wn Elect, 1968-70; Legal Secy, 1970-71; Ofc Mgr, Pirsch Brokerage Co, 1977-79; Supvr, Employmt, NWn Bell Telephone, 1979-81; NE St Senator, Dist 10, 1979-; Supvr, Commun Relats, NWn Bell Telephone, 1981-; Order of Wom Legis; Wom in

Mgmt Assn; cp/Univ of NE Omaha Parents Assn, Bd of Dirs; NE St Devel Disabilities Coun; Benson Repub Woms Clb; Omaha Area Coun on Alcoholism and Drug Abuse; Pres, NE Coalition for Victims of Crime; r/Presb; hon/Golden Elephant Awd; Outstg Legis Ldrship Awd, Nat Org for Victim Assistance, 1981.

PISKACEK, VLADIMIR RICHARD oc/Psychiatrist; b/Apr 13, 1929; h/1641 3rd Avenue, New York, NY 10028; ba/ Manhasset, NY; c/Dejan Gregory; p/ Frank and Ludmila Piskacek (dec); ed/ MD, Charles IV Univ Med Sch, Prague, 1956; Diplomate of Am Bd of Psychi and Neurology, 1968; Cert in Child Psychi, 1970; pa/Resident, Bellevue, NY Univ 1962-65, Mt Sinai Hosp 1962-65; Psychi Instr, Columbia Univ, 1967-68; Asst Dir, Madeline Borg Child Guid Clin, 1969-71; Med Dir, Nassau Ctr for Developmentally Disabled, 1972-74; Clin Asst Prof, Psychi, Cornell Univ, 1978-; Lectr, New Sch for Social Res, 1979; US-Tibet Comm, 1982; APA; AMA; hon/Pubs, *Psychiatric and Social Work Problems of Children of Interracial Marriages* 1973, "Les Orishas Urbains" 1982, Other Articles for Profl Jours; Recip, Awd Congresso Pan Americano de Hipnologia e Medicina Psicosomatica, Rio de Janeiro, Brazil, 1978; Dir of Med Specs; W/W E; DIB.

PISUNYER, F XAVIER oc/Medical Educator, Researcher; b/Dec 3, 1933; h/ 305 Riverside Drive, New York, NY 10025; ba/New York, NY; m/Penelope W; c/Andrea M, Olivia A, Joanna L; p/ James and Mercedes Pi-Sunyer, New York, NY; ed/BA, Oberlin Col, 1955; MD, Columbia Univ, 1959; MPH, Harvard Univ, 1963; Intern and Resident, St Luke's Hosp, 1959-60; Resident in Med, St Bartholomew's Hosp, London, 1961-62; Fellow in Med, Thorndike Lab, Harvard Med Sch, 1964-65; pa/ From Instr to Asst Prof of Med 1965-76, Assoc Prof of Clin Med 1976-78, Assoc 1965-, Columbia Univ; From Asst Att'g to Att'g Phys, St Luke's Hosp, 1965-; Dir of Div Endocrinology 1977-, Assoc Dir of Med 1983-, St Luke's-Roosevelt Hosp Ctr; Am Diabetes Assn; Am Soc Clin Nutrition; Endocrine Soc; Am Fdn Clin Res; Am Bd of Nutrition; Am Inst of Nutrition; Soc for Exptl Biol and Med; Harvey Soc; NY Acad of Med; Phys for Social Responsibility; cp/Amnesty Intl; Sierra Clb; ACLU; hon/Author, Over 120 Pub'd Articles; Fellow, USPHS, 1963-64; Fellow, NY Heart Assn, 1966-68; Sr Investigator, NY Heart Assn, 1968-72; Fogarty Intl Fellow, NIH, 1979-80; Mem, Nutrition Study Sect, NIH, 1983-; W/W E; W/W Frontier Sci and Technol; Am Men and Wom of Sci.

PITTMAN, EVELYN LaRUE oc/ Retired; b/Jan 6, 1910; h/1309 Northeast 56 Street, Oklahoma City, OK 73111; p/William Pittman (dec); Mrs Florence K Greer (dec); ed/BA, Spelman Col, 1933; Life Cert to Teach Music and Social Studies in OK, Langston Univ, 1938; Study of Composition w Robert Ward, Julliard Sch of Music, 1948; MMus, OK Univ; Pvt Study of Composition w Nadia Boulanger, Paris; Further Study at Columbia Univ; Perm Cert, St Ed Dept of NY, to Teach Public Sch Music on Any Level; pa/Org'd

Evelyn Pittman Choir, 1938; Started Writing Column, "Lady Evelyn Says" for *Black Dispatch* Newspaper, 1943; Served on Radio Comm in OKC, 1946; Dir of 350-Voice Interdenominational Choir, 1948-56; Joined Music Dept of Greenburgh Sch Dist, 1958; Directed the Westchester All-Co Choral Fest, 1965; Org'd Freedom Child Musical Grp Inc, 1976; Joined ASCAP, 1963; hon/ Pubs, *Rich Heritage*, a Book of Songs, Biogl Sketches and Pictures of 21 Afro-Ams and Their Contbns to the World 1944, "Sit Down, Servant," "Rocka Mah Soul," "Any How," "Nobody Knows the Trouble I See," "Joshua" 1949-56, "Trampin'" 1965, "I Love the Springtime" 1949, "We Love America" 1953; Pittman Sisters Sang on *Ed Sullivan Show*, OKC, 1953; Composed Folk Opera, "Cousin Esther," 1954; Recip, Spec Achmt Awd, Spelman Alumnae, 1959; Excerpts of "Cousin Esther" Given at Carnegie Recital Hall 1962, Played Over Radio Sta WNYX during Am Music Fest 1963; Composed "Freedom Child," a Musical Drama Portraying the Life of the Late Dr Martin Luther King Jr, 1970; "Freedom Child" Cast Toured So US, Norway, Sweden, Copenhagen, England, Scotland, Liberia, Ghana; Composed "Oklahoma's Jim Noble"; Set Up Music Composition Awd for $500 at Langston Univ, 1982; Voted into the Afro-Am Hall of Fame, 1983; Other Hons.

PIZER, ELIZABETH FAW HAYDEN oc/Composer; b/Sep 1, 1954; h/PO Box 42, Three Mile Bay, New York 13693; ba/Same; m/Charles Ronald; p/John (dec) and Ann Hayden, Watertown, NY; ed/NY St Regents Dipl and HS Dipl, Watertown HS, 1972; Student, Drama and Dance, Boston Conservatory of Music, 1972-75; pa/Self-Employed Accompanist/Coach, 1972-78; Accompanist/Coach, San Jose St Univ, 1978-80; Self-Employed Composer/ Musician (Pianist), 1980-; Self-Employed Free-Lance Radio Prodr, 1980-; Broadcast Music Inc; Intl Leag of Wom Composers, Chp 1982-; Am Music Ctr; Nat Leag of Am Pen Wom; Am Soc of Univ Composers; Composers Guild; MN Composers Forum; Am Wom Composers; Composers Forum; Nat Assn of Composers, USA; Nat Wom's Hall of Fame, Nat Hons Com 1984-; r/Epis; hon/Third Prize for Vocal Music, Nat Leag of Am Pen Wom Biennial Composition Contest, 1984; First Prize for Choral Music, Nat Leag of Am Pen Wom Biennial Composition Contest, 1984; Second Emminent Mention for "Traditional Sonnet Form" Category, Poets of the Vineyard Poetry Competition, 1983; Third Prize for "Theme Poem" Category, Poets of the Vineyard Poetry Competition, 1983; Hon Mention for Vocal Music, Composers Guild Composition Contest, 1983; Third Prize for Instrumental Music, Composers Guild Composition Contest, 1983; Num Other Hons; Contemp Concert Music by Wom: A Dir of the Composers the Their Works; Outstg Yg Wom in Am; W/W Am Music; World W/W Wom.

PLACE, IRENE oc/Professor Emeritus; b/Jan 27, 1912; h/12705 Southeast River Road, Portland, OR 97222; ba/ Portland, OR; m/Darold; ed/BA, Univ of NE, 1932; MA, Columbia Univ, 1933;

EdD, NY Univ, 1947; pa/Instr, Briarcliff Col, 1933-36; Instr, Marshall Univ, 1936-37; Asst Prof and Bus Tchr Tng Dept Hd, Univ of Toledo, 1937-43; Assoc Prof, Grad Sch of Bus Adm, Univ of MI Ann Arbor, 1943-66; Prof, Sch of Bus, Portland St Univ, 1966-80; Current Prof Emeritus of Bus Ed, Sch of Bus Adm, Portland St Univ; r/ Christian; hon/Pubs, *Records Management: Controlling Business Information* 1982, *Women in Management* 1980, *Executive Secretarial Procedures* 1980, *Opportunities in Office Management* 1979, "Simulation and In-Basket Exercises: Preparation for Expanding Career Opportunities" 1977, Num Others; Rackham S'ship, Univ of MI, 1950; Ford Foun S'ship, Univ of MI, 1963; Dist'd Ser Awd, Sys and Procedures Assn, 1968; Delta Pi Epsilon, Beta Kappa Chapt, 1975; Hon Mem, Am Records Mgmt Assn, 1980; World W/ W Wom; W/W Am Wom; DIB; 2,000 Wom of Achmt; Ldrs in Ed; Nat Register of Prom Ams.

PLANTE, ELIZABETH ADELINE oc/ Institute Director; b/Feb 21, 1915; h/ 1209 California Road, Eastchester, NY 10709; ba/Same; c/Barbara Ann Stavenik, Richard T Stavenik, Virginia Marie Braun; ed/Grad, Bronxville HS, 1932; Postgrad Courses in Chem and Biol, A B Davis HS, 1933; RN, Phila Gen Hosp, 1936; Att'd, NY Univ, 1954-55; BS Cand, Pace Univ, 1984; pa/Gen Duty, Roosevelt Hosp, 1937; Night Supvr, NY Hosp Westchester Div, Psychi, 1939-40; Dir of Nurses, Mt Vernon Convalescent Home, Geriatrics, 1942; Hd Nurse and Gen Duty, Mt Vernon Hosp, 1943-53; Vis'g Nsg Assn of New Rochess, 1954-55; Dir of Nsg, Saw Mill River Convalescent Home, Geriatrics, 1955; Dir of Nsg, Hebrew Home for Aged, 1956; Relief Nurse, Lawrence Hosp, 1957-68; Pvt Duty, Psychi, 1968-73; Appt'd to Adv Bd, Leighton Med Ctr, 1972; Relief Hd Nurse, Lawrence Hosp, 1973-; Num Lectures Given to Var Orgs, incl'g, Lic'd Practical Nsg Assn of Mt Vernon, Nat Hlth Fdn Sprg Conf, Canadian Schizophrenia Foun; cp/Huxley Inst; En Star; New Rochelle Garden Clb; PARC; AARP; hon/Pubs, "René, the Biography of a Schizophrenic," 1974; Newsletter for HIBR, 1976-.

PLATH, DOUGLAS FRANK oc/ Director of Adolescent Substance Abuse Program; b/Jan 9, 1940; h/72 Poe Street, Hartsdale, NY 10530; ba/White Plains, NY; m/Susan Klebanow; c/Scott Douglas, David Craig, Mai Melissa; p/ Frank and Margaret Plath, Lauderdale Lakes, FL; ed/AB, Rutgers Univ, 1962; MA, Seton Hall Univ, 1964; PhD, NY Univ, 1976; pa/Kessler Inst for Rehab, 1962-64; Commun Sers for the Blind, 1964-67; Mt Sinai Hosp, 1967-68; Yonkers Mtl Hlth Clin, 1968-80; Westchester Co Dept of Commun Mtl Hlth, 1980-; Greenburgh Narcotics Guid Coun, Bd of Dirs; The Deron Sch, Bd of Dirs; Woodlands HS S'ship Fund, Bd of Trustees; cp/The Dad's Clb, Bd of Dirs; r/Unitarian; hon/Pubs, "Accuracy of Perception of Counselors Toward Clients in Methadone Maintenance Treatment Programs," "Emergency Evaluation of Suicidal Patients in Outpatient Mental Health Centers"; W/ W E.

PLUESE, RONALD CHARLES oc/

Doctor of Chiropractic; b/Jan 27, 1937; h/964 Dogwood Avenue, Delray Beach, FL 33444; ba/Boca Raton, FL; m/Jeanne Susan; c/Karen Vollare, Rick; p/Mr and Mrs John Pluese, Delray Beach, FL; ed/ Student, Temple Univ, 1958; AS, DC, Nat Col of Chiro, 1962; mil/USAF; pa/ 23 Yrs of Chiro (19 Yrs in NJ and 4 Yrs in FL), Pluese Chiro Hlth Ctr; Am Chiro Assn, Charter Mem; FL Chiro Soc; FL Chiro Trust; Palm Bch Chiro Soc; Am Coun of Orthopedics and Nutrition; Am Col of Chiro Orthopedics; Nat Col of Chiro, Pres's Cabinet; Nat Col Alumni Assn; FL Coun of Orthopedics; ACA Coun on Roentgenology; Kimball Foun; Foun for Chiro Res and Ed; Nat Acad of Res Biochems; Am Acad of Nutritional Conslts; Rockley Res Acad; D Paul Reilly and Assocs; Acad for the Advmt of Chiro, VP; Profl Chiro Soc; Nat Anti-Trust Com; Coun of Chiro Ed; Royal Order of the Kings in Chiro; Coun of 100 of the AAC; cp/ Gtr Boca Raton C of C; Boca Raton Hist Soc; Caldwell Playhouse, Angels and Friends; Boca Raton Ctr of the Arts and Friends, Past Dir; ARC of Boca Raton, Chm of First Annual Ball 1982; Forum of Profl and Businesspeople of Boca Raton; Blue Lodge Masons; 32nd Deg Mason of the Consistory; Cresent Temple Shrine; Lighthouse Pt Yacht and Racquet Clb; Boca Raton Hotel and Clb; Mercedes-Benz Clb of Am; Fountain of Hlth Spa; r/Unity of Delray Bch, Dir; The 700 Clb; Foun of Christian Living; Eagles Clb, Robert Schuller; Helping the Chd, Jimmy Swaggart; Terry Cole Whittaker Min; Gold Coast Curcillo; hon/Outstg Achmt Awds, Nat Col of Chiro; Sigma Phi Kappa Frat, Chiropractor of the Yr, 1975.

PLUMMER, VERIAN DURHAM oc/ Elementary Teacher; b/May 4, 1937; h/ 6743 Cove Creek Drive, Charlotte, NC 28215; ba/Charlotte, NC; m/Robert H; c/Dawnalia A Ross, Robert H Jr, Gregory, Mark, Jeffrey; p/Mr Andrew L Durham Jr (dec); Mrs Annie B Durham, Charlotte, NC; ed/BA, cum laude, Johnson C Smith Univ, Univ of NC, 1965; Employmt Cnslr, Wilvar Inst, 1970; pa/Charlotte Commun Hosp; Charlotte Rehab Hosp Open House Drug Therapeutic Ctr; Marie G Davis Elem Sch; Morgan Elem Sch; Chantilly Elem Sch; Alpha Kappa Alpha Sorority; NEA; NC Assn of Ed; Student Ser Com; Primary Dept Chm, Chantilly Sch; Tchr, Adv Com; Supvr, Student Tchrs; cp/YWCA; U Appeal Campaign Rep; r/ Steel Creek AME Zion; hon/Ms Alpha Kappa Alpha, 1964; Tchr of the Yr, 1983.

POAGE, WALLER STAPLES III oc/ Architect, Urban Planner, Professor; b/ Apr 25, 1936; h/701-A West Banyon Court, Laredo, TX 78041; ba/Laredo, TX; m/Elizabeth Bock; c/Mary Elizabeth, Mary Margaret; p/Waller S Poage Jr (dec); ed/BArch w Minor in Urban Planning, VA Polytechnic Inst, 1960; pa/ Larson & Larson Archs, 1956-60; Cameron Fairchild & Assocs, Archs, 1960-61; Hayes, Seay, Mattern & Mattern, Archs, Engrs, Planners, 1961-63; Mackie and Kamrath, Archs, 1963-64; Leonard Gabert & Assocs, Archs, 1964-65; Waller S Poage & Assocs, Archs, 1965-73; Dales Y Foster & Assocs, Archs, 1973-75; Commun Planners Inc, 1975-82; The

Gondeck-Poage Ptnrship, Archs, 1982-; Instr, Univ of TX San Antonio, Dept of Arch, 1980-; AIA, 1965-; TX Soc of Archs, 1965-; Constrn Specifications Inst, 1967-; cp/Laredo C of C, 1975-; r/Epis; hon/Pubs, "Design of Radiation Fall-Out Shelters for New and Existing Buildings" 1966, "The Zero Base of Real Estate Activity" 1975; Outstg Residential Design, *House and Home Magazine*, 1966; Outstg Ser Awd, Houston Chapt, Constrn Specifications Inst, 1972; "Un Poquito Mas" Awd, Laredo C of C, 1980; W/W S and SW; Am Archs.

POBANZ, RITA BERNADETTE oc/ Registered Nurse; b/Oct 16, 1941; h/ 1349 Coral Place, Hampton, VA 23669; ba/Hampton, VA; m/Kenneth Walter; c/ Karen, Stephen; p/John Daniel (dec); Mary Robert Simpson Grady, New York, NY; ed/ABN w Hons, En NM Univ; pa/Staff Nurse, Gerald Champion Hosp, 1974; Critical Care Staff, Charge, IC Instr, Hampton Gen Hosp, 1974-79; Patient Ed Coor 1978-79, Critical Care Coor 1980-82, Critical Care Supvr 1979-80, Holy Cross Hosp; Asst Dir of Nsg, Coliseum Pk Nsg Home, 1982-; Hosp Vol, ARC, 1967-70; CPR Instr, Am Heart Assn, 1979-81; Am Assn Critical Care Nurses, Tidewater Chapt, Secy 1981, Pres-Elect 1982; Nat Leag of Nsg; Carolina-VA Soc Critical Care Med; cp/Ofc Chm, Fam Sers, USAF, 1961-62, Publicity Chm 1962-64; Den Ldr, CSA, 1970; hon/Phi Theta Kappa, 1974-; CCRN, 1978-; W/W Am Wom.

PODOLSKY, SAMUEL oc/Entrepreneur; b/Dec 20, 1945; h/Sierra Madre 450, Mexico City, DF 11000, Mexico; ba/Mexico City, Mexico; m/Paulette Levy; c/David Podolsky-Levy, Daniel Podolsky-Levy; p/Manuel Podolsky, Miriam Rapoport; ed/MBA, Wharton, Univ of PA, 1971; BA, CPA, UNAM, Mexico, 1969; pa/Mgmt Conslt, Mgr Mexico, Booz Allen & Hamilton, 1971-73; Sr VP, Banco de Comercio, Mexico, 1973-76; Fdr, Pres, Podolsky y Asociados, 1976-79; Fdr and Pres of Grupo Indust Polen, of Directron, of Mirada Opticos, 1979-; cp/Fdr and Pres, Wharton Mexico City Clb, 1973-77; hon/Grad, summa cum laude, UNAM, 1969.

POLAHA, JEROME MICHAEL oc/ Lawyer; b/Feb 21, 1940; h/115 Greenridge Drive, Reno, NV 89509; ba/Reno, NV; m/Esther Lee Eben; c/Erik, Jon, Michael, Kristofer; p/Andrew and Justine Polaha, Allentown, PA; ed/AA, Syracuse Univ, 1957; BA, Univ of NV, 1964; JD, George Wash Univ, 1968; mil/ USAF, Security Ser 1957-60; pa/Assoc, Breen & Young, Whitehead & Hoy, 1968-69; Washoe Co Public Defender, 1969-72; Ptnr, Grellman & Polaha & Coffin, 1972-75; Polaha, Conner, Semenza & Lutfy Ltd, 1980-81; Polaha & Conner, 1975-; NV Trial Lwyrs Assn, Bd of Dirs 1975-; Am Bd of Crim Lwyrs, Dir 1981-; Nat Assn Crim Def Lwyrs; CA Attys for Crim Justice; ATLA; CTLA; NBA; ABA; Intl Sierra; Toastmasters-Aquarian; Elks; Barristers Clb of NV, Pres 1974-76; r/Rom Cath; hon/Nat Hist Soc, 1964; Nat Lang Soc; Nat Hon Soc, Pi Kappa Pi, Univ of NV, 1964; Yg Lwyrs Achmt Awd, 1973-74; W/W W; W/W Am Law.

POLK, VIDET RICHARD oc/Gospel Song Writer, Teacher; b/Jun 1, 1918; h/ 2280 North Vega Drive, Baton Rouge,

LA 70815; ba/Pass Christian, MS; p/ John Jeff (dec) and Lola Singletary Polk, Pearl River, LA; ed/Att'd, Sch in Pearl River, LA, Stamps-Baxter Sch of Gospel Music; Pvt Music Lessons Under V O Stamps, Mr and Mrs J R Baxter Jr; pa/ Pres of Gospel Singers of Am Inc, 1957-; Pres, Nat Gospel Singing Conv, 1961, 1966, 1972; Former Part Owner and VP, Stamps-Baxter Music Co; Tchr of Gospel Music, 49 Yrs; AR, LA, TX Tri-St Singing Conv, Pres for 20 Yrs; LA St Gospel Singing Conv, 25 Yrs; Nat Singing Conv, 3 Yrs; Gospel Singers of Am, 26 Yrs, VP and Part Owner for 5 Yrs; Orgr of Govs Gospel Singing, 4 Sessions; hon/150 Gospel Songs Pub'd; Compiled Biographies of Gospel Song Writers 1971, Select Ch Songs 1969; Compiled Mod Studies of Gospel Music 1972, Living Songs # 1, 2, 3, 4, 5; Col on Staff of Govs Earl K Long, Jimmie Davis, John J McKeithen and Present Gov Dave Treen, All of LA, 1957-82; W/W.

POLLACK, STEPHEN J oc/Executive, Stockbroker; b/Aug 25, 1937; h/ 245 East 40th Street, Apartment 14E, New York, NY 10016; p/Harold S and Gladys H Pollack; ed/Grad, Hill Sch, 1956; BS in Ed, Wharton Sch of Bus and Fin, Univ of PA, 1960; mil/Served in AUS, Hon Discharge 1966; pa/VP, Investmts, Asst Br Mgr, Dean Witter Reynolds Inc, 1977-; VP, Retail Sales, Drexel Burnham Lambert, 1960-77; Intl Assn of Financial Planners; Assn of Investmt Brokers, Bd Mem; cp/Yale Clb; Town Clb; Atrium Clb; Yg Men's Philanthropic Clb, Mem of Bd; Schuykill Country Clb; Wharton Sch Clb of NY; Univ of PA Clb; Ionosphere Clb of En Airlines; Clipper Clb of Pan Am Airlines; Admirals Clb of Am Airlines; Ambassador Clb of Trans World Airlines; Eastside Yg Repub Clb; Knickerbocker Repub Clb; E Side Tennis Clb; Matterhorn Sports Clb; Amex Clb of NY; Whitney Mus Circle Mem; Bus and Profl Com for Illeitis and Colitis Foun; r/Sutton Place Synagogue; Temple Emanu-El, NY; Gotham B'nai B'rith, Mem of Bd; hon/Life Mem, Am Biogl Inst; W/W E; 2,000 Notable Ams.

POMEROY, DONALD GRANT oc/ Printing Company Executive; b/Jul 8, 1944; h/6130 Sharon Avenue, Newfane, NY 14108; ba/Newfane, NY; m/Phyllis Gale; c/Donald Grant II, Anthony Charles, Timothy Jasper; p/Charles and Irene Pomeroy, Newfane, NY; ed/AAS, Rochester Inst of Technol; pa/Printer, Rochester Inst of Technol, 1962-65; Prodn Asst, Rous & Mann Press Ltd, Toronto, 1965-69; VP 1969-81, Pres and Dir 1981-, Star Printing Inc; Tech Assn Graphic Arts; Printing House Craftsmen, 1972-; Intl Typographical Union, 1973-; cp/Commr, Lewiston Trail Coun, BSA, 1981-; Dir, Wn NY Chapt, Nat Safety Town, 1977-; Pres, Newfane JCs, 1976-77; Editor, NYS JCs, 1976-78; Com Mem, Troop 22, BSA, 1981; Order of the Arrow, BSA, 1981-; Treas, Newfane-Am Field Ser, 1982-; r/Epis; hon/St George Epis Awd, 1981; JC of the Yr, 1973; Cubmasters-Scouters Key, 1981; Dist Awd of Merit, BSa, 1983; W/W E.

POND, MARGARET PEGGY PINNER oc/Public Relations; b/Aug 30, 1931; h/7712 Harwood Place, Springfield, VA 22152; ba/Springfield, VA; m/

Samuel Barber Jr; c/Samuel Barber III, Donna Margaret Pond Tracy, Lee MacRae; p/Donald C (dec) and Anna Hall Pinner, Suffolk, VA; ed/Grad, Suffolk HS, 1949; Att'd, Greensboro Col 1949-51, Norfolk Bus Col 1951-52; pa/Tchr, Homebound Chd, Suffolk City Sch Sys, 1955-56; Tchr, Homebound Chd, Princess Anne Co Sch Sys, 1960-61; News Editor, *Southside Virginia News*, 1962-63; Editor-in-Chief, *Springfield Independent*, 1965-67; Asst Dir of Public Relats 1967-72, Dir of Commun Relats 1972-76, Fairfax Hosp; Dir of Corporate Public Affairs, Fairfax Hosp Assn, 1976-; VA Press Wom, First VP 1978-80, Pres 1980-82; VA Soc of Hosp Public Relats, Pres 1974-75; Chm of Public Relats Com, Tri-St Hosp Conv, 1973; Pres, Nat Capital Chapt, Hosp Public Relats Assn, 1971; Pres, No VA Press Clb, 1973; Reg Adv Bd, Am Soc of Hosp Public Relats, 1974; Dir, Reg 10, Nat Fdn of Press Wom; Public Relats Soc of Am, Nat Capital Chapt; VA Hosp Assn Com on Public Relats; cp/VA St Chm of Am Cancer Soc's Great Smokeout, 1979; Bd of Dirs, Fairfax Co Chapt, Am Cancer Soc, 1974-; r/Meth; hon/6 Nat Fdn of Press Wom Writing Awds; 66 VA Press Wom Writing Awds; 12 VA Soc of Hosp Public Relats Writing and Pub Awds; 2 Intl Assn of Bus Communicators Writing Awds; 1 IABC Best of VA Writing Awd, 1979; Nat Fdn of Press Wom Top 10 Writers Awd, 1970; Press Wom of the Yr, VA Press Wom, 1976; Cert of Apprec, Fairfax Co Med Soc, 1969; Cert of Apprec, Fairfax Co Rec Dept, 1967; Cert of Apprec, Dept of Def Dependents Sch, 1979; Fellow, Am Soc of Hosp Public Relats, 1982; W/W Intl Public Relats; W/W S and SW.

PONDER, ANN oc/Nursing Home Administrator; b/Feb 5, 1935; h/Route 10, Box 1103, Tyler, TX 75707; ba/ Tyler, TX; m/Roger; c/Susan Riddle, Andy Brown, Gary, Larry, Debra; p/ Mrs Mack Johns, Jacksonville, TX; ed/ Grad, Jacksonville HS, 1952; Att'd, Lon Morris Col, Henderson Jr Col, Tyler Jr Col; pa/Legal Secy, 1952-69; Admr, Colonial Manor Nsg Home, 1969-83; Admr/Owner, Clairmont, 1983-; Am Hlth Care Assn, TX Nsg Home Assn, 1969-; Medicare Com Chm, TX Nsg Home Assn, 1976-80; Medicare/Medicaid Com for TX Nsg Home Assn, 1978-; Pres, E TX Chapt of TX Nsg Home Assn, 1975; Sr Citizens Liaison Com, TX Nsg Home Assn, 1976; Secy, Smith Co Gov's Coun on Aging; Adv Bd for Nsg Home Admrs, Tyler Jr Col, 1979-; Co-Tchr, St Bd Review for Nsg Home Admrs, 1980-; Spkr at Var Classes and Orgs on Aging and Related Subjects, Several Sems on Death and Dying, 1969-; r/Bapt; hon/Pub, "I Stand Alone, Help Me to Walk"; TX Nsg Home Assn's Recip of Chapt Pres of the Yr Awd, 1975; W/W S and SW.

PONTIOUS, MELVIN F oc/College Professor of Music; b/Jul 11, 1931; h/ 3644 Sandia Drive, Peoria, IL 61604; ba/ Peoria, IL; m/Dorothy Anne; c/Linda Anne, Karen Lee; p/Vere and Fern Pontious (dec); ed/Bach of Music Ed, cum laude, Wichita Univ, 1956; Master of Music Ed, Oberlin Conservatory, 1958; EdD, Univ of IL, 1982; mil/AUS, Army Field Band, 1952-55; pa/Dir of Bands and Prof of Music, Bradley Univ,

1980-; Dir of Bands, LaSalle-Peru HS, 1970-80; Asst Dir of Bands, 1963-70; Dir of Bands, Lakeville Commun HS, 1958-63; IMEA, 1983-85; St Pres 1983-85, Pres-Elect 1981-83, Dist Pres 1976-78, IL Music Ed Assn; Editor, *Illinois Music Educator*, 1969-70; Fac Sponsor, Phi Mu Alpha, 1981-; Curric Com, 1981-; Fac Sponsor, Band Coun; Prin Trombone, Peoria Symph, 1982-; Prin Trombone, Peoria Civic Opera Orch, 1981-; r/Meth; hon/Author of Articles on Breath Support, IL *Music Educator, Music Journal*; Medal of Hon for Conducting, MW Nat Band and Orch Clin, 1973; Dr Wm Revelli Conductor's S'ship Awd, Intl Music Fest, Vienna, Austria, 1972; Conducting Intern F'ship, Univ of IL, 1975-76; Intl W/W Music; Dir of Intl Biog.

PONZILLO, STEPHEN JOSEPH III oc/Educational Administrator; b/Jan 16, 1947; h/Marsteph Hall, 4 Norgate Court, Cockeysville, MD 21030; ba/ Dundalk, MD; m/Marie Ione Petts; c/ Marie Kathleen, Holly Anne; p/Mr and Mrs Stephen J Ponzillo Jr, Dundalk, MD; ed/BS 1969, MEd 1972, Towson St Col; Addit Studies, Morgan St Col, Loyola Col, Johns Hopkins Univ, Univ of MD; pa/Laborer, Bethlehem Steel Co; Tchr, Social Studies, Grades 9-12, Sparrows Pt Mid-Sr High; Asst Prin, Dundalk Sr HS; NEA; MSTA; TABCO; CASE; SSAA Exec Bd; Am Hist Assn; Nat Hist Assn; Chm, KT Ednl Foun of MD; cp/Past Master, Liberty Lodge (Masons); Past Thrice Illust Master, Hiram Coun; Past Cmdr, Monumental Commandery KT; Shriner; Grand Master, MD Cryptic Masons; r/Meth; hon/ Sr Demolay, Dist'd Ser Medal, Chevalier; Outstg Yg Edr, Dundalk JCs; W/ W E; Commun Ldrs of Am.

POOLE, CYNTHIA ANN oc/ Teacher; b/Mar 23, 1946; h/30 Shaw Avenue, Silver Spring, MD 20904; ba/ Washington, DC; p/Mr (dec) and Mrs Nelson Poole, Silver Spring, MD; ed/ BA, Columbia Union Col, 1967; MA, Bowie St Col, 1975; pa/Classroom Tchr, Bldg Resource Tchr, Hd Tchr, DC Public Schs, Garrison Elem Sch, 1967-; Nat Alumni Assn, Pine Forge Acad, VP 1978-80; Wash Metro Alumni Assn, Pine Forge Acad, Pres 1980-; ASCD; cp/ MD Chapt, Breath of Life, Treas 1979; r/SDA.

POPE, DORIS LYNN NAYLOR oc/ Educator; b/Jan 26, 1944; h/Route 5, Box 105, Dunn, NC 28334; m/Earl Dalton; c/Earl Scott, Amy Lynn; p/Mr and Mrs Graham W Naylor, Dunn, NC; sp/Mrs Dalton Pope, Dunn, NC; ed/BSEd, E Carolina Univ, 1962-65; MAEd, E Carolina Grad Sch, 1980-82; pa/Tchr, Harnett Co Sch Sys, NC, 1962-83; NCAE, By-Laws Com, 1982-83; Delta Kappa Gamma Soc Intl; PTA, Var Coms; hon/Midway Beta Clb, 1961-62; HS Valedictorian, 1962; Delta Kappa Gamma Hon Tchr's Soc, 1979; E Carolina Univ Hon Roll, 1965.

POPOVICH, PAUL JOHN oc/Radiologist; b/Jan 26, 1928; h/150 Riverside Drive, Melbourne Beach, FL 32951; ba/ Melbourne, FL; c/Paul Jr, Adria, John Conan, Megan; p/John and Joesephine How Popovich (dec); ed/Undergrad, St Louis Univ Sch of Arts and Scis; MD, St Louis Univ Sch of Med, 1951; mil/ Capt, USAF; pa/Radiologist; Columbus Hosp, 1957-60; Pvt Pract of Radiol,

Delray Bch, FL, 1960-62; Dir of Radiol Dept, Sacred Heart Hosp, 1962-63; Dir, Dept of Radiol 1963-81, Radiologist 1963-, Holmes Reg Med Ctr; Am Cancer Soc; Pres, FL Radiological Soc, 1976-77; FL Councilor, Am Col Radiol, 1978-80; Pres, Brevard Co Med Soc, 1983; Chair, Com Radiologic Ser of ACR, 1980-82; Bd Assoc, FL Inst of Technol; cp/Pres, Melbourne Rotary Clb, 1974-75; Gov, Dist 699, Rotary Intl, 1980-81; Dir, Melbourne Area C of C, 1978-80; r/Cath; hon/Cit for Meritorious Ser, Rotary Intl, 1980; F'ship, Am Col of Radiol, 1978; W/W S and SW; W/W FL; Personalities of S.

POPOWICH, JOHN CHARLES oc/ Sheetmetal Shop Owner, Research and Development Work on Computers; b/ Mar 21, 1940; h/Box 147, Lake Hughes, CA; ba/Rock Stream, NY; m/Patricia A; c/John Charles Jr; p/John Charles (dec) and Anna Augusta Snyder Popowich, Rock Stream, NY; ed/A&E Course, Teteroboro Sch of Aeronautics, 1954-57; Att'd, Univ of MD 1958-61, Wagner Col; Contract Law Studies, Aaron Inst, 1964; A&E Refresher, LA Trade Tech, 1969; mil/USAF, 1957-61; pa/Buyer of Salvage and Metals, R J Cash Co, 1962-63; Prin, J&P Home Repairs, 1963-65; O/H of 720's, DC63 & Electras, Wn Airlines, 1965-67; O/H and Modification of F100s, C130s, C133s, C119s, Lear Siegler Inc, 1967-68; Sales Mgr, Singers Rug & Carpet Co, 1968-70; Aircraft Maintenance Dir, Flight Assoc Activs, 1970-73; Estimator/Reconstrn Supvr, Gunnell Aviation Inc, 1970-72; Sheet Metal Foreman, Ken Air Inc, 1971-72; VP, Pops Aero Inc, and Dean of Admissions for Pacific Air Travelers Sch (FAA Approved), 1972-74; Owner, The Tin Shop (R&D Wk, Mfr Aircraft Assemblies, Comml Sheet Metal Prods) 1975-81; Mfr Sets for Movie and TV Industs, incl'g, *Land of the Giants*; Currently Devel an Alert Sys for the Elderly; Devel Water Sterilizing Unit for Houlin Res Ctr, Aguamatic 1978, Water Power Disposal Unit; cp/Elected Mem, Flood Control Com 1979-81, Sewer Com 1979-81; DeMolay; r/Luth; hon/ Good Conduct, USAF; W/W CA.

PORTER, DOROTHY SUGGS oc/ County Extension Agent; b/Apr 29, 1934; h/857 McGuire Avenue, Paducah, KY 42001; ba/Paducah, KY; m/Samuel A; c/Arnold V, Vondra C; p/James and Evelyn Suggs (dec); ed/BS in Elem Ed 1956, MS in Elem Ed 1958, TN A&I St Univ; Further Study, Murray St Univ; pa/Elem Sch Tchr, Nashville Indep Sch Sys, 1959-60; Elem Sch Tchr, Paducah Indep Sch Sys, 1960-68; Elem Sch Tchr, Indpls Sch Sys, 1968-69; Co Ext Agt, 4-H, Univ of KY Cooperative Ext Ser, 1969-; KAE4-HA, Secy 1973-74; Purchase Area Profl Improvement Assn, Secy 1974-77, Pres 1983; ABWA; Alpha Kappa Alpha; Epsilon Sigma Phi; Nat Assn of Ext 4-H Agts; r/Bapt; hon/Pubs, *4-H on Wheels* 1976-83, *4-H Bowl-A-Lympics* 1980-83, *Backyard Camping* 1979, *Inexpensive/No Expense Toys for Children* 1979, *Gift Wrapping* 1978; NAE4-HA Dist'd Ser Cit, 1981; KAE4-HA Best Feature Story Awd and Outstg Teen Ldr Prog Awd; Epsilon Sigma Phi Activs Awd; KAEHE Prog Awd; Feltner Outstg Agt.

PORTER, MICHAEL LEROY oc/

PERSONALITIES OF AMERICA

Historian, Writer, Poet, Scholar, Essayist, Community Worker; b/Nov 23, 1947; h/3 Adrian Circle, Hampton, VA 23669; ba/Hampton, VA; p/Leroy and Doretha Porter, Hampton, VA; ed/BA, Sociol, VA St Univ, 1969; MA, Hist, Atlanta Univ, 1972; PhD, Hist, Emory Univ, 1974; Further Study, GA St Univ, Univ of CO, Univ of VA, Univ of HI, Kent St Univ, Stanford Univ, Vassar Col, Queens Col, Cambridge Univ; mil/ AUS, Hosp Corpsman, 1969-71; pa/Bk Teller, Chem Bk of NY, 1969; Sr Clk, Typist, Pers Dept, City of Atlanta, 1972; Asst Prof of Hist, WA St Univ Pullman, 1974-75; Asst Ednl Coor, Target Projs Prog, Newport News, VA, 1977; Asst Prof of Hist, Hampton Inst, 1977-80; Ins Exec, NC Mutual Ins Co, 1980-81; Security Ofcr, and Pvt Investigator, Old Dominion Security Inc, 1981-82; Intl Soc for Philosophical Enquiry; Served on 1 Hon Adv Bd, 2 Bds of Advrs, 2 Panels, 13 Edit Bds, 25 Bds of Dirs, 40 Policy Making Bodies; cp/Mensa; Repub Party; r/Bapt; hon/Author, 4 Theses, 3 Books, 74 Articles, 25 Poems, 24 Columns; Made 750 Speeches; Cited in 62 Books, 2 Intl Dics, 25 Intl Directories, 6 Mags, 186 Pubs; Hon Edit Adv Bd to the Nat Bd of Advrs of Am Biogl Inst; US Pres Achmt Awd, 1982; US Pres Hon Roll, 1982; Spec Awd, Nat Repub Congl Com, 1982; Recip, 4 Dipls, 8 Plaques, 20 Prizes, 75 Hon Lttrs, 1 Plate, 1 Ribbon, 1 Medal, 1 Paperweight, 8 Badges, 6 Orgl Decorations, 5 Lics, 7 Hon Rolls, 28 Cits, 1 Hon Course, 21 Times Dist'd (Total of 305 Awds); Intl Dic; Intl Intells; Intl Authors and Writers; Men of Achmt; Intl Profiles.

PORTER, PARKS CADMAN oc/ Assistant Superintendent, High School Principal; b/Dec 9, 1930; h/904 Valley Road, Kosciusko, MS 39090; ba/Kosciusko, MS; m/Anne Marie Hughes; c/ Sheila Anne, Glenn Hughes; p/Charlie Jefferson and Lena Frazier Porter (dec); ed/BS in Ed 1955, MS 1960, Delta St Univ; pa/Ath Dir, Monticello HS, 1955-60; Ath Dir, Lockard Elem Sch Prin, HS Prin, Indianola, 1960-70; Asst Supt, HS Prin, Kosciusko, 1970-; Nat Assns of Sec'dy Sch Prins; MEA; Phi Delta Kappa; cp/Lions Clb; Kiwanis Clb; Civitan Clb; Friends of the Lib; r/Bapt; hon/Deacon in Bapt Ch; Chm of Deacons, First Bapt Ch.

PORTUONDO, ALEIDA T oc/University Professor of Literature; b/Jun 11, 1929; h/10308 Lariston Lane, Silver Spring, MD 20903; ba/Washington, DC; p/José Tamayo; Carmen Amador; ed/ PhD, Lit and Romance Lang, 1975; Prof Ed, Havana, Cuba, 1953; BA, BSc, Havana Inst, Cuba, 1948; MA, Jour, Sch Journalist, 1952; ED 1952, MA in Social Wk 1954, Havana Univ; French Cert, Univ of Paris, France, 1955; MA, Spanish Lit, Cath Univ, 1967; pa/Tchr, Public Schs, Havana, 1948-55; Social Wkr, Supvr, 1955-61; Editor, "Azucar" Jour; Social Sci Prof, Havana Univ, 1957-60; Asst Prof, Grad Sch 1963-; Chm Spratlin Com 1976-, Tenure Com, Eval Com 1982-, Howard Univ; Lectr, Fed City Col, 1971-73; Pres, AATSP, 1974-76; Pres, Cireulo de Cultura Panamericano, 1981-; Dpty, CCP, 1981-; GWATFL, Secy 1978-80; Chm, Black Studies, 1980-83; r/Cath; hon/ Pubs, *Maria Montessori and the Contemporary Education* 1957, "Women in the Journal-

ism Profession" 1958, *The Judaism Influence of La Celestina* 1976, Others; Elected Mem, Academia de la Historia de Cuba, 1978; Cert and Medal, Cuban Assn of Journalists in Recog of 25 Yrs as Journalist, 1977; Sigma Delta Pi, 1970; World W/W Wom.

POSEY, JOSEPHINE McCANN oc/ Assistant Professor of Education; b/Sep 29, 1949; h/305 Shackleford Drive, Greenville, MS 39428; ba/Greenville, MS; m/Curtis Leon; c/Carlos Lenard; p/ Calvin and Aline McCann; sp/Willie E and Ruby Posey; ed/BS, Alcorn St Univ, 1969; ME 1973, Ed Spec 1976, EdD 1983, MS St Univ; pa/Elem Tchr, Wolfolk Elem Sch, Yazoo Co Sch Sys, 1969-71; Elem Tchr, Mt Olive Elem Sch, Covington Co Sch Sys, 1971-73; Elem Tchr, Leland Mid Sch, Wash Co Sch Sys, 1973-78; Col Instr, MS Valley St Univ, Bd of Inst of Higher Lng, 1978-81; Grad Asst, Dept Curric & Instrn, MS St Univ, 1981-83; Asst Prof of Ed, Alcorn St Univ, 1983-; Phi Delta Kappa; Mid-S Ednl Res Assn; Alpha Kappa Alpha Sorority; cp/Alcorn St Alumni Assn; MS St Univ Alumni Assn; hon/Outstg Yg Wom of Am, 1982; Meritorious Awd, MVSU, 1981; Silver Cup and Tray Presentation from Student Tchrs, MVSU, 1979, 1980; Neophyte of the Yr Trophy, AKA Sorority, 1969; 1st Place Trophy from Regional Spkg Contest, Yg People's Tng Union, 1966.

POSEY, RODERICK BURL oc/ Accounting Professor; b/Sep 1, 1953; h/ 115 Perry Lee Drive, Hattiesburg, MS 39401; ba/Hattiesburg, MS; m/Eula Dawson; c/Tarasha La Chelle, Jannelle Lynnette, James Ray; p/James Ray Posey (dec); Angeline Posey-Sullivan, Collins, MS; ed/BSBA w Highest Hons 1974, MS 1975, Univ of So MS; PhD, OK St Univ, 1980; pa/Assoc Prof of Acctg 1982-, Asst Prof 1979-81, Univ of So MS; Acting Asst Prof, OK St Univ, 1977-79; Asst Internal Auditor, Univ of So MS, 1980; Sr Auditor, Lewis and Assocs, CPAs, 1981-; VChm, Bd of Dirs, Pinebelt Area Commun Enhancement, 1983-; Lib Sers Com, 1982-; Tutorial Preven Prog, 1979-82; Acctg Curric Com, 1979-; Acctg Accreditation Com, 1981-82; Bus Curric Com, 1983-; cp/ Advr, Love, Salvation, Determination Choir, 1979-; r/Bapt; hon/Pubs, "Tax Benefits through Leasing" 1982, "Oil and Gas Disclosure Requirements" 1983, "Effects of Grading on the 'Curve' on Student Performance" 1982, "Internship and Co-op Programs in Accounting" 1981; Univ of So MS Hall of Fame, 1974; Outstg Grad, 1974; Outstg Acctg PhD, 1977; Outstg Acctg Prof, 1983; CPA Gold Medal, 1983; CPA Nat Sells Awd, 1983; Outstg Yg Men of Am.

POSPISIL, LEOPOLD JAROSLAV oc/Professor of Anthropology, Curator of Museum; b/Apr 26, 1923; h/554 Orange Street, New Haven, CT 96511; ba/New Haven, CT; m/Zdenka A; c/ Zdenka, Miraslava; p/Leopold J Pospisil (dec); Ludmilla Petrlak Pospisil, New Haven, CT; ed/Mat Ex 1942, JUC 1948, Czechoslovakia; BA, Willamette Univ, 1950; MA, Anthropology, Univ of OR, 1952; PhD, Anthropology, Yale Univ, 1956; pa/Tchg Asst, Dept of Anthropology, Univ of OR, 1950-52; Res Asst, Yale Peabody Mus, 1953-56; Instr in Anthropology 1956-57, Asst Prof 1957-60, Assoc Prof 1960-65, Prof 1965-, Yale Univ; Dir, Div of Anthro-

pology, Yale Peabody Mus, 1966-; Editor, Yale Publicity in Anthropology, 1975; Simon Vis'g Prof of Anthropology, Univ of Manchester; Fellow: Am Anthropological Assn, Sigma Xi, NY Acad of Scis; Pres, Czechoslovak Soc of Arts and Scis; Nat Acad of Sci; Fellow, Branford Col; r/Rom Cath; hon/Pubs, *Kapauku Appuans and Their Law* 1958, *Kapauku Papuan Economy* 1963, *The Kapauku Papuans of West New Guinea* 1963, *Kapauku Papuans and Their Law* 1964, *Anthropology of Law* 1971, *The Ethnology of Law* 1972; W/W Am.

POSTA, ELAINE L oc/Executive, Training Consultant, Lecturer; b/May 6, 1938; h/70 West 69th Street, New York, NY 10025; ba/New York, NY; p/ James and Frances Kukla Posta, Ligoneer, PA; ed/BS in Ed, Thiel Col, 1960; Cont'g Ed at Var Univs and Cols; pa/ Tchr, 1960-61; Grooming, Trans World Airlines, 1961-70; Dir, Flight Attendant Public Relats, TWA's Liason w the White House, The Erno Laszlo Inst, 1970-74; Nat Inst Conslt, NE Reg Dir, Dir of Public Relats, Revlon, 1974-75; Tng and Public Relats Conslt, Glemby Intl, 1975-79; Tng Dir, En Sales Mgr, Dir of Public Relats, Kree Intl; Pres and Fdr, The Image Inst, 1979-; NY Wom's Bus Owner's Assn; The Fashion Grp; Am Soc of Tng and Devel; Wom's Ec Devel Corps; Nat Spkrs Assn; Nat Assn Exec Females; cp/Vols for Chd; r/Fifth Ave Presb Ch; hon/Pubs, *Image Impact for the Professional Woman* 1981, *Image Impact for the Professional and Businessman* 1983, Articles in *Nation's Business* 1980, *Cosmopolitan* 1980, 1981, *Mademoiselle* 1980, 1981, *Glamour* 1983, Others, Many Maj Newspapers; Author, Tng Manuals in Field; Bushwick Commun Awd for Underprivileged Yg Blackwom's Employmt Tng Prog, 1969; W/W Am Wom.

POTENTE, EUGENE JR oc/Interior Designer; b/Jul 24, 1921; h/6634 Third Avenue, Kenosha, WI 53140; ba/Kenosha, WI; m/Joan; c/Eugene J, Peter Michael, John Francis, Suzanne Marie; p/Eugene Potente Sr; ed/PhD, Marquette Univ; Cert, NY Sch of Interior Design; mil/AUS, 1943-46; pa/Snap-on Tools Corp, 1946-47; Potente Decorating Co, 1948-58; Studios of Potente Inc, 1959-; Nat Pres, Interfaith Forum on Rel, Art and Arch, 1982-83; Nat Secy 1978-82; Treas, WI Chapt, Am Soc Interior Designers, 1981, 1982, 1983, Pres-Elect 1984; Bd Mem, Ctr Rel and the Arts, Wesley Sem; r/Rom Cath; hon/ Articles and Exhibs of Wk: *Your Church*, *National Sculpture Review*, *New Conversations*, *Commercial Remodeling*, *The Specifier*, *Interior Design*; St James Hon Awd, 1983; Columbus Day Spkr 1975; W/W MW; W/W Bus and Fin.

POTTER, EARL H III oc/Assistant Professor of Management; b/Oct 4, 1946; h/4 Allyn Street, Mystic, CT 06355; ba/New London, CT; m/Christine Ann Marshall; c/Margaret, Christopher, Bandon, Earl, Jamie; p/Earl H Jr and Dorothy Nelson Potter, North Kingstown, RI; ed/BA, cum laude, Wms Col, 1968; MS in Psych 1977, PhD in Psych 1978, Univ of WA; mil/LCDR, USCG, 1969-; pa/Opers Ofcr, USCGC, Sweetbrier, 1970-71; Pers Ofcr, USCGC, Northwing, 1971-73; Chief, Recruiting and Tng Bds, 13th Coast Guard Dist, 1973-76; Asst Prof, USCG

457

Acad, 197-; Am Psychol Assn; Acad of Mgmt; Phi Beta Kappa; cp/Big Brother/Big Sister of SEn CT, Bd Mem 1979-, Pres of the Bd 1980-82; Chair, Planning and Review Com, Hlth Sys Agy of En CT; r/Prot; hon/Author, Var Jour Articles; En CT Ofcr of the Yr, 1983; USN Commend Medal, 1973; Coast Guard Commend Medal, 1982; W/W E.

POTTER, MILES BUTTLES oc/Consulting Engineer; b/Jun 5, 1909; h/23 Jack Ladder Circle, Horsham, PA 19044; ba/Spring House, PA; c/Patricia Carol, Barbara Ann, Donna Helen, Miles Milton; p/Lewis Milton and Ruth Buttles Potter (dec); ed/Student, Gettysburg Col, 1927-29; BS, Bloomsburg Univ, 1933; Postgrad, Univ of DE 1951-53, Villanova Univ 1953-54; pa/Tchg, The Citadel, N GA Col, VMI, Wash & Lee, Villanova Univ, 1933-56; Assoc Dir of Res, Villanova Univ, 1950-56; Consltg Engr, Pres, Harris, Henry & Potter, 1956-72; Municipal Envir Assocs Inc, 1972-; Chm of Bd, MDD Corp, 1980-; Reg'd Profl Engr, PA, NY, NJ, ME, FL; Am Soc of Engrg Ed, Past Dir of Ednl Div; PA Consltg Engrs Coun, Past Ofcr; PA Soc of Profl Engrs, Past Pres of DE Co Chapt; PA Assn of Consltg Engrs, Past Ofcr; r/Meth; hon/Hon DSc, 1972; Engrs of Distn; Yg Men of Am; W/W E.

POTTER, RAESCHELLE JULIAN oc/Opera Singer; b/Sep 9; h/2403 Hewes Avenue, Gulfport, MS 39501; ba/Vienna, Austria; m/Dr Stephan L Deimel; p/Dr and Mrs Edward H Potter, Gulfport, MS; ed/Fulbright Grant, Vienna Acad of Music, 1972-73; MMus, So IL Univ, 1969; Voice and Opera Wkshop, Xavier Univ, 1967; pa/Opera Stage: Met Opera Studio (Compromario Soprano) 1969-72, European Debut (Countess "Figaro"), Schönbrunn Palace in Vienna 1973, Opernhaus Graz (Lyric Soprano) in Graz 1973, Debut at Vienna St Opera 1981, Switzerland, Luxemburg, Germany, Austria 1973-; TV: Debut, PBS's "Bayou Legend" 1980, Series of Concerts w Pierre Sallenger 1981; Delta Sigma Theta Soc, 1969; Mu Phi Epsilon, 1969; r/Bapt; hon/WGN Auditions Winner, 1969; Met Opera Auditions Nat Finalist, 1967; Grad Asst, Marjorie Lawrence, 1967-69; Recip, Met Opera Coun Grants, 1969-73; Fulbright F'ship to Austria, 1972-73; Comml for Japan Airways, 1971; Recording for Harvard Anthology of Music, 1968.

POTTER, ROBERT WALLACE JR oc/Principal; b/Aug 15, 1947; h/Lacy Road, Jaffrey, NH 03452; ba/Antrim, NH; m/Betsy Coleman; p/Robert Wallace and Mary Tilli Potter, Springfield, MA; ed/BA, cum laude, Hist, St Anselm Col, 1969; ME, Curric and Instrn, Keene St Col, 1978; pa/Tchr, St Catherine Sch, 1969-70; Tchr, Coach, St Patrick Sch, 1970-74; Tchr 1974-, Prin 1978-, Antrim Mid Sch; NEA, 1974-82; NH Edrs Assn, 1974-82; Conval Admrs' Org, 1978-, Treas 1981-; NH Assn of Sch Prins, 1982-; New England Leag of Mid Schs, 1979-; cp/Jaffrey C of C, 1982-, Corresponding Secy 1983-; Jaffrey War Meml Com Inc, 1983-; Secy-Treas; r/Rom Cath; hon/Pi Gamma Mu, Nat Social Studies Hon Soc, 1969; W/W E.

POU, J W oc/University Administrator; b/Jul 8, 1917; h/379 Sandstone Drive, Athens, GA 30605; ba/Athens, GA; m/Dr Emily Q; c/John W Jr, Constance P Yellowmoon, David M Quinn; ed/BS, NC St Univ, 1938; MS, Univ of WI, 1947; PhD, Cornell Univ, 1951; mil/AUS, WWI, Pacific Ocean Theater, 4 Yrs; Ret'd Lt Col, USAR; pa/Prof and Hd, Dairy Dept, Univ of MD, 1951-53; Prof and Hd, Dept of Animal Indust, NC St Univ, 1953-58; Dir, Cooperative Ext Ser, Univ of AZ, 1958-61; VP and Hd, En Reg Agribus Ofc, Wachovia Bk and Trust Co, 1961-75; Num Past Orgl Mbrships and Ofcs; r/Presb; hon/Pubs, "Land-Use Planning: What's Extension's Role?" 1977, "The Significance of Farm Management in Today's Agricultural Operations" 1972, Num Others; Recip, NC 4-H Alumni Awd, 1962; Univ of AZ Medallion Awd of Merit, 1961; Pitt Co U Fund Outstg Citizenship Awd, 1964; FFA Outstg Ser Awd, 1965; Greenville Civitan Clb Book of Golden Deeds Awd, 1966; Pres's Key Awd, Greenville C of C and Merchants Assn, 1969; Greenville Citizen of the Yr, 1970; Spokesman of the Yr Awd, Chevron Chem Co and Farm Chems Mag, 1974; Dist'd Alumni Awd, Sch of Agri and Life Scis, NC St Univ, 1977; Ldg Men in USA; W/W Fin and Indust; W/W S and SW; W/W Am; NC Lives; Am Men of Sci.

POUNDS, JANET LYNN oc/Research Chemist; b/Nov 29, 1944; h/3097 Baughman Road, Clinton, OH 44216; ba/Barberton, OH; m/Richard Miles Bowen; c/Kristina; p/Truman Edward and Marilynn Carlton Pounds; ed/BA in Chem 1966, MS in Organic Chem 1969, LA St Univ; pa/Grad Tchg Asst, LA St Univ Chem Dept, 1966-69; Sci Tchr, Baker Jr High, 1969-77; Chem Instr, So Univ, 1972-77; Res Chem, PPG Industs, Chem Div, Corpus Christi 1977-80, Barberton 1980-; Am Chem Soc, Organic Topical Grp Chair, Akron Sect 1981; cp/NOW, St Legis Coor, LA NOW 1973-74; St ERA Coor, LA NOW, 1974-75; Participant, 18th So Assem 1974, 20th So Assem 1976, Tulane Univ; Akron Ski Clb; hon/Pub, *Chemical Communications*, 1975; US Patent Application Filed Dec 1981; NIH MARC Res F'ship Awd Recip, 1978; W/W Am Wom.

POWELL, JAMES O oc/Professional Watercolor Artist; b/Jun 20, 1924; h/1408 Apache Drive, Richardson, TX 75080; ba/Richardson, TX; m/Jimmie Lee Pearce; c/Karen Ann, Nancy Catherine; p/Mr and Mrs Fred F Powell (dec); ed/BS in Math and Combined Scis, TX Wesleyan Col, 1948; Grad Wk in Math, Hardin-Simmons Univ, 1962; mil/Pilot, Light Bombardment, WWII; pa/Pan Am Petro Corp, 1948-60; Aircraft Sales and Corporate Pilot, 1960-78; Profl Artist, Transparent Watercolor, 1978-; Watercolor Tchr in Sch of Cont'g Ed, So Meth Univ; SWn Watercolor Soc, Pres 1976-77; Wn Art Assn, Adv Bd 1978 (Continuous); Artists and Craftsmens Assn, Bd Mem 1978-79; r/Bapt; hon/Artist in Residence, Mus of Native Am Cultures, 1980; Featured Artist, ND Intl Wn and Wildlife Show, 1983; Best of Show at Nat Wn Art Show, 1978, 1979, 1980, 1981, 1982.

POWELL, JOHN JAMES oc/Retired Methodist Minister; b/Sep 15, 1917; h/Route 1, Box 293, Mill Spring, NC 28756; ba/Mill Spring, NC; m/Irene Cook; c/Dr James L, Dr Martha J Powell Blackwell; p/Rev Hubert L and Margaret Hague Powell (dec); pa/Pastor: Main St (Rowan, Salisbury) 1938, Lee's Chapel (Greensboro) 1941, Lindsey St (Reidsville) 1943, Purcell (Charlotte) 1946, Thrift (Charlotte) 1950, Epworth (Concord) 1951, Boger City 1955, Mt Olivet (Concord) 1959, Calvary (Greensboro) 1960, Hoyle Meml (Shelby) 1963, First Ch (Sylva) 1965, Sedge Garden (Kernersville) 1969, Proximity (Greensboro) 1972, Oak-Grove-Salem (Rutherford Co) 1975, Concord-Hopewell (Catawba) 1979; Ret'd, Mill Sprg Circuit, 1983-; cp/Secy Staff, WNC Annual Conf; Secy, Comm on Archives and Hist, WNC Conf; Lions Intl; Mason; En Star; r/Meth; hon/Dist'd Alumni Awd, Brevard Col; Spec Ser Awd, Lions Intl, 1981; W/W Methodism; DIB.

POWERS, CYNTHIA MARIE oc/Commander; b/Nov 16, 1958; h/43 Del Tara, Jacksonville, AR 72076; ba/Jacksonville, AR; m/Shawn Peter; p/James and Donna Resler, Waukesha, WI; ed/BS, Fgn Lang, Univ of WI, 1979; MS, Opers Mgmt, Univ of AR, 1984; mil/USAF Ofcr, 1980-; pa/Customer Ser/Package Flow, U Parcel Ser, 1977-81; Sales Mgr, Waukesha Cheese House, 1980; Dpty Cmdr 1981-83, Cmdr 1983-, Titan ICBM Crew, USAF; Asst Dir, Aerospace Ed, Ark Wing, Civil Air Patrol, 1982; Dir, Aerospace Ed, Ark Wing, Civil Air Patrol, 1983; Nat Assn of Female Execs; cp/ARC, CPR Instr 1981-; hon/Nat Hon Soc, French, 1974-76; Nat Hon Soc, Spanish, 1974-76; Nat Hon Soc, German, 1974-76; Tchrs' Assn Nat Hon Soc, 1976; Outstg Yg Wom of Am.

POWERS, HUBERT PAUL oc/Accountant; b/Apr 7, 1906; h/803 H Northwest, Childress, TX 79201; ba/Childress, TX; m/Lula Mae Carter; c/Patsy Vee Powers Nichols, Paula Powers Jones; p/Si Thomas and Mary Dibbon Barker Powers (dec); ed/BA in Chem 1934, MA in Ed Adm 1938, TX Tech Univ; Postgrad in Psych, W TX St Univ, 1954-; pa/Prin of Rural Schs, Mitchell Co, TX, 1927-33; HS Prin, McCaulley, TX, 1935-39; Supt of Schs: McCaulley, TX 1939-43, Avoca, TX 1943-47, Throckmorton, TX 1947-54; Elem Prin, Childress, TX, 1954-71; Acct, Income Tax and Bkkpg Ser, 1971-; NEA; TSTA, Pres 5 Times; cp/Rotary, Pres 1980; Boy Scout Master, 8 Yrs; Farm Bur; Camp Fire Girls, Chm of Bd for 5 Yrs; Red Cross, Chm of Bd for 4 Yrs; Am Cancer Soc, Secy for 5 Yrs; r/Bapt; Sunday Sch Tchr for 25 Yrs; hon/Pubs, Thesis for MA Deg, Several Articles for Ednl Jours through the Yrs; Cit from Pres Roosevelt for War Effort; Del to St Conv, TSTA, 4 Times; Rep, Oil Royalty Owners, Before St RR Com; Cits (Plaques): ARC, Am Cancer Soc, Rotary, Childress Sch Bd; W/W S and SW.

POWERS, ROBERT M oc/Author; b/Nov 9, 1942; h/PO Box 12158, Denver, CO 80212; ba/Same; ed/Cert, Univ of Edinburgh, Scotland, 1968; BA, Univ of AZ, 1969; pa/Author, 1969-; Fellow, Royal Astronom Soc, UK; Royal Astronom Soc of Canada; Am Soc of Aerospace Pilots; Aviation Space Writers Assn; Authors Leag and Guild; hon/Pubs, Articles in All Maj Mags 1970-83; Books: *Planetary Encounters* 1978, *Shuttle: World's First Spaceship* 1979, *The Coattails* of God 1981, *Other Worlds Than Ours* 1983, *Shuttle* 1983, *Mars* 1984; Univ S'ship Hons, 1969; Best Book Awd, AWA, 1979; F'ship, Nat Endowment of Arts and Humanities, 1979; Three Time Winner, Best Book on Space, Aviation Space Writers, 1979, 1980, 1981; W/W Sci; Am Men of Sci; Contemp Authors; Men of Achmt; W/W Aviation.

POWERS, ROBERT N oc/Executive; b/Dec 23, 1922; h/11 Elizabeth Street, Port of Spain, Trinidad, W Indies; ba/ Houston, TX; m/Edna; c/Paul Ragan, Marsha Lane; p/Lewis R Powers (dec); ed/BS, OK St Univ, 1948; mil/103rd & 5th Inf Divs, 1943-46; pa/Drilling, Reservoir and Petro Engr (TX, OK, NM) 1948-56, Prodn Mgr (Venezuela and Libya) 1957-62, Chief Petro Engr (NY) 1963-69, Mgr, Ec 1970, Exploration and Prodn Coor (Iran) 1971-74, Pres and Gen Mgr (Holland) 1975-79, Pres and Gen Mgr (Trinidad) 1979-, Amoco Prodn Co (Intl); Chm of Num Chapts, Soc of Petro Engrs; API; ASME; Pi Tau Sigma and Sigma Tau, Hon Engrg Frats; Field Tested Num Patent Disclosures in Exploration and Prodn for Oil; r/Presb.

POZNIAK, RICHARD ALEXANDER oc/Director of Public Relations; b/Dec 7, 1947; h/11 Chester Road, Billerica, MA 01866; ba/Burlington, MA; m/Alexandra; c/Alexa, Jonathan; p/ Benjamin and Eleanor Pozniak, Hartford, CT; ed/BS, Bus and Indust Communs, Emerson Col; Exec Mktg and Mgmt Progs, Wharton Sch of the Univ of PA; pa/Dir of Public Relats, MA Hosp Assn, 1978-; Dir of Communs, The Ser Com, 1976-78; Dir of Public Relats, Babson Col, 1974-76; Dir of Public Relats, Bldrs Assn of Gtr Boston, 1972-74; Asst to Dir of Communs, Mayors Ofc, City of Boston, 1971-72; Dir of Public Info, Emerson Col, 1968-71; Bd of Dirs, Consumers Credit Cnslg Ser of En, MA, 1981-; Mem of Publicity, Clb of Boston, 1970-; Public Relats Soc of Am, 1975-; r/Rom Cath; hon/Author, Articles Pub'd in *Boston Globe* 1978, *Boston Herald Traveller* 1978, *Boston Magazine* 1979, *New England Business Journal* 1978-79, *The New Englander Magazine* 1979, *Boston Phoenix* 1978, *More Media Magazine* 1979; Bellringer Awd for Public Affairs, Publicity Clb of Boston, 1981, 1983; Intl Assn of Bus Communicators Gold Quill Awd for Excell in Public Affairs, 1982; W/W E.

PREBLE, MICHAEL ANDREW oc/ Art Museum Curator; b/Jul 27, 1947; h/12 Tremont Street, Portland, ME 04103; ba/Portland, ME; p/Mrs John J Johnston, Harahan, LA; ed/BA in Art Hist, Cornell Univ, 1969; MA in Humanities, CA St Univ Dominguez Hills, 1977; pa/Curator of Collections, Portland Mus of Art, 1981-; Curator of Exhbns and Collections, Huntsville Mus of Art, 1979-81; Exhbn Supvr, Muckentbaler Cultural Ctr, 1979; Dir, Art Gallery, Mt San Antonio Col, 1974-78; hon/Author, Num Art Criticisms and Exhbn Catalogues (*James Brooks, Theodore Wores, William Baziotes*); W/W Am Art; W/W E.

PRESLEY, S PATRICK oc/Member of Mississippi House of Representatives, Senior Public Affairs Representative; b/ Mar 1, 1951; h/10,600 Goodes Mill Lake Road, Pascagoula, MS 39567; ba/Jackson, MS; p/Mr and Mrs W L Presley, Pascagoula, MS; ed/BS in Metall Engrg,

MS St Univ, 1974; pa/Refinery Engr 1974-79, Spec Assignments, Reg Mktg Ofc 1979, Chevron USA; Corporate Ec Ofc, Standard Oil of CA, 1980; Govt Affairs Ofc and Wash Ofc 1981, Employee Relats Rep 1982-83, Sr Public Affairs Rep, MS Ofc, Mktg 1984-, Chevron USA; MS Ho of Reps, 1976-84; Chm, Univs and Cols Com, 1984; VChm, Trans Com, 1981-83; Other Com Assignments: Ways and Means, Conserv and Water Resources, Pensions and Public Hlth; hon/MS Ec Coun "Leadership Mississippi" Selection, 1981; MS St Univ Engrg Sch Hall of Fame, 1973-74; Intl Rotary Foun Awd, Grp Study Exch Prog to the Netherlands, 1982; W/W Am Govt; Outstg Yg Men in Am.

PRESTON, CLASSARAL DELORES oc/District Sales Manager; b/Jun 10, 1951; h/414 Colusa Way, Livermore, CA 94550; ba/San Leandro, CA; m/J P; p/Mr and Mrs R C McMillan, Prichard, AL; ed/BS, Ottawa Univ, 1974; One Yr of Grad Studies, OK St Univ; pa/Sales Rep 1976-78, Adm Asst (NY Ofc) 1978, Dist Acct Mgr 1978-80, Dist Mgr 1980-, Bristol Myers Co; Career Wom's Netwk; r/Bapt; hon/Participant in Jr Miss Pageant, AL, 1969; Queen of Beta Sigma Phi Sorority, 1974; Recip, HUD F'ship, 1973; Outstg Teenagers of Am.

PRESTON, RANDALL EDWARD oc/Health Care Entrepreneur; b/Jul 6, 1955; h/420 West Russell Street, Barrington, IL 60010; ba/Itasca, IL; p/ Samuel Preston Jr, Huntington, IL; Phyllis J Preston (dec); ed/BA, IN Univ, 1979; pa/Mktg Rep, Share Hlth Plan of IL; Chm of Bd, Reach (Res, Ed, Action, Change, Hlth) Sys Inc; r/Presb.

PREZIOSI, ROBERT CHARLES oc/ Savings and Loan Executive; b/Feb 6, 1946; h/18493 Southwest 83 Place, Miami, FL 33157; ba/Miami, FL; m/ Barbara Sue Brant; c/Lauren Marie, Carly Elizabeth; p/Emil C and Charlotte Rohder Preziosi (dec); ed/BA 1968, MEd 1972, FL Atl Univ; MPA 1976, DPA 1977, Nova Univ; pa/Tng Supvr, Burger Castle, 1969; Exec Dir, Yth Activs, 1970-74; Prog Admr 1974-78, Pers Dir 1978-80, Cath Ser Bur; Mgr, Staff Devel 1980-82, Current VP, Staff Planning and Devel, Am Savs & Ln; Am Soc for Tng and Devel, Miami Chapt, Treas 1981, Pres-Elect 1982, Pres 1983; Am Mgmt Assn, 1980-83; cp/Gtr Miami Ath Conf Ofcls Assn, Bd of Dirs 1973-78; VChm, Citizens Adv Com, Dade Co Public Schs, 1975-76; Charter Mem, Gtr Miami C of C; Ldrship Miami, 1979; Bd of Dirs, Jr Achmt, 1982-83; r/Rom Cath; hon/Man of the Yr, K of C, 1973; Contbn to Ed Awd, Dade Co Public Schs, 1975; W/W S and SW.

PRIBIC, NIKOLA R oc/Professor Emeritus; b/May 22, 1913; h/1940 Sageway, Tallahassee, FL 32303; ba/ Tallahassee, FL; m/Elizabeth; c/Rado; ed/Dipl, Univ of Zagreb, 1939; PhD, Univ of Munich, 1949; pa/Docent, Univ of Munich, 1949-61; Assoc Prof 1961-65, Prof 1965-82, Univ of TX Austin; AAASS; ATSEEL; Am Assn of 18th Cent Studies; Am Comparative Lit Assn; Nikola Tesla Meml Soc; Suedosteuropa Gesellschaft, Munich; SAMLA; MLA; r/Serbian Orthodox; hon/Author and Co-Author of Several Books, More Than 100 Reviews and Articles in the Field of Slavic and Comparative Lits;

Festschrift Under Pub for 70th Birthday, 1983; Prof Emeritus, FL St Univ; DIB; Intl Scholars Dir; Dir of Am Scholars; W/W Am Ed; W/W Scholars; W/W S and SW.

PRICE, GERALDINE McCRABB oc/ Business Owner, Consultant for Business and Government in Reading and Writing; b/May 7, 1940; h/1232 "H" Street, #1, Sacramento, CA 95814; ba/ Sacramento, CA; p/Howard James (dec) and Edna Eisle McCrabb, Stockton, CA; ed/AA, Stockton Col, 1957; BS 1967, MS 1972, Univ of UT; pa/Tchr 1961-70, Ed Conslt 1972-74, Granite Sch Dist; Dir, RDI of CA, 1975-83; Owner, Conslt, Price Assocs, 1977-; ASTD, Sacramento, SF, LA; cp/Wom's Netwk, Sacramento; hon/Nat Level Water Skier; Cert'd Ski Instr; Class "A" Racer; W/W.

PRICE, THOMAS ROWE III oc/ Public Relations Director; b/Dec 29, 1938; h/154 Rathton Road, York, PA 17403; ba/York, PA; m/Patricia Z; c/ Thomas Rowe IV; p/T Rowe Price, Baltimore, MD; ed/Att'd, McCoy Col-Johns Hopkins Univ, Wash Col; Dale Carnegie Human Relats, 1969; Pubs, PA St Univ, 1975; Mgmt Devel, PA St Univ, 1976-77; mil/USNR, Hon Discharge 1961; pa/Dir of Public Info, York Hosp, 1971-; News Dir, WORK-AM, 1966-71; Spec Events Dir and Prodn Asst, WVQM-FM, 1966; Announcer, WCOJ-AM, 1966; Announcer, WAQE-AM, 1963-65; Announcer, WFMD-AM & FM, 1962-63; Hosp Assn of PA; Am Soc for Public Relats; Am Hosp Assn; Assn of Am Med Cols, Grp on Public Affairs; Public Relats Soc of Am; cp/Bd of Dirs, Alzheimer's Disease Assn of MD, 1982-84; Adv Com, York Hosp Med Explorer Post, 1973-; Chm, Adv Com, Med Explorer Post, 1979-; Num Past Civic Activs; hon/Meritorious Achmt, Hosp Assn of PA, 1978; Third Place, Wom in Communication, 1980; First Place, Annual Report, Wom in Communication, 1981; Second Place, Annual Report, Wom in Communication, 1982; Cert'd, Am Soc for Hosp Public Relats, 1982; W/W E; Prom Public Relats Profls, Hlth Care Edition; W/W Public Relats.

PRICHARD, JACK HOUSER oc/ Senior Minister; b/Aug 13, 1921; h/5156 Meadow Crest, Dallas, TX 75229; ba/ Dallas, TX; m/Kathleen Cole; c/James, Mark, David, Kathy; ed/BA in Hist, OK City Univ; Div, Ch Hist, Princeton Theol Sem; ThM, Homiletics, Brite Div Sch; DD, TX Christian Univ; pa/ Ordained Min, Presb Ch, USA, 1945; Min, OK, 1945-50; Dir, Westminster Foun, and Univ Pastor, Univ of AZ Tucson, 1950-54; Assoc Pastor, First Presb Ch, Albuquerque, 1954-57; Pastor, Hemphill U Presb Ch, Ft Worth 1957-64, Grace First Presb Ch, Weatherford (TX) 1964-70, Churchill Way Presb Ch 1970-; Div Evang, U Presb Ch, 1961-62; Moderator, Presbyteries, El Reno-Hebart 1948-49, So AZ 1952-53; Stated Clk, Synod AZ, 1952; Grace Union Presb Chair Risk Evang, 1978-79; Chair Com, Ret'd Mins, 1977-78; Outreach Com, 1978-79; r/Presb; hon/ Contbr to Several Newspapers and Profl Jours; Pi Gamma Mu; Kiwanis; Lions; Exch; W/W Rel; Men of Achmt.

PRIEST, E LOUISE oc/Executive Director of Educational Corporation; b/

May 16, 1935; h/705 Forrest Glen Drive, Evansville, IN 47712; ba/Evansville, IN; p/Jesse and Laura Priest (dec); ed/BS, IN St Univ, 1977; Grad Wk in Clin Psych, George Mason Univ, 1978-79; pa/Exec Dir, CNCA (Coun for Nat Cooperation in Aquatics), 1980-; Asst Nat Dir of Water Safety, ARC, 1975-80; Nat Forum for Advmt of Aquatics, Chm 1982-84; AAHPER MW Chair-Elect 1983; AAHPERD Aquatic Coun, 1980-83; Mycological Assn of Wash, DC, Pres 1979-83; Consortium on PE and Rec for Handicapped, 1979-83; hon/ Pubs, *Adapted Aquatics*, ARC 1977, "Aquatics in 80's," CNCA 1980, 50 Profl Articles Pub'd by AAHPERD, NRPA, CNCA, Other Mags; Psi Chi Nat Hon Soc, Psych, 1975; Alpha Chi, 1976; OH Ho of Reps Commend, 1977; AAHPERD Ser Awd, 1982; IN Univ PA Hon Awd, 1983; W/W E; Am Biogl Inst; World W/W of Wom.

PRITCHARD, PAMELA oc/Director and Professor; b/Jun 18, 1949; h/PO Box 172, Talladega College, Talladega, AL 35160; c/Animah Eileen; p/Bernadine E Pritchard, Cols, OH; ed/PhD in Ed, OH St Univ, 1982; MA in Hist, Atlanta Univ, 1975; BS in Social Studies, OH St Univ, 1971; pa/Dir, Bolinga, Black Cultural Resources Ctr/Minority Affairs, Wright St Univ, 1982-; Grad Tchg Assoc, OH St Univ, 1979-82; Housing Conslt, Housing Opport Ctr, Cols, 1979; Cultural Resource Reviewer, OH Hist Soc, Cols, 1978-79; Hlth Investigator, Grady Hosp, 1973-77; ABWA; cp/Nat Coun of Negro Wom, Elected Ofcr 1981; Dayton Black Arts Com, Chm of Exhibs 1983; r/Bapt; hon/Phi Kappa Phi Nat Hon Soc, 1981; Grad Tchg S'ship, 1979, 1980, 1981; Outstg Yg Wom of Am.

PROCHNOW, VIRGINIA WILMA oc/Private Music Instructor; b/Mar 30, 1935; h/1420 South 34th Avenue, Yakima, WA 98902; ba/Same; ed/AA, 1955; BA, 1957; Grad Studies, 1968; pa/ Organist, Ctl Luth Ch, 1955-; Secy, USDA, 1955-57; Secy, Ctl Luth Ch, 1957-59; Pvt Music Instr, 1957-; Am Guild of Organists, Dean 1969-72, Sub-Dean 1974-76; Music Tchrs Nat Assn, 1957-; WA St Music Tchrs Assn, SE VP 1965-66, Organ Div St Chm 1978-; Yakima Val Music Tchrs Assn, Pres 1963-65, 1971-73, 1979-81; Chm, Daniel Pollack Wkshop, 1977-; Am Guild of Eng Handbell Ringers, 1980-; Commun Concert Assn, Bd of Dirs 1965-67; Col Concert Series Bd, 1969-, Secy-Treas 1974-; Allied Arts, Bd of Trustees 1971-73; Patrons of Music Bd 1971-73; Ladies Musical Clb, Pres 1974-75, VP 1973-74; Mem and Soloist, Yakima Symph Chorus, 1973-; r/Luth Brotherhood Area Communicator, 1979-; hon/2,000 Notable Ams; Personalities of W.

PROCTOR, CLAUDE OLIVER JR oc/Director of Education; b/Jun 9, 1938; h/1712 McCoy Place, Georgetown, TX 78626; ba/Austin, TX; m/Doris Stricker; c/Christopher Michael, Gabriel Marcus; p/Claude O Proctor Sr (dec); Helen Proctor Rawls, Aulander, NC; ed/Att'd, Davidson Col 1956-58, Syracuse Univ 1963; BGE, Univ of NE Omaha, 1966; MA, Univ of Notre Dame, 1974; Tchg Cert w Distn, SWn Univ, 1981; mil/ USAF 1958-80, Ret'd Maj; pa/Russian Linguist, USAF, 1958-66; Intell Ofcr, 1968-70; Chief of Fgn Lang Dept, USAF

Sch of Applied Cryptological Scis, 1971-72; Soviet Area Spec, Def Lang Inst, 1974-77; Asst Prof of Russian and Chm of Strategic Langs, USAF Acad, 197-80; Dir of Ed and Info, The Prosecutor Coun, 1980-; Intl Security Conslt, Floyd Purvis and Assocs Intl, 1983-; Gamma Theta Upsilon, 1966-; Am Coun for Tchrs of Russian, 1978-; TX Fgn Lang Assn, 1980-; AF Assn, 1975-; Assn of Former Intell Ofcrs, 1980-; cp/Merit Badge Cnslr, Lone Star Coun, BSA, 1980-; Bd of Dirs, Georgetown Sertoma Clb, 1982; Lions Clb, 1965-66, 1971-72; r/Luth; hon/Pubs, *Soviet Press Translation* 1980, *The Analysis of Soviet Press Propaganda: A Case Study of Press Polemics in the Sino-Soviet Conflict* 1960-69, 1973; Valedictorian, Russian Intermediate Course, Syracuse Univ, 1963; W/W S and SW.

PROCTOR, LINDA NADINE oc/ Educator; b/Dec 14, 1954; h/2029 North Woodlawn #622, Wichita, KS 67208; ba/ Wichita, KS; p/Mayo and Janet Proctor, Knoxville, TN; ed/BS, Univ of TN Knoxville, 1974; MS 1976, EdS 1981, Univ of GA Athens; pa/Little TN Ednl Cooperative, 1975; Knoxville City Schs, 1975-78; Univ of GA Athens, 1978-82; Inst of Logopedics, 1982-; CEC; Assn for the Severely Handicapped; r/Christian; hon/Grad'd w Highest Hons, Univ of TN, 1974; Kappa Delta Pi Hon Soc, 1973; Phi Kappa Phi Hon Soc, 1974; W/ W Am Wom.

PROUT, RALPH EUGENE oc/Physician, Medical Administrator; b/Feb 27, 1933; h/831 Linwood Street, Vacaville, CA 95688; ba/Vacaville, CA; m/Joanne; c/Michelle, Michael; p/Mr and Mrs Ralph Byron Prout (dec); ed/MD, Loma Linda Univ Sch of Med, 1957; BA, Loma Linda Univ Riverside Campus, 1953; MS, Hlth Adm, Columbia Pacific Univ, 1984; pa/Intern, LA Co Hosp, 1957-58; Resident, Internal Med, White Meml Hosp, 1958-60; Resident, Psychi, Harding Hosp, 1960-61; Pvt Pract, Napa, CA, 1961-63; St of CA Dept of Corrections, 1963-, Chief Med Ofcr 1968-; Am and CA Socs of Internal Med; Am Correctional Hlth Sers Assn, Nat and CA; cp/ Commonwealth Clb, SF; Native Sons of Golden W; r/Prot; hon/Alpha Omega Alpha, Epsilon Chapt of CA, 1957; Outstg Yg Men of Am; W/W World; W/ W Am; W/W W; W/W CA.

PROUTY, GARRY F oc/Psychologist, College Professor; b/Aug 21, 1936; h/ 5541 Allemong, Matteson, IL 60443; c/ Gwen Allyson; ed/BA 1959, MA 1962, Univ of Buffalo; Att'd, Univ of Chgo, 1962-66; pa/Chief Psychol for Kennedy Sch for Exceptl Chd, 1966-70; Prof of Mtl Hlth, Prairie St Col, 1970; Pvt Pract, Psychotherapy, 1968-; Am Psychol Assn; Am Orthopsychi Assn; Am Sociological Assn; Intl Assn for Mtl Imagery; hon/Pubs, "Pre-Therapy-A Method of Treating Pre-Expressive Psychotic and Retarded Patients" 1976, "Protosymbolic Method: A Phenomenological Treatment of Schizophrenic Hallucinations" 1977, "Hallucinatory Contact: A Phenomenological Treatment of Schizophrenics," "A Pilot Study of Pretherapy Method Applied to Chronic Schizophrenic Patients" 1979; Meth S'ship; Buffalo St Tchrs Col; Laverne Noys Scholar, Univ of Chgo; Tchg Fellow, Univ of Buffalo; Hon Fellow, Chgo Cnslg and Psychotherapy Ctr; W/W

MW.

PRUETT, SHARON HENSON oc/ Petroleum Landman; b/Jan 8, 1941; h/ PO Box 764, Quitman, TX 75783; ba/ Quitman, TX; c/Kevin W, Nancy C, Donna L; p/V E (dec) and Foy M Henson, Houston, TX; ed/BS in Sociol, E TX St Univ, 1977; Dipl, Durham Bus Col, 1965; pa/Secy 1972, Med Eligibility Wkr 1974, Proposal Devel Spec, Reg Planner, Dir of Data Sect 1978-80, Petro Landman 1980-, TX Dept of Human Resources; E TX Assn of Petro Landmen; Nat Assn of Female Execs; AAUW; Nat Acad of Polit Sci; cp/NOW; r/Bapt; hon/Pub, "State Policies and the Women's Movement," 1981; Pi Sigma Alpha, 1980; W/ W Am Wom.

PSANIS, MARIA VASILIOU oc/ Writer, Hostess; b/Dec 29, 1954; h/60 Oakwood Drive, South Windsor, CT 06074; ba/Simsbury, CT; p/Vasilios and Niki Psanis, South Windsor, CT; ed/AA, 1976; BA, 1979; pa/Has Wk'd for Fam Bus for Past 10 Yrs; Author, *The Free Inhibited Child* 1980, *Thoughts, Love and You* 1981, *Immortal Shadows* 1983; IPA; Nat Writer Clb; CT Writer Leag; Com of Small Mag Editors and Publishers; r/ Greek Orthodox.

PUCKETT, JAMES MANUEL JR oc/ Genealogist and Historian; b/Dec 8, 1916; h/1563 Runnymeade, Northeast, Atlanta, GA 30319; ba/Atlanta, GA; m/ Robbie Horton; c/James William (dec); p/James Manuel Sr and Alma Willkie Puckett (dec); ed/Att'd, W GA Col 1933-35, Emory Univ 1953-54; mil/USN (Gunner's Mate), WWII; pa/Mayor, Oakman, GA, 1937-39; Retail Merchant, 1937-42; Naval Ser, 1942-44; US Treas Ofcr, 1944-53; Public Acct and Pvt Investigator, 1954-63; Basic Res, Hist and Geneal, 1963-66; Feature Writer, *Georgia Genealogical Society Quarterly*, 1965-75; Writer, Lectr, Tchr, Conslt, to St and Var Agys, Cherokee Frontier Hist and Geneal; Foremost Authority, Cherokee Frontier Hist and Geneal; cp/Heraldry Soc; Ancient Monument Soc, London; SAR, St and Nat Ofcs 1965-75; Sons Confederate Vets, St and Nat Ofcs 1965-75; Order of Stars and Bars, St Cmdr 1966-70; Nat Hist Soc; So Hist Soc; GA Hist Soc; Nat Geneal Soc; GA Geneal Soc; Var Co Socs; Smithsonian Assoc; Nat Archives Assoc; Nat Trust for Hist Preserv; St Trust for Hist Preserv; Natural Hist; Nat Pks Soc; Soc of the Confederacy, Charter Mem; r/Prot; Personal Cit, US Chief of Pers, 1943; Gov's Staff, 1964-71; Legion of Merit Medal, Order of Stars and Bars, 1967; Dist'd Ser Medal, 1969; W/W S and SW; Nat Heritage Soc Annual.

PUCKETT, RICHARD E oc/Recreation Executive; b/Sep 9, 1932; h/1152 Jean Avenue, Salinas, CA 93905; ba/Ft Ord, CA; m/Velma Faye Hamrick; c/ Katherine Michelle Briggs, Deborah Alison Bolinger, Susan Lin, Gregory Richard; p/Vernon Elijah (dec) and Leona Bell Clevenger Puckett, Keno, OR; ed/BA, Public Ser, Univ of SF, 1978; Att'd, So OR Col of Ed 1951-56, Lake Forest Col 1957-58, San Jose St Univ 1973, Hartnell Jr Col 1960-70, Monterey Peninsula Jr Col 1960-70; pa/Asst Arts and Crafts Dir, Ft Leonard Wood, MO, 1956-57; Arts and Crafts Dir, Asst Spec Ser Ofcr and Mus Dir, Ft Sheridan, IL, 1957-59; Designed and Opened First

PERSONALITIES OF AMERICA

Ft Sheridan Army Mus, 1957-59; Arts and Crafts Dir, Ft Irwin, 1959-60; Arts and Crafts Dir, Ft Ord, 1960-; Directed Opening of First Presidio of Monterey, CA, Army Mus; Am Pk and Rec Soc; Salinas Fine Arts Assn; Monterey Peninsula Art Assn; Glass Arts Soc; r/ Prot; hon/One-Man Shows: Seaside City Hall 1975, Ft Ord Arts and Crafts Ctr Gallery 1967, 1973, 1979, 1981, Presidio of Monterey Art Gallery 1979; Exhib'd in MO, IL, CA; Art Wks in Pvt Collections in US, Canada and Europe; Designed, Conducted and Pub'd, Ft Ord Rec Survey, 1978; First Place, Dept of Army and AUS Forces Command Awds for Programming and Publicity, 1979, 1980, 1981, 1983; Prog Excell Trophy; 13 Awds for Outstg Perf; 1st and 3rd Place in Mod Sculpture, Monterey, CA, Fair Fine Arts Exhib, 1979; Multiple Ribbon Awds; W/W Armed Forces Rec; Artists of Renown; W/W W.

PUDDY, DONALD R oc/Chief of Flight Operations Systems Division, Flight Operations Directorate; b/May 31, 1937; h/221 Bayou View Drive, Seabrook, TX 77586; ba/Houston, TX; m/Dana C Timberlake; c/Michael R, Douglas A, Glenn L; p/Mr and Mrs L A Puddy, Ponca City, OK; ed/BS, Mech Engrg, Univ of OK, 1960; MBA, Univ of Houston, 1978; mil/USAF, Ellington AFB, 2nd Lt Assigned to High Altitude Res, 1960-64 (After 1964, Promoted to Capt); pa/Chief of Flight Opers Sys Div 1982-, Div Chief of Sys Div and Flight Dir for STS-2 1981-82, Flight Dir for STS-1 1978-81, Flight Dir for Approach and Landing Tests 1976-77, Br Chief, Mission Opers Br and Flight Dir for the Apollo Soyuz Test Proj 1974-75, Other Previous Positions, Lyndon B Johnson Space Ctr, NASA; AIAA; Pi Tau Sigma; Sigma Tau; Phi Kappa Phi; r/Prot; hon/ Sr Exec Ser, 1982; Outstg Perf Rating, 1982; NASA Exceptl Ser Medal, 1981 (STS-1); NASA Exceptl Ser Medal, 1978 (Shuttle Approach and Landing Test); Outstg Perf Rating, 1977; JSC Skylab Grp Achmt Awd, 1974; Other Hons; W/ W S and SW; W/W Govt; W/W Aviation and Aerospace; W/W Houston.

PULATI, EVALENE G M oc/Writer, Television Producer; b/Nov 20; h/PO Box 1404, Santa Ana, CA 92702; ba/ Same; m/Vito L; p/Bertha Massie, Palmdale, CA; ed/Bus Adm Course in Col; Med Asst Course in Pvt Sch; pa/ Med Asst in Ofc of MD, 15 Yrs; Owner, Operator of Antique Collectables Shop, 16 Yrs; Editor, Writer of Newslttrs for Var Orgs, 8 Yrs; Writer, Prodr, TV Programming, 4 Yrs; Pres, Nat Valentine Collectors Assn; Pres, Orange Co Antique Bottle and Collectables Clb; Secy, Numismatic Coun of Orange Co; Bd of Dirs, Ebell Soc of Santa Ana Val; r/Prot; hon/Pubs, *Illustrated Tin Container Guide* 1973, *Disneyana Price Guide* 1975; Editor, Quarterly Jour for Valentine Assn; TV Spec Awds, 1981-82, 1983; Mus Pkg Anquities Awd, 1974; Santa

Ana Wom of Yr, 1973; DIB; W/W World of Wom.

PULLEN, RICHARD OWEN oc/Lawyer, Communications Company Executive; b/Nov 6, 1944; h/5428 North 24th Street, Arlington, VA 22205; ba/Washington, DC; m/Frances G Eisenstein; p/ Dr Roscoe LeRoy Pullen (dec); ed/BA in Ed, Whitman Col, 1967; JD, Duke Univ Sch of Law, 1972; mil/USCG Resv, 1967-75; pa/Fin Mgmt Trainee, Gen Elect Co, 1967-69; Admitted to DC Bar, 1973; Sr Atty, Domestic Facilities Br, Common Carrier Bur 1972-79, Atty-Advr, Ofc of Opinions and Review 1979-81, Fed Communs Comm; VP, Corporate Devel, Contemp Communs Corp, 1981-; Am Bar Assn; Fed Bar Assn; r/Unitarian; hon/Num Rulemakings and Opinions for Fed Communs Comm; Chm, Wkg Grp "A" (Definitions and Terminology), Jt-Indust Govt Preparatory Grp for 1977 World Adm Radio Conf on the Broadcasting Satellite Ser; W/W S and SW.

PULLIAM, PAUL EDISON oc/Electrical Engineer; b/Jun 6, 1912; h/7916 Grandstaff Drive, Sacramento, CA 95823; ba/Sacramento, CA; m/Ila M Catrett; c/Carol Ann Pulliam Rolls, Paula Ann Pulliam Bermingham; p/ George Washington Pulliam (dec); Hattie Lucy Vaudeventer Pulliam (dec); ed/BSEE, Univ of MO Col of Engrg, 1951; Cert, Indust Col of the Armed Forces, 1958; mil/2nd Lt to Maj 1937-72, Ret'd, AUS; pa/Elect Engr: in Constrn of Powerhouse at Bull Shoak Dam 1951-52, in Devel of Redstone and Jupiter Weapon Sys (Chrysler Corp), in Outfitting, Tng, Start-Up and Oper of AEC's Gaseous Diffusion X-Placed (Goodyr Atomic Corp); Mech Plan Checker in Clark Co, NV; Bldg and Safety Depts, incl'g Las Vegas Strip; r/ Bapt; hon/Recip, Army Commend Ribbon, for Suggesting Use of Radar by the Field Artillery during WWII from Keesler Field, MS.

PURCELL, GWENDOLYN oc/Clinical Chemistry Analyst; b/Jul 5, 1933; h/ 1135 Corner Road, Southwest, Powder Springs, GA 30073; ba/Hiram, GA; p/ Thornton and Lou Etta Purcell (dec); ed/ BS in Biol, GA St Univ, 1964; pa/Dept and Shift Supvr, Linden Labs Inc, Upjohn Co, 1959-74; Chem Tech, ASPA, 1976; Chem Supvr, Cobb Gen Hosp, 1976-77; Chm Med Tech, Kennestone Reg Hlth Care, 1977-; Nat Registry Clin Chem; Am Assn for Clin Chem; Am Soc of Clin Pathologists; Nat Registry ASCP; r/Bapt; hon/S'ship and Attendance Awd, Univ of GA; Lab Employee of Yr, 1982; W/W Am Wom.

PURER, AL oc/Research Chemist; b/ Aug 13, 1934; h/306 Virginia Avenue, Lynn Haven, FL 32444; ba/Panama City, FL; m/Phyllis Jean; c/Ronda Kay, Karen Jean; p/Pete (dec) and Mary Ann Purer, Liberal, KS; ed/BS in Chem, Ft Hays St Univ, 1958; pa/Chem, Helium Activity, 1958-60; Res Chem, Helium Res Ctr,

1960-70; Res Chem, Naval Coastal Sys Ctr, 1970-; Am Chem Soc; cp/Panama City Dive Clb; Panama City Swim Assn, Treas 1978, Dir 1979; Panama City Swim and Tennis Clb; r/U Meth; hon/ Pubs, "Chromatographic Separation of the Nuclear Spin Isomers of Hydrogen and Deuterium Below 60ºK" 1971, "Separation of the Neon Isotopes by Cryogenic Chromatography" 1969, Others; US Bur of Mines Pub Cit, 1965; W/W S and SW.

PUTNAM, LARRY DEWAYNE oc/ Manager of Trust Department; b/Apr 15, 1936; h/3946 South Mission Oaks Drive, Chattanooga, TN 37412; ba/ Chattanooga, TN; m/Patsy Jo Pope; c/ Michael Dewayne, Michele Denise; p/ Louis Burna (dec) and Mamie May Putnam, Chattanooga, TN; ed/BS, Acctg, Univ of TN Chattanooga, 1958; Master of Trust Admin, NWn Univ, 1969; mil/AUS, Fin, 1959-61; pa/Sr VP and Trust Ofcr, Dept Hd, Commerce Union Bk, 1974-; Sr Trust Mktg Ofcr, Am Nat Bk and Trust Co, 1972-74; Trust Ofcr, Pioneer Bk, 1961-71; Estate Planning Coun of Chattanooga, Pres 1969; Am Inst of Bkg, Pres 1970; Lambda Chi Alpha Alumni Assn, Pres 1967; cp/ Chattanooga Opera Assn, Pres 1976-77; Bd of Dirs, Downtown YMCA; Bd of Dirs, Moccasin Bend Girl Scout Coun; Bd of Dirs, Girls Clbs of Chattanooga; Bd of Dirs, Sr Neighbors of Chattanooga, Treas 1982; Bd of Dirs, U Cerebral Palsy; r/Meth; hon/W/W Am Cols and Univs; Outstg Yg Men of Am; W/W S and SW.

PUTNAM, MICHAEL BROOKS oc/ United States Army Officer; b/Mar 4, 1947; h/8 Sherbrooke Drive, Princeton Junction, NJ 08550; ba/APO, NY; m/ Maria M; c/Patricia A; p/Frank W Putnam, Princeton Junction, NJ; ed/BS in Aerospace Engrg, WV Univ, 1970; US Marine Command and Staff Col, 1981; USACGSC, 1981; US Air Command and Staff Col, 1983; US Naval War Col, 1983; mil/AUS, 1970-; pa/Cmdr, Btry A, 2BN, 71 ADA, S Korea, 1974-75; Cmdr, HQ Btry, 3 BN, 67 ADA, W Germany, 1976-78; Opers Ofcr, HQ 3 BN, 67 ADA, W Germany, 1978-79; Pers Assignment Ofcr, AUS Milpercen, 1980; BN S-3, IBN, 59 ADA, W Germany, 1981-83; Asst G3 Tng 8 ID(M), W Germany, 1983-; AFA; AIAA; Am Mktg Assn; Am Mgmt Assn; AMI; MCA; MOWW; MCHF; NHA; NRA; NSSA; Outstg Am Handgun Awds Foun; NSI; Pi Kappa Alpha Frat; ROA; RUSI; Soc of the Third Inf Div, AUS; US Naval Inst; USSI; USFAA; AUSA; Armor Assn; ADPA; AFHF; WV Alumni Assn; VFW; AOC; WV Engrg Alumni; r/Epis; hon/Outstg Yg Man of Am, 1976; Scabbard and Blade, 1968; AUS Meritorious Ser Medal; AUS Commend Medal, 2 OLCs; AUS Achmt Medal; Nat Def Medal; AFEM; ASM; OSR; W/W Aviation and Aerospace.

461

Q

QUIBLE, ZANE KEITH oc/Professor; b/May 7 1942; h/1819 Liberty Avenue, Stillwater, OK 74074; ba/Stillwater, OK; m/Patricia Mandel; c/Christopher Zane; p/Mr and Mrs Kenneth Quible, Marriman, NE; sp/Mr and Mrs Stanley Mandel, Deerfield, IL; ed/BS 1964, MEd 1966, Univ of NE; PhD, MI St Univ, 1972; pa/Instr, SE MO St Univ, Cape Girardeau, 1966-70; Prof, MI St Univ, E Lansing, 1970-81; Prof Col of Bus, OK St Univ, Stillwater, 1981-; Mem: Pres Lansing MI Chapt, Adm Mgmt Soc, 1972-; Pres MI St Univ Chapt, Delta Pi Epsilon, 1966-; Pres-elect 1981-82, Mem 1972-81, MI Bus Ed Assn; Newslttr Editor 1982-85, Mem 1981-, Mtn-Plains Bus Ed Assn; Am Bus Commun Assn; Alpha Kappa Psi; Phi Delta Kappa; Phi Kappa Phi; r/Meth; hon/Author, Over 30 Profl Articles; Author of Texts, *Intro to Adm Ofc Mgmt*; *Intro to Word Processing*; *Intro to Bus Communs*; Dist'd Ser Awd, Alpha Kappa Psi, 1970; AMS Merit Awd, 1978; AMS Diamond Merit Awd, 1980; AMS 300 Clb Awd, 1982; W/W in S & SW.

QUIGLEY, CATHERINE LANGDON FOLEY oc/Technical Information Specialist; b/Apr 15, 1920; h/5309 Camberley Avenue, Bethesda, MD 20814; ba/Bethesda, MD; m/Stephen Timothy; c/Stephen Timothy Jr, Catherine Mary Q Wicks; Mary Carol Q Stevens; Eileen Abigail, Kevin Christopher, John Brennan; p/Ellen Brennan and John Robert Foley (dec); sp/Mary O'Leary and Stephen Cornelius Quigley (dec); ed/BA, Col of St Catherine, 1942; MS, Wayne St Univ, 1944; CGA, Intl Graphoanal Soc, 1965; Att'd Grad Sch & Var Courses, NIH, 1970-; Att'd Courses, Nat Lib of Med, 1980-; Other Addit Study; pa/Cereal Chem, Gen Mills Inc, Mpls, MN, 1944; Med Technol, Boeing Aircraft, Seattle, WA, 1944-45; Med Technol, Clin Ctr Blood Bk, NIH, 1968-71; Med Technol, Employee Hlth Ser Co, NIH, 1971-74; Med Technol, Applied Physics Sect, Dept of Nuclear Med, CC, NIH, 1974-80; Tech Info Spec, Nat Lib of Med, Bethesda, MD, 1980-; Mem: Mt, ASCP; Soc of Nuclear Med; Nat Treas 1960-62, Kappa Gamma Pi; Nat Secy & Exec Dir Nat Ofc 1979-83, Sigma Delta Epsilon; Chp & Parliamntn, EEO Adv Com, NIH; cp/Leag of MN Poets; Nat Mil Wives Assn; Nav Ofcr's Wives Clb, Wash DC; VPres Camera Clb, NIH; r/Rom Cath; hon/Author of Articles in Profl Jours incl'g: *Jour of Occupl Med*; *Lab Med*; Articles in Pubs of Soc of Nuclear Med & Intl Graphoanal Soc; Num Poems Pub'd; Valedictorian, Landroche Eng Awd, St Felix HS, 1938; 4 Yr S'ship, Kappa Gamma Pi, Iota Sigma Pi, Mary Carol Sci Awd, Col of St Catherine, 1938-42; Med Technol F'ship, Wayne St Univ, 1942-44; Guest-in-Residence, Col of Notre Dame, Belmont, CA, 1967-68; 2nd Prize Technol Sect, Soc of Nuclear Med, 1975; Grp Superior Perf Awds, EEO Adv Coun Awds, Quality Increase, HEW Suggestion Awds, NIH & Nat Lib of Med, 1968-; W/W of Wom.

QUILLEN, JAMES HENRY oc/Member of United States House of Representatives; b/Jan 11, 1916; h/1601 Fairidge Place, Kingsport, TN 37664; ba/Washington, DC; m/Cecile Cox; p/John A and Hannah Chapman Quillen (dec); ed/Hon LLD, Milligan Col, 1978; mil/USN, 1942-46, Lt; pa/Kingsport Press, 1934-35; *Kingsport Times*, 1935-36; Fdr & Pubr, *Kingsport Mirror*, 1936-39; Mem 1954-62, Legis Coun 1957, 1959 & 1961, Minority Ldr 1959-60, TN Ho of Reps; Mem 88-98th US Congs, 1st Dist Rep, TN; Ranking Minority Mem, House Rules Com; Mem, Repub Ldrship; Del-at-Large, GOP Nat Conv in SF, 1956; Del to GOP Nat Convs, 1964, 1968, 1972, 1976; Parliamntn, 1980 GOP Nat Conv, Detroit; cp/Past Pres Kingsport Lions Clb; C of C; Am Legion; VFW; Ridgefields Country Clb; Capitol Hill Clb; r/Meth; hon/Num Cits & Awds: Vets of WW I, Am Legion, VFW, Amvets, DAV; SAR Awd; Golden Age Hall of Fame Awd; Defender of Indiv Rts Awd; Ams for Constitl Action; Nat Bicent Medal; Am Revolution Bicent Adm; Watchdog of the Treas Awd & Guardian of Small Bus Awd, Every Cong since 1963; Nat Security Ldrship Awd; Am Security Coun; Featured in *Life & Rdr's Digest*; Num W/W & Other Biogl Listings.

QUIRICO, FRANCIS JOSEPH oc/Justice of Supreme Judicial Court of Massachusetts, Retired; b/Feb 18, 1911; h/1282 East Street, Pittsfield, MA 01201; p/Luigi and Lucia Giovanetti Quirico (dec); ed/LLB, NEn Univ Sch of Law, 1932; mil/USAF, 1942-46; pa/Law Pract, 1932-56; City Solicitor, 1948-52; Justice of MA Superior Ct, 1956-69; Justice of MA Spr Jud Ct, 1969-81; Recall Justice of Superior Ct, 1981-; Mem: ABA; Am Law Inst; Berkshire Co Bar Assn; Inst for Jud Adm; r/Cath; hon/400 Judic Decisions Pub'd, 969-81; Hon LLD Degs: NEn Univ, 1970; Suffolk Univ, 1971; Am Intl Univ of Springfield, 1974; WN N Eng Col, 1981; N Adams St Col, 1981; Num W/W & Other Biogl Listings.

QURAISHI, MOHAMMED SAYEED oc/Entomologist, Toxicologist; b/Jun 23, 1924; h/19813 Cochrane Way, Gaithersburg, MD 20760; ba/Bethesda, MD; m/Akhtar Imitaz; c/Rana, Naveed, Sabah; p/Mohammed Latif Quraishi (dec); Akhtar Jehan, Karachi, Pakistan; sp/Imitaz Mohammed and Nisar Begam Khan (dec); ed/BSc, Agra Univ, 1942; MSc, Aligarh Muslim Univ, 1944; PhD, Univ of MA, 1948; pa/Sr Mem, UN WHO Malaria Tm, 1949-51; Entomologist, Malaria Inst, Pakistan, 1951-55; Sr Res Ofcr, Pakistan Coun of Sci & Indust Res & Sr Sci Ofcr, Pakistan Atomic Energy Comm, 1960-64; Sr Sci, Ctl Treaty Org, Inst of Nuclear Sci, Tehran, Iran, 1960-64; Assoc Prof, Univ of Manitoba, Winnipeg, Canada, 1964-66; Hd Interdeptl Pesticide Residue Lab, ND St Univ, 1966-72; Prog Mgr Interdeptl Contract Proj THEMIS, Dept of Def, 1968-74; Chief Sci Biol, NY St Sci Ser, Albany, NY, 1974-75; Entomologist, Toxicologist, Chief Pest Control & Consultation Sect, NIH, Bethesda, MD, 1976-; Mem: Am Chem Soc; Pub Com, Edit Bd, Soc of Envir Toxicology & Chem; Entomology Soc of Am; r/Islam; hon/Author, Over 50 Sci Papers in Intl Sci Jours; Author of Book, *Biochem Insect Control: Its Impact on Economy, Envir & Natural Selection*, 1977; Merit S'ship, Aligarh Muslim Univ, 1942-44; Overseas S'ship, Govt of India, 1946-49; Num US & Intl Lecture Presentations at Acad & Sci Socs; Chp Equal Opport Com, ND St Univ Chapt NEA, 1973-74; Sigma Xi; Phi Kappa Phi.

R

RAAM, SHANTHI oc/Research Scientist; b/Nov 26, 1941; ba/Tufts University Medical Cancer Unit, Lemuel Shattuck Hospital, 170 Morton Street, Boston, MA 02130; ed/BS 1960, MS 1962, Univ of Madras, India; PhD, Univ of GA, 1973; pa/Res Assoc, Dept of Med Tufts Univ Sch of Med & Dir Oncology Lab Div, Lemuel Shattuck Hosp, Boston, MA, 1975-; Res Assoc, Tufts Cancer Res Ctr, Boston, 1976-; Postdoct Res Fellow, Tufts Cancer Res Ctr & Tufts Univ Sch of Med, Boston, 1973-; Res Asst Immunol 1972-73, Tchg Asst Microbiol 1970-72, Univ of GA; Tchg Asst Dept Microbiol, Med Col of GA, 1968-70; Instr Zool Dept, SIET Woms Col, Madras, India, 1966-67; Res Asst Dept Zool, Univ of Madras, India, 1962-64; Mem: Am Assn of Immunols; Am Assn of Cancer Res; Am Assn of Clin Oncologists; AAAS; Participant, Num Profl Sems; hon/Author & Co-Author Num Articles in Profl Jours & Sci Books on Immunol of Estrogen Receptors, Biochem & Clin Aspects of Cancer; Grantee: Am Cancer Soc; NIH; Recip Ekambaranathayyar Prize for 2nd Yr MS Prog & Best Student Awd for 1st Yr MS Prog, Univ of Madras; Mem, NCI Consensus Com for Steriod Receptors in Breast Cancer, Bethesda, MD, 1979; Res Awd Nat Am Cancer Soc, NIH, 1979-80, 1980-81, 1981-82, 1984-; W/W in Frontier Sci & Technol.

RAATZ, SHERRY SWETT oc/Vice Regent Rainer Chapter, Daughters of American Revolution; Wife and Mother; Former Entertainer; b/Sept 20, 1933; h/7500 27th Northeast, Seattle, WA 98115; ba/Seattle, WA; m/Charles F Jr; c/Robin Elaine, Roger Lockwood, Rondee Doreen, Reneé Josette; p/Lawrence L and Louise M Hanson Swett, Seattle, WA; sp/Charles Raatz Sr (dec); Gertrude L Raatz, Castro Val, CA; ed/BA, Univ of WA, 1955; mil/US Citizens Ser Corps, WW II; pa/Singer (age 4), "Uncle Frank's Chd's Hour," KJR Radio, Seattle, WA; Profl Singer (age 8), Perf'g at Palomar, Orpheum & Paramount Theatres, Jerry Ross Agy; Perf'd as "Sweetheart of the Army" for Armed Forces during WW II & Korean War at Stas in WA & OR & Num USO Clbs & Hosp Wards; Toured w Maj Bowes' Unit in Canada Bert Levy Circuit, 1942; Actress: "The Wom," Univ of WA Showboat Theatre, 1951; "Sing Out Sweet Land," Univ of WA Playhouse, 1952; "Rumplestiltskin," Univ of WA Chds' Theatre, 1952; Singer, Cabaret Concert Theatre, Hollywood, CA, 1955; "Joyride Musical Revue, Huntington Hartford Theatre, Hollywood, CA & Schubert Theatre, Chgo, 1956; Lead, TV Show "Sally," 1958; Lead, Live TV Matinee Theatre, "Mrs Moonlight," Burbank Studies, 1958; Secy to City Libn, Seattle Public Lib, 1960-61; cp/1st V Regent 1981-, Mem 1980-, Rainier Chapt, Nat Soc of DAR; Daughs of Fdrs & Patriots of Am, 1982; Freedoms Foun at Val Forge, 1982; r/Prot; hon/Illust'd Article "Piracy in Iceland," *The Am Scandinavian Review*, 1961; Wrote Theme Song, for Nat Soc of DAR, 1981; Wrote Theme Song, for Freedoms Foun, 1982; Direct Descendant, John Swett Fdr of Newbury, MA & John Darling Swett Am Revolution

War Patriot; Cert of Apprec, for 5,000 Hours of Entertainment to Ser-men during WW II, Seattle Civilian War Comm, 1943; Cert of Merit, Wash Ath Clb, 1943; Ltter of Thanks for Selling War Bonds, War Savs Staff, US Treas Dept, 1943; Alpha Chapt, Phi Beta Kappa 1955, Creat Drama Awd 1955, Grad cum laude 1955, Univ of WA; Other Awds & Hons.

RACHLIN, HARVEY BRANT oc/Author; b/Jun 23, 1951; h/252 Robby Lane, Manhasset Hills, NY 11040; ba/Same; p/Philip and Mazie Rachlin, New Hyde Park, NY; ed/BA, Hofstra Univ, 1973; pa/Author, 1977-; Mem: Am Soc of Composers, Authors & Pubrs; Am Guild of Authors & Composers; hon/Author, *The Songwriter's Handbook*, 1977; *The Ency of the Music Bus*, 1981; *Love Grams*, 1983; *The Money Ency*, 1984; Deems Taylor Awd, ASCAP, 1983; Outstg Ref Bk of Yr, Am Lib Assn; "Selected Bibliog," Copyright Ofc, Lib of Cong; W/W in E; Contemp Authors.

RADLAUER, EDWARD oc/Author, Illustrator, Photographer; b/Mar 3, 1921; h/PO Box 1637 Whittier, CA 90609; ba/Same; m/Ruth Shaw; c/David, Robin, Daniel; p/Kurt and Hulda Radlauer (dec); sp/Tracy and Ruth Shaw (dec); ed/BA, Univ of CA-LA; MA, Whittier Col; mil/AUS, 1941-43; pa/Tchr & Prin, 1950-68; Author, 1968-; Mem: Univ of So CA Assocs, 1975-; cp/Rotary Clb, 1960's; hon/Author, Illustr, Photog, Over 200 Chd's Books, Games, Cassetes, Filmstrips for use in Schs & Libs; Co-Recip (w Wife), Dorothy McKenzie Awd for Ser to Chd & Rdg, So CA Coun on Lit for Chd & Yg People, 1983.

RADLAUER, RUTH SHAW oc/Editor, Author; b/Aug 18, 1926; h/PO Box 1637 Whittier, CA 90609; ba/Same; m/Edward; c/David, Robin, Daniel; p/Tracy and Ruth Shaw (dec); sp/Kurt and Hulda Radlauer (dec); ed/BA, Univ of CA-LA, 1950; pa/Tchr, 1st Grade, Spec Ed, Adults (Parent Ed & Creat Writing), 1950-70; Editor, Elk Grove Books, 1971-; Author, Chd's Books; Mem: Authors Guild; So CA Coun on Lit for Chd & Yg People; r/Prot; hon/Author & Co-Author, Over 200 Books Incl'g 20 Titles on the Nat Pks, 1958-; Co-Recip (w Husband), Dorothy C McKenzie Awd for Ser to Chd & Rdg, So CA Coun on Lit for Chd & Yg People, 1983; Contemp Authors.

RAGLAND, SAMUEL CONNELLY oc/Industrial Engineer; b/Jul 12, 1946; h/280 North 71st Street, Scottsdale, AZ 85257; ba/Phoenix, AZ; m/Marilyn Margaret; c/Sherry Anne, David Michael; p/Julian Potter Ragland (dec); Stella (Thompson) Ragland; sp/John Thomas and Elizabeth; ed/BSBA, AZ St Univ, 1974; Cert'd MTM Analyst, Bruce Payne & Assocs Inc, 1970; pa/Industl Engr, 1st Interstate Bk of AZ, Phoenix, 1966-76; Industl Engr, Beckman Instruments, Scottdale, AZ, 1976-78; Mgmt Analyst, AZ Legis Budget Com, Phoenix, 1978; Industl Engr, Mgmt Sys ITT Courier Terminal Sys, Tempe, AZ, 1978-80; Proj Control Admr, Geno Host Corp, Phoenix, 1980-81; Sr Conslt, Arthur Yg & Co, Phoenix, 1981-82; Opers Analyst, City of Phoenix, 1982-; Mem: Chm Commun Ser 1983-84, Phoenix Chapt, AIIE; Assn for Sys Mgmt; cp/Dir, Merry Moppets of High-

land Inc, 1977-81; hon/Contbr, Var Articles to Govt Pubs; U Fund Exceptl Ser Awd, Mesa, AZ U Fund, 1970; W/W in W.

RAHMAN, MATIUR oc/Professor; b/Sep 1, 1940; h/122 Hazelholme Drive, Halifax, Nova Scotia, Canada B3M 1N5; ba/Halifax, Nova Scotia, Canada; m/Nasim Ara Rahman; c/Susan, Tarjin; p/Lutfur Rahman and Dumuni Chowki (dec); sp/Mrs Sahajadi Begum, Assam, India; ed/BSc 1962, MSc 1964, Gauhati Univ; DIC, Imperial Col, London, 1969; MPhil, London Univ, 1969; PhD, Windsor Univ, 1973; pa/Assoc Prof Applied Math, Tech Univ of Nova Scotia, Halifax, 1980-; Asst Res Ofcr Hydraulics Lab, Nat Res Coun, Ottawa, 1977-80; Adj Prof Math, Univ of Ottawa, 1977-80; Res Assoc Applied Math, Univ of Manitoba, Winnipeg, 1976-77; Res Prof Applied Math, Univ of Moncton, New Brunswick, Canada, 1973-76; Math Lectr, Univ of Windsor, Windsor, Canada, 1969-73; Tchg Asst Math, Imperial Col, London, UK, 1966-69; Math Lectr, Jorhat Engrg Col, Assam, India, 1964-66; Referee, Var Sci Papers for Profl Jours; r/Moslem; hon/Author, Over 40 Articles Pub'd in Profl Jours; Over 10 Tech Reports; Over 10 Profl Conf Papers; Curric & Acad Regulation Com, TUNS, 1980-; Convocation Com, London Univ, UK, 1969-; Canadian Applied Math Soc, 1980-; Asst Edir, *Intl Jour Math & Math Scis*, 1979-; Mem, Engrg Inst of Canada, 1974-.

RAHMAN, MOHAMMAD H oc/Allergist, Immunologist; b/May 6, 1937; h/1055 Dautel, St Louis, MO 63146; ba/St Charles, MO & Alton, IL; m/ANISF; ed/MD, Dow Med Col, Univ of Karachi Sch of Med; Cert'd: Am Bd of Allergy & Immunol; Am Bd of Pediatrics; Dipl Chd Hlth, Col of Phys & Surgs; Pediatrician, St Louis Hosp & St Charles Hosp; Instr Pediatrics, Wash Univ Sch of Med, St Louis; Instr, Fellow in Allergy & Clin Immunol, KS Univ Med Ctr, Kansas City, KS & Univ of MO Kansas City Sch of Med; Mem: Am Acad of Allergy & Immunol; Am Col of Allergists; Fellow, Am Assn of Cert'd Allergists; Fellow, Am Acad of Pediatrics; IMA, MO St, St Charles & St Louis Metro Med Socs; AMA; r/Islam; hon/Phys Recog Awd, AMA, 1974-80; W/W in MW.

RAHMAN, MUKHLES UR oc/Research Engineer; b/Jan 28, 1953; h/51 Woodside Drive, Penfield, NY 14526; ba/Rochester, NY; m/Sofia; p/AM Nawab Ali (Nur), Mymensingh, Bangladesh; sp/A Bari Khan, Mymensingh, Bangladesh; ed/BSC Engrg, UE&T, Pakistan, 1974; MSc, Univ of New Brunswick, Canada, 1977; MSc 1979, PhD 1981, Univ of WI-Madison; mil/Pakistan AF, 1974-75, Pre-Cadet Engr; pa/Res Asst & Tchg Asst: Univ of New Brunswick, Canada; Univ of Calgary, Canada & Univ of WI-Madison, 1975-81; Sr Res Engr, Eastman Kodak Co, Rochester, NY, 1981-; Mem: Soc of Exptl Stress Analysts; AIAA; cp/Lions Clb Intl; r/Islam; hon/Author of Var Pubs in Jours & SESA Conf Proceedings.

RAIMEY, TIBERTHA W oc/Retired Reference Research Librarian; h/1536 Northeast 33rd Street, Oklahoma City, OK 73111; ba/Oklahoma City; m/Isaac Raimey (dec); p/Albert and Katie Williams (dec); sp/Isaac and Elizabeth Raimey (dec); ed/Cert Lib Sci, St Benedictine Col, 1947; BS Sec'dy Ed & Lib Sci, OK St Univ, 1963; Grad Study, OK Univ, 1967-72; pa/Hd Libn Commun Br Lib Admr, Kay Co Bd of Ed, 1947-62; Ref Res Libn, OK Co Libs, OK City, OK, 1966-; Other Previous Position in Ponca City, OK; Mem: Recruitment, Am Lib Assn, 1959-61; Secy Ref Dept, OK Lib Assn, 1953; AAUW, 1963-; VChp, ONTA, 1944-47; Hd Chd's Libn, 1964-66; Chp Exec Coun, OFCWC, 1983-85; Other Var Org Positons; cp/ Life Mem, NAACP; YMCA; Grand Worthy Cnslr, Grand Ct Order of Calanthe, OK Juris, K of P, 1972-84; Ch Libn, Tchr Intermediate Dept 1967-83, Prayer Grp Ldr, Wom's Chorus 1972-, Recording Secy E Zion Dist 1980-83; r/Bapt; hon/Author of Article Pub'd in OK Lib Assn Bltn, 1965 on Fgn Libs & Mus; Outstg Commun Ser, AAW, 1954; Good Neighbor, U Meth Wom, 1954; Outstg Ser QBGC, 1982; Other Hons & Awds.

RAINES, MARGARET GORDON oc/Clinical Psychologist; b/Jan 9, 1928; h/1679 Cambridge Boulevard, Columbus, OH 43212; ba/Columbus, OH; m/ Alan John Markworth; c/Catharine R Wright, Barbara Campbell, Nancy Davis, Robert A Jr; sp/Eleanore Markworth, Westlake, OH; ed/BA, Middlebury Col, 1950; MA 1974, PhD 1979, OH St Univ; pa/Conslt to Commun Orgs, Columbus Area Mtl Hlth Ctr, 1972-78; Dir Psychol Sers, Integrity House Drug Treatment, 1978-81; Conslt, Psychol Devel, 1976-82; Pvt Pract Clin Psych, 1983-; Mem: Am Psychol Assn; OH Psychol Assn; Am Pers & Guid Assn; r/U Ch of Christ; hon/Author of Article on Anal of Male Drug Abusers; Am Men & Wom of Sci.

RAJAN, RENGA oc/Research Engineer; b/Jan 8, 1952; h/11822 North Fairhollow, Houston, TX 77043; ba/ Houston, TX; m/Komal N; c/Vikram; p/ Rajam and Kumudavalli (Raghavachari) Parthasarathy, India; sp/N S and Ranganayaki Vijayaraghavachar, India; ed/ BTech, Reg Engrg Col, Tiruchirapalli, India, 1973; MSChE, Clarkson Col of Technol, 1976; PhD, WV Univ, 1978; pa/Sr Res Engr 1981-, Res Engr 1979-80, Exxon Prodn Res Co, Houston, TX; Res Asst, WV Univ, Morgantown, 1976-78; Tchg Asst, Clarkson Col of Technol, 1974-76; Mem: AIChE, 1974-; r/Hindu; hon/Author, Over 5 Articles Pub'd in Profl Jours Incl'g: AIChE Jour; CEP Tech Manual; Intl Jour Heat Mass Transfer; 4 Assn Paper Presentations; Var Tech Reports; summa cum laude; Univ 1st Rank Gold Medalist; Num Other Hons; W/W in S & SW.

RAKICH, CHRISTA MARTIN oc/ Organist, Harpsichordist; b/Nov 11, 1952; h/19 Dwight Street, Boston, MA 02118; ba/Boston, MA; p/A Rakich and E C Martin, Southbury, CT; ed/BMus Organ, BA German, Oberlin Col, 1975; Hochschule für Musik und darstellende Kunst, Vienna, Austria, 1975-77; MMus Organ, N Eng Conservatory, 1979; pa/ Asst Univ Organist, Harvard Univ, 1978-81; Prof Organ, N Eng Conservatory, 1979-; Lectr in Organ & Harpsichord, Univ of CT, 1980-; Vis'g Artist (Harpsichord), Vat Pelt Col House, Univ of PA, 1981-; Mem: Exec Bd Boston Chapt 1981-83, Profl Status Com, Am

Guild of Organists; hon/Recordings: J S Bach Organ Wks, Clavierübung III, 1983; Bezzazian Perf Awd, Oberlin Col, 1971-75; Phi Beta Kappa, 1975; Pi Kappa Lambda, 1975; Fulbright Study Awd, 1975; Commencement Recitalist, Oberlin Col, 1975; 2nd Prize, Intl Organ Competition, Wks of JS Bach, Bruges, Belgium, 1976; Semi-finalist, Intl Organ Competition, Nürnberg, Germany, 1977; Grant-in-Aid, Austro-Am Soc, Boston, 1978; Featured Organist, Harvard Organ Sem on J S Bach, 1981; Featured Recitalist, AGO Convs, Worcester, MA & Richmond, VA, 1983; W/W: of Profl Wom, in Am Music.

RALSTON, BARBARA JO oc/School Counselor; b/Aug 8, 1955; h/509-B Savannah Street, Greensboro, NC 27406; ba/Ramseur/Franklinville, NC; p/Mr and Mrs Allan Ralston, Jamestown, NC; ed/ BA Psychol & Phy Ed, Univ of NC-Chapel Hill, 1977; MA Sch Cnslg, Appalachian St Univ, 1978; pa/Randolph Co Schs, Sch Cnslr 1978-, Coach & Ofcl 1978; NC Pers & Guid Assn; NC Sch Cnslrs Assn, Awds Com Fall 1983; cp/NC Peer Helper Assn; Sportime Raquet Clb; NCPHA Presenter; hon/Author Pubs in Peer Facilitator Qtly, Oct 1983; NCPHA News, Sprg 1983; Randolph Co Vol Awd, 1981; Served on St Task Force for Devel'g Peer Helper Progs, 1984; Psi Chi, 1976; NC Sch Cnslr's Assn Mid Sch Cnslr of the Yr, 1982.

RAMEH, CLÉA A oc/Professor, Department Chairman; b/Jan 9, 1927; h/ 3901 Cathedral Avenue Northwest, Washington, DC 20016; ba/Washington, DC; p/Abdon S Rameh (dec); Josephina A Rameh, Brazil; ed/BA 1947, Licentiate 1948, Especialization 1955, Univ of São Paulo; MS 1962, PhD 1970, Georgetown Univ; pa/Chm Dept of Portuguese 1979-, Assoc Prof Portuguese 1975-, Asst Prof Portuguese 1970-75, Georgetown Univ; Mem: Exec Com, Div Luso-Brazilian Lang & Lit 1981-, Del to Assem at Annual Meetings 1978-80, MLA; Mem Nom'g Com for VPres & Coun Mems 1979-80, Am Coun on Tchg of Fgn Lang; Am Assn of Tchrs of Spanish & Portuguese; Adv Coun Ofcl Rep of Georgetown Univ 1978-, NE Conf on Tchg of Fgn Lang; Pres 1981-, VPres 1980-81, Gtr Wash Assn of Tchrs of Fgn Langs; Co-Chm 1981-, Reg Coalition of Fgn Langs Orgs; hon/Author of 2 Books, Português Contemporâneo I & II; Editor, Semantics: Theory & Application; Author of Var Articles & Book Chapts; Phi Beta Kappa, 1969; Phi Lambda Beta, 1973; Proj Dir, US Dept of Ed Grant Communicative Competence in Portuguese, 1981-; Gulbenkian Foun Grant for Res in Portugal, 1980-81; W/ W: in Ed, of Wom in Ed; Dir of Am Scholars; DIB.

RAMIREZ-SMITH, OSCAR ALBERTO oc/Executive; b/Dec 23, 1949; h/8460 Southwest 27 Place, Davie, FL 33328; ba/Miami, FL; m/Patricia; c/Carla Beatriz, Claudia Patricia; p/Oscar Smith (dec); Coralia Ramirez, El Salvador, CA; sp/Nino and Marissa Panzacchi, El Salvador, CA; ed/Chem & Industl Engr, 1971; MBA, 1975; pa/Pres & CEO, IIM Corp, 1980-; S A Exec Dir, Compania Azucarera Salvadoreña, 1978-80; Asst to Chm of Bd, ADOC-El Salvador, 1978; Gen Mgr, Delicia S A De C V-El Salvador, 1975-77; Adm Mgr, Spec Projs Mgr, Anodizing Dept Mgr, Alcoa De Centroamerica S A, 1973-75; r/Cath; hon/Author,

Oper Manual for Alcoa De Centro Am; Hon Mention, Instituto Tecnol'gico y de Estudios Superiores de Monterrey, Mexico; W/W in World.

RAMOS DE JULIÁ, OLGA oc/Assistant Director Academic Affairs; b/Sep 22, 1923; h/553 Estocolmo, Caparra Heights, Puerto Rico 00920; ba/San Juan, PR; m/ Enrique J Santini; c/Enrique Guillermo, Luis Enrique, Juan Enrique; p/Luis Ramos Arroyo and Ana Andino Rodr'guez, Yabucoa, PR; sp/Enrique Ram'rez Pab'n (dec); Braulia Ram'rez Pab'n, R'o Piedras, PR; ed/BAE, Dipl Guid & Cnslg 1965, MA 1969, Univ of Puerto Rico; EdD, Nova Univ, 1982; pa/Tchr, Grades 1-6 & 7-9 Spanish & Social Studies, 1945-60; Sch Cnslr Guid & Cnslg Prog 1961-68, Gen Supvr Guid & Cnslg Prof 1969-71, Asst Dir Guid & Cnslg Prog 1972-73, St Dept of Ed; Cnslr 1972-73, Dir Guid & Cnslg Ofc Col of Ed 1973, Instr 1973-75, Ed Practicum Supvr Bilingual & Bicultural Consort 1976, Dir & Coor Consort for Bilingual & Bicultural Cnslrs 1974-76, Pt-time Instr 1977-79, Dir Ofc of Acad Affairs Ctl Adm Sum 1982, Asst Dir Acad Affairs Ctl Adm 1980-, Univ of PR; Dean of Acad Affairs, San Juan Tech Commun Col, 1978-80; Mem: Phi Delta Kappa; Am Pers & Guid Assn; 1 Term Pres, PR Pers & Guid Assn; PR Tchrs Assn; NEA; Secy PR Chapt, Profl & Bus Wom Assn; Participant, Num Profl Sems & Confs; cp/ARC; Nat Assn of Cancer; Exch Clbs of PR; Muscular Distrophy Campaign; Polio Campaign; r/Cath; hon/Author of Var Articles on Ed & Cnslg; Author, 5 Profl Assn Paper Presentations; Pres, PR Pers & Guid Assn; Secy-Treas Advy Coun, Adult Ed in PR; 1st Place Awd for Progs, Am Pers & Guid Assn; Legis Div Rep, Am Pers & Guid Assn; Recip, Var S'ships, Univ of PR; Del from Dept of Instrn, Career Ed Conf, St Louis, MO; Invited Mem, Ft Jackson Edrs Tour, 1980; Voc Advy St Coun, Univ of PR Sys; Pres Exch, Caparra Hgts Ech Clb; Del from Univ of PR, Panel on Non Verbal Commun & Hispanic Child, NY St; Spec Awd & Other Awds, PR Exch Clb.

RAMOS, ECHEVARRIA, SIXTO oc/ School Superintendent; b/Jan 1, 1933; h/ CL-15 Dr Morales Ferrer, Levittown, Cataño, Puerto Rico 00632; ba/Cataño, PR; m/Carmen Mir'; c/Carmen Ivette, Pedro Angel, Mayra Ivelisse, Sixto Alexis; p/Pedro and Crucita-Castañer Ramos, PR; sp/Casimiro and Ursual Mir' (dec); ed/BA, Social Scis & Ed, 1958; MA, Supvr & Sch Adm, 1969; DEd, Ednl Adm, 1980; mil/USMC, 1951-53; pa/Elem & Sec'dy Sch Tchr, 1957-70; Elem & Sec'dy Sch Prin, 1970-80; Asst & Sch Supt, 1980-82; Univ Prof, 1970-; Mem: Phi Delta Kappa, San Juan PR Chapt, 1980; World Future Soc, PR Tchr Assn of NEA, 1980; Pres Ednl Com, Uni Coop of PR, 1981; Assn for Supvn & Curric Devel, 1980; r/Cath.

RAMSHAW-REED, JANE oc/Health Insurance Broker; b/Mar 31, 1949; h/3940 Gresham #142, San Diego, CA 92108; p/ William G and Jean H Ramshaw, Albuquerque, NM; ed/TWA Flight Hostess Sch, 1969; Att'd Univ of NM, 1967-71; CLU Studies, The Am Col, 1979-80; pa/ Owner, Jane Ramshaw-Reed Enterprises, 1980-; Reg Dir, CA Pacific Ins, 1976-80; Sales Rep, Blue Cross/Blue Shield, 1974-75; Sales Rep, Clinton P Anderson Agy, 1973-74; Mem: Past Pres 1982-83, Num Other Postions & Coms 1976-, San Diego Assn of Life Underwriters; Hlt

Chm 1979-80, Bd of Dirs 1982-83, N San Diego Co Assn of Life Underwriters; VChm Hlth Com 1982-83, Other Coms, Nat Assn of Life Underwriters; Charter Bd Mem 1982-83, The Wom Life Underwriters Conf of NALU; Charter Pres, 1977-79, Soroptimist Intl of Tancho Bernardo; Charter Sgt-at-Arms, Toastmasters Intl, 1979; Bd of Dirs, Employee Benefit Coun, 1977-79; Indep Ins Agts Assn, 1980-; Nat Spkrs Assn, 1980; Grp Hlth Assn of Am, 1974-75; cp/Tm Dir for Jr Achmt Fund Dir, 1974; Clipped Wings, TWA, 1969-71; Editor, Sophomores Woms's Hon (SPURS), 1969; Chi Omega Sorority, 1967-69; Nat Hon Soc, 1966-67; hon/Author of Var Articles Pub'd in *The Ins Salesman*; & *CALU Underwriter*; Recip Num Awds, 1979-, Nat Assn of Life Underwriters; Recip Num Awds 1979-, CA Assn of Life Underwriters; Var Awds & Hons, Nat Assn of Hlth Underwriters; Qualifier for Co Conv 1982, Conv Spkr 1983, Allied Assocs; Qualifier for Co Conv 1979, Security Benefit Life Ins; Keynote Spkr Nat Conv 1978 & 1982, Life Ins Cashiers & Ofc Mgrs Assn; Recip Num Awds, San Diego Assn of Life Underwriters; Top Salesman Awd, Blue Cross/Blue Shield, 1975; S'ship, Albuquerque Pub Schs Col of Ed, 1970-71; Other Awds; W/W: of Am Wom, in CA, Among San Diego Wom; Outstg Wom of Am.

RANADIVE, NARENDRANATH SANTURAM oc/Professor; b/Sep 9, 1930; h/74 Cornerbrook Drive, North York, Ontario, Canada M3A 1H7; ba/Toronto, Canada; m/Kishori Mokashi; c/Salil, Madhuvanti; p/Santuram Ranadive (dec); Manoramabai Ranadive, Bombay, India; sp/Jagannath and Sarlabai Mokashi, Bombay, India; ed/BSc 1952, MSc 1957, Univ of Bombay; PhD, McGill Univ, 1965; pa/Anal Chem, Glaxo Lab, Bombay, India, 1958-60; Post-doct Fellow, McGill Univ, 1965-66; Post-doct Fellow, Scripps Clin & Res Fdn, CA, 1966-69; Assoc Prof, Univ of Toronto, 1973-; Mem: Inst of Immunol, 1971-; Am Assn of Pathols, 1969; Am Assn of Immunols, 1974; Canadian Soc for Immunol, 1971; AAAS; r/Hindu; hon/Autor, Over 48 Res Papers Pub'd in Profl Jours; 2 Chapts in *Inflammation, Immunity & Hypersensitivity*; Over 30 Abstracts; Govt of India Scholar, 1954-56; James Erwing Fellow, 1950-55; Med Res Coun of Canada Scholar, 1969-72; W/W in E; Am Men & Wom of Sci.

RANDHAWA, MARGUERITE BUNYARD oc/Manager & Owner of Travel Agency; b/Jun 29, 1919; h/7711 Broadway # 16B, San Antonio, TX 78209; ba/San Antonio, TX; p/Mr and Mrs Ben Bunyard (dec); sp/Mr and Mrs Ravindar Randhawa (dec); ed/BA, McMurray Col; Att'd Tokyo Lycium, Tokyo; Att'd Sophia Univ, Tokyo; Att'd Calcutta Univ, India; Att'd San Angelo Col & San Angelo Bus Sch; pa/Ct Reporter, Ctl Flying Tng Command, 1940-44; Ct Reporter, Maj War Crimes Trials, Tokyo, 1944-48; Precis Writer for UN Ec Comm for Asia & the Far E, Bangkok, Thailand, 1948-50; Free Lance Writer for Pubs Incl'g: *Colliers Ency*; Fdg Mng Editor, *The Sikh Review*, Calcutta, India, 1950-56; Mgr & Owner, Margarita's Travel Inc, 1956-; Instr, San Antonio Col & Our Lady of the Lake Univ; cp/Helped to Establish a Sch for Sikh Chd; r/Bapt; hon/Author, Var Articles, Short Stories, Movie & TV Scripts; 2 Booklets:

"Loose Ends" & "The Golden Temple of Amritsar"; Num Articles for Newspapers & Mags in Asia.

RANDISI, ELAINE MARIE oc/Senior Payroll Accountant; b/Dec 19, 1926; h/742 Wesley Way #1-C, Oakland, CA 94610; ba/Oakland, CA; C/Jeanine C Manson, Martha A Cheney, Joseph J, Paula M Small, Catherine E Tateo; George J, Anthony C; p/John D Fehd, Vacaville, CA; Alveta I (Raffety) Fehd (dec); ed/AA, Pasadena Jr Col, 1946; BS, Golden Gate Univ, 1978; pa/Sr Payroll Acct, 1983-, Sr Corp Acct 1979-83, Corp Acct 1978-79, Corp Buyer 1977-78, Corp Buyer Kaiser Industs Corp 1975-77, Asst Buyer 1973-75, Secy 1969-73, Raymond Kaiser Engrs, Oakland, CA; Consltg Astrologer; Lectr; Tchr; Am Fdn of Astrologers, 1981-; Bd of Dirs 1979-82, VPres 1979-80, Secy 1980-81, Ravenwood Homeowners Assn; VPres 1979, Spkrs Bur 1964-70, CA Assn for Neurol Handicapped Chd; cp/Com for Minority Bus Fair 1976, Bay Area Purchasing Coun, 1975-78; Practitioner-in-Tng for Ch of Rel Sci; Lectr on Astrology Monthly at Theosophical Soc, SF; Pres, Presentation HS Parents Clb, 1965-66; hon/Gianini S'ship for 3 Sems, Golden Gate Univ; Fac, Am Fdn of Astrologers Conv, Chgo, 1982; Life Mem, Alpha Gamma Sigma S'ship Soc & CA S'ship Soc; W/W of Am Wom.

RANFTL, ROBERT MATTHEW oc/Executive; b/May 31, 1925; h/PO Box 49892, Los Angeles, CA 90049; ba/El Segunda, CA; m/Marion Goodman; p/Joseph S Ranftl (dec); Leona G Ranftl, Santa Monica, CA; sp/John J and Helen S Goodman (dec); ed/BSEE, Univ of MI, 1946; Addit Grad Study, Univ of MI & Univ of CA-LA; pa/Corp Dir Engrg & Design Mgmt, Hughes Aircraft Co, 1951-; Pres & Consltg Exec, Ranftly Enterprises Inc, 1981-; Sr Proj Engr, Webster Chgo Corp, 1950-51; Hd Engrg Dept, Radio Inst of Chgo, 1947-50; Prod Engr, Russell Elect Co (Raytheon), 1946-47; Mem: AAAS; AIAA; Am Soc for Engrg Ed; IEEE; Inst of Mgmt Scis; Intl Platform Assn; NY Acad of Scis; Univs of MI & UCLA Alumni Assns; hon/Author of Book, *Res & Devel Productivity*, 1974 & 1978; Co-Author, *Productivity: Prospects for Growth*, 1981; Num Articles on Mgmt & Productivity in Profl Jours; Nat Awd for Book, *Res & Devel Productivity*, 1981; Mem Num Nat Coms & Panels Incl'g White House Conf on Productivity; Guest Lectr, Num Univs Incl'g CA Inst of Technol & Univ of CA; W/W: in W, in Engrg, in Technol Today, in Aviation & Aerospace; Am Men & Wom of Sci; DIB.

RANK, ARVILLA C oc/Independent Living Coordinator for Hearing Impaired; b/Apr 4, 1935; h/6358 South 20th Street, Milwaukee, WI 53221; ba/Milwaukee, WI; p/Peter and Agnes Rank, Luxemburg, WI; ed/BS, St Norbert Col, 1958; MS Bus Ed 1970, MS Spec Ed 1978, Univ of WI; pa/Gen Ofc Wk, St Norbert Col, De Pere, WI, 1955-58; Audit Reviewer, Employers Mut Ins Co of Wausau (Wausau Ins Co), 1958-61; Acct, St Agnes Hosp, Fond du Lac, WI, 1962-66; HS Bus Ed Tchr, St John's Sch for the Deaf, Milwaukee, WI, 1966-81; Indep Living Coor, SEn WI Ctr for Indep Living, 1981-; Mem 1966-, Pres 1981-, VPres 1980-81, Secy 1977-79; Ofcr of Milwaukee Chapt 7 1969-78; MW Reg Pres 1976-78, Past Pres 1978, w Intl

Cath Deaf Assn; Mem 1972-, Treas 1973-77, Trustee 1982-, Interpreter Cert Eval Tm 1980-, Nat Mem 1972-, WI Registry of Interpreters for the Deaf; Mem 1972-, Pres-elect 1983, Future Pres 1985, WI Assn of Deaf; Mem, Nat Assn of Deaf, 1972-; SE Reg Treas 1978-80, Mem & St Bd Mem 1978-, WI Disability Coalition; Mem 1974-, Treas 1978-81, WI Telecommuns for the Deaf Inc; Cont'g Ed Advy Bd, Milwaukee Hearing Soc, 1976-; Advy Bd, WI Div of Voc Rehab, 1981-82; Bd of Dirs 1976-79 & 1980-81, Nat Cath Ofc for the Deaf; Mem, Conv of Am Instrs for the Deaf, 1967-; Delta Pi Epsilon Bus Ed Frat, 1970-; Nat Bus Ed Assn, 1967-82; r/Cath; hon/Quota Intl Inc Dist 22 Deaf Wom of Yr for Outstg Achmts & Dedication to Ser, 1982; Recog For Outstg Commun Vol Ser, The Gtr Milwaukee Vol Action Ctr, 1983; Golden Hands Awd for Outstg Advy on Behalf of Hearing Impaired Citizens of WI, WI Assn of Deaf, 1983.

RANNEY, MARY ELIZABETH oc/Writer; b/Nov 10, 1928; h/13 River Ridge Road, Pisgah Forest, NC 26768; m/G Royal; c/Diane, Nancy; p/James (dec) and Erna Connell, Monmouth, IL; ed/Att'd Monmouth Col, 1946-47; CPS Rating, NSA, Study & Exam at Univ of Miami, 1974; pa/Fdr, Abortion Referral Ser of SW FL, 1972; Fdr, Planned Parenthood, Naples, FL Ctr, 1975; cp/Fdr, Ranney Chapt, Am Hibiscus Soc, Sr & Seedling Judge 1977; Fdr, Accordion Band of Naples, 1974; Pres, Meml Soc of SW FL, 1975-77; Fdg Ofcr, Naples Concert Band, 1972; hon/Copyright Brochure, *Abortion*, 1976; Author, *AHS Show Chairman Manual* 1979, *AHS Judges Manual* 1980; Selected Prominent Wom of Commun, 3 Times, 1977-79; Recog as Mover of the 70's in *Naples NOW Mag*, 1980; Recip Pres Awd for Ser to Soc, AHS, 1980; Life Story Feature in *Naples Star*, 1981; Featured in *Naples Daily News* for Hibiscus Res, 1981; Featured as Great Achiever in *Encore Edition* of *Naples Star*, 1982; Recip Life Mbrship for Ser to AHS, 1982; Hibiscus of Yr Awd for New Variety of Hibiscus Named for Granddaughter (Gina Marie), Pictured on Cover of Seed Pod Mag, 1982; Hon'd as Fdr of Ft Myers (FL) Nat Org of Wom at 10th Anniversary Celebration, 1982.

RAO, DANDAMUDI VISHNUVARDHANA oc/Nuclear Medical Physicist, Educator; b/Apr 5, 1944; h/26 Manger Road, West Orange, NJ 07052; ba/Newark, NJ; m/Sujata L; c/Saroja, Neeraja; p/Veeraraghavaiah and Sarojini Rao; sp/Rajamannar and Sarojini; ed/BS 1964, MS 1966, Andhra Univ; MS 1970, PhD 1972, Univ of MA; pa/Tchg Asst 1968-70, Lectr 1970-72, Univ of MA; Instr, Albert Einstein Col of Med, 1972-76; Asst Prof 1974-78, Assoc Prof 1978-, Univ of Med & Dentistry of NJ; Mem: Am Assn of Physicists in Med; Soc of Nuclear Med; NMR Imaging Soc; NY Acad of Scis; AAUP; NJ Med Physics Soc; Tech Expert, IAEA; r/Hindu; hon/Author, Num Articles in Profl Jours; Author of Text, *Intro to Physics of Nuclear Med, 1976; Editor, Physics of Nuclear Med: Recent Advances*, 1984; Vis'g Sci, Univ of Oxford, England, 1980; Prog Dir, AAPM Sum Sch; W/W: in World, in Frontier Sci & Technol.

RAO, GUNDU H R oc/Experimental Pathology; b/Apr 17, 1938; h/9333 Hyland Creek Road, Bloomington, MN 55437; ba/Minneapolis, MN; m/Yashoda

T R; c/Aupama T G, Prashanth T G; p/ H V Rama Rao and T S Annapoornamma (dec); sp/T N Ramachandra Rao and T N Kamalamma, Mysore, India; ed/BSc Tumkur, India, 1957; BSc 1958, MSc 1959, Univ of Poona, India; PhD, KS St Univ, 1968; pa/Res Asst, KS St Univ, 1965-68; Post-doct Fellow, TX A&M Univ, 1968-69; Post-doct Fellow, Univ of MN-St Paul, 1970-71; Post-doct Fellow 1971-72, Sci Dept of Pediatrics 1972-75, Asst Prof Lab Med & Pathol 1975-81, Assoc Prof Lab Med & Pathol 1981-, Univ of MN-Mpls; Mem: Am Heart Assn; Am Soc of Heamotology; Nat Acad Clin Biochem; Intl Soc of Thrombosis; Nat Coun on Thrombosis; cp/Bd of Dirs, India Clb of MN; Fdr & Mem, Sch of Indian Langs & Culture; Life Mem, Friends of Vellore; r/Hindu; hon/Author, Over 100 Pubs in Profl Jours; Fellow, Coun of Sci & Industl Res, India, 1960-65; Fellow, NIH, 1971-72; MN Affil Awd, Am Heart Assn, 1984; W/W: in Indian Immigrants, in Frontier Sci & Technol.

RAPPAPORT, MARGARET oc/Psychologist, Executive Director; b/Nov 16, 1942; h/509 East Sedgwick Street, Philadelphia, PA 19119; ba/Same; m/Herbert; c/Amanda and Alexander; p/Leo Williams, Tucson, AZ; Marie Williams, Buffalo, NY; ed/BA 1967, MA 1969, St Univ of NY; PhD, Univ of CO, 1971; pa/ Primary Tchr, Grades K, 1-4, 1961-65; Chd's Ser, Dept of Welfare St of CT, 1966; Clin Trainee, Prog for Emotional Disordered Chd, Buffalo, NY, 1966-68; Psych Trainee, VA Hosp, Buffalo, 1968-69; Curric Devel Prog, NY St Dept of Ed, 1968-69; Chwom, Human Relats Prog for Tchrs, Buffalo, 1968-69; Psych Trainee, CO Protective Sers Prog & Denver Pre-Sch Intervention Proj, 1970-71; Res Asst 1969 & 1970, Vis'g Asst Prof 1970-71, Univ of CO; Prog Devel, Early Detection & Cnslg in Tanzanian Elem Schs, 1971-73; Lectr, Univ of Dar es Salaam, Tanzania, E Africa, 1971-73; Exec Dir, Inst for Parent Child Sers, Phila, PA, 1978-; Ptner in Pvt Pract Psychol, Rappaport Assocs, Phila, PA, 1974-; Prog Devel Conslt, Prim Prev Infancy & Early Childhood, 1975-; Infant-Parent Prog Conslt, 1977-; Coor, Frontrunners Proj, 1980-; Lectr Primary Care 1977-79, Lectr Student Devel Prog at Ctr for Contemp Studies 1978-80, Lectr Mar & Fam Therapy Grad Courses 1979, Adj Fac Dept Psych 1974-, Temple Univ; Mem: NAEYC; DVAEYC; NEA; AAUP; Num Invited Spkg Presentations for Var Assns & Orgs; Var Media Experience, 1965-; cp/NOW; EMAN; hon/Author & Co-Autor of Books, *Changes in the Am Fam; Love, Limits & Lrng: A Pract Guide for Parents; Theories of Personality*, 1977; Manual for *Psychopathol: The Sci of Understanding Deviance*, 1975; Var Articles in Profl Jours & Assn Pubs Incl'g: *Jour of Ednl Psych; Intl Hlth Conf; Childbirth Ed Assn; The Am Psychol*; Other Pubs.

RAPPOPORT, KENNETH S oc/Sports Writer; b/Feb 14, 1935; h/29 Owens Road, Old Bridge, NJ 08857; ba/New York, NY; m/Bernice Goodman; c/Sharon, Felicia, Larry; p/Jack and Margie Rappoport, Old Bridge, NJ; ed/BS Jour, Rider Col; m/ AUS, 1957-59; pa/Reporter, Dorf Feature Ser, Newark, NJ 1960-61; Reporter, Doylestown, PA *Intelligencer*, 1961-63; Reporter Phila PA 1963-69, Sports Writer NY 1969-, AP; Mem: Baseball Writers Assn of Am; r/Jewish; hon/Author of 13

Books Incl'g: *Football's Spec Tms: Cowboys & Raiders*, 1982; *Doubleheader: Yankees & Dodgers*, 1982; *Pigskin Power*, 1981; *Super Sundays*, 1980; *Diamonds in the Rough*, 1979; *The Classic*, 1978; *Great Col Football Rivalries*, 1978; *Tar Heel: NC Basketball*, 1976; Others; Contbr to 5 Books Incl'g: *George Allen's 50 Greatest Games; A Cent of Champs*; Others; W/W in E.

RATAJCZAK, HELEN VOSS-KUHLER oc/Research Immunologist; b/ Apr 9, 1938; h/126 North Taylor, Oak Park, IL 60302; ba/Chicago, IL; c/Lorraine, Eric, Peter, Eileen; p/Max P Vosskuhler (dec); Marion M Vosskuhler, Tucson, AZ; ed/BS 1959, MS 1970, PhD 1976, Univ of AZ; pa/Asst Res, Univ of AZ SWn Clin & Res Inst, 1967-72; Res Tech & Student, Univ of AZ Hlth Sci Ctr, 1972-76; Asst Res Sci, Univ of IA Col of Med, 1976-78; Instr Eye & Ear Hosp 1978-80, Res Assoc 1980-81, Univ of Pgh; Asst Prof, Stritch Sch of Med, Loyola Univ, 1981-83; Res Immunol, IIT Res Inst, Chgo, 1983-; Mem: Am Chem Soc, 1957-59; Am Soc Microbiol, 1968-72; Sigma Xi, 1972-; Am Thoracic Soc, 1974-; Assn Res Vision Aphthal, 1979-80; Am Assn Immunol 1982-; AAAS, 1984-; NY Acad of Sci, 1984-; r/Rom Cath; hon/ Author & Co-Author, Over 13 Res Articles & 15 Abstracts Pub'd in Profl Jours; 8 Assn Conf Paper Presentations; Am Field Ser Exch Ser, 1954; Freshman Hon Mention, 1955-56; Spurs (Sophomore Wom's Hon), 1956-57; Phi Lambda Upsilon, 1972-73; Am Lung Asn F'ship, 1974-76; Post-doct F'ship, NIH, 1978; W/ WW in Frontier Sci & Technol.

RATLIFF, KATHY LORRAINE oc/ Supervisor and Testing Coordinator; b/ Sep 16, 1942; h/PO Box 925, Grundy, VA 24614; ba/Grundy, VA; p/Clyde Ratliff (dec); Maye Ratliff, Grundy, VA; ed/BA, Milligan Col, 1965; MEd, Univ of VA-Charlottesville, 1972; pa/Testing Coor & Supvr of Co Schs 1983-; Tchr 1963, Tchr Grade 12, Cnslr Grades 8-12, Asst Prin Garden HS & Garden Mid Sch 1974-83; Dir Early Childhood Devel Prog 4 Co Area 1973; Tchr Grundy HS 1970-73 & 1965, Grundy Jr HS & Grundy Elem Sch 1968-69, Hdstart Tchr 1967-69, Buchanan Co Public Sch Sys, Grundy, VA; Buchanan Co Bd of Supvrs, Manpower Prog CETA, 1979-81; Tchr, Southview Elem Sch, Roanoke Co Public Schs, 1967; Tchr, MacArthur Elem Sch, Ctr Twnship, Crowpoint, IN, 1966; Adj Instr, SW VA Commun Col, 1978-83; Mem: Reg Coor & Exec Bd, VA Coun of Social Studies; Nat Coun of Social Studies; Sec'dy Sch Prins & Asst Prins of VA; Buchanan Co Ed Assn; VA Ed Asn; NEA; cp/Bd of Trustees, Buchanon Co Public Lib; Bd of Dirs, Buchanan Co Chapt of Am Cancer Soc; Cp-chp, Buchanan Co ARC; Organist & SS Tchr, Grundy Ch of Christ; r/Ch of Christ; Outstg Yg Wom of Am; Notable Ams.

RAUCH, MARSHALL A oc/Executive, State Legislator; b/Feb 2, 1923; h/1121 Scotch Drive, Gastonia, NC; ba/Gastonia, NC; m/Jeanne Girard; c/John, Ingrid, Marc, Peter, Stephanie; p/Nathan A and Tillie P Rauch; ed/Grad, Duke Univ; mil/ AUS, WW II, ETO; pa/Chm of Bd, Pres & Dir, Rauch Indust Inc, Gastonia, NC; Dir & Treas, The E P Press Inc, Gastonia, NC; Dir, Majestic Ins Fin Corp, Gastonia, NC; Pres & Dir, P D R Trucking Inc, Gastonia, NC; Pres & Dir, Magic Ltd, Gastonia, NC; Mem NC St Senate, Dist

25, 1967-; Num Senate Coms Incl: Utilites Com, Higher Ed Com, Trans Com, Appropriations Com, Ways & Means, Spec Ways & Means, Fin Com, Mfg Com, Labor & Commerce Com, Num Others; cp/Mayor Pro Tem, City of Gastonia, 1952-54 & 1961-63; City Coun-man, Gastonia, 1952-54 & 1961-65; Chm, NC Hwy Study Comm, 1981; Chm, Legis Ethics Comm, 1981; Sports Facil Comm, 1977-80; Advy Com, NC Voc Textile Sch, 1970-71; Trustee, Univ of NC, 1969-73; Bd of Advrs, Gardner Webb Col, 1969-77; Big Brother, 1951-60; Sr Advr 1947-63, Dir 1964-71, Gastonia Boys Clb; Dir, Gastonia YMCA, 1959-62 & 1967-72; Dir, Salvation Army Boys Clb, 1963-71; Dir, Gastonia C of C, 1965-66; Bd of Govs, NC Jewish Home for Aged, 1968-70; Pres, Temple Emanuel, Gastonia, 1962-64; Num Other Commun Activs; r/Jewish; hon/Combat Inf Medal, WW II; Man of Yr, Gastonia C of C, 1957; Man of Yr, Gastonia Jr Wom's Clb, 1964; Man of Yr, Gaston co Omega Psi Phi, 1966; Man of Yr, NC Hlth Dept, 1968; Nat Red Cit, Nat Rec Assn, 1965; Nat Coun of Christians & Jews Brotherhood Awd, 1969; Man of Yr, Gastonia Red Shields Boys Clb, 1970; Human Sers Awd, NC Assn of Jewish Men & St of NC, 1980; W/W: in World Jewry, in S & SW, in Israel, in Am Polits; Ldg Men in US; Nat Register of Prominent Ams.

RAVEN, PETER H oc/Botanical Garden Director; b/Jun 13, 1936; h/2361 Tower Grove Avenue, St Louis, MO 63110; ba/St Louis, MO; m/Tamra Engelhorn; c/Alice Catherine, Elizabeth Marie, Francis Clark, Kathryn Amelia; p/Walter Francis and Isabelle Marion (Breen) Raven; ed/AB, Univ of CA-Berkeley, 1957; PhD, Univ of CA-LA, 1960; pa/ Post-doct Felow, NSF, at Brit Mus Natural Hist, 1960-61; Taxonomist & Curator, Rancho Santa Ana Botanic Garden, Claremont, 1961-62; Asst & Assoc Prof, Stanford Univ, 1962-71; Sr Res Fellow, New Zealand Dept of Sci & Industl Res, 1969-70; John Simon Guggenheim Meml Fellow, 1969-70; Dir MO Botanical Garden, 1971-; Engelmann Prof of Botany, Wash Univ-St Louis, Current; Adj Prof Biol, St Louis Univ & Univ of MO; VPres, CA Botanical Soc, 1968-69; Pres, Am Soc of Plant Taxonomists, 1972; Pres, Botanical Soc of Am, 1975; Pres, Soc for the Study of Evolution, 1978; Pres, Assn of Systematics Collections, 1980-82; Treas, Org for Tropical Studies, 1981-84; Pres, Am Soc of Naturalists, 1983; Pres, Am Inst of Biol Scis, 1983-84; VPres Devel, Org for Tropical Studies, 1984-; Num Past & Present Coms; Edit Bd Mem, Num Profl Jours; cp/Coun 1983-85, Mem 1977-, Nat Acad of Scis; Gov'g Bd, Nat Res Coun 1983-85; Fellow, Am Acad of Arts & Scis, 1977-; Fgn Mem, Royal Danish Acad of Scis & Lttrs, 1980-; Fgn Mem, Royal Swedish Acad of Scis, 1982-; Felow, CA Acad of Scis, 1964-; Fellow, AAAS, 1980-; Fellow, Linnean Soc of London, 1981-; Num Other Socs; hon/Author, Over 300 Titles Incl'g: Res Articles in Profl Jours & 9 Books; A P DeCandolle Prize, Geneva, 1970; Dist'd Ser Awd, Japan Am Soc of So CA, 1977; Awd of Merit, Botanical Soc of Am, 1977; Achmt Medal, Garden Clb of Am, 1978; Willdenow Medal, Berlin Botanical Garden, 1979; Hon Curator of Phanergams, Museo Nacional de Costa Rica, 1980-; Socio Hon, Sociedad Argentina de

Boв'nica, 1980-; Dist'd Ser Awd, Am Inst of Biol Scis, 1981; VPres, XIII Intl Botanical Cong, Sydney, 1981; Rudi Lemberg Travelling F'ship, Australian Acad of Sci, 1981; Joseph Priestly Medal, Dickinson Col, 1982l; Intl Envir Ldrship Medal, UN Envir Programme, 1982; Gold Seal Medal, Nat Coun of St Garden Clbs, 1982; Recip Var Hon DSc Degs: St Louis Univ, Knox Col & So IL Univ-Edwardsville .

RAVITZ, LEONARD J oc/Physician, Scientist, Professor; b/Apr 17, 1925; h/ 1459 Bayville Jct I-64, Willoughby Spit, Norfolk, VA 23503; ba/Norfolk, VA & NYC; p/Leonard Robert and Esther Evelyn Ravitz (both dec); ed/BS, Case Wn Resv Univ, 1944; MD, Wayne St Univ Col of Med, 1946; MS, Yale Univ, 1950; Cert'd, Am Bd of Psych & Neurol Inc, 1952; Addit Grad Tng; mil/AUS, 1943-46, Resv, 1946-; pa/Rotating Intern, St Elizabeth's Hosp, Wash DC, 1946-47; Jr/ Sr Asst Resident Psychi, Yale-New Haven Hosp & Asst Psychi & Mtl Hygiene, Yale Med Sch, 1947-49; Res Fellow to Prof Harold S Burr, Neuro-Anatomy Sect, Yale Med Sch, 1949-50; Sr Resident Neuropsychi 1950-51, Asst to Prof R Burke Suitt Pvt Diagnostic Clinic 1951-53, Duke Univ Hosp; Instr Neuropsychi & Asst to Prof R S Lyman, Duke Med Sch, 1950-51; Assoc Neuropsychi, Duke Univ, 1951-53; Vis'g Asst Prof & Asst to Prof R S Lyman, Meharry Med Col, Nashville, TN, 1953; Asst Dir & Prof of Ed in Charge Psychi & Neurol Tng, Univ of WY, 1953-54; Chief, Downey VA Hosp, N Chgo IL, 1953-54; Assoc Psychi Sch of Med & Hosp, Assoc to Prof Kenneth E Appel, Univ of PA-Phila, 1955-58; Secy/Treas 1956-63, Pres 1963-69, Euclid-97th St Clin, Cleveland, OH; Dept Asst Secy of Def in Charge of Hlth & Med, Aug-Sep 1958; Dir Tng & Res, En St Hosp, Williamsburg, VA, 1958-60; Pvt Pract Psychi, Norfolk, VA, 1960-; Conslt in Psych, Cleveland, OH, 1960-69; Conslt in Psychi, Upper Montclair, NJ, 1982-; Psychi & Conslt Div of Alcohol Studies & Rehab, VA Dept of Hlth (VA Dept Hlth & Mtl Retard), Norfolk, 1961-81; Staff, Med Ctr Hosps, Norfolk, VA, 1961-; Lectr Sociol (Criminology), Old Dominion Univ, Norfolk, VA, 1961-62; Conslt, Tidewater Epilepsy Foun, Chesapeake, VA, 1965-69; Spec Med Conslt, Frederick Mil Acad, Portsmouth, VA, 1963-71; Conslt, Old Dominion Res Foun, Norfolk, 1975-; Co-Prin Investigator, Nutrition Res Proj of Prof Ruth F Harrell, Old Dominion Univ, 1975-; Conslt, USPH Hosp Alcohol, Norfolk, 1978-; Asst Editor, *Jour of Am Soc of Psychosomatic Dentistry & Med*, 1980-83; Conslt, Nat Inst for Rehab Therapy, Butler, NJ, 1982-; Clin Asst Prof Psychi, Downstate Med Ctr, NYC, 1983-; Psych, Downstate Mtl Hlth Assocs, 1984-; Pt-time Psychi, Greenpoint Clinic, NYC, 1983-; Mem: Beta Chapt, Nu Sigma Nu; Yale Chapt, Sigma Xi; Fellow, Am Psychi Assn; Fellow, AAAS; Fellow, NY Acad of Scis; Charter Fellow, Am Soc of Clin Hypnosis; Fdg Pres, VA Soc of Clin Hypnosis; Fellow, Royal Soc of Hlth (London); Norfolk Acad of Med; VA Med Soc; cp/Num Lectrs & Demos, 1951-;Orgr, Var Profl Symps; hon/ Author, Over 35 Pubs Incl'g Articles in Var Profl Jours; Chapts in Books Incl "Systematic Exptl Extension of Field

Physics into Measurement of Emotional & Phy States,"*Proceedings of the 5th Intl Conf on Human Functioning*, 1982; Book in Preparation: *Electrodynamic Man: the Measurement of Emotions*; Discoverer of Field Correlates of Human Electrocyclic Phenomena Paralleling other Life Forms, Earth & Atmosphere & the Objective Assessment of Emotional & Phy States both United under Principle Defined in Terms of Field Intensity & Polarity; Featured Spkr, 14th Annual Meeting, Am Soc of Clin Hypnosis, 1971; Olive W Garvey Lectr, 5th Intl Conf on Human Functioning, 1981; Others; Cover Feature, *DukEngr*, 1951; Wks Translated into Spanish, May Issue *Archivos de Medicina Internacional*, 1952; Essay in *Main Currents in Mod Thought*, 1962; Mem, Pres's Com on the Handicapped, 1961-64; Diplomate, Am Bd of Psychi & Neurol; W/W in S & SW; Am Men of Sci; DIB; Other Biogl Listings.

RAY, C L oc/Texas State Supreme Court Justice; b/Mar 10, 1931; h/4800 Wild Briar Pass, Austin, TX 78745; ba/ Austin, TX; m/Janet Watson; c/Sue Ann Ray Culber, Robert E, Glenn, David Keller, Marcie Lynn, Ann Marie; p/C L Ray Sr (dec); sp/Marvin Watson, Texarkana, TX; ed/BBA, 1952, JD, 1957; mil/ USAF Resv, Lt Col; pa/Atty, Smith & Hall, Marshall, TX, 1957-60; Co Judge, Harrison Co, 1960-66; Ptner, Ray, Kirkpatrick, Grant, Dennis & Baxter, Marshall, TX 1966-70; Assoc Justice, Ct of Reps, 1966-70; Assoc Justice, Ct of Appeals, 1970-80; Justice, Supreme Ct of TX, 1980-; Mem: ABA; TX Bar Assn; Bd of Dirs, St Jr Bar Assn; VChm, Gen Pract Sect of TX Bar Assn; cp/JC's; Rotary Clb; Bd of Trustees, Wiley Col in Marshall; Scoutmaster, Chm of Dist, Bd of Dirs, Reg Prog Com Chm, Mem Nat Coun, BSA; r/Meth; hon/Grad, Nat Judicial Col, Univ of NE & Inst of Jud Adm, NY Univ; Outstg JC, 1960; Dist'd Eagle Scout, 1982; Silver Antelope & Beaver Awds; W/W: in Meth Ch, in Am Polits, in Am Law, in Am Govt, in TX, in S & SW.

RAY, SHIRLEY DODSON oc/Curriculum Director; b/Sep 20, 1929; h/Route 4, Box 186C, Robstown, TX 78380; ba/ Corpus Christi, TX; m/John Davis; c/Ellen Ray Stauffer, Daniel Dodson, John Andrew; p/P J Dodson (dec); Marjorie Dietz-Dodson, Austin, TX; sp/M C Ray (dec); Minnie Mugg Ray, Henderson, TX; ed/BA, Baylor Univ, 1950; MA, TX A&I Univ, 1964; pa/Curr Dir, Calellen ISD, 1978-; Conslt K-12, Ed Ser Ctr, Reg II, 1973-78; Coor for Elem Instrn, Corpus Chirsti ISD, 1970-73; Elem Math Conslt, 1966-70; Elem Tchr, Corpus Christi ISD, 1958-66; Adj Prof, Corpus Chrisit St Univ; NSF Tech Staff, TX A&I Univ; Metric Conslt for St; Mem: Nat Assn for Supvn & Curric; TX Assn for Supvn & Curric Devel; S TX Assn for Supvn & Curric Devel; Nat Coun of Tchrs of Math; Pres, TX Coun of Tchrs of Math; Pres, Coastal Bend Coun of Tchrs Math; TX Assn of Supvrs of Math; Assn of TX Profl Edrs; Phi Delta Kappa; r/Bapt; hon/Writer & Editor, Var Curric Pubs, Game Booklets & Activ Pamphlets; Outstg Edrs in Am; W/W in S & SW; Other Biogl Listings.

RAYMOND, EUGENE THOMAS oc/ Aircraft Engineer; b/Apr 17, 1923; h/ 25301-144 SE Kent, WA 98042; ba/ Seattle, WA; m/Bette Mae Bergeson; c/ Joan Kay Raymond Hibbs, Patricia Lynn,

Robin Louise; p/Mr and Mrs Evan J Raymond, San Diego, CA; sp/Mrs Arthur L Bergeson, Rogers, AR; ed/BSME, Univ of WA, 1944; mil/USNR, WW II, PTO, Lt; pa/Proj Design Engr, Gen Dynamics, 1963-66; Res Engr & Sr Grp Engr 1946-63, Sr Grp Engr, Sr Spec Engr & Prin Engr 1966-, Boeing Co; Mem: AIAA; Fluid Power Soc; Puget Soun Fluid Power Assn; Soc of Automotive Engrs Com A-6; Aerospace Fluid Power & Control Technologics; r/Luth; hon/Author, Over 20 Articles & Tech Papers, 1956-; Aircraft Edit Advy Bd, *Hydraulics & Pneumatics Mag*, 1960-70; Cert of Apprec, SAE Tech Bd, 1979; W/W in W.

RE, EDWARD DOMENIC oc/Federal Judge; b/Oct 14, 1920; h/305 Beach 147th Street, Neponsit, NY 11694; ba/New York, NY; m/Margaret Anne Corcoran; c/Mary Ann, Anthony John, Marina, Edward, Victor, Margaret, Matthew, Joseph, Mary Elizabeth, Mary Joan, Mary Ellen, Nancy Madeleine; p/Anthony and Marina (Maetta) Re; ed/BS 1941, LLB 1943, St John's Univ; JSD, NY Univ, 1950; Recip, Num Hon Degs; mil/USAF, 1943-47; pa/Instr of Law & Govt 1947-48, Law Prof 1951-69 (on leave 1961-69), Adj Prof 1969-, Dist'd Prof 1980-, St John's Univ; Prof Legal Aspects of Engrg, Pratt Inst, 1948-49; Vis'g Prof, Georgetown Univ Sch of Law, 1962-67; Adj Prof of Law, NY Law Sch, 1972-; Spec Hearing Ofcr, US Dept of Justice, 1955-61; Chm Fgn Claims Settlement Comm of US, 1961-68; Asst Secy St Ednl & Cultural Affairs, 1968-69; Judge 1969, Chief Judge 1977-, Chm Advy Com on Experimentation in Law, Fed Jud Ctr, 1978-; US Customs Ct; Chief Judge, US Ct of Intl Trade, 1980-; Mem 1958-69, Mem Emeritus 1969-, Bd of Higher Edn, NYC; Mem: Chm Sect Intl & Comparative Law 1965-67, Ho of Dels 1976-78, ABA; Bklyn Bar Assn; NYC Bar Assn; Pres, Am Fgn Law Assn, 1971-73; Pres, Fed Bar Coun, 1973-74; Pres, Am Soc Writers on Legal Subjects, 1978-79; Appellate Rules Advy Com 1976-, Jud Conf of US; Am Law Inst; Advy Com on Pvt Intl Law, US St Dept, 1981-; hon/Author, *Fgn Confiscations in Anglo-Am Law*, 1951; (w Lester B Orfield) *Cases & Mats on Intl Law*, Rev Edit, 1965; *Selected Essays on Equity*, 1953; *Brief Writing & Oral Argument*, 4th Rev Edit, 1977; *Cases & Mats on Equity*, 1967; *Equity & Equitable Remedies*, 1975; Contbr, Num Articles in Legal Jours; Col, Judge Advocate Gen's Dept (Ret'd); Decorated, Order of Merit, Italy; Recip, Bill of Rts Cit; Recip, Morgenstern Foun; Recip, Interfaith Awd; USAF Commend Medal; W/W: in World, in Am; Justices & Judges of US Cts.

READOUT, ROSALEE J oc/Instructor; b/Nov 24, 1936; h/2700 SE 27th Street Court, Choctaw, OK 73020; ba/ Choctaw, OK; m/David E; c/Judy Allene Ziller, Jerry Allen Stehman, Kathy L Potts; p/Floyd and Naomi King, W Liberty, OH; sp/Ellen D Readout, Council Bluffs, IA; ed/AA Med-mgmt, 1977; AA, 1978; BEd, CO St Univ, 1979; MBA Cand, Ctl St Univ; pa/Instr Bus & Ofc Ed, En OK AVC, 1982-; Clk-Typist Instr, Larimer Co AVC, 1978-82; Fashion Buyer/Coor, Joslins Dept Store, 1971-77; Ofcr Mgr, Owner, Stehman Distb'g Co, 1966-71; Underwriting Asst-Keypunch Operator, St Farm Ins Co, 1964-66; Mem: VPres Mbrship, OKC Chapt Intl Info/Word

Processing Assn & Intl Word Processing Specs, 1983; r/Prot; hon/Grad w 3.9 Avg, CO St Univ, 1979; W/W Am Wom.

REAVES, R LEE oc/Commisssion Director; b/Dec 10, 1909; h/400 North University # 713, Little Rock, AR 72205; ba/Conway, AR; m/Glenda Pittman; c/ Anne R Downs, Robin R Hawkins; p/Mr and Mrs B A Reaves (dec); sp/Mr and Mrs B A Pittman, Sparkman, AR; ed/AB, Univ of AR-Monticello; MA, Univ of AR-Fayetteville; pa/Fac, AR Sch for Blind, Little Rock AR, 1931-33; Supt of Schs, Hermitage, AR, 1936-51; Admr, Bradley Co Meml Hosp, 1951-53; Owner, Radio Sta KWRF, Warren, AR, 1953-59; VPres & Dir of Devel, Univ of AR-Monticello, 1959-63; Dir, AR Ed TV Netwk, 1963-; Mem: AR St Senator, 16 Yrs & Secy of AR St Senate, Past 18 Yrs; Phi Delta Kappa; Nat Assn of Ednl Broadcasters; Warren & Bradley Co Bds of Ed; cp/Bd Mem, Warren Industl Devel Comm; Stadium Comm, Little Rock; Past Pres, Warren C of C; VPres, Monticello C of C; Hon Doct Deg, Sioux Empire Col, IA; W/W in S & SW.

RECHNITZER, ANDREAS B oc/Technical Advisor to Oceanographer of the Navy; b/Nov 30, 1924; h/6368 Dockser Terrace, Falls Church, VA 22041; ba/Washington, DC; m/Martha Jeanne Mitchell; c/David Franklin, Andrea Jean, Martin Allan, Michael Jon; p/Ferdinand Martin & Dagmar Constance Rechnitzer (dec); sp/Frank and Ferol Mitchell; ed/BS, MI St Univ, 1947; MA, Univ of CA-LA, 1951; PhD, Univ of CA, Scripps Instn of Oceanography, 1956; mil/USN, Capt; pa/Res Assoc, Univ of CA, 1952-56; Deep Submergence Prog Coor, Nav Elects Lab, 1956-60; Dir Ocean Scis, N Am Aviation, 1960-70; Tech Advr, Chief of Nav Opers, 1970-; Mem: Fellow 1960-84, Chm Wash (DC) Sect of 1977, 1979 & 1981, Marine Technol Soc; Pres, Cedam Intl, 1967-76; VPres, Confedn Mondial Subacquatiques, 1961-68; VPres, Am Soc for Oceanography, 1967; Hon Life Mem, Nat Geographic Soc, 1960-; Hon Life Mem, Propellor Clb, 1960-; Num Other Positions & Consltgships; cp/Mem, NY Explorers, 1960-75; Cosmos Clb, Wash DC, 1971; Num Other Commun Activs; r/Prot; hon/Author, Num Articles & Papers in Profl Jours & Sci Pubs; Featured in Var Oceanography Books; Dir & Tech Advr, Var Motion Pictures; Disting Civilian Ser Awd, presented by Pres Eisenhower at White House, 1960; Richard Hopper Day Awd, Phila Acad of Scis, 1960; Gold Medal, Chgo Geographic Soc, 1960; Gold Medals, Underwater Photographic Soc; Num Other Awds & Hons; W/W: in West, in World, in Am Ed, in Underwater World; Am Men of Sci; DIB; Other Biogl Listings.

REDDY, CHADA S oc/Associate Professor of Toxicology; b/Nov 5, 1949; h/3205 Kohler Circle, Columbia, MO 65203; ba/Columbia, MO; m/Chaya C; c/Ramchandra C; p/Ramchandra C Sr (dec); Lalitha C Reddy, India; sp/Bhim D Reddy (dec); Ahalya D Reddy, India; ed/BVSc, AP Agri Univ, India, 1971; MS, AL A&M Univ, 1977; PhD, Univ of MS Med Ctr, 1980; pa/Vet Asst Surg, AP Dept of Animal Husbandry, India, 1972-73; Asst Prof Vet Preven Med, The OH St Univ, 1980-84; Assoc Prof Toxicology, Univ of MO-Columbia, 1984-; Mem: Am Vet Med Assn; Ctl OH Public Hlth Vet Assn; Assn of Am Vet Med Cols; hon/Author,

Var Articles Pub'd in Profl Jours; hon/ New Investigator Res Awd, Nat Inst of Dental Res, 1983-86; NIH Nat Res Ser Awd, 1978-80; W/W in Frontier Sci & Technol.

REDMOND, JOSEPH E oc/Executive; b/Apr 4, 1934; h/62 Longview Drive, Ridgefield, CT 06877; ba/Danbury, CT; m/Margaret R Redmond; c/Leslie, Jill C, Jan E; p/Thomas J and Mary A Redmond (dec); sp/Earl and Ruth Ash (dec); ed/BS, W Chester St Univ, 1962; Grad Sch, Univ of DE, 1962-65; mil/USN, 1956-57; pa/AI Dupont Schs HS Ec Tchr & Coach, Brandywine HS, 1962-66; Employmt Mgr, Atlas Chem Industs Inc, Wilmington, DE, 1966-70; Dir Employee Relats, Honeywell Info Sys Inc, Boston, 1970-72; Dir Pers Adm, PepsiCo Inc, Purchase, NY, 1972-77; Pres, J Redond & Assocs Inc, Danbury, CT, 1977-; Mem: Past Pres 1975-76, Employmt Mgmt Assn; Charter Mem, Nat Assn of Corp & Profl Recruiters; Am Mgmt Assn; Am Soc of Pers Admrs; cp/Danbury C of C; Am Legion; K of C; hon/Author, Anatomy of a Search-EMA Ref Guide, 1983; W/W: in E, in Fin & Indust.

REEB, RENE MARIE oc/Professor; b/ Dec 19, 1938; ba/2500 North State Street, Jackson, MS 39216; p/Conrad J Reeb III (dec); Kathryn John Dilliner Reeb, Belleville, IL; ed/BS, So IL Univ-Edwardsville, 1966; MN 1972, PhD 1981, Univ of MS; Nurse-Midwifery, Frontier Nsg Ser, 1968; Cert/Intern, Nurse-Midwifery, Downstate Med Ctr & Maternity Ctr Assn, 1969; pa/Staff Charge Nurse, St Elizabeth's Hosp, Belleville, IL, 1966-69; Staff Dist Nurse, Frontier Nsg Ser, Hayden, KY, 1968-69; Charge Nurse, Cénterville Twnshp Hosp, Centerville, IL, 1969; Nurse-Midwifery Clin Instr, 1969-72, Asst Prof & Dept Chm 1972-75, Assoc Prof Grad Prog 1977-, Univ of MS, Jackson, MS; Mem: Bd of Dir 1977-78, 1981-83, MS Nurses Assn; Chapt VPres 1979-80, Chapt Pres 1980-81, Am Col of Nurse-Midwives; ANA Coun on High Risk Perinatal Nsg; Nurses Assn of Am Col Ob & Gyn; Nat Leag Nsg; Intl Childbirth Edn Assn; Childbirth Edn Assn Netwk, Jackson, MS; r/Cath; hon/ Author, Var Nsg Articles in Profl Jours; Fac Medic Salute, Univ of MS, 1974; Phi Delta Kappa, 1981; W/W in S & SW.

REED, DAVID J oc/Optometrist, Bookstore Owner; b/Nov 6, 1944; h/602 Joyce Lane, Springfield, TN 37172; ba/ Springfield, TN; m/Janet Taylor; c/ Jennifer, Wesley; p/Katherine Walton, Nashville, TN; sp/Mr and Mrs H L Taylor, Elizabethton, TN; ed/Att'd Milligan Col, 1962-65; BS 1968, OD 1968, So Col of Optometry; mil/AUS, 1969-70, Vietnam, Capt; pa/Pvt Pract, Optometry, Springfield, TN, 1971-82; Owner, Springfield Optical Inc, 1981; Bookstore Owner, 1981-; Mem: Pres, Visual Perception, 1980; Bd of Dirs, TN St Optometric Assn, 1978-79; Pres, N Ctl Optometric Soc, 1981-82; Bd of Dir Sr Citizen Advy Coun, Am Optometric Assn; Phi Theta Upsilon; cp/Pres, Springfield Lions Clb, 1975; VCmdr, Am Legion Post 48, 1979-80; Scoutmaster, BSA, 1972-75; Robertson Co Mbrship Chm, GSA, 1981; r/Presb; hon/Eagle Scout; W/W in S.

REED, FRED WARREN oc/Professor, International Consultant; b/Sep 30, 1939; h/Sleeman Gulch, Lolo, MT 59847; m/ Susan Jane; c/Benjamin Ward; p/Fred W

and Norda R Reed, Billings, MT; sp/ Milton and Miriam Friedman, Clarks Green, PA; ed/BA, Univ of MT, 1965; MA 1970, PhD 1972, Univ of NC-Chapel Hill; mil/AUS, 1959-62; pa/Asst Prof Sociol, Univ of Chgo, 1972-75; Conslt for UNICEF Ethiopia 1975-76; Prof Sociol, Univ of MT, 1976-; Conslt, UNFPA Indonesia & Num Other Consltg Positions for Us Dept of ST, UNICEF, UNESCO & Many Countries, 1980-82; cp/City Coun of Missoula, MT, 1979-80; hon/Author, 2 Books: Pre-Testing Communs, 1974; Rejuvenating the Moribund Clin, 1974; Over 14 Articles & Reviews Pub'd in Profl Jours; Over 7 Papers Presented to Var Orgs & Confs; W/W in W.

REED, KATHLYN LOUISE oc/Chairperson and Professor; b/Jun 2, 1940; h/ 8800 Rolling Green, Oklahoma City, OK 73132; ba/Oklahoma City, OK; p/Herbert C Reed, Oklahoma City, OK; Ruth Krehbiel Reed (dec); ed/Att'd Univ of WI-Madison, 1958-61; BS, Univ of KS, 1964; MA, Wn MI Univ, 1966; PhD, Univ of WA, 1973; pa/Temp Supvr in Occupl Therapy, Vis'g Nurse Assn, Beloit, WI, 1964; Staff Occupl Therapist in Psychi, KS Univ Med Ctr, Kansas City, 1964-65; Student Tchr Occupl Therapy, Wn MI Univ, Kalamazoo, 1966; Acting Supvr Psychi Occupl Therapy, Univ of WA Hosp, Seattle, 1967; Occupl Therapy Instr 1967-70, Coor Grad Prog Occupl Therapy Dept of Phy Med & Rehab 1968-70, Field Ser Supvr Yth Ser Ctr 1971, Res Assoc & Conslt Exptl Ed Unit 1972-73, Univ of WA, Seattle; Vol Tutor, King Co Juv Ct, Yth Ser Ctr, Seattle, 1970; HEW Public Hlth Conslt, OH St Univ, 1970-71; Acting Instr Occupl Therapy, Univ of Puget Sound, Tacoma, WA, 1971; Chp & Assoc Prof Dept 1973-77, Chp & Prof 1977-, Dept Occupl Therapy, Univ of OK Hlth Scis Ctr; Conslt, Child Study Ctr, Oklahoma City, 1975-79; Conslt, OK St Dept of Hlth, 1976-77; Conslt in Orthopedically Handicapped, OK City Public Schs, 1980-81; Edit Bd, Occupl Therapy Jour of Res, 1981-82; Peer Review Panel for Rehab Res Engrg Ctrs, Nat Inst of Handicapped, 1983; Mem: Num Com Positions, Am Occupl Therapy Assn, 1964-; AAUP, 1981-; Treas, OK City Assn of Severely Handicapped, 1980-81; Am Soc of Allied Hlth Professions, 1980-; Am Assn for Higher Ed, 1980-; OK Coalition for Citizens w Disabilities, 1979-; OK Div, Coun for Exceptl Chd, Div for Chd w Lrng Disabilities, 1978-; Am Assn for Mtl Deficiency, 1973-; Am Assn for Ed of Severly/Profoundly Handicapped, 1978-; Num Other Orgs; cp/Num Univ of OK Coms; Num Other Commun Activs; hon/ Author, 2 Books: Models of Pract in Occupl Therapy, 1983; Concepts of Occupl Therapy, 2nd Edit, 1983; Over 15 Articles Pub'd in Profl Jours; Awd of Merit, AOTA, 1983; Fellow, Am Occupl Therapy Assn, 1975; Recip, HEW—RSA Traineeship, 1970-72; Elmer H Wild Awd, Wn MI Univ, 1966; W/W: of Am Wom, in S & SW, in Hlth Care; DIB; Commun Ldrs & Noteworthy Ams; Other Biogl Listings.

REEDY, THOMAS WAYNE oc/Minister; h/503 Northeast 23rd Street, Mineral Wells, TX 76067; ba/Same; m/ Kathleen Hethcock; c/Matthew, Thomas; p/Reba Juanita Reedy, Mineral Wells, TX; sp/Mr and Mrs Joe Krieg; ed/BA, Baylor Univ, 1977; MDiv 1980, DMin Cand

1983-, SWn Bapt Theol Sem; pa/Pastor, Cedar Sprgs Bapt Ch, 1976-78; Media Asst, Sagamore Hill Bapt Ch, 1977-80; Pastor, Bethel Bapt Ch, 1980-83; Chaplain, TX Dept of Mtl Hlth & Mtl Retard, Vernon Ctr, TX, 1983-; Pastor, Northside Bapt Ch, 1983-; Min & Student, 1983-; Mem: VPres Bd of Dirs, Hope Inc; cp/ Alpha Gamma Sigma; Public Relats Dir, Alpha Epsilon Chi; Treas, Zeta Phi Eta; PRSSA; Baylor Alumni Assn; US Judo Fedn; CA St Scholar; SCVA Hon Choir; r/So Bapt; hon/4.0 GPA DMin, SWn Bapt Theol Sem, 1981-; CA All-St Tenor, Lttrman; Bronze Medal, TX Intercol Judo Tour; Brown Belt; Dean's Hon Roll; Baylor Student Foun S'ship; Yg Commun Ldrs of Am.

REEPMEYER, MARIE CHRISTINA oc/Assistant Librarian; b/Oct 4, 1947; h/ 12 MacDonald Circle, Menands, NY 12204; ba/Albany, NY; p/Herman John and Marion Lula (Debien) Reepmeyer, Cohoes, NY; ed/AA, Stephens Col, 1967; BA, St Univ of NY-Buffalo, 1969; MLS, St Univ of NY-Albany, 1974; pa/Asst Libn, NY St Dept of Law, Albany, 1979-; Hd LEgal sers Libn, Legal Aid Soc, Albany, 1977-79; Wholesale Dir, We Care Mink Oil Prods, 1971-; Receptionist & Libn, Woodland Village Retirement Home, Troy, NY, 1977-80; Lib Aide, Mark Skinner Public Lib, Manchester, VT, 1976; Lib Aide, Cohoes Public & Tool Lib, 1970-71; Ctl Inlake Casewkr, Erie Co Dept of Social Sers, Buffalo, 1969-70; Mem: Corres'g Secy & Newslttr Typist & Editor 1980-82, Del at Cent Conv in Boston 1981, Teller NY St Div Conv 1983, Nom'g Com 1983-84, Albany Br, AAUW; Chm World Wk of Prayer 1982, Bd of Dirs Albany Br 1982-86, YWCA; r/Rom Cath; hon/Asst, Foun of Legal Sers Libns Newslttr, 1977; Study w 3rd Order Secular Carmelites (Pilgrimage to Fatima, Portugal), 1983; Life Mem, St Univ of NY Alumni Assn; W/W of Am Wom.

REESE, ANDREW JOEL oc/Attorney; b/May 5, 1945; h/249 West Gobbi Street #I, Ukiah, CA 95482; ba/Ukiah, CA; m/ Beatrix Pequeno; c/Elisabeth, Galen Coleman, Summersette Coleman; p/J H Reese (dec); Margaret Metcalf; sp/ Ernesto Hernandez (dec); Alicia Hernandez; ed/Hon-at-Entrance, Univ of So CA, 1963-64; BS, CA St Polytech Univ, Ponoma, 1972; JD, Harvard Univ, 1975; AS Bus & Real Est, Mendocino Col, 1979; mil/USAF, 1964-68; pa/Jr Field Engr, Philco-Ford Corp, 1969; Assoc, Pacht, Ross, Warne, Bernhard & Sears Inc Attys, 1975-76; Dept Dist Atty, Mendocino Co, 1976-79; Pract Atty, 1979 & 1981-; Ptner, Adams, Henderson & Reese Attys, 1980; Criminal Conflicts Atty, Mendocino Co, 1980-82; Mem: ABA, 1975-; CA St Bar Assn, 1975-; LA Co Bar Assn, 1975-76; Harvard Law Sch Alumni Assn, 1975-; Secy/Treas, Bd of Dirs, Mendocino Co Employees Fed Credit Union, 1974-75; Bd Mem 1979-80, Chm of Bd & Pres 1980-, Alcohol Rehab Corp; Interim Policy Advy Com, Mendocino Alcohol Proj, 1980; CA Dist Attys Assn, 1976-79; Mendocino Co Bd of Realtors, 1980; hon/W/W: in W, in Am, in World, in Fin & Indust.

REEVE, JACQUELINE ANNE oc/ Director of Nursing Service; b/Apr 10, 1951; h/PO Box 93, Jefferson, OH 44047; ba/Wickliffe, OH; p/James A and Thelma J Reeve, Jefferson, OH; ed/AA Nsg, Kent St Univ, 1971; Addit Ed, Kent St Univ & Cleveland St Univ; pa/Nsg Supvr,

Char-Lotte Nsg Home Inc, Rock Creek, OH, 1971-79; Tm Ldr, NEn OH Gen Hosp, N Madison, OH, 1979-80; Dir of Nsg, Con-Lea Nsg Home, Geneva, OH, 1980-81; Dir of Nsg, Good Samaritan Nsg Home Corp, E Peoria, IL, 1982; Dir Nsg Ser, Wickliffe Country Place, Wickliffe, OH, 1982-; Mem: Peer Review Surv Tm, OH Hlth Care Assn, 1981-; Cleveland Chapt, ACLU, 1971-; Nat Leag for Nsg, 1982-; Com for Dir of Nsg in Nsg Homes, Cleveland Area Citizens Leag, 1982-; Cleveland Area Citizenas Leag for Nsg, 1982-; Rescue Squad, Jefferson Vol Fire Dept, 1978-; r/Nondenom; hon/Nat Hon Soc, 1968; Quill & Scroll, 1969; W/W of Am Wom.

REEVE, DONALD CROPPER JR oc/ Executive, Corporate Chairman; b/Jan 29, 1943; h/1131 Hempstead Court, Westerville, OH 43081; ba/Columbus, OH; m/ Deborah Crooks; c/Heather Renee, Michael Scott, Thomas Adam; p/Ronald C and Aldus M Reeve, Columbus, OH; sp/Shirley Crooks, Winthrop Harbor, IL; ed/BSc, OH St Univ, 1967; MBA, Xavier Univ, 1972; mil/USAF, 1968-69; OH NG, 1965-68; pa/Chm 1982-, Pres & CEO 1979-82, Fdr, Adv'd Robotics Corp; Gen Mgr 1977-79, Mktg Mgr 1975-77, Prod Mgr 1974-75, Tektran Div Air Prods & Chems; Prod Planning Spec 1972-73, Prod Engr 1970-72, Proj Engr 1969-70, Devel Engr 1969, Gen Elect Co; Mem: Chm Chapt 5 Com AWS Handbook, Am Welding Soc, 1974-; Am Soc for Metals, 1975-; Soc of Mfg Engrs, 1981-; Robot Inst of Am, 1979-; Robotics Intl, CASA, 1982-; hon/Author, CAD/CAM Handbook, 1983; Var Articles in Profl Pubs & Papers to Orgl Confs; Small Bus Person of Yr, Small Bus Assn, 1981; W/W: in MW, in W.

REGAN, DONALD THOMAS oc/ White House Chief of Staff; b/Dec 21, 1918; ba/15th Street and Pennsylvania Avenue, Northwest Washington, DC 20220; m/Ann Gordon Buchanan; c/2 Sons, 2 Daughs; p/William F and Kathleen Regan (dec); sp/Mr and Mrs Buchanan (dec); ed/Att'd Harvard Col; mil/USMC, 1940-46, Lt Col; pa/Securities Exec, Merrill Lynch, Pierce Fenner & Smith Inc, 1946-81; Secy Dir & Adm Dir 1960-64, Exec VPres 1964-68, Pres 1968-71, Chm of Bd 1971-80, Chm Bd & CEO, Merrill Lynch & Co Inc, 1973-81; US Treas Secy 1981-85; Chief of Staff 1985-; Mem: Securities Investor Protection Corp, 1971-73; VChm Bd, NY Stock Exch, 1972-75; Bd Dirs, Beekman Downtown Hosp, 1969-73; Policy Com 1978-80, Bus Roundtalble; VPres Gov 1966-67, Investmt Bkrs Assn of Am; hon/Author, "A View from the Street," 1972; Fortune Mag's Hall of Fame for Bus Ldrship Awd, 1981.

REGAN, HELENE oc/International Banking Placement Specialist; b/Nov 12, 1938; h/4 Lexington, Avenue, New York, NY 10010; ba/Same; c/Scott Lawrence, Keith Martin, Andrea Beth; p/Abraham and Yetta Straussman; ed/Att'd Brandeis Study Grp; Att'g, Baruch Col, Currently; pa/Intl Bkg Placement Conslt to Intl Bkg Instns; Intl Bkg Placement Spec for Intl Bkg Opers, Fgn Exch & Money Mkt Traders, Fgn Exch & Money Mkt Brokers; hon/W/W of Am Wom, of Wom; Intl Book of Hon.

REGNIER, CLAIRE NEOMIE oc/ Business Consultant; b/May 2, 1939; h/ 7772 Woodridge, San Antonio, TX 78209;

ba/San Antonio, TX; m/James Lewis Pipkin Jr; p/Eugene Arthur and Claire J Regnier (both dec); ed/BS Jour, Trinity Univ, 1961; Lic'd, TX Real Est Broker; Pres, Metro Conslts, San Antonio, TX, 1981-, Exec Dir, San Antonio River (Paseo del Rio) Assn, 1968-81; Freelance Advtg & Public Relats Conslt, 1963-68; Mem: Intl Assn of Bus Communrs; Past VPres for Progs, Wom in Commun Inc; TX Public Relats Assn; TX Rec & Pks Soc; San Antonio Press Clb; Chm Var Coms 1977-83, Chm 1980-82, Centro 21 Downtown Revitalization Task Force, San Antonio; Mem San Antonio Pks & Rec Advy Bd, 1978-82; Rep, San Antonio River Corridor Com, 1976-82; cp/Mem, San Antonio & S TX Area Nat'l Kidney Foun Bd; Editor of Proceedings, VPres for Progs, Univ Roundtable; Coun on Intl Relats; Info Com, Altrusa Clb of San Antonio; Assoc Mem Var Coms, San Antonio Conserv Soc; Bd of Dirs 1977-82, Chm Public Relats Com 1971-82, Mem 1977-, San Antonio Area Coun GSA; Commr, Fiesta San Antonio Comm, 1970-81; VPres Pulic Relats, Nat Ldrship Conf 1982, Trin Univ Alumni Coun, 1973-76; hon/Editor & Pubr, Monthly Newspaper (20 pages & Circulation of 60,000); Contbr of Wkly Column, San Antonio Daily Metro Newspaper; Contbr, Num Articles to Var Area Mags; Awds of Excell for Editing Showboat 1970-74, Intl Assn of Bus Commrs, San Antonio Chapt; Pres's Cit for Outstg Ser as VPres for Public Relats, Trinity Univ Alumni Coun, 1976; Communr of Yr, Intl Assn of Bus Communrs, San Antonio Chapt, 1977; Hdliner Awd for Public Endeavor, Wom in Commun Inc, San Antonio Chapt, 1980; SW Reg Banner Awd for Excell in Commun, Wom in Commun Inc, 1981; W/W: of Am Wom, of S & SW; 2000 Dist'd Southerners; Outstg Yg Wom of Am; Intl Book of Hon; Other Biogl Listings.

REHBERG, IRENE LEE oc/Executive; b/Feb 22, 1946; h/20735 White Bark, Strongsville, OH 44136; ba/Medina, OH; m/John Thomas; c/Eric Lee; p/Kam Yee and Chan Heng (Ho) Lee, Strongsville, OH; sp/Jack Thomas and Mary Ellen (Lysaght) Rehberg, Cleveland, OH; ed/ BS, OH Univ-Athens, 1973; Addit Study, Lakeland Commun Col, 1973-75; pa/Res Asst to Dr Tong, OH Univ, Athens, 1971-73; Lang Instr (Chinese) 1973-77, Lakeland Commun Col; Res Chem 1973-78, Res & Devel Spec 1980, Fusion Inc; Profl Chem II, SCM Corp, 1977-78; Sr Dev Chem, Tremco Inc, 1978-80; Conslt 1982-, VPres & Dir 1980-, Elastic Mats Inc; r/Cath; hon/Author, Var Articles & Tech Papers Pub'd in Profl Jours & Presented at Assn Confs; S'ship Awds, Delta Phi Alpha German Hon Soc, OH Univ, 1971-73; Recip, US & Fgn Patents for Alumninum Single Component Brazing Paste, & Fluid Roof Coating; W/W of Am Wom.

REHFELD, DAWN ARLENE oc/Real Estate Broker; b/Feb 26, 1940; h/8417 Vicara Drive, Alta Loma, CA 91701; ba/ Arcadia, CA; m/Richard W; c/Dale Wallace, Dean Robert; p/Clinton L and Thelma E Ward, New Westminster, BC, Canada; sp/Edwin R and Ivy D Rehfeld (dec); ed/BA Real Est, La Verne Univ, 1970; Grad Wk, Univ of So CA, 1980-81; pa/Adm Asst to Exec VPres, FBC, 1970; Music Dept Hd, EMC Schs, 1972; Real Est Assoc, 1978; Assoc, Real Est Broker,

1981-; Mem: CA Assn of Rltrs (CAR), 1979-; Nat Assn of Rltrs (NAR), 1979-; Wom in Real Est (WIRE), 1982-; cp/Repub Wom Clbs, 1981-; Thauma Clb, 1968; r/ Prot; hon/Author, Var Articles Pub'd in *Mess Mag*; Thauma Awd of Excell, 1970; Music Voc Awd, FL St Col, 1969 & 1970; Gold Med Voc Sts, 1972; Spec Recog, 1975-79; Sales Awds, 1980-81, 1982; W/ W of Am Wom.

REICH, PAULINE C oc/Equal Opportunity Specialist, Asia Specialist; b/Nov 13, 1946; ba/Office for Civil Rights, US Department of Education, 26 Federal Plaza, New York, NY 10278; m/Brian Poon; p/Stanley G Reich (dec); Elsa Reich, Forest Hills, NY; sp/Hing-Shun Poon, Hong Kong; Lam-Tai (Chu) Poon (dec); ed/Cert Crit Langs, Princeton Univ, 1967; BA, City Col of NY, 1968; MA, CUNY, 1972; CORO Foun Public Affairs Ldrship Prog, NYC, 1981; JD Cand, NY Law Sch, 1981-; pa/Tchr Adult Indochinese Refugee Prog, NYC Bd of Ed, 1970-72, 1974-76, 1977-81; Instr: Isuada Col, Tokyo Wom's Christian Col Jr Col, Chuo Univ, Sophia Univ Intl Div Tokyo, Japan, 1972-74; Owner, Pvt Inst for Japanese Execs, NYC, 1974-76; Career Devel Conslt, Babel/Lau Ctr, Berkeley, CA, 1976-77; Equal Opportunity Spec, Post Sec'dy Ed Div, Ofc for Civil Rts, US Dept of Ed, NYC, 1978-; Mem: E Coast Dir 1981-, Nat Dir-elect, Indep Scholars of Asia (Affil Assn for Asian Studies); Chair, Intl Comparisons Com, Coun on Mun Perf, NYC, 1981-82; Japan Soc NYC; Assn for Asian Studies; Asia Soc NYC; CORO Assocs; ABA; Wom's Ec Roundtable; Wom's City Clb NYC; hon/Author, Num Articles on Japanese & Indochinese Lang, Lit, Employmt, Bus & Govt; Princeton & Carnegie Foun F'ship, Princeton Univ, 1966-67; NDEA Fellow, 1966-67; Japan Foun Fellow, Tokyo, 1973; W/W of Am Wom.

REICHLE, FREDERICK ADOLPH oc/ Vascular Surgeon, Professor; b/Apr 20, 1935; h/771 Easton Road, Warrington, PA 18976; ba/Philadelphia, PA; p/Albert and Ernestine Reichle (dec); ed/BA Col of Arts 1957, MD Sch of Med 1961, MS Biochem Sch of Med 1961, MS Surg Sch of MEd 1966, Temple Univ; Intern, Abington Meml Hosp, 1962; Residency, Temple Univ Hosp, 1966; pa/Chm Dept of Surg, Surg, Presb-Univ of PA Med Ctr; Prof Surg, Univ of PA; Assoc Att'g Surg, Epis Hosp; Assoc Att'g Surg, St Christopher's Hosp for Chd; Assoc Att'g Surg, Phoenixville Hosp; Conslt, Vets Hosp, Wilkes-Barre, PA; Conslt, The Germantown Dispensary & Hosp; Conslt, St Mary's Hosp; Mem: Am Surg Assn; Soc of Univ Surgs; Spec Site Visitor, Residency Review Com for Surg, Liaison Com on Grad Med Edn 1979, AMA; PA Med Soc; Am Soc of Contemp Med & Surg, 1981; The Royal Soc of Med, 1980; DE Val Vascular Soc, 1979; Am Col of Angiology, 1979; Am Inst of Ultrasound in Med, 1979; Am Physiol Soc, 1979; Fellow, The Col of Phys of Phila, 1979; Societe Internationale De Chirurgie, 1978; Surg Hist Soc, 1978; Sociedad De Cirujanos De Chile, 1982; Intl Cardiovas Soc, 1981; Assn of Prog Dirs in Surg; The Soc of Vascular Surg, 1977; Am Aging Assn; Surg Biol Clb; Am Diabetes Assn; Fellow, Am Col of Surgs, 1970; Sigma Xi, 1961; NY Acad of Scis, 1968; AAAS, 1968; Phil Acad of Surg, 1971; Num Other Orgs; cp/Site Visitor, Can-

adian Dept of Hlth & Welfare Progs Br, 1977; Lectures & Forums Com, Med Fac Senate, 1976-79; Spec Site Visitor, Inspection for Continuation of Gen Surg Residency Tng Prog, 1980; hon/Author, Over 80 Res Articles Pub'd in Profl Jours Inc'g: "Current Mgmt of the Hemorrhaging Cirrhotic Patient," *PA Med*, 1979; "Hemodynamic Patterns in Human Hepatic Cirrhosis: A Prospective Randomized Study of the Hemodynamic Sequelae of Distal Splenorenal (Warren) & Mesocaval Shunts," *Annals of Surg*, 1979; Others; Contbr, Over 9 Book Chapts Incl'g: "The Biol Fate of Arterial Grafts," & "Deterioration of Vein Grafts," in *Complications in Vascular Surg*, 1980; Contbr, Over 75 Astracts to Profl Jours, 1967-; Author, Over 125 Paper Presentations to Profl Orgs, Assns & Univs, 1961-; Var Conf Presentations Incl'g The 6th Annual Med Surg Conf of the Dept of Surg, Col of Phys, 1979; Full Tuition Competitive S'ship, Temple Univ, 1953; Nathan Lane Awd for Highest Student Achmt in Chem, Temple Univ, 1957; Col of Liberal Arts Grad Awd, Temple Univ, 1957; Grad summa cun laude, Temple Univ, 1957; F'ship in Nutrition, AMA Sum Med Sch, 1961; St Res Awd, Temple Univ Med Sch, 1961; Surg Res's Res Paper Awd, Phila Acad of Surg, 1966 & 1967; Gross Essay Prize, Phila Acad of Surg; Estab'd Investigatorship Grant, Am Heart Assn, 1973; Omega Alpha; W/W: in Am, in E, in Hlth Care, of Intells; DIB; Dir of Med Specs; Men of Achmt; Am Patriots of the 1980's; Num W/W, & Other Biogl Listings.

REID, JOHN KENNETH oc/Clinical Psychologist, Administrator; b/May 30, 1945; h/625 Morningside, San Antonio, TX 78209; ba/San Antonio, TX; p/Mr and Mrs Kenneth M Reid, Tulsa, OK; ed/BS 1967, MS 1971, PhD 1975, OK St Univ; Intern, Univ of TX Hlth Scis Ctr, 1975; pa/Psychol Assoc, OK Dept of Instrn, Social, & Rehab Sers, 1970-72; Tchg Asst, OK St Univ, 1972-73; Admn Asst, Psych Guid Clin, 1974; Resident Clin Psych 1974-75, Clin Asst Prof 1976-, Univ of TX Hlth Scis Ctr; Dir Psych Sers Admissions Unit 1975-77, Dir Psych Tng 1977-79, Dir Adolescent Psych 1979-, Asst Chief Psych 1977-, San Antonio St Hosp; Pvt Pract, 1975-; Adj Asst Prof, Trinity Univ, 1976-; Mem: Pres 1979-80, Bexar Co Psychol Assn; Pres Applied Div 1981-82, Chm Local Affairs 1978-79, Liaison Ofcr for Public Affairs 1982-85, TX Psychol Assn; cp/Bd Mem, Psych Cent Clb, 1982-85; Advy Bd, U Way Crisis Ctr, 1978-80; Bd of Trustees, San Antonio Free Clin 1979-81; Bd of Dirs, Halfway House, 1979-82; Bd of Dirs, Yth Alternatives, 1981-83; hon/Author, Psychol Articles Pub'd in Profl Jours & Presented at Convs & Spkg Presentations; Regents S'ship, OK St Univ, 1963; NIMH Spec Merit Awd, 1974; Ldrship Awd, San Antonio, 1982; Outstg Yg Men of Am; W/W in S & SW.

REID, NINA B oc/Utah County Recorder; b/Jul 7, 1933; h/280 East 300 South, Springville, UT 84663; ba/Provo, UT; m/Omer Arthur; c/Terry, Kim, Wendy Reid Hill; p/Royal Barney (dec); Lillie Barney, Springville, UT; sp/Omer H Reid, Springville, UT; Cecil Reid (dec); ed/Att'd Brigham Yg Univ; pa/UT Co Recorder, 1969-; Lady VPres 1974-75, Bd of Dirs 1975-76 & 1980-84, Secy Hum Sers Legis Com 1978-80, UT Assn of Cos; Pres, UT Assn of Co Recorders, 1980-81;

Election Com 1979-80, Land Records Com 1979-81, Chm 'Nat Land/Title Records Com 1982-, Nat Assn of Recorders & Clks; Del 4 Yrs, Corres'g Secy 2 Yrs, UT Co Wom's Legis Coun; Chm, Mtnlands Area Agy Coor Coun on Aging (Wasatch, Summit & UT Cos), 1975-79; Bd Mem 1978-, Pres Ctl UT Chapt 1982-83, Am Soc for Pulic Admrs; UT St Cadastral Mapping Cert Com; UT St Plat Standards Com; UT Co Boundary Commr, 1979-; Bd of Dirs, Mtl Hlth Assn of UT Co, 1980-83; UT St Human Resource Steering Com, 1979-81; Num Other Co & St Coms; cp/Num Positions, Springville Civic & Fed'd Fairs Bien Clb; Past Mem, Springville Coor Coun; Past Pres, Springville City Coun of Clb Pres; Past Mem, Springville Art Bd; Past Secy, Com on Chd & Yth; 2nd VPres, Nebo 1st Dict Fed'd Wom's Clbs; r/LDA (Mormon); hon/Recip, Nat Achmt Awd for Co Records Storage Prog, 1979; Recip, Nat Achmt Awd for Automated Land Recors Mgmt Sys, 1980; Recip, UT Assn of Co Ofcls Cert of Recog, 1978, 1981 & 1982; Recip, UT St Outstg Co Ofcls Awd, 1982; Recip, Outstg Yg Wom of Am Awd, 1965; Var Indiv & Ch Ldrship Awds.

REILLY, DOROTHY PRICE oc/ Instructional Facilitator; b/Aug 2, 1950; h/901 North Washington Street, Sylvester, GA 31791; ba/Sylvester, GA; m/ Joseph M; c/Martha Lucinda; p/Mr and Mrs Glen Price Sr, Wrightsville, GA; sp/ R J Reilly, Columbus, GA; ed/AA, Norman Col, 1970; BS 1972, MEd 1980, GA SWn Col; pa/Tchr, Gwinnett Co Bd of Ed, 1972-74; Tchr 1978-79, Title I Instrnl Supvr 1979-80, Elem Instrnl Facilitator 1981-, Worth Co Bd of Ed; Mem: GA Assn of Edrs; Nat Assn of Edrs; Worth Assn of Edrs; cp/Sylvester Jr Woms Clb; hon/Gamma Beta Phi Soc, 1971-.

REISMAN, JUDITH oc/Research Professor; ba/The American University, School of Education, 5010 Wisconsin Avenue, Northwest, Washington, DC 20016; ed/BA (Waived in Lieu of Profl Mass Media Experience) 1975, MA Spch Commun 1976, PhD 1980, Case Wn Resv Univ; pa/Res Prof Sch of Ed, Proj Dir & Prin Investigar Ofc of Juv Justice & Delinq Preven 1983-, Res in Media Sociol, Dept of Anthropology/Sociol 1981-83, The Am Univ, Wash, DC; Mem: AAAS; Am Assn of Composers, Authors & Pubrs; Am Fedn of TV & Recording Artists; Intl Commun Assn; NY Acad of Scis; OH Acad of Sci; The Hastings Ctr/ Inst of Soc, Ethics & the Life Scis; World Assn of Infant Psychi; r/Jewish; hon/ Author, Books Forthcoming: *A Scholarly Exam of the Kinsey Experiments on Child Sexuality*; *From Shirley Temple to Pretty Baby: The Journey of the Child*; Author/Co-Author, Num Articles Pub'd in Profl Jours; Num Lectrs, Symps, Confs & Sems on Men & Wom, Pornography, Rape, Violence, Media Influences on Chd, Sexuality, Marriage & Other Topics; Composer, Num Orig Songs & Media Mats for NBC-TV, Cleveland, OH; "Capt Kangaroo," CBS-TV; *Scholastic Mag*; Others; Recip Num Awds for Sound Filmstrip Series "Families," Incl'g: Dukane Annual Awd for Outstg Creat in Sound Filmstrip Prodn, " 1982; 1st Place Gold Camera Awd for "Making Rules," Industl Film Fest, 1982; 2nd Place Gold Camera Awd for "Lrng," Industl Film Fest, 1982; Bst Film, Filmstrip of Yr, *Lrng Mag*, 1981-82;

Silver Plaque Awd for "Making Rules," Intl Commun Fam Video Competition, 1982; Emmy Nom for Public Ser Spot "Pride in Country," NBC-TV, Cleveland, OH, 1976; 1st Place Winner for Local TV Series, 13th Public Relats Competition, Jewish Fam Ser, Fam Ser Assns, 1974; Best of 1965, Les Claypool, KPFC Pacifica, LA, CA, Best Songs Written in 1965; Dir of Dist'd Ams; 2000 Notable Ams; Intl Book of Hon.

REISMAN, SCOTT oc/Psychologist; b/Oct 9, 1951; h/Box 17324 Ft Lauderdale, FL 33318; ba/Ft Lauderdale, FL; m/Susan Greenberg Levy; p/Emanuel and Myra Reisman (both dec); sp/Irving Greenburg (dec); Judith Levy, Ft Lauderdale, FL; ed/BGS, OH Univ, 1974; MS 1977, MS 1980, Nova Univ; pa/Mtl Hlth Wkrs, Dade Co, FL, 1974-77; Prog Evalr, Nova Clins Inc, 1979-81; Adj Fac, Nova Col, 1981; Clin Assoc, Alan A Jaffe PhD & Assocs, Ft Lauderdale, FL, 1981-; Mem: Am Psychol Assn; Soc of Behavioral Med; Assn for Advmt of Behavior Therapy; FL Psychol Assn; Biofeedback Soc of Am; r/Jewish; hon/W/W in Frontier Sci & Technol.

REMICK, OSCAR EUGENE oc/College President; b/Aug 24, 1932; h/313 Maple Street, Alma, MI 48801; ba/Alma, MI; m/Emma L; c/Mark Stephen, John Andrew, Paul Thomas; p/Horace W Remick, Alma, MI; Blanche Rich Remick (dec); sp/Ezra L and Bufie H Lorance, Mineral Sprgs, AR; ed/AB, En Col of St Davids, 1954; BD, En Bapt Theol Sem, 1957; MA, Univ of PA, 1957; PhD, Boston Univ Grad Sch, 1966; pa/Instr, En Bapt Theol Sem, 1955-57; Min, U Bapt Ch, Topsham, ME, 1961-63; Instr, Bates Col, 1962-63; Min, Univ Ch of Christ, Paxton, MA, 1963-66; Prof 1966-69, Acad Dean & VPres 1968-71, Assumption Col; Pres Chautauqua Instn, Chautauqua, NY, 1971-77; Prof, St Univ of NY-Fredonia, 1977-80; Pres, Alma Col, Alma, MI, 1980-; Mem: Co-Fdr/Dir/Mem, Ecumenical Inst of Rel Studies, 1967-; MA Conf U Ch of Christ, 1963-71; VPres & Pres, Worcester Area Coun of Chs, 1969-71; cp/Dir & VPres, Jamestown YMCA, 1971-72; Dir, 1st Nat Bk, Jamestown, NY, 1972-77; Dir & VPres, Fredonia YMCA, 1978-80; Pres, Am Friends of the Jerusalem Soc for World F'ship, 1979-; Dir, Bk of Alma, MI, 1981-; Mem 1981-, Chm 1983, MI Coun for the Arts; r/Prot; hon/Author of Var Articles in Profl Jours Incl'g: *Mission; Inspection News*; Book: *Responding to God's Call*, 1970; Book Chapt: in *Chautauqua: A Ctr for Ed, Rel & the Arts in Am*, 1974; Fulbright Grant, 1958; Fulbright F'ship, 1967; Outstg Yg Man of MA, 1967; DD, Assumption Col, 1971; DD, Allegheny Col, 1974; W/W: in Am, in World; DIB; Outstg Edrs.

RENDER, SYLVIA LYONS oc/Consultant, Lecturer, Writer, Researcher; b/Atlanta, GA; h/6429 Princeton Drive, Alexandria, VA 22307; ed/BS Eng & Ed, TN A&I St Univ, 1934; MA, OH St Univ, 1957; PhD, George Peabody Col for Tchrs, 1967; Addit Grad Study; pa/Var Clerical & Profl Posts in St & Fed Agys & Newspaper Reporter, Columnist & Editor, Columbus OH, 1934-50; Dir of Out-of-St S'ship Aid Prog, Instr, Asst Prof, Assoc Prof & Prof Eng, FL A&M Univ, Tallahassee, 1950-62; Prof Eng, NC Ctl Univ, Durham, 1964-75; Guest Prof, George Peabody Col for Tchrs, Nashville, 1970; Conslt: Ford Foun, The Macmillan Co, So Assn of Cols & Schs, Nat

Endowment for the Humanities, George Wash Univ, Nat Urban Leag; Conductor: Wkshops in Afro-Am Lit, Durham Co Bd of Ed & Ldrship Dept, AUS Inf Sch Ft Benning GA; Manuscript Histn, Spec in Afro-Am Hist & Culture, Manuscript Div, The Lib of Cong, Wash, DC, 1973-82; Conslt, Lectr, Writer & Researcher, 1983-; Mem: Del Assem 1975-77, MLA; Nat Com 1970, 1971 & 1972, NCTE; S Atl MLA; Col Lang Assn; Soc for the Study of So Lit; Assn for the Study of Afro-Am Life & Hist; Lib of Cong Profl Assn; Assn for Documentary Editing; Charter Mem, Afro-Am Hist & Geneal Soc; Fdr & Past Pres, Lib of Cong Daniel A P Murray Afro-Am Culture Clb; Num Spkng Presentations, Var Univs & Orgs; cp/YMCA; YWCA; NAACP; Nat Urban Leag; Cub Scouts; Alpha Kappa Alpha Sorority; ARC; Local Chapts of UN Orgs; Durham Coun on Human Relats; Hopkins House, Alexandria VA; Var Cub Grps; hon/Author, Over 10 Articles in Profl Jours; Editor of Book, *The Short Fiction of Charles Chesnutt*, 1974 & 1981; Author of Book, *Charles W Chesnutt*, 1980; Anderson-Billy Hale Medal 1932, Alpha Kappa Alpha S'ship 1933, Phi Beta Tau (Alpha Kappa Mu) 1934, Class Valedictorian 1934, TN A&I Univ; Mary Mildred Sullivan Awd 1960, Kappa Delta Pi 1960, George Peabody Col S'ship 1960-61, So Ed Foun F'ships 1960-67, George Peabody Col; Sum Aws, Am Philosophical Soc, 1965; Grants, NC Ctl Univ Fac Res Com, 1966, 1969; Outstg Edrs of Am, 1972 & 1973; Felow Coop Prog in Humanities, Duke Univ & Univ of NC-Chapel Hill, 1961-68; Ford Foun Res & Writing Grant, 1970; Sr F'ship for Indep Study & Res, Nat Endowment for the Humanities, 1973; Outstg Ldrship & Contbn to Excell in Ed, Theta Allpha Chapt, Kappa Delta Pi, 1978; Vis'g Prof Black Exch Prog, Nat Urban Leag, 1980; Outstg Wom of Yr, NAACP, 1980; Participant, Inst for Editing of Hist Documents, Nat Hist Pubs & Records Comm, Univ of WI-Madison, 1981; Alumna of Yr, TN St Univ, 1982; Superior Ser Awd, Lib of Cong, 1982; W/W: of Wom, Among Black Ams, in S & SW, in Am Ed; Outstg Edrs of Am; DIB; Living Black Am Authors; Other Biogl Listings.

RENDON, LAURA I oc/College Administrator; b/Jul 31, 1948; h/517 Galveston, Laredo, TX 78040; ba/Laredo, TX; p/Leopoldo and Clementina Rendon, Laredo, TX; ed/AA, San Antonio Col, 1968; BA, Univ of Houston, 1970; MA, TX A&I Univ, 1975; PhD, Univ of MI, 1982; pa/Dir Nat Intervention Project, Border Col Consortium 1981-, Dir Coor'd Bilingual-Bicultural Studies 1975-79, Laredo Jr Col; Eng & Rdg Tchr, Laredo ISD, 1970-75; Mem: Am Assn of Commun & Jr Cols, 1983; Nat Chicano Res Netwk, 1983; Bd, Alternative Films, 1983; r/Cath; hon/Author, "Chicano Students in S TX Commun Cols: A Study of Student & Instn Related Determinants of Edl Outcomes," 1982; Var Articles in ERIC Clearinghouse for Commun Cols; Dissertation of Yr, Univ of MI Div of Higher Adult & Cont'g Ed, 1983; Appt'd Nat Bd of ERIC Clearinghouse for Commun & Jr Cols, 1983; W/W in TX Ed; TX A&I Alumni Dir.

RENO, JOHN F oc/Business Executive; b/Jun 5, 1939; h/31 Prospect Street, Winchester, MA 01890; ba/Burlington, MA; m/Suzanne McKnight; c/David

Findley, Anne McKnight; p/Alice F Reno; Macomb, IL; sp/David W McKnight, So Dartmouth, MA; ed/AB, Dartmouth Col, 1961; MBA, NWn Univ, 1963; mil/USAF; pa/Investmt Bk, G H Walker & Co, 1964-74; Pres, Dynatech Cryomed Co, 1974-77; VPres Corp Devel 1977-81, Grp VPres 1981-, Dynatech Corp; Mem: MA High Tech Coun, Currently; cp/Fdr & Dir, Winchester ABC, 1971-78; Dir, Winchester Savs Bk, Currently; Dir, Winchester Hosp, Currently; Dir, Mt Vernon Home, Currently; Small Bus Roundtable Syn, 1968-75; r/Unitarian; hon/Author, *Japanese Security Mkts*, 1963; Most Dist'd Grad Student in Fin, NWn Univ, 1963; Dist'd Yg Ams, C of C, 1972; W/W in Fin & Indust.

REYNOLDS, RICHARD SAMUEL III oc/Executive; b/Aug 8, 1934; h/309 Stockton Lane, Richmond, VA 23221; ba/Richmond, VA; m/Pamela Coe; c/Richard Samuel IV, Anne Brice, Katherine Louise; p/Richard S Reynolds Jr; sp/Robert and Dell Coe; ed/Att'd Woodberry Forest Sch, 1948-52; Att'd Princeton Univ, 1952-56; pa/Asst to Chm, Asst VPres, VPres & Dir, Robertshaw Controls Co, Richmond, VA; cp/Chm, Richmond Area, U Givers Fund Campaign, 1974; Fund Raising Chm, Richmond Area Mtl Hlth Assn, 1972; Chm, U Negro Col Fund Campaign, 1982; Bd of Dirs, Robert E Lee Coun BSA; Reynolds Homestead Advy Com; Nat Cont of Christians & Jes; Elected Ho of Dels, St of VA, 1975; r/Presb; hon/Bd of Trustees, VA Union Univ; Bd of Assocs, Univ of Richmond.

RHINEHART, DOUGLAS ARTHUR oc/Rehabilitation Services Administrator; b/Apr 19, 1942; h/600 Regional Court, 2-A, Flemington, NJ 08822; ba/Trenton, NJ; c/Andrea; p/Arthur Isaac and Ethel Oglesby Rhinehart (dec); ed/BA, LA Col, 1966; MSW, Rutgers Univ, 1977; pa/Peace Corps Vol, Am Peace Corp Rajkot, Gujaret, India, 1966-67; Voc Cnslr, Total Commun Action Inc, NO, LA, 1968; Asst Field Dir, Am Nat Red Cross, Osan AB, S Korea, 1968-70; Spec'd Asst to Dist Supt of Schs, Orleans Parish Sch Bd, NO, LA, 1970-71; Mktg Spec 1972-76, Prog Planning & Devel Spec 1976-, NJ Dept of Labor, Trenton, NJ; r/Luth; hon/Author, *Tng Guide for Rehab Profls*, 1980; *Wk Adjustment, Job Exploration & Job Seeking Skills: A Guide for Grp Ldrs*, 1981; Author, Var Articles; Nom Margaret Fairbairn Awd, Recog'g Indiv Achmt in Job Placement of Disabled, 1975; W/W: in E, of Intells; NASW Dir; Men of Achmt; DIB; Other Biogl Listings.

RHODES, DONALD FREDERICK oc/Research Physicist; b/Jul 1, 1932; h/439 Trestle Road, Pittsburgh, PA 15239; ba/Pgh, PA; m/Patricia J; p/Fred D Rhodes (dec); Irene M Rhodes, Somerset, PA; sp/Jules and Roberta Beaumariage; ed/Dipl, DeVry Tech Inst, 1951; BS 1954, MS 1956, Univ of Pgh; PhD, Pacific Wn Univ, 1982; mil/USN, 1958; USNR, 1958-65; pa/Res Asst Cyclotron Accelerator Lab 1953-54, Physics Instr Elect Measurements 1955, Univ of Pgh; Jr Engr, Ultrasonic Applications, Westinghouse Elec Corp, 1956-57; Physicist Nuclear Applications Sct Phy Sci Div 1958-65, Fdr Neutron Activation Anal Prog 1960, Co-Devlr Gulf Hydrogen Analyzer 1962-65, Res Physicist Chem Physics Sect Phy Sci Div 1966-73, Orgr of Radiation Protection Prog 1966, Chm Radionuclide Com 1966-68, Co-Devlr Guld Sulfur

Analyzer 1968-, Grp Ldr Nuclear Techniques Grp Anal Tech Dept 1973-79, Sr Res Physicist Elements Anal Sect Anal Tech Dept 1975-79, Develr Static Charge Reducer for Flowing Jet Fuel Streams 1975-76, Sr Proj Engr Elect & Measurements & Anal Instrumentation Sects Sys & Controls Dept 1979-, w Gulf Res & Devel Co; Pt-time Instr, Univ of Pgh, 1975-; Profl Radiotelephone Operator, Flight Instr for Var Aircraft, Ground Instr, & Pilot, Lic'd by Fed Aviation Adm, 1959-82; Mem: Lectr Pgh Sect for Ed of Sci Tchrs 1969, Am Nuclear Soc; Audit Com 1981, Ed Com 1982, Nom Com 1983, Wn PA Hlth Physics Soc; Cochm, Am Nuclear Soc & Hlth Physics Soc Jt Symp on Hazardous Waste Mgmt, 1982; Am Aircraft Owners & Pilots Assn; AF Assn, 1975; Aero Clb of Pgh, 1975; r/ Prot; hon/Author & Contbr, Over 15 Pub'd Articles to Profl Jours & Sci Book Pubs; Recip, 7 US Patents in Field; Industl Res IR-100 Awd for Sulfur Analyzer, 1968; Conslt Nuclear Technol, US Govt, 1973; Chm Interprofl Relatship Com, WN PA Hlth Physics Soc, 1977; Accident Preven Cnslr, Fed Aviation Adm, 1981-; Conslt on SRC Radotracer Tests, Exxon Co, 1981; W/W in Frontier Sci & Technol.

RICE, DOROTHY P oc/Medical Economist, Professor; b/Jun 11, 1922; h/1055 Amito Avenue, Berkeley, CA 94705; ba/ San Francisco, CA; m/John D; c/Kenneth D, Donald B, Thomas H; p/Gershon Pechman, Riverdale, NY; ed/Att'd Bklyn Col, 1938-39; BA, Univ of WI, 1941; pa/ Statl Clk, US Dept of Labor, 1941-42; Economist, War Prodn Bd, 1942-44; Labor Economist, US War Labor Bd, 1945-47; Hlth Economist, USPHS, 1947-49; Anal 1960-65, Dept Asst Commr for Res & Stats 1965-72, Soc Security Adm, Wash, DC; Dir, Nat Ctr for Hlth Stats, Hyattsville, MD, 1976-82; Regent's Lectr, Univ of CA-SF, 1982-; Mem: APHA; Am Statl Assn; Inst of Med/ Nat Acad of Scis; Am Ec Assn; Am Public Welfare Assn; AAUW; cp/Leag of Wom Voters; r/Jewish; hon/Author, Over 100 Articles in Profl Jours on Med Ecs, Cost of Illnes & Hlth Stats; Hon SCD, Col of Med & Dentistry of NJ, 1979; Pres Sr Exec Meritorious Awd, 1982; Asst Secy for Hlth Spec Recog Awd, 1982; Jack C Massey Awd for Achmt in Hlth Sers, 1978; Domestic Awd for Excell, APHA, 1978; W/W: in W, of Am Wom.

RICE, MARIE WALRATH oc/Retired; b/Apr 11, 1917; h/12220 5th Street #175, Yucaipa, CA 92399; ba/Same; m/Seward Nelson (dec); p/Milton Jane and Charlotte (McDonald) Walrath (dec); sp/Charles Irving and Flora (Geer) Rice (dec); ed/ Att'd Citrus Comm Col & Mt San Antonio Col; Grad, Nat Floral Inst, 1963; Att'd, Chgo Sch Restaurant Mgmt, 1963 & Inst of Broadcasting Arts, 1963; pa/ Jr Acct, Lux Clock Mfg Co, Waterbury, CT, 1939-43 & 1945-51; Acct, Pacific Telephone & Telegraph Co, Pomona, CA, 1944-45 & 1951-63; Supvr of Communs, Pacific St Hosp, Pomona, CA, 1964-72; Treas/Mgr, LA Grange Fed Credit Union, San Dimas, CA, 1974-81; Relief Mgr, Dallas Travelodge, Dallas, TX, 1982; Mem: Ret'd Public Employees' Assn, CA; Am Assn Ret'd Persons; Nat Assn Deaf; CA St Employees Assn; cp/Middlebury Grange, Middlebury, CT, 1950; San Dimas Grange, San Dimas, CA; San Dimas Subordinate Master, 1961; LA Co Pomona Grange Master, 1975; Reg Supt

of Jr Granges in CA, St Grange Dist 4, 1972-76; Jr Dir, CA St Grange, 1977-80; Dept St Master, CA St Grange, 1978; Orgr & 1st Pres, Grangers 7th; Deg Clb #3 for LA Co, 1968-71; Good Sam Recl Vehicle Clb; Commend of Sers, City of San Dimas, CA, 1960; Cert of Recog for Contbns for Promoting City, San Dimas, 1963.

RICH, MARIA F oc/Executive Director; b/Jun 18, 1925; ba/Central Opera Service, Metropolitan Opera, Lincoln Center, New York, NY 10023; m/Martin; c/Monica J; p/Richard and Else Koerner Fritz (dec); ed/Baccalaureate Deg, Stockholm, Sweden; pa/Asst Admr 1962-65, Adm Dir 1965-72, Exec Dir 1973-, Ctl Opera Ser, Metro Opera; Artistic Coor, Am Inst Musical Studies, Graz, Austria, 1979-81; Guest Lectr: Num Univs & Art Assns Incl'g: Columbia Univ; NY Univ; Univ of MD; Mem: Bd of Dirs, Nat Music Coun; Conslt: Nat Endowment of the Arts; Nat Opera Inst; Am Arts Coun; Pres's Coun of Arts Orgs; Intl Platform Assn; Coun of Nat Arts Orgs' Execs; hon/ Editor, W/W in Opera, 1976; Editor/ Author, Career Guid for the Yg Singer & 8 other Monographs on Opera & Arts Adm; Editor, Ctl Opera Ser Bltn; Contrbg Editor, Opera Qtly; Contrbg Author, Opera News, Musical Am; Am Musicologist; Others; 1st Recip, Verdi Medal of Achmt, Metro Opera, 1977; Spec Cit, Wom's Press Clb of NY; Rep at White House Conf of the Arts; W/W: in Am, in Am Wom, in E, in Am Music; Other Biogl Listings.

RICHARD, PAUL STUART oc/Corporate Executive, Marketing Consultant; b/ Oct 29, 1945; h/4801-210 Spencer Street, Las Vegas, NE 89109; ba/San Diego, CA; p/Lisle Francis and Bertha Marie (Allard) Richard; ed/Att'd Atlanta Bapt Col, 1970-71; pa/VPres Mktg, W Hobbs Ltd, Atlanta, 1974-78; Gen Mgr, Imperial Bronzelite Corp, LA, 1978-79; Sr VPres Gen Mgr, Brawn of CA Inc, San Diego, 1979-80; Dir, Wn Mktg Assocs Ltd, San Diego, 1980-81; Pres, Bullion Res N Am, LA, 1980-81; Pres, Fdr, Dollarplan Strategy Sems, Las Vegas, 1982-; Chm, Fdr, Christian Fin Enrichment Sems, Las Vegas, 1982-; Mem: Fac, San Diego St Univ Ext, 1982; Wkshop Ldr, Chm Fin Com, 1st So Bapt Ch; Hon Mem, Capt 1965-70, O L Davis Fire Co of Endwell, NY Fire Dept; VChm, Christian Bus-man's Com, San Diego, 1982; hon/ Author, Dollarplan Strategy, 1981; The Gospel of Christian Personomics, 1983; Adventures in Personomics, 1983; Contbr, Articles to Num Profl Jours; Recip, Outstg Awd for Achmt, Dale Carnegie 7 Assocs, 1972; W/ W in W.

RICHARDS, CHRISTINE-LOUISE oc/Author, Artist, Musician and Composer; b/Jan 11, 1910; h/Springslea PO Box 188, Morris, NY 13808; ba/Morris & New Berlin, NY; ed/Att'd Var Art Schs in US & Europe; pa/Fdr, Owner & Pres, Blue Star Music Pub'g Co, Morris & New Berlin, NY; Composer, Num Musical Pieces; Perfs Incl: Sammy Vincent's Orch of Pittsfield, MA & The Singing Strings Orch on Yankee Radio Netwk, Boston, MA; Author & Illustr, Chd's Lit; Num Painting Exhibns in Solo & Juried Art Shows Incl'g: Grand Ctl Art Galleries, NY; Oneonta, NY; Stockbridge, MA; Mem: Am Fedn of Musicians; Nat Assn of Composers; PA Acad of Fine Arts; Phila Art Alliance; Smithsonian Instn; Peale Clb of Phila; Phila Orch Assocs;

Metro Opera Guild; Academia Italia delle Arti e del Lavoro of Parma, Italy; Metro Mus of Art; Intl Biogl Assn; Am Biogl Inst; hon/Author of Chd's Books Incl'g: The Blue Star Fairy Book of Stories for Chd, 1950; The Blue Star Fairy Book of More Stories for Chd, 1969; The Blue Star Fairy Book of New Stories for Chd, 1980; Branches, 1983; Hon Dipl Master in Painting, Academia Italia-Intl Sems; 2nd Gold Medal for Artistic Merit; Prize of The Golden Centaur; Alumna of Phebe A Thorne Sch, Bryn Mawr Col, PA; Mem, Nightingale-Barnford Alumnae Assn, NYC; Silver Medal, Intl W/W in Commun Ser; W/W: in E, of Am Wom, in World, in Fin & Indust, in Art & Antiques; DIB; Other Biogl Listings.

RICHARDS, CORY DANA oc/Marketing Executive, Producer; b/Jul 30, 1955; h/536 North Sweetzer Avenue, Los Angeles, CA 90048; ba/Same; p/Alfred and Meryl Richards, Chatsworth, CA; ed/ BA high hon, Univ of CA-Santa Cruz, 1976; MBA, Cand; pa/Prodr, "Live from Gilley's," Syndicated Country Radio Show on 350 Radio Stas Natly; Promotion Dir, Hang Ten Intl, 1980; Prod Mgr, MCA Records, 1979-80; Mgr of Col Promotion, Mgr Retail Mktg Res, Macey Lipman Mktg, LA1978-79; Mktg Res Coor, Broadcast Wks, LA, 1977-78; Distbn, Proj Dir, Public Media Ctr, SF, 1974-77; Conslt to Entertainment Indust; Mem: Country Music Assn; cp/Fund Raiser, YMCA, 1978-81; r/Jewish; hon/ Grad w hons, Univ of CA-Santa Cruz, 1977; Hons on Thesis, 1977; Cowel Hlth Ctr Recog Awd, 1976; CA St S'ship, 1973-77; Book S'ship, 1973-77; W/W in Am Wom.

RICHARDSON, CHARLES R oc/ Facility Psychologist; b/Nov 2, 1926; h/ 4141 West Broadway Street, Louisville, KY 40222; ba/L'ville, KY; m/Dorothy B; c/Kevin, Rhonda; p/Charles and Alma Richardson (dec); ed/BA 1951, MA 1955, Post Grad Study, Univ of L'ville; Cert'd Psychol, 1969 & 1982; mil/USMC, Pfc 1944-46, 1st Lt 1951-53; USMCR, 1954-56, Capt; pa/Dir, CA Red Shield Boys Clb, 1953; Grad Asst Psych, Univ of L'ville, 1954; Asst to Dir, Servicemen's Ctr, 1955-62; Assembler, Gen Elect Appliance Pk, 1955-58; Social Wkr, L'ville and Jefferson Co Chd's Home, 1958-61; Child Welfare Wkr 1961-63, Psychol 1963-66, KY St Dept of Child Welfare; Coor Var Depts & Psychol, Reg Edn-Diagnostic Treatment Ctr, 1966-69; Residential Sers Supt, KY Dept of Child Welfare Ctl KY Reception Ctr, 1969-74; Residential Sers Supt, KY Dept for Human Resources, KY Chd's Home, 1974-79; Clin Treatment Coor, KY Dept for Human Resources, Bur for Social Sers, Div of Residential Sers, 1980-; Mem: KY Psychol Assn; KY Coun on Crime & Delinq; cp/Past Chm, Jefferson St Reg Voc & Ednl Advy Com; Past Bd Mem, Maryhurst Advy Co; Steering Com, Jefferson St Voc Tng Sch, 1982-; Steering Com, LaGrange Reformatory, 1982-; Human Sers Prog Advy Com, Jefferson Commun Col; Yth Allocation Com, U Way, 1976-; r/Bapt; hon/ Co-Author, "Techniques in Guided Grp Interaction Progs," in Child Welfare Leag Jour, 1972; 1st Black Commd'd Ofcr to Serve Active Duty in USMC; L'ville Dist'd Citizen Awd-Harvey Sloane, 1976; Jefferson Co Cert of Apprec-Hollenbach, 1977; Jefferson Co Schs Awd of

Merit-Van Hoose, 1972; Ranked #2 Amateur Tennis (black) Player in 50 & Over Div in US, Am Tennis Assn; W/ W in S & SW.

RICHARDSON, EMILIE WHITE oc/ Executive; b/Jul 8, 1929; h/1531 Northeast 51st Street, Ft Lauderdale, FL 33334; ba/Fayetteville, NC; c/Julie; p/Mr and Mrs Emmett White, Fayetteville, NC; ed/BA Anthropology, Wheaton Col, 1951; pa/w Co 1952-, Secy 1956-66, VPres 1967-74, Exec VPres 1975-79, Pres & CEO 1980-, Christy Mfg Co Inc; VPres, E White Investmt Co Inc, 1968-; Conslt, Aerostatic Industs, 1979-; Mem, Intl Platform Assn, 1983-; cp/VPres Public Relats 1974-76, VPres Mbrship 1977-78, Advy Bd 1978-, Ft Lauderdale Symph Soc; Freedom Foun; Ft Lauderdale Mus of Art; Beaux Arts; Americanism Chm 1971-72, Mem 1968-, E Broward Wom's Repub Clb; Green Val Country Clb; r/Presb; W/ W of Am Wom; Personalities of S; Intl Book of Hon; Other Biogl Listings.

RICHARDSON, GILBERT PAYTON SR oc/Executive Director; b/Nov 4, 1926; h/98 Lake Hunter Drive, Lakeland, FL 33803; ba/Annandale, Virginia; m/Lee Ann Gillen; c/Amy L, Gilbert P Jr, Susan Leigh; p/Claude Burns Richardson (dec); Doris Orton Richardson, Lakeland, FL; sp/Arlo Cisco Gillen (dec); Marjorie Stevenson Gillen, Dinuba, CA; ed/Att'd Mexico City Col, 1948; BA Hist, Sociol & Bus Adm, David Lipscomb Col, 1949; MA US Polit Hist, Sociol, Edn & Mgmt-Labor Relats, George Peabody Col, Vanderbilt Univ, 1951; Grad, US Air Univ Acad & Allied Ofcrs Sch, 1967; Residence Completed for PhD, Am Univ, 1956-59; mil/AUS, Italy, France, Switzerland, ETO, WW II; pa/Motion Picture Dir/ Writer of Industl Prodns, Tasco Motion Pictures Corp, Atlanta, 1952-53; Dir Admissions 1953-56, Instr Wn Civilization, Mgmt, Labor Relats 1956-57, Asst Prof Latin Am Hist, Polit Sci 1957-61, Chm Dept of Am Culture 1955-56, FL So Col; Pvt Resr, Lectr & Profl Spch Writer, Incl'g Res & Surveys in Argentina, Chile, Peru, Panama, Soviet Union, 1962-64; Asst Prof Hist & Polit Sci, Pepperdine Univ, 1964-66; Assoc Prof Intl Relats 1966-68, Prof Intl Relats 1968-70, Dean Inst on the Position of the US in World Affairs 1981-, US Def Intell Agy Grad Sch, Wash, DC; Exec Dir, Am Assn for Study of the US in World Affairs, Annandale, VA, 1978-; Mem: Assoc Exec Dir, Editor, Bd of Dirs 1957-61, Nat Clearinghouse Del 1957, FL Citizenship Clearinghouse; Intl Relats Com, Fac Grad Sch US Dept Agri, Wash DC, 1969-74; Lectr, No VA Commun Col, Alexandria, 1973-76; cp/Pres 1956-59, Chm of Bd 1960-62, Lake Reg Execs Clb; Pres, USWA Inst, Am Univ, 1956 & 1959, Wash, DC; Mem of Bd, Annandale Road Def Assn, 1980; VCmdr, Am Legion, Winter Haven, FL, 1955; VCmdr, Am Legion Post 4, Lakeland, FL, 1957; Intl Platform Assn, 1965; r/Ch of Christ; hon/ Author, *Our Rigorous Race to Russia*, 1963 & 1965; *Was Vietnam Am's Holy War?*; Author & Contbr, Num Articles on Intl Relats to Profl Jours, Newspapers & Mags; Subject of Num Interviews in Periods & TV; Pi Gamma Mu; Sigma Tau Delta; Cit Recip, Freedoms Foun, 1956; Dist'd Ser Awd & Outstg Yg Man of 1960, US Jr C of C; Recip Var Hon Doct Degs; Ext Travel for US Govt; W/W: in S & SW, in Wash; Men of Achmt; Ency

of Assn Execs; DIB.

RICHARDSON, JACQUELINE LEE oc/Technical Recruiter, Executive; b/Jul 21, 1951; h/3359 Bryan Avenue, Simi Valley, CA 93063; ba/Chatsworth, CA; m/Reginall L; p/Walter and Rosemary Dillery, Paynesville, MN; ed/Att'd Univ of MN, 1970-73; pa/Sr Tech Recruiter, Compdata, Costa Mesa, CA, 1978-79; Dir of Support Sers 1979-81, VPres Mktg 1981-82, Sys Software Inc, Anaheim, CA; Tech Recruiter, Pres, Computer Intell Co, 1982-; Mem: Nat Assn of Female Execs; cp/Chatworth C of C; Vol, Spastic Chds Foun; W/W of Am Wom.

RICHARSON, KAREN L oc/Lawyer; b/Sep 15, 1950; h/503-S Bashford Lane, Alexandria, VA 22314; ba/Washington, DC; pa/Mr and Mrs Lerohls, Alexandria, VA; ed/BA, Col of Wm & Mary, 1972; JD, Am Univ, 1978; LLM, George Wash Univ, 1982; pa/Atty, Ofc of Secy of Def, Wash, DC, 1980-; Atty, HQ's, Def Logistics Agy, Alexandria, 1978-80; Law Clk, Arnold & Porter, Wash, DC, 1975-78; Supvr, Prudential Ins Co, Wash DC, 1975-78; Mem: VA St Bar, 1979; US Ct of Appeals for Fed Circuit, 1981; 4th Circuit Ct of Appeals, 1982; US Supr Ct, 1982; Public Contracts Div 1979-, Former Dept Chm Cost Principles Subcom, ABA; Coun on Adm Law 1979-, Fed Bar Assn; Nat Contract Mgmt Asn, 1979-82; The Columbian Wom, George Wash Univ, 1983-; Dept of Def Sr Profl Wom's Grp, 1981-; Wom in Def, 1982-; cp/Wash Area Tennis Patrons, 1983-; Pres, Cameron Sta Tennis Clb, 1980; Tm Capt The Racqueteers, Michelob Light Leag Tennis, 1983; hon/Author, "The Application of the Ser Contract Act to ADP Ser Contracts- A Classic Case in Overregulation," in *ABA Public Contract News*, 1982; Recip, Pres Sports Awd in Tennis, 1980; Dist'd Yth Awd, Dept of the AUS, 1976; Dean's F'ship, Am Univ, 1977; Acad S'ship, Col of Wm & Mary, 1968; Hon Grad, Contract Atty's Course, Dept of the AUS, 1978; Outstg Yg Wom of Am Awd; W/W of Wom in Am.

RICHARDSON, RUTH DELENE oc/ Professor; b/May 27, 1942; h/2026 Greenbrier Road, Florence, AL 35630; ba/ Florence, AL; p/Mr and Mrs Daniel E Richardson, Florence, AL; ed/BS, Mars Hill Col, 1965; MS 1968, EdD 1974, The Univ of TN; pa/Tchr, LaFollete HS, 1965-66; Instr, Clinch Val Col, 1967-68; Instr, Univ of SC-Union, 1968-69; Instr, TN Wesleyan Col, 1969-71; Instr, Roane St Commun Col, 1971-73; Assoc Prof & Dept Chm, AL St Univ, 1974-75; Assoc Prof Sec'dy Ed, Univ of S AL, 1975-80; Assoc Prof Ofc Adm, Univ of N AL, 1980-; Mem: 2nd VPres 1982-83, Florence BPW Clb; Am Bus Commun Assn; Nat Bus Ed Assn; Chapt Secy 1982-83, Nat Assn of Female Execs; Nat Ed Assn; Delta Pi Epsilon; Omicron Tau Theta; Phi Delta Kappa; Pi Lambda Theta; r/Bapt; hon/Author of Book Chapt in *Imperatives in Voc Ed*, 1979; Article Pub'd in *SBEA Bltn*, 1981; EPDA F'ship, The Univ of TN, 1973-74; S'ship Awd, Clinch Val Col, 1962; W/W in S & SW; Outstg Yg Wom of Am; Other Biogl Listings.

RICHARDSON, STEPHEN A oc/ Professor; b/Jun 24, 1920; ba/Albert Einstein College of Medicine, 1300 Morris Park Avenue, Bronx, NY 10461; m/Marion Lyman; ed/Master Mariner, Brit Bd of Trade, 1946; BS, Harvard Univ, 1949; MS 1951, PhD 1954,

Cornell Univ; pa/Asst Dir, Assn for the Aid of Crippled Chd (AACC), 1956-69; Prof Dept of Pediatrics & Commun Hlth, Albert Einstein Col of Med, Yeshiva Univ, 1969-; Attached Wkr, Med Res Coun, Inst of Med Sociol, Univ of Aberdeen, Scotland, 1974-; Perinatal Res Com, Nat Inst of Neurol Diseases & Blindness, 1959-64; 3 Annual Profl Sems on Regulation of Growth in the Fetus & Child, WHO, Geneva, 1965-67; Conslt, Nat Inst of Child Hlth & Human Devel, 1967-; Chm Task Force on Psycho-social Deprivation & Social-emotional Devel, Nat Inst of Hlth & Human Devel, 1968-; Contl, WHO, 1969-; Res Adv Com, Planned Parenthood, 1963-72; Res Adv Com, Am Foun for Blind, 1963-75; Res Adv Com, Lexington Sch for Deaf, 1968-71; Mtl Retard & Tng Com, NICHD, 1968-71; Trustee, Easter Seal Res Foun, 1970-75; Conslt Editor, *Social Sci & Med*, 1972-; Assoc Editor, *Jour of Hlth & Social Behavior*, 1974-78; Bd of Dirs, NAC-PAC (New Alternatives for Chd), Blythedale Chd's Hosp, 1980-; hon/Author/Co-Author/ Editor of 4 Books: *The Mtly Retarded & Soc: A Social Sci Perspective*, 1975; *Mtl Subnormality in the Commun: A Clin & Epidemiological Study*, 1970; *Childbearing: Its Social & Psychol Aspects*, 1967; *Interviewing, Its Forms & Functions*, 1965; Contbr, Num Book Chapts; Over 80 Articles & Reports Pub'd in Profl Pubs; Frank Scott Guerrish S'ship, Harvard Col; Grad magna cum laude 1949, Phi Beta Kappa, Harvard Univ; Fellow for Adv'd Studies in Behavioral Studies; Cornell Univ Chapt, Phi Kappa Phi.

RICHARDSON, WILLIAM C oc/ University Administrator; b/May 11, 1940; h/16525 Shore Drive Northeast, Seattle, WA 98155; ba/Seattle, WA; m/ Nancy; c/Elizabeth, Jennifer; p/Henry B and Frances C Richardson, Sparta, NJ; sp/ John E Freeland, Waukegan, IL; ed/BA, Trinity Col, 1962; MBA 1964, PhD 1971, Univ of Chgo; pa/Assoc Study Dir Nat Opinion Res Ctr 1968-70, Grad Instr 1967-70, Res Assoc 1967-70, Res Asst 1965-67, Univ of Chgo; Adm Asst, NY Univ Med Ctr, 1963-64; Asst Prof Hlth Sers 1971-73, Prof Hlth Sers 1976-, Assoc Dean Sch Public Hlth & Commun Med 1976-81, Acting Dean 1977-78; Acting Chair, Dept of Envirot Hlth 1981, Dean Grad Sch & VProvost for Res 1981-, Univ of WA; Mem: Inst of Med; Fellow, APHA; Assn of Tchrs of Prev Med; Reg Advy Bd, WA/AK Reg Med Prog; Chair Ser Fellows Peer Review Bd NCHSR 1975-81, Ofc of Asst Secy for Hlth, Dept Hlth, Ed & Welfare; Mem 1977-81, Chm 1979-81, Coun on Res & Devel, Am Hosp Assn; Mem 1978-, VChm 1980-83, St Employees Ins Bd, St of WA; Adm Bd, Wash Archaeol Res Ctr, 1981-; Chm Policy Bd, WA Mining & Mineral Resources Res Int, 1981-; Com on Grad Student Fin Assistance, Assn of Grad Schs, Assn of Am Univs, 1982-; Bd of Trustees, Fred Hutchinson Cancer Res Ctr, 1982-; Conslt, Num, WA St & US Govtl Agys & Pvt Insts; Num Other Coms & Orgs; r/Epis; hon/Author & Co-Author, 7 Reports & Book Pubs Incl'g: *Consumer Choice & Cost Containment*, 1983; Over 40 Articles & Book Chapts Pub'd in Profl Jours & Hlth Sci Pubs; Trinity Whitlock Awd; Chgo-Trinity S'ship; Mary H Bachmeyer Awd, Univ of Chgo; Kellogg

Fellow; Beta Gamma Sigma; W/W in Am.

RICHMOND, DONALD KEITH oc/ Supervisory Grievance Examiner/EEO Investigator; b/Dec 21, 1950; h/2204 North Pickett Street #202, Alexandria, VA 22304; ba/Arlington, VA; p/Raymond and Mary Ann Richmond, Columbia, SC; ed/BA 1975, BS 1976, Rollins Col; MA Univ of OK, 1976; mil/US Coast Guard, 1969-79; US Coast Guard Resvs, 1976-; pa/Civil Rts Cnslr, Cmdr, 5th Coast Guard Dist, 1973-74; Instr Behavioral Scis Div, Dept of Def Race Relats Inst, 1974-76; Human Relats/Human Resource Mgmt Conslt, 1976-77; Exec Asst to Dir Ofc of Civil Rts 1979-82, Bldg Mgmt Asst Public Bldg Ser 1982, Gen Sers Adm; Shore Equal Opportunity Prog Conslt, Nav Material Command 1977-79, Supvry Grievance Examr/EEO Investigator, Ctl Field Div Nav Civilian Pers Command 1982-, Dept of Nav; Mem: Fed Mgrs Assn, 1980-; Am Soc for Public Adm, 1982-; Conf of Minority Public Admrs, 1982-; cp/Chd's Def Fund, 1981-; Fdg Mem, People for the Am Way, 1980; Common Cause, 1979-; ACLU, 1979-; Intl Transactional Anal Assn, 1977-79; Mtl Hlth Assn of Portsmouth, VA, 1977-79; Am Leag Post 190, Portsmouth, VA, 1977-79; Ctl Civic Forum, 1977-79; NAACP, 1973-; Num Other Commun Orgs; r/Prot; hon/Co-Author, Dept of Def Race Relats Inst Anthology Ref Book, *IQ, Race & Intell*; Dept of Def Secy's Jt Ser Commend Medal, 1976; Coast Guard Good Conduct Medal, 1973; Commandant's Coast Guard Achmt Medal, 1973; Nat Def Ser Medal, 969; Admr's Meritorious Ser Awd 1982, Commend Ser Awd 1981, Outstg Perf Rating 1980, Gen Sers Adm; Outstg Yg Man of Am.

RICHMOND, JOHN oc/Attorney; b/ Dec 10, 1907; h/1611 Bonita Avenue #2, Berkeley, CA 94709; ba/Same; p/Samuel and Sarah Smith Richmond (dec); ed/BS 1928, MS 1934, Univ of CA-Berkeley; LLB, Oakland Col of Law, 1942; mil/ USAAF, 1942-45; pa/Pres 1928-, Atty 1946-, Richmond Enterprises; Atty at Law, Pvt Pract, 1946-; Mem: CA St Bar Asn; Alameda Co Bar Assn; Berkeley-Albany Bar Assn; ABA; Fed Bar Assn; Fdr, Nat Lwyrs Clb, 1952; Fdr, Supr Ct Hist Soc, 1976; cp/Cmdr, VFW Berkeley Post 703, 1962; Pres, U Vets Coun of Berkeley, 1963; VFW of US Nat Mbrship Com, 1980-81; Co-Chm Lincoln & Wash Patriotic Prog 1962, Gen Chm Meml Sers 1963, Gen Chm Marin Pt Aquatic Pk 1963, City of Berkeley; Mem, Grand Lodge of Free & Accepted Masons of CA Sojourners Com, 1958-66; Master, Henry Morse Stephens Lodge # 541 Free & Accepted Masons, 1958; Affils w Var Masons, 1958-; hon/Hon PhD, Hamilton St Univ, 1973; USAAF Sponsored Study, Balliol Col, Oxford Univ, England, 1944; W/W: in W, in Fin & Indust, in World, in Commun Ser, of Intells; Intl Book of Hon; Nat Register of Prominent Ams & Intl Notables; Dir of Dist'd Ams; Num Other Biogl Listings.

RICHTER, JoLYNNE oc/Graduate Assistant, Master Tutor, Forensics Coach; b/Oct 25, 1952; h/PO Box 86, Cripple Creek, CO 80813; ba/Gunnison, CO 81230; m/(Bill) William Edwin; p/ Douglas Eugene and (Norma) Jeanne Gill, Arvada, CO; sp/Charles Eugene and (Wilma) Jean Richter, Arvada, CO; ed/ Att'd, Jefferson Co Adult Ed Ctr, Lakewood, CO, 1970; Att'd Univ of No CO,

Greeley, 1970-71; BA Eng Ed, CO St Univ, Ft Collins, 1974; MA Cand Ed & Commun Arts, Wn St Col, Gunnison, 1984-; pa/Grad Asst, Master Tutor & Forensics Coach, Divs of Humanities & Ed & the Lrng Ctr, Wn St Col, Gunnison, CO, 1983-; Tchr 7-12, Cripple Creek-Victor Sch Dist, Cripple Creek, CO, 1980-83; Master Tutor, Delta-Montrose Area Voc-Tech Sch, Delta, CO, 1977-80; Instr & Subs Tchr, Delta Co Jt Sch Dist 50, Delta, CO, 1975-80; Pvt/Spec Tchr/Tutor Deaf Ed, Delta & Eckert, CO, 1975-802; Ast & Subs Instr, Jefferson Co Sch Dist R-1, Lakewood, CO, 1969-75; Spec Tchr (Exptl), Thompson Sch Dist, Berthoud, CO, 1974; Spec Tchr & Asst (Exptl), Poudre Sch Dist, Ft Collins, CO, 1971-74; Previous Other Clerical Postions, 1969-74; Pvt Tutor, 1964-; Curricula, Progs & Resources Devel, 1972-; Wkshop Facilitation & Presentation in Areas of Ed, Commun & Mgmt, 1972-; Dir/Prodr, Var Plays & Musicals, 1974-; Mem: LIT; Kappa Delta Pi; CADRE; ASCD; CASCD; NCTE; Pi Kappa Delta; CASE; CLAS; CDSA; Sch Climate Pilot Tm Ldr, CO Dept of Ed, 1982-83; cp/Arvada Hist Soc; NB & PW; OES; Hon Rotarian; Right-to-Read, 1970-1980; FTA; FLA; Subcom Chp, Cripple Creek Accountability Com, 1982-83; Bd of Trustees 1980-83, VPres 1981-83, RIF Chp 1981-83; Franklin Ferguson Meml Lib; O'Leary Advy Coun, 1982-83; TEAMS; GSA, 1962-70; Campfire Girls, 1960-62; r/Prot; hon/Author/Contbr, Num Articles to Var Profl Pubs Incl'g: *CADRE*; Author, *Tales of Edgar Elephant* & Other Chd's Lit; Author, Num Creat, Lang, Drama, Commun Lrng Activ Guides for Chd & Chd's Wkshops; In Prog: *Wn St Col Viewbook*; Jr Rotarian; NHS; Nat Jr Hon Soc; Col Sr Wom's Hon; Panhellenic Hon; Hon Rotarian; Var Hon Rolls & Deans' Lists; LIT, 1973; KDP, 1981; Grad w Distn, CO St Univ, 1974; HS Grad Hons & Spkr; W/W in W.

RIDDELL, ALICE MARY oc/Drug Prevention/Intervention Progran Director; b/Aug 12, 1928; h/65-25 160 Street, Flushing, New York, NY 11365; ba/ Flushing, NY; m/Robert Lawrence; p/ Jeffrey Lawrence; -p/Arthur Edward Robertson (dec); Alice Mary McAuliffe Robertson, Flushing, NY; sp/William and Margaret Svenstrup Riddell (dec); ed/BA 1963, MS 1966, Cert Narcotics Inst 1968, Queens Col CUNY; PD, St John's Univ, 1973; pa/Dir Proj 25 Commun Sch Dist 25's Alcohol & Drug Prev/Interv Prog, Flushing, NY, 1971-; Dist Narcotics Coor, CSD 25, 1970-71; Guid Tchr, Advr & Tchr of Consumer Ed & Fam Living, JHS 218, CSD 25, 1963-70; Asst Prof Drug Abuse & Consumer Ed, Queens Col, 1970-78; Other Previous Positions; Mem: Pres, NY St Assn of Sch-Based Prev Profls, 1982-; Editor, *The Qtly* of NY St Assn of Substance Abuse Progs; Trustee & Bd Mem, Daytop Village Inc; Bd Mem, Col Pt Sports Assn; NY St Adv Coun on Substance Abuse, 1978-83; NYC Adm Wom in Ed; Chp, Citywide Coalition of Drug Dirs, 1972-74; Co-Chp Drug Abuse Task Force, Wom in Crisis Inc, 1982; Queens Boro Pres' Advy Coun on Alcohol & Substance Abuse; Chancellor's Advy Coun on Substance Abuse, 1981-; cp/ Num Other Commun Orgs & Activs; r/ Rom Cath; hon/Editor & Writer, Num Articles Pub'd in *The Qtly* of NYS Assn

of Substance Abuse Progs; Author, *A Handbook for Sch Staffs Re: Alcohol, Drugs-Possesion, Use, Abuse & Crisis*; Num Paper Presentations at Profl Confs; Phi Delta Kappa, St John's Univ; Frank De Silva Meml Awd for Outstg Contbns to the Field, 5th Annual NY St Conf on Substance Abuse, 1982; Congl Del, White House Conf on Chd, 1970; Presentor, 1st Intl Cong of Drug Ed, Montreaux, Switzerland, 1973; W/W in E.

RIDDICK, LAZETTA A oc/Consultant; b/Jun 20, 1948; h/835 Shadwell Drive, Houston, TX 77062; ba/Same; m/ Oliver W Jr; c/Le Titia J, Christopher D; p/Mr and Mrs Henry Church, Balto, MD; sp/Carmen Riddick, Balto, MD; ed/AS, Middlesex Commun Col, Bedford, MA, 1975; BS, Univ of MA, 1977; MA, Antioch Univ, 1981; pa/Conslt, 1983-; Reg Prod Sales Spec Digital Imaging Houston TX 1982, Prod Spec Digital Imaging Balto MD 1981, CGR Med Corp; Adm Fac, Coor of Prior Lrng Prog 1980-82, Antioch Univ; Dir Ednl Prog Devel 1978, Fellows, Read & Weber Inc, Hagerstown, MD; Tng Spec, Pfizer Med Sys, Columbia, MD, 1977-78; Acting Dir/Instr Radiologic Tech Prog, Bunker Hill Commun Col, Charleston, MA, a1975-76; Pt-time Instr Radiologic Tech Prog, Middlesex Commun Col, Bedford, MA, 1974-75; Instr Radiologic Tech Prog, Wash Techn Inst, Wash, DC, 1972-74; Staff Radiologic Technol, Johns Hopkins Hosp, Balto, MD, 1972-74; Staff Radiologic Technol, York Road Med Ctr, Timonium, MD, 1970-71; Pt-time Radiologic Technol, Ch Home & Hosp, Balto, MD, 1968-71; Mem: Am Registry of Radiologic Technols, 1971-; Nat Tech Assn, 1980-81; CAEL, 1980-81; Nat Assn of Female Execs, 1979-; cp/Chp Pack Co, 595, Cub Scouts; r/Cath; hon/ Author, "Eval'g the Radiologic Technol Student in the Cognitve & Psychomotor Domains," in *Mayflower*, 1975; Coor & Presenter, Num Intl & Intercultural Progs; Prog Emcee, Balto City Asian Fest, Hopkins Plaza, 1981; W/W of Am Wom.

RIDENHOUR, NANCY ANN oc/ Senior Systems Developer; b/Jan 22, 1954; h/3619 Colony Road, Apartment 6, Charlotte, NC 28211; ba/Charlotte, NC; p/Charles and Helen Ridenhour, Kannapolis, NC; ed/BS, Stats, NC St Univ, 1976; pa/Programmer, Cannon Mills, 1976-78; Programmer/Anal, Riegel Textile, 1978-80; Sr Sys Developer, 1st Computer Sers, 1st Union, Charlotte, NC, 1980-; Mem: AAUW, 1st Union Mgmt Assn; cp/Vol, Discovery Place Sci Mus, Charlotte; NC St Alumni Assn; NC St Univ Wolfpack Clb; r/Luth; hon/W/W in Am Wom.

RIDLEY-THORNBURY, LANI SUE oc/Marketing Manager; b/Mar 21, 1948; h/752 Oak Crest Drive, Sierra Madre, CA 91024; ba/Culver City, CA; m/Thomas Ray Thornbury; c/Jason Michael, Shane, Tod; p/Manuel Joseph Pedrini, Temple City, CA; Vera Jean Van Steenwyk Pedrini (dec); sp/James Pearson Thornbury, Oregonia, OH; Wilma Jean Warman, Middleton, OH; ed/BA, Univ of CA-LA, 1971; Tchg Credentials 1972, MA 1973, Univ of So CA; pa/Graphic Design/Comml Artist, Selected Free-Lance Advtg Art, LA, CA, 1966-77; Prodn Mgr/Comml Arts, Lloyd's Fashion Advtg, LA, CA, 1972-73; Advtg Prodn Mgr/Art Dir, McMahan's Furniture Co, Santa Monica, CA, 1973-75; Media Dir/ Prodn Mgr, Walgers & Assocs Advtg Inc,

Hollywood, CA, 1975-77; Acct Exec/ Media Dir/Prodn Mgr, Darryl Lloyd Advtg Inc, Encino, CA, 1977-78; Br Mgr/ Mktg Sales Mgr/Nat Acct Mgr/Maj Acct Mktg Rep, Prime Computer Inc, Culver City, CA, 1980-; Mem: Am Soc of Profl & Exec Wom 1981-, The Res Inst of Am 1979-, The Nat Assn of Female Execs 1980-, Wkg Wom's Soc 1979-, Assn for Wom in Computing 1982-, Data Processing Mgmt Assn 1982-, Career Guild 1980-, US Consumers Assn 1981-, Bkcard Holders of Am 1981-; cp/The Am Film Inst, 1982-; The Am Rose Soc, 1980-, Alpha Phi Sorority, 1966-; hon/Author of Mkt Res on the Top 8 Mini-Computer Cos in Mktplace; Top Prod'g Mgr in LA Dist Awd, Prime Computer Inc, 1983; The Field File Awd, Prime Computer Inc, 1982; $1 Million Record Breaker Awd, Prime Computer Inc, 1980 & 1981; Top Prodr in Wn Reg Awd, Prime Computer Inc, 1981; Rookie of Yr Awd, Prime Computer Inc, 1980; Exec Participation Awd, The Res Inst of Am, 1979; Sales Profl Participation Awd, The Res Inst of Am, 1979; Grad, magna cum laude, Univ of CA-LA, 1971; W/W: in CA, of Am Wom.

RIEDER, RICHARD WALTER oc/ Management Analyst; b/Feb 18, 1940; h/ 15565 Woodhollow Court, Reston, VA 22091; ba/Washington, DC; m/Edelgard Lestin; c/Stephanie E, Arnold F; p/Walter and Virginia (Lincoln) Rieder, Upland, CA; sp/Friedrich Lestin (dec); Ella Friedrich, Bonn, Germany; ed/BA, Yale Univ, 1961; MPA, George Wash Univ, 1970; MPA, Univ of So CA, 1976; mil/USN, 1961-66; USNR, Lt; pa/Nav Ofcr, 1961-66; Mgmt Anal, HQ's NASA, Wash, DC, 1966-; Mem: Am Soc for Public Adm; cp/Yale Clb of Wash, DC; VP/Elder, Good Shepherd Luth Ch, Reston, VA, 1977-81; BSA Troop, 1970; Swiss Clb of Wash, DC; SCAPA Praetors, Univ of So CA; r/Luth; hon/US Civil Ser Comm F'ship, Univ of So CA,, 1974-75; W/W in S & SW.

RIFKIN, SANDRA A oc/Interior Designer and Consultant; b/May 22, 1938; h/3864 South Quince Street, Denver, CO 80237; ba/Denver, CO; m/ Robert C; c/Terri Lin; p/Ervin Anderson (dec); Marguerite Anderson, Denver, CO; sp/Nathan and Bessie Rifkin, Far Rockaway, NY; ed/Grad, Bergman Art Inst, 1959; pa/Comml & Fashion Artist & Assoc, Guirys & Co, Denver, 1964-67; Owner, Pvt Design Studio, 1967-71; Owner, Design Assocs, 1971-; hon/ Designs for Num Pvt Residences and for Public Places which incl Proof of the Pudding (Denver, CO), Turn of the Century Restaurant and Night Club, The Lady and the Dove Restaurant and Night Club, Lyle Alzados Restaurant, Reflections Disco, The Parlour Disco, Julianos Restaurant, Miss Rosy Bottom Restaurant and Disco, The Charlie Horse Saloon, The Fresh Fish Company, Proof of the Pudding Restaurant & Night Club, and Knicks Saloon; Conslt for Hist Restoration.

RIFKIND, LAWRENCE JAY oc/Interim Chairman; b/Nov 1, 1951; h/751 North Indian Creek Drive, Apartment 259, Clarkston, GA 30021; ba/Atlanta, GA; m/Constance S; p/Mrs Estelle Rifkind, Harrison, NY; sp/Mr and Mrs Everett Sasser, East Point, GA; ed/BA in Spch 1973, MA in Spch Communication 1974, PhD in Communication 1975, FL

St Univ; pa/Instructor 1975-76, Asst Prof 1976-, Interim Chairman of Spch and Theater Dept 1981-, GA St Univ; GA Spch Communication Assn, 2nd VP 1978-79, Pres 1979-80; So Spch Communication Assn; Spch Communication Assn; Intl Spch Communication Assn; hon/Pubs: "Allow Yourself to Grow" (Guest Column in "The Georgia State University Signal") 1978, "The Development of an Outstanding Speaker Contest for the Freshman Level Speech Course" 1977-78, "An Analysis of the Inaugural Address of President James Earl Carter" 1978, "An Analysis of the Effects of Personality Type Upon the Risky Shift in Small Group Discussions" 1975, Others; Phi Kappa Phi; Omicron Delta Kappa; Alpha Lambda Delta; American Film Inst; Commun Ldrs and Noteworthy Ams; DIB; Intl W/W in Commun Ser; Intl W/W of Intells; Notable Ams; Personalities of the S; Men and Wom of Distn; Men of Achmt; Commun Ldrs of Am; 1980 Am Biogl Inst Am Registry Series; Am Biogl Inst Res Assn; Intl Book of Hon; IPA; 2,000 Notable Americans.

RIGBY, EUGENE TERRELL oc/University Graphics Illustrator; b/Feb 10, 1958; b/2470 Northwest 141st Street, Opa Locka, FL 33054; p/Eugene and Eddie Rigby, Opa Locka, FL; ed/AA, 1979; AS, 1979; BA, 1984; pa/Free-Lance Artist, FL Intl Univ, 1982-; Salesman, Bakers Shoes Corp, 1978-82; Student Govt Assn of FL Intl Univ, Chief Justice of Intl Ct 1983-84, Asst Elections Commr 1984, Public Relats Conslt of Intl Black Student Org 1983-84, Public Relats Conslt of Caribbean Student Assn 1983-84, Co-Chp of Social and Cultural Prog Coun 1983-84, Mem of Bd of Govs 1983-84, Chp of Homecoming Com 1983, Chp of Am Week 1983, Co-Chp of Intl Week 1983, Chp of Black Hist Week 1983, Mem of Black Hist Week 1982, Chp of Social and Cultural Prog Coun 1982-84, Asst Controller 1982-83, Senator 1982-83, Mem of Budget Com 1981-82, Consularie 1983; Student Govt Assn of Miami Dade Commun Col, Mem of Black Student Union 1978-79; hon/ Certs of Apprec: Coun on Chairs 1982, Ways and Means Com 1982, Mem of Bd of Govs 1982, Mem of Social and Cultural 1982, Outstg Ser as Senator 1982-83, Outstg Ser on Budget Com 1982-83; Plaques: Outstg Ser Mem of Social and Cultural Com 1982, Outstg Ser Chp of Social and Cultural Com 1983, Most Ldrship Ability 1982, Dist'd and Dedicated Ser for Black Student Union 1982, Student Ldrship Awd 1983.

RINALDO, MATTHEW JOHN oc/ Member of Congress; b/Sep 1, 1931; h/ 142 Headley Terrace, Union, NJ 07083; ba/Washington, DC; p/Ann and Matthew Rinaldo, Union, NJ; ed/BS in Bus Adm, Rutgers Univ; MBA, Seton Hall Univ, 1979; DPA, NY Univ; pa/Elected Pres, Union Twp Zoning Bd, 1963; Elected, NJ St Senate 1967, Re-Elected 1971; Elected, 12th Dist Congressional Seat 1972, Re-Elected 1974, 1976, 1978; Former Tchr, Labor Mgmt Relats, Rutgers Univ's Ext Div; Mem, House Com on Interst and Fgn Commerce, the House Select Com on Narcotics Abuse and Control (ex officio); Previously Served on House Bkg and Fin Com and Merchant Marine and Fisheries Com; Trustee, Bd of Dirs of the Paul Stillman Sch of Bus Adm, Seton Hall Univ; Trustee, Adv Bd of the Dept of Polit Sci, Kean Col; hon/Outstg Yg Man

of the Yr, JCs; Knight of the Yr, K of C; B'nai B'rith Citizen of the Yr Awd; Man of the Yr, UNICO Nat Chapts in Union, Plainfield and Maplewood, NJ; Recog for His Leading Role in Getting the 200-Mile Fishing Limit Enacted into Law, Rod and Gun Editors of Metro NY; Hlth Freedom Awd; Hon'd by NJ St Fireman's Mutual Benevolent Assn, the Cath War Vets, Hadassah, the Union Co Heart Assn, the Policemen's Benevolent Assn, the VFW, Am Legion, U Clergy of Vauxhall, the St Grand Jurors Assn, NJ St Police; W/W US; W/W Am Politics; W/W E; W/W Govt; Men of Achmt; W/ W Am.

RINGERT, WILLIAM F oc/Lawyer, State Senator; b/Jun 1, 1932; h/4170 Lenora, Boise, ID 83704; ba/Boise, ID; m/ Lynne K Bing; c/John Franklin, Beth Anne; p/Fred and Elizabeth Ringert, Buhl, ID; ed/BS in Agronomy, Univ of ID Moscow, 1953; Att'd, San Angelo Col, 1955; LLB, So Meth Univ, 1962; mil/ USAF, 1st Lt/Multi-Engine Pilot 1953-56; pa/Braniff Intl Airways, Dallas, TX, 1956-62; Anderson, Kaufman, Ringert & Clark, Boise, ID, 1962-; ID St Senator, 1982-; Participated in the Devel of the Grindstone Butte Proj (an Irrigation Proj in Elmore Co, ID), 1973-74; Currently Engaged in Irrigated Farming Opers on Land for Grindstone Butte Proj; Delta Theta Phi; ID Bar Assn; Agri Law Com on Gen Pract Sect.

RINI, LISA M oc/Supervising Recreation Specialist; b/Dec 29, 1951; h/4324 Corinth, San Diego, CA 92115; ba/San Diego, CA; m/Stephen S. Wallet; p/Mr and Mrs John A Rini, Willoughby Hills, OH; sp/George Wallet, Fresno, CA; Irene Wallet, Huntington Beach, CA; ed/BA in Hlth and PE, 1973; MEd in PE, 1974; PhD in PE, Spec Ed and Early Childhood Ed; pa/Supvg Rec Spec, Disabled Sers, San Diego Pk and Rec Dept, 1983-; Asst Prof, PE Dept, San Diego St Univ, 1979-83; Instr 1978-79, Grad and Adm Asst 1977-78, PE Dept, Univ of MN; Asst Prof, PE Dept, WA St Univ, 1975-77; Instr, PE Dept, Univ of WI LaCrosse, 1974-75; Grad Asst, PE Dept, Miami Univ, 1973-74; Am Alliance for Hlth, PE and Rec; Nat Assn for Yg Chd; Wom in Mgmt; cp/NOW; Several Local Orgs; Bds and Chapts Involving Disabled Citizens; CA Wom in Govt; hon/Pubs: "Perceptual Motor Development Equipment and Activities" (w P Werner) 1976, "The Relationship Between Selected Affective Variable and Motor Proficiency in Elementary School Children" 1982; Nom'd Tchr of the Yr, WA St Univ, 1976.

RINKER, DUDLEY HOUSTON oc/ Executive; b/Sep 18, 1953; h/Route 2, Box 240, Stephens City, VA 22655; ba/ Stephens City, VA; p/Ray D (dec) and Ruth B Rinker, Stephens City, VA; ed/ Grad, James Wood HS, 1972; Att'd: Lord Fairfax Commun Col, 9 Indepth Fruit Schs, Personnel Supvn Wkshops, Apple Safety Sem; Cert'd Pesticide Applicator; pa/Gen Labor for Ray Rinker (Prior to 1972); Prodn Mgr 1972-76, Gen Mgr 1976-79, Ray Rinker Estate; Gen Mgr, Secy, VP, Rinker Orchards Inc; VChm, VA Farm Bur Apple Mktg Com, 1984; VA Farm Bur Labor Com, 1984; Bd of Dirs 1976-78, VP 1979-80, Pres 1981-82, Past Pres 1983-84, Chm of Yg Farmers Com 1979-80, Chm of Mbrship Com 1979-80, Chm of Budget Com 1983-84, Chm of Land Purchasing Com 1983,

Frederick Co Farm Bur; VA Farm Bur St Resolutions Com, 1982; Rep, VA St Farm Bur Conv, 1981-83; Bd of Dirs 1982-84, Mem of Labor Com 1981, Chm of Camp Constrn Com 1982, Fruit Maturity Com 1983, Frederick Co Fruit Growers Assn; CoChm, S Frederick Agri Dist Orgl Com, 1981-82; Frederick Co Fruit Adv Com, 1979-84; The Old Time Apple Growers Assn, 1983-; Treas, Frederick Co Fruit Tour Com, 1980-83; Appt'd Mem, Selective Ser Bd, 1982-; Spkr, Intl Dwarf Fruit Tree Assn Annual Conv, 1981; Intl Dwarf Fruit Tree Assn, 1980-; VA St Hort Soc, 1968-; WV St Hort Soc, 1980-; Nat Coun of Agri Employers, 1982-; cp/Mem 1972-, Bd of Dirs 1976-80, 1981-, Pres 1980-81, Stephens City Lions Clb; Dist Chm 1980-82, Zone Chm 1983-84, Lions Intl; Del, VA St Lions Conv, 1974-83; Del, Lions Intl Conv, 1983; Host, Intl Dwarf Fruit Tree Assn Sum Tour, 1980; Host, VA Polytechnic Inst and St Univ Hort Student Tour, 1975-79; VP 1982-84, Secy-Treas 1979-82, Life Mem 1976, James Wood FFA Alumni; r/VChm of Adm Bd 1970-81, Supt of Sunday Sch Prog 1977-80, Secy 1971-78, Stephens City U Meth Ch; hon/Pubs: Articles in "The Great Lakes Fruit Growers News" (May 1981) and "Virginia Fruit" (Jul 1981); Outstg Yg Farmer of the Yr (Dist), 1983; Outstg Conservationist, Lord Fairfax Soil and Water Conserv Dist, 1982; Club Pres Awd, Lions Intl, 1982; Mem of the Yr, Stephens City Lions Clb, 1982; Hon Mem, Robert E Aylor Jr HS FFA, 1982; Outstg Yg Farmer, Winchester-Frederick Co JCs, 1977; FFA St Farmer Awd, 1972; FFA Student Awd, Puritan Clb, 1972; Personalities of Am.

RISCH, JAMES E oc/Attorney, President Pro Tem; b/May 3, 1943; h/5400 South Cole Road, Boise, ID 83709; ba/Boise, ID; m/Vicki L Choborda; c/James E, Jason S, Jordan D; ed/St John's Cathedral, Milwaukee, WI; BS in Forestry, LLD, Univ of ID Moscow, 1968; pa/Dpty Prosecuting Atty, Ada Co, ID, 1968-69; Chief Dpty Prosecuting Atty, Ada Co, ID, 1969-72; Ada Co Prosecuting Atty, 1972-74; St Senator for ID from Dist 18, 1974; Majority Ldr, ID St Senate, 1977-82; Pres Pro Tem, ID St Senate, 1983-; Ptnr, Risch, Goss, Insinger & Salladay Law Firm, 1975-; Tchr of Crim Law, Boise St Univ; Phi Delta Theta; Xi Sigma Pi; Past Pres, ID Prosecuting Attys Assn; Past Mem, Bd of Dirs, Nat Dist Attys Assn; Am Bar Assn; ID St Bar; Nat Dist Atty's Assn.

RISCHARD, MAUREEN McCLINTOCK oc/Homemaker; b/Jan 28, 1921; h/18901 East Dodge Avenue, Santa Ana, CA 92705; m/Theodore Eugene; c/Marilyn Rischard Franklin (Mrs Joel), Carolyn Rischard Fox (Mrs Tony), Vivienne Rischard Roberts (Mrs Buddy); p/Clarence Martin and Bertha Alice Goetz McClintock (dec); sp/Joseph Jacob and Marie Henco Rischard; ed/AB, cum laude, Fine Arts, Univ of So CA, 1942; cp/Ebell Soc of the Santa Ana Valley, Pres 1980-83; Katuktu Nsdar Registrar, 1970-85; Zeta Tau Alpha Sorority, Pres 3 Times; hon/Author: Centennial History of the Tustin Presbyterian Church 1884-1984 1984, McClintock Ancestors and Descendants 1979, Saddleback Ancestors 1969, Sepulveda Chapts; Editor, For King or Country, Vol I 1975, Vol II 1976, for Orange Co, CA, Genealogy Soc; 4-H Commun Ser Awd,

1978; Wom of the Yr, Ctl Orange Co Panhellenic, 1975; Wom of the Yr, City of Tustin, 1975; 30-Yr Pin as Girl Scout Adult 1980, Thanks Badge 1960, GSA.

RISLEY, ROD ALAN oc/Administrator; h/Box 230, Canton, MS 39046; ba/Canton, MS; m/Lynn Plimpton; p/Ralph and Pat Risley, Inman, KS; ed/AA, 1975; BBA, 1982; pa/Assoc Dir, Phi Theta Kappa Nat Hon, 1983-; Dir of Alumni Affairs, Phi Theta Kappa, 1978-83; Nat Pres, Phi Theta Kappa, 1974-75; Pres, Pi Kappa Alpha, 1976-77; Bd of Advrs, Lee's-McRae Col; cp/Kiwanis Clb; Madison Co Repub Party; hon/Pub, "Transfer Trauma" in Golden Key, Phi Theta Kappa; Phi Theta Kappa, 1974; Phi Theta Kappa Hall of Hon, 1978-; Nat Dean's List, 1982; Outstg Yg Man of Am, 1979, 1980, 1981, 1982; Pres Scholar, 1976; W/W Am Jr Cols; DIB; Personalities of S.

RITTER, MARY L oc/Interior Designer, College Instructor; h/349 Selby Lane, Atherton, CA 94025; ba/Same; m/Henry Jr; c/Caroline Victoria, Mark Henry; p/Gilbert M Loewe MD (dec); Alma N Loewe (dec); sp/Henry Ritter MD; Beatrice K Ritter; ed/BA, Leland Stanford Univ; Cert, Elem Drafting, NY Sch of Interior Design; pa/Edit Scout, NYC and Surrounding Area for: American Home, Better Homes & Gardens, Better Homes & Gardens Building Book, Better Homes & Gardens Christmas Book, Better Homes & Gardens Decorating Book, Family Circle, Farm Journal, Good Housekeeping, House Beautiful, Living for Young Homemakers, and Pathfinder, the Town Journal, 1951-56; Interior Decorator, Pvt Pract, SF and Peninsula, 1956-; Edit Scout, SF and Peninsula for: American Home, Better Homes & Gardens, Better Homes & Gardens Building Book, Better Homes & Gardens Christmas Book, Better Homes & Gardens Decorating Book, Better Homes & Gardens Kitchen Book, and Good Housekeeping, 1956-63; Instr, Engrg Technol, W Valley Commun Col, Cont'g Ed Dept, 1976; Instr, Canada Col, 1976; Instr, W Valley Col and Canada Col, 1977; WAIF-Intl Social Ser VP of Spec Events, 1969; Chm of WAIF-Intl Social Ser Spec Event, 1974; Nat Soc of Interior Designers; Am Inst of Interior Designers; WAIF-Intl Social Ser; Former or Present Mem: National Home Fashions Leag, IPA, Stanford Alumni Assn, SF Mus of Art; Bd Mem, No CA Peninsula Chapt, ASID, 1983; Representative of Sculptor Richard Lippold, 1983; cp/Mem, San Mateo Co Jr Mus Aux, 1956-; Former or Present Mem: CA Palace of Legion of Hon, SF Ballet Guild, Far W Ski Assn, Far World Ski Clb, Menlo Pk Tennis Clb, Eng Spkg Union; Chm, SF Host Com Dinner Dance Honoring the Consul Generals and Mayor Dianne Feinstein, 1979; Chm, March of Dimes Tribute to Beverly Sills Benefit, 1979; Mem, Exec Bd, SF Host Com, 1979; hon/DIB.

RIVENES, JAMES DIXON oc/Executive; b/Aug 20, 1935; h/44 Riverside Drive, Bozeman, MT 59715; ba/Bozeman, MT; m/Kay Sommers; c/James Sommers, Traci Jane; p/James H and Virginia Nelson (dec) Rivenes; sp/Ralph and Bresis Sommers; ed/BA, Univ of WA, 1953; mil/Capt, USMC; pa/J A Hogle, 1961-63; Goodbody & Co, 1963-70; Boettcher & Co, 1970-72; E F Hutton, 1972-73; E Wilbur Saunders & Co, 1973-76; Mgr, Investmt Mgmt & Res, 1977-; Pres, Rivenes & Assocs Inc, 1981-; Marine Corps Resv Ofcrs Assn, 1962-65;

cp/VP, Exch Clb, 1965; S Coast Hosp Adv Bd, 1968; VP, Mission Viejo Swim & Racquet Clb Bd, 1966; Dir, Mouton Nigud Water Dist, 1966-70; VP, Mission Viejo Men's Clb, 1967; Bozeman Pk & Rec Bd, 1974-81; Mem, Elks & Optimist Clbs; hon/Pubs: "Outstanding Brokers" in Wall Street Transcript (1982), "I'm My Own Best Client" in The Digest of Financial Planning Ideas (1982); Outstg Brokers of 1981 "Top 20"; W/W Fin and Indust.

RIVERA, HÉCTOR A oc/Executive; b/Apr 4, 1946; h/Arroyo C-5, El Remanso, Rio Piedras, PR 00926; ba/Rio Piedras, PR; m/Jeanette Biascoechea; c/Jeansselle, Joanne, Héctor Alcy; p/Héctor and Luz Delia; sp/Alcione and Conchita; ed/BSIE, 1969; mil/USAR, 6 Yrs, Hon Discharge; pa/Asst Ser Mgr, USI PR Inc; Parts & Ser Mgr, TAC Corp; Exec VP, Heridel Inc; Pres, Heridel Inc; AGC of Am, PR Chapt, Dir 1982; AWWA; hon/Pub, Thesis on IE, 1969; W/W in S & SW.

RIVERA, LESLIE ANN oc/Volunteer Coordinator; b/Mar 7, 1947; h/73 Edgewater Drive, Coral Gables, FL 33133; p/Jean MacIvor Rivera, Coral Gables, FL; ed/MA in Brit Lit, Wroxton Col of Fairleigh Dickinson Univ, 1978; MA in Hist, Univ of RI, 1977; BA in Hist, Univ of Miami, 1970; Student of Hist, Univ of CO 1967, Gulf Pk Jr Col 1965; pa/Social Studies Tchr, Carrollton Sch for Girls, 1970-72; Sales Rep, Bauder Fashion Col, 1972; Hist Dept Chp, Tchr of Hist and Eng, Our Lady of Lourdes Acad, 1973-74; Social Studies Tchr, W Miami Jr High, 1974-75; Instr of Eng, Miami Dade Commun Col, S Campus, 1978; Curatorial Asst, Hist Assn of So FL, 1978-79; Asst to the VP of Public Relats and Spec Events, Burdines Dept Store, 1980; Vol Coor/Spec Events and Fellows Liaison, Hist Assn of So FL, 1981-83; Dir, Vols in Agys (Corresponding Secy); Assn for Vol Adm; AAUW; cp/Jr Leag of Miami Inc; Vizcaya Decorative Arts Mus, Pres of LA Leag 1980, 1981; hon/W/W Am Wom; World W/W Wom.

RIZZI, ROSE ASSUNTA ANN oc/Independent Researcher; b/Aug 12, 1947; h/PO Box 1354, State College, PA 16804; ba/University Park, PA; p/Mr and Mrs Joseph Rizzi, Staten Island, NY; ed/BA, Villa Maria Col, 1968; MA, City Univ of NY at Richmond, 1972; DEd, PA St Univ, 1983; pa/Employed by the Stats Dept, PA St Univ, 1982; Wk'd as a Reporter at the 1981 Conv of the ASHE in Wash, DC; Wk'd as a Conslt w Dr L Jackson for Res Psychols Press Inc, 1980; Res Asst, Adm Asst to the Dir, Ctr for the Study of Higher Ed, PA St Univ, 1977; Employed as a Tchr in Eng Lit, NYC Public Sch Sys, 1968-72 (Jr High 1971, Curtis HS, New Dorp HS); Currently Employed as a Rdg Spec and Cnslr; Pres, Pi Lambda Theta, Alpha Kappa Chapt, a Nat Profl and Ednl Hon Soc, 1977; Pres, Villa Maria Col Alumnae Assn, NY and Metro Chapt, 1974-76; ASHE; AAHE; AACD; AERA; Gamma Chi Lambda Hon Soc; CCD; hon/Pub: Principles, Practices, and Alternatives in State Methods of Financing Community Colleges and an Approach to Their Evaluation: With Pennsylvania a Case State (S V Martorana and James Wattenbarger, w the assistance of David C Nichols, William Andre, and Rose Rizzi), 1978; Selected as One of 18 Students in the Nation to Serve as a Reporter at the 1981 ASHE Conv in Wash, DC; Selected in 1980 as One of

20 Students in the Nation to Attend the Sem on Nat Higher Ed Policy in Wash, DC (Sponsored by ASHE, AAHE, and ERIC Clearinghouse on Higher Ed); Elected Pres of Pi Lambda Theta, 1976-77; Chw of the Class of 1968 for Villa Maria Col S'ship Fund Drive, 1975; Elected Pres for 2 Yrs, NY Chapt of Villa Maria Col's Alumnae Assn, 1974-76; Selected for Mbrship in Gamma Chi Lambda Hon Soc for Super Achmts in Rdg, 1969.

ROADEN, ARLISS L oc/University President; b/Sep 27, 1930; h/Box 5007-TTU, Cookeville, TN 38501; ba/ Same; m/Mary Etta Mitchell; c/Janice Roaden Skelton, Sharon Roaden Hagen; p/Mr and Mrs J S Roaden, Corbin, KY; ed/EdD 1961, MS 1958, Ednl Adm, Univ of TN Knoxville; AB, cum laude, Eng, Carson Newman Col, 1951; mil/AUS Signal Corps, 1951-53; pa/Tchr, Elem Sch, 1949-50; Staff Asst, Univ Relats Div, Oak Ridge Inst Nuclear Studies, 1957-59; Asst Prof, Auburn Univ, 1961-62; Asst Prof, Assoc Prof, Prof, Sch of Ed, OH St Univ, 1962-74; Dir, Dean of Grad Studies, Acting Dean for Sch of Ed, Vice Provost for Res, Pres, TN Technological Univ, 1974-; Bd of Dirs, Am Bk & Trust; Chm, Bd of Govs, Phi Delta Kappa; St Rep, Am Assn of St Cols and Univs; Phi Kappa Phi; cp/Rotary; Lions Clb; BSA; Exec Bd, U Way; Bd of Dirs, Teen Challenge; hon/Editor, *Problems of School Men in Depressed Urban Centers*, 1969; Co-Author, *The Research Assistantship*, 1975; Cent Medallion for Dist'd Fac, OH St, 1970; Dist'd Alumnus, Cumberland Col, 1975; W/W Am; Outstg Personalities in the S; DIB; Book of Hon; Men of Achmt; Commun Ldrs of Am.

ROARK, JACQUELYN DeVORE oc/ Director of Admissions; b/Sep 12, 1950; h/100 Gracemont Drive, Greenwood, SC 29646; ba/Greenwood, SC; m/Walter Lynch III; c/Walter Lynch IV; p/Mr and Mrs W N DeVore, Greenwood, SC; sp/ Mr and Mrs W L Roark Jr, Greenwood, SC; ed/BS, Lander Col, 1972; MEd, Clemson Univ, 1975; pa/Admissions Cnslr 1972-73, Asst Dir of Admissions 1974-76, Dir of Admissions 1977-, Lander Col; Delta Kappa Gamma Soc Intl; Alpha Phi Intl Frat; Greenwood Personnel Assn; Am Coun of Higher Ed; APGA; Am Assn of Col Registrars and Admissions Ofcrs; Carolina and So Assn of Col Registrars and Admissions Ofcrs, (EOE, Chm 1978-79); cp/Bd of Dirs, Lung Assn; Greenwood Wom's Forum; Greenwood Wom's Clb; hon/Yg Careerist for Greenwood Co, BPW Clb; W/W Am Cols and Univs; Outstg Yg Wom of Am; World W/W Wom.

ROBBINS, DONALD S oc/Advanced Financial Planner; b/Aug 4, 1944; h/14321 Goldfish, Corpus Christi, TX 78418; ba/ Corpus Christi, TX; m/Amy Joyce; c/ Scarlet, Angela, Scott, Michelle; p/Mozell Ruby Robbins, Kosse, TX; ed/Grad, Lyford HS, 1962; pa/Duke & Ayers Inc, 1963-66; Self-Employed, Sales, Corpus Christi, 1966-68; Nat Life & Accident, 1968-69; Prudential Ins Co, 1969-75; Robbins & Assocs, 1975-79; E F Hutton, 1979-; VP, Investmts, Prudential-Bache Securities; hon/Prudential Pres Roundtable, 1972, 1974; Pres Cit, 1973; Intl Hon Clb, 1973; Ldrs Roundtable, 1973; Dist Man of the Yr, 1973; Million Dollar Roundtable, 1974, 1975, 1976, 1977; Security Life's Pres Clb, 1976, 1977, 1978; Security Life's Pres Roundtable, 1977,

1978; Security Life's Hon Coun, 1977, 1978; Security Life's Golden Spur, 1977, 1978; E F Hutton Century Coun, 1979, 1980, 1981, 1982; E F Hutton Pres Cabinet, 1980, 1981, 1982; Hutton Life Spec Awd, 1980; Hutton Financial Sers Ldg Financial Planner, 1981; Hutton Financial Sers Mktg Adv Coun, 1982; W/ W S and SW.

ROBERTS, DELNO M oc/Assistant Librarian for Public Services; b/Dec 31, 1920; h/849 East North 11th Street, Abilene, TX 79601; ba/Abilene, TX; m/ J W (dec); c/Jay Wheeler, Kathy F Brown; p/Mr and Mrs Reynolds M Wheeler (dec); sp/Mr (dec) and Mrs R L Roberts Sr, Abilene, TX; ed/Att'd, Martin Col, 1938-39; BA 1941, MEd 1973, Abilene Christian Univ; MLS, N TX St Univ, 1975; pa/Freshman and Sophomore Eng Tchr, Holliday HS, 1941-42; Clerical Ofc Wk (War Effort), Wichita Wire Products, 1944-45; Minister's Wife in Ser of Riverside Ch of Christ and Brightwood Ch of Christ, 1942-46; Exec Secy to Pres 1953-69, Exec Secy to Chancellor 1969-74, Asst Libn 1975-, Abilene Christian Univ; AAUW, 1965-, Newsletter Editor 1970-72, Recording Secy 1972-74; Charter Mem, Wom of ACU; Delta Kappa Gamma, 1981-; Am Lib Assn and SWn Lib Assn, 1975-; TX Lib Assn, 1974-; NTSU Alumni Bd, Sch of Lib and Info Sci, 1980-81; Secy, TX Lib Assn Interlibrary Loan Roundtable, 1980-81; hon/ Pubs: "Rich Heritage" 1959, "The Generous and the Honest Man" 1968, "The Radiance of Faith" 1968, "The Impact of OCLC Networking on Interlibrary Loans" 1977; Edit Asst and Typist for Husband's 200+ Rel Articles, 3 Commentaries, and 6 Study Guides; Valedictorian, Giles Co HS, 1941; Phi Theta Kappa (Jr Col Hon Soc), and Lettered in Basketball, 1938-39; ACU Hon Grad (Highest), 1941; Alpha Chi, 1941; Alpha Lambda Sigma and Beta Phi Mu (NTSU Hon Lib Sci Soc, Same on Nat Level), 1975-; AAUW S'ship, 1974-75; ACU Alumni Dir.

ROBERTS, JOHN ARNOLD oc/Engineering Manager; b/Jan 11, 1945; h/66 Westchester Drive, Picayune, MS 39466; ba/Picayune, MS; m/Mildred Ann; c/ Charles Alan Pfadenhauer; p/John C and Helen O Roberts, Hunnewell, MO; sp/ Bill Jayne, Burlington, IA; Rita Hanna Danville, IA; ed/BSME, Univ of MO Columbia, 1968; pa/Load, Assemble and Pack Engr 1968-71, Sr Engr 1971-74, Proj Engr 1974-76, Mason and Hanger, Burlington, IA; Load, Assemble and Pack Sr Proj Engr 1976-80, Deptl Engr 1980-82, Engrg Mgr 1982-, Mason Chamberlain Inc; Am Def Preparedness Assn, Bd of Dirs; Lake Pontchartrain Chapt, Am Def Preparedness Assn; hon/ W/W S and SW.

ROBERTS, STEVEN MAURICE oc/ Professional Counselor in Private Practice; b/Nov 2, 1949; h/PO Box 763, Woodville, TX 75979; ba/Same; c/Joseph Dylan; p/Huie Jr and Katherine Hayes Roberts, Dothan, AL; ed/BA in Rel Studies, Univ of AL, 1974; MS in Cnslg and Guid, Troy St Univ, 1977; mil/AL Army NG, 1970-76; pa/Psychi Aide, Bryce St Hosp, 1972-74; Cnslr, Wiregrass Mtl Hlth Ctr, 1974-77; Dir, Red River Co Satellite, Ark-Tex Ctr for Human Sers, 1977-78; Dir, Tyler Co Outpatient Clin, Deep E TX MHMR, 1978-82; Profl Cnslr in Pvt Pract, 1982-; APGA; AMHCA; cp/Lions Clb; r/Bapt; hon/W/

W S and SW.

ROBERTSON, GEORGE WILBER oc/ Consulting Agrometeorologist; b/Dec 20, 1914; h/Box 1120, Kemptville, Ontario, Canada K0G 1J0; m/Lucille Eileen Davis; c/Glenn Petrie, Shirley Leila Robertson MacMillan; p/Joseph D and Elizabeth Petrie Robertson; sp/George Evans and Jeanne Sasseville Davis; ed/BSc, Math and Physics, Univ of Alberta, 1939; MA, Physics and Meteorology, Univ of Toronto, 1948; pa/Completed w the Comm for Agri Meteorology of WMO (1983): Mem of a Wk'g Grp on Agrometeorological Sers in Devel'g Countries, Rapporteur on the Application of Models and Forecasting of Devel and Ripening of Crops, Mem of Task Force on Crop-Weather Models; Chaired Sci Sessions; Org'd Confs and Sects of Symposia; Conducted WMO Roving Sem on Agri Meteorology in Several Countries in Asia; Lectured at Instituto Agronomico, Campinas, Brazil, and Caribbean Meteorlogical Inst, Bridgetown, Barbados; Vis'g Profl Lectr, Univ of the Philippines, Manila, 1969-71; Assoc Mem of the Fac of Grad Studies, Univ of Guelph, 1978-80; Assoc Editor, *Journal of Applied Meteorology*, 1962-72; Edit Adv Bd, *Journal of Envir Research*, 1967-77; Canadian Consltg Agrologists Assn; Agri Inst of Canada; Ontario Inst of Agrologists; Canadian Soc of Agronomy; Canadian Meteorological and Oceanographic Soc; Am Meteorological Soc; Royal Meteorological Soc; Intl Soc of Biometeorology; AAAS; NY Acad of Scis hon/ Author, Num Pubs; Pres's Awd, Royal Meteorological Soc, Canadian Br, 1951; Darton Prize, Royal Meteorological Soc, 1955; Awd in Applied Meteorology, Canadian Meteorological Soc, 1966; W/ W E; W/W Brit Scists.

ROBERTSON, PATRICK WAYNE oc/ Funeral Director; b/Mar 10, 1955; h/310 South Jefferson, Clarendon, TX 79226; ba/Clarendon, TX 79226; p/Delbert W and Patsy Wallace Robertson, Clarendon, TX; ed/Hon Grad, Clarendon HS, 1973; Att'd, Clarendon Jr Col, 1973-74; Grad, Dallas Inst of Mortuary Sci, 1975; TX EMT, 1978; TX Cert'd Paramedic, 1979-; EMS Instr, 1980-; pa/Apprentice Funeral Dir and Embalmer, Robertson Funeral Dirs, 1973-74; Student Public Relats Asst, Clarendon Jr Col, 1973-74; Staff Employee 1975-76, Jr Ptnr 1976-, Roberson Funeral Dirs; Lic'd Funeral Dir and Embalmer; CEMS Assn, Past Pres (1 Yr); TX Assn EMT; Nat Assn EMT; cp/Vol, Clarendon Emer Med Sers, 1973-; Clarendon Vol Fire Dept, 1975-, Past Pres (1 Yr), Past Secy (2 Yrs); Rescue Squad, 1975-; TX A&M Fire Acad, 2 Yrs; Canyon FD Fire Acad, 2 Yrs; r/Christian; hon/ Eagle Scout; God and Country Awd; Order of the Arrow-Brotherhood Awd; Clarendon C of C Commun Ser Awd, 1980; Xi Lambda Xi Chapt, Beta Sigma Phi, People Helping People Awd, 1981.

ROBICHAUD, PHYLLIS ISABEL oc/ Art Teacher and Artist; b/May 16, 1915; h/1053 Lenox Circle, New Port Richey, FL 33552; m/Roger Joseph; c/George Wilmot Graham, William Henry Graham, Phyllis Mary Elizabeth Graham Watson; Peter Robert Burnett Graham; ed/Grad, Tutorial Col, Kingston, Jamaica, West Indies, 1933; Att'd, Munro Col (St Elizabeth, Jamaica) 1946, Ctl Tech Sch (Toronto, Canada) 1960-63, Anderson Col (Canada) 1968-69; pa/Secy to Supvr of 1940-50; Loans Ofcr and Cashier, Confdn Life Assn, Kingston, 1950-53; Tchr, Art, Jamaica Wel Ltd, 1963; Tchr, Art, Rec Dept, New Pt Richey, FL, 1969-77; Tchr, Art, Pasco Hernando Commun Col, New Pt Richey, 1977-; Mem and Past VP, Tampa Br, Nat Leag of Am Pen Wom; FL Fine Arts Guild; W Pasco Art Guild; VP, Holiday, FL, Lioness Clb; r/Cath; hon/Awd, T Eaton Co of Canada, 1961; Art Cert of Merit, Mayor of New Pt Richey, 1976; Plaque, New Pt Richey Rec Ctr, 1977; Awd, FL Heart Assn; World W/W Wom; Am W/W Wom; W/W Intells; Intl W/W; Many Others.

ROBINSON, DONNA MACKEY oc/ Artist and Instructor; b/Aug 29, 1951; h/ 1426 Parker Drive, Laurel, MS 39440; ba/ Same; m/Christopher Harold; p/James Wilson Mackey, Laurel, MS; sp/Mr and Mrs R H Robinson, Meridian, MS; ed/ Grad, R H Watkins HS, 1969; Grad, Jones Co Jr Col, 1971; Student, Liberal Arts, Art Instrn Sch, Minneapolis, MN, 1982; pa/Long Distance Operator, S Ctl Telephone Co, 1969-75; The Diamond Shop, 1977-78; Drafter, Schlumberger, Cased Hole Well Sers, 1978-81; Bd of Dirs, Jones Co Art Assn, 1983-84; cp/Ladies Aux of Fraternal Order of Police; YWCA, 1978-.

ROBINSON, JAMES C oc/Assistant Professor; b/Aug 28, 1945; h/Route 1, Box 190-B, Bowman, SC 29018; ba/Orangeburg, SC; m/Priscilla L; c/Jamaal C, Joel Perrin; p/Mr and Mrs Thomas E Robinson, Orangeburg, SC; sp/Rev and Mrs James Glover Jr, Bowman, SC; ed/BA, Morehouse Col, 1967; MEd, SC St Col, 1971; EdD, Univ of MA, 1973; mil/USN, 1968-69; pa/Social Studies Tchr, Bowman HS, 1967-68; Guid Cnslr, Guinyard Mid Sch, 1970; Asst Prof of Ed, Lincoln Univ, 1973-74; Dir, ACTION Prog, SC St Col, 1975-76; Asst Prof, Coor of Cnslr Ed, SC St Col, 1977-; APGA, 1977-; SC Pers and Guid Assn, 1977-; Assn for Rel and Value Interests in Cnslg, 1977-; Assn for Sch Cnslrs, 1977-; cp/Alston Wilkes Soc, 1975-; hon/Pubs: *South Carolina's Black Colleges: A Strategy for Survival* (dissertation) 1973, *Black Colleges: A Vital Necessity*, "Counseling the Right Brained Child," Others; Awd for Excell (Grad Student), Univ of MA, 1973; Outstg Tchr, Dept of Ed, Lincoln Univ, 1974.

ROBINSON, MARY LOIS CLARK oc/ Elementary Teacher; b/Jun 8, 1917; h/513 Graham Road, Danville, KY 40422; ba/ Danville, KY; m/John Earl; c/Betsy Lois, John Earl Jr, Patricia Ann; p/William Langford and Bessie Lee Lanter Clark (dec); sp/Walter Pascal and Beulah Surface Robinson (dec); ed/BS in Eng and Communication 1938, MA in Elem Ed 1971, Spec in Elem Ed 1975, En KY Univ; pa/Tchr, Stearns HS, 1938; Secy, Blue Grass Dept, Richmond, KY, 1943; Secy, Murray Tr Sch, 1952; Secy, Lex Ave Bapt Ch, 1962; Bkkpr, Danville HS, 1964-66; Tchr, Danville City Schs, 1966-; KY Gov's Coun on Tchr Ed and Cert, 1972-76; Pres, AAUW, 1974-76; Pres, Danville Ed Assn, 1974-75; Pres, Tchrs' Book Clb; Alpha Delta Kappa; Delta Kappa Gamma, Hon Tchrs' Grp (Pres); cp/KY Hist Soc; DAR; Filson Clb; KY Genealogical Soc; r/ Disciples of Christ; hon/Editor and Publisher of Poems by Nell Lanter Wells, 1979; Editor and Publisher of *Stories Out of This World* (by Students at Hogsett Sch); Author, *My Roots* (Lanter and Allied Fams), 1982; Recip, AAUW S'ship, 1967; Recip, Outstg Alumni Awd, En KY Univ,

1974.

ROBINSON, ROBBY oc/Model, Nutrition Consultant, World Champion Bodybuilder; b/May 24, 1946; h/PO Box 982, Venice, CA 90291; m/Elaine; c/Sherrie, Tonya, Robert III; ed/AA in Hlth and Nutrition, Tallahassee Jr Col; mil/AUS, 82nd Airborne Paratrooper Div; pa/ Model for Swimwear Spreads; Sems and Posing Exhbns, US and Europe; Guest Appearances, US and Europe; Promotional Wk as Rep of Weider Res Inst; Movie and TV Appearances: *Pumping Iron* 1977-78, *Stay Hungry* 1975, "Streets of San Francisco" 1976; Prodns: Posters and Photos, T-Shirts, Tank Tops and Chemise Vest Tops, Personal Diet and Tng Prog; Robby Robinson Bodybuilding Day Camps, 1979-80; Pvt Coaching; Tchr of Hlth and Nutrition, Alternative Acad, Watts; Jr HS Tchr of Rdg; Intl Fdn of Bodybldg; Weider Res Inst; hon/Pubs, Tng Manuals (1976): *Chest and Back Routine, Shoulder Routine, Leg Routine, Arm Routine,* Magazine Articles for *Muscle and Fitness* 1975-, Magazine Columns for *Muscle and Fitness* 1977-80, 1983; hon/Maj Titles: Mr Olympia (over 200 lbs), Mr Universe, Mr World, Mr Intl, Mr Am, Profl World Cup, Night of Champions, Best of the World; Key to the City of Pgh; Purple Heart, AUS; Dist'd Ser Cross, AUS; S'ship, Tallahassee Jr Col; Offers of Over 150 Other Col S'ships; Awds from Lincoln HS: All-Am Fullback, All-Am Track.

ROBSON, JOHN THEODORE oc/ Neurosurgeon; b/May 18, 1912; h/624 Crooked Creek Drive, Nacogdoches, Texas; ba/Nacogodoches, TX; m/Gail; c/ John, Burr, Leila, Hannah, Matthew; p/ Margaret Kelly (dec); ed/BA 1937, BS 1938, JD 1956, Univ of Washington; MS, Univ of MN, 1976; MD, Oregon, 1942; pa/Prof of Neurosurg, Univ of ND; AOA, Med Hon, 1942; Pres, MMHA; hon/ Author, Num Pubs.

ROCKEFELLER, JOHN DAVISON IV oc/Governor; b/Jun 18, 1937; m/Sharon Percy; c/Jamie, Valerie, Charles, Justin; ed/Att'd, Intl Christian Univ, Tokyo, Japan; Studied, Yale Univ; Grad, Harvard Univ; pa/Re-Elected Gov of WV in 1980 by 65,000 Votes (the First Dem Gov in the Hist of the St to Serve Two Consecutive Terms); Served as Chm, White House Conf on Balanced Nat Growth, the So Reg Ed Bd, and the Pres's Comm on Coal; Chair, Comm on Energy and the Envir of the Nat Govs' Assn; r/Presb.

RODGERS, MARC DAVID oc/Insurance and Accounting Executive; b/Dec 3, 1948; h/4625 Julington Creek Road, Jacksonville, FL 32223; ba/Jacksonville, FL; p/Arnie J Rodgers (dec); Marie Hooker, Valdosta, GA; ed/DSc in Acctg, Am Univ; pa/Sales Rep, U Inns of Am, 1970-71; Controller and Treas 1971-, Exec VP 1982-, Brandick Co & Assocs Inc; Exec VP, St Johns Ins Mgmt, 1982-; VP, St Johns Aviation, 1977-; Pres, Chm of the Bd, Adv'd Acctg Concepts, 1982; Nat Assn of Accts, 1976-; Ins Acctg and Stat Assn, 1978; Pres, Citizens for Mandarin Devel, 1981; hon/W/W S and SW.

RODMANN, DOROTHY P oc/Personnel Director; b/Dec 1, 1930; h/8428 Georgian Way, Annandale, VA 22003; ba/ Washington, DC; m/Horst; c/Leslie A, Karen L; sp/Charlotte Rodmann, Mainz, Germany; ed/BA 1954, Grad Wk 1954-55, George Wash Univ; pa/Pers Dir, Am Chem Soc, 1977-; Pers Mgr, Leag of

Cities/Conf of Mayors, 1972-77; Pers Asst, Employmt Mgr, NEA, 1959-72; Wash Pers Assn, 1973-; Conf of Instnl Admrs, 1979-; hon/Intl W/W Wom; W/ W Am Wom.

RODRIGUEZ, FRED HENRY JR oc/ Pathologist; b/Oct 5, 1950; ba/1601 Perdido Street, Lab Service (113), New Orleans, LA 70146; m/Susan M; c/Alison P, Fred H III, Kathryn L; p/Mr and Mrs Fred H Rodriguez Sr; sp/Mr and Mrs Ignatius Di George; ed/BS, Biol, Univ of NO, 1972; MD, LA St Univ Sch of Med, 1975; pa/Residency in Pathol, Charity Hosp, NO, 1975-79; Staff Pathol, VA Med Ctr, NO, 1979-; Asst Prof, LA St Univ Med Ctr, Dept of Pathol, 1980-; Dir, VA Med Ctr Sch of Med Technol, 1979-; Vis'g Pathol, Charity Hosp, 1979-; AMA; So Med Assn; Am Soc Clin Pathols; Internation Acad of Pathol, US-Canadian Div; Phi Eta Sigma Hon Frat; Beta Beta Beta Hon Soc; Phi Kappa Phi Hon Soc; Bd of Dirs, NO Ronald McDonald House; hon/Author of Co-Author of 20 Sci Papers in Var Jours; Biol Scis Awd, Univ of NO, 1972; Am Cancer Soc Grantee, 1974; AMA Phys Recog Awd, 1978, 1981; W/W Am Cols and Univs; W/W S and SW.

RODRIGUEZ, ILUMINADA R oc/ Administrator; b/Sep 13, 1935; h/2333 Hudson Terrace, Fort Lee, NJ 07024; ba/ New York, NY; m/Proculo Jr; c/Jed Luther, Jasmin Lucy Rodriguez Punla, Zinnia Joyce Rodriguez Tanglao; p/ Laureano Rovillos (dec); Catalina Floro; sp/Proculo Rodriguez Sr (dec); Eleuteria Cuizon; ed/Dipl in Nsg, Mary Johnston Col of Nsg, 1956; BS in Nsg, Philippine Wom's Univ, 1966; MPH, Johns Hopkins Univ, 1973; Fam Planning Nurse Practitioner Cert, NJ Col of Med and Dentistry, 1975; pa/Exec Dir, Fam Life/ Population Prog, Ch World Ser, 1976-; Adm Supr, Maternity and Fam Planning Div, Prince George Co Hlth Dept, MD, 1973-75; Fam Planning/Population Conslt, Govtl Affairs Inst, Wash, DC, 1972-73; Prog Ofcr/Tng Spec, Fam Planning Org of the Philippines, Manila, 1969-72; Tng Coor, Planned Parenthood Movement, Manila, 1964-69; Hd Nurse, Admitting/Outpatient Dept and Public Hlth, Mary Johnston Hosp, 1960-64; Participated as Del to Several Intl Population/Fam Planning Wk/Shops, Sem and Confs; hon/Intl Dir of Biog.

RODRÍGUEZ, MARÍA AMELIA oc/ Social Studies General Supervisor; b/ Mar 21, 1932; h/Santa Cecilia B-5, Caguas, PR 00625; ba/Hato Rey, PR; m/ Jose Enrique Torres; c/Ruth, Arlyn, Arnaldo; p/Ramón Rodríguez Acero; Amelia Rivera; sp/Flor and María Torres; ed/PhD Cand, NY Univ; PhD Cand, Caribbean Ctr for Postgrad Studies; MA 1968, BA in Sec'dy Ed 1965, BA in Elem Ed 1956, Normal Dipl 1950, Univ of PR; pa/Sec'dy Sch Tchr 1950-56, Elem Sch Tchr 1962-69, Elem & Sec'dy Sch Prin 1969-70, Social Studies Reg Gen Supr 1970-72, Social Studies Gen Supr 1970-, Dept of Ed; Psych Col Prof, Caguas City Col, 1980-; Affil Mem, Am Psychol Assn, 1976-; Assn for Supvn & Curric Devel, 1980-; Asociación de Maestros de PR, 1950-; NEA, 1950-; Conslt, Geriatric Ctr, 1980-; Nat Coun for the Social Studies; hon/Pubs: Master's Thesis, "Percepciones que tiene los estudiantes delas reglas escolares," Univ of PR (1968), & "Elementos Básicos de

Psicología," Dept of Ed (1974); S'ship, Univ of PR, 1950-52; S'ship, Dept of Ed, 1966-68, 1977-79; Fulbright Grant, 1980; W/W S & SW; Nat Dean's List.

RODRÍGUEZ ALCALÁ, MARÍA T oc/Doctoral Student; b/Oct 15, 1952; h/ 397 State Street, Apartment 9-A, Albany, NY 12210; p/José and María Isabel Rodríguez Alcalá, Ponce, PR; ed/ BA in Polit Sci 1973, JD 1976, Cath Univ of PR; MA in Intl Affairs, FL St Univ, 1978; Studying towards PhD, SUNY-Albany; pa/Admitted to the PR Bar, 1977; Pvt Pract of Law, Ponce, PR, 1978-80; Instr, Polit Sci Dept 1978-82, Asst Prof 1982, Cath Univ of PR; Phi Alpha Theta, 1972; Phi Alpha Delta, 1974, Vice-Justice 1975; Phi Delta Kappa, 1979; PR Bar Assn, 1977; Appt'd Mem to the Comm on Wom's Rts of the PR Bar Assn, 1980-82; Latin Am Studies Assn, 1981; Pi Gamma Mu, 1977; hon/Nat Dir of Latin Americanists, the Lib of Cong, 1981.

ROEBUCK, AUBREY LEANDER oc/ State Vocational-Technical Education Director; b/Jan 29, 1937; h/PO Box 3914, St Thomas, Virgin Isl 00801; ba/St Thomas, Virgin Isl; m/Edna; c/Bernard, Leander, Shawn; e/Ector Roebuck, St Thomas, Virgin Isl; sp/Roy and Eulalie Mahoney, Rio Rico, AZ; ed/BS, 1959 MEd, 1976; PhD, 1980; mil/ROTC; pa/ Lic'd Elect, 1981; Industl Arts Tchr, 1958-60; Voc Ed Instr, 1961-75; St Supvr, Trade & Industl Ed, 1976-79; St Dir, Voc-Tech Ed, 1979-; Vis'g Prof, Col of Virgin Isl; Mem: Pres, PTA; Chm, St Employmt Tng Coun; Chm St Occupl Info Coor Com; Am Voc Assn; cp/Lions Clb; r/Luth; hon/Author, *Assessment of Voc Ed in Virgin Isl*; Tchr of Yr, 1975; Outstg Ser Awd, 1981.

ROEDER, LARRY WINTER JR oc/ International Commodities Economist; b/ Dec 26, 1948; h/504 Bashford Lane, Apartment 201, Alexandria, VA 22314; ba/Washington, DC; p/Mr and Mrs Larry Winter Roeder; ed/BA, Culver-Stockton Col, 1974; MLS, Cath Univ, 1977; Post Grad Study, George Wash Univ, 1982-; mil/AUS, 1969-72; pa/Fgn Affairs Resr 1975-81, Fgn Affairs Ofcr (Intl Commodities Economist) 1981-, Dept of St, Wash DC; Chief, US Negotiating Tm on Elect Instruments 1983, Acting Permanent US Del 1983, COCOM, Paris; Mem: Mensa; Pi Kappa Delta; Sigma Tau Delta; Mid E Inst; Chm, Palestine-Israeli Wkg Grp of Sec of St's Open Forum, 1979-82; Bd of Dirs, Blair House Lib Foun, 1976-81; Conslt, Haya Arts Ctr Proj, Amman, Jordan, 1979-80; r/Rom Cath; hon/Num Spchs & Articles on E-W & the Mid E; Lund Forensic Awd, 1974; Cert of Apprec for Wk on Iran Hostage Crisis, Dept of St, 1981; Cert of Apprec for Wk on Habib Peace Mission, Dept of St, 1983; Pi Kappa Delta Awd, 1974; W/W in E.

ROGERS, CAROL J oc/System Consultant; b/Oct 3, 1940; h/3305 Shores Boulevard, Wayzata, MN 55391; ba/ Same; m/Donald Dee; c/Sue Ann Okun Vruno, Roxanne Leigh Okun Carlson, Wade William; p/John Edward Christensen (dec); Luella Grace Holland, Mpls, MN; sp/Otis Rogers and Mary Alice Minor, Wichita, KS; ed/Data Entry Cert, IBM, 1960; Modeling Dipl, Estelle Compton Inst, 1964; Profl Procedural Charting & Analyzation Cert, Stand Register, 1975; Documentation Preparation Cert, Manuals Corp of Am, 1978; pa/Indep Sys Conslt, Mpls, MN, 1978-;

Sys Flow Tech Anal, Super Valu Stores Inc, Eden Prairie, MN, 1974-78; Mktg Sers Coor, Naida's Girls Modeling Agy, Mpls, MN, 1970-72; Jewelry Sales, Demerest Sales, Phila, PA, 1971-72; Dir & Instr, Mary Lowe Modeling Sch, Mpls, MN, 1969-70; Upper MW Coor, (Pageants for MN, NE, ND, MI & WI), Miss Universe, 1967-71; MN Coor, Miss Am Teenager Pageants, 1965-69; Profl Model, Nat Promotional, 1965-72; Scheduling Coor, WTCN-TV, 1963-65; IBM Data Entry Spec, Hennipen Co Dept of Ct Sers, Mpls, MN, 1959-63; Mem: Netwk Dir 1983, Mem 1981-, Nat Assn for Female Execs; Pres 1983-84 & Var Positions w Agassiz Chapt, Am Bus Wom's Assn, 1982-; cp/ABIRA; Adv Coun, Sawyer Sch of Bus, Mpls, 1970; Modeling Instr & Spkr, MN Public Schs, 1969-71; SS Tchr 1980-84, Grace Luth Ch, Deephaven, MN, 1978-; r/Luth; hon/Won Trip to Bahamas, Nat Sales Contest of Demerest Sales, 1971; W/ W: Am Wom, of Wom, MW, Intells; Intl Register of Profiles; Dir of Dist'd Ams; Num Other Biogl Listings.

ROGERS, DOUGLAS GARY oc/Executive; b/Aug 13, 1942; h/2528 East Montebello Drive, Sandy, UT 84092; ba/ Midvale, UT; m/Marjorie Jean; c/Lisa Marie, David Mark; p/Elizabeth Rogers, Bountiful, UT; sp/Mr and Mrs Howard Sharp, SLC, UT; ed/Att'd Brigham Yg Univ-HI Campus; mil/USAF; pa/Exec VPres, Dir & Co-Fdr, Ad Media Intl, 1981-; Exec VPres & Dir, Common Carrier Advtg, 1978-80; Nat Tng Dir, Pertec Computer Corp, 1976-78; Wn Reg Tng Mgr 1972-76, Salesman 1969-72, 3M Co; Sales Mgr, *LA Times*, 1967-69; Mem: Am Platform Spkrs Assn; Sales & Mktg Execs Assn; Am Soc for Tng & Devel; Am Mgt Assn; r/Mormon; hon/Designed & Implementing Tng Progs for Num Cos; Former Recording Artist, w "The Coachmen"; W/W: in W, in Tng & Devel.

ROGERS, ROLF ERNST oc/Professor and Author; b/Aug 31, 1931; h/347 Vetter Lane, Arroyo Grande, CA 93420; ba/San Luis Obispo; p/Ernst and Philomena Rogers (dec); ed/MA 1968, PhD 1970, Univ of WA; USAF, 1951-55; pa/Prof, Univ of Alberta, Canada, 1970-75; Prof Mgmt, CA Polytech St Univ, 1975-; Vis'g Prof, Univ of So CA, 1981-82; Mem: Acad of Mgmt; Am Sociol Assn; hon/Author of 5 Books Incl'g: *Org & Mgmt*, 1983; *Corp Strategy & Planning*, 1981; *Orgl Theory*, 1975; *The Polit Process in Mod Orgs*, 1971; *Max Weber's Ideal Type Theory*, 1968; Num Articles in Profl Jours; Beta Gamma Sigma, 1968; Num W/W & Other Biogl Listings.

ROHLFS, JERRY MICHAEL oc/Businessman, Manager; b/Aug 18, 1946; h/ 1658 East 141st Avenue, Brighton, CO 80601; ba/Westminster, CO; m/Margaret Jane Robertson; c/Donald Maurice, Brandie Jean; p/Donald Henry and Edith Lois Rohlfs, Littleton, CO; sp/Dorman Maurice and Naida Birdene Robertson, Eagle, NE; ed/Grad, Littleton HS, 1964; Var Trade Ed; Asst Mgr, Safeway Corp, l1962-69; Sales, CO Delivery, 1969-71; Sales, Keebler Co, 1971-73; Owner/Mgr, A & R Assocs Inc, 1973-; cp/Dir & Chamber Ambassador, Westminster C of C; Bd Mem, Adams Co Bd of Adjustment; Appt'd, Westminster Trans Comm, 1982; Trustee, St Anthony Endowment Foun, 1984; Westminster Rotary Clb; N Metro Chamber; Repub Party Nom for Co Treas, 1982; Vol, USO; r/Presb; hon/

Bus-man of Yr, HS Pub'g Co, CO, 1982-83; Recog Cert Flight For Life, St Anthony Hosp Sys, 1982; Arch Awd, WOOD Inc, 1981; Bus-man of Yr Awd, Westminster C of C, 1980.

ROHRLICH, BEULAH F oc/Professor, Society President; b/Mar 1, 1929; h/226 Ridgecrest Road, Dewitt, NY 13214; ba/ Syracuse, NY & Washington, DC; m/ Iritz; c/Emily H (R) Graham, Paul E; p/ Abraham and Gertrude Friedman (dec); sp/Egon and Illy Rohrlich (dec); ed/BA, Queens Col, 1950; MA, Cornell Univ, 1951; PhD, Syracuse Univ, 1967; pa/Instr, Queens Col, 1952-53; Res Assoc, St Univ of IA, 1956-58; Vis'g Lectr, Syracuse Public Schs, 1964-65; Coor Spch Ed, Ford Foun Prog, 1964-65; Asst Prof 1967-72, Assoc Prof 1972-77, Prof 1978-, Syracuse Univ; Mem: Pres 1982-84, Pres-elect 1981-82, VPres 1980-81, Soc for Intl Ed Tng & Res (SIETAR); Chp Intercultural Commun Div, En Commun Assn, 1979-80; Mem-at-Large, NY St Spch Commun Assn, 1976-79; Chp, NY St BPW Assn S'ship Com, 1978-79; Pres Syracuse Univ Chapt, Phi Beta Kappa, 1975-76; cp/Conslt, Literacy Vols of Am, 1979-; hon/Author, Var Articles Pub'd in *Intl Jour of Intercultural Relats & Communique*; Author of Student Manual, *Interviewing*, 1977; Var Videotape Series; BA cum laude, 1950; Zeta Phi Eta Ser Awd, 1977; Phi Beta Kappa, 1950; W/W: of Am Wom, in Ed; Dir of Am Scholars; Contemp Personalities.

ROLWES, MARK S oc/Space Shuttle Flight Engineer; b/Mar 28, 1956; h/17030 Coachmaker, Friendswood, TX 77546; ba/Houston, TX; m/Mary K; p/Robert Rolwes, St Louis, MO; sp/Gerard Proctor, St Louis, MO; ed/BS, So Ill Univ-Edwardsville, 1979; pa/On-Orbit Attitude & Pointing Ofcr 1978-81, Sr Engr Shuttle Flight Opers 1981-, McDonnel Douglas Tech Sers Co; cp/Area Capt, Houston Mgmt Clb, 1979; Men's Soc, Mary Queen Ch, 1981-; r/Cath; hon/Nat Merit S'ship Lttr of Commend, 1974; Nat Hon Soc, 1974; 1st Shuttle Flight Achmt Awd 1981, Public Ser Grp Achmt Awd 1981, NASA; Outstg Yg Men of Am.

ROMAN, STANFORD A JR oc/Physician, Educator, Administrator; b/Nov 19, 1942; h/Goodfellow Road, RFD, Lynne, NH 03768; ba/Hanover, NH; m/ Mgina Lythcott; c/Maniyah; p/Mr & Mrs Stanford Roman, NY, NY; sp/Mr George I Lythcott, Madison, WI; ed/BA, Dartmouth Col, 1964; MD, Columbia Univ Col of Phys & Surgs, 1968; MPH, Univ of MI Sch of Public Hlth, 1975; pa/ Instr of Med, Columbia Univ Col of Phys & Surgs, 1972-73; Assoc Dir Ambulatory Care, Harlem Hosp Ctr, 1972-73; Asst Prof Med, Univ of NC-Chapel Hill, 1973-74; Dir Clin Sers, Hlthco Inc, Soul City, NC, 1973-74; Asst Prof Med & Sociomed Scis 1974-78, Asst Dean Sch Med 1975-78, Boston Univ; Dir Ambulatory Care Sers, Boston City Hosp, 1974-78; Dir, Boston Comprehensive Sickle Cell Disease Ctr, 1975-78; Lectr in Hlth Sers, Harvard Univ Sch of Public Hlth, 1977-78; Assoc Prof Commun & Fam Med, Georgetown Univ Sch of Med, 1978-81; Assoc Prof Commun & Fam Med, Howard Univ Col of Med, 1978-81; Med Dir, DC Gen Hosp, 1978-81; Assoc Dean for Acad Affairs 1981-, Assoc Prof Commun & Fam Med 1981-, Dartmouth Med Sch; Mem: Assn of Am Med Cols; APHA; AMA; Nat Med Assn; Nat Assn of Minority Med Edrs; Num Advy & Consltg Positions; Num Acad Coms; hon/ Author, Over 15 Articles Pub'd in Profl Med & Hlth Jours; Var Spkg Presentations at Assn Meetings & Confs; W/W: in Hlth, in Black Am, in E.,

ROMERO-BARCELÓ, CARLOS ANTONIO oc/Governor of Puerto Rico; b/Sep 4, 1932; h/La Fortaleza, Suan Juan, PR 00901; ba/Same; m/Kathleen Donnely; c/Carlos, Andres, Juan Carlos, Melinda; p/Antonio Romero-Moreno and Josefina Barceb' De Romero (dec); sp/ Walter and Rosemary Donnelly, NY; ed/ BA, Yale Univ, 1953; LLB, Univ of PR, 1956; pa/Atty, Pvt Pract, San Juan, PR, 1956-58; Mayor of San Juan, PR, 1969-77 (2 Terms); Gov of PR, 1977-, (2 Terms); Mem: Co-Fdr 1967, VPres 1971, Pres 1974-, New Prog Party of PR; Nat Govs' Assn; Chm, So Govs Assn, 1980-81; Coun on Fgn Relats; r/Rom Cath; hon/ Hon LLD, Univ of Bridgeport, 1977; Outstg Yg Man of Yr, JC's, 1968; James J and Jane Hoey Awd for Interracial Justice, Cath Interracial Coun of NYC, 1977; Spec Gold Medal, Spanish Inst NYC, 1979; Atty Gen's Medal for Public Ser, US Dept of Justice, 1981; W/W: in Am, in World, in Am Polits, in S & SW; Men of Achmt; DIB; Other Biogl Listings.

RONNE, EDITH MASLIN oc/Lecturer and Writer on Antarctic Affairs; b/Oct 13, 1919; h/6323 Wiscasset Road, Bethesda, MD 20816; ba/Same; m/Finn Ronne (dec); c/Karen Ronne Tupek; p/ Charles J and Elizabeth P Maslin (dec); sp/Martin and Maren Ronne (dec); ed/ Att'd Col of Wooster, 1936-38; AB Hist & Eng, George Wash Univ, 1940; pa/Nat Geographic Soc, 1940-41; Info Spec Ofc of Intl Info & Cultural Affairs, Dept of St, 1941-47; Histn & Mem, Ronne Antarctic Res Expedition, 1946-48; Expeditions to Spitsbergen, 1962 & S Pole, 1971; Num Worldwide Lectures; Mem: Bd, UN Assn, 1960's; Histn Columbian Wom, George Wash Univ, 1960's; ARCS, 1960's; Asst Treas, VPres, Pres 1978-81, Soc of Wom Geographers; Histn, VPres 1981-, Nat Soc of Arts & Ltters; Salvation Army Aux, 1976-; r/Epis; hon/Correspondent, N Am Newspaper Alliance Inc, in Antarctica, 1946-48; Num Articles 1959, on Spitsbergen 1962, on S Pole 1971-82; Annual Ency Article, *Americana*, *Britannica*, 1948-71; Revisions for *Funk & Wagnalls*; Editor & Reviewer, Num Books, 1950's & 60's; 1st Am Wom to Set Foot on Antarctic Continent; Dept of Def Medal for Antarctic Exploration; Carried Soc of Wom Geographers Flag to S Pole, 1971; Terr-A-Qua Earth Globe Presented to Nat Archives in Recog of Capt & Mrs Romme's Exploration & Sci Res in Antarctica; W/W: of Am Wom; Num Other Biogl Listings.

ROOK, RONALD COHICK oc/ Teacher; b/Sep 2, 1938; h/216 Forest Hill Drive, Havelock, NC 28532; ba/Havelock, NC; m/Maureen Joan Magenis; c/ Michael, Patrick, KellyAnn; p/Arnold G and Dorothy May Cohick (dec); sp/Eugen L Magenis, Coral Gables, FL; Frances Flanagan (dec); ed/BS, Springfield Col, 1961; USN Flight Tng, 1963; MA Pepperdine Univ, 1976; MA & Prin Cert, E Carolina Univ, 1983; mil/USMC, 1960-81, Trans Helicopter/Aircraft Pilot; pa/Dir & Tchr 1981-; Baseball Coach 2 Yrs, Football Coach 1 Yr, HS Soccer 1 Yr, Alternative Lrng Ctr, Havelock, Mid Sch; Career w USMC: Resv Pvt to Maj;

Sqdrn Pilot & Cmdr; Two Tours in RVN, UH34 Helicopters & KD130 Trans Aircraft; Air Liaison Ofcr w 26th Marine Regt in RVN; Mem: The Ret'd Ofcrs Assn; FRA; NEA; NCAE; cp/Springfield Col Alumni, 1979-80; r/Presb; Meritorious Ser Medal; Air Medal w 13 Stars; Vietnam Sers Medal; Nat Def Ser Medal; Armed Forces Expeditionary Medal; Vietnam Campaign Medal; Combat Action Ribbon; Pres Unit Cit w Palm; Sea Ser Devel Ribbon.

ROPER, STEPHEN DAVID oc/Professor, Consultant; b/May 30, 1945; h/1612 Garfield Street, Denver, CO 80206; ba/ Denver, CO; p/Ruth T Roper (dec); ed/ BA, Harvard Col, 1967; PhD, Univ Col, Univ of London, 1970; Postdoct, Harvard Med Sch, 1973; pa/Instr, Harvard Med Sch, 1970-73; Asst Prof 1973-79, Assoc Prof 1979-, Univ of CO Med Sch; Mem: Chapts Com, Neurosci Soc; Neurobiol Study Sect, NIH; Assn for Chemoreception Scis; Am Physiol Soc; Fdr & Chm, Rocky Mt Reg Neurosci; Am Assn of Anatomists; hon/Author, Var Articles Pub'd in Profl Jours; BA magna cum laude, Harvard, 1967; Fullbright Fellow, 1967-69; NSF Predoct Fellow, NSF, 1969; NIH RCDA, 1978-82; W/W: in Frontiers of Sci, in W.

ROSE, SANFORD SAMUEL oc/Executive; b/Feb 10, 1938; h/110 Northside Road, Bellevue, WA 98004; ba/Tacoma, WA; m/Paula Jean; c/Alisa, Michael, Megan; p/Mr and Mrs Al Rose, Seattle, WA; sp/Mr and Mrs Leslie Sussman, Tacoma, WA; ed/BA, Univ of WA; Var Am Mgmt Assn Sems; mil/AUS, Inf 415th Regt, Capt; ROTC; pa/Pres & Bd of Dirs, Jet Equip & Tools (Largest Pvt Industl Equip Importer), Tacoma, WA, 1958-; Bd of Dirs, Gen Metals Inc of Tacoma; Mem: Constrn Indust Mfrs Assn; Am Rental Assn; Spec Tools & Fasteners Distbrs Assn; Nat Tire Dealers Retreaders Assn; Assn of Equip Distbrs; Mat Handling Equip Distbrs Assn; World Trade Ctr; Am Importers Assn; Motor & Equip Mfrs Assn; Am Retreaders Assn; Am Voc Assn; Nat Trade Show Exhibrs Assn; US C of C; Nat Assn of Credit Mgmt; Tocama BBB; Var C of C's; cp/ Bellevue Ath Clb; Ctl Pk Tennis Clb; Seattle Symph; Seattle Art Mus; Bellevue Art Mus; Bd Mem, Paul Barlin Dance Theater; Jewish Fam Ser; Bd of Dirs & VPres, Coun of Ops Hertzl-Ner Tamid; Bellevue Boys & Girls Clb; Brotherhood of Elks; Other Commun Activs; hon/ Apprec Awd to Coach Rose, Bellevue Boys & Girls Clb; Jet Reps Awd, Outstg Boss; VPres Zeta Beta Tau Frat, Univ of WA; White Br Ctr, JC's of Am; Num HS, Jr HS & Col Awds; W/W: in Am, in World, in W, in Fin & Indust; Men of Achmt; DIB; Num Other Biogl Listings.

ROSENBERG, CLAIRE FREHLING oc/Professor; b/Aug 20, 1926; h/4915 Bancroft Drive, New Orleans, LA 70122; ba/New Orleans, LA; m/Samuel I; c/Ann, Robert; p/Joseph M and Lilian M Frehling (dec); ed/BS 1967, MEd 1973, DEd 1977, Univ of NO; pa/Assoc Prof 1981-, Asst Prof 1977-81, Instr 1974-76, Spec Lectr for Col Ed, Univ of NO; Orleans Parish Sch Bd & Sys, 1969-79; Mem: AAUP; Assn for Supvn & Curric Devel; Am Voc Assn; LA Assn of Edrs; LA Assn for Higher Ed; LA Assn for Supvn & Curric Devel; LA Bus Ed Assn; LA Voc Assn; Nat Bus Ed Assn; NEA; Ofc Sys Res Assn;

So Bus Ed Assn; Assn of Tchr Edrs; Assn of Records Mgrs & Admrs Inc; Am Bus Commun Assn; cp/Block Chm, Am Cancer Soc; Brandeis Univ Wom's Com; City of Hope Foun; Chd's Hosp Wom's Aux; Contemp Arts Ctr; Friends of the Cabildo; Friends of the Laudubon Zoo; Block Chm, Heart Assn; Spec Donor Unit, Jewish Welfare Fund; Block Chm, Mother's March for Cancer Soc; Mutliple Sclerosis Foun; Nat Coun of Jewish Wom; Registry of Interpreters for the Deaf; Tuberculosis Assn; Block Chm, U Way; Num Spkg Presentations; Others; r/ Jewish; hon/Author, Over 20 Articles Pub'd in Profl Jours & Brochures; Var Reports; Beta Gamma Sigma, 1981; Omicron Delta Kappa, 1981; Real Pro Awd, Futute Bus Ldrs of Am, Phi Beta Lambda, 1980; Cert of Apprec, UNO-Carver Complex of Schs Ptnership Prog, 1980; Pres 1980-83, VPres 1978-80, Phi Kappa Phi; Alpha Theta Epsilon, 1977; Secy 1976-78, Kappa Delta Pi; Phi Delta Kappa, 1975; Mayor's Commend, City of NO, 1970; Public Ser Awd, WTIX, 1968; VPres 1967-68, Phi Chi Theta; W/W: in S & SW, in Am, of Wom, of Intels; Other Biogl Listings.

ROSENBLUM, HAROLD oc/Senior Staff Consultant; b/Mar 30, 1918; h/1310 Webster Street, Orlando, FL 32804; ba/ Silver Spring, MD; m/Hannah B; c/ Lawrence J, Susan L (R) Shevitz, Ira F; p/Joseph and Sadie Rosenblum (dec); sp/ Anna Wrubel (dec); ed/BChE, The Cooper Union, 1943; MEE, NY Univ, 1951; Undergrad Study, CUNY & Polytech Inst of Bklyn; Grad Study, Univ of FL & Univ of Ctl FL; Postgrad Study, NY Univ; mil/USN, Elects Tech 3/C; pa/ Hd Radar Sys Design Grp, NY Nav Shipyard, 1941-54; Elects Tech, USN, 1945-46; Positions at Nav Tng Equip Ctr, Orlando, FL, 1954-74 Incl: Hd Flight Tnr Br, Hd Air Tactics Br, Hd Strike/Air Def Sys Tnrs Div, Hd Aerospace Sys Tnrs Dept, Asst Tech Dir Air & Land Warfare, Hd Sys Engrg Dept, Dept Dir of Engrg; Mgmt Engrs Conslt, k1974-; Dir of Tech Mktg, Applied Devices Corp, Kissimmee, FL, 1977-78; Sr Staff Conslt, Singer Co, Link Simulation Sys Div, 1980-; Sr Mem, IEEE; NY Acad of Scis; Sigma Xi; cp/Chm, Ctl FL Cath/Jewish Dialogue; Bd of Dirs, Congreg Oheu Shalom, Orlando, FL; Bd of Dirs, Temple Israel, Orlando, FL; Bd of Dirs, Marathon Jewish Commun Ctr, Douglastown, NY; Bd of Govs, Solomon Schechter Sch, Rego Pk, NY; Pres, Pathfinders Toastmasteer Clb, Orlando; Pres, PTA Jr HS, 1972, Queens, NY; Dir Sci Projs N Shore Hebrew Acad, Gt Neck, NY; hon/Author of Var Reports for Profl Symps & Confs Incl'g: Nat Security Industl Assn Radar Landmass Symp, 1963 & 1st Nav Tng Equip Ctr/Indust Conf, 1966; from USN: Outstg Perf Awd 1970, Lttr of Congrats 1966, Awd of Merit in Grp Achmt 1963 & 1965, Commend 1951, 1961 & 1965, Sustained Superior Perf Awd 1963 & 1964, Superior Achmt Awd 1963, Superior Accomplishment Awd, 1960, Beneficial Suggestion Awd 1949 & 1957, Lttr of Apprec 1953 & 1957; W/W: in Elect Indust Engrg, in S & SW, in Technol Today, in Am; Am Men & Wom of Sci; Men of Achmt; Intl Scholars Dir; DIB; Commun Ldrs & Noteworthy Ams; Dirof Dist'd Ams; Intl Book of Hon; Num Other Biogl Listings.

ROSENFELD, ROBERT A oc/Director of Internship Programs; b/Mar 28, 1950;

h/Apartment UT-18, 4100 Massachusetts Avenue Northwest, Washington, DC 20016; ba/Wash DC; m/Karen; p/Jack Rosenfeld (dec); Marjorie Rosenfeld, St Louis, MO; sp/Mr and Mrs A J Bradbury, Rugley, Staffordshire, England; ed/AB, Syracuse Univ, 1973; MArch, Univ of CA-Berkeley, 1976; pa/Nat VPres, Assn of Student Chapts/AIA, 1976-78; Asst Dir of Profl Devel Progs, AIA, 1978-80; Mem: CA Reg Dir, Assn of Student Chapts/AIA, 1975-76; Accreditation Vis'g Tm, Nat Arch Accrediting Bd, 1975 & 1978; hon/Author, Num Edl & Profl Articles for Profl Jours; Ser Awd, CA Coun/AIA, 1975; Ser Awd, Assn of Student Chapts/AIA, 1977; Bd of Dirs Spec Cit, AIA, 1978; W/W Among Students in Am Univs & Cols; Dir of Dist'd Ams.

ROSENKRANZ, ROBERTO PEDRO oc/Pharmacologist; b/Mar 30, 1950; ba/ Syntex Research, 3401 Hillview Avenue, Palo Alto, CA 94304; m/Heather Lynn Blum; p/George and Edith Rosenkranz, Mexico City, Mexico; sp/Jerry and Jocelyn Blum, Los Altos Hills, CA; ed/AB, Stanford Univ, 1971; PhD, Univ of CA-Davis, 1980; pa/Neurobiol Resr, Instituto Nacional De Neurologia, Mexico, 1971--72; Mexican Del, Intl Grp on Drug Legis & Progs, Geneva, 1971-73; Dir Res, Centro Mexicano de Estudios en Farmacodependencia, 1972-73; Res Fellow, Dept of Med, Stanford Univ, 1980-82; Staff Resr, Syntex Res, Palo Alto, CA, 1982-; Mem: AAAS; NY Acad of Sci; Soc of Neurosci; Am Soc of Pharms & Exptl Therapeutics; Wn Pharm Soc; hon/Author, Over 30 Contbns of Articles to Profl Jours on Pharm; Recip, 2 US Chem Patents; Conslt to Mexican Pres Lic. Luis Echeverria Alvarez; Mexican Del to Jt US-Mex Exec Conf on Drug Abuse & Planning, 1972; Mexican Del to UN Social Def Res Inst, Rome, 1971-72.

ROSOWSKI, SUSAN JEAN oc/Professor; b/Jan 2, 1942; h/1810 South 25th Street, Lincoln, NE 68502; ba/Lincoln, NE; m/James Ray; c/Scott Merritt, David William; p/William and Alice Campbell, Tucson, AZ; sp/Josef Rosowski (dec); Elva Rosowski, Stanton, CA; ed/BA, Whittier Col, 1964; MA, Univ of AZ, 1967; PhD, Univ of AZ, 1974; pa/Asst Prof Eng 1976-78, Assoc Prof Eng 1978-82, Univ of NE-Omaha; Assoc Prof Eng (Spec in Willa Cather), Univ of NE-Lincoln, 1982-; Mem: Bd of Govs, Willa Cather Pioneer Meml & Edl Foun; Exec Coun 1980-83, Wn Lit Assn; MLA; Univ of NE-Lincoln Orgs: Univ Sen, 1978-79; Grad Coun, 1977-80; Co-Dir, Willa Cather Nat Sem, 1983; hon/Co-Editor, *Wom & Wn Am Lit*, 1982; Author, Over 20 Articles & Reviews on Willa Cather in Num Profl Jours Incl'g: *Wn Am Lit*; *Prairie Schooner*; *Studies in Am Fiction*; Others; Articles on Congreve, Joyce & Atwood; Danforth Assoc, 1980-; Gt Tchr Awd, 1980; Dir of Am Scholars.

ROSS, CHARLES WORTHINGTON IV oc/Safety and Health Consultant; b/ Jan 27, 1933; h/18 Ferndale Road, Madison, NJ 07940; ba/Madison, NJ; m/Betty L Waldvogel; c/Holly Theresa, Kristna Lynn, Amy Louise, Carol Ann; p/Mr and Mrs Charles W Ross III, Frederick, MD; sp/Mr and Mrs Henry Waldvogel (dec); ed/Att'd Univ of MD, 1951-54; Att'd Syracuse Univ, 1962-63; BA, MA Occupl Saety & Hlth, NY Univ, 1973-76; mil/ USAF, 1954-68, Capt; pa/W USAF: Sr

Navigator, Ground/Explosive/Nuclear Safety Ofcr; Gen Mgr, Mgmt Recruiters Inc, Norfolk, VA, 1968-71; Reg Safety Mgr, Mobil Oil Corp, Scarsdale, NY, 1971-75; Corp Safety Mgr, Schering-Plough Corp, Kenilworth, NJ, 1975-79; Corp Mgr Safety & Hlth, Westvaco Corp, NYC, NY, 1979-81; VPres, IHI-Kemron Inc, Huntington, NY, 1982-83; Dir Safety Progs, WAPORA Inc (Sub of IHI), 1983-; Mem: Chm Profl Paper Awds Com, Am Soc Safety Engrs; Nat Safety Mgmt Soc; Sys Safety Soc; Safety Execs of NY; Profl Engr (CA);Cert'd Safety Proflcp/Rotary Intl, 1970-79; r/Epis; hon/Author, *Intro to Computerized Safety Data Sys*, 1984; Var Articles in Profl Jours; Tech Paper Awds, 2nd Place, Am Soc of Safety Engrs/Vets of Safety, 1980; W/W in E.

ROSS, CHARLOTTE P oc/Suicide Prevention and Crisis Center Director; h/445 Virginia Avenue, San Mateo, CA 944-2; b/Burlingame, CA; c/Beverly R Jamison, Sandra Gail; p/Joseph Pack (dec); Rose Pack, Shawnee Mission, KS; ed/ Att'd Univ of OK, 1949-52; Att'd New Sch for Social Res, 1952-53; pa/Exec Dir, Suicide Preven & Crisis Ctr, San Mateo Co, CA, 1966-; Instr Suicide Preven Sum Courses, SF St Univ, 1980 & 1981; Crisis Intervention & Suicide Preven Instr, Canada Col, 1980; Suicide Crisis Instr, Col of San Mateo, 1981 & 1982; Sem Instr, Sch of Ed, Univ of CA-LA, 1976; Cont'g Ed Sems 1971-75, NIMH Adv'd Tng Suicide Preven 1970, Univ of CA Sch of Med, SF; Edit Bd, *Suicide & Life-Threatening Behavior*, 1976-; Editor: *Newslink*, Bltn of Am Assn of Suicidology, 1975-77; Mem: Secy 1972-74, Gov'g Bd 1974-, Chm Reg IX 1975-, Accreditation Com, Am Assn of Suicidology; Mem 1967-, Secy Gen 1977-, Intl Assn for Suicide Preven; APHA, 1972-; CA Public Hlth Assn, 1972-; Mem 1978-, VPres 1980, Pres 1982, Assn of Short Doyle Contract Agys; cp/Reg Selection Panel, Pres's Comm on White House F'ships, 1975-78; Fdg Mem, Wom for Responsible Govt, 1978-; Chwom No CA Sect 1982-83, Sen Advy Com on Yth Suicide Preven; Pres 1974, Mem 1974-, Assn of U Way Agy Execs; Mem, Peninsula Press Clb, 1980-; Circlon, 1980-; Spkr's Bur, U Way of Am, 1969-78; hon/Author, Co-Author & Contbg Author, 3 Books Incl'g: *Eval Criteria for the Cert of Suicide Preven & Crisis Intervention Progs*, 1976; *Suicide in Yth & What You Can Do About It*, 1977; Articles in Var Profl Jours; Outstg Exec Aws, 1970; KABL Citizen of the Day, 1980; Outstg Ser Awd, 1969; Commun Achmt Awd, 1972; San Mateo Foun Awd, 1977; W/W: of Am Wom, of World; Personalities of W & MW.

ROSS, DENNIS K oc/Physics Professor; b/May 4, 1942; h/1411 Curtiss, Ames, IA 50010; ba/Ames, IA; m/Roberta; c/ David; p/Gerald and Ida Ross, Ogden, UT; ed/BS, CA Inst of Technol, 1964; PhD, Stanford Univ, 1968; pa/Asst Prof 1968-72, Assoc Prof 1972-77, Porf 1977-, Physics Dept, IA St Univ; hon/Author, Over 40 Res Articles Pub'd in Profl Jours; Nat Merit S'ship, 1960; Danforth F'ship, 1964; Woodrow Wilson F'ship, 1964; Num Other Biogl Listings.

ROSS, JEFFREY ALLAN oc/Political Scientist, Educator; b/Dec 24, 1947; h/ Brimfield Street, Clinton, NY 13323; ba/ Clinton, NY; m/Marjorie Appelson; c/ Craig, Eric, Brian; p/Joseph and Pearl

(Epstein) Ross; ed/BA, SUNY-Binghamton, 1969; PhD, Univ of MN, 1982; pa/NY St Regent's Fellow & Tchg Asst 1969-71, Res Asst 1971-73, Instr 1973, Univ of MN-Mpls; Huber Foun Fac Res Grantee 1973, 1974 & 1977, Mellon Foun Grantee 1974, Res Prof 1975-76, Kirkland Col, Clinton, NY; Govt Instr 1978-80, Asst Prof 1980-, Hamilton Col, Clinton, NY; Chm & Mem, Var Profl Panels; Am Polit Sci Assn; Exec Coun NE Polit Sci Assn; Intl Polit Sci Assn; Intl Studies Assn; VPres 1982-83, NY St Polit Sci Assn; Num Others; hon/Co-Author, *The Mobilization of Collective Identity: Comparative Perspectives*, 1980; Contbr & Reviewer, Articles to Num Profl Jours; Editl Bd, *Tchg Polit Sci*, 1971-81; Editor, *Hamilton Social Sci Review*, 1977-79; W/W E; Commun Ldrs of Am.

ROSS, JOHN MUNDER oc/Clinical Psychologist, Educator; b/Jun 20, 1945; h/ 277 West End Avenue, New York, NY 10023; ba/New York, NY; m/Katherine Ball; c/Matthew Munder Ball; p/Nathaniel Ross, NYC; Barbara Evangela Ross (dec); sp/Frederic J Ball Sr (dec); Mrs Frederic J Ball, Washington, DC; ed/BA, Harvard Col, 1967; MA 1973, PhD 1974, NY Univ; pa/Clin Assoc Prof Dept Psychi 1980-, Clin Asst Prof 1978-80, Downstate Med Ctr; Adj Asst Prof Psych in Psychi, NY Hosp, Cornell Med Ctr, 1980-; Clin Instr Dept of Psychi & Psych, NY Hosp, Cornell Med Col, 1978-80; Vis'g Asst Prof Dept Psychi, Albert Einstein Col of Med 1977-78, Asst Prof Dept Psych Ferkauf Grad Sch 1976-78, Yeshiva Univ; Adj Asst Prof, New Sch for Social Res, 1974-76; Adj Asst Prof Dept Psych, NY Univ, 1974-75; Asst Att'g Psych (Conslt & Supvn), Downstate Med Ctr, NY Hosp & Roosevelt Hosp, 1978-; Child Therapy Supvn, New Hope Guild, 1977-78; Pvt Pract Psychotherapy, 1975-; Res Conslt; Other Positions; Mem: Am Psychoanalytic Assn; Divs 12 & 39, Am Psychol Assn; Cands for Advmt of Psychoanalytic Ed; NY St Psychol Assn; AAAS; Phi Beta Kappa; Others; hon/ Author, Num Pubs in Profl Jours; Editor & Contbr, *Father & Child: Devel & Clin Perspectives*, 1982; Author & Spkr, Num Paper & Discussion Topic Presentations for Var Orgs, Assns & Instns; Dist'd Tchr Awd, Downstate Med Sch, 1979 & 1980; Most Outstg Book in Behavioral Scis, Scholarly & Profl Div Awd for *Father & Child*, Am Assn of Pubrs, 1982; John Harvard S'ships; Harvard Col S'ships; Detur Prize; Phi Betta Kappa; Adams House Crest; Signet Soc; Others; W/W: in E, in Frontier Sci.

ROSS, PATT JAYNE oc/Physician, Obstetrics & Gynecology; b/Nov 17, 1946; h/12214 Drakemill, Houston, TX 77077; ba/Houston, TX; m/Allan Robert Katz; sp/Mr and Mrs Milton Katz, Sunrise, FL; ed/BS, Depauw Univ, 1968; MD, Tulane Med Sch, 1972; pa/Asst Prof Dept Ob/Gyn 1976-81, Dir Adolescent Ob & Gyn 1978-, Dir Sophomore Ob & Gyn Phy Diagnosis 1977-, Assoc Prof Dept Ob/Gyn 1982, UT Med Sch-Houston; Bd of Dirs, Pituitary Foun, 1982; Sigma Xi; TX Med Assn; Assn of Profs of Ob & Gyn; Soc of Adolescent Med; Am Assn of Gyn Laparoscopists; AAAS; Tulane Alumni Assn; Johns Hopkins Alumni Assn; Assn for Wom Sci; r/Cath; hon/Author & Co-Author, Articles & Papers Pub'd in Var Profl Jours & Assn Pubs; Var Book Chapts; Beta Beta

Beta, 1966; Hon Citizen of NO, 1971; Sigma Xi, 1970; Outstg Lectr, 1978; Tchr of Yr, 1981; W/W: in Houston, Among Am Wom, in SW.

ROSSEL, SVEN HAKON oc/Professor; b/Oct 25, 1943; h/18725 65th Place Northeast, Seattle, WA 98155; ba/Seattle, WA; c/Eva Maria Katharina; p/Leon Hancke Rossel (dec); Maria Müller Rossel, Denmark; ed/PhD Comparative & Scandinavian Lit, Univ of Copenhagen, 1968; pa/Asst Prof, Univ of Hamburg, 1968-69; Asst Prof, Univ of Kiel, 1969-71; Res Fellow, Univ of Copenhagen, 1971-74; Assoc Prof 1974-80, Prof 1980-, Chm Dept Scandinavian Lang & Lit 1981-, Univ of WA; Mem: Soc of Advmt of Scandinavian Studies; Intl Assn of Scandinavian Studies; Medieval Assn of the Pacific; Arbeitsgemeinschaft Norden-Deutschland; Danish Folklore Soc; VPres 1976-77, Seattle Danish Clb; Bd, Nordic Heritage Mus, 1980-; r/Rom Cath; hon/Author, *A Hist of Scandinavian Lit 1870-1980,* 1982; *Scandinavian Ballads,* 1982; *Johannes V Jensen,* 1983; Co-Author, *Tales & Stories by Han Christian Anderson,* 1980; Num Other Books & Articles Pub'd in Profl Jours; Grundtvig Olrik Awd, 1976 & 1980; Denmark-Am Foun, 1980; WA St Spec Awd, 1981.

ROSZAK, BONNIE LOUISE oc/Nursing Administrator; b/Aug 9, 1944; h/345 South Doheny Drive # 207, Beverly Hills, CA 90211; ba/Santa Monica, CA; m/Rudy; c/Christopher Thomas; p/Cleo Groves, Paducah, KY; Ann C Hamm, Hendersonville, TN; sp/Rudolph Roszak (dec); Agnes Roszak, Denver, CO; ed/Dipl, Mtro Gen Hosp Sch of Nsg, Nashville, TN, 1965; BS Belmont Col, Nashville, TN, 1969; Post Grad Study, Univ of CO, 1978-; MA Prog, CA Coast Univ; pa/Dir Surg Nsg Sers, Santa Monica, Hosp Med Ctr, 1980-; OR Conslt, Pacific Hlth Resources, LA, 1980-; Dir of Surgs, Good Samaritan Hosp, Corvalis, OR, 1978-80; Dir Surg 1977-78, Asst Dir Surg 1976-77, Hd OR Nurse 1975-76, Rose Med Ctr, Denver, CO; Phys Asst, Mid TN Anesth, PC, Nashville, TN, 1973-75; Phys Asst, Anesth Assocs, Nashville, TN, 1972-73; Hd OR Nurse, Bapt Hosp, Nashville, TN, 1966-72; Staff Nurse Emer Room, Vanderbilt Univ Hosp, Nashville, TN, 1966; Cert'd ARC Nurse, 1966-; Chm Steering Com for Implementation of Quality Circles, Santa Monica Hosp Med Ctr; LA Chapt, Assoc of OR Nurses; CA Soc of Nsg Ser Admrs; r/Prot; hon/W/W in W.

ROTH, THOMAS JEROME oc/Financial Executive; b/May 14, 1930; h/7618 Leith Place, Alexandria, VA 22307; ba/McLean, VA; m/Louise Morton Cole; c/Margaret Morton, Elizabeth Cole; p/Raymond Frank and Elizabeth Marie (Brown) Roth; ed/BGE, Univ of Omaha, 1965; Postgrad Study, US Army Command & Gen Staff Col, 1968; mil/AUS, Enlisted 1951; Command Ofcr to Lt Col, 1970; Served in Korea & Vietnam; Assigned to Army Gen Staff & Jt Chiefs of Staff; Ret'd, 1976; pa/Dist Fin Mgr, Sperry Univac Comml Mktg, McLean, 1976-; cp/SAR; Am Legion; Mil Order of World Wars; Soc of Indust Pioneers; Belle Haven Country Clb (Alexandria); r/Presb; hon/Bronze Star Medal; W/W in S & SW.

ROTH-CAPPS, TERI ANNE oc/Teacher, Coordinator; b/Oct 9, 1952; h/485 31¼th Road, Grand Junction, CO

81504; ba/Grand Junction, CO; m/Jerrel W Capps; p/Herman and Florence L Roth, L'akewood, CO; ed/AAS, Mesa Col, 1970-72; BA, Univ of No CO-Greeley, 1977; pa/Presch/Kgn Tchr, Nav Commun Sta, Guam, 1972-75; Kgn Tchr, JC Nursery, Grand Junction, CO, 1977-78; Tchr/Coor, Presch & Deaf/Blind Progs, Grand Junction Reg Ctr, Grand Junction, CO, 1978-; Mem: Am Assn for Mtl Deficiency; Nat Assn for the Ed of Yg Chd; CO Assn for the Ed of Yg Chd; Wn Slope Assn for Ed of Yg Ch; Lb of Spec Ed; r/Luth; hon/Author of Article Pub'd in *Sensory World,* 1979; Publicity Chp 1982, Interagy Coun Chp 1983-84, Devel Tester 1979-, Child Find; W/W: in W, in Am; Personalities of W & MW.

ROTHENBERG, IRWIN Z oc/Laboratory Manager; b/Feb 17, 1944; h/2236 Evelyn Avenue, Memphis, TN 38104; ba/West Memphis, AR; p/Alex and Tillie Rothenberg, Hollywood, FL; ed/BS, Bklyn Col, CUNY, 1965; MS, CO St Univ, 1969; Med Tech, Good Samaritan Hosp Sch of Med Technol, Phoenix, AZ, 1973; pa/Staff Med Technol, Carl Hayden Commun Hosp, Tucson, AZ, 1974; Adm Technol, McKee Med Ctr, Loveland, CO, 1974-79; Lab Mgr, Crittenden Meml Hosp, W Memphis, AR, 1979-; Lab Mgmt Conslt, PIC Incorp, Memphis, TN, 1980-82; Am Soc of Clin Pathol; Am Soc for Med Technol; Clin Lab Mgmt Assn; Phi Kappa Phi; Sigma Xi; cp/ACLU; Intl Assn of Black & White Men Together; Black & White Men Together, Memphis; r/Jewish; hon/Prog Chm 1977, Pres-elect 1978, Denver Chapt, CO Soc for Med Technol; Med Technol Rep, CO PSRO, 1977-78; W/W: in S & SW; Men of Achmt; DIB; Other Biogl Listings.

ROTHMAN, JOHN oc/Clinical Research Scientist; b/Jun 11, 1948; h/Box 168 Burrell Road, Lebanon, NJ 08833; ba/Nutley, NJ; m/Patricia; c/Noah Christopher; p/Mr and Mrs Harold Rothman, Ctl Pk W, NYC; sp/Robert Murphy, Kensington, MD; ed/Att'd Univ of MD Sch of Bus, 1969-71; BA, Windham Col, 1971-73; MS, Tulane Univ Sch of Med, 1979; PhD, City Univ of LA, 1981; pa/Res Assoc, NO VA Hosp, 1977-79; Pharm Instr, Tulane Univ Sch of Med, 1978-79; Clin Lab Tech, St Charles Gen Hosp, NO, 1979-80; Clin Res Assoc, Revlon Care Grp, USV Labs, 1980-82; Interferon Med Res Assoc, Schering Corp, 1982-83; Clin Res Sci, Hoffman-La Roche Inc, 1983-; Mem: Am Soc for Clin Pharm & Therapeutics; Am Fedn for Clin Res; NY Acad of Scis; AAAS; Phi Chi; Sigma Xi; Neurosci Soc; Endocrine Soc; r/Jewish; hon/Author & Co-Author, Over 25 Abstracts, Articles, Res Reports & Papers Pub'd in Profl Jours & Presented at Assn Meetings; Undergrad Hons & Deans' Lists; NIH Predoct Tng F'ship; Outstg Student Res Awd Grant, Sigma Xi, l1978; Student Awd for Outstg Res, Am Fedn of Clin Res, 1979; Promising Student Awd, Tulane Univ Sch of Med, 1978 & 1979; W/W.

ROUNER, ARTHUR ACY JR oc/Preaching Minister; b/May 21, 1929; h/4526 Drexel Avenue South, Edina, MN 55424; ba/Edina, MN; m/Mary Sunderland Safford; c/John Newell, Kristen Safford, Thomasin Sunderland, Mary Elizabeth, Arthur Andrew; p/Arthur Acy Rouner Sr (dec); Elizabeth Stephens Rouner, Wellesley, MA; sp/Truman Sunderland Safford, Riverside, CT;

Naomi Brackett Safford (dec); ed/AB, Harvard Univ, 1951; Att'd New Col Edinburgh Univ, 1952-53; MDiv, Union Theol Sem,1954; DMin, Luther Theol Sem, 1978; pa/Min, Eliot Ch of Newton, MA, 1959-62; Sr Min, Colonial Ch of Edina, MN, 1962-; Other Previous Employmt; Mem: Moderator, Hampshire Assn of Congl Chs, 1954; Boston Del 1956, Omaha Del 1958, Gen Coun Congl Chs; Dir, Wayside House for Alcoholic Wom, 1965-70; Trustee, U Theol Sem, 1979-84; Dir, Ecumenical Inst, St John's Univ-Collegeville, MN 1984-; Del, U Ch of Christ Gen Synod, 1985; r/Congregationalist; hon/Author of 8 Books Incl'g: *Receiving the Spirit,* 1982; *Healing Your Hurts,* 1978; Others; Num Articles in Profl Jours & Newspapers Incl'g: *Christian Herald; Christianity Today; The Mpls Star; The Congregationalist;* Others; Paul Harris Fellow, Rotary Intl, 1982; Bush Foun Fellow, 1972; One of 10 Most Influential Clergy in Twin Cities, 1980; Others; W/W: in MW, in Rel.

ROUTSON, RONALD C oc/Soil Scientist; b/Dec 12, 1933; h/Benton City, WA; ba/Richland, WA; m/Mary Joan; Kelly Lynn; p/Chester A and L F Routson, Peshastin, WA; ed/BS 1958, PhD 1967, WA St Univ; mil/AUS, 1958-62; USAR, 1973-; pa/Sr Res Sci & Prog Mgr, Battelle PNL, 1967-77; Staff Soil Sci, Rockell Hanford Opera, 1977-; cp/Pres, Lions Clb; Benton Co Jr Fair Assn; 4-H Ldr, 10 Yrs; US Congl Advy Bd; r/Cath; hon/Author, Over 80 Articles & Tech Res Reports Pub'd in Profl Jours & Pubs; Nat Def Ed Fellow; 4-H Awd of Silver Clover; Chapt Farmer, FFA Awd; AUS Commend Medal; W/W in W; Men of Achmt; DIB.

ROY, ALVIN DAY JR oc/Assistant Industrial Relations Manager; b/Apr 24, 1947; h/Route 4, Box 386, Natchez, MS 39120; ba/Natchez, MS; m/Pamela McCaa; c/Teri Allise; p/Alvin and Dorothy Roy, Natchez, MS; sp/R B McCaa (dec); Lucille Hake, Bakersfield, CA; ed/BS, MS St Univ; MS, Univ of So MS, 1980; pa/Asst Industl Relats Mgr 1982-, Supvr of Stats Tng 1981-82, Industl Engr 1971-81, Engr Co-op Student1967-71, Armstrong Rubber Co, Natchez, MS; Mem: Inst of Industl Engrs; MTM Assn; Industl Mgmt Clb; r/Bapt; hon/Pt-time Instr Bus Adm, Univ of So MS.

ROYALL, CAMILLA BLAFFER oc/Oil Executive; b/Sep 8, 1941; h/1107 5th Avenue, New York, New York 10028; ba/Ft Lee, NJ; c/John Blaffer, Hiram Walker; p/Mrs W B Tramell, Houston, TX; sp/John H Blaffer, Houston, TX; ed/BA, Sarah Lawrence Col, 1963; MA, Columbia Univ, 1966; pa/Pres, Brit Am Petro, 1978-; Pres, Isis Devel, 1980-; Pres, Isis Intl, 1980-; Bd of Dirs, Kleen Vu Resources; cp/Trustee, Spoleto Fest Foun; r/Epis.

ROYER, MARTHA LOU oc/Educator; b/Feb 1, 1955; h/216 East Jefferson Street, Douglas, GA 31533; ba/Douglas, GA; m/Christopher F; c/John Christopher, Kathryn Lee; p/Mr and Mrs Karl K Dockery Sr, Douglas, GA; sp/Mr and Mrs John H Royer Sr, Guton, GA; ed/BSEd 1976, MEd 1978, EdS 1983, GA So Col; pa/Grad Asst Child Devel Lab Tchr 1976-77, Pt-time Staff Mem Div of Home Ec 1979-, GA So Col, Occupl Child Care & Devel Tchr, Glynn Co Bd of Ed, Brunswick, GA, 1978-81; 1st Grade Kgn Tchr, Coffe Co Sch Sys, Douglas, GA, 1981-; Mem: Pres, Beta Sigma Phi,

Currently; Nat Assn Ed Yg Chd; GA Assn for Yg Chd; GA Assn of Edrs; Coffee Co Assn of Edrs; cp/Yth Ldr, Bapt Ch; r/Bapt; hon/Author, "Inexpensive & Creat Lrng Mats & Activs (Ages 3-5), *Proceedings of Early Childhood Devel Inst*, 1982; Coffe Co Edr of Yr, 1984; Att'd GA Assn Yg Chd Conf, 1982; Conductor, Early Childhood Ed Wkshops.

ROYER, PAUL HAROLD oc/Professor; b/Sep 3, 1922; h/337 Lincoln Lane South, Brookings, SD 57006; ba/Brookings, SD; m/Ruth; c/Judith, Randall, Ronald, Peter; p/Paul and Grace Royer, Durham, NC; sp/Ray and Marie Duning, Richmond, IN; ed/BM 1947, MMus 1949, Col of Music, Univ of Cinc; mil/AUS, 1942-6, Bandsman; pa/Instr, Col of Music, Univ of Cinc, OH, 1947-50; Min of Music, Reid Ch, Richmond, IN, 1950-51; Prof, Huron Col, 1951-57 & 1958-68; Prof, SD St Univ, 1968-; Mem: Am Guild of Organists; SD St Pres 1972-76, W Ctl Div Pres & VPres 1976-80, Music Tchrs Nat Assn; r/Luth; hon/Composer: Choral, "Sing a New Song," SATB; "Echo Song," SATB & TTBB w Brass Quartet; Fanfare Fest for Band; Danforth Tchr Grants, 1957-58 & 1961; Nat Endowment for Arts Composition Grant, 1966; Composer in Residence, SD St Univ, 1972; Nat Endowment for Arts Grant, 1976.

ROYSTON, FANNIE oc/US Postal Clerk; b/Mar 1, 1919; h/3219 Ward Street, Pittsburgh, PA 15213; m/Moses; c/Charles M, Ada Bell Robinson; p/ Saunders and Fannie Mitchell (dec); sp/ Moses Royston (dec); ed/Catering & Dressmaking Deg, Art Inst; pa/Postal Clk 1968-75, ZMT Operator 1975-, US Postal Ser; cp/Advy Bd, WQED; Nat Achmt Clb; Bd Me, Poetry Forum; r/Bapt; hon/ Author, Num Pub'd Poems, 1968-; Var Poetry Rdgs on Radio & TV; Cert of Apprec, Rodent Control Proj, Allegheny Co Hlth Dept; Cert for Recog of Outstg Poetry, Poetry & Writers Guild, 1971; Commun Ser Awd, Nat Chapt JUGS Inc, 1975; Spec Adhmt Awd, US Postal Ser, 1976; Citizen of Yr, Kiwanis Clb of Oakland, 1973; Carter's Awd for Commun Achmt, 1974; Outstg Ser in Neighborhood Improvement, 1974; Dr Martin Luther King Awd, Hand in Hand Inc, 1975; Good Deed Awd & Better Block, 1977; Agape Awd, Hill House, 1977; Thank You Awd, Reach Out Supper Prog, 1979; Dedicated Gardener, 1964-; DIB.

ROZENBERGS, JANIS oc/Scientist; b/ May 6, 1948; h/5016 Appletree Drive, Roanoke, VA 24019; ba/Roanoke, VA; p/ Peteris Arvids and Austra Alers Rozenbergs, Thunder Bay, Ontario, Canada; ed/ BSc 1970, Hon BSc 1971, MSc 1974, Lakehead Univ, Canada; Dipl Eng 1975, PhD 1978, Johannes Kepler Univ, Austria; pa/Sr Sci, ITT Electro-Optical Prods Div, 1978-; Mem: Am Phy Soc; r/Luth; hon/Author, Num Articles in Sci Jours Incl'g: *Elect Commun*; *Proceedings of SPIE*; *Solid St Elects*; *Jour of Applied Physics*; Others; W/ W in Frontier Sci & Technol.

RUBEN, IDA G oc/State Legislator; b/ Jan 7, 1929; h/11 Schindler Court, Silver Spring, MD 20903; ba/Annapolis, MD; sp/L Leonard; c/Garry Dennis, Michael Keith, Scott Kevin, Stephen Derek; p/Sol and Sonia Esther Darman Gass (dec); sp/ Albert Ruben (dec); Estelle Jenny Ruben, Silver Spring, MD; ed/Att'd Sems: Univ of W FL; Univ of Pgh; Temple Univ; Wn

MD Univ; pa/Legis, MD House of Dels, 1974-; cp/Pres Indep Chapt 1959-60, Pres Dist 5 1971-72, Treas 1978-80, VPres 1980-, B'nai B'rith Wom Intl; Ser Guild of Wash; Legal Aid Soc; Acitv in Local, St & Nat Campaigns, 1964-; Dist'd Public Ser Awd, MD-DC Retail Ser Sta Dealers, 1979; Montgomery-Prince George's Cos Psychol Assn Awd for Outstg Wk in Field of Mtl Hlth, 1981; Anti-Defamation Leag's Wom of Commitment Awd, MD-DC Reg, 1982.

RUBIN, BERTHOLD oc/Professor Emeritus; b/Jul 10, 1911; h/4122 Fessenden Northwest, Washington, DC 20016; ba/Berlin, W Germany; m/Jutta Hildebrandt; c/Monte, Roxanne (R) Crews; p/Wilhelm and Anna B Zanger Rubin (dec); sp/Gustav and Käthe Hildebrandt (dec); ed/PhD 1938, PhD Habil 1941, Univ of Berlin; mil/Interpreter of Russian & Other Langs; pa/Prof & Dir, Insts of Balkanology, 1942-45; Editor, Insts for En Europe, Munich, 1951-57; Prof & Dir 1957-, Prof & Dir Byzantine Inst 1960-79, Prof Emeritus 1979-, Cologne Univ; Mem: German Archaeol Inst; Mid German Cultural Coun; cp/ Explorers Clb NYC; Fdr & Pres, Friends of CSU (Initiative for a 4th Party in W Germany); r/Prot; hon/Author, *The Age of Justinian (Das Zeitalter Iustinians)*, 1960; Other Books; Contbr, Num Essays & Book Reviews, 1964-; W/W: in Germany, in World; Other Biogl Listings.

RUBIO, PEDRO A oc/Surgeon; b/Dec 17, 1944; h/7800 Fannin # 201 Houston, TX 77054; ba/Houston, TX; c/Eddie, Sandra; p/Isaac and Esther Rubion; ed/ BS Escuela Nacional Perparatoria Numero Uno 1961, Med Surg Deg Facultad de Medicina 1962, Univ Nacional Autonoma de Mexico; pa/Chief Dept of Surg, Med Ctr Del Oro Hosp, Houston, TX, Currently; Mem: Bd of Dirs, Haris Co TEXPAC Bd, 1981-; Coun, Denta A Cooley Cardiovas Surg Soc, 1981-; cp/Bd of Dirs, Theatre Under the Stars, 1981-; Bd of Dirs, Houston Chambers Singers, 1981-; hon/Author, Over 105 Articles Pub'd in Profl Med Jours; Prod'd Sci Motion Picture, "Modified Human Umbilical Vein Graft as a Source of Circulatory Access in Chronic Hemodialysis, 1980; Outstg Surg Intern, Baylor Col of Med, 1970-71; Phys Recog Awd 1971 & 1973-82, AMA.

RUDD, HOWARD FREDERICK JR oc/Professor; b/Feb 28, 1944; h/2807 Sunset Avenue, Bakersfield, CA 93304; ba/Bakersfield, CA; m/Vicki Hill; c/ Kimberly Butterfly, Nathalie Ashley; p/ Howard F Rudd (dec); Louise M, Ft Lauderdale, FL; sp/John R and Ferne Hill, Brownfield, TX; ed/BSME 1965, MBA 1967, Syracuse Univ; DBA, TX Tech Univ, 1973; mil/USAF, 1967-71, Capt; pa/ Prof Mgmt, CA St Univ, 1973-; Instr, TX Tech Univ, 1972-73; Res Asst, TX Tech Univ Ctr for Mtl Retard, 1971-72; Asst Hosp Admr, USAF, 1967-71; Applications Engr, Sum 1967; Factory Planner, Sum 1965; Mem: Mem 1975-, Pres Reg IX 1978-79, VPres Reg IX 1977-78, Small Busj Inst Dirs Assn; The Acad of Mgmt, 1973-; Am Soc for Pers Admrs, 1974-; r/Meth; hon/Author of Articles, Var Pubs; Edit Advy Bd 1982-, *Jour of Small Bus Mgt*; USAF Commend Medal, 1971; Sigma Iota Epsilon, TX Tech Univ, 1969; SBA Dist Best Case Awd, 1979; W/W in W.

RUDOLPH, ANDREW HENRY oc/

Dematologist; b/Jan 30, 1943; ba/6560 Fannin # 724, Houston, TX 77030; m/ Mary Fox; c/Kristen Ann, Kevin Andrew; p/Mary M Rudolph, Southgate, MI; sp/ Mr and Mrs J W Fox, Houston, TX; ed/ MD, Univ of MI, 1966; Cert'd Am Bd of Dermatology, 1971; mil/USPHS, 1970-72; pa/Assoc Prof Dermatology, Baylor Col of Med & Chief Dermatology, VA Med Ctr, 1972-; Mem: Past Pres, Houston Dermatological Soc; Past Pres, Am Venereal Disease Assn; AMA; So Med Assn; TX Med Assn; TX Dermatology Congress; Royal Soc of Hlth; Assn of Mil Surgs of HS; Dermatology Foun; The Skin Cancer Foun; Assn of Mil Dermatologists; Others; hon/Author, Over 75 Pubs in Var Profl Med Jours & Books; Alpha Omega Alpha; Phi Kappa Phi; MD cum laude, 1966; Am Dermatological Assn Inc; W/W: in S & SW, in TX.

RUDOLPH, JAMES ROBERT oc/ Special Education Teacher; b/Mar 1, 1957; h/13108 Turquoise Northeast, Albuquerque, NM; p/Robert and Jean Rudolph, Albuquerque, NM; ed/BA 1980, MA 1981, Univ of NM; PhD Cand, Lehigh Univ, Currently; pa/Child Devel Spec, The Centennial Sch, Lehigh Univ, 1984-; Spec Ed Tchr, Albuquerque Public Schs, 1982-84; cp/Pres, Secy, Pledge Tnr, Intl Frat Coun Rep 1976-79, VPres 1978, Pi Kappa Alpha; Pres, Blue Key, 1978-80; Pres, Psi Chi, 1980-82; Pres & VPres 1981-82, Prog Dir 1980, Pi Lambda Theta; Bd of Dirs 1980, Chm of Bd 1980-81, Student Crisis Ctr; Phi Alpha Theta; Delta Tau Kappa; Alpha Kappa Delta; Phi Sigma Tua; Phi Delta Kappa; La Campanas Jr Hon; hon/Dean of Students Awd of Outstg Ser, 1978 & 1979; Pi Kappa Alpha Man of Yr, 1978; Nom, Nat Outstg Pi Kappa Alpha Undergrad, 1979; Nom, Outstg Greek Man, Univ of NM, 1979; Dean's Hon List, Col of Arts & Scis, 1978 & 1979; Appt'd Grad Com Del from Sch of Ed & Appt'd Cnslg Doct Advy Com, Lehigh Univ, 1983; W/ W Among Students in Am Univs & Cols; Intl Yth in Achmt; Commun Ldrs of Am.

RUEGSEGGER, PAUL MELCHIOR oc/Physician, Researcher; b/Jun 27, 1921; h/One Landon Terrace, Bronxville, NY 10708; ba/New York, NY; m/Freya Bund Wipf; c/Theodore Bernard, Christine Monica, Carole Suzanne; p/Paul and Frieda Beatrice (Schmocker) Ruegsegger (dec); sp/Haermann A Wipf (dec); Freya H (Walser) Wipf, Zurich, Switzerland; ed/ MD, Univ of Zurich, Switzerland, 1946; Diplomate, Am Bd Internal Med; Intern 1948-51, Resident 1951-52, Bellevue Hosp, NYC; Resident in Cardiol, Meml Sloan Kettering Cancer Cetr, NYC, 1952-53 & 1955-56; mil/USAF, 1953-55, Capt; Japan; pa/Asst Prof Clim Med, Cornell Univ Med Sch, NYC, 1959; Res Assoc, Sloan Kettering Inst, NYC, 1959-67; Att'd Phys: Meml Ctr for Cancer, NYC, 1959-69; NY Hosp, 1956-69; Res Dir, Med Imaging Lab (Biotronics Inst), NYC 1970-; Aero-Med Conslt, Swissair Lince, NYC, 1956-; Thermography Conslt, Trial Lwyrs Assn, NYC, 1982-; Conslt Med Imaging, Hoffmann-LaRoche Corp, Nutley, NJ, 1969-; Mem: NY Acad of Scis; Am Fedn Clin Res; Harvey Soc NY; NY Co Med Socl Am Acad Thermology; European Thermology Soc; Am Soc Intl Med; cp/ Zool Soc NY; NY Botanical Garden; Swiss Soc of NY; Gramatan-Vernon Lodge

#927, Mason; r/Prot; hon/Author, "Transaminase Tests," 1956; "Coronary Thrombolysis," 1959; "Walking EKG Stress Test," 1963; "Thermography of Pain," 1969 & 1981; Var Other Articles & Res Reports in Profl Pubs; Yg Investigator Awd, NHI, 1958; W/W: in W, in Frontier Sci & Technol.

RUF, KURTIS MATTHEW oc/Systems Analyst, Programmer and Controller; b/Mar 8, 1960; h/13700 Pflumm, Olathe, KS 66062; ba/Olathe, KS; ed/BS Univ of KS-Lawrence, 1982; MBA, Rockhurst Col, 1983; pa/Sys Anal/ Programmer, Ruf Corp, 1978–; Mem: Secy, Imprs Users Grp; r/Presb; hon/ Author, *Gensim Users Manual*, 1983; 1st Place, KS Univ Open Raquetball Tournament.

RULE, PATRICIA A oc/Librarian; b/ Oct 23, 1949; h/780 Dexter Street, Denver, CO 80220; ba/Denver, CO; p/ Emma Jane Mattson, Denver, CO; ed/BA Eng w Writing Emphasis, Metro St Col, 1984; pa/Libn, Rocky Mtn News; Author; Playwright: *The Park*, 1971; *There's Nothing More Obscene Than Plastic Lillies*, 1972; *The Metaphys Rainstorm Blues*, 1973; *Requiem 1/ 1*, 1976; Theater Reviews for *The Straight Creek Jour*; Theater Writer; *Capitol Ledger*; Articles for *Westworld & Bravo*; Reviews for *Rocky Mtn News*, 1978–; hon/4 Plays Prod'd at Changing Scene Theater; Short Story "Manhattan Winter," Pub'd in *Bloomsbury Review*, 1981; VPres's Hon Roll, Metro St Col, 1982; CO Scholar's Awd, 1982-1984.

RULON, PHILIP REED oc/Professor; ba/Dept of Hist, Northern AZ University, Flagstaff, AZ 86011; ed/BA, Washburn Univ, 1963; MA, KS St Tchrs Col, 1965; DEd Hist & Higher Ed, OK St Univ, 1968; Post-Doct Visitor, Univ of TX, Dept of Cultural Founs of Ed & Commun Col Ldrship Prog, 1974; mil/AUS, Quartermaster Corps; pa/Grad Asst Hist 1963-64, Asst Prof Hist NDEA Inst in Am Hist Sum 1967, EPDA Inst in Am Hist Sum 1969, Emporia St Univ; Grad Asst Hist 1964-65, Grad Asst Hist NDEA Inst in European Hist Sum 1965, Instr 1965-67, OK St Univ; Asst Prof Hist 1969-71, Assoc Prof 1971-80, Prof 1980–, Dir Annual Hist of Ed Inst 1969-73, No AZ Univ; Mem: Num Confs, Wkshops, Projs, Chm & Mem Num Coms, No AZ Univ; Var Positions w: Phi Alpha Theta; Ctr for the Study of the Presidency; Org of Am Histns; Nat Endowment for the Humanities; AZ Coun on the Humanities & Public Policy; Nat Advy Bd, Com on Hist in the Clrm; N Ctl Assn Eval Tms; Reg Dir, Nat Hist Day, 1981; Am Hist Assn; Wn Hist Assn; Num Others; hon/ Author & Co-Author, 5 Books Incl'g: *The Seven Ages of Christmas*; *Spkg Out: An Oral Hist of the Am Past Volumes I & II*, 1981; *Lttrs From the Hill Country: The Correspondence of Rebekah and Lyndon Baines Johnson*, 1981; *Compassionate Samaritan: The Life of Lyndon Baines Johnson*, 1981; Num Articles Pub'd in Profl Jours & Presented at Assn Meetings & Confs; Edit Bd, *Tchg Hist: A Jour of Methods*; Edit Bd, The *Histn*, 1974-79; Reviewer Var Hist Jours; Recip Num Grants, Lyndon Baines Johnson Foun; Am Hist Assn; The Col Bd; No AZ Univ; Var Com Positions w Phi Alpha Theta; Corres'g Secy Local Chapt, Phi Kappa Phi, 1982-83; Nat Bd of Advrs, Am Biogl Inst; W/W: in W, of Intells, in Ed; Contemp Authors; Dir of Am Scholars; Ldrs in Ed; The Writer's Dir; Men of Achmt; The

Am Registry; DIB; Num Other Biogl Listings.

RUNDELL, MALCOLM RAY oc/Academic Dean; b/Oct 9, 1935; h/11419 Sagepark, Houston, TX 77089; ba/Houston, TX; m/Barbara; c/Teresa, David; p/ C E and Bertha Rundell, Delhi, LA; sp/ C E and Anne Ball, Rustun, LA; ed/BS, LA Polytech Univ, 1957; MS, NWn Univ-Louisiana, 1963; EdD, Univ of Houston, 1975; mil/NG; pa/Chem & Physics Instr, Bossier City HS, 1957-62; Chem Instr, Pasadena HS, 1962-64; Chem Instr, Sam Rayburn HS, 1964-65; Chem Instr 1965-74, Chem Dept Chm 1974-79, San Jacinto Col Ctl; Acad Dean, San Jacinto Col S, 1979–; Mem: TX Jr Col Tchrs Assn; TX Assn of Col Registrars & Admissions Ofcrs; Phi Delta Kappa; TX Assn of Acad Deans & VPres; So Assn of Col Registrars & Admissions Ofcrs; Gulf Coast Area Instrn Ofcrs; cp/ Optimist Clb; Sageglen Commun Assn; r/Bapt; hon/Author, *Gen Chm Lab Manual*; Nom'd Piper Awd, 1975 & 1976; NSF Grantee, Oak Ridge Nat Lab, TN; W/W in S & SW.

RUNKEL, JANE ELIZABETH oc/Director of Career Planning and Placement; b/Aug 27, 1952; h/412 Ardmore, Ripon, WI 54971; ba/Ripon, WI; p/Paul D and Jean B Runkel, Port Washington, WI; ed/ BA, Ripon Col, 1974; MSW Univ of WI-Oshkosh, 1979; pa/Admissions Cnslr 1974-77, Asst Dean of Admissions 1977-79, Asst Dean of Admissions & Asst In Career Planning & Placement 1979-80, Dir Career Planning & Placement & Dean of Students 1980-82, Dir Career Planning & Placement 1982–, Ripon Col; Mem: Co-editor Spkrs Book 1982, Steering Com 1983–, Mem 1981–, Associated Cols of MW Woms Concerns Com; WI Career Planning & Placement Assn Histn, 1981–; WI Soc of Higher Ed Coor, 1980–; cp/ St Jr Sales Chair 1981-83, St Jr Mbrship Chm 1983-86, John Scott Horner Chapt Registrar, DAR; Nat Jr Mbrship Chm 1983-86, Chapt 2nd VPres 1983-86, Colonial Dames of 17th Cent; Nom Com 1981-83, Wau-Bun GSA; Secy, Ripon Study Clb, 1982-83; hon/ACE/NIP 5 St Prog; Outstg Yg Wom of Am; W/W of Am Wom.

RUSCH, MEDRA HALL oc/Public Library Bookmender; b/Apr 2, 1895; h/ 509 South 5th Avenue, Bozeman, MT 59715; ba/Bozeman, MT; m/Herman W (dec); p/John A Hall and Annie Louise Ivy (dec); sp/Robert and Augusta Rusch (dec); ed/Att'd OR St Col-Corvalis, Sum 1920; S'ship Sem in Nutrition, Univ of TX, 1922; BS Home Ec, MT St Univ; pa/HS Home Ec & Biol Tchr, Manhattan, MD, 1918-1919; HS Home Ec Tchr, Ft Benson, MT, 1919-1920; Grade Sch Hom Ec Tchr & Adult Course in Foods, Serving & Tailoring, Bozeman, MT, 1920-27; Gradesch, Jr HS & Adult Courses, Sioux Falls, SD, 1927-31; Bookmender, Bozeman Public Lib; Mem: Phi Upsilon Omicron; AAUW; cp/Fdg Mem, MIA; r/Presb; hon/ Phi Upsilon Omicron, 1917; S'ship for Hlth Wk in Bozeman, 1922; Ofcl Rep APHA to Nat Hygiene Cong & Nat Sanitary Inst, Margate, England, 1930; W/W: in W, of Am Wom; DIB; Other Biogl Listings.

RUSSELL, OSCAR CECIL "BUD" JR oc/Bank Executive; b/Nov 10, 1945; h/ 2733 Hudson Place, New Orleans, LA 70114; ba/New Orleans, LA; p/Oscar Cecil and Lovena Russell, Sr, Huntsville,

AL; ed/BS Biol, Univ of AL, 1964-68; Att'd GA St Univ Bus Sch, 1974-77; mil/USA, Capt, 1968-73; pa/Mgr of Proof/Encoding Dept 1973, Mgr Bkkpg & Customer Ser Dept, Asst VP, Mgr of Check Processing Ops & Adm Div 1977, Citizens & So Nat Bk, Atlanta, GA; Sr VP & Cashier, Ops Grp Exec, Hibernia Nat Bk, New Orleans, LA, 1977–; Mem, Past Pres, New Orleans Clearing House Assn, 1977–; Past Dir, Mem Exec Com, Louisiana-Alabama-MS Automated Clearing House Assn, 1977-82; Mem & Past St Treas, GA Alumni Assn; Phi Kappa Psi Frat, 1975-76; Bd Mem, Treas, New Orleans Ballet, 1982; hon/Army Commend Medal; W/W S & SW.

RUSSELL, RALPH TIMOTHY oc/ Executive; b/May 16, 1948; h/117 West Rosette Aveuen, Foley, AL 36535; ba/ Foley, AL; m/Sandra Schultz; c/Karen M, Kevin T, Kenton L; p/Mr and Mrs Ralph J Russell, Foley, AL; sp/Mr and Mrs Paul F Schultz, Foley, AL; ed/BS, Univ of AL, 1970; MBA, Univ of S AL, 1975; Chartered Property Casualty Underwriter, 1979; mil/AUS, 1971-72, Capt; pa/VPres, Baldwin Mut Ins Co Inc, 1972–; Mem: Chm Farm Underwriting Com, Nat Assn of Mut Ins Cos, 1981; cp/Pres, S Baldwin C of C, 1976-82; Pres, Foley Rotary Clb, 1978-79; Pres, S Baldwin U Way, 1980-82; Chm Bd of Dirs, Riviera Utilities, 1978-82; Reg Blood Sers Com, ARC, 1981-82; Nat VPres, Univ of AL Alumni Assn, 1978; r/Cath; hon/Contb'g Author, *Farm Underwriting Manual*; Merit Awd, Nat Assn of Mut Ins Cos, 1980; Outstg Yg Men of Am; W/W in Am Cols & Univs.

RUTH, PETER C oc/Executive and Consultant; b/Nov 23, 1944; h/894 Minnesota Avenue, San Jose, CA 95125; ba/San Jose, CA; m/Ruth Ann Allen; c/ Peter C II, Pamela B Musante, Paul M Musante, Robert R Musante; p/Leslie J and Lillie H Ruth (dec); sp/Harold John and Ruth Irene Adank, San Jose, CA; ed/ Att'd: USAF Inst; Univ of Paris; Heidelberg Univ; Univ of Tours; Elect Computer Programming Inst; W Val Col; Univ of PA-Phila; Allentown Col of St Francis de Sales; mil/USAF, 1962-70; pa/Elect Tech (Devel Engrg), Dat Pathing Inc, Sunnyvale, CA, 1970; Elect Tech, Engrg Assoc, Devel Engr, Sr Quality Engr, Test Engrg Sys Mgr, Spec Projs Proj Engr, Memorex Corp, Santa Clara, CA, 1970-75; Indep Conslt, Mgmt & Info Processing, 1973-81; Quality Engrg Mgr, Nat Semiconductor Corp, Santa Clara, CA, 1975; Proj Engr, Quality Assurance Mgr, En Reg Data Processing Ctr Mgr, Memorex Corp, King of Prussia, 1976-80; Adv'd Mfg Engrg Sr Conslt, Spec Mfg Opers Sr Conslt, Memorex Corp, Santa Clara, 1980; Fdr & Pres, Solutions Inc, Quakertown, PA, 1976-80; Exec VPres Spec Projs, Critical Path Solutions Inc, San Jose, CA, 1980–; Mem: Pres, Intl Francophiles An, 1966; Data Processing mgmt Assn, 1975-77; cp/Fdr, Franco-Am Clb, 1964; Pres, Ecurie Chatearoux, 1965-66; Fdr & Pres, Chateauroux Sports Car Clb, 1965-66; Fdr & Pres, Argenton Track Clb, 1966; PA Proj 81 Com, 1978-80; Quakertown Sch Dist Curric Review Com, 1979; r/Prot; hon/Author, Num Articles in Tech & Trade Jours; W/ W: in E, of Intells; Men of Achmt.

RUTTER, DAWN E oc/Retired Poet; b/Jul 28, 1921; h/7290 Larkdale Avenue, Dublin, CA 94568; m/John F Rutter (dec); c/Norma, Charles Frederick, Celia; ed/

Grad, Hammond HS, Hammond, IN; cp/ Dublin Woms Clb; Pres, Intl Longshoreman's Union Federated Aux, 5 Yrs; VFW Aux; POW, Poetry Org for Wom; World Poetry Soc; r/Prot; hon/Author of 3 Books: *Tears & Teacups*, 1979; *Kangaroos Pockets*, 1979; *Feathers on the Wind*, 1981; Poems Pub'd in Num Poetry Pubs in India, England, Australia, Canada & US; W/W of W.

RYAN, CLARENCE E JR oc/Technical Service Consultant; b/Jan 23, 1923; h/PO Box 247 Oak Forest, IL 60452; ba/ Peotone, IL; m/Josephine; c/Dorothy; p/ Mr and Mrs C E Ryan Sr, Warrenton, MO; sp/Mr and Mrs A Frankville, Rock Island, IL; ed/BS, St Ambrose Col, 1943; LLB, Blackstone & John Marshall Law Sch, Notre Dame Univ; Grad Wk: Univ of IL, Univ of AL, MI St Univ, Augustana Col; Cert'd Chem & Chem Engr, 1974-; mil/USNR, 1944, Ofcr, Retired; pa/Lab Tech, St of IL; Pharm, Aluminum Co fo Am, Davenport, IA; Chem, Aluminum Seal, Richwood, IN; Tech Dir, Caspero Tinplate; Gall Metal Inc & Metal Div; Weyerhouser Co, Fairview, WA; Tech Ser Conslt, Bennett Industs, 1978-; Mem: Am Chem Assn; AIA; Intl Platform Assn; cp/Am Def Preparedness Assn; Ret'd Ofcrs Assn; Nav Resv Assn; VFW; Grand Order of Moos; r/Cath; hon/Author, Var Tech Articles & Excerpts on Metal & Metal Coatings; Fellow, Am Inst of Chems, 1973-; Dir, Transcontl Intl Inc; Dir, Parenterprises; W/W: in MW, in Fin & Indust.

RYAN, JAMES WALTER oc/ Research Physician; b/Jun 8, 1935; h/ 3420 Poinciana Avenue, Miami, FL 33133; ba/Miami, FL; m/Una Harriett Scully; c/James Patrick Andrew, Alexandra Lynette Elizabeth, Amy Jean Susan; p/Lee W and Emma Elizabeth Haddox Ryan; ed/AB, Dartmouth Col, 1957; MD, Cornell Univ Med Col, 1961; DPhil, Oxford Univ, 1967; mil/USPHS, 1963-81, Cmdr; pa/Intern 1961-62, Asst Resident Med 1962-63, Montreal Gen Hosp, McGill Univ; Res Assoc, NIMH, NIH, 1963-65; Guest Investigator 1967-68, Asst Prof Biochem 1968, Rockefeller Univ, NYC; Sr Sci, Papanicolaou Cancer Res Inst, Miami, FL, 1972-77; Assoc Prof Med 1968-79, Prof Res Med 1979-, Dept of Med, Univ of Miami; Biochem Soc; So Soc for Clin Investigation; NY Acad of Sci; Fellow, Am Inst of Chems; Sigma Xi; Am Soc of Biol Chems; Divs of Biol Chem & Med Chm, Am Chem Soc; Coun on Cardiopulmonary Diseases, Coun for High Blood Pressure, Med Advy Bd, Am Heart Assn; Microcirculatory Soc; European Microcirculation Soc; r/Bapt; hon/Author, Num Profl Jour Articles Incl'g: "Comparative Study of 3 Parenteral Inhibitors of the Angiotensin Converting Enzyme," & "Metabolic Functions of the Pulmonar Vascular Endothelium,"; Smith, Kline & French Travelling F'ships, 1960; Wm Mecklenberg Polk Res Prize, Cornell Univ Med Res Col, 1960-61; Travel Awd, Rockefeller Foun, 1962; Res Prize, Montreal Clin Soc, 1963; Postdoct Fellow, USPHS, 1965-67; Wm Waldorf Astor Travelling F'ship, 1966; Spec F'ship, USPHS, 1967-68; Career Devel Awd, USPHA, 1968; Investigator, Howard Hughes Med Inst, 1968-71; Pfizer Travelling Fellow, Univ of Montreal, 1972; Vis'g Prof, Clin Res Inst of Montreal, 1974; Vis'g Fac Thoracic Disease Div, Dept of Internal Med, Mayo Clin, 1974; Invited Spkr for 500th Anniv of Univ of Uppsala, 1977; Holder, Num US Patents in Field; 42 Patent Applications Pending in 32 Countries; 2000 Notable Ams.

RYNIEWICZ, W SHERRY oc/Payroll Systems Consultant; b/Aug 5, 1931; h/ 40 Bloomfield Avenue, Windsor, CT 06095; ba/Same; c/Douglas, Dwight, Desiree, Debra-Lee; p/Warren Andrew Rinehart (dec); Marion W Rinehart; ed/ Att'd Univ of Hartford, 1973; pa/Saks 5th Avenue, NYC, 1955-56; Witco Chem Co, Paramus, NJ, 1960-62; Gen Motors Co, Englewood Cliffs, NJ, 1963-64; Green Manor Constrn Co, Manchester, CT, 1967-68; Sears Roebuck & Co, Manchester, CT, 1968-72; Dir Payroll, Univ of Hartford, Windsor, CT, 1972-82; Mem: Chm S'ship Fund, Univ of Hartford Wom's Leag; Dir Bd of Dirs & Chm Credit Com, Ctl CT Tchrs Fed Credit Union; cp/Asst Chm, Publicity Guild of Our Lady of St Bartholomew; r/Cath; hon/ W/W: of Wom, of Am Wom.

S

SABATELLA, JOSEPH JOHN oc/ Professor of Art and Dean of College of Fine Arts; b/May 5, 1931; h/2510 Northwest 30th Terrace, Gainesville, FL 32605; ba/Gainesville, FL; m/Ruth Anne Bernacki; c/John J, Steven L, Michael J, Joseph P, Philip A, Thomas F, Mary K, Clarissa L; p/John J and Mary R (dec) Sabatella, Chicago, IL; ed/BFA in Painting and Graphics 1954, MFA in Painting and Graphics 1958, Univ of IL; mil/1st Lt, Anti-Aircraft Artillery, AUS, 1954-56; pa/Higgins Handicrafted Glass Inc, 1954; Mgr, Elenhank Designers Inc, 1958-59; Prof of Drawing and Design 1959-66, Asst Dean of Col of Arch and Fine Arts 1966-74, Acting Dean of Col of Arch and Fine Arts 1974-75, Dean of Col of Fine Arts 1975-, Univ of FL Gainesville; Acad Affairs Admrs, 1967-75; Intl Coun of Fine Arts Deans, Exec Bd 1980-82; Comm on the Arts of Nat Assn of St Univs and Land-Grant Cols, 1977-; Phi Kappa Phi; Omicron Delta Kappa; Sigma Lambda Chi; cp/Bd of Dirs, U Way for Alachua Co, 1977-79; r/Rom Cath; hon/Artwk Exhib'd in Nat and Reg Juried Shows, 1955-75; Represented in Num Pvt Collections in US and England; Grand Awd, Painting, SEn Reg Exhbn, Jacksonville Fest of the Arts, 1963; Juror: Mr Thomas Messer, Dir of Guggenheim Mus; W/W Am; W/W Am Art; Personalities of S; Men of Achmt.

SABLE, RONALD KEITH oc/Military Officer; b/May 8, 1941; h/1915 Mason Hill Drive, Alexandria, VA 22307; ba/Washington, DC; m/Sandra; c/Ronna; p/Roy C Sable, Packwood, IA; Pauline E Sable, Keota, IA; ed/MS, 1976; BS, 1963; mil/Col USAF, Chief Air Opers, Secy Air Force Ofc of Legis Liaison; Acting Dir of Civil Air, Pres Advance Agt, 1974-78; Chif, US Contingency Plans, Mil Airlift Cmd, 1973-74; Instr Pilot C-141, Wing Exec Ofcr, Charleston AFB, SC, 1970-73; Chief of Tng & C-123K A/C, Air Commando's, Republic of Vietnam, 1969-70; Air Force Assn; Order of Daedalians; Am Assn of Airport Execs; Treas, Mason Hill Citizens Assn; Chd's Hosp, Wash DC Fund Raising Com; hon/Author, "The Deterrent Effect of Strategic Airlift," *Def Trans Jour*, 1980; "Civil Res Air Fleet: A Primer for Def & Indust," 1979; "Ldrship Styles, *Air Univ Review*, 1981; Var Free-lance Articles; St Louis Area Patriots Awd, 1977; George Wash Hon Medal, Freedom Foun, 1976; Dist'd Flying Cross, 1971; Air Medal (5); Meritorious Ser Medal (2), Air War Col Hon Grad; Nuclear Weapons Sch Hon Grad; W/W World.

SACARELLO, HILDEGARDE LOUISA ANNE STANINGER oc/Industrial Hygienist, Toxicologist; b/Feb 2, 1955; h/15828 Deep Creek Lane, Tampa, FL 33624; ba/Orlando, FL; m/ Raphael Matos; p/Rudolf John and Vina Florence Butkevich Staninger, Titusville, FL; ed/AA in Liberal Arts 1976, BS in Microbiol 1977, MS in Sec'dy Ed Sci 1980, Univ of Ctl FL; Indust Toxicology, Kensington Univ, 1982; pa/ Indust Hygienist, Martin Marietta Aerospace, 1981-; Indust Hygienist for the St of FL, Bur of Indust Safety and Hlth, 1980-81; Tchr, 10th-12th Grade Geometry, Elem Algebra and Gen Math, Merritt Isl High, 1979-80; Other

Previous Positions; AAAS; Am Soc for Microbiol; Am Indust Hygiene Assn; Am Inst of Biol Sci; Assn for Wom in Sci; Univ of Ctl FL Alumni Assn; hon/ Pubs, *Brevard County Secondary Schools Mathematics Curriculum Guide* 1980, *Ensio Fuswatti-Citrus Scab* 1976, *Asbestos in the Workplace* 1981, Others; Tranworld Airlines Sci Awareness Awd, 1970; Table Tennis Awd for Intermurals, 1970; Soccer Awd for Intermurals, 1970; Social Studies and Latin Awd, Astronaut HS, 1973; Chi Kappa S'ship for Col, Astronaut HS, 1973; Third Place for Ribbon, Season of Sailboat Racing for Titusville Yacht Clb, 1978; Recip, 3 Harry P Leu Free Enterprise S'ships for Sum of 1980, Univ of Ctl FL Ec Dept; W/W S and SW.

SACHS, CHARLES IRA oc/Writer, Maritime Historian, Photographer, Lecturer, Publisher, Film Producer; b/ Mar 9, 1944; h/3907 Vineland Avenue, Studio City, CA 19604; ba/Universal City, CA; p/Jack and Mirium Sachs (dec); ed/BS in Radio and TV, IN Univ, 1968; Grad Studies in Cinema, Syracuse Univ, 1969-70; mil/AF Ofcr, Active Duty 1968-72, Resv and Guard 1973-; pa/AF Ofcr, Top Secret Courier 1968-69, Audio Visual Ser Active Duty 1969-72; AF Ofcr, Resvs, Audio Visual Ser 1973-77; AF Ofcr, CA Air NG, Dir of Public Affairs 1977-83; Film Adv Bd, Steamship Hist Soc of Am; Fdr and Pres, Oceanic Navigation Res Soc, 1977-; r/ Jewish; hon/Pubs, *Sea Classics* 1982, Var Articles; Misc Intl Awds in Still Photo, 1968-69; Best Color Photograph of Yr, Aero Space Audio Visual Ser, USAF; W/ W CA; Ldrs in Am.

SACKMANN, I JULIANA oc/Astrophysicist; b/Feb 8, 1942; h/1230 Arden Road, Pasadena, CA 91106; ba/Pasadena, CA; m/Robert F Christy; c/Juliana Lilly Christy, Alexandra Roberta Christy; p/Emil Sackmann, Moerikestr, West Germany; Lilly Stelter, Vancouver, Canada; ed/Sr Matriculation, Bloor Col, 1959; BA in Physics 1963, MA in Astronomy 1965, PhD in Astrophysics 1968, Univ of Toronto; pa/Fac Assoc 1981-, Sr Res Fellow 1976-81, CA Inst of Technol; Res Assoc, Jet Propulsion Lab, 1974-76; Res Fellow, CA Inst of Technol, 1971-74; Res Assoc, Univ of Hamburg Observatory, 1971; Postdoct Fellow, Max-Planck Inst für Physik and Astrophysik, 1969-71; Postdoct Fellow, Univ of Göttingen, 1968-69; Am Astronom Soc, 1965-; Canadian Astronom Soc, 1978-; Intl Astronom Soc, 1968-; r/Meth; hon/Pubs, "Anatomy of Successive Helium Shell Flashes-Stationary Shell Burning?" 1980, "A Shortlived, Deep Convective Envelope for Highly Evolved Blue Supergiants?" 1978, Num Others; Nat Res Coun of Canada Postdoct F'ship, 1968-69, 1969-70; Alexander-von-Humboldt Awd, W Germany, 1970-71; Res Fellow, Caltech, 1971-74; Vis'g Assoc, Caltech, 1974-76; NRC Resident Assoc, JPL, 1974-75; NRC Sr Res Assoc, JPL, 1975-76; Num Other Hons; W/W of Am Wom; Am Men and Women of Sci; W/W in Frontier Sci and Technol; W/W in CA; W/ W in Technol Today; World W/W of Women.

SADKER, MYRA POLLACK oc/ Dean of School of Education; b/May 3, 1943; h/8608 Carlynn Drive, Bethesda, MD 20834; ba/Washington, DC; m/

David; c/Robin, Jacqueline; p/Louis and Shirley Pollack, Lauderdale Lakes, FL; ed/BA, Boston Univ, 1964; MAT, Harvard Univ, 1965; EdD, Univ of MA, 1971; pa/Asst Prof, Univ of WI Parkside, 1971-73; Assoc Prof 1973-79, Prof 1979-, Dean of Sch of Ed 1979-, Am Univ; hon/Pubs, *Sexism in School and Society* 1973, *Now Upon a Time: A Contemporary View of Children's Literature* 1977, *Teachers Make the Difference* 1980; Am Ednl Res Assn Wom Ed Awd, 1980; Univ of MA Wm Cosby Awd for New Frontiers in Ed; W/W Am Wom; Contemp Authors; DIB.

SADLER, ERNEST E oc/Executive; b/ May 15, 1932; h/405 Southwest Street, Anaheim, CA 92805; ba/Irvine, CA; m/ Maureen Sheila Downey; c/Kathleen Ann, Faith Eileen, Amy Lynn, Daniel Sean; p/Faith Robichaud, Anaheim, CA; ed/BA 1959, MS 1961, Univ of MA; mil/ USN 1949-54, ETO; pa/Res Asst, Univ of MA, 1958-61; Res Engr, N Am Rockwell, 1961-64; Mem of Tech Staff, Rockwell Intl, 1964-70; VP, Gen Mgr, Good Taste Ltd, 1964-70; VP of Opers, Dir, Unisen Inc, 1974-; Human Factors Soc; Am Psychol Assn; Soc Engrg Psychols; Sigma Xi; cp/AMVETS; VFW; r/Prot; hon/Author, Articles in Profl Jours, incl'g, *Journal of Applied Psychology*, *Human Factors Journal*, *Journal of Experimental Psychology*; DIB; Commun Ldrs of Am; Am Men of Sci; 2,000 Men of Achmt; W/W W.

SAHA, SUBRATA oc/Professor and Coordinator of Bioengineering; b/Nov 2, 1942; h/7601 Old Spanish Trail, Shreveport, LA 71105; ba/Shreveport, LA; m/Pamela; c/Sunil, Supriya; p/Dr Jaladhar Saha (dec); Mrs Sushama Saha; ed/BE, Calcutta Univ, 1963; MS, TN Technol Univ, 1969; Engr 1971, PhD 1973, Stanford Univ; pa/Engr in Consltg Firms, 1963-67; Res and Tchg Asst, TN Technol Univ 1968-69, Stanford Univ 1969-73; Res Assoc, Yale Univ Sch of Med, 1973-74; Asst Prof, Yale Univ, 1974-79; Assoc Prof 1979-84, Prof 1984-, LA St Univ Med Ctr; cp/India Assn of Shreveport, Pres 1983, VP 1982, Treas 1981, Secy 1980; VP, Intl Assn, Stanford Univ, 1972; Pres, Indian Assn, TN Technol Univ, 1968-69; r/ Hinduism; hon/Author, Over 200 Pubs in Nat and Intl Jours and Proceedings in Bioengrg, Biomechs and Biomats; Fullbright Awd, 1982; Res Career Devel Awd, NIH, 1978-83; US-India Exch of Scists Awd, 1978; Sigma Xi; W/W Frontier Sci and Technol.

SAHANI, ARISH K oc/Life Insurance Salesman; b/Mar 6, 1944; h/70-16 136 Street, KG Hills, NY 11367; ba/Rego Park, NY; m/Neena; c/Priya, Seema; p/ Krishan Lal Sahani, India; ed/BSc, Mech Engrg, 1965; pa/Life Ins Salesman, NY Life Ins Co, 1972-; Telco, India, 1966-71; r/Hindu; hon/Mem, Million Dollar Round Table, 1975-83.

SAHM, M JERE oc/Automation Planning and Research; b/Sep 12, 1934; h/ 2421 Elizabethtown Road, Elizabethtown, PA 17022; ba/Harrisburg, PA; m/ Gladys June Duffy; c/Kim Lori Sahm Welz; p/Mr and Mrs John Urban, Brownstown, PA; ed/BS, Franklin & Marshall Col, 1956; MBA, Creighton Univ, 1965; Armed Forces Staff Col, 1972; Indust Col of the Armed Forces, 1976; Air War Col, 1977; FBI Sys Security; EDP and Mgmt, Harvard &

Temple, 1981-82; mil/USAF 1957-79, 2nd Lt through Lt Col; pa/Indust Engr, Hamilton Watch Co, 1956-57; USAF, Position of Increasing Responsibility in Pers Mgmt and EDP, Last Position: Dir, Pers Sys and Data Processing, AF Resv Pers Ctr; Automation Planning and Res, Commonwealth Nat Bk, 1979-; Life Mem, AF Aid Soc; Ret'd Ofcrs Assn; Beta Gamma Sigma; Automation and Bkg Socs; Chp, Nat Computer Users Grp; Bk Spkrs Bur; cp/Polit Action Com; U Way Vol; Masons; Shriners; r/Epis Ch, Sunday Sch and Yth Grps; hon/ Perfect Grade Point Average, Grad Sch, 1965; Data Sys Mgr of Yr, 1974; Am Soc of Mil Comptrollers Awd for Outstg Perf, 1977; W/W W; W/W Fin and Indust.

ST DAWN, GRACE oc/Lecturer, Author, Poet, Lyricist, Crusader; h/340 Elliot Place, Paramus, NJ 07652; m/ Vincent Galasso; c/Richard Galasso; p/ Mr and Mrs P Seminerio (dec); ed/DDiv, 1980; Hon DHL, 1977; pa/Let It Be Known that I Have Grown So Close to God that No Man on Earth Can Surpass or Show Me How to Live in Peace with My Fellow Man Because I Have Reached that Plateau-to This End I Was Born; IPA, 1971; U World Poets Laureate Intl, 1973; r/Cath and All Rels; hon/Pubs, "The Gift of Peace" 1975, "Love God, Trust God" 1976, "God Gave Me His Peace" 1980; Am Poet w Bicent Dist, 1976; Poet Laureate of Spiritual Revelation, 1978; Cert of Merit for Outstg Lyrics, 1977; Awd for Outstg Ser to Commun and Notable Concern for All People, TIA, Edrs for World Peace, 1978.

ST JOHN, SUZANNE M oc/Psychotherapist; b/Mar 19, 1951; h/2991 West Schoolhouse Lane, Philadelphia, PA 19144; ba/Philadelphia, PA; p/ Roland C St John; Josephine G Baunhuber King; ed/BA 1973, MEd 1975, Trenton St Col; Phila Sch of Psychoanal, 1978-; Doct Cand, Union for Experimenting Cols and Univs; pa/Asst Psychi Social Wkr, Marlboro St Hosp, 1970; Asst Dir, Arrowhead Day Camp of YMCA, 1973-74; Grad Asst, Trenton St Col, 1973-75; Grp Facilitator, 1974-75; Psychotherapist, Humanistic Psychtherapy Studies Ctr, 1975-77; Prog Supvr of Partial Hospitalization Fam Ser Assn, Atl Co, 1977-79; Supvr of Grp Psychotherapy, NE Commun Ctr for Mtl Hlth/Mtl Retard, 1979-; Staff Psychotherapist, Phila Consultation Ctr, 1979-; Tchg Assoc, Phila Sch of Psychoanal, 1982-83; Assoc Mem, Am Psychol Assn; PA Psychol Assn; Am Exam Bd Psychoanal (NAAP); hon/W/ W E.

SAKS, JUDITH-ANN oc/Artist; b/ Dec 20, 1943; h/434 Hunterwood, Houston, TX 77024; m/Haskell Irvin Rosenthal; c/Brian Julien Rosenthal; p/ Julien David and Lucy-Jane Saks, Houston, TX; ed/Postgrad Wk, Univ of Houston, 1967; BFA, Painting and Sculpture, Newcomb Col, Tulane Univ, 1966; Att'd, Rice Univ 1962, TX Acad of Art 1957-58; pa/Curator of Student Art, Univ of Houston, 1968-72; Profl Artist, 1967-; Houston Mus of Fine Arts; Houston Art Leag; Artist Equity; cp/Lady Wash Chapt, DAR, Chapt Curator 1983-84; hon/Reproductions of Wks incl: Houston Assistance Leag (Painting Used on Cover of Prog, Invitation and Stationery) 1979, *Maersk*

Post (Larry Keller, Author) 1977, *Archives of American Art* 1980, *Port of Houston Magazine* Covers (Oct 1976, Jul 1976, May 1976, Oct 1975, Sep 1971), Others; Var One-Person Art Shows; Pt of Houston Auth's Am Revolution Bicent Proj Artist; W/W Am Art; World W/W Wom; W/W Am Wom.

SAKS, JULIEN DAVID oc/Retired; b/ Jun 10, 1906; h/735 International Boulevard, #93, Houston, TX 77024; m/ Lucy-Jane Watson; c/Judith-Ann Saks Rosenthal; p/Joseph and Amelia Rice Saks (dec); ed/Castle Hgts Mil Acad, 1922; BS in Engrg, GA Inst of Technol, 1926; Passed AL Bar Exam, 1934; MBA, Univ of AL, 1950; mil/AUS: Comm'd 2nd Lt 1934, Entered Active Duty (WW II) as 1st Lt, Post Chem Warfare Supply Ofcr 1940; pa/Subdividing Fam Property, 1946-48; Public Utility Conslt, John Bickley, 1951-53; Broker, Comml and Indust Real Est, 1954 to Retirement; Houston Bd of Rltrs, 1958-72; cp/Jewish War Vets of US, Nat Dpty Inspector 1981-82, 1982-83; Warren Zindler Post 590 Jewish War Vets Holocaust Chm; TX Talkers Toastmaster Clb, 1970-76; Houston Civil Def Vol Spkr to Clbs during Fall-Out Scare of 1960's; 12th Armored Div Assn; Navy Leag of the US, 1979-81; r/Ushers Corps, Congreg Beth Israel; Jewish; hon/Pubs, "Synthesis in Diphenyl Series II" 1929, "Are Introductions That Important?" 1975, *In the Beginning* 1978; Bronze Star Medal, Liberation of Colmar; ETO w 3 Battle Stars; Commend, Houston Jewish Commun Coun for Wk Done, 1974; Liberator's Cert, US Holocaust Coun, 1982; Am Jewish Archives.

SALADIN, KENNETH S oc/Biology Professor; b/May 6, 1949; h/112 Camellia Circle, Southwest, Milledgeville, GA 31061; ba/Milledgeville, GA; m/C Diane Campbell; c/Emory Michael, Lisa Nicole; p/Albert R Saladin, Santo Domingo, Dominican Republic; Jennie L Saladin, Kalamazoo, MI; ed/BS, Zool, MI St Univ, 1971; PhD, Parasitology, FL St Univ, 1979; pa/Asst Prof of Biol 1977-83, Assoc Prof of Biol 1983-, GA Col, Dept of Biol; Nat Ctr for Sci Ed, Bd of Dirs 1982-, Treas 1983-; AAAS, 1967-; Am Soc of Parasitologists, 1973-; Animal Behavior Soc, 1974-; Nat Assn of Advrs for the Hlth Professions, 1980-; SEn Assn of Advrs for the Hlth Professions, 1980-; SEn Soc of Parasitologists, 1973-; Assn of SEn Biologists, 1978-; GA Acad of Sci, 1978-; GA Coun for Sci Ed, 1980-, Charter Bd Mem, Treas 1983-, Editor 1982-; GA Sci Tchrs Assn, 1983-; cp/Big Brothers/Big Sisters of Am Inc, Bd of Dirs 1978-; ACLU, 1980-; Am Humanist Assn, 1974-; hon/ Author, 40 to 45 Papers and Abstracts in Parasitology, Popularized Sci, Hist and Politics of Fundamentalist Creationism, Premed Ed, in Sci Jours, Mags and Newspapers; Elon E Byrd Awd, SEn Soc of Parasitologists, 1978; Am Men and Wom of Sci; W/W Frontier Sci and Technol; Outstg Yg Men of Am.

SALADINI, VINCENT ROCCO SR oc/Teacher of Men's and Women's Fashion Design, Adjunct Assistant Professor of Men's and Women's Fashion Design; b/Dec 23, 1924; h/111 Pilgrim Drive, Clifton, NJ 07013; ba/ New York, NY; m/Viola E G; c/Denise Ann, Deborah Jean, Vincent Rocco Jr; ed/MA, Montclair St Col, 1973; BS, St

Univ of NY Oswego, 1971; mil/USN, 1943-46; pa/Tchr, HS of Fashion Indust, 1967-; Adj Asst Prof, Fashion Inst of Technol, 1975-; Dept Hd, Charles W Elbow, Clothiers, 1954-67; Cert'd Guid Cnslr, NY St, NYC, NJ; Exec Bd Mem, Journey Men's Tailor's Union, Local 195, 1955-65; U Fdn Tchrs Del, HS of Fashion Indust, 1977-78; U Fdn Consultative Com, HS of Fashion Indust, 1976-83; r/Rom Cath; hon/Copyright for Song, "Our Last Goodbye," 1970, Copyright for Four-Part Prog in Ladies Tailoring Techniques, 1982; US Achmt Acad Nat Adv Bd, 1983-.

SALAMONE, JOSEPH CHARLES oc/Professor of Chemistry, Dean of Science; b/Dec 27, 1939; ba/University of Lowell, 1 University Avenue, Lowell, MA 01854; m/Ann Beal; c/Robert Charles, Alicia Rebecca; p/Joseph John and Angela Barbagallo Salamone; ed/ Res Assoc, Univ of MI Ann Arbor, 1967-70; NIH Postdoct Fellow, Univ of Liverpool, 1966-67; PhD in Chem, Polytechnic Inst of NY Brooklyn, 1966; BS in Chem, Hofstra Univ, 1961; pa/ Asst Prof of Chem 1970-73, Assoc Prof of Chem 1973-76, Chm of Dept of Chem 1975-78, Prof of Chem 1976-, Acting Dean of Col of Sci 1978-81, Dean of Col of Sci 1981-, Univ of Lowell; Am Chem Soc, Div of Polymer Chem, Div of Polymeric Mats; Soc of Polymer Sci, Japan; Assoc Fellow, Am Acad of Ophthalmology; hon/Author of 85 Sci Papers in Polymer Jours on New Monomers and Polymers; Co-Author of 4 US Patents on Contact Lens Mats; Dist'd Alumnus, Polytechnic Inst of NY Brooklyn, 1984; Editor, *Polymer*, 1976-; Edit Adv Bd, *Journal of Polymer Science*, Polymer Chem Addition, 1974-; W/W Technol Today; W/W E; W/W Frontier Sci and Technol.

SALES, JAMES BOHUS oc/Attorney; b/Aug 24, 1934; h/14938 Bramblewood, Houston, TX 77079; ba/Houston, TX; m/Beuna M; c/Mark Keith, Debra Lynn, Travis James; p/Henry B and Agnes M Sales, Weimar, TX; ed/BS, Univ of TX, 1956; LLB w Hons, Univ of TX Sch of Law, 1960; mil/USMC, 3rd Bat, 9th Marines, 3rd Div, 1956-58; pa/Atty 1960-, Hd of Litigation Dept 1979-, Fulbright & Jaworski; Bd of Trustees, S TX Sch of Law, 1982-; Fellow, Am Col of Trial Lwyrs; Fellow, Intl Acad of Trial Lwyrs; Houston Bar Assn, Pres 1980-81; TX Assn of Def Lwyrs, VP 1978-80; St Bar of TX; Am Bar Assn; Houston Bar Foun, Bd of Dirs 1982-83; Adv Bd of TX Col of Trial Advocacy; Intl Assn of Ins Counsel; Fellow, Am Bar Assn; Fellow, TX Bar Foun; r/Cath; hon/Pubs, *Sales, the Law of Strict Tort Liability in Texas* 1977, Num Legal Articles; TX Bar Foun Awd for Outstg Writing, 1977, 1978; Univ of Houston Awd for Outstg Legal Writing, 1978; Houston Bar Assn Awd for Outstg Ldrship, 1976-77, 1977-78; W/W Am; W/W World.

SALISBURY, BART R oc/Political Scientist; b/Nov 29, 1955; h/11525 40th Avenue, Northeast, Seattle, WA 98125; ba/Seattle, WA; m/Gwen H R; ed/BA 1979, MA 1981, PhC 1983, Univ of WA; pa/Res Asst, Ctr for Law and Justice, 1979-81; Conslt, Ctr for Social Sci Computation and Res, 1981-83; Tchg Asst, Dept of Polit Sci, Univ of WA, 1983-84; Res Conslt: Proj Skills of Sch of Social Wk (Univ of WA), Behavioral Scis Inst, Jud Eval Surveys, Seattle-King Co Bar Assn, Tacoma-Pierce Co Bar Assn, News Proj of Dept of Polit Sci (Univ of WA); Am Polit Sci Assn; Wn Polit Sci Assn; Profl Assn of Scuba Instrs; Phi Theta Kappa; hon/Pubs, "Evaluation Voting Behavior: An Experimental Examination" 1983, 'Rational Choice: The Emerging Paradigm in Electra Studies"; Alfred A Barron Citizenship Awd, 1973; W/W W; W/W Am Jr Cols.

SALLAH, MAJEED "JIM" oc/ Self-Employed Land Developer, Builder, Restauranteur, Investment Trader in Stocks and Bonds; b/Aug 5, 1920; h/Hilltop Road, Gloucester, MA 01930; ba/Gloucester, MA; m/Aline Powers; c/Christopher M, Melissa R; p/ Habeeb Kyrouz Sallah (dec); Rose Karem Sallah (dec); ed/St Ann's Grammar Sch; Gloucester HS; mil/AUS, 1942-45; pa/Pres, Dir, Glo-Bit Fish Co, 1947-48; Pres, Live-Pak of OH Inc, 1947-51; Pres, Treas, Cape Ann Glass Co Inc, 1950-72; Pres, Cape Ann Rlty Corp, 1961; Pres, Maria's Restaurants, 1960-; Pres, Treas, Gloucester Hot-top Constrn Co, 1967-75; Trustee, Christopher Investmt Trust; Pres, Lutsal Inc, 1969-79; Pres, Lebanese-Am Bus-men's Clb; Treas, Lebanese Maronite Soc, 1965-69; Gloucester Assocs, 1960-62; Cape Ann Investmt Corp, 1965-; Pres, Cameron's Inc, 1981-; cp/Am Legion, 1945-82; Amvets, Life Mem, Charter Mem; Lions Clb; Elks; Hon Order KY Cols; r/Rom Cath.

SALSBURY, BARBARA GRACE oc/ Consumer Specialist, Author, Lecturer; b/Dec 27, 1937; h/651 West 40 North, Orem, UT 84057; ba/Orem, UT; m/ Larry P; c/Erin Scott, Sandi Grace Salsbury Simmons; p/Vincent J (dec) and Dorothy M Thayer; ed/Att'd, El Camino Col; pa/VP, Salsbury Enterprises, 1972-; Spec Fac, Brigham Yg Univ Cont'g Ed, 1972-; Consumer Spec, 1980-; St of UT Consumer Cong by Invitation of St Atty Gens Ofc; UT Authors Leag; r/LDS; hon/Pubs, *Plan or Panic, A Guide to Emergency Evacuation/72 Hour Survival* 1983, *Cut Your Grocery Bills in Half* 1982, *If You Must Work: Helps for Part-Time Homemakers* 1976, Others; Frequent Guest on TV and Radio Shows, incl'g, *Merv Griffin Show* and *Phil Donahue Show*; W/W W; Contemp Authors.

SALVADOR, SAL oc/Jazz Musician, Educator, Composer, Columnist; b/Nov 21, 1925; ba/1697 Broadway, New York, NY 10019; m/Catherine Dorinda Randall; c/Barry, Danny, Lorinda; p/Salvatore and Virginia Salvador; ed/Grad, HS; pa/Ldr, Sal Salvador Trio, 1947-49; Guitarist w Mundell Lowe and Terry Gibbs, NYC; Staff Musician, Columbia Records, NYC, 1950-52; Mem, Stan Kenton Big Band, 1952-53; Ldr, Sal Salvador Combo, 1954-80; Ldr, Colors in Sound, 1960-65; Owner, Danbar Records, Lorido Music Pubs, NYC; Accompanist, Robert Goulet, Carol Lawrence, Steve Lawrence, Edye Gorme, Paul Anka, Johnny Mathis, Leslie Uggams, Pat Boone, Tony Bennett, and Num Others; Appeared in Films, *Jazz on a Summer's Day, Blackboard Jungle*; Performed w Bill Evans, Herbie Hancock, Phil Woods, Billie Holiday, Sonny Stitt, Gerry Mulligan, Sarah

Vaughn, Ella Fitzgerald, Peggy Lee, Milt Hinton, Billy Taylor, Frankie Laine; Hd, Guitar Dept and Small Grp Jazz Dept, Univ of Bridgeport, 1970-; Ldr, Small Grp and Jazz Guitar Ensembles; Pvt Tchr, NYC, 1955-; Now w Sal Salvador/ Joe Morello Quartet; ASCAP; Nat Acad of Arts and Scis; Am Fdn of Musicians; r/Presb; hon/Author, *Sal Salvador's Single String Studies, Sal Salvador's Beginners Book for Guitar, Jazz for Two Guitars, Sal Salvador's Complete Chord Book, Technique for Beginners, Complete Guitar Method, Do It Yourself Course*, Others; Num Recordings; Recip, Num Awds, ASCAP; W/W E.

SALVATORI, VINCENT LOUIS oc/ Corporate Executive; b/Apr 22, 1932; h/ 8101 Birnam Wood Drive, McLean, VA 22102; ba/McLean, VA; m/Enid Joan Dodd; c/Leslie Ann, Robert Louis, Sandra Ann; p/Louis and Lydia Tofani Salvatori (dec); ed/BSEE, PA St Univ, 1958; mil/USAF, Sgt 1948-52; pa/High Speed Radio Operator, USAF, 1949-52; Electronic Inspector of Automation Sys, Automation Timing and Control Corp, 1952-54; Hd, Spec Detection Grp 1959-60, Hd of Microwave Techniques Sect and Antennae Lab 1960-63, Mgr of Passive ECCM Sys and DF Technique Progs 1963-67, HRB-Singer Inc; Mgr, Reconnaissance Sys Dept, Radiation Sys Inc, 1967-69; VP of Engrg 1969-73, VP of Technol 1973-81, Quest Res Corp; Exec VP of Technol and Planning, QuesTech Inc, 1981-; IEEE; Am Optical Soc; AIAA; Assn of Old Crows; hon/ Pubs, "A Rocket-bourne 400 KC TRC Receiver" 1958, "Factors Influencing Communications with Satellites" 1959, "Investigation into Microwave Multipath Interferometer" 1959, "Investigation of Luxembourg Effect Utilizing Cubic Function Solid State Devices" 1960; Patent, "Cubic Function Generation"; Engrg Hons Prog, PA St Univ; W/W Fin and Indust; W/W Frontier Sci and Technol.

SALZMAN, ERIC oc/Composer, Writer; b/Sep 8, 1933; h/29 Middagh Street, Brooklyn, NY 11201; m/Lorna Jackson; c/Eva Francis, Stephanie Beatrice; ed/ Studied w Morris Lawner, Otto Luening, Vladimir Ussachevsky, Jack Beeson; BA in Music, Columbia Univ, 1954; MFA, Princeton Univ, 1956; pa/Music Critic, *New York Times*; Music Dir, WBAI-FM, 1962-63, 1968-72; Music Critic, *New York Herald Tribune*, 1963-66; Asst Prof of Music, Queens Col, 1966-68; Critic, *Stereo Review*, 1966-; hon/ Compositions: *In Praise of the Owl* and *The Cuckoo, Foxes and Hedgehogs, The Peloponnesian WarFeedback, The Nude Paper Sermon, Ecolog*, Others; Fulbright F'ship.

SAMMONS, ROBERT ARDEL JR oc/ Behaviorist; b/Jul 20, 1945; h/119 Willow Way, Chapel Hill, NC 27510; m/ Diana Louise Walters; c/Jennifer Nerritt; p/Dr Robert A Sammons, Huntsville, AL; ed/Univ of NC Med Sch (Present); PhD, Univ of NC Greensboro, 1974; MS 1969, BS 1967, Auburn Univ; mil/USAF 1969-72, Capt; pa/Asst Prof, E Carolina Univ, 1977-80; Dir, Sopris Mtl Hlth Ctr, 1974-77; Co-Fdr, Rocky Mtn Conf on Behavior Modification; Ethics Com, CO Psychol Assn and NC Psychol Assn; Am Psychol Assn; Assn for Advmt of Behavior Therapy; hon/Psi Chi; Alpha Epsilon Delta; W/W S and SW.

SAMPLE, DOROTHY ELLIOTT oc/

Union President; b/Nov 1, 1938; h/3119 Prospect Street, Flint, MI 48504; ba/ Birmingham, AL; m/Richard; c/Richard Howard, Scott Elliott, Lisa DeAnne; p/ John Belton (dec) and Annie E Elliott, Brilliant, AL; ed/AB w High Distn 1966, MA 1967, PhD 1976, Univ of MI; BA, summa cum laude, Free Will Bapt Bible Col, 1961; ThD, Toledo Bible Col and Sem; pa/Tchr in Sec'dy Schs and Cols, Linden Commun Schs and Flint Commun Schs; Adj Prof in Psych, John Wesley Col, 1973-75; Ctr for Christian Studies, 1979-80; Piloted Jr High Gifted Ed Prog, Flint Schs, 1977; Profl Cnslr in Psychol Clin, Personality Dynamics, Flint and Southfield, 1977-81; Current Pres, Wom's Missionary Union, Aux to the So Bapt Conv; Free-Lance Conf Ldr and Spkr; hon/Pubs, *Life in the Fifth Dimension*, Mag Articles; Free Will Bapt Col: Valedictorian, Delta Epsilon Chi, Outstg Student Merit Awd from Fac, Lit Soc Awd, Yrbook Editor, Student Govt Ofcr, Elected Best All Around; Univ of MI: Among Top 10 Students in Grad'g Class, Phi Kappa Phi, Delta Kappa Gamma; W/W Am Wom; World W/W Am Wom; Personalities of W and MW.

SAMPSON, EVA B oc/Nursing Director of Student Health Service; b/Jul 31, 1932; h/PO Box 626, Pembroke, NC 28372; ba/Pembroke, NC; m/John W; c/ Ursula Kaye Freeman, Kelvin Dale, Karen Gale Suzanne; p/Clyde (dec) and Lillie Mae Brewington, Lumberton, NC; ed/RN; BS in Psych; BA in Sociol; Emer Med Tech; Emer Med Vehicle Operator; pa/Staff Nurse, Charity Hosp; Ofc Nurse for Gen Practitioner, 1956-66; Staff Nurse, SEn Gen Hosp, 1968-70; Nsg Dir, Student Hlth Ser, Pembroke St Univ, 1970-; Asst Dir, Fam Care Home; Vol Home Vis'g Nurse; Inser Ed; Instr, Pembroke Vol Rescue Squad; Trustee, NC Cancer Inst; Bd of Dirs, Nsg and Bloodmobile Prog, ARC; NC Hlth Study Com, Dept of Public Instrn; ANA; NC Nurses Assn; ARC Nurse; Sigma Sigma Sigma; NC Assn of Rescue Squads; Robeson Co Rescue Squads; cp/ Former Cub Scout Den Mother; r/ Former Sunday Sch Tchr; Bapt; hon/W/ W Am Cols and Univs; W/W Am Wom.

SAMUEL, PAUL oc/Physician; b/Feb 17, 1927; h/25 Nassau Drive, Great Neck, NY 11021; m/Gabriella Relly Zeichner; c/Robert Marc, Adrianne Jill; p/Adolf and Magda Zollner Samuel (dec); ed/Baccalaureat, cum laude, Kemeny Zsigmond Gymnasium, Budapest; MD, Trés Honorable, Univ of Paris Fac of Med; pa/Dir, Arteriosclerosis Res Lab, Long Isl Jewish-Hillside Med Ctr, 1969-; Adj Prof, Rockefeller Univ, 1971-81; Adj Prof of Med, Cornell Univ Med Col, 1979-; Clin Prof of Med, Albert Einstein Col of Med, 1981-; Fellow, Am Col of Cardiology; Am Col of Phys; Pres, Am Heart Assn, Nassau Chapt, 1980; Fellow, NY Cardiological Soc; r/Jewish; hon/Author, About 120 Pub'd Articles in Sci Jours and Books; Dist'd Achmt Awd, Am Heart Assn, Nassau Chapt; W/W Sci; W/W E.

SANDERLIN, CHRISTINE FAUST oc/Manager of Technical Training; b/ Oct 29, 1950; h/1971 Brookview Drive, Northwest, Atlanta, GA 30318; ba/ Atlanta, GA; p/Mr and Mrs Henry C Faust Jr, Atlanta, GA; ed/BA in Eng, Sprg Hill Col; pa/Tnr, Fed Resv Bk of

Atlanta, 1973-78; Proj Mgr 1978-79, Sr Proj Mgr 1979-80, Mgr of Tech Tng 1980-, Coca-Cola USA; Am Soc for Tng and Devel; Intl TV Assn; r/Cath; hon/ Golden Reel of Merit, 14th Annual Videotape Fest; W/W Am Cols and Univs; W/W S and SW.

SANDERS, CATHERINE de LORIS oc/Optometrist; b/Sep 30, 1925; h/215 Pat-Mar Square, Mullins, SC 29574; ba/ Mullins, SC; m/Lexton Ivy Cox; ed/ Att'd, Winthrop Col, 1943-44, 1944-45; OD, So Col of Optom, 1947; pa/ Secy-Treas, SC Optometric Assn, 1948-50; Pres 1950-51, Secy-Treas 1951-52, Pee Dee Optometric Assn; Am Optometric Assn, 1947-82; SC Optometric Assn, 1947-82; Pee Dee Optometric Assn, 1947-82; Optometric Ext Prog Foun, 1947-82; Art Frat, Kappa Pi; Optometric Sorority, Pi Kappa Rho; So Coun of Optom; cp/Metro Opera Guild; r/Presb; hon/W/W Am Wom; W/W S and SW.

SANDERS, DANIEL SELVARAJAH oc/Dean, Professor and Director of International Programs; b/Sep 18, 1928; h/1807 Vancouver Place, Honolulu, HI 96822; ba/Honolulu, HI; m/Christobel; p/David S (dec) and Harriet C Sanders, Sri Lanka; ed/BA, Social Scis, Univ of Ceylon, 1953; Dipl in Social Wk, Univ of Wales, 1958; MSW 1967, PhD in Social Wk 1971, Univ of MN; pa/Dean 1975-, Acting Dean 1974-75, Prof 1974-, Dir of Intl Progs 1974-, Assoc Prof and Asst to the Dean in Intl Progs 1973-74, Assoc Prof 1971-73, Univ of HI Sch of Social Wk; Spec Projs Conslt-Admr, Div of Child Wel, MN Dept of Public Wel, 1967-69; Other Previous Positions; Coun on Social Wk Ed; Nat Assn of Social Wkrs; Acad of Cert'd Social Wkrs; Nat Conf on Social Wel; Intl Coun on Social Wel; Intl Assn of Schs of Social Wk; AAAS; Intl Soc for Commun Devel; Inter-Univ Consortium for Intl Social Devel; r/Christian; hon/Pubs, *Education for International Social Welfare* 1983, *The Developmental Perspective in Social Work* 1981, Others; Wn Interst Comm on Higher Ed, Fac Devel Awd, 1973-74; Univ of MN Putman D McMillan Doct Dissertaion F'ship Awd, 1970-71; Inst of Intl Ed, Devel Fellow, US, 1966-67; World Coun on Chs, Ecumenical Scholar, US, 1965-66; Brit Coun Scholar, UK, 1957-58; W/W Hlth Care; W/W Rel; W/W Am; Intl W/W Commun Ser; W/W World; Intl W/W Contemp Achmt; Commun Ldrs of World.

SANDERS, GILBERT OTIS oc/ Research Psychologist, Consultant, Educator; b/Aug 7, 1945; h/2107 Tucker Terrace, Pittsburg, KS 66762; ba/ Pittsburg, KS; m/Doris Jean Young Cutchall; c/Lisa Dawn, Cecily; p/ Richard A and Evelyn Sanders, Oklahoma City, OK; ed/AS, Murray St Col, 1965; BA, OK St Univ, 1967; MS, Troy St Univ, 1970; EdD, Univ of Tulsa, 1974; mil/Tours in Vietnam, and Maj, USAR, 1968-72; pa/Dir of Ed, Am Humane Ed Soc and MA Soc for the Preven of Cruelty to Animals, 1975; Chm, Dept of Computer Sci and Dir of Computer Sers, Calumet Col, 1975-78; Res Psychol, AUS Res Inst, 1978-79; Engrg Psychol, AUS Tng and Doctrine Commands' Sys Anal Activity, 1979-80; Proj Dir/Res Psychol, Applied Sci Assocs, 1980-81; Res Psychol, Resv Compo-

nents Pers and Adm Ctr, 1981-83; Pvt Conslt in Behavioral Scis, 1981-83; Adj Prof of Bus and Psych, Columbia Col, Buder Campus, 1982-83; Assoc Prof, Col of Arts and Scis, Pittsburg St Univ, 1983-; Pres, SWn Behavioral Res and Mktg Co, 1984-; Pvt Cnslg Pract, 1984-; Prin Editor, *TRACOC Training Effectiveness Analysis Handbook*, 1980; Am Psychol Assn; AAAS; Human Factors Soc; TX Psychol Assn; OK Psychol Assn; KS Psychol Assn; MO Psychol Assn; Assn of Ednl Communication and Technol; cp/OK Hist Soc; Resv Ofcrs Assn; Masons; r/Bapt; hon/Author, *Statistics and Research for the Businessman* 1984, Num Res Reports; Hon Col, Gov's Staff of OK, 1972; Hon Ambassador for St of OK, 1974; Recip, Kavanough Foun Commun Bldr Awd, 1967; W/W MW; W/W Frontier Sci and Technol; W/W World.

SANDERS, GLORIA TOLSON oc/ Physical Therapy Educator, Researcher; b/Nov 17, 1944; h/1205 East 5th Street, Greenville, NC 27834; ba/Greenville, NC; p/Mattocks and Zeta Sanders, Hubert, NC; ed/Att'd, NC Wesleyan Col, 1962-65; BS in Phy Therapy, Med Col of VA, 1967; Student of Exptl Psych 1970-71, MS in Rehab Cnslg 1976, E Carolina Univ; mil/Maj, USAR, 1977-; pa/Staff Phy Therapist, Grady Meml Hosp, 1967-69; Staff Phy Therapist, Kennestone Hosp, 1969-70; Dir of Phy Therapy, Univ Hosp of Jacksonville, 1971-74; Assoc Prof, E Carolina Univ, 1974-; Am Phy Therapy Assn; NC Phy Therapy Assn; Delta Kappa Gamma Soc; r/Meth; hon/Pubs, "A Technique for Measuring Pelvic Tilt," "Sling Support during Pregnancy After Hemipelvectomy," *Lower Limb Amputations: A Guide to Rehabilitation*; Instr for Sigma Xi Res Soc Undergrad Res Awd, E Carolina Univ, 1980, 1983; Nom for Baethke/ Carlin Awd for Tchg Excell, APTA; Outstg Yg Wom of Am; W/W Frontier Sci and Technol; W/W World.

SANDERSON, SANDY oc/Principal Broker; b/Nov 28, 1944; h/1573 East 1425 North, Logan, UT 84321; ba/ Logan, UT; m/Howard; c/Mary Faith, Sara Love; p/Mildred Sanderson, Logan, UT; ed/BA 1965, MA 1966, Whittier Col; GRI, 1981; CRS, 1982; LTG, 1984; pa/Tchr 1966, Rdg Supvr 1967, Whittier, CA; Rdg Spec, BIA-UT, 1968; Cont'g Ed Dir, Logan, UT, 1969; Sales Assoc, Aloma Real Est, 1979-82; Fdr, Gold Key Real Est, 1982; Mgr, Wardley Better Homes and Gardens, 1983; Broker, Coldwell Banker Baugh Assocs, 1984-; Fdr, Logan Wom's Coun of Rltrs, 1982, First Pres; St Farm and Land, Secy-Treas 1982; St CRS Chapt Treas 1983-84; St WCR VP, 1983-84; Woms Coun of Rltrs; r/Quaker; hon/Recognized by Nat WCR as Nat Tnr in Ldrship Prog, 1984; Sales Assoc of 1981, Logan Bd of Rltrs; Million Dollar Seller, 1980, 1981, 1982, 1983; W/W W.

SANDFORD, VIRGINIA ADELE oc/ Speaker, Trainer, Seminar Leader; b/ Nov 29, 1926; ba/811 Fife Heights, Northeast, Tacoma, WA 98422; c/Susan L, Kaye E, James C; p/Fred (dec) and Lucille Wepfer; ed/Student, Univ of WA, 1946-49; pa/Tchr of Stringed Instruments, Puyallup Sch Dist, 1944-46; Exec Secy, Tacoma Sch Dist, 1972-75; Tchr, Ed Secy Prog, Clover Pk Voc-Tech, 1975-82; Spkr and Sem Ldr

of Own Bus, VA Sandford & Assocs; Profl Mem, Nat Spkrs' Assn; IPA; r/ Prot; hon/W/W W.

SANDIFER, ROBERT LOWRY oc/ Public Information and Education Officer; b/Aug 9, 1935; h/7816 Loch Lane, Columbia, SC 29206; ba/Columbia, SC; m/Sherry J; c/Steven L, Jodie S Davis, Robert Paul; p/Mr and Mrs C H Sandifer, Florence, SC; ed/BS, Clemson Univ, 1957; mil/AUS 1957-58, Capt FA; pa/Stat, USDA, SRS, 1958-67; Economist 1967-70, Public Affairs Ofcr 1970-, Soil Conserv Ser, USDA; CEA; EEASC; SCSA; NACD; CAPH; SCFOA; SCWF; r/Presb; hon/Conservationist of the Yr in SC, 1980; Conserv Edr of the Yr, 1979; Shrine Bowl Football Referee, 1981; Pres, SCSA, 1970, Nat Councilman 1978-81; W/W S and SW; Others.

SANDLER, BERNICE RESNICK oc/ Women's Rights Activist; b/Mar 3, 1928; ba/Association of American Colleges, 1818 R Street, Northwest, Washington, DC 20004; c/Deborah Jo, Emily Maud; p/Abe and Ivy Resnick, Hallandule, FL; ed/BA, cum laude, Brooklyn Col, 1948; MA, City Col of NY, 1950; EdD, Univ of MD, 1969; pa/Current Exec Assoc, Dir of Proj on the Status and Ed of Wom 1971-, Assn of Am Col; Dpty Dir of Wom's Action Prog, HEW; Ed Spec, US Ho of Reps' Spec Subcom on Ed; Exec Com, Inst for Ednl Ldrship, 1982-; Bd of Overseers, Wellesley Ctr for the Study of Wom in Higher Ed and the Professions, 1975-; Adv Bd, Weal Ednl and Legal Def Fund, 1980-; Bd, Ctr for Wom's Policy Studies, 1972-; Adv Com, Wider Opports for Wom, 1978-; Num Other Profl Mbrships; hon/Pubs, "Women in Administration: Seek and You Shall Find" or "Women Who Work in Administration-Why It Still Hurts to Be A Woman in Labor" 1979, "You've Come a Long Way, Maybe-Or Why It Still Hurts to Be a Woman in Labor" 1979, Num Others; LLD, Bloomfield Col, 1973; LLD, Hood Col, 1974; LHD, Grand Val St Col, 1974; LLD, RI Col; Rockefeller Public Ser Awd, 1977; W/ W Am Wom; DIB; Commun Ldrs and Noteworthy Ams; W/W Am Jewry.

SANDOK, THERESA HELEN oc/ Assistant Professor of Philosophy; b/ Nov 4, 1945; h/1600 Ruth Avenue, #5, Louisville, KY 40205; ba/Louisville, KY; p/Louis and Helen Sandok, Chetek, WI; ed/BA, magna cum laude, Col of St Thomas, 1969; PhD, Univ of Notre Dame, 1975; pa/Tchg Asst, Univ of Notre Dame, 1971-72; Vis'g Prof, Mt Senario Col, Sums of 1971, 1980; Asst/ Assoc Prof of Phil, Col of St Catherine, 1975-81; Asst Prof of Phil, Bellarmine Col, 1982-; Am Cath Philosophical Assn; Am Philosophical Assn; Intl Ctr for Lublin Univ Translations; KY Philosophical Assn; Nat Assem of Rel Wom; Nat Scholastic Hon Soc; Personalistic Discussion Grp; Soc for Wom in Phil; r/Rom Cath; hon/Pub, Translation from Polish into Eng of Chapts IV, VII, XII of *Jaczlowiek: Zarys antropologii filozoficznej* by Mieczyslaw A Krapiec, 1979; Ed Grant, KY Chapt of Intl Fdn of Cath Alumnae, 1983; Intl W/W Ed; Outstg Yg Wom of Am; W/W Am Wom; World W/W Wom.

SANDS, DONALD E oc/University Administrator; b/Feb 25, 1929; h/335 Cassidy Avenue, Lexington, KY 40502;

ba/Lexington, KY; m/Elizabeth S; c/ Carolyn Looff, Stephen R; ed/BS, Worcester Polytechnic Inst, 1951; PhD, Cornell Univ, 1955; pa/Res Assoc, Cornell Univ, 1955-56; Sr Chem, Lawrence Livermore Lab, 1956-72; Asst Prof of Chem 1962-65, Assoc Prof 1965-68, Prof 1968-81, Acting Dean 1978, 1980-81, Assoc Vice Chancellor 1981-84, Vice Chancellor for Acad Affairs 1984-, Univ of KY; Am Chem Soc; Am Crystallographic Assn; Sigma Xi; AAAS; NY Acad of Scis; KY Acad of Scis; r/Humanist; hon/Pubs, *Introduction to Crystallography* 1969, *Vectors and Tensors in Crystallography* 1982, About 50 Sci Articles and Num Other Pubs; Am Men of Sci; W/W S.

SANDS, M DALE oc/General Manager of Environmental Services; b/Feb 13, 1951; h/4837 Muirwood Drive, Pleasanton, CA 94566; ba/Dublin, CA; m/Debra Heath; c/Hilaria Elizabeth, Trenton Dale, Kendrick Duffy; p/ Maynard D and Claire T Sands (dec); ed/BS in Chem and Biol, Ctl MI Univ, 1973; MS in Envir Scis, Univ of MI, 1974; MBA in Process, CA St Univ Hayward; pa/Lab Mgr, Raytheon Co, Oceanographic and Envir Sers, 1974-77; Dir, Scis Dept, Oceanic and Engrg Opers, Interst Electronics Corp, 1977-81; VP, Marine Ecological Conslts, 1981; Gen Mgr, McKesson Envir Sers, 1981-; Am Chem Soc, Envir Chem Sect; Water Pollution Control Fdn; Am Chem Soc, Num Positions within Local Chapt Over Past 10 Yrs; r/Epis; hon/Author, Over 25 Tech Pubs and Presentations in Field of Envir Assessment Regarding Energy Prodn and Chemicals Mgmt; W/ W W; W/W Commun Ldrs.

SANFORD, LESLIE McHENRY JR oc/Naval Officer; b/Apr 20, 1946; h/359 Calle Navarro, Camarillo, CA 93010; ba/Pt Mugu, CA; p/Leslie M Sr and Aleeyne P Sanford, Ruther Glen, VA; ed/BS in Psych, BA in Eng, VA Polytechnic Inst, 1968; Grad Studies in Bus and Indust Psych, Univ of W FL, 1975-77; mil/Lt Cmdr, USN, 1965-; pa/ Enlisted in Naval Resv, 1965; Comm'd Ensign, 1968; Patrol Squadron Sixteen, 1969-70; Aviation Tng Command, 1970-72; Attack Squadron Seventy-Five, 1972-74; Instr, Aviation Tng Command, 1974-77; Aircraft Ferry Squadron Thirty-One, 1977-80; Naval Air Rework Facility, 1980-82; Tactical Electronic Warfare Squadron Thirty-Four, 1982-; Life Mem, Assn of Naval Aviation; Life Mem, AF Assn; Life Mem, Naval Inst; AAUP; Naval Aviation Exec Inst; cp/Charter Mem, Rotating Beacon Assn; Life Mem, Nat Rifle Assn; r/Meth; hon/5 Indiv Air Medals, 1972; Air Medal (11 Flight/Strike Awds), 1972-73; Navy Commend Medal (2 Awds), 1972; Navy Achmt Medal, 1977; Vietnamese Cross of Gallantry, 1972-73; Num Campaign Awds and Ribbons; W/W S and SW; Men of Achmt; Personalities of S; Jane's W/W Am Aviation.

SANFORD, RUTH COOPER oc/ Facilitator of Learning, Therapist, Columnist; b/Dec 26, 1906; h/2023 Cecilia Place, Seaford, NY 11783; ba/ Same; m/Daniel S; c/Mei-Mei E C; p/ Elden O Cooper (dec); Elma M Dorn (dec); ed/AB, Lebanon Val Col, 1930; MA, Tchrs' Col, Columbia Univ, 1937;

Postgrad Wk, NY Univ, Rutgers, Columbia Univ, 1952-65; pa/Tchr, Lakewood, NY, HS, 1930-36; Asst ot Secy, Tchrs' Col, Columbia Univ, 1937-40; Asst Prof, Guid Ofcr, WMD Col, 1945-49; Dir, Guid and Cnslg, Lakewood, NJ, HS, and W Hempstead Public Schs, 1954-73; Conslt, NY St Ed Dept, 1957-59; Adj Fac, Long Isl Univ and Hofstra Univ, 1973-; Interpersonal Growth, 1979-82; Facilitator, Person-Centered Intl Wkshops, 1978-; Staff, Person-Centered Lng Prog, 1980-; Columnist, Observer Newspapers, 1975-82; Bd of Dirs, Ctr for Interpersonal Growth, 1978-; APGA, Seaford Planning Coun; Assn for Humanistic Ed; Assn of Humanistic Psych; Alumni Assn Intl Hoose, NYC; cp/Chm, Seaford Renewal Prog; Bd of Dirs, Seaford C of C; r/ Eclectic; hon/Author, Res Reports and Profl Papers, incl'g, "Creativity, Intelligence and Achievement in West Hempstead Public Schools," "Nurturing Creativity in the Classroom," "Preparing Youth for a World of Change"; Co-Author, *Journey to the Heart of Africa* 1982, *Intimacy in a Person-Centered Way of Being* 1982; Lebanon Val Col Alumni Awd, Outstg Achmt in Ed, 1975; Peter Zenger Awd for Journalism and Public Ser, 1976; BSA Awd for Public Ser, 1976; Outstg Contribution to the Counseling Profession, NY State Guidance Association, 1976.

SANGER, ISAAC JACOB oc/Retired Artist from Graphics Section; b/Jan 8, 1899; h/3610 Riviera Street, Temple Hills, MD 20748; ba/Same; m/Marjorie Graybill (dec); p/Samuel Abraham and Rebecca E Sanger (dec); ed/Att'd, Bridgewater Col, 2 Yrs; BS, Fine Arts Ed, Tchrs' Col, Columbia Univ; Grad Wk, Sch of Painting and Sculpture, Columbia Univ, and Art Students Leag; mil/ WWII; pa/Arts Illustrator, Mil Air Transport Ser, USAF; Visual Info Spec, Graphics Sect, Public Hlth Ser, HEW, Wash, DC; Soc of Wash Printmakers; Illustrations in Books and Pubs, incl'g, *Land of the Free*, *Wood Engravings of the 1930's*, *Graphic Works of American 30's*, *American Prints from Wood*; r/Brethren; hon/Jt Prize, Phila Print Clb, 1929; Represented 4 Times in 50 Prints of the Yr; Included in the Fine Prints of the Yr, 1936, 1937; Hon Mention, Phila Print Clb, 2 Times; Cited for Outstg Achmt in Graphic Arts, Bridgewater Col, 1977; Prints incl'd in Perm Collections of Nat Collections of Fine Arts, Lib of Cong, and Other Public Collections.

SAN MIGUEL, MANUEL oc/Historian, Consultant; b/Sep 29, 1930; h/1214 Howell Creek Drive, Winter Springs, FL 32708; m/Sandra Bonilla-San Miguel; c/ Manuel, Ana Victoria; p/Manuel San Miguel Nazario (dec); Luisa Griffo-San Miguel; ed/Att'd, Univ of Puerto Rico 1947-51, Univ of PA 1966-68, Arts Student Leag 1968-69; mil/AUS Inf, Capt 1951-53; pa/Histn, US Nat Pk Ser, San Juan Nat Historic Site, US Dept of the Interior, 1953-63; Exec Secy, Acad of Arts and Scis, 1963-64; Devotes Full-time to Hist Consultation, Painting, Writing and Music Composition, 1964-; Acad of Arts and Scis, Puerto Rico Chapt; Ateneo de Puerto Rico; Augusto Rodriguez Foun; Mem and Conslt, Inst of Puerto Rican Culture and San Juan Nat Historic Site; Co-Fdr,

Galeria Oller Mus, NYC, and Carribean Art Gallery, Puerto Rico; Maj One-Man Shows in Painting: Univ of Puerto Rico, Inst of Puerto Rican Culture, Ateneo de Puerto Rico, Ponce Puerto Rico Mus, Houston Mus, NY Hispanic Mus; cp/ Lions Clb Intl; Disabled Am Vets, Life Mem; r/Rom Cath; hon/Author, Num Articles, Res Papers and Pamphlets Currently in US Nat Archives, 1959-; Commendable Ser Medal for Hist Res, Nat Pk Ser, US Dept of Interior, 1964; Cit for Commendable Ser in the Field of Interpretation, Nat Pk Ser, US Dept of Interior, 1964; Lion of the Yr, 1962-63; W/W S and SW; Ency of Puerto Rican Culture; Artists USA.

SANNELLA, JOSEPH L oc/Director of Research; b/Jul 27, 1933; h/2803 West Woodbridge, Muncie, IN 47304; ba/ Muncie, IN; m/Nancy Marshall; c/ Joseph A, Sueanne E, Stephen J; p/Dr and Mrs Theodore Sannella, West Concord, MA; ed/AB in Biochem Sci, Harvard Univ, 1955; MS in Chem, Univ of MA, 1957; PhD in Biochem, Purdue Univ, 1963; MBA, Fin, Univ of DE, 1969; pa/Supvr of Organic Res 1967-69, Mgr of Graphic Arts 1969-71, Supvr of Chem Res 1971-74, Dir of Res 1974-, Ball Corp; Ball Employees Credit Union, Bd of Dirs 1981-; Phi Lambda Upsilon; Sigma Xi; Alpha Chi Sigma; Nat Metal Decorators Assn; Soc of Plastic Engrs; cp/Muncie Kiwanis Clb; Muncie C of C; DE Co Easter Seal Soc for Crippled, Bd of Dirs 1979-; Ball Polit Action Com, 1976-; hon/Pubs, "Fractional Precipitation with Ethanol" 1965, "Phosphorylation of Amylose with B-Cyancethyl Phosphate" 1963, Others.

SANSONE, MARLEEN BARBARA oc/Artist, Arts Advocate; b/Nov 13, 1942; h/46 Stevens Street, East Haven, CT 06512; ba/Hartford, CT; m/Joseph A; c/David, Benjamin, Naomi, Eva Marie; p/Douglas and Mary Hoover (dec); ed/CAS, Studio Art, Wesleyan Univ; MA, Sociol of the Arts, Goddard Col, 1982; BA, Art Hist, Charter Oak Col; Student, Art Inst of Chgo, Albertus Magnus Col; pa/Exec Dir, CT Advocates for the Arts, 1979-; Grantsperson, U Way of Gtr New Haven, 1974-79; Arts and Crafts Instr, Wooster Square Creat Arts Wkshop, 1970-74; Pres, Cultural Arts Coun of E Haven; Pres, CT Chapt, Wom's Caucus for Art; Artwks Gallery; Bd Mem, Artspace Inc; Past Bd Mem, Shoreline Arts Alliance, U Theater of the Americas; r/Cath; hon/Pubs, "Politics and Policy" 1983, "The Case in Connecticut" 1983, Var Articles in *Connecticut Artists Magazine* 1979-82, 4 Wks of Art in *Aurora* 1980; Commission, Mural for Pk City Hosp; Purchase Prize, Juried Art Show, E Haven Town Hall; Selected for Num Juried Art Shows in CT and Chgo; DIB; Dir of Dist'd Ams; Foremost Wom of 20th Century.

SANTAELLA, IRMA VIDAL oc/ Justice of the Supreme Court of State of New York; b/Oct 4, 1924; h/800 Grand Concourse, Apartment 1J, Bronx, NY 10451; ba/Bronx, NY; c/ Yvette, Antonio Vidal; p/Sixta Thilet Vda Vidal, Ponce, Puerto Rico; ed/Grad, Acctg, Mod Bus Col, Ponce, 1942; Att'd, Univ of Puerto Rico Rio Piedras, 1945; BA, Polit Sci, Hunter Col; LLB 1961, JD 1967, Brooklyn Law Sch; pa/Present Justice, NY St Supr Ct; Chp, NY St Human Rights Appeal Bd, 1974-83; NY

St Human Rights Appeal Bd, 1968-73; Ptnrship, Senator Anthony A Gazzara, 1966-68; Dpty Commr, NYC Dept of Corrections, 1963-66; cp/Coalition of the Hispanic People, Nat CoChm; Chm, Puerto Rican Cancer Assn, NY Chapt; Chm, BSA, S Bronx Chd's Camp 41st Police Precnt; VChm, Cath Interracial Coun of NY Inc; Yth Crusade for Moral Rearmament and Nat Coalition of Hispanics, CO; hon/Author, 1,400 Legal Opinions on Human Rights; NY St Assem Resolution, 1972, 1982; Senate Resolution of the Commonwealth of Puerto Rico, 1982; Gov Hugh L Carey's Exec Message, 1982; Bronx Borough Pres's Cit of Merit, 1982; Puerto Rican Nat Forum Awd, 1982; Num Other Hons; W/W World; Intl Biogl Roll of Hon; World W/W Wom; IPA; Intl W/W Contemp Achmt; DIB; Intl Book of Hon.

SANTIAGO, MARGARET WALKER ALICEA oc/Museum Registrar; b/Oct 22, 1931; h/29 Tuckerman Street, Northwest, Washington, DC 20011; ba/Washington, DC; m/Ismael Alicea Sr; c/Carmelita A Williams, Ismael Alicea Jr, Fredric A, Cheryl A A; p/Lee Walker (dec); Mozell Murray, Pittsburgh, PA; ed/Att'd, A&T Col 1949, Cardoza Evening Sch 1956, USDA Grad Sch 1965, 1975, 1976, 1978, Am Univ 1971-72; Cert, Smithsonian Ofc of Pers Adm, Pers Mgmt for Supvrs, 1967; Cert, Smithsonian Ofc of Pers Adm, Supvrs Role in Equal Opport, 1973; Cert, Civil Ser Comm, An Intro to Automated Data Processing, 1974; Cert, Smithsonian Wkshop, Packing and Shipping Sem, 1980; pa/Clk-Typist 1960, Asst Supvr 1965, Supvr 1966, Supervisory Mus Tech 1970, Registrar for Nat Mus of Natural Hist 1977-, Smithsonian Instn; Conslt, AAM Mus Assessmt Prog, 1982; Smithsonian Registrars Coun; Am Assn of Museums; Registrars Com, AAM; Registrars Nom'g Com, 1980 Slate; NE Mus Conf; Registrars Com, NEMC; Afro-Am Mus Assn; Smithsonian Wom's Coun; Nat Coun of Negro Wom, Metro Area Sect; r/Bapt; hon/Cert, NAACP; Cert, Nat Coun of Negro Wom for Outstg Achmt; Plaque, Min of Info, Govt of Kuwait, 1981; Plaque, Gethsemane Bapt Ch for Outstg Ser through Song, 1980; Key to the City of San Jose, CA, 1980; World W/W Wom; Intl Registry of Profiles; Intl W/W Intells.

SANZ, ROBERT LOUIS oc/Consultant to the Oil Industry; b/Oct 21, 1947; h/6707 Chancellor Drive, Spring, TX 77379; ba/Houston, TX; m/Irene Randel; c/Regina Louise; p/Robert and Elaine B Sanz, Washington, DC; ed/Att'd, Mercersberg Acad; Student of Bus Adm, Vanderbilt Univ; mil/Mem, USN SEAL Team; pa/Pres, TX Energy Resv Corp, 1980-82; Exec VP, Langham Petro, 1978-80; Exec VP, Intercontinental Oil, 1977-78; Wash Rep for Var Petro Concerns, 1975-77; r/Cath; hon/W/W Oil and Gas.

SARAFIAN, ARMEN oc/University President; b/Mar 5, 1920; h/PO Box 1624, Glendora, CA 91740; ba/La Verne, CA; c/Norman, Winston, Joy; p/Kevork and Lucy Gazarian Sarafian (dec); ed/AB, magna cum laude, La Verne Col; MA, Claremont Grad Univ; PhD, Univ of So CA; LLD, La Verne Col; pa/Pres, La Verne Col (Now Univ

of La Verne), 1976-; Pres, Pasadena City Col, Supt of Pasadena Area Commun Col Dist, 1965-76; Adm Dean for Instrn, Pasadena City Col, 1959-65; Adj Prof of Commun Col Adm, Univ of So CA, 1968-78; Other Previous Positions; cp/Native Sons of the Golden W; Pasadena Arts Coun; S Pasadena Oneonta Clb; Arcadia Coor'g Coun; Pasadena Hist Soc; Patron, Pasadena Area Mexican-Am S'ship Com; r/Ch of the Brethren; hon/Life Mbrship, Gold Seal Bearer, CA S'ship Fdn; Hon Life Mem, Pasadena Coun of Parents and Tchrs; Hon Life Mem, Assoc'd Student Body of Pasadena City Col; Dist'd Commun Ser Awd, Pasadena Ed Assn; Conservation Merit Awd, CA Conserv Coun; Omicron Mu Delta Dist'd Ser Awd; Meritorious Ser Awd, Pasadena City Col Fac Senate; Citizen of the Day Awd, Sierra Madre City Coun; Phi Delta Kappa Spec Recog Awd; Ralph Story Awd for Outstg Ser to Ed; Pres-Emeritus, Pasadena City Col; Num Other Hons; W/W World; W/W Am; W/W CA; Men of Achmt; Contemp Personalities; 2,000 Notable Ams.

SARID, AKSEL oc/Research Institute Director; b/Jan 10, 1951; ba/1914 Wyndale #2, Houston, TX 77030; m/Roni Fern; c/Alyssa Rose, Lauren Michell; p/Salvator Lisi; Ines Rezzoable; ed/BA in Hlth, Med and Soc, City Col of NY, 1978; MS in Studies of the Future, Univ of Houston, 1983; MPH, Univ of TX Houston, 1984; mil/Vietnam Vet; pa/Aerospace Med Assn; APHA; World Future Soc; Nat Space Inst; r/Jewish; hon/W/W Fin and Indust.

SARKAR, NURUL H oc/Virologist in Cancer Research; b/Aug 5, 1937; h/1161 York Avenue, New York, NY 10021; ba/New York, NY; m/Rabeya; c/Atom, Tanya; p/Patan Uddin and Aleya Khatoon Sarkar, India; ed/BSc in Physics 1959, MSc in Biophysics 1960, PhD in Biophysics 1966, Univ of Calcutta; pa/Assoc Mem, Hd of Lab of Molecular Virology, Sloan-Kettering Cancer Ctr, 1973-; Assoc Prof of Biol, Sloan-Kettering Div, Grad Sch of Med Sci, Cornell Univ, 1981-; Hd, Div of Electron Microscopy 1972-73, Assoc Mem 1971-73, Assoc 1969-71, Instr for Med Res, NJ; Asst Prof of Res Pediatrics, Univ of PA Sch of Med, 1972-75; Breast Cancer Task Force Exptl Biol Com, NIH, 1976-79; Bd of Certification, Electron Microscopy Soc of Am, 1978-; r/Islam; hon/Author, About 100 Articles in Jours, Chapts in Several Books; Merit S'ship, 1953-57; Res Scholar, Biophysics Div, Saha Inst of Nuclear Physics, Calcutta, 1961-67; W/W E; W/W Technol Today; Men of Achmt.

SARKIS, VAHAK D oc/Professor of Chemistry; h/765 Bay Boulevard, Port Richey, FL 33568; ed/PhD in Chem, Walden Univ, 1982; MS in Chem, Adelphi Univ, 1961; BS in Chem, Am Univ, Cairo, 1957; pa/Prof of Chem, Pasco-Hernando Commun Col, 1985-; Prof of Chem, St Univ of NY, Fulton-Montgomery Commun Col, 1967-84; Vis'g Prof and Lectr in Chem, Erevan St Univ, Armenian USSR, 1973; Instr in Chem, In Charge of Chem Prog, Dowling Col, 1961-65; Instr in Chem, Massapequa HS, 1960-61; Instr in Chem (Pt-time), Long Bch HS, 1963; Tchg Fellow, Adelphi Univ, 1958-60; Consltg Chem, Fiber Glass Industs,

1980-81; Other Previous Positions; Am Inst of Chems, Fellow; Am Chem Soc; NY St 2-Yr Col Chem Tchrs Assn, Past Chm of No Sect; NEA, NY Edrs Assn; Fulmont Assn of Col Edrs, Past Pres; hon/Pubs, *The Chemistry of Cosmic Evolution-An Interdisciplinary Scientific Interpretation* 1984, "Photomicrography in Chemical Investigations" 1984, "Chemical (Optical) Microscopy Experiments for a General Chemistry Course" 1981, Others; Grant, Nat Foun for Improvement of Ed, Kodak and Nat Ed Assn, 1984; NSF Grant on Tchg Improvements in Col Chem, 1971-72; US Ofc Ed Grant to Publish Document on Mid E, 1970; Public Hlth Ser Grant in Cancer Res, 1959-60; Cottrel Foun Grant in Biopolymer Res, 1958-59.

SARNO, PATRICIA ANN oc/Science Department Chairman, Biology Teacher; h/49 South Balliet Street, Frackville, PA 17931; ba/Schuylkill Haven, PA; p/John T and Anna Sarno, Frackville, PA; ed/BS in Biol 1966, MEd in Biol Ed 1971, PA St Univ; Postgrad, Bucknell Univ 1968, Bloomsburg St Col 1970-71; pa/Programmer for Planetarium 1966, Tchr of Sci 1967, Pottsville Sch Dist; Tchr 1967-, Sci Dept Chm 1970-, Haven Sch Dist; Res Conslt on Ecol and Arachnology, PA St Univ, Schuylkill Campus, 1974-; PTO; NEA; PSEA; SHEA; AAAS; NABT; NSTA; PSTA; AIBS; PA Acad of Sci; Am Mus of Natural Hist, Fellow; Smithsonian Inst, Fellow; PA St Univ Alumni Soc; Phi Sigma; Delta Kappa Gamma; r/Cath; hon/Pubs, "A New Species of *Atypus*" 1973, "The Effect of Pesticides on House Spiders," Num Pubs Concerning Curric Devel, New Progs in Sci and Indep Study Progs; Contbr to *Bloodlines*, Jour on Dog Breeding; Election to Phi Sigma; Election to Delta Kappa Gamma; Dow Chem Co Grantee for "Effects of Pesticides on House Spiders"; Nom for PA Tchr of the Yr, 1976; W/W E; PA St Univ Alumni; Outstg Edrs of Am.

SARNOFF, LILI-CHARLOTTE oc/Sculptor; b/Jan 9, 1916; h/7507 Hampden Lane, Bethesda, MD 20814; ba/Same; m/Dr Stanley J; c/Daniela M Sarnoff Bargezi, Robert L; p/Baroness Robert von Hirsch (dec); Willy Dreyfus (dec); ed/Arbitur, Mommsen Gymnasium, Berlin; Grad, Reinmann Art Sch, Berlin; Att'd, Univ of Berlin, Univ of Florence; pa/Res Asst, Harvard Sch of Public Hlth, 1948-54; Res Assoc, Nat Heart Inst, 1954-59; Pres, Rodana Res Corp, 1959-61; VP, Catrix Corp, 1959-61; Trustee, Corcoran Gallery of Art; Dir, The Art Barn; cp/Wom's Com of the Wash Opera; Wom's Com of the Wash Performing Arts Soc; hon/Author, Many Sci Articles; Accademia Italia delle Arti e del Lavoro, "Medaglia d'Oro," 1980; W/W Am Wom; W/W Am Art; W/W E.

SATO, MAKIKO oc/Scientific Analyst; b/May 29, 1947; h/240 Anderson Avenue, Closter, NJ 07624; ba/New York, NY; m/Makoto; c/Tomokazu F; p/Masakazu Hayashi (dec); Yone Hayashi, Ashiya, Japan; ed/BS in Physics, Osaka Univ, 1970; MS in Physics 1972, PhD in Physics 1972, Yeshiva Univ; pa/Res Scist, Columbia Univ, 1978; Res Assoc, St Univ of NY Stony Brook, 1978-79; Sci Analyst, Sigma Data Sers Co, NASA Goddard Inst for Space Studies, 1980-; Am Astronom Soc and Its Div for

Planetary Scis, 1979-; Voyager Photopolarimeter Sci Team, 1980-; r/Buddhism; hon/Author, Articles in Sci Jours, incl'g, *Astrophysical Journal*, *Journal of Atmospheric Science*, *Science, Journal of Geophysical Research*; NASA Grp Achmt Awd, 1982.

SAUDER, WILLIAM C oc/College Professor; b/Jan 3, 1934; h/Route 1, Box 364, Lexington, VA 24450; ba/Lexington, VA; m/Nanalou West; c/Anne Elizabeth, William Henry Lee; p/Howard R and Lodema B Sauder (dec); ed/BS, VA Mil Inst, 1955; PhD, Johns Hopkins Univ, 1963; mil/USAF 1956-57, 2nd Lt, 1st Lt, Capt; pa/Instr, Asst Prof, Assoc Prof, Prof 1955-, Dept Chm 1979-84, Dept of Physics, VA Mil Inst; Conslt, Nat Bur of Standards, 1965-82; Am Phy Soc; Am Assn of Physics Tchrs; VA Acad of Sci; cp/Chm, Rockbridge Co Dem Com; r/Epis; hon/Author, Num Articles in Profl Jours; W/W S and SE; W/W Frontier Sci; Men of Sci.

SAUL, WILLIAM E oc/Dean of Engineering; b/May 15, 1934; h/Ponderosa Drive, Moscow, ID 83843; ba/Moscow, ID; m/Muriel; ed/BSCE 1955, MSCE 1961, MI Tech; PhD, NWn Univ, 1964; pa/Mech Engr, Shell Oil, 1955-59; Asst Prof, Civil Engrg, Univ of WI, 1964-67; Assoc Prof 1967-72, Prof 1972-84, Chm 1976-80, Civil Engrg, Univ of WI; Dean of Engrg, Univ of ID, 1984-; ASCE, Madison Br Pres 1978-80, WI Sect Pres 1983-84; Chm, Com on Res in Engrg Ed, 1982-; ACI; IABSE; ASEE; AAUP; hon/Author of Many Ednl Articles for Profl Jours; Hon Mem, Tau Beta Pi.

SAVAGE, FREDERICK RIDINGS oc/Insurance and Real Estate; b/Dec 31, 1944; h/521 Newport Avenue, Williamsburg, VA 23185; ba/Williamsburg, VA; m/Belinda Stublen; c/Thomas Littleton, Jennifer Peyton; p/Thomas Daley Savage (dec); ed/BS, Cornell Univ, 1967; mil/USN, NAS Oceana; pa/Innkeeper, Winegardner & Hammonds 1969-72, Holiday Inns Inc 1969-72; Pres, The Savage Agy, 1975-; Cornell Soc of Hotelmen; VALU;NALU; VAIIA; PIA; NAIIA; cp/Sertoma; Masons; Lee Soc of VA; r/Epis; hon/Personalities of S; W/W Fin and Indust; Biogl Roll of Hon.

SAVAGE, MICHAEL JOHN KIRKNESS oc/Executive; b/Oct 28, 1934; h/410 Greenwood Beach Road, Tiburon, CA 94920; ba/San Francisco, CA; m/Virginia; c/Matthew N; p/Leonard W H (dec) and Hilda C Fletcher Savage; ed/Att'd, Manchester Bus Sch 1965, Mid E Centre for Arab Studies 1966-67; MA in Ec and Law, Cambridge Univ, 1958; mil/2nd Lt, Royal Artillery, Brit Army, 1953-55; pa/Pres, BP AK Inc, SF, 1977; Pres, Sohio Petro Co, SF, 1978-82; Intl Dir, BP London, 1982; Pres, Merlin Petro Co, SF, 1983-; Bd of Trustees, AK Pacific Univ, 1982-; Bd of Trustees, SF Conservatory of Music, 1983-; hon/W/W W, W/W World of Oil and Gas.

SAVAGE, XYLA RUTH oc/Artist and Designer; b/Dec 17, 1937; h/12901 Chalfont Avenue, Fort Washington, MD 20744; ba/Washington, DC; m/John William Jr (dec); c/Mark Wayne, John Christian; p/Joel Frederick (dec) and Thelma Gladys Burgess Church, Norman, OK; ed/BA, Univ of OK, 1969; Att'd, USDA Grad Sch, 1971; pa/Interior Designer, Sears, Roebuck & Co, 1966-67; Hd, Tech Illustration Dept,

ITT, 1967-69; Supvr in Pubs Dept, NASA, 1969-71; Supvr of the Illustration Dept for the VA, 1971-72; Visual Info Spec Mgr, Forms Design and Visual Communs Dept, Bur of Labor Stats, 1972-; Instr for Forms Design, USDA Grad Sch, 1972-; Bus Forms Mgmt Assn; Printing Industs of Am; cp/Chm of Publicity for Band Parents, Ofcr in Parents Org for Sons' Schs; r/Christian Ch; hon/Awd for Contbns to the Revision of the Consumer Price Index, (Labor Dept Awd), 1978; Awd for Support of the Apollo XI Lunar Landing Mission from Goddard Space Flight Ctr, 1969; W/W E.

SAVITZ, FRIEDA JOYCE oc/Artist, Instructor; h/109 West Clankstown Road, New City, NY 10956; c/Nina Beth Laden, David Jan Laden; ed/BS, MA, Art, NY Univ; S'ship, Hans Hofmann Sch, 1954-55; Cooper Union, 1953-54; Hon Dipl, Universitai delle Arti, 1981; Hon Master of Painting, Accademia Italia, 1983; pa/Solo Exhbns: St Capital (Albany) 1983, AZ St Univ Tempe 1978, So VT Art Assn 1978, Hansen Galleries 1975-76, Others; Grp Exhbns: Salon of the Nations 1983, 4th Perm Exhbn of Palazzo delle Manifestazioni-Accademia Italia 1983-84, Intl Expo (Yugoslavia) 1983, 9th Intl Indeps of Prints (Yokohama, Japan) 1983, Guild Hall (E Hampton, NY) 1983, Smithsonian Nat Air and Space Mus 1984, Rutgers Nat Wks on Paper 1981-82, Others; hon/Author, Var Poems, Fables and Articles; World Culture Prize Statue of Victory, Centro Studiue Ricerche delle Nazioni, 1984; Intl Parliament for Safety and Peace Appt, Gold Medal for Artistic Merit, 1983; Num Other Hons; Intl W/W Intells; Commun Ldrs of Am; Book of Hon; 2,000 Notable Ams; Dist'd Ams.

SCARBOROUGH, KENNETH M oc/Executive; b/Apr 18, 1941; h/4144 Prescott, Dallas, TX 75219; ba/Dallas, TX; m/Lynn Wilford-Scarborough; c/Valerie, Christopher, Adam; p/M H Scarborough; Knovis Elizabeth Arnold; ed/BS in Polit Sci 1971, Postgrad and Grad Degs 1980, Inst for Org Mgmt, So Meth Univ; mil/Army Intell, 1962-65; pa/Chm and CEO, Scarborough Boot Co, 1979-; Assoc, The Jim Walsh Co, 1980-; Reg Public Affairs Mgr, US C of C, 1974-82; Legis Aide, Congressman Dale Milford, 1971-73; Dist Aide, Congressman Graham Purcell, 1968-71; C of C Execs Assns, TX, NM, AR, LA, MO, OK; E TX Execs and Secys Assn; N Dallas C of C Govtl Affairs Com; Bd of Advrs, Inst for Public Policy Res; cp/Bd of Advrs, Yale Lit Mag, New Am Patriots, Epis Foun for Drama; TX Prison F'ship; Dallas Friday Grp, 1979-; Dallas Study Grp, 1979-80; Boy Scouts Com of 30; Nom, Sons of the Republic of TX, 1981; r/Epis; hon/Pubs, "Buttons, Stickers and Campaigns I Have Been Attacked By" 1978, "Stress on the Campaign Trail" 1980; Outstg Ser Awd, TX C of C Execs Assn, 1982; W/W Cols and Univs; W/W S; Personalities of S; W/W Bus and Fin.

SCARITO, ELIZABETH A BAGNALL oc/Senior Process Engineer; b/Dec 4, 1952; h/Severna Park, MD; ba/1701 East Patapsco Avenue, Baltimore, MD 21226; m/Philip Raymond Jr; p/James J and Alice (Lidwin) Bagnall; ed/SBChE 1975, SMChe 1975, MA Inst of

Technol; pa/Sr Process Engr, FMC Corp, 1984-; Res Engr, FMC Corp, 1977-84; Devel Engr, CIBA-Geigy Corp, 1975-77; Mem: AIChE, 1975-; NJ Sect Treas, 1978-84, Soc of Wom Engrs; Pres 1982-83, VP Progs 1981-82, Secy 1979-81, MA Inst of Technol Clb of Princeton; Sigma Xi, 1975; Ednl Coun, MA Inst of Technol, 1981-; r/Rom Cath; hon/Pres's Awd, MA Inst of Technol Clb of Princeton, 1983; Patentee in Field, 1981, 1985; W/W Am Wom.

SCATTERGOOD, THOMAS W oc/Planetologist; b/Oct 3, 1946; h/505 Cypress Point Drive, Mountain View, CA 94043; ba/Moffett Field, CA; p/William and Grace Scattergood, Columbus, NJ; ed/BS in Chem, Univ of DE, 1968; MS 1972, PhD 1975, Chem, St Univ of NY Stony Brook; pa/Res Asst, St Univ of NY Stony Brook, 1972-76; NRC-NAS Res Assoc, NASA Ames Res Ctr, 1977-78; Res Assoc 1979-84, Adj Asst Prof 1984-, St Univ of NY Stony Brook; AAAS; AAS, Div of Planetary Scis; Am Geophy Union; Planetary Soc; Photographic Soc of Am; cp/Cypress Pt Lakes Homeowners' Assn, Pres 1983; Ctl Coast Cos Camera Clb Coun, Pres 1982; Cameraderie Camera Clb; r/Quaker; hon/Authored and Co-Authored 10 Articles in Profl Jours; W/W Frontiers of Sci; W/W World.

SCHACHTER, MICHAEL BEN oc/Medical Doctor; b/Jan 15, 1941; h/303 Phillips Hill Road, New City, NY 10956; ba/Nyack, NY; m/Marlene; c/Brian, Amy, Stefan; p/Saul Schachter, New York, NY; Ann Palestine Schachter (dec); ed/BA, Columbia Col, 1961; MD, Columbia Col of Phys and Surgs, 1965; Mixed Med/Surg/Pediatrics Internship, Hosp for Jt Diseases and Med Ctr, 1965-66; 3-Yr Residency in Psychi, Downst Med Ctr, Completed 1969; mil/Maj, MC, USAF, 1969-71; pa/Dir of Emer and Admissions, Rockland Co Mtl Hlth Ctr, 1971-72; Dir of Rockland Co Mtl Hlth Clin, 1972-74; Assoc Att'g in Psychi, Good Samaritan Hosp; MD and Psychi, Mountainview Med Assocs, Pvt Pract Specializing in Preven Med and Nutritional Treatment, 1974-; Am Acad of Med Preventics, Fellow; Acad of Orthomolecular Psychi, Fellow; Soc for Clin Ecol; Intl Acad of Preven Med; Intl Col of Applied Nutrition; Am Col of Nutrition; Am Holistic Med Assn; NY St Med Soc; Rockland Co Med Soc; AMA; Am Psychi Assn; Orthomolecular Med Soc; hon/Pubs, *The Food Connection* 1979, *Food, Mind and Mood* 1980; Appreciation Awd, Nat Hlth Fdn, 1979; Carolo Lamar Pioneer Mem Awd, AAMP, 1980; Awd of Merit, Am Acad of Craniomandibular Disorders, 1981; W/W E; Dir of Med Specs; Men of Achmt; Contemp Authors; Dir of Dist'd Ams; DIB.

SCHADE, CHARLANNE MURRAY oc/Reading Consultant; b/Mar 17, 1941; h/24 Beech Road, New Rochelle, NY 10804; ba/Larchmont, NY; m/Malcolm Robert; p/Charles and Anne Murray (dec); ed/BA 1963, MEd 1967, CPGS 1969, Univ of MA; pa/4th Grade Tchr 1963-67, 5th Grad Tchr 1967-68, Rdg Tchr 1968-69, Suffield, CT; Rdg Coor, Windham SE Supervisory Union, 1969-71; Prof of Ed, Windham Col, 1970-71; Conslt, Antioch Putney, VT, 1970-71; Conslt, Marlboro, VT, 1970-71; Rdg Conslt 1971-, Curric Coor

1973-81, Manaroneck, NY; Study Grp, Bd of Ed, Manaroneck, NY, 1979-80; IRA; Assn Supvn and Curric Devel; New England Rdg Assn; NY St Rdg Assn; Westchester Rdg Assn; AFT; Delta Kappa Gamma, Pres of Phi Chapt 1982-84; r/Epis; hon/W/W E.

SCHAEFFER, JEAN MAPLE-THORPE oc/Editor; b/Mar 15, 1915; h/ 3945 Oak Point Road, Lorain, OH 44053; m/Roy Edwin; c/John William, Tane Narda; ed/Valedictorian, Pontiac HS, 1933; 2-Yr Dipl, Ward-Belmont Col, 1935; pa/Fashion Coor of Crowley-Milner Co, Detroit, MI, 1939-44; r/Congregational; hon/ Author, 2 Articles, Book Reviews; Editor, International Platform Association Theatre Newsletter, *Talent.*

SCHAEFFER, LORRAINE DEY oc/ Assistant State Librarian; b/Dec 14, 1946; h/1892 Nekoma Court, Tallahassee, FL 32304; ba/Tallahassee, FL; p/ Joseph W and Hilda Ritchey Dey, Keystone Heights, FL; ed/BA 1968, MS in Lib Sci 1969, Grad Cert in Public Adm 1981, FL St Univ; pa/Ext Libn, Santa Fe Reg Lib, 1969-71; Public Lib Conslt 1971-78, Asst St Libn 1978-, St Lib of FL; Am Lib Assn, Coun 1982-86; Assn of Specialized and Cooperative Lib Agys, Bd of Dirs 1980-82; SEn Lib Assn, Bd of Dirs 1976-80; FL Lib Assn, Secy 1978-79; r/Meth; hon/Contbr to Pubs; Beta Phi Mu, 1969; W/W Am Wom; W/ W Lib and Info Sers.

SCHAFFNER, IRVING oc/Medical Doctor, Researcher, Acupuncturist; b/ Sep 10, 1930; h/1231 La Granada, Thousand Oaks, CA 91361; ba/Thousand Oaks, CA; m/Charlotte Elaine; c/ Daniel Lee, John David, Rivka Ann; p/ Sam and Mary Schaffner, Houston, TX; ed/BS, 1951; Att'd, Univ of IL, Roosevelt Univ, Univ of IL Col of Pharm; MD, Chgo Med Sch, 1956; Interned, VA Ctr, LA; Residency, Stanislaus Co Hosp; Postgrad Wk, Fed Aviation Adm; pa/Pvt Pract of Med, 1958-; Sci Editor, Thousand Oaks Broadcasting Co, 1965-70; Owner, Radio KNJO, 1964-70; Fdr, Conejo Val Commun Hosp, 1964; Med Dir, Grumman Aerospace; Med Dir, Bunker Ramo; Med Advr, Rockwell Intl; Assoc Prof, Drew Postgrad Med Sch; Ventura Co Med Soc; CA Med Assn; Indust Med Assn; Sr Fed Aviation Med Examr; Civil Aviation Med Assn; hon/ Kiwanis Clb of Thousand Oaks Layman's Awd; Outstg Ser Awd, SemTech Corp; Assoc, Chgo Med Sch; Humanitarian Awd, Optimist Clb; W/W W.

SCHAMBER, ANITA LOUISE oc/ High School Counselor; b/Jul 18, 1942; h/Route 3, 3 Pine Lane, Sheridan, WY 82801; ba/Sheridan, WY; m/Karel Ray; c/Mrs Dana Lynn Barton, Jill Suzanne Arney, Michele Louise Arney, Ryan Christopher Arney; p/Henry E Rohn, Highland, CA; Margaret M Lauffer, Great Falls, MT; ed/BA in Sociol and Polit Sci, Augustana Col, 1965; MEd in Ednl Psych (Cnslg), Univ of IL, 1967; pa/6th Grade Tchr, Myna Thompson Sch, 1965-66; Cnslr, Jefferson Jr High, 1967-68; Instr, Sheridan Col, 1971; Cnslr, Sheridan HS, 1979-; Am Sch Cnslrs Assn, 1979-; WY Sch Cnslrs, Pres 1981-82, 1983-84; Am Assn of Cnslg and Devel, 1979-; WY Pers and Guid Assn, Secy 1981-82; Nat Assn for Wom Deans, Admrs and Cnslrs; Career Planning and Adult Devel Netwk, WY

Rep; NEA; WY Ed Assn; Sheridan Co Ed Assn; AAUW; WY Writers; Range Writers; Chapt T, PEO, Past Pres; KKR Alumni, Past Pres; Univ of WY Alumni Assn, Life Mem; cp/WY Coun for Chd and Yth, Title XX Task Force; Career Fair; Friends of Lib, Life Mem; Civic Theatre Guild, Bd of Dirs 1968-71; r/ Presb; hon/Monthly Feature Articles in *Country Journal*, 1979-; Pubs, in *Wyoming Personnel and Guidance Journal* 1981, *Owen Wister Review* 1983; Kappa Delta Pi, Ed Hon, 1967; 1st Place, Non-Fiction, WY Writers Contest, 1982; Career Wom of the Yr Runner-Up, 1982; Outstg Yg Wom in Am; W/W W.

SCHARY, SUSAN oc/Artist; b/Aug 7, 1936; h/228 Saint Albans Avenue, South Pasadena, CA 91030; ba/Same; ed/BFA w Hons, Tyler Sch of Fine Arts, Temple Univ, 1960; pa/Tchr, Art, Harcum Jr Col, 1961-63; Held Painting, Drawing and Chd's Classes, Samuel S Fleischer Art Meml, 1967-68; Wks on Display: Louis Newman Galleries 1977-82, Ten CA Artists Salut the LA Bicent at CA Mus of Sci and Indust 1981, CA Mus of Sci and Indust 1976, Civic Ctr Mus 1968, 1971, 1974, Many Others; Exhbns in Phila: Samuel S Fleischer Art Meml Fac Exhbn 1968, Grabar Art Gallery 1967, Phila Artists Self-Portraits 1967, 100 Dist'd Phila Artists from 1840 to Present 1967, Univ City Arts Leag 1967, Phila Wom in Fine Arts Annual Exhbns at Moore Inst of Art 1962-66; Var Comms and Sculptures; IPA; Artist's Equity Assn; hon/ Dean's Prize in Student Exhbn, Tyler Sch of Fine Arts, 1958; B W Gottlieb Meml Prize, Samuel S Fleischer Art Meml Fac Exhbn, 1968; First Gimbel Awd for Art, Henry H Houston Elem Sch; Second Gimbel Awd and Gold Medal for Art, Phila HS for Girls; World W/W Wom; W/W Am Art; W/W Am Wom; Others.

SCHAUFELE, WILLIAM EVERETT JR oc/Association President; b/Dec 7, 1923; h/41 East 19th Street, New York, NY 10000; ba/New York, NY; m/ Heather Moon; c/Steven, Peter; p/Mr and Mrs William E Schaufele (dec); ed/ BA, Yale, 1948; MIA, Columbia Sch of Intl Affairs, 1950; mil/AUS, 1943-46; pa/Resident Ofcr, Pfaffenhofen/Ilm, Augsburg, Germany, 1950-52; Vice Consul, Duessldorf 1952-53, Munich 1953-55, Dept of St 1955-59; Consul, Casablanca, Morocco 1959-65, Bukavu, Zaire 1963-64; Zaire Desk Ofcr, Dept of St, 1964-65; Dpty Ofcr, Dir, Afl African Affairs, 1965-67; Ofc Dir, W Ctl African Affairs, 1967-69; Ambassador, Upper Volta, 1969-71; Dpty US Rep to UN Security Coun, 1971-75; Inspector Gen of Fgn Ser, 1975; Asst Secy of St for Africa, 1975-77; Ambassador to Poland, 1978-80; Current Pres, Fgn Policy Assn; Adv Coun, Columbia Univ Sch of Intl and Public Affairs; Dir, Helsinki Watch, Global Perspectives in Ed, Fgn Policy Assn; r/Prot; hon/Pubs, *Polish Paradox* 1980, Occasional Articles for *Christian Science Monitor*; Wilbur Carr Awd, Dept of St, 1980; Dist'd Alumni Awd, Columbia Sch of Intl Affairs; W/ W Am.

SCHEMMEL, RACHEL ANNE oc/ Professor; b/Nov 23, 1929; h/1341 Red Leaf Lane, East Lansing, MI 48823; ba/ East Lansing, MI; ed/BS, Clarke Col, 1951; MS, Univ of Iowa Iowa City; PhD,

MI St Univ; pa/Chd's Hosp, LA; From Instr to Full Prof of Human Nutrition, MI St Univ; Am Inst of Nutrition, 1972-; Brit Nutrition Soc; Am Dietetic Assn; Past Pres and Del, MI Dietetic Assn; Inst of Food Technologists; NY Acad of Scis; Soc of Exptl Biol and Med Edit Bd; AAAS; hon/Author, Over 100 Pubs in Refereed Jours, Chapts in Books; Editor, *Nutrition, Physiology and Obesity*; Sigma Xi, Current Pres of MI St Univ Chapt; Omicron Nu, 1952, Nat Treas; Dist'd Alumni Awd, Mt Mercy Col, 1971; W/ W; Am Men of Sci; W/W MW.

SCHIAVI, ROSEMARY FILOMENA oc/Educator; b/Feb 20, 1947; h/237 Stafford Avenue, Syracuse, NY 13206; ba/Syracuse, NY; p/Stefano and Rose Falso Schiavi, Syracuse, NY; ed/AA, Maria Regina Col, 1967; BA, Brescia Col, 1969; MS, Syracuse Univ, 1973; Doct Cand, Tchr Ed and Curric Devel, Syracuse Univ, 1983-; pa/Syracuse City Sch Dist: Edr 1969-83, Sci Ed Wkshop Facilitator for Admrs and Tchrs 1982, Lang Arts Com Mem and Curric Developer 1981-82, Gen Elem Ed Curric Eval Team Mem 1980-81, Orgr and Instr for Gifted and Talented Prog 1978-80, Acting Elem Sch Prin of Meachem Sch 1979, Social Studies Curric Com Mem and Curric Developer 1978-80, ESAA Team Mem and Commun Tchr Rep 1977-79, Rdg Com Mem and Curric Developer 1974-77, Sch Ecol Prog Dir at Meachem Sch 1974-83, Red Cross Instr at Meachem Sch 1974, Girls Softball Coach 1973-74, Participant in NSF's Wkshop in Regards to the Improvement of Sci Ed 1974, Developer for Profl In-Ser Ed Prog for Edrs 1982-83, 1977-78, 1974-75, 1969-71; Assn for Supvn and Curric Devel; Am Fdn of Tchrs; NY U Tchrs Assn; Syracuse Tchrs Assn, Bldg Rep 1972, 1975, 1976, 1977, 1980; Brescia Col Alumni Assn; Syracuse Univ Alumni Assn; Assoc'd Photogs Intl; hon/Syracuse Fdn of Wom's Clbs Awd, for Original Ed Prodn, 1975; W/W E.

SCHIAVONE, LUCREZIA CANTERINO oc/Educational Psychologist; b/ Jun 6, 1949; h/175 McLean Avenue, Yonkers, NY 10705; ba/Yonkers, NY; p/Antonio Emanuel and Matilde Canerino, Yonkers, NY; ed/BA, Ladycliff Col, 1971; MST 1973, PD 1979, Fordham Univ; pa/Tchr, NYC, 1972-73; Spec Edr to Emotionally Handicapped, Yonkers, NY, Sch Sys, 1973-; Tchr's Conf Day Wkshop Facilitator, 1976-79; Yonkers Fdn of Tchrs Bldg Del, 1974-77; Am Fdn of Tchrs Conv Del, 1976; Yonkers Fdn of Tchrs Newsletter Staff, 1975-76; PTA Rep, 1976-78; NY St Assn of Tchrs of the Handicapped, 1978-; r/Cath; hon/ John La Farge Gold Medal, 1964; Sociedad Honoraria Hispanica, 1966; Alpha Mu Gamma, 1970; Phi Delta Kappa, 1975; Kappa Delta Pi, 1976; Alpha Delta Kappa, 1977; DIB; Notable Ams; Commun Ldrs and Noteworthy Ams; W/W Child Devel Profls; Intl W/ W Commun Ser; Book of Hon; Intl W/ W Intells; World W/W Wom; Men and Wom of Distn.

SCHILD, RUDOLPH ERNEST oc/ Astronomer; b/Jan 10, 1940; h/99 Hesperus Avenue, Magnolia, MA 01930; ba/Cambridge, MA; m/Jane Struss; p/Kasimir and Anneliese Schild (dec); ed/BS 1962, MS 1963, PhD 1966, Univ of Chgo; pa/Postdoct Fellow, CA

Inst of Technol, 1967-69; Astronomer, Harvard-Smithsonian Ctr for Astrophysics, 1969-; Lectr, Harvard Univ, 1975-83; Am Astronom Soc, 1968-; Intl Astronom Union, 1971-; Harlow Shapley Vis'g Lectr, Am Astronom Soc, 1981-; r/Luth; hon/Author, 80 Sci Pubs to Profl Jours; Smithsonian Scholar, 1982-84; NASA Grantee, 1982-84; Smithsonian Res Foun Awd, 1976-77; W/W Sci and Technol.

SCHINKE, CECIL S oc/Consulting Engineer; b/Apr 26, 1947; h/3357 Chetwood Place, Dublin, OH 43017; ba/Dublin, OH; m/Terri L; c/Cecil W, Lynn M; p/R Siepierski, Livonia, MI; ed/ASME 1977, ASBA 1979, BSBA 1983, Franklin Univ; mil/Army, 1966-68; pa/Assoc Engr 1971-79, Proj Engr, Dir of Quality Assurance and Reliability and Mgr of Prod Liability 1979-83, IRD Mechanalysis; Self-Employed, 1983-; ASTM, Subcom Chm, Profl Mem, Nat Safety Coun; ASME; ASLE; Exptl Aircraft Assn; r/Epis; hon/Pub, "Evaluating Hydraulic Fluid" in *Machine Design*, 1983; W/W MW; W/W.

SCHLOSS, BRIGITTE oc/Coordinator of Native and Northern Education Teacher Education Program, Assistant Professor; b/Oct 3, 1927; h/337 Maplewood Place, Saint John's, Newfoundland A1E 4L8; ba/Saint John's, Newfoundland; p/Rev Erwin and Emy Ruppert Schloss (dec); ed/Tchr's Cert, Fribourg, Switzerland; BA in Ed, Meml Univ of Newfoundland, 1965; MA, Laval, 1969; PhD, Univ of Toronto, 1980; pa/Tchr, Finishing Sch, Switzerland, 2 Yrs; Tchr, All Grades, No Labrador Moravian Ch-Integrated Sch Bd, 20 Yrs; Asst Prof, Univ of Wn Ontario, 3 Yrs; Coor of Native and No Ed Tchr Ed Prog, Labrador; Asst Prof, Meml Univ, 1981-; cp/YWCA; r/Moravian; hon/Pubs, *Deux linguistiques* 1977, *The Uneasy Status of Literature in Second Language Teaching at the School Level: An Historical Perspective* 1981, Others, Book Reviews, Informal Articles, Articles on Native Tchr Ed Prog; Grad F'ships, Ontario Inst for Studies in Ed, 1971-74.

SCHMALTZ, ROY EDGAR JR oc/Professor of Art; b/Feb 23, 1937; h/1020 Whistler Drive, Suisun City, CA 94585; ba/Moraga, CA; m/Julia M; c/Liese Marlene, Jennifer Lynn, Gregory Jason; p/Roy and Mercedes Schmaltz, Seattle, WA; ed/BFA, summa cum laude 1963, MFA 1965, SF Art Inst; Att'd, Frye Mus Sch 1956-58, Otis Art Inst 1959-60, Univ of WA Seattle 1956-57, 1960-61, Akademie Der Bildenden Kunste 1965-66; pa/Lectr in Art, Col of Notre Dame, 1968-70; Lectr in Art, M H de Young Meml Art Mus, SF, 1969-70; Vis'g Artist-Grad Sems 1976-77, Vis'g Prof 1974, Lone Mtn Col, SF; Prof of Art, St Mary's Col of CA, 1969-; Exhbns: Crocker Art Mus 1982, TX St Univ 1980, AK St Mus 1981, Univ of HI Hilo 1983, Haggin Art Mus 1982, Huntsville Mus of Art 1982, Butler Inst of Am Art 1981, Springfield Art Mus 1980, Rutgers Univ 1979, Num Others; Perm Public Art Collections: Univ of HI Hilo, Mills Col, SF Art Inst, M H de Young Meml Art Mus, Hoyt Mus of Fine Arts, Contra Costa Co Art Collection, Frye Art Mus, Amerika-Haus; AAUP; SF Art Inst Alumni Assn; Dir, St Mary's Col Art Gallery, 1970-75;

Grad Prog Bd, Lone Mtn Col, SF, 1971-77; r/Cath; hon/Selected for Bay Area Artists Calendar, KQED TV, 1984; Purchase Awd, Walnut Creek Civic Art Ctr, 1982; Nat Awd, Chautauqua Inst, 1980; Vis'g Artist Lectures, Grad Prog, Lone Mtn Col, 1974; Fulbright F'ship, 1965; Seattle Art Assn Grant, 1957; Frye Mus Traveling F'ship, USA, 1957; W/W Am Art; W/W W.

SCHMERLING, ERWIN R oc/Assistant Director of Space Science; b/Jul 28, 1929; h/9917 La Duke Drive, Kensington, MD 20895; ba/Greenbelt, MD; m/Esther M; c/Susan D, Elaine M; ed/PhD in Radio Physics 1958, MA 1954, BA in Physics 1950, Cambridge Univ, England; pa/Asst Dir, Space Sci, NASA Goddard Space Flight Ctr, 1984-; Vis'g Scholar, Stanford Univ, 1983; Prog Chief, Space Plasma Physics, NASA HQs, 1964-82; Assoc Prof, Elect Engrg, PA St Univ, 1963-64; Fellow, IEEE; Chm, US Comm III, Intl Union of Radio Sci, 1969-72; Chm, Com on Space Res, COSPAR; Subcom C1, Earth's Upper Atmosphere and Ionosphere, 1982-; Electromagnetic Wave Panel Adv Grp on Aerospace Res and Devel; r/Jewish; hon/NASA Exceptl Ser Medal, 1979; NASA Sustained Superior Perf Awd, 1980; W/W Govt; W/W Engrg; Am Men and Wom of Sci.

SCHMIDT, CARL FREDERIC oc/Professor of Pharmacology Emeritus; b/Jul 29, 1893; h/1707 Great Springs Road, Bryn Mawr, PA 19010; ba/Philadelphia, PA; m/Elizabeth Viola Gruber (dec); c/Carl F Jr, Barbara Schmidt De Long; ed/AB, Lebanon Val Col, 1914; MD, Univ of PA, 1918; Hon DSc, Lebanon Val Col, 1955; Hon DSc, Univ of PA, 1965; Hon DSM, Charles Univ, Prague, 1965; mil/First Lt, Med Resv Corps, 1917-25; pa/Intern, Univ Hosp, Phila, 1918-1919; Instr in Pharm, Univ of PA, 1919-1922; Assoc in Pharm, Peking Med Col, 1922-24; Asst Prof of Pharm 1924-29, Assoc Prof 1929-31, Prof 1931-59, Prof-Emeritus 1959-, Univ of PA; Clin Prof of Pharm, Univ of S FL Col of Med, 1970-; Unitarian Med Mission to Germany, 1948; Physiol Study Sect, USPHS; Chm, Intl F'ships Com, 1964-65; USPHS, 1963-64; Drug Res Bd, Nat Acad of Sci, 1963-69; Nat Res Coun, 1947-50; Secy, Subcom on Oxygen and Anoxia, 1941-45; Chm, Subpanel on Med Aspects of Chem Warfare, 1948-50; Adv Panel on Physiol, Ofc on Naval Res, 1947-52; Intl Union of Physiol Sci, VP of Sect on Pharm 1959-65, Pres 1965-66; Conslt to Surg Chm, Life Ins Med Res Fund, 1954-55; Gen, AUS, and VA Vis'g Prof, Univ of Philippones, 1955; Res Dir, US Naval Air Devel Ctr, 1962-69; Chm, Pharm Study Sect, USPHS, 1947-51; Chm, Panel on Physiol Res and Devel Bd, 1948-50; r/Prot; hon/Author, Articles on Respiration, Cerebral and Coronary Circulation, Action of Chinese Drugs (incl'g Ephedrine), Kidney Function, and Aerospace Pharm in Profl Jours; Contbr, Bard's Textbook; Most Dist'd Alumnus, Univ of PA Med Sch, 1984.

SCHMITT, CARVETH JOSEPH RODNEY oc/Internal Auditor; b/Sep 10, 1934; h/538 North Pampas Avenue, Rialto, CA 92376; ba/San Bernardino, CA; m/Carolyn Sue; p/Clarence Charles Schmitt, San Bernardino, CA; Thelma

June White Schmitt (dec); ed/Dipl, Bus Adm/Acctg, Skadron Col of Bus, 1959; AA, San Bernardino Val Col, 1962; BS, Bus Adm, Univ of Riverside, 1970; MA, Univ of Redlands, 1975; Cert in Human Ser, Univ of CA Ext (Riverside), 1977; Postgrad Wk, Univ of CA Ext (Riverside), 1976-80; BS, Liberal Studies, Univ of St of NY Albany, 1977; BA, Social Sci, Thomas A Edison St Col, 1978; mil/USAF, 1954-58; pa/Acct, Barnum & Flagg Co, 1959-70; Stationers Corp: Credit Mgr 1970-77, Ofc Mgr/Credit Mgr 1977-83; Internal Auditor, Stockwell & Binney Ofc Prods Ctrs, 1983-; Pt-time Reg'd Rep, Inland Am Securities Inc, 1966-70; Pt-time Life & Disability Agt, Inland Am Life Agy Inc, 1966-70; Pt-time Reg'd Rep, Parker-Jackson & Co, 1970-73; Pt-time Reg'd Rep, LeBarron Securities Inc, 1974; Reg'd Rep, Ernest F Boruski, NY, 1956-61; cp/Anthenaeum, Univ of Redlands; Univ of Redlands Fellows; Fontana Tour Clb; M&M Tour Clb; Rosicrucian Order, AMORC; Val Prospectors; Am Philatelic Soc; Arrowhead Stamp Clb; CO Mining Assn; NW Mining Assn; NV Mining Assn; Gold Prospectors Assn of Am, Charter Mem; Nat Travel Clb; Nat Geographic Soc; Myrtle Bch Lodge 353 AFM; Nat Rifle Assn, Life Mem; Rex Alumni Assn; Thomas A Edison St Col Alumni Assn; Friends of the Lib Assn, Univ of Redlands; Univ of Redlands Alumni Assn; Repub; hon/CA Tchg Credential (Adult Ed, Bus Ed, Psych, Social Studies), 1981-86; CA Commun Col Instr Credential, Valid for Life; CA Commun Col Student Pers Wkr Credential, Valid for Life; Airman of the Month, AC&W Squadron, Myrtle Bch AFB, 1977; Good Conduct Medal, USAF, 1957; Nat Def Ser Medal, USAF, 1954; W/W W; W/W CA; DIB; Men of Achmt; Intl W/W Intells; Commun Ldrs of Am; 2,000 Notable Ams; Intl Book of Hon; Personalities of W and MW; 5,000 Personalities of the World; Commun Ldrs of the World; Dir of Dist'd Ams.

SCHNEIDER, GERALD E oc/Professor of Mechanical Engineering; b/Aug 21, 1949; h/81 Culpepper Drive, Waterloo, Ontario, Canada N2L 5K8; ba/Waterloo, Ontario, Canada; m/Joan Diane; c/Jeremy Glen, Joshua James; p/Nelda Schneider, Waterloo, Ontario, Canada; ed/BASc 1973, MASc 1974, PhD 1977, Univ of Waterloo; pa/Res Engr 1973-77, Asst Prof of Mec Engrg 1977-1981, Assoc Prof of Mech Engrg 1981-, Univ of Waterloo; Full Time On-Site Conslt, Aerojet Electro Sys, 1980; AIAA; ASME; AIAA Thermophysics Com, 1976-79, 1982-85; AIAA Pubs Com, 1980-; r/Luth; hon/Author, 43 Pubs in Sci Jours and at Confs, 3 Invited Chapts, 14 Sci Reports; WCI Fac Awd, 1968; Univ of Waterloo Fac Bursary, 1973; NRC S'ship, 1974; W/W Frontier Sci and Technol.

SCHNEIDER, HAROLD oc/Applied Mathematics and Engineering; b/Apr 8, 1930; h/855 Clara Drive, Palo Alto, CA 94303; ba/Sunnyvale, CA; m/Joan Shirley; c/Dr Lynn Dee, Steven Kalman; p/Kalman and Ethyl Schneider (dec); ed/PhD in Physics 1956, MS in Applied Sci 1954, BS in Physics 1951, Univ of Cinc; pa/Staff Engr, Lockheed Missiles & Space Co, 1978-; Prin Engrg Mem, RCA Corp, Missile & Radar Sys Design, 1978;

Sr Sys Analyst, Dynamics Res Corp, 1972-78; Staff, MIT Lincoln Lab, 1962-72; Aeronautical Res Scist, NASA Lewis Res Ctr, 1951-62; Soc of Sigma Xi, MIT Chapt, 1971-; Am Nuclear Soc, 1960; Soc of Indust and Applied Math; AIAA, 1967-; IEEE, 1983; NY Acad of Scis, 1979-80; AAAS, 1981-82; r/Jewish; hon/Author, 35 Formal Tech Pubs in Optimal Estimation, Optimal Control and Guidance, Re-entry Dynamics and Aerodynamic Force Modeling in 6 and 3 Degs of Freedom, Simulation and Error Analyses, Ballistic Missile Def, Neutron Transport Theory,"Parameter and State Estimation of Nonlinear Systems" 1981; Am Men of Sci; W/W Technol Today; W/W W.

SCHNEIDER, STEPHEN H oc/ Atmospheric Scientist, Author; b/Feb 11, 1945; ba/NCAR, PO Box 3000, Boulder, CO 80307; m/Cheryl K; c/ Rebecca E, Adam W; p/Samuel and Doris Schneider, New York, NY; ed/BS 1966, MS 1967, PhD 1971, Columbia Univ; pa/Postdoct Res Assoc, GISS, 1971-72; Postdoct Fellow 1972-73, Scist 1973-80, Sr Scist 1980-, Hd of Visitors Prog and Dpty Dir of Adv'd Study Prog 1980-, NCAR; Am Meteorological Soc; Am Geophy Union; AAAS; Fdn of Am Scists; Sigma Xi; Fellow, Scists' Inst for Public Info; hon/Pubs, *The Genesis Strategy* 1976, *The Primordial Bond* 1981, *The Coevolution of Climate and Life* 1984, 3 Edited Volumes and 100 Articles; W/W World; W/W Am; W/W W; W/W Technol Today.

SCHNEIDER-HALVORSON,BRIG-ITTE LINA oc/Professor of German; b/ Mar 4, 1935; h/3925 Rogers Road, Spring Valley, CA 92077; ba/San Diego, CA; ed/BA in German, Spanish and Eng 1967, MA in German 1969, San Diego St Univ; PhD in German, Univ of CA Riverside, 1978; pa/Legal and Exec Secy w Spec Assignments in Advtg, Public Relats, Translations, Mgr of Fgn Advtg, Düsseldorf, Germany; Assoc Prof of German, Univ of San Diego, 1971-; Pt-time Tchg Experience at Col Level, 1967-81; Tchg Asst in German, San Diego St Univ, 1969-81; Instr in German, San Diego Evening Col; Staff Editor, *Modern Austrian Literature Journal*, 1981-; Assn of Am Tchrs of German; AAUP; CA Tchrs Assn; Intl Arthur Schnitzler Res Assn; Intl Assn for Germanic Studies, Basel, Switzerland; r/Luth; hon/Pub, *The Late Dramatic Works of Arthur Schnitzler*, 1983; Grad w Hons and Spec Distn, San Diego St Univ, 1967; World W/W Wom; W/W Among San Diego; Dir of Am Scholars.

SCHOONER, EDWARD FRANCIS oc/Director of Transportation;b/Jun 18, 1924; h/Post Office Box 212, Chalfont, PA 18914; ba/Blue Bell, PA; m/Muriel V (Allen); c/Carol Jeanne Zieske, Edward Francis Jr; p/Edward D and Anna S, New York City, NY; sp/George and Gertrude Allen, New York City, NY; ed/Att'd Power Meml Acad, 1942; Acad Advance Traffic, 1953;Univ of WI, 1960; mil/AUS, 1942-45; pa/Passenger Rep, NY Ctl RR, 1946-50; Passenger Rep, Remington Rand Inc, 1950-52; Claims Supvr, 1952-55; Rate Auditor, 1955-56; Routing Mgr, 1956-58; Factory Traffic Mgr, Univac Div, Sperry Rand Corp, Ilion, NY, 1958-60; Gen Traffic Mgr, Utica, NY, 1960-65; Dir Trans, New York City (NY) 1965-68,

Blue Bell (PA) 1968-; Shippers Adv Bd, Am Airlines; ICC Parctioners; Past Chapt Pres, Nat Def Trans Assn; Past Pres, Univac Mgmt Assn; Nat Indust Traffic Leag; cp/Sustaining Mem, Republ Nat Fin Com; Past Chapt Pres, Delta Nu Alpha; Life Mem, DAV; Vets Battle of Bulge; hon/Decorated Bronze Star w Cluster, Purple Heart w Cluster, Dist'd Ser Cross, Expert Combat Infantryman Badge; W/W E.

SCHOTT, SALLY MARIA oc/Choral Director, Choral Consultant; b/Feb 7, 1943; h/2126 Possum Creek, Houston, TX 77017; ba/South Houston, TX; p/ Doris Sitler, Beggs, OK; ed/BMus, OK Col for Wom, 1964; Master of Music Ed, N TX St Univ, 1966; pa/Choral Dir, Pasadena Indep Sch Dist, 1965-; Choral Conslt, AMC Music; Sigma Alpha Iota Alumnae, Pres of Houston Chapt 1966; TX Choral Dirs Assn, First VP 1975-77; Music Edrs Nat Conf; Am Choral Dirs Assn; TX Music Edrs Assn, Pres 1984-85, VP and Vocal Div Chm 1981-83; TX St Tchrs Assn; NEA; r/ Meth; hon/Pubs, *Something to Sing About* (Volumes I, II & III), Workbook and Tchrs Guide for *Something to Sing About*, *Something to Sing About for Young Voices*, Num Articles for *Southwestern Musician*; Pasadena ISD Tchr of the Yr, 1979; Sigma Alpha Iota Ldrship Awd, 1966; Pasadena JCs Outstg Yg Edr, 1968; Outstg Yg Wom of Am; Foremost Wom of the 20th Cent.

SCHROEDER, JANICE JONES oc/ Program Director; b/Sep 15, 1935; h/ 75 Palmer Avenue, Kenmore, NY 14217; ba/Buffalo, NY; c/Karl, Cheryl, Don, John; ed/BS, 1969; MEd, 1975; PhD (Applied for); pa/Current Dir, Native Am Biling Prog, MBO-City Towananda; EEO Coor/MBO, Erie Co; Ed Cnslr, Erie Co; Res Analyst, Erie Co; Res Dir, NY St Ed; Exec Dir, Native Am CETA; Tchr, Kenmore W HS; Tchr, Niagara Commun Col; Tchr, Erie Commun Col; Chair, Erie Commun Col Ed Adv Bd; NY St Biling Assn, Nat Am Lang Del; Nat Biling Assn; Nat Task Force on Indian Langs; cp/Bd, YWCA; Media Coun, Channel 7; Bd of Dirs, Buffalo Engr Awareness for Minorities; hon/Pub, *Native American Bilingual Education*.

SCHROEDER, RITA MOLTHEN oc/ Doctor of Chiropractic; b/Oct 25, 1922; h/9870 North Millbrook, Fresno, CA 93710; ba/Fresno, CA; c/Richard, Andrew, Barbara, Thomas, Paul, Madeline; p/Frank Joseph (dec) and Ruth Jessie McKenzie Molthen, Fresno, CA; ed/DC, Palmer Sch of Chiro, 1949; DC, Cleveland Col of Chiro, 1960; Att'd, Immaculate Heart Col 1940-41, Univ of CA LA 1941-42; pa/Engrg Design Data Coor, Douglas Aircraft Co, 1941-47; Engrg Draftsman, Rural Electrification Adm, 1947-49; DC, Brooklyn, NY, 1949-59; DC, Fresno, CA, 1961-; Pres, Schroeder Chiro Inc, 1982-; Bd of Dirs 1979-80, Pres 1980-81, Pacific Sts Chiro Col; Intl Chiropractors Assn; CA Chiro Assn; Am Assn of Col Pres; cp/Fresno C of C; r/Rom Cath; hon/Outstg Ser Awd, Pacific Sts Chiro Col, 1981; Ambassador Awd, 1976; W/W Am Wom.

SCHROM, GERARD KILLARD oc/ Educator; b/Jul 18, 1947; h/816 Derwyn Road, Drexel Hill, PA 19026; ba/Concordville, PA; m/Carol Packer; p/Erwin

R Schrom, Middletown, DE; ed/BS, PA St Univ, 1969; Postgrad, Princeton Univ 1974-76, Cambridge Univ 1982; JD, Widener Univ, 1983; pa/Eng Tchr, Wakefield HS 1969-70, Hunterdon Ctl HS 1972-76; Pres, Schrom Constrn Co, 1976-78; Chm, Eng Dept, Garnet Val HS, 1979-; Am Bar Assn; DE Bar Assn; NEA; PA Ed Assn; Moot Ct Hon Soc; Phi Alpha Delta; Sigma Alpha Epsilon; VP, Garnet Val Ed Assn; Arbitrator, Am Arbitration Assn; hon/Author, Several Legal Articles and Legis for the St of DE; Am Jurisp Awd, 1982; Fed Bar Assn Awd, 1983; W/W E.

SCHUBERT, RUTH CAROL HICKOK oc/Contemporary Artist; b/ Dec 24, 1927; h/134 Dunecrest Avenue, Monterey, CA 93940; m/Robert Francis; c/Stephen Robert, Michelle Carol Schubert-Kump; p/Fay Andrew Hickok and Mildred Willimette, San Jose, CA; ed/Att'd, DeAnza Col, 1972, 1973; AA w Hons, Monterey Peninsula Col, 1974; BA w Hons and Distn, CA St Univ San Jose, 1979; pa/Owner, Casade Artes Studio Gallery, 1977-; Coun Res Dir, Monterey Peninsula Mus of Art, 1975-76; Invitation Exhbns: CA St Pk and Rec Sys, La Purisimo Mission, Lompoc 1977 and SF Bay Nat Wildlife Resv 1979; One-Wom Shows: Switzerland, Rome, Wells Fargo Bk, Monterey, Seaside City Hall Gallery, San Jose St Univ, Village Gallery, Lahaina Maui; Grp Shows: Sierra NV Mus of Art, Bard Hall Gallery Nat Exhbn, Rahr-W Mus, Nat Exhib (Manitowoc, WI), Rosicrucian Mus, SWA Hall of Flowers, SF Golden Gate Pk; Pres, Ctl Coast Art Assn, 1977, 1978, 1979; Pres, Nat Leag of Am Penwom, 1983; Artists Equity Assn; Am Watercolor Soc; Soc Wn Artists; SF, Kona and Lahaina Art Socs; Monterey Peninsula Watercolor; Pacific Grove Artists; Art Alumni, San Jose St Univ; MP Mus of Art; cp/En Star; Monterey Civic Clb; r/Epis; hon/Pub, "Dateline Italy," 1978; Permanent Collections: Monterey Peninsula Mus of Art, Muscular Dystrophy Assn (SF Ofc), Nabisco Brands (San Jose Ofc), San Jose St Univ; Recip, More Than 30 Art Awds in the US; W/W W; Artists USA.

SCHUETZ, CARY EDWARD oc/ Thermophysics Engineer; b/Dec 6, 1953; h/10961 Roebling Avenue, Los Angeles, CA 90024; ba/Hawthorne, CA; m/June; p/Celestine Edward Schuetz (dec); Doris M Schuetz, San Diego, CA; ed/BS, Mech Engrg, Univ of CA Santa Barbara, 1978; pa/Engr, Univ of CA Santa Barbara, 1976-78; Engr/Scist, McDonnell Douglas Corp, 1978-81; Sr Engr, Northrop Corp, 1981-; AIAA, 1978-; Nat Soc of Profl Engrs, 1979-; CA Soc of Profl Engrs, 1979-; hon/Pub, *CINDA Developments at Northrop Corporation*, 1982; Invented Thermoelectric Generator to Provide Automobile Electricity from Wasted Engine Exhaust Heat, 1978; One of Four Most Outstg Engrg Design Projs upon Conferment of Acad Deg, Univ of CA, 1978; W/W W; W/W Frontier Sci and Technol.

SCHULTZ, ALBERT BERRY oc/ Venemma Professor of Mechanical Engineering; b/Oct 10, 1933; h/1310 Glendaloch Circle, Ann Arbor, MI 48104; ba/Ann Arbor, MI; m/Susan; c/ Carl, Adam, Robin; p/George D and Belle Schultz, Philadelphia, PA; ed/BS

1955, Master of Engrg 1959, PhD in Mech Engrg 1962, Yale Univ; mil/USN, 1955-58; pa/Univ of DE, 1962-65; Univ of IL Chgo, 1965-83; Univ of MI, 1983-; Intl Soc for the Study of the Lumbar Spine, Pres; Bioengrg Div, ASME, Chm 1981-82; Am Soc of Biomechs, Pres 1982-83; US Nat Com on Biomechs, Chm 1982-; hon/Author, Over 60 Full-Length Sci Jour Articles on Orthopaedic Biomechs and Engrg Mechs; Phi Beta Kappa, 1955; Phi Kappa Phi, 1980; Tau Beta Pi, 1955; NIH Spec Res Fellow, 1971-72; NIH Res Career Reward, 1975-80; Am Men of Sci; W/W Frontier Sci and Technol.

SCHUNK, DALE HANSEN oc/Professor of Educational Psychology; b/Aug 14, 1946; h/8711 Ariel Street, Houston, TX 77074; ba/Houston, TX; m/Caryl Sue; p/Elmer C and Mildred A Schunk, Sun City, AZ; ed/BS in Psych, Univ of IL, 1968; MEd, Ed, Boston Univ, 1974; PhD in Ednl Psych, Stanford Univ, 1979; mil/USAF 1968-74, Served to Capt; pa/ Res Asst and Instr, Stanford Univ, 1975-79; Prof of Ednl Psych, Univ of Houston, 1979-; Am Psychol Assn; Am Ednl Res Assn; Soc for Res in Child Devel; SWn Psychol Assn; SW Ednl Res Assn; Univ of Houston Com for the Protection of Human Subjects; Many Coms in Univ of Houston Col of Ed and Dept of Ednl Psych; r/Meth; hon/ Author of Many Pubs in Profl Jours, incl'g, *Journal of Educational Psychology, Educational Psychologist, Journal of Personality and Social Psychology, Human Learning, Contemporary Educational Psychology,* Var Book Chapts; Early Contbns Awd in Ednl Psych, Am Psychol Assn, 1982; Grad w High Hons, Boston Univ, 1974; Grad w High Hons, Bronze Tablet, Phi Beta Kappa, Phi Kappa Phi, Univ of IL, 1968; W/W Frontier Sci and Technol.

SCHURR, AVITAL oc/Neuroscientist; b/Aug 23, 1941; h/1100 Timberoak Drive, Louisville, KY 40223; ba/Louisville, KY; m/Dafna; c/Barak, Hila, Ori; p/Aryeh (dec) and Esther Schurr, Jerusalem, Israel; ed/BSc, Agronomy, Hebrew Univ, 1967; MSc, Biochem, Tel Aviv Univ, 1970; PhD, Biol, Ben Gurion Univ, 1977; pa/HS Tchr, Israeli Min of Ed, 1968-77; Res Assoc, Author, Res Devel, Beer Sheva, Israel, 1970-77; Res Fellow, Baylor Col of Med, 1977-79; Res Assoc, Univ of TX Med Sch, 1979-81; Asst Prof, Univ of Louisville Sch of Med, 1981-; NY Acad of Sci, 1978-; Soc for Neurosci, 1979-; AAAS, 1981-; Am Soc of Anesthesiologists, 1983-; r/Jewish; hon/Author, Var Pubs; W/W Frontiers in Res and Devel.

SCHUSTER, MARVIN M oc/Physician; b/Aug 30, 1929; h/3101 Northbrook Road, Baltimore, MD 21208; ba/ Baltimore, MD; m/Lois; c/Roberta, Nancy, Catherine; p/Isaac Schuster (dec); ed/BA 1949, BS 1951, Univ of Chgo; MD, Univ of Chgo Sch of Med, 1955; pa/Instr in Med 1962-67, Instr in Psychi 1962-70, Asst Prof of Med 1967-69, Asst Prof of Psychi 1970-80, Assoc Prof of Med 1969-75, Prof of Med 1976-80, Prof of Med and Jt Appt in Psychi 1980-, Johns Hopkins Univ Sch of Med; Dir, Div of Digestive Diseases, Francis Scott Key Med Ctr, 1961; Asst Chief of Med, Balto City Hosps, 1962-67; Phys, Balto City Hosps, 1961-62; Other Previous Positions; Pres, MD Div of Am Cancer Soc; Am

Col of Phys; Am Physiol Soc; Am Soc for Internal Med; Am Gastroenterological Assn; Am Soc for Gastrointestinal Endoscopy; En Gut Clb; Phila Gastrointestinal Res Forum; Am Fdn for Clin Res; AAUP; MD Soc for Med Res; AAAS; Am Psychi Assn; Fellow, Am Geriatric Soc; MD Psychi Soc; AMA; Num Other Profl Mbrships; r/Jewish; hon/Author, 3 Textbooks, 14 Chapts in Textbooks, Over 150 Articles in Sci Jours; Diplomate, Am Bd of Internal Med, 1965; Fellow, Am Col of Phys, 1966; Fellow, Am Psychi Assn, 1976; W/ W World; W/W E; Men of Achmt; W/ W Frontier Sci and Technol.

SCHWABEL, MARY JANE oc/Chief Virologist, Nurse; b/Oct 9, 1946; ba/462 Grider Street, Buffalo, NY 14215; p/ Albert T Schwabel (dec); Doris K Schottin (dec); ed/BS, Daemen Col, 1968; MS, Canisius Col, 1975; AAS, Trocaire Col, 1983; pa/Chief Virologist 1980-, Sr Serology Tech/Supvr 1974-79, Res Asst 1968-74, Erie Co Lab; Wn NY Infection Control Soc; Am Soc for Microbiol, Nat and Wn NY; Am Public Hlth Assn; NY St Assn of Public Hlth Labs; NY St Public Hlth Assn; Erie Co SPCA; Nat Antivivisection Soc; r/Rom Cath; hon/Pubs, "A Comparison of Isolation and Identification Between Culterset and Conventional Cell Cultures" 1983, "A Study of Hemagglutination Inhibition, Fluorometric and ELISA Assays for Rubella Antibody Screening" 1981, "Comparison of Fluorometric and Hemagglutination Inhibition Assays for Rubella Antibody Screening" 1980, Others; Beta Beta Beta Biol Hon Soc, Elected 1968; W/W Am Wom.

SCHWAN, HERMAN PAUL oc/Professor, Scientist; b/Aug 7, 1915; h/99 Kynlyn Road, Radnor, PA 19087; ba/ Philadelphia, PA; m/Anne M; c/Barbara, Margaret, Steven, Catherine, Carol; p/ Wilhelm (dec) and Meta Schwan, Germany; ed/PhD in Biophysics 1940, Dr habil, Physics and Biophysics 1946, Univ of Frankfurt, Germany; pa/From Tech Asst to Assoc Dir, Max Planck Inst of Biophysik, Frankfurt, Germany, 1937-47; Res Scist, US Naval Base, Phila, 1947-50; From Asst Prof to Prof, Univ of PA, 1950-; Biomed Engrg Soc; Biophy Soc; IEEE, Fellow; AAAS, Fellow; Soc for Cryobiol; German Biophy Soc; Intl Fdn of Med and Biol Engrg; hon/Edison Medal, IEEE, 1983; US Sr Scist Awd, A V Humbold Foun, 1980; Mem, Nat Acad of Engrg, 1975-; Boris Rajewsky Prize for Biophysics, 1974; NIH-HEW Certs of Apprec for Sers on NIGMS Prog Proj Com 1966, and Nat Envir Hlth Coun 1972; IEEE Cert for Sers Rendered to Further the Objectives of the IEEE, 1968; Other Hons; W/W World; W/W USA; W/W E; W/W Engrg; Men and Wom of Distn; DIB; Intl W/W Intells; Intl W/W Engrg; Men of Achmt; W/W Technol Today; Am Men and Wom of Sci.

SCHWARTZ, DONALD oc/University Chancellor; b/Dec 27, 1927; h/21 Sanford Road, Colorado Springs, CO 80906; ba/Colorado Springs, CO; m/ Lois; c/Leanne, Mark W, Scott B, Bradley F; p/Ethel Schwartz, Colorado Springs, CO; ed/BS, Univ of MO, 1949; MS, MT St Univ, 1951; PhD, PA St Univ, 1955; mil/USCG, 1945; pa/Chancellor, Univ of CO Colorado Sprgs,

1978-; Chancellor, IN Univ-Purdue Univ at Ft Wayne,. 1974-78; VP and Acting Pres, St Univ of NY Col at Buffalo, 1971-74; Dean for Adv'd Studies, FL Atl Univ, 1970-71; Am Chem Soc; Sigma Xi; Phi Lambda Upsilon; Phi Delta Kappa; cp/AF&AM; hon/Author, Over 75 Pubs Dealing w Titanium Compounds, Humic Acids, Higher Ed; Num Grants; W/W Am.

SCHWARTZ, HERBERT oc/Institute Director; b/Mar 8, 1925; h/1963 Maurice River Parkway, Vineland, NJ 08360; ba/Vineland, NJ; m/Martha Scheepers; c/Simone L Hobert, David; p/Edward Schwartz (dec); ed/BA, 1942; Dipl, Chem, 1955; PhD, 1965; mil/AUS 1943-46, WWII; pa/Res Chem: Vineland Chem Co 1955-57, FDA 1957-58, Grad Hosp 1958, Inst Organic Chem TNO 1959-65; Dir, Biovivan Res Inst 1965-; Adj Prof of Organic Chem, Cumberland Co Col, 1969-75; Am Chem Soc; AAAS; r/Jewish; hon/Author, Articles in Profl Jours; 16 US Patents; W/W E; DIB.

SCHWEICKART, RUSSELL L oc/ Commissioner of Energy; b/Oct 25, 1935; ba/1516 9th Street, Sacramento, CA 95814; m/Clare W; c/Vicki, Russell, Randolph, Elin, Diana; p/George and Muriel Schweickart, Spring Hill, FL; ed/ BS in Aerospace Engrg 1956, MS in Aeronautics and Astronautics 1963, MIT; mil/USAF 1956-60, 1961-62, Fighter Pilot; pa/NASA Astronaut, NASA, 1963-74; Dir, NASA Ofc of Applications, NASA HQs, 1974-77; Asst to Gov Gerry Brown, Gov's Ofc, CA, 1977-79; Chm, CA Energy Comm, 1979-83; Soc of Exptl Test Pilots; AIAA; Sigma Xi; Explorer's Clb; Am Astronautical Soc; hon/Author, "No Frames, No Boundaries," Var Essays and Video Progs; NASA Dist'd Ser Medal, 1969; NASA Exceptl Ser Medal, 1973; Emmy, 1969; De La Vaux Medal, Fdn Aeronautique Internationale, 1970.

SCHWEITZER, GERTRUDE oc/ Artist, Painter, Sculptor; h/Studio, Stone Hill Farm, Colts Neck, NJ 07722; ed/Student, Pratt Inst, Acad Julian, Nat Acad of Design; Hon Dr of Fine Arts, Pratt Inst; pa/Public Collections: The Brooklyn Mus, Toledo Mus of Art, Hackley Art Gallery, Davenport Mun Art Gallery, Canajoharie Lib and Art Gallery, Norton Gallery and Sch of Art, Atlanta Art Assn Galleries, Witte Meml Mus, Montclair Art Mus, Mus of Mod Art (Paris), Num Others; Solo Exhbns: Montclairr Art Mus, Wash Water Color Clb, Cayuga Mus of Hist and Art, Potsdam Gallery of Art, Currier Gallery of Art, Bevier Gallery at Rochester Inst of Technol, Erie Public Mus, Cortland Lib, Norton Gallery and Sch of Art, Galerie Charpentier, Galleria Al Cavallino, Num Others; hon/Pub, *Peintures et Dessins,* 1965; Elected to Nat Acad of Design; Yth Friends Awd, Sch Art Leag and Bd of Ed, NY; First Am to Have One-Man Show at Galerie Charpentier, Paris; First Am to Be Represented in Albi Mus Contemp Collection, France; Represented in Pvt Collections in US, England, France, Denmark and Italy; Outstg Wom Artists of Am; W/W Am Wom; W/W World; W/W S and SW; W/ W E; World W/W Art and Antiques; DIB; Personalities of S; Outstg Wom Artists of Am; Num Other Biogl Listings.

SCHYCKER-BAILEY, NANCY oc/

Educator; b/Jan 4, 1941; h/14737 Calkin, Hacienda Heights, CA 91745; ba/Rosemead, CA; m/Jim D Bailey; c/Michael Vaughn; p/Fred Peter Kinn, Baldwin Park, CA; Better Lee Zamer, Rosemead, CA; ed/AA, 1960; BA, 1962; MA, 1972; PhD, 1983; pa/Tchr, LA Unified Schs, 1962-63; Tchr, Covina Val Unified Sch Dist, 1964-67; Tchr/Master Tchr 1967-73, Dir of Hd Start St Presch Prog 1973-80, Prin 1980-81, Garvey Sch Dist; Res Assoc, IA St Univ Sch of Ednl Adm, 1981-82; Reg Demonstration Tchr, Garvey Sch Dist, 1983-; Adj Prof, CA St Univ LA, 1983-; Ed Adv Com, Pasadena Area Commun Col Dist, 1974-75; Chp, Hd Start St Presch Coors' Coun; Ofc of the LA Co Schs Supt, 1979-80; r/Christian; hon/Pubs, *Creation and Testing of a Diagnostic-Prescriptive Staff Development Instrument for K-12 Teachers* 1983, *English as a Second Language Curriculum Guide* 1972, Ednl Articles; Dir of Dist Ams; W/W W.

SCOPER, DELL DICKINS oc/Homemaker; b/Sep 10, 1934; h/603 West 14th Street, Laurel, MS 39440; m/Vincent Gradie; c/Stephen Vincent, Cynthia Dell; p/Ruth T Dickins, Leland, MS; ed/BA, MS Col, 1956; cp/Wom's Missionary Union, SBC (Maj Ofcs in All Areas); Exec Bd, MS WMU, 1969-75, 1984-89; Regent, Nahoula Chapt, DAR; Bds of Dirs: Laurel YWCA, Jones Co ARC, Jones Co Cancer Soc, Laurel Commun Concert Assn; Laurel Jr Aux, Life Assoc Mem; r/Active Mem and Bible Tchr, First Bapt Ch of Laurel; hon/MS Col Alumni Assn: Pres 1980-81, Chm of Annual Fund 1981-82, Alumna of the Yr 1982; Laurel's Wom of the Yr Awd, 1980.

SCOTT, MAE RANKIN oc/Executive; b/Jan 1, 1940; c/Leslie Ann Scott Garris, William Eugene Jr; p/William Roscoe; Francis M and Annie Mae Dobbs Rankin Johnson; ed/Student, Ext Univ, AL, 1959-61; pa/Heritage Corp of NY, 1962-67; Asst VP 1967-73, Sr VP 1973-78, Exec VP 1978-, King's Way Mortgage Co, Miami; Corporate Secy, Veritas Ins Co, Alpha Inc; VP, Pan Am Mortgage Corp; Approved Underwriter, Fed Home Loan Bk, Fed Nat Mortgage Assn; Mortgage Bkrs Assn of S FL; Mortgage Bkrs Assn of Am; S FL Home Bldrs Assn; Nat Assn Rev Appraisers (Cert Rev Appraiser); Intl Inst of Valuers, SCV; Var S FL Real Est Bds; cp/Dem; Active, Preven of Blindness; r/Bapt; hon/Contbr, Articles to Pubs; W/W S and SW; W/W Am Wom.

SCOTT, RONALD LEE oc/Senior Area Counsel; b/May 17, 1951; h/7 Duke Street Mansions, 70 Duke Street, London W1 England; ba/London, England; m/Judy Combs; p/Homer Reese and Bessie Dean Scott, Ada, OK; ed/JD 1976, MA in Human Relats 1973, BA in Psych 1972, Univ of OK; pa/Var Atty Positions w Halliburton Sers and Subsidiary Halliburton Mfg and Sers Ltd, London, 1976-; Currently in Charge of Legal Dept for Europe, Africa and Mid E Regs of Halliburton; Am Bar Assn; OK Bar Assn; Intl Bar Assn; Petro Equip Suppliers Assn, Lien Law Com 1978-79; hon/Am Jurisp Awd, 1976; W/W S and SW.

SCRUGGS, JULIUS RICHARD oc/Pastor; b/Feb 1, 1942; h/3709 Battlefield Drive, Huntsville, AL 35810; ba/Huntsville, AL; m/Francina Bannister; c/

Jennifer Juliette; p/Rev and Mrs Earl Scruggs Sr, Toney, AL; ed/BA, 1965; MDiv, 1968; Doct of Min, 1975; pa/Pastored Several Chs; Prof of Old Testament, Am Bapt Col; Editor, Nat Bapt Publishing Bd; Current Pastor, First Bapt Ch; cp/NAACP; Urban Leag; PUSH; Huntsville Human Relats Coun; r/Bapt; hon/Pubs, *Meditations on the Church* 1976, *Baptist Preachers with Social Consciousness* 1978; Pastor of the Yr, 1978; Epsilon Theta Hon Soc; W/W Rel.

SCULL, WILLIAM DAVID oc/Business Owner; b/Aug 28, 1934; h/1109 Fulton Street, Raeford, NC 28376; ba/Red Springs, NC; m/Nora; c/Mike Peckham, Delaine Peckham, Judy, Randy; p/Mr and Mrs O H Scull, Raeford, NC; ed/HS Grad, 1952; mil/Navy, 1953-55; pa/Stock Clk to Mgr, A&P Tea Co, 1952-74; Town of Raeford, 1974-75; Owner, Piggly Wiggly, 1975-; cp/Pres, Red Springs C of C, 1972; Chm, Troop Com, Boy Scouts #404, 5 Yrs; Ch Sch Supt, 21 Yrs; r/Meth; hon/Recip, Dist'd Ser Awd, Jr C of C, Hoke Co.

SCZECHOWICZ, EDWARD STEVEN JR oc/Psychologist, Program Director; b/Apr 13, 1954; h/4630 Northwest 79th Avenue, 2-C, Miami, FL 33166; ba/Hialeah, FL; m/Brenda Lynn McCarter; p/Edward S Sczechowicz Sr, Spartanburg, SC; Mercedes Owens Sczechowicz (dec); ed/BA, Villanova Univ, 1976; MS 1979, PhD 1982, Univ of Miami; Intern, Phila St Hosp, 1979-80; pa/Pvt Pract, A&A Profl Cnslg Assocs, 1982-; Clin Dir, A&A Profl Cnslg Assocs Outpatient Sex Offender Rehab Prog; Psychol, Prog Dir, Vulnerable Unit, S FL St Hosp; Prog Clin Psychol, Dr Geraldine Boozer Sex Offender Rehab Prog, 1980-82; Am Psychol Assn, 1983, 1979-81; r/Cath; hon/Author of Articles for Profl Jours; Phi Kappa Phi Hon, 1975-; Univ of Miami Commend for Outstg Acad Excell, Clin Psych Grad Fac, 1977; Grad Clin Psych F'ship (3), 1977, 1978, 1979.

SEABORN, MARY MARGARET oc/Training Coordinator; b/May 11, 1953; h/1416 Glendale Drive, Marion, IN 46952; ba/Boston, MA; m/Joseph William Seaborn Jr; p/Rev George and Christine Nalley, Fountain Inn, SC; sp/Joe and Betty Seaborn, Six Mile, SC; ed/BA Elem Ed, Ctl Wesleyan Col, 1976; MA Elem Ed, En KY Univ, 1979; EdD Cand, Boton Univ; pa/Tchr, Boyle Co Elem, 1976-79; Tng Instr, Blue Cross, 1979-82; Tng Coor, Blue Cross, 1982-; Boyle Co Ed Assn; KEA; NEA; cp/Fac Wives F'ship of ENC, 1979-82; Blue Cross, Blue Shield Assn, 1979-; Cert'd Ventriloquist, Maher Inc, 1979-; hon/Outsg Yg Wom of Am, 1980; Furman Univ Scholar, 1972; Dean's List, Ctl Wesleyan Col, 1974-76; hon/Outstg Yg Wom of Am, 1980.

SEABROOK, MELISSE GILPIN oc/Manager of Special Services; b/Jul 7, 1948; h/4024C Palm Bay Circle, West Palm Beach, FL 33406; ba/Riviera Beach, FL; p/Richard B Gilpin, Atlanta, GA; Bettie Brownell Gilpin (dec); ed/HS Grad, Savannah, GA, 1965; pa/Operator, Ser Asst 1966, 1st Level Mgr, Grp Chief Operator 1968, Dial Ser Adm 1972, Dial Adm Electron Switchers 1973, Promoted to Ctl Ofc Foreman-Electronic 1976, Promoted to 2nd Level Mgr-Netwk Adm 1978, Mgr

of Spec Sers-Ctl Ofc 1982-, So Bell; Bell Spkrs Bur, 1977-79; Wom's Exec Wkshop; cp/Big Sister Prog, 1978-80; Zonta Intl, 1982-; Humane Soc, 1983; Zonta, Bd Mem 1983; U Way Com, So Bell, 1982; r/Presb; hon/W/W Am Wom.

SEAL, ASHER FOLEY SR oc/Executive; b/Mar 6, 1919; h/910 Gazelle Trail, Winter Springs, FL 32708; ba/Winter Park, FL; m/Henrietta D; c/Asher F Jr, Robert Howard (dec), Charles E; p/Jesse L Seal (dec); Eva A Seal, Lexington, KY; ed/Att'd, Univ of KY Lexington, Wn Univ, Bowling Green Univ, George Wash Univ, Am Univ; Grad Sch, USDA; Grad, Nat Acad of Broadcasting; mil/AUS, 1942-45; pa/VP, Treas, Bd of Dirs, Arjay Intl Corp; Pres, Chm of Bd, RHS Enterprises; Conslt, Winter Pk, FL; Former VP, Bd of Dirs, Treas, Arjay Mktg Corp; Edit Columnist, Mil and Var Newspapers, 1942-45; Spch Writing, Lectr, 1936-41; Edit Columnist, Pvt Pubs, 1947-49; Radio Script Writing and Acting, 1947-49; US Govt, Spec Assignment (Confidential), 1949-50; Spec Projs Mgmt and Financial Analyst; Liaison w Cong, Pvt Indust, White House, Intl and Fgn Ofcls, 1949-77; cp/32 Deg Mason-Shrine; YMCA; Former Mem, Exec Com, Repub Party; Former Mem, Nat and FL Sheriffs' Assns; Sheriff's Dept, VA; hon/Recip, 4 Awds and 6 Cits While w US Govt; Former KY Col.

SEARLES, JERRY LEE oc/Television Program Producer, Entrepreneur, Consultant, Humanitarian; b/Jul 6, 1931; h/1704 Maryland Avenue, East, St Paul, MN 55106; ba/Same; p/Leo K and Mary R Pendy Searles, St Paul, MN; mil/AUS, US and Korea, 1950-52; pa/Creator of Num Famous TV Shows, incl'g, "Let's Make a Deal" 1959, "Jeopardy!" 1962; Creator of Peace Corps Concept, 1954; Creator of Wash, DC, Moscow "Hotline" Concept, 1954; cp/Masonic Lodge; Scottish Rite, 32 Deg; Shriners; Am Legion; VFW; Disabled Am Vets; Intl War Vets Alliance; Amvets; Mil Order of the Purple Heart, NC, 1980-81; 40/8; Cooltes; Millionaires; Ath; r/Prot; hon/Author, Num Bus Adm, Advtg, Non-Fiction Mag Articles and Books; Conslt at White House to Pres Carter and Pres Reagan, 1979-; Presented Wreath at Tomb of Unknown Soldier, Arlington Cemetery, 1981; Awds, Jury of Freedoms Foun; Intl Man of Achmt, 1980-81; W/W World; W/W MW; W/W Am; W/W Fin and Indust.

SEBASTIANELLI, CARL THOMAS oc/Private Practice of Clinical Psychology; b/Dec 12, 1943; ba/Comprehensive Health Services Center, Suite 100, 1416 Monroe Avenue, Dunmore, PA 18509; p/Carlo and Antonia Antonelli Sebastianelli, Jessup, PA; ed/BS in Psych, magna cum laude, Univ of Scranton, 1965; MA in Psych, Temple Univ, 1967; Postgrad Ed in Clin Psych, Long Isl Univ (PhD Cand 1970); PhD in Clin Psych, Clayton Univ, 1983; pa/Pvt Pract, Clin Psych, Radio/TV Media Psychol, Psychol Wkshops, 1979-; Clin Psychol, Psychi Treatment Ctr 1977-79, Fam Therapy Ctr and Psychol Lab 1971-77 (Dir 1976-77), Chm of Psychol Forum 1974-76, Doct Internship 1970-71, Harrisburg St Hosp; Psychol, Fairview St Hosp, 1967-68; Adj Fac, PA St Univ and Univ of Scranton, 1979-; Nat Register of Hlth Ser Providers in Psych;

Am Psychol Assn; PA Psychol Assn, Chm of Public Info Com 1981-83; NEn PA Psych Assn, Secy 1980-82, Exec Coun 1982-; Soc of Behavioral Med; Am Acad of Behavioral Med; Acad of Psychols in Marital Sex and Fam Therapy; Biofeedback Soc of Am, 1979-82; PA Social Sers Union, St Bd Mem and S Ctl Chapt Pres 1974-75; r/Cath; hon/ Pubs, High School Anthology of Poetry 1960, Several Nonreferred Articles in Psych Pubs; "Enhancing the Diabetes Education" Awd, NE PA Chapt, Am Diabetes Assn; W/W E; Biogl Roll of Hon; 2,000 Notable Ams; Intl Bk of Hon.

SEDA, ANGEL L oc/Minister, Hospital Chaplain; b/Jun 10, 1910; h/1452 Ashford Avenue, Apartment 5-D, San Juan, Puerto Rico; m/Eva Mora; c/Angel L Jr, Eva Iris, Angela Luisa; p/Juan Seda-Velez (dec); Julia Matoa (dec); ed/ Tchr's Lic, 1926; Dipl, Evang Sem of Puerto Rico, 1932; BA, Univ of Puerto Rico, 1943; BTh, Evang Sem of Puerto Rico, 1945; MA, Tchrs' Col, Columbia Univ, 1948; MRE, Union Theol Sem, 1948; EdD, Columbia Univ, 1958; MTh, Evang Sem of Puerto Rico, 1972; mil/ Puerto Rican NG, ROTC, Army Resv, CAP; pa/Pastor, Balboa Presb Ch, Mayaguez, 1933; Pastor, Presb Ch, Las Marias, 1933-37; Chaplain, Presb Hosp, 1937-79; Vis'g Prof, Sch of Nsg 1942-70, Vis'g Prof of Psych and Sociol, Presb Hosp; Vis'g Prof of Pastoral Cnslg, Evang Sem of Puerto Rico, 1955-65; Orgr and Pt-time Pastor, Hildreth Meml Presb Ch, 1975-79; Presby of Puerto Rico, 1935-72; Presby of San Juan, 1972-84; Presb Synod of Puerto Rico, 1972-84; Evang Coun of Puerto Rico, 1945-84; Phi Delta Kappa, 1948-84; Col of Chaplains, 1948-84; Assn of Presb Mins, 1950-72; Alumni Assns of Univ of Puerto Rico, Columbia Univ, Union Theol Sem and Evang Sem of Puerto Rico; cp/Puerto Rico Chd's Com, 1958-73; Presb Hlth, Ed and Wel Assn, 1945-84; ARC, 1933-84; Mtl Hlth Assn of Puerto Rico, 1948-60; r/Presb; hon/Pubs, *Where the Physician and the Minister Meet* 1943, *Development of Hospital Chaplaincy in the United States-Its Implications for Puerto Rico* 1958, Spanish Translation of Values for Living 1979, 1980, 1981, Rel Hymns and Poems; Citizens Medal, Citizens Mil Tng Camp, 1928; First Prize, Evang Sem of Puerto Rico for Highest Grade Index, 1932; Del from Puerto Rico to Gen Assem of Presb Ch, 1937, 1977; Hon Guest at Quadrenial Meetings of Nat Org of Presb Wom, 1946, 1950, 1962; Del to Intl Conv in Japan, 1958; Appt'd Pastor Emeritus, Hildreth Meml Presb Ch, Presbytery of San Juan, 1984; Hon Plaque, Evang Missionary Crusade of Puerto Rico, 1984; Num Other Hons; W/W Am Ed; Personalities of S; DIB; Men of Achmt; Notable Am of Bicent Era.

SEEGAR, CHARLON IONE oc/ Assistant Professor, Social Scientist; b/ May 13, 1936; h/5 Lakeshore Loop, Augusta, GA 30904; ba/Augusta, GA; p/Wilner H Seegar (dec); Mrs Ione Lee, Augusta, GA; ed/BA, La Grange Col, 1959; MSW, Univ of NC Chapel Hill, 1964; pa/ARC, Ser to Mil Hosps: Ft Jackson (SC) Army Hosp 1959-61, USAF Hosp (Maxwell AFB) 1962-63, Ft Bragg Army Hosp 1964-65, 97th Gen Army Hosp (Frankfurt Am Main, Ger-

many) 1965-67, US Naval Hosp (Charleston, SC) 1967; Fam Planning Conslt, St Dept Fam and Chd Ser, 1967-69; Chief Social Wkr, Instr, Ob-Gyn, Maternal and Infant Care, Fam Planning Projs 1969-80, Assoc Prof of Nsg and Chm of Dept of Distributive Nsg, Asst Prof, Social Scist, Dept of Psychi 1980-, Med Col of GA; Acad Cert'd Social Wkrs; Nat Assn Social Wkrs; GA Hlth Care Assn; GA Soc Hosp Social Wkrs; Am Assn Sex Edrs and Therapists; Planned Parenthood Bd Dir, 1975-80; AAUW; Mtl Assn, Augusta; Mtl Hlth Assn, GA; cp/Pilot Clb, Augusta; So Christian Ldrship Conf; U Way, Gtr Augusta, Bd of Dirs 1980-; ACLU; LWV; Nat Assn Female Execs; r/Non-Denominational Christian; hon/ Pubs, "Social and Economic Aspects of Family Planning" 1968, "Planning and Implementing a Large-Scale Family Planning Program in Georgia" 1970; Commun Involvement Awd, Augusta, 1970; GA Social Wkr of Yr, 1977; W/ W Am Wom; World W/W Among Wom; Outstg Yg Wom of Am.

SEGAN, KENNETH AKIVA oc/ Artist, Draftsman and Printmaker; b/ Feb 19, 1950; ba/Studio 701, 909 4th Avenue, Seattle, WA 98104; p/Meyer and Barbara Graff Segan, Floral Park, NY; ed/BA, Art, So IL Univ, 1977; MFA, Printmaking and Drawing, Univ of MO, 1980; pa/Mus Collections: AR Arts Ctr, Dahl Fine Arts Ctr, DeCordova and Dana Mus, Judah L Magnes Meml Mus, MIT Mus, MN Mus of Art, Others; Univ and Lib Collections: Columbia Univ Law Sch, Harvard Univ Law Sch, Herrett Mus of the Col of So ID, Univ of IL Illini Union Collection, Univ of MN Katherine Nash Gallery, Others; Instnl Collections: Dallas City Hall, Jefferson Expansion Meml Nat Historic Site, Newman Ctr Cath Ch, NC St Bar, Pacific Sci Ctr, Seattle Aquarium, TX Law Ctr of TX St Bar Assn, Wesley Foun Ch; Corporate Collections: CL Sys Inc, First Interst Bk, Hillcrest Hosp, Long Isl Jewish-Hillside Med Ctr, Others; Solo Exhbns: AIA Gallery, Univ of IL Illini Union Gallery, Mittleman Jewish Commun Ctr, Springfield Art Mus, Polack Gallery, Arthead Gallery, Others; Grp Exhbns: NW Juried Art '83, Soc of Am Graphic Artists 60th Annual, Sep Competition, Anacortes Arts and Crafts Printmaking Exhbn, Pacific Sts Prints and Drawings, Others; r/Jewish; hon/W/W Am Art; W/W W.

SEGGEV, LYDIA NADLER oc/Psychologist, Psychoanalyst; b/Apr 11, 1937; h/24 Pine Drive North, Roslyn, NY 11576; c/Michael; p/Yehoshua and Henriette Nadler, Tel-Aviv, Israel; ed/ BA, Hebrew Univ, Israel, 1963; MA, Univ of MI, 1965; PhD, Syracuse Univ, 1971; Postdoct Dipl in Psychotherapy and Psychoanal, Adelphi Univ, 1979; mil/Israeli Army; pa/Pvt Pract, Psych and Psychoanal, 1975-; Psychotherapist, Long Isl Consltn Ctr, 1975-77; Dir, Eval, Title I Prog, Dist 9, Bronx, NY; Lectr, Hebrew Univ, 1971-72; Lectr, Tel-Aviv Univ, 1971-72; Lectr, St John's Univ, 1970-71; Bd, Nassau Co Psychol Assn; NY Soc for Clin Psychols; Am Psychol Assn; Soc for Res in Child Devel; Nassau Psychol Assn; Adelphi Soc for Psychotherapy and Psychoanal; NY St Psychol Assn; r/Jewish; hon/W/ W Am Wom.

SEIBEL, GEORGE HENRY JR oc/ Quality Assurance Specialist; b/Apr 21, 1921; h/Box 96-C-36, Route #1, Oakridge Estates, Eastaboga, AL 36260; m/ Estelle Lucille Gulley; c/Lorita Joeann, Georgeania Marie, Clifford George, Henry Curtis; p/George Henry Seibel (dec); Marie Sophia Johnson Seibel, Belleville, IL; ed/USAFI: Univ of IL, Univ of Omaha; Att'd, Univ of AK, Univ of NM; Att'd, Var Mil Schs; mil/USAF T/ Sgt (Ret'd); pa/Chief Instr, USAAC Drivers Sch; Aircraft Intercept Controller Instr; Elect Counter-Measures Instr; Conslt; USAF Detachment Cmdr; Ch Flight Opers Elect-Countermeasure; Elect Intell Anal, Spec; Other Profl Positions; Life Mem, Pearl Harbor Survivors Assn; Am Def Preparedness Assn; Nat Adv Bd, Am Security Bd; USAF Sgts Assn; AIAA; Am Fdn Govt Employees; cp/Smithsonian Assocs; Nat Geographic Soc; Nat Hist Soc; Early Am Soc; r/Nondenominational; hon/Var Inventions; Composer; Lttrs of Apprec and Fin Awd, USAF and AUS; Awd and Ceremonial Dinner for Assistance to People of Korea, Republic of Korea; Lttrs of Apprec: Cmdr Concord Nav Sta, AL Sheriff's Assn, Cmdr 2nd Coast Guard Dist, Dept Civilian Aviation, Republic of Costa Rica; Letter of Commendation, Errol L des Santos, Colonial Secretary, Port of Spain (Trinidad).

SEITZ, LAURA RUTH oc/Owner of Graphic Design Firm; b/Nov 29, 1951; h/28 Park Avenue, Venice, CA 90291; ba/Santa Monica, CA; p/John and Charlotte Collins Seitz, Dearborn, MI; ed/Student, Wn MI Univ 1969-72, LA Mun Art Galleries 1975-78, Univ of CA LA 1978; pa/Owner/Designer, Moonshadow Designs, 1974-77; Secy 1976-79, Acct Exec 1979-80, Acct Supvr 1980-81, Maher Elen Advtg; Sales Mgr, Sojourn Design Grp, 1981-82; Dir of Mktg, Anselmo Design Assocs, 1982-; LA Ad Clb; Nat Assn of Female Execs; Intl Assn of Bus Communicators; cp/ Red Cross First Aid Instr, 1974-75; Planned Parenthood Commun Edr, 1975-78; NOW Task Force, 1977; Muscular Dystrophy Olympics Steering Com, 1979; March of Dimes Superwalk Steering Com, 1981; hon/March of Dimes Battered Boot Awd, 1981; W/W W; W/W Am Wom.

SEKELLA, THOMAS CURRAN oc/ Engineering Manager; b/Aug 19, 1946; h/517 Larchmont Road, Elmira, NY 14905; ba/Elmira, NY; m/Barbara Elizabeth Yeadon; c/Jennifer Lynn, Jillian Elizabeth; p/Youston (dec) and Mary Catharine Curran Sekella, Elmira, NY; ed/Bach of Mech Engrg, Villanova Univ, 1968; pa/Jr Engr to Sr Engr, Electronic Fuel Injection Prod Devel, Bendix Corp, 1968-72; Sr Engr, Catalytic Converter Prod Devel, Corning Glass Wks, 1972-75; Sr Engr to Engrg Mgr, Electromagnetic Clutch and Brake Prod Devel, Facet Enterprises Inc, 1975-; ASME; Soc of Automotive Engrs; cp/ Elmira Cath Sch Bd, Chm of Fin Com 1979-; Past Bd Mem and Vol, Big Brother Prog; r/Rom Cath; hon/Several Patents through Career; Author, Tech Paper on Effect of Turbulent Flow on Catalytic Converter Efficiency Pub'd through SAE; Tau Beta Pi and Pi Tau Sigma, Engrg Nat Hon Socs; W/W E.

SELF, DONALD R oc/Marketing

Professor; b/Aug 10, 1944; h/Box 383, Brooklet, GA 30415; ba/Statesboro, GA; m/Mary Anne; c/Malda; p/Mr and Mrs Raymond R Self, Donna, TX; ed/BA 1965, MBA 1971, TX A&I Univ; DBA, LA Tech Univ, 1977; mil/USNR, 1961-64; pa/Assoc Prof, GA So Col, 1980-; Asst Prof, GA Col, 1977-80; Mgr of Mktg Res and Prod Planning, Burgess Inc, 1969-70; Pi Sigma Epsilon, Nat Dir 1982-; Assoc Editor, *Marketing Abstracts*, Jour of Mktg, 1981-; Editor, *Southern Traveler*, 1983-; Pres, GA Assn of Mktg Edrs, 1979-80; cp/Treas, Kiwanis Clb, 1980-; Secy, Town Planning Comm, 1980-82; hon/Active in Pub'g Scholarly Acad Articles; Outstg Prof, GA Col, 1977; Outstg Yg Men of Am.

SELF, HAZZLE L oc/Professor of Animal Science; b/Aug 1, 1920; h/2221 Clark Avenue, Ames, IA 50010; ba/Ames, IA; m/Martha; c/Linda Ann, Debra Jo (dec), Ann Marie, Michael Dow; p/H K (dec) and Ethel Self, Hico, TX; ed/AS, 1947; BS in Agri Ed, TX A&M Univ, 1948; MS in Animal Husbandry and Ed, TX Tech Univ, 1950; PhD in Genetics and Animal Sci, Univ of WI, 1954; mil/Army, 1944-46; pa/Asst Prof, Tarleton St Univ, 1948-52; Fellow, Univ of WI, 1952-54; Asst Prof, Univ of WI, 1954-59; Assoc Prof and Swine Spec, IA St Univ, 1959-61; Prof-in-Charge, Agri Exptl Sta, IA St Univ, 1961-; Am Soc of Animal Sci, 1952-, Prog Chair 1978; IA Forage and Grassland Coun, Bd of Dirs 1976-78, Pres 1978; Cert'd Animal Scist, 1976-; cp/Rotary Intl, 1959; r/Prot; hon/Author of Over 50 Sci Pubs in Profl Jours, Co-Author of 1 Book and Contbg Author to 4 Books, 1952-; Animal Mgmt Awd of Am Soc of Animal Sci, 1979; IA Cattleman's Apprec Awd, 1971.

SELLERS, CAROL oc/Lawyer; b/Mar 2, 1943; h/4412 North Wilson Street, Fresno, CA 93704; ba/Los Angeles, CA; m/James K Herbert; c/John, Kathie, Paul, Barry; p/George Grover and Mae Savage Sellers; ed/BA, Duke Univ, 1964; JD, cum laude, Whittier Sch of Law, 1976; pa/Tchr, HS Eng, Heber, UT, 1964-67; Fdr, Exec Dir, Fremont Scholastic Inst, SLC, 1967-71; Admr, Ofc of the Dean, Whittier Sch of Law, 1973-76; Admitted to CA Bar, 1976; Assoc, Firm of Katz, Granof, Palarz, 1976-78; Dir, Wn Div, Harcourt Brace Jovanovich Legal and Profl Pubs, 1977-81; Pres, Exec Dir, Harcourt Brace Jovanovich Multistate Wkshop, 1981-; Dean, San Joaquin Col of Law, 1982-; Lectr, Wom in Legal and Bus Professions, CA; Beverly Hills Bar Assn; Fresno Co Bar Assn; Assn Wom and Law Com, 1st Chm 1977; Am Bar Assn; hon/Angier B Duke Scholar, 1961-64; Beverly Rubens Gordon Scholar, 1972-76; W/W Am Wom.

SELLERS, GREGORY JUDE oc/Physicist; b/Jun 20, 1947; h/PO Box 296 C, Convent Station, NJ 07961; ba/Morristown, NJ; m/Lucia Sunhee Kim; p/Douglas L (dec) and Rita R Dieringer Sellers, Lynbrook, NY; ed/AB in Physics, Cornell Univ, 1968; MS in Physics 1970, PhD in Physics 1975, Univ of IL Urbana; pa/Physicist, Applications Devel, Allied Corp, 1976-; Sr Scist, B-K Dynamics Inc, 1974-76; Am Phy Soc; AAAS; IEEE; Soc of Plastics Engrs; r/Christian; hon/Co-Inventor w Following Patents: Adhesive Bonding Metallic

Glass, Electromagnetic Shielding, Testing of Thermal Insulation, Amorphous Antipilferage Marker, Amorphous Spring-Shield; Inventor Awd, Allied Corp, 1979; W/W Frontier Sci and Technol.

SELTZER, RONNI LEE oc/Physician Specializing in Psychiatry; b/Apr 24, 1952; h/245 East 63rd Street, New York, NY 10021; ba/Englewood, NJ; m/Gary Broder; p/Herbert M and Marian Willinger Seltzer, Roslyn Heights, NY; ed/Residency in Psychi, NY Univ Med Ctr/Bellevue Hosp, 1977-81; MS, Chgo Med Sch, 1977; BA, Syracuse Univ, 1973; Att'd, Wheatley Sch, 1969; pa/Pvt Pract Specializing in Psychi, 1981-; Med Staff, Englewood Hosp, 1981-; Tchg Asst, Psychi, NY Univ Med Ctr, 1980-; Am Psychi Assn; NJ Psychi Assn; En Psychi Res Assn; AMA; Bergen Co Med Soc; Am Med Wom's Assn; NJ Psychi Assn; Chgo Med Sch Alumni Assn; r/Jewish; hon/Pubs, "Monoamine-Oxidase-Inhibitor-Induced Rapid Cycling Bipolar Affective Disorder in an Adolescent" 1981, "Lithium Carbonate and Gastric Ulcers" 1981.

SELTZER, VICKI LYNN oc/Physician, Hospital Administrator; b/Jun 2, 1949; h/36 Bacon Road, Old Westbury, NY 11568; ba/Jamaica, NY; m/Richard S Brach; c/Jessica Brach, Eric Brach; p/Herb and Marion Seltzer, Roslyn Hgts, NY; sp/Herbert and Elizabeth Brach; ed/BS, Rensselaer Polytech Inst, 1965; MD, NY Univ Sch of Med, 1969; pa/Resident & Chief Resident in Ob/Gyn, Bellevue Hosp, 1973-77; Am Cancer Soc Fellow in Gyn Cancer, NY Med Col, 1977-78; Fellow in Gyn Cancer, Meml Sloan Kettering Cancer Ctr, 1978-79; Assoc Dir, Gyn Cancer, Albert Einstein Col of Med, 1979-83; Dir Ob/Gyn, Queens Hosp Ctr; VP, Wom's Med Assn of NYC, 1974-79; Fellow, Am Col of Obs/Gyns; NY Ob Soc; Coop'g Investigator, En Coop Oncology Grp, 1980-83; NY Cancer Soc; VChm, Cancer Com, Planned Parenthood Fdn of Am; VP, Alumni Assn, NY Univ Sch of Med, 1978-79; Fac Sen, Albert Einstein Col of Med; Chm, Hlth Care Com, Nat Coun of Wom, 1979-; hon/Author, "Natural Cytotoxicity in Malignant and Premalignant Cervical Neoplasia and Enhancement of Cytotoxicity with Interferon," *Gyn Oncology*, 1973; "Delayed Childbirth—How Late is Too Late," *Wom's Life*, 1981; "The Second Opinion—How and When to Get One," *Wom's Life*, 1982; Alpha Omega Alpha, Nat Med Hon Soc, 1972-; Nat Safety Coun Awd, 1978; Am Med Wom's Assn Cit, 1973; NY Univ Alumni Assn Awd, 1973.

SENG, MINNIE A oc/Retired Librarian, Editor; b/Nov 30, 1909; h/110 South Broadway #Q, Frostburg, MD 21532; p/Edward and Ella Pattie Seng (dec); ed/Att'd, Muskegon Commun Col, 1927-29; AB 1932, AB in Lib Sci 1935, MA in Lib Sci 1943, Univ of MI; pa/Asst Med Libn, Univ of IA, 1935-39; Order Libn, MI Univ of Technol, 1940-42; Hd Cataloger, CA St Univ Fresno, 1944-59; Editor, *Education Index*, H W Wilson Co, 1959-66; Hd Cataloger, St Ambrose Col, 1967-72; Periodical Libn, Frostburg St Col, 1972-74; Ret'd, 1974; AAUW; Am Hort Soc; Univ of MI Alumni Assn; cp/Frostburg Mus Assn; hon/W/W Am Wom; W/W E;

World W/W Wom; DIB; Personalities of S; Dir of Dist'd Ams.

SENNEMA, DAVID CARL oc/Museum Director; b/Jul 6, 1934; h/4008 Kilbourne Road, Columbia, SC 29205; ba/Columbia, SC; m/Martha Dixon; c/Daniel Ross, Julia Kathryn, Alice Dixon; p/Mrs Carl E Sennema, Grand Rapids, MI; ed/BA, Albion Col, 1956; mil/Army, 1957-58; pa/Mgr, Columbia Music Fest Assn, 1964-67; Fdg Dir, SC Arts Comm, 1967-70; Assoc Dir, Fed-St Ptnrship and Spec Projs Progs, Nat Endowment for the Arts, Wash, DC, 1971-73; Prof of Arts Adm and Dir of Commun Arts Mgmt Prog, Sangamon St Univ, 1973-76; Dir of SC St Mus, 1976-; cp/Columbia Rotary Clb; Carolina Coliseum Adv Com; Carolina Chorale, Chm of Bd; Mayor's Arts Coun Study Com, Past Chm; r/Meth; hon/Pubs, "Sure Hit Skit Kit" 1980, Articles; W/W Am Art; W/W S and SW.

SENNET, DIANE CAROL oc/Executive; b/Mar 28, 1948; h/460 East 79 Street, New York, NY 10021; ba/New York, NY; p/Bernard Sennet, New York, NY; ed/BA, Univ of TN, 1969; Att'd, Grace Downs Sch, 1970; pa/Supvr, Trans World Airlines, 1970-75; Pres, Sennet Sec Travel, 1975-; Air Traffic Conf of Am; Intl Air Transport Assn; Intl Passenger Steamship Assn; NY Assn of Wom Bus Owners; hon/Mem, Pan Am World Airways Adv Bd 1983-85, En Airlines Adv Bd 1983; W/W Am Wom.

SERTO, MICHELLE JEAN oc/Certified Public Accountant; b/Apr 1, 1949; h/6623 43rd Avenue, Kenosha, WI 53142; ba/Kenosha, WI; p/Ferdinand and Minnie Serto, Kenosha, WI; ed/BSBA, magna cum laude, Georgetown Univ, 1971; pa/Self-Employed in Public Acctg, 1978-; Mgr of Inventory Eval, Ladish Co, Tri-Clover Div, 1975-78; Staff Acct, Fiat-Allis Corporate HQs, 1974-75; Instr, Gateway Tech Inst, 1974; Asst to Divisional Controller, Ladish Co, Tri-Clover Div, 1972-74; Staff Auditor, Price Waterhouse & Co, 1971-72; Am Inst of CPAs; WI Inst of CPAs; Nat Assn of Female Execs; Racine-Kenosha Estate Planning Coun; AAUW; cp/Bd Mem, Current VP, St Joseph HS Inc, 1980-; Treas, Secy, Current VP, Quota Clb of Kenosha Inc, 1978-; Bd Mem, Secy, Current Treas, Parish Coun, 1981-; r/Rom Cath; hon/W/W Am Wom.

SESTINI, VIRGIL ANDREW oc/High School Biology Teacher; b/Nov 24, 1936; h/6618 West Coley Avenue, Las Vegas, NV 89102; ba/Las Vegas, NV; p/Santi and Merceda F Sestini, Las Vegas, NV; ed/BS in Ed, Univ of NV Reno, 1959; MNS, Univ of ID Moscow, 1965; Postgrad Studies, Univ of No AZ 1969, Univ of NV Reno 1972, OR St Univ 1963, AZ St 1967; mil/USAR, 1959-65; pa/Biol Tchr, Rancho HS, 1963-75; Biol Tchr 1976-, Sci Chm 1976-81, Bonanza HS; Nat Sci Tchrs Assn, St Mbrship Chm 1968-70; Nat Assn Biol Tchrs; Am Microbiol Soc; Am Inst of Biol Scis; Nat Sci Supvrs Assn, Nat Assn of Taxidermists; Book Reviewer, *American Biology Teacher*, 1970-80; r/Rom Cath; hon/Pubs, *National Science Teacher* 1981, *Spotlight on Education*, Var Articles; Rotary Clb Intl Hon Tchr, 1965; NABT Outstg Biol Tchr, 1970; NABT Outstg Biol Tchr,

Reg VIII, 1970; NSTA-STAR Awds, 1977, 1980; NSTA-OHAUS Awd, 1980; Pres Awd for Excell in Sci Tchg, NV St Winner, 1983; Excell in Ed Awd, NV St Dept of Ed, 1983; W/W W.

SEWER, PAULINE LUCIA oc/Instructor of Education; b/Jun 22, 1921; h/76B Estate La Valle, Saint Croix, United States Virgin Islands 00820; m/Myron; p/Jesse Ewing and Evelyn M Watley (dec); ed/BA in Elem Ed, Col of the Virgin Isls, 1972; MA, Early Childhood, Univ of CT, 1973; Cand for PhD in Ed, Univ of CT Storrs, 1982-83; pa/Instr in Ed and Supvr of Student Tchrs, Col of the Virgin Isls, 1973-81; Resource Person for Tchr Trainee Prog, 1974-75; Panelist and Thesis Presenter, Intl Ednl Conf at Univ of MA, 1981; US Dept of St Nat Fgn Policy Conf for Ldrs in Tchr Ed, 1981; Phi Delta Kappa; Pi Lambda Theta; World Ed F'ship of CT; Nat Coun of Negro Wom; AAUW; Assn of Tchr Edrs; BPW Clb of Christiansted; Former Ednl Conslt to Arawak Prog; Gov's Appointee to Govt Employees Ser Comm; Adv Bd, Panelist and Grp Ldr of "Emancipation a Second Look," A Cultural Heritage and Hist Study of Virgin Islanders, Bur of Libs; cp/ NAACP; r/Moravian; hon/Dr Barnett Frank Awd for Highest Grade Point Average for a Wom; Dr Barnett Frank Awd for Excell in Field of Study, Col of the Virgin Isls; Mem of Pres's Clb for 4 Yrs; BA, cum laude, Col of Virgin Isls, 1972; MA w Hons, Univ of CT, 1973; Morris de Castro F'ship for Doct Study, Govt of US Virgin Isls, 1978; First Fac of the Yr Awd, Col of Virgin Isls, 1974-75; BPW Clb of Christiansted Wom of the Yr, 1975; W/W S and SW; Personalities of S.

SHACHTMAN, TOM oc/Writer, Television Producer; b/Feb 15, 1942; h/ 12 West Tenth Street, New York, NY 10011; ba/Same; m/Harriet Shelare; c/ Noah Max, Daniel Shelare; ed/BS, Tufts Univ, 1963; MFA, Carnegie-Mellon, 1966; pa/Writer, CBS News, 1966-69; Asst Chief, TV Div, Nat Geographic Soc, 1969-70; Free-Lance Writer and TV Prodr, 1970-; Current Lectr in Film and TV, NY Univ; Writers Guild of Am, E; Authors Guild; hon/Pubs, *The Day America Crashed* 1979, *Edith and Woodrow* 1981, *The Phony War* 1982, *Decade of Shocks* 1983, *Growing Up Masai* 1981, *The Birdman of St Petersburg* 1982; Shubert Fellow in Playwriting, 1965; Golden Gate Awd, SF Film Fest, 1972; Gold Prizes, Atlanta and Virgin Isls Fests, 1972-75; 2 Gold, 1 Silver, NY Intl Fest, 1972-75; NY Area Emmy Awd, 1976; Num Other Awds for Films and TV Progs; Men of Achmt.

SHAFFER, BERNARD W oc/Mechanical and Aerospace Engineer, Educator; b/Aug 7, 1924; h/18 Bayside Drive, Great Neck, NY 11023; ba/Brooklyn, NY; m/Florence; c/Janet Ilene, Roberta Franceen; ed/PhD in Applied Math, Brown Univ, 1950; MSME, Case Inst of Technol, 1947; BME, Col of City of NY, 1944; mil/AF; pa/Prof, Mech and Aerospace Engrg, Polytechnic Inst of NY, 1973; Prof of Mech Engrg 1958-73, Assoc Prof 1953-58, Asst Prof 1950-53, Proj Dir of Res Div 1950-73, NY Univ; Res Assoc in Grad Div of Applied Math, and Engrg Instr, Brown Univ, 1947-50; Spec Lectr in Applied Mechs, Evening Session, Case Inst of Technol, 1946-47;

Aeronautical Res Scist, Flight Propulsion Res Lab, Nat Adv Com for Aeronautics, 1944-47; Mem of Adv Coun, Acad of Aeronautics; Appt'd by Nat Res Coun Assem of Math and Phy Scis to Com on Recommendations for AUS Basic Sci Res; Edit Adv Bd, *International Journal of Mechanical Sciences*; Reviewer: Applied Mechs Reviews, ASME, NSF, Nat Res Coun-Nat Acad of Scis; hon/ Author, Num Pubs; Recip, Richards Meml Awd, ASME, 1968; Elected to Tau Beta Pi, Pi Tau Sigma, Sigma Xi; ASME, Fellow; AIAA, Assoc Fellow; World W/ W in Sci from Antiquity to the Present; W/W Engrg; Am Men of Sci; W/W E; W/W Aviation and Aerospace; Intl Dir of Engrg Anal; Intl W/W Engrg.

SHAFFER, GARY LEE oc/Associate Professor of Education; b/Oct 24, 1942; h/83 Sharon Street, Harrisonburg, VA 22801; ba/Harrisonburg, VA; m/Donna Faye Daniels; c/Cheryl Lee, Leslie Faye; p/Harry L and Stella K Shaffer (dec); ed/EdD 1975, MS 1973, Univ of So MS; BS, Murray St Univ, 1964; pa/Assoc Prof of Ed, James Madison Univ, 1975-; Adj Fac, Univ of So MS, 1972-75; Public Sch Tchr, Middletown, OH, Sch Sys 1968-72, Montgomery Co, OH, Sch Sys 1964-68; Pres, Shenandoah Val Rdg Coun, 1981-82; Bd of Dirs, VA St Rdg Assn, 1981-82; Social Action Comm Chp, Col Rdg Assn, 1979-81; Delta Kappa; IRA; Col Rdg Assn; VA St Rdg Assn; VA Col Rdg Edrs; cp/Bd, Harrisonburg Kiwanis Clb, 1983-84; Kiwanis Intl; r/Meth; hon/Pubs, "Phonics: Yes or No?" 1984, "Commercial Television: Its Influence on Reading" 1983, "Commerical Television: Motivator for Reading Instruction" 1980, *Statewide Staff Development in Beginning Reading Competency: Final Report* 1979, "Preservice Teachers' Perceptions of Reading Instruction" 1978, Others.

SHAFFER, HOWARD JEFFREY oc/ Clinical Psychologist; b/Sep 1, 1948; h/ 171 Summer Street, Andover, MA 01810; ba/Boston, MA; m/Linda Marie; c/David Andrew; p/Milton and Ruth Shaffer, Medford, MA; ed/BA, Psych, Univ of NH, 1970; MS 1972, PhD 1974, Psych, Univ of Miami, FL; pa/Adv Bd and Fac, NEn Comprehensive Ser Inst, 1983-; Asst Prof of Psych in Dept of Psychi, Harvard Med Sch at Cambridge Hosp, 1982-; Fac, MA Psychol Ctr, 1980-; Chief Psychol, N Charles Inst for the Addictions, 1982-; Coor of Psychi Ed, Dept of Psychi, Harvard Med Sch at Cambridge Hosp, 1982-; Coun on Marijuana and Hlth, Nat Org for the Reform of Marijuana Laws, 1981-; Num Previous Positions; Am Acad of Polit and Social Scis, 1975-77; Am Psychol Assn, 1976-; AAAS, 1976-; Soc of Psychols in Addictive Behaviors, 1981-; hon/Pubs, "The Use of Contingency Contracts to Alter Self-Cutting in a Chronic Psychiatric Patient" 1983, "A Perspective for the Treatment of the Addictions" 1983, "How Did Addictive Behavior Become the Object of Clinical Assessment?" 1982, "Addiction Paradigms II: Theory, Research, and Practice" 1979, Others; Guest Editor, Spec Issue, *Advances in Alcohol and Substance Abuse*, 1983; *Classic Contributions in the Addictions* Selected as an Alternate Main Selection, Behavioral Sci Book Clb, Psychotherapy and Social Sci Book Ser, 1981; Phi Kappa Phi, Univ of Miami,

1974; H A Carroll Awd, Univ of NH, Dept of Psych, 1970; Univ of NH Undergrad Conf for Psychol Res, First Place, 1969; Psi Chi, 1968; W/W E; W/ W Frontier Sci and Technol.

SHAFI, MUHAMMAD IQBAL oc/ Associate Professor; b/Aug 23, 1943; h/ 525-Randolph North, Holly Springs, MS 38635; ba/Holly Springs, MS; m/ Fahmida I; c/Nadee I; p/Mohammad Shafi, Karachi, Pakistan; Ashrafunnisa Begum (dec); ed/BSc w Hons; MS; PhD; pa/Assoc Prof, Biol, Rust Col, 1980-; Postdoct Asst, Lectr, Univ of New Brunswick, Canada, 1978-79; Ecologist/ Biologist, Andre Marsan & Assocs and Dimension Envir Ltd, Montreal, Canada; Tissue Culture Assn, 1984-; Canadian Botanical Assn; Am Ecological Soc; Brit Ecological Soc, 1968-73; Quebec Assn of Biologists, 1974-76; Canadian Land Reclamation Soc, 1978-79; r/Islam; hon/Author, 7 Papers in Profl Jours, 1 Thesis and 5 Internal Reports for Govt Agys and Pvt Firms; Ontario Govt F'ship, 1969-70; Nat Res Coun of Canada Postdoct Asst'ship, 1978-79; Univ of Toronto Res Asst'ship, 1967-72; W/W Frontiers of Sci and Technol.

SHAH, SHIRISH K oc/Chairperson of Computer Systems and Engineering Technologies Department, Prof of Science; b/May 24, 1942; h/5605 Purlington Way, Baltimore, MD 21212; ba/ Baltimore, MD; m/Kathleen Long; c/ Lawrence; p/Kalyanbhai and Sushilaben Shah, Ahmedabad, India; ed/BS in Chem and Physics, St Xavier's Col, Gujarat Univ, 1962; PhD in Phy Chem, Univ of DE, 1968; Addit Grad Studies, Cornell Univ, Univ of MN, Johns Hopkins Univ; mil/8 Wks of Basic Tng, Bhosle Mil Sch, Nasik, India; pa/Asst Prof, Wash Col, 1967-68; Res Fellow, Univ of DE, 1964-67; Dir of Quality Control, Vita Foods, 1968-74; Asst Prof, Assoc Prof, Admr of Marine Sci, Food Sci and Voc Progs, Chp of Div of Tech Studies, Chesapeake Col, 1968-76; Prof of Sci, Coor of Acad Prog Devel, Chair of Tech Studies, Commun Col of Balto, 1976-; Com of Am Lung Assn of MD, 1971-80; Adv Com for Back River Waste Water Treatment Plant, 1980-; Sigma Xi; AVA; ATEA; MACJC; Basic Ed Coun; MACJC, VP 1977-78, Pres 1978-; r/Jain and Cath; hon/Pubs, "Studies in the Radiation and Photchemistry of Aqueous P-nitrosedimethyl Aniline" 1968, "A Model Food Science Technician Program" 1975, "Creation of Occupational Program Model in the Rural Community College," "A Native Returns to India" 1968, "India Today" 1975; Selected Outstg Edr, 1972; Pres of MD Assn of Commun and Jr Cols, 1978-; Editor, MACJC Newsletter, 1977-79; Outstg Edr at CCB Harbor Campus, 1977; CCB Nom for ACE F'ship, 1978; CCB Nom for Outstg Edr, Chem Mfg Assn, 1981; W/W E.

SHAHRYAR, ISHAQ M oc/Executive; b/Jan 10, 1936; h/1132 Tellem Drive, Pacific Palisades, CA 90272; ba/ Hawthorne, CA; p/Ahmad Ali and Zahra Shahryar (dec); ed/BS in Phy Chem, MA in Polit Sci, Univ of CA Santa Barbara; pa/Fdr, Pres, Solec Intl Inc, 1976-; Former Mem, 3-Man Team which Developed First Low Cost Solar Cell for Terrestrial Use, Spectrolab; Joined Halex Inc as Res Scist, 1971;

Joined Centralab as Sr Res Engr, 1968; From Engr to Prodn Supt, Continental Device Corp (Later Teledyne Semiconductor), 1961-66; Counsel to Chancellor, Univ of CA, 1981-; cp/Repub; r/ Moslem; hon/Inventor, Low Cost Solar Cell, 1972; Patentee, Photovoltaics Tech, 1977; W/W CA; W/W Frontier Sci and Technol.

SHAMSID-DEEN, ABDUR-RAHIM oc/Leader of Muslim Community (Imam); b/Feb 4, 1937; h/113 West Desert Drive, Phoenix, AZ 85041; ba/ Phoenix, AZ; m/Ummil-Kheer; c/Dirul, Darian, Mahasin, Jameelah, Malikah, Khadijah; p/Benjamin and Minnie Smith (dec); ed/BA in Rel and Islamic Studies, King Abdel-Aziz Univ, Jeddah, Saudi Arabia; Student of Law, La Salle Univ; Student of Music, Univ of Heildelberg, W Germany; Student of Public Relats, Mktg and Advtg, Embassy Enterprises; BA in Psych, IN St Sch of Metaphysics; Student of Lang, CO Col; mil/Army; pa/ Dir, Advtg and Public Relats, *Denver Blade Newspaper*, 1962-65; VP and Dir, Advtg and Public Relats, *Eastsider Magazine*, 1965-68; Chm of the Bd and Pres, S&S Enterprises, Afro Enterprises, *Afro Magazine*, Afro Advtg and Conslts, *Denver Chronicle* Newspaper, *Colorado Chronicle* Newspaper, *Phoenix Chronicle* Newspaper, *Black Gold Magazine*, 1967-73; Exec Dir, Fair Housing Ctr, Phoenix, 1979; Chaplain, AZ Dept of Corrections, 1976-84; Imam, Ldr of Phoenix's Muslim Commun; World Coun of Imams, 1977-84; Am Muslim Mission, 1972-84; Sales and Mktg Execs Intl, 1962-72; Nat Newspaper Publishers Assn, 1965-72; Denver Advtg Clb, 1962-72; Nat Fdn of Advertisers, 1962-72; Phoenix Islamic Mosque and Inst Proj, 1978-84; cp/Phoenix Union HS Dist Citizens Adv Coun; Denver C of C, 1962-72; r/Al-Islam; hon/Featured in *Black History and Achievement in America*, 1982; Chosen as One of AZ's Most Influential Blacks, 1982, 1983; Rel Awd of the Yr, 1977; Humanitarian Awd of the Yr, 1977; Police Apprec Awd and Commun Awd, 1972.

SHAND, KANDI oc/Writer, Entrepreneur; b/Nov 11, 1946; h/Route 2, Box 165, Ruckersville, VA 22968; ba/Same; m/Raymond Martin Stirling; c/Melissa, Trevor, Terry, Tammy; p/Mr and Mrs William Shand, La Habra, CA; ed/BA 1968, MBA 1972, Univ of CA LA; Tchg Credentials, Sec'dy 1970, Elem 1973; pa/ Tchr, HS, Jr High and Elem Sch; Owned, Bear Mt Furniture and Laguna Devel Co, Laguna, CA; Owned Target Pubs and Target Sales; Owner and Dist'd Breeder of Chinese Shar-Pei (Joss Kennels), and Currently on Bd of Dirs for Dace Pub'g, Puppy Patch Pet Shops, T T Pet Supplies, Shenandoah Prods, Bartholomew Candies; Chinese Shar-Pei Clb; Am Quarter Horse Assn; Alpha Phi Alumni Clb; cp/Green Co Wom's Clb; Active Supporter of 4-H Clbs; hon/Pubs, *Secrets to Success, Armando's Bartending Course, How to Start a Second Income and Make It Grow, Teach Your Child to Ski, Raise Your Child's IQ*, Var Articles; Grad, cum laude, Univ of CA LA; Wom of the Yr in Laguna Bch, 197; 4-H Supporter Awd, 1980, 1981.

SHANNON, ARRETTA oc/Assistant Chemical and Training Officer; b/Mar 9, 1958; h/7103 Flora Street, Kansas City, MO; ba/APO, NY; p/Shelby Shannon, Kansas City, MO; Loraine Shannon (dec); ed/BA in Polit Sci, Lincoln Univ, 1980; mil/ROTC, Lincoln Univ, 4 Yrs; Chem Sch, Ft McClellan, AL, 1980; Advance Camp, Ft Riley, KS; pa/7th Signal Brigade Asst Chem and Tng Ofcr, 1980-; Dpty Tng Standard Ofcr, 1981; Nurses Attendant, Lincoln Univ, Student Infirmary, 1976-78; Asst Libn, Page Lib, 1979-80; Nurses Attendant, Still Hosp, 1978-79; Student Govt Assn; Alpha Kappa Alpha Sorority, Treas 1979; Alpha Kappa Alpha, Correspondence Secy 1978, Wom's Dormitory Pres 1979, Wom's Dormitory Treas 1978; ROTC Color Guard, Cadet Sgt First Class, Flag Carrier 1979, Disciplinary Com Bd Mem 1978-79, Traffic Com Bd Mem 1978-79; Alpha Kappa Alpha Sorority Internship, Leggs Corp, Winston Salem, 1979; Alpha Kappa Alpha Ldrship Prog, Spencer, IN, 1978; r/Bapt; hon/Neophythe Awd, AKA Scholastic Achmt; AUS Tng, Army Letter of Apprec 1983, Mil Justice 1980; Spec Ct Martial Bd Mem, 1983; Dean's List, W/W Among Col Students, 1978-80.

SHAPIRO, CAROL SADIE oc/Plastic Surgeon; b/Sep 24, 1939; h/7822 Gingerbread Lane, Fairfax Station, VA 22039; ba/Woodbridge, VA; m/Donald E Morgan; c/Leslie M Morgan, Donald E Morgan Jr; p/Dr Charlotte Shapiro, Pittsburgh, PA; ed/BS, Univ of Pgh, 1961; MD, Med Col of PA, 1965; Plastic and Reconstructive Surg, Georgetown Univ Hosp, 1972; Clin Instr, Georgetown Univ, 1972-; pa/Solo Pract in Plastic and Reconstructive Surg, 1972-; Pres, Prince Wm Co Med Soc, 1980-81; Pres, Potomac Hosp Med Staff, 1980-82; Pres, Med Coun of No VA, 1981; r/Jewish; hon/W/W Am Wom.

SHAPIRO, IRWIN I oc/Center Director; b/Oct 10, 1929; h/17 Lantern Lane, Lexington, MA 02173; ba/Cambridge, MA; m/Marian Helen Kaplun; c/Steven, Nancy; p/Samuel and Esther Feinberg Shapiro (dec); ed/AB, Cornell Univ, 1950; AM 1951, PhD 1955, Harvard Univ; pa/Dir, Harvard-Smithsonian Ctr for Astrophysics, 1983-; Paine Prof of Practical Astronomy and Prof of Physics, Harvard Univ, 1982-; Sr Scist, Smithsonian Astrophysical Observatory, 1982-; Schlumberger Prof, MIT, 1980-; Phillips Visitor, Haverford Col, 1978; Morris Loeb Lectr on Physics, Harvard Univ, 1975; Sherman Fairchild Dist'd Scholar, CA Inst of Technol, 1974; Other Previous Positions; AAAS, Fellow; Am Astronom Soc; Am Geophy Union, Fellow; Am Phy Soc, Fellow; Intl Astronom Union; hon/Pubs, *Prediction of Ballistic Missile Trajectories from Radar Observations* 1958, "Limits on Arcsecond-Scale Fluctuations in the Cosmic Microwave Background" 1984, "Use of Space Techniques for Geodesy" 1983, "VLBI Observations of the Gravitational-Lens Images of Q0957+561" 1984, Num Others; Dannie Heineman Awd, Am Astronom Soc, 1983; NY Acad of Scis Awd in Phy and Math Scis, 1982; John Simon Guggenheim F'ship, 1982; Benjamin Apthorp Gould Prize of the Nat Acad of Scis, 1979; Other Hons; W/W Am; W/W E.

SHAPIRO, LINDSAY STAMM oc/ Architectural Curator, Professor, Writer; b/Nov 27, 1947; h/560 Riverside Drive, New York, NY 10027; m/David; p/Eugene and Eleanor Stamm, Rye, NY; ed/Att'd, Bryn Mawr Col 1965-66, Cooper Union Dept of Arch 1971-73; BA, Barnard Col, 1970; MArch, Columbia Univ Grad Sch of Arch and Planning; pa/Vis'g Lectr, Cooper Union Sch of Arch, 1982-; Dir of Exhbns, Inst for Arch and Urban Studies, 1981-83; Mng Editor, *Oppositions Books*, IAUS, 1979-81; Arch Conslt, McGraw-Hill Info Sys Co, 1977-79; Instr, Sch of Visual Arts, 1980-82; Curator, Inst for Art and Urban Resources, 1978-80; Rschr, Cooper-Hewitt Mus, 1978; Rschr, Arch Leag, 1977; Arch Designer, Peter Wilson Assocs, 1976-77; Other Previous Positions; Am Sect, Intl Soc of Art Critics, AICA, 1979-; Hon Mem, Soc of the Arts, Cooper-Hewitt Mus, 1979-; Fellow, Inst for Arch and Urban Studies, 1982-83; hon/Pubs, "On Interiority" 1981, "A Poetics of the Model: Eisenman's Doubt" 1981, "Vienna Moderne" 1979, "The Decorative Designs of Frank Lloyd Wright" 1978, Others; Barnard Sum Grant, 1969; Cooper Union Essay Prize, 1972; Kinne Sum Travelling F'ship, 1974; Ednl Facilities Labs Arch F'ship, 1979.

SHARMA, RAJENDRA M oc/Physician; b/Apr 29, 1949; h/319 North 8th Street, Vineland, NJ 08360; ba/Vineland, NJ; p/Devaki and Mulk R Sharma, New Delhi, India; ed/Pre-Med, 1968; MD, 1972; Diplomate, Am Col of Phys, 1978; pa/Resident in Med, Downstate Bklyn VA Hosp; Tchg Assoc, Rutgers Sch of Med at Cooper Med Ctr, 1983; Conslt in Nephrology and Med, Newcomb Hosp, Bridgton Hosp, Millville Hosp, 1980; Fellow and Instr in Med, Albany Med Col, 1975-77; Asst Prof of Med, Albany Med Col, 1977-80; AMA; Am Col of Phys; hon/Dir of Med Specs.

SHARMA, RAVINDRA NATH oc/ Head Librarian; b/Oct 22, 1944; h/147 Ridgewood Drive, Freedom, PA 15042; ba/Monaca, PA; m/Mithlesh; c/Nalini, Mohini; p/Baikunth Nat, Bambay, India; Gyan Devi (dec); ed/PhD, St Univ of NY Buffalo, 1982; MLS, N TX St Univ, 1970; MA in Hist 1966, BA w Hons in Hist 1963, Univ of Delhi; pa/Free-Lance Journalist, 1963; Reporter and Sports Correspondent, *The Canadian India Times*, 1967-68; Asst Libn, Col of the Ozarks, 1970-71; Reference Libn, Colgate Univ, 1971-81; Hd Libn, PA St Univ, Beaver Campus, 1981-; Pres, Kiddi Korner Child Devel Ctr, 1983-84; Treas, Asian/ Pacific Ams Lib Assn, 1982-84; Area Chm for So Asia, Intl Round Table of Am Lib Assn, 1983-; r/Hinduism; hon/ Pubs, *Indian Librarianship: Perspectives and Prospects* 1981, "India, Academic Libraries in" 1983, "Indian Library Association" 1983, "ALA at Philadelphia: A Report" 1982, "Library Instruction: An Opinion" 1982, Others; Del to Gen Ed Conf, PA St, 1982; W/W Lib and Info Sers; W/ W E.

SHARP, ANNE C oc/Artist, Painter, Art Teacher; b/Nov 1, 1943; h/20 Waterside Plaza, New York, NY 10010; ba/Same; p/Elmer Sharp, Eatontown, NJ; Ethel Hunter Sharp (dec); ed/MFA, Bklyn Col, 1973; BFA, Pratt Inst, 1965; pa/Art Tchr, Sch of Visual Arts 1978-; St Univ of NY Purchase 1983, Pratt Manhattan Ctr 1982-, NY Univ 1978; Wom's Caucus for Art; Artist's Equity Assn of Am; Wom in the Arts, Bd of

Dirs 1984; AAUW; Foun for the Commun of Artists; Am Film Inst; r/Epis; hon/Solo Art Shows: Eatontown Hist Mus 1980, "Art in a Public Space-Windows at Waterside" 1979, Contemp Gallery 1975, Pace Editions 1974, Others; Artpk, Lewiston, NY, Artist-in-Residence Grant, 1980; NY Foun for the Arts Artists Roster, 1983; VA Ctr for the Arts, Sweet Briar, Artist-in-Residence Grant, 1974; Tchg F'ship, Bklyn Col, 1972; W/W Am; W/ W Am Art.

SHARP, GLADYS MARIE oc/Writer; b/Mar 29, 1920; h/7520 Sprague, Anderson, IN 46013; ba/Anderson, IN; m/ Earl L; c/Edward Earl; p/James Edward Sexton, Ft Smith, AR; ed/Grad, Anderson HS, 1940; Att'd, Anderson Col; pa/Activs Dir, Nurse-Attendant, 16 Yrs (Wk'd through Nurses Registry), St John's Hosp, Commun Hosp, Nsg Homes, and Home Care of Patients; IPA; ABPW; Local Poetry and Writers Grps; SSF; cp/OES; Quest, Ldr; r/Unity; hon/Pubs, *The Undivided God, Chained to a Dream, The Two Angels-Twangela and Tarmela,* "Trust in a Dream,""Don't Say My Name," Var Poetry, Songs and Articles.

SHARP, SHARON BARTS oc/Special Assistant to the Governor on Women; b/Oct 7, 1939; h/1306 West Cedar Lane, Arlington Heights, IL 60005; ba/Chicago, IL; m/Donald L; c/Laura Sue, Christopher Barts; p/Edwin and Gertrude Barts, Arlington Heights, IL; ed/ Att'd, Holy Cross Ctl Sch of Nsg, 1957-59; AAS, Journalism, Harper Col, 1975; pa/Spec Asst to Gov on Wom, 1979-; Govt and Polit Writer, 1974-78; Elected, Elk Grove Twp Clk, 1977-79; Editor, *Elk Grove Township News,* 1975-77; Editor, *Illinois Federation of Republican Women News, Views and Issues,* 1977-78; Wom in Mgmt; Exec Clb of Chgo; cp/ Hon Co-Chair, ERA IL; IL Displaced Homemaker Adv Bd; Dir, LifeSpan; LWV; Arlington Hgts Friends of the Lib; Altrusa; Chgo Area Public Affairs Grp; City Clb, Chgo; Adv Com, Harper Col Wom's Prog; Friends of Harper Col; Support Chgo; NWn Univ Wom's Commun Adv Com; CoChm, RepubCtl Com of Cook Co; Chm, Wom's Div, Repub Ctl Com of Cook Co; Chm, Repub Cook Co Search Com; Dir, IL Fdn of Repub Wom; Pres, Wom's Nat Repub Clb; IL Wom's Polit Caucus; Repub Wom's Task Force; 12th Congl Dist Wom's Repub Clb; Chm, Cook Co Repub Cand Com; Chm, Cook Co Repub Reorg Com; Cook Co Repub Exec Com; CoFdr, Repub Wom for ERA; hon/Phi Theta Kappa; 1978 Repub Nom, IL Secy of St's Ofc; First Wom to Ever Win a Maj Statewide Nomination; Subject of Harper Col Polit Sci Film, "Female Political Candidate"; Subject of Public TV Film, "The Political Woman"; Charlotte Danstrom Wom of Achmt Awd, NW Suburban Chapt, Wom in Mgmt; W/W Am Commun Cols; W/W Am Polit; W/W Am Wom.

SHAW, L JEANETTE oc/Financial Planner; b/Dec 3, 1942; h/4228 South 4900 West, Salt Lake City, UT 84120; ba/Salt Lake City, UT; p/Donald and Corinne Shaw, Nashville, TN; ed/BS, 1965; MS, 1979; pa/Financial Planner, Wall St W, 1981-; Gen Agt, E F Hutton Life, 1981-; Financial Planner, Financial Estate Planners (Self-Employed), 1979-; Exec Dir, UT Nurses Assn, 1978; Am

Assn of MBA Execs, 1979-; Intl Assn of Financial Planners, 1982; Fdr and Pres, Legacy Unltd, 1982; cp/Treas, Beta Sigma Alpha (Civic Sorority), 1967; r/ LDS; hon/Author, 4 Pubs in Field; Beta Gamma Sigma, 1979; Phi Kappa Phi, 1979; Nat Dean's List, 1979; W/W Am Wom; World W/W Wom; W/W W.

SHAW, LOIS HOGUE oc/Workshop Presenter, Painter, Exhibitor; b/Aug 6, 1897; h/309 West Texas Street, Sweetwater, TX 79556; ba/Same; c/Elmer Earl, Marjorie Shaw Duffin, Patsy Shaw Fritz, Bill Sloan; ed/BFA, Mary-Hardin Baylor, 1924; Att'd, Chgo Art Inst 1921, Art Students Leag 1922; Pvt Student of John Sloan, NY, 1927; pa/Tchr of Art, Mary-Hardin Baylor 1920, 1921, 1922, McMurry Col 1924, 1925, 1926, ACC Col; Has Been Pres of Art Clbs; Mem, Stables Gallery, 1959; r/Presb; hon/Lois Hogue Shaw Trophy Presented to Adv'd Sr Art Student Each Yr; Many One-Man Shows; W/W Am Art.

SHAW, MARTIN ANDREW oc/Clinical and Clinical Child Psychologist; b/ Jan 27, 1944; h/160 South Middle Neck Road, Great Neck, NY 11021; ba/New York, NY; m/Dorothy K; c/Anatole B; ed/BS, NY Univ, 1966; MA, Dalhousie Univ, 1972; PhD, Univ of WI, 1977; Cert in Analytic Psychotherapy, Adv'd Inst for Analytic Psychotherapy, 1982; pa/ Art Tchr, NYC Schs, 1966-69; Art Therapist, Kingsbridge VA Hosp, 1969-71; Grad Tchg Asst, Supvr of Tchr Trainees, Dalhousie Univ, 1971-72; Psychometrician, Psychotherapist, NYC Bd of Ed, 1977-80; Staff Therapist, Staff Psychol, Adv'd Ctr for Psychotherapy, 1977-82; Clin/Child Psychol, Hlth Ins Plan, Mtl Hlth Ser, 1980-; Pvt Pract, Clin and Clin Child Psych, NYC and Great Neck, 1981-; Trustee, Signal Hill Ed Ctr Inc; Am Psychol Assn; NY St Psychol Assn; NY Soc of Clin Psychols; AAAS; hon/Contbr of Papers to Profl Jours and Confs in Psych; NY Univ Fdrs Day Awd, 1966; VA Commend, 1969; Pi Lambda Theta, Univ of WI Madison, 1977; W/W E; Am Psychol Assn Dir.

SHAW, STAFFORD EDGAR oc/ Yardmaster, Foreman; b/Apr 16, 1934; h/33103 35th Avenue, Southwest, Federal Way, WA 98023; ba/Tacoma, WA; m/Carolyn Sue Cox; c/Stafford Edgar Jr, Lacie Ann, Erin Cristene Ward, Rhonda Jean; p/Lacy Newton (dec) and Margaret Sizemore Shaw, Valdosta, CA; ed/Cook HS; mil/Army, 1952-56; pa/Trainman, NP Railway, 1956-66; Machinist, AC Finishing Co, 1966-68; Switchman, Foreman, Yardmaster, Tacoma Beltline, 1968-; UTU, Gen Chm 1972-74; Local 21 ILWU, 1976-77; Local 556 UTU; Formed, Indep Yardmasters of Tacoma, 1980, Gen Secy-Treas 1980-82; r/Bapt; hon/W/W W.

SHAW, SUSAN JEAN oc/Communications Specialist; b/Sep 30, 1943; h/5 Bryant Crescent 2K, White Plains, NY 10605; ba/Nyack, NY; c/Scott Lewis Einziger, Tamra Eileen Einziger; p/Mr Noah Shaw, Ft Lauderdale, FL; ed/Bach of Music Ed, Syracuse Univ, 1965; Att'd, Hunter Col 1965-66, Tchrs' Col of Columbia Univ 1966-69; Att'g, Alliance Theol Sem 1980-; pa/Music Ed Tchr, Westchester Co, NY, Public and Pvt Schs, 1966-73; Placement Cnslr, Fanning Pers, 1974-75; Pres, Communiscope Inc, 1976-77; Exec Dir, Dental

Hlth Sers, 1977-79; Free-Lance Conslt and Writer, Shaw Enterprizes Inc, 1979-81; Communs Spec, World Relief Corp, 1981-; Bryant Gardens Corp, Bd of Trustees, Secy 1981; Profl Bus Wom's Assn; Profl Christian Wom's Assn; Pi Lambda Theta; Sigma Alpha Iota; Wom in Min; cp/Christian Singles F'ship; r/ Hebrew/Christian; hon/Pub'd in *Christian Herald* 1981, *Touching Magazine* 1981, *The Alliance Witness* 1981, 1982, 1983, *Business Leader* 1976; Grad, cum laude, Syracuse Univ, 1965; Alliance Theol Sem S'ship, 1980; Ridgeway Alliance Ch S'ship, 1980; Thoman A Nelson S'ship, 1981; W/W Am Wom.

SHAW, WILLIAM JAMES oc/Assistant Professor of Psychiatry and Behavioral Science, Clinical Assistant Professor of Pediatrics; b/Mar 11, 1947; h/1506 Northwest 88th, Oklahoma City, OK 73114; ba/Oklahoma City, OK; m/Dr Catherine Jarvis; p/Mrs William J Shaw, Belleville, NJ; ed/BA, Iona Col, 1968; MA, Fairfield Univ, 1975; PsyD, Baylor Univ, 1976; pa/Asst Prof of Psychi and Behavioral Scis, Clin Asst Prof of Pediatrics, Univ of OK Hlth Scis Ctr, 1981-; Chief Psychol, OK Dept of Corrections, 1978-81; Adj Assoc in Crim Justice, OK City Univ, 1980-81; Adj Clin Instr, Psychi and Behavioral Scis, Univ of OK Hlth Scis Ctr, 1979-81; Adj Asst Prof of Ed, Univ of OK, 1977-78; Pvt Pract in Clin Psych, 1976-81; Other Previous Positions; OK St Bd of Examrs of Psychols, 1979-82, Chm 1981-82; OK Psychol Assn, Bd of Dirs 1977-79, Treas 1979-81, Chair, Mbrship Com 1977-79, Pubs Com 1976-78, Legis Com 1978-80; Chair, Pubs Com, SWn Psychol Assn, 1977-79, Editor of *New Bulletin* 1977-79; Am Psychol Assn; OK Mtl Hlth Assn; Soc of Behavioral Med; Am Acad of Behavioral Med; Soc of Adolescent Med; Pres, Grad Student Org, Baylor Univ, Dept of Psych, 1974-75; r/Cath; hon/Pubs, "Crime and Delinquency," "Sharing Life's Meaning: Finding Fulfillment in the Hospice,""Relaxation Treatment of Foot-fetish in an 8 Year Old Boy" 1979, "Psychothanatology and the Human Existence" 1977,"Toilet Training: What Do Parents Know, Anyway?" 1976, "The Behavioral Counselor's Approach to School Phobia" 1975; Cert of Apprec, Am Trial Lwyrs Assn, 1981; Diplomate, Am Acad of Behavioral Med, 1981; Dist'd Public Ser Awd, Div 18, Am Psychol Assn, 1979; Nat Register of Hlth Ser Providers in Psych; W/W S and SW.

SHEA, CHARLENE RIOPELLE oc/ Motivational Speaker and Consultant; b/Sep 3, 1934; h/121 Allied Street, Manchester, NH 03103; ba/Manchester, NH; m/Thomas; c/Valarie, Thomas, Gwen; p/George and Ruth Riopelle (dec); ed/BS, Ed and Psych; pa/First Grade Tchr in Germany, Okinawa, El Paso (TX), Highland (NJ), 14 Yrs; Dir of Sales Tng, Mary Kay Cosmetics, 7 Yrs; Motivational Spkr and Conslt, 3 Yrs; Pres, Charlene Shea Inc, a Motivational Spkr/Conslt Firm; Nat Spkrs Assn; IPA; Am Soc of Tnrs and Developers; cp/Dir, Bd of YWCA, Manchester; hon/Author, 4 Cassette Album, "Becoming Your Own Best Friend," 1982; NH Wom in Bus Advocate, Small Bus Adm, 1982; W/W Am Wom.

SHEALY, R CLAYTON oc/Clinical

Psychologist; b/Jan 22, 1952; h/1712 11th Place South, Birmingham, AL 35205; ba/Birmingham, AL; p/Mr and Mrs Ralph C Shealy, Newberry, SC; ed/BS, Univ of SC, 1974; MA 1977, PhD 1979, Univ of So MS; pa/Clin Psychol, Riverbend Ctr for Mtl Hlth, 1979-80; Asst Prof of Clin Psych, Depts of Psychi and Psych, Univ of AL B'ham, 1980-82; Pvt Pract of Clin Psych, 1982-; Am Psychol Assn; Div of Psychotherapy; SEn Psychol Assn; AL Psychol Assn; Assn of Lic'd Psychols in AL; Soc for Personality Assessmt; r/Luth; hon/Pubs, "Sleep Onset Insomnia" 1900, "The Effectiveness of Various Treatment Techniques on Different Degrees and Durations of Sleep Onset Insomnia" 1979; W/W S and SW; Personalities of S.

SHEDD, CARRIE McDONALD oc/Educator, Office Manager, Secretary, Writer, Poet; b/Nov 15, 1932; h/PO 516, Tuskegee Institute, AL 36088; ba/Tuskegee Institute, AL; m/Charles C; c/Gwendolyn T Dean, Vivian F Saunders; p/Oscar L (dec) and C B Howell McDonald, Chattanooga, TN; ed/BS w High Hons in Elem Ed, 1954; MS, Ed Adm and Supvn, 1961; PhD Student, OH St, 1970-71; Att'd, Newark St 1964, George Peabody 1965, Hampton Jr Col 1962-63; Cert, LCB McCray Sch of Bus, 1949; IBM Short Courses, 1950, 1960; Child Care, J A Andrew Hosp, 1949; Behavior Objective Writing, 1969; pa/Tchr, K-14, AL, NJ, FL, TN, 1954-59, 1963-67, 1969-70, 1972-76; Lab Sch Tchr, AL, 1964-67; Asst Coor, Tchr Ed, TICEP-OEO, 27 Ctrs, 8 Cts, AL, 1966; Tchr, French Conversation/Skits, Exp, Grades 2-6, AL, 1957-58; Col Reg Wk, AL, Sums 1956-59; Col Asst Reg and Registrar, AL, FL, 1959-63; Instr/Supvr of Tchrs, FL, OH, 1961-63, 1971-72; Col Co-op Ed Coor, AL, 1979-80; Ed Adm Secy, Dept of Bus, Tuskegee Inst, 1977-79, 1980-; Other Positions; Wom's Intl Conf, Recorder 1980; TI Indust/Cluster Recorder, 1980-82; Bus Mgmt Conf Publicity-Prog, 1983; HS 1950 Reunion Correponding Secy, 1980; Coalition of Wom, Recording Secy 1982; CEA, 1979-80; Soc for Profs of Ed; NAWDC; APGA; AAUP; AAUW; NCAWE; cp/SE Reg 50th Anniv Vice Chair, 1982; Daughs of Isis; VA Med Ctr Vol, 1981-; John Dewey Soc, 1972-74; ACLU, 1970-74; NAACP; r/AME; hon/Pubs, "Help Your Child How to Learn" 1973, "A Poetic Leisure" 1982, "Women in Business: A Look to the Future" 1981, "Our Schools: Us Is Askin' and We Be Beggin', Too!" (Poem), "Unwinding with---Poetry for Those Inclined to Unravel" 1983, "Women in Academe: Advancing and Enhancing a Brave New World" 1983, "Nostalgia of Rural Community Living" 1983, Others; Kappa Delta Phi, 1967; Pi Lambda Theta, 1971; 10 Yr Ser Awd, Girl Scouts, USA, 1968; AFS Hostess, Barbados, SA Students, NAACP Awd, 1981; W/W Among Students in Am Cols and Univs; W/W Am Wom; Intl Register of Profiles; Intl W/W Intells.

SHEEHAN, ROBERT JAMES II oc/Management and Economic Consultant; b/May 13, 1937; h/1606 Wrightson Drive, McLean, VA 22101; ba/Same; m/Marie Elizabeth Yoskovich; c/Stephanie Ann, Robert James III; p/Regis James and Helen Lillian Sheehan, Pittsburgh,

PA; ed/AB in Ec 1967, MA in Ec 1970, Postgrad Wk, Univ of Pgh; pa/VP, Regis J Sheehan & Assocs, 1983-; Staff VP, Nat Assn of Homebldrs, 1973-83; Dir of Rehab, Nat Assn of Homebldrs, 1967-73; Nat Assn of Profl Conslts; Nat Economists Clb; Nat Assn of Bus Economists and Adm Mgmt Soc; cp/Pres, Kent Gardens Elem PTA, 1975-77; Pres, Longfellow Intermediate PTA, 1977-79; Pres, Kent Gardens Rec Clb, 1978-81; Swimming Refereee, No VA Swimming Leag 1978-, Fairfax Co HS Leag 1982-; r/Rom Cath; hon/Author, Num Articles in Var Profl Jours, 1974-; Monthly Contbr to *Economic News Notes*, 1973-83; W/W E.

SHEEHE, LILLIAN CAROLYN oc/Painter; b/Oct 16, 1915; ed/BS, Art, IN Univ; Ceramics and Sculpture w Sheldone Grumbling; Majolica w Hugh Geise; Painting and Sculpture w George Ream; pa/Wk: "Court of Gabrielle" (Serigraph), "Trees at Christmastime in California" (Serigraph), 130 Glass-Fired Paintings and Sagged Bottle Collection; Num Other Art Wks; Area Art Coun Chm, 1975-83; cp/Chm, Cultural Affairs, Comm of C of C, Johnstown, 1975-82; Pres, Chrysanthemum Soc; r/Cath; hon/Pub, "I Dreamed in Glass"; A B Crichton Awd, 1979; Allied Artist Awd.

SHEEHY, THOMAS DANIEL oc/Director of Manufacturing Resource Planning; b/Dec 9, 1946; h/40 C3 Whitney Ridge Road, Fairport, NY 14450; ba/Rochester, NY; m/Lisa Mary; c/Christine Judith, Matthew Thomas; p/Bernard A Sheehy, Methven, MA; ed/BS, Bus Adm 1969, MBA 1974, Suffolk Univ; mil/AUS, 1970-71; pa/Res and Devel Engr 1969-71, Prodn Control Mgr 1972-77, Malden Mills Inc; Corporate Mgr, Prodn and Inventory Control 1977-80, Mgr of Mfg Resource Planning 1980-81, Dir of Mfg Resource Planning 1981-, Champion Prods Inc; Am Prodn and Inventory Coptrol Soc; Area Chm, Suffolk Univ Alumni Fund, 1975-77; r/Rom Cath; hon/Nat Conf, Am Prodn and Inventory Control Soc, Article on Prodn and Inventory Control, 1979; Article on Shop Floor Control, through Grad Sch of MI St Univ, 1983; Awd'd, CPIM (Cert'd Practioner of Inventory Management), 1982; W/W Fin and Indust.

SHEETZ, RALPH ALBERT oc/Attorney at Law; b/Jun 13, 1908; h/798 Valley Street, Enola, PA 17025; ba/Harrisburg, PA; m/Ruth Lorraine; c/Ralph Bert; p/(dec); ed/PhB, Dickinson Col, 1930; Univ of MI; BA, Univ of AL, 1933; JD, Univ Sch of Law, 1953; pa/Solicitor, Peoples Bk of Enola, 1935-75; Solicitor, E Pennsboro Twp; Asst Solicitor, First Class Twp, 10 Yrs; E Pennsboro Twp Planning Comm VChm; Zoning Comm Chm, 1959; PA Bar Assn, 1935; ABA; Legal Aid, By-Laws and Prog Coms in Cumberland and Dauphin Co; Soc Com, Dauphin Co, 1934-; Farrah Law Soc of Univ Sch of Law, 1975; Charter Mem, Century Clb of Univ of AL; Bd of Adjustments, Twp, Chm of Bd, 1959; Atty for Lwyrs Title Ins Corp, 1956; Atty, Commonwealth Land Title Ins Co, 1957; Enola Boys Clb, Treas, Atty, 1950; Pres, E Pennsboro Twp PTA, 1951, 2nd Term 1952; Atty, Hon Mem, Incorp Citizens Firs Co No 1, 1951; Secy, Treas, W Shore Reg Coor Com,

Cumberland Co, 10 Yrs; Atty for Employees Loan Soc, 10 Yrs; Spkr, Dedication of New PA Hwy Between Overview and Marysville, PA; Semi-Profl Baseball, W Shore Leag, 1926-36, Umpire; cp/Deg of Master Mason, Perry Lodge 458; F&AM of PA, 1930, Worshipful Master 1971; Bd of Dirs, Harrisburg Masonic Sch of Instrns, 1972; Rep, Perry Lodge No 458, Grand Lodge of PA; Rep, John P Henry Jr, Dist Dpty Grand Master of Grand Lodge of PA, 110; Harrisburg Forest No 43, Tall Cedars of Lebanon, 1930, Drill Team 1934-43; Life Mbrship, Muscular Dystrophy; Corres, Forest's Pub, "Cedar Park"; Histn, Harrisburg Forest No 43, Exec Com; Guest of Hon, Dinner and Dist Ceremonial of Tall Cedars, 50 Yr Emblem and Cert by Supreme Forest of US; Harrisburg Consistory, 32 Deg, Ancient Accepted Scottish Rite, Deg Wk: Zembo Temple, Ancient Arabic Order of Nobles of Mystic Shrine, Zembo Shrine Patrol; Zembo Shrine Luncheon Clb, York and Cumberland Co Shrine Clbs; Deg of Royal Arch Mason in Perseverance Royal Arch Chapt #21, Most Excell High Priest, 1947; Toastmaster, Dinner Held by Royal Arch Chapt, 1948; Degs of Royal and Select Master, Harrisburg Coun #7, Royal and Select Masters; Toastmaster for Testimonial Dinner, Ezra C Cassell, Puissant Dist Dpty Grand Master, Dist No 5, Royal and Sel Masters of PA, 1942; Rep, Harrisburg Coun No 7, Grand Coun of Royal and Sel Masters of PA, 1943; Order of Temple in Pilgrim Cmdry No 11, Knights Templer, Cmdr 1946; Rep, Pilgram Cmdry No 11, Tri-Annual Conclave of Knights Templer of the US, 1946; Toastmaster, Cmdr's Dinner in Harrisburg, 1946; Rep, Pilgram Cmdry No 11, Grand Commandery of Knights Templar of PA, 1947-48; Order of the Silver Trowel, Coun of Appt'd Kings of the Commonwealth of PA, 1948; Order of Penn Priary No 6, Knights of the York Cross of Hon, Annual Conclave; E Pennsboro Twp Repub Clb, 1936; Harrisburg C of C, 1950; E Pennsboro Twp Sr Citizens Century Clb, 1979; Harrisburg Coun No 499, Royal Arcanum of PA; Mem of Com of Laws, Session of the Grand Coun; Chm, Grand Coun on Laws; 49th Session of Grand Coun, Dist'd Ser Mem, 1979; Keystone Cir No 3; Life Mem, Grand Coun, 1982; Sel Ser Ofcl for Appeal Area No 4, PA; Assoc Legal Advr to Draft Bd No 2, 1941; hon/Past Thrice Illustrious Master's Cert, Hon By Harris Coun #7, Ofc of Thrice Illustrious Master, 1942; Red Ribbon Cert of Achmt, 1947; Past Cmdr's Cert, for Ser to Templary and Pilgrim Cmdry #11, Knights Templar, Harrisburg, St of PA, Eminent Cmdr; Cert's Copy of Resolution by Senator Edwin S Bower for Outstg Ser; Pin, Medal, Badge from HQs for Select Ser, Commonwealth of PA, WWII, 1946; Cert of Select Ser Sys for Ser; Cert for Apprec, Dwight D Eisenhower, 1957; Pin and Cert, John F Kennedy, 1963; 25-Yr Emblem and Cert, Lyndon B Johnson, 1968; Pin and Cert, Bryan V Pepitone, Dir of Select Ser, 1974; Advr to Registrants to Local Bd 55, Fed Bldg, Harrisburg, 1974; 30-Yr Emblem and Cert, Gerald R Ford, Pres of US, 1975; W/W Am; Nat Social

Dir; Intl W/W Intells; Men of Achmt; DIB; Book of Hon; Notable Ams; Commun Ldrs of Am; 2,000 Notable Ams; Intl Book of Hon; W/W Fremasonry.

SHEHAN, LAWRENCE CARDINAL oc/Former Archbishop of Baltimore; b/ Mar 18, 1898; h/408 North Charles Street, Baltimore, MD; ed/Doct in Sacred Theol, Urban Col, 1923; pa/ Ordained, 1922; Asst Pastor, St Patrick Parish, 1923-41; Named Admr, then Pastor, St Patrick Parish, 1941; Papal Chamberlain, 1939; Domestic Prelate, 1945; Bishop, 1945; Aux Bishop of Balto and Pastor of SS Philip and James Parish, Until 1953; First Bishop of Bridgeport, CT; Coadjutor Archbishop, Balto; Elevated to Cardinalate, 1965; Appt'd to Consistorial Congreg, 1965; Appt'd to Body of Pres of Second Vatican Coun, 1965; Mem of Congreg for the Doctrine of the Faith, 1965; Named as Papal Legate to 40th Intl Eucharistic Cong, 1973; hon/Nat Brotherhood Awd, Nat Conf of Christians and Jews, 1965.

SHEINBEIN, MARC LESLIE oc/ Clinical and Forensic Psychologist, Marriage and Family Therapist; b/Dec 11, 1945; h/8734 Clover Meadow Drive, Dallas, TX 75243; ba/Dallas, TX; m/ Andrea Riff; c/Amy Michelle, David Benjamin; p/Isadore and Gloria Sheinbein, Oklahoma City, OK; ed/BA, Vanderbilt Univ, 1967; MA 1969, PhD 1972, Univ of TN; Doct Internship in Clin Psych, Univ of OK Med Sch, 1971-72; mil/Regular Army, 1968; pa/ Asst Prof of Psychi, Univ of TX Med Sch at Dallas, and Chief Psychol, Chd's Med Ctr, 1972-75; Pvt Pract in Clin and Forensic Psych, 1975-; Pres of Hillel, Vanderbilt Univ, and VP of Alpha Epsilon Pi Frat, 1964-67; Am Psychol Assn; Dallas Psychol Assn; Nat Coun of Hlth Care Providers in Psych; Am Assn of Marriage and Fam Therapists; Dallas Assn of Marriage and Fam Therapists, Secy and VP; Adv Bd Mem to Jewish Fam Sers and to RACLD; r/ Jewish; hon/Author, Approx 25 Profl Articles, Papers and Chapts, and One Book Length Manuscript; Articles Pub'd in Profl and Lay Jours; Publishers' Prize in Psych, Am Psychol Assn Best Paper, 1973.

SHEINIUK, GENE oc/Information Services Management Consultant; b/ Feb 15, 1936; h/3712 Westwood Boulevard, Los Angeles, CA 90034; ba/Santa Monica, CA; c/Robyn, Michael; ed/BS, Factory Mgmt, NY Univ, 1957; MBA, Indust Mgmt, Univ of So CA, 1965; mil/ AUS; pa/Chm, Dey Consltg Grp, 1983-; Sr VP, Gottfried Conslts Inc, 1975-82; VP, Data Processing, Imperial Bk, 1973-74; Mgr, Main Hurdman, 1970-73; Prin, J Toellner & Assocs, 1967-70; Supvr, Ernst & Whinney, 1965-67; Sys Analyst, Tidewater Oil Co, 1961-65; Indust Engr, McCullough Corp, 1959-61; Indust Engr, Repub Aviation, 1958-59; Assn for Sys Mgmt, 1969-, Pres of So CA Chapt 1973-74; Wn Sys Conf, Gen Chm 1972; Inst of Mgmt Conslts, 1979-; r/Jewish; hon/ Author, Num Articles and Spchs to Civic and Profl Grps and Mags during Past 15 Yrs; ASM Achmt Awd, 1975; Cert in Data Processing, 1978; Cert'd Mgmt Conslt, 1979; MTM Cert, 1962; W/W W.

SHEIRR, OLGA oc/Artist, Painter, Printmaker; b/Jun 7, 1931; h/360 First Avenue, 11G, New York, NY 10010; ba/ New York, NY; m/Maurice Krolik; p/ Edward Sheirr (dec); Mrs Lillian Wetzler; ed/BA, Bklyn Col, 1953; Grad Studies, NY Inst of Fine Art, 1954; Intaglio Wkshop, 1961-63; Att'd, NY Univ 1963-64, Pratt Graphic Ctr 1965-70, Art Students Leag 1970-72; NY Tchr of Fine Art, HS Lic, 1970; pa/ Indiv Exhbns: Noho Gallery 1975, 1976, 1978, 1979, 1980, 1982, 1983, Cicchinelli Gallery 1982, Intl Art Exch 1962, 1963; Grp Exhbns: Fairleigh Dickinson Univ 1983, Springville Mus of Art 1983, 1981, Riyadh, Saudi Arabia 1982, BACA Annual Miniatures Competition 1982, Commun Gallery in NYC 1980, 1981, 1983, Cicchinelli Gallery 1980-82, Chelsea Artwk 1980, Num Others; Public Collections: Mus of City of NY, St Vincent's Hosp, Greenville Co Mus, NY Univ Hosp, Village Nsg Home; Noho Gallery, 1975-; Noho for the Arts, 1975-; Assn of Artist Run Galleries, 1976-; Wom in the Arts, 1977-; Coalition of Wom's Art Orgs, 1978-; NY Artists Equity, 1978-; Wom's Caucus for Art, NY Chapt 1981-, Nat Chapt 1982-; hon/Subject of Num Articles; W/ W Am Wom; Intl W/W Intells; Intl Book of Hon; World W/W Wom.

SHELTON, BESSIE ELIZABETH oc/ Educator, Educational Media Associate; h/PO Box 187, Cumberland, MD 21502; p/Robert Shelton (dec); Mrs Bessie Plenty Shelton, Lynchburg, VA; ed/ Dipl, US Sch of Music, 1955; BA, WV St Col, 1958; MS, St Univ of NY, 1960; Dipl, Universal Schs, 1971; Dipl, Beckwith Schs, 1972; Dipl, N Am Sch of Travel, 1972; Dipl, Nashville Sch of Songwriting, 1975; Addit Study, Chgo Conservatory of Music, NWn Univ, Univ of VA, VA Wn Col; mil/USN 1951-55, Pers Dept; pa/Yg Adult Libn, Bklyn Public Lib, 1960-62; Art and Music Libn, Circulation Libn, Asst Hd, Ctl Reference Div, Queens Borough Public Lib, 1962-65; Edr/Instrnl Media Spec, Lynchburg Public Sch Sys, 1966-74; Music Conslt, 1972-; Travel Conslt, 1972-; Res Spec, 1974-; Edr/Ednl Media Assoc, Bd of Ed of Allegany Co, 1977-; NEA; MD St Tchrs Assn; Allegany Co Tchrs Assn; Life Danae Mem, Intl Clover Poetry Assn; Life Mem, Vocal Artists of Am; Intl Entertainers Guild; Tri-St Commun Concert Assn; Am Assn of Creat Artists; AAUW; Nat Assn for Female Execs; cp/YWCA; Am Biogl Inst Nat Bd of Advrs; Am Biogl Inst Res Assn; r/Bapt; hon/Contbr of Poems to Clover Collection of Verse, Great Contemporary Poems, The Creative Artist Review, and Var Other Pubs; Achiever's Intl Merit Awd, 1980; Col Pres's Hon Roll, 1976; Sweetheart of the Day, Radio Sta WLVA, 1973; First Prize Vocal Talent Awd, 1969; BA Deg w Hons, WV St Col, 1958; Other Hons; Achievers Intl Record; Commun Ldrs and Noteworthy Ams; Commun Ldrs of Am; DIB; 5,000 Personalities of World; Intl Book of Hon; Intl Scholars Dir; Intl W/W Commun Ser; Intl W/W Intells; Num Other Biogl Listings.

SHELTON, NICOLINA SYLVESTER oc/Public Relations Executive, Journalist; h/21 Rhodes Street, New Rochelle, NY 10801; ed/Att'd, Columbia Univ, 1947; Student of Public Relats and

Creat Writing, Iona Col, 1966-67; Cnslr Tng Course, Am Soc of Travel Agts; pa/Dir of Wom's Mkt for Seagram Distillers Co, 1952-61; News and Info Spec, GAF Corp, 1971-73; Public Relats and Press Release Ofcr, Paul Andrews Assocs, 1973-80; hon/Contbr to Many Profl and Popular Newspapers and Mags; Article Writing Awd, Writer's Digest, 1970; Recip, Addit Awds from Publishers in Recog of Articles and Feature Stories; World W/W Wom.

SHEN, SINYAN oc/Music Director, Author, Erhu Recitalist; b/Nov 12, 1949; h/2329 Charmingfare, Woodridge, IL 60517; m/Yuan-Yuan Lee; c/Jia, Jian; p/ Shen Shao-Quan and Chen Tien-Siu, Singapore; ed/BS, Univ of Singapore, 1969; MS 1970, PhD 1973, OH St Univ; pa/Music Dir, Orch of the Chinese Music Soc of N Am, 1976-; Editor-in-Chief, Chinese Music, 1978-; Music Dir, NWn Univ Chinese Choir, 1974-77; Music Dir, OH St Univ Chinese Choir, 1970-73; First Violinist, OH St Symph, 1969-71; Concert Recitalist on the Erhu, 1963-; Chinese Music Soc of N Am, Pres 1976-; Music Dir of Orch 1976-; Am Phy Soc; AAAS; hon/Pubs, What Makes Chinese Music Chinese 1981, Superfluidity 1982, Others; Music Advr, Encyclopaedia Britannica, 1983-; Music Panel, IL Arts Coun, 1982-; Musical Artists Awd, 1982-83, 1983-84; Dist'd Ser Awd, OH Union, 1973; Fulbright Scholar, 1969; Nat Merit Scholar, Singapore, 1968; Distn in Violin Perf, Royal Schs of Music, London, 1968; Intl W/W Music.

SHEN, WEI-CHIANG oc/Associate Professor; b/May 3, 1942; h/11 Dartmouth Avenue, Needham, MA 02192; ba/Boston, MA; m/Daisy; c/Howard, Jerry; p/Tze-Ping Shen (dec); Yi-Ching Shen, Needham, MA; ed/BS, Tunghai Univ, 1965; PhD, Boston Univ, 1972; pa/Res Fellow of Biol Chem, Harvard Med Sch, 1972-73; Sr Res Assoc, Brandeis Univ, 1973-76; Asst Res Prof of Pathol 1976-80, Assoc Prof 1980-, Boston Univ Sch of Med; Am Soc of Cell Biol; Am Soc of Pharm and Exptl Therapeutics; Am Soc of Biol Chems; NY Acad of Scis; Prin 1983-84, Newton Chinese Lang Sch; r/Christian; hon/ Author of Many Sci Articles for Profl Jours and Books; Postdoct Res F'ship, MA Heart Assn, 1972-73; Cancer Res Scholar Awd, Am Cancer Soc, MA, 1982-; W/W Frontier Sci and Technol.

SHERARD, THOMAS ALEXANDER JR oc/Supervisor of Properties Development; b/Jun 23, 1954; h/937 Sardis Cove Drive, Matthews, NC 28105; ba/Charlotte, NC; p/Thomas A and Olivia H Sherard, Anderson, SC; ed/BS, Civil Engrg, Clemson Univ, 1976; pa/Jr Engr 1976-78, Asst Distribution Engr 1978-81, Distribution Engr (Supvr of Properties Devel) 1981-, Duke Power Co; cp/Unit Commr, BSA, 1980-81; Asst Dist Commr, BSA, 1982-; Free Enterpriser, Jr Achmt, 1982-; Yg Life Ldr, 1972-75; r/Presb; hon/W/W S and SW; Personalities of S.

SHERIDAN, PATRICK MICHAEL oc/Executive; b/Apr 13, 1940; h/6628 Walnutwood Circle, Baltimore, MD 21212; ba/Baltimore, MD; m/Jane L; c/ Mary, Patrick, Kelly, Kevin, James; p/ Paul (dec) and Frances Sheridan; ed/BA, Univ of Notre Dame, 1962; MBA, Univ of Detroit, 1975; mil/Capt, AUS; pa/

Pres and CEO, Am Hlth and Life Ins Co, 1981-; Pres and CEO, Sun Ins Sers Inc, 1978-81; Exec VP and COO, Sun Life Ins Co of Am, 1976-78; Exec VP, Alexander Hamilton Life Ins Co, 1973-76; cp/Pres, MI JCs; Treas, US JCs; Pres, Charlesbrooke Commun Assn; r/ Cath; hon/Outstg Yg Man of Yr, Detroit and One of Five for MI; W/W World; W/W Am; W/W Bus and Fin; W/ W E; W/W Ins.

SHERMAN, PATRICIA ANN oc/ Visiting Assistant Professor of Physical Education; h/112 Greene Way Apartments, Greenville, NC 27834; ba/ Greenville, NC; p/Frederick Daniel and Joye Elizabeth Sherman, Winona, MN; ed/BS in PE, Winona St Univ, 1964; MA 1968, PhD 1972, PE, Univ of IA; pa/Vis'g Asst Prof of PE and Men's and Wom's Div I-A Tennis Coach, E Carolina Univ, 1982-; Asst Prof of PE, Tennis and Basketball Coach, Dept of Hlth, PE and Rec, Winona St Univ, 1979-81; Asst Prof of PE, Tennis, Basketball and Volleyball Coach, PE Dept, Univ of WI River Falls, 1973-79; Asst Prof of PE, Tennis, Basketball and Volleyball Coach, PE Dept, Gustavus Adolphus Col, 1972-73; Instr, Tennis Coach, Wom's PE Dept, Univ of IA Iowa City, 1967-72; Other Previous Positions; AAUP; AAHPERD; NAGWS; NASPE; USTA; WTA; NWTA; Univ of IA Alumni Assn and PEM Alumni Assn; Winona St Univ Alumni Assn; Pirate Clb; hon/Pubs, "Sherman Untimed Consecutive Rally Test" 1979, "Tennis Bibliography" 1976-78, "Considerations for Warm Up and Match Play" 1976-78, "You've Come a Long Way Baby" 1975, Others; W/W MW; World W/W Wom; Commun Ldrs of Am; W/W MW.

SHERRARD, CAMILLA MONSEQUE oc/Retired School Principal; b/ Oct 10, 1913; h/3210 Auchentoroly Terrace, Baltimore, MD 21217; m/ Clifton Walter; p/George and Lenora White (dec); ed/Att'd, Coppin Col, 1937; BS, Morgan Col, 1945; Master's, NY Univ, 1952; Profl Dipl, Columbia Univ, 1957; Grad Studies, Cath Univ, 1951; pa/Tchr 1937, Supvg Tchr 1942, Tchg Prin 1956, Vice Prin 1958, Prin 1959 to Retirement in 1974, Balto City Sch Sys; Zeta Phi Beta Sorority, 1937; Arena Players Inc, 1967; Foun Bd, Coppin St Col, 1970; cp/MD St Arts Coun, 1981; r/Union Bapt Ch, 1947; hon/Dist'd and Outstg Personalities of S.

SHERREN, ANNE TERRY oc/Professor of Chemistry; b/Jul 1, 1936; h/10 South 108 Meadow Lane, Naperville, IL 60565; ba/Naperville, IL; m/William S; p/Edward Allison (dec) and Annie Lewis Terry, Spanish Fort, AL; ed/BA, Agnes Scott Col; PhD, Univ of FL Gainesville; pa/Instr of Chem 1961-63, Asst Prof of Chem 1963-66, TX Wom's Univ; Assoc Prof of Chem 1966-76, Prof of Chem 1976-, N Ctl Col; Iota Sigma Pi, Nat Pres 1978-81, Past Pres 1981-84; Am Chem Soc, 1958-; Am Inst of Chems, 1965-; Dir of IL Inst, 1976-; r/Presb; hon/Author, Var Pubs; IL Inst of Chems Hon Scroll Awd, 1984; Outstg Yg Wom of Am; Outstg Edrs of Am; Am Men and Wom of Sci; W/W MW; W/W Am Wom; Notable Ams of 1976-77.

SHERRICK, DANIEL NOAH oc/ Executive; b/Mar 28, 1929; h/14420 Lake Candlewood Court, Miami Lakes, FL 33014; ba/Miami, Lake, FL; m/Dora

Ann Moore; c/Renata Ann, Sherrick Dee; p/Conrad D and Helen Lorene Sherrick, Greenup, IL; ed/BS. Ed, w Hons, En IL Univ, 1956; mil/S/Sgt, USAF, 1948-52 (Korea); pa/Owner, MW Ins Agy, 1956-60; Supt of Agys, MW Life Ins Co, 1960-62; Asst VP, Gulf Life Ins Co, 1962-71; Pres, Bk of Carbondale, 1971-74; Pres, Prescription Lng Corp, 1974-76; Exec VP and Dir, Imperial Indust Inc, 1976-; Pres, Heritage Hills Homeowners Assn, 1973; cp/ Pres, C of C, 1959; Alderman, Pk Civic Assn, 1968; Pres, C of C, Carbondale, 1974; VFW; Am Legion; Past Cmdr, Elks; AF&AM; Scottish Rite; r/Pres, Ch Good Shepherd, 1974; Pres, Miami Lakes Congregational Ch, 1978, 1981, 1982; Prot; hon/W/W S and SW; W/W FL.

SHERRY, MARILYN MORIN oc/ Psychiatric Social Worker; b/Mar 25, 1935; h/23 Pontiac Road, West Hartford, CT 06117; ba/Farmington, CT; m/ Gerald B; c/Samuel M, Trudy M; p/Jacob Morin, Worcester, MA; Gertrude G Morin (dec); ed/AB, Clark Univ, 1956; MS, Simmons Col Sch of Social Wk, 1958; pa/Social Wkr, Child and Fam Sers, Manchester, CT, 1958-61; Social Wkr, Child and Fam Sers, Hartford, CT, 1965-70; Social Wkr, Fam Sers of New Britain, 1971; Social Wkr, E Hartford and Marlborough Public Schs, 1972-74; Social Wkr, St Dept of Social Sers, 1977-79; Geriatrics and Palliative Care, Mt Sinai Hosp, 1979-81; Psychi Social Wkr, Univ of CT Hlth Ctr, 1981-; Fdg Mem, CT Coalition of Social Wk Orgs; Nat Assn of Social Wkrs; Acad of Cert'd Social Wkrs; Nat Soc of Clin Social Wkrs; NE Soc for Grp Psychotherapy; cp/Adv Bd, YWCA Encore Prog; hon/ W/W Am Wom.

SHINDLER, JACK THOMAS oc/ Executive, General Counsel; b/Jan 18, 1924; h/1611 Palma Vista, Las Vegas, NV 89109; ba/Las Vegas, NV; p/Col Harold A Shindler (dec); ed/AB, Georgetown Univ, 1948; Att'd, Harvard Univ 1946-47, Univ of Louvain 1950; JD, LLB, IN Univ, 1963; mil/Lt jg, USNR, 1942-45; pa/Asst Atty Gen, IN, 1964; US Atty, Inpls, 1968; Law Pract, 1969; Current VP and Gen Counsel, The Thomas Co; Bar Assn; Bd Mem, Nye Co, Thomas Co, Francis Corp; cp/Am Legion; YMCA; St Rose of Lima Hosp; Theatre Guild, Houston, Las Vegas; r/ Rom Cath; hon/Publisher, The Needah News, WI; Author, Var Profl Articles and Books in Preparation; Freedom Foun, 1948; Liberty Foun, 1968; Am Legion, 1965; W/W; W/W W.

SHINNAR, REVEL oc/Distinguished Professor of Chemical Engineering; b/ Sep 15, 1923; ba/Department of Chemical Engineering, City College, New York, NY 10031; m/Mirguim; c/Shlomo, Meir; ed/PhD, Chem Engrg, Columbia Univ, 1957; Dipl Eng, Chem Engrg, Technion Haifu, Israel, 1945; pa/Var Positions in Indust, Israel, 1945-62; Assoc Prof of Chem Engrg, Technion Haifu, 1958-62; Res Assoc, Guggenheim Jet Lab, Princeton Univ, 1962-64; Prof of Chem Engrg 1964-, Dist Prof of Chem Engrg 1979-, City Col of NY; AIChE; ACS; AIAA; AAAS; NY Acad of Sci; r/Jewish; hon/Author, 80 Papers on Chem Reaction Engrg, Process Control, Process Ec, Crystallization

Mixing, Other Subjects; Alpha Chi Sigma Awd, AIChE, 1979; W/W Engrg; W/W E.

SHIPMAN, HARRY LONGFELLOW oc/Astrophysicist; b/Feb 20, 1948; h/346 Old Paper Mill Road, Newark, DE 19711; ba/Newark, DE; m/Editha Davidson; c/Alice Elizabeth, Thomas Nathaniel; p/Arthur L (dec) and Mary D Shipman, Hartford, CT; ed/BA, Astronomy, Harvard Univ, 1969; MS, Astronomy 1970, PhD, Astronomy 1971, CA Inst of Technol; pa/J W Gibbs Instr, Yale Univ, 1971-73; Asst Prof of Physics, Univ of MO St Louis, 1973-74; Asst Prof of Physics 1974-77, Assoc Prof of Physics 1977-81, Prof 1981-, Univ of DE; Harlow Shapley Vis'g Lectr, Am Astronom Soc, 1976-; Ed Ofcr, Am Astronom Soc, 1979-; Trustee, Mt Cuba Astronom Observatory, 1977-; Harvard Clb of DE, Schs and S'ship Com 1976-; r/Prot; hon/ Author, Over 60 Articles in Profl Jours, Black Holes, Quasars, and the Universe 1980, The Restless Universe: An Introduction to Astronomy 1978; NSF Grad F'ship, 1969-71; Guggenheim F'ship, 1980-81; Univ of DE Chapt, Sigma Xi, Dist'd Scist Awd, 1981; Univ of DE Excell in Tchg Awd, 1984; W/W E; W/W Technol Today; Am Men and Wom of Sci; Outstg Yg Men of Am.

SHIRAS, VIRGINIA ECHOLS oc/ Home Health Nursing Coordinator; b/ Feb 26, 1918; h/3 Rosemont Drive, Little Rock, AR 72204; ba/Little Rock, AR; m/ Pete (dec); c/Ginger, Kathleen Shiras Hickey; p/James and Eva Petterson Echols (dec); ed/BA, MO St Univ, 1940; BS in Nsg, Univ of Ctl AR, 1972; MA, Scarritt and George Peabody Col, 1943; Cert, CA Col in China, 1945; MsD, DD, Am Bible Inst, 1975; pa/Missionary, Meth Ch, 1943-45; Fac Mem, Univ of CA, 1944-45; Fac, Mtn Home, AR, Public Sch, 1950-69; Staff Nurse, USPHS Indian Hosp 1972, VA Hosp 1972-73; RN Dir, Merci Mobile Med Unit, AR Dept of Hlth and Ofc on Aging, 1973-74; Home Hlth Nsg Coor, AR Dept of Hlth, 1974-; Bd, Albert Pike Hotel, Little Rock; Bd, Public Hlth Nsg Assn of AR; cp/Adv Coun, Salvation Army, Little Rock; r/Christian; hon/ Pubs, "Influence of Prevailing Religions on Chinese Family Life" 1943, "Comparison of School Systems Around the World" 1967, "The Bible-Genesis to Revelation-Analagous to the Life of a Man" 1973, "Death Beliefs, Funeral Customs, Burial Practices" 1983; AR Tchr of the Yr, 1958; W/W Am Wom; AR Lives; Nat Social Sci W/W.

SHOEMAKER, HELEN E MARTIN ACHOR oc/Retired; b/Mar 24, 1915; h/ 707 Dresser Drive, Anderson, IN 46011; m/Robert N; c/Dianne Johnston (Mrs Robert), Lana Martin Dean (Mrs Winston); p/Earl L and Blanche Martin (dec); ed/AB, Anderson Col; pa/Resident Dir 1967-69, Dir of Alumni Sers 1969-72, Anderson Col; Mem, IN Ho of Reps from Madison Co, 1968-70; Legis Counsel, IN Cols and Univs, 1970-72; Spec Asst, Ctr for Public Ser and Cols, 1973-77; Spec Asst, Dean for Acad Devel and Cols, 1977-78; Secy-Treas, IN St Lib and Hist Expansion Bldg Comm, 1973-81; Adv Com, Georgetown Univ Grad Sch Acad in the Public Ser, 1976-82; Trustee, Anderson Col, 1978-; cp/Reg Comm, GSA, 1958-66; Adv Coun, Financial Aid to Students,

Ofc of Ed, HEW, 1976-78; VP, IN Fdn of Wom's Repub Clbs, 1945-46; Treas, Nat Fdn of Wom's Repub Clbs, 1947-51; Bd of Dirs, Urban Leag of Madison Co, 1967-76; Adv Com on Sex Discrimination, IN Civil Rights Comm, 1978-83; Bd of Dirs, Opportunities Industrialization Ctr Inc, Madison Co, 1980-; Bd of Dirs, Madison Co LWV, 1978-; Bd, St John's Med Ctr; hon/Hon LLD, Anderson Col, 1978; Wm B Harper Awd, Urban Leag of Madison Co; W/W Am Wom.

SHOENIGHT, ALOISE TRACY oc/Poet, Former Teacher; b/Nov 20, 1914; h/Route 3, Box 1107, West Riverwood Drive, Foley, AL 36535; m/Hurley F; c/Paul (Stepson); p/William F and Carrie Ellen Milhous Souers (dec); ed/BEd, En IL Univ, 1937; Grad Classes in Art, En IL Univ, Univ of MO; Writing Confs and Poetry Wkshops in IL, NC, AL, and NM; pa/Tchr, Wiley Brick Sch 1937-38, Tracy Elem Sch 1938-46; En IL Alumni Assn, Life Mem; Am Poets F'ship Soc, Hon Life; Pensters, Former Chaplain; Performing Arts Assn; Am Poetry Leag; Acad of Am Poets; cp/Nat Geographic Soc; Nat Ret'd Tchrs Assn; PEO Sisterhood; Foley Homemakers Ext Clb; Baldwin Sr Travelers Clb; Pleasure Isl Sr Citizens Clb, Charter Mem; r/So Bapt; hon/Pubs, "His Handiwork" 1954, "Memory is a Poet" 1964, "The Silken Web" 1965, "A Merry Heart" 1966, "In Two or Three Tomorrows" 1968, "All Flesh is Grass" 1971, "Beyond the Edge" 1973; W/W Am Wom; World W/W Wom; Intl W/W Poetry; 2,000 Wom of Achmt; W/W S and SW; Personalities of S; DIB; Intl Authors and Writers W/W; Nat Register of Prom Ams and Intl Notables; Num Other Biogl Listings.

SHOOK, ROBERT MICHAEL oc/Coordinator of Medical Staff Affairs; b/Mar 5, 1943; ba/1015 Northwest 22nd, Portland, OR 97229; m/Jacqueline P; c/Alexandra, Justin; p/William and Eleanor Downey Shook; ed/BS, No AZ Univ, 1966; MA, Portland St Univ, 1979; pa/Coor, Med Staff Affairs 1983-, Dir of Prog Devel 1980, Good Samaritan Hosp and Med Ctr; Dir of Developmental Disabilities, St of OR, Dept of Human Resources, 1975; Prog Dir, Contra Costa Co Med Sers, 1970; Assn for Retarded Citizens; Epilepsy Assn of OR; Am Assn on Mtl Deficiency, Past Pres of Reg I; hon/Pubs, *Program Actions for Children with Epilepsy*, 1984; W/W W.

SHORTER, JOHN WILLIAM oc/Engineering Executive; b/Mar 7, 1931; h/25156 Pico Vista Way, Sunnymead, CA 92388; ba/Norco, CA; m/Cynthia Ann; c/Jeffrey W; p/Ardith V and Louise F Lynn Shorter, Waynesboro, VA; ed/BS in Bus Adm, VA Tech and St Univ, 1954; MS, Sys Mgmt, Univ of So CA, 1978; Att'd, Command and Staff Col 1972, Air War Col 1974; mil/Lt Col, USAF, 1955-76 (Ret'd); pa/Engrg Exec, McLaughlin Res Corp, 1979-; Arnold Air Soc; Soc of Logistical Engrs; VA Tech Century Clb; Univ of So CA Alumni Assn; Air War Col Alumni Assn; AF Assn; TROA; cp/Kiwanis Clb, Past Pres; BSA Assn; Com-man, Soc of Scabbard and Blade; So CA Hist (ECV; Mason; Knight Templar; 32 Deg Scottish Rite; Shriner; OES; r/Meth; hon/Author, Var Tech Papers to Air War Col and Univ of So CA; US Meritorious Ser Medal; AF Commend Medal; Pres

Unit Cit; W/W Am.

SHOUN, SANDRA oc/Psychologist, Director of Assessment Services; b/Apr 20, 1946; h/5789 Winston Court, Apartment 261, Alexandria, VA 22311; ba/Washington, DC; p/Frances S Snyder, Johnson City, TN; ed/BS, E TN St Univ, 1968; MS 1977, EdD 1981, Univ of TN Knoxville; pa/Eng Tchr, Kingsport, TN, 1970-72; Adm Asst, E B Copeland & Co, 1973-75; Admissions Cnslr, So Benedictine Col, 1977-78; Res Assoc, Univ of TN Knoxville, 1979-82; Dir of Assessmt Sers, Intl Pers Mgmt Assn, 1982-; Am Psychol Assn; Am Ednl Res Assn; Pers Testing Coun; r/Bapt; hon/Pubs, "As Is the Principal" 1981, "Comparison of Husbands' and Wives' Perceptions of Marital Intimacy and Wives' Stress" 1982, "The Retirement Power in Education Project: An Evaluator's Perspective" 1981; Outstg Yg Wom of Am, 1981.

SHOWERS, JACK PAUL oc/Attorney at Law; b/Nov 18, 1945; h/235 River Drive, Lafayette, LA 70506; ba/Lafayette, LA; m/Pammela Kathryn Hammond; c/Elizabeth Hammond Gray; p/Mr and Mrs Jack Roy Showers (dec); ed/JD, LA St Univ, 1976; mil/USAR; pa/Sr Ptnr, Showers & Guidry, Attys at Law, 1977-82; Acting Mgr of Computer Sys, Blue Cross of LA, 1967-70; Bar of US Supr Ct; Bars of Var Fed Appellate and Dist Cts; Am Bar Assn; LA St Bar Assn; Assn of Trial Lwyrs of Am; LA Trial Lwyrs Assn; Aircraft Owners and Pilots Assn; Am Home Bldrs Assn; LA Home Bldrs Assn; cp/SW LA Mardi Gras Assn; r/Meth; hon/Dir of Dist'd Ams; Personalities of S; W/W S and SW; Men of Achmt.

SHREVE, GREGORY MONROE oc/Academic Dean, Executive; b/Aug 3, 1950; h/14649 Evergreen Drive, Burton, OH 44021; ba/Burton, OH; m/Joan M; c/Jessica C; p/J L Shreve, Columbia, SC; Rosi Shreve, Hilton Head, SC; ed/BA in Anthropology, 1971, MA in Anthropology and Linguistics 1974, PhD in Anthropology and Linguistics 1975, OH St Univ; Cert of Adv'd Study, Computer and Info Sci, Univ of Pgh, 1980; mil/Hon Discharge, USAR, 1971; pa/Univ Fellow 1972-75, Vis'g Asst Prof 1975, OH St Univ; Asst Prof 1975-80, Assoc Prof/Grad Prof 1980-, Asst to Dean 1980-81, Acad Dean 1981-, Kent St Univ; Pres, Structured Software Sys (Consltg Firm), 1982-; VP, Logitech Inc, 1984; Am Anthropological Assn; Am Folklore Soc; Assn for Computing Machinery; Soc for Hist Archaeol; Digital Equip User's Soc; Kent St Acad Computing Adv Com, Univ Chm; cp/U Way Info Line/Vol Sers Bur Steering Com, Geauga Co; Geauga Co Arts Coun, Pres 1981-83; hon/Pubs, *Genesis of Structures in African Narrative Vol I* 1975, *Genesis of Structures in African Narrative Vol II* 1984, "Form and Genre in African Folklore Classification: A Semiotic Perspective" 1980, "Images of Aging in Literature: An Annotated Bibliography" 1982, "The Bone Tool Industry at White Rocks: A Woodland Rockshelter" 1983, Others; Four-Yr AUS S'ship, 1968-72; Four-Yr Univ F'ship, OH St Univ, 1972-75; Am Men and Wom of Sci; W/W Frontier Sci and Technol.

SHUFF, LILY oc/Artist; ed/BA, MA, Hunter Col; Att'd, Columbia Univ, Bklyn Acad of Fine Arts, Art Students

Leag of NY; pa/Perm Collections: Metro Mus of Art (NYC), Yale Univ Art Gallery, Lib of Cong, Butler Inst of Am Art, Bezalel Nat Mus, Norfolk Mus of Arts and Scis, GA Mus of Fine Arts, Others; One-Man Shows: St Univ (Morrisville, NY) 1974, Holy Cross Sem 1972, Studio Angelico 1972, Pack Meml Gallery 1971, The Rosenberg Lib 1970, Univ of ME 1968, Others; Maj Exhbns: Butler Inst of Am Art, Bklyn Mus of Art, Whitney Mus of Am Art Art USA, Lib of Cong, Smithsonian Instn, Riverside Mus, Nat Acad of Design, Richmond (VA) Mus, Others; Artists Equity Assn; Audubon Artists; Am Color Print Soc; Allied Artists; Am Soc of Contemp Artists; CT Acad of Fine Arts; Hunterdon Co Art Assn; Nat Assn of Wom Artists; Other Profl Socs; hon/Allied Artists $200 Awd; Audubon Silver Medal, 1979; NSPC&A Acrylic, 1977; Elizabeth Morse Genius Prize, Nat Assn of Wom Artists, Casein, 1976; Doris Kreindler Meml Awd, Nat Soc of Painters in Casein, 1976; Grumbacher Prize, Nat Soc of Painters in Casein, 1973; Am Soc of Contemp Artists, Oil, 1970; Num Other Hons; W/W World; W/W Am; Archives of Am Art, Smithsonian Instn; Art Collectors' Almanac; Wom Artists in Am; W/W Am Art; W/W Am Wom; Num Other Biogl Listings.

SHUFORD, JAMES W oc/University Administrator; b/Aug 27, 1948; h/12008 Rockcliff Drive, Huntsville, AL 35810; ba/Normal, AL; p/Robert L and Cora R Shuford, Wetumpka, AL; ed/BS, AL A&M Univ, 1970; MA 1972, PhD 1975, PA St Univ; pa/Dean of Sch of Agri 1982-, Assoc Dean 1976-82, Acting Assoc Dean 1975-76, Grad Asst 1970-75, Res Asst 1974-75, AL A&M Univ; Univ Deans Coun, Curric Com; Soil Sci Soc of Am; Am Soc of Agronomy; cp/Kiwanis Intl; r/Prot; hon/Author of Several Articles for Profl Jours; Outstg Yg Men of Am.

SHULTZ, GEORGE PRATT oc/Chairman of Economic Policy Board; b/Dec 13, 1920; ba/2201 C Street, Northwest, Washington, DC 20520; m/Helena Maria O'Brien; c/2 Sons, 3 Daughs; p/Birl E Shultz; Margaret Pratt; ed/BA, Ec, Princeton Univ, 1942; PhD, Indust Ec, MIT, 1949; mil/Served in War, USMC, Pacific, 1942; Maj, 1945; pa/Fac, MIT, 1948-57; Sen Staff Economist, Pres's Coun of Ec Advrs, 1955-56; Prof of Indust Relats 1957-62, Dean 1962-69, Univ of Chgo; Prof of Mgmt and Public Policy, Stanford Univ Grad Sch of Bus, 1974; Secy of Labor, 1969-70; Dir, Ofc of Mgmt and Budget, 1970-72; Secy of the Treasury, 1972-74; Dir: Gen Motors Corp, Dillon, Read & Co Inc; Exec VP 1974-75, Pres 1975-79, Bechtel Corp; VChm, The Bechtel Grp, 1980; Chm, Pres's Ec Policy Bd, 1981-; hon/Pubs, *Pressures on Wage Decisions* 1951, *The Dynamics of a Labor Market* 1951, *Management Organization and the Computer* 1960, *Strategies for the Displaced Worker* 1966, *Guidelines, Informal Controls, and the Market Place* 1966, *Workers and Wages in the Urban Labor Market* 1970, *Economic Policy Beyond the Headlines* 1978; Hon LLD: Notre Dame Univ 1969, Loyola Univ 1972, PA 1973, Rochester 1973, Princeton 1973, Carnegie-Mellon Univ 1975; W/W.

SHUMATE, MINERVA oc/Insurance Underwriter; b/Mar 20, 1949; h/5421 Lincoln Boulevard, PO Box 477, Hudson, OH 44236; ba/Cleveland, OH; p/ Everett and Arthurine Shumate, Hudson, OH; ed/BA, OH No Univ, 1972; pa/Supvg Sr Analyst, Aetna Life and Casualty, 1979-; Risk Analyst, Reed Shaw Stenhouse, 1977-78; Sr Mktg Spec, Corroon and Black of IL Inc, 1975-77; Sr Underwriter, Home Ins Co, 1972-75; Ins Wom of Cleveland Inc, Second VP 1983-84, Ed Chm 1982-83, Mbrship Chm 1981-82; Nat Assn of Ins Wom Intl, 1980-, OH St Legis Chm 1981-82; cp/Kent Area Chapt, The Links, 1981-; Reader, Cleveland Soc for the Blind, 1981-; r/Ch of God; hon/ Outstg Yg Wom of Am, 1982.

SHUSTER, MALCOLM DAVID oc/ Engineer, Scientist; b/Jul 31, 1943; h/ PO Box 431, Glenn Dale, MD 20769; ba/Seabrook, MD; p/Samuel J and Sarah B Shuster (dec); ed/SB, Physics, MIT, 1965; PhD, Physics, Univ of MD, 1971; MS, Elect Engrg, Johns Hopkins Univ, 1982; pa/Tchg and Res Asst, Univ of MD College Park, 1965-70; Ingénieurphysicien, French Atomic Energy Comm, Paris, 1970-72; Wissenschaftlicher Asst, Univ of Karlsruhe, W Germany, 1972-73; Lectr, Tel-Aviv Univ, 1973-76; Vis'g Asst Prof, Carnegie-Mellon Univ, 1976-77; Sr Mem of Tech Staff, Computer Scis Corp, 1977-81; Staff Scist, Bus and Technological Sys Inc, 1981-; Adj Prof, Dept of Mech Engrg, Howard Univ, 1983-; Am Astronautical Soc, Sr Mem; AIAA, Nom'd for Assoc Fellow; Am Phy Soc; Brit Interplanetary Soc, Fellow; IEEE, Sr Mem; hon/Author, More Than 28 Pubs in Physics, Elect Engrg, and Aerospace Engrg; Currently Preparing a Book of "Spacecraft Attitude Estimation"; Bat-Sheva de Rothschild Foun Awd, 1974; NASA Grp Achmt Awd, 1981; Sigma Pi Sigma; Sigma Xi; Tau Beta Pi; W/W in E; W/W in Aviation and Aerospace.

SHUSTER, RONALD L oc/Retired, Amateur Poet; b/Dec 10, 1927; h/303 East Auglaize, Wapakoneja, OH 45895; p/Mr and Mrs George A Shuster (dec); ed/BA, Eng Lit, OH St Univ, 1951; Studied Lib Sci, Bowling Green, 1960's; mil/USAAC, 1946-47; USAF, 1958-59; pa/Martha Kinney Cooper Ohioana Lib Assn, Columbus; r/Prot; hon/Has Pub'd More Than 100 Poems in Var Poetry Mags and Anthologies, 1967-; Pubs, *The Ever-Increasing Dawn* 1973, *Sketches in Oil and Other Poems* 1973, *Fool's Histories and Other Prose Writings* 1974, *Poems Based on News-Items and Other Verses* 1975, *The Heck with 'The Wreck of the Hesperus' and Other Poems* 1976, *A Pretty Good Bunch* 1978, Others; Hon Mention, Bowling Green Dist S'ship Exam, 1945; Life Mem, Disabled Am Vets.

SHWEDO, JOHN JOSEPH oc/ Marine Electronics Company Executive; b/Apr 26, 1928; h/352 Washington Avenue, Pleasantville, NY 10570; ba/ New Rochelle, NY; c/Robin Goff, Amy Fernald, Gregory John; p/John J (dec) and Agnes Kelly Shwedo, White Plains, NY; ed/BA in Bus Adm, St Lawrence Univ, 1952; BA in Psych, Marymount Col, 1977; MDiv, Union Theol Sem, 1980; Att'd, Columbia Univ, 1980-81; Att'g, NY Theol Sem, 1982-; mil/AUS, 1946-48, 1952-53; pa/Sales Trainee, IBM, 1952; Mgr, Shwedo Electronics, 1954-57; Sales Rep, Radio Corp of Am, 1968-69; Sr Sales Engr 1969-70, Mfg

Rep 1971-75, Harris Corp; Ser Mgr 1975-76, Sales Rep 1977, Sales Mgr 1978-80, Sales/Mktg Dir 1981-, Griffith Marine Navigation; Cnslr, Westchester Coun on Alcoholism, 1976-; Assoc Chaplain, Bellevue Hosp, 1979-80; New Testament Lectr, Epis Interfaith Study, 1982-; Am Mgmt Assn; Nat Assn of Alcoholism Cnslrs; Nat Marine Electronics Assn; Maritime Assn of Port of NY; Nat Maritime Hist Soc; cp/Hellenic Am C of C; Nat Trust for Hist Preserv; Dpty Dir, Westchester Co Civil Def, 1964-66; Pres, Thompson Village Assn, 1967-68; Co-Fdr, Thompson Hist Assn; r/Ch Vestry, Epis Ch, Pomfret, CT 1966-67; Stockbridge, MA 1968-69; hon/Tau Kappa Alpha, Nat Debating, 1952; Student Senate, 1950-52; W/W E.

SIDDAYAO, CORAZON MORALES oc/Economist, Professor, Research Coordinator; b/Jul 26, 1932; h/1201 Wilder Avenue, Apartment 2704, Honolulu, HI 96822; ba/Honolulu, HI; p/Crispulo S Siddayao (dec); Catalina T Morales (dec); ed/PhD 1975, MPhil 1975, MA 1971, Ec, George Wash Univ; BBA, Univ of the E, Manila, 1961; pa/ Coor of Energy and Industrialization Proj, E-W Ctr, Resource Sys Inst, 1981-; Affil Prof of Ec (Grad Fac), Univ of HI, 1979-; Res Fellow, E-W Ctr, 1978-81; Sr Res Economist, Inst of SE Asian Studies, Singapore, 1975-78; Expert Conslt, US Fed Energy Adm, 1974-75; Other Previous Positions; Am Ec Assn; Intl Assn of Energy Economists; Soc of Policy Modelling; SE Asia Petro Exploration Soc; r/Rom Cath; hon/Pubs, *Critical Energy Issues in Asia and the Pacific* 1982, *The Supply of Petroleum Reserves in South-East Asia* 1980, Others, Articles in Profl Jours; Valedictorian w High Hons, Philippine Normal Col, 1951; Var F'ships and S'ships; Hon Soc in Ec, Omicron Delta Epsilon, 1973; Invited Spkr at Confs, incl'g Travel Grants; W/ W W; Am Ec Assn Dir.

SIEGEL, BETTY LENTZ oc/College President; b/Jan 24, 1931; h/3141 West Somerset Court, Southeast, Marietta, GA 30067; ba/Marietta, GA; m/Dr Joel H; c/David Jonathan, Michael Jeremy; p/Carl N (dec) and Vera Lentz; ed/BA, Wake Forest Col, 1952; MEd, Univ of NC, 1953; PhD, FL St Univ, 1961; Postgrad, IN Univ, 1964-66; pa/Asst Prof 1956-59, Assoc Prof 1961-64, Lenoir Rhyne Col; Asst Prof 1967-70, Assoc Prof 1970-72, Prof 1973-76, Dean of Acad Affairs for Cont'g Ed 1972-76, Univ of FL Gainesville; Dean, Sch of Ed and Psychol, Wn Carolina Univ, 1976-81; Pres, Kennesaw Col, 1981-; Am Psychol Assn; Am Ednl Res Assn; Nat Assn St Univs and Land Grant Cols; Phi Alpha Theta; Pi Kappa Delta; Alpha Psi Omega; Kappa Delta Pi; Pi Lambda Theta; Phi Delta Kappa; Delta Kappa Gamma; r/Bapt; hon/Pubs, *Problem Situations in Teaching* 1971, Articles in Profl Jours; Outstg Tchr Awd, Univ of FL, 1969; Mortar Bd Wom of the Yr, Univ of FL, 1973.

SIEGEL, VICTORIA oc/Mayor; b/ Feb 11, 1943; h/2 Hilary Drive, Bayville, NY 11709; ba/Bayville, NY; m/Edwin; c/Stephen Allan, Michael Joseph; p/ Philip and Teresa Capodiferro (dec); ed/ Att'd, IBM Inst, 1964; Grad, cum laude, Walton HS, 1960; pa/Aimcee Wholesale, 1960-66, in Charge of Warehouse Oper, Inventory Control (Domestic and Fgn)

1962-63, in Charge of Tabulating Ofc 1963-64, Supvr of Electronic Data Processing 1963-66; Village Trustee, 1978-82; NY Conf of Mayors, 1982; Village Ofcls Assns, 1978-; cp/VChm, Northshore Conservative Clb, 1972-78; Pres, W Harbor Estates Assn, 1972-; Pres, Bayville Sch Parent Coun, 1977-79, Trustee, Brian Piccolo Lodge, OSIA, 1980-; r/Cath.

SIERACKI, LEONARD MARK oc/ Executive; b/Apr 15, 1941; h/9421 Kilimanjaro Road, Columbia, MD 21045; ba/Columbia, MD; m/Martha Elaine; c/Jeffrey, Jennifer, Julie; p/Joseph L and Lillian J (dec) Sieracki, Meriden, CT; ed/Bach Mech (Aero) Engrg 1963, Master of Ocean Engrg 1970, Cath Univ; MBA, Johns Hopkins Univ, 1977; pa/Proj Engr, AUS's Harry Diamond Labs, 1963-67; Prog Mgr, Hydrospace Res Div EGG, 1967-70; Mgr, Applied Mech Div, Columbia Res Corp, 1970-74; Pres, Lorelei Corp, 1974-77; Pres, Tritec Inc, 1977-; Am Assn of Small Res Cos, 1981-; Am Def Preparedness Assn, 1981-; r/Rom Cath; hon/Contbr, 52 Tech Articles in Fluid Mechs, Ocean Engrg, Fluidics and Hydraulics; Author, *Handbook of Fluidic Sensors*, AUS, 1977; Prin Author, 3 Volume Series, *Submarine Cabled Systems Design and Planning Manual*, USN, 1976; Directed IR100 Proj, 1981; W/W Technol Today; W/W E; W/W Frontier Sci and Technol.

SIGLER, LOIS OLIVER oc/Teacher; b/Sep 8, 1923; h/4785 Rolling Meadows Drive, Memphis, TN 38128; ba/Millington, TN; m/W Virgil Jr; c/William Oliver; p/Willie Campbell and Lillie B Oliver (dec); ed/BS, E TN St Univ, 1944; MS, Univ of TN Knoxville, 1952; Postgrad Wk, Univ of TN Knoxville, 1952; Sec TN Univ; pa/Home Ec Tchr, Buchanan, VA, 1944-46; Area Supvr, Home Ec Ed, St Dept of Ed, VA, 1946-54; Asst Nat Advr, FHA and New Homemakers of Am, 1954-56; Nat Advr, FHA, Dept of Hlth, Ed and Wel, 1956-63; Coor, Fam Living Pilot Prog, 1963; Home Ec Tchr, Millington, TN, 1966-; Am and TN Home Ec Assns; Am and TN Voc Assns; Nat and TN Voc Home Ec Tchrs Assns; W TN Home Ec Ed Assn; Nat, TN, W TN and Shelby Co Ed Assns, NEA/NCATE Team Evaluator 1977-; r/Meth; hon/Omicron Nu; Pi Lambda Theta; Hon Mem, FHA; TN Home Ec Tchr of the Yr, 1975; DIB; World W/W Wom; W/W Am Wom; Intl W/W Commun Ser; Commun Ldrs of Am; Notable Ams of Bicent Era; Commun Ldrs and Noteworthy Ams; Dir of Dist'd Ams; Personalities of S.

SILVERMAN, BARRY G oc/Professor of Engineering, Research Institute Director; b/Jul 5, 1952; h/9653 Reach Road, Potomac, MD 20854; ba/Washington, DC; m/Fern Linda; c/Rachel, Joel; p/Joseph and Miriam Silverman; ed/BSE 1975, MSE 1977, PhD 1977, Univ of PA; pa/Asst Prof 1978-80, Assoc Prof 1980-, George Wash Univ; Sponsored Res Proj Dir for Num Public Sector Agys (incl'g, NASA, DOD, EPA, DOE, White House, US Cong), and Pvt Sector Orgs (incl'g, Brookings, GRI, Mathematical, CSC); Co-Admr or Co-Designer, 3 Master's Deg Progs; Dir, Inst for Artificial Intell, 1984-; Bd of Dirs, Def Sys Mgmt Col Inst, 1984-; Adv Bd, Senator John Glenn, 1983-; Bd of Dirs, IEEE Soc,

1985-; IEEE; TIMS; IIE; ACM; AAAI; Several Ofcs and Ldrship Trainee, UJA, 1979-; cp/Bd of Dirs, Holmes Run Civic Assn, 1980-83; r/Jewish; hon/Author of Over 30 Pub'd Papers in Jours and Books; Co-Author of 2 Books; Edit Bd Mem, 2 Jours; Reviewer for 6 Jours; Editor of Conf Proceedings; Sigma Xi; Sr Mem, IEEE, 1983-; Awd'd Tenure, George Wash Univ, 1982; W/W.

SILVERMAN, NEIL I oc/Obstetrician, Gynecologist; b/Jun 17, 1933; h/2 Nicole Drive, Media, PA 19063; ba/Ridley Park, PA; m/Barbara-Lee; c/Sara-Beth, David Sheldon; p/Mac (dec) and Florence Silverman, Hallandale, FL; ed/BA, Dickinson Col, 1954; MD, Univ of Basel, 1960; mil/Capt, MC, AUS, 1962-64; pa/Fellow, Toxemia Res, Kings Co Hosp, 1962; Chief Resident, Ob-Gyn 1966-67, Clin Assoc Prof, Ob-Gyn 1972-, Hahnemann Med Col; Chief, Dept of Gyn, Taylor Hosp, 1980-83; Am Col of Ob & Gyn, 1964-; Am Bd of Ob & Gyn, Diplomate 1969-; Royal Soc of Med, 1980-; Pan-Am Med Soc, 1975-; cp/Jaguar Drivers Clb; Jaguar Clbs of N Am; r/Jewish; hon/Pub, "The Role of Angiotensin in Toxemia," 1963; Grad, magna cum laude, Univ of Basel, 1960; W/W Am.

SILVEY, AGNES JOAN oc/Dietetic Consultant; b/Feb 28, 1922; h/7019 East 72nd Street, Tulsa, OK 74133; ba/Tulsa, OK; m/Howard Gordon (dec); p/Edward J and Margaret M Wolfe (dec); ed/BS, Marymount Col of KS, 1944; Dietetic Internship, CA Luth Hosp, 1944-45; Reg'd Dietitian, 1969; pa/Therapeutic and Adm Asst, Good Samaritan Hosp, 1945-50; Instr, Food and Nutrition, Marymount Col, 1948-49; Clin Dietitian, Cedars of Lebanon Hosp, 1950; Dist Nutritionist, LA Public Hlth Dept, 1950-67; Home Ser Dir 1950-67, Dietetic Conslt, Energy Sys Mktg 1967-, OK Natural Gas Co; OK Restaurant Assn; OK and Nat Foodser Assns; Tulsa City/Co Hlth Dept Food Coun Adv Com, 1967-69; Secy, OK Home Ec Assn, 1954-56; Secy, OK Dietetic Assn, 1960-61, Pres 1961-64, 1975-79; OK Del, Am Dietetic Assn, 1979-82, Area IV Coor; r/Cath; hon/Author, Articles in Hosp Mag; W/W Am Wom; W/W S and SW; DIB.

SIMMONS, ANITA RUTH oc/Principal; b/Apr 20, 1943; h/1578 North Atwood Drive, Macon, GA 31204; ba/Macon, GA; m/Craig Edward; c/Melanie Robinson, Danys Robinson; p/Mrs Ruby Hightower, Macon, GA; ed/BS, Biol, Stillman Col, 1965; MEd, Ednl Adm and Supvn, Univ of GA, 1973; pa/Tchr of Biol, Perry G Appling HS, 1965-67; Tchr of Adult Ed, Bibb Co Adult Ed Prog, 1965-; Profl Actress, Kaleidoscope Players, 1967-68; Tchr of Adv'd Biol, Dudley Hughes HS, 1968-70; Asst Prin, SW HS, 1970-79; Prin, Ballard A Jr HS, 1979-; Pres, PTA, Winship Sch, 1976, 1977; Chm of Bd, St Agnes Day Care Ctr, 1979-; Ad Hoc Com, Gov's Task Force on Adult Ed; GA Assn of Edrs; Bibb Assn of Edrs; Nat Assn of Edrs; GA Assn of Sec'dy Schs; r/Cath; hon/Salutatorian, 1961; Nat Drama Awd, 1964; Woodrow Wilson F'ship, 1964; Bibb Extra Spec Person, Macon Telegraph and News, 1982; Outstg Yg Wom of Am; W/W Am Wom.

SIMMONS, TROY WILLIAM oc/Management Consultant; b/Nov 13, 1927; h/13574 Paseo Del Mar, El Cajon, CA 92021; ba/Same; m/Pauline Mildred; c/Troy Jr, Karen Ann, Robert Wayne, Ronald Gene; p/Irish Jeannette Beyers Simmons, Rock Hill, SC; ed/Student, Old Dominion Univ 1962-63, Grossmont Col 1973-75, USN Supply Corps Sch 1959, USN Trans and Traffic Mgmt Sch 1961; mil/USN 1943-69, Adv'd through Enlisted Grades to Lt Cmdr; pa/Var Duties as Enlisted Storekeeper and Supply Ofcr, Dir of Supply Opers at US Naval Shipyard (Last Position), USN, 1943-69; Mgr, Mat Control and Traffic, Vetco Offshore Industs, 1969-71; Gen Supvr, Mat Sers, Solar Turbines Intl, 1971-74, 1978-80; Dir of Opers, Aldila Inc, 1975-78; Pres, W Coast Engrg Co, 1980-; Prodn and Inventory Control Soc; cp/Chm, Combined Fed Campaign, Pearl Harbor, 1967; VP, Treas, Little Leag Assn, Pearl Harbor, 1966-68; Neighborhood Commr, Kamehameha Dist Aloha Coun, BSA, 1966-68; Ret'd Ofcrs Assn; Masons; r/Assemblies of God; hon/Contributed Articles to Profl Jours, 1979; Dean's List, Grossmont Col, 1973-75; W/W Am; W/W W.

SIMON, SHELDON WEISS oc/Professor, Director of Center for Asian Studies; b/Jan 31, 1937; h/5630 South Rocky Point, Tempe, AZ 85283; ba/Tempe, AZ; m/Charlann Scheid; c/Alex Russell; p/Jennie Dim Simon, Birmingham, AL; ed/BA, Univ of MN, 1958; MA, Princeton Univ, 1960; PhD, Univ of MN, 1964; pa/Asst Dir, Ctr for Intl Relats, Univ of MN, 1961-62; Polit Analyst, US Govt, 1963-66; Asst Prof of Polit Sci, Univ of KY, 1966-75; Prof and Chm of Polit Sci 1975-79, Dir of Ctr for Asian Studies 1980-, AZ St Univ; Edit Bd Mem, *Asian Forum* 1976-80, *Asian Affairs* 1983-; r/Jewish; hon/Author, 50 Articles in Profl Jours, 5 Books (incl'g, *The Asian States and Regional Security* 1982) Phi Beta Kappa, 1958; Grad, summa cum laude, 1958; Woodrow Wilson Nat Fellow; W/W W; W/W Am Ed.

SIMONETTI, JOAN E oc/Manufacturing Manager; b/Aug 17, 1952; h/1903 West Taylor Street, Apartment 210, Sherman, TX 75090; ba/Sherman, TX; p/Col and Mrs L D Simonetti; ed/BS, Biol, Bethany Col, 1974; Completing MA in Indust Relats, Rutgers Univ, 1977-; pa/Mgr, Fibre Finishing, Johnson & Johnson, 1982-; Mgr, Suture Mfg 1980-82, Needle Mfg Supvr 1979-80, Ethicon Inc; Ptnr, Elizabeth T Lyons & Assocs, Mgmt Conslts, 1975-79; ASPA, 1979-; NAFE, 1981-; Link; Indust Relats Res Assn; cp/Former Bd Mem, YWCA of Ctl Jersey; hon/Freshman Biol Scholar, 1970; Cert of Nomination, Outstg Wom in Bus, Raritan C of C; W/W Am Wom.

SIMONS, ANNEKE PRINS oc/Professor, Painter; b/Feb 15, 1930; h/238 Ogden Avenue, Jersey City, NJ 07307; ba/Jersey City, NJ; p/Hugo and Charlotte Prins; ed/BA, Vassar Col, 1952; Att'd, Yale-Norfolk Sum Sch of Art, 1952; MAT, Harvard-Radcliffe, 1953; Boston Mus Sch, 1953-56; PhD, PA St Univ, 1968; pa/Prof, Jersey City St Col, 1967-; Grad Res Asst, PA St Univ, 1962-64; Senator-at-Large, Faculty Senate, Jersey City St Col, 1983-84; AAUP; cp/Asia Soc; hon/F'ship, Yale-Norfolk Sum Sch of Art, 1952; S'ship, Harvard-Radcliffe, 1952-53; Grad Sch F'ship, PA St Univ, 1964-65; Grant, Nat Endowment for the Humanities, 1975; Painting Owned by Metropolitan Mus; Print Exhib'd and Maintained by Metropolitan Mus of Art, NY; Painting Exhbns in Metro Area; Intl W/W of Intells; World W/W of Wom in Ed; Commun Ldrs and Noteworthy Ams.

SIMONS, DAN C oc/Entrepreneur; b/Jan 30, 1936; ba/1225 South Redwood Road, Salt Lake City, UT 84104; m/Sally Jane Anderson; c/8; p/Harold Earl and Fredda Simons; ed/Att'd, Univ of UT; Specialized Courses in Real Est, Nat Assn of Rltrs; Cert'd Real Est Cnslr, Nat Assn of Real Est Appraisers and Nat Assn of Review Appraisers; pa/Lic'd Salesman, Bettilyon Rlty Co, 1959; Salesmgr, Capson Investmt Co, 8 Yrs; Formed Real Est Conslts, 1968; Broker and Pres, Bettilyon and Simons Rltrs; Current Broker and Pres, Simons and Co, and Pres, Real Est Conslts; Capitalized and Org'd, Pioneer Dodge and Frontier Motors; Purchased and Sold Interest, Peck & Shaw, Buick, GMC, GMC Motor Coach and Rolls Royce; Org'd Geodyne II and Alpine Ltd; Bd, Val Mortgage Corp, UT Acad of Gymnastics and Am Intl Real Est; Has Lectured and Taught, Brigham Yg Univ, UT St Univ, Henagars LDS Bus Cols, and Others; Life Mem, URPAC, RPAC; cp/4-H; BSA; Little Leag; GSA; r/High Priest, Ch of Jesus Christ of LDS; hon/Salesman of the Yr, Salt Lake Bd of Rltrs, 1968; Rltr of the Yr, UT Assn of Rltrs, 1976; Omega Tau Rho; Life Awd, GSA; W/W Am DIB; Notable Ams.

SIMPKINS, BARBARA DIXON oc/Computer Assisted Instruction Coordinator; b/Sep 24, 1934; h/13207 Rhame Drive, Ft Washington, MD; ba/Washington, DC; c/Monti Lemans, Lubara; p/Rev Dr Joshua O Dixon (dec); Mrs Celestine F Dixon, Pensacola, FL; ed/Att'd, Cascadilla Preparatory Sch/Cornell Univ, 1948; BS, Fisk Univ/FL A&M Univ, 1954; Master of Music Ed, Temple Univ, 1955; EdD, Nova Univ, 1978; Further Study, Univ of UT, FL A&M Univ, Cath Univ of Am; pa/Supvg/Demonstration Tchr, Howard Univ and Univ of MD Student Tchr Prog, 1966-69; Music Tchr, Wash Jr HS, 1955-65; Elem Sch Music Tchr/Master Tchr, DC Public Schs, 1965-69; Cultural Enrichment Coor, Model Schs Div, DC Public Schs, 1969-75; ESEA Title I Field Supvr 1975-82, Computer Assisted Instrn Coor, ECIA Chapt 1 Prog 1982-, DC Public Schs; Instr, DC Tchrs Col 1966-68, Wash Jr Col 1965; MENC; DC MENC; Assn of Supvn and Curric Devel; CoChm, Ednl Conf; DC Affil Unit of Assn of Supvn and Curric Devel; DC Coun of Sch Ofcrs; Delta Sigma Theta Sorority; Phi Delta Kappa, Past VP; Prince George's Co Chapt, Jack and Jill of Am Inc; Orgr and First Pres, Prince George Co Chapt of Links Inc; cp/DC Chapt, Top Ladies of Distn Inc; Nat Coun of Negro Wom; r/Bapt; hon/Author, Wash Jr High Alma Mater and Fight Song, Copyright Lib of Cong; Dist'd Ser Awd Presented by Wash Jr HS Hon Soc, 1963; Queen of Pensacola, FL Fiesta of Five Flags, 1953.

SIMPSON, ALAN K oc/United States Senator; b/Sep 2, 1931; m/Ann Schroll; c/William Lloyd, Colin Mackenzie,

Susan Lorna; p/Milward L and Lorna K Simpson; ed/Att'd, Cranbrook Sch, 1950; BS, Law 1954, JD 1958, Univ of WY; mil/Comm'd as 2nd Lt, Began Active Ser 1954, Served in 5th Inf Div and 2nd Armored Div in Germany, Hon Discharge (1st Lt) 1956; pa/Elected to 96th Cong, Nov 1978; Served in Ho of Reps of WY St Legis, 14 Yrs; City Atty, City of Cody, and US Commr, 1959-69; Asst Atty Gen, WY, 1959; Am Bar Assn; Assn of Trial Lwyrs of Am; Pres, Univ of WY Alumni Assn, 1962, 1963; cp/ Chm, Com on Vets' Affairs; Mem, Jud Com, Envir and Public Wks Com; Chm, Jud Subcom on Immigration and Refugee Policy; Subcoms on Regulatory Reform and Cts; Chm, Subcom on Nuclear Regulation; Subcom on Envir Pollution; Subcom on Toxic Substances and Envir Oversight; Nat Repub Senatorial Com; Bd of Trustees, Buffalo Bill Hist Ctr; Bd of Dirs, Wn Arts Foun; Bd of Trustees, Gottsche Foun Rehab Ctr; Lifetime Mem, VFW; r/Epis Ch.

SIMS, JUNE CRENSHAW oc/Business Owner; b/Jul 22, 1928; h/4685 Devonshire Road, Dunwoody, GA 30338; ba/Marietta, GA; m/Frank Foster; c/Deborah Sims Massey; p/R J (dec) and Blanche Crenshaw, Dunwoody, GA; ed/Grad, Phillips HS, 1947; pa/ Secy, Brownell Tours; Housewife; Co-Fdr, Creations Etc, "Silk Florist"; Beta Sigma Phi; cp/Rainbow Girls; Cobb Co C of C, 1983; r/Presb.

SINGER, MARSHA A oc/Telecommunications Business Owner; b/Sep 24, 1954; h/296 Juanita Avenue, Pacifica, CA 94044; ba/San Francisco, CA; p/Mr and Mrs Edgar G Singer, San Francisco, CA; ed/Grad, Lowell HS, 1972; pa/ Owner and Salesmgr, The Cordless Phone Ctr, 1982-; Mgr, The Good Guys! (Retail Audio-Video), 1978-81; Pvt Investor in Real Est (Current); cp/ NOW; r/Jewish; W/W Am Wom.

SINGH, TEJA oc/Research Scientist; b/Jun 18, 1928; h/3620-106 Street, Edmonton, Alberta T6J 1A4; ba/Edmonton, Alberta; m/Lavinia Hall; c/K P, Sukhdeep Multani; p/Mr and Mrs Gian Singh (dec); ed/PhD 1966, MSc 1963, UT St Univ; BA, Punjab Univ, India, 1948; pa/Res Scist and Biometrician, No Forest Res Centre, Canadian Forestry Ser, Envir Canada, 1980-; Conslt on Envir Impact of Watershed Devel Projs, FAO, Rome, Italy, 1979; Watershed Mgmt Res Expert, FAO/UNDP, Tehran, Iran, 1977-78; Res Scist, Forest Hydrology, Canadian Dept of Envir and Fisheries, 1967-77; Res Ofcr, Watershed Mgmt Res, Canada Dept of Forestry, 1965-66; Math Tutor, UT St Univ, 1964; Res Asst, Watershed Mgmt, En Rockies Forest Conserv Bd, Canada, 1963; Res Asst, Ecol and Hydrology, UT St Univ, 1960-62; Forest Range Ofcr, Himachal Pradesh and Pubjab, India, 1951-59; Canadian Inst of Forestry; Am Geophy Union; Soc for Range Mgmt; Sigma Xi; Canadian Wildlife Fdn; New Zealand Hydrological Soc; Intl Soc of Soil Sci; Intl Water Resources Assn; cp/ Pres, Intl Clb; Pres, India Students Assn; Columnist (Intl Corner), *Student Life*; Fdg Dir, Secy, Singh Soc of Alberta; Fdg Mem, Am Students Acad; Asst Coach, Edmonton Minor Soccer Assn; hon/ Pubs, "Preliminary Operational Guidelines for Environmental Impact Studies for Watershed Management and Devel-

opment in Mountain Areas" 1979, "Watershed Management Research in Iran" 1979, "Iran Watershed Research Programme: Prerequisites and Research Priorities" 1979, "Statistical Calculations" 1978, "Streamflow Quality and Quantity Relationships on a Forest Catchment in Alberta, Canada" 1978, Others; Intl Student of the Yr (Robins Awd); Var Other Awds and Hons in Commun Life; Am Men and Wom of Sci; Men of Achmt; Intl Book of Hon; 5,000 Personalities of World.

SINGLETON, "J" ARTHUR oc/High School Social Studies Teacher; b/Oct 24, 1925; h/PO Box 5428, Virginia Beach, VA 23455; ba/Virginia Beach, VA; m/ Mary D; c/Arthur Wayne; p/William K Singleton, Columbus, MS; ed/BS in Ed, 1974; MS, Ed, 1979; mil/USN, 1943-74; pa/Aviation Machinist, Flight Engr, PBY, 1944; PB4Y, 1945; Ground Test Supvr in Aircraft Overhaul, 1946-49; Maintenance Supvn in Squadron, 1950-52; Ground Maintenance Instr, 1953-54; Squadron Maintenance Adm Tng CPO and Sr Flight Crewman, 1955-56; Flag and Staff, 1957-59; Comm Ensign LDO, Became Squadron Asst Main Ofcr, 1960-63; Naval Air Sta as Quality Assurance Ofcr, 1964-66; Comfair Power Plants Ofcr, 1967-69; Selected in Original 100 Ofcrs as Aviation Maintenance Duty Ofcr; AIMD Ofcr or Carrier, 1970-71; Squadron Maintenance Ofcr, 1972-73; Asst AIMD Ofcr, Naval Air Sta, 1973-74; Adv'd through Grades to LCDR, 1968; Served in Aviation Maintenance; Served in Pacific, S Atl, Iceland, Mediterranean, Cuba; Public Sch Tchr, 1975; Tchr, Social Studies, Bayside HS, VA Beach; NEA Conv Del, 1980, 1981, 1982; VCSS, 1976; Nat Coun of Social Studies, 1976; VA Bch Ed Assn, Treas 1980-81, Bd of Dirs; U Tchg Profession, 1975; cp/Pres, Tidewater Baseball Umpires Assn, 1957-58; Pres, IAABO Bd 225, 1958-59; Pres, SEn VA Football Assn, 1962-63; r/Tchr of Sunday Sch, Mem of Fin Com, Deacon, Trinity Bapt Ch; hon/Dist'd Flying Cross; Air Medal w Five Stars; Asiatic-Pacific Campaign Medal w Four Stars; Nat Def Ser Medal; Navy Expeditionary Medal; Am Campaign Medal; Armed Forces Expeditionary Medal, Cuba; W/W S and SW.

SINGLETON, WILLIAM EDWARD III oc/Director of Personnel; b/Mar 1, 1946; h/114 Northwood, Houston, TX 77009; ba/La Porte, TX; c/Katherine Elizabeth; ed/BA, TX Tech Univ, 1968; MEd, San Houston St Univ, 1973; EdD, Wn CO Univ, 1977; pa/Dir of Pers, La Porte ISD, 1983-; Asst Supt for Pers, N Forest ISD, 1978-83; Dir of Pers Sers, Aldine ISD, 1973-78; Asst Prin, Aldine Sr HS, 1972-73; Lectr on Staff Evals, Hiring, Hearings and Staff Termination; Bd of Dirs, TX Assn of Sch Pers Admrs; AASPA; TASPA; Phi Delta Kappa; cp/La Porte C of C, Commun/ Police Relats Com; NAACP; Past Mem, Vestry; r/Unity.

SINNEMAKI, ULLA ULPUKKA oc/ Registered Nurse, Director of Nursing, Health Executive; ba/South Cameron Memorial Hospital, Route 1, Box 227, Cameron, LA 70631; c/Markku Taneli, Sirkka Astrid; p/Otto William Spjut (dec); Kaisa Viola Siermala; ed/AA 1970, BA 1972, NY Univ; BS, St Univ of NY Stony Brook, 1976; MEd 1978, EdS

1979, MEd 1981, McNeese St Univ; pa/ Public Sch Tchr, Prin, Finland, 1948-50; HS (Mid Sch) Tchr, Finland, 1956-61; OR Asst, NY, 1965-72; Field Interviewer, US Bur of Census, NYC, 1973-75; Staff Nurse, LCMH, 1976-77; Hd Nurse 1977-80, Asst Dir of Nsg 1980, Dir of Nsg 1981-, SCMH; NLN; ANA; Nat Leag for Nsg; COIN; AECT; HEMA; ASCD; AAUP; AMBA; NAFE; AAUW; Suomi-Seura Home Hlth Care Adv Bd; cp/NOW; ACLU; Alcohol and Drug Abuse Preven of SW LA Inc, Team Mem; r/Cameron Parish, VP; r/Luth; hon/Am Sch Awd, 1966-67; NY Univ Ettinger Awd, 1970-72; W/W S and SW; Personalities of S.

SKAALEGAARD, HANS DIANA oc/ Marine Artist, Art Gallery Owner, Lecturer; b/Feb 7, 1923; h/25197 Canyon Drive, Carmel, CA 93923; ba/ Carmel, CA; m/Mignon Diana; c/Karen Solveig; p/Hanna Elis Fredrisen; ed/ Studied w Marine Artist Anton Otto Fishek, 1940's; Brief Attendence, Royal Acad of Copenhagen, Denmark; Silver Medal 1970, Gold Medal 1972, Tomasso Campanell Acad, Italy; Gold Medal, Academia Italia del Arti, 1980; pa/ Started Own Art Gallery, 1966; Has Had Over 50 One-Man Shows throughout CA, and in WA and OR; Bd of Dirs, Hist and Art Assn; Watch Stander, Maritime Mus; cp/First Hon Male Mem, Woms Monterey Civic Clb; Mem, Past Cultural Dir, Aasgaarden 112 Sows of Norway Lodge; Monterey Dir on Bd of Dirs, Monterey Navy Leag, Past 5 Yrs; r/Luth; hon/Cover and Article, *Palette Talk*, 1980; Cover, *Compass Magazine*, 1980; Am Artists of Renown; Intl W/ W Art and Antiques; Intl Dir of Arts; DIB; W/W Arts; World Biog; W/W Intl Commun Ser; Commun Ldrs and Noteworthy Ams; Num Other Biogl Listings.

SKAALEGAARD, MIGNON DIANA oc/Art Gallery Director, Real Estate Agent; b/Aug 27, 1923; h/25197 Canyon Drive, Carmel, CA 93923; ba/ Carmel, CA; m/Hans; c/Karen Solveig; p/Mr Frank Haack and Mrs Dorothy Feltus, Petaluma, CA; ed/Grad, HS; Att'd, Golden Gate Col; pa/Real Est Agt, Herold & Herold, 1961; Night Clb Singer during War Yrs; Owner, Skaalegaard's Square Rigger Art Gallery, 1966-; Real Est Assoc, 1961-; Dir on Bd of Dirs, Hist and Art Assn, 1973; Peninsula Mus of Art; Past Mem, Monterey Real Est Bd; Carmel Bd of Rltrs; cp/Monterey Civic Clb, 1966-, 13 Yr on Bd, Pres 1972-73, 1982-; Pres, Monterey and Pacific Grove Quota Clb, 1971; Social Dir, Sons of Norway Lodge, Aasgaarden 112, 1973; Friends of the Inst; Navy Leag of Monterey; Jesters the Fun Fund Raisers for Monterey; r/ Christian Principles; hon/Cert for "Historic Adobes," Painting Proj in 1969; Paintings Hung in Civic Clb; Notable Ams; Commun Ldrs of Am.

SKINNER, JASPER DALE II oc/ Prototype Equipment Company Executive; b/Jul 11, 1947; h/PO Box 94993, Lincoln, NE 68509; ba/Lincoln, NE; m/ Ethel Marie Baysinger; c/Cliti Eleta Nokomis; p/Lt Col Jasper and Marilyn Skinner, Lincoln, NE; ed/BA 1969, MS 1971, PhD 1974, Univ of NE Lincoln; pa/Ext Entomology Tech 1969-70, Botany Inst Lab Instr 1971, Res Assoc, Agronomy Dept 1974-75, Entomology Tech 1975, Univ of NE Lincoln; Asst

Entomologist, Intl Crops Res Inst for the Semi-Arid Tropics, Hyderabad, India, 1975-76; Dir, Chief Designer, Slaten and Tunlaw, 1976-; Sigma Xi; Phi Eta Sigma; Grad Student Assn, Univ of NE, VP 1972, Pres 1973; cp/Nat Rifle Assn; r/Luth; hon/Pubs, "A Note on the Discovery of the Male of *Acritochaeta distincta* Mall (Diptera, Muscidae)," "Attractants for *Atherigona* spp Including Sorghum Shootfly, *Atherigona soccata* Rond, Muscidae: Diptera" 1980; Regents Scholar, 1965; Undergrad Hons Prog, Biol, Polit Sci, Hist; NSF Undergrad Res Prog, 1969; NDEA Title 11 Fellow, 1970-73; Personalities of W and MW; W/W MW; Men of Achmt; W/W Intells.

SKINNER, JERRY ALLAN oc/Family Therapist, College Professor, Minister; b/Jun 28, 1958; h/12014 Coulson Circle, Houston, TX 77015; ba/Houston, TX; m/Cerise C; p/Floyd and Betty Skinner, Houston, TX; ed/BA, Baylor Univ, 1980; MA, Univ of Houston Clear Lake City, 1982; pa/Prof of Psych, So Bible Col; Min of Music, Centerwood Assem of God Ch; Fam Therapist, Fam Wks Inc; Family Therapist, Christian Cnslg Assocs; Am Assn for Marriage and Fam Therapy, Assoc Mem; SW Football Ofcls Assn; Pres, Lambda Chi Alpha Frat, Baylor, 1979-80; Lic'd Min, Assems of God, 1980-; cp/Royal Rangers Cmdr, 1980-82; r/Assem of God; hon/Dean's List, Baylor; Frontiersmans Camping Frat.

SKINNER, LARRY WARD oc/Executive, Marine Engineer, Chemical Consultant; b/Sep 15, 1942; h/#7 Skinner's Place, Savannah, GA 31406; ba/Garden City, GA; m/Marjorie Lynn Waters; c/Randall Lawrence, William Poole, Christopher Scott, Ceryl, Larry Ward II, Mary Ella; p/Ward Jones Skinner (dec); Thelma Alcedine Roach Skinner, Savannah, GA; ed/US Naval Acad Ext Grad in Marine Engrg and Lic in Diesel and Steam; AA; BS in Psych and Hist; Tchr's Cert for GA and SC Grad Sch, Univ of GA; Lic'd Pilot; Cert'd Underwater Surveyor; mil/US Coast and Geodetic Survey; pa/Fireman, USS Pierce, 1963-65; Grad Sch, 1965-68; Tchr, Asst Cnslr, Jasper Co HS, 1968-69; Prin, Patrick Henry Acad, 1969-70; Prin, Southside Elem Sch, 1970-71; Fdr and Prin, Nova Acad, 1971-72; Truck Driver and Fed Courier, 1972-77; Pres and Chm of Bd, Hedgetree Chem Mfg Inc, and Chem Conslt, 1978-; Composer of Music and Lyrics; Poet; Writer; Publisher; Phi Chi Frat; cp/Masonic Order Solomons #1, Consistory 32 Deg Mason; Shriner, Alee Temple; En Star Topai Chapt; GA Hist Soc; Area Rep and Host Fam for Am Scandinavian Student Exch Prog; J S Green Soc; r/Meth; hon/Writer of 8 Sch Currics, St Cert'd in GA and SC; AUS Heroism, 1969; Hon Mem, DAR; Hon Mem, Woms Soc of Christian Ser; Hons Awd from Swedish Min of Ed; W/W S and SW; Personalities of S.

SKLAR, RICHARD J oc/Executive; b/Nov 21, 1929; h/205 West End Avenue, New York, NY 10023; ba/New York, NY; m/Sydelle; c/Scott, Holly; p/William and Cecile Sklar, Brooklyn, NY; ed/BS, NY Univ, 1953; pa/Announcer, Sta WPAC, 1954; Copywriter, Prodr 1954-56, Prog Dir 1960, Sta WINS; Prog Dir, Sta WMGM, 1961; Prodn Dir 1962, Prog Dir 1963-72, WABC; Opers Dir, WABC and VP of Programming, ABC Owned Stas, 1973-76; VP of Programming, ABC Radio, 1976-; Adj Prof, St Johns Univ, 1973-; Intl Radio and TV Soc, Bd of Govs; Nat Assn of Broadcasters Radio Div Prog Conf Steering Com Fdg Mem; Radio Pioneers; cp/Sighted Advr, US Assn Blind Aths; Road Runners Clb of NY; hon/OH St Awd, 1971; Pres's Medal for Dist'd Ser, St Johns Univ, 1975; W/W Am; W/W World; Men of Achmt.

SKROWACZEWSKI, STANISLAW oc/Conductor, Composer; b/Oct 3, 1923; h/PO Box 700, Wayzata, MN 55391; m/Krystyna Jarosz; p/Pawel and Zofia Karszniewicz Skrowaczewski; ed/Dipl, Fac Phil, Univ of Lwow, 1945; Dipl, Facs Composition and Conducting, Acad Music, Lwow, 1945; Conservatory at Krakow, Poland, 1946; LHD, Hamline Univ 1963, Macalaster Col 1973; Doct, Univ of MN, 1979; pa/Composer, 1931-; *First Symphony and Overture for Orchestra* Written at Age 8, Played by Lwow Philharm Orch, 1931; Pianist, 1928-; Violinist, 1934-; Conductor, 1939-; Perm Conductor and Music Dir, Wroclaw Philharm 1946-47, Katowice Nat Philharm 1949-54, Krakow Philharm 1955-56, Warsaw Nat Philharm Orch 1957-59, MN Orch 1960-79; Guest Conductor, Europe, S Am, US, Japan, Israel, Australia, Canada, 1947-; Prin Conductor and Musical Advr Elect, Hallé Orch, Manchester, England; Union Polish Composers; Intl Soc Mod Music; Nat Assn Am Composers-Conductors; Am Music Ctr; Nat Soc Lit and Arts; Composer: 4 Symphonies, *Prelude and Fugue for Orchestra* 1948, *Overture* 1947, *Cantiques des Cantiques* 1951, *String Quartet* 1953, *Suite Symphonique* 1954, *Music at Night* 1954, *English Horn Concerto* 1969, Music for Theatre, Motion Pictures, Songs and Piano Sonatas; hon/Recip, Nat Prize for Artistic Activity, Poland, 1953; First Prize, Santa Cecilia Intl Concours for Conductors, Rome, 1956; Ricercari Notturni Awd, Kennedy Ctr, 1977; Conductor's Awd, Columbia Univ, 1973; Mahler-Bruckner Gold Medal of Hon, 1969; 4 Awds for Programming, MN Orch, ASCAP, 1961-79.

SLATE, CARL PHILIP oc/Professor of Missiology and Preaching; b/Oct 1, 1935; h/1105 Colonial Road, Memphis, TN 38117; ba/Memphis, TN; m/Patricia Anne Finch; c/Karen Marie Slate Guinn, Carla Joan Slate Greenwood, Carl Philip Jr; p/Mr and Mrs J C Slate, Hendersonville, TN; ed/BA, David Lipscomb Col, 1957; MA, Harding Grad Sch of Rel, 1961; DMiss, Fuller Theol Sem, 1976; pa/Fgn Ser w Chs of Christ, 1961-71; Asst, Assoc, Full Prof of Missiology, Harding Grad Sch of Rel, 1972-; Conslt to Missionary Grps in Guatemala, Brazil, Japan, Taiwan; Min w Chs of Christ in TN, KS, Great Brit; World Assn for Christian Communication; Soc for the Sci Study of Rel; Am Soc of Missiology; F'ship of Profs of Missions; r/Ch of Christ; hon/Author, Articles and Book Reviews in Profl and Rel Periodicals, Chaps in *The Church and the Future* 1972, *What the Bible Teaches* 1972; W/W Am Cols and Univs.

SLIMMER, VIRGINIA McKINLEY oc/Home Economics Administrator in Higher Education; b/Jun 21, 1932; h/Oak Grove Church Road, Rural Route #3, Benton, KY 42025; ba/Murray, NY; m/Myrl D; c/Jackie Slimmer Langholz, Kathy, Bruce; p/John W and Virga Pridy McKinley; ed/BS in Home Ec and Art, Ft Hays St Univ, 1969; MS in Interior Design and Clothing, KS St Univ, 1970; EdS in Adm and Supvn, Ft Hays St Univ, 1977; PhD in Higher Ed, IA St Univ, 1981; pa/Co-Owner and Mgr of Ranch, 1962-; Grad Adm Asst, KS St Univ, 1969-70; Instr, Ft Hays St Univ, 1970-71; Voc Home Ec Tchr, Plainville HS, 1972-74; Adv'd Clothing Tchr, Hays Sr High; Asst Alumni Dir, Ft Hays St Univ, 1977-79; Adm Asst to Dean, KS St Univ; Chair of Dept of Home Ec, Murray St Univ, 1982-; Nat Assn of Wom Deans, Admrs and Cnslrs; Am Ednl Res Assn; Am Assn for Higher Ed; Am Home Ec Assn; Phi Delta Kappa; Kappa Omicron Phi; Phi Kappa Phi; Phi Delta Gamma; Eval Netwk; r/Meth; hon/Pubs, "Evaluating Programs in Higher Education: A Conceptual Process" 1983, "Being in the Right Place at the Right Time: Strategies for Employment," "Evaluating a Program in Higher Education" 1983; Selected as Participant in Wkshop for Emerging Admrs in Home Ec, 1982; KS Home Ec Assn S'ship Winner, 1972; W/W Am Wom.

SLONEM, HUNT oc/Artist; b/Jul 18, 1951; h/87 East Houston, New York, NY 10012; p/Mr and Mrs C E Slonem, Manassas, VA; ed/BA, Painting, Tulane Univ, 1973; Att'd, Skowhegan Sch of Painting and Sculpture; pa/One-Man Shows: Alex Rosenberg Gallery 1983, Traveling Exhbn 1983 (Colegio de Architecto, Instituto Abraham Lincoln, Centro Equitoriana Norteamericano, Galeria Pardo Heeren), St Mary's Col 1983, Wks II Gallery 1982, Hunter Mus 1981, Stefanotti Gallery 1980, Martha White Gallery 1980, Others; Grp Exhbns: The Ressurection Show 1982, Hudson River Mus Annual 1982, Millican Gallery 1982, Weatherspoon Mus 1981, ABC No Rio 1981, Arsenal Gallery 1981, David Barnett Gallery 1981, Others; Public Collections: Acad of the Arts, Am Telephone and Telegraph, Borough Hall, Dayton Art Inst, Grey Gallery, Long Isl Hist Soc, Mint Mus, Mus of Mod Art, NO Mus of Art, Newark Mus, OK Art Ctr, Pt Auth, St Mary's Col, St Boniface Ch, Sidney Mus, Wichita Art Mus, St Nicolas Human Resources Ctr; hon/Featured in Num Articles; Awds: MacDowel F'ship 1983, Ragdale Foun 1983, Montalvo Ctr for the Arts 1983, Altos de Chavon 1983, Millay Colony for the Arts 1982, Greenshields Foun Grant (Painting) 1976, Painting Awd-Skowhegan Sch of Painting and Sculpture 1972, Rotary Intl Exch Student 1968.

SMARTSCHAN, GLENN FRED oc/Director of Curriculum; b/Dec 11, 1946; h/2442 Allen Street, Allentown, PA 18104; ba/Allentown, PA; m/Linda Susan Bastinelli; c/Erin Joy, Lauren Nicole; p/Mr Fred G Smartschan, Emmaus, PA; Mrs Joyce I Smartschan (dec); ed/BS in Ed, Hist and Comprehensive Social Studies, Kutztown St Col, 1968; MS in Ed, Temple Univ, 1972; EdD in Ednl Adm, Lehigh Univ, 1979; Social Studies Tchr, S Mtn Jr HS 1968-76, Asst Prin, Raub Jr HS 1976-78, Prin, Raub Jr HS 1978-80, Dir of Curric

1980-, Allentown Sch Dist; Nat Consortium on Testing; PA Assn for Supvn and Curric Devel; Nat Assn for Supvn and Curric Devel; Assn for the Gifted; Nat Bus Ed Assn; NE Conf on the Tchg of Fgn Langs; PA Sch Bds Assn, Assoc Mem; Coun for Basic Ed; Nat Assn for Gifted Chd; Am Assn of Sch Admrs; cp/Adv Com for Lehigh Co Hist Mus, 1980-; Lehigh Co C of C Ed Com, 1982-; Profl Adv Coun, March of Dimes, 1982-; hon/Pubs, "The Great American Textbook" 1982, "Rx for the Credibility Gap--District-Wide Final Examinations" 1983, Others; Recip, First Annual Matthew Gaffney Awd for Outstg S'ship, Lehigh Univ; W/W E.

SMEDLEY, RONALD FRANK oc/ Labor Relations and Human Resource Development; b/Mar 30, 1955; h/13601 East Sunset Drive, Whittier, CA 90602; ba/Los Angeles, CA; m/Julie Kay; p/ Charles and Theo Smedley, Kent, WA; ed/BA, Psych, Biola Col, 1979; MS, Indust Psych, CA St Univ Long Bch, 1981; pa/Pers and Tng Mgr, Advance Paper Box Co, 1982-; Self-Employed, Human Resource Devel Conslt, 1981-; Self-Employed, Free-Lance Profl Trumpet Player, 1978-; SW Dir of Tng and Pers, Kindercare Lng Ctrs Inc, 1981-82; Psi Chi, 1978-79; Grad Com, CA St Univ Long Bch, 1980-81; ASTD, 1982-; Pers and Indust Relats Assn, 1982-; Pers Testing Coun of So CA, 1980-; cp/AWANA Ldr, 1975-76; BSA, Life Scout 1967-70; r/Whittier Area Bapt F'ship, Career Class Coor, Ch Orch, Brass Ensemble, Pres Coun; hon/ Pub, *Selah* (Poems), 1979; BSA, Order of the Arrow, 1968; Rotary Sr Scholar, 1973; Am Legion Outstg Sr, 1973; W/ W W; Outstg Yg Men of Am.

SMELTZER, MARY SUSAN oc/Independent Artist, Pianist; b/Sep 13, 1941; h/8102 Tavenor, Houston, TX 77075; ba/Same; m/Dr Philip S Snyder; p/Mr and Mrs F C Smeltzer, Sapulpa, OK; ed/BM, OK City Univ, 1963; MM, Univ of So CA, 1964-69; Master Classes, Univ of So CA 1969, 1970-71, Sum 1971; pa/Poet; Painter; Sculptress; Artist-in-Residence, Instr of Humanities, Col of the Mainland, 1972-79; Profl Accompanist, Univ of Houston, 1972-73; Vis'g Piano Fac, Rice Univ, 1972-73; Pvt Instr, Piano, Theory, Pvt Studio, 1964-72; Piano Instr (Preparatory Div) 1966-69, 1970-72, Piano Instr (Pt-time Fac) 1966-69, 1970-72, Mt St Mary's Col; Piano Instr, First Congregational Ch, 1966-67; Piano Instr, VA Conservatory of Music, 1965-66; Other Previous Positions; hon/Fulbright Grant to Vienna; Van Cliburn Intl Piano Competition, US Rep and US Voice of Am Rep; MM Awd, Univ of So CA; MM, magna cum laude, Univ of So CA; Concerto Winner, Univ of So CA; CA Concert Artist Series Awd; Inglewood Yg Artist Awd; Nat Fdn of Music Clb Awd; OK Music Tchrs Assn Awd; Bloch Yg Artist Awd; Num Other Hons; W/ W Am Wom; Intl Book of Hon; DIB; 5,000 Personalities of World.

SMILARDO, MARGARET WATKINS oc/Hotel Manager; b/Sep 1, 1921; h/720 North Third Street, Milwaukee, WI 53203; ba/Milwaukee, WI; c/Darla, William Geno; p/Edgar and Nora Price Watkins (dec); ed/Grad, Jellico, TN, HS; mil/US Wom's Army Corp, 1945-48; pa/ Crosley Corp, 1942-45; Wk'd w Hus-

band in Hotel Mgmt, 1960-78; Mgr, WI Hotel, 1976-; Bd of Dirs, Milwaukee Hotel-Motel Assn; Notary Public; cp/ House Com, Milwaukee Press Clb; US Congl Adv Bd; Pres, Sunday Morning Breakfast Clb, First Wom Pres; Am Legion Post 448; En Star, Lake Pk Chapt 202; Milwaukee Traffic Clb; Toastmaster Intl; WI Clb.

SMILEY, CLEERETTA HENDERSON oc/Assistant Director of Home Economics Education; b/Jun 20, 1930; h/ 2209 Ross Road, Silver Spring, MD 20910; ba/Washington, DC; c/Consuela Angelia, Robert Edward, Lisa Kay, Joan Alyssa; p/Mrs Rebecca Ann Odom, Bessemer, AL; ed/BS in Home Ec, 1948; MS in Textiles, Clothing, Fam Life, 1970; Adv'd Study, 1971-; Dipl, Esoteric Sci and Psych, Am Univ, 1975; Cert, Admrs Ldrship Tng Acad, 1983; pa/Asst Dir of Home Ec, FHA/HERO St Advr, DC Public Schs, 1980-; Relief Soc Pres, Ed Coun, Ch of Jesus Christ of LDS, 1981-; Tchr, Home Ec and Yth Employmt Tng, DC Public Schs, 1962-80; Am Voc Ed Assn, 1981-; DC Voc Assn, 1981-; Nat Assn of Female Execs; World Modeling Assn; Life Mem, Nat Assn of Black Voc Edrs, 1980-; FHA/HERO Voc Yth Org; hon/Mrs DC to the Mrs Am Pageant; Mrs DC Savs Bonds to Mrs US Savs Bonds Pageant; Finalist, Mrs Am/Mrs US Savs Bonds, 1968; Harambees Mother of the Yr, 1970; Wash, DC, Blue Book of the Elite, 1970-; W/W Am Wom; W/W Among Blacks in the Washington Area; Personalities of S.

SMITH, ALBERT ALOYSIUS JR oc/ Electrical Engineer; b/Dec 2, 1935; h/11 Streamside Terrace, Woodstock, NY 12498; ba/Poughkeepsie, NY; m/Rosemarie Ann (dec); c/Denise, Matthew Patrick; p/Albert (dec) and Jean Smith, Yonkers, NY; ed/BSEE w High Hons, Milwaukee Sch of Engrg, 1961; MSEE w Hons, NY Univ, 1964; mil/USN, 1953-57; pa/Sys Engr, Adler Westrex, 1961-64; Adv Engr 1964-78, Sr Engr 1978-, IBM; IEEE Electromagnetic Environments Com, 1978-; Am Nat Standards Com C63 Subcom 1, 1980-; cp/Com Chm, Woodstock Boy Scout Troop 34, 1978-79; Com Chm, Woodstock Cub Pack 34, 1976-78; r/Rom Cath; hon/Author, 14 Papers Pub'd in Profl Jours, Book: *Coupling of External Electromagnetic Fields to Transmission Lines* 1977; Pres, Tau Omega Mu Hon Frat, 1961; IBM Invention Achmt Awd, 1979; IBM Div Awd, 1981; Milwaukee Sch of Engrg Alumnus Awd, 1981; W/W E.

SMITH, ALLIE MAITLAND oc/ Dean of School of Engineering, Professor of Mechanical Engineering; b/Jun 9, 1934; h/PO Box 1857, University, MS 38677; ba/University, MS; m/Sarah Louise Whitlock; c/Sara Leianne Smith Taylor, Hollis Duval, Meredith Lorren; p/Emma W Smith, Tabor City, NC; ed/ Bach of Mech Engrg w Hons 1956, MS 1961, PhD in Mech and Aerospace Engrg 1966, NC St Univ; pa/Dean of Engrg and Prof of Mech Engrg, Univ of MS, 1979-; Bd of Dirs Mem, MS Mineral Resources Inst, 1979-; Res Mgr, Sverdrup/ARO Corp, 1966-79; Adj Prof of Mech and Aerospace Engrg, Univ of TN Space Inst, 1967-79; Res Proj Engr, Res Triangle Inst, 1962-66; Asst Prof, Mech Engrg Dept, NC St Univ, 1961-62; Mem of Tech Staff, Bell Telephone

Labs, 1960-62; Other Previous Positions; AIAA, Assoc Fellow, Nat Terrestrial Energy Sys Tech Com 1978-; Nat Pubs Com 1979-, Nat Energy Activs Task Force 1976-; ASME, Tech Com K-12 on Aeronautical and Astronautical Heat Transfer 1975-; Am Soc of Engrg Ed; AAUP; hon/Pubs, *Radiation Transfer and Thermal Control* 1976, *Thermophysics of Spacecraft and Outer Planet Entry Probes* 1977, "Finite Element Analysis of Radiative Transport in Fibrous Insulation" 1983, "Determination of Radiative Properties from Transport Theory and Experimental Data" 1982, "Progress in Alternate Energy Resources" 1982, "1981 Technical Highlights in Terrestrial Energy Systems" 1981, Num Others; AIAA Nat Thermophysics Res Awd, 1978; Sigma Pi S'ship Awd, 1955; Sigma Xi; Phi Kappa Phi; Tau Beta Pi; Pi Tau Sigma; NY Acad of Scis; W/W S and SW; W/ W Am; W/W Aviation; W/W Engrg; Am Men and Wom of Sci; Num Other Biogl Listings.

SMITH, BARBARA JANE oc/ Teacher and Instructional Supervisor of English; b/Aug 23, 1941; h/1856 Whitbeck Road, Newark, NY 14513; ba/ Newark, NY; p/George and Alice Smith, Newark, NY; ed/BS in Elem Ed 1963, BS in Sec'dy Eng 1974, MS in Curric and Instrn 1981, Cert of Adv'd Study in Curric and Instrn 1982, Doct Wk in Curric and Instrn 1981-82, St Univ of NY Albany; pa/Fifth Grade Tchr 1963-68, 7th and 8th Grade Eng Tchr 1968-71, Newark Ctl Sch Dist; Sec'dy Eng Tchr 1971-, Instrnl Supvr of Sec'dy Eng 1974-, Newark Sr HS; Pres, Beta Theta Chapt, Delta Kappa Gamma Intl Soc for Wom Edrs, 1982-84; VP, Finger Lakes Eng Coun, 1968; Phi Delta Kappa; Nat Assn of Sec'dy Sch Prins; Assn for Curric Devel; NCTE; cp/Newark Country Clb; r/Bd of Christian Ed, Newark First Bapt Ch; hon/Recip, Intl S'ship, Delta Kappa Intl Soc for Wom Edrs, 1983; Recip, $3,000 Intl S'ship, Delta Kappa Gamma, to Be Used in Completing Doct Wk at St Univ of NY Albany, 1983; W/W E; Outstg Sec'dy Edrs of Am.

SMITH, BEULAH TAYLOR oc/ National Certified Counselor; b/Oct 25, 1934; h/932 Balboa Avenue, Cap Heights, MD 20743; ba/Washington, DC; m/Stanley Jr; c/Gail Denise, Stanley Keith, Joyce Irone; p/Stephen Thomas (dec) and Beulah Amanda Denkins Taylor, Washington, DC; ed/BS, DC Tchrs Col, 1957; MA, Fed City Col, 1972; Postgrad, Trinity Col 1977-81, Gallaudet Col 1978-81; pa/Tchr 1958-73, Open-Space Coor 1973-75, Communs Coor 1975-76, Cnslr 1978-83, DC Public Schs; Nat Cert'd Cnslr; DC Elem Sch Cnslrs Assn, Pres-Elect 1982, Pres 1983; APGA; DC Voc Guid Assn; Nat Capital Pers Guid Assn; DC Sch Cnslrs Assn; cp/Blacks in Gov 4; r/Bapt; hon/Cert, Excell Sers, Validation Tchr Competency Based Curric, 1977; Letter of Commend, Sers, Citywide Planning Comm, 1982; Cert, Nat Cert'd Cnslr, 1983; Var Plaques; W/ W E.

SMITH, CHARLES ROGER oc/Dean Emeritus, Professor; b/Mar 31, 1918; h/ 4873 Chevy Chase Avenue, Columbus, OH 43220; ba/Columbus, OH; m/ Genevieve Taylor; c/Ronald Roger, Debra A Beckstett, Eric William; p/C R Smith (dec); ed/DVM 1944, MSc 1946,

PhD 1953, OH St Univ; pa/Instr of Vet Physiol 1944-53, Asst Prof 1953-55, Assoc Prof and Chm 1955-57, Prof and Chm 1957-69, Res Prof 1969-, Dean Emeritus and Prof 1980-, OH St Univ Dept of Vet Physiol/Pharm; Dir, Ofc of Vet Med Ed, OH St Univ, 1969-72; Acting Dean 1972-73, Dean 1973-80, OH St Univ Col of Vet Med; Res Assoc, Physiol of Mammary Gland, Univ of MN, 1947; Asst Vet, Agri Experiment Sta and Div of Vet Sci, Res, Vet Physiol and Pharm, Purdue Univ, 1949, 1950, 1951; Vis'g Scholar, Res, Vet Cardiology, Univ of WA Col of Med, 1960; Col Res Com, 1981-; Am Vet Med Assn; Am Physiol Soc; AAAS; Am Heart Assn; Am Acad of Vet Physiologists and Pharmacologists; Phi Zeta; NY Acad of Scis; Acad of Vet Cardiology, Pres 1969-71; OH Vet Med Assn; Assn Am Vet Med Cols; r/Meth; hon/Author, Over 100 Articles in Profl and Sci Jours; Contbr to Several Textbooks; OH Vet of the Yr, 1979; Dist'd Alumnus Awd, OH St Univ Col of Vet Med, 1981; Ser Awd, OH Heart Assn; Res Awd, Ctl OH Heart Assn; Omega Tau Sigma Nat Gamma Awd, 1964; World W/W Sci; Outstg Edrs of Am; W/W Am; W/W MW; W/W World.

SMITH, DELORES PACE oc/Director of Family Services Division; h/3551 North Emerson Avenue, Indianapolis, IN 46218; ba/Indianapolis, IN; m/Rev Arthur Jr; p/George L (dec) and Ola Kale Pace, Grantville, GA; ed/BS, 1962; Cert'd Libn, 1967; pa/Tchr, Coweta Co Ctl HS, 1962-67; Casewkr 1972, Intensive Casewkr 1972, Supvr 1972-74, Supvr, Tng Ofcr 1974-75, Casewkr Supvr VI 1975, Asst Chief Supvr 1975-79, Acting Chief Supvr 1979-80, Div Dir 1980-, Marion Co Dept of Public Wel; Am Public Wel Assn; Delta Sigma Theta Sorority; cp/Forest Manor Multi-Ser Ctr, Bd of Dirs; Sounds of Music Ensemble; Chd's Mus; Wel Sers Leag; NAACP; Daughs of ISIS; En Star; Halcyon Temple #127; Nat Coun for Negro Wom, Indpls Sect; U Negro Col Fund, Urban Leag; Transafrica; Channel 20 WFYI; r/Ambassador Missionary Bapt Ch, Choir Mem, Ch Clk, Sunday Sch Tchr, Deaconess Bd; John Wesley Meth Ch; Pilgrim Bapt Ch; Choir Mem, Billy Graham Crusade; Puritan Bapt Ch; hon/Originated and Implemented Quality Control Prog to Reduce Error Rate; Originated, Designed and Org'd Procedural Notebook Where None Existed Before; One of Orgrs and Charter Mems of Ambassador Missionary Bapt Ch; Presented Wkshops on Public Wel to Local and St AFL-CIO Mems in St of IN; Appt'd by Mayor to IN Employmt and Tng Adv Coun, 1982; Num Other Hons; Outstg Black Wom in St of IN.

SMITH, DONNA LILIAN oc/Executive; b/Oct 8, 1944; h/PO 49193, Los Angeles, CA 90049; ba/Encino, CA; p/ Joseph and Mary Burke (dec); ed/AA, Fashion Inst of CA, 1970; Att'd, CA St Northridge Univ 1962-63; Spec Courses, Wharton Sch of Bus 197, NY Univ 1977, Univ of CA LA 1977, 1978; pa/Pres, Sems Intl, 1979-; Fashion, Meeting Conslt, 1971-; VP, Fashion Inst Design Mdse, 1969-78; Dir, Fashion Mdsg Inst, 1968-69; LA Costume Coun; Meeting Planners Intl, 1981-; Mbrship Sers Com, Assn of Indep Cols/Schs; cp/ LA Co Art Mus, 1974-; r/Rom Cath;

hon/Author, Many Ednl/Sys Manuals; W/W Am Wom; W/W W.

SMITH, DORIS DUNN oc/Teacher of Mathematics, Writer, Speaker; b/Aug 21, 1933; h/912 Hayward Street, Anaheim, CA 92804; ba/Fontana, CA; m/ Ralph Ray; c/A Glenn, Harriet L, Marcus R; p/D Harry Dunn, Anaheim, CA; Wilma K Dunn (dec); ed/PhD, Ed, Univ of Beverly Hills, 1980; MAT, Biol Sci, Univ of CA Irvine, 1973; BS, Biol and Math, Flora Macdonald Col, 1955; pa/Fontana Unified Schs, 1982-; Anaheim Union HS Dist, 1967-81; Newport-Mesa Unified Schs, 1965-67; Charlotte-Mecklenburg Schs, 1964-65; Belmont City Schs, 1962-64; St Pauls City Schs, 1955-57; Free-Lance Writer and Poet, 1978-; NEA; CA Tchrs Assn; Fontana Tchrs Assn; AAUW; Orange Co Sci and Engrg Fair Dir, 1978; Intl Wom's Writers Guild; cp/Toastmaster's Intl, Clb 550, Treas 1983; GSA, Ldr 1970; Far W Anaheim Bobby Sox Softball, 1969-71, All-Star Mgr and Coach; Wom's World Intl; r/Presb; hon/ Pubs, *Numbers Sci and You* 1973, *A Limb of Your Tree* 1983, "Thank You, Natural Mother" 1981, "Our Wedding Day" 1982; E I du Pont de Nemours Fellow, Univ of NC, 1956; First Class Girl Scout, 1943; W/W Am Wom.

SMITH, DOROTHY B oc/Hemodialysis Nurse; b/Aug 26, 1928; h/2004 Del Rio Drive, Richmond, VA 23223; ba/ Richmond, VA; m/John Douglas; c/Dr Reginald Alvis Booker; p/William R and Bessie Blount (dec); ed/Nsg Dipl, MCV Hosps; Grad, Maggie L Walker Sch of Beauty Culture, Wash, DC; Postgrad Courses in Pharm and Psychi Nsg, Ctl St Hosp; Res Course in Anatomy and Physiol of Renal Disease, VCU; pa/ Employee, MCV's Hosp, 25 Yrs, Scrub and Circulating Nurse in Gen Surg, Specializing in Chest Surg; Att'd Sems for Am Assn of Internal Organs; Pres, NCV Hosp Nurses Alumnae, 1963-65; Adv Bd, Nat Leag of Nurses; ARC Disaster Team II; Am Assn of Nephrology; Transplantation Nurses; ABWA; cp/Yg Wom's Christian Leag Inc, Secy 1980-82, Treas 1968-80, Pres; Jolly Wives Social Clb, Past Pres 1980-85, Treas; r/Del to VA Meth Conf, 1975, 1980; Pres of Nurses Unit, Asbury U Meth Ch; hon/First and Only Black Nurse to Do Res in Renal Disease at MCV; Commun Ser Awd, Sigma's Psi Phi Psi, for Outstg Wk in Commun, 1963.

SMITH, DOROTHY MADELAINE oc/Hotel Manager; b/Feb 21, 1922; h/ 11449 Airlane, Drive, #B, Bridgeton, MO 63044; m/William L (dec); c/ Anthony, Martin, Christopher; p/ Anthon J and Mabel Wollenzien Opstedal (dec); ed/BS 1941, MS, magna cum laude, Univ of WI; mil/Lt Cmdr, USNR, 1942-44; pa/Ofc Mgr, Pauly Rlty, 1973-76; DR Mgr, Concourse Hotel, 1976-77; Res Mgr, Edgewater Hotel, 1977-78; Front Desk Supvr, Holiday Inn, 1978-81; Asst Gen Mgr, Middletown, NY, 1981; ABWA, Pres of Badger Chapt 1978, Pres, Louis IX 1980; WI Alumni Assn; Phi Beta Kappa; Theta Sigma Upsilon; Kappa Alpha Theta; cp/ Bd of Dirs, New Hope Foun; Ret'd Ofcrs Assn; W Point Ofcrs Clb; Hosp Vol; r/ Luth; hon/WI Wom of the Yr, 1978; Spec Arrangements Chm, ABWA Reg Conv; CoChair, Cred Com, ABWA Nat

Conv, 1981.

SMITH, ENID oc/Social Service Administrator; b/Jan 12, 1935; h/152 Willow Street, Brooklyn, NY 11201; ba/ Brooklyn, NY; p/Ben D (dec) and Lea Alpert Smith, Albany, NY; ed/BS, Spec Studes, summa cum laude, St Francis Col, 1977; MA, Psych, Long Isl Univ, 1980; pa/Dancer, Choreographer, Tchr of Dance and Drama in Num Pvt Schs and Instns, incl'g Adelphi Acad (Bklyn), Sch of Creat Arts (Martha's Vineyard), Chapin Sch (Nightingale-Bamford, NYC), 1952-66; Public Relats Spec, The Bklyn Hosp, Staten Isl Hosp, Brookdale Hosp, NYC, 1974-79; Psychotherapist, Bklyn Psychosocial Rehab Inst, 1980-82; Dir, Bhrags Sr Citizens Prog, 1982-; Pvt Pract in Psychotherapy and Cnslg; Am Mtl Hlth Cnslrs Assn; APGA; r/Jewish; hon/Recip, Awd from Commun Agys Public Relats Assn, 1975; Nat Archives of Am Med Col for Excell in Med Ednl Public Relats; W/W E.

SMITH, G T oc/College President; b/ Nov 12, 1935; h/9631 Fleet Road, Villa Park, CA 92667; ba/Orange, CA; m/ Joni; c/Paul Brian, Sherry Lynn; ed/BA, Col of Wooster, 1956; MPA w Distn, Cornell Univ, 1960; LLD, Bethany Col, 1979; pa/Assoc Dir of Devel, Cornell, 1960-62; Dir of Devel 1962-66, VP 1966-77, Col of Wooster; Pres, Chapman Col, 1977-; Exec Com, Assn of Indep CA Cols and Univs; Indep Cols of So CA, Pres 1981-82; cp/Dir, Orange Co World Affairs Coun; Goodwill Industs of Orange Co; Nat Conf of Christians and Jews, Dir and Mem; Lincoln Clb; Pacific Clb; Balboa Bay Clb; Univ Clb, Wash, DC; r/Presb; hon/ Author, Pubs and Articles in Var Profl Jours; W/W Am; W/W Ed; W/W CA.

SMITH, GENEVIEVE GRANT oc/ Elementary School Principal; b/Dec 3, 1922; h/1825 South Pacific, Boise, ID 83705; ba/Boise, ID; m/Jasper William; c/Lawrence Jasper, Lynda Jean, Eldon Howard, Stanley Dayle; p/Lawrence Jessie (dec) and Melitta Mae Stiegelmeier Grant, Meridian, ID; ed/AA, Boise Jr Col, 1957; BA, NW Nazarene Col, 1964; MEd, Col of ID, 1969; pa/ Classroom, Vocal Music Tchr (Coor, Boise, ID), ISD, 1957-63; Adm Team Ldr, Lowell Sch, 1973-76; Asst Prin, Garfield Sch, 1976-78; Prin, Whitney Sch, 1978-; Active, Dist, St Ed Coms; Wkshop Instr; Supvr and Curric Devel, ID and Nat; ID Soc Indiv Psych; ID Assn Elem Sch Prins; Nat Assn Elem Sch Prins; ID Assn Sch Admrs; Boise Assn Sch Prins; Boise Ed Assn; ID Ed Assn; NEA; NW Wom in Ednl Adm; Alumni Assn, Boise St Univ; NW Nazarene Col Assn; Phi Delta Kappa; Delta Kappa Gamma; Phi Delta Lambda, Bd Mem 1970-; Cap Edrs' Fed Credit Union, Served as Secy, VP and Pres; cp/ Vista Neighborhood Housing Sers; Active, Num Fund Raising Coms; Yokefellows Assn; NOW; Boise Sch Equal Employmt Opport Com, 1979-; r/Prot; hon/Contbr, Articles to Local Newspapers; Recip, ID Gem Awd, ID Assn Elem Sch Prins, 1980; Life Merit Awd, ID St PTA, 1979; Red Apple Awd, Boise Sch Dist, 1975; Recip, Boss of the Yr Awd, Ada Co Assn Ednl Ofc Pers, 1983; Title IV-C Match Prog, 1980; W/ W W.

SMITH, HARRY V JR oc/Community College President; b/Aug 5, 1929; h/

915 Holly Street, Blytheville, AR 72315; ba/Blytheville, AR; m/Margaret Swann; c/Peggy Smith Herbst, Harry V III, Betty Grace, James Michael; p/Dr and Mrs Harry V Smith, Fayetteville, GA; ed/PhD, Commun Col Adm, FL St Univ, 1968; MEd 1954, BA in Math 1950, Mercer Univ; mil/2nd Med Bat, 2nd Inf Div, Korea; pa/Pres, MS Co Commun Co, 1975-; Exec Dean, Broward Commun Col, Ctl Campus, 1972-75; Exec Dean, Broward Commun Col, N Campus, 1971-72; Assoc Dean of Acad Affairs 1970-71, Asst Dean of Acad Affairs 1969-70, Chm of Div of Math and Sci 1968-69, Broward Commun Col; Assoc Prof and Hd, Dept of Math, So Tech Inst, 1955-66; Other Previous Positions; FL Voc Assn; Am Voc Assn; FL Assn of Commun and Jr Cols; Am Soc for Engrg Ed, Tech Inst Div; Am Assn of Higher Ed; Am Soc of Allied Hlth Professions; Other Profl Mbrships; cp/Rotary Clb; Intl Solar Energy Soc; r/Bapt; hon/Pubs, "The Mississippi County Community College, Large-Scale Demonstration Project: A Success Story" 1982, "The World's Largest Photovoltaic Concentrator System: A Case Study" 1981, Others; Alpha Phi Omega, 1949; Kappa Phi Kappa, 1949; Blue Key, 1950; M Clb, 1949-50; Boss of the Yr, NE AR Chapt, Nat Secys Assn, 1978; Num Other Hons; Outstg Edrs of Am.

SMITH, JANICE SHIRLEY oc/College Instructor of Nursing; b/Jan 29, 1937; h/770 Troy Court, Aurora, CO 80011; ba/Westminster, CO; p/E Burl (dec) and Cova Bolinger Smith, Springdale, AR; ed/MS in Med/Surg Nsg, Univ of CO Denver, 1970; BS in Nsg, Univ of CO Boulder, 1964; Dipl in Nsg, Sparks Meml Hosp Sch of Nsg, 1958; pa/Instr, Med/Surg Nsg, Commun Col of Denver, N Campus, 1977-; Instr, Coor and Dir of Div of Hlth Occupations, Commun Col of Denver, Auraria Campus, 1970-76; Instr, Presb Med Ctr Sch of Nsg, 1964-69; Staff Nurse, Psychi, CO Psychi Hosp, 1962; Staff Nurse, Team Ldr, Gen Rose Meml Med Ctr, 1961-62; Nsg Supvr and Dir of Inser Ed, Hillcrest Med Ctr, 1960-61; Staff Nurse, Team Ldr, Presb-St Luke's Med Ctr, 1959; Instr, Clin, 1958-59, 1959-60; Sigma Theta Tau, Pres of Alpha Kappa Chapt for 2 Yrs, Nom's Com Chp, Prog Planning Com; ANA; CO Nurses Assn, Bd of Dirs, St Mbrship Com; Dist 14, CO Nurses Assn, Pres for 2 Yrs, VP, Bd Mem, Nom'g Com Chp, Prog Com, Mbrship Com Chp; Involved Nurses for Polit Action in CO; NEA; CO Ed Assn, Local Chapt Rep; CO Voc Assn, Prog Planning Com for Annual Sum Conf; Am Voc Assn; Nat Leag for Nsg; CO Leag for Nsg, Prog Planning Com; cp/Cherokee Nat Hist Soc; r/Prot; hon/Selected to Sigma Theta Tau, Alpha Kappa Chapt of Nat Hon Soc in Nsg for Acad Excell, 1970.

SMITH, JERRY L oc/Attorney at Law, State Senator; b/Dec 6, 1943; h/5327 East 33rd, Tulsa, OK 74135; ba/Tulsa, OK; m/Sally Huye-Smith; p/Hollis C Smith (dec); Eulema M Dougherty, Tulsa, OK; ed/BA, OK St Univ; JD, Univ of Tulsa Sch of Law; pa/OK St Senate, 1980-; OK Ho of Reps, 1972-80; Atty at Law, 1971-; OK Bar Assn; Tulsa Co Bar Assn; OK Trial Lwyrs Assn; Nat Repub Legis Assn; Am

Legis Exch Counsel; cp/Trans Clb of Tulsa; r/Meth; hon/W/W Am Polit; W/W S and SW; Personalities of S; Outstg Yg Men of US.

SMITH, JOHN CARLTON oc/Superintendent of Schools; b/May 2, 1937; h/PO Box 1315, Hartselle, AL 35640; m/Martha L; c/Kenneth, Bill; p/Mr and Mrs John O Smith, Talladega, AL; ed/BS, Livingston St Univ, 1959; MEd, Auburn Univ, 1967; EdD, Univ of AL, 1971; mil/Army/NG; pa/Asst Coach/Tchr 1959-61, Hd Coach/Tchr 1962-67, Bullock Co HS; Hd Coach/Tchr, E B Erwin HS, 1967-68; Prin, Roy Stone Jr High, 1968-71; Asst Supt, Jackson Public Schs, 1971-73; Assoc Supt, Richland Dist I, 1973-75; Supt, Hartselle City Schs, 1975-; Am Assn of Sch Admrs, 1971-; AL Assn of Sch Admrs, 1975-; AL Coun for Sch Adm and Supvn, 1975-, Dist VP/Pres-Elect 1983; Nat Assn of Sec'dy Sch Prins, 1968-; Phi Delta Kappa, 1966-; cp/Kiwanis Intl, 1975-; Morgan Co Mtl Hlth Assn, Bd of Dirs 1975-78, Pres 1978; r/Bapt; hon/Pub, "The Relationship of the Superintendent and High School Principal in the Decision Making Process"; Citizen of the Yr, Hartselle Civitan Clb, 1983.

SMITH, JOSEPHINE MARSHALL oc/Vocational Counselor; b/Jun 6, 1932; h/1802 Lakeview Drive, Scottsboro, AL 35768; ba/Scottsboro, AL; m/Chester Lee Sr; c/Chester Lee Jr, Mary Jacqueline Smith LaRue, Patricia Louise; p/Richard Quention Marshall (dec); Mary Lucille Carter (dec); ed/Att'd, E MS Jr Col 1950-52, Univ of KY 1959-60, Campbellsville Col 1965-66, A&M Univ 1973-78, Univ of AL 1980; BS in Elem Ed, 1967; Master's Deg in Guid and Cnslg, 1976; A Cert, Adm and Supvn, 1977; AA Cert, Adm and Supvn, 1978; Adv'd Studies in Adm and Planning, 1980; pa/2nd Grade Tchr, Muldraugh, KY, 1959-60; 6th Grade Tchr, Scottsboro Jr High, 1967-75; 6th Grade Tchr, Scottsboro Elem Sch, 1975; 12th Grade Tchr, Govt and Ec, and Cnslr, 1975-77; Prin, 1977-80; Coor, Curric/Staff Devel, Area Chm for Ed, AAUW, 1976-78; SEA, Treas 1973-74, Pres-Elect 1974-75, Pres 1975-76; Treas, Delta Kappa Gamma, Rho Chapt, 1976-78; Fin Com, Beta St; r/Bapt; hon/W/W S and SW.

SMITH, SISTER KATHLEEN MARY oc/Dean of Student Services; b/Sep 26, 1945; ba/Mount Aloysius Junior College, Cresson, PA 16630; p/Michael W and Mary E Smith, New Hyde Park, NY; ed/BA, Col Misericordia, 1969; MA, IN Univ of PA, 1974; PhD, Univ of MI, 1982; pa/Dean of Student Sers, Mt Aloysius Jr Col, 1982-; Adm Intern, Suomi Col, 1981; Conslt, Title II Prog, MI Christian Col, Univ of MI Ext Ser, 1981; Interviewer, Univ of MI Psych Dept, 1981; Interviewer, Univ of MI's Ctr for the Study of Higher Ed Res on National Higher Ednl Assns, 1980; Instnl Res/Conslt, Title II Prog, Washtenaw Commun Col, 1979-81; Dir of Student Financial Aid/Lectr in Math, Mt Aloysius Jr Col, 1974-79; Patient Relats Coor, Mercy Hosp, 1974; Other Previous Positions; Sisters of Mercy Ser/Ldrship, Due Process Procedure-Arbitrator 1981-85, Fiscal Mgmt Comm 1982-, Corp of Sisters of Mercy of Cresson Bd Mbrship 1982-, Sisters of Mercy Formation Coun 1982-; Am Assn

of Commun and Jr Cols; Am Assn of Higher Ed; Assn for Study of Higher Ed; Mercy Higher Ed Colloquium; Nat Assn of Student Pers Admrs; Nat Assn of Student Financial Aid Admrs; PA Assn of Student Financial Aid Admrs; Univ of MI Students for Ednl Innovation; cp/KEY Specialized Foster Care Sers Inc, 1983-; r/Rom Cath; hon/Pubs, "Student Achievement and Open Admissions: Do Students Outcomes Fulfill the Promise of the 'Open Door'?" 1983, The Relationship of Community College Transfer Students' Characteristics to Their Baccalaureate Institutional Choice and Outcomes 1982; Pres's Comm on White House F'ships Reg Finalist, 1982-83; Univ of MI Sch of Ed Merit Awd, 1981-82; P I Merrill S'ship, 1980-81; Other Hons; W/W in Am.

SMITH, LOUISE SOMERS WINDER oc/Homemaker, Poet; b/Aug 20, 1912; h/Star Route Box P233, Hartfield, VA 23071; am/Capious Otway; c/Capious Otway, Lee Winder, Nan Somers; p/Alonzo Lee and Ruth Somers Winder (dec); ed/Grad, Newport News Bus Col, 1930; pa/Secretarial Position, Allan R Hoffman & Co, 1930-31; Secretarial Position, VA Facility, 1931-41, 1949-50; AZ St Poetry Soc, 1974-; Poetry Soc of VA, 1976-; Wash Poets Assn, 1974-; Wn World Haiku Soc, 1974-; Yuki Teikei Haiku Soc of USA and Canada, 1978-; Former Mem: Am Poetry Leag, Haiku Apprec Clb, PA Poetry Soc, Piedmont Lit Soc, Poets' Tape Exch; cp/Exec Bd, Allegheny Co Chapt, Muscular Dystrophy Assn Inc, 1957-72, Serving as VP, Chm, Ed Com, Spkr, Fund Raiser, Exec VP, Pres; IPA, 1967-69; Pgh Com on Employmt of the Handicapped, 1969-71; Rep, Muscular Dystrophy Assn Inc, to Annual Meeting, 1970; Pres's Com on Employmt of the Handicapped; r/Bapt; hon/Poetry Pub'd in Var Anthologies and Jours, 1929-; Haiku Pub'd (USA and Japan) in Var Poetry Jours, Quarterlies and Anthologies; Var Haiku Awds as Result of Contests of Var St Poetry Orgs; Recip, Dragonfly Haiku of the Yr Awd, 1981 (Winning Haiku Pub'd in "Haiku in English" Sect of Mainichi Daily News, Tokyo, 1982); Commun Ldrs of Am; W/W Am Wom; Wom of Canada; W/W E; World Notables.

SMITH, MARK CRAIG oc/Clinical Psychologist; b/Mar 28, 1953; h/310 West 88th Street, Apartment #8, New York, NY 10024; ba/New York, NY; p/Harold and Berenice Smith, Fort Wayne, IN; ed/BA, IN Univ, 1975; MA 1977, PhD 1979, CA Sch of Profl Psych; pa/Clin Psychol in Pvt Pract, 1983-; Dir of SR-One, S Bch Psychi Ctr, 1981-82; Clin Psychol, NH Hosp, 1979-80; Am Psychol Assn; Assn for the Advmt of Psych; cp/Psychols for Legis Action Now; ACLU; Amnesty Intl; Greenpeace; Mun Art Soc; Wildlife Foun; hon/Pub, "The Relationship Between Draw-A-Person Test Performance and Four Psychodiagnostic Groups," 1979; W/W E.

SMITH, NELLE CREWS oc/Nursing Education; b/Apr 12, 1925; h/1706 Hollywood Drive, Columbia, SC 29205; ba/Columbia, SC; m/William Clyde Jr; c/William Clyde III, Roy Crews, Margie Merrinelle; p/Roy Walter (dec) and Ruby Adcock Crews, Oxford, NC; ed/Att'd, Mars Hill Col 1943, Columbia

Hosp Sch of Nsg 1947; BS in Nsg 1976, Master of Nsg 1981, Univ of SC; pa/ Hd Nurse, Med Disease Unit 1947-49, Supvr of Surg Disease Unit 1949-51, Columbia Hosp; Hlth Room Supvr, A C Moore Sch, 1957-61; Nurse Spec, Columbia, 1961-66; Instr, Coronary Care Unit, Columbia Hosp, 1966-68; Hd Nurse, Coronary Care Unit, Providence Hosp, 1968-69; Instr 1969-76, Instr/ Coor 1977-81, Richland Nsg Prog; Instr, Assoc Deg Nsg Prog, Midlands Tech Col, 1981-; Nat Leag for Nsg, Agy Coun Mem 1977-81; SC Nurses Assn; ANA; Ctl Midlands Nurses Assn; Columbia Hosp Alumnae Assn; Univ of SC Alumni Assn; SC Tech Ed Assn; Am Heart Assn; SC Heart Assn; Sigma Theta Tau Nat Nurses Hon Soc; r/Bapt; hon/Sigma Theta Tau Nat Nurses Hon Soc, 1980; W/W Am Wom; World W/ W Wom.

SMITH, PAUL A oc/Executive; b/Jan 1, 1945; h/6105 Glenhurst Way, Citrus Heights, CA 95610; ba/Same; m/Nancy Fuller; c/Jeremy James, Emily Anne; p/ Paul L Smith, San Antonio, TX; ed/PhD 1982, MA 1981, Univ of Ctl CA; BA, San Diego St Univ, 1971; mil/USN, Hosp Third Class, 1962-68; pa/Chief, Pers Policy, Standard and Exams, CA Dept of Developmental Sers; Chief, Employee Tng and Devel, CA Dept of Developmental Sers; Affirmative Action Coor, CA Dept of Developmental Sers; Labor Relats Rep, San Diego Public Employees Assn; Current Pres, Profl Assault Response Tng; cp/Yth for Nixon, San Diego Co, 1968; r/Quaker; hon/Author, Several Profl Jour Articles; Awd of Merit, 1981; Outstg Profl Perf, 1979; Outstg Contbn and Prog, 1977; Outstg Yg Men of Am.

SMITH, RAYMOND F oc/Foreign Service Officer; b/May 31, 1941; h/1208 D Street, Southeast, Washington, DC 20003; ba/Washington, DC; m/Cynthia G; p/Catharine M Smith; ed/AB, magna cum laude, Temple Univ, 1965; MA 1966, PhD 1973, NWn Univ; mil/ 1959-62; pa/Labor Relats Examr, Nat Labor Relats Bd, 1968-69; Fdg Ser Ofcr, Dept of St, 1969-; Third Secy, Tunis Tunisia, 1970-72; Desk Ofcr for the Sudan, Wash, 1972-74; Chp, Secy's Open Forum Panel, 1974-75; Second Secy, Moscow, USSR, 1976-79; First Secy, Abidjan, Ivory Coast, 1979-82; Ofcr-in-Charge, Bilateral Relats Sect, Ofc of Soviet Union Affairs, 1982-; St Dept Rep, Treas, Secy, Am Fgn Ser Assn, 1972-75; hon/Author, Articles in *Foreign Service Journal, Open Forum, Journal of Peace Research, Journalism Quarterly;* Dist'd Ser Awd, Am Fgn Ser Assn, 1975; W/W World.

SMITH, ROBERT IRVINE II oc/ Chief of Engineer Resources Management Division; b/Nov 21, 1947; h/1035 South Holly Street, Columbia, SC 29205; ba/Jackson, SC; m/Elizabeth Anne Dominick; p/Robert I and Lorene Smith, Augusta, SC; ed/BS, Civil Engrg, 1976; BS, Mech Engrg, 1977; Master of Engrg, 1978; mil/USN, 1967-71; USNR, 1971-80; pa/Consltg Engrg, Jt Legis Com on Energy, SC Gen Assem, 1977-78; Self-Employed, Owner of Engrg Design and Testing Corp, 1978-80; Chief of Mgmt and Engrg Sys Br 1980-81, Current Chief of Engr Resource Mgmt Div, Directorate of Engrg and Housing; ASCE, Chapt

Secy-Treas 1974; ASME, Chapt Secy-Treas 1977, VP 1978; Pi Mu Epsilon, Secy-Treas 1975, Pres 1976; Pi Tau Sigma, VP 1979; Am Nuclear Soc, Treas 1980; cp/Boy Scouts of Am, Scoutmaster 1975-76; Order of the Arrow, BSA Lodge Chief, 1965; hon/ SC Gov's Palmeto Awd, 1981; ASME Dist'd Ser Awd, 1980; Univ of SC Dist'd Ser Awd, 1978; Eagle Scout Awd, 1965; Vigil Hon, 1966; Omicron Delta Kappa, 1979; Pi Mu Epsilon, 1975; Tau Beta Pi, 1980; Pi Tau Sigma, 1979; Hon Soc of Civil Engrs, 1980; Pi Sigma, 1981; Outstg Yg Men of Am; W/W Am Cols and Univs.

SMITH, ROBERTA ANN oc/Interim Dean, Associate Professor; b/Aug 11, 1944; h/1032 Belvidere Drive, Nashville, TN 37204; ba/Nashville, TN; c/ Elizabeth Pointer; p/Mrs Uarta Ann Pointer, Ft Myer, FL; ed/BSN, IL Wesleyan Univ, 1966; MSN, Univ of IL at the Med Ctr, 1969; PhD, Clin Psych, George Peabody Col, 1976; pa/Staff Nurse, IL St Psychi Inst, 1966-67; Instr, Univ of IL Col of Nsg, 1969-72; Dir of Geriatric Sers, Dede Wallace Mtl Hlth Ctr, 1976-78; Assoc Prof 1978-, Interim Dean 1983-, Vanderbilt Univ Sch of Nsg; Psychotherapist, Pvt Pract, 1978-; Bd of Dirs, Alive-Hospice of Nashville, 1981-; VP, Vanderbilt Wom's Fac Org, 1979-81; Exec Com, Vanderbilt Fac Senate, 1981-83, Secy 1982-83; Adv Bd, Vanderbilt Wom's Ctr, 1979-82; r/Prot; hon/Phi Kappa Phi, 1966; Sigma Theta Tau, 1968; Yg Wom of the Yr for TN, 1980; Carolyn Rupert Awd in Nsg; Hon Master's Thesis, Univ of IL.

SMITH, RUFUS HOWARD I oc/ Retired Educator; b/Jan 21, 1920; h/ #40-20th Avenue South, Birmingham, AL 35205; ba/Birmingham, AL; m/ Elizabeth Bloxom; c/Alfred Tyrone, Rufus Howard II, William, Corenza, Marion; p/Editor W H and Lizzie Wooden Smith (dec); ed/Cert, Selma Univ, 1939; BS, AL St Univ, 1942; MEd, Tuskegee Inst, 1953; LLD, Faith Col, 1983; pa/Instr, Selma Univ, 1946; Instr, B'ham Public Sch Sys, Lincoln 1946-54, Riley 1954-68, Wn-Olin High 1968-70, Phillips HS 1970-82; Chm of Social Studies Dept, Phillips High, 1972-82; Assem Chm, Voters Registration Coor, B'ham Cent Chm, Phillips, 1971; Tnr for TV Series at Phillips, "Youth Speaks Out"; Col Class Pres; NEA; AEA; BEA; Alpha Phi Alpha Frat; VP, Selma Univ Alumni Assn, B'ham Chapt; cp/Charter Mem, Phantom Knights Social Clb; r/ Bapt; hon/Author, Articles Pub'd Frequently in *Birmingham News, Birmingham World, Birmingham Times, Baptist Leader, Birmingham Post Herald;* Tchr of the Yr, Riley, 1964-65; First Ruuner-Up for St of AL Favorite Tchr, 1974; Cit, Zeta Phi Lambda Sorority, 1983; Nat Alumni Spkr, Selma Univ, 1983; Fdr's Day Spkr, ASU, 1984.

SMITH, RUTH CATHERINE oc/ Education Specialist; b/Jan 12, 1935; h/ 800 South Belgrade Road, Silver Spring, MD 20902; ba/Rockville, MD; m/Harold E (dec); c/Wanda Smith Person, Carlton Harold; p/Edward and Jessie Jackson (dec); ed/BS, DC Tchrs Col, 1956; MA, George Wash Univ, 1970; pa/DC Public Schs, 1956-61; Camden, NJ, Public Schs, 1963-64; Willingboro, NJ, Public Schs, 1964-67; Montgomery Co Public Schs, 1967-70; Ed Spec, Montgomery Co

Public Schs, 1970-; NEA; MCEA; MSTA; Nat Coun of Social Studies; Assn for Supvn and Curric Devel; Phi Delta Kappa; cp/African-Am Wom's Assn, VP; Nat Coun of Negro Wom; NAACP; Trans Africa; r/Bapt; hon/Pub, "Comparing and Contrasting the Educational System in Montgomery Co, MD, USA, and Kenya, East Africa," 1980; Spec Contbns to African-Am Affairs, African-Am Wom's Assn, 1981-83; W/W E.

SMITH, STANLEY ALLEN oc/Data Processing Consultant; b/Nov 27, 1952; h/5912 Walla, Fort Worth, TX 76133; ba/Fort Worth, TX; m/Jacqueline; c/ Nathaniel Reid, Zachary Alden; p/ George F and Mary Inez Smith, Tempe, AZ; ed/BS in Engrg, AZ St Univ, 1976; Postgrad Wk, SWn Bapt Theol Sem, 1977; pa/Programmer/Analyst, Nat Spinal Cord Injury Data Res Ctr, 1975-76; DP Supvr, Westmoor Mfg Co Inc, 1977-78; Programmer/Analyst, Priority Sys Inc, 1978; Owner, Designer Software Conslts, 1979-; VP, Mun Software Conslts Inc, 1980-; r/So Bapt; hon/Alpha Pi Mu, Indust Engrg Hon Soc; W/W S and SW.

SMITH, SYLVIA MAE oc/Medical Technologist; b/Sep 25, 1947; h/1290 West 24th Street, San Bernardino, CA 92405; ba/Apple Valley, CA; m/Peter J; p/J Clifford and Ieleen M Stone, San Bernardino, CA; ed/BA, CA St Col, 1969; Cert, Med Technol, VA Hosp Sch Med Technol, 1970; CA Lic, 1970; ASCP Registration, 1970; pa/Med Tech, Instr in Chem, VA Hosp, 1970-71; Supvr, Automated Chem and Serology, Instr of Chem, Urinanalysis, Immunol and Serology, Commun Hosp, 1971-75; Chief Tech, Clin Lab of San Bernardino, 1975-76; Chief Tech, Col Med Surg Sers, 1976; Staff Med Tech, St Mary's Desert Val Hosp, 1982-; Am Assn Clin Pathologists, Assoc Mem; CA Assn Lab Med Technol; r/Free Meth; hon/Nat Hon Soc, 1965; Bronze and Silver Medal in Eng Ballroom Dancing w Hons, 1966; W/W Am Wom.

SMITH, VIRGINIA BEATRICE oc/ College President; b/Jun 24, 1923; h/ President's House, Vassar College, Poughkeepsie, NY 12601; ba/Poughkeepsie, NY; p/Frank B Smith Sr, Seattle, WA; ed/BA 1944, JD 1946, MA in Labor and Ec 1950, Univ of WA; Postgrad Study, Ec and Law, Columbia Univ, 1947; pa/Pres, Vassar Col, 1977-; Dir, Fund for the Improvement of Postsec'dy Ed, US Dept of Hlth, Ed and Wel, 1973-77; Asst Dir 1967-71, Assoc Dir 1971-73, Carnegie Comm on Higher Ed, 1967-73; Coor of Public Progs, Inst of Indust Relats 1952-58, Instr, Univ of CA Ext 1952-60, Adm Analyst 1958-60, Asst to the VP 1962-65, Coor of Adm Policy Unit 1963-65, Asst VP 1965-67, Univ of CA Berkeley; Other Previous Positions; Dir, Assn of Am Cols, 1977-; Soc for Values in Higher Ed, Bd Pres 1981-; Mod Lang Assn, Comm on the Future of the Profession, Adv Bd 1981-; Trustee, Culinary Inst of Am, 1980-; Trustee, Carnegie Foun for Advmt of Tchg, 1980-; Am Assn for Higher Ed; Am Ednl Res Assn; Dir, Marine Midland Bks Inc; Am Coun on Ed, Nat Comm on Higher Ed Issues; Def Adv Com on Wom in the Sers; CA St Bar Assn; hon/ Pubs, *The Impersonal Campus* 1979, "City and Campus" 1975, "Individualized Self-Paced Instruction" 1974, "Assessing Experiential Learning: The Search for an Integrating Logic" 1974, Others; Hon LHD, DePaul Univ 1982, Alverno Col 1982, Hood Col 1977; Hon DHL, RI Col, 1978; Hon LLD, Ottawa Univ, 1974; Named One of 44 Ldrs in Am Higher Ed, *Change Magazine* Survey, 1975; Fulbright Scholar in England, 1956-57; Res Fellow, Inst of Labor Ec, Univ of WA, 1946; W/W Am; W/W Am Wom; 5,000 Personalities of World; World W/W Wom.

SMITH, WILBUR STEVENSON oc/ Executive; b/Sep 6, 1911; h/1630 Kathwood Drive, Columbia, SC 29206; ba/ Columbia, SC; m/Sarah Bolick; c/Sarah Jane Smith Cahalan, Margaret Paul, Dr Stephanie Elizabeth; p/George W and Rebecca S Smith (dec); ed/BS in Elect Engrg 1932, MS in Elect Engrg 1933, Univ of SC; Grad Study, Harvard Univ, 1936-37; Res Fellow, Inst of Labor Ec, 1936-37; Hon LLD, Univ of SC, 1963; Hon LHD, Lander Col, 1975; pa/Chm of the Bd 1976-, Chm of the Bd and Pres 1972-76, Pres 1952-72, Wilbur Smith and Assocs; Fac Mem and Assoc Dir, Yale Univ's Bur of Highway Traffic, 1943-68; Fac Mem, Traffic Engrg, Clemson Univ and Univ of SC (Pt-time), 1943-46; Coor, Traffic Studies and Trans Theory Courses, Fed Bur of Invest, 1943-46; Conslt on Trans to Ofc of Civil Def, 1943-46; Dir, Traffic Engrg Dept, SC Dept of Highways and Public Trans, 1936-43; Highway Engr, SC Dept of Highways and Public Trans, 1933-36; Chm, Eno Foun for Trans Inc; Nat Acad of Engrg; Am Road and Trans Bldrs Assn; Dir, Transportation Assn of Am; Dir, SC C of C; Dir, Highway Users Fdn for Safety and Mobility; Hon Mem, ASCE; Hon Mem, Inst of Transportation Engrs; Fellow, Am Consltg Engrs Coun; Trans Res Bd; Intl Road Fdn; Fellow, Instn of Civil Engrs, UK; Fellow, Instn of Engrs, Australia; Fellow, New Zealand Instn of Engrs; Fellow, Hong Kong Instn of Engrs; hon/ Author, Num Tech Reports, Papers and Bulletins; Dist'd Alumni Awd, Univ of SC, 1968; Roy W Crum Awd, Trans Res Bd, 1980; Theodore M Matson Meml Awd, 1965; Algernon Sydney Sullivan Awd, Univ of SC, 1978; Burton W Marsh Dist'd Ser Awd, Inst of Trans Engrs, 1982; Recip, First Highway Div Awd Presented by ASCE, 1982; Recip, 40-Yr Ser Awd, Am Soc of Safety Engrs, 1982; Recip, Dist'd Ser Awd, Sch of Engrg Alumni Assn, Duke Univ, 1982; Chi Epsilon, Hon Mem; Phi Beta Kappa; W/W Am.

SMITH, WILBURN ALEXANDER JR oc/Assistant Commissioner of Education; b/Aug 13, 1939; h/#10-1-13 Estate Charlotte Amalie, St Thomas, Virgin Islands 00801; ba/St Thomas, Virgin Islands; m/Viola Calistro; c/Andre Previn, Lurleen Marie, Lisa Anne; p/ Wilburn Alexander Sr and Elma Davis Smith, St Thomas, Virgin Islands; ed/ EdD, Rutgers Univ, 1979; EdM, IA St Univ, 1965; BS, AL A&M Col, 1960; pa/ Asst Commr of Ed 1979-, Territorial Dir for Voc and Tech Ed 1967-79, Coor for Voc and Tech Ed 1966-67, Asst Coor for Voc and Tech Ed 1963-66, Virgin Isls Dept of Ed; Indust Arts Ed Tchr, Charlotte Amalie HS, 1960-63; Phi Delta Kappa, 1965; Nat Assn of St Dirs of Voc Ed, 1967; Virgin Isls Voc Assn,

1960; Phi Beta Sigma Frat, 1958; Epsilon Pi Tau, 1965; Study Comm/Coun of Chief St Sch Ofcrs; cp/Dukes Clb Inc, 1959; r/Presb; hon/Pubs, "Economic Development Survey: Its Relevance to Future Ecnomic Planning and Development for the United States Virgin Islands," "Educational Reform: A Social Strategy for Survival in a Contemporary Caribbean" 1982; W/W Caribbean and W Indies.

SMITH, WILFRED CANTWELL oc/ University Professor; b/Jul 21, 1916; h/ 17 Jason Street, Arlington, MA 02174; ba/Cambridge, MA; m/Muriel Struthers; c/Arnold Gordon, Brian Cantwell, Julian Struthers, Rosemary Muriel, Heather Patricia Smith Hines; p/Mr and Mrs Victor Arnold Smith (dec); ed/PhD 1948, MA 1947, Oriental Langs, Princeton Univ; Student of Theol, Westminster Col, Cambridge, 1938-40; Res in Oriental Lang, St John's Col, 1938-40; BA w Hons in Oriental Lang, Univ of Toronto, 1938; Att'd, Upper Canada Col, 1924-33; pa/Prof of the Comparative Hist of Rel, Chm of Comm on the Study of Rel, Harvard Univ, 1978-; McCulloch Prof of Rel, Dept of Rel, Dalhousie Univ, 1973-78; Prof of World Rels, and Dir of Ctr for the Study of World Rels, Harvard Univ, 1964-73; Birks Prof of Comparative Rel 1949-63, Dir of Inst of Islamic Studies 1951-63, McGill Univ; Other Previous Positions; Fellow, Royal Soc of Canada; Fellow, Am Acad of Arts and Scis; Mid E Studies Assn of N Am; Am Soc for the Study of Rel; Canadian Theol Soc; Am Acad of Rel; Intl Cong of Orientalists; r/ Christian; hon/Pubs, *On Understanding Islam* 1981, *Towards a World Theology* 1981, *Faith and Belief* 1979, *Belief and History* 1977, Others; Hon DD, U Theol Col 1966, McGill Univ 1973, Univ of Edinburgh 1982; Hon LLD, Concordia Univ, 1979; Hon DLitt, Trent Univ, 1979; Hon DHL, Ctl MI Univ, 1980; Many Biogl Listings.

SMITH, WILLARD GRANT oc/Special Education Consultant; b/Jun 29, 1934; h/6879 Maverick Circle, Salt Lake City, UT 84121; ba/Price, UT; m/Ruth Ann; c/Deborah Sue Henri, Cynthia Lynn Koster, Andrea Kay Richards, John Charles; p/Frank C Smith, Binghamton, NY; ed/BS, magna cum laude, Univ of MD, 1976; MS 1978, PhD 1981, Univ of UT; mil/USAF 1953-76, Ret'd Master Sgt; pa/Spec Ed Conslt, SEn Ed Ser Ctr, 1983-; Exec Dir, UT Indep Living Ctr, 1982-83; Ednl Psychol, Jordan Sch Dist, 1978-82; AF Assn; AF Sgts Assn; Am Ednl Res Assn; Am Psychol Assn; Assn for Supvn and Curric Devel; CEC; Coun of Admrs of Spec Ed; Nat Assn for Indep Living, Pres-Elect 1984; Nat Assn of Sch Psychols; Nat Rehab Assn; Ret'd Enlisted Assn; r/Prot; hon/Pubs, "Drug and Alcohol Abuse: What You Need to Know" 1981, "The Development and Evaluation of a Social Competence Program for Behaviorally Handicapped Early Adolescents" 1981, "The Effect of Three Different College Curricula on Moral Development" 1978, "Issues in Independent Living for Disabled People in Utah and Education and Spec Education for Disabled People" 1983; Phi Kappa Phi Nat Hon Soc; Alpha Sigma Lambda Nat Evening Col Hon Soc; Dean's List, Univ of MD, 1975, 1976;

Scholastic Achmt Awd, Univ of MD, 1975; W/W W.

SMITH, WILLIAM (BILL) II oc/ Energy Conservationist, Building Safety Engineer; b/Nov 30, 1941; h/102 South Balsam Street, Denver, CO 80226; ba/Denver, CO; m/Sylvia Knight Morgan; c/William III, Maurice A; p/ William and Willie Mae Smith, Bay City, TX; ed/BS, Tuskegee Inst, 1964; Postgrad Study, Wash Univ of St Louis, 1968-70; mil/USNR, 1979; pa/Equip Engr, Boeing Co, 1964-67; Plant Design Engr, McDonnell Douglas Corp, 1967-69; Proj Engr, St Louis Co Govt, 1969-72; Div Engr, E I duPont de Nemours & Co Inc, 1972-74; Engrg Mgr, Westinghouse Corp, 1974-76; Bldg Safety Engr 1976-, Proj Admr 1977-, Energy Conservationist 1978-, Denver Public Schs; Am Soc of Safety Engrs; CO Assn of Sch Energy Coors; Am Assn of Blacks in Energy; Tuskegee Inst Nat Alumni Assn, Mem-at-Large; cp/Bd of Dirs, Denver Opports Indust Ctr, 1979-80; Nat Comm of Future of Regis Col; Mayor's Citizens Adv Com on Energy, 1980-; r/Rel Sci; hon/Pres Nat Awd for Energy Conserv, 1980; W/ W W; W/W Am.

SMITH, WILLIAM PRESTON JR oc/ Equal Opportunity and Human Resource Management Specialist; b/ Mar 26, 1948; h/301 G Street, Southwest, Washington, DC 20024; ba/Arlington, VA; p/William and B Mae Smith, Snow Hill, MD; ed/BS, Hampton Inst, 1970; MS 1976, PhD Cand, Emory Univ; Further Study, Yale Univ Grad Sch of Journalism, 1970; Att'd, IN Univ, 1972; mil/USAR, 1971-76; pa/Staff Supvr, Dept of Ed and Spec Projs, Hartford, CT, 1968; Reporter Intern, *The Hartford Courant*, 1970; Lang Arts Instr, Norwalk HS, 1970-74; Am Studies Advr, The Spanish Heritage Assn, 1973; Res Asst, Emory Univ, 1976; Instr of Eng 1976-78, Dir of Afro-Am Studies 1976-78, Morehouse Col; Instr of Humanities, Atlanta Univ, 1978; Instr of Humanities, Drexel Univ, 1979; Correspondent III, Colonial Penn Sers, 1979; EEO (Employmt) Spec, Aviation Supply Ofc, 1979-80; EO/ Human Resource Mgmt Spec, HQs, NAVSUPSYSCOM, 1980-; Am Mgmt Assn; Sigma Tau Delta Hon Soc; Blacks in Govt Inc; Nat Assn for Interdisciplinary Studies; Am Soc for Tng and Devel; cp/Nat Urban Leag; r/Prot; hon/ Pubs, "Miss Cynthie" 1978, "The Impact of Early 20th Century Migration on the Urban Church" 1979; Sustained Superior Perf Awd, 1982; Spec Achmt Awd, CHNAUMAT, 1982; Lilly Foun Fellow, IN Univ, 1972; Nat Endowment for the Humanities Fellow, Emory Univ, 1974-76; Intl Dir of African-Am Scholars; Outstg Yg Men of Am; W/W Among Students in Am Cols and Univs.

SMITHSON, BEATRICE ORR oc/ Housewife; b/Mar 28, 1904; h/8899 Orr Road, Galt, CA 95632; m/Otto Hayden; c/Charlene Orr Mathews; p/George and Mary MacFarlane Orr (dec); ed/Grad, Galt-Union HS, 1923; ba/d, Duford Bus Col, 1923-24; cp/Past Pres, Current Trustee, Galt Wom's Civic Clb; Rel-Rebekah Lodge #132, Mem for 59 Yrs, Vice Grand; Val Oaks Grange #365, 50 Yrs; Past Chm, Sacto Co Home Ec of Grange; r/Galt U Meth Ch, Ofcl Bd, Histn, Fin Com; Past Pres, Galt U Meth Wom; hon/Galt Citizen of the Yr, 1982.

SMYTH, DOROTHY L oc/Realtor; b/ Jul 4, 1934; h/192 Willow Road, Northwest, Albuquerque, NM 87107; ba/Albuquerque, NM; m/Leo R; c/Robert Leo, Lany Alan, Kathleen Ann Smyth Walsh; p/Joseph L (dec) and Grace Johnson, Albuquerque, NM; ed/Att'd, Univ of NM, 1954-57; BA, UTEP, 1969; Grad, Cert Designer, Albuquerque Floral Arts, 1976; Lic'd to Sell Real Est, New Real Est Inst and Comm, 1973; pa/US Post Master, 1957; Pvt Music Tchr, 1954-69; Kgn Tchr, El Paso, 1964-69; NM Lic'd Rltr, 1973-; Owner, Mgr, Smyth's Flowers and Greenhouse, 1976-79; Sales Mgr and Co-Owner, C-2/Robertson Inc, 1979-; Nat, St and Local Rltr Mem; Nat Wom's Coun of Rltrs; cp/Albuquerque Civic Symph, 1954-; Pres, Ext Clbs, Las Lunas, 1960-64; 4-H Ldr; Girl Scout Ldr; r/ Music Dir, WMS Pres, GA Ldr, YWA Dir, Bapt Chs in Las Lunas, Albuquerque, Las Vegas, NM, and El Paso; hon/Pub, "What Can Kindergarten Do for My Children?" 1968; NM Ext Ser, Outstg Ser, 1964; Albuquerque Bd of Rltrs Trophy for Sales Achmt, 1975; Many Certs for Com and Vol Wk for Albuquerque Bd of Rltrs, So Bapt, 4-H, Albuquerque Public Schs; W/W W.

SMYTHIES, JOHN RAYMOND oc/ Psychiatrist, Neuroscientist; b/Nov 30, 1922; ba/Neurosciences Program, UAB Medical Center, Birmingham, AL 35294; m/Vanna Maria Grazia; c/Adrian Greville, Christopher John Evelyn; ed/ MA 1955, MSc 1958, MD 1955, Cantab; DPM, London, 1952; MSc, UBC, 1955; FRCP, 1975; FRC Psych, 1970; FAPA, 1975; mil/Surg-Lt, RNVR; pa/Nuffield Fellow, 1955-57; Sr Registrar, Maudsley Hosp, 1959-61; Sr Lectr/Rdr, Univ of Edinburgh, 1961-73; C B Ireland Prof of Psychi Res, Univ of AL B'ham, 1973-; Fellow, Royal Soc of Med; Biophy Soc; Collegium Internationale Neuropsychopharmacologium; Am Col of Neuropsychopharmacology; r/Epis; hon/ Pubs, *Analysis of Perception* 1956, *Biological Psychiatry* 1971, *Brain Mechanisms and Behavior* 1970, *Psychiatry for Students of Medicine* 1976, *Schizophrenia* 1963, and 200 Sci Papers; Exhbn, Christs Col, Cambridge, 1941; Pres, Intl Soc of Neuropsychopharmacology, 1971-74; Secy, The Sherrington Soc, 1975-; W/W World.

SNAPP, J STEVENS oc/Director of Operations; b/May 30, 1935; h/2739 North Highland, Jackson, TN 38305; ba/ Jackson, TN; m/Malissa B; c/John, Scott, Melody; p/Charles V (dec) and Anne H Snapp, Greeneville, TN; ed/Grad, Greeneville HS, 1953; Tri-St Col of Med Arts Nsg, 1966; pa/Dir of Opers, Hlth Care Delivery Sys; Secy, TN Hlth Care Assn; Am Hlth Care Assn; Am Col of Nsg Home Admrs; Am Acad of Med Admrs; cp/Jackson Rotary Clb; r/Bapt; hon/W/W S.

SNAVELY, RICHARD MELLINGER oc/Executive Director of Radio Station and Youth Center; b/Jun 4, 1931; h/15 Alexander Street, Avoca, NY 14809; ba/ Bath, NY; m/Jacqueline D; c/Carol Ann Snavely Canaday, Richard Jr, G Randall, Ronald; p/Abram H (dec) and Anna Snavely, Bath, NY; ed/BA, 1954; pa/Exhb Rep for Billy Graham Evangelistic Film Assn, 1954-56; Ldr, Area Yth for Christ Inc, 1957; Exec Dir, Area Yth for Christ, 1957-; En Area VP, Yth for Christ Intl,

1972-73; Fdr and Exec Dir, New Life Homes-Snell Farm, 1973-; Fdr and Mgr, ECIK-FM Radio Sta, 1982-; Exec VP, Yth Evang Assn, 1980-; Editor, *Youth for Christ Reporter*; cp/Rotary Clb; Nat Rifle Assn; r/Prot; hon/Nat Yth for Christ Rural Dir of the Yr, 1962; En Yth for Christ Dir of the Yr, 1969; W/W E.

SNELGROVE, FRANCIS A oc/District Superintendent of Schools; b/Feb 14, 1925; h/411 Ridgecrest Drive, Camden, SC 29020; ba/Camden, SC; m/ Deltha B; c/Mrs Sandra Snelgrove Friddle, Mrs Delores Snelgrove Camp; Stepchd: Anita Karen Runyan, Melissa Yvonne Runyan, Keith Ladell Runyan; p/Horace E and Ruth Addy Snelgrove (dec); ed/BS, Newberry Col, 1945; EdM, Univ of SC Columbia, 1952; Profl Dipl, Columbia Univ, 1954; mil/WWII, AUS, 1945-47; pa/Supt 1977-, Asst Supt for Pers and Gen Adm 1971-77, Sch Dist of Kershaw Co; Supt, Camden Area I Schs, 1969-71; Prin, Camden HS, 1957-69; Prin, York HS, 1955-57; Asst Prin, Chapman HS, 1954-55; Other Previous Positions; Am Assn of Sch Admrs; Nat Assn of Sch Pers Admrs; NEA; Phi Delta Kappa; Kappa Delta Pi; cp/Am Legion; 4-H Clbs of Am; Lions Clb; r/Luth; hon/Dept of Army Cit for Exceptl Civilian Ser in Support of ROTC Progs, 1966-81; Outstg Supt Awd, SC Assn of Adult Ed Dirs, 1980; Dist'd Ser and Ldr Awd, 4-H Clbs of Am, 1981; W/W Palmetto St; W/W SE; W/W Ednl Adm; Ldrs of Am Elem and Sec'dy Ed.

SNELL, RICHARD oc/Executive; b/ Nov 26, 1930; h/4515 North Dromedary Road, Phoenix, AZ 85018; ba/Phoenix, AZ; m/Alice Wiley; c/Karen L, Marilyn E, Sarah J; p/Frank L Snell, Scottsdale, AZ; ed/BA, Stanford Univ, 1952; JD, Stanford Law Sch, 1954; mil/Inf Ofcr, AUS, 1954-56; pa/Ptnr in Law Firm of Snell & Wilmer, 1956-81; Chm of Bd, Pres, CEO, Ramada Inns Inc, 1981-; Dir, Wn Technols Inc, 1978-; Trustee, Am Grad Sch of Intl Mgmt, 1978-; Dir, AZ Public Ser Co, 1975-; Bd of Advrs, Col of Bus and Public Adm, Univ of AZ, 1982-; Adv Coun for Lodging, Restaurant and Tourism Adm, Col of Bus Adm, No AZ Univ, 1982-; Am Hotel and Motel Assn's Govtl Affairs Com, 1983-; Assn for Corporate Growth, AZ Chapt; AZ St, Maricopa Co and Am Bar Assns; cp/Phoenix Forty; Dir of AZ Reg, Nat Conf of Christians and Jews; r/Luth; hon/W/W W.

SNELLING, ROBERT GARRISON JR oc/Jeweler, Manufacturer; b/Sep 8, 1952; h/4706 Kendall Avenue, Gulfport, MS 39501; m/Laura S; c/Robert G III, Andrew Hyatt; p/Mrs Robert G Snelling Sr; ed/Grad, Gulfport E HS, 1971; Coast Guard Fire Fighting Sch, 1971; Course in Jewelry Repair 1978, Course in Adv'd Jewelry Repair 1979, Trenton Jewelry Repair Sch; mil/USCG 1971-74, Hon Discharge, Rank E-3 Cook; pa/Ins Salesman, Life of GA Life Ins Co, 1976-77; Mgr, Jeweler, Nacal Jewelry, 1977-80; Self-Employed Wholesale Mfg Jeweler, Owner, Bobby Snelling Jewelers, 1980-81; Self-Employed in Retail Jewelry Mfg, Owner, Coast Mfg Jewelers, 1981-83; Owner, Snelling Jewelers and Mfg, 1983-; r/Meth Men's Clb; hon/ Designer, Line of Rel Jewelry.

SNELSON, WILLIAM MITCHELL oc/Contractor; b/Jul 18, 1926; h/814

Garden of Eden, Sedro Woolley, WA 98284; ba/Sedro Woolley, WA; m/ Dolores Mary Simaz; c/Linda, Chris, Nancy, Susan, Julie, Mary, Barbara; p/ Frank D and Connie B Sluder Snelson (dec); ed/Grad, Sedro Woolley HS; mil/ Army/AF, 1945-46; pa/Supt and Plumbing Foreman, Snelson Cos Inc, 1946-57; Pres and Chm of Bd, Snelson Cos Inc, 1957-; VP, Point Indust Corp, 1982-83; Pres, S-L Resources Inc, 1983; Pres, Skagit Mining Ltd, 1983; Pres, Chm of the Bd, Snelson-Anvil Inc, 1974-83; Pacific Energy Assn; Pres, Distribution Contractors Assn, 1982, Served on Bd for 8 Yrs; Pres, Mech Contractors Assn, 4 Yrs, Served on Bd; Pipeline Contractors Assn; hon/W/W W.

SNODGRASS, W D oc/Writer, Teacher; h/RD #1, Erieville, NY; ba/ Newark, DE; c/Cynthia, Kathy (Stepdaugh), Russell; p/B D and Helen M Snodgrass (dec); ed/BA 1949, MA 1951, MFA 1953, Att'd 1953-55, St Univ of IA Iowa City; pa/Dist'd Vis'g Prof, Eng Dept, Univ of DE, 1979-; Vis'g Prof, Eng Dept, Old Dominion Univ, 1978-79; Eng and Spch Depts, Syracuse Univ, 1968-77; Eng Dept, Wayne St Univ, 1959-67; Eng Dept, Univ of Rochester, 1957-58; Eng Dept, Cornell Univ, 1955-57; Morehead Writers' Conf, 1955; Antioch Writers' Conf, 1958, 1959; Narative Poetry Wkshop, St Univ of NY Binghamton, 1977; hon/Pubs incl: *Magda Goebbels* 1984, *The Four Seasons* 1984, *Platoons and Files* 1983, *The Boy Made of Meat* 1983; *Six Minnesinger Songs* 1983, *These Trees Stand* 1982, *If Birds Build with Your Hair* 1979, *Traditional Hungarian Songs* 1978, *The Fuehrer Bunker Poems* 1977, *In Radical Pursuit* Essays 1975, *Heart's Needle* 1959, Others; Grant for Extended Res, Univ of DE, 1983-84; Sum Res Awd, Univ of DE, 1982; Cent Medal, Govt of Romania, 1977; Bicent Medal, Wm and Mary Col, 1976; Acad of Am Poets F'ship, 1973; Guggenheim F'ship, 1972-73; Nat Coun on Arts Sabbatical Grant, 1966-67; Miles Mod Poetry Awd, 1966; Ford Foun Grant for Study in Theatre, 1963-64; Guiness Poetry Awd, 1961; Pulitzer Prize in Poetry, 1960; Other Hons.

SNOW, HELEN FOSTER oc/Author, Genealogist; b/Sep 21, 1907; h/148 Mungertown Road, Madison, CT 06443; ba/Same; m/Edgar Parks; p/John Moody and Hannah Davis Foster (dec); ed/Att'd, Univ of UT 1925-27, Yenching Univ 1934-35, Tsinghua Univ 1935; Hon DLitt, St Mary's of the Woods Col, 1981; pa/Pubs, *The China Years* 1983, *Women in Modern China* 1967, 6 Other Trade Books, *The Saybrook Story*, *The Guilford Story*, *The Madison Story*, *The History of Damariscove Island in Maine, Notes on the Early History of Madison, CT, Special Research in Local and Family History* 1980, *Connecticut Research in Local and Family History* 1980; Soc of Wom Geographers, 1939-; r/Unitarian; hon/Nom'd for Nobel Prize for Peace, 1981; Contemp Authors; W/W Am Wom; Dir of Brit and Am Writers.

SNOWDEN, LILLIAN JOHNSON oc/Accountant; b/Dec 8, 1941; h/911 O Street, Northwest, Washington, DC 20001; ba/General Services Administration, 7th and D Street, Southwest, Washington, DC 20407; m/Ron; c/ Jacquelyn, Stephanie, Tio-Carmalita, Demetrius; p/Elijah Sr and Ruth L

Johnson, Monroe, LA; ed/BSBA in Acctg, ASBA in Mgmt, SEn Univ; pa/ Operating Acct; Staff Acct; Pers Ofcr; Ec Adv Coun, DST; Wash Alumnae Chapt, Delta Sigma Theta Sorority Inc; Mem, Secy, Bd of Govs, SEn Univ Alumni Assn; cp/Chair, En Reg Nom's Com; Fdr and Pres, Prograstive Chapt, FEW; VP and Secy, DC Nat Guard Enlisted Assn; Chair, Nat Army Enlisted Com; NAACP; NCNW; Bd of Dirs, GSA Fed Credit Union; Past Exec Dir, W St Ensemble, Wkshops Panelist in Area of Fin; hon/AUS Commend Medal; SEn Univ: Dist'd Meritorious Ser Awd; Whole Person Awd, Alumni Awd; Sheppard Pk PTA Awd of Apprec; Carroll High Alumni Pres Awd; Xi Zeta Chapt Pres Awd; GSA Public Ser Awd, Fed Credit Union; Wash Alumnae Chapt, DST Ser Cert; W/W Among Students in Am Cols and Univs; W/W Fin and Indust in Am.

SNYDER, JED C oc/Foreign Policy Specialist, Research Scholar; b/Mar 24, 1955; h/2201 L Street, Northwest, Apartment #602, Washington, DC 20037; ba/Washington, DC; p/David (dec) and Lynn Snyder, Bala Cynwyd, PA; ed/BA, Colby Col, 1976; MA, Univ of Chgo, 1978; PhD, Polit Sci/Intl Relats, Expected 1984; pa/Current Res Assoc, Woodrow Wilson Intl Ctr for Scholars; Current Guest Scholar and Profl Lectr in Intl Relats, Sch of Adv'd Intl Studies, Johns Hopkins Univ; Sr Spec Asst to Dir of Bur of Politico-Mil Affairs, US Dept of St, 1981-82; Asst Div Mgr, Pan Heuristics Div, R&D Assocs, 1979-81; Conslt, Rand Corp, Sci Applications Inc, 1979-81; Coun on Fgn Relats, NY; Intl Inst for Strategic Studies, London; Elected Fellow, Inter-Univ Sem on Armed Forces and Soc; AIAA; US Naval Inst; Acad of Polit Sci; Intl Studies Assn; r/Jewish; hon/ Author, Num Classified Pubs and Reports, Unclassified Articles in *New York Times*, *US Naval War College Review*, *Middle East Journal*; US Dept of St Superior Hon Awd for Wk in Crisis Mgmt, 1982; Commend for Excell, Secy of St Haig, 1982; Univ of Chgo Grad F'ship, 1978; W/W E; W/W Wash; W/ W Sect in Def and Fgn Affairs Handbook.

SOGLIERO, GENE SANDRA oc/ Senior Research Scientist, Statistician; h/324 Thames Street, #5, Groton, CT 06340; ba/Groton, CT; c/Stephen William, Christine Marie; p/Frank Cianfarani (dec); Sarah Taggart (dec); ed/PhD, Math Stats, Univ of CT, 1970; AM in Math, Brown Univ, 1954; EdB, Math/ Sci, RI Col, 1947; pa/Biostat (Sr Res Scists), Pfizer Ctl Res, 1982-; Math Stat, USCG Res and Devel Ctr, 1979-82; Asst Prof of Math, Trinity Col, 1978-79; Asst Prof of Stats, Univ of CT, 1977-78; Adj Prof, Univ of Hartford, 1977-78; Statistical Conslt, U Technols Res Labs, 1977-78; Sr Math Spec, U Technols Res Ctr, 1973-77; Prof of Math, Nat Univ of Zaire, 1971-73; Sr Mathematician, U Technols Res Ctr, 1967-71; Other Previous Positions; Inst of Math Stats; Math Assn of Am; AAAS; Am Statistical Assn; AIAA; Am Soc for Testing and Mats, Com Ell-Statistical Procedures in Chem; hon/Pubs, "Some Pattern Recognition Considerations for Low Temperature Luminescence and Room Temperature Fluorescence Spec-

tra" 1981, "Applications of DC Argon Plasma Emission Spectroscopy to Saline Waters: A Study of Enhancement Effects" 1980, "Fatigue Life Estimates of Mistuned Bladed Disks via a Stochastic Approach" 1980, "Key Control Assessment for Multivariable Systems" 1976, Others; Recip, Spec Achmt Awd for Accomplishments in Studies of DC Argon Plasma Emissions of Trace Metals, 1980; Cert of Recog for Participation in NASA-ASEE Sum Fac F'ship Prog, 1979; Kappa Delta Pi; Am Men and Wom of Sci.

SOLA-SOLÉ, JOSEP M oc/Chairman of Modern Languages Department; b/ Jul 18, 1924; h/6268 Clearwood Road, Bethesda, MD 20817; ba/Washington, DC; m/Montserrat D; c/Elisenda, Roger; p/Jordi (dec) and María, Spain; ed/MA, Univ of Barcelona, 1948; Elève Diplomé de l'Ecole Practique des Hautes Etudes, 1955; PhD, Univ of Barcelona, 1959; pa/Stagiaire, Centre National de la Recherche Scientifique, Paris, 1950-52; Lektor of Spanish, Univ of Tu³bingen, 1952-61; Assoc Prof of Spanish 1961-65, Ordinary Prof of Spanish 1965-, Chm of Spanish Sect 1966-78, Cath Univ of Am; Dir of Sum Course, Valencia, 1968-; Chm, Mod Langs Dept, Cath Univ of Am, 1978-; MLA; SAMLA; AATSP; CH; ALLC; ALDEEU; Dir, Sigma Delta Pi, DC; Del, Assem of Mod Lang Assn; Main Editor, *Ediciones Hispam*, *Biblioteca Universitaria Puvill*; Pres, Spanish-Am Cultural Exch Inc; Academia Norteamericana de Lengua Española; Corresponding Mem, Hispanic Soc of Am; Pres, I and II Gen Assem, ALDEEU; hon/Pubs, *Hispania Judaica* I, II, III 1981-83, *Judíos, árabes y marranos* 1983, *La Dança* General de la Muerto 1982, *Los sonetos "fechos al itálico modo" del Marqués de Santillana* 1980, Others, Articles in Var Periodicals Related to Semitic or Hispanic Studies; F'ship from French Govt, 1948-49; Miembro de Hon, Instituto Peruano de Altos Estudios Islámicos, 1960; Premio Nacional de Letras, Consejo Superior de Investigaciones Científicas, 1959; John Simon Guggenheim F'ship, 1967-68, 1976; Orden de Don Quijote, Sigma Delta Pi, 1982; DIB; ISD; W/W S and SW; DASCL; DAS; 2,000 Men of Achmt.

SOLBRIG, INGEBORG HILDEGARD oc/Professor of German; b/Jul 31, 1923; h/1126 Pine Street, Iowa City, IA 52240; ba/Iowa City, IA; p/Reinhold J and Hildegard M A Solbrig (dec); ed/ St Dipl, Chem, Germany; BA, summa cum laude, SF St Univ, 1964; MA 1966, PhD in Humanities and German 1969, Stanford Univ; pa/Schoeller Co, Osnabrück, 1951-58; Stazione Zoologica, Naples, Italy, 1958-59; Ditto Stoeckicht, Naples, 1959-61; Asst Prof, Univ of RI Kingston 1969-70, Univ of TN Chattanooga 1970-72, Univ of KY Lexington 1972-75; Assoc Prof 1975-81, Prof 1981-, Univ of IA; Gov's Com on German-IA Heritage; Mod Lang Assn of Germanic Studies; Am Assn of Tchrs of German; Assn of German Studies; Am Soc for 18th Century Studies; Goethe Soc of N Am, Fdg Mem; Goethe-Gesellschaft, Weimar; Deutsche Schiller-Gesellschaft; Am Coun for the Study of Austrian Lit; cp/ KY Col; hon/Pubs, *Hammer-Purgstall und Goethe* 1973, *Rilke heute* 1975, *Reinhard

Goering: Seeschlacht/Seabattle 1977, Num Articles, Contbns to Books, Reviews; Stanford Univ Fellow, 1965-66, 1968-69; Fellow, Austrian Min of Ed, 1968-69; Gold Medal, pro orientalibus, Austria, 1974; Old Gold Fellow, Univ of IA, 197; Sr Fac Res Fellow, Humanities, Univ of IA, 1983; German Acad Exch Ser, 1979; Am Coun of Lnd Socs, 1980; Num Am and Brit W/W Listings.

SOLIMAN, KARAM F A oc/Professor, Director of Division; b/Oct 15, 1944; h/2414 Blarney Drive, Tallahassee, FL 32307; ba/Tallahassee, FL; m/ Samia S; c/John K, Gina K, Mark K; p/ Mr and Mrs Farah Attia Soliman, Cairo, Egypt; ed/BS, Cairo Univ, 1964; MS 1971, PhD 1972, Univ of GA; pa/Asst Prof of Physiol and Pharm, Sch of Vet Med, Tuskegee Inst, 1972-75; Assoc Prof, Sch of Pharm, FL A&M Univ, 1975-79; Prof of Physiol and Pharm 1979-, Dir of Basic Sci 1982-, Col of Pharm, FL A&M Univ; Am Soc of Pharm; Am Physiol Soc; Soc for Exptl Biol and Med; Endocrine Soc; Intl Soc for Chronobiol; r/Christian Orthodox; hon/Pubs, "The Role of the Adrenal Gland in Ethanol Triglycerides Mobilization" 1984, "Circadian Variation in the Monoamine Oxidase Activity of Specific Rat Brain Area" 1984, "Circadian Variation of Beta Endorphin in Discrete Areas of the Rat Brain" 1984, "Chronopharmacology and Chronotoxicology of CNS Drugs: Interrelationships with Neuromodulators" 1983, Num Others; Awd'd, More Than $500,000 for Res Grants, NIH, NASA; Recip, Travel Awd to Address Toward Chronotherapy Meeting of Nagasaki, Japan, 1981; Recip, Endocrine Soc Awd to Attend 6th Intl Cong on Endocrinology, Melbourne, Australia, 1980; Recip, Awd from NATO to Attend the Advance Student Prog on Jet Lab, Hannover, Germany, 1979; Gamma Sigma Delta; Kappa Psi; Rho Chi; Other Hons; Personalities of S; Men of Achmt; W/W Am; W/W S and SW; W/W Frontier Sci and Technol; 2,000 Notable Ams.

SOLL, DAVID B oc/Ophthalmologist; b/Aug 9, 1930; h/1127 Devon Road, Rydal, PA 19046; ba/Philadelphia, PA; m/Jean Shtasel; c/Abby, Stephen, Warren, Adam; p/Hyman and Sara Soll, Brooklyn, NY; ed/BA, NY Univ, 1951; MD, Chgo Med Sch, 1955; Internship, Phila Gen Hosp, 1955-56; Ophthal Grad Course, NY Univ Postgrad Med Sch, 1956-57; Residency, Manhattan Eye, Ear and Throat Hosp, 1957-59; Cert, Am Bd of Ophthal, 1960; MS in Ophthal, NY Univ Postgrad Med Sch, 1963; mil/USPHS, 1959-61; pa/Conslt in Ophthal, Magee Meml Rehab Ctr, 1980-; Prof and Chm, Dept of Ophthal, Hahnemann Med Col and Hosp, 1974-; Vis'g Prof in Ophthal, Univ of Puerto Rico Dept of Ophthal, 1982-; Conslt in Ophthal, PA Hosp Dept of Ophthal, 1975-78; Conslt in Plastic Surg, PA Hosp; Surg in Ophthal, Presb-Univ of PA Med Ctr, 1972-78; Dir, Rolling Hill Hosp and Diagnostic Ctr Dept of Ophthal, 1969-; Dir, Phila Geriatric Ctr Dept of Ophthal, 1965-; Clin Affil, Dept of Surg, Chd's Hosp Div of Ophthal, 1961-; Att'g in Ophthal, VA Hosp, 1961-; Conslt in Ophthal 1975-77, Assoc Asst Att'g Ophthalmologist 1961-75, Phila Gen Hosp; Other Previous Positions; Am Col of Surgs,

Fellow; Am Acad of Ophthal and Otolaryngology, Fellow; Am Soc of Ophthalmic Plastic and Reconstructive Surg, Charter Fellow; AMA; PA Acad of Ophthal and Otolaryngology; Am Assn of Cosmetic Surgs; Am Acad of Facial Plastic and Reconstructive Surg; Am Assn of Ophthal; AAUP; Num Other Profl Mbrships; r/Jewish; hon/Pubs, "Vein Grafting in Nasolacrimal System Reconstruction" 1983, "45-Degree Angled Aspiration Tip with Sandblasted, Roughened Edge for Posterior Capsule Polishing" 1983, Num Others; Am Acad of Ophthal Hon Awd, 1977; Chgo Med Sch Dist'd Alumni Awd, 1979; Legion of Merit Awd, Chapel of Four Chaplains, 1979.

SONNENFELD, JANET MARLOFF oc/Attorney, Owner of Bankruptcy Firm; b/Feb 9, 1948; h/322 South Juniper Street, Philadelphia, PA 19107; ba/Philadelphia, PA; m/Marc J; p/Raymond James (dec) and Muriel Goodkin Marloff, Rumson, NJ; ed/BA, Eng Lit, George Wash Univ, 1970; JD, cum laude, Howard Univ Sch of Law, 1973; pa/Assoc, Drinker, Biddle & Reath, 1973-76; Assoc Counsel, Consumer Bkg, The Fidelity Bk, 1976-77; Pvt Pract, 1977-; Current Owner, Bankruptcy Firm; PA Bar Assn, Com on Drug and Alcohol Abuse 1978-; cp/Com-wom, Dem Party, 1974-76, 1978-82; Policy Com for Selection of Jud Cands, 1978-82; r/Cath; hon/Pubs, "Housing the Elderly" 1971, Num Bankruptcy Cases in Legal Ref Mats; W/W Am Wom.

SOO, CHARLIE H oc/Business Development Director, Consultant; b/Mar 24, 1945; h/1250 North Stone, Chicago, IL 60610; ba/Same; ed/MA, Bus Adm; Hon Doct; pa/Pres, Chgo Intl, 1960-65; Commr, IL Ec Devel, 1965-70; Exec Dir of Ec Devel Adm, MT, 1968-70; Dir, Chgo Ec Devel Corp, 1970-75; Projs Dir, City of Chgo Neighborhood Devel, 1975-81; Bd Mem, Chgo Assn of Commerce and Indust; Execs Clb of Chgo; Chgo Press Clb; Chm, Adv Coun, IL Future Bus Ldrs of Am; Asian Am Small Bus-men's Assn; cp/UN Assn; Others; hon/Chgo's Outstg Yg Man, 1967; City of Hope Outstg Ldrship Awd; IL Bus-man of Yr, 1979; Commended by IL Senate for Outstg Ser and Contbn to City and St, 1968; Outstg Yg Men of Am.

SORBO, PAUL J JR oc/Superintendent of Schools; b/Oct 31, 1927; h/15 Timber Lane, Windsor, CT 06095; ba/Windsor, CT; m/Marian K; c/Paul K, Kathleen, Thomas P, John E; ed/BS, Ctl CT St Univ, 1951; MS, Univ of CT, 1963; Adv'd Grad Study in Sch Adm, Univ of CT, 1962-70; mil/AUS, 1952-54; pa/Supt 1969-, Asst Supt 1965-69, Adm Asst 1963-65, Windsor Public Sch Dist; CT Assn of Sch Admrs, Pres 1981-82; Gtr Harford Coun on Ec Ed, Chm 1969-71; cp/Rotary Clb of Windsor, Pres 1976-77; Hartford Easter Seal Rehab Ctr, Bd of Trustees 1972-84, Pres 1977-79; hon/Vol of the Yr Awd, Hartford Easter Seal Rehab Ctr, 1979; Dist'd Ser Awd, Gtr Hartford Coun on Ec Ed, 1975; Wm Moriarty Awd, CEC of CT, 1983; W/W E.

SORICELLI, DUANE BARRY oc/Chairman of Division of Behavioral and Social Sciences, Associate Professor of Psychology; b/Jun 10, 1946; h/4036 Fairway Road, Lafayette Hill, PA 19444; ba/Gwynedd Valley, PA; m/Rosemary K; c/Cheryl Lynn, Donna Marie, Sandra Leigh, Duane Barry Jr; p/Frank (dec) and Ida Soricelli, West Pittston, PA; ed/PhD 1977, MA 1973, BA 1969, Psych, Temple Univ; pa/Grad Res Asst, Temple Univ, 1970-72; Sci Tchr, Emanuel Luth Sch, 1974-75; Grad Tchg Asst, Temple Univ, 1975-76; Asst Prof of Psych 1976-80, Chm of Dept of Psych 1978-80, Clarion St Col; Assoc Prof of Psych 1980-, Chm of Div of Behavioral and Social Scis 1981-, Gwynedd-Mercy Col; Am Psychol Assn; Div 1 of APA (Div of Gen Psych); En Psychol Assn; Coun of Undergrad Psych Depts; AAUP; cp/Chestnut Hill Commun Assn; Colonial Sch Dist PTO; Franklin Inst; Phila Zool Soc; Friends of Wm Jeanes Lib Assn; r/Prot; hon/Author, "Effect of Mass Loading and Arm-Movement Duration on Kinesthetic-Visual Intersensory Form Discrimination" 1979, Other Acad Papers; Co-Author, "Effect of Mass Loading on the Performance of a Linear Positioning Task," 1978; Acad S'ship and Grad Asst'ships for Doct Study, Temple Univ; W/W E; Am Psychol Assn Biogl Dir; Gwynedd-Mercy Col Calendar Biographee.

SOSHANA, AFROYIM oc/Painter; b/Sep 1, 1927; h/8 Barstow Road, Great Neck, NY 11021; c/Amos Afroyim; p/Grete Schuller, Great Neck, NY; ed/Art Student Leag, NY; Art Acad, Vienna; pa/One-Man Exhibs: Circle of Fine Arts 1948, Mod Art Gallery (Zurich) 1957-80, Hartert Gallery 1957, Henry Lidchi Gallery 1958, Gallery Edouardd Loeb 1958, O'Hana Gallery 1959, Gallery Barsinski 1960, Mus of Art (Sao Paulo) 1960, Bodley Gallery 1961, Mus Antibes 1961, Gallery de la Madeleine 1961, Ruth White Gallery 1967, Essen 1968, Moos Gallery 1969, Toronto 1970, Gallery Seiler-Statte 1970; Salons: Realites Nouvelles 1963, Jeunes Peintres 1963, Grands et des Jeunes 1964; Maj Wks: "Portrait of Giacometti," "Man Alone," "Birds in Flight"; Permanent Collections: Mus of Mod Art (Sao Paulo), Mus of Mod Art (Mexico), Salisbury Art Gallery, Fairleigh-Dickenson Univ, NYC Hosp; Num Pvt Collections; ICA; Am Assn of Artists; Arch Leag.

SOTIS, SHIRLEY ANN BURCH oc/Executive Director of Seminars; b/Apr 17, 1934; h/3733 Towndale Drive, Bloomington, MN 55431; m/Franc Andrew; c/Frank Joseph, Clifford Orlando; p/George William Burch, Dixon, IA; Norma Marie Hesse Oton (dec); ed/AA, Harbor Jr Col; BS, Univ of So CA; pa/Tchr, So CA Reg Occup Ctr; Tchr, El Camino Col (Evening), 1973-75; Financial Admr, MN Inst, 1975-78; Bus Admr, Control Data Inst, 1978-80; Exec Dir, Wkg Wom's Sems, 1980-; MN Med Grp Mgmt Assn; Nat Assn of Credit Mgrs; N Ctl Credit and Financial Mgmt Assn; Profl Bus Wom of Minnetonka; r/Luth; hon/Author, *Computerized Health Care*, AMA, 1977; Guest Lectr, Normandale Col, Univ of MN.

SOTO, ROGELIO ROY oc/Personnel Officer; b/Sep 21, 1946; h/94-581 Holaniku Street, Mililani, HI 96789; ba/Honolulu, HI; m/Ellen Asako; c/Stephanie Kiyomi, Kelsey Anne Yukie; p/Esteban and Helen Soto, Honokaa, HI; ed/Honokaa High and Elem Sch, 1952-64; Cert, Higher Acctg, Cannon's Col of Commerce, 1967; mil/AUS, 1967-69; pa/Acctg Clk, Hawaiian Homes, 1967-68; Gen's Aide, AUS, 1968-69; Bkkpg Machine Operator, Pers Clk to Pers Tech, Hawaiian Homes, 1970-; HI Govt Employees Assn, Assoc 1975-76, Excluded Unit 1976-, Del to Conv 1982-83; cp/Mililani Town JCs, Dir 1975-76, Pres 1976-77, Current Mem; HI JCs, Secy 1978, Prog Mgrs 1979-80; Mililani Town Assn, Dir 1980-86, VP 1982-84; Dem Party of HI, Mem 1976, Precnt Councilman, Mililani 1978-79, 1982-83, Pres 1977-78, Voter Registrar 1983, Del to St Conv 1976-83; HI Claims Assn, 1982-83; ARC/Ctl YMCA-Sustaining Mem, 1976-; HI JCs Intl Senatorship, 1983-84; W Oahu YMCA-Y's Men Clb, 1983-84; r/Mililani Bapt Ch, Human Resources Com 1983-86, Usher/Greeting Com 1983-; hon/AUS Commend Medal, 1969; Nat Def Ser Medal, 1969; Vietnam Ser Medal, 1969; Fam of the Yr Awd, Mililani Town JCs, 1977; JC of the Yr Awds, Mililani Town JCs, 1976, 1978; Outstg St Ofcr Awd, HI JCs, 1978; JCs Pres Awd of Hon, Mililani Town JCs, 1979-80; Recip of 3 Outstg Yg Persons Awd, HI JCs, 1980; DHHL Dir's Awd, Hawaiian Home Lands, 1980; Gov's Awd for Dist'd St Ser, Gov/DPS, 1980; JCs Intl Senatorship Awd, Mililani Town JCs, 1983; W/W W.

SOUDER-JAFFERY, LAURA MARIE TORRES oc/Research Consultant; b/Aug 15, 1950; h/PO Box 1651, Agana, Guam 96910; ba/Same; m/Syed Zaigham Shafiq Jaffery; p/Paul and Mariquita Souder, Agana, Guam; ed/PhD Cand, Dept of Am Studies, Univ of HI, 1979-; Master in Sociol, Dept of Sociol, Univ of HI, 1976; Bach in Sociol, Dept of Sociol, Emmanuel Col, 1972; pa/Curator, Guam Mus, 1983; Res Conslt (Self-Employed), 1979-; Tchr, Acad of Our Lady of Guam HS, 1974, 1979; Spec Asst for Cultural and Public Affairs, Ofc of the Gov, 1976-78; Ofc Admr, Dept of Commerce, 1973-74; Other Previous Positions; Charter Mem, Chamorro Studies Assn, 1976-; Smithsonian Assoc, Smithsonian Inst, 1976-; Oral Hist Assn, 1976-; Nat Geographic Soc, 1976-; Am Assn of Mus, 1977-; Nat Trust for Hist Preserv, 1977-; Archives Assoc, Nat Archives Trust Fund, 1977-; HI Am Studies Assn, Univ of HI, 1979-; Am Studies Assn, Univ of PA, 1981-; Gov's Task Force on Palace Restoration Proj, 1983-; hon/Pubs, "The Protectresses of Culture" 1977, "The Living Museum" 1976, Others; Cit for Outstg Contbn, Guam Meml Hosp Vols Assn, 1980; Cit for Outstg Contbn, Muscular Dystrophy Assn, 1977; Elected Del, Chp, Guam Delegation, White House Conf on Libs and Info Sers, 1979; E-W Ctr Deg Scholar Grant for PhD, Univ of HI, 1979-82; Other Hons; Outstg Yg Wom of Am.

SOWERS, MIRIAM R oc/Artist, Poet, Publisher; h/3020 Glenwood Northwest, Albuquerque, NM 87107; m/H Frank; c/Craig V, Keith A; p/Mrs Paul Hochstettle; ed/Att'd, Miami Univ 1940-44, Chgo Art Inst 1944-45, Univ of NM 1956; pa/Draftsman, Army Map Ser, 1944-45; Free-Lance Illustrator for NBC, Chgo, 1944-45; Owner,

Portrait-Painting Studio, Chgo, Findlay (OH), Albuquerque, 1944-; Owner, Symbol Gallery of Art, 1961-80; Delta Phi Delta Art Hon, Pres 1942; Kappa Delta Pi Ed Hon; Findlay Art Leag, Pres 1949; Mus and Grp Exhbns: Dayton (OH) Art Inst, Butler Art Inst, Akron Art Inst, Massilon (OH) Art Inst, Toledo Mus of Art, Canton (OH) Art Inst, The Little Studio (NYC); Num Others; r/ Christian Scist; hon/Pubs, "Parables from Paradise" 1975, "The Suns of Man" 1981; Prizes for Paintings; W/W Am Art; W/W Am Wom; W/W W; W/ W NM; Intl Dir of Arts; Num Other Biogl Listings.

SOZA, SHARON ELIZABETH oc/ Writer, Micro-Computer Consultant, Legal Researcher; b/Jun 21, 1945; h/PO Box 81, Yreka, CA 96097; ba/Same; m/ Albert Rudolph; c/Ravi Narayan Seth; p/Francis T and Mary E Newton, Groves, TX; ed/Survey of Sci Careers and Res Asst in Nutrition, NSF Grant, TX A&M, 1962; BS, Chem, Lamar St Col of Technol, 1968; Computer Sci, Univ of Houston, 1969; Film-Making and Videotape Documentaries, Rice Univ Media Centre, 1975; Spec Proj, Computer Skills Bk, Col of Siskiyous, 1978; MS and PhD, Columbia Pacific Univ (Tentative); pa/Newspaper Proof-reader, *Beaumont Enterprise Newspaper,* 1967-68; Tech Writer, Fed Elect/ITT, NASA, Houston, 1968-69; Sys Pro-grammer, TX Instruments, 1969-70; Sys Programmer, Conslt, Urban Sys and Sers, 1970-72; Sys Programmer, SCI Inc, 1972-73; Contract Conslt/ Programmer, TRW Sys, 1974; Min-icomputer Programming/Design/ Consltg; Micro-Computer Software Devel for Indep Software Vending; r/Comparative Rel: Blavatsky, Ghandhian Truth Firmness, Time Matrix Translation (Inter-Dimensional); hon/Pubs, *Toxin Release* 1977, "The State of Jefferson" 1975-82, "List-Master" 1975-82; Nat Merit Finalist, 1963; Hon Prog, Lamar Tech; W/W in CA; W/W of Am Wom.

SPAGNARDI, RONALD LEE oc/ Magazine Editor and Publisher; b/Apr 25, 1943; ba/1000 Clifton Avenue, Clifton, NJ 07013; m/Isabel; c/Lori Ann; p/Leo L Spagnardi, Bloomfield, NJ; ed/ Montclair Col, 1968; Berklee Col of Music, 1963; pa/Free-Lance Musician, 1968-70; Owner/Mgr, The Music Scene, 1970-77; Fdr and Pres, Editor/ Publisher, *Modern Drummer Magazine,* 1977-; Am Music Conf; Percussive Arts Soc; Nat Assn of Jazz Edrs; Soc of Profl Journalists; Pres's Assn; Am Soc of Mag Editors; cp/US C of C; r/Prot; hon/Pub, *Cross-Sticking for the Drumset,* 1976; W/W E.

SPANDORFER, MERLE SUE oc/ Artist, Educator; b/Sep 4, 1934; h/8012 Ellen Lane, Cheltenham, PA 19012; ba/ Philadelphia, PA; m/Lester; c/Cathy, John; p/Bernice Bank Altschul, Balti-more, MD; ed/Syracuse Univ, 1952-54; BS, Univ of MD, 1956; pa/Presently Tchg, Tyler Sch of Art; Paintings and Prints in Perm Collections: Mus of Mod Art (NY), Metro Mus of Art (NY), Israel Mus, Phila Mus of Art, Balto Mus of Art, Lib of Cong; Artist Equity; Col Art Assn of Am; Nat Art Ed Assn; Am Color Print Soc; r/Jewish; hon/16 One-Person Exhbns, incl'g Shows in NY and Japan; Exhib'd in Over 100 Grp Exhbns;

Outstg Art Edr, 1982; Phila Mus of Art Purchase Awd, 1977; Balto Mus of Art Gov's Prize and Purchase Awd, 1970; W/W Am Wom; W/W Am Art.

SPANGENBERG, KRISTIN LOUISE oc/Curator of Prints, Drawings and Photographs; b/Jun 3, 1944; h/1601 Clio Avenue, Cincinnati, OH 45230; ba/ Cincinnati, OH; p/Karl R (dec) and Ruth B Spangenberg, Palo Alto, CA; ed/AB, Univ of CA Davis, 1968; MA, Univ of MI Ann Arbor, 1971; pa/Asst Curator of Prints 1971-74, Curator of Prints, Drawings and Photographs 1974-, Cinc Art Mus; Print Coun of Am, 1972-; Am Assn of Mus, 1972-; r/Meth; hon/Pubs, *Homage to Maurits Cornelis Escher 1898-1972* 1973, *Eastern European Print-makers* 1975, *French Drawings, Waters and Pastels 1800-1950* 1978, *Color Photographs by Marie Cosindas* 1980, *The Cincinnati Art Museum Photography Collection* 1984.

SPARKMAN, LUCILLE WAHL oc/ Science Educator; b/Jul 4, 1920; h/Route 2, Box 636, Crystal River, FL 32629; ba/ Crystal River, FL; m/Thomas Ray (dec); c/Elizabeth Rae, Thomas Ray Jr; p/Mr and Mrs J G Wahl, Crystal River, FL; ed/BSVHE 1947, BAEED 1970, Univ of FL Gainesville; Att'd, Harding Univ; pa/ Vocational Homemaking, 1949-61; Homemaker, 1961-65; Elem Ed, 4th Grade, 1965-79; Elem Sci, 1980-83; NEA; FEA; CCEA; Nat Sci; Marine Sci Nat; cp/Am Legion Aux; Garden Clb; Jr Wom Clb; FL Leag of the Arts; March of Dimes, Chair; Cancer, Co Orgr; Heart Assn, Co Chair; Former GSA and CSA Ldr; Yth Ctr Orgr, 1955; r/Ch of Christ; hon/FHA Advr of Yr, 1954; Outstg Tchr in Am, 1972-73; Tchr of Yr, 1977-78; W/W S and SW; World W/ W Wom.

SPARKS, OTIS VERNON oc/Man-ager of Finance and Accounting; b/Jun 15, 1951; h/PO Box 277, McKee, KY 40447; ba/McKee, KY; m/Dinah Sue Yost; c/Ryan Ashley; p/Mr Gene Edward Sparks, Somerset, KY; ed/BS, Acctg and Bus, Union Col, 1974; pa/Asst Comptroller, So Dollar Stores Inc, 1974-75; Asst Ofc Mgr 1975, Ofc Mgr 1975-82, Fin and Acctg Mgr 1982-, Jackson Co Rural Elect Cooperative Corp; Pres, Phi Upsilon Beta, Union Col, 1973; Bus Mgr of Sch Paper, Union Col; KY Elect Cooperatives Accts Assn, Secy 1979, VP 1980, Pres 1981; cp/Pres, Jackson Co Little Leag, 1975-80; Exter-nal VP, Jackson Co JCs, 1977; Secy-Treas, Jackson Co Kiwanis Clb, 1976-78, VP 1979-80; r/Bapt; hon/W/W S and SW.

SPARROW, LYNNE ORSER oc/ Truck Transportation Executive; b/Dec 6, 1939; h/Route 2, Box 110, Gardiner, ME 04345; ba/Same; m/William B Sr; c/William B Jr, Patricia A, Deborah L; p/Ralph L (dec) and Charlotte Fogg Orser, North White Field, ME; ed/ Gardiner HS, 1958; Gates Bus Sch, 1959; Student, Univ of ME Augusta; pa/ Treas, W B Sparrow Forest Prods, 1969-; Treas, Sparrow Leasing Co of FL, 1970-; Fleet Operator, Refrigerated Food Express Inc, 1977-; Augusta BPW; cp/Gardiner Gen Hosp Wom's Bd, Secy 1969-70; Augusta Gen Hosp Aux, Secy 1979; ME Assn of Hosp Auxs, Secy 1980, Pres 1983-84; Gardiner Lib Assn; Augusta Wom's Clb; r/Prot; hon/Phi Theta Kappa, 1983; W/W E.

SPEARMAN, DAVID H oc/Veteri-

narian; b/Nov 16, 1932; h/PO Box 327, Easley, SC 29640; ba/Easley, SC; m/ Patsy C; c/Kathleen Elizabeth Spearman Daniel, David H Jr; p/David R (dec) and Elizabeth H Spearman, Easley, SC; ed/ BS, Clemson Univ; DVM, Univ of GA, 1956; pa/Cleveland Pk Animal Hosp, 1956-57; Self-Employed Vet, 1957-; Alpha Zeta; Alpha Psi; SC Bd of Vet Examrs; Fdr and Past Pres, Secy, Blue Ridge Vet Med Assn; cp/Easley Lions Clb, Past Pres and Intl Del; JCs, All Ofcs Except Pres; Pres, Pickens Co Fair; Pres, Pickens Co Foxhunters; Pendleton Farmers Soc; Chm, Easley Zoning Comm; r/Pres, Deacon, Chm of Pulpit and Organ Coms; hon/Key Man Awd, JCs; W/W S and SW.

SPEARMAN, PATSY C oc/Real Estate Broker; b/Aug 23, 1934; h/PO Box 327, Easley, SC 29640; ba/Green-ville, SC; m/David H; c/Kathleen Eliza-beth Spearman Daniel, David H Jr; p/ Lee Pierce (dec) and Jeanette Munn Cordle, Richmond, VA; ed/AA, Rich-mond Profl Inst of Col of Wm and Mary; Att'd, Univ of GA, 1953, 1954; Grad, Rltrs' Inst, 1978; pa/Cabell Eanes Advtg Agy, 1952-53; Univ of GA, 1954-56; Wk'd for and w Husband, 1956-78; Real Est Broker, C Dan Joyner & Co Inc, 1978-; SC Vet Aux; r/Presb; Past Pres, Wom of the Ch; hon/Recip, Num Awds from SC Eye Bk and SC Lions Clb for Obtaining Eye Donors; W/W S and SW.

SPEARS, JANET E oc/Business Pro-fessor, Sole Proprietor; b/Sep 5, 1933; h/RR 1, Sheffield, IL 61361; ba/Kewa-nee, IL; m/Keith A; c/Bruce, Roger, Darci, Paul; p/Enoch E and Marguerite Downey (dec); ed/AA, Black Hawk Col, E Campus; BS, Bradley Univ, 1980; Currently Wkg on MBA, St Ambrose Col; pa/Secretarial Positions: Kewanee Machinery Conveyor 1951-52, Wm E Trinke, Atty 1952-53, Walworth Co 1968-72; Adm Asst, Kewanee Public Hosp, 1972-75; Asst Pers Dir, Daven-port Osteopathic Hosp, 1980-81; Bus Mgr, Franciscan Med Ctr, 1981; Bus Prof, Black Hawk Col, E Campus, 1981-; Am Mgmt Assn; Soc for Advmt of Mgrs; Nat Assn of Female Execs; AAUW; Phi Chi Theta; cp/Kewanee Public Hosp Assn; Kewanee Art Leag; Henry Co Repub Wom; U Fairview Wom; Annawan Jr Wom's Clb, Pres 1964-65; r/Meth; Ch Liturgist; Sunday Sch Tchr; Mem of Adm Coun for Many Yrs; hon/Chris Hoer Scholar, Bradley Univ; W/W Am Wom.

SPEER, OLGA BURDICK oc/Health Food Store Operator; b/Sep 6, 1914; h/ Hoxbar Route, Box 183, Ardmore, OK 73401; ba/Same; m/Ralph Turner; p/ Roland (dec) and Clara Burdick, Ard-more, OK; ed/BS, Madison Col, 1941; pa/Food Ser Dir, Col Cafeteria, Madison Col, 1941-45; Therapeutic Dietitian, FL Hosp, 1945-47; Food Ser Dir, Ardmore Hosp, 1948-50, 1955-59 (Also Taught Nutrition); ARC Instr, 1956-65; Path-finder Ldr as Master Guide, 1939-67; r/SDA; hon/In Missionary Vol Ser, 1935-67; 28 Hons.

SPENCE, HENRY LOSTON oc/Engi-neer; b/Oct 26, 1943; h/1421 Palmetto Avenue, Virginia Beach, VA; ba/New York, NY; m/Pamela A Butler; c/Lau-rietta Sharaga, Adrienna Reil, Henry Loston Jr; p/Nehmiah E (dec) and Laura A Spence, Virginia Beach, VA; ed/ MSET, BSE, Columbia Pacific Univ,

1979-82; MSEE 1979, BSEE 1977, Metro Inst; ASET, Norfolk St Univ, 1971; Hon DDiv, 1977; mil/USN, 3½ Yrs; USAF, 4 Yrs; pa/Engr 1, Communication, ITT World Communication, 1981-; Sales Mgr and VP of Sales Distributions, SIA Inc, 1972-81; Sr Sys Engr, Telecommunication, Wn Union Corp, 1981-82; Engr Writer, Elect and Electronics, Westinghouse Elect Corp, 1980-81; Sys Engr, Tomahawk Cruise Missile, Vitro Lab Automation Industs Inc, 1979-80; Other Previous Positions; IEEE; AFCEA; Soc of Am Mil Engrs; Am Soc of Notaries; Am Entrepreneurs Assn; IAISP; cp/US JCs, Past Pres; Kawaida JCs, Past Chm; IPA; r/Bapt; hon/US Dept of Navy Plank Hon Awd, 1975; USS VA CGN-38; 4-Yr Appt, St Wide Notary of VA Gov Appt, 1978-82; W/W E.

SPENCE, LEWIS C oc/Corporate Executive; b/Jul 12, 1931; h/3084 Northwest 74th Terrace, Okeechobee, FL 33472; ba/Jupiter, FL; m/Katherine Jean; ch/Sharon, John, Robin, Lydia, Melody; p/John Lewis and Margarette Lea Spence (dec); sp/Thomas and Vera Nuttall, Riviera Bch, FL; ed/BLS Humanities & Scis, Univ of OK, 1966-67; Att'd Univ of MD, 1952; USAF Ext Inst, 1960-64; Voc Tech Inst, 1947; mil/USAF; 8th AF-Strategic Air Cmd, Korea, 1950-60; Spec Proj Engr in Charge of Ground Communs, AF Comm Ser Mid E, 1960-63; Spec Proj Engr in Charge of MARS, Dpty for Comm, Rank Capt OK Wing CAP, Ctl Comm Region HQs, OK, 1963-65; Asst Dir Comm, USAF, Adj Gen Staff, St of TX, 1965-66; Res & Devel Engr/Multi-band & Satellite Communs, USAFE, Mid E, 1966-67; Assignment, USAF, HQs AF Comm Ser, Scott AFB, IL, 1967-68; pa/Res & Devel Engr, Tracor Inc, 1966; Exec VP, Chief Res & Devel Engr, Dynamic Communs Inc, Riviera Bch, FL, 1969-75; Exec VP, Chief Res & Devel Engr, Tradewinds Labs Inc/Dynamic Comm Inc, Jupiter, FL, 1975-82; ARRL; MARS; CAP; Soc for Am Inventors; Palm Bch Inventors Soc; Mem Bd of Dirs, Ocean Measurements Inc; hon/AF Commend & Var Commends Assoc'd w 18 Yrs in USAF; Active Duty on 3 Continents; W/W FL; The Palm Bch Register; Personalities of S.

SPENCER, CAROLINE M oc/Senior Fashion Designer; b/Nov 22, 1932; h/10316 Wilkins Avenue, Los Angeles, CA 90024; ba/Hawthorne, CA; p/Harold Austin and Anna M Spencer (dec); ed/BFA, Mpls Col of Art and Design, 1955; Profl Designation in Bus Mgmt, Univ of CA LA, 1982; pa/Designer, Chd's Sportswear, Wonderalls, 1958-62; Sportswear Designer, Jr House of Milwaukee, 1962-63; Sr Fashion Designer, Clothes and Accessories for the Barbie Doll, Mattel Toys, 1963-; Fashion Grp Inc; Costume Soc of Am; Wom at Mattel; Mattel Mgmt Assn; Nat Assn Female Execs; cp/Marina City Clb; r/Rom Cath; hon/Keynote Spkr, Barbie Doll Collectors Conv, 1982; Guest Fashion Editor, Mademoiselle Mag, 1955; Recip, Best Toy Awd, Mattel Toys, 1973, 1977.

SPENCER, DEBORAH LYNN oc/Assistant Director of Nursing; b/Oct 17, 1954; h/PO Box 459, Grundy, VA 24614; ba/Grundy, VA; m/Joe; c/Cha-

rles Allen, Brian Edmond; p/Charles and Euline Anderson, Elkhorn City, KY; ed/Assoc Deg in Nsg, Morehead St Univ, 1975; pa/Charge Nurse, Hazard ARH, 1975-78; Charge Nurse, Drs Hosp, 1979; Asst Dir of Nsg, Inser Ed Dir, Nsg Quality Assurance Coor, Buchanan Gen Hosp, 1979-; hon/W/W Am Wom.

SPENCER, DIANNE WINTER oc/Public Relations and Marketing Firm Executive; b/Aug 15, 1936; h/15 West 84th Street, New York, NY 10024; ba/New York, NY; c/Sheba; p/George Wolters (dec) and Mary Enzweiler Winter; ed/St Joseph's Acad, 1950-54; Univ of Cinc, 1954-57; pa/Acct Rep, J Walter Thompson, 1961-62; VP, Schless & Co, 1963-67; VP, Dir, Strauchen & McKim, 1968-71; Acct Supvr, Manning, Selvage & Lee, 1975-79; Pres, Spencer-Wood Inc, 1979-; Pres's Assn; Am Mgmt Assn; Nat Home Fashions Leag; hon/W/W Am Wom.

SPERBER, PHILIP oc/Manufacturing Executive; b/Feb 29, 1944; h/30 Normandy Heights Road, Convent Station, NJ 07961; ba/New York, NY; m/Doreen Faye Strachman; c/Shoshana, Ryan, Sara; p/Sol and Sally Sperber, Deerfield Beach, FL; ed/BS, NJ Inst of Technol, 1965; JD, Univ of MD Sch of Law, 1969; pa/Sales Mgr, NJE Corp, 1965-68; Ptnr, Firm of Blair, Olcutt & Sperber, 1968-71; Admitted to MD Bar, 1970; VP, Cavitron Corp, 1971-77; Grp Exec, ITT, 1977-79; Pres, Refac Intl Ltd, 1979-; Chm, The Negotiating Grp, 1976-; CoChm, Ann Bus Inst, Fairleigh Dickinson Univ, 1974-76; Chief Instr, Am Negotiating Inst, 1976-80; Lectr, World Trade Inst, 1978; Lic'g Execs Soc, Trustee 197-79; Ultrasonic Indust Assn, VP 1975-77; Intl Execs Assn, 1980-; Am Inst Chem Engrs, Mktg Div 1980-; ASTM, Sect Chm 1976-77; ABA, Com Chm 1975-80; NJ Bar Assn, Councilman 1977-80; Am Arbitration Assn, Judge 1974-; Pres's Clb, 1983-; Sales Execs of NY; cp/Pres, Runnymede Hills Civic Assn, 1971-72; Pres, Consumer Clearinghouse, 1977-78; r/Jewish; hon/Author, Intellectual Property Management 1974, Negotiating in Day to Day Business 1976, The Science of Business Negotiation 1979, Corporation Law Department Manual 1981, Failsafe Business Negotiating: Strategies and Tactics for Success 1983, and Over 80 Pub'd Papers; Named Outstg US JC, 1966; Recip, Awds, NJ Writers Conf, 1974, 1979, 1981, 1983; Am Mktg Assn, 1975; Commend, Am Law Inst, 1976; Cit, Am Mgmt Assn, 1978; Outstg Alumnus Awd, NJ Inst Technol, 1981; W/W Am Law; W/W Engrg; Intl Authors and Writers W/W; Men of Achmt; W/W E; Contemp Authors; DIB; Am's Names and Faces; Notable Ams.

SPIEGEL, SUSAN LYNN oc/Manufacturing Firm Executive; h/159 Brookville Lane, Old Brookville, NY 11545; ba/Port Washington, NY; m/Maurice; c/Robert Wayne Flaxman, Stephen Mark Flaxman; p/Irving and Beatrice Jaffe, Boca Raton, FL; ed/BS, Boston Univ, 1964; Hofstra Univ Grad Sch of Ed; C W Post Univ Grad Sch of Bus; pa/Elem Sch Tchr, Long Bch, NY, 1964-67; Pres, Fashions by Appointment, 1967-71; Adm Asst, Peerless Sales Corp, 1967-71; Pres, N Shore Sales, 1971-74; Sales Mgr 1973-75, Mktg Dir 1975-78, VP of Opers and Control 1978-, U Utensils Co Inc; Bd of Dirs, Peerless

Aerospace, 1980-; NTSEA; BPAA; AMI; r/Jewish; Haddassah; hon/Boston Univ All Univ Dean's List, 1962; W/W Am Wom.

SPILLER, ELLEN BRUBAKER oc/Instructor of English; b/Jul 17, 1932; h/211 Rue Orleans, Baytown, TX 77520; ba/Baytown, TX; m/Samuel Christopher; c/Katherine Quesney, Georgianne; p/George Nunley (dec) and Lou Greathouse Brubaker, San Marcos, TX; ed/BJourn, Univ of TX Austin, 1954; MA in Eng, Univ of Houston Ctl Campus, 1965; MA in Col Tchg, Univ of Houston Clear Lake City, 1980; pa/Editor, Texas Future Farmer, 1955-57; Editor, House Organs, St Luke's/TX Chd's Hosps; Eng Tchr, Aldice Jr High, 1959-61; Eng Tchr, Waltrip Sr High, 1961-65; Instr of Eng, Lee Col, 1965-; TSCTA; Wom in Communs; AAUP; CCCC; CCTE; cp/Lee Col Wom's Clb, VP 1980-81, Pres 1981-82; r/Altar Guild of All Sts Epis Ch; hon/Author, Num Articles in Profl Jours; T R Larsen S'ship, Univ of TX, 1953; Exxon Excell in Ed; W/W S and SW; W/W Am Wom; Personalities of S; Commun Ldrs.

SPITZBERG, IRVING JOSEPH JR oc/General Secretary; b/Feb 9, 1942; h/7612 Winterberry Place, Bethesda, MD 20817; ba/Washington, DC; m/Roberta Frances; c/Edward Storm, David Adam; p/Dr and Mrs Irving J Spitzberg, Little Rock, AR; ed/BA, Columbia, 1964; BPhil, Oxon, 1966; JD, Yale, 1969; pa/Asst Prof, Pitzer Col and Claremont Grad Sch, 1969-71; Fellow, Inst of Current World Affairs, 1971-74; Vis'g Lectr, Brown Univ, 1974; Dean of the Cols 1974-79, Assoc Prof of Policy Studies and Ed 1974-80, St Univ of NY Buffalo; Gen Secy, AAUP, 1980-; Am Bar Assn; Bar of St of CA; AAAS; Intl Studies Assn; Assn for the Study of Higher Ed; hon/Editor and Author, The Exchange of Expertise: Counterparts and the New International Order 1978, Universities and the International Exchange of Knowledge 1979; Kellett Scholar, Oxford Univ, 1964-69; Fellow, Inst of Current World Affairs, 1971-74; W/W E; W/W W; Men of Achmt; DIB.

SPIVACK, BARBARA BENTZ oc/Director of Student Services; b/Nov 8, 1944; h/310 Stanmore Road, Baltimore, MD 21212; ba/Baltimore, MD; p/Peter and Catherine Bentz, Almont, MI; ed/Ed 1965, Student of Pers Adm 1969, MI St Univ; pa/Elem Sch Tchr, MI Public Schs, 1965-67; Occupl-Ednl Info Spec, MI St Univ, 1969-70; Asst to Dean for Student Pers Sers 1971-75, Coor for Student Devel Sers 1975-80, Dir of Student Sers 1980-, Univ of MD Sch of Nsg; Am Col Pers Assn, Directorate Body, Comm I 1976-79; MD Col Pers Assn, Pres 1977-78; APGA; MD Pers and Guid Assn; hon/Danforth Awd, 1962; Outstg Yg Wom of Am; W/W E; Outstg Personalities of S.

SPRAGUE, NANCY EASTER oc/Administrator of Reading; b/Jul 17, 1934; h/Hill Top Drive RD #3, Tunkhannock, PA 18657; ba/Tunkhannock, PA; c/William Lloyd, Douglas; p/Dr Stanley B Easter (dec); Mrs Helen C Easter, Tunkhannock, PA; ed/BS, Ed, PA St Univ; MS, Rdg Ed, Marywood Col; MS, Adm, Univ of Scranton; pa/Elem Ed, Shippensburg Schs, 1956; Elem Ed, New Rochelle Schs, 1956-58; Elem and Rdg Ed, Hasting-On-Hudson

Schs, 1958-60; Rdg Instr 1964-74, Admr of Rdg 1975-, Tunkhannock Schs; Pt-time Instr of Rdg, PA St Univ, Wilkes Barre Campus, 1970-78; Pt-time Instr of Rdg, Marywood Col, 1981; Nat Elem Prins Assn; PA Elem Prins Assn; Nat Assn for Curric Devel; PA Assn for Curric Devel; Nat Fed Coors Assn; PA Fed Coors Assn; NRA; PA Rdg Assn; NE Rdg Assn; cp/Merit Badge Cnslr, BSA; r/Presb; hon/Spkr, Chd and TV, NE Rdg Assn Conf 1981, PA Rdg Conf 1981, NY Rdg Conf 1981, World Rdg Conf 1982; Spkr, Rdg and Vision, NE Rdg Conf 1982, PA Rdg Conf 1982, PA Fed Coors Conf 1983; W/W E.

SPRECHER, LON oc/State Budget Director; b/Jun 3, 1952; h/4333 Bagley Parkway, Madison, WI 53716; ba/ Madison, WI; m/Sue; c/Megan; p/Mr and Mrs Les Sprecher, Prairie du Sac, WI; ed/BS 1974, MS 1975, MBA Course Wk, Univ of WI Madison; pa/St Budget Dir, St of WI Dept of Adm, 1982-; Exec Asst to Mayor of City of Madison, 1979-82; Dir of Div of Prog Mgmt, Dept of Adm, 1978-79; Envir Protection Analyst, St Budget Ofc, 1977-78; Univ of WI Analyst, St Budget Ofc, 1975-77; Adm Asst to Gov Lucey, 1974-75; WI Mun Fin Ofcrs Assn, 1980-82; Nat Assn of St Budget Ofcrs, 1982-; cp/Bd of Dirs, Exec Com, Madison Gen Hosp, 1981-83; WI Leag of Municipalities, Legis Com, 1980-82; Treas, Madison Christian Commun, 1979-81; r/U Ch of Christ; hon/Author, Num St Govt Pubs Pub'd by St Printing Ofc; "80 for the 80's," *Milwaukee Journal*, 1979; One of 10 Alumni of the Decade, Univ of WI Ctr Sys, 1983.

SPRINGER, ANDREA PAULETTE oc/Educator and Physical Therapist; b/Nov 20, 1946; h/411 East Highland, Kilgore, TX 75662; ba/Longview, TX; m/Alfred E IV; c/Alfred E V; p/Mr and Mrs W M Ryan, Leakey, TX; ed/BS, TX Wom's Univ, 1969; MS 1973, PhD 1977, Baylor Univ; pa/Phy Therapist: Dallas Soc Crippled Chd 1969-71, Convalescent Ctr 1971-72, Kerrville St Hosp 1973-74, Reg VII Ed Ser Ctr 1979-81, Longview ISD 1980-81; Presently Wkg as Phy Therapist, Smith Co Coop; Spec Lectr, LeTourneau Col; Asst Prof, Dept of Phy Therapy, Sch Allied Hlth Professions, LA St Univ Med Ctr; Am Phy Therapy Assn; Soc for Neurosci; Sigma Xi; cp/Assoc Mem, Evergreen Garden Clb; r/Bapt; hon/Pubs, "Motor Effects of Cholinergic Stimulation of the Globus Pallidus in Rats" 1975, "An Electromyographic Study of Neck Torsion in Cats Following Cholinergic Stimulation of the Globus Pallidus, Entopeduncular and Caudate Nuclei" 1980; Am Phy Therapy Assn, USPHS Grad Ed Trainee, 1972-73, 1974-76; Rocksprgs HS Valedictorian, 1965; W/W S and SW; World W/W Wom; Biogl Roll of Hon.

SPRINGER, WILLIAM L oc/Retired Congressman; b/Apr 12, 1909; h/900 West Park Avenue, Champaign, IL; m/Elsie Mattis; c/Katherine, Anne, Georgia; p/Otha L and Daisy E Springer; ed/BA, DePauw Univ, 1931; LLB, Univ of IL Law Sch, 1935; Hon LLD, Millikin Univ, 1953; Hon LLD, Lincoln Col, 1966, Hon LLD, DePauw Univ, 1972; pa/Began Pract of Law, Champaign, 1936; St's Atty, Champaign Co, 1940-42; Co Judge of Champaign Co,

1946-50; Elected to 82nd through 92nd Cong; Former Ranking Minority Mem, House Com on Interst and Fgn Commerce, and Num Subcoms; hon/Author, Public Law 480, Surplus Agriculture Trade and Development Act of 1954; Appt'd by Pres Nixon as Mem of Fed Power Comm, 1973; Appt'd by Pres Ford, Fed Election Comm, 1976.

SQUAZZO, MILDRED KATHERINE OETTING oc/Corporate Executive, Entrepreneur; b/Dec 22; h/721 Glenside Avenue, Berkeley Heights, NJ 07922; ba/Berkeley Heights, NJ; p/William John and Marie Margaret Fromm Oetting; ed/Student, Long Island Univ, 1946; Am Mgmt Assn, Intermittently, 1959-64; mil/Nurse Corps, AUS, 1946-47; pa/Secy-Treas, Purchasing Agt, Ofc Mgr, Kelite Corp, 1953-59; Adm Asst, Asst Sales Mgr, Electronic Tube Div, Burroughs Corp, 1960-61; Secy-Treas, Stanley Engrg Inc, and VP, Stanley Chems Inc, 1962-68; Pres, Ofcr, Chem-Dynamics Corp, 1964-68; Gen Admr, Purchasing Dir, Engrg Div, Richardson Chem Co, 1968-69; Owner, Operator, Berkeley Employmt Agt, Ofc Mgr, Berkeley Temporary Help Ser 1969-, and Berkeley Employmt Agy 1982-; Pres, MKS Bus Grp Inc, 1980-; Conslt, Mgmt, Pers Fin; Lectr in Field; Nat BPW Clb; hon/W/W E; W/W Fin and Indust.

SRIPADA, PAVANARAM KAMESWARA oc/Research Chemist; b/Jan 17, 1933; h/18 O'Rourke Path, Newton, MA 02159; ba/Boston, MA; m/Hemalatha; c/Meenakhi Lakshmi, Ramani Prakasa, Jagannadh Satya; p/Jagannadharao and Mahalarshmi, Rajahmundry, AP, India; ed/BSc w Hons 1952, MSc 1953, DSc 1959, Andhra Univ; pa/Res Assoc, Biophysics, Boston Univ Med Sch, 1981-; Res Assoc, Dept Nuclear Med, Univ of CT Hlth Ctr, 1976-81; Res Assoc, Dept Med Chem, Univ of RI Kingston, 1972-76; Lectr, Banting & Best Dept Med Res, 1968-72; Am Chem Soc; Chem Soc, London; r/Viswa Hindu Parishat; Hindu; hon/Author, 30 Pub'd Articles, Abstracts and Papers in Profl Jours; Elected Fellow, Royal Inst of Chem, 1969; W/W E.

SRIVASTAVA, RAMESH K oc/Plastic Surgeon; b/Feb 26, 1937; h/180 St George Place, Athens, GA 30606; ba/Athens, GA; m/Meena; c/Amitabh, Anurag; p/R Srivastava, India; ed/BSc 1956, MD 1961, Master of Surg 1964, Lucknow Univ; pa/Gen Surg Residency, Bklyn, NY, 1973-76; Plastic Surg Residency, Christ Hosp, 1978-80; Asst Surg, Shriners Burn Inst, 1976-78; Att'g, Athens Gen Hosp and St Mary's Hosp, and Plastic Surg Pract, 1980-; Am Burn Assn; So Med Assn; Med Assn of GA; Crawford Long Med Soc; Long Acre Destafno Med Soc; r/Hindu; hon/Pubs, "Shifting Neurovascular Flap for Reconstructing Amputated Digit," "Cardiac Infection in Burn Patients," "A Challenge to Resurface Major Burns"; Awd for Dedicated and Outstg Ser, Shriners Burn Inst.

STAFFORD, BETTY TRAMMELL oc/Instructor; b/May 26, 1931; h/Route 2, Box 345H, Gulfport, MS 39503; ba/Gulfport, MS; m/William M; c/Donna Stafford Stapp, William M Jr; p/George G (dec) and Bertha K Trammell, Gulfport, MS; ed/RN, Crawford Long Hosp, 1952; BSN, Univ of MS, 1969; MS, Univ

of So MS, 1979; pa/Staff Nurse, Gulfport VA Hosp, 1952-54; Charge Nurse, Gulfport Hosp, 1954-56; Charge Nurse, Univ of AR Med Ctr, 1958-66; Instr, MS Gulf Coast Jr Col, 1969-70; Instr, FL Keyes Jr Col, 1970-71; Inser Ed Coor, Eljon Val Hosp, 1971-72; Instr, MS Gulf Coast Jr Col, 1973-; ANA, 1953-; MS Nurses Assn, Dist 5, Treas, Bd, Del; NY Acad of Sci; Jefferson Davis Fac Assn; Epsilon Sigma Alpha; Sigma Theta Tau; Univ of MS Alumna; Univ of So MS Alumna; Counsel of Specs Psychi and Mtl Hlth Nsg; r/Handsboro Meth Ch; hon/Pub, "Correlation of Nurses Cognitive Knowledge About the Aged and Selected Demographic Variables with Nurses Attitude Toward and Interest in Assisting the Aged"; Psychi-Mtl Hlth Nurse of the Yr, MS, 1983; Sigma Theta Tau, 1979; Nat Hon Soc, 1949; Nat Music Hon Soc, 1949; W/W Am Nsg.

STAHELI, LANA RIBBLE oc/Counselor; b/Jun 21, 1947; h/2301 Fairview East #404, Seattle, WA 98102; ba/Seattle, WA; m/L T; c/Todd, Diane, Linda; p/Vercil and Mildred Ribble, Battle Creek, MI; ed/BA 1974, MEd 1976, Univ of WA; PhD, Union for Experimenting Cols and Univs, 1978; pa/Co-Fdr, Chp, Cnslr, Human Alternatives, NW, 1972-75; Pres and Mgmt Conslt, Profl Pract Cons/ts, 1975-78; Pres, Cnslr, Conslt, Staheli Inc, 1978-; Bd Mem, Univ Tutoring Ser, 1980-82; Fdr and Bd Mem, Rainier Foun, 1983-84; r/Unitarian; hon/Grad, cum laude, Univ of WA, 1974; W/W W.

STAMBAUGH, EDWARD E II oc/Licensed Clinical Psychologist; b/Mar 18, 1943; h/1004 Springfield Drive, Walnut Creek, CA 94598; ba/Pleasant Hill, CA; m/Elizabeth Louise; c/Edward E III, James C; p/Mr and Mrs Edward E Stambaugh, Spring Grove, PA; ed/Att'd, Franklin and Marshall Col, 1964; BA, Phil, Univ of UT, 1964; MDiv in Theol, MA in Pastoral Cnslg, Pacific Sch of Rel, 1970; BS, Psych, Abilene Christian Col, 1971; PhD, Clin Psych, Univ of TN, 1975; pa/Asst Prof, En MI Univ, 1975; Staff Psychol, Mtn Comprehensive Care Ctr, 1976; Dir of Mtl Hlth Sers, Lansdowne Mtl Hlth Ctr, 1977; Assoc Clin Prof of Psychi, Marshall Med Sch, 1980; Clin Conslt, Dept of Corrections, KY, 1980; Pvt Pract, Rafa Cnslg Assocs, 1980-; Am Psychol Assn, 1976; Am Soc of Clin Hypnosis, 1978; Intl Neuropsychol Soc, 1978; Nat Acad of Neuropsychols, 1979; Intl Soc of Hypnosis, 1980; Nat Assn of Alcoholism Cnslrs, 1980; Nat Epilepsy Foun, 1980; Soc of Pediatric Psych, 1981; AAAS, 1983; ISPE, 1981; cp/Mensa, 1979; r/U Ch of Christ; hon/Pubs, *Ecological Assessment of Child Problem Behavior* 1976, "Multimodality Treatment of Migraine Headache" 1977, "Hypnotic Treatment of Depression" 1977, "Audiotaped Flooding" 1978, "Hypnosis and Sports" 1978, "Transfer of Therapeutic Effects" 1979, "Waking State Suggestion" 1979, "Hemoperfusion for Chronic Schizophrenia" 1980, "When Hypnosis Casts Its Spell" 1980, "Burnout" 1980, "Executive Burnout Inc" 1980; W/W W.

STANFIELD, JAMES RONALD oc/Professor of Economics; b/Nov 22, 1945; h/2106 Kirkwood Court, Fort Collins, CO 80525; ba/Fort Collins, CO; m/Jacqueline Bloom; c/Bailey Thelma, Kellin Chandler; p/Tom Thornton and

Thelma Estelle S Stanfield (dec); ed/BA, MA, Univ of TX Arlington, 1968-69; PhD, Univ of OK, 1972; pa/Prof of Ec, CO St Univ 1974-, Univ of CA San Diego 1973-74, ID St Univ 1972-73; Assn for Social Ec, Exec Coun 1980-82; Assn for Evolutionary Ec, Edit Bd 1978-81, Bd of Dirs 1982-84; Omicron Delta Epsilon, Fac Advr and Reg Coor 1975-83; cp/Dist Coor, Kennedy for Pres, 1980; hon/Pubs, *Economic Surplus and Neo-Marxism* 1973, *Economic Thought and Social Change* 1979, Num Jour Articles; Omicron Delta Epsilon, 1969; H C Potter Awd, 1975; Semi-Finalist, Mitchell Prize, 1977; Fellow, Intl Inst of Social Ec, 1979; Outstg Yg Men of Am; Current Res in Social Ec.

STANILOFF, HOWARD MEDA oc/ Cardiologist, Epidemiologist; b/Sep 18, 1940; h/15825 Vose Street, Van Nuys, CA 91406; ba/Los Angeles, CA; m/ Robin Debra; p/Sidney and Ethel Staniloff, Richmond, British Columbia, Canada; ed/BSc w Hons 1970, MD 1973, Univ of Brit Columbia; MPH, Univ of CA LA, 1980; pa/Dir, Cardiac Rehab 1983-, Cardiologist 1980-, Cedars-Sinai Med Ctr; Adj Asst Prof of Med and Public Hlth, Univ of CA LA, 1980-; Royal Col of Phys and Surgs of Canada, Fellow 1977-; Am Col of Cardiology, Fellow 1979-; Am Heart Assn; Canadian Cardiovas Soc; Am Col of Phys; Soc for Epidemiologic Res; APHA; r/Jewish; hon/Author, Articles in Profl Jours; NIH Res Career Devel Awd, 1981-86; Men of Achmt; W/W CA; W/W W.

STANKIEWICZ, RAYMOND oc/ Industrial Engineer; b/Sep 3, 1934; m/ Ann F; c/Michael R, Raymond T, Stacy Ann; p/Benjimen and Stella Baer Stankiewicz; ed/Grad, Am Detective Tng Sch 1953, J Barns Detective Tng Sch 1953; Cert in Tool Design, St Univ of NY Farmingdale, 1960; BS in Indust Engrg, Allied Inst Technol, 1967; MSET, Am Wn Univ, 1982; mil/Served w AUS, 1951-54; pa/Fdr, Indust Engr, Am Engrg Model Co, 1959-; Coor, Suffolk Co Spec Olympics, 1982-; Bd of Dirs, Skills Unltd Inc, 1980-; Soc Plastics Engrs; LI Advtg Clb; Bohemia Bus and Civic Assn; LI Inst Archs; IPA; Constrn Specifiers Assn; Soc Am Mil Engrs; cp/Polish Inst Arts and Scis; Am Legion, Sgt-at-Arms 1960-61; Nat Rifle Assn; Nat Geographic Soc; Franklin Mint Collectors Soc; hon/Contbr, Articles; Winner, Var Sports Awds.

STANKOVICH, IVAN D oc/Consulting Engineer, Lecturer; b/May 22, 1924; h/324 San Carlos Avenue, Piedmont, CA 94611; ba/Piedmont, CA; m/ Valentina; c/Vadim; p/Dragoljub and Marta Stankovich (dec); ed/Grad, Mil Col, Odessa, USSR, 1948; Dipl, Mech Engrg, Inst of Technol, Moscow, USSR, 1959; Postgrad Study, Univ of CA Berkeley, 1967-68; pa/Var Positions in Mfg Indust, USSR, 1959-62; Proj Dir, Inst for Space Technol, Belgrade, Yugoslavia, 1965-66; Mfg Engr, Food Machinery and Chem Corp, 1967-68; Assoc Engr, Kaiser Engrs, 1968-74; Corp Staff Engr, Kaiser Aluminum and Chem Corp, 1974-82; Consltg Engr and Prin, W Gen Assocs; Pres, Consltg Engr Corp, 1983; ASME, Rep Mats Handling Engrg Div of Pacific Reg; AIME, Mem and Diplomate; Am Acad of Envir Engrs; hon/Author, *New Machines and Tools* 1971, *Machinery Handbook* 1964-66,

The Alumninum Industry in the Soviet Union 1978, Second Edition 1982, *The Aluminum Industry in East Europe and Communist Asia* 1980, *Mats Handling Handbook* 1983, Others, More Than 20 Articles; Reg'd Profl Engr, CA, WV; Holder, Patent in Field of Mat Handling; Lectr, CA St Univ Hayward Postgrad Sch of Bus and Ec.

STANLEY, BARBARA HREVNACK oc/Educator, Administrator; b/Aug 13, 1949; h/271 McMillan Road, Grosse Pointe Farms, MI 48236; ba/Detroit, MI; m/Michael; c/Melissa, Thomas; p/Mr and Mrs John Hrevnack, Hillside, NJ; ed/Grad, Hillside (NJ) HS, 1967; BA, Montclair St Col, 1971; MA 1975, PhD 1979, NY Univ; pa/Asst Prof, Dept of Psychi, Wayne St Univ Sch of Med, 1981-; Dir, Psychi, Ethics & Law Prog, Lafayette Clin (Detroit), 1981-; Clin Instr, NY Univ Med Ctr Dept of Psychi, 1980-81; Adj Asst Prof, NY Univ Dept of Psychol, 1979-80; Res Psychol, Hillside Div, Long Isl Jewish-Hillside Med Ctr, 1980-81; Pvt Pract in Clin Psychi, 1980-81; Clin Psychol, Long Isl Jewish-Hillside Med Ctr, 1978-80; cp/ Com for the Protection of Human Participants, Am Psychol Assn, 1983-86; Instnl Review Bd, Lafayette Clin, 1982-; Instnl Review Bd, Long Isl Jewish-Hillside Med Ctr, 1980-81; Nat Inst on Aging Task Force on "Senile Dementia of the Alzheimer's Type and Related Diseases: Ethical and Legal Issues Related to Informed Consent," 1981-82; hon/Long Isl Jewish-Hillside Med Ctr, Annual Sci Paper Contest Paper Awd, 1981; NIMH Traineeship; Psi Chi; New York Univ Asst'ship.

STANLEY, LUTICIOUS BRYAN JR oc/Field Service Engineer; b/Aug 26, 1947; h/PO Box 5386 WSB, Gainesville, GA 30501; p/Luticious Bryan and Frances Aileen Stanley, Gainesville, GA; ed/BS, Civil Engrg, So Tech Inst, 1974; Postgrad, GA St Univ, 1976-77; BS, Mech Engrg, So Tech Inst, 1982; mil/USAR, 1969-75; pa/Field Engr, Jordan, Jones and Goulding Inc; Proj Mgr/Engr, Mayes, Sudderth and Etheredge Inc, 1974-79; Ser Engr, Westinghouse Elect Corp, 1979-82; Prin, LBS Enterprises, 1982-; Am Water Wks Assn; Am Soc of Mil Engrs; ASHRAE; ASME; cp/Cobb Co Lions Clb; r/Christian Sci; hon/Author, Newspaper Articles, Articles in Field, Studies; Phi Theta Pi Scholar, 1968; Rookie of the Yr, Cobb Co Lions Clb, 1981; W/W S and SW.

STANLEY, SANDRA ORNECIA oc/ Educational Diagnostician, Researcher, Consultant; b/Jul 6, 1950; h/70 Madison Avenue, Jersey City, NJ 07304; ba/ Same; p/McKinley and Thelma Stanley, Jersey City, NJ; ed/BA, Ottawa Univ, 1972; MSEd, Univ of KS Lawrence, 1975; PhD, Univ of KS Med Ctr, 1980; pa/Dir and Hd Tchr, Salem Bapt Accredited Nursery Sch, 1972-73; Spec Ed Instr, Joan Davis Sch for Spec Ed, 1975-76; Instrnl Media/Mats Trainee 1976-77, Res Asst 1977-79, Univ of KS Med Ctr; Dir/Coor of Tng and Observation, Juniper Gardens Chd's Proj-Sch Res Unit, Bur of Child Res, Univ of KS KC, 1979-82; Ednl Diagnostician/Rschr/ Conslt, KC, 1977-; CEC; Coun of Lng Disabilities; Black Caucus-Minority Exceptl Chd, CEC; Assn for Supvn and Curric Devel; Easter Seal Soc for Crippled Chd and Adults of MO; Wom's

Ednl Netwk; Col Wom Inc; Nat Assn for Female Execs; Wom's Ednl Soc of Ottawa Univ; IPA; hon/Pubs, "How Much 'Opportunity to Respond' Does the Minority Disadvantaged Student Receive in School?" 1983, *Teaching Formats That Maximize the Opportunity to Learn: Parent and Peer Tutoring Programs*, Others; Achmt Recog, *Jersey Journal Newspaper*, 1981; Nom'd and Selected Student Grad Rep, Search Com for Chp, Dept of Spec Ed, Univ of KS, 1978-79; Hons, Comprehensive Exam, Univ of KS, 1978; Doct F'ship, Dept of Spec Ed, Univ of KS, 1977-79; S'ship, Col Wom Inc, 1977; Other Hons; W/W Among Students in Am Univs and Cols; 5,000 Personalities of World; Intl Biogl Roll of Hon; 2,000 Notable Ams; World W/ W Wom; Biogl Roll of Hon; Other Biogl Listings.

STAPLES, ALBERT FRANKLIN oc/ Dentist, Educator; b/Sep 3, 1922; h/2713 55th Terrace, Northwest, Oklahoma City, OK 73112; ba/Oklahoma City, OK; m/Virginia McManus; c/Sue Ellen, Craig Lawrence, Amy Jane, Allen Francis; p/Charles C and Bessie A Small (dec) Staples; ed/Att'd, Boston Univ, 1942-43, 1946-47; DMD, Tuft's Dental Sch, 1951; BSD 1954, PhD 1970, Baylor Univ Col of Dentistry; mil/AUS, 1942-46; USAF, 1951-53; pa/Clin Prof of Oral Surg 1954-57, Asst Prof 1961-63, Assoc Prof 1963-67, Spec Fellow in Physiol 1967-70, Baylor Col of Dentistry; Prof and Chm of Dept of Oral Surg, Univ of OK, 1970-; Univ Senate, Fac Appeals Bd, Curric Com, Exec Com, Col of Dentistry, Univ of OK; Am Dental Assn; Am Bd of Oral Surg; Am Col of Dentists; Am Assn of Dental Schs; Am Dental Soc of Anesthesiology; NY Acad of Scis; Sigma Xi; OKU; r/Rom Cath; hon/Articles Pub'd in *Texas Dental Journal*, *Oklahoma Dental Journal*, *Dental Association Journal*; Chapts in "Current Therapy in Dentistry," "Dental Clinics of North America," "Pain and Anxiety Control in Dentistry"; Best Clin Prof, Baylor Col of Dentistry, 1963, 1965; W/W Am; Am Men and Wom in Sci.

STARKERMANN, RUDOLF oc/Professor of Mechanical Engineering; b/ Apr 12, 1924; h/172 Riverview Drive, Fredericton, Canada E3B 5Y1; ba/ Fredericton, Canada; m/Rosmarie Pfister; c/Renate-Claudia, Brigitte-Esther; p/Auguste Starkermann, Zurich; ed/ Dipl Masch Ing 1950, Dr sc techn 1964, Swiss Fed Inst of Technol, Zurich; pa/ Consltg Engr, Brown, Boveri & Co, 1950-54; Sys Engr, Honeywell, 1954-56; Consltg Engr, Brown, Boveri & Co, 1956-70; Prof of Mech Engrg, Univ of New Brunswick, 1970-; Schweizerische Gesellschaft für Automatik; ASME; Intl Assn for Mathematical Modelling; Canadian Indust Computer Soc; Intl Assn of Sci and Technol for Devel; hon/ Author, 4 Books in Nonlinear and Multiple Automatic Control, 25 Pubs in Multiple Automatic Control, 35 Pubs in Applied Sys Theory in the Psycho-Social Realm; Gold-Level Judge in Figure Skating (Free Skating, Compulsory Figures and Dancing); W/W Ed; Intl W/ W Intells; Men of Achmt; Intl Register of Profiles; W/W Commonwealth; 5,000 Personalities of World; DIB.

STARKMAN, LAWRENCE J oc/Real Estate Developer, Appraiser, Broker; b/

Jan 3, 1946; h/2417 Central Park, Evanston, IL 60202; ba/Chicago, IL; m/ Nancy; c/Amanda, Abigail; p/Fred and Louise Starkman, Chicago, IL; ed/BA, Roosevelt Univ, 1968; MAI, Am Inst of Real Est Appraisers, 1978; pa/Current Pres, L Starkman & Assocs, Windsor Mgmt Co; Former Pres, Leason, Starkman & Co, 1972-81; Panel of Arbitrators, Am Arbitration Assn; Chgo Real Est Bd; Sustaining Mem, Landmarks Presv Coun of IL; Am Inst of Real Est Appraisers; Lic'd Real Est Broker; Instr, Ctl YMCA Col.

STARNES, PAUL M oc/Educator, Legislator; b/Dec 31, 1934; h/4004 Patton Drive, Chattanooga, TN 37412; ba/Chattanooga, TN; m/Mary Grace Feezell; p/James Albert (dec) and Helen Hudgens Starnes, Chattanooga, TN; ed/ BA, TN Wesleyan Col, 1957; MEd, Univ of Chattanooga, 1961; Hon DHL, TN Wesleyan Col, 1981; pa/Asst Supt and Bd Info Ofcr 1977-, Commun Relats Ofcr 1974-77, Hamilton Co Dept of Ed; Ho of Reps, St of TN: Mem of 88th, 89th, 90th, 92nd Gen Assems; Asst Prin, E Ridge Jr HS, 1971-74; Coor of Spec Projs, Hamilton Co Dept of Ed, 1969-71; Dean of Students, Hiwassee Col, 1964-69; Tchr, E Ridge HS, 1959-64; Tchr, McMinn Co HS, 1957-59; Hamilton Co Ed Assn; E TN Ed Assn, Exec Com, Pres; TN Ed Assn; NEA; Nat Sch Public Relats Assn, TN Chapt; TN Pers ad Guid Assn; Am Assn Sch Admrs; TN Assn Sch Admrs; Public Relats Soc of Am, Chattanooga Chapt; Phi Delta Kappa Ednl Frat; cp/Univ of TN Col of Med Adv Com of Chattanooga Clin Ed; Am Diabetes Assn, Gtr Chattanooga Chapt, Bd of Dirs; Chattanooga St Tech Commun Col, Bd of Assocs, Wom's Ctr Bd of Dirs; Chattanooga Area Hist Assn; Chattanooga Area Safety Coun; Kiwanis Intl, Num Ofcs; Other Civic Mbrships; r/McFarland U Meth Ch; hon/E Ridge Outstg Citizen Awd, 1976; Monroe Co's Most Outstg Man of the Yr, 1968; Most Outstg Yg Man in E Ridge, JC Awd, 1963; TN's Most Outstg Yg Tchr, JC Awd, 1962; E Ridge Most Outstg Tchr, JC Awd, 1962; W/W Govt; W/W Ednl Adm; Commun Ldrs and Noteworthy Ams; DIB; Personalities of S; Other Biogl Listings.

STARR, EVANGELINE oc/Estate Planning; b/Feb 24; h/306 Blanchard, Seattle, WA 98121; ba/Seattle, WA; p/ William P and Carrie Bell Thompson Starr (dec); ed/LLB, JD, cum laude, Univ of WA; AB, Univ of WA; pa/Dpty King Co Prosecuting Atty, 1935-41; Judge, Seattle Dist Ct, 1941-71; Estate Planning, 1971-; Phi Delta Legal Frat, Past Intl Pres, Hon Life Intl Pres 1970-; Phi Alpha Delta Law Frat Intl, Hon Life Mem of Intl Adv Bd 1980; Nat Assn of Wom Lwyrs, Assem Del 1972-80; Assn of Profl Mortgage Wom, Seattle, Parliamentarian 1964-; Past Pres's Assem, Pres 1973-75; Pres's Forum, Past Pres; Assn Univ Wom, Seattle, Pres 1971-73, Parliamentarian 1973-75, Hon Mem 1981; Nat Assn of Parliamentarians; Am Assn of Parliamentarians; Kappa Delta Sorority; Beta Sigma Phi Intl; Fdn of BPW Clbs, Past St Pres, Past Nat Legis Com Mem; cp/Zonta Intl, Seattle; Fdn of Wom's Clbs, Seattle, Pres 1978-80; Gov's Comm on Status of Wom, 1963-71, Wrote Legal Rights Sect

Report; Univ of WA Hosp Aux, Hon Bd Mem 1961-; hon/Nat Ser Awd, Nat Assn of Wom Lwyrs, 1972; Achmt Awd 1971, Hons Awd 1980, Assn of Profl Mortgage Wom; Achmt Awd in Law, Zonta Intl, 1983; Hons Awd, Fdn of Wom's Clbs, 1980; Achmt Awd, Past Pres's Assem, 1982; Recog Awd 1981, Hon 1984, Pres's Forum; F'ship Awd, Assn of Univ Wom, 1967.

STAUBLIN, JUDITH ANN oc/Financial District Manager; b/Jan 17, 1936; h/6115 Woodmont Boulevard, Norcross, GA 30092; ba/Atlanta, GA; c/Juli Jackson, T Scott Jackson; p/Mr and Mrs Fred Wiley, Anderson, IN; ed/Att'd, Ball St Univ 1954-55, 1969-70, Savs & Ln Inst 1962-67, Univ of GA 1974, Wright St Univ 1975; pa/Teller, Anderson Fed Savs & Ln, 1962-64; Data Processing Mgr 1965-70, Loan Ofcr 1970-72, VP 1972-74, Financial Sys Mktg 1974-76, NCR Corp; Financial Dist Mgr, Thrift Indust, So Data Ctrs, NCR Corp; GA Exec Wom's Netwk; cp/High Mus of Art; C of C; hon/W/W S and SW; W/ W Am Wom; W/W Fin and Indust; World W/W Wom.

STAVER, BRENDA H oc/Self Improvement Schools Owner and Operator; b/Mar 11, 1940; h/25073 Owens Lake, El Toro, CA 92630; ba/El Toro, CA; m/Robert L; c/Michael, Corey, Richard; p/Mrs Jewell Huffman, New Ellenton, SC; ed/Palmer Col; Patricia French Finishing Schs; pa/Ch Staff, Charleston, SC, 1961-62; Ch Staff, Miami, FL, 1963-65; Franchise Owner/ Operator, Image of Loveliness Self Improvement Schs, 1980-; cp/Toastmasters; Christian Wom's Clbs; Wom's Missionary Union; Reg BYW Dir, 1971; WMU Dir, 1973-79; Pres, WMU, CA, 1981; Bapt Jt Comm, 1981; hon/Author, Free-Lance Articles for Pubs of Wom's Missionary Union.

STEBINS, JANET H oc/Executive; b/ Jan 17, 1939; h/PO Box 37, Ansonia Station, New York, NY 10023; ba/New York, NY; p/Irving (dec) and Irma Stebins, New York, NY; ed/Att'd, LA City Col 1956-58, City Univ of NY 1958-62; Paralegal Cert, Long Isl Univ/ Bklyn Ctr, 1978; pa/Pres, Consumer Assistance Sers Inc, 1982-; Coor, Consumer Ed Progs, Phoenix House and Daytop Village, 1978-81; Free-Lance Legal Secy, 1971-79; Stewardess, Reservations Rep, U Air Lines, 1966-71; GET Consumer Protection Inc, Exec Dir 1971-; Am Coun of Consumer Interests, Consumer Ed Com 1982-; Soc of Consumer Affairs Profls, NY Chapt, 1978-; BPW; Netwks Unltd, Charter Mem 1980-; Am Arbitration Assn, Small Claims Arbitration, Adv Com 1983-; cp/NY Leag, Dir and Chair of Hospitality Com 1983-; IPA, 1980-; hon/ Consumer Ed Awd, 1974; W/W Am Wom.

STEELE, CHARLES oc/Retired, Consultant in Internal Medicine and Cardiology; b/Dec 1, 1905; ba/1 Wakefield Street, Lewiston, ME 04240; m/Ruby Mabell Cram; c/Charles William, Mary Louise, Richard Earl, Linda Maybelle; p/ William D and Katherine Louise Steele (dec); ed/AB 1927, MA 1929, Univ of MO; Att'd, Harvard Univ Med Sch, 1927-32 (Studies toward MD); Pathol Intern (1 Yr), Internal Med Intern (1½ Yrs), IV Med Ser, Harvard; Resident in Internal Med/Cardiol, Ctl ME Gen

Hosp, Lewston, 1934-35; mil/AUS, 1942-46 (Asst Chief Med Sers 67th Gen Hosp and Asst Chief to Chief Med Sers 121st Sta Hosp); Lt Col, Army Med Corps, 1942-56; Plans and Tng Ofcr, 1951-64; pa/Pvt Pract Med and Cardiol, 1937-42, 1956-81; Cardiol in Chief 1939-42, 1956-74, Sr Att'd Phys 1937-42, 1956-65, Chief of Cardiac Outpatient Clin 1952-74, Ctl ME Gen; Assoc Phys, ME Med Ctr, Portland, 1952-66; Conslt in Internal Med to Togus Vets Gen Surg and Med Hosp, 1947-78; Conslt in Cardiol, Rumford Commun Hosp 1948-68, Bath Meml Hosp 1948-68; Assn Mil Surgs, US; Charter Mem, Chapt Mil Order of World Wars; Resv Ofcrs Assn; Ret'd Ofcrs Assn; Androscoggin Co Med Soc; ME Med Assn; AMA; Am Heart Assn; Am Diabetic Assn; New England Heart Assn; Pan-Am Med Assn, Cert'd 1964; Intl Soc of Internal Med; Am Chem Soc, Med Sect; Am Soc of Internal Med; Soc of Internal Med of ME, Pres; ME Heart Assn, Pres; ME Arthritis Assn; Nat Rehab Assn; cp/Conslt, Div Hlth Mobilization, USPHS, 1960-70; Public Safety Coun of ME, 1954-74; St Dir #3, Responsible for Hlth Sers and Spec Weapons Def, 1957-70; Hlth Sers of US Civil Def Coun, 1955-70, Chm 1958; Civil Def Com, AMA, 1956-62; Rotary Intl; hon/George Wash Freedom Foun Awd, Freedom Foun of Val Forge, 1952; Scroll Awd, 333rd Gen Hosp, 1962; Gold Seal of Merit, ME Civil Def Coun, 1960; Outstg Commun Ser by Phys, Robins Co, 1964; Recog Awd for Outstg Ser Performed on Behalf of Soc, Am Soc of Internal Med, 1972; ME Heart Assn Cit for Outstg Public Ser, 1972; Plaque, US Civil Def Coun, Reg I, 1973; Commun Ldrs and Noteworthy Ams; W/W E; Who's Important in Med; Am Men of Med; Intl W/W Commun Ser; Commun Ldrs of Am; DIB; Dir of Dist'd Ams; 5,000 Personalities of World; Commun Ldrs of World.

STEELE, JAMES E oc/Clergyman; b/ Oct 13, 1934; h/1745 North Keystone, Chicago, IL 60639; ba/Chicago, IL; m/ Geraldine; c/Cerenthea Diana, Donnis LaRay; ed/BA, Liberal Arts and Sci, 1982; MS, Crim Justice, 1984; pa/ Pastorates: Chgo Cathedral 1979-, Chgo Tabernacle 1964-76, Riviera Bch 1963-64, Miamisberg 1961-62, Chgo Tabernacle 1956-58, Sesser 1955-56; Supt, IL Missionary Child Home, 1960; Dir, Yth Action, 1966-78; Chaplain, Cook Co Jail, 1979-80; Prin, Cathedral Acad, 1979-82; APGA; Am Assn for Cnslg and Devel; r/Ch of God; hon/ Pubs, "Please, Uncle Jim, Try One More Time" 1979, "Ministering to the Troubled" 1978, "Youth Ministry" 1975, "Little Appalacia's Steele Man" 1971, "Ministering to Youth in Trouble" 1969, "The Frustrated Church in a Multi-Cultural Society" 1984, *Feed My Sheep, Compassion, Youth and Drugs, I Have a Ghetto in My Heart, Darkness in Gangland.*

STEELE, JOYCE MARIE oc/Executive Director; b/Oct 17, 1957; h/2116 South Springfield, Chicago, IL 60623; ba/Chicago, IL; p/Mr and Mrs Robert Steele, Chicago, IL; ed/BA, Eureka Col, 1980; Seeking MBA, Roosevelt Univ; pa/Exec Dir, Joyce's Fine Arts; Corporate Loan Analyst, Harris Bk, 1980; Personal Clk, Sears & Roebuck, 1974-79; Fiscal Analyst, St of IL, 1982-;

Alpha Kappa Alpha Sorority; Artist for Congressman Washington; Eureka Col Alumni Clb; Nat Commerce for Wom; cp/Nat Coun of Negro Wom; r/Bapt; hon/Image Awd, 1982; Arts and Ed Awd, 1982; Commun Devel Awd, 1982; W/W Among Am Wom.

STEELMAN-BRAGATO, SUSAN JEAN oc/Public Relations; b/Aug 25, 1957; h/920 Walnut, San Carlos, CA 94070; ba/Foster City, CA; m/Larry Bragato; p/Claude and Leota Steelman, San Carlos, CA; ed/BA, Journalism, Polit Sci, Pepperdine Univ, 1980; pa/Dir of Communs, CA Beef Coun, 1982-; Acct Exec, DJMC Advtg, 1981; Reg Press Coor, Carter Mondale Re-Election Campaign, 1980; Sum Intern, White House Press Ofc, 1980; Congl Envir Standards Conf, 1978; Public Relats Soc of Am; Soc of Profl Journalists; Am Wom in Radio and TV; CA Wom for Agri; cp/Commonwealth Clb of CA; hon/Editor-in-Chief, *The Graphic* (Pepperdine Univ Col Newspaper) 1980, *Oasis* (Pepperdine Univ Mag) 1979, *Impressions* (Pepperdine Univ Yrbook) 1978; Soc of Profl Journalists Outstg Journalism Grad, 1980; Edit Ldrship Awd, Student Pubs, Pepperdine Univ, 1979; Outstg Yg Wom of Am; W/W W.

STEIGER, DALE ARLEN oc/Publishing Consultant; b/May 14, 1928; h/511 Forest Avenue, Rye, NY 10580; ba/New York, NY; m/Alyce; c/Christine, Maria; p/Mrs Eldred Pkoksch, La Crosse, WI; ed/BA, Chgo Acad of Fine Arts, 1951; Postgrad Studies, Drake Univ; Att'd, Iona Col; mil/AUS, 1946-48; pa/Art Dir 1956, Promotion Mgr 1958, Div Exec VP 1967, *Look* Mag Subscription Div; Assoc Pub Mktg Dir, *Saturday Evening Post*, 1971; Pres, Dale Steiger Assocs, 1972; Art Dir, Assn of IA, Co-Fdr, Pres 1962; Nat Art Dirs Assn, 1962; Des Moines Advtg Clb, 1958; Fulfillment Mgmt Assn, Pres, Chm 1978-80; r/Prot; hon/Author (w Others), *Handbook of Magazine Management*; Lee C Williams Awd, FMA, 1982; Art Direction Awds, 1962, 1963, 1964.

STEIN, JUDITH ELLEN oc/Museum Curator and Critic; b/Jun 27, 1943; h/2400 Waverly, Philadelphia, PA 19146; ba/Philadelphia, PA; m/Jonathan M; c/Rachel A; ed/PhD 1981, MA 1967, Art Hist, Univ of PA; BA, Art Hist, Barnard Col, 1965; pa/Staff Lectr, Phila Mus of Art, 1966-71; Instr, Tyler Sch of Art, 1971-78; Arts Reviewer, Nat Public Radio, 1979-83; Curator, PA Acad of the Fine Arts, 1981-; Col Art Assn; Intl Art Critics Assn; Wom's Caucus for Art; cp/Phila Barnard Alumnae Clb, Pres 1975-77; Bd Mem: The Print Clb 1981-, Wilma Proj Free Theatre 1978-79, Phila Art Alliance 1982-; hon/Pubs, "The Artists' New Clothes" 1983, "Contemporary American Realism" 1981, "Natural Disposition" 1981, "Portrait: Philadelphia" 1980.

STEINBERG, PATRICIA VIRGINIA oc/Consultant to Business and Industry; b/Mar 16, 1949; h/One Swarthmore Place, Swarthmore, PA 19081; ba/Same; m/Richard Leon; c/Richard Leon II, David John; p/Joseph and Dorothy Kusterbeck, Richmond Hill, NY; ed/BA, magna cum laude w Hons, Queens Col of the City Univ of NY, 1973; MA in Ed 1974, MS in Lib Sci 1975, Villanova Univ; PhD in Cnslg, Columbia Pacific

Univ, 1983; Intl Liaison Ofcr 1983-, Dir of Spec Projs 1983-, Hardware and Supply Co of Chester, PA; Ednl Conslt, Self-Employed, Swarthmore, PA, 1979-82; Ofc Mgr, Law Ofc of Richard L Steinberg, 1978-82; Tng Dir/Opers 1977-78, Staff Admr/Opers 1976-77, The Fidelity Bk; Math Tchr, Stetson Jr HS, 1976; Res Asst, Dept of Lib Sci, Villanova Univ, 1974-76; Res Asst to Rev L Rongione, Falvey Lib, Villanova Univ, 1974-76; Other Previous Positions; cp/Treas, Swarthmore Coun of Repub Wom, 1981-; Bd of Dirs, Swarthmore Rec Assn, 1981-82; Devel Chm, Sch Bd, The Sch in Rose Val, 1983-; hon/Pub, "Commentary on Bibliotherapy," 1975; Kappa Delta Pi; Psi Chi, VP for One Yr; Alpha Sigma Lambda; Deptl Hons in Psych; Kappa Phi Kappa; W/W E.

STENCHEVER, DIANE H oc/Social Worker; b/Aug 10, 1933; h/8301 Southeast 83rd Street, Mercer Island, WA 98040; ba/Seattle, WA; m/Morton A; c/Michael, Marc, Douglas; p/Hanford and Rose (dec) Bilsky, Hallandale, FL; ed/BS, Univ of Buffalo, 1955; MSW, Univ of UT, 1975; pa/Pvt Pract, Marriage and Fam Cnslg, Seattle and Renton, WA, 1977-; Grp Ldr, Divorce Lifeline, 1977-; Nat Assn of Social Wkrs; cp/Mercer Isl Country Clb; Pres, Woodland Pk Zoo Docents, 1983-84; hon/CoChm, March of Dimes, Shaker Hgts, OH, 1965.

STEPHENSON, ROBERT L oc/Archeologist; b/Feb 18, 1919; h/5831 Satchel Ford Road, Columbia, SC 29206; ba/Columbia, SC; m/Georgie E; p/George A and Myrtle L Stephenson; ed/BA 1940, MA 1942, Anthropology, Univ of OR; PhD, Anthropology, Univ of MI, 1956; mil/USMC, 1942-46, Resv to 1963; pa/Dir, Inst of Archeol and Anthropology, Univ of SC, and St Archeologist of SC, 1968-; Coor, NV Archeological Survey, 1966-68; Dir, River Basin Surveys, Smithsonian Instn, 1963-66; Chief, MO Basin Proj, River Basin Surveys, Smithsonian Instn, 1952-63; Other Previous Positions; Am Anthropological Assn, Fellow; AAAS, Fellow, Com Mem; Am Assn for St and Local Hist; Am Soc for Conserv Archeol, Com-man; Am Soc for Ethnohist; Antropological Soc of Wash, DC; Num Other Mbrships; hon/Pubs, "Frank H Watt: A Tribute" 1980, "Archeology in the South" 1976, Others; W/W S and SW; Personalities of S.

STEPP, RAYMOND WESLEY oc/Doctor of Optometry; b/Apr 27, 1947; h/108 Acorn Lane, Comanche, TX 76442; ba/Comanche, TX; m/Susan; c/Shawnna, Shelley; p/Ray (dec) and Helen Stepp, Zephyr, TX; ed/BA, SWn Union Col, 1969; OD, Univ of Houston, 1973; pa/Self-Employed, Solo Pract of Optom, 1973-; Am Optometric Foun; Better Vision Inst; NFIB; Am Optometric Assn; TX Optometric Assn; Mid TX Optometric Soc, Pres 1975-76; cp/Comanche C of C, Pres 1976-77; Bd of Dirs, Comanche Indust Foun, 1977-; Comanche Noon Lions Clb; r/SDA; hon/Outstg Yg Man of Am, 1977; W/W S and SW.

STERIAN, HENRY D oc/Executive; b/Oct 17, 1921; h/1067 Fifth Avenue, New York, NY 10128; ba/New York, NY; m/Christine Valmy; c/Countess Marina Valmy de Heydu; p/Sally Sterian, New York, NY; ed/BA, Law;

PhD, Ec; BA, Mech Engrg; pa/Dir, Chm of Bd, Parde Inc, Frankfurt, W Germany, 1963-72; Pres, Bioline Plus Sys Ltd, 1972-; Chm of Bd, Christine Valmy Inc, 1978-; Pres, Gt NY Chapt, People to People Intl Foun, 1983-; cp/Pres, U Roumanians for a Strong Am, 1978-; r/Jewish; hon/Pubs, *Biography of Giuseppe Garibaldy* 1957, *Monography of Great Britain* 1958.

STERN, PAULA oc/Senior United States International Trade Commissioner; m/Dr Paul A London; c/Gabriel Stern London, Genevieve Stern London; ed/BA, Goucher Col, 1967; MA, Reg Studies, Harvard Univ, 1969; MA 1970, MALD 1970, PhD 1976, Fletcher Sch of Law and Diplomacy; pa/Sr US Intl Trade Commr, 1978-; Legis Asst to Senator Gaylord Nelson, 1972-74; Guest Scholar, Brookings Instn, 1975-76; Sr Legis Asst to Senator Nelson, 1976; Intl Affairs Fellow, Coun on Fgn Relats, 1977-78; Bd of Dirs, Inter-Am Foun, 1980-81; Coun on Fgn Relats; hon/Pubs, *Water's Edge: Domestic Politics and the Making of American Foreign Policy* 1979, Num Articles on Domestic Affairs, Intl Trade, Fgn Policy, Mid E and Soviet Issues and the Wom's Movement; Recip, Alicia Patterson Foun Awd; Num Biogl Listings.

STERN, RICHARD EDWARD oc/Orthopaedic Surgeon; b/Nov 27, 1943; h/277 West End Avenue, New York, NY 10023; ba/New York, NY; m/Francine Martin; c/Remy Henri, Mariel Beata; p/Harry L and Rose K Stern, New York, NY; ed/BA, 1964; MD, 1968; mil/USAF, Maj 1973-75; pa/Clin Asst Prof, Orthopaedic Surg, Albert Einstein Col of Med; Att'g Orthopaedic Surg, Montefiore Med Ctr, 1976-; Police Surg, NYCHAP, 1976-; Hd Orthopaedic Surg, Replant Team, Montefiore Med Ctr; Fellow, Am Col of Surgs; Fellow, Am Acad of Orthopaedic Surg; Fellow, NY Acad of Med; Undersea Med Soc; r/Jewish; hon/Author of Many Orthopaedic Surg Articles for Profl Jours.

STERNLIEB, ANTONIA oc/Physician; b/Jun 10, 1915; h/7414 South Pine Park Drive, Lake Worth, FL 33463; p/Samuel and Dora Sternlieb (dec); ed/Grad, Gymnasium, Vienna, Austria, 1933; MD, St Univ Vienna, 1939; NY St Med Bd, 1946; pa/Dpty Med Supt, NYC Hosp, 1950-71; Asst Clin Psychi, Mtl Hygiene, Lebanon Hosp, 1957-68; Staff Phys, Royal Hosp, 1955-60; Bd of Govs, Nat Bus and Profl Coun, NY, 1964-67; AMA; FL Med Assn; Palm Bch Co Med Soc; r/Jewish; hon/Cert of Hon, Fordham Univ Alumni Assn for Dedicated Ser, 1950-64; US Treas Dept 25th Anniversary Awd; W/W Am Wom; Dir of Dist'd Ams; Personalities of S; W/W FL; Register of Palm Bch Co.

STERNS, PATRICIA MARGARET oc/Attorney and Counsellor at Law; b/Jan 30, 1952; ba/519 Eleven West Jefferson, Phoenix, AZ 85003; p/Lawrence Page and Mildred Dorothy Barbaras Sterns, Phoenix, AZ; ed/JD, Univ of AZ Tucson, 1977; BA, AZ St Univ Tempe, 1974; pa/Ptnr, Law Ofcs of Sterns & Tennen, Phoenix and Tucson, 1978-; Intl Inst of Space Law, 1979-; Am Soc of Instl Law, 1981-; AIAA, 1980-; Aviation/Space Writer's Assn, 1981-; AZ St Bar Assn, 1978-; Maricopa Co Bar Assn, 1978-; Am Bar Assn, 1980-; Maricopa Co Bar Assn Fam Law Com,

1982-; Am Bar Assn Aerospace Law Com, 1981-; Am Bar Assn Fam Law Sect, 1983-; Am Bar Assn, Intl Law Sect, 1980-; Am Dairy Goat Assn, 1981-; AZ Dairy Goat Assn, 1981-; r/Luth; hon/ Pubs, "Obligations of States in the Corpus Juris Spatialis: Fathoming Uncharted Waters" 1984, "Jurisprudential Philosophies of the 'Art of Living in Space'" 1983, "Institutional Arrangements: Foundations for Development of Living in Space" 1982, "Protection of Celestial Environments through Planetary Quarantine Requirements" 1981, Others; Cert of Outstg Ser, AZ St Legis, 1976; Phi Theta Kappa, Mu Sigma Chapt, 1971; AZ Law Review, 1975-76; W/W W; W/W Aviation and Aerospace; W/W Am Wom.

STEVENS, ELEANOR SANDRA oc/ Professional Services Executive; b/Nov 1, 1932; h/3530 Edgehill Drive, Los Angeles, CA 90018; ba/Los Angeles, CA; c/Fred W, Nathandra, Benjiman, Olaenaid; p/Benjiman Franklin and Mary Lou Smith (dec); ed/AS, Fresno St Univ, 1954; Student, Adult Ed, LA Trade Tech, 1972-73; pa/Disc Jockey, KGST-Fresno, 1954-55; Bkkpr, LA Co Assessor, 1961-69; Supvr, Holzman-Begue Real Est Co, 1969-73; Dist Mgr, U Sys Inc, 1973-77; Public Relats Conslt, Harold G Simon & Assocs, 1977-81; Pres, Owner, Stevens Personalized Sers, 1982-; Nat Assn Female Execs, 1982-; Wom's Referral Ser, 1983-84; cp/ St Anthony Grand Lodge; OES; r/Prot; hon/W/W in W.

STEVENS, MRS LaVERGNE BELDEN JR (RUTH MAXINE BURR) oc/Retired Educator; h/2740 Glenwood Road, Royal Oak, MI; m/LaVergne Belden Jr (dec); p/Clifford James Burr (dec); Evangeline Alberta Bowles (dec); ed/Undergrad, Univ of MI; BS, Music, Wayne St Univ, 1943; EdM (Plus 45 Hours), Wayne St Univ, 1953; pa/ Circulation Dept, *Washington Post*; Complaint Dept, Woodward and Lothrop, 1934; Interior Dept, PWA, 1934-47; Kgn Tchr, Detroit Bd of Ed, 1943-75; Life Mem, Beta Sigma Phi, Hon Soc, Wayne St Univ; cp/DAR, Ezra Parker Regent, 1981-83; St Pres, Huguenot Soc of MI, 1983-85; Mayflower Descendants of MI, Elder 1981-83; NSNE Wom, Past Dir, Recording Secy 1981-84; DAC, St Registrar 1979-82, Pres 1982-85; DCW, Recording Secy 1980-83; Colonial Dames XVII Cent, First VP 1981-83; Wom Descendants of Ancient and Hon Artillery; MI Soc Dames of the Ct of Hon, Flag Bearer 1981-83; NS of the US Daughs of 1812; Life Mem, OES #175; Life Mem, Forest Lake Country Clb; Lost Lake Woods Clb; Detroit Soc for Geneal Res; Linden Mills Hist Soc; NW Oakland Co Hist Soc; Oakway Symph Soc; Nat Soc Colonial Daughs of 17th Century; r/ Presb; hon/Pub, *Descendants of Thomas Bowles of Maryland 1758-1978*; Name Appears in *The Dodder Family Record, William R Macdonald and His Descendants, My Family Ancestors and Descendants, History of Freemasonry in Oakland County, MI, Ancestors of Robert Struble III, The Alice D Serrell Collection, Oakland County, MI, The Colonial Courier, The Hereditary Register of the USA, 1,600 Lines to Pilgrims; DAR Library Catalog*.

STEWART, CATHERINE oc/R&D Contract Monitoring; h/430 Marilyn

Lane, Redlands, CA 92373; ba/San Bernardino, CA; c/Kevin Charles Stewart Marker; p/Alexander P Stewart (dec); Marguerite L McCarron (dec); ed/ MS, 1960; AB, 1941; pa/Human Factors Proj Engr, TRW Def Sys Grp-NAFB, 1982-; Mgr and Fdr, Human Factors Grp, EG&G ID Inc, ID Nat Engrg Lab, 1978-82; Supervisory Auditor, Psychol, US Gen Acctg Ofc, 1976-78; Res Psychol, US Dept of Trans, 1974-76; Tech Staff, Mitre Corp, 1971-74; Conslt, 1970-71; Human Engrg Analyst, Boeing Co, 1960-69; Sch Psychol and Instr, Drummond Day Sch, 1949-58; Human Factors Soc, Founded Intermtn Chapt in ID, First Pres; Eval Res Soc; Assn for Wom in Sci; Am Nuclear Soc; cp/ Audubon Soc; Sierra Clb; hon/Pubs, "Human Reliability and Fault Tree Analysis" 1982, "Workshop: Design of Questionnaires" 1982, The Probability of Human Error in Selected Nuclear Maintenance Tasks" 1981, Others; W/ W Am Wom.

STEWART, ELIZABETH VICTORIA oc/Retired Professional Nurse; b/ Feb 20, 1910; h/77 Watkins Park Drive, Upper Marlboro, MD 20772; p/Mr and Mrs William Stewart (dec); ed/Dipl, Freedman's Hosp Sch of Nsg, 1933; BSNE, Cath Univ of Am, 1945; MS, Univ of MD Sch of Nsg, 1971-; pa/ Freedmen's Hosp: Staff Nurse 1939-41, Hd Nurse 1941-45, Relief Tchg Pediatrics 1945, Dept Supvr and Clin Instr, Med Sers 1945-50, Adm Nurse-Supvr, Med Sers 1950-54, Asst Dir, Relief 1954-58, Charge Supvr, PM 1953-61, Transferred to Sch-Student Hlth Dir and Instr, Trends I & II 1961-69, Sr Instr of Maternal Child Nsg 1969-71, and Archivist for Sch of Nsg; Nurse Spec, Exec Secy to Nurses' Examining Bd, DC, 1971; Asst Prof, Wash Tech Inst, 1972; Instr, P G Commun Col, 1973-76; APHA, 1978-; ARC, 1972-; Mtl Hlth Assn of MD, 1974-; Freedmen's Alumni Assn, 1935-; Cath Univ Alumni, 1950-; ANA, 1971-; DC Nurses' Assn, 1952-; Nat Leag for Nsg and DCLN, 1960-; cp/ Nat Trust for Hist Preserv, 1974; r/Epis; hon/Pubs, "Freedmen's Hospital in Historical Perspective and Its Effect Upon Nursing, 1862-1970," "The History of the Integration of the Negro Nurse into Diploma Schools of Nursing in the USA" 1971; Fac, Freedmen's Hosp Sch of Nsg, 1968: The Nightingale Emblem, "The Glowing Lamp"; Freedmen's Hosp Alumni Clb's Plaque: "Devoted Service to All Men," 1973; Edith M Beattie Awd, DC Nurse Assn, 1977; DCLN, "In Appreciation" 1974, "As Historian" 1981; "Service through the Years", Longview Bch Clb, 1981; Freedmen's Hosp Nurses Assn, Clbs, Nat Ofc, "As Historian," 1982; World W/W Wom; Intl Register of Profiles; Intl W/W Intells.

STEWART, GRACE oc/Educator, Administrator; ba/5101 Evergreen Road, Dearborn, MI 48128; c/Mark Wurster, Kevin Wurster; p/Marshall and Rachel Stewart, Rahway, NJ; ed/ PhD 1977, MA 1969, BA 1968, Wayne St Univ; pa/Dir, Focus on Wom Prog, Henry Ford Commun Col, 1978-; Instr 1974-78, Grad Asst 1968-72, Eng Dept, Wayne St Univ; Phi Beta Kappa; MI Wom's Studies Assn; Nat Wom's Studies Assn; Detroit Wom's Forum, Bd of Dirs; Nat Assn of Wom Deans, Admrs, Cnslrs; Mod Lang Assn; AAUW; cp/Bd

of Dirs, YWCA of Wn Wayne Co, 1980-83; r/Epis; hon/Pubs, "Mother, Daughter, and the Birth of the Artist as Heroine" 1979, "Albee's Festival Chant: Who's Afraid of Virginia Woolf?" 1976, *A New Mythos: The Novel of the Artist as Heroine* 1979; Colloquium, Wayne St Univ, 1968; Wayne St Univ F'ship, 1972, 1973, 1976; Henry Ford Commun Col Fac Lectureship Awd, 1982; W/W Am Wom.

STEWART, JAMES BENJAMIN oc/ Educator; b/Jul 18, 1947; h/100 Hartswick Avenue, State College, PA 16801; ba/University Park, PA; m/Sharon; c/ Kristin, Lorin, Jaliya; p/Reuben and Clora Stewart, Cleveland, OH; ed/PhD, Ed, Univ of Notre Dame, 1976; MA, Ec, Cleveland St Univ, 1971; BS, Math, Rose-Hulman Inst of Technol, 1969; pa/ Assoc Tech Studies Engr, Cleveland Elect Illuminating Co, 1969-74; Asst Prof of Ec and Dir of Black Studies Prog, Univ of Notre Dame, 1975-80; Asst Prof of Ec and Dir of Black Studies Prog, PA St Univ, 1980-; r/Bapt; hon/IL/IN Race Desegregation Assistance Ctr, Ctr Assoc 1979; W/W MW; Outstg Yg Men of Am.

STEWART, JOAN L oc/Editor; b/Oct 5, 1947; h/PO Box 696, Fort Benton, MT 59442; ba/Fort Benton, MT; m/John R; c/David Alan, Wesley Edward, Daniel Paul; p/Leland W and Doris E Nelson (dec) Overholser, Fort Benton, MT; Att'd, Univ of MO Columbia, Univ of MT Missoula; pa/Clk 1963-66, Assoc Editor 1968-77, 1979, Editor 1980-, River Press Publishing Co; cp/Chouteau Co Crimestoppers, Secy 1982, Pres 1983; Meml Ambulance QRU, 1979-; Chouteau Co EMS, Secy 1982; MT Emer Med Sers Assn, 1980-; Chouteau Co Jail Com, Secy 1983-; Chouteau Co Homemakers Coun, Pres 1979-83; Local Homemakers Clb, Pres 1979-; Police Magistrate, City of Ft Benton, 1970-72; CPR Instr, 1979-; r/Meth; hon/Grad, Nat Inst of Corrections, PONI, Boulder, CO, 1983; W/W W; W/W Am Wom.

STEWART, JOHN P oc/Center Director; b/Oct 14, 1934; h/29A Royal American Circle, Carlisle, PA 17013; ba/ Carlisle Barracks, PA; m/Mary Elizabeth; c/Mary Jane, Thomas, William, Frances, Elizabeth; p/Thomas and Frances Stewart, St Paul, MN; ed/BA, Polit Sci, Univ of MN, 1956; MPA, PA St Univ, 1976; mil/AUS; pa/Res Analyst, St of MN, 1956; Field Artillery Ofcr, 1957-58; Aviation Ofcr, 1959-62; Opers and Plans Ofcr, 1962-67; Combat Devel Ofcr, 1968-72; Battalion Cmdr, 1972-75; Dpty Cmdr, Corps Artillery, 1976-79; Fac, Air War Col, 1979-81; Dept Chm, Army War Col, 1981-84; Dir, Ctr for Land Warfare, 1984-; Army Aviation Assn; Assn of AUS; AF Assn; US Naval Inst; Am Space Foun; Tech Mktg Soc of Am; Pi Alpha Alpha; r/ Cath; hon/Author, Num Studies and Reference Texts Dealing w Mil Strategy, Mil Planning and Operations, Command and Control, and Def Budgeting; W/W Aviation and Aerospace.

STEWART, RONALD K oc/State Senate Minority Leader; b/Aug 16, 1948; h/PO Box 1442, Longmont, CO 80501; ba/Denver, CO; m/Dottie Martin-Stewart; p/William and Doris Stewart, Longmont, CO; ed/BA, Polit Sci, Univ of CO Boulder, 1974; Grad Studies in Hist, Public Adm, Univ of

Denver; pa/Elected to St Senate, 1976 (Re-Elected 1980); Elected Senate Dem Ldr, 1982; Gov's Comm on Public Broadcasting, 1976-77; Boulder Co Dem Chm, 1970-75; CO Dem St VChm and Mem of Dem Nat Com, 1977-79; Appt'd by Gov to Reapportionment Comm, 1981-; cp/Longmont Citizens' Adv Comm to Reg Trans Dist, 1974; Boulder Co Budget Adv Comm, 1975, Chm 1976; Longmont Symph Orch, 1976-77; Chm, Boulder Co U Way Bd, 1976; Boulder Co Pks and Open Space Adv Coun, 1977-82, Chm 1979; r/Prot; hon/Handbook of St Legis Ldrs; W/W Am Polit; W/W W; CO Legis Almanac.

STEWART, WILLIAM HAROLD oc/ Marketing Executive, College Dean, Clergyman; b/Apr 18, 1935; h/119 South St Marks, Chattanooga, TN 37411; ba/Chattanooga, TN; m/Bonnie Mai Spears; m/Candida; p/Harold Waltham and Mildred Sadie Hancock Stewart; ed/BS, NC A&T St Univ, 1960; MA, Ctl MI Univ, 1973; JD, Blackstone Sch of Law, 1977; DBA, Wn CO Univ, 1980; Hon DD, Laurence Univ, 1968; mil/Served w AUS, 1955-57; pa/Dept Mgr, Bancrofts Inc, 1960-62; Chief Cnslr, IL St Employmt Ser, 1962-66; Dir, Urban Demonstration Prog, Coop Leag of USA, 1966-69; Tng Dir, Gen Elect Co, 1969-70; Dir, City Demonstration Agy, 1970-71; Div Dir, HUD, 1971-75; Assoc Dir, Exec Sem Ctr, US CSC, 1975-78; Planning/Tng Exec, Div Power Utilization, TVA, 1978-80; Mgr, Commun Conserv Projs, 1980-; VP, Candida Intl, 1977-; Dean, Chattanooga Bapt Bible Col, 1981-; Assoc Min, Christian Ed, New Monumental Bapt Ch, 1978-; Chm of Bd, Chattanooga Area Minority Investmt Forum 1981-, Candida Grp 1982-; Pres, Rochdale Inst, 1978-80; Chm of Bd, Vista Devel Corp, 1980-81; Pres, Sun-Belt Assoc Industs, 1977-80; Nat Bar Assn; Chattanooga Area Bd of Rltrs; Planning Exec Inst; N Am Soc Corporate Planning; Am Acad Rel; Nat Assn Bapt Profs of Rel; Nat Assn Mkt Developers; Sales and Mktg Execs Intl; Profl Salespersons of Am; Nat Bus Leag; Alpha Kappa Mu; Kappa Delta Pi; Alpha Iota Alpha; Sigma Rho Sigma; Delta Mu Delta; Alpha Phi Alpha; cp/Chattanooga Area C of C; Optimist; Masons; hon/Outstg Bus Developer, Sun-Belt Assoc Industs, 1978; Recip, Awd of Merit, Affil Contractors of Am, 1974; Man of the Yr, Alpha Iota Alpha, 1971; Saslows Awd, 1960; Yth and Commun Ser Awd, Frederick Douglas Chapt, Hamilton Co Repub Party, 1981; Dist'd Citizen Awd, City of Chattanooga, 1981; W/W S and SW.

STIEFEL, BETTY KRAEUCHE oc/ Personnel Counselling, Registered Nurse, Executive; b/May 24, 1941; h/ 3117 Bay View Drive, Green Bay, WI 54301; ba/Green Bay, WI; m/William J; c/John Benjamin, James Gottfried, Elisabeth Kraeuche, William George; p/ George Roland Kraeuche, Stone Lake, WI; Delores Horst (dec); ed/RN, Mt Sinai Hosp Sch of Nsg, 1962; Univ of WI Milwaukee and Green Bay, 1962-63, 1969-; Patricia Stevens Career Col of Milwaukee, 1963; Harry Conover Sch, 1963-64; mil/Served to 2nd Lt, Nurse Corps, AUS; pa/Pres, Owner, Betty K Stiefel and Assocs, 1980-; Occupl 1965-79, Ofc/Pers Mgr 1976-79, Dir

1969-, VP, Secy 1976-, Stiefel Clothing Co; Vol Res Asst, Marquette Univ, 1962; Weekend Night Nurse, Ivanhoe Sanitarium, 1962-64; Staff Nurse, Med Surg Floor, to Asst Hd Nurse, Mt Sinai Med Ctr, 1962-64; Chm, Inser Progs, Mt Sinai Med Ctr, 1962-64; Model, Var Firms in Milwaukee, Chgo and Green Bay, 1962-78; Chm, Taping for the Blind and Visually Handicapped, Brown Co Lib, 1973-79 (Conslt 1981-); Editor and Publisher, Con Brio, Green Bay Symph Orch Wom's Guild, 1981-; cp/ Treas, Cnesses Israel Sisterhood, 1981-, Mem 1965-; Ella Sauber Chapt of Hadassah, 1965-; B'nai B'rith Wom, 1965-; Breen Bay Symph Orch Assn, Exec Bd Mem 1980-; Green Bay Symph Orch Wom's Guild, Ex Officio 1982-; NE WI Arts Coun, Charter Mem; NE WI Talent Ed Inc, Steering Com; Green Bay Suzuki Assn, Charter Mem; Brown Co Civic Music Assn; Sally Ariens Chapt, City of Hope; Green Bay Montessori Soc Inc; Ser Leag of Green Bay; Peninsula Music Fest, Sustaining Com 1970-, Showcase Displays 1970-, Properties and Equip 1971-; YWCA; U Way of Brown Co; Num Past Ofcs Held in Civic Orgs; r/Jewish; hon/Jaycettes Commun Apprec Awd, 1969; City of Hope Spirit of Life Awd; Betty Crocker Homemaker of the Future, 1959; W/W Am Wom.

STIEGHORST, JUNANN JORDAN oc/Seed Company Executive; b/Jun 8, 1923; h/2070 Foothills Road, Golden, CO 80401; ba/Same; m/Guenther Paul; c/Theodore Mark; p/John Wallace and Myrtle Harrison Jordan (dec); ed/BA in Lib Sci, BA in Eng, Univ of OK, 1946-47; Postgrad, So Meth, 1959-60; Creat Writing Ext Courses, Univ of OK, 1950's; pa/Stewardess, Braniff Airways, 1944-45; Advtg Copywriter, Model, Neiman Marcus, 1945-46; Dir of Charge Acct Promotion and Clientele, 1947-55; Advtg Copywriter, Wilhelm-Laughlin-Wilson, 1946; Dir, Public Relats and Clientele, Lichensteins, 1955-56; Clientele Dir, Joskes of TX, 1957-58; Chd's Libn, Jefferson Co Lib, 1967-69; Alpha Chi Omega Sorority, Pres Alumni Clb; Writers Roundtable, 1955; cp/DAR, St Chm Public Relats and Hon Roll, Nat VChm of Public Relats, Chapt Regent, 1971-84; Jr Ser Leag, 1959; r/Luth; hon/Pubs, "Bay City and Matagorda County: A History" 1965, "Colorado Historical Markers" 1978, "History of Mount Lookout Chapter NSDAR" 1984, "Salvage Archaeology at Golden Site 5JF12" 1973, Var Others; Outstg Book Awd, 1966; Num Nat Soc DAR Public Relats Awds, 1974-84; DIB; W/W Am Wom; W/W W; Intl W/W Intells.

STIEGLER, CHRISTINE B oc/Professor of Technology and Occupational Education, Consultant; b/Dec 9, 1940; h/8474 Farm Pond Lane, Maineville, OH 45039; ba/Highland Heights, KY; m/ James R; p/Mrs Ann L Brown, Red Springs, NC; ed/BS, Bus 1962, MA, Bus 1963, Appalachian St Univ; Att'd, Univ of FL 1966, FL St Univ 1967; EdD, Bus, Univ of No CO, 1969; pa/Conslt, CBS Conslltg Grp, 1981-; Prof, Technol and Occupl Ed, No KY Univ, 1978-; Lectr, Univ of Cinc, Raymond Walters Col, 1976-77; Lectr, Edgecliff Col, Mgmt Sci Prog, 1976-77; Editor, S-Wn Pub'g Co, 1972-77; Lectr, Univ of Cinc, Raymond

Walters Col, 1972-74; Other Previous Positions; Am Mgmt Assn; Adm Mgmt Soc; Am Soc for Tng Devel; Am Bus Communication Assn; Am Voc Assn; Delta Pi Epsilon; Nat Bus Ed Assn; Nat Assn of Tchr Edrs for Bus and Ofc Ed; KY Voc Assn; Other Profl Mbrships; hon/Pubs, "Cost Effective Letter Writing Techniques" 1984, Business Communication: An Administrative Approach 1984, Others; Bus Wom of the Yr, St of FL, 1965; Wom of the Yr, Leesburg, FL, 1966; Helen Eisenhower Awd, Outstg Yg Wom of Am, 1966; Nat Register of Prom Ams; W/W NC; W/W MW; W/ W Am Wom.

STILZ, CAROL KATHLEEN CURTIS oc/Writer, Educator; b/Jan 24, 1945; h/4625 Norcross Court, Southeast, Olympia, WA 98501; m/Clifford Louis Jr; c/Kathleen Jayne; p/Melvin and Maybelle F Curtis, OR; ed/BA, cum laude, Willamette Univ, 1966; Standard Tchg Cert, Univ of WA, 1974; pa/Eng Instr w Seattle Area Sch and Olympia Public Schs, 1969-76; Instr, Creat Dramatics, Holiday Crafts, Pks and Rec, and St Capitol Mus; Conslt, WA-OR Broadcasting; Instr for Writers' Wkshop, St Capitol Mus, 1980-; cp/ Thurston-Mason Co Bar Aux, Pres 1980-81, Prog Chm 1979-80; Chd's Orthopedic Hosp Guild, 1975-, Guild Secy 1982-83; Salvation Army Wom's Aux, Secy 1980-82; POSSCA, Secy, Bd of Dirs 1982-84; r/Epis; hon/Contbr and Mng Editor, Naturally Northwest, 1982; Author, Articles for Olympia News and Family Times; Mortar Bd, 1966.

STIMACH, JANET LOUISE oc/ Self-Employed Investor, Commercial Broker, Certified Property Manager, Consultant; b/Oct 29, 1939; h/1926 South Spokane Street, Seattle, WA 98144; ba/Seattle, WA; c/Craig B; p/Mr and Mrs Carl J Carulli, Seattle, WA; pa/ Comml Broker, Cert'd Property Mgr, Conslt, Wn Investmt & Mgmt Inc, 1973-; Cert'd Property Mgr, Neus Rlty, 1971-73; Property Mgr, Clark-Ruble & Assocs, 1970-71; Pt-time Instr, Lowry Real Est Sems, 1979-; Inst of Real Est Mgmt; Cert'd Bus Cnslrs; cp/IPA; Repub Nat Assn; r/Cath; hon/W/W Am Wom; W/W W.

STIMSON-DUFFIELD, DOROTHY B oc/Brokerage Company Executive; b/ Dec 31, 1917; h/161 Hendrie Boulevard, Royal Oak, MI 48067; ba/Detroit, MI; m/Robert W Duffield; c/Harry Richard, Jane S Schweitzer, Cynthia S Howe, Denise S Andersen, Scott Robert, Jeffrey Donald; p/Harry Joseph Brickwedd (dec); Marie A Ihlendorf (dec); ed/ PhB, Marygrove Col, 1940; Postgrad, Univ of MI; Att'd, NY Inst of Fin, Univ of PA, Wharton Sch, Oakland Univ; pa/ Stockbroker, Signal Corp Ground Signal Ser, 1941-45; Stockbroker, Bache & Co, 1960-65; Asst Mgr 1965-70, VP 1970-, Paine Webber Jackson & Curtis; Lectr, Bache & Co, Paine Webber Jackson & Curtis, Internationally; Wom in Fin; Ec Clb; Trustee, Marygrove Col; cp/Pres, Detroit Osteopathic Hosp Aux; Pres, Detroit Osteopathic Wom's Clb; Bd of Dirs, MI Osteopathic Wom's Clb; Am Osteopathic Wom's Clb; Zonta Intl; Detroit Golf Clb; Recess Clb; r/Rom Cath.

STINE, ANNA MAE oc/Executive; b/ Sep 6, 1938; h/215 Haddon Commons, Haddonfield, NJ 08033; ba/Riverside,

NJ; p/Mr and Mrs C L Stine, Monongahela, PA; ed/BS in Ed, 1959; Master's in Elem Ed, 1962; Elem Prin Cert, 1962; Rdg Spec, 1963; Postgrad, 1963-65; pa/ VP and Nat Sales Mgr, E 1978-, Reg Mgr, Nat 1975-78, Macmillan Pub'g Co; Conslt/Free-Lance Writer, 1965-75; Tchr/Supvr, Upper St Clair Sch, 1959-65; Keystone Rdg Assn; IRA; PSEA; NEA; Pres, Upper St Clair Tchrs Org; r/Rom Cath; hon/Donald McGrew for Excell in Conslt'g, 1967; Robert Hahn Awd for Excell in Writing and Conslt'g, 1965.

STOCKDALE, JAMES BOND oc/ Senior Research Fellow; b/Dec 23, 1923; h/6 Pearce Mitchell Place, Stanford, CA 94305; Stanford, CA; m/Sybil Elizabeth Bailey; c/James Bond, Sidney Bailey, Stanford Baker, Taylor Burr; p/Vernon Beard and Mabel Edith Stockdale (dec); ed/BS, US Naval Acad, 1946; MA, Stanford Univ, 1962; Hon Degs: Univ of So CA, Univ of MA, Salve Regina Col, Norwich Univ, The Citadel, Brown Univ; mil/Designated Naval Aviator 1950, Adv'd through Grades to Vice Admiral 1977; pa/Naval Aviator, 1950; Cmdr, Fighter Squadron 51, USS Ticonderoga 1963-64, Carrier Air Wing 16, USS Oriskany 1964-65; Sr Naval Ser Prisoner of War in Hanoi, 1965-73; Cmdr, Anti Submarine Warfare Wing, US Pacific Fleet, 1974-76; Dir, Strategy, Plans and Policy Div, Ofc of the Chief of Naval Opers, 1976-77; Pres, Naval War Col 1977-79, The Citadel 1979-80; Vis'g Prof, Hampden-Sydney Col, 1981; Sr Res Fellow, The Hoover Instn on War Revolution and Peace, 1981-; Acad Adv Bd, US Naval Acad; Trustee, US Naval Acad Foun; cp/SAR; Soc Cinc; Ends of Earth Soc; Explorers Clb; Am Mensa Soc; Congl Medal of Hon Soc; Pres Comm on White House F'ships; hon/ Pubs, "Principles of Leadership: A Western Perspective" 1983, "Educating Leaders" 1982, "Challenges to Individual Spirit" 1982, Others; W/W Am; Intl W/W Contemp Achmt; Am Biogl Inst; Commun Ldrs of World.

STOCKMAN, BENEVEST ADVARRDS oc/Chairman of Board, Owner; b/Dec 29, 1951; ba/Elm Street, Box-3, Eminence, KY 40019; p/John A Stockman (dec); Marry Victoria Stockman (dec); ed/PhD in Bus Fin; BS; BI; pa/Prof, Stanford Univ, 1968; Owner, Sacco Oil Co 1973-74, U Mortgage Co 1979-; Dir, First U Fund, Others; cp/ Yg Businessmen's Millionaires; No Hunter; Bow Hunter; No Yacht; Deer Hunters; Cattlemen's; r/Jewish; W/W S and SW.

STOCKTON, M DAVID oc/Family Physician; b/Mar 1, 1953; h/Proctor Hall Road, Box 220, Sewanee, TN 37375; ba/ Sewanee, TN; p/Mr and Mrs Marshall D Stockton, Knoxville, TN; ed/BA, magna cum laude, Univ of TN, 1975; MD, Univ of TN Ctr for Hlth Scis, 1978; Diplomate, Am Bd of Fam Pract, 1981; pa/Resident in Fam Pract, 1978-81; Pvt Solo Med Pract, 1981-; Clin Instr, Med Units, Chattanooga, 1983; AMA, 1983; Am Acad of Fam Pract, 1980-83; Bapt Med/Dental F'ship; Christian Med Soc; r/Bapt; hon/Pres, Franklin Co Med Assn, 1984.

STODDARD, ANN HARRIS oc/ Associate Professor; b/Jul 10, 1928; h/ 601 Osborne Street, St Marys, GA 31558; ba/Jacksonville, FL; m/William

Edward; c/Lynn, Brian; p/Mrs Tola Harris, St Marys, GA; ed/AB, Spelman Col, 1947; MA, Atlanta Univ, 1959; EdS 1973, EdD 1975, Univ of GA; pa/Assoc Prof, Univ of No FL, 1977-; Asst Prof, UPI, 1975-77; Conslt, NE and Okefenokee CESA, 1972-75; Asst Prof, Ed, Waters Col, 1971-72; Public Schs, 1954-71; Dir of Hd Start, 1967-68; NCSS; CUFA, Secy 1981, 1982; ACEI; ASCD; FCSS, Exec Dir; GCSS; AERA; EERA; PDK; AKA; MHA; NCNW; cp/ Gilman Hosp Auth, Secy 1981; Guale Hist Soc; r/Epis; hon/Author, Articles for Ednl Jours; Nat F'ship Fund Recip; W/W SE.

STOECKMANN, KENNETH PAUL oc/Rancher, Farmer, Land Company Executive; b/Mar 26, 1919; h/PO Box 2013, Pecos, TX 79772; ba/Red Bluff, CA; m/Ethel Dolores Infantas; c/Frances P Priest, Kenneth Paul, William R, Robert W; p/Paul Truman and Laura Vivian Lamont Stoeckmann; ed/Student, Sacramento Jr Col 1939, and Voc Schs; mil/Served w USAAF, 1943-45; pa/Capt, All Am Air Export, 1946-54; Fdr, Owner, Pres, Chm of Bd, Stoeckmann Ranches Inc, 1976-; Fdr, Owner, Chm of Bd, Stoeckmann Land Co Inc 1972-, Stoeckmann Farms Inc 1977-; hon/Decorated w Air Medal.

STOEGER, KEITH A oc/Consultant; h/Des Plaines, IL; ed/BS in Indust Engrg, MS in Ed, So IL Univ; mil/USMC, 6 Yrs; IL NG, 2 Yrs; pa/Assoc'd w Conslt'g Firm of S Michael Assocs; Soc of Mfg Engrs; Frequent Contbr to Telemktg Sems; cp/ VFW; IPA.

STOKES, ERIC GODFREY oc/Chief Executive Officer; b/Jul 6, 1949; h/654 Lucy Avenue, Teaneck, NJ 07666; ba/ Rochelle Park, NJ; m/Susan Lee Woldahl; c/Stephanie Alexandra; p/Josiah Taylor and Jane Diane Driscoll Stokes, Teaneck, NJ; ed/Student, Math and Bus, Fairleigh Dickinson Univ, 1967-72; pa/ Pres, E&M Bldrs, 1967-71; Controller 1972-78, CEO 1978-, SunRise Photo; Photo Mktg Assn; Assn Profl Color Labs; cp/Photo Merit Badge Cnslr, BSA, 1973-; r/Christ Epis Ch; hon/Contbg Editor, *Photo Weekly* 1978-, *Photo Marketing Magazine* 1978-; Notary Public, 1978-; W/W E.

STONE, ALAN J oc/College President; h/1307 Marseillaise, Aurora, IL 60506; ba/Aurora, IL; m/Jonieta J; c/ Kirsten K, Timothy McClain; p/Mr and Mrs Hubert Stone, Dakota City, IA; ed/ DMn 1970, MTh 1968, Univ of Chgo; MA, Univ of IA, 1969; BA, Morningside Col, 1964; pa/Pres, Aurora Col, 1975-; Dir of Devel, Univ of ME Orono, 1976-78; VP for Devel, WV Wesleyan Col, 1975-76; Chm, Consortium of W Suburban Cols; Pres, Assoc'd Cols of IL; Bd Mem: Fdn of Indep IL Cols and Univs, Consortium of Small Put Cols, Carlow Col, First Am Bk of Aurora; cp/ Bd Mem: Mercy Ctr for Hlth Care, Aurora C of C, Aurora U Way, Corridor's Ptnrs for Ed, No IL Communs Netwk; r/Meth; hon/Outstg Edr, 1970; Outstg Tchr, 1968; Univ of Chgo S'ship, 1966-70; W/W Am.

STONE, JOHN GREENVILLE oc/ Executive; b/Feb 26, 1938; h/PO Box 327, Weslaco, TX 78596; ba/Weslaco, TX; p/John G Stone (dec); ed/BS, Pre-Vet, NC St Univ, 1962; MS, Microbiol, Univ of NY, 1968; mil/AUS, Sp 2, 1955-57; pa/Processed Food Inspector,

USDA, 1962-65; Minute Maid Quality Control, 1965-67; Microbiologist, Coca-Cola Foods FL Citrus, 1967-69; Texsun Quality Control, 1969-70; Prodn Mgr 1970-76, VP 1976-, Texsun Corp; John Knox Village Corp, Pres 1980-, Fdg Bd of Dirs; Assn Photogs Intl, 1981; Nat Assn Underwater Instrs, 1981; TX Canners and Freezers Assn, Pres 1975-77; Rio Grande Val Hort Soc, VP 1982; cp/TX SCUBA Divers of the Lower Rio Grande Val, Fdr and Pres 1982; r/First Christian Ch, Bd of Dirs and Deacon 1980-.

STONEBRIDGE, JERRY BERT oc/ Construction Company Executive; b/ Jun 2, 1941; h/3329-S East Harbor Road, Langley, WA 98260; ba/Same; m/M Suzanne; c/Jerry Edward, Jeffrey Scott; p/H W and Phoebe Stonebridge, Freeland, WA; ed/BS, Zool, Chem, WA St Univ, 1963; Student, Computer Sci, Bioengrg, Bioelectromagnetics, Univ of WA, 1970-75; mil/USAF ROTC, 1959-62; pa/Res Asst, Dept of Rehab Med 1964-72, Res Assoc, Dept of Rehab Med 1972-78, Univ of WA; Pres, Stonebridge Constrn Co Inc, 1978-; Conslt for On-Site Sewage Disposal Sys and Their Mgmt, 1978-; Conslt for On-Site Waste Mgmt Adv Com for 4th NW On-Site Waste-Water Short Course, Univ of WA, 1982; Isl Co Tech Review Bd, 1980-82; cp/Pres, Freeland Commun Assn, 1980-82; Bd of Trustees, Saratoga Bch Commun Assn, 1982-84; hon/Pubs, "Experimental and Numerical Studies of the Temperature in a Human Leg Heated by Microwave Diathermy," "A Comparison of Stray Radiation Patterns of Therapeutic Microwave Applicators Observed Around Tissue Substitute Models and Humans–A Basis for Development of Safety Standards" 1978, "Development of a 915 MHz Direct-Contact Applicator for Therapeutic Heating of Tissues" 1978, "Evaluation of a Therapeutic Direct Contact 915 MHz Microwave Applicator for Effective Deep-Tissue Heating in Humans" 1978, Others; Bausch & Lomb Sci Awd and Grant, 1959-60; Nellie Martin Grant, 1960; Outstg Freshman Student, WA St Univ, 1960; First Place Prize for Res Exhib Presented at 50th Annual Conf of Am Phy Therapy Assn, 1973; Silver Medal, Second Place Overall for Sci Exhib, 50th Annual Session of Am Cong of Rehab Med, 1974; W/W Technol Today.

STONER, JAMES L oc/Executive Director; h/21 Taber Knolls, Pawling, NY 12564; ba/Pawling, NY; m/Janice; c/ Thomas Clark, Geoffrey Lloyd, James Douglas; ed/BS, Bethany Col, 1941; BD, MDiv, Yale Univ Div Sch, 1944; Hon DD, Bethany Col, 1958; pa/Current Exec Dir, Foun for Christian Living, and Spiritual Ldr for Holy Land Tours; Sr Min, Ctl Christian Ch, 1972-80; Asst Gen Secy for Exec Opers, Nat Coun of Chs, NYC, 1966-72; First Full-time Min of N Christian Ch, 1956-66; Dir, Univ Christian Mission, Fed and Nat Coun of Chs, 1947-56; Christian Ch Rep to TX Conf of Chs, Div of Christian Unity; Past Pres, Austin Conf of Chs; cp/1 of Nat Fdrs, F'ship of Christian Aths; Fdr and First Pres, Link Awd, Ridgewood, NJ (Recog'd Yth in Commun); Current Pres, Pawling Rotary Clb; Bd of Mgrs, New Milford Hosp; Bd of Dirs, Holiday Hills YMCA; C of C; 32 Deg Mason;

Shriner; hon/W/W Am; W/W Rel; Personalities of S; DIB; Men of Achmt; Intl W/W Commun Ser.

STONICK, VICTOR H oc/Executive; b/Feb 25, 1930; h/616 East 445 South, Orem, UT 84057; ba/Riyadh, Saudi Arabia; m/Patricia A; c/Cynthia, Lyndell, Mark, Timothy, Christopher, Amelia, Jennelle; p/Joseph and Mary Stonick, San Bernardino, CA; ed/Bach, 1956; mil/USAF; pa/VP, Trainex, Saudi Arabia Ltd, 1982-; Conslt, 1981-82; Grp Dir, WICAT, 1981-82; Pres, MCI, 1976-81; Exec VP, VARCON, 1976-78; Dir of Opers, NTS, 1975; Dir of Opers, HOLS, 1974-76; Prod/Dir, SCROC, 1969-72; Supvr, MP Gen Dynamics, 1967-69; Writer, Dir, No Am, 1965-67; Dir, Comm, Lyla Univ, 1964-67; Am Soc Tng and Devel; LANSPI; r/LDS; hon/ Produced Hundreds of Instrnl, Documentary and Informational Progs; W/ W W.

STOREY, MARK L oc/Manufacturing Manager; b/Aug 9, 1934; h/3714 Canyonland Drive, Baton Rouge, LA 70814; ba/Baton Rouge, LA; m/Jimmie Ann Greene; c/LeDena Ann, Mark Kevin, Kristi Lynn; p/Archie L and Virdie D Cork Storey, Tuscaloosa, AL; ed/BS, Elect Engrg, Univ of AL, 1965; mil/USAF, 1953-57; pa/Owner, Hunter, Storey & Hale TV Ser, 1957-60; Elect Engr, Rust Engrg Co, 1965-69; Process Engr, Mobil Chem Co, 1969; Proj Engr, Boise So Paper Co, 1969-71; Maintenance Supt 1971-76, Sr Proj Engr 1976-78, Mgr of Maintenance 1978-, Am Hoechst Corp (Formerly Foster Grant Co); LA Assn of Bus and Indust; Public Affairs Res Coun; LA Chem Assn; IEEE; Inst of Cert'd Mgrs, Cert'd Mgr; Intl Mgmt Coun, Pres, Div VI Secy; Univ of AL Alumni Assn, Baton Rouge Chapt Ofcr; cp/C of C; Baton Rouge Ballet Theater, Bd of Trustees; Former VP, Tuscaloosa, AL, Jr C of C; Former BSA Scoutmaster; r/Meth; hon/ W/W S and SW; Personalities of S.

STOTHART, ROBERTA BATES oc/ Museum Bookstore Manager; b/Mar 29, 1934; h/1553 Palisades Drive, Pacific Palisades, CA 90272; ba/Santa Monica, CA; c/Lisa, Camille, Anna, Elizabeth; p/ Dorothy Bates, Pacific Palisades, CA; ed/Att'd, Univ of AZ, 1953; 10 Yrs Travel and Study, Italy and Switzerland; Stanford Pub'g Course, Palo Alto, 1982; pa/Bookstore Mgr, Buyer, Publisher, The J Paul Getty Mus, 1974-; Mus Store Assn, Mem 1975-, Bd Mem 1981-83; r/ Epis; hon/Author, Articles in Mus Store Assn's *Must*, 1981-83; W/W Am Wom.

STOTT, KENHELM WELBURN JR oc/Zoologist, Author, Explorer; b/Aug 27, 1920; h/2300 Front Street, Apartment 402, San Diego, CA 92101; ed/ BA, Zool, Pomona Col, 1942; mil/ Epidemiologist, USNR, 1942-46; pa/ Curator of Mammals and Pubs 1946-48, Gen Curator 1948-54, Res Assoc 1961-82, Gen Curator Emeritus 1982-, San Diego Zoo; Life Fellow, Royal Geographical Soc, 1977; Life Fellow, Zool Soc of London, 1978; Life Fellow, CA Acad of Scis, 1981; Life Fellow, Explorers Clb, 1976; Fellow, Linnean Soc of London, 1980; Life Fellow, Royal Soc Prot Birds, 1978; Hon Trustee, Martin & Osa Johnson Safari Mus, 1976-; Trustee, Nat Underwater & Marine Agy, 1979; Conslt, US St Dept Wn Pac, 1980; Life Mem, IUCN, 1976;

Am Soc Mammalogists, 1941; Am Ornithologists Union, 1944; hon/ Author, 3,000+ Articles and Sci Papers, 2 Field Guides to S Pacific Fauna, Books: *Exploring with Martin & Osa Johnson* 1978, *Martin Johnson's Cannibals of the South Seas* 1980; Pijorn Zool Awd, 1941; Cit of Merit, Explorers Clb, 1977; Sweeney Medal, Explorers Clb, 1980; Dedication, Stott Explorers Lib, Johnson Safari Mus, 1980; Personal Commend and Decoration by Dalai Lama, 1978; Commend, Queen Elizabeth, 1980; Gold Conserv Awd, Zool Soc of San Diego, 1981; W/W W; W/W Am; Am Registry Series; Notable Ams; DIB; Men of Achmt; Am Men of Sci.

STOVALL, CATHERINE LOUISE oc/Restauranteur, Giftware Executive; b/Oct 31, 1955; h/5 Cornwallis, Irvine, CA 92714; ba/Anaheim, CA; c/Cara Marie De La Rosa, Jennifer Lauren De La Rosa; p/Jack K Stovall, Corona Del Marr, CA; Noyla G Augspurger, Phoenix, AZ; ed/BA, Anthropology and Liberal Studies, CA St Univ Long Bch; pa/Banquet Mgr, Stovall Motor Hotels, 1976-82; Owner, Mgr, Stovall Gift Shops, 1979-82; Pres, Delcourval Inc, 1981-; Owner, Mgr, Kingdom Gift Distributing, 1980-; Gen Mgr, Spaghetti Sta Restaurant, 1982-; Chief Financial Ofcr, Spaghetti Sta Inc, 1982-; AAUW; cp/NOW; GSA, 15 Yrs, Scout Ldr for 3 Yrs; Anaheim C of C; Anaheim Visitor and Conv Bur; r/Cath; hon/W/ W Am Wom.

STOVER, BONNIE oc/Bank Executive; b/Dec 19, 1949; h/1701 Glenbrook, Corsicana, TX 75110; ba/Corsicana, TX; c/Marissa D; p/Virgle E Widener, Corsicana, TX; ed/BS, TX Wom's Univ; Grad Studies, Univ of TX Arlington; Sch of Mortgage Bkg, Mortgage Bkrs Assn of Am; pa/VP, Mortgage Loan Dept, InterFirst Bk, 1978-; Secy/Treas 1976-, Dir 1979-, Old Reliable Mortgage Co Inc; Asst VP 1976-78, Supvr 1974-76, Mortgage Loan Dept, Inter-First Bk; Nat Assn of Bkg Wom, Treas, Heart of TX Grp, 1984; TX Mortgage Bkrs Assn, Loan Adm Com; Mortgage Bkrs Assn of Am; BPW Fdn Inc, Dist Dir 1982-83, 1983-84; Yg Career Wom, BPW Clb, 1978; Dir, Navarro Co Assn of Home Bldrs; cp/Dir, Corsicana Coun Camp Fire Inc; r/Bapt; hon/NABW S'ship Winner, 1981; W/W Am Wom.

STRAIN, JOHN WILLARD oc/Aerospace Test Manager; b/Dec 31, 1929; h/ 626 Oneida Drive, Sunnyvale, CA 94987; ba/Sunnyvale, CA; m/Elizabeth L Moment (dec); c/James Anthony, Mary Therese, Michael Douglas, Meagan Kathleen; p/John W and Agnes Gertrude Strain (dec); ed/BA, Univ of No IA, 1952; mil/AUS 1952-54, Physicist, Signal Corps; pa/Supvr, Rocket Power Plant Engr, White Sands Proving Ground, 1954-55; Mgr of SCTB 1960-63, Mgr of ETR/SV Support 1967-73, RPV Aquila Chief Test Engr 1975-79, Mgr of Factory Test, RPV Prog 1979-82, Div Mgr of Qualification/Test Engrg 1982-84, Aerospace Test Mgr 1984-, Lockheed Missiles and Space Co; AIAA; AAAS; Am Inst of Envir Scis; Assn of Unmanned Vehicle Sys, Treas of Redwood Chapt 1983; cp/Bd of Dirs, San Jose Civic Light Opera, 1971-73; Ldr, BSA, 1964; Pres, Fremont HS Featherettes, 1983-84; r/Cath; hon/ Assoc Editor, *Missile Away Magazine*,

1954-55; Assoc Fellow, AIAA, 1975; Sr Mem, Am Inst of Envir Scis, 1982; Alumni Ser Awd, Univ of No IA, 1981; W/W W; W/W Frontier Sci and Technol.

STRATMAN, MAXINE T oc/Bank Executive; b/May 22, 1938; h/Route #1, Box 170, Barneveld, WI 53507; ba/ Ridgeway, WI; c/Julie Lynn, Jodie Lynn; p/Mr and Mrs Max Theobald, Barneveld, WI; ed/Grad, Barneveld Public Sch, 1955; pa/Barneveld St Bk, 1956-: Job Tng (Bkkpr, Bkkpg Supvr, Teller), Asst Br Mgr 1969, Asst Cashier and Br Mgr 1973-79, Asst VP and Br Ofc Mgr 1980-; IA Co Bkrs Assn, Secy-Treas 1973-79; Nat Assn of Bk Wom, 1976-; NABW Hospitality Chp, 1980-81; cp/Meml Hosp Fund Campaign Chw, 1980; Chw, Ridgeway Salvation Army, 1981-; r/ Meth; Sunday Sch Supt and Tchr, 1970-75; Ch Treas, 1976-80; hon/W/W Am Wom.

STRAUSS, FRED oc/Association Executive; b/Mar 30, 1925; ba/Lincoln Park Chamber of Commerce, 11 West Illinois Street, Chicago, IL 60610; c/ Scott, Jonathan, Daniel, Craig; p/Solly and Fanny Wertheim Strauss (dec); ed/ Att'd, Purdue Univ 1943-44, DePaul Univ 1950-51, Wn Resv Univ 1952-53; Instr, Roosevelt Univ, 1982; Guest Lectr, Loyola Univ 1983, NEn IL Univ 1983; mil/AUS, Mil Intell Ofcr, 1944-48; pa/Owner, Fred Strauss Agy, 1953-58; Pres, Talent Corp of Am, 1958-60; Exec Prodr, Communs Corp of Am, 1960-67; Public Info Dir, Am Cancer Soc, 1967-82; Exec Dir, Lincoln Pk C of C, 1982-; Publicity Clb of Chgo, 1967-, Bd of Dirs 1974-80, VP 1977-78, Pres 1979-80; Bd of Dirs, Social Ser Communicators, 1978-; cp/Commun Adv Coun, St Joseph Hosp 1983, IL Masonic Hosp 1984; hon/Exec Prodr, "Last Full Measure of Devotion," Motion Picture, 1964; Co-Prodr, "Impossible Dream Come True," Motion Picture 1967, "Teens of the World," TV Film and Syndication 1967-82, "Telling a Child About Death," TV Syndication Talk Show 1965-66, Others; Chris Awd, Columbus Film Fest, 1964; Helen Cody Baker Awd, 1976-77; Nat Awd, Am Cancer Soc, 1970; Hon Cit, 1977; Publicity Clb of Chgo Dist'd Ser Awds, 1973, 1975; Purple Heart; 2 Battle Stars; Combat Inf Man's Medal; Bronze Star; W/W Public Relats; W/W MW.

STREET, DAVID RUSSELL SR oc/ School Superintendent; b/Oct 24, 1927; h/301 North Santa Cruz Boulevard, Eloy, AZ 85231; ba/Eloy, AZ; m/Betty M; c/David R Jr, Carol S, Jeffrey D, Elizabeth D; p/Pleasant J and Mary C Street (dec); ed/BA 1951, MA in Ed 1954, LA St Univ; PhD, Rockwell Univ of AZ, 1982; mil/AUS, 82nd Airborne, 1946-50; pa/Supt, Eloy Elem Dist #11, 1980-; Supt, Ashfork Unified Schs, 1977-80; Grad Res Assoc, AZ St Univ, 1975-77; Prin, Ganado HS, 1973-75; Asst Supt, Wilson Elem Sch Dist, 1968-73; Supt, Apache Junction Unified Schs, 1967-68; Prin, Window Rock HS, 1965-67; Supt, Sanders Unified Schs, 1962-64; Prin, Maurepas HS, 1955-62; NEA, 1962-; AZ Ed Assn, 1962-; Pres, Pinal Co Sch Supts Assn, 1983-84; r/ Rom Cath; hon/Pub, "The Effects of Locus of Control on Achievement and Test Performance in Undergraduate Students," 1982.

STREETEN, PAUL PATRICK oc/

528

Professor of Economics; b/Jul 18, 1917; h/21 Penniman Road, Brookline, MA 92146; ba/Boston, MA; m/Ann Hilary; c/Jay D Palmer (Stepson), Patricia Doria, Judith Andrea; ed/MA, Aberdeen, 1944; BA 1947, MA 1951, DLitt 1976, Oxford; Hon LLD, Aberdeen; mil/Hampshire Regt Commandos, Wounded 1943; pa/ Fellow of Balliol Col, Oxford, 1948-66, 1968-78; Dpty Dir, Gen Ec Planning Min of Overseas Devel, 1964-66; Acting Dir and Fellow, Inst of Devel Studies, Univ of Sussex, 1966-68; Prof, Univ of Sussex, 1966-68; Spec Advr, World Bk, 1976-80; Dir of Studies, Overseas Devel Inst, 1979-80; Dir, Asian Ctr, Boston Univ, 1980-; Soc for Intl Devel, Pres of Brit Chapt nd Coun Mem; Royal Ec Soc; Am Er Assn; Bd Mem, Commonwealth D vel Corp; cp/Royal Comm on Envir Pollution; hon/Pubs, *First Things First* 1981, *Development Perspectives* 1981, Others; Hon Fellow, Inst of Devel Studies, Sussex; W/W; Intl W/W; W/W E; W/W Authors.

STRETCH, SHIRLEY MARIE oc/ Assistant Professor of Clothing and Textiles; b/May 6, 1949; h/4604C 55th Drive, Lubbock, TX 79414; ba/Lubbock, TX; p/Lloyd and Roberta Stretch, Culbertson, NE; ed/PhD 1982, MBA 1977, OH St Univ; MS, KS St Univ, 1972; pa/Asst Prof, Dept of Clothing and Textiles, TX Tech Univ, 1980-; Grad Adm Assoc, Univ Col, OH St Univ, 1976-78, 1980; Asst Mgr, Direct Mktg Div, Ashland Petro Co, 1978-80; Instr, Dept of Home Ec, Bowling Green St Univ, 1973-75; Am Mktg Assn; Am Collegiate Retailing Assn; Assn of MBA Execs; Nat Assn of Female Execs; Am Home Ec Assn; Am Col Profs of Textiles and Clothing; Omicron Nu; Phi Upsilon Omicron; Pres, Bd of Dirs, Sunport Condominium, 1982-; cp/VP, W TX Ski Clb, 1982-83; TX Twisters Ski Clb, Treas 1983-84; r/Meth; Ednl Profl Devel Act Fellow, 1971-73; NE Gov's S'ship, 1969; Make It Yourself w Wool NE Rep, 1968; W/W Am Wom.

STRICKLAND, SANDRA HEIN-RICH oc/Nurse, Associate Professor; b/ Sep 18, 1943; h/206 North Willomet, Dallas, TX 75208; ba/Dallas, TX; m/ William C; c/William Henry, Angela Lee; p/Mr and Mrs Henry Heinrich, Victoria, TX; ed/BS, Univ of TX Sch of Nsg, 1965; MS, Univ of MD Sch of Nsg, 1969; Doct in Public Hlth, Univ of TX Sch of Public Hlth, 1978; pa/Clin Instr, Univ of TX Sch of Nsg, 1965-66; Staff Nurse, Hidalgo Co Public Hlth Dept, 1966-67; Supvr, TBC Control, TX Dept of Hlth, 1969-71; Instr, St Luke's Hosp Sch of Nsg, 1971-72; Instr, TX Wom's Univ Sch of Nsg, 1972-74; Dir of Nsg, Dallas City Hlth Dept, 1974-80; Assoc Prof, Grad Prog of Nsg, TX Wom's Univ, 1980-; Sigma Theta Tau; TX Public Hlth Assn; TX Nurses Assn; APHA; hon/W/ W S and SW.

STRINGHAM, JINX oc/Artist; b/Jan 20, 1926; h/Route 1, Box 455, Ellensburg, WA 98926; ba/Jackson, WY; m/ Robert D; c/Suzette Ruby, Holly Marie; p/Walter and Ruby Small (dec); ed/Grad, Auerswald's, Seattle, WA; pa/Owner, Operator, Wn Art Gallery, 1972-78; Originator and Dir, Nat Wn Art Show, 1972-78; Dir, Intl Wn and Wildlife Art Show, 1980; Mgr, Long's Studio Gallery, 1980-81; Advr, Intl Wn and Wildlife Art Assn Art Show, 1982-83;

Am Artists of the Rockies Assn, Advr 1982-83, Bd of Dirs 1984; r/Prot; hon/ Featured in Books: *Contemporary Western Artists, How to Feed a Starving Artist*; Silver Medallion, Presented by Fellow Artists in Apprec of Efforts on Behalf of Fellow Artists, 1981; Bronze Plaque, Intl Wn and Wildlife Assn, 1983; Key to City of Williston, ND, for Contbns to Cultural Devel of City, 1983.

STRINGHAM, JUDITH MITCHELL oc/Corporation Secretary and Treasurer; b/May 9, 1939; h/10 Dogwood Hill Road, Wappingers Falls, NY 12590; ba/ Wappingers Falls, NY; m/Varick Van Wuck Jr; c/Amanda Judith, Pamela Campion, Varick III, Rebecca Watson; p/William Joseph Mitchell (dec); Irene Campion, Poughkeepsie, NY; ed/AAS, Fashion Inst of Technol, 1959; BS, Cornell Univ, 1961; MS, St Univ of NY New Paltz, 1964; pa/Wk'd (While in HS and Col) as Day Camp Cnslr, Dept of Specialty Store Salesperson, Buyer's Asst, Pers Clk, Gen Ofc Secy for Small Newspaper; Tchr, Fishkill Elem, Lamar Elem and Presb HS, 1961-65; Secy-Treas, N Atl Equip Sales Inc, 1972-; Cornell: Alumni, Human Ecol Alumni, Chorus Soc (Charter); cp/Jr Leag of Poughkeepsie, Mem, Past Bd Mem; LWV, Mem, Past Bd Mem; Commun Chd's Theatre, Current Dir, Past Pres and Treas; Commun Experimental Repertory Theatre, Current Pres, Past Secy; Dutchess Co Arts Coun Adv Com, Past Secy and Bd Mem; Cunneen-Hackett Cultural Ctr, Current Secy, Charter Bd Mem; Co Players, Patron; Bardavon 1869 Opera House, Patron; Hudson Val Philharm, Charter Landmark Subscriber; Hudson River Sloop Clearwater, Mem, Past Crew; Dutchess Co Hist Soc; Fishkill Hist Soc; Dutchess Co Landmarks; Mt Gulian Soc; Mtl Hlth Assn; Century Circle of Vassar Brothers Hosp; Dutchess Co SPCA; Mid-Hudson Clb; Sec'dy Schs Com; Paul Harris Sustaining Mem of Rotary Foun; r/Dutch Reformed; hon/ W/W Am Wom.

STRONACH, DAVID BRIAN oc/ Archaeologist; b/Jun 10, 1931; h/815 Shattuck Avenue, Berkeley, CA 94707; ba/Berkeley, CA; m/Ruth; c/Keren, Tami; p/Ian David (dec) and Marjorie Stronach; ed/BA; MA; Att'd, Horace Mann Sch 1941, Gordonstoun Sch, Scotland 1945-50, Univ of Cambridge 1951-55; pa/Scholar, Brit Inst of Archaeol at Ankara, 1955-56; Fellow, Brit Sch of Archaeol in Iraq, 1957-60; Brit Acad Archaeological Attaché, Iran, 1960-61; Dir, Brit Inst of Persian Studies, 1961-80; Vis'g Prof, Univ of AZ, 1980-81; Prof of Near En Studies, Univ of CA Berkeley, 1981-; Hon VP, Brit Inst of Persian Studies, 1981; Fellow, Soc of Antiquaries of London, 1963; Fellow, German Archaeological Inst, 1973; Fellow, Explorers Clb, NYC, 1980; hon/Pub, *Pasargadae: A Report on the Excavations Conducted by the British Institute of Persian Studies*, 1978; Decorated Order of the Brit Empire, 1975; Recip, Prix Ghirshman, Academie des Inscriptions et Belles-Lettres, Paris, 1979; Sir Percy Sykes Meml Medal, Royal Soc for Asian Affairs, London, 1980; W/W; W/W World.

STUART, PAUL RICHARD oc/Executive; b/Jan 1, 1944; h/1747 East 3 Street, Brooklyn, NY 11223; ba/New

York, NY; m/Alice Descartes; c/Julie, Jane; p/John and Julia Stuart, Brooklyn, NY; ed/BS, Col of the City of NY, 1973; MBA w Hons, Long Isl Univ, 1975; mil/ AUS; pa/Field Engr, U Photocopy, 1967-78; Ser Mgr, Greenwald Industs, 1978-80; VP of Opers, U Photocopy, 1980-; Am Mktg Assn; IEEE; NY Acad of Scis; Intl Hon Soc in Ec; r/Epis; hon/ Medal for Highest Score in Mod Lang, 1973; Outstg Wk in Venture Capital Course, 1975; W/W Fin and Indust.

STUDLEY, HELEN ORMSON oc/ Artist, Poet, Writer, Designer; b/Sep 8, 1937; h/5020 Hazeltine, Sherman Oaks, CA 91423; ba/Sherman Oaks, CA; c/ William Harrison; p/Mr and Mrs Clarence Ormson, Elroy, WI; ed/Pat Stevens Sch; LA Val Col; pa/Free-Lance Artist and Writer; Graphic Designer; Child Devel, 1971; LA Public Schs, Hlth Sers, 1972-77; Owner of RJK Original Art, 1979-; Owner of Studley Soc for Illustrators and Artists; Epsilon Sigma Alpha Sorority, 1956-58; cp/GSA, 1959; Yahara Fishermen's Clb, 1955-58; City of Hope, 1968-72; Sons of Norway, 1972-; Repub; r/Luth; hon/Pubs, Chd's Book: *Tiger-Pooh Goes to the Circus* 1983, Aspen Series of Greeting Cards and Stationery Notes, Lithograph: "Love is All Colors" 1982; Represented in Num Public and Pvt Collections throughout the US, Norway, Sweden, Austria, Germany, Denmark, Philippines, Peru, Canada and England; W/W W; Artists USA.

STUDTMANN, ARNOLD DWIGHT oc/Clergyman, Professor of Natural Science; b/Jan 14, 1930; h/1516 East 11th Street, Winfield, KS 67156; ba/ Winfield, KS; m/Gwen Elaine Falkner; c/Paul, Barbara, Edward, Benjamin, Joel, Amy; p/Irwin C and Bertha Studtmann (dec); ed/BA, Valparaiso Univ, 1951; Theol Dipl, Concordia Sem, 1957; MS, IL Inst of Technol, 1970; MDiv, Concordia Sem, 1971; PhD, Nat Col and Grad Sch Div of E Coast Univ, 1979; EdD, Avon Univ, 1980; ThD, Windsor Univ Theol Sem, 1980; DREd, Intl Bible Inst and Sem, 1982; pa/Pastor, Zion Luth Ch, 1957-59; Physics/Chem Instr, Milwaukee Luth HS, 1960-63; Natural Sci/Math Prof, Concordia Tchrs Col, 1963-72; Physics/Chem Instr, Crete-Monee HS, 1974-79; Pastor, Christ Luth Ch, 1979-82; Prof of Math and Natural Sci, St John's Col, 1982-; Am Assn of Physics Tchrs; Ministerium of the Luth Ch-MO Synod, Bd of Adjudication; AAAS; Creation Res Soc; Luth Ed; cp/Kiwanis; BSA; r/Luth; hon/ Pubs, *A Lecture Syllabus for Quantum Mechanics* 1977, *A Lecture Syllabus for Mathematical Physics* 1976, *Science and the Scriptures* 1980, *Toward a Unified Cosmological Physics: The Reciprocal System of D B Larson* 1979, Others; Four Yr S'ship, Valparaiso Univ, 1948-51; NSF S'ship for Study of Physics Tchg, Marquette Univ, 1962-63; Phi Kappa Phi Hon Soc, 1959; Aid Assn for Luths S'ship in Theol, 1957; Am Men and Wom of Sci; Dir of Am Scholars; Men of Achmt; Intl W/W Intells.

STUMPF, STEPHEN A oc/Management Consultant, Business Professor; b/Dec 28, 1949; h/100 Bleecker Street, Apartment 11E, New York, NY 10012; ba/New York, NY; m/Alice Arnone; c/ Eugene Stephen; p/Richard W and Jacqueline M Stumpf, Rochester, NY;

ed/PhD in Mgmt/Orgl Behavior and Indust/Orgl Psych 1978, MPhil in Mgmt/Orgl Behavior 1978, NY Univ; MBA, Behavioral Sci, Univ of Rochester, 1972; BS, Chem Engrg and Mgmt, Rensselaer Polytechnic Inst, 1971; mil/ USAF 1971-75, Capt; pa/Assoc Prof of Mgmt and Orgl Behavior 1980-, Asst Prof of Mgmt and Orgl Behavior 1978-80, Instr of Mgmt 1977-78, NY Univ; Res and Consltg in Several Industs, incl'g, Communs, Chem, Ed, Fin, Pub'g, 1977-; Scist and Mgr, AF Aero Propulsion Lab, Wright Patterson AFB, 1972-75; Acad of Mgmt; Am Psychol Assn; Am Inst of Decision Scis; r/Cath; hon/Pubs, *Managing Careers* 1982, *Management Education: Issues in Theory, Research, and Practice* 1982, "The Relation of Participant Estimates to Objective Measures of Decision Effectiveness" 1981, "Group Decision Making: Combining Experiential Exercises" 1979, Num Others; Social Sci Res Coun Grant, 1981-82; NSF Res Initiation Grant, 1980-81; NY Univ Curric Devel Grant, 1981; NY Univ Res Challenge Fund Grant, 1980-81; Spencer Foun Grant, 1979-80, 1980-81; Nat Endowment for the Humanities Grant, 1978-82; S Rains Wallace Dissertation Awd in Indust and Orgl Psych, Am Psychol Assn, 1979; Herman E Krooss Outstg Dissertation Awd, 1978; Dept of Labor Doct Dissertation Grant, 1977-78; Beta Gamma Sigma Bus Hon; Tau Beta Pi Engrg Hon; Pi Lambda Upsilon Chem Hon; Rensselaer Achmt Awd; W/W E.

STYRES, KATHRYN SMELLEY oc/ Nursing Education; b/Apr 11, 1938; h/ Route 4, Box 106, Northport, AL 35476; ba/Tuscaloosa, AL; m/L Wayne; c/ Pamela Kay, Cynthia Leigh; p/Mr and Mrs Ervin C Smelley (dec); ed/MS, Nsg, MS Univ for Wom, 1977; BS, Nsg, Samford Univ, 1975; pa/Instr of Nsg, Shelton St Commun Col, 1982-; Fam Nurse Practitioner, Gordo Fam Pract Ctr, 1981-82; Asst Prof of Nsg and Fam Nurse Practitioner, Univ of AL, 1977-81; ANA; Nurse Practitioner Coun; r/Bapt; hon/Capstone Hon Soc, 1981; Sigma Theta Tau, 1982; W/W Am Wom; W/W Am Jr Cols.

SU, TSUNG-CHOW JOE oc/Ocean Engineering Educator and Researcher; b/Jul 9, 1947; h/8298 Brant Drive, Boca Raton, FL 33431; ba/Boca Raton, FL; m/ Hui-Fang Angie Huang; c/Julius Tsu-Li, Jonathan Tsu-Wei, Judith Tus-Te; p/ Chin-shui and Chen-lin Shih Su, Yuan-lin, Taiwan; ed/BS in Civil Engrg, Nat Taiwan Univ, 1968; MS in Aeronautics 1970, AeE in Aeronautics 1973, CA Inst of Technol; EngScD, Ocean Engrg, Columbia Univ, 1974; mil/2nd Lt, Chinese Army, 1968-69; pa/Grad Tchg/Res Asst, CA Inst of Technol, 1970-72; Res Asst, Columbia Univ, 1972-73; Naval Arch/Structural Engr, John J McMullen Assocs Inc, 1974-75; Asst Prof of Civil and Ocean Engrg, TX A&M Univ, 1976-82; Assoc Prof of Ocean Engrg, FL Atl Univ, 1982-; AIAA; Am Soc of Engrg Ed; ASME; ASCE; Am Acad of Mechs; Reg'd Profl Engr, TX; Appt'd Judge, 1983 St Sci and Engrg Fair, FL; hon/Tech Papers Pub'd in Jours; Elected Mem, Am Acad of Mechs, 1982; W/W S and SW; W/W Aviation and Aerospace; Personalities of S; W/ W Frontier Sci and Technol.

SUDDITH, ROBERTA LUCILLE oc/ Registered Nurse; b/Jun 30, 1945; h/ 9720 Hosler Road, Leo, IN 46765; ba/ Ft Wayne, IN; p/Effie L and Beaman Suddith (dec); ed/Dipl, Luth Hosp of Nsg, 1966; Student, St Francis Col, 1976-; pa/Staff Nurse, Luth Hosp, 1966; Asst Hd Nurse, Coronary Care Unit, Luth Hosp, 1968-71; Cardiovas RN Spec, 1971-; ANA; IN St Nurses Assn; Am Assn of Critical Care Nurses; Luth Hosp Sch of Nurses Alumni Assn; Am Heart Assn, Bd of Dirs; r/Luth; hon/ Am Heart Assn Good Heart Awd 1973, Bronze Ser Medallion 1974, Silver Ser Medallion 1975, Gold Ser Medallion 1977; W/W World; Personalities W and MW; Intl Biogl Dic; W/W Am Wom.

SUELTENFUSS, SISTER ELIZA-BETH ANNE oc/University President; b/Apr 14, 1921; h/411 Southwest 24th Street, San Antonio, TX 78285; ba/San Antonio, TX; p/Edward L Sueltenfuss (dec); Elizabeth Amrein (dec); ed/PhD 1963, MS 1961, Biol, Univ of Notre Dame; BA, Botany and Zool, Our Lady of the Lake Col, 1944; pa/Tchg, HS in OK and LA, 1942-49; Tchg, Sums 1940-49, Full-time 1949-59, Our Lady of the Lake Col; Chp of Biol Dept 1963-73, Adm Staff Mem to Superior Gen of Sisters of Divine Providence 1973-77, Pres 1978-, Our Lady of the Lake Univ; Bd of Dirs: Indep Cols and Univs of TX, Inst for Ednl Ldrship, Trim and Swim, SW Res Inst; Secy, TX Indep Col Fund, 1982-83; Indep Cols and Univs of TX Task Force for On-Going Res, 1982-; Pres, Higher Ed Coun of San Antonio, 1980-81; cp/Pres, San Antonio Chapt, Zonta Intl, 1982-; r/Cath; hon/ Pubs, "A Cytochemical Assay for Duck Hepatitis Virus Interferon" 1963, "Further Characterization of Agents Isolated from Normal Baboon" 1967; Featured as "Today's Woman" in *San Antonio Light*, 1982; Univ of Notre Dame Awd of the Yr, Achmt and Ldrship, 1978-79; W/W Fin and Indust; W/W Am Wom.

SUHOR, GERALYN ZIMMER oc/ Accountant; b/Jul 10, 1956; h/2405 Judy Drive, Meraux, LA 70075; ba/New Orleans, LA; m/John Gerard; p/Mrs Florence C Zimmer, Arabi, LA; ed/BS, Acctg, Univ of NO, 1978; pa/Pt-time Tax Acct, J K Byrne & Co, CPAs, 1982; Controller, George Kellett & Sons Inc, 1981-82; Sr Staff Acct, J K Byrne & Co, CPAs, 1978-81; Am Soc of Wom Accts; Reg'd Tchr and Judge, Nat Baton Twirling Assn; r/Cath; Active in Ch Functions, Lector and Eucharistic Min on Sundays; Mem of Liturgy Com, Adult Advr for Cath Yth Org; Wk w Yth for Archdiocese of NO; hon/HS Sch Spirit Awd; Cath Yth Org 5 Yr Ser Awd.

SULFARO, JOYCE A oc/Principal; b/ Oct 23, 1948; h/9011 Crescent Drive, Miramar, FL 33025; ba/West Hollywood, FL; m/Guy; c/Jacqueline A, Kristin Lynn; p/John and Mildred Monaco, Miramar, FL; ed/BA, Sociol, 1970; MA, Adm and Supvn; pa/Tchr, Resurrection Sch, Diocese of Bklyn, 1970-72; Tchr 1977-80, Vice Prin 1979-80, Prin 1980-, Annuciation Sch, Archdiocese of Miami; FL Leag of Mid Schs, 1979-80; NCTM, 1980-81; Nat Cath Ednl Assn, 1977-; ASCD, 1980-; Cath Edrs Guild, 1980-; cp/Nat Right to Life Com, 1982; r/Cath; hon/Author, *The Basket*, 1980; W/W S and SE; Per-

sonalities of S.

SULLIVAN, JOANN MARIE oc/ Co-Owner and Director of Medical Laboratory, Medical Technologist; b/ May 31, 1938; h/PO Box 7, Agana, Guam 96911; ba/Tamuning, Guam; m/ Thomas Roy; c/Michelle Ann, Renee Marie; p/Mr (dec) and Mrs J D Bracco, Butte, MT; ed/BS, cum laude, Carroll Col, 1960; Internship for Med Technol, Sacred Heart Hosp, 1959-60; pa/Univ of WA, 1960-63; Stanford Univ Hosp, 1963-64; Supvr, Guam Meml Hosp, 1964-65; Supvr, SDA Clin, 1965-67; Dir/Co-Owner, Phys Diagnostic Lab, 1972-; Am Soc of Clin Pathologists, 1960-; Am Soc of Med Technologists, 1960-; Am Cancer Soc Bd, 1971-78; Comprehensive Hlth Planning Bd, 1973-75; Blood Exch Bd, Pres 1977-79; Legis Task Force for Med Pract Act, Chm 1974; Adv Coun for MT Prog, Univ of Guam, 1975; Beta Sigma Phi, 1964-66; cp/PEACE Foun, 1975-; r/ Cath; hon/Hons Received for Civic Wk; W/W W.

SULLIVAN, KAREN HARRIS oc/ District Manager; b/Dec 12, 1954; h/ 3529 Tidal Marsh Drive, Jacksonville Beach, FL 32250; ba/Norcross, GA; c/ Lauren Marie; p/William Clinton (dec) and Elsie Jackson Harris; ed/BFA, 1976; pa/Famous-Barr Co: Dept Mgr 1976-77, Asst Buyer, Designer Sportswear Dresses and Accessories 1977, Dept Mgr, Designer Dresses, Coats, Furs and Sportswear 1977, Dept Mgr, Intimate Apparel 1978, Sr Assoc Buyer, Intimate Apparel 1979-81; Libson Shops: Dist Mgr 1981, Dir of Stores 1982, Gen Mdse Mgr 1982-83; Dist Mgr, J Riggings Inc, Div US Shoe Co, 1983-; Alpha Delta Pi Alumni Assn; r/Rom Cath; hon/ W/W Am Wom.

SUMMERS, MARSHA JOY oc/Administrative Supervisor; b/Dec 24, 1953; h/438 Skyline Drive, Daly City, CA 94015; ba/San Francisco, CA; p/James B (dec); Berniece B; ed/AA, 1973; BA, 1976; MA, 1984; pa/Receptionist, Mary's Help Hosp, 1972-77; ECE Instr, Jefferson Elem Sch Dist, 1978; Adm Supvr, SF St Univ, 1978-; Assn Supvn and Curric Devel; Basic Ed Assn; Student CA Tchrs Assn; Phi Delta Kappa; r/Rom Cath; hon/Pubs, "Drug Abuse and the School Age Child," "Alcohol Abuse and the School Age Child," "Child Abuse and How It Affects Achievement," "Reading Curriculum for Music"; Achmt Awd, Bk of Am, 1971; Mod Music Masters, 1971; Student CA Tchrs Assn, 1979, 1980; W/ W W.

SUN, ANTHONY oc/Venture Capital; b/Jul 8, 1952; h/1 Brown Avenue, Rye, NY 10580; ba/New York, NY; m/ Leslie Shao-Ming; c/Christopher C; p/ Chung-Ta Sun and Ching-Sin Ho, Kuala Lumpur, Malaysia; ed/SBEE 1974, SMEE 1974, EE 1975, MIT; MBA, Harvard, 1979; pa/Gen Ptnr, Rockefeller Fam and Assocs, 1979-; Engrg Mgr, Caere Corp, 1976-77; Product Line Mgr, TRW Inc, 1975-76; hon/Pub'd in World Hlth Org; Patentee.

SURI, TEJ PARTAPSINGH oc/Certified Public Accountant, Business Executive; b/Apr 13, 1922; h/6239 Morse Avenue, North Hollywood, CA 91606; m/Raj K; c/Manindar Partap Singh, Robina; p/Ishar Singh and Maya Wanti Suri (dec); ed/BSc, Panjab Univ,

1940; MBA, OH St Univ, 1961; CA Inst of Chartered Accts, India, 1946; PA Inst of CPAs, 1971; Passed Inter Exams of Inst of Cost and Mgmt Accts, UK 1951, Chartered Inst of Secretaries, UK 1956; pa/Plant Controller Assoc, Elect Indust Mfg Co, Calcutta, 1950-52; Comptroller, Carew and Co, Calcutta, 1952-61; Asst Fin Controller, Remington Rand, Calcutta, 1962-65; Controller and Treas, Frick India, New Delhi, 1965-67; Sr Acct, IU Intl Corp, 1968-81; Chm, CEO and CFO, Jolly, Singh & Suri Enterprises Inc, 1982; Am Inst of CPAs; PA Inst of CPAs; Nat Assn of Accts; Inst of Chartered Accts of India; cp/Dir, Treas, VP, Calcutta Jr C of C; Nat Treas and Dir, JCs India; Indo-Am Soc Eng Speaking Union; Treas, Calcutta Panjab Clb; Past Pres, Assn of Indians in Am; Fdr, Pres, India Assn of S Jersey; Fdr, Pres, Guru Nanak Sikh Soc of Del Val; Past Dir, Ctl Host's Lions Clb, Phila; r/Sikh; hon/Pubs, "Role of Electronic Data Processing in India's Industrial Development" 1961, "Qualifications, Traits, and Skills of an Ideal Executive" 1961; Stood First in Sr Yr BSc Class; W/W E.

SURRIDGE, ROBERT C III oc/Trust Officer of Corporate Business Development; b/Jun 3, 1951; h/1512 East Harvard Street, Glendale, CA 91205; ba/Los Angeles, CA; p/Dr and Mrs Robert C Surridge; ed/BA in Ed, San Diego St Univ, 1973; JD, Wn St Univ Col of Law, 1977; CA St Bar, Fed Dist Ct, So Dist, 1978; pa/Asst to the Pres, NBJ Real Properties Corp, 1977-78; Asst Counsel, Sea World Inc, 1978-82; Trust Ofcr, CA First Bk, 1982-; LA and San Diego Co Bar Assns; Am Bar Assn; Barrister's Clb; r/Cath; hon/Hons Cert, Wn St Univ Col of Law, 1976-77; W/ W Am Law; W/W Fin and Indust.

SUSLOV, ALEXANDER V oc/Writer, Lecturer; b/Apr 18, 1950; h/9023 Manchester Road, Silver Spring, MD 20901; m/Eugenia; c/Philip, Katherine, Alexandra; ed/PhD, Georgetown, 1984; Att'd, Georgetown Univ 1979-84, Moscow Inst of Lit 1972-75; pa/Editor, Moscow Tchrs' Inst, Moscow, USSR, 1973-74; Lit Secy, Writers' Union, Moscow, 1975; Refugee, 1976-79; Lang Instr, Dept of St, Wash, DC, 1980-81; Lectr, Georgetown Univ, 1982-84; Writer; IPA; r/ Orthodox; hon/Pubs, *Loosestrife City* 1980, *Swarm of Memory* 1984; Contemp Authors; Intl W/W Intells; DIB.

SUTHERLAND, HAL oc/Artist; b/Jul 1, 1929; h/21927 45th Avenue, Southeast, Bothell, WA 98021; m/Fay; c/ Lisa, Keith; p/Harold E and Doris Sutherland, Bothell, WA; ed/HS; mil/ USAF, 1947-50; pa/Film Dir and Prodr of Chd's TV and Fam Motion Pictures; Pudget Sound Grp of NW Painters; Am Artists of the Rockies Assn; r/Cath; hon/Featured in *Art/West Magazine*, Jan 1981; Featured Artist, *Artists of Reknown,* 1981; Artist/Dealer Awd, Plus Com Awd, Best of All Media, Mus of Native Am Cultures, Spokane, WA, 1981.

SUTPHIN, CECILE AYERS oc/Curriculum Specialist; b/Mar 25, 1921; h/ 81 Northwest 18 Street, Homestead, FL 33030; ba/Homestead, FL; m/Tellie Garst; c/Jonathan David; p/Mr Millard Ayers (dec); ed/BS, Radford Col, 1961; MEd, VA Polytechnic Inst, 1963; AdmS, Univ of Miami, 1971; EdSp, Nova Univ, 1978; DrEd, Heed Univ, 1981; pa/Eng

Tchr, Meml Jr HS, 1961-63; Tchr, Key W Sr HS, 1963-64; Tchr/Dept Hd, S Dade Sr HS, 1964-78; Tchr, Miami Dade Jr Col, 1970-71; Curric Spec, S Dade Adult Ed Ctr, 1978-; NEA; FL Ed Assn; Dade Co Tchrs of Eng; U Tchrs of Dade; Dade Co Tchrs Assn; Nat Assn Supvn and Curric Devel; FL Assn Supvn and Curric Devel; cp/St Textbook Adoption Com; US Power Squadron; r/Presb; hon/Author, Short Stories, *Radford Review*, 1968-74; Kappa Delta Gamma; Epsilon Tau Lambda; Pi Gamma Mu; Kappa Delta Pi; W/W S and SW; Personalities of S; World W/W Wom; Ldrs of Sec'dy Ed.

SVENTY, SISTER MARY AQUILINE oc/Supervisor of Mathematics; h/ 139 Gill Hall Road, Clairton, PA 15025; ba/Clairton, PA; p/Steven and Mary Sventy (dec); ed/EdB 1955, EdM 1961, Duquesne Univ; Master of Adm and Supvn, 1976; pa/Joined Vincentian Sisters of Charity, 1931; Tchr, Pgh Diocese, 1935-69; Prin, St Joseph Sch, 1966-69; Math Supvr, Clairton Public Sch, 1969-; NCTM; Assn Supvn and Curric Devel; r/Rom Cath; hon/John Carroll Univ Grantee, 1945; W/W E.

SWAMY, SRIKANTA M N oc/University Administrator; b/Apr 7, 1935; h/ 275 Des Landes, St Lambert, Quebec, Canada J4S 1V9; ba/Montreal, Quebec, Canada; m/Leela Sitaramiah; c/Saritha, Nikhilesh, Jagadish; p/M K Nanjundiah (dec); M N Mahalakshamma, India; ed/ BSc w Hons, Mysore Univ, 1954; DIISc, India Inst of Sci, 1957; MSc 1960, PhD 1963, Univ of Saskatchewan; pa/Sr Res Asst, India Inst of Sci, 1957-59; Sessional Lectr 1960-63, Res Asst 1959-63, Asst Prof 1964-65, Univ of Saskatchewan; Govt of India Scist, India Inst of Technol, Madras, 1963-64; Asst, Assoc, Full Prof, Tech Univ of Nova Scotia, 1965-68; Prof of Elect Engrg, Univ of Calgary, 1969-70; Prof 1968-69, Prof and Chm of Elect Engrg Dept 1970-77, Dean of Engrg 1977-, Concordia Univ; hon/Co-Author, *Graphs, Networks and Algorithms* 1981; Author/Co-Author, Over 100 Res Articles in Sci Jours; Fellow, IEEE, 1980; Fellow, Engrg Inst of Canada, 1981; Fellow, Inst of Engrs, India, 1979; Fellow, Inst of Electronics and Telecommunication Engrs, India, 1980; Fellow, Inst of Elect Engrs, UK, 1983; DIB; IBA Yr Book; Am Men and Wom of Sci; Others.

SWAN, HARRY KELS oc/Curator of Historic Museum; b/Nov 14, 1928; h/ 32 Elizabeth Street, South Bound Brook, NJ 08880; ba/Titusville, NJ; p/ Peter Kinney and Martha Anita Kels Swan (dec); ed/BS in Ed 1952, MEd, Grad Sch of Ed 1954, Passed Field Exam for EdD, Rutgers, The St Univ; pa/ Curator of Decorative Arts, Histn, Liberty Village Ltd, 1972-76; Curator, Wash Crossing St Pk, DEP, 1976-; Histn, Am Legacy Assn; Histn, VP, Wash Camp Ground Assn; Histn, Revolutionary Meml Soc; Bucks Co, PA, Hist Soc, Life; SAR; Voorhees Fam Assn; r/Prot (Reformed); hon/Pubs, *History of South Bound Brook, New Jersey* 1964, *Raritan's Revolutionary Rebel: Frederick Frelinghuysen* 1967, *American Revolutionary Riflemen* 1973; AMVETS Americanism, Histn Awd, 1983; SAR Heritage Awd, 1982; W/W E.

SWANSON, BARBARA JOAN oc/ Adult Reference Librarian; b/Aug 5,

1939; h/132 Franklin Court, Glendale, CA 91205; ba/Los Angeles, CA; p/ Louise E Swanson, Mission Viejo, CA; ed/BA 1961, MALS 1968, Univ of MN; pa/Bookmobile Libn, Hennepin Co Lib, 1962-68; Yg Adult Libn, Adult Reference Libn 1981-, LA Public Lib, Eagle Rock Br Lib; Am Lib Assn, 1962-; CA Lib Assn, 1969-; cp/Soroptimist Intl of Eagle Rock-Highland Pk, Pres 1980-81; hon/W/W W.

SWEENEY, JAMES EDWARD oc/ Communications and Electronics Officer; b/Jul 6, 1950; h/PO Box 38, Belleville, IL 62222; m/Hyang H; ed/BS, Math, En MI Univ, 1975; MA, Communication, Univ of No CO, 1979; mil/ USAF; pa/Fuel Spec, USAF, 1969-73; Chief Media Devel Br, HQ USAFSS, 1977-78; Chief Ed and Eval Br, HQ ESC, 1978-79; Chief of Maintenance, 1982 CS, 1980-81; Radar Eval Ofcr, 1954 RADES, 1981-; Armed Forces Communs and Electronics Assn; r/Prot; hon/ Am Legion Sch Awd, 1965; Pres, Student Coun, 1965; Highest Hon Grad, Cass Tech HS, 1969; Hon Grad, Chanute Tech Tng Ctr, 1969; Hon Student, En MI Univ, 1973-75; USAF Commend Medal, 1979; Life Patron, ABIRA; Dir of Dist'd Ams; Personalities of S; Biogl Roll of Hon; Intl Book of Hon; 2,000 Notable Ams.

SWEITZER, HARRY PHILLIPS oc/ Pastor; b/Jul 30, 1916; h/1392 Wasatch Boulevard, Salt Lake City, UT 84108; ba/Salt Lake City, UT; m/Margaret; c/ Paul, Mary, Jean; p/Benjamin and Agnes Sweitzer (dec); ed/BA, Muskingum Col, 1938; MDiv, McCormick Theol Sem, 1941; DD, Muskingum Col, 1972; pa/ Pastor: First Presb Ch (Kingfisher, OK) 1941-43, First Presb Ch (Chickasha, OK) 1943-45, Westminster Presb Ch (Mpls, MN) 1945-51, First Presb Ch (Grand Forks, ND) 1951-58, Ctl Presb Ch (St Paul, MN) 1958-73, First Presb Ch (SLC, UT) 1973-; Pres, St Paul Min Assn, 1965; Pres, Salt Lake Min Assn, 1977; Pres, Bd of Trustees, UT Presby, 1976-80; Moderator, Sinod of ND, 1954; Moderator, Presby of Pembina and St Paul; cp/Dir, Bush Foun, 1970-; Trustee, Westminster Col, 1973-77, 1979-; Dir, Westminster Col Foun, 1983-; Pres, Kiwanis Clb, Grand Forks, ND, 1954; Pres, Kiwanis Clb, SLC, 1984; Dir, Salt Lake YMCA, 1975-81; Trustee, Alcohol Foun of UT, 1975-; Dir, Bonneville Knife and Fork Clb, 1979-81; hon/Author, "Prospect Lists and the Neighborhood Plan," 1970; Pastor Emeritus, First Presb Ch, SLC, 1983; Personalities of W and MW; W/ W Rel; DIB; W/W Prot Clergy; Men of Achmt.

SWERGOLD, MARCELLE MINDLE oc/Sculptor; b/Sep 6, 1927; h/450 West End Avenue, New York, NY; ba/New York, NY; m/Maurice; c/Diane Botnick Henry, Gary, Paul Kogan, George Kogan; ed/NY Univ; Art Students Leag; Wax Harold Caster; pa/Sculptor, 1965-; Exhbns: Studio 12 1980, 1982, Fairleigh Dickinson Univ 1972, Cork Gallery, Philharm Hall, Lincoln Ctr, Audubon Artist Ann 1978, Allied Artists Nat Acad Galleries, New Brit Mus Am Art 1980, Others; Housewife; Exec in Castillo Dress Design; Artist Equity; NY Soc of Wom Artists, Pres 1979-81, Exec VP 1981; Contemp Artists Guild; r/Jewish Orthodox; hon/1st Prize,

Woms Art Gallery, 1977; W/W Am Art; W/W Am Wom.

SWETMAN, GLENN ROBERT oc/ University Professor, Author; b/May 20; h/PO Box 1162, Thibodaux, LA 70302; ba/Thibodaux, LA; c/Margarita June, Glenn Lyle Maximillian, Glenda Louise;. p/Mr and Mrs Glenn L Swetman, Biloxi, MS; ed/BS, MA, Univ of So MS; PhD, Tulane Univ, 1966; mil/ AUS Intell, Sgt; pa/Subst Copy Editor, Biloxi-Gulfport (MS) *Daily Herald*, Sum 1956; Instr, Univ of So MS, 1957-58; Instr, AR St Univ, 1958-59; Instr, McNeese Univ, 1959-61; Instr, USAF Bottstrap Prog, 1959-61; Instr, Col of Arts and Scis, Instr Univ Col, Spec Advr to Dept of Elect Engrg, Tulane Univ, 1961-64; Book Reviewer and Lit Conslt, Jackson (MS) *State Times*, 1961-62; Asst Prof, Univ of So MS, 1964-66; Assoc Prof, LA Tech Univ, 1966-67; Stringer Corres, Shreveport (LA) *Times*, 1966-67; Prof and Dept Hd, Nicholls St Univ, 1967-70; Prof of Eng, Nicholls St Univ, 1971-; Conslt, Union Carbide, Ormuba Corp, Offshore Res Ser; Consltg Editor, Scott Foresman, Paon Press, Burgess; Jt Author, *Poems 1961*, *The Pagan Christmas 1962*; Author, *Tunel de Amor 1973*, *Shards 1979*, *Concerning Carpenters 1980*, *Son of Igor 1981*, *Christmas 1981*, *A Range of Sonnets 1981*; Others; LA St Poetry Soc, Pres 1971, 1972, 1973-; Nat Fdn of St Poetry Socs, VP 1972-76, Pres 1976-77, Nat Mbrship Chm 1972-76; Col Writers Soc, VP 1970-71, Pres 1971-72, Exec Dir 1983-; So Lit Fest Assn, Exec Bd 1973-76, VP 1976-77; Intl Boswellian Inst, Exec Bd 1972; MLA; Am Studies Assn; Phi Eta Sigma; Sigma Tau Delta; ODK; LA Folklore Soc; Am Soc for Engrg Ed; Am Inst of Elect and Electronics Engrs; S-Ctl MLA; S Atl MLA; Soc for the Study of So Lit; Soc For the Study of So Lit; AAUP; UFCT, Chapt Pres, St VP, Nat Com to Resist Attacks on Tenure; Others; So List Fest Assn, VP and Exec Bd 1983-84, Pres 1984; cp/U Campus Min, Exec Bd; r/St John's Epis Ch, SS Fac 1968-72, Vestry 1969-73; hon/Recog in KQUE Haiku Contest, 1964; *The Green World* Brief Forms Awd, 1965; Col Arts Contest Awd, 1966; Hon Fellow, Intl Boswellian Inst, 1966; Yokosuka Black Ship Fest Haiku Awd, Japan, 1967; J Mark Press Awd, 1968; Order of Gracian, Intl Boswellian Inst, 1970; Outstg Edr of Am, 1971; Outstg Achmt Awd, UFCT, 1973; LA Poetry Soc Haiku Awd, 1977; W/W S and SW; Dir of Am Scholars; Intl Scholars Dir; DIB; Intl W/W Poetry; Dir Yg Am Authors; Contemp Authors; Others.

SWIFT, GAYLE CELESTE oc/ Director of Patient Services; b/Aug 1, 1943; h/9332 Coronet Avenue, Westminster, CA 92683; ba/ Westminster, CA; m/William F Jr; c/ Michele, David, Jennifer, Jeffrey; p/ Kenneth and Glynna Thomas, Anaheim, CA; ed/BS, Hlth Sci, Com-

mun Hlth Ed, 1976; MS, Hlth Sci, 1980; pa/Dir, Patient Sers, Nat MS Soc, 1980-; Pt-time Fac, CA St Univ Long Bch, 1979; Hlth Ed Conslt (Vol), CA St Univ Long Bch Student Hlth Ser, 1978-80; Subst Tchr, Anaheim Unified HS Dist, 1977-80; Soc for Public Hlth Ed; APHA; CA Assn for Physically Handicapped; AAUW; Adv Com for the Handicapped, City of Westminster, Chair 1982, 1983; r/Prot; hon/Nat Dean's List, 1980; Grad Dean's List, 1980; Phi Kappa Phi, 1979; World W/W of Wom.

SYED, SHAFI MOHAMED oc/ Manager of Materials and Purchasing; b/Feb 10, 1939; h/70 Trillium Cres, Barrie, Ontario, Canada L4N 5K3; ba/ Barrie, Ontario, Canada; m/Elisabeth Gertrude; p/Mr and Mrs Syed Abdul Bashir (dec); ed/BS w Hons, 1962; DSS, 1964; Dipl in Plastics Technol, Aachen, W Germany; mil/2 Yrs in India; pa/ Purchasing Mgr, Olsonite Corp, 1969-75; Mgr, Intl Purchasing, Automotive Div, Bendix Corp, 1975-78; Chm, Plastics and Chems, 1978-80, 1980-82; Corporate New Resource Devel, VW Canada Inc, 1982-; Soc of Plastic Engrs; Purchasing Mgmt Assn of Canada; cp/Barrie C of C; r/Islam; hon/Author, Var Tech Papers and Pubs in Modern Plastics; W/W Bus and Fin.

SYKES, MAYME JEAN PHARIS oc/ Educational Administrator; b/Feb 21, 1928; h/3305 Buckeye Lane, Temple, TX 76501; ba/Temple, TX; m/Stephen McKenzie; c/Stephen McKenzie, Sandra Jean; p/Henry Garland and Ethel Fern Mandeville Pharis; ed/BA, LA Col, 1949; MEd, Univ of Houston, 1954; pa/ Tchr, LA and TX Schs, 1949-53; Prin, Jefferson Elem Sch, 1973-; Conslt, Ednl Ser Ctr; NEA; Assn Supvn and Curric Devel; Nat Assn Elem Prins; Prins Res Assn; TX Tchrs Assn; TX Elem Prins Assn, Dist VP 1981-82, Dist Pres 1983-84; PEO; Phi Delta Kappa; Delta Kappa Gamma; Alpha Delta Kappa; cp/ Former Mem, City Comm on Safety; OES; Opti-Mrs, Past Pres; r/Meth.

SZE, ANDREW WEI-TSENG oc/ Investment Banker, Executive; b/Sep 27, 1926; h/9 Barnes Road, Tarrytown, NY 10591; ba/New York, NY; m/Sylvia H; c/Michael; p/Fau Hau and Tse C Sze, Shanghai, China; ed/BA in Ec, St John's Univ, Shanghai, 1946; MLitt in Indust Mgmt 1950, PhD in Ec 1951, Univ of Pgh; pa/VP, Thomson McKinnon Securities Inc, 1978-; Mem of Fac, Sch of Bus Adm, Fordham Univ, 1961-72; r/Cath; hon/W/W Fin and Indust.

SZEGHO, EMERIC oc/Retired Professor; h/215 Ross Avenue, Cambridge Springs, PA 16403; c/ Marika; ed/Lic at Law, Univ of Cernauti, Rumania, 1938; Doctor Juris Universi, Univ of Cluj, Rumania, 1947; Dipl of Atty-at-Law, Rumanian Bar Assn, Bucharest, 1941; pa/Pract'g Atty-at-Law and Jurisconslt, Timisoara, Sibiu, Rumania, 1941-60; Prof, Alliance Col, Cambridge Sprgs, PA, 1966-73

(Currently Ret'd w an Awd of Tenure); AAUP, Emeritus Mem; Am Security Coun (Nat Adv Bd); Fdr, Ctr for Intl Security Studies, Am Security Coun Ed Foun (Formerly Inst for Am Strategy); cp/Repub Pres Task Force, 1981; Fdg Mem, US Senatorial Clb, 1977-; IPA; Fellow, IBA; Mem, Nat Def Task Force; Life Mem, Repub Party; Life Mem, Repub Nat Com; r/U Presb Ch, Cambridge Sprgs; hon/Author, *Crime and Punishment: The Problem of Crime* and *The Way of Life and the Crime*; Book of Hon; Intl W/W Commun Ser; Intl W/W Intells; Intl Register of Profiles; Men of Achmt; DIB; W/W N Am; Notable Ams of 1976-77; Commun Ldrs and Noteworthy Ams; Intl Book of Hon; 2,000 Notable Ams.

SZOC, RONALD ZBIGNIEW oc/ Corporate and Operations Manager; b/ May 25, 1948; h/4607½-A MacArthur Boulevard, Northwest, Washington, DC 20007; ba/Washington, DC; p/Mr and Mrs Antoni Szoc, Chicago, IL; ed/ BA, Loyola Univ, 1970; MA, Univ of CA Santa Barbara, 1973; PhD, Loyola Univ, 1980; Sem in Structural Equation Modelling, Johns Hopkins Univ, 1981; pa/Computer Conslt, Loyola Univ Dept of Info Sys, 1973-77; Instr, Dept of Psych, Loyola Univ, 1973-77; Res Assoc, Michael Reese Hosp, 1975-76; Public Sector Spec, Westinghouse Public Applied Sys, 1977-78; Res Assoc, Ctr for Urban Affairs, NWn Univ, 1978-80; Sr Public Sector Spec, Westinghouse Public Applied Sys, 1980-83; Corporate and Opers Mgr, Ruesch Intl, 1983-; Am Psychol Assn, 1980-; Voting Mem, Am Sociological Assn, 1980-; Soc for the Psychol Study of Social Issues, 1980-; Assn for Computing Machinery, 1980-; Eval Netwk, 1980-; hon/Author, *Fear of Crime in Urban America 1979, Family Factors Critical to the Retention of Navy Personnel: Literature Review and a Tentative Causal Model 1981, Family Factors Critical to the Retention of Navy Personnel: Random Samples Constrained by Temporal Sampling Windows, Multiple Strata, and Equal Standard Errors, Family Factors Critical to the Retention of Navy Personnel: Final Report of Findings and Model Parameter Estimates 1982, "Producing Official Crimes: Verified Crime Reports as Measures of Police Output" 1980, "Producing Official Crimes and the Question of Service Equity" 1978, "Police Referral of Mental Health Patients: A Community Area Analysis" 1980, "Evaluating Productivity Improvement Programs: The Generation of Productivity Indicators and Their Use" 1982, "Development of the Westinghouse Roadmap for Navy Family Research" "Evaluation of Navy Family Services: A Summary" 1982, "Linkages between Family and Military Career Commitments" 1982, Others; Nat Merit Finalist, 1965; IL St S'ship Winner, 1966-70; Chp, Strategic Planning Subcom for Res, Westinghouse Elect; W/W E.

T

TABOR, HARRY BERNARD JR oc/ Marketing Executive; b/Mar 26, 1936; h/Route 5, Box 9, Louisville, MS 39339; ba/Starkville, MS; m/Vale; c/Tammy, Timothy, Deborah, Terri; p/Mr and Mrs Harry B Tabor, McCool, MS; sp/Mrs E H Finley, Louisville, MS; ed/BS, MS St Univ, 1958; MS Auburn Univ, 1964; pa/ MS Forestry Com, 1958-62; Res Asst, Auburn Univ, 1962-64; Instr, Abraham Baldwin Col, Tifton, GA, 1964-65; Staff Forester, TVA, Norris, TN, 1965-66; Mktg Mgr, Taylor Machine Wks, Louisville, MS, 1967-74; Self-Employed, 1974-81; VPres Mktg, FESCO, Starkville, MS, 1981-; Mem: Soc of Am Foresters; Nat Wildlife Fedn; Ch Equip Suppliers Coun, Am Pulpwood Assn, 1972; Div Chm, FPRS, 1969; Xi Sigma Pi; cp/Chapt Chm, Ducks Unltd, 1983; Pres, Lions Clb, 1972; SS Tchr; r/Meth; hon/Author, Over 7 Tech Papers & Articles Pub'd in Profl Jours & Presented at Assn Meetings Incl'g: "Machine Planting- Seedlings & Tubelings," Am Pulpwood Assn Lake Sts Meeting, 1983; Outstg Yg Men of Am; HS Salutatorian, 1954; Recip, Masonite Forestry S'ship, 1954-56.

TAHIR, ASH H oc/Physician; b/Sep 16, 1940; h/5831 Wright Road, New Orleans, LA 70128; ba/Same; m/Dixie Ann; c/Lisa, Michael, Ashley; p/Zia M Khan and Mumtaz Begum, Pakistan; sp/ Orvis and Mildred Webb; ed/BScl; MBBS, MRCP; FRCP; FACA; pa/Asst Dir & Sr Assoc Anesth, Charity Hosp, NO, 1970-75; Clin Assoc Prof Dept of Surg, Tulane Univ Sch of Med, 1972-75; Staff Anesth Meth Hosp, NO, 1975-; Mem: Am Soc of Anesths; Intl Anesth Res Soc; LA Soc of Anesths; Royal Col of Phys & Surgs of Canada; LA St Med Soc; Orleans Parish Med Soc; hon/ Contbr of Book Chapt, *Appraisal of Current Concepts in Anesth*; Author, Over 30 Sci Articles Pub'd in Profl Med Jours; Phys Recog Awd, AMA, 1969 & 1974; W/W in S & SW; Men of Achmt; Notable Ams of Bicent Era; Other Biogl Listings.

TALLEY, RONDA CAROL oc/ Assessment and Placement Coordinator; b/Nov 21, 1951; h/1114 Whetstone Way, Louisville, KY 40223; ba/L'ville, KY; p/Jack Howard and Ronda Mae McCoy Talley, L'ville, KY; ed/BS, Wn KY Univ, 1974, Grad Studyt 1976, Univ of L'ville, KY; PhD, IN Univ, 1979; pa/Coor-Assessment/Placement Sers, Exceptl Child Ed, Jefferson Co Public Schs, L'ville, KY, 1981-; Adj Prof, Univ of L'ville, KY, 1981-; Lrng Disabilities Resource Spec, Whitney Yg Elem, Jefferson Co Public Schs, L'ville, KY, 1980-81; Adm Intern, Bur of Ed for the Handicapped & Prin Investigator Tech Asst on Adm Strategies to Integrate Handicapped Students, 1978-80; Res Coor, Chd's TV Wkshop, NYC, Sum 1978; Res Asst, Ctr for Innovation in Tchg the Handicapped, IN Univ, Bloomington, 1977-79; Sch Psych Externs Supvr, Montroe Co Commun Sch Corp, 1977-78; Assoc Instr, Ed Psych Dept, Sch of Ed, IN Univ, Fall 1977; Res Asst, Prog Res in Integrated Multi-ethnic Ed (PRIME), Univ of CA-Riverside, Sum 1977; Lrng Disabilities Conslt, Bartholomew Co Spec Ed Coop, Seymour Commun Schs, 1976-77; Tchr of Chd w Lrng Disabilities, Jefferson Co Public

Schs, 1973-76; Res Conslt Dept of Ednl Res, WN KY Univ, 1974-79; Mem: AAUP; Am Ednl Res Assn; Div of Sch Psych, Am Psychol Assn; Coun for Admrs of Spec Ed, Coun for Ednl Diagnosticians, Coun for Exceptl Chd; Delta Kappa Gamma; Intl Assn of Applied Psych; Jefferson Co Assn of Sch Admrs; KY Assn for Psychols in the Schs; KY Coun for Admrs of Spec Ed; KY Psychol Assn; KY Soc of Psychols Inc; Nat Assn of Sch Psychols; Phi Delta Kappa; Wom in Sch Adm; r/Meth; hon/ Co-editor of Book, *Admrs' Handbook on Integrating Am's Mildly Handicapped Students*, 1982; Author & Editor, Over 50 Res Articles, Papers & Reports Pub'd in Profl Jours & Presented at Orgl Meetings; Num Assessment Wkshop Presentations; Chp Com for the Dirs of Sch Psychol Sers, Div of Sch Psych, Am Psychol Assn, 1982-; Invited Participant, Olympia Conf on the Future of Sch Psych, Oconomowoc, WI, 1981; Chp Student Affils in Sch Psych, Div of Sch Psych, Am Psychol Assn, 1977-82; Conslt Editor, *Behavioral Disorders*, 1978-81; Reg Editor 1978-81, Student Editor 1979-79, *The Sch Psychol*; Student Res Grant, Bur of Ed for the Handicapped, US Ofc of Ed, Dept of Hlth, Ed & Welfare, 1978-79; Alpha Chapt, Phi Delta Kappa, 1979; WHAS Crusade for Chd S'ships, Univ of L'ville, 1973; W/W: in S & SE, Among Wom, Among Students in Am Univs & Cols, in Sci & Technol.

TALLMAN, RUTH MARCHAK oc/ Aviation Corporate Executive; b/Jul 18, 1928; h/1973 Vista Caudal, Newport Beach, CA 9266-; ba/Santa Ana, CA; m/ Frank Gifford III (dec); p/Michael Marchak (dec); Mary Hosko Marchak, Newport Bch, CA; sp/Frank and Inez G Tallman II (dec); ed/Att'd Seton Hall Col; pa/Fashion Model, Blue Book Modeling Agy, Hollywood, CA; Secy to Controller & Pers Mgr, KTLA TV, Hollywood, CA; Owner, Tallmantz Aviation Inc, Frank Tallman's Movieland of the Air Aricraft Mus, John Waye Airport, Santa Ana, CA, Currently; Mem: Aero Clb of So CAl Nat Aeronaut Assn; Soc of Exptl Test Pilots; cp/ Rolls-Royce Owners' Clb; Orange Co Perf'g Arts; Sound of Music Chapt, Orange Co Music Ctr; Orange Co Master Chorals; Hollywood Stuntmen's Hall of Fame; Ladies Aux of the Whirley Girls; r/Rom Cath; hon/W/W: in Aviation & Aerospace, of Am Wom.

TAMAGNA, JOSEPH ANTHONY oc/Oral Surgeon; b/Mar 25, 1939; ba/ 421 Huguenot Street, New Rochelle, NY 10801; m/Katherine; c/Rosette, Kathy Jo, Nicholas, Joseph II; p/Nicholas and Rose Tamagna; sp/Demetrius and Katherine Scalzo; ed/BS, Iona Col, 1960; DDS, Columbia Univ Sch of Dental & Oral Surg, 1964; mil/USAR, 1968-74; Capt; Chief of Mass Casualty Exercises, 1970-72; pa/Self-employed Oral Maxillofacial Surg, Currently; Att'g in Oral Surg at New Rochelle Hosp & St Joseph's Hosp; Chief Resident, Fordham-Misericordia Hosp, 1966-68; Mem: Am Assnof Oral & Maxillofacial Surgs; Am Bd of Utilization & Quality Assurancel Am Col of Utilization Review & Quality Assurance; r/Rom Cath.

TAPPAN, SANDRA HAZEN oc/ Counselor, Teacher; b/Sep 25, 1940; h/

22 Rugg Street, St Albans, VT 05478; ba/Same; m/Walter H II; c/Suzanne E, Heidi L; p/Joseph and Elaine Rogow, Sarasota, FL; sp/Herrick and Eugénia Tappan (dec); ed/BA, Trinity Col, 1979; MS, Univ of VT, 1983; pa/Pvt Cnslg Pract, 1983-; Tchr, Commun Col of VT, 1982 & 1983; Owner, Choreographer & Tchr, Sandra Tappan Profl Sch of Dance, 17 Yrs; Cnslr, Cnslg Practicum, St Albans City Elem Sch, 1983; Cnslr, Cnslg Practicum, Cnslg & Testing Ctr, Univ of VT, 1982; Cnslr, Planned Parenthood of VT, St Albans, 1979-80; CRASH Cnslr, St of VT, 1977-79; Ldr & Orgr, Wom's Growth & Support Grps, 1980-82; Tchg Practicum 2nd Grade 1979, 4th Grade 1977, St Albans Town/City Elem Sch; Others; Mem: Assn of Pers & Guid, 1982 & 1983; VT Pers & Guid Assn, 1983; AAUW, 1982 & 1983; cp/Franklin Co Planning Comm, 1974-76; Talent Show Judge in Dance, Franklin Co, VT; Bd Mem, U Way; Choir Mem, Congl Ch, 1980-82; VPres, Tchr-Parent Org, City Elem, 1976; VPres, Autonoe Clb, 1972; Others; r/Prot; hon/Grad Sch Mini-grant for Res, Univ of VT, 1981; Presentation of Res, N Eng Ednl Res Org, 1982; Grad cum laude, Trinity Col, Burlington, VT; W/W in E.

TASTLE, WILLIAM JOHN oc/Director of Operations; b/Nov 3, 1946; h/512 West Wendell Street, Endicott, NY 13760; ba/Binghamton, NY; m/Geraldine Ann; c/Michelle L, Stephen W J; p/William C and Josephine P Tastel, Little Falls, NY; sp/Frank and Clelia Billerio, Westfield, NY; ed/BS 1972, MS 1977, SUNY-Fredonia; MBA, SUNY-Binghamton, 1983; Cert, Industl Devel Inst, Univ of OK, 1980; mil/AUS Spec Forces (Airborne), 1967-70; pa/Dir of Opers, Roberson Ctr for the Arts & Scis, Binghamton, NY, 1981-; Dir of Ec Devel, So Tier E Reg Planning Devel Bd, Binghamton, NY, 1979-81; Dir of Industl Devel Programming, Broome Co C of C & Industl Devel Agy, Binghamton, NY, 1978-79; Asst to Pres for Devel & Govtl Affairs, SUNY Agri & Tech Col, Delhi, NY, 1974-78; Asst Coor of Sponsored Res, SUNY-Fredonia, NY, 1972-74; Mem: Bd of Dirs, So Tier E Reg Planning Devel Be, 1976-78; Chml, DE Co Coun on the Arts, 1975-78; cp/Activs/Tng Chm, Exec Bd & Other Positions, BSA, 1972-; Bd of Dirs, BC Pops, 1982-; Fin Com, St Anthony of Padua Ch, 1980-; K of C, 1971-; 3rd Deg, 1973; r/Rom Cath; hon/Author, *Earthquakes & Related Features: Minimizing the Damage to Economic Devel in Conterminous US*, 1980; Eagle Scout, 1964; Ad Altare Dei, 1960; Alpha Phi Omega, 1971; Outstg Yg Men of Am.

TATOM, JUDITH (JUDY) E oc/ Welfare Supervisor; b/Aug 18, 1926; h/ Route 9, Box 295A Dothan, AL 36303; ba/Dothan, AL; m/Marx F; c/Marx F (Frank) II; D Margaret T May; p/W B and Margaret Overton Ellard (dec); sp/ E Marx Tatom (dec); Dora K Taton, Greenwood, FL; ed/BA, Univ of Montevallo, 1944; MSW, Univ of AL, 1979; pa/w St of AL: Casewkr, 1948-50; Child Welfare Wkr, 1950-52; Co Welfare Dir, 1952-54; Casewkr, 1963-64; Child Welfare Wkr, 1964-66; Casewk Supvr, 1966-79; Welfare Supvr III, 1979-; Mem: Am Bus Woms Assn; AL Conf of Social Wk; Child Welfare Leag; Pres,

AL St Employees Assn, 1977-79; Advy Bd, Headstart; AL Conf of Child Care; SE AL Yth Sers Bd; Human Sers Org; cp/Pilot Clb; r/Meth; hon/W/W of Am Wom; Personalities of S.

TAUTENHAHN, GUNTHER oc/ Composer; b/Dec 22, 1938; h/1534 3rd Street, Manhattan Beach, CA 90266; ed/Att'd Caldwell Col, NY; Pvt Study w E Applebaum & D Stalvey; pa/ Composer, Currently; Comm'd Wks Incl: "Suite for D/Bass," 1970; "Dorn Dance for Sax," 1972; "Two Oct Songs for Trumpet & Marimba," 1976; "Distance for SATB a cappella," 1977; "Sonata for Guitar," 1978; "Caprice Elegant for Flute & Accordion," 1979; "Fenton Follies for Flute,"1979; "By The Dawn's Early Light," 1980; "Miniature Duo for Flute & Accordion," 1980; "24 Sons," 1981; "Southboard Songs for Guitar," 1982; "Trumpet & Percussion Pieces," 1982; Others; Over. 15 Music Compositions Perf'd on Var Radio Progs, 1969-, Incl'g: KANU-FM, Lawrence KS; KRWG-FM, Las Cruces NM; KCRW-FM, LA CA; KSCM-FM, San Mateo CA; KGNU-FM, Boulder CO; Others; hon/Composer of Recorded Songs: "Back As Lovers," w Jo Ann Castle Vocals & Charlie McCoy Arranger & Conductor, Jach Assn, 1981; "Blue Chip Lady," w Jere Swaggerty & Charlie McCoy Arranger & Conductor, Kingdom Records, 1982; Author of Articles & Lectrs Incl'g: "The Importance of One," *Jour of MI Music Theory Soc*, 1974; "Fiber, Movements," Nat ASUC Conf, FL, 1978; "Remember the Present," 1982; Yg Am Composers' Awd, 1963; Charter Mem, Nat Assn of Composers of USA, 1975; Appt'd Mem, Manhattan Bch Cultural Arts Com, 1980; Standard Awd, ASCAP, 1982; Hon Appt as Bd of Advrs, Am Biogl Inst, 1981; Commemorative Mention Awd, Intl Biogl Ctr, 1978; Intl W/W in Music; Personalities of W & MW.

TAYLOE, MARJORIE oc/Harpist and Singer; h/4527 Kraft Avenue, North Hollywood, CA 91602; m/Ralph Chester Tayloe; c/Mary Eleen, David Chester & Triplets Sarah Lee, Susan Marie and John Dannie; p/John L and Eleanor (Jones) Zaerr; ed/Dipl, Samolloff Opera Acad, 1952; Att'd: Whittier Col;LA Val Col; Occidental Col; Addit Study in Europe; pa/Harpist, Phil Kerr's Harmony Chorus, 1949-53; Appearances as Organist & Harpist, Var Radio & TV Progs, in US & Fgn Countries; Perf'd 11 Concert Tours in Europe; Appeared in Seattle World's Fair Concert, 1963; Sung Var Opera Roles & was Star of "Music Until Midnight," a Radio Broadcast, 1948-62; Recording Artist, Yg Records; Soloist & Harpist, Beverly Hills Symph, 1962-; Builder & Player, 1st Welch Triple String Harp, US; Dir, Taloe Fam Ringers & Singers;Fdr & Dir, Musical Arts Acad, N Hollywood, CA, 1950; Mem: Chm, CA Eng Hand Bell Ringers Assn, 1974; Pres, Minstrel Harpers Soc Am, 1962-68; Am Harpist Soc; Eng Hand Bell Ringers Am; CA St Music Chm, Pen Wom Am; cp/DAR; Fdr, Triplet & Quad Clb, 1964; W Shore Music Clb; LA Opera Rdg Clb; So CA Componology Clb; r/Presb; hon/ Author, *The Harp in the Bible*, 1983; Articles Incl: "Irish Songs for Irish Harpers," "Hooked on the Harp," "Am Songs for Irish Harp Players," "The

Tayloe Fams of Eng"; Editor, Pubr, *A Harpers Notebook* & *The Irish Harp*; Other Pubs; Made Guiness World Book of Records, as Having the Largest Gathering of Triplets & Quads; Intl Biogl Assn; W/W: in W, of W, in Am Wom, in Am.

TAYLOR, GEORGE WILLIAM oc/ Executive; b/Jun 16, 1934; h/305 Dodds Lane, Princeton, NJ 08560; ba/Princeton, NJ; m/Cynthia; c/Susan, George, Deborah, Felicity; p/George W Taylor (dec); Myrtle Taylor, Floreat Pk, Wn Australia; sp/William and Winnifred Hatch (dec); ed/BE 1957, DEng 1981, Univ of Wn Australia; PhD, Univ of London, 1961; pa/Tech Staff, RCA Labs, 1962-70; VPres Res & Engrg, Princeton Mats Sci, 1971-75; Pres, Princeton Res Assocs, 1975-; Mem: Fellow, Inst of Engrs (Australia); Fellow, Inst of Elect Engrs (London); Sr Mem, IEEE; r/Epis; hon/Author, *Dielectrics & Their Applications*; 1979 & 1981; Intl Jours Editor, *Ferroelects & Display & Imaging Technol*; RCA Lab Awd, 1967; W/W: in W, in Bus & Indust; Am Men of Sci.

TAYLOR, JOHN MICHAEL oc/ Director of Public Utilities and City Engineering; b/Aug 25, 1950; h/203 North College Street, Henderson, NC 27536; ba/Henderson, NC; m/Judy Ann Harless; p/J M Taylor (dec); Mrs J M Taylor, Hight Point, NC; sp/Mr and Mrs Robert Atwood, Chula Vista, CA; ed/ AAS, Guilford Commun Col, 1971; Post Grad Wk, UNC-Wilmington; BS, NC St Univ, 1983; pa/Mgr & Dir: the Dept of Adm & Engr, the Dept of Public Utilities & Kerr Lake Reg Water Sys, Henderson, NC, 1980-; Asst to Co Engr, Asst to Co Mgr & Var Co Depts, New Hanover Co, Wilmington, NC, 1978-80; Constrn Supt of Downtown Devel at Elon Col, P J Coble Constrn Co, Burlington, NC, 1977-78; Constrn Supt for Broad Street Mall in High Point, Beaman's Projs Inc, Greensboro, NC, 1977; Constrn Supvr, S B Simmons Constrn & Grading, High Point, NC, 1976-77; Proj Admr, Davis, Martin, Powell & Assocs, 1972-76; Civil Engrg Tech, NC Dept of Trans, Winston-Salem, NC, 1970-72; Mem: Sems & Wkshops Com for NC Chapt 1982, Am Water Wks Assn; Am Public Wks Assn; NC Rural Water Assn; NC Water Wks Opers Assn; NC Water Pollution Control Assn; Fed Water Pollution Control Fedn; Solide Waste Mgmt Assn; Inst for Water Resources; Inst for Adm Mgmt; r/Wesleyan Meth; hon/Among 50 Finalists for Proj in New Hanover Co, NC, Rolex Awds for Enterprise, 1980; Best Constructed Proj using NC Brick Prods, NC Brick Assn, 1977; W/W in S & SW; Commun Ldrs of Am; Men of Achmt; Intl Book of Hon; Other Biogl Listings.

TAYLOR, SHARON KAY oc/Public Relations; b/Jul 6, 1945; h/5033 Montessa Street, San Diego, CA 92124; ba/ San Diego, CA; p/Mr and Mrs Glenn L Taylor, La Mesa, CA; ed/BA, MA, San Diego St Univ; BA Intl Mgmt, Thunderbird Grad Sch; pa/Public Communs Ofcr, Metro Transit Devel Bd, San Diego, CA, 1980-84; Editor, *Arts & Activs Mag*, 1978-80; Exec Asst, San Diego C of C, 1978-79; HS Jour Instr, 1970-76; Mem: Public Relats Soc of Am; Intl Assn of Bus Communrs; San Diego Press Clb; Public Relats Clb of San Diego; hon/ Author, Over 100 Free-lance Articles

Pub'd; Winner of Over 2 Dozen Awds Incl'g: Best Public Relats Prog, Best Brochure, Best Photo, Others, By Profl Orgs (Listed Above).

TAYLOR, SUSAN HAYMAN oc/ Director of Market Development; b/ Aug 10, 1948; h/96 Louise's Lane, New Canaan, CT, 06840; ba/Pleasantville, NY; m/Francis Mortimer Jr; c/Pamel Suzanne, John Nelson; p/Robert Charles Hayman and Carol Hope Wyman (dec); sp/Francis Mortimer Taylor (dec); ed/BS, Univ of KS, 1970; Cert, Cambridge Univ, England; pa/Tchr, Fauldhouse Jrs Sec Sch, Fauldhouse, Scotland, 1970; Correspondent, Playboy Intl, Chgo, IL, l1971-72; Dist Sales Mgr, Intl Liaison Mgr 1974-75, Spec Sales Mgr 1976, Trade Sales Mgr 1977, Dir Mkt Devel 1978-, Reader's Digest, Pleasantville, NY; Mem: AAP; ABA; ALA; AMA; CBA; Pubr's Ad Clb; Rel Pubrs Clb; r/ Meth; hon/Contbr, *Trade Book Mktg: A Pract Guide*, 1983; W/W: in Am Wom, in Fin & Indust.

TAYLOR, TIMOTHY DAVIES oc/ Psychotherapist; b/Jan 25, 1945; h/4416 North 27th, Tacoma, WA 98407; ba/ Tacoma, WA; p/Tom and Eleanor Taylor, Tacoma, WA; ed/BA, Ctl WA Univ, 1968; MEd, Univ of Puget Sound, 1975; PhD, US Intl Univ, 1980; mil/USAR, 1967-72; pa/Tchr, Public Schs, St of WA,1968-72; VPres, Ins Brokerage, 1972-81; Cnslr, Fam Cnslg Ser, 1975-; Pvt Pract Psychotherapist, 1981-; Mem: Am Assn of Marriage & Fam Therapists; cp/Big Brothers/Big Sisters; Chm, March of Dimes, 1980-81; Pres, W Tacoma Optimist Clb; Elks Clb 174; YMCA; r/Christian; hon/Optimist of Yr, 1977; W/W: of W, of Intells; Outstg Yg Men of Am; Personalities of W & MW.

TAZEWELL, CALVERT WALKE (WILLIAM STONE DAWSON) oc/ Writer, Historian, Genealogist, Retired Air Force Officer; b/Apr 13, 1917; h/ 3517 Sandy Point Key, Virginia Beach, VA 23452; ba/Virginia Bch, VA; m/ Theresa Hoey; c/Lyn Diane, Patricia Marie, Beverly Ann, William Bradford, Valera Marie, Sabrina; p/Calvert Walke and Sophie Good Tazewell (dec); sp/ Patrick and Katherine Hoey; ed/Att'd: Air Univ, Sophia Univ (Turkey), IN Univ, NY Univ, Fisk Univ, Old Dominion Univ; mil/Enlisted AUS, 1937; Transfered to USAF, 1948; Meteorologist & Communs-Elect Staff Ofcr of Maj Commands & Bases; Cmdg Ofcr, Sqdrns & Bases in US, Japan, Korea & Caribbean; Ret'd Lt Col, 1959; pa/Comml Multi-Engine Pilot; Civil Def Coor, Metro Dade Co, FL, 1961; Staff Mem, Hlth-Welfare-Rec Planning Coun, Norfolk, VA, 1964-65 Computer Mktg & Sys Spec, 1977-82; cp/Orgr & 1st Chm, Metro Dade Co, FL Public Lib Advy Bd, 1963-64; Fd & 1st Pres, Norfolk Hist Soc, 1965; Fd & 1st Pres, VA Hist Fed, 1967; Trustee, Assn for Preserv of VA Antiquities, 1967-69; Bd Mem, Boush-Waller-Tazewell House, Norfolk, VA, 1980-; r/Unitarian; hon/ Author, Var Articles on Hist, Elects & Nutrition Pub'd in Profl Periods in US & Gt Brit; Bronze Star Medal for Ser in China Campaign, WW II; Winner Competition, *Writers Digest*, 1974 & 1975; Nat Writers Clb, 1976; W/W in S & SW; The Blue Book; Men of Achmt; DIB; Other Biogl Listings.

TEAL, MELVIN FREDERICK oc/ Postal Police Officers Manager & Security Officer; b/Jan 21, 1934; h/6035 South Transit Road, Lockport, NY 14094; ba/Buffalo, NY; m/Dalefred A; c/Deborah Ann, Melvin Frederick, Jennie Lorraine; p/George Herbert and Jennie Louise Teal (dec); sp/James and Mabel Murray (dec); ed/Att'd Chaffee Jr Col, 1967-69; mil/USMC, 1953-56; pa/Security Ofcr in Charge & Mgr US Postal Police Ofcrs, US Postal Inspection Ser, 1975-; Protection Mgr, Montgomery Ward Co, 1970-75; Police Ofcr & Detective, Chino, CA Police Dept, 1966-70; Dpty Sheriff, LA Co, CA Sheriff's Dept, 1961-66; Police Ofcr, Detroit, MI Police Dept, 1956-61; Mem: Detroit Police Ofcrs Assn, 1956-61; Nat Assn of Postal Supvrs, 1977-; r/LDS; hon/Dean's Hon Roll, Chaffee Jr Col, 1967-69; Recip, Over 13 Commends for Meritorious Police Wk, 1956-70; W/W in W.

TEEPLE, EDWARD JR oc/Professor; b/Jan 23, 1951; h/1910 Overland Drive, Chapel Hill, NC 27514; ba/Chapel Hill, NC; m/Christine Ann Edelmann; c/ Luke, Erin; p/Mr and Mrs Edward J Teeple, Nutley, NJ; sp/Mr and Mrs Robert Edelmann, Mendham, NJ; ed/BS, Rutgers Univ, 1973; MD, Col of Med of NJ, 1977; Bd Eligible Anesth Exam, Univ of Miami Sch of Med, 1981; Intern, Overlook Hosp, Summit, NJ, 1977-78; Resident Anesth, Univ of Miami Sch of Med, Miami, FL, 1978-80; F'ship, Univ of NC Chapel Hill & NC Meml Hosp, 1980-81; pa/Asst Prof Anesth, Univ of NC-Charlotte; Assoc Dir, Anesth Pain Clin, Asst Prof Anesth 1981-, Univ of NC Sch of Med & NC Meml Hosp; Mem: Am Soc of Anesth; FL Soc of Anesth; Undersea Med Soc; NC Soc of Anesth; Intl Pain Soc; r/Cath; hon/ Author & Co-Author, Over 15 Articles Pub'd in Profl Med Jours incl'g: Anesth; Hosp Phys; Comprehensive Therapy; Others; Over 6 Presentations Presented at Var Profl Confs, Symps & Instns; Welhoffer Scholar 1969-73, Grad w High Hons 1977, Rutgers Univ; Chief Resident Anesth, Dept of Anesth, Univ of Miami Sch of Med, 1979-80; W/W.

TEETS, JOHN WILLIAM oc/Chairman & Executive; b/Sep 15, 1933; h/ 5303 Desert Park Lane, Scottsdale, AZ 85253; ba/Phoenix, AZ; m/Nancy; c/ Jerri, Valerie, Heidi, Suzanne; p/John W Teets Sr, Bull Shoals, AR; Maudie Teets, Elgin, IL; sp/Betty Yates, Myrtle Beach, SC; ed/Att'd Univ of IL; mil/AUS; pa/for Greyhound: Mgr of NY World's Fair Restaurants 1964, Pres Post House Opers & Horne's Enterprises 1965, Greyhound's Sers Grp of Cos 1980, Chm & CEO Armour & Co & Greyhound Food Mgmt Inc 1981, VChm 1980, CEO 1981-, & Chm 1982-, The Greyhound Corp; Pres, John R Thompson, 1968; 1968-76: Corp VPres, Canteen Corp; CEO, Bonanza Intl; Mem: Coun of 100; AZ St Univ Conf Bd; Bd of Govs, Coun for Nat Policy; Bd of Dirs, Grocery Mfrs Assn; Bd of Dirs, Getty Oil; Bd of Dirs, ConAgra; cp/VChm, NCCJ's 31st Annual Testimonial Dinner; Bd of Trustees, Intl Gold & Silver Plate Soc; Val Ldrship; Chm Steering Com, Christian Bus-man's Assn; r/Prot; hon/LLD, 1982; Foodser Operator of Yr, Intl Food Ser Mfrs Assn, 1980.

TELLER, EDWARD oc/Pysicist; b/Jan 15, 1908; ba/Hoover Institution, Stanford, CA 94305; Lawrence Livermore National Lab, PO Box 808 L—O, Livermore, CA 94550; m/Augusta Harkanyi (Mici); c/Paul, Susan Wendy; p/Max and Ilon (Deutsch) Teller (dec); ed/Att'd Karlsruhe Inst of Technol, Germany, 1926-28; Att'd Univ of Munich, Germany, 1928; PhD, Univ of Leipzig, Germany, 1930; pa/Sr Res Fellow Hoover Inst on War, Revolution & Peace, Stanford Univ, 1975-; Conslt & Assoc Dir Emeritus, Lawrence Livermore Nat Lab 1975-, Prof Emeritus 1975-, Prof 1970-75, Prof Physics-at-large 1960-70, Chm Dept Applied Sci Davis/Livermore 1963-66, Dir 1958-60 & Assoc Dir 1954-58 Lawrence Livermore Lab, Physics Prof 1953-60, Conslt Livermore Br Radiation Lab 1952-53, Univ of CA; Vis'g Prof, Arthur Spitzer Chair of Energy Mgmt, Pepperdine Univ, 1976-77; Asst Dir 1949-52, Physicist 1943-46, Los Alamos Sci Lab; Prof Physics 1946-52, Physicist 1942-43, Univ of Chgo; Physicist, Manhattan Engr Dist, 1942-46; Prof Physics, Columbia Univ, 1941-42; Prof Physics, George Wash Univ, 1935-1941; Lectr, Univ of London, 1934-35; Rockefeller Fellow (w Neils Bohr), Copenhagen, 1934; Res Assoc, Göttingen, 1931-33; Res Assoc, Leipzig, 1929-31; Mem: White House Sci Coun; Advy Bd, Fed Emer Mgmt Agy; Bd of Govs, Am Acad of Achmt; Conslt, Def Sci Bd Task Force; Panel Mem on Mil Res & Devel, Ctr for Strategic & Intl Studies; Fellow, Am Acad of Arts & Scis; Fellow, AAAS; BD of Govs, Am Friends of Tel Aviv Univ; Fellow, Am Nuclear Soc; Advy Bd, Ams for More Power Sources; Sr Mem, Intl Acad of Quantum Molecular Sci; Num Other Orgl Mbrships; hon/Author, Co-Author & Editor, of 12 Books Incl'g: Fusion, Volume I: Magnetic Confinement, 1981; Pursuit of Simplicity, 1980; Energy from Heaven & Earth, 1979; Nuclear Energy in the Devel'g World, 1977; Energy: A Plan for Action, 1975; The Miracle of Freedom, 1972; Gt Men of Physics, 1969; Constructive Uses of Nuclear Explosives, 1968; The Reluctant Revolutionary, 1964; The Legacy of Hiroshima, 1962; Our Nuclear Future, 1958; Structure of Matter, 1949; Num Other Articles Pub'd in Profl Jours; Recip, Num Hon Doct Degs: DSci, JD, PhD, DHL, DNSci, MD from Num Univs; Nat Medal of Sci, 1983; Am Acad of Achmt Gold Medal, 1982; Heritage Freedom Awd, 1982; ARCS Man of Yr, 1980; Am Col of Nuclear Med Gold Medal, 1980; A C Eringen Awd, Soc of Engrg Sci Inc, 1980; Semmelweiss Medal, 1977; Enric Fermi Awd, 1962; Thomas E White Awd, 1962; Am Acad of Achmt Gold Plate, 1961; Albert Einstein Awd, 1958; Joseph Priestly Meml, Dickinson Col, 1957; Harrison Medal, Am Ordnance Assn, 1955; Num Other Awds; W/W: in Am, in World; Dir of Dist'd Ams.

TEMIN, HOWARD M oc/Professor; b/ Dec 10, 1934; ba/450 North Randall, Madison, WI 53706; m/Rayla; c/Sarah, Miriam; ed/BA 1955, Hon DSci 1972, Swarthmore Co; PhD, CA Inst of Tech, 1959; Addit Study: NY Med Col, 1972; Univ of PA, 1976; Hahnemann Med Col, 1976; Lawrence Univ, 1976; Temple Univ, l1979; Med Col of WI, 1981; pa/ Prof Oncology 1969-, Alumni Res Foun Prof Cancer Res 1971-80, Am Cancer Soc Prof Viral Oncology & Cell Biol 1974-,

Harold P Rusch Prof Cancer Res 1980-, Steenbock Prof Biol Scis 1982, Prof Oncology McCardle Lab for Cancer Res 1982-, Univ of WI; Mem: Nat Acad of Scis; Am Acad of Arts & Scis; Am Soc Microbiol; Am Assn Cancer Res; Am Phil Soc; hon/Author, Over 170 Articles & Papers Pub'd in Profl Jours, 1953-; Lila Gruber Res Awd, Am Acad of Dermatology, 1981; Hon Mem, WI Acad of Scis, Arts & Lttrs, 1978; Ctl HS Phila Hall of Fame, 1976; Charlton Lectr, Tufts Univ Med Sch, 1976; Alumni Dist'd Ser Awd, CA Inst of Technol, 1976; Lucy Wortham James Awd in Basic Res, Soc of Surg Oncologists, 1976; Nobel Prize for Physiol, 1975; Albert Lasker Awd in Basic Med Res, 1974; Gairdner Foun Intl Awd, Toronto, 1974; G H A Clowes Lectrship Awd, Am Asn for Cancer Res, 1974; Dyer Lectr Awd, NIH, 1974; Mod Med Awd for Dist'd Achmt, 1973; Num Other Awds; Num W/W & Other Biogl Listings.

TEMPLIN, ETHELYN MERLE oc/ Nurse, Supervisor; b/Nov 2, 1928; h/1335 West 5th Street, Hastings, NE 68901; ba/ Grand Island, NE; m/William Samuel (dec); c/Samuel Ray, Daniel Caye (dec), Roger Lee; p/John Pearson and Odessa Merla (Hendrickson) Anderson, Hastings, NE; sp/William Henry and Elizabeth (Pankau) Templin (dec); ed/Att'd Hastings Col, 1947-48; RN, Mary Lanning Meml Hosp, 1950; BS Psychol, Kearney Col, 1976; Num Cont'g Ed Units; pa/Hd Nurse, Clin Instr, Hastings, NE, Regional Ctr, 1956-59; Staff Nurse & Supvr, VA Med Ctr, Grand Isl, NE, 1952-55; Hd Nurse, 1960-74; Staff Nurse Intensive Care, 1975-76; Staff Nurse & Supvr, 1976-; Nat Assn Orthopedic Nurses Assn; Assn Operating Room Nurses; Am Nurses Assn; Am Assn Urin Wom; cp/ Walk to Emmaus Pilgrimage Movement, 1983; Cert Reach to Recovery Vol Am Cancer Soc, 1974; NE Civil Defense Nurse, 1963-65; ARC; Mary Lanning Meml Hosp Alumnae Assn; Order En Star, Acacia Chapt #39; Former BSA Scout Instr for 1st Aid & Art; Recruiter, St John's Mil Sch, Salina, KS, 1976; Author Patient Tchg Booklets on Cancer & Epilepsy for Grand Isl VA, 1981; Yrly Presentation on Closed Circuit TV on Cancer, 1980-; hon/Cert of Recog, NE Nurses Assn Comm on Ed, 1976, 1978, 1980; Dist'd Ser Awd, 1977; W/W Am Wom.

TENNEN, LESLIE I oc/Attorney; b/ Aug 26, 1952; h/4717 East 2nd Street, Tucson, AZ 85711; ba/Tucson, AZ; p/ Edward and Elsie Tennen, Tucson, AZ; ed/BA 1973, JD 1976, Univ AZ; Att'd Hebrew Univ, Jerusalem, 1975; pa/Law Pract, Tucson, AZ, 1977-79; Ptner, Sterns & Tennen, Phoenix & Tucson, AZ, 1979-; Mem: St Bar of AZ, 1977; US Fed Dist Ct for Dist of AZ, 1979; Intl Inst of Space Law, 1978; AIAA, 1980; Aviation Space Writers Assn, 1980; Planetary Soc; Num Nat & Intl Lectrs in Intl Law & Aerospace Activs; cp/Exec Bd, Fedn of Aerospace Socs in Tucson; hon/Author & Co-Author, Over 12 Articles Pub'd in Profl Jours & Assn Proceedings Incl'g: Proceedings of Annual Colloquium on the Law of Outer Space; Highest Score, AZ Bar Exam, 1977; Judge Jessup Intl Moot Ct Competition, 1982 & 1983; W/W: in W, in Aviation & Aerospace.

TEODORU, CONSTANTIN VALERIU oc/Physician, Educator, Scientist; b/

Feb 14, 1915; h/86th St Jackson, Heights, NY 11372; ba/Same; m/Maria Mirella Ioanid; c/Nicolas-Dor, Dan-Eugene, Michael-Nicholas; p/Mihail and Viorica (Angelescu) Teodorus; ed/Intern & Resident, Brancovenesc Hosp, Bucharest, 1936-42; pa/Med Pract, Bucharest, 1939-48; Med Pract, Jackson Heights, NY, 1959-; Assoc Prof Physiol, Bucharest Univ, 1939-48; Hd Med Depts, ARC, Cath Welfare Conf, Rumanian Red Cross, Bucharest, 1946-48; Chief Physiol & Pharm Res Lab, Roussel Drug Co, Paris, France, 1949-52; Res Assoc, Charge Polio Proj, Mt Sinai Hosp, NYC, 1952-57; Hd Applied Physiol, Prin Investigator I, Albert Res Inst, Bklyn, 1957-64; Att'g Dept Med Chief, Long Term Med Care Div, Kingsbrook Med Ctr, Bklyn, 1964-71; Assoc Vis Phys, Kings Co Hosp, Bklyn, 1961-; Vis Phys, Assoc Dir Med, NY Univ Med Ctr & Goldwater Meml Hosp, NYC, 1972-76; Clin Assoc Prof Med, Downstate Med Ctr SUNY 1961-, & NY Univ 1974-; Mem: Am Physiol Soc; Am & NY Rheumatism Assns; Endocrine Soc; Soc Exptl Biol & Med; Gerontological Soc; Reticulo Endothelial Soc; AAAS; NY Acad Scis; Harvey Soc; hon/Author, Over 67 Papers & Sci Presentations Pub'd in Am & Fgn Intl Sci & Med Jours; Recip of Ribbon for Outstg Sers, ARC, 1947; Medal, Rumanian Red Cross, 1946; Diplomate, Bd of Internal Med Rumania; Fellow, ACP; NY Acad of Med; W/W in E.

TERRANOVA, GEORGE JOHN oc/Physician; b/Mar 1, 1943; h/Mine Hill road, West Redding, CT 06896; ba/Danbury, CT; m/Bianca Josephine Terranova; c/Lucas, Leah; p/Vincent Terranova, Flushing, LI, NY; sp/Fausto Piscionieri, Rome, Italy; ed/BS, Marquette Univ, 1965; MD, Univ of Rome, Italy, 1970; mil/USAF, Chief of Aeromed Sers, 1973-75, Maj; pa/Chm 1978-, VChm 1976-78, Full-time Emer Phys 1975-, Emer/Primary Care Dept, Danbury Hosp, Danbury, CT; Chief Emer Sers, White Co Commun Hosp, Monticello, IN, 1974-75; Full-time Emer Room Phys, Leonard Hosp, Troy, NJ, 1973-; Phys (Fam Pract) Coeyman's Med Ctr, Coeyman, NY, 1971-73; Att'g Phys, S End Commun Hlth Ctr, Albany, NY, 1972-73; Mem: Am Acad of Fam Phys, 1973-; Am Col of Emer Phys, 1973; Bd of Dirs 1980-, Secy 1979-, CT Chapt, Am Col of Emer Phys; Bd of Dirs, MWn CT Coun on Alcoholism; Bd of Dirs, Reg V, Emer Med Sers Coun; VPres Med Advy Bd, Reg V, Emer Med Sers Coun; Pres, CT Med Advy Bd, 1980-; Med Dir & Prog Dir, Paramedic Prog at Danbury Hosp; cp/Mem Var Danbury Hosp Coms; Ad Hoc Com on Affirmative Action; Full Att'g Danbury Hosp Med Staff; Am Heart Assn Task Force on ACLS; Danbury Coalition Agnst Rape; r/Cath; hon/Author of Var Articles Pub'd in Profl Med Jours & Pubs; Cert'd, Am Bd of Fam Pract, 1978-; Cert'd, Am Bd of Emer Med, 1981-; W/W in E; Men of Achmt.

TERRELL, ARA J'NEVELYN oc/Psychological Counselor, Radio Personality; b/Jan 5, 1909; h/510 South Burnside Avenue, MH, Los Angeles, CA 90036; ba/LA, CA; m/James A; c/James A Jr, Trisch (T) Diaz; p/James and Mabel Williamson (dec); sp/W H and Mary F Terrell (dec); ed/Att'd Baylor Univ; BS, Sue Ross Col, 1931; Tchr, Monahans, Iraan, Sheffield & Iredell, TX, 1933-41;

Lectr on Adult Ed, World Lit, Psych, Probs of Aging, LA Schs, 1948-68; "Coincidence Lady," Radio Prog, 1983; Fdr, The Mental Shop Inc; Fdr, The Book Reporters; cp/Friday Morning Clb, LA, 1950's; BPW Clb, 1983; Quota Clb, 1983; Self-help Presentations at Prisons; Others; r/Metaphysical Prot; hon/Author, *Is There A Law of Coincidence?*; *Your Three Bodies*; Playwright, *Suddenly Tomorrow*; Nom'd for Staff Position w Peace Corp by Lyndon B Johnson, 1963; Spkr, at Nat Assn of Tchrs, Wash DC, 1941; W/W; Hist Soc of CA.

TERRY, DAVID RAY oc/Higher Education Administration; b/Jun 28, 1935; h/5432 South 800 East, South Ogden, UT 84405; ba/Salt Lake City, UT; m/Joyce Hansen; c/Aleesa Solberg, David II, Dru; p/Elvin and Geraldine Larson Terry, Mack's Inn, ID; sp/Gy and Vendora Hansen, Idaho Falls, ID; ed/BS 1958, MS 1962, Brigham Yg Univ; PhD, Univ of IL, 1973; pa/Asst Commr, UT Sys of Higher Ed, 1981-; Industl Ed Res, 1977-81; Dean Allied Hlth, 1973-77; Dental Ed Res, 1971-73; Dept Chm 1968-70; Assoc Prof Microbiol 1965-70; Germ Warfare Res, 1962-65; Med Technol & Radiologic Technol, 1965-68; Mem: Num Coms, Am, Voc Assn; Num Coms, Am Soc for Allied Hlth Professions; cp/Chm, Neighborhood Commun Coun, 5 Yrs; BSA, 15 Yrs; Lay Bisop, 4 Yrs; r/Mormon; hon/Author, *Changing the Role of Voc Tchr Ed*, 1973; *Dental Care Tasks Perf'd by Dental Auxs*, 1973; Num Other Articles & Res Reports Pub'd in Profl Jours & Pubs; Nom, Outstg Citizen of S Ogden, 3 Yrs; Nom, Outstg Citizen of UT, 1983; W/W in W.

TESK, JOHN ALOYSIUS oc/Scientist, Engineer, Manager; b/Oct 19, 1934; h/13446 Pond Field Court, Highland, MD 20777; ba/Gaithersburg, MD; m/Regina Budzyn; c/John A W; p/Mrs Theresa V Tesk, Chgo, IL; sp/William Budzyn, Chgo, IL; ed/BS 1957, MS 1960, PhD 1963; NWn Univ; pa/Asst Prof, Univ of IL-Chgo, 1964-67; Conslt 1964-67, Asst Metallurgist 1967-69, Argonne Nat Lab; Asst Mgr Res & Devel 1969-70, Dir Res & Devel 1970-79, Dental Div Mowmedica Inc; Dir Ed Sers, Inst of Gas Technol, 1977-78; Gen Phy Sci 1978-, Grp Ldr 1983-, Dental & Med Mats, Nat Bur of Standards; Mem: Secy-Treas 1982-83, VPres 1983-84, Pres 1984-85, Wash Sect, AADR; Student Affairs Chm Chgo Chapt 1964-65, Memm 1955-, Am Soc for Metals; Others; Chm, ANSC, MD, 1981-; cp/Ch Bldg Com, 1973-75; Cub Scout Com Chm, 1982-83; Chm, USA TAG TC 106, 1981-; Others; r/Rom Cath; hon/Author, Num Articles Pub'd in Profl Jours & Chapts in Dental Textbooks; Holder of US Patents on Dental Mats; Sigma Xi, 1960; Granger Awd for Outstg Tchr, Univ of IL-Chgo 1965; W/W in MW; Am Men & Wom of Sci.

TETLIE, HAROLD M oc/Pastor and Missionary; b/Aug 24, 1926; h/Box 1607 Alice, TX 78332-1607; ba/Same; p/Harold B and Anne M Tetlie (dec); ed/BS, St Olaf Col, 1951; MBA, Univ of Denver, 1956; Doct Study, Cornell Univ, 1960-61; ThB, Luther Sem, 1965; mil/WW II, 1945-46, Philippine Isls; pa/HS Tchr, in MT, 1951-57; Instr, Pacific Luth Univ, Tacoma, WA, 1957-59; Pastor, Missionary, Christ the King Ch, Alice, TX, 1965-; Mem: Ministerial Alliance; Life Mem,

NEA; cp/JACS Coor, Alice, TX; Secy, Proj Area Com Urban Renewal; r/Luth Cath; Grad cum laude, St Olaf Col, 1951; Ser to Mankind Awd, Sertoma Clb of Corpus Christi; Personalities of S.

THAYER, EDNA I oc/Director of Nurses; b/Jul 25, 1923; h/7819 Ponce Avenue, Canoga Park, CA 91304; ba/Panorama City, CA; m/Charles A; c/Linda Louise; p/Charles E and Aude I (Messenger) Trask (both dec); ed/BSN, Elliot Commun Hosp Sch of Nsg, 1941-44; Reg'd Nurse; MA Nsg, Univ of CA-LA, 1953; mil/US Army Nurse Corps, 1944-45; pa/Supvr, Meriden CT Hosp, 1950; Supvr, Inst of Living, Hartford, CT, 1954-59; Tchr Ednly Handicapped Chd, Brockton Sch, 1972-78; Dir of Nurses, Canoga Terrace, Canoga Park, CA, 1979-80; Dir of Nurses, Corbin Hosp, Reseda, CA, 1981-82; Dir of Nurses, Sun Air Hosp, Panorama City, CA, 1982-; Mem: CA Nurses Assn; Nat Leag of Nsg Ed; ANA; cp/Am Legion; CA Cong PTA; BPW Clb; Emblem Clb; r/Bapt; hon/Golden Apple Awd, LA Unified Sch Dist; Lifetime Ser Awd, CA PTA; W/W of Am Wom.

THEINER, ERIC CHARLES oc/Clinical Psychologist; b/Sep 27, 1935; h/61 Belleair Drive, East Memphis, TN 38104; ba/Memphis, TN; m/Margaret Ann; c/Cynthia Gabrielle, Eric Post; p/Theresa Maria Theiner, Memphis, TN; sp/Mr and Mrs, M A Guill, McKenzie, TN; ed/BS, Manhattan Col, 1957; MA Syracuse Univ, 1960; PhD, Univ of Houston, 1966; mil/AF, 1960-69, USAR, 1973; pa/VAMC/Pvt Pract, 1972-; Mgr Assessment Sers, ITT, 1971-72; Sr Conslt, Ed N Hay, l969-70; Chief Psychol, Malcolm Grow USAF Hosp, 1968-69; Psychol, USAF, 1960-68; Mem: Pres, TN Psychol Assn, 1980-81; Pres, Biofeedback Assn of TN, 1980-81; Am Psychol Assn; Others; cp/BSA; BST; Others; Author, Over 21 Articles, 15 Papers & 20 Reviews Pub'd in Profl Jours; r/Rom Cath; hon/W/W: in SE, in Frontier of Sci.

THEROUX, MARJORIE E oc/Substitute Public School Teacher; b/Mar 7, 1918; h/8 Belleview Boulevard #102, Belleair, FL 33516; m/Paul Richard; c/David Jon, Gary Michael, Linda Sue; p/Mr and Mrs John D Withrow (dec); sp/Frank R Theroux (dec); Mrs Frank R Theroux, Clearwater, FL; ed/BS, Ctl MI Univ, 1939; Att'd Nat Col of Ed, Evanston, IL, 1940· pa/Kgn, Art & Elem Sch Tchr, MI, OH, NY, IL, CT, CA, FL, 1939-; Mem: Corres'g Secy & VPres-elect Jackson MI 1945-47, Fdr Royal Oak MI 1948-49, Fdr Westfield NJ 1954-59, Treas Westchester NY 1959-64, w Beta Sigma Phi; AAUW, 1973-75; cp/Bay City, MI Dow Chorus, 1943-45; Northsore, IL Harmonizers, 1976-81; Suncoast Singers, FL, 1982; Fed Wom's Clb, Var Sts, 1954-; Commonwlth Clb of CA, 1974-76; Eagle Forum, 1972-; Pro-Fam Forum, 1975-; Pro-Am 1973-76; Repub Wom's Clb, 1973-; Christian Wom's Clb, 1960-73; IL Chm 1972-73, CA Chm 1973-76, Fam Preserv; r/Bapt; hon/Phyllis Schlafly Eagle Awd, 1974; Intl Hon Cits, Beta Sigma Phi, 1955; Girl of Yr Awd, Zeta Nu Chapt (NY), Beta Sigma Phi, 1964; Cert of Awd for Conserv Res 1981 & Patriotic Efforts Cert 1982, Suncoast Conserv Union, FL.

THIBODEAU, DIANE (DEE) VIRGAL oc/Sales Director; b/Apr 6, 1943; h/2504 Cherrywood Road, Minnetonka,

MN 55343; ba/Bloomington, MN; m/ James; c/Troy, Chad, Nicole; p/Adeline Stroschein, Mpls, MN; sp/Agnes Thibodeau, Trenton, NJ; ed/BS, 1965; Grad Sch, 1982-83; pa/Tchr, Richfield Dist, 1965-67; Tchr, Robbinsdale Dist, 1967-82; Gen Mgr, Computer Lrng Ctr, 1982-83; Dir of Corp Sales, Schaak Elects, 1983-; Mem: Pres Wayzata Chapt Edrs of Gifted & Talented, 1981-82; Chp of Chapt Devel & Maintenance, MN Coun Edrs of Gifted & Talented; Wom in Computing; AAUW; MN Wom's Netwk; Nat Fedn of Tchrs; MN Fedn of Tchrs; Others; cp/Chief Negotiater, Robbinsdale Resv Tchrs, 1980-82; Omnibus Coor, Wayzata Sch Sys, 1981-82; Chp Ways & Means, Mpls Chd's Hosp, 1979-80; Fdr, Summ Pre-sch Bible Sch, St Joseph's Parish, 1975-77; NOW; Others; r/Rom Cath; W/W of Am Wom.

THOMAS, BARBARA S oc/US Securities & Exchange Commissioner; b/Dec 28, 1946; h/2500 Virginia Avenue NW, Wash DC 20037; ba/Washington, DC; m/ Allen L; c/Allen L Jr; p/Jules Singer (dec); Marcia Singer, Old Westbury, NY; ed/ BA, Univ of PA, 1966; JD, NY Univ, 1969; pa/Assoc w Law Firm, Paul, Weiss, Rifkind, Wharton & Garrison, NYC, 1969-73; Assoc w Law Firm, Kaye, Scholer, Fierman, Hayes & Handler, NYC,1973-77; Ptner in Law Firm, Kaye, Scholer, Fierman, Hayes & Handler, NYC, 1978-80; Commr, US Securities & Exchange Comm, 1980-; Mem: Ad Hoc Task Force on Intl Aspects of US Law, ABA; Intl Bar Assn; Com on Fed Regulation of Securities, ABA; NY St Bar Assn; Assn of Bar of City of NY; cp/Coun on Fgn Relats; Ec Clb of NY; Bd of Overseers, Wharton Sch of Fin; Trustee, Pace Univ; Dir, Inst for E-W Security Studies; Advy Coun, Wom's Ec Roundtable; Nat Advy Bd, The Am Univ; Fin Wom's Assn of NY; Trustee, Yth for Understanding; Advy Com, Nat Mus of Wom's Art; Trustee, Wash Opera; Dir, NY Univ Law Alumni Assn; Trustee, Univ of PA Alumni Assn of NYC; Univ of PA Alumni Coun on Admission; hon/ Author, Over 18 Articles Pub'd in Profl Jours & Newspapers; Named one of WETA-FM's Wom of Achmt, 1983; Outstg Ser in Govt Awd, Fin Mktg Coun of Gtr Wash, 1982; Am Jurisprudence Prizes for Excell 1976-69, Jefferson Davis Prize in Public Law 1969, John Norton Pomeroy Scholar 1968-69, Other Hons, NY Univ Sch of Law; W/W: in Am, in Am Law, in Am Politics, in Fin & Indust, of Wom; Outstg Yg Wom of Am.

THOMAS, FAYE EVELYN J oc/Intermediate Elementary Teacher; b/Aug 3, 1933; h/19353 East Bagley Road, Middleburg Heights, OH 44130; ba/Berea, OH; m/Archie Taylor (dec); p/Felton and Altee Johnson, Cullen, LA; sp/Hose and Ola Thomas, Cullen, LA; ed/AS Ba Univ, 1954; MSE, Univ of Ctl AR, l1971; MSE, Cleveland St Univ, 1979; Tchr, Cullen Elem Sch, Cullen, LA, 1957; Eng & Social Studies Tchr, Brown HS, Springhill, LA, 1952-70; Eng Tchr, Upward Bound Prog, Grambling St Univ, 1968; Eng Tchr, Springhill HS, Webster Parish Sch Bd, 1970; Elem Intermediate Tchr, Riveredge Elem Sch, Berea City Sch Dist, OH, 1971-; Mem: NEA; OH Ed Assn; Berea Ed Assn; NE OH Tchrs Assn for Supvn & Curric Devel; Charles Brown Soc Org; Berea Employees Sch Credit Union; Black Caucus, NEA; cp/People U to Save

Humanity; OH Motorists Assn; r/Bapt; hon/Intl Paper Foun Grant, Tuskegee Inst, Sum 1958 & 1960; NDEA Grant, Ctl MI Univ, Sum 1965; EPDA Grant in Early Childhood Ed, Univ of Ctl AR, 1970-71; W/W in MW; Biogl Roll of Hon.

THOMAS, JERRY WAYNE oc/Elementary School Principal; b/Jan 19, 1950; h/PO Box 127 Wingate, NC 28174; ba/ Same; m/Ann Lowery; c/Allison Leigh, Trenton Patrick; p/Hoyle J and Blake G Thomas, Marshville, NC; sp/Tom and Mildred Lowery, Wingate, NC; ed/AA Wingate Jr Col, 1970; BS, Appalachian st Univ, 1972; MEd 1977, Eds 1981, Winthrop Col; mil/AUS, 1972-74; pa/Tchr, Forest Hills HS, Union Co Bd of Ed, 1974-78; Prin Wingate Elem Sch, Union Co Bd of Ed, 1978-; Mem: Treas 1979, Monroe-Union Co Prins Assn, 1978-; Nat Assn Elem Sch Prins, 1982-; cp/Dir, Wingate Com Rec 1978-; Mbrship Chm, Pack Com Cub Scouts, BSA, 1980-; Plan Implementation Com, So Piedmont Hlth Sys Agy, 1980-; Treas, Union Co Babe Ruth Assn, 1979-; Secy 1982, Mem 1974-, Wingate JC's; r/Bapt; hon/Outstg Yg Edr, Wingate JCs, 1977; Outstg Yg Men of Am; W/W in S & SW; Personalities of S.

THOMAS, JOHN SULLIVAN JR oc/ Optometrist; b/Jun 8, 1925; h/416 Lee Street, Thomson, GA 30824; ba/Thomson, GA; m/Billie McMinn; c/David Moore; p/John Sullivan Thomas and Nell Moore Griffin (dec); sp/Sallie McMinn (dec); ed/DO, N Ga Col, 1944; OD, So Col of Optom, 1949; mil/USMC, 1944-46; pa/Optometrist, 1949-; Past Pres 10th Dist, Trustee, Treas, VPres, Pres, GA Optom Assn; Am Optom Assn; cp/Fdr, GA Motorist Visual Screening; Nat Rifle Assn; Pres, Kiwanis; Bd of Dirs, Bd of Trade; Charter Mem, 10-60's (IND Dev); Chm, McDuffie Co Mtl Hlth; Chm, McDuffie Co Red Cross; Chm Bd of Deacons, 1st Bapt Ch (3 Terms); Fdr & 1st pres, Thomson Archery Clb; Charter Mem, Bd of Dirs, VPres, 1st Fed Savs & Loan; VFW; Omega Delta; Beta Sigma Kappa; Sigma Alpha Sigma; r/Bapt; hon/ Optom of Yr, GA Optom Assn, 1960; Silver Anniv Awd, No Col of Optom, Chgo, IL, 1960; Recip, Purple Heart at Iwo Jima, 1946; W/W in S & SW.

THOMAS, STEPHEN PENN oc/Investment Banker, Director; b/May 2, 1940; h/8600 Elliston Drive, Wyndmoor, PA 19118; ba/Flourtown, PA; m/Mary Ann MacDonald; c/Ryan, Kiernan, Clarke; p/ Francis Thomas, Brielle, NJ; sp/W F MacDonald, Phila, PA; ed/BSBA, Georgetown Univ, 1969; mil/USMC, 1961-67, Pilot & Test Pilot; pa/Prin, Wyndmoor Assocs Ltd, 1983-; Chm of Bd, Cadec Sys Inc, 1983-; Dir, Doron Enterprises Inc, 1983-; Exec VPres, Fahmestock & Co, 1977-83; Pres, Rylge Corp, 1971-77; Asst Secy, 1st Wash Sec Corp, 1971; Asst to Mng Ptner, Ferris & Co, 1969-71; cp/ Broadstreet Clb NYC; Manasquam River Yacht Clb; Local Com, Ducks Unltd; hon/ Air Medal Awd, 6 Combat Stars, USMC; W/W in Bus & Fin.

THOMPSON, DAMON LEON oc/ Professor; b/May 14, 1930; h/638 4th Avenue, Williamsport, PA 17701; ba/ Williamsport, PA; m/Jean; p/Benjamin Franklin Thompson and Bertha May Kuntzman (dec); ed/Att'd Sinclair Col, 1953-54; BFA 1954-57, Postgrad Study 1958-59, OH St Univ; Att'd The Dayton Art Inst, 1958; MFA, Univ of IA, 1959-61;

Att'd Bucknell Univ, l1969; mil/AUS, Signal Corps, 497th Signal Photo Ser; Ft Monmouth, NJ & Karlsruhe, Kaiserslautern, Germany, 1951-53; pa/Clk-typist, Soundscriber, Wright-Patterson, AFB, 1949-51 & 1953-55; Asst Libn, OH St Univ, 1958-59; Comml Artist, 1958; Eng Instr, Marshal Univ, 1961-63; Eng & Jour Instr, Dakota St Col, 1963-64; Eng Instr, Slippery Rock St Col, 1964-67; Asst Prof Eng 1967-68, Prof Eng, Creat Writing, Am Art 1978-, Wmsport Area Commun Col, PA; Mem: NEA, 1970-; Wmsport Area Commun Col Ed Assn, 1968-; cp/ Jacques Cousteau Soc; Friends of J V Brown Lib, Wmsport, PA; Am Film Inst; The Smithsonian Instn; hon/Author of Num Short Stories, Poems, Novel Segment, Book Reviews incl'g: "Of Grandmother"; "Spring Comes"; "Autumn"; "Remembering the Wkshop"; "To Praise the Buzzard"; "Of Grinny"; "On the Joys of Preparing Sassafras Tea"; *Remembrance Is A Rapturous River*; "Of the Boy & Of Music"; "Of Fergy"; Intl Platform Assn, 1982; Medalist Awd, Columbia Univ as Advr for Col Lit Mag, Wmsport Area Commun Col, 1972; Lit Fellow 1960-61, Writing S'ship 1960, Univ of IA; 1st Prize for Short Story, Nat Soc Arts & Lttrs, Columbus, OH Br, 1959; Student Art Exhibn, 1956; HS Eng S'ship Test, 1947; HS Hist S'ship Test, 1946; Listed in *Sylvester Thompson, OH Pioneers & Descendents*; W/W: in E, in Am, of Intells; Men of Achmt; Commun Ldrs of Am; Num Other Biogl Listings.

THOMPSON, DAVID EUGENE oc/ Data Processing Executive; b/Dev 10, 1945; h/7508 West 98th Terrace, Overland Park, KS 66212; ba/Kansas City, MO; c/Michael David, Jonathan Paul, Daniel Ethan; p/Mauric E Thompson (dec); Charlotte Ruth Harrington Thompson, Phoenix, AZ; ed/BS 1968, Postgrad Study 1969, NWn Univ; Postgrad Study, Univ of MI, l1970-71; MBA, Rockhurst Col, 1982; pa/Programmer, Ford Motor Co, Chgo, IL, 1968-69; Fin Analyst, Dearborn, MI, 1969-72; Dat Processing Mgr, Norfolk, VA, 1972-77; Data Processing Exec, Kansas City, MO, 1978-; Mem: Mem 1982-, Bd of Dirs 1983-, Data Processsing Mgmt Assn; cp/Mem 1973-77, Treas 1975-76, Pres 1977, Hon Life Patron 1977, VA Bch (VA) Civic Chorus; Singles Min Mem 1978-, Treas 1981-82, CoChm 1982-83, Village Presb Ch, Prairie Village, KD; r/Presb; hon/W/ W in Fin & Indust.

THOMPSON, DONNIS HAZEL oc/ State Superintendent of Education; ba/ PO Box 2360, Honolulu, HI 96804; p/John William and Katherine Redmond Thompson (dec); ed/BS 1955, MS 1959, George Wms Col; DEd, Univ of No CO, 1967; pa/Prog Dir, Shiel House Cath Yth Org, Chgo, 1959-61; Chp Dept of PE, Hyde Pk HS, Chgo, 1956-61; Prof Ed & Asst Dir of Intercol Aths, Dir of Wom's Aths, Univ of HI, 1961-82; Supt of Ed, St of HI, 1982-; Mem: Bd of Dirs, US Coun Sports Com of Univ World Games, 1979-81; Admr, 1979 World Games, Mexico City; Pres 1977, Chp Var Coms, Assn of Intercol Aths for Wom; Chp SW Dist, Nat Assn of Girl's & Wom's Sports, Am Assn for Hlth, PE & Rec, 1975-76; Bd of Dirs, HI Public Broadcasting Auth; Advr, Num Coms & Couns, as Ex-officio Supt of Ed; Num Others; cp/Honolulu C of C; Fdr, Kaneohe Road Runners, 1970-73; HI St Org'g Com, Intl Wom's

Yr Conf; HI St Civil Rts Bd of Commrs; Bd of Dirs, Boys Clbs of Honolulu; Bd of Dirs, Honolulu Ballet; hon/Author, *Activs Handbook*, 1973; *Mod Track & Field for Girls & Wom*, 1971; *Wom's Track & Field*, 1969; Over 20 Articles Pub'd in Profl Jours incl'g: *Res Qtly*; *Wom's Sports*; *CAPHER Jour*; Others; Hon Fellow Awd, Nat Assn of Girls & Wom in Sports, 1981; Schuman Awd, for Contbns to Amateur Aths in St of HI, 1981; Delta Kappa Gamma; Female Edr of Yr Awd, Univ of No CO Alumni Assn, 1976; Spec Resolution Commend, for Univ of HI Wom's Ath Prog, 1976; Dist'd Ser Awd, HI St Chapt, Am Assn of Hth, PE & Rec, 1974; Dist'd Ser Awd, HI Ath Union, 1962; Cert of Ldrship, US Volleyball Assn; Others.

THOMPSON, EDWARD THOR-WALD oc/Editor-in-Chief; b/Feb 13, 1928; h/Guard Hill Road, Bedford, NY 10506; ba/Pleasantville, NY; m/Susan Jacobson; c/Edward T III, Anne B, Evan K, David S, Julie H; p/Edward K Thompson, Mahupac, NY; sp/Mrs Allan Jacobson, Washington, NJ; ed/SB, MA Inst of Technol, 1949; mil/USNR, 1950-60; pa/Mobil Oil Co, Beaumont, TX; Assoc Editor, *Chem Engrg Mag*, NYC, 1952-55; Mng Editor, *Chem Wk Mag*, NYC, 1955-56; Assoc Editor, *Fortune Mag*, 1956-60; Asst Mng Editor 1960-73, Mng Editor 1973-76, Editor-in-Chief & Exec Com 1976-, *Rdr's Digest*, Pleasantville, NY; Dir, *Rdr's Digest*, Assn; Trustee, *Rdrs's Digest* Foun; Mem: Am Soc Mag Editors; cp/Coun on Fgn Relats; Nat Bd of Trustees, Boys Clbs of Am; Mem of Corp, Chm Linguistics & Phil Vis'g Com, MA Inst of Technol; Com on Ed, Hudson Inst; Pension Com, Boys Clbs of Am Pension Trust; hon/Recip Golden Plate AWd, Am Acad of Achmt, 1977; W/W in Am.

THOMPSON, ERNESTINE LAVAN oc/Educational Consultant; b/Apr 30, 1929; h/6603 Ashland Drive, Austin, TX 78723; ba/Austin, TX; m/William M (dec); p/John Lavan (dec); Essie Lee Scott Lavan, Milano, TX; ed/BA, Samuel Houston Col, 1950; MA, Univ of MI, 1976; pa/Prog Dir, Temple USO, Temple, TX, 951-53; Case Wkr, MI Dept of Social Sers, Battle Creek, MI, 1953-55; Tchr, Pennfield Schs, Battle Creek, MI, 1959-70; Dir of Head Start, Calhoun Co, Intermediate Sch Dist, Marshall, MI, 1967-68; Cnslr, Wk Study Coor/Admr, Calhoun Area Voc Ctr, Battle Creek, MI, 1970-77; Conslt, TX Ed Agy, 1977-; Mem: Secy, Assn Retarded Chd, 1972-74; Manpower Advy Coun, Calhoun Co Bd Commrs, Marshall, MI, 1974; Chm Advy Bd, Huston-Tillotson Col Parent-Fam Life Ctr, Austin, 1979-; AAUS; Alpha Delta Kappa; cp/Dem; r/Bapt; hon/Pubs in Var Newwlttrs; Com Mem, City of Austin's Budget, 1981-82; W/W of Am Wom.

THOMPSON, JUDI oc/Executive Editor at Inst for Polynesian Studies; b/Feb 28, 1938; h/512 Oneawa Street, Kailua, HI 96734; ba/Laie, HI; c/Terri Anne, David Ross, Rebecca Jean, Michael Jai; p/Mrs William P (Jean) Blackmores, Kailua, HI; ed/BAE, Univ of FL, 1959; MA, Univ of HI, 1971; pa/Tchr, Le Jardin d'Enfants, 1968-69; Artist, Honolulu, 1968-72; Tchr, Yoga Col of India, Honolulu & SF, 1971-73; Tchr, Gateway Montessori, SF, 1972-73; Tchr Dept of Ed, Honolulu, 1975-80; Fdr, Dept of Ed Prog for Runaways, Hale Kipa, Honolulu, 1980; Assoc Editor 1980-81, Exec Editor 1981-, Inst for Polynesian Studies, Brigham Yg

Univ-HI Campus; Mem: Womin Scholarly Pub'g; SRF; Kappa Delta; Honolulu Acad of Art; cp/Smithsonian Soc; Ursenke Foun; Cousteau Soc; Honolulu Symph; r/Epis; hon/Author, *Hlthy Pregnancy the Yoga Way*, 1977; Co-Author, *Polynesian Canoes & Navigation*; 1980; Illustr, *Honolulu Zoo Riddles*; 1974; Illustr & Cover Designs for: *Two Tahitian Villages*; *Anuta*; *Brass Bands in the Pacific*; Editor, *Firehouse Ghost Tales of HI*; *Menehune Folktales*; Photog, Other Pubs; W/W: of Wom, in Oceana.

THOMPSON, LAURENCE C oc/Professor; b/Mar 11, 1926; h/959 Koae Street, Honolulu, HI 96816; ba/Honolulu, HI; m/Maranell L Terry; ed/AB, Middlebury Col, 1949; MA 1950, PhD 1954, Yale Univ Grad Sch; mil/AUS, Pvt to T/Sgt, 1944-46; USAR, Capt, Mil Intell, 1946-64; pa/Asst Instr Vietnamese, Yale Univ, 1953-54; Asst Dean, US Army Lang Sch (Def Lang Inst, 1954-56; Eng Instr 1957-59, Supvr Eng for Fgn Students 1958-59, Asst Prof Dept Far En & Slavic Langs & Lit 1959-62; Assoc Prof 1962-66, Supvr Vietnamese Lang Prog 1960-66, Chm Interdept Com on Linguistics 1960-61, Univ of WA, Seattle, WA; Prof Dept Linguistics, Univ of HI-Manoa, 1966-; Field Res, Amerindian Langs of Pacific NW, NSF, 1957-; Prin Investigator, Dics of NW Amerindian Langs, NSF & Nat Endowment for Humanities, 1974-; Chm Bd of Trustees, Univ of WA Archives, 1971-; Edit Bd Mem, *Intl Jour of Am Linguistics*, 1982-; Num Consltg Positions; Other Profl Activs: Mem: Linguistic Soc of Am; Am Oriental Soc; Intl Linguistic Circle; Am Anthropological Assn; Am Folklore Soc; Soc for Study of Indigenous Langs of the Americas; AAUP; hon/Author & Co-Author, Num Articles Pub'd in Profl Jours, Books & Other Pubs on Vietnamese Lang, Amerindian Langs & Linguistics.

THOMPSON, MARGARET DRODY oc/Businesswoman, Writer and Publisher; b/Apr 21, 1931; h/4528 Wyndale Avenue Southwest, Roanoke, VA 24018; ba/Roanoke, VA; m/K Reed; c/Larry Stephen, Fred Lamar; p/Harold Orson Drody, Atlanta, GA; Bernice Alice Floyd (dec); sp/Howard Thompson (dec); LaRue Head Thompson, Claxton, GA; ed/BMus Ed, Radford Col, 1970; Pvt Secy to SE Dist Sale Mgr, CF&I, Wickwire Spencer Steel, Atlanta, GA, 1950-54; Music Instr & Dir, Bedford Co, VA, 1970-71; Music Instr & Choral Dir, Roanoke Co, VA, 1971-80; Music Instr, VA Music Camp, Masanetta Springs, VA, 1972 & 1973; Fdr, Editor & Pubr, *Fam Assn Newslttr*, 1980-; Feature Writer, *Salem Times Register*, 1981-; Owner & Agt, Personally Yours Tours, 1982-; Mem: Vis'g Com, So Assn of Sch Accreditation for Music, VA; Mu Phi Epsilon; Kappa Delta Pi; cp/Fdr, Pres 1982, Clan MacIvor Soc of Am; 3rd VPres, Roanoke Chapt, UDC, 1982; Dir, Chd of Confederacy, 1982; Rebecca Motte Chapt, DAR, 1982; Nat Soc Colonial Dames XVII Cent; Huguenot Soc of SC; Dir, VPres, Recording Secy, Dir of Concert Series, Thursday Morning Music Clb of Roanoke, VA, 1959-63; Voter's Ser Chm, Leag of Wom Voters, 1959; Den Mother & Boy Scout Merit Badge Cnslr, 1956-68; Soloist, Green Meml Meth Ch, 1957-63; r/Disciples of Christ, Peachtree Christian Ch; hon/Author & Editor of Books: *Fam Assn Newsltr*; *Elizabeth Jane Lanier, Her Ancestors from Circa 1540, & Descendants to 1982*;

Rhythm & Rhym & the Sea; *My 1st Music Notebook*; *A Singing Primer for the Beginning Choral Student*; Num Newspaper Articles; Citizen Mother, Leag of Wom Voters, 1962; Guest Editor, *Roanoke World News*, 1962; Awd of Merit, SEn Conf of IEEE, 1979; Awd of Recog for Outstg Ser, Roanoke Co Ed Assn, 1980-81; Other Hons; Personalities of S.

THOMPSON, OPAL T oc/Nurse; b/May 27, 1928; h/1560 Litina Drive, Alamo, CA 94507; m/T Theodore; c/Stephanie Dawn, Kelly Lyn, Theron Treadway; p/Mrs Lena Treadway, Spindale, NC; sp/Mrs Theron Thompson, VA Bch, VA; ed/Dip, SC Bapt Hosp; AA, Univ of SC-Aiken, 1973-75; BSn 1976, MSN 1977, Med Col of GA; pa/Pvt Duty Nsg, Ft Jackson Base Hosp, 1949-50; Staff Nurse, Civil Ser, 1950-53; Nurse, Savannah River Plant, E I Dupont, Aiken, SC, 1953-60; Nurse, Univ Hosp, Augusta, GA, 1975-76; Instr, SC Col of Nsg, 1977-78; Instr, Univ of SC Div of Nsg, Aiken, SC, 1979-83; Dir Nsg, Blair House Inc, Augusta, GA, 1981-82; cp/Chancel Choir Mem, 1962-82, Grace U Meth Ch; Pres, Carolina Hosp Clb, 1962; Secy, N Augusta, SC Wom's Clb, 1963; Newcomers Clb; N Augusta Commun Choral, 1981-82; r/Meth; hon/W/W of Am Wom.

THORNBURG, FREDRIC EARL oc/Vocational Education Director; b/Dec 20, 1933; h/PO Box 442 Somerville, TN 38068; ba/Somerville, TN; m/Colleen Marie; c/Wade C, Fredric W, Emmett J, Cole A; p/E H Thornburg (dec); sp/Mr and Mrs J A Crowell, Odessa, NE; ed/BPS 1978, MS 1982, Memphis St Univ; mil/USN, 1952-73, CWO; pa/Industl Mech 1973-77, Tech Instr 1977-78, Dir Voc-Tech Ed 1978-, Fayette Co, TN; Mem: VPres 1981-82, Pres-elect 1982-83, Pres 1983-84, TN Coun Local Dirs of Voc-Tech Ed; Am Voc Assn; TN Voc Assn; W TN Voc Assn; Nat Coun Local Admrs; TN St Coun of Admrs; cp/Former Scoutmaster, Cubmaster Dist Comm, Explorer Advr, BSA; r/Prot; hon/W/W in S & SW; Personalities of S.

THORNTON, ELAINE R oc/Real Estate Association Executive; ba/Byrne and Rick, Inc, 128 West Scenic Drive, Pass Christian, MS 39571.

THORPE, ALMA LANE KIRKLAND oc/Religious Broadcaster; b/Dec 20, 1941; h/963 Beecher Street, Southwest, Atlanta, GA 30310; ba/Same; m/Jim Edward; c/Margie Ann; p/Pierce and Dolly Odessa (Pardue) Kirkland, Anniston, AL; sp/Almetha Inis Moore Thorpe, Anniston, AL; ed/Att'd Trevecca Nazarene Col, 1960-61; Att'd Columbia Sch of Broadcasting, 1974; pa/Black's Beauty Shop, 1953; Clk, W T Grants, Anniston, AL, 1957-59; Clk, for Dr James Carter, Anniston, 1959-60; Clk, Sears Roebuck & Co, Nashville, TN, 1960-61; AL Assn of Credit Execs, B'ham, AL, 1961-62; GA Assn of Credit Execs, Atlanta, GA, 1962-63; City of Atlanta Rec Dept, 1963; So Bell T&T, 1963-65; FCC Lic'd Broadcaster, 1974-; r/Prot, Holy Kingdom; hon/Participant: Miss Queen of So Horse Show, 1953; Miss Good Posture Queen, 1959-60; Miss Maid of Cotton, 1961; W/W of Am Wom.

THRAILKILL, MARGARET (PEGGY) A oc/Property Management; b/Jan 15, 1943; h/15616 Oak Valley Road, Romona, CA 92065; ba/La Mesa, CA; m/William C; p/John E and Peggy Paynoha, San Diego, CA; sp/William and Juanita Thrailkill (dec); ed/BA, Univ of San Diego, 1965; Postgrad Study, Univ of CA-San Diego, 1971-75; St of CA Tchr Credential Cert for HS & Jr Col; Real Est Lic, St of CA, 1979; pa/Tchr, Dept Chm, Cnslr, Our Lady of Peace Acad, San Diego, 1965-77; Operator, Mgr, Tyler Mall, Riverside, CA, 1978; Operator, Mgr, Fashion Val Shopping Ctr, San Diego, 1978-82; Tchr, San Diego Commun Col, 1982; Gen Mgr, Grossmont Land Co & Operator, Mgr, Grossmont Shopping Ctr, 1982-83; VPres, Grosssmont Land Co & Grossmont Shopping Ctr, La Mesa, CA, 1983-; Mem: Specific Plan Com, La Mesa-Grossmont, 1982-84; Itl Coun of Shopping Ctrs; AAUW; NAFE; cp/Trustee, Angles Unaware Foun, 1982; Bd of Dirs, Bd Mem, La Mesa C of C, 1984; r/Cath; hon/Tribute to Wom & Indust Awd, YWCA, 1982; W/W in W.

THRONER, GUY C oc/Section Manager of Ordnance Systems and Technology; b/Sep 14, 1919; h/2074 Nayland Road, Columbus, OH 43220; ba/Columbus, OH; m/Jean Holt; c/Richard H, Steven L, Carol (T) Peart; sp/O W Holt, Woodland, CA; ed/BS, Oberlin Col; Exec Prog, Grad Sch of Bus Mgmt, Univ of CA—LA; mil/USN, 1943-47, Lt; pa/Mgr Explosive Ordnance Br & Explosive Ballistics Br, Nav Ordnance Test Sta, 1947-53; Mgr Tactical Weapons Sys Div, Aerojet Gen Corp, 1963; VPres & Gen Mgr, Def Tech Labs, FMC Corp, 1964-74; VPres, Kilby Steel, 1964-74; Dir & Mgr, Info Prods Div, Omron Corp of Arm, 1974-79; Dir of Res & Devel, Vacu-Blast & Tronic Corp, 1974-79; VPres of Prodn & Engrg, Dahlman Inc, 1974-79; Section Mgr Ordnance Technol, Battelle Columbus Labs, OH, 1979-; Mem: Am Def Preparedness Assn; Sigma Xi; hon/ Author, 80 Tech Papers & Reports; Bronze Medal, Am Def Preparedness Assn, 1974; IR-100 Awd for Airborne Fire-fighting Sys for C-130, 1973; Order of St Barbara (Mil Order).

THURMON, JACK, JEWEL oc/Financial Services Executive; b/Aug 14, 1944; h/426 Rancho Bauer, Houston, TX 77079; ba/Houston, TX; m/Barbara Fern Henson; c/J Gregory, J Clarke, J Douglas; p/ Merida E and Agnes (Jones) Thurmon, Dallas, TX; sp/Samuel and Fern Henson (dec); ed/BS, So Meth Univ, 1967; MBA, Harvard Univ, 1969; mil/USAR; 1969-75, SFC; pa/Pres, Rimcor Inc, 1969-72; Pres, Houston Mut Agy Inc, 1972-; Pres, Jojoba Mgmt Inc, 1982-; cp/Fdg Dir, Meml Drive Acres Homeowners' Assn, 1981-; Trustee, Meml Drive Meth Ch, 1982-; Coaching Boys Sports; r/Meth; hon/W/W: Among Students in Am Univs & Cols, Among Profl Ins Agts, in Fin & Indust.

TIETKE, WILHELM oc/Gastroenterologist; b/Oct 15, 1938; h/2707 Westminster Way, Huntsville, AL 38501; ba/ Huntsville, AL; m/Imme Schmidt; c/ Cornelia, Claudia, Isabel; p/Wilhelm and Frieda Tietke; ed/MD, Univ of Goettingen, W Germany, 1968; Intern, Edward W Sparrow Hosp, 1970; Resident Internal Med, Henry Ford Hosp, 1971-73; Fellow Gastroenterology, 1973-75; pa/Vol Fac & Conslt 1976, Clin Asst Prof Internal Med 1979-, Univ of AL-Huntsville; Mem: Pres, Gastroenterology Assocs, PA & Huntsville, AL, 1979; Diplomate, Am Bd of Internal Med; Cert'd, Gastroenterology, 1981; AMA; AL Med Soc; Am Soc of Gastrointestinal Endoscopy; r/Luth.

TILDEN, LORRAINE FREDERICK

oc/"Alumni News" Writer; b/May 16, 1912; h/351 Oakdale Drive, Claremont, CA 91711; ba/Claremont, CA; m/Wesley Roderick; p/Milo Grover and Anna Hebert Frederick (dec); ed/AA, 1931; BA Spanish, 1948; MA Spanish Lit, 1954; PhD Studies, Univ of CA—LA & Univ of CA-Riverside; Addit Study: Universidad de Madrid, Spain; Universidad de Guanajuato, Mexico; SF St Col (Field Studies in Italy, Greece & Turkey); Cornell Univ; pa/Tchr, Eng Sch, Havana, Cuba, 1937-41; Tchg Asst, Scripps Col, 1950-52; Instr, Mt San Antonio Col & Chaffey Col, 1954-60; Tchg Fellow, Univ of CA—LA, 1956-57; Lectr, Claremont Men's Col, 1959-61; Assoc Prof Humanities, Upland Col, 1962-65; Tcrh of Spanish & Spanish Lit, Glendora HS, 1967-77; Dir Alumni Records Proj 1978-, "Alumni News" Writer 1983-, Claremont Grad Sch; Mem: St Arts Chm, AAUW, 1957-58; Pres, Claremont Grad Sch Alumni Assn, 1973-75; Treas Alpha Iota Chapt, Pi Lambda Theta, 1981-83; Pres, Town Affil Assn of Claremont, 1963-65; Pres, Rembrandt Clb of Pamona Col, 1981-82; cp/Var Positions, Pilgrim Congl Ch; r/Congregationalist; hon/Author, Num Drama, Music & Book Reviews Pub'd in MWn Newspapers & Mags, 1929-; Author, 6 Books of Verse, 1927-41; *Brief Life of José Asunción Silva*, 1954; Staff Mem, *Nat Printer Jour*, *IL St Register & IL St Jour*; Other Pubs; Hon Citizen, Guanajuato, Mexico, 1963; Dist'd Public Ser Cits, Claremont City Coun, 1964 & 1965; Best Single Proj Awd & Best Overall Prog Awd, People to People, 1964 & 1965; Pres's Awd for Dist'd Ser, Claremont Grad Sch, 1965; W/W: of Wom, in Poetry, in CA, in W, of Am Wom, in Am Ed; Commun Ldrs & Noteworthy Ams; Men & Wom of Distn; DIB; Num Other Biogl Listings.

TILLMAN, ANN COMBS oc/Homemaker & Bed & Breakfast Tour Guide; b/Mar 1, 1950; h/Winchester House, Natchez, MS 39120; ba/Natchez, MS; m/ C Randolph; c/Catherine, Clifford, Margaret, Rebecca; p/Mr and Mrs Carl w Combs, Natchez, MS; sp/Mr and Mrs Clifford Tillman, Natchez, MS; ed/Grad, Peabody Col, 1972; pa/Self-employed, Ann Tillman's Puppets & Toys, Nashville, TN, 1972-76; Bed & Breakfast Tour Guide at Her own Antebellum Home (Winchester House); Mem: Kappa Kappa Gamma; cp/Pilgrimage Garden Clb; Garden Clb of Am; r/Cath.

TINDAL, CAROLYN L oc/Nurse Consultant; b/Dec 5, 1946; h/3401 Yataruba Drive, Baltomore, MD 21207; ba/Washington, DC; p/Mr and Mrs Henry W Tindal, Balto, MD; ed/RN, Luth Hosp of MD, 1967; BSN, Hampton Inst, 1975; MS, Univ of MD, 1976; Doct Cand, Am Univ, Currently; mil/USAR, Maj; pa/ Staff Nurse, Luth Hosp, Balto, 1967-68; Hd Nurse, Univ of MD Hosp, Balto, 1968-73; Staff Asst to Dir, Johns Hopkins Hosp, Balto, 1976-77; Ed Spec, Howard Univ Hosp, Wash DC, 1977-79; Dir Cont'g Ed, Walter Reed Army Med Ctr, Wash DC, 1979-81; Nurse Consult, Tri-Ser Med Info Sys, Wash DC, 1981-; Conslt, Resource Applications Inc, Balto, 1981-; Mem: ANA; MD Nurses Assn; Sigma Theta Tau; Alpha Kappa Mu; MD Leag of Nsg; AAMI; r/Holiness; hon/ Contbr, Var Book Revies Pub'd in *Mil Med*, 1980 & 1981; Alpha Kappa Mu; Sigma Theta Tau; Purdue-Frederick Awd

for Adv'd Study; Outstg Yg Wom of Am; W/W Among Am Wom.

TINDALL, CHARLES W oc/Executive; b/Feb 7, 1926; h/5024 Ranch View Road, Ft Worth, TX 76109; ba/Ft Worth, TX; m/Raeia Jean Chandler; c/John Scott, Jerry Ann (T) Taylor, Angie Goodman, David Goodman; p/Lottie Belle Tindall, Kirksville, MO; sp/Mr and Mrs W I Chandler, Abilene, TX; ed/Att'd NE MO St Univ, 1946-48; BS, Univ of MO, 1950; CPA, 1953; mil/USMC, 1944-46; Iwo Jima; pa/Mng Acct, Price-Waterhouse, 1951-66; VPres & Treas, Sr VPres, Treas & CFO, Tandy Corp, 1966-; Mem: Am Inst of CPA's; TX Soc of CPA's; Ft Chapt of TX Soc of CPA's; Fin Execs Inst; Petro Clb of Ft Worth; Bd of Dirs: Pier 1 Imports Inc; TX Commerce Bk of Ft Worth; TX Greenhouse Co; cp/Bd Mem, Exec Com & VPres Fin, Ft Worth Ballet; Grp Chm, U Way of Tarrant Co; 1984 US Olympic Com; Shady Oaks Country Clb; Colonial Country CLb; Cent II Clb; r/Ch of Christ; hon/Purple Heart; W/W: in Am, in Fin & Indust.

TINDALL, MICHAEL EDWARD oc/ Administrative Director; b/Jan 9, 1950; h/ 11 Constitution Drive, Chadds Ford, PA 19317; ba/Chester, PA; m/Diane Perzchowski; p/Charles Edward and Margaret Irene Tindall, Fremont, OH; sp/Charles and Margaret Perzchowski, Ridley Pk, PA; ed/BA, Col of Wooster, 1972; Att'd Princeton Theol Sem, 1972-74; MSW, Rutgers Univ, 1975; MBA, Widener Univ, 1983; pa/Sem Dir, Today Inc, 1973-74; Psychi Social Wkr, Carrier Foun, 1975-77; Tm Ldr 1977-79, Asst Adm Psych 1979-81, Adm Dir Psych 1981-, Crozer-Chester Med Ctr, Chester, PA; Mem: Nat Assn of Social Wkrs; Am Pers & Guid Assn; cp/Dela Co Yth Aid Panel; r/Presb; hon/Author, Articles Pub'd in *Nat Conf on Social Welfare Bltns*, 1979 & 1980; BA w Hons, Col of Wooster, 1972; Grad cum laude, Rutgers Univ, 1975; W/W in E.

TINGEY-MICHAELIS, CAROL oc/ Professor; b/Sep 24, 1933; ba/Normal, IL; c/Richard, Blaine, Jim, Neil, Patricia; p/ Willis and Lola Tingey, Logan, UT; ed/ BSS 1970, MEd 1971, PhD 1976, Univ of UT; ca/Public Schs, SLC, 1970; Spec Ed Tchr, SLC, 1971-72; Clin Instr, Univ of UT, 1972-74; Dir of Staff Devel, USTS, Am Fork, 1974-75; Asst Prof, Univ of No IA, Cedar Falls, IA, 1975-77; Asst Prof, Trinity Col Wash DC, 1977-79; Asst Prof, Georg Mason Univ, Fairfax, VA 1978-79; Assoc Prof, NWn St, Natchitoches, LA, 1979-81; Assoc Prof, IL St Univ, Normal, IL, 1981-83; Mem: Fellow, Am Assn on Mtl Deficiency; Coun for Exceptl Chd; Down Syndrome Cong; Phi Kappa Phi; Assn for Severely Handicapped; hon/ Author, Var Handbbooks & Manuals: *Home & Sch Ptnerships in Exceptl Ed*, 1980; *Adaptive Behavior: Self Help*, 1979; *Adaptive Behavior: Socialization*, 1979; *Daily Living Skills*, 1981; *Commun Helpers*, 1981; *Handicapped Infants & Chd: A Handbook for Parents & Profls*, 1983; Num Profl Articles; Advy Bd, *The Exceptl Parent*; Alpha Lambda Delta, 1952; Phi Kappa Phi, 1970; MA F'ship Grant, 1971; Others; W/W of Am Wom.

TINTNER, ADELINE R oc/Independent Scholar; b/Feb 2, 1912; h/180 East End Avenue, New York, NY 10028; ba/New York, NY; m/Henry D Janowitz; c/Mary R Grinberg; p/Benjamin A Tintner (dec); ed/BA, Barnard Col, 1932; MA, Columbia Univ, 1933; pa/Asst to Fine Arts Dept,

1935; Lectr, Var Lit Subjects, 1973-; Mem: Barnard Alumni F'ship Com, 1932-85; Del, MLA, 1982-84; hon/ Author, Over 152 Articles Pub'd in Scholarly Jours & Books on Henry James, Edith Wharton & Others, 1972-83; Carnegie Scholar, 1935-; Other Hons; W/ W in Am Wom.

TIPTON, DOROTHY VELMA oc/ Businesswoman; b/Jul 20, 1914; h/9485 Southwest Inglewood Street, Portland, OR 97225; ba/Portland, OR; m/James Rains; c/Rains Lamarr, Gary Lee; ed/ Grad, Salem HS, 1933; Pvt Adv'd Vocal Tng; pa/Vocalist, Radio Sta KWJJ, Portland, OR, 1931-32; Staff Mem, Wn Paper Converting Co, Salem, OR, 1933-37; Ptnr, Tipton Barbers, 1968-; cp/Sunset Merchants Assn, Portland, OR, 1974-81; Garden Road Clb, Salem, OR, 1937-41; Pres, Gregory Hgts Elem Sch PTA, Portland, OR, 1946-48; Crescendo Clb, Portland, OR, 1948-50; hon/Cert of Merit, Circuit Ct of the St of OR, Wash Co, 1975.

TIPTON, GARY LEE oc/Executive; b/ Jul 3, 1941; ba/1085 Northwest Murray Road, Portland, OR 97229; p/Dorothy V Tipton, Portland, OR; ed/BS, OR Col of Ed, 1964; mil/OR Air NG; pa/Credit Rep, Standard Oil Co of CA, Portland, OR, 1964-67; Credit Mgr, Uniroyal Inc, Dallas, TX, 1967-68; Ptner, Bus Mgr, Tipton Barbers, Portland, OR 1968-; Mem: Co-fdr, Treas, Sunset Merchs Assn, 1974-81; Pres, Sunset Mall Merchs Assn Inc, 1982-; Intl Platform Assn, 1979-; Life Fellow, Intl Biogl Assn, Cambridge, UK, 1979-; cp/Repub Nat Com, 1980-; Sen Howard Baker's Pres Steering Com, 1980; The Smithsonian Soc, 1980; r/Prot; hon/Acad S'ship, OR Col of Ed, 1959; Small Arms Ecpert Markmanship Ribbon, OR Air NG, 1964; Cert of Dist'd Contbn, Sunset HS Dad's Clb, 1973 & 1974; Pres Achmt Awd, 1982; Cert Spec Recog, Sen Howard Baker's Pres Steeing Com, 1980; Cert of Attendance, 9th IBC Intl Cong on Arts & Communs, Cambridge, UK, 1982; Num Certs, Repub Nat Com & Repub Nat Congl Com, 1979-; W/W: of Intells, in Am, in Fin & Indust; Commun Ldrs of Am; Intl Book of Hon; DIB; Num Other Biogl Listings.

TIPTON, JAMES McCALL oc/Professor; b/Jul 20, 1948; h/1016 Hummingbird Drive, Waco, TX 76710; ba/Waco, TX; m/ Barbara Ann Miller; p/Mr and Mrs James Reed Tipton, Knoxville, TN; sp/Mrs Marie Miller, Sanford, FL; ed/BS, Univ of TN, 1971; MBA 1976, MA 1978, PhD 1981, Univ of FL; mil/AUS, 1971-74, Ofcr; pa/Asst Prof Bkg & Fin, Baylor Univ, 1980-; Tchg Asst Ec 1978-80, Public Utilities Res Ctr 1976-77, Univ of FL; Treasury Analyst, Chgo NW Trans Co, 1974; Mem: Am Fin Assn; Am Ec Assn; So Fin Assn; Fin Mgmt Assn; Wn Fin Assn; Wn Ec Assn; Wn Fin Assn; cp/ Kiwanis; Sigma Chi; r/So Bapt; hon/ Author, Var Pubs in Fin, Ec & Stats; Omicron Delta Epsilon; Fin Mgmt Assn Hon Soc; Omicron Delta Kappa; Outstg Public Utility Res Paper, 1978; W/W: in S & SW, in Fin & Indust; Personalities of S.

TODD, DIANN MAE oc/Information Systems Manager; b/Jun 18, 1955; h/39 Netto Lane, Plainview, NY 11803; ba/ Stamford, CT; p/Ralph and Mae Todd, Plainveiw, NY; ed/BS, Union Col, 1977; pa/Sys Analyst, Intl Gen Elect, 1977-78;

Tech Mgr, Gen Elect Info Sers Co, 1978-82; Corp Info Sys Mgr, VS Industs Inc, 1982-; Mem: Assoc Class Agt 1977-, Alumni Coun 1979-, NY Chapt Alumni Clb Bd 1980-, Exec Alumni Coun 1982-, Union Col; r/Prot; hon/Grad cum laude, 1977.

TODD, REBECCA ERLE TIPLER oc/ Organist, Music Teacher; b/Jul 11, 1941; h/2261 Ridgeland, Memphis, TN 38119; ba/Memphis, TN; m/Joseph Larry; p/ Thomas Earl and Lucille G Tipler, Grand Junction, TN; ed/BMus, Union Univ, 1963; MMus, George Peabody Col, Vanderbilt Univ, 1964; pa/Organist, Brook Hollow Bapt Ch, Nashville, TN, 1963-64; Organist, Tchr, 1st Bapt Ch, Kannapolis, NC, 1964-65; Organist, Music Secy & Music Tchr, Union Ave Bapt Ch, Memphis, TN, 1965-; Mem: Am Guild of Organists; Treas,Sigma Alpha Iota, 1962; Treas, Ch Omega, 1962; Treas, Camerata Music Clb, 1980-82; r/ Bapt; hon/Ldrship Awd, Sigma Alpha Iota, 1963; Alpha Chi Hon, 1962; W/W: in Am Univs & Cols, in S & SW.

TOEBE, DIANNE M oc/Professor; b/ Jul 4, 1948; h/8211 Pioneer Drive, Anchorage, AK 99504; ba/Anchorage, AK; m/Thomas L Fakler; p/John and Helen Toebe, Munsing, MI; ed/BS, Ctl MI Univ, 1970; MS, NY Med Col, 1972; PhD, US Intl Univ, 1982; mil/USAF, 1974-1980; pa/Staff Nurse, NYC, 1972-74; Flight Nurse, USAF, 1974-80; Asst Prof, Univ of AK-Anchorage, 1980-; Mem: ANA; Nat Leag of Nsg; Nat Assn of Ob-Gyn Nurses; Nat Med Aerospace Assn; hon/Author, Var Articles Pub'd in *Jour of Cont'g Ed in Nsg* & *Mobious*; Phi Kappa Phi, 1970; Grad magna sum laude, 1970; W/W in Aerospace & Aviation.

TOLLESON, (MRS) JOHNNIE STONE oc/Executive; b/Apr 6, 1945; h/ 907 Valley Road, Kosciusko, MS 39090; ba/Kosciusko, MS; m/William A (Billy); c/Tracey; p/Charlie J Stone (dec); Nannie C Stone, Kosciusko, MS; sp/W A Tolleston, Kosciusko, MS; Nell Gary, Jackson, MS; ed/Dipl I, Inst of Fin Ed; pa/ Teller/Secy 1973, Hd Teller 1974, Teller Supvr 1977, Asst Vpres & Mgr of Kosciusko Div 1981, VPres & Mgr of Kosciusko Div 1982-, Unifirst Fed Savs & Ln Assn; Mem: 2nd VPres, 1st VPres, Pres-elect 1982-84, MS Fed of BPW Clb; 2nd VPres, 1st VPres 1982-84, MS Lung Assn; Dir, Mid-St Mgmt Assn; Mid-MS Home Bldrs Assn, 1981-; Mid-MS Realtors Assn, 1981-; Num Other Orgl Mbrships; cp/Dir, Kosciusko-Attala C of C, 1982-84; Past Pres, Attala Co Univ, Am Cancer Soc; Friends of Lib; Dir/Chm, Kosciusko Miss Hospitality Pageant, 1976-; Chm, Attala Co Chapt, MS Lung Assn, 1976-; Chm, Annual SuperKids Event Fundraiser for MS Lung Assn, 1977-; Mem 1972-, Pres & Var Positions 1977 & 1981, Kosciusko BPW Clb; Dir/ Tchr SS Dept 1969-, Adult Choir Mem 1967-, Others Coms, 1st Bapt Ch; Others; r/Bapt; hon/Author, Num Feature Articles Pub'd in *MS Bus Wom* BPW Mag; Kosciusko BPW Wom of Achmt, 1979; Nom, Outstg Citizen of Attala Co, 1979, 1982 & 1983; Outstg Yg Wom of Am.

TOMIKAWA, SANDRA AKIKO oc/ School Psychologist; b/Jul 18, 1953; h/ 99-650 Aliipoe Drive, Alea, HI 96701; ba/ Kaneohe, HI; p/Isao and Grace (Komatsu) Tomikawa, Alea, HI; ed/BS, Univ of HI, 1974; MS 1976, PhD 1979, Univ of UT;

pa/Ednl Coor, Chd's Ctr, Honolulu, HI, 1975-76; Tchg Fellow Dept Psych, Univ of UT, SLC, 1977-79; Sch Psychol, St of HI Dept of ED, 1980-; Conslt, Naris Cosmetics, Honolulu, 1979-; Mem: Am Psychol Assn; HI Psychol Assn; Sch Cnslr Assn; Coun Exceptl Chd; HI Assn for Chd w Lrng Disabilities; Phi Sigma Rho Alumni Assn; cp/HI St Tennis Leag; r/ Christian; hon/Author & Co-Author, Articles Pub'd in Profl Jours; Nat Hon Soc Outstg Student of Am, 1971; Phi Beta Kappa & Phi Kappa Phi, Univ of HI, 1974; W/W of Am Wom.

TOMPKINS, DONALD ROBERT oc/ National Account Manager; b/Jun 9, 1941; h/60 Arthur Court, Port Chester, NY 10573; ba/Harrison, NY; m/Cherylee Ganzenmuller; c/Brian Dale, Kathleen Kim, Colleen Joy; p/Reed P Tompkins (dec); Lucille M Hunt, Selkirk, NY; sp/ John and Shirley Wallace, Morris Plains, NJ; ed/AAS Wn CT St Col, 1974; Postgrad Study, Fairleigh Dickinson Univ, 1977-79; mil/USN, 1960-64; pa/Positions w AT&T Long Lines: Engrg Supvr White Plains NY 1968, Opers Supvr 1968-71, Opers Cutover Chm 1971-73, Opers Cutover Chm Bridgeport CT 1973-75, Opers Mgr White Plains 1975-77, Indust Sales Mgr Newark NJ 1977-78; Nat Acct Sales Mgr White Plains 1978-80, Dist Mktg Mgr 1980-82; Nat Acct Mgr, Am Bell Inc, 1983-; Mem: Am Mgmt Assn, 1980-82; Telephone Pioneers, 1982-83; cp/Com Chm 1965-70, Scoutmaster 1970-78, Fairfield Co, CT, BSA; Sch Supt, Meth Ch, Danbury, CT, 1965-72; Sales/ Mktg Exec Clb, Westchester, 1982-83; Repub Pres Task Force, 1982-83; Cert'd Lay Preacher, Meth Ch, 1974-75; r/Meth; hon/Ptners in Profit Awd, 1980; Play to Win Awd, 1981; Mgr of Yr Awd, 1982; W/W: in World, in Fin & Indust; Personalities of E.

TONTZ, JAY L oc/Univ School Dean; b/Jul 20, 1938; h/602 Lomond Circle, San Ramon, CA 94583; ba/Haywood, CA; m/ Anne Deems; p/E Logan and Charlotte Tontz, Greensboro, NC; sp/Mr and Mrs Harold Deems, Clayton, CA; ed/BA, Denison Univ, 1980-; MS, NYSSILR-Cornell Univ, 1962; PhD, Univ of NC, 1966; mil/USAF, Capt; pa/Asst Prof Ec, USAF Acad, CO, 1966-69; Acting Assoc Dean Sch of Bus & Ec 1970-72, Chm Dept Ec 1972-73, Acting Dean Sch of Bus & Ec 1973-74, Dean Sch of Bus & Ec, 1974-, Fac Mem Dep Ec 1969-, CA St Univ-Hayward; Mem: Chm Bd of Trustees, St Rose Hosp, 1980-; Am Ec Assn; Wn Ec Assn; Nat Assn of Docts in US; hon/Author, Var Articles Pub'd in Profl Jours & Newspapers & Var Profl Reports Incl'g: "Reaganomics Offers New Hope for Future," *The Daily Review*, 1981; Delta Sigma Pi; Omicron Delta Epsilon; W/W in W; Commun Ldrs of Am.

TOPP, ALPHONSO AXEL JR oc/ Environmental Scientist; b/Oct 15, 1920; h/872 Highland Drive, Los Osos, CA 93402; ba/Same; m/Mary Catherine Virtue; c/Karen E, Susan J, Linda A, Sylvia R, Peter A, Astrid K, Heidi E, Eric L, Megan A, Katrina R; p/A A Topp Sr Indianapolis, IN; sp/W A Virute, Lebanon, IN; ed/BS, Purdue Univ, 1942; MS, Univ of CA-LA, 1948; Addit Study, 1951; mil/ AUS, 1940-70, Col; pa/w AUS: 2nd Lt, 1942; Capt, Command HQ Btry 13th Armored Div Artillery, WW II, ETO; Capt, 1st Counter Mortar-Counter Battery Radar Unit, Korea; LTC, Command 1st How Bn 19th Artillery, Schweinfurt, Germany, 1959; Col, Mil Advr to Shah of Iran, 1966-68; Inspector Gen, FC DASA, 1969-70; Envir Sci 1970-81, Chief 1981-, Radiation Protection Bur, St of NM; Mem: Assoc Mem, Sigma Xi, 1948-; Hlth Physics Soc, 1981-; Mem 1981-83, Emeritus Mem 1984, Chm Com E8 (Uraniim Mill Tailings), Conf of Radiation Control Prog Dirs; Lectr in Field; cp/BSA, 40 Yrs; r/Presb; hon/Author, *Regulations for Control of Ionizing Radiation*, St of NM, 1971 & Num Other Tech Reports; Legion of Merit, 1970; Bronze Star w 2 OLC, 1945, 1950 & 1951; Jt Sers Commend Medal; AUS Commend Medal; Korea Dist'd Unit Cit; W/W in W.

TORBET, LAURA oc/Writer and Artist; b/Aug 23, 1942; h/225 East 73rd Street, New York, NY 10021; ba/Same; m/Peter H Morrison; p/Earl B and Ruth C Robbins, Wayne, NJ; ed/BA, BFA, OH Wesleyan Univ, 1964; pa/Mng Editor, *Suburban Life* Mag, E Orange, NJ, 1964-65; Asst Public Relats Dir, U Funds NJ, Newark, 1965-67; Art Dir, Alitalia Airlines, NYC, 1967-69; Propr, Laura Torbet Studio, NYC, 1969-; Author, Num Books; Mem: Am Crafts Coun; Am Wom's Ec Devel Corp Clb; Nat Arts NYC; hon/Author & Co-Author, Over 18 Books incl'g: *The Virgin Homeowner's Handbook*, 1984; *The Inner Enemy*, 1983; *Helpful Hints for Hard Times*, 1982; *A Time for Caring*, 1982; *How To Fight Fair w Your Kids & Win*, 1980; *Squash: How to Play, How to Win*, 1978; *Superflier: The Air Travelers Handbook*, 1978; *The Complete Book of Mopeds*, 1978; *Fads: America's Crazes, Fevers & Fancies*, 1977; *The Complete Book of Skateboarding*, 1976; *The T-Shirt Book*, 1976; *How to Do Everything w Markers*, 1976; *Dic of Fgn Terms*, 1974; *Leathercraft You Can Wear*, 1974; *Clothing Liberation*, 1972; *Macrame You Can Wear*, 1972; Editor: *The Ency of Crafts*, 1980; *Helena Rubinstein's Book of the Sun*, 1979; W/ W: Among Wom, in Am Wom; Contemp Authors; Outstg Yg Wom of Am.

TORES, JOHN MAX JR oc/Corporate Safety Director; b/Jul 21, 1949; h/8403 Bodkin Avenue, Pasadena, MD 21122; ba/ Towson, MD; m/Janice Darlene; c/Angela Nicole, Andree Renee, John Michael; pa/ John Max Sr and Leona Mae Tores, Millersville, MD; sp/Kester H Sr and Christina Helen Kirk Greene, Glen Burnie, MD; ed/Att'd Catonsville Col, 1978; pa/Fire & Safety Ovcr, Dept of Hlth & Mtl Hygiene, St of MD, Springfield Ctr, 1972-74; Occupl Safety & Hlth Insp, Div of Labor & Indust, 1974-78; Safety Inspection Conslt, Mayor's Ofc of Safety, Balto, MD, 1978; Safety Engr, Aetna Ins Co, Balto, 1978; Exec Dir, Occupl Safety Sers, Pasadena, MD, 1978-79; Corp Safety Dir, The Arundel Corp, Towson, MD, 1979-; Mem: Lectr in Field; Occupl Safety & Hlth Inst; Safety Engrg Clb of MD; Chm Chesapeake Chapt, Nat Mem, Am Soc of Safety Engrs; Exec Com, Tech & Profl Socs; Dir, VPres Constrn & Utilities Div, Safety Coun of MD; Com Person-Safety, Nat Slag Assn; cp/Chm Balto Reg Chapt, ARC; Industl Relats Com, MD C of C; Bd of Dirs, Wee World Lrng Inc, Glen Burnie, MD; r/Luth; hon/ Apprec for Safety Lectr Awd, Safety Engrg Clb of MD, 1982; W/W in E.

TORIGOE, RODNEY Y oc/Psychologist; b/Feb 1, 1945; h/1258 Hind Iuka Drive, Honolulu, HI 96821; ba/Honolulu, HI; m/Bess M; c/Tiffany Kikue Nakamura; p/Samuel and Sueko Torigoe, Honolulu, HI; sp/Kikue Nakamura; ed/BS, 1968; MA, 1973; PhD, 1976; pa/Asst Clin Prof, Dept of Psychi, Univ of HI, 1980-; Chief, VA Psychol Ser, 1980-; Chief, VA Day Treatment Ctr, 1978-; Clin Psychol, Phoenix VA Med Ctr, 1976-78; Psychol Assn, AZ St Hosp, 1975-76; Affirmative Action Ofc, WICHE, 1973-74; Treas, HI Psychol Assn, 1981; cp/Pres Bd of Dirs 1981-, Mem Bd 1980-, The House Inc; Neighborhood Bd, 1981-83; r/En; hon/ Am Legion Awd, 1963; Hemenway S'ship, 1964-65; Star S'ship, 1965; NIMH F'ship, 1971-72; WICHE Awd, 1974; W/ W in W.

TORRES AYBAR, ANA MARÍA oc/ Special Services Director; b/Oct 25, 1935; h/Jardines Fagot Calles 3 #E15 Ponce, PR 00731; ba/Ponce, PR; p/Francisco J Torres, San Juan, PR; María P Aybar (dec); ed/BPhil, Siena Hgts Col, 1961; MS Adm & Supvn 1970 & Guid & Cnslg 1975, Barry Col & Cath Univ; PhD Cand, Nova Univ, 1982-; pa/Spec Sers Dir, Cath Univ of PR, Ponce, 1974-; Asst Supt of Cath Schs, San Juan & Caguas, 1971-74; Prin 1969-71, Tchr & Asst Prin 1957-65, San Anthony's Sch, Guayama, PR, Tchr & Asst Prin, Sacred Heart Acad, Santurce, PR, 1967-69; Sch Dir, the Parish Sch, San Juan de la Maguana, Dominican Repub, 1966-67; Tchr, Our Lady Queen of Martyrs Sch, Ft Lauderdale, FL, 1965-66; Prof, Barry Col, Miami FL, 3 Sums; Mem: AAUP; ASCD; PRASCD; PGA; PRPGA; Pres PR Chapt 1975-79, VPres Reg II 1977-79, Assn of Equality & Excell in Ed (AEEE); Phi Delta Kappa; APORE; Pres, Caribbean Assn Trio Progs (CATP), 1980-83; COR; Conslt to Var PR Schs & Progs, 1980-82; cp/Co-Fdr, Co-op Sys & Old Peoples Home, San Juan de la Maguana, Dominican Repub, 1966; r/Cath; hon/Author, 2 Articles Pub'd in *Familia y Escuela* Mag; 4 Other Articles Pub'd; Kappan of Yr, 1982; Edr of Yr, 1980; Outstg Contbn to Reg II, AEEE, 1978; Outstg Contbn for 5 ½ Yrs, CATP, 1980; Outstg Contbn to Commun, Dominican Repub, 1966; Other Hons; W/W in S.

TORRES-DÍAZ, MIGDALIA oc/ Attorney, Counselor at Law; b/Jun 2, 1946; h/Apartment 13-B Torre II, Guynabo, PR 00657; ba/Bayamón, PR; p/ Samuel Angel Torres; ed/BA, Univ of PR, 1967; JD, Inter Am Univ of PR Sch of Law, 1975; pa/Cnslr, Rehab Assn of Drug Addicts Inc, Rio Piedras, PR, 1967-68; Dir of Multiple Activs Ctr for Elderly People, Geriatric Comm, Dept of Hlth, PR, 1967-70; Cnslr, PR Telephone Co Traffic Dept, 1970-75; Atty at Law, Spec in Civil Law, 1975-; Atty Advr, PR Telephone Co & Pr Telephone Auth, 1975-; US Dist Court of PR, 1979-; US Ct of Appeals 1st Circuit, 1981-; Pres 1982-84, Secy 1980-82, Bayamon Jud Dist Chapt, PR Bar Assn; Bd of Dirs PR Legal Sers, San Juan, PR, 1983-84; cp/Secy Bd of Owners, Altavista Condominium, Guaynabo, PR, 1981-83; Bd of Dirs, Academia Disciplos de Cristo Inc, 1982-85; Legal Advr Bd of Dirs, Accion Social Egida Los Cantares Inc, 1981-; r/Prot; hon/Kappa Lamda Chapt, Phi Theta Kappa, 1964; Kappa Lamda Chapt, Phi Theta Kappa, PR Jr Col, 1964; Mem, *Law Review*, Inter Am Univ of PR, 1973-75; Awd of Recog, Iglesia Discipulos de Cristo Inc, 1981; Dist'd Wom of Yr, PR Telephone Co, San Juan, 1984.

TORRES-FLORES, GILBERTO oc/

Executive, Attorney at Law; b/May 22, 1933; h/Adonis 56 Street, Alto Apolo, Guaynavo, PR 00657; ba/Alto Apolo, Rio Piedras & San Juan, PR; m/Wilma G Vargas; c/Wilma M, Gisela L, Gilberto M; p/Pablo Torres, Aibonito, PR; María Flores (dec); sp/Felipe Vargas and Margarita Ortiz, Rio Piedras, PR; ed/BBA, Univ of PR, 1957; LLB, LD, Cath Univ of PR Sch of Law, 1966; mil/AUS, 1952-53; pa/Positions w Aguirre Complex: Asst Gen Mgr PR Opers 1969-70, Gen Coun, VPres & Secy Aguirre Co (A Trust) 1966-77, VPres, Secy & Treas Aguirre Co (A Trust) 1971-77, Trust Trustee 1978-, VPres, Treas, Secy Aguirre Corp 1966-77, Corp Dir 1978-; Sr Ptnr, Torres & Smith Law Firm, Guaynabo, PR, 1977-; Conslt in Field; Pres & Chm Bd of Dirs, Intcontl Minerals of PR Inc, 1982-; Mem: Admitted to PR Bar, 1966; US Supr Ct Bar, 1979; Superior & Supr Ct of PR; DC Ct of Appeal : PR Bar Assn; ABA; cp/Dorado Bch & Golf Tennis Clb; r/Cath; hon/Grad cum laude, Sch of Law, 1966; Recip, Francisco Parra Toro Medal, For Dist'd Student in Civil Law, Cath Univ of PR, 1966; W/W in S & SW.

TORRES-RENTA, DEADINA M oc/ Professor; b/Jul 9, 1935; h/12 Street, C-6 Reparto Universidad, San Germán, PR 00753; ba/San Germán, PR; p/Ernest and Esmeralda (Renta) Torres; ed/BA, Cath Univ of PR, 1956; MS, Fordham Univ; PhD, Univ of Madrid, Spain, 1962-63 & 1970-71; pa/Asst Prof Ed 1965-66, Asst Dean of Students 1966-68, Univ Coor 1968-69, Ath Univ Leag 1979-81, Univ Senate 1974-81, Assoc Prof Ed 1969-, Assoc Dean Acad Affairs 1979, Dean of Student Affairs 1979-81, Inter Am Univ of PR; Sec'dy Sch Tchr 1956-62, Sec'dy Sch Prin 1965, Dept of Public Ed, PR; Mem: Pres, Phi Delta Kappa, 1978-79; Alpha Delta Kappa; Comparative & Intl Ed Soc; Nat Assn of Student Pers Admrs; Asociación de Españoles en PR; Coor, Segundo Congresso Instituto Lexicografà Hispano-americano, 1981; Lectr in Field; Spkr, 4th WCCI World Conf on Ed, Univ of Alberta, Canada, 1983; cp/ Guide Tour to Europe, 1972-77; r/Rom Cath; hon/Author, Over 15 Articles Pub'd in Profl Jours, 1971-; Dist'd Dean of Student Affairs & Dedication of Student Govt Fest, Inter Am Univ, 1981; Dist'd Dean of Student Affairs 1980 & 1981, by Student Govt, Other Hons & Awds, Inter Am Univ; Recog Awd 1981, Dist'd Past Pres 1979, Other Awds, Phi Delta Kappa Chapt; Recog Awd, Univ of PR, 1980; Dist'd PR Student in Spain, PR Students Assn in Madrid, 1963; Rep Intl Students, Investmt of Chancellor of Univ of Burdeos (France), Univ of Madrid, 1963; Others; W/W in S & SW.

TOTTY, SHIRLEY EDWARDS oc/ Executive Director; b/Oct 15, 1937; h/ 2105 Vicki Drive, Birmingham, AL 35235; ba/B'ham, AL; m/Walker S; c/ Michael K, Gregory A; p/Raymond and Mae Belle Edwards, Bentonville, AR; sp/ Bessie Totty, Olive Br, MS; ed/BA, Univ of AR, 1959; pa/Welfare Wkr, TN Dept of Public Welfare, 1959-62; Social Wkr, Wn St Hosp, TN, 1962-65; Social Wkr, MS St Hosp, 1965-68; Social Wkr, Wyandott Co, KS Dept of Public Welfare, 1968-69; Dir RSVP 1973-81, Exec Dir 1981-, Positive Maturity Inc, B'ham, AL; Mem: VPres 1975, Pres 1979-80, AL Assn of RSVP Dirs; Bd of Dirs, AL Gerontological Soc, 1982; CoChm Mbrship Com, So Gerontological Soc; Bd of Dirs 1978-82, Pres 1982, AL Ofc of Voluntarism; cp/Gubernatorial Appt as Chm Advy Coun 1982, AL Ofc of Vol Citizen Participation; Ofcl Observer, White House Conf on Aging, 1981; Mayor's Com for Betterment of Handicapped, 1982; Secy, Coun of Exec Dirs of U Way Agys, 1982; Advy Coun, Univ of AL-B'ham Ctr for Aging, 1982; Zonta Intl, 1981-82; Area Advy Coun, B'ham Reg Planning Comm Coun on Aging, 1982; r/Bapt.

TOUZEL, TIMOTHY J oc/Professor; b/Nov 2, 1945; h/120 Reta Street, Conway, SC 29526; ba/Conway, SC; m/Susan Wingate; c/Jeremy Stuart, James Timothy; p/Stewart and Margaret Eicher Touzel (dec); sp/James and Bess Wingate, Nashville, TN; ed/BS 1969, EdD 1975, Univ of TN; MEd, Memphis St Univ, 1972; mil/USAR, 1968-74; pa/Asst Prof 1978-, Interim Dean 1982, Coastal Carolina Col, Conway, SC; Instr, Oak Ridge Schs 1975-78, Prog Dir Title I 1974-75, Shelby Co, TN; Instr 1973-74, Grad Tchg Asst 1973, Univ of TN; Tchr 1969-72, Hd Sci Dept 1971-72, Memphis City Schs; Mem: Am Ed Res Assn, 1972-; Assn for Supvn & Curric Devel, 1978-; Fdg Pres 1979, VPres, Mem 1979-, Math Advmt Coun of Horry-Georgetown Area; Nat Coun Tchrs of Math, 1978-; Nat Del 1982-83, Mem 1972-, Phi Delta Kappa; Res Coun for Diagnostic & Descriptive Math, 1979-; r/ Unitarian-Universalist; hon/Author, *Effective Tchg*, 1983; Editor, *MAC Newslttr*, 1981-82 & 1982-83; Var Articles Pub'd in Profl Jours Incl'g: *TN Tchr; TN Ed*; Others; Outstg Tchr Nom Tchr Ed, Coastal Carolina Col, Conway, SC, 1980-81; Phi Delta Kappa, 1973; Kappa Delta Pi, 1974; W/W in S & SW.

TOVSEN, JOAN ESTHER oc/Executive; b/Dec 3, 1950; h/Box 4-1975 Anchorage, AK 99509; ba/Anchorage, AK; p/ Oliver and Josephine Tovsen, Anchorage, AK; ed/Att'd Anchorage Commun Col & Univ of AK, 1969-72; Cert'd Grad, Dale Carnegie Human Relats & Public Spkg Course, 1979; pa/Procurement Clk, Misc Document Clk, Legal Clk, Bur of Land Mgmt, 1972-78; Pres & Propr, Anchorage Welcome Ser & Relocation Ctr, 1978-; Mem: Pres, City Hostess Intl Assn, 1982-83; Secy & Bd of Dirs, Advtg Fed of AK, 1982; cp/Hospitality Com, Anchorage C of C, 1981-; Fdr, AK Awareness Inst Inc, 1983-; r/Worldwide Ch of God; hon/Editor & Pubr: *Anchorage Street Map & Guide*, 1980 & 1983; *The Anchorage Blue Book: A Guide to Public Sers & Resources* (Volume 3), 1981; *The Anchorage Ec Compas: A Socio-Ec Profile*, 1981; W/W of Am Wom.

TOYOMURA, DENNIS T oc/Architect; b/Jul 6, 1926; h/2606 Manoa Road, Honolulu, HI 96822; ba/Honolulu, HI; m/ Charlotte Akiko; c/Wayne J, Gerald F, Amy J, Lyle D; p/Sansuke and Take Sata Toyomura; ed/BS, Chgo Tech Col, 1949; Postgrad Study: Univ of IL Ext, 1950, 1953 & 1954; IL Inst of Technol, 1954-55, Univ of HI, 1966-67 & 1973; mil/AUS, 1945-46; pa/Designer Draftsman, Hames M Turner, Hammond, IN, 1950-51; Designer Draftsman, Wimberly & Cook, Honolulu, 1952; Designer Draftsman, Gregg & Briggs, Chgo, 1952-54; Architect, Holabird, Root & Burgee, 1954-55; Prin Arch, Dennis T Toyomura, AIA, 1954-; Arch, Loebl, Schlossman & Ben-

nett, 1955-62; Secy, Dir, Maiko of HI Inc, 1972; Dir, Pacific Canal HI Inc, 1972-; Archtl Conslt, Honolulu Redevel Agy, Kapahulu Dist, City & Co of Honolulu, 1967-71; Fallout Shelter Analyst, Dept of Def; HI Bd Registration Profl Engrs, Archs, Surveyors & Landscape Archs, 1974-; Mem: Advy Com Drafting Tech, Leeward Commun Col & Univ of HI, 1968-81; WN Reg Del, Nat Coun Archtl Registration Bd, 1975-80; Nat Del, 1976, 1978, 1979 & 1980; Reg'd Profl Arch: IL & HI; Real Est Broker, IL; Ofc Mgmt Com 1977, Pract Mgmt Com 1978, Dir HI Soc 1973-74, Treas 1975, Other Coms, AIA; Am Concrete Inst; Acad of Polit Sci; Am Acad Polit & Social Scis; IL Assn Professions; AAS; ASTM; Reg Bd of Govs 1980-81, Coun Ednl Facility Planners Intl; Dir 1975, Treas 1976, Lyon Arboretum Assn; Dir 1973-, Treas 1976-77, Constrn Industl Leg Org; Kappa Sigma Kappa; cp/ Honolulu C of C; Chgo Nat Hist Mus; Chgo Art Inst; Malolo Mariners Clb; Treas 1964, Purser Clb; Pres 1965, Skipper Clb; r/Presb; Del Commr St Assem, Synod of IL, 1958; LA Presby, 1965; hon/Outstg Citizen Recog Awd, Consltg Engrs Coun of HI, 1975; W/W in Fin & Indust; Personalities of W.

TRAKIMAS, RAYMOND DOMINIC oc/Management Consultant; b/Oct 29, 1954; h/671 Stolle Road, Elma, NY 14059; ba/Pittsburgh, PA; m/Susan Maria Vitelli; p/Raymond Trakimas (dec); Ruth Trakimas, Buffalo, NY; sp/Quinton and Rita Vitellia, Phila, PA; ed/BSIE, MBA, Lehigh Univ; pa/Mgr 1982-, Sr Conslt 1980-82, Price Waterhouse; Sr Conslt, Arthur Andersen & Co, 1977-80; Mem: CPA; CDP; CCP; CMC.

TREIBLE, CAROL ANN oc/Professor; b/Feb 12, 1943; h/1601 East 19th Street, Georgetown, TX 78626; ba/Belton, TX; m/Kirk; c/Todd Mosher; p/Mr and Mrs Chas G Mosher, Vero Bch FL; sp/Mrs William B Treible, Newton, NJ; ed/BA, WV Wesleyan Col, 1964; MEd, Wright St Univ, 1968; Addit Grad Study: WV Univ; TX A&M; pa/Tchr & Dir, Wesley U Meth Kgn, Morgantown, WV, 1964-65; Tchr, Mud River Green Sch Dist, Enon, OH, 1965-69; Instr, Parkersburg Commun Col, Parkersburg, WV, 1970-72; Asst Prof Ed, WV Wesleyan Col, Buchannon, WV, 1972-77; Asst Prof Ed Univ of Mary Hardin-Baylor, Belton, TX, 1978-; Mem: Kappa Delt Pi; S'ship Chm, Delta Kappa Gamma; Phi Delta Kappa; IRA; VPres, Bell Co IRA Coun; Fac Assem Chp, Univ of Mary Hardin-Baylor, 1982-83; Commun Ed Bd, Georgetown ISD; cp/Conslt: WV Headstart Prog, 1965-68; Georgetown ISD; Killeen ISD, 1980-; cp/Coun Pres, Georgetown ISD PTA; Former Cubscout Ldr; Chp, Area March of Dimes, 1981-82; r/Meth.

TREMAYNE, LESTER (LES) oc/Actor; b/Apr 16, 1913; h/901 South Barrington Avenue, Los Angeles, CA 90049; ba/ Same; m/Joan Lenore Hertz; c/Walter Carl Christian (dec); Dorothy Alice Tremayne (Gwilliam) Lewellyn Henning, LA, CA; ed/Studied Greek Drama, NWn Univ, 1937-39; Studied Anthropology: Columbia Univ 1949-50 & Univ of CA-LA 1951-52; Addit Study; pa/Over 70 Yrs as Actor: In Films in England, 1917; In Films in Hollywood, 1951-; On Radio, 1931-; On TV, 1939-; Pop Radio Progs Incl: "The First Nighter," 1933-43; "Grand Hotel," 1934-40; "The Thin Man," 1945-50; "The Falcon," 1946-49;

"Betty & Bob," 1935-39; Orig Leading Man on "The Romance of Helen Trent,", 1934; Num Others; Broadway Appearance: Mem of Orig Cast in "Detective Story," 1948-49; TV Appearances Incl: "One Man's Fam," "Perry Mason," "Matinee Theatre," "Thin Man," "Bonanaza," "The Man & The City," Mr Mentor of Chd's TV Series "Shazam!"; Others; Films Incl: "The Racket," 1951; "The Blue Veil," 1952; "Francis Goes to W Point," 1951; "It Grows on Tress," 1952; "Dream Wife, " 1953; "I Love Melvin," 1952; "N by NW," 1958; "War of the Worlds," 1954; "A Man Called Peter," 1955; "Susan Slept Here," 1954; "The Lt Wore Skirts," 1958; "Story of Ruth," 1959; "Fortune Cookie," 1966; "Goldfinger," 1966; "Holy Wednesday," 1974; "Quest," 1982; Others; Narrator & Portrayer of Voices; Ednl Films; Industl-Comml Films; Documentary Films; Mem: Pres 1952-56, Hollywood Actors Coun; Bd of Dirs, LA Chapt AF Assn, 1966-; Charter Mem, Del 1st Conv 1938, Am Fedn Radio Artists; VPres, Nat & Local Mem, Bd of Dirs 1965-, Chm Var Coms, AFTRA; Past Chm, Actors Div, Wkshop Com, Acad of TV Arts & Scis; Screen Actors Guild; Prime Time Negotiations Com, AFTRA—SAG; Actors Equity; Life Mem, Actors Fund Am; Fdr, Incorporator, Charter & Life Mem, Past Bd of Dirs, Chm Audio Hist Com & Spkrs Bur, Pacific Pioneer Broadcasters; Host of "Nostalgia Nights"; Archaeol Inst of Am; cp/Lambs Clb NYC; Other Activs; hon/ Author, Res Paper on Archaeol; Blue Ribbon Awd for Best Actor of MO, *Box Ofc Mag*, 1955; Best Radio Actor in US, 1938; Recip, Industl Film Aws, 1968; Blue Ribbon Awd, Am Fest, 1964; Cert of Merit, Info Film Prodrs Assn, 1964; County Awd 1967, 1971, Finalist 1970; Andy Awd, Advtg Clb NYC, 1968; Cine Golden Eagle Awd, 1978; Awd of Merit, Braille Inst of Am, 1977; Named One of 3 Most Distinctive Voices in US, 1940; Num Others; W/W: in W, in Am, in World, of Intells; Men of Achmt; Other Biogl Listings.

TRENKA, MALARET HERMINIA oc/ Elementary School Prinicpal; b/Jul 6, 1925; h/Box 3957, Bayamón Gardens, Sta, PR 00620; ba/Bayamón, PR; m/ Vladimir; c/Karen Elizabeth; Laura Isabel; p/Pedro S Malaret (dec); sp/Bohumil Trenka (dec); ed/BA 1956, MA 1948, Bryn Mawr Col; pa/Psychometrician, Johnson O'Connor's Human Engrg Lab, 1947-48; Res Wkr, Univ of PA Press, 1948-50; Translator, Sharp & Duhme Inc, 1950-52; Prof Eng, Cath Univ, 1966-68; Eng & Hist Tchr 1968-69, Guid Coor 1969-80, Academia del Perpetuo Socorro; Tchr 1958-62, Prin 1980-81, St John Sch; Prin, Baldwin Sch, 1981-; Mem: Mid Sts Reg Coun Col Bd, 1980-81; Advy Com, Title IV Dept of Edn; Chm Coor Com, Cath Sch Guid Sers, 1976-77; Pers & Guid Assn; Pres 1976-79, VPres 1979-, Caribbean Cnslrs Assn; cp/Parti de Nuevo Progresista; hon/W/W in S & SW.

TRENT, DARRELL oc/Ambassador; b/ Aug 2, 1938; ba/Washington, DC & Wilmington, DE; m/June Yeardye; ed/BA, Stanford Univ, 1961; Att'd Intl Law Sch, The Hague, Netherlands; MA, Grad Sch of Bus, Columbia Univ, 1964; pa/Ambassador, 1983-; Chm US Civil Aviation Del, Negotiating w European Civil Aviation Conf Countries, 1983-; Chm of Bd & CEO, Rollins Envir Sers Inc, Wilmington,

DE, 1983-; Dpty Secy of Trans, Dept of Trans, 1981-83; Sr Res Fellow 1974-76 & Assoc Dir 1975-76, Hoover Instn, Stanford Univ; Dpty Campaign Mgr & Sr Policy Advr, Ronald Reagan's Pres Campaigns, 1976 & 1980; Dir, Pres-elect's Ofc of Policy Coor, 1981-82; Dept Dir & Dir, Pres Ofc of Emer Preparedness & Var Other Positions in Richard Nixon's Adm, 1970-74; Dept Asst to the Pres, 1969-70; Conslt to Pres; Commr of Gen Sers Adm's Property Mgmt & Disposal Ser; Chm of Bd & CEO, Var Previous Corps; Nat Security Coun; Cost of Living Coun; cp/Lic'd Pilot; Var Biogl Listings.

TREVER, JAMES EDGAR oc/Computer Systems Programmer; b/Sep 1, 1945; h/PO Box 4653 Pensacola, FL 32507; ba/Pensacola, FL; m/Mary S; c/Stephen, Elizabeth; p/Mr and Mrs John C Trever, Claremont, CA; sp/Lydia Stoan, Pensacola, FL; ed/Att'd Univ of So CA, 1964-67; BA, Baldwin Wallace Col, 1968; Postgrad Study, Brown Univ, 1971-72; EDS, Sys Engr Devel Sch, 1975; mil/USN, 1969-73, Nav Flight Ofcr; pa/Chief Ground Instr/ Flight Instr, Gunnell Aviation Inc, 1968-69; Sys Engr, Elect Data Sys Inc, 1974-78; Sys Engr, Shenandoah Life Ins Co, 1978-79; Computer Spec, USN, 1979-; Dir & Fdr, Cordo Enterprises, 1977-; Mem: VPres Pensacola Chapt, Data Processing Mgmt Assn, 1982; Bd Mem, Occidental Intl Masters Championships, 1977; cp/Res Assoc Vertebrate Paleontology, Nat Hist Mus of LA Co, 1969-; r/Meth; hon/Author, *Bibliog of Sabre-tooth Cats Plio-pleistocene N Am*, 1976; *All World Bibliog of Sabre-tooth Cats*, 1977; Tech Report; Num Articles Pub'd in Var Hobby Pubs on Trading Cards; Var Sci Achmt Awds, 1960-63; Dist'd Nav Grad, 1969; Nav Achmt Medal 1972; Dist'd Ser Awd, USN (Civilian), 1981; W/W in SE; Outstg Yg Men of Am.

TRIAS—MONGE, JOSÉ oc/Chief Justice; b/May 5, 1920; h/PO Box 4006 San Juan, PR 00905; ba/San Juan, PR; m/Jane Grimes; c/José Enrique, Peter James, J Arturo; ed/BA, Univ of PR, 1940; MA 1943, LLB 1944, Harvard Univ; JSD, Yale Univ, 1947; pa/Lectr, Univ of PR, 1947-66; Dpty Atty Gen, 1949, Atty Gen 1953-57, PR; Mem, Constitl Conv of PR, 1951-52; Mem, OAS, 1966-67; Mem, Nat Com of ACLU, 1958-74; Trustee, Superior Ed Coun 1962-72; Mem, Gov Comm Reform of Jud Sys PR; Chief Justice, Supr Ct of PR, 1974-; Mem: Royal Acad of Spanish Lang, PR Chapt, 1979; Société de Legislation Comparée, France, 1981; Assoc Mem, Intl Acad of Comparative Law, France, 1982; r/Cath; hon/Author, *El Sistem Judicial de PR*, 1978; Editor, *Las Crisis del Derecho en PR*, 1979; Editor, *El Sistem Constitl de PR Volumes 1 & 2*, 1979 & 1980; Var Articles Pub'd in Profl Law Reviews.

TRIMMER, DOROTHY ANN oc/ Nurse Educator; b/Jan 28, 1951; h/5301 North Camelhead Road, Phoenix, AZ 85018; ba/Tempe, AZ; m/William K P Li; p/Robert and Jane Trimmer, Irvington, NJ; sp/James Li; ed/BSN, Seton Hall Univ Col of Nsg, 1973; MSN, Hunter Col, City of NY Bellevue Sch of Nsg, 1976; pa/Instr of Nsg, AZ St Univ, 1982-; Instr Nsg, Univ of FL, 1981-82; Dir of Staff Devel, Riverside Gen Hosp, Secaucus, NJ, 1977-81; Instr, Passaic Co Commun Col, Paterson, NJ, 1976-77; Staff Nurse in Critical Care, St Barnabus Med Ctr

1974-75 & U Hosps of Newark Med Ctr 1973-74; CPR Instr, Am Heart Assn, 1978-; Mem: Chp, Hudson Co Coun of Inser Edrs, l1978-81; ANA; AACCN; ASHET; ASNA; cp/Former Girl Scout Ldr; r/Prot; hon/Author, Var Tchg Modules for Staff Devel, 1978-81; Cont'g Ed Lectures & Other Nsg Progs; Profl Nurse Traineeship, 1975-76; Grad magna cum laude, Hunter Col, 1976; NJ St S'ship, 1969-71; Nsg Grant, 1972; Seton Hall Univ Grant, 1973; Dean's List, 1970 & 1973; W/W in Am Wom.

TRINGALE, VINCENT JOSEPH oc/ Artist, Professor; b/Jul 15, 1923; h/47 Independence Drive, Woburn, MA 01801; ba/Boston, MA; m/Josephine Louise; c/Steven Vincent, Kevin Sebastian, Vincent Joseph Jr; p/Sebastian Tringale, Boston, MA; Rafaella Tringale (dec); sp/Jack and Anna Virginia Zuccala, Reading, MA; ed/BS, MA Col of Art, 1949; MA, Boston Univ, 1953; mil/AUS, WWII; pa/Prof of Art, Bunker Hill Commun Col, Boston, 1982, 1983-; Conducting Tours to Europe for Bunker Hill Commun Col; Art Tchr, Shurtlett Jr HS, 1949-50; Art Tchr, Chelsea Sr HS, 1950-53; Instr 1953, Asst Prof 1956, Assoc Prof 1957, Chm Art Dept 1957-78, Prof 1971, Boston St Col; Curric Com, Hon Com, Student Adv Yrbk, 1957-59; Grad Com; Pro Cont'g Ed Com, 1957-67; Tchr, Painting, Falmouth Artists Guild; Fdr, Chelsea Fine Art Classes, 1950-; Fdr, Tringale Studio of Art, 1965-; Nat Art Ed Assn, 1949-81; MA Art Ed Assn, 1949-81, Treas 1958-61; Copley Soc Boston, 1957-; Mus of Fine Arts, Boston, 1953-; Woburn Guild of Artists, 1965-; Falmouth Artist's Guild, Cape Cod, MA, 1963-; Annual Judge of Art Scholastic Awds, Boston Daily Globe, 1957-79; r/ Rom Cath; hon/Author of Num Pubs; Num Exhbts; S'ship Awd to MA Col of Art; Mus Sch Dist'd Ser Awd, 1981; Awds in Art Exhbts; W/W E.

TRIPLETT, ARLENE ANN oc/Assistant Secretary for Administration; b/Jan 21, 1942; h/6327 Beachway Drive, Falls Church, VA 22044; ba/Washington, DC; m/William K; c/Stephen, Patricia; p/ Vincent and Lorraine Jakovich, Delano, CA; sp/B C and Laura Triplett, Delano, CA; ed/BA, Univ of CA-Berkeley, 1963; pa/Budgets & Reports Analyst, Cutter Labs, Berkeley, CA, 1963-66; Controller, Citizens for Reagan, Wash DC, 1975-76; Dir of Adm, Repub Nat Com, Wash DC, 1977-80; Asst Secy for Adm, 1980-; Mem: Steering Com for the Pres's Mgmt Reform Initiative "Reform 88" White House Task Force for Wom; Appt'd by Pres, Task Force on Legal Equity for Wom; r/Cath.

TROEMEL, JEAN WAGNER (WIL-LHITE) òc/Artist; b/May 4, 1921; h/6 South Street, St Augustine, FL 32084; ba/ Same; m/Benjamin H; c/Benjamin H Jr, Robert E, Linda Lovelace; p/Ralph B Wagner (dec); Edna Macomber Wagner, W Palm Bch, FL; sp/Benjamin and Linga Troemel (dec); ed/Att'd: Art Students Leag NYC & Nat Acad of Design NYC, 1939-42; Norton Sch of Art, FL, 1943-44; Univ of NM, 1947 & 1948; pa/Asst Engr & Illustr, Univ of CA-Los Alamos, NM, 1946 & 1947; Art Instr, Ridge Art Assn, Winter Haven, FL; Jacksonville Art Mus, FL, 1966-68; Flagler Col, St Augustine, FL, 1971-73; Pvt Art Classes, 1973-; Self-employed Portrait Artist, 1973-; Mem: VPres 1957, Pres 1974-76, FL

Artist Grp Inc; Fdr 1949, Hon Life Mem, Ridge Art Assn, Winter Haven, FL; Secy & Treas 1979-80, Life Mem, St Augustine Art Assn; VPres, FL Fdn of Art, 1955-56; Life Mem, Art Students Leag of NYC, 1941; Cummer Mus of Art; Jacksonville Mus of Art, FL; r/Luth; hon/Over 12 Grp Juried & One Man Shows; Exhibns Incl: Univ of FL-Gainesville; Ringling Art Mus, Sarasota; Sarasota Art Assn; Norton Gallery of Art, W Palm Bch; Four Arts Soc, Palm Bch; Miami Bch Art Assn; Barry Col, Miami; St Petersburg Art Assn; FL Fed of Art; Tampa St Fair; Dixie Paper Co, Atlanta; SE Annual, Atlanta; FL So Col, Lakeland; Jacksonville Art Mus, FL; Ridge Art Assn, Winter Haven; FL Artists Grp; Stetson Univ, DeLand FL; Asheville NC Artists Guild; NM Art Mus; Denver Art Mus; B'ham Art Mus; Dallas Art Mus; St Augustine Art Assn; Flagler Col, St Augustine, FL; Wks in Num Pvt Collections; Recip Num Maj Show Awds for Portraiture incl'g: Ringling Art Mus; Sarasota Art Assn; Palm Bch Art Leag; 4 Arts Soc; FL Fedn of Art; FL Artists Grp Inc; Tampa St Fair; St Augustine Art Assn; Fellow, Royal Soc of Art, London, 1973-83; Kappa Intl, 1962; Other Hons; W/W of Wom.

TROY, JOHN JOSEPH oc/Executive; b/May 28, 949; h/3535 Winston Drive, Hoffman Estates, IL 60195; ba/Waukegan, IL; m/Susan Murray; c/Jennifer Anne, John Murray; p/Mr and Mrs John J Troy, Floral Park, NY; sp/Mr and Mrs Alva M Jones, Wauwatosa, WI; ed/BS, St John's Univ, 1970; MM, NWn Univ, 1982; CPA, PA, 1976; pa/Staff Auditor, Touche Ross & Co CPA, 1970-71; Sr Auditor, Clarence Rainess & Co CPA, 1971-73; Internal Auditor, Mobil Oil Corp, 1973-77; Internal Auditor, Ashland Oil Corp, 1977-78; Corp Controller, Hawthorn Mellody Inc, 1978-82; VPres Fin, Am Heritage Industs Inc, 1982-; Mem: Am Inst of CPA's, 1976-; Inst of Internal Auditors, 1977-; Am Mgmt Assn, 1978-; hon/W/W: in MW, in Fin & Indust.

TRUE, JUDITH NAPIER oc/College Teaching and Educational Consultant; b/ Aug 29, 1938; h/4643 Mountain Creek Drive, Roswell, GA 30075; ba/Dahlonega, GA; m/David W; ed/BA, Marshall Univ, 1960; BS 1964, MS 1967, FL St Univ; PhD, GA St Univ, 1974; pa/Tchr Hort Elem Sch 1960-62, Rdg Tchr Norcrest Elem Sch 1964-65, Broward Co Bd of Instrn, Ft Lauderdale, FL; Hd Resident Cnslr, S'ship House for Girls, FL St Univ, Tallahassee, 1962-64; Rdg Tchr Fernbank Elem Sch 1965-66, Rdg Conslt DeKalb Schs Rdg Ctr 1966-71, Rdg Spec & Vol Coor DeKalb Schs Rdg Ctr 1972-73, DeKalb Co Bd of Ed, Decatur, GA; Grad Tchg Asst & Pt-time Instr, GA St Univ, Atlanta, 1973-75; Assoc Prof Ed, N GA Col, 1975-; Mem: Co-Chm Parents & Rdg Com 1982-, US Mbrship & Org Com 1978-81, IRA Coor for St of GA 1976-79 & 1982-84, Local Coun Chp 24th Annual Conv-Atlanta, IRA; NCTE; Editor of *Focus* 1979-82, Edit Advy Bd for *GA Jour of Rdg*, 1981-, GA Coun of Intl Rdg Assn; Pres 1981-82, Chm Task Force on Competency Based Tchr Ed 1977-79, GA Coun of Rdg Profs; cp/Public Relats Co-Chm Annual Invitational Race 1982, Atlanta Ath Clb; Newslttr Editor, SEn Squash Rackets Assn, 1982-; r/Bapt; hon/Author, *Coors Handbook*, 1981; *N GA Col Prep of Preser Tchrs to Tch Rdg in Elem Sch* Report, 1976; Var Articles Pub'd in Profl Rdg Jours;

1979 Pres's Awd, GA Coun of Intl Rdg Assn; Dir, N GA Col Right To Read Tchr Ed Grant, 1975-76; W/W: in S & SW, Among Students in Am Univs & Cols.

TRUJILO, PAUL EDWARD oc/Instructor; b/Dec 15, 1952; h/PO Box 396, Peralta, NM 87042; ba/Belen, NM; m/Rita Alice Martinez; c/Erica Marie; p/Juan Del Dios and Reigna Trujillo, Belen, NM; sp/ Arnulfo and Eusebia Martinez, Grants, NM; ed/BS Elects, NM St Univ, 1976; MS Computer Engrg, Univ of NM, 1984; mil/ NM Army NG; pa/Houston Lighting & Power, 1973-74; Instr, NM St Univ, 1974-76; Edgerton, Germeshausen & Grier, 1976-81; Instr, Univ of NM, 1981-; cp/NM Poetry Soc, 1979-; Rio Grande Writers Assn, 1979-; r/Cath; hon/Author of Num Poems Pub'd in Jours Incl'g: *The Bi-lingual Review; Beacon Review; Poetry Now; Writers Forum; Maize; Encore; Vanderbilt Review;* Wks in Anthology, *A Ceremony of Brotherhood;* Others; Nom for Pushcart Prize in Poetry, 1980; W/W of Authors & Writers; Men of Achmt.

TRYBUS, RAYMOND J oc/Dean of Research Institute; b/Jan 9, 1944; h/8806 Altimont Lane, Chevy Chase, MD 20815; ba/Washington, DC; m/Sandra Noone; c/ David Noone, Nicole Alexandra; p/Fred Trybus (dec); Cecilia Trybus, Chgo, IL; sp/Dommy and Alice Noone, Shreveport, LA; ed/BS 1965, MS 1970, PhD 1971, St Louis Univ; pa/Dean of Res Inst & Prof Adm 1978-, Res Psychol & Dir of Demographic Studies 1972-78, Clin Psychol 1971-72, Gallandet Col, Wash DC; Clin Psychol, St Louis Jewish Employmt & Voc Ser, 1968-71; Mem: Am Psychol Assn; Intl Assn for Study of Interdisciplinary Res; Psych Sect Chp 1982-, The Von Bekesy Soc for Interdisciplinary Res in Deafness; Consltg Pyschol, MD St Mtl Hlth Prog for the Deaf, 1982-; r/Rom Cath; hon/Author, Co-Author & Editor, Over 21 Res Reports, Articles, Chapts & Books Incl'g: *Dir of Mtl Hlth Progs & Resources for Hearing Impaired Persons,* 1981-82; *Am Annals of the Deaf,* 1981; *Sign Lang & the Deaf Commun: Essays in Hon of Wm C Stokoe Jr,* 1980; *Life in Fam w Deaf Mems: Proceedings of the 5th World Conf in Deaf,* 1978; *TX St Survey of Hearing Impaired Chd & Yth: A New Approach to Statewide Planning, Monitoring & Eval of Spec Ed Programming,* 1978; *Am Annals of Deaf Dir of Progs & Sers,* 1977; *The Future of Mtl Hlth sers for Deaf People: Proceedings of the 1st Orthopsychi Wkshop on Deafness, Mtl Hlth in Deafness,* 1977; Others; Nat F'ship, WK Kellogg Foun, 1983-86; W/W: in E, in Frontier Sci & Technol.

TRZASKO, JOSEPH ANTHONY oc/ Psychologist; b/Jun 4, 1946; h/30 Lake Drive, Somers, NY 10589; ba/Dobbs Ferry, NY; m/Ann Elizabeth; c/Joshua Damon; p/Joseph A and Lottie M Trzasko, Bellerose, NY; sp/William G and Elizabeth M Kidd, Golden, CO; ed/BA, Univ of NH, 1967; MA 1969, PhD 1972, Univ of VT; Cert of Behavior Therapy, Behavior Therapy Inst of Psychi Sers Ctr, 1976; Postdoct Intern Mtl Retard, Ridge St Home & Tng Sch, CO Dept of Instns, 1980; pa/Prof Dept Psych 1969-, Dir Instnl Testing 1969-80, Mercy Col; Adj Prof Depts of Psych, Guid & Cnslg & Ed, LI Univ-Westchester Campus, 1978-; Psychol, St Dominic's Intermediate Care Facility for Develmtly Disabled & Mtl Retarded, 1980-; Consltg Psych, Jewish Guild for the Blind, 1982-; Pvt Pract Spec in Psychol Eval & Diagnosis; Mem: Am

Psychol Assn; Intl Coun Psychols; Westchester Co Psychol Assn; AAUP; Am Ednl Res Assn; r/Cath; hon/Author, Over 100 Internal Statl Reports while Dir of Insttl Testing, Mercy Col, 1969-80; Nat Def F'ship, Univ of VT, 1967-69; NSF Fac Res Participation Grant, Ed Comm of Sts/Nat Assessment Of Ednl Progress, 1976; Psi Chi; Pi Gamma Mu; Kappa Delta Pi; Lic'd Psychol, NY St, 1977-; W/W in E.

TSANG, N F h/27896 Adobe Court, Hawyard, CA 94542.

TSAU, WEN SHIUNG oc/Project Engineer and Inspector; b/Jul 22, 1946; h/516 Fossil Butte Drive (PO Box 2012), Kemmerer, WY 83101-1901; ba/Kemmerer, WY; p/Chun-Fu Tsau (dec); Yu-In Yang Tsau, Bklyn, NY; ed/BA Engrg & Arch, Tamking Univ, 1969; BSCE, NEn Univ, Boston, 1978; MSCE, Univ of WY, 1981; pa/Proj Engr/Inspector, Johnson-Fermelia & Crank Inc, 1981-; Grad Asst, Dept Civil Engrg, Univ of WY Grad Sch, 1979-80; Civil Engr, Taiwan Power Co, 1970-73; Mem: Nat Soc of Profl Engrs, 1977-; WY Soc of Profl Engrs, 1977-; ASCE, 1978; WYSCE, 1978; Concrete Reinforcing Steel Inst, 1981; Life Mem: Sigma Xi; Tau Beta Pi; hon/Author, "Optimization of Hybrid Girders," 1981; Sigma Xi, 1980; Tau Beta Pi, 1980; Grad S'ships & Asst'ships, 1979-80; Dean's List Scholar w Hon, 1976-78; W/W in W.

TSCHUMPERLIN, MARIE DOLORES ANN oc/Independent Contractor; b/Mar 27, 1945; h/PO Box 952 Salinas, CA 93902; ba/Salinas, CA; p/ Joseph Tschumperlin (dec); Lylyan Tschumperlin, Salinas, CA; ed/AA, Harnell Col, 1965; pa/Onion Buncher, J & A Farms, 1969; Indep Contractor for *St Anthony Messenger,* 1984-; Mem: Exec Coun 1965, Life Mem, Delta Psi Omega; cp/Madonna Dal Sasso Altar Soc; r/Cath; hon/Pub'd Poems in *Jean's Jour,* 1983-84; Others; Poet of Yr, J Mark Press, 1974; Intl W/W in Poetry.

TSUANG, MING T oc/Professor; Psychiatrist; b/Nov 16, 1931; ba/Butler Hospital, 345 Blackstone Boulevard, Providence, RI 09206; m/Huei Shiang Snow; c/John, Debby, Grace; p/Ping-tang Tsuang, Taiwan; Chhun-kei Lin, Taiwan; ed/MD; PhD; pa/Prof & VChm Dept Psych & Human Behavior, Brown Univ, Providence, RI, 1982-; Dir Psychi Epidemiology Res Unit & Assoc Med Dir, Butler Hosp, Providence, RI, 1982-; Prof, Staff Psych, IA City; Resr; cp/Bd Mem, MW Formosa Christian Foun; r/Trinity Christian Reform Ch, Elder; hon/ Sino-Brit F'ship Scholar; Res Grants Awd, NIMH.

TUCCI, MARK A oc/Educational Administrator; b/Dec 14, 1950; ba/ Katzenbach Sch for the Deaf, 320 Sullivan Way, West Trenton, NJ 08628; m/Carolyn; c/Nicholas, Anthony, Vincent; p/Mr and Mrs William F Tucci, Trenton, NJ; sp/Mr and Mrs Michael Bilecki, Trenton, NJ; ed/BS, 1972; MEd, 1978; Cert'd: Supt, Prin, Supvr, Tchr of Deaf & Hearing Impaired, Tchr of Handicapped, for Sts of NJ & NY; pa/ Tchr in Diagnostic Univ 1972-75, Tchr in Lower Sch 1975-76, Tchr in Med Sch 1976-82, Parent Ed/Public Info Coor, 1982-, Katzenbach Sch; Mem: Kappa Delta Pi; Phi Delta Kappa; Conv of Am Instrs of the Deaf; NJ Assn for Chd w Hearing Impairments; Past Pres, Katzenbach Tchrs Assn; Past Pres, Katzenb-

ach Chapt, NJ St Employees Assn; cp/ Scout Ldr, Commun Scouting Grp; r/ Cath; hon/Author, Var Articles Pub'd in Profl Jours; Num Photos Pub'd in Worldwide Salon Catalogs & Profl Jours; Sr Traineeship, 1971-72; Hon Cert, Gamma Zeta Chapt, Kappa Delta Pi, 1971; Num Awds for Photos; W/W in E.

TUCKER, WANDA HALL oc/Senior Managing Editor; b/Feb 6, 1921; ba/525 East Colorado, Pasadena, CA 91109; m/ Frank R; c/Frank R Jr, Nancy Irene; p/ Frank Walliston and Hazel G Smith Hall (dec); ed/AA, Citrus Col; pa/Sr Mng Editor, *Pasadena Star-News,* Currently; Mem: Sigma Delta Chi; Gtr LA Press Clb; cp/City & Co Affairs Coms; Pasadena C of C; Exec Bd, Pasadena Opportunites Industrialization Ctr; Advy Com, Pasadena Commun Col; r/Prot; hon/Writing Awd, Gtr LA Press Clb & CA Newspaper Pubrs Assn; Awd for Commun Ser, Wom's Civic Leag of Pasadena; Wom of Achmt, Pasadena Commun Col; Resolutions from Var Cities incl'g: Pasadena, Glendora, Duarte & Azusa.

TUDMAN, CATHI GRAVES oc/Musician; b/Nov 24, 1953; h/2246 North Jackson, Fresno, CA 93703; ba/Same; m/ Dennis P; c/Colleen Melissa; p/Mr and Mrs R E Graves, Fresno, CA; sp/Mr and Mrs Donald Tudman, Fresno, CA; ed/BA, CA St Univ-Fresno, 1978; Ryan Act Tchg Credential, 1978; pa/3rd Flute & Piccolo, Fresno Philharm Orch, 1976-; Piccolo, Santa Cruz Symph, 1981; Flute & Piccolo, Orpheus Chamber Ensemble, 1979-82; Music Tchr, Wash Colony Sch, 1978-80; Music Tchr, Monroe Elem Sch, 1978-79; Flute & Piccolo Fresno Swingphonic Band, 1972-83; Flute Instr, Fresno Philharm Music Camp, 1981-83; Flute Instr, La Sierra Music Camp, 1977; Marching Band Aud Grp Advr, CA St Univ-Fresno, 1974-78; Marching Bd Advr: McLane HS, Fresno, 1976; Sanger HS, Sanger, 1977; Fresno HS, 1981; Tranquility HS, 1982; Pvt Studio Flute Instr, 1971-83; Mem: Phi Kappa Phi; Pi Kappa Delta; Tokalon; Music Edrs Nat Conf; Ctl Sect, CA Music Edrs Assn; Coor, CMEA Ctl Sect Solo & Ensemble Fest, 1972-82; Fest Chm CMEA Ctl Sect, 191-82; Adjudicator, Fresno-Madera Counties Hon Band & Orchs, 1976-82; Col Pres 1975-77, VPres & Pledge Advr 1978, Chaplain 1975 & 1982, Alumni Secy 1981, Nat Chm (Friendship Corner) 1979-82, Mu Phi Epsilon; Nat Flute Assn; Music Tchrs Assn; Chm, Fresno Br, VOCE, 1981-83; cp/Fresno Musical Clb; Blue Key Ser Soc; r/Prot; hon/Perf'd Premier New Wk "Concerto for Flute & Strings" by Jose Brown, 1982; Participant, Master Class Hidden Val CA by Julius Baker Prin Flute w NY Philharm, 1981-83; Participant, Mas Class by Miles Zenter 1980, Toby Kaplan 1979, CA St Univ-Fresno; Soloist, Fresno String Orch, Bach's "Brandenburg Concerto #2," 1979; Soloist, Telemann "Suite in A Minor," "Kennan Night Soliloquy," "Chaminade Concertino," CA St Univ-Fresno Symph Orch, 1976-78; Soloist, MENC Wn Div Conv, SF, 1975; Nat Tour of Champs: Ypsalanti, MI 1972; Plattsburg, NY 1973; Finalist, Bolling Green, KY 1974; Only Double Qualifier (Estemp & Expres) to Nationals, 9er Invitational, Long Bch St Univ, 1973; 1st Place, Expository Spkg Wn Sts Assn, 1974; 1st Flute & Piccolo, Yg Ams in Concert, Nat Hon Band, 1971; Others; Outstg Yg Wom in Am.

TUDOR, JAMES P oc/State Police Lieutenant; b/Nov 20, 1946; h/6913 Yorkwood Drive, Little Rock, AR 72209; ba/Little Rock, AR; m/Melanie K Williford; c/Scotty; p/W A Tudor, Little Rock, AR; sp/C E Williford, Brinkley, AR; ed/Att'd Univ of AR, 1964-66; Profl Photo Credentials, NY Inst of Photo,1982; Att'd Police Photo Sems; pa/Lt 1982-, Asst Cmdr of Records Bur 1982, Cmdr of Public Info Sect 1980, Cmdr Commun Sect 1971, AR St Police; Mem: Associated Photogs Intl, 1981-82; AR Peace Ofcrs Assn; Past Pres, SEn Law Enforcement Telecommuns Sys; cp/Govs Comm on Sci & Technol; Govs Com on Resource Conserv; AR Archaeol Soc; r/Bapt; hon/ Author, *Treasure Res Techniques*; Editor, *Hist of the AR St Police*; Num Articles in Nat Mags; Ctl AR Police Ofcr of Yr, 1971; Outstg Yg Men of Am; W/W in S & SW.

TURBYFILL, ROBERT REEVES JR oc/ Genealogist and Compiler; b/Jun 13, 1947; h/309 Scott's Way, Augusta, GA 30909; ba/Augusta, GA; m/Ann Chafee; c/Robert R 3rd, James C, Laura F; p/ Robert R Sr and R Lucille, Augusta, GA; sp/James T Chafee (dec); Mary S Chafee, Augusta, GA; ed/Att'd Acad of Richmond Co, 1966; Att'd Augusta Area Tech Sch, 1968; Att'd So Bapt Theol Sem-Sem Ext, 1981-; pa/Compiler of Fam Hists; Preparer of Lineages (Spec So Fams) for: Nat Soc of DAR, Nat Soc SAR, Colonial Dames, Sons of The Confederate Vets; Compiler, Geneal Soc, 1978-; Mem: Bd of Mgmt 1980-82, Nat Soc SAR; Pres, Col Wm Few Chapt SAR, 1982-83; Nat Mem, Sons of Confed Vets, 1980-; Co-fdr, Brig Gen E Porter Alexander Camp 1286, Sons of Confederate Vets; cp/Col Grp Pres, 1966-67; Dir, Inner City Mission, 1967-68; Ofcl Bd 1966-69 & Steward, Trintiy on the Hill U Meth Ch; r/Meth; hon/Compiler, *Grandaddy's Turbyfills*, 1980; *Reeves Review Volume 2*, 1982; *Andrew Robeson of Scotland & His Descendants Volume 2*, 1983; *Some Descendants of Richard Warren of the Mayflower*, 1980; Awd for Outstg Perf on Nat Edni Devel Tests, NEDT, 1962; Mem, Mil Order of Stars & Bars, 1982; W/W in S & SW.

TURKAT, DAVID M oc/Psychologist; b/Apr 7, 1952; h/3221-I Post Woods Drive, Atlanta, GA 30339; ba/Atlanta, GA; p/Michael Turkat, Smyrna, GA; Phyllis Schiff Turkat (dec); ed/BA, Brandeis Univ, 1973; MA 1974, PhD 1978, LA St Univ; pa/Prog Eval Spec, Div of Mtl Hlth & Mtl Retard Commun Support Proj, Atlanta, 1978-80; Prvt Pract, Clin & Consltg Psych, 1979-; Mem: VPres, Assn for Med Psych, 1982-84; Am Psychol Assn, 1978-; Mtl Hlth Assn of GA, 1978-; cp/Access Atlanta, 1980; Gen Semantics Inst, 1978-80; hon/Author, Over 35 Articles Pub'd in Profl & Sci Jours; Fellow, Menninger Foun, 1980-82; Caber Awd, 1982; W/W in S & SW.

TURMAN, GEORGE F oc/Lieutenant Governor of Montana; b/Jun 25, 1928; h/1300 Stuart, Helena, MT 59601; ba/ Helena, MT; m/Kathleen H; c/Marcia (T) Bartlett, Linda (T) Madsen, Douglas, John, Laura; ed/BA Ec, Univ of MT, 1951; mil/AUS, 1951-53, Inf, Korea; pa/Var Positions, Fed Resv Bk of SF, 1954-63; Bus-man, Missoula, MT, 1964-70; Mayor of Missoula, MT, 1970-72; St Legislator, St of MT, 1973-74; Public Ser Commr, St of MT, 1975-80; Lt Gov, St of MT, 1981-; Mem, Num Orgl Mbrships & Commun Activs; r/Epis; hon/Combat Inf Badge, AUS; Others; W/W in W.

TURNBULL, DOREEN J oc/Systems Analyst; b/Jan 10, 1938; h/3620 Moreno Avenue, Space 52, La Verne, CA 91750; ba/Pasadena, CA; p/Dales and Juliet Turnbull, Laguna Hills, CA; ed/BS, Bus Mgmt, 1969; MBA, Claremont Grad Sch, 1984; pa/Sr Sys Analyst, Sunkist Growers Sherman Oaks, CA, 1968-74; EDP Sys Analyst, Ralphs Grocery Co, Compton, CA, 1974-77; Owner, DJT Consits, 1977-80; Proj Mgr, Sr Sys Analyst, Xerox Med Sys, Pasadena, CA, 1980-; Mem: Bd Mem 1982, Secy 1983, San Gabriel Chapt, Data Processing Mgmt Assn; Nat Assn of Female Execs; Am Mgmt Assn; Secy 1981-82, Treas 1983-84, Altrusa Clb of Arcadia; Bd Mem 1982-83, IS/DP Alumni; Wom in Mgmt; r/Epis; hon/W/ W of Am Wom.

TURNER, CARL JEANE oc/Electronics Engineer, International Business Development Executive; b/July 27, 1933; h/51 Harbor Park Drive, Centerport, NY 11721; m/Flossie Pearl Ingram; c/Kenneth Jeane, Marcia Lynne, Theresa Jeanette, Christopher Alan, Robin Jyne; p/Kenneth Albert and Lenna Faye Christopher Turner (dec); sp/James Newton Ingram (dec); Alice Jane West Ingram, Waco, TX; ed/BSEE, BSEd 1980, MBA 1982, PhD 1983, Columbia Pacific Univ; mil/USAF, 1950-72 (Ret'd); FL Air NG, 1948-50; CAP FL Wing, 1946-51; pa/Pres, Intermgmt Technol (Intl Bus Consits), 1983-; Intl Sales Mgr, Probe Sys Inc, Sunnyvale, CA, 1983; Mgr Export Mktg, Wn Div, GTE Sylvania Sys Grp, Mt View, CA, 1981-83; Mgr Intl Progs Planning & Control Applied Technol Div, Sunnyvale, CA 1981, Resident Mgr German Progs Ofc at AEG-Telefunken AG, Ulm, Germany 1979-81 (Itek Intl Corp, Lexington, MA), Prog Devel Mgr Optical Sys Div Athens, Greece 1978-79 (Itek Intl Corp, Lexington, MA), Sr Intl Mktg Rep Applied Technol Div Sunnyvale, CA 1976-77, Reg Mgr MidE Opers, Mgr Iranian Field Opers & Sr Field Ser Rep Applied Technol Div Tehran, Iran 1973-76, Field Ser Rep Applied Technol Div Sunnyvale, CA 1972-73, Itek Corp; Sr Engr/Analyst & Chief Instr, E-Systems Inc, Greenville, TX, 1977-78; Mem: Profl & Tech Consits Assn; Nat Assn of the Professions; IEEE; AF Assn; Armed Forces Communs & Elects Assn; Am Entrepreneurs Assn; cp/IPA; Assn of Old Crows; Order of Seasoned Weasels; Intl Biogl Assn; Nat Writers Clb; Sustaining Mem, Repub Nat Com; Repub Pres Task Force; Smithsonian Assocs; r/Bapt; hon/ Author, "An Intl Mktg Plan for a Def Elects Small Bus to Capitalize on its Fully Developed Prods, Sys & Sers," 1983; "The Mgmt Challenge to Coproducing High Technol Sys in Germany," 1983; "Establishment of a Br Ofc in Greece by Virtue of Law 89/378," 1982; Author/Editor, "Joint Elect Warfare Mgmt," 1978; George Wash Hon Medal, Freedoms Foun, 1965; Pres Achmt Awd & Pres's Medal of Merit, Ronald Reagan, 1982; PATCA; Multilingual: Eng, German, Japanese, Thai & Persian; W/W: in Fin & Indust, in Consltg, of Contemp Achmt; Commun Ldrs of Am; Intl Book of Hon; 2000 Notable Ams; Men of Achmt; DIB; Num Other Biogl Listings.

TURNER, DONALD PAUL oc/Inventor, Educator, Educational Publisher, Consultant; b/Jan 22, 1930; h/16 Bradley Court, Rockville, MD 20851; m/Doris Elizabeth Bozman; c/Rosemary, Dorene, Cheryl, Karen; p/Gilbert E Turner (dec); Mae B Williams, Westminster, MD; sp/ Isaac J Bozman (dec); Fannie A Roberts, Salisbury, MD; ed/BS, Ed, 1951; MA, George Wash Univ, 1961; mil/USAF, 1951-53; USAFR 2nd Lt- Capt, 1953-62; pa/Tchr: 1953-56, 1958-69 & 1974-84; Area 1 Elem Sci Tchr, Spec, Montgomery Co, MD, 1969-74; Ret'd, MD St Tchr Ret Sys, 1984; Fdr, Chm of Bd & Pres, Edu-Game Co Inc, T A Chesapeake Games, Rockville, MD, 1981-; Fdrs, Pres, Lern-a-skil Co, Rockville, MD, 1981-; Fdr, Pres, Inventors Mktg Coop, 1982-; Edni Pubr, 1982-; Edni Consltg, 1982-; Vol Emer Med Tech & Paramedic Asst, Takoma Pk & Rockville, MD, 1975-; Life Mem, NEA; Life Mem, MD Tchrs Assn; MD Home Edn Assn; Life Mem, Montgomery Co Edn Assn; Edni Sales Rep Assn in MD, DE & Wash DC; r/Prot; hon/Edni Pubr, Inventor of Instrni Games for Lrng Multiplication Tables; Holds Num Copyrights for Lrng Games in Var Edni Areas; Eagle Scout Awd, 1950; Scouter's Awd, 1961; Arrow Hd Awd, 1973; Commr's Key, 1975; Scoutmaster's Key, 1979; W/W in E; Men of Achmt.

TURNER, DOROTHA L oc/Office Manager and Art Instructor; b/Feb 23, 1927; h/Route 1, Box 311 Corning, AR 72422; ba/Reyno, AR; m/Filbert; c/Janice D (T) Garrett, Phylliss R (T) Wright, Gary W, Clarissa L (T) Russell; p/Carrel and Irene Hester, Datto, AR; ed/Grad, Corning HS, 1944; pa/Subst Tchr, Var Schs, 1944-64; Purchasing Agt, Johanson Shoe, Corning, AR, 1964; Bkkpr 1969-70, Ofcr Mgr & Secy/Treas 1975-81, Blackman Oil Co, Corning, AR; Indusrl Engr, Computer Programming, Corning Distbg Co, 1970-75; Ofcr Mgr, Pearcy Oil Co, 1982-; Art Instr, 1981-; cp/Var Ofcs in Home Demonstration Clbs, 1946-56; Rural Communs Clb, 1956-62; Ldr, 4-H Clb, 1957-66; Activ in Boys & Girls Local Sports Progs; Art Clb; Nat Rifle Assn; r/Bapt; hon/Nat Hon Soc, 1942; Artist of Mo, at Least Once Each Yr, 1979-83; Basic Art Instrn, Once a Mo, Local Elem Public Schs, 1983; W/W in Am Wom.

TURNER, HERMAN NATHANIEL JR oc/Educator, Mathematician; b/Nov 6, 1925; h/5917 Emma Avenue, St Louis, MO 63136; ba/St Louis, MO; m/Terrance Diane Parker; c/Anthony Cabot, Mark Courtney, Herman Nathaniel III, Erik Alexander, Marian Terese Simmons, Mariesta Marcella Simmons, Melita Diane Simmons; p/Herman Nathaniel Sr and Rosie Mae (Williams) Turner (both dec); ed/BS 1951, Grad Courses in Math & Ed 1951-52, Bradley Univ; mil/USMC, 1944-46, WW II S Pacific Area; pa/ Cartographic Photogrammetric Aide, Aeronautical Chart & Info Ctr, Photogrammetry Div, Topography Br, St Louis, MO, 1953-54; Math, White Sands Proving Ground, Flight Determination Lab, Data Reduction Br, Optical Reduction Sect, Las Cruces, NM, 1954-55; Math Tchr, Vaux Jr HS & Stoddart-Fleisher Jr HS, Phila, PA, 1956-59; Math Tchr, Wash Sr HS, Caruthersville, MO, 1961-62; Math Tchr, U Township HS, E Noline, IL, 1965-66; Math Tchr, NW HS, St Louis, MO, 1968-; Mem: Math Assn of Am, 1962-; Am Fedn of Tchrs, 1969-; Am Math Soc, 1977-; Pub Relats Com, NW HS, St Louis, 1978-; Math Tchr Cert: MO, IL, PA, NJ, NY; cp/Area Cmdr (w Wife), Area F, Reg 9,

Operation Brightside (St Louis Cleans-Up), St Louis, MO, 1982; Chm, Block Unit 962, Urban Leag, St Louis, MO, 1982-; Fellow 1979-, Nat Bd of Advrs 1982-, ABI; Fellow, Intl Biogl Assn, 1978-; Hon Fellow, Anglo-Am Acad, 1980-; Chm Public Relats Clb, Kiwanis Clb of E Moline, IL, 1965-66; Dem; r/ Presb; hon/Cert of Apprec, Kiwanis Clb of E Moline, IL, 1965; Cert of Merit, MOA, 1978; Cert of Merit, IWWCS, 1979; Cert of Merit, DIB, 1979; Scroll of Anglo-Am Acad, 1980; Tchr of Mo, (Chosen by Student Body), NW HS, Oct 1979; Tchr of Yr (Sr Class), NW HS, 1980; "Who's Who Via Its Students," NW HS Yrbook, 1981; Num Other NW HS Apprec Awds; Voice Spotlight on Commun Wkrs, Editor & Pubr of *Voice Mag*, St Louis, MO, 1982; W/W: in MW, of Commun Ser, of Intells, of Anglo-Ams; Men of Achmt; 2000 Notable Ams; Commun Ldrs of Am; DIB; Intl Book of Hon; Other Biogl Listings.

TURNER, LOYD LEONARD oc/Corporate Executive; b/Nov 5, 1917; h/3717 Echo Trail, Ft Worth, TX 76109; ba/Ft Worth, TX; m/Lee M; c/Terry Lee (T) Hollis; Loyd Lee; p/James R Turner (dec); sp/Charles Barr (dec); ed/BA 1939, MA 1940, Baylor Univ; Postgrad Study, Univ of PA, 1940-42; mil/USAAF, WW II, 1942-46; pa/Instr, Univ of PA, 1940-42; Public Relats Coor, Consolidated Vultee Aircraft Corp, 1946-48; Dir of Public Relats, Ft Worth Div, Gen Dynamics Corp, 1948-72; VPres, Tandy Corp/Radio Shack, 1972-; Pres N TX Chapt, Public Relats Soc of Am, 1977; Pres, Advtg Clb of Ft Worth, 1977-78; Trustee, Baylor Univ, 1980-; cp/Pres, Ft Worth Bd of Ed, 1965-71; Pres, Ft Worth Public Lib Bd, 1958-63; Pres, Rotary Club of Ft Worth, 1974-75; Pres, Casa Manana Musicals, 1978-80; r/Bapt; hon/Author, *ABC of Clear Writing*, 1954; Paul M Lund Public Ser Awd, Public Relats Soc of Am, 1980; Silver Medal, Am Advtg Fedn, 1981; Paul Harris Fellow, Rotary Intl, 1982; Other Hons & Awds; W/W: in Am, in World, in S & SW, in Fin & Indust.

TURNER, PATRICIA RAE oc/University Administrator; b/May 15, 1935; h/1506 Caper Lane, San Antonio, TX 78232; ba/San Antionio, TX; m/Donald H; p/James Ray and Linnie Maria Watson, Canton, TX; sp/John and Becky Turner, Greenville, TX; ed/BBA 1971, MBA 1974, E TX St Univ; Completed PhD Course Wk, TX A&M Univ; pa/Prog Coor Cont'g Ed 1970-72, Dir Student Devel 1974-76, E TX St Univ, Commerce, TX; Asst Dir Commun Ser, Mt View Col, Dallas, TX, 1972-73; Dir Div of Adult & Cont'g Ed, Angelo St Univ, San Angelo, TX, 1974; Assoc Dir Commun Ser, El Centro Col, Dallas, TX, 1976-77; Div Hd Spec Progs Tng Div 1978, Mgr S Ctl TX Reg Tng Ctr 1978-, TX Engrg Ext Ser, The TX A&M Univ Sys, San Antonio, TX; Mem: Voc Tech Tng Coun; Ec Devel Foun; City of San Antonio Industl Devel Bd; Alamo Area Coun of Govt A-95 Review Com; Reg Devel & Review Com; Nat Alliance of Bus Pvt Indust Coun; Num Others; cp/Gtr San Antonio C of C; San Antonio Arts Coun; Economic Urban Roundtable, U San Antonio; San Antonio Bd 3 Yrs Term, The Zonta Clb; Num Others; r/Bapt; hon/Editor, Contbg Author, *SCTRTC*; *Handbook for Employing the Handicapped*; Num Articles on the Handicapped, Pub'd in TX Rehab Comm TPEA

Monthly Newslttr & Dallas Commun Col Dist Inter-Com Newslttr; Var Funded Proposals, 1978-82; Cert of Apprec, US Dept of Nav; Appreciation Resolution, Bd of Regents of E TX St Univ; Today's Wom, San Antonio Light Newspaper, 1982; Am Soc for Tng & Devel W/W Tng Dir; WAVE; W/W: in S & SW, of Am Wom; Other Biogl Listings.

TURNER, ROBERT FOSTER oc/Government Official, Attorney, Author; b/ Feb 14, 1944; h/8222 La Faye Court, Alexandria, VA 22306; ba/Washington, DC; m/Debra H; p/Edwin W Turner, Homestead, FL; ed/BA, IN Univ, 1968; Grad Wk in Hist & Polit Sci, Stanford Univ, 1972-73; Grad Wk in Govt & Fgn Affairs 1979-81; JD, Univ of VA Sch of Law, 1981; mil/AUS, 1968-71, Capt, Armor, Vietnam; pa/Counsel, Pres's Intell Oversight Bd, The White House, 1982-; Spec Asst to Under Secy of Def for Policy, 1981-82; Assoc Dir, Ctr for Law & Nat Security, Univ of VA Law Sch, 1981; Legis Asst/Spec Asst to US Senator Robert P Griffin, 1973-79; Public Affairs Fellow & Res Assoc, Hoover Instn on War, Revolution & Peace, Stanford Univ, 1973-74; Mem: VA St Bar Assn; ABA; Am Soc of Intl Law; cp/US Chess Fedn; Jefferson Lit & Debating Soc; Nat Eagle Scout Assn; hon/Author, *Vietnamese Communism: Its Origins & Devel*, 1975; *Myths of the Vietnam War: The Pentagon Papers Reconsidered*, 1972; *The War Powers Resolution: Its Implementation in Theory & Pract*, 1983; Assoc Editor for Asia & Pacific 1973 & 1974 Editions (Contbr of 14 Chapts), *Yrbook on Intl Communist Affairs*; Sr Editor, *VA Jour of Intl Law*, 1980-81; Num Articles & Reviews Pub'd in Var Profl Jours; W/ W in S & SW; Contemp Authors; Other Biogl Listings.

TURNER, TERRANCE DIANE (PARKER) oc/Housewife, Mother, Secretary; b/Jun 7, 1947; h/5917 Emma Avenue, St Louis, MO 63136; ba/St Louis, MO; m/Herman Nathaniel Jr; c/ Marian Terese Simmons, Mariesta Marcella Simmons, Melita Diane Simmons, Anthony Cabot, Mark Courney, Herman Nathaniel III, Eirk Elexander; p/Marion Willand Sr and Esther Agusta (Hackett) Parker, Oakland, CA; sp/Herman Nathaniel Sr and Rosie Mae (Williams) Turner (both dec); ed/Keypunch Cert, O'Fallon Tech Ctr for Adult Ed, 1967; ba/Bindery Asst, Con P Curran Printing Co, St Louis, MO, 1970-72; John S Starks Printing Co, Manchester, MO, 1972-75; Pressperson, Lianco Container Corp, Bridgeton, MO, 1975-79; Area Cmdr (w Husband) Area F, Reg 9 Operation Brightside (St Louis Cleans-Up), St Louis, MO, 1982; Secy, Block Unit 962, Urban Leag, St Louis, MO, 1972-; Mem: Local 55, Intl Brotherhood of Bookbinders Assn, 1970-75; Graphic Arts Local 505, Master Printers of Am, 1975-79; cp/Vol, ARC, St Louis MO Bi-St Chapt; Annual Assoc, ABI; Mothers' Clb: Walnut Pk Sch 1971-77, Cupples Sch 1977-79, NW HS 1979-82, St Louis, MO; PTO, Wyland Elem Sch, Overland, MO, 1982-; Dem; hon/Lttr of Intro, Lianco Container Corp, 1979; Commun Ldrs of Am; 2000 Notable Ams; Personalities of W & MW.

TURNER, VANESSA JOAN oc/College Administrator; b/Jun 26, 1954; h/ 1840 Carriage Lane, Charleston, SC 294-7; ba/Charleston, SC; p/Artis Turner, Ridge Spring, SC; Sallie M Turner, NYC, NY; ed/BA, Univ of SC,

1976; MA Cand in Human Relats, Webster Univ; pa/Asst to VPres for Instnl Advmt, Col of Charleston, 1981-; Dir of Public Relats, Voorhees Col, 1979-81; Public Relats/Recruiter, Augusta Opportunities Industrialization Ctr, 1977-79; Subst Tchr, Riverside Mid Sch, 1977; pa/ Mem 1980-, Com on Intnl Relats 1983-85, Coun for Advt & Support of Ed (CASE); Instnl Rep 1981-, Am Coun on Ed-SC Wom in Higher Ed; cp/Treas 1975-76, Secy 1980, Alpha Kappa Alpha; YWCA, 1982-; Others; r/Bapt; hon/ Author & Editor, Var Pubs, Pamphlets, Brochures & Bltns for Var Instns; Nat Hon Soc, 1972; Among 50 Yg Ldrs of Future, *Ebony Mag*; Meritorious Ser Awd, U Negro Col Fund, 1979 & 1983; Outstg Yg Wom of Am; W/W Among Am HS.

TURNER, WELD W oc/Industrial Psychologist; b/Jul 25, 1931; h/601 East Rosemary Road, Apartment 3905, Largo, FL 33540; ba/New York, NY; c/Jean Ann, Alan Weld; p/Frank and Hazel Thirza (Weld) Prevratil (dec); ed/BS, UK St Univ, 1954; MS 1955, PhD 1959, Purdue Univ; mil/AUS, 1951-52; pa/Pers Eval Assoc, Gen Motors Inst, Flint, MI, 1955-60; Supvr Pers Res, B F Goodrich Co, Akron, OH, 1960-67; Sr Manpower Advr, Mobil Oil Corp, NYC, 1967-; Mem: MWn Psychol Assn, 1955; Am Psychol Assn, 1955-; Soc for Industl & Orgnl Psych 1955-; r/Unitarian Universalist; hon/ Author, Var Articles Pub'd in *Jour of Applied Psych*; Var Contbns to Industly & Orgnl Psych; W/W in S & SW.

TUTHERLY, LOIS R oc/Professor; b/ Aug 16, 1923; h/21 Orchard Road, Windsor, CT 06095; ba/Hartford, CT; m/ Herbert W; c/Nancy T Griffin, Diane F Resly; p/Clarence W and Etta W Pierce, Windsor, CT; sp/George C and Gertrude B Tutherly; ed/BS, Univ of Hartford, 1963; MS, Ctl CT St Univ, 1968; CAGS Dipl in Profl Ed, Univ of CT, 1975; pa/ Asst Prof, Gtr Hartford Commun Col, 1970-83; Asst Prof, Manchester Commun Col, 1968-70; Asst Prof, Univ of Hartford, 1965-68; Mem: Hon to Grad Bus Edrs, Delta Pi Epsilon, Beta Mu Chapt, 1972-; Hon Grad w Distn, Omicron Tau Theta, Zeta Chapt, 1980-; CMA, Am Assn of Med Assts; r/Christian; hon/Author, Articles Pub'd in *NBEA Forum & Profl Med Asst*; Textbook, *Adv'd Med Terminology/Med Transcription*, 1983.

TUTTILA, MARY ELLEN GLOVER oc/Boy Scout Leader; b/May 28, 1932; h/ 1828, West 169th Street, Hazel Crest, IL 60429; m/Jonas E II; c/John A Calderon, Nancy Calderon Krezman, Deborah Calderon Seaman, Jonas E III; p/Arthur Glover (dec); Margaret E Markel Glover; sp/Jonas I and Nola Thompson Tuttila (dec); ed/Grad, Thornton Twp HS, 1950; pa/Vet Asst, 1965-68; Mgr, Dino's Pizza Place, 1974-76; Mgr, Leeson's, 1976-80; Amway Sponsor; cp/Co-Chm Spring Camporee 1981, Chm Dist Cub Scout Phy Fitness Olympic Finals 1981, Den Ldr 7 Yrs, Den Ldr Coach, LR Pack 443 5 Yrs, Merit Badge Cnslr, IR Troop 443 5 Yrs, Orgr of New Pack 444 Markham, Asst Dist Commr, Cub Scouts; Orgr, Explorer Troop 443 Hazel Crest; Master Guide, Pathfinders; Affil Mem, Circuit Ct of Cook Co; Fam Ser & Mtl Hlth; Thornton Twp; Outreach; Respond Now; Active in PTA, 14 Yrs; Civil Def, 2½ Yrs; Precinct Capt; Sch Bd Competancy Tm; SS Tchr; LPN: Vol, Hazel Crest Lib; Bible Study Ldr; Num Other Activs; r/Prot;

hon/Arrowhead Awd, Cub Scouts; Dist Awd of Merit, 1981.

TUZIL, TERESA JORDAN oc/ Clinical Social Worker, Psychotherapist; b/May 13, 1948; h/3859 Tiana Street, Seaford, NY 11783; ba/Seaford, NY; m/ Joseph Stephen; c/Joseph IV, Brian Joseph; p/Lester F Jordan (dec); Kathleen Brady; sp/Joseph and Eleanore, Tuzil; ed/BA, St John's Univ, 1970; MSW, Hunter Col, 1973; Cert in Gerontology, Hunter/Brookdale, 1977; pa/Social Wkr, Salvation Army Foster Care & Adoption Sers, NYC, 1971-72; Sr Social Wkr, Jewish Assn for Services to the Aged, NYC, 1973-78; Prog Conslt, Commun Coun of Gtr NYC, 1978-79; Pvt Pract Psychotherapist, 1976-; Field Wk Instr, Hunter Col Grad Sch of Social Wk, 1975-78; Fieldwork Instr, Columbia Univ Sch of Social Wk, 1977-78; Mem: NASW, 1973-; ACSW, 1975-; Edit Staff, *Jour of Geronological Social Wk*, 1978-; r/Rom Cath; hon/ Author, Var Articles Pub'd in Profl Jours incl'g: *Social Wk*; *Jour of Gerontological Social Wk*; W/W of Am Wom.

TWEED-ARKUKSH, JANET oc/ Executive; b/Jul 5, 1941; h/15 West 12th 81, New York, NY 10011; ba/New York, NY; m/Jacob Arkush; p/George Swift Tweed (dec); Hilda Tweed Wigley, NJ; ed/BSBA, Montclair St Col, 1963; Grad Studies, Columbia Univ, 1963-65; pa/ Co-Fdr/Prin & Exec VPres, Gilbert Tweed Assocs Inc, 1972-; Co-Fdr/Prin, J G Tweed, 1967-72; Mgr of Tech Dept, Assoc, Dunhill Pers, 1967; Asst Pers Mgr, NY Express Sys, 1963-65; Instr, Katherine Gibbs Secretarial Sch; Mem: Nat Assn of Corp & Profl Recruiters; Am Soc for Pers Adm; Intl Assn for Pers Wom; hon/Co-Author, Chapt on "Recruitment, Eval, Selection & Retention of Sales & Mktg Pers," in *AMA Handbook*; "The Use of Conslts," & "Eliminating Turnover in the Sales & Mktg Depts," *Dow Jones-Irwin's Mktg Mgr's Handbooks*; Co-Author, Nonfiction Book *Boardwalk*; Featured in Num Articles in: *Fortune; The NY Times; The Wall Street Jour; Bus Wk*; W/W of Am Wom.

TWIGGS, DENNIS GLENN oc/ Psychologist; b/Feb 5, 1946; h/3232 Luther Street, Winston-Salem, NC 27107; ba/Winston-Salem, NC; m/ Tamara H; c/Jason Twiggs; p/James and Velra Twiggs, Morganton, NC; sp/Jay and Maxine Hatley, Concord, NC; ed/ BA, Appalachian St Univ, 1969; PhD, Tulane Univ, 1977; mil/AUS Spec Forces, 1969-72; pa/Psychol, Mexia St Sch, 1977-78; Psychol, San Antonio St Hosp/Sch, 1978-80; Psychol, Pvt Pract, 1980-; Mem: AAAS; Am Assn on Mtl Deficiency; Past Pres, Bd of Dirs,

Forsyth Co Assn for Retarded Citizens; Bd of Dirs, Piedmont Handicapped Assn; Sigma Xi; cp/Lions Clb; r/Bapt; hon/Author, Articles Pub'd in Profl Jours incl'g: *Sci; Am Jour of Phy Therapy; Phsyiol & Behavior*; AV Series on Strees & Biofeedback; Sigma Xi; Tchg F'ship, Tulane Univ; W/W in S & SW.

TYLER, JOANNA ARMIGER oc/ Psychologist; b/Jan 13, 1943; h/9647 Green Moon Path, Columbia, MD 21046; ba/Columbia, MD; c/ Christopher Blair; p/William James Armiger, Martinsburg, WVA; Marie Eileen Lowery, Victoria, TX; ed/BA 1971, MA 1973, CA St Univ-San Jose; PhD, Univ of MD, 1977; Post Doct Sems, Cath Univ of Am, 1981; pa/ Psychol, Pvt Pract, Columbia, MD, 1978-; Prin Proj Mgr, Arbitron Ratings (Subsidiary of Control Data Corp), 1981-83; Proj Mgr, Applied Mgmt Sers Inc, Silver Spring, MD, 1978-81; Sr Res Analyst, Teledyne Brown Engrg (Subsidiary of Teledyne Industs), Rockville, MD, 1976-78; Adj Asst Prof, Catonsville, Commun Col, 1973-78; Fac Staff, Univ of MD, Col Pk, MD, 1973-77; Fac Staff, CA St Univ-San Jose, 1972-73; Fam Planning Cnslr, Fam Planning Alternatives, San Jose, CA, 1972; CA Commun Col Cnslg Credential, 1973; CA Commun Col Tchg Credential, 1973; MD Lic'd Psychol, 1980; Mem: Am Pscyhol Assn, 1979-; MD Psyhol Assn, 1980-; Howard Co Drug Abuse Adv Coun, 1979-81; r/ Cath; hon/Author & Co-Author, Over 15 Articles, Papers & Reports Pub'd in Profl Jours & Presented at Assn Meetings; Undergard S'ship, Wom's Clb of San Mateo, CA, 1967; Grad cum laude, CA St Univ-San Jose, 1971; Phi Kappa Phi, 1971; Psi Chi, 1971; Grad F'ship, 1973-77; W/W of Am Wom.

TYRE, IRMA TYRE oc/Bank Manager; b/Jan 27, 1933; h/207 Burney Branch Circle, Blackshear, GA 31516; ba/Hoboken, GA; m/Carroll J; c/Dennis C, Debra T King; p/Felton and Myrtle Tyre, Screven, GA; sp/Silas and Annie Tyre (dec); ed/Grad, Screven HS, GA; pa/Teller, 1st Nat Bk, 6½ Yrs, Jesup, GA; Mgr, Citizens Bk, 9½ Yrs, Hoboken, GA; cp/SS Tchr, 1968; Acteen Tchr, 1967 & 1968; Blackshear Wom's Clb, 1973, 1974 & 1975; C of C, 1981-83; W/W: in GA, in Am.

TZINCOCA, REMUS oc/Conductor; h/632 Avenue Hervé-Beaudry, Laval, Montréal, Quebec, Canada H7E 2X6; ba/ Montréal, Canada; ed/Conservatory of Music, Iassy; Fac of Law, Iassy Univ; 1st Prize Conducting of Conservatoire National Supérieur de Musique de Paris; Study w Louis Fourestier, Jean Gallon & George Enescu; pa/Music Dir, Pat-

riarchal Cathedral, Bucharest; Insp, Labor Dept, Bucharest; Secy of Musical Studies, St Opera, Bucharest; Prof, Iassy St Conservatory; Choir Dir & Conductor, Iassy St Opera; Music Dir & Conductor, Laval (France) Philharm; Conducted Gala Concert in Paris Salle Pleyel, for UN Dels, 1948; Musical Asst to George Enescu; Judge in Jury, Conservatoire Nat Supérieur de Musique de Paris; Collaborated to Voice of Am; Guest-Conductor, Ipswich Music Fest, MA; Fdr & Music Dir, Newport Music Fes, RI; Fdr & Music Dir, Orch da Camera, NY; Conducted Num Concerts at: Carnegie Hall, Town Hall, Metro Mus of NY, Others; Conducted in N Am & Europe: NY Philharm, Cleveland Orch, London Philharm, Zurich Tonhalle, Montreal CBC, Paris-Colonne, Lamoureux & Pasdeloup Orchs, Orchestre Philharm de la Radio-TV Francaise, "Geroge Enescu" Philharm Bucharest, Radio-TV Orch Bucharest, Romanian St Opera Bucharest, Others; Invited Tchr of Conducting, Orch, Instrumental & Vocal Ensemble, Montreal Conservatoire; Prof, "Vincent-d'Indy" Superior Sch of Music, Montreal; Fdr & Artistic Dir, Montreal "Orch da Camera"; Mem: Canadian Assn of Pubrs, Authors & Composers; hon/ Freedom Baton from Gov of RI, Am Org "Crusade for Freedom"; Mem of Hon & Fdg Mem, Quebec Assn of the Consevatoire's Profs; Medal of St Indep of Romania; Considered by Intl Critics as a Gt Interpreter of Enescu, Beethoven & Wagner; W/W of Intells; Intl Register of Profiles; Men of Achmt; DIB; Personnages Contemporains.

TZVETIN, IVAN DIMITROV oc/ Architect; b/Apr 6, 1929; h/6412 Hagen Boulevard, El Cerrito, CA 94530; ba/ San Francisco, CA; m/Ellen Yamada; p/ Dimitri Ivanov Tzvetin (dec); Elena (Velcheva) Tzvetin, Sofia, Bulgaria; ed/ BArch, St Polytech Uiv, Sofia, Bulgaria; pa/Sr Designer in Arch & Urban Design, Itis & Glavproj, Sofia, 1953-63; Designer, City Planner Gravereaus & Denieul, Marti, Paoli, Paris, 1964-66; Arch Designer, McCue Boone, Tomsick Archs, SF, CA, 1967-70; VPres Design, Anshen & Allen, SF, CA, 1970-82; Ptnr, Anshen & Allen, SF, CA, 1982-; Mem: Am Inst of Archs; Others; r/Greek Orthodox; hon/Competition Projs & Biogl Info Pub'd in the Daily Press & Profl Mags in 15 Countries; 2nd Prize, Intl Design Competition for Monument, Mus & Plaza, Playa Giron, Cuba, 1963; 1st Prize, Intl Design Competition for Civic Ctr Plaza, SF, 1965; 1st Prize, Intl Competition for Landmark of City of Melbourne, Australia, 1980; W/W in W.

U

UEHLING, BARBARA STANER oc/
University Administrator; b/Jun 12,
1932; h/Chancellor's Residence, Francis
Quadrangle, Columbia, MO 65211; ba/
Columbia, MO; m/Stanley Johnson; c/
Jeff, David; p/Roy W and Mary Elizabeth
Hilt Staner, Wichita, KS; ed/BA, Univ
Wichita, 1954; MA 1956, PhD 1958,
NWn Univ; pa/Mem Fac, Oglethorpe
Univ, 1959-64; Mem Fac, Res Fellow,
Emory Univ, 1964-69; Adj Prof, Univ
RI, 1969-71; Mem Fac 1970-71, Acad
Dean 1972-74, Roger Williams Col;
Dean Arts & Scis, IL St Univ, 1974-76;
Provost, Univ OK, 1976-78; Chancellor,
Univ MO, 1978-; Dir, Merc Bancorp Inc;
Adv, Dir, Merc Trust Co; Dir, Meredith
Corporation; Bd Dirs, United Way;
Trustee, Carnegie Coun Advmt Tchg;
NIMH Fellow, 1966-69; Mem, AAHE,
Past Pres; Dir, Nat Coun Ednl Res; Dir,
Am Coun Ed; Mem Adv Coun Pres;
Assn Gov'g Bds; Mem, Edit Bd, Nat
Forum Mag, Phi Kappa Phi; hon/Auth
of Num Pubs incl'g "Meeting the
Demands of the Future" *Ednl Record*
1978, DHL, Hon, Drury Col, 1978; LLD,
Hon, OH St Univ, 1980; W/W: Am, MW;
DIB; Am Men Wom Sci; Men Achmt.

UGOAGWU, BARBARA JACKSON
oc/Biology-Chemist; b/Jun 24, 1952; h/
809 Kostner, Matteson, IL 60443; ba/
Chicago, IL; m/Marcel Chukwuma; c/
Vanlynette Chinyere; p/Louis and
Elizabeth Davis, Chgo, IL; sp/Emmanuel
and Florence Ugoagwu, Nigeria, W
Africa; Cook Co Grad Sch Med, Lab
Cert, 1969; AS, Ctl Y Col, 1973; BS,
Roosevelt Univ, 1977; Harvard Univ,
Hlth Career Cert, 1976; IL Inst Technol;
pa/Clin Chem Tech, IL Masonic Hosp,
1969-70; Med Res Supvr, IL Inst Tech-
nol Res Inst, 1970-71; Supvr, Dept
Hlth-Lead Poision Screening, 1972-76;
Med Coor, Blue Cross/Blue Shield,
1978-; AAUW; Am Chem Soc; cp/Park
K Forest S Wom's Assn; Blue Cross/
Blue Shield Commun Med Conslt; Cntrl
Y Col, Cnslr, Student Affairs; Harvard
Univ Alumni; Roosevelt Univ Alumni;
Phi Theta Kappa; Nat Hon Soc; Delta
Tau; r/Rom Cath; hon/Harvard Hlth Ed
Corps S'ship; Dewitt Wallace Foun
Merit S'ship; Phi Theta Kappa Nat Hon
Soc; W/W Am Wom.

ULREY, CHARLES FRANKLIN oc/
Retired Bandmaster, General
Manager-Retail Music Business; b/Nov
10, 1923; h/2171 NE 44th Court,
Lighthouse Point, FL 33064; ba/Ft
Lauderdale, FL; m/Patricia Dort; c/
Marie Eileen, Carol Louise; p/Lena Mae
Ulrey, Columbus, OH; sp/Mr and Mrs
H E Williams, Boynton Beach, FL; ed/
BS, OH St Univ, 1949; MME, FL St
Univ, 1957; Post Grad, Univ FL, FL
Atlantic Univ; mil/AUS, 1943-45; pa/
Band, Orch, Chorus, Brian HS,
1949-51; Band, Sanford HS, 1951-52;
Band, Ladora HS, 1951-52; Band, Orch,
Chorus, Canal Winchester HS, 1952-55;
Band, Pompano Bch HS, 1957-70; Band,
Pompano Bch Mid Sch, 1970-79; Pres
1966-67, St Dir & HS Chm 1962-66,
Parliamentarian 1962-66, Dist Chm
1969-70, 1972-73, FL Bandmasters
Assn; Dist Contest Adjudicator, March-
ing & Concert Bands, Solo & Ensemble,
1962-; St Chm, Assoc Mbship Chm, Am
Sch Band Dirs Assn; Nat Conv Exhibs,
Chm; r/Meth; hon/Phi Beta Mu; Kappa

Kappa Psi; Dir & Clinician, Broward Co
& Palm Bch Co, FL-Mid Schs Hons Bd;
Intl W/W; DIB; Biographical Roll Hon;
Men Achmt; Dir Dist'd Am.

**UNDERWOOD, JOANNA
DEHAVEN** oc/Executive Director,
Environmental Research Organization;
b/May 25, 1940; h/138 East 13th Street,
New York, NY 10003; ba/New York,
NY; m/Saul Lambert; c/Jonathan W
Lambert, Katherine A Lambert; p/Louis
Ivan and Helen Guiterman Underwood;
ed/Semester Diploma, Sorbonne, 1965;
BA, Bryn Mawr Col, 1962; pa/Fdr &
Exec Dir, INFORM, 1973-84; CoDir &
Editor, Coun Economic Priorities,
1970-72; AV, Planned Parenthood,
World Pop, 1968-70; Bd Mem, NY St
Energy Res & Devel Auth; Bd Mem,
Correctional Assn NYC; Adv, Ofc Tech
Assessmt; Energy Adv Comm, Aspen
Inst; Fellow, Scist Inst Public Info; cp/
Mem, US Assn Clb Rome; hon/Author
of "Paper Profits" 1971; W/W: Am, Am
Wom.

UNDERWOOD, NANCY MAE oc/
Occupational Safety and Health Engi-
neer; b/Dec 29, 1944; h/1637 Veteran
Avenue Number 9, Los Angeles, CA
90024; ba/Lynwood, CA; c/Apryl; p/
Jennie Espie, Century, FL; ed/BS 1974,
Tchg Credential Accident Preven,
Public Safety, Drivers Tng 1975, CA St
Univ LA; Cert Proficiency Engrg/
Occupl Safety & Hlth, 1975; Cert
Proficiency Occupl Safety & Hlth
Mgmt/Engrg, 1977; MA, CA St
Univ-LA, 1982; MS, Univ SF, 1981; pa/
Owner, Operator, Nancy's Safety Tng
& Consultation Firm, 1982-; Pt-time
Fac, Conslt, CA St Univ-LA, 1982-; Mgr
Safety, Northrop Aircraft Grp,
1978-82; Mgr Safety, Hydraulic Res,
1977-78; Tchr, LA Unified Sch Sys,
1976; Safety Engr, Travelers Ins Co,
1975-76; St Advr Res/Ed, US Congl Adv
Bd; Nat Safety Coun; Am Soc Safety
Engrs; Am Indust Hygiene Assn; Nat
Assn Female Execs Inc; Am Soc Profl
& Exec Wom; cp/CA St Univ—LA
Alumni Assn; Intersafe, Assn Safety
Profls; OES; Daugh Isis Deg; Amaranth
Deg; r/Christian Sci; hon/Author of
Num Pubs; W/W: Am Wom, Wom, W;
Personalities W & MW, World.

**UNRUH, BARBARA JoANNE
(SLAMA)** oc/Educational Administra-
tor; b/May 31, 1939; h/728 South 10th
Avenue, Brighton, CO 80601; ba/
Brighton, CO; m/Stanley R; c/Scott S;
p/Joseph and Noreen Slama, Pilot Pt,
TX; sp/Arline Unruh, Brighton, CO; ed/
BS 1961, ME 1970, Phillips Univ;
Postgrad Studies, Univ No CO
1976-84; pa/Elem Tchr, Enid OK,
1961-65; Jr HS Tchr, HS Libn, Sterling
CO, 1965-68; Jr HS Eng Tchr, Dept
Coor, Vikan Jr HS, 1968-75; Jr HS Asst
Prin, Acting Prin, 1975-79, Vikan Jr HS;
Asst Prin 1979-83, Prin 1983-, Brighton
HS; Assn Supvn Curric Devel; CO Assn
Sch Execs; Nat Assn Sec'dy Sch Prins;
cp/Kappa Delta Pi; Alpha Delta Kappa;
r/First Christian; hon/Editor of
"Update" Newslttr; Edr Yr, Brighton
CO; W/W: W, Among Am Cols & Univs;
Admr Yr, Brighton Assn Ednl Ofc Pers;
St Admr Yr, CO Assn Ednl Ofc Pers.

**URBANCZYK, ANDREW AUGUS-
TUS** oc/Author, Scientist, Adventurer,
Inventor; b/1936; h/Post Office Box
1099, Montara, CA 94037; m/Krystyna
Dorota Saborowska; ed/MS, Chem &

Physics, Univ Gdansk, 1960; pa/Conslt
to Num Inst & US Govt; Self Employmt;
cp/Slocum Soc, 1980; Maritime Authors
Union, 1968; hon/Author of Num Pubs;
Nums Listings incl'g W/W.

UREY, DONALD A oc/Chairman,
Department of Pastoral Studies; b/Sep
10, 1935; h/43 Homestead Road, Levit-
town, PA 19056; ba/Langhorne, PA; m/
Delores; c/Karen; p/Beatrice Urey,
York, PA; ed/BA, Wash Bible Col, 1959;
MA, Columbia Bible Col, 1966; DMin,
Wn Conservative Bapt Sem, 1980; pa/
Pastor, Ctl Bapt Ch, 1959-61; Pastor,
Calvary Bible Ch, 1961-65; Dean Stu-
dent Affairs, Prof, Lancaster Bible Col,
1967-74; Pastor, Faith Calvary Ch,
1969-73; Pastor, First Bapt Ch, 1974-75;
Gen Dir, Berean Mission Inc, 1975-80;
Chm, Pastoral Studies Dept, Phila Col
Bible, 1980-; Bd Mem, Barbados Bible
Inst, 1978-; Assn Christian Deans &
Cnslrs Men, 1976-80; Chm, En Indep
Ch Mission, 1974-75; r/Bapt; hon/
Author of Num Pubs incl'g "Messages
on Altars of Abraham" 1977; Outstg
Edrs Am.

URKA, MARTIN CHARLES oc/Nat-
ural Resource Specialist; b/Nov 11,
1924; h/3854 Monte Vista Avenue,
Cedar City, UT 84720; ba/Cedar City,
UT; m/Peggy; c/Meggen, Wendy, Preston, Polly; p/Anton and Anna Urka
(dec); sp/Walter and Estelle Crane (dec);
ed/Cert, Agri Tech Inst MI St Univ,
1948; Addit Credits, 1948-75; mil/S/Sgt
Inf in Italy, 1944-46; M/Sgt SIG Corps
FA, USAR, 1953-56; pa/Soil Conserv
Aid & Tech; USDA, Soil Consers Ser,
1948-53, 1954-64; Gen Motors Corp,
1953, Aircraft Assem; Soil Conservationist 1964-71, Dist Conservationist
1971-75, Soil Scist 1975-79, US Soil
Conserv Ser; USDI Bur Indian Affairs,
1979, Soil Scist; Land Opers Ofc,
Owyhee NV, 1981; Nat Res Spec, 1983,
Cedar City UT; SCSA; SSSA; ASA; cp/
Lions Clb; FFA; r/Prot; hon/Author of
Num Pubs; Recip Outstg Perf Awd,
1962; Sustained Perf Awd; Num Spec
Recog incl'g by Secy Interior, FFA,
Calhoun Soil Conserv Dist; W/W.

UTLEY, LINDA KAY CHALFANT
oc/Teacher of Spanish; b/Oct 9, 1943;
h/123 El Camino Way, Ft Washington,
MD 20744; ba/Washington, DC; c/
Charles V Jr, Yvette Melissa; p/Mr and
Mrs Fred Chalfant, Clay, NY; ed/BA,
1965, Vassar Col; MS, 1971, George-
town Univ; pa/Spanish Tchr, DC Public
Schs, 1965-; Lang Spec, Latin for
Modern Sch, 1972-; Instr, Dept Ednl &
Psychol Foun, Univ DC, 1982-;
Co-Organizer, Chm, Fgn Lang Action
Grp, 1978-80; Am Assn Tchrs Spanish
& Portuguese; Am Coun Tchg Fgn
Langs; Gtr Wash Assn Tchrs Fgn Langs;
DC Assn Supvn & Curric Devel; DC
Coun Tchrs Eng; Wash Scholastic Press
Assn; Wash Tchrs Union; r/Rom Cath;
hon/S'ship, Vassar Col; W/W Am Wom.

**UZODINMA, MINTA LaVERNE
SMITH** oc/Director, Nurse-Midwifery,
Education; b/Mar 29, 1935; h/2832
Gretna Green Drive, Jackson, MS
39209; ba/Jackson, MS; m/John Eze; c/
Chinwe LaVerne, Chika Diane, Eze
Allan, Amechi John; p/Dorothy
LaVerne Cherry, Clinton, MS; ed/BS,
St Univ IA, 1957; Cert Nurse-
Midwifery 1970, MN 1975, Univ MS
Med Ctr; pa/Staff Nurse 1957, Hd
Nurse 1962, Univ Hosp; Clin Instr, IA

Meth Hosp, 1958; Instr In-Ser Ed 1968, Staff Nurse-Midwife 1970, Dir Nurse-Midwifery Ser 1971-74, Instr Nurse-Midwifery Ed 1976, Asst Prof Dept Ob-Gyn 1979, Asst Prof Sch Nsg 1981, Dir Nurse-Midwifery Ed Prog 1982, Univ Med Ctr; ANA; NAACOG; CEAMJ; Am Cancer Soc; Am Col Nurse-Midwives; MS Bd Nsg; cp/LWV; r/Bapt; hon/Pubs; Sr Student Awd, IA Plumbers Wom's Aux, 1956; Exceptl Ser Plaque, Farish St Bapt Ch, 1980.

V

VACCARO, ANNE oc/Hairdresser and Councilwoman; b/Mar 22, 1930; h/Road 4, Box 602, Newton, NJ 07860; ba/Newton, NJ; m/Joseph Thomas; p/Peter (dec) and Helen Sokol, Newton, NJ; ed/Wom's Garment Trades; Robert Fiance Inst Hair Design, 1950; pa/Hairdresser and Makeup Artist; Plan Bd Mem, 1973; Plan Bd Chm, 1974; Coun-wom, 1974-83; Grants Wom, 1979-82; Bus Profl Wom, 1973-83; cp/NJ Leag Mun; Pres, 1962-63, VFW Aux; Zonta Corres Secy, 1980-83; Way Home Drug Abuse Org; r/Byzantine; hon/W/W Am Wom.

VALENTA, JANET ANNE oc/Prevention Education Coordinator; b/Sep 22, 1948; h/3115 Draper Street Southeast, Warren, OH 44484; ba/Youngstown, OH; m/Mario; c/Nan; p/Frank A and Ann Shenk, Euclid, OH; sp/Anton (dec) and Antica Valenta, Zamask, Yugoslavia; ed/BA, Cleveland St Univ, 1970; Master's Cand Sch Planning, Univ Cinc; pa/Preven Ed Coor, Alcoholic Clin Youngstown, 1979-; Owner, Mgr Wrought Iron Retail Shop, 1978-79; Dir Preven Ed, Trumbull Co Coun Alcoholism, 1973-78; Nat Assn Preven Profls, 1977-; Nat Public Hlth Caucus Chp, 1978; cp/Publicity Chm, Trumbull Art Guild Bd, 1974-76; r/Cath; hon/Yg Bus & Profl Wom Yr Nom, 1978; Outstg Yg Wom Am; World W/W Wom.

VALLÉE, RUDY oc/Entertainer; m/Eleanor; p/Charles Alphonse and Katherine Lynch Vallée; ed/Att'd Univ ME; Grad, Yale Univ, 1927; mil/USN, 1917; pa/Singer & Musician, Heigh Ho Clb, NYC; Radio Personality, The Fleischmann Hour; Performer, Villa Vallee Supper Clb; Performer, Paramount Theatres NYC; Actor, George White's Scandals, 1931; Actor of Num Plays & Motion Pictures.

VAN DERBUR, MARILYN oc/Speaker; b/Jun 16, 1937; h/1616 Champa Street, Suite 210, Denver, CO 80202; ba/Same; ed/Grad, Univ CO; pa/Personality, TV & Radio; Competitor, Nat AAU Swim Meets & Univ CO Ski Team; Horse Tnr; Guest Lectr Num Grps incl'g, Gen Motors, IBM, Kodak; Devel Marilyn Van Derbur Motivational Inst Inc; Former Mem, Pres Adv Coun Adult Ed; hon/Miss Am; Outstg Wom Spkr Am; Only Wom to Receive Spkrs Hall Fame Awd; Spec Recog as Miss Am by Andy Rooney on "Sixty Minutes".

VANDERSTAY, OTTO RANDOLPH oc/Director of Electronic Engineering/Telecommunications; b/Jan 17, 1933; h/443 Edwards Place, Glendale, CA 91206; ba/Los Angeles, CA; m/Jacqueline Paulette; c/Natalie Michelle, Rachelle Monique; p/Addie Byrd St Clair, Rio Dell, CA; sp/Marcel Dochet, France; ed/Univ TX, 1951; Univ Houston, 1956; Upper IA Univ, 1983; mil/USAF, 1953-61, Sgt; CA St Mil Resv, Capt, 1981; pa/Dir Electronic/Telecommuns, Chd's Hosp LA, 1980-; Sr Test Engr, Conslt, DuPont Instruments, 1978-80; Nat Ser Mgr, Vitek Instruments, 1978; Pres & Gen Mgr, Evaporation Apparatus Inc, 1976-78; Resv Ofcrs Assn; Assn AUS; NG Assn; Assn Advmt/Med Instrumentation; Assn Field Ser Mgrs; r/Cath; hon/Author of Num Pubs; W/W: CA, W.

VANDEVER, LOIS ARLENE oc/President, "Invest in Yourself Inc", Wellness Seminars; b/Apr 17, 1931; h/835 West Geddes Circle, Littleton, CO 80120; ba/Littleton, CO; c/Vincent James; p/Rev Russell D and Thelma E Laycock (dec); ed/BSN, Univ Denver, 1959; PNP, Univ CO Sch Med & Nsg, 1970; pa/Sem Devel & Ldr, Invest in Yourself, 1980-; Conslt, St Dept Hlth; Nsg Conslt, Univ CO, 1974-80; CO St Bd & Nsg Lobbyist, Nsg Assn CO St Legis, 1970-73; Coor, Hlth Ser, Cherry Creek Sch; Am & CO Nurse Assn; cp/Zonta Clb Englewood; Jefferson Co Wellness Adv Bd; Univ Denver Alumni Assn Bd; Friends Nsg Bd; Cent C of C Com; r/Epis; hon/Author of Num Pubs; Article Recog on Wellness Prog; 1st Nurse to become PNP; Devel Sch Hlth Prog; W/W Am Wom.

VAN EERDEN, NEIL oc/Executive Vice President; b/Jun 22, 1932; h/370 Indian Road, Wayne, NJ 07470; ba/New York, NY; m/Eleanor; c/Kristen, Heidi, Peter; p/Peter and Louise Van Eerden, Ogden, UT; sp/Hedwig Kobs, Franklin, MA; ed/Weber Col, 1958; BS, Boston Univ, 1960; mil/USAF, 1952-56; pa/Exec VP, Victor of Milano Ltd; Pres, Van Eerden & Assocs, 1981-; VP Sales, CoParel Inc, 1978-81; Dir Sales, Faberge Inc, 1965-77; NE Cosmetic Assn; cp/Bd Dirs, Weber Col Alumnae Assn; Pines Lakes Assn; r/Prot.

VAN ETTEN, RD MARGUERITE RUBY BAGGETT oc/Registered Dietitian; b/Jul 2, 1921; h/460 Southwest 131 Avenue, Fort Lauderdale, FL 33325; ba/Miami, FL; c/Janel Anne, Vicki Tina, Karen Lynette; ed/BS, Univ OK, 1945; Dietetic Internship, St Lukes Hosp, 1946; MS, Nova Univ, 1981; pa/Relief Adm & Therapeutic Dietitian, Chestnut Lodge, 1949, 1950; Adm Dietitian, Montgomery Co Jewish Commun Inc, 1949; Relief Therapeutic Dietitian, Suburban Hosp, 1954-63; Vol, Dial-a-Dietitian, 1963-72; Conslts Dietitian, Altheia Woodland Nsg Home, 1964; Clin Dietitian, Clin Preceptor, Coordinated Undergrad, Dietetics Progs Dietitians & Dietetic Assts, St Michaels Hosp & Univ WI Coordinated Undergrad Prog, 1972-73; Conslts Dietitian, St Jude's Nsg Home, 1972-73; Dir Dietary Sers, S FL Bapt Hos, 1973-74; Public Hlth Nutrition Conslt, St FL Hlth & Rehab Sers, 1974-; Am Dietetic Assn; FL Dietetic Assn; Broward Co Dietetic Assn; Am Dietetic Assn Conslts Dietitians Hlth Care Facilities; FL Dietetic Assn Conslts Dietitians Hlth Care Facilities; FL Assn Hlth & Social Sers Inc; Am Coun Sci & Hlth; cp/FL Coun Aging; Num Commun & Polit Activs incl'g Organizing Secy, Nat Soc DAR; Pres Elect, Broward Co Dietetic Assn; Am Assn Ret'd Person; hon/S'ship, Univ OK, 1943-46; W/W S & SW.

VAN GLABEK, MARCE G oc/Realtor/Appraiser; b/Jul 15, 1932; h/3N 514 Lincoln Drive, St Charles, IL 60174; ba/St Charles, IL; m/Edward A; c/William Alan, Christine Marie; p/Stanley F (dec) and Celia Holtz, Chicago, IL; sp/Ed (dec) and Minnie Van Glabek, St Charles, IL; ed/Grad Rltrs Inst, 1976; Cert'd Residential Spec, 1979; Cert'd Appraiser-Sr, Am Assn Cert'd Appraisers, 1980; pa/Owner, ERA Van Rlty, 1973-; Rltr, Grossklag Agy, 1966-73; Rltr, Aim Rite

Rlty, 1962-66; ABWA, Fox River Chapt, Pres, 1978-79; cp/Dir, Zonta Intl Bus Wom's Grp; St Charles C of C, 1977-, Pres; Fox Val Bd Rltrs, 1974, Pres; r/Rom Cath; hon/Rltr Yr, 1981; Wom Yr, 1978, ABWA; St Charles Chronicle Newspaper, Smile of Yr, 1977.

VANN, SAMUEL LeROY oc/Professional Artist; b/Sep 16, 1952; h/PO Box 344, Trumansburg, NY 14886; b/Same; p/Mr and Mrs David Vann, Trumansburg, NY; ed/BA, Fort Lewis Col, 1973; pa/Num Collections incl'g Everson Mus Art, Menninger Foun; Instr in all Mediums; Lectr; Juror for Several Reg Art Exhibs; Asst to Dir, Chautauqua Inst Ctr Arts, 1979-80; Num Exhibs; r/Bapt; hon/W/W: Am Cols & Univs, Am Art; Intl Biog; Chautauqua Inst, Cora B Tustin S'ship; VA Ctr Creat Arts, F'ship; Granted Residency on Ossabaw Isl, Ossabaw Foun; Recip So Tier Arts Assn "NY St Artisan's Awd" Artist Div.

VAN RAALTE, POLLY ANN oc/Reading Specialist and College Educator; b/Sep 22, 1951; h/26 Meadow Lane, Lawrence, NY 11559; ba/Inwood, NY; p/Byron and Enid Van Raalte, Lawrence, NY; ed/BA, Beaver Col, 1973; MS, Univ PA, 1974; Spec Ed Cert, W Chester St Col, 1977; pa/Lectr, Adelphia Univ, 1979-83; Rdg Spec, Lawrence Public Schs, 1978-83; Rdg Spec, Abington Sch Dist; Title I Rdg Supvr, Salvation Army Ivy House, 1977; Lang Arts Coor, Main Line Day Sch & Mitchell Sch, 1975-76; Title I Rdg Tchr 1974-75, Title I Rdg Supvr 1975, W Deptford Sch Dist; Camp Cnslr, Camp DeBaun, 1969, 1972-74; IRA, 1973-83; DE Val Rdg Assn, 1974-78; NCTE, 1976-83; Assn Supvn Curric & Devel, 1978-83; Nassau Rdg Coun, 1978-83; cp/Cooper Hewitt Mus, 1981-82; Friends of Carnegie Hall, 1981-82; Friends of Am Ballet Theatre, 1982-83; Whitney Mus Art, 1980-83; Metro Mus Art, 1980-83; Mus Mod Art, 1981-83; Beaver Col Annual Fund Chp, 1973-83; r/Judaism; hon/Author of Num Pubs; Pi Lambda Theta; Kappa Delta Pi; W/W in E.

VAN SANTVOORD, RICK oc/Secondary School English Teacher; b/Apr 19, 1935; h/2 Emerald Drive, Glen Cove, NY 11542; ba/East Norwich, NY; m/Irena; c/Alexander L; ed/BA 1957, MS 1958, Hofstra Univ; Sec'dy Sch Adm, NY Univ; Oxford Univ England; pa/Friends Acad 1958-66, Vernon Sch 1967-, Tchr Sec'dy Sch Eng; Intl Mil Music Soc; cp/The Holland Soc; Sons of Revolution; Underhill Soc Am; Sustaining Mem, Detroit Concert Band; Nassau Co Hist Soc; hon/Author of Num Cover Notes incl'g "Heritage of March"; Composer of Num Marches incl'g "Poughkeepsie" (dedicated to Robert Hoe), "Portledge" (supressed by Composer), "R B H" (dedicated to R B Hall), "Invincible" (dedicated to composer's wife), "IMMS" (dedicated to Intl Mil Music Soc), "Prince David" (dedicated to David C Christman, Dean, New Col, Hempstead, NY, "The Kremlin-Overture" (dedicated to Alexander Glazounov); Phi Delta Kappa, 1962; Dic Intl Biog.

VAN THIEL, DAVID H oc/Physician, Professor of Medicine; b/Sep 5, 1941; h/Road 3, Box 78, Tarentum, PA 15084; ba/Pittsburgh, PA; m/Judith S; c/Lisa, Mike, Krista; p/J M Van Thiel, Redondo

Bch, CA; ed/MD, Univ CA-LA, 1967; mil/USPHS, 1969-71; pa/Clin Assoc Endocrinology Br 1969-70, Clin Assoc Reprodn Res Br 1970-71, NIH; Residency 1971-72, Res Fellow 1972-73, Univ Hosp Boston MA; Instr Med 1973-74, Asst Prof Med 1974-78, Assoc Prof Med 1978-82, Chief Gastroenterology 1979-, Dir Gastroenterology Lab 1978-, Prof Med 1982-, Univ Pgh Sch Med; Diplomat, Nat Bd Med Examrs; Am Col Phys; Am Fdn Clin Res; Res Com, Pubs Com, Councilor, Am Assn Study Liver Diseases; Ctl Soc Clin Res; Am Med Soc Alcoholism; The Endocrine Soc; AAAS; NY Acad Sci; Am Soc Clin Invest; Gastroenterology Res Grp; Alpha Omega Alpha; MW Gut Clb; Bd Dirs, Am Liver Foun; Assoc Editor, Jour Studies Alcohol; Mem, Soc Andrology; Edit Bd, Currents in Alcoholism; Adv Bd, British Jour Alcohol & Alcoholism; Mem, Biomed Res Grant Review, NIAAA; Edit Bd, Hepatology; r/Cath; hon/Author of Num Pubs; Recip USPHS Cancer Devel Awd; Pres, MW Sect, AFCR, 1981-82; Num Grants & Coms.

VARGAS, ARMANDO JR oc/Recreation Coordinator; b/Feb 27, 1954; h/ 1520 West Windsor Street, Tucson, AZ 85705; ba/Tucson, AZ; p/A R and R M Várgas, Tucson, AZ; ed/BA 1976, Master's Public Adm 1983, Univ AZ; pa/ Clk 1976-77, Prog Aide 1977-79, Adm Asst 1980-82, Rec Coor 1983-, Univ AZ Student Union; Am Assn Cnslg & Devel, Div Am Col Pers Assn, 1981-; Assn Col Unions, Intl, 1980-; Chp Pub Com, Student Union Activs Bd, 1975-76; Num Positions in Una Noche Plateada Inc; cp/Open-Inn Inc, 1977-80; AZ Hist Soc; Friends Tucson Pops Orch; Friends Tucson Public Lib; Nat Geographic Soc; Smithsonian Assocs; hon/Am Legion Aux, Andrew P Martin Meml S'ship, 1972; Gen Res Scholar & S'ship, Univ AZ, 1973; Univ S'ship Hons, 1972-73; Tucson Lodge, Frat Order Police S'ship, 1974-75; Mexican-Am S'ship Foun S'ship, 1975; E T Koehler Awd, Student Union Activs Bd, 1976; W/W W.

VARZANDEH, JAVAD oc/Assistant Professor of Quantitative Management; b/Mar 23, 1951; h/Post Office Box 2930, State University, AZ 72467; ba/ Jonesboro, AR; p/H Varzandeh, Seattle, WA; ed/BA, Tehran Univ, 1972; MA, St Mary's Univ, 1976; PhD, OK St Univ, 1981; mil/AUS; pa/Asst Acct, San Antonio TX, 1976; Asst Prof Ec 1979-80, Asst Prof Quantitative Mgmt 1980-, AR St Univ; cp/Beta Gamma Sigma; Jonesboro C of C; Omicron Delta Epsilon; r/Moslem; hon/Author of Num Pubs; Hon Soc in Ec, 1976 & 1980.

VATANDOOST, NOSSI MALEK oc/Art Consultant, Art Instructor, Artist; b/May 22, 1935; h/105 Country Club Drive, Hendersonville, TN 37075; ba/Madison, TN; m/Ira; c/Debbie, Cyrus; p/Mahtaban and Abdullah Malek, Teheran, Iran; ed/BA, Wn KY Univ; MI St Univ; pa/Elem & Sec'dy Tchr, 1971-72; Art Dir & Tchr, Nossi Sch Art, 1972-; cp/Hendersonville Arts Coun; Art Guild Hendersonville; Smithsonian Assocs; Intl Platform Assn; r/ Muslim; hon/Num Art Awds; W/W Am Wom; World W/W Wom; Commun Ldrs Am; Personalities S.

VAUGHAN, RICHARD A oc/Chartered Life Underwriter; b/Jul 18, 1946; h/12 Timbercreek, Sherman, TX 75090; ba/Sherman, TX; m/Terence; c/Shannon, Elizabeth, Todd; p/John W (dec) and Margaret Ann Vaughan; Univ TX; N TX St Univ; pa/Chartered Life Underwriter (CLU); Am Col; Instr, Life Underwriters Tng Coun; Spkr Num Estate & Tax Planning Sems & Wkshops; Nat Spkg Tour, 1980-81, Fed Pubs; Past Dir, Texoma Assn Life Underwriters; Fdr & Dir, Consol Printing Co Inc; Million Dollar Round Table; cp/Bd Dirs, Am Cancer Soc; Dir Publicity, United Fund; Sherman Fund, Austin Col; Pres, Univ TX Ex-Students Assn; Past Dir, Salvation Army; Sherman City Coun; Dir, Texoma Reg Planning Comm Coun Govts; hon/W/ W: Bus & Fin, S & SW, World; Personalities S; Mensa.

VAUGHN, RUTH WOOD oc/Professional Author/Playwright; b/Aug 31, 1935; h/Box 1565, Bethany, OK 73008; ed/BA, MA, PhD; pa/Pub'd Author, 1957-; Col Prof, Bethany Nazarene Col, 1968-76; Wom Communication Intl; Pi Lambda Theta; Theta Sigma Phi; Intl Platform Assn; hon/Contemp Authors; W/W: Am Authors, S & SW, Am Wom; Worlds W/W Authors; Intl Authors' & Writers' W/W; Outstg Eds Am; Personalities W & MW; DIB; World W/W Wom.

VENIT, WILLIAM B oc/ Broker-Consultant; b/May 28, 1931; h/ 4850 North Monticello Avenue, Chicago, IL 60625; ba/Chicago, IL; m/Nancy Jean; c/April Ann, Steven Louis; p/Ida (dec) and George Venit, Elkland, MO; sp/Carl (dec) and Fanny Carlson, Chgo, IL; ed/Univ IL; mil/AUS, Qtrmaster; pa/ Pres, Chm Bd, Cordnot Inc, 1951-73; William Lamp Co, William Wire Inc, William Roma Wire, 1973-79; William B Venit Sales, 1979-; MSWV Inc, 1980-; cp/Dir, Jewish Peoples Inst; Lamp & Shade Inst; r/Jewish; hon/World W/W; W/W Fin & Indust.

VER BECKE, W EDWIN oc/Artist, Writer, Poet; b/Jul 21, 1913; h/840 8th Avenue, Suite 6M, New York City, NY 10019; ba/Same; m/Countess Eugenia (dec); ed/BA, Univ MN; Duluth Tchrs Col; Mpls Sch Fine Arts; Ordained UCM Order, CA; pa/Instr, Univ MN, 1935; Gallery Dir, Owner Galleries by Sea, 1945-51; Theatre Dir, 1951-55; Display Artist, Sachs NYC, 1970-75; City Soc Dir, NYC, 1980-82; Cort Theatre NY, Appearance, 1982 Tour; Dramatist Guild Am; Poetry Soc Am; Min, Psychic Universal Ch Master; r/Prot; hon/ Author of Num Pubs incl'g "Poems of Spirit" 1945; "Line in Painting" 1950; Nat Art S'ship, Mpls Sch Fine Arts, 1932; Maxwell Anderson Drama Awds, 1950; Nat Playwrights Dir; Men Achmt.

VERYHA, WASYL oc/Librarian; b/ Jan 3, 1922; h/215 Grenadier Road, Toronto, Ontario M6R 1R9; ba/ Toronto, Ontario; m/Oksana; c/ Andrew Zenon, Luba Irene, Peter Wasyl, Olena Daria; p/Iva and Irena (dec); sp/Arestea Albota; ed/BA 1959, BLS 1961, Univ Toronto; MA, Univ Ottawa, 1968; mil/Ukrainian Nat Army, 1943-45; pa/Edr, 1961-76; Libn III, Hd, Slavic Unit, Bibliographic Processing Dept 1976-, Libn, Order Dept 1961-64, Libn, Catalogue Dept 1964-76, Wn Langs Sect, Univ Toronto Lib; Shevchenko Sci Soc Canada, Bd Dirs, 1975-;

Nat Exec, VP 1978-, Ukrainian Nat Fdn Canada; Univ Toronto Fac Assn; Am Assn Advmt Slavic Studies; Am Lib Assn; r/Ukranian Cath; hon/Author of Num Pubs incl'g "Along the Roads of World War II" 1980, 1981; Men Achmt; Intl Scholars Dir; Dir Libns US & Canada.

VERZINO, WILLIAM JOHN JR oc/ Chemist; b/Oct 28, 1940; h/32 Upshur Road, Annapolis, MD 21402; ba/Annapolis, MD; m/Judith Ann; c/William John, Robert Lee, Anthony James, Patricia Margaret; p/William J and Regina M Verzino (dec); sp/Calvin and Margaret L Massey, Albuquerque, NM; ed/BS, Muhlenberg Col, 1962; MS, John Carroll Univ, 1967; PhD, CO St Univ, 1970; mil/USN, 1962-64, Ensign, 1982-84, Cmdr; pa/Sr Res Chem, Am Enka Corp, 1970-74; Exch Res Chem, Enka-Glanzstoff, AG Obernburg, 1972-73; Mem, Tech Staff, Aerospace Corp, 1974-78; Acting Assoc Grp Ldr, Los Alamos Nat Lab, 1978-82; Asst Prof, Chem Dept, US Naval Acad, 1982-Pres; Fellow, Am Inst Chem, Cert'd; Mem, Am Chem Soc; Royal Soc Chem; Naval Resv Assn; Resv Ofcrs Assn; Fleet Resv Assn; r/Cath; Author of Num Govt Reports & Profl Jour Articles; Phi Kappa Phi; NSF Fellow; W/ W W.

VICKREY, JAMES F oc/President, University Montevallo; b/Feb 2, 1942; h/Flowerhill, Montevallo, AL 35115; ba/ Montevallo, AL; c/John; p/Mrs F G Murray, Montgomery, AL; ed/BA 1964, MA 1969, Auburn Univ; PhD FL St Univ, 1972; Cert Inst for Ednl Mgmt, Harvard Univ, 1974; Addit Studies; pa/ Pres, Univ Montevallo, 1977-; Exec Asst to Chancellor & Dir Public Affairs, St Univ Sys FL, 1975-77; Asst Pres & Dir Univ Relats, Univ S FL, 1971-75; Adm Asst to Exec VP, FL St Univ, 1970-71; Instr & Dir Forensics, Auburn Univ, 1965-68; Author Num Articles Profl Jours; Communs Conslt; Former Mem Nat Freedom of Spch Comm, SCA: Nat Govt Relats Com, Coun for Advmt & Support Ed; Am Assn St Cols & Univs; Others; cp/Spkr Civic Orgs; Tampa C of C; Auburn Alumni Clb; Downtown Redevel Com; Ednl Com, Fine Arts Coun; Others; r/Bapt; hon/Exceptl Achmt Awd, Coun for Advmt & Support Ed; Univ Fellow, FL St Univ; Doct Hons Sem Participant, SCA; Phi Delta Phi Awd; S Allen Edgar F'ship; Alegernon Sydney Sullivan Awd, Auburn Univ; Phi Kappa Phi; Omicron Delta Kappa; Others.

VIDAL, JULIO oc/Political Science Instr; b/Aug 1, 1952; h/113-B Santa Maria, Ponce, PR 00731; ba/Ponce, PR; p/Miguel A Vidal and Lydia E Vazquez, Ponce, PR; ed/ABD, St Univ NY; MA, FL St Univ, 1975; BA, Cath Univ PR; pa/Departamento de Servicios Sociales, 1975; Polit Sci Instr, Cath Univ PR, 1976-79, 1981-; Am Polit Sci Acad; Polit Sci Acad; Latin Am Studies Assn; Am Soc Public Adm; Ctr Cuban Studies; cp/ Phi Delta Kappa; Pi Gamma Mu; r/Rom Cath; hon/Author of Num Pubs; Pi Gamma Mu; Phi Delta Kappa; Nat Dir Latin Americanists; W/W S & SW; Dir Scholars & Spec Third World Studies; Grad F'ships, St Univ NY.

VIERA, GRELA S oc/Quality Assurance Officer, Satellite Office Manager; b/Sep 5, 1950; h/4409 Berkshire Manor

Drive, Number 1323, Tampa, FL 33614; ba/St Petersburg, FL; c/Jose C Jr, Frank J; p/Ary and Odalina Hernandez, Miami, FL; ed/AA, Miami Dade Commun Col, 1973; Att'd Univ FL, FL Intl Univ; pa/ Clerical 1972-74, Ser Rep 1974-76, Claims Rep 1976-77, Mgmt Intern Prog 1977-79, Opers Ofcr 1979-81, Quality Assurance Ofcr, Satellite Ofc Mgr 1981-, Social Security Adm; Fed Hlth & Safety Coun, 1981-; Nat Assn Female Execs, 1981-; Tampa Bay Fed Exec Assn, 1982-; cp/Quota Intl, 1978-79; St Pauls Cath Ch, 1982; Pierce Jr HS Booster Clb, 1981; NW Little Leag, 1983; r/Cath; hon/Spec Achmt Awd, Dept Hlth & Human Sers, 1976; Companerismo from Image Org Awd, 1976; Cert Recog, Channel 2, Miami FL, 1975; Lttr Commend, Social Security, 1975; W/W Am Wom.

VINCENT, CLARE oc/Museum Curator; b/Aug 30, 1935; h/326 East 85th Street, New York, NY 10028; ba/New York, NY; p/Lorena C Vincent, Neshanic Station, NJ; pa/BA, Col William & Mary, 1958; MA, Inst Fine Arts, 1963; Cert Mus Tng, Inst Fine Art & Metro Mus Art, 1963; pa/Asst to Curator Decorative Arts, Cooper Union Mus for Arts Decoration, 1961; Curatorial Asst, Wn European Arts 1962-67, Asst Curator 1967-72, Asst Curator European Sculpture & Decorative Arts 1972-, Metro Mus; Am Sect, Antiquarian Horological Soc, VP, 1977-; Sci Instrument Comm; Intl Union Hist & Phil of Sci, 1981-; Societe International de l'Astrolabe, 1976-; Furniture Hist Soc, 1966-; Col Art Assn, 1959-; Hist Sci Soc, 1974-; Renaissance Soc Am, 1970-; hon/Author of Num Pubs; Phi Beta Kappa; Lord Botetourt Medal, Col William & Mary; W/W: Wom, Am Wom; Dir Am Scholars; Outstg Yg Wom Am.

VINCENT, HAL WELLMAN oc/ Investor, Rancher, Pilot; b/Sep 24, 1927; h/24321 Lakeview Lane, El Toro, CA 92630; ba/Ashland, OR; m/Virginia Bayler; c/David Bayler, Dale Wellman, Deborah Kathryn Minder; p/Mrs Glenn Vincent, Laguna Hills, CA; sp/Gen and Mrs W L J Bayler, Santa Ana, CA; ed/ Student Navy V-5 Prog, Wn MI Col, Colgate Univ, 1945; BS, US Naval Acad, 1950; Postgrad Marine Ofcrs Basic Sch, 1950; Flight Sch, 1952; Test Pilot Sch, 1955; Navy Fleet Air Gunnery Sch, 1958; AF Fighter Weapons Sch, 1959; Indsl Col, 1969; mil/Commd 2nd Lt, USMC, 1950; Adv'd Through Grades to Maj Gen, 1974; Rifle & Machinegun Platoon Cmdr, Camp Lejeune, NC 1951; Fighter Pilot, El Toro, CA & Korea, 1953-54; Test Pilot Flight Test Div, Patuxent River, MD, 1955-57; Ops Ofcr, Sqdrn Asst & Fighter Pilot, El Toro, 1958-59; Conventional Weapons Proj Ofc Naval Air Weapons Test Ctr, China Lake, CA, 1960-62; Sqdrn Ops & Exec Ofcr, El Toro & Japan, 1962-64; Aviation Spec Marine Corps Amphibious Warfare Presentation Team & Staff Ofcr, Quantico, VA, 1965-66; CO 2nd Marine Aircraft Wing Fighter-Attack Sqdrn, Beaufort SC, 1967-68; Exec Ofcr, Marine Aircraft Grp, Vietnam, 1969; Logistics Staff Ofcr, Fleet Marine Force Pacific, HI, 1970-72; CO, Marine Aircraft Grp, Yuma, AZ 1972-73; Chief of Staff, 3rd Marine Aircraft Wing, El Toro, 1973-76; Dpty Chief of Staff Plans & Policy, to

Comdr in Chief Atlantic, Norfolk, VA, 1976-78; Comdg Gen, 2nd Marine Aircraft Wing, Cherry Point, NC, 1978-80; Dpty Comdg Gen, Fleet Marine Force Atlantic, Norfolk, 1980-81; Investor, 1981-; Flight Test Pilot, Preliminary Pilot, Evaluator New Mil Aircraft; Marine Corps Aviation Assn; Mem, SAR, Soc Exptl Test Pilots; Early Pioneer Nav Aviators; Marine Corps Assn; Order of Daedelians; Mach 2 Clb; 1000 Miles Per Hour Clb; Clbs Army-Navy Country; Army-Navy Town; hon/Contbr Num Articles on Tactics & Conventional Weapons Delivery, Flight Test Stability & Control to Var Mil Pubs; Invented Triple Ejector Rack for Delivery of Conventional Bombs, 1961; Devel Fighter Tactics in F8 & F4 Aircraft, 1958-69; Flew 165 Models of Fgn & US Aircraft, 1953-82; 1st Marine to Fly Mach-2, 1958; Decorated Legion of Merit w Two Gold Stars, DFC; Bronze Star w Combat V; Air Medal w Star & Numeral 14; Jt Sers Commend Medal (US); Hon Medal 1st Class; Cross Gallantry w Gold Star (Republic of Vietnam); W/W Am, World.

VIRGO, JULIE CARROLL oc/Executive Director, Association of College and Research Libraries; b/Jun 14, 1944; h/5288 Geddes Road, Ann Arbor, MI 48105; ba/Chgo, IL; m/Daniel T Carroll; p/Archibald Noolan, Australia; ed/Lib Assn Australia, Registration Cert, 1965; AM 1968, PhD 1974, MBA 1983, Univ Chgo; pa/Exec Dir, Assn Col & Res Libs, 1977-; Dir Ed, Med Lib Assn, 1972-77; Lectr, Grad Lib Sch, Univ Chgo, 1968-; Am Soc Info Sci; Cont'g Lib Ed Netwk; Am Mgmt Assn; Am Soc Assn Execs; Med Lib Assn; Spec Libs Assn; Am Lib Assn; AAAS; hon/Author of Num Pubs; Am Soc Info Sci Doct Dissertation Awd, 1975; Nat Lib Med Grant, 1973-75; HEA Title 11B F'ship, 1969-72; W/W: MW, Am, Am Wom.

VIZENOR, GERALD ROBERT oc/ University Teacher; b/Oct 22, 1934; h/ Native Am Studies, 3415 Dwinelle Hall, Univ CA-Berkeley, 94720; ba/Same; m/ Laura Hall; c/Robert Thomas; p/Clement William Vizenor and LaVerne Harsch (dec); sp/Philip and Phyllis Hall, Upminster, Essex, England; ed/BA, Univ MN, 1960, Grad Study Harvard, Univ MN; mil/AUS, 1953-55; pa/Edit Writer, Mpls Tribune; Col Tchr, Univ MN; Col Tchr, Univ CA-Berkeley; hon/Author of *The People Named the Chippewa* 1984, *Matsushima* 1984, *Earthdivers* 1982, *Wordarrows* 1978, Num Articles & Books; Bush Ldrship Awd, Mpls, MN; Contemp Am Authors.

VOELKLE, WILLIAM M oc/Curator of Medieval and Renaissance Manuscripts; b/Mar 27, 1939; h/451 East 84 Street, New York, NY 10028; ba/NY, NY; p/Mrs Lina Voelkle, Endicott, NY; ed/MA, SUNY-Binghamton; MA, Columbia, 1965; pa/Dir Visual Resources, SUNY-Binghamton, 1966-67; Asst Curator of Medieval & Renaissance Manuscripts, Assoc Curator, Curator 1983, Morgan Lib, 1967-; CAA; hon/ Author of Num Pubs incl'g *The Spanish Forger*, 1978; Cit from Art Libs Soc NY, 1981; Boston Craftsman Clb Awd.

VOGEL, WILLIAM ALBERT oc/ Executive Director; b/Jul 27, 1924; h/ 211 Second Street, Denton, TX 76201; ba/Denton, TX; m/Glenice R Hopkins; c/Gary M, Mary A, Nancy J, Susan E,

Theresa L, Joseph S, Jacqueline Lee; p/ Victor and Mary Grillot Vogel (dec); sp/ James and Ellen Morgan Hopkins (dec); ed/Att'd Parsons Jr Col, 1942-43; Intl Corres Schs, 1959; pa/Num Positions incl'g Gen Bkkpr, Chief Clk Corp Acctg, Mgr Cost & Res, Mkt RR Co, 1947-69; Exec LSL Grp Cos, Chm Bd, Pres, Sr VP, Dir, 1970-74; Pvt Pract Ins & Securities Sales, 1974-77; Ex Dir, Mean Green Eagle Clb (Ath Fund Raiser), N TX St Univ, 1977-; Nat Assn Securities Dealers; Nat Assn Ath Fund Raisers; cp/ K of C, 1945-, Past Grand Knight 1979-, Trustee 1975-81; United Comm Travelers Am, 1967-, Past Grand Cnslr St Pres 1977; St Patrick's Sch Bd, 1955-57; Pres, BSA Coun Troop 602, 1960-64; Secy, St Patrick's Parish Coun, 1965; Bd Dirs, Krassovska Ballet Jennessee, Dallas, 1980; r/Cath; hon/Man of Yr, LSL Grp Cos, 1972; Man of Yr, United Comm Travelers Am, TX Grand, 1976; N TX St Univ Talon Spirit Awd, 1982; W/W: 4-H Clb, Railroading, S & SW.

VOISINE, JOAN MARY oc/Artistic Administrator; h/11391 Thorpe Road, Richmond, BC, Canada, V6X 1J5; b/ Vancouver, BC; m/Gerald; p/Mr and Mrs C W Day, Stevenage Herts, UK; sp/Mr and Mrs R Voisine (dec); pa/ Personal Asst to Tech Dir, Royal Opera House, London, 1960-67; Exec Secy to Comptroller, O'Keefe Ctr, Toronto, 1967-68; Admr, Burlington Ofc Ctr, 1968-70; Art Admr, Vancouver Opera, Vancouver, 1971-; r/Ch England.

VOLPÉ, ROBERT oc/Physician, Professor; b/Mar 6, 1926; h/3 Daleberry Place, Don Mills, Ontario, M3B 2A5; ba/ Toronto, Ontario; m/Ruth; c/Catherine Lillian, Elizabeth Anne, Peter George, Edward James, Rose Ellen; p/Dr and Mrs Aaron G Volpe (dec); sp/Harry Pullian; ed/MD, Univ of Toronto, 1950; FRCP, 1956; FACP, 1965; mil/RCNVR, 1943-45; p/Sr Res Fellow, Dept of Med, Univ Toronto, 1957-62; Asst Prof 1962-68, Assoc Prof 1968-72, Prof 1972-; Att'g Staff, St Joseph's Hosp, 1957-66; Active Staff, Wellesley Hosp, 1966-; Dir, Endocrinology Res Lab, Wellesley Hosp, 1968-; Phys-in-Chief, 1974-; 1st Pres, Canadian Soc of Endocrinology & Metabolism; Pres, Am Thyroid Assn; Gov, Am Col of Phys; Endocrine Soc; Am Fdn Clin Res; NY Acad Sci; Royal Soc of Med; European Thyroid Assn; Latin Am Thyroid Assn; r/Jewish; hon/Goldie Medal for Med Res, Univ Toronto, 1971; St-of-Art Lectr, Endocrine Soc, 1975; St-of-Art-Lectr, Dept Med, Univ Toronto, 1981; Hon Mbrship, Soc Endocrinology & Metabolism Chile; W/ W: Am, World, Commonwealth; Am Men & Wom Sci.

VON SELDENECK, JUDITH ANN CROWELL oc/Interior Design Consultant, Educator; b/Feb 12, 1945; h/85 Middlebrook Street, Harrisonburg, VA 22801; ba/Same; m/Roger D; c/Jeffrey Dean; p/Mr and Mrs Robert K Crowell, Richmond, VA; sp/Mr and Mrs Bradford K Cross, Waynesboro, VA; ed/AA, Averett Col, 1965; BA, Westhampton Col, 1967; Cert, NY Sch Interior Design, 1971; pa/Tchr, Augusta Co VA, 1967-69; Asst to Designers, Yg Assocs, ASID, 1969-70; Self-Employed Interior Design Conslt, 1971-; Tchr Interior Design, Balto Co Adult Ed, 1976-78; Tchr Bus Eng & Interior Design,

Patricia Stevens Career Col, 1979; Design Instr, Harrisonburg Rec Dept, 1980-; Subst Tchr, Harrisonburg City, Rockingham Co, 1981-; DAR; cp/ Westhampton Col Alumnae Bd; Lynchburg Jr Wom's Clb; Harrisonburg Jr Wom's Clb; r/Prot; hon/Girl of Month, Shenandoah Dist Jr Dir's Clb, 1982, Harrisonburg Jr Wom's Clb; W/ W S & SW.

VOOBUS, ARTHUR oc/Professor; b/ Apr 28, 1909; h/230 South Euclid Avenue, Oak Park, IL 60302; ba/ Chicago, IL; m/Ilse Luksep; c/Ruth, Eti; p/Karl Ed Voobus (dec) and Linda Helene Voobus, Oak Park; ed/Cand BTh, ThM, DTh; pa/Manuscript Res in Syrian Orient; Discoverer of Unknown Manuscript Sources; Author 91 Books & 300 Articles in Intl Scholarly Jours; cp/Antibolshevik Bloc of Nations; r/ Evang Luth; hon/Intl Acad Scis & Lttrs; Royal Acad Belgium; F'ships: JS Guggenheim Meml Foun, Am Coun Learned Socs; Am Phil Soc; Nat Endowmt for Humanities; 40 Lead'g Intl Scholars Pub'd "A Tribute to Arthur Voobus: Studies in Early Christian Lit & Its Envir, Primarily in the Syrian East" (1977).

VOORTHUYZEN, PETER oc/ Scientist, Clergyman, Musician; b/Jan 5, 1927; h/113 Ball Avenue, Canastota, NY 13032; ba/Same; p/Jacob Marinus Voorthuyzen and Jannetje van Dam Doorntjes (dec); pa/Anal Res Chem, Bird's Eye Deepfreeze, 1947-49; Anal Res Chem, Agri St of the Dutch Govt, 1949-50; Anal Prodn Control Chem, Elektro Oxygen & Hydrogen Factories, 1950-52; Res Chem, Philips Dutch Pharms, 1952-58; Res Chem, Chem Res Assocs Inc, 1958-59; Res Chem, Merck Sharp & Dohme, 1960-61; Min Positions: Golden Hills Ch Melrose MA, 1964, First Bapt Amherst NH, 1964-68, Fed'd Ch N Litchfield ME, 1968-70, Bapt Ch Plains Litchfield ME, 1968-70, Bapt Ch Sabattus ME, 1970-76, Bapt Ch Canastota NY, 1977-79, Freelance Writer, Spkr, Tchr; Am Chem Soc, 1958-; cp/Intl Platform Assn, 1980; Rotary Intl, 1978-; r/Christian; hon/ Author of Num Pubs; Byington F'ship, 1964-65; ABI; IBC; Notable Ams; Noteworthy Ams & Commun Ldrs; Book of Hon; Dist'd Ams; W/W E.

VOSLER, DEBORAH LYNN oc/ Biology Teacher, Volleyball Coach; b/ Mar 16, 1957; h/3344 Birch Place, Cheyenne, WY 82001; ba/Cheyenne, WY; p/Robert C Vosler, Rock River, WY, Eileen Vosler, Guernsey, WY; ed/ AA, En WY Col, 1977; BS, Cameron Univ, 1979; EdM, SWn OK St Univ, 1980; pa/Biol Instr, Volleyball & Basketball Coach, Sch Dist #1, 1980-81; Water Safety Instr, Night Supvr, Mun Pool, 1980-81; Grad Asst, Hon Fellow, Hd Wom's Volleyball Coach, SWn OK St Univ, 1979-80; Adult Ed Instr/Life Guard, 1979; WY Coaches Assn; WY & Nat Sci Tchrs Assns; Cheyenne & Nat Tchrs Ed Assn; CPR & Water Safety Instr, ARC; r/First Christian; hon/ Sigma Tau Delta, 1978; Student Ed Assn; Phi Kappa Phi; Summa Cum Laude Grad; WCCAC Volleyball Champs; Outstg Freshman Eng Hon Student; Pres Hon Roll, 1975-79; Commun Ldrs of Am; Intl Yth in Achmt; W/W Amg Students in Am Jr Cols; Nat Dean's List.

VOTAPKA, RICHARD BRUCE oc/ Professional Civil Engineer; b/Sep 4, 1948; h/873 Southeast Lance Street, Sebastian, FL 32958; ba/Vero Beach, FL; m/Linda Louise Kauffman; c/Kenneth, Kevin, and Keith; p/Richard W and Pauline J Votapka, Vero Beach, FL; sp/ John M and Mary J Kauffman, Selmsgrove, PA; ed/BS, NEn Univ, 1971; pa/Jr Design Engr 1971-72, Asst Track Supvr 1972-73, Bessemer & Lake Erie RR; Design Engr, GHQ Inc, 1973-75; Acting City Engr & Engr III, Vero Beach, FL, 1975-77; Proj Engr, Bleindorf & Assoc, 1977-; Coun-man, City of Sebastian, FL, 1981-83; Mem, Bd Trustees, Sebastian River Med Ctr, 1983-85; Mem, Bd Trustees Sebastian United Meth Ch; Mem, Nat Soc Profl Engrs; Am Soc Civil Engrs; FL Engrg Soc; Soc Am Mil Engrs; Am Waterwks Assn; Pres, Am Soc Civil Engrs, 1976-77; cp/Planning & Zoning Comm Mem, City of Sebastian, 1977-78; MC for Dedication of Am Soc Civil Engrs Dist 10 Outstg Civil Engrg Achmt Awd for Cape Kennedy Space Shuttle Runway, 1978; r/Meth, Sebastian United Meth Ch; Adm Bd Mem 1979-81, Financial Secy 1980-81; Pres & Fdr, 1980-81, Sebastian United Meth Men; Secy,

Melbourne Dist United Meth Men, 1980-81; hon/Engr Yr Awd, 1978, Am Soc Civil Engrs; W/W S & SW.

VU, BAO HUU oc/Medical Doctor; b/ Apr 11, 1934; h/9708 Louisville Avenue, Lubbock, TX 79423; ba/Lubbock, TX; m/ Luuphuong T Pham Vu; c/Khanh, Huan, Han, Edward Chuong; p/San HUU and Cu Pham Vu, Saeto, CA; sp/ Uoc Trong Pham (dec) and Khang Thi Dang, San Jose, CA; ed/BS, 1954, Hanoi Vietnam; MD, 1963, Saigon Vietnam; Cert'd Diplomate, Am Bd Fam Prac, 1978; mil/Armed Forces, S Vietnam, 1954-75; pa/Army Surg, 1963-64; Sch Aerospace Med, Brooks AFB, 1964; Wing Surg, Dispensary Comdr, AF, 1964-68; Adv'd Course Aerospace Med, 1969, Brooks AFB; Asst Surg Gen, Vietnamese AF, 1970-72; Comdr, Vietnamese AF Med Ctr, 1972-75; Staff Phys, Luth & Mennonite Deaconess Hosp, Beatrice, NE; Staff Phys & Chm, Med Record & Infection Control Coms; Aerospace Med Assn; Am Heart & Lung Assn; Nat Assn VA Phys; Am Med Assn; r/Buddhist; hon/Author of "Place des Examens Virologiques dans le Diagnostic de la Poliomyelite Anterieure Aigue", 1963; 20 Mil Decorations incl'g Nat Order; Am Med Assn Phys Recog Awds; W/W MW; Intl W/W Intells.

VUONG, KENNY SIU oc/President, Insurance Agency; b/Feb 8, 1945; h/ 3423 Brighton Street, Rosemead, CA 91770; ba/Los Angeles, CA; m/Dinh Sy San; c/Vaygi, Nhavan, Taivan, Kietvan, Boigi, Nancy; p/Hai Phuc Vuong and Duc Tran An, LA, CA; sp/Kim A Tran and Mui Tai Hoang, IA; ed/Tu Do Sch, Vietnam, 1961; Lam Tran Eng Comml Sch, Vietnam, 1965; pa/Sales Engr, Universal World Trade Co, 1972-73; VP, Arinco Advtg, Printing, Decorating Co, 1973-75; Sales Rep 1978-79, Sales Mgr 1979-81, Metro Life Ins Co; Pres, Kenny Vuong Ins Agy, 1981; Fellow Intl Biographical Assn; VP, Am Chinese Vietnamese Friendship Assn; Mem, Nat Assn Life Underwriters; Mem, Indep Ins Agts & Brokers Assn; Notary Public; hon/Ldrship Conf Awd, Metro Life Ins Co, 1980; W/W: in W, USA; Men Achmt; Dic of Intl Biog.

PERSONALITIES OF AMERICA

W

WADDINGTON, BETTE HOPE (Elizabeth Crowder) oc/Violinist; b/Jul 27, 1921; h/2800 Olive Street, Saint Louis, MO 63103; ba/St Louis, MO; p/John and Marguerite Crowder Waddington (dec); ed/AB, Univ of CA, 1945; MA, SF St Univ, 1953; Gen Elem & Sec'dy Tchg Credentials, CA; Jr HS Libnship Credentials, CA; Life Credentials Mus & Art, CA Jr Cols; Grad Wk: San Jose St Univ, 1953-55; Univ of CA; Juilliard; SF St Univ; Addit Pvt Studies; pa/Violinist, St Louis Symph, 1958-; cp/Alpha Beta Alpha Alumnae of Univ of CA, San Jose St Univ & SF St Univ; r/Presb; hon/ S'ship, Juilliard, 1950; Concert Mistress, Univ of CA Symph, 1945; Mem, Carmel Bach Fest Orch, 1946-49; Concert Mistress, Peninsula Symph, Redwood City, CA, 1956-58; W/W: of Am Wom, in MW, in World, of Contemp Achmt, in Am Music; DIB; 2000 Notable Ams; Num Other Biogl Listings.

WADE, BEN F oc/College Provost; b/Jul 20, 1935; h/112 West Col Street, Bridgewater, VA 22812; ba/Bridgewater, VA; m/Janice W; c/Andrea M, Laurel F; p/Mr and Mrs Frank H Wade (dec); sp/J A Wine, Bridgewater, VA; ed/BA, Bridgewater Col, 1957; MDiv, U Theol Sem, 1960; STM, Boston Univ, 1961; MS, Columbia Univ, 1966; PhD, Hartford Sem Foun, 1966; pa/Phil & Rel Instr, Shenandoah Col; Prof of Theol & Lib Dir, U Theol Sem; Prof of Phil & Rel, James Madison Univ; Dean of Col, Brevard Col; Dean of Col, FL So Col; Pres, Westmar Col; Provost, Bridgewater Col; Mem: AAUP; Lambda Soc; Theta Chi Beta; r/Prot; hon/"God as Personal & Transpersonal in the Thought of Paul Tillich & L Harold DeWolf"; Other Articles & Book Reviews; Sr Hon S'ship, U Theol Sem; Hartler Fellow & Tchg Fellow, Hartford Sem Foun; W/W in Am Cols & Univs; Outstg Edrs of Am.

WADE, JULIA HOWARD oc/Interior Designer and Furniture Store Owner; b/Dec 2, 1928; h/412 Baxter Lane, San Augustine, TX 75972; ba/San Augustine, TX; m/Nelsyn Ernest Brooks; c/Sylvia Laureen W Drake, Lise France W Crouch, William Alan, David Eugene; p/Mr and Mrs S E Howard, Pineville, LA; sp/Mrs W M Wade, San Augustine, TX; ed/BA, Baylor Univ, 1948; Studied Art & Drama, Baylor Univ in Paris, 1952; Cert, Home Furnishings Cnslr, SWHFA, 1980; pa/Dir, Chd's Theater, San Augustine, TX, 1948-52; Pt-owner, Augus Theater, San Augustine, 1948-58; Eng Tchr, S A HS, 1948; Bible Tchr, HS, 1955; Ptner, Decorator, Advtg Mgr & Buyer, Nelsyn Furniture Store, 1958-; Lectr, Interior Design & Hist; Writer of Pageant, 1967; Mem, SW Home Furnishings Assn, 1968-; Nat Assn of Female Execs; Nat Trust for Hist Preserv; TX Old Missions & Fts Restoration Assn; Life Mem, Baylor Alumni Assn; cp/Hist Chm, 8 Co Bd Devel Assn, 1975; Chm Bd of Dirs 1983-, Bd Mem 1980-, San Augustine Public Lib; Med Bd of Devel, E TX Bapt Col, 1978-; DAR; S A Co Hist Comm; Pres, Heritage Clb, 1963; Others; r/Bapt; hon/"S A Hist Pageant," 1967; Num Articles on Interior Design in Papers & Mags; Outstg Small Retailer, SWHFA, 1979; Pres Awd, C of C, 1973;

Public Ser Awd, Rotary Clb, 1980.

WADE, NEIL H oc/Head Geotechnical Engineer; b/Apr 11, 1936; h/240 Valhalla Crescent, NW, Calgary, Alberta, Canada, T3A2A1; ba/Calgary, Alberta; m/Louise M; c/N Kevin, Jonathan A; p/Mr and Mrs Paul R Wade, New Brunswick, Canada; ed/BSc, Univ of New Brunswick, 1959; DIC, Imperial Col, London, England, 1963; PhD, Univ of London, England, 1963; pa/Sr Geotech Discipline Engr, Civil Engrg Dept, Monenco, Calgary, Alberta, 1980-; Guest Lectr Geotech Engrg, Univ of Alberta & Univ of Calgary, 1980-; Supvr, Geotech Sect 1975-80, Sr Geotech Engr 1971-74, BC Hydro & Power Auth, Vancouver, Brit Columbia, Canada; Vis'g Prof Geotech Engrg, Dept of Civil Engrg, Univ of CA-Davis, 1975-80; Exec Engr, Klohn Leonoff Conslts Ltd, 1974-75; Sr Soils Engr, Hd Soil Testing Sect, TAMS Intl Corp, Tarbela Dam Proj, W Pakistan, 1968-71; Sr Soils Engr, Tippetts-Abbett-McCarthy-Stratton, NY, 1967-68; Assoc Prof, Sch of Civil Engrg, GA Inst of Technol, Atlanta, GA, 1964-67; Acting Asst Prof, Dept of Civil Engrg, Univ of CA-Berkeley, 1963-64; Grad Res Student, Imperial Col, Univ of London, 1959-63; Mem: Assn of Prof Engrs, Geols & Geophysicists of Alberta; Assn of Profl Engrs of Brit Columbia; Engrg Inst of Canada; ASCE; Canadian Geotech Soc; Past Chm & Past Treas, Vancouver Geotech Grp; Intl Soc of Soil Mechs & Foun in Engrg; r/Prot; hon/Author, Over 12 Tech Papers Pub'd in Profl Jours & Other Pubs; Ford Foun Residency in Engrg Pract, 1967-68; NSF Res Initiation Grant, 1965-67; GA Tech Matching Res Grant, 1965-67; GA Tech Instl Res Grant, 1965-66; NASA-GA Tech Equip Grant, 1965; NRC (Canada) Spec S'ship for Grad Study in United Kingdom, 1959-61; Others; W/W: in W, in Commonwlth; Am Men & Wom of Science.

WAGNER, ALAN B oc/Executive; b/Jun 8, 1938; h/1523 Lakewood Court, Lexington, KY 40502; ba/Lexington, KY; m/Lynn F; c/Brian, David, Beth Lynn; p/Robert E and Anna M Wagner, Hagerstown, MD; sp/W D and Helen T Wynant (dec); ed/BES, Johns Hopkins Univ, l1960; MS 1962, PhD 1965, Case Wn Resv Univ; pa/Mgr 1965-70, Dir 1967-70, Div VPres 1970-73, Corp VPres 1973-77, Intl Minerals & Chems Corp, Northbrook, IL; Pres, Fed Mining Co, Inc, Lexington, KY, 1979-82; Pres, Wagner Mgmt Corp Inc & Hilliard-Lyons, Wagner Assocs, Lexington, KY, 1982-; Mem: Am Mgmt Assn; ASME; AAAS; Dir, KY Coal Assn; cp/Bd of Trustees, Union Col of KY; Bd Mem, Ctl KY Concert & Lectr Series, Lexington; Greenbriar Golf Clb, Lexington; hon/Alfred P Sloan Nat Foun Scholar, 1959; Johns Hopkins Univ Scholastic Awd, 1960; Sigma Xi, 1962; ASHRAE Hommers Addam's Awd, 1963; W/W: in Fin & Indust, in S & SW, in World.

WAGNER, ANDREW JAMES oc/Meteorologist; b/Apr 12, 1934; h/7007 Beverly Lane, Springfield, VA 22150; ba/Washington, DC; m/Betty Ritenour; p/Andrew and Ruth M Wagner (dec); sp/E R (Tommy) and Doris Ritenour, Harrisonburg, VA; Ed/BA, Wesleyan Univ, 1956; MS, MA Inst of Technol,

1958; pa/Res Meteorologist, US Weather Bur, 1965-67; Meteoroligist (Forecasting), Envir Sci Ser Adm, 1967-71; Meteoroligist (Forecasting & Climate Res), Nat Oceanic & Atmospheric Adm, 1971-; Adj Prof of New Testament Greek, Whole Word Theol Sem, 1981-82; Mem: Am Meteorol Soc; Am Geophy Union; Royal Meteorol Soc; Am Sci Affil; Nat Weather Assn; Mgr-at-large, Wash Acad of Scis, 1982-; cp/Pres 1977-79, VPres 1979-81, Lake Beverly Forest Civic Assn; 3rd VPres & Chaplain, Fairfax Resolves Chapt, SAR, 1979-; Advr, Explorer Post 1001; r/Congregl; Elder & Trustee, 1968-; hon/Author, Over 55 Papers Pub'd in Profl Pubs Incl'g: Monthly Weather Review; Weatherwise; Bltn Am Meteorological Soc; W/W in S & SW; Other Biogl Listings.

WAGNER, LOIS MYRL oc/Retired; Investor, Writer and Study Group Director; b/Nov 26, 1910; h/455 E Ocean Boulevard, Apartment 316, Long Beach, CA 90802; m/Howard W Wagner (dec); ed/BEd 1953, MEd 1952, Univ of CA-LA; Gen Sec'dy Credentials, Univ of Redlands; Grad in Marriage Cnslg, Inst of Fam Relats; Ordained Min, Practr, Now-Clear Universal Ch; Grad of Classes, Assoc, Fdr's Ch of Rel Sci; pa/Retired; Investor, Writer; Religious Sci Study Grp Ldr, Director; Adult Tchr of Dressmaking, San Bernadino Evening HS; Tchr, 8 Subjects, VPrin, Templeton Union Higher Sch, 1933-37; Jr & Sr HS Tchr, LA City Schs, 1937-71; World Traveler; Lectr; Gen Ofc Wk; Hom Economist Spec; Mem: Am Home Ec Assn; AAUW; Profl Writers Leag; Intl Platform Assn; Ch Rel Sch; OES; CA Ret'd Tchrs Assn; Nat Ret'd Tchrs Assn; NEA; Sunset Srs Clb; Helen Matthewson Clb; Alumni-UCLA S'ship Grp; Dir, Sci of Mind Study Grp, 1984-; hon/Re-write of Novel in Progress; Num Articles, Plays, Poetry, Metaphysical Writings; Girls Leag S'ship, San Bernadino HS, 1928; Nat S'ship in Fin, UCLA, Ins Inst, 1953; Nat Del, Nat Conv of AAUW, Seattle, 1975; 3rd Awd, Poetry Contest, Profl Writers Leag, 1984; W/W: of Wom, in Am; DIB; Dir of Dist'd Ams; Personalities of W.

WAGNER, MARGARITA DOLORES oc/Manufacturer, Lecturer and Writer; b/Jul 15, 1903; h/1256 Tiffancy Circle, West Palm Springs, CA 92262; ba/Palm Springs, CA; c/Maynard S McHenry; ed/Var Courses: L'Ecole L'Union Francaise; Sacred Heart Convent; Sophie New Comb Col; pa/Edl & Creator of Cosmetic Oils made from Extracts of Nuts, Fruits & Vegetables; Mem: Fdr & Pres, Sans Soucy Celebrity Jrs Aux; Contbg Mem, Asst Leag Social Ser; r/Cath; hon/Writer of Var Articles; Num Recog Hons, for her Cosmetic Creations.

WAGNER, PAUL ANTHONY JR oc/Philosopher, Professor; b/Aug 28, 1947; h/2622 Plymouth Rock Drive, Webster, TX 77598; ba/Houston, TX; m/Karen Anne Seroka; c/Nicole Seroka, Eric Paul, Jason George; p/Paul H and Mary K Wagner, LaGrange Pk, IL; sp/George and Eleanor Seroka, Hollywood, FL; ed/BS, NE MO St Univ, 1969; MEd 1971, MA 1976, PhD 1978, Univ of MO; mil/USAR, 1970; MO NG, 1971-76; pa/Internal Expeditor, Gen Motors Electromotive Div, 1970; Phil Instr, Moberly Jr Col; Instr Phil of Ed & Cnslg Psych,

554

Univ of MO-Columbia, 1974-78; Instr, Humanities & Social Sci, MO Mil Acad, 1978-79; Asst Prof, Univ of Houston-Clear Lake City, 1979-; Book Reviewer, *Houston Post*; Mem: Am Phil Assn; Brit Phil of Sci Assn; Phil of Sci Assn; Phil of Ed Soc; SW Phil of Ed Soc; SW Assn of Edrs of Tchrs of Sci; Phi Delta Kappa; Kappa Delta Pi; Am Ednl Studies Assn; John Dewey Soc; Conslt, Local Sch Dists on Gifted Ed & Phil for Chd, 1978-; Var Col Coms; cp/VChm, City of Columbia, MO Human Rts Comm, 1976-78; Correctional Ed Assn; SS Tchr, Mary Queen Cath Ch, Friendswood, TX, 1980-; Others; r/Rom Cath; hon/Author, Over 50 Articles & Book Chapts Pub'd in Profl Jours, 1977-; Vis'g Scholar, Stanford Univ, 1981; Atrium Circle Dist'd Scholar Awd, 1982; Omar E Robinson S'ship, 1969; Graessle S'ship, 1968; MO NG Medal of Commend, 1975; Grad Tchg Awd, Univ of MO-Columbia, 1977; Fellow, Phil of Ed Soc, 1980; W/W: in Am Cols & Univs, in S & SW; Dir of Am Scholars; Dir of Am Phils.

WAIHEE, JOHN oc/Lieutenant Governor; b/May 19, 1946; ba/State Capitol, Honolulu, HI 96813; m/Lynne Kobashigawa; c/John IV, Jennifer; p/John Waihee (dec); Mary Waihee, Kuhio Village, Kamuelo-Waimea, HI; ed/Grad, HI Mission Acad, 1964; BA, Andrews Univ; MA Urban Planning, Ctl MI Univ; JD, Univ of HI Law Sch, 1976; pa/Asst Dir Commun Ed, Benton Harbor, MI; Prog Evalr & Planner, Honolulu Model Cities Prog; Sr Planner, City & Co Ofc of Human Resources; Pvt Pract Law, Firm of Shim, Sigal, Tam & Naito, 1976-79; Pvt Pract Law, (Own Firm) Waihee, Manuia, Yap, Pablo & Hoe; Del & Maj Ldr, Constitl Conv, 1978; Elected to St Ho of Rep, Salt Lake-Kaliki Area, 1980; Mem, Ho Policy Com, 1980; Lt Gov, St of HI, 1982-.

WALDEN, KATHRYN CARROLL oc/Teacher, Civic Leader; b/Apr 5, 1910; h/PO Box 355, Headland, AL 36345; ba/Headland, AL; m/Arthur D (dec); c/David Carroll (dec); Gwendolyn W Hand; p/Marvin and Lula Carroll (dec); sp/David and Maude Walden (dec); ed/BS Home Ec, Univ of Mentevallo, 1931; Att'd Univ of AL, 1956-58; pa/Home Ec Tchr, 1939-; Kgn Tchr, 1944-48; cp/Dist Ofcr, Wom's Grp of Meth Ch, 1955-57; Pres, Wom's Grp Headland Meth Ch, 1952-53; Pres, Headland Study Clb, 1958; Pres, Homemakers Clb, 1959; Reagent, Robert Griers Chapt, DAR, 1957; Wiregrass Mtl Hlth Assn, 1976-82; Elder Hostel, 1980-81; Home Ec Com, AL Dept of ED, 1982; Mem, AL ASHRAM Com, 1981-82; r/Meth; hon/Foun Set Up for Hom Ec HS Grads for 4 Yrs of Col, 1977; Foun Set Up for Mtl Hlth, 1982; Foun Set Up for Meth, 1982; Foun Set Up for Landmark Pk, 1982; Cert of Apprec, Mth Hlth Assn, 1978-80; Mem, IntlNew Thought Alliance, 1981; Att'd Inst of Rel Sci, 1978-80; World Traveler; Other Hons; W/W; Commun Ldrs of Am; Intl Register of Profiles; Book of Hon; Other Biogl Listings.

WALDEN, LINDA L oc/Attorney; b/Aug 16, 1951; h/7117 Wood Hollow, Austin, TX 78731; ba/Austin, TX 78711; p/Mr and Mrs L L Walden Jr, Dallas, TX; ed/BA, TX Wom's Univ, 1972; JD, St Mary's Univ, 1975; pa/Asst Atty Gen,

St of TX, 1979-; 1st Asst Dist Atty, 1977-79; Asst City Atty, City of Amarillo, 1976-77; pa/Altrusa Intl; TX Wom's Polit Caucus; Travis Co Wom's Bar Assn; hon/Co-Author, *TX Prosecutor's Trial Manual*, 1978; Cert'd Crim Law Spec, St Bar of TX; W/W of Am Wom; Blue Book of Panhandle.

WALDMANN, JOHN JOSEPH oc/Executive; b/Jul 31, 1936; h/2129 Knickerbocker Drive, Charlotte, NC 28212; ba/Charlotte, NC; m/Veronica; c/Madalina, George; p/Lon Vlaguiand Ecaterina Vlagiu, Romania; sp/Ion and Ioana Botezat (dec); ed/MSC, Univ of Bucharest, 1962; PhD, Bucharest Acad of Sci, 1969; pa/Res Chem, Ctl Res Chem Ctr, Romania, 1962-64; Sr Res Chem 1964-68, Grp Ldr 1968-74, Inst of Phy Chem, Div of Ctl Res Chem Ctr; NSF Spec Intl Fellow, NC St Univ, Raleigh, 1971-72 & 1973-74; Sr Res Chem, Ciba-Geigy Co, Ardsley, NY, 1974-75; Grp Ldr, SCP Div, Henkel Inc, 1976-78; Grp Ldr, Water Treatment Div, The Bouligny Co, Charlotte, NC, 1978-81; VPres of Res & Devel Div, Enwright Res Co, Charlotte, NC, 1981-; Mem: Am Chem Soc; Water Pollution Control Fedn; Repub; r/Presb; hon/19 Pubs in Intl Chem Jours, 1962-80; Recip, 22 Intl Patents in Chem Field, 1962-80; Recip Awd, Acad of Sci of Romania, 1974; W/W in Am, in S & SW.

WALK, DARLENE M oc/Data Analysis Director, Consultant; b/Jun 3, 1950; h/PO Box 53067 New Orleans, LA 70153; ba/New Orleans, LA; p/Donald W Walk, Pillow, PA; Lois L Walk, NO, LA; ed/BA 1972, MA 1974, Univ of SWn LA; Post Grad Study, Tulane Univ, 1973-81; pa/For City of NO: Urban Policy Spec I, Ofc of Policy Planning; Proj Mgr, Data Anal Unit, 1974-76; Urban Policy Spec II, 1976-77; Proj Mgr, Planning & Data Units, 1977-78; Dir, Neighborhood Profiles Proj, 1978; Coor, Data Anal Unit, 1979-; Urban Policy Spec III, 1980-; Data Conslt, 1979-; Mem: Am Planning Assn; Am Polit Sci Assn; So Polit Sci Assn; Am Hist Assn; Am Mgmt Assn; Am Acad of Polit & Social Sci; So Sociol Soc; LA Chapt, Metro Sect, Am Planning Assn; Urban & Reg Info Sys Assn; Am Philatelic Soc; cp/Bocage Civic Assn; Friends of the Audubon Zee; NO Mus of Art; hon/Author & Editor, Over 15 Citizen & Neighborhood Data Pubs; Sr Awd, AAUW, 1972; Meritorious Proj for *Neighborhood Profiles*, LA Am Planning Assn, 1982; Phi Kappa Phi, 1971; Sigma Tau Delta, 1969; Kappa Delta Pi, 1969; Pi Gamma Mu, 1970; Phi Sigma Alpha, 1973; Pi Mu Epsilon, 1970; Alpha Lambda Delta, 1969; W/W: in Am Cols & Univs; in S & SW; Outstg Yg Wom in Am; Other Biogl Listings.

WALKER, CAROLINE ANN oc/Utility Comapany Manager; b/Nov 16, 1944; h/2515 Thorndyke Avenue West #5, Seattle, WA 98199; ba/Seattle, WA; p/Charles Leonard Walker, Kent, WA; Ann Phyllis Walker, Kent, WA; ed/BA, Univ of WA, 1966; MA, Univ of CA-LA, 1968; Proj Mgr Treas & Fin Ec Anal 1983-, Staff Spec Bus Mktg Support Opers & Bus Revenue Forecasting 1982-83, Staff Spec Bus Mktg Support Opers & Line Mktg Objective Setting Process 1981-82, Staff Spec Bus Mktg Prod Tracking & Anal 1979-81; Mkt Admr Bus Mktg & Bus Sys Selling &

Implementation 1979; w Pacific NW Bell, Seattle, WA; Staff Spec, AT&T, Seattle, WA, 1983; Reg Economist Seattle, WA 1978-79 & 1971-73, Ec Anal LA, CA 1969-70, AUS Corp of Engrs; Proj Coor, WA/AK Reg Med Prog Tacoma, WA, 1974-75; Ec Anal, Congl Res Ser, The Lib of Cong, Wash DC, 1970-71; Mem: Seattle Economists Clb, 1979-; Alumni Assn of Univ of WA, 1973-; Wom's Univ Clb, 1981-; World Trade Clb, 1983; Sustaining Mem, Wash Repub Party, 1983-; Public Interest Com, Adm Subcom, Pacific NW Bell Wash-PIC, 1981-; World Affairs Coun, 1983; cp/Henry Art Gallery Assn, 1983; Seattle Art Mus, 1983; Seattle Sailing Clb, 1982; Wash Ath Clb, 1979-; r/Christian; hon/Lectr on Navigation Ec, at 13th Annual Pacific NW Reg Ec Conf, 1979; Sponsored St Initiative 322, 1976; Won WA St Supr Ct Appeal vs Secy of St to put Antiflouridation Initiative on the Ballot; W/W of Am Wom.

WALKER, DONNA RAE BOYD oc/Business Co-Owner; b/May 10, 1932; h/4804 Burning Tree Drive, Baytown, TX 77521; ba/Baytown, TX; m/L Douglas; c/Ronna Janice Walker Martin, LaRisa Diane Walker Briles; Mark Douglas; p/Robert Ben and Gladys Pauline Hoover Boyd (dec); sp/James Luther Walker (dec); Bessie Frances Douglas Walker Rogers (dec); ed/Var Short Courses; pa/Allocation of Requested Monies for Radar & Radio Sites, OKC Air Material Area, 1950-53; Co-owner w Husband, Admr, Acctg & Tax Bus, 1956-; cp/Gov 1984-85, 1st Lt Gov 1983-84, 2nd Lt Gov 1983, 3rd Lt Gov 1981, Projs Div Coor for Dist 1980, TX Dist Pilot Clb Intl; Pres 1979-80, 1st VPres 1978-79, 2nd VPres 1977-78, Treas 1971-72, Dir 1980-81, Baytown Chapt Pilot Clb Intl; C of C, Baytown; OES; Mothers Agnst Drunken Drives (MADD); Baytown Citizen's Safety Coun; PTA; POTC; Little Leag; Polit Activs; r/St John's U Meth Ch, Adm Bd; hon/NHS, HS; Bronze Medal, St Music Contests, HS; Dist's Outstg Clb Awd, 1979-80; Marguerite Dimerling Clb Achmt Awd, 1980; Citizen of Wk, Baytown Radio Sta, 1983; Donna Walker Day & Presented Key to City, Mayor of Port Arthur, TX, Oct 4, 1983; Donna Walker Day, Mayor of Nederland, TX, Oct 5, 1983; Ser Placque, Baytown Pilot Clb, 1979-80; Other Pilot Clb Awds; Other Hons.

WALKER, DUDLEY J oc/Medical Sciences Liaison; b/Jul 1, 1945; h/1565 East Bank Drive, Marietta, GA 30067; c/D Jennings Walker Jr; ed/BS, The Citadel, 1967; pa/w Upjohn Co: Med Sci Liaison, Infectious Diseases, 1980-; MSL Hypersensitivity Diseases, 1979-80; MSL Infectious Diseases 1978-79; Hosp Sales, Jackson, MS, 1976-79; Host Sales, Charlotte, NC, 1973-76; Gen Sales, Atlanta, GA, 1972-73; Gen Sales, Fayetteville, NC, 1969-72; Tchr, Spartanburg, SC, 1968-69; Tchr, Charleston, SC, 1967-68; Mem: Am Soc for Microbiol; Profl Picture Framers of Am; cp/Mbrship Chm, Ducks Unltd, 1981 & 1982; Pres, The Quacker Box Inc, 1980-; r/Epis; hon/Class Ofcr, HS; Dean's List, Col; Outstg Yg Man of Am, 1980; W/W in S & SW.

WALKER, GEORGE E oc/Administrative Assistant; b/Jan 25, 1940; h/828

Monique Court, Cedar Hill, TX 75104; ba/Cedar Hill, TX; m/Linda Kay; c/Eli Samuel; p/Mr and Mrs J O Morgan (dec); sp/Mr and Mrs Norris Cheves, Bridgeport, TX; ed/BS, Cumberland Col, 1966; MEd, E TX St Univ, 1978; mil/USN, 1960; pa/Elem Tchr, Mt Hlthy (OH) ISD, 1966-71; Jr HS Coach, 1968-71; Elem Tchr, Cedar Hill (TX) ISD, 1971-79; Coach, 1973-78; Acting Prin, 1977; Asst Prin, 1977-78; Elem Sch Prin, 1979-82; Adm Asst, 1982-; TX Mem, Nat Assn Elem Sch Prins; TX Elem Sch Prins & Supts; Phi Delta Kappa; cp/Cedar Hill C of C; r/Bapt; hon/W/W in S & SW.

WALKER, JOHN JAMES oc/Research and Development Chemist; b/Jul 4, 1935; h/2952 Greenrock Trail, Doraville, GA 30340; ba/Atlanta, GA; m/Charlene Carlson; c/Rache Lynne, Nathan Scot, Samuel Trent; p/Thomas M Walker (dec); Sylvia P Walker, Holdrege, NE; sp/Henry D Carlson (dec); Judith M Carlson Sumney, NE; ed/BS, Univ of NE, 1958; MS, Atlanta Univ, 1968; Phd, GA Inst of Technol, 1973; mil/AUS, 1958-60, Germany; pa/Instr, Omaha Public Schs, 1960-62; Instr, Louisville, NE Public Schs, 1964-66; Instr, Clark Col, Atlanta, GA, 1967-68; Pt-time Instr, GA Inst of Technol, 1968-73; Chief Chem, Hysam Corp, Atlanta, 1973-81; Res Chem, I Schneid Inc, Atlanta, 1981-; Mem: Am Chem Soc; GA Chem Soc; Fellow, Am Inst of Chems; AAAS; Phi Epsilon Kappa; r/Christian & Missionary Alliance Ch, Elder; hon/Author, "Synthesis of Barbituric Acid & Derivatives"; NSF Foun Grant; Atomic Energy Comm Grant; Pres S'ship in Chem; W/W in S & SW, in GA; Am Men & Wom of Sci.

WALKER, LINDA DOWLING oc/Production Foreman; b/Jun 13, 1952; ba/200 South 24th Street, Billings, MT 59101; m/Philip D; p/J Robert Dowling (dec); Eleanor Peterson, Missoula, MT; sp/Floyd and Margaret Walker (dec); ed/BS Voc Rehab & Cnslg, En MT Col, 1979; Epilepsies & Medications Cert, St of MT, 1981-; Devel Disabilites Client Programming Tech Cert, St of MT, 1982-; pa/Yth Home Cnslr, Billings Chd's Receiving Hom, 1979-80; Chd Devel Tech, Yellowstone Boys Ranch, 1980; Prod Foreman of Needletrades, Small Assem & Wood Assem, Billings Wkshop, 1980-; Mem: Am Pers & Guid Assn, 1980-; AAUW, 1980-; Nat Voc Guid Assn, 1980-; r/Cath; hon/Bd Mem, Postal Custome's Coun, 1983-; Cert Uses & Abuses Assertiveness & Confrontation, St of MT Dept of Instns; W/W in W.

WALKER, LORNA ANN oc/Nutritional/Allergy Consultant; b/Jun 19, 1950; h/11091 NW 21st Court, Sunrise, FL 33322; ba/Lauderhill, FL; m/Philip Mac; c/Brent Alan; p/Orville H and Clara M Hussey, Naples, FL; sp/Murray and Marilyn Walker, Butler, GA; ed/BS, Univ of RI, 1971; Med Technol, Newport Hosp; MS Cand in Nurtition & Metabolic Studies, Antioch Intl Univ; pa/Med Technol, Chula Vista CA Commun Hosp, 1972-74; Med Technol, Tri-Cos Blood Bk, Santa Barbara, CA, 1974; Instr Lab Scies, Charron Wms Col, Ft Lauderdale, FL, l1981-82; Nutritional/Allergy Conslt, Sunrise, FL, 1979-; Nutritional/Allergy Conslt, Chiropract Care Ctr, Lauderhill, FL,

1982-; Bd of Dirs & Lectr/Conslt, Hypoglycemia Res Foun Inc; Am Soc of Clin Pathols, 1972-; Am Soc of Med Technol, 1976-78; Intl Acad Nutritional Conslts; Human Ecol Action Leag; r/Rom Cath; hon/Author, Var Articles for Hypoglycemia Res Foun; Recip New Engrg Soc Awd for Promotion of Arts & Scis; Lambda Tau Hon Med Technol Soc Awd, 1968; W/W of Am Wom.

WALKER, T URLING oc/Mayor; b/Jan 31, 1925; h/1170 Ives Street, Watertown, NY 13601; ba/Watertown, NY; m/Mabel Brooks; c/Mrs Constance W Monroe, Thomas H Jr, Laurel E; p/Thomas A and Clara U Walker (dec); sp/Harry F and Mabel I Brooks, Watertown, NY; ed/Att'd Wash & Jefferson Col, 1946-47; BSME, Case Inst of Technol, 1951; Grad Wk: Oswego St, Syracuse Univ & Bucknell Univ; mil/USAF, 1944-46, PTO, Sgt & Crew Chief; pa/Mayor, City of Watertown, NY, 1984-; Self-employed, 1975-83; Exec Secy, Watertown Foun Inc, 1972-75; Assoc Coor Housing, Watertown Urban Mission, 1971-72; Asst Prof Engrg Scis, Jefferson Commun Col, Watertown, 1963-70; 7th & 8th Grade Math Tchr, N Jr HS, Watertown, 1962-63; Engr & Dir of Safety Watertown Div, NY Air Brake, 1951-60; Others; Mem: Watertown Bd of Ed; ASME; Bd Mem, Jefferson Commun Col Foun; Pres of Bd, Neighbors of Watertown Urban Mission; Chm of Bd, Creg Corp; Pres, Ives Hill Land Co; VChm, Clarkson Col Entrepreneural Corp; Others; cp/Planned Parenthood of No NY; Bd of Trustees, YMCA; GSA; Rotary Clb; Bicent Com; Advy Bd, Salvation Army; Jefferson-Lewis Sch Bd Assn; U Way of Jefferson Co; Jefferson Co Repub Com; Watertown C of C; Others; r/Presb; hon/Shapiro Awd for Citizen of Yr, 1983; No Country Cit, St Lawrence Univ, 1983; Silver Beaver Awd, BSA, 1983.

WALKER, U OWEN oc/Engineer; b/Oct 9, 1925; h/PO Box 1224 Albuquerque, NM 87103; ba/Same; p/James N and Amy Wimberly Walker (dec); ed/BE, Yale Univ, 1946; mil/USN, 1943-46; pa/Engr, S & W Constrn Co, 1946-53 & 1970-72; Engr, Def Depot, Memphis, TN, 1953-70; Engr, Memphis Dist AUS Corp of Engrs, 1973-76; Engr, Nav Sta Mayport, 1976-79; Engr, USMC Logistics Base, 1979-81; Engr, USDI, 1981-84; Mem: ASCE; CPE, AIPE; CEM, AEE; CM, ICPM; CRM, ICRM; APM, PAI; Nat Dir/Com-man, Chapt Orgr/Pres/Editor, AIPE, 1965-70; St/Local Sect Chm/Com-man, NSPE, 1965-67; Others; r/Bapt; hon/Author of Var Tech Report Papers; Plant Engr of Yr, 1968; Richard H Morris Medal, AIPE; Mr Indust Awd, Editors of IMPO Mag, 1969; W/W: in Engrg, in Technol Today, in W, in S & SW.

WALLACE, BETTY ABERNATHY oc/Teacher and Author; b/Jun 28, 1926; h/30 Woodlawn Avenue, Hampton, GA 30228; ba/McDonough, GA; m/William Andrew Jr; c/Rebecca Abernathy (Mrs Rob Chapman), Janet Lynn (Mrs Phillips Bradley), William Scot; p/Thomas J Abernathy (dec); Emily Frances Glenn Abernathy, Gastonia, NC; sp/Wm Andrew and Edna Wallace (dec); ed/Att'd, Agnes Scott Col, 1944-46; BFA, Univ of GA, 1948; Postgrad Wk: GA St Univ; Tift Col; W GA Col; DT-4 Art,

1971; DT-4 Elem, 1977; DT-4 Gifted, 1980; pa/Art Tchr, 1950; Pianist, Hampton Sch of Ballet, 1960; Pub'g Poet, 1965-84; Elem Edr, 1966-80; Tchr of Gifted, 1980-84; Author, 1984; Mem: VPres, Local AAUW, 1957-58; NEA & GAE, 1966-84; Chapt Music Chm, Delta Kappa Gamma Intl, 1978-84; Charter Mem, GA St Poetry Soc, 1980-84; cp/Ch Pianist/Organist, 1957; Secy, Wom of the Ch, 1948-50; Chancellor Choir, Pianist, Organist & Singer, 1958-66; r/Meth; hon/Author, Through a Time Sieve, 1984; Num Other Pubs in Lincoln Log; Poetry Scope; GA Life; The Hampton News; The Writer; Am Bard; NY Herald-Tribune; & Var Anthologies; Awds for Poetry Incl: "Retreat W/O Maximilian," Daniel Whitehead Hicky Nat Awds, 1983; "Beyond Other Seasons," "Indigo Reverie," The Io Moth," IL St Poetry Soc, 1982 & 1983; "House of The Muses," Nat Fed of St Poetry Socs, (MA), 1980; "The Bayeux Tapestry," "House of The Muses," GA St Poetry Soc, 1980; Edward Shorter Awd for Painting, Univ of GA, l948; Hon Mention, GA St Exhibn, 1948; Art S'ship, Univ of GA, 1947; 2nd Place Orig Piano Compostion, NC Fedn of Music, 1944.

WALLACE, DEBORAH SUE oc/Professor, Special Education Coordinator; b/Apr 16, 1947; h/2727 Godby Road, Apartment O-8, Col Pk, GA 30349; ba/Atlanta, GA; p/Richard and Mary Wallace, Westerville, OH; ed/BSEd, OH Univ, 1969; MA 1974, PhD 1976, OH St Univ-Columbus; pa/Assoc Prof Dept of Spec Ed, Coor Spec Ed Adm Prog, GA St Univ, Atlanta, 1976-; Instr, Kent St Univ, Sums 1976-; Tm Ldr, Parent Tng Prog Exceptl Chd Dept 1976, Grad Res Assoc, Student Tchr Supvr & Sem Instr 1975-76, Tm Ldr Indiv'd Instrn Wkshops Sum 1975, Grad Res Assoc, Coor of Thurber Sch Proj 1974-75, Eval Tm Coor Sum 1974, Grad Res Asst Lng Disabilities Proj 1973-74, OH St Univ; Conslt, Lrng Disabilities & EMR Wkship Div of Spec Ed, OH Dept of Ed, Sum 1974; Math & Rdg Tchr, Lancaster, OH, Sum 1972; Math & Biol Tchr, Lancaster, OH, Sum 1971; Tutor, Neurologically Handicapped, Lancaster, OH, 1970-73; Other Positions; Mem: Coun for Exceptl Chd, 1973-; Coun for Chd w Behavior Disorders, 1973-; Div for Chd w Lrng Disabilities, 1973-; Tchr Ed Div, 1977-; GA Coun for Admrs in Spec Ed, 1977-78; Pi Lambda Theta, 1975-; GA St Univ Fac Advr, Kappa Delta Epsilon, 1982-; cp/Chm Policy & Procedures Com 1981-, Bd of Dirs 1980-, Tommy Nobis Ctr for the Mtly Retarded, Marietta, GA; Advy Bd Mem, Morehouse Col Atlanta Univ, Paraprofl Prog, 1979-; NAACP, 1978-; Pres 1978-79, VPres 1977-78, Fulton Co Yg Dems GA; Alt Nat Com Wom, GA Yg Dems, 1978-79; Others; r/Meth; hon/Author, Num Articles, Manuals, Media Prods & Other Pubs on Skill Devel & Ed; Nom, Am Coun on Ed Fellows in Acad Adm, 1982; Tommy Nobis Ctr Ser Awd, 1982; Alumni Foun Tchg Awd, GA St Univ, 1981; Intl Wom's Yr Recog Recip, 1977; Martha Holden Jennings Scholar, l972; W/W in Am Wom.

WALLER, JERRY JIM oc/Agronomist; b/Jun 23, 32; h/2103 Pamela, Temple, TX 76502; ba/Temple, TX; m/Dixie Sue; c/Don, Bob, Jim, Carol; p/John R Waller (dec); Hazel McMillan,

Ben Franklin, TX; sp/D S and Anna Lue Long, Groesbeck, TX; ed/AA, Paris Jr Col, 1951; BS, E TX St Univ, 1953; MS TX A&M Univ, 1961; MRA, Univ of MT, 1976; mil/AUS, 1954-56; pa/Trainee, USDA/Soil Conserv Ser, Stephenville, TX, 1953; Soil Conservationist, DeLeon, TX, 1953-54; Soil Conservationist, Groesbeck, TX, 1956-59; Range Conservationist, Goldthwaite, TX, 1960-61; Asst Agri Ext Agt, TX Agri Ext Ser, Greenville, TX, 1961; Soil Conservationist, Waco, TX, 1961-65; Dist Conservationist, Big Spring, TX, 1965-66; Agronomist, S TX & Gulf Coast of TX, Alice, TX, 1966-67; Agronomist, N Ctl & NE TX, Denton, TX, 1967-72; St Agronomist, Bozeman, MT, 1972-76; St Agronomist, Temple, TX, 1976-; Mem: Am Soc of Agronomy; Soil Conserv Soc of Am; TX Chapt Am Soc of Agronomy; Cert'd Profl Agronomist; Cert'd TX Chem Applicator; cp/ Master Mason, Royal Arch Mason, Royal & Select Master Mason, Knight Templer Mason; Shriner, OES; Hon, Order of Demolay; BSA Ldr, 1968-75; Little Leag Baseball Coach, 1967-76; Yth Coun & Usher, 1st Meth Ch, Temple, TX; r/Meth; hon/Author, *Estab'g Perennial Grasses Along Hwy Rts-of-Way During the Sum Mos*, 1961; *A Field Manual to Adopt the Universal Soil Loss Equation in MT*, 1976; *TX Erosion Handbook (Wind & Water)*, 1978; *Ec Anal of Conserv Tillage*, 1980; McWherter Agri S'ship, 1950-51; Res Asst S'ship, 1960-61; USDA-SCS Grad Sch Selection, 1975; USDA-SCS Cert of Merit, 1978; USDA-SCS Outstg Perf Awd, 1981; W/ W in S 7 SW.

WALLING, JOHN B oc/Executive; b/ Oct 5, 1928; h/5613 Trail Lake Drive, Ft Worth, TX 76133; ba/Ft Worth, TX; m/Bobbie Marie Boggs; c/Danny Michael, John Scott, Candace Walling Davis; p/Wade Hampton and Ida Walling, Munday, TX; sp/Mahlon Boggs (dec); Ruby Boggs, Ft Worth, TX; ed/ Att'd TX Univ, 1946; BS, Mwn Univ, 1949; Att'd NY Univ on Boy's Clb S'ship, 1949; Grad Wk, TX Univ-Austin, 1951 & 1952; pa/Prog Dir, Boy's Clb of Wichita Falls, TX, 1948-49; Coach, St Champ Basketball Tm, 1949; Ednl Dir, Floral Hgts Meth Ch, 1949 & 1950; Mem, TX St Legis, 1951-59; Pres, World Oil & Gas Corp, 1958-66; Chm of Bd, Appalachian Coal & Timber, 1966-69; Pres, Everman Success Inc (Owned & Managed Blackstone Hotel, Ft Worth), 1968-72; Conslt, Wedgco Inc, Jay-Bo Inc & Cadasco Inc, 1976-78; Pres 1978-86, Conslt 1980-, Chm of Bd 982-, Fluid Lift Intl Inc; Indep Creat Designer & Inventor, 1963-; Legis Coms: TX St Oil, Gas & Mining Com; Chm, Common Carriers Com; Spec Schs Com; Water Conserv Com; r/Prot; hon/Co-Author, TX Turnpike Act; TX Securities Act; Author, Nat Gas Ec Waste Bill; Inventor of Oil Indust Prodn Sys; Recip, 4 Patents in Field; Del, So Gov's Conf, 1958; Appt'd Mem 1981, VChm 1982, Elected 5 Yr Term on Bd of Dirs 1983, UN-USA; W/W: in Am, in SW; in Fin & Indust.

WALLIS, BEN A JR oc/Attorney, Rancher, Hunting Preserve Operator; b/Apr 27, 1936; h/1363 Inwood Park, San Antonio, TX 78216; ba/San Antonio, TX; c/Ben III, Jessica; p/Ben and Jessie Longbotham Wallis, Llano, TX; ed/BBA, Univ of TX, 1961; JD, Univ of

TX Sch of Law, 1971; Post Grad Study, So Meth Univ Sch of Law; Admitted to Pract: US Supr Ct; US Cts of Appeal for DC, 5th Circuit, 8th Circuit, 11th Circuit; US Dist Cts for Wn, No, So Dists of TX & DC; TX Supr Ct; DC Ct of Appeals; pa/Pvt Pract, Llano, TX, 1966-68; Investigaor-Prosecutor, St Securities Bd, 1968-72; Pvt Law Pract, Dallas, TX, 1972; VPres Devel, Clb Corp of Am, Dallas, 1973; Assoc Counsel, US House of Reps Com on the Judiciary Impeachment Task Force, Wash DC, 1974; Pvt Law Pract, San Antonio, 1975-; Rancher & Hunting Preserv Operator, 1962-; Mem: Sect on Taxation, ABA; Theta Phi Legal Frat; Delta Sigma Pi; St Bar of TX; DC Bar Assn; Fed Bar Assn; Assn of Trial Lwyrs of Am; San Antonio Bar Assn; Dallas Bar Assn; Nat Cattlemen's Assn; cp/Guest Lectr for Var Orgs; r/Bapt; hon/Author & Editor, *Your Property Newslttr*, 1977-81; Num Land Use and Property Rts Spchs & Pubs; Chm, Nat Land Us Conf, 1979-81; Counsel, Nat Assn of Property Owners, 1976-81; Mem, Gov's Area-wide Planning Advy Com, 1975-78; Pres, Inst for Human Rts Res; W/W in Am Law; Other Biogl Listings.

WALLS, SALLY A oc/Personel Manager; b/Oct 5, 1951; h/3232 Maryland Avenue North, Crystal, MN 55427; ba/ Mpls, MN; p/Donald and Joyce Walls, Richfield, MN; ed/BA 1974, MA 1975, Univ of MN; pa/Pers Mgr, Gen Mills Inc, 1982-; Dir of Pers, Calhoun's Collectors Soc, 1980-82; Pers Mgr 1978-80, Employmnt Admr 1975-76, The Pillsbury Co; Pers Adm Mgr, Poppin Fresh Pie Shops, 1976-78; Mem: Twin Cities Pers Assn, 1980-; Am Soc of Pers Adm, 1980-; cp/VPres Bd of Dirs 1978-, Mem-at-Large Bd of Dirs 1976-77, Nat Coun Del 1978 & 1981, Gtr Mpls Girl Scout Coun; Safety Instr, ARC, 1975-; hon/God & Commun Awd, GSA.

WALMAN, JEROME PREISER oc/ Psychotherapist-Hypnotist; b/Jun 19, 1937; h/400 E 59th St (9F), New York, NY 10022; ba/Same; m/Mary Joan; p/ Ralph Pranara; ed/WV Univ; Boston Univ; Berkely Sch of Music; pa/Practicing Psychotherapist, Hypnotist, Music Therapist, 11 Yrs; Dir, Memory Improvement Ctr of Am; Conslt, Meditation & Mental Improvement Ctr & Rdg Improvement & Speed Rdg Ctr; Hypnosis Sers, US Dept of Def & NY Univ Med Sch; hon/Author, Var Articles Pub'd in Var Profl Qtlys & Mags; Author of a Musical; Prodr of Acclaimed TV Series, "Enterprises Unltd Presents"; Prodr, Broadway & Off-Broadway Musicals.

WALSH, BARBARA KLINCK oc/ Project Manager, Commercial Development; b/Jun 13, 1941; h/700 Foxcroft Circle, Marietta, GA 30067; ba/Atlanta, GA; m/Jerry; c/Michael, David, Christopher; p/Hannah D Klinck, Garden City, SC; ed/Grad, Green Mtn Col, 1961; pa/Proj Mgr, Kern & Co, 1983-; Mktg Mgr, So Sites Inc, 1981-83; Dir of Sales, Sheraton-By-the-Sea, Jekyll Isl, GA, 1979-81; cp/Pres & Co-Fdr, Atlanta Ronald McDonald House, 1977-; Bd of Dirs, Yg Matrons Circle of Tallulah Falls Sch, 1980-83; Bd of Trustees, Metro N Yth Soccer Assn, 1980-; hon/Alpha Delta Pi, 1981; Outstg Clbwom, Town & Co Jr Wom's Clb,

1974; W/W in Am.

WALSH, CHARLES RICHARD oc/ Banker; b/Jan 30, 1939; h/9 Blueberry Lane, Oyster Bay, NY 11771; ba/ Hicksville, NY; m/Marie Anne Goulden; c/Kevin Charles, Brian Richard, Gregory Michael; p/Charles J Walsh (dec); Anna Ellen Walsh, Ridge, NY; sp/James and Mathilde Goulden (dec); ed/BS, Fordham Univ, 1960; MBA, St John's Univ, 1966; mil/USAR, 1960 & 1961-62; pa/Credit & Collection Mgr, Texaco Inc, NYC, 1961-67; Mgr of Credit Res, Trans World Airlines, NYC, 1967-712; Dir of Br Opers, Avon Prods Inc, NYC, 1971-74; VPres 1974-80, Sr Pres 1980-, Mfrs Hanovers Trust Co, NYC; Mem: Dir, En Sts Monetary Sers, Lake Succes, NY, 1978-; Chm of Bd, En States Monetary Sers, 1978; Ch Exec Com, Am Bkrs Assn Bk Card Div, 1982; Former Chm Consumer Bking Div, NY St Bkrs Assn, 1977-82; Cert'd Consert Credit Execs; Am Mgmt Assn; NY Credit & Fin Mgmt Assn; cp/Forest Ests Clb; Repub; r/Rom Cath; hon/W/W: in World, in Fin & Indust.

WALSH, DANIEL EUGENE oc/Elementary Principal; b/Mar 12, 1944; h/ Union Square B-8, Madison, SD 57042; ba/Madison, SD; m/Janette; c/Katherine Elizabeth, Kelly Jean, Jennifer Marie; p/ Loretta Katherine Walsh (dec); sp/ Henry and Rosella Wagner (dec); ed/BS 1966, MA 1971, Univ of SD-Vermillion; pa/6th Grade Tchr & Coach 1966-82, Elem Prin 1982-83, Lake Ctl Schs, Madison, SD; Area Rep Worldbook Childcraft Intl, Sum 1974-78; Rec Supr, Amerts-Madison, SD, Sum 1979-83; Elem Prin, Garfield Elem Sch, Madison, SD, 1983-; Mem: NEA, 1966-; SD Ed Assn, 1966-82; Madison Ed Assn, 1966-82; SD Assn of Elem Sch Prins, 1982-; Treas, Madison Ed Assn, 1968-70; cp/Interlakes Yth Coun, 1965-75 & 1983; Elks Clb, 1967-83; SD Coaches Assn, 1981-83; Little Leag Baseball Coach, 3 Yrs; VFW Teener Baseball Coach 13 Yrs; Elks Yth Softball Coach, 1 Yr; r/Rom Cath; hon/Outstg Yg Edrs, Lake Co Area, 1971; Life Mem, SD PTA, 1974; Top Sales Rep for En, ND & SD, Worldbook/Childcraft Intl, 1975; Plaque of Apprec for Coaching, VFW Teener Baseball, 1976.

WALSH, DANIEL STEPHEN oc/ College Professor and Management Consultant; b/Dec 3, 1941; h/91 Armstrong Drive, Clark, NJ 07066; ba/ Newark, NJ; m/Lois D; c/Lorraine E, Kevin P, Maureen P; p/Vincent D and Marie F Walsh, Clark, NJ; sp/Harry and Dorothy (dec); ed/BSME, 1963; MBA, 1969; MS Sys Engrg, 1974; mil/USAF, 1st Lt; pa/Supermkts Gen Corp, 1971-83; Delicia Corp, 1970-71; Merek & Co, 1967-70; Staff Indust Engr; Sys Analyst; Mgr Opers Res; Mgr Spec Projs; Mem: The Inst of Mgmt Scis; Opers Res Soc of Am; AIIE; Assn of Computers Users; cp/Mem, Twp Planning Bd; r/Rom Cath; hon/Pub'd Over 10 Tech Papers & articles; Guest Lectr, Rutgers University; Sem Ldr; Cert'd Profl Engr; Alpha Pi Mu; Alpha Iota Delta; Howard Begg F'ship; W/W in E.

WALSH, SARA ELIZABETH (ECHART) oc/Professor; b/Dec 11, 1938; h/9023 Gaylord #102, Houston, TX 77024; ba/Houston, TX; p/Faye Echart, Hondo, TX; ed/BS 1960, MS 1962, E TX St Univ; Doct Credits, Univ of Houston; pa/Exec Secy, VPres, E TX St Univ, 1960-62; Hd of Bus Dept & Tchr, N Shore Sr HS, Galena Pk, TX, 1962-65; Tchr, S TX Jr Col, Houston, 1965-74; Asst Prof & Supvr Info Proc Ctr, Univ of Houston-Downtown Col, 1974-; Mem: 1st Exec VPres & 1st Dir of Ed/Historian, Intl Info Word Processing Assn, 1980-81; Corres'g Secy, Delta Pi Epsilon, 1982; Secy-Treas, TX Bus Ed Assn, 1980; Intl Assn Word Processing Specs; Gamma Phi Beta; AAUW; r/Bapt; hon/Co-Author, "Dress for Success," in TX Bus Ed Assn The Edr, 1982; Outstg Mem of Yr, Intl Info Word Processing Assn, 1981-82; Hon Soc Cert, 1980-81; Hon Soc Plaque, 1981-82; Num Other Awds; W/W: of Wom, in Am Cols & Univs, in Ed, in S & SW, of Intells; Commun Ldrs of Am; DIB; Other Biogl Listings.

WALTERS, CAROL WELCH oc/Educator; b/Jan 11, 1944; h/4750 North Sheridan, Chicago, IL 60640; ba/Chgo, IL; m/Malcolm George; c/Richard George, Kevin Charles; p/Benjamin F Welch, Jacksonville, FL; ed/Att'd Carson-Newman Col, 1961-62; Att'd Inst of Cultural Affairs, 1967-70; pa/Dir, Tng Inc, 1975-; Conslt, Inst of Cultural Affairs, 1970-75; Mem, Nat Bus Ed Ass, 1976-; cp/Bd of Dirs, Oak Brook Assn of Commerce & Indust, 1980-82; r/Christian; hon/Author, Tng Inc Curric Manual, 1980; Imaginal Ed for Adults, 1979; Selected for Exemplary Tng Prog, US Dept of Labor, 1981; W/W: of Am Wom, of Wom.

WALTERS, DAVID W oc/Real Estate Broker; b/May 22, 1948; h/5614 Forestview Road, Little Rock, AR 72204; ba/Little Rock, AR; m/Marha B; c/David Jr, Stacie D; p/Mr and Mrs Eddie L Walters, Little Rock, AR; sp/Mr and Mrs Willie Blake, West Helena, AR; ed/BSBA, University of AR-Pine Bluff, 1970; pa/Store Mgmt, The Kroger Co, 1970-76; Newspaper Pubr, The Consumer Newspaper, 1972-75; Dir of Intake & Assessment, CACETA Prog, 1975-80; Real Est Broker, Walters & Assocs Realtrs, 1980-; Mem: Bd Chm, Carver YMCA Bd of Dirs, 1977-80; Bd Mem, Metro YMCA Bd of Dirs, 1977-; cp/Pres, Vols in Public Schs (VIPS); Scoutmaster, Troop 73 Little Rock, AR; SS Tchr, Mt Zion Bapt Ch; r/Bapt; hon/Commun Ser Awd, KARK Channel 4 & Gov's Ofce of Vols, 1980; Outstg Yg Men of Am.

WALTERS, JUDSON V oc/Retail Merchant, Farmer; b/Jun 25, 1911; h/Route 1, Box 113, Laurel, MS 39440; ba/Laurel, MS; m/Marjorie Poole; c/Diane Everitt, Patricia Rogers; p/Archie and Etta Coker Walters (dec); sp/H H and Viola Poole (dec); ed/Dipl, Wayne Co HS, 1936; ed/AL Shipbldg Co; pa/Pipe Fitter; Owner, J V Walters Grocery; Farmer, Horses, Broilers & Cattle; Mem: ASCS Bd; Farm Bur Bd; Dixie Elect Assn; Walking Horse Breeders Assn; Cattlemen's Assn; cp/Mason; Steward & Trustee, Antioch Meth Ch; hon/Meth.

WALTERS, KAY LYNN oc/Executive; b/Nov 27, 1942; h/2816 Lakeshore Drive, Arlington, TX 76013; ba/Richardson, TX; c/David Ryan, Stephen Paul; p/LaVerne Clawson, Big Spring, TX; ed/BA Eng, Univ of TX-Arlington, 1974; MBA, So Meth Univ, 1978; pa/Proj Ldr, Bk of A Levy, Ventura, CA, 1966-68; Proj Ldr, 1st Data Processing, Big

Spring, TX, 1968-70; Proj Ldr, Results Inc, Dallas, TX, 1970-72; Dir of Applications Sys, ENSERCH Corp, 1973-80; Mgr of Devel 1980-81, VPres 1981-, Perf Assocs (Software Devel Firm); Mem: So Meth Univ MBA Assn; r/Bapt; hon/W/W of Am Wom.

WALTERS, LARRY MACON oc/Executive and Representative; b/Mar 27, 1947; h/Route 3, Box 465, Ellisville, MS 39437; ba/Laurel, MS; m/Diann Cheeks; p/Macon H and Aline Walters, Laurel, MS; sp/Jimmie and Carmen Cheeks, Ellisville, MS; ed/AA, Jones Co Jr Col, 1967; BA, Univ of So MS, 1969; mil/AUS, 1969-71; VietNam Vet; pa/VPres Machine Mgr & Authorized IBM Typewriter Rep, Ofc Supply Co, Ellisville, MS, 15 Yrs; cp/Univ of So MS Alumni Assn; Marvin Stanton Post, Am Legion; Bd of Dirs, 20/20 Hunting Clb; Pres 1982-83, Bd of Dirs 1983-84, Ellisville Lions Clb; r/Meth; hon/Hattiesburg's Dist'd Salesman's Awd, Sales & Mktg Execs Com, 1974; Husband of Yr Awd, Beta Sigma Phi, 1978 & 1981; 25th Inf Div of Tropic Lightning; Purple Heart; Bronze Star; AUS Commend Medal; VietNam Ser Medal; Outstg Yg Men of Am.

WALTON, FERNIE ALBERT oc/Minister and Master Barber; b/Jan 17, 1924; h/PO Box 7249, Jacksonville, NC 28540; ba/Jacksonville, NC; m/Joyce I (dec); c/Robert E, Ava M; p/Lige and Hallie Stewart (dec); sp/Eslie and Nora Walton (dec); ed/Dipl, Richlands HS, 1941; Grad, Shuffords Inst of Barbering, 1947; Att'd SWn Bible Col, 1956-57; mil/USN, 1941-47, WW II; pa/Pastor, Sneads Ferry Pentecostal Holiness Ch, 1961-63; Pastor, Hood Meml Pentecostal Holiness Ch, 1963-77; Ord'd Freewill Holiness Camp Ground, Clinton, NC, 1980; Pastor, Jacksonville Freewill Holiness Ch, 1980-81; Pastor, Warsaw Freewill Holiness Ch, 1981-; As a Jacksonville Barber: Ser Barber Shop, 1947-49; Farmers Barber Shop, 1949-59; Owner & Mgr, Plaza Barber Shop, 1954-63; Mgr, Northwoods Barber Shop, 1963-; Mem: Exec Secy, Onslow Co Chapt; Assoc'd Master Barbers of Am; Chaplain USS Washington-BB56, Reunion Grp; Past Chaplain, Burton-Cowell Post 265 Am Legion; Am Battleship Assn; cp/Smithsonian Inst; Intl Platform Assn; VFW; r/Holiness; hon/Author, From Death Unto Life, 1977; 13 Battle Stars & 8 Ser Ribbons in WW II; Served on USS Brinkley Bass-DD 887 in Japanese Occup Forces w Asiatic Fleet, 1946; Hon Lt Gov of NC (Appt'd by Jimmy Green), 1977; Fellow, Intl Biogl Assn, 1983; W/W of Intells; Men of Achmt.

WALTON, VINCENT MICHAEL oc/Principal Engineer; b/Oct 23, 1949; h/2116 Bataan Road # B, Redondo Beach, CA 90278; ba/Torrance, CA; m/Mary Elizabeth; p/Mr and Mrs Norman John Walton, Bremerton, WA; sp/Mrs Edward Francis McGuire, Philadelphia, PA; ed/BSEE 1973, MSEE 1975, Univ of WA; Postgrad Study, Stanford Univ, 1978; pa/Tech Staff, Boeing Aerospace Co, 1973-75; Dept Staff Engr, TRW Sys Grp, 1975-81; Prin Engr, Measurement Anal Corp, 1981-; r/Non-denom; hon/Author, Over 10 Tech Pubs in Instrument Fault Detection, Gimballed Pointing Control Sys, Multirate Sampled Data Anal & St of Art High Accuracy

Gimballed Optical Payload Control Sys; Grad cum laude; Tau Beta Pi; W/W in Aviation & Aerospace.

WAMPLER, CECIL L oc/County Treasurer; b/Jun 25, 1937; h/Route 1, Box 323, Mt Crawford, VA 22841; ba/Harrisonburg, VA; m/Dorothy K; c/Gina; p/J Harold Wampler (dec); Edith Wampler, Mt Crawford, VA; sp/John Kuykendall (dec); Amelda Kuykendall, Ft Seybert, WV; ed/BA, Bridgewater Col, 1959; mil/VA NG, 1960-66; pa/Asst Co Treas 1961-75, Co Treas 1976-, (Elected in Gen Elections 1975, 1979 & 1983) Rockingham Co, VA; Mem: Treas's Assn of VA, 1976-; cp/Pres, Mt Crawford Ruritan Clb, 1969; Treas 1974-76, Dist Gov 1983, Rockingham Dist #9 Ruritans; r/Ch of Brethren; hon/20 Yrs of Ser w Rockingham Co, 1981.

WANG, LEONARD FONG-SHENG oc/Professor; b/Jul 4, 1950; h/Route 4 Box 132 Central, SC 29630; ba/Clemson, SC; p/Gen-Ming Wang and Nan-Fan Wang Hang, Taiwan; ed/BA 1971, MA 1973, Soochow Univ; MS 1977, PhD 1980, Purdue Univ; mil/ROC MP, 1973-75; pa/Asst Prof Ec, Wright St Univ, 1980-82; Asst Prof Ec, Clemson Univ, 1982-; Vis'g Res Fellow, Chung-Hua Inst for Ec Res, Sum 1983; hon/Author, Num Articles Pub'd in Profl Jours incl'g: So Ec Jours; Jour of Macroecs; Jour of Ec Studies; Bltn of Ec Res; Phi Tau Phi, 1974; Beta Gamma Sigma, 1980; W/W of Sino-Am.

WANGBERG, ELAINE GREGORY oc/Professor; b/Aug 4, 1942; h/1603 Chimney Wood Lane, New Orleans, LA 70126; ba/NO, LA; m/Devon J Metzger; c/Brigitte, Leslie; p/Bradford and Freda Gregory; sp/Leo and Evelyn Metzger; ed/BS, Univ of MN, 1964; MA 1970, PhD 1979, Univ of MI; pa/Clrm Tchr, Robbinsdale Public Schs, MN, 1964-66; Rdg Tchr & Conslt 1971-74, Lang Arts Conslt 1974-79, Staff Devel Spec 1978, Ann Arbor Public Schs, MI; Asst Prof 1979-81, Assoc Prof 1982-, Univ of NO, LA; Mem: IRA; Am Ednl Res Assn; Assn for Supvn & Curric Devel; So Ednl Res Assn; NCTE; LA for Supvn & Curric Devel; Mem of Var Coms, Phi Delta Kappa; hon/Author, Over 20 Articles Pub'd in Profl Jours incl'g: Jour of Tchr Ed; Rdg Horizons; Rdg Improvement; The Rdg Tchr; Others; One of Top 10 Grads, Col of Ed, Univ of MN, 1964; Phi Delta Kappa; Pi Lambda Theta; Outstg Dissertation Awd, Tchr Ed, Univ of MI, 1979-80; W/W in S & SW.

WARD, ALBERT L oc/Minister; b/May 5, 1910; h/Route 2, Box 27, Cookeville, TN 38501; m/Ruth; c/Dean W Thomas, Jean W Burchett, John Albert, Edward L; p/Mr and Mrs Fate Ward (dec); sp/Mr and Mrs H C Gentry (dec); ed/8th Grade Ed; Addit Courses, The Am Correspondence Sch; Addit Courses, TN Polytechnic Univ; pa/Minister, Throughout 12 SEn Sts, 51 Yrs; r/Ch of Christ; hon/Rel Staff Writer, the Dispatch Local Daily Newspaper; Author, Var Rel Pamphlets for Ch of Christ; 50 Yrs in Pulpit Hon, 1982; Leather Bible for Sers, Sycamore Ch, Cookeville, TN, 1983; Gold Watch for Ser, Bethlehem Ch of Christ, 1983; Hats Off to Albert Ward, Local Radio Sta; Celebrated 50th Wedding Anniv, 1979.

WARD, DIANE KOROSY oc/Attorney, Managing Partner; b/Oct 17, 1939; h/16503 Avenida Florencia, Poway, CA

92064; ba/San Diego, CA; m/R Michael Walters; c/Christopher LaBruce, Samantha Martha Thompson; p/Theodore L and Edith B Korosy, Cotte Madera, CA; sp/Robert E and Dorothy M Walters; ed/AB, Heidelbero Col, 1961; JD, Univ of San Diego Law Sch, 1975; pa/Mng Ptner, Ward & Howell Attys, 1978-79; Mng Ptner, Walter, Howell & Ward, 1979-82; Mng Ptner, Walters & Ward, 1982-; Mem: VPres & Dir, Oak Broadcasting Sys Inc, 1983; ABA; CA & San Diego Bar Assns; cp/Pres, Bd of Dirs, Green Val Civic Assn, 1979-80; Pres, Bd of Dirs, Soroptimist Intl of Rancho Bernardo; Pres, Los Amados Aux Chd's Home Soc; Pres, Fdr, Profl & Exec Wom of the Ranch; Lectr, Ctr for Cont'g Ed, San Diego St Univ, 1983-84; r/Epis; hon/ W/W: in CA, in W, Among San Diego Wom.

WARD, JAMES E oc/Manager of Systems & Programming; b/Sep 5, 1951; h/PO Box 633 Pass Christian, MS 39571; ba/Gulfport, MS; m/Barbara A; c/Dawn Renée, Brian James, Brandi LaRae, Joshua Shane; p/Charles and Elsie Ward, Hamilton, OH; sp/Jon and Kay Blevins, Hamilton, OH; ed/Deg in Sys Anal, Miami Univ (OH); mil/AUS, 1970-78, Vietnam Vet; pa/DataProcessing Mgr, Leshner Corp, 1978-79; Sys Mgr, Graham Energy, 1980-81; Mgr of Sys & Programming, Indal Aluminum, Gulfport, MS, 1981-; Mem: Pres, S MS Chapt, Data Processing Mgrs Assn, 1983-84; cp/Secy, VICA, 1968; r/Prot; hon/Bronze Star, 1971; AUS Commend Medal, 1977.

WARD, MARGARET MOTTER oc/ Violist; b/Sep 21, 1928; h/1101 Playford Lane, Silver Spring, MD 20901; ba/ Washington, DC; m/Robert Paul Jr; c/ Eva Lynne Motter, Phoebe Motter Baldini, Antonia Lee Motter, Charles Frederick Motter; p/Gerrit Van Ringelesteyn (dec); Dorris Van Ringelesteyn, Grand Rapids, MI; sp/R P and Sara Ward (dec); ed/Att'd MI St Univ, 1946-49; MusB, Eastman Sch of Music, Univ of Rochester, 1952; pa/Violist, Grand Rapids Symph (MI), 1942-51; Violist Fac Quartet, MI St Univ, 1947-49; Violist, Rochester Philharm (NY), 1951-53; Instr of Violin & Viola, Univ of NC-Chapel Hill, 1953-56; Violist, Miami Symph (FL), 1962-64; La Quartette, Miami, 1963-64; Prof of Violin & Viola, Conservatoire Nationale du Liban, Beirut, 1964-66; Pvt Tchr Violin & Viola, Wash, DC, 1967-78; Viola Instr, Montgomery Col, 1970-74; Violist, Kennedy Ctr Opera House Orch, Wash DC, 1971-; Violist, Wolf Trap Filene Ctr Orch, 1971-; Violist, Balto Symph, 1973-74; Mem: Am Camerata for New Music, 1974-; Fdr & Violist, New String Art Quartet, 1982-; r/Prot; hon/W/W: in Music, of Am Wom.

WARD, ROBERT A JR oc/Executive; b/Sep 25, 1943; h/393 Ski Trail, Kinnelon, NJ 07405; ba/Butler, NJ; m/ Nancy Prescott; c/Victoria, Jennifer, Robert; p/Robert A Ward Sr (dec); Edith A Ward, Kinnelon, NJ; sp/Robert Prescott; Adela Prescott (dec); ed/BA, Yale Univ, 1959; mil/USMC, 1959-61; AUS, 1962-72, Capt; pa/Acct Exec, US Trust Co of NY, 1959-63; VPres, Fdr & Dir, Progressive Mktg Ser of NY, 1963-64; Co-Fdr, VPres & Dir, Coin Depot Corp,

Elizabeth, NJ, 1963-68; Pres, J S Riley Co, Wayne, NJ, 1965-70; Pres, Pompton Lakes Tele Answering Ser, 1968-; Pres, Dir & Co-Fdr, C G W Enterprise, 1969-; Pres, Devon Pub'g Co, 1977-78; Pres, Lithe Four Printing Co, Butler, NJ, 1976-; Pres, B E K Inc, Wayne, NJ, 1968-; Pres, Carelli, Glynn & Ward Advtg, Butler, NJ, 1983-; Mem: Bd of Trustees, PENPAC of Commerce & Indust Assn of NJ; NJ Mfg Assn; Bus & Profl Advtg Assn; Dir, N Jersey Ad Clb; cp/Police Commr, Kinnelon, 1978-; Councilman, Borough of Kinnelon, 1978-; Sr Warden, St David Epis Ch, Kinnelon, 1978-; Dir, Yale Clb of Montclair; Bd of Trustees, Inner City Ensemble, Patterson, NJ; SAR; Huguenot Soc; Co-Pres, Kinnelon Home & Sch Assn, 1977-78; Bd of Govs, Morris Area Girl Scout Coun, 1979-81; r/Epis; hon/W/W: in E, in Advtg.

WARNER, CRYSTELLE H oc/Social Service and Public Relations; b/Dec 5, 1926; h/525 Alexander Street, Jonesboro, LA 71251; ba/Jonesboro, LA; c/ Jack L Jr, Johnny N; p/Johnny Haynes (dec); Narvel Mayfield Haynes, Shongaloo, LA; ed/Dipl, Shongaloo HS, LA; pa/Employee, Dairy Queen Indust, 20 Yrs; Public Relats Advr, Pine Belt Commun Action Agy; Supvr of Homemaker & Respite Sers, Jackson & Winn Parishes, Am Commun Sers; 1st Wom Coun Mem, Town of Jonesboro, Elected 2 Consecutive Terms, 1978-; Mem: LA Assn for Retarded Citizens; Bd of Dirs, N Ctl LA Promotion Assn; NE LA 3-Rivers Tourist Assn; Others; cp/Chm Coun on Aging, Jackson Parish, 1973-75; Appt'd Liaison for Jackson Parish Handicapped & Disabled; Appt'd Legis Coun Mem, Rep Jackson Parish; Bd of Dirs 3 Yrs, Mgr 1 Yr, Jackson Parish C of C; Other Commun Ser Activs; r/Meth; Pres Hodge U Meth Wom 1976-78, Dist Ofcr Bd of Global Mins of U Meth Wom 1976-78, Adult Coor 1982, Jonesboro U Meth Ch; hon/ Hon Secy of St of LA; Hon St Rep of LA; Achmt Awd, Town of Jonesboro; Ombudsman Awd, Nsgn Home Vol; Outstg Ser Awd, Jackson Parrish Coun on Aging; Hist Awd for Commun Preserv, N S DAR.

WARNER, W KEITH oc/Professor; b/ Sep 6, 1930; h/899 East 2730 North, Provo, UT 84604; ba/Provo, UT; m/Vila J; c/Karen Stone, Janice Dabling, Randall, Neil; p/Wilson A Warner, SLC, UT; Eva L Warner (dec); sp/Asael R and Mable Jenks (both dec); ed/BS 1958, MS 1959, UT St Univ; PhD Cornell Univ, 1960; mil/AUS, 1953-55; pa/Asst Prof of Rural Sociol 1960-66, Assoc Prof of Rural Sociol 1966-69, Prof of Rural Sociol 1969-71, Univ of WI; Prof of Sociol, Brigham Yg Univ, 1971-; Mem: Am Sociol Assn; Pres 1973-74, VPres 1971-72, Rural Sociol Soc; Fellow, UT Acad of Scis, Arts & Lttrs; r/Ch of Jesus Christ of LDS; hon/Editor, Rural Sociol, Volumes 33 & 34, 1968 & 1969; Author, Num Sociological Pubs incl'g Articles in Profl Jours, Book Chapts & Reports. Selected to Give 11th Annual Dist'd Fac Lecture, Brigham Yg Univ, 1974; Outstg Ed of Am, 1972 & 1974-75.

WARREN, JEFFREY CLARY oc/Clinical Psychologist and Dean; h/7511 High Avenue, La Jolla, CA 92037; ba/San Deigo, CA; c/Adam Bernard; p/Bernard W Warren (dec); Florence S Warren,

Encino, CA; ed/BA 1971, MA 1974, PhD 1976, Univ of CA-Santa Barbara; Assessing & Influencing Consumer Behavior, World Trade Inst, 1982; pa/ Clin Psych, Tri-Commun Ser Sys, 1976-; Dir, Edwards Inst for Adv'd Study, 1980-; Sr VPres, Gride Res Corp, 1981-; Exec Pubr & Editor, Tri Press Pubrs, 1982-; Bd of Dirs, Sr VPres, Grid Ltd, 1980-; r/Jewish; hon/Author, Accurate Perception of Nonverbal Commun, 1976; S'ship, Univ of CA-Santa Barbara, 1969-71; S'ship, Val Col, 1967-69; W/ W in W; Other Biogl Listings.

WARREN, RICHARD E oc/Executive; b/Jan 27, 1942; h/345 Baskin Drive Southwest, Marietta, GA 30064; ba/ McDonough, GA; m/Cynthia W; c/ Deborah Marie, James L Kendrick III; p/Ernest Reynolds and Marina (Echevirra) Warren; ed/BCS, Loyola Univ of S, 1970; mil/USAF, 1960-64; pa/Pres, Henco Advtg Agy, 1983-; Dir of Advtg, Snapper Power Equip Co, 1983-; Sr Reg Acct Supvr, J Walter Thompson, Atlanta, 1979-83; Reg Acct Mgr, Mace Advtg Agy Inc, NO, 1977-79; Pres & Gen Mgr, Warren Advtg Agy, NO, 1976-77; Advtg Acct Exec, Ladas Agy, 1974-77; Bus Mgr 1968-69, Exec Dir 1969-71, Intl Dir Gen 1971-74, Public Affairs Conslt 1974-75, Info Coun of the Americas; Sales Ofc Mgr, Avoncraft Dir, Avondale Shipyards Inc, 1964-68; Editor, Singles Critique, 1974-79; Mem: Am Legion; Am Fedn of Police; Italian Cultural Soc; Radio Free Asia; Info Coun Ams; Adm Mgmt Soc; cp/Exec Dir, LA Epilepsy Assn, 1976-77; Conslt, Patrolman's Assn, NO, 1969-76; Prodr, "Spirit 76" Intl TV Series, 1973; Prodr, TW Series, "Sportsman's Paradise," 1976-77; Prodr, Jerry Lewis/MDA Telethon, NO, 1970-73; Conslt, Metro Public Relats, 1973-74; Michael The Archangel Police & Fire Legion, 1976; Orgr, Jefferson Parish Am Revolution Townhall Bicent Prog, 1973-74; Coor, Freedoms Foun-Yg Men's Bus Clb Awds Presentation, 1972-73; Celebrity Chm, Miss NO Pageant, 1973-74; Judge, Baton Rouge Pageant, 1973; Bd of Dirs: Muscular Dystrophy Assn, Goals to Grow Foun, Crippled Chd's Hosp; SAR; So Karate Assn; Yg Men's Bus Clb of Gtr NO; NO C of C; Loyola Univ Alumni Assn; Cross Keys; Mason; hon/ Contbr, Num Articles to Profl Jours; Cit of Merit, Profl Bus Wom of Am, 1970; Outstg Bur Chm, Yg Men's Bus Clb, 1969; Cert of Apprec, NO Public Sch Sys, 1971; Merit Cit, Am Fedn of Police, 1972; Loyalty Day Awd, VFW, 1970; Merit Cit, Exec Clb of NO, 1970; Cert of Apprec, Kiwanis Clb, 1969; Merit Awd, Info Coun of Ams, 1968; Plaque of Apprec, Alton Ochsner Med Foun, 1970; Plaque of Merit, Muscular Dystrophy Assn; Keys to Cities, Cert of Merit: NO 1973, Westwego 1977, Hammond 1975, Houma 1975, Morgan City 1977, Lafayette 1977, Alexandria 1977, Shreveport 1977, LA; Key to City, Chattanooga, TN, 1982; Num Other Hons; W/W: in Am, in S & SW; Men of Achmt.

WARRICK, ALAN EVERETT oc/ Judge; b/Jun 18, 1953; h/509 Burleson, San Antonio, TX 78202; ba/San Antonio, TX; m/Cynthia; c/Alan II, Whitney Blair; p/John Warrick, NO, LA; Geri Crisman, Woodridge, NJ; sp/Joe and Cecelia Scott, San Antonio, TX; ed/BA,

Howard Univ; JD, IN Univ Sch of Law; pa/Judge, Mun Ct, City of San Antonio, 1982-; Atty, Branton & Mendelsohn Inc, 1978-82; Intern, Marion Co Prosecutor's Ofce, Indianapolis, IN, 1977-78; Campaign Aide, US Senator R Vance Hartke, Indianapolis, IN, 1976-77; Civil Rts Spec, IN Civil Rts Comm, Indianapolis, IN, 1975-76; Res Asst, Jt Ctr for Political Studies, Wash DC, 1972-74; cp/Pres, Dignowitty Hill Area Neighborhood Assn, 1982-; Bd of Dirs, San Antonio Fest Inc, 1982-; 3rd VPres, NAACP, San Antonio Br, 1980-81; Exec Com, U Negro Col Fund, 1980-81; Bd of Dirs, San Antonio Symph, 1980-81; Area Adv Coun, Small Bus Assn, 1980-81; Ldrship Prog of San Antonio C of C to Help Develop Yg Ldrs in Commun, 1979-80; Bd of Dirs, Parliamentn, Ella Austin Commun Ctr, 1979-80; Bd of Dirs, San Antonio Eastside Ec Devel Corp, 1982-; Omega Psi Phi; Phi Alpha Delta; Van Courtlandt Social Clb; Master Mason, A F&AM; r/Rom Cath; hon/Author of Article, "Black Wom in Electoral Politics," in *Focus* from the Jt Ctr for Polit Studies, 1973; Assoc Editor, *IN Law Review*, 1977-78; 1st Place Awd Winner, ABA Reg Moot Ct Competition, 1978; Phi Beta Kappa, Howard Univ, 1975; Pi Sigma Alpha, 1974; W/W: Among Students in Am Univs & Cols, in S & SW.

WARSHAUER, ITENE CONRAD oc/Attorney; b/May 4, 1942; h/505 East 79th Street, New York, NY 10021; ba/New York, NY; m/Alan M; c/Susan; p/A Alfred Conrad, Portchester, NY; ed/BA, Univ of MI, 1963; LLB, Columbia Law Sch, 1966; pa/Ofcr, NY St Mtl Hlth Info Ser, 1st Jud Dept, 1966-68; Assoc, Chadbourne, Park, Whiteside & Wolff, NYC, 1968-75; Mem, Anderson Russell Kill & Olick, P C, NYC, 1975-; Mem: Jud Com, Bar Assn of NYC, 1982-; Com on Mtl Hygiene 1978-, Chwom Subcom Mtly Disabled & the Commun 1978-82, NY St Bar Assn; Com on Torts, ABA; Def Res Inst Com on Multidist Litigation; Panel of Arbitrators, Am Arbitration Assn, 1973-; NY Acad of Scis, 1980-; Am Mgmt Assn, 1982-83; Wom's City Clb of NY; NY St Bar, 1966-; US Dist Ct So Dist NY, 1969-; Us Ct of Appeals for 2nd Circuit, 1969-; US Supr Ct, 1972; hon/Author of Article Pub'd in *Notre Dame Jour of Legis*; Var Books incl: *Grp Def: The View form the Cos; Litigation Mgmt Techniques; Methods to Effetively Manage Complex Multi-party Disputes, Resolution & Avoidance of Disputes*; KY Col; CPR Leg Prog Significant Pract Achmt Awd; W/W in Am Law.

WASS, HANNELORE LINA oc/Professor; Book and Journal Editor; b/Sep 12, 1926; h/6014 Northwest 54th Way, Gainesville, FL 32606; ba/Gainesville, FL; m/Harry H Sisler; c/Brian C; ed/BA, Tchrs Col, Heidelberg, W Germany, 1951; MA Human Devel 1960, PhD Ednl Psych 1968, Univ of MI; pa/Prof Ednl Psych & Assoc Ctr for Gerontological Studies 1975-, Assoc Prof Psych Foun of Ed 1971-74, Asst Prof 1969-71, Univ of FL, Gainesville; Editor, *Death Ed*; Consltg Editor, *Ednl Gerontology*; Consltg Editor of Book Series on Death Ed, Aging & Hlth Care for Hemisphere & McGraw-Hill Intl Pubrs; Assoc Prof 1965-69, Fac Headstart Tng Sum 1967, En MI Univ Ypsilanti, MI; Res Assoc

for Prof Flanders 1967-68, Fac Hum Relats Wkshop Sum 1960, Fac NSF Wkshop Sum 1959, Supvg Tchg 1958-64, Univ of MI, Ann Arbor; Elem Tchr, Pittsfield, MA, 1957-58; Coor of Engl Lang Instn, German-Am Sch Relats Advr, Mannheim City Schs, Germany, 1954-57; Mid Sch Tchr Exptl Prog, Fgn Lang Instr, Supvr & Sch Camp Coor, 1952-57; Tchr Trainee, Cultural Exch Prog, US Ofc of Ed, Wash DC, 1951-52; Elem Tchr, Mannheim, Germany, 1947-51; Mem: Am Psychol Assn; Intl Wk Grp in Death, Dying & Bereavement; The Gerontological Soc; Intl Bd of Advisers, Forum for Death Ed & Cnslg; Bd of Trustees, The Ctr for Thanatology Res & Ed Inc; The Foun of Thanatology; Nat Coun on Aging; So Gerontology Soc; FL Coun on Aging; Soc for the Psychol Study of Social Issues; The Menninger Foun; Am Ednl Res Assnl; Assn for Humanistic Ed; NEA; cp/Bd of Dirs, Tnr, Vol, N Ctl FL Hospice Inc; Bd of Dirs, Gainesville Chapt of the Compassionate Friends; Bd of Dirs, Meml Soc of Alachua Co; Alachua Gen Hosp Corp; r/Meth; hon/ Editor & Co-Editor 8 Books; Author, Over 10 Book Chapts & 40 Jour Articles; Co-Prin Investigator, NIA Grant w Stein Gerontological Inst, 1981-83; Prin Investigator, HRS Tng Grant, St of FL, 1978; Res Support, Univ of FL Grad Sch, 1974; Minisabbatical, Winter Qtr, Ofc of Instrnl Resources, 1974; Fac Released Time for Res, Inst for the Devel of Human Resource & Col of Ed, 1973; Prin Investigator, USOE—NIE Small Contract Res Grant, 1972; Sum Fac Res Awd, Univ of FL, 1971; Prin Investigator, EDPA F'ship Grant, En MI Univ, 1968; US Ofc of Ed Traineeship, Cultural Exch Prog, 1951-52; W/W: in SE, of Am Wom, in Frontier Sci & Technol, of Wom; Ldrs in Ed; DIB.

WATASA, KINICHI oc/Real Estate Broker; b/Jun 12, 1926; h/1224 Lucia Court, Santa Maria, CA 93454; ba/Santa Maria, CA; m/Maureen Catherin (2nd); c/Cheryl Lynn, Kenneth Dean, Christopher John; p/Mr and Mrs George K Watase, HI; sp/Mrs Mary Dreyfus, SF, CA; ed/AA, LA City Col, 1953; Att'd LA St Col & UCLA; Att'd Revac Investmnt Inst, Denver, 1970; Real Est Strategy & Tactics Prog for Cont'g Ed, Univ of So CA, 1981; mil/ AUS, 1945-47; pa/Pres, Watase Realty Inc, 1968-74; Pres, Santa Barbara Land Co Inc, 1981-; Real Est Broker, Kenland Devel Inc, Torrance, CA, 1968-74; Real Est Salesman, Jones & Goodglick & Assocs, Inglewood, CA, 1964-68; cp/ Uptown Pres, Japanese Citizen Leag, 1959; Hearing Examr, LA Police Comm, 1959-67; Neighborhood Commr, Hollywood-Wilshire Area Coun BSA, Vestry, St Mary's Epis Ch, 1962-64; r/ Epis; hon/Cert of Apprec, St Mary's Epis Ch, 1965.

WATERS, HARRY G oc/Registered Professional Industrial Engineer; b/Sep 28, 1908; h/600 A Cauthen Way, Signal Mt, TN 37377; ba/Same; m/Anne D Waters; c/2 Sons & 1 Daugh; ed/LLB, 1929; AS, 1943; pa/Bk Employee, St Treas Dept, St of CT; Drayyo Shipyard; Time Study Industl Engr, Miller Co; Method Engr & Type of Method, Elmer Adwane Co; Mgmt Conslt, Brit, CT, 20 Yrs; Div Hlth & Safety, Sholze Tannone, 10 Yrs; Mem: Am Soc of Safety

Engrs; Chatanooga Engrg Soc; TN Val Chapt, Am Industl Hygienist Assn; r/ Presb; hon/Life Mastor, Am Contract Bridge Leag; W/W in S & SE.

WATERS, RAYMOND WOOLSEY oc/Executive; b/Sep 8, 1924; h/20 Carmel Avenue, Salinas, CA 93901 & Route 5, Box 250, Magnet Cove, AR 72104; m/Rowena Kimzey-Cohan; c/Stephen Wesley (dec); Douglas Joseph; John Kimzey Cohan, Thomas Alan Cohan, Mark Randolph Cohan, Jeffrey Scott; p/ Wesley Waters Sr and Myrtle Dora (Woolsey) Prickett; ed/Traffic Engr, NWn Univ; BS, Univ of WI; LLB, Chgo Law Sch; MS, George Wash Univ; MS, Command & Gen Staff Mil Col; mil/ US Army Air Corp, 1940-45; Police, 1945-50; Mil Police Corp, 1950-57; Police Liaison Ofcr, Metro Tokyo Police, 1953-55; Provost Marshall, Camp Drake, in Japan, 1954-56; Dept Commandant, Ft Leavenworth, KS, 1956-57; Provost Marshall, Ft Ord, CA, 1950-52; pa/Criminologist, 1958-73; Exec VPres, Oceanview Cablevision, 1973-77; Exec VPres, Hudson-Cohan Pub'g Communs Co, 1973-; Pres, KTMR Enterprises Inc, 1977-; Pres, Foun for Human Achmt, 1976-; Reg'd Polled Hereford Breeder & Land Develr, 1977-; cp/Hot Springs Country Clb, Hot Springs, AR; Carmel Val Racquet Clb, Carmel Val, CA; Kiwanis; Elks; hon/Author, NAAFI, Mat & Text w Course Mat in Police, Ins, Ins Adjusting, Fire & Criminology.

WATERS, ROWENA JOYCE KIMZEY-COHAN oc/Executive; b/Dec 15, 1931; h/20 Carmel Avenue, Salinas, CA 93901 & Route 5, Box 250, Magnet Cove, AR 72104; m/Raymond W; p/ Joseph Wood and Jalina Jane (Thomas) Kimzey; ed/Att'd Henderson St Univ, 1948; pa/Adm Asst to Pres, Salinas Broadcasting Corp & Successor Corp, Ctl CA Commun Corp, Salinas, CA, 1951-71; Dir, Secy-Treas, Ctl CA Communs Corp, Salinas CA, 1967-71; Pres, Ocean View Cablevision Inc, Seaside, CA, 1970-77; Hudson-Cohan Pub'g & Communs Co, Salinas, 1970-; VPres, KTMR Enterprises Inc, Magnet Cove, AR, 1978-; cp/Treas, Salinas Val Meml Hosp Aux, 1962-65; Dir, AR Easter Seal Soc, 1978-; Trustee, York Sch, Monterey, CA, 1977-; Carmel Val Racquet Clb, CA; Hot Springs Country Clb, AR; Life Mem, Monterey Hist Soc, CA; Life Mem, Intl New Thought Alliance; hon/Spec Citizens Awd, Marina, CA; Butterfly Awd, Pacific Grove, CA.

WATERS, THOMAS LYLE oc/College Teacher; b/Mar 11, 1929; h/PO Box 459, West Sand Lake, NY 12196; ba/ Loudonville, NY; m/E Yvonne; c/ Timothy, Wendy; p/T L Waters (dec); Lucile Taylor Waters, West Sand Lake, NY; ed/BEEE, 1953; MS Sys Mgmt, 1973; MS Ed, 1975; PhD, 1981; mil/ AUS, 1953-76; Ret'd Lt Col, 1976; pa/ Asst Dir Cont'g Engrg Ed, George Washington Univ, 1977-78; Coor Ctr for Corea Ser, RPI, 1978-80; Asst Prof Math & Stats, Siena Col, 1981-; Mem: CPL & Sr Mem, Soc of Logistics Engrs; Soc of Am Mil Engrs; Charter Mem, NACADA; AAHE; Life Mem, Am Def Preparedness Assn; Life Mem, DAV; Life Mem, The Ret'd Ofcrs Assn; AUSA; r/Luth, MS Synod; hon/Author, *Defended Area Model I*, 1962; Legion of Merit, 1970; 2 Bronze Stars, 1966 &

1967; Meritorious Ser Medal, 1973; 3 AUS Commend Medals, 1962, 1964 & 1966; W/W: in E, in TX; 1000 Outstg Ams.

WATSON, ALTA GLADYS oc/Professor; b/Dec 4; h/1325 North East 56th Street, Oklahoma City, OK 73111; ba/ Langston, OK; m/Emanuel M (dec); c/ John R, Kenneth C, Glenda Watson Moss; p/Mr and Mrs Elmer C Brown (dec); sp/Mr and Mrs L M Watson (dec); ed/BS, Langston Univ; EdM 1954, PhD 1974, Univ of OK; pa/Prof of Ed 1974-82, Coor & S'ship-Ldrship Enrichment Prog 1975-82, Chp Elem Ed Dept 1978-82, Kappa Delta Pi Advr 1978-80, Elem Ed Clb Advr 1975-82, Student Ed Assn Advr 1977-82, Langston Univ, Langston, OK; Mem: NEA; OK Ed Assn; OK Assn of Cols of Tchr Ed; OK Assn of Tchr Edrs; Kappa Delta Pi; Univ of OK Chapt, Phi Delta Kappa; Alpha Kappa Alpha Sorority; The OK City Links Inc; r/Meth; hon/Author, "A Study of The Hist Devel of Tchr Cert in OK"; Outstg Wom of Yr, Alpha Kappa Alpha, 1976.

WATSON, ANDREA LOUISE oc/ Economist; b/Apr 22, 1947; h/1380 Sacramento, San Francisco, CA 94109; ba/SF, CA; p/John C and Julia L (Avery) Watson, Kingston, MA; ed/BA, Univ of MA, 1969; MA, Johns Hopkins Sch of Adv'd Intl Studies, 1972; pa/Economist 1980-, Sr Analyst 1978-80, Bechtel Fin Sers; Res Assoc, Intl Res & Technol, McLean, VA, 1974-78; Intl Bk Ofcr, Citibk, NYC, 1972-74; Mem: VPres, Nat Assn of Bus Economists; VPres SF Chapt, Soc for Intl Devel; World Affairs Coun; Commonwlth Clb; Corp Planners Assn; r/Unitarian; hon/ Author, Num Govt Pubs & Book Reviews, 1974-; W/W of Am Wom.

WATSON, GREGORY H oc/Executive; b/Jul 16, 1948; h/5340 Holmes Run Parkway, Suite 215, Alexandria, VA 22304; c/Andrew Daniel; p/Robert J and Anne B Watson, Tenafly, NJ; ed/BA, Taylor Univ, 1970; MS, Univ of So CA, 1975; MA, Antioch Sch of Law, 1983; Dipl, Nat Def Univ, 1981; mil/USN, 1971-77, Lt; USNR, Lt Cmdr; pa/Sr Analyst & Reg Mgr, Atlantic Anal, 1977-78; Profl Staff, Ctr for Nav Anal, 1978-80; Prog Mgr, USNR, 1980-83; Pres, ASW Inc, 1983-; Mem: Mil Opers Res Soc, 1977-; Opers Res Soc of Am, 1975-; Acoustical Soc of Am, 1981-; r/ Prot; hon/Author, Num Classified Reports & Articles; Grad Fellow, Am Univ, 1970-71; W/W in S & SE; Personalities of S.

WATSON-FREILINGER, IDA M oc/ Student; b/Apr 30, 1943; h/7365 South Washington Street, Littleton, CO 80122; m/Michael J; c/Suzanne Marie, Steven Michael; sp/Mr and Mrs O P Freilinger, Aurora, IL; ed/BA Cand, Metro St Col; pa/Concesion & Dressing Room Supvr, Willows Pool, Oakmont, PA, 1958-60; Editor & Writer, The Oriole, 1960-61; Clk, Typist, Secy-Stenographer, Gulf Res 7 Devel Co, Harmarville, PA, 1961-68; Vol Typist, Soc Sers, Price, UT, 1974; Writer, Shuttle, Spindle & Dyepot, Handweavers Guild of Am Inc, 1979-; Editor Voices of Auraria 1982-, Editor Windmils & Wishing Wells 1983, Ofc Mgr & Poetry Editor Metrosphere 1983-, Metro St Col, Denver, CO; Mem: Poetry Soc of CO, 1984-; Var Coms, Rocky Mtn Weavers

Guild, 1977-; Handweavers Guild of Am, 1977-; cp/Writers Bloc Lit Clb, 1983-; St Andrew Soc, 1981-; Altar & Rosary Soc, All Souls Ch, Englewood, CO, 1983-; r/Cath; hon/Author, Over 17 Poetry Pubs in Var Lit Mags & Collections; 2 Articles, for Shuttle, Spindle & Dyepot; Listed in Art Index of Shuttle, Spindle & Dyepot.

WATSON-MILLER, INGRID FRAN oc/Spanish Teacher; b/Jul 4, 1949; h/ 3917 13th Street Northwest, Washington, DC 20011; ba/Washington DC; m/ George E Miller III; c/Sean Gregory; p/ Mr and Mrs Dempsey Watson, Wash, DC; ed/BA, NC Ctl Univ, 1971; MEd, Howard Univ, 1982; pa/Subst Tchr, DC Public Schs, 1971-73; Spanish Tchr, Dept Chm, 1977 & 1983 Sr Class Sponsor, Span Clb/Spanish Hon Soc Sponsor, Cheerldrs Sponsor 1973-77, DC Public Schs, 1973-; Mem: Am Assn of Tchrs of Spanish & Portuguese; Assn for Supvn & Curric Devel; AAUW; Gtr Wash Area Tchrs for Lang; Treas, T Roosevelt HS Alumni Assn, 1979-81; DC Assn for Retarded Citizens; Recording Secy 1972-74, Corres'g Secy 1976-77, VPres 1977-78, Pres 1978-79, DC Chapt NC Ctl Univ Alumni Assn; Alpha Kappa Alpha Sorority; Reporter 1970, Asst Advr 1972-75, Advr 1975-76, VPres 1976-80, Parliamentn 1981, Mbrship Chm 1982, UDC; Var Ch Orgs; r/Bapt; hon/Alumnus of Mo, DC Chapt NC Ctl Univ, 1972; Recog Plaque for Grad Adv to No Atlantic Reg, Alpha Kappa Alpha, 1977; W/W: Among Am Cols & Univs, in E; Outstg Yg Wom in Am.

WATT, EDWARD WILLIAM oc/ Cardiovascular Physiologist, Director; Sep 25, 1937; ba/Schumpert Medical Center, 915 Margaret Place, Shreveport, LA 71120; m/Barbara Kay; c/John, David; ed/Inst of Bkrs Dipl, City of London Col, 1961; DEd, Southampton Univ, UK, 1964; BSc, NWn St Univ, 1966; MSc, Univ of TN, 1967; PhD, Univ of MI, 1970; NIH Postdoct Fellow, Human Biol, PA St Univ, 1971; mil/Brit Army, 3 Yrs; pa/Dir Cardiac Rehab, Schumpert Med Ctr Shreveport, LA, 1981-; Dir Human Perf Lab Preven Med Inst, Clin Physiol, Dept of Med, GA Bapt Med Ctr, 1973-81; Adj Prof Biol, GA St Univ; Res Assoc Dept Physiol, Emory Univ Sch of Med; Co-Dir, Prev Cardiol Clin, Atlanta, GA; Others; Mem: Nat Exercise & Heart Disease Proj & Adv Com NIH, 1974-77; Fellow Coun on Circulation, Cert'd Hlth Support (CPR) Instr, Am Heart Assn; Am Physiol Soc; Past Chm Public Ed Com, GA Heart Assn; hon/Author, Over 40 Articles Pub'd in Profl Med Sci Jours; Brit Army & Intersers 1 Mile Champ; Brit Univs Cross Country (6 Miles) Champ, 1963; Gulf Sts Conf 1 Mile, 2 Mile & Cross Country Champ, 1966; NCAA All Am Awd, 1966; Other Biogl Listings.

WATTS, MARIE ELIZABETH FUR-TULA (MITZI) oc/Artist, Executive; b/ Feb 17, 1936; h/PO Box 12227, Dallas, TX 75225; ba/Same; m/Cleal T Jr; c/ Cleal T III, Milan, Elizabeth, Lawrence; p/Milan (dec) and Marie Eichinger Furtula, Dallas, TX; ed/St Mary's Col, Notre Dame; pa/Acting & Fdg Ofcr VPres, CEO, HFCO Inc Coal Mining & Mfg, 1971-; CEO, H F Constrn Co Inc Heavy Gen Constrn, 1962-; Artist in

Painting, Sculpture, Chinese Brush Painting, Ceramics; One Wom Shows: Georgetown Gallery, Atlanta, GA; Lynn Kottler Gallery, NYC; Florence Gallery, Dallas, TX; Miller-Simonson, Dallas, TX; Grp Shows: Hyatt Regency, Wash DC; Mark A Gallery, Teaneck, NJ; Hyatt Regency, Indianapolis, IN; Exhibited Juried Shows: Chgo Arts Inst; Bal Mus (Muncie, IN); AR Art Ctr; Dallas Mus Fine Arts; Perm Collections: St Mary's Col, Notre Dame, IN; Ursuline Acad, Dallas, TX; Crippled Chd's Hosp, Dallas; Var Pvt Collections; Mem: Art Conslt; Past VPres, TX-AR Fin Arts Comm; Art Show Judge for TX-AR Area; cp/VPres, Prestencrest Repub Wom; Repub Exec Bd, 1962-64; Dist Dir, TX's Largest Congl Dist, 1962-63; Chm Patrons Bd, Intl Acad of Phil; Ursuline Acad Sch Bd, 1977-79; Ursuline Acad Alumni Bd, 1971-74; Other Commun Activs; r/Cath; hon/W/W: of Bus & Fin, of Wom, of Intells; Dir of Dist'd Ams; 2000 Notable Ams; Num Other Biogl Listings.

WAXMAN, DAVID oc/Executive Vice Chancellor; b/Feb 7, 1918; h/5800 Mission Drive, Mission Hills, KS 66208; ba/Kansas City, KS; m/Jane Z; c/Gail, Michael, Dan, Ann, Steve, Abby; p/ Meyer Waxman (dec); Fannie Waxman, Kansas City, MO; ed/BS Chem, Syracuse Univ, 1942; MD, Syracus Col of Med, 1950; mil/USAFR, Pilot, Flight Surg, Ret'd Maj Gen; pa/Positions w Univ of KS Col of Hlth Scis & Hosp: Instr of Internal Med 1961-64, Asst Prof Preven Med & Commun Hlth 1964-67, Asst Internal Med 1964-69, Assoc Prof Preven Med & Commun Hlth 1967-71, Assoc Prof Internal Med 1969-77, Dir Dept of Med Outpatient Ser 1970-74, Asst Dean 1970-71, Assoc Dean for Student Affairs 1971-72, Dean for Students 1972-74, VChancellor for Students 1974-76, VChancellor 1976-77, Dept Exec VChancellor 1977, Prof Internal Med 1977-, Exec VChancellor 1977-; Staff Appts: Bapt Meml Hosp, Kansas City, MO; Kansas City VA Hosp, MO; Menorah Hosp Med Ctr, MO; Res Hosp Med Ctr, MO; Univ of KS Bell Meml Hosp, KS; Mem: KS Med Soc; Jackson Co Med Soc; Wyandotte Co Med Soc; Fellow, Am Col of Phys; Royal Acad of Med of Valencia; Alpha Omega Alpha; Others; r/Jewish; hon/ Author, Over 20 Articles Pub'd in Profl Med Sci Jours; Dist'd Ser Medal, 1978; Legion of Merit w OLC; W/W.

WEATHERSBY, A (AUGUSTUS) BURNS oc/Emeritus Professor; b/May 19, 1913; h/210 Bishop Drive, Athens, GA 30606; ba/Athens, GA; m/Olive Hammons; c/Richard Michael, Robert Benton; p/Augustus Benton Weathersby (dec); Louie Burns Weathersby, Tylertown, MS; ed/BS 1938, MS 1940, PhD 1944, LA St Univ; mil/USN, 1942-62; pa/Entomologist, Dept of Agr, LA, 1940-42; Entomologist-Parasitologist, USN, 1942-62; Epidemiology, 3rd Marines, S Pac, 1943-45; Med Res, Cairo, Egypt; Spec Advr, Min of Hlth, Tehran, Iran, 1946; Nav Med Res Inst, Bethesda, MD, 1947-55; Nav Forces, Far E (Japan), 1956-67; Res, Bethesda, MD, 1958-62; Fac, Univ of GA, 1962-83; Mem: Chapt Pres, Phi Kappa Phi, 1976-77; Pres, SEn Soc of Parasitologist, 1975-76; Sigma Xi; Gamma Sigma Delta; Var Entomology, Parasitology &

Tropical Med Assns; cp/Orgr & Pres, Fedn of Commun Assns, 1967-; Pres & Coach, Little League Baseball, 1970-74; BSA; r/Bapt; hon/Author, Over 46 Articles Pub'd in Profl Jours; *Lab Manual for Med Entomology (Sect II)*, 1958; Chapt, in *Cinemicrography in Cell Biol*, 1963; Chapt, in *Invertebrate Immunity*, 1975; Phi Kappa Phi; Excellent Tchrs, Univ of GA, 1981; Dist'd Achmt Awd in Tchg, Entomology Soc of Am, SE Br, 1982; H H Ross Tchg Awd, 1982; W/W: in E, in S & SW, in US, in Frontier Sci & Technol; Am Men & Wom of Sci; Pioneers in Sci; Men of Achmt; DIB; Commun Ldrs of Am; Other Biogl Listings.

WEAVER, ROSE S oc/Technical Researcher; b/Sep 13, 1953; h/115 Bethun Circle, Oak Ridge, TN 37830; ba/Oak Ridge, TN; p/Anne Mae Weaver, Oak Ridge, TN; ed/BS Ed/ Sociol, Berea Col, 1975; Pt Student in Bus Adm, Univ of TN-Knoxville, 1977; Repub Pers Cert, Pers Mgmt; pa/Tech Resr 1977-, Info Asst 1975-77, Union Carbide, Oak Ridge Nat Lab, TN; Descriptive Analyst-DOE/TIC, 1974-75; Pers Cnslr, Repub Pers, 1974-75; Social Wkr, Planned Parenthood, 1974; Mem: VPres & Ed Chm, Treas 1982-83, Commun Chp Scarboro Commun Ctr 1981-, NAACP; One Imperative Chp, Planned Parenthood Assn, 1983; Exec Bd, Alpha Kappa Alpha Sorority, 1983; Exec Bd Mem, Hodegos, 1983; Bd of Dirs, Fundraising & Public Relats Coms, Planned Parenthood, 1983; Am Soc of Info Sci; AAG, TN Spec Grp, 1981-; cp/Past Commun Devel Chp, Mbrship Ch, Exec Mem & Asst Precinct Chp, Anderson Co Dem Party; Histn, Exec Com 1981-83, Anderson Co Dem Wom; Exec Bd, YWCA, 1979-; Spurgeon Chapel, 1982-83; Ch Yth Choir Dir, Supt Buds of Promise 1980-83, Trustee 1981-82, Missionary Dept Asst 1982-83; Secy, Black Artists Collectively, 1983; Troop Ldr, Girl Scouts, Tanasi Coun, 1980-81; Min Chp, Randy Tyree Gubernatorial Campaign, 1981-82; r/AME Zion Meth; hon/ Author Var Tech Reports, *Underground Housing in E TN*, AGA meeting in L'ville, KY, 1981; *Trans Engergy Bibliog*, TN St Univ, 1980; *Industl Energy Conserv*, 1980; *Envir Impact Assessment in Alcohol Fuel Plants in LA, OK & IN*, *Trans Energy Data Book*, 1979-81; *Trans Sys Utilization Br Report*, 1983; Other Reports; Editor of *A Collection of Black Poetry*, 1983; Delto Dem Mid Yr Meeting, Phila, 1982; Del to TN St Dem Meeting, 1979-82; Ch Del/Wkr, AME Zion Ch, 1979; Del to Missionary Annual Meeting, AME Zion Ch, 1980; Commun Ser Awd, Union Carbide, 1982; Safety Liaison Pers Info Div, Oak Ridge Nat Lab, 1983; Outstg Yg Wom; W/W in Am.

WEBB, LEOTA F oc/Manager; b/Nov 2, 1932; h/2523 Larwood Drive, Charleston, WV 25302; ba/Charleston, WV; c/Keith Alan, John Scott, Kelly Rae; p/ Mr and Mrs John V Behen, Swampscott, MA; ed/Ext Courses, Harvard Univ, 1951; Att'd Berlitz Sch of Lang, 1951; pa/Exec Secy, John Hancock Mut Life Ins Co, Boston, MA, 1950-56; Exec Secy 1956-76, Gen Sers Ofc Mgr 1976-79, Mgr Ofc & Spec Sers 1979-, Columbia Gas Transmission Corp, Charleston, WV; Mem: Am Mgmt Assn, 1979-; Intl Word Processing Assn, 1981; Zonta Intl

Clb, 1979-; r/Prot; hon/W/W in S & SW.
WEBBER, MUKTA MALA oc/Associate Professor and Director of Research; b/Dec 5, 1937; h/903 Cypress Drive, Boulder, CO 80303; ba/Denver, CO; m/Patrick John; c/Michelle Mala; p/ H S Maini, India; ed/BSc, 1957; MSc, 1959; Att'd Nat Cancer Inst of Canada, Univ of Saskatchewan; PhD, Queen's Univ, 1963; Dipl in Elect Microscopy, Univ of Toronto, 1978; pa/Canada Res Sci, Roswell Pk Meml Inst, Buffalo, NY, 1962-63; Lectr, Histology & Embryology, Dept of Anatomy, Queen's Univ, 1963-65; Res Assoc, Urogenital Oncology, Queen's Univ & Kingston Gen Hosp, 1965-68; Sr Instr 1971, Asst Prof & Dir of Res 1972-78, Asst Prof Biochem, Biophy & Gen 1977-79, Assoc Prof & Dir of Res 1978-, Div of Urology, Univ of CO Hlth Scis Ctr; Mem: Cadre Mem; Nat Prostatic Cancer Proj; Nat Cancer Inst; NIH Dept of Hlth & Human Sers; AAAS; Am Assn of Cancer Res; AM Soc for Cell Biol; Elect Microscopy Soc of Am; NY Acad of Scis; Sigma XI; Sci Res Soc of N Am; Tissue Culture Assn Inc; AAUP; hon/Author, Over 70 Sci Papers & Reviews, 1960-; Editor, *In Vitro Midels for Cancer Res*; Reveiwing Editor, *In Vitro*, Jour of the Tissue Culture Assn Inc, 1980-81; Am Urological Assn Res Awd, 1966; Sci Exhibit 1st Prize 1973, 1974, 1975, Am Urological Assn; Intl Can Res Tech Transfer Awd, Intl Union Against Cancer, Geneva, 1980; Var Res Grants, Am Can Soc & Nat Cancer Inst, 1972-; W/W in W; Am Men & Wom of Sci.

WEBSTER, BURNICE HOYLE oc/ Physician and Thoracologist; b/Mar 3, 1910; h/2315 Valley Brook Road, Nashville, TN 37215; p/Thomas J and Martha Ann Melton Webster; ed/BA, MD, Vanderbilt Univ; PhD, FL Res Inst; BSC, STD & BD; mil/Dir, USPHS; Chm, Med Selective Ser for TN & Nat Security Agy for TN; Ofcrs' Resv Assn; pa/Med Dir, Nashville Hlth Care Ctr; Med Dir, Univ Hlth Care Ctr; Mem: Pres, TN Long Care Phys Assn; Nashville Acad of Med; TN St Med Assn; Am Thoracic Soc; TN Lung Assn; Nashville Soc of Internal Med; Fellow, Nashville Cardiovas Soc; Am Col of Chest Phys; Am & Intl Cols of Angiology; Am Acad of Tuberculosis Phys; Brit Soc of Parasitology; Intl Soc of Cardiol; Royal Soc of Med; cp/Mastor Mason; Super Excel Mason; K Templar; Shriner; Order of Elks; Order of Immaculate; K of Hon; Prior of Prior of Franklin, Royal Yugoslavian Hospitaller Order of St John Jerusalem; Pres & Nat Trustee, Andrew Jackson TN & Nat Soc of SAR; Dpty Pres, Nat Soc of Sons of Colonial Wars; 2 Term Cmdr-in-Chief, Sons of Confederate Vets; Cmdr Gen John Hunt Morgan Chapt, Hon Cmdr Gen Nat Soc, Order of Stars & Bars; r/Epis; Prelate, So Epis Ch; hon/Author, Over 50 Papers Pub'd in Sci Jours; Num Nat & Intl Prog Appearances; Var Hon Degs Incl: DLit, DhumLet, LLD, DD & DCE; F'ships Incl: Am Col of Chest Phys; Am Col of Angiology, Am Gerontological Soc, Am Geriatric Soc, Royal Soc of Hlth; Phi Beta Kappa; Delta Phi Alpha; Alpha Omega Alpha; Phi Beta Pi; Silver Stethescope Awd; Dist'd Phys & Thoracologist Awd; The Dist'd Ser Awd, Arthritis Foun; Wisdom Awd of Hon; Lib Bicent Awd; So Hermitage Awd; J Edgar Hoover Awd; KY Col; TN

Col; AL Col; GA Col; W/W: in TN, in US; Nat Register of Prominent Ams; Intl Inst of Commun Ser; Book of Hon; Nat Social Dir; Other Biogl Listings.
WEED, HELENE MEISSEL oc/Educator; b/Aug 22, 1942; h/2207 Nagle Road, Erie, PA 16510; ba/Erie, PA; m/John Harold; c/Elizabeth Ann, Jennifer Marie; p/Mr and Mrs Fred Meissel, Ft Myers, FL; sp/Mr and Mrs Harold Weed, Erie, PA; ed/BS 1964, MEd 1966, Edinboro St Col; pa/4th Grde Tchr 1964-72, Subst Tchr 1972-82, Harbor Creek Sch Dist; 5th Grade Tchr, Luther Meml Lrng Ctr, 1982-; Mem: NEA, 1964-72; PSEA, 1964-72; Harbor Creek Tchrs Assn, 1964-72; Delta Kappa Gamma, 1984; r/U Meth.

WEEKS, CLIFFORD M oc/Public School Administrator; Arranger, Composer and Trombonist; b/Apr 15, 1938; h/20 Fells Avenue, Medford, MA 02136; ba/Hyde Park, MA; m/Lynn (dec); c/ Clifford M Jr, Michele Lynn; p/Vernal and Adeline Weeks, Spring Valley, NY; ed/Profl Dipl (Arranging & Composition), Berklee Col of Music, 1962; BMus 1963, MMus 1975, Boston Conservatory; CAGS Ednl Adm, Boston St Col, 1977; Addit Study, N Eng Conservatory; pa/Music Edr, Boston Public Schs, 1963-72; Coor of Instrumental Music 1975-79, Asst Prin 1979, Adm Asst to Commun Supt 1979-, Boston Public Schs; Arranger, Composer, Trombonist for Profl Artist; Jazz Studies Dir, Nat Ctr of Afro-Am Artists, 1970-73; Mem: Iota Chi Chapt, Omega Psi Phi; Basileus, Cambridge, MA, 1970, 1972; Treas, Black Edrs Alliance of MA, 1973-76; MEMC; cp/JC's, 1975; r/U Meth; hon/ Music Composition: Triptych for Tuba & Piana, 1971; 4 Stage Band Compositions & Arrangements, 1976; Dean's List (4 Semesters), Boston Conservatory; Grad cum laude, Boston Conservatory, 1963; Omega Man of Yr, 1973; Black Edrs Alliance Awd for Excel in Ed, 1976; Dic of Am Composers.

WEEKS, PHYLLIS ERLENE oc/Public School Teacher; b/Mar 21, 1934; h/ Route 1, Box 54, Balko, OK 73931; ba/ Balko, OK; c/Charles, Earl Lyn; Irene (Daug-in-Law); Alison (Grand Daugh); p/S A and Elsie Pugh, Balko, OK; ed/ BS Home Ec 1958, BS Elem Ed 1967, OK Panhandle St Univ; pa/Sch Tchr, Adams, OK, 1961-62; Kgn Tchr, Balko, OK, 1967-72; 2nd Grade Tchr, Balko, OK, 1973-; Mem: NEA; OK Ed Assn; OK Rdg Assn; High Plains Rdg Coun; Beaver Co Ed Assn; cp/Secy, Balko Apostolic Faith Ch; r/Apostolic Faith; hon/Outstg Home Ec Student, 1958; Co Tchr of Yr Rep, 1979; W/W of Am Wom.

WEICK, FRED ERNEST oc/Retired Aeronautics Engineer, Consultant; b/Jul 14, 1900; h/2 Dolphin Drive, Vero Beach, FL 32960; m/Dorothy Jane Church; c/Donald Victor, Elizabeth Jane, Richard Fred; ed/BSME, Univ of IL, 1922; mil/AUS SATC, 1918; pa/ Draftsman, Air Mail Ser of PO Dept, 1922-23; Supt, Yackey Aircraft Co, 1923-24; Jr Aero Engr, Bur of Aeronaut Nav Dept, 1924-25; Aero Engr, Nat Advy Com for Aeronaut, 1925-29; Chem Engr, Hamilton Aero Mfg Co, 1929-30; Aero Engr, NACA, 1930-36; VPres Engrg, Engrg & Res Corp, 1936-48; Prof & Res Engr, TX AA&M Col Sys, 1948-57; Dir, Piper Aircraft Devel Ctr, 1957-69; Ret'd; Mem: VPres

Aero, Fellow, SAE, 1936; Hon Fellow, AIAA; ASME; Quiet Birdmen; VPres, FL Aero Clb, 1936; Exptl Aircraft Assn; AOPA; Life Mem, TX Aerial Applicators Assn; Hon Life Mem, Flying Engrs; U Flying Octogenarians; Tau Beta Pi; Sigma Zi; Pi Tau Sigma; Phi Kappa Phi; Sigma Gamma Tau; cp/Rotary Clb, 1939-; Pres, Vero Bch Clb, 1961-62; hon/Author, *Aircraft Propeller Design*, 1930; Over 60 NACA Tech Reports & Notes; Num Tech Aeronaut Articles Pub'd; Sylvanus Albert Reed Awd, 1944; Fawcett Aviation Awd, 1945; Puffer Awd, Nat Agri Aviations Assn, 1972; Laura Tabor Barber Air Safety Awd, 1975; Listed as Significant Contbr to Flight Technol, Nat Air & Space Mus of Smithsonian Instn; W/W in Aviation.

WEIDA, DONNA LEE oc/Computer Company Executive; b/Oct 29, 1939; h/14241 Utrillo Drive, Irvine, CA 97714; ba/Irvine, CA; c/Mark, Traci, Teri; p/Donald L and Leila J (Sweet) Klackner; ed/AA, Orange Coast Col and Saddleback Col, 1980; BS, Bus Adm & Computer Info Sys, CA St Univ-Fullerton, 1983; pa/Secy, K L K Mfg Co, Logansport, IN, 1957-60, 1963-65; Secy, Sch of Ed, MI St Univ, 1962-63; Secy, Sch of Fine Arts, Univ of CA-Irvine, 1966-69; Co-orgr, Plaza Vet Clin, Upland, CA, 1969-70; Mgr, Bob Bondurant Sch H Perf Driving, Ontario Motor Speedway, CA, 1970-73; Chuck Jones Racing, Costa Mesa, CA, 1973; Exec Secy, Dana Steel, Newport Bch, CA, 1974; Estimator/Ofc Mgr, Hardy & Harper, Tustin, CA, 1975-76; Controller/Mgr, Gillen/Kloss Advtg , Newport Bch, 1977-78; Purchasing Admr, Butler Housing, Irvine, CA, 1979; Controller, X Mark Corp, Costa Mesa, 1980-81; Corp Secy, Adm Mgr, Pers Sys Tech Inc, Irvine, CA, 1982; Fdr, Owner, Numbers & Words, Irvine, CA, 1982-; Mem: Nat Assn Female Execs; Am Soc Profl & Exec Wom; Beta Sigma Phi; cp/Repub; r/Epis; hon/W/W of Am Wom; Personalities of W & MW.

WEINSTOCK, HELENE SUZETTE (KARLIN) oc/Psychotherapist and Marriage, Family, Child Counselor; b/Apr 26, 1935; h/Fountain Valley, CA; ba/Huntington Bch, CA; m/Donald J(ay); p/Bernard L Karlin (dec); Betty E (Balter) Karlin, Canoga Pk, CA; sp/Irving A and Rose (Primack) Weinstock, Camarillo, CA; ed/AA 1954, AB 1955, MA 1958, CPhil in Hist 1969, Univ of CA-LA; MA Psych, CA St Univ-LA 1980; pa/Tchr, Mt Vernon Jr HS, LA City Schs, 1958-61; Public & Profl Ed Coor, Riverside, CA Mtl Hlth Assn, 1967-73; Psych Asst, Leonard I Schneider PhD & Assocs, Newport Bch, CA, 1976-78; Psych Cnsltr, Huntington Bch, CA Commun Clin, 1978-80; Psych Cnslr, Non-profit W Co Cnslg Ctr, 1980-81; Cnslt & Supvr of Interns & Trainees, W Co Cnslg Ctr, 1981-; Pvt Pract Psychotherapist & Marriage, Fam & Child Cnslr, Huntington Bch, CA, 1981-; Mem: Am Assn for Marriage & Fam Therapy; So CA Assn for Marriage & Fam Therapy; CA Assn of Marriage & Fam Therapists; Orange Co Chapt, CAMFT; Am Psych Assn; Wn Psychol Assn; CA St Psychol Assn; Nat Assn for Poetry Therapy; Coor Com for Wom in Hist Prof; Wn Assn of Wom Histns; Phi Beta Kappa; Psi Chi; Pi Gammu Mu; Phi Alpha Theta; Pi Sigma Alpha; Alpha

Mu Gamma; Alpha Lambda Delta; cp/Mem, Bd of Dirs & Num Coms, Riverside Mtl Hlth Assn; Var Coms, Riverside Co Mtl Hlth Advy Bd; Riverside Co Mtl Hlth Action Com, 1968-72; Riverside Co/Commun Drug-Abuse Action Com, 1970; Riverside Co Mtl Hlth & Mtl Retard Com, 1972; Num Other Coms in Riverside Co, CA; r/Judaism; hon/Author of Pub'd Poems & Articles, *Voices: The Art & Sci of Psychotherapy*, Jour of Am Acad of Psychotherapists; *Pudding Mag*, Nat Assn for Poetry Therapy; Nat Def Fgn Lang F'ships in Afrikaans, Sum 1964, 1964-65, 1965-66; Mabel Wilson Richards Grad Scholar in Polit Sci, Univ of CA-LA, 1955-56; Mem, Num Hon Socs; W/W: in W, in CA.

WEISHEIT, RICHARD LANE oc/Certified Public Accountant, Executive; b/Jan 27, 1951; h/10210 Chisholm Trail, Dallas, TX 75243; ba/Dallas, TX; m/Margaret Lynette; p/Mr and Mrs O G Weisheit Jr, Tyler, TX; sp/Nancille Willis, Dallas, TX; ed/BBA, TX Tech Univ, 1973; CPA, 1978; pa/Staff Acct, Frank Began CPA, 1973-77; Sr Acct, Isham P Nelson CPA's, 1977-78; Pres, Richard L Weisheit PC, CPA's, 1978-; Mem: Public Relats Com & Taxpayer Ed Com, Dallas Chapt of CPA's, 1979-81; Dallas Discussion Ldr, Peer Grp of CPA's, 1982; cp/Yg Repubs; Treas, 500 Inc of Dallas, 1981-82, 1982-83; r/Meth; hon/Author of Article on Tax Equity & Fiscal Responsibility Act of 1982 in *Big B Acctg & Tax Manual*; Outstg Yg CPA's in Dallas, 1979-80; W/W in S & SW.

WEISSINGER, MARY HAZEL MATTINGLY oc/Teacher; b/Nov 4, 1927; h/Georgiana Plantation Box 333, Cary, MS 39054; m/Charles Hyde; c/Charles Hyde Jr, Guy Mattingly, MaryAnne W Smith, Elizabeth Hansford, Thomas Leland, Hazel Shanahan; p/Guy Leland Mattingly, Greenville, MS; Hazel Shanahan Mattingly (dec); sp/Harry McElroy Weissinger (dec); Ethel Powers Weissinger, Cary, MS; ed/BS, MS Univ for Wom, 1949; Grad Study: Univ of AL; Univ of MS; MS St Univ; pa/Clrm Tchr; cp/Pres, MS Soc Colonial Dames XVII Cent, 1977-79; Sr Pres 1974-80, Sr Chaplain 1978-81, MS River Soc Chd of Am Revolution; Libn, St Soc DAC, 1978-81; Libn, James McBride Chapt, DAC, 1981-85; 1st V Regent, Belvidere Chapt, DAR, 1980-83; Gov Thomas Welles Chapt, Colonial Dames XVII Cent, 1983-85; r/Rom Cath; hon/Wom of Achmt, BPW Clb, 1969; Dream Girl, Pi Kappa Alpha; Other Hons; W/W of Wom; Personalities of S; The Hereditary Register of US.

WELCH, FERN STEWART oc/Public Relations Consultant, Writer; b/Aug 13, 1934; h/7511 East Berridge Lane, Scottsdale, AZ 85253; ba/Phoenix, AZ; m/Kenneth A; c/Joni Stewart Olsen, Susan Stewart Caldwell, John D Stewart; p/Mrs E L DeMente Phoenix AZ; ed/AA, Phoenix Col, 1953; Att'd: AZ St Univ, 1965; Bellevue Commun Col, 1967; Lake Wash Commun Col, 1968; pa/Writer, Reporter, Columnist, *Sammamish Val News*, Redmond, WA, 1967-71; Staff Writer, Asst Public Relats Dir, The 1st Nat Bk OR, Portland, 1971-72; Asst Public Relats Dir 1972-73, Public Relats Dir 1973-77, The AZ Bk, Phoenix; Fdr & Pres, Fern Stewart & Assoc, 1977-;

Mem: Nat & Phoenix Chapts, Public Relats Soc of Am; Intl Assn of Bus Commrs; Wom in Commun Inc; Arizonians for Cultural Devel; cp/Scottsdale Ctr for the Arts; Val Shakespearel; AZ Hist Soc; Friends of Channel 8 (PBS); Phoenix Country Clb & the Plaza Clb; Bd of Dirs, Ctl AZ & Maricopa Co Chapts, ARC; Bd of Dirs, Compas; Scottsdale Girls Clb; r/Presb; hon/Author, Num Bus-related & Freelance Articles Pub'd in Maj Nat Newspapers & Mags Incl'g: *LA Times*; *Seattle Times*; *Am Bkr*; *Phoenix Mag*; *Wn Bkr*; *Entree Mag*; *AZ Living*; Others; Awds of Merit & Excel, Intl Assn Bus Commrs, 1975-77; Merit & Best of Indust Awds, Fin World, 1975; Awds for Excel in Public Relats Vol Efforts During Floods, ARC, 1980 & 1981; W/W in W.

WELLS, VALDA E oc/Management Services; b/Jun 23, 1935; h/36-19 Bowne Street, Flushing, NY 11354; ba/Flushing, NY; p/William F and Valda Baldwin Wells; ed/BA Ec, New Sch for Social Res, 1967; Addit Grad Studies; pa/Edit, Layout & Copy Editing, Subscription Fulfillment, w Prentice-Hall, Harcourt Brace & *Saturday Review*, 1964-67; Res Assoc Trade Policy 1967-73, Conslt Trade Policy Devel 1973-75, Mgr Intl Res Progs 1975-80, Gen Elect Co, NYC; Pres, Wellspring (Mgmt Consltg Co), NYC, 1980-; Co-Dir, CW Assocs (Mgmt Sers Co), NYC, 1983-; Mem: Nat Assn of Female Execs; Am Soc of Profl & Exec Wom; AAUW; Intl Platform Assn; Indep Citizens Res Foun; r/Presb; hon/Author & Co-Author Over 15 Articles Incl'g: "Polit & Mil Strategy in WW III," 1981; "Effect of Exch Rates on Dollar Valuation of World Exports," 1980; 'The Generalized Sys of Preferances," 1980; "Progress in Intl Trade Documentation," 1979; "Opports for the 1980's (Intl Trade Negotiations)," 1978; Others; W/W of Am Wom.

WELSCH, JAMES LESTER oc/Municipal Judge; b/Oct 2, 1917; h/707 North Frontier Street, Bloomfield, NM 87413; ba/Bloomfield, NM; m/Grace Warner; p/W F Welsch (dec); sp/W F Warner (dec); ed/BS, Purdue Univ, 1942; MA, LA St Col, 1954; Addit Grad Study; mil/USN, US & PTO, 1942-46, Lt (JG); Korean Police Action, 1951-52, Lt; USNR, Lt; Cmdr, USNR Unit, Fairbanks, AK, 1949-50; Cmdr, US Coast Guard Aux, Farmington, NM, 1969-72; pa/Safety & Plant Protection Ofcr, Alumninum Co of Am, Lafayette, IN, 1940-42; Safety Mgr, Vigo Ordinance Plant, Esslinger-Misch Contracting Corp, Terre Haute, IN, 1942; Instr, Purdue Univ, W Lafayette, IN, 1940-42; Instr, DePauw Univ, Greencastle, IN, 1943; Br Mgr & Asst Secy Nat City Br, San Diego Pacific Title Co, San Diego, CA, 1946-49; Dir of Athletics & Hd of PE Dept, Univ of AK, 1949-50; Dir of Industl Relats Elects Div, The Nat Cash Register Co, Hawthorne, CA, 1952-55; Dir Industl Relats & Acting Prodn Mgr Mercast Mfg Corp La Verne 1955-56, Dir Industl Relats La Verne 1956-57, Plant Sers Mgr Sums Gyroscope Corp Santa Monica 1958, The Atlas Corp of NY; Safety Mgr, Kaise Aluminum & Chem Corp, Halethorpe, MD, 1956; Asst Prof Bus & Ec, En NM Univ, 1957-58; Asst Prof Industl Mgmt, CA Wn Univ, San Diego, CA, 1958-63; Prin, Chilchinbeto Day Sch, US Bur of Indian

Affairs, Chilchinbeta, AZ 1963-66; Sci Tchr, Hermosa Jr HS, Farmington, NM, 1966; Supt, Dolores Public Schs, Dolores, CO, 1967-68; Proj Dir, Montelores Multicultural Ctr, Cortez, CO, 1968-69; Asst Prin, Farmington HS, Farmington, NM, 1970-71; Real Est Salesman, Foutz Real Est, Farmington, NM, 1971-73; Asst Prin, Bloomfield HS, Bloomfield, NM, 1971-74; Realtor, Broker, Co-Owner, Realty 1, Bloomfield, NM, 1973-; Guid Cnslr, Dzilth-na-odith-hle Commun Sch, US Bur of Indian Affairs, Bloomfield, NM, 1974-76; Supvry Guid Cnslr, Huerfano Dorm, US Bur of Indian Affairs, 1976-80; Realty Spec, Rts Protection Jun Area Ofc 1980-81, & Supvry Realty Spec, AK Native Claims Settlement Act (ANCSA) Projs Ofc, Juneau Area Ofc, Anchorage, 1981-83; Mun Judge, Bloomfield, NM, 1984-; Mem: AK Chapt, Am Soc of Safety Engrs, 1982-; Mesa Verde Chapt, CO Pres 1979-80, Life Mem, Phi Delta Kappa; Nat Assn of Realtors Wash DC, 1971; Ed Com 1979-80, Realtors Assn of NM, Santa Fe, 1971-; San Juan Co Bd of Realtors, 1971-; NM Sch Admrs Assn, Santa Fe, 1971; NM Pers & Guid Assn, Albuquerque, 1974; cp/Dir San Juan Co Chapt, ARC, 1980; Dir, San Juan Co Mus Assn, 1977-79; Dir, Bloomfield C of C, 1977-79; Spec Dpty Sheriff, San Juan Co, 1974-; Chm 74th Precinct, San Juan Co, Repub Party, 1973, 1974 & 1984; Mason; K Templar; OES; Nav Resv Assn; Ret'd Ofcrs Assn; Am Legion; VFW; Lions Clb; Rotary Intl; Kiwanis Intl; FFA; Rainbow for Girls; BSA; Num Other Commun Activs; r/Prot; hon/Var Pubs, "Industl Mgmt Ed-Present and Future"; *Col News & Views*; Cert of Ser, US Dept of Interior, 1983; Admiral, The TX Nav, St of TX, Galveston; Spec Act Awd, Navajo Areas, US Dept of Indian Affairs, Dept of Interior; Order of Red Cross of Constantine, St Sophia Conclave, NM; Others; W/W in W.

WELTERS, GWENDOLYN HEASTIE oc/Elementary Assistant Principal; b/Apr 30, 1924; h/2900 Northwest 50th Street, Miami, FL 33142; ba/Miami, FL; m/Warren W Sr; c/Bernard C, Martha A, Warren W III; p/Raymond C Heastie (dec); Lena H Heastie, Miami, FL; sp/Peter and Martha Welters, Key West FL; ed/BS, FL A&M Col, 1943; MA, Columbia Univ, 1962; pa/Secy 1943-57, Elem Tchr 1957-59, Douglas Elem Sch; Elem Tchr 1959-63, Rdg Tchr 1963-65, Bethune Elem; Elem Tchr, W Lab Sch, 1965-68; PLATS Tchr, Johnson Elem, 1968-69; Elem Tchr, Olinda Elem, 1969-70; Rdg Tchr, Bright Elem, 1970-74; Adm Asst, Westview Elem, 1974-77; Mem: Past Mem, Basileus, Alpha Kappa Alpha, 1976-77; Nat Dir, Intl Trends & Sers 1982-84, Treas Gtr Miami Chapt 1978-81, The Links Inc; Local Chm, Alpha Kappa Alpha Nat Conv, 1974; Chm Wom's Activs, Alpha Phi Alpha Nat Conv, 1975; FL Assn of Sch Admrs; Assn for Supvn & Curric Devel; r/Cath; hon/25 Yr Soror 1976, Soror of Yr 1974, Alpha Kappa Alpha; W/W in S & SW.

WENBERG, BURNESS G oc/Professor; b/Jul 14, 1927; h/2608 Rockwood, East Lansing, MI 48823; ba/Lansing, MI; p/Mrs H L Wenberg, Beach, ND; ed/BS Dietetics & Home Ec, Univ of ND, 1949; MS Nutritional Ed, OH St Univ, 1957;

Cert Dietetic Intern, VA Hosp Hines, IL, 1949-50; pa/Assoc Prof & Coor Undergrad Dietetic Curric Dept of Food Sci & Human Nutrition, MI St Univ, E Lansing, 1973-; Assoc Prof & Dir Dietetic Intern Sch of Home Ec, Univ of WA, Seattle, 1970-72; Asst Prof Med Dietetics 1968-69, Asst Dir Sch of Allied Med Profs 1966-68, Asst Prof Med Dietetics 1961-66, Instr 1957-59, OH St Univ, Columbus; Asst Prof, SD St Col, Brookings, 1959-61; Tchr Cut Bk HS, Cut Bank, MT, 1954-56; Staff & Head Dietition, Kammehameha Schs, Honolulu, HI, 1952-54; Staff & Hd Dietitian, VA Hosp, LA, CA, 1950-52; Dietetics Conslt, Var Univs, Towns & Projs; Mem: Am, MI & Lansing Dietetic Assns; Am & MI Home Ecs Assns; Am Soc of Allied Hlth Profs; Am Ed Res Assn; Am Assn on Higher Ed; Nutrition Today Soc; Soc for Nutrition Ed; MI Public Hlth Assn; MI League for Human Sers; Secy 1963-65, Pres-elect & Pres 1965-67, Columbus (OH) Dietetic Assn; Secy, OH Dietetic Assn, 1968-70; Var Coms, Am Dietetic Assn; Var Coms, Am Diabetes Assn; Nutrition Com, MI Diabetes Assn, 1976-; Var Coms, MI Dietetic Assn; Other Commun Activs; Num Orgl Presentations; r/U Ch of Christ; hon/Author, *Intro to Hlth Professions*, 1972; *Dynamics of Clin Dietetics*, 1982; 2 Book Chapts & 4 Monographs; Over 10 Articles Pub'd in Profl Jours; Phi Upsilon Omicron, Univ of ND; Delta Kappa Gamma Awd for Outstg Grad Sr in Ed, Univ of ND, 1949; Phi Kappa Phi, MI St Univ, 1980.

WERNER, JANE BROOK oc/Tibetan Specialist, Asian Art Consultant; b/Oct 14, 1931; h/61 Grove Street, New York, NY 10014; ba/Same; m/Lobsang Nyima Aye; p/June McCallen, Bronxville, NY; sp/Wangchuk Dolma Aye (dec); pa/Asst Dir, YLHS India, 1963; Asst Dir, Am Emer Com for Tibetan Refugees, NY, 1962; Dir of Asian Dept ACEP, NY, 1968; Dir of Public Relats to His Holiness the Dalai Lama, Ofc of Tibet, NY, 1970; Fdr & Dir, Tibetan Cultural Inst, 1976-; Former Curator, Jacques Marchais Mus, SI, NY, 1972; Mus Conslt, Newark Mus, 1974; Christie's Spec in Tibetan & Himalayan Art, London, Paris, Brussels & Amsterdam, 1980; Mem: Appraiser's Assn of Am; Himalayan Coun of the Asia Soc, NY; r/Mahayana Buddhist; hon/Translations of Medieval Tibetan; Author, "An Hist Outline of the Sakyapa Sect," 1963; "The Jalsey Lalay of the Sakya Pandita," 1974.

WERT, JONATHAN MAXWELL JR oc/Management Consultant; b/Nov 8, 1939; h/916 Town Lane, Port Royal, PA 17082; ba/Harrisburg, PA; m/Monica Kay Manbeck; c/Jonathan Maxwell III, Kimberly Dee; p/Jonathan and Helen Wert, Port Royal, PA; sp/Miriam Manbeck, Mifflintown, PA; ed/BS 1966, MS 1968, Austin Peay St Univ; PhD, Univ of AL, 1974; mil/USMC, 1958-61; pa/Energy Conslts Inc, 1983-; PA Dept of Commun Affairs, 1982-83; PA St Univ, 1977-81; Energy/Envir Conslt, 1975-77; TN Val Auth, 1971-75; Bays Mtn Pk, Envir Ctr, 1969-71; PA Dept of Forests & Waters, 1968-69; Mem: Num Profl Assns, Advy Couns & Coms; r/Luth; hon/Author, Over 40 Pubs on Envir Quality, Planning, Mgmt & Conserv; Am Motors Conserv Awd, 1976; W/W:

in World, in Am, in E, in S & SW; Men of Achmt; DIB; Commun Ldrs & Noteworthy Ams.

WESLEY, JANICE MARION oc/Administrative Assistant; b/Mar 16, 1943; h/Middleburg Road, Liberty, KY 42539; ba/Camden, NJ; p/Charles E Wesley, Liberty, KY; ed/AA, Lindsey Wilson Jr Col, 1964; AB, En KY Univ, 1966; Att'd: Spalding Col 1973-78; Univ of L'ville 1979; Univ of KY 1980; pa/Elem Tdchr, Liberty, 1962-68; Social Wkr, Liberty, 1968-78; Adm Asst, Watson Lumber Co Inc, 1978-79; Disaster Loan Asst, Mobile, AL, 1978-80; Asst Loan Ofcr & Documents Examr, NO, LA, 1980-81; Legal Documents Examr & Asst Loan Ofcr, Denver, CO, 1981-; Document Examr, Fargo, ND & Sioux Falls, 1982; Adm Asst, Respond Inc, Camden, NJ, 1982-83; cp/Wom's Repub Clb; VPres, Woms Clb of Ctl KY; Sierra Clb; Casey Co War Meml Hosp Aux; U Way; r/Meth.

WESLEY, THERESSA GUNNELS oc/Writer, Director of Writing Lab; b/Sep 2, 1945; h/14508 Sara Lynn Drive, Little Rock, AR 72206; ba/Pine Bluff, AR; m/John W; c/Dwayne, Rashida, Kameelah, Jameel, Crystal; p/Fred Gunnels, Morrilton, AR; Florence Gunnels (dec); sp/Walter Wesley, Springfield, AR; Carries Wesley (dec); ed/BA, Philander Smith Col, 1962; MA, Kent St Univ, 1972; pa/9th & 10th Grades Eng Tchr, Springfield Public Schs, 1967-69; 7th & 10th Grades Eng Tchr, Pulaske Co Sch Sys, Little Rock, AR, 1969-70; Eng Instr, Univ of WI, 1972-74; Dir of Career Devel, Philander Smith Col, Little Rock, AR, 1975-78; Eng Tchr, Little Rock Public Schs, 1980-83; Writer, Dir of Writing Lab, Univ of AR-Pine Bluff, 1983-; cp/Zeta Phi Beta Sorority; 1st Bapt Ch-Highland Pk; r/Bapt; hon/Author, *Black Am Writers Past & Present: A Biogl & Bibliogl Dir*, 1975; Outstg Ref Book, Select Co, of Am Lib Assn, 1975; Personalities of S & SW; 2000 Notable Ams; Book of Hon; Other Biogl Listings.

WEST, BILL GRAYUM oc/Professional Speaker; b/May 24, 1930; h/2138 Park Willow, Katy, TX 77450; ba/Houston, TX; m/Ann; c/Jason; p/Mr and Mrs Kade West, Vernon, TX; sp/Mrs Dorthy Radnor, Houston, TX; ed/BA, 1951; ThD, 1957; pa/Pastor, 1st Bapt Ch, Alamulgee, 1958-65; Pastor, River Oaks Bapt Ch, Houston, 1965-72; Assoc Prof, Houston Bapt Univ, 1972-75; Profl Spkr, 1975-; Mem: Am Soc for Tng & Devel; Nat Spkrs Assn; hon/Author, 4 Books: *Free To Be Me*, 1971; *How To Survive Stress*, 1981; *Platform To Sucess*, 1982; *Successful Supvn Step By Step*, 1982; Over 100 Articles in Nat Pubs; W/W: in S & SW, in Fin & Indust; Intl Authors & Writers W/W.

WEST, DOROTHY ANNE oc/Speech Pathologist and Educational Consultant; b/Mar 21, 1936; h/976 Baird Drive, Baton Rouge, LA 70808; ba/Baton Rouge, LA; c/Jeffrey W Freeman; p/Philip W West, Baton Rouge, LA; ed/BS 1958, MEd 1973, LA St Univ; pa/Spch & Hearing Therapist, St Helena Parish Schs, 1959-61; Asst to Dean of Wom, LA St Univ, 1961-66; Spch & Hearing Therapist, E Baton Rouge Parish Schs, 1966-82; Compliance Conslt & Spch Pathol/Ednl Conslt, E Baton Rouge Parish Schs, 1982-; Mem: Pres, Mortar Bd Alumnae Assn,

1960-62; Bd of Dirs, Diamondhead Commun Assn, 1980-81; Bd of Dirs 1978-82, Secy-Treas 1978 & 1979, Pres 1980, 1981 & 1982, Lakeside Villa Condominium Assn; Phi Delta Kappa; S'ship Chm 1965-69, Nom'g Com 1968-70, Povince IX Col Chm 1970-75, Awds Chm 1975-79, Gamma Zeta Chapt' Pledge Advr 1959-60, Advy Bd Chm 1960-61 & 1979-82, S'ship Advr 1978-79, Baton Rouge Alumnae Chapt Panhellenic Del 1969-70, Pres 1982-, Delta Gamma Frat; hon/Delta Gamma Cable Awd, 1980; Delta Gamma Foun Name Grant; Outstg Yg Wom of Am; W/W in S & SW; Commun Ldrs of Am; Other Biogl Listings.

WEST, EARL IRVIN oc/Minister, Teacher; b/May 18, 1920; h/722 North Payton Road, Indianapolis, IN 46219; c/ Robert Earl, Timothy Eugen; p/Tena West, Indianapolis, IN; ed/BA, George Pepperdine Col, 1943; MA 1945, BD 1948, ThM 1950, Butler Univ Sch of Rel; PhD, IN Univ, 1968; pa/Min, Franklin Rd Ch of Christ, Indianapolis, IN, 1957-; Tchr Harding Grad Sch of Rel, 1968-; r/Ch of Christ; hon/Author, *Life & Times of David Lipscomb*, 1953; *Search For Ancient Order* Vol I 1949, Vol II 1953 & Vol III, 1975; *Elder Ben Franklin: Eye of the Storm*, 1983; Apprec Dinner, By AL Christ Sch of Rel, 1983; Personalities of S.

WEST, JOHN C oc/Attorney; b/Aug 27, 1922; h/176 Mooring Buoy, Hilton Head Island, SC 29928; ba/Hilton Head Isl, SC; m/Lois Rhame; c/John Carl Jr, Douglas Allen, Shelton Simmons; ed/ BA, The Citadel, 1942; LLB, Univ of SC, 1948; mil/AUS, 1942-46, Maj; pa/Ptnr, Law Firm of West, Holland, Furman & Cooper, Camden, SC, 1947-70; Ptner, Law Firm of West, Cooper, Bowen, Beard & Smoot, Camden, SC, 1975-77; Law Firm, John C West, PA, Hilton Head Isl, SC, 1981-; Dist'd Prof of Med E Studies, Univ of SC, 1981; St Senator, St of SC, 1954-66; Lt Govr, St of SC, 1966-70; Gov, St of SC, 1971-75; Ambassador to Saudi Arabia, 1977-81; Mem: Phi Beta Kappa; Bd of Trustees, So Ctr for Intl Studies; Bd of Dirs, Donaldson, Lufkin & Jenrette; Bd of Dirs, Whittaker Corp; Bd of Dirs, Circle "S" Industs Inc; Bd of Dirs, Vinnell Corp; cp/Dem; r/Presb; hon/AUS Commend Medal; K Cmdr, Order of Mert, Fed Repub of Germany.

WEST, KENNETH LAFE oc/Alcohol and Drug Counselor; b/Aug 15, 1939; h/Box 446, Mackay, ID 83251; ba/Elko, NV; c/Jeri Diane; p/Mr and Mrs Lafe West (dec); ed/AA Elects, Col So ID, 1971; AA Cnslg, Otero Jr Col, 1979; Att'd ID St Univ-Pocatello; mil/AUS, 1957-58; mil/USAF, 1962-65; pa/Vol Probation/Parole Ofcr, Elko, NV; Alcohol/Drug Cnslr, 1983-; Owner, Wn Silver Inc, Mining Co; Owner/Ptner, Gen Mgr, Moonwalker Inc, 1981, 1983; Gen Mgr, Owner, Dir, Attitude Awareness Ctr, 1979-81; Secy, Moonwalker Foun, 1981-83; Probation Ofcr, Custer Co, ID, 1981, 1983; Newspaper Columnist, *The Post Register*; Guest Columnist, *ID St Jour*; cp/Am Legion; DAV; Lions Intl; Masonic Lodge #19 (Mackay, ID); Edr, ID St Univ, 1980-81; Host, Radio Show, KID Radio, Idaho Falls; Num Guest Appearances on KID-TW; hon/ Congl Nom to West Point, 1957; W/W in W.

WESTBROOK, VIRGINIA GRAY oc/Retired English Teacher; b/Jan 30, 1916; h/8116 Eastern Avenue Northwest, Washington, DC 20012; m/Fred E; c/Anita W McClendon, Fred E Jr; p/Lula Hammond Gray, Washington DC; sp/ Mr and Mrs A W Westbrook (dec); ed/ BA, Lane Col, 1938; MS 1936, Linguistic Spec 1963, TN St Univ; Adv'd Study, Univ of TN; pa/Eng & Music Tchr, Memphis & Shelby Co Bd of Ed, 1938-45; Eng Tchr, Bd of Ed, Nashville, TN, 1946-73; Mem: Secy, Chm Ed Com, 1974, AAUW; Bd Mem, Ed Ch, Dir 1980 Census Contest for DC Students, DC Leag of Wom Voters; Secy 1976, Ch Wom U; Life Mem, Anti Basileus, Reporter, Public Relats Chm, Chm Music Com, Alpha Kappa Alpha Sorority, 1944-; Spiritual Editor of Epistle Newslttr, Deaconess Bapt Ch; Focus Bd, Wide Horizon Support Grp for DC Schs; Vol Tutor in Eng Skills, Operation Rescue for DC Elem Pupils; r/ Christian-Bapt; hon/Author, Units (Unipacs) on Eng Grammar; Editorials; Poems; Outstg Contributions to Sorority, Xi Omega & Alpha Delta Omega Chapts, Alpha Kappa Alpha.

WESTERFIELD, WILLIAM (BO) A oc/University Professor and Administrator; b/Mar 1, 1947; h/376 Milagra Drive, Pacifica, CA 94044; ba/San Francisco, CA; p/Richard A and LaValle Slater Westerfield, Overlea, MD; ed/BA 1970, MA 1971, Univ of MD; PhD, Wayne St Univ, 1976; pa/Acting Chair Theatre Arts Dept 1983-, Assoc Prof 1974-, SF St Univ; Pres, BOWEST Talent & Modeling Agy, 1979-82; Mng Dir, Chd's Theatre Wing, Santa Rosa Sum Theatre, 1977; Exec Dir, No CA Chd's Theatre Fest, 1976 & 1977; Asst to Dir of Public Relats, Wayne St Univ, 1972-74; Other Previous Positions; Mem: URTA Fellow 1972-74, Mem 1968-, Am Theatre Assn; Gov Reg 8 1978-80, Mem-at-Large 1977-78, Nat Awds Com 1979 & 1984, Mem 1974-, Chd's Theatre Assn of Am; US Del to Intl Cong in Madrid 1978, Mem 1976-, (ASSITEJ) Intl Chd's Theatre Assn; cp/ Wk w Num Adult & Chd's Theatre Arts Progs & Orgs; r/Luth; hon/Assoc Editor, *Chd's Theatre Review*, 1980-; Author of Var Articles Pub'd in *Chd's Theatre Review*; Contbg Author, *How to Produce a Succeful Chd's Theatre Fest*, 1976; *Training the Actor for Participation Theatre*, 1977; *Emergence of An Americanized Form of Theatre-in-Ed*, 1977; Co-Author, *A Kidsum Night's Dream*; Hilberry F'ship, Wayne St Univ, 1972-74; Acting S'ship, Univ of SC, Sum 1968; Grant, Arts AK Artist-in Residence Prog, 1980; Others; W/W: in Am, in W; Outstg Yg Men of Am; Noteworthy Ams of Bicent Era; DIB.

WESTON, J FRED oc/Professor; b/ Feb 6, 1916; h/258 Tavistock, Los Angeles, CA 90049; ba/LA, CA; m/June Mildred; c/Kenneth F, Byron L, Ellen J; p/David and Bertha (Schwartz) Weston (dec); sp/Charles and Mildred Sherman (dec); ed/BA 1937, MBA 1942, PhD 1948, Univ of Chgo; mil/AUS, 1943-45; pa/Instr 1940-42, Asst Prof 1945-48, Sch of Bus, Univ of Chgo; Ec Conslt to Pres, Am Bkrs Assn, 1945-46; Prof Mgrl Ec & Fin, Grad Sch of Mgmt, Univ of CA-LA, 1949-; Mem: Pres, Am Fin Assn, 1966; Pres, Wn Ec Assn, 1960; Am Ec Assn; Econometric Soc; Am Statl Assn; Royal Ec Soc; Fin Analysts Soc;

Pres, Fin Mgmt Assn, 1980-81; r/Presb; hon/Author, Books: *Mgrl Fin*, 1981; *The Impact of Large Firms in the US Economy*, 1973; *Scope & Methodology of Fin*, 1968; *Essentials of Mgrl Fin*, 1979; *Intl Mgrl Fin*, 1972; *Fin Theory & Corp Policy*, 1979; Ford Foun Res F'ship, 1961-62; McKinsey Foun Grant, 1965-68; Gen Elect Foun Grant, 1972-82; Pres, Am Fin Assn, 1966; Pres, Wn Ec Assn, 1959-60; Pres, Fin Mgmt Assn, 1979-80; W/W in CA.

WESTOVER, DAVID ARTHUR oc/ Executive; b/Apr 13, 1950; h/Kingsbury Road, Walpole, NH 03608; ba/Keene, NH; m/Cynthia; c/Robert; p/Arthur Westover, Port St Lucie, FL; Edna Westover (dec); sp/Robert and May Graves, Walpole, NH; ed/BA Psych, Keene St Col, 1972; Cert'd Ins Cnslr, 1976; pa/Underwriter, Peerless Ins Co, 1972-75; Treas and Comml Accts Spec, Clark Ins Agy, 1975-; cp/Bd of Dirs, Big Brothers & Big Sisters Monadnock Reg; Bd of Dirs, Monadnock U Way; Bd of Dirs, Keene Day Care Ctr; Past Pres, Keene JCs; Past St Treas, NJ JCs; r/Luth; hon/NH JC of Yr, 1977; Clint Dunagan Meml Awd, US JCs, 1980; Outstg Yg Men of Am.

WETHINGTON, THOMAS DEWEY oc/Engineer; b/Dec 5, 1926; h/1305 Melmart Drive Bartlesville, OK 74003; ba/Bartlesville, OK; m/Jennevieve Laverne Rieke; c/Lynette Diane, Susan Marie, David Thomas, Karen Rae; p/ Herbert Omer and Jenny Marie Smith Wethington (dec); sp/Ray Enos and Esther G Schmidt Rieke (dec); ed/BSME, Univ of CO, 1950; MSEngrg, TX Tech Univ, 1971; mil/USAAF, 1945; pa/ Inspector, Cadillace Motor Div, Gen Motor Corp, Detroit, MI, 1950; Wholesale Clk, Crane-O-Fallon Co, Pueblo, CO, 1950-51; Time Study & Methods Engr, Gates Rubber Co, Denver, CO, 1951-57; Assoc Design Engr Waco, TX 1957, Assoc Design & Maintenance Engr 1958-60, Sr Mech Engr 1960-63, Chief Mech Engr 1963-72, Chief Maintenance Planner 1972-75, Maintenance & Sers Supt Borger, TX 1975-78; Phillips Petro Co, Phillips, TX; Prin Constrn Planning Engr, Philips Petro Co, Bartlesville, OK, 1978-; ASME, 1949-51; AIIE, 1954-57; Bartlesville Engrs Clb, 1981-82; cp/Dir, VPres & Pres, Borger JC's, 1958-62; Borger C of C, 1972-78; Co Conv Del, Dem Party, 1958-72; St Conv Del, Repub Party, 1976; CoChm Pubs & Recogs Coms, TX Tech Dad's Assn, 1972-82; Bartlesville Geneal Soc, 1981-82; Com Mem to Estab Voc Tech Sch, Pt-time Fluid Mechs Instr 1972-76, Frank Phillips Jr Col r/Prot; hon/W/W in S & SW.

WEWER, DEE J oc/Executive; b/Apr 27, 1948; h/0226 Kings Row, Carbondale, CO 81623; ba/Aspen, CO; m/Ira E Litke; p/Gene and Juanita Wewer, San Antonio, TX; sp/Mae Litke, Miami, FL; ed/BS, Univ of So MS, 1969; MA, Am Univ, 1974; Doct Wk, Georgetown Univ, 1981-82; PhD Cand, The Union Univ; pa/Employee w Dixie Press, Biloxi, MS, 1968-70; Tchr, St Martin Public Sch, Biloxi, 1970; Editor, Newspaper of Nat War Col, Ft McNair, Wash DC, 1971-73; Press & Scheduling Assoc & Coor, Nat Fedn St Chm, Ofc of Chm, Repub Nat Com, Wash DC, 1972-73; Conslt, Nat Wom's Ed Fund, Nat Wom's Polit Caucus, 1973-74; Gen Mgr, Press, Printing Sers Unltd, Wash DC, 1975;

Instr, Inst of Polits, Harvard Univ, Boston, 1976; Media Dir/Prodn, Mgr/ Creat Grp Hd, Bailey, Deardourff & Assocs, Wash DC, 1975-76; Dir Mktg/ Acct Supvr, Weitzman & Assocs, Wash DC, 1976-78; Dir Mktg, Britches of Georgetown, Wash DC, 1978-79; Instr, Col of Bus Mgmt, Univ of MD, Col Pk, 1980-; VPres Public Affairs, AMF Hd Sports Wear, Columbia, MD, 1979-81; Exec VPres, Sport-Obermeyer, Aspen, CO, 1982-; Conslt in Field; Mem: Ski Industs of Am; Wom in Advtg & Mktg; Am Wom in Radio & TV; Am Mgmt Assn; Advtg Clb; Art Dirs Clb; NOW; hon/Author of Poems Pub'd in *Am Poet's Anthology*; Recip, Creat Design Distn, Andy, Printing Industs Am, 1981; Dist Merit Awd, Advtg Clb of NY, 1980; Arts Dirs Clb of Met, Wash DC, 1980; Cleo Awds, 1979; Outstg Wkg Wom, *Glamour Mag*, 1978; Nat Newspaper Nat Creat Awd, 1974; W/W: of Am Wom, in W.

WHEELER, BEVERLY GAIL oc/Medical Doctor, Psychiatrist; b/Jul 15, 1952; h/2552 Madison Road #4, Cincinnati, OH 45208; ba/Cincinnati, OH; p/Mr and Mrs Jesse L Wheeler, Springfield, VA; ed/BS, Emory Univ, 1974; MD, Med Col of VA, 1978; Postgrad Med Tng in Psychi 1978-82, F'ship in Geriatric Psychi 1982-84, Univ of Cinc Med Ctr; pa/Admitting Psych, Rollman's Psychi Inst, 1980-; Adj Clin Instr, Dept of Psychi 1982-83, F'ship in Geriatric Psychi Dept of Psychi 1982-84, Univ of Cin Med Ctr; Staff Psychi in Conslt Liaison Psychi, Cinc VA Hosp, 1982-83; Mem: AMA; Am Med Wom's Assn; Am Psychi Assn; OH Psychi Assn; Cinc Acad of Med; Assn for Advmt of Psychi; r/Presb; hon/Phi Sigma Hon Soc for Biol Res, 1973; Hon Res in Biol, Emory Univ, 1973-74; Upjohn Achmt Awd for Most Outstg Intern, Univ of Cinc Med Ctr, 1979; Chief Resident in Psychi, Univ of Cinc Hosp, 1982; W/W in Am Wom.

WHEELOCK, SHARON MARIE oc/ Newspaper Publisher; b/Jun 23, 1938; h/Box 134, Hyannis, NE 69350; ba/ Hyannis, NE; c/Robyn Reneé, James Sidney, Londa Sue, Chris Marie, Lance Michael; p/Milton D Thomas, Englewood, CA; Lois Mae (Jone) Thomas Mansfield, No Platte, NE; ed/Public Schs in Denver, CO & Hyannis, NE; pa/ Writer 1957, Chief Reporter 1962, Mgr & Editor 1974, Owner, Pubr & Editor, 1976-, Grnat Co News; Mem: NE Writers Guild; Nat Fedn of Press Wom; NE Press Assn; Intl Clover Poetry Assn; Soc of Am Poets Sigma Delta Chi; r/ Bapt; hon/Author of Wkly Newspaper Column, "Sass & Sentiments"; Poetry Pub'd in *Best Am Poems*, 1967; *Clover Collections & Verse; 20th Cent Poets & Their Poems*; 3rd Prize, Clover Poetry Contest; W/W of Am Wom.

WHELAN, PAUL ANDREW oc/Clinical Psychologist; b/Dec 12, 1943; h/PO Box 592, Monticello, IN 47960; ba/ Monticello, IN; m/Karen Mary Hammill; p/Alden and Lucille Whelan (dec); sp/Frank and Margaret Hammill, Kalamazoo, MI; ed/BA, Lawrence Univ, 1966; MA, Wn MI Univ, 1969; PhD, Univ of UT, 1974; pa/Parole Agt, Dept of Corrections, Milwaukee, WI, 1966-67; Asst Prof, Buffalo St Col, Buffalo, NY, 1973-76; Dir Clin Psych, Smoky Mtn Area Mtl Hlth Ctr, Bryson City, NC, 1976-82; Dir Clin Psych, Carroll-White Mtl Hlth Ctr, Monticello,

IN, 1982-; Mem: Bd of Dirs, Autistic Soc of Wn NY, 1974-75; Bd of Dirs, IN Psych Assn Polit Action Com, 1982; cp/ Chm, Commun Schs Com, 1976-82; Swain Co/Bryson City Planning Bd, 1980-82; Bd of Dirs, Tecumseh Area Planned Parenthood, 1982; Pres, Bryson City Rotary Clb, 1981; r/Meth; hon/Phi Kappa Phi, 1973; Outstg Edrs of Am; W/W in S & SW.

WHIPPLE, CAROL OWEN oc/Ranching and Business Consultant; b/Apr 11, 1940; h/Route 2, Box 370 Canyon, TX 79015; ba/Amarillo, TX; m/Gordon; c/ Laura, Randall, Katherine; p/Wiley Ducoe Owen (dec); Mrs W D Owen, Amarillo, TX; sp/Floyd Whipple (dec); Mrs Floyd Whipple, Waynoka, OK; ed/ Undergrad Wk: Univ of AZ & W TX St Univ; pa/Owner-Operator, Creekwood Ranch (Horses & Cattle), 1960-; Corp Dir 1976-78, Corp Secy 1978-80, OK Stud Inc (Horsebreeding), Purcell, OK; Corp Secy 1975-79, Pres 1979-, Rowel Inc (Small Comml Bldgs & Property Mgmt); Owner & Operator, A New Idea Furniture Leasing, 1979-80; Pres, Sun Tans Unltd Inc, 1979-81; Ptnr, Whipple Assocs (Bus & Mgmt Consltg Ser), 1981-; Mem: Nat Assn of Female Execs; Am Soc of Profl & Exec Wom; Intl Entrepreneur Assn; Fedn of Indep Bus; Am Qtr Horse Assn; Appaloosa Horse Clb Inc; cp/Kappa Alpha Theta; Pres, Amarillo Girl Scout Coun, 1974-84; r/Presb; hon/Thanks Badge, Highest Hon Given Vols by GSA, 1978; W/W of Am Wom; World W/W of Wom.

WHITE, CALVIN EDDY oc/Research Animal Scientist; b/Jul 17, 1943; h/ Route 2, Box 2280, Live Oak, FL 32060; ba/Live Oak, FL; m/Patricia Parker; c/ Emily Elizabeth; p/James A White Sr, Scott, AR; ed/BS 1970, MS 1972, PhD 1978, Univ of AR; mil/USAF, 1961-65; Capt, USAR; pa/Res Animal Sci, Univ of FL, IFAS—AREC, Live Oak, 1978-; Grad Ast, Univ of AR, Fayetteville, AR, 1975-78; Ecologist II, AR Dept of Pollution Control & Ecol, Little Rock, AR, 1972-75; Mem: Am Soc of Animal Sci; Sigma Xi; Gamma Sigma Delta; r/ Ch of Christ; hon/Author, Num Sci Articles Pub'd in Profl Jours & Num Experiment Reports; Var Pop Articles; Contbg Author, Chapt in Toxicological Textbook; Pres Outstg Unit Awd, 1963; AUS Commend Medal, 1983; Nat Def Ser Medal, 1965.

WHITE, GERALD E oc/ Safety-Health Manager; b/Sept 1, 1923; h/1 Hearthstone Drive Reading, PA 19606; ba/Boyertown, PA; m/Betty A; c/Barry Lee, Nancy Jean; p/LeRoy J and Miriam White, Shillington, PA; ed/BS Chem, Albright Col, 1948; Postgrad, Temple Univ, 1954; Participant Textile Machine Wks Coop Prog, WY Polytech Inst, 1946; mil/AUS, 1943-46, ETO; pa/ Chem, Foreman Safety Engr, Safety-Hlth Mgr, Beryllium Corp & Succesor Firms: Kaweck Berylco Indust Inc & Divof Cabot Corp, Reading, PA; Mem: Am Soc of Safety Engrs; Nat Safety Coun; Bekrs Co Mfg Assn Safety-Hlth Grp; cp/Advy Bd, Hawk Mtn BSA, 1960-; Bd of Dir 1968-, Pres 1975-81, Hope Rescue Mission; Bd of Dirs 1954-58, St Safety Chm 1956, Jr C of C; Pres, James U Ch of Christ, 1980-82; Other Commun Activs; r/ Prot; hon/Recip, Commun Ser Cit, PA Acad of Opthol & Otolaryngology,

1967.

WHITE, IRMA REED oc/Librarian Assistant for International Law Firm; h/4000 Massachusetts Avenue Northwest, Apartment 331, Washington, DC; ba/Washington, DC; m/Wilford L (dec); p/Eustace Glen and Martha Soper Reed (dec); ed/BA, Univ of CP, 1919; pa/Eng Instr, Univ of CO, 1922-24; Report Writing Instr, Harvard Sch of Bus Adm, 1926-28; Asst Chief Field Sect, Edit Rationed Foods Lttr, Ofc Price Adm, 1943-47; Public Info Spec, Bur of Census & Ofc Secy of Commerce, 1958-71; Dir Press Room, Cost of Living Coun, 1971-74; Libn Asst, Mayer, Brown & Platt, 1975-; Mem: Nat Press Clb; Nat Leag of Am Pen Wom; Am News Wom's Clb; Intl Coun Smal Bus; hon/Author, "Do You Know Your Economic ABC's?," Dept of Commerce Best Seller Series; Articles Pub'd in: *Am Heritage; Ency Brittanica; Ency Americana; Christian Sci Monitor; London Times*; Awd for Outstg Achm, Ofc Price Adm, 1945; Meritious Ser Awd, Bur of Census, 1959; Silver Medal for Dist'd Ser, 1964; Awd for Creat Commun, Dept of Commerce, 1965; 3 Awds for Excell in Commun, Fed Edits Assn, 1965, 1966, 1970; Cert of Merit, Patent Law Assn of SF, 1966; Nat Achmt Awd, Nat Leag of Am Pen Wom, 1966; Outstg Ser Awd, Cost of Living Coun, 1972, 1973; Public Ser Awd, Small Bus Adm, 1978; Intl Coun Small Bus, 1978; W/W: of Am Wom, in E; World W/W of Wom; DIB; 2000 Wom of Achmt.

WHITE, JACK LESLIE III oc/Executive; b/Mar 4, 1948; h/2202 Surrey Lane, Bossier City, LA 71111; ba/Bossier City, LA; m/Joanne Marie; c/Jocelyn Marie; p/Ellen Mae White, Republic, PA; sp/ John Russi, Brownsville, PA; ed/BS, Cornell Univ, 1970; MA, Bowling Green St Univ, 1974; MA, Harvard Univ, 1980; mil/USAR, 1966-71, 1st Lt; pa/Salesman 1970-72, Sales Mgr 1972-74, Fin Analyst 1974-76, W R Grace & Co; Dir of Mktg, Bird & Son Inc, 1976-80; VPres Mktg & Sales, McElroy Metal Mills Inc, 1980-; Mem: Am Mgmt Assm, 1976-; AMBA, 1974; Bd of Dir, Quadco, Boston, MA, 1980-; Bd of Dirs, Expansil Inc, NYC, 1981-; Planning Execs of Am, 1979-; cp/Diplomat, Shreveport C of C; r/Rom Cath; hon/Author of Num Articles Pub'd in: *Metal Bldg News; Farm Bldg News; Am Economist*; Var Local Newspapers & Reg Trade Pubs; Top 10 Outstg Ldrs in Metal Bldg Indust, 1981; W/W in Am.

WHITE, LAWANDA JEANNE oc/ Animal Control Officer and Pound Master; b/Jan 18, 1945; h/Route 10, Box 73 Claremore, OK 74017; ba/Claremore, OK; m/Stanley R; c/Kimberley Gail Engel, Keith Robert Engel, Karl Gorden Engel; p/Calvin Edwards, Jay, OK; Jessie M Phellips (dec); sp/Mr and Mrs George White, Vinita, OK; ed/Cake Decorating & Baking & Adv'd Sewing, Kirkwood Col, Cedar Rapids, IA; pa/ Collins Radio & Gen Mdse Mgr, Warehouse Mkt, Cedar Rapids, IA; Newspaper Columnist, Mays Co, OK; Cake Decorator, Tiffney's Bakery, Tulsa, OK; Cake Decorator, Warehouse Mkt, Claremore, OK; Baker & Cake Decorator, Safeway Bakery, Claremore, OK; Pound Master, Police Dept, Claremore, OK; Mem: Humane Soc, Rogers Co, 1981; Am Kennel Clb, 1983; Assem of

God Ch, 1979; r/Prot.

WHITE, LOUISE HUMPHRIES oc/ Writer and Publisher; b/Mar 30, 1926; h/3286 Wetherbyrne Road, Kennesaw, GA 30144; ba/Kennesaw, GA; m/Verlin Ralph; c/Carol L W Kelly, V Ralph Jr; p/Ernest Christ and Mary Elder Humphries (dec); sp/Guy L White (dec); Gladys Hefley White, Prague, OK; ed/BA Eng, Centenary Col of LA, 1962; MEd Cnslg, GA St Univ, 1971; pa/Employmnt Cnslr, Yt Opport Ctr, LA St Employmnt Ser, 1965-68; Master Cnslr GA St Bur of Employmnt Security, Dept of Labor, 1968-78; Owner, Cnslg Assocs Profl Ofc; Atlanta, GA, 1978-80; Writer & Pubr of Hist Pubs, Archive Press, Kennesaw, 1982-; cp/Treas 1980-83, Kennesaw Hist Soc; GA Trust for Hist Presv; Northside Wom's Clb; Chm Arts Dept, GEWC, 1979-80; Daughs of King, Cathedral of St Philip Epis Ch; hon/ Writer & Pubr of Book on Early Hist of Kennesaw GA & Its Fdrs; Jongleurs Dramatic Awd, Shreveport, LA, 1962; US Cath Conf for Selfish Devotion to Resettlement of Indo-Chinese Refugees, 1975-77; W/W in S & SE; DIB.

WHITE, MARGARET ELIZABETH oc/Insurance Agent; b/Dec 23, 1920; h/ 4305 Pensacola Court, Dallas, TX 75211; ba/Dallas, TX; m/Femme Sole; p/Russel Worley White (dec); Margaret McGaha White, Dallas, TX; ed/Dipl, Metro Bus Col, 1940; Cert of Achmt, Dallas Col of So Meth Univ, 1955, 1956; Cert of Achmt, El Centro Commun Col, 1973; pa/Secy-Ins Solicitor, Cairns-Blakeley & Co, Dallas, TX, 1959-62; Ins Agt, Asst to Pres, Gen Aviation Underwriting Corp, Dallas, TX, 1936-64; Sole Owner & Agt, Fire & Casualty/Personal, Margaret E White Ins Co, 1964-; Ofcr Mgr, Asa Hunt Inc, Dallas, TX, 1978-82; Mem: Pres, SW BPW Clbs, 1977-78; Chm Hallmark Art Contest, Dallas Fdn of Wom's Clbs, 1970-71; Former Mem: Zeta Gamma Chi; Beta Sigma Phi; Dallas Assn of Ins Wom; cp/Pres, Wom's C of C, Dallas, 1967-68; Spec Advr, Dallas Public Lib Lrng Prog, "Remembering and Writing," 1980; Dallas Comm on Status of Wom, 1979; VPres, Cliff Hills Repub Wom's Clb, 1979; Charter Mem, Kessler Pk Repub Wom's Clb,1983; Oak Cliff Soc of Fine Arts; Oak Cliff C of C, Dallas; Meth Hosps of Dallas "Lifeline"; Dallas Coun on World Affairs Wom's Grp; Sponsor, Lone Star Coun of Camp Fire Girls Inc, Dallas, 1981; r/ Meth; hon/Wom of Yr, SW BPW Clb, Dallas, 1978; W/W of Am Wom.

WHITE, ROBERT EDWARD oc/ Manager & Supervisor; b/Nov 27, 1928; h/7614 Southwest 7th Place, North Lauderdale, FL 33068; ba/Ft Lauderdale, FL; m/Betty Lucille Tice; c/Walter Reed, Robert E; p/Francis Wheaton White (dec); Katherine Rankin Rowton White Smith, N Lauderdale, FL; sp/Glen Aldrich and Ethel Lawrence Rumery Tice (dec); ed/USAF Sr NCO Acad, 1960; Courses in Mgmt & Elects, Dept of Def; Radio Communs Technol, Commun Col of the AF, l977; Minicomputer & Microprocessor Technol, Capitol Radio Engrg Inst, 1982; mil/ USAF, 1946-77, Ret'd Chief Master Sgt; pa/Var Positions as Elects Tech & Shop Supvr 1946-56, Sr Tech Advr Directorate of Sys Eval, HQ's of AF Communs Ser 1966-77, USAF; Sr Engr, Harris

Corp R F Commun Div, Rochester, NY, 1977-78; Mgr/Supvr, OKI Elects of Am Inc, 1978-; Mem: IEEE, 1977-; Armed Forces Communs & Elects Assn, 1976-; VFW, 1979-; AF Sgts Assn, 1974-; NCO Assn, 1977-; cp/Treas, Palm Bch Soc of Am Inventors, 1982; r/Prot; hon/Patent: Co-Inventor "Improvements in & Relating to Teleprinter Apparatus"; Bronze Star Medal, 1972; Meritorious Ser Medal w OLC, 1972, 1977; W/W: in S & SW, in Aviation & Aerospace.

WHITEHAIR, CHESTER LOUIS oc/ Aerospace Engineering Executive; b/Jan 28, 1936; h/8681 Shannon River Circle, Fountain Valley, CA 92708; ba/El Segundo, CA; m/Mary Kathryn Horsney; c/Anne Michele, Robert Scott; p/ Berry Morgan Whitehair, St Petersberg, FL; Margaret Beatrice (Fairfax) Whitehair, San Leandro, CA; sp/ Andrew Jr and Anna Teresa (Stydahar) Horsney; ed/BS Aeronaut Engrg, Univ of WV-Morgantown, 1959; Addit Engrg & Mgmt Study: Univ of CA-LA, Pepperdine Univ, The Aerospace Corp; mil/ USMCR, E4, 1956-62; pa/Mech Designer, Whitehair's Machine Shop, Clarksburg, WV, 1956-59; Instr Aircraft Detail Design, WV Univ-Morgantown, 1958-59; Missile Propulson Design Engr (Thor, Sky Bolt & Nike Zeus), Douglas Aircraft Co, Santa Monica, CA, 1959-62; Designer 1st Semi-submerged Solid Rocket Nozzle for Skybolt, 1960; Chief Design Engr Metals Div, SuperTemp Corp, Santa Fe Springs, CA, 1962-63; Var Tech & Mgmt Positions, Space Launch Vehicles, The Aerospace Corp 1963-78, Prin Dir of Intertial Upper Stage 1978-, El Segundo, CA; Advr, USAF Space Div on Titan III Space Launch Vehicle, 1963-73 & Space Shuttle Inertial Upper Stage 1973-; Mem: AIAA, 1959-; AF Assn, 1984; cp/Repub; r/Rom Cath; hon/ Author of The Aerospace Corp Report "Titan IIIC SSLV-5 # 12 Payload Fairing Failure Report," 1969; Lucy Bailey S'ship, 1954; Am Legion Student Ldrship Awd, 1954; Inst of Aeronaut Scis Best Student Paper Awd, 1959; USAF Sys Command Outstg Achmt Awd, 1966; USAF Commend Lttrs, 1975, 1978, 1980, 1981 & 1982; W/W: in W, in Aviation & Aerospace.

WHITELEY, MARILYNN MAXWELL oc/Educator; b/Apr 17, 1929; h/ 971 Linden Hall Road, Chattanooga, TN 37415; ba/Chattanooga, TN; m/William K Whitley (dec); c/Margaret K, Janet W Sullivan, Kenneth M; p/M W Maxwell, Greenville, NC; Thelma M Maxwell (dec); sp/Kenneth F Whiteley (dec); Jean E Whiteley, Greenville, NC; ed/BS, E Carolina Univ, 1949; MEd 1975, EdD 1981, Univ of TN; pa/Tchr, S Edgecombe HS, Tarboro, NC,1949-51; Tchr, Chattanooga & Hamilton Co Schs, 1966-74; Rdg Spec in Fed Progs, Chattanooga Public Schs, 1974-; Adj Prof in Curric & Instrn, Univ of TN-Chattanooga, 1980-; Mem: Phi Delta Kappa; Delta Kappa Gamma; IRA; NCTE; Assn for Supvn & Curric Devel; AAUW; U Tchg Prof; r/Meth; hon/ Author, "A Semantic Description of Selected 1st Grade Basal Rdg Textbooks Using Case Grammar," 1981; Alpha Chapt S'ship, Delta Kappa Gamma, 1975; Sabbatical Leave, 1978-79; W/W: in S & SW, in Chattanooga.

WHITEMAN, BETTY B oc/Retired

Teacher, Museum Attendant; b/Jun 2, 1914; h/Box 218 Richey, MT 59259; m/ George D (dec); c/Dewey Dean, Peggy Louise W Ganzeveld, Sharon Elizabeth W Canfield, Janice K W Louser; ed/ Grad, St Normal Sch, 1937; Elem Life Cert, 1942; BS, Wn MT Col, 1976; pa/ Tchr, Richland & Dawson Cos, MT, 1933-42 & 1955-57; Tchr, Richey Elem Sch, 1950-54 & 1957-78; Collector of Info & Photos of Area Homesteaders for, Mus Archives, Richey; cp/ Secy-Treas, Richey Hist Soc, 1970-84; Treas, Richey Hlth Ctr, 1975-79; VPres, Richey Sr Citizens, 1980-84; Chaplain 1978-80, VPres 1980-83, Am Legion Aux; Secy, U Meth Ch, 1981-84; r/ Meth; hon/Author, Honyacker's Heritage-A Hist of Richey, MT, 1981; Richey's Outstg Citizen, 1974-75; Runner-up 1979, Cand 1980, (DIANA) Dist'd Intl Acad of Noble Achmt; W/W: of Wom, of Intells.

WHITFIELD, BRIAN THOMAS oc/ Chiropractor; b/Jul 9, 1952; h/13 Chapel Hill Drive, Plymouth, MA 02360; ba/ Plymouth, MA; p/Frederick Arthur Whitfield, Eufaula, OK; Phyllis Inez Whitfield, San Diego, CA; ed/BS, 1981; Doct of Chiro, 1981; pa/Section Player, Fresno Philharm, 1974-78; Doct of Chiro, 1981-; Mem: Linus Pauling Inst, 1979-; MA Chiro Soc, 1982; Am Chiro Assn, 1982; cp/Class Pres 1978-81; Delta Tau Alpha, 1979-81; Pres 1981, Mem 1978-81, Toastmaster Intl; Plymouth C of C, 1982; r/Christian; hon/ Band Am Awd in Art, 1970; Class Pres Plaque, 1981; Outstg Student Awd, 1981; Clin Lecture Series, 1981; W/W: Among Am HS Students, Among Am Cols & Univs.

WHITLEY, ONA RUTH oc/Retired Emeritus Bacteriologist; b/Dec 6, 1898; h/1000 East Franklin Street, Monroe, NC 28110; p/Amis David N and Elizabeth (Belle) Whitley (dec); ed/BA, Queens Col, 1920; AB 1924, Postgrad Study in Botany 1926-27, Univ of NC-Chapel Hill; MSc, Sch of Hygiene & Public Hlth, Johns Hopkins Univ, 1934; pa/HS Sci Tchr, 1920-23; Hd Sci Dept, Chapel Hill HS, 1924-29; Botany & Biol Instr, Univ of NC-Chapel Hill, Sums 1924-27; Asst Bacteriologist, Cultural Lab, MD St Dept of Hlth, 1930-36; Assoc Bacteriologist & Bacteriologist-in-charge, St Br Lab, Hagerstown, MD, 1936-39; Sr Bacteriologist & Mycologist, Montgomery, AL, 1942-46; Sr Bacteriologist & Mycologist, Dir of Diphtheria & Mycology Labs, IN St Bd of Hlth, Indianapolis, IN, 1946-61; Mem: Secy & Treas IN Br 1952-54, Soc of Am Bacteriologists; NY Acad of Sci; AAAS; APHA; Fellow, Royal Soc of Hlth; cp/Wom's Rotary Clb of Indianapolis; hon/Author of Var Articles Pub'd in Profl Jours Incl'g: Jour of Sab & Clin Med, 1934 & 1935; Am Jour of Hygiene, 1936; Public Hlth Reports, 1949; Gold Medal in NC St Spelling Contest, Davidson Col, 1916; Rep Queen's Col, at Inauguration of Russel J Humbert as Pres of DePauw Univ, Greencastle, IN, 1952; Cit, IN St Bd of Hlth, 1961; Rep Univ of NC-Chapel Hill, at Inauguration of Thomas E Corts as Pres of Wingate Col, 1974; Outstg Alumna Awd, Queen's Col, 1975; Hon Fellow, Anglo-Am Acad of Cambridge, England, 1980; W/W: in S & SW, in MW, of Am Wom, of Intells; Ldrs in Am Sci;

NC Lives; DIB; Notable Ams of Bicent Era; Men & Wom of Distn; Num Other Biogl Listings.

WHITLOCK, RUTH H S oc/Professor, Choral Music Educator; b/May 10, 1934; h/2712 6th Avenue, Fort Worth, TX 76110; ba/Ft Worth, TX; m/Robert Edward; c/Karen W Williams, Robert Edward III, Harold McIntosh Summers; p/Harold G Hendricks (dec); Lucile McKee Hendricks, McAllen, TX; sp/R E Whitlock (dec); Mrs R E Whitlock, Austin, TX; ed/BA, Newcomb Col of Tulane Univ, 1955; MA, Occidental Col, 1970; PhD, N TX St Univ, 1981; pa/TX Choral Music Tchr: Georgetown ISD, 1955-58; Austin ISD, 1958-59; Edinburg Co ISD, 1959-67; McAllen ISD, 1970-72; Carrollton-Farmers Br ISD 1972-73; Assoc Prof Choral Music Ed, N TX St Univ, 1973-; Mem: Kappa Alpha Theta; Music Edrs Nat Conf; TX Music Edrs Conf; TX Music Edrs Assn; Am Choral Dirs Assn; TX Choral Dirs Assn; Mu Phi Epsilon; r/Epis; hon/ Author, *Choral Insights* Gen Edition & Renaissance Edition, 1982; Var Articles Pub'd in Profl Jours; Theodore Presser S'ship, 1953; Alpha Sigma Sigma, 1953; Outstg Fac Awd, 1980; Mu Phi Epsilon Doct Grant, 1980; Pi Kappa Lambda, 1979; W/W: in Am Univs & Cols, in Am, in Music; TX Wom of Distn.

WHITNEY, MYRNA-LYNNE oc/ Integrated Logistics Support Engineer; ba/Canoga Park, CA; m/Richard Abbott; p/Edmund and Sylvia Prasloski, Ventura, CA; ed/BA, CA St Univ-Northridge, 1971; MS, Ctl MO St Univ, 1975; mil/USAF, 1971-74; USAFR, Maj, 1975-; pa/Secy 1962-69, Methods & Procedures Analyst 1976-77, Envir Hlth & Safety Engr 1977-79, Sys Safety Engr 1979-81, Integrated Logistics Support Engr 1981-, Rocketdyne, Rockwell Intl, Canoga Pk, CA; Mem: Am Soc of Safety Engrs; Sys Safety Soc; Phi Kappa Phi; Resv Ofcrs Assn; r/Rel Sci; hon/Meritorous Ser Medal, USAF, 1974; 1st OLC to Meritorious Ser Medal, 1984; W/W: in W, in Am.

WHITNEY, VIRGINIA K oc/Educator; b/Feb 6, 1927; h/502 Orchard St, Aztec, NM 87410; c/Barbara Peterson, James Thomas; p/Clare V Koogler, Aztec, NM; ed/BS 1959, MEd 1965, Adams St Col; pa/Sci Tchr 1959-62, Libn 1962-, K Jr HS, Aztec, NM; Mem: Pres, NM Sch Libns, 1972-73; Pres, NM Media Assn, 1982-; NM St Legis Com, NEA, 1973-79; St Pres, Kappa Kappa Iota Ednl Sorority, 1962-65; cp/St Ctl Com 4 Yrs, Del to Nat Conv 1984, Repub Party; Pres, San Juan Co Repub Wom, 1984; r/Meth; hon/Author, *Wom in Ed in NM*, 1977; *Koogler Fam of VA*, 1969; Westinghouse Sci S'ship, 1944; Fellow, NM Acad of Sci, 1973; Delta Kappa Gamma St Awd, 1982; W/W: of Am Wom, in Polits; DIB; Other Biogl Listings.

WHITTEMORE, EDWARD WILLIAM oc/Executive; b/Dec 25, 1922; h/ 22 Flying Cloud Road, Dolphin Cove, Stamford, CT 06092; ba/New York, NY; m/Jeanne McConnochie; c/Edward William Jr, Jeannette L; p/Harold Clifton Whittemore (dec); Florence Veronica (Stratton) Whitemore; ed/BA, Columbia Col, Columbia Univ, 1947; mil/ USAF, 1943-45; pa/Var Positions 1947-72, Exec VPres 1970-72, Wilson

Jones Co, Chgo; Exec VPres 1972-75, Pres & COO 1975-77, Pres & CEO 1977-78, Swingline Inc, NYC; Dir 1977-, VPres Sub Adm 1978-79, Exec VPres Opers 1979-80, Chm & CEO 1981-, Am Brands Inc, NYC; Mem: Chm Res Com 1968-70, VPres & Chm Mfrs Div 1969-70, Nat Ofc Prods Assn; Dir, Wholesale Stationers Assn, 1970-72; Pres, Bus Records Mfrs Assn, 1971-72; cp/Exec Com, The Pres's Pvt Sector Survey on Cost Control, 1982-; VChm Bd of Visitors, Columbia Col; Columbia Univ; Dir & Chm of Exec & Fin Coms, Police Ath Leag Inc; The Ec Clb of NY; NY Yacht Clb; hon/Patentee, Binder & Compression Mechanism; John Jay Awd for Dist'd Profl Achmt, Columbia Col, Columbia Univ, 1982; W/ W: in Am, in Fin & Indust; Other Biogl Listings.

WHITTINGTON, MARGARET ANN oc/Executive; b/Aug 3, 1948; h/ 14972 Paddock Street, Sylmar CA 91342; ba/Valencia, CA; m/Edward A Wagner; p/David Kelsey Whittington, Gibsonia, PA; sp/Ruth M Wagner Bridgeville, PA; ed/Att'd Blackburn Col, 1967-68; Att'd Communn Col of Allegheny Co, 1971-72; pa/Student Employmnt Coor, Carnegie-Mellon Univ, Pgh, PA, 1975-77; Admissions Asst, CA Inst of Arts, Valencia, CA, 1977-80; Adm Mgr, G W Smith & Assocs Inc, Valencia, CA, 1980-82; Exec VPres & Controller, US Fin Conslts Inc, Valencia, CA, 1983-; Mem: Trustee on Bd of Trustees, CA Inst of Arts, 1978-79, 1979-80; VPres, SCV Career Wom's Netwk, 1983-84; NOW, 1973-; r/Presb; hon/Spec Cert, Grad Sch of Photog, CA Inst of Arts, 1979; Spec Recog/Student Coun, CA Inst of Arts, 1980; W/W: in CA, in W.

WICKWIRE, PATRICIA JOANNE NELLOR oc/Consultant; h/2900 Amby Place, Hermosa Bch, CA 90254; ba/ Same; m/Robert James; c/William James; p/William McKinley Nellor (dec); Clara Pautsch Nelor, Charter Oak, IA; ed/BA, Univ of No IA, 1951; MA, Univ of IA, 1959; PhD, Univ of TX-Austin, 1971; Addit Grad Studies; pa/Tchr, Ricketts ISD, IA, 1946-48; Tchr & Cnslr, Waverly-Shell Rock ISD, IA, 1951-55; Rdg Conslt, Hd Dorm Cnslr, Univ of IA, 1955-57; Tchr, Sch Psychol, Coor of Psychol Sers, Dir of Student Sers & Spec Ed, S Bay Union HS Dist, CA, 1962-82; Lectr, Loyola-Marrymount Univ, CA, 1980-; Conslt, CA St Dept of Ed; Indep Const in Mgmt & Ed; Mem: Pres, Exec Bd, CA Assn for Measurement & Eval in Guid, 1981-; Exec Bd, CA Assn of Sch Psychols, 1981-83; Exec Bd, Assn of CA Sch Admrs, 1977-81; Exec Bd, CA Pers & Guid Assn, 1977-78; Pres, LA Co Admrs of Pupil Sers, 1974-79; Pres, Exec Bd, LA Co Pers & Guid Assn, 1977-80; Pres, LA Co SW Admrs of Spec Ed, 1976-81; CA Exec Bd, AAUW, 1965-70; Chm of Bd, CA St Univ-Dominguez Hills, 1981-; Exec Bd, CA Interagy Mtl Hlth Coun, 1968-72; World Future Soc; Nat Assn of Female Execs; Am Psychol Assn; Am Pers & Guid Assn; Am Assn of Sch Admrs; Am Assn for Measurement & Eval in Guid; cp/Exec Bd, VPres, Bd Cities Symph Assn, 1970-82; r/Luth; hon/Author, *The Acad Achmt & Lang Devel of Am Chd of Latin Heritage*, 1971; Contbr, Num Articles to Profl Jours, Mags &

Newspapers; Achmt Awd in Jour, 1950; Achmt Awd in Eng, 1951; S Bay Wom of Yr, 1978; Pi Lambda Theta; Psi Chi; Sigma Alpha Iota; Kappa Delta Pi; Alpha Phi Gamma; W/W: in CA, in W, of Am Wom, Among Sch Dist Ofcls; DIB; Other Biogl Listings.

WIDISS, ALAN I oc/Lawyer, Educator; b/Sep 28, 1938; h/316 Kimball Road, Iowa City, IA 52240; ba/Iowa City, IA; m/Ellen Louise Magaziner; c/Benjamin L, Deborah Anne, Rebecca Elizabeth; p/ Al and Rose H (Sobole) Widiss; ed/BS 1960, LLB 1963, Univ of So CA; LLM, Harvard Univ, 1964; Admitted to CA Bar, 1963; pa/Tchg Fellow, Harvard Univ, 1964-65; Asst Prof Law 1965-68, Assoc Prof 1968-69, Prof 1969-78, Joseph R Witte Prof 1978-, Univ of IA; Vis'g Prof, Univ of So CA & Univ of San Diego; Dir, CLRS Mass No-Fault Auto Ins Study, 1971-76; Trustee, Univ of IA Sch of Rel, 1976-; Chm, Johnson Co Citizens Advy Com for Reg Trans Study, 1971-75; Mem: ABA; CA Bar Assn; Am Law Inst; Am Assn of Law Schs; Order of Coif; Phi Kappa Phi; Delta Sigma Rho; hon/Author, Editor (w Others), *Arbitration: Comml Disputes, Ins & Tort Claims*, 1979; *No-Fault Auto Ins in Action: The Experiences in MA, IL, DE & NY*, 1977; *A Guide to Uninsured Motorist Coverage*, 1969; *Uninsured & Underinsured Motorist Ins, Volume I*, 1984; Contbr, Num Articles to Law Jours; W/W in World.

WIEGLER, BARRY ALLAN oc/Consulting Firm Executive; b/Jun 17, 1938; h/6162 Pat Avenue, Woodland Hills, CA 91367; ba/Santa Monica, CA; m/ Deanna; c/Laurie, David, Michael, Lisa, Shera; p/Paul Wiegler (dec); Marie Wiegler, LA, CA; sp/Mr and Mrs Robert Hamilton, Pilot Rock, OR; ed/Att'd Santa Monica Col, 1956-59; BBA, Woodbury Univ, 1965; MBA, CA St Univ-LA, 1967; mil/USAFR, 1956-65; pa/Assoc VPres, Security Pacific Nat Bk, LA, CA, 1961-69; Mgr Fin Indust Planning, Gen Elect Computer Div, Phoenix, AZ, 1969-71; Dir Res & Planning, MSI Dat Corp, Costa Mesa CA, 1971-72; VPres in SF1973-80, VPres in LA 1980-81, Sr VPres 1981-82, Gottfried Conslts Inc, CA; Pres, Bd of Dirs & Co-Fdr, Key Conslts Grp Inc, Santa Monica, CA, 1983-; Mem: Trustee & Chm of Bd, EDP Steering Com; Ofc Automation Advy Com, Woodbury Univ, LA; cp/Rotary Clb of SF; r/Jewish; hon/Phi Gamma Kappa, 1964; Ctl Data Processor, 1965; Jr Col Tchg Credential, 1965; W/W: in CA, in W.

WIEMANN, MARION R JR oc/Biologist and Microscopist; b/Sept 7, 1929; h/PO Box E, Chesterton, IN 46304; ba/ Chesterton, IN; c/Tamara Lee; p/Marion R and Verda Peek Wiemann Sr, Chesterton, IN; ed/BS, IN Univ, 1959; Course Completion Certs 1967, 1968, 1970, 1971, Formal Tng Microscopy, McCrone Res Inst, Chgo, IL; AN(P), Na Tech Tng Ctr, Jacksonville, FL, 1952; AD "A", Na Tech Tng Ctr, Memphis, TN, 1952; mil/USN, 1951-53; pa/ Histo-Res Tech 1959, Res Asst 1959-62, Res Tech 1962-64, Res Tech 1965-67, Sr Res Tech 1967-70, Res Technol 1970-79, Univ Chgo; Sci Tchr, Westchester Twp Sch, Chesterton, IN, 1964-66; Prin, Marion Wieman & Assocs, Consltg, Res & Devel, Chesterton, IN, 1979-; Mem: VPres 1969-70, Pres 1970-71, St Microscopal Soc of IL;

AAAS, 1983-; Intl Platform Assn, 1983-; Life Mem, Field Mus of Natural Hist, 1967-; Other Sci Socs; cp/Former Commr, BSA; Life Mem, ABIRA, 1983-; hon/Contbr, Num Articles to Profl Jours Incl'g: *Am Biol Tchr; Jour Dental Res, Jour Periodontol; Oral Med; Oral Pathol; The Microscope*; Photomicrographs Pub'd in *Ency Britanica; TransVision Atlas of Hlth; Sci Yr; World Book Sci Annual*; Num Others; Scouters Key 1968, Arrowhead Hon 1968, BSA; Awd of Merit, Soc for Tech Commun, 1973; Dist'd Tech Communr, 1974; S'ships, McCrone Res Inst, 1968; Dean's Hon List, High Scholastic Achmt, 1952, 1956; Fellow, Royal Microscopical Soc, 1971; Nat Advr, ABIRA, 1982-; Cit, Marquis W/W, 1981; W/W in MW; Awd of Merit, ABI, 1982; Dedication of Intl Book of Hon, 1983; Notable Am Awd, 1983; Cert of Merit, Intl Biogl Ctr, 1983; Commun Ldrs of World; W/W of Intell; Dir of Dist'd Ams; World Biogl Hall of Fame; Num Other Biogl Listings.

WIER, RAYMOND DAVID JR oc/ Certified Public Accountant; b/Aug 25, 1947; h/1449 Richland, Abilene, TX 79603; ba/Abilene, TX; m/Cindy Harrison Wier; c/John Matthew, Jordan Leigh; p/Mr and Mrs Raymond D Wier, Odessa, TX; sp/Mr and Mrs Earl P Harrison, Abilene, TX; ed/BA, Baylor Univ, 1969; MS, Abilene Christian Univ, 1979; mil/USAF, 1969-81, Capt; pa/Intell Ofcr 1969-73, Navigator C130 1973-81, USAF; CPA Budget & Forecasting Acct, W TX Utilites Co, Abilene, TX, 1982-; Mem: Am Inst of CPA's; TX Soc of CPA's; Nat Assn of Accts; Soc of Petro Accts; cp/Kiwanis; r/Bapt; hon/ AF Commend Medal for Combat is SE Asia, 1973; God & Country Awd, BSA, 1964.

WIEWIOROWSKI, EDWARD IGNACY oc/Chemical Engineer; b/May 10, 1931; h/3620 Rue Andree, New Orleans, LA 70114; ba/Braithwaite, LA; m/Irena Sobolewska; c/Martin Charles, Maria Gertruda; p/Karol Ignacy and Gertruda (Pluszkiewicz) Wiewicrowski (dec); sp/Franciszek Sobolewska (dec); Maria (Urbanek) Sobolewska; ed/ BSChE, MSChE 1956, PhD Chem Engrg 1965, Gdansk Inst of Technol, Poland; pa/Asstship 1954-63, Fac Mem 1963-72, Gdansk Inst of Technol, Gdansk, Poland; Pvt Pract in Chem Engrg & Conslitg, Gdansk & Warsaw Poland, 1964-72; Sr Res & Dev Engr, Amax Nickel, Braithwaite, LA, 1973-; Mem: Lic'd Profl Engr, LA, 1980; Nat Soc of Profl Engrs; LA Engrg Soc; Am Inst of Metal Engrs; Am Chem Soc; AIChE; Polish Chem Soc; Assn Engrg Polish Chem Indust; r/Cath; hon/ Author, 50 Papers Pub'd in Profl Jours; US & Europe Patents in Field of Chem Engrg & Hydrometallurgy; Naturalized Citizen, 1978; W/W in S & SW.

WIGGINS-JONES, KATHLYN YVETTE oc/Communications Systems Representative; b/Dec 16, 1950; h/22 University, Buffalo, NY 14214; ba/ Buffalo, NY; m/Young B Jones; c/ Anayet; p/Mack C Sr and Texana R Wiggins, Memphis, TN; sp/Willis Jones, Lake Providence, LA; Katie Howard (dec); ed/BS, 1972; MS, 1974; Doct Cand; pa/Communs Sys Rep 1981-, Mktg Adm 1977-81, Commun Conslt 1974-77, NY Telephone Co; Mem: Am Mktg Assn; Curric Devel & Instrnl

Media Clb; Nat Assn of Female Execs; Exec Urban Leag; NAACP; Alpha Kappa Alpha; r/Bapt; hon/Author, *Telecommuns Info for the Blind & Visually Impaired*, 1981; Video: "Intro to Bell Mktg Dept," 1981; W/W of Am Wom.

WIGLEY, JEAN M oc/Homemaker, Volunteer, Fiber Artist; b/Apr 4, 1931; h/5735 Westbrook Road, Minneapolis, MN 55422; m/Robert J; c/Michael, Thomas, Kristin (dec); p/K O Christianson (dec); Marian Christianson, Decorah, IA; sp/M R Wigley (dec); Myrtle Wigles, Mpls, MN; ed/Att'd Mankata St, 1949-51; Grad in Related Art, Univ of MN, 1967; pa/ Self-employed Fiber Artist & Tchr, Vol, Currently; Home Economist, Pillsbury Co, 196-68; Ofc Mgr, Water Prods Co; Mem: Pres Bd of Dirs 1981-83, Bd of Dirs 1978-84, Mem Num Coms, Mmpls Area YWCA; Pres Ch Coun 1983, VPres 1980-82, Calvary Luth Ch of Golden Val; Nat Trainer, YWCA; Secy & one of Fdrs, Twin City Chapt, The Compassionate Friends (A Support Grp for Bereaved Parents); Vol Trainer, "I Can" Trainer (a Nat Interagy Collaboration for Vol Devel; Funding Com, Vols for MN; Past Pres, PEO Chapt DJ; cp/Mem Num Arts & Wom's Orgs; r/Luth.

WILBER, DONALD BLAINE oc/ Minister/Pastoral Counselor; b/Oct 5, 1952; h/1006 Burgundy Place, Prosser, WA 99530; ba/Prosser, WA; m/Janet M; c/Eric, Charles, Ty; p/M Blaine and S June Wilber, Ontario, OR; sp/Lester and Mary Scott, Ontario, OR; ed/BA, NW Nazarene Col, 1976; MA Cnslg, Col of ID, 1980; PhD Cnslg Psych, Columbia Pacific Univ, 1982; pa/Min & Pastoral Cnslr, Ch of Nazarene, Harper, OR, 1976-79; Yth Min & Cnslr, Ontario, OR, 1975-76; Min & Pastoral Cnslr Coun, ID, 1979-80; Hlth Crisis Cnslr Intern, Mtn States Tumor Inst, Boise, ID, 1980; Pvt Pract Cnslg, Ontario, OR, 1980-82; Min/Pastoral Cnslr in Pvt Pract, Prosser, WA, 1982-; Mem: Christian Assn of Psychol Studies; Am Orthopsychi Assn; Am Assn of Cnslg & Devel; Am Mtl Hlth Cnslrs Assn; VPres, Coun Min Assn, 1979; Prosser Min Assn; r/Nazarene; hon/Author, Var "Insight" Column Articles for Local Newspaper; Ordained Min, 1978; W/W in W.

WILDER, LISA FAYE oc/Certified Public Accountant; b/Aug 18, 1956; ba/ Blytheville, AR; c/Misty L Eubanks; p/ John Wilder Sr, Kennet, MO; Suzanne Garrett, Nashville, TN; ed/BS Acctg, AR St Univ, 1981; pa/CPA, Sr Acct, Block, Kelly & Co, Currently; Jr Acct, Robert Stiles & Co, 1981; Mem: AICPA; ASCPA; AWSCPA; r/Meth; hon/Dean's List, AR St Univ; NHS, Kennet HS; Cert of Recog, Univ of MO.

WILDMAN, SUZANNE BLAN-CHARD oc/Composer, Educator; b/Jan 4, 1940; h/27 Pine Street, Manchester, MA 01944; ba/Manchester, MA; c/ Helen LeRoy, Ben H II; p/Helen L Pirnie, Manchester, MA; ed/AB Classics, Stanford Univ, 1958; AB, SF Conservatory of Music, 1957; Att'd Am Sch of Music, Fontainbleau, France, 1965; pa/Tchr of Elem Piano, SF Conservatory, 1963-64; Pt-time Sales Clk, Macy's, SF, CA; Inventory Taker, The Emporium; Mem: Leag of Wom Voters of SF; Met Opera Raffle; UNICEF; Am Security Coun; Stanford Univ Alumni Assn; Repub

Town Com, Manchester, MA; Foster Parent "Happy Child" Taiwan, 1975-81; cp/Pebble Bch Clb, Carmel, CA; Bath & Tennis Clb, Manchester, MA; Revolutionary Ridge Book Clb, Concord, MA; Advry Mem, Marquis Biogl Lib Soc; r/Christian Sci; hon/Music Compositions Incl: "Preludes 1 & 2" Perf'd at Palace to Legion of Hon, SF, 1961; "Prelude 3 & Fugue" Perf'd at Temple Emmanuel, SF, 1961; "The Gov Proposes," 1962; "5 Christmas Duets for Tchr & Beginner," 1968.

WILDS, BOBBY oc/Branch Director of Club; b/Sep 22, 1947; h/2509 Pine Street, Tampa, FL 33607; ba/Tampa, FL; c/Darrolyn, Michelle, Bobby Jr; p/Jettie B and Minnie Wilds, Tampa, FL; ed/ Att'd FL A&M Univ, 1966-68; Addit Tng; mil/AUS, 1968-70, Supply Sgt; pa/ Tng & Job Experience Spec, Tampa Concentrated Employmnt Prog (TECEP), 1970-71; Pre-Trial Spec & Cnslr, A L Nellum & Assocs, 1971-72; Job Develr, Human Resources Devel Prog, 1972-74; Job Develr/Cnslr 1974-75, Chief Cnslr Ctl Intake 1975, Prog Dir Chemotreatment Ctr 1975, Drug Abuse Comprehensive Coor'g Ofc (DACCO); Investigator, Ofc of Public Defender Hillsborough Co, 1975-78; Dir Jose Llaneza Br, Boys & Gils Clb of Gtr Tampa, 1978-; Mem: Cert'd Instr, Am Coaching Effectiveness Prog, 1982; Cert'd Instr, Nat Yth Sports Coaching Assn, 1983; cp/Football Coach, Police Ath Leag, 6 Yrs; Ath Dir, Tampa Eagles Football Inc, 8 Yrs; Cert'd Notary Public, 19 Yrs; Proj Ldr, FL Dem Party, 1974; Dept Supvr Election Ofc, Hills Co, 1974; Treas, Police Advy Com, 1975; Tampa JC's, 1977; Asst Varsity Football Coach, Tampa Bay Tech, 1980; Num Spkg Presentations; hon/Tampa Bay Blacks Most Influential, 1983; Coach of Yr, Ath Dir of Yr, Tampa Eagles; Coach of Yr, PAL; Awd for Devel of Black Talent, Tampa Urban Leag; Awd for Ser to Commun in Yth Football, Tampa Golf Clb; Awd for Dedication, Tampa Eagles; Awd for Ser on Oratorical Contest, Optimist Clb of Ybor City; Ser Awd, HRS, 1982; Ser Awd, Belmont Hgts Little Leag Nat Champs, 1981; Ser Awd, Coop Ed Clb, Robinson HS, 1980; Cert of Apprec for Outstg Ser, 5th Annual KY Sch of Alcohol Studies; Citizen of Day, Citizens Fed Savs & Ln Assn & WPLP/Talk Radio 57.

WILES, MICHAEL ROBERT oc/ Chiropractic Educator; b/Feb 15, 1951; h/Rural Route 1, Locust Hill, Ontario, Canada L0H1JU; ba/Toronto, Ontario, Canada; m/Janice Isobel; c/Timothy Matthew; ed/Doct of Chiro, CMCC, 1976; BSc, Univ of Toronto, 1979; Med, Brock Univ, 1983; pa/Asst Dean 1982-, Chm Dept of Chiro Sci 1978-, Resident Chiro Sci 1976-78, CMCC; Assoc Editor, *Jour of Canadian Chiro Assn*, 1978-83; Mem: Am Chiro Assn; Canadian Chiro Assn; AAHM; hon/Author, Num Profl Papers, Edits & Lttrs Pub'd in *Jour of CCA, Jour of MPT* & Other Profl Jours; Jack Nosle Prize (Highest Acad Standing in Med Class), Brock Univ, 1983; W/W: in Chiro, in Commonwlth; Intl Book of Hon.

WILHELM, WILLA METTA oc/ Retired Educator; b/Sep 10, 1912; h/ 85501 Jasper Pk Road, Pleasant Hill, OR 97455; m/George A; c/Daren Lyle (dec);

p/Charles and Margaret Logsdon (dec); sp/George and Amelia Wilhelm, Junction City, OR; ed/BS 1933, MEd 1941, Univ of OR; pa/Jr HS Instr, Sprague River, OR, 1934-35; Instr, Canyonville HS, OR, 1935-37; Instr, Junction City HS, OR, 1937-41; Bus Ofc, Corvair Corp, San Diego, CA, 1942-45; Instr 1945-46, Supt 1946-47, Riddle HS, OR; Instr 1947-61, Media Spec 1961-77, Lowell HS, OR; r/Cath; hon/Recip Int 1st Place Awd, Lowell HS Newspaper Broadcaster; Quill & Scroll Awds, 1948-49, 1949-50; Personalities of W & MW; Commun Ldrs of World.

WILKINS, ROBERT MASON oc/Physician, Rancher; b/Apr 18, 1937; h/Route 4, Dry Lake Road, Nampa, ID 83651; ba/Nampa, ID; m/Gloria (Jaci); c/Robert Bruce, Marguerite Davis; p/Robert Bruce Wilkins (dec); Marguerit Edwards, Durham, NC; sp/Mr and Mrs Frederick Heil (dec); ed/AB Eng, Univ of NC, 1959; MD, Bowman-Gray Sch of Med, Wake Forest Univ, 1963; Intern, Univ of CO, 1963-64; F'ship in Gastroenterology 1964-65, Resident in Med 1977-78, Duke Univ Med Ctr; mil/USN, 1965-67; pa/Pvt Pract Gastroenterology, Durham, NC, 1969, 1972; Conslt Gastroenterologist, VA Hosp, Fayetteville, NC, 1969-71; Assoc Commun Hlth Scis, Duke Univ Med Ctr, 1969-72; Pvt Pract Gastroenterology, Med Ctr Phys, PA, Nampa, ID, 1972-; Clin Asst Prof of Med, Univ of WA, Seattle, 1977-; Mem: Fellow, Gov for ID 1984-88, Am Col of Phys; Diplomate, Am Bd of Internal Med; Fellow, Am Col of Gastroenterology; Am Gastroenterology Assn; AMA; So Med Assn; SW Dist ID Med Soc; ID Med Assn; ID Soc of Internal Med; Pres, Wn Sts Angus Assn; Pres, ID Angus Assn; Others; r/Epis; hon/Author, Over 10 Papers Pub'd in Profl Jours & Presented at Assn Meetings; Morehead Scholar, Univ of NC, 1955-59; W/W in W.

WILKINSON, THOMAS LLOYD JR oc/Materials Engineering; b/Dec 14, 1939; h/6908 Park Avenue, Richmond, VA 23226; ba/Richmond, VA; m/Maxine Doyle; c/Margaret Carter, Thomas Douglas; p/Gladys M Wilkinson, Lynchburg, VA; sp/Mr and Mrs M E Doyle, McKinnley, VA; ed/BS, VA Commonwlth Univ, 1963; MC, Univ of Richmond, 1976; pa/Sr Devel Proj Dir 1980-, Proj Dir 1973-80, Sr Devel Engr 1967-73, Devel Engr 1966-67, Test Engr 1963-66, Reynolds Metals Co; Mem: Soc for Advmt of Material & Process Engrg; Adhesives Coun Soc of Mfrg Engrs; VChm Richmond Chapt, Am Soc for Metals; Secy, Am Soc for Testing & Mats Adhesives Com; Modern Plastics Mgmt Advy Coun, 1979-81; cp/Theta Chi; Pres, Duntreath Civic Assn, 1979; Precinct Capt, 1980; r/Presb; hon/Author, 4 Books: Aluminum Assn Booklet T17 "Weldbonding—An Alternative Joining Method for Aluminum Auto Body Alloys", 1978; Aluminum Assn Booklet T14, 1975; Reynolds Metals Co Tech Bltn, 1981; Reynolds Co Tech Handbook, 1966; Over 15 Articles & Papers Pub'd in Profl Jours & Presented at Assn Meetings; W/W in S & SW.

WILKS, JACQUELIN H oc/Counselor; b/Jan 18, 1950; h/Route 3, Shawnee, OK 74801; ba/Shawnee, OK; m/Tom; c/David, Brian; sp/Milton and Bernice Wilks, Bastrop, LA; ed/BS, LA Col,

1972; Att'd So Bapt Theol Sem, 1974; Att'd SE MO St Univ, 1977; MAT, OK City Univ, 1982; Adv'd Reality Therapy Cnslg, OK Univ, 1982; Cnslg Cert, Ctl St Univ, OK, 1982-83; pa/Coor of Student Pers, Gordon Cooper Voc-Tech, Shawnee, OK, 1982-; Dir of Tutorial Prog, Instr 1980-82, Dir of Admissions & Fin Aid 1979-80, OK Bapt Univ, Shawnee, OK; 6th Grade Sci Tchr A D Simpson Sch 1976, 1st Grade Tchr Bertrand Elem Sch 1975, Charleston R-1 Sch Dist, Charleston, MO; Kgn Tchr Doyle Elem Sch 1974, E Prairie R-2 Sch Dist, E Prairie, MO; Eng & Rdg Tchr, Pine Bluff HS, AR, 1972; Secy to VPres Installment Ln Dept, Nat Bk of Commerce, Pine Bluff, AR, 1972; Singer & Spkr in Foun Singers, LA Moral & Civic Foun, Baton Rouge, LA, 1970; Instr, Triple D Guest Ranch, 1969; Secy to Admr, Allen Parish Hosp, Kinder, LA, 1968; cp/Tutor, Prog in Own Home for Chd under Juris of Juv Ct, Jefferson Co, AR; Grp Cnslg Session Ldr, Juv Ct, Jefferson Co, AR; Repub; Mini Basketball Clin, Charleston, MO Girls Basketball Tm; r/Bapt; hon/Superior Sum Student, Hd Cheerldrs, Miss LA Col Finalist, Homecoming Ct, May Ct Finalist, Campus Favorite, LA Col.

WILLIAMS, ANNIE RUTH oc/Executive; b/Dec 24, 1934; h/13068 Sutton, Cerritos, CA 90701; ba/Cerritos, CA; p/Erwin Stevens, Atlanta, GA; Rosie Sturns, Long Beach, CA; ed/BS 1971, MS 1972, Fresno St Univ; MS, CA St Univ-LA, 1976; pa/Pres, Owner, Rehab Mgmt Spec Inc, 1978-; Supvr, Profl Cnslr Inc, 1977-78; Fac/Asst Prof, CA St Univ-LA, 1975-77; Inser Instr, VA Hosp, 1972-75; Asst Prof, Fresno St Univ, 1971-72; Mem: Ed Chp, CARP, 1980-82; Com Chp, CPGA, 1980-82; Ad Hoc Minority Exec Secy, 1974-77; Dir, CA St Retention Prog; Chm, Ethnic Ed Com; r/Prot; hon/Author, Nurses Attitude toward Therapeutic Abortion Patients; Grad magna cum laude, Fresno St Univ, 1972; Best Oratory Awd, HS; W/W: of Am Wom, Among Black Wom in CA.

WILLIAMS, BARBARA ELIZABETH WOMACK oc/Guidence Counselor, Licensed Professional; b/Feb 4, 1938; h/5556 McVitty Road, Roanoke, VA 24018; ba/Roanoke, VA; m/Leon Franklin; c/Mark Franklin, Alice Kathleen, Stephanie Todd; p/William A and Margaret K Womack, Huntsville, AL; sp/Frank and Louise Williams, Callao, VA; ed/BA 1966, MEd 1968, Am Univ; Postgrad Studies, Univ of VA, VA Polytech Inst & St Univ, Radford Univ; pa/Mil & Security Ofc HQs, Redstone Arsenal, Huntsville, AL, 1956-57; In Charge of Maintenance of Fgn Students, US Dept of Agri, Wash DC, 1957-59; Tchr Eng, Humanities & Psychol, Glenvar HS, Roanoke, VA, 1968-72; Guidance Cnslr, Hidden Valley Jr HS, 1972-; Lic'd Profl Cnslr, 1974-; NEA; VA Ed Assn; Secy, VA Assn of Tchrs of Eng; Chm Profl Ser, Roanoke Co Ed Assn; Roanoke Valley Mtl Hlth Assn; Roanoke Area Personnel & Guid Assn; Nat Coun Tchrs of Eng; VA Personnel & Guid Assn; cp/Fdr, Farmingdale Civic Leag; hon/Americanism Awd, Nat Sojourners; Ldrship Awd, Elks Clb; Cited by Secy of Agri for Outstg Ser to Attache Commun; Personalities of S; W/W: Am Wom, S & SW; 2000 Notable Ams; Intl W/W Wom.

WILLIAMS, BETTY C oc/Ranch Owner and Investor; ba/The Triple "W" Ranch, Route 3, Box 260, Lindale, TX 75771; c/Joy Lynne Williams; p/William Purvis Cox (dec); Jewel Lena Hering George, Hawkins, TX; pa/Owner/Mgr, Triple "W" Ranch, near Tyler, TX; Investor in Comml Real Est Incl'g Ofc Bldgs & Land; Dir, Bk of E TX; r/Meth; Mem: Am Mgmt Assn; Nat Assn of Female Execs; cp/Dallas Coun on World Affairs; Les Femmes du Monde, Dallas; Timberlawn Foun, Dallas; Fdg Patron, TX Bus Hall of Fame, Tyler, TX; Holly Tree Country Clb, Tyler; Willow Brook Country Clb, Tyler; Plaza Clb, Tyler; Petro Clb, Tyler; The Listeners Book Clb, Dallas.

WILLIAMS, CHARLES MOLTON oc/Mortgage Banking Executive; b/Jun 21, 1930; h/3924 Royal Oak Drive, Birmingham, AL 35243; ba/Birmingham, AL; m/Hope; c/Charles Molton Jr, John Thomas Hunter, John White, Kate Hope; p/Elliot Tuttle and Gertrude Molton Williams (dec); sp/John M and Kate Hope White, Uniontown, AL; ed/BS, Wash & Lee Univ, 1952; Grad Wk, Univ of AL; mil/AUS, 1952-54; pa/Var Ofcs, Ins VPres 1954-68, Pres & CEO 1968-78, Chm of Bd 1978-, Molton, Allen & Williams Inc; Mem: Bd of Dirs, The Bapt Hosp Foun of Birmingham Inc; Dir, Nat Bk of Commerce, 1980-; Mortgage Bkrs Assn of Am & AL; Past Pres, Mrtgage Bkrs Assn of AL; Yg Pres' Org, 1972-80; Dir Edward Lee Norton Ctr for Cont'g Ed, Birmingham-So Co, 1979-; cp/Pres, Birmingham Fest of Arts Assn, 1979; Bd of Visitors, Montreat-Anderson Col, 1981-; Advy Coun, Salvation Army Home & Hosp, 1978-; Exec Bd Birmingham Area Coun, BSA, 1979-; Dir, Birmingham Boys' Clb, 1979-; Kiwanis Clb; Redstone Clb; Newcomen Soc of Am; Relay House; Jefferson Clb; Country Clb of Birmingham; Shoal Creek Country Clb; Quarterback Clb; The Clb; r/Presb; hon/W/W: in S & SW, in Fin & Indust, in the World; The Am Bkr; Dir of US Bkg Execs; Men of Achmt; Other Biogl Listings.

WILLIAMS, CHERIE DAWSON oc/Professor; b/Mar 1, 1947; h/5420 East 113th Place South, Tulsa, OK 74136; ba/Tulsa, OK; m/Eddie Anthony; p/Dona M Dawson, Tulsa, OK; ed/BS 1968, MA 1970, EdD 1972, Univ of Tulsa; pa/Instr 1971-72, Asst Prof 1972-81, Assoc Prof 1982-, Oral Roberts Univ; Mem: Phi Gamma Kappa; Kappa Delta Pi; NEA; OK Ed Assn; Secy-Treas, OK Assn of Tchr Edrs; Intl Acad of Preven Med; Secy, Oral Roberts Univ Fac Senate; Pres Tenured Fac, Oral Roberts Univ, 1981-83; Am Assn of Tchr Edrs; OCCETE; AERA; r/Pentecostal; hon/Author, "The Commun as a Sci Resource," in Sci & Chd, 1982; F B Parriott Fellow, 1969-70; Univ Scholar, 1964-68; Outstg Edr of Am, 1974.

WILLIAMS, CLARKSTON GUSTAV oc/Author and Tax Accountant; b/Dec 11, 1940; h/Route 1, Box 532, West Point, MS 39773; ba/West Point, MS; c/Christian Eric, Victory Rene; p/Daniel Abel Williams (dec); Inse Virginia (Hazelwood) Williams, West Point, MS; ed/Grad, AUS Engr Sch, 1960; BSBA, MS St Univ, 1968; Grad, H & R Block Tax Sch, 1974; mil/AUS, 1958, 1960-61, 1975; pa/Chief Ofc Clk, IL Ctl RR,

Jackson, MS, 1968-69; Hist Tchr, Canton, MS Acad, 1969-70; Hist & Ec Tchr, Faith Christian HS, Collingwood, NJ, 1970-72; Social Studies Tchr, Greenville MS Christian Sch, 1972-73; Owner, The Tax Man, West Point, MS, 1973-; Owner, The Book Hut, West Point, MS, 1973-; Owner, Paul Revere Press, 1975-; Mem: Soc for the Admvt of Mgmt, 1964-68; Alpha Phi Omega, 1965-; Nat Hist Soc, 1972-74; r/Pentecostal Ch of God; hon/Pubr & Compiler: *Handbook on God & Country,* 1975; *Handbook on Liberty,* 1976; Author, *How to Fail in Marriage: Be the Ruler of the Roost & Your Wife Might Become Your Ex,* 1981; Cong of Freedom Liberty Awd, 1975 & 1976; W/W in S & SW.

WILLIAMS, DENNIS BUCHER oc/Actor; b/Aug 21, 1944; h/11684 Ventura Boulevard, Ste 124, Studio City, CA 91604; ba/Beverly Hills, CA; p/Mr and Mrs A W Bird, Stilwell, KS; ed/Att'd Shawnee Mission W Jr Col; Att'd Kansas City Jr Col; BA Theatre & Drama, Univ of KS; pa/Motion Pictures: "Synthetic Fuel Conspiracy"; "Silent Movie"; "Truce in the Forest"; "Paved w Gold"; "Born of Water"; TV: "Gypsy Warriors"; "Operation Petticoat"; "Bionic Wom"; "Mary Hartman, Mary Hartman"; "Maude"; "Nancy Walker Show"; Movies of the Wk: "Spec Olympics Spec"; "Jour From Darkness"; "Halls of Anger"; "Dennis Williams Show"; Theatre: "Spec Olympics"; "Beautiful People of Am"; "Star Spangled Girl"; "Oklahoma"; "Hope Sch"; "Fantastiks"; Mem: Screen Actors Guild; AFTRA; AEA; AGVA; Spec Olympics; Christian Chds Fund; Actors & Others for Animals; Am Film Inst; Hollywood Heritage; Motion Picture Relief Fund; Permanent Charities Com; hon/Author of Screenplay, "Sunset Heaven," 1978; Presv of Arts Awd, Am Film Inst, 1976; Cert of Apprec, Anaheim C of C, 1977; Nat Gold Key for Art, 1963; Nat Gold Key for Art, 1963; Kennedy Foun Spec Awd, 1983; Golden Eagle Best Actor Awd, Munich Film Fest, 1978; Bronze Halo Awd, So CA Motion Picture Coun, 1983; W/W in Theatre; Personalities of W & MW; Noteworthy Ams.

WILLIAMS, DOUGLAS oc/Management Consultant; b/Oct 13, 1912; h/7612 Horizon Drive, PO Box 941, Carefree, AZ 85377; ba/Carefree, AZ; m/Esther Grant; c/Penelope W Winters, Grant T; p/Marjorie T Williams, Greenwich, CT; ed/AB, Cornell Univ, 1934; MBA, Harvard Univ, 1936; mil/AUS, WW II, Lt Col; pa/Air Reduction Co, 1936-37; Stat, Am Inst of Public Opinion, 1938; Mkt Res Conslt, Elmo Roper Co, 1939-40; Assoc Dir, Nat Opinion Res Ctr, Univ of Denver, 1940-42; Pres, Douglas Williams Assocs, NYC & AZ, 1948-; Mem: Pres, Commun Chest, Larchmont, NY, 1959; Bd of Mgrs, West Side YMCA, NYC, 1957-60; cp/Larchmonst Yacht Clb; Winged Foot Golf Clb; Union Leag; Desert Forest Golf Clb; AZ Harvard Bus Sch; r/Epis; hon/Author, "The Ed of Employees," for Am Mgmt Assn, 1953; *Survey of Small Bus,* US Dept of Commerce, 1957; "Employee Attitude Surveys," Sect in *Handbook of Bus Adm,* 1967; *Cornell Univ Survey,* 1969; Num Other Articles Pub'd in Profl Jours & Bus Mags; W/W: in W, in Fin & Indust.

WILLIAMS, EDDIE ANTHONY oc/

Business Systems Manager; b/Oct 2, 1947; h/5420 East 113th Place South, Tulsa, OK 74136; ba/Tulsa, OK; m/Cherie Anna; p/Mr and Mrs Eddie Ray Willams, Tyler, TX; sp/Mrs Dona Dawson, Tulsa, OK; ed/BS, Univ of TX-Arlington, 1970; MBA, Univ of Tulsa, 1978; pa/Programmer, Standard Oil of IN, Tulsa, OK, 1970-73; Sr Programmer Analyst, The Mentor Corp, Tulsa, 1973-75; Sr LSys Analyst, The Williams Cos, Tulsa, 1975-79; Mgr Bus Sys, C—E NATCO, Tulsa, 1979-; Mem: Lic'd Sales Assoc, OK Real Est Comm; Assn for Sys Mgmt, 1976-; cp/Conserv Dem; r/Pentecostal; hon/Sigma Iot Epsilon; Dean's List, Univ of TX-Arlington; W/W in S & SW.

WILLIAMS, GLORIA LOUISE oc/Communication & Government Security Officer; b/May 31, 1932; h/304 Emma Jane, Rockwall, TX 75087; ba/Garland, TX; p/Lonnie and Louise Williams (dec); ed/Att'd Prairie View A&M Univ, 1950-51 & 1953-54; pa/Maid 1960-63, Mail Clk 1963-66, Pers Clk 1966-68, Security Admr 1968-71, Security Ofcr 1971-77, Varo Inc, Garland, TX; Communs & Govt Security Ofcr, EEO/Affirmative Action Prog, 1977-80; cp/Bd of Dirs, Rockwall YMCA, 1977-81; Rockwall Growth Com, 1977-78; Tour Guide for Ch Tours; r/Bapt; hon/Active in Getting Swimming Pool for Black Commun, 1960's; Recip James S Cogswell Awd, Varo Inc, 1975 & 1981.

WILLIAMS, MAMIE ALETHIA oc/Pastor; b/Aug 13, 1950; h/1031 East Monument Street, Baltimore, MD 21202; ba/Balto, MD; p/John W Williams, Sumter, SC; Mrs John W Williams (dec); ed/BA, Claflin Col, 1972; MDiv, Wesley Theol Sem, 1978; pa/Pastor, Cent U Meth Ch, 1982-; Pastor, Calvary U Meth Ch, 1977-82; Sum Investment Wkr, SC Annual Conf, 1983; Coor, NW Parish Ed Min WA Ctl Dist, 1976-77; Other Previous Employmnt; Mem: Steering Com, Balto Conf Bd of Pensions, 1982; Balto Clergy & Laity Concerned, 1982; Nat Bd of Black Meths for Ch Renewal, 1976-80; Gen Bd of Ch & Soc, 1976-80; Ordained Elder, 1979; Ordained Deacon, 1976; Lic'd to Preach, 1974 & 1975; Other U Meth Ch Coms; cp/Balto Br, NAACP; Pres, Bd of Dirs, Wash Innner City Self-Help, 1979-; Pres, Bd of Dirs, Common Capital Fund, 1980-; Co-Convener Wash Br, Wom's Intl Leag for Peace & Freedom, 1980-82; Bd of Dirs, Metro Wash Planning & Housing Assn, 1981-82; Interim Dir 1980-82, Pres, Bd of Dirs 1981-82, Calvary Bilingual Day Care Lrng Ctr; Nat Black Hook-up of Black Wom Inc, 1979-80; Convenor, Multi-ethnic Task Force on the ERA, 1979-80; 14th Street Proj Area Proj, 1977-80; African Am Wom's Assn, 1979-80; Bd of Dirs, Planned Parenthood of Wash, 1979-80; DC Cong of Parents & Tchrs Assn, 1978-79; Num Public, Radio & TV Appearances; r/U Meth; hon/Mamie A Williams Day, Wash DC City Coun Resolution, Jun 6, 1982; Las Amigas' Ser Awd, 1982; Columbia Hgts Commun Ser Awd, 1977-78; WISH, 1982; Crusade Scholar, 1976, 1978; Choir Recog 4 Yrs in Col; Am Legion Awd, 1972; Plaque, UNCF Ser Awd, 1970; Simon P Montgomery Awd, 1970; Pres S'ship, 1970; Dean's

List, 1970; Cent Medallion, 1968; Am Ledion Medallion, 1968; Outstg Yg Wom in Am; Other Awds & Hons.

WILLIAMS, PEGGY FOWLER oc/Management Consultant; b/May 8, 1933; ba/PO Box 7173, Dallas, TX 75209; c/Leigh Ann, Walter Lochran; p/Leon Dockrey Fowler (dec); Annie Bell (Williams) Dodd, Baylor Co, TX; ed/BS, N TX St Univ, 1954; MBA, Rollins Col, 1963; Cert of Adv'd Study, Am Grad Sch of Intl Mgmt, 1980; pa/Mgmt Consltg, Owner, Williams Consltg Sers (Formerly Moranz Consltg), 1963-; Employed w TX Instruments, 1957-58; w Temco Aircraft, Dallas, TX, 1951-53 & 1955-57; HS Math Tchr, Arlington, TX, 1953-54; Mem: Nat Assn of Female Execs; Am Mgmt Assn; AAUW; cp/Listeners Clb; Bonnie Blue Flag Chapt, UDC; Dallas Hist Soc; r/Epis; hon/CPS Designation Awd, Nat Secys Assn Intl, 1965; GRI Designation Awd, TX Assn of Realtors, 1978; W/W of Am Wom.

WILLIAMS, PEGGY LENORE oc/Assistant Performance Director; b/Nov 5, 1948; h/1909 Jefferson Street, Madison, WI 53711; ba/Washington, DC; p/Madison, WI; ed/Att'd Univ of WI-Madison, 1970; Grad, Ringling Bros & Barnum & Bailey Circus Clown Col, 1970; pa/Positions w Ringling Bros & Barnum & Bailey Circus (RBBB): Profl Circus Clown RBBB, 1970-79; Staff Instr, RBBB Clown Col, 1973-; Advance Clown (Public Relats), 1973-80; Coor Ednl Sers Dept, RBBB Circus, 1980-81; Asst Perf Dir Blue Unit, RBBB Circus, 1981-; Mem: Nat Asns Female Execs, 1980-; Circus Fans of Am, 1977-; r/Ch of Jesus Christ of LDS; hon/Appearances on Over 100 Local & Nat TV Shows & in Num Mags; 1st Female Asst Perf Dir in Circus Hist; 1st Female Grad of RBBB Clown Col; W/W of Am Wom.

WILLIAMS, RICHARD LEE JR oc/Business Executive, Psychologist; b/Sep 13, 1943; h/425½ East 4th Claremore, OK 74017; ba/Same; c/Richard, Tracey, Michael; p/C L and Julie Williams, Ocean Springs, MS; ed/BA, Univ of W FL, 1969; MS 1972, PhD 1979, Univ of So MS; mil/AUS, 1961-64; pa/Nuclear Test Tech 1964-69, Sys & Test Engr Nuclear Power Div 1972, Litton Industs; Engr Nuclear Power Div, Westinghouse Col, 1969-71; Conslt, St of MS, Jackson, 1972-74; Pvt Pract Industl Conslt, Employee Asst Progs, Jackson, 1974-; Pres, Williams Oil, Gas & Mining Corp, Tulsa, OK, 1980-; Pres, Williams Fgn Mining Opers Inc, Tulsa, 1980-; Psych Lectr, NE St Univ, Tahlequah, OK, 1980-; Hypnosis/Psych Lectr, Claremore, Jr Col, OK, 1980-; Diplomate, Am Acad Behavioral Med; Am Psychol Assn; OK Psychol Assn; Tulsa Psychol Assn; cp/Meth Clb; Elks; r/Meth; hon/Author (w Gutsch & Sizemore) *Sys of Psychotherapy,* 1978; Sr Editor, *Occupl Alcoholism Progs,* 1974; Grad Fellow, Univ So MS, 1969-72, 1977-79; W/W in S & SW.

WILLIAMS, ROBERT BRUCE oc/Library Director; b/Oct 21, 1942; h/107 South 8th Street, Williamsburg, KY 40769; ba/Williamsburg, KY; p/Bruce V Williams (dec); Ada Gillian Williams, Williamsburg, KY; ed/BA Cumberland Col; AM George Peabody Col for Tchrs, EdD Cand, Vanderbilt Univ; pa/Dir, Public Lib, Corbin, KY, 1965-74; Fellow, Grad Sch of Lib Sci, George Peabody

Col for Tchrs, 1975-76; Hd Ref Dept, Univ of TN-Nashville, 1976-79; Hd Libn & Dir Lib Sers, Cumberland Col, 1979-; Mem: Am Lib Assn; KY Lib Assn; TN Lib Assn; SEn Lib Assn; Am Soc for Info Sci; AAUP; Coun of Indep Am Cols & Univ Libns; KY Bapt Col Lib Netwk; Bet Phi Mu; r/Disciple of Christ; hon/ Editor, *KY Rel Heritage Series*, Cumberland Col; Editor, Peabody Lib Sch *Forum*; T J Roberts Ldrship Prize, Cumberland Col; George Peabody Fellow; Andrew Mellon Foun Grantee; Outstg Fac Awd, Cumberland Col Student Govt Assn; W/W in S & SW.

WILLIAMS, ROSE A oc/Marketing, Public Relations, Special Productions; b/ Sep 24, 1949; h/3129 West Flournoy, Chicago, IL 60612; ba/Chgo, IL; p/Bealie and Louise Williams (dec); BS Ed, 1971; pa/Sr Proj Mgr, Spec Mkt Sers Inc, 1982-; Pres, Rose & Assocs, 1980-; Dr of Mkgtg, Chgo Defender Newspaper, 1979-80; Ecec Asst, Bk Mktg Assn, 1974-79; Mdsg Mgr, Playboy Enterprises, 1970-73; Mem: Publicity Clb of Chgo; Am Mgmt Assn; Nat Assn of Media Wom; Chgo Fashion Exch; Netwk Dir, Nat Assn for Female Execs; Chm Publicity, Spkrs Bur; cp/Undergrad Advr, Delta Sigma Theta, 1978-80; Chgo PBS Sta WTTW; Provident Hosp Wom's Aux, 1980-83; NAACP, 1977-; 1992 World's Fair Com; r/Cath; hon/ Govs Awd, 1981; Public Ser Awd, Nat Coun Negro Wom, 1978; Chgo Black Gold Recip, 1983; Dept of Labor Wom's Bur, 1981 & 1982; Nat Assn of Female Execs, 1982; Outstg Yg Wom of Am; W/W of Am Wom.

WILLIAMS, SHIRLEY ANN oc/ Teacher; b/May 10, 1954; h/4006 Tiffin Street, Houston, TX 77026; ba/Houston, TX; p/Mrs Blossom H Williams, Houston, TX; ed/BS 1975, MS 1978, Pairie View A&M Univ; PhD, Pacific Wn Univ, 1981; pa/Art Instr, Ctl Houston, YMCA, 1973-74; Asst to Dean of Sch of Agri, Prairie View A&M Univ, 1978; Tchr, Conslt-Facilitator, Houston ISD, 1976-; Mem: Parliamentn, Phi Delta Kappa; Intl Human Relats Assn; Houston Assn for Supvn & Curric Devel; Houston Coun of Ed; Houston Tchrs Assn; PTA; r/Meth; hon/Author, *A Study of Sibling Attitudes Toward the Mtly Retarded Child*; W/W of Am Wom.

WILLIAMS, VERNON B JR oc/ Retired Urban Consultant; b/Jul 17, 1908; h/7026 South Saint Lawrence Avenue, Chicago, IL 60637; ba/Chgo, IL; m/Naomi S; c/Vernon B III; p/Vernon B and Edith S Williams (dec); sp/ Jeremiah P and Lena G Williams (dec); ed/BS, IL Inst of Technol, 1937; MA Ednl Adm, Univ of Chgo, 1939; pa/ Telephone Supvr, 1941-45; Telephone Mgr, 1945-49; Ofc Mgr, 1949-53; Comml Mgr, Comml Engr Rate Analyst; Asst Staff Supvr; Public Relats Asst; Commun Relats Mgr & Pers Supvr; cp/Past Pres, Frontiers Intl; Lions Intl; Past Pres, Chatham Lions; Chgo Area Proj; Beatric Caffrey Yth Ser; Halfway House Com & Intl Visitors Ctr; Chm, Wash Pk Fund Drive; South Side Div, March of Dimes; Num Other Commun Activs; r/Jewish; hon/Invited Participant, Joint Civilian Orientation Conf #39, 1969.

WILLIAMS, WILBUR E oc/Sales and Marketing Director, Lawyer; b/Oct 2, 1947; h/Urb. Ponce de León, Calle 20 #308, Guaynabo, PR 00657; ba/San Juan, PR; m/Myriam Capó; c/Mayrim M, Bilmarie, Wilbur G; p/Wilber E and Matilde Ortíz Williams; sp/Aristides and Margarita Martir Capó; ed/BBA, 1969; JD, 1971; mil/PR Army NG; pa/Profl Med Rep, Upjohn Intl, 1965; Profl Hosp Prods Rep 1972, Dist Sales Mgr 1975, Div Mgr Hosp Prods Div 1979, Abbott Labs; Sales & Mktg Dir, PR & Caribbean, Schering del Caribe Inc, 1982-; Mem: Past Pres PR Chapt, Am Mktg Assn, 1981-82; Am Mgmt Assn, 1979-; Past Pres, Nu Sigma Beta Frat; Isla Verde, PR; Clb Deportivo de Ponce; Lions Clb; r/Cath; hon/Ser Awd, PR NG, 1964.

WILLIAMS, WILLA ETTA MITCHELL oc/Elementary Teacher; b/Apr 17, 1934; h/7900 Crenshaw Boulevard, Apartment D, Inglewood, CA 90305; ba/LA, CA; p/Lucille Williams, LA, CA; ed/AA, LA City Col, 1954; BA, CA St Univ-LA, 1958; MA, Azusa Pacific Col, 1979; pa/Grades 2 & 3 Tchr, 75th St Sch, LA Unified Sch Dist, 1958-64; Spec Ed Tchr, Parmalee Avenue Sch, LA Sch Dist, 1965-67; Tchr, Raymond Ave Sch, LA Unified Sch Dist, 1968-71; Tng Tchr for Pepperdine Univ, 1968-71; Hoffman Rdg Lab Tchr, 59th St Sch, LA Unified Sch Dist, 1972-76; Grade 4 Tchr 1977-80, Bilingual Grade 4 Tchr 1981-84, Marvin Ave Sch, LA Unified Sch Dist; Mem: NEA; CA Tchrs Assn; U Tchrs of LA; Alpha Kappa Alpha; Nat Assn of Col Wom; Phi Delta Kappa; Intl Toastmistress; Nat Assn of Supvn & Curric Devel; cp/Las Comunicadores; LA Music Assn; Marvin Ave PTA; Marvin Ave Advy Coun; LA In-School Scouting; Num Guest Spkg Presentations; Num Other Sch & Commun Coms & Activs; r/U Meth, St Mark's U Meth Ch; hon/Author, Poetry; U Way Ser Awd, 1983; Phi Delta Kappa Ser Awd, 1983; Marvin Ave PTA Ser Awd, 1982; Coor, Urban Impacted Sch Activs; Num Other Hons & Awds.

WILLIAMS, YVONNE ELAINE oc/ Home Economics Teacher; b/Oct 13, 1944; h/1720 Applewood Ridge Court, Colorado Springs, CO 80907; ba/Colorado Springs, CO; m/Lawrence Richard; c/Jeremy Za; p/William Dean and Martha LaVerne Sams, Rush, CO; sp/Vearl and Josephine Williams (dec); ed/BS, Bob Jones Univ, 1966; MA, Univ of No CO, 1968; Postgrad Wk, Univ of CO-Colorado Springs, 1980 & 1983; pa/ Home Ec Tchr, Kit Carson Sch Dist, Kit Carson, CO, 1966-68; Hom Ec Tchr, Elkhart HS, Elkhart, KS, 1968-73; Home Ec Tchr, Russell Jr HS Colorado Springs, CO, 1974-75; Hom Ec Tchr & Dept Chm, Doherty HS, Colorado Springs, CO, 1975-; 2nd VPres Rho Chapt, Delta Kappa Gamma, 1980-84; cp/Judge, CO Beef Cook-Off, Local & Dist Competions; Judge, Clothing Exhibits, El Paso Co Fair; Gifted & Talented Parent Grp, Lincoln Elem Sch, 1980-83; Asst Cub Scout Den Mother, BSA; Bible Sch Tchr, Calvary Bapt Ch, 1982-83; r/Prot; hon/Recip, Bob Jones Univ Outstg Achm in Home Ec Awd, 1966; Yg Career Wom of Elkhart, KS, 1969; Outstg Yg Wom of Am; W/W: Among Students in Am Cols & Univs, in W.

WILLIAMSON, NANCY D oc/Nurse Educator & Clinical Nurse Coordinator; b/Sep 26, 1944; h/1725 Sourwood Place, Charlottesville, VA 22901; ba/Charlottesville, VA; m/John Rollen; c/John Russell, Jennifer Leigh, Jessica Marie; p/ Elmer Charles and Agnes Marie Onten Burk, McDonald, KS; sp/John Russell Williamson (dec); Lois Foshee Williamson, Augusta, GA; ed/Dipl in Nsg, Wichita St Joseph Sch of Nsg, 1965; BSN 1977, MSN 1979, Med Col of GA; pa/ Clin Nurse Coor & Asst Prof 1983-, Instr Sch of Nsg 1980-83, Relief Nsg Supvr Univ Hosp, 1981-82, Univ of VA Hosps, Blue Ridge Gerontology/Oncology Unit & Univ of VA Sch of Nsg, Charlottesville, VA; Nsg Instr, Johnson Co Commun Col, Overland Pk, KS, 1979-80; Nsg Instr, Augusta Area Tech Sch, 1975-76; Staff Nurse Intensive Care & Coronary Care Unit, St Joseph Hosp, Augusta, GA, 1969 & 1975; Charge Nurse ER, St John's Hosp, Salina, KS, 1970-71; Staff Nurse ER, Monmouth Med Ctr, Eatontoron, NJ, 1970; Charge Nurse Intensive Care & Coronary Care Unit, Commanchee Co Hosp, Lawton, OK, 1969; Designed, Estab'd & Hd Nurse Coronary Care Unit 1967-69, Hd Nurse Intensive Care Univ 1966-67, Charge Nurse Med-Surg Unit 1965-66, Asst Nurse ORN 1963-65, St Joseph Hosp, Wichita, KS; Nurse Aide, Med-Surg-Ob Unit, St Anthony's Hosp, Dodge City, KS, 1962-63; Mem: Num Univ, Nsg & Hosp Coms; ANA; VA Nurses Assn; Var Positions w Beta Kappa Chapt, Sigma Theta Tau; Cert'd CPR Instr, Am Heart Assn, 1980-; cp/Sustaining Mbrship Chp, Girl Scout Troop 401, 1981; Conductor Vol, Adult Diet Clin for Overweight Clients, Karlsruhe, Germany, 1973-74; Vol Cnslg Ser, AUS Ser-men, Karlsruhe, Germany, 1973-74; Num Other Ser Activs; r/ Cath; hon/Author, *Handbook for Univ of VA Sch of Nsg Students in Albemarle Co Schs*, 1981 & 1982; Co-Author, "Factors Affecting Employmnt of Grads of Univ of VA Sch of Nsg from 1978-80," 1982; Author, Var Wkshop Presentations, Nsg Assessment Tools & Other Orgl Paper Presentations; Sigma Theta Tau, 1979; 100 Hours Pin, ARC, 1973; Career Girl, Bus & Profl Wom's Assn, 1967; 2nd VPres, KS St Student Nurses' Assn, 1964-65; W/W of Am Wom.

WILLIS, JOHN PATRICK oc/Chemical Research Manager; b/Mar 10, 1947; h/101 Brimstone Lane, Sudbury, MA 01776; ba/Same; m/Tientje Jane; p/Mary C Willins, Albany, NY; sp/Hans H Dirzuwent, Rensselaer, NY; ed/BS, Iona Col, 1969; MS, SUNY-Oswego, 1974; PhD, Univ of CT, 1977; pa/Mgr of Chem Research, Nova Biomed Corp, 1980-; Postdoct Resr, Univ of MN, 1979-80; Res Chem, Uniroyal Inc, 1977-79; Res Chem, Winthrop Labs, 1970-72; Mem: Fellow, Am Inst of Chems, 1982-; Am Chem Soc, 1970-; Electrochem Soc, 1975; Am Assn of Clin Chem, 1982-; NY Acad of Sci, 1981; hon/Author, Num Profl Pubs in Field, Patentee in Field, 1982; Res Foun Fellow, Univ of CT, 1976; Sigma Xi, 1976; Phi Kappa Phi, 1976; Phi Lambda Upsilon, 1974; W/W in E.

WILSON, ARTHUR JESS oc/Clinical Psychologist; b/Oct 25, 1910; h/487 Park Avenue, Yonkers, NY 10703; ba/ Same; m/Lillian; c/Warren David, Anton Francis; p/Samuel Louis and Ann Gilbert Wilson (dec); ed/BS 1935, MA 1949,

PhD 1961, NY Univ; LLB, St Lawrence Univ, 1940; JD Bklyn Law Sch, 1967; mil/USN, 1944-46, Classification Spec; pa/Pvt Pract Clin Psych, 1973-; Clin Psychol, VA Hosp, Montrose, NY, 1968-73; Dir, Manhattan Narcotic Rehab Ctr, NYC, 1967-68; Dir of Rehab, Westchester Co Med Ctr, Valhalla, NY, 1948-67; Supvr of Voc Rehab, NY St Ed Dept, NYC, 1942-44; Mem: Am Psychol Assn; NY St Psychol Assn; Kappa Delta Pi; Phi Delta Kappa; Epsilon Pi Tau; hon/Author, *The Emotional Life of the Ill & Injured*, 1950; *A Guide to the Genius of Cardozo*, 1939; *The Wilson Tchg Inventory*, 1941; Contbr, Num Articles to Profl Jours; Elected, NY Acad of Scis; Fdrs Day Awd for Achmt, NY Univ, 1961; Hon Mem, Intl Mark Twain Soc, 1950; Westchester Author, Westchester Co Hist Soc, 1957; W/W in E, in Am Ed; Am Men of Sci; DIB.

WILSON, BRENDA COKER oc/ Attorney; b/Jun 25, 1952; h/Apartment 45B, 4259 22nd Avenue Southwest, Naples, FL 33999; ba/Naples, FL; m/ George A II; p/Paul and Helen Coker, Naples, FL; sp/Mr and Mrs George Wilson, Cinc, OH; ed/BA, Univ of No IA, 1974; JD, Univ of Tulsa, 1977; pa/ Sole Pract'g Atty, The Legal Ctr, Naples, FL, 1980-; Assoc Atty, Firm of Rhodes & Tucker, Marco Isl FL, 1978-80; Legal Intern, Tulsa Co Legal Aid Soc, Tulsa, OK, 1976-78; Mem: Yg Lwyrs Div, FL Bar Assn; ABA; Collier Co Bar Assn, 1978-83; Co-Chm Law Day Com 1981, Bd of Dirs 1981-83, Treas 1981-83, Nat & FL Assn of Wom Lwyrs; cp/Bd of Dirs 1979-83, VPres 1982-83, Abuse of Naples Inc; Past Pres, Sun Coast Chapt, Am Bus-wom's Assn; Leag of Wom Voters; Zonta Intl Inc; Co-Fdr, Naples Profl Wom's Netwk; Dem Wom's Clb; Orig'g Mem, Collier Co Rape Crisis Prog; Bd of Dirs, Planned Parenthood; Co-Chm, Com to Re-elect the Gov, 1982; Num Orgl Spkg Presentations; Other Commun Activs; r/ Presb; hon/Jaycettes Outstg Yg Wom of Marco, 1981; Exec Dir's Awd, Cath Ser Bur, 1981; Salute to Wom, Wom Achiever of Collier Co, 1983; W/W: of Wom, in Am Law; Personalities of S.

WILSON, BYRDIE BRUNER oc/ Executive Director; b/Sep 13, 1922; h/ 78 Country Club Boulevard, Town House 244, Worcester MA 01605; ba/ Marlboro, MA; p/Joseph M and Mary Luther Bruner (dec); ed/BS, NC Clt Univ, 1944; Nsg Dipl, Harlem Hosp Sch of Nsg, 1951; MSN, NY Univ Dept of Nsg Ed, 1959; pa/Exec Dir, Assabet Val Home Hlth Assoc Inc (Non-profit Commun Hlth Agy), Marlboro, MA, 1976-; Adm Supvr & Conslt, Webster-Dudley Samaritan Assoc Inc, MA, 1976; Prog Dir, Fam Nurse Practitioner Prog, Worcester Hahnemann Hosp, MA, 1974-75; Dir Nsg, Maternity & Fam Planning Ctr, Bronx, NY, 1970-74; Adm Supvr 1959-70, Staff Nurse 1953-58, Vis'g Nurse Ser of NY; Staff Nurse, Newborn Nursery, Harlem Hosp, 1951-52; Mem: APHA; ANA; Bd of Dirs, Pres, Baypath Sr Citizens Sers, Framingham, MA, 1980-; Profl Advy Com, Hahnemann Rehab Ctr, 1980-; r/ Prot; hon/W/W: of Wom, in Hlth Care.

WILSON, CHARLES WILLIAM oc/ Physician, Psychiatrist; b/Aug 12, 1916; h/4655 Basque Drive, Santa Maria, CA 93455; ba/Same; m/Frances Preshia

Stephenson; c/Charles William II, Walter Stephen, Cherrie, James Robin; p/ Jacob Resor and Estella Cherrie Wilson (dec); ed/BA, Wichita Univ, 1938; MD, Kansas Univ, 1942; Intern, Harper Hosp, Detroit, MI, 1942-43; Resident Phys Neurology, Univ Hosps, Iowa City, IA, 1946-47; Resident Phys Psychi, Ctl St Hosp, Norman, OK, 1964-67; mil/ USN, 1943-46, Lt (Sgt), MC; pa/Pvt Pract Psychi & Med Hypnosis: Ponca City, OK 1967-71 & Santa Maria, CA 1971-; Psychi Dir, Mtl Hlth Ctr for Students, OK St Univ, Stillwater, OK, 1968-71; Staff Psychi at Commun Mtl Hlth Ctrs: Attascadero St Hosp 1975-79, San Luis Obispo, CA 1973-75, Santa Maria, CA 1971-72, Ponca City, OK 1967-71, Gen Pract & Pvt Pract Phys & Psychi: La Crosse, KS 1962-64; St Francis, KS 1947-62; Mem: Am Psychi Assn; So CA Psychi Soc; Acad of Parapsychol & Med; The Soc for Clin & Exptl Hypnosis; Intl Soc of Hypnosis; AMA; Var St & Co Med Socs in KS, OK & CA; Charter Mem, The Am Soc of Clin Hypnosis; Pres, NW KS Med Soc, 1951; cp/Scoutmaster, Explorer Ldr, Scouter Tnr & Other Positions, BSA, 23 Yrs; Pres St Francis, KS 1955, Ponca City, OK, Rotary Intl, 19 Yrs; Lions Clb; Elem Sch Bd, St Francis, KS; Am Legion; Masonic Lodge; OES; Men of Webster; Phi Lambda Psi; Delta Upsilon; Phi Beta Pi; Toastmaster Intl; AAAS; r/Meth; Lay Ldr, Meth Ch, La Crosse, KS; Com Mem 1st Meth Ch, Norman, OK, SS Tchr, Meth Ch, Ponca City, OK; hon/Author, *Stop Bedwetting!*, 1979; Cit, Nat PTA; Eagle Scout Awd, Silver Explorer Awd, Scoutmasters Key & Wood Badge, BSA; Ext Prof, CA Polytech St Univ, San Louis Obispo, CA; Instr, Allan Hancock Col, Santa Maria, CA; The Intl Platform Assn; Resr & Develr of 4 Rapid Psychotherapies; W/W: in CA, in W, in Am, in World, of Intells, of Commun Ser, of Contemp Achmt; Men of Achmt; Men & Wom of Distn; Intl Dir of Dist'd Psychotherapists; Inl Book of Hon; DIB; Num Other Biogl Listings.

WILSON, CLARENCE JR oc/Personnel Manager; b/Sep 19, 1952; h/D-4 Bellwood Apartments, Laurel, MS 39440; ba/Taylorsville, MS; m/Phyllis Beatrice Williams; c/Caralisa, Carmen; p/Clarence and Maggie Wilson, Talladega, AL; sp/Williams & Louvenia Gilmore, B'ham, AL; ed/BA, B'ham So Col, 1975; pa/Measurer & Lister, H L Yoh Appraisal Co, 1975-76; Social Wkr, Dept of Pensions & Security, 1976-78; Asst Pers Dir, Crown Textile Co, 1978-83; Pers Mgr, GA Pacific Corp, 1983; cp/ Div Chm 1979-83, Bd'of Dirs 1981, U Way; Chm, U Meth Men's Grp, 1983; Treas, Kappa Alpha Psi Frat Inc; Talladega Alumni Assn, 1982-83; Bd Mem, Pittard Voc Sch, 1982; r/Meth; hon/ Outstg Yg Men Nom, Talladega JC's, 1981; Outstg Yg Man of Am, US JC's, 1983.

WILSON, DEIRDRE oc/Theatre/ Dance Education, Drama Therapist, Counselor, Choreographer & Performer; b/Feb 21, 1945; h/Northeast 1050 "B" Street, Pullman, WA 99163; m/Douglas John Hammel; c/Devon; p/ Joseph H Wilson; Audrie Ilene Branin (dec); sp/John and Norma Hammel; p/ AA, Grossmont Col, 1977; BA, Antioch Univ, 1979; MEd 1983, MA Theatre

1983, Doct Cand Cnslg, WA St Univ; Addit Tng & Study; pa/Perf'g Experience: Ballet Soloist, SF Opera, 1972-75; Ballet Soloist, SF Sprg Opera Theatre, 1974-75; SF Ballet, 1972-74; Demi-Soloist, Dance Spectrum, SF, 1974-75; Soloist, SF Dance Theatre, 1973-75; Prin Dancer "Tommy," Seattle Opera Co, Seattle, 1972-; Opera Ballet, Pasadina Opera Co, Pasadina, 1970-; Am Consert Ballet, LA, 1967-70; Musical Theatre/Theatre Experience: Prin Dance/Featured Vocalist, "Tommy," Seattle Opera Co, 1972; Co-star in "Showboat" Supporting Role in "Carousel," Louis & Yg Prodns, Intl St Dept Goodwill Tour of S Am, 1967; Supporting Role in "Carousel," Sacramento Music Circus, 1967-; Supporting Role in "Carousel," Fresno Music Circus, 1967-; Ensemble & Featured Dancer in Var Prodns, Val Music Theatre, Woodland Hills, CA, 1965-66; Ensemble Var Prodns, Carousel Theatre, West Covina, CA, 1965-; Dancer in "Here's Love," San Bernadino Civic Light Opera, 1964-; Dancer & Featured Performer Var Prodns, San Diego Civic Light Opera, 1961-64; "Galileo," Old Globe Theatre, San Diego, CA, 1964-; Films: "How To Succeed in Bus w/o Really Trying," 1967; "Hold On," 1967; Tchg Experience: ½-time Grad Tchg Asst, Dept of Spch/Theatre Arts Current, Dept of PE 1980, Dept of Ed Sum 1980, WA St Univ; Dir, Owner & Admr, Acad of Ballet, Pullman, WA, Currently; Instr, Ballert Folk, Moscow, ID, 1980-; Instr, SF Dance Theatre, 1974-75; Instr, Ed Mock Studios, SF, 1974-75; Num Courses & Wkshops in Drama Therapy; Choreography: Dir & Choreographer, WA Jr Concert Ballet, Currently; Var Prodns w WA St Univ & SF Opera; Mem: Actor's Equity Assn; Am Guild of Musical Artists; Nat Assn for Drama Therapy; Am Pers & Guid Assn; Phi Delta Kappa; cp/Dir, Pocket Players, 1983-; Chm, Disabled Sers Advy Coun, 1978; Advy Bd, Exploring Fam Sch, 1977-78; Senate (Grad Rep), WA St Univ Senate, 1980; Others; hon/ Author, *Intro to Theatre for the Aged Disabled*, 1977; *Adaptive Theatre: Theory & Methods*; Fed Grant Recip, to Devel & Dir the San Diego Theatre for the Disabled, 1978; Grante, RA From the Ofc of Grants, Res & Devel, WA St Univ, 1982; Grantee, WA Comm for the Humanities; W/W in W.

WILSON, FRANCES PRESHIA oc/ Psychiatric Nurse and Homemaker; b/ Mar 13, 1919; h/4655 Basque Drive, Santa Maria, CA 93455; ba/Santa Maria, CA; m/Charles W; c/Charles William II, Walter Stephen, Cherrie W Pedigo, James Robin; p/Walter P Stephenson (dec); Grace M Stephenson, Menlo Pk, CA; ed/BS, RN, Univ of KS, 1940; pa/Instr & Asst Dir, Sch Nsg, Axtell Christian Hosp, Newton, KS, 1940-41; Admr & Chp Student Hlth Prog, Grace Hosp, Detroit, MI, 1941-43; Ofcr Nurse, Norton, KS, 1944-46; Instr Psychi Nsg, Ctl St Hosp, Norman, OK, 1964-67; 1st Chp Geriatric Nsg Div, OK St Nurses Assn, 1964-67; Psychi Nurse, Co-Cnslr & Receptionist for Psychi (Husband), 1971-; Mem: AAUW; Alpha Chi Omega; ANA; Nat Leag for Nsg Ed; ARC Nsg Ser; KS St Nsg Assn, 1960-64; MI St Nurses Assn, 1941-43; OK St Nurses Assn, 1964-71; Pres

1951-53, Mem 1947-62, NW KS Nurses Aux; cp/Water Safety Instr & Chp Water Safety Prog, Cheyenne Co, KS, 1948-62; Key Tnr, Brownie Ldr, Camp Nurse, GSA; OES; Rotary Anns; Am Legion Aux; PTA; Fellow, Intl Platform Assn; Others; r/Prot; Life Mem & Pres, Wom's Soc Christian Ser; SS Tchr; Ordained Min; hon/Co-Resr & Co-Develr (w Husband), 4 Very Rapid Psychotherapies; Hon DDiv; Nat Hon Soc; Sigma Theta Tau Nat Nsg Frat; Most Outstg Girl Scouter Cheyenne Co, St Francis, KS; W/W of Wom; Dir of Dist'd Ams.

WILSON, LOWELL HENRY oc/Real Estate Developer and Insurance Marketing; b/May 24, 1932; h/217 Fairway West, Tequesta, FL 33458; ba/Miami, FL; m/Joan Ann; c/Joel, Jeff; p/Harry W Wilson (dec); sp/Henrietta Cloase, Hobe Sound, FL; ed/Att'd Drake Univ; pa/Self-employed in Cnstrn Bus, 1953-58; Pres & Prin Var Real Est Corps in IA, MO, KY & VA, 1958-; Fdr & VPres, Life Ins Mktg Corp, Ofcs in 15 Sts, 1972-; Past Pres, JJAA; cp/Blue Lodge, York Rite, Scottish Rite, Masons; Charter Mem & Past Potentate, AMARA Shrine Temple; r/Presb; hon/Var W/W & Other Biogl Listings.

WILSON, THOMAS JOSEPH JR oc/Optomestrist; b/Dec 28, 1916; h/202 Canebreak Lane, Simpsonville, SC 29681; ba/Simpsonville, SC; m/Doris An (Bender); c/Maureen Louis (W) Wersinger, Thomas Joseph III, John Romuald, James Michael; p/Thomas Joseph Sr and Rose Esther (Solari) Wilson (dec); Leslie Colby and Miriam Gertrude (Michael) Bender (dec); ed/BS, Univ of PA, 1960; OD, So Col of Optometry, 1963; mil/USN, 1938-60, Med Dept; pa/Pvt Pract Optom, Charleston, SC, 1963-74; Dept Hd & Prof of Optom Technol, Greenville Tech Col, Greenville, SC, 1974-79; Pvt Prac Optom, Simpsonville, SC, 1979-; Mem: Am Optom Assn; SC Optom Assn; Appalachian Optom Soc; Optom Ext Prog; Optom Foun; Omega Delta Optom Frat; cp/US Nav Inst; FRA; Am Legion; r/Rom Cath; hon/Author, Num Articles Pub'd in Profl Optom Pubs; Pres, Charleston Co Optom Assn, 1964-66; Chm, Armed Sers Com, SC Optom Assn, 1967-70; Frs, Dept of Optom Technol, Greenville Tech Col, Greenville, SC, 1974; Optom Conslt, USAF Base Hosp, Charleston, 1964-68; Subnormal Vision Conslt, VA Hosp, Columbia, SC, 1977-79; Gov's Comm for Consolidated Govt Charleston Co, 1964-66; Recip Dedicated Public Ser Awd 1974, Outstg Ser to Profession of Optom Awd 1979, SC Optom Assn; VPres, Alpha Chapt, Omega Delta Intl Frat, 1963; W/W in S & SW.

WILSON-THOMAS, SANDRA ELAINE oc/Circuit Designer; b/Feb 11, 1943; h/95 West Calaveras, Altadena, CA 91007; ba/LA, CA; m/A Douglas Thomas; c/Vincent Charles, Michael DeWayne, Rosalyn Walker; p/Mr and Mrs Harry M Jackson, Kansas City, KS; Mrs Aline Sloan, Kansas City, KS; sp/Mr and Mrs L T Thomas (dec); ed/AA, Kansas City Col, 1962; BA Bus, BA Psych, Univ of KS, 1978; pa/Supvr, Nat Bellas Hess, 1964-65; Engrg Aid, AT&T, 1964-77; Circuit Designer, Pacific T&T, 1978-; Mem: Pres, Ctl Coun, Telephone Pioneers of Am; cp/Music Coor, Lincoln

Avenue Bapt Ch, 1979-84; Wom's Aux; Pasadena Boys Clb; r/Bapt; hon/Outstg Wom of Am; W/W: in W, of Am Wom.

WILTSE, CHLORYCE J oc/Computer Software Programmer, Marketer and Speaker; b/Nov 25, 1933; ba/Volberg, MT; m/Gary L Wiltse; c/Mark Wiltse, Lynn Braswell; p/Carl Ode and Leila Gibbs Ode, Tempe, AZ; sp/Earle Wiltse, DeKalb, IL; Erma Wiltse (dec); ed/BS, Univ of NE-Lincoln, 1955; Adv'd Wk: IA St Univ; Univ of MT; Mt St Univ; pa/Home Ec Instr, Osceola HS, Osceola, NE, 1955-57; Rural Tchr, Billup Sch, Powder River Co, MT, 1957-58; Home Ec & Computer Sci Instr, Powder River HS, Broadus, MT, 1964-83; Computer Software Prodr, Tchr & Spkr, Clo's----Line, Volberg, MT, 1982-; Mem: Am Home Ec Assn; Treas 1980-82, MT Home Ec Assn; Phi Upsilon Omicron; Omicron Nu; Gamma Alpha Chi; Delta Kappa Gamma; Kappa Delta; Wm 1977, OES; WIFE; Mortar Bd; Alpha Lambda Delta; Phi Sigma Chi; r/Luth; hon/Author, Computer Software under Clo's----Line Copyright: "The Cost Study Prog," "The Calorie Study Prog," "Recipe Search," "The Two-Income Lifestyle Study," "Clrm Potpourri"; Book/Software: Apples for the Tchrs; MT Hom Ec Tchr of Yr, 1975; Outstg Sec'dy Edr of Am, 1974; Broadus Outstg Yg Edr of Yr, 1976; Tchr, Nat Winning Class of Fleischmann Yeast Menu Planning Contest, 1969; Nat Runner-up, Share-the-Hlth Contest, 1980; Top FHA Chapt in MT, 1968 & 1973; W/W in W.

WIMMER, GLEN ELBERT oc/Professional Engr and Management Consultant; b/Feb 16, 1903; h/3839-48 Vista Campana South, Oceanside, CA 92056; ba/Same; m/Mildred G McCullough; c/Frank Thomas; ed/BSME 1925, MSME 1933, IA St Univ; MBA NWn Univ, 1935; mil/USAR, Ofcr Active 1925-28, Inactive to 1938; pa/Draftsman, GE Co, Ft Wayne, IN, 1925-29; Asst Engr, Wn Elect Co, Chgo, IL, 1929-32; Mech Engr Instr, MI Col Mining & Technol, 1936-37; Machine Designer, Firestone Tire & Rubber Co, Akron, OH, 1937-38; Engr in Charge of Design, Ditto Inc, Chgo, 1938-39; Asst to Chief Engr, Victorgraph Corp, Chgo, 1939-40; Designer of Tools & Machinery, Pioneer Engrg & Mfg Co, Detroit, MI, l940-41; Designer & Checker, Assoc Designers, Detroit, MI, 1941-42; Designer & Checker, Engrg Ser Corp, Detroit, MI, 1942; Checker & Asst Supt, Design for Norman E Miller & Assocs, Detroit, MI, 1942; Engrg Checker, Lee Engrg Co, Detroit, MI, 1942-45; Hd Design & Devel Dept, Cummins Perforator Co, Chgo, 1943-45; Staff Engr Charge of Design & Devel, Tammen & Denison Inc, Chgo, 1945-58; Instr of Cost Anal, Evening Course, IL Inst of Technol, Chgo, 1946-47; Engr, Barnes & Reinick Inc, Chgo, 1958-60, 1961-68; Devel Engr, B H Bunn Co, Chgo, 1960-61; Pvt Pract, 1968-; Mem: Dir, IL Engrg Coun, 1958-66; Soc of Automotive Engrs; Soc Mfg Engrs; Computer & Automated Sys Assn; IPA; Delta Chi; Cert'd, Nat Bur Engrg Bds; cp/Am Def Preparedness Assn; Life Mem, IBA; r/Meth; hon/W/W: in Engrg, in MW, in W, in CA, in Technol Today; Ldrs in Am Sci; Intl Blue Book World Notables; Nat Social Dir; Soc Dirs of US & CA;

The Blue Book; IL Lives; 2000 Men of Achmt; 2000 Notable Ams; Dir of Dist'd Ams; DIB; Intcontl Biog Assn; Men of Achmt; Personalities of W & MW; CA Register; Intl Register of Profiles; Intl W/W of Intells, Commun Ser; Commun Ldrs of Am; Am Patriots of the 1980's; Am Registry; CA W/W in Bus & Fin; Notable Ams; Commun Ldrs & Noteworthy Ams; Notables of the Bicent Era; Profiles of Freedom (Impressions of the Am Hist Soc); Men & Wom of Distn; Book of Hon.

WINBORN, LOIS DIANE MOYER oc/Principal; b/May 7; h/5390 Sherwood Drive, Katy, TX 77449; ba/Katy, TX; c/Wendy Diane, Rebecca Marie; p/George and Lois Moyer, La Marque, TX; ed/BS, Univ of TX; MEd, Univ of Houston 1973; pa/Tchr, Houston ISD; Tchr, Alief ISD, 1971-76; Asst Prin 1976-78, Prin 1978-, Katy ISD; Mem: TX Elem Prins & Supvrs Assn; TX Assn for Curric & Devel; cp/DAR; Daugh of Am Colonists; Colonial Dames of XVII Cent; Descendents of Colonial Clergy; Order of Huguenots; r/Epis; hon/W/W in S & SW; The Balliet Fam; Soc of Discendents of Colonial Clergy.

WINFIELD, ARLEEN DENT oc/Public Administration; b/Jul 14, 1932; h/3512 Jeff Road, Landover, MD 20785; ba/Washington, DC; m/Emeile I Jr; c/Tawana Tolson Hinton; p/Emily F Dent, Forestville, MD; sp/Lillie G Winfield, Norfolk, VA; ed/BS, Hampton Inst, 1965; Addit Study: George Wash Univ & NIH Grad Sch in Immunology/Virology, 1965-68; Bus Adm, Univ of MD, 1971-73; Num Certs for Def Intell, Profl, Mgrl & Exec Courses, 1967-80; pa/Microbiol Intell Analyst 1965-68, Microbiol 1968-70, Dept of AUS; Sci/Math Tchr, Prince George's Co, MD Schs, 1970-71; Social Sci Res Analyst 1971-75, Social Sci Advr 1975-79, Career Devel Advr, Social Sci Advr 1979-, Wom's Bur, US Dept of Labor; Mem: Leag of Wom Votes, 1966-67; Am Pers & Guid Assn, 1974-77; Chair, Dept of Labor Employee Awds Com, 1975-77; Bus & Profl Wom's Assn, 1975-79; cp/Chair, Civic Assn Planning Com, 1975-78; Co Civic & Coun Rep for Budget, Assessment & Tax Com; Study Dir, Pres Carter's Task Force on Wom Bus Owners, 1977-78; Wash DC Hampton Inst Alumni Assn; Bd of Dirs, Interfaith Commmuns Cable Netwk, 1982-83; r/Meth; hon/Author, Careers for Wom in the '70s, 1972; "Engrg Today & Tomorrow: Wom Needed Too," in Proceedings of Engrg Foun Conf, 1973; Facilitating Career Devel for Wom & Girls, 1973; "The Bottom Line: Unequal Enterprise in Am," Sect of Pres Report, 1978; Co-Author, Wom in Apprenticeship: A Tng Wkshop, 1980; Num Other Articles Pub'd in Profl Jours & Newspapers; Num Radio, TV & Public Spkg Presentations; Deptl Hons, 1965; Spec Achmt Awd, Dept of Labor, 1978; Num Certs, Lttrs of Apprec from Var Orgs Incl'g: Dept of AF, Dept of AUS, NASA, GSA; Invited Spkr, NC Tar Heel Girls St, Univ of NC-Greensboro, Am Legion Aux, 1972-82; Legal Def Fund Wash Com; Hampton Inst Alumni Dir.

WINKLEMAN, GLORIA PAULINE oc/Teacher and Private Elementary Grade Tutor; b/Nov 18, 1944; h/88 Coachman Drive South, Freehold Township, NJ 07728; ba/Perth Amboy, NJ; m/

Edward M Jr; p/Richard and Minnie Santillo, Pompton Plains, NJ; sp/Edward W Winkleman Sr, Garwood, NJ; Marguerite Winkleman (dec); ed/BA, Paterson St Col, 1966; Tchg Related Courses & Sems on Cont'g Ed Basis; pa/1st Grade Tchr, Perth Amboy Bd of Ed, 1966-; Elem Rdg & Math Tutor, 1966-; Mem: NJ Ed Asn; Am Fedn Tchrs, AFL-CIO #857, 1966-; cp/Mbrship Chp, Sea Rayders Inc; Downs Collectors Clb, 1981; Goebel Collectors Clb, 1978-81; r/Cath; hon/Musical Participant, World Music Fest, Kerkrade, Netherlands, 1962.

WINSKI, LOUISE F oc/Staff Biologist; b/Jun 20, 1950; h/1090 Bayless Place, Engleville, PA 19403; ba/West Point, PA; p/Ladislaus and Florence Winski, Phila, PA; ed/BSc in Med Technol, Phi Col of Pharm & Sci, 1972; pa/Staff Biol, Merck, Sharp & Donne, 1975-; Med Technol, Lower Bucks Hosp, 1972-75; Mem: Am Soc of Clin Pathols; Reg'd Med Technol & Affil Mem; cp/Exec Coun, Polish Intercol Clb of Phila, 1983; Bd of Dirs, Alumni Assn of Phil Col of Pharm & Sci, 1983-84; r/Rom Cath; hon/W/W: Among Students in Am Cols & Univs; Among Am Wom.

WIRTHS, WALLACE RICHARD oc/Executive; b/Jul 7, 1921; h/Wantage House, Compton Road, Rural Delivery 3, Sussex, NJ 07461; ba/Same; c/Harold John, Ung N Le; p/Rudolph and Dorothy Wirths (dec); ed/BS, Lehigh Univ, 1942; Att'd Fordham Law Sch, 1943; Addit Courses: NY Univ, Stevens Inst, Rutgers Univ, Upsala Col; mil/USNR, 1950-54; pa/Aluminum Co of Am, 1943-54; Sylvania Elect Co, 1954-56; Westinghouse Elect Corp, 1956-81; Pres, Wantage Galleries Inc, 1981-; cp/Nat Coun on Crime & Delinq, 1966-; Past Chm Essex Co Chapt, NJ Employers Legis Com, 1959-; VPres of Wantage Twnship Com, Sussex Co Repub Com, 1962-; Sussex Co Soil Conserv Dist, 1967-; NJ Farm Bur, 1960-; NJ Agri Soc, 1969-; Life Mem, Sussex Co Hist Soc; Sussex Co SPCA, 1974-; Exec Com, Sussex Co Arts Coun, 1973-; Pres, Unique Homeowners, 1973-; Life Mem, Alexander Linn Hosp Assn; KY Col, 1973-; No NJ Lehigh Alumni Clb, 1964-; Repub Congl Clb, 1972-; Sustaining Mem, Repub Party, 1970-; Reg Hlth Planning Coun, 1979-; Pres Advy Bd, Upsala Co, 1980-; Num Other Coms & Commun Activs; r/Prot; hon/Author of Newspaper Column, "Candidly Spkg," 1970-82; Book: *Candidly Spkg*, 1982; Conserv Farmer of Yr, Sussex Co Soil Conserv Dist, 1975; Host for the Pres, 1972; Fund Raising Prog Awd, Sussex Co Cancer Soc, 1975; Ortho Nat Commun Ser AWd, Chevron, 1976; Commun Ser Awd, Westinghouse Corp, 1976; Donated 1 Million Dollar Sussex Campus to Upala Col, 1978; Sussex Co Citizen of Yr, Radio Sta WSUS, 1979; Outstg Big Brother of Yr, 1978; Outstg Commun Ser Cit, Wantage Twnship, 1978; Hon Doc of Laws, Upsala Col, 1981; Cert of Recog, Nat Repub Congl Com, 1982; Nat Repub Victory Cert, 1979; Awd of Apprec, Repub Nat Com, 1982; Others; W/W: in E, in World, in Fin & Indust, in Commun Ser, of Intells; Men of Achmt; DIB; Other Biogl Listings.

WISE, JANIE DENISE oc/Executive;

b/Dec 15, 1945; h/5020 Puritan Circle, Tampa, FL 33617; ba/Tampa, FL; p/Joseph W Wise (dec); Kathryn S Wise, Lakeland, FL; ed/BA, Univ of KY, 1970; MA, Univ of L'ville, 1972; pa/Pres, Effective Communs (Exec Consltg Firm), 1980-; Communs Spec, Sales-Mktg, 3M Co, 1978-80; Communs Spec, Public Affairs, Tri-Co Alcoholism Sers, 1975-78; Pvt Pract Psychol, 1973-75; Cnslr, Public Affairs, Hillsborough Co Alcoholism Sers, 1972-73; Commun Relats Spec, L'ville, KY, 1971-72; Tchr, 1970-71; Nat Mgmt Conslt; Guest Spkr in Field; FL Rep, Nat Cong for Ofc of Wom, Wash DC; Dir, FL Task Force on Wom & Alcohol; cp/Pilot; hon/"People on the Move," Tampa Bay Area, 1982; Outstg Yg Wom of Yr, St of KY; W/W in Am Wom.

WISEMAN, JAY DONALD oc/Executive and Business Owner; b/Dec 23, 1952; h/6429 South 300 East, Murray, UT 84107; ba/Bountiful, UT; m/Barbara Taylor; c/Jill Reva, Steve Jay; p/Donald Wiseman; Reva Wiseman Peterson, Provo, UT; sp/L Eugene and Helen Taylor, Midvale, UT; ed/Att'd UT St Univ, 197-72; Att'd Univ of UT, 1975-77; pa/Estimator 1976-81, VPres 1981-, A&T Heating; Pres, Owner, Jay Wiseman Photo, 1977-; Mem: IPPA; RMPP of Am; PP of Am; PSA; r/LDS, Mormon, Missionary in Finland; hon/Recog of Photos in *The Profl Photog*, Jul, Oct & Nov, 1983; 1st Place, RMMPA, 1982; 1st Place, IPPA, 1981, 1982 & 1983; Best of Show, IPPA, 1982; Masters Trophy, IPPA, 1982; 75% of Prints Entered Accepted, PP of Am Intl; 88% of Prints Entered Accepted & 3 Hon Mentions, TCC Intl Salon, 1983; W/W in W.

WISLER, NORMAN E oc/Marketing Communications Executive; b/Mar 26, 1943; h/2139 Clay Street, Phila, PA 19130; ba/North Wales, PA; m/Marcia; p/Norman Wisler, Phila, PA; sp/Rose Rosen, W Palm Bch, FL; ed/BS, Temple Univ, 1964; Dipl, Charles Morris Price Sch of Advtg & Jour, 1965; pa/Copy Contact, Tricebock Advtg, Huntington Val, PA, 1965; Advtg Asst, KSM Div, Omark Industs, Morrestown, NJ, 1965-67; Advtg Mgr, Amchem Prods Inc, Ambler, PA, 1967-73; Reg Mktg Mgr, Hitchcock Pub'g Co, Wheaton, IL, 1973-83; Advtg Acct Mgr, Leeds & Northrop Instruments, N Wales, PA, 1983-; Mem: Asst Treas 1972-73, Treas 1973-74, Chm Clins & Sems 1968-70, Dir 1968-72, Hospitality Chm 1978-80, Auditing Chm 1973-75, CBC Com Chm 1980-83, Dir 1980-82, Secy 1983-, Bus Profl Advtg Assn; r/Rom Cath; hon/Contbr, Var Bus-Related Articles to Trade Pubs, 1967-73; Cert'd Bus Communr (CBC) Designation; Bus Profl Advtg Assn, 1980; Alumnus Awd, Charles Morris Price Sch of Advtg & Jour, 1965; W/W: in World, in Fin & Indust.

WITCHER, SETH LAMAR JR oc/Surgeon; b/Mar 28, 1950; h/101 Pompano, Galveston, TX 77550; ba/Galveston, TX; m/Martha Jane; c/Jennifer, Trey; p/Mr and Mrs S L Witcher, Clifton, TX; sp/Mr and Mrs M E Keath, Sabinal, TX; ed/BA 1972, BS 1974, Baylor Univ; Doct of Dental Surg, Univ of TX Dental Sch, 1979; pa/Yth Dir 1970-71, Interim Pastor 1971-72, Kopperl Bapt Ch, TX; Resident, Audie

Murphy VA Hosp, San Antonio, TX, 1979-80; Pvt Pract Gen Dentistry, Hondo, TX, 1980-82; Resident, Oral & Maxillofacial Surg, Galveston,TX, 1982-; Mem: Am Dental Assn; TX Dental Assn; Xi Psi Phi, 1975-79; Univ of TX Dental Sch-San Antonio Alumni Assn; Life Mem, Baylor Alumni Assn; Baylor Lttrman's Assn, 1972-; cp/Asst Scoutmaster Troop 376, Clifton, TX, BSA; Baylor Univ C of C, 1970-74; Coach, Clifton Little Leag Baseball; Pres, Hondo Little Leag, 1981-82; Hondo C of C, 1980-; A Capella Choir, Baylor Univ, 1968-72; r/Mem 1970-75, Mid-wk Meal Com 1974-75, Fin Com 1974-75, SS Tchr for 4 & 5 Yr Olds 1974-75, 7th & James Bapt Ch; Mem 1975-80; Yth (11th & 12th Grades) SS Tchr 1976-78, Manor Bapt Ch, San Antonio; Mem 1980-82, Deacon Selection Com 1980-81, Pastor Search Com 1981-82, 1st Bapt Ch, Hondo; Ch Choirs, 1972-80; Current Mem, 1st Bapt Ch, Galveston; hon/Author of Var Dental Surg Articles Pub'd in Profl Jours; NHS, 1965-68; Eagle Scout 1967, God & Country Awd 1968, BSA; TX Yth Safety Coun, 1967; All-Dist Band, 1967-68; All-Reg Band, 1968; Reg Qualifier, Ready Writing, 1966-68; St Alt, Ready Writing, 1968; Reg Qualifier, Persuasive Spkg, 1968; Hon Grad, 1968; St Qualifier, Solo & Ensemble Contest, 1967; Mosby S'ship Awd, 1979; *Dental Mgmt Mag* Advy Staff, 1981-82.

WITTELES, ELEONORA MEIRA oc/Physicist; b/Jul 14, 1938; h/4714 Browndeer Lane, Palos Verdes, CA 90274; ba/LA, CA; p/Salomon and Rivka Komornik Witteles (dec); ed/BS 1962, MS 1963, Fordham Univ; MS, NY Univ, 1965; PhD, Yeshiva Univ, 1969; pa/Asst Prof, Bar-Ilan Univ, Israel, 1970-72; Indep Conslt, 1972-80; Sr Res Sci, Atlantic Richfield Co, 1980-; Mem: Am Phy Soc; AAAS; IEEE; IEEE Engrg in Med & Biol Soc; IEEE Magnetics Soc; The Com on the Status of Wom in Physics; hon/Author, *Inventions in Med Instrumentation & Cryogenic Instrumentation*; Num Articles Pub'd in Profl Jours in Field of: Solid St Physics, Applied Mat Sci & Superconductivity; Post Doct F'ship, Bar-Ilan Univ, 1969-70; Res F'ship, Yeshiva Univ, 1967-69; W/W of Am Wom.

WOECKENER, JAME M PACHURA oc/Registered Dietician; b/Dec 15, 1949; h/3405 La Selva Drive, San Mateo, CA 94403; ba/Stanford, CA; m/Michael C (dec); p/Edward P Pachura (dec); Helen (Grabski) Pachura, Mosinee, WI; ed/BS, Univ of WI, 1972; MS, Univ of IA, 1976; Dietetic Intern, Univ of IA Hosp & Clins, 1972-73; Reg'd Dietician, 1973-; pa/Reg'd Dietician, Univ of IA Hosp & Clins, 1973-76; Conslt Dietician for Nsg Homes, IA, 1974-76; Clin Instr in Dietetics Sch of Home Ec, Univ of WI-Stevens Point, 1976-77; Food Ser Admr I & Dir of Dietetic Interns, Univ of WI Hosp-Madison, 1977-80; Asst Dir of Dietetics/Nutritional Sers, Stanford Univ Hosp, Stanford, CA, 1980-; Mem: Am Dietetic Assn; Am Hosp Assn; Am Soc for Parenteral & Enteral Nutrition; CA Dietetic Assn; Chm Quality Assurance Com, San Jose Peninsula Dist Dietetic Assn, 1982-84; Clin Nutrition Mgmt Pract Grp; Am Soc for Hosp Food Ser Admrs; Omicron Nu; Sigma Zeta; Other Previous Profl Assns; r/Rom Cath; hon/Co-Author, "Urinary

Urea-Nitrogen Ratio as an Index of Protein Nutrition in Diabetic Pregnancy," in *Jour of OB & Gyn*, 1978; Internship, S'ship, WI Dietetic Assn, 1972; S'ship, Alpha Delta Alpha Dietetics Clb, 1972; Traineeship Grant, Dept of Hlth, Ed & Welfare, 1973-76; W/W in W.

WOHL, EMANUEL oc/Insurance Broker; b/Oct 11, 1920; h/3150 Rochambeau Avenue, New York, NY 10467; ba/ New York, NY; p/Samuel and Fannie Wohl (dec); ed/BS, Col of City of NY, 1943; MS, NY Univ, 1948; Bus Adm, Alexander Hamilton Inst, 1954; LLB, LaSalle Ext Univ, 1969; pa/Chemist, Keto Chem Co, LI, NY, 1943-44; Chem, Radio Receptor Co, NYC, 1944-48; Res Chem, Sylvania Elect Prods Inc, Boston, MA, 1948-49; Sr Chem, Galvanic Prods Corp, Val Stream, NY, 1952-53; Ptner, Riviera Wine & Liquor Co, Bronx, NY, 1954-61; Abstractor, Chem Abstracts Sers, Am Chem Soc, Columbus, OH, 1963-64; Reg'd Rep, Becker, Nagler & Weisman Inc, Bronx, NY, 1963-67; Ins Broker-Agt, Securities Broker-Dealer, Paramount Brokerage Co, Bronx, NY 1969-; Mem: Nat Assn of Securities Dealers Inc; Am Chem Soc; cp/Dem Co Com, 1967 & 1968; Participant, White House Conf on Small Bus, 1979; Bd of Dirs, NY Univ Gard Sch of Arts & Sci Alumni; Intl Clarinet Soc; hon/Author, "Studies w N-Acetyl Phenylisopropylamine Derivatives (Olefin-Nitrile Condensation)"; W/W in Fin & Indust.

WOJCIECHOWSKA, CÉCILE CLOUTIER oc/Professor and Writer; b/ Jun 13, 1930; h/44 Farm Greenway, Don Mills, Ontario, Canada, M2A 3M2; ba/ Toronto, Ontario, Canada; m/Jerry; c/ Maria, Eve; ed/BA 1951, MA 1953, Licence es Lettres 1953, Dipl d'Etudes Supérieures 1954, Laval Univ; Doct in Esthétique, Univ of Paris, The Sorbonne, 1962; MPh, McMaster Univ, 1978; MTh, Univ of Toronto, 1981; pa/ Prof of Latin, Greek, Spanish & Fr Lit, Marymount Col, Quebec, 1955-58; Prof of Fr & Quebec Lit, Univ of Ottawa, 1958-64; Prof Aesthetics, Fr & Quebec Lit, Univ of Toronto, 1965-; Guest Prof, Laval Univ, Sums 1969-72; Vis'g Prof, Queen's Univ, Fall Sem 1980; Mem: MLA; Am Assn of Tchrs of French; Assn Canadienne des Professeurs de Francais; Société des Ecrivains Canadiens; Société des Poetes; Pen Clb; Assn des Anciens de l'Université de Paris; Société d'Esthétique de Paris; Am Soc of Aesthetics; Brit Soc of Aesthetics; Assn des Ecrivains de Langue Francais; Intl Platform Assn; cp/Participant in Num Confs; Num Lectr & Spkg Presentations; r/Cath; hon/Author, Books of Poetry Incl: *Mains de Sable*, 1960; *Cuivre Et Oies*, 1964; *Cannelles Et Craie*, 1969; *Paupieres*, 1970; *Cablegrammes*, 1972; *Chalevils*, 1979; *Springtime of Spoken Words*, 1979; Num Articles, Reviews & Wks of Translations; Médaille D'argent de la Société des Ecrivains Francais, Paris, 1960 (Prix Jugé par Jean Cocteau); Prix du Concours de la Comm du Centenaire, Ottawa, 1967; Others.

WOLAVER, LYNN E oc/Dean for Research; b/Mar 10, 1924; h/1380 Timberwyck Court, Fairborn, OH 45324; ba/Wright-Patterson AFB, OH; m/Arah-Dean S; c/Stephen A, Rick S; p/Mr and Mrs Lendle H Wolaver (dec);

sp/Mrs Arthur H Scheele, Springfield, IL; ed/BS 1949, MS 1950, Univ of IL; PhD, Univ of MI, 1964; mil/USAAC, 1944-46; pa/Positions at Wright-Patterson AFB, OH: Engr, Wright Air Devel Ctr, USAF, 1950-56; Applied Math 1956-65, Dir 1966-71, Aerospace Res Labs, USAF; Dean for Res, AF Inst of Technol, USAF, 1971-; Mem: Soc of Industl & Applied Math (SIAM); IEEE; Biofeedback Soc; Fellow, Brit Interplanetary Soc; MWn Simulation Coun; AAAS; Am Soc for Engrg Ed; cp/ Fairborn, OH Planning Bd; r/Luth; hon/ Author, *Mod Techniques in Astrodynamics*, 1970; Over 60 Papers in Field of Navigatin, Astrodynamics, Nonlinear Sys, Modeling Physiol Sys, 1950-80; Meritorious Civilian Ser Awd, USAF, 1979; Eta Kappa Nu, 1949; Tau Beta Pi, 1970; Sigma Xi, 1974; Outstg Tchr 1978-82; W/W: in MW, in Govt; Am Men & Wom of Sci; DIB; Ldrs in Am Sci; Outstg Ldrs in Ed.

WOLENS, MICKEY EARL oc/Corporate Purchasing Manager; b/Jan 6, 1937; h/3500 Williams & Mary Road, Birmingham, AL 35216; ba/B'ham, AL; m/ Mary Bobbie Wolens; c/Jason Zachary, Heather Lynne; p/Cyril Wolens (dec); Elaine Wolens, Corsicana, TX; ed/BBA 1982, MBA 1982, Pacific Wn Univ; Att'd Num Mgmt Sems, 1974-80; mil/AUS Armored Div, 1958-61, SP4 (CPL); pa/ Purchasing Mgr 1979 & 1982-, Asst Mgr of Purchasing 1980-82, B E & K Constrn Co, B'ham, AL; Procurement Mgr 1976-79 & 1979-80, The Litwin Corp, Houston, TX; Purchasing Mgr 1974-76, Mgr of Inspection, Expediting & Traffic 1974, Proj Purchasing Agt 1973-74, Davy Powergas Inc, Lakeland, FL; Sr Buyer, Hess Oil Virgin Isl Corp, St Croix, Virgin Isl, 1973; Purchasing Agt 1970-73, Supvr of Field Inspectors/ Expeditors 1969-70, Asst Purchasing Agt 1967-69, The M W Kellogg Co, Houston, TX; Sr Buyer, Trinity Industs Inc, Dallas, TX; Cert'd Purchasing Mgr (CPM), Nat Assn of Purchasing Mgmt Inc; Purchasing Mgmt Assn of AL Inc; Chm Mbrship Com 1983, Assoc'd Bldrs & Contractors of AL Inc (ABC); W/W in S & SW.

WOLF, JACK oc/Insurance and Financial Planning; b/Nov 9, 1934; h/2927 Robinson Road, Missouri City, TX 77459; ba/Houston, TX; m/Marlene; c/ David, Michael, Stephen; p/Joseph Wolf (dec); Mary Wolf, Kansas City, MO; ed/ BA, Univ of MO, 1956; Chartered Life Underwriter (CLU), Am Col of Life Ins, 1972; mil/AUS; pa/Agt & Gen Mgr, Jack Wolf, CLU Ins, 1967-; Mem: Am Soc of CLU, 1972-; Million Dollar Round Table, 1980-; cp/VPres 1983-84, E Ft Bend Kiwanis Clb; Life Master, Am Contract Bridge Leag, 1959-; Qualifying Mem, Million Dollar Round Table, 1980-84; TX Ldr's Round Table, Lone Star Ldr, 1983; W/W in SW.

WOLF, SEYMOUR SY oc/Executive; b/May 12, 1921; h/2245 Vistact, Northbrook, IL 60062; ba/Northfield, IL; m/ Ellie; c/Susan, Stephen, Charles; p/ Charles and Mae Wolf (dec); sp/David & Gussie Schreiber (dec); ed/LLB, NWn Univ, 1948; Att'd Col of Pacific; mil/ AUS, 1941-45; pa/VPres, Selected Brands Inc; Pres, Ceramic World; Pres, S C Ltd; cp/Magistrate, Niles Twnship; Staff Profl, US Golf Acad; World Golf Hall of Fame; Canadian Football Assn;

r/Jewish; hon/Ideaism Awd, City Hope; Cert of Apprec, City Hope; W/W; W/ W in MW; Personalities of MW.

WOLFE, CHARLES EDWARD oc/ Methodist Clergyman; b/Nov 7, 1931; h/3100 Shiloh Road, Hampstead, MD 21074; ba/Same; m/Helen Bickel; c/ Christian, Hawley, Lewis, David; p/Mrs Harley Strawer, Zephyrhills, FL; ed/BA, No IA Univ, 1952; BD, Austin Presb Theol Sem, 1958; DMin, Wesley Theol Sem, 1977; mil/AUS, 1966-69, Chaplain, VietNam Ser 1967-68; AUS Command & Gen Staff Col; DC NG Chaplain Corps, Lt Col Ret'd; pa/Adj Prof, Wn MD Col, Current; Bible Instr, Course of Study, Wesley Theol Sem, Current; Pastor, Shiloh Meth Ch, Hampstead, MD, 1977-; Pastor, W End Presb Ch, Albany, NY, 1971-76; Pastor, 1st Presb Ch, Killeen, TX, 1960-66; Assoc Pastor, Delmar Meth Ch, NY, 1968-69; Chaplain, AUS, 1966-69; Mem: Soc Biblical Lit; r/Meth; hon/ Presenter of Scholarly Papers at Nat & Reg Meetings; Author, *Homecoming: 1st Person Sermons*, 1979; *The 7 Words From the Cross: A Commentary*, 1980; *Exegesis of the Biblical Texts for the Spec Days Exegetical Resource*, 1982; "Exegetical Resource," for *Pulpit Resource*; Scholarly Jour Awd 1983, Fac Book Awd 1980, Wn MD Col; W/W in Rel; NG Register; DIB; Commun Ldrs of Am; Men of Achmt.

WONG, BETTY JEAN oc/Educatinal Administrator; b/Mar 15, 1949; h/1137 Woodfield Drive, Jackson, MS 39211; ba/Jackson, MS; p/Mr and Mrs Henry Wong, Greenville, MS; ed/BS Ednl Psych, MS St Univ, 1971; MEd Guid & Cnslg, Delta St Univ, 1973; pa/Career Devel Spec, Greenville mun Separate Sch Dist, 1973-74; Instnl Mats Spec for Career Ed 1974-76, Res Spec 1976-77, Res Curric Spec, Res/Curric Unit 1977-79, MS St Univ; Coor of Res, Curricula, Tchr Ed 1979-80, Asst Dir Supportive Sers Sect Voc Div 1980-, St Dept of Ed; Mem: St Exec Bd, MS Pers & Guid Assn; Am Pers & Guid Assn; MS Voc Assn; Nat Policy Bd Guid Sect 1982-84, Planning Com for Nat Conv 1984, Am Voc Assn; Handbook Chp 1976, AAUW; Nat Voc Guid Assn; MS Voc Cnslrs Assn; cp/Jackson Symph Leag; Jackson Arts Alliance; New Stage Theatre; r/Bapt; hon/Author of Career Ed Mats & the Job Placement Handbook for Voc Cnslrs in MS; Commun Advy Coun, EBCE Itawamba Jr Col; One of 15 Outstg Wom in US in Voc Ed, Am Voc Assn, 1983; W/W: in S, of Wom; Personalities of S; Notable Ams.

WONG, OTTO oc/Epidemiologist/ Biostatistician; b/Nov 14, 1947; h/111 Clyde Drive, Walnut Creek, CA 94598; ba/Berkeley, CA; m/Betty; c/Elaine, Jonathan; p/K Wong, Toronto, Canada; sp/B Yeung, Tucson, AZ; ed/BS, Univ of AZ, 1970; MS, Carnegie-Mellon Univ, 1972; MS 1973, ScD 1975, Univ of Pgh; pa/Sr Epidemiligist, Envir Hlth Assocs, 1981-; Dir of Occupl Res, Biometric Res Inst, Wash DC 1980-81; Dir of Epidemiology, Tabershaw Occupl Med Assocs, 1978-80; Asst Prof Epidemiology, Georgetown Univ Sch of Med, 1975-78; Mem: Am Col of Epidemiology; Am Statl Assn; Biometric Soc; Soc for Epidemiol Res; APHA; Soc for Clin Trial; Soc for Occupl & Envir Hlth; hon/ Author, Num Articles Pub'd in Profl Jours Incl'g: *Intl Jour of Epidemiology*; *Jour* of Occupl Med; Jour of Chronic Diseases; Am Jour of Clin Nutrition; Brit Jour of Industl Med; Intl S'ship Recip, Univ Scholar, Univ of AZ; Pi Mu Epsilon; Phi Beta Kappa; Grad BS magna cum laude; W/W: in CA, in W.

WOOD, ARLETTA RENEE oc/Executive; b/Apr 19, 1945; h/2418 Homestead Drive, Silver Spring, MD 20902; ba/Washington, DC; ed/BSBA, Howard Univ, 1967; pa/Exec Secy to Dept Hd, OH Dept of Ed, 1963-64; Adm Secy to Hd Botany Dept, Howard Univ, 1964-66; Adm Asst, Exec & Adm Secy Var Locations, 1967-79; Adm Secy, Air Trans Assn of Am, Wash DC, 1979; Fdr & Pres, Affil Enterprises Inc (Artists Mgmt & Fin Brokerage), Silver Spring, MD, 1967-; Pres, B I Prodns, 1971-79; Pres Renee's Beauty Boutique, 1974-79; Mem: Air Transport Assn; Pres 1980-81, Am Employees Assn; Am Soc Profl & Exec Wom; UN Assn US Pres's Assn; Am Mgmt Assn; Intl Platform Assn; Am Lyceum Assn; Am Film Inst; Am Fedn of Musicians; cp/Nat Trust Hist Presv; Smithsonian Instn; Spiritualist Clb; Toastmasters Intl; hon/ "Arletta Renee Day," Proclamation by Mayor Marion Bradley of Wash DC, Jan 8, 1982; W/W: in S, in A, in World, of Wom, Among Black Ams, in Fin & Indust; Dir Dist'd Ams; 2000 Notable Am Personalities.

WOOD, CHARLES NEWBOLD oc/ Self-Employed; b/Jan 16, 1943; h/Mill House Farm, 31 West Fourbridges Road, Long Valley, NJ 07853; ba/Same; p/ Wilfrid and Charlotte Wood (dec); ed/ Att'd St Bernards Col; BA, MA, PhD, Yale Univ, 1966; pa/Self-Employed, Mill House Farm & Horse Farm (Cedar Hill Farm); Doct of Psych; r/High Espc; hon/ Racing, Riding & Sailing; NY Social Register.

WOOD, FAY S oc/National Sales Manager; b/Aug 22, 1945; h/61-20 Grand Ctl Parkway, Forest Hills, NY 11375; ba/New York, NY; c/Deborah S, Esther L; p/Paul H Wiener, Phila, PA; sp/Dorothy B Berkowitz (dec); BA, PA St Univ, 1967; Grad Exec Mgmt Courses RCA Corp, 1977; pa/Nat Sales Mgr 1982-, Quantech Corp; Pres, Full Line Repairs Ctrs Inc, 1979-82; Reg Sales Mgr RCA Ser Co, 1976-79; VPres Sales, P H D Hearing Ctrs Inc, 1972-76; Dist Sales Mgr, Beltone Hearing Aid Ctrs, 1970-72; Sales Rep, Real Est of PA, 1968-70; Mem: AAUW; Bus & Profl Wom; NAFE; Wom Bus Owners; Leag of Wom Voters; cp/B'nai B'rith; NYC Comm on the Status of Wom; r/Jewish; hon/Articles Pub'd in HFD Retailing Hom Furnishings; Sales & Mktg Mgmt Mag; Master Conslt Awd, 1975; Reg Mgr of Yr Awd, 1979; 1st Deg Black Belt, Tae Kwan Do, Karate, 1975; W/W of Am Wom.

WOOD, KATHERINE E oc/Social Worker; b/Jul 4, 1950; h/331 North Hass, Frankenmuth, MI 48734; ba/Bay City, MI; m/Michael (dec); c/Jared M Wood; p/Maurice and June Finger, Frankenmuth, MI; sp/Harold Wood and Cynthia Rose, Rose City and Clio, MI; ed/BA, Valparaiso Univ, 1971; MSW, Wayne St Univ, 1976; pa/Tchr's Aide, Nursery for Emotionally Impaired Chd, S Bend, IN, 1971; Sch Social Wkr, Grand Blanc & Goodrich Sch Dists, MI, 1972; Subst Tchr, Frankenmuth, Clio & Birch

Run Sch Dists, MI, 1973-74; Clin Social Wkr & Pre-intake Wkr, Bay Area Guid Ctr, Bay City, MI 1976-81; Pvt Pract Cert'd Social Wkr, Bay City, MI, 1982-; Mem: Nat Assn of Social Wkrs, 1971-; Wom's Chair 1982-84, VPres in Charge of Programming 1983-85, AAUW; r/ Prot; hon/Play & Observation Rms Dedicated in Her Name, Bay Area Guid Ctr, MI, 1981; W/W: in Am Wom, in World of Wom.

WOOD, LARRY (MARYLAIRD) oc/ Journalist, Educator; h/6161 Castle Drive, Oakland, CA 94611; c/Mary, Marcia, Barry; p/Edward Hayes and Alice (McNeel) Small; ed/BA 1938, MA 1940, Univ of WA-Seattle; Postgrad Study 1941-42, Cert in Photo 1971, Stanford Univ; Postgrad Wk in Jour: Univ of WI, 1971-72; Univ of MN 1971-72; Univ of GA 1972-73; Univ of CA-Santa Cruz, 1974-76; pa/By-line Columnist, Oakland Tribune, SF Chronicle, 1946-; Contbg Editor: Mech Illus, 1946-; Popular Mech, 1948-; Feature Writer Wn Reg: Christian Sci Monitor, CSM Radio Syn & Intl News, 1973-; Des Moines Register & Tribune Syn, 1973-; Contbg Editor, Travelday Mag, 1976-; Author, Contbg Editor: Fodor Guides, David McKay Co, NYC, 1982; (Book) SF, 1982; Charles Merrill Co Sci Series 1982-83; Bell & Howell (Charles Merrill, USA) Worldwide Editions of Focus On Sci, 4 Books, 1983-; Reg Corres: Spokane Mag; CA Corres, Money Mag; Portland Oregonian; Seattle Times Sunday Mag; Far W Contbg Editor, Fashion Showcase, Dallas; Byline Feature Writer, Photog, Parade Mag, 1960-; Feature Writer Industl Progress: CA Today, 1977-; E/W Netwk, 1982-; Feature Writer, Chevron USA, 1982; Feature Writer Motorland Pubs: AAA Travel Mag-No CA & AAA Travel Mag-So CA; Wk for Syn Feature Synopses on Radio Stas, CSM Radio News Ser; Freelance Writer Var Mags Incl'g: Times Mirror Co Syn; Knight Ridder Syn; Linguapress France; Parents; Sports Illus'd; Ocean & Seas Frontiers; Accent; People on Parade; House Beautiful; Am Home; Others; Dir Public Relats, No CA Assn Phi Beta Kappa, 1969-; Asst Prof Jour, Envir Sci & Pub Relats, San Diego St Univ, 1975-; Other Positions; Mem: Intl Assn of Bus Commrs; Coun for Advmt in Sci Writing; Nat Acad of TV Arts & Scis; CA Press Wom; Public Relats Soc of Am; Am Mgmt Assn; Nat Exec Bd Mag Div 1979-, Nat Chm Travel Writing Contest for Am Univ Students 1978-, Am Assn Edn in Jour; Advtg & Mktg Assn; Nat Assn Sci Writers; Travel Writers of Am; Soc Profl Jours; Nat Press Clb; Sigma Delta Chi; CA Writers Clb; Num Other Orgs; cp/Secy, Oakland Jr Arts Ctr, 1962-; Trustee, CA St Pks Foun, 1976-; Other Commun Activs; hon/Author, Eng for Social Living: Tell the Town; Principles of Sci Series (4 Books); Feature Writer (Bus & Sci) Honoree, Chevron USA & Oakland C of C, 1983; Cit, Nat Pk Ser, 1976; Nat Headline Awd, Mercury News, 1979 & 1980; NOAA Cit, 1981 & 1982; Wks Selected for CA Rm, Oakland Public Lib & NW Rm, Univ of WA Lib; Num Other Hons & Awds; W/W of World.

WOOD, LINCOLN JACKSON oc/ Aerospace Engineer and University Professor; b/Sep 30, 1947; ba/Jet Propulsion Lab, 4800 Oak Grove Drive, Pasadena, CA 91109; p/William Hulbert

and Sarah Brock (Strumsky) Wood; ed/ BS, Cornell Univ, 1968; MS 1969, PhD 1972, Stanford Univ; pa/Bechtel Instr in Engrg 1972-74, Lectr in Sys Engrg 1975-76, Vis'g Asst Prof of Sys Engrg 1976-78, Vis'g Assoc Prof of Sys Engrg 1978-, CA Inst of Technol, Pasadena, CA; Staff Engr, Sys Anal Lab, Space & Communs Grp, Hughes Aircraft Co, El Segundo, CA, 1974-77; Tech Staff 1977-81, Tech Grp Supvr (Future Mission Studies Grp) 1981-, Navigation Sys Sect, Jet Propulsion Lab, CA Inst of Technol; Conslt to Var Aerospace Cos, 1972-74 & 1979; Mem: Sr Mem, Space Flight Mech Com 1980-, Am Astronaut Soc; AIAA; AAAS; IEEE; Assoc Editor, Jour of the Astronaut Scis, 1980-83; Jour of Guid, Control & Dynamics, 1983-; cp/Del, CA Dem Coun Conv, 1978; VPres & Dir 1980-, LA Stanford Bachelors; Pres, Seal & Serpent Soc, 1967-68; LA Co Mus of Art; Cornell & Stanford Alumni Assns; hon/Author & Co-Author Over 30 Tech Papers on Interplanetary Navigation, Trajectory Optimization, Gravity Field Estimation & Control Theory; Sigma Xi; Tau Beta Pi; Phi Kappa Phi; Phi Eta Sigma; Dean's List, 1964-68; NSF Trainee, 1968-72; W/ W: in CA, in W, in Aviation & Aerospace; Men of Achmt; Commun Ldrs of Am; DIB; Dir of Dist'd Ams; Num Other Biogl Listings.

WOOD, RONALD WILSON oc/ Engineering Management; b/Nov 17, 1943; h/6267 North Lausanne Drive, Mobile, AL 36608; ba/Pascagoula, MS; m/Janith Carolyn; c/Christopher Darby, Heather Michelle; p/Frank W and Renee S Wood, Farmington, NH; sp/Harold W and Freta Maine, Kinsington, CA; ed/ BSME, Worcester Polytech Inst, 1965; MBA, Univ of S AL, 1976; pa/Staff Asst to Dir of Design Engrg 1982-, MGR US Nav Res & Devel Studies 1980-82, Proj Mgr 1978-80, Sec Mgr 1974-78, Sr Engr 1969-74, Ingalls Shipbldg Co, Pascagoula, MS; Engr, Elect Boat Co, 1965-69; Mem: Local Coun, Am Soc of Nav Engrs; ASME; Soc of Nav Archs & Marine Engrs; Am Def Preparedness Assn; cp/Coach & Bd Mem, Springhill Dixie Boys Baseball; r/Epis; hon/W/W in S & SW.

WOOD, SANDRA E oc/Systems Analyst Programmer; b/Jun 27, 1944; h/ PO Box 303, Big Island, VA 24526; ba/ Big Island, VA; p/Mr and Mrs W L Wood Dr, Big Isl, VA; ed/Exec Secy Cert 1970, Cert'd Profl Secy 1972, Phillips Bus Col; BA 1982, MBA Cand, Lynchburg Col; pa/Sales Clk, G C Murphy, 1962; Sales Clk, Baldwin's, 1962-63; Secy, Schewels Furn Co, 1963-64; Secy, C W Hancock & Sons Inc, 1964-66; Secy in Var Positions 1966-74, Data Processing Supvr/Programmer 1974-76, Sys Anal Programmer 1977-, Owens IL Inc; Mem: Secy, Exec VPres, Pres, Data Processing Mgmt Assn, 1977-; CRS Assocs, 1972-; Chapt Treas, Chapt 1st VPres, Chapt Pres, Sem Chm, Chapt Conv Del, Div Com Chm, Coor 1982 SE Dist Conf, Profl Secys Assn; Participant, Wom's Focus, 1983; cp/Secy, Bedford Co Trans Safety Comm, 1974-; r/Meth; hon/Interviewed in Data Mgmt Mag, 1981; Valedictorian HS Sr Class; Chapt Secy of Yr, 1970; Outstg Alumni, Phillips Bus Col, 1972; Gold Key Hon Soc 1982, Grad cum laude, Lynchburg Col; Beta Clb, 1961-62; NHS; Outstg

Yg Wom of Am; W/W of Am Wom.

WOODARD, MARSHA BROWN oc/ Minister of Christian Education; b/Mar 22, 1949; h/5610 Enright Apartment 108, St Louis, MO 63112; ba/St Louis, MO; p/Mr Portia Brown, Univ City, MO; Mrs Laura Brown, St Louis, MO; ed/BA, Ottawa Univ (KS), 1971; MDiv, Eden Theol Sem, 1980; pa/Tchr, Franklin Co Day Care, Ottawa, KS, 1971-73; Tchr, Webster Groves Day Care, 1973-76; Dir Acad of Urban Sers, Child Devel Ctr, 1976-77; Dir, James E Cook Nursery, 1977-80; Min of Christian Ed, Antioch Bapt Ch, 1980-; Mem: Exec Coun 1981-85, Ch Wom U Metro St Louis; 2nd VPres, Metro Min Alliance, 1983; Secy 1982, Bd Mem, Early Child Care Devel Corp; Nat Coun of Christians & Jews; Clergy Support Com, The Opports Industrialization Corp; cp/ YWCA; r/Bapt; hon/Author of Var Articles Pub'd in Ch Wom Mag, 1983; Chd's Tchr SS Pub'g Bd, 1983; Commun Ser Awd, OES, 1982; Outstg Yg Wom of Am.

WOODS, GLORIA JEAN SUGGS oc/ Administrative Assistant; b/Dec 19, 1948; h/5601 Hamil Road #227, Houston, TX 77039; ba/Houston, TX; m/ Arthur Allen; p/George Lee and Clarice (Cassidy) Suggs, Durham, NC; sp/Uhl and Marcella Woods, Ooltewah, TX; ed/ BA, NC Ctl Univ, 1971; MA, Howard Univ, 1972; EdD 1982 & Current Postgrad Wk, TX So Univ; pa/Tchr, Bd of Ed, Norwalk, CT, 1973-76; Tchr 1976-80, Adm Asst for Asst Supt of Pers 1980-, N Forest ISD, TX; Mem: TX Assn of Sch Pers Admrs; TX ST Tchrs Assn; Assn of Supvn & Curric Devel; Nat Assn Female Execs; Am Assn of Sch Pers Admrs; r/Bapt; hon/Outstg Fac Rep, N Forest ISD, 1980; Ms NC Ctl Univ Band, 1970; W/W of Am Wom.

WOODS, JONATHAN CARL oc/ Engineer, Executive; b/Aug 11, 1939; h/ Two Breakers Isle, Laguna Niguel, CA 92677; ba/Huntington Bch, CA; m/Janet Sue Parker; c/Christine, Nicola, Jonathan; p/Carl S Woods, Gallipolis, OH; Rugh C Woods, San Gabriel, CA; sp/ Helen Parker, Mission Viejo, CA; ed/ Cert in Paint Technol, LA City Col, 1962; AA, E LA Col, 1962; BS, Univ of Redlands, 1980; mil/USMC, 1962-65; pa/Fdr & Pres, Engard Coatings Corp, Huntington Bch, CA, 1964-; Formulating Coating Chem, Mobil Chem Corp, Azusa, CA, 1963-64; Formulating Coating Chem, Magna Corp, Santa Fe Springs, CA, 1961-63; Mem: Nat Assn of Corrosion Engrs; Am Soc for Testing & Mats; Nat Paint & Coatings Assn; LA Soc for Coating Technol; Am Water Wkrs Assn; cp/Reg Comm, Coach & Referee, Am Yth Soccer Org; Mission Viejo Gymnastics Acad Booster Clb; Poorer Man's Poker Clb of Laguna Bch; r/Luth; hon/Active Mem of ASTM Subcom Do1-43 which Prepared the Manual of Coating Wk for Light-Water Nuclear Power Plant Primary Containment & Other Safety Related Facilities, 1979; W/W: in CA, in W.

WOODS, POWELL oc/Lawyer; b/Jan 19, 1922; h/411 South Britt, Siloam Springs AR 72761; ba/Siloam Springs, AR; m/Lola Lavoy Keener; c/Lola Lavoy (Mrs Steve Walthour), John Powell III; p/John Powell and Mabel Fairfax Hon Woods (dec); sp/Orlando Roswell and Myrtle Harris Keener (dec); ed/BS, Univ

of AR-Fayetteville, 1948; LLB, AR Law Sch-Little Rock, 1950; mil/AUS, 1943-45; pa/City Atty, Siloam Springs, 1960-62 & 1973-75; Mun Judge, Siloam Springs, 1963-64; Gen Pract, Currently; Mem: ABA; Benton Co Bar Assn; AR Bar Assn; Comml Law Leag; cp/ Secy-Treas, Siloam Springs Salvation Army, 1962-81; Rotary Clb; Isaac Walton Leag; Am Legion; NW AR Geol Soc; Benton Co Hist Assn; r/Meth; W/ W in S & SW; AR Lives.

WOODWORTH, GENE BOSWELL oc/Teacher; b/Oct 11, 1926; h/704 Madison Street, Manchester, TN 37355; ba/Tullahoma, TN; c/Jill, Camille, Patricia, John; p/Carl and Vida Langford Boswell, Manchester, TN; ed/ BS 1968, MA 1975, Mid TN St Univ; pa/Tchr, Tullahoma TN Sch Sys, 1968-; Mem: Assn for Supvn & Curric Devel; NEA; TN Ed Assn; Med TN Ed Assn; Past Pres, Tullahoma Ed Assn; cp/ Tullahoma Hist Assn; Bus & Profl Wom Manchester; r/Meth; hon/S'ship, Freedom Foun, 1979-80; S'ship, NSF, 1978 & 1981; Panel Mem, NSF Grant Awds, 1980; W/W: in S & SW, in Am; Personalities of S.

WOOLARD, GILBERT GARLAND JR oc/Educator, School Administrator; b/Sep 23, 1929; h/108 Valley Court, Camden, SC 29020; ba/Camden, SC; m/ Betty Heath; c/Garland, Becky, David; p/G G and Inez Woolard (dec); sp/Henry and Lilian Heath (dec); ed/BS, MA, E Carolina Univ, 1951; EdD (EPDA Fellow), NC St Univ, 1973; Postgrad Wk: Univ of CA; Univ of SC; Clemson Univ; Ball St Univ; mil/USAF, 1951-56, Jet Fighter Pilot/Instr, Korea; pa/Prin, Bushy Fork Sch, 1951; Mgr, Woolard Furniture Co, Williamston, NC, 1956-63; Mgr, Kimbrell's Furniture Col, Camden, SC, 1964-68; Dir, Kershaw Co Voc Ctr & Dist Voc & Adult Ed Progs, Camden, SC, 1968-; Ednl Conslt & Adj Prof: Univ of SC & Var Gvt Agys & Fgn Countries; Mem: AASA; AVA; AEA; NAPCAE; Phi Delta Kappa; ACE; Camden Merchs Coun, 1967; SC Voc Dirs Assn, 1974; SC Voc Assn, 1979; Former Commandant of Cadets, SC Civil Air Patrol, 1968-72; Num Other Ednl & Aviation Coms & Orgs; cp/Past Pres: Williamston Kiwanis, U Fund, C of C, 1960; Scoutmaster; Commr; Ch Bd & Tchr, Williamston, 7 Yrs; r/Meth; hon/Author, Master Craftsman-Master Techr, Some Got To Fly, Num Other Ednl Articles; Yg Man of Yr, Williamston JC's, 1960; Silver Beaver Awd, BSA, 1963; Num Dist'd Sers Awds; SC Legis Commend, 1976; SC Voc Edr, 1979; W/ W: in S & SW, in Aviation, in Ed.

WOOLLIAMS, KEITH RICHARD oc/Arboretum and Botanical Garden Director; b/Jul 17, 1940; h/47-722J Ahuimanu Loop, Kaneohe, HI 96744; ba/Haleiwa, HI; m/Akiko; c/Frank Hiromi, Angela Misako; p/Gordon and Margaret Woolliams, England; sp/ Toshio and Nobuko Narita, Japan; ed/ Grad, Royal Botanic Gardens, Kew, UK, 1963; Var Certs in Horticulture, Royal Horticulture Soc; Cert of Arborculture, Royal Forestry Soc of England & Wales; pa/Hd Res Sta, Univ of London, UK, 1963-65; Horticulturist, Hotel Grp, Bermuda, 1965-67; Curator, Botanic Garden, Dept of Forests, Div of Botany, Lae, Papua, New Guinea, 1967-68; Studied Horticulture/Botany in Japan,

1969-70; Horticulturist & Supt, Pacific Tropical Botanical Garden, Kauai, HI, 1971-74; Horticulturist 1974-80, Dir 1980-, Waimea Arboretum & Botanical Graden, Oahu, HI; Mem: Res Affil, Bishop Mus (Botany), Honolulu, HI; Am Assn Botanic Gradens & Arboreta; Am Horticulture Soc; Royal Horticulture Soc, London; Pres 1980, HI Botanical Soc; hon/Editor 1973-, Notes From Waimea Arboretum 10 Volumes to Date; Author, Var Horticulture Articles Pub'd in Profl Jours & Pub'd Ednl Series: "Waimea Arboretum Foun (HI Plants for Cultivation)"; W/W in W.

WOOTEN, JOAN GUYMON oc/ Elementary Instructor; b/Dec 14, 1949; h/Route 8, 112 North Kerns Drive, Gulfport, MS 39503; ba/Gulfport, MS; m/Michael Lynn; c/Jeffrey Michael; p/ Mr and Mrs Martin L "Bud" Watson, Wesson, MS; sp/Roy L Wooten, Brittany, LA; Sally Wooten, Collin, MS; ed/ AA, Copiah-Lincoln Jr Col, 1969; BS, Univ of So MS, 1971; MA 1979, AAA 1980, Wm Carey Col; Extended Studies, Gulf Park, 1980; pa/Tchr, Harrison Ctl Elem Sch 1971-75; Tchr, Bel-Aire Elem Sch, 1975-; Hd Tchr, Title I, 1979; Adult Ed Tchr, 1981-; Mem: NEA; MS Ed Assn; Harrison Co Tchr Assn; Assn Supvn & Curric Devel; Nat Math for Elem Tchrs; FTA; Phi Delta Kappa; cp/ Grade Chm 1972-75, Hospitality Chm 1972-75, Wesley Foun; r/Meth; hon/ Author, "A Study of the Effects of Adding Phonetic Instrn to a Basal Rdg Prog"; Moose Lodge S'ship, 1967; W/ W: in S & SW, in Am Ed.

WORD, AMOS JARMAN III oc/ Architect; b/Mar 10, 1949; h/101 Gillon Drive, Birmingham, AL 35209; ba/ B'ham, AL; p/Mary David Word, Inverness, MS; ed/Att'd Univ of MS, 1967-69; Att'd Delta St Univ, Sum 1969; BA, Auburn Univ, 1973; pa/Grad & Arch, Brewer Godbold & Assoc, Clarksdale, MS 1973-78; Arch, Blondheim, Williams & Golson, B'ham, AL, 1978-79; Assoc, The Ritchie Org, B'ham, AL, 1979-; Mem: AIA, 1978-; Cert, Nat Coun of Arch Registration Bd; r/Bapt; hon/AIA Cert of Recog, Participation in Cont'g Ed; W/W in S & SW; Personalities of S.

WORDELL, EDWIN HOWLAND oc/ Artist; b/Aug 27, 1927; h/6251 Lorea Drive, San Diego, CA 92115; ba/Same; m/Marie C; c/Cathryn L (W) Murduck, Thomas A; p/Edwin H Wordell (dec); Cathryn Burns, Largo, FL; sp/Josephine D Cunningham, San Diego, CA; ed/BS, San Diego St Univ; mil/USN, 1945-49; pa/Journeyman Meat Cutter, 1949-61; Crim Invest, IRS, 1961-82; Artist, 1956-; Mem: Beta Gamma Sigma; Nat Watercolor Soc; Rocky Mtn Watermedia Soc Watercolor W; Pres 1975-76, San Diego Watercolor Soc; Pres, San Diego Art Inst, 1978-79; hon/Wks in Permanent Collection, UT St Univ, Logan, UT, 1982; Wk Exhibns: Missoula Mus of Arts, Missoula, MT, Aug 1982; Univ of WI, Whitewater, WI, May 1982; Westmoreland Co Mus of Art, Greensburg PA, Sum 1982; San Bernardinao Co Mus, San Bernardino, CA, Oct 1982; Nat Arts Clb, NYC, Mar-Apr 1983; FL A&M Univ, Tallahassee, FL, Jun 1983; Atlanta Meml Arts Ctr, Atlanta, GA, Jul-Aug, 1983; Owensboro Mus of Fine Art, Owensboro, KY, Aug-Sep 1983; Salmagundi Clb, NYC, Nov 1983;

Greenville Mus of Art, Greenville, SC, Jan-Feb 1984; hon/Hon Mention Awd, Traditional Show, Fine Arts Inst, San Bernardino Co Mus, CA, 1983; Invitation, W Pub'g Co's "W's/83 Art & the Law," Nat Traveling Exhibit, 1983-84; 1st Awd, San Diego Watercolor Soc Mbrship Exhibit, CA, 1982; Hn Mention Awd, Wn Fedn 7, Pueblo Grand Mus, Phoenix, AZ, 1982; 1st Awd, San Diego Watercolor Soc Mbrship Exhibn, CA, 1981; 1st Awd, St Mark's Lenten Art Fest, San Diego, CA, 1981; Painting Selected for Nat Traveling Exhibit, Nat Watercolor Soc's Open Annual Show, 1980; 2nd Awd, Nat Watercolor Soc Mbrship Exhibit St Mary's Col, LA, CA, 1980; Juror's Cash Awd, San Diego Watercolor Soc, CA, 1979; Nat Watercolor Soc Cash Awd, Watercolor W XI Exhibit, Riverside, CA, 1979; W/W: in W, in Am.

WORK, WILLIAM ALEC oc/Professional Artist; b/Nov 21, 1951; h/304 Ridgewood Drive, Tullahoma, TN 37388; ba/Same; m/Linda Carolyn; c/ Matthew Peter, Benjamin Andrew, Seth Adam; ed/Att'd Motlow St Commun Co, 1980-81; pa/Profl Artist, 1974-; Mem: Tullahoma Fine Art Ctr, Tullahoma, TN, 1983; Assoc Mem, So Watercolor Soc, 1983; Intl Assn for Quality Circles, 1983; Gamma Beta Phi Hon Soc, 1980-81; cp/Num Public Spkg Presentations; r/Christian; hon/Wk in Exhibns: 83rd Annual Open Watercolor Exhibn, Nat Arts Clb, NYC; 10th Ihntl Dogwood Fest Art Show, Atlanta, GA.

WORRELL, GAIL G oc/Medical Illustrator; b/Apr 11, 1946; h/3850 Clifton Avenue, Cincinnati, OH 45220; ba/ Cinc, OH; m/Bruce S; p/Wayne and Gloria Garrett, Amelia, OH; sp/Charles and Lee Worrell, Lehigh Acres, FL; ed/ BS in Design, Univ of Cinc, 1969; pa/ Graphic Designer, Alpha Designs Inc, 1969-73; Med Illustr Supvr, Good Samaritan Hosp, 1973-; Freelance Designer; cp/Soroptimist Intl of Cinc, OH; hon/Illustr, *Vascular Surg*, Volume 2; Contbg Illustr to Num Med Textbooks; 2nd Prize, OH Med Assn Exhibit, 1977; Bronze Plaque, OH Med Assn, 1978; Hull Awd, AMA, 1980; Tulsa Art Dir Show, 1977; 1st Prize, Am Occupl Med Assn Exhibit, 1976; W/W of Am Wom.

WORTHAM, JEANETTE STRATTON PORTER oc/Mathematics and Curriculum Specialist; b/Apr 3, 1931; h/ 1902 Warrington Way, Louisville, KY 40222; ba/L'ville, KY; m/1st, L Glenn Collins (dec); 2nd, Francis L; c/Patrick Glenn Collins, Susan Jean Collins; p/ Herbert and Ethel Thomas Russell, Liberty, KY; sp/Fonrose Wortham (dec); Eva Decker Wortham, L'ville, KY; ed/ AA, Lindsey Wilson Col, 1950; BS 1952, MA 1953, En KY Univ; NSF Grants: Univ of ID, 1958-59; Ctl WA Univ, 1964; Univ of Puget Sound, 1965; Univ of L'ville, 1980; pa/Elem Tchr, Casey Co, KY Schs, 1949; Math Tchr, Versailles HS, KY, 1952-56; Math Tchr, San Diego Unified Schs, 1957; Mat & Hist Tchr, Moscow HS, ID, 1957-60; Math Tchr, Clover Pk HS, Tacoma, WA, 1960-65; Math Tchr, Jefferson Co, KY Schs, 1966-69; Math Conslt/Spec, Jefferson Co Schs, 1969-; Elem Math Instr, Univ of L'ville, 1974-80; Mem: Life Mem, NEA; Pres 1981, Gtr L'ville Chapt, En KY Univ Alumni Assn; Pres 1982, Gtr

L'ville Coun of Tchrs of Math; Pres Xi Chapt 1982-84, Delta Kappa Gamma; KY Coun & Nat Coun of Tchrs of Math; Nat Coun of Supvrs of Math; KY Assn of Ednl Supvrs Exec Bd, 1981-83; KY & Jefferson Co Assn of Sch Admrs; ASCD; CUE; NSDAR; cp/Filson Clb; Casey Co Hist Socs; hon/W/W: in KY, in S & SW; Personalities of S.

WORTHEN, BLAINE RICHARD oc/ Professor; b/Oct 10, 1936; h/175 Quarter Circle Drive, Logan Rural Free Delivery, UT 84321; ba/Logan, UT; m/ Barbara Allen; c/Jeffrey Allen, Lynette (W) Penrod, Bradley Wade; p/Grace M Worthen; ed/BS 1960, MS 1965, Univ of UT; PhD, OH St Univ, 1968; pa/Prof & Hd Dept of Psych, UT St Univ, Currently; Dir, Wasatch Inst for Res & Eval, Currently; Dir Div of Eval, Res & Assessment 1975-78, Dir Ofc Res & Eval Sers 1973-75, NW Reg Ed Lab; Asst & Assoc Prof Ednl Psych & Co-dir Lab of Ednl Res, Univ of CO, 1969-73; Asst Prof Ednl Res & Devel 1968-69, Assoc Dir Eval Ctr 1967-69, OH St Univ; Mem: Am Ednl Res Assn, 1965-; Am Psychol Assn, 1969-; Interam Soc of Psych, 1983-; Nat Wkg Grp on Eval, 1968-; Nat Eval Netwk, 1975-; Rocky Mtn Psychol Assn, 1983-; UT Psychol Assn, 1980-; r/LDS (Mormon); hon/ Co-Author of 4 Books Incl'g: *Ednl Eval: Theory & Pract*, 1973; *Measurement & Eval in the Schs*; Author of Over 11 Pub'd Book Chapts Incl'g: "Jour Entries of an Eclectic Evalr," in *Applied Strategies for Curric Eval*, 1981; "Prog Eval," in *Intl Ency of Ed: Res & Studies*, 1983; Author of Over 23 Articles & 3 Reviews Pub'd in Profl Jours Incl'g: *Contemp Psych; Ednl Eval & Policy Anal; Ednl Ldrship; Ednl Resr; Ednl & Psychol Measurement; Jour of Ednl Measurement; Jour of Ednl Res; Jour of Higher Ed; Jour of Sch Psych; Jour of Tchr Ed; Res in Higher Ed*; Other Pubs Incl: 11 Set of Media or Print Tng Mats; 5 Tests or Test Reviews; 67 Res & Eval Reports or Tech Papers; Flesher Fellow for Outstg Grad Student in Ed, OH St Univ, 1968; Awd for Best Eval Study (Eval of HS 3-2-1 Prog), Am Ednl Res Assn, 1977; Outstg Conslt Awd, Assn for Supvn & Curric Devel, 1982; W/W in W; Contemp Authors.

WRENTMORE, ANITA KAY oc/ Lecturer of Mathematics; b/Dec 3, 1955; h/103 Ramona Avenue, Newark, OH 43055; ba/Newark, OH; p/Mr and Mrs Lloyd Wrentmore, Logan, OH; ed/BS 1978, MS 1979, OH Univ; pa/Instr of Math 1983-, Guest Lecturer of Math & Computer Sci 1981-, Ctl OH Tech Col; Instr of Math, OH St Univ-Newark, 1980-83; Guest Lectr of Math & Computer Sci, Denison Univ, 1980; Mem: Phi Kappa Phi; Delta Pi; VPres, Publicity Chm, Newark Coun Tchrs of Math; Nat Coun Tchrs of Math; OH Coun of Tchrs of Math; Math Assn of Am; Am Math Soc; Sch Sci & Math Assn; OH Math Assn of 2-yr Cols; Ctl OH Chapt, Assn for Computing Machinery; Assn for Individualy Guided Ed; Coun for Basic Ed; OH Assn for Supvn & Curric Devel; Assn of Tchr Edrs; Nat Ret'd Tchrs Assn; OH Assn of 2-yr Cols; AAUW; cp/Licking Co BPW Clb; YWCA; Venus Chapt #76, OES; W/W: in MW; 2000 Notable Ams; Commun Ldrs of World; Dir of Dist'd Ams; DIB; Personalities of MW.

WRIGHT, ESTELLE VIOLA oc/ Artist, Sculptor; b/Sep 28, 1905; h/226 West 138th Street, New York, NY 10030; ba/Same; m/William McKinley Wright (dec); p/Elijah and Elicia (Butler) Harrison (dec); sp/Thomas and Augusta Wright (dec); ed/Att'd Art Student Leag of NYC; Nat Acad of Design; Newark Mus S'ship; Nat Acad Sch of Fin Arts: Studied w Carl Schmitz & Ellen Kay-O-Berg; pa/Pvt Modelling Monitors of Mbrship Class, Art Student Leag, 1955-79; ARC Metro Area, 1950-67; Chd's Aid Soc Tchr, 1948-50; Spec Tchr, Bd of Ed, 1970-72; Art Wks Incl: Relief of Ethel Morgan, Designer & Singer, 1979-80; Bas-relief of Christ & His Disciples, The Commun Ch, Lake Placid, NY; Bronze Bust of Eubie Blake in Schomberg Collection, Mus of City of NY, 1960; Bronze Bust of Dr Adolphous Anderson, Sch of Podiatry, Temple Univ, Phila, PA, 1966; Portrait Bust of Mary McClod Bethune, Public Sch 92; Bust of Hippocrates, 1961; Bust of Noble Sissle, 1960; Wk Included in Num Exhibits Incl'g: "Forever Free" Art by African Am Wom 1862-1980, IL St Univ; Lever House Black Hist Mo, 1981; Others; cp/Mem Frederick Douglas Chapt, John Beoron Meml Assn; Wom's Coun of Bklyn; r/Rosicrucian Anthroposophic Leag; hon/Author of 4 Articles & Lttrs to Students of the Rosicrucian Anthroposophic Leag; Meritorious Ser Cert, Bklyn Wom's Coun, 1963; Sculptor S'ship, NY Acad of Design, 1962; Nat Sculptor S'ship, 1962; W/W: in E, of Wom; DIB.

WRIGHT, LANCE SANDERS oc/ Psychiatrist, Psychoanalyst, Child Psychiatry; b/Mar 9, 1923; h/4028 Filbert Street, Philadelphia, PA 19104; ba/Phila, PA; m/Barbara Ramsay; c/Deborah Jean, Rebecca Ann, Lance S III, Wayne Arthur; ed/BC, MS St Univ, 1943; MD, Univ of TN, 1946; MED, Univ of MI, 1948; mil/USPHS, 1951-52; pa/Dir Tng Child Psychi, Devereux Sch, 1957-60; Dir Child Psychi, Montgomery Co Mtl Hlth Clin, 1959-61; Sr Att'g Psychi, Psychi Institute, PA Hosp, 1961-; Assoc Prof Child Psychi, Hahnamann Med Univ, 1970-; Assoc Dir, Grp Psychotherapy, Phila Guid Hosp, 1956-76; Dir, Psychi Sers Inc, 1970-; Mem: Pres, Phila Assn of Adolescent Psychi, 1968; Pres, DE Val Grp Psychotherapy Assn, 1974; Med Dir, Tri-Co Foun Ctr, 1960-76; Fdg Mem, Assn of Holistic Hlth; Fdg Mem, Am Holistic Med Assn; Fdg Mem, Am Soc Adolescent Psychi; Fellow, Am Psychi Assn; Fellow, Am Grp Psychotherapy Assn; Fellow, Am Orthopsychi Assn; Pres, N Am Reg Col, World Univ; r/Prot; hon/Author, *Silva Mind Control*, 1976; Conslt, *Aftermath of Rape*, 1978; *Grp Psychotherapy Probational Sex Offender*, 1974; *Talking Grp Therapy 11 Yr Old Boys*; DLit, World Acad of Arts & Culture, 1981; Fellow, Am Psychi Assn, 1966; Fellow, Am Grp Psychotherapy Assn, 1981; Res Fellow, World Univ, 1978; 2000 Notable Ams.

WRIGHT, LINDA J oc/Executive; b/ Dec 14, 1949; h/8360 Greensboro Drive, Rotunda 3-118, McLean, VA 22102; ba/ Falls Ch, VA; m/Kelly W Jr; p/Eugene F and Rosemary M Kemph, Chgo, IL; sp/Mr and Mrs Kelly W Wright Sr, Swordscreek, VA; ed/Att'd Loretto Hgts Col, 1967-69; Att'd Univ of IL, 1970-71; pa/Asst to VPres, Busey 1st

Nat Bk, Urbana, IL, 1969-72; Spa Mgr, Sales Tng Supvr, Venus & Apollo Hlth Clb, 1973-76; Owner, Retail Plant Store, 1967-77; Sr VPres Comml Lending, Town & Country Bk & Trust Co, 1977-; Mem: Secy of Bd of Dirs, Town & Country Bk & Trust Co; Chm No VA Grp 1981, Nat Assn of Bk Wom; cp/Dir & Treas, No VA Local Devel Corp; Dir & VPres, Fairfax Co C of C; Exec Com, Fairfax/Falls Ch U Way; Mem, Fairfax Hunt; Pvt Pilot; r/Rom Cath; hon/W/W: in S & SW, of Am Wom.

WRIGHT, MARY L oc/Educator; b/ Jul 26, 1947; h/11930 Midlake Drive, Dallas, TX 75218; ba/Dallas, TX; p/Giles C and Nancy Van Sant Wright, Dallas, TX; ed/BA 1972, MEd, So Meth Univ; EdD Cand, E TX St Univ; pa/Art Tchr, Dallas ISD, 1973-74; Art & Remedial Rdg Tchr, Dallas ISD, 1974-76; Rdg Resource Tchr, Dallas ISD, 1976-79; Intern Ldrship Tng Prog, Dallas ISD, 1976; Lang Arts, Social Studies Tchr, Dallas ISD, 1979-82; Rdg Clin Tchr, Sums, 1975-77 & 1979-80; Mem: Phi Delta Kappa; IRA; Assn of Supvn & Curric Devel; r/Epis; W/W in S & SW; Personalities of S.

WRIGHT, RICHARD A oc/Professor; b/Jan 16, 1953; h/751 East Euclid Street, McPherson, KS 67460; ba/ McPherson, KS; m/Sharon Bowman; c/ William; p/Ruth Wright Kite, McPherson, KS; sp/Mr and Mrs L E Bowman, Vienna, VA; ed/BS, James Madison Univ, 1973; MA, OH Univ, 1975; Addit Grad Study: PA St Univ & IN Univ; pa/ Asst Instr, IN Univ, 1976-78; Asst Prof Sociol, McPherson Col, 1979-; Mem: Am Sociol Assn; MW Sociol Soc; Am Soc of Criminology; hon/Author, 1 Book, 3 Chapts in Books; 15 Articles & 25 Book Reviews in Profl Jours; Prof of Yr Awd for Excell in Tchg, McPherson Col, 1983; 1st Prize Winner, No Ctl Sociol Assn Grad Student Paper Competition, 1976; Var Biogl Listings.

WRIGHT, WILBUR ERNEST oc/ Administrator; b/Jul 23, 1932; b/Stanford University Medical Center, Stanford, CA 94305; c/Diane, Stephen, Jeanine, Brian; p/Wilbur Samual and Marie Ernestine (Clarke) Wright, Rockledge, FL; ed/BS, St Peter's Col, 1955; MSS, Fordham Univ, 1958; Public Hlth Adm, Univ of OK, 1965; JD, SF Law Sch, 1984; mil/AUS, 1st Lt; USPHS, Comdr; pa/Dir Dept of Clin Social Wk, Stanford Univ Med Ctr, 1982-; Public Hlth Social Wk Conslt, CA Dept of Hlth Sers, 1981-82; Mtl Hlth Admr, SF Coun of Chs, 1980-81; Secy Gen Coun of Intl Progs, US St Dept, Wash DC, 1978-80; Exec Dir, Mtl Hlth Bd of Ctl FL Inc, Orlando, FL, 1975-78; Hd Dept of Social Wk, Royal Perth Hosp, Wn Australia, 1974-75; Dpty Hd Dept of Social Wk, Alfred-Monash Univ Hosp Dept of Preven & Social Med, Fawkner Pk Commun Hlth Ctr, Prahran, Victoria, Australia, 1973-74; Conslt/Dir of Resource Devel, OBECA/Arriba Juntos- Commun Devel Corp, Cath Charities (Archdiocese of SF), 1972-73; Dir of Ser & Rehab, CA Div of Am Cancer Soc, SF, 1968-72; Dir of Social Wk, Scripps Meml Hosp, LaJolla, CA, 1966-68; Sr Med Social Wkr, Univ of CA-San Diego & San Diego Co Hosp, 1965-66; Conslt/Hlth Ser Ofcr 1962-65, Med Ser Corp Ofcr 1959-62, USPHS,

Wash DC; Fam Cnslr, U Fam & Chd's Soc, Plainfield, NJ, 1958-59; Mem: Fellow, APHA; Fellow, Royal Soc of Hlth, UK; Fellow, Soc for Clin Social Wk; Assn of Mtl Hlth Adm; Am Hosp Assn; Soc for Hosp Social Wk Dirs; Others; Conslt & Guest Lectr in Field; cp/Participant on Num Local Coms & Bds; r/Anglican; hon/Author, Var Articles Pub'd in Profl Jours; Var Reports, Prog & Ser Guides, Handbook & Manual for Profl Socs & Govt Agys; W/W: in CA, in S & SW, in MW, in Hlth Care; in Commun Ser; Commun Ldrs & Noteworthy Ams.

WRUSCH, MICHAEL MANFRED oc/Interior Designer; b/Oct 26, 1957; ba/Palos Verdes Estates, CA 90274; p/ Gerhard and Margot Wrusch, Utica, MI; ed/BA, MI St Univ, 1980; Interior Designer, Martha Shinn Interiors, Okemos, MI, 1978-80; Sr Interior Designer, Carlton Wagner Designer, Palos Verdes, CA, 1980-81; Prin Designer, Michael Wrusch Designs, Palos Verdes Ests, CA, 1981-; Mem: Am Soc of Interior Designers (ASID), 1981-; cp/Nat Trust for Hist Presv, 1984; r/ Luth; hon/Author of Articles Pub'd in "MI Lifestyle," *Detroit Free Press*, 1981; "Home Sect," *LA Times*, 1981; Decorative Arts & Arch S'ship, MI St Univ, 1979; Omicron Nu Ldrship Awd, 1979; Sandpiper Awd for Dist'd Ser, 1982; Mem, Phi Kappa Phi, 1980; Mem, Omicron Nu 1978; W/W in W.

WU, TSE CHENG oc/Research Associate; b/Aug 21, 1923; h/14-E Dorado Drive, Morristown, NJ 07960; ba/ Morristown, NJ; m/Janet Ling; c/Alan Leo, Anna Mae, Bernard Jay; ed/BS, Yenching Univ, 1946; MS, Univ of IL, 1948; PhD, IA St Univ, 1952; pa/Res Chem, E I DuPont De Nemour & Co, 1953-60; Res Chem, Gen Elect Co, 1960-71; Sr Res Chem, Arbor Inc, 1971-77; Res Assoc, Allied Corp, 1977-; Mem: Am Chem Soc; Alpha Chi Sigma; cp/Troy Arts Guild; Morris Co Art Assn; hon/Author of Over 21 Articles Pub'd in Sci & Tech Jours; Holder of 30 US Patents in Field; Gold Medallion Awd for Inventions, Gen Elect Corp, 1967; Phi Kappa Phi; Phi Lambda Upsilon; Sigma Xi; W/W: in E, Technol; DIB.

WYATT, WILSON W SR oc/Attorney; b/Nov 21, 1905; h/The 1400 Willow Apartment 1205, Louisville, KY 40204; ba/L'ville, KY; m/Anne K Duncan; c/ Wilson W Jr, Mary Anne, Nancy (W) Zorn; p/Richard H and Mary (Watkins) Wyatt (dec); ed/Att'd, Bellarmine Col & Univ of L'ville; pa/Atty, Law Firm of Wyatt, Tarrant & Combs; Mayor, City of L'ville, 1941-45; Housing Expediter & Admr, Nat Housing Agy, 1946; Chm Bd of Trustees, Univ of L'ville, 1951-55; Lt Gov, St of KY, 1959-63; Mem: ABA; KY Bar Assn; L'ville Bar Assn; cp/Pres, L'ville C of C, 1972; Pres 1973-75, Chm Nat Conf on Govt 1976-78, Nat Mun Leag; Chm US Sts Circuit Judge Nom'g Comm, 6th Circuit Panel, 1977-80; Chm of Bd, Reg Cancer Ctr Corp, 1977-84; Chm Bd of Trustees, Bellarmine Col, 1979-82; Chm, Ldrship L'ville Foun, 1979-81; VChm, KY Ec Devel Corp, 1984-; Chm, L'ville Commun Foun, 1984-; Chm, Ldrship KY, 1984-; r/Presb; hon/Personal Campaign Mgr of John F Kennedy in KY and Adlai E Stevenson Pres Campaigns; Pres Emissary, From Pres Kennedy to Pres

Sukarno, Indonesian Oil Negotiations, Tokyo, 1963; Man of Yr, Advtg Clb of L'ville, 1973; Lwyr of Yr, KY Bar Assn, 1976; Lwyr of Yr, L'ville Bar Assn, 1981; W/W in Am; Best Lwyrs in Am; Num Other Biogl Listings.

WYCKOFF, CHARLOTTE oc/Educational Administrator; b/Oct 8, 1934; h/ 5333 Amethyst Alta Loma, CA 91701; ba/Cucamonga, CA; m/Bill; c/Robert, Shir, Paul, Brandy, Joseph; p/Ray L and Ruth Charlotte (McLain) Murphy; ed/ BA, LaVerne Col, 1974; MA, CA St Univ-San Bernardino, 1977; Postgrad Study US Intl Univ-San Diego; pa/Fdr & Dir, CA Lrng Ctrs, Rancho Cucamonga, 1967-; Prof, Chaffey Commun Col, Rancho Cucamonga, 1973-; Coor Tng Progs, Casa Colina Hosp, Pomona, CA, 1975-76; Advy Bd, Bonita HS, San Dimas, CA, 1975-77 & Pomona HS, 1975-77; Admr, Claremont (CA) Collegiate Sch, 1977-; Mem: Advy Bd, Pomona HS & Bonita HS; Am Pers & Guid Assn; Nat Soc Autistic Chd; Nat Assn Edn of Yg Chd Assn; Humanistic Psychols; CA Assn of Spec Schs; Nat Assn for Edn Yg Chd; Pre Sch Assn; CA Assn Sch Psychols & Psychometrists; CA St Psychol Assn; CA Assn Neurol Handicapped Chd; Doctorial Soc Clb; Altrusa Clb.

WYDLER, HANS ULRICH oc/Intl Lawyer; b/Nov 11, 1923; h/945 5th Avenue, New York, NY 10021; ba/ Same; m/Susan Hart; c/Hans Laurence, Steven Courtney; p/Grethe A Wydler Baker, OR; sp/Marjorie E Hart, NYC; ed/BS 1944, BME 1947, BIE 1949, OH St Univ; MS, MA Inst of Technol, 1948; LLB, Harvard Law Sch, 1951; mil/USN, 1944-46; pa/Intl Lwyr, Conslt, Hans U Wydler, 1966-; Sr VPres, Security Nat Bk, Huntington, NY, 1973-74; VPres, Mfrs Nat Bk of Detroit, Detroit, MI, 1964-65; Ass VPres, Chem Bk, NYC, 1958-64; Atty, Fin Conslt, Trustee, Louis J Hunter Assocs, Boston, MA, 1951-57; Mem: MA Bar Assn; ABA; NY Co Lwyrs' Assn; Reg'd Profl Engr; US Treas Dept (Tax) Pract; Life Mem, Acad of Polit Sci; ASME; Nat Soc of Profl Engrs; Dir, Buning Intl Inc; Dir, Volume Mdse Inc; r/Rom Cath; W/W: in E, in Fin & Indust; DIB; Royal Blue Book.

WYERS, MARY ELLEN oc/University Dean; b/May 15, 1938; h/3405 Ashford, Ft Worth, TX 76133; ba/ Arlington, TX; m/Patrick Z; c/Randolph Zane, Suzanee Abell; p/Hazel M Abell; Charlottesville, VA; sp/Ruth O Wyers, Ft Worth, TX; ed/BSN, Univ of VA, 1959; MEd, TX Christian Univ, 1972; MSN, Univ of TX-Austin, 1981; EdD, Nova Univ, 1976; pa/Hd Nurse, Univ of VA Hosp, 1961-62; Med-Surg Coor, So Bapt Hosp Sch of Nsg, 1963-66; Asst Nurse Admr, John Peter Smith Hosp Sch of Nsg, 1967-71; Asst Prof & Dir of Cont'g Ed 1971-76, Assoc Prof & Assoc Dean Sch of Nsg 1976-, Univ of TX-Arlington; Mem: ANA; Dist #3 Secy & Exec Bd 1982-84, TX Nurses Assn; NLN; Com of Nom, TX LN; Univ Orgs: Eval Com, Undergrad Curric Com, Grad Progs Com, Grad Studies Com, Interprog Coun, Adm Coun, NLN Self Study Steering Com, Asst Dean Search Com; cp/Allocation Sub-com, U Way of Gtr Tarrant Co, 1981-; Bd Mem, Pres Elect 1983-84, Arlington Div, Am Heart Assn; Bd of Dirs, ARC, 1983-84; Mayor's Com on Employmnt of the

Handicapped, 1983-84; Forum Ft Worth; r/Meth; hon/Author, Var Articles, Prog Reports, Studies & Res Presentations Pub'd in Profl Pubs & Presented to Profl Orgs; Sigma Theta Tau; Hazel M Jay Res Awd, 1983; Univ of TX Res Awd, 1983; Ldrship Ft Worth, 1980; Site Visitor, CBHDP, 1982-.

WYMAN, RICHARD H oc/Property Management/Leasing; b/Aug 5, 1946; h/206 Prospect Street, Framingham, MA 01701; ba/Boston, MA; m/Mary Ellen; c/Michelle, Christine; p/Majorie Wyman, Winchester, MA; sp/Mr and Mrs Joseph Stanley, Framingham, MA; ed/BA, Univ of ME, 1969; MBA Babson Col, 1973; Fellow, Life Mgmt Inst Ins Ed Prog, 1979; Cert'd Life Underwriter Prog; pa/Property Mgmt/Leasing 1982-, Property Mgmt/Leasing 1979-82, Investmnt Acctg 1977-78, Computer Sys Devel & Var Positions 1969-76, Prudential Ins Co, Boston, MA; Ptnr, RELM Income Properties, 1982-; Pt-time Broker Comml Div, Dallamora Realtors, Framingham, MA, 1982-; Mem: N Eng Coun Shopping Mall Mgrts, 1979-; MA Property Investors; cp/Fin Advr, Jr Achmt; Boston C of C; Gov King's Mgmt Task Force 1979, Adv Com, Dept of Revenue; Ins Acctg Instr; Auction Fundraiser Com (Chm for Prudential Ctr/Back Bay 1981), Channel

2; W/W: in World, in Fin & Indust; The Am Registry.

WYNDEWICKE, KIONNE ANNETTE oc/Teacher; b/Mar 28; h/533 East 33rd Street, Chicago, IL 60610; ba/Chgo, IL; p/Clifton Thomas and Missouria Jackson Johnson (dec); ed/BS, IL St Univ, 1960; MEd, Nat Col of Ed, 1982; pa/Casewkr, Cook Co Dept of Public Aid, 1960; Tchr, Chgo Bd of Ed, 1961-; Mem: CARA; ISTA; Spch Commun Assn; CABSE; IPA; Corres'g Secy, Installation Co-chm, Ad-book Co-chm, Publicity Chm & Co-chm, Vol Ser, Dinner Dance, PWA of Provident Hosp; cp/Luth Ch Wom; r/Luth; hon/One of 25 Black Wom in Chgo to Receive a Kizzy Awd from Womafest, Beatrice Caffney Yth Ser Inc, 1978; Outstg Commun Ser Awd; W/W: in MW, of Am Wom, World of Wom, of Commun Ser; 2000 Notable Ams; Intl Register of Profiles; Book of Hon; Personalities of W & MW; DIB.

WYNNE, RICHARD THOMAS oc/Agricultural Meteorologist; b/Jul 31, 1951; h/104 Pleasant Apartment 217, Bryan, TX 77801; ba/College Sta, TX; p/Walter David (dec); Ethel Elizabeth (Lauffer) Wynne, Minooka, IL; ed/BS, No IL Univ, 1973; MS, IA St Univ, 1976; pa/Agri Meteorologist, NOAA/Nat Weather Ser, 1976-; Mem: Am Agron-

omy Soc; Soil Sci Soc of Am; Am Meteorological Soc; Nat Weather Assn; Toastmaters Intl; cp/TX A&M Sailing Clb; Brazos Sailing Clb; r/Rom Cath; hon/SAR Awd, 1969; W/W in S & SW.

WYSZYNSKI, VALENTINE ADAM oc/Executive; b/Dec 24, 1941; h/PO Box 1558, Belen, NM 87002; ba/PO Box 2012, Las Cruces, NM 88004; m/Elizabeth Kathleen DeWitt; c/Brian Lee DeWitt, Tonia Rae DeWitt; p/Genevieve Wyszynski, Cicero, IL; sp/Lenora Robinson, Las Cruces, NM; ed/BSEE, NM St Univ, 1980; mil/USAF, 1964-70, S/Sgt; pa/Pres, Tierra Communs Sys, 1980-; Graphics Conslt, Nifty-Five Pubs, 1983-; Sound-Video Designer, NM St Univ Drama Dept, 1977-81; Reg Sales Mgr, Combined Ins Co, 1973-76; Ldr of the "Majestics" Rock n' Roll Grp, 1959-64; Mem: Soc of Broadcast Engrs, 1981-; Satellite Antenna Spec Assn, 1982-; Nat Assn of Christains in Social Wk, 1980-; cp/St Dir, Newslttr Editor, Romeoville/IL JCs, 1969-73; r/7th Day Adventist; hon/Orig Music Composed for: Tony Awd Winner "Chd of a Lesser God," 1980; The "Majestic Kid," 1981 (written by Mark Medoff); "Nightlife" Columnist Entertainment Guide, 1982-83; Spoke Awd 1970, Best Newslttr 1971, IL JCs; 500 Clb, Ford Motor Co, 1971; W/W in SW.

Y

YAMANASHI, WILLIAM SOIC-HIRO oc/Associate Professor Radiology; b/Jul 12, 1943; h/107 East G Street, Jenks, OK 74037; ba/Tulsa, OK; m/Sandra L; c/Allison S; p/Minoru and Fuyo Yamanashi, Tokyo, Japan; sp/Calvin Noltee (dec) and Eula Mae Atkins; ed/BA, Andrews Univ, 1966; PhD, MIT, 1969; pa/Sr NMR Physicist & Assoc Prof, Radiol, City of Faith Med & Res Ctr, Oral Roberts Univ Sch Med, 1983–; Asst Prof, Asst Biomed Engr, MD, Anderson Hosp & Tumor Inst, Univ TX, 1980–83; Asst Prof Adj, Physiol, Baylor Col Med, 1982–; AAAS; Soc Magnetic Resonance Med; Soc Magnetic Resonance Imaging; IEEE; Radiation Res Soc; Assn Univ Radiologists; Am Assn Physicists Med; Bioelectromagnetic Soc; Am Phy Soc; Am Chem Soc; r/Christian Ch; hon/Author of Num Pubs; Cum Laude, Andrews Univ, 1966; Phi Lambda Upsilon; W/W Am Col & Univs.

YAO, CHRISTOPHER KANG-LOH oc/System Engineer, Audio Distribution Systems, IBM; b/Apr 4, 1941; h/885 Windsor Trail, Roswell, GA 30076; ba/Atlanta, GA; m/Becky J; c/Jenney, Mary; p/Huang-Jui (dec) and Shu-Mei Yao, Roswell, GA; sp/David and Phoebe Jung, Indpls, IN; ed/BS, Univ KS, 1966; MS, Union Col, 1978; pa/Jr Metallurgist, Mat Engr, Mfg Quality Engr, Prod Devel Engr, Mat Mgmt Programmer, Facility Sys Analyst, Audio Sys Engr, IBM, 1967; Sys Engr, 1981-82, Audio Dist Sys; Am Soc Metals; Am Soc Ceramics; cp/Pres, Atlanta Chapt, Nat Assn Chinese-Ams, 1979; hon/Author of "Gen Purpose Automation Exec" 1981.

YASSA, GUIRGUIS F oc/Senior Analyst Systems, Chase Manhattan Bank; b/Oct 1, 1930; h/RD 1, Box 178, Sussex, NJ 07461; ba/New York, NY; m/Laila; c/Elham, Medhat, Magdi, Laura Marie; p/Fahmy Yassa (dec); sp/Naguib Nosseir (dec); ed/B Eng 1951, MSc 1964, Dipl Stats 1966, Cairo Univ; ITC Photogrammetric Eng, Netherlands, 1956; PhD, Cornell Univ, 1973; pa/Topographic Engr 1951-53, Photogrammetric Engr 1953-65, Hd Photogrammetric Sect 1965-67, Survey Egypt; Sr Lectr, Intl Inst Aerial Survey, 1967-69; Tchg Asst, Cornell, 1962-72; Systems Analyst, Dir Mapping, Robinson Aerial Surveys, 1973-79; Sr Programmer, Analyst, Chase Manhattan Bk, 1980–; Am Soc Photogrammetry; Am Soc Civil Engrs; Sigma Xi; Coptic Orthodox; hon/Author of Num Pubs; Talbert Abrams Awd, Am Soc Photogrammetry, 1975; W/W E.

YATES, EDWARD CARSON JR oc/Aerospace Engineer; b/Nov 3, 1926; h/3800 Chesapeake Avenue, Hampton, VA 23669; ba/Hampton, VA; m/Carleen Wells; c/Barry Wells; p/Edward Carson and Estelle Yarborough Yates (dec); sp/Roy Leon and Eula Simpson Wells, Altavista, VA; ed/BS 1948, MS 1949, NC St Univ; MS, 1953, Univ VA; PhD, VA Polytechnic Inst, St Univ, 1959; pa/Aerospace Engr, NASA/NACA Langley Res Ctr, 1949–; Lctr Physics, VA Polytechnic Inst & St Univ, 1959-67; Adj Assoc Prof, NC St Univ, 1964-75; Professorial Lectr, George Wash Univ,

1968–; Assoc Editor, Jour Aircraft, 1972-78; Assoc Fellow, Am Inst Aeronautics & Astronautics; hon/Author of Num Pubs; Phi Eta Sigma; Phi Kappa Phi; Sigma Xi; Num S'ships, 1947, 1948; NASA Perf Awd, 1964; Fed Aviation Adm Cit, 1964; NASA Grp Achmt Awd, 1967; NASA Apollo Achmt Awd, 1969; NASA Spec Achmt Awd, 1982; NASA Exceptl Ser Medal, 1982; W/W: S & SW, Govt, Technol Today, Aviation & Aerospace, Aviation, Frontier Sci & Tech; Am Men & Wom Sci; Men Achmt; Dict Biography; Intl W/W Engrg.

YEARGAIN, BETTY JAN oc/Banker; b/Jul 20, 1942; h/13723 Woodthrush, Choctaw, OK 73020; ba/Midwest City, OK; m/Virgil L; c/Marvie Allen Dunn III; p/Edgar J and Audrey B Fisher, Walnut Grove, MS; sp/Virgil E Yeargain (dec) and Marilee Yeargain Walters; pa/Sr VP & Cashier, Security Bank & Trust Co, 1983–; Sr VP, Cashier, Adv Dir, So Bk & Trust Co, 1978-83; Opers Ofcr, Choctaw St Bk, 1977-78; Asst VP, Employmt Mgr, Fidelity Bk NA, 1969-77; Exec Secy, Security Bk, 1968-69; Am Inst Bkg; Nat Assn Bk Wom; Ctl OK Clearinghouse Assn; r/Bapt; hon/Bkr Yr, 1975, Am Inst Bkg; W/W: Am Wom, Intl Intells.

YEN, PETER T oc/Professor and Director, International Business Institute; b/Sep 22, 1937; ba/Saint Bonaventure, NY; ed/BA, NCU; MA, CA St Univ; PhD, Univ SF; Post Doct, Univ CA-LA; mil/AUS; pa/Prof, Sch Bus, St Bonaventure Univ; Exch Prof, Univ W FL, 1980; Vis'g Scholar, Grad Sch Mgmt, Univ CA-LA, 1979; Prof Mktg & Mgmt, NCU, 1976-79; Asst Prof Mgmt, HD Devel, VA Polytechnic Inst, 1975-76; Am Mktg Assn; Mgmt Sci Assn; Mem & Bd Dir, Mktg Res Assn; Acad Mgmt; Acad Intl Bus; Fellow, Intl Acad Mgmt; r/Cath; hon/Author of Num Pubs; Grant Nat Behavior Sci Coun; Hon Citizen, Pensacola FL; Cultural Exch Awd; Intl W/W Intell; Men Dist'd; W/W Ed.

YODER, DAVID HARVEY oc/Housing and Real Estate Development; b/Oct 10, 1931; h/Winona Court, Morgantown, WV 26505; ba/Morgantown, WV; m/Ruby Jeanelle Shenk; c/Jon David, Robert Eliott; p/G Ernest Yoder, Salisbury, PA; sp/C W Shenk, Elida, OH; ed/BA, Goshen Col, 1957; MA, WV Univ, 1965; PhD Cand, Univ Vienna, 1965; Vienna Acad of Music, 1962; Vis'g Scholar, Univ of Graz, Vienna, 1965; pa/Dean of Students, Wn Mennonite Prep Sch, 1953-54; Student Asst, Goshen Col, 1956-57; Grad Asst, WV Univ, 1963-64; Designer, Housing Constrn, 1966–; Supvr, Real Est Mktg & Sales; Bd of Dirs, N Ctl WV Home Bldrs Assn, 1976–; 1st VP 1976, Pres 1977-80; Chm Com on Legis & Govtl Affairs, Home Bldrs of WV, 1978-80; Bd Dirs, Nat Assn of Homes Bldrs, 1978–; St Home Bldrs Rep, House & Senate of WV, 1978-80, Rep to US Cong, 1979; 1st VP 1979-82, Pres 1983-84, WV Home Bldrs Assn; Chm Com on Mortgage Fin, 1980–; Expert Conslt for Home Bldg Indust to US Cong, 1979; Appt'd by WV Legis to its Task Force on Housing, 1981; Pres, Pineview Rlty Inc; Exec VP, Allegheny Devel Corp; Secy/Treas, Pineview Supply Corp; Treas, Allegheny Real Est Sales Inc; cp/C of C; hon/

Bldr of the Month Awd, 1972; Outstg Bldr of the Yr, 1973; Cert of Merit for Outstg Contbns to Bldg Indust, 1976; Mbr of the Yr Awd, WV Home Bldrs Assn, 1980; W/W: Fin & Indust, S & SW; Men of Achmt.

YODER, PAUL TIMOTHY oc/Physician, Family Practice, District Overseer-10 Churches; b/Feb 24, 1928; h/1047 Stuart Street, Harrisonburg, VA 22801; ba/Harrisonburg, VA; m/Daisy Agnes Byler; c/Debra Ann, Daniel Wayne, Paul Timothy Jr, Judith Carol; p/David Samuel and Savilla Bender Yoder; sp/Jesse D (dec) and Agnes Gunden Byler, Topeka, IN; ed/BS, 1950, En Mennonite Col, 1950; MD, George Wash Univ Med Sch, 1955; Att'd En Bapt Sem, 1968; MPH, Johns Hopkins Univ Sch Public Hlth & Hygiene, 1972; pa/Phys, 1977–; Med Missionary, En Mennonite Bd Missions & Charities, 1956-77; Proj Dir, Awash Commun Hlth Sers, 1972-77; Med Ofcr, Med Secy, 1968-72; Med Dir 1962-63, 1968-71, Staff Phys 1957-60, Acting Med Dir 1956-57, Haile Mariam Mammo Meml Hosp; Med Dir, 1963-66; Med Dir, Deder Hosp-Ethiopia, 1960-61; Staff Phys, Blue Ridge 1961-62; Med Soc VA, Rockingham Co Med Soc; Am Acad Fam Phys; Christian Med Soc; Mennonite Med Assn; Diplomate Am Bd Fam Pract; Mennonite Hlth Assn; cp/George Wash Gen Alumni Assn; Alumni Assn Johns Hopkins Univ; r/Prot; hon/Author of Num Pubs; Alumnus (w Wife) of Yr, En Mennonite Col, 1982; Am Med Assn Phys' Recog Awd, 1980, 1983; Election to King-Kane Obstetrical Soc.

YONKERS, WINIFRED FRANCES oc/Reading Specialist; b/Sep 30, 1939; h/2011 Hannon Street, Hyattsville, MD 20783; ba/Washington, DC; m/Mervyn Leroy; c/Pamela Marie, Vernon Lee; p/Wilfred Lawrence (dec) and Mary Frances Haddock, Pittsburgh, PA; sp/Earl H and Isabella Yonkers, Pittsburgh, PA; ed/BS, Univ Pgh, 1961; MA, George Wash Univ, 1967; pa/Elem Tchr, Pgh Public Schs, 1961-63; Elem Tchr, DC Public Schs, 1963-67; Rdg Spec, DC Public Schs, 1967–; Curric Writer, DC Public Schs, Sum 1982; IRA; cp/Alpha Kappa Alpha; Pi Lambda Theta; Lewisdale Civic Assn; Lewisdale, Univ PK Boys & Girls Clb; r/Prot.

YOO, JANG HEE oc/Professor of Economics, Economic Analyst; b/Feb 11, 1941; h/3219 Nuttree Woods Drive, Midlothian, VA 23113; ba/Richmond, VA; m/Chong Cha; c/Alex, Kenneth; p/Jong Ja Jung, McLean, VA; sp/Mr and Mrs Changsop Song, Gwachon, Korea; ed/BA, Seoul Nat Univ, 1963; MA, Univ CA-LA, 1969; PhD, TX A & M Univ, 1973; Spec Prog in Public Ec, MIT, 1979; mil/ROKA, Lt, (Korea); pa/Res Asst, Ec Res Ctr 1963-65, Prof 1981-82, Seoul Nat Univ; Res Assoc, Human Resource Res Ctr, USC, 1969-70; Asst Prof Ec, Clark Univ, 1972-76; Assoc Prof 1976-81, Prof 1981–, VA Commonwealth Univ; Am Ec Assn; Prog Com Mem, Nat Tax Assn; Assoc Mng Editor of Jour Ec Devel; Chm Sessions, Nat Tax Assn Conv, Wn Ec Assn Conv, SWn Soc Sci Assn Conv, Korean Economists Assn Meeting; r/Presb; hon/Author of Num Pubs incl'g "Macro Cross Elasticities in Disequilibrium Adjustments" *Korean Economic Review* 1976; Grantee of Soc Sci

PERSONALITIES OF AMERICA

Res Coun & Am Coun of Learned Soc, NSF, Am Coun Life Ins, Economic Planning Bd; W/W S & SW; Am Economic Assn Listings.

YORK, GEORGE WOLTZ oc/Sales Executive; b/Sep 2, 1940; h/714 Enchanted River, Spring, TX 77373; ba/ Houston, TX; m/Emily Miriam Slayton; c/Janet Lyn, William Tuck; p/Mr and Mrs Guy Aytca York, Atlanta, GA; sp/ Mrs Olive Dixon Philpot, Memphis, TN; ed/Univ GA, 1958-59; BIE, GA Inst Technol, 1966; Postgrad, Univ Houston, 1968-69; pa/Tech Sales Rep 1969-, Area Mgr 1980-, Tech Conslt 1980-, York Div Borg Warner Corp; ASME; ASH-RAE; cp/GA Tech Alumni Assn; Sigma Nu; US JCs; Num Sports & Social Clbs; r/Presb; hon/Provided Tech Asst for "Design of Mech Refrigeration Sys" 1967; York Div, Borg Warner Sales Hall of Fame; Pres' Hon Clb Awd; Salesman of Yr Awd; Spec Recog Awd; W/W in S & SW.

YOUNG, EULALIE BARNES oc/ Social Services Consultant; b/Oct 24, 1942; h/4157 Brookfield Drive, Sacramento, CA 95823; ba/San Bernardino, CA; m/James Leonard; c/Shawn Arlene McGee, Darren Lance McGee, Jayanna; p/Roy and Lucille Woods Barnes, New Orleans, LA; ed/BA, So Univ, 1966; MS, St Univ NY, 1976; pa/Supervisory Rec Spec, Dept Army, Fort Polk, 1967-72; Prog Coor, YMCA/Model Cities Teen Ctr, 1972-74; Student Intern, VA Hosp, 1974-76; Prog Coor, BUILD Wk Assessmt Ctr, 1976-77; Sr Rehab Cnslr, CA St Dept Rehab, 1978-80; Soc Ser Conslt, CA St Dept Social Sers, 1980-; Am Pers & Guid Assn; Nat Rehab Assn; Assn Black Psychol; cp/CA Coor, Nat Hook-up Black Wom; Aware of Wom; r/Bapt; hon/Outstg Achmt Awd, CA St Dept Rehab, 1980; W/W of Am Wom.

YOUNG, LEO F oc/Mail Order Dist; b/Nov 20, 1944; h/8319 South Breeze, Houston, TX 77071; ba/Houston, TX; m/Willie C; c/Tyrone, Elisabeth, Bruce; ed/AA Electroncis; mil/USCG Resv; pa/ Gen Mgr, Williams & Son Inc, 1974-82; Owner, Baabys Ltd Record Sales, 1970-74; Clk, A & P Supermkt, 1970; cp/Chm, Riceville Civic Assn Inc; r/Bapt; hon/Author of "Breath Freshener", " Hlthy Pets" 1981; Gulf Coast Commun Ser Awd; Dept Energy Cert 1981; W/ W in Business.

YOUSSEF, KAMAL A oc/Physician, Laboratory Executive; b/Sep 15, 1933; h/Sorter 6548, West Palm Beach, FL 33405; p/A M and L Y Mansour Youssef; ed/MD, Cairo Univ, 1957; DMSc, 1964; Intern, Min of Hlth Hosps, Egypt, 1958-59; pa/Med Tech, Manhattan Med & Dental Assist Sch, NYC, 1969-70; Res Assoc, So Bio-Res, FL So Col, Lakeland, 1970-71; Resident in Pathol, Bapt Meml Hosp, Jacksonville, 1971-72; Resident in Pathol, Misericordia & Meth Hosp, 1972-74; Fdr, Pres, Mycogel Labs Inc, Bkly, 1975-; Am Soc for Microbiol; Nat Soc for Human & Animal Mycology; Med Mycological Soc of the Ams; Med Mycological Soc of NY; Fdr, Pres, World Nutrition Islamic Foun; hon/Presentation to Egyptian Med Assn Clin Soc, 1957; Discovered 7 Novel Species of Amoeba; 33 Patents Worldwide; Presentation, Nat Cancer inst, 1973; Recip, Sci Achmt Awd from U Scists & Inventors of the US; World W/W; W/W in Fin & Indust.

YUGOVICH, JOHN oc/Electrical Designer; b/May 12, 1952; h/30900 Ridgeway, Farmington Hills, MI 48018; b/Same; p/Mr and Mrs Michael Yugovich, Dearborn, MI; ed/Henry Ford Commun Col, 1972; Lawrence Inst Technol; pa/Elect Designer, Diclemente-Siegel Engrg Co, 1970-79; Pres, Yugovich Enterprises, 1979-83; cp/Mem, Detroit Bldrs Exchg Vol Wkr for Sarah Fisher Home for Underpriviledged Chd, 1982-; r/Cath; hon/Pres Elect, Dale Carnegie Class, 1981; Cert Merit for Training & Employing the Handicapped.

YUNICE, ANDY ANIECE oc/ Research Scientist and Associate Professor; b/Jan 2, 1925; h/2325 Morgan Drive, Norman, OK 73039; ba/Oklahoma City, OK; m/Lillian; c/Carla, Paula, and Laurie; p/Asad and Mona Yunice, Lebanon; sp/Mitchel and Najla Saleeby; ed/BA, Am Univ Beirut, 1948; MS, Wayne St Univ, 1958; PhD, OK Univ, 1971; pa/Res Instr, WA Univ, 1958-69; Asst Prof Med & Physiol, 1971-77, OKC, OK; Assoc Prof & Dir Trace Metal Lab, 1977-, OK Univ & VAMC; Am Physiol Soc; Am & Intl Soc Nephrology; Sigma Xi; r/Christian; hon/ Author of Num Pubs; Awd for Graduate Studies, 1969; W/W in S & SW; Am Men & Women of Science.

Z

ZAJICEK, BARBARA J oc/Vice President-Business Manager Health Care, Medical Management; b/Jan 12, 1932; h/619 Hillside Road, Glenview, IL 60025; ba/Des Plaines, IL; m/Albert F; c/Gregg Hahn, Lisa Jeffries, Dana Hahn; p/Gale E (dec) and Thelma B Allen, Ft Myers, FL; sp/Rudy and Anastasia Zajicek (dec); pa/Ofc Supvr, Asst to Pres, Larry Smith & Co, 1970-74, 1976-77; Asst to Pres, Devel Control Corporation, 1974-76; Bus Mgr, EMSCO Ltd, 1978-; VP, MW Med Mgmt Inc, 1982-; Sr VP 1983-84, Emer Med Mgmt Assn, 1978-; Nat Assn Freestanding Emer Ctrs, 1982-; r/Luth; hon/Pres' Scholar, Oakton Commun Col, 1980; W/W Am Wom.

ZALESKI, MAREK BOHDAN oc/ Immunologist, University Professor; b/ Oct 18, 1936; h/95 Willow Green, Tonawanda, NY 14150; ba/Buffalo, NY; p/Stanislaw and Jadwiga Zaleski; ed/MD 1960, DMS 1963, Med Acad-Warsaw Poland; mil/Polish Army Resv, 1st Lt Med Corp; pa/Instr 1955-60, Asst Prof 1960-69, Dept Histology, Sch Med Warsaw; Res Asst Prof 1969-72, Assoc Prof 1976-78, Prof 1978-, Dept Micro-biol, St Univ NY; Asst Prof 1972-75, Assoc Prof 1975-76, Dept Anatomy, MI St Univ; Vis'g Scist 1965, Inst Exptl Biol Genetics, Czechoslovak Acad Sci; Brit Coun Scholar, 1966-67, Queen Victoria Hosp-England; Polish Anatomic Soc; Transplantation Soc; Intl Soc Exptl Hematology; Am Assn Immunologists; NY Acad Sci; Buffalo Collegium Immunol; Ernest Witebski Ctr Immunol; Edit Com, Immunological Communs; cp/Solidarity & Human Right Assn; r/Rom Cath; hon/Author of Num Pubs; Recip Num Grants incl'g NIH, 1976-; W/W: Am, World, Technol Today; Men Achmt; Dic Bibliog.

ZAMONSKI, STANLEY WALTER oc/Museum Director and Curator; b/ Aug 7, 1919; h/800 South Vellejo, Denver, CO 80223; ba/Golden, OH; m/ Barbara Helen; p/Stanley W and Cecilia (Zamojski) Zamonski (dec); sp/Forrest I Stewart (dec); Mildred K Stewart, Dallas, TX; ed/Att'd N Eng Aircraft-Wentworth Inst, 1940-42; Att'd MIT, 1942-43; Addit Study, Georgetown Univ; mil/USAAC, Pilot, 2nd Lt, B-24 Bomber, PTO; pa/ Engrg-Draftsman, Airway Manual, 1946-47; Engrg-Draftsman, CO Dept of Hwys, 1947-55; Free Lance Photog-writer, 1950-70; Photog, Jefferson Sentinal Press, 1955-70; Prof of Photo-jour, Instituto Allenda, San Miguel Allenda, Mexico, 1970-72; Engrg-Draftsman, Denver Planning Dept, 1973-78; Curator, Buffalo Bill Meml Mus, Golden, CO, 1978-; Mem: Nat Writers Clb; Polish Inst of Arts & Scis; CO Authors Leag; CO—WY Assn of Mus; Am Assn of St & Local Hist; Wn Hist Assn; Denver Press Clb; Am Coun of Polish Culture; cp/Dpty Sheriff, Denver Wnrs, 1982; Treas, Denver Art Clb, 1950; CO Hist Assn; Denver Hist Assn; Indust Jefferson Co; Chm of Comm Lakewood; hon/Author of Over 100 Articles Pub'd in Newspapers & Mags; Books Incl: *The 59'ers, Roaring Denver*, 1961-83; *The Westernaires*, 1967; *Buffalo Bill- His Life & Legend*, 1981; *Grunwald*, 1982; *Denver City*, 1982;

Gentleman Rogue, 1984; *Padre Polaco*, 1984; Decorated Air Medal w 2 OLC; Braum Awd, Denver Art Dirs & Advtg Assn, 1959; CO Press Photog, 1965-67; Nat Press, 1967; Buffalo Bill Tent Awd, 1982; W/W: in W, of Wn Histns, of Contemp Authors.

ZAMPIELLO, RICHARD SIDNEY oc/Executive, Copper Industry; b/May 7, 1933; h/Woodbury Road, Washing-ton, CT 06793; ba/Waterbury, CT; m/ Helen Shirley Palsa; c/Geoffrey R; p/ Sidney and Louise Zampiello, Hamden, CT; sp/Anna Palsa, Washington, CT; ed/Bach, Trinity Col, 1955; MBA, Univ Bridgeport, 1961; pa/Westinghouse Elect Corp, 1955-64; Exec VP, Ullrich Copper Inc, 1964-71; Sr VP, Gerald Metals Inc; GMP Div; ASME; AIME; SME; cp/Mining Clb; Yale Club; Copper Clb; Wash Clb; Delta Kappa Epsilon Clb; r/Cath; hon/Author of Num Pubs; W/ W E.

ZEHEL, WENDELL EVANS oc/ General Surgeon; b/Mar 6, 1934; h/553 Harrogate Road, Pittsburgh, PA 15241; ba/Pittsburgh, PA; m/Joan; c/Lori, Wendell; ed/BA, Wash & Jefferson Col, 1956; MD, Univ Pgh, 1960; mil/USAF, 1961-63, Capt; pa/Gen Surg, 1968-82; Am Col Surgs; AMA; Nat Adv Bd Am Biographic Inst; NY Acad Sci; Assn Advmt Med Instrumentation; AAAS; hon/W/W E; Noble Personalities Am; Dir Dist'd Ams; 2000 Noble Ams; Intl Register Profiles; Intl W/W: Intells, Commun Ser.

ZEITCHICK, ABRAHAM A oc/ Security Director; h/1280 East 86th Street, Brooklyn, NY 11236; Married; 2 Chd; pa/Dir of Security Guards; Lic'd Pvt Investigator; Employed w Kings Co Dist Atty's Ofc; Ins Broker; Mutual Fund Salesman; cp/Commun Planning Bd; Bklyn Jewish Coun; VP, Flatbush Commun Coun; Chm, W Remsen Civic Assn; Pres, Remsen Hgts Jewish Ctr; VP, Jewish Nat Fund; Dir, Child Guild Clinic; B'nai B'rith; K of P; Others; hon/ Man of the Month, Holy Fam PTA; BSA; Oscar, Dist Commr's Key, Scout-ers Key, Order of Arrow, Silver Beaver; Appt'd to Am Fdn Police; Others.

ZELAZO, NATHANIEL K oc/Presi-dent and Chief Executive Office; b/Sep 28, 1918; h/1610 North Prospect Avenue, Milwaukee, WI 53202; ba/ Milwaukee, WI; m/Helene Fishbein-Ret; c/Ronald E, Annette R; p/Morris (dec) and Ida Zelazo, Queens, NY; sp/David and Rose Mihaly Fishbein-Ret; ed/BS, City Univ NY, 1940; MSME, Univ WI, 1957; Postgrad Studies, Columbia Univ; Hon Doct Engrg Deg, Milwaukee St Engrg; mil/USN Dept; pa/Pres & CEO, Astronautics Corporation Am, 1959-; Dir Res, Devel Avionics Div, 1955-59; VP, United Aircraft Corporation, 1952-55; Regent & Mem Corporate Bd, 1979-, Milwaukee Sch Engrg; Chm, 1983-84, WI Elect Assn; Milwaukee Sch Engrg, Elect Engrg Technol Indust Adv Com, 1983-84; Assoc Fellow, AIAA; Sr Mem, IEEE; Nat Soc Profl Engrs; Am Soc Nav Engrs; Am Helicopter Soc; Navy Leag US; AF Assn; Engrs & Scist Milwaukee Inc; Physics Clb Milwaukee; Armed Forces Communs & Elects Assn; hon/IEEE, Cent Medal; Milwaukee St Engrg, Hon Deg; Albert Einstein Awd, 1982, Am Technion Soc; Employer of Yr Awd, Dept Def; Billy Mitchell Awd, AF Assn; Small Businessman Yr WI,

Small Bus Adm; W/W: Aviation, Fin & Indust, Technol Today, Am; WI Men Achmt; Biographical Dir Computer Graphics Indust.

ZELLER, VIRGINIA G M oc/Public Relations, Real Estate Investments; h/ 1701 Park Avenue, Baltimore, MD 21217; m/Leon H (dec); p/John Gordon Mitchell (dec) and Mrs J Gordon Mit-chell, Charlotte, NC; ed/BS; MS, 1983, Johns Hopkins Univ; pa/Fdg Pres, Advtg Assn of Balto; cp/Past Pres, Balto Opera Guild Inc; Fdg Pres, MD Action for Foster Chd Inc; hon/1st Nat Awd for Org'g MD Action for Foster Chd "Model" for the Country, HEW, 1974; J Hochreiter Awd for Foster Chd Commun Ser.

ZEMEL, HELENE LEVEY oc/Associ-ation Executive; b/Jan 3, 1947; h/102-40 67th Road, Apartment 3W, Forest Hills, NY 11375; ba/New York, NY; m/ Leonard S; p/Theodore (dec) and Sylvia Levey, Rosedale, NY; sp/Abraham and Sandra Zemel, Delray Beach, FL; ed/BA, Hofstra Univ, 1968; MA, Queens Col, 1972; MBA Cand, NY Inst Technol; pa/ Piano Instr & Concert Pianist, 1968-77; Asst Admr Soc/Coun Adm 1977-78; Admr Conf Activs 1978-, IEEE; Record-ing Secy 1981-82, Treas 1982-83, Bd Dirs 1983-85, Del NY St Conv 1983, NY Leag BPW; Budget & Fin Com Mem, 1982-83, Meeting Planners Intl; r/ Jewish; hon/Piano Recitals incl'g Lincoln Ctr; Sigma Kappa Alpha; Tchg F'ship, Queens Col; Cum Laude, Hofstra Univ; W/W Am Wom.

ZERR, RITA GREGORIO oc/Direc-tor, Teaching Assistantship Program Elementary Schools; b/Jun 9, 1928; h/ 4759 Knight Drive, New Orleans, LA 70127; ba/New Orleans, LA; m/George James; c/Jeanne Rita, Gary George; p/ Fred (dec) and Clothilde Gregorio, New Orleans, LA; sp/George B Zerr, Metairie, LA, and Ida B Piro (dec); ed/ BA, Newcomb Col, 1948; MA, Tulane Univ, 1959; PhD, Univ So MS, 1970; pa/Food Chem, Charles Dennery Inc, 1948; Elem Tchr, New Orleans Public Schs, 1948-66; Adj Fac, Ctr Tchr Ed, Tulane Univ, 1961-67; Instr, Newcomb Col, 1967-71; Assoc Dir 1967-68, Dir 1968-, Coor Elem Ed, Asst Prof 1971-, Tchg Asst'ship Prog Elem Schs, Tulane; VP 1976-77, Pres-Elect 1977-78, Pres 1978-79, LA Coun Social Studies; Res Editor, 1983-84, Intl Assn Pupil Pers Wkrs; Nat Coun Social Studies, Prog Com, 1974-75; Assoc Curric & Superv, Am Ednl Res Assn; cp/Fac Sponsor, Nominations Com 1982-84, Chm Nom-inations Com 1984-86, Kappa Delta Pi; r/Rom Cath; hon/Author of Num Pubs incl'g "The Mid Sch Potential Dropout: A Proactive Approach" *Jour Intl Assn Pupil Pers Wkrs* 1983; Pres Cit, Nat Soc Perf & Instrn, 1972; Personalities of S; DIB; World W/W Wom; W/W Social Studies.

ZIBRUN, STEPHEN MICHAEL oc/ President, Telemarketing Consultancy Firm; b/Aug 1, 1945; h/346 South 48th Avenue, Bellwood, IL 60104; ba/Bel-lwood, IL; m/Carol Ann Salerno; c/ Michael, Jennifer; p/Stephen John and Elizabeth Behrendt Zibrun, New Port Richey, FL; sp/Dominic and Mary Salerno, River Forest, IL; ed/BA, Bus Adm, 1968; MBA, IL Benedictine Col, 1982; mil/USNR, 1968-70; pa/Pres, S Michael Assocs, 1981-; Mgr, Corporate Communs, Mark Controls Corporation, 1980-81; Advtg Dir, Patten Indust Inc, 1979-80; Advtg Mgr, 1968-79; Cert'd Bus Communicator, Bus/Profl Advtg Assn; cp/Bellwood C of C; Bellwood Zoning Bd Appeals; r/Rom Cath; hon/Author of Num Pubs; W/W: in MW, in Consltg.

ZIMBAL, CAMILLA K oc/US Probation Officer; b/Jun 25, 1949; h/1679 State Highway 121, Apartment 801, Lewisville, TX 75067; ba/Dallas, TX; p/ Mr and Mrs Ray W Zimbal, May, TX; ed/BS, Howard Payne Univ, 1971; MS, Abilene Christian Univ, 1980; PhD, TX Wom's Univ; mil/AUS, 1st Lt; pa/US Probation Ofcr, Mtl Hlth Spec, US Probation No Dist TX, 1979-; St Parole Ofcr, St Bd Pardons & Parole, 1977-79; Adjutant & Chief Alcohol/Drug Mgmt Preven & Control Prog, US Army, 1975-77; Adj Fac Criminal Justice, TX Wom's Univ, 1982-; Instr, Dallas Commun Col Prog, 1979-80; Tnr, St Parole Ofc, 1978-79; Instr, US Army, 1975-77; Eng Tchr, Bangs HS, Bangs, TX, 1972-75; TX St Tchrs Assn; TX Correctional Assn; Am Correctional Assn; Fed Probation Ofcrs Assn; Fed Law Enforcement Ofcrs Assn; Am Sociological Assn; TX Mtl Hlth Assn; TX Profl Cnslrs; cp/Public Spkr, Rape Crisis Ctr, 1979-; Commun Ed, Dallas Public Sch Sys Corrections, 1979-; Coun Govts, Public Spkr Crim Aspects & Progs of Rehab, 1980-; Dallas Coun Alcoholism, Commun Treatment Prog, 1980-; Dallas Mtl Hlth Assn, Public Spkr Mtl Illness Corrections, 1981-; r/Ch of Christ; hon/Author of Num Pubs incl'g "Hiring Wom Ex-Offenders: What We Can Do", Fed Probation, 1983.

ZIMMER, THERESA MAGDALENA oc/Assistant Professor in College of Business; b/Dec 16, 1951; h/239 Arlington Drive, Lake Charles, LA 70605; ba/ Lake Charles, LA; p/George C (dec) and Florence C Zimmer, Arabi, LA; ed/BS 1973, MEd 1977, Univ of New Orleans; PhD, N TX St Univ, 1981; pa/Secy, LSUNO, 1971-73; Secy, Blue Plate Foods, 1973-74; Bus Tchr, Andrew Jackson HS, 1974-81; Asst Prof, McNeese St Univ, 1981-; St Bernard Assn Edrs, Sch Rep, 1975-77; LA Assn Bus Ed, St Treas, 1982-84; Nat Bus Ed Assn; AAUW; cp/Phi Chi Theta, Pres, 1973; Delta Pi Epsilon; Phi Kappa Phi; Phi Delta Kappa, Nat Col Assn of Secy; Kappa Delta Pi; SASA; LVA; r/Cath; hon/Author of "Tchg the Alphabet & Num Keys Concurrently in HS Typewriting Classes" Alpha Epsilon Res 1983; Outstg FBLA Advr; Conslt & Spkr, Word Processing & Ofc Sys.

ZIMMERMAN, FRANCIS ADDIE oc/Training Instructor, Public Relations Department of Labor; b/Oct 10, 1924; h/9706 Hayes, Overland Park, KS 66212; ba/Kansas City, MO; m/Eugene R (dec); c/Donald E, Nancy C Giller, Robert J, Laura L; p/Dewey J (dec) and Louise F Howell, Kansas City, KS; ed/ Park Col, 1941-44; Rockhurst Col, 1972;

Univ of MI; Univ of Houston; pa/Dir Public Relats & Co Orgr, Am Cancer Soc, 1959-60; Public Relats, MO Employmt Ser, 1962-75; Instr & Art Dir, Reg Tng Ctr, US Dept Labor, 1975-80; Employer Coor, 1980-; Intl Assn Pers; Mgr, Employmt Security; Am Soc Tnrs; Nat Assn Female Execs; cp/Nelson Gallery Art; Kansas City C of C; Urban Leag Gtr KC; Personal Dynamics Assn; Pk Col Alumni Assn; Art Dirs Clb KC; Lioness; KC PTA Bd; Bd Dirs, Shawnee Mission HS; r/Unity; hon/W/W of Am Wom.

ZINIAK, MADELINE oc/Television Producer, Journalist; b/Jun 2, 1956; h/ 24 Tarlton Road, Toronto M5P 2M4, Ontario; ba/Don Mills, Ontario; p/Mr and Mrs M Ziniak, Toronto, Ontario; ed/BA, Univ of Toronto, 1979; Ryerson Polytech Inst, 1980; Royal Conservatory Music; Cable TV, 1980-; cp/ Ontario Adv Coun, Multiculturalism & Citizenship, Chp Media & Communs Com; Canadian Ethnic Jour & Writers Clb; Byelorussian Wom's Com; r/Byelorussian Orthodox; hon/Author of "Don't Overlook Mkt Served by Ethnic Media" 1980; The Canadian Acad Cultural Exch, 1980; Canadian Ethnic Jour Awd, 1982; World W/W of Wom.

ZOOK, MARTHA HARRIS oc/Director Nursing; b/Nov 15, 1921; h/1109 Johnson Street, Larned, KS 67550; ba/ Larned, KS; m/Paul W; c/Mark Warren, Mary Elizabeth Hughey; p/Dwight Thacher and Helen Houston Harris; sp/ Elizabeth Zook, Larned, KS; ed/Dipl, Meriden Hosp Sch Nsg, 1947; BA, Stephens Col, 1977; mil/Cadet Nurse Corps; pa/Staff Nurse, Watkins Meml Hosp, 1948-49; Nsg Supvr, Larned St Hosp, 1949-53; Sect Supvr, 1956-57; Dir Nsg, 1958-61; Sect Nurse Sedgwick Sect, 1961-76; Clin Instr, Nsg Ed, 1976-77; Dir Nsg Ed, 1977-83; Dir Nsg, 1983-; Clin Nurse for Podiatrist, 1953; Sect Supvr Dillon Bldg, Larned, KS, 1957-58; ANA; KS Nurses Assn; Nat Leag Nsg; KS Leag Nsg; St Bd Nsg (Mtl Hlth Tech Exam Com); Nat Assn Human Ser Edrs; AAUW; r/Cath; hon/ W/W of Am Wom.

ZUCKERMAN, STUART oc/Medical Director, Clinical Professor; b/Feb 18, 1933; h/6700 Atlantic Avenue, Ventnor, NJ 08406; ba/Ventnor, NJ; p/George Zuckerman, Atlantic City, NJ, and Cassie Zuckerman (dec); ed/BS, Univ Al, 1954; DO, Phila Col Osteopathic Med, 1958; Rotating Intern, 1958-59; pa/ Psychi Fellow, Resident, Phila Mtl Hlth Clin, 1959-62; Psychoanal Studies Inst 1959-62, Chief Resident 1962; Chief, Div Neuropsychi, Grandview Hosp, Dayton, OH, 1962-65; Asst Med Dir, Chief Chd's & Adolescents Unit, NJ St Hosp, Ancora, 1967-70, Chief Outpatient Dept, Atlantic City, 1970-72; Pract in Neuropsychi, 1965-76; Fdg Prof Psychi, Sch Med, Marshall Univ, 1977-78, Clin Prof 1979-; Chief Mtl Hygiene, VA Hosp, Huntington, WV,

1978-79; Liaison Psychi, VA Med Ctr, Perry Pt, MD, 1979-; Med Dir, Mtl Hygiene Clin Ocean Co, Toms River, NJ 1980-; Consltg Psychi, 1977-; Conslt, Chd Study, Spec Sers, S Jersey Sch Sys; Nom Com, Mtl Hlth Assn Atlantic Co, 1972-75; Hosp Insp Team, Am Osteopathic Assn, 1971-75; Bd Dirs, Atlantic Co Fam Sers Assn, 1968-74; Cape May Co Drug Abuse Coun; Diplomate, Am Osteopathic Bd Neurol & Psychi; Am Nat Bd Psychi; Fellow, Royal Soc Hlth; Intl, Am, MD, Psychi Assns; Am NJ Public Hlth Assns; Am Osteopathic Assn; AAUP; Am Soc for Law & Med; Am Acad Forensic Scis; Am Assn Acad Psychi; Am Col Emer Phys; Am Acad Psychotherapists; Am Assn on Mtl Deficiency; Acad Psychosomatic Med; NJ, CA Assns Osteopathic Phys & Surgs; NJ Hosp Assn; Am Voc Assn; Am Assn Grp Therapy; Assn Mil Surgs US; Am Assn Psychi Admrs; Am Assn Adolescent Psychi; World Med Assn; Am Assn Mtl Hlth Admrs; Am Assn Gen Hosp Psychis; Am Phys F'ship Assn for Res Nervous & Mtl Diseases; Atlantic Co Osteopathic Med Soc, Pres 1970-72; Assoc Editor, Bulletin of Am Col Neuropsychis, 1963-70; hon/Author of Num Profl Pubs; W/W: in Am, in E, in MW; World W/W.

ZYBINE, ALEK oc/Choreographer, Ballet Master; b/Jun 2, 1934; h/Av San Francisco 3388, Col, Chapalita, Guadalajara, Jal, Mexico; ba/Same; m/Violette; c/Nadya, Olivia; p/Lilia Zybina, Great Barrington, MA; sp/Uros and Zora Zelich, Daytona Beach, FL; ed/Universidad Autonoma de Mexico; Dance Studies w Hypolite Zybine, Anatole Vilzac, Edward Caton, Anthony Tudor, Matt Mattox; pa/Danced, Choreographed for TV & Movies, 1951-55; Danced w Ballet Russe de Montecarlo in USA, 1956-58; Soloist, Metro Opera NYC, 1958-60; Ldg Dancer Dallas Liric Opera, 1961; Ldg Dancer, Kovach, Rabowsky Co, 1961-62; Assoc Dir, Choreographer, Tchr & Dancer, Nassau Civic Ballet, 1962-70; Headed Creation & Dir of Folklore Grp Sent to Olympic Games in Mexico, 1968; Guest Leading Dancer in Port Au Prince under Lavinia Williams, 1972; Dir, Fdr, "New Breed Dancers Ltd", 1973-75; Headed the Dance Dept for Min of Ed in Bahamas, 1973-75; Choreographed "Misa Caribe" 1975; Est'd Academia del Ballet Guadalajara, AC, 1975; Dance Tchr, Folklorie Grp of Univ Guadalajara, 1975; Dir, Dance Dept, Bellas Artes, Jalisco, 1982; Dir, Official Dance Co, Jalisco, 1983; r/ Russian Orthodox; hon/1st Prize Dance Contest, Instituto Nacional de la Juventud Mexicana, 1952; Presented to Queen Elizabeth II as Pres of Festival of Arts & Crafts in Nassau, 1966; 1st Father/Daughter Team, Intl Ballet Competition in Varna, Bulgaria; Men of Achmt; Intl W/W of Intells; Dic of Intl Biography.

ADDENDUM

ASHTON, KATE PEGGY oc/Editor, Professor, Speech Consultant; b/Sep 11, 1948; h/5046 Ducos Place, San Diego, CA 92124; ba/San Diego, CA; p/Lester Leopold, Boca Raton, FL; Louise Monroe, Hartwood, VA; ed/BS in Spch Communication 1970, MA in Platform Arts 1972, Bob Jones Univ; MA in Spch Communication, San Diego St Univ, 1979; pa/Instr, Bob Jones Univ, 1970-72; Asst Prof, Christian Heritage Col, 1972-76; Prof, San Diego City Col, 1976-83; Editor, *Where* Mag, 3M, 1980-83; Spch Conslt, Marine Corps, San Diego Gas & Elect & Pacific Telephone; Wn Spch Assn, 1985; Communicating Arts Grp, 1982; r/Prot; Hon/Pubs, "Take Home Pictures" in *Where* Mag, 1982; "Coping w Student Criticism" in *Guide* 1977; & *Emily* 1972; W/W: Am Wom, Among Cols & Univs.

BURKES, DORIS S HAMILTON oc/ Retired Educator; b/Apr 23, 1914; h/ Route 3, Box 255, Laurel, MS 39440; m/Grady B (dec); p/Oscar D and Era Magee Simmons (dec); ed/BS 1937, MA 1954, Univ of So MS; pa/Civilian Employeee, USAAC, 1944-45; Tchr, Voc Home Ec, Moselle 1937-40, Brandon 1940-41, Hattiesburg 1941-42, Jones Co Schs 1945-54, Laurel City Schs 1954-71; Supervisory Tchr, Univ of So MS, 1941-42, 1947-71; Jones Co Tchrs Assn, Pres 1953-54; MS Home Ec Assn, Treas 1964; Delta Kappa Gamma Soc, Zeta St Pres 1965-67; BPW Clb; Laurel Clrm Tchr; Laurel Ed Assn, Pres; Pres, MS Voc Home Ec Tchrs, 1968-70; MS Voc Assn, 1970-71; MS Ret'd Tchrs, 1982-83; cp/MS 4-H Adult Ldrs Coun, Pres 1952-53; Altrusa Clb, Pres, Laurel 1957-58, 1970-73; Red Cross Bd & Tchr, 1946-; MS Chgo Clb, 1983-84; Farm Bur, Bd & Wom's Chair; Coun of Aging, Chair, Adv Com 1982; SS Tchr; hon/ Articles in Newslttrs as St Pres; 4-H Ldrship Awd, 1953; MS 4-H Alumni Recog Awd, 1954; Named Wom of Achmt, BPW Clb, 1975; Diana Awd, 1978; Zeta St Delta Kappa Gamma Outstg Sers Awd, 1979; W/W: in Am Ed, of Am Wom, in S & SW, in US; Commun Ldrs of Am; DIB.

YOUNG PERSONALITIES OF AMERICA

A

AARON, GRACE A oc/Graduate Student; b/Feb 9, 1961; h/11622 Pawnee Drive Southwest, Tacoma, WA 98499; p/Mr and Mrs Russell K Aaron, Tacoma, WA; ed/Grad, Clover Park HS; BA, MS Univ for Wom, 1983; Att'g MS St Univ, MPPA expected 1984; cp/MS Univ for Wom Student Govt VP; Phi Kappa Phi; Student Senate Pres, MS Univ for Wom; Mng Editor, MS Univ Wom Newspaper; MS Univ for Wom Literary Mag Editor; Sigma Delta Chi, Soc for Profl Jour, Pres; Wom in Communs, VP; Gamma Beta Phi, Pres; Mortar Bd; Treas, Jr Class Honorary; Sigma Tau Delta, English Hon Soc; r/Meth; hon/Dean's & Pres' List, MS Univ for Wom; Grad magna cum laude, 1983; F'ship to MS St Univ, 1983-84; HS Hon Grad; Ray A Furr Jour S'ship; W/W Among Students in Am Univs & Cols; Intl Youth in Achmt; Commun Ldrs Am; Nat Dean's List; g/MPPA, 1984; Position in St or Fed Govt.

ABEL, MICHAEL A oc/Chef; b/Jan 17, 1965; h/Route 4, Box 74-D, Piedmont, AL 36272; ba/Gadsden, AL; p/James B Jr and Rachel F Abel, Piedmont, AL; ed/Sprg Garden HS; pa/Dock Instr, Browns Transport Co, 1979-80; Hdchef, Asst Mgr, The Other Office, 1981-84; Pres, FFA, 1980-83; Lib Asst, 1982-83; HS Ftball; Jr HS & HS Basketball; HS Class Treas; r/Bapt; hon/FFA Pres; Chapt Farmer, 1982; Greenhand Awd, 1980; Lib Asst Awd, 1983; g/Computer Programmer & Repair.

ABELE, KAREN ANN oc/Student; b/May 17, 1962; h/3223 Ramsgate Road, Augusta, GA 30909; p/Dr and Mrs Donald C Abele, Augusta, GA; ed/BA, Converse Col, 1984; cp/Crescent Pres, 1981-82; Yrbk Editor, 1982-83; Alpha Lambda Delta, VP 1981-82; Mortar Bd, VP 1983-84; House Bd, Dorm Pres 1982-83; Chm of House Bd, 1983-84; Student Gov't VP, 1983-84; r/Presb; hon/Milliken Scholar, 1980-84; CRC Freshman Chem Awd, 1981; Fac S'ship, 1982-84; Converse Scholar, 1982-84; Jr Marshal, 1982-83; W/W; Nat Dean's List; g/Med Sch of the Med Col of GA.

ABNER, TROY ALLEN oc/Student, Part-time Photographer; b/Jan 21, 1963; h/General Delivery, Kay Jay, KY 40906; p/Troy and Phyllis Abner, Kay Jay, KY; ed/Knox Central HS, 1981; Eastern KY Univ, 1981-82; Union Col, 1982-84; pa/Ofc Asst, John C Dixon, Atty, 1980-81; Ofc Asst, Milton Townsend, VP, Union Col, 1982-83; Photog, Union Col, 1983-; cp/Treas 1980, VP 1981, Future Bus Ldrs of Am; Barrister's Soc, Pre-Law Org, 1981-82; Treas 1982, VP 1983, Phi Beta Lambda Pre-Profl Bus Org; Student Governing Bd, 1982-83; Acad Policy Comm, 1982-83; Gamma Beta Phi Nat Hon, Mem 1982-83, Reporter 1982; St VP 1983; Commmun Registry for Sharing Sers, 1982-83; r/Bapt; hon/Eng Composition Awd, 1983; Phi Beta Lambda Outstg Mem Awd, 1983; St and Reg Awds in Bus Law, 1980-81; Sr Bus Student Awd, 1981; Hon Roll, 1979-81; Dean's List, 1981-83; W/W; Am's Outstg Names and Faces; Nat Dean's List; Soc for Dist'd Am Students; g/Degs in Bus, Psych, and Sociol; Attend Law Sch; Return to Appalachia for Practice.

ABNEY, CARRIE GAIL oc/Student; b/Jan 13, 1966; h/Kaye Street, Route 5,

Berea, KY 40403; p/Mr and Mrs William E Abney, Berea, KY; ed/Att'g HS; pa/Cashier, Druther's Restaurant, 1983; cp/Nat Hon Soc, Reporter 1983; Sr Beta Clb, VP 1982-83; FHA, Treas, Pres, 1980-83; Student Govt VP, 1982-83; Sr Class Secy, 1983; Pep Clb, Treas 1980-84; Future Bus Ldrs of Am, Secy 1983; Colorguard Squad Co-Capt, Capt, 1980-84; *The Pirate* Monthly HS Newspaper; HS Yrbook; r/Bapt; hon/HS Health Awd; Jr HS Math Bowl Team, 1983; Homecoming Court 1st Runner-up; FHA Sophomore Sweetheart Attendant; Del to KY Girls' St, 1983; W/W Among Am HS Students; g/Attend Col with Major in Home Ec to become Teacher.

ABRAHAM, MARTIN A oc/Graduate Student; b/Feb 18, 1961; h/14-3A Cheswold Boulevard, Newark, DE 19713; p/Sam and Barbara Abraham, Levittown, NY; ed/Gen Douglas MacArthur HS, 1978; BSChE, Rensselaer Polytechnic Inst, 1982; Att'g Univ of DE; pa/Co-op Student, ARCO Chem Co, 1980-81; Summer Intern, Stauffer Chem Co, 1982-83; cp/AIChE; ACS; Colburn Clb; hon/Tau Beta Pi, 1981-; Phi Lambda Upsilon, 1981-; Univ of DE F'ship, 1982-; W/W in Am Cols and Univs; Commun Ldrs of Am; g/PhD, Chem Engrg at Major Univ.

ABRAMS, MARY TOMMIE oc/Student; b/Nov 13, 1960; h/732 Amelia Street, Newberry, SC 29108; p/Mr and Mrs George Carter Abrams, Newberry, SC; ed/Newberry HS, 1979; BA, Newberry Col, 1982; pa/Middle Sch Drama Tchr, 1982-83; cp/Alpha Psi Omega Hist; Phi Gamma Nu Editor; Intervarsity Christian F'ship Prog Coor; Christian Coun; Presb Ch SS Tchr; DAR; Bus Mgr *The Indian*; hon/Cardinal Key; Outstg Theatre Freshman/Sr On-Stage/Off-Stage Supporting Awds; W/W in Am Cols and Univs; g/Grad Study, Presb Sch of Christian Ed; Christian Edr.

ADAIR, DENNIS W oc/Senior Internal Auditor; b/Jan 4, 1955; h/4436 Pasture Drive, Elizabethtown, PA 17022; ba/Hershey, PA; m/Bonnie L; c/Matthew C; p/William and Alma Adair, Ephrata, PA; sp/Theodore and Mildred Dietrich, Akron, PA; ed/Att'd PA St Univ, 1973-75; BS, Elizabethtown Col, 1977; pa/Auditor 1977-80, Sr Info Conslt 1980-81, Arthur Andersen & Co; Sr Internal Auditor, Hershey Foods Corporation, 1981-; Am Inst CPAs; PA Inst CPAs; r/United Ch Christ; hon/Acad S'ship, Elizabethtown, 1976, 1977; PA Inst CPAs S'ship, 1977; Investmt Awd, Wall St Jour, 1977; Elected as Cand for Sch Dir, 1983.

ADAMEC, JAMES C oc/Student, Electrician; b/Feb 1, 1957; h/c/o Forte Certland Home, Apt 5A, Lexington Avenue, Mohegan, NY 10547; m/Margaret; p/Kenneth E Adamec, Stamford, CT; Joan C Gall Adamec, Danberry, CT; sp/Charles Sammann Jr, Katonah, NY; ed/John Jay Sr HS, 1975; AAS, Westchester Commun Col, 1982; Fordham Univ, 1978-80; cp/HS Varsity Ftball; Fordham Univ Student Govt; IEEE; HS Varsity Ski Racing Tm; hon/Dean's List; W/W Amg Students in Am Cols & Univs; Commun Ldrs of Am; g/BSEE, PE, R&D Eng.

ADAMIK, JASON MICHAEL oc/Student; b/May 16, 1962; h/3309 Oak

Hill Drive, Garland, TX 75043; p/Wayne and Joan Adamik, Garland, TX; ed/S Garland HS, 1980; Att'd TX A&M Univ, 1980; Att'g N TX St Univ, Music Major; cp/HS Band, 1976-80; Key Clb, Treas 1978; Chem Clb, 1977-80; French Clb, 1978-79; Beta Clb, 1978-80; Math Tm, 1979; Biol Clb, 1976-79; Active in Cath Student Commun of N TX St Univ & TWU, 1981-83; Soc for Creative Anachronism, NTSU, 1982; r/Cath; hon/Illustrated Book on Early Am Hist; Illustrated 3 Annual HS Literary Mags; HS Sr Class Pres, 1980; Highest Score in HS, Nat Math Exam, 1980; All-City Band, 1979-80; Medals in UIL Music, 1979-80; Art Editor of *Libertas*; Art & Lit Pub, 1978-79; Rotary Clb Student of the Month, Twice, 1980; N TX St Univ First Freshman Classical Guitar Major, 1981; g/Bach's Deg in Art or Chem; Use Scientific & Artistic Abilities in Career in Scientific Res.

ADAMS, ALESIA SUZANNE oc/Student; b/Mar 15, 1964; h/Route 2, Box 2, Clover, SC 29710; p/George S Adams, Gastonia, NC; Brenda M Burgin, Clover, SC; ed/Att'g E Carolina Univ; cp/Ch Choir; SS Pres; UMYF; 4-H Reporter; Varsity Basketball, Volleyball; hon/Scholar/Ath Awd; Outstg Sr S'ship; g/Vet Med.

ADAMS, AMY R oc/Sales Representative; b/May 10, 1960; h/2011 Estrada Parkway #134, Irving, TX 75061; p/Mr and Mrs Richard D Adams, Orange, TX; ed/Little Cypress-Mauriceville HS, 1978; BBA Fin, TX A&M Univ, 1982; pa/Student Asst, TX A&M Univ Lib Circulation Div, 1979-82; Aquatics Dir & Swim Instr, YMCA of Orange, TX, 1979-80; Sales Rep, CompuShop, 1983-; cp/Teens Aid Retarded, Pres 1978; Spec Olympics; Nat Hon Soc; Cath Yth Org; HS Tennis Tm; Student Govt; Fin Assn; Lib Staff Assn; Intramural Sports; Little Sister, Pi Kappa Phi Frat; r/Cath; hon/Hon Grad; Am Legion Citizenship Awd, 1978; Ath Boosters Clb S'ship, 1978; Dist'd Student, TX A&M, 1982; g/Store Mgr, CompuShop; MBA, Bus Computing Sci.

ADAMS, LESTER LEE oc/Student; b/Jan 25, 1963; h/905 Wall Street, Galena, KS 66739; p/Lester L and Doris L Adams, Galena, KS; ed/Galena HS, 1981; Pgh St Univ; cp/Order of DeMolay, Past Master Cnslr; Jr Class VP; Sr Class Pres; Yrbook Co-Bus Mgr; Sigma Phi Alpha Pres; Boy's St Supr Ct Justice; Cherokee Co Repub Ctl Com-man; Yg Repub Party Secy/Treas; Straight A Hon Roll; KU Hon Student; hon/St Scholar of KS; St of KS St Scholar S'ship; Lambda Sigma; Kappa Mu Epsilon; Alpha Mu Gamma; Dean's Hon Roll; Math S'ship, David Wright Meml S'ship; W/W Amg Am HS Students; Intl Yth In Achmt; Yg Commun Ldrs of Am.

ADAMS, MARY CAROLYN oc/Student; b/Oct 17, 1966; h/Box 121A, Jeremiah, KY 41826; p/Jimmy Ray and Jean Adams, Jeremiah, KY; ed/Att'g Letcher HS and Letcher Co Area Voc Ed Center, Bus Ofc Dept; cp/Future Bus Ldrs of Am, 1982-84 (Pres, 1983-84); r/Bapt; hon/Hon Roll, 1980-84; Write Articles for Sch Newspaper, 1983-84; g/Attend Col, Bus Adm; Manage Own Bus Firm.

ADAMS, PENELOPE RENEE oc/Student; b/Sep 25, 1963; h/4 Trailridge

Lane, Route 7, Edwardsville, IL 61761; p/Mr and Mrs Luther Holst, Edwardsville, IL; ed/Collinsville HS, 1981; Att'd Greenville Col, Psych; Att'd IL St Univ, Music Therapy; pa/Clerical Secy, May Dept Stores, 1981; Secy, McDonnell Douglas, 1982; Recreational Aide, Music Tchr, Huddleson Bapt Chd's Home, 1983; cp/Collinsville HS Band, Bassoon Player; Flag Corps, Capt; Newspaper, Yrbook, Staff Mem; Greenville Col, Singing Gp, Cornerstone, Pianist; Yrbook, Staff Mem; Il St Univ, Student Christian F'ship; Music Therapy Clb; Alpha Gamma Delta Sorority; Ch Organist; r/Bapt; hon/Miss Collinsville, 1983; running, Miss IL, 1984; g/ BS, Employmt, Music/Music Therapy.

ADAMS, RUTHIE COLEMAN oc/ Nursing Supervisor; b/Mar 6, 1957; h/ Post Office Box 2148, Natchez, MS 39120; ba/Natchez, MS; m/Johnny E III; p/Joe and Rosie Shepherd, Macon, MS; sp/Luther and Willie Adams, Shubuta, MS; ed/BSN, 1979; pa/GN Staff Nurse, St Dominic Hosp, 1979; RN Staff Nurse, Hinds Gen Hosp, 1979; RN Instr, Alcorn St Univ, 1981-82; RN Nsg Supvr, Humana Hosp, 1981-; MS Nurse Assn; ANA; Chi Beta Phi Hon Sci Frat; r/ Meth; hon/Deans List, MS St Univ, 1976; Sr Campus Beauty, William Carey Col Sch Nsg, 1978-79.

ADAMS, SHEILA DAWN oc/Spanish Teacher; b/Nov 20, 1962; h/1400 West Blue Starr, #1-J, Claremore, OK 74053; p/John and Pat Adams, Oologah, OK; ed/Oologah HS, 1980; BA Spanish, OK St Univ, 1983; pa/Spanish Tchr, Oologah HS, 1983-; cp/Oologah Clrm Tchrs Assn; OK Ed Assn; Nat Ed Assn; OK Fgn Lang Tchrs Assn.

ADAMS, SHIRLEY LORRAINE (LORI) oc/Student; b/Jul 7,1962; h/74 Bahama Circle, Tampa, FL 33606; p/ Bruce Waldo and Shirley Bowman Adams, Tampa, FL; ed/Grad, Tampa Prep Sch; Att'd Yale Univ; cp/Asst Num Plays, Artist for Sets & Playbills, Yale Univ; HS Student Coun; Spec Olympics Asst; Piano, Bach Fests, Yrly; GSA; r/ Prot; hon/Valedictorian; Scholastic Art Awd, Gold Key; Nat Merit Scholar; Most Valuable Tennis Player, 4 Yrs; Full S'ship (declined), Eckerd Col; Intl Yth in Achmt; W/W Amg Am HS Students.

ADAMSON, ANGELA ALLYN oc/ Student; b/Mar 20, 1961; h/305 Dundee Road, Glencoe, IL 60022; p/R Christina Adamson, Glencoe, IL; ed/New Trier Twp HS E, 1970; Univ of Notre Dame; cp/Fdr, Dir, Abiogenesis Dance Collective; Photo Editor, Scholastic Mag; Pres, Photo Clb; Newspaper Art Columnist; Arts & Lttrs Student Adv Coun to the Dean; Staff Asst, Notre Dame/St Mary's Theatre; hon/Notre Dame Scholar; Dean's List; W/W Amg Am HS Students; g/MFA or MA in Dance or Arts Adm.

ADAMSON, TERRIE ELAINE oc/ Teacher, Coach; b/Aug 5, 1953; h/1419 Shady Lane, #403, Bedford, TX 76021; p/Mrs T J Adamson, Jr, Brenham, TX; ed/ HS, Brenham, TX, 1971; BS, TX Christian Univ, 1975; Att'd Univ of Salzburg, Austria, 1979-80; Att'd Univ of St Andrews, Scotland, 1982; pa/ Teacher, Coach, Richland HS, 1976-; Cnslr, Am Inst for Fgn Studies, 1978-; cp/Ch Choir; Softball Leag; r/Epis; hon/ HS Tennis Tm, 1967-71; First Dist Doubles, Jr. Davis Cup Tour Invitation,

Reg Finalist 1968, Dist Finalist 1971; HS Basketball Tm, 1968-71; St Quarterfinalist, 1971; Col Tennis Tm, 1971-74; Conf Conslt, 1972; Col Basketball Tm, 1973-75; Commun Ldrs of Am; g/Write Best-selling Book.

ADKINS, CARL EDWARD oc/Student; b/Jul 30, 1965; h/319 Kennedy, Middleton, TN 38052; p/Mr and Mrs Larry C Adkins, Middleton, TN; ed/ Middleton HS, 1983; Att'g Memphis St Univ; pa/Sta Attendant, Vicker's Delta Ser Ctr, 1981-82; Factory Worker, Dover Elevator Corp, 1983; cp/HS Beta Clb, Mem 1980-83, Pres, 1983; HS Basketball Scorekeeper, 1980-83; Sr Class Pres; Selected Most Likely to Succeed; r/Bapt; hon/Hugh O'Brian Yth Ldrship Foun Rep, 1980; First Pl Acctg 1982, Mr Future Bus Exec, Top 10% of Class 1977-83, Bus Day Conf, Freed-Hardeman Col; g/Maj in Acctg, CPA.

ADKINS, CURTIS ELWOOD oc/ Student; b/Sep 29, 1960; h/6451 Naldo Lane, Franklin, OH 45005; p/Curtis and Audrey Adkins, Franklin, OH; ed/HS, 1978; BA, Warner So Col, 1982; pa/Yth Pastor, First Ch of God, 1979; Yth Pastor, Chapelwood Ch of God, 1980-81; Yth Pastor, First Ch of God, 1982; Yth Pastor, Helm St Ch of God, 1983; cp/BSA Jr Asst Scoutmaster; NHS; Mu Alpha Theta; German Clb; Pres, Ch Yth F'ship; Chm, Acad Excell Com; Fund Raising Com; Student Body Pres; Varsity Soccer; hon/Nat Dean's List; Intl Yth in Achmt; W/W in Am Cols & Univs; Commun Ldrs of Am; Outstg Col Grads; g/Biblical Studies; Pastoral Min; Psychol; Christian Ed; Master's Deg; MDiv.

AGEE, CONNIE LYNN oc/Sr Secy, Dean of Col of Social and Behavioral Sci in Bus 1974; b/Aug 20, 1956; h/ Route 6, Frazerwood, Richmond, KY 40475; p/W J and Nannie Agee, Richmond, KY; ed/Madison Ctl HS, 1974; En KY Univ; Madison Co Voc Sch in Bus, 1974; cp/Pres, Reg Treas, FBLA; Beta Clb; Madison Co Voc Sch FBLA Clb; hon/Cert of Recog; Secretarial-Stenographic Awd; Intl Yth in Achmt; Phi Kappa Phi Awd for High Scholastic Achmt, 1982; Yg Personalities of the S; Commun Ldrs of Am; g/ Bus Adm Deg.

AGEE, DAWN LYNN oc/Student; b/ Jun 27, 1964; h/Rural Route #3, Richmond, KY 40475; p/Donald and Jeanette Agee, Richmond, KY; ed/Madison Ctl HS, Att'g En KY Univ; pa/Telephone Conslt, Olan Mills Studio, 1981; Clothing Clk, Heck's Dept Store, 1981-82; Shoe Salesperson, Adams Shoe Store, 1982-83; cp/Jr Beta Clb; Sr Beta Clb; Hlth Careers Clb; Pep Clb; FBLA; ARC Vol; Cancer Crusade and Mar of Dimes; Bapt Ch Yth Grp; Assn'l Yth Grp; 4-H Clb, Choral Grp; Ch Choir; Pres, Bapt Ch Yth Grp; r/So Bapt; hon/Eng Merck Awd; Hon for Dist'n, HS; Acad Excell Awd; Baton Twirling Hon Awd, 1975; Third Runner-Up Twirling Contest, 1976; March of Dimes Yth Participation Awd; St Finalist, Miss Teen Pageant; St Finalist, Miss U Teenager Pageant; g/ Maj in Bus Adm; Work for Maj Corp.

AGEE, NANCY DENISE oc/Student; Part-time Cashier; b/Dec 12, 1964; h/ 1505 Randy Drive, Cookeville, TN 38501; p/Don and Irene Agee, Cookeville, TN 38501; ed/Cookeville HS,

1983; Att'g, TN Tech; pa/Arts and Crafts Tchr, Parks and Rec, 1978-80; Salesperson, Don's Antiques, 1980-82; Salesperson, Armand's Dept Store, 1983; Cashier, Food Town Grocery Store, 1983; cp/Basketball, 1976-83, Capt 1978-79, 1983; Softball, 1976-83, Capt 1978-79, 1983; FHA Clb; Secy, DECA; Secy, Jr and Sr HS Classes; C Clb, Sigma Delta Sigma Soriorty; g/Maj in Home Ec; Own Real Est Ofc.

AGUILERA, RAYMOND OTTO oc/ Student; b/Jul 13, 1963; h/1724 West Melrose Street, Chicago, IL 60657; p/ Ramon and Margot Aguilera; ed/St Patrick HS, 1981; Lewis Univ; pa/ Firefighter, Tri-St Fire Dept; Admissions Peer Cnslr, Orientation Ldr Incoming Freshmen Prog, Resident Asst, Lewis Univ; cp/Nat Jr Hon Soc; Nat Hon Soc; Key Clb VP; Student Coun VP & Pres; Wrestling; Ftball; Spanish Nat Hon Soc; Curric Com; Yth Grp Secy; Ch Folk Grp; Candy Stripers-IL Masonic ER; Singer, Westmont Hlth Ctr; Diplomat, Mid-W Model UN, 1983; Communs Chp, Student Govt, 1983; hon/Nat Dean's List, 1983; Univ Dean's List, Hon Roll, 1983; W/ W Among Am HS Students; Cambridge Student Search; Kiwanis Citizenship Awd; Commun Ldrs of Am; Intl Students in Achmt; g/Majs in Polit Sci, Public Adm; Intl Polit.

AHO, KATHERINE WINDSOR oc/ Graphic Designer; b/Jul 5, 1961; h/B-3 Sturbridge Square, Blacksburg, VA 24060; m/David; ed/Dipl, HS, 1979; BFA, VA Commonwealth Univ, 1983; pa/Graphic Designer, Advantage Advertising Agy, 1983-; cp/Pres, Inter-Varsity Christian F'ship, VA Commonwealth Univ Chapt 1980-81, Missions Coor 1981-82; Sum Mission Wk in Philippines, 1981; hon/Ruth Hibbs Hyland Awd; g/Overseas Mission Wk.

AKAR, NABIH NABIH b/Jan 12, 1959; h/22087 Barton Road, Grand Terrace, CA 92334; p/Nabih and Nadia Akar, Grand Terrace, CA; ed/Univ So MS; BS 1981, MA 1983, Univ CA; pa/ Internship, Dept Finance, Riverside, CA; Pres, Chm Publicity for Soc Advmt Mgmt, 1980-82; Mem, Am Prodn & Inventory Control Soc, 1980-82; hon/ Nat Dean's List, 1981; Cert Achmt, Soc Advmt Mgmt, 1981; London Awd, Inst Anglo-Am Studies, 1981; g/PhD in Fin; Ldg Ofcr in Bkg Indus.

AKERS, BRENDA LACHELLE oc/ Student; b/Mar 18, 1964; h/209 Cindy Place, Goodlettsville, TN 37072; p/Mr and Mrs Akers, Goodlettsville, TN; ed/ Goodlettsville HS, 1982; Att'g Univ TN, 1982; pa/Full-time Student, Univ TN; FFA St Farmer, 1982; Secy 1983-84; r/ Bapt; hon/FFA St Farmer 1982; FFA Star Chapt Farmer Awd, 1982; W/W Among Am HS Students; Commun Ldrs Am; g/Marketing Major.

AKIYAMA, JULIE S oc/Graduate Student; b/Jan 17, 1957; h/1147 South Windsor Boulevard, Los Angeles, CA 90019; p/John and Dorothy Akiyama, LA, CA; ed/LA HS, 1975; BA, CA St Univ-LA, 1980; MA, Pepperdine Univ, 1983; PhD Prog, St Louis Univ; pa/ Psych Intern, Asian Pacific Cnslg & Treatment Ctr, Hollywood Mtl Hlth, 1982; Tchr's Asst, Pepperdine Univ, 1981-83; Therapeutic Intern, Beverlywood Mtl Hlth Ctr, 1982-83; r/Christian; hon/Nat Dean's List, 1980; Ephebian Soc, 1975; g/PhD in Clin Psychol; Child Psychol.

ALDERMAN, LOUIS CLEVELAND III oc/Computer Sys Tech Support Engineer; b/Oct 7, 1955; h/3011 Falling Brook Drive, Kingwood, TX 77339; p/ Louis C Jr and Anne A W Alderman, Cochran, GA; ed/Cochran HS, 1973; AS, Mid GA Col, 1975; BEE, GA Inst Tech, 1977; pa/TX Reg'd Profl Engr; Chd of Am Revolution, Charter Pres; SAR; Nat Assn of Eagle Scouts; Magna Charter Barons; hon/Eagle Scout; STAR Student; Salutatorian; Hon Grad; Beta Clb; Phi Theta Kappa; Wallace Harris Meml S'ship; Burgoyne Gibson Moors Meml S'ship; Dean's List; St of GA, Univ GA Cert of Merit; St of GA Gov Hon Prog, Math; W/W Am Jr Cols; g/MBA.

ALDRIDGE, SABRINA KAYE oc/ Student; b/May 18, 1960; h/Route 2, Box 224A, Moulton, AL 35650; p/ Hansel and Martha Aldridge, Moulton, AL; ed/Lawrence Co HS, 1978; BA, Univ AL, 1982; Att'g Athens St Col for BS Ed; pa/Reporter, *The Moulton Advertiser*, 1984; Secy, Calhoun Commun Col, 1984; Reporter, *The Huntsville News*, 1982; Sigma Delta Chi; Soc Profl Journalists; r/Ch of Christ; hon/Athens St, Miss Merry Christmas, 1983; Outstg Yg Ams, 1979; Nat Dean's List, 1979; US Senate Yth Prog, 1978; g/ Master's Deg, Tchg.

ALEMAR, DEBRA CARTER oc/ Switchboard Operator; b/Mar 5, 1959; h/3325 Galindo Street, Oakland, CA 94601; m/Carlos R; p/Mr and Mrs B J Carter; ed/HS Dipl, Patten Acad of Christian Ed, 1977; BA, Patten Col, 1981; ETTA Cert, 1981; pa/Registrar, Patten Col, 1980-82; Switchboard Operator, Retirement Home, 1983-; Food Sers Cashier, 1983; cp/VP, HS; VP, Secy, Col; Symphonette; Co-Editor of Sch Paper; Sunday Sch Tchr; Tchr's Asst; AACRAO; Col Singers Orch II; r/Christian Evang; hon/Nat Dean's List, 1981; Grad, cum laude; Gold "P"; Silver and Gold "A," 1977; W/W Among Sudent in Am Univs and Cols; W/W Among Dist'd HS Students.

ALEXANDER, ALPHA VERNELL oc/ Associate Athletic Director; b/Jun 9, 1954; h/870 North 28th Street, Apartment 216, Philadelphia, PA 19130; p/Mr and Mrs Alexander (dec); ed/Jefferson Sr HS, 1972; BA, Col of Wooster, 1976; Master's Deg 1978, Doct Deg 1981, Temple Univ; pa/Assoc Ath Dir 1983-, Acting Wom's Ath Dir 1982-83, Temple Univ; AAHPER; PA AHPER; Nat Assn for Girls and Wom in Sport; Black Interested Coaches; Psycho/Sociol Sport Interactions Lab, Temple Univ; Wom Sport Foun; Site Dir, USFHA Olympic "D" Camp, Temple Univ; Ad Hoc Com Wom Ath; Search Com, HPERD Outdoor Facilities Coor; Pers Com Mem Wom Ath; Grad Student Rep, Dean's Search Com; Records Custodian of Wom Intercol Ath Pers Com; Chm of Wom Intercol Ath Pers Com; Wom Intercol Ath Res Coun; Dir of Grad Student Assn Coffee Shop; Participant, EAIAW Reg 1-B Basketball Tourn; Minority Recruitment Prog for PE; Full-time Wom Sports Info Dir; hon/ Pub, *Black Women in Sport*, 1981; Outstg Wooster Student; Martindale Compton S'ship; Outstg Yg Wom of Am; Intl Yth Achmt; Basketball Awd; Dir of Dist'd

Ams; g/To Help Minority Wom.

ALEXANDER, ANDREA ALICIA oc/ Student; b/Jul 23, 1967; h/204 Edgemont Street, Easley, SC 29640; p/ Barron and Lynn Alexander, Easley, SC; ed/Easley HS; cp/French Clb, Secy 1983-84; Jr Class Secy, 1983-84; Student Coun, 1983-84; Student Coun-Homeroom Pres, 1982-83; r/ Presb; Interact Handbell Choir at Ch, 4 Yrs; hon/Participant in Clemson Univ Biol Merit Exam, 1983; Participant in Miss Teen of SC Pageant, 1983; g/To Attend Either the Univ of AL or Clemson Univ and Maj in Bus Adm or Computer Sci.

ALEXANDER, CAROLYN JEAN oc/ Student; b/Dec 21, 1960; h/1524 Dade Street, Augusta, GA 30904; p/Ms Agnes Alexander, Augusta, GA; ed/Dipl, Acad of Richmond Co, 1978; BS, Biol, Clark Col, 1982; Student, NC A&T Univ, 1983-; pa/Subst Tchr, Acad of Richmond Co, 1982-83; Res, "Invivo Location of R6K Plasmids in *E coli*," Morehouse Col, 1981-82; Res, "Regulation of Phosphotidylcholine Biosynthesis," Purdue Univ, Sum 1981; Beta Kappa Chi Sch Hon Soc, Secy; cp/Acad of Richmond Co, Exec Coun Secy 1977; Red Cross Vol, 1973-; Vol Tutor, 1982-; r/Born Again Christian; Ch Pianist, 1976-81; hon/Undergrad Access to Res Careers S'ship, 1980-82; Alpha Kappa Mu Hon Soc, 1980; Beta Kappa Chi Sci Hon Soc, 1981; g/To Attain PhD in Biol and Become a Biomed Scist/Rschr.

ALEXANDER, DON L oc/Associate Professor of Mathematics; b/Feb 22, 1948; h/582 Ashville Road, Montevallo, AL 35115; ba/Montevallo, AL; p/Dr and Mrs W A Alexander, Covington, TN; ed/BS 1970, MA 1972, PhD 1979, Univ of AL; pa/Asst Prof of Math 1974, Assoc Prof of Math 1981, Univ of Montevallo; AL Tchrs of Col Math; Univ of Montevallo Fac Coun, Secy; cp/Bd of Dirs, AL Soccer Leag; Montgomery Caps Soccer Team; Univ of Montevallo Ultimate Frisbee Team, Fac Advr; Univ of Montevallo Soccer Clb, Fac Advr; B'ham Track Clb; Porsche Clb of Am; hon/Pubs, "Concerning Equivalences of Almost Continuous and Connectivity Functions of Baire Class I on Peano Continua" 1979, "Blocking Sets and Almost Continuous Functions" 1979; Univ of Montevallo Merit Awd Recip, 1982.

ALEXANDER, FRED JR oc/Student; b/Mar 28, 1965; h/2307 Briargrove Drive, Charlotte, NC 28215; p/Fred and Dilsie Alexander, Charlotte, NC; ed/ Grad, Garinger HS, 1983; cp/Student Body Pres, 1982-83; Nat Hon Soc, 1982-83; Math Hon Soc, 1982-83; Treas, Exec Com, 1981-83; Pres, Bible I, 1982-83; Pres, French Clb, 1980-81; Sophomore Class Treas, 1981-82; Jr Marshall, 1981-82; Sci Clb, 1982-83; Varsity Baseball, 1980-81, 1981-83, 1982-83; Band, 1980-81, 1981-82, 1982-83; Coun of Concerned Citizens, 1982-83; Master Knight, Knights of Pythagoras, 1982-83; hon/Civitan Awd, 1983; Grad Panhellenic Coun Outstg Sr, 1983; Charlotte Post Top 10 Srs, 1983; Mr Garinger, 1983; Garinger Super Sr, 1983; Voted Most Intellectual, 1983; Highest Batting Average Awd, 1982; Proj Excell at Davidson Col, 1982; INROADS Prog, 1983; Ranked 10th of 484, 1983; W/W Academics; W/W

Music; g/To Attend NC St Univ.

ALEXANDER, RONALD EDDIE oc/ Student; b/Mar 28, 1962; h/Route 2, Box 48, Salem, SC 29676; p/Mr and Mrs Bea Alexander Jr, Salem, SC; ed/ Tamassee-Salem HS; BA, Furman Univ, 1984; pa/Govt Relats Intern at 70,001 LTD, Wash Ctr Internship Prog, Sprg Term, 1983; Sum Yth Employmt Cnslr, Pre-Employmt Coor, Field Coor, CETA-Share, Sums 1982-83; Yth Dir, Salem Bapt Chm, Sums 1981-82; cp/Vol Wk in Var Polit Campaigns; Col Ednl Ser Corps, 1980-84, Div Hd 1982-84, May Play Day CoChp 1982, Coor 1981-84; Yg Dems Clb, 1980-84; Reorg'd Clb and Served as Pres 1982-84; Bapt Student Union, 1980-84, Prog Chm 1983-84, Min Chm 1982-83; Col Bowl Team Mem, 1982-84; Bread for the World, 1980-84; Furman Univ Hunger Alliance, 1982-84; r/So Bapt; hon/Voted the Alfred S Reid Outstg Jr Male, 1983; Elected Mem, Quaternion Clb, 1983-84; Recip, Doyle Meml S'ship, 1980-84; Recip, Furman Scholar S'ship, 1980-84; Recip, Class of 1965 S'ship, 1983-84; Dean's List Each Term; Omicron Delta Kappa Ldrship Hon, 1983; Dist'd Ams; W/W Among Students in Am Cols and Univs; g/To Attend Law Sch and Become Involved in Politics.

ALEXANDER, RUTH ANN oc/Student; b/Jan 6, 1965; h/Route 1, Box 47, Mt Crawford, VA 22841; p/R V and Phyllis L Alexander, Mt Crawford, VA; ed/Sch Dipl, 1983; Assoc of Fine Arts, So Sem Jr Wom's Col, 1985; pa/Stage Mgr, Shenendoah Val Choral Soc, 1983; cp/Turner Ashby Concert Choir, 1979-83, Libn 1981-83, Secy 1982-83; Turner Ashby Band, 1979-83, Libn 1982-83; Turner Ashby Forensic Team, 1974-83; Turner Ashby Drama Clb, 1979-83; So Sem Drama Clb, 1983-84; r/Luth; hon/Turner Ashby Outstg Vocal Music Student Awd, 1983; Music Hon Awd, 1980-83; VA Lions Clb Band S'ship Contest, Vocal Div, 1st Place Awd, 1981-83; W/W Am HS Students; g/To Attain a BA in Music Ed at Bridgewater Col.

ALEXANDER, THEODORE M III oc/Computer Operations Intern; b/Sep 15, 1961; h/3148 Kingsdale Drive, Atlanta, GA 30311; ba/Hapeville, GA; p/T M Jr (dec) and Janis B Alexander, Atlanta, GA; ed/HS, The Westminster Sch, 1980; Seeking Deg in Computer Sci w a Bus Minor, Morehouse Col; Subsequently Seeking an MBA at Emory or Stanford; pa/Salesman, Programmer, Datamart Inc, 1979; Computer Sci Apprentice, Res Ctr for Sci and Engrg, 1980; Computer Reservationist, The Day Co, 1981; Computer Opers Intern, First Atlanta Bk, 1982-; Alpha Phi Alpha Frat, Chapt Treas 1982-83; cp/NAACP, Life Mem; Jack & Jill of Am Inc, Chapt Secy 1980; Engrg Clb at Morehouse, Com Chp 1980; HS: Tennis Team 1977-79, Chess Team 1977-78, Computer Sci Clb 1977-80; Col: Tennis Team 1980; r/Congregational; hon/Hon Roll at Morehouse, Fall Semester 1980 and Sprg Semester 1981; Dean's List, Sprg Semester 1981; NAACP, Act-So Sci Awd, 1979; g/To Own or Co-Own a Fortune 500 Co in the Area of Computer Applications and to Further His Investmt Skills amd Knowledge.

ALEXANDER, YOLETTE UDA oc/ Unemployed; b/Mar 23, 1958; h/3616

7th Court, Wylam, Birmingham, AL 35224; p/Lloyd L and Emma Alexander, Birmingham, AL; ed/Ensley HS, 1976; Miles Col, 1976-78; BA, Social Wk, Univ of Montevallo, 1981; cp/NASW; Social Wk Clb; Afro-Am Soc; Sociol Clb; Am JA Soc; Electron Clb Treas; Acad Hon Roll; Bapt Ch SS Tchr; Asst Yth Dir; Yg Adult Usher Bd, Secy; Girl Scout Ldr, Cahaba Girl Scout Coun, 1982-83 (Troop #229, Jrs); hon/Friends of Miles Col S'ship Awd; Nat Dean's List; Outstg Yg Wom of Am; Commun Ldrs of Am; g/Master's Deg in Social Wk; Social Wkr.

ALFORD, KEITH ANTHONY oc/Salesperson; b/Dec 6, 1961; h/815 Pine Street, Columbia, SC 29205; ba/Florence, SC; p/Ethel J Finley, Columbia, SC; ed/HS Dipl, Dreher HS, 1979; BA, Hist and Sociol, Coker Col, 1983; pa/Columnist, *Black News*, 1977-79; Intern, Darlington Co Dept of Social Sers, 1980; Intern, SC St Dept of Social Sers, 1981; Intern, Midlands Human Resources Devel Comm, 1982; Practicum in Social Sers, Darlington Co Dept of Social Sers, 1983; Salesperson, Belk Dept Store, Magnolia Mall; cp/Coker Col: Commr Ser Org, F'ship of Christian Students, Student Admissions Com, Coker Singers, Student Rep to Lib Com, Student Rep to Acad Standards Com, Publicity and Calendar Chp, Sophomore Class Pres 1980-81, Student Govt Assn Pres 1981-82, 1982-83, Coker Col Union Exec Bd Mem, Bd of Govs Mem; r/Bapt; hon/Charles Kirkland Dunlap Scholar, 1982-83; Coker Col Dean's List, Sprg 1980, Fall 1980, Fall 1982, Sprg 1983; W/W Among Students in Am Univs and Cols; Nat Dean's List; Intl Biogl Centre; g/To Earn a Master's Deg in Social Wk; To Wk as a Protective Sers Wkr in the Fam Sers/Protective Ser Div of the Dept of Social Sers.

ALGARY, KATHRYN ELIZABETH oc/Student; b/Aug 18, 1962; h/20 Stonehaven Drive, Greenville, SC 29607; p/Dr and Mrs William P Algary, Greenville, SC; ed/Grad, J L Mann HS, 1980; BS, Winthrop Col, 1984; pa/Co-op Position at Bigelow-Sanford Inc; Full-time Employee, Pers Dept, Bigelow-Sanford Inc, Sum 1983; cp/Social Chm, Panhellenic Coun, Winthrop Col, 1983; Pres, Delta Zeta Sorority, Winthrop Col, 1983; Alpha Kappa Psi Bus Frat; r/Presb; hon/Dean's List, Winthrop Col, 1983; Recip, Hons Key in HS; g/To Attain an MBA Deg.

ALLEGRETTI, EDWARD PHILIP oc/Student; b/Jan 31, 1962; h/12500 Poppy Lane, San Jose, CA 95127; p/Mr and Mrs John M Allegretti, San Jose, CA; ed/Grad, Piedmont Hills HS, 1980; Student, San Jose St Univ; pa/Res Asst, NASA/Ames, Sum 1980; Asst Mgr, Wilson's Suede and Leather, Sum 1982; Asst Supvr, Nat Communs Inc, Sum 1983; cp/Phi Alpha Theta, Intl Hon Soc in Hist; Alpha Lambda Delta, Nat Hon Soc; Soc for Advmt of Mgmt; Italian-Am Heritage Foun; San Jose St Univ's Bd of Gen Studies, 1981-83; Fdr and Pres, Yth Grp, Italian-Am Heritage Foun, 1982; r/Trustees Bd, Hd Usher, Alum Rock Covenant Ch, 1983; hon/Dean's Hon List, 1982, 1983; Alumni Assn Dean's S'ship, 1981; Commends from Mayor Hayes of San Jose and Congressman Mineta; Intl Yth in

Achmt; W/W Commun Ldrs; g/Fin Maj w Career Goal of Bus Mgmt.

ALLEN, BONNIE ROSE oc/Farmer; b/Mar 14, 1958; h/Route 1, Box 202, Pinetops, NC 27864; ba/Macclesfield, NC; p/James and Mildred Allen, Pinetops, NC; ed/Grad, S Edgecombe HS, Pinetops, 1976; Att'd, E Carolina Univ, 1976-78; pa/Asst Mgr, Deena Casuals Clothing Store, Tarboro, NC, 1978-79; Farmer, 1979-; Floor Mgr, B&F Tobacco Warehouse, Rocky Mount, NC, 1983-; NC Farm Bur (Yg Farmers) St Adv Com Mem, 1982-83; cp/HS Beta Clb, 1973-76; HS Math Clb, Secy 1975-76; r/Bapt; W/W Among Am HS Students; g/To Attend USDA Tobacco Grading Sch; To Attend Ednl Farming Progs in Near Future.

ALLEN, BRONWYN JAYE oc/Student; b/Jun 25, 1966; h/Lynn at 25th Street, Big Spring, TX 79720; p/Mr and Mrs Robert J Allen, Big Spring, TX; ed/HS Grad, 1984; cp/Pres, Nat Jr Hon Soc, 1980; Nat Hon Soc, 1982-83; Student Coun, 1981, 1984; Class Treas, 1981, 1982; Girl's Choir Treas, 1981; French Clb Treas, 1981, 1982; Tri-Hi-Y Yth in Govt Treas and Publicity Chm, 1981, 1982, 1983; Basic Jr C of C, 1982-83, 1983-84; Hosp Jr Vol (Candy Striper), 1981, 1982; Baseball Home Run Honeys, 1982, 1983; r/1st Christian Ch; Ch Handbell Choir, 1978-83; Ch Chancel Choir, 1980, 1981; Christian Yth F'ship, 1981-83; Chi Rho (Jr High Ch Yth Grp), 1978-80; hon/Am Legion Awd, 1980; Soc of Dist'd Am HS Students, 1981, 1982, 1983; US Achmt Acad Awd in French, 1982; Quaternion 1st Place in French, 1983; Sum Sci Sem, USAF Acad, 1983; Jr Statesmen Foun Sum Sch, Wash, DC, 1983; Oddfellows UN Pilgrimage for Yth, 1983; Tri-Hi-Y Dist and St Convs, 1981, 1982, 1983; W/W Big Sprg HS; W/W Among Am HS Students.

ALLEN, ELIZABETH HOPE oc/Student; b/Nov 22, 1960; h/3905 Third Place, Northwest, Rochester, MN 55901; p/Paul and Beverly Allen, Rochester, MN; ed/Grad, John Marshall HS, 1979; BA, Carleton Col, 1983; pa/Pt-time, Sum Help Positions; cp/Sierra Clb, 1982-; AAU Swim Team, 1976-78; Student Coun Rep; Hosp Vol; r/Meth; hon/Nat Hon Soc, 1978-; Nat Merit Commend, 1979; Mortar Bd, 1982-; #1 in Class; Dean's List; Cross Country Team; W/W Among Am HS Students; Commun Ldrs of Am; g/To Attend Div Sch and Study Comparative Rels at the Grad Level; To Attain an MDiv and PhD.

ALLEN, FREDERICK LEWIS oc/Part-Owner of Business; b/Feb 25, 1957; h/PO Box 264, Polson, MT 59860; ba/Polson, MT; p/Warren G and Marjorie H Allen, Minot, ND; ed/Minot Sr HS, 1975; BCS 1978, BS 1980, Minot St Col; MA in Eng, Univ of ID, 1983; pa/Sales/Stock, Sharks Clothiers, 1975-76; Sales, Yg Am Inc, 1976-80; Eng Instr, Cambridge HS, 1980-81; Tchg Asst, Univ of ID, 1981-83; Pt-Owner, Recording Studio; cp/NHS; Gov's Coun on Yth in ND; hon/Mng Editor, Cartoonist, *Rock* (Student Pub); Student Assn Pres, HS; Pres's Hon Roll; Nat Dean's List; W/W Am Cols and Univs; g/PhD in Eng.

ALLEN, JEAN RENEE oc/Head Waitress; b/Sep 13, 1963; h/Route 654

Birchwood Apartments, Apartment 13-H, Cloverdale, VA 24077; ba/Daleville, VA; p/Mr and Mrs Calvin R Allen, Monroe, VA; ed/Adv'd Dipl, Amherst Co HS, 1981; Dipl, Wilma Boyd Career Sch, 1982; Att'd, Ctl VA Commun Col, 1981; pa/Waitress, Madison Hgts Pizza Hut; Hd Waitress, Daleville Pizza Hut; cp/March of Dimes Walkathon, 1978-79; Am Cancer Soc, 1980; Lynchburg Tng Sch and Hosp Vol; Amherst Co Jr High Softball, 1977; Pep, Spanish, Tri-Hi-Y Clbs, 1979; Pep Clb, Tri-Hi-Y (Secy), 1980; Pep, Tri-Hi-Y (Secy), Varsity Clbs, 1981; Band, Clarinet, 1976-81; Rifles, 1979-81; Co-Capt 1980, Capt 1981, Sabre; Drill Team, 1981; r/U Meth Yth F'ship, Secy; hon/Miss U VA Teenager Articles, 1979; Miss Botetourt Pageant Articles, 1981; Adv'd Dipl, 1981; Perfect Attendance, 9 Out of 12 Yrs of Sch; 4-H Hons, Blue Ribbons, 1974 (1), 1975 (3), 1976 (3), 1974 (Red, 2), 1975 (1), 1976 (Purple, 1); Miss U VA Teenager, 1980 (3rd Runner-Up); Miss Botetourt, 1981 (1st Runner-Up); g/To Attend Cosmotology Sch.

ALLEN, LISA CORBETT oc/Student; b/Feb 13, 1965; h/3309 Evans Street, Greenville, NC 27834; p/Mr and Mrs Kenneth Allen Sr, Greenville, NC; ed/Grad, D H Conley HS, 1983; Student, Math Ed, Campbell Univ; pa/Var Farm Jobs for Kenneth Allen & Son Farms, 1977-82; Cashier/Hostess, Jack's Steak House, 1981-82; cp/HS Chorus, 1979-80; Student Coun Assn, 1979-80; Lit Clb, 1979-80, 1981-82; Nat Hon Soc, 1981-83; Mu Alpha Theta, 1981-83; Future Bus Ldrs of Am, 1980-81, 1982-83; Bi-Chem-Phy, 1980-81; Spanish Clb, Pres 1982-83; Quill and Scroll, 1982-83; r/Free-Will Bapt; Ch Yth Grp, Secy and Treas 1981-82; hon/Pres S'ship to Campbell Univ; Recip, Prospective Tchr S'ship; Loan Fund Recip, Marshal, 1982-83; Hon Sr; g/To Become a Math Tchr.

ALLEN, ROBERT EARL oc/Student; b/Feb 9, 1960; h/Route 1, Box 350 C, Drummonds, TN 38023; p/Robert and Sue Allen, Drummonds, TN; ed/Millington HS, 1978; Assoc in Applied Sci (Drafting and Design Technol), NW MS Jr Col, 1982; Current Student, Univ of TN Martin; cp/MCHS, Rodeo Clb Pres 1976-77, 1977-78; NWJC, Tech Soc 1980-81, Pres 1981-82; AG Clb, 1980-81, 1981-82; Rodeo Team, 1980-81; Phi Theta Kappa, Pres 1981-82; UP Senate, 1981-82; UTM Rodeo Clb, 1982-83, 1983-84; IEEE, 1983-84; r/Bapt; hon/Pres Lists, NWJC, Fall 1981; Grad'd on Dean's List, 1982; Rodeo S'ship, NWJC, 1980-81, 1981-82; Rodeo S'ship, UTM, 1983; g/Deg, Elect Engr in Technol.

ALLEN, RODNEY HOLT oc/Student; b/Oct 22, 1952; h/207 Truman Drive, Fayetteville, NC; p/J T Allen Jr, Fayetteville, NC; ed/Pine Forest Sr HS, 1970; NC St Univ, 1970-72; Baylor Univ, 1976; Hlth Ser Command Phys Subst Course; cp/Sponsor, WUNC TV and Radio Repub Nat Com; AUS Spec Forces; Hon Grad, Phys Subst Course; Pershing Rifles; BSA; hon/Author, USASF Phys Subs Tests and Ref Volumes; Army Meritorious Ser; Army Commend; Eagle Awd, BSA; g/MD Deg w Ob-Gyn.

ALLEN, SUSAN KAY oc/Registered

Nurse; b/Jun 22, 1959; h/5018 11th Avenue, Northeast, Seattle, WA 98105; p/Mr and Mrs Richard G Allen, Redding, CA; ed/Los Altos HS, 1977; BSN, Pacific Luth Univ, 1981; pa/Med-Surg Staff Nurse, VA Mason Hosp, 1981-; Hosp Quality Assurance Com; WA St Nurses Assn; ANA; cp/Univ Singers; r/ Luth Ch Choir; hon/Grad, summa cum laude; Nat Dean's List; Am Biogs; g/ Adult Practitioner or Instr in Nsg.

ALLEN, WILLIAM RICHARD oc/ Student; b/Oct 18, 1957; h/130 South Estes Drive, Chapel Hill, NC 27514; p/ Mr and Mrs Junior R Allen, Abingdon, VA; ed/Chilhowie HS, 1976; BS, Emory and Henry Col, 1980; Univ of NC Chapel Hill; cp/Basketball; Track; Hi-Y; Beta Clb; NHS; Band; Monogram Clb; Sigma Mu; Am Phy Soc; hon/Grad, magna cum laude; Nat Merit Scholar; Col Phy Awd; Nat Dean's List; Intl Yth in Achmt; Soc of Dist'd Am HS Students; g/Doct in Physics.

ALLENSWORTH, DEANETTE FAYE oc/Student; b/Oct 20, 1962; h/PO Box 123, Plainville, IL 62365; p/John and Betty Stout, Plainville, IL; ed/Seymour HS, 1980; NE MO St Univ; pa/Univ Res Asst, NM St Univ, Sprg 1983; cp/Pep Clb Band; All-St Band; Band Pres; Student Coun; Elem Ed Clb; Intramural V'ball; Softball; Basketball; HS Lttrman's Clb; Girl's Ath Assn; Basketball Capt; Track; Softball; V'ball; Pep Clb Pres; Elem Ed Clb, Treas; Floor Pres, NM St Univ, 1983-84; Alpha Phi Sigma Hon Frat; Campus Vols; r/Akers Chapel Christian Ch; hon/HS Student of the Yr; HS Co-Valedictorian; Univ Dean's List; IL St Scholar; Pres's Hon S'ship, 1983-84; Intl Yth in Achmt; Yg Commun Ldrs of Am; g/Elem Tchr.

ALLISON, LESA HOKE oc/Student; b/Mar 7, 1961; h/1405 Stadium View Drive, Murray, KY 42071; m/Doug; p/ Charles Robert and Peggy Beale Hoke, Almo, KY; ed/Calloway Co HS, 1979; BA, Radio-TV, Murray St Univ, 1983; pa/Customer Ser Dir, K-Mart Corp, 1979-83; Student Wkr, Murray St Univ Extended Ed Ofc, 1980; cp/Newswriter for Murray St Univ TV 11 News; Calloway Spch Team, 1978 St Champs, VP 1979; Nat Forensic Leag, 1976-79; Students in Action for Ed, 1977-79; Alpha Delta Pi Social Sorority; Sigma Chi Little Sisters; Hostess for "Friday Magazine" Prog for Murray St Univ-TV 11 News; FCC 3rd Class Lic; hon/4th KY St Spch Team, 1978; Dean's List, 1979; Calloway Spch Team Hall of Fame, 1979; hon/W/W Among HS Students; g/To Become a Broadcast Journalist, and Then a Reporter-Anchor.

ALLISON, DONALD HALASZ oc/ World Bank Official; b/Mar 29, 1955; h/1623 33rd Street, Northwest, Washington, DC 20007; ba/Washington, DC; p/Harry and Agnes Allison; ed/BA, Ec, Univ of CA Berkeley, 1977; MBA, Harvard Bus Sch, 1979; Dipl in Devel Ec, Oxford Univ, 1980; pa/Assoc, Lewis Bouley & Assocs, 1979-81; Financial Analyst, US Synthetic Fuels Corp, 1981; World Bk Ofcl, 1981-; hon/Co-Author, *The Real World War*, 1982; Phi Beta Kappa, 1977; Baker Scholar, Harvard Bus Sch, 1979; Grad w Distn, Oxford Univ, 1980; Former Eagle Scout; Outstg Yg Men of Am Awd, 1983.

ALLISON, LYNDA M oc/Student; b/

Oct 27, 1961; h/1005 Buckingham Circle, Atlanta, GA 30327; p/Mrs M F Eve, Atlanta, GA; ed/The Lovett Sch; BA in Communs and Jour, Brenau Col, 1983; pa/Free-Lance Writer and Photog; Equestrian Sci Instr for Brenau Col, 1981-82; cp/Brenau Nom'g Com, 1979-80; Alpha Chi Omega Sorority, VP of the Pledge Class; Brenau Rec Assn; Exec Bd, Brenau F'ship Assn; Exec Cabinet, Annual and Newspaper Staff; Phoenix Soc Debutante, 1980-81; Brenau Panhellenic Assn, Secy; r/Anthem Cath; hon/Author, Articles in *Georgia Journal*, 1981, 1982; HGH Sr Hon Soc, 1983; W/W in Am Cols and Univs; W/ W Intl Frats and Sororities.

ALLOWAY, JAMES EUGENE oc/ Student; h/821 North Central, Parsons, KS 67357; p/William S Fouts, Parsons, KS; ed/Parsons HS, 1982; Student of Hist and German, Univ of KS; cp/Nat Hon Soc, 1981-82; Pres of PHS Chess Clb, 1981-82; Nat Forensic Leag, 1979-82; Student Coun Rep at Large, 1981-82; Jud Bd of Battenfeld S'ship Hall, 1983; r/Bapt; Bapt Yth F'ship, 1979-82; hon/Outstg Hist Student, PHS, 1982; Recip, Caroline B Spongler German S'ship, 1983; Bd of Regents Scholar, 1982; Dewey S'ship Recip, 1982-83; Anschutz S'ship Recip, 1982-83; KU S'ship Hall Mem, 1982-84; W/W Am HS Students; g/To Work in Archives.

ALSOBROOK, ALICE E oc/Student, Secretary; b/Apr 5, 1963; h/Box 132, Highway 55, Cusseta, AL 36852; ba/ Troy, AL; p/Mrs John N Alsobrook, Cusseta, AL; ed/HS Dipl, Lee Acad; AA, Troy St Univ; pa/Secy, E AL Med Ctr, 1980; Secy, Bill Fuller, Atty at Law, 1981, 1982; Bkkpg Clk, Farmers and Merchants Bk, 1982; Secy, Botts & Ray Inc, Civil Engrs and Surveyors, 1982-; cp/Alpha Gamma Delta Social Sorority; Sigma Chi Social Frat, Little Sister; Gamma Beta Phi Hon Soc; r/Prot; hon/ Alpha Gamma Delta, Pledge of Yr 1981; W/W; g/Secy/Paralegal.

ALSOBROOK, MARY ANNE oc/ Student in Graduate School; b/Apr 6, 1961; h/PO Box 26, Cusseta, AL 36852; ed/HS, Lee Acad; Bach Deg, Early Childhood Ed, Univ of AL, 1982; pa/ Proof Operator, Auburn Nat Bk, 1983-; Teller, Bkkpr, F&M Bk, 1979-82; Cnslr, Camp ASCCA for E AL Mtl Hlth, 1978; Secy, Country and Comml Properties; cp/Kappa Delta Pi, Ed Hon; Assn for Chd Intl; Beta Clb; Anchor Clb; Delta Zeta Sorority, Asst Treas; r/Bapt; Inducted, Kappa Delta Pi, 1983; Dean's List, Univ of AL; Miss Lee Acad, 1979; W/W Among Am HS Students; Commun Ldrs of Am; g/To Teach Kgn or First Grade.

ALSTON, WARREN DELANO oc/ Student; b/Apr 5, 1962; h/RR 1, Box 28-A, Awendaw, SC 29429; p/Mr and Mrs Timothy Alston Sr, Awendaw, SC; ed/Lincoln HS, 1981; Univ; cp/Basketball; Ftball; Gov Scholar; hon/Valedictorian; NHS; Best All-Around Student; Spkg Contest Awd; 1st Place, Math Fair; W/W Among Am HS Students; Soc of Dist'd Am HS Students; g/Law, Math, Sci, Phil, Engrg.

ALTENHOF, SHIRLEY ELAINE oc/ Student; b/Oct 30, 1960; h/Route 2, Box 687, New Braunfels, TX 78130; p/Mr and Mrs Howard A Altenhof, New Braunfels, TX; ed/Seguin HS, 1979; BS

cum laude in Agri Ec; TX A&M Univ, 1983; pa/Sum Intern, TX Bk for Cooperatives, 1981; Ofc Asst, Prodrs Cooperative Mktg Assn, 1980; cp/Bd of Trustees, Nat Alpha Zeta Foun, 1982-83; TAMU Placement Adv Coun and Student Orgs Bd, 1981-83; TAMU Col of Agri Student Coun, 1982-83; Pres 1982-83, Treas 1981-82, TAMU Agri Ec Clb; Secy, TAMU Nat Agri-Mktg Assn, 1980-81; Histn, Photog, TAMU Jr Hon, 1981-82; Phi Kappa Phi Scholastic Hon; Gamma Sigma Delta Agri Hon, 1983-; Mortar Bd Sr Hon, 1982; Lambda Sigma Sophomore Hon, 1980; Alpha Lambda Delta Freshmen Hon, 1980; r/Luth; hon/Nat Alpha Zeta Agri Hon Top S'ship Recip, 1982-83; TAMU Spirit Awd, 1983; TAMU Undergrad Fellow, 1982-83; TAMU Col of Agri Sr Merit Awd, 1983; TAMU Dept of Agri Ec Fac and Student Outstg Sr Awd, 1983; W/W Among Students in Univs and Cols; Outstg Yg Ams; g/Law Sch.

ALTICE, TAMMI LYNN oc/Student; b/Mar 23, 1963; h/Route 1, Box 475, Wirtz, VA 24184; ba/Radford, VA; p/ Wilford and Betty Altice, Wirtz, VA; ed/ HS, 1981; Student, Radford Univ; pa/ Post Ofc Clk, Radford Univ (Wk/Study S'ship for 2 Yrs); CRT Operator, Blue Cross and Blue Shield; cp/Nat Hon Soc; Spanish Clb; FBLA; Math Clb; Alpha Lambda Delta; Kappa Mu Epsilon; r/ Meth; hon/Alpha Lambda Delta, 1982; Kappa Mu Epsilon, 1983; Spanish Clb S'ship, 1981; Local S'ships, 1981, 1982, 1983; Nat Hon Soc; W/W; Intl Yth in Achmt; g/To Be a Computer Programmer or Analyst.

ALVAREZ, GIL oc/Manager for Sistemas de Riego; b/Nov 5, 1954; h/Calle Terrazas #4, Colonia Juarez 31857, Chihuahua, Mexico; ba/Chihuahua, Mexico; p/Mr and Mrs David Alvarez, Chihuahua, Mexico; ed/Academia Juarez AC, 1973; BS 1979, MS 1981, Sul Ross St Univ; pa/Br Mgr for Intl Commerce Corp; Mgr for Sistemas de Riego, JEFE; cp/Student Govt Ofc; Delta Tau Alpha, Pres; Alpha Chi; Rodeo Clb; Interviewed as Example Student in Documentary TV Film about Sul Ross Univ; r/Ch of Christ of LDS; hon/Intl Yth in Achmt; Nat Dean's List; W/W Am Cols and Univs; g/Ranch Operation.

ANCHELL, THEODORE JAMES JR oc/Electrical Engineer; b/Oct 5, 1961; h/ 8485 San Rafael, Charlack, MO 63114; ba/St Louis, MO; ed/Luth HS W; Valparaiso Univ; Enrolled in Wash Univ Grad Engrg Prog (Wkg toward MSEE Deg); pa/Engr, McDonnell Douglas Aircraft Co, 1983-; IEEE; cp/Phi Sigma Epsilon; Choral Soc; Alpha Lambda Delta; Overseas Study Prog; hon/Phi Beta Kappa Awd; Dean's List; Valparaiso Univ Sr Hons; Valparaiso Univ High Hons; g/Elect Engrg Deg.

ANDERBERG, MICHELLE RENEE oc/Student; b/Feb 12, 1961; h/7621 Route 20 West, Galena, IL 61036; p/Mr and Mrs Richard Anderberg, Galena, IL; ed/Galena HS, 1979; Coe Col; cp/Pres, GSA Troop; Q&S; Delta Delta Delta; Track; Band; hon/W/W Among Am HS Students; g/RN; BSN; Wk in Neonatal ICU.

ANDERSON, DALYN DEE oc/Graduate Student; b/Mar 4, 1960; h/3804 Booth #11, Kansas City, KS 66103; p/ Mr and Mrs David B Anderson, Drexel,

MO; ed/Shawnee Mission NW HS, 1978; Bach Deg, KS St Univ, 1982; Grad Student, Spch Pathol, KS Univ; cp/AKL Little Sister; Spch Pathol Clb; Boyd Hall Bible Study, Publicity Ofcr; Univ Prog Coun; 4-H Camp Cnslr, Adv Bd Mem, Oil Painting Ldr; Designed, Painted Nursery Mural for Ch; AFS Host; Student Govt Elections Helper; Kappa Alpha Theta, Rush Advr 1983; Dancer, *Hello Dolly*, Theatre in the Pk; hon/1978 Miss Bo Peep; 1978 Miss 4-H; Phi Kappa Phi; Nat 4-H Sheep Winner S'ship; Golden Key Hon; Kappa Alpha Theta Grad S'ship Winner, 1982; Selected for UAF, Grad Stipend; g/Spch Pathol Deg.

ANDERSON, GRAHAM THOMAS oc/Flight Test Analysis Engineer; b/Oct 22, 1961; h/5503 Mesagrove Avenue, Whittier, CA 90601; ba/PO Box 2507, Pomona, CA 91766; ed/AS, Don Bosco Tech Inst, 1980; BS, Engrg Technol, CA St Polytechnic Univ, 1982; pa/Flight Test Anal Engr, Gen Dynamics, Pomona Div, 1982-; cp/1st Trombonist in Col Band; Pks and Rec; Hosp; Yth Grp; hon/Tau Alpha Pi, 1982.

ANDERSON, JUDY PAGE oc/Student; b/Jan 15, 1962; h/632 Wilson Street, Roanoke Rapids, NC 27870; p/Rev and Mrs Austin Anderson, Roanoke Rapids, NC; ed/Roanoke Rapids HS, 1980; BA, Psych, Meredith Col, 1984; pa/Psych Prof's Asst, Meredith Col, 1982; Reservation and Sales Agt, World-Wide Sheraton Reservations, 1982; NC Dept of Adm Intern, NC St Govt, 1983; cp/HS: Drum Majorette 1980, Keywanettes (Treas 1980), French Hon Soc; Col: Meredith Christian Assn 1980-81, Psych Clb 1980-83, VP of Psych Clb, Co-Chair of Carolinas Psych Conf 1983; Am Psychol Assn, 1983; r/Christian; hon/Pubs, "Teacher's Reading Patterns to Children 2 & 4 Yrs" 1983, "Effects of Stimulus Familiarity on Semantic Memory" 1982; Psi Chi Induction, 1983; Kappa Nu Sigma Induction, 1983; g/To Attend Grad Sch; To Wk w Inmates in Correctional Instns.

ANDERSON, KAREN RENEE oc/Student; b/Apr 14, 1963; h/Box 27, Jackson, MN 56143; p/Harold and Helen Anderson, Jackson, MN; ed/Jackson HS, 1983; Student, Mankato St Univ; cp/Co 4-H Fdn Treas; German Clb; Sch Newspaper, Annual Staff; Chorus Declamation; Alpha Chi Omega Asst Rush Chm and Histn; Col Flag Corps, 1982, 1983; Little Sister to Alpha Tau Omega, 1982; hon/Lions Clb "Extra Curric Activs Student of the Yr"; MN 4-H Key Clb Awd; Intl Yth in Achmt; W/W Among HS Students; g/To Complete Course Wk in Scandinavian Studies, and Find Suitable Career in It.

ANDERSON, KATHY LYNNETTE oc/Student; b/Mar 30, 1967; h/Route 2, Box 300-A, Fuquay-Varina, NC 27526; p/Leon and Teresa Anderson, Fuquay-Varina, NC; ed/Student, HS; cp/Basketball; Softball; Tennis; French Clb; Pep Clb; FBLA; Class Ofcr; Beta Clb; Cheerldr; Monogram Clb; Student Coun Ofcr; hon/Intl Fgn Lang Awd, 1982; Hist Awd, 1982; Geometry Awd, 1982; Typing I Awd, 1983; AG Eng II Awd, 1983; Algebra II Awd, 1983; Perfect Attendance Awd, 1980-83; Nat Ldrship and Ser Awd, 1983; US Achmt Acad; Commun Ldrs of Am; g/RN.

ANDERSON, KRISTEN DAWN oc/

Student; h/Route 10, Box 372, Morganton, NC; p/Mr and Mrs Charles W Anderson, Morganton, NC; ed/Freedom HS, 1981; Appalachian St Univ; cp/Anchor Clb Pres; NHS; Mar Band; ASU Mar Band; Gamma Beta Phi, 1982, 1983; Compass Clb, Pres (Charter Clb) 1983; r/U Meth Ch F'ship Secy; hon/Valedictorian, Freedom HS, 1981; Yth Apprec Wk Awd, Breakfast Optimists; Hon'd as One of Top 10 Students in Jr Class at ASU, 1983; g/To Become a Tchr of Spec Students; To Share My Humanity w Others to Make the World Better for Them.

ANDERSON, LAURA KAY oc/Teacher; b/May 23, 1961; h/RR #1, Box 21, Gladstone, IL 61437; ba/Wellsville, MO; p/Mr and Mrs L A Anderson, Gladstone, IL; ed/Grad, Union HS, 1979; BS, Elem Ed, Culver-Stockton Col, 1983; pa/3rd Grade Tchr, Wellsville-Middletown Schs, 1983-; cp/Student SMSTA; AWS, Treas and Pres; Student Intramural Dir, 2 Yrs; Ball Girl for Men's Basketball Team; Alpha Chi, Hon Scholastic Frat, VP; McDonald Hall Secy, 2 Yrs; Acad Coun Mem; Cross Country Team; hon/Col Homecoming Queen, 1982; 2nd in Dist in Cross-Country, 1982; I Dare You, 1979; Soc of Am Dist'd HS Students, 1979; Most Served Points in Volleyball, 1977; Coaches Attitude Awd, 1978; Valedictorian, 1979; Grad, magna cum laude, 1983; Outstg Female of Col Sr Class, 1983; Wood Citizenship Awd, 1983; W/W Am Cols and Univs; W/W Among HS Students; g/Grad Wk.

ANDERSON, LEROY JR oc/National Direct Student Loan Operations Manager, Business Owner; b/Apr 14, 1960; h/2608 La Salle Street, Charlotte, NC 28216; ba/Winston Salem, NC; p/Mr and Mrs Leroy Anderson Sr, Charlotte, NC; ed/Dipl, W Charlotte Sr HS, 1978; BA in Bus Adm, Morehouse Col, 1982; pa/Nat Direct Student Loan Operations Mgr, Wachovia Sers Inc, 1983-; Bus Owner, Synergy Intl, 1980-; cp/BSA, Troop 107, Scoutmaster (Univ Pk Bapt Ch); Morehouse Col Nat Alumni Assn; Metrolina Morehouse Alumni Clb; NC Yg Dems; r/Bapt; hon/Morehouse Col, Hon Roll 1979-82, Dean's List 1979-82, Dept of Ec and Bus Adm Hons 1982, Morehouse Aux Prize 1982; W/W Among Students in Am Univs and Cols; Outstg Yg Men of Am; Yg Commun Ldrs of Am; Intl Yth in Achmt; Nat Dean's List; g/Cert'd Financial Planner; MBA Deg (Mgmt).

ANDERSON, LORI CHOYCE oc/Student; b/Oct 25, 1963; h/Route 2, Box 67, Indian Trail, NC 28079; p/George Thomas and Margaret Jean Wyatt Anderson; ed/Sun Val HS; BA in Human Sers w Double Emphasis in French and Sociol, Wingate Col; Wkg on Master's Deg in Clin Cnslg, The Citadel; cp/Rainbow Girls Past Worthy Adv, Grand Cross of Color Bearer; Past Grand Page; Spec Recog for Wk; Jr Civitans, Civitan of the Yr 1979, Miss Civitan for Sun Val, 3rd Runner-Up at Miss NC Jr Civinette; Spec Olympics; Gov Sch; Spec Ldrship Conf; U Co Quiz Bowl Team; High Q Bowl Team; Homecoming Ct; Yrbook Staff; Pep Clb; French Clb; Math Clb; Sci Clb; Passed Cecchetti Grade V; TV Appearances; Charlotte Ballet Theatre; r/Prot; hon/Marshal, Wingate's 1983 Graduation;

NHS; French NHS; Nat Ed Devel Tests Awd; Cert of Excell in Adv'd Placement Calculus and Eng; Num S'ships for Var Sources; Lttrs of Congratulations from U Co Supt B Paul Hammack and Congressman Bill Hefner; Outstg Sr in Acad; Valedictorian; Personalities of S; Commun Ldrs of Am; Intl Yth in Achmt; g/To Incorporate the Uses of Self-Expression and Humor w Cnslg.

ANDERSON, PAMELA YVONNE oc/Student; b/Aug 3, 1962; h/230 Keowee Trail, Seneca, SC 29678; ba/Greenville, SC; p/Mr and Mrs James M Anderson, Seneca, SC; ed/Grad, Seneca HS, 1980; Student, Furman Univ; cp/Beta Chi Biol Clb, 1981-83; Alpha Epsilon Delta, 1982-83; All Committed Together, 1981-83; Girl's Soc, Rush Chm 1983; Inter Clb Coun, 1981-83, VP 1982-83; Montague Living Lng Ctr, 1981-83; Ser Corp CESC, 1981-83; Jr Acad of Sci, 1977-80, Pres 1979-80; Student Coun, 1978-80; Beta Clb, 1976-80; Debating Clb, 1976-80; r/Bapt; hon/Dean's List, Furman Univ, 1980-83; Salutatorian, HS, 1980; Rotary Scholar, 1976, 1977, 1979, 1980; Sci Awd, 1980; Math Awd, 1980; Furman Scholar, 1979; Gov's Scholar, 1979; PC Jr Fellow, 1979; Beta Chord, 1980; g/BS in Biol; BS in Pharm; PharmD.

ANDERSON, PATRICK DEAN oc/Student; b/Nov 25, 1960; h/1278 Briarwood Drive, San Luis Obispo, CA 93401; p/Regina Anderson, San Luis Obispo, CA; ed/San Luis Obispo Sr HS; BS, Food Sci, CA Polytechnic St Univ; pa/Lab Tech, Sum Wk; cp/Food Sci Clb, Polyroyal Chm, Clb Photg, 1980-; Order of the Arrow, 1976-; r/Cath; hon/Boys' St, Hon Scout; W/W Among HS Students; Commun Ldrs of Am; g/MBA.

ANDERSON, PAUL LEON oc/Student; b/Mar 17, 1962; h/2608 La Salle Street, Charlotte, NC 28216; p/Leroy Sr and Veola C Anderson; ed/Dipl, W Charlotte Sr High, 1980; BBA, NC Ctl Univ; DTh, Theol Sem; Received Lic, The Gospel Min, 1983; cp/Bus Mgr, Sch Newspaper, 1983-84; Reporter/Writer/Columnist, Sch Newspaper; Pres, Jr Ushers; Bus Dr; MVP Basketball; Var Tennis, Soccer; Asst Coach, Var Basketball; r/Christian; hon/Jr HS Citizenship Hon; Outstg Christian Ser Awd; g/MBS.

ANDERSON, ROBERT JOSEPH oc/Student; b/Aug 8, 1960; h/1525 Robert Hardeman Road, Winterville, GA 30683; p/Dr and Mrs James L Anderson, Winterville, GA; Mrs G L Anderson, Lawrence, KS; ed/Grad, Cedar Shoals HS, 1979; Grad, Univ of GA, 1983; cp/Pianist, GA Jazzband II; Campus/Commun Relats Chm, Phi Gamma Delta; Phi Eta Sigma, Freshman Hon; Kappa Delta Big Brother; Univ of GA Karate Clb; Beta Clb; Nat Hon Soc; Initiations Chm, Jr Classical Leag; Lttr, Swimming; Cedar Shoals Jazzband; hon/Biftad, Highest Hon for Freshman or Sophomore Male, Univ of GA; Phi Eta Sigma; Nat Hon Soc; Dean's List; 3rd in Latin Derivation, St Competition; Hons Prog Participant, Univ of GA; Outstg Commun Ldrs; Personalities of S; g/BBA and MBA in Mgmt Info Sys.

ANDERSON, TRACY KAY oc/Student; b/Aug 9, 1960; h/15 Capri Drive, Mankato, MN 56001; ba/Same; p/John R and Judith M Anderson, Abaco,

Bahamas; ed/Student, Bus Adm, Mankato St Univ; Mankato W HS; cp/Alpha Chi Omega, Pres 1982-83, 1983-84; Intl Bus Org, 1983-84; g/To Obtain an Entry Level Position in Credit Mgmt/Intl Bus.

ANDERSON, VERTUS DUANE oc/Registered Pharmacist; b/Jan 30, 1958; h/300 Pirie Drive, #3, Hiawatha, IA 52233; ba/Cedar Rapids, IA; m/Carol Lynn; c/Joshua Michael, Sara Ashley; p/Ray and Dorothy Anderson, Yanktun, SD; ed/Yankton Sr HS, 1976; BS in Pharm, SD St Univ, 1982; pa/Chief Pharm/Mgr, Revco DS Inc Store #3015; Pharm Intern, Hosp; Reg'd and Lic'd in KS and IA; cp/Am Hon Soc; Kappa Psi Regent, Treas; VP, Phi Lambda Upsilon; Rho Chi Hist; hon/S'ship Hon, Kappa Psi; Nat Dean's List; Recip, 1982 Bristol Awd; g/Greater Involvement in Politics, Especially of Repub Party.

ANDREWS, CHRISTOPHER CHARLES oc/Student, Part-time Library Page; b/Jan 6, 1966; h/Route 2, Box 118, Seneca, SC 29678; ba/Seneca, SC; p/Mr and Mrs Charles Andrews, Seneca, SC; ed/Grad, Seneca Sr HS, 1984; pa/Lib Page, Seneca Br Lib, 1982-; cp/YMCA Basketball Leag, 1975-81; Oconee Jr Bowling Leag, 1976-83; Beta Clb, 1979-83; Rotary Interact Clb, 1982-83; Am Field Ser Clb, 1980-83; Student Coun Eighth Grade Pres, 1979-80; Newspaper Staff, *Patriot Press*, 1979-80; Copy Editor, Yrbook Staff, *Seneconian*, 1982-83; r/Bapt; hon/Rotary Intl Scholar, 1979, 1980, 1981, 1982; Furman Univ Scholar, 1983; Presb Col Jr Fellow, 1983; Boys St Participant, Palmetto, 1983; Math Awd, 1977, 1978, 1979, 1980; Var Other Acad Awds; W/W Among Am HS Students; g/BS in Computer/Info Sys, and MS in Hotel or Bus Adm, Leading to Career in Hospitality Indust as Sys Analyst.

ANDREWS, TRACEY LYNN oc/Student; b/Dec 21, 1964; h/5 Hiawatha, Jackson, TN 38305; p/Mr and Mrs G E McCullar, Jackson, TN; ed/Old Hickory Acad, 1983; Student, Jackson St Commun Col; cp/Chorus; Cheerldr; Yg Life; r/Meth; hon/Best All Around, 1983; Art and Spanish Hons, 1979-81; Hon Roll, 1978-83; F E Wright Meml Foun S'ship, 1983-84; g/Area of Communs and/or Photo.

ANESHANSEL, ROBERT THOMAS oc/Student; b/Jul 18, 1963; h/9145 Pontage Street, Massillon, OH 44646; p/Mr and Mrs Charles Aneshansel, Massillon, OH; ed/Grad, Jackson HS, 1981; Student, OH Univ; pa/Lawn Care Maintenance, St Jacobs Luth Ch, 1979-83; Lang Lab Supvr, OH Univ, 1981-83; cp/Stark Co Beekeepers Assn, 1974-83; Nat Jr Bowling Cong, 1973-78; Trials Inc, 1978-81; r/Luth; hon/OH Univ Ultimate Frisbee Team Sectional Champs, 1983; g/Career in Hosp Adm.

ANGOWSKI, JOAN DOLORES oc/Student; b/Jul 10, 1960; h/66 Mohr Avenue, Bloomfield, NJ 07003; p/Theodore and Anne Angowski, Bloomfield, NJ; ed/St Mary HS; BS in Elem Ed, Seton Hall Univ; Cert in Spec Ed and Early Childhood Ed; Current Student, Montclair St Col; pa/Lng Ctr Tchr, Glen Ridge Mid Sch, Glen Ridge, NJ; NJ Ed Assn; Co-Fdr, Secy, Elizabeth Ann Seton Ed Assn; Kappa Delta Pi; cp/Asst Editor, SHU Newsletter; Galleon Yrbook Writer; hon/Valedictorian; Dean's List; *The Dean's List*; Grad, summa

cum laude, Seton Hall Univ, 1982; g/Master's Deg in Lng Disabilities, Montclair St Col.

ANSCHUTZ, LUCY ANN oc/Student, Para-Professional for Crisis-Intervention; b/Apr 10, 1961; h/PO Box 190, Russell, KS; p/Willis D Anschutz, Dorrance, KS; Mary Anna Anschutz, Russell, KS; ed/Dorrance HS, 1979; BA, Ft Hays St Univ, 1983; Accepted for Master's Prog in Clin Psych, Ft Hays St Univ, 1983; pa/Undergrad Res Asst to Dr Cameron Camp for Gerontology Study, Ft Hays St Univ, 1982-83; cp/SGA Senator, 1982-83; French Clb; Forensic Team; Bd of Dirs, Hays Commun Helpline; cp/Dean's Hon Roll; Psi Chi Nat Psych Hon Soc; Alpha Lambda Delta Nat Hon Soc; Nat Residence Hall Hon; Resident Hall Assn, Treas, Exec Coun; Am Yth Foun; Russell Co Asst 4-H Dog Ldr; hon/Intl Ambassador to Europe; Mortar Bd Treas; Phi Kappa Phi Hon Soc; Grad, magna cum laude, Ft Hays St Univ, 1983; Ft Hays St Univ Wom's Fac S'ship; Mortar Bd S'ship; Commun Ldrs of Am; W/W Am Cols and Univs; g/Crisis-Intervention or Gerontology.

ANSELME, BRADLEY JAY oc/Jeweler; b/Apr 20, 1959; h/202 South Taylor, Pryor, OK 74361; ba/Pryor, OK; m/Faye; p/Mr and Mrs Lloyd Anselme, Pryor, OK; ed/Pryor HS, 1977; AA, NEn OK A&M Jr Col, 1979; BS, OK St Univ, 1981; r/Luth; hon/4th Place, Nat Col Powerlifting Meet, 1980; 2 Time St Col Powerlifting Champion and Outstg Lifter, 1978, 1979; Eagle Scout, 1976.

ANSPACH, KEITH MARLIN oc/Graduate Student; b/Nov 22, 1959; h/402 Heights Avenue, Tullahoma, TN 37388; p/Mr and Mrs E E Anspach, Tullahoma, TN; ed/Tullahoma HS, 1977; AS, Math, MSCC, 1980; BS, Computer Sci, MTSU, 1982; cp/Assn of Computing Machinery; Nat Rehab Assn; hon/Pres's Awd, MSCC, 1980; Top 10 Grad'g Sophomores, MSCC, 1980; Math Awd, MSCC, 1980; Honeywell Math and Computer Sci Awd, MTSU, 1982; B H Goethert Scholar, Univ of TN Space Inst, 1982-84; g/MS in Computer Sci, UTSI.

ANTHONY, MICHAEL LEE oc/Senior Analyst; b/Dec 9, 1958; h/11 Cocodrie Court, Kenner, LA 70062; ba/New Orleans, LA; ed/Oscar H Wingfield HS, 1976; AA, Hinds Jr Col, 1978; BS, Indust Engrg, MS St Univ, 1980; pa/Co-op Engr, Gen Elect, Jackson Glass Plant, 1978-80; Sr Analyst, Arthur Andersen & Co, NO Ofc, 1980-83; Am Inst of Indust Engrs; Am Prodn and Inventory Control Soc, Publicity Chm 1982; cp/Col: Phi Theta Kappa (VP), Phi Kappa Phi, Kappa Mu Epsilon (Pres), Alpha Pi Mu, Tau Beta Pi, Omicron Delta Kappa, Blue Key, Elderly Statesman, Kappa Alpha, MSU Fashion Bd, 2-Yr Basketball Letterman in Jr Col; HS: 3-Yr Basketball Letterman, Class Pres 1975, Student Coun 1974-76, Nat Hon Soc, Mu Alpha Theta, Jr Classical Leag; hon/HS: Bkkpg Awd 1976, Salutatorian, Class of 1976; W/W Among Am Jr Cols; Outstg Yg Men of Am; g/To Attend Grad Sch; To Attain a Position That is Challenging.

ANTISDEL, WENDY PATRICE oc/Student; b/Apr 2, 1962; h/721 Craig Avenue, La Canada, CA 91011; p/Albert L and Frances P Antisdel, La Canada,

CA; ed/La Canada HS, 1980; Att'g, Occidental Col; cp/SOAR Prog, Col; Student Affil, Am Chem Soc; Tennis Team; hon/S'ships, La Canada Rotary Clb, La Canada Thursday Clb, Commun S'ship Foun; Awd for Perfect GPA, HS; Math Awd, Sci Awd, French Awd, Eng Awd, 1980; Flight #3 Doubles Champion, 1983 NCAA Div III Nationals; SCIAC All-Conf Selection, 1983; W/W Am HS Students; Intl Yth in Achmt; g/A Career in Engrg or Computer Sci.

ANTONIO, STEVEN-ANTHONY oc/Student; b/Mar 15, 1962; h/29 High Point Circle, Franklin, NJ 07416; p/Mr and Mrs Steve Antonio, Franklin, NJ; ed/Franklin HS, 1980; Co Col of Morris; cp/HS Football Team Quarterback; Capt, Varsity Basketball Team; Girls Softball Umpire for Franklin City; hon/Hon Roll; Am Legion Boys' St Del; Intl Yth in Achmt; W/W Among Am HS Students; g/Bus Mgmt.

ARCENTALES, CARMEN ELIZABETH oc/Student; b/Jun 5, 1964; h/2111 Third Avenue, #1, New York, NY 10029; p/Maria Isabel Ortiz, New York, NY; ed/Charles Evans Hughes HS, 1982; Att'g, Hofstra Univ; pa/Cashier, Food Emporium, 1980; Student Peer Cnslr, EPIC, NY Inst of Technol, 1980-81; Adm Asst, Ctr for Housing Ptnrships, 1981-82; cp/Treas of Sr Class, 1982; Secy of Hon Soc, 1982; Hd, Trip Com for Srs, 1981-82; hon/U Fdn of Tchrs S'ships, 1982; Max Horowitz Meml Awd, 1982; Margaret MacAleenan Character Awd, 1982; Nat Hon Soc, 1980, 1981, 1982; W/W Among Am HS Students; g/BA in Jour/Broadcasting.

ARCHER, AMBER LYNN oc/Student; b/May 13, 1962; h/2911 Patterson Avenue, Key West, FL 33040; p/Mr and Mrs Glynn Archer Jr, Key West, FL; ed/Key W HS, 1980; AA, FL Keys Commun Col, 1982; BA, FL Atl Univ, 1983; cp/FL Student Ldrship Assn for Tchr Edrs; HS Cheerldr; Treas, Beta Clb; Interact, Keyettes; KWHS Yrbook Staff Editor; Order of Rainbow for Girls, Worthy Advr; hon/Sr Class Ser Awd; Outstg Sr; Anchor Lodge Best All Around Sr; g/Elem Edr.

ARCHER, CATHERINE SUSAN oc/Student; b/May 23, 1962; h/115 West Mariposa, San Antonio, TX 78212; p/William Archer, San Antonio, TX; Lorraine Archer, San Antonio, TX; ed/Incarnate Word HS, 1980; BA, Univ of TX Austin, 1984; pa/Ofc Cashier, Handy Andy, 1978-81; File Clk, Univ of TX Austin, 1981-83; Camp Cnslr, TECABOCA, 1983; Tour Guide, TX Capitol, 1983; cp/Legion of Mary, Secy, Treas, VP, 1974-81; Student Coun Rep, 2 Yrs; Sophomore Class Secy; Yg Dems Secy; Booster Clb; Tchrs and Students Interested in Polit Sci; Communication Dir, Campus Min; Cath Student Assn, Secy; Student Govt Com-Person; Vol Campaign Wkr; hon/Voice of Dem Spch Contest, 3rd Place, 1980; NHS, 3 Yrs; Hon Roll, 4 Yrs; High Hon Roll; Ranked 7th in Grad'g Class; Dean's List, 1982; W/W Among Am HS Students; Intl Yth in Achmt; g/To Teach HS; To Attend Grad Sch; To Join Jesuit Vol Corps.

ARCHER, JACKIE DEE oc/Student; b/Apr 29, 1964; h/105 Vine Street, Princeton, WV 24740; p/Jackie L and Carolyn H Archer, Princeton, WV; ed/Princeton HS, 1982; cp/FBLA; r/First Ch of God; hon/Hon Roll; Consistent A's in Typing I; Most Outstg Typist in Typing II; Perfect Attendence Awd; Student Coun Rep; Accepted for Accelerated Prog at Blfd St Col; A T Massey S'ship, 1982; Most Outstg Bus Student, 1982; Shorthand II Awd, 1982; g/Legal Secy.

ARCHER, KEVIN GERARD oc/Student; b/Dec 17, 1961; h/535 Wolcott Avenue, Beacon, NY; p/Mr and Mrs Edward D Archer, Beacon, NY; ed/Beacon HS, 1979; Cath Univ; pa/Cath Univ Engrg Res Lab Asst, 1982-; cp/Resident Advr; Intramural Ath; Eagle Scout; AIA; Civil Engrg Soc; ASCE; Nat Eagle Scout Assn; Football, Track Varsity Capt; r/Rom Cath; hon/Spec Scout Ser Corps to 141st Eucharistic Cong; Lion's Clb Citizenship Awd, 1979; Soc of Dist'd Am HS Students, 1978-79; Nat Hon Soc; Cardinal Spelman Yth Awd, 1978; Scholar-Ath, 1979; W/W Among Am HS Students; g/Arch and Civil Engrg, Bldg Constrn Technol.

ARCHER, MAUREEN E oc/Student; b/Sep 16, 1963; h/535 Wolcott Avenue, Beacon, NY 12508; p/Mr and Mrs Edward D Archer, Beacon, NY; ed/Beacon HS, 1981; Att'g, Marywood Col, 1981-; pa/Pt-time Clk, Drug Store, 1978-81; Sum Toll-Collector, NY St Bridge Auth, 1982-83; cp/Girl Scouts, First Class, 1971-81; Hon Soc, 1980, 1981, VP 1981; Varsity Track and Field, 1979-80; Varsity Basketball, 1979-81; Varsity Volleyball, 1979-81, Co-Capt 1981; Varsity Tennis, 1981; Col: Varsity Volleyball 1982, Varsity Basketball 1981, 1982, Orientation Com 1983, Phi Beta Lambda 1981, 1982; r/Rom Cath; hon/MVP, Volleyball, 1980, 1981; Most Improved Player, Basketball, 1980-81; Col Co-MVP, Basketball, 1982; g/BS in Bus and Acctg.

ARIAS, ESTELLA oc/Student, Teller; b/Aug 9, 1965; h/618 West Gibbs, St Johns, MI 48879; p/Victoria Arias, Gibbs, MI; ed/Dipl, St Johns HS, 1983; Student, Prensg Prog, Lansing Commun Col, 1983-; pa/Hosp Vol, CMH, 1980-82; McDonald's Employee, 1982-83; Teller, Clinton Bk & Trust, 1983-; cp/FCA, 1982-83, VP; Student Coun Rep, 1979-81; Class Ofcr, 1979-83, VP 1981-82, Pres 1982-83; Red Cross Blood Drive, 1980-83; Nat Hon Soc, 1982-83; VFW Spch; Rock-A-Thon Chair; Spec Olympics; Proj Outreach, Ldr Forum; Career Fair; r/Cath; hon/Outstg Coun Mem, 1980-81, 1982-83; Homecoming Queen, 1982-83; Social Ser Hon Cert, 1980-81; DAR Citizenship of Yr, 1982-83; Girls St, 1982; Wilson S'ship Winner, 1983; MI St Comp Scholar, 1983; W/W Among Yg Ams; g/Nsg, Occupl Therapy, Spec Ed.

ARIAZ, CHERYL LYNN oc/Student; b/Aug 15, 1960; h/227 Wessington Place, Hendersonville, TN; p/Louie and Doris Ariaz, Hendersonville, TN; ed/Grad, White House HS, 1978; Vol St Commun Col, 1980-81; Grad, Jo Susan Modeling Sch, 1982; Att'g, Belmont Col; pa/Former Legal Secy; cp/Pres, Alpha Omega F'ship; Secy, Alpha Chi, 1984-85; hon/Dean's List; Ranked 5th, HS Grad'g Class; Hon Roll, HS, 4 Yrs; Intl Yth in Achmt; W/W Among Am HS Students; Yg Personalities of S; g/Communication Arts w Specialization in Theatre and Drama; To Become Fashion Conslt or Makeup Artist.

ARIAZ, TANYA LEAH oc/Student; b/May 9, 1962; h/227 Wessington Place, Hendersonville, TN 37075; ba/Washville, TN; p/Mr and Mrs Louie Ariaz, Hendersonville, TN; ed/White House HS, 1980; Vol St Commun Col; Jo Susan Modeling Sch; cp/Alpha Omega; Christian Wom Clb; Ch Choir; Soloist in Ch; Singer, Legal Secys Benefit; hon/Vocal S'ship Student, Belmont Col, 1982-; Outstg Minority Talent Roster; Yg Personalities of S; W/W Am Jr Cols; g/Gospel Music; Piano and Voice Instr.

ARMBRISTER, DENISE LaVON oc/Student; b/Dec 14, 1963; h/RR 1, Zurich, KS 67676; p/Arthur and Jacqueline Armbrister, Zurich, KS; ed/HS Dipl, 1982; cp/Home Ec Clb; Trojans Recruiting Admissions Clb; Phi Theta Kappa; Pep Clb; FHA; P Clb; Forensics; Powder Puff Football; Band; Tennis; Track; March of Dimes Collector; Coop Yth Ldrship Conf; r/St Johns Luth Ch; Luth Leag Pres, Secy; hon/Pres's Hon Roll, Fall 1982, Sprg 1983; NHS; Rural Elect Yth Tour; KS Hon Student; Hon Roll; Commun Ldrs of Am; Nat Dean's List; g/Acctg.

ARMBRUSTER, TRACEY LEE oc/Student; b/Nov 2, 1964; h/53 Hallsdale Drive, Louisville, KY 40220; p/Robert C and Dolores Armbruster, Louisville, KY; ed/Hon Grad, Jeffersontown HS, 1982; Att'g, Centre Col; cp/Kappa Alpha Theta, Active; Kappa Alpha Theta, Chaplain 1982-84; Key Clb, Treas and Pres; Sr Class Secy; Sr Exec Bd; FHA, Chapt Reporter, Pres; Thespian Soc; Nsg Home Vol; Bagpipes in Commun Band; March of Dimes Yth Com; Beta Clb; German Clb; Pep Clb; Helper of the Blind through Example; r/Epis; hon/Miss U Teenager Pageant, 1982: 1st Place Essay, Citizenship Awd, Miss Congeniality, 2nd Runner-Up Overall; Ideal Pledge, Kappa Alpha Theta; Campus Guide, Centre Col; Intl Key Clb Steven Sapaugh Awd, 1982; WLRS Radio Sta Joseph B Robinson Awd, 1982; Mtl Hlth Assn Louisville Chapt Awd, 1982; Trustee Scholar, Centre Col, 1982; Jeffersontown Rotary Clb Awd, 1982; Andy Hutson Key Clb Awd Nom, 1982; Bell Awd, 1983-84; Best All-Round Key Clubber; W/W Among Am HS Students; Outstg Commun Ldrs of Am; g/To Obtain a Degree in Clin Psych, Specializing in Helping Parents of Handicapped Chd.

ARMSTRONG, CURTIS DUANE oc/Student; b/Jan 7, 1966; h/Route 2, Box 113, Vaiden, MS 39176; p/Mr and Mrs Curtis Armstrong, Vaiden, MS; ed/Grad, Ethel HS, 1984; cp/Class Pres, 3 Yrs; Pres, VICA, 2 Yrs; Beta Clb; Am Legion Boys' St Rep; hon/Nat Merit Semi-Finalist; Am Legion Boys' St Sch Rep, 1983; Sci Fair Winner, 1982, 1983; Awds in All Acad Areas, 1981-; Woodmen of the World Am Hist Awd, 1983; Nat Hon Roll, 1983; W/W Among Am HS Students; g/To Maj in Computer Engrg; To Obtain a Doct in His Chosen Field; To Concentrate on Res and Gain Entry into the Space Prog.

ARMSTRONG, PHILIP CHRISTIAN oc/Student; b/Nov 25, 1961; h/127 Monte Rey Drive, Los Alamos, NM 87544; p/Philip E and Roberta D Armstrong, Los Alamos, NM; ed/Los Alamos HS, 1980; NM St Univ; cp/VP for Adm, Residence Hall Assn, Sprg 1982; IEEE, Pres-Alumni Ave; Student Senate; Senator, Residence Halls Assn; hon/Engrg Dean's List; Crimson Scholar; Soc of Dist'd Am HS Students; g/Elect Engr in Stereo Components.

ARNOLD, AMY oc/Student; b/Dec 20, 1962; h/61010 Candle Path, Plano, TX 75023; ba/Houston, TX; p/Jerry Clinton and Judy Ann Johnson Arnold, Dallas, TX; ed/Grad, DeSoto HS, 1981; Att'g, Rice Univ; cp/Drill Team, 2 Yrs; VP and 4-Y Mem, French Clb; Future Tchrs of Am, 3 Yrs; Powder Puff Football, 2 Yrs; Secy, Homecoming Chm, Student Coun, 1 Yr; Yth in Govt; hon/Pres's Hon Roll, Rice Univ, Sprg 1983; Nat Merit Commended Scholar; Nat Hon Soc; Secy-Treas, Mu Alpha Theta; French Hon Soc; Valentine Queen, HS, 1981; Jan Sr Spotlight Awd; Nat Dean's List; Intl Yth in Achmt; W/W Among Am HS Students; g/To Pursue a Master's Deg in Sociol after Completing BA in Sociol and Managerial Studies.

ARNOLD, SUZANNE M oc/Student; b/Aug 10, 1963; h/Route #8, Box 427, Lebanon, TN 37087; p/Mr and Mrs Claude A Arnold, Lebanon, TN; ed/Grad, Mt Juliet Sr HS, 1981; Student, David Lipscomb Col 1981-83, Mid TN St Univ 1983-84; cp/Lebanon Sound and Light Co; Handweavers Guild of Nashville; Theta Tau, DLC Ladies Social Clb; 4-H Clb; Hon Clb; All-Stars; Wash, DC, Citizenship Short Course; Intl Thespian Soc; Dactylology Clb; Good News Singers; Col, HS Paper Staff; r/Ch of Christ; hon/Dean's List, DLC, Fall 1982; Pres, Classroom for Yg Am; NHS; Ldrship S'ship; W/W Among Am HS Students; g/Communs Deg.

ARNOLD, TONYA HEACOCK oc/Student, Secretary; b/Jul 21, 1964; h/712 North Indiana Road, Weatherford, OK 73096; ba/Weatherford, OK; m/Jeff; p/Gary and Delores Heacock, Woodward, OK; ed/HS Dipl, 1982; Student, SWn OK St Univ, 1982, 1983; pa/Lockstone Funeral Home Inc, 1983; Woodward Florist and Catering, 1980, 1981, 1982; U Supermkts, 1982; cp/Drama Clb; Red Cross Blood Mobile Vol; Ch Wkr; r/Nazarene; hon/W/W Among Am HS Students; g/Nsg and/or Mortuary Sci.

ARONSON, LISA SHEPARD oc/Latin Americanist; b/Aug 24, 1961; h/66 Hickory Hill Road, Tappan, NY 10983; p/Shepard and Muriel Aronson, Tappan, NY; ed/New Lincoln Sch; BA, Cornell Univ, 1982; pa/Writer; Assoc Editor, *Scienceland Magazine*, 1982; Asst, Dir, Dept of Latin Am Affairs of the Anti-Deferation Leag of B'nai B'rith, 1983; cp/Columnist, *Cornell Daily Sun*; Editor, *Ithaca Women's Anthology*; Phi Beta Kappa; Hon Soc, Com on US/Latin Am Relats; hon/Kram Prize in Wom Studies; White Prize; Col Scholar; g/Journalist and/or Writer.

ARNOVITZ, TAMARA KAY oc/Student; b/Aug 13, 1965; h/Route 2, Berea, KY 40403; p/Presley Arnovitz, Berea, KY; ed/HS Grad W Distn; Att'g, En KY Univ; cp/KY St Poetry Soc; Lexington Poets; Girls St; Beta Clb; r/Jewish; hon/Hon Mention for Poem, *World of Poetry*, 1983; Poem Pub'd by *Reaching* Mag, 1983; Winner of Golden Leaf Pageant in Cooperation w KY Tobacco Farmers and Madison Co C of C; Hon Roll; Hon Certs; W/W Among Am HS Students 1983, Yg Commun

Ldrs of Am 1983, Intl Yth in Achmt (Cambridge, England); Intl Biogl Centre; W/W Among Am HS Students; g/ To Become a Writer.

ARRINGTON, BILLY WAYNE oc/ Student; b/Mar 7, 1963; h/Route 5, Box 296, Gate City, VA 24251; ba/Berea, KY; p/Cecil and Bethel Arrington, Gate City, VA; ed/Grad, Gate City High, 1981; Indep Deg in Musical Theatre, Berea Col, 1985; pa/From Ofc Clk, to Hd Sound Tech, to Publicity Mgr, Jelkyl Drama Ctr, Berea Col, 1981-84; cp/Pres, Nat Hon Soc, GCHC, 1980-81; Pres, Berea Players, 1982-83; VP, Berea Players, 1983-84; Treas, Co-Ldr, New Life Singers, 1982-84; Pres, Drama Clb, GCHS, 1979-81; Jr Civitan, GCHS, 1979-81; Parliamentarian of Student Coun, GCHS, 1980-81; Hon Grad, GCHS, 1981; r/Indep Bapt; hon/Fleur de Lis, 1982; Alpha Psi Omega, 1982; Berea Players' Hall of Fame, Tech, 1982; Johnson-Hilliard Cup for Best Performer, Sum 1983; GCHS Spch and Drama Awd, 1981; Berea Col Dean's List, 1982-84; g/To Complete Deg in Musical Theatre; To Pursue a Career as an Entertainer.

ARROYO-RIVERA, FREYA M oc/ Safety Engineer; b/Jan 14, 1960; h/1 Lincoln Place, Apartment 6A, North Brunswick, NJ 08902; ba/Ft Monmouth, NJ; p/Remy Arroyo-Segarra, Rio Piedras, Puerto Rico; ed/Colegio del Espiritu Santo, 1977; BS, Chem Engrg, Univ of Puerto Rico, Mayaguez Campus, 1982; pa/Intern in Safety, Darcom ITC, 1982-83; Safety Engr, Army Safety Ofc at Cecom; Am Inst of Chem Engrs, VP 1982; Soc of Wom Engrs, Treas Asst 1980; cp/VP, Grad'd Class of Chem Engrg, 1982; Colegio de Ingenieros y Agrimensores de Puerto Rico; hon/Cert of Hon of Engrg Sch, 1978-80; g/Future Grad Courses on Bus Adm and Indust Engrg.

ASHBURN, MICHELE RANEE oc/ Student; b/Jul 9, 1962; h/Rt DeGraff, MN 56233; p/James and Patricia Ashburn; ed/Kerkhoven-Murdock-Sundberg HS, 1980; AA, Willmar Community Colllege, 1982; Student, Univ of MN Minneapolis; cp/Band; Cheerleader; Volleyball Manager; Track Team; Annual Staff Mem; Theatre; B Hon Roll; Letter Clb; 4-H, Photog, Secy, Co-Ambassador, Co-Jr Ldr, Dir; Phi Theta Kappa; hon/4-H Key Awd; Min-Norske Exec Mem; g/Public Relats Deg; Flight Attendant.

ASHE, PAMELA YVONNE oc/Student; b/Feb 10, 1967; h/Route 66, Box 79, Cullowhee, NC 28723; p/Mr and Mrs Donald Joe Ashe, Cullowhee, NC; ed/Camp Lab Sch, Class of 1985; pa/ Student Employee, Food Sers Dept, Wn Carolina Univ, 1981-; cp/Girl Scouts, 1978-80; FHA, 1981-82; r/Bapt; hon/ Incl'd in *United States Achievement Academy Official Yearbook* 1984, *The Sylva Herald* 1983, *The Asheville Citizen Times* 1983; US Achmt Acad Nat Ldrship and Ser Awd, 1984; Typing I Awd, 1982; Typing II Awd, 1983; Most Profl Jr Vol, 1983; Most Hours Wk'd by Jr Vol (211), 1983; g/Bus Adm, Info Sys.

ASHFORD, IVY JEAN oc/College Graduate; b/Jan 16, 1962; c/Devunya Denise; p/Mr and Mrs James G Ashford, Ackerman, MS; ed/Grad, Ackerman HS, 1980; AS, Mary Holmes Jr Col, 1983; cp/Pres, Afro-Wom; VP, Mary Holmes

Concert Choir, 1982-83; Mem: Phi Theta Kappa, Drama Clb, Mary Holmes Concert Choir; r/Bapt; hon/Outstg Concert Awd, 1983; Music Awd, 1983; g/Singer or RN.

ASHMORE, LESLIE MARIE oc/ Financial Analyst; b/Mar 20, 1956; h/ 4916 West Chicago, Rapid City, SD 57701; ba/Rapid City, SD; m/Daniel Eugene; c/Kathryn Marie; p/Vincent and Shirley Henderson, Rapid City, SD; ed/Grad, Stevens HS, 1974; BS, Acctg, Univ of SD, 1978; pa/Acct, Univ of SD, 1978-79; Sys Acct 1979-82, Financial Analyst 1982-, Black Hills Power and Light Co; AAUW; Univ of SD Alumni Assn; Alpha Xi Delta; ABWA; r/Luth Ch; hon/Alpha Lambda Delta, 1975; Guidon, 1976; W/W Cols and Univs; Intl Yth in Achmt; Yg Commun Ldrs of Am; g/Sr Corporate Mgmt.

ASHOOH, VERONICA MERCEDES oc/Student; b/Aug 28, 1964; h/3800 Towanda Road, Alexandria, VA 22303; p/Joseph P Sr and Gloria D Ashooh; ed/ Grad, Thomas A Edison HS, 1982; Student, Polit Sci, James Madison Univ; pa/Inst of Mod Procedures, Basic Ednl Opport Grant Prog, 1980, 1982, 1982-83; Cashier on Computer Terminal, W Bell and Co, 1981-82, 1982-83; cp/Informative Spkr, VA JCs 1980, Arcadames Toastmistress Clb 1981, Fairfax Co Sch Bd 1981, Cath Yth Org 1979-82; Polit Campaign Wkr; Phi Mu Frat Intl, Jr Exec; James Madison Pre-Legal Soc; James Madison Inner-Hall Coun and Hall Coun Exec; James Madison Intl Relats Soc; Thomas Edison Forensic Team, 1979-82, Secy-Treas; Spch Team Capt, VP, Pres; Thomas Edison Student Govt, 1979-81; Thomas Edison *Erudite* Staff Editor, 1981-82; Thomas Edison Eng Team Co-Capt, 1980-81; hon/Extra-Curricula Activs Awd, 1980-82; Selected to Participate in a Pres Classroom for Yg Ams, Am Univ, 1981; Selected to Participate in Hugh O'Brien Ldrship Sem; Univ of Richmond 1980 St Finalist, Century II Ldrship S'ship; Nat Forensic Leag Double Distn, Merit S'ship, Georgetown Univ Forensic Inst; Nat Hon Soc; Govs Sch for the Gifted, Nom; Nat Sci Merit Awd Winner in US Achmt Acad, 1982; DAR Essay Contest Winner, 1977; DAR Citizenship Awd, 1981; Soroptomists Intl S'ship; VFW Awd; W/ W Am HS Students; Yg Commun Ldrs; g/Govt, Polits, Law.

ASKEW, JAMES KEITH oc/Student; b/Mar 27, 1961; h/414 Franklin Street, Roanoke Rapids, NC 27870; p/Mr and Mrs James Earl Askew, Roanoke Rapids, NC; ed/Dipl, Roanoke Rapids HS, 1979; BA, Ec, Univ of NC Chapel Hill, 1983; Att'd, NC St Univ, 1979-81; pa/Var Sum and Wk Study Jobs; cp/Spanish Clb, 197; Hosts Tutoring Prog, 1979; Univ of NC Bowling Team, 1982-83; Intramural Basketball Team Capt, 1980; Bowling Leag Secy and Team Capt, 1983; So Intercol Bowling Cong, 1982-83; Am Jr Bowling Cong, 1978-81; Univ of NC Gen Alumni Assn, 1983-; r/Bapt; hon/ Recip, Student Stores S'ship Based on Merit and Financial Need; g/To Attend Law Sch.

ATHERTON, JEFFREY ALAN oc/ Student, Self-Employed Programmer; b/Jan 4, 1963; h/Route 4, Valley View Drive, Mount Washington, KY 40047; p/Mr and Mrs S G Atherton, Mount

Washington, KY; ed/Grad, Bullitt Ctl HS, 1981; Att'd, KY Polytechnic Inst, 1982-83; Att'g, Watterson Col, 1983-; pa/Cashier, Mt Wash Key Mkt, 1978-80; Line Ser Tech, Bowman Field, 1980, 1981; Laborer, Linco Shell Prods, 1982-83; Self-Employed Computer Programmer, 1983-; cp/KPI Student Coun; KPI Pres's List; Watterson Pres's List; hon/Perfect GPA at KPI.

AULT, CYNTHIA KAY oc/Administrative Assistant; b/Dec 19, 1958; h/ 8100 Balcones #217, Austin, TX 78759; ba/Austin, TX; p/Mr and Mrs William C Ault, Corpus Christi, TX; ed/Grad, Richard King HS, 1977; BS, Baylor Univ, 1981; pa/Subst Tchr, Austin ISD, 1981-82; Auditor, Am Lung Assn, 1982; Adm Asst, Co-op Advtg Sers, 1983; Adm Asst, Capital Trust Corp; cp/FCA; Ath in Action; Baylor Sch of Ed Assn; Tennis Team; Meth Home Tutor; Psych Clb; French Clb; Coronets; hon/VA Graves Ogilvie S'ship; Dean's Hon Role; NHS; Hon Role; g/Master's Deg in Ed/ Earth Sci; Study/Travel in Australia.

AUSBURNE, OZZIE LEE oc/Student, Child Counselor; b/Dec 25, 1964; h/ 2502 Holloway, Midland, TX 79701; ba/ Midland, TX; p/Mr and Mrs H L Ausburne, Midland, TX; ed/Grad, Midland HS; pa/YMCA Child Cnslr, 1979-82; Kgn Tchrs Aid, Midland ISD, 1982-83; Sum Camp Cnslr, Pk and Rec, 1983; YMCA Child Cnslr, 1983-; cp/HS: Jr Coun (Pres) 1981-83, 100 Clb 1980-81, Student Coun 1980-83, Pres's Cabinet 1982-83, French Clb (VP) 1980, Home Ec Cooperative Ed (Pres) 1982-83; Col: Student Senate 1983-84, Cheerldr 1983, Mascot 1983-84, BSU 1983-84, Spirit Clb 1983-84, Pres of Students Against Child Abuse; r/Bapt; hon/HECE Tchrs Aide Tng Cert, City of Midland, 1982-83; PTA S'ship, 1983-87; Drama Letter, 1980-81; Acad Letter, 1983; HECE St Rep, 1983; W/W Among Am HS Students; g/To Finish Her Freshman and Sophomore Yrs at Midland Col, and to Complete Her Jr and Sr Yrs at E TX St Univ (Majoring in Ed w a 2nd Maj or Minor in Psych); To Be a Tchr/Cnslr.

AUSTIN, JON NICHOLAS oc/Student; b/Aug 12, 1959; h/2625 West Ardmore Place, Peoria, IL 61604; p/Mr and Mrs Harold H Austin, Peoria, IL; ed/Manual HS, 1977; BA, Bradley Univ, 1981; Student, NY Univ, 1982-; pa/Lib Clk, NY Univ, 1982-83; Grad Asst, Mus Studies Dept, NY Univ, 1983-84; cp/Am Assn of Mus, 1981-; Peoria Hist Soc, 1976-; Citizens Com to Preserve Jubilee Col; IL and Gen Soc of Mayflower Descendants; Archivist-Citizens Com to Preserve Jubilee Col; Am Assn for St and Local Hist; r/Meth; hon/Grad, cum laude; Phi Alpha Theta; g/Mus Studies or Hist Soc Adm.

AWTREY, MARGARET CATHERINE oc/Assistant Manager; b/Dec 17, 1960; h/1711 North Chatham Avenue, Siler City, NC 27344; ba/Burlington, NC; p/Grant and Melba Awtrey, Siler City, NC; ed/Jordan Matthews HS, 1979; BA in Commun w Emphasis on Psych, Univ of NC Wilmington, 1983; pa/Internship w Snelling and Snelling Employmt Agy, 1983; Asst Mgr, Eckerd Drug; cp/VP of Commun Clb, Univ of NC Wilmington, 1981-82; Public Relats Chp, Commun Clb, Univ of NC Wilmington, 1982-83; r/So Bapt; b/Master's in Commun; Public Relats.

AYERS, BARBARA GAIL oc/Art Director; b/Feb 20, 1960; h/837 Isthmus Court, San Diego, CA 92109; ba/San Diego, CA; ed/BA, Graphic Design, San Diego St Univ, 1983; AA, Jour, Grossmont Col; Grad, Monte Vista HS, 1978; pa/Art Dir, KUSI Channel 51 TV; Acct Supvr, Inman & Assocs, Mktg/Advtg and Public Relats, 1982-83; Personal Bus Prods Greeting Cards; Art Dir, David Grant Inc, Advtg and Public Relats, 1982; Free-Lance Designer/ Photog, 1979-; Art Dir, *San Diego Daily Transcript*, *La Mesa Courier, Tierrasanta Bulletin*, 1980-82; Photog, Can-U-Antiq-Us Portrait Studio, 1978-80; Asst Mgr, May Co Portrait Studio, 1979; Promotion Dir, *The G Newspaper*, Grossmont Col, 1979; Am Mktg Assn; Assn for Multi-Image, Bd Mem; Communicating Arts Grp; cp/San Diego Mus of Art; San Diego St Univ 1st Place; Wom of Distn, Grossmont Col; Editor, Newspaper Won Gen Excell at 1980 CA Jour Assn of Commun Col; Won On-the-Spot Feature and Sports Photo, CA Jour Assn of Commun Col; 2nd Place Photograph, Pepperdine Jour Competition; HS Art Dept Awd; Intl Yth in Achmt; Commun Ldrs of Am; g/Design of Promotional Graphics for Outdoor-Oriented Org or Mag.

AYERS, WILLIAM YURI oc/Student; b/Feb 20, 1969; h/113 Marsey Lane, Birmingham, AL 35209; p/Emma Ayers, Birmingham, AL.

AYNES, JEFFREY ALAN oc/Student; b/Dec 5, 1966; h/14282 Northeast 50, Choctaw, OK 73020; p/Mr and Mrs Teddy G Aynes, Choctaw, OK; ed/Jones HS; Student, Small Bus Mgmt, En OK Co Voc Tech; pa/Checker, Venture, 1983-84; Stocker, TG&Y, 1983; Groomer, Dreessen's Dog Grooming, Sums of 1980, 1981, 1982, 1983, 1984; Distributive Ed Clbs of Am, Parliamentarian 1983-84; Teen Age Repub; Dir, EOC TARS, 1984; Band; r/So Bapt; hon/W/ W; g/Ch Related Wk.

B

BABB, LYNDA JEAN oc/Student; b/ Nov 15, 1963; h/3202 Overton Crossing, Memphis, TN 38127; p/Charles and Billie Babb, Memphis, TN; ed/Trezevant HS, 1982; cp/ARC; TN Ofc Edn; Art Clb; Ofc Asst; r/Christian; hon/Acad Excell in Sci; Jr HS Hon Soc; W/W Among Am HS Students; Commun Ldrs Am; g/Col Secy Course; Art Course.

BACON, DOUGLAS RICHARD oc/ Medical Student; b/Jan 28, 1959; h/5101 Clearview Drive, Williamsville, NY 14221; ba/East Setauket, NY; p/Drs Paul and Margaret Bacon, Williamsville, NY; ed/Williamsville E HS, 1977; BS cum laude 1981, BA cum laude 1981, St Univ NY-Buffalo; Stony Brook Sch Med, St Univ NY, MD Expected 1985; 1981-83; The Immigration & Naturalization Ser, 1981-; Am Med Student Assn, 1981-; Fam Pract Clb, 1981-; NY St Med Soc, 1981-; Student Mem, AMA, 1982-; Vol, Emer Rm, Millard Fillmore Suburban Hosp, 1980-81; Vol, Hist of Med Rdg Grp, 1982-; cp/Undergrad Hist Coun, 1980-81; Hons Coun Fdr, 1979-81; Secy, Alpha Epsilon Delta; Sr Advr, Phi Eta Sigma, 1980-81; Treas, Alpha Lambda Delta, 1978-79; r/U Meth; hon/ John T Horton Undergrad Hist Essay Prize, 1980; 100 Hour Vol Pin, Millard Fillmore Suburban Hosp, 1981; W/W Among Am HS Students; Intl Yth in Achmt; Commun Ldrs of Am; W/W Among Students in Am Univs & Cols; Am Soc Anesthesia Preceptee, 1983; g/ Anesth.

BADGETT, KENNETH WOLTZ oc/ Student; b/Jul 3, 1965; h/Route 2, Box 532, Dobson, NC 27017; p/Mr and Mrs Samuel W Badgett, Dobson, NC; ed/ Surry Ctl HS, 1983; to Attend Wake Forest Univ; pa/Yth Advr, Surry Friends of Yth; 2nd VP, Explorer Post 580; Treas, NHS; Eagle Scout; Jr Asst Scout; Vars Track, Cross Country; Editor, Yrbk; hon/Boys' St Del; Century III Ldrship Awd; DAR Good Citizen NC & SEn Div (7 Sts); g/Pre-Med; W/W and Soc Dist'd Am HS Students.

BAER, BARBARA SUE b/Jan 7, 1963; h/345 S North Street, Maugansville, MD 21767; p/L Jason and Arlene L Baer, Maugansville, MD; ed/N Hagerstown HS, 1981; Brandeis Univ, 1982; pa/ Student; cp/Hon Clb & Hon Soc; Pres, Ch Yth Grp; Secy, Yth & Govt Clb; Pep Clb; French Clb; All-Country Orch; Wn MD Reg Hons Orch; hon/Student Intern, Gifted & Talented Prog, HS; MD Dist'd Scholar; S'ship, Signal Oil Co; W/W Among Am HS Students, 1979-80, 1980-81; g/ Pediatrician.

BAGLEY, MARY CAROL oc/College Instructor; b/Mar 11, 1958; h/12539 Falling Leaves Court, St Louis, MO 63141; ba/St Louis, MO; p/Mr and Mrs Robert E Bagley, St Louis, MO; ed/ Lutheran HS N, 1976; BA 1980, MA 1982, Univ MO-St Louis; pa/Instr, St Louis Commun Col; Instr, Maryville Col, 1982-; Gtr St Louis Eng Tchr's Assn, 1982-; AAUP; NCTE; UMSL Senate; pa/Homecoming Ct; Miss Teenage Am Cand; Features; Fine Arts & Photog Editor, Current Newspaper; KWMU Radio Announcer; hon/Pub in "MO Grand & Memorable Theatres", Contbg Editor "St Louis Bride" Mag;

Student Affairs Awd at UMSL; Magna Cum Laude Grad; W/W Am Cols & Univs; Outstg Wom Am; g/to Receive PhD in Eng.

BAILEY, BAMBI LYNN oc/Student; b/Nov 10, 1964; h/210 Park Street, Grayson, KY 41143; p/Dallas Bailey, Olive Hill, KY and Glenna Bailey, Grayson, KY; ed/E Carter HS, 1982; Attend Transylvania Univ; cp/Grayson Softball Leag; Student Activs Bd; Sigma Kappa Sorority, Treas & House Chm; Jr Panhellenic Coun; Transylites-Admission Ofc Tour Guides; Circle K; Wom's Ath Assn; Panhellenic Newslttr; Intrammural Sports; hon/Hon Secy St; Acad Scholar, Transylvania Univ; W/W Among Am HS Students; Commun Ldrs Am; g/to Tch in HS & Coach Basketball.

BAILEY, ELIZABETH ROANN oc/ Student; b/Feb 5, 1962; h/214 York Road, Greenville, NC 27834; p/Dr Donald Etheridge and Betty Dyson Bailey, Greenville, NC; ed/Junius H Rose HS, 1980; Univ NC-Chapel Hill; cp/Delta Sigma Pi-Profl Bus Frat; Phi Eta Sigma-Freshman Hon Soc; Beta Gamma Sigma-Acad Bus Frat; Beta Alpha Psi-Acad Acctg Frat, VP 1983-84; Phi Beta Kappa; r/Presb; hon/Univ NC-Chapel Hill Nam Am Wom's Soc CPA S'ship, 1983; g/CPA.

BAILEY, JACK MARKUS oc/Realtor; b/May 12, 1961; h/1233 Guilford College Road, Jamestown, NC 27282; ba/ Greensboro, NC; p/Jack and Margie Bailey, Jamestown, NC; ed/Wn Guilford HS, 1979; BS, High Pt Col, 1983; Lic Real Est Broker, Dan Mohr Real Est Sch, 1983; pa/Courtesy Clk, Food World, 1977-79; Stock Room Clk, Guilford Mills, 1980; Ofc Mgr, Jack C Bailey Bldrs, 1983; Rltr Assoc, Russ Rlty, 1983-; cp/HS Activs, Student Coun, VICA Clb, Ftball, Track, VP Men's Ath Clb; Col Activs, Track, Bapt Student Union; Col & Careers Dept; Greensboro Bd Rltrs; r/Bapt; hon/HS Ath Hons in Track; Pres Singles Dept; g/to become Small Bus Owner & Real Est.

BAILEY, JACQUELIN oc/ Pre-Kindergarten Teacher; b/Jan 29, 1961; h/2121-B Fitzroy Drive, Columbus, OH 43224; ba/Columbus, OH; ed/ Erwin HS, 1979; BS, Winston-Salem St Univ, 1983; pa/Tchrs Aide, CETAI-SYEP, 1976-82; Sales Clk/Cashier, Pic 'N Pay Shoes, 1980-82; Lib Tech & Asst, Winston-Salem St Univ, 1980-81; Secy/ Receptionist, Images 'N Fashion, 1983; Pre-Kgn Tchr, Edu-Care Guid Ctr; cp/ Students NEA; Winston Salem St Univ Alumni Mem; Big Brother/Big Sister; Nat Edrs Book Clb; Supts Yth Coun, 1979; Inter-Clb Coun Pres, Erwin HS, 1978; Student Govt Assn, 1979-81, Winston Salem St Univ; r/Meth; hon/ W/W Among Am HS Students; Outstg Ser & Ldrship Awd; Deans List; g/Public Schs, Ednl Based Pub Co.

BAILEY, JANET L oc/Graduate Student; b/Jul 11, 1958; h/Post Office Box 1085, San Juan, TX 78589; m/Joe Edward; c/Karen Jo and Janet Lynn; p/ Mr and Mrs Sidney Ford, San Juan, TX; sp/Mr and Mrs Luther Bailey, San Juan, TX; ed/PSJA HS, 1976; BBA, Pan Am Univ, 1981; MBA Prog at Pan Am Univ; pa/ADAP Inc 1979-80, 1981-82 TREBCO Inc 1980-81, Computer Programmer; VP, DR Hunt Computer Conslts, 1982-83; Computer Conslt,

Steve Glass & Assoc, 1983; Grad Tchg Asst, Pan Am Univ, 1983; cp/Beta Gamma Sigma, Charter Pres, 1980-81; Alpha Chi; Kappa Delta Pi; TX Student Assn, VP, 1982-83; Pan Am Univ Student Assn; Grad Senator, 1982-83; Am Soc Pers Adm; r/Bapt; hon/W/W Among Students Am Univ & Cols; Nat Dean's List; Yg Commun Ldrs Am; to Attend Nat Sem Beta Gamma Sigma; g/MBA, PhD in Computer Sci, Univ Prof.

BAILEY, JOE EDWARD oc/Sales, Business Forms; b/Jan 15, 1954; h/Post Office Box 1085, San Juan, FL 78589; m/Janet Lou Ford; c/Karen Joe and Lynn; p/Luther and Gladys Bailey, San Juan, TX; ed/Atlantic Airline Sch, 1973; Pan Am Univ, BBA, 1983; pa/Area Sales Rep, Gulf Bus Forms, 1981-; cp/ Sorensen PTA, 1981-83; HIDALCO Co Dpty Registar, 1982; Am Soc Pers Adm; Data Processing Mgmt; Pan Am Univ Student Assn; TX Student Assn; Alpha Chi; Beta Gamma Sigma; r/Bapt; hon/ Acad S'ships; Nat Deans List; Dean of Students Ldrship Awd; Commun Ldrship Awd; Yg Personalities Am; W/ W Am Univs & Cols; g/Pers Mgmt Indust Psychol.

BAILEY, MARSHA GAYLE b/Sep 28, 1963; h/Post Office Box 147, LaCenter, KY 42056; p/Mr and Mrs Alvin Lynn Bailey; ed/Ballard Meml HS, 1981; Wn KY Univ; pa/Student; cp/Band; Flag Corps; Rifle Corps; Beta Clb; Future Tchrs Am; FHA; Yrbook Staff; Broadcasting Clb; Secy, Freshman Class; Del, KY Girls' St; Pulp & Paper Tech Wkshop; Alpha Phi Omega Ser Frat; VP, Little Sisters, 1983; Phi Eta Sigma Freshman Hon Soc, 1982; Jr & Sr Plays; Showcase Musical; Softball; hon/Recog, Pres of Wn KY Univ; Chosen to Participate in Fac Mentor Prog, Wn KY Univ, 1983; Dean's List; Am Outstg Names & Faces; W/W Among HS Students; g/Bus Mgmt.

BAILLARGEON, PETER PAUL oc/ Teacher of the Severely Handicapped; b/Apr 30, 1955; h/10 Circus Place, Brunswick, ME 04011; ba/Brunswick, ME; p/Calix and Betty Baillargeon, Old Town, ME; ed/BS, Univ ME, 1976; EdM, Univ VT, 1982; pa/Tchr, SAD Num 58, 1976-77; Tchr, Multiple Handicap Ctr, 1977-78; Tchr, Brunswick Sch Sys, 1978-; cp/CEC; Applied Behavioral Anal; Assn Severely Handicapped; Indep Assn Retarded Citizens; r/Cath; hon/Kappa Delta Pi; Alpha Chi Nat Hon Soc; Corinne Morrison Strong S'ship, Fine Arts Achmt; g/Doct Studies in Ed of Handicapped.

BAIN, ALTON DEEMS b/Jun 3, 1960; h/200 East Ivey Street, Lillington, NC 27546; p/Mr and Mrs Edgar R Bain, Lillington, NC; ed/Cape Fear Christian Acad, 1978; BA, Duke Univ; Univ of NC Sch Law; pa/Student; cp/Pi Sigma Alpha; Phi Eta Sigma; FCA; Var Golf; VP, Col Dorm; Student Legis; Hon Roll; r/Presb; hon/Phi Beta Kappa; Summa Cum Laude Grad; Pres, 1st, 2nd Yr Law Class; g/Law.

BAIN, CLINTON DWIGHT oc/Graduate Student; b/Aug 2, 1960; h/Box 576 Clarcona, FL 32710; ba/Lynchburg, VA; m/Sheila Campbell; p/Clinton and May Bain, Orlando, FL; sp/Hollis and Evelyn Campbell, Kissimmee, FL; ed/Heritage Prep Sch, 1978; Valencia Commun Col,

1980; Heritage Col, 1981; Pastoral Cnslg Inst, 1982; Liberty Bapt Sem, 1984; pa/Crisis Cnslr, Thomas Rd Bapt Ch, 1983-84; Area Rep, Marlena Fashions, 1982-83; Spch/Drama Tchr, Heritage Prep Sch, 1980-82; Promo Mgr, Hidden Hills Energy Corporation, 1982-; Spkr, Success Motivation Inst, 1980-81; cp/Student Body Pres, Yrbook Editor, Liberty Bapt Sem; Admin VP, Toastmasters, 1981; Heritage Sch Photog; Varsity Sports Announcer "Voice of Heritage Prep"; r/Bapt; hon/Student Body Pres, Liberty Bapt Sem, 1983-84; W Orange Co Sertoma Col Student of Wk; 20th Century/Fox Screen Test for "M*A*S*H"; W/W HS Students; Outstg Yg Men Am; Intl Yth Achmt; g/Doct in Psychol.

BAINS, DEBRA LOIS oc/Teacher; b/Aug 10, 1960; h/2601 Dillard, Shreveport, LA 71104; p/Mr and Mrs J C Bains, Shreveport, LA; ed/Bach, LA Col, 1983; pa/Tchr, West Shreveport Sch, Caddo Parris Schs; Assn Chd Ed Intl; r/So Bapt; hon/W/W Among Am Col & Univ; Dean's List; g/to own Chd's Theatre.

BAKER, ANNE THERESA oc/Substitute Teacher Day Care; b/Oct 11, 1961; h/457 Derwyn Road, Drexel Hill, PA 19026; ba/Media, PA; p/Dr and Mrs Richard Baker, Drexel Hill, PA; ed/BA, St Joseph's Univ, 1983; pa/Cook & Cashier, Wendy's Hamburgers, 1980; Infant Home Care, 1981; Operator, Am Telephone, 1982; Subst Tchr, Tchr, Delco Child Day Care Assn; Saleswom, Fuller Brush Co, 1983; Tchr, Nativity BVM; cp/HS Student Coun Ofcr; Yth Commun Ser Corps; Nat Hon Soc; Commun Action Prog; Balto Housing Proj & Campus Min; Alpha Sigma Nu; r/Cath; hon/Treas Nat Hon Soc, 1978-79; Spanish Nat Hon Soc; Secy, Alpha Sigma Nu, 1982-83; Dean's List; W/W Yg Ldrs; g/Tchg, Open Day Care Ctr.

BAKER, CHARLOTTE MAUREEN oc/Student; b/Jul 7, 1962; h/Post Office Box 9234, Winter Haven, FL, 33881; p/Mr and Mrs Maurice F Baker, Auburndale, FL; ed/Auburndale Sr HS; Attends Troy St Univ; pa/Cnslr, Auburndale City Rec Dept, 1980-82; Tutor Horsebackriding, Social Folk & Sq Dance, Troy St Univ; Cnslr & Dir, Lake Howard Fitness & Hlth Clb, 1983; cp/Gamma Beta Phi Soc; Daugh Crossed Swords; Troy St Univ Volleyball; HPER, VP, 1983; r/Presb; hon/Theta Chi Frat Dream Girl, 1983; Volleyball All-St, 1981; Volleyball All Gulf S Conf, 1982; W/W Among Am HS Students; g/Master's Deg in Exercise Physiol.

BAKER, DANA LYNN b/Jan 9, 1958; h/5816 D Hunting Ridge Lane, Charlotte, NC 28212; p/Mr and Mrs Donald H Baker, Covington, VA; ed/Alleghany Co HS, 1976; BS, Berea Col; pa/Asst Hd Nurse; cp/Nurses Assn Am Col Ob & Gyn; NHS; Nat Leag Nsg; Sun Sch Tchr; Pres, Yth Org; GSA; Red Cross Vol; Basketball, Tennis, Track; hon/HS Hon Grad; Soc of Dist'd Am HS Students; Commun Ldrs Am; W/W Among Am HS Students; g/Master's Deg Nsg.

BAKER, JOE R JR oc/College Student; b/May 17, 1963; h/2101 30th Avenue, Vero Beach, FL 32960; ba/Lakeland, FL; p/Joe R and Joyce W Baker, Vero Beach, FL; ed/Vero Bch Sr HS, 1981; Attends FL So Col; pa/Vero Bch Police Traffic Dir, 1978-81; Bk Teller,

Security Guard, First Bankers of Indian River Co, 1982-83; cp/Lambda Chi Alpha Frat; Student Coun Pres; Student Govt Senator; Student Govt Treas; Omicron Delta Kappa; r/1st Christian Ch; hon/Dean's List; Outstg Sophomore; Nat Hon Soc; W/W Among Am HS Students; g/BA in Polit Sci; Law Deg.

BAKER, JOHN M oc/College Student; b/Oct 4, 1963; h/1322 Shorehaven Drive, Garland, TX 75040; ba/Greenville, SC; p/Donald M and Janet M Baker, Garland, TX; ed/Garland Christian Acad; Attends Bob Jones Univ; cp/HS Sr Class Pres; Letterman, Ftball, Basketball, Baseball; r/Indep Bapt; hon/Nat Hon Soc; All Conf Hons (Ath); g/Ch Adm/Proficiency Camp Wk.

BAKER, MICHAEL S oc/Student; b/Jul 10, 1962; h/1358 Walton Way, Norcross, GA 30093; m/Carla; p/Mr and Mrs Gerald Baker, Mayfield, KY; sp/Mr and Mrs Allen Willoughby, Mt Sterling, KY; ed/Freed-Hardeman Col; Attends GA St Univ; cp/Editor, "HonorRole", 1982-83; So Reg Hons Coun Newslttr; Social Clb; Hons Assn; Sophomore Rep; Public Relats Com Chm; Del, Nat & So Reg Hons Coun Convs; Sports Edit & Student Sports Info Dir; hon/Pres's List; W/W: Among Am HS, Music; Personalities of S; g/BBA Deg Mgmt.

BAKER, RELEATA EVELYN oc/Student; b/May 28, 1967; h/Route 2, Box 489-A, Rose Hill, NC 28458; p/Linwood and Mamie Baker, Rose Hill, NC; ed/Attends Wallace Rose Hill HS; cp/Charity Mid Sch Jr Beta Clb; Am Legion Post Jr Aux; Deca 4-H Clb; Wallace-Rose Hill Girl's Monogram Clb; Math Clb; Marching Band; Athletic Clb; Softball Team; Charity Mid Sch Newspaper Staffer; Annual Staff; hon/All-Co Band; All-State Band; Nat Guild Piano Players; Semi-Finalist, NC Sch Sci & Math; Jr HS & Sr HS Hon Roll; Att'd Bennett Col in Accessing Math; g/to attend UNC-Chapel Hill w deg Computer Sci.

BAKER, STEPHANIE YVONNE oc/Student; b/Feb 19, 1964; h/Post Office Box 570, Sanford, FL 32771; p/Mr and Mrs Stewart Baker, Sanford, FL; ed/Seminole HS; Attends Univ FL; cp/Univ FL Gospel Choir; r/Christian; g/Deg Microbiol & Cell Sci, Med Sch.

BAKER, SUSAN MARIE oc/Houskeeper; b/Jan 3, 1963; h/Route 2, Box 4490, Rapid City, SD 57701; ba/Rapid City, SD; p/Mr and Mrs Edward B Baker, Rapid City, SD; ed/Douglas HS, 1981; cp/Secy 1979-80, Mem 1978-79, FHA; Pres 1979-80, 80-81, FTA; r/Bapt; hon/W/W; Worlds W/W; Commun Ldrs Am; Yg Personalities Am.

BAKER, VANESSA DENISE oc/Student; b/Oct 3, 1964; h/800 Hill Road, Kingsport, TN 37664; p/Mr and Mrs Samuel Ralph Baker, Kingsport, TN; ed/Sullivan Co HS, 1982; Attends E TN St Univ; cp/Beta Clb; Pres 1981-82, Hon Clb Pres, 1982, All Stars 1979-82, Vol Ldr 1983, Alumni Ser Corps E TN St Univ 1982-83, 4-H; FHA, Secy, 1982; Jr Adv Bd Appalachian Fair, 1981-82; Sch Newspaper, 1979, Editor; Am Home Ec Assn; r/Bapt; hon/1981 St Winner 4-H Breads Proj; 1981 Del Nat 4-H Cong; 1982 Del Nat 4-H Conf; 1982 Danforth "I Dare You" Awd; 1981 Outstg Sullivan Co 4-H'er; W/W Among Am HS Students; Commun

Ldrs Am; Intl Yth in Achmt; g/Dietician.

BAKER, VERNA LEIGH oc/Graduate Student; b/Oct 21, 1963; h/3050 Kirklevington Drive, Number 59, Lexington, KY 40502; p/Thursie Baker, Burdine, KY; ed/BBA, En KY Univ, 1984; pa/Acct, Hearthstone Tavern & Pub, 1984; Student Intern, Lexington-Fayette Urban Co Govt, 1983; Bkkpr/Programmer, United Carr Enterprises, 1982; cp/Acctg Clb, Mem 1981-84, Pres 1983-84; Sigma Tau Pi, Mem 1982-84; Treas & Com Chm 1983-84; Phi Kappa Phi, The Gamma Beta Phi Soc; r/Bapt; hon/En KY Univ Pres S'ship, 1980-84; Amick & Helm S'ship, 1983-84; Nat Dean's List; W/W: Among HS Students, Among Am Cols & Univs; g/Career in Public Accounting.

BALDREE, DAVID FRANKLIN oc/Student; b/Feb 28, 1966; h/708 Branton Drive, Shelby, NC 28150; p/J D and Margaret Baldree, Shelby, NC; ed/Shelby HS; cp/Drama Clb, VP 1983, Pres 1984; Nat Thesbian Hon Soc, 1982, 1983, 1984; Orch 1978-84; Nat Hon Soc, 1983, 1984; Marshall 1983, 1984; Spanish Clb, 1982, 1983; Shelby H Theater Tech Crew, 1982, 1983, 1984; Chorus 1981, 1984; Band 1982, 1984; r/Bapt; hon/Mars Hill Choral Clin 1982, 1983; NC All Honors Chorus, 1982; NC All-State Chorus, 1983; Gov's Sch NC, 1983; Drama Clb Ser Awd, 1983; g/College.

BALDRIDGE, SCOTT ALAN oc/Electrician; b/Apr 25, 1964; h/1358 Woodside Drive, San Luis Obispo, CA 93401; p/Mr and Mrs Robert Charles Baldridge; ed/San Luis Obispo Sr HS, 1982; Ch Sem Grad, 1982; cp/Cross Country, Wrestling, Basketball, Softball, Volleyball Teams; Pres, Student Coun; Pres, ASB; HS Sophomore Activs Com; HS Accreditation Student Coms Coor; Chm of Accreditation Adm Subcom; Student Cong Rep; Sr Patrol Ldr; Treas, Scout Patrol; Basketball Coach; Volleyball Coach; Ch Co Volleyball Spec; hon/Eagle Scout; Freshman Outstg Citizenship Awd; CA Sch Fdn Seal Bearer; 4th Pl, 125 lb & Under Weight Class in 5th Annual San Luis Obispo Weight Lifting Tourn; CA Polytech St Univ Indust Arts Show, 3rd Pl, Mech Drafting; HS Tiger Pride Awd; Duty to God Scout/Ch Awd; Commun Ldrs Am; Intl Yth Achmt; g/18 Mo Mission for Ch of Jesus Christ of LDS; Col.

BALDRIDGE, STEVEN KENT b/Apr 25, 1964; h/1358 Woodside Drive, San Luis Obispo, CA 93401; p/Robert C and Sherie W Baldridge; ed/San Luis Obispo Sr HS, 1982; pa/Student; Painter; cp/Jr HS Student Body Pres; Student Coun; Student Cong; InterClb Coun Rep; Chm, Student Cong; Sr Class Pres; Sch Bd Ambassador; Designer, Crew Foreman; Homecoming Float; Jt Orgr, Homecoming Skits; Morgan Volleyball Team; HS Swim Team; Drama Clb; HS Ch Newspaper; Accreditations Sch Philosophies & Goals Chair; Pres Clrm Mem; Treas Ch Grp; Ch Single Adult Ldr; r/Ch of Jesus Christ LDS; hon/Freshman Outstg Sr Awd; Freshman S'ship Awd; Eagle Scout; Commend Student Nat Merit S'ship Foun; Seal Bearer, CSF; Joseph S Locheran Latin Essay Awd; Leroy Farrar Ath Scholar; Duty to God Awd; Tiger Pride, Acad Hon; W/W Am HS Students; Commun

Ldrs Am; g/18 Mo Mission for Ch; Law.

BALDWIN, DENISE KATHLEEN oc/ Student; b/Jul 26, 1955; h/505 Bonnie Drive, Ozark, AL 36360; m/David A; c/ Thomas D, Kristin S; p/Raymond J Lore Sr, Princeton, FL and Harriet T Lore, Feasterville, PA; sp/Thomas E and Evelyn L Baldwin, Memphis, TN; ed/ Miami Sr HS, 1973; AS 1982, AAS 1983, Enterprise St Jr Col; mil/AUS, 1973-76, Data Processing Spec; pa/Paste-up Artist, Ace Letter Ser, 1972-73; AUS, Data Processing Spec, 1973-76; Student (Troy St Univ), Homemaker, Mother, 1978-; cp/Swimming Team, Hon Soc; Hostess Clb; Flagette Band Mem; St John's Cath Wom's Clb; Non-Commissioned Wives Clb; r/Cath; hon/Army Commend Medal & Good Conduct Medal, 1976; Hons Grad, Enterprise St Jr Col; g/Bach Deg Computer Sci.

BALDWIN, KATHLEEN MARIE oc/ Student; b/Jun 28, 1962; h/1404 Dogwood, Mt Prospect, IL 60056; ba/Chgo, IL; ed/John Hersey HS; DePauw Univ, 1984; Univ Strasbourg, 1984; pa/Asst to VP, Starline Corporation, 1982; Switchboard/Mail/Ofc Clk, Equitable Life Assurance Soc, 1981; Accounts Receivables Clk, Ser on Wheels Hosp Supply, 1981; cp/VP Sr Class; Varsity Cheerleading Capt; S'ship Chm; Alpha Chi Omega Mem; Mgmt Fellows Prog; Intramurals Rep; r/Cath; hon/IL St Scholar; Inaugural Class of DePauw Univ Mgmt Fellows Prog; W/W Among Am HS Students; g/Mgmt Position or Financial Conslt Position.

BALL, BETH ANN oc/Student; b/Oct 6, 1966; h/1059 Riverside Drive, Battle Creek, MI 49015; p/Earl and Betty Ball, Battle Creek, MI; ed/Lakeview HS, 1984; pa/Vol Clerical Wk, Calhoun Co Hlth Dept, 1983; Cashier, McDonald's, 1983-; Babysitter; Swim Team, Syncronized Swim Team; Yrbook Staff; Bapt Yth Grp; r/Bapt; hon/Sch Newspaper Pubs; Hon Roll; g/to Attend Col.

BANICK, PAUL DAVID oc/Student; b/Sep 5, 1961; h/6 Sand Hill Road, Stanhope, NJ 07874; p/Paul and Kay B Banick, Stanhope, NJ; ed/Pope John XXIII HS, 1979; BS magna cum laude 1983, Villanova Univ, 1983; pa/Analytical Chem, Phila Gas Wks, 1982; Tchg Asst in Chem, Villanova Univ, 1982; Pvt Tutor in Chem, 1982-83; cp/Resident Student Assn; Villanova Univ Astronom Soc; Physics Clb; Alpha Epsilon Delta; Pres, Sigma Pi Sigma; Sigma Phi Epsilon; Am Chem Soc; Lakeland Rescue Squad; Villanova Chem Soc; Villanova Univ Curric Coun; Pi Mu Epsilon Math Hon Soc; Lakeland Diving Squad; Ch Custodian; Polit Campaign Photog; hon/Author of "Black Holes" Adv Sci Pub, 1982; Res Grant from NASA; CRS Press Awd for Excell in Chem; Dean's List; Salutatorian; Phi Kappa Phi; Am Chem Soc Awd in Chem; W/W Am Cols & Univs; Nat Deans List; Med Sch Grant; g/Georgetown Med Sch.

BANKS, LORI LEANN oc/Student; b/Aug 24, 1964; h/Route 2, Box 17, Meadows of Dan, VA 24120; p/Harlon and Betty Banks, Meadow of Dan, VA; ed/Patrick Co HS, 1982; VA Polytech Inst & St Univ; pa/Nat Pk Concessions; Mabry Mill Interpreter; cp/Lady Hokie Cheerleader, VPI, 1983-; Nat Beta Clb; Monogram Clb; Band; Gymnastics

Team (Most Improved); Cheerldg CoCapt, Capt; Student Coop Assn Secy; Jr Marshal; 4-H Adult Ldr; Heart Assn; MS; Bapt Ch; Fitness Awds; Spec Olympics Chm; hon/Homecoming Queen, Rep; Soc Dist'd Am HS Students; W/W; Yg Commun Ldrs Am; g/ Computer Sci Maj.

BANKS, PAMELA oc/LSM Clerk; b/ Aug 29, 1961; h/5758-A Saloma, St Louis, MO 63120; ba/St Louis, MO; p/ Elnora B Mitchell, St Louis, MO; ed/ Northwest HS & Ohallon Tech, 1978; Att'g Forest Park CC; UMSL, 1979; pa/ Clk/Typist, Corps of Engrs, 1977, 1978; LSM Clk, Main Post Ofc, 1978-; cp/Yg Lwyrs Sect, Bar Assn; FBLA; Proj Close-up; Jr Achmt; Col Prep; Sigma Gamma Rho Sorority Inc; Barbizon; Exclusively Eric Model; r/Bapt, Grace Bapt Gospel Chorus; hon/Nat Merit Lttr, 1977; Nat Hon Roll, 1976; W/W Among Am HS Students; Intl Yth Achmt; g/Corporation Law, Modeling.

BARAKAT, ABDEL-RAOUF IBRA-HIM b/Oct 3, 1964; h/4315 Leesville Road, 24 H, Raleigh, NC 27612; p/ Ibrahim A and Siham I Barakat, Raleigh, NC; ed/HS, 1981; NC St Univ; pa/ Salesman, The Cheese Shop, 1979-; cp/ Bd Dirs Am Freedom Assn; Raleigh Chess Clb; Sci Clb; NHS; French Clb; Am Space Foun; Broughton Commun Assn; r/Muslim; hon/Spkg Contest Trip Winner; Engrg Freshman Hon Soc, Phi Eta Sigma & Alpha Lambda Delta; Engrg Hon Soc; NC Scholastic Chess Champ; W/W Am HS Students; Intl Yth Achmt; Commun Ldrs Am.

BARBEIRO, THOMAS EUGENE oc/ Room Service Waiter/Student; b/Jul 12, 1961; h/1409 West 3rd Street, 1-A, Chico, CA 95926; ba/Lake Tahoe, NV; p/Eugene and Katherine Barbeiro, Auburn, CA; ed/Att'd Sierra Col, 1979-81; CA St Univ, 1981-82; Butte Col, 1983-; pa/Fam Owned Bus, 1978-; Intern Employee, CA Dept Economic & Bus Devel, 1980; Supvr, Waiter, Sambo's Restaurant, 1978-81; Cook/Food Prep, Ranch House Restaurant, 1981; Waiter, Cook, Fredrico's Mexican Restaurant & Loung, 1981; Room Ser Waiter/Cashier, Harrah's Hotel/Casino, 1982-83; r/Bapt; hon/Kiwanis/Key Club Ser Awd, 1977; W/W Among Am HS Students; g/Civil Engrg Deg, Peace Corp.

BARBOUR, CATHY ANN oc/Nurse; b/Dec 31, 1959; h/1139 N Church Street, Apt B-4, Greensboro, NC 27401; ba/Greensboro, NC; p/Frank Barbour, Angier, NC and Florence Barbour, Dunn, NC; ed/Dunn HS, 1978; BS, UNC-Chapel Hill, 1983; pa/RN Applicant, Moses Cone Hosp, 1983-; HS, Jr Tri-HY-Y, FHA, Sci Clb, FBLA, Beta Clb; Col, Resident Hall Govt, NCMH, Student Hlth Action Com Clin; Orient Cnslr, Student Nurses Assn; Student Advocacy Com; r/Bapt; hon/Dean's List; S'ships incl'g James M Johnston Nsg S'ship; Order of Silver Key; DAR Good Citizenship Awd Nom; Commun Ldrs Am; g/Grad Sch, Nurse Practitioner.

BARBOUR, JULIA DONETTE oc/ Student; b/Apr 27, 1966; h/Route 3, Box 400, Benson, NC 27504; p/Mr and Mrs Barry Barbour; Benson, NC; ed/S Johnston HS, 1984; cp/Track, Monogram, F'ship Christian Ath; Quill & Scroll; Palladium; Nat Hon Soc; Pep Clb; Acad Superbowl; r/Bapt, Ch Choir, Ch

Yt Grp; hon/Hist & Sci Awd, 1982; Nat Jour Awd, 1983; Homecoming Ct, 1981; Outstg Freshman; Gov's Sch Nom; W/ W Am HS Students.

BARDEN, CHIFFON oc/Student; b/ Nov 4, 1965; h/718 Mallory Street, Forrest City, AR 72335; p/Mr and Mrs Roosevelt Barden, Forrest City, AR; ed/ Forrest City HS; cp/Eureka Civic & Soc Clb; Beta Clb; r/Bapt; hon/Yg Black Am; R & R Res Outstg Students; W/W Am HS Students; Miss Black Teenage World, St Francis Co; g/Lawyer.

BARDIS, BYRON GALEN b/Jan 21, 1967; h/2533 Orkney, Toledo, OH 43606; p/Dr and Mrs Panos D Bardis, Toledo, OH; ed/Ottawa Hills HS, 1985; cp/BSA; Beer Can Collectors Am, 1978-; Toledo Jr Orch, 1979-82; Toledo Yth Orch, 1982-85; hon/Num Pubs incl'g "To Pres Reagan" (poem, w Jason Bardis), *The News World*, 1981, "Chem Wizard" 1985; Enrichment Math for Gifted, 1978; Hon Classes, 1979-85; Photog, "Arrowhead", 1981-82; Geometry Contest, 7th out of 550, 1982; Semifinalist, Nat Merit S'ship Competition, 1984; W/W Am HS Students.

BAREFOOT, ELIZABETH NICOLE oc/Student; b/Dec 22, 1966; h/Route 6, Box 48, Dunn, NC 28334; p/Mr and Mrs Hilton R Barefoot, Dunn, NC; ed/Att'g HS; cp/Beta Clb; 4-H; Chp for Perf Arts for 4-H; Harnett Co Arts Coun; Sch Chorus; Sch Tennis Team; Basketball; Cheerleader; r/Prot, Ch Choir; hon/ Hdmaster's List; Soc of Dist'd HS Students; Nom for Intl Fgn Lang Awd; Rec'd Rel Awd at Sch; Class Secy/Treas; Gov's Sch Dance; NC Perf Arts Troupe for 4-H; Nat French Contest in NC; g/ Col.

BARFOOT, RANDY LYNN oc/Student; b/Mar 3, 1962; h/4704 Bridle Path Lane, Greensboro, NC 27410; ba/ Charlotte, NC; p/Mr and Mrs James H Barfoot, Greensboro, NC; ed/Walter Hines Page HS, 1980; UNC—Charlotte, 1984; pa/Sales Clk, Blumenthal's Mens & Boys Wear, 1977-81; Acctg Clk, Ciba Geigy Corporation, 1981-82; Lifeguard, UNC-Charlotte, 1982-; cp/Delta Zeta Sorority, Social Chm, Hist, & Chaplain; ARC Blood Drives; Vol, Spec Olympics; Fund Raising, Am Diabetes Assn; UNC-Charlotte Intramurals; Vol, Charlotte NC Rehab Hosp; Mem, AIESEC; r/Judaism; hon/HS-One of most Outstg Srs; Student Coun; W/W Among Am HS Yth, Among Greensboro NC Yth; g/Grad Sch, Pursue Career in Mktg & Advtg.

BARGER, GRACE oc/Mother, Wife, Student; b/Jan 4, 1946; h/Route 2, Box 462, Atoka, TN 38004; m/David L; c/ David L Jr, Anthony A; p/Mrs Celia Chaney, Chula Vista, CA; sp/Mr and Mrs D C Sitz, Floresville, TX; ed/ Waipahu Adult Sch, 1969; Trend Setters Intl Beauty Sch, 1971; San Joaquin Delta Jr Col; Att'g Memphis St Univ; cp/Gamma Beta Phi Nat Hon Student Org, Pres, 1983-84; hon/Dean's List, San Joaquin Delta Jr Col; Dean's List, Memphis St Univ; Lttr Commend, Chief of Naval Opers, 1974; g/Maj-Intl Bus & Fgn Lang.

BARGER, KARLENE oc/Missionary; b/Dec 28, 1959; h/Star Route, Box 33, Preston, ID 83263; p/Donald N Barger; ed/Preston HS, 1978; Assoc Deg, Ricks Col; BS, Brigham Young Univ, 1982; cp/ Girls Track, Editor Sch Paper; Pres,

Home Ec, Rick's Col; Lambda Delta Sigma; Sigma Delta Omicron; r/Ch of Jesus Christ LDS, Pres Wom Assn; hon/ Nat Hon Soc; Intl Yth in Achmt; FHA; Phi Kappa Phi; 4-H Watch Awd, Most Outstg; Pres Awd; g/Home Ext Agt.

BARGER, NORMA RAY oc/Special Ed Teacher; b/Jun 4, 1961; h/1004 Jefferson Davis Boulevard, Apartment 214, Fredericksburg, VA 22401; ba/ Spotsylvania, VA; p/Raymond (dec) and Christine S Barger, Eagle Rock, VA; ed/ James River HS, 1979; BS, James Madison Univ, 1983; pa/Spec Ed Tchr, Spotsylvania Co HS, 1983-84; cp/NTA, 1983-84; Student Ed Assn, 1979-83; CEC, 1980-83; Yth Assn Retarded Citizens, 1980-83; r/Meth; hon/Grad 5th HS Class, 1979; Magna Cum Laude, James Madison Univ, 1983; W/W Among Am HS Students; g/to Cont'd Study in Spec Ed.

BARLOW, DANA SCOTT oc/Medical Student; b/Apr 4, 1957; ed/Aurora HS, 1975; BS, Lynchburg Col, 1980; Post Grad Wk, VPI & SU, 1981-82; cp/ Nat Beta Clb-HS, 1975; Am Med Assn; r/Bapt; hon/Dean's List, 1978-80; W/W Among Am HS Students; g/Neurosurg.

BARLOWE, AMY b/Jan 20, 1952; h/ 754 Mill Street, Southeast, Salem, OR 97301; p/Sy and Dorothea Barlowe; ed/ A G Berner HS, 1970; BM 1975, MM 1976, Juilliard Sch; Juilliard Pre-Col Div, 1969-70; Meadowmount Sch Music, 1969-76; pa/Concert Violinist/Violist; Fdr, Sr Hons Baroque Ensemble; Fdr-Dir, Williamette Univ Pre-Col Div of Music; Concert Master Salem Symph; Local 99, Lectr, Classes for Commun, Local 802; Fdr, Sprg String Fest; Recitals as Soloist & Violinist with OR Trio-Perf throughout W Coast in Addition to Commun; Solo & Duo Recitals, E & W Coasts; Radio & TV; cp/ASTA; OMTA; hon/Author of "Sprg Thing on a Shoestring" ASTA Jour, 1982, "A Guide for Enjoyable Listening", 1983; Helena Rubinstein Foun S'ship; Atkinson Fund Grants; NW Area Grant; F'ships, Meadowmount Sch; NHS; Great Neck Symph & Massapequa Symph S'ships; W/W Am Wom; Intl Yth in Achmt; W/W Am Music (classical); Merit Awd, Williamette Univ, 1983; Sabbatical, 1983; g/Attain Recording Contracts, Maj Recitals, Perfs in Maj Cities; Continue Transcribing Lit for Solo Violin.

BARNES, ALEXANDER FREDERICK oc/Technical Writer; b/Feb 24, 1955; h/Millcreek Apartment 18, 2732 Park Avenue, Petersburg, VA 23805; ba/Petersburg, VA; m/Michele Anne; p/ Mr and Mrs F S Barnes, Rome, NY; sp/ Mr and Mrs M A Capani, Binghamton, NY; ed/H H Arnold HS, 1973; BS 1980, MA 1982, St Univ NY; mil/USMC, 1974-77; ANG, 1977-83; pa/Crew Chief & Artifact Analyst, Public Archaeol Facility, 1980-82; Tech Writer, Diversified Data Corporation, 1982-; Soc Logistics Engrs, 1982-83; Co Mil Hists, 1982-83; Marine Corps Leag, 1977-80; cp/Cortland Rugby Ftball Clb, 1978-80; St Univ NY Cortland, Anthropology Clb, 1977-80; St Univ NY Binghamton, Anthropology Grad Org, 1980-82; r/ Presb; hon/Author of "Losing the Buckland Races", Mil Images 1980, "Indoor Tow Tng", Inf, 1982; Magna Cum Laude, Dean's List; USMC Good Conduct Medal; NY St Medal for Ser

in & of Civil Auth; NATO Commend; NY St Mil Commend Medal; Commun Ldrs Am; g/Logistics Engrg & Tng.

BARNES, ALICE ELIZABETH oc/ Student; b/Jun 22, 1962; h/461 Dewey Street, Delphos, OH 45833; p/Harvey and Ladonna Barnes, Delphos, OH; ed/ St John's HS, 1980; AA, OH St Univ, 1982; pa/Res Asst, OH St Univ, 1981-82; Student Tchg, Shawnee Elmwood, Elida Elem, 1981, 1982; Pvt Tutoring, 1983; Mem, SNEA, 1981-82; cp/Pres, OH St Univ, Lima Student Adv Com, 1981-82; Rep, Alpha Lambda Delta, Phi Eta Sigma, OH St Univ Reg Affairs Com, 1981-82; Mem, Chimes, 1982-83; Mem, Phi Kappa Phi, 1983; r/ Mormon; hon/Author of Pubs; OH St Univ Dean's List, 1980-83; Alpha Lambda Delta & Phi Eta Sigma; Chimes; Phi Kappa Phi; Buckeye Awd & Summa Awd, 1982; W/W; Intl Yth in Achmt; Commun Ldrs Am; Am Outstg Names & Faces; g/to help others in Achieving Gtr Self-Knowledge.

BARNETT, DUANE ALAN oc/Student; b/Jul 9, 1965; h/Route 1, Normandy, TN 37360; p/Mr and Mrs James T Barnett, Normandy, TN; ed/Shelbyville Ctl HS, 1983; cp/4-H, Treas, Countywide Clb; r/Luth; hon/Nat Hon Soc, 1982-83; W/W Among Am HS Students; g/Vet Med.

BARNETT, KELLY DENISE oc/Physical Therapist Aid; b/Dec 7, 1963; h/ Route 2, Box 68, Kevil, KY 42053; ba/ Paducah, KY; p/Mr and Mrs William C Barnett, Kevil, KY; ed/Georgetown Col, 1981; Paducah Commun Col, 1982-83; Union Univ, 1983-85; cp/Ch Choir; Yth Commun Chorus; Little Ch Ldr; Puppet Min; Acteens; FCA; BSU; FHA; Annual, Newspaper Staff; Broadcasting Clb; HS Chorus; Jr/Sr Play Cast Mem; Flag Corp; Rifle Corp; Phy Therapy Vol; hon/Beta Clb S'ship; FTA S'ship; Outstg Mem, FHA; 2nd Pl, FHA Creed Contest; Citizenship Awd; Hon Grad; W/W Among AM HS Students; Commun Ldrs Am; g/RN Prog, 1983-85.

BARNETT, THOMAS COOPER JR oc/Student; b/Nov 27, 1964; h/Post Office Box 152, Hernando, MS 38632; ba/Hernando, MS; p/Mr and Mrs Milton Smith, Hernando, MS; ed/Att'g Hernando HS; cp/Varsity Ftball, 2 Lttrs, Most Improved Player; Most Outstg Defensive Back, Player of Wk; Spanish Clb; Rotary Clb Intl Ldrship Conf Rep; Reg Jr Sci & Humanities Symp; Pan Am Pageant Spkr; MS Sci & Math Exam; r/Bapt; hon/Writes Basketball Article, DeSoto Co Tribune; Nat Hon Soc; Quill & Scroll; 3rd in Sr Class; Nat Sci Merit Awd; W/W Among Am HS Students; g/Mech or Elect Engrg.

BARONE, MARK ANTHONY oc/ Student, Graduate Research Assistant; b/May 2, 1960; h/800 West Oak, Ft Collins, CO 80521; ba/Ft Collins, CO; p/Mr and Mrs Salvatore Barone, Tonawanda, NY; ed/BA, 1982, Canisius Col; Presently MS Student at CO St Univ; pa/Lab Instr; Mem, Intl Embryo Transfer Soc; Treas, Wn NY JA Assn; Beta Beta Beta; Campus Programming Bd; New Student Orient Com; Vol, Med Ctr; hon/NHS; Canisius, NYS Regents S'ships; Dean's List; Nat Dean's List; Intl Yth in Achmt; Grad, Magna Cum Laude; W/W Among Students; g/Res Scist.

BARR-DUFFY, VICKI LYNN oc/ Student; b/Aug 4, 1958; h/9831 Greenmoor Drive, New Haven, IN 46774; m/ Robert Thomas; p/Mr and Mrs Harley E Barr, New Haven, IN; sp/Thomas E (dec) and Ruth Duffy, Rocky River, OH; ed/New Haven HS, 1976; BS, IN Univ, 1981; Master's Prog at IN Univ; Order Entry & Invoicing Clk; cp/German Clb; Alumni Clb, IN Univ; Vol, Inner City Missions; Vol, Eng Dept, HS; Judge, New Haven HS Homecoming Parade; hon/Nat Col Dean's List; IN Univ Acad S'ships & Dean's List; Yg Commun Ldrs Am; Yg Personalities Am; g/Tchng Career.

BARRETT, LESLIE ELIZABETH oc/ Student; b/Sep 4, 1965; h/129 Vance Avenue, Cedartown, GA 30125; p/Mr and Mrs William R Barrett, Cedartown, GA; ed/Cedartown HS, 1983; cp/Band HS, 1979-83; Hon Soc, 1979-83; Sci Clb, 1979-83; Key Clb, 1979-83; Band Sect Ldr, 1979-83; r/Bapt, First Bapt Ch; hon/GA Cert Merit, 1982; Band Mem of Mo; Yth of Mo; Hon Grad; Outstg Student in Humanities; Sr Hist Awd, 1983; Freshman Sci Awd, 1980; g/ Engrg.

BARRETTE, JEANNINE R oc/Salesperson; b/Apr 12, 1960; h/1097 Mendon Road, Woonsocket, RI 03895; ba/Providence, RI; p/Lucien and Blanche Barrette, Woonsocket, RI; ed/Woonsocket HS; BA, Anna Maria Col, 1981; pa/Corp Brothers, 1983-; CO-OP Credit Union, 1981-; cp/Sophomore Rep, Student Acad Affairs Com; Jr Rep, Resident Life Com; Writer, Images; Yrbook Staff; hon/Dean's List, 1977-81; The Dr Bernadette Madore Awd for Acad Excell for #1 Grad, 1981; Nat Dean's List; Intl Yth in Achmt; Yg Commun Ldrs of Am; Dir Dist'd Ams; g/MBA.

BARRINGER, JUDY LYNN b/Aug 23, 1963; h/155 Pearce Parkway, Pearl River, NY 10965; p/Mr and Mrs W C Barringer, Pearl River, NY; ed/Pearl River HS, 1981; King's Col; pa/Student; MENC, Secy, VP; United Students Assn Cnslrs; cp/Choral & Sr Play Accompanist; Band Secy, Rep; Drama Clb; Yrbook Staff; Col Choir; NHS; Ch Yth Grp; Col Musical Min; hon/Col Pres S'ship; MENC S'ship, 1983; Paula Boheveskv Perf Arts S'ship; Col Acad S'ship; g/Bus Adm.

BARSTOW, JUDY KAY b/Oct 11, 1957; h/4820 Eagle Street, Denver, CO 80239; ba/Denver, CO; m/Charles Alden Jr; c/Jennifer Diane; p/Lewis Bowman, Logansport, IN; ed/Lewis Cass Jr-Sr HS, 1976; BS, IN St Univ, 1981; pa/Paralegal Secy; Housewife; cp/ NHS; Sigma Kappa Pres; Alpha Lambda Delta; Pamarista; Nat Secy Assn; Diving Coach Vol; hon/The Dean's List; Outstg Yg Wom of Am; W/W Am Cols & Univs; g/Fam; Civil Ser Wk.

BARTH, FELICIA BETH oc/Student; b/Apr 6, 1961; h/Route 1, Box 163-A, Comfort, TX 78013; p/Mr and Mrs Felix Louis Barth, Comfort, TX; ed/Comfort HS, 1979; AA, Schreiner Col, 1981; BBA, Univ TX, 1983; pa/Secy 1982, Reporter 1983, Fritztown Sqs; cp/Secy, WOW Grove 6932; Herman Sons; Acctg Clb; German Clb; Fritztown Sqs; Fam Dance Clb; Tennis, 1975-76; Tm Mem 1975-76, Mgr 1976-77, Track; Basketball Mgr, 1975-76 & 1978-79; Parliamentn, Drama Clb, 1975-79; Spanish

Clb, 1975-79; Mem 1975-79, Libn 1977-78, Asst Drum Maj 1978-79, Band; hon/Lttr & Capt, Volleyball Tm, HS; Flute Solo (1st Pl 1975-78 & 1978-79, 2nd Pl 1976-77), Flute Ensemble (1st Pl 1977-78 & 1978-79, 2nd Pl 1975-76), Spelling (1975-79), Prose Rdg (1975-76), News Writing (1978-79), Num Sense (1975-76), Univ Interscholastic Leag; All-Dist Band, 1975-79, Dist Winner 1976-77 & 1978-79; All-Reg Band, 1976-77 & 1978-79; Most Outstg Musician Trophy, 1978-79; Ranked 10th, Grad'g Class, 1978-79; Acad Dean's Hon Mention Roll, 1979-82; W/W Among Am HS Students; Intl Yth Achmt; Yg Personalities S; Personalities Am; Yg Commun Ldrs Am; World W/W Wom; Intl Register Profiles; g/CPA.

BARTMAN, KELLI A oc/Registered Nurse; b/Jul 2, 1960; h/Route 1, Box 208, Perkiomenville, PA 18074; ba/Allentown, PA; ed/Boyertown Area Sr HS, 1978; BSN, WV Wesleyan Col, 1982; pa/Cnslr, Pottsgrove Sch Dist Rec, 1978-80; Nsg Asst, Grandview Hosp, 1981-82; RN, Leigh Val Hosp Ctr, 1982-; Jr Rep 1980-81, Pres 1981-82, Student Nurses Wesleyan; Student Nurses Devel Com, 1980-82; cp/Alpha Delta Pi; Col Field Hockey & Basketball; Basketball, Volleyball Intramurals; r/Luth; hon/Sigma Theta Tau; Sigma Theta Tau Ways & Means Com; Wesleyan Freshman S'ship; Wesieyan Hon S'ship; g/Masters Prog, Critical Care Course.

BARTYLLA, JAMES ROBERT oc/Public Accountant; b/Dec 20, 1961; h/West 220 South 3731 Hidden Court, Waukesha, WI 53186; p/Mr and Mrs Donald H Bartylla, Waukesha, WI; ed/Waukesha South HS, 1979; BBA, Univ 1983, Univ WI-Whitewater; pa/Pres, Fin Assn, 1982; Pres, Silver Scroll Hon Soc, 1982-83; Acad Adv, 1982; Vol Income Tax Asst Prog, 1983; Beta Gamma Sigma Scholastic Hon Soc, 1982-83; Dean's Adv Coun, 1982; Law Soc; Beta Alpha Psi Profl Acct Frat; Phi Eta Sigma; Phi Kappa Phi; Acct Tutor, Noncompensatory; hon/Donald Beattie Univ WI Col Bus & Ec S'ship, 1982; Arthur H Carter Am Acctg Assn S'ship, 1983; 2nd Pl NAA Student Manuscript Contest, 1983; Hon Mention, Beta Alpha Psi Student Manuscript Contest, 1983; Nat Dean's List; Intl Yth Achmt; W/W Among Students Am Univs & Cols; Commun Ldrs Am.

BARTYLLA, THOMAS EDWARD oc/Student; b/Aug 6, 1964; h/West 220, South 3731 Hidden Court, Waukesha, WI 53186; p/Mr and Mrs Donald H Bartylla, Waukesha, WI; ed/Waukesha South HS, 1982; Att'g Univ WI; pa/Karate Instr, Four Winds Taekwondo Acad, Waukesha YWCA, 1981-; Profl Ednl Conslt, 1983, SWn Co; VP Undergrad Student Adv Com, Univ WI; r/Rom Cath; hon/Phi Eta Sigma Freshman Hon Soc; VP, Phi Eta Sigma, Student of Mo, Physics-Sci Dept, Waukesha S HS; g/Fin & Mgmt BBA Deg.

BASDEN, ALFRED DARRELL oc/Student; b/May 26, 1966; h/Post Office Box 747, Beulaville, NC 28518; p/Alfred and Vernell Basden, Beulaville, NC; ed/East Duplin HS, 1984; cp/Career Exploration Clb Am, Pres; Sci Clb; Masquerators; Spanish Clb; FTA; Baseball; Basketball; Ftball; Monogram Clb; hon/All Conf Baseball, 1983; Outstg Sr,

1983; Spanish Awd, 1983; g/to become SBI Agt or Hwy Patrolman.

BASS, ANNA LEE oc/Student; b/Jun 8, 1967; h/Route 1, Post Office Box 214, Seaboard, NC 27876; p/Mr and Mrs Robert D Bass Jr, Seaboard, NC; ed/Halifax Acad, 1985; cp/Beta Club, VP; Student Govt, VP; Monogram Clb; Basketball; Softball-All Conf; r/Cath; hon/Soc Dist'd Am HS Students; MVP, Basketball, 1983; All-Conf Softball, 1983; g/Law.

BASS, MERRIAM ALEXANDER oc/Photographer/Writer; b/Sep 14, 1951; h/1200 Union Street, Brunswick, GA 31520; ba/Same; m/J Richard; p/Mrs Carlton Alexander, St Simons Isl, GA; ed/Brent Sch, 1970; BA, St Andrews Presb Col, 1974; AB, Daytona Bch Commun Col, 1979; pa/Coor of Promo, Montreat Conf Ctr; cp/Profl Photog of Am; Profl Photog of GA; Profl Photog of FL; Daytona Bch Photog Soc; SS Tchr, Presb; Ch Newslttr Editor; Pictorial Dir Com; Stewardship Com; r/Presb; hon/"Presb Survey", 1982, 1983; "Presb Wom", 1983; High Hon Grad, Daytona Bch Commun Col; W/W: Am Cols & Univs, Am Jr Cols; Commun Ldrs Am.

BASTIN, LOUIS DEAN b/Dec 23, 1962; h/RR 1 Box 87, Selden, KS 67757; p/Mr and Mrs Dean Bastin, Selden, KS; ed/Golden Plains HS, 1981; AA, Colby Commun Col, 1983; Att'g KS St Univ; pa/HS-Hon Roll; Ch Yth Grp Pres; Forensics; Sch Plays; Basketball, Track, Baseball; Band; Choir; Sophomore Class Pres; Jr Class Treas; Student Coun Pres; Cub Scouts; Am Legion Boys St; Col-Phi Theta Kappa, Nat Hon Soc; Gold Keys Ser Org, Pres; Col Baseball; cp/Cowboys for Christ; MDA Dance-a-thon; r/Mem Rexford Commun Ch; hon/St of KS Scholar; KS Hon Student; Pres Scholar; W/W Among Students Am Jr Cols; Nat Dean's List; Pres Hon Roll; Commun Ldrs Am; Intl Yth Achmt.

BATCHELOR, PATRICIA ANN oc/Payroll Clerk; b/May 31, 1962; h/68 East Grove, Morocco, IN; p/Mr and Mrs Larry Batchelor Sr, Morocco, IN; ed/N Newton HS, 1981; IN Bus Col, 1982; pa/Payroll Clk, Remington Freight Lines; cp/4-H; FBLA; NHS; Indep Res, Study, Royal Neighbors Am; hon/W/W Among Am HS Students; Intl Yth Achm; Outstg Am Names & Faces; Yg Commun Ldrs Am.

BATES, WILLIAM RANDALL oc/Student; b/Dec 14, 1962; h/Post Office Box 213, Spring Arbor, MI 49283; ba/Same; p/Gerald and Marlene Bates; ed/Wn HS, 1981; Att'g Sprg Arbor Col; pa/UPS; Box Factory; Camp Maintenance; Rest Home; Pres, Freshman HS Class; VP, Soph Class; Student Coun; Ch Yth Grp Ldr; Prefect of Dorm; Campaign, Election Wkr; Pres, Freshman Col Class; Student Cong Chm; Constitutional Review Com; Parliamentn, Student Cong, Col; Freshman Devel Ldr; Rugby, Soccer; Competition Writer; r/Free Meth, Sun Sch Tchr; hon/Citizenship Awd; Meritorious Ser & Dedication to Student Cong Recog; g/Law or Diplomatic Wk.

BATGOS, JOANNA b/Jan 1, 1964; h/796 Worthington Road, Wayne, PA 19087; p/Mr and Mrs James Batgos; ed/Conestoga Sr HS; Amherst Col; pa/Student; cp/AFS; Wom's Rugby Team;

Student Housing Liason; hon/Nat Merit Finalist; Sr Class Treas; Chm, Baccalaureate Com; W/W Among Am HS Students; Commun Ldrs Am; g/Psychol.

BATISTE, AMY LEILANI oc/Student; b/Jul 9, 1965; h/709 Fawndale Lane, San Antonio, TX 78239; ba/San Antonio, TX; p/Lt Col and Mrs H E Batiste Jr, San Antonio, TX; ed/Theodore Roosevelt HS, 1983; pa/Pres, Freshman Class; VP, Sophomore Class; VP, Pres, Student Coun; Asst Drum Maj; Chm, Elect Com, Pres Clb; Chm, Homecoming; Rough Rider Band; Secy, NE Student Coun Assn; Mem, NE Indep Sch Dist-Sch Pride Com; Pres, Sr Troop 11; Alamo Assn Student Couns; r/United Meth; hon/Num Univ Interscholastic Leag Music/Acad Awds; Roosevelt HS Miss Teen Optimist; Outstg Student Coun Mem Awd; Am Legion, Outstg Girl Awd; g/Career in Corporate Communs.

BATSON, STEVE WESLEY oc/Assistant to President, Director of Planning; b/Aug 20, 1946; h/2418 Westgate Drive, Commerce, TX 75428; ba/Commerce, TX; m/Sara James; p/Mr and Mrs John T Batson, Macon, GA; ed/Lanier HS, 1965; BA, Mercer Univ, 1970; EdM 1974, EdS 1978, GA Col; pa/Asst to Pres, Dir of Planning, E TX St Univ; Kiwanis of Statesboro; GA Acad Sci; Soc of Univ & Col Planning; Assn of Inst Res; Nat Assn of Sec'dy Sch Prins; Nat Assn Biol Tchrs; Nat Org on Legal Problems of Ed; hon/Outstg Yg Alumni, GA Col; GA Power Ldrs of Tomorrow Prog; Outstg Grad Paper, Sci Ed Div, GA Acad of Sci Annual Meeting; g/Higher Ed Am, Tch & Pub in Area of Ed Law.

BATTIN, KIMBERLY SUE oc/Student; b/Aug 6, 1960; h/77 Finlay Place, Vailsburg, NJ 07106; m/Cristian Gibson; p/Mr and Mrs Dale E Battin, Belle Mead, NJ; sp/Mr and Mrs Jay Decker, Peninsula, OH; ed/Walton Comprehensive HS; BS, Marshall Univ, 1981; Med Sch, Univ Med & Dentistry of NJ; cp/Senator, Pres Pro Tem, Student Govt; Chm, Rules Com, Fac Eval Com; RHGA Rep; Chi Beta Phi; Gamma Beta Phi; Tutor, Chem, Phys; Blood Drive Wkr; r/Meth; hon/Dean's List; W/W Am Cols; g/Pediatrician.

BATTLE, JULIET LEE oc/Clerk, City of Milwaukee, Bureau of Forestry; b/Sep 11, 1957; h/1836 East Pryor Avenue, Milwaukee, WI 53207; ba/Milwaukee, WI; m/Clyde O; p/Mr and Mrs Frank T Lee, Greendale, WI; sp/Mr and Mrs O C Battle, Milwaukee, WI; ed/Greendale HS, 1975; BA, Carroll Col, 1979; MS, Univ WI, 1981; pa/Clerk, City of Milwaukee; Am Pers & Guid Assn; Nat Rehab Assn; cp/Phi Alpha Theta; VP, Pres Beta Rho Chapt; r/Rom Cath; hon/Author of "Badgers for a Free KS: The WI KS Emigrant Aid Soc" *Milwaukee Hist*, 1979; Sigma Epsilon Sigma; Phi Eta Sigma; Kappa Delta Pi; Delta Sigma Nu; Pres S'ship; RSA Traineeship; Intl W/W Wom; Dic Intl Biography; g/Rehab Cnslr.

BATTLE, RENEE oc/Student; b/Feb 15, 1964; h/3901 Suitland Road, Suitland, MD 20746; p/Percy and Blanche Battle, Suitland, MD; ed/Suitland Sr HS, 1982; Wheaton Col, 1986; cp/HS-Acad Hon Roll; VP, Hon Soc; VP, Sr Class; Spanish Hon Soc; Spanish Clb; Lttrman's Clb; Drill Tm; Student Govt

Rep; Clb Coun; hon/Intl Fgn Lang Awd; Yg Am of the Mo; W/W Among Am HS Students; g/Law Sch, Patent Law.

BATTLES, OSCAR EUGENE oc/Student; b/Mar 18, 1962; h/Route 5, Box 325-A, Gadsden, AL 35903; p/Mr and Mrs M E Battles, Gadsden, AL; ed/Hokes Bluff HS, 1980; Jacksonville St Univ; Att'g Univ AL; pa/Vol, The Chd's Hosp AL, 1982-83; Peer Adv, Univ AL, 1983; Univ AL Biol Clb; cp/VP, Key Clb; Beta Clb; VP, SGA; Am Legion Boys' St; Pres, Jr Class; Cnslrs S'ship to Jacksonville St Univ; Dean's List; hon/Phi Eta Sigma; Intl Yth Achmt; W/W Among AM HS Students; Alpha Epsilon Delta; Personalities of Am; Commun Ldrs Am; g/Med.

BATTO, ELIZABETH BERNADETTE oc/Student/Secretary; b/Feb 25, 1961; h/1115 North LBJ-A 4, San Marcos, TX 78666; p/Raymond and Elizabeth Batto, Bandera, TX; ed/Bandera HS, 1979; BS, 1984, SW TX St Univ; pa/Teller, Secy, Bkkpg, 1st Nat Bk; Secy, SW TX Univ-Sch of Ed; Assn Guid Assocs; TX St Tchrs Assn; cp/SW TX; Assoc Student Govt; Residential Ofcr; Nat Hon Soc; r/Cath; hon/Dist'd Am HS Students; Commun Ldrs Am; Doane Scholar; g/Bus Tchr or Cnslr.

BAUER, MARY LELIA oc/International Program Officer-State Department; b/Dec 5, 1958; h/1201 South Courthouse Road, Number 201, Arlington, VA 22204; ba/Washington, DC; p/Mr and Mrs John Bauer, Rochester, MI; ed/Avondale Sr HS, 1977; BA, Aquinas Col, 1981; pa/Sr Biling Asst, Am Motors, 1982-83; Intl Progs Ofcr, State Dept, 1983-; Tchg Asst; cp/Pi Delta Phi; Lambda Iota Tao; Pres, French Clb; VChm, Commun Senate; Acad Assem; Campus Min; Student Tutor; Lib Com; Commun Action Vol of Aquinas; Secy, Residence Hall Coun; hon/Valedictorian, 1977; Summa Cum Laude Grad; Monsignor Bukowski Outstg Sr Awd; Commun Ser Awd; W/W Col; Commun Ldrs Am; g/MS-French Linguistics.

BAUER, ZANE RANDELL oc/Student; b/Dec 14, 1965; h/Mason Route, Box 92, Llano, TX 78643; p/J W Bauer, Llano, TX; ed/Att'g HS; cp/Jr Maine-Anjou Assn; Varsity Ftball & Golf; FFA; Nat Hon Soc; FTA; Jets; TCCA; Am Yorkshire Assn; Am Jr Maine, Anjou Assoc; r/Luth, St James Luth Ch; hon/Dist & Local Star Greenhand; High Ranking Freshman & Sophomore; Dist Reporter for FFA; g/Deg Animal Sci.

BAUGHMAN, TERRY W oc/Electronics Engineer; b/Feb 15, 1960; h/Post Office Box 182, Chambersburg, PA 17201; p/Mr and Mrs Robert G Baughman Sr; ed/Chambersburg Area Sr HS, 1978; BSEE, Penn St Univ, 1982; pa/cp/NHS; APS; Ski Clb; IEEE Pres; Eta Kappa Nu; Tau Beta Pi; Pi Mu Epsilon; Phi Eta Sigma; Dorm House Treas; Intramural Sports; hon/Eta Kappa Nu Outstg Soph EE Student; ca/Dean's List; Nat Dean's List; W/W Among Am HS Students; Commun Ldrs Am.

BAUGHMAN, WILLIAM ALLEN oc/Staff Counselor and Graduate Student; b/Mar 23, 1959; h/6078 Cherokee Valley Lane, Lithonia, GA 30058; ba/Avondale Estates, GA; m/Diana M; p/Mrs Clara Hillard, Fleming, PA; sp/Mr and Mrs Albert Jakstadt, Cinc, OH; ed/

BA, Cedarville Col, 1981; MEd, GA St Univ, 1983; pa/Mtl Hlth Staff mem, Strawberry Fields Inc, 1980; Mtl Hlth Spec, Peach Ford Hosp, 1981-82; Staff Cnslr, First Bapt Ch, 1983; Student Asst, Grad Res Asst, Grad Tchg Asst, GA St Univ, 1982-83; APGA; r/Bapt; hon/Intl Yth Achmt; Commun Ldrs Am; GA St Dean's List; g/PhD in Clin Psych; Lectr, Publisher, Tchr; Pvt Cnslg Pract.

BAUGHN, KRISTI ANN oc/Student; b/Jun 6, 1966; h/6390 Duquesne Drive, Pensacola, FL 32504; p/Oran H and Bobbie Baughn, Pensacola, FL; ed/Woodham HS; Gulf Breeze HS; cp/Num Coms in HS incl'g Homecoming, Prom; Num Expositions w Exch Students; HS Student Coun; Yth Ch Grp; Ch Basketball Team; r/Meth; hon/Newspaper Article "The Exch", 1984; Acception by Ednl Foun for Fgn Studies to be Exch Student in France; MIP Basketball; W/g/Polit.

BAUMAN, ROBIN ADELE b/Nov 4, 1959; h/651 West Melrose, Chicago, IL 60657; p/Gerald and Harriett Bauman, Chgo, IL; ed/Mather HS, 1977; BA, Univ IL, 1982; Univ Jerusalem, 1977-78; Inst for Yth Ldrs; pa/Public Relats Dir for Pvt Tele-Communs Firm, Chgo; cp/Pres, Assn Mvts for Israel; Mvt for Zionist Fulfillment; Yth Group Advr; Am Israel Public Affairs Com; Mng & Feature Editor of *Chicago Ilini*; hon/Cir Student Ser Awd; Acad S'ship; Dean's List; Intl Yth in Achmt.

BEAMON, SHARON ANN oc/Student; b/Oct 31, 1965; h/Post Office Box 844, Kinston, NC 28501; ba/Same; p/Rev and Mrs Willie E Beamon, Kinston, NC; ed/Att'g HS; cp/Girl Scouts, 1970-83; 4-H, 1980-83; SGA, 1980-83; Band, 1982-83; Co Chorus, 1980-82; r/Bapt; hon/Voted Most Likely to Succeed; Senate Page, 1983; Straight "A" Student, 1-6 Grades.

BEAN, MICHAEL CHRIS b/Jun 22, 1958; h/523 Crossway Avenue, Murfreesboro, TN 37130; p/Mr and Mrs Colonel Bean, Murfreesboro, TN; ed/Oakland HS, 1976; BS, Mid TN St Univ, 1980; Univ of TN Spare Inst; pa/Sci Programmer/Anal w Sci Applications Inc; cp/MTSU Pres; St Dir for TN, Nat Exec Com of Gamma Beta Phi; MTSU Sigma Clb; MTSU Hon Prog; MTSU Jr Vars Tennis TM; SAI Tennis Tm; Huntsville Indust Tennis Leag; hon/Most Outstg Hon Student, MTSU; Intl Yth in Achmt; W/W in Am Cols & Univs; g/Master's Deg in Computer Sci; Programming/Anal Wk for Sci Applications Inc.

BEARD, CHERYL JUANITA oc/Student; b/Mar 24, 1961; h/1372 Dewitt Street, Augusta, GA 30901; ba/Nashville, TN; p/Mrs Rosa T Beard, Augusta, GA; ed/Acad Richmond Co, 1979; BA, Fisk Univ, 1983; cp/Alpha Kappa Alpha, VP, Chaplain, 1982; Fisk Univ Ushers, Hd Usher, 1982-83; Mod Black Mass Choir; Fisk Univ Choir; GA-Fisk Clb, Pres 1980-81, Treas 1982-83; Hons Coun Jr Rep, 1981-82; r/Christian; hon/W/W Among HS Students; SADAKA Great Potential Awd, 1979; Dist'd Am HS Students; g/Deg in Psychol, Psychol, Mgmt.

BEASLEY, MARK ANDERSON oc/Minister and Seminary Student; b/Jun 15, 1958; h/1906 Bethesda Avenue, Durham, NC 27703; ba/Durham, NC; m/Susan Annette Mauney; p/Anderson

C Beasley, Colfax, NC, and Peggy R Beasley, Kernersville, NC; sp/Marvin and Sue Mauney, Stanley, NC; ed/SEn Bapt Theol Sem, 1981-; BA, Wingate Col, 1981; E Forsyth Sr HS, 1976; pa/Min Yth & Chd, Page Rd Bapt Ch, 1981-; Min Yth, First Bapt Ch Mooresville, 1981; Chaplain Intern, Presby Hosp Charlotte, 1980; Min Yt, Colfax Bapt Ch, 1980; Min Yth, Morven Bapt Ch, 1979; Min Yth, Thompsonville Bapt Ch, 1978; cp/Wingate Vol Dept, 1977-81; Colfax Vol Fire Dept, 1973-77; r/So Bapt; hon/Outstg Yg Men Am; W/W Am Cols & Univs; W/W Am HS; g/MDiv deg.

BEAUFORT, BARBARA LYNNETT oc/Student; b/Feb 22, 1964; h/Route 2, Box 162-A, Vanceboro, NC 28586; p/Marie Beaufort, Vanceboro, NC; ed/Craven Commun Col; pa/Cashier/Clk, Montgomery Ward, 1981; Appt Secy, Park Way Studios, 1982; Secretarial Asst, NEn NC PSRO Inc, 1982-83; cp/DECA, Secy, 1980-81, 1981-82; FBLA, 1980-82; SGA Treas, 1981-82, Mem, 1980-81; Bible Clb, 1980-81, Pres, 1981-82; DECA Alumni VP, 1982-83; SGA Col, 1982-83; r/Holiness; hon/Jr Marshal, 1981; Outstg Sr, 1982; W/W Am HS Students; Yg Com Am; Outstg Mktg & Dist Ed Student; Nat Hon Soc Nom; g/Computer Field.

BECK, DEBORAH CAROL oc/Student, Retail Assistant Manager; b/Oct 28, 1961; h/Route 4, Box 230, Albertville, AL 35950; ba/Boaz, AL; p/Doyle and Carol Beck, Albertville, AL; ed/Boaz HS, 1980; Snead St Jr Col, 1980-82; Univ AL-Huntsville, 1982-; pa/Salesclk, 1978-81; Engrg Asst, 1982-83; Retail Asst Mgr, Doe Spun, 1983-; cp/Acad Modeling; FHA; FCA; Vol Alcohol & Drug Abuse Ctr; ARC Vol; Student Govt; r/Prot; hon/Co-Author of "On Orbit TPS Inspection"; W/W Among Am HS Students; Beta Clb; Dean's List; Mu Alpha Theta Student Govts; Lee Mathis S'sh;p; Gene Buffington S'ship; g/Applied Math Maj, Computer Sci Minor.

BECKER, KEVIN PAUL oc/Head Basketball/Tennis Coach; b/Oct 22, 1958; h/730-23 Street, Bismarck, ND 58501; p/Louis and Lois Becker, Bismarck, ND; ed/St Mary's Ctl HS, 1977; AA, Bismarck Jr Col, 1979; BA, Chamainade Univ of Honolulu, 1981; cp/Vol Charles Hall Yth Home; Basketball Referee; Yth Ftball Coach; YMCA-MO Val Fam; HS Student Constit Com; HS Student Coun; Jour; Col Intramurals; Intercol Softball & Basketball; hon/Hon Student; Nat Dean's List; Basketball MVP, All-St; Col Ath Awd; Intl Yth in Achmt; W/W All Am; g/Grad Wk in Guid & Cnslg; Coach Basketball; Yth Involvement.

BECKER, RANDI ELLEN oc/Student; b/Mar 1, 1964; h/102 One Sugarloaf Court, Baltimore, MD 21209; p/Stanley L and Rita L Becker, Balto, MD; Pikesville HS, 1982; Att'g Drexel Univ; cp/HS-Varsity Sports, Lacrosse, Field Hockey, Basketball, Wrestling Mgr, Track & Field Soccer; Student Govt Assn, Secy; Pres, United Synagogue Yth; Chiz UK Amono Congregation; Commerce & Engrg Soc; Intramural Capt, Volleyball Team, Drexel Univ; VP, Freshman Class, Drexel; Varsity Lacrosse Team, Drexel; r/Jewish; hon/Col S'ship; g/Deg in Commerce &

Engrg.

BECKNER, JENNIE LEE oc/Student; b/Oct 9, 1961; h/404 Edgewood Drive, Nicholasville, KY 40356; p/Mr and Mrs Ernest Dan Beckner, Nicholasville, KY; ed/Jessamine Co HS, 1979; BA, En KY Univ, 1983; Univ KY Law Sch, 1986; pa/Census Enumerator, US Bur Census, 1980; Indust Engr Clk, Donaldson Co Inc, 1981; Dispatch Clk, Malone & Hyde, 1982; Prodn Control Clk, Donaldson Co Inc, 1983; cp/HS-French Clb Pres; Jr Beta Clb; Mu Alpha Theta Clb; Flag Corps; Spch Clb; Kappa Delta Tau; Kappa Delta Pi; Sigma Tau Delta; Col Pentacle/Mortar Bd; Student Rep United Way Com; Tutor; r/Ch of Christ; hon/HS-Eng Awd; French Awd; Beta Awd; Ret'd Tchrs S'ship; Christian Appalachian S'ship; En Foun S'ship; Cert Achmt; Flag Bearer; Dean's List; Nat Dean's List; W/W; g/Law.

BEDRICH, PRISCILLA RUTH oc/Payroll Timekeeper; b/Aug 7, 1958; h/5751 South Normandy Avenue, Chicago, IL 60638; ba/Chgo, IL; p/Charles and Mildred Bedrich, Chgo, IL; ed/John F Kennedy HS, 1977; AAS, Richard J Daley Col, 1980; pa/Audit Clk, Sears Roebuck & Co, 1977-78; Acctg Temp, Accountemps, 1980-82; Payroll Timekeeper, Wilson Jones Co, 1982-; hon/Daley Col Deans & Hons List; Kelly Girl Awd; Nat Dean's List.

BEERS, SCOTT ALLEN oc/Cost Analyst; b/May 6, 1958; h/106 Short Street, Trafford, PA 15085; ba/Monroeville, PA; m/Kay Elaine; p/Mr and Mrs Albert A Beers, Greenville, PA; sp/Mr and Mrs William F Baker, Meadville, PA; ed/Reynolds HS, 1976; BA, Youngstown St Univ, 1980; pa/Mgmt Trainee 1980, Jr Cost Analyst 1981, Cost Analyst 1982, Bessemer & Lake Erie RR; Nat Hon Soc, Concert Band, HS; Alpha Kappa Psi Profl Bus Frat, Secy, 1979; r/Meth; hon/Summa Cum Laude; Dist Dir Inst Fed Taxation S'ship; Commun Ldrs Am; g/Grad Sch for MBA.

BEGALKA, TIMOTHY PAUL oc/Horticulturist; b/Feb 19, 1960; h/Box 181, Clear Lake, SD 57226; ba/Same; p/Mr and Mrs Leon Begalka, Clear Lake, SD; ed/Clear Lake HS, 1978; BS, SD St Univ, 1982; pa/Sodak Gardens; Nurseryman, Grower, Landscaper; FFA Alumni, Secy 1983; Clear Lake Commun Playhouse, Pres 1979-83, Dir 1982-83; Phi Kappa Phi; Alpha Xi, VP 1981; Farm House Frat, Bus Mgm 1980, Treas 1981; Alpha Zeta; Mortar Bd; Gamma Sigma Delta; Alpha Tau Alpha; Kappa Delta Pi; r/WI Synod Luth; hon/High GPA at Farm House Frat; Grad of Dale Carnegie Course; Co-Ed Broom Hockey Champ, 1982; W/W among Am HS Students; Soc Dist'd Am HS Students; Nat Register Commended Scholars.

BEGNAUD, WANDA HEBERT oc/Assistant Professor; b/Jul 24, 1952; h/110 Karen Drive, Lafayette, LA 70503; ba/Lafayette, LA; m/Henry Lionel Jr; p/Mr and Mrs Morris J Hebert, Baton Rouge, LA; sp/Mr and Mrs Henry L Begnaud, New Iberia, LA; ed/MS, LA Tech Univ; BS, Univ of SWn LA; RD, Lafayette Gen Hosp & Our Lady of Lourdes Hosp; pa/Asst Prof 1980-, Instr 1979-80, Lab Asst & Dietitian Dir 1976-79, Univ of SWn LA; Dietetic Traineeship, Lafayette Gen Hosp & Our Lady of Lourdes Hosp, 1975-76; Am

Dietetic Assn; LA Dietetic Assn Newslttr Editor, 1980-82, Prog CoChm 1980; Lafayette Dietetic Assn, Pres 1982-83, Pres Elect 1980-82, Prog Chm 1980-81; Initiator 1980, Chm 1980-, Secy 1978-80, Dial a Dietitian Prog; USL Alumni Assn; Home Ec Alumni, Chapt Secy 1979-81, Treas 1977-79; Omicron Nu; Nutrition Today Soc; Nutrition Ed Soc; Univ of SWn LA; Coor Inst Food Ser Tchg Prog, Our Lady of Lourdes Hosp & USL, Coor Dist IV Golden Yam Contest, Coor LA Cattlemen's Assn Beef Cook-Off, Coor Undergrad Prog Devel Comm, Chm Home Ec Rally Com, S'ship & Awds Com, Curric & Catalog Com, Equal Employmt Opport Com, Agri Student Coun Advr; Mayor's Com on Needs of Wom; cp/Am Cancer Soc Vol; Am Heart Assn Vol; Lafayette Diabetes Assn Conslt; hon/Author of Num Pubs; Phi Kappa Phi Hon Soc; LA Dietetic Assn, Recog Yg Dietitian of 1982; Recog Yg Dietitian 1978-81; Yg Commun Ldrs of Am; Personalities of S; Outstg Yg Wom of Am.

BEHRENS, BRETT ALLEN oc/Sports Photographer; b/Jun 29, 1962; h/2741 Lakeshore Lakeport, CA 95453; ba/Lakeport, CA; m/Candi; p/Mr and Mrs Walter H Behrens, Lakeport, CA; sp/Mr and Mrs Norman Essex, Los Molinas, CA; ed/Clear Lake HS, 1980; Brooks Inst Photo Sci, 1982; pa/Lake Co Record-Bee 1982-, AP 1982-, SF Giants 1983-, Golden St Warriors 1982, Photog; Lake Co Spec Olympics Coach; hon/Lions Clb Spch Contest, 1979, 1980; Top 10 Sports Photogs No CA, 1982-83; Dean's List, Brooks Inst, 1980-82; All Star, Lake Co Adult Softball Assn, 1982; Commun Ldrs Am; W/W Among Am HS Students; g/Sports Illustrated Cover Photo & Photo Staff.

BELCHER, JIMMI LYNN oc/Student; b/Dec 4, 1965; h/Route 4, Box 45 Pinnacle View, Berea, KY 40403; p/James and Barbara Belcher, Berea KY; ed/Dipl, Madison Ctl HS, 1983; Att'g Berea Col (Math Maj), 1983-; Mem, Beta Clb, 5 Yrs; Mem, Pep Clb; r/Bapt; hon/Math Awd, Home Ec Awd & Grad w High Distn, Madison Ctl HS, 1983; Recip, Nat Merit Sci Awd, 1983; W/W Among Am HS Students.

BELCHER, JUDITH LEE b/Sep 19, 1962; h/301 Asbury Circle, Easley, SC 29640; p/Mr and Mrs Thomas E Belcher; ed/Easley HS, 1979; BA, Furman Univ, 1983; cp/NHS; Bldrs Clb; Univ Singers; Big Sister Prog; Orient Staff; Furman Univ Yrbk Staff; Col Ed Ser Corps; hon/Top 10 in Grad Class; Internship, Public Relats Dept, Greenville Hosp Sys; 1 of 2 HS Srs to Attend Sem on Ec, Univ SC; Dean's List; g/Customer Ser Rep, Orders Tile & Distributing Co.

BELCHER, PHILIP BURGESS oc/Student; b/Jul 31, 1960; h/201 Overhill Road, Walterboro, SC 29488; p/Posey and Jean Belcher, W'boro, SC; ed/Grad, Barnwell HS, 1978; Att'g Furman Univ, 1978-; cp/Mgr, Furman Singers; Pres, Pi Gamma Mu; Omicron Delta Kappa; Prog Chm, Bapt Student Union; Sum Missionary to Taiwan, 1981; Chaplain's Asst, Greenville Gen Hosp; Archaeological Excavation at Tel Dan Israel, 1982; hon/Article in "The Student" 1982; Omicron Delta Kappa; Dean's List, 9 or 10 Terms; Pi Gamma Mu; HS Valedictorian; Phi Beta Kappa, 1982; Quaternian Clb, Furman Univ, 1982; Middler

Theol Awd, SWn Bapt Theol Sem, 1983; Dean's List; Personalities of S; g/Tchg, Law Sch.

BELEVICH, JEFFREY JOSEPH b/Sep 1, 1962; h/4406 West Run Road, Homestead, PA 15120; p/Duane D and Jean Belevich, Homestead, PA; ed/Bishop Boyle HS; Embry-Riddle Aeronaut Univ; pa/Student; cp/Ftball & Golf Teams, HS; Choir, Band; BSA; Altar Boy; hon/Dean's List; 3rd Pl Hon in Class, HS; 2nd Pl Hon in Sci, Math; Achmt Awd; g/Aeronaut Sci.

BELKNAP, SUSAN MARIE oc/Graduate Nurse; b/Dec 11, 1962; h/Route 2, Box 40A, Sherman, TX; ba/Sherman, TX; p/Mr and Mrs W L Belknap, Sherman, TX; ed/Howe HS, 1981; Grayson Co Jr Col; pa/Secy; cp/Jr Vols, Hosp; 4-H Pres, Secy, CoDel; Explorer's Clb; TSNA; FHA; Band; Ctr St Ch of Christ; hon/4-H Gold Star Girl; Band Most Spirited Girl; FHA St Rep; g/Masters in Sci.

BELL, LOUISE HELEN oc/Staff Assistant at the White House; b/Oct 6, 1959; h/3246 Q Street, Northwest, Washington, DC 20007; ba/Washington, DC; p/Dr and Mrs Robert L Bell, Coatesville, PA; ed/Linden Hall Sch for Girls-HS, 1976; BA, Washington & Jefferson Col, 1980; pa/Staff Asst, White House, 1982-; Corres Analyst, White House, 1981-82; Communs Spec, Pres Inaugural Comm, 1980-81; cp/Delta Gamma Nat Frat, Treas 1979-80; Art Barn Assn; Renaissance Wom; Yg Repubs; Activs Editor, Yrbk; Wom's Varsity Field Hockey; Linden Hall Class of 1976, Class Rep; Student Govt; Lttrman's Clb; Wom Coun; Mgr, Men's LaCrosse Team; r/Presb; hon/Internship w Morgan Maxfield Economic Forecaster, 1980; Mrs Haubner Activs Awd, 1976; W/W Am HS Students; Yg Commun Ldrs; Yg Personalities Am; Outstg Yg Wom Am; Intl Outstg Yth; g/Grad Sch for MBA, Career in Polits.

BELL, NORCOTT ESTANCIA oc/Student; b/Oct 2, 1965; h/4906 Bragg Boulevard, Fayetteville, NC 28303; p/Mrs Norcott E Bell, Fayetteville, NC; ed/Seventy-First HS, 1983; Att'g NC Ctl Univ; cp/Secy, Sr High Voices Choir; Fayetteville/Cumberland Co Yth Coun; Debate Team; Pep Clb; Drama Clb; French Clb; r/Bapt; hon/Lettered in Debate; Chancellor's S'ship & Tuition S'ship, 1983; Nat Merit S'ship Finalist; Hon Grad; g/Bus Info Sys, Computer Programmer.

BELL, SUSAN ELAINE oc/Student; b/Aug 6, 1962; h/Route 1, Box 96-1, Jones, OK 73049; ba/OKC, OK; p/Mr and Mrs John W Bell, Jones, OK; ed/Jones HS, 1980; Univ OK Hlth Sci Ctr; r/Meth; hon/Hon Soc, Hon Roll, HS; Student Foun, Phi Eta Sigma, Hon Roll, Col; W/W; United Meth Student F'ship; g/Deg Occupl Therapy.

BELL, WARREN SNOWDEN oc/Student; b/Dec 14, 1963; h/Maple, NC 27956; m/Malia Christine Wells; p/Mr and Mrs Horace W Bell Jr, Maple, NC; sp/Mr and Mrs Don Wells, San Diego, CA; ed/Currituck Co HS; Elect Computer Programming Inst; cp/Boys Clb of Am; Cub Scout, BSA; Crawford Vol Fire Dept; Boys' St; Secy, Rep, Freshman Class; Rep, Jr Class; Student Coun; Ftball; Quarterback Senator; Baseball; All-Conf Ftball; r/Bapt; hon/Citizenship Awd; Sr Beta Clb; Hon Roll; W/W Am

HS Students; g/Digital/Computer Tec.

BELLA, ISABELITA R oc/Student; b/ Dec 5, 1963; h/330 Lakewood Drive, Butler, PA 16001; p/Dr and Mrs Romeo Bella, Butler, PA; ed/Butler HS, 1981; Bryn Mawr Col; pa/Fashion Stylist, Beeline Fashions, 1983; cp/Pres, Explorers Rep Cabinet; 1st VP of Candystriping; Secy, Explorers Post for Med; Tennis Teams; Vol Tutor; Flute Player for Ch; Morris Dancing; Dancer in Folk Fest; r/Rom Cath; hon/1st Pl, Jr Acad of Sci, Reg, 2nd Pl, St; Soroptimist Commun Ser Awd; Hon Roll; W/W; Am Outstg Names & Faces; g/MD.

BEMBRY, DEBORAH ELAINE oc/ Administrator, Professor; b/Apr 15, 1953; h/Post Office Box 185, Bourbonnais, IL 60914; ba/Kankakee, IL; p/Joe and La-Donia Bembry, Hawkinsville, GA; ed/Hawkinsville HS, 1971; BS, Albany St Col, 1974; MEd, Univ IL, 1975; PhD, Univ IA, 1978; pa/Asst Prof Ed, Asst to VP Acad Affairs, Olivet Nazarene Col, 1981-; Asst Prof Ed & Adm, Asst to Pres, TN Tech Univ, 1978-81; Cnslr, Univ IA, 1977-78; Eric Profile Conslt, Univ IA, 1975-77; AAUW; cp/Phi Delta Kappa; r/Nazarene, Wildwood Ch Nazarene, Pres of Local Nazarene Yth Intl, 1982-, Choir Mem; hon/Corporate Mem AAUW; Magna Cum Laude Grad; W/W Wom; W/W Am Cols & Univs; Outstg Yg Wom; g/Cert as Spec in Developmental Ed.

BENDALL, VALERIE RHEA oc/Student; b/Sep 6, 1962; h/3236 Dundale Road, Birmingham, AL 35216; p/Mr and Mrs James O Bendall, Birmingham, AL; ed/W A Berry HS, 1977-80; BS, 1985, Auburn Univ; cp/Student Govt Assn, Secy Public Relats, 1983-84; Alpha Omicron Pi Social Sorority; Omicron Delta Kappa; Hlth & Hosp Adm Org, Secy 1982-85; Sigma Nu Little Sister, 1981-84; r/Meth; hon/Nat Maid of Cotton, 1984; AL Maid of Cotton, 1983; W/W Am Cols & Univs; Dean's List; g/ Careers in Modeling, Hosp Adm.

BENEFIELD-WILLIAMS, DEBBIE KAY oc/Student; b/Mar 6, 1963; h/117 South Lincoln, Hobart, OK 73651; m/ C E Jr; p/Mr and Mrs Richard G Benefield, Anadarko, OK; sp/Mr and Mrs C E Williams Sr, Lawton, OK; ed/ Anadarko HS, 1981; Univ Sci & Arts of OK; pa/Commls on KTJS/KQ-106 Radio; FBLA; NHS; St Hon Soc; Chem Clb Reporter; Drama Clb; Biol Pre-Hlth Sci Clb Pres; Student Union Activs Bd VP; Student Union Renovations Com; hon/S'ship in Chem to USAO; Awds in Ec, Drama, Algebra, Sci; Pi Gamma Mu Hon Soc; Lifetime Mem, Intl Sociol Hon Soc; W/W; Yg Personalities of S; Outstg Names & Faces; g/Social Worker, Writer.

BENGTSON, CYNTHIA SHAWN oc/Actuary, Mutual Omaha; b/Dec 6, 1960; h/824 Lincoln Road, Number 206, Bellevue, NE 68005; ba/Omaha, NE; p/ John E and Myra J Bengtson, Bellevue, NE; ed/Bellevue East HS, 1978; AS, York Col, 1980; BS, Univ NE, 1982; cp/ Acapella Choir; Vocal Ensembles; GATA Social Clb Ofcr; Phi Beta Lambda Ofcr; Phi Theta Kappa Ofcr; Alpha Ch; Parliamentary Procedure Team; Tutor; Ch Softball; r/Ch of Christ, Yth Grp; hon/Dean's List; Nat Dean's List; Intl Yth in Achmt; W/W Am Jr Cols; Soc of Dist'd Scholars; Commun Ldrs; g/MA

in Acctg.

BENNETT, JOHN REAGAN b/Sep 11, 1963; h/507 Union Street, Brownsville, PA 15417; p/Delilah W Ray, Brownsville, PA; ed/Brownsville Sr HS, 1981; CA Univ PA; pa/Student; cp/PA Yth Ed Assn; Yrbook Advtg Staff; Drama Clb; Tour Guide, Brownsville Hist Soc; Vol Wkr, Muscular Dystrophy Bike-a-Thon; hon/Intl Yth in Achmt; W/ W Am HS Students; Yg Commun Ldrs Am; g/Bus Adm & Mgmt.

BENNETT, JOY LYNN oc/Student; b/May 5, 1964; h/Route 1, Box 273, Lost Creek, WV 26385; p/Mr and Mrs Robert J Bennett, Lost Creek, WV; ed/S Harrison HS, 1982; Fairmount St Col; pa/ Crew Mem, McDonald's; cp/Pres, Sr Class; Pres, NHS; VP, Student Coun; Band; Choir; All-St Choir; r/Meth; hon/ Salutatorian; Harrison Co Bk S'ship; DAR Awd; W/W; Am Outstg Names & Faces; Soc Dist'd Am HS Students; g/ CPA.

BENNETT, KELLY EVANS oc/Student; b/Jan 11, 1963; 215 South Hill Drive, Christiansburg, VA 24073; m/ Richard W; p/Roger and Judy Evans, Covington, VA; sp/Bill and Opal Bennett, Covington, VA; ed/Alleghany Co HS, 1981; Hollins Col, 1981-83; BA, VPI & St Univ, 1985; cp/Nat Hon Soc; Key Clb; Varsity Clb; Gymnastics Team; Ponpon/Flag Squad; Class Ofcr; VP, Student Govt; CoCapt Gymnastics; Hollins Outdoor Prog, 1981-82; CoChm, Inter-Clb Coun; r/Prot, Secy, Ch Yth Grp; hon/Wom's Col Invitational Art Exhbn, Sweet Briar Col, 1983; Nat Hon Soc; Outstg Accomplishment in Art; W/W Among Am HS Students; Soc Dist'd Am HS Students; g/BA Studio Art.

BENNETT, SUSAN CAROL oc/Graduate Student; b/Jun 30, 1960; h/1100 Reinli Street, Number 148, Austin, TX 78723; p/Ralph O and Lois M Bennett, Prattville, AL; ed/Prattville HS, 1978; BBA, Univ Montevallo, 1982; Univ TX-Austin; Am Mktg Assn; cp/Chi Omega Sorority, 1979-82; Student Govt Assn, Pres 1981-82; Panhellenic Coun, VP 1981; Res Hall Assn, Exec Secy 1979-81; Univ TX Ldrship Bd, 1982-83; Omicron Delta kappa; Phi Kappa Phi; Sigma Tau Delta, VP; r/Prot; hon/Charles E Prathro S'ship; Outstg Yg Wom Am; Dean's List; Outstg Mktg Student; W/W Among Students Am Univs & Cols; g/Master's Deg Bus Adm.

BENSON, BARTLEY HOWELL oc/ Dental Student; b/Apr 27, 1961; h/2061 Cobana, US 1, Memphis, TN 38107; m/ Katherine Heath; p/Dr and Mrs Howell O Benson, Winchester, TN; sp/Mr and Mrs Floyd Heath, Belvidere, TN; ed/ Franklin Co HS, 1979; BA, Univ TN, 1983; cp/Phi Beta Kappa, 1982; Phi Kappa Phi, 1982; r/Meth; hon/Top Grad in Liberal Arts at Univ TN; God & Country Awd, 1974; g/Dentist.

BENTEL, MARIA ELISABETH b/Oct 19, 1965; h/23 Frost Creek Drive, Locust Val, NY 11560; p/Frederick R and Maria A Bentel, Locust Val, NY; ed/St Paul's Sch, 1983; Harvard Col Sec'dy Sch, 1981; 1st Exch Student, Sekei Sch, 1981-82; cp/Reporter/Fgn Corres to Sch Newspaper; Debating Soc; Japan Clb; Italian Clb; Outing Clb Bd Mem; Contbr, St Paul's Mag; hon/ Hon Student; Hons Grad, Summa Cum Laude, St Paul's Sch, 1983; g/E Asian

Studies.

BENTEL, PAUL LOUIS b/Jun 13, 1957; h/23 Frost Creek Drive, Locust Val, NY; p/Frederick and Maria Bentel; ed/Phillips Exeter Acad, 1975; BA 1979, MArch 1982, Harvard Univ; PhD Cand, Tchg Fellow; cp/Editor-in-Chief, *Harvard Architecture Review*; Graham Foun F'ship; Fac Advr; Tchg Fellow; Ogrg, Envir Arts Grp; hon/Num Awds in Sculpture, Graphic Arts; Langley Prize for Achmt in Arch; MArch w Distn, 1982, Harvard Grad Sch; David McCord Prize; Graham Foun S'ship; g/PhD Arch Hist; Profl Career, Arch; Tchr of Arch.

BENTLEY, DEBORAH LYNN oc/ Research Technician; b/Oct 9, 1958; h/ 402 Wood Street, Midvale, UT 84047; ba/Salt Lake City, UT; p/Arthur and Jean Bentley, Midvale, UT; ed/Hillcrest HS, 1977; BS, Univ UT, 1982; pa/Res Tech, Univ UT, 1982-; Med Records Clk, St Marks Hosp, 1981; Nurses' Asst, Univ, Hosp, 1979-80; Res Lab Asst, Greenwood Genetic Ctr, 1978; Tech Processing Clk, Salt Lake Co Lib, 1976-77; Lambda Delta Sigma Sorority; Med Explorers; Yg Wom's Midvale Civic Assn; Biol Student Adv Com; r/LDS; hon/Intl Yth in Achmt; W/W Among HS Students; Nat Cand, AMA Recog Plan; Adv'd Study S'ship; Biol Dept S'ship; Elks Nat Foun Awd; Nat Exploration Awd; Univ UT Hons Prog; Outstg Yg Wom Am; g/Grad Studies in Hlth Psychol.

BENTON, KRISTI LYNN b/May 26, 1965; h/Bena, VA 23018; p/Mr and Mrs Julius D Benton Jr, Bena, VA; ed/ Gloucester HS, 1983; cp/Student Coun Assn Treas, Reporter, Asst Secy; Beta Clb; Drama Clb; Forensics; 4-H; Band; Madrigals; "D'Otisingers"; Key Clb; Rep Party of VA Wkr; Bapt Ch Yth Grp; Flag Corps Capt; Co Jazz Ensemble; Spring Musical; hon/10th, Nat Talent Competition, Notre Dame Univ; Dist VIII Reg Chorus & Band; W/W Among Am HS Students; Intl Thespian Soc; Nat Beta Clb Nat Conv Spec Talent Competiton, 1st Pl Winner, 1983; g/Attend VA Tech, Maj Arch.

BENZINGER, MARGARET GARDNER oc/Director of Merchandising & Special Events; b/Aug 13, 1958; h/1315 Broadway Road, Lutherville, MD 21093; ba/Balto, MD; p/Mr and Mrs James F Benzinger, Lutherville, MD; ed/ Dulaney Sr HS, 1976; Towson St Univ, 1980; pa/Mktg Dir, Merchandising & Spec Events Dir, Balto Blast Soccer Team, 1980-; cp/Pres, Secy, Forensic Union, 1978-80; Sr Class VP, 1980; Secy, Pi Kappa Delta, 1979-80; Balto Blast Booster Clb Adv, 1984; r/Presb, Timonium Presb Ch; hon/Dean's List, 1980; Deg Excell, Pi Kappa Delta Nat Tour, 1979; MD St Champ Debater, 1980; Yth in Achmt; W/W Among Am Cols & Univs; Commun Ldrs Am; Personalities Am; g/Excell in Mktg & Promotional Field.

BERGER, ANITA LYNN oc/Internal Auditor; b/Oct 1, 1958; h/Route 3, Box 89, Lake Charles, LA 70605; ba/Lake Charles, LA; m/Richard L; p/Mr and Mrs Louis C Gordon, Oberlin, LA; sp/ Mr and Mrs B G Berger, Lake Charles, LA; ed/Oberlin HS, 1976; BS 1980, MBA 1984, McNeese St Univ; pa/Asst Controller, Lake Charles Mem Hosp; cp/Phi Chi Theta; Am Mktg Assn; FBLA; GCE; Beta Clb; NHS; Wom Hon

Grads of Am HS; hon/WT Burton S'ship; AM Legion Awd; Intl Yth in Achmt; W/W: Among Am HS Students, in Am Cols & Univs; Commun Ldrs Am; g/Cert'd Internal Auditor Exam.

BERGER, AUDREY MARILYN oc/Clinical Psychologist; b/Nov 2, 1955; h/1844 Crittenden Road, Apartment 3, Rochester, NY 14623; ba/Rochester, NY; p/Alexander and Elaine Berger, Brooklyn, NY; ed/BA, 1976, St Univ NY-Binghamton; MA 1978, PhD 1981, Univ IA; pa/Assoc Psychol, Rochester Reg Forensic Unit, Rochester Psychi Ctr, 1983-; Psychol, Pt-time Pvt Pract; Assoc Psychol, Secure Care Unit, Rochester Psychiatric Ctr, 1981-83; Psychol Intern, Strong Meml Hosp, Univ Rochester Sch Med & Dentistry, 1980-81; Am Psychol Assn; Rochester Area Assn Clin Psychol; Genesee Val Psychol Assn; cp/Amnesty Intl; r/Jewish; hon/Author of Num Pubs incl'g "Characteristics of Child Abusing Fams" *Handbook of Fam Psychol & Psychotherapy;* 1976 Hon Mention, The Danforth Foun; 1976, Phi Beta Kappa; Highest Univ Hon, St Univ NY, 1976; Hons in Psychol, St Univ NY, 1976; NY St Regents S'ship, 1972; Outstg Yg Wom Am; W/W Frontier Sci & Technol.

BERGER, JOY SUSANNE oc/Student/Musician; b/Nov 27, 1959; h/806 Camellia Road, Augusta, GA 30909; ba/Louisville, KY; p/Mr and Mrs J R Berger, Augusta, GA; ed/Grad, Savannah Christian Sch, 1977; BM, Samford Univ, 1981; Wking on Master's Ch Music; pa/GA Bapt Ch Music Dept, 1983, 1984; Prof's Asst, 1984-85; Num Pt-time Music Positions; Dorm Supvr, Aspen Sum Music Fest, 1983; Instr Prep Piano Dept, Samford Univ Sch Music; cp/Student Govt Senator Sch Music, Adm/Student Coms, Minnesingers Accompanist, Univ Chorale, Col Choir, Delta Omicron, Phi Mu Alpha Little Sister, Residence Hall Progs, Campus Min Fam Ldr, The Joyful Sound Vocal/Piano/Drama Duo, Samford Univ; Num Ch Music, Yth & Col Activs; Student Coun VP, HS; Many Music-Related Grps; Sr Class Ofcr; r/So Bapt; hon/Author of "Gifts", *The Student* 1984, "Yth-Led Worship: God Gives Me Confidence" *Equipping Yth* 1985; GA Gov's Hons Prog; GA Bapt Yth Music Camp Hon Camper, 1976; GA All-St Piano; Intl Guild Piano; VP, Nat Hon Soc; Chorus Accompanist; Drama & Typing Awds; Sr Superlative; Presser Foun S'ship; Samford Perf'g Arts Prog Concerto-Aria Perf; Dean's List; High Class Hons; Omicron Delta Kappa; Phi Kappa Phi; Alpha Lambda Delta; Chaplain, Hypatia Hon Soc; Pi Kappa Lambda; Homecoming Ct, 1981; Outstg Yg Wom Am; Dir Dist'd Am; W/W Univs & Cols.

BERGER, NANETTE SUE oc/Student and Nursing Aide; b/Apr 14, 1963; h/63363 Dogwood Road, Mishawaka, IN 46544; p/Harold and Ferne Berger, Mishawaka, IN; ed/Bremen HS, 1981; Att'd Bethel Col; pa/Wking at Retirement Home & at Bethel Col; cp/Hand Bell Choir; Ch Choir; r/Prot; hon/W/W; Yth for Understanding to Switzerland, 1981; Ldrs of Tomorrow, 1982; Intl Yth in Achmt; Commun Ldrs Am; g/Nurses Tng.

BERGIN, NANCY ANN oc/Academic Counselor; b/Mar 11, 1955; h/RFD 1, Box 455, Dover, NH 03820; ba/Durham, NH; p/Dr and Mrs John W Bergin, Bedford, MA; ed/Bedford HS, 1973; BA, Bowdoin Col, 1977; MS, Univ WI, 1980; pa/Acad Cnslr, Whittemore Sch Bus & Ec, Univ NH, 1982-; Dir Cooperative Ed, Lyndon St Col, 1981-82; Asst Dir Cooperative Ed, Middlesex Commun Col, 1980-81; Asst to Hd Tutor, Dept Sociol, Harvard Univ, 1978-79; NH Wom in Higher Ed, Admin, 1982, 1983; Vol Mediator for Dover Juv Diversion Prog, 1983; NE Assn Cooperative Ed, 1980-82; NE VT Indust Ed Coun, 1981; Am Voc Assn, 1983; hon/Dean's List; James Bowdoin Scholar; Phi Beta Kappa; g/Grad Study in Occupl/Career Ed & Adult Devel.

BERMÚDEZ-PAZO, ANA L oc/Professor; b/Feb 19, 1960; h/W-24-A-C-19, Glenview Gardens, Ponce, Puerto Rico, 00731; ba/Ponce, PR; p/Mr and Mrs Pedro Bermudez, Ponce, PR; ed/BA, Cath Univ, 1981; MSW, St Louis Univ, 1983; pa/Tchr Asst, New Hope Lrng Ctr, 1981-82; Social Wkr, Vol Legal Sers, 1983; Prof, Cath Univ, 1983-; Pi Gamma Mu, 1980; Local Ofc at Cath Univ PR; r/Presb; hon/W/W Among Students in Am Univ & Cols; Excell Trophee, 1978; Cum Laude Grad; Highest Pt Average, Cath Univ, 1981; g/Social Work.

BERNARD, ZOE E oc/Dental Coordinating Assistant; b/Apr 9, 1961; h/218 Sunny Lane, Lafayette, LA 70506; b/Lafayette, LA; p/Davy L and Gwen J Bernard, Lafayette, LA; ed/Lafayette HS; Pursuing BS, in Biol-Chem; pa/Student Lab Tech, Lafayette Charity Hosp, 1980-81; Dental Coor'g Asst, 1981-84; Premed Soc, Biol Soc, Sailing Clb, SWn LA Univ; Lafayette Nat Hist Mus & Planetarium Assn; Student Intern for Univ Med Ctr Rape Crisis Ctr; Lafayette Oral Cancer Conf; BSA; Wom's Repub Clb Lafayette; r/Epis; hon/Coun for Devel French in LA S'ship Recip for One-Mo Study Prog in Angers, France, 1980; S'ship Nom for One-Mo Study Prog in Montpellier, France; SWn LA Univ Hons Prog; g/Career in Dental Hygiene.

BERNHARDT, DARCY GWEN oc/Student; b/Nov 1, 1963; h/Route 1, Champion, NE 69023; ba/Same; p/Don and Joann Bernhardt, Champion, NE; ed/HS, 1982; Att'g Pepperdine Univ; cp/FFA Pres, Secy; Y Teen Pres; 4-H Pres; Cheerldr; Miss NE Teen, Miss NE Teenworld Pageants; Repaired Pk Benches, Bathroom, Basement; 4-H St Livestock Judging Team; HS Student Coun Del; I-Clb, 1980-82; hon/4-H Wash Citizenship Focus, 1981; Homecoming Royalty; Prom Royalty; Intl Yth in Achmt; Yg Commun Ldrs Am; W/W Am HS Students; g/Study Social Sers or Bus.

BERNHARDT, KURT oc/Student; b/Jan 12, 1962; h/Rural Route 1, Champion, NE 69023; p/Don and JoAnn Bernhardt, Champion, NE; ed/Chase Co HS, 1980; AA, NE Jr Col, 1982; pa/Chase Co 4-H Livestock Judging Team Coach, 1983; Farmer w Don Bernhardt; cp/4-H, Jr Ldr Reporter, 1980, Mem 1970-80; Imperial FFA, 1976-83, Com Chm 1978-79, Reporter 1979, Secy 1980, Alumni 1983-; Student Coun; Secy, NE Jr Col Aggies, 1981; hon/FFA Am Farmer, 1983; CO St Univ, Wn Stockshow Assn S'ship, 1983; Chase Co 4-H Alumni Awd, 1983; Imperial FFA

Greehand, 1977; Imperial FFA Chapt Farmer, 1978; NE St FFA Farmer, 1980; Outstg FFA Sr Ofcr, 1980; Chase Co 4-H Livestock Judging Team, 1978, NE Jr Col; Nat Champ Livestock Judging Team; W/W Among Am HS Students; Intl Yth in Achmt; g/Become Successful Farmer.

BERNIER, NADINE JACQUELINE b/Jan 20, 1961; h/10542 Avenue E, Chicago, IL 60617; p/James and Michaeleen Bernier, Chgo, IL; ed/Geo Wash HS, 1979; Loyola Univ, 1981; pa/Claim's Examr, US RR Retirement Bd, 1983; cp/News Editor, HS Newspaper; Quill & Scroll; Poems Pub'd in HS Lit Mag; hon/W/W Among Am HS Students; g/Write Book for Pub.

BERRY, ALAN BROADUS oc/Lieutenant, US Army; b/Feb 11, 1961; h/750 Starlight Drive, Atlanta, GA 30342; ba/Ft Bliss, TX; ed/Ridgeview HS; Bach Aerospace Engrg, GA Inst Technol, 1983; mil/Army Air Def Artillery; pa/Lt, AUS, Commissioned 1983; cp/Capt, Civil Air Patrol, 1974; Aircraft Owners & Pilots Assn, 1981; Am Inst Aeronautics & Astronautics, 1981; Tau Beta Pi, 1982; Sigma Gamma Tau, 1982; Soc Am Mil Engrs, 1983; r/Epis; hon/Dist'd Mil Grad, 1983; Fgn Legion Awd Acad, ROTC, 1982, 1983; Engrg Excell Awd, Soc Am Mil Engrs, 1983; g/Master's Deg in Aerospace Engrg.

BERRY, CYNTHIA MILLS oc/Student; b/Jul 31, 1962; h/910 Randall Drive, Mt Pleasant, SC 29464; m/John A; p/Mr and Mrs Charles H Mills Jr, Mt Pleasant, SC; ed/Wando HS, 1980; BA, Erskine Col, 1984; cp/Athenian Lit Soc, Social Com; Bus Clb; Atlanta Lit Soc; Phi Alpha Theta; r/Meth, Meth Yth F'ship; hon/AAUW Govt Awd, 1983; Bernard L Poole Govt Awd, 1983; AAUW Hist Awd, 1984; Garnet Circle; Erskine Scholar; Dean's List; Phi Alpha Theta; Soc Dist'd Am HS Students; W/W Am HS Students; g/Grad Sch for MPA.

BERRY, JIMMY DARRELL oc/Student; b/Mar 13, 1963; h/805 West Fifth Street, Clarksville, TX 75426; p/Mr and Mrs W F Berry, Clarksville, TX; ed/Clarksville HS, 1981; Att'g Stephen F Austin St Univ; cp/Acctg Clb, Fin Clb, Stephen F Austin St Univ; Phi Eta Sigma; Bapt Student Union; Nat Hon Soc, 2 Yrs; r/Col Ave Bapt Ch, Usher; hon/Phi Eta Sigma; Del, Boys St, 1980; Alpha Chi; Beta Gamma Sigma; Omicron Delta Epsilon; W/W Among Am HS Students; Intl Yth in Achmt; g/Acct w CPA Cert; Own Acctg Firm.

BERRY, MARILYN DIANE b/Apr 3, 1960; h/1046 Sharon Copley Road, Wadsworth, OH 44281; p/John W and Laurel A Berry, Wadsworth, OH; ed/Highland HS, 1978; BS, Heidelberg Col, 1982; pa/Serving w Peace Corps, Sierra Leone W Africa, 1983; Marine Fisheries, 1982; cp/OH Conserv & Outdoor Ed Assn; Am Mus of Nat Hist; Sharon Ctr U Meth Ch Yth Rep to Coun on Min, Lay Witness; Total Student Devel Prog Peer Facilitator; Cir K Corres Secy, VP, Dir Euglossian Soc Treas, Rush Co-Chm; King Hall Dorm Coun Social Chm; Volleyball Team; Spch Team; Ftball Stat; Biol Fac; Col Chorus; hon/Outstg Freshman Biol Maj; IRHC Resident Life Awd; A G Mcquate Awd; US Yth Conserv Corps; Cleveland Metro-Pks; Col Geol Lab Asst; Beta

Beta Beta; Kappa Delta Pi; Pi Kappa Delta; Tower Laureat S'ship; g/Involvement w Num Outdoor, Envir, Conserv Ed Progs.

BESSON, RONALD MARK oc/ Alarm Technician; b/Nov 15, 1961; h/ 406 Reagan Street, Pineville, LA 71360; ba/Alexandria, LA; p/Mr and Mrs Thomas B Besson, Sr; ed/HS, 1979; BA, NE LA Univ; cp/Student Coun; NHS; Band; Parish Hon Band; Acad Hon Roll; Phi Kappa Phi; Cum Laude Grad, NE LA Univ, 1983; T H Harris S'ship; Alpha Phi Sigma; W/W Am; g/LA St Police Ofcr.

BEST, BARBARA ELLEN oc/Student; b/May 27, 1965; h/CPO 42, Berea, KY 40404; p/Bill and Irmgard Best, Berea, KY; ed/Berea Commun HS, 1983; cp/Nat Beta Clb; NHS; Soccer Mgr; Marching & Concert Band; Sun Sch Tchr; Commun & Col Theatre; hon/ DAR Good Citizen, 1983; KY Girls St, 1982; Jour Awd, 1983; BCHS Student Hall of Fame, 1983; Wkly Student of Wk; W/W Among Am HS Students; Commun Ldrs; g/Theatre.

BETTIS, STEPHEN BLAIR oc/Student; b/Jan 10, 1960; h/Route 1, Box 197, Loudon, TN 37774; p/Howard and Dorothy Bettis, Loudon, TN; ed/Loudon HS, 1978; pa/Equipment Oper, Monterey Mushroom Co, 1979-83; Gemtron Corporation, 1983; r/Bapt; hon/All-Am HS; All-Co Basketball; All-E Tchr; Ldg Dist Scorer; Best All-Around Loudon Co, 1978; Most Improved, 1977; All-Am HS Ath, 1978, Hammer Pubs; g/Bus Mgmt.

BEVERAGE, GLENNA EVON b/May 1, 1964; h/Route 2, Box 671, Bridgeport, WV 26330; p/Glen and Yvonne Beverage, Bridgeport, WV; ed/Bridgeport HS, 1983, Att'g WV Univ; cp/4-H; Bapt Yth Grp; Candystriper; 150 Hrs of Vol Wk; hon/Harrison Co Spelling Champ; WV St Spelling Champ; Citizenship Awd; NHS; Valedictorian; W/W Among Am HS Students; g/CPA.

BIDDIX, PENNY D b/Jun 21, 1961; h/Route 5, Box 641, Kings Mountain, NC 28086; p/Mr and Mrs James W Biddix, Kings Mtn, NC; ed/Kings Mtn Sr HS, 1979; Att'd Ctl Wesleyan Col, 1980-81; BA, Univ NC-Charlotte, 1983; Cert'd K-3 Tchr; cp/Dir Jr Assem; Asst Dir Chd's Choir; Asst Dir CYC; Mem Yg Believers; r/Wesleyan; hon/W/W Among Am HS Students; Outstg Yg Ams; Pres List at UNCC; g/Tchg, Master's Deg Spec Ed, Deg in Art Ed.

BIEHLER, DARREN FOSTER oc/ Student; b/Sep 17, 1962; h/A-20 The Village Green, Chapel Hill, NC 27514; p/Dale and Dana Biehler, Newton, NC; ed/Newton-Conover HS; Univ NC-Chapel Hill; pa/Nsg Asst, NC Meml Hosp, 1983; Hosp Attendant, Catawba Meml Hosp, 1982; Zool Lab Tchg Asst, UNC-Chapel Hill, 1982; cp/Alpha Epsilon Delta; Col Repubs of UNC-CH; Dir of Publicity for Carolina Ath Assn; Chm IM-REC Coun at UNC-CH; r/ Luth; hon/HS-Lttr in Track & Wrestling; Col Varsity Track, Gymnastics Clb; Olympic Weightlifting; Dean's List; Atlantic Coast Conf Acad Hon Roll; UNC-CH Intramural Ath Yr; Varsity Lttr Track; g/Career: Phys, Ortho Surg.

BIERNAT, CATHERINE MARIE oc/ Computer Scientist; b/Aug 30, 1961; h/ 40 Howell Street, Buffalo, NY 14207; ba/Buffalo, NY; p/Mr and Mrs Leon J

Biernat, Buffalo, NY; ed/Riverside HS, 1979; BA, St Univ NY-Buffalo, 1983; pa/Assoc Computer Scist, Arvin/Calspan Adv'd Technol Ctr, 1983-; cp/Phi Beta Kappa; Student Coun; Key Clb; Co-Editor, Sch Newspaper; NHS; Salutatorian; Computer Sci Undergrad Student Assn Secy-Treas; Cir K Clb Pres; Phi Eta Sigma; Assumption Ch Parish Coun; Assumption Folk Grp; hon/Circle K Outstg Pres Awd; Bausch & Lomb Sci Awd; Grace Capen Meml S'ship; Am Legion Awd; Intl Yth in Achmt; Outstg Yg Wom Am.

BIESER, JOANNE MARIE b/Jun 29, 1962; h/300 1st Street, Mendota, IL 61342; p/Donald and Patricia Bieser, Mendota, IL; ed/Mendota Twp HS, 1980; ASA, IL Val Commun Col; No IL Univ; cp/Vars Band Pres; Concert Band Hd Secy; Flag Corp Co-Capt, Capt; Steering Com; Prom Chm; Ch Yth Grp Secy-Treas; Chm, Main Money Raising Event; Phi Theta Kappa; Ofc Hist; hon/Girls' St Participant; Dean's List; W/W Among Am HS Students; g/ Bus Adm-Mktg.

BIFULCO, ANNA MARIE oc/Student; b/Aug 10, 1958; h/448 Eldert Lane, Brooklyn, NY 11208; p/Vincenzo and Patricia Bifulco, Bklyn, NY; ed/Saint Michael HS, 1976; BS, Saint Joseph's Col, 1980; cp/Phi Alpha Theta; VP, Secy, & Senate Rep; St Joseph's Col; Sacristan, Polit Affairs Clb; Rel Affairs Com; Sci Clb; Phi Mu; NHS; r/Cath; hon/NY St Regents S'ship, 1975; Betty Crocker "Fam Ldr of Tomorrow"Awd, 1976; Gen Excell Aw from St Michael's HS, 1976; Nat Dean's List; Phi Mu; W/W Among Am HS Students; Intl Yth Achmt; g/Med.

BIGGS, LISA DIANNE b/Sep 30, 1964; h/1116 Bath Avenue, Ashland, KY 41101; p/Mr and Mrs Robert G Biggs; ed/Paul G Blazer Sr HS, 1982; Att'g Anderson Col; cp/HS Band Hist, 1981-82; JA VP Mktg, 1980-81; FBLA Reporter, 1981-82; Ch of God Girls Basketball Tm; Ch Puppet Min; Ch Choir; hon/Nat Band Assn Awd; W/W Among Am HS Students; Commun Ldrs Am; g/Bus Ed Deg.

BILBREY, DONNA MARIE oc/Student; b/Feb 21, 1966; h/400 Price Street, Livingston, TN 38570; p/Mr and Mrs James Lelon Bilbrey, Livingston, TN; ed/ Livingston Acad HS; Barbizon Sch Modeling; cp/Vol Wk-Nsg Home, Public Lib, Pacesetters; GSA; Ch Acteens; Jr HS Basketball, Volleyball; 4-H Clb; HS Spanish Clb; Eighth Grade Play Cast; r/Bapt; hon/Jr HS Class Salutatorian; 15 Ribbons in Art Competitions; 1st Pl in Scrapbook Competition; 5th Pl in Spch; Participated in Two Sch Operas at TN Technol Univ; Sch Perfect Attendance Awds; Acad Hon Roll; Sch Track Meet Awd; 1st Pl for 4-H Demo Spch; Participated in TN St Finals of Mod Miss Pageant; g/Attend Col.

BILLER, JERRY LYNN II oc/Student; b/Mar 29, 1966; h/Post Office Box 1168, Nokomis, FL 33555; p/Jerry and Rhoda Biller, Nokomis, FL; ed/Venice HS, 1984; pa/Mason, Kaufman Masonry, 1981-83; Carpenter, Brittain & Berdon Constrn, 1984; Life Guard, YMCA, 1984; cp/Key Clb Mem, 1982; Spanish Clb Pres, 1983; Sr Cnslr, DeMolay, 1982-83; Student Govt Senator, 1984; Boy's St Cand, 1981-84; Wrestling Team Capt; r/Presb; hon/Am HS Ath,

1982; Num Wrestling Awds incl'g S'ship to Bloomsburg Univ, Dist Champ 1982, 1983, 1984, Jr Olympic Champ 1983, HS Most Valuable Wrestler 1982, 1983; Grand Nat Champ, 1982; Cultural Exch Team, 1981, 1982; Nat Zone AAU Champ; FL Assn AAU Champ; Num Track Awds incl'g Dist Champ, 1983, 1984; HS Decathalon Record Holder, 1983; 3rd in Dist, 1982; Pres Phy Fitness Awd; Varsity Lttrman; Sport Lttrman; Red Belt-Tae Kwon Do; Venice HS Most Outstg Ath; g/to Enter Pre-Law at Bloomsburg Univ; to Qualify as Mem of 1988, 1992 Olympic Wrestling Team.

BILLIAN, MARTHA BOWERS oc/ Student; b/Jun 25, 1964; h/920 Peachtree Dunwoody Court, Atlanta, GA 30328; p/Douglas C Billian, Atlanta, GA, and Jane Ray Taylor, Savannah, GA; ed/N Sprg HS, 1982; Att'g Stephens Col; pa/Mktg Dept; Asst Golf World Mag, 1982, 1983; Pt-time Delivery Person, Harts & Flowers Florist, 1982; cp/Class Treas 1981, Yrbk Sports Editor 1982, Hon Prog, Yglife, FCA, Basketball Stat, Girl's Soccer Team, HS; Pillsbury Hall VP & Hall Mgr 1983-84, Phoenix Debutante Soc, Stephens Col; r/Bapt; hon/Articles Concerning Phoenix Soc in Sandy Sprgs/Northside Neighbor; Nat Merit Commended Student; Outstg Sr Nom; Acad Hon Roll; Pillsbury Hall Spirit Ring; Ten Ideals Recip; g/Deg in Bus Adm.

BILLINGS, SHARON ANN oc/Peace Corps Volunteer; b/Oct 28, 1959; h/ 9300 Vaughn Place, Lanham, MD 20706; p/Mrs Genevieve L Billings, Lanham, MD; ed/DuVal Sr HS, 1977; BA, High Pt Col, 1980; MA, Am Univ, 1982; pa/Peace Corps Vol in Tanzenia E Africa, 1983; cp/Nat Hon Soc Pres, HS; Alpha Delta Theta, Secy, Chaplain; SGA, Com Chm, Class Legis; Christian F'ship Teams; Ascension Luth Ch Soc Min Chp, SS Tchr, Missions Bd Mem; Bread for the World, Intern; hon/Pi Alpha Alpha; Sigma Delta Pi; Alpha Chi; W/W Am Cols & Univs; Intl Yth in Achmt.

BILOTTO, JAMES ANTHONY oc/ Army Officer, 1st Lieutenant; b/Dec 5, 1950; h/5908-1 Fisher Avenue, Ft Hood, TX 76544; ba/Ft Hood, TX 76544; m/ Deborah D; c/James R, Tina M, Joseph C; p/Mr and Mrs James T Bilotto, Beaver, PA; sp/Mr and Mrs Richard D Sprecker, Beaver, PA; ed/Beaver Area HS, 1968; Assoc, Data Processing, Beaver Co Commun Col, 1980; mil/ USAR, 1970-80, AUS, 1981-; pa/Tech, USAR, 1973-81; Ofcr, AUS, 1981-; cp/ Resv Ofcrs Assn; Chem Ofcrs Assn; Assn of AUS; r/Rom Cath; hon/Army Commend Medals, 1976 & 81; Ten-Yr SVC Awd, 1980; DA Cert Achmt, 1983; W/W Am Jr Col; Intl Yth in Achmt; Yth in Achmt; Commun Ldrs Am; g/MBA Deg, Sr Ofcr in Mil.

BINDSEIL, CHERYL LYNN oc/Student; b/Sep 29, 1965; r/Route 3, Box 521, San Antonio, TX 78218; p/Dan and Carolyn Bindseil, San Antonio, TX; ed/ Canyon HS; cp/Chm Coman Co 4-H Coun; Pres Comal Co 4-H Exch Clb, VP Oakridge 4-H Clb; Pres Future Tchrs Am; Secy Nat Hon Soc; Mem CHS German Clb; Bracken Vol Fire Dept Ladies Aux; 1st Chair Flute & Piccolo in HS Band; r/Luth; Triumphant Luth Ch; hon/Am Legion Awd; WOW Awd; Straight "A" Awds; TX All-St

Lions Band; 4-H Awds; W/W Am HS Students; Third Runner-up to Miss Antonio TEEN; Comal Co Farm Bur Queen & Dist 10 Farm Bur Queen.

BING, PAMELA GALE oc/Student; b/Oct 20, 1959; h/Route 1, Enterprise, KS 67441; p/Duane and Martha Bing, Enterprise, KS; ed/Enterprise Acad, 1978; Union Col; cp/Student Senator, Chm of Allocations Com for Assoc Student Body; Usher Coor for Campus Min; Vol Tchr, Country of Haiti; hon/ Awd in Communs Union Col; High Hon Grad, HS; W/W Among Am HS Students; g/Double Maj, Bus Adm & Behavioral Sci.

BINGHAM, DONNA LYNN oc/Student; b/Oct 21, 1966; h/Route 4, Barbourville, KY 40906; p/Mary Ann and Don Bingham, Barbourville, KY; ed/HS, 1984; cp/Cheerldr, 1973-84; Chorus, 1978-84; r/Bapt; hon/Music Awd, 1984; Hon Student, 1984; Sportsmanship Awd, 1984; Cheerldg Awd, 1984; Most Valuable Cheerldr, 1984; Best All Around Cheerldr, 1983; Top 20 out of 212 Students, 1984; W/W Among Am HS Student; Soc of Dist'd HS Students.

BIRDWELL, KIMBERLY KAYE oc/ Student; b/Oct 26, 1966; h/Route 1, Box 175, Cookeville, TN 38501; p/Charlotte and Donald Pierce, Cookeville, TN; ed/ Cookeville HS; cp/Pres, Voc Indust Clbs Am; r/Ch of Christ; g/USAF, Career in Cosmetology.

BISCHOF, PATRICE JOANNE oc/ Secretary/Paraprofessional Dean of Students; b/Oct 3, 1961; h/8001 West Balmoral, Chicago, IL 60656; ba/Chgo, IL; p/Albert and Joanna Bischof, Chgo, IL; ed/Resurrection HS, 1979; BA, DePaul Univ, 1983; pa/Secy/Paraprofl, DePaul Univ Assoc Dean Students, 1983-; Dance Instr, Le Ballet Petit Studio Dance, 1979-; Writing Tutor, DePaul, 1981-83; Water Safety Instr, Park Ridge, 1978-; Pubs Editor, Forkosh Meml Hosp, 1982; Reporter, Pioneer-Pickwick Press, 1980-82; cp/ Blue Key Nat Frat Pres, 1982-83; Mem, Delta Sigma Epsilon & Kappa Gamma Pi Hon Frats; r/Rom Cath; hon/Author of Wkly Newslttr, Qtrly Mag & Public Ser Announcements, Forkosh Hosp; Author of Num Pubs; Hon Grad, DePaul Univ; 1st Pl Features Story *DePaulia*; W/W Among Am Cols & Univs & HS; g/Perf'g Arts Mgmt, Public Relats.

BISCHOPING, DENISE ANN oc/ Applications Analyst; b/Aug 4, 1961; h/ 5083 River Road, Scottsville, NY 14546; ba/Rochester, NY; p/George and Nancy Bischoping; ed/Wheatland-Chili HS, 1979; BA, Potsdam Col; cp/Dorm Coun; hon/Pi Mu Epsilon; Valedictorian; Pres List; g/Math Maj, Computer Sci Concentration.

BITTO, PAMELA ANN oc/Student; b/Apr 4, 1964; h/Route 1, Box 149 B, White Post, VA 22663; ba/Williamsburg, Va; p/Carl Peter and Shirley Pearl Bitto, White Post, VA; ed/James Wood HS, 1982; Col of William & Mary, 1986; cp/Key Clb Treas, Proj Chm; Octagon Clb Pres; NHS; NFL; Debate; SCA; Big Sister; Sci Clb Treas; Sch Musical; Forensics; Art Clb; French Clb; Fgn Lang Clb; Kids are Our Concern Bd of Dirs; Math Team; Thespian Clb; Blood Donor; Col Repubs; Circle K; r/Cath; hon/Valedictorian; Rotary Clb Ldrship S'ship; C of C Commun Ldr; Armstrong

Foun S'ship; NHS Acad S'ship; Key Clb-Intl Spch Finalist; W/W Am HS Students; Commun Ldrs Am; g/Ec, Bus Maj Corporate Law.

BLACK, CARL ANTHONY oc/Student; b/Sep 22, 1963; h/Route 2, Box 252, Burkesville, KY 42717; p/Billy F and Gloria J Black, Burkesville, KY; ed/ Cumberland Co HS, 1982; Wn KY Univ, 1982-83; Somerset St Voc-Tech Sch; cp/ Beta Clb; 4-H; AJBC Bowling Assn; UMYF Pres; BSA; APE Prog; Cumberland Co Gifted & Talented Students Prog; Track; Jr Class Secy; Sr Class Most Dependable; r/Meth; hon/Hon Roll; Soc of Dist'd Am HS Students; W/ W Among Am HS Students; Yg Commun Ldrs Am; g/Computer Sci Deg.

BLACK, LAURELL LAURENT oc/ Dec 13, 1959; h/318 West Alpine Street, Santa Ana, CA 92707; ed/AA, Santa Ana Col, 1982; BA, Sonoma St Univ, 1984; Mem: Publicity Chm, Am Mktg Assn; Statewide Ednl Rts Netwk; NAACP; hon/Editor/Fdr, *The Black Student's Voice*, Sonoma St Univ; W/W Among Students in Am Cols & Univs.

BLACKLIDGE, FRANKIE LEE oc/ Student; b/Nov 9, 1957; h/212 Baldwin Avenue, Belen, NM 87002; p/Frank Edward and Ann Emerson Blacklidge, Belen, NM; ed/Thoreau HS, 1975; AA, NM St Univ, 1982; NM Inst Mining & Technol; cp/Tutor, Handicapped Students; Student Supvr, Summer Yth Prog; Dir, Tchr, Play & Art Projs; hon/ Cert of Achmt, Col S'ship Bd; Intl Yth in Achmt; W/W in Am Jr Cols; The Nat Register of Col Grads; g/Petro Engr, Metall Engr.

BLACKWELL, GLORIA DIANE oc/ Programmer; b/Jan 5, 1960; h/2513 Kendall Drive, Charlotte, NC 28216; ba/ Gaithersburg, MD; p/Mr and Mrs Leroy Blackwell, Charlotte, NC; ed/W Charlotte HS, 1978; BA, Univ NC-CH, 1983; pa/Programmer, IBM Corporation, 1983-; Supvr Guest Relats, Carowinds, 1976-83; Baton Instr, Charlotte Pk & Rec, 1979-80; cp/Nat Soc Black Engrs, 1980; Assn Computing Mach, 1981-82; r/Meth; hon/Order of Lion, 1978; Hon Clb Ldrship Awd in Commun, 1980; 3rd Pl Winner of Students Reg Tech Symp, 1983; g/Grad Sch, MBA, Mgr at IBM.

BLACKWELL, PAMELA J oc/Student; b/May 16, 1963; h/Route 2, Box 172, Westminster, SC 29693; p/Dewitt and Arvilla Blackwell, Westminster, SC; ed/Oakway HS, 1981; Assoc Deg, Mktg, Tri-Co Tech Col, 1983; cp/Sr Beta Clb, F'ship of Christian Ath, VP Sr Class, Capt of Cheerldg Squad, HS; Mktg Rep of Student Govt Assn, Tri-Co Tech Col; r/Christian; hon/Nat Dean's List; HS Hon Roll; Tri-Co Tech Col Dean's List; US Achmt & Acad Nat Awds; g/Career in Retailing as Fashion Buyer.

BLAILOCK, SHARI B oc/Student; b/ Apr 19, 1963; h/Route 1, Box 43AA, McComb, MS 39648; p/Mr and Mrs Jack Blailock, McComb, MS; ed/McComb HS, 1981; SW MS Jr Col; cp/Secy, Nat Hon Soc; Nat Jr Hon Soc; Future Bus Ldrs Am; Sr Rep, Student Coun; Quill & Scroll; Mu Alpha Theta; Art & Bus Edit, Annual Staff; Bus Edit, SW MS Jr Col *Whispering Pines*; Dynamics SW Chorus; r/Ch, Yth Coun & Yth Choir, Asst Edit Ch Yth Newspaper, Camp Sunshine, Vacation Bible Sch; hon/SW MS Jr Col Hall of Fame; Valedictorian; Chorus Awd; Whispering Pines Awd;

Eng Awd; Phi Kappa Phi; Highest Hon in the Bus Col; Coun of Cardinal Newman Hall; BSU; PTA St & Nat Cultural Art Awd; Distributive Ed Clbs Am Awd; Mktg Awd; Denman Hall of Fame; Supt's Scholar; Dean's List; W/ W in Acads & Activs; W/W Am HS Students; Outstg Names & Faces; Intl Yth in Achmt; g/deg in Dietetics.

BLAIR, BRUCE ALAN oc/Accountant; b/Aug 5, 1960; h/132 El Paso Boulevard, Apartment I, Manitou Springs, CO 80829; ba/Colorado Springs, CO; p/Mr and Mrs Marvin Blair, Coffeyville, KS; ed/Fredericktown OH HS, 1978; BBA, Kent St Univ, 1982; pa/Acct, Ofcs Am Inc, 1983-; cp/Acctg Assn; Beta Alpha Psi; Intramural Basketball; Acctg Tutor; r/Prot; hon/Hon Col; Scholar in Residence S'ship; Nat Dean's List; g/MBA Acctg, Help the Less Fortunate.

BLAIR, STANLEY SCOTT b/Oct 22, 1962; h/5 Hawkins Lane, Willingboro, NJ 08046; p/Mr and Mrs Stanley J Blair Jr, Willingboro, NJ; ed/Holy Cross HS, 1981; L'Universite du Quebec a Trois-Rivieres, 1982, 1983; Currently Enrolled at Gardner-Webb Col; cp/ Dormitory Dir; Student Asst, GWC Dept of Fgn Langs & Lit; GWC Ofc of Admissions; Editor GWC Lit Mag; Edit Editor, GWC Newspaper; Intl Brotherhood Clb; GWC Freshman Orient Prog; Pres, French Clb; VIP Day Tour Guide; Student Registration Asst; HS Ftball & Track; Future Phys Clb; Chief Editor CYO Newspaper; Little Leag Baseball Coach; Capt, Track Team; hon/NHS; Lttrs in Ftball & Track; NJ St Senate Cit; GWC Sophomore Scholastic Achmt Awd; 3rd Pl 1983 GWC Poetry Contest; Commun Ldrs Am; GWC Dean's List; Holy Cross HS Eng Awd; GWC French Awd; W/W Am HS Students; g/Col or Univ Prof.

BLAIR, TERRY L oc/Director of Bands & Choral Activities; b/Jan 21, 1961; h/101 South 7th, Albany, MO 64402; ba/Albany, MO; p/Mr and Mrs Glenn D Blair, Cameron, MO; ed/ Cameron R-1 HS, 1979; BME, Ctl Meth Col, Cum Laude, 1983; pa/Dir Bands & Choral Activs, Albany HS, 1983; MENC; MO Music Edrs Assn; MO St Tchrs Assn; cp/Phi Mu Alpha Nat Comm on Standards, 1982-85; Sigma Pi Epsilon Hon Soc; UN Pilgrimage for Yth; Yg Columbus XX; People-to-People Intl; KC Am Legion Reg Band; Cornet Band; Commun Band; Jazz Fest Coor; r/Bapt; hon/E P Puckett Hall of Sponors S'ship; Selecman Achmt Awd, Outstg Grad, 1983; Outstg Sr, 1983; Ctl Meth Col Hons Wk; Nat Dean's List; W/W Am Univs & Cols; Commun Ldrs Am; Intl Yth in Achmt.

BLAKEMAN, LORI ANN oc/Student; b/Dec 27, 1965; h/47 Pathfinder Drive, Sumter, SC 29150; p/Mr and Mrs Gary Blakeman, Sumter, SC; ed/Sumter HS, 1984; pa/Pt-time, Baskins-Robbins Ice Cream, 1984-; cp/Student Body Pres, 1983-84; VP Nat Hon Soc; Art Editor for Mag; Copy Editor of Yrbook; Marching Band; Jr Class Pres; r/Luth; hon/*Signature* Mag, 1983, 1984; *Paragon* Yrbook, 1982, 1984, *Signature* Calendar, 1983, 1984; Fac Citizenship Awd; Acad Achmt; Winthrop Ldrship S'ship; Rotary Outstg Ldrship Awd; Elks Clb Student of-the-Mo; W/W Among Am

HS Students; g/Deg, Interior Design.

BLALACK, JINNI LEIGH oc/Graduate Student; b/Sep 16, 1960; h/417 Lennanwood Avenue, Covington, TN 38019; ba/Murfreesboro, TN; p/Walter L Blalack, Hughes, AK, Virginia B Smith, Covington, TN; ed/Rosemark Acad, 1978; BS, Union Univ, 1981; Wking Towards MA at Middle TN St Univ; pa/Cashier, K-Mart, 1978-79; Salesclk, J C Penney, 1979; Ofc Clk, Big K-Wal Mart, 1980-; cp/Cheerldr, 1974-78, Union Univ; Psychol Clb, 1978-81, 1981-83; Sociol Clb, 1978-81; Pi Gamma Mu, 1980-81; Student Mem, Am Psychol Assn; Psi Chi, 1983; r/Bapt; hon/Union Univ S'ship; The Tipton Co Jr Aux S'ship; g/to Obtain MA Clin Psychol & Pursue a Career in Field.

BLALACK, PAULA DAWN oc/Student; b/Sep 8, 1965; h/Route 3, Box 321, Brighton, TN 38011; p/Mr and Mrs W E Blalack Jr, Brighton, TN; ed/Rosemark Acad; cp/Capt Basketball Team; Capt Volleyball Team; r/Bapt; hon/W/W Am HS; Nat Track Winner; Mod Miss Teenage Am; Basketball Queen; Mat Contest Participant; Spch Participant; All Tour Team; MVP Player; g/Phy Therapist.

BLALOCK, TOM J oc/Student; b/Sep 29, 1961; h/2700 Shoreridge Avenue, Norman, OK 73069; m/Michelle; p/Mr Tom Blalock, Guthrie, OK, and Mrs Ray G Wikkel, OKC, OK; sp/Dr and Mrs Jim Sotterlee, OKC, OK; ed/Putnam City HS, 1979; BS, OK St Univ, 1983; cp/Delta Tau Delta; Interfrat Coun Jud Bd Chief Justice; Gamma Gamma; OK St Univ Alumni Assn; r/Christian; hon/Dean's Hon Roll; Gamma Gamma, Top 1% Greeks; W/W Among Students in Am Univs & Cols; Delta Tau Delta Arch Chapt Awd for Scholastic Excell; Bob Cox Awd, Outstg Mem; Outstg Yg Men Am; g/Law Sch.

BLANCHETTE, SUSAN MARIE oc/Law Student; b/Jan 2, 1960; h/RFD 4, Smith Hill, Winsted, CT 06098; p/Mr and Mrs Robert G Blanchette Sr, Winsted, CT; ed/Gilbert Sch, 1978; BS, Wn CT St Univ, 1982; Att'g Wn NE Col Sch of Law; cp/SGA; Crim Justice Assn; Pres, Wom Ath Assn; Chm, Sch Tutoring Com; Resident Asst; Juv Probation Ser; Varsity Volleyball; Varsity Badminton Freshman Orient Com; Freshman Curric Com; Rec Res; Student, WNEC Law Sch Resident Advr; Patrolman, CT Dept of Envir Protection; Adm Clk, Superior CT, CT Jud Dept; r/Cath; hon/Nat Dean's List; Nom for 1980 Harry S Truman S'ship; Intl Yth in Achmt; Commun Ldrs Am; g/Atty, Legal Investigator.

BLANCO, NANCY LEIGH oc/Student; b/Apr 3, 1964; h/Route 1, Box 508, Killeen, TX 76541; p/S J and Nancy H Blanco, Killeen, TX; ed/Ellison HS, 1982; TX A & M Univ; pa/Secy, Lakeside Hill Land Sales, 1980; Teen Bd Model, Barry's Dept Store, 1981-82; Life Guard/Asst Swimming Instr, Killeen TX, 1982, 1983; Typist, TX A & M Univ Meml Student Ctr, 1983-1984; cp/Opas, TX A & M Cultural Soc, 1982-83; TX A & M Acctg Soc, 1982-83; VP, Sr Class; Student Coun Senator; Secy, Keywanettes; Drill Team; Rep, St Student Coun Conv; ARC Vol; Jerry lewis Telethon; r/Cath, Ft Hood Chapel Cath Ch; hon/Secy, NHS; Voted "Most Likely to Succeed"; Miss Ellison HS; 2nd

Runner-Up, Jr Miss Pageant; 1st Runner-Up, Miss Jubilee Contest; 2nd Runner-Up, Harker Hgts Miss Flame Contest; Princess in TX A & M Cotton Ct, 1982, 1983; TX A & M Dunn Hall Sweetheart, 1982, 1983; Commun Ldrs Am; g/CPA or Cert Math Tchr.

BLANCO, TERESA SUE oc/Student; b/Apr 17, 1966; h/Route 1, Box 508, Killeen, TX 76541; p/Silviano Joe and Nancy H Blanco, Killeen, TX; ed/Ellison HS, 1984; pa/Teen Bd Model/Clk, Dillard's Dept Store, 1982-84; cp/Jr Nat Hon Soc, 1979-80; Spanish Clb, 1980-81; JV Emeralds Drill Team, 1980-81; Varsity Band, 1980-84; Student Coun Rep, 1980-84; Varsity Emeralds Drill Team, 1981-84; Keywannettes, 1980-84; Jr Class Pres, 1982-83; Sr Class Pres, 1983-84; Future Homemakers Am, 1980-81; r/Cath; hon/Jr Nat Hon Soc, 1979-80; Represented EHS at Hugh O'Brian Student Coun Conv in Dallas, 1981-82; Voted "Class Favorite" 1981-82; Jr Class Pres, 1982-83; Sophomore Class VP, 1981-82; Sophomore Keywanette Rep, 1981-82; Sophomore Emerald Rep, 1981-82; Dillard's Teen Adv Bd, 1982-84; Sr Class Pres, 1983-84; 1983 Heart of TX Smile Girl; Yg Personalities Am; g/Attend TX A & M Univ, Maj in Computer Sci.

BLAND, FENTON LEE JR oc/Student; b/Mar 7, 1962; h/1103 East Booker Circle, Petersburg, VA 23803; ba/Petersburg, VA; p/Mr and Mrs Fenton L Bland Sr, Petersburg, VA; ed/Petersburg HS, 1980; VA St Univ; pa/William N Bland & Son Funeral Home Inc, 1975; Turner-Bland Funeral Home Inc, 1977; cp/Kappa Alpha Psi Frat; Mem VA Unit So Christian Ldrship Conf, NAACP; r/Bapt; hon/Articles Pub'd in Newspaper; Outstg Yg Virginian; Polemarch Awd of Achmt, Ft Lee Chapt; g/to become a Mortician.

BLANKENSHIP, JOHN WILLIAM III oc/Student; b/Apr 18, 1966; h/6758 Brandon Mill Road, Atlanta, GA 30328; p/John Jr and Joan Blankenship, Atlanta, GA; cp/BSA; Nat Hon Soc; Nat French Hon Soc; Jr Achmt-VP Fin; Sch Band; Nat Beta Clb; r/Bapt, First Bapt Ch Sandy Srgs Yth Coun, Ch Choir & Handbell Choir; hon/Hon Roll; Nat Hon Soc; Eagle Scout Awd; g/Engrg Deg.

BLANKENSHIP, PHILIP ARTHUR oc/Student; b/Oct 30, 1962; h/145 Chateau Terrace, Apartment 20, Athens, GA 30606; p/C A Jr and Kermetta Libby Blankenship, Atlanta, GA; ed/Crestwood HS, 1980; Univ GA; pa/Interned w GA Dept Human Resources, Ofc of Frad & Abuse, 1983; cp/Ftball, Track Team, Beta Clb, HS; Phi Eta Sigma, Golden Key Hon Soc, Delta Sigma Pi, Col; r/Prot; hon/Univ GA Dean's List; g/Pursue Career in Bus.

BLANTON, BRENDA GAIL oc/Editor/Writer; b/Jun 6, 1956; h/915 Ewing Boulevard, Apartment A2, Murfreesboro, TN 37160; ba/Nashville, TN; p/Sammie L and Ruby Blanton, Unionville, TN; ed/Commun HS, 1974; BS, Mid TN St Univ, 1978; pa/Newspaper Reporter; Soc Profl Jours; Editor/Writer in Ofc of Public Relats, United Meth Communs, 1983-; Reporter & Photog, Shelbyville Times-Gazette, 1978-83; cp/Past Treas Mid TN St Univ Chapt, Sigma Delta Chi; Gamma Beta Phi; Tau Omicron; Rel Public Relats Coun; r/

United Meth; hon/JCs Outstg Yg Wom of 1982; Gene Graham Awd in Jour; Gamma Beta Phi Grad Awd; g/Free-lance Writer; Outstg Yg Wom of 1982 in Bedford Co, TN; W/W Am Cols & Univs.

BLANTON, KATHI SUE b/Feb 10, 1964; h/1209 Lynn Street, Cumberland, KY 40823; p/Dale and Sharon Blanton, Cumberland, KY; ed/HS, 1982; AAS, 1983, SE Commun Col; Bus Ed, En KY Univ; cp/FBLA Hist; NHS Secy; Nat Beta Clb; Co-Editor, Sch Newspaper; Annual Staff; Cheerldr; FHA; Pep Clb; SE Commun Col Student Coun, VP, 1982-83; r/Bapt; hon/Phi Theta Kappa, 1983; Voted Miss Success of Sr Class; US Nat Jour Awd; W/W Among Am HS Students; Soc Dist'd Jr & Commun Col Students; g/Bus Tchr.

BLEDSOE, MYRA ANN oc/Sales Clerk; h/3912 Hillcrest Court, Huntsville, AL 35805; ba/Huntsville, AL; p/Mr and Mrs Elgan F Bledsoe, Huntsville, AL; ed/S R Butler HS, 1978; N AL Col Commerce, 1980; pa/Clk, West Huntsville Cleaners, 1978-80; Bkkpr, The Shoe Den, 1980-81; Sales Clk, Murphy's Mart, 1981-; cp/Nat Hon Soc, 1977-78; Quill & Scroll, 1977-78; hon/Soc of Dist'd Am HS Students; W/W Among Students in Am Jr Cols; Intl Yth in Achmt.

BLISS, JUDITH ANN oc/Student; b/Nov 11, 1959; h/5101 East Farmhurst Road, Lyndhurst, OH 44124; p/Mr and Mrs Jack C Bliss, Lyndhurst, OH; ed/Charles F Brush HS, 1978; John Carroll Univ, Cum Laude, 1982; cp/SS Tchr; Eng Clb CoChm; Pre-Law Soc Secy; Lambda Iota Tau VP; Hon Com Student Rep; r/Bapt; hon/Hon Scholar, John Carroll Univ; Outstg Eng Scholar, 1982; Alpha Sigma Nu; 3rd Out of 690 in HS Grad Class; W/W Among Students in Am Cols & Univs; Nat Dean's List; Yg Commun Ldrs Am; Intl Yth in Achmt; g/Atty.

BLIZZARD, DIANE oc/Software Engineer; b/Jul 9, 1961; h/Raleigh, NC; ba/Raleigh, NC; p/Mr and Mrs Earl D Blizzard, Beaulaville, NC; ed/E Duplin HS, 1979; BS, Univ NC-Greensboro, 1983; pa/Software Engr, Telex Terminal Communs, 1983; cp/Assn Computing Mach, 1983-; Pi Mu Epsilon, 1982-; hon/W/W in Music; Outstg Sr; Assoc Editor of Yrbook; Nat Hon Soc; Pi Mu Epsilon; Grad Magna Cum Laude; Math S'ship; Univ Marshal; g/Master's Deg in Computer Sci.

BLOCK, LISA VICTORIA oc/Student; b/Feb 1, 1962; h/1410 Pinecroft Drive, Sugar Land, TX 77478; ba/College Station, TX; p/Carl and Geraldine Block, Sugar Land, TX; ed/John Foster Dulles HS, 1980; TX A & M Univ, 1984; cp/Phi Kappa Phi; Sigma Gamma Epsilon; Newman Assn; Geol Clb; Outdoor Rec Com, PR Chm; r/Cath; hon/Outstg Jr Awd Col of Geosci, TX A & M Univ, 1983; Nat Dean's List; g/Recieve Deg in Geol & Geophysics.

BLOHM, ROBERT CHANCY oc/Student; b/Aug 2, 1964; h/2248 Rando Lane Northwest, Atlanta, GA 30318; p/Mr and Mrs William H Blohm III, Atlanta, GA; ed/Northside HS; NC St Univ; pa/Pt-time, YMCA, Field Maintenance, 1980-82; Gen Warehouse Wkr, Fun Co, 1980-82; cp/Soccer, Cross Country, Math Team, Acad Team, Computer Sci Clb, Humanities Coun,

Homeroom Rep, HS; BSA; Tech Assn of Pulp & Paper Indust; Student Spkrs for Animals Anonymous, Christian Sci Org, Col; r/Christian Sci; hon/Chem Awd, 1980; Top Eng Student; Brown Book Awd; Most Valuable Def Player, Soccer; Excell in German Awd; Bausch & Lomb Hon Sci Awd; Physics Awd; Math Dept Cup; Nat Hon Soc; Dean's List; g/Double Engrg Deg.

BLOMQUIST, PRESTON HOWARD oc/Medical Student; b/Aug 13, 1960; h/4922 Finley Drive, Austin, TX 78731; p/Mr and Mrs Gilbert V Blomquist, Austin, TX; ed/Grad L C Anderson, HS, 1978; Bach Engrg Sci, Univ TX-Austin, 1982; Univ TX SW Med Sch; cp/HS Valedictorian; Tau Beta Pi; Mortar Bd; Friar Soc; Phi Eta Sigma; Trombone Sect Ldr, Longhorn Band; IEEE; Nat Eagle Scout Assn; hon/Phi Kappa Phi Fellow; Nat Merit Scholar; Golden Key Nat Hon Soc Outstg Sr Awd; Dist'd Col Scholar; Univ TX Cactus Outstg Student; Engrg Scholar; Kappa Kappa Psi; Longhorn Alumni Band Awd; g/MD.

BLOMQUIST, VICKI JEAN oc/Student; b/Apr 27, 1963; h/4922 Finley Drive, Austin, TX 78731; p/Mr and Mrs Gilbert V Blomquist, Austin, TX 78731; ed/L C Anderson HS, 1981; Univ TX-Austin; pa/Mgr, Remodeling Contractor's Ofc, 1983; Teen Bd Model, Foley's Dept Store, 1980-81; Cashier & Model, Yaring's Wom's Fashion Apparel Store, 1979-80; cp/Phi Eta Sigma, Nat Exec Com Mem 1982-84, Pres Univ TX Chapt 1982-83, Adv 1983-85; Longhorn Band; Beta Gamma Sigma; Golden Key Nat Hon Soc; Alpha Kappa Psi; Orange Jackets; r/Meth; hon/Hons Prog in Col of Bus; Recip Endowed Pres S'ship, 1981-85; Longhorn Alumni Band S'ship, 1983; Valedictorian; Dean's List; Intl Yth Achmt; g/Pursue a Career in Data Processing & Anal.

BOATMAN, JEFFERY PAUL oc/Student; b/Feb 23, 1963; h/Post Office Box 2347, Spartanburg, SC 29304; b/Clemson, SC; p/William and Mary F Boatman, Spartanburg, SC; ed/Spartanburg HS, 1981; BS, Clemson Univ (Expected); cp/HS Band: VP, Bowling Leag; IEEE; Ftball; Baseball; Water & Snow Skiing; Ski Clb; Tiger Band; hon/W/W; Personalities of S; g/Computer Engr & Bus Exec.

BOATZ, JERRY A oc/Graduate Student; b/Nov 16, 1959; h/101 Esteran Drive, Bismarck, ND 58501; p/Robert and Dorothy Boatz, Bismarck, ND; ed/Underwood HS, 1978; BA, BS, 1983, Minot St Col; cp/Phi Sigma Pi, Treas; Beta Gamma Phi Pres; Student Assn; hon/Summa Cum Laude, Minot St Col; Valedictorian; Am Legion Citizenship Awd; Nat Dean's List; W/W Among Am HS Students; g/PhD in Theoretical Chem.

BODINE, JEFFREY PHILIP oc/Student; b/Apr 21, 1963; h/6415 North Valentine, Fresno, CA 93711; p/Dr and Mrs Robert Bodine, Fresno, CA; ed/HS, 1981; CA St Univ-Fresno; pa/Stat, Salvation Army ARC, 1981-83; cp/Alpha Gamma Omega, Alpha Chapt Neophyte Pres & VP, 1981-82; r/Presb; hon/US Nat Band Awd Recip, 1980-81; Crouch S'ship, 1982-83; W/W Am HS; Intl Yth in Achmt; Commun Ldrs Am; g/Sys Analyst/Data Base Mgmt.

BOEHM, MICHELLE CARLA oc/Student; b/Oct 11; h/208 Kingsridge Boulevard, Tullahoma, TN 37388; b/Knoxville, TN; p/Mr and Mrs Karl F Boehm, Tullahoma, TN; ed/Tullahoma HS; Univ TN; pa/Lifeguard, 1979; Asst Secy, Micro-Craft Inc, 1980; Sales Clk, Caster Knoft Dept Store, 1981-; Secy to Interfrat Coun at Univ TN, 1983-; cp/Gamma Beta Phi; Golden Key Hon Soc; Nat Hon Soc; Comm of Wom; r/Cath; hon/Nat Hon Soc; Gamma Beta Phi; Golden Key; Comm of Wom; Motlow St Commun S'ship; GE S'ship.

BOGGESS, MARTIN BINION (BIN) oc/Waiter/Chef; b/Sep 15, 1959; h/607 3rd Street South, Columbus, MS 39701; ba/Columbus, MS; p/Mrs J E Boggess, Columbus, MS; ed/S D Lee HS, 1977; BS, 1983, MS St Univ; pa/Asst Mgr, Army-Navy Dept Store, 1980; Asst Mgr, Kelly's Seafood, 1981; Waiter & Chef, Annie's Restaurant, 1983-; cp/Student Govt Assn, 1972; F'ship of Christian Ath, 1974; Pres, Chess Clb, 1975; VP of Goodwill Org, 1976; Cavalier at MS Debutante Soc, 1979; Mem of Columbus Pilgrimage Ct, 1977; r/Cath; hon/MS St Univ Dean's List; Mem, Nat Dean's List; g/Seeking Entry Level Mgmt Position or Sales Position w a Pharm Co.

BOGGS, GREGORY ALAN oc/Student; h/Post Office Box 316, Cumberland, KY 40823; p/Charles B Boggs, Cumberland, KY; ed/Cumberland HS; cp/Basketball; Baseball; Ftball; Beta Clb; Sci Clb; Pres Sci Clb; FCA; Annual Staff; hon/Moorehead St Univ Ath S'ship; Moorehead St Univ Regents Acad S'ship; Dan Forth Citizenship Awd; Chem Symp Cumberland Col; Nat Baseball Awd; All Reg Baseball; All-Dist Baseball; All-St Ftball; W/W Among Am HS Ath; Profiles of Am Students; Dist'd Am HS Students; g/Chem Engr.

BOLGER, CHARLES JR oc/Systems Analyst, Student; b/Feb 22, 1952; h/1518 Robinson Avenue, Willow Grove, PA 19090; m/Davida; c/David; p/Rev Charles and Mary Bolger Sr, Philadelphia, PA; sp/David and Rita Hudson, Philadelphia, PA; ed/Univ PA, Grad Profl Devel Prog; BBA, Temple Univ, 1974; BA, Inst Computer Sci, 1971; Olney HS, 1969; pa/Sys Analyst III, Sun Co, 1977-; Pt-time Data Processing Instr, Commun Col Phila, 1980-82; Pres & Fdr, Tri-Precision Sers Inc, 1982-; Pres & Fdr, Ribbons Devel Co, 1980-; Computer Programmer, Scott Paper Co, 1976-77; Computer Programmer, Kranyley & Co, 1975-76; Sr Choir Dir, 1966-, Christian St Bapt Ch; Chd's Choir Dir 1976-, Bd Deacons 1978-, Secy to Bd Deacons 1981-, Worship & F'ship Comm Dir 1982-, Ch Financial Secy 1979-, 19th St Bapt Ch; Temple Univ Intercol Gymnastic Team, 1972-74; r/Christian; hon/Author of "Uses of Teleconferencing: An Info Mgmt Tool"; W/W Among Students in Am Univs & Cols; Phila City Champ on Side Horse Event, 1969; Phila Jr Olympics Champ on Side Horse Event, 1969; YMCA St Champ on Side Horse Event, 1969; Temple Univ Sch Bus, Outstg Orgnl Ser Awd, 1974; Outstg Yg Men Am; Temple Univ Dean's List.

BOLLING, JAMES ROY JR oc/Student; b/Nov 15, 1963; h/3210 Ashby Street, Roanoke, VA 24015; p/Mr and Mrs J Roy Bolling SR, Roanoke, VA; ed/Patrick Henry HS, 1982; Emory & Henry Col; pa/Computer Lab Asst, Roanoke City Public Schs, 1983; cp/Alpha Phi Omega; Local Theatre Group; Property Master for Emory & Henry Players; Mem, Emory & Henry Concert Choir; r/Meth; hon/Salutatorian; Hon Rol of Emory & Henry Col; Outstg Freshman Math Awd; Commun Ldrs of Am; W/W Am HS Students; g/Computer Sci.

BOLTON, DAVID H oc/Minister; b/Feb 24, 1958; h/861 South Glencliff Drive, Number 90, La Habra, CA 90631; ba/Anaheim, CA; p/Mrs Alta Bolton, Fairfield, CA; ed/Reg Bapt HS, 1976; BA, Bapt Bible Col, 1980; MDiv, Talbot Theol Sem, 1983; Master's of Theol Prog at Talbot Theol Sem; pa/Pastor, Bethel Bapt Ch; cp/Rel Ser Holder in Convalescent Hosp; Interim Pastor; Dir, Grace Bible Inst; Deacon, Ch; Tchr of Yg Married Couples in Ch; r/Prot; hon/Kappa Tau Epsilon; Scotty Alexander Meml Awd in Homiletics; Louis T Talbot Meml S'ship Awd; Sr Sermon, Talbot Sem; Nat Dean's List; Intl Yth in Achmt; g/PhD in Biblical Studies, Min, Col Prof.

BOLTON, MATTHEW MICHAEL oc/Student; b/Dec 31, 1961; h/439-B Hill Street, Henderson, TN 38340; m/Taryn Danette Naylor; p/Mike and Judy Bolton, Henderson, TN; ed/Chester Co HS, 1980; BS, Freed-Hardeman Col, 1984; Univ TN, Ctr for Hlth Sci, Col of Med; pa/Pt-time Asst Sales, Fin Mgr, Bolton Ford Inc; cp/HS Ftball, Basketball, Track; HS Student Body Pres, Class Pres; Student Govt; Sci Clb; r/Ch of Christ; hon/Ath w highest GPA; Civitans Yg Citizen of Yr Awd; All Vol Conf Ftball; Gov's Trophy Match Winner; Dean's List & Pres List.

BOLTON, TARYN DANETTE (NAYLOR) oc/Technical Specialist; b/Nov 28, 1960; h/439-B Hill Street, Henderson, TN 38340; ba/Henderson, TN; m/Matthew M; p/Dr and Mrs B J Naylor, Henderson, TN; sp/Mr and Mrs Mike Bolton, Henderson, TN; ed/BS, Freed-Hardeman Col, 1982; Chester Co HS; pa/Tech Spec, Freed-Hardeman Col, 1983-; Co Ext Agt Trainee, 1982; Mgr of Lodge, Chickasaw St Pk, 1979; Craft House Supvr, Short Mt Bible Camp, 1980; cp/Sophomore Class Treas; Jr Class Secy; Pres's List; Alpha Chi; Annual Staff; Chorus; Bus Mgr for Makin Mus Prodn; Interface Ldr; r/Ch of Christ; hon/W/W Among Am Cols & Univs; Personalities of S; g/Home Ec Ext Agt.

BONEY, ROCK ANTHONY oc/Student; b/Apr 8, 1966; h/254 Sloan Street, Wallace, NC 28466; p/Lynn and Peggy Boney, Wallace, NC; ed/Pender Acad; cp/Sr Class Pres, 1983-84; Beta Clb VP, 1983; Asst Editor Sch Yrbook, 1982-84; Spanish Clb, 1980-82; Secy/Treas Jr Class, 1982-83; r/Bapt; hon/Moly Newspaper Weather Summary; Nat Fgn Lang Awd Winner in Spanish; NC Govs Page; ECU Gifted-Talented Sum Sci Camp; W/W Am HS Students; Nat Ldrship & Ser Awd; g/NC St Univ w Maj in Meteorology.

BONEY, YVETTE oc/Student; b/Sep 2, 1965; h/Route 1, Box 281-B, Willard, NC 28478; p/Mr and Mrs William I Boney Jr, Willard, NC; ed/Union HS, 1983; cp/Black Student Union; 4-H Clb Pres, 1977; Drama Clb; Future Bus Ldrs Am, 1982-83; Yth Orgs United; r/

Worldwide Ch of God; hon/Acad Ldrship & Excell, 1979-80; Dipl in Social Mus, 1983; g/to become a RN.

BONNEMANN, SONYA JOAN oc/Student; b/Jan 1, 1964; h/127 Lake Shore Drive, Richmond, KY 40475; p/Heinz Bonnemann, W Germany, and Joan Boewe, Richmond, KY; ed/Model Lab HS, 1982; Univ KY; pa/Cashier, McDonald's, 1981-82; Pt-time Desk Wkr, AV Med Lib, 1982-; Tch Flute Lessons Pvt; cp/Sigma Alpha Iota; Editor; Lambda Sigma Soc; Univ KY Orch, Marching Band, Symph Wind Ensemble; r/Disciple of Christ; hon/Dean's List; Best Pledge Awd of Sigma Alpha Iota; Nat Hon Soc; Outstg Bandsman Awd; KY All-St Band; Am Musical Foun Band Hons; Am Outstg Names & Faces; W/W Music; Intl Yth in Achmt; g/to Maj in Music Perf.

BORONSTEIN, TRACY oc/Student; b/Sep 23, 1962; h/1185 Sailfish, Hitchcock, TX 77563; p/Hymie and Esther Boronstein, Hitchcock, TX; ed/LaMarque HS, 1981; BA, Austin Col, 1984; Wking on MEd; VP, Yg Dems; Secy SEA; Pi Lambda Sigma; Nat Hon Soc; Yrbook Staff; VP, Fgn Lang Clb; Anchor Clb; r/First Bapt Ch, Mem; hon/Hon Grad; VFW Voice of Dem S'ship; *Lamarque Times* Jour Awd; W/W Among Am HS Students; Personalities of S; Intl Yt in Achmt; g/Career in Spec Ed.

BORST, MARY ELIZABETH b/Jul 23, 1954; h/4705 Rista River Road, Ft Worth, TX; p/Leo A and Kathleen A Borst, Wichita, KS; ed/Bishop Carroll HS, 1972; BS, KS Newman Col, 1976; MS, TX A & M Univ, 1977; cp/AIIE, Pres 1982-83, VP, Treas, Secy; Alpha Pi Mu; Sigma Zeta; Kappa Gamma Pi; hon/Acad S'ship; Acad Achmt Awd; Dean's Hon List; Dir of Dist'd Am; The Anglo-Am W/W; The Am Registry Series; Book of Hon; Outstg Yg Wom of Am; Commun Ldrs & Noteworthy Am; Men & Wom of Distn; DIB; Notable Am; Personalities of the W & MW; Personalities of Am; W/W: Am Cols & Univs, of Am Wom; World W/W of Wom.

BOSLEY, DONALD CHRISTOPHER oc/Student; b/Feb 16, 1967; h/310 Pin Oak Drive, Richmond, KY 40475; p/Kenard Sr and Henretta Bosley, Richmond, KY; cp/Beta Clb, 1983-84; Chess Clb, 1983-84; M Clb (Lttrman) 1982-84; Pep Clb, 1984; Sci Clb, 1983-84; Spanish 1982-84; Jr Class Pres 1984; Sophomore Class Pres 1983; Freshman Class Pres 1982; r/Bapt; hon/HS Ftball Co-MVP 1983; All-Ctl KY Conf 1st-Team in Ftball 1984; Ldrship Awd in Ftball 1983-84; All-44th Dist Basketball Team 1983; Golden Glove in Baseball 1982-83; Eng Awd, 1982-83; Sci Awd, 1982; Spanish Awd 1982-83; Algebra I Awd, 1982; g/to Maj in Area of Math.

BOSLEY, RICHARD ALAN b/Oct 22, 1963; h/3908 Shiloh Avenue, Hampstead, MD 21074; p/Mr and Mrs Kenneth L Bosley, Hampstead, MD; ed/N Carroll HS; Towson St Univ; ca/SGA; Spanish Clb Treas & Pres; Tennis Team; Concert Band; Marching Band; NHS; Exec Com, Class of 81; All Country Band; Spanish Awd; hon/Dean's List, Towson St Univ; St of MD Scholastic Merit Awd; MD Dist'd Scholar Awd; W/ W Among Am HS Students; Commun Ldrs Am; g/Mass Communs.

BOST, CRYSTAL RENEE oc/Student; b/Jul 2, 1966; h/258 Broad Drive, Concord, NC 28025; p/Mr and Mrs Ernest Bost, Concord, NC; cp/Bible Clb; Gold Key Soc; Treas, Student Body; r/Bapt, First Bapt Ch; hon/Bible I Awd, 1981; Bible II Awd, 1982; Girls' St, 1983; Nat Hon Soc.

BOSTIC, HEUGUETTE b/Jun 10, 1962; h/Route 3 Box 860, Moncks Corner, SC 29461; p/Willie Jr and Bertha Lee Bostic; cp/Volleyball; Student Coun Pres; Jr Class Marshall; 4-H; Jr Usher in Ch; Secy, Univ Engrg Soc; Editor, Lit Mag; Beta Clb; Blood Dr Asst; Foods & Nutrition Tchr for Chd; Angel Flight, Asst Pledge Tnr, 1983; hon/Nat Achmt S'ship for Outstg Negroes; Edgar A Brown Scholar; Gov Scholar; Intl Yth Achmt; Commun Ldrs Am; g/Computer Engrg.

BOSTON, ETHEL NADINE oc/Cashier; b/May 15, 1961; h/1506 Avenue E, Ensley, Birmingham, AL 35218; ba/B'ham, AL; p/Mr and Mrs Corey Boston, SR, B'ham, AL; ed/P D Jackson, Olin HS; BS, Miles Col; pa/Spch Therapist Asst, 1979-; Ofc Asst Bus Affairs 1982-82, Ofc Asst Career Placement 1982-83, Miles Col; Cashier, DAV Thrift Store, 1982-; cp/Alpha Kappa Alpha Sorority Inc; Y Teens Social Clb; Jackson-Olin HS Choir, Sect Ldr 1977-79; Miles Col Gospel Choir; Vol Chd's Hosp, 1975-80; Social Wk Vol, B'ham Fam Ct; Soc Wk Vol, W Clyde Williams Terr Apts; r/Bapt; hon/Felix Mendelssohn Awd, 1978-79; W/W Among HS Students; Cert of Achmt; Cert of Achmt in Music; Cert of Achmt in Ofc Asst; Nat Dean's List; W/W Among Col Students; g/MSW at Univ AL-B'ham.

BOTWINIK, LEON oc/Programmer, Anal; b/Jan 9, 1959; h/5775 Wentworth, Cote St Luc, Quebec H4W2S3; p/David and Silvana Botwinik, Cote St Luc, Quebec; ed/Bialik HS, 1976; Vanier Col; Concordia Univ, 1982; cp/Editor, Ed Mag; Bd of Dir, Jewish Public Lib; Pres, Co-Fdr, Computer Clb; Yiddish TV Prog Yth Del; Author, Yiddish Sci-Fiction Nov; hon/Awds, Recog, Num Yiddish Essays, Stories; Ath Lttrs; g/Computer Animation; CAD-CAM; Computer Ed; Software Engrg; Yiddish Writing; Bring Yiddish & High Tech Closer Together.

BOURGAULT, DENNIS PAUL oc/Student; b/Jul 2, 1962; h/19 Walnut Street, Danvers, MA 01923; p/George A and Irene M Bourgault, Danvers, MA; ed/Danvers HS, 1980; Univ of Redlands; cp/Univ Redlands Jud Coun, Polit Sci Ctr Mem, Polit Sci Dept Adv Com, Film Commr, Post Card Campaign, US Demo Campaign Com; Cath Newman Clb Pres; Sch-Wide Christian Ldrship Coun Rep; San Bernardino Diocese Campus Min Adv Coun; Danvers HS Students for Kennedy for Pres, Coor; Danvers Precnt Capt, Kennedy for Pres; hon/Pi Gamma Mu; Omnicron Delta Kappa; Mortarbd; Outstg Student Asst, Armacost Lib; Vahe Proudian Interdisciplinary Hon Prog; Hon at Entrance; Arthur B Willis Scholar; Nat Dean's List; NHS; French Hon Soc; Intl Yth in Achmt; g/Polit Sci Deg, Pre-Law.

BOW, JONATHAN DAVID oc/Attorney; b/Aug 30, 1957; h/3610 Avenue R, Lubbock, TX 79412; ba/Lubbock, TX; m/Elizabeth Lansford; c/Scarlet; p/Jack T

Bow, Alpine, TX; sp/Joyce Lansford; ed/HS 1975; BS, Sul Ross St Univ, 1980; JD, TX Tech Sch Law, 1983; pa/Staff Atty; cp/TX Yg Lwyrs Assn; hon/W/W Am Cols & Univs; W/W Am Law Schs.

BOWDEN, BARBARA BROWN oc/Student; b/Apr 21, 1967; h/Route 5, Box 370, Harrisonburg, VA 22801; p/Charles L and Faye E Bowden, Harrisonburg, VA; ed/Turner Ashby HS; cp/Ofcs Clb Secy 1981, Clb Pres 1982, Belmont 4-H Clb, 1977-84; r/United Meth; hon/Pub'd *Bea-Bee's Bread Basket* 1983; Yth Sweepstake Winner 1979, Teen Sweepstake Winner 1982, Rockingham Co Fair; 1st Runner-Up, Teen Sweepstake, VA St Fair, 1983; VA 4-H All Star; Nat Hon Soc.

BOWDISH, FANNIE BETH oc/Student; b/Apr 1, 1962; h/Rural Route 1, Leonard, MO 63501; p/Kathleen Bowdish, Leonard, MO; ed/N Shelby, 1980; Cert, Law Enforcement Photo, 1981; Crim Justice, 1982; BS, Crim Jus, 1984; pa/Desk Staff Wkr, MO Hall, 1983-84; Ch Tchr, 1977-80; cp/Explorers 81; FHA 1970-80; Treas, FBLA, 1979; Student Coun Treas 1979, Pres 1980, Class Treas 1980; Asst Yrbook Editor, 1980; Spartan Clb, 1980-82; Lambda Alpha Epsilon, 1982-84; Jr-Sr Plays 1979-80; Chorus, 1976-80; Cheerldr, 1978; Track Mgr, 1976; Sign Lang Clb, 1983-84; r/Christian; hon/Homecoming Queen Card, 1976; Valentine Queen 1980; Prom Queen 1980; 3rd Place Yrbook Queen, 1980; Friendliest Sr Awd, 1980; Hon Student, 1980; Cadet Common Awd, 1981-82; Dir Dist'd Ams; g/Deg Crim Justice, to be a Juv Ofcr or Probation Ofcr.

BOWEN, LINDA ELAINE oc/Piano Instructor; h/Route 5, Box 335, Rock Hill, SC 29730; ba/Rock Hill, SC; p/Rev and Mrs Charlie Bowen, Elko, SC; ed/Williston-Elko HS, 1978; BMus, Winthrop Col, 1982; pa/Hd Piano Instr, Sullivan Music Ctr, 1980-; Profl Accompanist, 1982-; cp/SC Piano Fest Assn, 1980-; Phi Kappa Phi, 1982-; Concert, Jazz & Pep Band, Winthrop Col; VP Student Adv Bd, Music Dept; hon/Pres List, Grad Marshall, Winthrop Col; Rock Hill Music Clb Awd, 1979; Hogan Music Awd, 1982; Var Acad S'ships; g/to own & Operate Music Studio.

BOWEN, YVONNE RENA oc/Cashier; b/Oct 26, 1964; h/Box 196, Crittenden, KY 41030; ba/Florence, KY; p/Russell K and Barbara Bowen; Crittenden, KY; ed/Grant Co HS, 1982; Barbizon Sch Modeling, 1980; Associated Schs Inc, 1983; pa/Pt-time Cashier, Long John Silver's, 1983-; cp/Bowling; Horseback Riding; Brownie Scout; Ch Softball; Yth Choir; Acteen Pres, Secy-Treas; Boy Scout Bake Sales; Drill Team; Band; Grant Co Fair Beauty Pageant; Teens for Christ Reporter; hon/Beta Clb; Miss Congeniality; Perfect Attd; Hon Roll; W/W Among Am HS Students; g/Travel Agt.

BOWERS, LISA CAROLYN oc/Student; b/Sep 28, 1964; h/Route 3, Box 39, Selmer, TN 38375; p/Mr and Mrs J E Bowers Jr, Selmer, TN; ed/HS, 1982; cp/TN Vol Girls' St, Cnslr, 1982, 1983; Beta Clb; Intl Clb; Christian Yth Org; SS Tchr; Mod Music Masters; Mar of Dimes Walk-a-Thon; Yg Dem; Am Legion Jr Aux; hon/Hons Student Assn; W/W in Music; W/W Among Am HS Students; Soc of Dist'd Am HS Students; Soc of Dist'd Am HS Students; g/Grad from MTSU w deg in Info Sys & Acctg.

BOWMAN, JOAN ELIZABETH oc/ Computer Programmer; b/Nov 16, 1960; h/19850 CR 226, Fostoria, OH 44830; ba/Findlay, OH; p/Mr and Mrs Raymond Bowman, Fostoria, OH; ed/ Arcadia Local Sch, 1979; BS, Bowling Green St Univ, 1983; cp/4-H Pres, Secy, Treas, Jr Ldrship, Advr; Yrbk Layout Editor; Student Coun; NHS; Alpha Lambda Delta; Phi Eta Sigma; Univ Activs Org; Mar Band; All-Co Band, Chorus; 3rd, Dist Voice of Democracy Contest; Student Keynote Spkr, CoGovt Day; Pres, Yth Grp; hon/Phi Beta Kappa; VP, Kappa Mu Epsilon; Phi Kappa Phi; Mortar Bd; Fac Achmt Awd Computer Sci; Martin Essex Sch for the Gifted; Nat 4-H Citizenship Short-course; 1 of 10 Finalists, Bowling Green St Univ Ourstg Jr Competition; Yg Commun Ldrs; Intl Yth Achmt; g/ Computer Programmer.

BOWSER, JOANN oc/Student; b/ Nov 28, 1966; h/2837 Fordwood Drive, Charlotte, NC 28208; p/Mr Terry W and Gladys C Bowser, Charlotte, NC; ed/Charlotte Cath HS; cp/Track Team; French Clb; r/Bapt; hon/1st and 2nd Hons, 1982; g/Psychol.

BOYCE, KIMBERLY ANNE oc/ WCLF Channel 22; b/Mar 14, 1961; h/ 1014 Inman Terrace, Winter Haven, FL 33881; ba/Clearwater, FL; p/Mr and Mrs Richard Boyce, Winter Haven, FL; ed/Evangel Christian Sch, 1979; Univ S FL; pa/Vocalist, Ctl Sound Studio; On the Air Personality, WTWB Radio; Assoc Prodr, "Action 60's", WCLF Channel 22; Profl Singer; Newscaster, PTL Satellite Netwk; hon/Miss Manatee Co, 1983; W/W Among Am HS Students; Salutatorian; Nat Hon Soc; g/perf Contemp Christian Music & TV.

BOYD, KIMBERLY REBECCA oc/ Student; h/1015 South Howard Circle, Tarboro, NC 27886; b/Nov 27, 1961; p/ Mr and Mrs T Chapman Boyd Jr, Tarboro, NC; ed/Tarboro HS, 1980; BA, Univ NC, 1984; cp/Zeta Tau Alpha Wom's Frat; Theta Tau Chapt; Derby Wk Fund-Raising Chm; NC Student Acad Sci; French Clb; Proj Chm; Drama Clb; Jr Mtl Hlth Assn; Nat Hon Soc; r/Epis; hon/Chief Marshal, 1979; E Carolina Univ Hons Sem in Sci 1979; E Carolina Univ Math Contest, 1978, 1979, 1980; Most Studious, 1980; Valedictorian, 1980; NC Gov's Sch Nom; Outstg Sr; W/W Among Am HS Students; g/Advtg Agy.

BOYDEN, KAREN VANESSA oc/ Legal Assistant; b/Nov 4, 1961; h/101 Liberty Road, Apartment E, Bergen-field, NJ 07621; ba/New York, NY; p/ Carl and Genolia Boyden, Bergenfield, NJ; ed/Woodrow Wilson HS; Col Prep, 1978; BS, AS, Bluefield St Col, 1980; pa/Legal Asst, 1981; Files Clk, VA Hosp, 1980; Cashier & Sales Clk, Fashion Bug Clothing Store, 1977-80; Clk Recep-tionist, Bluefield St Col, 1982; Clk Receptionist, Media Ctr, Bluefield St Col, 1979; cp/Delta Sigma Theta Sor-ority Inc; Pres, 1981-82; Col Campus Newspaper, 1982; r/Bapt; hon/Nat Hon Soc, 1978; Alpha Chi Nat Hon S'ship Soc; Magna Cum Laude Grad; S'ship from St of WV; g/Law Sch.

BOYER, ROGER LEE oc/Associate Engineer, Nuclear Safety Analysis; h/

9930 Sagegreen, Houston, TX 77234; ba/Houston, TX; m/Julia Y; p/Glenn and Twila Boyer, Palmyra, MO; sp/John and Anna Yuhas, Sugar Creek, MO; ed/ Palmyra HS, 1976; BS-Mech Engr 1981, BS-Nuclear Engr 1981, MS-Nuclear Engr 1983, Univ MO-Rolla; pa/Asst Engr, Union Elect Co, 1980-82; Assc Engr, Houston Lighting & Power, 1983-; cp/Beta Sigma Psi; Interfrat Coun; Blue Key; Cir K; Nat Soc of Profl Engrs; MO Soc of Profl Engrs; Am Nuclear Soc; ASME; Repub Nat Com; Am Soc of Heating, Refrig & Air Conditioning Engrs; Beta Chi Sigma; Theta Tau; Key Clb; Yng Engrs & Scist; r/Luth; hon/Author of "Analyzing & Predicting Nat Circulationg for a SNUPPS's PWR Using RETRAN-01" 1983; Inst Nuclear Power Opers F'ship, 1982; Tau Beta Pi, 1982; Alpha Nu Sigma, 1982; Eagle Scout w Silver Palm; Am Legion Americanism Awd; Bausch & Lomb Sci Awd; Mo Am Legion Boy Scout of Yr; W/W Am Cols & Univs; Intl Yth in Achmt;; Nat Register of Outstg Col Students; Commun Ldrs Am; g/Nuclear Engrg; Fam; Promote Scouting; Mgmt Position.

BOYETTE, LAWRENCE JOYNER oc/Student; b/Mar 4, 1959; h/1703 Beaumont Drive, Greenville, NC 27834; p/Dr Joseph G and Mrs Evelyn L Boyette, Greenville, NC; ed/J H Rose HS, 1977; BA, Univ NC-Chapel Hill, 1983; pa/Journeyman Electrician, Brown & Root Constrn, 1979-80; Guitarist, Jazz Plus Band, 1982-83; cp/ Ftball; hon/Nat Hon Soc; Phi Eta Sigma; Phi Beta Kappa; Nat Merit S'ship Finalist; Rush Rhees F'ship, Univ Rochester; W/W Among Am HS Stu-dents; g/PhD in Hist, Career as Histn.

BOYLES, SANDRA KAY b/Jan 14, 1953; h/2950 Bixby Lane, Apartment A304, Boulder, CO 80303; p/J W and Louise Boyles, OKC, OK; ed/NW Classen HS, 1971; BMus 1976, MMus 1977, Univ OK; Att'g Univ CO; pa/Pvt Piano Tchr; cp/Am Musicology Soc; Music Tchrs Nat Assn; Cert'd Piano Tchr; Sigma Alpha Iota; Greenpeace; Alpha Gamma Delta; Jr Music Clb of OK, Pres, 5th VP; hon/S'ship, Am Col of Musicians; Nat Guild of Piano Tchrs Paderewski Medal; W/W in Music; World W/W of Wom; Commun Ldrs Am; g/Completion of Doct Musical Arts Deg.

BRACKETT, LYNN ELIZABETH oc/ Student; b/Nov 14, 1962; h/PO Box 14, Lawndale, NC 28090; p/Mr and Mrs Woodrow Lafay Brackett, Lawndale, NC; ed/Grad, NS, 1981; Wn Carolina Univ; cp/Nat Hon Soc; Beta Clb; Spanish Hon Soc; Spanish Clb; Quill & Scroll; Volleyball; Basketball; Keywannettes; Jr Class Pres; Sr Class Treas; Student Coun; Delta Zeta Sorority, S'ship Chm 1983, Pres 1984; Mortar Bd Sr Hon Soc; Alpha Lambda Delta Hon Soc; Student Marshal Clb; Mem, Cullowhee Connec-tion; F'ship Christian Aths; Newspaper Staff; r/Lawndale Meth Ch; hon/WCU Freshman Math Awd, 1982; WCU Panhellenic S'ship Awd, 1983, 1984; Delta Zeta Province XXI S'ship Awd, 1984; Patrons of Quality S'ship; Charles I Dover S'ship; Barrier Salutatory S'ship; Lawndale Wom's Clb S'ship; Exch Clb Yth of Mo; g/Maj in Computer Sci & Math.

BRADNER, JOEL L oc/Student; b/

Apr 18, 1966; h/Route 1, Box 207, Gladys, VA 24554; p/Mr C E Bradner, Gladys, VA, and Mrs D C Bradner, Restburg, VA; ed/William Campbell HS, 1984; Lynchburg Col; pa/Farming; Computer Programmer, Oper, Conslt, William Campbell HS Guid Dept, 1983-84; Pt-time Employmt at Local Restaurant, 1982-83; cp/Student Govt; FFA; KVG; Sci Clb; Nat Beta Clb; Spanish Clb; r/Bapt; hon/Valedictorian of Class; Recip of Gtr Lynchburg Area Hon S'ship; NMSQT Lttr of Commend; 1983 VA Gov's Sch for Gifted; Cert for Outstg Achmt in Computer Sci, Eng, Jour, Adv'd Math, Biol, Chem, Physics; W/W Am HS Students; g/Jt Maj in Computer Sci & Bus Adm.

BRADSHAW, RITA LYNN oc/Stu-dent; b/Sep 23, 1961; h/Rural Route Number 4, Frankfort, IN 46041; p/Mr and Mrs Mike Reppert, Frankfort, IN; ed/Clinton Ctl HS, 1980; Anderson Col; pa/Bkkpr, Hoosier Stockyards Inc, 1980-; Resident Asst 1981-82, 1982-83, Acctg Grading & Lab Asst 1983-84, Anderson Col; cp/Search Grp Ldr, 1983-84; HS Class Pres; Choir Pres, 1979-80; Student Coun; Hon Soc VP, 1979-80; r/Prot; hon/DAR Good Citizen 1980; Elks Yth Hon Day Participant, 1980; Girls' St Rep; I Dare You Awd, 1979; Arion Awd, 1980; Dean's List; W/ W Am HS Students; Nat Dean's List; g/CPA, Hoosier Stockyards Inc as Bkkpr/Acct.

BRADY, LORI GAIL oc/Student; b/ Dec 2, 1968; h/Route 3, Box 330, Tullahoma, TN 37388; p/Ray and Janie Brady, Tullahoma, TN; ed/Franklin Co HS; cp/Jr Beta Clb; Adv Coun, F'ship of Christian Aths, 1983-84; r/Bapt; hon/ 8th Grad Scholastic Awd; Hon Roll; Most Studious; Top 10% in Nation on Nat Ednl Devel Test, 1984; g/to attend TN Technol Inst, Career in Engrg.

BRAGG, SUSANNE BETH b/May 31, 1956; h/Post Office Box 31882, Phoenix, AZ 85046; m/Ronald Lee; c/Venessa Joan; p/Donald and Joan Sockrider, Phoenix, AZ; ed/Paradise Val HS, 1974; BS, The Univ of AZ, 1978; Master's of Cnslg, AZ St Univ, 1982; cp/Paradise Val Ed Assn; Gifted Students Com; Campo Bello PTA; Fac Adv Com; Social Chm for Fac, kachina Jr Wom Clb-GFWC, Pres, Mem at Large; AFWC-JM, Chm Bylaws Com; Paradise Val Jr WC, Social Chm 1982-; Campo Bello Sch, Grade Level Rep, 1982-83; CoChm Contests; AFWC Ctl Dist Chm; Ed Dept Shephard of the Hills Cong Ch; Extracurric Intl Spa; hon/Phi Kappa Phi; Finalist, Clb Pres of the Yr; Intl W/W in Wom; Intl W/W in Am; g/Cnslg; Corp Job; PhD.

BRAGG, STACY ANNE oc/Public Relations Consultant; b/Oct 31, 1961; h/1405 West Monmouth Court, Rich-mond, VA 23233; p/Mr and Mrs John P Bragg, Richmond, VA; ed/Douglas Southall Freeman HS, 1979; BA, Elon Col, 1983; pa/Public Relats Conslt, 1983-; cp/Sigma Sigma Sigma; Intl Assn Bus Communicators; r/Presb; hon/ Articles Pub'd in *Burlington Daily Times News*, *Greensboro Daily News*, *Alamance-Orange Enterprise*; Sigma Tau Delta; Dean's List; Nat Dean's List; Highest GPA in Sigma Sigma Sigma; Yg Personalities of Am.

BRAHMSTEDT, ALICIA KAY oc/ Graduate Student; b/Apr 21, 1961; h/

935 Glenwood Drive, Cookeville, TN 38501; p/Dr and Mrs Howard Brahmstedt, Cookeville, TN; ed/BMus Ed, TN Technol Univ, 1983; MMus Ed, Univ IL, 1984; pa/Tchg Asst, Univ IL, 1983-84; Flag Instr, Smith-Walbridge Camps, Syracuse IN, 1983; Dir of Marching Illini Band, Univ IL; Accompanist & Pvt Piano Instrn, 1980-83; Dance Instr, Alicia's Sch of Dance, 1977-80; Flag Instr, TN Technol, 1980-83; Choreography Work, Sum Theater & Chd's Theater Grps; cp/Alpha Delta Pi; MENC; r/Cath; hon/W/W Am Cols; W/ W Am HS Students; Mortar Bd Ser Org; Phi Kappa Phi; Num Awds & Hons.

BRAMES, ELISA MARIE oc/Student; b/Nov 18, 1962; h/13026 South McArdle Road, Monroeville, IN 46773; p/ Joanne Brames, Monroeville, IN; ed/ Heritage HS, 1981; Indiana Univ-Purdue Univ; pa/Lib Clk Law Firm, Ft Wayne IN; cp/Concert Choir, Spanish Clb, Heritage Scholastic Soc, Copywriter for Yrbook, Class Secy, HS; r/Rom Cath; hon/C of C Awd, 1981; Hoosier Scholar, 1981; Chancellor's List at IN Univ-Purdue Univ, 1982; g/to Maj in Bus Adm.

BRANDON, LISA ANN oc/Student; b/Aug 12, 1966; h/Route 1, Manchester, TN 37355; p/Mr and Mrs Billy C Brandon, Manchester, TN; ed/Manchester Ctl HS, 1984; cp/Beta Clb, 1980-84; Spanish Clb, 1982-84; Student Coun, 1980, 1982-84; Band, Majorette, 1981-84; Track Varsity, 1980-84; Basketball, 1980-84; Kappa Chi Omega Sorority 1981-84; r/Ch of Christ; hon/ All Star-Softball, 1981-83; All Tour-Softball, 1983; Fball Homecoming Attendant, 1983; Coffee Co Fairest of the Fair, 1983-84; W/W Among Am HS Students; g/Motlow Col, RN, Anesth.

BRANSCOM, DAVID DOUGLAS oc/Student; b/Feb 5, 1963; h/Route 1, Box 192, Fincastle, VA 24090; ba/ Lexington, VA; p/Mr and Mrs Frederick D Branscom, Fincastle, Va; ed/Lord Botetourt HS; mil/ROTC Cadet; r/ Presb; hon/Lord Botetourt HS, Outstg Ath, Nat Hon Soc; DAR Good Citizen Awd, Nat Conf of Christians & Jews Awd, F'ship of Christian Aths Awd; Wash & Lee Univ, Dept of the Army Superior Cadet Awd, James S Wood Prize in German, Mil Order of the World Wars Awd; g/Math Maj, to become Army Ofcr.

BRANSON, ALLISON U oc/Leasing Representative; b/Dec 23, 1958; h/53 West Emerson, Melrose, MA 02176; ba/ Woburn, MA; p/Mark and Jean Branson, Glens Falls, NY; ed/Salem Ctl Sch, 1975; Mt Holyoke Col, 1980; Rotary Exch Student, 1975-76; pa/Stockbroker, Dean Witter Reynolds, 1980-84; Leasing Rep, Continental Financial Resources, 1984-; cp/US Combined Tng Assn; Editor, 1975; Soccer Team, 1978-79; hon/MHC Chem Awd, 1979; DAR Good Citizen, 1975; Regents S'ship, 1975; Hon Soc, 1975.

BRASHER, JERRY WAYNE oc/Executive; b/Jun 10, 1954; h/Post Office Box 15689, Baton Rouge, LA 70895; ba/ Baton Rouge, LA; p/Mr and Mrs Tallie John Brasher Sr, Madison, MS; ed/Ctl HS, 1972; BS, MS St Univ, 1980; AA 1980, AS 1976, Hinds Jr Col; mil/AUS, 1972-74; pa/Pres, Galactica Sports/Med Indust, 1983-; Indust Engr, Cameron

Iron Wks, 1980-83; TX Soc Profl Engrs; Am Inst Indust Engrs; Soc Mfg Engrs; Am Soc Metals; Iron & Steel Soc; r/ Christian; hon/Patents incl'g Optical Distance Finder, Force Converter, Force Positioner; Tau Beta Pi; Alpha Pi Mu; Phi Kappa Phi; Phi Theta Kappa; Army Commend Medal; Good Conduct Medal; Nat Def Ser Medal; Lifetime Cannoneer of the 1st Armored Div Artillery; Cert of Tng; Cert of Awd; Cert of Safety; Biographical Roll of Hon; Intl Yth Achmt; Commun Ldrs of Am; Outstg Yg Men of Am; W/W in S & SW; Dir of Dist'd Ams; g/PhD in Physics & Work in Res.

BRASWELL, CRYSTAL REBECCA oc/Student, Salesperson; b/Aug 5, 1964; h/310 Smith Road, Mt Holly, NC 28120; ba/Gastonia, NC; p/James D and Reva C Braswell, Mt Holly, NC; ed/E Gaston HS, 1982; Belmont Abbey Col; pa/ Salesperson, Mr Darrell Farley; cp/Jour Staff; Pres, Sun Sch; Pres, Tng Union; Sun Sch Yth Coun; Ch-wide Yth Coun; Gaston Co Hlth Dept Fam Planning Adv Coun Teen Com; TAPS; Art Soc; Spanish Clb; FTA; Commun Ser; r/Bapt; hon/Lit Mag, 1982; Newspaper Article, 1982; Acteens Queen & Queen w Septor; W/W Among Am HS Students; Commun Ldrs of Am; g/BA Computer Sci, Computer Programmer.

BRAUNING, DONALD RAY JR oc/ Student; b/Jun 8, 1962; h/282 Kinsman Court, Cincinnati, OH 45238; p/Donald and Dell Brauning, Cincinnati, OH; ed/ Oak Hills HS, 1980; Col Preparatory, Acctg; No KY Univ, 1985; cp/Pi Kappa Alpha Frat, Secy Rush Com 1981, Asst Treas 1982, Treas 1982-83, Pres 1984; Student Govt, Univ Affairs Com, 1983-84; r/Cath; hon/Pi Kappa Alpha Calendar, 1982-83, Sales/Promotions; Piano S'ship, 1980-81; Nom'd Pike of Mo, 1983; Nom'd for Undergrad Mem to Supreme Coun Pikes, 1983; g/CPA; Start own Bus/Acctg Firm.

BRAWLEY, JAMIE BLANCHE oc/ Student; b/Jan 7, 1962; h/4655 Mahoning Road, Newton Falls, OH 44444; p/ James and Janet Brawley, Newton Falls, OH; ed/SE HS, 1980; Kent St Univ; pa/ Mgr, Jamie's Restaurant, 1976-; cp/ Varisty Basketball; Volleyball; Track; Softball; Class Pres; Student Coun; Pepsi-Cola Hotshot Basketball Team; Horse 4-H, 1976-80; hon/Col Dean's List, 1983; Mem, Nat Dean's List; Mem, Beta Gamma Sigma; MVP Awd, All-Star Team in Softball; Dean's List, 1981; W/W Among Am HS Students; Intl Yth in Achmt; Commun Ldrs of Am; g/Deg in Bus Mgmt & Ec.

BRAY, KATHI DAWN oc/Student; b/ Sep 15, 1964; h/1000 North Chowning, Edmond, OK 73034; ba/OKC, OK; p/ Mr and Mrs Marlin Bray, Norman, OK; ed/Wn Hgts HS, 1982; Att'g Ctl St Univ; pa/Waitress, Cashier, Ken's Pizza, 1978-81; Hostess, Steak N Ale Restaurant, 1981; Cashier, Commonwealth Theatres Inc, 1981-; Apex Temp Sers, 1983-; cp/Student Senate, Ct St Univ; Col DECA, VP; Delta Zeta Social Sorority, S'ship Chm, Rush Cnslr; Daughs of Diana of Tau Kappa Epsilon Frat; hon/Alpha Lambda Delta Freshman Hon Soc; Top Ten Freshman of Ctl St Univ; Dean's Hon Roll; Outstg Pledge & S'ship for Delta Zeta Sorority; Nat So Reg Rep for Nat Prog Devel Coun for Col Div of DECA.

BRAY, LESLEY LYNN oc/Student; b/ Oct 5, 1964; h/Rural Route 1, Box 712, Noblesville, IN 46060; p/Philip D and Helen Bray, Noblesville, IN; ed/Westfield HS; Att'g IN Ctl Univ; cp/VP Student Coun, 1979-83; Band Secy, 1982-83; French Clb, 1982-83, VP; Spanish Clb; FCA, 1980-83; Editor of Newspaper, 1983; Nat Hon Soc, 1981-83; Drama Clb, 1982-83; r/Meth; hon/Outstg Student, 1978; Am Legion Awd, 1980; W/W Awd; USNAA Art Awd; g/Maj in Phy Therapy & Sports Med.

BRAY, PERRY LYVONNE oc/Student; b/Aug 26, 1961; h/Box 14, Roundhill, KY 42275; p/Mr and Mrs Samie Bray, Roundhill, KY; ed/Edmonson Co HS, 1979; BS 1984, MS 1985, Wn KY Univ; cp/Rec Ldr, Tennis Attendant, Bowling Green Pks & Rec Dept, 1983-; Sports Clb Coor, Pt-time Admr 1981-83, Facility Supvr 1982, Student Secy 1979-81, Wn KY Univ Campus Rec Dept; Hilltopper Hundred Clb, 1979-82; cp/KY Rec & Pk Soc; Wn KY Univ Rec Majs Clb; Nat Intramural-Rec Sports Assn; Univ Ctr Bd; Spec Olympics Vol; r/Bapt; hon/Sports Clb Com, Nat Intramural-Rec Sports Assn; Com Chp, KY Special Olympics; Pres's List; Signs & Decorations Chm, 1981; Pres, FBLA, 1978-79; W/W Among Am HS Students; Intl Yth in Achmt; Yg Personalities of S; g/Wk as Sports Clb Coor at Maj Univ.

BRAYNARD, PENNY JEANETTE oc/Emergency Medical Technician; b/Jul 13, 1962; h/3807 South Hopkins, Number 20, Titusville, FL 32780; ba/ Titusville, FL; p/Mr and Mrs Herbert H Braynard II, Melbourne, FL; ed/Ctl Cath HS, 1981; Brevard Commun Col, Cert Emer Med Technol, 1982; pa/ Danish Interiors Inc, 1978; Counter Help, Wendy's, 1979; Counter Help, McDonald's, 1979-80; Salesclk, Sears, 1980; Bakery Clk, Publix Palm Bay Danish Bakery, 1981; Dietary Aide, W Melbourne Hlth Care Ctr, 1981; Cashier, Melbourne Fruit & Produce Inc, 1981; Ranger, Space Ctr Campground, 1982-; cp/Pres, Secy & Treas, GSA; Jr Aux, J E Holmes Reg Med Ctr; Special Olympics; Instr for First Aid & CPR, ARC; HS Mem, Brain Bowl, Key Clb, French Clb, FHA, Drama, Liturgy, Dance & Drill Team; r/Rom Cath; hon/ Hon by Gov Bob Graham on Becoming 1st Class Girl Scout; Hon by Aux at J E Holmes Reg Med Ctr for Vol Over 700 Hours, 1980-81; W/W Among Am HS Students; W/W Among Intl HS Students; Yg Ldrs of Am; Commun Ldrs Am; g/Cert of Fire-Tng; Paramed Prog.

BRAZIEL, MARTEN LEIGH oc/Student; b/Jul 1, 1959; h/Route 1, Box 359, Pitts, GA 31072; p/Delano R and Barbara C Braziel, Pitts, GA; ed/Wilcox Co HS, 1977; BMus, GA So Col, 1981; GA Studies Abroad Prog, 1979; Am Conserv, 1980; cp/Opera Theatre; Statesboro Symph; Savannah Symph Orch; Kappa Delta; Gamma Beta Phi VP; Phi Kappa Phi; Delta Phi Alpha VP; Sigma Alpha Iota Treas; hon/Music S'ship; Magna Cum Laude Grad; GA Gov Hon Prog; Star Student S'ship; g/ Profl Opera/Oratorio Career in Europe; Vocal Technique Tng; Drama Wkshops; Repertoire Classes; German, French Study.

BREED, GWEN ELIZABETH oc/

Student; b/Apr 18, 1961; h/4319 Wickerfield Drive, St Louis, MO 63128; p/David and Lorraine Breed; ed/Lindbergh HS, 1979; St Louis Univ; cp/Awana; GSA; Camp Cnslr; Bible Quiz Team Capt; Pre-Med Clb; Explorers; Candy Striper; Nurse Aide; Spanish Clb; Intervarsity Christian F'ship; Med-Tech Clb; hon/Chd & Ambassador of Christ; Awana Meritorious Awd; 1st Class Girl Scout; g/Med Tech, Med.

BRENEMAN, CINDY LaVERNE oc/Media Consultant; b/Jan 14, 1961; h/6924 Delta Lake Drive, Charlotte, NC 28215; ba/Charlotte, NC; p/Carl David Sr and Nancy C Breneman, Charlotte, NC; ed/BA, Univ NC-Greensboro, 1983; pa/Univ NC-Greensboro Dorm Receptionist, 1980; Olsten Temp, Barclays Am, Charlotte, NC Mktg/Advtg Dept, 1981; Creat Temp, First Union Bk & McDevitt & Street; Munn & Assocs, Inc, 1983; cp/Charlotte Yth Ah Clb; Cheerldr, 1977; Basketball 1978; The Little Theatre of Charlotte, 1978; Student Govt Secy, 1979; Jour Clb, 1978-79; Camera Clb 1979; Math Clb 1979; Drama Clb, 1977-79; FTA, 1979; Photog Ftball Team; Newspaper Staff Photog & Writer, 1978-79; Editor for Feature Mag; Col WUAG-FM Radio News Announcer & Disc Jockey, 1979-82; Elliott Univ Coun Mem, 1979-83; Spec Events Com Mem & Exec Staff Mem, 1980; Pres, Alpha Chi Omega, 1980-82; Zeta Xi Chapt, Charter Mem, 1982; UNCG Senate Mem, 1979, 1982; Univ Media Bd Mem, 1982; hon/The Little Theatre of Charlotte, Best Supporting Actress in *Camelot*, *Flowers for Algernon*, 1978; HS Best Actress, 1978, 1979; W Stanly Player of the Yr, 1979; NHS, 1978; Nom for Gov Sch in Theatre Arts, 1978; Pheiffer Col 3 Credit Hrs SPEC in Theatre Arts, 1977; Golden Chain Hon Soc, 1982, 1983 Nom for Outstg Sr, Ser Awd for Senate Activs; Sr Awds in Jour, Drama & Ser; g/Master's Deg in Advtg, Public Relats w Background in Eng & Writing; Position in Public Relats or Media Consltg.

BREWER, LINDA HAASE oc/Youth Ministry; b/May 21, 1957; h/720 South 6th Street, Montebello, CA 90640; m/Rev Brian David; p/Robert L and Violet M Haase, Olympia, WA; sp/Ronald L and Maxine Brewer, Sweet Home, OR; ed/Olympia HS, 1975; AA, BA, NW Col, 1981; Gen Cert, Am Inst of Bkg, 1978; pa/Teller 1976-81, Note Teller 1981-83, Seattle Trust; cp/March of Dimes; FBLA Pres; ASB Treas; Student Coun; Senate; Jr Class Secy-Treas; World Outreach Min; ASB Coun; Cnslg Intern; Yth Camp Dir; S/B Yth Camp Cnslr; hon/Outstg Bus Student of Yr; NW Col Dean's List; Outstg Yg Wom of Am; W/W Among Students in Am Cols & Univs; g/Christian Ed; Cnslg Min.

BRICHETTO, ANNETTE HELENE oc/Student, Assistant Bookkeeper; b/Dec 12, 1960; h/2054 West Foster Avenue, Chicago, IL 60625; p/Paul and Marie Brichetto, Chicago, IL; ed/Roald Amundsen HS, 1978; BS, DePaul Univ, 1982; cp/Rho Delta Pi, Pledge Class Pres, Rush Com, Treas, Pledge Chm, Ad Book Chm; Homecoming Dance Com, Publicity CoChm, Dance/Reservations CoChm; Inter-Sorority Coun, Pres, Del, Dance Com; Blood Drive

Chm; Intramural Sports; Homecoming Dance Com; Orient Com, Carnival Chm, Grp Ldr; Mgmt Clb; hon/Blue Key Nat Hon Frat; DePaul Univ Competitive Scholar; Outstg Sr Ldr Awd; Delta Sigma Pi Little Sister; Phi Kappa Theta Little Sister; W/W Am Cols & Univs; g/MBA.

BRICKEY, JANICE KAY MAGNUSEN oc/Housewife, Mother; h/Route 2, Box 120-G, Rockwood, TN 37854; m/Ralph E; c/Sara Ruth; p/Mr and Mrs William H Magnusen, Newport News, VA; sp/Louella R Brickey, Harriman, TN; ed/Burt Commun HS, 1970; Roane St Commun Col; BA, Univ TN, 1983; cp/Nat Hon Soc; r/Christian; hon/Highest Hons Dean's List, Univ TN, 1980; Dean's List, Roane St Commun Col, 3 Times; Nat Dean's List.

BRIDGES, LISA JOY oc/Student; b/Dec 26, 1967; h/29 Mennonite Lane, Newport News, VA 23602; p/Mr and Mrs Charles D Bridges, Newport News, VA; ed/Menchville HS; pa/Over 100 Hours Vol Wk at Hampton Convalescent Ctr; hon/Outstg Citizenship Awd, 1982; Nat Jr Teen, 1982; g/Career as Mortician; Own Funeral Home.

BRIGHTMAN, CHARLES RAYMOND oc/Student; b/Mar 10, 1962; h/100 Woodlawn Place, Tullahoma, TN 37388; p/Mr and Mrs Jerry L Brightman, Tullahoma, TN; ed/Tullahoma HS, 1980; AS, Motlow St Commun Col, 1982; Att'g Mid TN St Univ; pa/Microcraft Inc, 1978-82; First Fed Savings & Loan Assn, 1982; cp/Assn MBA Execs Inc; r/First Christian; hon/Dean's List at Motlow St; Jack K Adams S'ship Awd in Mktg, Mid TN St Univ; g/MBA w Emphasis in Mktg; Career in Advtg.

BRITT, BETTY ANN oc/Student; b/Feb 3, 1962; h/Route 2, Box 265, Angier, NC 27501; p/Mr and Mrs J B Britt, Angier, NC; ed/Harnett Ctl HS, 1980; cp/Ch Yth Choir; Yth Coun; Band; Beta Clb; Math Clb; Sci Clb; Latin Clb; Biomed Clb; Student Coun; hon/Charles B and Alma Dark Howard S'ship; Hon Grad; All-Co Band; Outstg Bus Driver Awd; Commun Ldrs Am; g/BS Biol, Grad Sch in Med.

BRIZENDINE, JAMIE RENEÉ oc/Student, Intern; b/Jan 20, 1962; h/Route 1, Guthrie, KY 42234; ed/Todd Co HS, 1980; Univ GA, Fashion Mdsing, 1983; pa/Internship, Davison's, 1983; 4-H Clb, 1971-80, Nat Congress, Proj Ldr, Camp Cnslr, Fund Raising Activs; Spkr for Rotary Clb & FHA; Angel Flight, 1980-81; Alpha Chi Omega Sorority, VP of Pledge Class, 1982; Candy Striper, 1978-79; Phi Gamma Delta Little Sister, Treas 1982; NY Fashion Study Tour, 1983; r/Ch of Christ; hon/Miss KY United Teenager, 1979; KY Farm Bur Queen, 1979; Miss Univ GA Agri, 1980; Valedictorian, 1980; Nat Hon Soc, 1980; g/Retail Mgmt, Fashion Promotion, Advtg.

BROCK, JONATHAN EUGENE oc/Student; b/Jan 3, 1966; h/105 Sunset Drive, Easley, SC 29640; p/Hamilton E and Barbara Owen Brock, Easley, SC; ed/HS; cp/Wn Reg Band, 1980, 1981, 1982; Student Coun, 1982; Arrow of Light, 1977; r/Christian; hon/Essay Contest, 1982; Gov's Sch for Arts, 1983; g/Maj Eng, Creat Writer.

BROCK, RUTH ELLEN oc/Traveling Collegiate Secretary; b/Jun 17, 1960; h/

201 Vanderbilt Lane, Cowan, TN 37318; ba/Atlanta, GA; p/J R and Virginia McKowan Brock, Cowan, TN; ed/Franklin Co HS, 1978; BBA, Mid TN St Univ, 1983; pa/Teller, Franklin Co Bk, 1981-83; cp/Alpha Delta Pi Sorority, Pledge Ed VP; Mid TN St Univ Panhellenic Assn, 2nd VP, Treas; Am Soc Pers Adm, Prog Dir, 1982-83; Md TN St Univ Gen Sessions Ct Justice, 1982-83; Gamma Beta Phi Hon Soc, 1979-83; Tau Omicron Wom's Hon Soc, 1980-83; Rho Lambda Greek Wom's Hon Soc, 1981-83; Mid TN Associated Student Body Cabinet, 1980; Kappa Alpha Little Sister, 1981-82; Pres Classroom for Yg Ams Alumnae Assn; hon/Dorothy Shaw Ldrship Awd, 1983; W/W Among Am Cols & Univs; Nat Dean's List; g/MBA; Pers Mgmt.

BROCKHOFF, MARY ANNE b/Dec 8, 1960; h/Route 2, Box 369, Conover, NC 28613; p/William and Jean Brockhoff, Conover, NC; ed/Newton Conover HS, 1979; BS, Univ NC-Charlotte, 1983; mil/Navy Nurse Corps; pa/Halman's Nursery, 1975; Cashier, Hardee's, 1979-83; Nurses Asst, Catawba Meml Hosp, 1981-82; cp/Student Nurses Assn; Sigma Theta Tau; Intramural Sports; r/Cath; hon/Louis Armstrong Jazz Awd, 1979; Music Merit Awd, 1979; Sigma Theta Tau, 1983; W Among Am HS Students; g/Navy Nurse Corps.

BROOKS, BARBARA ANN oc/Student; b/Feb 14, 1964; h/113 Main Street, Post Office Box 470, Ridgeley, WV 26753; c/James Robert; p/Mrs Elizabeth Ann Brooks, Ridgeley, WV; ed/Frankfort HS, 1982; Potomac St Col; cp/Sch Activs; hon/Lion's Clb Citizenship Awd; DAR Citizenship Awd; W/W Among Am HS Students; Dir of Dist'd Ams; Intl Yth in Achmt; g/Mech Engrg.

BROOKS, GEORGE BENJAMIN JR oc/Vice President, Director of Research & Development; b/Sep 28, 1955; h/5040 Comanche Drive, Number 115, La Mesa, CA 92041; ba/Scottsdale, AZ; p/Dr and Mrs G Benjamin Brooks, Phoenix, AZ; ed/E HS, 1973; BS, AZ St Univ Tempe, 1980; MS Cand, 1984, San Diego St Univ; pa/Bio/Phy Sci Tchr, USDA Water Conserv Lab, 1979-81; Asst Mgr, McDonald's Oper Co, 1981-82; Staff Biologist, Aquatic Fish Farms AZ, 1981-82; Indep Aquatic Resources Consult, 1982-; VP Res & Devel, Aquatic Food & Energy Sys Intl, 1984-; Nat Tech Assn; Marine Technol Soc; cp/World Mariculture Soc; CA Aquaculture Assn; Elem Inst Sci, Bd Dir; San Diego Coun Black Engrs, Bd Dir; Kappa Alpha Psi Frat; Sigma Xi; r/Presb; hon/Co Author, "Simulation of a Low Cost Method for Solar Heating an Aquaculture Pond" Energy in Agri, 1983; Cited as One of 50 Upcoming Yg Ldrs of the 80's, Ebony Mag, 1983; Black Scist Yr, St of AZ, 1984, AZ Coun Black Engrs & Scists; g/PhD Univ CA Davis-San Diego St Univ Co-op Prog.

BROOKS, JAMES HENRY oc/Student; b/Dec 14, 1965; h/1121 East Irvine, Richmond, KY 40475; p/Henry and Peggy Brooks, Richmond, KY; ed/Madison HS, 1983; pa/Yth Employmt, Univ KY Biochem Dept, 1982; cp/Beta Clb, Treas, 1982-83; Sci Clb, 1981; Quill & Scroll Clb, Pres, 1981-82; F'ship Christian Students; Newspaper Staff, Editor, 1981-82; NAACP, 1982; r/

Missionary Bapt; hon/WOW Awd; US Achmt Acad Awd in Bus Ed; Nat Soc Math Engrs Awd, 1983; Cumberland Col S'ship; Soc of Dist'd HS Students, 1981-83; W/W Among Am HS Students; g/Maj in Premed Biol; Doct Deg.

BROSS, JAMES BEVERLY JR oc/Student, Part-time Accountant; h/7 Thomas Lane, Box 497 CWC, Central, SC 29630; ba/Ctl, SC; p/Dr and Mrs James Bross, Ctl, SC; ed/D W Daniel HS, 1980; BA, Ctl Wesleyan Col, 1984; pa/Pt-time Acct, D Ken Whitener Acctg Sers, 1983-; Pulmonary Function Tech, Dan River Woodside Mills, Liberty Med Clin, 1981-; cp/Ctl First Wesleyan Ch Bd Adm; Ctl Wesleyan Col Student Govt Assn; S C Delta Chapt, Alpha Chi Hon Soc; Student Mem, Nat Assn Accts; r/Prot; hon/Ctl Wesleyan Col Student Govt Assn Pres, 1983-84; Alpha Chi Hon Soc, VP, 1984; Outstg Yg Men Am; W/W Am Univs & Cols; g/BA-Acctg, Bus Adm, Psychol; CPA; Financial Mgmt.

BROTHERS, HENRY J II oc/Student; b/Sep 17, 1957; h/401 Robert Road, Slidell, LA 70458; p/William C and Sally S Brothers, Slidell, LA; ed/Slidell HS, 1975; BA, Tulane Univ, 1979; Geo Wash Univ, JD Expected 1984; cp/BSA Eagle Scout, Order of the Arrow, Vigil Hon, Camp Cnslr, Asst Scoutmaster; Key Clb Treas; Capt, Ftball, All-Dist Team; VP, Assoc Student Body, Tulane; VP, Kappa Alpha Order; Dorm Advr; hon/Omicron Delta Kappa; Kappa Delta Phi; g/Law Pract.

BROWN, BRENDA BRITT oc/Adjunct Faculty; b/Sep 30, 1951; h/Route 6, Box 900, Brookhaven, MS 39601; ba/Hattiesburg, MS; c/Shay; p/Mr and Mrs W D Britt Sr, Brookhaven, MS; ed/Brookhaven HS, 1969; Assoc's Deg w hons, Copiah-Lincoln Jr Col, 1971; BA w hons 1981, Master's Deg 1984, Univ So MS, 1983, 1984; cp/VP 1980-81, Pres 1982, Secy 1983, Logos (Phil) Clb; Lambda Iota Tau; Phi Delta Rho; hon/Grad Tchg Asst'ship, Pres's List 1980 & 1981, Dean's List 1978-80, Univ So MS; Outstg Phil Student And Hon Grad, Copiah-Lincoln Jr Col; g/PhD in Phil or Eng; Univ Prof.

BROWN, BRIDGET A oc/Student; b/Jun 8, 1966; h/2690 Lake Road, Tucker, GA 30084; p/Mr and Mrs Eugene F Brown, Tucker, GA; ed/Marist Col Prep; Mercer Univ, Profl Voice Classes; pa/Sales Rep, Davison's, 1983-; Waitress, Cashier, Hickory House, 1983-; cp/Drama Clb, 1980-83; Ski Clb, Pres, 1982; Thespien Soc, Pres 1982, 1983; FCA, 1983; Yrbook Editor, 1980-83; Photog Editor, 1982, 1983; Varsity Drill Team, 1980, 1981; Varsity Swim & Diving Team, 1982, 1983; GA Retard Ctr, Ednl Dir, 1982, 1983; r/Bapt; hon/Intl Thespian Soc; Miss GA Teen Pageant Semi-Finalist, "Miss Congeniality", 1983; Won 3rd in St, 4th in Reg Voice Competitions; W/W Among Am HS Students; g/Voice Perf Maj; Tch Col & Perf St Operas.

BROWN, CAROLYN M oc/Attorney; b/May 7, 1957; h/3711 Holland Apartment 203, Dallas, TX 75219; ba/Dallas, TX; m/James L Jackson II; p/Everett and Hazel Brown, Somerset, KY; ed/Somerset HS, 1975; BS, Univ KY, 1979; JD, Univ KY Col Law, 1982; pa/Atty, Thompson & Knight; Am Trial

Lawyrs Assn; Dallas Bar Assn, Exec Coun & Prog Com, Envir Law Sect, 1984; Am Bar Assn, Nat Resources Law Sect, 1982-; TX Bar Assn, Envir & Nat Resources Assn, 1983-; TX Bar, 1982; Bar for the No Dist TX, US Dist Ct, 1982; cp/Staff Mem, *KY Law Jour*; Chp Tech Com, Moot Ct Bd; Pres, Alpha Xi Delta; hon/Co Author of "Obtaining Permits for Indust Wastewater Discharges: A Statutory & Regulatory Overview", 1983; Outstg Third Yr Mem, Moot Ct Bd; Omicron Delta Kappa; 1st Alt, Moot Ct Nat Team; Cert of Merit Landscape Design, KY Chapt Am Soc Landscape Archs; Am Bar Assn Awd for Excell in Study of Land Use Plan'g; g/Atty dealing w Envir Law & Litigation.

BROWN, DANIEL CLAYTON oc/Student; b/Feb 27, 1961; h/214 Welch Road, Nashville, TN 37211; p/Edward Clayton and Jacquelyn Marsh Brown, Nashville, TN; ed/Grad, HS, 1979; Mid TN St Univ; Vanderbilt Univ; pa/Airbrush Artist, Opryland USA; cp/Univ Debate Team; Pledge Dir, Kappa Alpha Order, 1982; Freshman/Sophomore ASB Senator; Del, TN Intercol St Legis; Asst Scoutmaster, BSA; Gamma Beta Phi; Col Repubs; Univ Hons Prog; r/Christian; hon/Eagle Scout, BSA; Top Salesman, Gold Awd, "I Wanna Win" Awd, SWn Co; Gamma Beta Phi; Best Pledge, Kappa Alpha Order; Nat Hon Roll; Nat Dean's List; Intl Yth in Achmt; g/Law Sch.

BROWN, DARRYL DeWYNN oc/Student; b/Aug 7, 1963; h/Rural Route 1, Box 158, Laurel, IN 47024; p/Melvin D Brown (dec) and Clara E Brown, Laurel, IN; ed/Laurel HS, 1981; Ball St Univ; cp/Pres Pro Tem Ball St Univ Student Senate, Chm Election Bd, Chm Univ Sers Com, Univ Senate Student Welfare Coun Mem; Del Nat Model United Nations; Ball St Col Bowl Champs; Intramural Softball Capt; Nat Hon Soc, Nat Hon Soc Play-Actor; Bus Editor, Yrbook; Spanish Clb; Chess Clb; Newspaper; Basketball; Basketball Mgr; Student Ctr Gov'g Bd; hon/Century III Cert Merit, 1981; Admitted to Ball St Univ w Distn, 1981; Citizenship Awd; Math Awd; I Dare You Awd; Kappa Kappa Kappa S'ship; Mem, Hons Col; W/W Among Am HS Students; Soc of Dist'd Am HS Students; Am's Outstg Names & Faces; g/Deg in Polit Sci; Deg in Law.

BROWN, DEBRA GAIL oc/Student, Grad Instructor; b/Dec 19, 1959; h/816 Ouachita Circle, Little Rock, AR 72205; ba/Univ MS; p/Mr and Mrs James D Brown Sr, Little Rock, AR; ed/Little Rock Hall HS, 1978; BSEd, 1981; MSEd, 1982; Wking on PhD; pa/Grad Asst, Ouachita Bapt Univ, 1981-82; Upward Bound Instr 1982, Grad Instr 1982-84, Univ MS; cp/Sigma Tau Delta Eng Hon Soc, 1982-84; NCTE; MS Coun Tchrs Eng, 1982-84; Freshman Class Treas; Assn Wom Students; Secy, Pres 1981-82, Kappa Delta Pi; Pres, Chi Delta Social Clb, 1980; r/Christian; hon/Profile of "Fool" to be included in *Am Comic Mags*; Outstg Tchr in Tng, OBU, 1981; Pres's List, 1981; Kappa Delta Pi Ed Hon Soc; Ouachita Homecoming Contestant; Nat Dean's List; W/W; g/Master's Deg; Career Tchg Eng & French; Doct.

BROWN, ERIC LEE oc/Student; b/

Feb 29, 1964; h/Post Office Box 8, Benson, NC 27504; ed/HS; Assoc Printing Technol; cp/BSA, Eagle Scout; F'ship of Christian Ath; Cross Country Track; Wrestling; r/Meth; hon/Hon Roll Student, HS & Col; Hon Rel; Kitty Hawk Hon Soc; All Conf; Most Outstg Ath in HS; Stanley Coats Awd, 1982; Excell in Aths; Nat S'ship Trust Fund; g/Plant Mgr at Printing Firm.

BROWN, GREGORY DEAN oc/Assistant Manger of Convenience Store, Freelance Photography; b/Jan 18, 1961; h/Box 7, Liscomb, IA 50148; m/Tamara; p/Mr and Mrs Jerry Brown, Conrad, IA; sp/Mr and Mrs Gerald Hilsabeck, Liscomb, IA; ed/Beaman-Conrad-Liscomb HS, 1979; AAA, Hawkeye Inst of Tech, 1981; cp/BSA; Baseball; Ftball; Track Tri Capt; Instrumental & Vocal Music; Drama; Thespians VP; Am Legion Boys St; Profl Photog of IA; IA Pres Photog; Ctl IA Camera Clb; r/United Meth, Conrad United Meth Ch; hon/Eagle Scout Awd; Am Legion Boys St; Intl Yth in Achmt; Commun Ldrs Am; g/Wk with Kids.

BROWN, JAMES KEITH oc/Student, Research Assistant; b/Aug 15, 1962; h/J-9 Kingswood Apartments, Chapel Hill, NC 27514; p/Mr and Mrs James Clifton Brown, Siler City, NC; ed/Jordan Matthews HS, 1980; Univ NC-Chapel Hill; pa/Fed Correctional Inst, 1983; Res Asst Pulmonary Med, 1982; Asst, Univ NC Dental Sch in Sterilization, 1980-81; Asst, 1979; cp/Num HS Activs incl'g Beta Clb, Reporter, Bible Clb, Songldr, Sgt-at-Arms, Monogram, Chorus, French Clb, Music Clb, Student Coun-Pres, Ftball; Num Rel Activs incl'g Ldr at UNC-CH, Choir, F'ship Com, Outreach Com, Intl Relats Com, Bapt Student Union; Num Commun & Vol Activs incl'g UNC-CH Glee Clb, Cleft Palat Clin, Freshman Orient Cnslr, Big Buddy Coor, Commun Links Com Mem, Campus Y Mem; r/Bapt; hon/Hons Grad HS; Outstg Student Body Pres & Mem; Beta Clb Mem; Dean's List; g/Psychol/Zool Maj; Doct in Clin Psychol.

BROWN, KAREN LEE oc/Kelly Girl/Lay Minister; b/Oct 31, 1957; h/6721 Irving, Denver, CO 80221; m/David G Brown; p/Fred and Dorothy J Butterfield; sp/Richard H and Alice M Brown, Denver, CO; ed/Arvada W HS, 1975; BS, Bethany Nazarene Col, 1983; pa/Kelly Sers Employee, 1983-84; Dir Chd's Mins, 1983-; Dir of Vacation Bible Sch; cp/Circle K, Bethany Nazarene Col; r/Nazarene; hon/Nom & Cand for Secy & Pres Exec Coun, Circle K; Dorm Resident Advr; Yg Personalities; Nat Dean's List; g/Deg in Rel Ed; Chd's Min or Christian Ed Dir, Nazarene Ch.

BROWN, KENNETH M oc/Comptroller; b/Nov 17, 1953; h/50 East Middle Street, Gettysburg, PA 17325; ba/Worcester, MA; m/Rebecca Gustafson; c/Johanna Elizabeth; p/Walter D and Elizabeth S Brown, Belle Mead, NJ; sp/E Donald and Jean H Gufstafson, West Chester, PA; ed/Montgomery HS, 1971; BA, Antioch Col, 1976; MS, Shippensburg Univ, 1982; pa/Fdr, Netwk Trucking, 1976; Fdr, Sq Records, 1979; Systems Engr, Mandex Inc, 1982; Programmer, Dept of Energy: Residential Energy Consumption Survey, 1983; Comptroller, Worcester Mag, 1983; cp/Mem, Assn Computing Machinery; g/

MBA & PhD in Computer Sci.

BROWN, MAURICA ANN oc/Student; b/Dec 25, 1965; h/Route 1, Box 143, Michie, TN 38357; p/Mr and Mrs Randall M Brown, Michie, TN; ed/Adamsville HS, 1984; cp/Beta Clb, VP & Pres; A-Clb, Class Ofcr, VP, Secy, Treas; Basketball; Mascot-Ftball; Student Govt, VP; Annual Staff; r/Bapt; hon/Soc of Dist'd Am HS Students; W/W Among Am HS Students; Homecoming Queen, 1983; Class Favorite, 1983; Homecoming Ct, Basketball & Ftball, 1982; g/Maj in Pre-Med in Col.

BROWN, MICHAEL WAYDE oc/Electrician's Helper, Automobile Mechanic; b/Aug 4, 1960; h/Route 1, Box 271, Telford, TN 37690; p/Mr and Mrs H G Brown, Telford, TN; ed/David Crockett HS, 1978; AAS, Tri-Cities St Tech Inst, 1980; cp/Beta Clb; hon/Ranked 14 of 260, 3.67 GPA, HS Grad'g Class; St Farmer Deg, Future Farmers of Am; Grad w Highest Hons, 3.91 GPA, Tri-Cities St Tech Inst; g/Co-Owner of Automotive Repair Shop w Father.

BROWN, PATRICIA DENEICE oc/Graduate Student; b/Oct 20, 1959; h/Route 1, Box 151, Forest Home, AL 36030; p/Mr and Mrs Ambenne Brown, Forest Home, AL; ed/Greenville HS, 1978; BA, AL St Univ, 1982; pa/Lab Asst 1979-82, Tutor-Cnslr 1982, Lab Instr 1982-, AL St Univ; cp/Senator for Student Govt, 1982; Spec Sers Clb, 1979-83; S'ship Chp for Bessie Benson Hall; Beta Kappa Chi Hon Soc, Pres; Bapt Student Union, 1980; r/Bapt; hon/Hon Student; Nat Dean's List; Student of Yr; W/W Among Student in Am Cols & Univs; g/Wk in a Cancer Res Lab; PhD.

BROWN, RUSSELL GREGORY b/Oct 5, 1966; h/910 Westwood Drive, Tullahoma, TN 37388; p/Manuel and Glenna Brown, Tullahoma, TN 37388; ed/Tullahoma HS, 1984; cp/Tullahoma Atari Computer Users Grp; Mu Alpha Theta, 1983-84; Nat Hon Soc, VP, 1983-84; French Clb, 1980-84; r/Presb; hon/1st Place, 1983, TN Math Tchrs Assn Stwide Geometry Contest; TN Hons List in Math, 1984; Nat Merit Scholar, 1984; W/W Among Am HS Students; Nat Hon Role; g/Elect Engrg, Computer Sci.

BROWN, SANDY oc/Student; b/Feb 20, 1966; h/H C 85, Box 2900, Isom, KY 41824; p/Donald and Louise Brown, Isom, KY; ed/Whitesburg HS, 1984; Att'g Lee's Col; cp/Christian Ath Clb, 1980-84; Runner's Clb, 1983-84; r/Holiness; hon/Most Ath, 1979-80; All Dist Team, 1982-84; St Runner-up, 1983; All St Team, 1983; Miss Clutch, 1984; WHS Basketball Awd, 1984; All St Hon Mention, 1983; Most Talented in Sr Class, 1984; Girls Classic All Tour, Boone Co Recorder, 1984; One on One Champ, Lady Eagle Camp, 1982; 3 on 3 Champ, Lee's Col, 1984; MVP Field Events, 1984, WHS; g/Deg in PE.

BROWN, SHARON WAKEFIELD oc/School Psychologist; b/Nov 9, 1954; h/Post Office Box 275, Albertville, AL 35950; ba/Guntersville, AL; m/William Ray Jr; c/William Ray III; p/Mrs Ann S Garmon, Panama City, FL; ed/Albertville HS, 1972; BS, Univ AL, 1974; MEd, GA St Univ, 1976; pa/Therapist-Chd's Sers, Calhoun Cleburne Mtl Hlth Bd Inc, 1977-79; Sch Psychometrist, Marshall Co Bd Ed, 1979-; Am Psychol Assn;

AL Psychol Assn; Am Assn Sch Psychols; AL Assn Sch Psychols; cp/Ladies Civitans; United Daughs of Confederacy; r/Meth; hon/Nom, Yg Career Wom, 1982.

BROWN, SUSAN LEIGH oc/Secondary School Teacher; b/Aug 24, 1954; h/Route 2, Box 354, Jasper, AL; p/Mr and Mrs H C Brown; ed/Carbon Hill 1972; AS, Walker Jr Col, 1973; BS 1975, MA 1976, Univ of N AL; cp/Sponsor of HS Beta Clb, HS Red Cross Blood Dr; Ser Jackson & Perkins Rose Res Panel; NEA; UNA Christian Student Ctr; Walker Co Ed Assn Sem, Bldg Rep; AL Ed Assn; Secy, Alpha Omicron Pi; Sociol Clb; Hist Clb; UNA Alumni; Sponsor of Acad Team; hon/Nom for Yg Careerist Awd; Nom, Outstg Yg Wom of Am; g/Doct in Hist.

BROWN, TONY M oc/Executive; b/Jun 26, 1954; h/19811 Brightstone, Humble, TX 77338; ba/Humble, TX; m/Renay Powell; p/Mr and Mrs Dan M Brown, Odessa, TX; sp/Mr and Mrs Eddie I Powell, Humble, TX; ed/Odessa Permian HS, 1972; Abilene Christian Univ, 1976; pa/Wn Area Sales Mgr, PA Inc, 1978-80; VP, Potrox Energy Corporation, 1980-81; Pres, Mint Energy Corporation, 1981-83; cp/Student Adv Bd, 1973; Humble Area C of C; Assoc Mem, Indep Petro Assn of Am; Former Mem, Soc of Petro Engrs, 1980; r/Kingwood Ch of Christ; hon/MVP, Tennis, Abilene Christian Univ.

BRUCE, MELISSA GAIL oc/Student; b/Jun 28, 1965; h/Route 1, Box 476, Gray, KY 40734; p/Gale and Virgie Bruce, Gray, KY; ed/Knox Ctl HS, 1983; Att'g En KY Univ; pa/Pt-time Wk; Secretarial Wk for Fin Co & Atty; cp/Beta Clb, Secy 1982-83; Spanish Clb, Rep, 1980-83; Layout Editor of the *Centralian*, 1983; 4-H Clb; Queen Cand in Daniel Boone Fest; Cand in Homecoming, 1980, 1982, 1983; Cand in Valentine Contest; Gamma Beta Phi; r/Bapt; hon/Nat Hon Soc; Num Awds in HS incl'g Spanish Awd, Yrbook Awd, Hon Roll Awd; Ranked 6th in Graduating Class w a 4.1 GPA; Dean's List in Col; g/BBA, CPA.

BRUCE, JOHN ROBERT oc/Computer Programmer/Analyst; b/Jul 29, 1961; h/742 5th Street West, Huntington, WV 25701; ba/Russell, KY; p/Mr and Mrs John R Bruce Jr, Huntington, WV; ed/Huntington HS, 1979; BS, Marshall Univ, 1983; Marshall Univ Marching Band, 1979-83; r/Presb; hon/Dean's List, 4 Yrs; Gamma Beta Phi; Nat Hon Soc, HS; Assn for Computing Machinery; W/W Among Am HS Students; g/MBA at Marshall Univ.

BRUMBELOW, BETSY KAY oc/Student; b/Oct 19, 1963; h/Route 14, Box 346, Tyler, TX 75707; p/Mr and Mrs William E Brumbelow, Tyler, TX; ed/Chapel Hill HS, 1982; Tyler Jr Col; pa/Pt-time Bkkpr, E TX Constrn Prods Inc, 1982-83; cp/Hd Cheerldr in HS, 1981-82; Pres, Future Tchrs Am, 1982; Editor, HS Yrbook, 1981-82; Tennis Team; r/So Bapt; hon/HS Hon Grad, 1982; Nat Hon Soc, 1981; Col Phi Theta Kappa, 1983; DAR S'ship, 1983; Pres & Dean's List, 1983; Outstg Eng Student, Tyler Jr Col; W/W Among Am HS Students; g/Polit Sci Maj.

BRUNS, PEGGY SUE oc/Systems Engineer; b/Oct 23, 1960; h/5616 Abrams Road, Dallas, TX 75214; ba/

Richardson, TX; p/Lawrence and Alice M Crain, Williford, AR; ed/William HS, 1977; BBA, AR Col, 1981; pa/Systems Engr, Elect Data Systems, 1981-; cp/Vol Income Tax Asst; Phi Beta Lambda; Nat Dean's List; hon/Bus Awd, AR Col, 1981.

BRYAN, KATHRYN DALE oc/Student; b/Aug 17, 1962; h/405 West Salisbury Street, Pittsboro, NC 27312; p/Mr and Mrs Clinton E Bryan, Jr, Pittsboro, NC; ed/Northwood HS, 1980; Meredith Col; pa/Ch Organist, Pittsboro Bapt Ch, 1979-80; Ch Organist, Highland Bapt Ch, 1981-; cp/Am Guild of Organists; Freshman Rep to Legis Bd, Meredith Col; r/Prot; g/BMus w Applied Study in Organ & Ch Mus Cert.

BRYAN, KIMBERLY DAWN oc/Student; b/Oct 19, 1965; h/Post Office Box 293, Hartselle, AL 35640; p/Mr and Mrs Marshall J Bryan, Hartselle, AL; ed/Hartselle HS, 1984; cp/Mixed Chorus, 1981; Girl's Chorus, 1982; Concert Chorus, 1983, 1984; Show Choir, 1983, 1984; Marching & Concert Band, 1981, 1982; Pep Band, 1981, 1982; Scorekeeper, HS Girl's Basketball Team, 1981; Scorekeeper, HS Wrestling Team, 1982, 1983, 1984; Reporter, Future Bus Ldrs Am, 1984; VP, Delta Sigma Phi, 1984; Yth Rep, Ch Coun, 1983; Yth Mem, Ch Rec Com, 1983; Soloist, Ch Choir; Mem, Girls-Bapt Ch Basketball Team, 1980-84; Sum Wkr in Day Camp, 1981, 1982; r/Bapt; hon/Lettered in Band; Solo & Ensemble Awds, 1981, 1982; Spanish Clb, 1982, 1983; First Alt, Morgan Co Fair (Beauty Pageant), 1983; Winner, Miss Princess Theater Beauty Pagean, 1983; Winner, Miss Christmas Pageant, 1983; First Runner-up as Model of the Mo for December, 1983; First Alt, Miss Valentine Pageant, 1983; Winner, Miss Spring Beauty Pageant, 1983; Talent Winner, Morgan Co Cinderella Miss Pageant, 1983; Beauty Winner, Miss Autumn Pageant, 1983; W/W Among Am HS Students; g/Public Relats, Music.

BRYAN, MARGARET KELLY oc/Student; b/Dec 24, 1966; h/Route 1, Box 268, Teachey, NC 28464; p/Mr and Mrs Lee Bryan Jr, Teachey, NC; ed/Wallace-Rose Hill HS; cp/Nat Jr Beta Clb, Treas, 1981; Math Clb, Secy/Treas, 1983-84; r/Wesleyan Meth; hon/Am Legion Sch Awd; Nat Jr Beta Clb; Nat Hon Soc; g/Col.

BRYANT, CAROL ANN oc/Clinical/Research Dietitian; b/Jan 27, 1955; h/230 Arlington Avenue, Lexington, KY 40508; ba/Lexington, KY; p/William and Lillian Bryant, Taylorsville, KY; ed/Taylorsville HS, 1973; BS, Berea Col, 1977; MS, Univ KS, 1978; Clin Dietitian, Univ KS, 1978; Clin Dietitian-Renal Specialty, Univ KY, 1981-83; Outpatient Clin Dietitian 1983-84, Spec Diagnostics Treatment Unit 1984-, VA; Am Dietetics Assn; KY Dietetics Assn; Bluegrass Dietetics Assn; cp/Civitan; Donor to Muscular Dystrophy, March of Dimes; hon/Pub of Res, JPEN; KY Col Dean's List; BPW Clb Yth Awd; HS Hon Student; Betty Crocker Awd, 1973; W/W Among Am HS Students; Intl Yth in Achmt; g/Res & Edr at Col Level.

BRYANT, DARLA MARIE oc/Dental Hygienist; b/May 9, 1961; h/4712-L Dansey Drive, Raleigh, NC 27604; ba/Raleigh, NC; p/Mr and Mrs Joseph A

Bryant, Roanoke Rapids, NC; ed/Roanoke Rapids HS, 1979; BS, Univ NC-Chapel Hill, 1983; pa/Pvt Pract Dental Hygienist, 1983; Pt-time Sales Clk, Ivey's Dept Store; ADHA; NCDHA; SADHA; cp/French Hon Soc; Pep Clb; Fgn Exch Student Com; r/Bapt, Acteens, Secy, VP, Pres, Pianist; hon/Dist'd HS Students; g/to own Hygiene Pract.

BRYANT, KELVIN SEBRON oc/Student, Computer Operator; b/Sep 26, 1964; h/5219 Foxfire Road, Fayetteville, NC 28303; p/William M and Lizzie Irene Bryant, Fayetteville, NC; ed/HS, NC St Univ; pa/Busboy, Red Lobster, 1980-82; Computer Oper, NC St Univ, 1982-83; cp/ROTC; United Student F'ship; Mu Alpha Theta Math Clb; hon/Nat Hon Soc; Ft Bragg Bowling Champ; Hon Co Commr during Yth Wk, 1982; Dean's List; Black Achmt Awd, 1983; g/Deg in Computer Sci.

BRYANT, KEVIN LEE oc/Student; b/Feb 21, 1964; h/2925 Redford Drive, Owensboro, KY 42301; p/Rev and Mrs Delbert L Bryant, Owensboro, KY; ed/Owensboro HS, 1982; Univ Chgo, 1982-83; Univ KY; cp/HS Rifle Team; ROTC Color Guard; ROTC Drill Team; Ch Softball Team; Col Fencing Team; Col Lacrosse Clb; r/Bapt; hon/Nat Hon Soc; Alcoa Foundation Achmt S'ship Nom; Wn KY Univ Chem S'ship Competition, 5th Pl, 1982; US Army Scholastic Achmt Awd, ROTC, 1979-82; Century III Ldrship Competition Awd Winner, 1982; Bausch & Lomb Sci Awd, 1982; JW Snyder Meml Sci Awd, 1981; SAR Mil Sci Achmt Awd, 1982; JCs Outstg Yg Kentuckian, 1983; Honoree, Am Acad Achmt; US Army Superior Cadet, ROTC, 1979-1982; Am Outstg Names & Faces; g/Deg in Elect Engrg and/or Computer Sci.

BRYANT, LYNN ANNETTE oc/Student; b/Aug 15, 1966; h/600 Grove Crest Road, Pryor, OK 74361; p/Gayle and Janice Bryant, Pryor, OK; ed/Pryor HS; pa/Waitress, Karen Wilson, 1982; Lifeguard, Swimming Instr, 1983; cp/Ftball & Basketball Cheerldr, Capt Ftball Squad, 1982-84; Track, 1981-83; Student Coun, 1982-83; Thespians, 1982-83; Nat Forensic Leag, 1983; r/Meth; hon/Nat Hon Soc, 1982-83; Ftball Royalty, Jr Attendant, 1982; Broke 4 Sch Track Records, 1983; Sr Class Pres, 1983-84; Placed 2nd in the 3200 Meter Relay at St Meet, 1983; W/W Among Am HS Students; g/to attend Univ OK.

BRYANT, VINCENT DONNELL oc/Student; b/May 28, 1963; h/3333 North 54th Street, Milwaukee, WI 53216; ba/West Point, NY; p/Earl Alan and Margaret Jinwright Bryant, Milwaukee, WI; ed/John Marshall HS; BS (Expected) US Mil Acad; mil/AUS, Cadet USMA; cp/HS Ftball, Team Capt; Baseball; r/AME/Bapt; hon/Parachutists Badge, US Army Airborne Sch, 1983.

BRYNN, JONATHAN oc/Actor; b/Jan 21, 1964; h/Box 2174, Palm Beach, FL 33480; p/Donald and Brynn Meyers, Toledo, OH; ed/Palm Beach Jr Col; pa/MC; Star of "Surfing USA"; Wkly Spch Aquatic TV Series for Cable; Star of "Gayna & FL", 1984; cp/Am Surfing Assn; YMCA; ARC; Sierra Clb; Screen Actors Guild; LA Ath Clb; Kona Kai Clb; Raquet Ball of Am; r/Epis; hon/Pub include *A Brief Hist of Surfing*, 1983; All

Am Surfer, 1982, 1983; All World Surfer, 1983.

BUCCI, BARBARA ELLEN oc/Self-Employed Word Processing, Computer, Data Entry; b/Dec 21, 1959; h/4101 Five Oaks Drive, Number 20, Durham, NC 27707; ba/La Jolla, CA; p/Barbara Echols, Durham, NC; ed/Carolina Friends, 1976; Emory Univ, 1978; BA, Univ NC-Chapel Hill, 1982; pa/Retirement Planning, Money Mkt Sales & Secy, 1980-82; Ivestmts Ofc Mgr, 1982-83; Self-Employed, 1983-; cp/Kappa Alpha Theta Sorority, 1978-80; Big Sisters of San Diego, 1983-; Tarrey Pines Racquetball Clb, 1983-; c/Cath; hon/Nutritional Res, 1980, *Common Sense Guide to Eating*; W/W Am Col & Students; Yg Commun Ldrs; Intl Yth Achmt.

BUCHANAN, TERRY LEE oc/Student; b/Apr 11, 1960; h/2415 Fairbanks Drive, Clearwater, FL 33546; ba/Richmond, VA; m/Carol Moore; p/Vincent W and Marguerite L Buchanan, Clearwater, FL; sp/Vernon L and Dorothy C Moore, Richmond, VA; ed/Clearwater HS, 1978; BA, Eckerd Col, 1984; MA, Presb Sch Christian Ed, 1984; pa/Student Assoc Pastor, Lakewood United Meth Ch, 1982-83; Yth Coor, Mt Pisgah United Meth Ch, 1983-84; Yth & Yg Adult Dir, Christ Ch United Meth, 1984-; cp/Commun Ldrship Prog; Nat Hon Soc; F'ship of Christian Aths; Student Tchr; Rschr in Rheumatoid Arthritis; Omicron Delta Kappa Residential Advr, 1980-81; Pres's Task Force, 1980-82; Campus Min; Early Chd Ed Internship, 1979; Vet Med Internship, 1979; r/United Meth; hon/Merit S'ship at Duke Div Sch, 1982-83; Hons Grad at Eckerd Col; HS Salutatorian; Hons S'ship, 1978-82; CRC Outstg Freshman Chem Awd, 1979; Nat Dean's List; Intl Yth in Achmt; W/W Among Am HS Students; Yg Personalities of S; Men of Achmt Awd; g/MDiv; Yth Min, Christian Camp Dir or Christian Cnslr.

BUCHER, HELEN ANN BLANKENSHIP oc/Teacher; b/May 30, 1958; h/106 Cross Brook Drive, Brunswick, GA 31520; ba/Brunswick, GA; m/David Eugene; p/Dr and Mrs J W Blankenship, Houston, TX; sp/Mr and Mrs Calvin Bucher, De Soto, TX; ed/Stratford Sr HS, 1976; BS, Bethany Nazarene Col, 1980; pa/Tchr, Dean Jr HS, 1980-81; Tchr, Brunswick Christian Acad, 1981-; Student Ed Assn; TX St Tchrs Assn; cp/Local Hist, 1977; Local Pres, St Secy & VP, 1978; Local Pres, 1979; Alpha Lambda Delta Secy, 1977; Cardinal Key Hist, 1978; r/Ch of the Nazarene; hon/Cum Laude Grad, 1980; Mortar Bd Hon Soc, 1979; Dean's S'ship, 1976-79; Georgiana Bayles McDaniel Ed S'ship, 1979; Commun Ldrs Am; g/EdM.

BUCHTMAN, ROGER JOSEPH oc/Director, Financial Planning Reporting & Analysis; b/Sep 10, 1956; h/Rural Route 3, Churubusco, IN 46723; p/Joseph FJ and Bernice Buchtman, Churubusco, IN; ed/New Haven HS, 1974; AB, St Francis Col, 1978; pa/Cost Acct 1978-79, Financial Analyst 1979-80, Acctg Mgr 1981-82, Mgr Financial Planning Reporting & Analysis 1982-83, Dir Financial Planning Reporting & Analysis 1983-, Starcraft; IN Assn CPAs; Inst Mgmt Acctg; cp/Ft Wayne Univ Clb; Single Cath Adult Clb; Sigma

Lambda Frat; Commentator, Spec Min, St John Bosco Cath Ch; hon/CPA; Delta Epsilon Sigma; St Francis Col Bus Dept Acad Achmt Awd; Intl Yth in Achmt; Commun Ldrs Am; g/MBA/Fin.

BUCKLEY, DAVID WAYNE oc/Assistant Minister; b/May 13, 1958; h/1837 Farmer Road, Sanford, MI 48657; ba/Midland, MI; m/Jeanne Marie Honeycutt; c/Holly Michelle; p/Mr and Mrs George Buckley, Littleton, CO; sp/Rev and Mrs John Honeycutt, Denver, CO; ed/Silver St Bapt HS, 1976; BA, Bob Jones Univ, 1980; Grad Wk at Bob Jones; pa/Asst Pastor, Calvary Bapt Ch, 1981-; cp/Bd Dirs, Gilman Sprgs Bapt Camp, 1982-; cp/Pres, Min Class, Bob Jones Univ; Chaplain, Soph, Jr & Sr Classes; Pres, Chaplain , Secy, Theta Kappa Nu; Pres, Jr & Sr Classes in HS; r/Bapt; Christian Ldrship Awd; Yth Coun; Basketball; Baseball MVP; Softball; Strom Thurmond Citizenship Awd; Theta Kappa Nu Man of Yr; W/W Among Students in Am Cols & Univs; Intl Commun Ldrs Am; g/Sr Min.

BUCKLEY, STEVEN MICHAEL oc/Student; b/Oct 14, 1967; h/15406 Lindita Drive, Houston, TX 77083; p/Mr and Mrs R J Buckley, Houston, TX; ed/Christian Brothers HS, 1982; Strake Jesuit Col Prep, 1983-; cp/Intramural Sports, 1981-; Soccer Clb, Goalie; Hockey Team, Goalie; Spanish Clb; Bicycle Racing Clb; Go Brothers Pep Clb; r/Rom Cath; hon/Father Parham's Rel Writing Awd, 1980, 1981; B Hon Roll, 1982; g/Maj in Computer Sci, Career in Soccer.

BUCKLEY, TIMOTHY JOSEPH oc/Student; b/Mar 19, 1964; h/15406 Lindita Drive, Houston, TX 77083; p/Richard and JoAnn Buckley, Houston, TX; ed/Christian Brothers HS, 1982; Att'g Univ MO; pa/Internship at Radio Sta KODA-FM 99 Houston TX, 1983; cp/Pi Kappa Phi Frat; Senator in the MO Students Assn Student Govt; Intramural Sports; SGA Commr of Intramurals; Swim Team; Newspaper, Annual Staffs; Yg Polit Scists; Close-Up; TN Yth Legis; Nat Ldrship Inst Ldrship Conf; Mu Alpha Theta; Spanish Clb; Vol. Dem Nat Conv; BSA Order of Arrow; Memphis Amateur Hockey Leag; r/Rom Cath; hon/Writer for the *Maneater* Student Newspaper, Univ MO, and for the *Savitar* Sch Yrbook; Hons Classes; Twice Named Winner of the Univ MO Alumni Assn; Memphis Chapt S'ship; W/W Among HS Students; Commun Ldrs of Am; g/Deg in Jour.

BUCKHAM, MARIT JOHANNE oc/Student; b/Oct 9, 1956; h/1517 Jones Drive, Number 18, Ann Arbor, MI 48105; p/Harold Strandheim, Norway; Solfrid Heim, Norway; m/William C; ed/GED, 1975; Bellevue Col, 1979; BA, Psychol & Eng, 1982; Univ MI; cp/Am Norwegian Student Assn; hon/Psi Chi Nat Hon Soc in Psychol; Frances M Edwards S'ship; Golden Key Hon Soc; Nat Dean's List; Class Hon; Intl Yth in Achmt; Commun Ldrs Am Awd; g/Clin Psychol.

BUDD, DEBORAH LYNN oc/Student; b/Nov 4, 1966; h/11 Ascot Drive, Freehold, NJ 07728; p/Dale and Lilly Budd, Freehold, NJ; ed/Freehold Twp HS; pa/Paper Carrier, Asbury Pk Press; Hosp Vol, Freehold Area Hosp, 1980-82; Babysitting, Homemakers, 1978-84;

Packed Corn, Buckley Farms, 1980; Freehold Twp Rec Spec Cnslr, Freehold Twp Rec Assn, 1982-83; Softball Umpire, 1983; cp/Gymnastic Mgr, 1980; HS Basketball Team, 1980-82; Track Team, 1982; Softball Team, 1983-84; Basketball Mgr, 1983-84; Secy for Yth Bd, 1980-81; Parish Coun Yth Del, 1980-84; Parish Yth Grp Pres, 1982-84; Yth Facilitator, 1983; Eucharistic Min, 1983-84; Parish Nursery Org, 1980-84; r/Cath; hon/Pope John Paul II Ldrship Awd, 1983; Pres I, II, III, IV Awds, 1978-81; Coach Awd, 1981; Merit Awd, Best All Around, 1979; g/Maj in Psychol in Col.

BUIE, MELAINE KAYE oc/Student; b/May 29, 1964; h/Post Office Box 912, Denton, NC 27239; p/Mr and Mrs Carl Buie, Denton, NC; ed/Denton HS, 1978-82; Univ NC-Greensboro; cp/Pagette, Ho of Reps; Beta Clb; FHA Histn; GSA, CABS Asst Secy-Treas, Secy, Yg People's SS Class; Asst GS Ldr, 1983; hon/FHA Merit Awd, 1981-82; GS Gold Awd, 1982; Austin Finch S'ship, 1982, 1983; Shorthand Awd; Perfect Attendance Awd; g/Bus Tchr.

BULCAVAGE, CHRISTA ANNE oc/Student; b/Jul 31, 1962; h/336 Sycamore Road, West Reading, PA 19611; p/Joseph and Elizabeth Bulcavage, W Reading, PA; ed/Holy Name HS, 1980; King's Col; pa/Pt-time Secy/Clk, Reading Hosp, 1978-80; Pt-time Computer Oper, Rockwell Intl, 1981-83; cp/Treas, Bus Ad/Mktg Clb, 1983-84, Mem, 1982-83; Cantor for Sacred Heart Ch; Mem, Campus Min; King's Col Volleyball; Intramural Basketall; Softball Team Publicity Chm for Min; r/Cath; hon/Winner of Nat Hist Day Contest, 1980; NHS; Spanish Hon Soc; Coach's Trophy, Basketball; Dean's List; W/W Among Am HS Students; Commun Ldrs Am; Yth in Achmt; Biog of Berks Co Artists; g/Mktg, Assoc Deg Info Sys.

BULLOCK, BYRON SWANSON oc/Assistant Director/Counselor; b/Aug 4, 1955; h/5024 North Tupelo Turn, Wilmington, DE 19808; ba/Newark, DE; m/Antoinette Langston; c/Melanie Nicole; p/Rev and Mrs Robert E Johnson, Danville, VA; sp/Mrs Cornelia Davis, Phila, PA; ed/Northwest Cath HS, 1973; BA, Lincoln Univ, 1977; MA Prog at Univ DE; pa/Cnslr on Admissions, Lincoln Univ, 1977-79; Asst Dir/Cnslr, Proj Upward Bound, 1979-; Mid-En Assn Ednl Opport Prog Pers; DE St TRIO Org; DE Pers & Guid Assn; cp/Gamma Theta Lambda Chapt S'ship Chp, Xi Omicron Chapt Grad Advr, Alpha Phi Alpha Frat Inc; Big Brothers of DE; r/Meth, Simpson United Meth Ch; hon/Alpha Phi Alpha Frat Inc; Xi Omicron Chapt Ldrship Awd; Dean's List Lincoln Univ; Outstg Eng Maj of Yr, Lincoln Univ; Elizabeth H Train Meml Prize in Oratory; Outstg Yg Man of Am.

BUMGARNER, SHELIA ANN oc/Independent Historian, Researcher; b/Apr 15, 1958; h/233 Rader Street, Burlington, NC 27215; p/D Y and Frances Bumgarner, Burl, NC; ed/Hugh M Cummings III Sr HS, 1976; Appalachian St Univ, 1976-78; BA, Elon Col, 1981; MA, Univ NC, 1983; pa/Coor of Wom's Hist 1982-83, Res Asst 1981-82, Univ NC-Greensboro; Lib Asst, Elon Col, 1980-81; cp/Watauga Col; Elon Col Mem Phi Alpha Theta, 1979; Pi Gamma

Mu & Alpha Chi, 1980; Org of Am Histns, 1981; Nat Trust for Hist Preserv, 1980; UNC-G Mem of Grad Student Assem; Org of Am Hist & Nat Trust; r/Presb; hon/Phi Alpha Theta; Alpha Chi & Pi Gamma Mu; Marshall 1980 Elon Col Commencement; Recip of Pi Gamma Mu S'ship for Grad Studies; S'ship Study Tryon Palace Symp; Personalities of S; g/to go into Res.

BUNCH, ELIZABETH ANNE oc/Student; b/Jun 5, 1964; h/Route 1, Box 63, Elkwood, VA 22718; ba/Ashland, VA; p/Carter A Jr and Lucy Botts Bunch, Elkwood, VA; ed/Culpeper Co HS, 1982; Randolph-Macon Col; cp/Tri Hi Y, VP; Latin Clb, VP; Sunday Sch Dir & Tchr; Bible Sch Tchr; 4-H Dairy Clb, Secy; GSA; Madrigal Chorus; r/Bapt; hon/Nat Hon Soc Secy; VA Girls' St; Nat Merit S'ship Hon Mention; Randolph-Macon Col Choir.

BUNCH, SUSAN KAY oc/Student; b/Apr 21, 1966; h/Route 1, Box 63, Elkwood, VA 22718; p/C A Jr and Lucy Botts Bunch, Elkwood, VA; cp/Octagon Clb; Latin Clb; Homeroom Rep to SCA; Treas of Jr Class; Pres of Jr Nat Hon Soc; Girls' Ath Assn; French Clb; Tennis & Hockey Teams; Bible Sch & Sunday Sch Tchr; r/Bapt; hon/VA Girls' St, 1983; W/W Among HS Students.

BURCH, CHARLES JR oc/Accountant; b/Aug 9, 1960; h/15215 Blue Ash Drive, Number 123, Houston, TX 77090; ba/Woodlands, TX; p/Charles Burch Sr, Southfield, MI; Vernell Burch, Detroit, MI; ed/Southfield HS, 1978; BS-Magna Cum Laude, NC A & T St Univ, 1982; pa/Peat, Marwick, Mitchell & Co, 1982-83; Mitchell Energy & Devel Corporation, 1983-; Pres, Sr Class; Pres, Beta Gamma Sigma; Pres, MI Renaissance Inc; VP, Alobeaum Soc; Treas, NC Fellows Exch; Nat Assn Black Accts; Houston Area Urban Leag; NC A & T Alumni Assn; Student Pres, Alpha Lambda Delta; Treas, Alpha Kappa Mu; Treas, Alpha Chi; hon/Alpha Kappa Mu; Alpha Chi; Alpha Lambda Delta; Outstg Col Grads; W/W Among Students in Am Univs & Cols; Nat Dean's List; Yg Personalities of S; Intl Yth in Achmt; g/MBA & CPA; Public Acct.

BURGESS, JEFFREY WAYNE oc/Student; b/Aug 12, 1965; h/Route 1, Box 148, Livingston, TN 38570; p/Mr and Mrs Haskell P Burgess, Livingston, TN; ed/Livingston Acad, 1984; mil/USAF, 1984; cp/BSA; r/Presb; hon/Eagle Scout, 1983; Order of the Arrow, 1982; God & Country, 1982; Yg Personalities of S; g/AF Pilot.

BURKE, AMY oc/Student, Piano Teacher; b/Jun 27, 1966; h/Post Office Box 168, Myra, KY 41549; p/Mr and Mrs Edmund H Burke Sr, Myra, KY; ed/HS, 1984; cp/Band; Co-ed Y Chaplain; Chess Clb; Teen Missions Intl; r/Bapt; hon/US Achmt Acad; W/W Am HS; Most Outstg Piano Student.

BURKE, PATRICIA ANN oc/Trial Attorney; b/Jan 31, 1954; h/1600 South Eads Street, Number 636-S, Arlington, VA 22202; ba/Washington, DC; m/Michael A Kuhlmann; p/Mr and Mrs Joseph M Burke, Binghamton, NY; sp/Mr and Mrs A Donald Kuhlmann, Conyers, GA; ed/Binghamton N HS, 1972; BA, Univ Notre Dame, 1976; JD, Cath Univ Am Law Sch, 1979; pa/Trial

Atty, Interstate Commerce Comm, 1982-; Atty, Advr, 1980-82; Indexer, US Rwy Assn, 1979-80; Intern, US Securities & Exch Comm, 1979; Legal Tech, US Gen Acctg Ofc, 1978; Am Bar Assn; Fed Bar Assn; DC Bar; St Bar of CA; Wom's Trans Sem; Student Bar Assn; Moot Ct Assn; Cath Univ Law Review; cp/Notre Dame Rowing Clb; Univ Notre Dame Alumni Assn; hon/Law Review Cert; Student Bar Assn Awd; Moot Ct Assn Cert; Notre Dame Scholar; Dailey Meml S'ship; Dean's List; Nat Hon Soc; Girls St.

BURKET, JOHN F oc/Building Construction; b/Feb 5, 1960; h/Post Office Box 3322, Vero Beach, FL 32964-3322; p/Mr and Mrs Richard J Burket, Vero Beach, FL; ed/Bach Bldg Constrn, Sch of Bldg Constrn, Univ FL, 1983; Vero Bch HS, 1979; pa/Carpenter, Suncrete Corp, Sanford FL; Carpenter, Richard J Burket Inc, Vero Bch FL; Pt-time, Site Layout & Landscaping Techniques, Tippin Landscaping; Public Relats, Walt Disney World of Orlando, 1978; cp/Sigma Lambda Chi; Student Contractors & Bldrs Assn; Assn Gen Contractors; r/Cath; hon/GPA 3.6; Grad w Hons; Sigma Lambda Chi; Phi Eta Sigma; Freshman Hon S'ship; W/W Col; g/Entry Level Mgmt Position in Constrn Indust.

BURKS, CHRIS ANN oc/Graduate Physician's Assistant; b/Jun 27, 1961; h/Box 252, Iaeger, WV 24844; p/Allen and Nancy Burks, Iaeger, WV; ed/Iaeger HS, 1979; BS summa cum laude, Alderson-Broaddus Col, 1984; cp/H Bd Majorette, HS Band; Secy, Pep Clb; French Clb; 4-H Clb; SAE; FMLA; Secy & Rep, Student Coun; Secy & Histn, Keywanettes; Alpha Sigma Tau; Assn Wom Students; Student Ldrship Com; Am Acad Phys Assts; r/VP, Meth Yth F'ship; Coun on Min; Circle K Clb, 1983-84; hon/VP, Nat Hon Soc; Pres S'ship; Am Legion Awd; Gamma Beta Phi; Girls St; Hon Roll Dean's List; All-County; All-Area Band; Co & Reg Sci Fair; Co Math Field Day; Awds in Algebra, Adv'd Math, French, Spch, Typing, World Cultures, Biol & Adv'd Biol; Know Your Co Govt Day; Student Coun Ser Awd; Majorette Trophies; Homecoming & Snowflake Queens; Am's Outstg Names & Faces; Nat Dean's List; Bruce McLaughlin S'ship for Outstg PA Student; Acad Awd for 4.0 GPA; Sprg Fest Princess, 1983; Personalities of S; Am Outstg Names & Faces; g/Phys' Asst.

BURKS, DEBORAH ANN oc/Proof Transit Operator, Student; b/Dec 14, 1963; h/2944 Lawndale Avenue, Cincinnati, OH 45212; ba/Cinc, OH; p/Mr and Mrs Curtis Burks, Cinc, OH; ed/Woodward HS, Wn Hills HS, Queen City Voc Ctr; Cert of Completion, Law Enforcement Tng & Spec Assignments from Wn Hills/Queen City Voc Progs; Univ Cinc; pa/Security Agt, RIC Consits & Sers; Data Processing Proof Transit Operator, Ctl Trust Co NA; cp/YMCA Commun Volleyball Leag, Varsity Basketball, 1980-82; Jr Class Secy, 1981; Mem of Jr Achmt, 1979-81; Mem of Najac Assn, 1980; Grand Girls Assem St of OH, 1979-; r/Bapt; hon/Articles in Num Pubs; Commend of Security Agt Assignments, 1981; Dale Carnegie S'ship, 1981; Outstg Detective Wk, 1982; Most Outstg Law Enforcement

Prog W Hill HS, 1982; Grand Royal Queen, St of OH, 1982-83; Proclamation from the City of Cinc for Ldrship, Deborah Ann Burks Day, Apr 23, 1983; g/Law.

BURNETT, BARBARA ANN oc/Student; b/May 12, 1966; h/851 Kenwood Lane, Jonesboro, GA 30236; p/Arnold and Vicki Burnett, Jonesboro, GA; cp/Beta Clb; Math Clb; Swim Team; Student Coun Homeroom Rep; Angelflight Drill Team; ROTC Ofcr; r/Jewish; hon/Nat Hon Soc; Ldrship Awd from the US Navy; W/W Among Am HS Students; g/Col, AF.

BURNETT, SANDRA oc/Staff Writer; b/Oct 29, 1959; h/Post Office Box 95, Madison, MS 39110; ba/Jackson, MS; p/Mr and Mrs Tommie Lewis Burnett, Madison, MS; ed/Madison-Ridgeland HS, 1977; Canton Votech Ctr, 1977; BA, Tougaloo Col, 1981; pa/Receptionist, Newspaper Prodn Co, 1981-82; Staff Writer, Clarion Ledger Newspaper, 1982-; Jackson Assn Black Jour, Secy; Nat Chapt Black Jour; cp/Three-Way Inn Softball Team; China Grove AME Ch Choir, VP; hon/Awded Excell Writer in Jour; Nat Yth in Achmt; Personalities of S; Nat Dean's List; g/Deg in Paralegal Tng.

BURNS, MARY JANE oc/Special Education Teacher; b/Jan 24, 1959; h/Route 1, Box 237-C, Auburn, KY 42206; ba/Russellville, KY; m/Robert A Gates Jr; p/Mr and Mrs Robert A Gates, Sr, Nashville, TN; ed/Auburn HS, 1977; BS 1981, MA 1982, Wn KY Univ; cp/Student Coun for Exceptl Chd VP; SNEA; KY Reg V Spec Olympics; "Fit by 8" Fitness Prog for Chd; FHA; Beta Clb; Student Coun VP; hon/Magna Cum Laude Grad; Dean's List; Nat Dean's List; Outstg Yg Wom in S; Commun Ldrs in Am; KY St Special Olympics Coach; Intl Yth in Achmt; g/Tch Spec Ed; Area Coor for Spec Ed.

BURRELL, DONNA DENEÉ oc/Student; b/May 14, 1962; h/2629 Portland Street, Number 208-B, Los Angeles, CA 90007; p/Mr and Mrs James Burrell, Richmond, VA; ed/Armstrong HS, 1980; Univ So CA; pa/Lib Asst, Univ So CA, 1980-81; Pt-time Ofc Wkr, 1981; cp/ARC, Student Coun, Homeroom Rep; Y-Teens; Student Guid Clb; Pres, 1979-80, DECA; Hlth Clb; Photo Clb; r/Prot; hon/Cert Ldrship from DECA, 1980; Hon Roll; Chosen to Represent Sch on Ldrship Coun formed by City Ofcls; Attendance Cert; g/MBA, to become an Entrepreneur.

BURRELL, MARCUS A oc/Student; b/Nov 4, 1967; p/Dewitt Burrell and Bettye F McKinney, West Helena, AR; cp/Basketball, Ftball, Track, Am Legion Baseball; NAACP; r/Bapt, First Bapt Ch Jr Choir, Sunday Sch; hon/MVP Baseball, 1978-81; Student of Mo; Two-Yr Lttrman in Ftball; First Yr Lttrman in Basketball, Track; Hon Roll; g/Math, Profl Baseball Player.

BURT, ANN LOUISE oc/Student; b/Sep 26, 1962; h/608 Oxford Oaks Lane, Oxford, MI 48051; ba/E Lansing, MI; p/Mrs George Burt, Oxford, MI; ed/Lake Orion Commun HS, 1980; MI St Univ, 1980-81, 1983-; Lansing Commun Col, 1981-83; Secy, Editor, Dragon Yrbook; Del, Am Legion Aux Girls St; Lake Orion Assem No 51, Grand Rep to St of FL, Grand Choir, Intl Order

Rainbow for Girls; Lansing Commun Col Mktg Clb; Am Mktg Assn; Nat Assn; OES Grand Cross Color; Intern, St MI Ho of Reps; Intern, Ingham Co Probate Ct; Lit Mag Staff Mem; Sr Mag Staff Mem; HS Govt Del; Hon Roll; Ski Clb; r/Epis; hon/Intl Yth in Achmt; W/W Among Am HS Students; Commun Ldrs Am; Yg Commun Ldrs; g/Bus, Law Ofc Adm, Legal Asst.

BURT, BARBARA JEAN oc/Nursing Instructor; b/Oct 23, 1956; h/622 Newcastle, Sherwood, AR 72116; ba/Little Rock, AR; m/David; p/Mr and Mrs Sidney G Ezell, Booneville, AR; sp/Mr and Mrs Edwin Burt, North Little Rock, AR; ed/Booneville HS, 1974; BS, Harding Univ, 1979; Coronary Care Course; Respiratory Care Course; Wkg on Master's in Nsg, Univ AR; pa/Nsg Instr, Bapt Sch Nsg, 1982; Pt-time Staff Nurse, Meml Hosp; CPR Instr for ARC; Nat Leag Nsg; cp/Sigma Theta Tau; HSNA; ASNSA; NSNA; r/Ch of Christ Bible Class Tchr, Visitor of Elderly, Shut-Ins, Hosp; Org of Activs for Yg People in Ch; hon/Tips & Timesavers Sect in Nsg, 1982; Num Articles on Med Errors; Outstg Holland Campaigner; Magna Cum Laude Grad; Alpha Chi; Michele Warren Nsg S'ship; Dean's List; Salutatorian; Hon Student; Sr Class VP; Rotary Clb S'ship; Creat Writing Awd; g/Outstg Yg Wom Am; Intl Yth in Achmt; g/Master's Deg in Nsg; To Live Eternally in Heaven w God.

BURT, TAMERA K oc/Waitress; Student; b/Apr 14, 1962; h/603 Philippine Street, Taft, CA 93268; c/Stephanie Renee; p/Richard and Cordelia Burt, Taft, CA; ed/Taft Union Sch, 1980; Taft Jr Col, 1981; Cal St-Bakersfield; pa/Tutor, Taft Col, 1980-82; Tchr Aide, Roosevelt Sch, 1981; Hostess, Marie Callendars, 1982; Waitress, Gentieus W, 1982-83; Waitress, Safaris W, 1983-; cp/Past Worthy Advr 1979, 1981, Intl Order Rainbow for Girls; Intl Order Jobs Daughs; OEA; DeMoby Princess; Chorale Pres; Pres Alpha Gamma Sigma; r/Epis; hon/Nat Sch Orch Awd; Nat Sch Choral Awd; Scholastic Hons Taft Col; W/W Music; Am Outstg Names & Faces; g/Elem Sch Tchr.

BUSBY, LAURA EILEEN (MARTIN) oc/Student; b/Nov 24, 1966; h/Route 1, Box 208, Salado, TX 76571; p/Mr and Mrs Jerry Dean Busby, Salada, TX; ed/Salado HS; pa/Vol Ser, Scott & White Hosp; cp/FHA; Basketball; Track; Yth Clb; r/Bapt; hon/Miss Congeniality, Waco Miss TEEN Contest, 1983; W/W Girl's PE; Hon Roll; g/Lab Technol.

BUSBY, REYNETTE MICHELLE oc/Student; b/Aug 14, 1965; h/207 Carolina Avenue, Easley, SC 29640; p/Mr and Mrs Ray M Busby, Easley, SC; ed/Easley HS, 1983; cp/Nat Hon Soc; Student Coun; Interact Clb; Pageant Participant; Sci Bowls at Lander & Converse Col; r/Meth; hon/Lead Role in HS Play Prodn; Marshal in Grad Ceremony; Top Ten Acad Awds; g/Deg in Chem Engrg.

BUSCH, ANN M HERBAGE oc/Registered Nurse; b/Jan 24, 1958; h/330 North Mathilda, Apartment 302, Sunnyvale, CA 94086; ba/Stanford, CA; m/John Patrick; p/Robert Canfield and Mary Magdaline Herbage, Roseburg, OR; sp/Robert and Sodelbia Busch, Grants Pass, OR; ed/Roseburg Sr HS, 1976; BSN, Univ Portland, 1980; pa/

Anatomy Physiol Lab Asst, Univ Portland, 1980; Nurses Aide, Mercy Med Ctr, Roseburg, OR, 1977-80; Staff Nurse II, Charge Nurse on Surg Floor Night Shift, Mercy Med Ctr, 1980-81; Staff Nurse IV on Acute Care Surg Floor, Stanford Univ Hosp, 1981-; cp/Com for Recog of Nsg Achmt, 1981-82; Blue Key Nat Hon Frat, Pres 1979-80, VP 1978-79; Delta Epsilon Sigma, Omicron Chapt Secy, 1979-80; Wom's Antioch, Ldr 1978-80; Student Nurses of OR, 1978-80; Sch of Nsg Counsel, Soph Rep, 1977-78; Dorm Counsel, VP & Act'g Pres 1977-78; Univ Dir Staff, 1979-80; Univ Yrbook Staff, 1977-78; Campus Min Outreach Prog, 1976-80; Univ Wind Ensemble, 1st Oboist, 1976-78; Commun Orch, Oboist, 1976-78; ASUP Tchr Ed Com, 1976-77; ASUP 75th Anniv Planning Com, 1976-77; Saga Food Com, 1977-78; Yg Adult Grp, St Joseph's Cath Ch, 1976-81; r/Rom Cath; hon/Univ Portland Hons at Entrance, 1976; BPOE Nat Foun "Most Valuable Student" S'ship, 1976; Univ Portland Scholastic S'ship, 1976-80; Student Address, Univ Portland, 1980; Blue Key Nat Hon Frat, 1st Female Pres at Univ Portland; Delta Epsilon Sigma; Nat Dean's List; W/W Among Students in Am Univs & Cols; Nat Register of Outstg Col Grads; Commun Ldrs of Am; Intl Yth in Achmt; g/Grad Study in Nsg, Career as Nurse Clin Spec in Gastrointestinal Nsg & as Tchr on Univ Level.

BUSHART, CHARLES RAE oc/Computer Programmer; b/Jan 12, 1961; h/Romulus, MI 48174; p/Mr and Mrs Charles E Bushart, Maybee, MI; ed/HS, 1979; BS, En MI Univ; pa/Computer Programmer, F X Coughlin Co, 1981-; cp/NHS Pres; Ch Yth Coun; Jr Varsity & Varsity Ftball; Freshman Class Pres; Christian Ser Brigade; hon/Regents S'ship; Dean's List; W/W Among AM HS Students; Commun Ldrs of Am; g/Computer Field.

BUSHMIRE, BRYAN LEE oc/Student; b/Aug 26, 1962; h/302 West Grant Street, Houston, PA 15342; p/Mr and Mrs Anthony Arnone, Houston, PA; ed/Chartiers-Houston HS, 1980; BA, Edinboro Univ, 1984; cp/Phi Eta Sigma, Treas, 1982; Alpha Chi, 1983-84; Russian Clb, VP, 1982-83; Col Bowling Team, Capt, 1983-84; Asst Editor Col Newspaper, 1983-84; Dobro Slovo, Pres, 1983-84; hon/Nat Hon Soc, 1978; Dean's List, 1980-83; W/W Am HS; Intl Yth in Achmt; g/Govt Wk, Fgn Corrrespondent.

BUSTAMANTE, MICHAEL JOHN oc/Student; b/Aug 22, 1961; h/1700 South Stoneman, Alhambra, CA 91801; ba/Monterey Pk, CA; p/Eliseo R Bustamante-Armida, Alhambra, CA; ed/Cantwell HS; E LA Col; pa/Pt-time Batch Control Oper, Auditing Dept Clk, Sears, Roebuck & Co, 1982; cp/Associated Student Pres, E LA Col; LA Col Coun, External Affairs, Legis Dir; So CA Commun Col Assn, Bd Dir; r/Cath; hon/Hons Grad, Cantwell HS; g/Bus Ec Maj, Career in Law.

BUTLER, ALICE ELAINE oc/Student; b/Dec 21, 1963; h/Route 3, Box 48, Martinsburg, WV 25401; p/Robert S and Virginia S Butler, Martinsburg, WV; ed/HS, 1982; cp/Lttrman in Basketball & Track; Pres, Class of 1982; Pres, Student Body; Pres, 4-H Clb; VP,

Meth Yth F'ship; hon/WV Hort Princess, 1982-83; WV Dairy Princess, 1982-83; 4-H All Star Pin, 1982; W/W Among Am HS Students; g/Bus Deg; Own Store.

BUTLER, JAMES KEITH oc/Graduate Student; b/Oct 31, 1961; h/Route 2, Box 197-A, Ramer, TN 38367; p/Mr and Mrs James H Butler, Ramer, TN; ed/McNairy Ctl HS; BS, Union Univ; pa/ Undergrad Res Asst, Univ AL, 1982; cp/ Sigma Alpha Epsilon, Pres 1983, VP 1982, Pledge Edr 1983, Correspondent 1982, Warden 1981; Sigma Zeta, Pres, 1983; Kappa Mu Epsilon, VP 1983; Men's Dorm, VP, 1981; Prexy Clb; BSA, Jr Asst Scout Master; r/Bapt; hon/Best Pledge for Sigma Alpha Epsilon; Outstg Chem Student; Chem Res Awd; Nat Registers for Outstg Col Grad; W/W; g/Indust Res or QC Chem.

BUTTS, DEAN MICHAEL oc/Student; b/Jan 5, 1966; h/Route 1, Box 115, Teachey, NC 28464; p/Mrs Betty P Butts, Teachey, NC; ed/Wallace-Rose Hill HS, 1983; NC St Univ; cp/Nat Hon Soc, 1982-83; Spanish Clb, 1982-83; Math Clb, 1982; Men's Varsity Tennis, 1982-83; r/So Bapt; hon/Gov's Sch Nom, 1981, 1982; NC Sch Sci & Math Nom, 1981; NC Vet's S'ship, 1983; g/Deg in Acctg.

BUTZ, DONALD JOSEPH oc/ Research Scientist; b/Oct 3, 1958; h/100 East Frambes Avenue, Apartment B-4, Columbus, OH; p/Mr and Mrs Donald E Butz, Caledonia, OH; ed/River HS, 1977; BSAAE, OH St Univ, 1981; cp/ Am Inst of Aeronautics & Astronautics Columbus Sect Student Pres, Public Relats Chm, Newslttr Chm; Am Def Preparedness Assn; Inf Assn; Sigma Gamma Tau; hon/Assoc Mem, Sigma Xi Sci Res Soc; John Dale Donoran S'ship; Am Inst of Aeronautics & Astronautics Columbus Sect Student of the Yr.

BYRD, CAROL LYNETTE oc/Student; b/Sep 10, 1964; h/1609 Inglewood Drive, Burlington, NC 27215; p/Robert and Chattie Byrd; ed/Walter Williams HS; Att'd Randolph-Macon Wom's Col; cp/Ch Choir; Keywanettes; Yth F'ship; Yth Adv Coun; Bible Sch Tchr; Bell Choir; Spanish NHS; Yth Coun; Homeroom Secy, Treas; Sch Chorus; hon/ NHS Secy, NC; Highest Spanish I & II Avgs; W/W Among Am HS Students; g/Rel Cnslg.

BYRD, DERRICK WAYNE oc/Administrative Assistant; b/Sep 6, 1960; h/ 131 East Prospect Avenue, Mount Vernon, NY 10550; p/Louise Byrd, New York, NY; ed/Mt Vernon HS, 1977; Lib Art Deg, Mercy Col, 1980; Empire St Col, 1980-; pa/Congl Staff Asst, 1977-79; Asst Supvr Tutorial Prog 1979, Asst Supvr Yth Employmt Ser 1979, Yth Advocate, Prog Coor 1980-82, Mt Vernon Yth Bd; Ednl Cnslr, Urban Leag of Westchester, 1979; Recording Secy, 3rd VP, Mt Vernon HS PTA; Mem, United Way of Westchester; Coalition for Better Ed; NAACP; Dem City Com; Mid Sts Steering Com; United Negro Col Fund; r/Meth Epis, Trustee Bethel AME Ch; hon/Manhattan Coun of Chs Dist'd Citizen Awd; United Negro Col Fund; Outstg Yg Man of Am; g/Polit, Tchg, Admr, Commun Ser.

BYRD, ELAINE INEZ oc/Student; b/ Feb 21, 1963; h/Route 1, Box 144, Fulton, KY; p/Richard and Ruby Byrd, Fulton, KY; ed/Hickman Co HS, 1981; Murray St Univ; cp/Murray St Univ Varsity Cheerldr; Sigma Sigma Sigma Soc Sorority; Pi Kappa Alpha Frat Little Sister; Murray St Univ Student Ambassador; Pres, Sci Clb; VP, Beta Clb; Student Coun; Sr Homecoming Queen; Co-Edit Yrbook; Campus Favorite; VP, Pep Clb; r/Ch Wkr; hon/Gamma Beta Phi; Alpha Lambda Delta; Alpha Chi; Sigma Pi Sigma; Omicron Delta Kappa; HS Valedictorian, 1981; Pres S'ship, Murray St Univ; Yrbook Awd; Eng Awd; Am Hist Awd; Most Likely to Succeed; g/Maj Engrg Physics.

BYRD, JUDITH ELAINE oc/Student; b/Nov 5, 1964; h/55 Hickory Place, Livingston, NJ 07039; p/Robert L and Jo Ann Byrd, Livingston, NJ; ed/HS, 1982; Rutgers Univ; r/Bapt.

BYRD, LAURA ELAINE oc/Minister of Recreation; h/33 Summit, Shreveport, LA 71129; ba/Shreveport, LA; p/ Dr Ronald J Byrd, Baton Rouge, LA, and Annie T Byrd, Shreveport, LA; ed/ Southwood HS, 1977; LA Col, 1981; BA, LA St Univ; pa/Min Rec, Highland Bapt Ch, 1982-; Grad Asst Leisure Sers, LA St Univ, 1981-82; YMCA Daycamp Asst Dir, 1981; Jr HS Activs Assoc, Emmanuel Bapt Ch, 1980-81; cp/LA Alliance of Hlth, PE, & Rec; r/So Bapt; hon/Bapt Basketball Leag MVP, 1973, 1974, 1975, 1977; LA Bapt Student Union All St Basketball Team, 1981; LA Col Homecoming Ct Maid; g/SWn Bapt Theol Sem.

BYRUM, JULIE oc/Student; b/Sep 10, 1965; h/1143 Mona Drive, Charlotte, NC 28206; p/Mr and Mrs Lloyd Byrum, Charlotte, NC; ed/Independence Sr HS, 1983; pa/Salesperson, Ivey's, 1983; cp/DECA, 1983; Patriot Singers, 1983; Lttr Girl, 1981-83; r/Cath; hon/W/W HS Students; g/to be Fashion Dir.

C

CABUHAT, CYNTHIA MACHADO oc/Student; b/Aug 17, 1963; h/846 Worthington Street, San Diego, CA 92114; p/Ernest M and Irene M Cabuhat, San Diego, CA; ed/Grad, Mt Miguel HS, 1981; Att'g San Diego St Univ; cp/CSF Secy; Hosp Vol; Marching Bd; Jazz Band; Dixieland Band; Pep Band; Symph Band; Orch; Clarinet Sect Ldr; Univ Marching Band; Nat Student Nurses Assn, 1983; hon/Bk of Am Cert in Music; Outstg Sr Girl in Music Dept; Life Mem, CSF, 1981; W/W Among Am HS Students; Commun Ldrs of Am; g/ Nsg Deg; Nurse Practitioner Lic.

CACKA—ADAMS, ELIZABETH SUE oc/Animal Health Technician; b/ Aug 13, 1962; h/4245 Third Avenue, San Bernadino, CA 92407; ba/San Bernadino, CA; m/Thomas M Adams; p/Frank and Norma Cacka, San Bernadiono, CA; sp/Bob and Nadine Eck, Phoenix, AZ; ed/Grad, Pacific HS, 1980; Att'd U Hlth Careers Inst, 1982; Att'd Val Col, San Bernardino & San Bernardino St Col; pa/Ofc Tech, Lady Markells, 1979-82; Clk, Mad Greek, 1981; Reg'd Animal Hlth Tech, Northside Vet Clin, 1982-; Reg'd Animal Hlth Tech; cp/Bike-a-thon Jr Chm, Cancer Soc; Zonta Clb; Vol, at Convalescent Homes; Min Pin Clb of Gtr LA; NRA; Intl Handgun Metallic Silhouette Assn; r/ Mormon; Nat Hon Soc S'ship; Grad w Highest Hons; CSF Chords & Tassels; NHS Chords & Tassels; W/W Among Am HS Students; g/Elem Tchr.

CADDELL, STACY LYNN oc/Student; h/1350 East Northern Apartment 342, Phoenix, AZ 85020; p/Mr and Mrs Gilbert W Caddell, Las Vegas, NV; ed/ Grad, Bonanza HS, 1983; Currently Att'g, DeVry Inst of Technol; cp/Nat Hon Soc, 1981-83; Photo Clb; Flag Twirler; Capt 1982-83, Co-Capt 1981-82, Flag Tm; Candy Striper; Blood Donor; hon/NV Classified Sch Employees Assn S'ship; g/BS Deg; Computer Sys Analyst.

CADENA—ANGEL, HECTOR FABIO oc/Student; b/May 18, 1956; h/ 143-06 Barclay Avenue, Flushing, NY 11355; p/Santiago Cadena (dec); Mariela Angel de Cadena, Flushing, NY; ed/ Grad, John Browne HS, 1975; BA, Queens Col of City of NY 1982; Att'd Polytech Inst of NY; cp/Mem, AIChE; Pres, Student Coun; Alpha Phi Omega; US Chess Fedn; Pres, Coun of Latin Am Orgs of Queens Col; Assn of Latin Am Students; Col Student Assn Acad Senator at Large, 1977; Nat Student Assn Del; Flushing Boys' Clb Cnslr & Coach; hon/Alumni Assn S'ship; Student Assn Meritorious Ser Awd; Arista; Nat Hon Soc; NY St Regents S'ship; W/ W in Am Cols & Univs; Intl Yth in Achmt; g/MA in French; Adj Lectr, Queens Col.

CADOW, STANTON LEE oc/Aide to Governor of Louisiana; Intergovernmental Liaison Officer; b/May 20, 1958; ed/E Jefferson HS, 1975; LA St Univ, 1978; BA, SEn LA Univ, 1982; pa/Aide to Gov of LA, Edwin W Edwards; Appt'd by Gov to Staff, Intergovt'l Liaison Ofcr, Gov's Staff; New Auto Sales; cp/ LA Yg Dems; St Bd of Dirs, 6th Congl Dist; Alumni Advr, Beta Pi Chapt of Theta Xi Frat; Election Commr, Chm, Gov Comm on U Way; Hi-Y Yth Legis

Alumni Advr; Theta Xi Mem 1978-, Pres, VP, Secy, Nat Com Chm, 3-Time Nat Del, Pledge Dir 1978-; Student LA Assn of Ed 1978-82, Chapt Pres, Parliamentn, Bd of Dirs, St VP, 1979-82; Student NEA, 2-Time Nat Bd of Dirs, Cong Contact Tm, 3-Time Nat Del 1978-82; SEn LA Univ SGA, 1978-82, Sen, Sen Chm 1978-79, Parliamentn, Exec Asst to Pres 1979-80, Govt Liaison Ofcr, Univ-City Rel Com Chm 1981-82; Col Dem, Fdr, Chapt Pres 1982; KSLU Radio Sta, News, Music Dir 1982; LA MS Soc, St Bd of Reg 1978-80; NEA, Nat Bd of MS Soc, St Bd of Reg 1978-80; NEA, Nat Bd of Dirs, Resolutions Com 1981-82; LA St Dem Party, St Conv Alt Del 1982-; LA Assn of Student Coun, Ldrship Wkshop Conslt Staff 1972-80, Asst Exec Dir 1973-80; ARC, WSI, 1976-81; Col Dem of Am, St Coor 1982; r/Rom Cath; Yg Dems of LA Nat Comm-man; hon/Theta Xi, Ben Franklin Most Scholastic Pledge 1978; Student LA Assn of Ed, Most Outstg Mem 1980; W/W Amg Students in Am Univs & Cols; Intl Yth in Achmt; SEn LA Univ, Green S Awd for Outstg Ser 1978, 1979, 1980, 1981, Dean's List; Most Outstg Male Greek 1981; Commun Ldr of Am; White House Spec Briefing on Dept of Ed for Student Ldrs, Del, 1980; Outstg Yg Men of Am.

CAFFEY, STEVEN DALE oc/Machinist; b/May 14, 1963; h/Rural Route 1 Box 152, Pryor, OK 74361; ba/Tulsa, OK; p/Wayne and Dorothy Caffey, Pryor, OK; ed/Grad, Pryor HS, 1981; Att'd NEn Area Vo-Tech/Machine Shop, 1981; AA Numerical Control Programming, OK St Tech, 1983; pa/ Machinist, Green Country Machine Shop, Claremore, OK, 1980; Machinist, NEn Area Vo-Tech, Pryor, OK, 1980-81; Machinist, Dover Corp, Morris Div, Tulsa, OK, 1983-; cp/Mem, Voc Clbs of Am, 1980-81; Mem, Soc of Mfrg Engrs; r/Bapt; hon/Articles Pub'd in *Outdoor Life*; *Computer*; *Mfg Engrg*; 2 Yrs Perfect Attendance Awd, NEn Area Voc-Tech, 1980-81; 98-100% Attendance Awd, OK St Tech, 1981-83; 3rd Place, Machine Shop Dist Contest, 1980 & 1981; 6th Place 1980, 9th Place 1981, OK St Machine Shop Contest; g/ Numerical Control Programmer w Co; Owner of Machine Shop.

CAIN, THERESA ANNETTE oc/ Student; b/Sep 14, 1967; h/Route 1 Box 17N, Chelsea, AL 35043; p/Earl and Betty Cain, Chelsea, AL; ed/Att'g Sr, at Chelsea HS, 1985; cp/Beta Clb; Jr Beta Clb; Chaplain, FHA; Chaplain & VPres, Student Govt; Math Clb; Jr HS Cheerldr; Hd, Varsity Cheerldr; Basketball; Soc of Dist'd HS Students; r/So Bapt; hon/Miss AL U Teenager, 1983; Miss Chelsea HS, 1981; Jr Miss Chelsea HS, 1980; Jr Miss Cheonet, 1980; Talent Winner, Shelby Co Cinderella Teen; W/ W Among Am HS Students; g/Attend Col; Wk in A Breigh Mission Field Comm'd by the So Bapt.

CALDWELL, CYNTHIA KAY oc/ College Student; b/June 13, 1957; h/ Route 3, Box 653, Wichita Falls, TX 76308; p/HD Caldwell, Wichita Falls, TX; ed/Grad, Iowa Pk HS, TX, 1976; Att'g Sr, MWn St Univ; pa/Bkkpr & Payroll Clk, Crawford Painting & Drywall Co, 1975-77; Acquisitions Clk, Stephen F Austin St Univ, 1978; Acctg Dept, Water Utilities & Tax Dept, City

of Abilene, TX, 1979-81; Teller, SW Nat Bk, Wichita Falls, 1982-83; cp/Pres, Univ Secretarial Assn, 1982-83; Treas/Sec, Ch of Christ Bible Choir at MWn St Univ, 1981; r/Ch of Christ; hon/Nom, Outstg Wom of MWn St Univ, 1983; g/Deg in Ofc Adm.

CALDWELL, MELISSA B oc/Staff Nurse-intern; b/Nov 17, 1961; h/Apartment 1902 Lincoln Green, New Garden Road, Greensboro, NC 27410; m/Marshall Neill; p/Mr and Mrs Worth T Bridges, Mooresville, NC; sp/Mr and Mrs Ralph Henry Caldwell, Greensboro, NC; ed/Grad, Mooresville Sr HS, 1980; BS Nsg, Univ of NC-Greensboro, 1984; pa/Staff Nurse-intern, Moses Cone Hosp, Greensboro, NC, 1984; Student Nurse-aide, Wesley Long Hosp, Greensboro, 1983-; cp/Water Safety Instr, ARC, 1978-; Vol, Wk w Deaf in Sign Lang; Past Mgr of City Pool; Past Lifeguard, Univ of NC-Greensboro Pool; Vol, Cancer Drive Fund & Heart Fund; r/Bapt; h/Dean's List, Univ of NC-Greensboro, Fall, 1983.

CALHOUN, DENETRA EVON oc/ Student; b/Aug 30, 1963; h/654 Collinwood Avenue, Montgomery, AL 36105; p/Mr and Mrs Calvin Calhoun, Montgomery, AL; ed/Grad, Sidney Lanier HS, 1981; Att'g Sr, AL St Univ, 1985; pa/Pt-time Clk, Christian Benevolent Ins Co, 1977; Pt-time Salesperson, Brooks Fashions of NYC; Pt-time Musical, The Revelation Bapt Ch; cp/ Treas, Student Govt Assn, 1982-83; Chaplain, Delta Sigma Theta, 1983-84; r/Bapt; hon/The Dean's List, AL St Univ, 1981-; The Nat Dean's List, 1983-84; g/BA in Music w Minor in Eng.

CALHOUN, GERALD JOSEPH oc/ Student; b/Mar 28, 1961; h/2390 Ridgewood Drive, Madisonville, KY 42431; p/Sherrell J and Elizabeth J Calhoun, Madisonville, KY; ed/Grad, Madisonville-N Hopkins HS, 1979; BE, Vanderbilt Univ, 1983; cp/Vanderbilt Prison Proj, 1980-83; Treas, Commun Ser Chm, Alpha Phi Omega; Parliamentn 1981-82, Pres 1982-83, Gamma Beta Phi; Cath Coun Mem; Pres, Soph Rep, Vanderbilt Cath Commun Engrg Coun; hon/Winston Churchill F'ship, Cambridge Univ, 1983; Tau Beta Pi F'ship, 1983; Fdrs Medalist, Vanderbilt Univ, 1983; Omicron Delta Kappa, 1982; Eagle Scout; James Stewart Jr Hon S'ship; Mortar Bd; g/Study Control Engrg & Opers at Cambridge Univ.

CALHOUN, TRACY ANN oc/Student; b/Feb 1, 1963; h/915 Spring Street, Grand Saline, TX 75140; p/Mr and Mrs Dave Calhoun, Grand Saline, TX; ed/ Grad, Grand Saline HS, 1981; AA, Tyler Jr Col, 1983; Att'g, TX A&M Univ, 1983-; cp/Phi Theta Kappa; FHA, 1977-79; FTA, 1978-80; Secy/Treas 1980, Mem 1979-81, Spanish Clb; VPres, Photo Clb, 1980-81; Student Coun Rep, 1978-81; Asst Editor 1979-80, Photo Editor 1980-81, Yrbook Staff, 1979-81; hon/Grad w Hons & Math Dept Awd, HS, 1981; Grad magna cum laude, Tyler Jr Col, 1983; W/W Among Students in Am Jr Cols; Nat Dean's List; g/Aerospace Engrg.

CALIENES, NORA F oc/Teacher and Medical Secretary; b/Apr 12, 1962; h/ 526 West 114th Street, New York, NY 10025; ba/New York, NY; p/Frank F Calienes, W NY, NJ; ed/Grad, Meml HS, 1980; BA Fgn Lang Ed, Fairleigh Dickinson Univ, 1983; pa/Med Secy Asst, Fermin Leon MD, 1979-81; Dental Asst, Bkkpg & X-Ray Tech, Miller & Beals, DDS, PA, 1981-83; Bkpg, Customer Relats, Adv'd Res Hlth, 1983; Med Secy & Transcriber, J C Baez MD, 1983-; Pt-time Choreographer, Social Events, 1980-; cp/Am Assn of Tchrs of Spanish & Portuguese; Rape Intervention Prog, St Luke's Roosevelt Hosp; r/Cath; hon/ Dean's List & Acad Hons, Fairleigh Dickinson Univ, 1981-83; 2nd Hons, HS, 1980; Dean's List; Nat Piano Playing Auditions, 1972-81; HS Rep in TV Dance Prog, 1977; Sonatina Awd, Piano Guild, 1980; W/W Among HS Students; Yg Personalities of Am; Commun Ldrs of Am; g/Complete Pre-dental Requirements for Dental Sch.

CALKINS, BENJAMIN oc/ Attorney-at-Law; b/Jan 20, 1956; ba/ 1800 Huntington Bldg, Cleveland, OH 44115; m/Lindsay N; c/Sarah N; p/Mr and Mrs Evan Calkins; sp/Mr and Mrs E Noble, Wellesley, MA; ed/Grad, Hamburg Ctl Sch, 1974; AB, Harvard Col, 1978; JD, Univ of MI Law Sch, 1981; pa/LBJ Congl Intern to US Rep Jack F Kemp, 1975; Corp Intern, W R Grace & Co, 1977; Sum Assoc, Hodgson, Russ, Andrews, Woods & Goodyear, Buffalo, NY, 1979; Sum Assoc, Sidley & Austin, Chgo, 1980; Sum Assoc, Herrick & Smith, Boston, 1981; Sr Law Clk to US Dist Judge Julian A Cook Jr, Detroit, 1981-83; Assoc, Squire, Sanders & Dempsey, Cleveland, OH, 1983-; Mem, DC Bar Assn; ABA; cp/Audubon Soc; Chm, Student Advy Com of John F Kennedy Inst of Polits, Harvard Col; Pres, HS Student Coun; Dist Curric Com, HS Human Relats Coun; Contl Dorset Clb; Editor, *Harvard Crimson*; r/Presb; hon/Author, "Waiver of Rgt to Arbitrate, An Issue for the Ct or the Arbitrator?" in *The Arbitration Jour*, 1982; "The Emerging Due Diligence Standard for Filing Delayed Notice of Appeal in Fed Cts," *Willamette Law Review*, 1983; Grad cum laude, Univ of MI Law Sch; Sr Judge, Writing & Advocacy Prog, Univ of MI Law Sch; Order of the Coif; Sr Editor, *MI Law Review*; Commun Ldrs of Am; g/Law; Polits.

CALLAHAN, KATIE M oc/Writer; b/ Aug 17, 1965; h/30219 Flanders Drive, Warren, MI 48093; p/Mr and Mrs Joseph J Callahan, Warren, MI; ed/Grad, Bishop Foley HS, 1983; pa/Clk/Typist, Kmart Intl HQ's, Troy, MI; cp/Sci Clb, 1980-83; Girls' Ath Assn, 1981-83; Nat Hon Soc, 1982-83; Intl Clb, 1983; Track Tm, 1980-83; Venturian Staff, 1980-83; Mem, 6 Sr Coms, 1983; r/Cath; hon/ Pub'd Poem, *Nat Poetry Press*, 1983; Genevieve Wreggelsworth Writing Awd, 1983; S'ship Awd, 1983; Grad HS cum laude, 1983; 3rd Place, Bishop Foley Writing Contest, 1983; Soc of Dist'd Am HS Students; W/W Among Am HS Students; g/Attend UCLA, Major in Theatre Arts.

CALVERT, ROBERT OWEN JR oc/ Graduate Student; b/Mar 29, 1961; h/ 1253 Church Street Apartment 1, Decatur, GA 30030; ba/Atlanta, GA; p/ Mr and Mrs R O Calvert Sr, Atlanta, GA; ed/Grad, Henderson HS, Chamblee, GA, 1979; Grad, Lenoir-Rhyne Col, 1983; Att'g, Emory Univ; cp/Nat Hon Soc; Varsity Cheerldr; Marching Band; Chi Beta Phi; Theta Xi; hon/Grad magna

cum laude, Lenoir-Rhyne Co, 1983; Dean's List, 8 Semesters; Mu Sigma Epsilon; Nat Merit S'ship; Hons S'ship; Univ of GA Cert of Merit; Outstg Cheerldr; Nat Dean's List; Outstg Yg Men in Am; g/Tchg at Lenoir-Rhyne Col.

CAMPBELL, ANNELLA DIANE oc/ Lead Customer Accountant; b/Jul 7, 1960; h/1419 Corry Road, Memphis, TN 38106; ba/Memphis, TN; p/Ulysses Campbell, Memphis, TN; Ola Elion, Memphis, TN; ed/Dipl, Hamilton HS, 1978; BS 1981, MBA 1983, Jackson St Univ; pa/Lead Customer Acct, Merrill Lynch Reg Oper Ctr, 1983-; Bkkpr, Merrill Lynch Brokerage Firm, 1982-83; Registrar, Mid MS Girl Scout Coun, 1981; Res Asst, Chem Dept, Jackson St Univ; cp/Mem, Nat Assn of Media Wom; Alpha Mu Gamma Fgn Lang Soc; Phi Kappa Phi; GSA; Alpha Lambda DElta; hon/Valedictorian, Jackson St Univ, 1981; Miss Nat Assn of Media Wom, 1979-80; Chosen by MS Consortia to do Res in Barbados W Indies, Sum 1981; Recip, Kellogg's Grant to Participate Mass Communs Orientation Prog, Sum 1978; g/Pursue Fin Career of Stock Mkt Bus.

CAMPBELL, CAROLYN JAYNE oc/ Student; b/Mar 30, 1963; h/Route 1 Box 101, Hampstead, NC 28443; ba/Wilson, NC; p/Mr and Mrs Morris Campbell, Hampstead, NC; ed/Grad, Topsail HS, 1981; Att'g, Atlantic Christian Col; pa/ Sch Busdriver, Pender Co Bd of Ed, 1979-81; Cashier, Red & White Supermkt, Surf City, Sums 1980-83; Cashier, Heart of Wilson Motor Inn, Winter & Fall, 1981-83; Self-employed Distbr, Fay Swafford Origs, 1983-; cp/ Secy-Treas, Freshman Class, 1981-82; Senator Sophomore Class, 1982; Atlantic Christian Col Senate Mem, 1981-83; Columnist for Co Newspaper, *The Pender Chronicle*; Miss Topsail Island, 1983; Columnist, Atlantic Christian Col *Collegiate*; Mem, Yg Repub Clb, 1981-82; g/BSBA w Minor in Eng; Position in Retail Mgmt.

CAMPBELL, ELIZABETH ANN oc/ Student; b/Apr 26, 1962; h/2957 Princess Anne Crescent, Chesapeake, VA 23321; ba/Harrisonburg, VA; p/Don and Laura Lou Campbell, Chesapeake, VA; ed/Grad, Wn Br HS, 1980; Att'g Sr, James Madison Univ, 1984; cp/GSA, 1968-83; HS: Chorus, 1976-80; VPres, Am Field Ser, 1976-80; Student Life Sect Reporter, Photog Coor, Editor-in-Chief, Yrbook Staff, 1977-80; Col: Yrbook Staff (Acad & Index Sect Editor), 1980-82; Hall Coun Rep, 1983; Psych Clb, 1983; Vol, Crisis Hotline, 1983; hon/1st Class Awd, GSA, 1976; Nat Hon Soc, 1979-80; Quill & Scroll Nat Hon Soc, 1979-80; Outstg Ser Awd, 1980; Dean's List, James Madison Univ, Fall 1981 & 1982 & Spng 1981; VA Music Camp S'ship, 1976; Girl Scout Wider Opport, 1976; Jr Miss Contestant (Poster Contest Winner), 1980; Yrbook Rep to Miss Madison Contest, 1981; Psi Chi Psych Frat, 1983; g/MS Cnslg Psych; Sch or Col Psychol.

CAMPBELL, JEFFREY P oc/Student; b/Oct 14, 1962; h/904 Wildwood Drive, Kings Mountain, NC 28086; p/George N and Myrtle L Campbell, Kings Mtn, NC; ed/Grad, Kings Mtn Sr HS; BSChE, NC St Univ; cp/AIChE; Tau Beta Pi Nat Engrg Soc; hon/Phi Eta Sigma, 1980; Phi

Kappa Phi, 1983; Chem Engrg Merit S'ship, 1982; W/W Among Am HS Students; g/Attend Med Sch for MD.

CAMPBELL, JULIE DAWN oc/Student; b/Mar 25, 1966; h/Route 1 Box 189 Mt Crawford, VA 22841; p/Mr and Mrs Everett Campbell, Mt Crawford, VA; ed/Grad, Spotswood Sr HS; cp/Co Pres 1983, Co Vpres 1982, All Star VPres 1983 & 1984, F-H; Pres, FHA, 1984; Brethren Dist Yth Cabinet; VPres, Mt Pleasant, Yth Grp, 1984; r/ Brethren; hon/Pubs in *Shenandoah Ripple*, Monthly Newslttr; Harrisonburg-Rockingham C of C Ednl S'ship, 1983; Nat Achmt Acad, 1983; VA St All Star, 1982; VA Photog (Poultry) Exhibit, 1983; St 4-H Presentation Winner, 1982; Nat Awds; US Achmt Acad, 1983-84; g/Attend En Mennonite Col; Fashion Designer.

CAMPBELL, PHILIP DEAN oc/Criminal Justice Reporter; b/Dec 13, 1961; h/PO Box 136, Darlington, SC 29532; p/Mr and Mrs Philip P Campbell, Darlington, SC; ed/Grad, St John's HS; Att'g, Univ of SC Col of Jour; pa/Legis Reporter for: *Darlington News & Press, The Berkeley Dem, The Hilton Hd Isl Packet* The Georgetown Times, *The Holly Hill Observer*; WOLS Radio-Florence & WESC-Greenville, 1984; Tech Writer Intern, Policy Mgmt Sys Corp, Columbia, SC, 1984; St House Legis Reporter: *Darlington News & Press, Berkeley Dem, Cheraw Chronicle, Pageland Progressive Jour*, 1983; Legis Reporter for Other Newspapers; Election Stringer: CBS, WIS-TV (NBC) Columbia & Florence Morning News; Mem, Sigma Delta Chi; cp/Asst Dir, Miss So 500 Pageant Com; r/Bapt; hon/Univ of SC Col of Jour's George A Buchanan S'ship, 1982-83; Dean's List, Univ of SC; Track Tm Lttrman; Holder of 3 Sch Distance Running Records; Lttrman, Cross Country Tm; Personalities of S.

CANNON, CYNTHIA ANNE oc/ Student; b/Oct 1, 1964; h/116 Cornelison Road, Richmond, KY 40475; p/Mr and Mrs Dean C Cannon, Richmond, KY; ed/Grad, Madison Ctl HS, 1982; Att'g, Univ of KY; cp/Beta Clb; All-Reg Band; All-Co BAnd; Univ of KY Choristers; Univ of KY Wesley Foun; Choir; Show Choir; Pep Band; Concert & Symph Band; Hlth Careers Clb; Fgn Lang Clb; Drama Clb; Pep Clb; U Meth Yth F'ship Grp; Foster Music Camp; hon/Superior Rating in Solo & Ensemble Contest, En KY Univ, 1981; US Achmt Acad Awd for Nat Ldship & Ser, 1983; Yg Commun Ldrship Awd, 1982; Hon Roll; magna cum laude Latin Awd; 50 Word Typing Awd; US Achmt Acad Eng & Creat Writing Awd; KY-OH All-St Chorus; Spirit Awd for Outstg Choral Musician; W/W: Among Am HS Students, in Music; Commun Ldrs of Am; g/DMDPSC in Dermatol or Orthodontics.

CANOVAI, TONI LYNN oc/Industl Engineer; b/Oct 21, 1960; h/125 Foust Road, Graham, NC 27253; p/Mr and Mrs Peter Canovai Jr, Graham, NC; ed/ Grad, Graham HS, 1978; BSIE, NC St Univ, 1982; pa/Industl Engr, (Coop Ed Prog w NC St Univ), No Telecom, 1980-81; cp/Bus Mgr, *So Engr Mag*, 1982; Treas, Inst of Industl Engrs, 1982; Nat Soc for Profl Engrs, 1980-83; Tau Beta Pi, 1982-83; Engrs' Coun, 1982; Alpha Pi Mu, 1981-82; Bowen Dorm House

Coun, 1979-82; Secy, HS Jr & Sr Class Yrs, 1977-78; HS Civinettes, 1976-78; hon/Author, "Lrng," Pub'd in *So Engr Mag*; K of St Patrick's Awd, 1982; Dean's List, 3 Semesters; g/MS in Industl Engrg; Consltg Industl Engr.

CANROBERT, LAURA MARIAN oc/ Medical Technology Student; b/Nov 14, 1960; h/PO Box 696, Conover, NC 28613; p/Mr and Mrs C W Canrobert, Conover, NC; ed/Grad, Newton-Conover HS, 1979; BSMT, High Pt Col, 1983; Att'g Med Tech Prog, Bowman Gray Sch of Med; pa/STAT Lab Wkr, NC Bapt Hosp, Winston-Salem, 1983; cp/HS: Volleyball; Basketball; Softball; Band; Beta Clb; Interact Clb; Varsity Clb; Col: Pep Band; Luth Assn; Pres Scholar; Tm Before Self Awd, HS Volleyball, 1976, 1977 & 1978 & All-Conf 1978; Tm Before Self Awd, HS Softball 1979 & All-Conf 1977 & 1979; Acad Ath of Yr, 1979; Pres, Beta Clb, 1979; Chief, Jr Marshal, 1978; Valedictorian, 1979; Pres S'ship & Jr Marshal, High Pt Col, 1982; W/W of Am; g/Med Technol.

CANTU, IRMA IRIS oc/Student; b/ Nov 29, 1965; h/PO Box 867, Freer, TX 78357; p/Edmonduno A and Oralia Cantu, Freer, TX; ed/Att'd Beverly Miller Sch of Dancing; Att'd Miss Majorette Baton Acd; Att'd Twirling Camp & 4-H Ldrship Lab, TX A&L Univ; Band Camp, TX Luth Col; Att'g, Freer HS; cp/Secy & Reporter, 4-H Clb; FHA; Spanish Clb; Student Coun; Nat Hon Soc; Freer Buckaroo Band; Majorette, Buckaroo Band; Vol Wk, Freer C of C; Freer Handicapped, Band Boosters; 4-H Clb Concession Stand; Miss Freer Beauty Pageant, 1981; r/ Cath; hon/Num Awds, Medals & Trophies in Twirling, Clarinet Solos, Trios & Ensembles, 1979-82; 1st Place Food Div, Duval Co Fair Co Food Show & 2nd Overall, 1980; 1st Place Art Drawing, Duval Co Fair, 1980, 1981 & 1982; 1st Place Sewing Div, Duval Co Fair, 1981; 1st & 2nd Place in Dist, Co & Dist Food Show; 3rd Place & 2nd Overall Co Dress Revue; Safety Hunting Patch; 4-H Dist'd Method Demo Open Class 3rd Place, 1981; 1st Place Handcraft 1981, 2nd Place Sewing & Food Div 1982, Duval Co Fair; 4-H Gold Star Winner; Freer HS Queen; Num Other Hons & Awds.

CAPANI, BERNADETTE MARIE oc/ Social Worker; b/Nov 25, 1958; h/76 Bennett Avenue, Binghamton, NY 13905; ba/Binghamton, NY; p/Michael and Antoinette Capani, Binghamton, NY; ed/Grad, Binghamton Ctl HS; BA Sociol, SUNY-Cortland, 1980; pa/Social Wkr, Willow Point Nsg Home, Binghamton, NY, 1980-; cp/Notary Public for NY St; r/Cath; g/Pursue MSW.

CAPPAERT, STEVEN MICHAEL oc/ Student; b/Jul 20, 1961; h/5411-11th Avenue A, Moline, IL 61265; p/Mr and Mrs George D Cappaert, Moline, IL; ed/ Grad, Moline Sr HS, 1979; BSC 1983, MS Cand, DePaul Univ; cp/HS: Student Newspaper; Capt, Debate Tm, 1978-79; Yrbook; Col: Student Newspaper; Recording Secy, Beta Alpha Psi, 1983-84; Pres, Phi Eta Sigma, 1980-81; Pres, Alpha Lambda Delta, 1980-81; Beta Gamma Sigma; VPres, Delta Mu Delta, 1983; Delta Epsilon Sigma; Kappa Gamma Pi; Blue Key; r/Rom Cath; hon/ HS: Nat Hon Soc; IL St Scholar; Quill

& Scroll; Col: Arthur J Schmitt Scholar; Hon Acctg Prog; Dean's Awd, 1983; Grad summa cum laude, 1983; Nat Dean's List; W/W Among Students in Am Univs & Cols; g/Pursue MS Accountancy.

CAPPIELLO, ANTHONY PETER JR oc/Student; b/Jun 30, 1964; h/Route 17 Sparks Road, Knoxville, TN 37931; ba/ Nashville, TN; p/Anthony P Cappiello (dec); Mrs A P Cappielo (Mildred), Knoxville, TN; ed/Grad, Webb Sch of Knoxville HS, 1982; Att'g, Vanderbilt Univ; Real Est Lic, St of TN, 1983; pa/ Affil Broker in Real Est, ERA, Gilco Realty, Oak Ridge, TN, 1983-; cp/ Freshman Rep 1982-83, Sophomore Rep 1983-84, Vanderbilt Student Govt Assn; Nat cum laude (HS); Sigma Nu Frat; Webb Sch Class Agt for Class of 1982; Alumni Contact Ofcr, Sigma Nu, Fall 1983; Star Scout, BSA; 1st U Ch Knoxville Teen Bd; Pres, Sr Class; Spkr, World's Fair, 1982; Varsity Soccer; HS Mock Trial Tm; Student Coun RepHS; r/Meth; hon/Nat cum laude Soc, 1982; Lttrman, SoccerI W/W Among Am HS Students; Commun Ldrs of Am; g/Maj, Ec; Minor, Bus; Atty; Polits.

CARAWAY, MIDGE D oc/Student; b/Mar 4, 1968; h/PO Box 327 Rose Hill, NC 28458; p/Mr and Mrs Kirk D Carawan, Rose Hill, NC; ed/Att'g Sophomore, Wallace-Rose Hill HS; Student Coun Rep; FBLA Clb; Tennis Tm; Stats for JV Football Tm; Warsaw Jr Music Clb; r/Bapt; g/Pursue Bus Deg.

CARDA, JUANITA MARIE oc/Computer Operator; b/Apr 19, 1960; h/1622 Grayson, Hobbs, NM 88240; ba/Hobbs, NM; m/Shaun Louis Carda; p/J W and Lois McLemore, Hobbs, NM; sp/Steve and Shirley Carda, Hobbs, NM; ed/ Grad, Hobbs HS, 1978; AAS, NM Jr Col, 1980; Att'd, The Univ of TX-Permian Basin, 1981; pa/Computer Operator, Univ of TX-Permia Basin, 1981; Computer Operator, Gulf Oil Co, 1982-; pl/ Pers Dir, Jr Achmt, 1977-78; Phi Theta Kappa, 1980; Student Rep, Salary Tm for NM Jr Col, 1980; r/Christian; hon/ Dist'd Grad, NM Jr Col, 1980; W/W Among Am Jr Cols, 1979-80; ABI; g/ PhD in Psych; Social or Clin Psychol.

CARDEN, ELIZABETH oc/Student; b/Jul 29, 1967; h/Lake Hills, Tullahoma, TN 37388; p/Milner and Martha Carden, Tullahoma, TN; ed/Att'g Sr, Tullahoma HS; pa/Employee, Highland Racquet Ctr; cp/Ch Yth Grp; Tennis Tm; Student Coun; Editor-in-Chief, Newspaper Staff; Sub-Deb Sorority; Basketball; French Clb; r/Meth; hon/ Most Improved Tennis Player, 1984; *High Mag*, Salesman, 1982-84; All Tour Tm Basketball, 1982; W/W Am HS Students; g/Maj in Broadcasting; Sports Commentator.

CARDEN, SUSAN ELAINE oc/Student; b/Mar 20, 1963; h/1510 Creighton Place, Tullahoma, TN 37388; ba/Greenville, SC; p/William H and Mildred Carden, Tullahoma, TN; ed/Grad, Tullahoma HS, 1983; Att'g Furman Univ; pa/Secy & Customer Ser Clk, Tullahoma Utilities Bd, Sums 1981-83; cp/Furman Singers; BSU Counm, 1982-84; r/Bapt; hon/Pi Eta Sigma, 1982; Kappa Delta Epsilon, 1983; g/Deg in Music Ed.

CARLIN, VICKI MICHELLE oc/ Student; b/May 6, 1965; h/Route 2 Box 352 Ramer, TN 38367; p/Mr and Mrs

E R Carlin, Ramer, TN; ed/Grad, McNairy Ctl HS, 1983; Att'g Sophomore, Memphis St Univ, 1985; cp/HS: Beta Clb; Sophomore Class Reporter; Intl Clb Reporter; Pep Clb; Lib Grp; Annual Staff; Col: Annual Staff, Memphis St Univ, 1983; r/Presb; hon/Typing Awd, 1981; Acctg Awd, 1982; g/Deg in Acctg; CPA for Exec Law Firm.

CARMICHAEL, ELMA J MIXON oc/ Charge Tech; b/Feb 21, 1949; h/3458 Monte Carlo, Dallas, TX 75224; ba/ Dallas, TX; m/Freddie; c/Zorana Renita; p/Minni Mixon, Waldo, AR; sp/Luegene Carmichael, Charleton, MS; ed/Grad, Westside HS, 1967; AA, El Centro Col, 1980; Att'd Univ of TX, 1981; pa/X-Ray Techn, Forest Ave Hosp, 1967; Assem Wkr, TX Instruments, 1969; Ser Tech, Charge Person, Parkandland Hosp, Dallas, TX, 1972-; cp/Vol, Ch Jail Min Prog, 1980-; r/Meth; hon/Cert for Supvr of Mo, 1981; 11 Yrs Awd Plaque, Parkandland Hosp, 1983; g/Var Courses of Study in Acctg, Programming, Mgmt, Ec, Real Est; Mgr of Mat Ser, Parkandland Hosp.

CARMICHAEL, LAWRENCE RAY oc/Law Student; b/Oct 22, 1958; h/PO Box 1023, Somerset, KY 42501; ba/ Somerset, KY; p/Virginia Black, Somerset, KY; ed/Grad, Somerset, HS, 1977; AA, Communs, Somerset Commun Col, 1979; BBA, Univ of KY, 1981; pa/Juv Intake Ofcr, 1981-83; Investor, Commonwlth Atty's Ofc, 1979; Intern, Congl Ofc, Wash DC, 1980; Juv Ofcr, Pulaski Dist Ct, 1981; cp/Am Trial Lwyrs Assn; Student Div, ABA; Phi Alpha Delta; Col Newspaper Staff Editor, 1978-79; St Chm, KY Col Repub Foun, 1980-82; Univ of KY Student Govt Senator, 1980-81; Phi Beta Lambda; Am Mktg Assn; Asst Scout Master, BSA, 1982; Nat Eagle Scout Assn; Am Bowling Leag; KY Yg Repub Foun; r/Prot; hon/KY Col, 1979; Eagle Scout, 1974; Intl Yth in Achmt; W/W in Am Polits; Yg Commun Ldrs; Yg Personalities of Am; g/Law Pract.

CARNES, GREGORY NATHAN oc/ Science Teacher; b/Jul 31, 1958; h/300 Harrison Street, Troy, OH 45373; ba/ Troy, OH; p/Mr and Mrs Joseph P Carnes Jr, Troy, OH; ed/Grad, HS, 1976; BS; pa/Sum Computer Sci Instr, Troy City Sch, 1983-; Mem: NEA; OEA; Dist Rep, WIEA; TCEA; cp/Ch Dir & SS Tchr; Yg Min; St Musician; PA of W; Alt Bldg Rep 1982-83, Elem Needs Com 1982-83, TCEA; Dean of Ed Selection Com; Peer Advr; Miami Univ (OH) Gospel Singers; Sr Class Pres; Student Coun Pres; hon/Nat Dean's List; Intl Yth in Achmt; W/W in Am Cols & Univs; Outstg Yg Men in Am; g/Instr, Ldr in Ed.

CARPENTER, "KATHY" ANN oc/ Student; b/Aug 30, 1965; h/115 Bates Avenue, Cherryville, NC 28021; ba/ Boone, NC; p/Fred Raeford and Geraldine B Carpenter, Cherryville, NC; ed/ Grad, Cherryville HS, 1983; Att'g, Appalachian St Univ, 1983-; pa/Sales Clk, Carpenter's Gift Shop; cp/French Clb; FBLA; Interact; Secy; Jr Heart Bd; Math Clb; Chorus; Pep Clb; Sci Clb; Student Coun; Chenoca Staff; Sales Staff; Guid Asst; Band; r/Meth; hon/ Gov's Page; Homecoming Student Coun Rep; W/W.

CARPENTER, LISA LYNN oc/University Student; b/Nov 19, 1964; h/

Route 4, Box 793, Lincolnton, NC 28092; p/Mr and Mrs B Hugh Carpenter, Lincolnton, NC; ed/Grad, Bessemer City HS, 1983; Att'g, Univ of NC-Greensboro, 1983-; cp/HS: Jr Civitan Clb; Beta Clb; Secy, Spanish Clb; Dram Clb Histn; FHA; Student Coun Reporter; Band Secy; All-St Band Mem; VPres 1981, Pres 1982, Rep 1983, Gaston Co 4-H Coun; Clogging Clovers 4-H Clb; Yth Pres 1982, Ldr of Yth Band, Bethel Luth Ch; Vol, ARC, 1980; r/Luth; ho/HS: Drum Maj, 1982; Marshal, 1981; Chief Marshal, 1982; Valedictorian, 1983; Orch Mem, Gov's Sch of NC, 1982; Outstg Voc Student, 1983; Quiz Bowl; Clothing/Textile Awd, 1981; 3rd Place Dist Typing Contest, 1982; Outstg 4-Her of Gaston Co; Dist & St 4-H Talent Winner, 1981 & 1982; Morehead S'ship Non; Elks Nat Foun S'ship; 4-H Devel Fund S'ship; Patterson Meml Fund S'ship (Luth); NC Ext Homemakers S'ship; Univ of NC-Greensboro James M Johnston S'ship; W/W Among Am HS Students; g/Maj: Home Ec in Bus & Commun Sers; Home Economist in Ext Sers; Host Consumer Show; Wk in Mass Media.

CARR, BEVERLY AYERS oc/Registered Nurse; b/Nov 5, 1953; h/111 Poplar, Martin, TN 38237; m/Kenneth William; c/Kenneth William II (Will); p/Mr and Mrs Hubert Ayers, Doniphan, MO; sp/Mr and Mrs James Doncho, Martin, TN; ed/Grad, Doniphan Sr HS, 1971; Dipl, Bapt Meml Hosp Sch of Nsg, 1974; BSN, Univ of TN-Martin, 1980; mil/USAR, 1978-79; pa/Staff Nurse 1974-77, Charge RN 1977-78, City of Memphis Hosp Crit Care; Fac Dept of Nsg, Univ of TN-Martin, 1980-82; Mem, AACN, 1976-78; cp/Vol, ARC, 1977-; Epis Ch Wom; Mem 1978-, Pres 1981-83, Weakley Co Med Aux Assn; Area Cor 1980-81, Dir 1983-85, Mem 1979-, Pilot Clb; Brownie Ldr, 1980-82; Day Camp Wkr, 1980-82; r/Epis; hon/Grad cum laude, Univ of TN-Martin, 1980; One of 6 Outstg Sr, Bapt Meml Hosp, 1974; Cert'd Crit Care Nurse, AACN, 1978-80; Outstg Yg Wom of Am; g/Complete MA in Nsg.

CARR, ELLEN WEST oc/Student; b/Jan 24, 1966; h/4755 Lafayette Avenue Northwest, Atlanta, GA 30327; p/Mr and Mrs James C Carr, Atlanta, GA; ed/Grad, Riverwood HS, 1984; pa/Pt-time Kennel Wk, Sandy Springs Animal Clinic, Atlanta, 1982-83; Pt-time Wk, Kiddie City Store, Atlanta, 1983-; cp/HS: Jr Civitan Clb, 1981-83; Interact Clb, 1983; Beta Clb, 1982-83; Secy, Nat Hon Soc, 1983; French Nat Hon Soc, 1982-83; 2nd VPres, Intl Clb, 1981-83; Volleyball Tm, 1982; Cross Country, 1981; Track Tm, 1980-83; Photo Editor, Yrbook Staff, 1982-83; Marching Band & Drill Tm; Candystriper, St Joseph's Hosp, 1982-83; Big Sister/Big Brother Prog, 1983-84; Atlanta Hist Soc, 1982; r/Meth; hon/Track Coach's Awd, 1980; Cross Country Most Valuable Sophomore, 1981; GA Cert of Merit, 1983; The Sewanee Awd for Excell, 1983; Hon Roll, 1980-83; Erskine Fellow, 1983.

CARRAGHAN, DONALD ALAN oc/Photographer; b/Dec 6, 1961; h/339 West Stree, Bethlehem, PA 18018; ba/Edinboro, PA; p/Mr and Mrs Robert W Carraghan, Bethlehem, PA; ed/Grad, Liberty HS, 1979; BA Polit Sci/Hist,

Edinboro Univ, 1983; pa/Photog, Public Relats Dept, Edinboro Univ, 1982-; cp/Pres, Alpha Chi Rho Frat; Col Senate; Dorm Coun; Yrbook Staff; Bd of Trustees; Disc Jockey & Gen Mgr, WFSE—FM, Univ Radio Sta; r/Prot; hon/Dean's List, l1983; Eagle Scout, BSA; Outstg Student Ldr S'ship, 1983; Student Ser Awd, 1981-83; Outstg Yg Commun Ldrs; g/Govt Adm; Polits.

CARROLL, BARBARA ANN oc/Statistical Assistant; b/Nov 23, 1956; h/72 Graystone Lane, Levittown, PA; p/John and Elizabeth Carroll, Levittown, PA; ed/Grad, Woodrow Wilson HS, 1974; BS, W Chester St Col, 1978; Att'd Rutgers Univ, 1982; oc/Stat Asst II, Stat Asst III 1983-, ETS; cp/Secy, PA Students in Math; Exec Bd, PA Coun of Tchrs of Math; ACE; PSEA; NCTM; Anderson Math Clb; Pres, Secy, Elem Maj Math Clb; hon/Grad magna cum laude; Kappa Delta Pi; Intl Yth in Achmt; W/W Among Students in Am Univs & Cols; Commun Ldrs in Am; g/Fortran/Cobol.

CARROLL, RICKY L oc/Student/National Park Employee; b/Jan 29, 1962; h/Route 2 Box 242, Smiths Grove, KY 42171; p/Bonnie J Jones, Portland, TN; ed/Grad, Edmonson Co HS, 1980; Att'g, Wn KY Univ; pa/Student; Employee, Mammoth Cave Nat Pk, 1980-83; cp/Mem, 2 Hist Socs; VPres, Sr Class; Prom Com; Beta Clb; SAE Clb; Editor, Newspaper; r/Missionary Bapt; hon/Writer & Pubr 2 Books about Hist of Edmonson Co, KY; Compiled Manual, for Mammoth Cave Pk; Art III Awd, 1981; Scholastic Jour Awd, 1980; W/W Among Am HS Students Commun Ldrs of Am; Intl Yth Ldrs; Yg Personalities of S; g/Communs & Radio Broadcasting Deg; Wk for US Govt.

CARSON, ROBYN ANNETTE oc/Student and Secretary; b/Mar 1, 1963; h/PO Box 201, Redwater, TX 75501; ba/Texarkana, TX; m/Norman H; p/Mr and Mrs Henry E Fagan, Redwater, TX; ed/Grad, Redwater HS, 1981; Att'g Texarkana Commun Col; Acad of Perf'g Arts, 1981; pa/Bk Teller, Guaranty Bond St Bank, 1981-82; Secy to Mgr, Texarkana Security Inc, 1982-; cp/FFA 4 Yrs; Cheerldr, 5 Yrs; Track Tm, 5 Yrs; Basketball, 5 Yrs; Yrbook Staff, 2 Yrs; Sch FFA Show Tm, 4 Yrs; r/Meth; hon/FFA Sweethart; Girls' St Rep; Hd Cheerldr; Lone Star Farmer Awd; Secy, FFA; 3 Yrs St Forrestry Tm; Homecoming Maid; W/W in Am HS Students; Personalities of S; g/Get Real Est Broker's Lic & Own a Co.

CARTER, CATHERINE ANN oc/Student; b/Apr 18, 1964; h/Route 3 Box 3571, Blackshear, GA 31516; ed/Grad, HS, 1982; cp/Pres, Jr Class; Pres, 4-H DPA Clb; 2nd Hon Grad; STAR Student; Dist 4-H Fashion Revue Winner; 4-H Fashion Bd; Beta Clb; Math Tm; Co-Ed Y Clb; Co-Editor, Yrbook; Ch Adult Choir; Girl's Golf Tm; Ofcr, Student Home Ec Assn, 1983; hon/Alpha Lambda Delta; Gamma Beta Phi; Top 5% of Freshman Class, Univ of GA, 1982-83; W/W Among Am HS Students; Soc of Dist'd Am HS Students; Am Outstg Names & Faces; g/Maj in Hom Ec; Housing Design & Property Mgmt.

CARTER, GLENDA F oc/Doctoral Student; b/Mar 13, 1955; h/1667 University Terrace #625, Ann Arbor, MI

68104; ba/Ann Arbor, MI 48109; p/Mrs Mae Bell Carter, Delhi, La; ed/Grad, Ctl HS, 1973; BA Psych, Grambling St Univ, 1976; MS Ednl Psych 1977, EdS Ednl Psych 1980, St Univ of NY-Albany; PhD Cand in Higher Ed Adm, Univ of MI; pa/Cnslor & Placement Coor, Dept of Human Resources, 1977-80; Asst VPres for Acad Affairs, Grambling St Univ, LA, 1980-82; Grad Res Asst, Ctr for Study of Higher Ed, Univ of MI, 1980-; Mem: NAACP; Soc of Col & Univ Planning; Assn for the Study of Higher Ed; Nat Bapt Cong of Am; r/Bapt; hon/Author of Article Pub'd in *Jour of Social & Behavioral Sci*, 1983; Pi Gamma Mu, 1974; Danforth S'ship Nom, 1975; Grad summ cum laude, 1976; Outstg Col Perf Awd, 1976; W/W Among HS Students; Outstg Yg Wom of Am; g/Acad Adm; VPres Acad Affairs.

CARTER, JUDY BURLESON oc/Student Teacher; b/Jun 25, 1952; h/129 Glendale Drive, Elkin, NC 28621; ba/Ronda, NC; m/Mickey B Carter; c/Christopher, Amy, Matthew; p/Mr and Mrs Kenneth B Burleson, Albermarle, NC; sp/Mr and Mrs Mitchell Carter, Albermarle, NC; ed/Grad, W Stanley HS, 1970; AS, Wingate Col, 1972; BS, Appalachian St Univ, 1983; pa/Secy, Chatham Mfg, 1976-77; Receptionist/Secy, Dybak, 1973-77; Student Tchr Hom Ec, E Wilkes HS, 1983; Mem: Pres 1978-79, Beta Sigma Phi; Kappa Omicron Phi; Alpha Phi; Am & NC Hom Ec Assn; r/Bapt; hon/Girl of Yr 1979, Sister of Yr 1982, Beta Sigma Phi; Recip, Madge Rhyne Student Tchg S'ship, Appalachian St Univ; g/Tchg Position in Home Ec; Pursue MA Deg.

CARTER, LAURA RUTH oc/Student; b/Dec 16, 1968; h/12451 Eastwood Drive, Choctaw, OK 73020; ed/Att'g HS, 1983-; Writing Student, OK Sum Art Inst; cp/Jr VP, Jr Pres, Sr VPres, Sr Pres, 4-H Clb; St Hon Soc, 1981-83; r/Meth; hon/Author Var Short Stories: "Save the Burros," "No Place for a Dog," in *Accent on Yth*; NPJH Art Awd, 1982; Lang Arts Awd, 1981-82; C of C Scholastic Awd, 1981; St Hon Soc; 4-H Medals in Sheep, Public Spkg & Photo; g/Maj in Art; Writer & Artist.

CARTER, OSCARA LYNNE oc/University Student; b/Sep 29, 1963; h/Route 3 Box 77, Wallace, NC 28466; p/Mr and Mrs Oscar T Carter, Wallace, NC; ed/Grad, Wallace-Rose Hill HS, 1981; AA, Peace Col, 1983; cp/Peace Col Student Govt; Pres, Sigma Delta Mu; FCA; Phi Theta Kappa, 1982-83; PSCA; hon/Salutatorian; Marshall; DAR Good Citizen, 1981; UN Good Citizen, 1981; ABWA S'ship, 1983; g/Attend NC St Univ; Maj in Acctg; CPA.

CARVER, JANET ANITA oc/University Student; b/Apr 19, 1961; h/1701 Redbird Trail, Touchton Woods, Douglas, GA 31533; ba/Athens, GA; p/James Henderson and Marie Carver, Douglas, GA; ed/S GA Col; Att'g, Univ of GA; pa/Photog Asst, Ronald Goodman Photos, 1978, 1979 & 1980; Salesperson, Carol's Shop, 1977-78; Salesperson 1980-81, Bkkpr 1980-81, Belks Dept Store; Subst Tchr, 1981; Cashier, Danny's Pizza, 1981; Receptionist, Registrar Ofc 1982, Cashier Col Bookstore 1982, Resident Asst Shannon Hall 1981-82, S GA Col; cp/Anchor Clb (HS), 1978; Future Bus Ldrs Clb (HS), 1978-79; Coffee HS Drill

Tm, 1977-78; Social Com & Sunshine Com, Gamma Phi Beta, 1982; r/Bapt; hon/Gamma Phi Beta Covergirl, *Pointer* Mag, 1983-84; Social Butterfly Awd, Gamma Ohi Beta, Gamma Phi Beta Rep for Univ of GA Calendar Girl; Dancer for Gamma Phi Beta Rush Skit; Nat Dean's List Book, 1983; g/Early Childhood Ed Tchr.

CASARES, LEIGH ANN oc/Student; b/Mar 14, 1965; h/410 N Main Apt 3, Madisonville, KY 42431; p/Lazaro Casares Jr, Madisonville, KY; Katie W Casares, Madisonville, KY; ed/Grad, Madisonville-N Hopkins HS, 1983; cp/Beta Clb, 1980-83; Pres, VPres, Tri-HI-Y, 1980-83; Secy Student Coun, 1980-82; Secy, Hist Clb, 1981-82; VPres, Biol Clb, 1980-83; Chem Clb, 1980-81; hon/Class Marshall, 1982; Morehead St Pres Merit S'ship, 1983; Class Histn, 1983; Finalist Pres S'ship, 1983; g/Attend Morehead St Univ, BS in Math & Computer Sci.

CASSEY, BRIAN KEITH oc/Student; b/May 28, 1963; h/RFD 1 Box 26, Swords Creek, VA 24649; p/Mr and Mrs Cecil Casey; ed/Grad, Honaker HS; Att'd SW VA Commun Col; Att'g Univ of VA; pa/Wkr, Univ of VA Food Sers, Observatory Hill, 1981-82; cp/Yg Repub; Marching & Concert Bands; Hi-Y Clb; 7th out of 100 in Grad Class; Yrbook & Newspaper Staff; Drum Maj; SCA; Model Gen Assem; Model UN; hon/2nd Place Vinton Drum Maj; Most Improved HS Musician; Quill & Scroll; Soc of Dist'd HS Students; W/W Among Am HS Students; Intl Yth in Achmt; Commun Ldr of Am; g/Deg in Psych & Psychi w background in Law & Archaeol.

CASEY, CAROL ANN BARBARICK oc/Therapeutic Supervisor, Diet Clerk; b/Jan 29, 1960; h/189 Old Hickory Boulevard, Apt G-4, Jackson, TN 38305; m/David Patrick; p/Robert Lunsford and Eleanor Lillian Barbarick, Washington, MO; sp/Leo Patrick Casey (dec); Lola Casey Strubberg, Union, MO; ed/Grad, Wash HS, 1978; AA, E Ctl Col, 1980; BS, SW MO St Univ, 1982; pa/Supvr/Diet Clk, St John's Mercy Hosp, Wash, MO; Therapeutic Supvr/Diet Clk, Jackson-Madison Co Gen Hosp, Jackson, TN; cp/Co Volleyball, Jackson-Madison Co Gen Hosp; Jr Public Relats Ofcr, Sr VPres, Am Soc of Pers Mgmt; Phi Theta Kappa Alumni; Candy Striper; 1st Christian Ch; Wrestling Scorekeeper; Girls Football; Volleyball; FBLA; Jr Prom Com; hon/Food Ser Editor, Jackson-Madison Co Gen Hosp; Hon Grad; Franklin Co Mercantile Bk S'ship; Bus Dept S'ship; NHS; Hon Roll; Top 15 % of Grad Class; Dean's List; Intl Yth in Achmt; Am Outstg Names & Faces; W/W in Am Jr Cols; Commun Ldrs of Am; g/MBA Deg; Hosp Mgmt.

CASSTEVENS, CHARLES FRANKLIN JR oc/College Student; b/Jan 25, 1964; h/Route 1, Box 337, Jonesville, NC 28642; p/Mr and Mrs Charles F Casstevens, Jonesville, NC; ed/Grad, Starmount HS, 1982; Att'g, Wingate Col; pa/Pianist, Mineral Springs Bapt Ch, 1981-82; Pres, Boonville Jr Music Clb, 1981-82; Sr Crewperson, McDonalds of Elkin, 1981-; cp/Nat Fedn of Music Clbs, 1974-81; HS: Drama Clb; Social Studies Clb; VPres, Spanish Clb, 1981-82; Capt, Men's Varsity Tennis Team, 1982; Col:

Phi Beta Lambda; Music Edrs Nat Conf; Concert Choir; Christian Student Union; r/So Bapt; hon/Yg Commun Ldrship, 1982; NHS, 1981-82; All-Conf Tennis NW AAA, 1980-81; Sch Winner Cent III Ldrs, 1981; 2 Gold Trophies; Nat Fedn of Music Clbs; McDonalds All-Am Tm Sect Winner, 1983; Soc of Dist'd Am HS Students; W/W Among Am HS Students; g/BS Deg in Music/Bus.

CASTLEBERRY, BRENDA C oc/Student; b/Nov 27, 1962; h/1115 West Bridge Street, New Braunfels, TX 78130; p/Mr and Mrs Dan E Castleberry, New Braunfels, TX; ed/Grad, New Braunfels HS, 1981; Att'g, SW TX St Univ; pa/Pt-time Med Secy, for Drs A E Rath Jr and T C Brever, New Braunfels, TX; cp/Phi Eta Sigma, 1982; *Unicorn* Yrbook Staff, 1979-81; Ofc Ed Assn, 1980-81; Theta Epsilon Nu 1979-81; NHS, 1980-81; r/U Pentecostal; hon/Editor 1981, Asst Editor 1980, *Unicorn* Yrbook; Grad from HS in top 10% of Class; Rotary Outstg Student; S'ships Incl: Delta Kappa Gamma; FTA; W Point Pepperell; BPW; Dean's List, SW TX St Univ, 1981-83; g/Deg in Bus Ed w minor in Math; HS Bus Tchr.

CASTO, LISA MARIE oc/Student; b/Nov 9, 1962; h/Route 4 Box 143 Gallipolis, OH 45631; p/Mr and Mrs Larry E Casto Sr, Gallipolis, OH; ed/Grad, Gallia Acad HS, 1981; Att'g Rio Grande Col & Commun Col; pa/Salesperson, Paul Davies Jewelers, 1980-83; cp/Pres, Treas & Advr, 4-H, 1972-; Tri-HI-Y, 1979; Debate Tm, 1980-81; Gallia Script Art Editor; hon/Outstg 4-H Clb Mem, 1980; W/W Among Am HS Students; Intl Yth in Achmt; Commun Ldrs of Am; g/Deg in Elem Tchg & Interior Design.

CASTRO, VINCENT EDWARD oc/Student; b/Jul 25, 1962; h/460 Grand Street, New York, NY 1002; p/Gladys Castro, New York, NY; ed/Grad, La Salle Acad, 1980; BS, St Joseph's Col; cp/Yth F'ship; HS Band; HS Newspaper Reporter; HS Yrbook Reporter; Nat Rifle Assn; r/Christian; hon/NHS, 1980; Cardinal Hayes Hon Soc, 1976-80; Outstg Student Awd, 1978; Soc of Dist'd Am HS Students; W/W Among Am HS Students; Yth in Achmt; g/Pursue MD.

CATALDO, CHET WILLIAM oc/Pastor; b/Jul 6, 1955; h/331 North Olatheview Road, Olathe, KS 66061; ba/Olathe, KS; m/Jodi; c/Jeremiah, Tobin; p/Mr and Mrs Robert Cataldo, Williams, MN; sp/Mr and Mrs Arthur Carpenter, Beeville, TX; ed/Grad, Garden City Sr HS, 1973; BA, Friends Bible Col, 1982; MA in Rel Studies, Ctl Bapt Theol Sem, 1983; mil/USN, 1973-77; pa/Fry Cook, Buzz Inn, 1972-73; Wkr, Green Lumber Yard, 1977-78; Alco-Receiving Mgr, 1978; Pastor, Belpre Bapt Ch, 1978-81; Pastor, Olathe Gen Bapt Ch; cp/Col Soccer Tm, 1981; Pres, Missionary Prayer F'ship, 1979; Rec Indoor Soccer; r/Bapt; hon/Author, Var Articles Pub'd in *Gen Bapt Messenger* Mag; Poem Pub'd in *Power* Mag; Eagle Scout, 1973; Grad summa cum laude, 1981; Pres Grant, Ctl Bapt Theol Sem, 1982; Nat Dean's List; Intl Yth in Achmt; W/W Among Students in Am Univs & Cols; g/To Serve the Lord & Spread the Word of the Gospel; PhD in Rel.

CATANIA, ANTHONY JR oc/Student; b/Nov 12, 1962; h/9290 Northwest 19th Place, Sunrise, FL 33322; p/Anthony and Patricia Catania, Sunrise, FL; ed/Grad, Piper HS, 1980; BS, Univ of Miami, 1984; pa/Med Student; Nsg Asst, Dept of Surg, Plantation Gen Hosp, Sums 1980-83; cp/Key Clb; Pres, Future Med Ldrs of Am; Marching & Jazz Bands; City Softball Leag, 1980-83; Karate; Vol, Plantation Hosp; VPres, Bowling Leags, 1978-83; Symph Band (Percussion), Univ of Miami, 1983; hon/NHS; Soc of Dist'd Am HS Students; W/W Among Am HS Students; Intl Yth in Achmt; Yg Commun Ldrs; Yg Personalities of Am; g/Complete Med Sch; Pediatrician.

CATO, JOHN EDWARD JR oc/Student; b/Sep 19, 1964; h/407 Cobblestone Court, Charlotte, NC 28210; p/John and Lucille Cato, Charlotte, NC; ed/Att'g HS; pa/Pt-time Cashier, Kroger Sav-on, 1981-; cp/Pres, Jr Achmt, 1982; Pres, German Clb, 1982; Pres, ARC, 1982; VPres, Jr Exec Coun, 1982; VPres, Computer Clb, 1982; Pres, Explorers, 1983; Olympic Marching Band, 3 Yrs; Editor, of Sch Mag; VPres, Sr Class; Reporter, Sch Newspaper; Homeroom Rep; Guid Rep; r/Bapt; hon/Beautillion Militaire; Most Productive Wkr, Kroger, 1983; W/W Among Am HS Students; g/Radio or TV Broadcasting; News Broadcaster.

CAUDILL, DONALD W oc/Doctoral Student; b/Jul 31, 1958; h/723 East Powell River Drive, Norton, VA 24273; p/Mr and Mrs Alfred Caudill, Norton, VA; ed/Grad, J J Kelly HS, 1976; BS, Berea Col, 1980; MBA, Morehead St Univ, 1981; Att'd VA Tech Inst; DBA Cand, Memphis St Univ; oc/Instr of Mktg; Mem: Assn of MBA Execs; Am Mktg Assn; Appalachian Writers Assn; Acad of Mktg Sci; cp/Freshman Class Ofcr; Parliamentn, Secy, VPres, Pres, Phi Beta Lambda; Chm, Campus Activs Bd; FCA; Track Tm; Swim Tm; Student Assn; Pre-Law Clb Ofcr; Berea Players; Sports Editor, Col Newspaper; Yrbook Staff; r/Elder, Christian Ch of God; hon/Mr Futre Bus Exec; Jr NHS; S'ship Com, Berea Players Hall of Fame; Alpha Psi Omega; Dean's List; W/W in Phi Beta Lambda; g/Prof; PhD Mktg; Conslt; Bus-man; Writer; Public Servant.

CAUL, PAULINE ANN oc/Student; b/Nov 13, 1963; h/PO Box 413 Covington, VA 24426; p/Mr and Mrs A B Caul, Covington, VA; ed/Grad, Alleghany HS, 1982; cp/4-H Hon & Sr Clb; 4-H All-Stars of VA; Med Explorers; Future Med Practs; Teen Vol, of Alleghany Reg Hosp; Spanish Clb; NHS; r/Presb; hon/Nat Merit Finalist; Salutatorian; 6th Dist Rep to VA Model Exec Govt Conf; g/Erskine Col; Med Col VA; Phy Therapy.

CECIL, CYNTHIA MARIE oc/Student; b/6653 Vesta Brook Drive, Morrow, GA 30260; b/Dec 10, 1966; p/Dean and Carol Cecil, Morrow, GA; Att'g Morrow HS; pa/Ormond's Fashion Advr, 1983; Ormond's Loss Preven, 1983; cp/Secy, Beta Clb; Secy, NHS; A & B Hon Roll; FHA; St Rep; Swim Tm; Most Ded'd; Drama Clb; Thespian Soc; Homeroom Rep, Student Coun; Morrow Flag Corps; FCA; Key Clb; r/Cath; hon/1st Runner-up Sweetheart Princess, 1980; Sweetheart Queen, 1981; Homecoming Ct: Sophomore Princess,

1981; Jr Princess, 1982; Homecoming Queen 1983; Outstg Ser Merit Awd in Band & Color Guard, 1983; Miss Teen St Rep, 1983; Miss Congeniality; W/W Among Am HS Students; g/Eng Maj; News/Editing.

CERBULIS, KARLIS ANDREJS oc/ Grain Farm Manager; b/Jul 10, 1959; h/ Rural Delivery 2, Box 940, Boyertown, PA 19512; p/Mr and Mrs Janis Cerbulis, Boyerstown, PA; ed/Att'd, Boyertown Area Sr HS, 1977; Att'd Lettishes Gymnasium, Münster, W Germany, 1978; BS Agronomy, PA St Univ, 1982; pa/Ptner 1974-, Full Time Mgr 1982-83, in Crop & Beef Farm w Father; Soil Res Asst, PA St Univ, 1982; Mgr, 1500 Acre Grain Farm, Germantown, MD, 1983-; cp/Initiator & Co-Chp, 1st & 2nd Annual N Am Baltic Yth Cong, 1981-83; Exec Com, Latvian Yth Assn, 1980-81; Treas, PA St Ag Clb; Com Chm, PA St Agronomy Clb, 1980-82; Treas, VPres, Pres, Phila Latvian Yth Assn, 1975-79; Phi Kappa Phi, 1981-83; Life Mem, Golden Key; Gamma Sigma Delta, 1982-83; Am Soc of Agronomy, 1983; Crop Sci Soc of Am, 1983; Soil Sci Soc of Am, 1983; r/ Luth; hon/PA St Univ Soil Judging Tm: 1st Place, Indiv NE Reg Contest, 1981; 5th Place Tm, 1981; Nat Soil Judging Contest, 1982; Sr Student Awd, NW Br Am Soc of Agronomy, 1982; PA Forage & Grassland Coun S'ship, 1981; Harry S Truman Meml S'ship, PA Semi-finalist, 1980; Eva B and G Weidman Groff Meml S'ship, 1981; Grad w Highest Distn, PA St Univ, 1982; Intl Yth in Achmt; Outstg Yg Men of Am; Commun Ldrs & Noteworthy Ams; g/MA Deg in Agri Ec.

CHADWELL, BARBARA SUE oc/ University Student; b/Oct 15, 1963; h/ 5119 Tulip Drive, Fayetteville, NC 28304; p/Mr and Mrs John D Chadwell, Fayetteville, NC; ed/Dipl, Douglas Byrd Sr HS, 1981; Att'g, E Carolina Univ, 1985; Wk Study w Sch of Nsg Dept, E Carolina Univ, 1983-; Loan Investigation Dept, Ft Bragg Fed Credit Union, 1982; Sales Promotion, Coca-Cola Bottling Co, 1981-82; cp/HS: Pres 1981, NHS, 1980-81; Keywannettes Ser Clb, 1980 & 1981; Co-Capt 1980 & 1981, Track Tm, 1979, 1980 & 1981; Basketball Tm, 1979; Volleyball, 1978, 1979 & 1980; Col: Phi Eta Sigma, 1981; Hon Prog, 1982 & 1983; r/Bapt; hon/HS: Most Outstg Art Student, 1979, 1980 & 1981; Most Ded'd Track Mem, 1979; CIT Acad Awd, 1979; Gov's Sch Nom for Art, 1980; Chem I Awd, 1980; Keywannette Ser Awd, 1980; Chief Grad Marshall, 1980; All-Conf, Sect & Reg in Track, 1979, 1980 & 1981; St Track Meet Participant, 1980; Lrdship Awd for Track, 1981; Coach's Awd for Track, 1980; Best All Around Volleyball Player, 1980; Homecoming Queen, 1980; High Acad Achmt Awd, 1981; Hon Grad, 1981; F D Byrd Scholar Ath Awd, 1981; Yg Wom of Yr Awd, Exch Clb of Gtr Fayetteville, 1981; g/BS Home Ec, Housing & Mgmt; MS Deg Home Ec.

CHADWELL, FAYE ANN ox/Student; b/Dec 9, 1961; h/5119 Tulip Drive, Fayetteville, NC 28304; p/Mr and Mrs John D Chadwell, Fayetteville, NC; ed/ Dipl, Douglas Byrd Sr HS, 1980; Att'g, Appalachian St Univ; pa/Wk-Study w Circulation Dept, Belk Lib, Appalachian St Univ, 1981 & 1983-; Switchbd Operator/Receptionist, Perkins Motors Inc, Sum 1982; Wn Pub'g Co, Sum 1980 & 1981; cp/HS: VPres, Beta Clb, 1978-79;

NHS, 1979-80; Participant, Gifted & Talented Prog, 1979-80; Capt, Volleyball, 1980; Co-Capt, Softball, 1979 & 1980; Basketball, 1977-78; Col: Univ Hon Prog; Appalachian St Univ Hon Clb; Gamma Beta Phi, 1981-; Alpha Chi Scholastic Hon Frat, 1982-; Wom's Varsity Softball, 1981-82; hon/HS: Biol Awd, 1978; DAR Hist Awd; "I Dare You" Awd; Grad Marshall; NC Gov's Sch Nom, 1979; Outstg Sr Hon Grad; Co-Winner Outstg Art IV Awd; Florence Kidder Meml S'ship, 1980; Mid-S 4 A All-Conf Volleyball & Softball Tm, 1979-80; MVP Softball, 1979; Best Spiker, Volleyball, 1979; Col: Appalachian St Univ Dean's List; Participant Hons Day for Scholastic Achmt, 1982; g/BA Deg in Eng w Minor in Phil/Rel; Grad Sch.

CHADWELL, LARRY DANIEL oc/Oil Exploration; b/Jan 26, 1958; h/8938 West Dartmouth Place, Lakewood, CO 80227; ba/Denver, CO; m/Teri Lynn; p/John and Ruth Chadwell, Fayetteville, NC; sp/ Charles and Phyllis Williams, Lakewood CO; ed/Dipl, Douglas Byrd HS, 1976; BSBA, Appalachian St Univ, 1979; pa/ Oper Engr, Geophy Ser Inc, Lakewood, CO, 1980-; NC Real Est Broker, 1977-; c/Pres, Key Clb, 1976; Chief Justice, Student Ct, Appalachian St Univ, 1978-79; Student Coun; r/Bapt; hon/ Outstg Key Clubber, 1974 & 1976; Outstg Sr, D Byrd HS, 1976; W/W Among Col Students.

CHADWICK, ROBERT LANE oc/ Student; b/Aug 7, 1964; h/6336 Burgundy Road South, Jacksonville, FL 32210; p/William Robert Chadwick, Jacksonville, FL; Nancy G Chadwick, Jacksonville, FL; ed/Dipl, N B Forrest HS, 1980; Att'g FL Jr Col; cp/Sons of Confederate Vets; Kirby Smith Camp; US Capitol His Soc; Smithsonian Assocs; FFA Reporter; Linder Geneal Tour to Brit; Aerospace Ed Ofcr, Alt Cadet Adv Coun Rep, Civil Air Patrol; Unit Mbrship Bd; Sqdrn Grievance Com; Unit Activs Prog Com; Cadet Activs Planning Com; French Clb; Annual Staff; Drama Clb; Charter Mem, St George's Soc of Jacksonville; FL Mem, Soc of War of 1812; SAR; The Huguenot Soc of FL; The Huguenot Soc of the Fdrs of Manakin in the Colony of VA; Mil Order of the Stars & Bars; The Mus of So Hist; Aberdeen & N East Scot Fam Hist Soc; hon/Music Awd; Awd of Merit; FFA Deg of Greenhand; Participant in Parliamentn Procedure; Ornamental Horticulture Contest, Land Judging.

CHAFFINS, JAMES ALLAN oc/Berea College Student; b/Oct 3, 1964; h/CPO 307, Berea, KY 40404; p/George Washington Chaffins, Livingston, TN; Reto Jean Chaffins; ed/Grad, Livingston, Acad, 1982; Att'g, Berea Col; pa/Apprentice in Pottery; cp/Assoc Editor, The Daily Vulture, Col Newslttr; Publicity Mgr & DJ of Col Radio Sta, WDNA; Exhib'g Students Art Leag, 1983; The Vulture Proud Fire Entertainment Com; hon/Best Art Student, Livingston Acad, 1983; Recog Awd, Garden Clb, 1982; Mem, "Fleur de Lis" Hon Soc, 1983; g/Attend Grad Sch in Art; Travel in London & Australia; Art Res.

CHAMBERS, STEPHEN GRADY oc/ Air Force Academy Student; b/Sep 9, 1964; h/5512 Hidden Valley Road, Greensboro, NC 27407; p/Mr and Mrs Joseph D Chambers, Greensboro, NC; ed/Grad, Lucy C Ragsdale HS, 1982; Att'g USAF Acad; cp/Jr Varsity & Varsity Cross Country, 1978-82; Jr Varsity Tennis,

1978-79; Jr Varsity & Varsity Wrestling, 1978-82; Beta Clb; French Clb; NHS; hon/ All-County Band, 1979-82; All-St Band, 1981-82; Chosen for Nat Math Test, 1981; Varsity Lttr, Ranked in top 7 Runners, Cross Country; Varsity Lttr in Wrestling; Dean's List, Spring Semester, USAF Acad; g/Deg in Civil Engrg, USAF Acad; Attend Pilot Tng Sch.

CHANCE, AMY NELL oc/Commercial Loan Analyst; b/Nov 6, 1959; h/5421 94th Street, Lubbock, TX 79424; ba/Lubbock, TX; m/Robert D; p/Mr and Mrs Walter L Watson, New Phila, OH; sp/Mr and Mrs Bill Chance, Shamrock, TX; ed/Grad, New Philadelphia HS, 1978; Att'd OH Val Col; BSBA, Lubbock Christian Col, 1982; pa/Sr Loan Analyst, 1st Nat Bk, 1982-; Money Mgmt, Security Nat Bk, 1982; cp/ Students in Free Enterprise, 1981-82; Christliche Damen Social Clb, 1980-82; Pres Ambassadors, 1981-82; Com on Free Enterprise, Lubbock C of C; Meistersinger Chorus; Mtntop Singers; hon/Grad magna cum laude, 1982; Alpha Chi Nat Hon Soc; Acad Achmt Awds, 1982; Nat Dean's List; Intl Personalities; W/W Among Students in Am Univs & Cols; g/Comml Loan Ofcr.

CHANCELLOR, HERBERT CHARLES oc/Student; b/Jun 27, 1963; h/PO Box 38 Cullowhee, NC 28723; p/Paul and Etheree Chancellor, Cullowhee, NC; ed/ Grad, HS, 1981; Att'g Wn Carolina Univ; mil/USAR, 2nd Lt in Indiv Ready Resv; cp/Pres, Student Industl Distbn Org (SIDO), Spring Semester, 1984; r/Bapt; hon/Student Industl Distbn Org S'ship, So Industl Distbn Assn, 1983; g/Industl Distbr.

CHANEY, TERESA YVONNE oc/ Rural Mail Carrier; b/Sep 10, 1961; h/ Route 9, Box 287-2, Shelby, NC 28150; ba/Shelby, NC; p/Mr and Mrs Alvin Glen Chaney Sr, Gastonia, NC; ed/Grad, Hunter Huss HS, 1979; AA Deg in Postal Mgmt, Bus Adm & Acctg, 1982 & 1983; pa/Salesman, Belks Dept Store, 1979; Salesman, Easy Living Furniture Co, 1979; A V Booking Clk, Gaston Co Schs, 1980; Rural Mail Carrier, US Postal Ser, Shelby, 1980-; cp/Gamma Beta Phi Hon Soc; hon/W/W Among Am HS Students; g/Postmaster Career.

CHANG, HOWARD F oc/Student; b/ Jun 30, 1960; h/711 Dwight Street, Springfield, MA 01104; p/Joseph J and Mary H Chang, Springfield, MA; ed/Dipl, Roy C Ketcham Sr HS, 1978; BA, Harvard Univ, 1982; MA Public Affairs, Woodrow Wilson Sch of Public & Intl Affairs, Princeton Univ, 1985; JD Cand, Harvard Law Sch; pa/Sum Assoc, Steptoe & Johnson Law Firm, Wash DC, 1983; Sum Intern, Senator Wm Proxmire, Wash DC, 1982; Proctor, Harvard Sum Sch, Cambridge, MA, 1981; Sum Intern, Dem Nat Com, Wash DC, 1980; hon/ Grad cum laude Gen Studies, 1982; John Harvard S'ships, 1980-82; Harvard S'ship for Acad Achmt of Highest Distn, 1979; Nat Merit S'ship, 1978-82; Valedictorian; g/Public Ser Career.

CHAPMAN, BRAD J oc/Student; b/ May 7, 1966; h/614 Shore Drive, Ocean Springs, MS 39564; p/Mr and Mrs F W Chapman, Ocean Springs, MS; ed/Att'g HS; r/Cath; hon/US Achmt Acad for Art Achmts, 1983; W/W in Am HS Students; Dist'd Am HS Students; g/Attend Univ of So MS; Maj in Art (Sketching); Career in USMC.

CHAPMAN, JEFF W oc/Student; b/Jan

30, 1966; h/3145 Woodsen Circle, West Columbia, SC 29169; p/Jeff C and Christa Chapman, W Cola, SC; ed/Grad, Brookland-Cayce HS; cp/1st Lt, Band; French Clb; Explorers; Hon Roll; Sr Hon Soc; Mu Alpha Theta; NHS; r/Meth; hon/ Nat Hon Roll; Jr Marshall, 1983; Dir of Dist'd Ams; W/W Among HS Students; Yg Personalities of Am; g/Pursue Mech Engrg Deg, Univ of SC.

CHAPMAN, KAREN LEIGH oc/University Student; b/Apr 24, 1964; h/104 Kentucky Drive, Darlington, SC 29532; ba/Durham, NC; p/Stewart C and Maureen C Chapman, Darlington, SC; ed/ Grad, St John's HS, 1981; cp/YMCA Swim Tm, 1974-77; Florence Civic Ballet, 1972-75; Pep Clb, Block SJ, 1978-81; Anchor Clb, 1978-81; Student Coun, 1978; HS Varsity Tennis Tm, 1978-81; Editor, HS Newspaper, 1980-81; Pi Beta Phi, 1982-; r/Epis; hon/Valedictorian, St John's HS, 1981; Dean's List, Duke Univ, 1982 & 1983; Hugh O'Brien Ldrship Awd; Furman Scholar; PC Jr Fellow; Att'd SC Gov's Sch, 1980; g/Deg in Ec.

CHAPMAN, NANCY oc/Student and Part-time Spa Instructor; h/3145 Woodsen Circle, W Cola, SC 29169; p/Jeff C and Christa Chapman, W Cola, SC; ed/ Grad, Brookland-Cayce HS; Att'g Univ of SC; pa/Pt-time Instr, Spa Lady, 1981-; cp/Capt 1980-81, Mem 1978-81, Gymnastic Tm; Asst Drum Maj; Flag Capt; Hosp Candy Striper; Mu Alpha Theta; Jr NHS; NHS; r/Meth; hon/MVP, Gymnastyics Tm, 1978-81; SC St Gymnast, Best All Around, 1978-81; Dean's List, Univ of SC; W/W Among Am HS Students; Soc of Dist'd Am HS Students; Intl Yth in Achmt; Commun Ldrs of Am; Dir of Dist'd Ams; g/Become a Corp Lwyr.

CHAPMAN, ODRIE MARIA oc/Law School Student; b/Oct 12, 1961; h/292 Hermer Circle, Northwest Atlanta, GA 30311; p/Mr and Mrs W B Chapman, Atlanta, GA; ed/Dipl, HS, 1979; BS, Spelman Col, 1983; Att'g Duke Univ Law Sch, 1983-; pa/Olston Temporary Agy, 1975 & 1978; Intern, NAACP, 1979-81; Salesperson, J P Allen, 1982-83; Intake Pers, Neighborhood Justice Ctr, 1983; cp/ NAACP, 1979-83; Cath Yth Org; Alpha Kappa Alpha, 1982-83; Spelman Col Nat Alumnae Assn; UNCF, 1979-83; YWCA, 1981-83; Eng Clb; Polit Sci Clb; Pre-Law Soc; Student Govt; Orch; Homecoming Queen; r/Rom Cath; hon/Harry S Truman Scholar, 1982; Awd of Excell, 1979; Sigma Tau Delta, 1982; Pi Sigma Alpha, 1981; Sr Hon Soc, 1983; W/W Among Students in Am Univs & Cols; Commun Ldrs of Am; g/Lwyr; Judge; Supr Ct Justice.

CHAPPEL, SANDRA KAY oc/Student; b/Apr 29, 1967; h/Route 1 Box 2 Garvin, OK 74736; p/Homer Chappel, Garvin, OK; ed/Att'g Valliant HS; cp/ Basketball, 1978-83; Beta Clb, 1982-83; Student Coun, 1982-83; Band, 1981-82; Chorus, 1982-83; Cheerleading, 1982-83; r/Bapt; hon/NHS, 1982; Acad Awd in Eng I, 1982; g/Attend OK St Univ; Phy Therapist or Computer Sci.

CHAPPELL, PAUL NEWTON oc/Sales Representative; b/Sep 10, 1959; h/PO Box 453 Senoia, GA 30276; ba/New York, NY; p/John and Shirley Chappell, Senoia, GA; ed/Grad, E Coneta HS, 1977; Assoc Bus Adm & Assoc Public Adm, Mid Ga Col, 1980; AB Ec, Univ of GA, 1982; pa/Sales Rep, Ortho Pharm, 1983; Sales Rep, Bali

Co, 1983-; cp/Civitan; Rotoract; Phi Theta Kappa; Gamma Beta Phi; Phi Beta Lambda; Univ of GA Football, 1980-82; Student Govt Assn; Student Activs Com; Student Adv Coun to Bd of Regents; hon/ Nat Dean's List, 1980; W/W Among Students in Am Univs & Cols; Intl Yth in Achmt; g/Pursue MBA; Attend Law Sch.

CHARVAT, JANE MARIE oc/Student; b/Sep 21, 1966; h/PO Box 97 Norfork, AR 72658; p/Mr and Mrs Harold Charvat, Norfork, AR; ed/Grad, Norfork HS, 1984; pa/Waitress, Whispering Woods Resort, 1980-83; McDonald's, 1982-83; cp/ 1982-83: Treas, FHA; VPres, Drama Clb; VPres, Sr Beta Clb; VPres, Jr Class; Basketball; r/Meth; hon/1982-83: Eng, Hist, Chem & Algebra Awds; Acad Hon Roll; All Bi-Co Basketball; W/W Among Am HS Students; g/Attend Univ of AR.

CHAVEZ, ORLANDO oc/Certified Substitute Teacher; b/Mar 14, 1958; h/ 2881 Northwest 5th Street Miami, FL 33125; p/Mr and Mrs Frank O Chavez, Miami, FL; ed/Grad, Bishop Kearney HS; Att'd, Miami-Dade Commun Col; BBA, Fl Atl Univ, 1983; cp/Voter Registrations Dpty; Phi Beta Lambda Bus Soc; Miami-Dade Fencing Clb; Pres, Phi Theta Kappa; FL Atl Univ Fencing Clb; hon/FL Blue Key Commun Col Ldrship Awd; Talent Roster for Minority Students; W/ W Among Commun Col Students; Nat Dean's List; Intl Yth in Achmt; g/PhD in Law.

CHEEK, EDWIN B oc/Student; b/Apr 27, 1964; h/PO Box 502 Mars Hill, NC 28754; ba/Winston-Salem, NC; p/Edwin R and Pauline B Cheek, Mars Hill, NC; ed/Grad, Madison HS, 1982; Att'g Wake Forest Univ; pa/Vessel Sanitation Engr, Epicure Sers Inc, 1981 & 1982; Asst to Min of Music, Mars Hill 1st Bapt Ch, 1981-82; cp/Mars Hill Commun Devel Org, 1977-82; 4-H NC Wn Dist Reporter, 1982-83; Dist Rep, 4-H, 1980-82; HS: Math Clb, 1982; Tennis Tm, 1982; Band, 4 Yrs; Wake Forest Univ Marching Band, 1983; Alpha Phi Omega, Wake Forest Univ, 1983; r/Bapt; hon/Artist, Mars Hill Jr HS Yrbook, 1978; Artist, Madison HS Yrbook, 1981; L R Harril S'ship, 1982; "I Dare You," Awd, 1979; 1st Place Winner, 4-H NC Wn Dist Proj Record, 1980 & 1981; NC Forestry Camp Del, 1979; Reg Resource Devel Conf Del, 1980; NC Elect Cong Del, 1981; g/Pursue Social Sci Deg; Tchg.

CHEN, SUSAN CHUN-YAO oc/Student; b/Nov 23, 1963; h/1614 Shreen Court, San Jose, CA 95124; p/Roseann Chang, San Jose, CA; ed/Grad, Pioneer HS, 1981; Att'g Univ of Santa Clara; cp/ Treas, Chem Clb; Class Rep, Freshman, Sophomore, Jr and Sr Classes; Treas, Jr Class; Hon Roll; CSF; Student Coun; Leo Clb; Orch; Sch Musical; Commun Wkr; Lib Aid; Ofc Aid; Volleyball; Tennis; Nat Piano Playing Auditions; Invest-in-Am No CA Coun Awd; Asian-Pacific Student Union; hon/Perfect Attendance Awd; 1st Place, Swimming & Archery; Mary Roche Strobel S'ship, 1983-84; Univ of Santa Clara S'ship; Nat Guild of Piano Tchrs HS Dipl Awd; W/W Among Am HS Students; g/Genetic Engrg.

CHENEY, REBECCA LYNN oc/Student; b/Apr 7, 1963; h/5290 Morganton Road, Fayetteville, NC 28304; p/David Cheney, Fayetteville, NC; ed/Grad, Reid Ross HS, 1981; Att'g Coker Col, 1981-; cp/Choreographer, Reid Ross "Har-

mony," 1978-81; Drum Maj, Reid Ross Marching Band, 1979-81; Vocalist, Reid Ross Stage Band, 1980-81; Spanish Clb, 1978-79; Drama Clb, 1979-81; Commr, Coker Col, 1982-83; Secy Interior, Reid Ross Student Coun, 1980-81; Pres, Intl Thespian Soc, 1980-81; All-St Band, 1978; Hons Chorus, 1980; Instrumentalist's Mag Awd, 1981; Outstg Sr, 1981; hon/ Editor for Orgs, Reid Ross Annual Staff, 1980-81; NHS, 1979-81; Intl Thespian Soc, 1980-81; Dean's List Coker Col, Sprng 1983; The Nat Dean's List; W/W in Music; W/W Among Am HS Students; g/BA Dance; Minor in Computer Sci; Computer Graphics.

CHEREPSKI, MARY ANN oc/Speech Pathologist; b/Feb 10, 1960; h/16 Nottingham Road #3, Little Rock, AR; ba/Little Rock, AR; p/Mr and Mrs A L Cherepski, Blytheville, AR; ed/Grad, Blytheville HS, 1978; BSE, Ar St Univ, 1981; MS, Univ of AR for Med Scis, 1983; pa/Grad Asst, Dr Sakina Drummond, 1981-82; Spvr of Spch Path Dept, Hot Springs Rehab Ctr, 1983; Spch Pathol, Fulbright Elem Sch, 1983-; Spch Pathol, Home Hlth Care, 1983-; Mem: Am Rehab Assn, 1983-; Nat Student Spch & Hearing Assn, 1980-; cp/Phi Kappa Phi; Chi Omega Alumni Clb, 1981; r/Cath; hon/ Author, "Linguistic Anal of Adult Dysphasics: Utilization of Pictograms," 1983; Phi Kappa Phi, 1981-; Gamma Beta Phi, 1980-81; Outstg Spch Pathol Sr, 1983; F'ship to Linguistic Inst, Univ of MD, 1982; Pres's Scholar, 1981; W/W Among Am Univ & Col Students; g/Open Spch & Hearing Clinic; Pvt Pract.

CHERRY, HARRIET ROSE oc/Architect Intern; b/May 23, 1960; h/1770 Saxon Place, Atlanta, GA 30319; ba/Atlanta, GA; p/Mr and Mrs Martin Cherry, Orlando, FL; ed/Grad, Boone HS; BArch, Ga Inst of Technol; pa/Draftsman, Fam Assoc, Brian Austin, Sums 1979 & 1980; HD Lifeguard, GA Inst of Technol Ath Complex, 1982; Intern Arch, Wm Fuller, The Fuller Grp/Arch, 1982-83; Intern Arch, Rabun Hatch & Dendy, 1983-; cp/ HS Nat Hon Soc; HS Varisty Gymnastics Tm; Ballet Royal Sr Co; FL Yth Orch, 1970-78; Emory Univ Orch, Currently; r/Jewish; hon/Pub'd, "Corbu Villas," 1980; g/Pursue MA in Arch; Reg'd Arch.

CHESSON, FRED LOUIS III oc/ Student; b/Nov 25, 1960; h/634 West Main Street, Williamston, NC 27892; p/ Mr and Mrs Fred L Chesson Jr, Williamston, NC; ed/Grad, Williamston HS, l1979; Att'd Univ of NC-Chapel Hill, 1979-80; BSBA, E Carolina Univ, 1983; pa/Pt-time, Ofc Asst, E Carolina Univ, 1982-83; Census Enumerator, US Dept of Commerce, Williamston, NC, Sum 1980; Supply Rm Clk, Marin Co Bd of Ed, Williamston, NC, Sum 1980; cp/HS: Band; Dance Band; Yrbook Rep; Orgs Editor & Subscription Editor, Annual Staff; French Clb; Student Coun Rep, Pin Clb; Bd of Dirs, Treas, Key Clb; Student Coun; NHS; VPres, U Meth Yth F'ship; Col: Phi Sigma Pi; Social Com Co-Chm, Phi Beta Lambda Bus Frat; Beta Kappa Alpha Bkg & Fin Frat; r/Meth; hon/HS: SES Student to Salzgitter, W Germany; Jr-Sr Waiter; Commencement Marshal; Sci Hons Sem; Hon Grad; NHS S'ship; Col: Univ Marshal; Archie R Burnette S'ship for Outstg Fin Majs; NC Tuition S'ship; Beta Gamma Sigma Nat Scholastic Hon Soc for Bus Adm; Phi Kappa Phi Hon Soc; Dean's List; All A's List; g/

Complete Grad Studies in Bus; Fin Planning & Mgmt Career.

CHILDERS, SHERRY ANN oc/Student; b/Sep 24, 1959; h/164 11th Street Northeast, Taylorsville, NC 28681; p/ Terry A and Brenda Childers, Taylorsville, NC; ed/Grad, Alexander Ctl HS, 1977; AA, Mitchell Commun Col. 1982; Att'g, Univ of NC-Greensboro; cp/VPres Hon Coun, Mitchell Commun Col, 1981-82; r/Presb; hon/Hon Grad; Phi Theta Kappa Frat, Mitchell Commun Col; Cert of Outstg Achmt, Kiwanis Assn of Statesville, NC, 1982; g/BS in Ed (Math); MA & PhD in Ed.

CHILDRESS, ALBERT FRANKLIN oc/Student; b/Nov 20, 1963; h/1819 Rugby Road, Charlottesville, VA 22901; p/James F and Georgia H Childress, Charlottesville, VA; ed/Grad, Charlottesville HS, 1982; Att'g, Harvard Col; pa/ Landscaper, Tay Gwaltney, 1981; Cashier, McDonald's, Sum 1982; Custodian, Univ of VA, Sum 1983; cp/2nd VPres, Charlottesville, Teen Dem; Charlottesville-Albermarle Yth Adv Bd; Yth Comm; Vol Supvr, Chd's Rehab Ctr; Varsity Debate; Varsity Tennis; Battle of the Brains; Hist, NHS; French Clb; hon/ Nat Merit Finalist & Semifinalist; 1st in Sr Class; Harvard Book Awd for Acad Achmt; Jr Classical Leag; Maxima Cum Laude, Nat Latin Exam; Awd for High Achmt in Chem; USA Challenge & Change; Gov's Sch for the Gifted, 1980; Semifinalist, Johns Hopkins Univ Study of Math Precocious Yth, 1976; g/Intl Lwyr.

CHILDS, RENEE McFADDEN oc/ Student; b/May 23, 1963; h/PO Box 28, LaGrange, TN 38046; m/Gaylon Roy; p/ Mr and Mrs W H McFadden, Martin, TN; sp/Mr and Mrs R W Childs, Memphis, TN; ed/Grad, New Madrid HS, 1980; BS Home Ec, Univ of TN-Martin, 1983; pa/ Water Safety Instr, Camp Pinecrest, Memphis, TN, Sums 1981 & 1982; Resident Asst in Dorm, Univ of TN-Martin Housing, 1982-83; cp/Student TN Ed Assn, 1983; VPres, Am Home Ec Assn, 1982; Treas, Alpha Delta Pi, 1981-83; Phi Kappa Phi; Phi Upsilon Omicron; r/Presb; hon/Univ Ser Awd, 1982; Outstg Home Ec Student, 1981; Hancock S'ship, Univ of TN-Martin, 1982; Phi Upsilon Omicron S'ship, 1981; Nat Dean's List; W/W Among Am HS Grads.

CHIN, LAI NGAI oc/Graduate Student; b/Sep 14, 1956; h/2238 Grand Avenue, San Diego, CA 92109; m/Maria Kathy Zuazua; p/Lai Shee Ngee, Singapore; sp/Xuan Zuazua, San Antonio, TX; ed/Beatty Sec'dy Sch, 1975; BA, Our Lady of the Lake Univ, 1982; Att'g Univ of CA-San Diego; mil/Sgt, Singapore Arm Forces; pa/Sales Mgr, Sound Elect Ctr, 1976; Pt-time Tchg Asst, Out Lady of the Lake Univ, 1980-82; Pt-time Lab Asst, SW Foun for Res & Ed, 1982; cp/Pres, Sigma Zeta; Alpha Chi; hon/Dean's List; Pres Scholar, Our Lady of the Lake Univ; Intl Yth in Am; Yg Commun Ldrs; Personalities of S; g/MS at Scripps Inst of Oceanography.

CHIN, LINDA G oc/Senior Staff Nurse; b/Jul 13, 1958; h/37 Nery Street, Apartment 21, New York, NY 10002; ba/ New York, NY; p/Sing Quon Chin and So Keen Yee, New York, NY; ed/Chem Dipl, Bklyn Tech HS, 1976; BS Nsg 1980, MA Nsg Ed 1982, NY Univ; pa/Staff Nurse Genital-Urinary 1980, Staff Nurse

Neurosurg 1982-83, Sr Staff Nurse Neurosurg 1983-, NY Univ Med Ctr; Mem: ANA, 1983-; NY St Nurses Assn; Neurosurg Critical Care Nurse's Assn; Chinese Am Student Org, 1980; Vol, ARC, 1976; r/Prot; hon/USPHS Title II S'ship, 1980-81; NY Univ Sch of Ed S'ship; 1978-80; Martin Luther King Jr S'ship; 1976-78; Regents S'ship, 1976-80; Intl Yth in Achmt; Nat Dean's List; Commun Ldrs in Am; g/Dir of Nsg.

CHIPMAN, TERESIA MARIE oc/SSG in US Army and Student; b/Dec 28, 1956; h/511 Gunter Street, Ozark, AL 36360; ba/Ft Rucker, AL; m/Paul S; c/Steven Paul; p/Zane D Isakson, Milton-Freewater, OR; Audrey R Badgley, N Bend, OR; sp/Claude Lewis Chipman (dec); ed/Grad, Marshfield HS, 1974; Att'g Troy St Univ; mil/AUS, SSG, 1975-; pa/Nurse's Aide, Fir Crest Nsg Ctr, N Bend, OR, 1974; Instr Utility Helicopter Br, AUS, Ft Rucker, AL, 1975-; cp/ NHS, 1974; r/Prot; hon/Hon Grad, Primary Ldrship Course, 1979; AUS Achmt Medal, 1982; HS Acad Hon Roll, 1971-74; 8th Grade Hist Awd, DAR, 1971; g/Pursue Bus & Computer Sci Degs.

CHOCHREK, THOMAS JOHN oc/ Graduate Student; b/May 12, 1961; h/ 14241 Cleveland Avenue, Posen, IL 60469; ba/Lincoln, NE; p/Mr and Mrs Edward Chochrek, Posen, IL; ed/Grad, Bramen Commun HS, 1979; BS, Bradley Univ, 1983; pa/Adm Asst, Ofc of Campus Activs & Progs, Univ of NE-Lincoln, 1983-; cp/Chml, Student Govt; VPres, Student Body; VPres, Secy, Programming Bd; Columnist, The Bradley Scout; Histn, Phi Gamma Delta; Treas, Omicron Delta Kappa; r/Rom Cath; hon/Pub'd in Am Col Poets, 198-; Olive B White S'ship; Tom Connor Meml S'ship; W/W Among Students in Am Univs & Cols; Outstg Yg Men of Am; Commun Ldrs of Am; Nat Register of Outstg Col Grads; g/MA in Ednl Adm.

CHOONG, MAI LENG oc/Student; b/ Mar 20, 1958; h/PO Box 276 Cotuit, MA 02635; ba/Urbana, IL; p/Choong Chow, Ipoh, Malaysia; Wong, Yuet Ling (dec); ed/Higher Sch Cert of Ed, Anglo-Chinese Sch, Ipoh, 1977; Att'd Meth Girl's Sch, Ipoh; BSc Bus Adm, Berea Col, 1982; Att'g, Univ of IL-Urbana-Champaign; pa/ Grad Asst, Arch Lib, Univ of IL-Urbana-Champaign, 1982-84; Student Ref Libn, Berea Col, 1978-82; Front Desk Clk, Boone Tavern Hotel, 1981-82; cp/ Secy, Cosmo Clb of Berea Col, 1979-82; Lib Com, 1981; Student Rep, 1981; r/ Christian; hon/Phi Kappa Phi, 1981-82; Elizabeth D Gilbert F'ship in Lib Sci, 1982; Kenneth H Thompson S'ship, 1982; Wom of Dept Lib Sci, 1981; g/MS Lib & Info Sci; Mgmt Position.

CHRISTENSEN, BARRY KEITH oc/ Student; b/Dec 12, 1962; h/460 West 800 South, Apartment 10, Richfield, UT 84701; p/Richard K Christensen, Glenwood, UT; Linda Christensen, Richfield, UT; ed/Grad, Richfield HS, 1981; Att'g Dixie Col; cp/Sophomore Class Rep; FFA Clb; Football Tm; Wrestling Tm; Track Tm; Distributive Ed Clb; hon/Var Trophies in Racing Events; W/W Among Am HS Students; Intl Yth in Achmt; g/Pursue Law Sch after Acctg & Bus Mgmt Deg.

CHRISTMAS, KIMBERLY ALTA-MESE oc/Senior Medical Records Technician; b/Jun 17, 1962; h/6335 Landover Road #202, Cheverly, MD 20785; ba/

Washington, DC; p/Dorothy J Christmas, Cheverly, MD; ed/Grad, Fairmont Hgts HS, 1980; AA Med Records Technol, Prince George's Commun Col, 1984; pa/ Cashier, House of Fine Fabrics, 1981; Clk, Def Communs Agy, 1979-84; Coder, George Wash Univ Med Ctr, 1984-; Mem: DC Chapt, Am Med Record Assn; r/Bapt; hon/Alain Locke Chapt, NHS, 1980; Grad w Hons, Prince George's Commun Col, 1984; Intl Yth in Achmt; Personalities of S; g/Pursue BS, George Wash Univ.

CHRISTOPHER, RANDALL STEVEN oc/Part-time Youth Minister and Student; b/Oct 30, 1958; h/Route 1 Irvine, KY 40336; p/William Christopher, Interlachen, FL; Lucille Birch, Winchester, KY; ed/Grad, George Rogers Clark HS, 1976; Att'g, En KY Univ; pa/Pt-time Yth Min; Student; cp/Basketball Ofcl; Missionary to Haiti; Gospel Singer; Dir, Ch Basketball Leag; hon/Dean's List, En KY Univ; Outstg Yg Men of Am; Yth Ldrs Awd, ABI; g/BS Elem Ed.

CHRUSTIC, GRACE ANN oc/Horticulture Instructor; b/Jan 3, 1957; h/9 South Ridge Drive West, Canyon, TX 79015; ba/Canyon, TX; p/Jan and Anna Chrustic, Piscataway, NJ; ed/Grad, Piscataway HS, 1975; BS, Cook Col, Rutgers Univ, 1979; MS, VA Inst of Technol, 1982; pa/Instr, Plant Sci Dept, W TX St Univ, 1983-; Mem: Am Soc for Horticulture Sci, 1980-; AAUW; Co-Advr, Alpha Zeta; cp/WTSU Rec Clb; VA Tech: Pi Alpha Xi; Advr, Chi Delta Alpha; NHS, 1975; r/Cath; hon/Author, Var Articles Pub'd in Profl Jours Incl'g: Proceedings of So Nurserymen's Assn Res Conf; Proceedings Czechoslovak Soc of Arts & Scis; Jour of Am Soc of Horticulture Sci; Others; g/Curator for a Botanical Garden.

CHUN, ADA TERESA oc/Student; b/ Apr 27, 1965; h/1049 Oakdale Lane, Arcadia, CA 91006; ba/New Haven, CT; p/Mr and Mrs John S Chun, Arcadia, CA; ed/Grad, Arcadia HS, 1983; Att'd Harvard Sum Sch, 1982; Att'g, Yale Univ; cp/Vol & Benefits Chm, Arcadia Meth Hosp; Bur Chm, Help Our Yth Clin; Jr Exch Clb; HS: Pres, French Clb; VPres, Kiowas; Tall Flags Tm; Apache TV New Anchorwom; Student Cong Rep; NHS; CA Scholastic Fedn; Hd of Art Sect, Yrbook Staff; Class pres; Pep Comm; Voted "Most Likely to Succeed"; hon/CA St Ambassador to Hugh O'Brien Yth Foun Intl Ldrship Sem, 1983; Miss So CA Nat Teenager, 1983; San Gabriel Val's Jr Miss, 1983; W Coast Miss Nat Teenager Citizenship S'ship; 1982; 1st Runner-up, Miss CA U Teenager, 1982; 2nd Runner-up, Miss So Ca Nat Teenager, 1982; CA Jr Miss Top Scholastic Achmt Awd, 1983; Verdugo Wom's Clb Ldrship Awd; Bk of Am Achmt Awd; Nat Merit Finalist; Am Acad of Achmt Nom; Winner, 7 Spch Competitions; 3 Miss Congeniality Awds; Num Piano Perf's & Competitions; Other Prizes; W/W Among Am HS Students; Intl Yth in Achmt; Commun Ldrs of Am; g/Medical Career.

CHYTIL, SALLY oc/Student; b/Jun 17, 1965; h/1412 26th Avenue, Vero Beach, FL 32960; p/Mr and Mrs Thomas V Chytil, Vero Bch, FL; ed/Grad, Vero Bch Sr HS, 1983; Att'g, Indian River Commun Col; pa/Pt-time Sales Clk, J Byron's, Vero Bch; cp/HS: Perf'd in Musicals, "Oklahoma," & "No, No Nanette"; Varsity Chorus; FBLA; Humanities Alliance; Publicity Mgr, Chorus, 12th Grade; hon/

Author of Article Pub'd in *Arrowhead* Yrbook; Kappa Kappa Iota S'ship, 1983; g/Deg in Elem Ed & Photog.

CIANCIOSI, VANDA oc/Academic Secretary and Interpreter/Translator; b/ Jul 20, 1961; h/663 North 65th Street, Philadelphia, PA 19151; p/Domenico and Anna M Cianciosi, Phila, PA; ed/Grad, W Phila Cath Girls HS, 1979; BA French, St Joseph's Univ, 1983; pa/Acad Secy, AFROTC Ofc, 1983–; Freelance Italian Interpreter/Translator, Berlitz Translation Ser, 1983–; Ofc Aide, St Joseph's Univ at US Dist Cthouse, 1979-81; Var Positions w Wk-Study Prog, St Joseph's Univ; cp/Italian Clb, 1979-82; Public Adm Assn, 1980-81; St Joseph's Univ Singers, 1980-81; Cartoonist, Sch Newspaper, 1980-82; Treas 1982-83, Spanish Clb, 1981-83; GER Com, 1981-83; St Joseph's/ Mexican Student Exch Prog, 1981; Fed Ct Clks Assn, 1981-82; Campus Min, 1982-83; r/Rom Cath; hon/Alliance Francaise S'ship, 1982-83; Clair Fam Vital S'ship, Sprg 1983; French Awd, 1983; Dean's List; Alpha Sigma Nu; Yg Commun Ldrs of Am; W/W on Wom; Intl Yth in Achmt; W/W Among Am HS Students; g/Career in Govt dealing w Nat &/or Intl Relats.

CINNAMON, LAURA ANN oc/Executive; b/Jan 23, 1962; h/204 Ridgelawn Avenue, Morristown, TN 37814; ba/ Morristown, TN; m/Larry M; p/Bob and Carol Defilippo, Sunrise, FL; sp/A Frances Cinnamon, Morristown, TN; ed/Grad, Plantation HS, 1980; Att'd, Carson-Newman Col, 1981-83; pa/ VPres, of Small Firm; cp/HS Band; Yth Chm, Polit Campaign; Bapt Student Union Choir; Sunrise Yth Grp; r/Bapt; hon/W/W Among Am HS Students; Yg Personalities of S; g/Exec Position w Large Firm.

CIRCEO, DAVID CHARLES oc/Student; b/Oct 26, 1964; h/35 Whittaker's Mill, Williamsburg, VA 23185; p/Mr and Mrs Richard B Circeo, Williamsburg, VA; ed/Grad, Walsingham Acad HS, 1982; Att'g, Old Dominion Univ; pa/Restaurant Cook, Busch Gardens, 1980-83; Bellman, Williamsburg Hilton Hotel, 1983; cp/ Kingsmill Swim Tm, 1982; Old Dominion Swim Tm, 1982-83; Capt, Kingsmill Swim Tm, 1983; Soccer; Tennis; SCA; Class Treas; Key Clb; Christian Awakening; r/Cath; hon/Hon Roll; MVP, Swimming; W/W Among Am HS Students; g/Biol Deg; Pre-Dental.

CLAEYS, ROSANN oc/Mechanical Engineer; b/Jul 27, 1959; h/23825 Anza Avenue #112 Torrance, CA 90505; m/ Henry Michael; p/Lawrence G Miloscia, Newark, NJ; ed/Grad, Archbishop Walsh HS, 1977; BSME, NJ Inst of Technol, 1981; pa/Mech Engr; Mem: ASME, Instrument Soc of Am; cp/NHS; Adm VPres, Student Senate; Sigma Pi; Contbr, Sch Paper; Bid Taker, PBS Sta; Vol Blood Donor; g/Broaden Ed.

CLARK, BONNIE LEIGH oc/ Free-lance Broadcaster; b/Feb 2, 1961; h/ 1104 Oakwood Avenue, Bryan, OH 43506; p/Harold and Joan Clark, Bryan, OH; ed/Grad, Bryan HS, 1977; AA 1980, BS 1981, The Defiance Col; MA, Bowling Green St Univ, 1982; pa/Grad Tchg Asst, Bowling Green St Univ, 1981-82; Asst Prog Dir, Music Dir, Defiance Area News Dir, Disc Jockey, Sales, WBNO AM-FM Radio, Bryan, 1977-81; Dir, Defiance Col Radio Sta; cp/Wom in Communs; Delta Pi Chapt, Alpha Xi Delta; Defiance

Commun Band; Bryan City Band; r/ Wesley U Meth Ch, Choir Mem, Mem Bell Choir & Lay Ldr; hon/Outstg Grad Student, 1981-82; BS magna cum laude, Alpha Chi; Pi Kappa Delta; Qualified for & Competed in Nat Forensics Tourns, 1979, 1980 & 1981 (Ranked in Top 10% in Nat); Grad from HS in 3 Yrs; NHS; Best Actress Awd, HS; Nat Dean's List; Dist'd Yg Ams; g/Mgr of Radio Sta.

CLARK, EMILY LYNN oc/Tutor and Student; b/Jul 17, 1963; h/908 Lakeview Drive, Kingston, TN 37763; p/DeRita C Lindsey, Kingston, TN; ed/Grad, Harriman HS, 1981; AS Pre-Med, Roane St Commun Col, 1983; Att'g, Univ of TN-Knoxville; pa/Self-employed Tutor, Math & Sci; cp/Chm of Student Fee Bd, 1983; St Bd of Regent's Pres Coun, 1983; Discipline Com, 1983; Student Govt Pres; HS: Annual Staff; Band; Ch Yth Choir; Beta Clb Pres; Drama Clb; Key Clb; Interact Treas; VPres, Student Coun; Tennis Tm; Sch Reporter; hon/Gamma Beta Phi, 1983; Nat Dean's List, 1983; Beta Clb S'ship; Gerald D Moore S'ship; Dean's List; Rotary Student of the Mo; Homecoming Hon Ct; W/W Among Am HS Students; Intl Yth in Achmt; W/W in Am Jr Cols; g/Complete Chem & Pre-med Deg.

CLARK, JAMES MICHAEL oc/Student; b/Oct 27, 1960; h/120 South Allen Avenue, Chanute, KS 66720; ba/Chanute, KS; p/Melvin and Anne Clark, Chanute, KS; ed/Grad, Bridgewater-Raritan HS, 1978; AA, Neosho Co Commun Col, 1982; Att'g, Wichita St Univ, 1982–; pa/Security Guard, Supvr of Guards, Raritan Val Investigations, 1977-79; Grp Ldr, Woodmark Inc, 1979-81; cp/Adm of Justice Clb; Phi Theta Kappa; r/Cath; hon/Dean's Hon Role, Neosho Co Col, 1980-82; Pres S-ship, Wichita St Univ, 1982-84; Dean's Hon Roll, Wichita St Univ, Sprg 1983; W/ W: in Am Jr Cols, in Intl Yth; g/Deg in Adm Just w Spec in Security; Security Mgr.

CLARK, JEROME oc/Free-lance Artist; b/Sep 23, 1964; h/4921 Theodore Avenue, Saint Louis, MO 63115; p/J T and Emma Lee Hines Clark, St Louis, MO; ed/Grad, NW HS, 1982; Att'g, Vatterott & Sullivan Ednl Ctr, 1984–; cp/ Comml Artist; Comml Art Tchr, Mathew-Dickeys Boys Clb, Sum Classes, 1982–; Cartoonist, Grail Newspaper, 1981; Cartoonist, Metro Happenings, 1982; Artist, Designer, 1982–; Cartoonist, Behavior Change Corp, 1983–; Art Displays & Exhibns Incl: 15th & 16th Annual Art Displays, AFO Am Arts Fest of Zeta Sigma Chapt, Sigma Gamma Rho Sorority Inc, 1983 & 1984; Walnut Pk Lib, 1983; Vaughn Cultural Ctr Art Clb, 1984; Jewish Ctr for the Aged, 1981-84; AFO Am Arts Fest of City Hall of St Louis, MO, 1983 & 1984; Others; cp/Quill & Scroll; *Trident* Newspaper Staff, 1980-82; NW HS Yrbook Cartoonist, 1981; r/Bapt; hon/Photo, *Augus* Newspaper; hon/Merit Awd, AFO Am Zeta Sigma Rho Art Fest; Cert of Merit as "Best Artist," Elem Sch, 1978; Citizenship Awd, Elem Sch, 1978; W/W Among Am HS Students; g/Comml Art Status.

CLARK, LANITA CHERYL oc/Student; b/Feb 5, 1963; h/Route 7, Box 378, Cookville, TN 38501; ba/Nashville, TN; p/Cecil and Andrea Clark, Cookeville, TN; ed/Grad, Rickman HS, 1981; BS, David Lipscomb Col, Vanderbilt Univ,

1984; pa/Resident Asst in Fanning Dorm, David Lipscomb Col, 1982-83; cp/Beta Clb, 1977-81; FHA, 1977-81; NEA; TN Ed Assn; Student TN Ed Assn; Am Hom Ec Assn; TN Home Ec Assn; Student Sect, David Lipscomb Col Home Ec Assn; r/ Ch of Christ; hon/Vol, Girls' St Del, 1980; Hom Ec Awd, 1981; Annual Staff Awd, 1981; W/W Among Am HS Students; g/ Marry; Missionary Wk in Papua, New Guinea.

CLARK, RICHARD D oc/Student; b/ Sep 12, 1962; h/2420 Bolivar Street, Owensboro, KY 42301; p/George D and Margaret Clark, Owensboro, KY; ed/ Grad, Owensboro Sr HS, 1981; Att'g, Univ of Evansville; cp/Evansville Philharm Orch; Evansville Chamber Orch; Univ of Evansville: Orch, Choir, Jazz Ensemble, Dixieland Band, Singing Aces, Studio Recording Orch, Phi Mu Alpha; r/Bapt; hon/All-St Orch, 1979-81; 1st Sophomore Hons Recital, Univ of Evansville; Music Maj S'ship, 1982-85; HS Hon Grad; g/Music Ed Tchr; Perf w Orch; Tch Pvt Lessons.

CLARK, STEPHANIE ELIZABETH oc/Student; b/Apr 9, 1958; h/215 Johnson Street, Blackshear, GA 31516; p/Foster and Ineta Clark, Blackshear, GA; ed/ Att'g, Pierce Co HS; cp/4-H Mem, 4 Yrs; FFA; FHA; r/Bapt; hon/1st Place 1978, 2nd Place 1980, Sci Fair; 1st Runner-up, Miss Pierce Co HS, 1983.

CLARK, WENDY ANN oc/Hairstylist, Manager; b/Apr 1, 1963; h/5641 Middle Ridge, Madison, OH 44057; ba/Chardon, OH; p/Mr and Mrs John E Clark Sr, Madison, OH; ed/Grad, Madison HS, 1981; Dipl, Auburn Career Ctr, 1981; pa/ Hd Cashier, Burger King, 1979-81; Hairstylist, Fazio's Hairstylists, 1981–; cp/ Rainbow for Girls; Secy, VICA; hon/1st Place, Sect Styling Contest; Top 18 of OH Styling Contest; W/W Among Am HS Students; Intl Yth in Achmt; g/Own Hairstyling Shop.

CLARKE, STEPHANIE ANN oc/Elementary School Teacher; b/Oct 18, 1957; h/Oswald Harris Court, Building 31, Apartment 271, St Thomas, Virgin Islands 00801; p/Mr and Mrs Ruth Clarke, St Thomas, VI; ed/Grad, Charlotte Amalie HS; BS Elem Ed, Bethune-Cookman Col, 1983; pa/3rd Grade Tchr, Dept of Ed, St Thomas, VI; Mem: Delta Kappa Pi; cp/Baseball; Track; Volleyball; Pres, Treas, Math Clb; Secy, Intl Clb; St Timothy's Yth F'ship; Miss Intl; Vol, Sum Camp; Vol Tchr Ser; hon/ Kappa Alpha Mu; Miss Delta Kappa Pi, 1982-83; Grad, magna cum laude, 1983; Spec Olympics Cert; Var Math, Eng & Sci Awds; Nat Dean's List; Pres Scholar; Acad Merit S'ship; W/W Among Students in Am Univs & Cols; Intl Yth in Achmt.

CLARY, KENNETH LEWIS oc/Student; b/Apr 3, 1963; h/310 West 5th Avenue, Lawrenceville, VA 23868; p/Mr and Mrs Herbert L Clary, Lawrenceville, VA; ed/Grad, Brunswick Sr HS, 1981; ASBA, Chowan Col, 1983; cp/HS: Tri-Hi-Y; Pres, Ecology Clb; Tennis Tm; Col: Phi Theta Kappa; Student Govt Assn; Rotary Clb; Secy, Rotaract; Dorm VPres; Circle K; Rock Ch Audit Com & Pianist; r/Meth; 1983: Cert for Outstg Ser, Phi Theta Kappa; Cert for Outstg Ser, Student Govt Legis; Cert for Outstg Ser, Rotaract Ofcr; W/W Among Students in Am Jr Cols; Pursue Bus Adm & Mgmt Deg.

CLATTS, KAREN ANNE oc/Nursing

Student; b/Sep 8, 1964; h/Route 1, Box 137, Penhook, VA 24317; p/Robert L and Gazella M Clatts, Penhook, VA; ed/Grad, Franklin Co HS, 1982; Att'g, Patrick Henry Commun Col; pa/Marine Laborer, Lakeside Marina, Penhook, VA, 1982; Wk-Study w Public Relats Ofc, Patrick Henry Commun Col, Martinsville, VA, 1983; Secy, Ctl Boat & Trailer Sales, Bassett, VA, 1983; Wk-Study w Dean of Fin Ofc, Patrick Henry Commun Col, 1983-; cp/Pres, St Victoria's Cath Ch Yth Grp, 1980-82; HS: Histn 1982, Mem 1978-82, FBLA; Flag Corp, 1980-82; Pom-Pom Squad, 1979; FCA, 1978; Tri-Hi-Y, 1978; Col: Student Govt Assn, Patrick Henry Commun Col, 1983-84; 8th Grade Rel Tchr, St Victoria's Cath Ch; hon/Franklin Co HS Rep, Sprg Reg Conf, 1982 FBLA Event, Salem, VA, 1982; Flagbearer, Hon Guard, 1981; Dean's List 1982-83, Hon List 1983, Patrick Henry Commun Col; Full Tuition S'ship, Circle K Clb, Fall 1983; g/Reg'd Nurse; Complete AS Deg; Pursue BS Deg.

CLAYTON, CHRISTINE MELISSA oc/Student; b/Feb 1, 1964; h/Box 281 Ft Ashby, WV 26719; p/Jeanne Clayton, Ft Ashby, WV; ed/Grad, Frankfort HS, 1982; Att'g, Potomac St Col, WV Univ; cp/NHS, 1982; Sigma Phi Omega, 1983; Singers; Concert Band; Mu Alpha Theta; AFS; FCA; Math Field Day; Enrichment Prog; Prom Com; Sr Class Play Stage Crew; SS Kgn Tchr; r/Pentecostal; hon/Hon Roll; Dean's List, 1982-83; W/W Among Am HS Students; Yg Commun Ldrs of Am; g/Deg in Computer Programming Technol.

CLAYTON, LESLIE JOE oc/Electrical Engineer; b/May 4, 1961; h/9455 Skillman #1711, Dallas, TX 75243; ba/Dallas, TX; p/Mr and Mrs Joe H Clayton, Elmwood, TN; ed/Grad, Smith Co HS, 1979; BSEE, TN Technol Univ, 1983; pa/Design Engr, TX Instruments, 1983-; cp/TN Technol Univ Hon Prog; Student Rep, Chm 1982-83, Hon Coun; Engrg Joint Coun Rep, IEEE; Secy-Treas, Assoc Scholars Guild; Treas 1982-83, Eta Kappa' Nu; Kappa Mu Epsilon; Alpha Lambda Delta; Omicron Delta Kappa, 1982-83; r/Bapt; hon/Grad magna cum laude, TN Technol Univ, 1983; ALCOA, TN Technol Univ Dept: Jere Whitson Meml & Edwina Oldham Meml S'ships; US Pres Cert of Merit; WATTec's Charles H Fox S'ship, 1982; 5th in Statewide Contests, HS Math & 7th in Algebra II; W/W Among Students in Am Univs & Cols; Intl Yth in Achmt; Commun Ldrs of Am; Men of Achmt; Personalities of S.

CLEMENT, PHYLLIS LAVERNE oc/Tutor, Hostess; h/215 North Pine Street, Seneca, SC 29678; m/Vincent DeWayne Moorehead; p/Johnnie M Clement, Seneca, SC; ed/Dipl, HS, 1979; BA Eng, Berea Col, KY, 1983; pa/Hostess/Waitress, Red Lobster, Sum & Fall 1984; Adm Secy, Col of Engrg, Clemson Univ, 1983; Eng Tutor & Revisor, Tri-Co Tech Col, 1983-84; Student Secy 1980-81 & 1982-83, Commun Cnslr 1981-82, Berea Col, KY; cp/VPres 1982-83, Bd Mem 1977-79, Chapel Choir, Berea Col, KY, 1979-84; Basketball, 1976-77; r/Christian Bapt; hon/Modified & Revised, *Annual Report for Industl Dept*, Tri-Co Tech Col; Am Legion Sch Achmt Awd S'ship, 1979; Most Talented Sr, Class of 1979; g/MA Communs; Career Cnslr.

CLEVENGER, KELLY SUE oc/Stu-

dent; b/Dec 12, 1963; h/Box 51-A Halls Road, Colliers, WV 26035; p/Mr and Mrs Robert Clevenger, Colliers, WV; ed/Grad, Brooke HS, 1982; Att'g, WV No Commun Col; cp/Spanish Clb, 1978-82; Med Careers Clb, 1980-82; Latin Clb, 1981-82; Chem Clb, 1980-82; NHS, 1981-82; r/Prot; hon/Hon Roll, 1978-82; W/W Among Am HS Students; Commun Ldrs of Am; g/AA Deg in Respiratory Therapy Technol.

CLIFTON, BARBIE ELOISE oc/Student; b/Jun 10, 1966; h/Route 1 Box 75, Faison, NC 28341; p/Mr and Mrs Francis Clifton, Faison, NC; ed/Grad, Hobbton HS; cp/Bus Driver's Clb, 1983; Monogram Clb, 1982-83; Beta Clb, 1983; Marshal, 1983; Sci Clb, 1982-83; Fgn Lang Clb, 1983; Annual Staff, 1982-83; Band, 1981-83; Stats for Varsity Basketball Tm, 1983; r/Bapt, Piney Grove Bapt Ch; hon/Gov's Sch, 1982; St 4-H Demonstration Winner, 1982; E Carolina Gifted & Talented Sc Camp, 1979; Appalachian St Univ Gifted & Talented Sci Camp, 1981; Hugh O'Brian Outstg Sophomore, 1982; Jr Marshal, 1982-83; Runner-up, Hobbton HS Pageant, 1983; g/Attend Univ of NC Pharm Sch; Pharm.

CLINE, MARLA MARIA oc/Student Information Assistant; b/Jan 16, 1963; h/Route 2 Box 3 Lawndale, NC 28090; p/Mr and Mrs Hoyte Cline Jr, Lawndale, NC; ed/Grad, Burns HS, 1981; Att'g, Univ of NC-Greensboro; pa/Clerical Aid, M & J Fin Corp, Sum 1980; Telephone Solicitor & Deliveryperson, Shelby JC's, Sum 1981; Lifeguard, Cleveland Rural Rec Ctr, Sum 1981 & 1982; Info Desk Asst, Elliot Univ Ctr, 1982-83; cp/HS: Spanish Clb; Hon Soc; Beta Clb; NHS; FCA; Col: Alternative Focus, 1981-82; Fire Marshall for Moravian Love Feast, 1982-83; r/Bapt; hon/Pres Clrm S'ship, 1980; NHS/Beta Clb S'ship, 1981; Dean's List, Univ of NC-Greensboro, 1982; g/Nsg Maj; Surg, Maternity or Pediatric Reg'd Nurse; Hlth Care Cnslg.

CLINE, MURRY EDWIN oc/Student; b/Oct 29, 1964; h/228 McCollum Drive, Forrest City, AR 72335; p/Billy M Cline, Forrest City, AR; ed/Grad, Forrest City HS, 1982; pa/Rodman, Cline & Frazier Engrg, Sum 1982 & 1983; cp/FCA; Beta Clb; Mu Alpha Theta; r/Meth; hon/Co-Capt, All-St & All-Conf in Basketball, 1982; Campus Personality in HS; W/W Among Am HS Students; g/Deg in Civil Engrg.

CLOWNEY, WANDA DENISE oc/Cashier, Student; b/Jan 25, 1963; h/315 Wood Avenue, Kannapolis, NC 28081; p/Jessie J Clowney, Kannapolis, NC; Margie Hollis, Kannapolis, NC; ed/Grad, A L Brown HS, 1981; Att'g, Univ of NC-Asheville; oc/Cashier; cp/Pres, Yth Dept, Vpres, Secy, Bible Clb; Track; Session House Rep; Monogram Clb; FBLA; Pep Clb; Dean's Page; hon/Minority Presense S'ship; hon/Acad Hon Roll; W/W Among Am HS Students; Yg Commun Ldrs of Am; g/Nsg Maj; Reg'd Nurse.

CLYBURN, GAIL LYNNE oc/Student; b/Jul 29, 1963; h/254 North Blake Road, Norfolk, VA 23505; p/Mr and Mrs Raymond G Clyburn Sr, Norfolk, VA; ed/Dipl, Granby HS, 1981; AS, Chowan Col, 1983; pa/Pt-time Mgmt Trainee, Tidewater Agts Fin Co Inc, 1978-; Pt-time, Smith & Wms Funeral Home, 1982-; cp/HS: Tm Capt 2 Yrs, MVP 2 Yrs, Swimming & Diving Tm; Pres

Keyettes, 1980-81; Alpha Pi Epsilon, Chowan Col, 1981-83; Treas, Phi Theta Kappa, 1982-83; Student Govt Assn, 1981-83; VPres of Missions & Outreach Org, Bapt Student Union, 1981-83; Student Admissions Rep, Chowan Col, 1981-83; r/Bapt; hon/Highest Scholastic Avg, Freshman, Chowan Col, 1981-82; Order of the Silver Feather, Chowan Col, 1982-83; Superior Citizenship Awd, Chowan Col, 1982-83; Recip, Var S'ships; W/W: Among Am HS Students, Among Students in Am Jr Cols; g/Bus Deg, James Madison Univ; Enter Ins Indust.

COBB, JILL WHITE oc/Part-time Servomation Employee; b/Oct 19, 1961; h/1604 Chase Circle, Roanoke Rapids, NC 27870; p/Mr and Mrs Clifton W Cobb, Roanoke Rapids, NC; ed/Grad, Roanoke Rapids HS, 1980; Att'g, E Carolina Univ; cp/HS: Drum Maj 1979-80; Band, 1975-80; Track, Girls Ath Assn, 1976-78; Col: PE Majs Clb, 1982-83; E Carolina Band, 1980-83; NC Alliance for Hlth, PE, Rec & Dance, 1982-83; r/Meth; hon/Essay Awd, Rotary Clb, 1977; g/BS Deg in PE.

COBB, LESA MAE oc/Student; b/Apr 8, 1968; h/Route 1 Sunset, SC 29685; p/Melvin and Vallie Mae Powell Cobb, Sunset, SC; ed/Att'g Picken HS; 13 Yrs of Dance: Ballet, Tap, Modern & Jazz; Musical Theatre, Painting; pa/Clemson Ballet Co; Fain Sch of Dance; cp/Pres, 4-H Elect Clb, 1982-85; Easley Commun Theatre; Greenville Little Theater; 4-H Puppeteer w Shady Grove Bapt Ch Puppet Theatre; hon/"I Dare You Awd," 1984; Num Certs of Hon & Awds, in SC 4-H Depts: Photog, Ldrship, Child Care, Home Envir, Debating, Elect, Wood Sci, Citizenship Achmt; Superior Rating in Solo & Ensemble on Flute, SC Music Edrs Assn; Recip, Num Trophies, Ribbons & Awds for Paintings; Teen Miss Pickens Co, 1981-82; W/W Among Am HS Students; Personalities of S; g/Own a Ballet Co.

COBBS, TRACY L oc/Student; b/Sep 5, 1966; h/111 Marshall Street, Hartselle, AL 35640; p/Mr and Mrs James A Cobbs, Hartselle, AL; ed/Grad, Hartselle HS, 1984; Att'g, Univ of AL; pa/Employee, McDonald's, 1983-; cp/Mem, Gifted Class, 1980-84; Scholar's Bowl, 1982 & 1983; r/Bapt; hon/Nat Merit Semifinalist S'ship, 1983; NHS, 1983; Acad Hon Roll, 1980-83; Pres Awd S'ship & Alumni S'ship, Univ of AL, 1983; W/W Among Am HS Students; g/French & Russion Lang Maj; Wk as Interpreter at UN.

COCHERES, SHERRY LYNN oc/Medical Student; b/Apr 11, 1955; h/15306 Seven L Trail, Helotes, TX 78023; ba/San Antonio, TX; p/Thomas and Jacquelyn Cone Cocheres, Helotes, TX; ed/BS, TX A&M Univ; Att'g, Univ of TX Hlth Ser Ctr; mil/USAFR, Capt, 5 Yrs Active Duty; pa/Med Technol, Am Soc Clin Pathols; Am Med Student Assn; AMA; hon/Grad cum laude from TX A&M Univ, 1977; Awd'd Commend Medal & Achmt Awd from AF.

COCO, JOSEPH JEFFREY oc/Student; b/Jan 29, 1962; h/Shady Drive, Rural Delivery 2, Moscow, PA 18444; p/Thomas Anthony and Irene Coco, Moscow, PA; ed/Grad, Scranton Prep Sch, 1980; Att'g, Villanova Univ; pa/Salesman, Wohl Shoe Co, 1978-80; Computer Operator, Univ of Scranton, 1981; Engrg Intern, Dept of Trans, Commonwlth of PA, 1982; cp/ASME; Pledge Marshal,

Sigma Nu Nat Frat, 1982-83; Yth F'ship, 1978-79; r/Rom Cath; hon/Dean's List; Villanova Univ, Fall Semester, 1983; Dist Champ 100 Meter High Hurdles, 1980; Capt, Track Tm, 1980; Ch Lector; Ch Wkr; Commun Ldrs of Am; Yg Commun Ldrship Awd, 1982; Intl Yth in Achmt; W/W Among Am HS Students; g/Mech Engr.

COHEN, DANIEL LAWRENCE oc/ Congressional Legislative Director; b/Jul 16, 1958; h/2004 Browns Lane, Ft Washington, MD 20744; m/Christine Louise Smith; p/Gerald Robert and Davene Shirley Cohen, Milwaukee, OR; sp/ Gordon and Dorothy Smith, Council Bluffs, IA; ed/Grad, Rex Putnam HS, 1975; BS, Willamette Univ, 1978; Att'd, Georgetown Univ; pa/Legis Dir, Cong-man Hoe McDade, 1983-; Asst to the Treas, The Heritage Foun, 1982-83; Treas, USA Foun, 1983-; cp/VPres for Govtl Affairs, US Yth Coun; Fgn Affairs Dir; Col Repub Nat Com; OR CoChm Draft Form Com; Campaign Conslt; Com for Survival of Freg Cong; St Chm, Col Repub; St Chm OR Repub Assn; GOP Ward Dir; r/Jewish; hon/Mem of Yr, OR Col Repub; Outstg Yg Men of Am.

COHEN, MARC ALAN oc/Dental School Student; b/Jun 12, 1961; h/1017 Oakmont Place #4, Memphis, TN 38107; p/Jule B and Edith Cohen, St Louis, MO; ed/Grad, Lakewood HS, 1978; Att'd CO Sch of Mimes, 1978-79; Att'd TN Technol Univ, 1979-82; BS Chem Engrg, Dental Study, Univ of TN Ctr for Hlth Scis; pa/ AIChE, 1980; Am Student Dental Assn, 1982; Am Dental Assn, 1982; Treas 1981-82, Mem 1980-82, Sigma Chi; Delta Sigma Delta, 1984; r/Jewish; hon/NHS, 1976-78; CERI S'ship, 1978; Outstg Sr, Math Dept, 1978; Nat Merit S'ship Finalist, 1978; Outstg Yg Men of Am; Personalities of S; g/Dentist.

COHENOUR, GRETCHEN A oc/ Teaching Assistant; b/Mar 12, 1955; h/ 916 East Gorham, Madison, WI 53703; ba/Madison, WI; m/John D Short; p/Mr and Mrs F D Cohenour, Babourville, KY; sp/Mr and Mrs George Short, Wichita, KS; ed/Dipl, Knox Ctl HS, 1973; BA Dance, Rockford Col, 1976; MFA Dance, Univ of WI-Madison, 1984; pa/Tchg Asst, Dept of PE & Dance, Univ of WI-Madison; Mem: Nat Dance Assn; Am Assn Hlth, PE, Rec & Dance, 1983-84; WI Dance Coun, 1982-84; r/Prot; hon/ Blanche Trilling F'ship, Univ of WI, 1983-84; Hanya Holm Dance S'ship, CO Col, 1976; Outstg Yg Wom of Am, 1976-77; MA Artists Foun Choreography F'ship Finalist, 1982; g/Univ Tchr; Artistic Dir of Own Dance Co.

COLE, DOUGLAS JAMES oc/Law Student; b/Sep 8, 1960; h/3863 Rodman Street Northwest, Apartment D-52, Washington, DC 20016; p/Ken and Konny Cole, Oak Ridge, TN; ed/Dipl, Oak Ridge HS, 1978; BA Hist, Mid TN St Univ, 1983; Att'g, Wash Col of Law, Am Univ; cp/Pres, Gamma Beta Phi; VPres, Pi Gamma Mu; Pres, Phi Alpha Theta; Pres Hons Coun, Mid TN St Univ; Soc of Profl Jours Sigma Delta Chi; Kappa Alpha; Edit Editor, Sidelines; Undergrad Coun; TN Intercol St Legis; Senator; r/ Prot; hon/Author, "A Brinfornian View of the Islamic Revolutionin Iran," 1983; S'ship Recip, Wash Col of Lae, 1983; Douglas C Carlisle Awd for Outstg Student Legis, 1981; Grad w Hons cum laude, 1983; Outstg Grad, Mid TN St

Univ, 1983; Intern w TN Gen Assem, 1983; Hon Roll, 1983; Nat Dean's List; Yg Commun Ldrs; W/W; g/Complete Law Sch; Intl Bus Law in Mid E.

COLE, DUNELL MARIE oc/Dietary Aide; b/May 8, 1963; h/910 10th Street #23, Lebanon, OR 97355; ba/Lebanon, OR; m/Timothy A; p/Mr and Mrs Daryl E Baker, Lebanon, OR; sp/Mr and Mrs Don Cole, Jefferson, OR; ed/Grad, Lebanon Union HS, 1981; pa/Dietary Aide, Lebanon Commun Hosp, 1980-; cp/ Vol, 1st Christian Ch; Yth Chorus; Treas, Keywanettes; Ofc Aide; r/Christian; hon/ NHS; Intl Yth in Achmt; W/W Among Am HS Students; Yg Commun Ldrs of Am; g/Phys, Surg.

COLE, RICKEY L oc/Student; b/Aug 10, 1966; h/Route 2 Box 231 Ovett, MS 39464; ba/Ellisville, MS; p/Mr and Mrs Robert L Cole Sr, Ovett, MS; ed/Grad, S Jones HS, 1984; cp/Nat Beta Clb, 1978-84; HS Band, 1978-83; VPres 1982-83, Pres 1983-84, HS French Clb, 1978-84; Hon Roll, 1978-84; Drama Clb, 1983; Sci & Math Tour Tm, 1982-84; Boys' St, 1983; r/So Bapt; hon/Dist 8 Am Legion Oratorical Contest Winner, 1982-83; Most Outstg Legis, Am Legion Boys' St; DAR Good Citizen, 1983-84; Cent III Ldr, 1983; Nat Merit Semi-finalist, 1983-84; 9 HS Acad Awds; Nat Merit Hon Roll; W/W Among Am HS Students; g/BA Deg in Polit Sci; Law Deg; Atty & Polits.

COLEMAN, ELAINE A oc/Student; b/ Oct 8, 1963; h/3114 Audubon Court, Sugarland, TX 77478; p/Mr and Mrs Robert O Coleman, Sugarland, TX; ed/ Dipl, Dulles HS, 1982; Att'g, Baylor Univ; cp/TX All-St Band (Clarinet), 1981 & 1982; Most Outstg Soloist, Univ of Houston; Dean's Hon Roll; Baylor Univ Golden Wave Band; Baylor Symph Band; Gamma Beta Phi; hon/Grad, magna cum laude, Dulles HS, 1982; 3.95 GPA, Baylor Univ; g/Attend Med Sch; Cardiovas Surg.

COLEMAN, GWENDOLYN JONES oc/Nursing Student; b/Nov 4, 1959; h/ Route 2 Box 492 Martin, TN 38237; ba/ Martin, TN; m/Charles R (Ray); p/Mr and Mrs Ernie Jones, Danville, GA; sp/Mr and Mrs Brooks Coleman, Martin, TN; ed/ Dipl, W Laurens Sr HS, 1977; AA Nsg-RN, Univ of TN-Martin, 1984; mil/ AF, 1977-81, Security Police, Canine Handler; pa/Nsg Asst, Sum 1983, RN 1984-, Vol Gen Hosp, Martin, TN; Mem: Student Nurses Assn, 1982; cp/Pres 1982-, Bapt Yg Wom (Ch); Phi Kappa Phi, Univ of TN-Martin, 1983-; r/Bapt; hon/ 4-H Key Clb Awd, 1976; USAF Commend Medal, 1980 & 1981; Phi Kappa Phi, 1983; g/MA Deg in Nsg; Nsg Tchr.

COLEMAN, PAMELA LYNETTE oc/ Student; b/Nov 9, 1961; h/PO Box 11203, Louisville, KY 40212; ba/Frankfort, KY; p/Mr Dave Coleman, L'ville, KY; ed/Dipl, Ahrens HS, 1979; BS, KY St Univ, 1983; Cert, L'ville Modelling Agy; cp/Treas, Jr Class; Treas, Sophomore Class; Gamma Sigma Sigma, 1980-83; Pres, Zeta Phi Beta Sorority Inc, 1982-83; Flag Girl; hon/ Lady-in-Waiting; Pres, Fgn Lang Hon Soc; "Miss T-Bred," 1979-80; "Miss Bapt Student Union," 1980-81; 2nd Runner-up, "Miss Phi Beta Sigma"; 1st Runner-up, "Miss Black & Gold"; W/W Among Am Cols & Univs; g/Complete Polit Sci Maj; Attend Law Sch.

COLEMAN, VENESSA EUGENIA oc/ Student; b/Oct 10, 1966; h/PO Box 1058 Seneca, SC 29769; p/James H Coleman

(dec); Mrs Hattie R Coleman, Seneca, SC; ed/Dipl, Seneca HS, 1984; pa/Bus Driver, 1982-84; cp/Intermediate Beta Clb; Secy (Freshman & Sophomore Yrs), FHA; Bus Drivers Clb; Nom, Palmetto Girls St; Actic Dir, UMYF, St James U Meth Ch; r/Meth; hon/Article on Girls St, 1983; Hon Roll, Freshman & Sophomore Yrs; W/W Among Am HS Students; g/Deg in Spch Pathol; MA Deg.

COLES, PATRICE MICHELLE oc/ Student; b/Mar 3, 1964; h/48 Campbell Road, Madison, TN 37115; p/Mr and Mrs Roland W Coles, Madison, TN; ed/Grad, Castle Hgts Mil Acad, 1982; Att'd Mt Holyoke Col, 1982-83; hon/Salutatorian; Acad Achmt Insignia; NHS; g/Maj in Med.

COLLADO, DAISY oc/Product Development Assistant; b/Nov 2, 1959; h/105 Pinehurst Avenue, Apartment 47, New York, NY 10033; ba/New York, NY; p/ Mr and Mrs Felix Collado; ed/Dipl, Mother Cabrini HS, 1978; AAS Fashion, Buying & Mdsg, Lab Inst of Mdsg, 1980; BS Mktg, Fashion Inst of Technol, 1983; pa/For Borghese: Prod Devel Asst, Revlon Inc & Ultima II, 1983-; Intern in Prod Devel Area Spring 1983, Intern in Mktg Area Beauty Care Div, Fall 1982, Revlon Inc; Asst Buyer for Intimate Apparel, Frederick Atkins Inc, 1980-81; Asst Mgr Jr Sportswear, Alexander's Dept Store, 1979-80; Salesperson for Men's Dress Shirts, Saks 5th Ave, 1978-79; cp/CoPres Fashion Bd, Lab Inst of Mdsg, 1979-80; r/Cath; hon/Grad cum laude, 1983; Saks 5th Ave Awd in Fashion Coor, 1980; W/ W Among Students in Am Jr Cols; Yg Commun Ldrs of Am; Intl Yth in Achmt; g/Mktg Career in Cosmetics Indust; MBA in Mgmt/Bus.

COLLETT, CAMILLE oc/Resident Intern; b/May 31, 1957; h/188 Q Street, Salt Lake City, UT 84103; ba/SLC, UT; m/Peter R Conwell; p/Robert W Collett (dec); Mary J Collett; sp/Walter and Catherine Conwell; ed/Dipl, Cherry Creek HS, 1975; BA, Westminster Col of SLC, 1979; Att'g Univ of UT Col of Med, 1983-; pa/Fam Pract Resident, 1983-; Mem: Phys for Social Responsibility; AMA; Am Med Wom's Assn; Sigma Xi; ACLU; Am Acad of Fam Pract; hon/Neison R Bank Awd for Outstg Sr, 1979; Outstg Sr in Natural Scis, 1979; W/W Among Students in Am Univs & Cols; g/Fam Pract Phys.

COLLIER, COLLETTE ELIZABETH oc/Student; b/Nov 18, 1966; h/142 Virginia Avenue, Richmond, KY 40475; p/Hugh and Sharron Collier, Richmond, KY; ed/Grad, Model Lab HS, 1984; pa/ Paper Carrier, Richmond Daily Register, 1975-81; Dance Instr, Fontaines World of Daince, Fall-Spring 1982-83; Food Handler, Burger King, 1983-; cp/Key Clb, 1981-82; Beta Clb; Cross Country; Track; Jr Miss Pageant Contestant; Editor, Sch Newspaper, 1982; Soc of Dist'd Am HS Students; r/Mormon; h/3rd Runner-up, Homecoming Contest, 1982; 3rd Runner-up, Local Am Legion Spch Contest; W/W Among Am HS Students; g/Deg in Elem Ed w Minor in PE.

COLLIER, DERONDA ROCHELLE oc/Graduate Student; b/Jun 4, 1962; h/ 9216 Marlboro Circle, Louisville, KY 40222; p/Mr and Mrs Ronald N Collier, L'ville, KY; ed/Dipl, En HS, 1980; BA, Union Co, 1984; Att'g, IN Univ-Bloomington; cp/Chapt Pres 1982-83, KY St Pres 1983-84, Gamma

Beta Phi; VPres 1983-84, Student Senate; Secy 1982-83, Pres 1983-84, Beta Chi Alpha Sorority; Iota Sigma Nu; Wom's Volleyball, 1980-81; Union Col Choir, 1980; L'ville YthChoir, 1980; r/Bapt; hon/ Dean's List, 1980-84; Iota Sigma Nu Awd for Freshman w. Highest GPA, 1980-81; Freshman Composition Awd, 1980-81; Gamma Beta Phi Hon Awd for Highest Overall GPA, 1981-82; S'shipJr Eng Awd, 1982-83; Union Col Rep to KY Mtn Laurel Fest, 1982; g/MA in Eng, PhD.

COLLINS, CHARLES LOWELL oc/ Student; b/Dec 17, 1962; h/1850 Oak Park Avenue, Menlo Park, CA 94025; p/ Nancy W Collins, Menlo Pk, CA; ed/Dipl, Menlo Atherton HS; Att'g San Diego St Univ; cp/Tm Capt, Soccer; Tennis; Varsity Football; hon/Most Inspirational Player; All-Leag Soccer; SPAL Hon Mention; Outstg Kicker Awd; Am Outstg Names & Faces.

COLLINS, COURTENAY GAY oc/ Student; b/6000 Winterthur Drive, Atlanta, GA 30328; b/Sep 20, 1962; p/ Mr and Mrs William C Collins, Atlanta, GA; ed/Dipl, Riverwood HS; Att'g, Converse Col; pa/Dance Capt, Performer, Crystal Pistol Show, 6 Flags Over GA, 1981; Performer, Theater of the Stars ("Oklahoma"), Atlanta, GA; Miss Atlanta, 1983; 2nd Runner-up, Miss GA Pageant, 1983; Miss Dekalb Co, 1984; Performer, USO Tour in Europe, Dept of Def, 1983; Mem: SEn Theatre Conf; cp/Mortar Bd; Chd of Am Revolution; Phoenix Soc; NY Cotillion Debutante; r/ Meth; hon/Mortar Bd, 1983; Delta Omicron; Dean's List, 1980-83; Outstg Yg Wom of Am; g/Complete MA Deg; Profl Singing & Acting Career.

COLLINS, PAMELA RUTH oc/Student; b/Feb 27, 1966; h/1703 Country Club Drive, Tullahoma, TN 37388; p/ Frank and Ruth Collins, Tullahoma, TN; ed/Dipl, Tullahoma HS, 1984; cp/Former Girl Scout, GSA; Intl Thespian Soc; Press Clb; Student Coun; Zeta Lambda Chi; French Clb; Christian Yth F'ship; Performer: "Hansel & Gretal," "Dr Doolittle," "The Princees & the Pea," "A Christmas Carol," "Beauty & the Beast," "Ten Nights in a Barroom," "The Music Man," "The Dark Side of the Moon," "Anything Goes," "Bye Bye Birdie," Worked on Set & Stage: "Maime," "Pippin"; Vol, Spec Olympics; r/Prot; hon/ Reporter 1981, Secy 1982, New Editor 1983 & 1984, Sch Newspaper; 2nd Place in Paino, French Contest, 1982; Superior Rating, Statewide Piano Contest, 1981; Superior Rating, Solo & Ensemble Fest, 1981; Cert of Merit, Jour Wkshop, Univ of TN, 1982; Recipient of Pin, For Wking Num Hours in Theatre Arts, 1983; 2nd Place in Poetry Contest, 1979.

COLLINS, THOMAS BRYAN oc/Field Engineer; h/503 Janice Street, Enterprise, AL 36330; ba/Ft Rucker, AL; p/John B and Jane L Collins, Sylva, NC; ed/Dipl, Sylva-Webster HS; AA in Elect Engrg Technol, BSEE, DeVry Inst of Technol; pa/Preloader, UPS, 1981; Landscaping, 1982; Bench Tech, All Computer Ser, 1983; Ser Tech, Nichels Inc, 1983; Field Engr, Singer Link Flight Simulation Div, 1984-; cp/Cross Country Tm, 2 Yrs; Wrestling Tm, 4 Yrs; Football Tm, 1 Yr; r/Meth; hon/Pres List, 1982 & 1983; Dean's List, 1980-82; g/Continue Study in Elects; Mgl Sys w Singer Link.

COLLINS, WILLIAM ROBEY oc/ Student; b/Jan 29, 1965; h/1850 Oak Park,

Menlo Park, CA 94025; p/Nancy W Collins, Menlo Pk, CA; ed/Dipl, Judson HS; cp/1st String Ftball, Soccer, Baseball; Baseball St Champ Tm; hon/Intl Soccer Cup, Helsinki; Outstg Track Awd.

COLÓN, SHERRY JEAN MARTIN oc/Librarian & Student; b/Feb 15, 1963; h/4600 Twin Oaks Drive, Apartment 315, Pensacola, FL 32506; m/Alexis A; p/Gary and Jean Martin, Pensacola, FL; sp/Isolina Lopez, New York; ed/Dipl, Escambia HS, 1981; Att'g, Pensacola Jr Col; pa/Page (Book Shelver), Book Mender, W FL Reg Lib; Copy Clk, Libn, *Pensacola News Jour*; cp/Anchor Clb, 2 Yrs; Swim Tm; Histn, L'Alliance Francaise & Beta Clb, 1981; NHS; Quill & Scroll, 2 Yrs; French Hon Soc; hon/Yrbook Editor, 1980-81; Stage Mgr Sch Plays, 1980 & 81; Jour Superlative Awd, 1980-81; W/W Amg Am HS Students; Intl Yth in Achmt; Personalities of S; g/Complete Ed; Wk in Mass Media.

COLSON, YOLANDA LEE oc/Student; b/Apr 8, 1960; h/Rural Route 2 Box 144, Byron, MN 55920; p/Thomas A and Shirley A Colson, Byron, MN; ed/Dipl, Byron HS, 1979; BS Biomed Engrg, Rennsselaer Polytech Inst, 1983; cp/ Student Rep, Trustee's Facilities & Fin Com, 1982-83; Chm, Rennselaer Ath Bd; VChm, Med Adv Com; Ath, Rec, PE, Intramural Bd; Intercol Wom LaCrosse Clb; Sailing Tm; Cross Country; Track Most Valuable Runner; Basketball; hon/ Tau Beta Pi; Dean's List; W/W Among Students in Am Univs & Cols; Commun Ldrs of Am; g/Attend Mayo Med Sch; Pursue MD & PhD, Surg Spec.

COLVILLE, SANDRA oc/Student; b/ Sep 18, 1960; h/5500 Elder Street, Moss Point, MS 39563; p/Flim R and Margaret Colville, Moss Pt, MS; ed/Dipl, Live Oak Acad HS, 1978; Att'g, Univ of So AL; cp/Jr & Sr Class Pres; Beta Clb; Annual Staff; Univ of So AL Math Review Bd; hon/Valedictorian; Dean's List; Acad Betterment Contest Awds; W/W Among Am HS Students; Intl Yth in Achmt; Commun Ldrs of Am; Personalities of S; g/Math Deg.

COMER, CHARLES MURPHY oc/ Student; b/Feb 23, 1963; h/Rural Route 2 Mays Lick, KY 41055; p/Mr and Mrs William T Comer, Mayslick, KY; ed/Dipl, Mason Co HS, 1981; AS, Maysville Commun Col, 1983; Att'g, Univ of KY; cp/Col: Pres 1984, Reporter 1983, Univ of KY 4-H Clb; Agribus Clb, 1984; Farm House Frat, 1983-84; Area Pres (Licking River Area) 1981-82, Area Rep to KY St Teen Coun 1980-82, Mason Co Pres 1979-81, VPres 1978-79, Clb Pres r/Cath; hon/Outstg 4-Her, Mason co, 1978; 4-H Awd of Excell, 1977 & 1981; KY Rep to Nat 4-H Conf, Wash, DC, 1982; g/4-H Ext Agt.

COMER, JANEY LOUISE oc/Student; b/Dec 24, 1964; h/708 Gay Street, Holden, MO 64040; cp/Secy/Hist, FHA; FTA; Thespians; Hon Choir; Candy Stripers; Capt, Holden Yth For Christ; r/Bapt; hon/Cand, Eagleball Queen, 1982; St Finalist, MO U Miss Teenager, 1982; g/Vocal Music Maj.

COMER, MATTHEW JOSEPH oc/ Student; b/Jul 7, 1967; h/Route 2, Box 237, Mayslick, KY 41055; ba/Maysville, KY; p/William T Comer, Mayslick, KY; ed/Att'g, Mason Co HS; cp/4-H: County Teen Coun Pres, 1982-84; Area Teen Coun Pres, 1983-84; Area Teen Coun

Secy, 1982-83; Area Rep to St Teen Co, 1983-84; 2nd VPres, FFA, 1983-84; Pres, Ch Yth Grp, 1982-84; r/Cath; hon/Yth Contest Winner, Co & Dist Farm Bur, 1983; Co 4-H Awd of Excell, 1983 & 1984; Outstg 4-Her, Co 4-H, 1983; Sr Sheep Proj Winner, Co & Area 4-H, 1983-84; g/Deg in Agri Ed; Agri Tchr & Farmer.

COMFORT, DERRICK MARK oc/ Student; b/Nov 19, 1960; h/525 Chesapeake Avenue, Stevensville, MD 21666; p/Mr and Mrs William M Comfort, Stevensville, MD; ed/Dipl, Queens Anne's Co HS, 1979; Dist'd Hon Grad, AUS Ofcr's Cand Sch, 1982; Hon Grad, Inft Ofcr Basic Course, 1983; mil/MD AUS NG, 1979-; pa/Detachment Comdr, CoC 2/175th Inf MDARNG, 1983; Asst Dir, Queen Anne's Co Civil Def Dept, 1983; Platoon Ldr, 1982; Repub Nom, MD Ho of Dels, 1982; Squad Ldr, 1981; Tm Ldr, 1981; cp/Chm, The Free St Lobby, 1982; US Def Com, 1983; Nat Rifle Assn; N Am Hunting Clb; Fdr, Kent Isl Body Bldg Clb, 1978; Fam Protection Lobby, 1981; Capt, Christian Ser Brigade #6401, 1980; r/Christian; hon/Authored Article, "The True Profl," 1983; Intl Hon Soc for HS Jours, 1979; Dist'd Hon Grad, AUS Ofcrs Cand Sch, 1982; The Erickson Trophy, Sons of Liberty Bowl, 1982; Hon Grad, Inf Ofcr Basic Course, 1983; Yg Commun Ldrs of Am; g/Deg in Jour; Prodr.

COMFORT, PAUL WILLIAM oc/ College Student; b/Jun 10, 1965; h/525 Chesapeake Avenue, Stevensville, MD 21666; p/William and Shirley Comfort, Stevensville, MD; ed/Dipl, New Covenant Christian Acad En Shore, 1983; Att'g, Chesapeake Col; pa/Pres & Fdr, Greenshore Sers, 1982-; Appt'd by Gov to Advy Com, Ofc of Chd & Yth, 1981-84; cp/ Exec Ofcr, Christian Ser Brigade #6401, 1983; Del, Gov's Yth Advy Coun, 1983-84; Queen Anne's Co Chd's Coun, 1983-84; r/New Covenant; hon/Chief Editor 1983, Editor-in-Chief 1982, *Acad Edition*, the HS Newspaper; Tireless Dedication, Fam Protection Lobb, 1981; 1st Place Male Oratory, ACE Reg Conv, 1983; Senatorial S'ship, 1983; Extraordinary Christian HS Students, 1983; Yg Commun Ldrship Awd, ABI, 1983; g/Polit Sci Maj; JD; Enter Polits.

CONCANNON, PAUL DEAN oc/ Student; b/May 10, 1959; h/4821 North 47th Street, Omaha, NE 68104; p/Daniel G Concannon (dec); Edna P Concannon, Omaha, NE; ed/Dipl, Omaha N HS, 1977; BS Arch Studies, Univ of NE-Lincoln, 1981; MArch, Univ of KS, 1984; pa/ Draftsman, Omaha Public Power Dist, Sum 1978 & 1979; Draftsman, Ambrose Jackson & Assocs, Sum 1980; Intern Arch, Leo A Daly Co, Sum 1981; Grad Tchg Asst & Adm Asst, Univ of KS, Sum 1983; c/Advr 1981-, Mem 1976-80, Order of DeMolay; Alpha Rho Chi, 1982-83; Illuminating Engrg Soc of N Am, 1983-; Grad Yr Rep, Arch Student Coun, 1982-83; r/Luth; hon/HS Sophomore Scholastic Awd, Omaha Exch Clb, 1975; Eagle Scout, 1976; Dean's List, 1977-78; Phi Eta Sigma, 1978; Chevalier, Order of DeMolay, 1979; Tau Sigma Delta, 1981; Intl Yth in Achmt; Commun Ldrs of Am; g/Profl Arch Lic; Envir Sys in Arch Firm.

CONE, DEBORAH ANN oc/Student; b/Mar 17, 1963; h/2560 Delk Road Apartment O-11 Marietta, GA 30067; p/ Mrs Frances M Cone, Marietta, GA; ed/ Dipl, James H Hammond HS, 1980; Att'd

Inst for Fgn Study, 1978; Att'd Presby Col, 1979; BA, Purdue Univ, 1984; cp/VPres, SSO, Anchorette Soc, 1983; Communs Ofcr, Tomahawk; Student Legal Aid; Sociol Clb; Pre-Law Clb; Purdue Fencing Clb; Gold Peppers; Purdue Col Repubs; Old Masters Hostess; Freshman Orientation Com, 1982-83; Judicial Bd, 1982-83; Purdue Tae Kwon Do Clb, 1981-82; Pres, Delta Chil Little Sisters; r/Epis; hon/Phi Eta Sigma, 1981; Phi Kappa Phi, 1983; Golden Key, 1983; Nat Merit Scholar; Palmetto Girls St; W/W Among Am HS Students; Soc of Dist'd Am HS Students; Commun Ldrs of Am; g/Attend Law Sch; Spec in Intl Law.

CONGLETON, CAROL LYNN oc/Student; b/Dec 27, 1966; h/PO Box 145 Richmond, KY 40475; p/Jerry and Virginia Congleton, Richmond, KY; ed/Dipl, Madison Ctl HS, 1984; cp/HS Student Coun; Beta Clb; Fgn Lang Clb; HS Girls' Golf Tm; FCA; HS AV Clb; Pep Clb; r/Disciple of Christ; hon/Att'd, KY's 1st Gov's Scholar's Prog; KY's Golden 100; Nat Sci Merit Awd; Gov's Yth Merit Awd; HS Hon Student; 2nd Place Latin, St Fgn Lang Competition; 1st & 3rd Place Latin (Artwk), 3rd Place Written Proficiency, Reg Fgn Lang Competion; W/W Among Am HS Students; g/Pursue Deg in Engrg.

CONGROVE, AUDREY MAE oc/Secretary; b/Feb 27, 1963; h/1736½ St Mary's Avenue, Owensboro, KY 42301; ba/Owensboro, KY; p/Betty Congrove, Dawson Springs, KY; ed/VocDistributive Ed Dipl, W Hopkins HS, 1981; Bus Adm & Acctg, Owensboro Jr Col of Bus, 1983; pa/Secy, Cardinal Fed Savs & Ln Assn, 1983-; Asst Secy & Libn, Newton Parrish Sch, 1982-83; cp/Press, DECA, 1979-81; Rec Ldr, FHA, 1979-80; hon/Outstg Student in Distributive Ed; 1st Alt, People's Security Fin S'ship; W/W Among Am HS Students; Intl Yth in Achmt; Yg Commun Ldr of Am; Personalities of S; g/Nursery Sch Tchr.

CONKLIN, BRENDA A oc/Financial Analyst; b/Aug 23, 1957; h/3155 Rochambeau Avenue, #8A, Bronx, New York 10467; ba/New York, NY; p/Patricia Schwartz, Punta Gorda, FL; ed/Dipl, Glen Rock Jr/Sr HS, 1975; BSBA, Univ of DE, 1979; pa/Restaurant Mgmt, Far W Sers Inc, 1979-80; Fin Anal, Mfrs Hanover Leasing Corp, 1980-; cp/Press, VPres, Bus & Ec Col Coun; Chaplain, Social Ser Histn, Alpha Phi; Undergrad Cabinet; Student Govt Budget Bd; Soph Rep, Univ of DE Col Coun; Notary Pub; r/Prot; hon/Mortar Bd; Pres, Omicron Delta Kappa; Quaker Oats Foun S'ship; g/MBA in Fin.

CONNAWAY, ROBERT WALLACE oc/Computer Programmer, Artist; b/Nov 5, 1956; h/7 B Street, St Augustine, FL 32084; p/Charles E and Ina M Connaway, St Augustine, FL; ed/BA, Flagler Col, 1978; BT, Univ of N FL, 1981; pa/Computer Programmer; Artist; Cert'd Pvt Pilot; cp/Exptl Aircraft Assn; St Augustine Art Assn; Aircraft Owners & Pilots Assn; hon/Grad cum laude, Flagler Col; Comm'd Mural, St Augustine Mun Airport; W/W: Among Students in Am Univs & Cols, in Aviation & Aerospace; g/Pursue MA Deg in Bus Adm.

CONNOR, LISA CHARLENE oc/Student; b/Aug 7, 1965; h/PO Box 62 Daleville, VA 24083; p/Mr and Mrs H W Conner, Daleville, VA; ed/Dipl, Lord Botetourt HS, 1983; Att'g, James Mad-

ison Univ; cp/NHS; FBLA; Band; Domestic Exch; Ch Yth Grp; r/Bapt; hon/Class Marshall, 1980 & 1982; Valedictorian of Class, 1983; Band Capt, 1982-83; Lttr'd in NHS, 1981-83; Hon Roll, 1979-80 & 1982-83; US Nat Band Awd; g/Complete Acctg Deg; CPA.

COOK, LUCY LINDA oc/Student; b/Jan 25, 1965; h/1908 43rd Avenue, Gulfport, MS 39501; ed/Dipl, Gulfport HS, 1982; Att'g, Jefferson Davis Jr Col; pa/Pt-time Clk, Coast Fed Savs & Ln Bk, 1982; Pt-time Dental Asst, w Dr James D Price, 1983; cp/Jefferson Davis Student Coun; Freshman VPres; Sophomore Pres; Editor, Jefferson Davis Newspaper; Jr Advr, Mademoiselle Clb; HS Tennis Tm, 1980-82; r/Presb; hon/Freshman Maid & Freshman Beauty 1982, Sophomore Maid & Sophomore Beauty 1983, Jefferson Davis Jr Col; Miss Congeniality, Jefferson Davis Pageant, 1983; Patti Palmer Awd in Tennis, 1981; W/W Among Am Jr Col Students; g/Deg in Spec Ed w Minor in Music.

COOK, RICHARD ALLAN oc/Student; b/Feb 25, 1966; h/Route 2 Box 45-A, Ruther Glen, VA 22546; p/Mr and Mrs James P Cook, Ruther Glen, VA; ed/Dipl, Caroline HS, 1984; pa/Line Wkr 1981-82, Cashier Foreman 1983, Kings Dominion; Employed, NCCI, Nat Card Control Inc, 1983-; cp/FFA, 1979-84; Sci Clb, 1980; Pres Carolie Chapt 1982-83, Reporter Caroline Chapt 1981-82, Reporter Caroline Mid Sch Chapt 1979-80, FFA; VPres, St FFA, 1983-84; r/Bapt; hon/Articles Pub'd in *Caroline Progress*, 1983; St Farmer Deg, Sum 1983; Hon Roll; g/Pursue Acctg Deg; CPA; Wk for Large Farm Org.

COOK, TAMARA JEANNETTE oc/Computer Consultant; b/Nov 1, 1959; h/707 New Street, Graham, NC 27253; p/Mr and Mrs Edward Lee Cook Sr, Graham, NC; ed/Dipl, Graham HS, 1978; BA Eng, Elon Col, 1983; pa/Computer Conslt, Info Technol Corp, 1984-; Legal Asst, Vernon, Vernon, Wooten, Brown & Andrews, PA, 1983-84; Tutor 1980-83, Deptl Asst 1981-83, Elon Col; Ovt Tutor, Burlington, NC, Sprg 1981, Fall 1982 & Sprg 1983; Cashier, Wendy's Restaurants, Sum 1981-Sum 1982; Secy/Receptionist, SEn Inst & Investmt Co Inc, 1979-81; Secy, Somers-Pardue Ins Agy, Sum 1978-Winter 1979; cp/Mem, Alamance Co Arts Coun, 1983-84; Lit Editor 1982-83, Asst Editor 1981-82, *Colonnades* Mag; Secy, Student Union Bd, 1982-83; Liberal Arts Forum, 1981-82; Lyceum Com, 1981-83; Hon Prog Planning Com, 1980-83; Assoc Justice, Hon Ct, 1982-83; Fac & Course Guide Com, Student Govt Assn, 1981-83; NC Student Legis, 1982-83; r/Bapt; hon/Stratford Acad S'ship; Rudd Acad S'ship; VPres, Omicron Delta Kappa; VPres, Sigma Tau Delta; VPres, Phi Alpha Theta; VPres, Theta Alpha Kappa; Recording Secy, Pi Gamma Mu; W/W Among Students in Am Univs & Cols; Nat Dean's List; Nat Register of Outstg Col Grads; Commun Ldrs of Am; Personalities of S; g/Pursue MA Deg (Possibly PhD) in Eng; Tch on Col Level.

COOK, VICKI LYNN oc/Student; b/Dec 6, 1963; h/Route 3 Zebulon, NC 2759; ed/Dipl, So Nash Sr HS, 1982; cp/Beta Clb, 1980-81 & 1982; r/Prot; hon/Moorehead Scholar, 1981-82; Hon Grad, 1982; g/Atty at Law.

COOPER, DEIDRA LYNN oc/Student, Mar 23, 1961; h/5824 Springfield

Place, Ellenwood, GA 30049; ba/Statesboro, GA; p/Mr and Mrs James E Cooper, Ellenwood, GA; ed/Dipl, Morrow Sr HS; BBA Mktg Cand, GA So Col; cp/Pres 1981-82 & 1982-83, Sigma Alpha Iota, 1980; Pi Sigma Epsilon, 1983; r/Bapt; hon/Gamma Beta Phi, 1980; Soc Dist'd HS Students; g/Complete Deg in Mktg w Emphasis in Music Bus.

COOPER, GEORGE MICHAEL oc/Student; h/Route 1 Box 118-B Chouteau, OK 74337; ed/Dipl, Chouteau HS, 1984; cp/Pres, Student Coun; Computer Clb; Track; VPres, Band; Drum Maj, AH Band; Nat Ldrship Conf, 1980; Acad Wkshop at W Pt, 1983; r/Prot; hon/3rd Place, Dist Voice of Dem; St Hon Soc, 1979-84; Most Likely to Succeed; Physics, Computer Sci & Eng II Awds; 4th Place, Dist Debate Contest; g/Attend W Pt; Pursue Deg in Engrg.

COOTES, HEIDI ELAINE oc/Student; b/Aug 16, 1963; h/1209 Constant Springs, Austin, TX 78746; p/Joyce Brooks, Austin, TX; ed/Dipl, Weslake HS, 1981; Att'g, Univ of TX, 1981-; cp/Phi Eta Sigma; IEEE; SWE; Ofcr, Sect Ldr, Longhorm Band; Tau Beta Sigma; hon/Nat Dean's List, 1982 & 1983; Col of Engrg Hon Roll, 1982 & 1983; Phi Eta Sigma; W/W Among Am HS Students; Soc Dist'd Am HS Students; g/Pursue Deg in Elect Engrg; Computer Engr.

CORNETT, PHILIP WADE oc/Student; b/May 14, 1964; h/Route 19, Box 202, Tyler, TX 75706; p/George Leland and Francis Judy Cornett, Tyler, TX; ed/Dipl, John Tyler HS, 1979; cp/Sci Clb, 1978-79; r/Cath; hon/Presentation of Mason Metrics, Mass & Energy, 1981-82; Commun Ldrs of Am; g/Pursue Deg in Physics & Chem.

CORNWELL, TAMARA LYNETTE oc/Student; b/Nov 23, 1963; h/107 Martin Road, Glen Burnie, MD 21061; p/Wayne M and E Jean Cornwell, Glen Burnie, MD; ed/Dipl, Old Mill Sr HS, 1981; Att'g, Anne Arundel Commun Col; pa/Pt-time Cashier, S & N Katz Castelberg's Jewelers, Winter 1982-83; cp/Choir; Vocal Ensemble; Girls' Chorus; NHS; Mod Music Masters; FBLA; Harundale Presby Ch Choir; Glen Burnie Pk Improvement Assn; Concert Assn; Vol, Leukemia, Heart Assn; r/Presb; hon/Dean's List, Anne Arundel Commun Col; Scholastic Merit Awd; Music Participation Cert; W/W Among Am HS Students; The Nat Dean's List; Commun Ldrs of Am; g/Complete Math/Sci Deg; PhD & Prof of Higher Math.

CORRELL, BLAINE S JR oc/Student; b/Apr 23, 1964; h/311 Robin Drive, Cardinal Hills Estates, Somerset, KY; p/Blaine S Sr and Dolores Correll, Somerset, KY; ed/Dipl, HS, 1982; Att'g, KY Col; cp/Varsity & Jr Varstiy Football; Varsity Basketball; Sr Class Pres; Yg Dem Clb; 1st Bapt Ch Yth Mission Tour; r/Bapt; hon/Nat Ath S'ship Soc of Sec'dy Schs, KY Col; W/W Among Am HS Students; Yg Commun Ldrship Awd; g/Bus Adm Maj; Comml, Industl Land Devel.

CORSELLO-EAMES, MARANATHA MARLENE oc/High School Teacher/Audio-Visual Supervisor; b/May 16, 1958; h/1249 Seabreeze Boulevard, Ft Lauderdale, FL 33316; ba/Hollywood, FL; m/Kevin James Eames; p/Mr and Mrs Joseph D Corsello, Ft Lauderdale, FL; sp/Mr and Mrs James Eames, Tucker, GA; ed/Dipl, Ft Lauderdale HS, 1976; BA

Theatre 1980, BA Communs 1982, FL St Univ; pa/HS Tchr/AV Supvr, Sheridan Hills Christian Sch, 1983-84; Videographer, KMV-TV, 1982; Audio Engr, FL Public TV, 1981; Tchr's Asst, FL St Univ, Col of Communs, 1980; Radio Announcer, WFSU-FM, 1980-82; Radio Announcer, WAFG, 1979; Videographer, FSU Video Ctr, 1978-79; cp/ Am Film Inst; r/Christian; hon/Dean's List; Intl Yth in Achmt; Yg Commun Ldrs of Am; Yg Personalities of S; Dir of Dist'd Ams; g/Wk in Film, TV &/or Radio.

CORYELL, LAWRENCE HEATH oc/ Student; b/Sep 5, 1963; h/8716 Eugene Place, Alexandria, VA 22308; p/Ritchie and Carol Ann Coryell, Alexandria, VA; ed/Dipl, Ft Hunt HS, 1981; Att'g, Randolph-Macon Col; pa/Contact Staff Teller, Dominion Nat Bk, Vienna, VA, Sum 1983; cp/Admissions Hometown Netwk Staff, Randolph-Macon Col, 1982-83; Intramural Softball; Randolph-Macon Col Mixed Chorus; BSA; Order of the Arrow; Commun Band; Waynewood Swim Tm; Latin Clb; Swim Tm Capt; Track Tm; Crew Capt; Semaphore; 1st Chair Coronet, Bugler; Marching Band; Symph Band; Pep Band; Col Repub; Del, Dist Co St Conv; Page, St Conv; Musical Solos; Intramural Soccer; Basketball; r/Presb; hon/Eagle Scout; Eta Sigma Phi; Dean's List; W Among Am HS Students; Intl Yth in Achmt; g/Ec/Bus Study.

COTTON, NANCY E oc/Instrumental Music Educator and Choral Music Educator; b/Mar 12, 1954; h/PO Box 105 Rosedale, IN 47874; ba/Rosedale, IN; p/ Mr and Mrs James W Cotton, Richmond, KY; ed/Dipl, Madison Ctl HS, 1972; BA Music Ed 1976, MA Music Ed 1981, En KY Univ; Post-Grad Study, IN St Univ; pa/Music Edr, Leslie Co Bd of Ed, Hyden, KY, 1976-79; Music Edr, Berea Commun Schs, Berea, KY, 1979-81; Music Edr, SW Pk Commun Sch Corp, Rosedale, IN, 1981-; Choir Dir, 1st Christian Ch, Clinton, IN, 1982-; Mem: Am Choral Dirs Assn; Secy, Delta Omicron, En KY Univ, 1975-76; Intl Clarinet Soc; IND St Sch Music Assn; Music Edrs Nat Conf; Nat Band Assn; Pk Co Band; Terre Haute Choral Soc; Wom Band Dirs Nat Assn; cp/Conductor, Cnslr, The US Col Wind Band European Concert Tour, 1983; Del, KY Edrs Assn, Leslie Co Sch Sys, 1977-78; HS: Pres, Fgn Lang Clb, 1971; Secy, Nat Beta Clb, 1971; Att'd Morehead Band Clin, 1971 & 1972; All-Est Band, 1972; r/1st Christian; hon/S'ship, Nat Beta Clb, 1972; Eng Awd, 1972; Grad w High Distn, 1972; Dean's List, En KY Univ, 1975-76 & 1979-81; Milestone Sr Cit Awd, En KY Univ, 1975-76; Hon Citizen, Hazard, KY, 1978; W/W Among Am HS Students; g/Continue Study in Music & Music Ed.

COUCH, CAPP M oc/Student; b/Dec 29, 1965; h/Box 1588 Ozona, TX 76943; p/Joe and Alice Couch, Ozona, TX; ed/ Dipl, Ozona HS, 1984; cp/Chapt Pres, FFA, 1982 & 1983; Chapt Pres, Concho Dist Secy, 4-H, 1983; W TX Rep, 4-H TX Sect Yth Range Wkshop, 1983; r/ Cath; hon/Hon Roll, 1980-84; Livestock Proficiency Awd, FFA, 1981 & 1982; Chapt Farmer, FFA, 1983; Showmanship Hon, 1981-83; Citizenship Awd, 1981-83; Ldrship Awd, 1981-83; Gold Star, 1983; Danforth; in 4-H: Star

Greenhand, 1980-81; Outstg Grass Judger Crockett Co, 1982 & 1983; g/ Attend NM Mil Inst; TX A&M Univ; Agri Ext Agt.

COUCH, MICHAEL JESSE oc/Student; b/Oct 30, 1963; h/Box 1588 Ozona, TX 76943; p/Joseph B and Alice H Couch, Ozona, TX; ed/Dipl, Ozona Sr H, 1982; Att'g, NM Mil Inst; pa/ Recruiter, NM Mil Inst, 1982-83; Student Contract, Army Basic Camp, Ft Knox, KY, Sum 1982; cp/Concho Dist Ofcr 1981, Ozona Chapt Pres 1982, FFA; BSA, 1974-82; Eagle Scout & Order of Arrow, 1979-; Lttrman, Football; Karate Clb, NM Mil Inst, 1983; Rodeo Tm, NM Mil Inst, 1982; Color Guard, NM Mil Inst, 1982; Cadet Capt 1983, Troop Cmdr, NM Mil Acad; r/ Cath; hon/Valedictorian, HS, 1982; FFA: Star Chapt Greenhand, 1979; Star Chapt Farmer, 1980; Lone Star Farmer Deg, 1981; Dekalb Awd, 1982; 4-H: Gold Star Awd, 1982; Var Awds & Hons in Agri, 1979-82; S'ship, USAR; g/ Attend, TX A&M Univ; Pursue Computer Sci Deg.

COULTHARD, DEBBIE DELORIS oc/Medical Technologist; b/Feb 21, 1958; h/217 S Silver Lamoni, IA 50140; m/James Dale; c/Julie Renae, James Matthew; p/Carl Lemke, Adair, IA; sp/ Dale Coulthard, Lamoni, IA; ed/Dipl, Adair Casey Commun HS, 1976; BS, Graceland Col, 1980; Grad, IA Meth Med Ctr, 1981; pa/Med Technol; Mem: ASCP; NCA; hon/NHS; Intl Yth in Achmt; W/W: Among Am HS Students, Among Student in Am Univs & Cols.

COURTNEY, CORY HUGHES oc/ Student; b/Jul 21, 1963; h/2003 Williamsburg, Denton, TX 76201; p/Mr and Mrs Robert C Courtney, Denton, TX; ed/Dipl, HS, 1981; Att'g, TX A&M Univ; cp/VPres, HS Student Coun; Croos Country Tm; Track Tm; Pres, Yth F'ship; Freshman Aide, TX A&M Student Govt; Coun Asst, Dir of Internal Sers 1983-84, Exec VPres of Adm 1984-85, TX A&M MSC Coun; Yth Agnst Cancer; hon/Recip, Aileen S Andrew Foun S'ship; NHS; Dist'd Ser to Denton HS Awd; Top 10; Math Awd; Del, TX TX Boys' St; Sphinx/Polaris Freshman Ldrship Grp, 1982; Harold W Gaines Outstg Ser Awd, 1984; Soc of Dist'd Am HS Students; Intl Yth in Achmt; Commun Ldrs of Am; W/W Among Am HS Students; g/Pursue Deg in Med & Engrg & Succesfully Combine the Two.

COUTURE, ELIZABETH ANN oc/ Student; h/5 Melvin Drive, Greenville, SC 29605; b/Jul 27, 1962; ba/Due West, SC; p/Mr and Mrs Paul Couture, Greenville, SC; ed/Dipl, Southside HS, 1976-80; Att'g, Erskine Col, 1980-83; pa/Spec Events Dir, City of Greenville Rec Dept, Sums; cp/VPres, Chi Lamda Sigma Literary Soc, 1983; Omicron Delta Kappa, 1983; Tri Beta, 1983; Varsity Basketball, 1980-83; Varsity Softball, 1981-83; Sigma Tau; r/Cath; hon/Dean's List, 1982-83; MVP Basketball, 1981-83; Capt, Basketball Tm, 1983-84; Capt, Softball, 1984; Player of Yr, Dist 6 NAIA, Basketball, 1982; Nat Player of Wk, NAIA, Basketball, 1982; All-Dist Basketball, 1981-83; g/Col Tchr & Coach.

COVERDALE, AMY RUTH oc/Student; b/Apr 28, 1963; h/200 Losey Street, Scott AFB, IL 62225; p/Robert

and Norma Coverdale, Scott AFB, IL; ed/Att'd Mascoutah HS, 1978-80; Att'd Vanden HS, 1981; Dipl, Mascoutah HS, 1981; Att'g, Univ of MO-Columbia; pa/ Pt-time Shoe Salesperson & Cashier, Garlands Dept Store, 1979-80; Pt-time Cashier, Base Exch, Sum 1983; Pt-time Model w Model Mgmt, St Louis, 1983-; cp/HS: Varsity Tennis Player, 1978-81; Varsity Clb, 1979-80; Fashion Bd, Univ of MO, 1983; Assn of Clothing & Textiles, 1983; Area E VCmdr 1983, Angel Flight, Univ of MO; hon/Miss Teenage CA, 1980; Rep US in Miss Teenage Intercontinental Pageant, 1981; Miss Vacaville, CA, 1981; Saluki Ambassador to So IL Univ, Carbondale, 1980; g/Deg in Bus/Mktg; Wk in Mktg, Promotions & Public Relats.

COVERDALE, LISA MAURINE oc/ Student; b/Aug 21, 1961; h/200 E Losey, Scott AFB, IL 62225; ba/Columbia, MO; p/Robert and Norma Coverdale, Scott AFB, IL; Dipl, Mascoutah Commun HS, 1979; Att'g, Univ of MO-Columbia; pa/ Beauty Conslt & Nail Techn, Natural Cosmetics, Sum 1979-81; Sales Clk, AUS/AFB Exch Sers, Sum 1982; Pianist, Good Times Dinner Theatre, Sprg 1980; cp/Sigma Delta Chi, 1984; VPres Pledge Class, Zeta Tau Alpha, 1980; Little Sister, Alpha Tau Omega, 1980; Col Intramurals, 1980-81; Cmdr 1983, Angel Flight, Secy, FCA, 1979; VPres, Beta Clb, 1979; Varsity Clb, 1979; Pep Clb, 1979; Yrbook Staff, 1979; r/Meth; hon/1st Runner-up, Miss IL, 1983 as Miss Collinsville, 1982; 2nd Runner-up & Miss Congeniality in Miss at Sweetheart Pageant, 1983; Toured w Miss IL, USO Review, Sum 1981; 4th Runner-up, Miss IL as Miss Kaskoskia Val, 1980; HS: MVP, Girls' Tennis Tm, 1978; Varsity Lttr in Tennis, 1976-78; Varsity Lttr in Softball, 1976-77; Homecoming Queen, 1978; Prom Ct Attendant, 1979; Hon Roll, All 4 Yrs; Outstg Yg Wom of Am; W/W Among Students in Am Univs & Cols; g/Complete Jour Deg; TV Reporter, Anchorwom.

COVERT, AIMEE oc/Student and Model; b/Jul 19, 1963; h/816 Potomac Avenue, Sacramento, CA 95833; p/Mr and Mrs Tom Covert, Sacramento, CA; ed/Dipl, Grant Union HS, 1981; Att'g, CA St Univ; cp/Jr Achmt; March of Dimes Fundraisers; YMCA; Track & Field; NHS; CSF; French Clb; Drama Clb; Block G Clb; hon/Cert of Hon, CA St Univ; Perfect Attendance Awd; Acad Hon Roll; Hon Block; Chevrons; Spec Commend, W/W Among Am HS Students; g/Model.

COX, CATHERINE COY oc/Student; b/Oct 26, 1966; h/1279 Miller Drive, Richmond, KY 40475; ba/Same; p/Nelson and MaryLou Cox, Richmond, KY; ed/Dipl, Madison Ctl HS, 1984; pa/ Waittress, Ponderosa Steak House, Sum 1982; cp/FCA; Ctl Girls Ath Clb; Beta Clb; Hon Soc; Jr & Sr Class Reporter, 1982-84; Cornerstone Ministry; Student Coun; r/So Bapt; hon/Madison Co Jr Miss Pageant; Madison Ctl Homecoming Queen Cand; Outstg Teens of Am; W/W Among Am HS Students; g/ Pursue Deg in Commun Disorders or Spec Ed.

COX, GINA LYNN oc/Student; b/Sep 29, 1964; h/9120 Leesburg Pike, Vienna, VA 22180; p/Mr and Mrs Gene E Cox, Cedar Bluff, VA; ed/Richlands HS, 1982; Att'd Clinch Val Col, 1½ Yrs;

Att'g, No VA Commun Col; pa/Vol Candystriper 1980, Lab Aide 1981-82, Clinch Val Commun Hosp; cp/Little Sister Epsilon Epsilon Chapt, Pi Kappa Phi; Ch Choir; Commun Choir; HS Class Couns; Freshman & Sohomore Class Treas; Band; CoCapt, Flag Corp, 1980; Majorette, 1979; Key Clb; Tornado Clb; Interclb Coun; ICT; Pres, VICA, 1982; Volleyball; Men's Basketball & Baseball Stat; Varsity Football Cheerldr; Model UN; r/Bapt; hon/PE Awd, 1979; Snow Queen Attendant, 1981; Hon Roll, 1979-82; ICT-1 Lttr, 1982; Jewell Smokeless Coal Corp S'ship, 1982; Yg Commun Ldrs of Am; W/W Among Am HS Students; g/Med Tech.

COX, KIMBERLEY PAIGE oc/Student; b/July 29, 1961; h/1514 Shannon Circle, New Braunfels, TX 78130; m/ Michael Gene; p/Ernest R Adams, Charleston, SC; Gayle Watson Thacker, Clute, TX; sp/Mr and Mrs Walter E Cox, Wichita Falls, TX; ed/Dipl, S H Rider HS, 1979; AA, Brazosport Col, 1982; pa/ Cashier/Clk, Joske's of Houston, Lake Jackson, TX, 1981-82; Secy/Typist, Manpower, Clute, TX, Sum 1979, Sprg 1980; cp/Berea HS, Greenville, SC: Freshman Class Coun, 1975; VPres, Freshman Class; French Clb; Pep Clb; S H Rider HS: Tri-Hi-Y & French Clb, 1976-78; Tennis Assts, 1977-78; Goal Post Decorators, 1978-79; Spanish Clb, 1978-79; VPres Social Clb, Rider Ranglers Drill Tm; NHS; r/Bapt; hon/ NHS, 1979; Stand-out, Stand-in Secy Awd, Manpower Inc, 1980; AA w Hons, 1982; g/BSBA Deg; CPA.

COX, PAUL ALEXANDER oc/Student; b/Oct 14, 1961; h/209 Ridglea, Midland, TX 79701; ba/Midland, TX; p/ Don and Rosemary Cox, Midland, TX; ed/Dipl, Midland HS, 1980; AS, Otero Jr Col; pa/Desk Clk, Dellwood Lanes; cp/VPres, 1st Choir; r/Cath; hon/Capt, Baseball Tm, 1980; All-Tour 1st Basemen, Tour of Champs; Tm MVP; Pres List, 1980-82 & Dean's List, Otero Jr Col; W/W in Am Jr Cols; g/Attend TX Tech Univ; Deg in Engrg.

COX, RICKY G oc/Geologist; b/Apr 19, 1958; h/2824 Shandon, Midland, TX 79701; ba/Midland, TX; ed/Dipl, Midland HS, 1976; BS 1980, MS 1982, TX Tech Univ; pa/Res Asst, TX Tech Univ, 1979-81; Tchg Asst, Dept of Geoscis, TX Tech Univ, 1981-82; Mem 1978-, Pres 1980-81, Sigma Gamma Epsilon; Gamma Theta Upsilon, 1981-; VPres 1981-82, Mem 1979-82, Student Chapt Am Assn of Petro Geols; Am Ass of Petro Geols, 1979-; Am Soc of Photogrammetry; r/Christian; hon/Dean's List, Angelo St Univ, 1976-77; Dean's List, TX Tech Univ, 1980; W/W Among Students in Am HS.

COX, TIMOTHY DIRK oc/US Army National Guard; b/Jun 8, 1962; h/7 Dubonnet Place, Durham, NC 27704; p/Bobbie Lee and Jennie Mae Cox, Durham, NC; ed/Dipl, No HS, 1982; mil/Combat Telecommuns Ctr Operator Course, Ft Gordon, GA, 1982; pa/ Pt-time USAR NG, 1980-; HS Bus Driver, 1981-82; Profl Male Model, "Male Lapel," 1983; 7th Kyu (Green Tip), Am Shorin Ryu Karate Assn, 1982-; cp/HS Homeroom Pres 10th & 11th Grade; Ecology Clb, 1981-82; Ser Clb, 1981-82; FCA, 1981-82; Monogram Clb, 1980-82; Sr Class VPres;

Wrestling Conf Champ, 1980-81; Football Mgr, 1980; Track Mgr, 1980; Cmdrs Classic, 10,000 Meter Run (42 Minutes, 39 Seconds), 1983; Baseball Mgr, 1981-82; r/Meth; hon/Hon Mil Occupl Tng Spec, 1982; Cert Achmt Awd, Maximum AUS Phy Readiness Test, 1981 & 1982; 3rd Battalian Funeral Detail Achmt Awd, Ft Gordon, GA, 1982; Selected for Tng in 1984 Olympic Biathlon; g/Male Model; Deg in Elect Engrg or Computer Tech.

COY, KIMBERLY CAROL oc/Nurse; b/Dec 19, 1960; h/892 West Main Street, Richmond, KY 40475; ba/Lexington, KY; p/John M Coy, Richmond, KY; Peggy M Coy, Richmond, KY; ed/Dipl, Model Lab Sch, 1978; BS Nsg, En KY Univ, 1982; pa/Britt's Dept Store, 1976-77; Wendy's, 1977-81; Nurse Aide, Pattie A Clay Hosp, 1981-82; Nurse, Albert B Chandler Med Ctr, 1983-; cp/Panhellenic Del, Kappa Delta Sorority; Pres, Baccalaureate Student Nurses Assn, 1982; Bloodmobile Chm, ARC, 1981-82; Order of Omega; HS Tennis Tm, 1975-78; r/Prot; hon/NHS, 1977-78; Order of Omega, 1981-82; Kappa Delta GPA Awd, Sprg 1981; Soc of Dist'd HS Students; W/W: Among Am HS Students, Among Students in Am Univs & Cols.

CRABILL, MARGARET REBECCA oc/Student; b/Dec 17, 1964; h/221 Orchard Street, Strasburg, VA 22657; p/Ralph H and Rebecca Y Crabill, Strasburg, VA; ed/Dipl, HS, 1982; Att'd, Lord Fairfax Commun Col; Att'g, Brigham Yg Univ; cp/4th Place St (Spelling), Forensics, 1982; Softball Scorekpr; Treas, Candystriper Treas; Beta Clb; GSA; Thespian Clb; French Clb; Secy, Tri-Hi-Y; Photog Clb; Concert & Stage Band; Gifted & Talented Prog; Annual Editor; FBLA; Hopwood Sum Scholar Prog; Med Explorers; Track; Pop Quiz Tm Capt; Fairfax Follies; Col: Pres Freshman Class; Student Govt Assn; Drama Clb; Student Govt Advy Com; Curric & Instrn Com; Spec Registration Com; r/Ch of Jesus Christ of LDS; hon/Yth Grants Proj, 1981; St Winner, UDC Essay Contest, 1980; Col Bd S'ship Recip, 1982; Dean's List, Fall, Winter & Sprg Qtr, 1982-83; NMSQT Lttr of Commend, 1982; Hon Grad; W/W Among Am HS Students; Yg Commun Ldrs of Am; g/Deg in Communs.

CRAFT, TAMMY GAIL oc/Grill Person and Cashier; b/May 17, 1965; h/ Route 4, Box 84, Troutville, VA 24175; ba/Troutville, VA; p/Dennis and Eunice M Cook, Troutville, VA; ed/Dipl, Lord Botetourt HS, 1983; pa/Grill Person, Cashier, McDonald's, 1982-; cp/FBLA, 1982-83; Lib Media Clb, 1980-83; r/ Holiness; hon/Hon Roll in Roanoke Times & World News, 1979-83; Am Bus Wom's Assn S'ship, 1983; Cert in Acctg, 1981-82; g/Pursue Deg in Acctg; CPA.

CRAFT, VANESSA JEAN oc/Student; b/Sep 13, 1961; h/2100-I Foxridge Apartments, Blacksburg, VA 24060; p/ Collins D and Jean R Craft, Fincastle, VA; ed/Dipl, Lord Botetourt HS, 1979; Att'd Roanoke Col, 1979-80; BA Ec, Hollins Col, 1983; Att'g, VA Polytech Inst & St Univ; cp/Student Govt Assn, 1980-81; Legis Com, 1980-81; Jr Achmt Advr, 1982-83; r/Meth; hon/Phi Beta Kappa, 1983; Omicron Delta Epsilon, 1982; Hon Student, 1980-83; Wall Street

Jour Awd, 1983; Fac Awd for Acad Excell, 1983; g/Res & Tchg of Ec.

CRAIG, REBECCA SUE oc/Student; b/Dec 10, 1962; h/Route 4 Box 128 Pickens, SC 29671; Jane Craig, Pickens, SC; ed/Dipl, Pickens Sr HS; Att'd, Anderson Jr Col; Att'g, Univ of GA; pa/ Salesperson, Turner's Jewelers; Salesperson, William A Hoffman Ltd; Concession Attendant, Myrtle Bch St Pk; Waitress, Ship's Bounty Restaurant; cp/ Pres, Sr Class, 1981; Capt, Volleyball St Champs, 1981; All-St Volleyball; Anderson Col Sophomore Senate, 1982; Anderson Col Social Bd; hon/Voted, Miss Anderson Col; W/W Among Am Jr Cols; g/Pursue Deg in Home Ec & Jour; Wk in Public Relats Field.

CRANFORD, KAREN L oc/Engineer and Model; b/Jul 19, 1960; h/1228-L Archdale Drive, Charlotte, NC 28210; p/Jerry B and Dorothy D Cranford, Mocksville, NC; ed/Dipl, Davie HS, 1978; Grad, Barbizon Sch of Modeling, 1978; Deg in Math & Bus Adm, Catawba Col, 1982; pa/Machinist, Cranford Machine & Weld, 1974-82; Model, Actress, Dancer, Jan Thompson Agy, 1979-; Engr, So Bell Telephone Co, 1982-; cp/Piedmont Players; VPres, Alpha Chi; Bad Apple Staff; Commerce Clb; Student Christian Assn; Media Bd; Chm, Col Union Bd Ideas & Issues Com; hon/Dean's List; Pres Hon Roll; Beta Clb; NHS; W/W: Among Am HS Students, Among Students in Am Univs & Cols; Register of Outstg Col Grads; Yg Commun Ldrs of Am; g/Modeling, Acting Career.

CRANIS, PETER F oc/Student; b/Apr 8, 1962; h/2553 Alafayu Trail, Orlando, FL 32826; p/Mr and Mrs Bernard Wiseman, Melbourne, FL; Paul Cranis, Locust Valley, NY; ed/Dipl, Eau Gallre HS, 1980; AA, Brevard Commun Col, 1982; BA Communs, Univ of Ctl FL, 1984; pa/Sports Editor Fall 1982, Sales Rep Sprg 1983, Future Newspaper; Student Escort, Univ Ctl FL Police Dept, 1983-84; cp/Bd of Pubs, Future Newspaper, Univ of Ctl FL; Phi Theta Kappa; Phi Kappa Phi; hon/Pres Hon Roll, Fall 1983; g/Free Lance Writing; Orgnl Commun.

CRAWFORD, BRET EDWARD oc/ Student; b/Jun 22, 1966; h/127 Highland Forest Drive, Aiken, SC 29801; ed/Att'g S Aiken HS; cp/Annual Staff, 1981-83; Math Tm, 1982-83; Marching, Symph, Pep & Stage Bands, 1980-83; Tennis Tm, 1980-83; City Leag Soccer, 1978-83; Basketball, 1973-83; Swim Tm, 1973-82; r/Christian; hon/SC Gov's Yth Advy Coun, 1982-83; Att'd Gov's Sch for the Arts, 1982; John Philip Sousa Awd, 1982; Jr & Sr All-St Band, 1981 & 1983; g/Pursue Deg in Music or Engrg.

CRAWFORD, JEFFREY ALAN oc/ Student; b/Mar 26, 1966; h/PO Box 264, Cotter, AR 72626; ba/Cotter, AR; p/Mr and Mrs Gene Crawford, Cotter, AR; ed/Dipl, Cotter HS, 1984; cp/VPres 1983-84, Pres 1982-83, Mem 1981-, Dist Treas 1982-83, FBLA; Student Coun, 1982-83; Beta Clb, 1981-; Class Pres, 1982-83; Basketball, 1978-82; VPres 1981-82, Sci Clb; r/Ch of Christ; hon/DAR Citizship Awd, 1980; Rotary Clb Yth Merit Awd, 1982; Geometry Awd, 1982; Danforth Awd, 1983; W/ W Among Am HS Students; g/Pursue MBA; Career in Bus & Polits.

CRAWFORD, KOLON MALACILE

oc/Mental Health Coordinator, Student; b/Feb 13, 1956; h/6307 North 104th Street, Milwaukee, WI 53225; p/ Mr and Mrs Ernest M Crawford, Detroit, MI; ed/Dipl, Mackenzie HS, 1974; BS, KY St Univ Sch of Bus, 1980; Att'd Wayne St Univ, 1980; Att'd Atlanta Life InsCo 4th Career Sales Acad, 1980; Att'd US Dept of Army Ammunition Sch & Ctr; Att'g Maranatha Bapt Grad Sch of Theol; pa/Mtl Residential Hlth Coor, 1982-83; HS Tchr, Calvary Bapt HS, 1983; Inner City Yth Min; cp/Baseball & Football Tms; Yth Dir, Teen SS Tchr, Treas & Trustee, Nsg Home Min, Milwaukee Bapt Ch, 1983; Asst Baseball Coach, Maranatha Bapt Bible Col, 1982; Basketball Tm, Baseball Mg/Coach, Milwaukee Bapt Ch, 1983; r/Fundamental Bapt; hon/NHS; Salutatorian; HS Math Awd; Intl Yth in Achmt; Yg Commun Ldrs of Am; W/W Among Students in Am Univs & Cols; g/Pastor.

CRAWFORD, LAURIE ANN oc/ Student; b/Mar 9, 1965; h/15 King Street, Selma, AL 36701; p/Mr and Mrs Bobby Crawford, Selma, AL; ed/Dipl, Dallas Co HS, 1983; Att'g, George C Wallace St Commun Col; cp/Secy, Beta Clb, 1981-83; Corres'g Secy 1980-81, VPres 1981-82, Student Coun; Cheerldr, 1981-82; Hd Cheerldr, 1982-83; Annual Staff, 1980-81 & 1982-83; Secy, FHA, 1979-80; Co Secy & Pres, 4-H Clb; r/Ch of Christ; hon/ Wkly Area Newspaper Sch Report, 1981-82; Homecoming Ct, 1979-80 & 1980-81; Class Favorite, 1978-79 & 1979-83; Jr Miss Contestant, 1982; Miss Nat Teenager St Finalist, 1983; Class Salutatorian, 1982-83; 4-H Clb Washington Citizenship Trip Winner, 1981; Girls St, 1982; Voice of Dem Winner, 1982; g/Pursue Deg in Computer Sci.

CRAWFORD, ROBERT K oc/Manager Trainee; b/860 Murfreesboro B14, Nashville, TN 37217; ba/Nashville, TN; p/Norman and Betty Crawford, Daniels, WV; ed/Dipl, Shady Spring HS, 1981; AA Bus Adm, Beckley Col, 1983; Sales Clk, Nat Record Mart Inc, 1979-83; Mgr Trainee, So Ctl Music Sales Inc, 1983-; cp/NHS; hon/Bus Awd; Cert of Hon; "I Dare You Awd"; Grad magna cum laude, Beckley Col; Nat Dean's List; Yg Commun Ldrs of Am; Nat Register of Outstg Jr & Commun Col Students; W/W Among Am HS Students; g/Mgr, Retail Record Outlet.

CRAWLEY, CLINTON ANDRE oc/ Student; b/Oct 21, 1961; h/Route 2 Box 34-A5 Spring Hope, NC 27882; p/Mr and Mrs Lenward Crawley, Spring Hope, NC; ed/Dipl, So Nash Sr HS; Grad, E Carolina Sch of Bartending; cp/ Upsilon Zeta Chapt, Omega Psi Phi Frat Inc; r/Bapt; hon/MVP in Football, 1978 & 1979; Tony Joyner Awd S'ship, 1979; Attend E-W All-Star Game; Record Holder of HS 100 Yard Dash, 440 Relay & 880 Relay; g/Prodn Mgmt of Maj Corp.

CREA, LOREN ANTHONY oc/Student; b/Sep 11, 1962; h/Box 130 Greencreek, ID 83533; p/Mr and Mrs Ralph W Crea, Greencreek, ID; ed/Dipl, Prairie HS, 1980; BS, Univ of ID, 1984; mil/USAF ROTC, Pilot Cand; cp/Notary Squire, Columbian Squires, 1976-80; Am Soc of Agri Engrs; Cadet Maj, Dpty Cmdr of Resources, AFROTC, Univ of ID; Student Coun Rep; Notary Secy;

Yrbook Student Life Staff; 4-H Ldr; All-St Band; r/Lector, Cath Ch; hon/ Grad w High Hons, 1980; Dean's List, Univ of ID; Petro Power Awd; Citizenship Awd; Band Dir Awd; Vet Sci Awd; Freshman Band Awd; Baseball, Football Lttr; Student Body Pres; S'ship to 4-H Cong; W/W Among Am HS Students; Dist'd Cadet, AF; g/Pilot, USAF.

CREECH, MARTHA LOUISE oc/ Student; b/Oct 25, 1964; h/HCR 3, Box 863, Cumberland, KY 40823; p/Owen and Sue E Creech, Cumberland, KY; ed/ Att'g, Cumberland HS; pa/Clk, Maloney's Discount Store, 1982; cp/Bapt Student Union, 1982-83; Love-in-Action, 1982-83; hon/HS Newspaper Articles; Dean's List, 2 Semesters; W/W Among Am HS Students; g/Maj in Eng; Career in Writing or Public Relats.

CRENSHAW, SHERYL DIANE oc/ Student; b/Feb 21, 1963; h/2511 Jester, Stafford, TX 77477; p/Robert A and Kay E Crenshaw, Stafford, TX; ed/Dipl, J F Dulles HS, 1981; Att'g SWn Univ; pa/ Student Union Artist, SWn Univ, 1983-84; Pt-time Hostess, Saga, 1982-84; Sales Position, SWn Co, 1983; Salesclk, Joske's, 1981; Cashier, T G & Y, 1979-80; cp/Songldr, Wesley F'ship, 1982-84; VPres Alpha Chapt, Alpha Chi, 1984; Sigma Delta Pi, 1982-84; Opera Theatre, 1982-83; Extraordinaires Music Ensemble, 1983-84; Ctl Austin Model UN Bloc Advr, 1983; Amigos Vet, Honduras, 1979; Sophomore Advr, 1982-83; r/Nondenom; hon/ Gen Acad S'ship, SWn Univ; Career Foun S'ship; Dean's List; W/W Among Am HS Students; Dir of Dist'd Ams; g/BA Intl Studies; Sec'dy Cert in Spanish & Math.

CREWS, JOEY G oc/Student; b/Feb 15, 1967; h/223 Powers Drive, Easley, SC 29640; p/Mr and Mrs Joe T Crews, Easley, SC; ed/Att'g, Easly HS; pa/ Landscaping Asst, Anthony Fatale, Sum 1983; cp/Easly HS: Varsity Football; Varsity Track Tm; Jr Varsity Football; Student Coun; Pep Clb; Interact; FCA; Ch Basketball Tm; r/Bapt; hon/Pres Phy Fitness Awd (4 Times), 1977-78; Best Back, 1979-80; Nat Math Exam, 1984; g/Pursue Engrg Deg at Clemson Univ.

CRIBBS, MICHAEL KEVIN oc/Computer Programmer/Analyst; b/Sep 5, 1960; h/1836 Burgundy Street, New Orleans, LA 70116; p/Mr and Mrs Ralph E Cribbs Sr, Ft Pierce, FL; ed/Dipl, John Carroll HS, 1978; BS Math, Loyola Univ of New Orleans, 1983; pa/Tchg Asst Dept of Math 1979-80, Student Asst Dept of Alumni Affairs 1981, Student Asst Dept of Acad Sys 1982-83, Loyola Univ; Computer Programmer/Anal, OAO Corp, 1983-; Chm Lib Com, St Anastasia Parish Coun 1977-78; HS: VPres, Student Coun, 1977-78; NHS, 1975-78; Spanish Clb, 1975-78; Staff 1975-78, Editor 1978, Veritas Yrbook; Cath Thespian Soc, 1976-78; Col: VPres, Pi Mu Epsilon, 1982-83; Am Math Soc, 1983; r/Rom Cath; hon/ Salutatorian, 1978; Spanish Awd, 1975-78; Am Lit/Hist Awd, 1976; Theol Awd, 1977; Hugh O'Brien Yth Ldrship Awd, 1975; Col: Pi Mu Epsilon Awd, 1983; W/W: Among Am HS Students, Among Students in Am Univs & Cols; g/PhD in Applied Math.

CRIDDLE, BARRY DAYTON oc/ Student; b/May 20, 1965; h/Route 3 Box

190, Houston, MS 38851; ba/Booneville, MS; p/Mr and Mrs Jerry Criddle, Houston, MS; ed/Dipl, Houston HS, 1983; Att'g, NE MS Jr Col; pa/Pt-time Employee, Union Camp Container Div, Houston, MS; cp/HS: Pres, Beta Clb 1983; Del Pres & Coun Rep, MS Model Security Coun, 1983; Soloist, Marching Band, 1983; Concert Band; Soloist, Jazz Band, 1982-83; Gifted/Talented Class; Ch Yth Grp; r/So Bapt; hon/MS Star Student Awd, 1983; Spec Hon Grad, 1983; Tm Capt, MS Math & Sci Tour, 1983; Band Coun, 1982-83; Most Improved Bandsman, 1981; Outstg Band Achmt Awd, 1983; Most Intell, 1983; Most Talented, 1983; MS St Band Clim, 1983; Mid-S Band Clin, 1983; Prophecy Com, 1983; Weitzenhoffer Foun S'ship Winner; Homecoming Com, 1981; Homecoming Queen Escort, 1983; Soc of Dist'd Am HS Students; W/W Among Am HS Students; US Achmt Acad Awd Winner, 1983; g/BS Chem Engr or Physics; Pursue MD.

CRIVELLO, CHRISTINE MARIE oc/ Computer Keyboard Operator; b/Sep 13, 1965; h/390 Seneca Avenue, Middlesex, NJ 08846; ba/Hillsborough, NJ; p/Thomas J and Stephanie Crivello; ed/ Dipl, Middlesex HS, 1983; pa/Computer Keyboard Operator, Thomas Crivello & Kenneth B Worden, 1983; cp/HS: Varsity Softball; Varsity Basketball; Varsity Field Hockey; Student Coun; Jr & Sr Prom Com; hon/Norman Seip Awd, for Outstg Student; g/Own Sporting Goods Shop.

CROOK, BECKY ANN oc/Industrial Engineer; b/Jul 16, 1958; h/461 Douglas Street, Janesville, WI 83545; ba/Janesville, WI; p/Mr and Mrs Virgil Crook, Janesville, WI; ed/Dipl, Joseph A Craig Sr HS, 1976; BIE, Gen Motors Inst, 1981; pa/Co-op Student, Gem Motors Assem Div, 1976-81; Indust Engr, Gen Motors Assem Div, 1981-; Student Libn, Janesville Public Lib, 1973; Desk/ Wkr, Gen Motors Inst, 1976-78; cp/St Dir 1982, Mbrship Dir 1983, Janesville Wom JC's; AIIE VPres, Janesville Area Singles Inc, 1979; VPres 1978, Pres 1979, Bd of Govs, Gov 1977, VGov 1976, Asst Gov 1976, Soc of Wom Engrs; GMTE Student Relats Staff Student Res & Devel Chm, 1979; GMTE Spec Events Staff: Winter Carnival Chm 1978 & Picnic Door Prize Chm 1979; Intervarsity Christian F'ship; Intramural Football, Basketball, Bowling, Backgammon, Volleyball; Sportsman Clb; Firebirds; Tech Sailors; Theta Phi Alpha-Stores/Commun Mgr, 1978; Steard 1979 & 1980, Steward Standards Com, 1980; Rock Co 4-H Ldr; St Mark's Luth Ch Choir & Yth Cnslr, 1981; Pres, Genuine Risk Investmnt Clb, 1982; Leag Sgt-at-Arms, Wom Intl Bowling Cong, 1982; Vol Instr, ARC; Fin Com, Indep Order of Foresters, 1983; r/Luth; hon/Rock Co 4-H Hon Mem; W/W Among Students in Am Univs & Cols; Intl Yth in Achmt; Commun Ldrs of Am.

CROOKE, DARCELLE FRANCES oc/Occupational Therapist; b/Aug 21, 1956; h/59 Grissing Court, Cedar Grove, NJ 07009; p/Mr and Mrs Walter B Crooke, Cedar Grove, NJ; ed/Dipl, Meml HS, 1974; BA, Caldwell Col, 1978; MS, Boston Univ, 1981; pa/Occupl Therapist for Hand Surg, John F

Kennedy Med Ctr, Edison, NJ, 1982-; Occupl Therapist, Hand Rehab Sers, Union, NJ, 1981-82; Mem: Am Soc of Hand Therapists; Am Occupl Therapy Assn; Arthritis Foun; cp/Adult & Fam Life Com, U Ch of Christ; Commun Ch of Cedar Grove; hon/Margaret Yardley Foun F'ship; Delta Epsilon Sigma; Commun Ldrs of Am; Intl Yth in Achmt; W/W Among Students in Am Univs & Cols.

CROSS, JANE ELLEN oc/Law Student; b/Aug 6, 1961; h/300 1st Avenue, Apartment 4G, New York, NY 10009; p/Thomas E Cross Sr, Queens, NY; Dolores E Cross, New York, NY; ed/Dipl, Claremont HS, 1978; Att'd, Univ of Madrid, Spain, 1981-82; BA, Univ of CA-Davis; Att'g, Univ of MI Law Sch; pa/Sum Res Intern, Surrey & Morse, 1980; Res Intern, Prof Homer Angelo, Univ of CA-Davis Law Sch, Winter & Sprg 1982; Sum Res Aid, Ofc Gen Sers, Counsel's Ofc, Sum 1982; cp/Am Field Ser; Spanish Clb; Pilgrim F'ship; CA Scholastic Fedn; Field Hockey; Basketball; Badminton; MV Ath in Jr Varsity Track & Field, 1978; VPres Davis Chapt, Alpha Kappa Alpha Sorority, 1982; Black Am Law Student Alliance; Intl Law Soc; r/Presb; hon/Nat HS Inst, 1976; Dept Awd for Outstg Achmt in Spanish, 1976; Bk of Am Awd for Fgn Langs, 1978; Life Mem, CA Scholastic Fedn, 1978; Prin Hon Roll, 1978; Am Field Ser Exch Student to Kenya, Sum 1978; Phi Beta Kappa; Pi Sigma Alpha; Deptl Cit for Outstg Perf in Intl Relats; Intercommun Alliance Netwk Awd for Highest Scholastic Achmt Among Black Grad Srs; Dean's List for 6 Qtrs, Univ of CA-Davis; Alpha Kappa Alpha Ldrship Prog & Grad S'ship; Soc of Dist'd Am HS Students; W/W Among Am HS Students; g/Atty, Spec in Intl Law.

CROWE, TINA LANEE oc/Student; b/May 18, 1966; h/15952 State Route 81 Dunkirk, OH 45836; p/Floyd and Marleen Crowe, Dunkirk, OH; ed/Dipl, Hardin No HS, 1984; Att'g, Columbus Col of Art & Design; cp/Hon Soc, 1982-84; Hon Ct, 1984; Sophomore Class Treas, 1981-82; Jr Class Secy, 1982-83; Sr Class Secy, 1983-84; Dola Slick Chicks 4-H, 1975-83; Treas 1981-82, Secy 1982-83, 4-H; Hardin Co Creat Arts & Crafts Guild, 1983; HS Volleyball, 1980-84; Basketball 1980-84; Track, 1981; Cheerldr, 1980-84; Band, 1979-82; French Clb; Varsity Clb; r/Meth; hon/Freshman Attendent, 1980; Homecoming Queen, 1983; Buckeye Girls St Rep; Girls St Roster Cover Winner (Top Designer); Best of Show, Hardin Co Art Show, 1982; Hardin Co Jr Fair Queen, 1983; Champ & Resv Champ, OH St Fair Fine Arts Show, 1983; Participant, Gov's Art Show in Columbus, 1981-82 & 1982-83; Bowling Green Scholastic Art Show Winner of 2 Gold Seals, 1983-84; Teenager of the Mo, 1983-84; Teenager of the Yr for Hardin No HS, 1984; Nat Scholar/Ath Awd, 1984; McDonalds All-Star Dist 8 Volleyball Tm, 1983-84; McDonalds All-Star Dist 8 Basketball Tm, l983-84; g/Pursue Study in Art.

CROWE, TONYA LOUISE oc/Student; h/15952 State Route 81 Dunkirk, OH 45836; p/Floyd Jr and Marleen Crowe, Dunkirk, OH; ed/Att'g, Hardin No HS; pa/Farm Wk, 1979-84; Baby

Sitter, 1980-84; Supvr, The Dunkirk Pk Crafts & Rec Prog, 1982 & 1984; cp/Ch Yth F'ship; Dunkirk Sum Softball Tm, 8 Yrs; Varsity Track, 1 Yr; Varsity Basketball, 3 Yrs; Varsity Volleyball, 2 Yrs; Cheerldrs, 4 Yrs; Baseball Stat, 1 Yr; Varsity Clb, 3 Yrs; French Clb, 3 Yrs; March & Concert Band, 3 Yrs; Squad Ldr, 1984; Trail Blazers Horse Clb, 1 Yr; 4-H Clb, 9 Yrs; Secy 2 Yrs; VPres, 2 Yrs; Hon Soc, 1984; r/U Meth; hon/Most Steals Awd 1982-83 & 1983-84, Basketball; Free Throw Winner & Hot Shot Winner, Delphas Camp Basketball, 1982-83; Def Spec Awd, Volleyball, 1983; Findlay Camp Hustle Awd, Volleyball, 1981; OH Univ Camp All-Star Volleyball, 1982; Outstg Awd 983, St Awd & Outstg Awd, 4-H; 4 Yr All-Star Player, Softball; g/Deg in Elem Ed &/or PE; Coach.

CROWNOVER, DANNY KENNETH oc/Housing Rehabilitation Specialist; b/Apr 12, 1955; h/609 South 4th Street, Gadsden, AL 35901; ba/Gadsden, AL; p/Kenneth Andrew and Mildred Louise Harris Crownover, Gadsden, AL; ed/Dipl, Gadsden HS, 1973; BA, Univ of AL, 1978; Grad Wk, Jacksonville St Univ; Cert, for Inspections, Specification Writing & Cost Estimating, 1980; Cert'd, Specification Writing for Rehab, Commun Rehab Tng Ctr, 1983; Cert'd, Housing Rehab Inspector, So Bldg Code Cong Intl Inc, 1981; pa/Draftsman, Copeland Glass Co, 1979-80; Housing Rehab Spec, City .of Gadsden, 1980-; cp/Pres, Gadsden HS Arts Clb, 1972-73; Univ of AL Alumni Assn, 1978-; Writer/Photog/Artist: Edit Staff, Univ of AL *Crimson & White* 1977-78, *AL Post* 1977-78, *Gadsden Times, Etowah News Jour;* Histn, Gadsden Art Assn, 1978-79; AL Solar Enrgy Coalition, 1980-81; Nat Spelogical Soc, 1979-; Gadsden Grotto, 1979-81; Lectures, for Num Civic Orgs; Gadsden Jaycees, 1984-; Editor, Gadsden Jaycees Newsletter, 1984-; VP Trails, AL Appalachian Assn, 1984-; Bd Mem, Etowah Co Meml Com, 1984-; Noccalula Civitan Clb, 1983-84; Usher Com, Legion Fields Stadium, Birmingham, AL, 1984-; r/Ch of Christ; hon/Author, *Black Creek: So Lookout Mtn,* 1983; Selected to St of AL Bicent Comm, 1973; Num St & Local Art Achmt Awds, 1967-; Selected to Design Cober of *ROTC Mag,* 1978; Intl Yth in Achmt; g/To Extend Ednl Background toward Doct; Be More Instrumental in City Planning.

CRUGER, LESLIE A oc/Medical Social Worker; b/Sep 15, 1958; h/14 South Mechanic Street, Cumberland, MD 21502; ba/Cumberland, MD; p/Mr and Mrs William H Cruger, Boonsboro, MD; ed/Dipl, Boonsboro Sr HS, 1976; AB, Hood Col, 1980; MSW, Sch of Social Wk & Commun Planning, Univ of MD, 1983; LGSW, MD St, 1983; pa/Med Social Wkr, Med/Surg Ward & Home Hlth Sers, 1984-; Drug Cnslr, VA Opt Clin-Drug Unit, Balto, MD, 1983; MD St Archival Asst Intern, Sum 1980; Res Asst in Social Wk, "Moral & the Elderly," 1982; MSW Student, Balto-VA Med Ctr, 1982; cp/Hood Choir, 1976-80; Choir Pres, 1979-80; Wash Co Hist Soc, 1975-82; BPW Clb, 1984; hon/HS Grad w Hons & Danforth Awd, 1976; Hood Dean's List, 1977-80; Convocation Hons, 1980; Nat Dean's List, 1980; Yg Achievers' Awd, ABA,

1981; Commun Ldrs of Am; Personalities of S; g/Wk in Med or Geriatric Setting as LCSW.

CRUSE, RANDY LEE b/Aug 24, 1961; h/Route 1 Albertson, NC 28508; p/Mr and Mrs Walter Lee Cruse, Albertson, NC; ed/Dipl, E Duplin HS, 1979; BS Agri Engrg & Agri Ed, NC St Univ, 1983; pa/Dairy Records Processing Ctr 1981-83, Poultry Sci Dept Sprg & Sum 1982, NC St Univ; cp/Agri Ed Clb & Agri Engrg Clb, NC St Univ; r/Holiness; hon/Gamma Sigma Delta, 1980; Alpha Lambda Delta, 1981; Alpha Tau Alplha, 1982; Kappa Delta Pi, 1981; Phi Kappa Phi, 1983; g/Wk in NC.

CRYSLER, SOPHIA G T b/Apr 3, 1959; h/311 Grays Lane, Haverford, PA 19041; p/Mrs R Godwin Crysler, Haverford, PA; ed/Dipl, Shipley Sch, 1977; AB, Sweet Briar Col, 1981; MA Fgn Affairs, Univ of VA, 1983; pa/Tchg Asst Dept Govt & Fgn Affairs Fall & Sprg 1981-1982 & 1982-83, Res Asst & Libn White Burnett Miller Ctr of Public Affairs 1982-83, Univ of VA; Staff Asst, Speedy Offset Printing, Sum 1979 & 1981; Freelance Calligrapher, 1975-80; cp/Monitor Recording for the Blind; Treas 1982-83, Grad Student Assn, Univ of VA; Jud Com Chwom, Sweet Briar Col, 1980-81; Food Sers, 1980-81; Student Govt Treas, 1979-80; Sophomore Class Pres, 1978-79; Sweet Briar Col News Staff, 1977-78; Tau Phi; r/Epis; hon/Phi Beta Kappa, 1981; Nat Merit Scholar, 1977-81; Czarra Awd for Ldrship, 1981; Manson Awd for Ldrship & Acad Achmts, 1980; Richards Awd for Ldrship, 1979; Dean's List, 1977-81; DuPont F'ship; Lassen F'ship; W/W Among Students in Am Cols & Univs; g/Govt Ser in Fgn Affairs.

CUAREZMA-TERAN, JORGE ANTONIO oc/Research Assistant; b/Apr 23, 1954; h/University Village Apartment 26-D, Starkville, MS 39759; ba/Mississippi State, MS; m/Jacqueline Otero; p/Anoldo and Nidya Cuarezma, Nindin', Nicaragua; sp/Guillermo and Marlene Otero, San Salvador, El Salvador; ed/Salesiano Col "Don Bosco"; HS Dipl, Masaya-Nicaragua, 1967-71; Agronomy Deg, Pan-Am Agri Sch, Honduras, 1972-74; MSc Crop Protection, Univ of PR, 1979-80; PhD Plant Pathol, MS St Univ, 1981-83; pa/Res Asst, MS St Univ, 1981-; Vis'g Res Assoc, CIAT-Cali, Colombia, Sum 1983; Res Asst, Dept Crop Protection, Univ of PR, 1979-80; Nematologist, W Germanic Tech Mission in Nicaragua, Sum & Fall 1978; Tech Asst, Nat Bk of Nicaragua, 1976-78; Res Techn, Ctl Bk of Nicaragua, 1975-76; Mem: Am Phytopathol Soc; Org of Tropical Am Nematologist; Soc of Nematologists; MS Assn of Plant Pathols & Nematologists; r/Cath; hon/Co-Author, "Study on Native Hardwood & Softwood in Nicaragua," 1976; Var Abstracts Pub'd in Profl Jours; Pan-Am Agri Sch, 1972; F'ship, Cordiplan, Venezuelan Govt, 1977; F'ship, Inst Goethe W German Govt, 1979; Co-Winner Awd, Am Phytopathol Soc, 1980; AID F'ship, 1981; g/Continue Res on Sorghum Diseases in MS.

CULP, DIANA G oc/Lawyer; b/Feb 27, 1957; h/1350 Avolencia Drive, Fullerton, CA 92635; p/Mr and Mrs Rollin Lee Culp, Fullerton, CA; ed/Dipl, Fullerton Union HS, 1975; AB, Occidental Col, 1979; JD, Harvard Law Sch, 1983; pa/Law Clk, Hon Richard A Gadbois Jr, US Dist Ct, CA, 1983-84; Law Clk, Hon John J Gibbons, US Ct of Appeals, 3rd Circuit, 1984-; cp/ Campaign Wkr; AAUW; Am Cancer Soc; Public Relats Com, C of C; Num Public Spkg Presentations to HSs & Jr HSs; Res Asst; hon/Var Newspaper & Mag Articles Pub'd; Phi Beta Kapp; Col Scholar; Grad summa cum laude; Pres, Psi Chi; Alpha Theta; Grad cum laude, Harvard Law Sch; Recip, Addison-Brown Prize.

CUMMINS, RHONDA D oc/Associate Computer Operator and Student; b/Dec 17, 1962; h/10305 Oak Creek Drive, Greenville, TX 75401; p/Herbert and Betty Cummins, Greenville, TX; ed/ Dipl, Greenville Sr HS, 1981; Att'g E TX St Univ; pa/Assoc Computer Operator, E-Sys Inc, 1982-; cp/Secy, Phi Eta Sigma, l982; Alpha Lambda Delta; SW Basketball Officiating Assn; NHS, 1980-; E TX St Univ Bapt Student Union Exec Coun, 1983-84; Fin Mgmt Assn; Student Advy Coun; r/Bapt; hon/ Author of Article Pub'd in *Greenville Herald Banner*, 1983; Dean's List; Top Ten Grad, 1981; Homer H Tate S'ship; Nat Dean's List; W/W Among Am HS Students; Intl Yth in Achmt; Yg Personalities of S; Yg Commun Ldrs of Am; g/BA Deg from E TX St Univ; Pursue MA Deg, Hardin-Simmons Univ.

CUNDIFF, PAMELA JOYCE oc/ Business Owner and Manager; b/Apr 29, 1960; h/524 East Boone Road, Eden, NC 27288; ba/Eden, NC; p/J Herbert and Joyce S Cundiff, Rocky Mt, VA; ed/ Dipl, Franklin Co HS, 1978; Travel Indust Dipl, SEn Acad, 1982; pa/VPres, Gen Mgr, Travel Consults Inc, 1982-; Mgr, Rockingham Travel Ser, 1980-82; Asst to VPres, World Travel Ser, Roanoke, VA, 1979-80; Cnslr, World Travel Ser, Tanglewood, Roanoke, VA, 1978-79; cp/Ski Clb; BPW Clb; r/Bapt.

CUNNINGHAM, ELLYN RUTH oc/ Campus Crusade for Christ Staff; b/Oct 29, 1961; h/401 Devonia Street, Harriman, TN 37748; ba/Arrowhead Springs, CA; p/Mr and Mrs E D Cunningham, Harriman, TN; ed/Dipl, HS, 1979; BS Animal Sci, Univ of TN, 1984; pa/Staff, Campus Crusade for Christ; cp/Beta Clb Ofcr; Student Govt Ofcr; Band; Num Others; hon/Univ of TN: Dean's List; Exec Coun, Pres 1982-83, Dir of Rush 1981, Panhellenic Coun; Outstg Greek, 1982-83; Mortar Bd; Scarabbean Hon Soc; Torchbearer, 1983; Omicron Delta Kappa; Rho Lambda; Alpha Zeta; Gamma Beta Phi; g/Become a Vet.

CUNNINGHAM, JOHN CRIS oc/ Student; b/Apr 25, 1965; h/10031 Clairemore Place, Charlotte, NC 28216; ba/Charlotte, NC; p/Mr and Mrs J C Cunningham; ed/Dipl, No Mecklenburg HS, 1983; Att'g, Johnson C Smith Univ; pa/Pt-time Energy Conslt, Solar Therm RII of Charlotte; Mgr Trainee Intern, Consolidated Coin Caterers, Charlotte, NC, 1983; cp/NHS, 1983; Student Govt, 1982-83; Introads, Charlotte, 1983; Nat

Latin Hon Soc, 1981-83; Smallwood Presb Ch Yth Coun Pres, 1983; Ch Choir & Musician, 1982-83; r/Presb; hon/Sports Writer 1982, Sports Editor & Hd Columnist 1983, Sch Newspaper; *Charlotte Post* All-Star Scholar, 1983; Duke S'ship, Johnson C Smith Univ, 1983; 10 Yr Nat Winner, Nat Piano Playing Auditions, 1983; Soc of Dist'd Am HS Students; g/Deg in Bus Adm & Computer Sci.

CUNNINGHAM, PAUL V oc/Student; b/Jul 1, 1960; h/74 Rockland Avenue, Yonkers, NY 10705; p/Francis J Jr and Joan P Cunningham, Yonkers, NY; ed/Iona Prep; AS, Westchester Commun Col, 1982; BS Ec, Clarkson Col of Technol, 1984; pa/External Data Processing, Manhattan Savs Bk, 1979-81; Temp Sales Rep, Nabisco Brands Inc, 1983; cp/Jr Achmt; VPres of Public Relats & Commun Affairs, Alpha Beta Gamma, Fall 1981; House Pres, Zeta Chi Zeta Frat; Alumni Assn, Westchester Commun Col; Cinema IO, Clarkson Col; r/Rom Cath; hon/Alpha Beta Gamma S'ship, 1983; Westchester Commun Col Grad Hons, 1983; Dean's List, Westchester Commun Col, 1981-82; Clarkson Col Trustee S'ship, 1983; g/Decision Making Position in a Fortune 500 Corp.

CURCIO, SHEILA MARGARET oc/ Student; b/Feb 23, 1965; p/Charles and Dora Curcio; ed/HS Dipl, 1983; pa/ Proof 1 Data Processing, U So Bk; cp/ CYO, 1980-82; Secy, DECA, 1983; Mu Alpha Theta, 1982-83; NHS, 1981-83; r/Cath; hon/Girls' St Star Student, 1983; Homecoming Maid, 1983; Homecoming Nom, 1981-82; Hall of Fame, 1983; 3rd Place ABC Competion; 2nd Place Fin & Credit Competition; Hon Grad, 1983; W/W Among Am HS Students; Nat Register of Outstg HS Students; g/Deg in Med.

CURRIN, BENA L oc/Student; b/Apr 8, l1966; h/833 North Peninsula Drive, Daytona Beach, FL 32018; p/Mr and Mrs H L Currin, Daytona Bch, FL; ed/ Dipl, Seabreeze Sr HS, 1983; Att'g CA Inst of Technol; cp/Seabreeze Latin Clb, 1980-83; Model UN Clb, 1982-83; Sch Div Pres, 983; All-St Orch, 1980-83; All-Co (Volusia) Orch, 1978-83; NHS, 1983; Jr Classical Leag, 1980-83; hon/ Nat Merit Finalist, 1983; 1st Place Co Latin Declammation, 1982; 1st Place Co Soc Studies Media Proj, 1982; Bausch & Lomb Sc Awd, 1983; Co Pride Sci Awd, 1983; Cert of Mert, FL Math Leag, 1983; W/W Among Am HS Students; Am Outstg Names & Faces; g/Deg in Elect Engrg.

CURTH, MICHAEL E oc/Investment Broker; b/Oct 13, 1959; h/803 East Main Street, Eaton, OH 45320; ba/Springfield, OH; p/Mr and Mrs Howard I Curth, Eaton, OH; ed/Dipl, Glandorf HS; Att'd Wright St Univ; Att'd The OH St Univ-Columbus; pa/Investmnt Broker, 1st Investors Corp; Sales Rep, Douglas Industl Co; Asst Mgr, Halle's Precious Jewels Salon; cp/Scoutmaster, Dist Exec Com, BSA; Univ Senate; Dir Reg Affairs, The OH St Univ; Mission-

ary for LDS, Leeds, England; r/LDS; hon/Eagle Scout; Yg Personalities of Am; Intl Yth in Achmt; g/Deg in Polit Sci; Open Investmnt Firm.

CURTIS, A BRENT oc/Student; b/Jul 29, 1966; h/218 Limestone, Maysville, KY 41056; p/Ed Curtis, Wilkesboro, NC; Gayle Curtis, Maysville, KY; ed/Dipl, St Patrick's HS, 1984; Att'g, Wn KY Univ; r/Cath; hon/Del, KY Boys' St, 1983; Selected to SPOKE Conf, 1983; Selected to Ball St Jour Wkshop, 1983; Winner in Math & Eng, US Achmt Acad, 1983; Layout/Design Editor, *The Leprechaun* Sch Newspaper, 1983-84; A Hon Roll, 1981-84; W/W Among Am HS Students; Soc of Dist'd HS Students; g/Deg in Bus Adm.

CURTIS, ELIZABETH DELL oc/ Student; b/Mar 14, 1966; h/151 Gary Street, Gulfport, MS 39503; p/Dawson and Shirley Curtis, Gulfport, MS; ed/ Dipl, Harrison Ctl HS, 1984; cp/Pres, New Horizons 4-H Clb, 1982; Pres, Astra Clb, 1982-83; Nat Beta Clb, 1981-84; French Clb, 1981-84; NHS, 1981-84; Football Cheerldr, 1982-83; Mu Alpha Theta, 1982-84; Student Coun Rep, 1981-82; r/So Bapt; hon/2 Poems Pub'd in the *Phoenix* Sch Lit Mag & Article in Sch Newspaper; Optimist Clb Essay Awd, 1981; Optimist Clb Oratorical Awd, 1982; Supvrs Essay Awd, 1981; Am Legion Oratorical Awd, 1983; Eng & Hist Awd, 1982; Soc of Dist'd Am HS Students; g/Become a Lwyr.

CUTTERIDGE, RONDA LYNETTE b/Sep 16, 1961; h/1006 West Heerdink Avenue, Evansville, IN 47710; p/William E and Jean Cutteridge, Evansville, IN; ed/Dipl, Ctl HS, 1979; BSBA, IN St Univ, 1983; Secy in Sch of Bus, Univ of Evansville, 1979-80; Res Asst & Student Asst, IN St Univ, 1980-; cp/ VPres, Distributive Ed Clb of Am, 1978; Pres, Ofc Ed Assn, 1979; Editor, *Centralian*, 1979; Pres, Delta Zeta Sorority, 1981; VPres, Student Union Bd; Leag of Profl Wom; Psych Clb; Registration Advy Com; Nat Assn for Col Activs; r/Cath; hon/Author of Presentation, Annual SEn Psych Assn, 1983; Hon Roll, 1975-79; Dist, St & Nat Ofc Ed Assn Awds, 1979; Dist & St Distributive Ed Clb of Am Awds, 1978; Kiwanis Awd, 1979; Rotary Clb Awd, 1979; W/ W: Among Am HS Students, Among Students in Am Cols & Univs; Outstg Yg Wom of Am; g/Complete MBA Deg.

CYPERT, JENNY L oc/Marketing Coordinator; b/Jun 17, 1961; h/1217 C East 15, Ada, OK 74820; ba/Ada, OK; p/Bob and Mollyann Cypert, Ardmore, OK; ed/Dipl, Armore HS, 1979; BS Mktg, OK St Univ-Stillwater, 1983; pa/ Mktg Coor, 1st Nat Bk & Trust Co, Ada, OK, 1983-; Ser Rep, SWn Bell Telephone, Stillwater, OK, 1982-83; Teller, 1st Nat Bk, Ardmore, OK, 1979-82; cp/ Ada C of C; Soroptimist Intl; BPW Clb; Pres, Delta Sigma Pi, 1982-83; r/So Bapt; hon/Outstg Mktg Student 1983, Outstg Bus Sr 1983, Outstg Jr 1982, OK St Univ; BPW Yg Careerist, 1983; W/W Among Am Cols & Univs; g/MA Deg in Bus Assn; Become Pres of a Bk.

D

DALE, DAVID MARK oc/Student; b/ Sep 6, 1965; h/Route #1, Box 231, Calhoun, TN 37309; p/Mr and Mrs Donald Dale, Calhoun, TN; ed/Grad, Charleston High, 1983; Att'g, Cleveland St Commun Col; cp/Sch Football, 1979-83; Pres of Sr Class, 1983; Editor of Sch Paper; Annual Staff; Yth for Christ, Treas; Capt, F'ship of Christian Aths; 4-H; Boys' St Del; r/Bapt; hon/ Outstg Teenager of Am, 1982; Soc of Dist'd HS Students; W/W; g/To Maj in Computer Sci and to Become a Sys Analyst; To Attend Univ of TN.

DALMONT, KENT WAYNE oc/Student, Rancher, Loan Assistant; b/Feb 7, 1963; h/Route 1, Box 95, McAlester, OK 74501; p/Mr and Mrs Orville Dalmont, McAlester, OK; ed/Indianola HS, 1981; Student, OK St Univ; pa/Loan Asst, Farmers Home Adm; Rancher; cp/Pres, Indianola FFA; OK Hon Soc; hon/OK St Farmer; W/W Among Am HS Students; Intl Yth in Achmt; Yg Commun Ldrs of Am; g/Mktg, Agri Ec Deg; Minor in Computer Sci.

DALY, KATHLEEN MARIE oc/Student; b/Aug 2, 1962; h/2360 Paddock Lane, Reston, VA 22091; p/Mark and Suzanne Daly, Reston, VA; ed/Grad, Rochester HS, 1980; Student, Univ of GA; pa/Resident Asst, Univ of GA, 1982-83; Univ of GA Orientation Ldr, 1983; cp/HS: Cheerldg, Swimming, Sr Coun, Yrbook, Symph Band, Hon Roll, NHS; Col: Alpha Chi Omega Sorority, Univ Union, Communiversity, Student Recruitment Team, Student Affairs; r/ Cath; hon/Dean's List, 1981; Nat Merit Commended Sr, 1980; Outstg Acad Achmt, 1980; W/W Among HS Students; g/Career w Intl Govt.

DANIEL, CAROLYN CHRISTINE oc/Student; b/Sep 24, 1965; h/Route 1, Box 346, Martin, TN 38237; p/Maj Michael Wayne and Mary Lilly Daniel, Martin, TN; ed/Att'd, Mannheim HS, Germany, 1979-80; Grad, Westview HS, 1983; Student, Univ of TN Martin; cp/Active Participant, Girl Scouts, 8 Yrs; Vol Wkr at Vol Gen Hosp, 1983; r/Bapt; hon/Fannie G and Arthur Hedgecock Awd, 1983; Am Legion S'ship, 1983; US Achmt Acad; g/A Career as a Fashion Designer.

DANSER, TIMOTHY LEE oc/Student; b/Dec 9, 1963; h/Route 13, Box 41, Morgantown, WV 26505; p/Mr and Mrs Leroy E Danser; ed/Univ HS, 1982; WV Univ; cp/Co-Editor, Bus Mgr, *Little Monticola*; Pres, Quill and Scroll; Chm, Univ HS Bd of Pubs; Student Coun; FBLA; Photog Clb; French Clb; Reporter, Bus Mgr, *Golden Hawk*; Advtg Mgr, *Rebel*; Rush Com, Phi Kappa Alpha Frat, Alpha Theta Chapt; hon/Most Outstg Journalist; Esprit Français, French Hon Awd; Mr USA Teen Finalist, 1982; W/ W Among Am HS Student; g/To Open a Chic Clothing Shop.

DARBY, DONNA E oc/Administrative Secretary; b/Jan 22, 1959; h/3400 Custer, #2103, Plano, TX 75023; ba/ Dallas, TX; p/Mr and Mrs Marvin G Darby, Southlake, TX; ed/Carroll HS, 1977; Assoc, Secretarial Sci, Tarrant Co Jr Col, 1980; pa/Adm Secy, Rockwell Intl, 1984-; Secy, Richardson Savs & Ln, 1983-84; Adm Secy, Rockwell Intl, 1981-83; Exec Secy, Alan H Smith Consltg Engrs, 1978-81; Ofc Ed Assn,

1978-80, Histn 1979-80; r/Bapt; hon/ Ofc Ed Assn: 2nd TX St Competition in Word Processing, Adm Secy 1979-80, 3rd TX St Competition and 2nd Nat Competition in Word Processing, Correspondent Secy 1978-79; Outstg Yg Wom of Am.

DARNELL, KRISTEN K oc/Student; b/Aug 25, 1966; h/836 Forest Drive, Cookeville, TN 38501; p/Gary and Sandra Darnell, Cookeville, TN; ed/ Manhattan HS; pa/Waitress, Manhattan Country Clb, 1982-83; Pt-time Help, NWn Mutual Ins, 1980-82; Logo Design, Aggie Transfers, 1981; cp/ Varsity Cheerldr, 1980-84; Freshman Class VP, 1980-81; Sr Student Cong Rep, 1983-84; French Clb, Secy 1982-83; Nat Hon Soc, 1980-84; Beta Clb, 1983-84; AFS, 1981-83; Pep Clb, 1980-84; Track, 1981; r/Meth; hon/ Cookeville Jr Miss, 1983; Local Yth Senate Winner, 1983; Commended Nat Merit, 1983; Gold Key Winner, Scholastic Art Awds, 1980; 6 Class and St Awds in St of KS S'ships; NCA Awd of Excell, 1983; W/W Among Am HS Students; g/To Attend Either the Univ of TN or Vanderbilt Univ; To Study Computer Graphics, Communs.

DASGUPTA, INDRANIL BABU oc/ Student; b/May 24, 1960; h/104 Simca Lane, Wilmington, DE 19805; p/Dr and Mrs S P Dasgupta, Wilmington, DE; ed/ Grad, Alexis I duPont Sch, 1978; BA, Phil, Duke Univ, 1982; pa/Rschr, Alzheimer's Disease for US House Subcom on Hlth and Long Term Care, 1983; Burn Ctr Vol, Univ of NC, 1982; Hosp Vol, 1978-82; Wk'd w Muscular Dystrophy Chd, 1981; cp/Pre-Med Soc, 1977; Sigma Alpha Epsilon; ASDU (Duke Student Govt) Rep, 1979; ASDU Jud Bd, 1980; Varsity Soccer Clb, 1978; HS Phi Beta Kappa; r/Meth; hon/HS Class Valedictorian, 1978; Congl Intern for US Senator Claude Pepper, 1983; Peter Jefferson Meml Awd, 1978; Boys' St, DE, 1977; Rep, HS, in Phil Sci Fair, 1977; W/W Among Am HS Students; g/MD/MBA w Ambitions of Serving in Rural Area Hosps in US and Improve Med Care in Area.

DASHNER, BRENDA JANE oc/Student; b/Sep 28, 1966; h/1020 Trinidad Avenue, Ft Pierce, FL 33450; p/Gerald and Patricia Dashner, Ft Pierce, FL; ed/ Grad, Ft Pierce Ctl HS, 1984; cp/HS Keyette Clb, 1981-84; HS Swimming, Nat Hon Soc, 1982-84; Jr Class Pres, Girl Scouts USA, 1973-78, 1980-84; Pres, Sr Girl Scouts Assn, 1983, 1984; Swim Team Capt, 1983, 1984; Nat Hon Soc, Secy 1983-84; r/Cath; hon/Star Student for Ft Pierce Ctl HS, 1983; Mem, Am Legion Aux, FL Girls' St, 1983; Pt St Lucie News Scholar-Ath, 1983; W/W Among Am HS Students; g/Study Nsg at Univ of FL; Career as Surg Nurse.

DAUBENSPECK, ANDREW DEAN oc/Student; b/Apr 23, 1963; h/8630 West 46th Avenue, Wheat Ridge, CO 80033; p/Mr and Mrs Forest C Daubenspeck, Wheat Ridge, CO; ed/Grad, Wheat Ridge Sr HS, 1981; Student, Univ of CO, 1981-; pa/Crew Person, McDonald's of Wheat Ridge, 1978-; cp/ Vineyard Christian F'ship; Atari Clb; AF ROTC, Cadet; Var Activision Clbs; Nat Hon Soc; Calvary Temple; Capt, Coach, Pres, Volleyball Team; Pres, Ch Yth Grp; Coach, McDonald's Softball Team;

hon/AF ROTC S'ship; Top 6 Percent of Grad'g Class; Commun Ldrs of Am; Intl Yth in Achmt; Personalities of Am; W/ W Among Am HS Students; g/Elect Engrg Deg; Comm in USAF as 2nd Lt.

DAUGHERTY, KARLA KAY oc/ Claims Analyst; h/106-A Pecan Valley, Granburg, TX 76048; ba/Dallas, TX; p/ Bill R and Martha Daugherty, Granbury, TX; ed/Grad, Haltom HS, 1977; BBA, N TX St Univ, 1982; pa/Claims Analyst, Southland Life Ins Co; TX St Tchrs Assn; NEA; Nat Bus Ed Assn; TX Real Est Comm; cp/Student Ed Assn; Pi Omega Pi, Pres 1981-83, VP 1982; Chi Omega Frat, Pledge Class Secy 1980, Chapt Correspondent 1981, Song Ldr 1982, 1st Place in Greek Sing Song 1982, Chapt Photog; r/Bapt; hon/Beta Gamma Sigma, 1982; Order of Omega; No TX St Perfect GPA Hon Roll, 1981; NTSU Dean's List, 1978, 1979, 1980, 1981; Pi Omega Pi; Alpha Lambda Delta; Phi Eta Sigma; W/W Among Am HS Students; W/W Among Am Cols and Univs; Nat Dean's List; g/Advance in the Ins Bus.

DAVIDSON, LINK MITCHEL oc/ Student; b/Jan 22, 1962; h/1235 Euclid Circle, Portland, TX 78374; p/Mike T and Joyce K Davidson, Portland, TX; ed/ AA, summa cum laude, Del Mar Col, 1982; pa/Activs of Daily Living Tech, Ada Wilson Hosp of Phy Med and Rehab; Tutor of Geog and Spanish, Del Mar Col; cp/Phi Theta Kappa Alumni Assn, Epsilon of TX Chapt; Mensa; People-Animal Wel Soc; Edgar Allan Poe Soc; r/Luth; hon/Outstg Student, Biol Dept; Outstg Student, Eng Dept; Outstg Student, Geog Dept; Phi Theta Kappa, 1982; Exxon Co USA S'ship; Hall of Fame, Del Mar Col, 1981-82; C J Davidson Foun, 2-Yr S'ship; Epsilon of TX Phi Theta Kappa Alumni Assn; Nat Dean's List, 1980-81, 1981-82; Dean's Hon Roll; W/W Among Am Jr Col Students.

DAVIS, CHRISTINA KAYE oc/Singer; b/Nov 21, 1959; h/PO Box 399, Newport, TN 37821; ba/Same; p/Mr and Mrs Robert K Davis, Newport, TN; ed/ Grad, Cosby HS, 1977; BA in Music Ed, BA in Applied Voice, Berea Col, 1982; pa/Singer, Reach Out Singers, Outreach for Christ Intl, 1983; Music Dir, A Christian Min in the Nat Pks, Flaming Gorge, UT, 1982; Music Dir, ACMNP, Yellowstone Pk, WY, 1980; cp/Col: Mortar Bd Hon Soc, Col Choir (Sr Pres), Chamber Singers, Harmonia Soc, New Life (Weekend Concerts), Mt Spirit Bd (Weekend Concerts), Country Dancers (Weekend and Extended Trips); r/ Christian; hon/Salutatorian, HS, 1977; Red Foley Music Awd, New Life, 1980; g/Studio Musician, Profl Singer.

DAVIS, CINDY KAY oc/Student; b/ Jun 13, 1966; h/Route 1, Box 23, Minor Hill, TN 38473; p/Mr and Mrs Alton Davis, Minor Hill, TN; ed/Giles Co HS; cp/French Clb, 1980; TN Ofc Ed Clb, VP 1983; Student Coun Rep, 1983-84; Sub-Deb, Reporter, VP, Pres, 1981-84; r/Ch of Christ; hon/Fairest of the Fair, Giles Co, 1983; Hon Roll; W/W Among Am HS Students; g/To Attend Col and Study Psych.

DAVIS, DANNY L oc/Student; b/Jul 22, 1966; h/8513 Southwest 76th, Oklahoma City, OK 73169; p/Danny and Mary Davis, Oklahoma City, OK; ed/Grad, Mustang HS; cp/Football; Nat

Hon Soc; Baseball (All Co Team as Jr); OK Hon Soc; hon/Att'd Boys' St, 1983; Att'd AF Acad's Sum Sci Sem, 1983; W/W Among Am HS Students; g/To Pursue a Career in Aeronautics at AF Acad.

DAVIS, DUANE MYRON oc/Student; b/Nov 9, 1964; h/2101 Rupp Street, Baltimore, MD 21217; p/Leroy Davis, Calverton Heights, MD; Saundra Davis, Baltimore, MD; ed/Loyola Sr High, 1982; Student, Franklin & Marshall Col; pa/Mktg and Sales Rep, Am Future Sys; Mktg and Sales Mgr, Seal-O-Matic; cp/BSU of Loyola High, 1980-82 (VP); BSU of Franklin & Marshall Col, 1982-83; Student Govt of Loyola High, 1981 (Class Pres); Varsity Basketball for Loyola High, 1979-82 (Capt); Varsity Basketball for Franklin & Marshall Col, 1982-83; Wkr, Local Soup Kitchen for Underpriveledged; hon/Headmaster's Medal Winner for Contbns to BSU, 1982; MVP of Basketball Team, 1982; W/W Among Am HS Students; Yg Commun Ldrs of Am; g/Maj in Ec.

DAVIS, JAMES J oc/Student; b/Nov 25, 1960; h/11610 Willis Drive, Savannah, GA 31419; p/Earl B and Gracie P Davis, Savannah, GA; ed/Savannah Christian HS, 1979; Grad, GA So Col, 1984; cp/Charter Mem of Key Clb, 1979; Kappa Alpha Order, Histn; Kappa Alpha, 1981-83; Punter on GA So Col First Football Team, 1982; Football and Track in HS; r/Bapt; g/To Obtain GA Real Est Lic; To Work in the Area of Bkg, Investmts, or Real Est.

DAVIS, ROBIN RAY oc/Student; b/Feb 1, 1965; h/Route 3, Box 266, Benson, NC 27504; p/Mr and Mrs Ralph B Byrd, Benson, NC; ed/Grad, S Johnston HS, 1983; Student, Univ of NC Chapel Hill, 1983-; pa/HS Bus Driver, Johnston Co Schs, 1981-83; cp/Nat Hon Soc, 1980-83; French Clb, Sgt-at-Arms 1980-83; Sci Clb, 1981-83; Fine Arts Clb, 1979-83; Bus Drivers Clb, 1981-83; S Johnston Chorus, 1979-83; S Johnston Small Ensemble, 1979-83; Acad Superbowl Team, Team Capt 1982-83; r/Christianity; hon/Commencement Marshal, 1982; Outstg Underclassman Awd in French; Outstg Underclassman Awd in Chorus, 1982; Prom Waiter, 1981; Won Johnston Co Acad Superbowl Championship, 1983; Morehead S'ship Nom, 1983; Sch Winner, Century Ldrs Prog, 1983; Att'd, Gov's Sch of NC, 1981; Outstg Sr Awd in Eng, Outstg Sr Awd in Chorus, Outstg Sr Awd in Acad Superbowl, 1983; Banner Post 109 Am Legion S'ship Recip, 1983; Class Salutatorian; W/W Among Am HS Students; Commun Ldrs of Am; g/Pharm Maj at Univ of NC Chapel Hill.

DAVIS, SHERRY A oc/Emergency Medical Technician Secretary and Bookkeeper; b/Nov 7, 1959; h/Route #3, Box 890H8, Birmingham, AL 35214; ba/Birmingham, AL; m/Jeffrey W; p/Mr and Mrs Oscar Tidwell, Nauvoo, AL; ed/Grad, Carbon Hill HS, 1978; Att'd, Walker Col 1978-79, Walker St Tech Col 1980 (Emer Med Tech Basic Level I); BS in Psych, BS in Crim Justice, Univ of AL B'ham, 1982; pa/Secy/Bkkpr, Suburban Ambulance Ser, 1980-; Interviewer Over Telephone Concerning Personal Assets, So Res Interviewing, 1979; Vol, Jasper, AL, Mtl Hlth Ctr, 1979; Cashier, Nauvoo Trade Ctr,

1975-80; cp/Anthropology Clb, 1979; Stars and Bars Yrbook Staff, 1979; Maurice W Commun Ctr, 1980; Intl Figure Salon, 1983; r/Primitive Bapt; hon/Nearly New Foun S'ship, 1979; g/PhD in Clin Psych.

DAVIS, SHERRY LYNN oc/College Student; b/Mar 13, 1965; h/RFD #1, Rutherford, TN 38369; ba/Rutherford, TN; p/Gerald D and Linda B Davis, Rutherford, TN; ed/Gen Deg, BHS, 1983; Wk'g on BS in Natural Resource Mgmt, Univ of TN Martin; cp/4-H Clb Mem, 1975-79; Beta Clb Mem, 1980; Beta Clb Treas, 1981; Beta Clb Secy, 1982; FHA Mem, 1980; FHA Chaplain, 1981; FHA Pres, 1982; FHA Sub-Reg VP, 1982; r/Meth; hon/DAR Good Citizen, 1983; Hon Student, 1980-83; Dist'd Am HS Students; W/W Among Am HS Students.

DAVIS, SUE ELLEN oc/Student; b/Nov 7, 1964; h/1564 Willshire Drive, Colorado Springs, CO 80906; ba/Dodge City, KS; p/Carole A Davis, Colorado Springs, CO; ed/HS Dipl, 1983; cp/Nat Hon Soc, Parliamentarian 1982-83; Intl Relats Clb, VP 1982-83; Interact, Pres 1982-83; Social Sers Com; Drill Team; hon/Hon Card, 1983; Hewlett-Packard S'ship, 1983; Foley Nsg S'ship, 1983; Acad S'ship, St Mary of the Plains Col, 1983; g/BS in Nsg.

DAWSON, JOHN DAVID III oc/Student; b/Mar 22, 1964; h/Route 2, Box 180, Supply, NC 28462; p/Mr and Mrs John David Dawson Jr, Supply, NC; ed/W Brunswick HS, 1982; Student, Biol, Univ of NC Wilmington; cp/Band; Chorus; Sci Clb; NHS; Hlth Occups Students of Am; Student Coun; Yth Coun; Hosp Vol; Meth Ch Yth Mem on Adm Bd; NC Gov's Sch Nom; hon/Gov's Yth Vol Awd, 1982; Dean's List, Univ of NC Wilmington, 1982-83; Yth Awd Nom; Outstg Ser Awd; Marshal, HS Grad Exercises; g/Phys.

DAY, JENNIFER ANN oc/Teacher; b/Dec 30, 1957; h/127 Arlington Avenue, Providence, RI 02906; p/Mr and Mrs Frank J Day; ed/St Patrick HS, 1976; BS, RI Col, 1980; Fairfield Univ; pa/Tchr; cp/Christian Encounter Team; Basketball Team; Vol Tchr Aide; Col Softball Team; Math Clb; Student Union Bd of Dirs; Yrbook; hon/Grad, cum laude; Hon in Student Tchg; Emin Ldrship Awd; RI St Scholar; RI Hon Soc; Intl Fdn of Cath Alumnae Awd; Intl Yth in Achmt; W/W Among Students in Am Cols and Univs; g/Devel and Implement Pre-Sch Prog.

DAY, KATHLEEN M oc/Student; b/Feb 10, 1964; h/1614 Baltimore Drive, Richardson, TX 75081; p/George and Mary Day, Richardson, TX; ed/Grad, Berkner HS, 1982; Student, Univ of Dallas; pa/Adm Asst, Shamrock Rltrs, 1983; cp/Secy, Whiz Quiz Team; Mu Alpha Theta; VP, Univ of Dallas Pre-Law Clb; UIL Mock Trial Team; Latin Clb; Spanish Clb; Keywanettes; Intramural Football Team; hon/Pubs, "Everson Walls: Rams to Riches" 1981, "Christ, Chapin Live" 1983; Nat Merit Commended Student; Finalist, Dallas/Ft Worth Notre Dame Alumni Clb Jr of the Yr Awd; Winner, TX Scholar S'ship, Univ of Dallas; HS Hon Grad, Hon Roll; g/Law Deg; Enter Pvt Pract w Specialty in First Amendment Law.

DAY, TAMMY ADELLA oc/Part-time Promotional Girl, Student; b/

Jun 15, 1963; h/Route #1, Old Fort, TN; ba/Cleveland, TN; p/Rev and Mrs Hoyt Day, Old Fort, TN; ed/Dipl, Polk Co HS, 1981; Gen Bus Deg, Cleveland St Commun Col, 1983; pa/Promotional Girl, Johnston Coca-Cola Co, 1982-83; cp/Phi Beta Lambda, Pres 1982-83; Phi Theta Kappa, 1982-83; Bat Girl for Cleveland St Baseball Team, 1983; r/Bapt Denomination; hon/Listed on Dean's List Every Quarter Attended at Cleveland St, 1981-83; Cleveland St Homecoming Queen, 1983; Salutatorian of Grad'g Class, 1981; Soc of Dist'd Am HS Students; W/W Among Am Jr Cols; Am Biogl Inst.

DAYHOFF, WILLIAM EUGENE oc/Student; h/902 South Florence, Claremore, OK 74017; p/Bill and Thecia Dayhoff; ed/Grad, HS, 1984; pa/Lifeguard, Elks Lodge; Projectionist, Martin Theatre's; Delivery Pers, Smith Furniture; Stock Pers, Hobo Discount Foods; cp/Tres, Sci Clb; Math Clb; Pres, Engrg Clb; r/Bapt; hon/W/W Among Am HS Students; Eagle Scout, 1984; g/Computer Engrg at OK St Univ.

DEALY, JOSEPH BRUNO oc/Student; b/Oct 31, 1961; h/Route 2, Box 2321, La Grande, OR 97850; p/J Edward and June S Dealy, La Grande, OR; ed/La Grande HS, 1980; OR St Univ; cp/Phi Eta Sigma, 1981; Alpha Lambda Delta, 1981; Phi Kappa Phi Hon Soc, 1983; Thespians; German Clb; Earth Sci Clb; Student Coun Sophomore Class Rep; Assoc Student Body Public Relats Ofcr; Presb Yth F'ship; Intramural Sports; hon/Hon S'ship; Nat Merit Finalist; Acad Hon Roll; W/W Among Am HS Students; Am's Outstg Names and Faces; Intl Yth in Achmt; g/Sec'dy Math/Computer Sci Tchr.

DEAN, JAMES JOSEPH oc/Student; b/Mar 3, 1963; h/4910 Dean Street, Ft Myers, FL 33905; p/Mr and Mrs William A Dean, Ft Myers, FL; ed/Riverdale HS, 1981; At'g, Univ of S FL; cp/HS Student Coun Rep, 3 Yrs; HS Spanish Clb, 1 Yr; Mu Alpha Theta, 2 Yrs; Del, FL Am Legion Boys St; Track Team, 3 Yrs; Cross Country, 3 Yrs, Capt for 2 Yrs; Univ Ctr Activs Bd; Bapt Campus Min, Pres 1984; Pre-Law Soc, 1981-84, Chm of Lecture Com; hon/Valedictorian; Sophomore Class Pres; Jr and Sr Class Treas; VP, Pres, Nat Hon Soc; Wash Intern, Congressman L A Bafalis; Edison Commun Col Sum Scholar Awd; Outstg Lang Arts, Math and Fgn Lang Student; Outstg Am Lit and Social Studies Student; Outstg Eng and Social Studies Student; DAR Good Citizen Awd; Am Legion Sch Medal Awd; Ft Myers Metro C of C Superior Student Awd; Pres's Endowed S'ship; Hons at Entrance, Univ of S FL; Omicron Delta Kappa, 1983; Phi Kappa Phi, 1983; Nat Dean's List, 1982, 1983; Dean's List, 1981-84; Personalities of S; g/Deg in Polit Sci and Ec; Law Sch; Law Pract or Polit Career.

DEANES, ANTHONEY SULLIVAN oc/Student; b/Dec 14, 1966; h/Route 1, Box 199, Cedar Bluff, MS 39741; ba/Same; p/Mrs Willie Jean Deanes, Cedar Bluff, MS; ed/W Clay Co HS; cp/Student Govt Treas, 1982-83; Jr Class Pres, 1982-83; FFA Secy, W Clay High, 1982-83; Bus Mgr for W Clay Yrbook, 1982-83; Boy Scout, 1979; 4-H Mem; Palo Alto Choir Treas; Jr Class Prom Com; r/Palo Alto MB Ch and Choir;

Bapt; hon/US Student Coun Awds, 1982-83; W/W Among Am HS Students; g/To Obtain Doct Deg in Gen Physics.

DeCICCO, DANIEL JOSEPH oc/Student; b/Jun 17, 1965; h/12505 Caswell Lane, Bowie, MD 20715; ba/Atlanta, GA; p/Mr and Mrs B T DeCicco, Bowie, MD; ed/Grad, Eleanor Roosevelt Sci and Technol Ctr, Eleanor Roosevelt HS, 1983; Student, GA Inst of Technol; cp/HS Soccer, 1978-82, Varsity Capt 1982; HS Wrestling, 1978-83, Varsity Capt 1983; Student Govt Rep, 1978-83; Drama Clb Tech Crew, 1982; r/Rom Cath; Altar Boy, 1974-83; Master of Ceremonies (High Mass), 1978-83; hon/Johns Hopkins Mathematically Precocious Yth, 1978; HS Soccer MVP, 1983; Nat Merit S'ship Quarterfinalist, 1982; Martin-Marietta Full Tuition S'ship, GA Inst of Technol, 1983; Intl Yth in Achmt; g/To Earn a Bach's Deg in Elect Engrg from GA Inst of Technol.

DEDEAUX, VALENTINE M oc/Student; b/Sep 3, 1966; h/203 Swanson Avenue, Pass Christian, MS 39571; p/Mr and Mrs Marcus A Dedeaux, Pass Christian, MS; ed/HS; pa/Nat Beta Clb; French Clb, Treas; Drama Clb, VP; Sci Clb; Student Coun; Yrbook Staff; Slam Clb; Beautification Soc; Quiz Bowl Homecoming Com; CYO; r/Cath; hon/Perfect GPA, 10th-12th Grades; Superior Underclassman Achmt Awd; Spec Hon Student; French I Awd; Eng IV Awd; VFW Voice of Dem; Biol Awd; Jr Class Pres; Homecoming Ct Princess; Sophomore Class Favorite; Supt's Hon Roll; Homeroom Pres, VP, Secy-Treas; Miss Teen of MS Titleholder; Soc of Dist'd Am HS Students; W/W Among Am HS Students; US Achmt Acad Nat Awds Yrbook; g/Maj in Acctg; Law Deg.

DEIS, CARROLL LOUISE oc/Office Manager; b/Apr 28, 1958; h/45 South Wyoming Avenue, Ardmore, PA 19003; p/Mr and Mrs Howard Deis Jr, Hazleton, PA; ed/Hazleton HS; AS, Harcum Jr Col; BS, W Chester St Col; pa/Ofc Mgr, Dr Landman; Pt-time Sci Instr, Harcum Jr Col; Cert'd Dental Asst; cp/Harcum Sch Day Student Pres; SGA; Dental Adv Bd, Jr Col; hon/Grad, cum laude; Dean's List; Dist'd Yg Am; Intl Yth in Achmt.

DE LA NOY, LAWRENCE THOMAS oc/Student; b/Mar 26, 1965; h/4845 East Fairmount, Phoenix, AZ 85018; p/Judy De La Noy, Phoenix, AZ; ed/Wn HS; Student, Deury Sch of Technol; pa/Pt-time in Testing Microchips, Intel; r/Cath; hon/Letter in Chess; g/Electronics Tech.

del CANTO, NATALIA HAMATI oc/Student; b/Mar 11, 1966; h/2703 Atlanta Drive, Silver Spring, MD 20906; ed/Student, Stone Ridge Country Day Sch of the Sacred Heart; cp/Mem, "It's Academic," 1981-83; Swimming Team, 1983; Student Commun Governance; r/Rom Cath; hon/1st Place at MD Music Tchrs Assn Piano Competition, 1974; Hon Student, Stone Ridge; g/To Attend Col and Study Music/Intl Law; To Become a Lawyer or a Translator, Concert Pianist.

DELGADILLO, JOSE BALTAZAR oc/Student; b/Jul 11, 1962; h/1106 Wisconsin Street, Muscatine, IA 52761; ba/Same; p/Mr and Mrs Baltazar Delgadillo, Muscatine, IA; ed/Student,

Muscatine HS; AA, Muscatine Commun Col, 1983; pa/Gen Maintenance Sum Job, 1978; Clerical/Receptionist Job, 1979; Leadman Position, Packer Sanitation Sers, 1980; Employee, IA E Ctl TRAIN, an Abstract Co, 1978, 1979; Salesman, Payless Shoe Source, 1982; cp/Fdr, Hispanic Student Assn, 1981; Host and Prodr, "Notas Musicales," a Locally Produced Cablevision Show; r/Cath; g/Job w an Ins Co.

DELLINGER, DREW ERIC oc/Student; Business Consultant; b/Jul 13, 1960; h/909 College Drive, Milton, FL 32570; p/Dean Wesley Sr and Dorothy Detter Dellinger, Milton, FL; ed/Milton HS, 1978; AA, Pensacola Jr Col, 1980; BS 1982, MBA 1984, Univ of W FL; cp/Am Mktg Assn; Univ of W FL Mktg and Ec Student Soc Pub Dir; Adm Bd, PJC SGA; Milton HS Sr Class Pres; r/Milton First U Meth Ch Assoc Lay Ldr; Asst SS Supt; Fin Com, Pastor-Parish Relats Com; hon/Pub'd in Best-Loved Contemporary Poems, 1979; Phi Kappa Phi Hon Frat, 1982; Univ of W FL Bus Col MBA F'ship, 1982; Univ of W FL Foun Fac Merit S'ship; Dean's List; PJC Ldrship Awd; Pres's List; Foun S'ship; Best Salesman Student, 1980; Commun Ldrs of Am; Intl Yth in Achmt; Nat Dean's List; W/W Am Jr Cols; W/W Am Univs and Cols; g/To Be Hired as VP, Gen Mgr of Canvas Ctr Unltd; Wk w Advtg Agy, St and Local Govt; Col or Univ Instr.

DEL VILLAR, GEORGE oc/Medical Student; b/Oct 11, 1955; h/28 Dekalb Avenue, White Plains, NY 10605; p/Andres and Fortunata Del Villar, White Plains, NY; ed/White Plains HS, 1974; AA, Biol, FL Keys Commun Col, 1980; BA, Biol, Southampton Col, 1982; cp/Corps of Engrs Res Proj; FL Dept of Natural Resources Spiny Lobster Res Proj; Southampton Hosp Emer Room Vol; hon/Talent Roster, 1979-80; Study Awd, 1980-81; Commun Ldr Awd, 1982; Intl Yth in Achmt Awd, 1981; W/W Among Students in Am Jr Cols; g/Dr.

DE MINE, ROBERT MARTIN JR oc/Student; b/Sep 6, 1961; h/283 North Highway 54, Jonesboro, GA 30236; ba/Dahlonega, GA; p/Mr and Mrs Robert M De Mine Sr, Jonesboro, GA; ed/Grad, Jonesboro Sr High, 1979; Student, Mgmt, N GA Col; mil/USAR, Br Combat Engrs; cp/AF JROTC, 3 Yrs, Grp Cmdr 1979; Army ROTC, N GA Col, 4 Yrs; r/Bapt; hon/Comm'd, USAR/EN, 1983; g/BBA in Mgmt; Serve in USAR.

DENEKA, DAVID ALAN oc/Student; b/Aug 1, 1965; h/4704 Cedar Rose Drive, Millington, TN 38053; ba/Millington, TN; p/Mr and Mrs Harry Deneka, Millington, TN; ed/Grad, Rosemark Acad, 1983; pa/Asst Mgr, Fred's of Millington, 1981-83; cp/Beta Clb; R-Clb; Pep Clb; Nat Hon Soc; Baseball Team; Basketball Team; r/Bapt; hon/Valedictorian, 1983; W/W; g/Pre-Med.

DENNIS, LEAH DIANE oc/Student; b/May 29, 1966; h/401 North Star Drive, Route 4, Hernando, MS 38632; p/Mr and Mrs Joe Dennis, Hernando, MS; ed/HS Student; cp/Nat Hon Soc; Quill and Scroll; Eudora First Responders; r/First Bapt Ch, Adult Choir; g/Maj in Acctg at a Col in MS.

DENT, JANEECE LICHTE oc/Student, Law Clerk; b/Oct 9, 1960; h/Rural

Route 2, Box 92, Lexington, MO 64067; m/C Russell; p/Forrest and Gladys Lichte, Lexington, MO; ed/Lexington HS, 1979; BS in Bus Adm, Ctl MO St Univ, 1982; JD, Univ of MO KC Sch of Law, 1985; pa/Law Clk, Carl E Laurent, PC, 1983-; Phonathon Participant, Ctl MO St Univ, 1982; Ad Salesperson, Ctl MO St Univ Muleskinner, 1980-81; Secy, Aull, Sherman & Worthington Law Firm, 1978-81; cp/KC Civic Orch, Violinist 1982-; Univ of MO KC Law Review, 1983-; Staff Mem, The Urban Lawyer, 1983-; Nat and MO St Assn of Parliamentarians, 1980-; Am Bar Assn; Christian Legal Soc; MO Assn of Trial Attys; r/U Ch of Christ Gen Synod, Asst Moderator 1983-85; hon/Charno Awd for Outstg Female Grad, Ctl MO St Univ, 1982; Grad, summa cum laude, 1982; Ranked 6th in 151 after 1st Yr in Law Sch; Phi Kappa Phi Hon Soc; Commun Ldrs of Am; Intl Yth in Achmt; W/W Am Cols and Univs; Nat Dean's List; g/Lwyr.

DENTON, JOHN ANTHONY oc/Student; b/Jan 10, 1965; h/4707 Crockett, Midland, TX 79703; p/John and Joanne Denton, Midland, TX; ed/Grad, Robert E Lee HS, 1983; cp/Nat Hon Soc; Indust Arts Clb; JETS; Key Clb; Student Coun Rep; Yg Life; Football (Lettered 2 Yrs); Baseball (Lettered 2 Yrs); Football Capt, 1983; All Dist Football, 1983; Nat Hon Soc Sweetheart, 1983; Jr Lion of the Wk; r/St Stephens Cath Ch; hon/DAR Good Citizen Awd, 1983; W/W Among Am HS Students; g/Mech or Petro Engrg.

DeSONIER, ROANNE KAY oc/Registered Nurse; b/Aug 14, 1958; h/8512 Bellingham, Dallas, TX; p/Mr and Mrs William Allen Riley; ed/Big Sprg HS; BS, Baylor Univ; pa/RN; Am Assn of Critical Care Nurses; cp/Chi's Wom Ser Clb; Alpha Tau Delta; Baylor Nsg Hon Soc; Inreach Dir, YMI; Treas, Sci Clb, Bible Clb; Outstg Choir Mem; BSU Freshman Coun; Basic Tng Bible Study Ldr; Dallas Geol and Geophy Aux.

D'ESPOSITO, LOUIS V J oc/Student; b/Feb 13, 1960; h/57 Storer Avenue, Pelham, NY 10803; ba/Potsdam, NY; p/Francis and Yolanda D'Esposito, Pelham, NY; ed/Pelham Meml HS; AS, Westchester Commun Col, 1981; BS, Clarkson Col, 1982; cp/Vol Town Fireperson; Vol Police Asst; Repub Com; St Joseph's Funding Com Coach; Pelham Little Leag Baseball; Dean's Adv Coun, Clarkson Col; Soc for the Advmt of Mgmt; Delta Chi Delta; Alpha Beta Gamma; Dean's List; Drucker Soc; hon/Clarkson Col Trustee S'ship; g/To Become Chief Exec Ofcr of Own Corp and to Bring It to Level of Fin Activ Consistent w Mbrship on NY Stock Exch.

DETHERAGE, CHERYL KAY oc/Student; b/Mar 11, 1966; h/PO Box 516, Barbourville, KY 40906; p/Joe and Clara Detherage, Barbourville, KY; ed/HS Grad; cp/Lib Clb, VP 1980; Spanish Clb, 1980-83; Beta Clb, 1983-84; r/So Bapt; hon/Homecoming Freshman Princess, 1980; Homecoming Queen, 1984; KY Homecoming Queen St Finalist, 1984; g/Maj in Psych; To Become an Airline Stewardess and Psychol.

DEVERS, CASH LESTER oc/Student; b/Mar 31, 1963; h/18 North Cherokee, Pryor, OK 74361; p/Nelson and Deloris Devers, Pryor, OK; ed/

Grad, Pryor HS, 1981; Assocs Deg, Rogers St Col, 1983; Currently Enrolled, NEn St Univ; mil/Airman 1st Class, Air NG (Security Spec); hon/ Nom'd for Boys' St, 1980; Cadet, Lawman Acad (Sponsored by Elks and OK Hwy Patrol), 1980; Awd'd Acad S'ship, Rogers St Col, 1981, 1982; W/ W Am Jr Cols; g/Tchr.

DeVORE, JULIA CAROLINE oc/ Student; b/Jun 4, 1965; h/712 Logan Court, Greenwood, SC 29646; ba/ Greenwood, SC; p/Mr and Mrs William N DeVore, Greenwood, SC; ed/Hon Grad, Greenwood HS, 1983; Enrolled at Lander Col; pa/Student Asst, Greenwood/Abbeville Reg Co Lib, 1981-83; Student Asst, Lander Col Admissions Ofc, 1983-; cp/Beta Clb, 1977-79; Nat Hon Soc, 1980-83; Oasis, 1979-80; Varsity Basketball Cheerldr, 1979-80; Annual Staff Reporter, 1977-79; r/ Presb; Yth Choir; hon/Outstg Freshman for Wk in Eng and Sci; 2nd Runner-Up, Jr Miss Greenwood, 1982; Lander Col Acad S'ship Winner, 1983; W/W Among Am HS Students; g/Maj in Computer Sci at Lander Col; Maj in Computer Engrg at Clemson Univ.

DeVRIES, LAURA H oc/Student; b/ Aug 14, 1966; h/215 Country Club Boulevard, Battle Creek, MI 49015; p/ Robert and Eleanor DeVries, Battle Creek, MI; ed/HS Student; cp/Vol, Battle Creek Art Ctr Sum Camp, 1983; Vol, Battle Creek Y-Ctr Day Camp, 1983; Lakeview HS Girls Swim Team, 1980-; MI Luth Yth Org Dist Rep, 1982-; Lakeview HS Fish Clb, 1980-; Lakeview HS Aqua Sprites, 1982-; Yth Gives Vol, 1983; Lakeview HS Yrbook Staff, 1982-; Lakeview HS Marching Band, 1981; r/St Peter Luth Ch Yth Grp, 1980- (Secy); hon/Lakeview HS Aqua Sprites Swim Bd, 1983; Lakeview HS Girls Swim Team Varsity Awd, 1980, 1981, 1982; Soc of Dist'd Am HS Students, 1983-; g/Study to Be a Lower Elem or Pre-Sch Tchr.

DeVRIES, ROBERT S oc/Student; b/ May 24, 1962; h/215 Country Club Boulevard, Battle Creek, MI 49015; p/ Robert A and Eleanor R DeVries, Battle Creek, MI; ed/Dipl, Lakeview Sr HS, 1980; BA, Albion Col, 1984; pa/Adm Intern, Pennock Hosp, 1982; Res/Eval Analyst, Starr Commonwealth Schs, 1982; Adm Intern, MI Hosp Assn, 1983; cp/Delta Tau Delta Frat, Pres; Omicron Delta Epsilon, Ec Hon, VP; F'ship of Christian Aths, VP; Big Brothers, Big Sisters; Ec/Acctg Tutor; Luth Student F'ship; Albion Col Concert Band, Marching Band, Brass Choir, Orch, Wind Symph; Detroit Free Press Intl Marathon Finisher; r/Luth; hon/Webster Merit S'ship, 1980; Mortar Bd, 1983; Dean's List, 1982; Dist'd Am HS Students; g/Attend Grad Sch in Hosp Adm.

DEWALD, HOWARD DEAN oc/ Graduate Student; b/Aug 11, 1958; h/ 915 South Mesquite Street, #13, Las Cruces, NM 88001; p/Mr and Mrs Derold Dewald, Casper, WY; ed/ Natrona Co HS, 1976; BS, Chem, Univ of WY, 1980; Presently Enrolled in Doct Prog, Electroanalytical Chem, NM St Univ; cp/Key Clb, 1975-76; Circle K Intl, 1976-82, Rocky Mtn Dist Gov 1978-79, Intl VP 1979-80; Kiwanis Intl, Kiwanis Clb of Mesilla Val, 1982-, Pres-Elect 1982-83, Pres 1983-84; Am Chem Soc, 1981-; hon/Pubs, "Potential Scanning

Voltammetric Detection for Flow Injection Systems" 1983, "Deposition of Metals at a Flow-Through Reticulated Vitreous Carbon Electrode with On-Line Monitoring of the Effluent" 1982, "Dual Coulometric-Voltammetric Cells for On-Line Stripping Analysis" 1983, "Anodic Stripping Voltammetry of Heavy Metals with a Flow Injection System" 1983, Others; Pres's Awd, Circle K Intl, 1980; Outstg Tchg Asst, NM St Univ Dept of Chem, 1982; W/ W Among HS Student; Outstg Yg Men of Am; g/Postdoct Wk; A Career in Acads or Res.

DeWALT, DERRICK W oc/Student; b/Aug 6, 1961; h/2817 Bancroft Street, Charlotte, NC 28213; p/Ms Barbara DeWalt, Charlotte, NC; ed/Grad, Independence HS, 1979; Att'd, Morristown Jr Col, 1979-80; Att'g, Lawrence Univ, 1981-; cp/HS: NAACP, Psych Clb, Treas of Monogram Clb, Order of the Patriot; Jr Col: Dorm Adv Coun; Univ: Spec Events Com, Pres of Black Org of Students, Co-Fdr of Lawrence's First Male Cheerldg Squad; hon/Varsity Letter, Dist Championship Team, 1977, 1978, 1979; Most Valuable Player as Varsity Basketball Capt, 1978; All-Conf Hons, 1978; Mt Carmell Bapt Ch Yth Ser Awd, 1979; Most Friendliest Person at Sch, 1979; Inducted into Order of the Patriot, 1979; Earned Letter in Varsity Basketball, 1980; Recip, 2 Named S'ships, Rev Irving H Carpenter Meml S'ship, Sadie D Cornelius Endowed S'ship Fund, 1980; 2nd Runner-Up in Mr Morristown Pageant, 1980; Earned Letter in Varsity Basketball, 1981, 1982; Recip, Class of 1969 Book Awd, 1982, 1983; Harriet S Tubman Awd, 1982; Arthur C Denny Meml S'ship, 1982, 1983; Pres's Prize, 1983; Most Inspirational Player, 1983; g/To Break into Sports Journalism by Way of Writing, Broadcasting, Reporting or Scouting; Master's Deg in Am Studies or Ednl Psych at Peabody Col of Vanderbilt.

DIAMOND, JOHN N oc/Assistant Majority Leader; b/Nov 12, 1954; h/ 18600 Broadway, Bangor, ME 04401; ba/Augusta, ME; m/Elizabeth; p/Mr and Mrs N J Diamond, Bangor, ME; ed/ Bangor HS, 1973; BA, Univ of ME, 1977; pa/Asst Majority Ldr, ME Ho of Reps, 1982-; St Rep, 1980-; Reporter, *Lewiston Daily Sun*, 197-78; Reporter, ME Public Broadcasting, 1976-77; cp/Dem St Com, 1979-; Bd Mem, Big Brothers-Big Sisters; St VP, Jimmy Fund; En Reg Coun on Alcohol and Drug Abuse; Chm, Penobscot Co Dem Com; Chm, ME Caucus of Dem Co Chairs; r/Prot; hon/Husson Col Outstg Commun Ser Awd Recip, 1983; Outstg Yg Men of Am; W/W Am Polit.

DICKENS, TIA LANEE oc/Student; b/Aug 4, 1967; h/PO Box 235, Lone Oak, TX 75453; ba/Lone Oak, TX; p/Mr and Mrs Charles Dickens, Lone Oak, TX; ed/Lone Oak High; pa/Checker, Piggly Wiggly Food Store, 1983-; cp/Lone Oak Drill Team; Tennis; Basketball; Student Coun; Ofcr, FHA; r/Bapt Ch Softball Team; hon/Elected Class Favorite, 1981; Awd'd 3rd Place in Doubles in Tennis, 1981; 2nd Runner-Up and Reg Qualifier in Tennis, 1982; g/Phy Ed.

DICKERSON, RUSSELL S oc/Student; b/Sep 21, 1963; h/615 Turner Boulevard, Grand Prairie, TX 75050; ba/ Arlington, TX; p/Lt CDR and Mrs Jaime

E Dickerson, Grand Prairie, TX; ed/ Grad, Grand Prairie HS, 1981; Att'd, Univ of Dallas, 1981-82; Att'g, Univ of TX Arlington; pa/Res Asst, Embryology Lab 1983-84, Lab Asst, Comparative Vertebrate Anatomy Lab 1984, Univ of TX Arlington; cp/Col J Barret Soc (Recording Secy), Chd of the Am Revolution, 1978-81; HS Newspaper Staff, 1980-81; VIL Competitions, 1980-81; Math Clb, Sci Clb, 1979-81; Whiz Quiz, 1980-81; Track, 1980-81; Key Clb, 1980-81; Alpha Chi, 1983-; Univ of TX Arlington Biol Soc, 1983-84; Med/Dental Preparatory Assn, 1983-84; hon/Hon Mention, Grand Prairie ISD Sci Fair, 1980; Hon Roll; Eagle Scout, BSA, 1980; Hon Roll, Univ of Dallas, 1981; Hon Roll, Univ of TX Arlington, 1982, 1983; TX Scholars Prog, Univ of Dallas ($4,000 S'ship), 1981; Univ of TX Arlington $400 Acad S'ship, 1983; W/W Among Am HS Students; g/MD.

DICKEY, CANDACE RENEE oc/ Student, Clerk; b/Sep 19, 1966; h/125 Taylor Street, Trenton, TN 38382; ba/ Trenton, TN; p/Sammy and Janice Dickey, Trenton, TN; ed/HS Student; pa/Clk, Clothing Store, 1979-81; Concession Wkr, Theatre, 1981; Disc Jockey, 1982; Modeling for Local Photog, 1982; Present Clk in Dollar Store; cp/Cheerldr, 1978-83; Capt, Beta Upsilon Mu Sorority, 1980-83; Beta Clb, 1976-83; Nite Lite Commun Theatre, 1982-83; Newspaper Staff, 1982-83; Drama Clb, 1981-83; r/Bapt; Finalist in Miss TN Teen All-Am, 1982; Homecoming Rep, 1981; Homecoming Royalty, 1983; 2nd Maid of Miss Trenton, 1983; Contestant in Mid-S Yth Talent Contest, 1979; Finalist in Miss TN Teen All-Am Pageant, 1982; 1st Maid, Miss TN Dixie, 1982; W/W Among Am HS Student; g/Performing, Modeling, Singing; Psych.

DICKINSON, IAN ROBERT oc/ Cadet; b/Jun 19, 1963; h/4413 St Andrews Circle, Las Vegas, NV 89107; p/Robert C and Sheila L Dickinson, Las Vegas, NV; ed/Wn HS, 1981; mil/Cadet, USAF Acad; cp/Master Councilor, New S DeMolay Chapt; NHS; 1st Sgt and Sqdrn Cmdr, AFJROTC Unit; hon/Pres Scholar; Outstg Cadet; AFJROTC Ldrship Awd; g/Hon Grad, USAFA; Master's Deg in Computer Sci; Profession as Ofcr.

DICKSON, DOUGLAS WYNN oc/ Student; b/Jul 23, 1955; h/9022 East Prospect, Indianapolis, IN 46239; p/ Charles F Dickson; Ruth J Range; ed/ Arsenal Tech HS, 1973; Jarvis Christian Col; cp/Jr Class Pres; Co-Pres, Techoir; Lttrman, Track and Cross-Country; VP, SGA; Alpha Kappa Mu; r/Soloist, Ch; hon/Mrs W B Skinner S'ship Fund; Pres Scholar; Hon Discharge, USN; g/ PhD in Theol from Univ of Chgo.

DIDRIKSEN, CALEB H III oc/Attorney; b/Nov 3, 1955; h/2103 Calhoun Street, New Orleans, LA 70118; ba/ New Orleans, LA; m/Megan L Conway; p/Caleb H Jr and Eleanore A H Didriksen, Wellesley, MA; ed/BS in Engrg, Univ of IL Urbana, 1977; JD, Tulane Univ Sch of Law, 1982; pa/Proj Control Engr, Anchor Hocking Corp, 1977; Assoc Atty, McGlindrey, Stafford, Mintz & Cellini, 1981; Am Bar Assn; LA Trial Lwyrs Assn; r/Meth Ch Assns; hon/Var Positions at Ch; Acad Hons;

Tau Beta Pi; Gamma Epsilon; Eagle Scout; g/Wk Hard and Enjoy Life.

DIGNES, LORI MARIE oc/Student; b/Dec 27, 1963; h/4201 Greenview Drive, Denair, CA 95316; p/Mr and Mrs Larry B Dignes, Denair, CA; ed/Grad, Denair HS, 1982; Currently Enrolled, Modesto Jr Col; pa/Photo Clk, Stanislaus Co Fair, 1981, 1982; cp/HS Basketball, 3 Yrs; HS Track, 4 Yrs; HS Basketball Statkeeper; HS Drama Clb; HS Outing Clb; HS FHA; HS Block "D" Clb; HS Acad Decathlon; HS Jr Ldrship; HS Yrbook; HS Journalism; HS CA S'ship Fdn; Denair Boosters Clb; r/Prot; hon/HS Acad Decathlon, 3rd Place, Eng, 1981; HS CA S'ship Fdn Life Mem, 1982; HS Citizenship Awd, 1982; HS Gratton Grange S'ship, 1982; HS Bk of Am Achmt Awd, Social Sci, 1982; HS Jr Ldrship, 1981; Hon Roll; Coaches Awd, Track, 1982; Other Track Medals, 1979-82.

DIGNES, SHEILA MARGARET oc/Student; b/Jun 3, 1962; h/4201 Greenview Drive, Denair, CA 95316; p/Larry B and Betty M Dignes, Denair, CA; ed/Grad, Denair HS, 1980; Student, CA St Col, 1980-; pa/Var Babysitting Jobs, 1976-; Photo Clk, Stanislaus Co Fair, 1981, 1982; cp/Pep Clb Mem, 1976; HS Band Mem, 1976-78; CA S'ship Fdn Mem, 1976-80; CA S'ship Fdn Secy, 1980; Basketball Statistician, 1978-80; Track Scorekeeper, 1978-80; Student Body Secy, 1980; Drama Clb Mem, 1976-80; Jr Ldrship Del, 1979-80; r/Prot; hon/Valedictorian, 1980; Denair Lion's Clb S'ship, 1980; Denair Unified Tchrs Assn S'ship, 1980; Bk of Am Plaque Winner for Liberal Arts, 1980; CA S'ship Fdn Mbrship, 1980; CA St Col, Stanislaus Dean's List, 1980, 1982; W/W Among Am HS Students; g/Psychol Concentrating in Sch Psych.

DILLARD, MARY VIRGINIA oc/Student; h/110 Glassy Mountain Street, Pickens, SC 29671; ba/Charleston, SC; p/James A and Virginia B Dillard, Pickens, SC; ed/Pickens Sr High; Student, Col of Charleston; pa/Pt-time Employee, Dillard's Funeral Home 1979-82 (Delivery Ser), Jack's Wholesale Bait 1982 (Laborer); cp/Jr Am Legion; Girls St; HS: Student Govt, Interact Clb, Art Clb, Sr Class Secy, Spanish Clb, Sci Clb, Basketball, Volleyball, Softball, Track; Col: Basketball, Volleyball, Alpha Delta Pi Sorority; r/Meth; hon/Girls St Senate; HS Basketball MVP, 1980, 1981, 1982; All-Conf, 1980, 1981, 1982; Volleyball, All-Conf, 1981, 1982, N-S All Star; Softball, 1980, 1981, All-Conf; Track, Upper-St, 1979; Voted Best Sr by Fac; g/To Continue Ed in Field of Polit Sci; Law Deg.

DIMENSTIEN, MINDY EVE oc/Dental Student; b/Mar 23, 1961; h/1424 11th Street South, Apartment E, Birmingham, AL 35205; p/Mrs F Dimenstien, Columbus, GA; ed/Brookstone Sch, 1979; BS w Hons, Newcomb Col of Tulane Univ, 1983; Currently Enrolled, Univ of AL Sch of Dentistry; cp/Sigma Delta Tau, House Mgr 1979-83; Alpha Epsilon Pi, Little Sister 1979-83; Tri Beta; Alpha Epsilon Delta, Secy 1982-83; ADSA; Am Heart Assn; B'nai B'rith Hillel; Pre-Med Soc; r/Jewish; hon/Pub, "A Histologic Examination of *Light lethal*, a Homozygous Mutation of *Xenopus laevis*"; Grad w Deptl Hons, 1983; Alpha Lambda Delta; Alpha

Epsilon Delta; Tri Beta; Dean's List; W/W Among Students in Am Univs and Cols; Yg Personalities of S; W/W; g/To Grad from Dental Sch and to Pract Dentistry.

DIODATO, ANDREA ELIZABETH oc/Student; b/Sep 17, 1962; h/31 Van-Ness Road, Beacon, NY 12508; p/Mario J (dec) and Laura Diodato; ed/Mt St Mary HS, 1979; Mt St Mary Col; cp/Drama Clb; Pep Squad; Spanish Clb; JNHS; NHS; r/Rom Cath; hon/Dean's List, 1983; Nat Biog Inst; W/W Among Am HS Students; g/Psychol.

DiPAOLO, BYRON RICHARD oc/Student; b/Dec 29, 1960; h/1322 Fern Avenue, Reading, PA 19607; p/Mr and Mrs Joseph DiPaolo, Reading, PA; ed/Holy Name HS, 1978; BS, Alvernia Col, 1982; pa/Tchg Asst, Lehigh Univ; cp/Sci Clb; hon/Am Inst of Chemists Awd, 1982; Reading Chemists Clb Awd, 1982; magna cum laude Hons, 1982; Nat Dean's List; Intl Yth in Achmt; Commun Ldrs of Am; g/PhD in Chem.

DISS, MARILYN RUTH oc/Student; b/Aug 21, 1961; h/PO Box 664, Lumpkin, GA 31815; p/Mr and Mrs Jesse W Diss, Lumpkin, GA; ed/Dipl, Grace Christian Acad, 1979; BA in Practical Christian Tng, Bob Jones Univ, 1983; cp/HS: 10th Grade Homecoming Queen, Class Secy, Spanish Clb, Choir, Asst Editor for Yrbook, Basketball; Col: Lit Soc (Sgt of Arms), Ath Dir, Chaplain Asst Prayer Capt, Sports 1, 2, 3, 4, Ext Grp at Nsg Homes; Cnslg, Juv Detention Ctr; r/Indep Bapt; hon/10th Grade Homecoming Queen, 1977; Pingpong Champion, 1979; Voted Most Spirited on Basketball Team, 1982; Placed 4th Overall at Sch, Pingpong Championship (Recip of Ribbon); g/LPN, GA Tech Sch.

DITTMER, DALE ROBERT oc/Student; b/Dec 27, 1961; h/14008 Melton Street, Burton, SC 29902; p/Mr and Mrs Robert W Dittmer, Burton, SC; ed/Battery Creek HS; Citadel; cp/Sigma Tau Delta, 1983, Hon Com 1983-84; Sports Editor, *The Brigadier*, 1983-84; Yrbook Staff; Drama Clb; All-Conf Football; Football Capt; Pres Classroom; hon/Valedictorian; Dean's List, 1980-81, 1981-82, 1982-83; Am Legion Awd for Acad Excell, 1983; Regimental Activs Ofcr, 1983-84; Citadel Scholar Recip; W/W Among Am HS Students; Commun Ldrs of Am; g/AF Missilier; MBA; Master's in Eng; Law or Tchg and Coaching.

DiVALL, MICHELLE ANNETTE oc/Portfolio Assistant, Department Secretary; b/Nov 8, 1961; h/8825 Nantucket, Wichita. KS 67212; ba/Wichita, KS; p/Frank L and W Louise DiVall, Arkansas City, KS; ed/AR City HS, 1979; AA, Cert in Data Processing, Cowley Co Commun Col, 1981; Wk'g towards Bus Adm Deg, Wichita St Univ; pa/Secy, Samford Stover Agy, 1978; Secy, St Farm Ins, 1979-80; Teller, Trust Investmts as Portfolio Asst, 4th Nat Bk, 1981-; cp/Tiger Action Clb, 1979-81; SGA, 1979-81; Chrldr, CCCC, 1979-81; HS Student Coun, 1978-79; r/Epis; hon/1st Runner-Up, Queen Alalah, CCCC; W/W Among Student in Am Jr Cols; Intl Yth in Achmt; g/Wk'g towards Having Her Own Bus.

DIVERSE-DIEZ, MARIE DENNISSE oc/Student; b/Jan 1, 1959; h/BB11 Daisy Street, Alt de Boringuen Cdns, Rio Piedras, Puerto Rico 00926; p/Ramon a

Diverse-Ufret and Lucila Diez-Lopez, Rio Piedras, Puerto Rico; ed/Free Sch of Music of San Juan City, 1975; BS, Univ of Puerto Rico, 1978; Profl Modeling Course, Barbizon's Sch of Modeling, 1974; cp/GSA; Eng Tchg TV Progs; Eng Fest Participant; Painting Competition; Free Sch of Music Bd; Sel to Ed Public through TV Drug Addiction Progs; Sci Fair Participant; Chorus; Orch; Acad Competitions; Univ of Puerto Rico Band; Red Cross Vol; Pre-Med Students Org; Vol Wk on Sci Exhib; hon/magna cum laude; High Hon Grad; Musical Hon, HS; Semifinalist, Acad Competition; Perfect Attendance; Soc of Dist'd Am HS Students; g/MD.

DIXON, GLYNIS MICHELLE oc/Student; b/Jan 1, 1966; h/404 North Gordon Street, Douglas, GA 31533; p/Mr and Mrs Dennis Dixon, Douglas, GA; ed/Coffee HS, 1984; cp/Tennis; FHA; Student Coun; Matrix Clb; Beta Clb; Letter Clb; Drama Clb; Math Team; Editor-in-Chief of Yrbook; Girl Scouts; r/Bapt; Girls' St; GA Cert of Merit Winner; Presb Col Jr Fellow Awd; Girl Scout Silver Awd; Prins Hon Roll; Tennis High Point Winner; W/W Among Am HS Students; g/Engrg, Math and Sci.

DIXON, JOHN MARK oc/Student; b/Jun 4, 1965; h/Route 4, Box 619, Magnolia, AR 71753; p/Mr and Mrs Kenneth Dixon, Magnolia, AR; ed/Grad, Magnolia HS, 1983; pa/Magnolia Feed Co; Constrn Wkr for Payne & Kellar; cp/F'ship of Christian Aths; Football; r/Bapt; hon/Mu Alpha Theta, Pres; Nat Hon Soc; Student Coun Rep; Hon Roll, All HS Semesters; 2 Yr Letterman in Football; Outstg Lineman in 7AAA St Playoff Football Game; 7AAA All Conf Hon Mention; W/W Am HS Students; g/Petroleum Engr.

DIXON, PHILATHEA ANN oc/Administrative Assistant; b/Apr 24, 1959; h/1501 Brown Boulevard, Greensboro, NC 27401; ba/Greensboro, NC; p/Mr and Mrs Bruce Dixon Jr, Magnolia, NC; ed/Dipl, James Kenan HS, 1977; BA in Eng, NC Ctl Univ, 1981; MS in Ednl Psych and Guid, NC A&T St Univ, 1984; pa/Adm Asst, Aux Sers, NC A&T St Univ, 1982-; Clk-Typist, Dept of Elem Ed and Rdg, NC A&T St Univ, 1981-82; Salesperson, J C Penney Inc, 1980-82; cp/Alpha Kappa Alpha Sorority Inc; Univ Eng Clb; Treas, Dormitory; Dormitory Student Resident Asst; Univ Ex-Umbra Magazine Staff; HS Math Clb; HS Student Coun; HS FHA, VP; r/Holiness; hon/Dean's List Student, 1978-81; Eng S'ship, 1978; W/W Hon Mention Among Cols and Univs; g/To Attain EdD in Guid.

DIXON, SAMPSON ELI oc/Student; b/Aug 18, 1961; h/Route 1, Box 211-E, Magnolia, NC 28453; p/Bruce and Annie Dixon, Magnolia, NC; ed/Grad, James Kenan HS, 1979; BA in Computer Sci, E Carolina Univ, 1983; mil/USAF; Active 3 Months; AF ROTC, E Carolina Univ, 4 Yrs; pa/Currently Wkg for USAF in 5131B Career Field, Computer Sys Devel Ofcr; cp/HS: Basketball for 2 Yrs, Track for 3 Yrs, Football for 3 Yrs, Pres of Sophomore and Jr Classes, Secy of Sr Class; Col Football, E Carolina Univ; r/Bapt; hon/Outstg Back Awd, 1978; g/To Complete Master's Deg in Bus Adm, While Making Capt in USAF.

DIXSON, RODRIQURESS oc/Student Administrative Clerk; b/Mar 4, 1963; h/917 Ouachita, El Dorado, AR 71730; p/Jimmie Dixson, West Covina, CA; Lela Dixson, El Dorado, AR; ed/Strong HS, 1981; Pre-Registered Nsg Maj, Miles Col; pa/Adm Clk, US Dept of Housing and Urban Devel, 1982-; Yth Choir, Ch Pianist, Thirgood Meml CME Ch, 1981-82; Clk-Typist, So CA Edison Co, 1981; cp/VP, Eta Nu Chapt, Delta Sigma Theta Sorority Inc, 1982-83, 1983-84; Bus Mgr, Jr Class, 1983-84; Miles Col Debate Team, 1984; Spec Ser Clb, 2nd Attendant Rep for Homecoming, 1981-82; Miles Col Steering Com, 1982; Dormitory Coun of Ofcrs, 1982-84; OES #352, 1983; Miles Col Homecoming Com and Subcom Chp and Mem, 1981, 1982, 1983; hon/Dean's List, 1983; Hon Roll, 1981, 1982; Miss Miles Col, 1983-84; W/W Among Students in Am Univs and Cols; Intl W/W Frats and Sororities; W/W Among Am HS Students; g/To Obtain a BS in Registered Nsg and to Specialize in Ob & Gyn; To Obtain a Master's and a Doct Deg in Registered Nsg.

DJUREN, JOHN IVAN oc/Instructor; h/1004 9th Street, Northwest, Waverly, IA 50677; p/Mrs Marjorie Djuren, Waverly, IA; ed/Hampton HS, 1975; BA, Wartbug Col, 1979; MA, Newport Univ, 1983; Med Spec Dipl, 1975; pa/Anal/Programmer, Instr, Bus Inst of Technol, 1983-; Pt-time Orderly, Bartels Luth Home, 1976-83; hon/MA Thesis: "Relevant Problems in Industrial Psychology"; Nat Dean's List; Commun Ldrs of Am; Intl Yth in Achmt; g/PhD in Clin Psych.

DOBSON, MARY ELIZABETH oc/Lifeguard; b/Apr 20, 1966; h/160 Gunston Drive, Lexington Park, MD 20653; p/Mr and Mrs Joe Dobson, Lexington Park, MD; ed/Great Mills HS; pa/Lifeguard; cp/Secy, Ch Yth Grp; Swimming Instr, Swim Team; Drum Maj, Band; Student Adv Coun Rep, Bd of Ed, 1983-84; hon/Class Rep; MD All-St Jr Band; Tri-City Hon Band; Sportsmanship Awd, St Mary's Col Racquetball, Swim Team.

DODSON, DENISE LYNN oc/Unemployed; b/Aug 6, 1961; h/Route 16, Box 75, Medina, TX 78055; p/Jerry and Diana Dodson, Medina, TX; ed/Medina HS, 1979; Deg in Ofc Adm, Abilene Christian Univ, 1983; cp/HS Basketball and Track; HS Beta Clb, Secy; HS Student Coun, Secy; Kappa Delian Shri Social Clb, 1980-83; hon/Valedictorian, 1979; Am Hist Awd, 1979; Acad S'ships, 1979; Dean's Hon Roll, Abilene Christian Univ; W/W Among Am HS Students; Soc of Dist'd HS Students; g/To Obtain a Secretarial-Clerical Job in a Co w Possible Advmt to an Exec Position.

DODSON, JUDITH DENEEN oc/Student; b/Sep 20, 1964; h/Route 1, Box 170-A, Sandy Ridge, NC 27046; p/Mr and Mrs Ray Odean Dodson, Sandy Ridge, NC; ed/N Stokes HS, 1982; Att'g, Rockingham Commun Col, 1982-; cp/4-H Horse Clb, Pres; SGA, Rep; Monogram, Camera, French, Latin and FHA Clbs; Jr Class Pres; Prom Chp; hon/W/W Among Am HS Students; W/W Among Am HS Students Second Yr Awd; Yg Commun Ldrs of Am; g/Bus Adm Maj.

DOLFINI, MICHELLE ANNE oc/Student; b/Oct 16, 1962; h/Route 1, Box 516, Goode, VA 24556; p/Mr and Mrs Robert J Dolfini, Goode, VA; ed/Grad, Jefferson Forest HS, 1980; BA, Hollins Col, 1984; pa/Tutor, Writing Ctr, Hollins Col (Present); Tchr's Asst, Res Methods in Polit Sci, Hollins Col, 1983; Student Asst, Polit Sci Dept, Hollins Col, 1980-82; Legal Internship, Thorpe & Rowe, PC, 1981; cp/Hollins Coalition for Peace, 1982-84; Com on Wom's Issues, 1983; Orchesis, 1983-84; Resident Asst, 1982-83; Coor of Wom's Sem Day in Conjunction w Spec Progs under Dean of Students, 1984; hon/Phi Beta Kappa, 1983; Omicron Delta Kappa, 1983; Hollins Scholar, 1983; Dean's List, 1980-83; Ranked Second in Class, 1982-; Recip, Sarah Griffith Cheney and Wm Coates S'ship, 1980-84; Student Rep to Fgn Affairs Conf, Naval Acad, 1983; Student Rep to 13th Annual Symp Sponsored by Ctr for the Study on the Presidency, 1982; g/To Obtain PhD in Polit Sci; To Teach Polit Sci on the Col Level (w an Emphasis on Wom's Studies).

DOMINGUEZ, JOEY ANTONIO oc/Student, Teacher; b/Jun 17, 1962; h/308 Upson Drive, Devine, TX 78016-2639; p/Tomasa M Espinosa, Devine, TX; ed/Grad, Devine, HS, 1980; Student, TX A&I Univ; pa/Percussion Instr, Lytle HS, 1982-83; Percussion Dir, Lytle HS Ensemble, 1983-; cp/Kappa Kappa Psi, Secy 1981, Treas 1982, Pledgemaster 1981-82; Phi Mu Alpha; r/Cath; hon/Yg Personalities of S; Intl Yth in Achmt; Commun Ldrs of Am; Biogl Roll of Hon; W/W Am HS Students; g/2 Degs: 1 in Music and 1 in Bus.

DONALDS, BETH KAREN oc/Accountant; b/Nov 24, 1957; h/36-23 Ferry Heights, Fair Lawn, NJ 07410; ba/New York, NY; p/Howard Donalds (dec); Elinor Schocket, Fairlawn, NJ; ed/Grad, Fair Lawn HS, 1975; BS in Acctg, Trenton St Col, 1979; MBA in Acctg and Taxation, Fairleigh Dickinson, 1983; pa/Sr Acct in Charge of Reinsurance and Pension 1984-, Accts Payable Supvr 1983-84, Home Life Ins; Financial Acct 1982-83, Jr Acct 1980-82, Lonza Inc; Staff Acct, Six Star Cablevision, 1979-80; cp/N Jersey Singles Coun; g/Controller.

DONALDSON, GREGORY LLOYD oc/Actor; b/Sep 21, 1954; h/1900 North Sycamore Avenue, Los Angeles, CA 90068; ba/Same; p/Lester Lloyd Donaldson, Tulare, CA; Mary N Wilson, Santa Cruz, CA; ed/Grad, Monterey Bay Acad, 1972; BFA, Musical Theatre Dance, US Intl Univ, 1982; pa/Actor; Messenger, Live Wires, the Singing Telegram People; Actors Equity Assn, 1st Nat Tour; cp/Soloist in Ch; Pro Musica Treas; hon/Starlight Star Awd; Inland Empire Awd; Mayr Foun S'ship; Nat Dean's List; W/W Among Students in Am Cols and Univs; Commun Ldrs of Am; g/Actor, Singer, Dancer for Stage, Film, TV, Commls.

DOOMEY, MICHELLE DENISE oc/Student, Waitress, Cashier, Model; b/Aug 28, 1966; h/514 South Townville Street, Seneca, SC 29678; ba/Seneca, SC; p/Roger and Barbara Doomey, Seneca, SC; ed/Student, Seneca Sr HS; pa/Child Care, Twin Oaks Child Care, 1977-81; Cashier, The Clothes Rack, 1982; Waitress, Cashier, Hostess, Po Folks, 1983-; Var Modeling Jobs; cp/Student Coun, 3 Yrs; AFS Clb; Drama Clb; Fgn Foods Clb; Band, 4 Yrs; Oconee Commun Theatre Yth Bd, 1983; Sr Rep, Band; Beta Clb, 6 Yrs; Softball, 1981; r/Cath; hon/Outstg Sci Student, 1 Yr; Beta Clb, 6 Yrs; W/W Among Am HS Students; g/To Go to Col and Maj in Spch and Theatrics, Minor in Bus.

DORITY, VICKIE LEE oc/Student; b/Jun 21, 1962; h/337 Bea Street, Hernando, MS 38632; p/Arline Buie, Hernando, MS; ed/Dipl, Hernando HS, 1980; NW Jr Col; MS St Univ; cp/Phi Mu Alpha Sinfonia, Sweetheart 1982-83; Band, 1972-73; Freshman Class Rep, 1976; Libn, 1978-79; Flag Corps, 1978-82; Music Edrs Nat Conv, 1981-83; C of C Vol; Chorus, 1978-80; Spanish Clb, 1978-80; Christian F'ship Clb, 1977-78; Hist Clb, 1977-78; Jr Optimist Clb, 1976-77; VBS Tchr; hon/Nat Hon Soc, 1978-79, 1979-80; MSU Upperclassman Acad S'ship, 1983-84; Phi Theta Kappa, 1981-83; Freshman and Sophomore Homecoming Maid Nom; Miss NWJC Nom, 1983; SGA Exec Coun Secy 1981-82, Jud Coun Pres 1982-83; St Finalist, Miss Teen MS, 1979; Intells, 1980; Ldrship S'ship, 1981; Phi Theta Kappa S'ship, 1983-84; Pres's List; Soc of Dist Am HS Students; W/W Among Am HS Students; Commun Ldrs of Am.

DORRIS, CHERYL IRENE oc/Student; b/Oct 19, 1963; h/1335 Glendale Street, Lakeland, FL 33803; p/Mr and Mrs Gale J Dorris, Lakeland, FL; ed/Col Prep Deg, Lakeland Christian Sch, 1981; BS in Sci Ed, Bob Jones Univ, 1985; cp/Nat Hon Soc, 1978-81, Histn 1980, Treas 1981; Ldr, Awana Yth Clb; Assn of Christian Tchrs, 1981-84; r/Ch Yth Grp, Treas 1981; r/Bapt; hon/Salutatorian, 1981; Am Legion Citizenship Awd, 1981; W/W Among Am HS Students, 1980, 1981; Personalities of S; g/BS in Sci Ed w Biol Proficiency; To Teach in Christian Sch.

DORRIS, MARTI JO oc/Student; b/Nov 5, 1963; h/5459 Lickton Pike, Goodlettsville, TN 37072; p/Mr and Mrs John Martin Dorris, Goodlettsville, TN; ed/Goodlettsville HS, 1982; cp/Phi Mu Frat for Wom; Volleyball Team; European Study Tour; FCA Nat Conf; PIVOT; Ofc Wkr; Bookstore Wkr; Citizen's Adv Com; Sch Sci Fair; Jr Show; hon/Pres S'ship from Lambuth Col; Dean's List; Eng Awd; NEDA Awd; Hon Roll; Acad Excell in Sci; Ser Awd; TN Proficiency Test Awd; Vol St Math Contest; Civitan Essay Contest Silver Medalist; NJHS; Glee Clb Libn; 4-H Clb Com Chm; Student Coun Com Chm; FCA; Newspaper Sports Editor, Co Editor; Alumni Awd; NHS Secy-Treas; Vol Girls St Del; Valedictorian; W/W Among Am HS Students; g/Music Therapy.

DORSEY, CAROL ELLEN oc/Student; b/Feb 8, 1963; h/Route 1, Box 12-11, Tifton, GA 31794; p/Mr and Mrs Newell E Dorsey, Tifton, GA; ed/Grad, Tiftarea Acad, 1981; AS in Med Technol, ABAC, 1983; Student, Columbus Col; cp/Capt, Tennis Team; Wom's Tennis Team, 1982, 1983; Quarterfinalist, NJCAA Nats, 1982; Treas, Beta Clb; hon/Hon Student, 1982, 1983; Dean's List, Columbus Col, 1984; Salutatorian, Beta Clb, 5 Yrs; Scholastic Hon Grp, 5 Yrs; Biol Awd; Physiol Awd; DAR Hist Awd; Scholar Ath; 3rd Place, Lit Essay; 3rd Place, Lit Trio; Col Dean's List; Lttr

5 Yrs, 6th in St Discus, Track; Lttr, Cheerldg, 3 Yrs; Most Outstg Perf, Spirit Awd, Lttr 5 Yrs, 2nd in Reg 3 Yrs, Tennis; Nat Dean's List; Personalities of S; W/W Am Jr Cols; Soc of Dist'd Am HS Students; g/Med Technol.

DORSEY, ROBIN LEE oc/Consultant, Analyst, Architect; b/Dec 4, 1959; h/525 Dunning Street, Williamsburg, VA 23185; ba/Columbia, MD; p/Robert C and Audrey M Dorsey, Williamsburg, VA; ed/Classical HS, 1978; BArch, Howard Univ, 1982; Fallout Shelter Analyst, Emer Mgmt Inst, 1983; pa/Conslt in Radiation Technol, 1982-; Free-Lance Arch Designer, 1983-; hon/Dean's List, 1978-82; Nat Dean's List, 1979-81; Intl Yth in Achmt; Yg Personalities of S; Commun Ldrs of Am; g/To Attend Grad Sch of Arch Design; To Become a Reg'd Arch and Structural Engr.

DORTA-DUQUE, JORGE JESUS oc/Student; b/Mar 31, 1961; h/5645 Southwest 87 Street, Miami, FL 33143; p/Jorge E and Maria L Dorta-Duque, Miami, FL; ed/Columbus HS, 1979; BA, Univ of Miami, 1983; Presently Att'g Univ of S FL Col of Med; cp/Student Orient Ser; Fdn of Cuban Students; Spec Asst to Acad Affairs Com of Student Body Govt Senate; Jackson Meml Hosp Vol; hon/Phi Kappa Phi Hon Soc, 1983; Psi Chi Hon Soc, 1982; Alpha Epsilon Delta Pre-Med Hon Soc, VP 1982-83; Golden Key; g/MD.

DOSSETT, MARK RICHARD oc/Installer of Marble Bathroom Fixtures; b/Feb 26, 1960; h/209 South 24th Avenue, Hattiesburg, MS 39401; ba/Hattiesburg, MS; p/James Roland and Allie Dossett, Southaven, MS; Betty Jo Dossett, Hattiesburg, MS; ed/Grad, Hattiesburg HS; pa/Marble Installer, L&G Tile and Marble Co, 1982-; Oil Drilling Rig Wkr, Penrod Drilling Co, 1981-82; Oil Drilling Rig Wkr, Platform Well Ser Inc, 1981; cp/Little Leag Baseball, Police Dept Team, 1970-72; r/Beginner, Primary and Jr Choirs, Main St Bapt Ch, 1964-71, Boys Missions 1968; r/Bapt; hon/Associational Winner, Lebanon Bapt Assn Explorers Bible Drill, 1971; Vacation Bible Ser Cert, Main St Bapt Ch, 1967-68, Jr Choir Cert 1969-71; Team Trophy, Little Leag Baseball, Police Dept Team, 1972; Dir of Dist'd Ams; g/To Return to Oil Field or Off Shore Drilling for Oil.

DOTSON, YOLANDA DENISE oc/Graduate Student; b/Aug 12, 1960; h/2191 Bent Creek Way, Southwest, Atlanta, GA 30311; p/Mr and Mrs William L Dotson, Cleveland, OH; ed/Dipl, Shaw HS, 1978; BA, AL St Univ, 1982; MA, Atlanta Univ, 1984; pa/Hd Cashier, Pekoc Hardware, 1976-78; Biol Lab Asst, AL St Univ, 1978-82; Rschr, Molecular Biol, Atlanta Univ, 1982-84; cp/Student Govt Assn, AL St Univ, 1978-82; Delta Sigma Theta Sorority Inc, 1979; Spec Ser Clb for Tutoring Slow Lng Chd, 1978-82; BDSA, Atlanta Univ, 1982-84; r/Bapt; hon/W/W Among Col Students; W/W Among Wom in Am; g/To Complete Grad Sch and Take Up Employmt at Leading Res Co.

DOUCET, JOHN PHILIP oc/Student; b/Feb 23, 1962; h/210 Palmetto Lane, Golden Meadow, LA 70357; p/Herman J (dec) and Dora R Doucet,

Golden Meadow, LA; ed/S Lafourche HS, 1980; LSU, 1980-81; Nicholls St Univ; pa/Tutor; cp/Nicholls Chem Scis Soc, Pres 1982-83; Alpha Chi Sigma; SGA Rep, LSU, 1980-81; SGA Senator, Nicholls St, 1982-83; KC; Holy Name Local Chapt; LA Jr Acad of Sci Pres; Nicholls Pre-Med Assn; Nicholls Sci Soc; Band; Nat Jr Sci and Humanities Symp; Intl Sci and Engrg Fair; hon/Poetry Pub'd in Nicholls St Univ Lit Mag, 1982, 1983; Salutatorian; Outstg Cath Yth, K of C; Hon Grp, Westinghouse Nat Sci Talent Search; g/MD.

DOVER, TRACY RENEE oc/Part-time Worker, Student; b/Sep 7, 1964; h/1203 Ridgemont Avenue, Shelby, NC 28150; ba/Shelby, NC; p/Donald and Betty Dover, Shelby, NC; ed/Dipl, Burns HS, 1982; Student, Gaston Col, 1982-; pa/Customer Ser, Burger King, 1981; Short Order Cook, Dayne's Shingle Shak, 1981-; cp/Cheerldr; Beta Clb; Nat Hon Soc; FCA; Student Coun Rep; Outing Clb; SME; IEEE; hon/Nat Hon Soc, 1982; HS Dipl, 1982; Jefferson Standard S'ship, 1983; W/W Among Am HS Students; g/Electronics Engr.

DOWELL, DANICE NANETTE oc/Student; b/Feb 13, 1962; h/508 Davis Drive, Kingston, TN; p/James W and Alma T Dowell, Kingston, TN; ed/Grad, Roane Co HS, 1980; Gen AS, cum laude, Roane St Commun Col, 1982; cp/Soc of Profl Journalists, Sigma Delta Chi, 1983; Student Editor, Roane St Commun Col Newspaper, 1981-82; Student Meml Awds Com, 1981-82; Reporter, Gamma Beta Phi, 1981-82; r/Ch of Christ; hon/Gene Scandlyn Outstg Freshman Awd, 1981; Outstg Humanities Student, 1981; Home Ec Awd, 1980; Outstg Yth, Optimist, 1979-80; Intl Yth in Achmt; Commun Ldrs of Am; W/W Among Students in Am Jr Cols; CIRCA Editor's Awd, Roane St Commun Col, 1982; g/Continue Ed in Jour at Univ of TN.

DOWNING, GWENDOLYN oc/Surgical Assistant to Orthopedic Podiatrist; b/Aug 26, 1960; h/1008 East Selma Street, Dothan, AL 36301; ba/Dothan, AL; p/Morris and Janelle Downing, Dothan, AL; ed/Dothan HS, 1978; BS, Troy St Univ, 1981; pa/Tutor; Surg Asst to Orthopedic Podiatrist; cp/Gamma Beta Phi; Phi Theta Kappa; Ch Pianist; Guid Cnslr, Ch Yth Grp; NHS; Student Actions for Ed Pres; Interclb Coun; Jr Engrg and Tech Soc; hon/Grad, summa cum laude; Nat Dean's List; Intl Biogl Ctr Inclusion; W/W Among Am Jr Cols; Commun Ldrs of Am; g/Cnslg Sers Clin.

DRAGON, PETER C oc/Broadcast Journalist; b/Jun 4, 1958; h/12 Maple Crest Circle, Holyoke, MA 01040; ba/Springfield, MA; p/Mrs Helen Dragon, Holyoke, MA; ed/Holyoke HS, 1976; Assocs Deg, Telecommuns, Sprgfield Tech Commun Col, 1978; BS, Broadcast Jour, Emerson Col, 1980; pa/Prodr/Anchor/Reporter, WAGM TV 8, 1980; Prodr/Anchor/Reporter, WSBA TV 43, 1980-81; Reporter/Anchor, WGGB TV 40, 1981-; cp/Nat Hon Soc, 1976; Holyoke Yth Baseball Leag (Coach-Umpire), 1976-82; Emerson Indep Video, 1978-80; Val Press Clb, 1982-83; NABET, AFL-CIO,1981-83; r/Cath; hon/Soc of Profl Journalists, Sigma Delta Chi, First Place Mark of

Excell Awd, TV Spot News, 1980.

DRAHOZAL, THOMAS JOSEPH oc/Restaurant Employee; b/Mar 15, 1961; h/637 28th Street Court, Southeast, Cedar Rapids, IA 52403; p/Mr and Mrs Jerry Drahozal, Cedar Rapids, IA; ed/George Wash HS, 1979; AS, St Gregory's Col, 1981; BA in Hist and Sec'dy Tchg Cert, Coe Col, 1983; pa/Lighting Tech 1979-80, Chief Lighting Tech 1980-81, St Gregory's Col; PJM Landscaping Enterprise Inc, 1981; Godfather's Pizza, 1982-; cp/K of C, 3rd Deg, 1979-; Tchr Asst, 1981-82; Varsity Soccer, 1980-81; Intramural Basketball, 1981; Softball, 1980-81; Floor Hockey Team Capt, 1980-81; Player on Godfather's Pizza's Softball Team, 1982-83, Capt 1983; St Gregory's Alumni Assn; hon/St Gregory's Dean's List, 1979-81; Acad Hons from St Gregory's, 1981; Coe Col Dean's List, 1982-83; Nat Dean's List, 1979-80, 1981-82, 1982-83; Intl Yth in Achmt; Yg Commun Ldrs.

DRAUGHON, KAREN HENDERSON oc/Student; b/Apr 3, 1966; h/135 Pine Lake Drive, Atlanta, GA 30327; p/Clyde and Lyn Draughon, Atlanta, GA; ed/Student, Riverwood HS; cp/Key Clb, 1982, 1983, Secy-Treas 1983; French Hon Soc, Pres 1982-83, 1983-84; Drill Team, 1981, 1982, 1983, Capt 1983; Atlanta All Star Drill Team, 1982-83; Cross Country Running Team, 1980, 1981, 1982; Fgn Lang Clb, 1980-84; Sch Chorus, 1982-83, 1983-84; r/Ch Choir, 1980-84, Secy-Treas 1983; Presb; hon/Accepted into Talented and Gifted Prog, 1980-84; Nat Hon Soc, 1983-84; Lead Role, French Play (Won 2nd Place in HS Competition), 1983; Asked to Try Out for All-St Chorus by Sch Chorus Dir; g/Maj in Bus w Minor in Fgn Langs; Wk for an Intl Bus, Corp.

DRAUGHON, RUTH ANN oc/Assistant Manager of Property Management Department; b/Mar 14, 1961; ba/PO Box 310, Fayetteville, NC 28304; p/Mr and Mrs James A Draughon; ed/Douglas Byrd Sr HS, 1979; BMus, Univ of NC Greensboro; pa/Asst Mgr of Property Mgmt Dept, U Rlty; cp/Nat Assn of Wom in Constrn, 1983; r/Presb; hon/Nat Merit S'ship Finalist, 1979; Kathryn Smith Reynolds Scholar, 1979-81; Selected for Gov's Sch in Music, 1978; Nat Dean's List; W/W Am HS; g/Performance (Music/Drama).

DRECHSLER, DAVID EDWIN oc/Second Round Draft Choice; b/Jul 18, 1960; h/PO Box 77, Cleveland, NC 27013; p/Thomas and Ann Drechsler, Cleveland, NC; ed/Grad, W Rowan HS; BS, Bus Adm, Univ of NC Chapel Hill; pa/2nd Round Draft Choice, Green Bay Packers; Pt-time Constrn for Piedmont Agri-Sys; Security for Zack's Bar and Restaurant; cp/HS Football, Basketball, Track; Student Coun; Sr Class Pres; Col Football, Track; Order of the Golden Fleece; Order of the Grail; r/Presb; hon/HS Football All-St, 1977; All-Am Col Football, 1982, 1983; Patterson Medal, Outstg Sr Ath at Univ of NC; g/MBA or Law Deg.

DRIVER, FRANK MICHEL oc/Jeweler; b/Jul 24, 1963; h/PO Box 15, Richland, SC 29675; ba/Seneca, SC; p/Philip F and Rebecca H Driver, Richland, SC; ed/Grad, Seneca HS, 1981; Grad Gemologist Deg, Gemological Inst of Am; pa/From Jewelry Repairman, to Hand Engraver, to Diamond Appraisals, to Stone Identification, W W Thraves Jeweler's, 1978-; cp/Keowee Sailing Clb; r/Meth; g/To Own Retail or Wholesale Bus; To Travel Around the World Buying and Selling Stones.

DROGIN, ELLEN BARBARA oc/ Research Assistant, Student; b/May 25, 1960; h/3519 Everton Street, Wheaton, MD 20906; p/Mr and Mrs Howard M Drogin, Wheaton, MD; ed/Wheaton HS, 1978; BA, Math and Rec, w Hons, Hood Col, 1982; Pursuing Master's Deg in Rec Adm and Planning, Univ of MD; pa/Res Asst, Univ of MD, 1982-; Nat Rec and Pks Assn; MD Rec and Pks Assn; cp/Montgomery Area Sci Fair Com; Coor, Am Heart Assn Jump Rope for Heart; Pres, Grad Rec Soc, Univ of MD; Hood Col: Class of 1982 Pres, VP of Rec and Pks Soc, Peer Advr, Treas of Rec Assn, Acad Affairs Com, Acad Standing Com, Student Life Com, Badminton Team, Energy Coun, Choir; hon/Mortar Bd, 1982; Hood Col Scholar, 1981-82; Convocation Hons, 1980-82; MRPA Outstg Student, 1981-82; Hood Col Ionic Soc, 1980; Intl Thespian Soc; Govs Cit, 1982; W/W Among Students in Am Cols and Univs; Commun Ldrs of Am; g/Master's Deg in Rec Adm and Reg Planning.

DUBIS, FRANK MICHAEL II oc/ Student; b/Nov 10, 1963; h/100 Renau Boulevard, Summerville, SC 29483; p/ Frank Michael and Patricia Ann Dubis, Summerville, SC; ed/Summerville HS, 1982; Currently Enrolled in Pre-Engrg Prog, The Citadel Evening Col; cp/ YMCA, Basketball 1980, Soccer 1980; Jr Engrg Tech Soc, 1982; Spanish Clb, 1982; r/Bapt; hon/Cert of Merit, Sci, 1977; Hon Roll, 1977; Cert of Perfect Attendance, 1978, 1979, 1980, 1981; Norton Co Safety Prods Div S'ship, 1983; W/W Among Am HS Students; g/Elect Engr.

DUFF, CANDACE GAYLE oc/Student; b/Dec 12, 1965; h/Dixie Lee Village, Lenoir City, TN 37771; ba/ Lenoir City, TN; p/Mr and Mrs Harold Boyd Duff, Lenoir City, TN; ed/Grad, Lenoir City HS, 1983; Att'g, Univ of TN Knoxville, 1983-; Grad, Rasnic's Modeling Sch, 1983; Att'd, Lenoir City Sch of Ballet Arts, 1974-83; pa/Sales Clk, Cashier, Supvr, Wal-Mart, 1982; cp/Nat Hon Soc, 1981-83, VP 1983; Eng Hon Soc, 1982-83; French Clb, 1982; Lit Clb, 1980-82; Math Clb, 1980; Interact Clb, 1983; Lenoir City HS Band, 1976-83; r/Treas, UMYF, Cardwell U Meth Ch, 1979-; hon/Recip, Frederick T Bonham S'ship, 1983; Teenboard Presentee, 1982; g/Maj in Bus Adm, Univ of TN.

DUFFY, MARK ELTON oc/Faculty Assistant; b/Aug 30, 1954; h/33 Lathrop Street, Madison, WI 53705; ba/Madison, WI; m/Evelyn G; p/Arthur and Shirley Duffy, South Bloomingville, OH; ed/ Worthington HS, 1972; BS in Physics, Purdue Univ, 1976; PhD in Physics, Univ of WI Madison, 1983; pa/Fac Asst, Univ of WI Dept of Physics; cp/Ofcr, Beta Sigma Psi Frat, Purdue Univ, 1974-76; r/Calvary Luth Chapel, Bd of Dirs 1983, 1982, 1979, 1978, 1977; Ofcr, Univ Luth Chapel, 1974-76; hon/Pubs, "Prompt Muon Neutrino Production in a 400 GeV Proton Beam Dump Experiment" 1983, "Dimuon Production by Nuetrinos in the 15-foot Bubble Chamber" 1980, Others; Phi Beta Kappa, 1976; Phi Kappa Phi, 1975;

Sigma Pi Sigma, 1975; Phi Eta Simga, 1973; Commun Ldrs of Am; Intl Yth in Achmt; g/Employmt in Physics in a Res and Devel Indust.

DUGGAN, WILLIAM PATRICK oc/ Student; b/Jun 18, 1959; h/1 Frear Avenue, Troy, NY 12180; ba/Troy, NY; p/Mr and Mrs Robert F Duggan, Middletown, NY; ed/John S Burke Cath HS, 1976; BS 1980, MS 1982, Pursuing PhD in Nuclear Engrg, Rensselaer Polytechnic Inst; pa/Instr, Rensselaer Polytechnic Inst, 1983-; Engr, Stone & Webster Engrg Corp, 1982-83; cp/Mystic River Rugby Clb; Student Govt Grand Marshal; Pres, Student Body; Trustees' Student Affairs Com; Student Senate; Sr Class VP; Bd of Dirs, Friends of the Folsom Lib; Alumni Class VP; Am Nuclear Soc; hon/Phalany; Tau Beta Pi; W/W Among Students in Am Cols and Univs; Yg Commun Ldrs of Am; g/PhD in Nuclear Engrg (Specialty-Fusion Engrg).

DUHIG, SUSAN CAROLINE oc/ Student; b/Jun 27, 1963; h/7250 Twin Branch Road, Northeast, Atlanta, GA 30328; p/Mr James J Duhig Sr, Atlanta, GA; ed/Grad, N Sprgs HS, 1981; BA in Eng, Emory Univ, 1985; pa/Res Asst, Dr Martin Shapiro, Psychol/Lwyr, Emory Univ, 1982-83; cp/HS: Debate Team, Math Team, Beta Clb, VP of Latin Clb; Col: Secy of Into Atlanta Com, Affairs Editor of Emory *Phoenix*, Amnesty Intl, Writer for the Emory *Wheel*, Barkley Forum Debate Soc, Hon Coun, Intl Exch Prog, Spanish Clb; r/Rom Cath; hon/ HS: Nat Hon Soc, Valedictorian, Harvard Book Awd; Col: Sigma Tau Delta, Alpha Epsilon Upsilon, Truman S'ship, John G Stipe Soc, Turman Scholar, Nat Merit Scholar; g/Law Sch; Going into the Judiciary.

DUKES, PAULA ANN oc/Student; b/ Aug 9, 1966; h/PO Box 152, Raleigh, MS 39153; p/John H and Ruby Fay Dukes, Raleigh, MS; ed/Grad, Raleigh HS, 1984; cp/Beta Clb, 1983-84; Hist Clb, 1982-83; Future Bus Ldrs of Am, 1983-84; FHA, Hero Chapt, 1982-83; Cheerldr, 1983-84; Reporter of Her Class, 1981-82; Homecoming Maid, 1983-84; Raleigh HS Chorus, 1982-83; r/Bapt; g/To Attend Jones Jr Col and Univ of So MS; Maj in Data Processing.

DUMONT, TRACEY ANN oc/Student; b/Nov 9, 1963; h/190 River Farm Drive, East Greenwich, RI 02818; p/ Roland and Ellen Dumont, East Greenwich, RI; ed/HS Dipl, 1982; Student, Nurses Prog, Univ of RI; ba/Fayva Shoe Store, 1982-; cp/Spec Olympics Vol, 1981-82; Vol for E Greenwich Rec Dept; Track; Volleyball; Yrbook Clb; NHS; Powder Puff Football; r/Cath; hon/Jr Achmt Awd; NHS; W/W Among Am HS Students; Yg Ldrs of Am; g/Grad w BS Deg; Wk in Pediatrics Dept.

DUNAWAY, NANCY ALICE oc/ Student; b/Sep 22, 1965; h/244 Cumberland Avenue, Barbourville, KY 40906; p/Milton and Adrian Dunaway, Barbourville, KY; ed/Grad, Knox Ctl HS, 1983; cp/Nat Beta Clb; US Achmt Acad; Tennis Team, 1982; Spanish Clb, 1983; FHA; r/Meth; hon/Hon Roll Student, 1983; Homecoming Queen, 1983; Voted Best Looking in Sr Class, 1983; W/W Among Am HS Students; Soc for Dist'd Am HS Students; g/ Dentistry.

DUNBAR, MICHAEL VANCE oc/

Student; b/Sep 5, 1961; h/642 Crothers Memorial Hall, Stanford, CA 94305; p/ Mrs Frank Dunbar, Atlanta, GA; ed/ Dipl, Westminster HS, 1979; Bach of Aerospace Engrg, GA Inst of Technol, 1983; Pursuing MS, Aeronautical Engrg, Stanford Univ; mil/Comm'd 2nd Lt, USAF; pa/Intern for Senator Sam Nunn, 1983; cp/Canterbury Assn, VChm 1982-83; Arnold Air Soc, Adm Ofcr 1980-82; Inter-Varsity Christian F'ship, GA Inst of Technol, Small Grp Ldr 1982-83; GA Inst of Technol Varsity Rifle Team; r/Christian; hon/ Phi Epsilon Sigma, 1979; Sigma Gamma Tau, 1981; Tau Beta Pi, 1983; Gamma Beta Phi, 1982; g/Serving in the AF; Wk'g at NASA.

DUNCAN, SYLVIA KAYE oc/Assistant Director of Admissions; b/Jun 7, 1959; h/PO Box 1160, Buies Creek, NC 27506; ba/Buies Creek, NC; p/Billy M Duncan, Whiteville, NC; Marian W Duncan, Lake Waccamaw, NC; ed/ Waccamaw Acad, 1977; BA, Eng, Univ of NC Wilmington, Campbell Univ, 1982; Att'd, Campbell Univ Sch of Law, 1982-83; pa/Asst Mgr, Merle Norman Cosmetics, 1980; Circulations Asst, Randall Lib, Univ of NC Wilmington, 1978-80; Salesperson, Lenny's Men's Clothes, 1977-78; Asst Dir of Admissions, Campbell Univ; cp/Toastmasters; Assoc Editor, *The Lyricist*; Witness, 1983 Client Cnslg Competition; Clk, 1983 Moot Ct Competition; Secy-Treas, Campbell Univ Yg Dems; Mabel Powell Eng Clb; Univ Pubs Bd; r/Bapt; hon/ Dean's List; W/W Among Am HS Students; g/Return to Sch for Further Study in Eng.

DUPEE, LEIGH DeFOREST oc/Student; b/Jul 13, 1963; h/South Stream Road, Bennington, VT 05201; p/Mr and Mrs DeForest Dupee, Bennington, VT; ed/Mt Anthony Union HS, 1981; N Adams St Col; pa/Computer Conslt, N Adams St Col, 1980, 1981, 1982; r/Prot; hon/W/W Among Am HS Students; Yg Commun Ldrs of Am; Intl Yth in Achmt; g/Wk in the Field of Ergonomics.

DUPREE, ANNIE PEARL oc/Student; h/Nov 2, 1964; h/904 Coffield Avenue, Tarboro, NC 27886; ed/Student, Tarboro HS; cp/Cheerldr, 1981; HS Band, 3 Yrs; Majorette, 2 Yrs; Jr Ebonette; Student Coun Rep; Hon Soc; Tchr, Baton at Rec Ctr; Tutor of Small Kids; r/Ch Choir; Piano Player for Ch and Sunday Sch; Bapt; hon/Nat Hon Soc, 1983; Class Princess, 3 Yrs; g/Computer Programmer, Computer Sci.

DUPREE, DAVID EDWARD oc/ Student; b/Nov 17, 1960; h/412 North Prospect Avenue, Redondo Beach, CA 90277; p/Mr and Mrs James E Dupree, Redondo Beach, CA; ed/Grad, Redondo Union High, 1979; Engrg Maj, Univ of CA LA; pa/Workroom Supvr, Electronic Convs Inc, 1979-81; Math Tutor, El Camino Commun Col, 1982; Field Engr, IBM, 1983; cp/Univ of CA LA Computer Clb; hon/Letterman, Water Polo and Swimming, Redondo Union High, 1976-79; 2 CIF Gold Medals, Varsity Competitive Swimming, 1977, 1978; Un Sung Hero Awd, Electronic Convs Inc, 1980; g/Grad Degs in Computer Design and Engrg, and Career in Same Field.

DUPREE, JACKIE MARSHELLE oc/ Student; b/Aug 20, 1967; h/Route 2, Box 209, Lexicross Bel, TN 37306; p/Ernestine Johnson, Lexicross Bel, TN; cp/Beta

1983-85; Student Coun, 1983-84; Pep Clb, 1982-85; Indust Arts Clb, 1983-84; Newspaper Staff, 1983-85; r/SDA; h/ Sch Jour; g/Engrg (Mech or Arch).

DuPRIEST, DARLENE oc/Student; b/Aug 4, 1964; h/1321 Walters Street, Covington, TN 38019; p/Jerry DuPriest, Covington, TN; Carleen Mathis, Covington, TN; ed/Covington High, 1982; Currently Enrolled, Union Univ; pa/ Mgr of Pool and Proshop, Covington Country Clb, 1981, 1982; *Jackson Journal*, 1983; cp/HS: Band, Flag Corps (Co-Capt), Annual Staff; Pep Clb (Pres), Student Coun (Secy and Parliamentarian), Drama Clb, French Clb; Col: Upsilon Chapt of Chi Omega; r/Bapt; hon/Nat Hon Soc; Del to Girls St; Salutatorian; W/W Among Am HS Students; g/BS in Acctg; CPA.

DUTSON, NATALIE oc/Student; b/Sep 11, 1963; h/625 South 500 West, Delta, UT 84624; p/George E and Sandra Dutson, Delta, UT; ed/Grad, Delta HS, 1982; Currently Att'g Brigham Yg Univ for BFA in Illustration; cp/Feature Twirler, BYU Cougar Marching Band; Perf in 2 Consecutive Holiday Bowls; Perf on Local, Reg and Nat TV; Competes Nationally in Twirling; HS Cheerldr, 3 Yrs; HS A Cappella and Madrigal Choirs; HS Feature Twirler; HS Art Sterling Scholar; Nat Hon Soc; hon/HS Valedictorian; Miss Millard Co; 1st Runner-Up in Brigham Yg Univ Homecoming Royalty, 1982; Art and Acad S'ships to Brigham Yg Univ; W/W Among Am HS Students; Am HS Aths; Am's Outstg Names and Faces; W/W in Baton Twirling; g/Grad from Brigham Yg Univ w BFA in Illustration and Minor in Psych; To Continue Tchg Baton Twirling.

DuVALL, KIMBERLY DAWNNE RAY oc/Student; b/Aug 18, 1961; h/7007 Lemay Road, Rockville, MD 20851; ba/Harrisonburg, VA; p/James E and Carol J DuVall, Rockville, MD; ed/Dipl, Richard Montgomery HS; Secretarial w Shorthand Cert 1981, Gen Bus Student Cert 1981, Montgomery Col;

Att'd, Shepherd Col; BS, James Madison Univ, 1983; pa/Word Processing Operator, R Keigher, Atty, 1981; Sales, Lord and Taylor, 1980-81; Spa Instr, Fitness World, 1980; Receptionist/Typist, P J Nee Furniture Co, 1977-80; cp/Nat Hon Soc, 1977-79; Phi Theta Kappa, Montgomery Col, 1980-81; Affil, Am Psychol Assn, 1983; Treas, House Coun, Miller Hall, Shepherd Col, 1981-82; Exec Com, Student Govt Assn, HS, 1977-79; Pompon Squad (Drill Team, HS), 1976-79, Capt 1977-79; Madrigal Singers, HS, 1978-79; Choir, HS, 1978-79; Choir, Shepherd Col, 1981; Sellerettes Dance Grp, 1979; Choir, HS, 1978-79; Choir, Shepherd Col, 1981; r/Bapt; hon/HS: Hon Roll, Nat Hon Soc, St of MD Scholastic Merit Awd, Outstg Bus Student of the Yr 1979; Montgomery Col: Dean's List, Chancellor's Hon Awd, Phi Theta Kappa; Shepherd Col: Dean's List, Ella Mae Turner S'ship, Shepherd Col S'ship; g/Maj in Psych and Minor in Secretarial Adm; To Wk in the Area of Interpersonal Relats, Cnslg Areas.

DYER, STACY RUTH oc/Student; b/Nov 20, 1963; h/2543 Harrison Street, Paducah, KY 42001; p/Ruth A Dyer, Paducah, KY; ed/Paducah Tilghman HS, 1981; BS, Murray St Univ; Cert'd Emer Med Tech; pa/Pt-time Sum Orientation Cnslr; Umpire, Baseball and Softball; cp/HS: Student Coun (Secy), Yrbook Staff (Sports Editor, Editor-in Chief), Sr Class Secy, Exec Bd, Student Rep to PTSA Ways and Means Com, Biol Clb (Pres), Spanish Clb (VP), Key Clb, Public Address and Stats, Football Homecoming Queen Ct, Basketball Homecoming Queen Ct, Sambiki Saru Sorority, Girls' Golf Team, Girls' Track Team, St Champions, Usher 10, Wrestling Stat, Letterman's Clb; Col: Omicron Delta Kappa (VP), Alpha Lambda Delta (VP), Gamma Beta Phi, Beta Beta Beta, Pre-Med Clb, Ethics Com Rep, Sigma Sigma Sigma Social Sorority (Treas, Pledge Class Pres, Fdr's Day Chp), Student Ambassador, Order of Omega, Pi Kappa Alpha Little Sister (Pledge Class Treas), Varsity Cheerldr (Bus

Mgr, Capt), Jud Bd, Bioethics Com (Secy), Undergrad Res, Intramurals, Softball, Flag Football, Swimming, Volleyball, Basketball, Co-Ed Softball, Co-Ed Basketball; r/Handbell Choir, Bible Sch Tchr, Cumberland Presb Yth F'ship (VP); hon/HS: Jr Rotarian II, Harvard Book Awd, Girls' St Del, Reg Yth Salute Winner, Am Awd for Nat Yth Ldr, Dutchess of Padukah, Nat Hon Soc, Page for KY Gen Assem, Valedictorian, Most Outstg Biol, Hist and Overall Sci Student, Dist'd Student Awd, DAR Citizenship Awd, Alpha Kappa Alpha Outstg Ser Awd, Num Other HS Hons; Col: Pres S'ship, Outstg Intramural Player, Dean's List, High S'ship; W/W Among Am HS Students; Am's Outstg Names and Faces; g/MD.

DYSON, DENISE O oc/Student; b/Sep 7, 1962; h/6481 Swan Arc, Norfolk, VA 23513; p/Ms Olivia M Dyson, Norfolk, VA; ed/Norview HS; Student, Old Dominion Univ, 1980-; pa/Computer Operator 1978-80, Supvr 1980-, Tidewater Trading Post Inc; cp/Pres, Old Dominion Univ Chapt of Nat Tech Assn, 1983-; Pres, F'ship of Minority Engrs and Scists, 1982-; Assoc Justice, ODU's Hon Coun, 1983-84; hon/Voted Most Outstg Mem Awd, 1983; W/W Among Students in Am Cols and Univs; g/BS in Mech Engrg; MS and PhD in Engrg.

DZUPIN, NANCY JANE oc/Executive; b/Oct 7, 1954; h/98-40 64th Avenue, Rego Park, NY 11374; ba/New York, NY; p/John and Anna Dzupin; ed/Acad Dipl, Seward Pk HS, 1972; BS, cum laude, Marymount Manhattan Col, 1976; MBA, Pace Univ, 1980; pa/Exec VP 1983-, Corporate Mgr 1981-83, First Sers; cp/Pace Univ Alumni Assn, 1980-; Chm, 1776 Conservative Clb, 1982-; Exec Com Mem, NY Co Conservative Party; Treas, Clemons for Assem Campaign, 1980; St Senate Cand, 27th ed, 1982; hon/U Fdn of Tchrs Col S'ship, 1972-76; NYC Mgmt Intern, NYC Fin Adm; W/W Among Students in Am Cols and Univs; Commun Ldrs of Am.

E

EADS, DOUGLAS EDWARD oc/ Student; b/Aug 28, 1964; h/Box 8, Windsor, KY 42565; p/James and Janet Eads, Windsor, KY; ed/Grad, Casey Co HS, 1982; Student, Somerset Commun Col; pa/News Reporter, WJRS, 1983; cp/ Pres, Cumberland River Yth Assn, 1980-81; Pres, 4-H Clb, 1976-77; Offensive Guard and Defensive Tackle, Football Team, 1978-80; Football, Basketball Stat; Pres, Bapt Yth Assn; Songldr, Bapt Yth Assn; Asst Sports Editor 1982-83, Sports Editor 1983, *The Mirror*; r/Ch Usher; Bapt; hon/KY Intercol Press Assn for Sports Articles; W/W Among Am HS Students; g/BA in Broadcasting.

EASON, JOSEPH SMITH JR oc/ Director of Occupational Therapy; b/ Jun 12, 1954; h/217-4th Street, Manchester, GA; ba/Warm Springs, GA; m/ Linda Sue Streeter; c/Ashley Marie, Casey Rene, Joseph Smith III; p/Joseph S Sr and Imogene Battle Eason, Ellaville, GA; ed/BS, Med Col of GA; pa/Staff Occupl Therapist, GA Retard Ctr, 1979-80; Sr Occupl Therapist 1980-83, Dir of Occupl Therapy 1983-, Roosevelt Inst; Nat, St and Dist Occupl Therapy Assns, 1977-; Nat and GA Rehab Assns, 1982-; cp/Scoutmaster, BSA, Troop 143, 1981-; r/Manchester First U Meth Ch Ofcl Bd, 1982-; hon/Grad, cum laude, Med Col of GA, 1977; Wood Badge, God and Country Awds, BSA; g/Eventual Pvt Pract Providing Occupl Therapy Sers in a Rural Commun.

EASON, KIMBERLY CLARK oc/ Student; b/Oct 1, 1965; h/1006 Hilton, Aiken, SC 29801; p/Charles R and Carol K Eason, Aiken, SC; ed/Att'd, May River Acad 1981-82, Brookstone Sch 1977-80, Presb Col 1982-83; Att'g, Univ of SC, 1983-; cp/Brookstone Sch Choir and Handbells, 1977-80; Nat Beta Clb, 1981; Class Ofcr: Treas 5th, Secy-Treas 6th, Secy-Treas 8th, Treas 9th, Treas 10th, Pres 12th; r/Bapt; Yth Coun and Yth Choir VP, 1979-80; hon/Awd for Acad Excell in Calculus, Dean's List, Presb Col; Sr Superlatives: Most Talented, Most Likely to Succeed, Best Dressed; Miss GA Pageant Dancer, 1980; Miss Columbus Pageant, Singer 1975, 1977, Dancer 1978; Miss Beaufort Pageant, Singer 1981, 1982, 1983, Dancer 1981, 1982; Contestant, Miss Teen All-Am Pageant 1979, Miss Azalea Pageant 1982, 1983; Chosen for "Carolina Alive" at USC, 1983; May River Acad Hon Roll, 6 Quarters, 1981-82; Miss Azalea, 1983; GA All-St Chorus, 1979-81; 2nd Place Reg AA Lit Meet Girls' Solo, 1980; Beaufort Water Fest Talent Show, 1st Place, 1980-81; All-Student Chorus USA, European Tour, 1982; $4000 Voice S'ship to Presb Col; Soc of Dist'd Am HS Students, 1981-82; g/Bus Maj; Profl Singing while Achieving Success in Bus.

EATON, PATRICIA A oc/Student; b/ Jan 21, 1963; h/1411 Evans Street, Morehead City, NC 28557; p/Mr and Mrs John H Eaton II, Morehead City, NC; ed/W Carteret HS, 1981; E Carolina Univ; cp/Co-Ed Intramurals, Volleyball, E Carolina Univ; Wom's Glee Clb, E Carolina Univ; Cheerldg; Student Coun; Sophomore Class VP; Jr Class Pres; Sch Newspaper, Assoc Editor; Homecoming Cand; Heart Fund Cand;

FCA; Pep Clb; Singers Choir; French Clb; Girls Aux St; NC Student Legis; r/Ch Choir; hon/Am Legion Ser Awd; Soc of Dist'd Am HS Students; W/W Among Am HS Students; g/BS Deg in Art.

EBRON, MICHELLE J oc/Part-time Employee of Dietary Medical Center; b/ Oct 11, 1960; h/1218 Davenport Street, Greenville, NC 27834; p/Mr and Mrs James Hopkins, Greenville, NC; ed/Dipl, Farmville Ctl HS, 1978; BA, Politi Sci, Johnson C Smith Univ, 1983; pa/Food Ser Wkr, Charlotte Meml Med Ctr, 1981-; Cashier, Charlottetown Cinema; cp/Vol Tutor for Charlotte Area Lit Leag, 1983; Staff Reporter, Polit Sci Clb, 1981-83, 1977-78; VICA; Ofc Asst and Staff Reporter, HS News; r/AME Zion; hon/2nd Runner-Up for Ms Greenville Contest; Elected to Nat Dean's List, 1981-83; g/To Gain Experience in All Phases of Law and Politics w the Ultimate Goal of Becoming a Crim Lwyr.

ECHAUS, MARGUERITE M oc/ Piano Teacher; b/Apr 30, 1958; h/ Apartment 302, 1266 West 13th Avenue, Vancouver, British Columbia, Canada V6H 1N6; p/Mr and Mrs Ramon R Echaus, Vancouver, British Columbia; ed/Georgetown Visitation Convent, 1976; BMus in Piano, Cath Univ of Am, 1980; Master of Music Ed w Kodaly Emphasis, Holy Names Col, 1985; pa/ Yamaha Piano Tchr, 1983; Canadian Music Edrs Assn; Brit Columbia Music Edrs Assn; Nat Guild of Piano Tchrs; Kodaly Inst of Canada; Carl Orff Canada; hon/Grad, magna cum laude; Pi Kappa Lambda; Sigma Alpha Iota Hon Cert; Nat Dean's List; W/W Among Am HS Students; Intl Yth in Achmt; Commun Ldrs of Am; g/Music Spec in Elem Schs.

EDIRISINGHE, JANAKA oc/Industrial Engineer; b/Jul 2, 1958; h/700-A, South Chapman Street, Greensboro, NC 27403; ba/Greensboro, NC; m/ Khulsum; p/Albert and Yasawathi Edirisinghe; sp/Mr and Mrs Bunchy Gunasekara; ed/BSc, MSc, Indust Engrg, NC A&T St Univ; pa/Wkg Dir, Albert Edirisinghe Electronics Ltd, 1982-83; Wkg Dir, Lanka Optical Industs Ltd, 1982-83; Wkg Dir, Albert Edirisinghe Opticians Ltd, 1982-83; Overall Supvr, NC A&T St Univ Dept of Indust Engrg, 1981-82; Instr, NC A&T St Univ Dept of Indust Engrg, 1980-81; Other Previous Positions; Nat Soc of Profl Engrs; cp/Assn of Cornell Lettermen Ath and Col Swimming Team; Intramural Sports; A&T Student Indust Cluster Assn; Student Rep to Dept of Self-Study Com, Intl Student Affairs Ofc; Student Rep for Sch of Engrg; hon/Pubs, "A Heciristic Approach for Module Scheduling in a Distributed Computer"; Grad, summa cum Laude; Beta Kappa Chi; Hon Roll; /Nat Dean's List; AIIE Awd, S'ship; Olin Corp Awd, S'ship; Tau Alpha Tau; Johnson Wax Corp Awd, S'ship; Alpha Phi Omega Awd; Student Indust Cluster Assn; W/W Among Students in Am Univs and Cols; Intl Yth in Achmt; g/ Wkg at So Optical as Quality Control Engr.

EDMISSON, KENNY W oc/Student; b/Feb 10, 1965; h/125 Louise Drive, Dickson, TN 37055; ba/Oxford, GA; p/

Kenneth W and Joyce K Edmisson, Dickson, TN; ed/Dickson Co Sr HS; Emory Univ; pa/Lifeguard, J Dan Buckner Mun Pool, 1979-80; Nsg Staff, Goodlark Med Ctr, 1981-; Lifeguard, Emory Univ, 1983-84; cp/Am Heart Assn, BCLS Instr, Tnr, Bd of Dirs, CPR Com Chm, Dist 6 Asst Chm; ARC, Water Safety Instr, Multi-Media First Aid Instr, Modular CPR Instr; Rotaract Treas; r/Ch of Christ; hon/Math, Sci, Bus, 1980; Sci, 1981; Sci, 1982; Math, Sci, 1983; Grad w Beta Hons; W/W Among Am HS Students; Personalities of S; g/BA in Eng and Biol, Minor in Chem; MD.

EDMONDS, MARK BRADLEY oc/ Medical Student; b/May 17, 1959; h/ 2209 Northwest 46th, Oklahoma City, OK 73118; ba/Oklahoma City, OK; p/ Aaron and Ruth Edmonds, Chouteau, OK; ed/HS Dipl, 1977; AS in Biol, Connors St Col, 1979; BS in Cardiorespiratory Sci, Univ of OK Hlth Scis Ctr, 1981; Med Student, OK Univ Med Sch, 1983-; pa/Respiratory Therapy Supvr, OK Chd's Meml Hosp, 1980-82; Respiratory Flight Therapist on the Neonate Flight Team, Dept of Human Sers, St of OK-Mediflight, 1982-83; Am Assn for Respiratory Therapists; Am Med Student Assn; AMA; Editor, Nat Am Assn of Respiratory Therapist's Student Sect Newsletters, 1980-81; r/ Cath; hon/Outstg Biol Student, Connors St Col, 1978-79; BS w Spec Distn, OK Univ, 1981; Nat Dean's List, 1979-80; Dist'd Student Awd, OK Univ, 1978-79; Jr Col Ldrship S'ship, 1980; Pres's Hon Roll, 4 Semesters; Dean's Hon Roll, 5 Semesters; W/W Am Cols and Univs; g/Grad from OK Univ Med Sch in May 1987; Residency in Pediatrics or Emer Med; Set Up Pract in Tulsa, OK.

EDWARDS, JANE ALISON oc/ Undergraduate Student; b/Jul 28, 1961; h/714 Fletcher Street, Cedartown, GA 30125; ba/Mt Berry, GA; p/Mr and Mrs C W Edwards, Cedartown, GA; ed/ Cedartown Comprehensive HS, 1979; Grad, Berry Col, 1984; cp/Hon Soc, 1975-79, Secy 1975-76; French Clb, 1975-79, Reporter 1978-79; Chorus, 1975-77; Lib Clb, 1976-79, Pres 1977-79; Lib Aide, 1976-79; Pres's Clb, 1977-79; Lambda Sigma, Sophomore Hon Soc, 1980-81; Phi Alpha Theta, Omicron Epsilon Chapt, 1982-; AAAS, 1978-79; Nat Space Inst, 1977-; Planetary Soc, 1981-82; Early Am Soc, 1977-; Oceanic Soc, 1978-79; r/Bapt; hon/ A-Average Awd, 1975-79; Berry Math Meet, 1977; Eng Awd, 1978; Gov's Hons Nom, 1977-78; Eng Lit Awd, 1979; Outstg Student in the Humanities, 1979; Grad'd 2nd in Class of 263, 1979; Recip, 4-Yr Acad S'ship to Berry Col, 1979; Recip, Lila Laughlin Carlisle S'ship, Berry Col, 1981-82; Recip, Eva Cook Ware S'ship, Berry Col, 1982-83; W/W Among Am HS Students; g/ Pursue Adv'd Deg in Hist, w a Career in Hist Res.

EDWARDS, TERI LYN oc/Student; b/Mar 11, 1962; h/110 West 7th Street, Pecatonica, IL 61063; p/Richard and Carol Edwards, Pecatonica, IL; ed/ Pecatonica HS, 1980; Bradley Univ; cp/ Acctg Students Assn, 1982-; Phi Chi Theta, 1982-; HS Class Secy; NHS VP; Quill and Scroll; Clb; Math Clb Pres; HS Newspaper Staff; Yrbook Writer,

Typist; Band; Basketball; Football, Basketball Stat; Ofc Aide, HS; Intramural Volleyball; Hospitality Corps Floor Rep; Alpha Lambda Delta, Phi Eta Sigma Secy; r/St John's Luth Ch Yg Peoples Soc Secy; Growing in Christ Yth Grp Pres; hon/Beta Alpha Psi, Reporting Secy 1982-; Beta Gamma Sigma, 1982-; Phi Kappa Phi, 1982-; IL St Scholar, 1980; Valedictorian; DAR Good Citizenship Awd; Dean's List; W/W Among Am HS Students; g/BS in Bus and Acctg; CPA.

EFTHYVOULOS, NICHOLAS oc/Microprocessor Design Engineer; b/Mar 29, 1958; h/PO Box 50244, Pasadena, CA 91105; ba/Sun Valley, CA; p/George Efthyvoulos, Harare, Zimbabwe; ed/Allan Wilson Tech High, 1978; BS, CA St Univ LA, 1982; mil/1977-78; pa/Microprocessor Design Engr, Dynatrol Nat, 1982-; IEEE, Chapt Pres 1980-82; Tau Beta Pi, Treas 1981-82; Eta Kappa Nu, VP 1981-82; Engrg Student Coun, Treas 1980-82, Phi Kappa Phi; ASME; SAME; r/Ch of God; hon/Hon Mention, LACES Outstg Engrg Student, 1983; SAME Outstg Engrg Student, 1980; Zimbabwe Govt S'ship; W/W Among Students in Am Univs; Intl Yth in Achmt; g/Res in Biomed Engrg for the Handicapped; MS and PhD in Robotics and Control Sys.

EGGER, PATRICIA ANNETTE oc/Student; b/Oct 25, 1964; h/Route 3, Box 262, Russell Springs, KY 42642; p/Mr and Mrs Elmer Egger, Russell Springs, KY; ed/Russell Co HS, 1982; Russell Co Voc Sch, 1982; cp/Band; Flag Corps; Drill Team; Pep Clb; FBLA; Hlth Occups Students of Am, Parliamentarian; Teens Who Care; NHS; hon/Perfect Attendance; Profiles of Outstg Yg Ams; W/W Amg Am HS Students; g/X-Ray Tech.

EGGERS, CYNTHIA ANNE oc/Student; b/May 28, 1963; h/236 Printz Avenue, Essington, PA 19029; p/Mr and Mrs Earl H Eggers; ed/Interboro HS, 1981; Millersville Univ of PA; pa/White Manor Country Clb, 1981; Millersville Univ Weather Sta, 1983-; Intern, WGAL-TV, 1984; cp/Student Senator, Millersville Univ of PA, 1983-84; Student Senator Advr to Fac Senate, 1983-84; NJHS, NHS, 1976-81; Latin Clb, 1977-82; Math Clb, 1981; Marching Band, 1977-81; Concert Band, 1977-81; Jazz Band, 1977-78; Chorus, 1977-81; Mini Chorus; Crossmen Drum and Bugle Corps, 1981-83; AFS Secy, 1980; German Clb, 1981; Hon Roll, 1970-81; Vol, 1979-81; Earth Sci Clb, 1981-; r/Epis; hon/Outstg Vol Awd, 1980; Optimist Awd, 1980; Band Key, 1981; Num Acad Achmt Awds for Classes in HS; W/W Among Am HS Students; Intl Yth in Achmt; g/Master's Deg in Meteorology; Wk for NASA or Other Form of Govt Agy.

EGGERT, KATHERINE E oc/Student; b/Nov 20, 1962; h/PO Box 2487, Houston, TX 77252; ba/Same; ed/Grad, Russell HS, 1980; BA, Rice Univ, 1984; pa/Editor, Sci Pubs Dept of Univ of TX M D Anderson Hosp and Tumor Inst, 1983; Tutor, Rice Univ Eng Dept, 1983-; cp/Rice Univ: Elections Col 1982-83, Undergrad Tchg Com 1983-84; Hanszen Col: Master Selection Com 1981-82, Communs Chm 1983-84, Orientation Wk Coor 1983-84; r/Luth; hon/Pres's Hon Roll, Rice Univ, All Semesters;

Lady Geddes Prize for Writing, Rice Univ, 1982; Hanszen Col Fellow, 1983; Beinecke Meml Scholar, 1983; Phi Beta Kappa, 1983; W/W Among Students in Am Univs and Cols; g/Professorship in Eng Lit.

EGLAND, LINDA RUTH oc/Student; b/Oct 27, 1966; h/203 Edgehill Drive, Battle Creek, MI 49015; p/Mr and Mrs Franklin Egland, Battle Creek, MI; ed/Grad, Lakeview HS, 1984; cp/Tchrs Aide, Sum Sch, 1983; Vol, Calhoun Co Hlth Ctr, Gen Ofc Wk, 1983; Fish Clb, 1981, 1982, 1983, Secy 1983; HS Newspaper Staff, 1982-83; HS Girls' Varsity Swim Team, 1980-83; Yth Gives Vol, 1983; HS Syncronized Swim Team, 1982-83; HS Girls' Jr Varsity Track Team, 1980; HS Band, 1980, 1981; r/Luth; Luth Yth Org Coun, 1983; hon/HS Girls' Swim Team, Co-Capt 1983; Most Improved Swimmer, 1980, 1981; HS Hon Roll; HS Girls Syncronized Swim Team Bd, 1984; Am Soc of Dist'd HS Students; g/Col Ed at 4-Yr Univ/Col.

EHRLICH, DAVID GURNEY oc/Legislative Assistant; b/Dec 11, 1957; h/502 F Street, Washington, DC 20002; p/William and Patricia Ehrlich, Grosse Point Park, MI; ed/Grosse Point S HS, 1976; BA, Univ of MI, 1981; pa/Legis Asst, Congressman Bruce A Morrison (CT-3), 1983; Legis Asst, Congressman Charles B Rangel (16-NY), 1983-; cp/Com Concerned w World Hunger; Theta Xi; Intl Relats Soc; Undergrad Polit Sci Assn; Univ of MI Sailing Clb; Kalamazoo Col Band; Orch; Ragtime Ensemble; MI St Univ Repertory Band; Local Jazz Band; Grosse Pt Jr Symph; Grosse Pt Symph, 1975-76; Nuclear Weapons Freeze Campaign, 1982; Kennedy Campaign Wkr; Emer Room Vol; Sr Class Pres; Student Senator; Kathleen O'Reilly Campaign Wkr; Betty Crocker Fam Life Knowledge Awd; Lttrman, Cross-Country, Track; hon/Recip, High Hons in Polit Sci, Univ of MI.

EICHELBERGER, PHILIS LAVORN oc/Radio Air Personality, Public Service Director; b/Feb 21, 1961; h/2102 20th Avenue, Apartment #6, Gulfport, MS 39501; ba/Gulfport, MS; p/Lavorn Eichelberger, Louisville, MS; ed/Grad, Louisville HS, 1978; BS, Mass Communs, Jackson St Univ, 1981; pa/Air Personality, Public Ser Dir, WTAM-AM, 1981-; Announcer, WJMI-FM, 1980-81; cp/Am Cancer Soc, Harrison Co Unit, Public Info, 1982- (Current Chp); r/Bapt; hon/Certs of Apprec for Support, Biloxi Pks, Rec and Cultural Affairs (Jul 1982, Dec 1982), and Gulfcoast Commun Action Agy (Aug 1983); g/Public Relats/Prodn Mgr for Large Firm.

EIKENES, DEBRA JEAN oc/Nursing Student; b/Nov 18, 1964; h/34 Thorney Avenue, Huntington Station, NY 11746; p/Torgrim and Jean Eikenes, Huntington Station, NY; ed/HS Grad, 1982; Grad, WV Wesleyan Col, 1986; cp/Girls' Ldrs Clb, 1980-82; Prom Com, 1981-82; Field Hockey Team, HS, 1977-81; Col Field Hockey, 1983; Sophomore Class Pres, Col, 1983; Student Nurses of Wesleyan, 1982-86; r/Exchange Free Ch; 10th Place, Miss Norway Contest, 1982; g/BS and RN; Master's Deg in a Specialized Field of Nsg.

EISENHAUER, DEE HERMES oc/

Student; b/Sep 20, 1959; h/1401 North College, Apartment D-14, Claremont, CA 91711; ba/Claremont, CA; m/John A; p/Mary Lou and Norman Hermes, Paradise, MT; ed/Grad, Plains HS, 1977; BS, Rocky Mtn Col, 1980; Equiv of MDiv, Sch of Theol, Claremont, CA, 1984; pa/Intern Min, Altadena Congregational Ch, 1983; Asst Min, Claremont U Ch of Christ, 1983; Intern Min, Claremont U Ch of Christ, 1982; Senate Aide, MT St Legis, 1981; Day Care Aide and Tchr, 1980; Asst to the Chaplain, Rocky Mtn Col, 1978; cp/Sch of Theol Student Coun Ofcr, 1981-82; Chp, Starthrowers Min Grp, Rocky Mtn Col, 1979; Chp, Hunger Task Force, Rocky Mtn Col, 1978-79; Plains HS Student Coun Rep, 1976; r/Christian; hon/Finalist in Wilshire Preaching Awd Competition, Sch of Theol, 1984; Recip, Cooper S'ship, 1981-84; W/W Among Am Cols and Univs; W/W Am HS; g/DMin; Ordained Min.

EISMAN, MERLE ROSE oc/Television Unit Manager; b/Aug 31, 1957; h/100 Coburn Woods, Nashua, NH 03063; ba/Boston, MA; p/Hy and Adri Eisman, Glen Rock, NJ; ed/Glen Rock Jr Sr HS, 1975; Att'd, Carnegie-Mellon Univ, 1975-76; BA, Mass Communs, Emerson Col, 1979; pa/Prodn Asst, "The New Action Four," WBZ-TV, 1978; Acctg Asst, WBCN-FM, 1979-80; Acctg Asst 1980, Unit Mgr of "Sports and Specials" 1981, Unit Mgr of "Frontline" 1982-, WGBH-TV.

ELAM, VANESSA GAY oc/Secretary and Receptionist; b/Mar 2, 1961; h/Route 6, Box 367, Lenoir City, TN 37771; p/Mr and Mrs James R Elam, Lenoir City, TN; ed/Lenoir City HS, 1979; BBA, Acctg, Mid TN St Univ, 1983; pa/Campus Rep for Beckers Review Course, 1982-83; Resident Hall Asst, MTSU, 1982-83; Secy/Receptionist, Burton M Rudolph MD, 1979-; Salad Girl, Kings Inn Restaurant; Waitress, Twin Lantern Restaurant; cp/Beta Alpha Psi, 1981-83, Correspondence Secy 1982; Acts Soc, 1980-83; Am Soc of Wom Accts, Charter 1982-83, Secy-Treas 1982-83; Sigma Iota Epsilon, 1980-83; Gamma Beta Phi, 1980-83; Delta Mu Delta, 1981-83, VP 1981-82, Telephone Com Chm 1982; Bapt Student Union, 1979-83; Wesley Foun, 1980-83; r/Bapt; hon/Dean's List, Sprg 1982, Fall 1982, Sprg 1983; Hon Roll, Sprg 1983; S'ship Awd, Govt Acts Nashville Chapt, 1982; W/W Among Student in Am Univs and Cols; Nat Dean's List; W/W; g/CPA.

ELLENBERG, MARY NAN oc/Student; b/Mar 6, 1966; h/PO Box 1, Richland, SC 29675; p/Henry C and Claudia Ellenberg, Richland, SC; ed/Grad, Seneca HS, 1984; cp/Jr Beta Clb, Pres 1979-80; Sr Beta Clb, 1982-83; Creat Writing Clb, 1981-84; Varsity Basketball, 1980-84; Varsity Softball, 1983-84; Seneconian Yrbook Staff, Copy Editor 1982; r/Meth; hon/Rotary Scholar, 1978-83; Furman and Presb Col Scholar, 1983; Sem for Tomorrow's Ldr, 1983; All-Conf Basketball Awd, 1982-83; Selected for Palmetto Girls' St, 1983; W/W Among Am HS Students; g/To Study Vet Med or Related Fields.

ELLERBE, FRANCES BEZANSON oc/Student; b/Apr 28, 1963; h/1723 Catawba Street, Fayetteville, NC 28303; ed/AA, St Mary's, 1983; BA,

Bryn Mawr Col, 1985; pa/Waitress; Tutor in Rdg; Student Asst, St Mary's Col Lib; Gift Wrapping at Thalhimer's; cp/St Mary's Col Ensemble, 1981-83; Section Editor, St Mary's Annual, 1981-82; r/Epis; hon/Valedictorian, St Mary's Col, 1983; Semi-Finalist, Nat Dean's List S'ship Competition; Winner of Music Awd and S'ship, St Mary's Col, 1982-83; Niles Medal for Citizenship, 1983; g/Hist Maj w Concentration in Math.

ELLIOTT, MARY EMILY oc/Student; b/Mar 29, 1964; h/Route 4, Stanford, KY 40484; p/Taylor and Betsy Elliott, Stanford, KY; ed/Grad, Lincoln Co HS; Student, En KY Univ; pa/Pt-time Asst Libn, 1981-; r/Presb; hon/Annie Peek Martin and Henry Franklin Martin Meml S'ship, 1983-84; g/2nd or 3rd Grade Elem Tchr.

ELLIOTT, VICTORIA BEARD oc/Teacher; b/Oct 19, 1957; h/14114 Barryknoll, Houston, TX 77079; ba/Houston, TX; m/Dr Gerald A; p/Mr and Mrs Frank Beard, Houston, TX; ed/Stratford Sr HS, 1976; BA, Houston Bapt Univ, 1980; MA, Univ of Houston, 1982; pa/Tchr, Acting and Pantomime, Sch for Theatre Arts, 1982; Tchr, Eng, Drama, Spch, Pantomime, Paul Revere Mid Sch, 1982; cp/Asst Dir, First Bapt Ch Christmas Pageant, 1983; Univ of Houston Mime Troupe; Drama Dept Activs; Sunday Sch Dir, Pre-Sch Div of First Bapt Ch; Houston Shakespeare Fest; r/Bapt; hon/Grad, cum laude, Houston Bapt Univ, 1980; Omicron Delta Kappa; Alpha Chi; Alpha Psi Omega; W/W Among Students in Am Univs and Cols; Yg Commun Ldrs; Intl Yth in Achmt; g/Doct Deg in Eng.

ELLIS, CINDY LEA oc/Director of Private Kindergarten and Childcare Center; b/Apr 26, 1957; h/1808 West Midway, McKinney, TX 75069; p/J D and LaVelle Ellis, McKinney, TX; ed/McKinney HS, 1975; BA, Baylor Univ, 1979; pa/Dir of Pvt Kgn/Childcare Ctr; cp/Plano Commun Theater; Dem Party; Handgun Control Lobby; MD Vol w Shadow Chd; Baylor Alumni Assn; Vol, TX Epidemic; Com Mem, McKinney Circus Fair; Camp Cnslr; Theater Grp, Prodn Staff; Campaign Vol; Sum Wk w Ch Yth; g/Writer of Chd's Lit, Resource Books.

ELLIS, LAWRENCE THOMAS JR oc/Student; h/382 Burnt Hill Road, Skillman, NJ 08558; p/Lawrence and Shirley Ellis, Skillman, NJ; ed/The Lawrenceville Sch; BA in Phil, Univ of NC Chapel Hill, 1983; pa/Archaeol Intern, "La Mairie de Vienne" (France), Free-Lance (Egypt), Sum 1982; Legal Intern, Dickstein, Shapiro & Morin, Sum 1981; cp/Carolina Student Union, Pres 1981-82; NC Fellows Prog; Carolina Black Student Movement, Bd Mem 1979-81; Epis Diocese Mission to Haiti, Instr and Interpreter, 1981; The Lawrenceville Sch, Secy for Class of 1979; r/Christian; hon/Rhodes Scholar-Elect, 1983; John Motley Morehead Foun Scholar, 1979-83; Phi Beta Kappa, 1981; Order of the Golden Fleece, 1982; Chancellor's Awd for Outstg Jr Man (Ernest L Mackie Awd), 1982; g/Study of Theol and Phil at Oxford Univ, England; Career in Filmmaking, Writing, Commun Affairs.

ELLIS, LUCINDA oc/Student; b/Aug 17, 1952; h/1406 Southwest 12th

Avenue, Gainesville, FL 32601; p/Locke and Susan Rand Ellis, Melbourne, FL; ed/Acad Deg, Vero Bch HS, 1970; AA, Pensacola Jr Col, 1981; BS, Biol/Pre-Profl, Univ of W FL, 1983; Student, Univ of FL Sch of Vet Med; Pvt Pilot Lic, 1973; pa/Vet Asst, Airport Animal Hosp, 1978-83; Rdr, Div of Blind Sers, 1978; Bkkpr, Univ of W FL, 1978; Ranch Hand, Smith & Sons Ranch, 1977; Receptionist, Chiro Ctr Clin, 1976-77; cp/Phi Theta Kappa, Treas 1980; Pensacola Wildlife Rescue, 1978-83; Nat Wildlife Rescue and Sanctuary of FL Inc, 1982-83; Piper Flying Clb, 1973; Caterpillar Clb, 1973; Sci Fair Helper, PJC, 1968-69; Tutor, PJC, 1978-81; Green Peace; hon/Univ of W FL Mascot; Capt Thunder, Univ of Marine Patrol; Grad w Hons, Pensacola Jr Col, 1981; 1st Place, Wom's Archery, PJC, 1980; W/W Among Students in Am Jr Cols; Intl Yth in Achmt; Commun Ldrs of Am; g/To Finish Vet Sch; To Make Significant Contbn to Mankind.

ELLIS, PATRI ELIZABETH oc/Student; b/Aug 23, 1966; h/Route 6, Box 171, Louisville, MS 39339; p/Mike and Libby Ellis, Louisville, MS; ed/Louisville HS, 1984; pa/Waitress, Pizza Hut, 1981; Ofc Clk, Byer Appraisal Sers, 1983-84; cp/Girl Scouts, 1974-84; Art Clb, 1982; Symphonic Band, 1981-84; LHS Rifle Corp, 1980; Majorette, 1981-84, Hd for 1 Yr; Physics Clb, Treas 1983-84; Beta Clb, 1980-84; Sci Clb, 1982-83; Vica Clb, 1983-84; FDA Clb, 1983-84; Tennis Team, 1981-83; Basketball, 1980; r/Ch Choir, Secy 1983-84; hon/Sr Homecoming Maid, 1983; Winston Co Jr Miss, 1983-84; r/Meth; g/Engr.

ELTING, SHEILA RAE oc/Software Engineer; b/Jun 24, 1957; h/10245 Des Moines Way South 205, Seattle, WA 98168; p/Wayne and Ruby Lovgren, Laurel, MT; ed/HS Dipl, 1975; BS, MT St Univ, 1979; pa/Software Engr, Boeing Aerospace Co; Assn for Wom in Computing, VP; cp/Kappa Alpha Theta Jr Alumni Clb, Pres; Kappa Alpha Theta Sr Alumni Clb, Career Chm; Boeing Employees Concert Band, VP.

ELWOOD, REBECCA LYNN oc/Student; b/Apr 14, 1965; h/1819 Clark Street, Spring Lake, NC 28390; p/Mr and Mrs Joe D Elwood, Spring Lake, NC; ed/Wn Harnett HS, 1983; Student, Campbell Univ, 1983-; cp/Student Govt Assn, Pres; Beta Clb; Drama Clb, VP; French Clb, Secy; Inner Clb Coun, Secy; Sci Clb, Reporter; Newspaper, Clb Editor; Guid Aide; r/Bapt; hon/Valedictorian, 1983; Chief Marshal, 1982; Gov's Sch of NC (Math), 1982; Morehead S'ship Nom, 1983; Pres S'ship, 1983; Student of the Yr, 1983; W/W Among Am HS Students; g/Maj in Trust Mgmt at Campbell Univ.

EMERSON, SHERI S oc/Graduate Student; b/Apr 11, 1963; h/7847 US 23 South, Ossineke, MI 49766; p/William and Caryl Emerson, Ossineke, MI; ed/Alpena Sr HS, 1980; AA, Ferris St Col, 1981; BS in Bus Adm, summa cum laude, Ferris St Col, 1983; cp/City Band; Civic Orch; Yth Bowling Leag; Marching, Symph Bands; Masquers Clb; NHS; Homecoming Ct; Adm Mgmt Soc; Profl Frat Assn; Phi Gamma Nu Profl Bus Sorority, Histn; Nom'd to Omicron Delta Kappa Nat Hon Soc; r/Epis; hon/Runner-Up, Alpena Area Jr Miss Pageant; Voted Most Likely to Succeed;

Grad, 2/737, HS; Omicron Delta Kappa Outstg Student Awd, 1983; Dean's List Every Term; Cert of Recog Each Yr; Phi Gamma Nu Grad'g Sr w Highest GPA Awd, 1983; W/W Among Am HS Students; W/W Intl; g/Corporate or Real Est Lwyr.

EMFINGER, REBECCA LEIGH RILES oc/Clinical Dietitian; b/Jul 28, 1960; h/Route 3, Box 89-A, Meadville, MS 39653; ba/Meadville, MS; m/Dalton Lynn; p/Rev and Mrs John L Riles, Ocean Springs, MS; ed/Grad w Hons, Ocean Sprgs HS, 1978; BS, Univ of So MS, 1982; pa/Nutritionist II, MS St Bd of Hlth, 1982-83; Clin Dietitian, Franklin Co Meml Hosp, 1983-; Am Dietetic Assn; MS Dietetic Assn; Univ of So MS Alumni Assn; r/Bapt; hon/Yg Personalities of S; Intl Yth in Achmt; g/Raise a Fam; Serve the Commun; Be the Best Dietician She Can Be.

EMIDY, LINDA ANN oc/Nurse Researcher; b/Jul 15, 1949; h/836 South Loomis Street, Chicago, IL 60607; ba/Chicago, IL; p/Raymond E and Mildred M Emidy, North Smithfield, RI; ed/Woonsocket HS, 1967; AB, RI Col, 1971; MA, Ball St Univ, 1974; BSN 1977, MSN 1980, DNSc 1983, Rush Univ; pa/Nurse Rschr; APHA; ANA; Am Gerontological Soc; Am Biofeedback Soc; IL Biofeedback Soc; cp/Sigma Theta Tau; Big Sisters of Am; Nsg Home Visits to Elderly; Peace Corps Vol; r/Cath; hon/Sigma Theta Tau; Rush Univ Local Hon Soc; Wom Bd S'ship; RI Hon Soc; g/Operate Commun Based Wellness Ctr for Hlth Maintenance and Disease Preven.

ENABNIT, MELINDA ANN oc/Student; b/Jan 16, 1961; h/Route #1, Box 14R, Marble Rock, IA 50653; p/Bob and Leona Enabnit, Marble Rock, IA; ed/Rockford HS, 1980; Student, Wartburg Col; cp/Coach for Softball, 1982; Basketball, Volleyball; Softball; Slowpitch Team; All-Star Team in Slow Pitch; Col; Golf, Track, FBLA; Vol Wk, Mr ABC at Marble Rock; 4-H; hon/Top Hon Student in HS, 1980; Chapt Sweetheart for FFA, 1980; VP, FFA, 1980; Many 4-H Awds, 1970-80; NHS; W/W Among HS Students; g/CPA or Wk w Computers.

ENDRESS, PAMELA JO oc/Court Reporter; b/Oct 1, 1955; h/RR 1, Edelstein, IL; p/Mr and Mrs John Endress, Edelstein, IL; ed/Princeville HS, 1973; Midstate Col, 1979; pa/Ct Reporter; hon/Perfect GPA; Valedictorian; Ct Reporting Outstg Achmt Awd; Intl Yth in Achmt; Nat Dean's List; W/W Among Students in Am Jr Cols.

ENGEL, DINAH KATHRYN oc/Student; b/May 17, 1966; h/Artemus, KY 40903; p/Rev John E and Wanda H Engel, Artemus, KY; ed/Grad, Knox Ctl HS, 1984; Att'd Spec Prog, Lincoln Meml Univ, 1983; cp/FTA, 1980-83; Beta, 1981-84; Spanish Clb, 1980-84; FHA, 1981-84, Treas 1984, Reporter 1983; Yrbook Staff, 1984; r/Bapt; hon/US Achmt Acad Spanish Awd, 1981; Nat Hon Roll Soc, 1984; All-Am High Acad Awd, 1984; Nat Sci Merit Awd, 1984; Valedictorian, 1984; Jour, 1984; Spanish, 1984; Math, 1984; Most Dependable, 1984; Most Intell, 1984; Hon Student, 1984; Physics, 1984; W/W Among Am HS Students; g/Math.

ENGELKEN, LuANN MARIE oc/Information Specialist; b/Dec 3, 1958;

h/611 2nd Avenue South, Humboldt, IA 50548; p/Edwin and Aletha Engelken, Earlville, IA; ed/Dipl, Maquoketa Val HS; BS, IA St Univ; pa/Info Spec, Corn Belt Power Coop; cp/JC Wom, Pres; 4-H Ldr; Coach, Co Dairy Judging Team; ISU Vol, Public Relats Chm; Agri Commun of Tommorrow; Ag Coun Secy; ISU Dairy Sci Clb Secy; Alpha Kappa Lambda Little Sister; IA Holstein Princess Alt; r/Cath; Sunday Sch Tchr, St Mary's; hon/Ag Ser Awd, IA St Univ; Dairy Yth Spec Awd; Alpha Zeta Agri Hon; Key Wom, 1983; Intl Yth in Achmt; Commun Ldrs of Am; Outstg Yg Wom of Am; g/Agri Jour.

ENGLE, DEBRAH LYNN oc/ Teacher; b/Jan 6, 1957; h/2095 Westchester Circle, Apartment 3, Memphis, TN 38134; ba/Memphis, TN; p/Mrs Wenona Engle, Jackson, TN; ed/HS, Old Hickory; BS, Elem Ed, Univ of TN Knoxville; MEd, Curric and Instrn, Memphis St Univ; pa/Day Camp Ldr, Jackson Rec and Pk Dept, 1980; Reservation Agt, Holiday Inns Inc, 1981, 1982; Tchr, Memphis City Schs, 1980-; Kappa Delta Pi, Hon Ednl Frat; cp/Alpha Omicron Pi, Social Sorority, Memphis Alumnae Pres 1983-84; Beta Clb, 1973-75; Mu Alpha Theta, 1974-75; Quill and Scroll, 1974-75; r/Christian; hon/Outstg Yg Wom of Am.

ENGLISH, LISA LeANN oc/Student, Student Teacher; b/Mar 7, 1963; h/9417 Album, El Paso, TX 79925; ba/Same; p/ Mr and Mrs James M English, Shepherd, TX; ed/Grad, Shepherd HS, 1981; Student, Univ of TX El Paso; pa/Student Tchr in Theory of Music and Composition of Music; Tchr of Piano, Flute, Clarinet, Organ, Guitar, Saxiphone; hon/Intl Yth in Achmt; Commun Ldrs of Am; g/Composer.

ENSLEY, MARTHA ANNETTE oc/ Student; b/Jan 9, 1961; h/17 Virginia Avenue, PO Box 223, Fieldale, VA 24089; p/Trula H Ensley, Fieldale, VA; ed/Grad, G W Carver HS, 1979; BA, Meredith Col, 1983; MSW, VA Commonwealth Univ, 1984; cp/Pres, Meredith Student Govt Assn, 1982-83; Var Vol Positions; Silver Shield Hon Ldrship Soc, Meredith Col, 1982-83; Kappa Nu Sigma, Meredith Col, 1982-83; Student Govt Pres, G W Carver HS, 1978-79; r/U Meth; Ch Wk; hon/Outstg Yg Wom of Am; W/W Among Students in Am Univs and Cols; World W/W Wom; Personalities of S; Commun Ldrs of Am; Intl Yth in Achmt; W/W Among Am HS Students; g/Human Ser or Ch-Related Occup.

ERICKSEN, LISA MARIE oc/Student; b/Sep 23, 1965; h/14019 Pine Street, Trona, CA 93562; p/Reynold and Patricia Ericksen, Trona, CA; ed/Trona HS, 1983; Student, Pomona Col; pa/ Pt-time Secy, Desert Engrg Co, 1981-83; cp/Student Coun; HS Sophomore Class Secy; HS Jr Class Pres; Kommerce Klub; Pep Clb; Mathletes; r/ Meth; hon/Trona Chapt Pres, Nat Hon Soc, 1982-83; CA S'ship Fdn, 1980-83; Bk of Am Achmt Awd, 1983; Teenager of the Month, 1983; Sr Class Salutatorian; Gemco Ec Finalist, 1983; W/W Am HS Students; Soc of Dist'd Am HS Students; g/Maj in Biol; Career as Genetic Researchist or Pediatrician.

ESHELMAN, JENNIFER LYNN oc/ Miss Pennsylvania; b/Mar 30, 1960; h/ 836 Chestnut Street, Hegins, PA 17938;

ba/Altoona, PA; ed/BS, Music Ed, PA St Univ, 1982; pa/Pt-time Secy/Receptionist, Twin Val Farmers Exch, 1974-78; Lifeguard, Tri-Val Commun Pool, 1977; Sales Rep, Twin Val Farmers Exch, 1982-83; Miss PA, Miss PA S'ship Pageant Assn, 1983-84; Min of Music, Traveling and Performing in All Denominations in a Duet, 1983-; Over 1000 Shows w Semi-Profl Singing Grp, Re-Creation, 1978-82; r/Choir Dir, Christ Commun U Meth Ch, 1983; hon/ Full S'ship to PA St Univ through Re-Creation; Miss Pocono, 1982; Miss PA, 1983-84; Semi-Finalist in NATS Prog, 1982; Selected to Phi Lambda Theta Hon Frat; Grad, summa cum laude.

ESPENSHADE, NANCY JEAN oc/ Registration Clerk; b/Aug 31, 1962; h/ 630 Humphrey Court, Harrisburg, PA 17109; ba/Harrisburg, PA; p/Walter A and Frances L Espenshade, Dauphin, PA; ed/Dauphin Co Voc Tech Sch, 1977-80; pa/Sales Clk, Kinney Shoe Corp, 1978-79; Sales Clk, Pomeroy's, 1979-81; Registration Clk, Commun Gen Osteopathic Hosp, 1981-; cp/ DECA, 1978-80; Am Cancer Soc, 1980; Student Coun Secy, 1980; Cooperative Ed Com, 1980; Band, 1974-77; Chorus, 1974-77; Sr Class Com, 1980; Voc Indust Clbs of Am, 1977-79; Am Hon Soc/Hon Roll, 1977-80; r/Prot; hon/Am Hon Soc/Hon Roll, 1977-80; W/W Among Am HS Students; Intl Yth in Achmt; Yg Commun Ldrs of Am.

EVANS, DAWN SANDERS oc/ High-School Math Teacher; b/Apr 29, 1960; h/601 Anderson Road, Hawkinsville, GA 31036; ba/Eastman, GA; m/ John Joseph; p/Mr and Mrs Ed Sanders, Eastman, GA; ed/Grad, Dodge Co HS, 1978; AA, Mid GA Col, 1980; BS, GA Col, 1982; pa/8th Grade Math Tchr, Pulaski Co Mid Sch, 1982-83; HS Math Tchr, Dodge Co HS, 1983-; PAGE; r/ Presb Ch, Bible Sch Asst; hon/Gov's Hons Prog in Math; Dean's List, Mid GA Col, 4 Quarters, GA Col, 3 Quarters; hon/Grad, HS and Mid GA Col; g/Master's Deg by 1986; Teach Col Math.

EVANS, MARGARET ELIZABETH oc/Student; b/Jun 12, 1963; h/947 Maple Street, Clarksdale, MS 38614; ba/ Hollins College, VA; p/Mr and Mrs Allen C Evans, Clarksdale, MS; ed/Lee Acad, 1981; Student, Hollins Col; cp/ Nat Hon Soc, 1979-80, 1980-81; Drama Clb, 1979-80; Gourmet Cooking Clb, 1978-79; Art Clb, 1978-79; Hunting Clb, 1980-81; Mu Alpha Theta, 1979-81; Math Clb; Pep Squad, 1975-78; Quill and Scroll, 1979-80; Girls' St, 1980; Lee Show Assem, 1980-81; Homecoming Assem, 1978, 1980; Powder Puff Football, 1980; Sr Play Crew, 1981; Annual Staff, 1979-80, 1980-81; r/ Meth; hon/Hon Grad, 1981; Hall of Fame Nom, 1981; Nat Hon Soc, 1979-81; ABC Participant, 1, 2, 3, 4; Dist and St Awd in Chem, 1979-80; Hon Student, Sprg 1982, Fall 1982; Dean's List; g/To Wk in a Computer-Related Field.

EVANS, PHILLIP KARL oc/Minister, Evangelist; b/Jun 14, 1959; h/2111 Cynthia Lane, Shreveport, LA 71118; ba/Same; ed/Wossman HS; Wk'g on BA, Master's, Doct (Theol and Psych); mil/ Col ROTC, LA Col, 2 Yrs; pa/Min, Evangelist, Shreveport So Hills Bapt

Ch, Union Bapt Ch, First Bapt Ch; Min of Music and Yth, Brownville Bapt Ch; Ordained to Min; cp/LA Moral and Civic Foun, St VP; LA Teenage Libns Assn; r/Bapt; hon/Started Preaching at Age 9; Lic'd to Gospel Min at Age 15; Ordained to Preach at Age 21; Num Hons Wkg and Cnslg Yg People; g/To Do All I Can To Make This a Better World for Those Who Will Follow Me; ThD and PhD in Psych and Theol.

EVERETTE, SHARON oc/Student; b/ Oct 4, 1966; h/507 Beasley Street, Tarboro, NC 27886; p/Mr and Mrs James Leroy Everette, Tarboro, NC; ed/ Tarboro High, 1984; pa/Organist, Batts Chapel Bapt Ch Jr Choir, 1974-; Jr Organist, Union Bapt, 1978-79; Jr Organist, St Stephens Bapt; cp/Pres, Tau-ette Clb; Girl Scouts; Percussion Capt of HS Band; Jazz Band; Jazz Vocal Ensemble; Cheerldr; Commun Yth Grp; Pres, Jr Usher Bd; r/Bapt; hon/ Tarboro-Edgecombe Jr Miss Contestant, 1983; Jr Miss Las Amigas, 1982; Commun Ldrs of Am; W/W Among Am HS Students; g/Attend E Carolina Univ; Attain BA in Music Ed; Become a Music Tchr.

EVERSMAN, JANIS ELLEN oc/Student; b/Dec 31, 1964; h/208 Whispering Pines, Enterprise, AL 36330; p/Capt and Mrs James F Eversman Jr, Enterprise, AL; ed/Enterprise HS, 1982; Att'd, Enterprise St Jr Col; Student, Univ of S AL; pa/Tutor, Enterprise St Jr Col, 1983; Lifeguard, Enterprise Rec Ctr, 1983; cp/Hlth Explorers, 1980; Math Clb, 1979-82, Secy 1981-82; Math Team, 1979-82; Prep Bowl, 1982; Nat Hon Soc, 1981-82; EHS Marching 1979-82, Concert 1979-80, Symphonic 1980-82, and Stage 1980-81 Bands; Pit Band "Damn Yankees," 1981; Enterprise Keynotes Jr Music Clb, 1981-82, Treas; ESJC Scholar Bowl, 1982-83; Phi Theta Kappa, 1983; Compass Clb, 1982-83, Secy; ESJC Commun Band, 1982-83; Alpha Epsilon Delta, 1983-84; Beta Beta Beta, 1984; r/Luth; hon/Top 10 Percent at Graduation, EHS, 1982; Bausch and Lomb Sci Awd, 1982; ESJC Acad S'ship, 1982; Solo and Ensemble Two-time Medalist, 1981; USA Pres S'ship, 1983; g/Deg in Biol/Zool w Planned Grad Study in Anatomy and/ or Physiol.

EVERY, THERESA ROSE oc/Student; b/Jun 7, 1963; h/Box 178 A Mountain View Avenue, Rosendale, NY 12472; p/James C and Joan A Every, Rosendale, NY; ed/HS, 1981; Assoc Deg, Bus Adm, 1983; cp/Instr, Swimming, Water and Bicycle Safety; Lectr, How to Save Energy; 4-H Teen Ambassador, Teen Ldr; Yth F'ship; Ch Choir; All-St Chorus; Area All-St Band; Shandaken Theatrical Soc; Chosen for Sound of Am European Tour Choir; French Clb; hon/Hon Soc, 1981; Am Legion Achmt Awd; Rondout Val S'ship; Commun Ldrs of Am; W/W Among Am HS Students; Mem, Intl W/W.

EZELL, JONATHAN PAUL oc/Student; b/Apr 3, 1961; h/407 Gold Street, Shelby, NC 28150; p/Dr and Mrs J M Ezell, Shelby, NC; ed/Shelby HS, 1979; BS, Acctg, Wingate Col, 1983; pa/ Survey Crew, St Hwy Dept, 1979, 1980, 1981; Acct Dept, Machine Bldrs and Design Inc, 1982; r/Bapt; hon/Pres of Col Repubs, 1982; Pres's Forum, 1982; Dean's List, 1982; Welding Awd in HS, 1979; g/MBA; CPA.

F

FAIN, THOMAS ALTON JR oc/ Assistant Band Director; b/Jul 10, 1958; h/3400 Custer Road, 1106, Plano, TX 75023; p/Mr and Mrs Thomas Alton Fain Sr, Baytown, TX; ed/Robert E Lee HS, 1976; BS, Lamar Univ, 1980; pa/ Asst Band Dir, Bowman Mid Sch, 1981-; cp/Plano Commun Band; Phi Mu Alpha; Lamar Univ Homecoming Steering Com; Gamma Zeta Chapt of Kappa Kappa Psi, Nat Hon Band Frat, Pres 1978-80; r/Prestonwood Bapt Ch, Brass Choir Dir; hon/Annual Awd for Lamar Univ Symph Band's Most Outstg Bandsman; Sect Ldr, Lamar Symph Band; hon/ Blue Key, Nat Hon Frat, 1979; Phi Eta Sigma, Nat Hon Soc, 1976; Acad Hon Grad; Outstg Yg Men of Am; g/Excell in Public Sch Music.

FALCONI, ALINA oc/Personnel and Payroll Officer; b/Aug 29, 1956; h/2715 South Kolin Avenue, Chicago, IL 60623; ba/Chicago, IL; p/Juan and Carmely Falconi, Chicago, IL; ed/Grad, Nicholas Senn HS, 1975; BS, Mgmt, Univ of IL, Chgo Circle Campus, 1982; pa/Pers Ofcr, Chgo Uniform Mfg Co, 1982-; cp/ Salvation Army, La Villita Corps; r/ Bapt; hon/Alpha Lambda Delta Hon Soc, 1976; Dean's List, 1976.

FALCONI, CECILIA DEL ROSARIO oc/Student; b/Nov 3, 1957; h/2715 South Kolin Avenue, Chicago, IL 60623; ba/Chicago, IL; p/Juan F and Carmely Falconi, Chicago, IL; ed/Dipl, Nicholas Senn HS, 1976; BA 1982, MFA 1984, Univ of IL Chgo; pa/Secretarial Aids, Pilsen-Little Village Commun Mtl Hlth Ctr, 1977; Clk Typist, Mgmt Devel Progs 1979-80, Clk Typist, Ofc of Student Employmt 1981, Asst to the Secy, Ofc of Student Affairs Adm 1981-, Univ of IL Chgo; cp/The Salvation Army, La Villita Ch, 1982-, Active Mem and Tchr; 700 Clb Mem, 1981-; World Vision, Ptnr 1981-; Gospel Missionary Union, Ptnr 1980-; Phi Kappa Phi Nat Hon Soc, 1982-; r/ Christian; hon/Grp Shows: Montgomery Ward Gallery 1982, Col of Art and Arch Gallery 1980, 1982, Montgomery Ward Gallery 1983, Ecuadorian Leag 1983; Nicholas Senn HS Hon Roll, 1975; Univ of IL Hon Roll; Phi Kappa Phi Nat Hon Soc, Univ of IL Chgo Chapt Achmt Recog Awd, 1983; Yg Commun Ldrs of Am; Outstg Yg Women of Am; Intl Yth in Achmt; g/To Exhib in Latin Am and Europe; To Work in Mus and Teach Art.

FALUSKI, LAURIE LYNN oc/Sales; b/Feb 7, 1963; h/10229-127th Place North, Largo, FL 33543; ba/St Petersburg, FL; p/George L and Dorothy J Faluski, Largo, FL; ed/Northside Christian HS; AA in Bus Adm, St Petersburg Jr Col; pa/Stock, U-Neda Vending, 1979-80; Sales (Comm), Burdines, 1980-; cp/Yrbook Staff, 1978-80; Editor of Yrbook, 1981; Sunshine Unltd (Puppet Grp); r/First Christian Ch of Seminole; Sunday Sch Tchr; hon/Jour Awd, 1981; Quill and Scroll, 1981; Dist'd Am HS Students; W/W Am HS Students; Personalities of S; g/Hosp Adm.

FALWELL, JEAN ANN oc/Student; b/ Nov 7, 1964; h/6023 Piedmont Place, Lynchburg, VA 24502; p/Dr and Mrs Jerry L Falwell, Lynchburg, VA; ed/ Lynchburg Christian Acad, 1982-; Lib Bapt Col; cp/Pre-Med Soc, Activs Coor

1983-84; Circle K, 1984; Chamber Choir, 1983-84; Red Cross Vol, 1983-84; NHS Secy; Sr Class Pres, 1982; Varsity, Jr Varsity Cheerldg; Pep Clb; Tennis Team Co-Capt; Yrbook Staff; Spanish Clb, 1982-83; r/Indep Bapt; hon/Freshman Biol Awd, 1983; Dean's List, 1982-84; Valedictorian, 1982; Fdr's Awd, 1982; Specialized Awds in Math, Bus, Spanish, Govt, Sci; Superior Ratings, 6-Yr Gold Cup in Piano; Intl Guild Mem, 1976-82; Fine Arts Contest, 1st Place, 1982; Coach's Awd, Tennis, 1982; Bland S'ship Reg Winner, 1982; Highest Hons, K5-12; W/W Among Am HS Students; Yg Commun Ldrs of Am; Dir of Dist'd Ams; g/Attend Univ of VA and Study Med.

FARRAR, JEFFREY KEITH oc/Student; b/Oct 14, 1961; h/PO Box 370, Winfield, AL 35594; ba/Winfield, AL; p/ Harlon and Martha Farrar, Winfield, AL; ed/Winfield HS, 1980; Currently Enrolled, Auburn Univ; Att'd, Herzing Inst of Computer Technol, 1982-83; mil/NG; pa/Teller, Ctl Bk, 1980-81; Teller 1981-82, Hd Teller 1982-83, MetroBank; cp/JV Varsity Football, 1977, 1978; r/Bapt; hon/Jr Hon Soc, 1978; Sci Fair Winner, 1977; Neither Tardy Nor Absent the Entire Yr, 1979; g/To Receive Comm as 2nd Lt through ROTC at Auburn Univ while in Pharm Sch.

FARRAR, SUZANNE oc/Student; b/ Jun 24, 1966; h/Route 3, Box 230, Lillington, NC 27546; p/Thomas and Jean Farrar, Lillington, NC; ed/Grad, Wn Harnett HS, 1984; Student, Appalachian St Univ; cp/4-H, Co Reporter 1980, Histn 1981, Secy 1982, Pres 1981, 1982, Dist Reporter 1983-84; Sch Lib Clb, Pres 1983-84; Sch Drama Clb, VP 1983-84; Sch Paper, Editor 1983-84, Bus Mgr 1982-83, 1983-84; r/Meth; hon/ Outstg Sr Co 4-H'er, 1983; Outstg Jr 4-H'er; 4-H "I Dare You" Recip; W/W Among HS Students; g/Maj in Communication.

FARRELL, TERESA LYNN oc/Student; b/Feb 5, 1965; h/6000 West 70th Street, Apartment 2601, Shreveport, LA 71129; p/Vonda L Farrell, Shreveport, LA; ed/Grad, Friendship Acad HS, 1983; Student, NE LA Univ, 1983-; pa/ Secy, Downtown Garage, 1982; Secy, Frymaster Corp, 1983; cp/F'ship of Christian Aths, 1983; Student Coun, Histn 1982, 1982; Yrbook Staff, 1982, 1983; Choir, 1983; Cheerldr, Capt 1982, 1983; Class VP, 1981, 1982; Barbizon Modeling Agy, 1983; r/Christian; hon/ All-Dist Choir, 1983; W/W Among Am HS Student; Soc for Dist'd Am HS Students; g/To Receive Deg in Acctg and To Fall Back on This After Fulfilling a Modeling Career.

FAULKNER, JULIE LANE oc/Student; b/Aug 6, 1966; h/830 Park Street, Southeast, Ardmore, OK 73401; p/Mr and Mrs Bob Faulkner, Ardmore, OK; ed/HS Grad; Student, OK St Univ; pa/ Receptionist, CPA, 1982-83; Lifeguard, 1982; Salesperson, Sporting Goods Store, 1984-; cp/Leaflets Study Clb, 1982-83; OK Hon Soc, 1980-84; Nat Hon Soc, 1982-84; Jr Class Ofcr, 1982-83; Sophomore Class Ofcr, 1981-82; Student Coun, 1982-83; FCA Mem, 1981-84; Spanish Clb, 1981-83; Sci Clb, 1981-83; Yth Activity Coun, 1982-83; Gifted and Talented Prog, 1982-83; r/Bapt; hon/Sophomore Win-

ter Sports Queen, 1981-82; Jr Winter Sports Queen Cand, 1982-83; Mat Maid, 1981-82; Hd Mat Maid, 1982-83; Supts and Prins Hon Rolls, 1980-84; Finalist for Both Miss OK Teenager Pageant and OK Miss TEEN Pageant, 1984; g/To Grad from a Top-Ranked Univ w Deg in Bus Fin; To Wk for a Large Corp and Wk w Many Different Aspects of the Bus Field.

FAUST, CLARK WESLEY oc/Student; b/Oct 24, 1962; h/9 River Oaks Drive, New Braunfels, TX 78130; p/ Betty Faust, New Braunfels, TX; ed/ Grad, Canyon HS; Currently Enrolled, SW TX St Univ; pa/Truckdriver, Brauntex Mats Inc, 1981; Utility Man, Servtex Mats Inc, 1982; cp/Charter Mem, Kappa Kappa Psi, Hon Band Frat; hon/Recip, Dept of Music's Awd for Acad Excell; Nat Dean's List, 1981-82, 1982-83; g/ To Perform Music Professionally; To Teach Music.

FAUST, TANYA MARIE oc/Student; b/Apr 14, 1963; h/1800 Rickety, Tyler, TX 75703; p/Dr and Mrs Peter Faust, Tyler, TX; ed/Grad, Robert E Lee HS, 1981; AA, Tyler Jr Col, 1983; cp/Robert E Lee HS Band, 1978-81; Tyler Jr Col Band, 1981-82; Phi Theta Kappa, Secy 1982-83; r/Cath; hon/Rotary Yg Citizens Awd, 1983; Grad w High Hons, Tyler Jr Col; Nat Dean's List, 1982, 1983; W/W Among Students in Am Jr Cols; g/BS in Pharm.

FAYARD, MARY MELISSA oc/Student; b/Feb 21, 1964; h/2401 Palmer Drive, Gulfport, MS 39501; p/Lt Col and Mrs Fred E Fayard Jr, Gulfport, MS; ed/Grad, Gulfport High, 1982; Currently Att'g, MS Gulf Coast Jr Col, Jefferson Davis Campus; cp/French Clb, 1980, 1981; Nat Hon Soc, 1981, 1982; Band, 1979, 1980, 1981, 1982; Band Coun, 1st Lt 1982; Phi Theta Kappa, 1982, 1983; Student Coun, Exec Secy and Tri-Campus Exec Secy 1983, 1984; Rifle Corps in Band, 1980, 1981, 1982; Rifle Capt 1981, 1982; r/Cath; hon/ Salutatorian of HS Grad'g Class; Voted Friendliest in W/W Elections, 1982; Tau Beta Sigma Band Awd, 1982; W/W Among HS Student; W/W Among Am Jr Col Students; g/Math Maj w Computer Sci Minor.

FELICE, STEPHANY A oc/Student; b/Nov 8, 1963; h/43 Lyceum Street, Geneva, NY 14456; p/Mr and Mrs Anthony D Felice, Geneva, NY; ed/ Geneva HS, 1981; AAS, Rochester Inst of Technol, 1983; cp/Varsity Clb, 1978-81; r/Cath; hon/St Finalist, Miss NY St U Teenager Pageant, 1979; Cert of Excell in HS Acctg/Bkkpg, 1981; W/ W Among Am HS Students; Intl Yth in Achmt; Yth in Ldrship; g/Bach Deg in Acctg; To Become an Auditor for the Fed Govt.

FELKER, ANTHONY MICHAEL oc/ Student; b/Jan 21, 1963; h/418 South Santa Clara, New Braunfels, TX 78130; ba/Austin, TX; p/Ruth C Felker, New Braunfels, TX; ed/New Braunfels HS, 1980; BA in Bus Mktg 1984, BJ in Communs 1984, Univ of TX Austin; pa/ Waiter, Faust Hotel; Dishwasher, New K's Tennis Ranch; Sales, Sherwin-Williams; Sales, Prodr's Coop; Crew Chief, McDonald's; cp/Am Mktg Assn; New Braunfels JCs; Intramural Tennis and Softball; hon/Pres Endowed S'ship; Phi Eta Sigma; Dean's Hon List, 7 Semesters; #4 in HS Class; W/W Am

Students.

FENNELL, JOE DON oc/Student; b/ Jul 6, 1966; h/3309 Oakgrove, Midwest City, OK 73110; p/Don C and Nanci L Fennell, Midwest City, OK; ed/MW City HS; cp/Nat Hon Soc, 1980-84, Exec Bd 1983-84; HS Baseball Team; r/Bapt; hon/OK Boys St Del, 1983; Att'd Yth Citizenship Sem, OK Christian Col, 1983; Acad Achmt Awd, OK St Univ Alumni Assn, 1983; g/Study of Engrg.

FERGUSON, CHARLES DOUGLAS oc/Student; b/Aug 15, 1966; h/Route 5, Box 355, South Fulton, TN 38257; p/ Mr and Mrs Clifford Ferguson, South Fulton, TN; ed/HS; cp/Obion Co 4-H Hon Clb; W TN 4-H All-Stars; TN 4-H Hon Clb; St Jude's Hosp Collector; Lion's Clb Telethon; Dist 4-H Camp Cnslr; Yth Grp Wkr; r/Bishop St Ch of Christ; hon/Bus Mgr, 1984 Yrbook; Voice of Dem, 3rd C, 1982; TN Boys St, 1983; TN St 4-H Winner, 1983; TN Jr HS Winner in 4-H Horse Proj; Jr HS 4-H Ldrship in TN, 2nd; Hon Student; g/Vet Sci or Res.

FERGUSON, ERIC HOWARD oc/ Student; b/Jun 21, 1962; h/Route 3, Box 374, Rocky Mount, VA 24151; p/Mr and Mrs Howard C Ferguson, Rocky Mount, VA; ed/Franklin Co HS, 1980; BA, Govt, Univ of VA; pa/Subst Tchr, Franklin Co Sch 1981-83; Sum Employee, E I duPont Co, 1983; cp/VA Senate, Page 1977; VA Ho of Dels, Bill Room Attendant 1979-82; Chm, Univ of VA Student Legis Com, 1982-83; Pres, VA Student Assn, 1983-84; Treas, VA Student Assn, 1982-83; Univ of VA Pres Adv Com on Master Plan 1983-84, Commun Cols 1982-83, Univ Housing 1981-82; Univ of VA Alumni Assn Life Mbrship Drive Steering Com, 1982; John B Minor Pre-Legal Soc, 1981-82; HS Jr Class Treas; HS Sr Class VP; Chosen Most Likely to Succeed, HS Sr Class; Snow Creek Rescue Squad, Vol, 1st Lt Jr Squad 1979-80; r/Dir, Vacation Bible Sch of Mt Carmell Bapt Ch, 1980-83; hon/Public Speaking Awds in 4-H and HS Forensics; Chosen to Live on The Lawn, Univ of VA, 1983-84; 13-Yr Old Baseball All-Star, 1975; Dean's List, 1982; Nat Hon Soc, Franklin Co HS; I Dare You Awd, 4-H Ldrship, 1979; Outstg Yg Ams; g/To Go to Univ of VA Law Sch and Eventually Be Active in VA Polits.

FERGUSON, EVELYN LELA oc/ Student; b/Apr 5, 1961; h/19 Henry Street, Roanoke Rapids, NC 27870; p/ Mr Alfred L Ferguson Sr (dec); Mrs Phyllis D Ferguson, Roanoke Rapids, NC; ed/Roanoke Rapids HS, 1979; BA, Psych, Univ of NC Chapel Hill, 1983; pa/Res Asst, Dr H L Rheingold, Univ of NC Chapel Hill, 1982-83; cp/Vol, John Umstead Hosp, Dr Robert Johnson, 1982; Intervarsity Christian F'ship, 1982-; French Hon Soc, 1977-79; r/Bapt; hon/French Hon Soc, 1977; Medlin S'ships, 1979; Dean's List, Fall 1980, Fall 1981, Sprg 1982, Fall 1982, Sprg 1983; Intl Yth in Achmt; g/To Eventually Obtain Master's Deg in Psych.

FERGUSON, JEFFREY WILLIAM oc/ Student; b/Jul 8, 1965; h/Route 1, Box 108, Wirtz, VA 24184; p/James and Joyce Ferguson, Wirtz, VA; ed/Grad, Franklin Co HS, 1983; Student, Univ of VA; cp/Concert and Marching HS Bands; Ferrum Col Jazz Band; Carolina Blues Drum and Bugle Corps; Ch Brass

Quartet; Wrestling Team; Varsity Football; Pres, Nat Hon Soc; VP, Spanish Clb; Marched w Phila Crossmen Drum and Bugle Corps, 1983; hon/ Salutatorian, 1983; Student of VA's Gov's Sch for the Gifted; Nom'd to McDonalds All-Am HS Marching Band; Mem, E TN Univ Hon Band; Drum Maj; St Acad Medal Receiver in Chem and Math; Tied for #1 Class Rank; g/To Attend MIT and Maj in Nuclear Physics.

FERGUSON, STEPHANIE KAY oc/ Student; b/Sep 2, 1964; h/Route 5, Box 355, South Fulton, TN 38257; p/Mr and Mrs Clifford Ferguson, South Fulton, TN; ed/HS, 1982; cp/Page for Rep John Tanner in TN Legis; 100 Spchs to Civic Clbs, Yth Grps; Beta Clb Reporter; Student Coun Rep; Pres, Obion Co 4-H Hon Clb; Scribe, W TN All-Stars; Sr Class Rep; Var Charities; hon/Perfect GPA, HS; Del to Nat 4-H Cong in Chgo; Editor, HS Yrbook; Gov Cabinet, TN Girls' St; S'ships: Fulton (KY) Rotary, UT Alumni 1982-83, Walking Horse Tnrs Aux 1983-84; g/Bus Maj, Univ of TN Martin.

FERN, DAVID EDWARD oc/Student; b/Feb 4, 1963; h/13217 Ingleside Drive, Beltsville, MD 20705; p/Edward M and Betty C Fern, Beltsville, MD; ed/ High Pt HS, 1981; Univ of MD; cp/BSA Order of the Arrow; Phi Kappa Tau Frat, Treas and Mbrship Ofcr; Student Mem, Soc of Mfg Engrs; r/Bapt Ch Yth Grp; hon/Eagle Scout; Eastman Kodak Co Intl Sci and Engrg Fair Awd; W/W Among Am HS Students; g/Univ of MD Deg in Prodn Mgmt and Indust Technol.

FERNANDEZ, NINA SUE oc/Library Technician; b/Jul 30, 1960; h/604 Royal Drive, Jacksonville, NC 28540; ba/Camp Lejeune, NC; p/Mr and Mrs R L Fernandez, Jacksonville, NC; ed/White Oak HS, 1978; AA, Jour, Coastal Carolina Commun Col, 1980; BA, Eng, Berea Col, 1982; pa/Reference/Interlib Loan, Berea Col-Hutchins Lib, 1981-82; Cataloging Tech, Circulation Tech, Base Spec Sers, Rec Fund, MCB-Base Gen Lib, Bldg 63, 1982-; cp/Nat Hon Soc, 1977-78; Reporter, NHS, 1978; Phi Theta Kappa, Alpha Beta Pi Chapt, 1980-; Sigma Tau Delta, Psi Pi Chapt, 1982-; Cath Yg Adult Min, 1982-; Vol CCD Tchr, 1982-; Newspaper Staff, CCCC, 1978-79; Annual Staff, BC, 1980-81; Newman Clb, 1980-82; Campus Min Orientation Team, BC, 1981; Lib, Math, Pep Clbs, WOHS; Adv Spch Clb, WOHS, VP 1977; r/Cath; hon/HS Marshall, 1976-78; Eng Cert, WOHS, 1977; Spanish I, II, III, IV Awd, WOHS; Latin Am Awd, WOHS, 1975-76; African Culture Awd, WOHS, 1975-76; g/ Master's in Medieval Eng Lit; Author of Chd's Plays or Books.

FERNANDEZ, RICHARD EDWARD oc/Student; b/Apr 9, 1957; h/3824 Motor Avenue, #40, Culver City, CA 90230; ba/Los Angeles, CA; p/Charles R Fernandez, Slidell, LA; Joyce Mouzakis, Marina Del Rey, CA; ed/Marion Abramson HS, 1974; Loyola Univ of the S, 1983; Pursuing PhD in Chem, Univ of So CA; mil/USMC 1974-78, SSgt (E-6); pa/Tchg Asst, Univ of So CA, Fall 1983; Tchg Asst, Res Asst, Univ of So CA, Sprg 1984; cp/Am Chem Soc, Student Affil 1979-83, Pres 1981-83, Mem 1983-; Beggars Frat, Lifetime Mem, Sgt-at-Arms 1980-82; hon/Hon Discharge, USMC, 1980; Merck Index

Awd, 1981; Am Inst of Chems Awd, 1983; g/To Attain PhD in Organic Chem and Pursue Basic Chem Res.

FETTERMAN, DAVID MARK oc/ Senior Administrator, Anthropologist, Education Evaluator, Lecturer; b/Jan 24, 1954; h/3208 Alameda de las Pulgas, Menlo Park, CA 94025; p/Elsie Fetterman, Amherst, MA; ed/BA, BS, AM, AM, PhD, Stanford Univ; pa/Sr Admr; Anthropologist-Ed Evaluator; Lectr; Chm, Com for Anthropology and Ed Ethnography/Ed Eval Div; Chm, Stanford Geneal Soc; Chm, Chinese Studies Soc; cp/Parochial Sch Tchr; Pres, Photo Clb; Chm, Kibbutz Commun; Asst Prog Dir, Sr Citizen Day Care Ctr; hon/Phi Beta Kappa; Eval Res Soc Awd; NY Acad of Sci; Nat Dist'd S'ship Awd.

FEY, CAROLYN ELIZABETH oc/ Student; b/Mar 22, 1967; h/50 Lark Lane, New Braunfels, TX 78130; ed/HS Student; cp/4-H, 1976-84, Pres, VP, Histn, Coun Del; Ch Yth Grps, 1981-84; Hosp Vol Grp, TEAMS, 1979-84, Pres; NHS, 1983-84; Student Coun, 1981-84; Class Pres, Freshman Yr, 1981-82; r/ Cath; hon/Am Legion Outstg Student, 1981; Rep to Nat Yth Range Forum, 1984; Comal Co Fair Queen, 1983-84; NHS, 1983-84; g/Maj in Plant Genetics at TX A&M Univ; PhD in Plant Genetics.

FIELD, SALLY JANE oc/Administrative Assistant; b/Jul 24, 1958; h/829 South Walnut, Springfield, IL; p/Harley V Jr and Mary Jane Field; ed/HS, 1976; BA, En IL Univ, 1979; pa/Adm Asst, Ofc of the Gov of IL; cp/Sigma Sigma Sigma Rush Com; Phi Beta Chi Pledge Tnr, Chapt Advr; Del to Model UN; Univ Jud Bd; Pemberton Hall Coun Mem; r/St John's Luth Ch; hon/W/W Among Students in Am Cols and Univs; Intl Yth in Achmt; g/Adm Position in St, Fed or Local Govt.

FIELDS, DAVID ALAN oc/Student; b/Apr 29, 1961; h/521 Rapids Street, Roanoke Rapids, NC 27870; ba/Cullowhee, NC; p/Mr and Mrs Howard A Fields, Roanoke Rapids, NC; ed/Grad, Roanoke Rapids Jr Sr HS, 1979; Student, Wn Carolina Univ; mil/USMC Ofcr Cand Sch, 1983; cp/Crim Justice Clb, 1982-83, VP; Semper Fidelis Soc, 1983; Outing Clb, 1983, 1984; r/Bapt; hon/Lettered in Varsity Football, Roanoke Rapids HS; Dean's List, 1981, 1982, 1983; g/Crim Justice Maj Seeking Employmt w Fed Govt.

FIELDS, LARRY NEWTON JR oc/ Student; b/Nov 8, 1964; h/145 Johnson Street, Red Springs, NC 28377; p/ Frankie Fields, Red Springs, NC; Dot Armstrong, Red Springs, NC; ed/Red Sprgs High; Emer Med Tech, Robeson Tech Col; pa/Milliken Mills, 1981-82; Woods Dept Store, 1982; Pembroke St Univ Emer Med Care (Security), 1983-; cp/BSA, Scoutmaster; Red Sprgs Stage Band, Reporter 1981-83; r/Bapt; hon/ Gold Music Awd, 1983; Emer Med Tech, 1983; W/W Among Am HS Students; g/To Go into Med Res, Especially Cancer Res.

FIGUEROA, MARIJOY DADO oc/ Student; b/Dec 12, 1963; h/565 Henry Drive, LaVale, MD 21502; p/Dr and Mrs Augusto Figueroa, LaVale, MD; ed/ Grad, Bishop Walsh HS, 1982; WV Univ, 1982-83; Univ of MD Balto Co, 1983; pa/Wk in Phys's Ofc, Sums 1978-82; Taught Piano, 1980; cp/Marching and Jazz Band, Secy 1980, Pres 1981; Candystripping, Treas 1980; Folk Grp; Am Field Ser; Commun Involvement Coun; Drama Clb; Thespian Soc; Nat Hon Soc; Ofc Aide; Ski Clb; Pit Orch; Sch Lit Mag; r/Rom Cath; hon/Hon Roll, 1978-82; Hood Piano Fest Finalist, 1981; Cumberland Music and Arts Clb S'ship Winner, 1980; Shennandoh Finalist, 1982; g/Maj in Nsg.

FIKAC, PEGGY RUTH oc/Reporter; b/Mar 20, 1961; h/709 Lamar Place, 210, Austin, TX 78752; p/Mr and Mrs Leonard H Fikac, New Braunfels, TX; ed/New Braunfels HS, 1979; Univ of TX Austin, 1979-83; pa/Reporter, Austin Bur of Freedom Newspapers Chain, 1983-; Intern for *The Copperas Cove Leader-Press*, Sum 1982; Sigma Delta Chi, Soc of Profl Journalists, 1982-; Phi Kappa Phi, 1982-; Alpha Lambda Delta, 1980-; r/Cath; hon/Norris G Davis S'ship, 1982; UT Pres S'ship, 1979.

FINCHER, LEE S oc/Insurance Agent; b/Dec 17, 1956; h/1155 Pond Ridge Drive, Riverdale, GA 30296; ba/Atlanta, GA; m/Steven M; p/Jo Anne Evans, Fairburn, GA; ed/Clayton Jr Col, 1983; M D Collins HS, 1974; LUTC, 1983; IIA, INS-21, 22, 23, 1979; Currently Enrolled in CLU Studies; pa/Ins Clk, Ivey & Co of Athens Inc, 1976-78; Customer Ser Rep and Prodr, Athen Insurers Inc, 1978-81; Ins Agt, Metro Ins Co, 1981-83; Formed Own Agy, Affil'd w The Bkrs Life of IA, Broker through Athens Insurers, Fincher Ins Agy Inc, 1983-; Nat Assn Ins Wom, 1976-; Tri-Cities Life Underwriters Assn; cp/Red Cross CPR Instr, 1978-; Tutor, Adult Rdg for Clayton Co Dept of Fam and Chd's Sers, 1981-; GA Wom's Polit Caucus, 1980-; Adv Coun 1983; VP, So Metro Assn, 1982; Clayton Co C of C, Pacesetters Com 1981-; hon/NAIW-LACE Reg Ldrship Clayton Grad, 1983; Ldrs' Conf, Metro Ins Co, 1982; Ins Wom of Athens, Speak Off Winner 1982, Rookie of the Yr 1979; g/Build My Own Agy to $500,000 Premium Volume; Complete My BA Deg from GA St Univ; Complete My CLU Studies.

FINKELSTEIN, STUART M oc/Student; b/May 19, 1960; h/26130 West 12 Mile #324, Southfield, MI 48034; ba/Ann Arbor, MI; p/Selma Finkelstein, Southfield, MI; ed/JD Cand, Univ of MI Law Sch, 1985; BBA w Distn, Univ of MI Sch of Bus Adm, 1982; pa/Current Sum Assoc, Skadden, Arps, Slate, Meagher & From, Attys; Acctg Tchg Asst, Univ of MI, 1983-84; Sum Assoc, 1983; Auditing Intern, Morof, Sheplow & Weinstein, CPAs, 1982; Auditing Intern, Plante and Moran, CPAs, 1981; Legal Clk, Roth and Dean, Attys at Law, 1979; Univ of MI: Elected Pres of Grad Sch of Bus Adm's Student Coun, Resident Advr in Mosher-Jordan Hall for 2 Yrs, Elected Pres and Treas of Mosher-Jordan House Coun, Elected Treas of Univ Residence Hall Coun, Student Participant in Vol Income Tax Assistance Prog; hon/Cert of Merit, Univ of MI Sch of Law's Writing and Advocacy Prog, 1983; Univ of MI Class Hons, 1978-81; Am MENSA Ltd, 1981-; St of MI Competitive S'ship, 1978-82; Korvettes Annual S'ship, 1978; Nat Dean's List, 1980; Financial Mgmt Assn Nat Hon Soc, 1981-82; Beta Alpha Psi,

Nat Hon Acctg Frat, 1980-82; Passed Entire Uniform CPA Exam, 1982; Outstg Yg Men of Am.

FINLEY, TERRENCE AUGUSTUS oc/Student; b/Mar 21, 1966; h/470 Mobile Street, Mobile, AL 36607; p/Mrs Ira Finley; ed/Student, Murphy HS; cp/Student Coun, Sr Class Pres; Yth Dept Pres; Yg Adult Choir Pres; Jr Achmt, VP of Prodn; r/Bapt; hon/Ldrship Scholar, Univ of AL, 1983; g/Maj in Arch, Univ of Houston.

FINNELL, B SCOTT oc/Minister; b/Jun 22, 1956; h/738 Show Place, Grand Prairie, TX 75051; ba/Grand Prairie, TX; c/Amanda Kay; p/Birly and Lawana Finnell, Grand Prairie, TX; ed/S Grand Prairie HS, 1974; BA, Baylor Univ, 1978; Att'g, So Bapt Theol Sem, 1981-82; MA, Baylor Univ, 1983; pa/Min of Yth, Pk Lake Drive Bapt Ch, 1978-80; Min of Yth/Ed, N Cheyenne Bapt Ch, 1980-81; Pastor, New Haven Bapt Ch, 1982; Yth Cnslr, Waco Ctr for Yth, TX Dept of Mtl Hlth/Mtl Retard, 1983; r/So Bapt; hon/Pubs, *Significance of the Passion in Luke*, 1983; Personalities of S; g/PhD in New Testament.

FISHER, PAIGE DALTON oc/Student; b/Jul 22, 1962; h/Route 2, Box 236, Fincastle, VA 24090; p/Mr and Mrs Duane Fisher, Fincastle, VA; ed/Grad, Lord Botetourt HS, 1980; Att'g, Radford Univ, 1980-; cp/HS Wrestling and Girls' Basketball Cheerldr, 1978-79; Pres of HS Art Clb, 1979, 1980; Circle K Clb, 1981-82; 4-H, 1973-78; Nat Hon Soc, 1979, 1980; Hon Student Assn, Secy 1982-83; NEA Assn and Student Ed Assn, 1982-83; r/Meth; hon/Var 4-H Achmt Awds, 1973-78; Art Awd, HS, 1979, 1980; Nat Hon Soc, 1979, 1980; Kappa Delta Pi, Ed Hon, 1983; W/W Among Am HS Students; g/BS Deg in Upper Elem Ed.

FLANAGAN, EDWARD GREYTON oc/Student; b/Nov 23, 1960; h/Route 8, Box 710, Greenville, NC 27834; p/E Graham Jr and Ellen Taylor Flanagan, Greenville, NC; ed/HS Deg, VA Epis Sch, 1979; BA, Eng, St Andrews Presb Col, 1983; Currently Enrolled, Pitt Co Tech Inst; cp/JV Wrestler, Sophomore Football, JV Track and Field, 1976-77; Varsity Wrestler, JV Track and Field, 1977-78; Varsity Wrestler, Track and Field, JV Baseball, 1978-79; DJ for St Andrews Radio Sta, Elected Suite Ldr in Mecklenburg Dorm on St Andrews Campus, 1979-80; DJ at St Andrews, Re-Elected Suite Ldr in Mecklenbrug Dorm, Elected Pres of St Andrews Col Repubs, 1980-81; DJ at St Andrews, Re-Elected Suite Ldr, Re-Elected Pres of Col Repubs, Reporter for St Andrews' Paper, "The Lance," 1981-82; Re-Elected Suite Ldr, Sci Editor for Col Paper, "The Lance," Mem of St Andrews Pep Band, 1982-83; Asst Baseball Coach for Greenville Prep Leag, 1981; Asst Baseball Coach for Greenville, Babe Ruth Leag, 1982; g/Field of Communication (Computers or Pub'g).

FLANAGAN, EILEEN MARY oc/Student; b/Nov 22, 1965; h/300 Battleground Avenue, New Bern, NC 28560; ba/Havelock, NC; p/Mr and Mrs Lawrence J Flanagan, New Bern, NC; ed/Havelock HS; cp/Cath Yth Org, 1980-83; Catechism, 1980-83; Med Explorers, Secy 1981-82; Jr Beta Clb, 1980-82; Track Mgr/Scorekeeper, 1981;

Wayne Commun Col Math Contest Participant, 1981; Parish Bd of Ed, 1981-83; Nat Hon Soc, 1982-83, Pres 1983-84; Jr Civitan, 1981-83, Histn 1983-84; CYO Volleyball, 1982; Powder Puff Football, 1981, 1983; Mtl Olympics, 1982, 1983; Vol, Nuclear Med Dept, New Rochelle Hosp Med Ctr, 1982; Annual Staff, 1980-84; Sci Clb, 1981-83, Pres 1983-84; Prom Com, 1983; Ch Lector/Commentator, 1982-83; Pt-time Job, 1982, 1983; Student Coun, Jr Class Rep 1982-83, Sr Class Rep 1983-84; Elections Chm 1983-84; Photo Clb, Pres 1983-84; r/Cath; hon/Freshman Eng Awd, 1981; 2nd Place, Annual Civitan Writing Contest, 1983; E Carolina Univ Scholars Weekend Participant, 1983; Gov's Sch Nom, 1983; Hopwood Sum S'ship Prog at Lynchburg Col, 1983; Morehead S'ship Nom, 1983; Outstg Sr, 1983; W/W Among Am HS Students; g/To Attend Col and Maj in Chem/Biol.

FLASCH, BARBARA ANN oc/Student; b/Jul 5, 1962; h/1639 Clarence Street, St Paul, MN 55106; p/Henry and Mary Ann Flasch, St Paul, MN; ed/Hill-Murray HS, 1980; Student, Mankato St Univ, 1981-; cp/HS Concert Choir, Track, Student Coun; Mankato St Univ Intercultural Student Ctr Adv Com, 1983; Dale Carnagie Course, 1978; Grad Asst, 1979; Jr Achmt, 1977-80, Co-Pres 1978-80; Achievers Assn, Pres 1977-80; Up w People, 1980-81; Alpha Chi Omega, 1981-, 1st VP 1981, Chaplain, Songldr, Parliamentarian 1983, 2nd VP 1982; Mankato St Student Ambassadors Assn, 1981-, Pres 1983-84; Mankato St Univ Student Senate Communs Adv Com, 1983-84; Mankato St Univ Residential Life Advr, 1981-83; Toastmasters Yth Ldrship, 1979; r/Cath; hon/HS Hon Roll, 1976-80; Pres of the Yr, Jr Achmt, 1980; S'ship Recip, Dale Carnagie Course 1978, Jr Achmt 1980, Mankato St Mass Communs Inst 1983; Mankato St Univ Dean's List, 1981-83; Toastmaster's Yth Best Spkr Awd, 1980; g/Mass Communs/Public Relats Maj; Minor in Bus Adm and Spch Communication; Public Relats Practitioner.

FLATT, BEN ANDERSON oc/Student; b/Feb 17, 1962; h/313 East Fort Street, Tullahoma, TN 37388; p/Ben and Judy Flatt, Tullahoma, TN; ed/Grad, Tullahoma HS, 1980; BS in Computer Sci, David Lipscomb Col, 1984; pa/Retail Salesman (Present); Computer Lab Tech, 1982-; Packaging Clk, 1982; Respiratory Therapy Tech, 1981; Pharm Tech, 1978-80; cp/Sigma Phi Omega, Treas 1979-80; Phi Beta Lambda, Chaplain 1983-; Pi Alpha Chi, Secy 1983, Current Pres; Band; Stage Band; Pep Band; r/Ch of Christ; hon/Best Soloist, Jazz, 1980; Featured Soloist Clinician, Concert, 1980; Outstg Yg Men of Am; g/MBA.

FLATT, MALEAH ANN oc/Student; b/May 6, 1962; h/Route 4, Box 286A, Livingston, TN 38570; p/Mr and Mrs E Leon Flatt, Livingston, TN; ed/Livingston Acad, 1980; BS Nsg, TN Technol Univ; pa/Col Wk-Study Prog, 1983-, Sch of Nsg, TN Technol Univ, Cookeville, TN; cp/Future Homemakers of Am, 1976-77; Beta Clb, 1978-80; Yth Conserv Bd, 1979-80; 4-H Clb, 1976-77; 1st VP 1983-84, 2nd VP 1982-83, Treas 1981-82, Del 1982 & 1983 TN Assn of

Student Nurses Conv, Mem 1980-84; Mem Awds Com 1982-83; TN Assn of Student Nurses, TTU Chapt; Nat Student Nurses Assn, 1980-84; Student Body Org, TTU Sch of Nsg, 1980-84; hon/Ardean Coleman S'ship, 1983; Girl's St Alternate, 1979; 3rd Pl in Yth Conserv Bd Dist Speech Contest, 1979; #10 in Top Ten of Grad'g Class, 1980; g/Continue Ed & Receive Master's Deg in Nsg.

FLETCHER, LISA KAY oc/Student; b/Jun 8, 1966; h/40 Lakeview Road, Livingston, TN 38570; p/Mr and Mrs Harold Fletcher, Livingston, TN; ed/Livingston Acad, 1984; pa/Lifeguard, City of Livingston, 1981-83; cp/Sci Clb; Spanish Clb; Basketball Mgr; Softball Mgr; Rainbow Girls; r/Meth; hon/Beta Clb; TTU Math Contest; W/W Among Am HS Students; g/Maj in Elect Engrg.

FLINT, LAURIE ANN oc/Medical Student; b/Jul 17, 1960; h/7113 Falcon Street, Annandale, VA 22003; ba/Norfolk, VA; p/Mrs Kemper S Flint, Annandale, VA; ed/Thomas Jefferson HS, 1978; BA in Chem, Univ of VA, 1982; Currently Att'g En VA Med Sch; cp/HS: Ch Choir, Christian Yth F'ship, Sch Newspaper Typist; Col: Madison House Med Sers Vol and Pediatric Prog Dir 1981-82, Alpha Phi Omega Ser Frat; Med Sch: Co-Editor of Student Handbook, Vol at Crestwood Clin; hon/HS: Hon Roll, 1974-78, Quill and Scroll 1982, Nat Jr Hon Soc 1976, Nat Hon Soc 1976, Valedictorian 1978; Col: Intermediate Hons 1980, Dean's List 1980, 1981; W/W Among Am HS Students.

FLORA, NORMA LEIGH oc/Student; b/Jul 1, 1966; h/Route 4, Box 104, Rocky Mount, NC 27801; p/Mr and Mrs John Mark Flora, Rocky Mount, NC; ed/HS Student; cp/Concert and Marching Band; Nat Jr Hon Soc, 2 Yrs (Treas); Nat Hon Soc; Future Bus Ldrs of Am; French Clb; Sci Clb, Treas; Quiz Bowl; r/Bapt; Citizenship Awds, 1980-82; Typing I, 1981-82; Acctg I, 1981-82; Outstg Achmt in Biol Sci, 1981-82; Outstg Achmt in Algebra I, 1980-81; 2 Awds for Being Semifinalist for Sch of Sci and Math, 1981-82; NC and Local Hist Awd, 1980-81; Phy Sci, 1980-81; Outstg Achmt in Geometry, 1981-82; g/To Study the Biol Scis in Col and to Have a Career in This Area.

FLORES, MARIA DeJESUS oc/Data Transcriber; b/Feb 13, 1963; h/PO Box 273, Helotes, TX 78023; ba/San Antonio, TX; p/Miguel V and Margarita Flores, Helotes, TX; ed/Grad, John Marshall HS, 1981; Att'g, San Antonio Col; pa/Eagle Life Ins Co, 1980-84; Data Transcriber, Kelly AFB, 1984-; Ofc Ed Assn (VOE); hon/Citizenship Awd; Spanish Hon Soc; W/W Among Am HS Students; g/Bus Adm.

FLOWER, DAVID ARTHUR oc/Student; b/Mar 10, 1962; h/230 Danbury Lane, Northwest, Atlanta, GA 30327; p/Mr and Mrs E E Flower, Atlanta, GA; ed/Grad, Riverwood HS, 1980; BS, Bus Adm (Mktg Mgmt Concentration), FL So Col; cp/Delta Sigma Pi Nat Bus Hon; Omicron Delta Kappa Nat Ldrship Hon; FSC Student Govt Assn, VP; FSC MS6A-AWS Jud Bd Chm; Theta Chi Frat; Polk Co Dept of Juv Rehab, Big Brother; r/Cath; hon/W/W Among Students in Am Cols and Univs; g/Pharm Sales/Sales Mgmt.

FLOYD, TAMMIE GALE oc/Student; b/Nov 13, 1962; h/305 8th Avenue, Northwest, Winchester, TN 37398; ba/Old Hickory, TN; p/Mr and Mrs Bobby Wells, Winchester, TN; ed/Grad, Franklin Co HS, 1981; AS, Engrg and Computer Sci, Motlow St Commun Col; Currently Enrolled, TN Technological Univ; pa/Pt-time Engrg Draftsman and Computer Programmer, Arnold Engrg Devel Ctr, 1983; cp/Nat Hon Soc, 1978-81; Nat Beta Clb, 1976-81; Editor, HS Newpaper, 1980-81; Hons Editor of HS Annual, 1980-81; Classroom Rep, Student Coun Com, 1979-80; Newspaper Staff, 1977-81; hon/Top Finalist, Jr Miss Pageant, 1980-81; Recip, Perfect Attendance Awd, 1974-81; Recip, DAR Awd and Metal, 1978; Recip, Excell in Eng I and Gen Bus Awd, 1978; Freshman Cheerldr, 1978; 3rd Runner-Up in 1981-82 Homecoming Ct at Motlow; Nat Soc of Profl Engrs, Motlow Chapt, 1981-82; VP, Nat Soc of Profl Engrs, 1982-83; Pres, Gamma Beta Phi Hon Soc, 1982-83; Sophomore Senator, Motlow Student Govt Assn, 1982-83; Elected Miss Motlow, 1982-83; Most Outstg Gamma Beta Phi Mem, and Recip of $200 S'ship and Plaque, 1982-83; W/W Among Students in Am Jr Cols; W/W Among HS Students; r/Epis; g/To Continue Ed and Receive BS in Either Elect or Chem Engrg and Computer Sci; Complete Master's Deg and Become a Profl Engr.

FOGLEMAN, MARTHA SPIER H oc/Wife; b/Aug 1, 1961; h/119 Beverly Place, Greensboro, NC 27403; m/James Ray Fogleman; c/Karen Anne, Laurie Melinda, Keith David, Lynne Denise, Robyn Barber; p/William D and Martha H Holloman, Scotland Neck, NC; ed/Hobgood Acad, 1975-77; St Mary's Col, 1977-79; Lake Erie Col, 1979-81; BA, Polit Sci, Univ of NC Greensboro, 1982; pa/Camp Cnslr, Robin Hood, 1979-80; Clk, Kroger Deli, 1981-82; Bartender, B B West, 1982-83; cp/HS Basketball Team, 1975-77; St Mary's Col Basketball and Softball Teams, 1977-79; Lake Erie Volleyball Mgr, Col Sophomore Class Pres 1981, Student Govt Secy 1980; hon/Sportsmanship Awd, LEC Basketball, 1980; Little Mother of the Yr Awd, LEC, 1980; g/Master's in Communs, Public Relats; Job.

FONG, KENNETH WAYNE oc/Trust Investment Officer; b/Nov 5, 1955; h/2020 Silver Avenue, Las Vegas, NV 89102; p/Wing and Lilly Fong, Las Vegas, NV; ed/Clark HS, High Hons, 1974; BS, Bus Adm w High Distn, Univ of NV Las Vegas, 1978; MBA, SF St Univ, 1982; pa/Mgr, Retailing, Sears, Roebuck and Co, 1978-80; Tchg Asst, Sch of Bus, SF St Univ, 1981; Trust Investmt Ofcr, Val Bk of NV, 1982-; Am Inst of Bkg, 1982-; Am Bkrs Assn, 1982-; Assn of MBA Execs, 1980-; cp/Chinese Student Assn, Univ of NV Las Vegas, Chm 1975, Treas 1976; VP, Sunrise Hosp Explorer Scouts, 1973-74; r/Elder, First Presb Ch, 1982-; Sunday Sch Tchr, First Presb Ch, 1982-; Rep Col Coun, Presb Ch in Chinatown, SF, 1976; hon/Pubs, Poem "Forgiveness" in *American College Poetry Anthology 1976*, Poem "If Distorted" in Joyce Kilmer Meml Nat Poetry Contest 1981 and in *Rocky Mountain Poetry Quarterly*; Phi Kappa

Phi, Univ of NV Las Vegas, 1977-78; Psi Chi, Univ of NV Las Vegas, 1977; Phi Lambda Alpha, Univ of NV Las Vegas, 1975; Nat Student Exch Prog to Univ of HI Honolulu, 1976-77; W/W Among Students in Am Univs and Cols; Men of Achmt; Intl Yth in Achmt; Nat Dean's List; g/Corporate Bkg and Investmts.

FONG, PAUL YEE oc/Student; b/Aug 2, 1963; h/4431 Northeast 20th Avenue, Oakland Park, FL 33308; p/Walter and JoAnn Fong, Oakland Park, FL; ed/Grad, NE HS, 1981; Student, Univ of FL; pa/Sales Clk, Colonial Garden Shoppes, 1979; cp/Mu Alpha Theta, Treas 1980, VP 1981; Nat Hon Soc, Treas 1980, VP 1981; Sr Class Treas, 1981; Grad Nite Chm, 1981; Col: Chinese Clb, Phi Eta Sigma, Delta Upsilon Frat (VP of Pledge Class 1981, Histn 1982, 1983, Rush Com 1982, 1983, Soccer 1981, 1982, Racquetball 1982); hon/Harvard Book Awd, 1980; Most Outstg HS Student, N Broward Co, 1981; W/W Among Am HS Students; g/Computer and Info Scis.

FONTENOT, NIGEL MARK oc/Chemist; b/Apt 23, 1961; h/Route 2, Box 151, Englewood, TN 37329; ba/Nashville, TN; p/Mr and Mrs Derien Fontenot, Englewood, TN; ed/Dipl, McMinn Ctl HS, 1979; Grad, cum laude, David Lipscomb Col, 1983; pa/Chem, TN St Envir Labs; Am Chem Soc; cp/Student Coun, 3 Yrs; Pres, Student Coun; VP, Mu Alpha Theta; Beta Clb; Yth Affairs Dept, McMinn Co; hon/Elks Clb Student of the Month; Grad Top 10 Percent, 6th in Class of 200; S'ship from Top 10 Percent (from High ACT Scores); Mu Epsilon Delta, Local Pre-Med Frat; Quarter Finals Awd, Wake Forest Debate in Novice Div; Preacher; g/Attend Med Sch to Obtain an MD and Specialize in Some Field of Med.

FORBES, DAVID GERALD oc/International Attorney; b/May 23, 1956; h/7825 Southwest 57 Avenue, #C, South Miami, FL 33143; p/Marc and Ina Claire Jaeger, Gainesville, FL; ed/Dipl, Gainesville HS, 1974; BA, German w Cert in European Studies, summa cum laude 1978, MA in German 1979, Univ of FL Gainesville; Rheinische Friedrich-Wilhelms Universitat, Bonn, Fed Republic of Germany, 1976-77; JD, Holland Law Ctr, Univ of FL Gainesville, 1982; pa/Practicing Atty in Intl/Corp/Comml/Bkg Law, 1984-; Fdr, Ptnr, Anda Ven Enterprises, 1981-84; Grad Tchg Asst'ship, Dept of Germanic and Slavic Langs and Lits, Univ of FL, 1978-79; Am Bar Assn, 1984-; FL Bar Assn, 1984-; Affil, Intl Bus Law Com, FL Bar, 1982-84; Phi Delta Phi, 1982-; cp/Moral Re-Armament, 1983-; Repub Pres Task Force, 1981-; US Congl Adv Bd, 1983-84; Phi Kappa Phi, 1979-; Omicron Delta Kappa, 1979-; ACLU, 1979-; hon/Highest Grades in Oral Argument; Brief in Appellate Advocacy; Student Govt Cabinet Dir; Univ of FL Intl Law Soc; Phi Delta Phi; Affil, Intl Bus Law Com; Other Hons; Intl Yth in Achmt; Intl Register of Profiles; g/Improve Relats and Co-operation between Indust and Soc Internationally and Domestically through Personal Diplomacy, Bus Consultation, Legal Pract and Personal Friendship.

FORD, JOHN EDWARD oc/Associate Pastor; b/Jan 26, 1958; h/20 West

Linden, Logansport, IN 46947; ba/ Logansport, IN; p/Robert and Josephine Ford, Hobart, IN; ed/Hobart Sr HS, 1978; BS, Ball St Univ, 1980; Currently Enrolled, Christian Theol Sem; pa/ Actor-Singer; Drama Coach, John Robert Powers Sch; Dist Mgr, *Gary Post Tribune*; cp/Repertory Theatre at CTS; CTS Cantors; Univ Theatre Actor-Singer, Cast; Tchr Asst; Ball St Choral Union; U Min Pres; Thespian Troupe; Genisius Players; Rhythmyx Swing Choir; Ch Soloist; r/U Meth; hon/ Palmer S'ship; Theatre Achmt Awd; 1st Rating, NISBOVA St Vocal Competition; g/Ordination as Min in U Meth Ch.

FORD, STAN oc/Student; b/Sep 22, 1958; h/6838 Raymond, University City, MO 63130; ba/Salzburg, Austria; p/Stanley L and Mamie L Ford, University City, MO; ed/Univ City Sr HS, 1975; So IL Univ at Edwardsville; BM, MM, St Louis Commun Col, 1982, Student, The Mozarteum, Salzburg, Austria; pa/Prof of Piano, Forest Pk Commun Col, 1981-83; Prof of Piano, So IL Univ at Edwardsville, 1980-83; cp/ Nat Yth Pres of Nat Assn of Negro Musicians; Disciplinary Review Bd at SIUE; Phi Kappa Phi; Pi Kappa Lambda; r/Bapt Ch of the Holy Communion, Asst Choir Master; hon/Martin Luther King Jr Awd; Competitive Grad F'ship Awd; Ruth Slenczynka Piano Perf Awd; Lena Rivers Dancy Awd; Republik Osterreich Bundesministerium S'ship, 1983-84; g/Artist Dipl in Piano at Mozartium; Concert Pianist; Teach on Univ Level; Doct of Music, Piano Perf.

FORGACS, LINDA MARY oc/Documentation Support Specialist; b/May 24, 1959; h/1400 Regal Road, Clearwater, FL 33516; ba/Tampa, FL; p/Lois A Forgacs, Clearwater, FL; ed/Arts and Scis Dipl, Largo HS, 1977; BA in Eng, Clearwater Christian Col, 1981; pa/ Feature Writer/Contbg Editor, *Christian Community Chronicle* Newspaper, 1976-77; Night Computer Operator, Largo Diagnostic Clin, 1979-80; Pre-Sch Tchr Aid, Grace Day Nursery, 1980; Clk Typist II, Hillsborough Co Data Processing, 1981-82; Documentation Support Spec, Hillsborough Co Data Processing, 1982-; cp/Col Choir, 1979-80; r/Indep Bapt; Adult Choir, Hillsdale Bapt Ch, 1978-; Pre-Sch Tchr, Hillsdale Bapt Ch, 1978-; hon/Valedictorian, 1981; W/W Among Am Univs and Cols; Intl Yth in Achmt; Commun Ldrs of Am; Personalities of S; Nat Dean's List; Dir of Dist'd Ams; g/ Acquire Addit Tng in Data Processing Field through Col Courses and On-the-Job Tng.

FORTENBERY, ROBERT EUGENE oc/Campus Coordinator; b/Nov 1, 1958; h/1309 Live Oak, Commerce, TX 75428; ba/Commerce, TX; p/Mr and Mrs Ellis C Fortenbery, El Paso, TX; ed/BS in Ed, Univ of TX El Paso, 1982; Burges HS, 1976; pa/Campus Coor, Bapt Gen Conv of TX, 1982-; Inventory Spec, Retail Grocery Inventory, 1981-82; Gymnastics Instr, Champion Studios, 1977-82; PE Tchr/Coach, Jesus Chapel Christian Sch, 1977-78; Staff Ldr, Baskin-Robbins 31 Flavors, 1975-7; cp/UTEP Gymnastic Clb; UTEP Volleyball Clb, Championship Teams 1977; 1981; UTEP Cheerldr, 1977-81; Hd Cheerldr 1980-81; UTEP Bapt Student Union, 1980-82; UTEP

Deptl Ser; r/So Bapt; hon/Distributive Ed Clbs of Am Male Student of the Yr, Burges HS Chapt, 1976; Col of Men of Mines from UTEP, 1982; Outstg Yg Men of Am; g/Wkg w Col Students as Programming Advr or BSU Dir.

FOSHEE, CARLYN DIANE oc/Sales Coordinator; b/Oct 8, 1959; ba/6721 Portwest Drive #150, Houston, TX; p/ Mr and Mrs George Foshee, Galena Park, TX; ed/Grad, Galena Pk HS, 1978; BBA, San Houston St Univ, 1981; pa/ Sales Coor, Harrison Boulle; Houston Sales, Behring Intl Inc; cp/Sam Houston St Univ Bearkat Twirler; Alpha Lambda Delta Nat Hon Soc; Alpha Chi; Pres, Golden Key Nat Hon Soc; JC Wom; hon/ Outstg Mktg Sr, 1981; W/W Among Students in Cols and Univs; g/To Become VP of Opers.

FOSTER, DIANNE ELIZABETH oc/ Student; b/Dec 24, 1962; h/2706 West Overhill Road, Peoria, IL 61615; ba/ Indianapolis, IN; p/Wes and Roberta Foster, Peoria, IL; ed/Grad, Peoria HS, 1980; BS, Pharm, Butler Univ, 1985; pa/ Nat Pharm Coun Sum Intern, Lederle Labs; Apprentice Pharm, Bogard Drug Inc; cp/Phi Delta Chi, Profl Pharm Frat, VP of Pledge Class 1981, Chaplain 1982, Pledge Master 1983, Conv Del 1982, Com Chair 1981, 1984; Blue Key Sr Hon Frat, Pres 1984; Alpha Phi Omega Ser Frat; Butler Univ Hons Soc and Hons Prog, 1980-84; r/Meth; hon/Freshman Chem Awd, 1981; Rho Chi Recog Cert, 1983; Rho Chi Pharm Hon, 1984; Dean's List, 1980-84; Ctl IL Pharm Assn Polen S'ship, 1983; Mortar Bd Sr Hon Soc, 1983; Chimes Jr Hon, 1982; Alpha Lambda Delta Freshman Hon, 1980; g/ Career in Pharm Indust or Adv'd Specialized Deg in Hosp Pharm.

FOSTER, KAREN oc/Student; b/Jan 21, 1964; h/Belmont College, Box 632, Nashville, TN 37203; p/Jesse and Linda Foster; ed/Grad, Clarksville HS, 1982; pa/Salesclk, La Baguette, 1983; cp/NHS, 1980-82; Beta Clb, 1978; Anchor Clb, 1980-81; GSA; Ch Yth; Ch Grp Missionary Trip; Sch Musicals, 1979-81; Blood Donor; r/So Bapt; hon/W/W Among Am HS Students; Yg Commun Ldrs of Am; Yg Personalities; g/Music Bus.

FOUCHI, DANA RAY oc/Medical Student; b/Nov 17, 1960; h/1900 Perdido Street, Apartment A93, New Orleans, LA 70112; p/Frank E Fouchi, Metairie, LA; Sheila Fry Hornbostle, Waxhaw, NC; ed/Archbishop Rummel HS, 1978; BS in Biol, Loyola Univ, 1982; Med Student, LA St Univ Med Ctr; pa/ Computer Operator, E Jefferson Gen Hosp, 1980-; Blood Bk Extern, Charity Hosp of NO, 1983-; Med Examr for Hooper Holmes, 1983-; Am Med Assn; LA St Med Soc; Orleans Parish Med Soc; Am Acad of Fam Phys; Am Med Students Assn; cp/Intl Student Assn, 1980-82; Spec Ednl Sers, Tutor 1981; Mardi Gras Coalition, Medic 1981; VP, Mu Alpha Theta, 1976-77; Editor-in-Chief, HS Newspaper, 1977-78; Pres, Nat Hon Soc, 1977-78; Dir of LSUMC Concert Band, 1983-84; Med Sch Sect Editor for Yrbook, 1983-84, Photog 1982-84; Pres, Alpha Sigma Nu Nat Jesuit Hon Soc, 1981-82; Pres, Blue Key Nat Hon Frat, 1981-82; Secy, Beta Beta Beta Nat Biol Hon Soc, 1980-81; Dir of Fin for SGA, 1981-82; Loyola Liaisons; Cardinal Key Nat Hon

Sorority; r/Cath; Lector and Eucharistic Min, 1980-82; hon/Competed in St Rally, Chem, 1977; Selected for Boys' St, 1977; Rev John H Mullahy SJ Awd for Outstg Acad Achmt, Integrity and Ldrship in a Sci Grad, 1982; Edmonds Foun S'ship Recip, 1983; Pres Scholar at Loyola, 1978-82; Dean's List, 1978-82; Nat Merit Scholar, 1978-82; Res F'ship and Grant from Am Heart Assn, 1981; Valedictorian of 324 Grads, 1978; K of C Cath Yth Ldrship Awd, 1978; Cert for Being a One Gallon Blood Donor, 1983; W/W in Am HS Students; Nat Register of Outstg Col Grads; g/ MD; Pract Med and Teach.

FOURMAN, GARY LEE oc/International Production Technical Support Pharmacist; b/Sep 5, 1955; h/5666 Powderhorn, Kalamazoo, MI 49009; m/ Janet L; p/Mr and Mrs Daniel K Fourman, Indianapolis, IN; ed/Warren Ctl HS; BS in Pharm, Purdue Univ, 1978; pa/Intl Prodn Tech Support Pharm, Upjohn Co, 1980-; Developmental Pharm, Upjohn Co, 1978-80; IN Pharm Assn Del; MI Pharm Assn; Am Pharm Assn; cp/Fairway Coop Alumni Assn, Pres; Whitegate Farms Assn, Treas; Purdue Student Housing Corp, Treas, Pres; Fairway Coop, VP, Pres; r/First Bapt Ch, Deacon, Trustee; hon/Pub, "Start-Up of Sterile Products Production in International Facilities," 1983; Phi Eta Sigma; Phi Kappa Phi; Rho Chi; g/Obtain MBA.

FOURSHEE, PAUL EVANS oc/Carpenter; b/Aug 21, 1959; h/PO Box 952, Cadiz, KY 42211; ba/Cadiz, KY; p/Mr and Mrs Thomas Fourshee, Cadiz, KY; ed/Trigg Co HS, 1977; pa/Carpenter, Fourshee Constrn Co, 1977; cp/Thomas and Bridges Assn, Bd of Dirs 1978-83; Trigg Co Hist and Preserv Soc, Bd of Dirs 1983; Pennyrile Arts Coun Inc, Theatre Arts Com 1982-83; So KY Indep Theatre Inc, Charter Mem and Bd of Dirs 1983; Pennyrile Players Commun Theatre, 1982; r/Bapt; hon/ Pub, *The Past Remembered*, 1982.

FOWKE, IVA ELAINE oc/Student; b/ Mar 26, 1966; h/2124 Baden Court, Morrow, GA 30260; p/Mr and Mrs F L Fowke Jr, Morrow, GA; ed/Morrow HS, 1984; cp/Band, 1976-84 (VP); Flag Corps, Co-Capt 1982-84; Nat Hon Soc, 1981-84; Student Coun, Rep 1984; Beta Clb, 1980; 4-H Co Pres, 1980-81; Sci Clb, Prog Chair 1982-83; Key Clb, 1983-84; FCA, 1983-84; Drama, 1980; Ch Yth Grp, 1982-84; r/Bapt; hon/ Homecoming Ct, 1983-84; 4-H Co Pres; UGA S'ship Recip, Band, 1980; Most Outstg Bandsman, 1980; Gov Hons Nom, 1981; French Superlative, 1980; Hugh O'Brien Yth Foun Scholar, 1982; All-St Band, 1980-82; Sr Superlative, Most Respected; W/W Among Am HS Students; g/Corporate Lawr.

FOX, FRANCES JO oc/Student; b/Jul 14, 1966; h/PO Box 450, Jellico, TN 37762; p/Joseph C (dec) and Charlotte Fox, Jellico, TN; ed/Jellico HS, 1984; cp/ Cheerldr, 5 Yrs, Capt for 2 Yrs; Homecoming Queen, 1981; FHA Clb VP, 1981; Class Pres, 1982; Class Favorite, 1982; 4-H Clb, 2 Yrs; Beta Clb; Beta Clb Treas; Pep Clb; Co-Editor, Sch Newspaper, 1983; r/Bapt; hon/Hon Roll, 3 Yrs; Perfect Attendance Awd, 9 Yrs; Spelling Awd, 2 Yrs; 2 Piano Music Awds; W/W Among Am HS Students.

FOX, JAMES EMERY oc/Student; b/

May 11, 1967; h/14370 SH 37 R2, Forest, OH 45843; p/Paul E and Anna M Fox, Forest, OH; cp/St Contest Choir; Marching Band; Solo and Ensemble Band; St Contest Band; Concert Band; Concert Choir; Musical Stage Prodns, HS; Yrbook; Yrbook Editor; Prom Chm; Quill and Scroll; Nat Hon Soc, 1982-84; r/U Meth; hon/Nat Hon Soc, 1984; Quill and Scroll, 1983, 1984; g/Advtg or Comml Art.

FOX, MARY ELLEN oc/Attorney; b/ Aug 8, 1956; h/14370 SH 37 RR#2, Forest, OH 43843; ba/Sandusky, OH; p/Paul E and Anna M Fox, Forest, OH; ed/Riverdale HS, 1974; BA 1978, JD 1981, OH No Univ; pa/Assoc, Stansbery, Shoenberger & Scheck, Attys at Law, 1981-; City Solicitor, Village of Nevada, 1982-; Wyandot Co Law Libn, 1982-; Am Bar Assn, 1981-; OH Bar Assn, 1981-; Wyandot Co Bar Assn, 1981-, VP 1983; cp/Student Bar Assn; Hon Soc; Quill and Scroll; Univ European Choral Choir; Phi Alpha Delta; ONU Chorus Secy; Alpha Xi Delta, Alumnae Pres 1983-84, Advr for Collegiates, Province Secy; hon/ Editor-in-Chief, Yrbook; Intl Yth in Achmt; W/W Among Students in Am Cols and Univs; Commun Ldrs of Am.

FOYE, MICHAEL LOUIS oc/Product Specialist; b/Jul 4, 1956; h/2924 Olden Oak Lane, #304, Auburn Heights, MI 48057; ba/Rochester, MI; p/Mr and Mrs Louis Foye, Burnsville, MN; ed/Walpole HS, 1974; BA, Ec, KS Univ, 1978; MBA, Fin/Acctg, Univ of MI, 1980; pa/Prod Spec 1981-, Adm Analyst 1980-81, Centronics Data Computer Corp; Budget and Planning Intern, Control Data Corp, 1978, 1979; cp/Rochester JCs, Dir of Commun Action 1982-83; Jr Achmt Advr, 1981-82; Col Repubs, 1974-76; Golf Team, HS, 1971; Delta Tau Delta Frat, Treas and Secy 1977, Housing Secy 1976; Ch Folk Grp, 1980-; r/Cath; hon/HS Hon Roll, 1970-74; Nat Hon Soc, Col Hons; HS Polit Sci S'ship; Ec S'ship, 1978; Univ of MI Alumni Forum, 1982.

FRACASSO, KATHERINE LOUISE oc/Student; h/Route 6, Box 76, Summerville, SC 29483; p/Leo P and Carolyn J Fracasso, Summerville, SC; ed/Summerville HS; Student, Limestone Col, 1983-; pa/Receptionist, Secy, Darkroom Wk, Ed's Photo, 1983; Bus Driver, Summerville Sch Dist #2, 1981-83; Bus Driver and Art Spec, Camp Joy, 1983; Bus Driver and Jr Cnslr, Camp Joy, 1982; Employee, Burger King, 1981; cp/ Summerville HS Jr Achmt, Insight Clb, Student Action for Ed, Glee Clb, Concert Choir, 1982-83; Mu Alpha Theta, 1981-82; Latin Clb, 1980-81; r/ Bapt; Ch Choir, 1980-83; Sunday Sch Tchr for Grades 5 and 6 Boys, Ch Tng Yth Pres, 1982-83; Ch Tng Yth Secy, 1981-82; hon/PTA Art Contest, 4th Place Awd, 1976; Recip, 1st Place Awd for Art Contest Sponsored by First Fed Savs & Ln Assn, Charleston Coastal Carolina Fair; Recip, Awd for Outstg Ser to Summerville HS Insight Clb, 1983; Recip, Limestone Hons Trustee S'ship; g/BA, Art and Ed; Comml Art, Tchg or Missions Wk.

FRANCK, THEODORA MARIE CONOPEOTIS oc/Teacher; b/Jan 31, 1957; h/1712 18th Avenue, Apartment 3, Rock Island, IL 61201; ba/East Moline, IL; m/Carsten H II; p/Theodore and

Nicky Conopeotis, Waukegan, IL; ed/N Chgo Commun HS, 1975; BA, Augustana Col, 1979; pa/Govt Tchr, Rock Isl HS, 1979; Psych and Govt Tchr, U Twp HS, 1979-81, 1982-; Varsity and Sophomore Cheerldg Coach, U Twp HS, 1979-81; Mgmt Trainee, N Shore Savs & Ln Assn, 1981-82; cp/Pres and Intramural Dir, Chi Omega Gamma Sorority, 1977-79; Rep to Inter-Sorority Coun, 1977-79; Col Bd of Mgrs, 1978; Psi Chi, 1978-; NEA-IEA, 1979-; Yth Cnslr; r/Greek Orthodox; hon/Pubs, "Teaching Methodology to High School Psychology Students through the Study of Motor Skill Learning" 1979, Psych Curric Guide for Gen and Col Prep HS Students 1983; Nat Psych Hon Soc, Psi Chi, 1978; Nat Sr Hon Soc, Mortar Bd, 1978; Freshmen Hon Soc, Topper's, 1976; Grad, cum laude, Augustana Col, 1979; W/W Among Am HS Students; g/MBA, Univ of IA.

FRANKE, MARY REBECCA oc/Elementary Music Teacher; b/Dec 21, 1961; h/1179 Fernwood Drive, Schenectady, NY 12309; ba/Voorheesville, NY; p/Mr and Mrs Donald A Franke, Schenectady, NY; ed/Niskayuna HS, 1979; BMus, magna cum laude, Westminster Choir Col, 1983; pa/Subst Tchr in Var Public Sch Sys, 1983; Elem Music Tchr, Voorheesville Elem Sch, 1983-; Music Edrs Nat Conf; Pi Kappa Lambda Nat Music Hon Soc; cp/Pres, Class of 1983, Westminster Choir Col, 1982; r/Luth; hon/Westminster Choir Col Achmt Awd, 1979; Aid Assn for Luths All-Col S'ship, 1979; Dean's List, Sprg 1980, Sprg 1982; g/Master's Deg.

FRANKEL, LAURA ANNE oc/Student; b/Apr 10, 1964; h/210 Cumming Drive, Brunswick, MD 21716; p/Gene Frankel, New York, NY; Pat Frankel, Brunswick, MD; ed/Brunswick HS, 1982; Student, Univ of MD Balto Co; pa/Biol Aide, Ft Detrick; cp/ Editor-in-Chief, Sch Newspaper; NHS VP; French Clb Secy; Student Coun Reporter; G&T Prog; Hon Roll; Latin Hon Soc; B Awds; Drama III; Musicals; Glee Clb; r/Meth; hon/MD Dist'd Scholar Semi-Finalist; Leonard F Thornton Prize; W/W Among Am HS Students; W/W Among Intl HS Students; g/Biochem.

FRASER, DOUGLAS W oc/Labourer; b/May 29, 1958; h/1 Gibson Avenue, Grimsby, Ontario L3M 1G8; p/Robert Fraser, Grimsby, Ontario; ed/Dipl, Grimsby Sec'dy Sch, 1978; Grad of Media Fundamentals, Sheridan Col, 1981; pa/Fruit Picker, Bain's Fruit, 1970-78; Greenhouse Wkr, R Jordan Greenhouses, 1979-80; Food Preparation/Dishwasher, Village Inn Steakhouse, 1981; Machine Operator, Grimsby Packaging, 1982; cp/Hamilton T'ai Chi Assn, 1983-; hon/Contbr, Once a Month Column in Grimsby Independent Newspaper (Local Art Criticism); hon/ Best in Show Awd, Grimsby Art Fest, 1982; Bronze Awd for Painting, Grimsby Art Fest, 1982.

FRAZIER, KATHLEEN oc/Student; b/Apr 2, 1965; h/Route 5, Box 453, Magnolia, AR 71753; p/Murlene Frazier, Magnolia, AR; ed/Walker HS, 1983; cp/Sr Class Treas; Student Coun Rep; Yrbook Staff, 1983; Homecoming Hon Maid; Girls' St Del, 1982; r/Meth; hon/Acad Hon Roll, Acctg, Ofc Pract, 1983; W/W Among Am HS Students;

g/To Attend So AR Univ and Maj in Computer Sci.

FREASE, SHERRY LYNNE oc/Divisional Sales Manager; b/Mar 15, 1960; h/578-106 Chinkapin Trail, Newport News, VA 23602; ba/Hampton, VA; p/ Mr and Mrs Gary W Frease, Fayetteville, NC; ed/Cape Fear HS, 1978; Gen Studies, Univ of NC Greensboro; Hardbarger Jr Col of Bus, 1980; pa/ Divisional Sales Mgr (Sr Exec), Miller & Rhoads, 1983-; Area Sales Mgr 1981-83, Sales Supvr 1980-81, Belk; Salesperson, Capitol Dept Store, 1979-80; cp/Christian Wom's Bus and Profl Clb; HS All St Band 1975, 1978, All Co Band 1976-78; HS Beta Clb, 1977-78; Asst Editor, HS Annual, 1978; HS Sr Class Secy; HS Band Pres; Tri-Hi-Y, 1978; r/Prot; hon/HS Marshal, 1977; Scholastic Excell Awd, 1977; HS Hon Roll, 1976-78; Hardbarger Jr Col Hon Grad, 1980; Intl Yth in Achmt; W/W Among Am HS Students; g/ Fashion Bus Mgmt.

FREELS, ANNE ELIZABETH oc/ Student; b/Jan 2, 1964; h/3800 Primrose Place, Paducah, KY 42001; p/Mr and Mrs William C Freels, Paducah, KY; ed/ Grad, Paducah Tilghman HS, 1981; BS in Fin, Murray St Univ, 1985; cp/Key Clb; Quill and Scroll, Pres; The Tilghman Bell; Alpha Omicron Pi Sorority; Panhellenic Del; r/Epis; hon/HS Salutatorian; Yth Salute; Highest Pledge Grade; Bd of Regents S'ship, 1981; Soc of Dist'd HS Students; W/W Am HS Students; g/Complete Fin Deg, Obtain MBA and Be a Bk Pres Before Reaching the Age of 35.

FREEMAN, CATHERINE ELAINE oc/Counselor; b/Oct 18, 1956; h/823 Florida, Joplin, MO 64801; p/Mr and Mrs John Freeman, Elk City, KS; ed/ Elk Val HS, 1974; BA 1978, MS 1979, Pittsburg St Univ; pa/Cnslr; MO St Coor, Nat Orientation Dirs Assn; Nat Assn Student Pers Admrs; MO Col Pers Assn; cp/Team Capt, MO So St Col Alumni Fund Drive; Sponsor, Col Repubs; Pittsburg St Univ Alumni Assn; Vol Polit Campaign Wkr; U Way Team Capt; Grad Student Assn, Rep to Grad Coun; r/U Meth Ch; hon/Pres Hon Roll; Omicron Delta Kappa; Phi Kappa Phi; Psi Chi; Intl Yth in Achmt; W/W Among Students in Am Univs and Cols; Commun Ldrs of Am; g/Terminal Deg in Higher Ed Adm; Adm Position in Student Affairs.

FREIHOFER, GRETCHEN ANNETTE oc/Student; b/Jun 7, 1961; h/19 Paul Hesser Drive, Lakeside Park, KY 41017; p/Fred and Pamela Freihofer, Lakeside Park, KY; ed/HS, St Henry, 1979; BA, cum laude, Mass Communs/ Public Relats, No KY Univ, 1983; cp/ Alpha Chi Hon Soc; Public Relats Student Soc of Am; Student Govt Public Relats Dir; Delta Zeta; Panhellenic Pres; Music Fest Com; Student Pub Bd; Hoxworth Blood Dr; Search Com, Dean of Commun Ser; Muscular Dystrophy and Easter Seals Telethon; Commencement Com; Com to Select Outstg Srs in Communs; Greek House Task Force; Homecoming Pub Com; r/Cath; hon/ Univ Ser Awd, 1983; Outstg Sr in Communs, 1983; Student Govt Ser Awd, 1983; Pres Ser Awd, 1983; Alpha Delta Sigma Hon Soc, 1983; Dean's List; Delta Zeta Rose Ct, Highest GPA Awd; Student Govt Dedication Awd; W/W

Among Students in Am Cols and Univs; Outstg Yg Wom of Am; Nat Register of Outstg Col Grads; Outstg Yg Commun Ldrs of Am; g/Career in Mass Communs and Public Relats.

FRERE, JOSEPH BENEDICT oc/Student; b/Mar 18, 1964; h/Box 27, Bel Alton, MD 20611; p/Mr and Mrs John E Frere Sr, Bel Alton, MD; ed/St Mary's Ryken HS, 1982; cp/Pres, Ch Yth Org; Ch Parish Coun; Liturgy Com; Co Softball Leag; 4-H; Class Rep; Ch and Commun Wkr; Yth F'ship; Spanish Clb; Intramural Sports; hon/Serra Clb for Outstg Ser; Hon Roll; Prin List; Col Commend List; Cert of Hon; Cert of Hon for Math; W/W Among Am HS Students; g/Acctg Maj and Computer Sci Minor, Loyola Col.

FREULER, SANDRA GAIL oc/Student; b/Feb 21, 1963; h/2516 Beechwood Drive, Tarboro, NC 27886; p/Mr and Mrs Daniel A Freuler, Tarboro, NC; ed/Grad, Tarboro HS, 1981; Student, Salem Col; pa/Pers Clk, Polylok Corp, 1979; Sum Jobs, Tarboro Rel Book and Music Store, 1980-83; cp/Staff Writer, *Salemite*, 1982-83; Intervarsity Clb, 1982-83; Student Govt Assn, Salem Col Secy 1983-84; r/Prot; hon/Nat Hon Soc, 1980-81; Alpha Lambda Delta, 1981-82; Pres Awd, Freshmen w Highest GPA, 1982; Marshal, One of Top Seven GPAs in Jr Class, 1983-84; Dean's List, Salem Col, Every Semester; Soc of Dist'd Am HS Students; g/BA Deg in Psych and Sociol from Salem Col; Grad Sch in Psych at Univ of NC Chapel Hill.

FRIEDLANDER, JANET A oc/Student; b/May 17, 1962; h/2014 North Jackson, Waukegan, IL 60085; p/Daniel and Shirley Friedlander, Waukegan, IL; ed/Waukegan E HS, 1980; BA, Purdue Univ, 1984; pa/Mgr, 19th Hole, Meshingomesia Country Clb, 1983; cp/Kappa Delta Rho Little Sister, VP; Purdue Swim Team Mgr; Alpha Delta Pi Sorority, 1982, Social Chm 1982-84; Rhi Soc, 1982-84, Treas 1983-84; Clb Mgr Assoc 1982-84; Chm, Proj and Enterprises, Intramurals; B'nai B'rith Yth Org Pres, Sum Prog Chm, Sum Conv; Campus Scout; JA Treas; Water Ballet Clb Secy-Treas, Pres; Future Nurses Pres; W Clb; GSA Bd Del; Brownie Scout Ldr; Homecoming Ct; hon/Statler Foun S'ship, 1983; Outstg Female Student of the Yr, Exec Clb of WKGN; Outstg Yg Am; Intl Yth in Achmt; g/Maj in Restaurant, Hotel and Instnl Mgmt; Own a Restaurant.

FRITSCH, CARLA E oc/Theology Teacher; b/Dec 10, 1958; h/15207 Madison Avenue, #309, Lakewood, OH 44107; ba/Lakewood, OH; p/Blanche Fritsch, Parma, OH; ed/Cleveland Ctl Cath HS, 1976; BA, John Carroll Univ, 1980; Currently Pursuing MA, John Carroll Univ; pa/Sophomore and Jr

Theol Tchr, Retreat Team Mem, St Augustine Acad, 1980-; cp/Spriritual Dir, Play, 1981-82; Vol Prog Coor, Kaleidoscope, 1981-82; Adult Catechist Formation Prog Tchr, 1983; Operative, Cleveland Cath Diocese; g/MA in Rel Ed; Diocesan Level Adm Position in Rel Ed.

FRONABARGER, DEBORAH ANN oc/Student; b/Aug 9, 1959; h/615 Natchez Trace Drive, Lexington, TN 38351; m/Ben W (dec); c/Angela Kay; p/Otto and Kathy Britt, Lexington, TN; ed/HS, 1977; BS, Mech Engrg Technol, 1983; pa/Tech Clk, Gould EMD Inc, 1981-82; Engrg Clk, R K Weir and Assocs, 1980-81; Soc of Mfg Engrs Student Chapt, Secy-Treas 1983-84; Am Inst of Indust Engrs, 1979-82; cp/Phi Theta Kappa Hon Frat, 1979; r/Meth; hon/Soc of Mfg Engrs S'ship, 1983; Engrg and Engrg Technol Deptl Awd, 1983; W/W Among Am HS Students; g/To Wk as Mfg Engr; Move into Mgmt.

FRULAND, DARCY DAWN oc/Adaptive Education Instructor; b/Jul 29, 1958; h/8946 West Lynx 27, Milwaukee, WI 53225; ba/Brown Deer, WI; p/Mr and Mrs Orven Fruland, Sheridan, IL; ed/Newark Commun HS, 1976; BA, Carthage Col, 1980; pa/Adaptive Ed Instr, Hearthside Rehab Ctr; Assn for Retarded Citizens, Milwaukee Chapt; cp/IL Pk and Rec Assn; WI Pk and Rec Assn; Soccer Track; Student Activs Bd; Union Rec Com Chm; Student Govt; Student Jud Bd; Wind Symph; Luth Yth Encounter Weekend Team; Pi Delta Chi; Yrbook Assoc Editor; hon/Beta Beta Beta; Blue Key; W/W Among Students in Am Cols and Univs; Intl Yth in Achmt; g/Wk w Geriatric Mtly Retarded.

FUGATE, EDWARD W oc/Student, Student Pastor; b/Aug 22, 1956; h/300 East Cherry Street, New Paris, OH 45347; ba/Same; m/Adina Sue; p/Claude and Arminda Fugate, Enon, OH; ed/Greenon High; BA, Rel, Berea Col; Att'g, U Theol Sem; pa/Ins Agt, Sales Mgr, Commonwealth Life Ins Co, 1979-82; Student Pastor, St Paul U Meth Ch, 1982-; cp/Kiwanis Intl; Col: Berea Col Country Dancers 1974-78, Student Body VP 1976-77, Dorm Senator on Student Coun 1977-78; r/U Meth; g/To Successfully Complete Sem and Enter the Parish Min.

FULGHAM, VICTORIA ADRIANNA oc/Student; b/Apr 9, 1962; h/452 Calhoun Street, West Point, MS 39773; p/Mrs Loyce Fulgham, West Point, MS; ed/W Pt HS, 1980; Student, Fashion Mdsg and Bus, MS Univ for Wom; pa/Tng Modeling Squad Dir, 1983; Modeling Squad Asst, 1982; cp/Circle K, Secy 1982-83; Students of Home Ec Assn; Am Home Ec Assn; Fashion Grp, Pres; Mam'selle Social Clb; Black List Social

Clb; Phi Beta Lambda; Capt of MUW Modeling Squad; r/Bapt; hon/Amblin Fashion Awd, 1983; 15th Grad'g HS Student, 1980; g/BS Deg in Mdsg; BS Deg in Bus; Master's Deg in Bus.

FULLER, ETHEL KAY oc/Student; b/Dec 28, 1963; h/13 Dunkard Avenue, Westover, WV 26505; p/Howard L and Aurora Fuller, Westover, WV; ed/BSJ, News/Edit Jour, 1985; cp/Alpha Phi Omega Nat Ser Frat, Ushering Chp, Publicity Dir, 1st VP; Pres, of Profl Journalists, Sigma Delta Chi; WV Univ Student Adm; PACETEC Assn; *Daily Athenaeum* Reporter; r/Meth; hon/Pres's Awd, Alpha Phi Omega.

FULLER, RICHARD BRIAN oc/Student; b/Jan 11, 1966; h/Route 1, Box 15, Liberty, SC 29657; p/Richard D and Sandra Fuller, Liberty, SC; ed/HS Grad, 1984; cp/VP, Student Body; Pres, Teenagers Against Substance Abuse; Block L Clb; Football; Baseball; Track; Am Legion Baseball; r/Bapt; hon/Best Back, Football, 1980; Pickens Sentinel Player of the Wk, Sep 24, 1982; Sentinel Defensive Player of the Wk, Sep 30, 1983; Most Valuable Player, Baseball, 1982; Best Defensive Back, Football, 1982; g/To Study PE in Col.

FULP, JEFFREY CHRISTIAN oc/Graduate Student; b/Aug 4, 1961; h/2032-D Quail Forest Drive, Raleigh, NC 27609; p/Mr and Mrs William Melvin Fulp, Winston-Salem, NC; ed/R J Reynolds Sr High, 1979; BA, Univ of NC Chapel Hill, 1983; Master of Textiles, Mats and Mgmt Expected, NC St Univ; pa/Coach, Choreographer, Univ of NC Formation Dance Team, 1982-; Costume Shop Asst'ship, Dept of Drama, Univ of NC Chapel Hill, 1980-83; Ballroom Dance Dept, Univ of NC Chapel Hill, 1982, 1983; Costume Shop Asst, "Young Washington," 1980; Assoc Costumer, "Unto These Hills," 1981; Asst Costumer/Designer, "Hatfields and McCoys," "Honey in the Rock," 1982; cp/Nat Hon Soc; Dir, Coach, Choreographer for Univ of NC Chapel Hill Formation Dance and Exhib Team; r/Moravian; hon/Nat Hon Soc, 1979; Var Hons and Awds in Ballroom Dance Competitions, incl'g, 2nd Place in US Tournament of Dance, 1978, and So Competitions; g/Wk in the Field of Textiles, Particularly in Fashion World; Continue Ballroom Tchg/Dancing.

FUNK, MICHAEL DUANE oc/Student; b/Jun 22, 1962; h/Rural Route 2, Box 116, Manito, IL 61546; p/Fred and Lois Funk, Manito, IL; ed/Pekin Commun HS, Pekin, IL, 1981; Currently Att'g, IL Wesleyan Univ, Bloomington, IL; cp/HS Football, Track, Wrestling; r/SDA; hon/Nat Hon Soc; W/W Among Am HS Students; Intl Yth in Achmt; Commun Ldrs of Am; g/Med Deg.

G

GADDIS, DOUGLAS CLAYTON oc/Student; b/Apr 12, 1965; h/2257 North Stratford Drive, Owensboro, KY 42301; p/Kenneth and Nancy Gaddis, Owensboro, KY; ed/Apollo HS, 1983; cp/Owensboro Choral Soc, Soloist 1981-83; Nat Beta Clb, 1981-83; KY Wesleyan Col Opera Theatre, 1982; Theatre Wkshop of Owensboro, 1982; Apollo HS Pep, Marching, Concert, Jazz Bands, 1979-83; r/So Bapt; 3rd Bapt Ch Choir, Handbell Ensemble, Wind Ensemble, 1983; Wesleyan Hgts Meth Ch Choir, Handbell Ensemble, 1983; hon/ Nat Merit Commend, 1982; Nat Hon Soc, 1982-83; Apollo HS Hon Roll, 1981-83; W/W Among Am HS Students; Soc of Dist'd Am HS Students; Am Achmt Acad; W/W Music; g/To Attend Univ of KY, then IN Univ; Maj in Applied Music; Career in Singing Opera.

GAETANO, MARIO ANTHONY JR oc/Instructor of Music; b/Oct 28, 1955; h/PO Box 1090, Cullowhee, NC 28723; ba/Cullowhee, NC; m/Tammy Phillips; ed/BM, St Univ of NY Potsdam, 1977; MM, E Carolina Univ, 1978; pa/Instr of Percussion and Dir of Jazz Ensemble, Wn Carolina Univ, 1979-; Orch Dir, Ballston Spa HS, 1978-79; Percussive Arts Soc; Nat Assn of Jazz Edrs; Am Fdn of Musicians; r/Cath; hon/Pubs, "Prelude for Marimba," "Song of the Libra" (for Solo Vibraphone); Finalist in Yg Artist Competition, Nat Assn of Composers, USA, 1984; g/DMA, Memphis St Univ, 1985.

GAFFNEY, PATRICIA ANNE oc/ Student; b/Jan 23, 1957; h/55 Brauch Avenue, Rochester, NY 14618; ba/ Boston, MA; p/Mr and Mrs Patrick Gaffney, Rochester, NY; ed/Our Lady of Mercy HS, 1975; BS, Bucknell Univ, 1979; pa/Internal Auditor, CBS Inc, 1979-80; Sr Acct, Arthur Andersen & Co, 1980-83; cp/Sr Class Pres; Jr Class VP; Sr Class Treas, Secy; Resident Asst for Dorm; Prodn Mgr, Student Newspaper; Sr Gift Drive Investmts Com; Class Agt for Bucknell Annual Fund; r/ Rom Cath; hon/Grad, cum laude; Mortar Bd; Delta Mu Delta; W/W Am HS Students; g/Financial Mgmt after Obtaining MBA from Harvard Bus Sch.

GAIN, DANIELLE RAE oc/Student; ed/Att'g, Villanova Univ; hon/Pres's List and Dean's List, DE Co Commun Col, 1983; Intl Register of Profiles; g/Polit Sci Maj Pursuing a Career in Law or Law Enforcement (FBI).

GALLAGHER, JAMES ROBERT oc/ Farmer; b/Sep 2, 1963; h/Maitland, MO 64466; p/Mr and Mrs Eldon Gallagher; ed/Nodaway-Holt-Graham HS, 1980; pa/Full-time Farmer at Age 19; cp/ Basketball Team; Student Coun; FFA Proj; hon/FFA Deg; DeKalb Awd; g/Am Farmer Deg.

GALLAGHER, TAMMY A oc/Student; h/Route 2, Box 210, Morrison, TN 37357; p/Mr and Mrs Thomas E Gallagher, Morrison, TN; ed/Grad, Warren Co Sr High, 1981; Att'd, Univ of TN Knoxville, 1981-83; BS, SpecEd/Severe/ Profound, Vanderbilt Univ, 1985; cp/ CEC, VP 1984-85; Impact, 1983-85; SGA Presents Com, 1984-85; Vucept Acad and Transfer, 1984; Intramural Football and Softball, Vanderbilt Univ; Univ of TN: Alpha Xi Delta Sorority,

Asst Corresponding Secy, Pledge Tnr, Mbrship Chm, 1981-83; Treas, Future Tchrs Am; Treas, F'ship Christian Aths; Histn and Treas, Demoiselle Sorority; Tri-Hi-Y; Sci Clb; Creat Writing Clb; Vol, ARC; GSA; Vol, Humane Soc; hon/ Mortar Bd, 1984; Intl Exch Student, 1981; Exch Teen of Month, 1981; Top 5% Class; Nat Hon Soc; Perfect Attendance Awd, Jr Yr; W/W Among Am HS Students; Soc of Dist'd Am HS Students; Personalities of S; Intl Yth in Achmt; g/Wk w Emotionally Disturbed; Wk w Autistic Chd through Spec Ed; Wk in Autism Res Prog.

GAMBLE, WANDA ELAINE oc/Law Enforcement Specialist; b/Apr 21, 1960; h/PSC Box 3913, Beale AFB, CA 95903; ba/Same; p/Mr Edward F Gamble Sr, Montgomery, AL; Mrs Flossie Stephens, Montgomery, AL; ed/HS Dipl, Sidney Lanier HS, 1978; BS, Govt, Auburn Univ, 1982; mil/USAF, 1980-87; pa/Coach, Bellingrath Jr High, Montgomery Pks and Rec, 1979-83; Law Enforcement Spec, USAF-AD, 1983-; cp/Alpha Kappa Alpha Sorority; Bellingrath Adv Coun; Alpha Kappa Alpha; Omni Clb for Black Interest; hon/Grad w Hons, Auburn Univ; Harry S Truman Awd; W E B Dubois Awd; Outstg Coach Awd; g/Lwyr; Public Admr; Public Ofcl.

GARCIA, EDUARDO ANTONIO oc/Student; b/Jan 6, 1963; h/911 Ferdinand Street, Coral Gables, FL 33134; p/Dr and Mrs Eduardo L Garcia, Coral Gables, FL; ed/Grad, Christopher Columbus HS, 1981; BS, Univ of Miami, 1984; Att'g, Univ of Miami Sch of Med, 1984-; pa/Am Cancer Soc Res Fellow, Papanicolaou Cancer Res Inst, 1983; cp/ Phi Kappa Phi, 1982; Golden Key Nat Hon Soc, 1982; Phi Beta Kappa, 1983; Alpha Epsilon Delta, 1983; Hosp Vol; Vol, March of Dimes, Leukemia Soc, Am Heart Assn; Med Vol, Univ of Miami Lifelines Hlth Fair, 1982; Judge, Dade Co Sci and Engrg Fair; hon/Pres Hon Roll, 1981, 1982, 1983; Dean's List, 1981, 1982, 1983; Liceo Cubano's Gran Orden Martiana, 1982; Cruzada Educativa Cubana's Dipl de Hon Juan J Remos, 1982; Alpha Epsilon Delta Outstg Sr Awd, 1983-84; Finalist, Nat Sci Talent Search for Westinghouse Sci S'ships and Awds, 1981; Outstg Scist Bringing Hon to St, FL Foun for Future Scists, 1981; Hon Mention for Sci Ser to Commun, Miami Herald Silver Knight Awds, 1981; Pres Scholar, Univ of Miami; Delta Theta Mu, Univ of Miami; Commun Ldrs of Am; Personalities of S; g/Career in Acad Med.

GARDNER, LLOYD YANCEY oc/ Student; b/Jan 22, 1963; h/902 Hyland Avenue, Williamston, NC 27892; p/L Stancil and Angeline D Gardner, Williamston, NC; ed/Williamston HS, 1981; Currently Enrolled, E Carolina Univ; cp/ Col: Phi Eta Sigma, Phi Beta Lambda (VP, Pres, NC St Histn), Phi Sigma Pi Nat Hon Frat (Com Chm), Pi Omega Pi; HS: Nat Hon Soc, Key Clb (Pres), Tennis Team, Band (Jr and Sr Drum Maj), Annual Staff; r/Prot; hon/Col: Marjorie Harrison Freshman S'ship Awd, Lena Ellis Sophomore Awd, W/ W in Phi Beta Lambda, Most Outstg Ser (Phi Beta Lambda), Univ Marshal, All A's List, Dean's List; HS: Nat Hon Soc S'ship, French Awd, C B Morrison S'ship, Marshal, Jr-Sr Waiter, Hon

Grad, Drum Maj Awd; g/Bus Ed/Mktg Distributive Ed w Future Advmt in the Field of Ed; Minor in Bus Adm.

GARDNER, MELISSA SUSAN oc/ Student; b/Nov 18, 1966; h/Route 1, Box 312, Richmond, KY 40473; p/Rex and Connie Gardner, Richmond, KY; ed/HS Grad, 1984; pa/Asst to the Dir of Woodwkg Symps, Berea Col, 1982, 1983; cp/French Clb Pres, 1982, 1983; Beta Clb Pres, 1983; Peer Cnslr VP, 1983; FBLA VP, 1983; Nat Hon Soc, Sr Class VP 1983-84; Jr Class Pres, 1982-83; r/Ch of God; hon/Hugh O'Brien Ldrship Sem, 1982; Jr Marshall, 1983; W/W Among Am HS Students; g/To Maj in Bus Adm at Berea Col.

GARRETT, DEIDRE LYNNE oc/ Student; b/May 4, 1961; h/522 University Parks Drive, Apartment #815, Waco, TX 76706; p/Charles and Eleanor Garrett, Garland, TX; ed/S Garland HS, 1979; BA, Austin Col, 1983; Student, Baylor Law Sch, 1983-; cp/Am Mensa Ltd; Sherman Symph Orch; Austin Col Jazz Ensemble; DAR; Daughs of Republic of TX; DAC; hon/Hons Thesis, 1982-83; John and Rachael Heard F'ship in Rel, 1982-83; Grad w Hons in Phil, Austin Col, 1983; Commun Ldrs of Am; g/Law Sch Graduation.

GARRISON, MICHAEL SHAWN oc/ Banjo Teacher, Student; b/Oct 20, 1966; h/1968 North Dixie, Cookeville, TN 38501; ba/Cookeville, TN; p/Mr and Mrs Haney Garrison, Cookeville, TN; ed/Grad, Cookeville HS; pa/Banjo Tchr, L&M Music Store, 1982-; r/Bapt; hon/ 1st Place in Banjo Contest, Ralph Sloan Day, 1983; 2nd Place, Jamestown, TN, Arts and Crafts Fest, 1983; Winner, Yth Talent Contest, 1983; g/To Become a Profl Musician; To Get into the Country Music Field.

GARSIDE, COLLEEN oc/Director of Student Activities, Night Manager; b/ Mar 17, 1958; h/1132 North Ross, Oklahoma City, OK 73107; ba/Edmond, OK; m/Steven L; c/Jamee Donn; p/James K and Sherry Packer, North Ogden, UT; ed/AS; BS; MEd; pa/Loan Note Ofcr 1981, Adm Secy 1980-81, OK St Regents for Higher Ed; Cheerldr Advr, Weber St Col, 1979-80; Gymnastics Instr and Coach, Rhythm Connections, 1977-80; Cert'd Ski Instr, Powder Mtn, UT, 1977-80; Dir of Student Activs; Night Mgr; Kappa Delta Pi; Phi Kappa Phi; Profl Ski Instrs of Am; Assn of Col Unions-Intl; r/LDS; hon/Outstg Grad, Sch of Humanities; Outstg Yg Wom of Am; World W/W Wom; Nat Dean's List; g/To Get a Doct Deg and Teach Communication Classes on the Col Level.

GARY, PAUL GRAY oc/Student; b/ Oct 11, 1964; h/Route 8, Box 36, Granbury, TX 76048; ba/Granbury, TX; p/Richard A Gray, Granbury, TX; ed/ Grad, Granbury HS; cp/Granbury FFA, Pres; FBLA, Parliamentarian; r/Bapt; hon/Nat Hist Awd; Lone Star Farmer; Rotarian Awd; g/To Attend Col and Maj in Bus.

GARZIA, MARIO RICARDO oc/ Member of Technical Staff; b/Mar 6, 1955; h/52 Harvey Avenue, Lincroft, NJ 07738; ba/Homdel, NJ; m/Marjorie Ann; c/Daniel Ricardo, Nichole Andrea; p/ Ricardo and Julia Garzia, Akron, OH; ed/BS 1975, MS 1977, Univ of Akron; PhD, Case Wn Resv Univ, 1982; pa/ Mem of Tech Staff, Bell Labs, 1982-; Sci Programmer, Babcock and Wilcox

Co, 1976-82; Pt-time Lectr 1978-80, Tchg Asst 1975-76, Dept of Math, Univ of Akron; IEEE (Assoc Editor of Modeling Newsletter), 1978-; SIAM, 1980-; AMS, 1977-; ORSA, 1974-76; hon/ Authored and Co-Authored More Than 10 Tech Papers Appearing in Tech Jours and Conf Proceedings; Pubs in *International Journal of Control*; Pi Mu Epsilon, 1976; Perfect GPA, PhD Studies; Intl Yth in Achmt; Commun Ldrs of Am; g/To Apply Tech Background in Chosen Career.

GASTON, RALPHETTE oc/Student; b/Feb 23, 1962; h/10119 South Calumet, Chicago, IL 60628; ba/Chicago, IL; ed/ John Marshall Harlan HS, 1979; Bach Deg, Crim Justice, Bradley Univ, 1982; Paralegal Cert, Roosevelt Univ, 1983; pa/Togetherness w Yth Intern, Ctl IL Crim Justice Comm, 1981-82; Tutor, Tri-Co Urban Leag, 1981; Ofc Clk, R Gaston's Auto Body, 1981; Cashier and Prodn Ldr, Inner City Foods (Burger King), 1979; cp/Nat Tech Assn, Resume Com 1980; Black Student Alliance, Secy 1980; Alpha Phi Omega Ser Frat, Fund Raising Com 1982; Pre-Law Clb, 1982; Pres, Jr Block Clb, 1978-79; Jr Class Treas, 1978; Culture Clb, 1978; Pres, HS Band, 1978; Drama Clb, Stage Mgr 1982; Model UN, 1977-79; hon/Nat Hon Soc, 1977-79; Outstg Student in Math, 1979; Prin Scholar, 1979; Acad Hon Roll, 1976-79; Dist'd Am HS Student, 1977; W/W Among Am HS Students; g/To Pursue a Rewarding Career as a Lwyrs Asst in Crim Litigation and Pract Crim Law at the "Grass Roots" Level.

GAZALEH, NICHOLAS EARL oc/ Student; b/Oct 21, 1968; h/Route 1, Box 123 D, Wallace, NC 28466; p/Mr and Mrs Zaki N Gazaleh, Wallace, NC; ed/ Student, Wallace-Rose Hill HS; cp/Boy Scout, 1978-, Sr Patrol Ldr, Life Scout; Cub Scout, 1974-78, Den Ldr 1977; Beta Clb, 1981-83, Treas 1983; Student Coun, 1981-84, VP 1983, St Conv Del 1984; Govt and Ec Clb, 1983-84, VP 1984; Football, 1981-83; Baseball, 1978-84; hon/Hon Roll; God and Country Awd, 1976; Arrow of Light, 1977; John T Smith Meml S'ship, 1981; US Achmt Acad, Sports, 1982; US Achmt Acad, Ldrship and Ser, 1983; g/Computer Sci and Bus Maj.

GEARY, CAROL JEAN oc/Loan Department Employee, Student; b/Mar 25, 1965; h/126 Lakeview Drive, Mount Washington, KY 40047; ba/Mount Washington, KY; p/Michael S and Barbara J Geary, Mount Washington, KY; ed/Grad, Bullitt E HS; Student, Bus Adm and Fin, Univ of Louisville; pa/ Loan Dept Employee, Peoples Bk; cp/ Beta Clb; Pep Clb; FBLA; FCA; Newspaper, Annual Staff; Track Team; Bapt Ch Softball Team; Prom Com; Ch Yth Coun; Basketball Stat; Hon Roll; hon/ Valedictorian, 1983; Eugene H Smith S'ship-Alternate, 1983; US Achmt Acad Bus Awd; 6th Place, Semi-St Competition, Track, Mile Relay; W/W Among Am HS Students; g/Grad, Univ of Louisville Sch of Bus; CPA.

GEBHARDT, SUSAN ANN oc/Student; b/Aug 16, 1961; h/7011 Adams Street, Guttenberg, NJ 07093; p/Mr and Mrs Robert Gebhardt, Guttenberg, NJ; ed/N Bergen HS, 1979; BA, Eng, summa cum laude, Caldwell Col, 1983; cp/ Editor-in-Chief, *The Kettle*, Col Newspaper, 1982; Dorm Coun Treas, 1982;

Campus Min, Eucharistic Min 1980-83; Circle K, VP 1980; Legis Coun, SGA Seat 1979-83; Resident Asst, 1980-83; Curric Com, 1979-83; r/Rom Cath; hon/ Alpha Chi NHS, 1982; Sigma Tau Delta, Profl Eng Frat, 1981-83; Wom in Min Awd, 1983; Soc of Col Journalists, Kappa Gamma Pi, 1983; Delta Epsilon Sigma, 1983; Eng Dept Awd, 1983; Nat Dean's List; W/W Among Am Univs and Cols; Intl Yth in Achmt; Commun Ldrs of Am; g/MA, Eng, Wn IL Univ; Tchg Asst'ship.

GEIGER, JANE NOREEN oc/Student; b/Oct 9, 1965; h/2609 Vestario Forest Place, Birmingham, AL 35216; p/ Mr and Mrs George W Geiger, Birmingham, AL; ed/Vestario Hills HS, 1984; cp/Jr Civitan Mem, 1981-82; Freshman Clb, 1980-81; SGA Rep, 1980-81; Sophomore Class Pres, 1981-82; Jr Class Girls' VP, 1982-83; FCA Pres-Elect, 1983-84; French Hon Soc Pres-Elect, 1983-84; Nat Hon Soc; Varsity Tennis and Volleyball, 1980-84; r/Bapt; hon/Century 21 Speedtypist, 1982; B'ham-So Col Sum Scholar, 1983; AL Key Clb Dist Sweetheart, 1983; Girls' St Del, 1983; 1st Place, Vestaria Tennis Tournament, Singles Div, 1982; Miss Reveille Pageant, Top 10 and Evening Gown Winner; g/Bus Maj; French Lang Minor.

GEORGE, BARBARA JENNIFER oc/ Student; b/Mar 6, 1962; h/18 Barnard Place, Elizabeth, NJ 07208; p/Lawrence and Ellen George, Elizabeth, NJ; ed/Dipl, Hillside HS, 1980; Student, Cornell Univ; cp/Alpha Kappa Alpha Sorority Mem; Minority Student Advr, Cornell; Orientation Cnslr; Yth Rep Stewardship Com; Future Phys Clb Secy; Girls' St Del; Color Guard; Black Bio Tech Assn; Gyn Clin Vol; Sr Coun Mem; Ahura Kumba Dance Ensemble; hon/ NHS; BPW S'ship; W/W Among Am HS Students; Intl Yth in Achmt; g/Med Sch.

GEORGE, JESSE ROMERAL oc/ Student; b/Apr 26, 1963; h/Route 5, Box 180, Magnolia, AR 71753; ba/State University, AR; p/Mr and Mrs Jesse James George, Magnolia, AR; ed/HS Grad; cp/U Voices Gospel Choir of AR St Univ, Chaplain; Master Mason, St John Lodge #456; Lead Staff Mem of AR St Univ; r/Jr Deacon, Bethlehem Bapt Ch; hon/Class Pres, Magnolia High, 1981; Pres, AR St Univ Union Bd, 1983-84; g/Maj in Jour/Public Relats; Rep for a Maj Corp.

GEREK, JOSEPH MICHAEL JR oc/ Cost Accountant and Analyst; b/Oct 9, 1958; h/885 Bears Den Road, Youngstown, OH; ed/Chaney HS, 1976; Youngstown St Univ; BA, Col; pa/Cost Acct/Analyst; cp/VP, Alpha Tau Gamma; Treas, Alpha Phi Delta; Student Govt; Intl Lions Clb; Treas, Polit Campaign for City Coun; hon/NHS; Voted Outstg Acctg Student; W/W Among Students in Am Cols and Univs; g/MBA in Mgmt; Corp Controller/ Upper Level Staff Mgmt.

GERMANY, PAMELA GAIL oc/Student; b/Jul 6, 1965; h/Box 122BB, Stantonville, TN 38379; p/Mr and Mrs J D Germany, Stantonville, TN; ed/ Grad, McNairy Ctl HS; cp/Beta Clb, 3 Yrs, Secy; Freshman Class Treas; Sophomore Class Treas; Sr Class Secy; Pep Clb; Student Govt Assn; Christian Yth Org; Chd's Choir Dir; Ch Libn; r/ W Shiloh Bapt Ch; hon/Cheerldr,

1979-83; Hall of Fame, 1983; Done Most for MCHS, 1983; Girls' St Del, 1982; Miss McNairy Ctl 1st Maid, 1982; Cheerldr Capt, 1983; Am Hist and Govt Awd; W/W Among Am HS Students; US Achmt Acad Nat Awds Yrbook; g/ To Attend Memphis St Univ and Maj in Bus Mgmt.

GERSTEN, JOEL IRWIN oc/Professor; b/Mar 18, 1942; h/28 Edgemount Road, Edison, NJ 08817; ba/New York, NY; m/Harriet; c/Samuel, Bonnie, Sarah, Eli, Rena; ed/Bronx HS of Sci, 1958; BS, City Col of NY, 1962; MA 1963, PhD 1968, Columbia Univ; pa/ Mem of Tech Staff, Bell Telephone Labs, 1968-70; Prof, City Col of NY, 1970-; Fellow, Am Phy Soc; Phi Beta Kappa; hon/Author, Approx 80 Pubs in Standard Physics Jours.

GESSEL, MICHAEL D oc/Press Secretary; b/Oct 15, 1954; h/803 Maryland Avenue, Northeast, Washington, DC 20002; ba/Washington, DC; p/Mr and Mrs Edwin Gessel, Dayton, OH; ed/ Grad, Colonel White HS, 1972; BA, Univ of PA, 1978; Radcliffe Pub'g Procedures Course, 1978; pa/Press Secy to Rep Tony P Hall, 1981-; Legis Asst to Rep Robert T Mastui, 1979-80; Staff Asst to Rep Charles W Whalen Jr, 1978; Assn of House Dem Pres Assts; cp/ Wash Area Bicyclist Assn, Pres; Univ of PA Clb of Wash, DC, VP; Philobiblon Clb; Intl Assn of Master Penmen, Engrossers and Tchrs of Handwriting; hon/Golden Spoke Awd, Wash Area Bicyclist Assn, 1979; Charles Fine Ludwig Awd, Philomathean Soc, 1978; John Frederick Lewis Awd, Philomathean Soc, 1975; g/Publisher.

GEST, TERRI ANN oc/Student; b/Jan 7, 1963; h/267 Spring Pines Drive, Spring, TX 77386; p/Ronald A and Barbara A Gest, Spring, TX; ed/Grad, J L McCullough HS, 1981; Att'g, Sam Houston St Univ; cp/Alpha Kappa Psi Profl Bus Frat, 2nd VP, Pledge Tnr, 1984-85; Ofc Ed Assn; Profl Acctg Clb; hon/Outstg Voc Ofc Ed Student, Jr and Sr Yrs; W/W Among Am HS Students; Intl Yth in Achmt; Commun Ldrs of Am; g/Bach of Acctg Deg, 1985; CPA.

GHARAGOZLOO, SHAHRAM oc/ Student; b/Jun 6, 1956; h/1712 Canyon Drive, #C, Columbia, MO 65201; m/ Elham Salari; ed/HS, 1974; BS in Mech Engrg 1979, MS in Nuclear Engrg 1983, Univ of MO Columbia; pa/Res Asst, Nuclear Engrg Dept, Univ of MO Columbia, 1982-; Am Nuclear Soc; r/ Islam; hon/1st Place in Am Nuclear Soc Student Design Competition, 1981; g/ Nuclear Engr.

GIBBS, DONNA ANNETTE oc/Public Relations Director; b/Mar 28, 1963; h/Route 1, Box 76, Newton, MS 39345; ba/Decatur, MS; p/Mr and Mrs Harvey H Gibbs, Newton, MS; ed/Newton Co Acad, 1981; AS, E Ctl Jr Col, 1983; pa/ Secy to the Dean of Students 1982; Public Relats Dir 1983-, E Ctl Jr Col; Bkkpr, First Nat Bk of Newton, 1983; cp/Sr Class Treas; Editor of HS Annual, 1981; VP of HS Hon Soc, 1981; Secy of NCA Student Coun, 1981; Editor of Paper Staff, 1981; VP, ECJC Student Body Assn, 1983; VP, ECJC Chapt of Phi Theta Kappa, 1983; r/Bapt; NCA Salutatorian, 1981; Achmt and Acad S'ship to ECJC, 1981; Most Intell and Most Likely to Succeed, 1981; ECJC Players Acting Awd, 1983; ECJC Singers Awd, 1983; ECJC Beauty, 1983; W/ W in Am HS; W/W in Am Jr Cols; g/ Return to Col and Obtain a Bach Deg and Perhaps a Master's Deg.

GIBSON, VALERIE S oc/Student; b/ Sep 19, 1961; h/8009 Springflower Road, Cola, SC 29204; p/Mr Henry Gibson, Cola, SC; Mrs Darlgene F Gibson, Cola, SC; ed/Dipl, Sprg Val HS, 1979; BA, Early Childhood Ed, Univ of SC, 1983; pa/Proof Operator 1978, Wk Distribution Clk 1979, Error Corrections Clk 1980, Proof Operator 1981-83, First Nat Bk Opers Ctr; cp/ SC Assn of Chd Under Six, 1983-; Blue Birds; Brownies; Girl Scouts; Cadettes; Candy Striper, Richland Meml Hosp, 1978; Beta Clb, 1976-77; Bapt Student Union, 1979-81; Softball; Piano; r/Bapt; g/Teach 3rd Grade.

GIDEON, ELLEN ELAYNE oc/Student; b/Feb 9, 1963; h/217 Marshall Street, Palmer, TX 75152; p/Mr and Mrs A J Gideon, Palmer, TX; ed/Grad, HS, 1981; Assoc in Gen Ed, Navarro Jr Col, 1983; Att'g, E TX St Univ; cp/Am Soc for Pers Adm, ETSU; Student Activs Bd, ETSU; r/Fundamental Bapt Ch Choir; hon/Dean's List, ETSU, Fall 1983; Ldrship S'ship, 1981-82; Nat Dean's List; g/Bach of Bus in Pers Mgmt.

GILBREATH, JENNIFER KAREN oc/ Student; b/Aug 11, 1966; h/Route 1, Box 286, Mount Hope, AL 35651; p/Mr and Mrs Charles Dennis Gilbreath, Mount Hope, AL; ed/Mt Hope HS, 1984; Currently Enrolled, John C Calhoun St Commun Col; cp/HS Varsity Basketball, 1980-84; HS Volleyball, 1984; HS Tennis, 1984; HS Varsity Cheerldr, 1982-83; HS Pres of FHA Clb, 1983-84; HS Secy-Treas of Beta Clb, 1983-84; Editor of HS Yrbook, 1983-84; Capt of Basketball and Volleyball, 1984; r/Bapt; DAR Good Citizenship Awd, 1983; Woodman of the World Hist Awd, 1983; Chem Awd, 1983; Miss MHHS, 1984; Hustle Awd in Basketball, 1984; Valedictorian, 1984; Tennis S'ship for Col, 1984-85; g/Deg in Elem Ed.

GILBREATH, ROBERT MARTIN oc/Student; b/Mar 15, 1967; h/1203 North 151 East Avenue, Tulsa, OK 74116; p/Mr and Mrs Jack Gilbreath, Tulsa, OK; cp/FAC; French Clb; AFS; Basketball; Football; Track; Yth Grp, Ch; Nat Hon Soc; St Hon Soc; Supt Hon Roll; r/Luth; hon/All Rogers City Football; Holds Sch Record, Longest Run, Most Passes (Football); St Record for Longest Run from Line of Scrimmage, 98 Yds (Football); Dist'd Am HS Students; g/Dentistry.

GILES, STEPHEN WARREN oc/ Student, Lifeguard; b/Jan 17, 1968; h/ 308 West "K" Street, Erwin, NC 28339; p/Mr and Mrs Sherrill Giles, Erwin, NC; ed/Student, Erwin HS; pa/Lifeguard, Dunn Moose Lodge, 1983-84; cp/Key Clb, VP 1983-; Spanish Clb, 1982-; Beta Clb, 1984; Monogram Clb, 1982-; Football Team, 1982-; Basketball Team, 1982-; Tennis Team, 1983-; Golf Team, 1984; r/Meth; hon/Algebra Awd, 1983; Hist Awd, 983; Gov's Sch Nom, 1984; NCSSM Nom, 1984; Hist Bowl Capt, 1983; Spanish Hon Soc, 1984; Boy Scout Arrow of Light Awd, 1981; US Achmt Acad; Soc of Dist'd Am HS Students; g/To Maj in Chem Engrg at NC St Univ; To Receive Master's Deg in Chem Engrg.

GILHULY, SHANNON JONES oc/

Marketing Manager; b/Mar 16, 1955; h/ SR Box 31206, Fairbanks, AK 99701; ba/ Fairbanks, AK; m/Alan F; p/Byron and Pat Jones, Cordova, AK; ed/Cordova HS, 1973; BA in Ofc Adm, Univ of AK Fairbanks; MBA, AZ St Univ, 1980; pa/ Mktg Mgr, Systronics Inc, 1982-; Res Analyst, NW Alaskan Pipeline Co, 1981-82; Res Asst, Univ of AK, Instnl Planning, 1980-81; Adm Asst to Pres, Univ of AK, 1977-79; cp/Phi Kappa Phi, Asst Secy-Treas 1976-77; Pres Search Com, Univ of AK, 1977; Wom's Ath Assn, 1976, 1977, Pres; Univ of AK Intercol Basketball Team, 1973-77, Co-Capt; Choir of the N, 1973-78; Fairbanks Wom Basketball Assn, 1978-83; Arctic Winter Games Basketball Team, 1978; Wom's Volleyball Team, 1981-83; r/Epis; hon/Marion Boswell Outstg Wom Grad Awd, 1977; Nat Merit Scholar, 1973; Valedictorian, 1973; Elks Yth Ldrship Awd, 1972; Elks Most Valuable Student Awd, 1974; Tuition and Acad S'ship, AZ St Univ, 1979-80; Intl Yth in Achmt; W/W Among Am HS Students; W/W Among Students in Am Cols and Univs; g/CPA; CMA; Pursue Career in Managerial Acctg and Consltg.

GILLESPIE, LORI SUSAN oc/Graduate Nurse; b/Sep 19, 1961; h/422 Woodland Drive, Livingston, TN 38570; ba/Same; p/Mr and Mrs Richard Gillespie, Livingston, TN; ed/Livingston Acad; BS in Nsg, TN Technological Univ; pa/Grad Nurse in Obstetrics, Cookeville Gen Hosp, 1983-; TTU Nsg Hon Soc; r/Meth; hon/Nsg Sch Agape Awd; g/Specialize in Obstetrical Nsg; Master's in Nsg.

GILLIS, BEVERLY ANN oc/Student; b/Dec 20, 1963; h/601 East Ethel, Douglas, GA 31533; p/Mr and Mrs D J Gillis, Douglas, GA; ed/HS Dipl, Citizens Christian Acad, 1981; Jr Col Deg, S GA Col, 1983; cp/Student Sum Missionary, GA Bapt Conv, 1982; Sum Yth and Chd's Dir, 1st U Meth Ch, 1983; Bapt Student Union, Music Chm 1981-82, Pres 1982-83; Student Govt Assn, Off Campus Rep; r/Bapt; hon/ Best All Around, 1983; Most Outstg BSU Student, 1982, 1983; Dean's List, 1982, 1983; HS Homecoming Ct, 1979-81, Queen 1981; Col Homecoming Ct, 1983; Track MVP, 1980, 1981; Sr Superlative, 1981; Hon Roll; W/W Am HS Students; W/W Am Jr Col Students; Nat Dean's List; g/Col Deg in Christian Ed; Attend Sem.

GILREATH, AMY SUZANNE oc/ Student; b/Jul 23 1963; h/PO Box 153, Church Hill, TN 37642; p/Thomas and Carol Gilreath, Church Hill, TN; ed/Ch Hill HS, 1977-80; Vol High, 1980-81; Student, Music Ed, En KY Univ, 1981-84; cp/Delta Omicron, 1982-84, Dir of Publicity; Gamma Beta Phi, 1983-84; Kappa Delta Pi, 1984; Fac Brass Quintet, 1983-84; Symphonic Band, 1982-84; Orch, 1982-84; Brass Choir, 1981; Jazz Band, 1982-83; r/ Meth; hon/S'ship from Intl Trumpet Guild to Attend the Conv, 1983; Mem, All Am Col Marching Band, EPCOT, 1982; Winner, Concerto Competition, 1982-84; Winner, KY Music Tchrs Assn Brass Div, 1983; Winner, Brass Competition, So Div for Music Tchrs Nat Assn, 1984; Dean's List, 1981-83; W/W Am HS; Intl Yth in Achmt; Nat Dean's List; g/Master's in Trumpet Perf; Play

Professionally.

GINN, SHANNON ELIZABETH oc/ Student; b/Jan 11, 1965; h/3301 Seven Mountain Drive, Fayetteville, NC 28306; ba/Fayetteville, NC; p/Fred L and Elizabeth T Ginn, Fayetteville, NC; ed/ Fayetteville Acad, 1983; pa/Pt-time Food Ser, Nicho's of NC, 1982-83; cp/ HS Sr Class Secy; Volleyball, Capt; Soccer; Swimming; Sci Clb; Intl Clb; Keywanettes; Student Coun; Basketball Scorekeeper; Nat Hon Soc, Secy; hon/ All Conf Volleyball Team, 1982; USMA Invitational Acad Wkshop, 1982; DAR Awd, 1981; Nat Merit Scholar Contest Finalist, 1983; Hon Roll, 1980-83; W/ W Among Am HS Students; Soc of Dist'd Am HS Students; g/Deg in Biol or Math.

GIORDANO, GINA MARIA oc/ Student; b/Oct 28, 1966; h/1322 B Binney Drive, Ft Pierce, FL 33449; p/ Mr and Mrs John F Giordano, Ft Pierce, FL; ed/John Carroll HS; pa/Peppermint Patti's Day Care Ctr, 1979-83; Sears, 1983-; cp/Girl Scouts; Anchor Clb; Pep Clb; Cheerldr; Batgirl; r/Cath; hon/ Civics Awd, 1980; Typing Awd, 1981; Eng Awd, 1981; Spanish II Awd, 1982; W/W Among Am HS Students; Dist'd Am HS Students; g/To Attend Stetson or Univ of FL; Maj in Polit Sci or Computer Sci; Lwyr.

GISH, CHRISTINE HEPBURN oc/ Student; b/Feb 27, 1960; h/Route 7, Box 79, Hopewell Junction, NY 12533; p/M Kaylor Gish, Tuckahoe, NY; Robin Birdfeather, Hopewell Junction, NY; ed/ Austin Commun Col, 1980-81; BA in Mid E Studies 1984, BS in Med Technol 1985, Univ of TX; pa/Info Staff, TX Union, Univ of TX, 1980-82; Acad Peer Cnslr, Ofc of Student Financial Aid, Univ of TX, 1982-83; Lab Asst, Dept of Microbiol, Univ of TX, 1983-; cp/ Microbiol-Med Tech Student Soc; Alternative Mid E Studies Soc; Amnesty Intl Univ Balkan Choir, Fdg Mem; r/Prot; hon/Best in Persian Lang, Dept Mid E Studies, 1982; Dean's List, 1983; Golden Key Nat Hon Soc, 1983; Liberal Arts Foun S'ship Recip, 1983-; g/Employmt in Hosp; Possibly Pursue MD in Pathol.

GISLER, DANA LYNN oc/Student; b/Mar 12, 1964; h/2032 Old Lexington Road, Danville, KY 40422; p/Rev and Mrs Albert Gisler, Danville, KY; ed/ Adv'd Dipl, Boyle Co HS, 1982; pa/ Dining Room Hostess, Arby's, 1983; Data Word Processor Operator, Rexnord, 1983; cp/Beta Clb; Pres, Yth Coun; Treas, Jr Class; Team Capt, Heart Fund Collection; Madrigal Choir Secy, Pianist; Cheerldg Capt; Musical Dramas; Track; Gamma Beta Phi, Hon Acad Soc; Sign Lang Team Mem, Bapt Student Union; Sang w Grp Which Traveled Around KY, OH and VA, 1982-83; hon/DAR Awd; Best All-Around Freshman, Soph, Jr Student; St Voice Contest; Talent Div Winner, KY Jr Miss Pageant; Chosen to Sing Nat Anthem, St Basketball Tournament; KY Reg Winner in All-Am Col Talent Search, 1983; Chosen to Sing for KY St Evang Conf, 1983; Soloist for Univ Prodn of *The Messiah*, 1982; Nat Dean's List; W/ W Among Am HS Students; g/To Get a Master's Deg in Musical Perf; Profl Singer.

GISLER, DAVID ALBERT oc/Student; b/Aug 16, 1966; h/2032 Old Lexington Road, Danville, KY 40422; p/

Albert J and Ruby M Gisler, Danville, KY; ed/HS Grad; cp/Beta Clb; SCORE; Pep Clb; Football Team; Baseball Team; Yth Scholar, Am Pvt Enterprise Sem; r/Bapt; hon/Freshman Ath of the Yr; Sophomore Class Treas; All-St Chorus, 1982; Acad Letter, 1981-82, 1982-83; W/W; g/To Attend Col and Wk Toward Pre-Med Deg and Then Get MD; Fam Pract.

GLESNER, RONALD GLENN oc/Dairy Farmer; b/Feb 10, 1963; h/RD 4, Box 465, Newville, PA 17241; p/Mr and Mrs J Glenn Glesner, Newville, PA; ed/Big Sprg HS, 1981; pa/Dairy Farmer, Employed by Father; Big Sprg Yg Farmers; Big Sprg Agri Adv Coun; PA Farmer's Assn; S PA AAA; cp/Newville Lions Clb; Mifflin Grange; Newville Ambulance Clb; BSA, Secy of Adv Coun; Student Coun; W PA Fire Co; r/First U Presb Ch Yth F'ship Treas; hon/Lion's Clb Student of the Month; Keystone Farmer Awd; God and Country Awd; W/W Am HS; Commun Ldrs of Am; Intl Yth in Achmt; g/Wkg for Cumberland Val Cooperation in Newville.

GLOVER, CARLA ONEIDA oc/Free-Lance Writer; b/Jun 19, 1960; h/4630 Ripley Street, Davenport, IA 52806; p/Selmer M and Theresa W Glover, Davenport, IA; ed/Davenport Ctl HS, 1978; BS, Bowie St Col, 1981; pa/Free-Lance Writer; Film Talk Show Co-Host; cp/Assoc Editor, Bowie St Newspaper; Alpha Kappa Mu; VP, Public Relats Student Soc of Am; Softball Team Left Field; 1st Clarinet, Band; hon/Intl Yth in Achmt; Nat Dean's List; W/W Among Students in Am Cols and Univs; g/Screen Play Writer/Dir.

GODDARD, SUSIE EVELYN oc/Student; b/Jan 3, 1965; h/10100 Northeast 10th Street, Oklahoma City, OK 73130; p/Kenneth and Neoma Goddard, Oklahoma City, OK; ed/Grad, Choctaw HS, 1983; Grad, Pk Ave Modeling Sch, 1981; Current Student, Ctl St Univ; pa/Secretarial Wk, Dispatcher, Goddard Concrete (during Sums); Pt-time Modeling, Pk Ave Modeling Agy; cp/Delta Zeta Sorority; Feature Twirler, Choctaw HS, 1980-83; Feature Twirler, Ctl St Univ; r/Ch of Christ; hon/Outstg Twirler, Six Flags Music Fest, 1982; First and Second Place Awds, St Fair of OK, 1978, 1980, 1981; A and B Hon Roll, Choctaw HS, 1983; g/Oral Communs/Broadcasting Maj; Continuation of Modeling Career.

GODWIN, WENDELL L oc/Student; b/Mar 16, 1962; h/503 East Bradley, Pauls Valley, OK 73075; p/Mr and Mrs Theron Godwin, Pauls Valley, OK; ed/BS, Bus Adm Mgmt, E Ctl OK St Univ, 1984; Att'd, Westfield St Col 1982, E Ctl OK St Univ 1980-81; pa/Inventory Controller, Ms Kathy Wyckoff, 1980-83; Gen Shop Mech, Mr J B Stallings, 1982; Maintenance, Dr Howard Thomas, 1979-80; cp/ECU Student Senate Pres, 1983-84; Senate Jr Rep, 1982-83; Pres Ldrship Class; OK Intercol Legis; Pres, Exch Student Clb; Phi Beta Lambda Bus Frat; Pi Kappa Alpha Frat; Former Exch Student; F'ship of Christian Aths; Dean's Hon Roll; ECU Bowling Team; Spec Olympics Vol; r/Trinity Bapt Ch; g/Maj in Bus Adm; Double Minor in Mgmt and Computer Sci.

GOEBEL, JIL THERESE oc/Product Marketing; b/Apr 5, 1958; h/750 State Street, #317, San Diego, CA 92101; ba/La Jolla, CA; p/Robert L Goebel, San Diego, CA; Mary K Goebel, San Diego, CA; ed/Will C Crawford HS, 1976; BBA, Univ of San Diego, 1980; MBA, Univ of San Diego, 1982; pa/Strategic Mktg, TRW; Prod Mktg, TRW; Am Mktg Assn, VP of Progs, Pres-Elect; Assn of MBA Execs; cp/AMA Commun Involvement Com; Alpha Kappa Psi, VP, 2 Nat Convs; Alumni Assn, Univ of San Diego; Colina Cnslg Ctr, Bd of Dirs, Secy; Phi Alpha Delta; Beta Gamma Sigma; Alpha Mu Alpha; Kappa Gamma Pi; San Diego Elect Netwk, Ways and Means Com; San Diego C of C; San Diego Adv Bd on the Status of Wom; Wom's Opports Wk, Com Mem; Delta Epsilon Sigma; r/Bd of Deacons, E San Diego Presb Ch; Sunday Sch Tchr; hon/Grad w BBA in 3½ Yrs, summa cum laude; 3rd in Class of Over 600 Students, HS; Intl Yth in Achmt; Commun Ldrs of Am; g/Wk in the Field of Advtg and Public Relats; Become Communs Mgr of a Corp.

GOERZ, DAVID JONATHAN III oc/Student; b/Jan 9, 1963; h/10938 Strathmore Drive, Los Angeles, CA 90024; p/Mr and Mrs David J Goerz Jr, Menlo Park, CA; ed/Woodside HS, 1981; BS, Physics, Univ of CA LA, 1985; pa/Geologic Field Asst, US Geological Survey, 1980-; cp/Phi Kappa Sigma Frat, 1982-; UCLA Lacrosse, 1982-; UCLA Crew, 1981-82; Student Rep to Dist Coor Com; Secy, Student Rep, Woodside Site Coun; Chief Justice to BOSA; Tennis; Football; Track; Yg Life; CSF; Prin's, Dean's Lists; r/Presb Ch; hon/PTSA S'ship; US Geological Survey Spec Achmt Awd; CSF, Life Mem, 1981; Most Effort, UCLA Crew (Fr), 1982; Intl Yth in Achmt; Commun Ldrs of Am; W/W Among Am HS Students; g/Grad Sch in Physics w a Career in Applied Physics Res.

GOFF, KAREN RAE oc/Student; b/Oct 27, 1965; h/Route 1, Box 246-B, Cedartown, GA 30125; ba/Cedartown, GA; p/Joel T and Sharon R Goff, Cedartown, GA; ed/Acad Dipl, Cedartown HS, 1983; cp/Cheerldr, 1980, 1981, 1982, 1983; Sci Clb, Fin Chm 1982-83; Math Clb, Pres 1982-83; Key Clb, 1981, 1982, 1983; Hon Soc, 1979, 1980, 1981, 1982, 1983; r/Bapt; hon/Gov's Hon Prog, 1982; GA Cert of Merit, 1982; Hall of Fame, Cedartown HS, 1982; W/W Among HS Students; g/Study Med; Become a Pediatrician.

GOLDEN, HERECE ANJEANETTE oc/Physical Therapy Aide and Student; b/Sep 28, 1964; h/3405 Keller Road, Temple, TX 76501; p/Ms Billie Jean Golden, Temple, TX; ed/Grad, Temple HS, 1982; Att'g, Temple Jr Col; Will Be Att'g, TX Wom's Univ, Fall 1985; pa/Tchrs Aide, Temple REACH Ctr, 1979; Cashier, K-Mart, 1980-81; Phy Therapy Aide, Scott & White Meml Hosp, 1981-; cp/Hlth Occups Students of Am, 1981-82; Phi Theta Kappa, 1982-83; r/Bapt; hon/Top Quarter Hon Grad, Temple HS, 1982; Superior, First and Second Ratings in HOSA; Temple HS Symphonic Band w Hons of Dist Band, 1978-79; Dist-Reg Band, 1979-80, 1981-82; Solo and Ensemble Medals, 1978-79, 1979-80, 1980-81, 1981-82; Zeta Phi Beta Debutante, 1982; Lions

Clb S'ship, 1982-83; Dunbar Meridith Alumni S'ship, 1982-84; Rotary Clb Sch, 1983-84; W/W Among Am HS Students; g/Career as an Occupl Therapist.

GOLDEN, TERA MARIA oc/Student; b/Aug 17, 1965; h/2012 Kaye Street, Seneca, SC 29678; p/Fred Golden Jr, Seneca, SC; Rose Marie Golden (dec); ed/Grad, Seneca HS, 1983; Currently Enrolled, Clemson Univ; cp/Yg Girls Aux, Pres 1981; HS Track Team, 1980-83; HS Band, 1980-83; JV Cheerldr, 1980; Student Coun Rep, 1980; Beta Clb, 1980; Interact Clb, 1982-83; HS FHA, Pres 1981, VP 1982; r/Bapt; hon/Semi-Finalist for Black Merit Scholars, 1982; W/W Among Am HS Students; g/Deg in Computer Engrg.

GONNILLINI, GLORIA ANN oc/Student; b/Jan 4, 1960; h/Route 5, Box 225-A, Natchez, MS 39120; c/Tracy; p/Mr and Mrs Louis Gonnillini, Natchez, MS; ed/Adams Co Christian Sch; Copiah Lincoln Jr Col, 1982-84; pa/Key Punch Operator, 1977-79; Lab Tech, 1981-82; Secy, 1983-84; cp/Pres, Student Govt Assn, 1983-84; Pres, Circle K, 1983-84; Jud Com, 1983-84; Staff Photog for Col Yrbook and Newspaper Staff, 1983-84; Phi Theta Kappa, 1983-84; r/Cath; hon/Outstg Ldrship Awd for Pres of Student Govt Assn and Pres of Circle K, 1984; Student of the Month, Dec 1983; Outstg Ser on the Annual Staff; g/Secy.

GONZÁLEZ, ELIZABETH ANN oc/Customer Service Representative; b/Jan 9, 1959; h/1613 Tulip, McAllen, TX 78501; m/Israel; c/Christina Suzanne; p/Mr and Mrs Jesse M Torrez, McAllen, TX; ed/Roma HS, 1977; TX Wom's Univ; Pan Am Univ; pa/Customer Ser Rep, Dial Fin Corp; cp/HS Student Coun, Treas, Pres; Nat Hon Soc, Treas; FHA, Secy, Pres, VP; Band, Twirler, Drum Majorette; Alpha Kappa Psi, Pledge Class Secy, Pledge Master, VP, Chaplain; Alpha Phi Omega, Pledge Class Secy; hon/Hon Roll; Best All-Around HS Student; FFA Sweetheart; FHA Ser Awd; Fac S'ship; Pan Am Univ S'ship; Alpha Kappa Psi Outstg Pledge; Dean's List; Miss PAU 1st Runner-Up; Soc of Dist'd HS Students; W/W Among Am HS Students; Intl Yth in Achmt; W/W Among Students in Am Cols and Univs; g/BBA in Fin.

GOOCEY, ANTHONY VAUGHN oc/Student; b/Jul 6, 1964; h/109 Crestview Road, Russell, KY 41169; p/Mr and Mrs Richard Goocey, Russell, KY; ed/HS, 1982; cp/Intramural Flag Football, Volleyball and Basketball, Cedarville Col, 1982-83; Ch Basketball; Vocal Ensemble; Teen Choir; Band; Prayer Grp; Sum Ch Camp Wkr; FCA; hon/Most Courteous Teen of the Yr, Sch; Cert for Straight A's in Algebra I and II; W/W Among Am HS Students; g/BS in Nsg.

GOODMAN, CONSTANCE BETH oc/Student; b/Sep 3, 1963; h/54 Levering Circle, Bala Cynwyd, PA 19004; p/Mr and Mrs Marvin Goodman, Bala Cynwyd, PA; ed/Grad, Lower Merion HS, 1981; Grad, George Wash Univ, 1985; pa/Data Tech, Ctr for Cognitive Therapy, Univ of PA, 1982; Lab Res Asst in Behavioral Neurosci, Univ of PA, 1983; cp/Col: Pre-Med Soc 1982-83, Intramural Volleyball 1982-83; HS:

Volleyball 1978-80, Softball 1979-81, Ser Leag, B'nai B'rith; Planned Parenthood Fdn of Am, 1982-83; hon/Col: Alpha Epsilon Delta 1983, Psi Chi 1983, Phi Eta Sigma 1982, Dean's List; HS: Nat Hon Soc 1980-81, Hon Roll, Most Valuable Player (Volleyball) 1979; W/W Among Am HS Students; Intl Yth in Achmt; Commun Ldrs of Am; g/Maj in Pre-Med and Psych; Career in Clin Med.

GOODMAN, MICHAEL R oc/Student; b/Dec 15, 1961; h/Box 1023, 414 Brazos, Forney, TX 75126; p/Bobby and Darlene Goodman, Forney, TX; ed/ Forney HS, 1979; AA, Henderson Jr Col, 1981; Baylor Univ; pa/Yth in Achmt; cp/Sum Missionary, CA, 1982; Alpha Phi Omega, Sprg VP 1983; Baylor Univ Welcome Wkend, Steering Com 1982, Participant 1983; Band; Drum Maj; Band Coun; Student Coun; OEA/VOE St Pres Cand, Sgt-at-Arms, Parliamentarian; Ch Wk; Yth Cnslr; Jr Col Student Senate; Phi Theta Kappa; Exec Coun, Social Concern, Baylor Student Union; hon/Jour S'ship, Baylor Univ, 1982; People Who Serve People Awds; Ofc Ed Assn Extemporaneous Spkg, 2nd Area St Participant; McCurry, Band, OEA/ VOE S'ships; Intl Yth in Achmt; g/BBA, Radio/TV/Mktg, 1983; Enter Ft Worth SWn Sem, 1984.

GOODSON, DEREK EDWARD oc/ Student; b/Mar 26, 1967; h/1111-59 Terrace, Ft Smith, AR 72904; p/Don and Linda Goodson, Ft Smith, AR; ed/Grad, Northside HS, 1985; cp/Nat Jr Hon Soc; Secy-Treas, Jr Optimist Clb, 1981-82; Key Clb, Treas 1983-84; Sophomore Coun; Student Coun; Tennis Team; USTA; r/Prot; hon/Nat Jr Hon Soc; Nat Hon Soc, 1983-84; Hon Roll; Lettered in Tennis; Soc of Dist'd Am HS Students; g/Career in Either the Field of Computer Sci or Chem Engrg; Attend Univ of AR.

GORCZYCA, MARIANNE CAMILLE oc/Associate Software Programmer and Analyst; b/Feb 23, 1961; h/3051 North Avers Avenue, Chicago, IL 60618; ba/Chicago, IL; p/Jerome T and Lillian R Gorczyca, Chicago, IL; ed/ Good Counsel HS, 1978; BS, DePaul Univ, 1982; pa/Assoc Software Programmer/Analyst, Standard Oil, 1982-; Math Assn of Am; Assn for Computing Machinery; cp/Blue Key; Delta Epsilon Sigma; Alpha Lambda Delta, Secy; Phi Eta Sigma; Student Govt Rep; Only Student Seat on Curric Revision Com; Student Rep to Math Dept; Fac Promotion Bd; Reporter, DePaul Univ; r/Ch Guitar Grp; Ch Choir; hon/Student Govt Awd; Student Ldrship Awd; Alpha Lambda Delta Awd.

GORE, LYNNE DENISE oc/Floral Designer; b/Dec 21, 1961; h/Route 2, Box 128, Mt Pleasant, SC; p/Mr and Mrs Robert R Gore, Mt Pleasant, SC; ed/ Wando HS, 1980; Col of Charleston, 1981; pa/Floral Designer, Blanche Darby Florist, 1981; Mgr, Pic-A-Daisy Flower Shop, 1982; Floral Designer, Carolina Floral, 1983; cp/GSA; Bapt Ch Nursery Wkr; Vol, Several Area Sr Citizen's Homes; Sci, French Clbs; Yrbook Staff; Hon Roll; Jr Com; Lit Mag; Ofc Asst; Guid Monitor; Attendance Monitor; Hon Grad; hon/Poem Pub'd in Lit Mag, 1976; Story Pub'd in *The Electric Press*, 1977; NHS; Soc of Dist'd Am HS Students; W/W Among Am HS Students; Yg Commun Ldrs of Am; W/

W; g/To Own and Manage Own Flower Shop.

GORDON, FRANK WILLIAM oc/ Student; b/Oct 3, 1965; h/340 Paul Street, Harrisonburg, VA 22801; p/Mr and Mrs John R Gordon, Harrisonburg, VA; ed/Harrisonburg HS, 1984; pa/Grill Operator, McDonald's, RAHE Inc, 1983-; Computer Conslt, NHS, Harrisonburg HS, 1983-; cp/Nat Hon Soc; Math Team; Hon Coun; SCA; Boy Scouts; Order of the Arrow, BSA; Nat Eagle Scout Assn; Sr Class Treas; Cross Country Team, Team Capt 1980-83; Track Team; Pop Quiz Team, Team Capt 1981-83; Spanish Clb, 1982; r/Epis; hon/NCTE Achmt Awd in Writing, 1983; NSTA-NASA Shuttle Student Involvement Proj, 1982 (Reg Winner); Nat Merit Semi-Finalist, 1983; Eagle Scout w Gold Palm, 1981; VA Boys' St, 1983; W/W Among Am HS Students; g/Med Res; Chem Maj (Undergrad).

GORDON, KAREN HOPE oc/Student, Telephone Operator; b/Sep 16, 1961; h/1150 Homeside Avenue, Cincinnati, OH 45224; ba/Cincinnati, OH; p/Martha F Gordon, Cincinnati, OH; ed/ Dipl, Aiken Sr HS; Mech Engrg Technol Assoc Deg, Univ of Cinc, OMI Col of Applied Sci; pa/Gardener, SYTP, 1975; Asst Secy, IRS, 1977-78; Secretarial Co-op 1978-79, Engrg Co-Op 1980, 1980-81, Proctor & Gamble; Engrg Co-op, Structural Dynamics Res Corp, 1981-82; Asst Plant Engr, Formica, 1982; Telephone Operator, Execucall, 1981-; cp/Nat Soc of Black Engrs, Secy; Soc of Wom Engrs, Pres; Soc of Mfg Engrs, Treas; cp/Cheerldr; Student Tribunal Mech Rep; Greivance Com Student Rep; Sr Class Rep; Bus Ofc Ed Secy, Parliamentarian, Banquet, Homecoming Chm; Drama Clb; Sch Paper; Student Coun Rep; hon/Adm Mgmt Soc Awd; Soc of Wom Engrs Scholastic Achmt; Awd of Distn; Cert of Merit, Voc Ed; Voc Triple A Awd; Nat Soc of Black Engrs Supportive Mem Awd; Bus Ofc Ed Most Likely to Succeed; Most Outstg Mem Awd, Soc of Wom Engrs, 1982; Intl Yth in Achmt; Commun Ldrs of Am; g/Remain a Jehovah's Witness; BS Deg in Mech Engrg Technol; Engrg Position in Well Established Engrg Firm.

GOSSAGE, KIMBERLY ANN oc/ Student; b/Apr 24, 1964; h/115 North Hickory Road, Sterling, VA 22170; p/ Mary D Gossage, Sterling, VA; ed/Pk View HS, 1982; Presently Att'g George Mason Univ; cp/Chm, Yth Coun of Ch; VP, Spanish Clb; Secy, NHS; Pres, Ch Girls' Grp; Varsity Soccer; All-Co Softball; hon/W/W Among Am HS Students; Commun Ldrs of Am; g/Maj in Physics; Career in Aviation.

GOSSARD, JULIE KAY oc/Elementary Teacher; h/Rural Route One, Box #106, Sheridan, IN 46069; ba/Noblesville, IN; p/Max and Judith Gossard, Sheridan, IN; ed/Marion-Adams HS, 1976; BS, IN St Univ, 1980; Grad Asst, IN St Univ, 1981-82; pa/Rdg Tchr 1982-83, 4th Grade Tchr 1983-84, Noblesville Schs; Hoosier Assn of Sci Tchrs; Assn for Childhood Ed Intl; cp/ ISU Sparkettes, 1976-80, Corporal 1978-79, Sgt 1979-80, Sparkette Alumni 1980-; ISU Blue Berets, 1977-80; Jr Union Bd, 1976-78; Delta Gamma Frat, S'ship Chm 1976-77, Recording Secy 1977, 1978, 1979, Rush Cnslr 1977-78; ISU Alumni Assn; Delta

Gamma Frat Alumni; hon/Blue Key; Outstg Student Tchr in Indpls Area, 1980; Sparkettes, Miss Pep 1977-78, Miss Congeniality 1978-79; Outstg Upperclassman, 1979-80; ISU Union Ser Awd, 1977, 1978, 1979, 1980; Rose Hulman Inst Lambda Chi Alpha Calendar Girl, 1979-80; Job's Daughs Majority Lifetime Mem; Miss Boone Co Runner-Up, 1977; Boone Co Pork Queen, 1978; Delta Gamma Most Outstg GPA, 1977-78; Most Improved GPA, 1977-78; Outstg Delta Gamma, 1977-78, 1978-79; W/W Among Students in Am Cols and Univs; Outstg Yg Wom of Am; Yg Commun Ldrs of Am.

GOSSELIN, LONNETTE JOY oc/ Teacher, Student; b/Sep 12, 1959; h/ West 2535 Riverview Drive, Coeur d'Alene, ID; p/Mr and Mrs Wesley R Hanson, Coeur d'Alene, ID; ed/Coeur d'Alene Sr HS, 1977; BS, Univ of ID; Master's, Guid and Cnslg; pa/Tchr; cp/ Alumni Relats Bd Secy, Social Chm, Treas; Hon Prog; Intermural and Co-Rec Sports; Valkyries Univ ID Student Recruitment; Theta Chi, Little Sister, VP, Secy; Vandal Cheerldr; r/ Presb Ch; hon/Grad, cum laude; Frosh Wom of the Yr; Intl Yth in Achmt; g/ Tchr, Cnslr, Elem Grades.

GOUVEIA, JULIE ANN oc/Student; b/Apr 8, 1962; h/923 Shannon Drive, Fayetteville, NC 28303; p/Emanuel Teixeira and Jean C Gouveia, Fayetteville, NC; ed/Reid Ross Sr HS, 1980; Att'g, Appalachian St Univ; cp/Bat Adjudant, JROTC, 1980; Pres, Explorer Post 774, 1980; Spanish Clb, 1979-80; Pep Clb, 1979-80; Bowling Team, 1982-83; Phi Mu Sorority, 1982-; Teen Rep, Commun Life Prog, 1978; Track Team, 1977; Cath Yth Org, 1978-80; Phi Mu, 1982-, Mbrship (Rush) Dir, Photo Dir, Songldr, Public Relats Com; r/Cath; hon/Math Awd, 1977; Am Legion Mil Excell, ROTC, 1978; Nat Sojourners, 1979; 1st Runner-Up, Mil Ball Queen, 1979; Queen of Mil Ball, 1980; Most Sch Spirited Student, 1980; Dean's List, 1982; W/W HS; g/Maj in Media Advtg; Minor in Mktg; Wk in Sales or Advtg.

GRACE, DEBORAH J oc/Student; b/ Dec 9, 1963; h/216 Packinghouse Road, Kingsport, TN 37660; p/Rev and Mrs Sherman Grace, Kingsport, TN; ed/ Grad, Sullivan N HS, 1982; Student, King Col; cp/Jr Achmt, 1979-82, VP of Adm 1980-82; Beta Clb, 1980-82; Drama Clb, 1978-82; Band, 1978-82; Pep Band, 1978-82; Wind Ensemble, 1980-82; Majorette, 1979; Drill Team, 1981-82; Jr Classical Leag, 1981; Col Choir, 1982; r/Freewill Bapt; hon/ Dean's List, 1981-82; Jr Achmt: VP of Adm of the Yr 1981-82, Exec Awd and Jr Exec Awd 1982, Achiever Awd 1981, $500 S'ship; 4-Yr $3,500 S'ship, Dr Manfred Gutzke S'ship Fund; g/Fgn Lang Maj; Govt or Tchg Career; Grad Wk.

GRADY, ROBERTA MICHELE oc/ Student; b/Aug 16, 1962; h/Route 1, Box 105, Seven Springs, NC 28578; p/Mr and Mrs Robert S Grady, Seven Springs, NC; ed/E Duplin HS, 1980; Att'g, NC St Univ; cp/FFA, Pres 1978-80, Secy 1977-78; Agri Ed Clb, Secy 1981, Reporter 1982, Pres 1983; Nat Hon Soc, 1980; r/Presb; hon/I Dare You Awd, 1979; Dekalb Outstg Ag Student, 1980; Outstg Sr, 1980; g/Agri

Tchr.

GRAHAM, DEBRA SUE oc/Student, Radio Announcer; b/Nov 19, 1965; h/ RR 1, Ida Grove, IA 51445; p/Robert and Marilyn Graham, Ida Grove, IA; ed/ HS Grad, 1984; pa/Stock Person, Pantry Supermkt, 1977-82; Page, IA Ho of Reps, 1983; Radio Announcer, KIDA, 1982-; cp/Capt, Football, Wrestling; Capt, Basketball; Cheerldr; Drill Team Choreographer; 4-H St Coun, Co Coun, Boys' and Girls' Clb Pres; Newspaper Editor; Nat Hon Soc; Gold Hon Roll; Pork Princess; Pork Queen; Track Letterman; Chorus; Swing Choir; Freshman VP; Jr Secy; Meth Yth F'ship; Sprg Plays, Musicals; r/Prot; hon/4-H St Coun, 1983-84; Ida Co Pork Queen, 1983-84; IA Ho of Reps Page, 1983; Commun Ldrs of Am; g/Corporate Exec; Politician; Ec Maj and Polit Sci Minor at Harvard; Harvard Law Sch.

GRAHAM, MARK'EL DWAIN oc/ Student, Musician; b/Jan 2, 1966; h/ Route 2, Box 75, Willard, NC 28478; p/Robert and Shirley Graham, Willard, NC; ed/Dipl, Pender HS, 1984; Dipl in Music, Nat HS, 1984; pa/Sch Bus Driver, Pender Co Bd of Ed, 2 Yrs; Musician for Several Ch Orgs; Performances at Univ of NC Wilmington, SEn Commun Col, NC Sch of the Arts, Univ of NC Greensboro, Several HS and Music Orgs; Nat Piano Playing Auditions, 9 Yrs; Sacred Arts Wkshop; r/Original U Holy Ch of Am Inc; hon/Nat HS Music Dipl; Pell Grant, Univ of NC Greensboro; Min S'ship, Univ of NC Greensboro; Outstg Achmt, Univ of NC Wilmington; Delta Sigma Theta Sorority; Omega Phi Si Sorority Sch and Talent Awds; W/W Among Am HS Student; g/Master of Music Ed; Doct Deg in Music; Profl Performing Artist; Deg in Drafting, Basic Composition.

GRANDSTAFF, T RAY oc/Student; b/Jan 5, 1967; h/Route 3, Box 616 F, Greenwood, AR 72936; p/Mr and Mrs Carl Grandstaff Sr, Greenwood, AR; ed/Student, Greenwood HS; cp/VP, Beta Clb; Student Coun; Pres, F'ship of Christian Aths, 1983-84; r/First Bapt Ch, Yth and Men's Choir, Drama, Yth Coun Ofcr, Outstg Ch Camper 1982, 1983, All Star Baseball Team at Ch Camp 1983, 1984; hon/Univ of AR Basketball Camp, Most Valuable Player, 1982; Undefeated Football Season, 1981; Football Dist Champs, 1981, 1982; Basketball: Dist Champs 1982, Undefeated Conf and Dist Champs 1983, Undefeated Conf Champs 1984; Track: Dist Champs 1981, 1982, 1983, 1984; Holder of Several Sch Records (in Long Jump, High Jump, 100 Yard Dash, 220 Yard Dash, 440 Yard Dash, 880 Yard Relay, 440 Yard Relay), 4 Dist Records in 1982, Won 12 High Point Meet Awds; Has Over 165 Track Medals and Awds; Boys' Clb: Set New St Record in 440 Yard Relay, Second in St in Long Jump; Ramsey Relays: Set New Record in 220 Yard Dash (Still Stands), 1979; Listed as an Outstg Ath, *Arkansas-Texas Football Magazine*, 1984; W/W Among Am HS Students; Dist'd Am HS Students; g/ Sports Med and Rel.

GRANT, BRADFORD C oc/Architect; b/Aug 22, 1953; h/1335 Clay Street, #11, San Francisco, CA 94109; ba/Oakland, CA; m/Toni Wynn; p/Mr and Mrs George Grant Jr; ed/MArch,

Univ of CA Berkeley, 1981; BArch, CA Polytechnic St Univ, 1976; pa/Assoc Proj Arch, Commun Design Collaborative, 1982-; Arch-Designer, MBT Assocs, 1979-82; cp/Bd of Dirs, Bay Area Urban Leag; r/Bapt; hon/W K Kellogg Fellow, 1983-86; CA St Affordable Housing Competition, 1981.

GRANT, CATHERINE oc/Teacher; b/Apr 2, 1958; h/Sunrise Apartments, #W-49, Sandersville, GA 31082; m/ Rudy A; c/Kareeshemah A Mountain; p/Mr and Mrs Mack Mountain Sr, Sandersville, GA; ed/Dipl, Wash Co High, 1976; BS, Ft Val St Col, 1980; MA, OH St Univ, 1981; pa/Wash Co Bd of Ed, 1983-84; Hancock Co Bd of Ed, 1981-83; GA Assn of Edrs; Alpha Kappa Alpha; Phi Alpha Theta; Alpha Kappa Mu; r/Pine Hill Bapt Ch; hon/Hon Student; Hon Grad; Alpha Kappa Mu; Phi Alpha Theta; Nat Dean's List; W/ W Among Students in Am Univs and Cols; g/Curric Dir.

GRANT, MICHAEL DANIEL oc/ Student; b/Jun 5, 1962; h/200 Prinz, San Antonio, TX 78213; p/Michael D and Helen L Grant, San Antonio, TX; ed/ Robert E Lee HS, 1980; BS, Zool, TX A&M Univ; Att'g, Univ of TX Med Sch at Houston; cp/TX A&M Univ Emer Care Team; Phi Eta Sigma; Pre-Med/ Pre-Dental Soc; Intramural Football, Baseball; Blue J Aux Pres; Jr Classical Leag Pres; NHS; Jr Engrg Tech Soc; Phi Kapa Phi Hon Soc, 1983; Beta Beta Beta Biol Hon Soc, 1983; r/Cath; hon/Outstg Mem, TX A&M Emer Care Team, 1983; Intl Yth in Achmt; g/Practicing Phys.

GRAVES, FARRELL DEAN oc/Student; b/Dec 16, 1963; h/3614 Northfield Place, High Point, NC 27260; p/Mr and Mrs Farrell D Graves Sr; ed/T Wingate Andrews HS; Student, Duke Univ; cp/ High Pt Yth Coun; NHS; Spanish Hon Soc Pres; Beta Clb; Sci Clb; Spanish Clb; Yrbook Staff; hon/Merit Awd, Scholastic Poetry Competition; 2nd, NC Student Acad of Sci; Gov's Sch of NC; g/ Phil/Rel Maj; PhD.

GRAVITT, DONNA RENEE oc/ Director of Residence Life; b/Dec 8, 1956; h/Box 1101, Columbia College, Columbia, SC 29203; ba/Cola, SC; p/ Rinnard and Christine H Gravitt, Columbia, SC; ed/Assoc of Bus, Midlands Tech Col; BA, MEd, Univ of SC; pa/Dir of Residence Life, Columbia Col; Fdr, SC Housing Ofcrs Assn, 1981; SC St Chp 1982, St Edit 1980, SEn Assn Housing Ofcrs; r/Covenant Presb Ch; hon/Dean's List, Midlands Tech Col and Univ of SC; Delta Zeta; Phi Kappa Sigma Little Sister; Alpha Lambda Delta Nat Hon Frat for Wom; Miss SC Hemisphere, 1977; Carolina Coquettes, Univ of SC Marching Band; W/W Among Am HS Students; Personalities of S.

GRAY, ERIC BRIAN oc/Student; b/ Mar 12, 1963; h/1001 West Gandy, Denison, TX 75020; p/Mr and Mrs William S Gray, Denison, TX; ed/Grad, Subiaco Acad, 1981; Att'g, Univ of Dallas, 1981-; pa/Instrument Repairman, Mr Wm Orrick, 1983, 1982; Lib Exec Help, Mrs Nettie Baker, 1981-82, 1982-83, 1983-84; Customer Sales Rep, Jack in the Box, 1980; Mtn Man and Indian Crafts Handiman, Mr Barry Hardin, 1979; cp/Intramural Sports Capt, HS; HS Server/Lector Soc; Actor, HS Plays; Intl Thespian Soc; Assn of

TX Profl Edrs, 2nd VP 1984-85; hon/ Valedictorian, 1981; Induction, Intl Thespian Soc; 2 Math and 2 Latin Gold Medals; King Foun Scholar Prog, 1983-84, 1984-85; Accepted to Univ of Dallas Ed Dept, 1983; g/Bach Deg in Sec'dy Ed; Teach German and Math.

GRAY, LARRY LORSE oc/Certified Public Accountant; b/Jun 26, 1955; h/ Route #5, Box #134, Salem, MO 65560; ba/Rolla, MO; p/L W and Eula Gray, Salem, MO; ed/Salem HS, 1973; BS, Acctg, Univ of MO Columbia, 1977; CPA, 1978; Live Permit to Pract, CPA, 1979; pa/CPA, Alfermann, Haynes & Gray, CPA, 1978-80; Ptnr in Firm, Alfermann, Gray & Co, CPA; Delta Sigma Pi; Beta Alpha Si; cp/JCs, 1978-80; Optimist Clb, 1980-; r/Bapt; hon/Outstg Yg Am Awd, 1980.

GRAY, MARIA DAWN oc/Student; b/Jan 19, 1967; h/PO Box 146, Ramer, TN 38367; p/Mr and Mrs James P Gray, Ramer, TN; ed/Grad, McNairy Ctl High; cp/Beta Clb, 1981, 1982, 1983; Student Govt, 1983-84; Treas 1983-84; HS Basketball Team, 1981-82, 1982-83, 1983-84; r/Cath; hon/Outstg Female Student, 1980-81; g/To Attend Col and Maj in Computers.

GRAY, TONI oc/Lawyer; b/Mar 18, 1955; h/1701 Winfield Street, Einfield, KS 67156; p/Mr and Mrs Wallace Gray, Winfield, KS; ed/Winfield HS, 1973; BA, SWn Col, 1976; JD, Georgetown Univ Law Sch, 1981; Admitted to KS and NJ Bars; pa/Instr, Embry-Riddle Aeronautical Univ, 1983-; KS Bar Assn; Mtl Disabilities Law Reporter; cp/Investigator Vol, Mtl Hosp; r/Yg Adult Coor, Meth Ch; hon/Grad, summa cum laude; Tutor, Georgetown Univ Law Ctl; Asst Editor, *Collegian*.

GRAYSON, DEANNE ELIZABETH oc/Housewife, Student; b/May 14, 1963; h/6756 103rd Street, #37, Jacksonville, FL 32210; m/David Berton; c/Karah Loren; p/Kenneth Elliott and Vonda Lee Kaplan, Orange Park, FL; ed/Hons Dipl, Orange Pk HS, 1981; FL St Univ, 1981-82; St Johns River Commun Col, 1982-83; mil/AUS 1982-83, Signal/ Security Spec; cp/Alpha Chi Sigma, 1982-; Girl Scouts, Ldr for Jr Troop 1982-83; Navy Wife's Clb, 1983-84; "Skilled" and "Ready around the Clock" Soldier Clb, 1983; NHS, All A's Chm; Latin Clb; Latin Hon Soc; German Clb, Treas; Varsity Cheerldr, Capt; Mensa, Chd's Coor; Forensics; Model UN; Ja Lit Mag; Math Clb, Publicity Chm; hon/ Marksman-Mile Medal, 1983; Sharpshooter, Grenade Medal, 1983; Co B Soldier of the Month, 1983; Grad w Hons in SIG/SEC Spec Course, 1983; Army Cert of Achmt, Softball Armed Forces Day, 1983; Supt's Awd for Top 10 Grad'g Class; 1st Place Derivatives I Dist Latin Forum; 2nd Place Derivatives I St Latin; 3rd Place Math Field Day, Duval Co, Metrics; 4th Place in Sch in Nat Math Exam, 1980; Pres Phy Fitness; W/W Among Am HS Students; Intl Yth in Achmt; g/BS in Chem; Being a Good Mother and Wife.

GREEN, BRIGITTE LENORE oc/ Secretary; b/Jun 20, 1964; h/1615 Pierce Street, Sandusky, OH 44870; m/Sgt H Curtis Churchwell; p/James L and Marjorie L Green, Sandusky, OH; ed/ Grad, Sandusky High, 1982; Student of Bus, Firelands Col; Hon Grad, Patricia Stevens Career Col and Finishing Sch,

1983; pa/Secy to Dean of Wom, Patricia Stevens Col; Ofc Asst, E F Hutton; Secy, Walter R Wagner, Atty; Other Positions; cp/Grand Royal Queen, Girls' Assem St of OH, 1984; VP, U Black Students, 1981; VP, NAACP Yth Grp, 1980; Pres, Sr Ofc Ed Clb, 1982; Intl Clb, 1979-82; Secy, Ebenezer Yth Grp, 1981; Sandusky High Student Coun, 1981; Student Senate, Patricia Stevens, 1983; Chorus and Dance Clb, Patricia Stevens, 1983; r/Bapt; hon/5th Place in Reg 7 OOEA Contests, Prepared Spch, 1980; 1st Place in Grand Assem Oratorial Contest, 1980-82; 1st Place in Reg 7 OOEA Contests, Legal Occup, 1982; 3rd Place in Reg 7 OOEA Contests, Receptionist, 1982; Acad Hons, Patricia Stevens Career Col, 1983; g/Help Others; To Be Able to Do Any Job That is Given to Me.

GREEN, DOLLY M BRADFORD oc/ Student, Secretary; b/Feb 13, 1951; h/ Route 2, Box 111, Bellevue, TX 76228; ba/Wichita Falls, TX; m/Kirby J; c/ Jennifer A, Kristina L; p/W T Bradford, Burkburnett, TX; ed/Burkburnett HS, 1969; BBA, MWn St Univ, 1983; pa/Ofc Clk, Bkkpr, Town and Country Mobile Homes Inc, 1969-71; Receptionist and Secy, Parker Square Savs & Ln, 1971-73; Secy, Carter McGregor, 1982-; cp/MSU Secretarial Assn, Treas 1982-83; r/Bapt; hon/Nom'd Outstg Wom of the Yr, MSU, 1983; Outstg Grad Ofc Adm, MSU, 1983; g/Teach HS Bus; Voc Ed and Career Cnslg.

GREEN, JONATHAN DAVID oc/ Graduate Student; b/Jul 21, 1959; h/ 517-B South Hafner, Stillwater, OK 74075; ba/Stillwater, OK; p/Mr and Mrs Carl Green, Richmond, KY; ed/Madison Ctl HS, 1977; BS 1981, MS 1983, Univ of KY; pa/Res Asst, Univ of KY, 1981-83; Res Asst, OK St Univ, 1983-; cp/So Weed Sci Soc; Soil Conserv Soc of Am; Track; FFA, Pres, Reg Secy; UK Agronomy Clb, Pres; Col Soil Judging Team; Agri Student Coun; Agronomy Review Com; r/Bapt; hon/Grad Student Paper Awds, So Weed Sci Soc, 1982, 1983; Grad Student Paper Awds, N Ctl Weed Sci Soc, 1981; Am Soc of Agronomy Student Awd; Gildea Foun S'ship; Phillip-Morris S'ship; W/W Am HS; Intl Yth in Achmt; g/PhD in Crop Sci (Weed Sci).

GREEN, KYLA KATHLEEN oc/Student; b/Jun 29, 1965; h/Route 1, Box 31, Medina, TX 78055; p/Mr and Mrs Timothy Z Green, Medina, TX; ed/HS Grad, 1983; pa/Sales Clk, Collins of TX, 1981-82; Micro Film, Bandera Elect Coop, 1982; cp/Nat Beta Clb, 1980-83; Basketball, Track, Volleyball, 1980-83; Tennis, Wom's Softball Leag, 1981-83; Yth Rodeo, 1980; hon/Nat Sci Merit Awd, 1983; Gifted and Talented Yth, 1981; All-Dist Basketball, 1982, 1983; Reg Track, 1980-83; Reg Basketball, 1982; Acad Awd, Social Studies, 1982; W/W Among Am HS Students; US Achmt Acad Nat Awds Yrbook; g/ Attend Col or Univ on Basketball S'ship; Maj in Nutrition, Minor in PE; Career as a Sports Nutritionist.

GREEN, LAURA GAYLE oc/Student; b/Jul 11, 1963; h/413 Wilson Street, Rocky Mount, VA 24151; p/Mr and Mrs Fred C Green, Rocky Mount, VA; ed/ Hon Grad, Franklin Co HS, 1981; Att'd, Bluefield Col, 1981-83; Att'g, Ashland Col, 1983-; pa/Unskilled Laborer,

Guyer-Roberts Mfg Inc, 1981, 1983; Yth Choir Pianist, First Bapt Ch; cp/HS Bible Clb, 1978-81, Pres 1979-81; HS Newspaper Staff, 1980-81; Bluefield Col Choir, 1981-83; Ashland Col Choir, 1983-84; Ashland Col Marching Band, 1983; Music Tchrs Nat Assn, 1983-84; r/So Bapt; Nat Hon Roll, 1981-82; W/ W Among Am HS Students; W/W Among Students in Am Jr Cols; g/Bach and Master's Degs in Piano Perf; Teach Piano and Music Hist in a Col Situation.

GREEN, RONALD DAVID oc/Student; b/Jun, 17, 1961; h/1503 Toms Creek Road, Blacksburg, VA 24060; ba/ Same; p/Mr and Mrs C M Green, Troutville, VA; ed/Lord Botetourt HS, 1979; BS, VA Polytechnic Inst and St Univ, 1983; pa/Vet Asst, Botetourt Vet Hosp; Farm Mgr, Green Angus Farms; cp/Block and Bridle Clb, VPI & SU, Pres 1982-83; Alpha Gamma Rho Frat, VPI & SU, Secy 1983; Alpha Zeta; VA 4-H All Stars; FFA Alumni Assn; r/Catawba Val Bapt Ch, Fin Mem; hon/Outstg Jr, Block and Bridle Clb, 1982; Ruby Dew Lloyd S'ship, 1982; Ashe Lockhart S'ship, 1982; Num Other S'ships; W/W Among Am Univs and Cols; Outstg Yg Men of Am.

GREENE, YVONNE oc/Clerical; b/ Sep 28, 1957; h/3707 Buford Highway, Northeast, Apartment #6, Atlanta, GA 30329; ba/Atlanta, GA; p/Mr and Mrs James Greene Jr, Darlington, SC; ed/St John's High, 1975; BA in Crim Justice Adm, Benedict Col, 1979; MS in Urban Govt Adm, GA St Univ, 1983; cp/Delta Sigma Theta Sorority, Corresponding and Recording Secy 1978-79; Alpha Kappa Mu Hon Soc, 1977; Delta Sigma Theta Sorority Alumni; HS: Sr Class Histn; Nat Hon Soc; Col: Student Govt Assn 1975-76, Sophomore Class VP 1976-77; hon/Alpha Kappa Mu Hon Soc, 1978; Grad, cum laude (BA); W/ W Among Am Cols and Univs; g/To Wk in the Area of Govt Relats for a Maj Corp; To Eventually Wk in Govt Mgmt.

GREENWOOD, JOHN MURRAY III oc/Student; b/Apr 30, 1962; h/PO Box 728, El Campo, TX 77437; p/Mr and Mrs John Murray Greenwood Jr; ed/El Campo HS; Univ of TX Austin; pa/M D Anderson Sum Prog in Biomed Sci, 1980; Camp Staff/First Aid, BSA, 1981; Mayo Clin Student Interim Prog, 1982; Resident Asst, Student, Univ of TX Austin, 1983; cp/Jr Lion; Jr Rotarian; Am Legion Boys' St; Delta Epsilon Phi; Sci Clb; Spch and Drama Clb, Parliamentarian; Intl Thespian Soc; Select Choir; Madrigal Singers; Men's Quartet; Nat Eagle Scout Assn; Order of the Arrow Ceremonial Clan, Chapt Chief, Vice Chief; VFW Voice of Dem Awds; Alpha Epsilon Delta; Alpha Phi Omega; Phi Eta Sigma; Alpha Lambda Delta; Pro Deo Et Patria; Campus Crusade for Christ; Concert Chorale; Beta Beta Beta; Golden Key Nat Hon Soc; r/Evang Christian; hon/Nat Merit Scholar; Vigil Hon, Order of the Arrow; TX Music Ed Assn TX All-St Choir; W/ W Among Am HS Students; Am's Outstg Names and Faces; Intl Yth in Achmt; Yg Commun Ldrs of Am; g/BS in Zool; BA in Biol; Psych BA Requirements; Med Sch.

GREER, CERITA YVETTE oc/Student; b/Jun 9, 1963; h/885 East Drive, Memphis, TN 38108; p/Rev and Mrs Clarence Greer, Memphis, TN; ed/Dipl,

Treadwell HS, 1981; cp/Alpha Kappa Mu Nat Hon Soc; Pres, Delta Sigma Theta Sorority, Theta Pi Chapt; r/Meth; hon/W/W Among Am HS Students and Aths; Dir of Dist'd Ams; g/To Attend Grad Sch and Study Pharmocognosy.

GREER, LEO CURTIS JR oc/Teacher, Coach, Guidance Counselor; b/Mar 12, 1957; h/Route 3, Box 260, Highway 76, Springfield, TN 37172; ba/Nashville, TN; m/Kristi Lynn Thornton; c/Joshua Curtis; p/Leo and Evelyn Greer, Hendersonville, TN; ed/Goodpasture HS; BA, Social Studies, David Lipscomb Col; MA, Oral Communication, Abilene Christian Univ; pa/Asst Instr of Spch, Abilene Christian Univ, 1979-81; Tchr, Coach, Beech HS, 1981-82; Agt, St Farm Ins, 1982-83; Tchr, Coach, Guid Cnslr, Nashville Christian Sch, 1983-; r/Flat Rock Ch of Christ, Min; Rivergate Ch of Christ, Asst Min; hon/Grad Asst in Spch, Abilene Christian Univ, 1979-80; Pres, HS Alumni Assn, 1979-80; Senator at Large, David Lipscomb Col, 1978-79; Ideal Student, HS, 1974-75; Outstg Yg Men of Am; W/W Among Students in Am Univs and Cols; g/Col Edr; PhD, Persuasion, Rhetoric and Public Address.

GREGORY, TEENA DENISE oc/ Student; b/Nov 22, 1963; h/Route 1, Dixon Springs, TN 37057; p/Clovis and Jeanette Gregory, Dixon Springs, TN; ed/Grad, Trousdale Co HS, 1982; Current Student, Cumberland Col of Lebanon; cp/HS Sr Class Secy, 1981-82; 4-H, 1978-82; FHA, 1978, 1980-82; 4-H Clb Pres, 1978; 4-H Hon Clb, 1978-82; 4-H All Stars, 1979-82; Sch Newspaper Staff, 1980-82; Annual Staff, 1980-82; Chorus, 1982; Cato Commun Ctr Secy, 1981-82; Sr Play Cast, 1982; Beta Clb, 1981-82; r/Song Ldr, Dixon Creek Missionary Bapt Ch, 1979-83; hon/ Highest Freshman Average, 1979; Friendliest and Best Personality, 1982; Nat Eng Merit Awd, 1982; Salutatorian, 1982; Sprg Queen Attendant, 1982; FFA Queen Attendant, 1982; FHA Tattered Tailor Awd, 1982; W/W Among Am HS Students; g/Bus Maj; To Study Computers and Become a Computer Programmer/Operator.

GREGORY, WILLIAM GEORGE oc/ United States Air Flying Training Officer; b/May 14, 1957; h/6436 Westwood Drive, Lockport, NY 14094; ba/ RAF Lakonheath, England; m/Mary Beth Harney; p/William and Kathleen Gregory, Lockport, NY; ed/Lockport Sr HS, 1975; BS, USAF Acad, 1979; MS, Columbia Univ, 1980; 60% Completed, MS in Mgmt, Troy St Univ; pa/493TFS Flying Tng Ofcr, 1983-; cp/Eagle Scout; YMCA Camp Ongahsa Staff; hon/CO Coun of Engrs Silver Medal Winner; NY St OTYM Finalist; Boston Marathon; Dist'd Grad, USAF Acad; Guggenheim F'ship, Columbia Univ; Placed 525th in London Marathon, 1983; W/W Among Students in Am Cols and Univs; g/USAF Test Pilot Sch; NASA Space Shuttle Prog.

GRICHNIK, JAMES MICHAEL oc/ Student; b/May 10, 1961; h/6540 Bellows Lane, #1301, Houston, TX 77030; ba/Houston, TX; p/James Grichnik, Elk Grove, IL; Corinne Grichnik, Park Ridge, IL; ed/Grad, Maine Twp HS S, 1979; AB, Chem and Biol, Wash Univ, 1982; pa/Res, Dr Farrand, Loyola-Stritch Sch of Med, 1981; Res,

Dr Mary-Dell Chilton, Wash Univ, 1981; cp/Hematology Vol, Luth Gen Hosp, 1980; Emer Room Vol, Resurrection Hosp, 1980; r/Cath; hon/Chem Dept Awd, Maine Twp HS; Nat Hon Soc, 1979; Grad, summa cum laude, 1982; Phi Lambda Upsilon, 1982; Med Scist Tng Prog, NIH Funded(MD, PhD), Full F'ship; g/Cancer/DNA Res; MD; PhD.

GRIFFIN, KAREN LYNN oc/Student; b/Spe 16, 1960; h/PO Box 280, Crossnore, NC; ba/Greensboro, NC; p/Mr and Mrs Raymond L Griffin, Crossnore, NC; ed/Avery Co HS, 1978; BA, Communication Arts/Theatre, Appalachian St Univ, 1983; MFA, Design/ Tech Theatre, Univ of NC Greensboro, 1985; pa/Tech Asst 1980, 1981, 1982, Shop Supvr 1982-83, Univ Theatre, Appalachian St Univ; Asst Tech Dir 1982, Tech Dir 1983, The Liberty Ct Outdoor Drama; Tech Dir, Univ of NC Greensboro (Aycock Auditorium), 1983; cp/Alpha Psi Omega, Hon Dramatic Soc, Secy 1981, VP 1982, Pres 1983; Playcrafters, 1981-83; hon/Theatre Excell Awds, 1980-83; Cratis Williams Theatre S'ship, 1982-83; Theatre Excell Awd, The Liberty Ct, 1982; g/ Wk and Train People in the Field of Theatre.

GRIFFIN, LOVEY DEANE oc/Student; b/Dec 19, 1962; h/219 Nunn Street, Havelock, NC 28532; p/George and Jewell Griffin, Havelock, NC; ed/Havelock HS; Att'g, Meredith Col; pa/Jo-Eds Florist, 1978-80; Acctg Apprentice, Craven Co Hosp, 1982; NC Bapt Assem, 1983; cp/Havelock HS Hon Soc; Future Bus Ldrs of Am; Future Tchrs of Am; Glee Clb, 1978-80; Band Lettermen, 1979-80; SMENC, 1982-83; r/Bapt; hon/Cast of "Lost in the City"; Cast of "Peter Pan"; Spanish Awd, 1983; S'ship Recip; g/After Receiving Music Ed Deg, I Plan to Teach K-12 Choral Music and Possibly Band; I Also Plan to Resume Wk on My Acctg.

GRIFFITH, MARVIN SCOTT oc/Student; b/Dec 10, 1962; h/618 Hunt Avenue, Trenton, NJ 08610; p/Mr and Mrs Glen Smith, Trenton, NJ; ed/Hamilton W HS, 1981; Presently Att'g, Rutgers Univ; pa/Computer Operator, Middlesex Co Col, 1982; Telephone Interviewer, R H Broskins Mktg Res Firm, 1983; Ticket Sales Reservationist, People's Express Airlines, 1984; cp/Am Legion Boys' St, 1980; r/Bapt; hon/ Excell through Ed S'ship, 1981; Pres, Eta Epsilon Chapt of Kappa Alpha Psi Frat Inc, 1983-84; Intl Yth in Achmt Awd; W/W Among Am HS Students; Commun Ldrs in Am; g/To Pursue a Career as a Mktg Analyst; To Attend Law Sch or Obtain an MBA.

GRIMES, MARSHELLE KAE oc/Student; b/Mar 23, 1965; h/54 North Mahoning Avenue, Alliance, OH 44601; p/Ms Cheryl L Grimes, Alliance, OH; ed/Alliance HS; Student, Findlay Col; cp/Yth NAACP; Girls' Assem, OES; St Grand Ofcs: Grand Princess Exchequer 1982-83, Grand Royal Princess 1983-84; Local Ofcs: Princess Guide 1978-79, Royal Queen 1979-82; HS: Key Clb 1982-83, Track Team 1981-83, Basketball 1979-81, Spirit Clb 1979-83, Lib Aide 1982-83, Boys' Basketball Stat 1982-83, Prom Com 1981-82, Blood Day Support Com Chp 1982-83, Barn Bash Com; Col: Black Student Union

1983-84, Student Govt Assn 1983-84, Freshman Class Pres 1983-84, Softball Team 1983-84; r/AME; hon/Elected to St Ofc for Girls' Assem, St of OH, Sponsored by OES, 1982, 1983; g/Bach Deg in Mktg; Career in Mktg.

GRISELL, MARGARET KATHLEEN oc/Student of Engineering; b/Dec 27, 1964; h/15707 Oak Road, Carmel, IN 46032; p/Ted Wood and Barbara Gail Grisell, Carmel, IN; ed/Grad, Westfield HS, 1983; Student of Engrg, Purdue Univ; cp/Yrbook Staff, 1982-83; Student Coun Rep, 1981-83; Booster Clb, 1979-83; French Clb, Spanish Clb, 1979-82; Cheerldr, 1979-80; Nat Hon Soc, 1981-83; Track Stat, 1981; hon/ Teamstest Mem, 1982, 1983; Geometry Awd, Biol Awd, French Awd, 1981; French Awd, Algebra Awd, 1980; Chem Awd, Computer Math Awd, 1982; Pre-Calculus Awd, 1983; Class Histn, 1983; Hoosier Scholar Awd, 1983; g/To Acquire a Chem Engrg Deg and Pursue Chem.

GRISSOM, ARTHUR TAYLOR JR oc/Utilities Engineer; b/Oct 26, 1952; h/ 711 Williamsboro Street, Oxford, NC 27565; ba/Butner, NC; m/Claudette Hilton; p/Mr and Mrs Arthur T Grissom Sr, Oxford, NC; ed/J F Webb HS, 1971; E Carolina Univ, 1972; Att'd, NC St Univ, 1974-76; mil/AUS; pa/Utilities Engr, US Dept of Justice, 1976–; Rehab Therapist, Murdoch Ctr, 1972-74; cp/ Granville Co Rescue Squad, Secy 1978; Granville Co Wildlife Clb; Beta Clb, E Carolina; Ath Clb, E Carolina; Nat Hon Soc, Webb HS; r/Bapt; hon/Life Awd, BSA, 1964; Pres, Flat River Royal Ambassadors, 1968-69; NHS, 1968-71; Outstg Yg Farmer of Am, 1983; Employee Awd, US Dept of Justice; Campbell Univ S'ship, 1971; MVP, VA Leag, 1969; Outstg Yg Men; g/To Continue to Be a Successful Farmer; To Remain Active in Commun Affairs; To Hold Public Ofc.

GROCE, KIMBERLY DIANNE oc/ Student; b/Aug 14, 1967; h/Route 1, Box 49B, Belvidere, TN 37306; p/Roy and Sandra Groce, Belvidere, TN; ed/Huntland HS; cp/Beta, Editor of Paper, Mem for 3 Yrs; Cheerldr, 6 Yrs, Capt Sr Yr; FFA, Secy 1984; 4-H Dist Showmanship, 3 Yrs; 4-H, Hon Reporter, 1983, VP and Scout 1984; 4-H All Stars; VP, Huntland 4-H Clb, 1984; Pres of Sophomore Class; r/Bapt; hon/Recip, 4-H Vol St Awd; Dist 4-H Steer Showmanship 1981, 1983, 1984; g/Attend Col and Study to Become a Vet or a Phy Therapist.

GROEPLER, FREDERICK MATTHEW oc/Student; b/Aug 4, 1966; h/ PO Box 613, Kentfield, CA 94914; p/ Mr and Mrs Frederick Groepler, Kentfield, CA; pa/Life Guard, Mt Tam Racquet Clb; cp/Model UN; Participant, Atl Pacific Math Competition, 3 Yrs; r/ Luth; hon/Brother Alfred Brousseau Math Awd, 1982; Hons Chinese Lang Student, 1982; Redwood HS Acad Decathalon (1 of 6 Students Representing Sch); Hons Math and Sci throughout Sch Career; HS Computer Sci Tchr.

GROSS, KATHLEEN ANN oc/Student; b/Dec 29, 1960; h/54 Sunset Drive, Streator, IL 61364; p/James D and Marilyn A Gross, Streator, IL; ed/ Streator Twp HS, 1979; No IL Univ (w Hons), 1983; cp/Univ Hon Prog; Lambda Sigma; Newman Ctr; No IL Guides;

Omicron Delta Kappa, VP, Pres; Phi Sigma; Residence Hall VP; Student Coun; NHS; German Clb; Sr Bowl Capt; Track; Tennis; hon/Nat Merit Commend Student; Acad Finalist S'ship; W/ W Among Am HS Students; Intl Yth in Achmt; Commun Ldrs of Am; g/MD w Career in Pract, Res and Tchg.

GROSS, MARY ELIZABETH oc/ Assistant Professor of Clinical Pharmacy; b/Nov 20, 1957; h/1826 Roundhill Terrace, Charleston, WV 25314; ba/ Charleston, WV; m/James L Martin; p/ Mr and Mrs Henry T Gross, Monee, IL; ed/Peotone HS, 1975; BS, Drake Univ, 1980; PharmD, Univ of UT, 1982; Grad Gerontology Cert, Univ of UT, 1982; pa/Asst Prof of Clin Pharm, Sch of Pharm, WV Univ, 1982–; Am Col of Clin Pharm, 1982–; Am Assn of Cols of Pharm, 1982–; Gerontological Soc of Am, 1982–; ASHP Geriatric SIG Midyr Planning Com, 1983; ASHP Geriatric SIG Reviewer, 1983; Substance Abuse Adv Coun, Shawnee Hills Mtl Hlth/ Retard Ctr, 1982–; Total Parenteral Nutrition Com, Secy/Editor of Newsletter 1982–; hon/Pubs, "Alcohol Abuse Among Geriatrics" 1983, Others; Merck Clin Pharm Awd, Univ of UT, Col of Pharm, 1982; Grace P Swinyard Meml S'ship; SAPHA Outstg Mem; Drake Univ Col of Pharm Fac Awd; W/ W Among Cols and Univs; Outstg Yg Wom of Am; g/Expand Wk in the Area of Geriatrics.

GROTH, GARY MITCHELL b/Aug 20, 1964; h/28015 Oaklar, Saugus, CA 91350; p/Mrs Ethel Groth Leigh, Saugus, CA; ed/Saugus HS, 1982; oc/ Student; ca/ARC Yth Disaster Action Tm Tng Wkshop; ARC Yth Ldrship Devel Ctr; ARC Yth Coun, Yth Disaster Action Tm & Coalition for Improved Sch Funding; ARC Yth Coun VP, Retreat Co-Dir, Pres, Intern; Freshman Class VP; Supt Student Adv Coun VP; Assoc Student Body VP, Pres; Track/ Cross-Country Tm; Student Coun; Sch Campus Improvement Prog; NHS; hon/ HS Outstg Ser Awd; Boys' St Alt; Pres Clrm for Yth Ams, Nom; Sen Yth Prog; ARC Outstg Ser in a Disaster Relief Operation Awd; U Way Yth Ldrship Awd; DAR Good Citizen Awd; Santa Clarita Val JCs Outstg Yg Teenager LA Co Outstg Ser Awd; g/Public Adm, Polits.

GUARNIERI, MICHAEL STEPHEN oc/Student; b/Jul 22, 1962; h/11 Hampshire Lane, Stamford, CT 06905; p/Mr and Mrs Michael Guarnieri, Stamford, CT; ed/Grad, Westhill HS, 1980; BS in Acctg, Fairfield Univ, 1984; cp/Student Mem, Nat Assn of Accts; Sustaining Mem, Repub Nat Com; VP, Fairfield Univ Col Repubs; r/Rom Cath; hon/ Polit Editor, *Fairfield Mirror*; Editor-in Chief, *Republican Review*; Nat Semi-Finalist, Jr Achmt, 1980; Bus Student of the Yr, Westhill HS, 1980; Recip, Nat Assn of Accts S'ship, 1983; Recip, Arthur Andersen & Co S'ship; Dean's List, Fairfield Univ; g/To Enter the Profession of Public Acctg and to Remain Politically Active.

GUERNSEY, BRIDGET SUE oc/ Assistant Director of Student Activities; b/Oct 4, 1957; h/521 Kelly Avenue, Apartment E, Wilkinsburg, PA 15221; ba/Pittsburgh, PA; p/Mr and Mrs William Richardson, Richey, FL; ed/Hobart Sr HS, 1975; BS, Ball St Univ, 1979;

Univ of Cinc; pa/Asst Dir of Student Activs, Univ of Pgh; cp/Greek Affairs Coor; Alpha Chi Omega Alumni Clb, Chapt Pres, VP; Venture Ser Org; Ball St Panhellenic Coun VP; Mortar Bd; Blue Key; Admissions Coor Team; hon/ Outstg Sr, Alpha Chi Omega; Outstg Sr Girl, HS; Outstg Yg Wom of Am; W/W Among Students in Am Cols and Univs; g/Cnslg in Ed or Bus.

GUESMAN, KIMBERLY JO oc/Critical Care Nurse Clinician; b/Oct 24, 1959; h/Apartment #205, 5426 Fifth Avenue, Pittsburgh, PA 15232; ba/ Pittsburgh, PA; p/Mr and Mrs Harold Guesman, Scottdale, PA; ed/Southmoreland HS, 1977; BS in Nsg, WV Wesleyan Col, 1981; pa/Staff Nurse in Coronary Care Unit 1981-83, Critical Care Nurse Clinician (Presently), Shadyside Hosp, Pgh; Sigma Theta Tau, VP 1979-80; CPR Instr; r/Meth; hon/Sigma Theta Tau, Nat Nsg Hon Soc, 1979-; W/W Am Col Students; Nat Register of Outstg Col Grads; g/MS in Nsg w Cardiovas Concentration, Univ of Pgh.

GUIDROZ, JAN RENEE oc/Student; b/Sep 12, 1966; h/Route 2, Box 510, Carencro, LA 70520; p/Mr and Mrs Bryan Guidroz, Carencro, LA; ed/Grad, Carencro HS, 1984; pa/Swimming Lesson Tchr, Ages 3-5 Yrs, 1983; Lifeguard, 1983; cp/Class Pres, 1980-81, 1982, 1983; Student Coun Pres, 1983, 1984; Cheerldr, 1980-81, 1982; Hd Cheerldr, 1983-84; Art Clb, 1980-81; Bearbacker Com, 1980-81, 1982, 1983, 1984; Sr Class Rep, 1983-84; Newspaper Staff, 1982-83; Spirit Squad, 1982-83; Softball Team, 1980-81, 1982, 1983; r/Cath; hon/Most Outstg Cheerldr, 1980-81; Teen of the Wk, Daily Advertiser, 1983; Class Favorite, 1980-81, 1981-82, 1982-83; Class Sweetheart, 1980, 1981, 1982, 1983; Key Clb Sweetheart, 1982, 1982, 1983; Homecoming Ct, 1982-83; Track Ct, 1981-82; Optimist Awd, 1980-81; Student Coun's Hardest Wkr, 1983; Bearbacker of the Month, 1980, 1981, 1982, 1983; Hon Roll, 1980-81, 1982; W/W Among Am HS Students; g/Attend Univ of SWn LA; Phy Therapist.

GULLEY, JEFFREY JAMES oc/Student; b/May 26, 1963; h/Route 1, Box 61, Tollesboro, KY 41189; p/Mr and Mrs James L Gulley, Tollesboro, KY; ed/ Grad, Tollesboro HS, 1981; BA in Govt

and Paralegalism, Morehead St Univ, 1985; pa/Legal Res Asst, Buddy R Salyer Law Firm, 1983-; cp/Sigma Nu Frat, Cmdr 1984-85, Pledge Marshal 1983-84, Recorder 1982-83; Phi Alpha Delta Law Frat, Treas 1983-84; Polit Sci Clb, Prog Coun; Miss MSU S'ship Pageant Exec Com, Dir of Publicity 1983-84, 1984-85; MSU Student Assn, VP 1983-84, Public Relats Dir 1982-83; Co Chm, Dems Together '83, Statewide Polit Campaign; r/Christian; hon/MSU Pres Merit S'ship, 1981-85; MSU Sci Fair Reg S'ship, 1981-85; Allie Whittington Yg Meml Awd as Outstg Polit Sci Student, 1984-85; Pres's List, 1981-83; Dean's List, 1983-84; Phi Kappa Phi Hon Soc; Sigma Nu S'ship Silver Key, 1983; Intl Yth in Achmt; W/W; Soc of Dist'd HS Students; g/To Attend Law Sch at Col of Wm and Mary; To Pract Corporate Law and Invest in Real Est.

GULLIFORD, JEFF J oc/Boxboy, Paperboy; b/Feb 28, 1965; h/719 Detroit Avenue, Vancouver, WA 98664; ba/ Vancouver, WA; p/Jim and Marj Gulliford, Vancouver, WA; ed/HS Grad, 1984; pa/Paperboy, *Columbian*, 1980-; Boxboy, Food Warehouse, 1982-; cp/ Football; Soccer; Baseball; Scouting; Tennis; Water and Snow Skiing; Golf; Basketball; hon/Jr HS: Team Capt (Football, Soccer, Basketball), Most Inspirational-Soccer Awd, MVP-Soccer Awd, Outstg Musician Awd, Outstg Student Awd; HS: Nat Hon Soc 1983, All Conf Kicker 1982, All Star Team Kicker (*The Oregonian*) 1982, All St Kicker 1982, All Star Tiger Cage Basketball Capt 1982-83, Pre-Season All St Kicker 1983, 2nd Place-Fred Meyer Cup Tournament Soccer Team, All Conf Kicker and Defensive Back 1983, and Hon Mention Receiver (*The Oregonian*), Sportsmanship Awd (Football) 1983, Gold Cup Leag Champion (Soccer) 1983; Eagle Scout, BSA; Superior Rating, Percussion Solo; g/To Attend Col Either through an Ath S'ship or Some Other Form of S'ship; Deg in Engrg.

GUMPEL, CRAIG SCOTT oc/Student; b/Jan 21, 1965; h/104 Cresci Boulevard, Hazlet, NJ 07730; ed/Raritan HS; Currently Enrolled, Rutgers Univ; pa/Cnslr, Pythian Camp, 1980, 1981; Chef, York Steakhouse, 1982; Cashier/ Sales, Sears Roebuck & Co, 1982-; hon/

W/W Yg Adults; b/PhD in Ec.

GUNNARSSON, GUNNAR KRISTINN oc/Student; b/Apr 8, 1964; h/635 Ridge Road, Salisbury, MD 21801; p/ Mr and Mrs G K Gunnarsson, Salisbury, MD; ed/Grad, James M Bennett Sr HS, 1982; Presently Att'g, Univ of DE; pa/Coldwater Seafood Corp, Sums of 1983, 1982, 1981, 1980; cp/Bethany Luth Yth Org; Yg Life of Salisbury; Campus Crusade for Christ, Univ of DE; Varsity Tennis; Varsity Golf; Marching and Concert Bands; Jazz Band; r/Luth; hon/All-En Shore Symphonic Band, 1980, 1982; St Scholastic Merit Awd, 1982; W/W Among Am HS Students; W/W Music; Commun Ldrs of Am; g/Elect Engrg Deg, Univ of DE.

GUNNING, SHARON FRANCES oc/ Student; b/Sep 25, 1963; h/24 Pecan Way, Natchez, MS 39120; p/Mr and Mrs Louis Gunning, Natchez, MS; ed/Grad, Cathedral High, 1981; Current Student of Acctg, MS St Univ; cp/HS Yrbook, Copy Editor; Col: Alpha Chi Omega Sorority (Asst Rush Chm 1982, 3rd VP 1983-84), Angel Flight (Comptroller 1984); hon/Pres's List, Fall 1981, Sprg 1982, Fall 1982, Fall 1983; g/To Be a CPA in a Large Firm.

GUTSCHENRITTER, DENISE LYNN oc/Teacher; b/May 30, 1956; h/ Box 324, Fairfax, MO 64446; ba/Fairfax, MO; m/Kevin Smith; p/Mr and Mrs Delmus Gutschenritter, Coin, IA; ed/S Page HS, 1974; AA, IA Wn Commun Col, 1976; BS 1978, MS 1980, NW MO St Univ; pa/1st Grade Tchr, Fairfax R-111 Schs, 1978-; NW St Tchrs Assn, 1978-; Fairfax R-111 Commun Tchrs Assn, 1978-, Treas 1980-82, VP 1982-83; Assn Mem, NRTA Div of AARP, 1979-; Mu Lambda Chapt, Beta Sigma Phi, Corresponding Secy 1981-82, Ext Ofcr 1982-83; cp/Histn, Jaycettes, 1981-; r/Cath; hon/Nom'd MO St Tchr of the Yr, 1983-84; Nom'd, Outstg Edrs Awd, NW Dist of MSTA, 1983-84; Grad w Highest Hons, 1976, 1978, 1980; Dean's List; Kappa Delta Pi; Lake Gidley, Spec Awd, SMSTA Outstg Jr, Acad Renewal and IA Cent S'ships; Miss Congeniality Awd and Sportsmanship Awd, 1977; Chosen Most Versatile of Sr Class, S Page HS; Pres, All-Am Teams, Perfect Attendance, K-12; Intl Yth in Achmt; Outstg Yg Wom of Am; Commun Ldrs of Am; Dir of Dist'd Ams.

H

HAAKE, LORI SUE oc/Student; b/ Apr 1, 1963; h/714 Vincent Drive, Taylor Mill, KY 41015; ba/Richmond, KY; p/Mr and Mrs Robert O Haake, Taylor Mill, KY; ed/Grad, Scott HS, 1981; Student, En KY Univ, 1981-; pa/ Lifeguard, Taylor Mill Swim Clb, 1982-83; cp/Pi Beta Phi Frat, 1982-; Student CEC, 1982-; Gamma Beta Phi Soc, 1983; NHS; Orch; Yth Choir; Band; Varsity Cheerldg; Yrbook Staff; hon/ Dean's List, 1982-83; Hon Grad; Nat Dean's List; Nat Hon Roll; W/W Among Am HS Students; g/Elem Ed, Spec Ed Study.

HABEEB, VALERIE BURKE oc/Student; b/Oct 22, 1959; h/2910 Keith Drive, Sanford, NC 27330; ba/Sanford, NC; m/Mark S; p/Arnold and Eileen Burke, Elizabethtown, KY; ed/E Hardin HS, 1977; Elizabethtown Commun Col, 1979; Bellarmine Col, 1982; pa/Taught Cheerldg Clins, Aerobics at Spa; Wk'd at Husband's Bus, Mr Gatti's; cp/VP, Pres, Newman Clb of Commun Col; Cheerldr; Min of Eucharist, Bellarmine Col; Campus Min; Sum Camp Dir; March of Dimes; Homecoming Chm; KY Bluegrass Sports Fest Chm; r/Cath; hon/Hon Roll; Intl Cheerldg Foun Div Dir; Homecoming Queen; W/W Among Students in Am Jr Cols; W/W Among Students in Am Cols and Univs; g/Elem or Kgn Tchr; Profl Homemaker.

HACKETT, DAVID ROGER oc/ Office of Christian Community Intern; b/Aug 14, 1956; h/295 North Madison, 14, Pasadena, CA; p/Mr and Mrs D Paul Hackett, Puyallup, WA; ed/Gov John R Rogers HS, 1975; BA, Univ of WA, 1979; Fuller Theol Sem; pa/Ofc of Christian Commun Intern; cp/Student Body Pres, Fuller Theol Sem, 1983-84; U Presb Vol Missionary in Korea; Royal Asiatic Soc; Univ of WA Mortar Bd Hon Soc; Korean Univ Lectr; Contbr, Korean Univ Text on Eng Composition; MV Jour, HS Paper; Editor, HS Paper; hon/ Plaque, Moderator of Presb Ch of Korea; Plaque, Soong Jun Ofc of the Pres; En Star Tng Awd; g/Profl Christian Min.

HAHN, COLETTE CAMILLE oc/ Student; b/Dec 6, 1961; h/300 Banbury Avenue, Elk Grove Village, IL 60007; p/Nicholas and Camille Hahn, Elk Grove Village, IL; ed/Elk Grove HS, 1979; BSC, DePaul Univ, 1983; cp/Theta Phi Alpha, Pres; Alpha Lambda Delta; Phi Eta Sigma; Beta Alpha Psi, VP of Adm 1983-84; Beta Gamma Sigma; Delta Epsilon Sigma; Delta Mu Delta; Blue Key; hon/Dean's List; Quill and Scroll; Nat Dean's List; W/W Among Students in Am Cols and Univs; g/CPA; Master's Deg in Acctg; Intl Acctg Firm Position.

HAHN, NICHOLAS GEORGE oc/ Accountant; b/Sep 20, 1960; h/300 Banbury Avenue, Elk Grove Village, IL 60007; p/Nick and Camille Hahn, Elk Grove Village, IL; ed/Elk Grove HS, 1978; BSC, DePaul Univ, 1982; pa/Staff Acct, Coopers & Lybrand, 1982-; IL CPA Soc, 1982-; Ledger and Quill Soc, 1982-; cp/DePaul Univ Century Clb, 1983; Parish Basketball Team; DePaul Univ Booster Clb, 1983; Alpha Chi; Univ Cheerldr; Campus Tour Guide; Orient Com Chm; Sports Media; Prog Coun; Intramural, Inter Fraternal Sports; Parish Softball Team; Acctg

Hon Student; Dean's List; r/Rom Cath; hon/DePaul Sr Ldrship Awd, 1982; Bob Neu Meml S'ship; Blue Key; Delta Mu Delta; W/W MW; W/W Am Cols and Univs; g/MBA, Univ of Chgo; Ptnr, Coopers & Lybrand.

HALBERT, REBECCA LEE oc/Assistant to Vice President of Marketing; b/ May 14, 1961; h/1235 Josey Street, Huntsville, TX 77340; ba/Huntsville, TX; p/B G and Avis Halbert, New Braunfels, TX; ed/Grad, New Braunfels HS, 1979; BA, Jour, Sam Houston St Univ, 1983; pa/Asst to the VP of Mktg, First Nat Bk, 1983-; Col: Orange Keys (Secy 1982-83), Delta Tau Delta Little Sister, Alpha Chi, Delta Phi Alpha, Wesley Foun (Exec Bd Mem for 4 Yrs), Beta Sigma Phi (Charter Pres 1983), Residence Hall Assn (Parliamentarian 1980-81); r/Meth; hon/Alpha Chi Hon Soc; Delta Phi Alpha German Hon Soc; SHSU Dean's List; Perfect GPA Awd; Student Govt S'ship, 1983; Annie Gibbs Meml Awd; Golden Key Nat Hon Soc, Secy-Treas 1983; W/W Am Cols and Univs; Nat Dean's List; g/To Enter the Field of Public Relats Either for a Small Public Relats Firm or for a Larger Co.

HALE, JOHN GREGORY oc/Communications Consultant; b/Feb 6, 1958; h/3225 South Main, PO Box 931, Vidor, TX 77662; p/Mr and Mrs Ralph Hale Jr, Vidor, TX; ed/Vidor HS, 1976; BS, Lamar Univ, 1980; pa/Communs Conslt; cp/Band; Choir; Student Coun; Drama; Newspaper Editor; Univ Band; Pres Staff; Student Affairs Coun; Student Org Com; Aux Budget Com; Setzer Student Ctr Gov Bd; hon/TX Chapt, Nat Sch Public Relats Assn Communs Contest Winner, 1983; Sabine Area Advtg Fdn S'ship; Fentress Foun S'ship; W/W Among Students in Am Cols and Univs; Intl Yth in Achmt.

HALEY, DAVID BRIAN oc/Student; b/Nov 23, 1964; h/3855 Thresher Street, Owensboro, KY 42301; p/John and Mary King Haley, Owensboro, KY; ed/Grad, Apollo HS; cp/Varsity A Clb; FCA; Football; Baseball; Basketball; Hockey; r/Bapt; hon/Football Awds: Leading Scorer 1980, 1981, 1982, Best Offensive Back 1980, 1981, 1982, Best Defensive Back 1982, All Big 8 Running Back 1981, All Big 8 Safety 1982, All Big 8 Kicker 1981, All City Defensive Back 1982, MVP 1981, 1982, All City Running Back 1981, 1982, All St Hon Mention 1982, All St Hon Mention (Kicker, Running Back and Defensive Back) 1981, 1982; All Big 8 Baseball, 1982; Mr Apogee, Homecoming King, Most Athletic, 1983; Hon Roll; Soc of Dist'd Am HS Students; W/W Am HS; g/Go to Col and Earn a Deg in Elect Engrg Technol.

HALL, AMHERIC MIGUEL oc/Student; b/Nov 1, 1964; h/322 Fairwood Avenue, Charlotte, NC 28203; p/ Donald and Polly Hall, Charlotte, NC; ed/Grad, Myers Pk HS, 1983; Att'g, Duke Univ; cp/Boy Scout, 1972-77; Jr Camp Cnslr, Camp Bethlehem, 1982; r/ Rom Cath; Altar Boy, Our Lady of Providence, 1972-78; hon/Gail Stovall Meml S'ship to Attend Duke Univ; g/ Marine Biologist.

HALL, BEVERLY LYNN oc/Student; b/Aug 23, 1967; h/Route 1, Box 422-A, Willard, NC 28478; p/Mr and Mrs Donald Ray Hall, Willard, NC; cp/Class Secy, 1981-82; Volleyball, Basketball,

Softball, 1981, 1982, 1983; Harrell's Crusader Ensemble; Pianist for Sch Plays, 1980-81, 1982-83; Pianist for HS Chorus; r/Bapt; Pianist for Ch Worship and Adult Choir; hon/Rookie of the Yr, 1981-82; All-Conf Basketball, 1982-83; g/Maj in Bus.

HALL, HOMER GLENN III oc/Student; b/Oct 19, 1965; h/480 Ingram Drive, Asheboro, NC 27203; p/Mr and Mrs Homer G Hall Jr, Asheboro, NC; ed/Asheboro HS, 1983; Student, Univ of NC Chapel Hill; p/Stamey's Jr, 1981; Rose's, 1981-; cp/HS: Baseball, Tennis, Key Clb; Mu Alpha Theta (Treas), Sr Sci Clb (Treas), Spanish Clb; r/Bapt; hon/Optimist Awd, 1980; Jr Marshal, 1982; Nat Hon Soc S'ship Awd, 1983; g/Pre-Med; MD.

HALL, HUGH WOOD oc/Volunteer in Mission; b/Jun 5, 1961; h/534 Brookwood Terrace, Griffin, GA 30223; p/Dr and Mrs J Denny Hall, Griffin, GA; ed/ Griffin HS, 1979; BS, Biol, Presb Col, 1983; pa/Vol in Mission (Tchg Chem, Biol and Eng to HS Boys), Zaire, Prog of Presb Ch; cp/HS: Basketball, Key Clb, Boys' St, Student Coun Yth Del, Hon Grad; Col: Sigma Nu Frat, Student Coun, Biol Soc, Freshman Orientation Bd, Acad Hon Roll; r/Presb; Presb Ch Softball Team, HS; hon/Eagle Scout; Asst Scoutmaaster to Nat Jamboree, 1979; g/To Attend Med Sch.

HALL, MARCIE ELAINE oc/Student; b/Aug 1, 1962; h/405 Orchard Avenue, Rocky Mount, VA 24151; ba/Salem, VA; p/Mr and Mrs Lawrence W Hall, Rocky Mount, VA; ed/Franklin Co HS, 1980; Assoc Deg, Ferrum Col, 1982; Bach Deg, Roanoke Col, 1984; pa/Fast Food Waitress, Good Food Shoppe, 1977; Cook/Cashier, Ben Franklin, 1978; Clk/ Cashier, Mack's Variety Store, 1979; cp/ VA Student Ed Assn; VA Rdg Assn; HIS Distributive Ed Clbs of Am; Mixed Chorus; r/Bapt; hon/Dean's List, 1982; Fac List of Hon Mention, 1983; Dean's List, 1983; W/W Among Students in Am Cols; g/Elem Sch Tchr.

HALL, RODERICK ASHLEY oc/ Student; b/Feb 20, 1964; h/Route 3, Box 77, Christiansburg, VA 24073; p/William and Priscilla Hall, Christiansburg, VA; ed/Auburn HS, 1982; VA Tech; pa/ Sports Info Student Asst, VA Tech; cp/ Christiansburg Stock Clb; Quill and Scroll; Basketball; Tennis; Debate; Forensics; Annual Staff; Photog; Newspaper Editor; Beta Clb, Treas; Spanish Clb, VP; Col Clb Reporter; Boys' St of VA; SCA Chaplain; US HS Jour Soc; r/Fin and Stewardship Com, Christ Luth Ch; Ch Coun; Pulpit Search Com; hon/St Debate Champion, 1982; Most Outstg Jour Student, AHS; Tennis Team MVP, 1981, 1982; Straight A Hon Roll; Dean's List, VA Tech, 1982-83; Rotary Clb Code of Ethics Awd, 1982; Most Outstg Debator, HS, 1982; 2nd Place Spkr Awd, St Debate Tournament, 1982; Most Conscientious and Dependable Jour Student; g/Stock Analyst; Deg in Fin and Ins.

HALL, TRICIA H oc/Student; b/Mar 8, 1961; h/17 Cathy Drive, Newport News, VA 23602; p/Tom and Margaret Hall, Newport News, VA; ed/Denbigh HS; BS, Christopher Newport Col, 1983; pa/Shop Supvr, Busch Gardens (Present); Aerobics Instr, City of Newport News, 1983; Pk Informationist, City of Newport News Pk, 1981-82;

Math Tutor, Jacksonville Univ, 1981; Supvr, Baskin Robbins, 1978-81; cp/ ACM Clb; hon/Alpha Chi Hon Soc, VA Zeta Chapt, Christopher Newport Col, 1981; Miss Congeniality, HS Pageant, 1978; Jr and Sr Hon Soc, HS, 1976-79; Outstg Yg Wom of Am; g/A Job in a Computer Related Field.

HALL, VIRGINIA LEIGH oc/Student; b/Sep 25, 1962; h/PO Box 741, Talladega, AL 35160; p/Mr and Mrs Robert D Hall, Talladega, AL; ed/ Talladega Acad, 1980; AS, Jefferson St Jr Col, 1982; Att'g, Auburn Univ, 1982-; cp/Jefferson St; Hd Jeffersonette; Diamond Doll Hostess for Baseball Team; Delta Zeta Social Sorority; Sorority Football, Basketball and Softball Teams; Auburn Ed Assn; Auburn Assn of Childhood Ed; Student Coun; Beta Clb Treas; Cheerldr, Hd; Ldr of Disco Eagles; Bus Staff; Girls' Basketball Team; Sch Newspaper; Vol Entertainer for Nsg Homes, Clbs; hon/Jefferson St Homecoming Alt; Miss Talladega Acad, Most Valuable Cheerldr, Basketball Player; W/W Among Am HS Students; W/W Among World Achievers; Personalities of S; Commun Ldrs of Am; g/ Doct Deg in Elem Ed; Tchr.

HALLIBURTON, DEANA RAE oc/ Student; b/Nov 21, 1964; h/Fulda, Germany; p/Tony Halliburton, Austin, TX; Patricia Jackson, Fulda, Germany; ed/HS Grad, 1983; pa/Nurses Aid, Meadowview Care Ctr, 1980; Cnslr, Dependent Yth Activs, 1981; Secy, Morale Support Fund, 1982; cp/Jr Class, 1981-82; Dorm Coun, 1981-82; Class Secy, 1978-79; Dorm Activity Dir, 1982-83; Band, 1977, 1978, 1979, 1980; Sr Class, 1982-83; Newspaper Staff, 1978-79; r/Ch of Christ; hon/Student Coun, 1978-79; Miss Friendliest, 1979; Basketball Mgr, 1983; g/Maj in Law; Become a Lwyr; Move into the Field of Govt.

HALSELL, LINDA LOU oc/Student; b/May 8, 1965; h/Route 1, Box 64, Rickman, TN 38580; p/Mrs Ilene Halsell, Rickman, TN; ed/HS Grad, 1983; cp/FHA; Chapt Pres; Beta Clb Pres; Sr Class Pres; 4-H Clb Pres; MYF VP; r/ Meth; TN Tech Univ Acad S'ship, 1983; Overton Co Ed Assn S'ship, 1983; W/ W Among Am HS Students; Soc of Dist'd HS Students; g/Maj in Home Ec Ed.

HALSEY, VICKY LYNN oc/Student; b/Mar 4, 1964; h/Route 1, Box 56, Max Meadows, VA 24360; p/Mr and Mrs William F Halsey, Max Meadows, VA; ed/Grad, Ft Chiswell HS, 1982; Currently Enrolled at Wytheville Commun Col; cp/FHA, 1978-79; Jr Beta Clb, 1979-80; Beta Clb, 1981-82; Sci Clb, 1979-81; Student Coun Assn, 1981; Annual Staff, 1979-82, Editor 1981; 4-H, 1977; Volleyball Team, 1979; r/ Bapt; hon/Perfect Attendance Awd, 1978, 1980-82; Pres Phy Fitness Awd, 1977; PE Awd, 1977; Cert of Hon, Hon Student, 1977; The Soc of Dist'd Am HS Students, 1980-82; W/W Among Am HS Students; Commun Ldrs of Am; Dir of Dist'd Ams; Intl Yth in Achmt.

HAM, DEBORAH TERESE oc/Student; b/Feb 3, 1964; h/Route #2, Box #159, Hickory, KY 42051; p/Mr and Mrs William H Ham, Hickory, KY; ed/Grad, Symsonia HS, 1982; Student, Murray St Univ; cp/FHA, Chapt Reporter, Parliamentarian, Reg I Secy; Ch Yth

F'ship, Secy-Treas; Springer Hall, Hall Coun Rep; r/Bapt; hon/Conservation Essay Winner, 1979; St Homemaker Deg, 1981; Chapt Homemaker Deg, 1980; Jr Homemaker Deg, 1979; Reg I FHA Del to KY St Foodarama Conf; W/ W; Soc of Dist'd Am HS Students; g/ Home Ec Voc Ed Maj; Murray St Univ.

HAMBLIN, JAMES ROE oc/Student; b/Mar 27, 1962; h/Route 1, Box 235, Covington, TN 38019; ed/Covington HS, 1980; Att'g, Univ of TN Martin; cp/HS FFA; Eagle Scout; Pres, Univ Agri Clb; Alpha Zeta Ofcr; Alpha Zeta Nat Hon Soc; Alpha Gamma Rho Agri Frat; Sch Student Govt, Asst VP; Univ of TN Martin Newspaper Staff; r/Cumberland Presb; Sunday Sch Supt; hon/Univ of TN Martin Gooch S'ship; God and Country Awd, BSA; g/Maj in Agri Sci; Career in Agri Sales.

HAMILTON, TERRIE LYNN oc/ Secretary, Receptionist; b/May 14, 1963; h/908 Center Street, Apartment E, Asheboro, NC 27203; ba/Asheboro, NC; p/Mrs Ann Patterson, Siler City, NC; ed/Grad, Jordan-Matthews HS, 1981; Assoc Deg of Applied Sci in Travel and Tourism, Asheboro Bus Col, 1983; pa/Secy, Receptionist, Asheboro Ophthal Assocs Inc, Drs Robert O Handley and Alan S Luria, 1981-; Cashier and Pharm Asst, Revco Drug, 1979-81; cp/ Beta Clb, 1978-81; Student Coun, Secy-Treas 1980-81; Spanish Clb, Pres 1981; Pep Clb; Girls' Monogram Clb; Hon Soc, Col; r/Meth; hon/Pres Awd, Assn of Indep Cols and Schs, 1983; Grad, cum laude, 1983; g/Career in Travel and Tourism.

HAMLIN, CHRISTOPHER MAURICE oc/Clergyman; b/Oct 9, 1959; h/ 954 Village Green Lane, 1006-1, Pontiac, MI 48054; ba/Pontiac, MI; m/ Elizabeth Ann Dixie; p/Herman and Doris Hamlin; ed/BA, Morehouse Col, 1981; MDiv, Colgate Rochester/Bexley Hall/Crozer Theol Sem, 1984; pa/ Curator, Howard Thurman Black Ch Student Resource Room, 1981-84; Asst Prot Chaplain, Univ of Rochester, 1982-84; Min of Yth and Ed, Trinity Bapt Ch, 1984-; Nat Bapt Conv USA Inc; Nat Conf of Black Seminarians; cp/ Macon-Mid GA Morehouse Alumni Clb; r/Christian; hon/Nat Dean's List; W/W Among Students in Am Cols and Univs; Outstg Yg Men of Am; Intl Yth in Am; Commun Ldrs of Am; g/PhD in Historical Theol, Liberation Theol; Teach on Col or Sem Level.

HAMMER, TRACEY LYNN oc/Student; b/Sep 13, 1965; h/Route 2, Box 410-T, Atoka, TN 38004; p/Mr and Mrs R P Hammer, Atoka, TN; ed/Grad, Munford HS, 1983; BBA, Austin Peay St Univ, 1987; r/Luth; hon/Nat Hon Soc, 1978-83; Valedictorian of HS Grad'g Class, 1983; Math, Eng and Home Ec Awds for Acad Performance Over 4-Yr HS Period; W/W Among Am HS Students; g/BBA w Maj in Acctg; CPA.

HAMMOND, JENNIFER L oc/Law Student; b/Nov 28, 1960; h/176 Fair Hill Drive, Elkton, MD 21921; p/Mr and Mrs Harry E Hammond, Elkton, MD; ed/ Elkton HS; BA, Wash Col; Student, Univ of Balto Sch of Law; pa/Bkkpr, Baker & Thomey, PA.

HAMMOND, RAYMOND PATTON oc/Student; b/Aug 31, 1964; h/ Route 5, Box 200, Troutville, VA 24175; p/Mr and Mrs A P Hammond III,

Troutville, VA; ed/Hon Grad, Lord Botetourt HS, 1982; Emer Med Sys Tng Prog: Shock Trauma Tech, Cardiac Tech; cp/Am Fdn Local 165 Big Band, 1979-82; Del to Jr Classical Leag Conv, 1981; Sci Mus; 4-H Clb; Leag of Am Wheelmen; Lighter than Air Soc; Profl Assn of Diving Instrs; Troutville Rescue Squad, Vol, Chaplain 1983, 2nd Lt 1984; Troutville Vol Fire Dept; Tri-Beta, Hon Biol Soc, 1982-84; Latin Clb, Treas 1982; Class Rep, 1978-82; Debate Team, 1978; Nat Forensic Leag; Jr Classical Leag, 1981-82; Sci Clb, 1978-82; Marching, Jazz, Concert and Pep (Capt 1979-82) Bands; r/Indep Bapt; hon/Hon Roll, 1978-82; Roanoke Col Hon Mention, 1983; Jr Scholar, Roanoke Col, 1981; Nat Hon Soc, 1981-82; Nat Latin Hon Soc, 1982; 1st Place, Sci Fair, 1978; 2nd Place, Bland Music Competition, 1978; US Band Awd, 1982; W/W Among Am HS Students; g/Biol Maj; Paramedic or Emer Med.

HAMMOND, TIMOTHY SCOTT oc/Student; b/May 26, 1963; h/381 Lynn Street, Kingsport, TN 37665; p/Shelby and Nellie Mae Hammond, Kingsport, TN; ed/Lynn View HS, Grad, Sullivan N HS; Current Student, Univ of TN; cp/NHS; Beta Clb; Jr Engrg and Tech Soc Treas; Octagon Clb VP; Sigma Beta Delta; Sch Photog; Teen Scene Photog; Track; hon/Yth Apprec Cit; Cand, Fgn Studies Prog; Sci Fair Hon Mention; Perfect Attendance Record; TN Scholars Prog; Optimist Clb S'ship; David Leonard Assocs S'ship; Hon Dipl; W/W Among Am HS Students; g/Profl Arch/ Illustrator/Designer.

HAMMONDS, CHIPPETTA MAURICE oc/Field Underwriter; b/Mar 6, 1955; h/200 Bentree Lane, #C-15, Florence, SC 29501; ba/Same; m/Doris W; p/Robert Hammonds Sr, Darlington, SC; Johnnie Mae Hammonds (dec); ed/ Dipl, Lamar High; BS, Sociol, Francis Marion Col, 1977; pa/Pers Asst, Sonoco Prods Co, 1979; Share Draft Mgr, Sonoco Prods Co, 1980; Field Underwriter, NY Life, 1982-; cp/U Way, 1979-83; Florence Co Yg Dems, Pres 1983; Francis Marion Col Alumni Assn, VP 1983; Alpha Phi Alpha Frat, Corresponding Secy 1983; SC Yg Dems Black Caucus, Chm 1981, 1982; NAACP, 1983; Bushua Foun, 1983; hon/Alpha Phi Alpha Chapt Man of the Yr; Alpha Phi Alpha Greene Awd, 1983; Outstg Yg Men of Am; Yg Commun Ldrs of Am; Personalities of S; W/W Among Students; g/Self-Employed Conslt.

HAMMONS, WENDELL LEWIS JR oc/Student; b/Jun 9, 1966; h/Route 1, Box 217, Flat Lick, KY 40935; p/Wendell Lewis Sr and Betty K Hammons, Flat Lick, KY; cp/Knox Clt HS Varsity Football; Nat Beta Clb; Spanish Clb; r/ Bapt; hon/DAR US Hist Awd, 1984; Hon Student, 1984; Social Studies Awd, 1984; g/Attend Univ of KY; Maj in Acctg; Law Sch.

HANDSHAW, AMANDA LaVERNE oc/Student; b/Nov 19, 1963; h/1305 Mariner Street, Franklin, VA 23851; p/ Mr and Mrs Jesse P Handshaw, Franklin, VA; ed/Grad, Franklin HS, 1982; Student, Hampton Inst; cp/Beta Clb, 1980-82; Yrbook Staff, 1980-82; Photo Clb, 1981-82; SCA, 1978-80; Pres Cabinet, 1979-80; Hon Soc, 1977-78; FHA, FBLA, 1978; Gospel Chorus,

Chaplain 1980-81, VP 1981-82; Secy of Sr Class, 1982; Sr Coun, 1982; Yg Adult Choir and Usherboard of House of Prayer, 1978-, Secy 1978-; J H Ensemble Chorus, 1980-; Nat Choir of AFCO-GLO, 1978-; Secy of Sunday Sch, 1978-; r/Pentecostal Holiness; hon/Hon Grad, 1982; Freshman Hon Student, Hampton Inst; Nat Merit S'ship Recommendations, 1981; VFW Voice of Dem Awd Cit, 1982; Hampton Inst S'ship Recip, 1982, 1983; g/Maj in Fine Arts w Emphasis and Deg in Photo and Fashion Design.

HANNAY, SCOTT PAUL oc/Missionary; b/Jan 23, 1957; h/Box 15665, West Palm Beach, FL 33406; ba/ Port-au-Prince, Haiti; p/Jack Hannay, Tullahoma, TN; ed/Grad, Union Sch, 1975; Att'd, Olivet Nazarene Col; pa/ Ser Mgr, Culkin's Marina, 1977-79; Mech Tng Dir for Voc Sch, Compassion Intl, 1979-81; Missionary, Dir of Devel, Dept World Mission Ch of the Nazarene, 1981-; cp/Diving Clb of Port-au-Prince, 1982; Circle K Clb, 1976; Student Ser Com, Student Govt; Yg Adult Ldr, Ch Grp Ldr, 1981-; r/ Ch of the Nazarene; hon/Outstg Yg Men of Am.

HANNES, ROSEMARY ANN oc/ Student; h/3071 Bellaire Lane, Oshkosh, WI 54901; p/Mr and Mrs Walter J Hannes, Oshkosh, WI; ed/High Hons Grad, Oshkosh N HS, 1979; Univ of WI Oshkosh, 1979-83; Marian Col, 1983; pa/Restaurant Mgr, Mike's Place Fam Restaurant, 1981-; Waitress, Mike's Place, 1977-81; cp/Bd of Dirs, Winnebago Co Zool Soc, 1979-; Key Clb, 1976-79, Secy 1977-78, Pres 1978-79; Nat Hon Soc, 1978-79; Circle K Intl, 1979-, Clb Pres 1980-81, Dist Secy-Treas 1981-82, Dist Gov 1982-83; 4-H, Mem for 10 Yrs; r/Cath; hon/ Optimist Yth of the Month, 1978; 4-H Key Awd, 1978; MW Reg Outstg 4-H Vet Sci Proj Winner, 1978; Gov's Cert of Recog for Outstg Achmt, 1979; W/ W Among Am HS Students, 1979; g/Career in Nsg, Surg Nsg.

HANSEN, BRENDA LEEAN oc/Student; b/Jul 14, 1963; h/2425 Johnston Drive, La Junta, CO 81050; p/Don and Barbara Hansen, Cheraw, CO; ed/ Cheraw HS, 1981; AS, Otero Jr Col, 1983; cp/Freshman Secy-Treas; Jr Secy-Treas; Sr VP; Sr Sweetheart Queen; r/Meth; hon/Hon Roll; Pres Hon List, 1981, 1982; Acad S'ship; Excell Student Awds in Psych, Earth Sci, Biol, Art; Dean's Hons List, 1983; Miss OJC, 1983; Pres's S'ship to CO St Univ; Grad, Otero Jr Col, magna cum laude; W/W Among Students in Am Jr Cols; Commun Ldrs of Am; g/Deg in Elect Engrg.

HANSEN, DIANNA LYNN oc/Student; b/Mar 30, 1965; h/1350 East Northern Avenue, Apartment 342, Phoenix, AZ 85020; p/Don Hansen, Holyoke, CO; Barbara Hansen, La Junta, CO; ed/Dipl, Cheraw HS, 1983; Currently Enrolled, DeVry Inst of Technol; cp/Volleyball; Basketball; Powder Puff Football; Girls' St Del; Student Body Secy-Treas; 4-H Pres; hon/Acad Hon Roll; Pins in Physics, Geometry, World Hist, Eng; $12,000 Full S'ship to DeVry Inst of Technol for Computer Sci, 1983; Valedictorian of HS Grad'g Class, 1983; W/W; Am's Outstg Names and Faces; g/Deg in Computer Sci or Genetic Engrg; Com-

puter Programmer in Bus Wkg Up to Sys Analyst.

HANSEN, MARY LOUISE oc/Student; b/Nov 6, 1961; h/1205 Carolina Avenue, Roanoke Rapids, NC 27870; p/ Mr and Mrs L P Bowen, Roanoke Rapids, NC; ed/Roanoke Rapids HS, 1980; AA, Halifax Commun Col, 1982; Att'g, E Carolina Univ; cp/FBLA, 1980; Student Govt Assn, Halifax Commun Col, 1982; r/Prot; Ch: Christians in Action, Taught 3, 4, and 5-Yr Olds (Jesus and Me Session); hon/Dean's List, Halifax Commun Col, Winter 1981 and 1982; Pres List, Halifax Commun Col, Sprg 1982; Hon Roll, E Carolina Univ, Fall 1982; Alpha Delta Kappa S'ship, Halifax Commun Col, Fall 1981; g/BS in Intermediate Ed.

HANZ, BRUCE KEITH oc/Student; b/Dec 29, 1962; h/1381 Rivercrest Drive, New Braunfels, TX 78130; p/ Alton and Virginia Hanz, New Braunfels, TX; ed/Canyon HS, 1981; pa/Ranch Hand, Udo Bruemmer, 1976-79; Butcher, Wuest's Supermkt, 1980-81; Ranch Hand, Arnold Moos, 1981; Ranch Hand, Udo Bruemmer, 1982-; cp/FFA; Comal Co Yg Farmers; r/Prot; hon/HS Nat Hon Soc, 1979; SW TX St Univ Dean's List, Fall 1983, Sprg 1984; g/Deg in Agri Ed w Cert to Teach.

HARDEN, BRENDA GALE oc/Student; b/Apr 4, 1964; h/Route 2, Box 63, Burkesville, KY 42717; p/Mr and Mrs Ray C Harden, Burkesville, KY; ed/ Student, Wn KY Univ, 1982-; Grad, Cumberland Co HS, 1982; pa/Nsg Asst, Clinton Co War Meml Hosp, 1983; cp/ KY Assn of Nsg Students, 1982-83; Beta Clb, Secy; r/Meth; Pianist, Bear Creek UMC; hon/Dean's List, 1982-83; Pres's List, 1982-83; Perfect GPA; S'ship from Wn KY Univ; Res, Chem Awd; W/W; g/BSN; Wk as RN at Clinton Co War Meml Hosp.

HARDGE, TAMMY OLIVIA oc/ Student; b/Jul 19, 1964; h/3951 Grimes Road, Irving, TX 75061; p/Imogene Rogers, Irving, TX; ed/Thomas Jefferson HS, 1982; Student, Univ of TX Austin, 1982-; pa/Paralegal, Palmer, Palmer & Coffee; cp/Black Student Assn, 1982; Mentor Prog, Univ of TX; Minority Student Ser Ofc in Conjunction w Univ of TX Profs, 1983; Assn of Legal Students; Law Explorers; Student Govt; Humanities Clb; Dallas Yth Adv Coun; Govt and Law HS Intern; Polit Campaign Wkr; Pres Elect Wkr; hon/NHS; Best Spkr, 1st Round of Govt Law Mock Trial Competition; Bronze Good Citizenship Awd; SAR; W/ W Among Dist'd HS Students; g/Acctg/ Pre-Law Maj.

HARDY, STEPHANI LAYNE oc/ Actress, Singer; b/Jun 13, 1957; h/18912 Santa Mariana, Fountain Valley, CA 92708; p/Mr and Mrs Vernon E Hardy, Fountain Valley, CA; ed/Fountain Val HS, 1975; BFA, Baylor Univ, 1979; cp/ Lead Singer/Dancer/Tnr, Baxter's St Dinner Cabaret; Leading Actress, So CA Conservatory Theatre, Curtain Call Dinner Theatre, Bigfork Sum Playhouse; cp/Cheerldr; Homecoming Princess; Class Favorite; Omega Delta Kappa; Alpha Lambda Delta; Gamma Beta Phi; Campaign Wkr; r/Trinity Bapt Ch Soloist; hon/Bk of Am Achmt Awd; Toured Japan as Singer; g/Musicals.

HARGIS, CLAYTA JOYCE oc/Student; b/Jun 2, 1962; h/Box 213, Palmer,

TN 37365; p/Clayton D and Margaret J Hargis, Palmer, TN; ed/Grundy Co HS, 1980; Student, MTSU; cp/Basketball, 1976-77; Basketball Mgr, 1978; OES, Tracy City Chapt 266; r/Prot; hon/ Grad'd in Top 20, HS; Pep Clb; Glee Clb; Lib Clb; FHA; Nat Dean's List.

HARGIS, KATHY LEE ODA oc/ Student; b/Dec 28, 1966; h/Box 213, Palmer, TN 37365; p/Clayton D and Margaret J Hargis, Palmer, TN; ed/HS Student; cp/Basketball, 1979-80; Most Valuable Player, 1980; Basketball Mgr, 1981-82; Beta Clb; Pep Clb; FHA; Cheerldr, 1975-79; r/Bapt; hon/Most Adv'd Music Awd, Piano, 1980; Perfect Attendance Awd, 2 Yrs; Nat Hon Soc, 1981-; Most Outstg Cheerldr, 1977; Music Awd, Most Talented, 1981.

HARMAN, MARK EVAN oc/Student; b/Apr 12, 1965; h/PO Box 366, Collbran, CO 81624; p/Mr and Mrs Emery E Harman, Collbran, CO; ed/ Grad, Plateau Val HS, 1983; Currently Enrolled, Brigham Yg Univ; cp/Student Coun VP, 1981-82; Sr Class Pres, 1982-83; Lettered in Band, 1980, 1981, 1982, 1983; Lettered in Varsity Basketball, 1982-83; Coun Mem, Co 4-H; Many Ldrship Positions in Boy Scouts; Staff Mem, Nat Staff at Nat Boy Scouts Jamboree, 1981; r/LDS; hon/BSA: Eagle Scout 1978, Palms to Eagle Scout, "On My Hon" Awd 1978, "Duty to God" Awd, 1980; W/W Among Am HS Students; Intl Yth in Achmt; Yg Commun Ldrs of Am; g/Intl Lwyr.

HARMAN, MICAH ALEXANDER oc/Student; b/Feb 18, 1967; h/5771 Highway 330, Box 366, Collbran, CO 81624; p/Emery and Bonnie Harman, Collbran, CO; ed/Student, Plateau Val HS; cp/Football, 2 Yrs; Basketball, 2 Yrs; Band, 3 Yrs (Letter 3 Yrs); Track, Varsity Letter; r/LDS; hon/BSA: Eagle Scout, 8 Palms, "On My Honor," "Duty to God"; Intl Yth in Achmt; g/Attend Brigham Yg Univ; Pre-Med; MD.

HARPER, MICHELLE EARLENE oc/ Student, Swimming Instructor, Lifeguard, Theatre Employee; b/Aug 8, 1965; h/523 Paul Street, Harrisonburg, VA 22801; p/Rhonda S and James R Harper, Harrisonburg, VA; ed/Grad, Harrisonburg HS, 1983; Att'g, Bridgewater Col; pa/Theatre Employee, Roth 1-2-3 Theatres, 1982-; Food Ser Catering, James Madison Univ, 1982-83; Lifeguard/Swimming Instr, Bridgewater Col, 1983-; cp/Yth Adv Coun Pres, Harrisonburg Rec Dept, 1982-83, Mem 1981-83; Nat Hon Soc, 1982-83; Talented and Gifted Students Org, 1981-83; F'ship Christian Aths, 1979-81; Harrisonburg HS Girls' Softball Team, 1979-83; Harrisonburg HS Girls' Basketball Team, 1979-82; r/ Meth; hon/Nat Hon Soc, 1982-83; First Recip, Jack Wages S'ship, Bridgewater Rotary Clb, 1983; Second Team All-Dist Softball Team, 1982, 1983 (Indiv Hon); Co-Capt, Girls' Softball Team, 1983; VA St AA Girls' Basketball Championship Runner-Up, 1981 (Team Hon); g/ Hlth and PE Tchr; Wk w the Handicapped.

HARPER, QUITA FISHER oc/Recent Graduate; b/Oct 18, 1960; h/1701 West Boulevard, #L-3, Charlotte, NC 28208; m/Gilbert Sr; c/Gilbert Jr; p/Elder and Mrs Kilmer P Fisher Sr; ed/Dipl, Pamlico Co HS, 1979; BA, Johnson C Smith Univ, 1983; cp/Alpha Kappa Mu,

1981-83; Alpha Chi, 1981-83, Treas; Beta Kappa Chi, 1983; Hons Prog, 1979-83; YWCA, 1979-80, Secy; Student Christian Assn, 1979-83, Miss SCA, VP; Liston Hall Coun, 1979-80, Pres; R W Johnson Spiritual Choir, 1979-83, Secy; r/Christianity; Luard S'ship Semi-Finalist, 1980-81; Bruce Bernard Joe Humanitarian Awd, 1983; Leroy E Sargeant Psych Awd, 1983; Bd of Trustees S'ship, 1983; Highest Acad Average, 1979-83; Fgn Lang Awds, French, Spanish, 1979-81, 1982-83; Nat Dean's List; Nat Register of Outstg Col Grads; W/W Among Students in Am Cols and Univs; g/After Furthering My Ed in the Discipline of Psych, w a Concentration in Cnslg, I Intend to Seek Employmt in the Area Abetting Chd and Adults.

HARPER, SUSAN ANNETTE oc/ Student; b/Aug 19, 1965; h/Route 1, Box 51, Dayton, VA 22821; p/Mr and Mrs Norman Harper, Dayton, VA; ed/ Student, Deaf Div, VA Sch for the Deaf and Blind; cp/SCA, 1982-83; Cardinal Letter Clb, 1982-83; r/Brethern; cp/ Homecoming Queen, 1983; g/Col; Computer Sci.

HARRELL, MARY VONDA oc/Student; b/Oct 13, 1963; h/1908 Cheltenham Lane, Columbia, SC 29206; ba/ Columbia, SC; p/John and Mary Harrell, Columbia, SC; ed/Grad, Sprg Val HS, 1981; Currently Att'g, Univ of SC; pa/ Adm Asst, Cambridge Plan Cnslrs Ofcs of Columbia; cp/Gamma Beta Phi, 1983, 1984; USC Marching Band, 1982-84; One Voice Choir Mem, 1983, 1984; Ch Basketball Team, 1982; r/First Bapt Ch of Columbia, 1982-84; hon/HS Hons, 1978-81; VP of Nat Hon Soc; Pres, Logos Bible Study; Featured Percussionist in Marching Band; Most Talented in Sr Class; Most Talented of Miss SV Pageant; Selected Outstg Sr; Jr Marshall; Girls' St Nom; Sr House Rep; Hon Roll; Converse Col Lrdship Awd; S'ship Winner for Trip to Europe; Num Piano Awds, Nat Fdn of Music Clbs; Col: Student Marshall, Chosen for May Ct, Rep on Jud Com, Dean's Hon List, Percussionist in Columbia Col Wind Ensemble, Gamma Beta Phi Hon Soc, Selected as Mem of USC Marching Band, Dean's List, Finalist and Miss Congeniality in Miss Columbia Pageant, Most Sportsmanship on Ch Basketball Leag; g/BA in Jour/News Edit w Emphasis in Mgmt; Deg from Univ of SC's Law Sch.

HARRELL, VICKI RENE oc/Student; b/Feb 22, 1962; h/1908 Cheltenham Lane, Columbia, SC 29206; p/Ret Lt Col John and Mary Harrell; ed/Sprg Val HS, 1980; Voc Secretarial Tng Grad, 1980; Student, Univ of SC; cp/Edit Cartoonist, Newspaper for Univ of SC, 1982; Marching Band, Col, 1982-83; Jerry's Angel for Promotional Commls and Telethon, Muscular Dystrophy Telethon; Outstg Achmt in Art Awd; Vol, Heart Fund; Vol Wkr w Handicapped; F'ship Christian Aths; Model, Benefit Show for Handicapped Citizens; Vol Debater, Annual Brit Union Debates, Univ of SC; Radio Vol, War on Cancer; March of Dimes Telethon; Piano Entertainer, Columbia Christmas Parade; Treas, NHS; Pres, Art Coun; r/Singles Choir, Bapt Ch; hon/1st Runner-Up, Miss SC Pageant, 1983; S'ship Talent Awd Winner, Miss SC Pageant, 1983;

Univ of SC Homecoming Queen, 1983; Miss Columbia, 1983; Soc of Dist'd Am HS Students; g/Wk as an Advtg Exec and Eventually Own My Own Advtg Co.

HARRILL, MARIA SUSANNE oc/ Student; b/Sep 24, 1963; h/1301 Morningside Drive, Maryville, TN 37801; p/ Mr and Mrs Walter Harrill, Maryville, TN; ed/Grad, Maryville HS, 1981; Student, Univ of TN Knoxville, 1981-; pa/Employee, Gateway Bookstore; Lab Asst, Dept of Anthropology; cp/Phi Eta Sigma Hon Soc, 1982; Alpha Epsilon Delta, Pre-Med Hon Soc, 1983; Gamma Beta Phi Hon Soc, 1983; Anthropology Dept Rep to Dean's Student Adv Coun; Liberal Arts Standing Coms, Hons, Individualized Progs; MENSA; Marching, Pep, Concert Bands; Col Wind Ensemble; New Providence Choir; NHS Secy; Beta Epsilon Pres; Mu Alpha Theta; Co-Editor, Annual; AFS; Top 10 Percent; Hon Roll; All-USA Marching Band; UT Hon Band; E TN All-St Band; Asst Dir, Jr Class Play; hon/Fredrick Bonham S'ship; Col Scholars Prog; Andrew D Holt Alumni S'ship; John Philip Sousa Awd; Intl Yth in Achmt; W/W Among Am HS Students; Yg Commun Ldrs of Am; g/Career in Cranio-Facial Surg.

HARRILL, STEVEN KENT oc/Student; b/Jun 3, 1964; h/763 Lowery Street, Shelby, NC 28150; p/Mrs Martha A Harrill, Shelby, NC; ed/Shelby HS, 1982; Currently Enrolled, NC St Univ; cp/HS: Tennis, French Clb (VP), NHS, Hi-Q Bowl; Col: NC Fellows, Student Senate, Col Bowl Chm, Intramural Awd, Univ Choir (Accompanist), Coun of Humanities and Social Scis; r/ Meth; hon/HS: Belk S'ship (Presb Col), Nat Competitive Exam S'ship (Univ of Dallas), Pres Classroom; W/W Among Am HS Students; Yg Commun Ldrs of Am; g/Deg in Tech Writing and Editing; Jour Sch.

HARRINGTON, SCOTT LOWERY oc/Student; b/Dec 24, 1961; h/114 Laurel Hill Drive, Natchez, MS 39120; p/Mr and Mrs James A Marlow Jr, Natchez, MS; ed/S Natchez-Adams HS, 1979; BA in Jour, LA St Univ, 1983; pa/ Student Reporter, LSU *Daily Reveille*, 1983; Asst to Supvr, LSU Ath Dept, 1983; cp/Acacia Frat; HS Key Clb, Secy-Treas 1978-79; Nat Hon Soc; Hon Col, HS Hon Roll; r/Bapt; hon/Charles Edison Yth Fund S'ship Winner from LSU to Am Polit Jour Conf in Wash, DC, 1983; Most Outstg HS Sports Writer in MS, MS Sports Writers Assn, 1979; Served as Spkr Pro-Tem, Ho of Reps, MS Yth Govt Affairs, 1979.

HARRIS, DAVID BOND oc/Student; b/Jul 2, 1961; h/Route 10, 101 Greenbrier Drive, Richmond, KY 40475; p/ Bond and Barbara Harris, Richmond, KY; ed/BMus, Vocal Perf, En KY Univ, 1983; Grad Acceptance, Juilliard Sch of Music, Manhattan Sch of Music, NWn Univ; pa/Cinc Opera Co, 1980-82; Frequent Soloist in Local Ch Sers and Weddings, 1978-83; Pvt Voice Tchr, 1982-83; cp/Italian Clb, 1981-83; Progress Staff Writer, 1983; hon/Lexington Singers F'ship Awd, 1982; Nat Assn of Tchrs of Singing Contest Winner, 1979-82; Lima Vocal Competitions, 1982; Delta Omicron Music S'ship, EKU, 1982; Jane Campbell and Irene Muir Music Dept S'ships for EKU,

1979-82; Other Hons; Nat Col Dean's List.

HARRIS, ELIZABETH ANNE oc/ Student; b/Apr 20, 1963; h/Route 6, Box 459, Dickson, TN 37055; ba/Gallatin, TN; p/Mr and Mrs Russell E Harris, Dickson, TN; ed/Dipl, Dickson Co HS, 1981; pa/Secy, Dickson Co Ins Agy, 1979; Receptionist, Fireman's Fund Ins Agy, 1980; Personal Secy, Bi-Rite Janitoral Supplies, 1982-83; cp/Dickson Co Girls' Basketball Team, 1977-80; Beta Clb, 1980-81; Sci Clb, 1980; TN Tomorrow, 1981; Lit Clb, 1979; FCA, 1979-80; Hist Clb, 1979-81; r/Bapt; hon/ Grad'd 7th in Class of 436, 1981; Selected to Attend Pres Classroom in Wash, DC, 1981; Am Hist Awd, 1980; W/W Am Jr Cols; g/Maj in Ofc Occups; Career as an Exec Secy.

HARRIS, JANA LYNN oc/Student; b/ Nov 11, 1964; h/PO Box 892, Ozona, TX 76943; p/Charles W and Nancy N Harris, Ozona, TX; ed/Dipl, Ozona HS, 1982; Student, Wn TX Col; pa/Adm Asst, Holman Kennedy and Assocs, 1981; Sales Clk, Ozona Boot and Saddlery, 1981; Announcer, KRCT Radio; cp/Jour Press Clb, 1982-83; Phi Theta Kappa, 1983, Co-Histn 1983-84; r/Prot; hon/Assoc Editor, *The Western Texan*, 1982-83; Pres's List; Finalist for Outstg Female Student, 1983; Outstg Acad Student in Mass Communs and Jour, 1983; 2nd Place, News Feature, Rocky Mtn Collegiate Press Assn; Hon Mention, News Feature, TX Intercollegiate Press Assn; g/To Continue Ed at WTC and Then Gain a Deg in Mass Communs at a 4-Yr Col.

HARRIS, JOAN MARIE oc/Student; b/Apr 1, 1962; h/Route 2, Box 926, Thomasville, NC 27360; ba/Lexington NC; p/Mr and Mrs R G Harris, Thomasville, NC; ed/Grad, Ctl Davidson Sr HS, 1980; AA, Davidson Co Commun Col, 1982; Student of Bus Mgmt, Univ of NC Wilmington; cp/Past Jr Civinettes; HS Spanish Clb Treas; Vol Wkr for Spec Olympics for Retarded Chd; hon/Mem, Phi Theta Kappa; W/ W Among Am HS Students; Personalities of S; g/Maj in Bus Mgmt; MBA.

HARRIS, LEE ELLEN oc/Student; b/ Dec 5, 1965; h/608 Pine Lane, Bowling Green, KY 42101; p/Freeland Jr and Patricia B Harris, Bowling Green, KY; ed/Bowling Green HS, 1984; cp/Jr Class Pres, 1982-83; Nat Hon Soc, 1982-84; Beta Clb, 1981-82; r/First Bapt Ch Yth Choir Libn, 1981-82; hon/KY Yth Merit Awd, 1983; KY Govs Scholar, 1983; Nat Merit Letter, PSAT-NMSQT Achmt, 1982; W/W Among Am HS Students, 1983; g/To Study at Vanderbilt Univ; Grad Sch in the Field of Chem Engrg.

HARRIS, RAYMOND DOUGLAS JR oc/Operations Research Analyst; b/ Nov 6, 1959; h/9136 Pepperdine, Midwest City, OK 73110; ba/Tinker AFB, OK; m/Edie R; p/Mr and Mrs Raymond D Harris Sr, Montgomery, AL; ed/ Kubasaki HS, Okinawa, Japan, 1977; BS, Math, AL St Univ, 1982; mil/USAF; 1982-; pa/Sci Res Analyst, USAF, 1982-; TAFB Co Grade Ofcrs Coun, 1982-84; 552 AWACD Spkr's Bur, 1982-84; cp/ Black Am Heritage Coun, 1983-84; r/ Bapt; hon/Grad, summa cum laude, 1982; AFROTC Dist'd Mil Grad, 1982; W Randolph Lovelace Meml Awd, 1982; Co Grade Ofcr of the Quarter Nom, 1983; W/W in Am Cols and Univs; Nat

Dean's List; Yg Ldrs of Am; g/Grad Deg in Opers Res and in Bus Adm.

HARRIS, SHARON FELICIA oc/Student; b/Feb 2, 1966; h/802 East Baker Street, Tarboro, NC 27886; p/Mr James Harris, Philadelphia, PA; ed/Grad, Tarboro HS, 1984; cp/NAACP, Secy; Jr Engrs Technol Soc; Pep Clb; Student Govt; r/Bapt; hon/S'ship, Com of Ed, to Attend Sum Camps during Sums of 1982, 1983; Acad Hon Roll, 1982-83; W/W Among Am HS Srs; g/To Attend NC St Univ and Maj in Engrg.

HARRIS, SHEILA A oc/Student; b/Aug 12, 1962; h/1213 Norfolk, VA 23405; p/David E III and Jacqueline L Harris, Glendale, AZ; ed/Ctl Sr HS, 1980; Old Dominion Univ; cp/Nat Urban Leag, 1982-83; VP, F'ship of Minority Engrs and Scists; Cross-Country; Indoor and Outdoor Track; AFJROTC; NHS; SHS; Salutatorian; St Champ, 1,000 Yard Run; Female Ath of the Yr; Outstg Sr; Danforth's "I Dare You" Awd; Students for the Devel of Black Culture; ASME; NSBE; BSU; Fdr, Harambe; hon/S'ship, NACME; Intl Yth in Achmt; W/W Among Am HS Students; g/BS, Mech Engrg; Aeronautical Res.

HARRIS, SHEILA LaNAY oc/Student; b/May 10, 1962; h/3425 North Audubon Road, Indianapolis, IN 46218; p/Mr and Mrs Herbert L E Harris, Indianapolis, IN; ed/Dipl, Arlington HS, 1980; Att'd, Andrews Univ, 1980-82; Att'g, IN Univ Sch of Music, 1982-; pa/Second Violin, Twin Cities Symph Orch, 1980-82; cp/Andrews Univ Symph Orch and String Ensemble, 1980-82; IN Univ Symphs, Sums 1981-82, 1982-; Lilly Endowment Ldrship Prog, 1979-80; Perf in Violin, Chds Mus Lilly Theater, Indpls Chd Mus, 1980; Active, Ch Wk; French, Sci, Thespians Clbs, 1977-79; Gtr Indpls Yth Symph, 1975-80; IN All-St Hons Orch, 1978-79; Human Relats Com Chm, 1976-80; IN Univ Symph Orch; Mu Phi Epsilon, Chorister 1983-; Passed Upper Divisional Exam in Violin Perf, 1983; Pi Lambda Theta Nat Hons and Profl Assn in Ed, 1982, 1983-; r/SDA; hon/Initiated into Mu Phi Epsilon, 1984; Nat Hon Soc; Hon HS Grad, 1980; St of IN House Page, 1977; Mohlon and Irene Hamel Music S'ship Endowment Fund to Andrews Univ, Matched by Twin Cities Symph, 1980-82; Hon Maj Awd "A" Average in Music, 1980; Concert Orch Awd, 1980; IN Assn Solo Contest, Reg and St, 1977-80; IN St Ensemble; Concert Orch and Choir String Ensemble; String Quartet and Girls' Chorus Contest (St), 1977-80; Tour Ensemble of Andrews Univ, Soloist (Rep of Andrews Univ); W/W Among Am HS Students; Intl Yth in Achmt; Commun Ldrs of Am; Dir of Dist'd Ams; Sr Editor, Yrbook, 1980; Feature Editor, Sch Paper, 1980; Cert in Jour; g/Col Prof; Concert Violinist for Maj Symph Orch; Mem of Maj Symph Orch; BME and Violin Perf Music Degs; Master's Deg; Doct Deg; Study Violin in Europe and Perform.

HARRIS, SHIRLEY D oc/Certified Public Accountant; b/Feb 2, 1959; h/Route 3, Box 920, Jay, FL 32565; p/Mr and Mrs Fletcher R Harris, Jay, FL; ed/Jay HS, 1977; AA, Pensacola Jr Col, 1979; BA, Univ of W FL, 1980; pa/Staff

Acct; Am Inst of CPAs; FL Inst of CPAs; Phi Kappa Phi; Phi Theta Kappa; Fin and Acctg Clb; cp/Circle K; r/Ch Pianist; hon/Elijah Watts Sells Silver Medal; FL High Grade Awd for CPA Exam; Dean's List; Pensacola Jr Col Fac S'ship Awd; PJC Intro to Bus Awd; Intl Yth in Achmt; Commun Ldrs of Am.

HARRIS, TAMMY JANE oc/Student; h/Route 1, Box 1, Littleton, NC 27850; p/Mr and Mrs Lindsay H Harris, Littleton, NC; ed/Grad, Halifax Acad, 1983; Enrolled, Atl Christian Col; cp/Varsity Girls' Basketball and Softball; Student Govt Assn, Treas; Class Treas; Voyager Staff, Bus Mgr; Anchor Clb, VP, Pres; r/Bapt; hon/Best All Around Girl, 1983; MVP, Varsity Girls' Basketball and Softball, 1981-82, 1982-83; All-Conf Varsity Girls' Basketball and Softball, 1981-82, 1982-83; W/W; Dist'd Am HS Students; g/Maj in Phy Therapy.

HARRISON, FREDERICK WILLARD JR oc/Student; b/Jan 5, 1964; h/600 South Haughton, Williamston, NC 27892; p/Mr and Mrs Frederick W Harrison Sr, Williamston, NC; ed/Grad, Williamston HS, 1982; Att'g, Campbell Univ; cp/Key Clb, 1978-82; French Clb, 1979-81; WHS Band: Concert 1978-82, Marching Competition 1979-81, Dance Band 1980-81, Wind Ensemble 1981-82; WHS Beta Clb, 1981-82; Wildlife Clb, 1981-82; WHS Yrbook Rep and Orgs Editor, 1981-82; UMYF, 1978-82, Pres 1981-82; Martin Commun Band, 1982; Campbell Univ Circle K; CU Social Sci Clb; CU Col Repubs; r/U Meth; hon/WHS Beta Clb S'ship, 1982; Sandy Menager Awd, 1982; Scott-Ellis S'ship, Campbell Univ, 1982; Williamston Lioness Clb S'ship, 1982; g/BA in Hist; Law or Grad Sch; Career as Atty, Hist Rschr or Tchr.

HARRISON, REGINA INGRID oc/Student; b/Oct 10, 1966; h/6465 Rabun Road, Morrow, GA 30260; p/Glenn and Inge Harrison, Morrow, GA; ed/HS Grad; Student, GA Inst of Technol, 1984-; pa/Ballet and Tap Tchr, Hutcheson Dance Acad, 1982-83; Fast Food Wkr, Chick-Fil-A, 1983-84; cp/F'ship of Christian Aths; Key Clb; Jr Beta Clb; Nat Hon Soc; Student Govt Rep; Chapel Choir; Flag Corps/Drill Team; Band; Chorus; r/Bapt; hon/A and AB Hon Rolls, 1978-84; 2nd Place, GA St Sci and Engrg Fair, 1982; GA Cert of Merit (Top 5% of Class), 1983; Homecoming Ct, 1982, 1983; US Nat Ldrship Merit Awd; W/W Among Am HS Students; W/W Among Christian HS Students; g/To Receive a Deg in Computer Engrg from GA Inst of Technol.

HARRISON, ROBERT DAVID (SKIP) oc/Data Processor Programmer and Operator; b/Apr 30, 1963; h/303 Highway 1417 South, #N-12, Sherman, TX 75090; ba/Sherman, TX; p/Mr and Mrs Dean Harrison, Greenville, TX; Mr and Mrs Morris Capps, Greenville, TX; ed/Grad, Greenville HS, 1981; Grad w Distn, TX Inst, 1983; Student, Grayson Co Col, 1984-; pa/Programmer/Operator, Redrill Inc, 1983-; cp/Gymnastics; Flippers Gym Team, Garland, TX; Spinners Gym Team, Greenville, TX; hon/Freshman Class Treas; Hon Roll; Student Coun; Sports Editor, Sch Newspaper; W/W Am HS Students; Intl Yth in Achmt; Dir of Dist'd Ams; g/To Maj in Acctg and Become a CPA.

HARRISON, RUTH ANNE oc/Stu-

dent; b/Nov 7, 1963; h/414 Forrest Hill, Grand Prairie, TX 75051; p/Charles and Diana Harrison, Grand Prairie, TX; ed/Grad, S Grand Prairie HS, 1982; Student, E TX St Univ; pa/Montgomery Ward's Wendy Ward Model, 1976-79; Lifeguard, Grand Prairie Pks and Rec, 1980, 1981, 1982; Cook, Butch's Barn, 1983; Waitress, Ken's Pizza, 1983-; cp/Wendy Ward Model, 1976-79; Red Cross Swimming Instr, 1976-; Ft Worth Mayors Outstg Yth of Am Awd, 1979-80; FTA Parliamentarian, 1978-79; Drill Team, 1979-80; Hon Band, 1979-82 (Percussion Bassoon); Flag Corps, 1980-82; Newspaper Staff, 1980-81, Features Editor 1981-82; Lit Mag Staff, 1981-82; Tau Beta Sigma Band Sorority, Initiated 1982; E TX St: Flag Corps 1982-83, Dance Line 1983-84, Orch Bassoon 1982, Woodwind Choir Bassoon 1982; r/Meth; hon/Ft Worth Mayor's Outstg Yth of Am, 1979-80; Superior Medal, E TX St Sum Camp, 1980, 1981; Best Aux Corps, HEB Marching Contest, 1980; UT Arlington Newspaper Sem, 3rd Place in Headline Writing, 1982; Outstg Attendance Awd, 1980-82; Music S'ship to E TX St (Bassoon), 1982; g/Mktg Deg w Emphasis on Fashion Msdg; Own Store.

HARRISON, STACEY ANDORA oc/Student; b/May 5, 1965; h/Route 15, Highway 14, Greenville, SC 29607; p/Mr and Mrs Wesley V Harrison, Greenville, SC; ed/Mauldin HS, 1982; Student, Gardner-Webb Col; cp/Nat Hon Soc; VP, Future Bus Ldrs of Am; Mauldin HS Chapt; Varsity Cheerldr, MHS; Vol, Greenville Bapt Assn; r/So Bapt; Sunday Sch Tchr; Assoc Dir, Sr Adult Ch Grp; hon/Mauldin HS Hon Grad, 1982; Miss SC U Teenager, 1983; Sr Superlative, Best Personality, 1982; W/W Among Am HS Students; Commun Ldrs of Am; g/To Study Radio/TV Broadcasting; To Have TV Talk Show.

HARRY, CYNTHIA RANDALL oc/Student; b/Aug 30, 1959; h/6650 Shady Brook Lane, #4223, Dallas, TX 75206; m/Dwight Vincent; p/Rev and Mrs Lamar Randall, Pensacola, FL; ed/Dipl, Escambia HS, 1977; BS, Mech Engrg, So Univ, 1981; Currently Enrolled, OH St Univ; pa/Sum Engr, Procter & Gamble, 1981; Sum Co-op, Union Carbide, 1980; Sum Intern, Procter & Gamble, 1979; cp/Am Soc of Mech Engrs, 1978-81; Soc of Wom Engrs, 1979-81, Secy 1979-80, VP 1980-81; Student Govt Assn, Senator 1979-80; Pi Tau Sigma Hon Frat, 1979-81, Pres 1980-81; Alpha Chi Nat Hon Soc, 1980-81; Alpha Kappa Mu Nat Hon Soc, 1980-81, Secy 1980-81; Alpha Kappa Alpha Sorority Inc, 1978-; Epistoleus-Tamiouchos, 1979-81; r/Bapt; hon/Grad and Profl Opports F'ship, 1981-; Engrg S'ship, 1977-81; Grad, cum laude, 1981; Alpha Kappa Alpha Sorority S'ship, 1977; Dean's List, 1978-81; W/W Among Am HS Students; g/MS in Mech Engrg.

HART, BILL J JR oc/Law Student; b/Mar 15, 1961; h/4417 Montecello, Enid, OK 73701; p/Mr and Mrs B J Hart Sr, Enid, OK; ed/Enid HS; BA, Univ of OK; Currently Enrolled, Univ of OK Law Sch; pa/Asst to the Chief Economist, US Ho of Reps Budget Com, 1981; Asst to Senator Don Nickles, 1982; Res Asst, Carl Albert Ctr for Congl Studies, 1982-83; Economist, Univ of OK Ctr for

Ec Res; cp/Phi Beta Kappa; Omicron Delta Epsilon; Am Bar Assn, Law Student Div; Am Polit Sci Assn; Am Enterprize Inst; Am Ec Assn, Conf on the Atl Commun; hon/Top 10 SRS, 1983; Big Man on Campus, 1982; 6 Times on Pres Hon Roll; Ewing F'ship, 1981; Bass S'ship, 1982; VP of Student Body, 1980-81; Pres, First Yr Law Class, 1983; g/JD; LLM; Intl Law; Constitutional Law.

HART, BRIAN JACK oc/Student; b/ Jun 23, 1960; h/8100 Morley, El Paso, TX 79925; ba/Bloomington, IN; p/Mr and Mrs John F Hart, El Paso, TX; ed/ Dipl, W H Burges HS, 1978; BMus, En NM Univ, 1982; Wkg on MMus, Musicology, IN Univ; pa/Tchg Asst 1984-, Res Asst 1982-84, IN Univ Sch of Music; cp/Phi Kappa Phi; Blue Key; Mem and Deacon, Univ Bapt Ch; Mem and Past Bible Study Ldr, IN Univ Bapt Student Union; hon/Elizabeth Corwin Music S'ship; Consecutive S'ships for Semester for Perfect GPA; Read Paper, 9th Conf of Soc for Baltic Studies in Montreal, 1984; Read Papers, IN Univ Musicology Colloquium, 1984; Dean's List; W/W; Intl Yth in Achmt; g/To Obtain Master's and Doct Degs in Music Hist; To Teach Music Hist in a Univ.

HART, CLIFFORD AWTREY JR oc/ Student; b/Aug 11, 1959; h/189 West Queens Road, Williamsburg, VA 23185; p/Clifford A Sr and Janet E S Hart, Williamsburg, VA; ed/MA in Fgn Affairs, Univ of VA, 1983; BA in Intl Affairs and Russian Studies, Mary Wash Col, 1980; pa/Instr in Soviet Govt, Sweet Briar Col, 1983; UVA Darden Intern, US Dept of St, Ofc of Soviet Union Affairs, 1982; Grad Tchg Asst, Univ of VA, 1981-82; Staff Asst for Fgn Affairs and Def Policy, Ofc of US Senator Joseph R Biden Jr, 1980; cp/ UVA Govt Dept Grad Students Assn, Pres 1982-83, Secy 1981-82; Mary Wash Col Intl Relats Clb, Pres 1979-80; Com on Disarmament, Nat HS Model UN, Dir 1979; Student Govt, Senator 1977-78; r/Prot; hon/Phi Beta Kappa, 1980-; Pres's Fellow in Govt, Univ of VA, 1980-83; UVA Colgate W Darden Intern, Dept of St, 1982; Mortar Bd, 1979-80; Dean's List, 1976-80; W/W Among Students; Nat Register of Outstg Students; g/US Govt Ser in the Fgn Relats Field.

HART, GARY LEE oc/United States Air Force Pilot; b/Apr 22, 1959; h/12 Old Farm Road, Marietta, GA 30067; p/Mr and Mrs Roy J Hart Jr, Marietta, GA; ed/Grad, Joseph Wheeler High, 1977; Att'g, Marion Mil Inst, 1977-78; BS, Mil Hist, USAF Acad, 1982; mil/USAF, 1978-; pa/USAF Pilot, 1983-; cp/AFJ-ROTC Squadron Cmdr; BSA, 1973-77; Pres, Prot Coun; Prot Choir; Pres, Bowling Leag; Repub Nat Com, 1980-; hon/Eagle Scout, 1975; Nat Hon Soc, 1976; Phi Theta Kappa, 1978; Supt's List, 1980-82; John C Fey Awd, 1982; Outstg Grad in Mil Hist, 1982; Grad w Mil Hons, 1982; Intl Yth in Achmt; g/Career as AF Ofcr; Master's Deg in Hist.

HART, TAMMY DARLENE oc/Purchasing Director; b/Feb 17, 1959; h/ Route 2, Campobello, SC 29322; ba/ Greenville, SC; p/Mr and Mrs Anthony G Hart, Campobello, SC; ed/Grad, Chapman HS, 1977; BA, Eng, Erskine

Col, 1981; pa/Purchasing and Receiving Clk, Monsanto Co, 1981; Purchasing Secy 1981-82, Food and Beverage Controller 1982-83, Dir of Purchasing 1983-, Hyatt Regency Greenville; cp/ Cheerldr, Erskine Col, 1978; Philomelean Lit Soc, 1978-81, Secy 1979-80; Secy-Treas, Jr Class, 1979-80; Jud Coun, 1980-81; Elections Com, 1980-81; r/Bapt; hon/Hon Grad, 1977; g/Further Career in Purchasing w Future Goals in Pers.

HARTELT, CHRISTINE CLARE oc/ Student; b/Sep 27, 1963; h/Route 1, Mount Vernon, IA 52314; p/Martin A and Sherry L Hartelt, Mount Vernon, IA; ed/Mt Vernon HS, 1982; cp/Editor, Yrbook; St Dist Spch Contest Participant; Yth Rep on Ch Bd of Ed; Pre-Sch Tchr, Ch Rel Ed Prog; Fgn Exch Student; hon/St of IA Scholar; Rotary Clb Exch Student; Writing Contest Winner; g/Fgn Correspondent; Journalist; Translator.

HARTFIELD, VIALLA BERNICE oc/ Student; b/Jun 5, 1961; h/Route 3, Box 369, Purvis, MS 39475; p/Mr and Mrs Roy Hartfield, Purvis, MS; ed/Grad, Purvis HS, 1979; BA in Spanish, summa cum laude, Univ of So MS, 1983; pa/ Tchg Asst, Univ of So MS, 1981-82; Spanish Tchr, Hattiesburg Preparatory Sch, 1982-83; cp/Alpha Lambda Delta; Mu Phi Epsilon, Chorister 1980; Omicron Delta Kappa; Phi Kappa Phi; Hons Student Assn, VP 1982, Rep to Hons Coun and to Nat Col Hons Coun; So Reg Hons Coun; Student Rep to Search Com for New Acad VP, USM; r/Pianist, Tabernacle Bapt Ch; hon/Univ Scholar; Recip, Pulley, Pulley & Gough S'ship 1980, Alumni Foun S'ship 1982, Rotary Intl Grad S'ship for 1 Yr's Study at Univ of Salamanca 1983-84; Outstg Spanish Student, 1982; Dean's List and Pres's List; Nat Dean's List; Outstg Yg Wom of Am; Outstg Yg Ldrs of Am; g/Grad Wk.

HARTSOCK, DION ERIC oc/Student; b/Mar 1, 1963; h/3610 Northwest 21st Street, Lauderdale Lakes, FL; p/ Bernard and Grace Burl, Ridgeley, WV; ed/Bishop Walsh HS, 1981; Att'd, Allegany Commun Col; AS, Ft Lauderdale Col, 1983; mil/PFC, USAR; cp/ Bishop Walsh HS Band Hon Guard; Cumberland Ski Clb; Cancer Dancer Marathon Runner-Up; Operation Driver Excell Runner-Up; Bishop Walsh Alumni; Puppeteer; Drama; Usher; Outreach Ldr; Volleyball Team; Scuba Schs Internation, Adv'd Open Water Diver; r/Graceland Bapt Ch; hon/Dean's List; Intl Yth in Achmt; W/W Among Am HS Students; Commun Ldrs of Am; g/Mgr, Own Hotel or Restaurant.

HARTWELL, HELENE MILBY oc/ Student; b/May 14, 1962; h/1803 Maberry, Midland, TX 79705; p/Mr and Mrs Charles Hartwell, Midland, TX; ed/Dipl, Midland HS, 1980; Student, Univ of TX Austin, 1980-; cp/Mortar Bd, Histn 1983-84; Omicron Delta Kappa, 1983-84; Orange Jackets, Pledge Tnr 1983-84; TX Union Spec Events Com, Secy 1982-83; Kappa Kappa Gamma, Pres 1983-84, Big-Little Sister Ofcr 1982-83, Pledge Class Pres 1980-81; hon/Dean's List; Univ Sweetheart Finalist, 1983; Spooks Most Spirited Pledge, 1982; Most Outstg Jr 1983, Braun Maynard Awd 1983, Most Outstg Sophomore 1982, Kappa Kappa

Gamma; Intl Yth in Achmt; g/Acctg or Law; Judge.

HARTZOG, WENDY VIRGINIA oc/ Student; b/Oct 27, 1964; h/PO Box 127, Hilda, SC 29813; p/Daniel Edward and Cheryl D Hartzog, Hilda, SC; ed/Dipl, Blackville-Hilda HS, 1982; Misc Courses, Denmark Tech Col, 1982; Student, Univ of SC Allendale, 1982, 1983; cp/HS: Jr Beta Clb, Nat Sr Beta Clb, French Clb, Bus Drivers Clb, FHA, Annual and Yrbook Staffs (Reporter), Sch Newspaper (Typist); Col: Sociol Clb (Mem, Proj Com), Girls' Softball Team; Woodmen of the World Life Ins Soc; WOW Sum Camp, Jr Ldr; Hilda F'ship Clb; Hilda Vol Fire Dept; 4-H Clb; Hilda Girl Scouts; Town of Hilda Fest Activs; r/So Bapt; hon/Barnwell Co 4-H Clb Co Bake-Off Winner, 1976; Cert of S'ship Awd, 1976, 1977, 1978, 1979, 1980, 1981, 1982; Math Cert of Awd, 1978; Home Ec I Awd, 1979; Am Legion Aux Palmetto Girls' St Del, 1981; Presb Col Jr Acad Achmt Awd, 1981; Augusta Col Cert of Acad Achmt Awd, 1981; Marshal, Grad Exercises, HS, 1981; Nom'd for Competition in Miss TEEN St Beauty Pageant, 1980, 1981, 1982, 1983; Nom'd for Competition in Miss Nat Teenager Beauty Pageant, 1980, 1981; W/W Among Am HS Students; Intl Yth in Achmt; Yg Commun Ldrs of Am; Yg Personalities of S; Nat Dean's List; g/ Elem Ed/Early Childhood Maj.

HARVEY, SALLY ANN oc/Recreation Supervisor; b/Feb 19, 1955; h/1800 Teasley Lane, #114, Denton, TX 76201; ba/Farmers Branch, TX; p/Mr and Mrs C E Harvey, Appomattox, VA; ed/ Appomattox Co HS, 1973; BS in Rec Adm, Radford Univ, 1978; pa/Therapeutic Spec 1978, Asst Yth Supvr 1979-80, Sr Citizen Ctr Supvr 1980-81, Danville Pks and Rec; Rec Supvr, Farmers Br Pks and Rec, 1981-; TX Rec and Pks Soc, Ways and Means Com Mem 1982-; N TX Res Assn, 1982-; cp/ CoChm, Publicity Com 1978, Chm, Publicity Com 1979, Exec Bd Mem 1979, 2nd VP, Exec Bd Mem, Publicity Com Chm 1980-81, Fest in the Pk Inc; Publicity Chm, Victorian Danville, 1979-81; Intramural Bd, Intramural Supvr and Ofcl, Radford Univ, 1975-78; Com on Wom, Radford Univ, 1976-77; Alumnae Assn, TX Wom's Univ, 1982-; r/Presb; hon/Outstg Yg Wom in Am; g/Coordinate and Supervise Activs for Sr Citizens in a Retirement Village Setting.

HASBROUCK, JEANNE MARIE oc/ Student; b/Jun 22, 1962; h/290 Route 32 North, New Paltz, NY 12561; p/Mr and Mrs Henry Hasbrouck, New Paltz, NY; ed/New Paltz Ctl HS, 1980; Barrington Col; En Nazarene Col, 1982; Elem Ed w Emphasis in Spch Pathol, St Univ of NY New Paltz, 1984; cp/Vol Wk, Mentally Retarded Teens, BOCES, 1983; cp/Nat Student Spch Lang Hearing Assn; Co Band; Co Choir; Concert, Marching Band; Yrbook Staff; Accompanist, Jr Choir, Yth Grp; Care Nursery; Yth Grp; Field Hockey; Volleyball; Hon Roll; Prin's List; AFS; Walk-a-Thon for World Hunger; GSA; Evan Assn; Field Placement for Christian Ed; Tutor; r/ Nazarene; hon/Lion's Clb S'ship; NY St Sch Music Assn; Commun Ldrs of Am; Intl Yth in Achmt; W/W Among Am HS Students; g/Master's Deg in Spec Ed.

HATCH, PATRICIA DARLENE oc/

Student; b/May 28, 1967; h/2609 Dunn Avenue, Richmond, VA 23222; p/Rev and Mrs William I Hatch Sr, Richmond, VA; ed/Grad, Marshall-Walker HS, Henderson Alternative Unit, 1985; cp/Spanish Hon Soc, 1982-; Battle of the Brains Team, 1983-84; Sci Clb, 1983-84; Key Clb, 1983-84; Spanish Clb, VP 1983-84; r/Meth; hon/US Bus Ed Awd, 1984; US Nat Ldrship Merit Awd, 1984; Acad All-Am, 1984; Sum Ec Inst Participant, 1984; Outstg Citizenship Awd, 1984; Acad Pin (Scholar Roll), 1984; Anatomy in Med Awd, 1984; Soc of Dist'd Am HS Students; W/W AMong HS Students; US Achmt Acad; Nat Hon Soc; g/To Attend a 4-Yr Univ and Receive a BS in Chem; To Attend Med Sch and Concentrate on Pediatrics.

HATCHETT, DONNA RAY oc/Student; b/Jan 14, 1960; h/Route 2, Penhook, VA 24137; p/Mr and Mrs Kenneth Hatchett, Penhook, VA; ed/Franklin Co HS; Att'd, Longwood Col 1978-79, Patrick Henry Commun Col 1980-81; BS, Social Wk/Sociol, Averett Col, 1983; pa/Internship (Social Wkr), Roman Eagle Nsg Home 1981, So VA Mtl Inst 1983; cp/Spanish Clb, 1976-77; Tri-Hi-Y, 1976-77; Nat Hon Soc Clb, 1977-78; Bapt Student Union, 1981-83; Therapeutic Rec Clb, 1978-79; Alpha Delta Mu, Averett Col, 1982-83; Social Wk Clb, 1981-83; r/Brethren; hon/Nat Hon Soc, 1977-78; Dean's List, 1974-78, 1978-79, 1981-83; Alpha Delta Mu; Nat Dean's List Cand, 1982-83; g/To Become a Med and Clin Social Wkr.

HATHAWAY, DOUGLAS WAYNE oc/Mechanical Engineer; b/Oct 18, 1957; h/845 Paularino #B108, Costa Mesa, CA 92626; ba/Irvine, CA; m/Joan; p/Carl and Wylene Hathaway, Costa Mesa, CA; ed/Coronado HS, 1975; BS, Harvery Mudd Col, 1980; MBA, Pepperdine, 1984; cp/Fluor Running Clb, Pres 1981, VP 1982; Col Track and Field, Capt 1980; Col Football; HS Track and Field; HS Football; Col Yrbook; Co-ed Softball, Capt 1982; OTL; r/Prot; hon/All-Conf T&F, 1979, 1980; Player of the Wk, 1978; Grad w Distn, H Mudd Col; Intl Yth in Achmt; W/W Among Students in Am Cols and Univs; Commun Ldrs of Am; g/Security in All Aspects of Life.

HATLEY, CARL BRENT oc/Student; b/Jul 8, 1959; h/PO Box 22, Lone Grove, OK 73443; p/David and Jean Hatley, Lone Grove, OK; ed/Dipl, Lone Grove HS, 1977; AS, Murray St Jr Col, 1979; BA, OK Bapt Univ, 1981; EdM, SEn OK St Univ, 1984; cp/Missionary Journeyman Tchr to Mexico, Fgn Mission Bd of So Bapt Conv; Student Coun Pres; Jr Col Student Senate Pres; Phi Theta Kappa Histn; BSU Pres; BSU Coun, Chm of Intl Student Mins; Varsity Cross-Country; Mortar Bd; Omicron Delta Kappa; Assn of Resident Men; Royal Ambassador Cnslr; Co-Orgr, City Wide Interdenominational Crusade; HS Sports; hon/Grad, summa cum laude; Mr Murray St Col; Co-Valedictorian; W/W Among Students in Am Jr Cols; W/W Among Students in Am Cols and Univs; g/Elem Ed w View towards Biling Ed and Overseas Employmt.

HAUPT, CRYSTALA EAGLE oc/Student; b/Jun 8, 1961; h/200 East Munn Street, Apartment 4, Dawson Springs, KY 42408; m/David Bryant; p/

Mr and Mrs Richard Eagle, Madisonville, KY; ed/Grad, Madisonville N Hopkins HS, 1979; Bach of Music Ed, Piano, Murray St Univ, 1983; pa/Tchr, Pvt Piano, 8 Yrs; cp/KY Music Tchrs Assn, Student Chapt, 4 Yrs; SMENC, Ednl Prog; r/Pentecostal; Dir, Chd's Choir, Lighthouse Pentecostal Ch; hon/Vocal Music Awd, HS, 1979; All-St Chorus Mem (Superior Rating), 1979; Quad-St Chorus Mem, 1979; All-Dist Chorus Mem, 1978; Vocal Soloist (Superior Rating), 1979; g/Elem Gen Music Tchr; Own Piano Studio.

HAUSE, EVAN ROBERT oc/Student; b/Apr 22, 1967; h/2208 Charles Street, Greenville, NC 27834; p/Robert Luke III and Karen McCann Hause, Greenville, NC; ed/Att'g HS; cp/Elmhurst Elem Concert Band, 1977-79; Greenville Mid Sch Concert Band, 1979-80; Aycock Jr High Concert Band, 1980-82; J H Rose High Marching Band, 1981-82; J H Rose High Concert Band, 1982-83; En Yth Orch, 1981-82; Little Leag Baseball, 1976-79; Babe Ruth Baseball, 1981-82; E B Aycock Jr High Football, 1981; E Carolina Univ Sum Music Camp, 1980, 1981; E B Aycock Jr High Stage Band, 1980-81; J H Rose High Sch Stage Band, 1982-83; En Symphonette, 1981, 1982; hon/NC En Dist Jr High All-St Band, 1981, 1982; Sr High All-St Band, 1983; Elected to Attend 1982-83 Gov's Sch; Superior Rating in NCMEA Solo and Ensemble Contest.

HAWK, LYNDA JOY oc/Student; b/Jun 27, 1963; h/313 Steele Road, Slidell, LA 70458; p/Mr and Mrs David F Hawk, Slidell, LA; ed/John Overton HS, 1981; Currently Enrolled, St Mary's Dominican Col; cp/Col: Yg Repubs (Sch Coor 1982-83), Student Govt Assn (VP 1982-83, Secy 1982, Freshman Rep 1981), Newspaper Staff, Student Govt Rep 1982, Eng Colloquium 1982-83, Alpha Iota Delta 1981-83, Phi Alpha Theta 1982-83, Cardinal Key 1983, Peer Advr 1983; HS: Forensics Clb (Secy 1980-81, Active Mem 1978-81), Student Govt (Parliamentarian 1980-81, Student Rep 1978-80), Nat Beta Clb 1978-81, Nat Hon Soc, 1980-81, Yrbook Staff (Org Editor 1980-81); r/Cath; hon/Harry S Truman Scholar from LA, 1983; 2nd Place, Nat Forensics Leag Nat Student Cong, 1981; 1st Place, Nat Forensics Leag TN Dist Cong, 1981; 2nd Place, Nat Forensics Leag, TN Dist Debate Tournament, 1980, 1981; Top 10 Metro-Nashville Forensics Leag, 1981; g/Maj in Hist, Bus; Career in Govt; Grad Study.

HAWKINS, ANDREW FROST oc/Student; b/Jun 4, 1964; h/921 Belvedere Drive, Gallatin, TN 37066; p/Mr and Mrs J W Hawkins, Gallatin, TN; ed/Grad, Gallatin Sr HS, 1982; Student, B'ham So Col; cp/Field Coor, Mtn TOP (TN Outreach Prog), 1983; Student Govt Assn Freshman Rep, 1982-83; Triangle Clb, 1983-84; Kappa Alpha Order (Social Frat); Constable, Sumner Co, TN; r/Meth; hon/Dean's List, 1983; Alpha Tau Omega Barney Monaghan Awd, 1983; Pres Hons S'ship, 1982; W/W; g/Pre-Med, Bus Adm Maj.

HAWKINS, GREGORY SCOTT oc/Student; b/Dec 9, 1965; h/29 Bentwood Drive, Piedmont, SC 29673; ed/HS Grad; cp/Band, Freshman and Sr Yrs; Wrestling, Freshman Yr; Ch Softball and Basketball; r/Wesleyan; hon/Fur-

man Scholar, 1983; Erskine Fellow, 1983; US Hist Awd, 1983; Band Awd, 1981; All-City Band, 1981; First Place, Sci Fair, 1981.

HAYDEN, PATRICIA JEAN oc/Student; b/Oct 3, 1961; h/3563 Maddox Lane, Lexington, KY 40511; ba/Owensboro, KY; p/Arthur E Sr and Joann Hayden, Lexington, KY; ed/Bryan Sta Sr High, 1979; BA in Psych and Art, KY Wesleyan Col, 1984; cp/SGA, Senator 1979-80, 1980-81, 1982-83; Cheerldr, 1979-80, Co-Capt 1981-82, Capt 1982-83; Bd of Pubs, Chp 1982-83; Gymnastics Team, 1976-79, Capt 1978-79; r/Cath; hon/110% Awd for Gymnastics, 1978-79; Homecoming Queen, 1983; Sr Art Awd, 1979; W/W Amongs Students in Am Cols and Univs; g/Art Therapist and Child Psychol.

HAYES, CHRISTIE POLLOCK oc/Accountant; b/Mar 16, 1961; h/Route 4, Box 56, Pulaski, TN 38478; ba/Pulaski, TN; p/Mr and Mrs Rand Hayes, Pulaski, TN; ed/Dipl, Giles Co HS; AA, Martin Col; BS in Bus Adm, Acctg, Auburn Univ; pa/Acctg Dept, First Nat Bk; cp/Phi Kappa Phi; Alpha Gamma Delta Social Sorority; Beta Alpha Psi Nat Acctg Hon; Beta Gamma Sigma Bus Hon; r/Presb.

HAYS, JUDITH MEYER oc/Music Teacher; b/Feb 2, 1957; h/1402 Ports-O-Call Drive, Palatine, IL 60067; p/Mr and Mrs Marlin H Meyer, Litchfield, IL; ed/Warren HS, 1975; Carthage Col, 1979; Univ of IL; pa/Music Tchr; MENC; Am Choral Dirs Assn; cp/Palos Village Players; All Sts Ch Choir; Chd's Choir; Yrbook Editor; Class Pres; Col Choirs; hon/Grad, summa cum laude; Alpha Lambda Delta; Sigma Lambda; W/W Among Students in Am Cols and Univs; g/Master's Deg in Music Ed.

HAYS, PATRICIA CAROL oc/Director of Preschool and Children's Ministries; b/Jan 11, 1955; h/4823 El Gusto, San Antonio, TX 78233; ba/Jonesboro, AR; p/Lt Col and Mrs C Allen Hays, San Antonio, TX; ed/Douglas MacArthur HS, 1973; BS, Elem Ed, Baylor Univ, 1977; Master of Rel Ed, SWn Bapt Theol Sem, 1983; pa/Dir of Presch Chd's Mins, First Bapt Ch, 1983-; Presch Dir, Ridgecrest Bapt Conf Ctr, 1983; Ch Tng Equipper, Bapt Gen Conv of TX, 1982; Presch Fac, Glorieta Bapt Conf Ctr, 1981; Asst Min of Childhood Ed, Trinity Bapt Ch, 1980; Tchr, Dallas ISD, 1979-80; TX St Tchrs Assn; Nat Ed Agy; cp/Nat Hon Soc; Future Tchrs of Am; Student Rel Ed Assn; BSU Puppet Team; r/Trinity Bapt Ch, Yth Choir, Mission Trips, Sunday Sch Tchr, Camp Cnslr, VBS Tchr; Home Ec Awd, 1973; Merit Awd, 1973; George Vakey S'ship, 1973; Angelo St Univ S'ship, 1973; Dean's List, 1981; Commun Ldrs of Am; Outstg Yg Wom of Am.

HEACOCK, TERI ANN oc/Student; b/Aug 8, 1967; h/2219 Santa Fe, Woodward, OK 73801; p/Gary and Delores Heacock, Woodward, OK; r/Nazarene; hon/Student of Today, 1978; Basketball, 1980, 1981; g/Acctg Maj w Computer Minor.

HEADRICK, SHARON oc/Student; b/Dec 9, 1962; h/1127 Chestnut Street, San Bernardino, CA 92410; p/Paul and Delores Headrick, San Bernardino, CA; ed/Aquinas HS; Presently Att'g, CA St Univ San Bernardino; pa/Swim Instr,

Pool Mgr 1983, Swim Instr, Lifeguard 1982, Rialto YWCA; Lifeguard 1981-82, Rec Ldr 1981-82, Pks and Rec Aide 1980, City Pks and Rec, San Bernardino; Student Aide, San Bernardino Co Reg Pks Dept, 1979-80; cp/MECHA, 1981; r/Cath; hon/Hon Roll, 1979-81; Commun Ldrs of Am; Intl Yth in Achmt; W/W Among Am HS Students; g/BS in Biol; BA in Spanish; Pediatrician.

HEARN, D DeLYNN oc/Chemist; b/ Apr 25, 1961; h/61 Crain Drive, Bryant, AR 72022; p/Mr and Mrs Jerry B Hearn, Bryant, AR; ed/Bryant HS, 1979; AR Tech Univ; cp/ATU Commun Choir; Chem Clb; Am Chem Soc Student Affil; Cardinal Key; Alpha Chi Pres; Student Activs Bd; Fine Arts Com Chm; Chm of Bd; Student Senate Exec Bd; hon/ Sum Undergrad Res Participant; Dean's List; Dorm Perf S'ship; g/Indust Chem Mgmt.

HEARN, DEBORAH D oc/Student; b/Apr 2, 1963; h/3235 North Federal Highway, Fort Pierce, FL 33450; p/Mr and Mrs William Hearn, Ft Pierce, FL; ed/Grad, Ft Pierce Westwood HS, 1981; AA, Indian River Commun Col, 1983; Student, Univ of S FL; pa/Public Relats Rep, Public Info Ofc, Indian River Commun Col, 1981-83; cp/Compass Clb, Pres; Phi Theta Kappa, VP; Nsg Home Vol; Nat Hon Soc, Corresponding Secy; Beta Clb, Secy; Keyettes, Treas, VP; Student Coun; Inter-Clb Coun; Varsity Clb; Cheerldr, Co-Capt; Jr Class Pres; 4-H Clb, Pres; r/Prot; hon/Miss IRCC Cand; FL Blue Key Nom; St Lucie Co Fair Gingham Girl, 1983; Valedictorian, 1981; Homecoming Queen Cand; Prom Queen, 1981; Num Other HS Hons; Chosen as Intern in Wash, DC, for Congressman Skip Bafalis; Girls' St; 4-H Dist Talent Awd; Hons Prog, Univ of S FL; Finalist, Miss FL Nat Teenager, 1981; Num S'ships Received; W/W Among Students in Am Jr Cols; W/W Among Am HS Students; Soc of Dist'd Am HS Students; g/Mktg Maj w Minor in Computer Info Sci.

HEARNE, HOLLY ANN oc/Student; b/Jun 21, 1964; h/600 Regency Drive, Salisbury, MD 21801; p/Mr and Mrs Earl W Hearne, Salisbury, MD; ed/Grad, Parkside HS, 1982; cp/PE Majs Clb, 1982-83; Am Alliance for Hlth, PE, Rec and Dance, 1983; VA Alliance for Hlth, PE, Rec and Dance; GSA; Hosp Vol; Wicomico Co Hlth Com; U Meth Yth F'ship, Secy-Treas; Varsity Clb; hon/ Lttr, HS Track, Basketball, Volleyball and Softball; NHS; St Finalist, Miss MD Nat Teenager, 1980; Royd Mahaffey S'ship; John H Dulany Meml Inc S'ship Grant; Hon Mention, Elks Most Valuable Student Awd; Parkside Ram Awd; Sr Ath Awd, Parkside HS; W/W Among Am HS Students; Yg Am Aths; Commun Ldrs of Am; g/Sec'dy PE Tchr and Coach.

HEARNE, STEVEN EDWARD oc/ Student; b/Dec 6, 1962; h/600 Regency Drive, Salisbury, MD 21801; p/Mr and Mrs Earl W Hearne, Salisbury, MD; ed/ Parkside HS, 1981; Univ of MD; cp/ Alpha Delta Lambda Hon Soc; Alpha Chi Sigma Frat; BSA; U Meth Yth F'ship, Pres, VP, Treas; SGA Rep; Yrbook Sports Editor; Wicomico Co Yth Coun; Varsity Clb; Lttrman, Basketball, Football; French Clb; Capt, Basketball Team; hon/Eagle Scout, BSA; Med Soc S'ship; Elks Aux S'ship; Elks Nat Foun

Most Valuable Student Awd; Royd Mahaffey S'ship; Sam Seidel Basketball Awd; Parkside Ram Awd; St of MD Scholastic Merit Awd; Parkside Sr Ath Awd; Royd A Mahaffey Achmt Awd; Soroptimist Yth Citizenship Awd; Gen MD St S'ship; NHS; Alpha Lambda Delta Soc; Yth Apprec Wk Awd, Optimist Clb; MD Dist'd Scholar Awd; Chancellor Scholar, Univ of MD; W/W Among Am HS Students; Am's Outstg Names and Faces; Commun Ldrs of Am; g/MD.

HEATH, SUSAN D oc/Student; b/Jul 25, 1963; h/PO Box 211, Gates, TN 38037; p/Mr and Mrs Ray D Heath, Gates, TN; ed/Grad, Halls HS, 1981; Att'g, Lambuth Col; cp/Beta Clb, 1979-81; Lib Clb, 1977-80, Secy 1978-79; French Clb, 1977-79; FHA, 1977-78; Deca, 1979-81; Phi Mu Frat, 1982-83, Recording Secy 1983, Room Chm 1983; 4-H; Sci Clb; r/Pentecost; hon/Most Sch Spirited, 1981; Best Phi Awd, Phi Mu, 1982; 3rd Place, St Deca Competition; 3rd Place Medallion, Reg Deca Competition; Dist'd Ser Plaque, Lib Clb; Hon Student; Commun Ldrs of Am; g/BS in Data Processing.

HEATWOLE, JANET M oc/Student; b/Feb 14, 1965; h/Route 8, Box 68, Harrisonburg, VA 22801; ed/En Mennonite HS, 1983; Att'g, En Mennonite Col; cp/Student Coun Org, Rep 1979; VP of Freshman Class, 1980; VP of Sophomore Class, 1981; Chm of Social Com, 1981; Sr Class Pres, 1983; VP of VA Conf Yth Cabinet, 1983-84; r/ Christian; hon/Nat Hon Soc, 1982; Nat Sci Merit Awd, 1982; Outstg Contbn to En Mennonite HS Awd, 1983; Music Deptl Awd, 1983; Col Prog S'ship to En Mennonite Col, 1983; g/Music and Math Ed; HS Tchr.

HECHT, KAREN BARBARA oc/ Student; b/Jun 3, 1962; h/16 Lindron Avenue, Smithtown, NY 11787; p/ Conrad and Elaine Hecht, Smithtown, NY; ed/Regents Dipl, Smithtown HS W; Att'd, Geheseo St 1980, Dowling Col 1981, 1982, 1983-84, Univ of S FL 1982, 1983; BA, Dowling Col, 1984; pa/Subst Tchr, 1983-84; Tchr, ABC Daycare, 1983; Pvt Piano Tchr, 1979-; Drama Tchr, Sch Enrichment Prog, 1978-80; Aerobics Tchr, Var Dance Studios, 1981-82; cp/Candystriper, St John's Hosp, 1977; AHRC Mem and Com Chp, 1977-80; Vol Spec Olympics, 197-80; Vol Tutor, 1983-84; g/Elem Ed Tchr; Master's Deg.

HECHT, MARJORIE G oc/Student; b/Apr 4, 1964; h/16 Lindron Avenue, Smithtown, NY 11787; p/Conrad and Elaine Hecht, Smithtown, NY; ed/ Smithtown HS W; Att'd, St Univ of NY Geneseo; Currently Enrolled, Dowling Col; pa/Salesgirl, Spencer Gifts, 1980-; Tchr Aide, Coop of Cooperative Ed Sers, 1983; Other Previous Positions; cp/ AHRC, Mem and Com Chp; Spec Olympics; Nat Thespian Soc; Class Coun, 1980-81; Career Exploration and Deca Clb; hon/Sch Ser Awd Cert, Class of 1982; g/Fashion Msdg; Bach Deg in Mktg and Bus.

HEES, DANA RENEE oc/Student; b/ Apr 8, 1962; h/Route 1, Box 155, Manor, TX 78653; p/Kermit and Lydia Hees, Manor, TX; ed/Pflugerville HS, 1980; Currently Enrolled, TX A&M Univ; pa/ Student Intern, TX Bk for Cooperatives, 1983; cp/Agri Ec Clb, Pres

1983-84, Sr Brochure CoChm 1982-83; Alpha Zeta, Refreshment Chm; Col 4-H Clb, Publicity Chm 1981-82, Student Agri Coun 1983-84; Nat Agri-Mktg Assn; Saddle and Sirloin; Fowler Hall; Residence Hall Assn; Cap and Gown, 1983-84; r/U Ch of Christ; hon/Salutatorian of HS Class, 1980; Dist'd Student and Dean's Hon Roll, Univ; Outstg Freshman, 1981; Initiation Awd, 1982; Outstg Jr in Agri Ec Clb, 1983; Wkhorse Awd, Alpha Zeta, 1983; Phi Kappa Phi; Gamma Sigma Delta; 4-H Gold Star Awd, 1980; W/W Among HS Students; g/Deg in Agri Ec.

HEIDINGER, CLORINDA ROSE oc/ Student; b/Feb 11, 1961; h/918 North Glenn Avenue, Siler City, NC 27344; p/Mrs Rosemarie Heidinger, Siler City, NC; ed/Jordan-Matthews HS, 1979; Currently Enrolled, Univ of NC Greensboro; pa/Profl Supervisory Wk in Quantity Food Ser Mgmt, UNC-G's Campus Cafeteria; cp/Girls' Monogram, VP; Future Christian Aths; Spanish Clb, VP; Cheerldr; Track; Pep Clb; Food-N-Nutrition Clb; r/Luth; hon/ Marshal, 1978; Hon Roll; Beta Clb, Reporter; Outstg Sr; Acad Awd, Social Scis; Hon Grad; Dean's List; Mose Kiser Acad S'ship; Omicron Nu, Editor; W/ W Among Col Freshmen; g/BS in Foods and Nutrition.

HEIDLAGE, VICKIE ANN oc/Student; b/Sep 20, 1963; h/PO Box 781, Claremore, OK 74018; p/Robert and Pat Heidlage, Claremore, OK; ed/Grad, Claremore HS, 1981; AS, Rogers St Col, 1983; Animal Sci/Pre-Vet Maj, OK St Univ; pa/Pt-time Sales Clk, Willman's Inc 1980-84, Bob Heidlage Photo 1983-84, Rena's Cards and Gifts 1978-80; cp/OSU Block and Bridle, Activs Chm 1984; Horse Judging Team, OSU, 1983; Livestock Judging Team, OSU, 1984; Animal Sci Student Adv Coun, OSU, 1983-84; Am Quarter Horse Assn; 4-H Ldr; Phi Theta Kappa, RSC, 1982-83; RSC Jazz Band, 1981-83; RSC Hlth and Life Scis Clb, Pres 1982-83; OK Pinto Horse Assn; r/Cath; hon/High Indiv Overall Am Quarter Horse World Col Horse Judging Contest, 1983; Miss Pinto OK, 1981-83; Dean's Hon Roll, OSU, 1983; Pres's Hon Roll, RSC, 1981-83; Pres Scholar, RSC, 1982-83; Nat Dean's List, 1983; W/W Among Am HS; W/W Jr Cols; g/Vet Med.

HEINEN, STEVEN GLENN oc/Student; b/Jul 1, 1965; h/Route 1, Box 68, Talala, OK 74080; ed/Oolagah HS; Student, Univ of OK; ed/Rogers Co Bk, Jr Bd of Dirs 1982-83; HS Band Pres; Nat Forensic Leag VP; Beta Clb Pres; Student Coun Chaplain; Soccer Team; Lambda Chi Alpha Frat; r/Ch of Christ; hon/OK St Hon Soc, 1979-83; Valedictorian, 1983; NROTC S'ship Recip; R Boyd Gunning Scholar; St Class A Debate Champion, 1982; Selected for Gov's Inaugural Band, 1983; W/W Among Am HS Students; Soc of Dist'd Am HS Students; Am's Outstg Names and Faces; g/Deg in Fin; Attend Law Sch; Bkg or Fgn Ser.

HEINZ, CYNTHIA ELLEN oc/Registered Nurse, Staff Nurse; b/Feb 15, 1956; h/RR #10, Box 82B, Columbia, MO 65202; ba/Columbia, MO; m/ Robert D; c/Jennifer P; p/Anton and Patricia Zoubek, Wood Dale, IL; ed/ Driscoll HS, 1973; BSN, Loyola Univ,

1977; pa/Staff Nurse, Orthopedic/ Rehab Unit, Grant Hosp, 1977-78; Staff Nurse, Mtl Hlth Unit, Mercy Med Ctr, 1978-79; Staff Nurse IV, Univ of MO Med Ctr, Rusk Rehab Ctr, 1979-; Assn of Rehab Nurses, 1979-83; Am Geriatrics Soc, 1980-83; Nat Leag for Nsg, 1981-83; Am Med Writers Assn, 1982-83; Columbia Commun Band, 1981-83; r/Cath; St Gertrude Ch Choir, 1977-79; Sacred Heart Ch Choir, 1979-83; g/Attend Grad Sch for MSN in Psychi Nsg.

HELICZER, SONYA BEATRICE oc/ Student; b/Apr 10, 1963; h/3303 59th Avenue Southwest, Seattle, WA 98116; p/Robert Michael and Maria Teresa Heliczer, Seattle, WA; ed/Mt Miguel HS, 1981; Univ of WA Exptl Col, 1982; Summit Univ, 1984; pa/LIFE Student Lit Tchr, 1978-79; Bonita Vista High Commun Ser Prog, Wkr w Handicapped Students, 1979-80; Sea World Salesperson, 1980; Infant Food Preparation, Montessori Intl, 1983-84; cp/St Germain Keepers of the Flame Frat; ASB Pres, 1978; Sophomore, 1979; Student Cong, 1978-81; Jud Coun, 1978-79; Hon Roll, 1976-81; Freedom Foun, 1979; H O'Brian Ldrship Foun, 1979; Yg Am Foun, 1980; Student Rep; Student Spkr, 1978-81; Oboist, Solo and Woodwind Quartet, 1976-79; Poetry and Lit Grps, 1980-81; Spch Team, 1978-79; Eng Hons; Speciality Corps, 1978-80; Drill Team Lt, 1979-80; Orch and Marching Band, 1976-79; r/Rom Cath-Jewish; hon/Salutatorian, 1981; Outstg Student of the Yr Awds; Outstg Student of San Diego, Outstg Student Freshman; Outstg Sophomore; Prin Lttr of Commend for Outstg Achmt, 1978-81; Trust S'ship Awd, 1981; Bk of Am Outstg Achmt in Eng, 1981; Intl Yth in Achmt; Commun Ldrs of Am; W/W Am HS Students; Dir of Dist'd Ams; g/Commun and Liberal Arts; Public Ser.

HELMS, LILA HARPER oc/Student; b/May 12, 1962; h/Route 3, Box 378, Darlington, SC 29532; p/Mr and Mrs Ernest L Helms Jr, Darlington, SC; ed/ Grad, St John's HS, 1980; Student, Univ of SC; cp/HS Tennis, Basketball, Softball; HS Hon Soc, Math Clb; Col: Gamma Beta Phi, Phi Alpha Theta (Pres 1982-83); r/Bapt; hon/MVP, Tennis, 1978-79, 1979-80; Best Def Player, Basketball, 1979-80; Columbia Col Trustee Scholar; Winthrop Scholar, HS; Nat Dean's List; g/Double Maj in Hist and Intl Studies; Grad Sch.

HENDERSON, JOSEPH SCOTT oc/ Student; b/Dec 18, 1967; h/142 East Clement Street, Wallace, NC 28466; p/ Mr and Mrs Robert Henderson, Wallace, NC; ed/Grad, Wallace Rose Hill HS, 1985; pa/Henderson Roofing Co, 1980-83; cp/JHS Softball; JHS Beta Clb; HS Student Coun Rep; HS Spanish Hon Soc; r/Bapt; hon/Am Legion Awd, 1980; Lang Arts Awd, 1980; Nat Spanish Exam Awd, 1982; NC Sch of Sci and Math Semi-Finalist, 1983; g/Computer Engr.

HENDERSON, JULIA DIANE oc/ Registered Nurse in Coronary Care Unit; b/Aug 16, 1961; h/3110 South Jefferson, Apartment 3C, Springfield, MO 65807; ba/Springfield, MO; p/Mr and Mrs T J Henderson, Mountain Home, AR; ed/Grad, Mtn Home HS, 1979; BSN, Harding Univ, 1983; pa/RN in Coronary Care Unit, St John's Reg

Hlth Ctr; cp/Harding Univ Student Nurses Assn, 1982; Omega Phi Social Clb, 1979-83, Devotional Dir; Red Cross Blood Drive Vol, 1981-83; MHHS Band, 1976; Beta Clb, 1976-79; Omega Phi Basketball and Softball Team, 1980-82; r/Ch of Christ; hon/Harding Univ Dean's List, 1982-83; DAR Citizenship Awd, 1979; W/W Most Intelligent; W/W Am HS; g/To Continue Wkg in CCU until 1985; MSN or Law Sch.

HENDERSON, KATHLEEN MARTIN oc/Head Nurse of Cardiac Surgery; b/Apr 6, 1957; h/5832 West 78th Street, Los Angeles, CA 90045; ba/Los Angeles, CA; m/Kenneth F; p/Mr and Mrs Donald A Martin, Costa Mesa, CA; ed/ Grad, Costa Mesa HS, 1975; AA, Pre-Nsg, Orange Coast Col, 1977; BS, Nsg, Univ of CA LA, 1979; pa/Orange Coast Col Lab Asst, 1976-77; Sr Nurses Aide, Univ of CA LA Med Ctr on Surg Nsg Unit, 1978-79; Clin Nurse, Univ of CA LA Med Ctr OR, 1979-80; Asst Hd Nurse, Cardiac Surg, Univ of CA LA, 1980; Hd Nurse, Cardiac Surg, Univ of CA LA OR, 1980-; Assn of OR Nurses, 1979-, Publicity Com 1980-81; cp/CA S'ship Fdn, 1973-75, VP 1974; Alpha Gamma Sigma, 1977; Orange Coast Col Crew Team Coxwain, 1975-76; Mu Alpha Theta, 1975-77; Student Nurses, Univ of CA LA, 1977-79, Soc Com Chair 1978-79; Alpha Tau Delta, 1977-, Bd Mem 1979-81; Sigma Theta Tau, 1979-; Permanent Mem, Alpha Gamma Sigma, Mu Alpha Theta, Sigma Theta Tau; hon/S'ship from Mercy Gen Hosp Wom's Aux, 1977; S'ship, Bk of Am, 1977; Grad w Hons, 1975; Intl Yth in Achmt; Grad w Hons, 1977; g/Master's in Nsg and/or Adm within Five Yrs; Position in Field; To Continue and Grow in Field of Study.

HENDERSON, RUTH ELAINE oc/ Hospital Chaplain; b/May 14, 1955; h/ #4 Windsor Drive, Tuscaloosa, AL 35404; ba/Tuscaloosa, AL; p/James A and Dorothy E Henderson, Hodges, SC; ed/Greenwood HS, 1973; BA, Bapt Col, 1977; MDiv, SEn Bapt Theol Sem, 1980; Clin Pastoral Ed, 1980-81; pa/Student Chaplain, GA Reg Hosp, 1980; Chaplain Residency, Carraway Meth Med Ctr, 1980-81; Asst Dean of Student/Activs, Bapt Col, 1982-83; Chaplain, Druid City Hosp, 1983-; Assn for Clin Pastoral Ed, 1980-; cp/Alpha Rho Omega, 1973-77, Pres 1975-76; BCC Wom's Tennis Team, 1975-77; BCC Choir, 1973-77; Bapt Student Union, 1974-77; SGA, 1973-77; Wom's Residence Assn, Pres 1975-77; r/So Bapt; hon/May Queen, 1977; Pres, Sr Class, 1976-77; Chp for Spec Events, Homecoming, May Day, MS BCC, W/W Among Am Cols and Univs.

HENNING, CYNTHIA JEAN oc/ Student; b/Nov 4, 1964; h/4808 Glencoe Drive, Cheyenne, WY 82009; ba/Torrington, WY; p/Ernest S Henning, Cheyenne, WY; m/Mr and Mrs C H Hope, Cheyenne, WY; ed/Grad, Cheyenne E HS, 1983; Att'g, En WY Col; cp/Volleyball, Basketball and Track Teams (Lettered 3 Yrs in Each), 1980-83; German Clb, 1983; Nat Hon Soc, 1982-83; r/ Christian; hon/Nat Hon Soc, 1982-83; US Achmt Acad Awd Winner for PE, 1982; All-Star Team for Wyo-Braska for Volleyball, 1983; All Tournament Team, 1979; Hon Roll; g/Maj in Sec'dy

Ed; Coach a HS Volleyball Team; Play Volleyball at Univ Level.

HENNRICH, SAM E oc/Student; b/ May 18, 1963; h/406 West Osborn Street, Sparta, IL; m/Dorothy Michelle Grafton; c/Christina Kay; p/Mr and Mrs Sam W Hennrich, Sparta, IL; Assoc, Automotive Technol, John A Logan Col; pa/Self-Employed Mechanic; cp/JCs; hon/Intl Yth in Achmt; W/W Among Am HS Students; Commun Ldrs of Am; g/Auto Tech Study.

HENSLEY, ELIZABETH JANE oc/ Student; b/Sep 29, 1963; h/Box 63, Paint Lick, KY 40461; p/Boyd and Doris Hensley, Paint Lick, KY; ed/Garrard Co HS, 1981; Student of Bus, Computers, En KY Univ; cp/FFA, Secy 1980-81; Softball, 1978-79; NHS; SAE; r/Meth Ch, MYF; hon/Citizenship Awd, 1978; FFA: Secy St Silver Awd, S'ship Awd, Ldrship Awd; Perfect Attendance, 10 Yrs; MVP, Softball, 1979.

HERNDON, DALE COLLINS JR oc/ Student; b/Dec 28, 1964; h/3840 North Stratford Road, Northeast, Atlanta, GA 30342; p/Mr and Mrs Dale C Herndon, Atlanta, GA; ed/Grad, N Fulton High; pa/Salesman/Stockboy, Ath Attic, 1983; Asst to Contractor, Universal Properties and Investmt Corp, 1979-83; cp/Boy Scouts, Sr Patrol Ldr, Ldrship Corp, Order of the Arrow; Meth Yth F'ship; Soccer, Capt 1983; Cross Country, Reg 1982; Golf, Reg 1982; Student Coun; Studio Theater; Latin Clb; HS Yrbook, 1981-82; r/Meth; hon/Hon Roll, 1981, 1982; Eagle Scout, 1983; Acad Excell Pin; GA Cert of Merit; Most Improved Student, 1982; Nat Latin Exam, magna cum laude; Cert of Commend, Atlanta Bd of Ed, 1983; S'ship to Freedoms Foun at Val Forge, 1981; W/W Among Am HS Students; g/Grad from Emory Univ.

HERRING, JAMES BARTON oc/ Student; b/Mar 8, 1963; h/Route #2, Box 150, Glasgow, MO 65254; p/Jimmy and Ruth Herring, Glasgow, MO; ed/ Kemper Mil Sch; Assoc Art Deg, Kemper Mil Sch and Col; cp/Track Team; Baseball Team; Marching Band, 6 Yrs; Hd Ofcr, Color Guard; Boys' St; Cadet Col, ROTC; Mil Hon Soc; Att'd, ROTC Camp; Kappa Alpha Frat; Staff of Sch Paper, 3 Yrs; Photog for Sch Paper; r/Meth; hon/First Cadet to Speak at Fdrs Day at Sch; Spkr, Rotary Clb; Band Played in Cherry Blossom Parade in Wash, DC; Aid-de-Camp to Pres of Mil Sch; Pres, Encore Clb; W/W HS Students; W/W Jr Cols; g/Maj in Agri.

HESS, CONNIE LOU oc/Student; b/ Nov 17, 1963; h/RR 2, South Haven, KS 67140; p/Mr and Mrs James P Hess, South Haven, KS; ed/HS, 1982; No OK Col; cp/Commun Yth Grp; U Meth Yth F'ship; Pres; GSA; FHA; GGA; FCA; Y-Teens; NHS; Pep Clb; Band; Pom Pon Girl; Lib, Lng Resource Com, Col; Ag Clb; Col Bowl; Volleyball; Basketball; Track; hon/FFA Sweetheart; Mission Ed Tour; Tchrs S'ship Awd; g/Pharm.

HEWETT, BENJAMIN JASON oc/ Student; b/Aug 30, 1960; h/Route 1, Box 179, Fort White, FL 32038; p/Mr and Mrs R H Hewett, Fort White, FL; ed/ Dipl, Rolling Green Acad, 1978; AA, Lake City Commun Col, 1984; pa/ Aircraft Mech, Aero Corp, 1979-83; cp/ BSA; Ch Choir; Ch Softball; HS Football; Letterman; r/Meth; hon/Beta Clb; Soc of Dist'd Am HS Students; Intl Yth in Achmt; W/W Among Am HS Students; g/Maj in Sys Anal, Minor in Sec'dy Ed, Univ of FL.

HEWITT, DEBORAH JEWEL oc/Student; b/Jun 20, 1968; h/2014 Winmar Lane, Conley, GA 30027; p/Clifford S and Doris W Hewitt, Conley, GA; ed/Grad, Forest Pk HS, 1985; pa/Pianist, Calvary Bapt Ch (Since Age 13); Has Played and Sung for Weddings and a Number of Chs; cp/Sr Class Treas; Band; Symphonic and Marching Band; Chorus; Nat Hon Soc, Pres; r/Bapt; hon/Outstg Sci and Hist Student; Social Sci Symp Participant; GA Cert of Merit; GA Inst of Technol Dist'd Sci Scholar Awd; Presb Col Jr Fellow Awd; GA Miss Nat Teenager Pageant (11th Among Top 10 in Talent); Allst Chorus; Gov's Hons in Choral Music; Dist Lit Team, Female Vocalist; Outstg Choral Student and Dirs Awd; W/W Among Am HS Students; g/Further Study and Dual Careers in Vocal Music and Psychi.

HICKS, AMY C oc/Graduate Student; b/Oct 6, 1959; h/1100 Reinli Street #148, Austin, TX 78723; p/Mr and Mrs D W Hicks, Tallassee, AL; ed/Reeltown HS, 1978; BBA, Univ of Montevallo, 1982; MBA, Univ of TX Austin, 1984; cp/Chi Omega Sorority, 1978-82, VP; Student Govt Assn, Pres pro tempore 1982; Omicron Delta Kappa, VP 1981-82; Vol Cnslr, AL Girls' St; r/Prot; hon/Phi Kappa Phi, 1982; UM Alumni Hons Scholar, 1982; Sr Elite in Mktg, 1982; W/W Among Students in Am Univs and Cols; Nat Dean's List; Outstg Yg Wom of Am; g/Position w Maj Firm in Mktg or Public Relats.

HICKS, JAMIE D oc/Student; b/Aug 16, 1960; h/821 Boston Street, Memphis, TN 38114; p/Mr and Mrs T E Hicks Jr, Memphis, TN; ed/Melrose HS; BS, Lane Col; MBA, TN St Univ, 1985; cp/Pres, Jr and Sr Classes, Col; VP, NAACP; VP, Phi Beta Lambda; Pres; Alpha Phi Alpha; hon/Dean's List; W/W Among Intl Students; W/W Among Students in Am Cols and Univs; g/CPA.

HICKS, JENNIFER MARIA oc/Student; b/Dec 13, 1965; h/3612 Playground Road, Caruthersville, MO 63830; p/Mr and Mrs Roy Alfred Hicks, Caruthersville, MO; ed/Caruthersville HS; cp/Freshman Homeroom Pres, Freshman HR Student Coun Rep, 1980-81; Sophomore Class Reporter, Sophomore HR VP, 1981-82; Band, 1980-83; Majorette, 1980-83; Majorette Capt, 1982-83; Future Bus Ldrs of Am, 1982-83; Future Tchrs of Am, 1982-83; French Clb, 1980-83; Harlequin-Thespians, 1980-83; Var Plays, 1981, 1982, 1983; r/Prot; hon/Voted Most Sophisticated in Class, 1982, 1983; 1982 Miss Arts and Crafts Teen Queen; One of Five St Finalists in Miss Teen MO; One of Five Finalists in Miss MO Bootheel; 2nd Place Winner in Ms FBLA in Dist; US Achmt Acad for Nat Ldrship and Ser Awd; W/W Among Am HS Students; US Achmt Acad for Nat Band Awd; g/To Attend AR St Univ; Maj in Acctg; CPA.

HIDALGO, PETER GUSTAF oc/Student; b/Apr 15, 1963; h/324 North Orangecrest, Azusa, CA 91702; ba/Azusa, CA; p/Mrs M E Lindman, Azusa, CA; ed/Dipl, Azusa HS, 1981; AA, Citrus Commun Col, 1983; BS, CA St Univ Fullerton, 1985; pa/Coor of Student Activs, Citrus Col; Asst Purchasing Agt, Citrus Col, 1982; Supvr,

Telecommuns Dept, World Vision Intl, 1981; Asst Mgr, KFC Corp, 1980; cp/Circle K Clb, Pres 1983; Alpha Gamma Sigma, Treas 1983; Christian Clb, VP 1982; VP, Citrus Col ASB, 1981-83; Legis Liaison, Citrus Col ASB, 1983; Yth Coun Pres, 1981; HS Newspaper Editor, 1980; Civitan Clb VP, 1979; r/Prot; hon/Fac Assoc Achmt Awd, Citrus Col, 1983; Pres's Dist'd Student Awd, Citrus Col, 1983; Bk of Am Achmt Awd, 1982; Outstg Clb Mem Awd, 1983; Man of the Yr, Citrus Col, 1983; WW Among Am HS Students; Yth in Achmt; Commun Ldrs of Am; g/Maj in Communs; Ednl Admr; Col Pres.

HIGGINBOTHAM, JAMES ROBBIE oc/Student; b/Aug 6, 1966; h/115 Oak Coulee Drive, Lafayette, LA 70507; p/Mr and Mrs Robert N Higginbotham, Lafayette, LA; ed/HS Grad, 1984; cp/Football, 1980-82; Wrestling, 1980-82; Baseball, 1980-84; Key Clb, 1981-84, VP 1983-84; Student Coun, 1981-84, VP 1983-84; Sci Clb, 1983-84; Nat Hon Soc, 1983-84; r/Cath; hon/Citizen of the Yr Awd, 1983-84; W/W Among Am HS Students; g/Maj in Bldg Arch or Chem Engrg.

HIGGS, PATRICIA JANE oc/Computer Systems Analyst Supervisor; b/Oct 30, 1957; h/3331 Summit Boulevard, #46, Pensacola, FL 32503; ba/Pensacola, FL; p/Mr (dec) and Mrs J D Higgs, Gulf Breeze, FL; ed/Gulf Breeze HS, 1975; AA, Pensacola Jr Col, 1977; BS 1979, MBA 1981, Univ of W FL; pa/Mgmt Asst, S Ctl Bell, 1978-79; Computer Sys Analyst II, Univ of W FL, 1979-82; Computer Sys Analyst Supvr, Univ of W FL, 1982-; cp/Phi Kappa Phi; RLDS Wom; Cerebral Palsy Camp Cnslr; r/Reorg Ch of Christ of LDS Activs; hon/Cert in Data Processing; UWF Exemplary Employee Bonus Awd; Grad, summa cum laude; Phi Theta Kappa; Phi Kappa Phi; Nat Dean's List; Intl Yth in Achmt; Commun Ldrs of Am; g/DP in Mgmt Consltg; PhD in MIS; Tchg MIS in a Univ.

HIGHTOWER, MICHAEL CRAIG oc/Student, Marine Option Midshipman; b/Apr 27, 1962; h/3722 Canterbury Lane, Metairie, LA 70001; p/Mr and Mrs Harold F Hightower, Metairie, LA; ed/Darlington Sch, 1980; BA in Ec, VA Mil Inst, 1984; mil/NROTC, Marine Option Midshipman; pa/Mod Appliance and Sales Inc, 1980-81; cp/Soc of Yg Economists, 1980-84, Pres; NROTC Unit, 1980-84; Investmt Clb, 1982-83; Pubs Bd; Commanding Ofcr, VMI Marine Detachment, 1983-84; Cadet Symp Com; HS: Track 1976-80, Cross Country 1976-80, Letter Clb 1978-80; r/Epis; hon/Academically Dist'd, 1981-82; Omicron Delta Epsilon, 1982-84; Dean's List, 1981-83; HS Hon List, 1976-80; Wm Lee Covington Meml S'ship, 1979; W/W Am Cols and Univs; g/MBA; Career in Bkg.

HILL, JAMES PIERCE JR oc/Futures Trader, Student; b/Aug 30, 1957; h/Post Office Box 488, Asheboro, NC 27204-0488; p/Dr and Mrs James P Hill, Asheboro, NC; ed/Grad, Asheboro HS, 1975; BA, Wake Forest Univ, 1979; MA, Appalachian St Univ; pa/Optometric Asst; Govtl Intern, City of Asheboro, 1980; Futures Trader, Self-Employed, 1981; cp/Karate Clb; Ch Choir; Ch Adm Bd; YMCA Basketball; Dem Party; Fund Raising; Marching Band; Pep Band; Jazz

Ensemble; Wind Ensemble; Concert Band; Pres, VP, Band; Co-Dir, Pep Band; Sci Clb; Ecol Clb; Spirit Clb; French Clb; Latin Clb; r/First U Meth Ch, Chair of Social Concerns Wk Area 1983-; hon/Pi Gamma Mu, 1981; Pi Sigma Alpha, 1982; Outstg Sr in HS Yrbook; Jr H Beta Clb; John Philip Sousa Band Awd; Intl Yth in Achmt; Col Register; Commun Ldrs of Am; g/Doct in Law; Public Ser Career in Govt.

HILL, KENNETH EDWARD oc/Student; b/Dec 13, 1965; h/322 Brookside Drive, Danville, KY 40422; p/Mr and Mrs Sidney T Hill, Danville, KY; ed/Grad, Boyle Co HS; cp/Beta Clb; 3-Yr Letterman in Football; Spanish Clb, Treas; Student Coun, 4 Yrs, Treas; Pep Clb; Freshman, Sophomore, Sr Class Pres; Jr Class Treas; Ch Yth Coun; 1 Yr Letter in Baseball; r/Cath; hon/DAR Good Citizen Awd, 1980; Best Spanish Student Awd, 1982; Acad Letter Awd, 1982-83; Am Pvt Enterprise Sem Scholar, 1983; W/W Among Am HS Students; Soc of Dist'd Am HS Students; g/Col Deg.

HILL, REGINA LaVERNE oc/Student; b/Jul 1, 1964; h/705 Harrison Street, High Point, NC 27260; p/Mr and Mrs McKinley Hill Jr, High Point, NC; ed/Grad, T W Andrews HS, 1982; Pursuing a BSBA in Acctg, Wn Carolina Univ, 1982-; Asst Res Analyst, Wn NC Tomorrow (WNCT); Resident Asst, 1984; Atari Computer Camp, 1983; Towne Twin Theater, 1981-84; cp/Wn Carolina Univ Inspiration Choir, Wn Gold; Org of Ebony Students, Secy 1983-84; Cooperative Ed Clb; Volleyball; Softball; Beta Clb; Anchor Clb; NAACP; Band; Miss Jabberwock, 1980; Treas, Meml Yg Adult Choir; Pres of Choir; VP, Meth Yth F'ship; r/Meth; hon/Dean's List, 1984; Nat Hon Soc; g/Maj in Mgmt and Mktg.

HILL, WALTER LEE oc/Student; b/Dec 13, 1955; h/712 East Eighth Street, Charlotte, NC 28202; ba/Charlotte, NC; p/Mr and Mrs Roosevelt Hill, Charlotte, NC; ed/GED, 1977; Ctl Piedmont Commun Col; Currently Enrolled, Johnson C Smith Univ; cp/HS Pres, CHEOO; Tae Kwon Do Soc; Silver Dragon Kung-Fu Soc; Jr High Class Pres; Jr High Student Coun Delegation; hon/Piedmont Col Acad Hon Roll; Johnson C Smith Acad Hon Roll; Johnson C Smith Awd of Acad Achmt; g/AA Deg in Jour; BA Deg in Communication Arts, Jour.

HILLS, HAROLD JR oc/Administrative Trainee; b/Sep 20, 1961; h/701 Maple Street, Brooklyn, NY 11203; ba/Syracuse, NY; p/Harold Hills Sr and Mary Hills-Jamerson, Brooklyn, NY; ed/Norman Thomas HS for Comml Ed, 1979; BS, Spch Communs, Syracuse Univ, 1983; pa/Word Processor, Hlth Studies Dept, Syracuse Univ, 1982-83; Ofc Mgr, Hon Edolphus Towns for Cong Campaign HQs, 1982; Yth Rec Coor, E NY Devel Corp, 1981; cp/Pres, Yth Lay Leag, 1976-78; Tenor Soloist, Temple Choir, 1975-81; Yth Coor, U Christian Front for Brotherhood Chapt 139, 1978-79; r/Berean Missionary Bapt Ch; Asst Songldr, Sunday Sch Dept, 1979-; hon/Dean's List, Sprg 1982, Fall 1982; Hon'd by the Ofc of Minority Affairs for Outstg Scholastic Achmt, 1982, 1983; Cert Winner for the Nat Urban Leag's Essay Contest, 1981.

HINDMAN, TIMOTHY WILLIAM oc/Student; b/Jun 4, 1963; h/HC 70, Box 45, Hay Springs, NE 69347; p/Mr and Mrs Delmer Hindman, Hay Springs, NE; ed/Grad, Rushville HS, 1981; Presently Att'g, Univ of NE; pa/Gen Farmhand; cp/ASME; Tau Beta Pi, Engrg Hon; HS Football and Basketball, Mgr and Statistician; HS Freshman Class Secy; HS Band; Swing Choir; FFA Secy; F'ship of Christian Aths Secy; All Sch Play; r/Rom Cath; hon/Hazel V Emley S'ship, 1983-84; Inter-HS Scholastic Contest, 1978-81; Nat Hon Soc; Cornhusker Boys' St, 1980; HS Hon Roll; HS Sr Class Eng, Math, Sci Awds; Co Govt Day, 1979-80; HS Class Valedictorian; Dean's List; 4-Yr Univ of NE Regents S'ship; W/W Among Am HS Students; W/W Music; Intl Yth in Achmt; g/Deg in Mech Engrg.

HINDS, SHEERY RENE oc/Student; b/Nov 17, 1962; h/1713 Richland, Abilene, TX 79603; p/Lt Col Paul T and Charlene Hinds, Abilene, TX; ed/Abilene HS, 1981; Student, Hardin-Simmons Univ; pa/File Clk in Radiol, Hendrick Med Ctr, 1981-; Secy, TX Drilling Co, 1981; Teller, First Nat Bk, 1980; cp/Future Bus Ldrs of Am, Pres 1980-81; r/So Bapt; hon/W/W Among Am HS Students.

HIRAYAMA, DAVID TSUYOSHI oc/Student; b/Aug 21, 1963; h/2120 Bangor Way, Anaheim, CA 92806; p/Tsutomu and Miyoko Hirayama, Anaheim, CA; ed/Grad, Katella HS, 1981; Student, Univ of CA Irvine; cp/BSA, 1974-81; HS Sr Assemblyman, 1980-81; HS Newspaper, 1980-81; CSF Mem, 1978-81; Vol Wk at Anaheim Free Clin, 1981; SEYO; Basketball; Baseball; hon/Eagle Scout, 1981; HS Salutatorian, 1981; CSF Gold Seal Bearer, 1981; g/Master's Deg in Elect Engrg.

HIRST, ERIK M oc/Student; b/Oct 26, 1965; h/PO Box 331, Walhalla, SC 29691; p/Mr and Mrs Jack M Hirst, Walhalla, SC; ed/Grad, HS, 1984; pa/Pt-time Drywall Helper, Walhalla Drywall; cp/Nat Beta Clb, 1982-83; HS Basketball, Football, Track; Block W Clb; Hon Roll, 1980-81, 1982-83; hon/USAA Nat Awd Winner in Fgn Langs, 1982-83; Am Legion Sch Awd, 1983; Palmetto Boys' St, 1983; Basketball Acad Awd, 1983; g/Deg in Computer Sci at Univ of Clemson.

HIRV, KELLY ANN oc/Student; b/Jul 12, 1967; h/Route 3, Box 31, Gloucester, VA 25061; p/Eino and Myrna Hirv, Gloucester, VA; ed/Grad, Gloucester HS, 1985; cp/Cheerldr, 1981-83; Chorus, 1981-82; Triple Rive Sub-Dist Yth Grp, 1981-83, Treas; Rappahanock Dist Yth Grp, Secy-Treas 1982-83; Nat Hon Soc, 1983; Musical "Godspell," 1983; r/Meth; hon/Hon Roll, 1979-83; g/Maj in Computer Sci at VA Polytechnic Inst; Computer Programmer.

HIVELY, VICKI D oc/Licensed Practical Nurse; b/Aug 10, 1951; h/Route 2, Box 58, Viola, AR 72583; m/Doyle D; c/April Michelle, Rachel Amanda; p/Harry and Nova Honeycutt, Calico Rock, AR; ed/Grad, Calico Rock HS, 1969; Grad, Ozarka Vo-Tech Sch of Practical Nsg, 1982; Upward Bound Prog, 1967-68; pa/Nurse's Aide, Good Samaritan Village, 1980; Nurse's Aide, White River Convalescent Home, 1981; LPN, White River Convalescent Home, 1983-; AR Nsg Home Assn; r/Prot; hon/

HS: Editor of Sch Paper, Bus Mgr of 1969 Yrbook; Citizenship Awd, Lion's Clb, 1969; Pres, Spans Clb, 1981-82; Ranked 4th in AR St Bd Nsg LPN Tests; g/To Attend RN Sch in Future.

HO, TRANG THITHU oc/Student; b/Dec 17, 1962; h/2102 Counter Point, Houston, TX 77055; p/Mr and Mrs Tam Van Ho, Houston, TX; ed/Dipl, Sprg Br HS, 1980; Att'g, Univ of Houston Ctl Campus (Pharm Maj); cp/Tennis Team; Mu Alpha Theta; Future Tchrs of Am; Chums Clb; Nat Hon Soc; French Clb, Secy; r/Buddhist; hon/Nat Hon Soc, 1979-80; W/W Among Am HS Students; Intl Yth in Achmt; g/To Become a Pharm; To Attend Grad Sch.

HOBBS, JANET E oc/Credit Analyst; b/Dec 3, 1960; h/7200 Rockledge Drive, Charlotte, NC 28210; ba/Charlotte, NC; p/Mr and Mrs Harry M Hobbs Jr, Charlotte, NC; ed/S Mecklenburg HS, BA, Univ of NC Charlotte, 1983; pa/Credit Analyst, NCNB, 1983-; Cashier, Winn Dixie, 1976-83; cp/UNCC Student Body Pres, 1982-83; Treas, UNC Assn of Student Govts, 1982-83; Omicron Delta Kappa Hon; NC Student Legis, 1981-83; r/Presb; hon/UNCC Student Govt Awd, 1983; Cindy Holmes Awd for Outstg Mem of Omicron Delta Kappa, 1983; Outstg Yg Wom of Am.

HOBGOOD, M LaVERNE GHOLSTON oc/Charge Nurse; h/6420, Apartment 2, Countryside Drive, Charlotte, NC; ba/Charlotte, NC; m/Angelo; p/Moris Gholston, Jacksonville, NC; Lucille Able Gholston, Charlotte, NC; ed/Grad, Harry P Harding HS, 1976; BSN, Univ of NC Charlotte, 1981; pa/Nurse on Med Unit, Mercy Hosp, 1981-82; Charge Nurse on Surg Unit, Mercy Hosp, 1982-; Sigma Theta Tau Nsg Hon Soc; cp/Secy, Mt Peace Sunday Sch and Bapt Tng Union Quarterly Dist Cong; Deborah Chapt, OES; Chp, Nsg Guild of Faith Meml Bapt Ch; Ch Choir Pianist and Organist; r/Bapt; hon/Sigma Theta Tau Nsg Nat Hon Soc; Nat Hon Soc; 12-Yr Perfect Attendance Awd, 1976; Band Awd; Panhellenic Awd; W/W Among Am HS Students; Outstg Teenagers of Am; g/To Further Ed in Nsg Field.

HOCK, THOMAS GORDON oc/Student; b/Mar 1, 1964; h/18 Josh's Way, Landenberg, PA 19350; p/Mr and mrs Thomas Hock, Landenberg, PA; ed/Grad, Weir HS, 1982; Att'd, Columbus Col of Art and Design; pa/Cook, McDonalds, 1982; Animal Care, DuPont's Haskell Labs, 1983; cp/Intl Thespians Soc; Nat Hon Soc, Coun Mem; Student Govt; Debate Team; Meth Yth F'ship; r/Christian; hon/Pennies for Arts Awd; Intl Yth in Achmt; W/W Among Am HS Students; g/Put Cartooning Abilities to Use and/or Form a Rock and Roll Band.

HODGES, CLAYTON G oc/Student; b/Sep 16, 1961; h/Route 5, Box 592, Rocky Mount, VA 24151; p/Mrs Louise E Hodges, Rocky Mount, VA; ed/Att'g, Old Dominion Univ; AS, Ferrum Col, 1982; Gen Dipl, Franklin Co HS, 1979; pa/Staff, Ferrum Col, 1982; Gen Utility Pers, Continental Homes, 1981; Lab Tech/Biol, EPA, Ferrum Col, 1980; Gen Utility Pers, Erath Veneer Corp, 1979; cp/Phi Beta Lambda, 1981-82; Ferrum Col Firefighters Clb, 1981-83; Riddick Hall 3rd Floor Hall Rep, 1981; Ferrum Col Dean's List, 1982; Franklin Co, VA,

Fed Credit Union Mem, 1979-; Franklin Co, VA, Credit Union Auditors Com, 1981; r/Bapt; hon/Ferrum Col Dean's List, 1982; g/Baccalaureate Deg in Bus Adm/Mgmt, Old Dominion Univ; MBA; Start a Bus.

HODGES, SIMUEL WARD oc/Student; b/Nov 15, 1961; h/214 Spring Avenue, Murfreesboro, NC 27855; p/Richard Sr and Jessie Hodges, Murfreesboro, NC; ed/Murfreesboro HS, 1980; AS, Chowan Col, 1982; Currently Enrolled, E Carolina Univ (Acctg Maj); pa/Salesperson; cp/DECA VP; Spanish Clb; DECA Advr; Day Student Org; hon/Dean's List, E Carolina Univ, 1983; Acad Achmt Awd; Hon List; W/W Am Jr Cols; Commun Ldrs of Am; g/Acctg.

HOFFMAN, BRENDA JOYCE oc/Intern in Internal Medicine; b/Sep 4, 1957; h/Route 1, St Charles, KY 42453; ba/Charleston, SC; p/John and Joy Hoffman, St Charles, KY; ed/S Hopkins HS; BS, Murray St Univ, 1979; MD, Univ of KY Col of Med, 1983; pa/Phys, Med Univ of SC, 1983-; cp/HS: Beta Clb (Pres), French Clb, Pep Clb, Newspaper, Yrbook, Basketball; Col: Beta Beta Beta (VP), Alpha Omega, Dorm Coun (Secy), Basketball, Football, Softball, Profl Wom's Clb; Med Sch: AMSA (Rep), Curric Com, Class Ofcr; hon/Alpha Omega; Alpha Omega Alpha; Dean's List; W/W Among HS Students; W/W Among Col Students; g/Internal Med.

HOFFMAN, HENRY JOHN oc/Computer Engineer; b/Oct 14, 1956; h/10209 Snyder Road, Monroeville, IN 46773; p/Richard and Carolyn Hoffman, Steelville, MO; ed/Heritage HS, 1975; BS, IN Inst of Technol, 1980; pa/Computer Engr, ITT; IEEE, Pres; Soc of Auto Engrs; cp/Student Bd Secy, VP; Sigma Phi Epsilon Alumni Bd Pres; Basketball; Football; Volleyball; Cross Country; r/St John Luth Ch Choir; hon/Iota Tau Kappa Freshman Engrg Awd; Ft Wayne IN Engrs Wk S'ship; W/W Among Students in Am Univs and Cols; g/Bus for Self./

HOKE, JENA LEE oc/Student; b/Jun 25, 1963; h/Route 1, Box 6, Almo, KY 42020; p/Charles R and Peggy Hoke, Almo, KY; ed/Grad, Calloway Co HS, 1981; Currently Enrolled, Murray St Univ; cp/Beta Clb, 4 Yrs; Pep Clb, 4 Yrs; Students in Action for Ed, 4 Yrs; Girls' Varsity Track Team, 4 Yrs; Girls' Varsity Basketball Team, 4 Yrs; Med-Tech Clb; r/Active Mem, Scotts Grove Bapt Ch; hon/Outstg Girls' Track Awd, 1980, 1981; Best Attitude Awd, 1980, 1981; Capt, Girls' Basketball Team, 1981; Capt, Girls' Track Team, 1981; Recip, Bd of Regents S'ship, 1981; Homecoming Queen, 1981; g/Maj in Med Technol; Wk in a Clin Lab or an Indust Lab.

HOKE, RAYMOND F II oc/Pharmacy Student; b/Dec 24, 1959; h/817 North Kansas, Weatherford, OK 73096; p/Robert E (dec) and Sheila W Hoke, Weatherford, OK; ed/Weatherford HS; Currently Wkg on BS in Pharm and BA in Chem, SWn OK St Univ; pa/Pharm Extern, Wycoff Drug, 1979-; cp/BSA, Eagle Scout, Vigil Mem of Order of the Arrow; Kappa Psi Pharm Frat, Secy of Delta Beta Chapt; SWn Am Pharm Assn; German Clb, Pres 1981-82; Alpha Phi Omega Nat Ser Frat, Histn of Psi Upsilon Chapt; BSU; Key Clb Pres, Secy; Nat Hon Soc; FBLA; FTA; Student

Coun; Citizenship Freedom Forum; Band; Marching Band; Golf Team; r/So Bapt; hon/Outstg Freshman Biol Student, Arthur Shuck Awd, 1980; Tom Duncan Awd, Key Clb, 1978; Vigil Hon in Order of the Arrow, 1981; Eagle Scout, 1975; Acad Achmt Awd; 2nd Place, OK Hist Div of SWn Interscholastic Meet; g/To Become a Reg'd Pharm in Sts of OK and TX; Grad Wk in Pharm.

HOLCOMBE, HOLLY LYNN oc/ Student; b/Dec 3, 1962; h/8 Arial Street, Easley, SC 29640; p/Edward and Bessie Holcombe, Easley, SC; ed/Grad, Easley HS, 1981; Student, Furman Univ; cp/ Green Wave Pep Clb; Nat Hon Soc; Furman Univ Chorus; Bapt Student Union; Intervarsity Christian F'ship; Phi Eta Sigma, 1981-82; r/Bapt; hon/Superior Wk in Ec, Psych, Geometry, Acctg; Top 10% of Grad'g Class; Commend from Congressman Butler Derrick and Senator Strom Thurmond of SC; W/W Among Am HS Students; g/Doct in Psych; Wk in Social Sers, Humanities.

HOLDER, CHERYL JAGGERS oc/ Math Teacher; b/Nov 1, 1954; h/10600 Six Pines #515, The Woodlands, TX 77380; ba/Spring, TX; m/E Paul; p/Mr and Mrs William Jaggers, Beaumont, TX; ed/Forest Pk HS, 1973; BS, Ed, Baylor Univ, 1977; MA, Sam Houston St Univ, 1981; pa/Tchr, Klein ISD, 1977-81; Tchg Asst, Baylor Univ, 1981-82; Instr, McLennan Commun Col, 1982; Tchg Asst, TX A&M Univ, 1982-83; Tchr, Klein ISD (Present); Alpha Lambda Delta, 1973-; Kappa Delta Pi, 1976-77; Gamma Beta Phi, 1977-; TX St Tchrs Assn; NEA; r/Bapt; hon/Grad, magna cum laude, Forest Pk HS 1973, Baylor Univ 1977; Alpha Chi, 1976; g/To Teach at the Col Level; To Publish Short Stories.

HOLDER, EUGENE PAUL oc/Scientist; b/Sep 1, 1954; h/10600 Six Pines Drive #515, The Woodlands, TX 77380; ba/The Woodlands, TX; m/Cheryl Jaggers; p/Mr and Mrs E E Holder, Beaumont, TX; ed/French HS, 1972; BS 1979, MS 1981, Sam Houston St Univ; PhD, Baylor Univ; pa/Scist, Betz Labs Inc; Pres, L E King Chem Soc; TX Acad of Sci; Am Chem Soc; NSF Cnslr; hon/ Pub, "Measurement of Viscosity of Clay and Organo--Clay Dispersions Under High Pressure," 1983; Alpha Chi; Golden Key; Intl Yth in Achmt; W/W Among Students in Am Univs and Cols; Commun Ldrs of Am; g/Indust Mgmt; Univ Univ.

HOLLAND, KENNY VAL oc/Student; b/Jul 7, 1962; h/Route 2, Box 71, Mansfield, AR 72944; p/Val and Buna Mae Holland, Mansfield, AR; ed/Mansfield HS, 1980; AA, Westark Commun Col, 1982; Currently Enrolled, Tulsa Univ (Maj in PE); cp/F'ship of Christian Aths; Bapt Clb, Treas; Sch Newspaper, Editor "Tiger's Tale"; Tnr for All Athletics at MHS; r/Christian; hon/ NJCAA Basketball Champion Team, Westark; Recip, Tuition S'ship to Westark; Recip, Ath Tng S'ship to Tulsa Univ; Awd'd MO Val Conf Championship Ring while at Tulsa Univ; Selected to Wk w New England Patriots at Tng Camp; g/To Hold the Position of Ath Tnr on a HS, Col or Profl Level.

HOLLAND, SCOTT DOUGLAS oc/ Student; b/Oct 4, 1964; h/6 Rosewood Lane, Newport News, VA 23602; p/Mr and Mrs J Alvin Holland, Newport

News, VA; ed/Menchville HS, 1982; Currently Enrolled, VA Polytechnic Inst and St Univ; cp/VPI Bapt Student Union; VA Jr Acad of Sci Pres; Nat Hon Soc, Treas; Bapt Yth Coun; HS German Clb VP; Model UN VP; hon/VA Gov Sch for the Gifted; NASA Cert of Outstg Achmt in Aerospace Res; 1st Place, VA Social Studies Fair; Dean's List, VPI, 1982-83; W/W Among Am HS Students; Commun Ldrs of Am; g/Maj in Aerospace and Ocean Engrg; PhD in Engrg; Res in Fluid Mechs.

HOLLETT, JOSEPH LAWRENCE oc/ Air Force Officer; b/Feb 16, 1961; h/170 Celestia Court, Port Saint Lucie, FL 33452; ba/Offutt AFB, NE; m/Taria; p/ Mr and Mrs Roger Hollett, Port Saint Lucie, FL; ed/Ft Pierce Ctl HS, 1979; BS, Mil Hist, w Mil Hons, USAF Acad, 1983; mil/USAF, 1979-; r/Epis; hon/Salutatorian; MVP, HS Swim Team; Outstg Cadet Squadron Cmdr, 1983.

HOLLEY, RANDALL LEE oc/Student; b/Jan 30, 1965; h/Route 1, Box 56, Henry, VA 24102; p/Mr and Mrs Charlie E Holley, Henry, VA; ed/Grad, Franklin Co HS, 1983; Att'g, Elon Col, 1983-; cp/Cub Scouts, 1975-76; Rec Baseball and Basketball, 1974-81; French Clb, 1979-81; Peer Ldrship Grp, 1980-81; Nat Hon Soc, 1980-83; Stage Band, 1980-83; VP 1981-82, Pres 1982-83, Band; hon/Best Sport in Basketball, 1976; Best Sport in Baseball, 1978; HS Hon Roll, 1979-83; Band Ser Awd, 1981; Ranked 11th in Sr Class of 485; g/Deg in Computer Sci.

HOLLIMAN, DEENA BETH oc/Dental Assistant; b/Jan 27, 1959; h/Route 3, Forsyth, GA 31029; ba/Forsyth, GA; p/Elizabeth K Holliman, Forsyth, GA; ed/Monroe Acad, 1977; Tift Col, 1981; pa/Dental Asst; cp/Varsity Tennis Team; Alpha Chi; Alpha Lambda Delta; VP, Bus Adm Clb of Tift Col; r/Ebenezer U Meth Ch; hon/Grad, summa cum laude; Div III All-St Tennis Team Awd; W/W Among Students in Am Univs and Cols; g/Dental Sch.

HOLLINGSWORTH, PHILIP ANDREW oc/Student; b/Aug 13, 1964; h/Route 2, Box 24, Ramer, TN 38367; p/James and Faye Hollingsworth, Ramer, TN; ed/HS Grad, 1982; Att'd, NE MS Jr Col, Stephen F Austin St Univ; Att'g, Memphis St Univ; pa/Inspector, ITT Telecommuns; cp/Football, 2 Yrs; Col; All Star, MS Jr Col, 1983; r/Bapt; hon/S'ship; g/Bus Mgmt; Become Part of a Firm.

HOLLINS, BETTY ANN oc/Student; b/Aug 12, 1965; h/1015 East Edgerton Street, Dunn, NC 28334; p/Johnny (dec) and Betty Hollins, Dunn, NC; cp/Beta Hon Clb; Marching Band; Drill Team; Close Up Clb; Student Coun; Bus Clb; r/Dunn U Christian Yth Movement; Pres, Christian Yth Coun, Trinity AME Lion Ch; Yth Usher Bd; Secy of Ch Sch; Missionary Yth Dept; Yg Adult Choir; hon/1st Place in Ofc Procedures, Bus Competition Day, 1983; Del to Beta Clb Conv, 1983; g/Col.

HOLMES, DEBORAH FAY oc/City Carrier; b/Jan 25, 1956; h/6800 Rasberry Lane, #301, Shreveport, LA 71129; p/Warren B and Ruthie J Holmes, Shreveport, LA; ed/Hon Grad, Booker T Wash HS, 1973; Assoc Deg in Natural Sci (Biol) 1981, Assoc Deg in Natural Sci (Med Lab Tech) 1982, So Univ Shreveport (Both Degs w Hons); mil/

USAFR, 1973-75; cp/Student Coun Rep, 1973; Student Govt Assn Pres, 1979-80; Afro-Am Soc, 1978-82; Sophomore Class Pres, 1980-81; VP, Zeta Phi Beta Sorority, 1981-82; Med Lab Tech Clb, 1982; Biol Clb, 1980-82; r/Bapt; hon/Nat Dean's List Scholar, 1978-80; Hon Student, 1978-82; Am Yth in Achmt; W/W Among Am Jr Cols; g/To Become One of the World's Most Renowned Mech Lab Techs in the Field of Res.

HOLMES, JEFFERY MOUNT oc/ Student; b/May 7, 1963; h/Route 1, Box 75, Goshen, AL 36035; p/J F and Helen Holmes, Goshen, AL; ed/HS Dipl; Troy St Univ; cp/Band; Choir; Col Band; Sch Paper, Yrbook; Eng Clb; Gamma Beta Phi Hon Soc, Troy St Univ; hon/Eng Awd; Dean's List, 1983; Comml Awd; Most Outstg Musician; W/W Among Am HS Students; Soc of Dist'd Am HS Students; Intl Yth in Achmt; g/Maj in Bus Adm/Fin.

HOLMES, KATHLEEN MARIE oc/ Student; b/Jul 31, 1956; h/928 West Alaura Drive, Alden, NY 14004; BS, Westminster Col, 1978; Brigham Yg Univ; Currently Wkg towards a Master's Deg in Social Studies Ed, St Univ Col at Buffalo; cp/Phi Alpha Theta; Alpha Chi; Vol, Spec Olympics; Co-Author, Title XX Grant for Handicapped Prog; Commun Ed Adv Coun; Granite Dist Handicapped Ser Adv Coun; hon/Co-Tchr of the Yr, Granite Dist Commun Schs, 1980; Intl Yth in Achmt; W/W Among Students in Am Univs and Cols; g/Geneal; Write Professionally; Pursue Doct; Teach on Col Level.

HOLMSTROM, CHERYL DENISE oc/Student; b/Nov 17, 1963; h/616 36th Avenue, Vero Beach, FL 32962; p/ Robert D and Dorothy Holmstrom, Vero Beach, FL; ed/Grad, Vero Bch Sr HS, 1981; Grad, Wheaton Col, 1985; Wash Semester Prog, Am Univ, 1983; pa/Internship, Senator Lawton Chiles' Ofc, Wash, DC, 1983; cp/HS: Student Coun, Meth Yth F'ship (Pres); Col: Freshman Student Govt Rep, Sophomore Class VP, Newscaster on WETN, Christian Ser Coun, Am Assn of Evang Students; Concerned Citizens Against Drugs; r/Meth; hon/DAR Citizenship Awd, 1981; Sr Exch Clb Dist Girl of the Yr, 1981; Nat Hon Soc, 1979-81; First Runner-Up, Vero Bch Jr Miss Pageant; W/W Am HS Students; g/Polit Sci Maj w Ec and Hist Emphasis.

HOLSHOUSER, VERA ELLEN oc/ Registered Nurse; b/Apr 13, 1959; h/ 4803 Hummingbird Lane, Memphis, TN 38117; ba/Memphis, TN; p/Mr and Mrs John H Holshouser; ed/Grad, Memphis Harding Acad, 1977; AA, Nsg Prog, Univ of TN Martin, 1980; Presently Att'g, Memphis St Univ for Baccalaureate Deg in Nsg; pa/RN, Coronary Care Unit, Jackson Madison Co Gen Hosp, 1980-81; RN, Critical Care Unit, Bapt Meml Hosp E, 1981-; Clin Nsg Instr on Med-Surg Unit, St Joseph Hosp Sch of Nsg, 1983; cp/Active Mem, Alpha Omicron Pi, 1977-80, Held Ofcs 1978-79, Sisterhood Chm 1979-80, Keeper of the Ritual; Little Sister, Alpha Tau Omega Frat, 1978-80; Col Activs; Secy of Student Govt, 1976-77; Nat Hon Soc; hon/Guest Spkr, 1979 Graduation Class, Memphis Harding Acad; Recip, Nsg S'ship, Univ of TN Martin, 1979; Recip, Jr Hon Mbrship, Sigma

Kappa Sigma Sorority, 1976.

HOLT, GAYLE LYNNE oc/Registered Nurse; b/Aug 16, 1960; h/1609 Corona, Austin, TX 78723; ba/Austin, TX; p/Victor F and Mildred S Holt, Granbury, TX; ed/Grad, SW HS, 1978; BS in Nsg, Univ of TX Austin Sch of Nsg, 1982; pa/Operating Room Nurse, Bailey Square Surg Ctr, 1983–; Assn of Operating Room Nurses, 1983; cp/Nat Hon Soc, 1977-78; Gymnastics Team, 1976-77; Varsity Cheerldr, 1977-78; Orch, 1975-76; r/Luth; hon/W/W Am HS Students.

HOLT, NANCY ELIZABETH oc/Recent Graduate; h/307 Golfer's Lane, Nashville, NC 27856; ed/Dipl, Williamston HS, 1979; BS, Univ of NC Chapel Hill, 1983; cp/Yg Dems at UNC, 1979-80; Social Chm, Parker Dorm, UNC, 1980-81; r/Bapt; hon/All St Band, 1978, 1979; John Phillip Sousa Band Awd, 1979; Student Exch Ser to Germany, 1978; g/To Wk w a Firm in Their Mktg Dept and Have a Challenging Position.

HOMISAK, CAROL ANN oc/Assistant Office Manager; b/Feb 15, 1955; h/840 Fischer Street, #9, Glendale, CA 91205; ba/Hollywood, CA; p/Mr and Mrs Andrew Homisak, Gouldsboro, PA; ed/N Pocono, 1973; Orange Coast Col, 1974-75; AS 1979, AA w Hons 1980, Daytona Bch Commun Col; BSBA, cum laude, Univ of Ctl FL, 1982; pa/Registration Asst, 1978-80; Computer Terminal Operator, 1982; Bookstore Mgr and Internal Facilities Mgr, 1980-82; cp/Phi Theta Kappa; Mu Rho; Col of Bus Rep to Daytona Bch Com for Student Govt, UCF; Phi Beta Lambda; Motorcycle Expo Supvr; hon/Nat Dean's List; Commun Ldrs of Am; Intl Yth in Achmt; g/Pursue MBA and Seek a Mgmt Position at the Corporate Level.

HOOKS, BERNADINE oc/Tutor; b/Apr 29, 1958; h/515 North 86th, East Saint Louis, IL 62203; ba/East Saint Louis, IL; p/Rosetta Hooks, Lebanon, IL; ed/Lebanon HS; AA, Liberal Arts, St Commun Col; BA, Psych, SIU Edwardsville; pa/Tutor/Cnslr, St Commun Col, 1980–; Am Soc of Pers Adm; cp/Pathfinders Yth Org; Psi Chi, Nat Psych Hon Soc; hon/Nat Dean's List, 1980-81; Valedictorian Awd of Excell, 1982; W/W Among Am Commun and Jr Cols; Outstg Commun and Jr Col Students; g/Indust Psychol.

HOOPER, TAMMY SUE oc/Student; b/Dec 2; h/RR 9, Southern Hills, Richmond, KY 40475; p/Mr and Mrs Vernon E Hooper, Richmond, KY; ed/Madison Ctl High, 1983; Student, En KY Univ; cp/Madison Ctl Band; Girl Scouts; Homeroom Rep, Sr Yr in HS; r/Christian; hon/USA Achmt of Merit, 1983; Pres S'ship, 1983; Soc of Dist'd Students; g/Deg in Physics and Math Ed; Tchr.

HOOVER, THERESIA MARIE (TERRI) oc/Student; b/Mar 20, 1963; h/Box 81829-USC, Columbia, SC 29225; p/J W Hoover, Houston, TX; N H Hamilton, Summerville, SC; ed/Grad, Summerville HS, 1981; BS, Univ of SC, 1985; pa/Co-Mgr, Pool Bar and Restaurant, 1984; Cash Register Operator, Wendy's Hamburgers, 1981-83; Other Previous Positions; cp/Wade Hampton Dorm Govt Pres, 1983-84; Bates M Treas, 1984-85; USC Wom's Rugby VP, 1983-85; Mortar Bd Hon Frat; Golden

Key Hon Soc; Chm, Student Govt Summit Fund Drive; RSD Fin Com; Ski Clb; r/Epis; USC Outstg Govt Ofcr, 1983; Outstg Residence Hall Ser Awd, 1983-84; Best Dorm Govt Trophy, 1983-84; Dean's List; Employee of the Month, Wendy's, 1981; Rugby Player of the Month, 1984; Hall of Fame, HS, 1981; Nat Dean's List; Outstg HS Students; g/Double Maj in Mgmt and Mktg; Master's Deg in Intl Bus.

HOOVER, THOMAS WAYNE oc/Student; b/Jun 14, 1961; h/38 Windsor on the Marsh, Savannah, GA 31406; p/Mr and Mrs L H Hoover, Savannah, GA; ed/Savannah Christian Preparatory Sch, 1979; BA in Jour/Advtg, Univ of GA, 1983; pa/Acad Internship, Pringle Dixon Pringle Advtg and Public Relats; cp/Tau Kappa Epsilon Social Frat, 1979-83, Pledge Tnr; Univ of GA AAF/ Advtg Clb; Univ Student Jud-Justice; Univ Student Union; r/Meth; g/To Gain a Position w Growth Potential w an Advtg Agt.

HOPF, JAMES FREDRIK oc/Student; b/Dec 21, 1961; h/39 Willow Drive, Chapel Hill, NC 27514; m/Julie B; p/Mr and Mrs William H Hopf, Jones, OK; ed/Conestoga Sr HS; BA in Govt, Campbell Univ, 1983; Student, Univ of NC Sch of Law; cp/Bapt Student Union; Student Govt Assn Rep, 1981-82; NC Student Legis, Campbell Univ Delegation Pres 1981-82; Varsity Soccer Team; r/So Bapt; hon/Phi Eta Sigma, Pres 1980-81; Epsilon Pi Eta, 1980; Omicron Delta Kappa, 1982; Phi Beta Kappa, 1982; Omicron Delta Kappa Pres Cup Recip, 1981; Pres S'ship, Col; W/W Am Cols and Univs; g/Finish Law Sch; Enter Legal Career.

HOPKINS, BONNIE JEAN oc/Student; b/Jan 1, 1962; h/1943 Northbrook Avenue, Macon, GA 31201; m/Donald Warren Kester; p/Mr and Mrs Joseph Roger Hopkins, Macon, GA; ed/Grad, Ctl HS, 1980; BA in Sociol and Human Relats, High Pt Col, 1984; cp/SGA Jr Class Pres; Alpha Phi Omega, Secy, Social Chm; Phi Mu Ritual Chm, Mbrship Chm; Resident Asst, High Pt Col; Am Humanics Student Assn, Banquet Com Chm, Annual Events Chm; Student Union; Bapt Student Union; Monitor, USDA; Del to Phi Mu Nat Conv; Intern, Cherokee Coun, BSA; Law Explorer Post Treas, Pres, St Pres of Exploring, BSA; Vol, Uwharrie Coun, BSA; Asst Den Ldr, Unit Commr, Coun Exploring Comm; Intern, Ctl GA Coun, BSA; USN Yth Coun; Del to Nat Explorer Pres Cong, 4 Yrs; r/Bapt; hon/Commun Ldrs of Am; g/BSA Dist Exec.

HORD, JEFFREY DALE oc/Student; b/May 13, 1963; h/Route #1, Tollesboro, KY 41189; p/Mr and Mrs Arthur D Hord, Tollesboro, KY; ed/Grad, Tollesboro HS, 1982; BA in Chem, Univ of KY; pa/Newspaper Correspondent, *Maysville Ledger-Independent*, 1980-81; Nsg Asst, UK Med Ctr, 1983; cp/UK Hons Prog, 1981–; Phi Eta Sigma Freshman Hon; Lambda Sigma Hon Frat; Lances Jr Men's Hon, 1981; Haggin Hall Dorm Coun; Alpha Epsilon Delta Pre-Med Hon; UK Student Affiliates of the Am Chem Soc; r/Christian; hon/Valedictorian of 1981 Grad'g Class; UK Pres S'ship, 1981; David Longnecker S'ship, 1982, 1983; UK Dean's List, 1981, 1982, 1983, Sprg 1983; En KY Univ Achmt Awd, 1981; W/W Among Am HS

Students; Intl Yth in Achmt; Soc of Dist'd HS Students; Nat Dean's List; g/ Med Sch; Gen Practitioner.

HORSLEY, WENDY GAIL oc/Student; b/Nov 17, 1963; h/Route 6, Box 139, Rocky Mount, VA 24151; p/Mr and Mrs Walter J Dalton, Rocky Mount, VA; ed/Grad, Franklin Co HS, 1982; Currently Enrolled in Dental Prog, VA Wn Commun Col; pa/Pt-time Operating Room Asst, Friendship Manor; Switchboard Operator, Admitted Patients, Franklin Meml Hosp; File Clk, Roanoke Neurological Ctr; cp/Secy of Dental Class, 1983-84; Am Dental Assn, 1983-84; Muscular Dystrophy Vol; TAD Grp; SCA Ofcr, 1980; FBLA, 1979-82, Parliamentarian 1980-81; Franklin Co Flag Corp, 1980-81; Med Explorers Troop, 1978-79; Candystriper, 1978-80; r/Bapt; hon/ABWA S'ship Awd, 1982; Muscular Dystrophy Best Sport Awd, 1981, 1983; Muscular Dystrophy Best Pair Awd for Cnslr, 1983; Am Love Run Awd, 1983; Jerry Lewis Labor Day Telethon Awd, 1983; Nom'd to Serve on Exec Com for Muscular Dystrophy Assn; g/Grad from Dental Sch; Attend Univ of NC for Specialty Prog.

HORTON, JENISE LENONA oc/Student; b/Feb 4, 1962; h/PO Box 551, Pittsboro, NC 27312; p/Lenon and Jean Horton, Pittsboro, NC; ed/Grad, Northwood HS, 1980; Cleveland St Univ, 1980-81; BS, Social Wk, Univ of NC Greensboro, 1984; pa/Probation/Parole Internship, Pre-Release and Aftercare, 1983; Cashier and Biscuit Baker, Hardee's, 1977-83; Unit Cnslr, Camp Ginger Cascades, 1983; Sr Choir Pianist, New Hope Bapt Ch, 1978-80; Other Previous Positions; cp/Vol Job Devel Asst, Offenders Aid and Restoration, 1982; Vol Ct Observer, Rape Crisis Ctr, 1981; Nat Assn of Social Wkrs, St Chapt, Bd of Dirs; Undergrad Student Rep, 1983-84; Piedmont Dist Steering Com 1983, Nat Assn of Social Wkrs; Nat Assn of Social Wkrs Student Org, Univ of NC Greensboro; Neo-Black Soc, Univ of NC Greensboro, Publicity Com 1982; Voc Indust Clb of Am, Pres 1978-80; Craft Clb, Pres 1979-80; Student Coun, VP 1979-80, VP of Jr Class; Northwood High Marching/ Concert Band, Drum Maj 1980, Bass Clarinetist 1977-80; Softball Team, 1977-78; Tennis Team, 1978; Track Team, 1979; r/New Hope Bapt Ch, Yg Adult Choir Mem 1973–, Secy of Yg Adult Choir 1977-78; hon/Shivers Meml S'ship, Dept of Social Wk, Univ of NC Greensboro, 1983-84; Nom, Univ of NC Greensboro Social Wk Dept for Nat Assn of Social Wkrs Student Rep, 1983; Most Outstg Publicity Com Mem Awd, Neo-Black Soc, 1983; Cert of Recog for Devoted Ser, New Hope Yg Adult Choir, 1982; Chatham Co Outstg Sr, *Chatham County Herald*, 1980; Music Awd, Recog of Outstg Achmt, Perf and Accomplishment, 1980; Exhbn of Art, Chatham Co Ct House, 1980; Most Acad in Eng Grammar, Univ of NC Chapel Hill Upward Bound Prog, 1979; Most Contbg Rdg/Vocabulary, Univ of NC Chapel Hill, 1979; Hon Roll, Univ of NC Chapel Hill, 1979; Most Improved Student, French II, 1978-79; Good Sportsmanship and Attitude Awd, 1978; Safe Driving Awd, Northwood

High, 1980.

HOULDITCH, CHARLENE oc/Student; b/Jun 22, 1966; h/Route 2, Box 380, Carbon Hill, AL 35549; p/John H and Carolyn L Houlditch; ed/Grad, Carbon Hill HS, 1985; r/Bapt; hon/Miss AL Teen USA Pageant, 1983; Recog in Achmt Cert, First Bapt Ch of Carbon Hill, 1983; Cert of Achmt for Excell in Modeling, Pageant Place, 1982; Third Alternate, Miss Hilltop Echoes, Carbon Hill HS, 1982; Sportswear Winner, Miss Am Dream Girl, 1982; 1st Alternate to Modeling, Miss Am Dream Girl Pageant, 1982; Parade Queen Over Mule Day, 1982; Miss October Photogenic Winner, 1982; Miss Christmas Angel Pageant All Over Beauty Winner, 1982.

HOUSE, JANICE LEE oc/Student; b/Dec 18, 1965; h/RR 2, Box 92, Oldtown, MD 21555; ba/Cumberland, MD; p/Mr and Mrs Ronald L Coffman, Oldtown, MD; ed/Dipl, Oldtown HS, 1983; AA (Mtl Hlth Assoc), Allegany Commun Col, 1985; pa/Pt-time Cashier, McDonalds, 1983-; Student Intern, Finan Ctr, 1982; cp/FHA, VP; 4-H, Secy; Christ Ambassadors; Chorus; Ushers, Pres; Green Thumb Clb, Pres; Bus Capt; Student Coun, Treas; Newspaper Staff, Editor; Yrbook, Ad Editor; Missionettes, Pres; Candystriper; Bible Quiz Team; Ofc Aid; r/Prot; hon/Sch Ath Letter; 2 Sch Activ Awds; 2 Cheerldg Awds; 2nd Place, Voice of Dem; Music Awd; Drama Awd; Cheerldg Awd; Extracurricular Activs Awd; Century III S'ship Awd; Sch Ser Awd; W/W Among Am HS Students; g/St Police Radio Dispatcher.

HOUSE, PAMELA LYNN oc/Secretary; b/Aug 7, 1963; h/RR 2, Box 92, Oldtown, MD; c/James David; p/Mr and Mrs Ronald Coffman, Oldtown, MD; ed/Oldtown HS, 1981; Allegany Commun Col; pa/Secy/Bkkpr, Sears, Roebuck & Co, in Cooperation w Martin Constrn Co, 1982; Student Secretarial Intern, Thomas B Finan Ctr, 1982; Student Intern Exploring the Field of Mtl Hlth, Thomas B Finan Ctr, 1980; Secy for Vice Prin, Oldtown HS, 1979-81; Ofc Aide, Oldtown HS, 1977-81; cp/Christ Ambassadors; Missionettes, FHA, Clb Reporter and Reg Reporter 1978-79; Jr and Sr High Chorus Mem and Piano Accompanist; Piano Accompanist for Sch Prodn of "The King and I"; Sr Class VP; Freshman, Sophomore Class Pres; Ushers Clb, Pres; 4-H Clb, Pres, Secy, Activs Dir, Ldr; Fire Patrol Mem; Bus Capt Mem; Candystriper; Cheerldr; JV Basketball Scorekeeper; Editor, Sch Newspaper; Circulation Mgr, Sch Yrbook; r/Prot; hon/Nat Secys Assn Best Comml Student; Voice of Dem 2nd Place; Miss Missionette; Ofc Asst Awd; Hon List; Hon Roll; 4-H Queen; Fire Queen Attendant; ACC Shorthand Contest Cert; Ldrship Awd; Sch Activs Awd; W/W Among Am HS Students; g/Secy Sci Maj.

HOUSE, VALERIE LORRAINE oc/Student; b/May 20, 1968; h/518 Chestnut Street, Darlington, SC 29532; p/Mr and Mrs George House, Darlington, SC; ed/HS; cp/Florence Ballet Co; Ch Choir; Student Coun; Class Rep; hon/Yth of the Yr, Bethel AME Ch, 1978; Beginners Violin Awd, 1978; Small Fry Girls Track Awd, 2nd Place; Perfect Attendance Awd, 1978-81; Soil and

Water Conserv, 1979; Arts and Crafts, 1979; Mite Girl Running Broad Jump, 1981; Good Citizenship, 1980; Fashion Show 1st Runner-Up, 1981; Most Fashionable Awd, 1982.

HOUSEHOLDER, GINA MARIE oc/Student; b/Jun 7, 1964; h/16 Plum Tree Lane, Williamsport, MD 21795; p/Mr and Mrs F P Householder, Williamsport, MD; ed/Williamsport HS, 1982; Att'g, Shepherd Col; cp/Shepherd Col Polit Sci Assn, 1983-84; HS Freshman and Sophomore Class Pres; VP, Student Govt, 1982; HS Radio Staff, 1982; French Clb, 1982; Ski Clb, 1982; Jr Class Play, 1981; Yrbook Rep, 1979-82; Christmas Dance Chp, 1982; Student Govt Elections Chp, 1982; Editor-in-Chief, Sch Newspaper, 1982; HS Yrbook Staff, 1982; r/Cath; hon/Nat Hon Soc, 1981-82; MD Scholastic Merit Awd, 1982; Am Newspaper Publishers Assn Scholastic Jour Awd, 1982; HS Sr Class Most Actively Involved, 1982; W/W Among Am HS Students; Yg Commun Ldrs of Am; g/Deg in Polit Sci; Career in Law.

HOUSER, KAREN YVONNE oc/Computer Programmer and Analyst; b/Aug 16, 1958; h/44 Pennsylvania Avenue, Watsontown, PA 17777; ba/Milton, PA; p/Mr and Mrs Wayne M Houser, Watsontown, PA; ed/Warrior Run HS, 1976; Clapham HS, S Africa, 1976; AS, Williamsport Area Commun Col, 1980; pa/Programmer Trainee, Stoehmann Brothers Co, 1980; Computer Programmer Tech, Eastman Kodak Co, 1980; Programmer/Analyst, Weis Mkts Inc, 1980-82; Programmer/Analyst, Am Home Foods, 1982-; W Br Data Processing, 1984; cp/HS Basketball; Hockey; HS Am Field Ser Clb; YEA Clb; Col Football; Judo; Volleyball; Am Field Ser Adult Chapt, 1977-80; Intl Interviewing Com, 1980-81; Am Field Ser Intl Chapt, 1976-82; r/Presb; hon/Tchrs' Achmt Awd, Col Graduation, 1980; AFS Exch Student to S Africa, 1976-77; Intl Yth in Achmt; Commun Ldrs of Am; W/W Among Am HS Students; W/W Among Students in Am Jr Cols; g/To Earn a BA Deg in Computer Sci.

HOWARD, DONNA MARIE oc/Student; b/Jun 9, 1965; h/Route 4, Box 75, Radford, VA 24141; p/Mr and Mrs Donald E Howard, Radford, VA; ed/Grad, Christiansburg HS, 1983; Att'g, Univ of VA, 1983-; pa/Secy, Dept of Human Nutrition and Foods, VA Polytechnic Inst and St Univ, 1982-83; cp/Class Secy; FBLA Reporter; Student Coun Secy; Nat Hon Soc Pres; Beta Clb; Math Clb, Treas; Monogram Clb; Bleacher Bums; Grad Com; Prom Com; Girls' Ath Assn; Spanish Clb; Pep Clb Exec Bd; Latin Clb; Track; Scorekeeper, Boys' Track Team; r/Cath; hon/Gov's Sch for the Gifted and Talented; Hugh O'Brian Yth Ldrship Conf; Radford Univ Omicron Delta Kappa Book Awd; Most Likely to Succeed in Sr Class, 1983; Homecoming Ct, 1983; Am Assn of Univ Wom Awd, 1983; Outstg Bus Student Awd, 1983; W/W Among Am HS Students; g/Bach's Deg, Acctg/Computer Sci, Univ of VA.

HOWARD, SHARON J oc/Attorney; b/Jul 31, 1954; h/1516 Oakwood Drive, Norman, OK 73069; p/Wilma Howard, Ponca City, OK; ed/Ponca City HS, 1972; BA 1976, JD 1981, Univ of OK;

pa/Atty; OK Bar Assn; OK Co Bar Assn; Org for Advmt of Wom in Law; Phi Delta Phi; cp/Nat Wom's Polit Caucus; LWV; hon/Dem Nom, OK Ho of Reps; Nathan Burkan Copyright Law Competition Winner; Mng Editor, *Oklahoma Law Review*.

HOWARD, VIVIAN ALYCIA oc/Student; b/Aug 22, 1967; h/1316 West Second Avenue, Pine Bluff, AR 71601; p/Judge and George Howard Jr, Pine Bluff, AR; ed/HS Student; pa/Asst Gymnastics Instr, Early Childhood Acad Day Care, 1982; Fashion Writer, *Ebony Forum*, 1981-82; cp/Pres of Sophomore Class, 1982-83; French Clb Treas, 1982-83; French Clb Pres, 1983-84; Cross Country Team Mgr, 1983; Lang Bd, 1983-84; Top Teens of Distn, Journalist/Histn 1983-84; Jr Social and Art; Jack and Jill; Cath Yth Org; r/Cath; hon/Miss Black Teenage World, Pine Bluff, 1983; Miss Black Teenage World, AR, 1983; 1st Runner-Up, Nat Miss BTW.

HOWE, STEPHEN WILLIAM oc/Social Worker, Supervisor; b/May 29, 1956; h/223 Stanmore Road, Baltimore, MD 21212; ba/Baltimore, MD; m/Leigh Thompson; p/Mr and Mrs William Howe, Liverpool, NY; ed/NY St Regents Dipl, 1974; AA, Herkimmer Co Commun Col, 1976; BA, Lycoming Col, 1978; MSW, Univ of MD, 1980; pa/Asst Yth Dir and Day Camp Profl Dir, Utica YMCA, 1973-78; Student Intern, Balto Dept of Social Sers, Protective Sers for Chd, 1979; Student Grant, HELP Resource Proj of MD, 1979; From Staff Asst to Sr Staff Asst to Supvr, Foster Care Review Bd of MD, 1980-; Am Public Wel Assn, 1980-; cp/Lycoming Col: Alpha Phi Omega, Pres of Sociol/Anthropol Clb, Student Assn 1978-80; HS: Student Coun 1972-74, Concert Band and Stage Band 1970-74; r/Meth; hon/Pub, "Special Curriculum Necessary to Prepare Agency Managers," 1976; Bishop Wm Perry Eveland Prize, 1978; Durkheim Awd, 1978; Dean's List, 1974-78; Phi Theta Kappa, 1975; YMCA Nat Ldr F'ship, 1974.

HOWELL, DELECTRA MAUNEKA oc/Student; b/Oct 4, 1966; h/1110 Frederick Street, Shelby, NC 28150; p/Alpheus B and Helen R Howell, Shelby, NC; cp/Pep Clb; Nat Hon Soc; Beta Clb; Civinettes; Red Cross Clb; French Clb; Band, All-St Band for 1983; Proj Uplift; Student Coun; Jr Marshall; Vol for Salvation Army; Ballet; Jazz; Welch's Sch of Dance Theatre; Chosen to Attend Gov's Sch, St Andrews Presb Col; r/Wash Bapt Ch, Mem of Choir, Usher, Mem of ACT Teen Clb, Sunday Sch; hon/All-St Band; Outstg Sophomore; Hugh O'Brian S'ship; Outstg Piano and Organ Student; Asst Pianist and Dir of Chd's Choir, Wash Bapt Ch.

HOWELL, STEVEN JAMES oc/Student; b/Apr 10, 1967; h/Route 1, Box 283A, Lamar, SC 29069; p/Mr and Mrs Willie J Howell, Lamar, SC; Presently Att'g, Lamar HS; cp/Lamar Elem Student Coun, 1978-79; Nat Beta Clb, 1979-; HS Basketball, Football, Baseball; HS Student Coun; Elem Student Coun Pres; Jr High Beta Clb Pres; Nat FFA Mem; Am Legion Baseball Pitcher and First Baseman, 1982; r/U Meth; hon/Jr HS MVP in Football, 1981; Lamar High's Acad Hon Roll; Recip, Hugh O'Brian Yth Foun Ldrship Awd; g/Deg from Univ of SC; Possible Future in Baseball.

HOYER, JESSE LEE oc/Student; b/ Jun 20, 1960; h/201 Birchwood, Easley, SC 29640; ed/Easley Sr HS, 1978; Currently Enrolled, GA Inst of Technol; pa/Co-op Student, US Bur of Mines, 1978-81; Student Asst, GA Tech Lib, 1983; cp/Am Ceramic Soc, Student Br, Secy 1982-83; Co-op Clb I; Soc of Wom Engrs; hon/Keramos, Ceramic Engrg Hon, 1982; Tau Beta Pi, 1983; Gamma Beta Phi, 1983; Briaerean Soc, 1981; Corning Glass Wks S'ship; Daniel Foun S'ship; W/W Among Am HS Students; g/Bach's Deg in Ceramic Engrg.

HUBBERT, DEWAYNE ALLEN oc/ Student; b/Oct 15, 1963; h/Route 2, Box 38, Fayette, AL 35555; p/Larry and Libby Hubbert, Fayette, AL; ed/HS; Student, Brewer St Jr Col; cp/Nat Hon Soc, 1980-82, VP 1982; F-Clb, 1982; AL Jr Cattlemen's Assn Secy, 1980; *Tiger Rag* Newspaper Staff, 1980-81; *Echo* Yrbook, 1981-82; r/Bapt; hon/1st Place, AL FFA Dairy Prodn Contest, 1982; Fayette Co Yth Achmt Winner, 1982; Pres, FFA, 1979-80, 1981-82; Editor, *Echo* Yrbook, 1982; AL Jersey Yth Achmt Winner, 1982; Feb Fayette Exch Clb Yth of Month, 1982; Fayette Exch Clb Yth of Yr, 1982; W/W Among Am HS Students; g/Maj in Dairy Sci, MS St; Doct Deg.

HUBER, JANE KRISTEN oc/Student; b/Sep 25, 1964; h/5002 Woodmark Drive, Greensboro, NC 27407; ba/Terre Haute, IN; p/Mr and Mrs Ronald L Huber, Greensboro, NC; ed/Grad, Ragsdale HS, 1982; Presently Att'g, IN St Univ; pa/Secretarial, Ronald Huber, 1981-83; Sales, Inatural Cosmetics, 1981-; Tchg, Baton Lessons, 1981-; cp/ Beta Clb, Pres 1981-82; Nat Hon Soc, 1981-82; Juniorettes Ser Clb, 1980-82, Treas 1982; Concert and Marching Bands, Secy 1981; Featured Baton Twirler, 1979-82; ISU Featured Twirler, 1982-86; Gamma Phi Beta Social Sorority, Public Relats Chm; Jr Union Bd, IN St Univ, 1983-84; r/Meth; hon/Full Ath S'ship to Attend IN St Univ as Feature Baton Twirler, 1982-86; Alpha Lambda Delta Freshman Hon, 1983; Dean's List, Fall 1982; Spirit of Am Intl Show Team Mem; Ofcl Goodwill Ambassador of the US while in Ireland Performing; g/Maj in Acctg; Minor in Ec; CPA; Wk for a Large Corp in Tax Acctg.

HUBER, MICHAEL GREGORY oc/ Student; b/Sep 29, 1963; h/2353 Chalet Drive, Rochester, MI 48063; p/Col and Mrs Thomas H Huber, Rochester, MI; ed/Rochester Adams HS, 1981; Currently Att'g, Albion Col; cp/Delta Tau Delta Frat, 1982; Interfrat Coun, 1982; Albion Col Hons Prog, 1981; Nat Hon Soc, 1979 (VP); Key Clb, 1980 (Secy); Adams High Wrestling Capt, 1980; Adams High Cross Country, 1980; St Irenaeus Yth Grp, 1980; hon/Phi Eta Sigma Hon, 1982; Albion Col Dean's List, 1982; Albion Col Webster S'ship, 1981; Scholar of Great Distn, 1981; g/ To Attend Med Sch upon Grad'g from Albion Col.

HUCH, DONNA LYNN oc/Student; b/Oct 16, 1962; h/317 Lamar Avenue, Hattiesburg, MS; p/Mr and Mrs Donald W Huch, Hattiesburg, MS; ed/Oak Grove HS, 1980; Univ of So MS; pa/ Co-op Ed, Phy Scist, US Naval Ocea-

nographic Ofc, 1982, 1983; cp/Delta Zeta, Treas 1982-83, Pres 1983; Gamma Beta Phi, 1982; Order of Omega, 1983; Red Cross Aux; Hon Student Assn; Kappa Mu Epsilon; Pres List Scholar; Secy-Treas, Pi Delta Phi; hon/Phi Kappa Phi, 1983; Omicron Delta Kappa, 1983; Phi Delta Rho, 1983; Univ Scholar; Alpha Lambda Delta; Phi Eta Sigma; Nat Dean's List; Commun Ldrs of Am; g/ Bach Degs in French and Math; Oceanographer/Mathematician w US Naval Oceanographic Ofc.

HUFFSTETLER, MICHAEL DAVID oc/Student; b/Feb 16, 1965; h/1380 Battle View Northwest, Atlanta, GA 30327; p/Mr and Mrs Dwight Huffstetler, Atlanta, GA; ed/HS, 1983; cp/ Cross Country; Soccer; Track; Rifle Team; Sr Class, Co-Pres; Student Govt; Beta Clb; Nat Hon Soc; German Clb; Acad Bowl; Pres, JROTC Ofcrs Clb; Sch Newspaper; Top 5%; Buckhead Soccer Leag; Empty Stocking Fund Dr, JROTC, 1980-82; Meth Yth F'ship, 1979-82; Yg Life, 1981-82; hon/Valedictorian, 1983; Atlanta Jour Cup, 1983; Rotary Clb S'ship, 1983; AF ROTC S'ship, 1983; Elks Clb Awd, 1983; Good Citizenship Awd, GA JCs, 1983; Legion of Valor Bronze Cross for Achmt, JROTC 1st ROTC Reg, 1982; Gov's Hons Prog, German, 1982; Hugh O'Brian Ldrship Sem, St Level, 1981; MVP, Cross Country, 1981; g/Arch Deg.

HUGHES, ERIC WILLIAMSON oc/ Student; b/Dec 21, 1966; h/Route 2, Box 416, Baxter Springs, KS 66713; p/Julie S Hughes, Baxter Springs, KS; cp/ Football; Hon Choir; Band; r/Presb; g/ Col at MO So St Col.

HUGHES, MARY ANN oc/Teacher; b/May 6, 1959; h/5850 West Gulf Bank Road, 1108, Houston, TX 77088; p/Mr and Mrs Clyde E Hughes, Baytown, TX; ed/Ross S Sterling HS, 1977; BS, Baylor Univ, 1981; Lee Col; pa/Tchr; cp/Choir; Capt, Drill Team; Treas, Lioness Clb; Nat Hon Soc; Student Govt; Circle K Clb; Kappa Delta Pi; Gamma Beta Phi; BSEA; ATPE; Alumni Assn; hon/Grad, cum laude, Baylor Univ and Ross S Sterling HS; g/Master's Deg in Ed.

HUGHES, THOMAS WILLIAM-SON oc/Student; b/Oct 1, 1964; h/ Route 2, Box 416, Baxter Springs, KS 66713; p/Julie S Hughes, Baxter Springs, KS; ed/Grad, HS, 1983; r/ Presb; hon/Outstg HS Students of Am; g/Comml Pilot Tng after BS Deg from MO So St Col.

HULL, DEE ANNE oc/Student; b/Jun 3, 1966; h/5954 Twilight Trail, Morrow, GA 30260; p/Mr and Mrs David Hull, Morrow, GA; ed/Morrow Sr HS; cp/ Pres, Ch Yth Grp, 1984; JV Softball, 1981; JV Basketball, 1982; Hon Roll; Key Clb, 1983-84; Intl Clb, 1983-84; FCA, 1983-84; Varsity Feature Twirler, 1980-84; r/Luth; hon/Sr Miss Majorette of SE, 1984; Miss Majorette of IL, 1983; St Solo and Strut Champion, 1983; 3rd in Sr World Solo Championships, 1983; World Champion Solo Twirler, 1979-80; World's Fair Twirling Champion, 1982.

HUMMEL, DEBRA ARLENE oc/ Student; b/Jan 28, 1962; h/Route 1, Box 84, Allons, TN 38541; ba/Cookeville, TN; p/Norman and Sally Hummel, Allons, TN; ed/Celina High, 1980; TN Tech Univ, 1984; cp/TN Tech Home Ec Assn, 1982, 1983, Pres 1984; Am Home

Ec Assn, 1983-84; Phi Kappa Phi Hon Soc, 1983-84; Col Chorále, 1983-84; Ch Choir Dir, 1981-82; r/Bapt; hon/Phi Kappa Phi Freshman Awd, 1981; TTU Wkstudy S'ship, 1980-84; McCory Rapid Am Sch, 1980-84; Home Ec Sch, 1983-84; TTU Fac Sch, 1983-84; g/Maj in Home Ec w Emphasis in Fashion Msdg and Ed; Career as a Co Agt or a Tchr.

HUMPHRIES, CLYDE EDWARD JR oc/Security Officer; b/Aug 23, 1960; h/ 812 Surrey Drive, Shelby, NC 28150; ba/Clover, SC; p/Clyde and Evelyn Humphries, Shelby, NC; ed/Shelby HS, 1978; Student, Criminal Justice and Law Enforcement, Wn Carolina Univ, 1983; pa/Security Ofcr, Duke Power Co, 1983-; r/Bapt.

HUNT, CAROL CHRISTIAN oc/ Flight Attendant; b/Feb 14, 1961; h/ 3902 Shadowood Parkway, Northwest, Atlanta, GA 30339; ba/Atlanta, GA; p/ Mr and Mrs A Bruce Hunt; ed/Tucker HS; Att'd, TX Christian Univ; BA, Jour, Univ of GA, 1983; pa/Sales and Adm Asst, Cohn & Wolfe Inc, 1983; Flight Attendant, Delta Air Lines Inc, 1983-; cp/Univ of GA Yg Alumni Coun; Atlanta Yg Life Yth Ldrs; Student Alumni Coun, VP for Public Relats and Spec Events; Student Jud; Delta Delta Delta; Intl Assn of Bus Communicators; Public Relats Student Soc of Am; Student Recruitment Team; Athens Cancer Aux; Kappa Sigma Frat Little Sister, Sweetheart Ct; Greek Wk CoChp; r/Presb; hon/Fac Awd for Acad Excell in Public Relats, 1983; Highest Acad Average in Jour Grad'g Class; Delta Delta Delta Sarah Ida Shaw Awd First Runner-Up, 1983; Homecoming Queen, 1981; Miss Greek Wk, 1981; Mortar Bd; Blue Key, Secy-Treas; Order of Omega; Phi Kappa Phi Nat Hon Soc; Kappa Tau Alpha Hon Soc; Palladia Wom's Secret Hon Soc, Pres; George H Boswell Jour S'ship; Delta Delta Delta Pott Foun S'ship; GA Alumni Soc S'ship; Carol V Winthrop Panhellenic S'ship; Acad Achmt S'ship; TCU; Other Hons; W/W Among Am HS Students; g/To Pursue Interests in Interior Decorating Area.

HUNT, DERRICK R oc/Student; b/ Feb 12, 1966; h/804 Regency, Longview, TX 75604; p/Raymon and Sylvia Hunt, Longview, TX; ed/HS Student; cp/ Student Coun, 1979-80, 1980-81, 1981-82; F'ship of Christian Aths; Pine Tree HS Chorale Choir; Player, Pine Tree HS Football Team; Baseball; r/Epis; hon/Nat Jr Hon Soc; All Reg Choir, 8th and 9th Grades; Capt, 9th Grade Pine Tree Jr High Pirates Football Team; g/ To Play Profl Football.

HUNT, JAY D oc/Student; b/Nov 6, 1962; h/805 Westwood Drive, Tullahoma, TN 37388; ba/Martin, TN; ed/ Tullahoma HS, 1980; BS in Biol, Univ of TN Martin, 1984; pa/Resident Asst, UTM Housing Dept, 1981-84; cp/UTM Chapt, Mu Epsilon Delta, Pres 1983-84; UTM Chapt, Student Affils of Am Soc, VP 1983-84; r/Meth; hon/BS w Hons, 1984; US Achmt Acad Nat Hosp Ldrship and Ser Awd, 1984; g/Attain a PhD in Molecular Biol.

HUNT, LISA LORAINE oc/Student; b/Oct 16, 1967; h/Route 2, Box 174B, Buchanan, VA 24066; p/Robert C and Barbara R Hunt, Buchanan, VA; ed/ Presently Att'g, James River HS; cp/

SCA Pres, 1984-85; Jr Varsity Volleyball Capt, 1983; GAA, 1982, 1983, 1984; FCA, 1982, 1984; Debate Team, 1982; Annual Staff, 1982; Sch Play, 1984; Homecoming Com, 1983; JV Basketball Stat, 1983; Am Angus Assn; VA Jr Angus Assn; 4-H: Lauderdale Commun Clb 1979-83, Botetourt Co Livestock Clb 1983-84, Sr 4-H Clb 1982-, Hon Clb 1982, All Stars 1984, Teen Ldr 1982-, Pres 1979, 1980, 1982, Secy-Treas, Reporter 1980-84, Livestock Judging Team 1980-84, Jr Stockman's Team 1980-84; r/VA Presb Ch Fin Com; Ch Choir; Sunday Sch Class Treas; hon/St Winner, Achmt Record Book, 1983; Del to Nat 4-H Cong, 1983; Tapped All Stars, 1984; Del to St 4-H Cong, 1982-84; Outstg Jr 4-H'er, 1981; Outstg Sr 4-H'er, 1983; Novice Beef Showmanship Champion, 1982; Sheep Showmanship Champion, 1983; St Elect Cong Del, 1982; St Wool Contest, 3rd, 1982; g/To Attend a 4-Yr Col; Maj in Public Relats or Related Field.

HUNTER, ANN MARIE oc/Student; b/Mar 19, 1963; h/Route 2, Box 333, Gray Court, SC 29645; ba/Due West, SC; p/Mr and Mrs M P Hunter, Gray Court, SC; ed/Grad, Laurens Dist 55 HS, 1981; Student, Erskine Col; cp/Pres, Student Coun; Editor, Sch Newspaper; Pep Clb; Key Clb; Spirit Com; Drama Clb; Nat Hon Soc; Pres, VFW Girls' Aux; hon/Selected Student of the Month; Won Voice of Dem Contest for Laurens Co, 1980; Articles Cited as Excellent when Sch's Lit Mag Won Dist and St Hons, 1980; J B Kennedy Scholar, 1981; Superior Performer on NEDT; Presb Col Jr Fellow; Rep to Girls' St (Elected Senator and Party VChm and Was an Alternate for Gov's Sch); Cnslr, Girls' St; Elected Most Likely to Succeed; g/To Grad from Erskine and Enter Law Sch.

HUNTER, GAIL LYNNE oc/Student; b/Mar 8, 1962; h/529 Alder Avenue, Birmingham, AL 35214; ba/Birmingham, AL; p/John F and Alvenia P Hunter, Birmingham, AL; ed/HS Dipl, P D Jackson Olin, 1980; Student, Univ of AL B'ham; Cashier, All-Around Employee, McDonald's, 1979-82; Secy, Care Fair, 1983; Clk, GSA Fed Telecommuns, Fed Bldg, 1983-; cp/Marching Band, 1977-80; Jour, Publicity, 1979-80; DECA, 1978-80; Govt (GSA) Student, 1979-80; Spanish Clb, 1979-80; Choir, 1979-80; Heart Donation Vol, 1984; Polit Campaign Vol, 1983; r/Bapt; Ch Jr Usher Bd's Secy, 1978-80; hon/Miss First Bapt, 1983-84; Perfect Attendance, 1971-80; DECA, 1980; Musician (Flexibal), 1980; Choir, 1980; Spelling Bee, 1975; W/W Among Am HS Students; g/Maj in Bus Adm; Further Knowledge of Communs.

HUNTER, SAMUEL LEE oc/Student; b/Mar 21, 1957; h/Route 4, Box 48, Rupert, ID 83350; ba/Rupert, ID; m/Mary Carol; p/Mr and Mrs Royal Hunter, Rupert, ID; ed/HS, 1975; AA, Math, Engrg, Arts and Sci, Ricks Col, 1981; Brigham Yg Univ; cp/Student Chapt, ASCE; BSA; Basketball, Baseball in Ch Leag; r/LDS; hon/Eagle Scout; Lttrman, Track, Cross Country; Hon Roll; Top Math Student in HS; Hon Soc Mem; Grad'd in Top 10 of Class; W/W Am; Intl Yth in Achmt; g/Master's Deg in Civil Engrg.

HURBAN, PENNY G oc/Student; b/

Dec 19, 1961; h/888½ Oglethorpe Avenue, #16, Athens, GA 30606; p/Effie A Hurban, Cols, GA; pa/Kendrick HS, 1980; Presently Att'g, Univ of GA; cp/Pres, Intl Relats Clb; French Clb; Lit Clb; Student Coun; Sr Class Coun; Model UN; Nat Hon Soc; Editor, Sch Maj; Marching Band; hon/Nat French Hon Soc; Cert of Merit for French; Hon Roll; W/W Among Am HS Students; g/AB in Romance Langs; Law Sch; Judge.

HURST, DEBRA LOUISE oc/College Student; b/Mar 12, 1962; h/221 Beverly Drive, Lafayette, LA 70503; p/Larry G Hurst, Lafayette, LA; ed/HS Grad, 1980; Grad from Dancing Sch, 1980; pa/Restaurant Cashier; Cook; Waitress; Hostess; Fast Food Restaurant Cashier and Cook; Day Care Ctr Wkr; cp/Secy, Hlth and PE Maj's Clb, 1982, VP 1983; Treas, Hd of Social Com, Kappa Delta Pi Hons Ed Frat, 1983; Secy, Delta Psi Kappa Hons PE Frat, 1982, Pres 1983; Drum Capt, 1980; Bible Study Grp; Varsity Track and Field Team; Asst Track Coach; Dance Tchr; Horseback Riding Tchr; Flag Football Team; Basketball Team; Volleyball Team; USL's Physically and Mentally Handicapped Prog; 4-H Clb; GSA; r/Rom Cath; hon/Hon'd at Ed Banquet, 1982, 1983; Recip, Hugh Duncan McLaurin S'ship for Outstg Achmt in Hlth and PE, 1983; Scholastic Letter, 1980; Track and Field Letterman, 1980; Acad Hon Roll, 1980, 1982, 1983; W/W Among Am HS Students; Intl W/W; Intl Yth in Achmt; g/Hlth and PE Tchr for Elem Students; Adaptive PE Tchr; Coach; Master's Deg in Exercise and Sports Sci.

HURST, MARNIE LEANN oc/Student; b/Feb 27, 1966; h/Route 3, Box 223, Town Creek, AL 35672; p/Mr and Mrs Larry D Hurst, Town Creek, AL; ed/Grad, HS, 1984; cp/Beta Clb; Student Coun; Annual Staff; Majorette; Band; Class Ofcr; r/Bapt; hon/Hd Majorette, 1983-84; VP, Beta Clb and Student Coun, 1983-84; Annual Staff Co-Editor; Class Pres, 1983, 1984; St Finalist in Miss AL USA Pageant; W/W Among Am HS Students; g/Maj in Acctg; Minor in Polit Sci; Law Sch.

HURT, HENRY E oc/Assistant Manager; b/Oct 23, 1958; h/Route 4, Box 100, Bedford, VA 24523; ba/Bedford, VA; p/Mr and Mrs Wiley H Hurt, Bedford, VA; ed/Staunton River HS, 1977; BS in Indust Arts Technol and Mgmt, Berea Col, 1981; pa/Student Pers Asst, Berea Col, 1981; Mgr Trainee 1982, Asst Mgr 1982-, Advance Auto Co; cp/Chess Clb, VP; Student Coun Assn, Rep; Track and Cross Country Teams; Student Life, Asst Dorm Dir; Energy Com, Chm; r/Bapt; hon/Berea Col Labor Awd, 1978; Awd, Cross Country, 1981; Bapt Assn S'ship, 1977; g/Co Div Mgr; Master's Deg in Bus Mgmt.

HUSBAND, PHILLIP LYLE oc/Student; b/Sep 25, 1962; h/Route 4, Box 208, Meridian, MS 39305; p/Billy Ford and Barbara Ann Byrd Husband, Meridian, MS; ed/Dipl, NE Lauderdale HS, 1980; AA, Meridian Jr Col, 1982; BBA, MS St Univ, 1984; pa/Resident Asst, MS St Univ Div of Student Affairs, 1983; cp/Treas and Fin Chair, Inter-Sch Coun, 1983-84; Col of Bus and Indust Coun, 1983-84; Pi Sigma Epsilon, 1983; Gamma Iota Sigma, 1983; Pre-Law Soc, 1980; hon/Phi Kappa Phi, 1983; Omi-

cron Delta Kappa, 1982; Phi Theta Kappa, 1980; Hall of Fame, 1983; W/W Among Students in Am Univs and Cols; Intl Yth in Achmt; g/Law Sch.

HUTCHINS, ELIZABETH McNEILL SOMERVILLE oc/Teacher; b/May 21, 1956; h/Route 4, Box 282A, Culpeper, VA 22701; ba/Culpeper, VA; m/Ronald B; p/Mr and Mrs Winston M Somerville, Culpeper, VA; ed/Culpeper Co HS, 1974; BA, Mary Wash Col, 1978; pa/Tchr; cp/HS and Col Yrbook Editor; Nat Hon Soc; Chm, Bd of Pubs; Pi Gamma Mu; Kappa Delta Pi; Phi Alpha Theta Pres; Hosp Vol; Fredericksburg Singers; Student Govt Rep; Tri-Hi-Y; Residential Coun Unit Chm; Tutor, Mtly Retarded Chd; r/Bapt; hon/Grad, cum laude; Almont Lindsay Awd; W/W Among Students in Am Univs and Cols; Yth in Achmt; Outstg Yg Wom in Am; g/Tchg; Commun Ser Prog Activs; Master's and PhD Degs; Raise a Fam.

HUTCHINSON, BRENDA I oc/Composer; b/Jun 15, 1954; h/405 East 13th Street, New York, NY 10009; ba/New York, NY; p/William Hutchinson, Lambertville, NJ; Mary Ann Byrnes, Newtown, PA; ed/BFA, Music, Carnegie-Mellon Univ, 1976; MA, Music, Univ of CA San Diego, 1979; pa/Assoc Dir/Tech Advr, Harvestworks Inc, 1980-; Administrative Asst, Patchworks, 1980-; Exhib Developer, The Exploratorium, 1978-82; Other Previous Positions; Commissions incl: Music for the Film, *Liquid Sky*, Num Dance Perfs, Video, Slide and Photographic Presentations; Perfs Presented at The Bourges Fest, The Exploratorium, Exptl Intermedia Art Foun, The Montreal Film Fest, Larry Richardson Dance Gallery; cp/Vol, Bronx St Psychi Hosp, 1982, 1983; hon/Pub, "The Spoken Narrative and Sounds from Life as Musical Resources," Univ of CA San Diego, 1979; Artist-in-Residence, Morningside Outpatient Ctr, 1982-83; Artist-in-Residence, PASS, 1983; g/To Continue Wk as Composer; To Make an Extended Tour of China; To Become More Competent in Computer Programming.

HUTTON, ROBIN LYNN oc/Student; b/Mar 17, 1964; h/62 Hunsley Hills Boulevard, Canyon, TX 79015; p/Mr and Mrs Robert Hutton, Canyon, TX; ed/Grad, Canyon HS, 1982; Jr Fin Maj, W TX St Univ; pa/Sum Secy, Indust Ed and Technol Dept, W TX St Univ, 1980-83; Student Secy, Alternative Energy Inst, W TX St Univ, 1982-; cp/WTSU Buffalo Belles; WTSU Student Foun; Alpha Kappa Psi, Assoc Class Secy 1983; Bapt Student Union; Chd of the Am Revolution, Pres 1981-82, VP 1980-81; r/So Bapt; hon/Don and Sybil Harrington Hon S'ship, 1982; Allie Collins Meml S'ship, 1982; Residence Hall S'ship, 1982; WTSU Organ S'ship, 1982; First Bapt Ch S'ship, 1983; Hon Grad, Canyon High, 1982; Nat Hon Roll; Soc for Dist'd Am HS Students; g/Fin Maj Wkg towards a Career in Bkg.

HUTTON, TERRY JOE oc/Senior Accountant; b/Aug 4, 1957; h/7473 East 30th Place, Tulsa, OK 74129; ba/Tulsa, OK; m/Wilda Diane; p/Mr and Mrs Clifford E Hutton, Tulsa, OK; ed/Meml HS, 1975; BSBA, Tulsa Univ, 1979; MS, OK St Univ; pa/Sr Acct; OK Soc of CPAs; AICPA; Tulsa Chapt of CPAs; cp/Pres Clb; Pres, Acctg Clb; Exec Coun,

Col of Bus; Fin Clb; Fund Raising Chm, Mortar Bd; VP, Scroll; VP, Lantern; Phi Eta Sigma; Student Assn; OK St Tchg Asst; Grad Student Coun; U Way Vol; Homecoming Vol; Yg Tulsans; Ambassadors for Friendship; r/Ch of First Born; hon/Tulsa Univ Bus'man; Phi Kappa Phi; Beta Gamma Sigma; Atl Richfield Acad Excell Awd; Fac Hon Medal; Fac Hon S'ship; Col Register; Delta Sigma Pi S'ship Key Recip; Phi Gamma Kappa; Pres Hon Roll; CPA Exam Pass; OK St Univ Devel Foun; S'ship; W/W Among Students in Am Univs and Cols; Commun Ldrs of Am.

HYRE, G SERENA oc/Student; b/Dec 15, 1959; h/2949 C Cottage Place, Greensboro, NC 27405; p/Roy and Goldie Hyre, Buckhannon, WV; ed/ Grad, Freedom Area HS, 1978; BSN, WV Wesleyan Col, 1984; pa/Nurses' Asst, St Joseph Hosp, 1983-84; Student Nurse Tech, VA Hosp, 1983; Nurses' Asst, Holbrook Nsg Home, 1982; WV Student Nurses' Assn; Nat Student Nurses' Assn; Mem and Ofcr, Student Nurses of Wesleyan; Mem and Ofcr, Epsilon Delta Chapt, Sigma Theta Tau, Nat Nsg Hon Soc, 1983; r/Christian; hon/Dean's List, 1981, 1982; Mason Crickard S'ship, 1982-83, 1983-84; Recip, Outstg Scholar Cert from Gov Rockefeller IV, 1983; g/Master's in Anesthesia.

I

IATAURO, PATRICIA SUE oc/Musician, Music Instructor; b/Feb 4, 1956; h/621 Nicholas, Socorro, NM 87801; m/Michael A; c/Michael James; p/Mr and Mrs James M Huddleston, York, PA; ed/York Cath HS, 1974; BS, NM Inst of Mining Technol, 1977; cp/AAUW; Col Music Soc; Socorro Pvt Music Tchrs Assn; Dir, NMIMT Theatre Arts Soc; Vocalist in Area Chs; Perf in Local Prodns; hon/Grand Champ, 1972 Capitol Area Sci & Engrg Fair; 4th Pl, Intl Sci & Engrg Fair; Num Awds from AUS, USN, & NASA; Intl Yth in Achmt; g/Perf w Maj Opera Com or Symph Orch as Singer or Conductor.

IGNATOFF, JANICE GAIL b/Oct 11, 1964; h/6214 Lymbar, Houston, TX 77096; p/Mr Jay Ignatoff, Houston, TX and Carole Ignatoff (dec); ed/Westbury Sr HS, 1982; pa/Feature Reporter, KTRK TV; cp/VP, Nat Forensics Leag; Nat Hon Soc; FBLA; Sr Homeroom Pres, Student Coun; hon/Semifinalist Nat Dean's List S'ship Prog, 1982-83; 1st Pl, Oration, City Spch Tour; 1st Pl, Optimist Oratorical Contest; PA Announcer, Fondren Jr HS & Westbury Sr HS; Nat Dean's List; W/W; g/TV Anchorwom News Broadcasting.

ILLIG, TOMMIE AUTHOR (PFC) oc/United States Army; b/Aug 27, 1963; h/Post Office Box 252, Crystal Springs, FL 33524; p/Mr and Mrs Jimmie Dale Illig, Crystal Springs, FL; ed/HS, 1981; Livingston Univ; Univ Ctl FL; mil/Ft Gordon, Communs; pa/Platoon Ldr-Basic Tng, Ft McClellan, 1984; cp/Pres, Varsity Clb, 1981; Assn of AUS; Pres, Ath Clb, 1980-81; Jr Nat Hon Soc; Ftball, 9 Yrs; Track, 4 Yrs; Basketball, 1 Yr; Wrestling, 1980-81; hon/Trainee of the Cycle, 1984; Most Valuable Player of Yr, Ftball, 1979-80; Varsity Clb Pres; Hon Roll; *Tampa Tribune* Player of Wk Ftball, 1979-80; W/W Among Am HS Students; Intl Yth in Achmt; Personalities of S; g/Army Career, Airborne, Ofcr Cand Sch.

IMMROTH, KATHLEEN MARIE oc/EDP Auditor; b/Oct 2, 1956; h/362 Atlantic Avenue, Trenton, NJ 08629; ba/New Brunswick, NJ; ed/St Anthony HS, 1974; BSc 1978, MBA 1983, Rider Col; pa/EDP Auditor, Johnson & Johnson, 1982-; Sys Engr, NCR Corp, 1979-82; Programmer Analyst, Johnson & Johnson, 1979; cp/Phi Chi Theta, VP & Recording Secy, 1975-78; Pres, Treas, Assn for Computing Machinery, 1977-78; r/Rom Cath; hon/Omicron Delta Kappa; Nat Hon Soc, 1973-74; W/W in Am Cols & Univs; Outstg Yth in Achmt, 1981; W/W of Yg Wom, 1982.

INGRAM, BONITA LYNNE oc/Student; b/Jul 5, 1962; h/Post Office Box 143, Cloverdale, VA 24077; ed/Lord Botetourt HS; pa/Sales Clk, Roses Dept Store, 1978-80; Salesperson, Wrangler Wranch, 1980-81; Salesperson, Country Legend, 1981; Sum Yth Dir, N Roanoke Bapt Ch, 1982; cp/SAM, 1982-83; Nat Hon Soc, 1978-80; Drama Clb, 1976; FBLA, 1978; Track Team, 1976; Gymnastics Team, 1976-78; r/Bapt; hon/Hon Grad, 1980; Hon Card Holder, 1980; Outstg HS Students; Outstg Students of S; S'ship from Botetourt Co Wom's Clb; All-Round Favorite Yth of N Roanoke Bapt Ch, 1980; g/CPA.

INGRAM, TRUDY MACHELLE oc/Student; b/Apr 28, 1965; h/Route 3, Box 526, Selmer, TN 38375; p/Mr and Mrs John Ingram, Selmer, TN; ed/McNairy Ctl HS, 1983; cp/Beta Clb, 1979-83; Pep Clb, 1979-83; Intl Clb, 1979-83; FHA, 1979-81; Ofc Ed Assn, 1981-83; Annual Staff, 1981-83; Christian Yth Org, 1980-82, Secy, 1982; Prom Com, 1982; Cheerldr, 1979-83, Capt, 1982-83; r/Bapt; hon/Miss McNairy Ctl HS, 1982; Most Dependable, 1982; Sr Class Favorite, 1982; Hall of Fame, 1982; Miss Congeniality, 1982; Salutatorian, 1983; Picwick Elect Co Essay Winner, 1982; Capt, Cheerldg Squad, 1982-83; W/W Among Am HS Students; g/Jackson St Commun Col, Bus Adm, Exec Secy in Bkg Field.

IRIGOYEN, EDNA EMILIA oc/Student; b/Dec 24, 1962; h/6111 Teague (PO Box 10585), El Paso, TX 79996; p/Pablo and Bertha D Irigoyen, El Paso, TX; ed/HS, 1981; Univ TX-El Paso; cp/Pres, Nat Hon Soc; Ldrship Devel Prog, Univ TX-El Paso; Rdg Tutor for Fellow Students; hon/Dean's List; Yth Apprec Awd, 1980; Valedictorian, 1981; Most Outstg Jr Awd, 1980; Salute to Teenagers Awd, 1981; Most Studious Awd, 1981; Student of the Month, Mar 1981; Soc of Dist'd Am HS Students; W/W Among Am HS Students; Personalities of S; Ldrs of Am; g/Mod Langs Deg in French, Russian & Spanish.

IRVIN, DIANE ANITA oc/Student; b/Nov 9, 1964; h/539 Spoleto Drive; p/Mr and Mrs Robert G Irvin; ed/Marymount HS, 1982; cp/Varsity Tennis, Volleyball, Basketball, Track, & Golf; Capt Varsity Volleyball & Basketball; Jr Mannequin Assisteens Leag; Pep Clb; Girl's Ath Assn; Jr Class Pres; Sr Class Pres; hon/Acad Hon Roll; CA S'ship Fdn; 1st Team All Leag Volleyball & Basketball; CSF; g/Computer Sci Study.

ISENBERG, LAURA LEE oc/Student; b/Jul 6, 1965; h/370 Elden Drive, Atlanta, GA 30342; p/Richard and Betty Isenberg, Atlanta, GA; ed/Ridgeview HS, 1983; pa/Sunday Sch Tchr, 1978-83; Hosp Vol, Over 300 Hrs Wkg Time; cp/Pres, French Nat Hon Soc, 1981-83; French Clb, 1980-83, Pres 1982-83; Beta Clb, 1981-83; Nat Hon Soc, 1982-83; Gov's Hon Prog, French, 1982; Anchor Clb, 1982-83; Student Coun, 1981-82; Sr Coun, 1982-83; Jr Class Pres, 1981-82; Sophomore Class VP, 1980-81; hon/Nat Alliance Francaise Writing Awd, 1979-80; 2nd Pl Fgn Lang Assn of GA Spkg Contest, 1980-81, 1981-82; Optomist Clb Teen of Mo. 1983; Hon Roll, 1979-83; S'ship to Am Univ, 1983; g/Col Maj of French & Jour.

ISAAC—TIMMONS, DENISE PAULETTE oc/Registered Nurse; b/Oct 28, 1954; h/224 SW 4th Avenue 5, Miami, FL 33130; ba/N Miami Beach, FL; m/Richard Earl; c/Latressa Lynette, April Tawana, Lucinda Mariah; p/Mr and Mrs Arthur Timmons, Miami, FL; ed/Miami Sr HS, 1972; AA 1978, AS 1980, Miami Dade Commun Col; Nurse's Asst, Dade Co Public Sch, Adult Ed, 1974; pa/Pres, Praises Fine Hats & Accessories Inc; cp/Phi Theta Kappa; Missionary, Deaconess, House of God; Miracle Temple Apostolic Faith; Move God Choir; Yth VP, House of God Miracle-Temple; r/Holiness; hon/Pres Phy Fitness Awd; Col Bd Talent Roster

S'ship; Nat Hon Soc; Yg Commun Ldrs of Am; g/to Praise God, Seek Success w Praises Fine Hats & Accessories Inc.

ITZOE, DONNA MARIE oc/Student; b/Mar 28, 1967; h/5619 Teresa Street, Columbus, GA 31907; p/Carmela Itzoe, Columbus, GA; ed/Kendrick HS; cp/Newspaper Staff, Exec Editor; Student Coun, VP; Intl Order of Rainbow for Girls; French Hon Soc; Intl Relats Clb, VP; Quill & Scroll; Math Leag; Jour Explorer Post; r/Rom Cath; hon/Most Outstg Eng Student; Most Outstg Jour Student; Outstg Math Student; Outstg Social Studies Student; Best News-Feature Story; Third Pl, Sr HS Writing Competition, 1983; Third Pl, Muscogee Co Lit Meet, 1983; US Nat Math Awd, 1982, 1983; W/W Fgn Langs, 1983; Intl Fgn Lang Awd, 1983; US Nat Jour Awd, 1983; Nat Ldrship & Ser Awd, 1983; Hon Roll, 1982, 1983; Top Five Percent of Class, 1982, 1983; g/Col, Career in Jour.

IVES, DWIGHT SUMMERS oc/Foreign Student Advisor, Graduate Student; b/Mar 20, 1954; h/720 Embassy Drive, Summerville, SC 29483; ba/Charleston, SC; p/Mr and Mrs D H Ives Jr, Summerville, SC; ed/Summerville HS, 1972; Col of Charleston, 1972-78; BS, Bapt Col, 1981; pa/Fgn Student Adv, 1982-; Stock Clk, Frozen Food Mgr, Cashier, Payroll Courier, Bag Boy, Summerville Piggly Wiggly, 1970-81; Gas St Attendant, Gate Gas St Hwy, 1974-76; Stock Clk, 17-A; Hardware Store Stock Clk, Port City Hardware, 1977-78; Field Rep & Instr, Nat Col Repub, 1981; AV Staff, Bapt Col at Charleston, 1982; cp/Nat Assn Fgn Students, 1982-; St Chm of SC Fdn Col Repubs, 1983-; White House Staff Aid, 1983; Treas, Student Govt Assn, Bapt Col, 1980-81; Pres, Men's House Coun, 1979-80; Pres, Bapt Col Repub Clb, 1980-81; VP, Psi Kappa Phi, 1980-81; Copy Writer, Cutlass Annual Staff, 1979-80; Sr Senator, Student Govt Assn, Bapt Col, 1979-80; Columnist & Reporter, "Buc'n Print" Campus Newspaper, Bapt Col, 1979-81; Mem, Pres Cabinet, 1980-81; Exec Coun, 1980-81; Bapt Student U, 1979-80; F'ship of Christian Aths, 1979-80; Tri Psi Chi, 1980-81; New Student Orient Com, 1979-81; Sound & Stage Crew, 1979-80; Bapt Col Activs Bd, 1978-81; Co-Fdr, Bus Clb, 1980-81; Rep, Nat Entertainment & Campus Activs, 1980; Disc Jockey, Bapt Col Activs Bd, 1979-80; Film Tech, Bapt Col Activs Bd, 1979-81; Geol Lab Asst, Bapt Col of Geol Dept, 1978-80; Geol Clb, Col of Charleston, 1977-78; Rep, SC St Col Repub Fdn, 1980-81; Mem Yth for Reagan Com 1980, Reagan Steering Com, 1980; Precinct Pres, Dorchester Co Yg Repubs, 1973-74; N Area Chm, Charleston Co Yg Repubs, 1972-74; Master Mason, Summerville Masonic Lodge, 1975-; Mem Intl Order of DeMolay, 1973-; Advr 1976-77, Reg Depty St 1974-75, Intl Order of DeMolay; Vol for Archaelo Team, St of SC Pks, 1982; Summerville Bapt Ch Choir, 1968-71; BSA, 1966-68; r/Bapt; hon/Outstg St Col Repub for SC, 1981; Intl Order of DeMolay, 1975; Rep DeMolay Awd, 1974; Past Master Councilor's Meritorious Ser Awd, 1974; St Finalist for SC in Liberty Life's Scholastic Contest, Blue Ribbon & Gold Key Awds, 1966; 1st Pl AAA Div,

Summerville Greenwave Band, 1972; W/W Among Students in Am Univs & Cols; Outstg Yg Men of Am; Register of Outstg Grads; Intl Yth in Achmt; Am's Outstg Names & Faces; Commun Ldrs of Am; Intl Yth in Achmt; Dir of Dist'd Ams; Author, "Clone's Corner", *The Buc 'n Print*, 1980-82; g/Career as a Corporation Pers Mgr.

IYER, SIDDHARTH PICO oc/Writer; b/Feb 11, 1957; h/254 Park Avenue South, Apartment 11-F, New York, NY 10010; ba/New York, NY; p/Raghavan and Nandini Iyer, Santa Barbara, CA; ed/Eton, 1970-74; BA 1978, MA 1982, Magdalen Col; AM, Harvard Univ, 1980; pa/Tchr/Tutor, Harvard Univ, 1980-82; Free Lance Writer, 1978-; Writer/Rschr, *Let's Go* Travel Books, 1981-82; Staff Writer, *Time*, 1982-; cp/Public Lectures, Plays Writer; Free-Lance Writer; Harvard Clb of NY; hon/Articles in Num Pubs incl'g *Time*, *The Nation*, *Saturday Review*, *London Mag*; Demyship, Magdalen Col; King's S'ship, Eton; Tchg F'ship, Harvard; g/Writing, Tchg.

J

JACKSON, ABBIGAIL b/Dec 14, 1962; h/Box 156, Artemus, KY 40903; p/James T Jackson Jr, Artemus, KY; ed/Knox Ctl HS, 1980; BS, En KY Univ, 1983; cp/Spanish Clb; Beta Clb; Pep Clb; En KY Univ MT & MLT Clb, Secy/Treas; r/Bapt; hon/HS Spanish & Eng Awd; Hon Student; Top Ten; Dean's List; g/Specialize in Chem, Med Technol.

JACKSON, C KELLY oc/Student; b/Jan 9, 1974; h/2320 White's Mill Road, Sumter, SC 29150; p/Mr and Mrs John H Jackson Jr, Sumter, SC; ed/HS, 1982; cp/Citadel Rod & Gun Clb, Secy; Westminster Yth F'ship, Treas; Blood Drive Com; Citadel Boating Adv Com; r/Prot; hon/Pres Awd for Creat Yth Devel, Citadel Sum Camp For Boys, 1983; W/W Among Am HS Students; g/Biol Maj.

JACKSON, CATHERINE PATRICIA oc/Word Processor Operator II; b/Feb 17, 1960; h/1005 East Brooks, Apartment C, Norman, OK 73071; ba/Norman, OK; p/Frank and Patricia Jackson, Springdale, AR; ed/Springdale HS, 1978; BFA, Univ OK, 1982; Columbia Col, 1978-79; pa/Word Processor Operator-Info Sys Progs 1982, Clk Typist-Botany/Microbiol 1982-83, Student Clk Typist-Chem Engrg 1981-82, Student Asst-Botany/Microbiol 1981, Univ OK; Student Secy, Maintenance Ofc, Columbia Col, 1979; Clk Typist, Univ Food Ser, Univ AR, 1978; Dancer in Num Prodns incl'g "High Button Shoes", "Gypsy", "Kiss Me Kate", "OK"; cp/Alphi Phi Social Frat, Corres'g Secy 1981, Pledge Class Treas 1979, Standards Com 1980-82; OU Ballet Co, 1979-82; Campus Chest, Treas, 1980; Winter Welcome Wk-All Campus Bash Chm, 1979; Campus Commun Govt Rep, 1978; Yrbook Staff, Acad Sect Editor; Ski Clb; Columbia Col Dance Co; r/Meth; hon/Dean's Hon Roll, Univ OK; Dean's List, Columbia Col; Columbia Col Dance S'ship; g/Dance, Arts Adm.

JACKSON, FRANCOIS oc/Teacher; b/Feb 11, 1952; h/C-4 Dillingham Heights, Richmond, KY 40475; ba/Lexington, KY; p/Mr William A and Mrs Heneritta Jackson, Richmond, KY; ed/USN, Yeomen Refresher Tng, Adm Cert, 1978; BA, Berea Col, 1970-79; BA, En KY Univ, 1979-82; Univ Cinc, 1978-80; mil/USN; pa/Yeomen Interpreter, Adm, USN, 1973-77; Berea Col Prog Dir, 1977-79; Fayette Co Sch Tchr, 1982-; cp/Dir, Ebony Players, 1979-; Tchr, Fed Corrections Inst, 1982; Opera Dir, Nat Endowment Arts, 1982; Perf, Ed TV, 1975-76; Dir, Richmond Dance Ensemble, 1979-82; Dir, Miss Black Richmond Pageant, 1979; Campus Act Bd; Upward Bound, 1970-79; En KY Univ Ensemble, 1979-82; Dir of Traveling Troup, *Mahalia*, 1983; r/Bapt; hon/Most Outstg Yg Men of Am; Nat Forensic, St Oral Interpreter Champ, 1975; Berea Col Outstg Civic Student; Owens-Dodson Poetry Awd, 1980; En KY Univ, Most Outstg Student, 1983.

JACKSON, IVY MARGARET oc/Unit Secretary, Student; b/Nov 1, 1962; h/518 Frisco Road, Pensacola, FL 32507; ba/Pensacola, FL; p/Harold T Booth and Billie Jean Booth, Pensacola, FL; ed/Pensacola HS, 1981; Cert, Unit Secy Prog, Pensacola Jr Col, 1982; pa/Unit

Secy, Peadiatric Unit, W FL Hosp, 1983; cp/Ladies Aux Fleet Res Assn; Renaissance Fitness & Hlth Spa; Editor Yrbook; r/Ch of Christ; hon/W/W Among Am HS Students; Poetry Contest; g/to become a Phy Therapist.

JACKSON, JERRY WEST oc/Student; b/Jun 7, 1965; h/9005 Coralberry Place, Richmond, VA 23229; p/Mr and Mrs Jerry Jackson, Richmond, VA; ed/Monroe HS, 1983; USAF Acad; cp/Monroe HS Band; Interact Clb; French Clb; Future Tchrs Am; Sci Clb; Am Field Soc; CD & Co (Sch Spirit Clb); Ch Leag Basketball; Jr Varsity Basketball; Participated in Num Progs incl'g Appalachian St Univ Sum Sci Prog, NC St Nuclear Sci & Technol Prog for Rising Srs, Close Up-Wash DC; r/Yth Choir, HS Hand Bell Choir, Yth Coun Rep, First Bapt Ch; hon/Nat Hon Soc; Rotary F'ship to Attend Close Up, Wash DC, 1982; Finalist in Selection for NC Sch of Sci & Math; Nom'd NC Gov's Sch; Co-wide Hugh O'Brien Ldrship Awd, 1981; Rotary Ldrship Camp, 1981; Wingate Col HS Math Contest, 1961, 1982; Class Marshall; Furman Univ Scholar Nom.

JACKSON, LESLIE LOUISE oc/Student, Pt-time Waitress; b/Dec 5, 1964; h/369 Westover Drive, Granbury, TX 76048; ba/Granbury, TX; p/Ronald and Pat Jackson, Granbury, TX; ed/Granbury HS; pa/Waitress/Hostess, Cuckoo's Nest Restaurant, 1981-83; Secy, 1980; cp/Varsity Basketball, 1981-82, 1982-83; Tutor; r/Meth, Sunday Sch Tchr, Acton Meth Ch; hon/Salutatorian; Nat Hon Soc, 1981-; g/Med.

JACKSON, LORI KAY oc/Student, Pt-time Retail Sales; b/Jul 17, 1963; h/Route 1, Box 1417, Arp, TX 75750; ba/Tyler, TX; p/Mr and Mrs E R Jackson Jr, Arp, TX; ed/Chapel Hill HS, 1981; AA, Tyler Jr Col, 1983; Univ TX-Austin; cp/Phi Theta Kappa, 1982-83; Math-Sci Clb, 1978-81; Band, 1977-81; Nat Hon Soc, 1980-81; Drafting Clb, 1979-81; Student Cong, 1980-81; hon/George W Pirtle Engrg & Sci S'ship, 1983-84; Gilley Swift Engrg S'ship, 1982-83; CRC Press Freshman Chem Awd, 1982; Outstg Physics Student, 1982-83; Rotary Clb Awd, 1981; DAR Good Citizen Yr, 1981; W/W Among Am HS Students; W/W in Music; W/W Among Am Jr Cols; Nat Dean's List; g/Engrg.

JACKSON, MARSHELL RENA oc/Student; b/Nov 18, 1966; p/Josh Jackson, Sawyerville, AL, and Mrs Eddie Mae Jackson, Birmingham, AL; ed/P D Jackson-Olin HS; pa/Elderly Aide, JCCEO, Pratt City Commun Ctr, 1982; cp/Marching & Concert Band, 1982-; FBLA, VP, 1983-84; Session Room Pres 1982-83; VP 1983-84; Bus Ed I, Pres, 1982-83; Bus Ed II, VP, 1983-84; r/Bapt; hon/Top Student in Bus Ed I, 1982-83; Outstg Sophomore in Marching Band, 1982-83; 1st Attendant to Ms Sophomore, 1982-83; 2nd Attendant to Ms Jr, 1983-84; Contestant in Miss AL Co-Ed Pageant, 1983-84; g/TN St Univ, Law.

JACKSON, MARTIN ERIC oc/Student; h/2048 West 16th Street, Jacksonville, FL 32209; p/Mattie Jackson, Jacksonville, FL; ed/Edward H White HS, 1980; Att'g Bethune Cookman Col; cp/Basketball Team; VP, Gamma Theta Chapt of Kappa Alpha Psi Frat Inc; r/Bapt; hon/Hon Student; All-Star at Stetson Univ Basketball Camp, 1979; Selected to 49 of 100 Players in FL, 1979;

g/Mktg.

JACKSON, MONICA MICHELLE b/Oct 3, 1965; h/1562 Cypress Drive, Radcliff, KY 40160; p/Mr and Mrs Thomas L Lee, Radliffe, KY; ed/N Hardin HS, 1983; cp/Pep Clb; Hist Clb; French Clb; Lttrman's Clb; Track Team; Presch VBS Tchr; Elect Return Helper; hon/Nat Merit S'ship Finalist; Olin Corporation S'ship Recip; St Ec Sem; Ath Lttr for Track; W/W Among Am HS Students; g/Ec.

JACKSON, TERESA ANN oc/Medicare Auditor; b/Feb 1, 1960; h/1984 Oberlin Court, Number 205, St Louis, MO 63146; ba/St Louis, MO; m/Larry R; p/Mr and Mrs W D Blair, Farmington, MO; sp/Roger N Jackson, Cheyenne, WY, and Doris F Jackson, Hallsville, MO; ed/Farmington Sr HS, 1978; BS, Ctl Meth Col, 1982; pa/Medicare Auditor, Blue Cross Assn, 1982-; cp/Phi Beta Pres, Treas; Zeta Psi Lambda; Omicron Delta Kappa; Delta Mu Delta; Beta Epsilon; Concert Band; Pom-Pom Corps; hon/Curator's Scholar; Outstg Mktg Student; W/W in Am Cols & Univs Nom; g/CPA in Growing Co.

JACOBMEIER, JON JAY oc/Student; b/Sep 30, 1965; h/1312 Meadow Lane, Wayne, NE 68787; ba/Provo, UT; p/Vern and Doris Jacobmeier, Wayne, NE; ed/Carroll HS, 1983; Brigham Yg Univ; pa/Foreman, 1977-83; Bean Walking/Baling Hay, 1980-83; Constrn, 1978; Mgr, 1977-83; cp/Team Capt Wrestling; Band; Stagehand; 4-H; Coach for Wrestling Clb; Ftball; Track; r/Meth; hon/Nat Hon Soc; Phi Eta Sigma; All-Area Team Wrestling, 1979-83; Sr Class Rep; g/Telecommuns or Theater & Cinematic Arts.

JACOBS, HORACE oc/Research Technician; b/Jun 9, 1959; h/3512 Gazella Cir, Fayetteville, NC 28303; ba/Washington, DC; p/Fannie Jacobs, Fayetteville, NC; ed/Westover Sr HS, 1978; A, Univ NC-Wilmington, 1983; pa/Res Aide, Coastal Zone Resources, 1983; Res Aide, Univ NC-Wilmington, 1983; cp/Clb Ftball Team Mem; r/Bapt; g/Social Res.

JACOBS, JACKIE L oc/Executive Director; b/Jul 8, 1953; h/431 Plaza Drive, Binghamton, NY 13903; ba/Binghamton, NY; p/Jenny Dornbusch Jacobs, Middletown, NY; ed/Middletown HS, 1971; St Univ NY-Binghamton; pa/Exec Dir, 1983, Jewish Fdn of Broome Co Inc; Asst Dir Planning & Allocations 1982-83, Planning Assoc 1979-82, United Way Broome City; Owner/Proprietor, Green Intl Enterprises, 1976-79; cp/Bd Dirs, NY-PA Hlth Sys Agy; Bd Dirs, Com Planning & Evaluation Com, CORE Agy Commun Support Sys; Broome Co Envir Mgmt Coun; Selective Ser Sys Draft Bd; Rotary; Yg Dems Broome Co; Morning Knights Toastmasters; BSA, Troop Ldr; r/Jewish; hon/Publisher, *The Reporter*; W/W Am HS; Outstg Yg Men Am; W/W World Ldrs.

JAEHNEN, CAROL SUE oc/Manager, Student; b/Mar 29, 1962; h/Route 2, Box 351-A, Covington, TN 38019; ba/Covington, TN; p/Edwin C and Ann Jaehnen, Covington, TN; ed/Covington HS, 1980; Memphis St Univ; Barbizon Modeling Sch; pa/Swing Mgr 1982-; Salesperson/Crew Chief 1980-82, McDonald's; cp/Student Secy, Covington HS, 1979; r/Cath; hon/Nat Hon Soc;

Top Ten in HS; 6th in Class; Dean's List, Memphis St Univ; g/Mktg Maj, BBA Deg.

JAFFE, KENNETH ALAN oc/Student; b/Jan 6, 1955; h/285 Central Park West, New York, NY 10034; ba/Same; p/Joseph and Nora Jaffe, New York, NY; ed/Walden HS, 1973; Columbia Col; Penn St Univ; BA, Hunter Col, City Univ NY, 1980; pa/Grp Tchr, Little Star of Broome St, 1982; Asst Tchr, Chd'd Day Care Ctr, 1981-82; Asst to Nora Jaffe on Sculptural Reliefs of Horses made for Decorator Karl Springer & Larry Gelbert; cp/NY Artist's Equity, 1982; Columbia Judo Clb, 1974-75; r/Jewish; hon/Crafts Maj, 1973, Walden HS; Intl Yth in Achmt; g/NY Inst Technol, Computer Graphics; Career as Artist.

JAFFE, WILLIAM B oc/Student; h/6 Macopin Avenue, Montclair, NJ 07043; ba/New York, NY; p/Julian (dec) and Miriam Jaffe, Montclair, NJ; ed/Montclair HS, 1980; Yeshivat Ha Mivtar, 1980; Columbia Univ, 1980-82; Hebrew Univ, 1982-83; pa/Temp Ofc Help, Radius Inst, 1982; Cnslr, Camp Young Judea, 1981; J, Levine Book Co, 1981; Montclair Public Lib, 1978-79; cp/Editor, *Mountaineer*, Montclair HS; Columbia Earth Coalition, 1980-82; Columbia Judo Clb, 1980-82; r/Judaism; hon/Author of "Ex-Refusenik: Jewish Activists in Peril" *Jewish Student Press Ser*, 1981, "A Yg Man Looks at the Yg Man in I B Singer's Stories", *Jewish News Yth Supplement-Spectrum*, 1981; g/Course of Study, European Hist.

JAKUB, CHERYL ANN oc/Student; b/Apr 6, 1965; h/Route 13, Box 329, Bowling Green, KY 42101; p/Joseph and Bernice Jakub, Bowling Green, KY; ed/Warren Ctl HS, 1983; Purdue Univ; cp/Beta Clb; FCA; Student Coun Rep; Feature Twirler; Flutist, Concert Band; Yng Life; UCP Telethon, Childfest, Boys Clb Benefit Perfs; Hosp Vol; JA VP; hon/Miss Majorette of KY; Nat Math Awd; 1st Runner-Up, Jr Miss; Jr Miss Scholastic Awd; W/W Among Am HS Students; W/W in Baton Twirling; g/Maj in Elect Engrg.

JALUFKA, KELLY RENEE oc/Student; b/Oct 12, 1962; h/Box 41, Blessing, TX 77419; p/Billy Jalufka and Evelyn Luker; ed/Tidehaven HS, 1981; Univ TX; cp/FTA; FHA; Coun of Pres; Lang Arts; Alpha Phi Omega; Cheerldr; Editor, Sch Newspaper; hon/Nat Hon Soc; Phi Eta Sigma; LG Balfour Awd; U/L St Competitor; Miss THS; Phi Beta Chi; All-Dist Volleyball; All-Dist Basketball; W/W Among Am HS Students; Soc Dist'd HS Students.

JAMES, BRENDA GAY oc/Student; b/Sep 10, 1983; h/Route 2, Box 188, Hopkins, SC 29061; p/Mr and Mrs Charles W James, Hopkins, SC 29061; ed/Lower Richland HS, 1983; Coker Col; pa/Pt-time Cashier, Mr Bunky's, 1981-; cp/4-H Horse Prog, 1976-82; Beta Clb Mem, 1979-81; VP 1980, Pres 1981, FBLA; Student Govt Assn Senator, 1982; Commr, Ser Org to Coker Col, 1983; Rho Alpha Nu Pres, 1982; SGA VP, 1983; r/Bapt; hon/Top Fifteen Hon Student, 1979; Hon Student; Outstg Mem, FBLA, 1981; Outstg Bus & Ofc Ed Student, 1981; Awd for Sers Rendered as SGA Senator, 1982; g/Bus Mgt Maj.

JAMES, HELENA CAROL oc/Student; b/Apr 16, 1966; h/Route 1, Mt View Est, Berea, KY 40403; p/Shirley Castle, Berea, KY; ed/Madison Ctl HS, 1984; Bus Voc Sch; cp/Secy F'ship of Christian Aths, 1983; Treas, Sr Beta, 1984; Secy, Tribe & Pep Clb, 1984; VP Jr Beta Clb, Ctl Girl's Ath Clb, 1981; Girl's Basketball, 1980-83; Cheerldr, 1980-83; hon/Acad Hon Roll, 1981-84; Optimist Clb Awd, 1983; KY St-wide Hist Comp, 1983; g/Deg in Computer Tech.

JAMES, SONYA ELAINE oc/Student; b/Nov 16, 1962; h/Post Office Box 395, Burgaw, NC 28425; ba/Mars Hill, NC; p/Mr and Mrs J W James Jr, Burgaw, NC; ed/Pender HS, 1981; Mars Hill Col; pa/Hlth Asst, Reade's Grocery, 1979-81; Cnslr, Camp Kirkwood, Camp Albemarle, 1982; Tutor/Cnslr, Mars Hill Col Upward Bound Prog, 1983; cp/Pres, Hlth Occups; Chm, Sprg Dance Com; Chm Clb; Sr Float Com; Drama Class Queen; Baily Mt Cloggers; Dance Co; Pi Sigma Phi; r/Presb; hon/Drama Class Rep, 1980; Freshman Class Rep, 1978; Baily Mt Cloggers, 1982; Advr's Aid, 1980-81; g/PE, Teach.

JAMIESON, WILLIAM MARK oc/Student; b/Apr 3, 1964; h/3141 Curzon Avenue, Memphis, TN; p/Mr and Mrs Oliver M Jamieson Jr, Memphis, TN; ed/Oakhave HS, 1982; GA Inst Technol; cp/BSA; TN Mock Trial Competition; Hon Soc Pres; Indust Arts Clb VP; Del, Yth Conf; Yrbook Staff; Mod Music Masters; Ch Coun on Min; Yth Choir; Cable TV Prod; hon/Nat Merit S'ship; Salutatorian; Most Likely to Succeed; g/Aerospace Engrg.

JARRELL, ELIZABETH ANN oc/Student; b/Oct 13, 1965; h/1235 East Colonial Drive, Salisbury, NC 28144; p/Mr and Mrs H Joe Jarrell, Salisbury, NC; ed/Salisbury HS, 1983; NC St Univ; cp/Keywanettes Parliamentn, ASTRA Treas; French Clb, AFS; Chm Student Coun Com, 1983; Homeroom VP, 1982; Bapt Ch Yth Grp & Volleyball Leag; r/Bapt; hon/Nat Hon Soc; Hons Assem; Hon Roll; Ec Awd, 1983; Debutane Ball, 1983; g/BA Deg in Spch-Communs.

JASINSKI, LAURIE EILEEN oc/Student; b/Sep 19, 1964; h/24 Ridge Drive, New Braunfels, TX 78130; ba/New Braunfels, TX; p/Richard A and Laurie J Jasinski, New Braunfels, TX; ed/New Braunfels HS, 1983; SW TX St Univ; pa/Legal Secy, 1982-84; cp/Nat Hon Soc; French Clb; Newspaper Staff; Phi Eta Sigma; Alpha Lambda Delta Hon Soc; r/Cath; hon/Articles in *Univ Star*, SW TX St Univ; Valedictorian, 1983; Elk's Teen of Yr, 1983; Dean's List; C J Davidson S'ships, 1983, 1984; W/W Among Am HS Students; g/Eng Maj, Freelance Writer & Songwriter.

JAVORSKY, SUE oc/Student; b/Mar 18, 1966; h/117 Old Bay Road, Biloxi, MS 39531; p/Mr and Mrs Joseph Javorsky, Biloxi, MS; ed/Mercy Cross HS; cp/Baseball, Ftball Mgr; Student Coun Rep; Nat Hon Soc Mem; Mu Alpha Theta Clb; Gayfers Teen Bd; Corres Secy & Histn of So Miss Clb; r/Cath; hon/Superior Hon Roll; US Achmt Awds in Algebra II, Biol; W/W Among Am HS Students; Soc Dist'd Am HS Students; g/Attend LA St Univ.

JEFFERSON, MARTHA S b/Feb 5, 1960; h/Route 3, Rocky Mount, VA 24151; p/Stephen Ashford Jefferson, Sr, Rocky Mount, VA; ed/Franklin Co HS, 1978; Emory & Henry Col, 1978-80; VA Intermont Col, 1980-81; BS, Radford Univ, 1981-83; pa/Radiol Receptionist, Bristol Meml Hosp, 1980-81; cp/Delta Mu Delta; Phi Kappa Phi; r/Christian; g/MBA, Career in Prodn Mgmt.

JEFFREY, MICHAEL DAVID oc/Student; b/May 24, 1965; h/4414 White Oak, Nacogdoches, TX 75961; p/Kay Jeffrey, Nacogdoches, TX; ed/Nacogdoches HS, 1983; pa/Labor, Indian River Intl, 1981; Stocker, Gibson's, 1981-83; cp/Key Clb, 1980; Meth Yth Org, Treas, 1982-83; Band, 1979-83; Nat Hon Soc, 1982-83; Tennis Team, 1982-83; r/Meth; hon/JC's S'ship, 1983; Rotary Student Guest, 1983; All-Reg Band, 1983; W/W Among AM HS Students, 1982-83; g/Attend Stephen F Austin St Univ.

JEHN, JUSTIN ANTHONY oc/Lifeguard, Student; b/Nov 11, 1966; h/863 Wayman, Taylor Mill, KY 41015; ba/Taylor Mill, KY; p/James and Janet Jehn, Taylor Mill, KY; cp/Cross Country Team, 1980, 1981, 1982; Sch Swim Team, 1980-83; French Clb, 1981-82; YMCA Swim Team, 1982, 1983; Sum Swim & Diving Team, NKSL, 1981-84; Yth Baseball & Basketball; r/Cath; hon/Recommended for Outstg Teens Am & W/W Among Am HS Students; Hons in Sch Cross Country & Swimming, 1982, 1983; Hons in Sum NKSL Swim & Diving, 1982-83; King of Mardi Gras Sch Dance; g/Col, Establish Career Contracting.

JELASIC, JAMES LESTER oc/Professional Piano Accompanist/Vocal Coach; b/Nov 6, 1957; h/23126 Lawrence, Dearborn, MI 48128; ed/Dearborn HS, 1975; BMus, En MI Univ, 1980; Fgn Exch Student, Univ Warwick (England), 1978; MMus, Univ MI, 1982; pa/Intern Coach/Accompanist, MI Opera Theatre, 1983; Recital Tour, Vocal Accompanist-Munich W Germany, 1983-84; Fulbright Scholar, Paris France, 1984-85; Pvt Tutoring w M Dalton Baldwin incl'g W Coast Recital Tour of Eng, 1985; cp/Mem in Stoic Soc & Mortar Bd, Nat Hon Socs, 1979; En MI Univ Madrigal Singers, Pres, 1976-78; Tours, UK, NH, NC; r/Cath; hon/En MI Univ Campus Ldr Awd, 1977-79; En MI Univ Dillman Mus S'ship, 1975-77; Piano Techs Guild Reg Competition Winner, 1975; Soloist w Detroit Symph Orch; W/W Among Am HS Students; g/Recital Tour, Univ Professorship in Accompanying.

JENKINS, DANA NANETTE oc/Agency Rep, Receptionist; b/May 3, 1957; h/4230 Shopton Road, Charlotte, NC 28210; p/Carroll O Jenkins, Charlotte, NC, and Ann E Jenkins, Robbinsville, NC; ed/Olympic HS, 1975; BA, Gardner-Webb Col, 1978; Master's of Hum Devel & Learning-Cnslg, Univ of NC, 1982; pa/Therapist, Bapt Cnslg Ctr, 1981-; Agy Rep, Bapt Chd's Homes, 1978-81; Am Assn Pastoral Cnslrs; cp/Min Bd of Assocs; Woodlawn Bapt Ch; Choir Pianist; Yth SS Wkr; Media Ctr Creat Spec Dir; Cnslr, Bapt Cnsl Ctr; Sr Adult Wk, Hot Lunch Prog; Retreat Ldr, Wkshop Coor; Alumni Assn Col; Fam Enrichment Ldrship; APGA; hon/Kappa Delta Pi; Outstg Yg Wom of Am; W/W Among Students Am Univs & Cols; Commun Ldrs Am; Intl Yth in Achmt; g/Cnslg in Ch Related Inst; Doct in Cnslg Field; Indep Psychotherapy

Pract; Doct in Case Psychol.

JENKINS, JEFFREY VAN oc/Student; b/Mar 4, 1956; h/2010 Seaton, Apartment 4, Manhattan, KS 66502; p/ Dr and Mrs Hal L Jenkins, Tempe, AZ; ed/Tempe HS, 1974; So Meth Univ, 1978; KS St Univ; mil/USAF; pa/Pt-time Tennis Instr, 1972-75; Computer Programmer, QC, Rockwell Intl, 1978-79; Missile Combat Crew Cmdr, USAF; cp/ BSA; Lttrman in Tennis; Jr Class Treas; Sr Class VP; Key Clb Pres; Sports Editor Sch Paper; German Clb; Dope Stop Cnslr; Kappa Sigma Frat, VP, Pledge Tnr, Little Sister Ldr; AF ROTC; SMU Yg Repubs; Meth Ch Volleyball Team; r/Meth; hon/Eagle Scout, 1973; God & Country Awd, 1972; Capt of Safety Patrol, 1970; Joe Sellah Awd Tennis Instr for Most Dedicated Player on HS Team, 1974; AF ROTC S'ship, 1974; Missile Crew Selected as Strat Air Commands, Missile Crew of Mo, 1982; Named as Outstg Performer during 3901st Strat Missile Eval Squadron Eval, 1982; g/Vet Sch at KS St Univ.

JENKINS, LORI ANN oc/Elementary Tchr; b/Mar 9, 1961; h/Route 2, Bittner's Number 43, South Sioux City, NE 68776, ba/Macy, NE; m/Robert; p/ Mr and Mrs William Duncan, Ionia, IA 50645; sp/Dr and Mrs C M Jenkins, Capake Falls, NY; ed/New Hampton HS, 1979; BA, NWn Col; pa/Tchr, Macy Public Sch, 1983-; cp/Newspaper Staff, Yrbook Editor; Soc Fgn Langs; Ch Wkr; Yrbook Staff in Col; Fgn Lang Frat; Future Tchr's Clb; r/Christian, Missionary Alliance; hon/Fgn Lang Frat, Pres 1982-83, Secy 1980-81; Summa Cum Laude Grad, 1979; St of IA Scholar, 1979; Outstg Eng Student, 1979.

JENKINS, LOTTIE BELL b/Oct 30, 1961; h/Route 1, Box 149-L, Hardeeville, SC 29927; p/Rev and Mrs James Jenkins, Hardeeville, SC; ed/W Hardeeville HS, 1979; BA, Morris Col, 1983; pa/Clerical Asst, Savannah Voc Tech Col, 1984-; Richards St Ctr; Clerical Asst, Savannah St Col, 1983; Upward Bound Tutor, Cnslr; Art Tchr, 1982; cp/ Pres, LeGare Hall Senate, 1982-83; Reporter of Peer Cnslr Clb, 1982-83; Bapt Student Union Reporter, 1982-83; Treas, VP, Alpha Kappa Alpha Sorority Inc; r/Bapt; hon/O R Reubeun Scholar, 1982-84; Dean's List, 1981-84; Nom'd Outstg Yg Wom in Am, 1983; Miss Morris Col, 1983-84; W/W Among Students in Am Univs & Cols, 1982-84; g/Social Sers Pers Cnslg Prog.

JENKINS, TIMOTHY E oc/Student; h/217 Poplar Drive, Elizabethtown, KY 42701; ba/San Rafael, CA; p/Mr and Mrs Anthony Jenkins, Elizabethtown, KY; ed/Elizabethtown Cath HS; BS 1977, BA, BMus, En KY Univ, 1984; MMus, 1985; pa/Pit Pianist/Arranger, TV in OH, 1979-84; Cruise-ship Pianist/ Arranger, 1982; Organist/Choir Dir, PRESIDIO; Accompanist for Opera Wkshop, NATS, 1982-84; cp/Mensa, 1969-; Am Guild Organists; Nat Forensics Leag; Ruby Mem; r/Cath; hon/ "Rikki-Tikki-Tavi", Rudyard Kipling Presentation for the Blind, NRH for the Lions Foun; Full S'ship to SF Conservatory; MCAT, 1981, Top 10% of US; NEDT Scholar, 1973; W/W; Mensa.

JENKINS, TRACEY LYNNE oc/Student; b/Nov 27, 1965; h/5970 Pleasant Hill Road, Hernando, MS 38632; ba/ Same; p/Mr and Mrs Florida Jenkins,

Hernando, MS; ed/Hernando HS; pa/ Cashier, Big Star; cp/Quill & Scroll Clb, Pres; Student Coun; Co-Editor Sch Newspaper, *Tiger Print*; Ensemble & Chorus; Drama Clb; FLBA, Secy/Treas; r/Bapt; hon/Article for *The Desoto Times*, 1983; Nat Spch & Drama Awd; Nat Jour Awd; Selected as Best Citizen by HS Fac; W/W Among Am HS Students; g/ Col.

JENKINS, TRINA FAYE oc/Student; b/Feb 19, 1967; h/Box 113, Ermine, KY 41815; p/Mr and Mrs James Day, Ermine, KY; cp/Cheerldr; r/Prot; hon/ Num Ath Awds; Majorette Awd, 1978; Softball, MVP, 1978; g/to attend Col.

JENKINS, TROY ALLEN oc/Student; b/Mar 23, 1962; h/Route 2, Box 66-A, Keyser, WV; p/Mr and Mrs Ward W Jenkins, Keyser, WV; ed/Keyser HS, 1980; AA, Potomac St Col, 1982; WV Univ; cp/Mineral Co 4-H; Potomac St Col Cir K; Mineral Co & WV 4-H All-Stars; WV Univ Chapt, IEEE; hon/ Outstg AFJROTC Cadet; "I Dare You" Awd; Intl Yth Achmt; Commun Ldrs Am.

JENNINGS, DEBRA ANN oc/Student; b/Oct 7, 1959; h/Route 1, Box 70, Forkland, AL 36740; ba/Columbus, OH; p/Azer Lee Neal, Forkland, AL; ed/ Paramount HS, 1978; BS, AL St Univ, 1982; Master's Deg, OH St Univ; pa/ Systems Analyst, Robins AF Base; cp/ Alpha Kappa Delta, 1982; AL Zeta Chapt Awd, PI Gamma MU; Alpha Kappa Mu; Pi Gamma Mu; Lambda Alpha Epsilon; CRJ Assn; Myles A Paige Sociol Clb; Sigma Gamma Rho; r/Bapt; hon/Soc S'ship Medal; One Yr F'ship to OH St Univ, 1982-83; Dean's Awd, 1982; W/W Among Students in Am Univs & Cols; g/Use the Skills Attained to make for a Better Soc.

JENSEN, MELODI KAY oc/Pension Administrator; b/Dec 22, 1957; h/1008 2nd Avenue South, Clear Lake, IA 50428; ba/Mason City, IA; p/Mr and Mrs Dale W Jensen, Kimballton, IA; ed/ Elk Horn-Kimballton HS, 1976; BA, Augustana Col, 1980; TV & Radio Braodcast Tng, Brown Inst, 1981; pa/ Pension Admr, Banker's Life; News Reporter & Weather Person, KDIX TV, 1981-82; cp/HS Hon Soc; Choir & Band; Ldg Roles in Drama; Pres, FHA; HS Softball; Dean's List; Bible Sch Tchr, Ch Choir; Drama Dir, 1976-80; Col Chorale; Solo Vocal Wk, Elem Drama Judge; r/Luth; hon/Phi Rho; Sch Hall of Fame for Vocal Music; Nat Hon Soc; Best Actresss Awd; Irene Ryan Acting Awd; Chi Epsilon; Soc of Dist'd Am HS Students; W/W: Among Am Music Students, Students in Am Univs & Cols; Intl Yth in Achmt; g/To Further Ed in Spch/Drama Field, Possibly Attaining Tchg Cert.

JERNIGAN, CAROL ROSE oc/Student; h/Route 6, Box 60, Dunn, NC 28334; p/Mr and Mrs Bobby S Jernigan, Dunn, NC 28334; ed/Midway HS; cp/ Christian Yth Grp; 4-H Clb; FHA, Reporter 1982-83, VP 1983, Pres 1984; Reach Out Clb, Commun Sers, 1981-82; Beta Clb; Midway HS, VP 1982-83, Pres 1984; Sampson Co Beta Clb, 1982-84, Pres 1984; Varsity Clb, 1982-84; F'ship Christian Aths, 1983-84, Pres; Pep Clb, 1981-84; Sci Clb, 1982-83, Secy; French Clb, 1983, Secy; Varsity Basketball, 1982-83; Varsity Softball, 1981; Student Coun Rep, 1983; Class Pres, 1983;

r/Prot; hon/Eng I Awd, 1981; Phy Sci Awd, 1981; US Hist Awd, 1982; Geometry Awd, 1982; French I Awd, 1982; Biol Awd, 1982; ECU Math Contest Participant, 1981; NC Gov's Sch-W Student, 1982; ECU Scholar's Wkend Nom, 1983; Chief Marshall, 1983; Eng III Awd 1983; French II Awd, 1983; Chem Awd, 1983; g/Col, Med Sci.

JERNIGAN, NANCY LEA oc/Speech and Hearing Coordinator; b/Jun 6, 1957; h/2265 Hidden Hills Drive, Apartment C-2, Dayton, TN 37321; ba/Dayton, TN; p/Mr and Mrs Lee E Jernigan; ed/ Jackson Ctl Merry HS; BA, Univ TN; pa/Spch Therapist, Rhea Co Dept Ed, 1981-82; Spch & Hearing Coor, Rhea Co Dept Ed, 1982-84; cp/TN Spch & Hearing Assn; Delta Zeta; Intl Bd Mem; VP, Delta Zeta; Histn & Intramurals Chm; Basketball; Track; Mu Alpha Theta; hon/Col Register of Socially Prominent Col Students; Nat Hon Soc; Commun Ldrs Am; W/W Among Am HS Students; g/Master's Deg; Admr in Public Sch Sys.

JERNSTROM, DONALD LEON II oc/Student; b/Jul 1, 1963; h/1926 Pollock Lane, Zephyrhills, FL 34248; p/Donald and Joan Jernstrom, Zephyrhills, FL; ed/ Zephyrhills HS, 1981; AA, Pasco Hernando Commun Col, 1982; pa/Student Asst, Univ FL Instrnl Mats Sers, 1984; cp/Phi Theta Kappa; VP, Phi Beta Lambda; Parliamentn, Student Govt Assn; Basketball; Coach, 4-H Poultry Judging Team; Agri Ed Soc, VP, 1982; Agri Coun Alt Rep 1983-84, Rep 1984-85, Chm of Share Phone-A-Friend Com 1984; Poultry Sci Clb, Pubs Ofcr 1982-83, Pres 1983-84, Secy 1984-85; hon/4-H "I Dare You" Awd; Am Legion Boy's St Spirit of Boy's St Awd; Am Legion Sch Awd; Rendleman Agri S'ship; FL Feed Assn S'ship, 1982; Ralston Purina Co SAM Prog Alt Cand, 1983; Dean's List; Moor Man Co Fund S'ship, 1983; Nat Dean's List; Nat Feed Ingredient Assn S'ship, 1984; Agri Ed Soc Outstg Jr Awd, 1984; Share Phone-A-Friend Outstg Ldrship Awd, 1984; g/Master's Deg in Agri & Ext Ed.

JESSUP, LESLIE JANE oc/Student; b/ May 10, 1962; h/815 Old Mill Road, Chapel Hill, NC 27514; p/Ben F Jessup Jr, Wallace, NC 28466; ed/Wallace-Rose Hill HS, 1980; Univ NC-Chapel Hill; cp/ Beta Alpha Psi; r/Bapt; hon/James M Johnston S'ship, 1982-84; Dean's List; W/W Among Am HS Students; g/CPA.

JEWELL, RHONDA MARIE oc/Student; p/Mar 7, 1967; h/Box 424, Five Fork Road, Liberty, SC 29657; ba/ Liberty, SC; p/Benny and Phyllis Jewell, Liberty, SC; ed/Liberty HS; pa/Pt-time Receptionist, Velo-Enterprises; cp/ Student Coun Rep; Hd Majorette; Feature Twirler; Bible Clb; r/Bapt; hon/ Miss Majorette of SC, 1983; Band Awd, 1983; Beginner Band Mem of Yr, 1983; Chorus Awd, 1981; Num Trophies & Medals in Baton Twirling; g/RN.

JEWELL, RUSSELL PARRISH oc/ Student, Pt-time Recreation Dir; b/Dec 19, 1957; h/Route 4, Easley, SC 29640; ba/Greenville, SC; p/Mr and Mrs Sam Jewell, Easley, SC; ed/Wren HS, 1976; AS, Montreat-Anderson Col, 1981; BA, Mars Hill Col, 1983; pa/Four Color Graphic Artist, Martin Printing Co, 1978-79; cp/Ftball; HS Track; Col Tennis; Col Track; Greenville Art Guild; r/Prot; hon/Author of *My Friends* *at the Zoo;* 1976 Pole Vaulting St Champ; 1976 Most Dedicated Track; 1976 Best All Around Sr; 1976 Most Dependable Sr; 1975 Boys St; 1980 Dean's List; 1982 Greenville Co Frisbee Golf Champ; g/ EdM, Tch on Col Level.

JIMENEZ, ARACELI oc/Student; b/ Nov 22, 1960; h/3005 Salinas, Laredo, TX 78040; ba/Same; p/Eduardo and Hortensia M de Jimenez, Tamaulipas, Mexico; ed/Raymond & Tirza Martin HS, 1979; AA, Laredo Jr Col, 1982; BS, Laredo St Univ, 1984; cp/Nat Hon Soc, 1978-; Spanish Nat Hon Soc, 1978-; FHA, 1979-; Phi Theta Kappa, 1980-; Sigma Delta Mu, 1980-; Yg Commun Ldrship, 1981-; Talent Roster of Minority Students, 1981-; N Am Mbrship in Am Biographical Inst Res Assn, 1984-; r/Cath; hon/1978, LISD Awd 1st Pl Certamen "Carta A Mi Madre"; Laredo Jr Col Acad Excell Awd, 1979; Cert of Congratulation by the St Rep, 1979; Talent Roster Cert of Achmt, 1981; Yg Personality of Am Awd, 1982; Outstg Yg Ldrship Awd, 1982; Soc of Dist'd Am HS Students; Nat Register of Outstg Jr & Commun Col Students; Intl Yth in Achmt; Yg Personalities of the S; Personalities of Am; Commun Ldrs of Am; World W/W of Wom; Commun Ldrs of World; Biographical Roll of Hon; DIB; Two Thousand Notable Ams; W/ W: Among Am HS Students, Among Students in Am Jr Cols; g/Sec'dy Ed.

JOHNKOSKI, JOHN ANTHONY oc/Student; b/May 14, 1962; h/52 Traverse Street, Battle Creek, MI 49017; p/Mrs Elizabeth Johnkoski, Battle Creek, MI; ed/Battle Creek HS, 1980; Albion Col; cp/Beta Beta Beta; Delta Delta Delta Frat, Acad Chm; Interfrat Coun on Housing Regulations; Albion Col Jud Bd; Albion Col Periodical Life Staff; Albion Ambulance Ser, Vol EMT; r/Presb; hon/Dean's List; g/Med Sch.

JOHNSON, ALECIA JAYNE oc/ Music Teacher; b/Aug 24, 1956; h/1805 West 18th Street, Little Rock, AR 72202; ba/Marianna, AR; p/Mr and Mrs John D Johnson, Jr, Little Rock, AR; ed/ Hall HS, 1974; BMus 1979, BMus Ed 1980, Henderson St Univ; pa/Music Tchr, 1981-; Hd Residence, Pines Hall, Henderson St Univ, 1981; Receptionist, Social Security Adm, 1978; Tutor/ Cnslr, Upward Bound, Philander Smith Col, 1977; cp/Delta Omicron Intl Music Frat; AEA-NEA; Lee Co Ed Assn; Sigma Gamma Rho Sorority Inc; NAACP; r/ Bapt; hon/Miss Kappa Alpha Psi, 1975; SWn Reg Undergrad of Yr, 1976; Annie Neville Talent Awd, 1976; W/W in Am Cols & Univs; g/Opera Audition, Pursue Doct in Vocal Perf.

JOHNSON, ARNETTA MAE oc/ Elementary Teacher; b/Feb 1, 1946; h/ 231 West Johnson Street, Camden, AR 71701; ba/Magnolia, AR; p/Mr Azell Johnson, West Palm Beach, FL; Mrs Minnie C Johnson, Camden, AR; ed/ Lincoln HS, 1963; AMN Col, 1969; pa/ Elem Sch Tchr, Magnolia Public Schs, 1969-; AEA; NEA; ACTE; cp/Delta Kappa Gamma; Pres of MEA, 1982-83; Past Secy, 1980; Past Secy & Pres of AAUW; r/Bapt; hon/Recipe Pub'd in *Potpourri of Cookery,* 1981; Camden News Bake Off, 1977-82; Cooking Awd from *So Living Mag,* 1981; Outstg Yg Wom Am.

JOHNSON, BARRY EDWIN oc/

Student; b/Apr 28, 1965; h/6902 Fieldcrest Road, Baltimore, MD 21215; p/Mr and Mrs Cecil E Johnson; ed/NWn Sr HS; cp/Nat Jr Hon Soc; Nat Hon Soc Treas, VP; BSA Highest Unit Ldr; Nat Conf of Christians & Jews; Metro Yth Coun, Balto City Rep; Assoc Student Cong of Balto City; Legis Lobbyist to MD Gen Assem; hon/Balto City Comm on Aging Retirement Ed, Jr Hall of Fame, Hon Mention; Am Legion Citizenship Awd; Most Outstg Student Ldr of Balto City; Wildcat Awd, Highest Sch Hon Awd; Student Commr, Balto City Sch Bd; Recip, MD Gov's Awd for Acad Excell, 1983; Balto City Sch Bd Awd for Acad Achmt, 1983; Eagle Scout, BSA, 1983; W/W in MD; g/Deg in Acctg, Polit.

JOHNSON, BRODIE IVORY oc/ Software Programmer; b/Jul 2, 1953; h/ 2808 Wyeth Avenue, Durham, NC 27707; ba/Durham, NC; m/Michelle; c/ Jermaine; ed/Cath HS, 1971; BS 1975, MS 1977, Memphis St Univ; pa/Pastor, Ebenezer Bapt Ch; Instr, Durham Tech Inst; Database Adm Spec, No Telecom; cp/Durham Interdenomination Ministerial Alliance; Soc Mfg Eng; Assn Indust Engrg; Soc Mil Engrs; r/Bapt; g/ Software Programmer, Indust Engr.

JOHNSON, CAROL JEAN oc/Student; b/Jul 27, 1966; h/63 Bon Air Circle, Jackson, TN 38305; p/Mr and Mrs Harold Johnson, Jackson, TN; ed/Jackson Ctl-Merry HS; pa/Recorder for Jackson TN; Coca-Cola; Clk, Ofc Wkr, Kisber's Dept Store; cp/Kappa Beta Chi Sorority; Mu Alpha Theta; Nat Hon Soc; Tennis Team; Cheerldg; Mascot; Latin Clb; Ch Leag Basketball; Colorguard; Rifle Squad for Band; Congl Page; r/Bapt; hon/Awd Excell Nat Hist Day Contest; Hons Student; W/W Am HS; g/to attend Univ TN.

JOHNSON, DAVID WILLIAM oc/ Student; b/May 9, 1963; h/5519 Firethorn Court, Cincinnati, OH 45242; p/ Philip C and Kathleen I Johnson, Cinc, OH; ed/Indian Hill HS, 1981; BA, Princeton Univ, 1985; cp/Ch Choir; Ch Softball; BSA; Nat Eagle Scout Assn; Princeton Univ Singers, Conductor Asst; Princeton Univ Band; Princeton Univ Opera Theatre; Musica Alta; Intramural Softball; r/Presb; hon/Valedictorian; Eagle Scout; Rensselaer Polytechnic Inst Med, 1980; NCTE Achmt Awds in Writing Finalist, 1981; W/W Among Am HS Students; Intl Yth in Achmt; g/Economist, Novelist, Prof.

JOHNSON, GREGORY RAYMOND oc/Student; h/Route 3, Box 596, Ridgeway, VA 24148; ba/Blacksburg, VA; p/ George R Johnson, Ridgeway, VA; ed/ Ridgeway-Drewry Mason HS, 1981; VA Tech; cp/BSA; Ch Grp; Varsity Basketball; Baseball; Ftball & Golf; Jr Play, 1980; Intramural Sports; Alpha Zeta Hon Frat; r/Bapt; hon/All Dist Reg & St Ftball; W/W; Am Outstg Names & Faces; g/Dentistry.

JOHNSON, HOWARD ARTHUR JR oc/Operations Analyst; b/Jul 25, 1952; h/309 Yacht Club Drive, Northeast, Fort Walton Beach, FL 32548; ba/ Arlington, VA; m/Teresa Thirsk; p/Mr and Mrs Howard A Johnson Sr, Ft Walton Bch, FL; sp/Mr and Mrs Charles K Thirsk, Ft Walton Bch, FL; ed/ Choctawhatchee HS, 1970; BA, Univ KS, 1974; mil/USN, 1974-78; pa/Sr Opers Analyst, Elect Inter Tech Inc, Dpty to US Dir Plans & Budgets, Min

Def & Aviation, 1981-; Opers Res Analyst, Armament Sys Inc, 1980-81; Opers Res Analyst 1977-78, Engrg Ofcr 1974-77, USN; cp/Tau Kappa Epsilon; Sr Class Pres; Student Coun; Aerospace Clb; LEO Clb; German Hon Soc; r/Prot; hon/Author of "Comparisons of Guerilla Strat in China & Vietnam", 1974, "The Soviet Union & Cuba 1960-63", 1974; Snyder Boot Awd, "Guerilla Warfare in SE Asian, Latin Am, & Africa", 1974; Navy ROTC S'ship to Univ KS; Nat Sojourners Awd for Americanism; Rep to US Naval Acad Fgn Affairs Conf, 1974; Hon Role; g/ MA Intl Studies/Interdisciplinary Policy Anal; MA in Mgmt.

JOHNSON, JACKLYN TRACY b/Jan 27, 1961; h/646 Powhatan Drive, Madisonville, KY 42431; p/Jack H (dec) and Gracie M Johnson, Madisonville, KY; ed/Madisonville N Hopkins HS, 1979; BA, Campbellsville Col, 1983; pa/Sum Wkr, Hopkins Co Social Security Adm, 1979; Sum Missionary to NY, So Bapt Home Mission Bd, 1980; Sum Wkr Hopkins Co Bur for Social Sers, 1981; Dorm Cnslr, Campbellsville Col, 1982; cp/Teens Who Care, VP, 1979; r/ Christianity; hon/Author of "Your Loving Spirit", 1978; Jr Achmt Exec Awd, 1977-79; Ofcr of Yr, 1978; Beta Clb, 1976-79; W/W Among Am Cols & Univs; g/So Bapt Fgn Mission Bd Journeyman to Honduras as Secy, 1983-85.

JOHNSON, JAMES KENNETH oc/ Student; b/Jan 30, 1957; h/101 Bremer Street, Fayetteville, NC 28303; p/Ms F E Johnson, Fayetteville, NC; ed/Pine Forest Sr HS, 1976; Dipl, Fayetteville Tech Inst, 1979; Meth Col, 1980; BS, Univ NC-Charlotte, 1983; pa/Rschr, Piedmont Waste Rech, Urban Inst, Univ NC-Charlotte, 1982-83; Civil Engrg Tech, Ft Bragg, NC Directorate of Engrg & Housing, 1982; Maintenance Mechanic, Bordeaux Mgmt, 1980; Electrician's Helper, Watson Elect Constrn Co, 1979; Vending Mechanic, Simmons Brothers Amusements, 1976-78; Am Soc Civil Engrs; Profl Engrs NC; Nat Soc Profl Engrs; cp/Tau Beta Pi; r/Prot; hon/Meth Col Dean's List; Chancellor's List, UNC; Engrg S'ship Recip; Commencement Marshall, 1982; g/Obtain Registration as Profl Engr.

JOHNSON, JOSEPH BENJAMIN JR oc/Student; b/May 28, 1965; h/28 Albert Spears Drive, Sumter, SC 29150; ba/ Greenville, SC; p/Mr Joseph B Johnson Sr, Sumter, SC, and Mrs Rubye J Johnson, Sumter, SC; ed/Sumter HS, 1983; cp/BSA, 1973-83; 4-H, 1980-83; Teenldr; Yg People's Dept of the AME Ch; Assn of Furman Students, 1983-84; Freshman Class Pres; Furman Univ Student Leag for Black Culture, 1983-; Furman Univ Marching Band, 1983-; Jazz Ensemble, 1983-; Concert Band, 1983-; Gospel Ensemble, 1983-; Jr Engr Tech Soc, 1979-83; Sumter HS Debating Clb; HS Awareness Clb; Boys' Clb Basketball Team; r/AME, Mt Pisgah AME Ch; hon/Eagle Scout of BSA, 1979; Mem of Champ SC St 4-H Debating Team, 1983; SC St FFA Public Spkg Winner, 1982; SC Palmeto Boys' St, 1982; SC Gov's Sch for the Arts Scholar, 1982; Mem of the SC SE Reg Band, 1983; Mem of US Col Wind Band, Sumter HS, 1983; Bandsman of the Yr; Sumter Elks Post #855 Teenager of the

Mo, 1983; Most Talented Awd of Sumter HS Chorus, 1983; Recip of the Sumter Chapt of Omega Psi Phi Frat Talent Awd & S'ship; 2nd Pl Winner in the SC St Talent-O-Rama Contest, 1983; Recip of a Music S'ship to Furman Univ, 1983; g/BA Deg in Eng or Mus; Public Relats.

JOHNSON, MONICA LYNN oc/Student; b/Mar 31, 1965; h/1202 Mills Avenue, Gulfport, MS 39501; ba/Hattiesburg, MS; p/Isaac (dec) and Jessie Mae Johnson, Gulfport, MS; ed/HS, 1983; pa/Tutor, Yth Ser Bur, CETA, 1981; Shelver, Gulfport-Harrison Co Lib, CETA, 1982; cp/W Gulfport Civic Clb; Garden Pk Med Explorers Post 264, 1980-83, 2nd VP, 1982; Jr Red Cross Clb, Sci Clb, 1982-83; Ujoma Clb, 1980-81; Reformed Univ F'ship, 1983; r/Bapt; hon/Cert Awd, Red Cross Clb, 1983; Cert of Awd, Participation in the Am Legion Aux Nat Pres S'ship Prog, 1st Pl in St, 1983; Cert of Merit, MS Gulf Coast Pan Hellenic Coun, 1983; g/Nsg.

JOHNSON, PATRICIA ANN oc/Student; b/Dec 31, 1961; h/Route 4, Box 501, Siler City, NC 27344; ba/Siler City, NC; p/Mr and Mrs Rexford Johnson, Siler City, NC; ed/Jordan Mathews HS, 1980; Univ NC-Greensboro; pa/Sales Clk, Belk Yates; cp/Acctg Clb, 1983; Omicron Delta Epsilon, 1983; Beta Clb; Spanish Clb; FTA; r/Pentecostal Holiness; hon/Nat Dean's List; Dean's List; Kathryn Smith Reynolds S'ship; Hist Awd; g/BS in Acctg, CPA.

JOHNSON, PATRICIA DAY oc/Computer Operator; b/May 31, 1964; h/4026 Wake Forest Highway, Durham, NC 27703; ba/Durham, NC; p/Patsy Johnson, Durham, NC; ed/So HS, 1982; pa/Computer Operator, Powe, Porter & Alphin, PA, 1982-; Secy, So HS, 1982; cp/Jr Marshall; Nat Hon Soc VP; Quill & Scroll Secy; Student Coun Secy; Yrbook Assoc Editor; Hon Roll; A P Hist Quiz Bowl; Calendar Com for Durham Co Schs; r/Bapt; hon/Outstg Sr, 1982; Most Conscientious Sr, 1982; Morehead S'ship Nom; W/W Among Am Teenagers; g/Elem Ed Deg.

JOHNSON, RAY GRANTHAM oc/Administrative Bookkeeper; b/Oct 11, 1959; h/Post Office Box 219, Wallace, NC 28466; ba/Wilmington, NC; m/Mary Ann D; p/Mr and Mrs W Ray Johnson, Wallace, NC; sp/Dr and Mrs Cesar J Diaz, Wallace, NC; ed/Wallace-Rose HS, 1977; NC St Univ, 1977-78; Pitt Commun Col, 1979; AAS, 1982, 1983, James Sprunt Tech Col; Owens Elect Supply Co; Computer Lab Asst, James Sprunt Tech Col, 1982; Tenter Frame Operator, Collin & Aikman, 1979-80; Dye Machine Loader, J P Stevens, 1978; Order Selector, N & W Wholesale, 1977; cp/Ftball, Basketball, Baseball, Tennis, Monogram Clb, Chess Clb, Pres of Spanish Clb, HS; SGA Senator, Alumni Assn Com, Rec Com, Tennis Coach, James Sprunt Tech Col; r/Meth; hon/Dean's List; All-Conf Softball; g/Acctg, Univ.

JOHNSON, ROSLYN oc/Student; b/Sep 13, 1966; h/2816 Dalecrest Drive, Charlotte, NC 28213; p/Mr and Mrs Willie Johnson, Charlotte, NC; ed/HS, 1984; cp/Inroads/Charlotte, 1982-84; Jr Achmt, Pers Corporate Secy, 1983, 1984; French Clb, 1983, 1984; Student Coun, 1983-84; r/Apostolic, Jr Adult

Ushers; hon/Jr Marshall for HS Grad, 1983; Att'd UNC-Chapel Hill, 1983 for Proj Uplift; Att'd US Naval Acad, 1983 for Engrg, Sci Sem; Att'd UNC-Charlotte for Inroads/Charlotte, 1983; Nat Hon Soc; Soc Dist'd Am HS Students; g/to Attend Duke Univ, Deg in Engrg, Computer.

JOHNSON, SHIRLEY KATHERINE b/Oct 28, 1960; h/6845 Melville Drive, Chesterfield, VA 23832; p/Dr and Mrs Hugh G Johnson, Algiers, Algeria; ed/Baccalaureat, Lycee Descartes, Algiers, Algeria, 1979; AS 1981, BS 1983, Ferrum Col; pa/Math Tutor 1980-81, Admissions Aide/Col Tour Guide 1983, Ferrum Col; Intern Animal Keeper, Maymont Foun, 1982; Vol, Smithsonian Insect Zoo, 1981; Kennell Asst, Mudlick Kennels, 1983; Salesperson, Hickory Farms, 1983; Subst Tchr, Roanoke VA City Schs, 1984; cp/Phi Theta Kappa, 1980-81; Smithsonian Assocs, 1980-; National Geographic Soc, 1984; Russian Clb & Chorus, Ferrum Col, 1980-83; Alpha Mu Gamma; Reporter, Phi Theta Kappa; r/United Meth; hon/Freshman Biol Awd, 1979-80; Wn Civilization Hist Awd, 1979-80; Hons Rel Course, 1980; Dean's List, 1979-80; Nat Dean's List; Phi Theta Kappa, 1980-81; Alpha Mu Gamma; Merit S'ship; W/W Among Am Jr Cols; Commun Ldrs Am; Intl Yth in Achmt; Personalities of S; g/Mus Curator.

JOHNSON, TRACY ANGELITA oc/Student; b/May 26, 1966; h/110 West Ruffin Street, Mebane, NC 27302; p/Mr and Mrs Thomas Johnson, Mebane, NC 27302; ed/En Alamance HS; pa/Cashier, Hardee's, 1981; Cahsier, Rite Aid Pharm, 1982; Dental Apprentice, Dental Res Ctr UNC-Chapel Hill, 1983; cp/Choral, Drama Clb, 1980-81; Spanish Clb, 1982-83; Civinettes, 1982-83, Chaplain, 1983; Explorer's Post Clb for Med, 1983, Secy/Treas; r/Bapt; hon/Gov's Sch Nom for Spanish, 1983; Nat Hon Soc, 1982-83; g/Col, Med.

JOHNSON, VIVIAN EVADNA oc/Student; b/Jan 19, 1961; h/1805 West 18th, Little Rock, AR 72202; ba/Arkadelphia, AR; p/John D Jr and Janie A Johnson, Little Rock, AR; ed/Hall HS, 1979; Henderson St Univ; pa/Asst Dir, Henderson St Univ-BSU Gospel Choir, 1981-83; Pianist/Organist, St Paul AME Ch, 1979-83; cp/Delta Omicron Mus Frat; Gamma Beta Phi Hon Soc; Sigma Gamma Rho Sorority Inc; r/Bapt; hon/Miss Alfresco, 1980-81; Miss CBS, 1981-82; Miss Henderson St Univ, 1st Runner-up, 1982; Student Govt Senator, 1983; Homecoming Queen at Henderson St Univ, 1982; Best Actress Awd, 1977; Sophomore Rep, Nat Assn Tchrs of Singing, 1st Pl, 1982, 2nd Pl, 1983; W/W Among Am HS Students; W/W Among Cols & Univs; g/Broadway, TV.

JOHNSON, WINNIE GAY oc/Speech, Language Pathologist; b/Oct 4, 1956; h/137 Cove Drive, Rocky Mount, NC 27801; ba/Tarboro, NC; m/Phillip Luther; p/Mr and Mrs Daniel Robert Gay, Fountain, NC; sp/Mr and Mrs E Ray Johnson, Rocky Mount, NC; ed/Farmville CT HS, 1974; BS, E Carolina Univ, 1978; Master's Wk, 1981-82; pa/Spch/Lang Pathol, Edgecombe Co Schs, 1978; NC Spch & Hearing Assn; Spch & Hearing Area Res Exch; cp/Parent-Action Grp for Handicapped

Chd; Vol for Special Olympics; Duke Sum Spch Camp Wkr; Alpha Xi Delta Sorority; r/Bapt, First Bapt Ch; g/Master's Deg Spch; Lang & Auditory Pathol.

JOHNSTON, JEFFREY oc/Editor-Troy St University Yearbook; h/Route 2 Box 53A, Ariton, AL; ba/Troy, AL; p/Thomas B Jernigan, Ariton, AL; ed/Ariton HS, 1981; Troy St Univ; cp/Beta Clb; Am Leg Boys St; DAR Good Citizen Awd; Ariton Jr Hist Soc Pres; Sr Class Pres; AL Jr Acad of Sci; hon/Editor Troy St Univ Yrbook; Ariton HS Student Yrbook Coun; George C Wallace Ldrship S'ship; Ariton Public Sch Sys Hutto Awd; Taylor Pub'g Co Yrbook Editors Awd; Sports Assoc Troy St Univ Yrbook; Gamma Beta Phi Soc; Bus Mgr Troy St Univ Yrbook; Intl Yth in Achmt; W/W Among Am HS Students; Commun Ldrs of Am; Yg Personalities of S; g/Bus Adm Degs, Troy St Univ.

JOHNSTON, LEIGH AMBA oc/Student; b/Dec 10, 1965; h/210 Nandina Road, Gulf Breeze, FL 32561; ba/Pensacola, FL; pa/Godfather's Pizza; Chick-fil-A; cp/Student Coun; Interact, 1982-83; Sister Cities Intl, 1980-94; r/Bapt, First Bapt Ch, Social & Outreach, Social Chm, Alto Sect Ldr; hon/Participated in Jr Miss, Santa Rosa Co, FL; g/Univ FL, Acctg, Law.

JOHNSTON, SHANNON SHERWOOD oc/Administrative Program Director; b/Oct 20, 1958; h/1709 1/2 Bruce Drive, St Simons Island, GA 31522; ba/Brunswick, GA; p/Dr (dec) and Mrs Albert S Johnston Jr, Florence, AL; ed/Coffee HS, 1977; BA, Univ of the S, 1981; pa/Commun Progs Dir, YMCA of NW AL, 1980-83; Assoc Dir of Progs, Cooperative Campus Min, Univ of N AL, 1981-83; Adm Prog Dir, Boys Clb of Glynn Inc; cp/Glynn, Brunswick Coun for the Arts; Boys Clb Profl Assn, FL-GA, Chapt; Exec Com, Frat Chapt Alumni Assn; Sponsorship Drive, Christian Chd's Fund; Pres, Beta Theta Pi; Pres, Univ Choir; Varsity Track Team; Vol, St & Local Polit Campaigns; Univ Col Bowl Team; Campus Jour; Student Govt; Commun Concert Series Com; Commun Sum Orch; Ch Coms; hon/Phi Beta Kappa; HS Valedictorian, 1977; Omicron Delta Kappa; Blue Key; Beta Theta Pi; Nat S'ship-Ldrship Awd; Am Legion's HS Awd; Rhodes S'ship St Finalist; Intl Yth in Achmt; Commun Ldrs of Am; Nat Register of Outstg Col Grads; Personalities of S; g/Epis Priesthood; Doct in Phil/Theol Studies.

JOI oc/Student; b/Mar 4, 1968; h/Filbert and Charles Streets, Palmyra, NJ 08065; p/Sherry A M Piergrass, Palmyra, NJ; ed/Burl Co Col Theater & Wkshop; pa/"Annie", "Square Balloon", "Gypsy"-Angela Lansbury Nat Tour, Ginza Theater-Tokyo Japan, Theatre; Mike Douglas Show, NHK Studio-Tokyo Japan, USO Shows, Dutch Inn-Lake Buena Vista, March of Dimes, TV Appearances; "Blow Out", "Honky Tonk Freeway", "King of the Gypsies", "Raging Bull", "Ida's Song", Film Appearances; "Two Dreams", "Sing A Song of Sunbeams", "A Song Worth Singing", "My Honey", Recordings; Modeling, Fashion Grp, Graphics, Off the Rax; Am Alphabet Book; Indust, Milliken Breakfast Show, 1979/80;

Commls; Appeared Regulary, Peter Sklars "Profl Chd's Revue"; cp/Equity; ALTRA; SAG; AGVA; Jr Am Legion Post 156; g/Teen Ambassadress.

JOLLIFF, KARA ANN oc/Student; b/May 5, 1966; h/19014 Quail Run Drive, Little Rock, AR 72209; p/Charles and Barbara Jolliff, Little Rock, AR; ed/McClellan HS; cp/McClellan Scotia Choir; Sr All-Region Choir; Sch Choir Accompanist; Concert Band; Handbell Chor; Spanish Clb; Highland Band; Vocal Jazz Ensemble; r/Bapt; hon/W/W Among Am HS Students; Nat Hon Soc Drama Awd Winner; Talent Awd Winner, Piano Solo, Miss McClellan HS Pageant; Talented & Gifted Prog; g/Career in Music or Psychol.

JONES, AMY ELIZABETH oc/Student; b/Nov 28, 1962; h/1709 Crooks Court, Grand Prairie, TX 75051; p/Johnny L and Barbara A Jones, Grand Prairie, TX; ed/Grand Prairie HS, 1981; pa/Log Ride, Six Flags Over TX, 1978; Crew Chief, McDonald's, 1978-81; Teller, Mercantile Bk Grand Prairie, 1981-; Student Aid, TX Tech Univ Lib, 1983-; cp/Nat Hon Soc; Choir Ofcr; Spirit Boosting Chm; Drill Team; Student Coun; Gamma Beta Phi, Secy; r/Ch of Christ; hon/G H Turner S'ship; Salutatorian; g/Bkg & Fin Maj.

JONES, BARBARA LYNN oc/Staff Physical Therapist; b/Sep 7, 1961; h/4155 Essen Lane, Apartment 189, Baton Rouge, LA 70809; ba/Baton Rouge, LA 70809; p/Mr and Mrs Forrest Allen Jones, McComb, MS; ed/McComb HS, 1979; AA, SW MS Jr Col, 1980; BS, Univ of MS Med Ctr, 1982; pa/Phy Therapy Aide, Dr's Hosp of Jackson, 1981; Staff Phy Therapist, Our Lady of the Lake Reg Med Ctr, 1982-; cp/Am Phy Therapy Assn, Nat & St Chapts, 1980-; r/Bapt; hon/Nat Jr Hon Soc, 1976; Nat Hon Soc, 1979; Phi Theta Kappa, Omicron Delta Chapt; Phi Kappa Phi; Am Oustg Names & Faces; Nat Dean's List; Intl Yth in Achmt; Commun Ldrs of Am; g/To Earn a Master's Deg in Phy Therapy Studies.

JONES, CARLOS L oc/Student; b/Jun 29, 1961; h/2115 Owens Street, Number 4, Tallahassee, FL 32301; ba/Tallahassee, FL; p/Carlos and Vernesser M Jones, Phila, PA; ed/Ctl HS, 1979; FL A & M Univ; pa/Intern, US Home Corp, 1980; Ptnr, Handyman's Home Improvement Ser, 1983-; cp/Pres, Bilalian Student Alliance, 1982-83; Student Govt Senator, FL A & M, 1979-81; HS Ftball & Track; r/Al Islam; hon/Pres Lttr of Recog, US Home, 1980; Nationally Commended Student; g/Deg in BA.

JONES, CHARLES HAMILTON JR oc/Student; b/Feb 27, 1964; h/700-F Blue Street, Mt Sinai Apartments, Fayetteville, NC 28301; p/Mr Charles Hamilton Jones Sr, Balto, MD; and Ms Willie Delories Jones, Fayetteville, NC; ed/Seventy-First HS, 1982; NC St Univ; cp/NC St Pre-Vet Clb; HS, Marching Band, Concert Band, Nat Hon Soc, Mu Alpha Theta Clb, Sci Clb, Drama Clb, Med Explorer Post #737, Intl Clb & Key Clb; r/Rom Cath; hon/Cert for Acad Excell as Afro-Am Student, 1983; Cert of Apprec for Ser in the NC St Pre-Vet Clb, 1983; g/BS in Zool, NC Sch of Vet Med.

JONES, CLARISSA INEZ oc/Student; b/Apr 4, 1961; h/537 East Avenue Northeast, Atlanta, GA 30312; p/Mr and Mrs Clarence R Jones, Atlanta, GA; ed/Northside HS, 1979; BS, Fisk Univ, 1983; pa/Asst Secy, Atlanta, 1979; Survey Tech, MARTA, 1980; Sum Teller, First Atlanta Bk, 1981, 1982; cp/Fisk Jubilee Singers; Zeta Phi Beta Sorority Inc, VP & Treas, 1982-83; Jud Bd of Sr Class; Univ Choir; GA Fisk Clb; Dormitory Floor Cnslr; Fisk Music Clb; r/AME, Yg Peoples Dept; hon/Nat Hon Soc; Nat Beta Clb; Acad Awd for Excell; Hon Roll; g/Maj Course of Study, Mgmt.

JONES, GARETH WELKIN oc/Student; b/Jul 17, 1965; h/Route 4, Box 219, Westminster, SC 29693; p/David TS Jones, Westminster, SC; cp/Track; Beta Clb; W Oak Newspaper, Prospective Editor-in-Chief; r/Prot; hon/1983 Furman Scholar; 1st Pl Sci Fair, 1982, Sr Div; 1st & 3rd Art Contest, 1982; 2nd Pl Essay Contest, 1983; Star Student, Highest Average in Jr Class, 1983; g/Elect Engrg.

JONES, GREGORY DWAYNE oc/Student, HUD Legal Div; b/Jul 30, 1961; h/17 Peachtree Street, Headland, AL 36345; ba/Birmingham, AL; p/Jo Ann Jones, Headland, AL; ed/Headland HS, 1979; BSBA, Miles Col, 1984; pa/Legal Div Clk, Dept HUD, 1982-; Apprentice, Dept Engrg & Housing, 1982; Bacon Cutter, Sunnyland Foods Inc, 1979-80; cp/Pres, Phi Beta Lambda; Keeper of Records, Exchequer of Kappa Alpha Psi Frat Inc; Chm of Miles Col Debate Team; Reporter, Miles Col Newspaper Staff; Pres of Jr Class; r/Bapt; hon/Dean's List; Hon Roll; Pres Scholar's List; Semi-Finalist in AL Law Inst Intern Prog; Hon Lt Col, Aide-de-Camp; W/W Among Students in Am Univs & Cols; Intl W/W in Frats & Sororities; g/JD, Establish own Consltg Firm.

JONES, JAMES LEONARD III oc/Student; b/Jul 2, 1966; h/Post Office Box 421, Sylva, NC 28779; p/Robert W and Mary C Ginn, Sylva, NC; ed/Sylva Webster HS; cp/Nat Hons Clb, 1982-83; VP, Math Clb, 1982-83; Spanish Clb, 1981-82; r/Prot; hon/Geometry 1981-82, Algebra 1981-82, Ldrship 1982-83, Ldrship & Ser 1982-83, US Achmt Acad Awd; S'ship to Univ NC—Asheville, Sum Sch of Engrg, 1982-83; W/W Among Am HS Students; VP, Math Clb, 1983-84; Nat Hons Clb, 1983-84; g/Attend Wn Carolina Univ, Pre-Engrg.

JONES, JOHN TERRY (JT) oc/Student; b/Sep 17, 1961; h/Route 3 Box 341, Princeton, WV 24740; p/James W and Audrey P Jones, Princeton, WV; ed/BS, Concord (in Progress); Mem, Bulmershe/Concord Exch Grp on Study/Travel Prog to Eng, Sum 1984; cp/Mem, Nat Geographic Soc, 1976-84; Supporting Assoc Mem, Nat Repub Congl Com, 1981-84; GOPAC, 1981-84; Am Polit Sci Assn Mem, 1982-84; St Advr, Am Security Coun Foun, 1982-84; Nat Repub Com Mem, 1983-84; WV Polit Sci Assn Mem, 1983-84; Acad of Polit Sci, 1983-84; NCPAC, 1984; Reagan-Bush '84 Vol, 1984; So Polit Assn, 1984; Concord Col SGA Commuters' Com Chm, 1983-85; Concord Col Polit Sci Clb, Pres, 1982-85; Concord Col SGA Bd of Dirs, 1983-84; Student Rep to the Col Bd of Advrs, 1984-85; PHS Baseball Team, 1977-74; JCC Softball Team, 1983-84; PJHS Tennis & Track Teams, 1974-76; Concord Col

SGA Defensive Driving Com, 1983-85; Concord Col Ctr Renovation Com, 1983-85; r/Bapt; hon/Baseball & Tennis Lttrman; Best Camper, Teen Wk Fountain of Life Camp, 1979; W/W Among Students in Am Univs & Cols; Personalities of S; g/MS in Geog at Univ KY.

JONES, JULIA LEIGH oc/Student; b/Mar 28, 1961; h/3341 Coliseum, Apartment C, New Orleans, LA 70115; p/Dr and Mrs Herbert Jones, Blytheville, AR; ed/Blytheville HS, 1979; BA, So Meth Univ, 1983; pa/Lab Tech, 1977-79; Lab Asst, 1981-83; cp/Phi Mu Frat, VP 1980-81, House Mgr 1982-82; Col Repubs, Prog Chm 1981-83; Phi Eta Sigma, Pres 1980-81; Tri Beta Biol Hon, Pres 1981-82; Sailing Clb; Chem Soc; hon/Phi Beta Kappa; Outstg Col Repub; Phi Mu Lady; Order of Omega; Harold Jesky Chem S'ship; Phi Lambda Upsilon; Magna Cum Laude; g/Med.

JONES, KAREN DAWN oc/Student; b/Oct 17, 1963; h/5609 River Bluff Drive, Suffolk, VA 23435; ba/Portsmouth, VA; p/Mr and Mrs T K Jones, JR, Suffolk, VA; ed/John Yeates HS, 1982; Col of William & Mary; pa/Secy/Bkkpr, Air Comfort Inc, 1979-; cp/Ladies Softball, 1979-; Col & Career Sunday Sch Class Mem, 1982-; Varsity Cheerldr Capt; Yrbk Staff Sect Ldr; Beta Clb Secy; Yth Adv Coun Pres; Tidewater Scholastic Achmt Team; Yth Choir; Spanish Clb; Student Coop Assn; Interclb Coun; Interact Clb; FBLA Secy; r/Bapt; Nansemond River Bapt Ch; hon/Most Valuable Varsity Cheerldr, 1981-82; Valedictorian, 1982; Most Likely to Succeed, 1982; Softball Player of the Wk, 1983, Currents; VA Gov Sch for the Gifted; W/W; Soc for Dist'd Am HS Students; g/Govt Maj, Biol Minor.

JONES, KEVIN DIMP oc/Student; b/Sep 28, 1963; h/Route 2, Box 188, Mansfield, AR 72944; ba/Fayetteville, AR; p/Donald and Freda Jones, Mansfield, AR; ed/Mansfield HS, 1981; Univ AR; pa/Photographs Unltd, 1982-83; cp/4-H, Co VP 1979, Co Pres 1980-81, St Reporter 1980, St Pres 1981, Col Pres 1983; Farm House Frat, Pledge Tnr; Student Senate; Bd Agri Home Ec Assn; UAM Pubs; Chm, Univ Ar Activ Day; UAM Annual, 1981; r/Ch of Christ; hon/St 4-H Hall of Fame; Dean's List; S'ship, Ross Foun Conserv Sch; Ross Foun 4-H Forestry Sch; Farm Bur S'ship; Photography S'ship; Nat & St FFA Bands; Whirlpool S'ship; St 4-H Proj Winner, 1981; W/W Am Students; Outstg Yg Musicians.

JONES, MARCUS DONELL oc/Student; b/Jul 28, 1967; h/Route 2, Box 209, Ruther Glen, VA 22546; p/Rev and Mrs E L Jones, Ruther Glen, VA; ed/Caroline HS; cp/Pres of Freshman, Sophomore, & Jr Class; 8th Grade Pres of SCA; Intermediate Basketball; NAACP; r/Bapt; hon/Nat Hon Soc; Runner-up Optimist Oratorial Contest; Runner-up Dist Forensics Competition; g/Bio-Med Chem or MD.

JONES, MARY LOU oc/WLIT Radio; b/Jul 19, 1958; h/109 Parkdale Road, Steubenville, OH 43952; ba/Steubenville, OH; p/Thomas C and Mary M Jones, Steubenville, OH; ed/Cath Ctl HS, 1976; Att'd Univ Steubenville; AAS, OH Univ, 1980; pa/Air Personality, WSTV, WRKY-FM Radio, Steubenville, 1979-80; Prog Dir, Public Ser Dir, Ofc Mgr, Air Personality, Telephone Salesperson, WLIT Radio, 1981-; cp/Campus Communication Sys; OH Univ Bkkpr, 1979-80; r/Rom Cath, St Peter's Cath Ch Adult Choir, 1974-; hon/Nom'd for Outstg Radio-TV Student, OH Univ, 1980; OH Univ Radio-TV S'ship Alt; Dean's List; Hon's List; W/W Among Am HS Students; W/W Among Students in Am Jr Cols; Intl Yth in Achmt; g/Mgmt Position at a Radio Sta in a Maj Mkt.

JONES, MELANIE LOUISE oc/Student; b/May 27, 1966; h/Route 2, Box 188, Mansfield, AR 72944; p/Donald and Freda Jones, Mansfield, AR; ed/HS, 1984; pa/Self Employed, Raise Reg'd Hampshire Sheep; cp/St 4-H VP, 1984; Sebastian Co 4-H Pres; Dayton 4-H VP, 1984; Co Secy/Treas, 4-H, 1982; Co 4-H Reporter, 1983; Dayton Clb Ofcr, 1976-84; FHA, 1982-83; Secreterial Clb; Paper Staff; r/Ch of Christ; hon/Band Hons St 3 Excell, 4 Superior; St 4-H Teen Star; St 4-H Ambassador; St Coor Wash Focus; Mem St 4-H Performing Arts Troupe 4 Yrs; Majorette; W/W Am Teenagers; W/W Am Music; g/to become an Ext Agt.

JONES, MICHAEL R oc/Student; b/Jan 17, 1964; h/414 Sunrise Drive, Forest City, AR 72335; ba/Same; p/Eugene Jones, Forest City, AR; cp/Basketball; r/Ch of God; hon/All Day S'ship to Jr Col.

JONES, RICHARD oc/Student; h/Post Office, Box 531201, Grand Prairie, TX 75031; p/John and Mary Jones, Haughton, LA 71057; ed/Princeton HS; So Univ; N TX St Univ; cp/Nat Assn Accts; Am Mgmt Assn; g/Mgmt in Acctg or Pers Adm.

JONES, ROBIN DELMA oc/Associate Nuclear Engineer; h/1145 Fox Hill Drive, Apartment T-12, Monroeville, PA 15146; ba/Monroeville, PA; p/Mr and Mrs Robert M Jones, Huntsville, AL; ed/Huntsville HS, 1978; Bach Nuclear Engrg, GA Tech, 1982; pa/Nuclear Design Engr, Westinghouse's Nuclear Fuels Div, 1982; cp/Am Nuclear Soc, 1978-82; VP Recruitment; NE Rep of SGA; Col Repubs; Jr Achmt Advr; r/Ch of Christ; hon/DAR Excell in Am Hist Awd, 1978; Hons Grad, GA Tech; g/Nuclear Engrg or Computer Sci.

JONES, STEPHEN MICHAEL oc/Student, Farm Worker; b/Mar 7, 1964; h/Route 2, Box 143, Pittsboro, NC 27312; p/Alvis & Nova Jones, Pittsboro, NC; ed/So Alamance HS, 1982; NC St Univ; cp/Pres, Nat Hon Soc, 1981-82; Jr Engrs, 1981; Co-Counsel Pres, Latin Clb, 1982-82; Marshal Co-Chief, 1981-82; FFA Secy, 1979-80; Men's Softball Team, 1980-; r/So Bapt; hon/Gov's Sch, 1981; Morehead Nom, 1982; Math Awds, 1981-82; Bus Driver of Yr, 1982; Voted Most Intell, 1982; Ruritan S'ship Awd, 1982; NC St Merit Scholars Finalist, 1982; NC Sch Sci & Math Nom, 1979; Hons Math Prog, 1982-83; Dean's List, 1982-83; g/Deg in Biol & Agri Engrg.

JONETT, SUSAN J oc/Student; b/Jun 6, 1957; h/508 E Maple Street, Spencer, WI 54479; p/Mr and Mrs Ronald M Jonett, Spencer, WI; ed/Spencer HS, 1975; St Joseph's Sch for Histologic Technique, 1979; pa/Student Mgr, Saga Food Ser, 1979-; cp/Assoc Mem, Tri-Beta, 1982-; EM Tech, UWSP, 1983-84; r/Luth; hon/W/W Among Students in Am Univs & Cols; Alt Badger Girl's St, 1974; 2nd at St in Track, 1975; Intl Yth in Achmt; g/Med Res, Biol Art.

JORDAN, MARY JOAN oc/Student; b/Jul 10, 1964; h/Route 5, Box 136, Northlakes, Hickory, NC 28601; p/John R Jr and Jane T Jordan, Hickory, NC; ed/S Caldwell HS, 1982; Appalachian St Univ; Univ NC-Chapel Hill; cp/French Clb; Mu Alpha Theta; Beta Clb; Student Coun Rep; Contestant, Caldwell Co Fair Pageant; r/Presb; hon/Nat Merit S'ship Semi-Finalist; Morehead Nom; Gov Sch of NC; Dean's List; W/W in HS; g/Computer Sci Maj.

JORDAN, MELANIE ELAINE oc/Student; b/May 18, 1963; h/Route 1 Eagle Bluff East, Jacksboro, TN 37757; p/James D and Patricia Jordan, Jacksboro, TN; ed/Campbell Co Comprehensive HS, 1981; Univ of TN; pa/Lead Supvr, World's Fair-Knoxville TN, 1982; Asst Mgr, Pizza Hut, 1983-; cp/Pom Pom Squad; Pep Clb; Art Clb Treas; Beta Clb; Yth Coun Secy; Band; Flag Corp; TOEC; 4-H; Owls for Christ; Lib Clb; Daugh of the Diamond, Treas; hon/Miss TN Teenager Finalist; Sweetheart Beta Theta Pi Frat, 1983; Art Awd, 1981; HS Hist Awd, 1981; Yg Commun Ldrs of Am; Yth in Intl Achmt; W/W Among Am HS Students; g/Univ TN-Knoxville, Sem Study.

JORDAN, RACHEL FAY oc/Student; h/Route 1, Box 279-C, Centre, AL 35960; p/Wallace and Sylvia Jordan, Centre, AL; cp/Hlth Occups Students of Am, Histn, 1983-84; FHA; 4-H Clb, Secy, 1980-81; Parent-Tchr Org; Spanish Clb; r/Holiness; hon/Outstg Student Awd, Eng, 1982; Perfect Attendance Awd, 1981; Teen Talk Awd, 1983; Awd for Most Money in a Rockathon; g/RN.

JOSEPH, STEPHANIE oc/Student; b/Oct 11, 1966; h/Route 10, Box 216, Easley, SC 29640; p/Anton Joseph, Greenville, SC, and Patricia Joseph, Easley, SC; ed/Wren HS; cp/Jr Varsity 1981-82, Varsity 1982-84, Cheerldr; Jr Rep 1982-83, Sr Class Seey 1983-84, Student Coun; ARC, 1982-83; Fashion Clb, 1982-83; Lttrman Clb, 1982-83; Pep Clb, 1981-82; Track, 1981; r/Cath; hon/Erskine Col Jr Fellow, 1983; Furman Univ Scholar, 1983; W/W Among Am HS Students, 1982-83; g/Furman Univ, Psychol.

JOSEPHSON, DARYL CRAIG oc/Student; b/Jul 23, 1960; p/Mannie Josephson (dec) and Sheila Josephson-Stecker, Lawrence, NY; ed/

Long Bch HS; BA, Crane Sch Music-Potsdam Col Arts & Sci; BS, Clarkson Col Technol; cp/Co-Chm Cub Sound; AV Tech-WCKN TV; Sound Tech-WTSC Radio; Physics Clb; IEEE, 1982-84; hon/Dean's List; Nat Dean's List; W/W Col; Intl Yth Achmt; Trustee's S'ship.

JOUETT, JOHN HOWARD oc/Student; b/Oct 16, 1965; h/Route 6, Manchester, TN 37355; p/John and Judy Jouett, Manchester, TN; ed/Manchester Ctl HS, 1983; Att'g TN Technol Univ; r/Ch of Christ; hon/L J Sverdrup Engrg S'ship; Murray, OH Engrg S'ship; Devel Foun S'ship from TN Technol Univ; g/Maj in Mech Engrg at TN Technol Univ.

JUDD, DENNIS L oc/Attorney; b/Jun 27, 1954; h/402 East 1500 South, Naples, UT 84078; ba/Vernal, UT; m/Carol Lynne; c/Lynne Marie, Amy Jo, Tiffany Ann, Andrew Chilberg; p/Derrel W and Leila Judd, Provo, UT; sp/John Chilberg (dec); Donna Rasmussun; ed/Morgan HS, 1972; BA summa cum laude 1978, JD 1981, Brigham Young Univ; Ptnr, Law Firm of Bennett & Judd, 1983-; Atty, Law Firm of Nielsen & Senior, 1981-83; Pt-time Instr, Polit Sci, Brigham Young Univ, 1980; Law Clk, McKeachnie & Allred, 1980; Congl Intern Congressman Jim Santini, 1977; Legis Intern UT St House of Reps Majority Whip Edison Stephens, 1977; cp/Mayor Pro Tem, City of Naples, 1983-; Mem, Naples Zoning & Planning Comm; Chm, Naples City Bd of Adjustment, 1983-; City Coun, City of Naples, 1982-; Dpty, Uintah Co Atty, 1982; Vernal Area C of C, Govt Affairs Com, 1981-82; Chief Justice, BYU Student Supreme Court, 1978-81; Chm, BYU Delegation, UT Intercol Assem, 1977, 1980; Chm, ASBYU Student Relats Coun, 1978-79; Sr Class VP, 1971-72; HS Yrbook Editor in Chief, 1971-72; Nat Hon Soc Pres, 1971-72; r/Mormon; hon/Hinkley Scholar Polit Sci, BYU, 1977-78; Phi Eta Sigma; Phi Kappa Phi; W/W Among Students in Am Univs & Cols; Intl Yth in Achmt; W/W in Am HS; Outstg Teenagers of Am.

JUMONVILLE, SUSAN LYNN oc/Student; b/May 12, 1965; h/8816 Whitaker Avenue, Sepulveda, CA 91343; p/Felix Joseph Jr and Marilu Jumonville, Sepulveda, CA; ed/James Monroe HS; cp/Ice Skating Inst of Am, 1975-; US Figure Skating Assn, 1976-; r/Meth; hon/Gifted Prom of the LA Unified Sch Dist, 1971-83; Grad as a Silver Seal Bearer from James Monroe HS, 1983; Homecoming Princess, 1982-83; Mem of the US Figure Skating Assn, Ice Angels Drill Team, 1981-83; Rec'd 19 Trophies, 35 Medals for Competitive Ice Skating, 1976-82; Awd of a Silver Tray for Most Artistic Perf in the Sierra NV Championships, 1982; Rec'd Achmt Awd in Poetry, 1980; g/Grad w Major in Computer Sci; Join Ice Show; Tch Ice Skating.

K

KABA, KIMBERLY KAY oc/Student; b/Apr 13, 1964; h/501 South Wyoming, Plainville, KS 67663; p/Mr and Mrs James Kaba, Plainville, KS; ed/Grad, Plainville HS, 1982; pa/Ft Hays St Ambassador, 1982-83; Housekeeper; Bkkpr; cp/Pom Pon Squad; Student Coun; Pep Clb; FHA; Nat Hon Soc; CYO; Tennis; Class Ofcs; P Clb; Student Exch; Homecoming Queen; Meml Union Ambassador, Ft Hays, 1982-83; hon/KS Univ Hon Student; Hon Roll; W/W HS Students; g/RN.

KADEL, TERRI CECILE oc/Office Manager; b/Aug 18, 1955; h/2665 Pleasant Valley Road, Mobile, AL 36606; ba/Same; m/Dr Roy E; p/Lt Col and Mrs Max H Spangler, Jefferson City, MO; ed/Jefferson City Sr HS, 1973; BS in Ed, Univ of MO Columbia, 1978; Grad Wk, Univ of MO Columbia, SE MO St Univ; pa/Receptionist and Ballroom Dance Instr, Fred Astaire, 1983; PE Tchr, Potosi Elem Sch, 1978-82; Asst Girls' Volleyball Coach, Potosi HS, 1978-81; Receptionist, Univ of MO Columbia, 1977-78; Tutor, Kinesiology, Trampoline, Gymnasics, Ice Skating, Univ of MO Columbia, 1975-77; Am Alliance Hlth, PE, Rec and Dance; AL Assn HPERD; Kappa Delta Pi; Intl Assn of Hlth Rschrs, Pres; r/Epis; hon/Bronze, Profl Ballroom Dance, 1983; Pre-Gold Ice Dancer, USFSA, 1981; USFSA Intermediate Free Style, 1981; Tri Penta, 1976-78, VP 1977; Ruby J Cline S'ship; Dean's List; W/W Cols and Univs; Intl Yth in Achmt; g/Complete Grad Wk in Adapted PE.

KAESER, HEIDI SUZANNE oc/Teacher and Curriculum Director; b/Sep 5, 1956; h/221 Crescent Avenue, East Peoria, IL 61611; ba/Peoria, IL; p/Mr and Mrs Gilbert Kaeser, East Peoria, IL; ed/MA 1982, BS 1979, Bradley Univ; Assoc in Arts and Sci, IL Ctl Col; E Peoria Commun HS, 1974; Grad Asst, Col of Ed 1980-82, Hd Tchr, Child Study Ctr 1980-82, Bradley Univ; Pre-Kgn Tchr and Curric Dir, Presch Ctr, Rogy's Gingerbread House Presch, 1981-; CIBAC; Pi Lambda Theta, VP 1982-83; Phi Delta Kappa; Am Assn of Univ Wom; cp/Town and Gown Clb; hon/Grad Asst'ship, Bradley Univ Col of Ed, 1980-81, 1981-82; W/W Among Students in Am Univs and Cols; g/Teach Sec'dy Ed or Art at Col Level.

KAESER, JULIE JUSTINE MAGDALENA oc/Student; b/Aug 20, 1962; h/221 Crescent Avenue, East Peoria, IL 61611; p/Mr and Mrs Gilbert R Kaeser, East Peoria, IL; ed/E Peoria Commun HS, 1980; BS, Constrn, Bradley Univ, 1984; cp/Sigma Lambda Chi, Treas 1983, Secy 1982; Sigma Alpha Iota, Secy 1982-83, VP 1983-84; Province Day Chm 1983, Frat Ed Chm 1981-82; Mortar Bd, Pres 1983-84; Soc of Wom Engrs, 1981-83; Ctl IL Yth Symph, 1976-82; AFS Student Bd, 1979-80; Bradley Intramurals, 1980-81; French Clb, VP 1978-79; Chem Clb, 1978-80; Orch, Secy 1979-80, Concert Mistress 1979-80; r/Prot; hon/Nat Hon Soc, 1980; IL St Scholar, 1980; Sterling Merit Awd, 1980; Nat Sch Orch Awd, 1980; Mortar Bd, 1983; Constrn Dept Sophomore S'ship Awd, 1982; Otto Baum Corporate S'ship, 1981-84; Soc of Wom in Constrn S'ship, 1983-84; W/W

Among Am HS Students; W/W Among Am Col Students; g/Profl Constrn Mgr.

KAMMER, ALICE ANN oc/Sales Merchandiser; b/Sep 5, 1959; h/1729-204 Gosnell Road, Vienna, VA 22180; ba/Farmingdale, NY; p/Mr and Mrs Max L Kammer, Bluefield, WV; ed/Bluefield HS, 1977; WV Univ, 1977; BS, Bus Mgmt/Mktg, Bluefield St Col, 1981; pa/Asst Mgr, Village Card Shop, 1978-81; Ofc Clk, Kammer Furniture Co, 1981; Cosmetic Conslt, Stone & Thomas, 1981-82; Sales Merchandiser, Del Labs, 1982-; cp/Mktg Clb, 1977; Phi Beta Lambda, 1979-81; Cheerldg Squad, 1978-79; Alpha Xi Delta Sorority; Accreditation Com; Acad Com; Mercer Co Humane Soc; Wash, DC, Humane Soc; r/Jewish; hon/Alpha Chi, 1980; Grad, cum laude, 1981; Miss Phi Beta Lambda, 1980-81; Miss Congeniality, 1980; Miss Poise, 1980; Sales Merchandiser, 1983; W/W Am Cols and Univs; Am Biogl Inst; g/Continue Career in Cosmetics in Mgmt/Mktg Relats.

KANDYBOWICZ, IRENA M oc/Eligibility Technician; b/Feb 3, 1959; h/131 Vought Place, Stratford, CT 06497; ba/Bridgeport, CT; p/John and Josephine Kandybowicz, Stratford, CT; ed/Andrew Warde HS, 1977; BA, Social Wk and Native Am Studies, Dakota Wesleyan Univ, 1980; pa/Eligibility Tech (Casewkr), St of CT, Dept of Income Maintenance, 1981-; NASW, 1980-; Social Wk Clb, 1977-80, Pres 1979-80, Public Relats/Histn 1978-79; cp/Fdn of Dem Wom, 1981-, Recording Secy 1982-; Harmonettes, 1981-82; r/Rom Cath; hon/Dean's List, 1977-80; BA, magna cum laude, 1980; Cert, Heart Assn, 1977; Intl Yth in Achmt; Commun Ldrs of Am; g/Grad Studies in Social Wk, Univ of CT; Elected to US Senate.

KANE, ROBIN EDWARD oc/Student; b/Feb 12, 1963; h/PO Box 716, Cullowhee, NC 28723; p/William D and Linda O Kane, Cullowhee, NC; ed/Student of Ocean Engrg; mil/Sr, USCG Acad; cp/USCG Acad Varsity Crew, Co-Capt; r/Rom Cath; hon/Best All Round Sr, 1981; Hon Grad, 1981; W/W HS.

KANITZ, LORI ANN oc/Student; b/Jan 20, 1965; h/2504 West Fort Worth, Broken Arrow, OK 74012; p/Russell and Carolyn Kanitz, Broken Arrow, OK; ed/Grad, Union HS, 1983; pa/Sales Clk, B Dalton Booksellers, 1981-82; Presch Tchr, Nat Child Care Ctr, 1982-83; pa/Mayor's Yth Coun, Auto Bd to Yg Vols in Action 1981-82; Yg Vols in Action, 1981-82; Drill Team, Lt, Capt; Cross Country Track, 1 Yr; Student Coun, 2 Yrs; Jr Bd; Sr Bd; Sr Class Secy; Nat Hon Soc, 2 Yrs; Spanish Clb, 2 Yrs; F'ship of Christian Aths, 1 Yr; Campus Life, 1 Yr; Yth Alive, Yth Min, 1 Yr; r/Luth; hon/Masonic Lodge Student of Today, 1980; Outstg Freshman Sci Student, 1980; Outstg Freshman Hist Student, 1980; Hugh O'Brian Ldrship Alumni, 1981; First Runner-Up, OK St Drill Team Competition, Indivs, 1982; Union HS Del to OK Girls' St, 1982; Other Hons; W/W Am HS Students; W/W Am Drill Teams; g/To Attend the Univ of OK, Majoring in Phy Therapy; Career as Phy Therapist.

KASIANOWICZ, JOHN JAMES oc/Graduate Student; b/Apr 22, 1957; h/205 Oakes Street, Port Jefferson, NY 11777; ba/Stony Brook, NY; m/Rachel

Helene; p/John E and Antoinette M Kasianowicz, Quincy, MA; ed/Quincy HS, 1975; BA in Physics w Distn, Boston Univ, 1979; MA in Physics, St Univ of NY Stony Brook, 1981; Grad Res Asst, Dept of Physiol and Biophysics, SUNY Stony Brook, 1983-; Prof of Physics, En Nazarene Col, 1982-83; Grad Res Asst, Dept of Physiol and Biophysics 1981-82, Grad Tchg Asst, Dept of Physics 1981, Grad Tchg Asst, Dept of Math 1979-81, SUNY Stony Brook; NSF Sum Res Prog, 1979; Tchr Asst 1978-79, Res Asst 1978-79, Dept of Physics, Boston Univ; Darkroom Tech, Sch of Ed, Boston Univ, 1976-78; cp/CYO Basketball, 1972-73; Student Coun, 1972-75, Pres 1974-75; Explorer's Clb, Astronomy, 1973-75; Reg Adv Coun, 1974-75; Boston Univ Physics Clb, 1975-79, Pres 1978-79; Mortar Bd Nat Hon Soc, Secy 1978-79; Boston Computer Soc, 1982-; hon/Yth Fitness Awd, 1972; NEDT Awd, 1972; Quincy Citizen's Envir Bd Awd, 1972; Am Legion Awd, 1972; Quincy HS Cert of Merit, 1974; MA Boys' St, 1974; Student Govt Day Awd, 1975; Jr Class S'ship, 1975; Grossman Foun Awd, 1975; Elks Awd, 1975; Winner, Photographic Contest (7 Awds), 1974; Winner, Photographic Contest (3 Awds), 1976; Buzz Orio S'ship, 1975-76; Boston Univ S'ship, 1975-79; Boston Univ Alumni Awd, 1979; Boston Univ Col Prize for Excell in Physics, 1979; Mortar Bd Hon Soc, 1978-79; W/W Among HS Students; Nat Col Register; g/Prof of Physics; Res in Physics and Biophysics.

KASIANOWICZ, RACHEL HELENE HULT oc/Systems Analyst; b/Sep 9, 1957; h/65 Phillips Street, Wollaston, MA 02170; ba/North Quincy, MA; m/John; p/Rev and Mrs Bertil E Hult, Wollaston, MA; ed/Quincy HS, 1975; BS in Music Ed, BA in Hist, En Nazarene Col; Sys Anal Cert, Grumman Data Sys Inst; Enrolled in St of the Art Prog, NEn Univ; pa/Sys Analyst, State Street Bk & Trust Co, 1982-; Programmer Analyst 1981-82, Sr Prodn/Copy Editor for *The Journal of Chemical Physics* 1980-81, Am Inst of Physics; cp/Dean of Am Guild of Organists, 1981-82; Boston Computer Soc and IBM Sci Sub-Grp, 1982-; Long Isl Symphonic Choral Assn, 1980-81; Pres, Nat Hon Soc, 1974-75; hon/Winner, LI Level Competition of Am Guild of Organists, 1981; Hist Deptl Hons, Phi Delta Lambda Hon Soc, 1979; Winner of Music Competition, S'ship Recip, 1975; Am Biogl Inst; g/PhD, Organ Perf.

KASITZ, COLLEEN oc/Student; b/Apr 1, 1966; h/Box 672, Route 7, Richmond, KY 40475; ba/Richmond, KY; p/Louis Jr and Mary Kay Kasitz, Richmond, KY; ed/Student, Madison Ctl HS; pa/Cashier, Winn Dixie; cp/Ctl Girls' Ath Clb; Fgn Lang Clb; Sr Beta Clb; Jr Class Histn, 1982-83; St Mark Yth Grp; r/Rom Cath; hon/US Achmt Acad Awd Winner in Sci; High Distn Awd, Madison Ctl, 1983; Hon'd w Distn, Madison Ctl, 1982; US Achmt Acad Yrbook; g/To Attend Col; Maj in Math.

KATCHMER, MICHAEL ANTHONY oc/Student; b/Nov 26, 1956; h/27 Blue Rock Street, Millersville, PA 17551; p/Geo and Pauline Katchmer, Millersville, PA; ed/Penn Manor HS, 1974; BA, Susquehanna

Univ, 1978; BA, Millersville St Col, 1981; PhD, IN Univ; cp/Univ Theatre; Univ Exptl Theatre; Opera Wkshop; Univ Choir; Chapel Choir; Fest Choir; Football; Alpha Psi Omega, VP; Classics Clb; Cantor, Ch; Gratis Perfs, Actors' Co of PA, Fulton Opera House Foun; Ch Softball; hon/Public Perf of Several Original Plays; Intl Yth in Achmt; W/W Among Students in Am Univs and Cols; Commun Ldrs of Am; g/Prof of Classics.

KATTMANN, NANCY SUE oc/Student; b/Oct 31, 1963; h/113 Saratoga Waye, Vienna, VA 22180; p/R H and Doris B Kattmann, Vienna, VA; ed/James Madison HS, 1982; cp/Ski Clb; Softball; Pom Pon Squad Secy; Yrbook; Lit Arts Mag; SGA Cabinet; Candystriper; Ch Grp Treas; Powder Puff Football; Cert CPR, Lifeguard/Pool Mgmt; hon/W/W Among Am HS Students; g/Forestry/Wildlife Devel.

KATZ, GILBERT oc/Student; b/Apr 21, 1962; h/439 Washington Street, Brookline, MA 02146; ba/Boston, MA; p/User and Mina Katz, Brookline, MA; ed/Hons Dipl, Brookline HS, 1979; BS in Elect Engrg, summa cum laude, Boston Univ, 1983; Cand for MD, Boston Univ Sch of Med, 1987; pa/Tchg Asst, Boston Univ Col of Engrg, 1981-83; Engrg Tech, AUS Corps of Engrs, 1982, 1981; Clk, Bay St Ser, 1980, 1979; cp/Tau Beta Pi, 1981; Undergrad Engrg Assn, Sci Advr; Boston Univ Volleyball Clb; Co-Fdr, Boston Univ Engrg House; HS Basketball 1979, 1978, Tennis 1979, 1978, 1977; HS Math Team, 1976-79; Intl Clb, 1975-79; r/Jewish; hon/Tau Beta Pi, 1981; Dean's List, 1979-83; Nat Merit Scholar, 1979-83; Nat Hon Soc, HS, 1978; Outstg Perf in Math Team, 1979; Finalist in Math Olympiad, 1978-79; g/Orthopedics or Internal Med.

KAUFMAN, JOEL oc/Student; b/Nov 2, 1960; h/11 Dahlia Street, Warwick, RI 02888; p/Eli and Bernice Kaufman, Warwick, RI; ed/Pilgrim High, 1978; BA, Providence Col, 1982; JD, Duke Univ, 1985; pa/US Senate Intern; Legal Intern; cp/Student Fac Curric Com; r/Jewish; hon/Reynolds Scholar, 1982.

KAYE, NEIL SCOTT oc/Student; b/Jun 1, 1958; h/RD 1, Voorbeesville, NY 12186; ba/New Scotland, NY; p/Jesse and Shirley Kaye, North Miami Beach, FL; ed/Phillips Exeter Acad, 1976; BA, Skidmore Col, 1980; Student, Albany Med Col; cp/Skidmore Rowing Clb Fdr; USRA Ygest Assoc Ofcl, EMT for NYS; Camp Shelley Maintenance, Dir; Jewish Student Union; Dorm Residence Staff; Long Range Planning Com; Saratoga Emer Corps; Hebrew Tchr; Student Rep to Lib Com; r/Jewish; hon/Bronze Medal, Empire St Games, 1982; USDAN Meml Prize for Excell in Mod Hebrew; W/W Am Univs; Intl Yth in Achmt; g/MD; Psychiatry.

KAZALEH, FADWA ANN oc/Coordinator of Research and Evaluation; h/1040 Martinique Road, Jacksonville, FL 32216; ba/Jacksonville, FL; p/Saed Elias and Salwa Bajalia Kazaleh, Jacksonville, FL; ed/BA, Univ of FL; MS, PhD Cand, FL St Univ; pa/Coor of Res and Eval, Duval Co Sch Bd; Am Ed Assn; FL Ed Res Assn; Comparative Intl Ed Soc; Duval Co Mtl Hlth Assn; Psi Chi; hon/Biling Fellow, FL St Univ, 1978-81; W/W S and SW; World W/W Wom; Personalities of S.

KEA, CATHY DENISE oc/Candidate for Doctor of Philosophy; b/Feb 12, 1954; h/1824 Tennessee, Apartment 4, Lawrence, KS; ba/Lawrence, KS; p/Mr and Mrs William J Kea, Durham, NC; ed/Dipl, Durham HS, 1971; BA, NC Ctl Univ, 1975; MS, Univ of WI La Crosse, 1976; Doct Student, 1981-; pa/Tchr, Univ Instr, NC St Conslt Div for Exceptl Chd; Coor of Proj ACSES, 1983-84; CEC; Black Caucus for Spec Ed; Div for Chd w Lng Disabilities; Delta Sigma Theta Sorority Inc, Advr for Undergrad Chapt; Alpha Kappa Mu Hon Soc; Div on Career Devel; r/Bapt; hon/Post-Baccalaureate F'ship, Univ of KS, 1982-83, 1983-84, 1984-85; Delta Sigma Theta Sorority Inc S'ship, 1982-83; Outstg Yg Wom of Am; g/To Train Tchrs to Effectively Teach Exceptl Chd.

KEARNEY, GERARD JOSEPH JR oc/Research Assistant; b/Apr 11, 1957; h/803 Elmwood Drive, Shelby, NC 28150; ba/Charlotte, NC; p/Gerard Joseph Kearney Sr, New Haven, CT; Anna Kearney Longley, North Haven, CT; ed/Notre Dame HS, 1975; Univ of NC Charlotte, 1983; mil/USN, 1977-83 (Hon Discharge); pa/Orderly, Arden House of Hamden Convalescent Home, 1974-75, 1977; Franciscan Friar, Franciscan Order of Friar's Minor Conventual, 1975-77; Rel Prog Spec, USN, 1977-81; Gen Psych Lab Proctor, 1982-83; Res Asst, "Memory in the Adult and Aging," UNCC Psych Dept, 1982-; cp/HS Cross Country, Track, Glee Clb, Spanish Clb, Current Events Clb, Confraternity of Christian Men Clb; St Hyacinth Col and Sem Freshman Class Dean, 1976-77; Guantanamo Bay Chapt, GSA, Troop Ldr, Coun Treas/Mem, 1979-80; Steering Com, Diocese of Charlotte, NC's Peace and Justice Comm's Prison Min, 1982-83; UNCC Alumni Assn, 1983; r/Rom Cath; hon/Full Acad S'ship to Notre Dame HS, 1971-75; US Naval Sta, Guantanamo Bay, Cuba, Petty Ofcr of the Month, 1981; Yale Univ Acad S'ship, 1981-82; Brycie Baber Acad S'ship, 1982-83; Phi Kappa Phi Hon Soc, 1982; Grad, cum laude, 1983; Hon Discharge, 1983; g/Fam Sers Psychol in US Civil Ser; PhD in Clin Psych.

KEATING, JOHN FRANCIS JR oc/Attorney; b/May 3, 1954; h/906 Cherokee Street, New Orleans, LA 70118; ba/New Orleans, LA; p/John F and Eleanor E Keating, Shelton, CT; ed/St Joseph HS, 1972; AB, Cornell Univ, 1976; MA, Univ of MD, 1981; JD, Tulane Univ, 1982; pa/Proj Mgr/Sys Analyst, Gen Elect Co Ctr for Adv'd Studies, 1976-79; Nat Security Conslt, Congl Budget Ofc, US Cong, 1980; Law Clk, McGlinchey, Stafford & Mintz, 1981; Law Clk, Hon Patrick Carr, US Dist Judge, 1982-; Am Bar Assn; CT Bar Assn; NY Bar Assn; Am Judic Soc; cp/Cornell Rowing Assn; Cornell Lightweight Crew; HS Varsity Football and Track; r/Rom Cath; hon/Pub, "The Jones Act Does Not Bar Recovery of Nonpecuniary Damages Under the General Maritime Law," 1981; Nat Hon Soc; Barnum Fest King Cand, 1972; Cornell Dean's List; JD, cum laude; Notes and Comments Editor, *The Maritime Lawyer.*

KECK, KARLA MAY oc/Teacher; b/May 23, 1960; h/RR 1, Clay City, IL 62824; ba/Louisville, IL; ed/Clay City Com Unit 10, 1978; AS, Olney Ctl Col, 1980; BS, En IL Univ, 1982; pa/Tchr, N Clay Elem; Kappa Delta Pi; SCEC; IL Rdg Assn; En IL Univ Rdg Coun; IL HS Assn; cp/CoChm, Heart Dr; Vol Softball Coach; hon/Valedictorian, Tchr's Ed S'ship for Spec Ed; IL St Scholar; g/EdM.

KEDROWSKI, KAREN MARIE oc/Student; b/Jan 29, 1964; h/Route 2, Box 129, Little Falls, MN 56345; ba/Minneapolis, MN; p/Henry and Clara Kedrowski, Little Falls, MN; ed/Grad, cum laude, Little Falls Commun HS, 1982; pa/Nurses' Aide, Luth Sr Citizens' Home, 1980-81; Chem Tutor, 1982; Lib Aide, Col of St Catherine Lib, 1982-83; St Ho of Reps Intern, 1983; Maintenance and Custodial Pers, Univ of MN, 1983-84; cp/Jr Vol, St Gabriel's Hosp, 1977-79; MN Music for Yth, 1978; Polit Activs, 1979-84; Caucus and Conv Attendee, 1980, 1982, 1984; Camp Wk, Rep Stephen Wenzel, 1982, 1984; Close-Up Alumni Assn, 1983-; Upper MW Artists Assn, 1983-84; VP, HS French Clb, 1978-82; Other Orgl Activs; r/Rom Cath; hon/1st Annual Charles D Martin Spch S'ship, 1982; Spkr of the Yr, 1982; Star Voting St Solo/Ensemble Contest, 1982; Reg High Score, All-St Band Auditions, 1981; Alt Flute, MN All-St Band, 1981-82; Dean's List, Col of St Catherine and St Cloud St Univ, 1983; Num Other Hons; W/W Among Am HS Students; g/Polit Sci/French Majs; Career as Polit Analyst/Commentator or Politician.

KEELS, FAITH MARIA oc/Student; b/Dec 23, 1963; h/378 Mooneyham Road, Sumter, SC 29150; p/Mr and Mrs Harold Keels, Sumter, SC; ed/Dipl, Sumter HS, 1981; Student, Benedict Col; cp/Soc of Physics Students, 1981-84; Army ROTC Drill Mem, 1983-84; Student Govt Assn, Rep 1983-84; Alpha Chi Nat Hon Soc; Alpha Kappa Mu Nat Hon Soc; Sigma Pi Sigma Nat Hon Soc; YMCA; r/Penecostal Holiness; hon/G L Scurry S'ship Recip, 1982-83; AUS ROTC S'ship Recip, 1983; Nat Dean's List, 1981-82, 1982-83; W/W Among Am Cols and Univs; g/Computer Engrg Maj; 2nd Lt in AUS's Engrg Corps.

KEETER, JEFFREY PERRY oc/Student; b/Jul 30, 1959; h/1101 Raleigh Street, Elizabeth City, NC 27909; ba/Buies Creek, NC; p/Mr and Mrs N C Keeter, Elizabeth City, NC; ed/NEn HS, 1977; BS, Pre-Law and Hist, cum laude, Campbell Univ, 1981; JD, Campbell Univ Sch of Law, 1984; pa/Clk, LeRoy, Wells, Shaw, Hornthal & Riley, 1983; Reservationist/Bkkpr/Handyman, Beacon Motor Lodge, 1981-82; Resident Dir for Campus Dorm, Campbell Univ, 1981; cp/Am Bar Assn, Law Student Div, Law Ofc Ec Sect; Epsilon Pi Eta Hon Soc; Omicron Delta Kappa Nat Hon and Ldrship Soc; St Grad Sch Rep, Col Fdn of Yg Dems; Phi Alpha Delta Law Frat; Intramural Client Cnslg Competition; Case Writer, Ct Calendar Editor, *Campbell Law Observer;* Chief Justice of Hon Ct, Campbell Univ Sch of Law; r/Bapt; hon/Dean's List, 5 Semesters; Grad, cum laude; Top 5 Outstg Col Dems in NC, 1980-81; Pres, Campbell Univ Yg Dems; Exec Coun, NC Fdn of Col Dems; Pres Envir Awd, 1977; Baseball; Eagle Scout Awd, 1974;

W/W Among Students in Am Univs and Cols; g/Pract Law in NC.

KELLER, MICHAEL AARON oc/ Student; b/Aug 24, 1969; h/Route 2, Box 202, Belvidere, TN 37306; p/Bobby and Carolyn Keller, Belvidere, TN; ed/HS Student; cp/F'ship of Christian Aths; Beta Clb, VP; Editor, S Jr High Newspaper; Student Against Driving Drunk; r/Bapt; hon/Outstg Student Awd; Hon Student; Indust Arts Awd; Reg Math Contest, 3rd Place; F'ship of Christian Aths Awd; Top 10% Nedtest; Artistic Awd; Phy Sci Awd; Math and Eng Excell Awd; g/Col.

KELLER, STEFFANIE LYNN oc/ Student; b/Jan 30, 1968; h/4906 Catalpha Road, Baltimore, MD 21214; p/ James and Linda Keller, Baltimore, MD; ed/Currently Enrolled, Seton HS; pa/ Telephone Operator, Greetings and Rdgs, 1983-; cp/Jr High: Pres of Student Coun; HS: Secy of Action Coun, Sophomore Class Bd; Drama Troupe, Marian Assn; r/Cath; hon/Acad S'ship to Seton HS; g/Deg in Med.

KELLEY, KEVIN MORRIS oc/Student; b/Dec 12, 1962; h/223 Orchard Road, Orinda, CA 94563; p/Tad Dewitt and Joan Mae Kelley, Orinda, CA; ed/ Miramonte HS, 1981; Wkg towards BA in Zool, Univ of CA Berkeley; pa/ Pt-time, Copy Quick, 1980-81; Real Wood Prods, Sum 1982; Mech, U 76, 1981-82; cp/HS French Hon Soc; Pop Warner Football, 1975-76; HS Football, 1979-81; HS Track; HS Tennis; Univ of CA Berkeley Pre-Med Soc; Univ of CA Berkeley Intramurals; Univ of CA Berkeley Kappa Alpha Order, Financial Ofcr; Chi Psi; Delta Delta Delta, Poseidon Man, Univ of OR; hon/1st Place, Sci Fair, 1976; Dean's List; Pop Warner Football Awd, 1975-76; W/W Among Am HS Students; Intl Yth in Achmt; Dir of Dist'd Ams; g/To Pursue a Career in Med or Res in Molecular Biol or Related Fields.

KELLEY, PAULA RENEE oc/Student; b/Apr 19, 1982; h/Route 6, Box 83, Martin, TN 38237; p/Paul and Martha Kelley, Martin, TN; ed/HS Dipl; BS, Elect Engrg Technol, Univ of TN Martin, 1984; pa/Univ of TN Martin Bookstore Employee, 1980-84; cp/VP, IEEE, 1983-84; VP and Secy, Zeta Tau Alpha, 1981-83; r/First Bapt Ch; hon/ Outstg Yg Am Wom; g/To Obtain a Job in the Field of Elect Engrg Technol; To Perform My Best and Strive to Learn More.

KELLY, DAVID ANTHONY oc/ Student; b/Aug 8, 1961; h/Route One, Green Meadows, Rond du Lac, WI 54935; ba/Oshkosh, WI; m/Kathleen Ann Williams; p/Raymond J Kelly Jr, Rond du Lac, WI; June K Kelly, Rond du Lac, WI; ed/Grad, Horace Mann HS, 1979; Polit Sci and Spch Maj, Univ of WI Oshkosh; cp/Circle K Intl, Intl Pres and VP, Dist Gov, Lt Gov, New Clb Bldg Chm, Chapt Mbrship Growth and Activity Chm; Oshkosh Student Assn, Senator for 2 Yrs, Assemblyman, VP pro tempore, Legis Affairs Dir; Alpha Lambda Delta Hon Soc, Secy; Theatre Student Assn, Pres; r/Luth; hon/ WI-Upper MI Key Clb Dist Outstg Lt Gov Awd, 1979; Key Clb Intl Robert F Lucas Outstg Lt Gov's Awd, 1979; WI-Upper MI Key Clb Dist Gov's Silver Star Awd, 1981; IN Circle K 1982, WI-Upper MI Circle K 1983, Dist Gov's

Diamond Awd; g/BS Degs in Spch and Polit Sci; Deg in Orgl Mgmt; To Found MW Ldrship Inst Inc.

KELLY, KEVIN JAMES oc/Student; b/Feb 27, 1962; h/1757 Southeast Dominic Avenue, Port Saint Lucie, FL 33452; p/Hugh P Kelly, Port Saint Lucie, FL; ed/John Carroll HS, 1980; Spanish and Social Sci Maj, Stetson Univ; pa/ Stock Clk, K-Mart, 1980; Sales Asst, Construx, 1978, 1979; cp/Phi Eta Sigma; Green Circle; Phi Alpha Theta; Pt St Lucie Disaster Com; Pres, Spanish Clb; Nat Hon Soc; Interact; Hons Prog; Varsity Tennis, HS; Student Govt Assn, Stetson; hon/Top Hons Student, Stetson, 1981, 1982; Outstg Jr in Hist, 1983; Highest GPA, Freshman, Sophomore and Jr Yrs at Stetson; Valedictorian, HS; Am Legion, HS; W/W; Soc of Dist'd Am HS Students; Commun Ldrs of Am; g/ Study Abroad; Law Sch.

KELLY, MARIA PATRICIA oc/Student; b/May 21, 1967; h/121 Banbury Circle, Greenville, NC 27834; p/Paul and Patricia Kelly, Greenville, NC; ed/ HS Student; cp/Cath Yth Org; Jr Achmt; Rose High Chorus; Drama Clb; HS and USS Swim Teams; r/Cath; hon/ Chosen for Admission to NC Sch of Sci and Math, 1983; 2 HS Letters for Swimming, 1981-82, 1982-83; 3rd Place, Algebra II Contest, Elizabeth City St Univ, 1983; Outstg Jr Achiever, Nat Jr Achiever Travelshp to Nat Conv, 1983; g/Deg in Chem Engrg.

KELLY, NATALIE KAY oc/Student; b/Jan 29, 1963; h/4621 Northwest 47th Avenue, Ocala, FL 32675; p/Charles and Evelyn B Kelly, Ocala, FL; ed/HS Dipl, Ocala Vanguard, 1981; AA, Ctl FL Commun Col, 1983; Att'g, FL St Univ; cp/1980 Homecoming Queen of Ocala Vanguard HS; Cheerldr, 9 Yrs; Girls' St, 1980; Miss VHS Pageant, 1979, 1980; Pres, JCL; CFCC: Variations Singing Grp 1982-83, Circle K Clb 1982-83, Capt of Cheerldrs 1982-83, F'ship of Christian Aths 1983, Student Govt 1983, Graphic Artist for "Patriot Press" 1983, Prodn Coor 1983, Phi Theta Kappa (Secy 1983); FSU: Phi Theta Kappa Alumni 1984, Focus 1984, Design Corps 1984, Advtg Clb 1984; hon/Hon Grad; Outstg Sr; Comml Art Awd, 1980-81; Jr Classical Leag Awd, 1980-81; Phi Theta Kappa, 1982, 1983; CFCC Art S'ship, 1983; Nom'd for FL Blue Key, 1983; Marshall Hamilton S'ship to FSU, 1983, 1984; U Daughs of the Confederacy S'ship, 1984; W/W Latin; W/W Am HS Students; Intl Yth in Achmt; Am Yth in Achmt; Personalities of S; Nat Dean's List; W/W Among Am Jr Cols; g/To Grad from FL St Univ w Maj in Visual Communs; To Wk for an Advtg Agy or a Large Design Firm.

KELLY, PAMELA RENEÉ oc/Student; b/Sep 10, 1967; h/West St Route 269-A, Wallace, NC 28466; p/Tilma and Anselma Kelly, Wallace, NC; cp/4-H; Cheerldr; Math Clb; Hon Soc; Spanish Clb; Student Coun; r/Disciple; hon/ Trophies in 4-H (Outstg 4-H'er, 2 Yrs); Awd, Cheering Sum Sch S'ship (2); Chosen to Attend the NC Sch of Sci and Math; g/Engr or Dr.

KELSO, TOM LEE oc/Student; b/Feb 22, 1956; h/Route 3, Savannah, MO 64485; p/Frank and Delores Kelso, Savannah, MO; ed/Savannah HS, 1974; MO Wn St Col, 1980; TX A&M Univ;

cp/Yg Dem of Andrew Co; Eagle Scout; MS Dance Marathon Subcom Chm; Secy-Treas, The Way Intl of Bryan, TX; hon/Dean's List; Intl Yth in Achmt; W/ W Among Students in Am Univs and Cols; g/Word Over the World Ambassador; The Way Corps.

KENEMER, KIMBERLY DEE oc/ Student; b/Oct 1, 1968; h/2919 Botany Drive, Jonesboro, GA 30236; p/Jerry and Sandra Nash, Jonesboro, GA; ed/ Student, Morrow Sr High; cp/Beta Clb, 1981-83; F'ship of Christian Aths, 1982-83; Girls' Basketball Mgr, 1981-83; Computer Clb, 1981-83; r/ Bapt; hon/Nat Sci Merit Awd Nom, 1982, 1983; Most Outstg 8th Grade Student Awd, 1982; Nom for Most Outstg 9th Grade Student, 1983; All A Hon Roll, 1980-83; Nat Merit Acad Yrbook.

KENNEDY, MARY REBECCA oc/ Operator; b/Apr 19, 1963; h/304 Crestview Drive, Martinez, GA 30907; ba/ Augusta, GA; p/Mr and Mrs William E Kennedy, Martinez, GA; ed/Dipl, Evans HS, 1981; Profl Modeling Dipl, Barbizon Sch of Modeling, 1982; pa/Cashier, Ye Olde Grocery Store, 1981; Model, The Barbizon Agy; Operator, The Krystal Co; cp/FHA, VP, Histn, Pres; Girls' Chorus; 4-H, VP; Cheerldg; GSA; Red Cross Aide; Student Coun; Ch Wk; hon/ St Finalist in Miss GA Nat Teenager Pageant, 1981; Hollywood Spotlite Photo Awd, 1982; Offer of Nashville Music Prodns Recording Contract, 1978; Invitation to Am Acad of Dramatic Arts, NY, 1982; Intl Yth in Achmt; W/W Among Am HS Students; Commun Ldrs of Am; Personalities of S; g/ Paralegal Asst; Actress and/or Singer.

KENNEDY, NINA GAMBLE oc/ Concert Pianist; b/Jul 1, 1960; h/2417 Gardner Lane, Nashville, TN 37207; ba/ New York, NY; p/Matthew Kennedy and Anne Gamble, Nashville, TN; ed/ McGavock Sr High, 1978; Att'd, Curtis Inst of Music, 1978-79; BMus, Temple Univ, 1982; Att'g, Juilliard Sch of Music, 1982-; pa/Appeared as Piano Soloist w Orchs in Nashville 1974, 1978, 1983, Savannah 1975, Memphis 1976, Jackson (MS) 1976, Kingsport 1976, Phila 1982, NY 1981, 1982; Concertized throughout the US, the Bahamas, S Am; Performed on Nationally Televised *Young Artists' Series*, 1976; Mem, Settlement Music Sch Piano Fac, Phila, 1979-82; r/Bapt; hon/TN Arts Comm Artist's Grant, 1983; Juilliard Tuition S'ship, 1982; Nat Soc of Arts and Lttrs Awd, 1982; Pro Arts Soc S'ship, 1982; Sigma Alpha Iota Awd, 1982; W/W Among Am HS Students; Soc of Dist'd Names and Faces; g/Tchg Position as Prof of Piano at a Col of Music or a Conservatory.

KENNEY, STEPHEN MARTIN oc/ Evangelist; b/Sep 21, 1961; h/203 West 7th Street, Lobelville, TN 37097; ba/ Lobelville, TN; m/Leslie Karen; p/ Robert Eugene and Lois Jean Kenney, Woodsfield, OH; ed/Woodsfield HS, 1979; ABS, OH Val Col, 1981; Att'd, OH St Univ; pa/Located Evangelist, Lobelville Ch of Christ, 1983-; r/Ch of Christ; hon/Paul Rusen S'ship, 1979; Highest ACT Score in Co, 1979; Nat Hon Soc; Nat Dean's List; Outstg Yg Men of Am; Commun Ldrs of Am; g/ Attend David Lipscomb Col and Maj in Communs; Wk for Nat Security; Mission Wk in France.

KENNEY, SUSAN RACHEL oc/Student; b/Mar 31, 1968; h/Route 4, Box 66, Woodsfield, OH 43793; p/Robert E and Lois J Kenney, Woodsfield, OH; ed/HS Student; cp/4-H, 7 Yrs, Treas for 2 Yrs, Secy 1983, Jr Fair Bd; FHA, 2 Yrs, News Reporter; r/Ch of Christ; hon/Spelling Bee Champ, 1982; Second Highest Math Average, 1982; g/To Attend a 2-Yr Col.

KERESTER, JOHN THOMAS oc/Student; b/Jun 24, 1964; h/1305 Kingston Avenue, Alexandria, VA 22302; p/Thomas P and Barbara L Kerester, Alexandria, VA; ed/Bishop Ireton HS, 1982; Sum Study, Univ of Paris, Sorbonne, 1983; Student, Swarthmore Col; cp/VP, Key Clb; Editor, Sch Newspaper; Ch Organist; Model UN; Debate Team; Congl Intern; Lifeguard; Rusk Inst, NYU Med Ctr, Pre-Med Intern; r/Rom Cath; hon/Eagle Scout; Dean's List; NH Hon Soc; Mu Alpha Theta; g/Polit Sci and Phil Maj; Law Sch.

KERN, BRENDA SUE oc/Neonatal Staff Nurse; b/Jul 5, 1956; h/7548 Wyandotte, Kansas City, MO 64114; ba/Kansas City, MO; p/August W and Shirley M Kern, Sainte Genevieve, MO; ed/Dipl, Valle HS, 1974; BSN, Avila Col, 1978; pa/Neonatal Staff Nurse, Chd's Mercy, 1982-; Clin Oncology Nurse, Davidner Hematology-Oncology Clin, 1980-82; Clin Lab Supvr, KC Med Grp, 1979-80; Neonatal Staff Nurse, Chd's Mercy, 1978-79; ABWA; Sigma Theta Tau, Histn 1978-80; Oncology Nurse Soc; ANA, Dist #2 Bd Mem 1978-80, 1980-82; MO Student Nurse Assn, Pres; NSNA; Delta Epsilon Sigma; cp/Wom's Ldrship Inst; Vol Cancer Soc Spkrs Bur; KC Royals Fan Accommodations, 1979-82; KC Chiefs Press Box, 1979-83; r/Cath; St Elizabeth Parish; hon/Avila Medal of Hon, 1978; Ariston Awd, Avila Col, 1978; Commun Ldrs of Am; W/W Among Am Univs and Cols; g/Med Sch.

KERN-FOXWORTH, MARILYN oc/University Professor; b/Mar 4, 1954; h/1014 Forest Heights Drive, Knoxville, TN 37919; ba/Knoxville, TN; m/Gregory Foxworth; p/Mrs Manella LouBertha Dickens Kern (dec); Jimmie Kern (dec); sp/Beulah Foxworth, Evergreen, NC; hon/Outstg Yg Wom of Am; g/Write 2 Bks: *An Historical Perspective of Blacks in Advertising, Ebonessence: The Expression of a Black Wom through Verse.*

KERNS, RHONDA LYNN oc/Student; b/May 8, 1959; h/3034 South Union Avenue, Chicago, IL 60616; p/James and Diane Kerns, Chicago, IL; ed/St Mary of Perpetual Help, 1976; BA 1980, MA 1982, DePaul Univ; cp/Mem, Edit Bd, *Essays and Ideas: A Journal of Critical Thought;* Nat Scholastic Hon Soc for Cath Cols and Univs; Polit Sci Dept Student Rep; hon/Highest Hon Grad; Grad w Distn; Schmitt F'ship in Phil; DePaul Competitive S'ship; g/Law Deg.

KERNS, TANA MACHELLE oc/Student; b/Jul 5, 1965; h/Route 1, Box 126, Salina, OK 74365; p/Kenneth and Joyce Kerns, Salina, OK; ed/HS Grad; Student, OK St Univ; pa/Waitress, Spanish Gardens 1983, Dairy Queen 1981; Secy, Salina Spavinaw Telephone Co, 1982, 1983; Maps and Spec Collections, Lib, OK St Univ, 1983-84; cp/Basketball, 4 Yrs, Capt for 1 Yr; Track, 4 Yrs, Capt for 2 Yrs; Softball, 1 Yr; Cheerldr, 4

Yrs, Capt for 1 Yr; FHA, Treas 1982, VP 1983; Yrbook Staff, 2 Yrs, Editor for 1 Yr; Outstg Acctg and Eng Student; FCA Mem; r/Freewill Bapt; hon/Hon Soc, St and Nat, 1980, 1981, 1982, 1983; Girl Citizen; Valedictorian, Sr Class; Homecoming Queen, HS; Homecoming Attendant, 1981-82; Student Coun Pres, 2 Yrs; Pres Ldrship Coun, OK St Univ; g/Acctg Maj, OK St Univ.

KERNSTINE, MITCHELL WRIGHT oc/Student; b/Aug 7, 1966; h/PO Box 755, Warsaw, NC 28398; p/Van and Ann Kernstine, Warsaw, NC; cp/BSA; Monogram Clb; Pep Clb; VP, Drama Clb, 1984; Tennis Team; Mgr, Varsity Football; hon/US Nat Bus Ed Awd; Voice of Dem Contest Sch Awd; Nat Hon Soc; US Nat Ldrship Merit Awd, 1984; US Nat Sci Merit Awd, 1984; Rotary Student of the Month, 1983; Hons Eng Awds; C P Hist Awd; Personalities of S; Soc of Dist'd Am HS Students; g/To Attend NC St Univ and Maj in Computer Sci.

KERR, JEAN oc/Pharmacist; b/Mar 22, 1959; h/2001 Aden Road, Apartment 121 Fort Worth, TX 76116; ba/Fort Worth, TX; p/Mr (dec) and Mrs Claude D Kerr, Hartsville, TN; ed/Trousdale Co High, 1977; Pre-Pharm, Univ of TN Knoxville, 1977-79; BS in Pharm, Univ of TN Ctr for the Hlth Scis; pa/Pharm Resident, Ft Worth Osteopathic Med Ctr, 1982-; Pharm Tech, VA Med Ctr, 1980-82; Staff Pharm, NW Hosp, 1983-; Rho Chi Nat Pharm Hon Soc; Lambda Kappa Sigma Pharm Frat; Phi Delta Chi Pharm Frat; Am Soc of Hosp Pharm; Gamma Beta Phi Hon Soc; Phi Iota Sigma Freshman Hon Soc; r/Ch of Christ; hon/Ethyl J Heath Key, 1982; Rho Chi Nat Pharm Hon Soc, 1981; W/W Among Students in Am Cols and Univs.

KERR, WILLIAM LAMAR oc/Student; b/Dec 21, 1965; h/PO Box 706, Mountain Home, AR 72653; p/Dr and Mrs Robert L Kerr, Mountain Home, AR; ed/HS Grad, 1984; cp/Marching and Concert Band; Basketball; Tennis; Math Team; Choir; Chamber Singers; VP, Med Explorers Post #1, 1982-83; r/Bapt; Choir; "Chara" (Auditional Singing Ensemble); hon/Att'd 4th Annual AR Gov's Sch for the Gifted and Talented, 1983; W/W Among Am HS Students; g/Attend Univ of AR Fayetteville and Study Pre-Med; MD.

KEYS, THOMAS CRAIG oc/Student; b/Aug 12, 1965; h/Route 5, Box 36, West Point, MS 39773; p/Mr and Mrs C T Keys Jr, West Point, MS; ed/W Pt HS; cp/Mu Alpha Theta (Math Clb), 1981-82; Nat Hon Soc, 1981-83; W Clb, 1980-83, Pres 1981-82; F'ship of Christian Aths, 1980-83; Scouts, 5 Yrs; UMYF; Tennis Team, Grade 8; Baseball, 9-10; Basketball, 8-11; Football, 9-12; r/Meth; hon/MVP, One-on-One Champ, MSU Basketball Jr High Camp; Hon Roll; Algebra I Awd; Undefeated Jr High Football Team; AA MS Football Championship; All-Little Ten, All-Dist, All-Star Game (Football); Grant-in-Aid to MSU in Football; US Achmt Acad; g/Agri Ec.

KEZON, MARTINA MARIE oc/Assistant Dean of Students; b/Apr 14, 1958; h/Hanover College, Hanover, IN 47243; ba/Same; p/Ann Marie Kezon, Oak Lawn, IL; ed/Maria HS, 1976; BA, Carroll Col, 1980; MA, Bowling Green

St Univ, 1982; pa/Frat/Sorority Advr, Univ of Toledo, 1980-82; Asst Dean of Students, Hanover Col, 1982-; Nat Assn of Wom Deans, Admrs and Cnslrs; APGA; ACPA; cp/Vol, Red Cross; Girl Scout Ldr, Cadette Troop; hon/Hon Mem, Kappa Delta Sorority, 1983; Mortarboard, 1982; Phi Alpha Theta Hon, 1978; Mayor Daley Yth Awd, 1976; W/W Among Students in Am Univs and Cols; Outstg Yg Wom of Am; g/PhD; To Become Dean of Students/VP at a Liberal Arts Col.

KHAN, SELINA oc/Student; b/Aug 1, 1963; h/Calle Uroyan AD4, Mayaguez, Puerto Rico 00709; ba/Same; p/Dr and Mrs Winston Khan, Mayaguez, Puerto Rico; ed/Acad of the Immaculate Conception; HS Dipl, 1981; Univ Student; cp/Commun Wkr; 4-H Clb; Math Clb; r/Cath; hon/Rel, 1978; Lib and Conduct, 1979; Math, Sci, 1980; Spanish, 1983; W/W; Commun Ldrs of Am; g/Engrg and Computer Sci.

KHAN, SHEREEZA oc/Student; b/May 31, 1965; h/Calle Uroyan AD-4, Alturas de Mayaguez, Puerto Rico; p/Dr and Mrs Winston Khan, Mayaguez, Puerto Rico; ed/Acad of the Immaculate Conception HS; Univ Student; cp/4-H Clb; Chess Clb; Math Clb; Sci Clb; Eng Spch Clb; r/Christian; hon/Math; Sci; Entered Univ in 3rd Yr of HS.

KHAN, WINSTON JR oc/Student; b/Oct 15, 1967; h/Calle Uroyan AD 4, Mayaguez, Puerto Rico 00074; p/Dr Winston and Joan Khan, Mayaguez, Puerto Rico; ed/Acad of the Immaculate Conception and Commun Sch; Dipl, Grammar Sch, AIC; HS Student; cp/Chess Clb, 1982-; Math Clb, 1982-; r/Cath; hon/Excell in Math, Sci Technol; g/Computer Engr.

KHATENA, MOSHE oc/Student; b/Sep 4, 1961; h/8 Tally Ho Drive, Starkville, MS 39759; p/Dr Joe and Nelly Khatena, Starkville, MS; ed/Currently Enrolled, MS St Univ; Att'd, Univ of MD Col Pk; cp/AIIE, 1981-; US Chess Fdn, 1976-; VICA, 1978-79; MS Karate Assn, 1981-; Alpha Pi Mu, Indust Engrg Hon Soc, 1983-; US Tennis (Table) Assn, 1979-; r/Judaism; hon/VICA St Champs, 1979, Clb Bus Procedure; Cross Country, Lettered 1977; WV All-Star Champs (Baseball) 1975, Leag Champs 1974-77; Karate, 2nd Yellow Belt Lt Wt 1982; Chess, US Jr Open Co-Champ 1981, Nat Master 1980; MS Speed Chess Champ, 1977-80; W/W; g/Wkg in the Mgmt Area as an Indust Engr; Wkg towards a Grandmaster Title in Chess and Blackbelt in Karate.

KHAWAJA, AZMATUL oc/Student; b/Sep 3, 1959; h/669 West Delavan, Buffalo, NY 14222; p/Ismat and Anwar Khawaja, Buffalo, NY; ed/Riverside HS, 1977; BA, D'Youville Col, 1981; Att'g, St Univ of NY Buffalo; pa/Budget Clk, Erie Co Hlth Dept, 1981-82; Res Student, Roswell Pk Meml Inst, 1975, 1980; Receptionist, D'Youville Col, 1979-80; cp/Med Clb, 1977-79; Hockey Team, 1980, Co-Capt, Volleyball Team, 1979-80; hon/D'Youville S'ship, 4 Yrs; Dean's List; Volleyball Championship, 1980; Nat Dean's List; Intl Yth in Achmt Awd, 1980; Yg Commun Ldrship Awd, 1981; Intl Yth in Achmt; g/MBA from SUNY Buffalo.

KHORSHAHIAN, ANNE MILLER oc/Student; b/Sep 24, 1960; h/1905 Robbins Place, Austin, TX 78705; m/

698

Farhad; p/Keith William Miller (dec); Frances Jensen; ed/Grad, summa cum laude, Margaret Hall Sch, 1978; 1st Deg, Université de Dijon, France, 1981; Presently Att'g, Univ of TX Austin; cp/Thespian, 1975; VP, Art Clb, 1979; Art Editor, *Pulse*, 1979; r/Epis; g/Dr of Gen Surg.

KIDD, ANN MARIE oc/Student; b/Jul 5, 1964; h/Route 2, Box 209, Enterprise, MS 39330; p/Paul Kidd, Enterprise, MS; ed/Dipl, Enterprise HS, 1982; Deg in Liberal Arts, Jones Jr Col, 1984; pa/Unit Secy, Riley's Meml Hosp, 1983; cp/Cheerldr, 1980-82; Beta Clb, 1977-82; Basketball Team, 1977-82; Touch of Gold, 1982-84; Maroon Kyphoon, Col Lair, 1982-83; r/Bapt; hon/HS Hon Roll; Fac List, 1982-83; Pres's List, 1983-84; S'ship to Jones Jr Col, 1982; g/BS in Nsg.

KIDD, LYNDEN LOUISE oc/Law Student; b/May 7, 1959; h/459 North 9th Street, Laramie, WY 82070; p/Mr and Mrs D Thomas Kidd, Casper, WY; ed/Natrona Co HS, 1977; AA, Stephens Col, 1979; BA, Univ of WY, 1981; pa/Intern, Congressman Dick Cheney, 1980; Grad Asst, Instr, Dept of Communs, Univ of WY, 1982-83; Resident Student Advr, Desk Hostess, Stephens Col, 1978-79; cp/Kappa Kappa Gamma Philanthropy Chm, VP of Search and Interviewing Sel Com; Pres, Search and Screening Com; ASUW Senator; ASUW Jud Coun; Student Atty Bd Chm; Student Bd of Appeals; Sigma Chi Little Sister; Appropriations Com; Student Info Ser Com; hon/Mortar Bd Treas; Omicron Delta Kappa; W/W Among Students in Am Univs and Cols; Nat Register of Outstg Col Grads; Intl W/W in Achmt; Commun Ldrs of Am; g/MA in Communication; Completion of Law Study.

KILLIAN, CHARISSE DIANNE oc/Student; b/Apr 15, 1966; h/PO Box 847, Athens, GA 30603; p/Alfred and Marlene Killian, Athens, GA; ed/HS Student; cp/Yrbook Staff; Student Coun; Marching Band Drill Team; Beta Clb; Ch Choir; Ch Usherboard; Ch Yth Dept; r/Bapt; hon/Miss Athens Jr Talented Teen, 1980; Miss GA Talented Teen, 1980; Sci Awd, 1981-82; Social Studies Awd, 1981-82; Hon Roll, 1981-82; Homecoming Ct, 1980, 1981, 1982; 2nd Place Essay Contest; Miss Debutante for Christ, 1981.

KIMPSON, MILTON G oc/Student; b/Jan 11, 1961; h/2233 Manse Street, Columbia, SC 29203; ba/Decatur, GA; p/Mr and Mrs Milton Kimpson, Columbia, SC; ed/Columbia HS, 1979; BS in Ec, Wofford Col, 1983; Student, Emory Univ Sch of Law, 1983-; cp/Omega Psi Phi, 1976-; Wofford Col Student Govt, 1982-83; Wofford Col Nat Alumni Assn, 1983-; Black Law Students Assn; r/Bapt; hon/Phi Beta Kappa, 1983; summa cum laude, 1983; Omega Psi Phi Scholar of the Yr, 1983; Charles F March Awd in Ec; W/W Among Students in Am Cols and Univs; W/W HS; g/Law; AUS.

KINBACK, KEVIN MICHAEL oc/Student; b/Aug 13, 1962; h/King College, Bristol, TN 37620; p/G M and J A Kinback, NJ; ed/Lenape Val Reg HS, 1980; Co Col of Morris, 1978-82; Mt Empire Commun Col, 1981; BS, Biol and Chem, King Col, 1984; cp/King Col Choir, 1980-84; Secy; Lakeland Emer

Squad, 1980-84, Chm of Blanket Toss Com; Eagle Scout, BSA; ARC, ANA CPR Instr; WSI; Soccer, 1982; Sci Clb; Psych Clb; r/Orthodox Presb; Ch of Covenant; hon/Highest Achmt Awd in Physics, King Col, 1983; EMT Cert'd, 1980; US Col Wind Bands, 1980; Ser to Sch and Commun Awd, 1980; Am Legion NJ Boys' St, 1979; CC Music S'ship, 1982; Manford Guteke S'ship, 1982; Dean's List, KC, 1983; Treas, KC SCA, 1984-85; Rep, SC SCA, 1982-83; W/W Among Am HS Students; g/MD.

KINCAID, KARLENE DENISE oc/Student; b/Apr 30, 1961; h/RR #3, Box 276, Richmond, KY 40475; ba/Berea, KY; p/Mr and Mrs F H Kincaid, Richmond, KY; ed/Madison Ctl HS, 1979; BA in Directing and Set Design, Berea Col, 1984; pa/Asst Sound Tech 1980, House Mgr 1980, Make-Up and Properties 1981, Make-Up 1982-83, Dir and Set Designer 1981, Grip 1982, Set Designer (3 Plays) 1982, Fog Machine Operator 1982, Stage Mgr 1983, Berea Col's Dramatics Dept; cp/HS Drama Clb, 1977; Berea Players, 1980, 1981, 1982, 1983; Alpha Psi Omega, 1983; The Living Bk, 1982; r/Bapt; hon/Dist'd Achmt Awd, 1979; Berea Players Ser Awd, 1980; Labor Day Dramatics Deptl Awd, 1983; W/W Among Am HS Students; g/BA in Directing and Set Design; Return to Sch.

KINCER, THOMAS GLENN II oc/Student; b/Aug 28, 1962; h/Box 89, Cromona, KY 41810; p/Thomas Glenn Sr and Vonda A Kincer, Cromona, KY; ed/Fleming-Neon High, 1980; Berea Col (Class of 1984); pa/Sum Employmt, SE Coal Co 1981, Daniel Boone Med Clin 1983; cp/Sin The' Karate Clb; Beta Beta Beta Biol Soc; Phi Kappa Phi; Sipple's Gym; r/Bapt; hon/Tri Beta; Phi Kappa Phi; Outstg Wkr in CETA; Lillian Webb S'ship; Outstg Wkr in Berea Col Labor Prog; 8 Col Semesters on the Dean's List.

KING, ALISON SUZANNE oc/Student; b/Feb 7, 1965; h/47 Rutland Street, Boston, MA 02118; p/James and Rayeanne King, Boston, MA; ed/Grad w Distn in Drama and Music, Beaver Country Day Sch, 1983; Student, Skidmore Col; cp/Num Ribbon Winner, Agri Fair, 1976-80; Housemgr of Beaver Country Day Drama Clb, 1981-83; Prog Cover Designer for Drama Clb, 1979-83; g/Film; Theatre; Psych.

KING, BEATINA GAY oc/Student; b/Oct 3, 1965; h/315 Hillcrest Street, Dresden, TN 38225; ba/Martin, TN; p/Mr and Mrs Herbert P King, Dresden, TN; ed/Grad, Dresden HS, 1983; Student, Univ of TN Martin, 1983-; pa/Operator of IBM Computer, Dresden Discount Drugs, 1982-; cp/Pre-Pharm Clb, Univ of TN Martin, 1983; Nat Beta Clb, Dresden Chapt, 1981-83, Pres 1983; Futurian Clb, 1981-83, Reporter 1982; Meth Yth F'ship, 1978-83, Secy 1981, VP 1982-83; Editor of HS Yrbook, 1983; Correspondent for *Dresden Enterprise*, 1982, 1983; r/Meth; hon/Valedictorian, 1983; Student of Distn, 1981, 1982, 1983; Univ of TN Math Contestant, 1980, 1982.

KING, CRAIG HUNTER oc/Collector in Business Office; b/Aug 24, 1961; h/2827 Soniat Street, New Orleans, LA 70115; ba/New Orleans, LA; p/Mr and Mrs Willie King, New Orleans, LA; ed/Grad, So Univ, 1985 (Maj in Bus Adm

and Computer Sci); pa/Collector, Eye, Ear, Nose and Throat Hosp, 1984-; Acct Exec, Westside Shuttle Co, 1983-84; Adm Asst, Endosa World Trade Intl, 1982-83; Mgr-in-Tng, The Foot Locker, 1981-82; cp/Pres, Treas, Dean of Pledges, Alpha Phi Alpha Frat Inc; VP, Student Govt Assn, So Univ; Computer Sci Clb, NAACP; Pre-Alumni Ambassador Clb; Phi Beta Lambda Bus Clb; NO Bus Leag; Afro-Am Culture Com; r/Bapt; Pres, Yg Deacon Bd, Fairview Bapt Ch; hon/Hon Roll, So Univ; Dist'd Student Awd, SGA; NO Sickle Cell Anemia Foun Inc Cert of Apprec; Outstg Yg Men of Am.

KING, DORLISA DAWN oc/Student; b/Mar 26, 1965; h/515 Greenhill Drive, Siler City, NC 27344; p/Dr and Mrs Charles C King, Siler City, NC; ed/HS Dipl, 1983; cp/Beta Clb, Secy 1981-82; French Clb, Treas 1982-83; Bible Clb, VP 1982-83; J M Concert Choir, Accompanist 1981-83; Mensa; r/Prot; hon/NEDT Certs, 1979, 1980; PSAT/NMSQT Commended Scholar; Marshall at Grad, 1981; Chief Marshall, 1982; Nat Merit Awds, Eng and Chem; NC Gov's Sch, 1982; Duke S'ships, Alumni and NC Hon; Soc of Dist'd Am HS Students; W/W; g/4 Yrs of Undergrad Study at Duke Univ.

KING, FLORENCE ELIZABETH oc/Student; b/Sep 23, 1960; h/Route 2, Box 24, Fairhope, AL 36532; p/Mrs H M King Jr, Fairhope, AL; ed/Fairhope HS, 1978; BA, Mus, Univ of Montevallo, 1982; Wkg towards MLS, FL St Univ; pa/Entertainer/Waiter, Musicana Enterprises, 1982; Cataloger, Univ of S AL Biomed Lib, 1980; Other Previous Positions; cp/Phi Alpha Mu, 1980; Phi Alpha Theta, 1980; Sigma Tau Delta, 1980, VP 1981; Omicron Delta Kappa, 1980; Concert Choir, 1978-82; Chamber Choir, 1979-82; hon/Dean's List, Univ of Montevallo, 1978, 1981; Nat Hon Soc, HS, 1976-78, Secy 1977-78; Outstg Vocalist, HS, 1978; W/W Am Cols and Univs; g/Career in Lib Sci.

KING, INDLE GIFFORD JR oc/Accountant; b/Jul 17, 1961; h/Victoria Park Apartments, #2303, 8600 South Course Drive, Houston, TX 77099; ba/Houston, TX; ed/Mercer Isl HS, 1979; BBA, Univ of WA, 1983; pa/Sum Internship, Arco Oil Co, 1982; Sum Internship, John Fluke Electronics Mfg Co, 1981; Pk Mgr 1980, Pk Maintenance 1979, Redman Pk and Rec Dept; Acct, Shell Oil, Pipeline Div; Elected to Phi Beta Kappa, 1983; Mercer Isl HS Student Coun Rep, 3 Yrs; Ofcr, Pi Kappa Psi, 1979-82; Bd Mem, Mercer Isl Yth Sers, 1976-79; Letter and Mem, St Champ Tennis Teams, Mercer Isl HS, 1976-78; Mem, N Mercer Jr HS Soccer Team, 1973-75; Sch Band, 1973-79; r/Prot; hon/Eagle BSA Awd, 1976; 1st Place Awd, Craft Belleaue Arts and Crafts Fair, 1975; Jr Life Saver, 1976; Alpha Kappa Psi; g/To Compliment Bus Background w MBA and Law Deg.

KING, JULIE ANNE oc/Student; b/Oct 1, 1965; h/1969 Troy Road, Dyersburg, TN 38024; p/Dr and Mrs Elton King, Dyers, TN; ed/Grad, Dyersburg HS, 1981; Presently Enrolled in Bus Ed, Univ of TN Martin; cp/HS: F'ship of Christian Aths, Spanish Clb (Treas), Math Clb (Treas), Pep Clb, Student Coun, Alpha Delta Kappa Sorority

(Sophomore Rep), Philanthropic Chm (Pres, Nat VP), Sophomore Class Rep; Col: Student Tchr Ed Assn, Alpha Omicron Pi Sorority (Asst Corresponding Secy, VP, Pres); r/Bapt; hon/Best Big Sister of Alpha Omicron Pi, 1982; g/ Tchr of Acctg, Ec.

KING, KENNITH WAYNE oc/Student; b/Apr 1, 1964; h/General Delivery, Rowe, VA 24646; p/Elbert C and Lucille S King, Rowe, VA; ed/Garden HS; cp/ Football, 1978-80; hon/Hon Roll, 1979-82; Mr Hustle, 1979; 2nd Place, Essay Contest; Hi-Y Clb; Basketball; Track; Hunting and Safety Clb; VICA; W/W; g/Mining Tech.

KING, PAIGE PHYLLIS oc/University Student; b/Dec 29; h/5075 West Mercer Way, Mercer Island, WA 98444; p/Mr and Mrs Indle King, Mercer Island, WA; ed/Mercer Isl HS, 1981; Student of Ballet, Cornish Sch of Fine Arts, 7 Yrs; pa/Internship, John Fluke Electronics Mfg Co, Indust Design Dept, 1983; cp/Alpha Gamma Delta, 1981-83; Mercer Isl Yth Sers Student Bd Mem, 1978-81; HS: Student Coun, Cheerldr, Drill Team, Flutist; r/Presb; hon/Outstg Art Student in St of WA, 1980-81; Mercer Isl Visual Arts Leag S'ship and Most Promising Art Student, 1981; g/ Art Maj at Univ of WA; Indust Designer.

KINGREN, JOHN FRED oc/Accountant; b/Jan 15, 1960; h/1156 Burdette Street, Roanoke, AL 36274; p/Mr and Mrs Carl Kingren; ed/Handley HS; BS, Samford Univ; pa/Acct, Price Waterhouse, 1982-; cp/Jr Achmt, Advr; Alpha Kappa Psi, Pres; Assn of Bus Majs, VP; Hon Coun, Student Rep; Samford Acctg Assn Fdg VChm; Student Assn, Secy/ Senate; Editorials Page Editor, Columnist, *The Samford Crimson*; hon/Phi Kappa Phi; Omicron Delta Kappa; Assn of Bus Majs Dist'd Ser Awd; Alpha Kappa Psi S'ship Awd; AL Soc of CPAs Acctg Achmt Awd; Nat Acctg Assn Hon Student Mbrship; Highest Class Hons, 1978-82; Velma Wright Irons Awd; Outstg Yg Men of Am; W/W Among Students in Am Cols and Univs; Commun Ldrs of Am; Intl Yth in Achmt.

KINNEY, MARTHA ELIZABETH oc/ Student; b/Aug 25, 1963; h/2270 Toxaway Drive, Sumter, SC 29150; p/Ch Maj and Mrs James W Kinney, Sumter, SC; ed/Woomera HS, S Australia, 1980; BA w Hons, Polit and Rel, Converse Col, 1984; mil/Army ROTC, 1982-84; cp/ Student Govt Assn, 1983-84; Mortar Bd, 1983-84; *Conversationalist*, Bus Mgr 1980-82; Pi Gamma Mu, 1982-84; SC St Student Legis, Senator 1981-84; r/ Rom Cath; hon/Presentation to SC Acad of Rel, 1984; Trustee Merit Scholar, 1980-84; Best Grad'g Sr in Polit, 1984; MVP in Softball, 1980; MVP in Soccer, 1980; Patrons Awd for Soccer, 1980; Nat Dean's List, 1981; W/ W Among Students in Cols and Univs; g/2nd Lt in AUS; Prof of Polit Phil at a Maj Univ.

KINSFATHER, REUBEN DANIEL oc/Savings Department Manager; b/Oct 9, 1947; h/205 Glen Brook Drive, New Braunfels, TX 78130; ba/Seguin, TX; m/ Jean D; c/Sara Anne, Michael Vaughn; p/Reuben and Martha Kinsfather, Bastrop, TX; ed/Grad, New Braunfels Sr HS, 1965; Bach of Applied Arts and Scis, SW TX St Univ, 1983; pa/Acctg Sers Supvr 1969-78, Div Pers Mgr

1978-83, Symons Corp; Savs Dept Mgr, Seguin Savs Assn, 1983-; Inst of Financial Ed, Chapt #25, Bd of Dirs 1984; cp/ New Braunfels Conserv Soc, Dir 1975-78, Treas 1977-78, Mem 1966-83; New Braunfels Wurst Assn, 1975, 1976; r/Epis.

KIRCHER, CARL CONVERSE oc/ Chemist; b/Jan 9, 1956; h/500 South Madison, #7, Pasadena, CA 91101; ba/ Pasadena, CA; p/Mr and Mrs Carl Kircher, Yuma, AZ; ed/Kofa HS, 1974; BS, Univ of AZ, 1978; PhD, MI St Univ, 1982; pa/Chemist; cp/Acad Coun; Student Coun; Grad Coun; Band; Alpha Phi Omega, Pres, Secy, Treas; Kappa Kappa Psi, Secy; Sophos; Chain Gang; Blue Key; MENSA; BSA; r/Lay Rdr, Epis Ch; hon/Eagle Scout; NSF Grad F'ship; W/ W Among Students in Am Univs and Cols; g/Anal Chem Career.

KIRKLAND, HOWARD F oc/Student; b/Sep 5, 1966; h/Route 2, Box 291, Zion Ridge Road, Loudon, TN 37774; p/Mr and Mrs Referd E Kirkland, Loudon, TN; ed/Grad, Loudon HS, 1984; pa/Clk, Simpson Grocery, 1980-81; Pharm Tech, Myers-Evans Drug Co, 1981-84; Dry End Operator, Union Carbide Corp, 1984; Reporter, WLNT Radio, 1983-84; Cameraman and Electronic Graphics Operator, WBIG-TV9, 1983-84; cp/HS Class Pres, 4 Yrs; Nat Hon Soc, Pres 1984; Student Coun, Pres 1984; F'ship fo Christian Aths; Jr Classical Leag, Treas 1982; Student Cafeteria, Adv Com, Ring Selection Com; TN Tomorrow Clb; Scanner Assn of N Am, 1984-85; Yrbook and Newspaper Staffs; r/So Bapt; hon/Class Valedictorian, 1984; TN Am Legion Boys' St, 1983; Wash Wkshops Congl Sem, 1983; NSEC Acad All-Am, 1984; Univ of TN Neyland Scholar, 1984-88; DAR Good Citizen Awd; Intl Assn of Machinists S'ship, 1984-88; W/W Among Am HS Students; US Achmt Acad; g/Study Pre-Med at Univ of TN Knoxville; Med Sch.

KIRKMAN, ALLEN JR oc/Instructor of Missile Combat, Crew Commander; b/Dec 17, 1957; h/12 Anamosa Street, Rapid City, SD 57701; ba/Ellsworth AFB, SD; m/Cynthia Gail; p/Mr and Mrs Allen Kirkman Sr, Norfolk, VA; ed/ Norview Sr HS, 1976; BS, NC Ctl Univ, 1980; MPA, Univ of SD, 1984; Squadron Ofcrs Sch, 1983; mil/Lt, USAF; pa/Dpty Missile Combat Crew Cmdr; Sr Dpty Missile Combat Crew Cmdr, Sp Command Post; Missile Combat Crew Cmdr; Instr Missile Combat Crew Cmdr; Instr Missile Combat Crew Cmdr, Asst Sect Chief; Life Mem, AF Assn; Jr Ofcrs Coun Mem; Resv Ofcrs Tng Corps Cmdr; cp/Alpha Phi Alpha Frat; Beta Kappa Chi, Nat Hon Soc; ARC CPR Instr; r/Bapt; hon/Dist'd Grad, Resv Ofcrs Tng Corps; AF Achmt Awd; Marksmanship Awd; Combat Crew Readiness Medal; Grad, cum laude; g/AF Logistics Plans and Prog Ofcr; PhD in Mgmt Res Field.

KISER, MICHAEL ROBERT oc/Electronics; b/May 1, 1963; h/3103 Warbler Street, Montgomery, AL 36108; ba/ United States Air Force; m/Suzan Danielle Benton; p/Walter and Christine Kiser, Montgomery, AL; ed/Jefferson Davis HS, 1981; Student, Auburn Univ; mil/Electronics, USAF; cp/Sr Patrol Ldr, BSA; Band Pres; Nat Hon

Soc; Mu Alpha Theta; French Hon Soc; Engrg Dorm Intramural Teams, Volleyball, Football, Basketball, Softball, Auburn Univ; hon/Naval ROTC S'ship; Elbridge A Stuart S'ship; W/W Among Am HS Students; g/Nuclear Ofcr in Navy.

KITCHEL, KIMBERLY E oc/Student; b/Sep 21, 1961; h/Box 1943, Fairview Heights, IL; p/Donald Kitchel, Fairview Heights, IL; Shirley Kitchel, Fairview Heights, IL; ed/Belleville Twp HS E, 1979; IN St Univ; cp/Delta Sigma Pi; En Star; Acctg Clb; Big Brother/Big Sister; Alpha Phi; German Clb; Blue Beret; hon/Phi Sigma Iota; Alpha Lambda Delta; German Consulate Awd; g/CPA.

KITCHEN, EDWARD MAURICE oc/ Student, Teacher; b/Jan 3, 1959; h/1003 Lotus Drive, Natchez, MS 39120; p/Lt Eddie Kitchen Jr (dec); Evelyn R West; ed/S Natchez Adams High; BS, Chem, cum laude, Tougaloo Col, 1979; pa/ Tchr, Sec'dy Sch, Nigeria, 1982-83; Res Asst, Electrochem, Monsanto Chem, 1978; Asst Hydrologist, US Geol Survey, 1979; Asst Computer Programmer, Yale Univ, 1977; cp/Phi Beta Sigma Frat Inc, Hd of Social Action; r/Love; g/Be a Witness of the Word of God; Med.

KLEIN, BETHANY LYNN-MARIE oc/Student; b/Jul 21, 1964; h/1842 Monticello Drive, Granbury, TX 76048; p/Philip and Barbara Klein, Granbury, TX; ed/Granbury HS, 1982; Fine Arts Maj, SWn Univ; cp/Nat Hon Soc, 1980, 1981, 1982, Pres 1982; Basketball; Track; Student Coun, Treas 1982; FCA, 1980, 1981, 1982; FTA, 1981, 1982; r/ Rom Cath; hon/Yg Rotarian, 1982; Most Valuable Player, Basketball, 1982; All-Dist Basketball, 1982; Hon Mention, TX HS Art Comp, 1982; 2nd Best of Show, PPCC Art Show, 1983; Best All-Around Student, 1981-82; W/W HS Students; W/W Hist; Yg Artists.

KLEIN, CARA LYN oc/Student; b/Jul 16, 1964; h/Box AG, Spirit Lake, IA 51360; p/Dr and Mrs Alfred L Klein, Spirit Lake, IA; ed/Spirit Lake HS, 1982; Att'g, IA St Univ; cp/Okoboji Music Factory Swing Choir, 1978-82; HS Band and Chorus, 1978-82; HS Cheerldr, 1978-82; Drama Clb, 1978-82; Booster Clb, 1978-82; Letterwinner's Clb, 1978-82; r/Epis; hon/Miss Teenworld, 1982; Gamma Phi Beta; Hon Roll Student; Miss IA Teenworld, 1981; Miss IA U Teenager, 1980; Golden Eagle Awd, Am Acad of Achmt for Promise of Greatness; Yg Commun Ldrs of Am; g/To Grad from IA St Univ w a Deg in Bus and Public Relats.

KLEINE, MARY CHRISTINE oc/ Student, Farmer; b/Nov 23, 1962; h/ Route 3, Box 81A, Troy, MO 63379; p/Casper and Barbara Kleine, Troy, MO; ed/Buchanan HS, 1981; BS in Agronomy, Univ of MO Columbia Sch of Agri, 1985; pa/Farm Labor and Home Improvement, Parents' Farm, 1977-82; Vet Apprentice, Wright City Vet Clin, 1979-80; Warren Co Farmers Mkt (Self-Employed), 1980-82; Sales, Supplies, Inventory, Wilcoxen Ofc Supply, Sum 1982; cp/MO Mule Skinners Soc, Charter Mem 1982; Warren Co Farmers Mkt Assn, 1981, 1982, 1983, Treas 1981-82; FFA, 1977-81; Spch/Drama Clb, 1978-80; Spanish Clb, 1978-79; UMC Pre-Vet Clb, 1981-82; Agronomy Clb, 1982; Assoc'd Humane Socs, 1978-84; Mule Hist Proj, 1982; Am Soc of Agronomy, 1982, 1983, 1984; r/Cath; hon/FFA Area Foun Awd, 1st Place, 1980; Gold Medal, FFA Dairy Prods Judging Team St, 1979; MO Assn of Fairs Spch Contest St Finalist, 1979; VFW Voice of Dem Spch Area Winner, 1979; Nat Humane Awd for Spch Assoc'd Humane Socs, 1979; Spanish Poetry Declamations, 2nd Place St, 1979; Outstg Spanish Student, 1979; Top Sch Letter, Spch/Drama Clb, 1979; FFA Blue Ribbon (Yth Fair), Silver Ribbon (St Fair), Car Ramps, 1980; Hon Roll, 1977-81; Perfect Attendance, 1980; Complimentary Letter, Gene Roddenberry, Star Trek, 1979; Spch Printed, Humane News, Assoc'd Humane Socs, 1979; Spch and News Items, Toy Free Press, 1977-81; 1st Place Spch in Spanish Tri-St, 1979; Patent on Novelty Motor Vehicle, "Buggy Hop," Assoc Inventor, 1981; S'ship for Res on Warm and Cool Season Grasses, Blue Stem Seed Co, 1984; W/W Fgn Langs in MWn HS; Commun Ldrs of Am; Dir of Dist'd Ams; Biogl Roll of Hon; Intl Yth in Achmt; W/W Among Students in Am Univs and Cols; W/W Among Am HS Students; g/DVM; Agronomy Spec.

KLEINPETER, MYRA ANNETTE oc/ Student; b/Jun 10, 1962; h/739 Staring Lane, Baton Rouge, LA 70808; ba/Same; p/Dr Milton H Kleinpeter, Baton Rouge, LA; Dr Eva B Kleinpeter, Baton Rouge, LA; ed/Grad, So Univ Lab Sch, 1980; BS, So Univ, 1984; pa/Res in Biomed Scis Prog, Meharry Med Col, 1981; Sum Acad Advmt Prog, Univ of NC Chapel Hill, 1982; MBS Prog, So Univ, 1982; cp/Beta Beta Beta, 1982-84, Pres; Biol Clb, 1980-84, Pres; Assn for Wom in Sci, 1982-84; Delta Sigma Theta Sorority, VP 1982-84; Port City Assn; Jack and Jill of Am Inc; All Am Yth Hon Musicians; So Univ Hons Prog, 1980-84; Sr Rep; Yg Am Bowling Alliance; Assn for Wom Students; Pre-Med and Pre-Dent Clb; hon/Phi Sigma, 1982-84; Beta Beta Beta, 1982-84; Alpha Kappa Mu, 1983-84; Alpha Chi, 1983-84; Pi Mu Epsilon, 1983-84; S'ship, E Baton Rouge Parish Assn Aux; Chancellor's Scholar; So Univ Dean's List; Nat Dean's List; Intl Yth in Achmt; W/W; Commun Ldrs of Am; g/To Attend Med Sch and Pursue a Career in Med.

KLINE, SCOTT MARSHELL oc/ Student; b/May 14, 1963; h/2530 Old Orchard Lane, San Antonio, TX 78230; ba/New Haven, CT; p/Mr and Mrs Fredric Kline, San Antonio, TX; ed/ Dist'd Hon Grad, Winston Churchill HS, 1981; BA in Polit Sci, Yale Univ, 1985; cp/Yale Ski Team; Yale Debate Assn; Bus and Ec Forum; Yale Record; Berkeley Col Coun; Optimist Clb; Nat Hon Soc; Yg Lwyrs Assn; r/Jewish; hon/ Nat Merit Finalist, 1981; TX St Champion, Extemp Spkg, Readywriting, 1981; Yth in Commun Ser, 1981; 70+ Spch and Debate Awds, 1978-83; W/W Among Am HS Students; Outstg Am Names and Faces; g/To Attend Law Sch and Pursue a Career as an Atty Concentrating in Corporate Litigation.

KLINE, STACEY BETH oc/Student; b/Jan 20, 1968; h/2530 Old Orchard Lane, San Antonio, TX 78230; p/Mr and Mrs Fred Kline, San Antonio, TX; ed/ Student, Winston Churchill HS; cp/ Class Ofcr; B'nai B'rith Yth Org; Underclassmen's Hon Soc; Nat Forensic Assn; DECA; r/Jewish; hon/2nd Place,

St Optimist Intl Oratory Contest, 1983; Pres of Student Body, Jackson Mid Sch, 1981-82; Prin Awd, 1980, 1981, 1982; Supt's Awd, 1982; Var Spch Hons/ Awds, Freshman and Sophomore Yrs of HS; VP, Freshman Class; Pres, Sophomore Class; HS Recognized as Outstg by Pres Reagan as Far as Excell in Ed, 1983.

KLINE, TERI A oc/Executive Director; b/May 12, 1959; h/700 Felder Avenue, Montgomery, AL 36106; ba/ Montgomery, AL; p/Dr John A Kline, Montgomery, AL; Robert Mauksch, Columbia, MO; ed/Jefferson Davis HS, 1977; BA, Auburn Univ, 1980; pa/Exec Dir 1981-, Exec Asst 1981, AL St Chiro Assn; Public Relats Coun of AL, 1981-, Bd of Dirs, Montgomery Chapt 1983; So Public Relats Fdn, 1981-; AL Coun of Assn Execs, 1981-; Am Soc of Assn Execs, 1981-; Assn of Chiro Execs, 1981-; Chiro Editors' Guild, 1981-; Intl Assn of Bus Communicators, 1983; Meeting Planners Intl, 1981-82; cp/ Montgomery Area U Way, Bd of Dirs 1983, Public Relats Chm 1983; Kappa Alpha Theta Alumni Clb, 1981-; Philanthropic Ednl Org, 1979-; r/First Bapt Ch, 1981-, Single Adult Coun Chm 1983, Public Relats Com 1983, Vocal Ensemble 1983; hon/Soroptimist Yth Citizen Awd; Dean's List; Outstg Actress Awd; Commun Ldrs of Am; g/ To Continue Wk in the Area of Assn Mgmt w Possibility of Pursuing MBA Deg.

KLINK, MAXINE ANN oc/Student; b/Apr 5, 1963; h/Route 1, Salisbury, PA 15558; p/Mrs Gretchen Minick, West Salisbury, PA; ed/Grad, Salisbury-Elk Lick HS, 1981; Att'g, Frostburg St Col, 1981-; cp/Camp Colstin, Camp Harmony, 1982; Model, Lennox E 1982-, Naturalizer Shoes 1982, Country Clb Mall 1982-, Mary Carol Shop 1982; cp/FSC Hon Prog; Dance Co; Ski Clb; Class Pres; Sch Newspaper Editor; Varsity Cheerldg Capt; Quill and Scroll; Student Coun; Prom Chm; Jr and Sr Class Plays; Band; Chorus Coun Chm; Yrbook Copy Editor; Lib Staff; Dixettes; Bible Sch Tchr; Camp Cnslr; Dist Yth Choir; All-Co Band; GSA; Columnist in Commun Newspaper; Hons Student Assn, 1982-, Pres 1983-84; Kittenettes Drill Team, 1982-83; Wn MD Dance Co; MD Coun for Dance; NCTE; MD Student Ed Assn; FSC Student Ed Assn; Phi Eta Sigma Hon Soc; r/Ch of the Brethren; Sunday Sch Tchr; hon/Maple Princess 1st Runner-Up; Delta Kappa Gamma S'ship; Salutatorian; Hist Awd; Citizenship Awds, DAR, Soroptimist, Keystone Girls' St; Miss Frostburg St Col, 1983; Miss Allegany Co, MD Pageant Finalist, 1983; Recip, Elisabeth Hitchins Meml S'ship and Phi Delta Kappa S'ship, 1983; Scholastic Journalist Awd, 1981; I Dare You Awd, 1980; Cert of Merit for Perf on Century II Ldrs S'ship Test, 1981; W/W Among Am HS Students; Commun Ldrs of Am; Intl Yth in Achmt; g/Maj in Elem Ed; Minor in Dance; BS; EdM; Tchr of Elem Students.

KLOESEL, DAVID WAYNE oc/Student; b/Feb 10, 1960; h/4500 Robin Lane, Midland, TX 79707; p/Mr and Mrs Joe A Kloesel, Midland, TX; ed/Grad, Robert E Lee HS, 1978; BA, Advtg/ Public Relats, TX Tech Univ, 1983; pa/ Campus Rep for TX Tech Univ, Muse

Air, 1983; cp/Pres, Pickwick Players; Yg People's Perf'g Co of Midland Commun Theatre; Pres, Student Coun, HS; Lambda Chi Alpha Frat; Public Relats Student Soc of Am, 1981-82, 1982-83; Lubbock Cultural Affairs Coun, 1983; r/Cath; hon/Outstg Nat Forensic Leag Mem, 1978; Dean's Hon List, 1983; Mag Layout Selected for Nat Col Competition, 1983; Personalities of S; g/Seeking Position in Public Relats and Advtg in the Entertainment Indust.

KLOEWER, DENISE MARIE oc/ Proof Operator; b/Dec 6, 1962; h/Route 1, Box 275, Underwood, IA 51576; p/ Mr and Mrs Leonard Kloewer, Underwood, IA; ed/HS, 1981; AA, IA Wn Commun Col, 1983; pa/Proof Operator; cp/Basketball; Volleyball; Choir; Marching Band; Flag Twirler; Annual St Columbanus Chili Supper Wkr; Underwood Cent Wkr; hon/Nat Hon Soc; Dean's List; W/W Among Am HS Students; Intl Yth in Achmt; Commun Ldrs of Am; g/Acctg.

KLUTTZ, ELIZABETH YORKE oc/ Student; b/Aug 26, 1965; h/311 William Street, Kannapolis, NC 28081; p/Dr and Mrs Robert F Kluttz, Kannapolis, NC; ed/Grad, A L Brown HS, 1983; cp/Ecol Clb, 1980; Tennis Team, 1980; Student Coun, Female Rep 1980; Citizenship Com, Chm 1980; Explorer Post 9, VP 1981, 1982, 1983; Y-Girls in Action, VP 1981; Marching Band, 1981, 1982, 1983; Symphonic Band, 1981, 1982, 1983; Fgn Lang Clb, 1981, VP 1982; Adv Coun, 1981, 1982, 1983; Yrbook Staff, 1983; Juniorettes, 1982, 1983; Omega Delta Phi Sorority, 1982, 1983; Hist Clb, 1983; Chm, A L Brown HS Sr Assem, 1983; Homecoming Com, 1983; r/Bapt; hon/ Cannon Jr HS Christmas Princess, 1980; Sophomore Class VP, 1981; Sophomore Class Valentine Princess, 1981; Jr Class VP, 1982; Jr Class Valentine Princess, 1982; Jr Class May Day Dance Coor, 1982; Sr Class Treas, 1983; Sr Hall of Fame, 1983; Miss Brown Hi, 1983; Homecoming Ct, 1983; Marching Band Letter Girl, Co Chief 1983; Varsity Basketball Cheerldr, 1983; Hon Letter, 1982, 1983; Hon Grad, 1983; Kannapolis Miss Merry Christmas, 1983; Nat Hon Soc, 1983; Debutante, Shelby Jr Charity Leag Debutante Ball, 1983; Peace Col; Peace Col; g/To Attend Peace Col and Univ of NC Chapel Hill.

KNAPP, PAULA ANN oc/Secretary Specialist; b/Aug 19, 1963; h/Route 2, Box 2273, Melrose, FL 32666; ba/ Gainesville, FL; p/Joseph G and Judy Knapp, Melrose, FL; ed/Grad, Hawthorne Jr Sr High, 1981; Att'd, Santa Fe Commun Col; pa/Sales Clk, K-Mart, 1980-82; Clk Typist, Univ of FL Pers, 1982-83; Secy II, Dept of Ec, Univ of FL, 1983-84; Secy Spec, Univ of FL Alumni Affairs, 1984-; cp/Future Bus Ldrs of Am; Sr Beta Clb; Annual Staff Typist; Ofc Aide Helper; Ch Wk; r/ Alliance; hon/W/W Among Am HS Students; Personalities of S; g/Adm Asst.

KNIERIEM, JO ANNE RAY oc/Systems Analyst; b/Sep 30, 1961; h/1318 Wood Park Drive, Kennesaw, GA 30144; ba/Atlanta, GA; m/Richard Keith; p/Mr Robert R Ray Jr, Mableton, GA; Mrs Robert R Ray Jr, Marietta, GA; ed/Dipl w Hons, Wheeler HS, 1978; BBA, cum laude, GA So Col, 1981; pa/

So Reg Sys Coor, Hercules Inc, 1982-83; Sys Analyst, GA Power Co, 1983-; GA Power Acctg Profls Assn, 1984; cp/Delta Sigma Pi Pledge Class Secy; CEI Chp and Fund Raising Com Chm; DPMA; Gamma Beta Phi; GA Soc Safety Com and Campus Life Enrichment Com; r/Meth; hon/Delta Sigma Pi Undergrad of the Yr, Epsilon Chi Chapt; Beta Gamma Sigma Charter Mem, 1981; Nat Dean's List, 1980, 1981; GSC Excell S'ship Awd, 1980, 1981; GSC Pres's Scholar, 1978-79; W/W Among Am Cols and Univs; Yg Personalities of S; g/To Pursue an Active Career in Sys Anal and Design; Master's Deg in MIS/Acctg; To Join Local DPMP and Delta Sigma Pi Chapts.

KNIGHT, AMY LEIGH oc/Piano Teacher; b/Mar 12, 1965; h/PO Box 121, Fayette, AL 35555; ba/Same; p/Charles and Ruth Knight Buckner, Fayette, AL; ed/Grad, Fayette Co HS, 1983; cp/Future Tchrs of Am, Histn; Future Bus Ldrs of Am; FHA, Pres; Band; Chorus, Libn; Echo Staff, Asst Ad Editor; r/Free Will Bapt; hon/Most Outstg Home Ec Student; FBLA Talent Winner; All-St Band; All-St Chorus; W/W Among Am HS Students; g/To Be a Piano and Eng Tchr.

KNIGHT, ANGELA J oc/Dental Assistant Student; b/Jan 18, 1965; h/Route 1, Box 200-A, Staley, NC 27355; p/Mr and Mrs Bob Knight, Staley, NC; ed/Grad, Jordan Matthews HS, 1983; Dental Asst Student, Univ of NC Chapel Hill; pa/Receptionist and Pt-time Asst, Dr Hal H Smith Jr, 1981-82; cp/Class Secy, 1981; Ofc Aid, 1982; Secy, Hlth Occups Students of Am, 1982-83; Girls' Ensemble Choir, 1981-82; r/Bapt; g/To Aquire Cert in Dental Asst'g and Possibly Specialize in Orthodontics.

KNIGHT, CHERI oc/Composer, Philosopher, Goatherd; b/Aug 4, 1956; h/316 Mill Valley Road, Belchertown, MA 01007; ba/Same; p/Edward W Knight MD, Merrit Island, FL; Ruth Knight, Canaan, NY; ed/HS Dipl, Berkshire Sch, 1974; Phil Maj, Whitman Col, 1975-77; BA, Music, Evergreen St Col, 1982; pa/Composer; Philosopher; Goatherd; New Music Alliance; Am Dairy Goat Assn; Nat Saanen Breeders Assn; Lost Music Network; hon/Musical Compositions which Appear on Record Albums: "Water Project #2261," "Tips on Filmaking," "Primary Colors," "Hear/Say"; g/To Operate a Comml Goat Dairy; To Write Music and Explore Sound Ideas.

KNIGHT, TRACY JEROME oc/Optometrist; b/Mar 17, 1958; h/5480 Illahee Road, Northeast, Bremerton, WA 98310; p/Mr and Mrs Richard M Knight; ed/E Bremerton HS, 1976; BS, Pacific Univ, 1981; OD, Pacific Univ Col of Optom, 1983; pa/OD, Puget Sound Vision Clin, 1983-; Am Optometric Assn, 1979-, Sports Vision Sect 1981-; WA Optometric Assn, 1983-; Col of Optometrists in Vision Devel, 1981-; Better Vision Inst, 1983; Optometric Ext Prog Foun, 1980-; Am Optometric Foun, 1983-; hon/Pub, "Histological Changes and Clinical Implications of Light Damage to the Retina," 1982; hon/Nat Dean's List; Intl Yth in Achmt; Outstg Yg Men of Am; Commun Ldrs of Am; g/To Provide Vision Care to the Commun through the Profl and Ethical Pract of Optom.

KNOPP, PHYLLIS MARY oc/Student, Laboratory Assistant; b/Jan 27, 1962; h/1620 15th Avenue, Seattle, WA 98122; ba/Seattle, WA; p/Mr and Mrs Clarence T Knopp, Seattle, WA; ed/Dipl, John F Kennedy Meml HS, 1980; BS in Psych, Seattle Univ, 1984; pa/Counter Person, Shift Ldr, Shift Mgr, Jack in the Box, 1978-80; Counter Person, Tng Coor, Adm Asst, Shift Mgr, McDonalds, 1980-82; Stats Tutor for Seattle Univ's Lng Resource Ctr, 1982-; Lab Asst, Puget Sound Blood Ctr, 1982-; cp/Secy-Treas, Intl Thespian Soc, 1978-80; Nat Hon Soc, 1979-80; Intl French Hon Soc, 1978-80; Publicity Dir, New Student Orientation, 1982; Pres, Alpha Sigma Nu, 1983; Peer Advg on the Col Experience, 1983; hon/Best Thespian, 1979; Alpha Sigma Nu, Nat Jesuit Hon Soc, 1983; Recip, Seattle Univ Merit Grant, 1980-83; Nom'd, Naef S'ship, 1983; W/W Among Am HS Students; g/Master's Deg; PhD; Clin Psychol.

KOEPP, WARREN POWELL oc/Student; b/Jan 20, 1965; h/Box 7, Salt Flat, TX 79847; ba/Lubbock, TX; p/W Philip and Marsha P Koepp, Salt Flat, TX; ed/HS; pa/Sales Rep, Everglades Natural Hist Assn, 1980-81; Bldg Salvage, George Temple, 1980; Radio Dispatcher, TX Hwy Dept, 1982; Maintenance Tech, TX Hwy Dept, 1983; cp/Nat Hon Soc, 1981-83, VP 1982-83; Mu Alpha Theta, 1980-81; Mensa, 1980-83; Student Coun, Pres 1982-83; Math and Sci Team, 1981-83; r/Christian; hon/Valedictorian, 1983; Outstg Sr Math Student, Sci Student and Eng Student, 1983; Pres Scholar Finalist, 1983; Univ Scholar, 1983-84; 3rd St Sci, 1983; W/W; W/W Am HS; g/BS in Math; Master's Deg; Doct Deg.

KOHLER, JAN M oc/Student; h/14464 South Dixie Highway, Monroe, MI 48161; p/Mr and Mrs John W Kohler, Monroe, MI; ed/HS Dipl, Monroe HS, 1979; Acctg Maj, Univ of Toledo; cp/Nat Assn of Accts, 1983; Freshman Resident Orientation Guide, 1981; Univ "Y," 1979-81; r/Cath; hon/Univ of Toledo Hon S'ship, 1979; Dean's List, 1979, 1982; g/Take the CPA Exam before Graduation.

KONDONASSIS, JOHN I oc/Student; b/Sep 10, 1956; h/512 Manor Drive, Norman, OK; p/Alex and Pat Kondonassis; ed/Interlochen Arts Acad, 1974; BM, DePauw Univ, 1980; cp/Pi Kappa Lambda, Nat Music Hon Soc; Chamber Music; Orch; Russian Lang Clb; Phi Eta Sigma; Mu Phi Epsilon; hon/DePauw Univ Presser Foun S'ship; Univ of TX S'ship; g/Profl Orch Mbrship; Chamber Music Involvement.

KOSTENKO, JANE FRANCES oc/Graduate Assistant; b/Jun 21, 1958; h/1424 5th Street, Southwest, Minot, ND 58701; p/Mr and Mrs Harold Kostenko, Minot, ND; ed/HS, 1976; BA, Minot St Col, 1979; MS, Millersville St, 1981; pa/Grad Asst; cp/Pres, Student Assn; Phi Sigma Pi; Editor, Col Newspaper, Yrbook; Pres, Grad Student Org; Soc for Col Jour; Wom Chorus; Student Rep, Fac Senate; Chm, Fin Comm; VP, Sci Clb; NSF; SOS Res Team; Col Photog; hon/Nat Assn of Geol Tchrs S'ship; Intl Yth in Achmt; W/W Among Students in Am Univs and Cols; g/PhD in Sci Writing; Travel.

KOZA, MONA LYNN oc/Installment Loan Securities Clerk; b/Oct 14, 1962; h/6100 Vine D-23, Lincoln, NE 68505; ba/Lincoln, NE; p/Mr and Mrs Norman Koza, Silver Creek, NE; ed/Dipl, Silver Creek High, 1980; Assoc Deg in Bus Adm w Distn, Lincoln Sch of Commerce, 1982; pa/Pt-time Asst, Union Catalogue, NE Lib Comm, 1981-82; Hist Card Clk 1982, Securities Clk, Installment Lending Div 1982-, First Nat Bk and Trust Co of Lincoln; Adm Mgmt Soc, 1981-82; ABWA, 1983-; Am Inst of Bkg, 1982-; cp/Track; Volleyball; Basketball; Pep Clb; SC Clb; Cheerldr; Swing Choir; Sophomore Class Treas; Yrbook Staff; r/Cath; hon/HS: 4-Yr Hon Roll Student, Ranked 3rd in Class; W/W Among Am HS Students; g/To Continue Career in Bkg while Furthering Ed in That Area; Bk Ofcr.

KOZLOWSKI, RICHARD R oc/Youth Worker; b/Jan 14, 1961; h/15 Linwood Place, Lynn, MA 01905; ba/Malibu, CA; p/Vivian Lazurek, Lynn, MA; ed/Lynn Classical HS, 1979; N Shore Commun Col, Computer Electronics 1983, Human Sers/Rec Ldrship 1979-80; pa/Grp Facilitator, LA Unified Sch Dist Student to Student Interaction Prog, 1983-84; Asst Dir, The Original Computer Camp, 1982-83; Tutor in Computer Lab, N Shore Commun Col, 1983; Temp Ofc Wkr, Temp Force, 1981-83; Envir Edr, Cape Cod Outdoor Ed Ctr, 1981-82; Unit Dir, Camp Rotary, YMCA, 1980-81; Cnslr, Lynn Boys' Clb, 1975-80; hon/W/W Among Am HS Students; Intl Yth Ldrs; g/To Wk in an Outdoor Ed Setting that Covers Human Relats and Current Technol as Well as Envir Awareness as Part of the Curric.

KRAFT, RICHARD LEE oc/Attorney; b/Oct 14, 1958; h/2001 South Sunset Avenue, Apartment G-125, Roswell, NM 88201; ba/Roswell, NM; p/Charles H and Marguerite Kraft, South Pasadena, CA; ed/S Pasadena HS, 1976; BA in Fgn Ser/Hist 1980, JD 1982, Baylor Univ; pa/Hd Student Mgr, Baylor Univ Dining Sers, 1979-82; Atty, Sanders, Bruin & Baldock, PA, 1982-; Am Bar Assn, 1980-; cp/Baylor Univ C of C, 1978-80; Baylor Univ Parliamentarian, 1979; Baylor Univ Bear Mascot Tnr, 1979-80; Zeta Tau Alpha Beau, Theta Omicron Chapt, 1978-82; r/Christian; hon/Phi Alpha Theta, Nat Hon Frat, 1978; Recip, Frank M Wilson Meml S'ship, Baylor Univ, 1982; Dean's List, Baylor Law Sch, Winter 1981-82.

KRAMER, KRISTI K oc/Professional Home Economist; b/Sep 10, 1961; h/640 Monte Vista, Sheridan, WY 82801; p/Donald Kramer, Ranchester, WY; Marcia Powers, Sheridan, WY; ed/Tongue River HS, 1979; BS, Univ of WY, 1983; pa/Profl Home Economist; Am Home Ec Assn, Pres, Publicity Chm; cp/Col 4-H Secy, Publicity Chm; FHA Dist Chm; Student Coun; hon/St Winner, 4-H Clothing Nat Report Form; Intl Yth in Achmt Nom; W/W Among Am HS Students; g/Ext Agt.

KREIDER, ANGELA CAROL oc/Student; b/Dec 11, 1963; h/Route 10, Box 13, Harrisonburg, VA 22801; p/John H and Sara E Kreider, Harrisonburg, VA; ed/Grad, En Mennonite HS, 1982; Currently Enrolled, En Mennonite Col; pa/Bkkpr, Kreider Machine Shop, 1981; Cnslr, Highland Retreat Mennonite Camp, 1982, 1983; cp/HS

Track, Basketball, Volleyball, Cross Country; HS Orch, Touring Choir, Student Newspaper (Sports Editor); HS Freshman Class Treas; Col Volleyball, Track; Col Chamber Singers, Jazz Band; Editor-in-Chief, Col Student Newspaper, 1984; r/Christian, Mennonite; hon/HS Acad Hon Roll; Nat Hon Soc, 1981; Salutatorian, 1982; HS Sci Dept Awd, 1982; Nat Merit S'ship Finalist, 1982; Pres Scholars Prog Finalist, 1982; Nat Sci Merit Awd, Winner, 1982; EMC Pres's S'ship Recip, 1982-86; US Achmt Acad Awds Yrbook; Am's Outstg Names and Faces; g/Deg in Eng Ed, Psych.

KRIEGER, KENNETH VINCENT oc/ Student; b/Oct 7, 1964; h/3115 North Park Drive, Missouri City, TX 77459; p/Charles and Edith Krieger, Missouri City, TX; ed/John Foster Dulles HS, 1982; Presently Att'g, TX A&M Univ; cp/Sci Clb, 1981-82; Jr Engrg and Tech Soc, 1981-82; Nat Marine Mammal Stranding Netwk, 1982-84; Intermural Softball, 1983-84; Dorm Assn, 1982-84; Sch Newspaper, 1983-84; r/Cath; hon/ Jr Engrg and Tech Soc S'ship, 1982; Dist'd Student List, 1982; Dean's List, 1983; Phi Eta Sigma; Nat Dean's List; g/Res in Marine Biol.

KRIER, PAUL ANTHONY oc/Student, Musician; b/Jan 20, 1962; h/107 Emerald Drive, Storm Lake, IA 50588; p/Mr and Mrs Andrew Krier, Storm Lake, IA; ed/Storm Lake Sr HS, 1980; BM, Applied Music, Univ of SD, 1984; pa/Piano Tchr, Univ of SD Arts Outreach Prog, 1983-84; cp/Mu Phi Epsilon, Profl Music Frat; SD Music Tchrs Assn; Vermillion Area Piano Tchrs Assn; Mortar Bd; Omicron Delta Kappa; Buena Vista Commun Theatre Actor, Musician, Choreographer; HS Choirs; HS Band; Spch Clb; Orch; Thespian Clb; Cherokee Symph; Univ of SD Choirs; Univ of SD Orch; Black Hills Playhouse; hon/MTNA, Alt Winner, 1982; Elected into Mortar Bd and Omicron Delta Kappa; Winner, SD Fdn of Music Clb's Yg Artist Auditions in Piano, 1983; Am Legion Awd; Chopin Piano Awd; Cherokee Symph Concert Competition Winner; g/Concert Pianist; Tchr at a Univ.

KRITCHER, KAREN MARIE oc/ Student; b/Apr 15, 1963; h/1780 US 31 North, Petoskey, MI 49770; p/Stan and Marge Kritcher, Petoskey, MI; ed/Grad, Petoskey Sr High, 1981; AS, N Ctl MI Col, 1983; pa/Clk, Jo Ann's Fabric, 1981;

Dept Hd, Cashier, Clk, Giantway Dept Store, 1981-; cp/4-H, 4 Yrs; 4-H Ldr, 3 Yrs; Marching Band, 3 Yrs; Symphonic Band, 3 Yrs; r/Rom Cath; hon/ 4-H Ldrship Awd, 1980; ROTC Finalist, 1981, 1982; Sewing Awds, 1981-83; Music Awds, 1976-80; W/W HS Students; Intl Yth in Achmt; Commun Ldrs of Am; Yg Commun Ldrs; g/RN; MD.

KRYJAK, MICHAEL ANTHONY oc/ Research Assistant; b/Feb 7, 1955; h/32 North Catherine Street, Shenandoah, PA 17976; p/Paul (dec) and Sylvia T Kryjak, Shenandoah, PA; ed/Dipl, Cardinal Brennan HS, 1972; King's Col, 1974; Bloomsburg St Col, 1975; Trinity Col, 1975; BA w Hons, Schiller Col, 1976; Grad Study, Univ of Leeds; Cert, Ec, Henry George Inst, 1981; pa/Res Asst, PA St Univ, 1981-83; Com Mem, Shenandoah Downtown Task Force, 1979-81; Secy-Treas, Shenandoah Merchants Assn; Indep Ednl Conslt, 1978-81; Lib Staff, Schiller Col, 1975-76; Security Aide, Dept of Security, Bloomsburg St Col, 1974-75; cp/Am Sociol Assn; Brit Broadcasting Corp World Ser Radio Clb; Free and Accepted Masons, Lodge 511; Hlth Sys Agy of NEn PA; r/Cath; hon/Recip, Carl Schurz Volksmarch Medal, 1976; Invited to Participate in En Sociol Assn's Annual Meetings, 1982, 1983; Am Govt Registry Series; Commun Ldrs of Am; Intl Yth in Achmt; g/To Remain in Ednl Res or Adm.

KUBIAK, GREG D oc/United States Senate Field Representative; b/Dec 12, 1960; h/2518 West Brooks, #1, Norman, OK 73069; ba/Oklahoma City, OK; p/ Curtis and Pearl Kubiak, Spencer, OK; ed/Mt St Mary HS, 1979; BA, Polit Sci, Univ of OK Norman, 1983; pa/Field Rep for US Senator David L Boren, 1983-; cp/Pres, Mt St Mary Alumni and Friends Assn, 2 Yrs; OK Univ Pres's Ptnrs; Pi Sigma Alpha, Polit Sci Nat Hon; r/Cath; hon/Gold Letzeiser Medal, Univ of OK, as Top Sr Male; Pres, Univ of OK Students Assn; Nora V Wells Awd, Univ of OK Pres's Ldrship Clb; W/W Among Col and Univ Students; g/To Attend Law Sch in Wash, DC.

KUCHEROV, MICHAEL FREDERICK oc/Student; b/Oct 11, 1963; h/5033 North 35th Street, Arlington, VA 22207; p/Alexander and Renate Kucherov, Arlington, VA; ed/Grad, Bishop O'Connell HS, 1981; Student, Col of Wm and Mary, 1981-; cp/Esperanto Soc of Wash, DC; hon/Elected to

Alpha Lambda Delta and Phi Eta Sigma; "It's Academic" Team Mem, HS; St Finalist (Twice), Optimist Oratorical Contest; Quality Control Mgr in Jr Achmt Prog; Semi-Finalist in Nat Merit Competition; Gifted and Talented Prog; 2 Gold Medals, Latin Exam; Commun Ldrs of Am; W/W Among Am HS Students; g/Maj in Ec; Enter Fgn Ser.

KUENZLE, KATHYJO WINEFRED oc/Teacher; b/Dec 1, 1955; h/748 Dace Lane, Saint Louis, MO 63125; p/Charlotte Kuenzle, Saint Louis, MO; ed/HS, 1974; BS, 1978; pa/Tchr; Assn for the Ed of Yg Chd; cp/OES; Intl Order of Job's Daughs; Gamma Sigma Sigma; Nat Hon Soc; hon/Gamma Sigma Sigma Nat Outstg Sister; Intl Yth in Achmt; W/W Among Students in Am Univs and Cols; Commun Ldrs of Am; Outstg Yg Wom of Am; g/MS in Early Childhood Ed.

KULIK, JOSEPH MICHAEL oc/Lawyer; b/Sep 17, 1957; h/121 Lorish Road, McKees Rocks, PA 15136; ba/Pittsburgh, PA; p/Joseph J (dec) and Katherine Kulik, McKees Rocks, PA; ed/ Montour HS, 1975; BA, summa cum laude, Duquesne Univ, 1978; JD, Duquesne Univ Sch of Law, 1981; pa/ Ofc of the Dist Atty of Allegheny Co, 1980-18; Assoc'd w Law Ofcs of Peter J King, 1981-; Self-Employed in Areas of Tax Consultation and Labor Negotiation; Am Bar Assn; Assn of Trial Lwyrs of Am; PA Trial Lwyrs of Am; PA Trial Lwyrs Assn; PA Bar Assn; Allegheny Co Bar Assn; cp/Nat Sch Bd Assn; Montour Sch Bd, 1977-, Secy 1984; Bd of Dirs, Parkway W Area Tech Sch, 1978-, Treas 1982-; r/Cath; hon/ Cit of Recog, St of MI, 1971; Detroit Renaissance Awd, 1980; Outstg Yg Men of Am; Yg Commun Ldrs; Intl Yth in Achmt.

KYLE, TERRY L oc/Student; b/Jan 4, 1962; h/PO Box 197, Taylor, AR 71861; p/Mr and Mrs Randall Kyle, Taylor, AR; ed/Taylor HS, 1980; Currently Enrolled, So AR Univ (Eng Maj); cp/ Alpha Hon Soc, Pres 1981-82; Talley Hall, Pres 1983-84; Alpha Chi, Pres 1983-84; Student Govt Del, 1981-82; Phi Beta Lambda, 1980-84, Local and St Parliamentarian; SAU Student Foun, 1982-84; r/Bapt; hon/Dean's List, 1980-83; First Place in PBL St Parliamentary Procedure Contest, 1983; Outstg Resident in Regard to Acad Achmt in Talley Hall, 1983; W/W Among Students in Am Cols and Univs; g/To Attend Law Sch upon Graduation.

L

LACKEY, MARGARET NELL oc/ Student; b/Jul 11, 1965; h/440 Old Creek Road, Northeast, Atlanta, GA 30342; p/Dr and Mrs Dixon A Lackey, Atlanta, GA; ed/Marist Sch, HS; Agnes Scott Col; pa/Pt-time Employmt as Tchr's Aide, Holy Innocents Epis Sch, 1981; Waitress, Canterbury Ct Retirement Home, 1982; Glass Oven Bakery, 1983; Vol, GA Retard Ctr, 1982; cp/ Editor of HS Newspaper; First Co Mem of So Ballet of Atlanta; Nat Hon Soc; Jr Classical Leag; Emmaus; r/Cath; hon/ S'ship to Agnes Scott Col, 1983; Class Medal for 10th & 11th Grade, 1981, 1982; Subject Awd for Latin, 1981, 1983; GA Cert of Merit Winner, 1982; Hon Roll Cert, 1979, 1980; Dean's List Cert, 1981-83; Nat Hon Soc, 1981; Valedictorian of Marist, 1983; Catherine Littlefield Ballet Awd, 1982, 1983; g/Vet Med.

LADD, PAULA MONZELL oc/Student; b/Jul 28, 1963; h/Rural Route 1, Box 260, Cadiz, KY 42211; p/Mr and Mrs Henry Philip Ladd I, Cadiz, KY; ed/ Grad, Trigg Co HS, 1981; Att'g Univ Louisville; cp/4-H, 3 Yrs; Brownie 2 Yrs, Jr Girl Scout 3 Yrs, GSA; Secy, Art Clb; Alpha Phi Alpha Frat Inc, Angel Pres, 1984, Angel Parliamentn; Secy, Jr Choir; Asst Secy, Bapt Tng Union; Track; Cross Country; Trick or Treat for UNICEF, 1981; hon/Omega Calendar Pageant, 2nd Runner-Up-Miss February; Contestant, Miss Black Wn KY Pageant; g/Phy Therapist.

LADNIER, PATRICIA oc/Student; b/ Feb 8, 1962; h/Post Office Box 165, 1917 Ladnier Road, Gautier, MS 39553; ba/ Lamoni, IA; p/Mr and Mrs Willie Ladnier, Gautier, MS; ed/Graceland Col; Pascagoula HS, 1980; pa/Historic Site Interpretor, Sum 1983; Intern for Congressman Trent Lott, Sum 1982; Tutor, Graceland Col Spec Sers, 1980-83; cp/Editor, Harry S Truman Alumni Assn Newslttr; Atara House Pres, 1983-84; Student Acad Coun Pres, 1982-83; Col Repubs Pres, VP, 1980-82; Graceland *Tower* Editor, News Editor, 1981-82; Mu Gamma Theta Cand; r/ Reorganized Ch of Jesus Christ of LDS; hon/Harry S Truman S'ship, 1982; Graceland Col Lrdrship Grant, 1980-84; Graceland Col Acad S'ship, 1980-84; Century III Ldrs S'ship, 1980; US Senate Yth Prog S'ship, 1979; Nat Dean's List; W/W Among Am HS Student; g/Law Deg & Master's Deg in Intl Relats.

LAFFOON, VIRGINIA RUTH oc/ Student; b/Jan 17, 1966; h/312 Poplar Street, Dawson Springs, KY 42408; p/ Mr and Mrs Lawrence R Laffoon, Dawson Sprgs, KY; ed/Dawson Sprgs HS, 1984; cp/HS Yrbok Staff, Asst Editor & Bus Mgr, Editor of 1984 Yrbok; Nat Beta Clb, Co VP, 1984; FHA; Pep Clb; Art Clb; HS Choir; r/ SDA, Tchr of Kgn Sabbath Sch Class at Hopkinsville SDA Ch; hon/KY's Golden 100 Mem; 3rd Pl Nat Sci Awd; 3rd Pl Social Sci Awd; Nat Career Guid Wk Poster Contest, 1st Pl Winner; US Achmt Acad Mem, Math Awd, Govt & Hist Awd, Bus Ed Awd, Ldrship Awd; W/W Among Am HS Students; g/CPA.

LAIR, MICHAEL PAUL oc/Associate Programmer-Analyst; b/Nov 12, 1959; h/3413 27th Street Northwest; Canton,

OH 44708; ba/Canton, OH; p/Robert L and Zovinar N Lair, Canton, OH; ed/ BA, Malone Col, 1981; pa/Underwriter Trainee, Westfield Ins, 1981-82; Assoc Programmer-Anal, The Timken Co, Corp Sys Dept, 1982-; cp/Student NEA, 1980 Pres; Malone Col Chorale, 1977-79; Malone Players, 1977-80; Yrbk Staff Photog, 1979-81; Sch Newspaper Photog & Feature Column Writer, 1979-81; Sunday Sch Supt, Sixteen St John's U Ch of Christ, 1977-78; Intl Brotherhood of Magicians & Secy of Local Chapt, 1981-; r/U Ch of Christ; hon/Cleveland Wizards' Conclave Magic Contest, 3rd Pl Close-up Winner, 1983; Author, "Parade", *The Linking Ring*, 1982; Spec Merit Cert for Article in *The Linking Ring*, 1982; Sigma Zeta Math & Sci Hon, 1979-81; Cum Laude Grad of Malone Col, 1981; W/W Among Students in Am Univs & Cols; Intl Yth in Achmt; Commun Ldrs of Am; Men of Achmt; g/Assoc Programmer-Anal, Corp Sys Dept of The Timken Co.

LAKES, MARILYN oc/Student, Salesperson; b/Mar 16, 1961; h/ Route 8, Box 13, Airport Road, Richmond, KY 40475; p/Mr and Mrs H A Lakes, Richmond, KY; ed/Madison Ctl HS, 1979; AA, BS, EN KY Univ, 1983; pa/Circuit Ct Adm Asst, 1981; Salesperson, Rose's Dept Store, 1982-; Asst to Commonwealth's Atty for Madison & Clark Counties, 1982; cp/Drama Clb; Pep Clb; Chorus; Fgn Lang Clb; FBLA; Pres 1978-79; Assn of Law Enforcement, 1981-; Secy, Nat Pres Alpha Phi Sigma; hon/Hon Roll; Dean's List; Nom for Milestone/Outstg Sr Awd at En KY Univ, 1982; Dist'd Achmt Awd, 1979; Secretarial Stenographic Awd, 1979; Perfect Attendance Awd, HS, 1975-79; Intl Yth in Achmt; W/W in Am Cols & Univs; g/Univ KY Law Sch.

LaLUZERNE, LORI ANN-ZIRBEL oc/Registered Nurse, Emergency Room; b/Aug 28, 1960; h/621 West Spruce Drive, Sturgeon Bay, WI 54235; ba/ Sturgeon Bay, WI; m/Steven W; c/ Andrew S; p/Ralph and Marilyn Zirbel, Sturgeon Bay, WI; sp/Wendell and Elaine LaLuzerne, Sturgeon Bay, WI; ed/Sturgeon Bay HS; BS, Univ WI-Eau Claire; pa/RN-Med/Sur Area, Emergency Room, Door Co Meml Hosp, 1982-; ANA; cp/Pres, Door Co Nurse's Assn, 1983-84; Broadway Showchoir Mem, 1977-78; Supporting Actress Musical "Pajama Game", 1977; Intramural Basketball Player, 1974-78; r/Cath; hon/Hon Grad HS; Alpha Lambda Delta; Phi Kappa Phi; Sigma Theta Tau; Outstg Sr Nsg Student, 1982; Magna Cum Laude, 1982; PEO Wom's S'ship, 1981; g/to Continue in Emer Room Wk.

LAM, BUN-CHING oc/Teacher; b/ Jun 26, 1954; h/208 78th Avenue East, Seattle, WA 98112; ba/Seattle, WA; p/ Chi-Wang Lam; ed/BA, Chinese Univ Hong Kong, 1976; MA, PhD, Univ CA-San Diego, 1982; pa/Instr of Music, Cornish Inst, 1982-; Tchg Asst, Univ CA-San Diego, 1976-81; cp/Coor, New Perf Grp, 1982; hon/First Awd, NW Composer's Symp, 1983; Finalist, Music Today Fest, Tokyo, 1982; Composition Awd, Aspen Music Fest, 1980; Piano Awd, 1979; 1st Prize, Song-Writing Contest, Hong Kong, 1976.

LAMB, JOE THOMAS oc/Student; b/ Mar 18, 1965; h/Route 4, Box 303, Berea, KY 40403; p/Floyd Lamb, Berea,

KY, and Betty Stephens Lamb, Berea, KY; ed/Madison Ctl HS; cp/FFA; hon/ Rec'd Poultry Prodn Awd, 1982; Rec'd FFA Welding Trophy; FFA Auctioneering Champ, 1983-84; 1st Pl Blue Ribbon; Purple Championship Rosette & Auctioneering Trophy, 1983; Honored by Berea Rotary Clb for Ser to Clb & Commun Having Conducted the Clb's Annual Benefit Auction, 1980; Rec'd Rotary Ser Plaque; 1st Pl Winner for 4 Yrs at Annual FFA-4-H Tobacco Show; Rec'd 1st Pl Plaque & Blue Ribbon at Univ KY Annual Field Day each Sprg at Lexington in Gen Farm Auctioneering Contest, 1980-83; Rec'd 3rd Pl Ribbon at St Fair in Louisville in Stwide FFA Tobacco Auctioneering Contest, 1980, 2nd Pl in 1981, 1982.

LAMBDIN, LAURA YVONNE oc/ Student; b/Nov 20, 1963; h/Route 6, Box 319, Natchez, MS 39120; p/Mrs W P Lambdin, Natchez, MS; ed/Trinity Epis HS; Univ AL-Capstone Hon Prog; LA Tech Univ-Rome Italy, MS St; pa/ Giftwrapper, Ullmans, 1978; Giftwrapper, Sales, Benoists, 1979-82; Interior Decorating Dept, H F Byrne, 1981; Interior Decorating, Beth Miller Interiors, 1984; cp/Natchez Pilgrimage Garden Clb; ASID; Chi Omega Social Sorority, Rush Ofcr; r/Presb; hon/ Gamma Beta Phi; Alpha Zeta; Kappa Omicron Phi; Dean's List; Natchez Pilgrimage Queen, 1984; Nat Dean's List; W/W Among Am HS Students; US Acad Achmt; g/Deg in Interior Design from MS St.

LANCASTER, WANDA LYNN oc/ Graduate Student, Clinical Faculty; b/ Aug 4, 1956; h/3440 Congress Avenue, Indianapolis, IN 46222; p/Melvin and Louise Lancaster, Shelby, NC; ed/ Shelby Sr HS, 1974; Cabarrus Meml Hosp Sch Nsg, Dipl, 1976; BSN, Univ NC-Charlotte, 1981; MSN, IN Univ, 1983; pa/Clin Fac Mem, IN Univ Sch Nsg, 1983; Res Asst, Riley Chd's Hosp, 1981-82; Mtl Hlth Nurse, Piedmont Area Mtl Hosp, 1981; Patient Ed Coor, Mecklenberg Mtl Hlth, 1977-80; Mtl Hlth Nurse, Piedmont Area Mtl Hlth, 1976-77; ANA; IN St Nurse's Assn; MW Nsg Res Soc; Grad Student Nurse's Assn; cp/Cabarrus Animal Protection Soc Invest, 1980-81; r/Meth; hon/ "Fankhauser & Lancaster Medication Prog", NC Dept Human Resources, 1979; Sigma Theta Tau, 1981; W/W Among Students in Am Univs & Cols; g/Mtl Hlth Nurse Clin Spec.

LAND, SHELIA KAY oc/Student; b/ May 10, 1967; h/Post Office Box 212, Haymond, KY 41810; p/Ova and Earnestine Land, Haymond, KY; ed/Fleming Neon HS, 1985; cp/Jour Clb; Fleming Neon Band; Pep Clb; Bible Clb, Pres; g/Cosmetologist.

LANDERS, SHARON L oc/Assistant to Mayor of New York City; b/May 18, 1953; ba/New York, NY; ed/BS, St Univ NY-Stony Brook, 1974; JD, Albany Law Sch, Union Univ, 1977; Cert Completion, Envir Mgmt Inst, USC, 1979; pa/ Asst Counsel, NYS Dept of Trans, 1977-82; Prog Asst, Trans Gov's Ofc, 1982-83; Asst to the Mayor of NYC, 1983-; hon/Contbg Author, "An Assessmt of the Motor Vehicle Inspection Prog for CA"; Co-Author, "Obtaining Economic Hardship Exemption: Fact or Fiction"; Reg Finalist, Pres' Comm on White House F'ships, 1983-84; Cert of Apprec for Outstg Ser During the 1980 Winter Olympics, 1980; Cert of Recog from the Am Lung Assn; Silver Key in Recog of Outstg Accomplishment, 1976.

LANDIS, JEFFERY A oc/Announcer for WYFR; b/Mar 24, 1959; h/1905 East Grand Avenue, Number 13, Escondido, CA 92027; ba/Oakland, CA; m/Donna J; p/Donald and Susanna Landis, Hayward, CA; sp/Harold and Shirley Camping, Almeda, CA; ed/BRE, Reformed Bible Col, 1981; MAR, Westminster Theol Sem, 1984; pa/Announcer/Prodr, Fam P Stations Inc, 1981-; r/Presb.

LANDRETH, BEVERLY CHARLENE oc/Student; b/Apr 8, 1963; h/Post Office Box 1092, Etowah, NC 28729; p/Mr and Mrs Billy H Landreth, Etowah, NC; ed/Rosman HS, 1981; Wingate Col; pa/Pt-time, Seeker Lure Co, 1983; cp/HS Band; Wingate Col Music Camp; Bible Clb; HS Sr Class Secy; Yrbook Staff; *The Bengal* Bus Mgr; Christian Student Union; MENC, Treas; r/Bapt, Ch Organist, Choir Dir; hon/Outstg Home Ec; Good Citizenship Medal; *The Gate* Orgs Editor; Soc of Col Jours; Dist'd Am HS Students; g/Music-Bus Deg, Music Mdsing.

LANDRY, LISA ANN b/Apr 28, 1966; h/30329 Garry, Madison Heights, MI 48071; p/John and Suzanne Landry, Madison Hgts, MI; ed/Bishop Foley HS, 1984; cp/Madison Hgts Pks & Rec Dept Rep for Bishop Foley, 1982; Sci Clb Treas; Track & Cross Country, 1981; Ski Clb, 1981-82; Flag Corp in Marching Band, 1982; r/Cath; hon/Hon Roll; Mech Drafting Reg Hons, 1982; Most Valuable Player, 1983; W/W Am HS; g/Attend a Univ in Law or Med.

LANDRY, RANDY VINCENT oc/Student; b/Sep 23, 1963; h/1701 Kerry Street, New Port Richey, FL 33552; p/Mr and Mrs Edward Mazdzer, New Port Richey, FL; ed/Gulf Comprehensive HS, 1981; AA, St Petersburg Jr Col; cp/Nat Hon Soc; Spanish Hon Soc; HOSA; Hlth Clb; Phi Theta Kappa, 1982-83; Pre Med Soc, 1983; r/Cath; hon/Pres' Hon Roll; Nat Hon Soc; Spanish Hon Soc; A-B Hon Roll; Jr Nat Hon Soc; Psych Awd; Hlth Ser Aide Awd; Geometry Awd; Sci Fair Awd; W/W Among Am HS Students; g/BA in Biol & Chem, Med Sch.

LANDS, DONALD GENE oc/Student; b/Mar 25, 1957; h/3317 Baumann, Midland, TX 79703; p/Jerry L Lands, Sr, Midland, TX; ed/BBA-Fin, 1982; cp/Student Coun Rep, Midland HS, 1973; FFA, VP 1974-75; TX Tech Fin Assn, 1982; TX Tech Petro Landman Assn, 1982; r/Bapt; hon/Most Popular, Midland HS, 1975; Jr Class Favorite, Midland HS, 1974; St Farmer, FFA, 1975; Dean's Hon Role, TX St Univ, 1978; g/Ofcrs Tng Prog at First City Nat of Midland.

LANE, CANDY NELL oc/Student; b/Jul 2, 1964; h/406 Nola Lane, Pinehurst, TX 77362; p/Mr and Mrs Pablo Martinez, Pinehurst, TX; ed/Magnolia HS, 1982; Nat Hon Soc; March of Dimes Walk-a-Thon; Mu Alpha Theta, 1983; Ch Wkr; Yth F'ship; Sch Choir; Drama Clb; FHA; Choir Secy; hon/Perfect Attendance Awd; Best Supporting Actress, 1982; ROTC 3 Yr S'ship, 1983; Transfer S'ship from Sam Houston St Univ, 1983; Yg Commun Ldrship Awd, 1982; Commun Ldrs Am; W/W Among Am HS Students; g/Med Technol.

LANE, DAVID WILLIAM oc/Student; b/Jul 29, 1965; h/Route 2, Box 178, Waynesboro, TN 38485; p/William C and Barbara B Lane, Waynesboro, TN; ed/Wayne Co HS, 1983; mil/USN; cp/F'ship of Christian Aths; Beta Clb; Ftball; Track & Field; BSA; French Clb; Band; Adv'd Math Clb; r/So Bapt; hon/Christian Ath of Yr, 1983; Dist 10-A 1st Team Offensive Tackle, 1982-83; NROTC, 4-Yr S'ship Winner; Sr Class Secy, 1983; W/W Among am HS Students; g/Engrg at Vanderbilt Univ.

LANE, KIMBERLY LYNN oc/Student; b/Nov 18, 1964; h/Route 1, Box 123, Pinetops, NC 27864; p/Mr and Mrs Joseph L Lane, Pinetops, NC; cp/Pres, 1982-83, Art Clb, 1980-81; French Clb, 1981-83; r/Bapt; hon/Hons S'ship to Atlantic Christian Col; Citizenship Awd, 1979-82; W/W Among Am HS Students; g/Major in Comml Art at Atlantic Christian Col; Advtg Media.

LANE, LESLIE LEIGH oc/Student; b/Jul 4, 1965; h/6749 Wendy Jean Drive, Morrow, GA 30260; p/Mr and Mrs H R Lane, Morrow, GA; ed/Morrow HS, 1983; cp/Pres, Nat Hon Soc, 1982-83; Mem, Key Clb, 1980-83; Mem, Co-Ed Y Clb, 1981-83; Cheerldr; Homeroom Rep, 1980-83; F'ship of Christian Aths, 1980-83; Baseball Mgr, 1981-82; Pres, Beta Clb, 1979-80; Gifted Prog; Spec Olympics Asst; r/Bapt; hon/Hon Roll; GA Cert of Merit Winner; Jr Princess, 1981-82; Homecoming Queen, 1982-83; Miss Morrow HS, Beauty Pageant, 1981-82; Miss Mustang, 1982-83; Booster Clb Scholastic Awds, 1981-83; Biol Awd Winner, 1980-81; Nat Merit Ldrship Awd, 1982-83; W/W Among Am HS Students; g/Attend Berry Col.

LANE, MELODAE DAWN Self-Employed, Mary Kay Beauty Consultant; b/Jan 16, 1958; h/1511-B Antoinette Avenue, Charlottesville, VA 22903; m/Dwight Denman; c/Dallas Denman; p/Mr and Mrs Willard H Smith, Parkville, MO; sp/Mr and Mrs Claire Lane, Blanchard, IA; ed/Park Hill HS, 1976; BS, NW Mo St Univ, 1980; pa/Resident Asst, 1979-80; Announcer, KXCV Radio, 1979-80; Front Desk Clb & Operator, KC Hilton Hotels, 1976-80; KMA Radio Reporter, 1980; KFEQ Radio Reporter, 1981; Traffic Dir, KXCV Radio, 1982; cp/Gymnastics Clb; Pep Clb; Student Coun Coor Bd; FHA, First VP, 1975-76; Trojan Newspaper Editor 1974-75, Copy Editor 1975-76; Winter Sports Cheerldr, 1975-76; Nat Hon Soc, 1975-76; 102 River Clb Publicity Chm, 1977; Tau Kappa Epsilon, Daugh of Diana, 1978; Alpha Sigma Alpha Fundraising Chm, 1978; Cardinal Key, 1979; KDLY Radio News Dir, Music Dir, News Editor, 1978-80; Beta Sigma Phi, 1983; SW Iowa Theater Grp, 1980-81; r/LDS; hon/Acad S'ship; W/W: Among Am HS Students, Among Students in Am Univs & Cols.

LANEY, LEIGH AUDREY oc/Student; b/Feb 20, 1962; h/Post Office Box 765, Magee, MS 39111; p/Mrs L R Laney, Magee, MS; ed/Magee HS, 1980; cp/Univ So MS; cp/Delta Gamma Hist; Lambda Sigma; Phi Chi Theta; Angle Flight; Soc for the Advmt of Mgt; ASB Senator; Magee's Miss Hospitality; hon/Scholastic All-Am Hon Soc; Editor, Histn 1981, Activs Chm 1982, Delta Gamma Sorority; Intl Yth in Achmt; Hons Grad Magee HS, 1980; Commun

Ldrs Am; g/Intl Bus Major.

LANG, SHERRY LYNN oc/Geriatric Nursing Assistant; b/Jun 16, 1962; h/4220 Maple Grove Road, Hampstead, MD 21074; ba/Manchester, MD; p/Mr and Mrs Ervin M Lang, Hampstead, MD; ed/N Carroll HS, 1980; Geriatric Nsg Tng, Cert, 1980; Travel Tng Associated Schs Inc, Cert, 1982; Catonsville Commun Col; pa/Geriatric Nsg Asst, Long View Nsg Home, 1980-; cp/Spanish Clb; Am Field Ser Clb; Choral Music Prog, Co & St Choruses; Charter Mem, N Carroll Choral Booster Clb, Secy, 1980-83; r/Prot, Ch of the Brethren, Yth F'ship, Secy 1978, VP 1979-80, Pastoral Needs Study Com 1981-82, Secy of Bldg Needs Study Com, Secy of Hist Steering Com, Del to Ch's Dist Conf, Mem of Jubilation Grp; g/Deg in Fgn Langs.

LANGFORD, LISA LYNN oc/Pt-time Waitress, Student; b/Dec 4, 1964; h/Route 1, Post Office Box 4, Rickman, TN 38580; p/Mr and Mrs Alvin E Walker, Rickman, TN; ed/Rickman HS, 1983; pa/Pt-time Waitress, Western Sizzlin, 1983-; cp/Sr Class Secy, 1982-83; Beta Clb Reporter; "R" Clb Pres, 1982-83; Softball Team, 1980-83; Volleyball Team, 1981-83; Annual Staff, 1981-83; Sophomore Class Reporter, 1981-83; Spanish Clb, 1982-83; Jr Bd Dirs Secy, Livingston's First Nat Bk, 1982-83; r/United Meth; hon/W/W Among Am HS Students; Eng Awd, 1983; Valedictorian, 1983; Guy B Copeland S'ship; g/Pre-Phy Therapy, TN Technol Univ.

LANGLEY, STEPHANIE LYNNE oc/Student; b/Feb 19, 1966; h/408 Pearl Street, Hartselle, AL 35640; p/Mr and Mrs James J Eisner, Hartselle, AL; ed/Hartselle HS, 1984; cp/B-Team Cheerldr, 1981-82; Varsity Cheerldr, 1982-83; Head Varsity Cheerldr, 1983-84; Concert Chorus, Showchoir "The Hartselle Performers"; Student Coun Rep, 1980-81; HS Musical "Bye Bye Birdie", 1983; r/Sparkmam Ch of Christ; hon/Modeling S'ship; Placed in Top 10 at Miss Point Mallard, Spirit of Am Fest; Morgan Co Jr Miss, 1984; Miss AL Darling of 1983; Nom'd to W/W Among Am HS Students; g/to Pursue Career in Computer Technol; to attend Univ AL.

LANGLEY, WILLIAM ALLEN oc/Student; b/Apr 13, 1963; h/1709 Cornell Road, Jacksonville, FL 32207; p/Mr and Mrs James C Langley, Jacksonville, FL; ed/Wolfson HS, 1981; Univ FL; cp/Kappa Alpha Order, S'ship Ofcr; Interact Clb, 1979-81; Remex Rowing Clb; Treas, Sr Men, 1981; r/Meth Yth F'ship Prog; hon/W/W Among Am HS Students; Personalities of the S; g/Mech Engrg Deg.

LANKFORD, LAURENE oc/Student, Mother/Wife; b/Feb 21, 1954; h/104 Ravenwood Circle, Dickson, TN 37055; m/Jerry Wayne Jr; c/Carina, Jerry Wayne III; p/Thomas (dec) and Dolores Wolenski, Hazel Park, MI; sp/Rev and Mrs Wayne Lankford, Dickson, TN; ed/Dickson HS, 1978; r/Free Will Bapt; hon/Dean's List; g/BS Deg in Early Childhood.

LANSFORD, ELIZABETH R oc/Attorney, Independent Practice; b/Nov 19, 1956; h/3005 Manioca Road, Lubbock, TX; ba/Lubbock, TX; p/William N (dec) and Joyce Lansford, Lubbock, TX;

ed/Monterey HS, 1974; BBA, TX Tech Univ, 1980; JD, TX Tech Univ Sch Law, 1983; TX Bar Assn; TX Yg Lwyrs Assn; cp/Nat Assn of Accts; hon/Phi Delta Phi; Nat Dean's List; g/Gen Law Pract.

LAPPE, DONNIE GENE oc/Attorney; b/Nov 19, 1955; h/2111 Avenue C, Brownwood, TX 76801; ba/Brownwood, TX; p/Alfred S and Muriel Lappe, Brownwood, TX; ed/Grad, Brownwood HS, 1974; BA, Howard Univ, 1977; JD, Baylor Law Sch, Baylor Univ, 1980; pa/Practicing Atty, Donnie Lappe & Ronnie Lappe Atty-at-Law, 1980~; Mem: ABA, TX Bar Assn, (Secy & Treas) Brown Co Bar Assn; Lic'd to Pract in: TX Supr Ct & Lower Ctrs; US Ct of Appeals; Fed Dist Ct; cp/Pres's Adv Coun, 1977; Mem, Lions Clb; r/Ch of Christ; hon/ Author of Num Poems Pub'd in Lit Mags; Alpha Chi, 1977; Alpha Lambda Delta, 1976; Pi Gamma Mu, 1976; Nat Hon Soc; Pres's List; W/W Among Students in Am Cols & Univs; Men of Achmt; Personalities of S; Other Biogl Listings.

LAPPE, RONNIE DEAN oc/Attorney; b/Nov 19, 1955; h/211 Avenue C, Brownwood, TX 76801; ba/Brownwood, TX; p/Mr and Mrs A S Lappe, Brownwood, TX; ed/Grad, Brownwood HS, 1974; BA Eng & BA Douglas McArthur Acad of Freedom, Howard Payne Univ, 1977; JD, Baylor Law Sch, Baylor Univ, 1980; pa/Practicing Atty, Donnie Lappe & Ronnie Lappe Atty-at-Law, 1980~; J of P, 1982~; Mem: ABA, TX Bar Assn, Brown Co Bar Assn, TX Yg Lwyrs Assn; Mem: Am Ajudicure Soc, Wright-Holmes Law List, Comml Law Leag of Am; cp/Mem, W Ctl TX Coun of Govts; Mem, Pvt Indust Coun; Chm, TX Sesquicent Com for Brown Co; Lions Clb; r/Ch of Christ; hon/ Author of Num Poems & Articles Pub'd in Lit Qtrlys & Mags; Nat Hon Soc, 1973; Class Salutatorian, 1974; Alpha Lambda Delta, 1975; Pi Gamma Mu, 1976; Alpha Chi, 1976; Pres's List, 1974-76 & 1979; Grad in Top 3, Howard Payne Univ, 1977; W/W Among Students in Am Cols & Univs; Commun Ldrs of Am; Intl Yth in Achmt; Other Biogl Listings.

LaROCHE, DOUGLAS WARREN oc/Student; b/Jun 13, 1961; h/Post Office Box 233, Crescent, GA 31304; ba/Athens, GA; ed/McIntosh Acad, 1979; Brunswick Jr Col; Univ GA; cp/ Crescent Bapt Baseball, Basketball Teams; GA Chapt, Nat Multiple Sclerosis Soc; BSA; Theatre Group; Lit Mag Mng Editor; Math Bowl Team; Hon Prog; Y Clb; Spanish Clb; Sci Clb; Interclb Coun; HS Play; Steering Com; Tennis; hon/Mng Editor of *Traditions Unltd*, Scholastic Achmt Awd Winning Pub; Sci Fair Winner; Eng, Sci, Art Awds; Commun Ldrs Am; W/W Among Am HS Students; Intl Yth in Achmt; g/Advtg/Mktg Major, Univ GA.

LARSEN, KATHRYN ANN (BAKER) b/May 9, 1957; h/3217 Putty Hill Avenue, Parkville, MD 21234; m/ Lawrence Michael; p/Cornelia K Baker, Largo, FL; sp/Lawrence E Larsen, Balto, MD, and Rita S Larsen (dec); ed/Largo HS, 1975; BS, Wake Forest Univ, 1979; mil/AUS, 1979-83; pa/Served in Fin Corps, AUS, 1979-83; 1st Lt, AUS; CPT, AUS; cp/Ofcrs Christian F'ship; Phi Beta Kappa; Acctg Soc; Alpha Phi Omega, Treas; Intervarsity Christian F'ship; Band; CPT Color Guard; Intl Soc; Sertomaettes Ser Org; Ch Choir; r/ Prot; hon/Magna Cum Laude, 1979; ROTC S'ship; AM Pullen Acctg Awd, 1979; Phi Beta Kappa, 1979; CPA Exam; Superior Sophomore Cadet; AUS, ARCOM; HS Hon Soc; Other Biogl Listings; g/Intended Career Area, CPA.

LATZ, RONALD STEVEN oc/Student; b/Aug 9, 1963; h/6850 Harold Avenue North, Golden Valley, MN 55427; p/Robert and Carolyn Latz, Golden Val, MN; ed/Univ of WI; Am Univ, 1983; pa/Intern, Am Enterprise Inst for Public Policy Res, Sum 1983; Intern, Am Univ Wash Semester Prog, Fall 1983; Sales Conslt, Dayton's Dept Store, 1980-84; cp/Zeta Beta Tau Frat Secy 1983, S'ship Chm 1982-83; Mortar Bd, 1983-84; Soc of the Mace, 1983-85; Phi Eta Sigma, 1982; B'nai B'rith Yth Org Intl VP 1979-80, Chapt Pres 1979-80; Gtr Twin Cities Yth Symphs, 1978-80; US Col Wind Band European Tour, 1981; Univ of WI Hons Prog; Vol Campaign Wkr, 1982 MN Gubernatorial Campaign of Warren Spannaus; Univ of WI Jazz Ensemble, 1981-84; r/Jewish; hon/Dean's List, Univ WI, 1981-83; Sophomore Hons, Univ WI, 1982; Finalist, Wash Crossing Foun S'ship Contest, 1981; Nat Merit S'ship Competition Commend Scholar, 1981; NHS, 1979-81; B'nai B'rith Yth Org Silver Shield of David Awd, Intl Life Mbrship, 1980; Hon Grad w Distn, Lindbergh HS, 1981; All-Am Hall of Fame Hons; Optimist Clb S'ship Awd, 1979; Am Legion Sch Awd Prog, Hon Mention; Lindbergh HS Hon Roll, 1980-81; MN St HS Leag Music Contests Superior Rating, St Contest Solo & Quartet, 1980; Yg Commun Ldrs of Am; Intl Yth in Achmt; W/W Among Am HS Students; Intl W/W Frats & Sororities; g/ Maj in Polit Sci; Attend Law Sch; Atty, Polits &/or Govt Ser.

LAUE, SCOTT KEVIN oc/Student; b/ Nov 11, 1960; h/5510 Blackthorn Drive, Rockford, IL 61107; p/Louis and Jacqueline Laue, Rockford, IL; ed/Guilford HS, 1979; BS, Bradley Univ, 1983; cp/Activs Coun of Bradley Univ, Asst Concert Coor 1981, Concert Coor 1982, Financier 1983; Student Activs Budget Review Com, 1980-83; Undergrad Assn; Delta Upsilon Frat; Am Mktg Assn; Soc for Advmt of Mgmt; Pre-Law Clb; hon/Eagle Scout, 1975; Nat Hon Soc, 1978-79; Omicron; Delta Kappa Ldrship Hon Soc, 1981-83; Yg Personalities; Commun Ldrs of Am; Bradley Univ Recog Recip, 1981, 1982, 1983; All Univ Tennis Champ; All Univ Golf Runner-up; W/W Among Am Cols & Univs; g/Pursue Law Career.

LAUGHTER, TARA CHARLEEN oc/ Student; b/Mar 7, 1964; h/3202 Ellsworth Drive, Greenville, NC 27834; p/ Joseph and Mabel Laughter, Greenville, NC; ed/Rose HS, 1982; St Mary's Col; cp/Swim Team; Keywanettes; Art Clb; hon/1st Pl Ceramics Div & Poetry Div, Assn Indep Schs NC; Lttr, Swim Team, Intl Yth in Achmt; g/Industrial Psychol.

LAWRENCE, KIMBERLY DAWN oc/ Student; b/Feb 8, 1966; h/1120 Second Street, Blue Ridge, VA 24064; p/Mr and Mrs Joey L Lawrence, Blue Ridge, VA; ed/Lord Botetourt HS, 1984; cp/Ch Grp; Softball; Basketball; Lettered Volleyball; Lettered Track; r/So Bapt; hon/Homecoming Ct; Queen; Blue Ridge Dist Volleyball Champs; Reg III Volleyball Champs; 4th in St Volleyball Tour; g/ to Attend Col.

LAWSON, DANA ALEX oc/Attorney; b/Jun 27, 1958; h/1926 South Jefferson Street, Casper, WY 82601; ba/ Same; p/Dan A and Darel Lawson, Casper, WY; ed/Kelly Walsh HS, 1976; BS, Univ of WY, 1980; JD, Univ of WY Col of Law, 1983; pa/Casper Area C of C, 1977-80; Polit Advr & Legal Intern, Bryan E Sharratt, 1981; Legal Intern, Bagley, Hickey, Evans & Statkus, 1982; cp/Albany Co Dem Ctl Com Treas; WY Nat Com'man for Yg Dem of Am; Pres, Univ Campus Dems; WY St Legis, Legis Intern; Student Tchg Asst, Univ Sci Dept; WY Kennedy for Pres Com; r/ First Bapt Ch; hon/Nat Dean's List; Outstg Yg Men of Am; Intl Yth in Achmt; W/W Among Am Law Students.

LAWSON, MARK ALAN oc/Student; b/Sep 13, 1962; h/379 North Perkins Road, Memphis, TN 38117; p/ Dr and Mrs James W Lawson, Memphis, TN; ed/Briarcrest Bapt HS, 1980; BSEE, Christian Brothers Col, 1984; cp/NHS; Mu Alpha Theta; Concert Chorus; Memphis Symph Chorus; Tau Beta Pi, Secy; IEEE, Secy; Alpha Chi; r/Meth; hon/HS Dir Awd; Dean's List; 10 Top Rising Srs; Top 20 Scholars; Eagle Scout; Outstg Jr Citizen; Hon Roll; W/ W Among Am HS Students; Soc of Dist'd Am HS Students; g/Med, Biomed Engrg.

LAWTON, JOSEPH JAMES III oc/ Student; b/Aug 24, 1963; h/Route 5, Box 507, Hartsville, SC 29550; p/Joseph J II and Penn A Lawson, Hartsville, SC; ed/ Choate Rosemary Hall, 1977-81; Duke Univ, 1981-85; pa/Byerly Hosp, Sum 1982; Transport, Recovery Rm, Duke Univ Hosp; Nurse's Aid, 1982; cp/ Varsity Golf, 1977-81; Capt, Golf, 1981; Student Govt, Election Com Chm, 1981; Duke Univ Sailing Clb, 1983; French Clb, 1983; Chapt Secy, Beta Theta Pi, 1983; r/Epis; hon/Grad w Hons in Eng, French, Math; 7th in CT on Natl French Exam; Layman Prize, 1978; Dean's List & Class Hons at Duke, 1982-83; g/Pre-Med, French Major; Med Sch.

LAY, GREGORY ALLEN oc/Student, Employee of Lay Tree & Brush Co; b/ Oct 3, 1964; h/General Delivery, Baileys Switch, KY 40905; p/Kenneth and Judy Lay, Bailey's Switch, KY; ed/Knox Ctl HS, 1983; Col Law Enforcement, En KY Univ; cp/Gamma Beta Phi Hons Soc; r/ Bapt; hon/W/W Among Am HS Students; Soc of Dist'd Am HS Students; Nat Dean's List; Dean's List; g/BS in Police Adm.

LAY, VICTOR HALL oc/Student; b/ Oct 15, 1965; h/Route 2, Box 329, Waynesboro, TN 38485; p/Mr and Mrs Joseph V Lay, Waynesboro, TN; ed/ Wayne Co HS; pa/Farm Wk; cp/Marching Band Secy, Band Counsel, Chm; Adv'd Math Clb, Pres; Secy, FFA; Treas, Sr Ofcr; r/Ch of Christ; hon/US Achmt Acad, 1982; Essay Awd, 1982; g/to become an Astronaut; Aerospace Study.

LEACH, CYNTHIA DIANE oc/Student; b/Nov 9, 1958; h/7419 Gerald Drive, Middleburg Heights, OH 44130; ba/Cleveland, OH; ed/PhD Cand, Case Wn Resv Univ; MS 1982, BA 1980, Anderson Col; pa/Res Assoc, Mgmt Sci Grp, Standard Oil of OH; cp/Opers Res Soc Am; Inst of Mgmt Sci; VP, Student

Chapt of ORSA at Case Wn Univ; r/ Prot, Organist, Music Coor, Sun Sch Tchr, Lakeview Ch of God; hon/Omega Rho Hon Soc; Alpha Lambda Delta; Alpha Chi; Sigma Zeta; Kappa Mu Epsilon; Grad Magna Cum Laude w Hons in Math; W/W Among Students in Am Univs & Cols; W/W Among Am HS Students; g/complete PhD; Opers Res Analyst.

LEACH, LYNNETTA JANE oc/Medical Social Worker; b/Apr 10, 1958; h/ 10206 Independence Boulevard, Number 22, Parma Heights, OH 44130; ba/Middleburg Hgts, OH; m/Mark Ronald; p/Leonard and Elsie Snuffer, Parma Hgts, OH; sp/Ronald and Marilyn Leach, Middleburg Hgts, OH; ed/Valley Forge HS, 1976; BSW, Anderson Col, 1980; MSSW, Univ Louisville, Kent Sch of Social Wk, 1981; pa/ Med Social Wkr, SW Gen Hosp, 1982-; Med Social Wkr, Marymount Hosp, 1982; Cnslr, Shelter House for Runaway Yth, 1980-81; Med Social Wkr, Luth Hosp, 1980; Bob's Pro Shop, 1979-80; Nat Assn Social Wkrs, 1980-; cp/Cnslr of Sr Yth, Lakeview Ch of God; Pres, Anderson Social Wkrs, 1979-80; Pres, Arete Pep, 1979-80; Vol at Juv Detention Ctr; Vol in Probation; Wom of the Ch of God; Ctr for Public Ser; Tri-S Yth Cnslg Missions; Anderson Wom's Track Team; Gtr Cleveland Oncology Social Wkrs; r/Prot; hon/Miss Congeniality, Jr Miss Pageant; Intl Yth in Achmt; Outstg Yg Wom of Am; Nat Yth in Achmt; Nat Dean's List; g/PhD; Dir of a Social Ser Dept in a Hosp; Pvt Pract.

LEACH, MARK RONALD oc/Student; b/Mar 3, 1961; h/7419 Gerald Drive, Middleburg Heights, OH 44130; p/Mr and Mrs Ronald Leach, Middleburg Hgts, OH; ed/Midpark HS, 1979; BS, Case Wn Resv Univ; pa/Res Asst, Case Wn Resv Univ, 1981; cp/Tau Beta Pi Hon Soc; Student Mem, IEEE; r/Prot; hon/HS Valedictorian; Nat Merit Finalist; Dean's High Hon List; Smith S'ship; OH Bd of Regents S'ship; W/W Among HS Students; g/MS in Sys Engrg.

LEATHERS, TERRI LYNN oc/Student; b/Jan 26, 1962; h/Meadowbrook Ulg B 131, Ponca City, OK 74601; p/ R Max Leathers, Ponca City, OK; B Ann Leathers, Ponca City, OK; ed/Ponca City HS, 1980; OK City Univ; pa/ Conoco Inc, 1981-83; cp/Gamma Phi Beta Sorority; Softball Team, Volleyball Team, OK City Univ; FCA; r/1st Ch of God; hon/Rookie of Yr, Volleyball 1981; Mem, OK Jr Olympic Volleyball Team; Most Valuable Player, Softball, 1981; Volleyball & Softball S'ship; W/W Among Am HS Students; g/Gen Bus Maj.

LEE, AMELIA BETH oc/Staff Nurse in General Medicine; b/Mar 8, 1961; h/ Route 2, Box 157-A, Benson, NC 27504; ba/Benson, NC; p/Mr and Mrs Kenneth M Lee, Benson, NC; ed/S Johnston HS, 1979; BS, Cum Laude, Atlantic Christian Col, 1983; pa/Nurse Extern Sum 1983, Staff Nurse, Pitt Co Meml Hosp; cp/Atlantic Christian Col Nsg Hon Soc; VP, ACC Sr Nsg Class, 1983; ACC Bapt Student Union, 1980-81; 3 Yr Lttrwom on the ACC Softball Team, 1981-83; ACC Col Band, 1982; Student Nurses Assn, 1981-83; Nat Leag for Nsg, 1983; Co-Capt ACC Softball Team, 1982-83; r/Bapt; hon/Marshal at Atlantic Chris-

tian Col Dept of Nsg Pin Presentation, 1982; Most Valuable Player Awd Softball, 1983; Most Outstg Sr Nsg Student of 1983 Awd; W/W Among Students in Am Univs & Cols; g/Master's Deg in Geriatric Nsg.

LEE, BARBARA MARY oc/Student; b/Sep 2, 1965; h/7 Winchester Drive, Freehold, NJ 07728; ba/Canton, NY; p/ Mr and Mrs Robert E Lee, Freehold, NJ; ed/The Peddie Sch; St Lawrence Univ; pa/Self Employed Photog; Student; cp/ Pres, Outing Clb; Mng Editor, Peddie News; Photog for Yrbook & Paper; Drama Clb Publicity Dir; Chm, Winter Carnival; Chm, Sprg Carnival; Field Hockey & Softball; Pres, Ch Yth Grp; r/Cath; hon/Num Articles Pub in HS Paper; Grad Cum Laude, 1983; Hon Soc; Walter H Annenberg Awd; g/BA Eng; Law Sch.

LEE, BRENDA STEWART oc/Student; b/Jun 8, 1961; h/5143 North Oak Street, Kansas City, MO 64118; ba/ Kansas City, MO; m/R Douglas; p/Mr and Mrs Richard Stewart, Purdy, MO; sp/Mr and Mrs Bob Ward, Westplains, MO; ed/Purdy HS, 1979; BA, Baylor Univ, 1982; MDiv Student, MWn Bapt Theol Sem, 1983-; pa/Co-Employed as Ch Planters, Home Mission Bd of the So Bapt Conv, 1984-; cp/Chi's Wom's Ser Org, 1981-82; Histn, 1981; Parliamentn, 1982; Pledge Capt, 1982; Wom in Min; Secy, Treas, 1984-85; r/So Bapt; hon/MFA S'ship, 1979-80; Acad S'ship, 1982; Pres S'ship, 1983-84; Betty Seats Meml S'ship, 1984-85; W/W Among Am HS Students; g/MDiv; PhD.

LEE, ERIKA SUE oc/Student; b/Jan 12, 1964; h/607 North Avenue C, Kermit, TX 79745; p/Jerry and Linda Lee, Kermit, TX; ed/Ozona HS, 1982; Att'g Wn TX Col; pa/Sales Clk, Clayton's Village Drug, 1980; Sales Clk, Tchr Store, 1981; Secy, Farmers Ins Agy, 1982; cp/Band, Secy 1981-82; HS Newspaper Editor, 1981-82; Annual Staff, 1981-82; Press Clb, 1982-83; Wn TX Newspaper Staff, 1982-83; Phi Theta Kappa Hon Soc, 1983; Tennis, 1980-82; r/Bapt; hon/Num Articles in Sch Newspaper; Cheerldr, 1981-82; Class Treas, 1981-82; Newspaper Editor, 1981-82; Band Secy, 1981-82; Hon Grad, 1982; Wn TX News Editor & Cartoonist, 1982-83; Best Citizen, 1982.

LEE, IVY HENRIETTA oc/Student; b/Feb 10, 1962; h/2-D South Street, Charleston, SC 29403; ba/Raleigh, NC; p/2-D South Street, Charleston, SC; ed/ Charles A Brown HS, 1980; St Augustine's Col, 1984; cp/Alpha Kappa Alpha Sorority Inc, Tamiouchos, Parliamentn; Dean of Pledgees; Kappa Delta Pi Nat Ed Hon Soc; Nat Tech Assn, Corres Secy 1983-84; Student Govt Assn Legis Mem, 1982-84; Hlth Careers Clb, Treas, 1983; PE Majors Clb, 1984; Pen Newspaper, Reporter & Photog; OEA; Jr & Sr Hon Soc; Beta Clb; Photo Clb; r/Cath; hon/Kappa Delta Pi Nat Ed Hon Soc; Alpha Kappa Mu Nat Hon Soc; Deans List; United Negro Col Fund; Meharry Med Col & Fisk Univ PreMed Sum Inst; Soc Dist'd Am HS Students; g/Grad Sch, Public Hlth; wk w Nat Inst Public Hlth & Mtl Hlth.

LEE, JANNA oc/Student; b/Oct 12, 1963; h/Post Office Box 63, Enterprise, MS 39330; p/Nettie Mallard Davis, Stonewall, MS; ed/Enterprise HS, 1981; Jones Co Jr Col, 1981-82; AA, Meridian

Jr Col, 1984; pa/Salesperson, Clk, Shirt Closet; Editor, Meridian Jr Col Student Newslttr; cp/Corres Secy, Phi Theta Kappa, Nu Upsilon Chapt, 1983; Cheerldr; Beta Clb, 1978-81; FHA, 1978-81; Student Coun Reporter, 1980-81; Secy, REC Clb, 1981; BSU, 1981; Meridian Jr Col Activs Bd; MIC Singers; r/Meth; hon/Nu's Notes, Newslttr for Phi Theta Kappa; Pres' List Scholar; Homecoming Queen, 1980-81; Salutatorian, HS; Miss Hospitality for Town of Enterprise, 1981-82; Intl Yth in Achmt; W/W Among Am HS Students; g/Communs Major.

LEE, JEANETTA L oc/Student; b/Apr 21, 1966; h/Post Office Box 131, Milford, VA 22514; p/Christopher and Jeanetta Lee, Milford, VA; ed/Carolina HS; cp/Student Coun Pres, VP 1982-83, Secy 1981-82; NAACP Yth Mem; Nat Hon Soc; hon/1st Class Girl Scout, 1980; Hugh O'Brien Yth Foun Ldrship Conf; Sum Transition & Enrichment Prog; g/Pediatrician.

LEE, JOSEPH THOMAS oc/Assistant Foreman; b/Dec 11, 1959; h/7 Winchester Drive, Freehold, NJ 07728; p/Robert and Margaret Lee, Freehold, NJ; ed/BA, Bucknell Univ, 1982; Att'g Hofstra Univ Law Sch; pa/Sum Delivery Driver, *Daily Racing Form*, 1982-; cp/Omicron Delta Kappa; Mortar Bd; Instr, Bucknell Univ Kung Fu Clb; Peer Cnslr; Programming Chm, Univ Coor Com on Human Sexuality; Alpha Phi Omega; Treas, Ph Lambda Theta; r/Cath; hon/Phi Eta Sigma; Omicron Delta Kappa; W/W Among Am HS Students; g/Master's Deg in Psychol; Law Deg.

LEE, KAREN DENISE oc/Student; b/ Jan 6, 1963; h/Post Office Box 33, Kuttawa, KY 42055; p/Keith and Bonnie Lee, Kuttawa, KY; ed/Lyon Co HS, 1981; Att'g Murray St Univ; cp/Kappa Delta Pi, VP 1984; Alpha Chi; Gamma Beta Phi; Alpha Lambda Delta; Student NEA; Secy, Beta Clb; Treas, FHA; Secy, Beta Clb; Pep Clb; r/Meth; hon/Outstg Sr; Most Intell, Sr W/W; Home Ecs Awd, 3 Yrs; Typing I Awd; W/W Among Am HS Students; g/Elem Ed.

LEE, KITTIE SUSAN oc/Active Duty in the USAF as a Professional Military Officer, Professional Registered Nurse; b/Feb 29, 1960; h/Buckhannon, WV 26201; ba/Belleville, IL; m/Ronald G; p/ David and Margaret Palchik, Bloomfield, CT; sp/Bert and Macel Lee, Buckhannon, WV; ed/BS, WV Wesleyan Col, 1983; Bloomfield HS, 1978; mil/ USAF, 2nd Lt; pa/Staff Nurse, St Joseph's Hosp, 1983; Profl RN, Profl Mil Ofcr, USAF, 1983-; cp/Sigma Theta Tau Nat Hon Soc of Nsg; Student Nurses of Wesleyan; r/Prot; hon/Grad w Hons, 1978; USAF Ldrship Awd, 1983; g/MS in Nsg.

LEE, PAULA KAY oc/Student; Paraprofessional; b/Feb 27, 1964; h/5532 West Vernon Avenue, Phoenix, AZ 85035; ba/Phoenix, AZ; p/Paul and Wanda Lee, Phoenix, AZ; ed/DeVry Inst of Tech; cp/Maryvale HS German Clb Assoc Student Clbs Rep; Maryvale HS HERO Clb Chapt Pres; Maryvale HS HERO; hon/HERO of the Yr, 1982; AZ HERO St Ofcr of the Yr, 1982; Dean's List; Yg Ldrs of Am; g/Computer Programmer.

LEE, ROBERT HANNA oc/Student; b/ h/2826 Haynes, Midland, TX 79705; p/ Midland, TX; ed/Robert E Lee HS; TX

A & M Univ; cp/BSA; pre-Med Soc TX A & M; hon/Eagle Scout, 1977; HS Hon Grad, 1982; Gifted & Talented Prog of TX, 1976-78; g/Pre-Med Student; MD.

LEE, SHERRYE PATRICIA oc/Student; b/Nov 1, 1964; h/Route 1, Box 400, Dunn, NC 28334; p/Mr and Mrs Billy S Lee, Dunn, NC; ed/Midway HS; cp/Pres Sr Class; Secy Jr Class; VP Sophomore Class; Student Coun VP; Sci Clb Ofcr; French Clb VP; Beta Clb Secy; Book Clb Reporter; Annual Staff; r/Bapt; hon/Chief Marshall, 1982; Outstg Sr,1983; Att'd Gov's Sch, 1981; Att'd Close-Up, 1981; Flute Sect Ldr in Band, 1982; Finalist, NC St Univ S'ship, 1983; Rec'd UFCW S'ship, 1983; g/NC St Univ Sch of Agri & Life Sci; Master's or Doct in Genetics.

LEE, WANDA MAE oc/Student; b/Mar 11, 1963; h/Route 6, Box 246, Dunn, NC 28334; p/Warren D and Judy W Lee, Dunn, NC; ed/S Johnston HS, 1981; Univ NC-Chapel Hill; pa/Res Tech, Biol Sci Res Ctr, 1982-83; cp/Student Am Pharm Assn,1983-84; 3-Yr Mem of Student Govt in HS, 1978-81; Mem, Nat Hon Soc, 1979-81; r/So Bapt; hon/Salutatorian Sr HS, 1981; Drum Major & Pres of Band in HS, 1980-81; Morehead Nom, 1982; g/BS Deg in Pharm.

LEEPER, STEPHANIE CHRISTMON oc/Medical Student; b/Aug 4, 1961; h/Route 3, Apartment 3, Lynn Road, Johnson City, TN 37601; m/Keith Anthony; p/Mr and Mrs James E Christmon, Manchester, TN; sp/Mr and Mrs Earl Leeper, Church Hill, TN; ed/Ctl HS, 1979; TN Technol Univ, 1982; BS, E TN ST Univ, 1983; Att'g Quillen-Dishner Col Med, E TN St Univ; pa/Head Resident of Dorm, TN Technol Univ, 1981; Resident Advr 1982-83, Spec Progs Dept Tutor 1982-83, E TN St Univ; cp/Chem-Med Clb, 1981-82; Alpha Kappa Alpha Sorority, Inc, 1981-82; Secy, Grammateus/Epistoleus; Alpha Lambda Delta Hon Soc,1981; Am Chem Soc, 1982-83; Am Acad of Fam Phys, 1983; r/Christian; hon/Alpha Lambda Hon Soc; Dean's List, 1979-82; Mortar Bd, 1982; g/Primary Care or Pediatrics.

LEGER, JAIME ADAM oc/Student; b/Aug 6, 1965; h/5243 Ardelle Street, Stockton, CA 95205; p/Mrs Valerie J Leger, Stockton, CA; ed/Franklin HS, 1983; Att'g San Joaquin Delta Jr Col; cp/HS Wrestling; Jr Achmt, VP; r/Greek Orthodox; Franklin HS Acad Achmt Awd; Jr Achmt Cert Awd; Outstg Citizenship Awd; Cert of Completion, Voc Ed Prog; Jr Achmt Ofcr of Yr Finalist Awd; Jr Achmt Cert of Accomplishment Awd; W/W Am HS Students; Outstg Yths; g/Law Sch; Law.

LEGROS, SANDRA LYNN oc/Accountant; b/Sep 27, 1961; h/1915 State Road 59 L11, Kent, OH 44240; ba/Kent, OH; p/Larry and Janet Legros, Deerfield, OH; ed/BBA, Kent St Univ, 1983; SE HS, 1980; pa/Acct, Kent St Univ; cp/Beta Alpha Psi; KSU Acctg Assn; Alpha Xi Delta; Intl Order of Rainbow for Girls; Quill & Scroll; Mod Music Masters; r/Meth; hon/OH Bd of Regents Acad S'ship, 1980-84; KSU S'ship, 1982-84; Dean's List, 1981; Beta Alpha Psi Acctg Hon; W/W Am HS Students; g/CPA, MBA.

LEIGH, WILLIAM LEWIS III oc/Student; b/Jul 8, 1964; h/5634 Mt Gilead Road, Centreville, VA 22020; p/Lewis Jr and Rosalie Leigh, Centreville, VA; ed/Robinson Sec'dy Sch; Univ VA; cp/The Archeological Soc VA; Am Angus Assn; Co of Mil Histns; Nat Hon Soc; Key Clb; Wrestling Team; No VA Relic Hunters Assn; Ftball & Track Team; 4-H Staffing Task Force; VA St 4-H Pres, 1982-83; CoChm St 4-H Ldrship Citizenship, Commun Resource Devel Component Com; VA 4-H Coun; St 4-H Ambassador; r/Meth; hon/"4-H Ldrship Survey: A Baseline Study of Vol Involvement in 4-H Programming", 1980; USA Del to Canadian Nat 4-H Conf; VA Del to Nat 4-H Conf; Most Likely to Succeed; Fac Awd; Co Sch-Commun Relats Awd; VA Gov Sch for the gifted; Outstg Bus Student Area IV Schs; Most Outstg Jr Awd; "I Dare You Awd"; W/W Among Am HS Students; Commun Ldrs of Am; g/Law.

LEININGER, MARVIN JAMES JR oc/Engineer; b/Jan 10, 1961; h/462 North Wickham Road, Apartment 270, Melbourne, FL 32935; p/Mr and Mrs Marvin J Leininger, Huntington Valley, PA; ed/Lower Moreland HS, 1978; BS, Penn St Univ, 1982; MS, Stanford Univ, 1983; pa/Sr Engr, Harris Corporation, 1983; cp/Stanford Symph Orch & Jazz Band; Symph Blue Band; Mar Blue Band; Phi Mu Alpha Sinfonia; Soc of Engrg Sci; Phi Mu Alpha Jazz, German & Dixieland Bands; r/Christian; hon/Outstg Freshman Engrg Awd; Pres Freshman Awd; Tau Beta Pi.

LEIPPRANDT, DOUGLAS J oc/Student, Beverage Manager; b/Apr 11, 1962; h/Post Office 312, Williamston, MI 48895; p/Robert and Diana Leipprandt, Williamston, MI; ed/Williamston HS, 1980; No MI Univ, 1984; pa/Asst Mgr, Star of Chgo; cp/Am Mktg Assn, VP; Eagle Scout Coun, BSA; Explorer Post; H S Student Coun; r/Williamston United MethCh; hon/Eagle Scout; Dean's List; g/BS Mktg; MBA.

LEMMON, CAROLYN ANN oc/Student; b/Sep 1, 1963; h/401 Saddle Tree, New Braunfels, TX 78130; ba/Ft Worth, TX; p/Mr and Mrs Joe B Lemmon, New Braunfels, TX; ed/New Braunfels HS, 1981; cp/Band, Sect Ldr & Capt, 1980-81; Nat Hon Soc; Asst Editor of HS Yrbook; Univ Symph Orch; Mid-TX Flute Clb; Mu Phi Epsilon, Histn; Tom Brown/Jarvis Living-Lrng Expt, Secy; Disciple Student F'ship; r/Meth; hon/TX All State Band; Twelve Superior Univ Inter-Scholastic Leag Solo & Ensemble Ratings; Most Outstg Girl in Jr & Sr HS Band; New Braunfels Music Study Clb S'ship Winner; Rotary Outstg Student, 1981; Dean's Hon List; Dick Hanley Meml Acad Achmt Awd; Phi Kappa Lambda Hon Recital; W/W Among Am HS Students; g/BMus Deg in Flute Perf, BS Elem Ed.

LEMOINE, MELANIE M oc/Registered Nurse; b/May 24, 1961; h/204 N Demanade Drive, Lafayette, LA 70503; ba/Lafayette, LA; p/John D Lemoine, Lafayette, LA; ed/Lafayette HS, 1979; BSN, Univ SWn LA, 1983; pa/Charge Nurse 1983–, Nurse Aide IV 1982-83, Nurse Aide II 1981-82, Pharm Clk 1979-81, Lafayette Gen Hosp; cp/SWn Assn Student Nurses, 1981-83, Histn 1982-83; LA Assn of Student Nurses, 1981-83; Student Nurses Assn, 1981-83; Alt Del to the SNA St Conv; ANA; LA Nurses Assn; Sigma Theta Tau; r/Cath; hon/Sigma Theta Tau, 1983-84; Awd for SASN Yrbook, 1982-83; W/W Among Am HS Students; g/Master's in Pediatric Nsg.

LEMOINE, ROBERT EDWARD oc/Licensed Practical Nurse; b/Mar 25, 1961; h/52 Riddle Street, Manchester, NH; m/Valerie J; p/Richard J (dec) and Lillian Lemoine, Norwich, CT; sp/Mr and Mrs Herbert Horne, Ledyard, CT; ed/Norwich Free Acad, 1979; Norwich Reg Voc Tech Sch; cp/Asst Scoutmaster; VP, Pract Nurse Ed Prog; Hosp Vol; r/Cath; hon/Eagle Scout; Intl Yth in Achmt; W/W Among Am HS Students; g/ADN.

LEMONS, MARTY H oc/Student; b/Nov 16, 1962; h/Route 1, Box 176, Madison, NC 27025; ba/Pembroke, NC; p/Harvey C and Ella Louise Lemons, Madison, NC; ed/S Stokes HS; Pembroke St Univ; cp/Beta Clb; Basketball, Ftball, Track & Cross Country in HS; Ch Softball Team; Cnslr for Ch Yth Grp; r/Bapt; Most Valuable Track, Cross-Country; Most Improved; Competed in NAIA Nationals; g/Qualify for the 1988 Olympics.

LeMOSY, ELLEN KAY oc/Student; b/Aug 30, 1963; h/514 S Hickory Street, Melbourne, FL 32901; ba/Orlando, FL 32816; p/Frederick L and Joan S LeMosy, Melbourne, FL; ed/Melbourne HS, 1980; BS, Univ Ctl FL, 1984; pa/Res Asst 1982-84, Pt-time Wk as Circulation Dept Asst 1981-82, Univ Ctl FL; cp/Pre-Profl Med Soc, 1981-84; Pres 1983-84, Secy 1982-83; Acad Peer Advisement Team, 1983-84; Wesley Foun, 1980-82, VP 1982; Am Mensa, 1980–; r/Christian; hon/Delta Tau Kappa; Omicron Delta Kappa; Phi Kappa Phi; Nat Merit S'ship; Acad Excell Awd; Alumni Assn S'ship; Grad Summa Cum Laude; W/W Among Students in Cols & Univs; g/MD/PhD in Immunol/Pediatrics.

LEMPESIS, COSTA PETER oc/Teacher; b/Sep 9, 1957; h/1334 Bryjo Place, Charleston, SC 29407; p/Gus and Canela Lempesis, Charleston, SC; ed/Middleton HS, 1975; BA, Univ of SC; The Citadel; cp/NEA; Scoutmaster; Staff, Camp Barstow, BSA; Staff, Camp Merrimac; Vol, Hotline; hon/Teenager of the Mo; Yth Ldrs Intl; W/W Among Am HS Students; g/To Be the Best in Chosen Field of Ed.

LENAGHAN, DONNA DISMUKE oc/Youthworker; b/Nov 28, 1954; h/8418 Lynwood Place, Chevy Chase, MD 20815; m/Michael J; p/Mr and Mrs C V Fraser Jr, Old Hickory, TN; sp/Mary Lenaghan; ed/Dupont Sr HS, 1972; BA, Salem Col, 1976; Univ MO; pa/Yth Coor, Chevy Chase Presb Ch, 1983–; Prog Conslt, Nat Hemophilia, Nat Red Cross Ldrship Prog; cp/Bd Dirs, Metro Wash Area, 1983-86; Bd Deacons, CCPC, 1983-86; Assn of Vol Admrs; GSA Vol; U Way Vol; Vol Safety Instr, Red Cross; Metro Coun on Aging; Campfire Vol; r/Presb; hon/Mayors Coun on Yth Devel; Intl Yth in Achmt; Outstg Yg Commun Devel; Commun Devel World; g/Profl Conslt in Prog Devel & Adm.

LENZ, VICTORIA YOUNG oc/Student; b/Apr 17, 1962; h/507 Riverside Drive, New Braunfels, TX 78130; p/Mr George M Lenz, Maryland Hgts, MO; ed/Klein HS, 1980; Att'g SW TX St Univ; cp/Varsity Volleyball; HS Volleyball, Tennis Teams; r/Meth; hon/Grad Cum Laude, 1980, HS; Dean's List, SW TX St Univ, 1982; g/Indust Relats.

LEONG, DEBORAH JOYCE oc/Student; b/Feb 15, 1962; h/134 High School Avenue, Cranston, RI 02910; p/Fook J and Anne Leong, Cranston, RI; ed/ Cranston E HS, 1980; Boston Col; cp/ Spanish Clb Treas; Nat Hon Soc; RI Hon Soc Math Team; Chem Team; Guid Aide; Med Arts Clb; Spanish Hon Soc; Sch Newspaper; Asian Clb; Computer Acad; hon/Author of "Penny", *Am Col Poets Anthology*, 1981; Magna Cum Laude Nat Latin Exam Cert; Dean's List; Intl Yth in Achmt; W/W Among Am HS Students; Yg Commun Ldrship; g/BS Computer Sci.

LERMA, LOUISE KATHLEEN oc/ Student; b/Feb 26, 1961; h/521 Airport Road, Number 205, Santa Fe, NM 87501; p/Wilfred Lerma, Espanola, NM; Gloria Lerma, Sante Fe, NM; ed/Espanola Val HS, 1979; Univ of NM; pa/Res Asst, Fetal Alcohol Syndrome Res; cp/ Nat Student Exchg to Bowling Green St Univ; NM St Lions Band; Vol, Glaucoma, Diabetes, High Blood Pressure Clinic; Capt, Flag Corps; r/Rom Cath; hon/Valedictorian; Univ NM Pres/Alumni S'ship; Univ NM Varsity Cheerldr; W/W Among Am HS Students; g/MD, RN, Univ of NM.

LeROY, CLARE MARIE oc/Student; b/Aug 7, 1962; h/127 South Fulton Avenue, Sturgeon Bay, WI 54235; ba/ Milwaukee, WI; p/Francis and Elly LeRoy, Sturgeon Bay, WI; ed/Sturgeon Bay HS; Att'g Univ WI-Eau Claire; cp/ Phi Beta Lambda, 1982-84, Treas 1983-84; Beta Gamma Sigma, 1983-84; Phi Kappa Phi, 1984; Wom's Chorus I, 1980-84; Social Coor, 1983, Pres 1983-84; r/Cath; hon/Beta Gamma Sigma Hon, 1983; Phi Kappa Phi Hon, 1984; MIS S'ship, 1984; Dean's List, 1980-84; g/Mgmt Info Sys Maj; Career as Sys Analyst.

LESHER, ARTHUR BRECHT III oc/ Electronics Instructor; b/Jul 27, 1960; h/ 1829 Colony Drive, Colony Park, Wyomissing, PA 19610; ba/Norfolk, VA; p/Mr and Mrs Robert W Blotz, Wyomissing, PA; and Mr and Mrs Arthur B Lesher Jr, Jim Thorpe, PA; ed/ Exeter Township HS, 1978; Elect Tech "A" Sch, 1979; Instr Tng Sch, 1983; mil/ Elect Tech 2nd Class, USN Seaman; pa/ Sch Command NTC, Great Lakes, 1978-79; Elect Tech 3rd Class, USS Johnston, 1979-80; Elect Tech 2nd Class, FLTCORGRU, 2 NAB LCRK, VA, 1980-83; Instr ET Sch FTC Norfolk VA, 1983-; cp/Jr Achmt of Reading & Berks Co, 1975-78k; Exeter Twp HS Yrbook Staff Photog, 1977-78; Little Leag Coach, 1981; Lansford Elks Lodge 1337, 1982-; Studebaker Driver's Clb, 1983-; r/Luth; hon/EXETER Twp HS Yrbook Photo, 1977-78; Jr Achmt Annual Reports, 1976-78; Outstg Yg Businessman, 1978; Del Nat Jr Achmt Conf, 1978; Sailor of the Qtr; W/W Among Am HS Students; Commun Ldrs of Am; Yth in Achmt; g/Deg in Elect Engrg; to Own a Business.

LESLIE, CARL EVANS oc/Teacher; b/Apr 25, 1956; h/Route 2, Box 345-C, Lawndale, NC 28090; p/Mrs Odessia Leslie, Lawndale, NC; ed/Burns HS, 1975; Livingstone Col, 1979; KS St Univ, 1982; UNCC, Adm Cert; pa/Tchr, Gaston Co Sch; cp/Alpha Phi Alpha;

Mosaic Masonic Lodge; NAACP, Co-Chm Ed Com; Livingston Col Alumni Pres; r/AME Zion; hon/Hon Grad, Livingstone Col; NCAE's S'ship, 1975; Outstg Yg Men Am; Intl Yth in Achmt; Commun Ldrs Am; g/Doct Deg; Col Tchg.

LEVITT, RICHARD KAORU oc/ Student; b/Jan 4, 1965; h/153 Riversville Road, Greenwich, CT 06830; p/Martin Levitt, Greenwich, CT; ed/Greenwich HS, 1983; Att'g Fordham Univ; cp/Pres, World Hunger Action Grp, 1982-83; Greenwich HS Prog Team, Activs Coun, 1982-83; Key Clb Intl; Students Helping Our Commun; Hotline Agy; hon/Acad Hon Roll, 1982-83; Greenwich Co Day Sch Tennis Awd; Readak Rdg Achmt Awd; Pres Physical Fitness Awd; Commun Ldrs Am; g/Theatre Arts Deg.

LEWIS, JAY oc/District Executive, BSA; b/Jul 17, 1958; h/610 Broken Arrow, Roswell, NM 88201; ba/Roswell, NM; m/Shauna; p/Mr and Mrs John D Lewis, Denton, TX; sp/Mr and Mrs Bill Martin, Burleson, TX; ed/ Denton HS, 1976; BA, Baylor Univ, 1980; pa/Dist Exec, Longhorn Coun BSA, 1980-83; Dist Exec, Conquistador Coun BSA, 1983-; cp/Rotary Intl; Sigma Chi Alumni Assn; Roswell Baylor Clb; r/Prot; hon/Eagle Scout, 1974; Baylor Outstg Sr Man, 1980; g/Public Relats w Yth Related Agy.

LEWIS, KENNETH LYNN JR oc/ Student; b/Jul 19, 1962; h/Box 291, Trenton, GA 30752; p/Mr and Mrs Kenneth L Lewis Sr, Trenton, GA; ed/ NW GA HS, 1980; Univ of GA; cp/ Wesley Foun, Pres; BSA; 4-H; Student Coun; Beta Clb; Newspaper Staff Editor; Track Team; Tennis Team; Bands; Ag Eng Clb; Wesley Foun Music Coor; hon/Eagle Scout; Valedictorian; Master 4-H'er; I Dare You Awd; John Philip Sousa Awd; GA Sect ASAE Student Achmt Awd; Intl Yth in Achmt; Commun Ldrs of Am; Personalities of Am; Soc of Dist'd Am HS Students; W/ W Among Am HS Students; g/BS Agri Engrg.

LEWIS, LORI ANN oc/Student; b/ Mar 4, 1968; h/HCR 3-Box 707 Cumberland, KY 40823; p/Mr and Mrs Sammy R Lewis, Cumberland, KY; ed/ Cumberland HS; cp/FHA, 1982; Secy, Bapt Yth Org, 1982; Mem, SECC Commun Choir, 1982; r/Bapt; hon/Acad Hon Roll, 1982; US Achmt Acad Sci Awd Winner, 1983; g/Bus Deg.

LEWIS, ROBERTA MAYE oc/Salon Owner, Student; b/Apr 25, 1963; h/Box 36, Centerville, KS 66014; ba/Centerville, KS; p/Mrs Rolland Lewis, Centerville, KS; ed/Prairie View HS, 1981; Fort Scott Commun Col, 1982; Johnson Co Commun Col; cp/SS Tchr, Secy; Parade Chm, Centerville Day; 4-H Pres, Secy, Treas, Coun Mem; Ofc Aide; Mgr, Volleyball, Track, Basketball; Student Dir Play, Musical, Stage Band Secy; hon/ Nat Hon Soc; KS Key Awd 4-H; Intl Yth in Achmt; W/W Among Am HS Students; g/Sales Rep for Maj Co.

LEWIS, ZOE LYNN oc/Student; b/ Apr 15, 1967; h/Route 2, Box 119E, Cheraw, SC 29520; p/Mr and Mrs Richard M Lewis, Jr, Cheraw, SC; ed/ Cheraw HS; cp/Treas, Girl Scout Cadette; Sr Planning Bd, Sr Girl Scout; Mem of Student Govt Assn; Bible Clb; Ch Choir; Nat Jr Hon Soc; Lib Asst; AV

Aid; French Clb; r/Bapt; hon/Francis Burch Awd, Highest Average in Class, 1982-83; US Achmt Acad, Geometry, Algebra II; US Nat Ldrship Awd, 1983; French Awd, 1983; Typing, 1983; NEDT, 1983; Perfect Attendance, 1982, 1983; g/to attend the Bapt Col of Charleston.

LIGHT, ALLISON KAY oc/Student; b/Aug 8, 1963; h/121 South Florida Street, Buckhannon, WV; p/Mr and Mrs William B Light, S FL, Buckhannon, WV; ed/Buckhannon-Upshur HS, 1977-81; WV Wesleyan Col; pa/WV Wesleyan Col Lib, Cnslg & Placement Ofc; cp/Alpha Lambda Delta, 1982-83; Phi Beta Lambda, 1981-83; Nat Hon Soc, 1979-81; VP, Natl Hon Soc, 1980-81; Rhododendron Girls St, Sum 1980; UMYF Pres, 1980-81; Mem of Bugettes, 1979-81; Wesleyan Activs Com, 1981-; r/Meth; hon/Grad 6th in Sr Class, 1981; Alpha Lambda Delta, 1982-83; Am Legion Citizenship Awd, 1981; Outstg Teenager of Mo, 1980; Nat Hon Soc, 1979-81; W/W Among Am HS Students; g/Bus Adm Maj.

LIGHT, DANA LYNN oc/Student; b/ Nov 20, 1962; h/2007 Crestview, Kilgore, TX 75662; p/Mr and Mrs J B Light, Kilgore, TX; ed/Kilgore HS, 1981; AA, Jacksonville Col, 1983; cp/Pres, Nat Hon Soc; Pres, FTA; Student Coun Senate Aide, HS; Choral Dept Pianist, HS, 4 Yrs; Secy/Treas 2 Yrs, Pres 2 Yrs, Nat VP 1 Yr, St Girls' Missionary Aux; Phi Theta Kappa, 1981-83; Circle K Clb; Accompanist for Choral Dept; Accompanist for TX A & M Univ Wom's Chorus; r/Bapt; hon/Freshman Class Treas, 1981-82; Student Govt Treas, 1982-83; Homecoming Queen, 1983; Student of the Wk, 1981-82; Dean's List; DAR Good Citizen; Dist Future Tchr of Yr; Valedictorian; Best All-Around Girl; W/W in Music; g/Tch Eng.

LIGHT, DIANA J KELLEY oc/Sales Representative; b/Dec 11, 1955; h/53 Ophelia Drive, Maumelle, AR 72118; ba/Same; m/Paul E; p/Mr and Mrs Howard A Burleson, Elsberry, MO; ed/ Louisiana RII, Louisiana, MO, 1974; BS, AR St Univ, 1981; Master's of Applied Psychol, Univ AR, 1984; pa/Sales Rep, Adv'd Care Prods Div, Ortho Pharm Corp, 1984-; Territory Mgr, Intl Playtex Inc, 1981-84; cp/Am Cancer Soc Vol; Psi Chi, Treas; Gamma Beta Phi; Bd Mem Jonesboro Helpline; Wom of the Moose; Nat Hon Soc; Yrbook Editor; Secy, Student Coun; hon/MO Curators Scholar, 1974; Nat Dean's List, 1980-81; Hon Grad, 1981; Intl Yth in Achmt; W/W Am Cols & Univs; Personalities of S; g/to Obtain MA in Psychol.

LIJEWSKI, TIMOTHY MARK oc/ Student; b/Aug 29, 1963; h/3356 Van Ohsen Road, Summerville, SC 29483; ba/Spartanburg, SC; p/George Anthony and Elizabeth Alice Lijewski, Summerville, SC; ed/R B Stall HS, 1981; Wofford Col; pa/Cnslr, Camp Joy, Sum 1982-83; Cnslr, Wofford Gifted Prog, Sum 1982-83; Lib Employee, Wofford Col, 1981-83; cp/Campus Union of Wofford Col, 1982-; Jud Comm, 1983-84; Treas, Inter Frat Coun, 1983-84; Treas, Pi Kappa Alpha Frat, 1983-84; Cheerldr, 1982-83; cp/Cath Yth Org; Yth Choir, Ch; Varsity Soccer; Treas, Nat Hon Soc; Pres, Mu Alpha Theta; SGA; Student Coun; r/Cath; hon/Hall of Fame Mem,

HS; Wofford Scholar; Furman Scholar; Presb Scholar; W/W Among Am HS Students; Soc of Dist'd Am HS Students; g/Pediatrician.

LILES, SARAH ANN b/Jul 30, 1956; h/Route 2, Box 199, Polkton, NC 28135; ba/Wadesboro, NC; p/Mrs Mary Ann Staton, Polkton, NC; ed/Bowman Sr HS, 1974; BS, Winston-Salem St Univ, 1978; pa/Staff Nurse 1978-79, Public Health Nurse II 1979-83, Anson Co Hosp; cp/Nat Assn Univ Wom, 1981-83; Burnsville Social Clb; Yth Sers Agy, VP 1983; NC Child Safety Passenger Assn, 1983; NC Public Hlth Assn, 1982; r/ Bapt; hon/Nat Hon Soc, 1971-74; Hon Roll, 1974-75; g/Master's Deg in Pediatric Nsg.

LIN, CHING—CHING LAURA oc/ Student; b/Aug 12, 1962; h/6743 Crest Road, Rancho Palos Verdes, CA 90274; p/John and Margaret Lin, Rancho Palos Verdes, CA; ed/Palos Verdes HS, 1980; Wking Towards BSBA, Univ So CA; pa/ Pre-Med Secy, Sch of Lttr, Arts, & Sci, Sum 1982; Showcase Mgr, 520 Giftware Ctr, Sum 1981; cp/Trojan Marching Band, Uniform Staff 1981, Secy 1982; Student Senate, Student's Affair Com Chm, 1983; Student Musical Prodn, 1982-83; Jt-Ednl Proj Commun Ser, 1983; hon/Recip of Music Perf Awd/S'ship, 1981-83; Alpha Lambda Delta; Beta Gamma Sigma; Golden Key Nat Dean's List; g/Law Sch; CPA or Lwyr.

LINCOLN, RUTH ANN oc/Student; b/Aug 30, 1962; h/10890 Northvale Road, Route 4, Hernando, MS 38632; p/Mr and Mrs William R Lincoln, Hernando, MS; ed/So BaptEd Ctr, 1979; Union Univ; cp/Alpha Chi; Footlights Drama Clb; Little Sister, Alpha Tau Omega; FCA; BSU Secy; Dorm Coun VP; Miss Union Univ Pageant Contestant; Chm, Ticket Sales, Backstage Crew; Cheerldr; Vol, Ctr for Enrichment of Handicapped Chd & Spec Olympics; hon/Nat Dean's List; W/W Among Am Cols & Univs; Grad Magna Cum Laude, 1983; g/Master's of Spec Ed.

LINDER, LEESA ELAINA oc/Coordinator of Safety/Security; b/Apr 28, 1959; h/Route 3, Box 737, Salisbury, NC 28144; ba/Concord, NC; p/Mr and Mrs James Linder, Salisbury, NC; ed/S Rowan HS; AAS, Davidson Co Commun Col; BS, Univ NC-Charlotte; pa/ Telecommunicator, Salisbury PD, 1978-79; Tchr/Cnslr, Commun Ser Prog, NC Dept Corrections, 1981-82; Coor Safety & Security, Phillip Morris USA, 1982-; cp/Crim Justice Clb, 1980-82; Facilities & Students Affairs Com, 1980-81; Sophomore Senator of Student Govt Assn, Davidson Co Col, 1978-79; LAE Crim Justice Frat, 1977-82; Treas, LAE, 1977-78; r/Luth; hon/Res Concerning the Magisterial Function was Incl'd in *An Annotated Bibliog of NC Crim Justice Res*; Dean's List; g/Master's Deg in Crim Justice.

LINDLEY, ELIZABETH ADAMS oc/ Student; b/Jul 10, 1963; h/4811 Estrella Street, Tampa, FL 33609; p/Carlyn C Lindley, Tampa, FL; ed/Tampa Prep Sch, 1980; Harvard/Radcliffe Col; cp/Nat Forensic Leag; Nat Cath Forensic Leag; Intl Thespian Soc; Harvard Intl Relats Coun; Model UN; Harvard Students Helping Students; Leverett Arts Soc; hon/Pres Scholar in Theatre Arts; Nat

Forensic Leag Nat Champ in Oral Interpretation; Nat Cath Forensic Leag Nat Champ in Cong Debate; g/Career in Exptl Psychol or Mtl Hlth Adm.

LINDSEY, BOBBY CLARK oc/Student; b/Apr 2, 1964; h/Brookside Drive, Linden, TN 37096; p/Mrs Lillian Qualls, Linden, TN; ed/Perry Co HS, 1982; pa/ Ofc Pers 1979-81, Lifeguard 1982, Maintenance 1983, Camp Linden, TN Bapt Conv; cp/Perry Co HS Basketball, Baseball, 1980-82; Alpha Phi Omega Nat Ser Frat, TN Tech Univ, Sectional Rep & Sports Chm, 1983-84; r/So Bapt; hon/Best All Around, 1982; HS MVP Baseball, 1982; Most Ath, 1982; All-Midstate Class A, Third Team, 1982; Best Ath, Alpha Phi Omega, 1983; Capt, HS Basketball, 1982; HS Sr Class VP; W/W Among Am HS Students; g/ Bus Mgmt Maj, Systems Analyst.

LINDSEY, STEVEN LEE oc/Student; b/Apr 1, 1966; h/222 Cherokee Circle, Cedartown, GA 30125; p/Terry and Jean Lindsey, Cedartown, GA; ed/ Cedartownn HS, 1984; cp/VP, Jr & Sr Class, 1982-84; Student Coun, 1981-84; FCA Clb; Key Clb; Yth Coun; r/Bapt; hon/Math Awd/Nat Mert; Lettered 3 Yrs Each in Ftball, Baseball, Basketball; Bulldog Awd; Golden Helmet Awd; Exch Clb Yth of Mo; Optimist Clb Yth of Mo; W/W Among Am HS Students; g/GA Tech-Aerospace Engrg.

LING, KRISTIN oc/Student; b/Sep 29, 1965; h/502 Jeff Davis, Waveland, MS 39576; p/Edwin R and Ingrid J Ling, Waveland, MS; ed/Coast Epis HS, 1984; cp/Pres, Nat Hon Soc, 1983-84; Student Dir of Hancock Co MS, C of C, 1983-84; Secy, Sr Class, 1984; Mu Alpha Theta Nat HS & Jr Col Math Hon Soc, 1983-84; HS Spanish Clb & Physics Clb, 1983-84; r/Prot; hon/Valedictorian & Star Student, 1984; Rec'd S'ships to Coast Epis HS; Awd for High ACT Scores, 1983; Colleen Queen of Waveland Civic Assn at Annual St Patrick's Day Celebration; magna cum laude, 1982; Nat Latin; Nat Merit S'ship Finalist; Alpha Hon Roll; r/Prot; hon/ W/W Among Am HS Students; Soc of Dist'd Am HS Students; g/Chem &/or Envir Engrg.

LINTON, LOUCINDY DENISE oc/ Student; b/Apr 25, 1965; h/1010 West Indiana, Midland, TX 79701; p/Mr and Mrs Dalton E Linton, Midland, TX; ed/ Midland HS, 1983; cp/Band, Chaplin & Homecoming Duchess; Ch Choirs & Yth F'ship; Softball; Majorette; Ch Orch; r/Indep Bapt; hon/Twirling, 3 Lttrs; Debate, 1 Lttrs; Yth Merit Awd, Rotarians; 2nd Runner-Up in W TX Nat Teenager Pageant; W/W Among Am HS Students; Soc Dist'd HS Students; g/ Attend Baylor Univ, Maj in Acctg.

LISLE, CURTIS RAYMOND oc/ Student; b/Oct 4, 1963; h/1010 South Patrick Drive, Indialantic, FL; ed/ Melbourne HS, 1981; GA Inst of Technol; pa/Power & Signal Systems Inc; DBA Systems Inc; cp/Band; Mun Band; Theta Xi; Presb Ch; GA Inst of Technol Band; GA St Univ Wind Ensemble; hon/ NHS; Soc of Dist'd Am HS Students; W/W Among Am HS Students; Kodak Scholars Prog S'ship; g/Res/Design Engr on Computer-Based Sys.

LIST, LESLIE SHANNON oc/Secretary; b/Oct 22, 1959; h/108 Dorchester Road, Louisville, KY 40223; p/Kenneth and Jacqueline List, Louisville, KY; ed/

En HS; En KY Univ, 1978; Sullivan Jr Col of Bus, 1980; cp/French Clb; Pi Beta Phi; Student Bd; FBLA; Yth Bd & Choir at Ch; Candystriper; hon/Pres Cup Awd; Dean's List; W/W Among Students in Am Jr Cols.

LISZEWSKI, RITA MARIE oc/ Design Automation Engineer; b/Jul 13, 1958; h/9700 North 37th Place, 303, Plymouth, MN 55441; p/Mr and Mrs Edmund Liszewski, Lublin, WI; ed/ Gilman HS, 1976; BS, Univ of WI, 1981; cp/Assn for Computing Machinery; Honeywell Wom Coun; VP, Assn of Computer Users; Nat Hon Soc; MENC; 4-H Clb; hon/Nat Merit S'ship Finalist; Valedictorian; W/W Among Students in Am Cols & Univs; g/Tech/Proj Ldrship.

LITRA, GREGORY FRANCIS oc/ Student; b/Jul 12, 1962; h/2355 Chinquepin Drive, Sumter, SC 29150; b/ Spartanburg, SC; p/Mr and Mrs H J Litra, Sumter, SC; ed/Sumter HS, 1980; BA, Wofford Col, 1984; pa/Law Clk, A Shedrick Jolly III, Atty-at-Law, 1983-; cp/Pre-Law Soc, Pres, VP; Pi Kappa Alpha Frat, VP, Exec Com, Rush Chm; Ec Soc; Pubs Bd; SC St Student Legis, Dist 4 VP, Del Chm; Wofford Col Band; Wofford Col Glee Clb, Chaplain; r/Rom Cath; hon/*Jour* Lit/Art Mag, Editor, Asst Editor, Edit Bd; Ruth Wynn Wickware Scholar, 1980-84; Nat Merit Scholar Finalist, 1980; Carolina Scholar, 1980; Dean's List, 1980-84; Buckey Nat Hon Frat, 1983-84; Pi Gamma Mu Sci Hon Frat, 1984; g/Law Sch.

LITTERAL, DEBORAH KAYE b/Mar 10, 1964; Route 2 Box 105, Bluefield, WV 24701; p/B Lewis and Myrtle C Litteral, Bluefield, WV; ed/HS, 1982; cp/ Choir Ensemble; Keywanettes; Pep Clb; Bible Clb; Student Coun; Secy, Sophomore Class; Treas, Jr Class; VP, Pres, UMYF; Secy, FBLA; hon/1st Runner-Up, Miss WV Nat Teenager Pageant; Musical Prodn Participant; Mercer Co Jr Miss Pageant Miss Mercer Co Jr Miss; WV Jr Miss Physical Fitness Awd; Voted Miss Mercer Co, 1982-83; Am's Outstg Names & Faces; Soc of Dist'd Am HS Students; W/W Among Am HS Students; g/Social Wk.

LITTLE, JOHN PAUL oc/Student; b/ Mar 22, 1965; h/1930 Manning, Philadelphia, PA 19103; p/John and Phyllis Little, Berea, KY; ed/Berea Commun HS; New Sch of Music; cp/HS Band; VP French Clb; Intl Horn Soc, 1980-83; Richmond KY Wind Ensemble, 1981-83; r/Quaker; hon/Nat Adv Bd of Accent Mag; Superior Rating for Solo in St Solo & Ensemble Contest, 1981-; Superior Rating for Solo in St Contest, Mem of Blue Lake in Bavaria Band, 1983; Superior Rating for Solo in Contest, Mem of All-St Band; Principal Horn in Sum Mus Inst at the Univ of Cinc, 1982; Voted Most Talented Boy, John Phillip Sousa Awd, Prin Horn in All-St Orch, 1983.

LITTLE, KATRINA G oc/Minister of Youth; b/Feb 11, 1961; h/Route 2, Box 59M, Statesville, NC 28677; p/Roberta G Little, Statesville, NC; ed/W Iredell HS, 1979; BA, Wingate Col, 1983; pa/ Public Relats, Motor Vehicle Lic Plate Agy, 1975-79; Yth Min, First Bapt Ch-Belmont NC, 1980-82; Yth Min, New S River Bapt Assn, 1983; cp/Class Rep, 1976-77; Lib Aide; Student Coun; Editor, Yr Book; FBLA, Secy; Keyettes; Spanish Clb; Beta Clb; r/Bapt; hon/Hon

Roll; Outstg Sr; Nom'd for Soc Dist'd Am HS Students; W/W Among Am HS Students; Dean's List; Col Hon Grad, Cum Laude; g/Phd Psychol.

LITTLE, RICK RAY oc/Educator, Author; b/Nov 9, 1955; h/2388 Hampstead Drive, Columbus, OH 43229; ba/Columbus, OH; m/Lisa Lee; p/Dick and Dottie Little, McComb, OH; ed/Findlay Col; pa/Pres, Fdr, The Quest Nat Ctr, 1975-; cp/Assn for Supvn & Curric Devel; Bd Mem, Nat Drug Abuse Found; Nat Fdn Parents for Drug-Free Yth; hon/Co-Authored w Bill Cosby, "You Are Somebody Spec"; Num Articles in Mags & Newspapers; Ser to Mankind Am; Sertoma Clbs of NW OH & MI; Outstg Yg Man in Am; W/W in the MW; Personalities in W & MW.

LITTLEFIELD, MARY ELIZABETH oc/Student; b/Mar 15, 1966; h/847 Country Club, Selmer, TN 38375; p/Mr and Mrs Gregory Littlefield, Selmer, TN; cp/Beta Clb; Student Govt Assn; Spanish Clb; Pep Clb; r/Bapt; hon/VP Sr Class; Cheerldr; Homecoming Royalty; Class Favorite; Hon Roll.

LITTLETON, CHARLENE oc/Student; b/Feb 17, 1964; h/Route 1, Box 311, Broxton, GA 31519; p/Ernest and Ella Mae Littleton, Broxton, GA; ed/Broxton HS, 1982; S GA Tech & Voc Sch, 1983; pa/Pt-time Secy Job Placement Ofc, Student Secy Instrnl Ser Ofc, Student Secy Dean of Students Ofc, 1983, S GA Tech; cp/Gifted Class, 1976-81; FHA, 1979-82; 4-H; r/Bapt; hon/Rec'd High Achmt SRA Cert, 1981; GA Occupl Awd Ldrship Nom, 1982; Rec'd S'ship Awd from Profl Secys Intl, 1983; g/Assoc's Deg in Bus Ed; CPA.

LLOYD, LINDA LAVERNE oc/Student; b/Sep 28, 1961; h/Post Office Box 7, Sharon, MS 39163; p/Mrs Johnnie Lloyd, Sharon, MS; ed/Velma Jackson HS, 1979; BA, Jackson St Univ, 1983; cp/Pierian Lit Soc, 1981-83; Alpha Chi, 1983; Phi Kappa Phi, 1983; Sigma Tau Delta, 1982; Mass Communs Clb; WJSU Radio Sta; News Editor, *Blue and White Flash*; Alpha Lambda Delta; Pres List; SS Tchr; hon/Valedictorian, 1983; Recip of Book Awd, 1983; Finalist in Jackson St Univ Competition for Rhodes Scholar; Dean's List; Nat Dean's List; Intl Yth in Achmt; W/W Among Students in Am Cols & Univs; g/Prof; Eng Study.

LO, MARY CHIA-HWA oc/Student; b/Nov 15, 1961; h/121 Wettermark, Nacogdoches, TX 75901; p/Houston, TX; ed/Jacksonville HS, 1980; Stephen F Austin St Univ, 1983; cp/Am Chem Soc, 1981; Nat Assn Accts, 1983; r/True Jesus Ch; hon/Shamrock Oil Acctg S'ship, 1983-84; Beta Alpha Psi; Alpha Chi; Phi Eta Sigma; g/Acctg; Law Sch.

LOBBY, MARISSA ELIZABETH oc/Student; b/Mar 8, 1965; h/331 Union Avenue, Middlesex, NJ 08846; p/Harry and Marilyn Lobby, Middlesex, NJ; ed/Middlesex HS, 1983; cp/Class Ofcr, 1979-83; Varsity Field Hockey, 1979-83, Capt 1983; Jr Varsity Track, 1980; Pom Pom Squad, 1980-82; Marching Band, 1979; Concert Band, 1979-81; Jr Prom Com, 1982; Sr Ball Com, 1983; German Clb, 1979-82; r/Cath; hon/Nat Hon Soc; NJ Girls' St Del, 1982; DAR Rep, 1983; AAUW's Awd, 1983; Middlesex NJ JCs Outstg Merit Awd, 1983.

LOCKE, SHANNA LEIGH oc/Student; b/Oct 7, 1963; h/909 West Cherry Avenue, Selmer, TN 38375; ba/Martin,

TN; p/Mr and Mrs E L Locke, Selmer, TN; ed/McNairy Ctl HS, 1981; Univ TN-Martin; cp/Zeta Tau Alpha, Chm of Communs; Univ TN Social Wk Clb; Yg Repubs; FHA; Pep Clb; Beta Clb; Intl Clb; Intl Clb Coun; FTA, VP; Christian Yth Org; Alpha Delta Kappa, Pledge Class Pres; Yrbook Staff, Advtg Editor; Yrbook Co-Editor, Features Editor; Copy Cat's (Drama Clb); Prom Com; Sr Follies Com; r/Meth; hon/Poetry Pub'd in *Windmills*, 1981-82, *Spirit*, 1981-82; Student's Excell, 1981; Awd for Ser & Dedication to the Class of 1981; OES; Eng Acad Awds; Pickwick Elect Essay Contest, 3rd Place Winner; W/W Among Am HS Students; Intl Yth in Achmt; g/BS in Social Wk.

LOFTIS, KERRY LANTZ oc/Student; b/Nov 7, 1966; h/2405 Poinsett Highway, Greenville, SC 29609; p/Mr and Mrs Dwight A Loftis, Greenville, SC; ed/Travelers Rest HS; cp/Golden Regiment Band, 1980-84; r/Bapt, Locust Hill Bapt Ch Yth Choir; hon/Drum Major of the Golden Regiment Band, 1983; Best Overall Drum Major, Furman Tropicana Music Bowl IV, 1983; Best Drum Major, Spartanburg Co Band Fest, 1983; Hon Roll; g/Drum Major; Computer Sci & Computer Design.

LOGAN, TERI KAY oc/Missionary, Assistant Apartment Complex Manager; b/Oct 13, 1956; h/1411 Southwest 67 Avenue Apartment 16, Miami, FL 33144; p/Rev and Mrs Nelson J Logan, Broken Bow, NE; ed/Granite Falls HS, 1974; BS, Calvary Bible Col, 1978; pa/Public Relats Recruitment Secy, Typesetter for Calvary Bible Col, 1977-79; Missionary, 1980-; cp/Puppet Min w Chd, incl'g Shows, Corres Course & Pen Pal Clb w Main Puppet; hon/HS Valedictorian, 1974; Granite Falls Alumni S'ship, 1974; Granite Falls PTA S'ship, 1975; Lions Clb S'ship, 1974; Bill Stanton S'ship, 1974; Col Valedictorian, 1978; Nat Hon Soc; I Dare You Awd; *Reader's Digest* Awd; Delta Epsilon Chi; W/W Among Am HS Students; W/W Among Students in Univs & Cols; Intl Yth in Achmt; Commun Ldrs of Am; Personalities of S.

LOLLIS, TERESA JO oc/Student; b/May 13, 1964; h/Route 7, Box 16, Easley, SC 29640; p/Mr and Mrs Grady Lollis, Easley, SC; ed/Easley HS, 1982; cp/SC Scholastic Press Assn, Piedmont Area Rep 1979-80, Second VP 1980-81, Pres 1981-82; *Tsunami*, Bus Mgr & News Editor; Ftball, Basketball Cheerldr; Interact Ser Clb; French Clb, Pres; Sci Clb, Secy/Treas, VP; *Search*, Lit Mag; Secy, Explorers Post 237; Outdoor Clb; Inter-Varsity Christian F'ship; Col Ednl Ser Corps; r/Bapt; hon/Author of "Behind Every Good Writer is a Good Copy Editor", *Scholastic Focus*, 1981; Nat Hon Soc; Sci Bowl Capt, First Pl Math Contest, Sci Olympiad at Converse Col; First Pl Adv'd Extemporaneous Oration, First Place French Skit, Fgn Lang Fest; Student of Mo; SC Scholastic Press Assn, Outstg Ser Awd; Phi Beta Kappa Awd; Math Awd; French Awd; Bill Davey Awd for Writing; Gov's Sch; Girls' St; Furman Scholar; Presb Col Jr Fellow; *Tsunami*, Most Valuable Staff Mem; Dean's List, Straight A's, Furman Univ; Phi Eta Sigma; W/W Among Am HS Students; g/Maj in Psychol; Clin Psychol.

LONG, ADRIAN ROSE oc/Student;

b/Sep 26, 1966; h/710 Hycliffe Drive, Richmond, KY 40475; p/John and Marilyn Long, Richmond, KY; ed/Model HS, 1984; pa/Pt-time Receptionist, En KY Univ Tennis Ctr, 1983-84; cp/Student Coun, VP & Treas; Art Clb, VP; Yth Grp; Tennis Team, Co-Capt; Sch Swing Choir; Nat Hon Soc; Ctl KY Yth Orch; Ch Chorus; Yrbook Staff; r/Presb; hon/Madison Co Jr Miss, S'ship Awd; KY Jr Miss S'ship Awd; US Nat Ldrship Merit Awd; Nat Merit Semi-Finalist; Outstg Eng & French Student; Student of Wk; W/W Among Am HS Students; Soc of Dist'd Students; g/Oberlin Col.

LONG, KAREN FELICIA oc/Student; b/Sep 1, 1964; h/2665 Hightower Court, Atlanta, GA 30318; p/Mr and Mrs Ralph Long Jr, Atlanta, GA; ed/Frederick Douglas HS, 1982; TX Christian Univ; pa/Six Flags Mdse Cashier, Sum 1981; Intern, Citizens & So Nat Bk, Sum 1982, 1983; cp/Inroads Atlanta Inc, 1982-83; TX Christian Univ Films Colm; TX Christian Univ Black Student Caucus; r/Bapt, Union Bapt Ch Yth Choir; hon/Harvard Book Awd, 1981; Vanderbilt Book Awd, 1982; H O Smith Valedictory Awd, 1982; St Sci Cong, 2nd Pl Awd, 1982; En Airlines Essay Contest Finalist; 1st Pl Regency Talent; g/Career in Performing Arts, Dance; Computer Sci.

LONG, MARK ALEXANDER DIETTERICH oc/Student, Counseling Psychologist; b/Jul 29, 1954; h/640 East Broadway Avenue, Apartment 4, Morgantown, WV 26505; ba/Morgantown, WV; p/Dr Lewis M K Long, Alexandria, VA; ed/Fort Hunt HS, 1972; BA, Earlham Col, 1976; MEd, James Madison Univ, 1977; EdD Cand, WV Univ, 1981-; mil/USN, Psychol; pa/Psychol, USN, 1983-; Lectured Instr, WV Univ, 1981-83; Mtl Hlth Cnslr; Fairfax-Falls Ch Commun Sers Bd, 1980-81; Mtl Hlth Cnslr, Arlington Commun Residences, 1979-80; Insight Mtl Retard Cnslr, 1979-80; cp/APGA; AABT; r/Unitarian; hon/Psychol Assessmt Computer Prog, 1983; Grad w Acad Hons & Dept Hons, 1976; g/Psychol.

LONG, MARK R oc/Bank Secured Lending Consultant; b/Oct 3, 1956; h/444 St James Place, Chicago, IL 60614; p/Virginia Palen Long, Dixon, IL; ed/Dixon HS, 1974; BS, No IL Univ, 1978; MM, NWn Univ, 1982; cp/Pres, Beta Gamma Sigma; Treas, Mortar Bd; Phi Kappa Phi; Pi Kappa Delta; Pres, Univ Resident Hall; Toastmasters; Forensics; Chgo Alliance of Bus Vol; r/Rom Cath; hon/St & Nat Public Spkg Champ; Beta Gamma Sigma's Outstg US Bus Student; Am Inst Bkg Dist Conf Keynote Spkr; Intl Yth n Achmt; The Col Register; Nat Dean's List; Commun Ldrs Am; W/W Among Students in Am Univs & Cols.

LOOPER, LISA ANN oc/Student; b/Sep 17, 1966; h/Route 2, Box 104, Loudon, TN 37774; p/Lane and Peggy Looper, Loudon, TN; ed/Loudon HS, 1984; cp/Jr Classical Leag; FHA; Student Coun; Nat Cheerldr Assn; March of Dimes Capt; Nat Student Govt Awd Mem; Pep Clb; r/Bapt; hon/Loudon Co Jr Miss, 1984; W/W Among HS Students; St Del, Ofcr & Student Coun Mem, 1981-84; Teen Bd Presentee, 1983; Nat Hist & Govt Awd; g/Public Reltats Maj.

LOPEZ, MARIA ELIZABETH oc/ Missionary, Teacher; b/Jul 30, 1958; h/ 506 Fourth Street, Calexico, CA 92231; ba/Calexico, CA; p/Mr and Mrs Santiago Lopez, Waynesville, NC; ed/Tuscola HS, 1976; BA, Greensboro Col, 1980; pa/Missionary/Tchr, Neighborhood House, 1982-; Pre-sch Tchr, 1st Meth Kgn, 1980-82; cp/Yth Cnslr, United Meth Yth-Calexico; Jr Ch Dir; NHS; Pianist, Chd Choir; Student Cnslr; Chm, Campus Min Task Force; NC Student Legis, Senate Clk, Bill Com Chm; SGA Parliamentn, Secy; SNEA; r/United Meth; hon/Hispanic, Asian, Native Am S'ship; DAR Good Citizen Awd; W/W Among Students in Am Cols & Univs; Commun Ldrs Am.

LORONA, KAREN ANN oc/Student; b/Feb 16, 1965; h/134 St Charles Avenue, Biloxi, MS 39530; p/Mr and Mrs Manuel Lorona, Biloxi, MS; ed/ Biloxi HS, 1983; Perkinson Jr Col; cp/ Cheerldr, 1983; Secy/Treas, 1983; r/ Cath; hon/Hon Grad HS, 1983; g/ Computer Sci Maj.

LOWMAN, HENRY BERNARD oc/ Student; b/Jun 14, 1962; h/4 East 32nd Street, Baltimore, MD 21218; p/Dr and Mrs Cecil B Lowman, Newberry, SC; ed/Newberry HS, 1980; Johns Hopkins Univ; cp/Am Chem Soc, Pres 1983-84; HS Rotary Clb Pres, 1979-80; Sci Clb Pres, 1978-79; Key Clb Pres 1979-80; Band & Orch; Jr & Sr Beta Clbs; r/Luth; hon/1978 4th Grand Awd, Int Sci & Engrg Fair; 1980 Carolina Scholar S'ship Awd; 1979-80, McDonald's All-Am HS Band; Nat Dean's List; g/PhD Biochem.

LOWRIMORE, PAMELA ELAINE oc/Student; b/Jan 5, 1961; h/Post Office Box 497, Jackson, SC 29831; p/Rev and Mrs Ralph T Lowrimore, Jackson, SC; ed/Branchville HS, 1979; Univ SC; BA, Columbia Col, 1983; pa/Student Asst, J Drake Edens Lib, Columbia Col, 1979-83; Student Intern w Downtown Action Coun, Columbia C of C, 1982; Student Intern, So Ednl Communs Assn, 1982; Slide Show Script, 1983; cp/ Wesley F'ship Pres, 1983-83, Campus Meth Grp; Student Christian Assn Cabinet Mem, 1980-83, Treas 1980-81; Sigma Tau Delta Mem; *Criterion*, Publicity Chm; Mem Student Pubs Com; r/United Meth; hon/Author of "The Silent Scream", *Post Script*, 1982; Num Articles; HS Salutatorian, 1979; Nat Beta Clb Mem, 1976-79; Dean's List, Columbia Col, 1982; W Foun S'ship Recip; W/W Nom; g/Communication Arts Maj.

LOWRY, ELIZABETH GRACE oc/ Student; b/Jul 3, 1966; h/215 Cloverbrook Drive, Jamestown, NC 27282; ba/ Greensboro, NC; p/Mr and Mrs Ivan Lowry, Jamestown, NC; ed/Ragsdale HS; pa/Carolina Travel, 1983-; cp/Beta Clb, VP; FBLA; French Clb; Juniorettes; French Hon Soc, Treas; Nat Hon Soc; HS Basketball, Tennis; HS Band; r/Pres, Hand Bell Choir, Yth Choir, Witness Com, Yth F'ship, Pulpit Nom'g Com; hon/Ragsdale Yrbook Staff, Acad Staff, Acad Editor; Girls' St, 1983; Gov's Sch, 1982; Most Acad of Class in 1978, 1980; Most Valuable Player, Little Leag Basketball Team, 1980; "A" Hon Roll; Superior Plus Rating at Nat Piano Playing Auditions, 1983; All Co Band, 1981; Jr Marshall, 1983; g/Master's Deg in Computer Sci; Systems Analyst.

LUCAS, KAREN LEE oc/Student; b/

Jan 30, 1964; h/190 North Mill Road, Atlanta, GA 30328; p/Mr and Mrs Robert W Lucas, Atlanta, Ga; ed/N Sprgs HS, 1982; Stephens Col; cp/Nat Hon Soc; Secy/Treas, Sr Beta Clb, 1982; Alpha Lambda Delta, 1982-83; r/Cath; hon/Dean's List, 1982-83; Nat Dean's List; g/Broadcast Communs, Producing TV & Video.

LUCAS, KELLY F oc/Auditor; b/Jan 14, 1961; h/1900 Bushford Manor Lane, Number 1322, Louisville, KY 40218; ba/ Louisville, KY; p/Clarence Lucas, Louisville, KY; ed/Seneca HS, 1978; BS, KY St Univ, 1982; oc/Auditor, Capital Holding Corporation, 1982-; cp/Big Brothers/Big Sisters of Kentuckiana Inc; Profl & Bus Wom's Assn; Vol Red Cross; VP, Delta Sigma Theta; Marching Band; Phi Beta Lambda; hon/Grad Magna Cum Laude, 1982; Rec'd Rookie Big Sister of the Yr Awd, 1983; Outstg Freshman Awd, Alpha Kappa Mu; KY St Univ Acad S'ship; Nat Dean's List; Outstg Yg Wom of Am; g/MBA, Univ Chgo.

LUCITO, DONNA MARIE oc/Student; b/Jul 28, 1962; h/650 Buffalo Avenue, Calumet City, IL 60409; p/ Anthony and Patricia Lucito, Calumet City, IL; ed/Thornton Fractional N HS, 1980; Wn IL Univ; cp/Pres, Girls Clb; VP, Spch & Debate Clb; Treas, DECA; St Ambassador DECA; Drama Clb; Intl Thespian Soc; Feature Editor; HS Newspaper; Quill & Scroll; Phi Kappa Theta; SGA; WJU Student Ambassador; Hall Govt Secy; Badminton, Tennis Teams; VP, Alpha Omicron Pi; Secy, Student Alumni Coun; Student Orient Bd Ldr; r/Cath; hon/Sigma Iota Epsilon Mgmt Hon; Nat Order of Omega, Secy/ Treas; NHS; Intl Yth in Achmt; W/W Among Am HS Students; Commun Ldrs Am; g/Mgmt Maj.

LUCKO, ELLEN RAYE oc/Elementary Music Teacher; b/Sep 16, 1960; h/ Route 1, Box 322, Cameron, TX 76520; ba/Spring, TX; p/Monroe and Lowvica Lucko, Cameron, TX; ed/C H Yoe HS, 1979; BMUSE, TX Tech Univ, 1983; pa/ Student Tchg, Evans Jr HS, Wester Elem, 1983; Field Study (SPACE), Iles Elem Sch, 1982; Student Observation, Evans Jr HS, 1982; Subst Tchr, Rosebud Elem Sch, 1980; cp/Libn, TX Tech Band, Band Camps, 1980-83; Ch Camp Cnslr, Master's Wkshop, 1978, 1979; Ch Organist & Trumpet Performer; MENC, Pres of Tech Chapt; Tau Beta Sigma, Pres 1982-83, Secy 1981-82; Mortar Bd, 1982-83; Phi Kappa Phi, 1982; Alpha Lambda Delta, 1980; Omicron Delta Kappa, 1982; Marching Band 1979-83, Varsity Band 1981-83, Brass Band 1979-80, Symph Orch 1980-81, TX Tech; r/United Ch of Christ; hon/ Num S'ships incl'g TX Tech Univ Music Dept, TX Tech Univ, TX Tech Dad's Assn, Alcoa Foun, United Steelwkrs Am, Farm Bur; Nat Hon Soc; W/W Among Am Students in Cols & Univs; Nat Dean's List; g/Music Tchr; Grad Sch.

LUGINBYHL, JAMES WESLEY oc/ Ofcr in USAF; b/Jan 20, 1958; h/1676 Tidal Wave, Cannon AFB, NM 88101; ba/Cannon AFB, NM; m/Debbie LaVonne Odom; c/James Anthony; p/ Robert I and Irene Luginbyhl, Stinnett, TX; sp/James Odom, Amarillo, TX; ed/ Palo Duro HS, 1976; BS, TX Tech Univ, 1980; MS, AF Inst of Technol, 1981; mil/

USAF, 1st Lt, 1980-; pa/Chief of Engrg Design 1982-, Chief of Envir & Contract Planning 1982, Chief of Constrn Mgmt 1981-82, USAF, Cannon AFB; cp/ NM Soc of Profl Engrs; r/Bapt; hon/ "Simulation of Runoff from an AFB Using a Programmable Calculator", *AFIT Pub* LSSR, 1981; Tau Beta Pi, Chi Epsilon Hon Soc, 1979; Sigma Iota Epsilon Mgmt Hon Soc, 1981; Nat Dean's List; W/W Among Am HS Students; Eagle Scout, 1972; g/Supervising Engrg Projs & Tech Pers.

LUM, GEORGE ENGLISH IV oc/ Student; b/Jul 10, 1964; h/605 Orchard Road, Jasper, AL 35501; p/Mr and Mrs James G Lum, Jasper, AL; ed/Walker HS, 1982; Walker Col; cp/Nat Jr Hon Soc; Beta Clb; FCA; Math Clb; Key Clb; HS Freshman Basketball & Ftball; Varsity Ftball, Golf; Ch Basketball Team; Col Intramural Ftball & Basketball; r/Presb; hon/Mem of 1981 St Champ Golf Team; Geddes Self Awd, 1982, Highest Ath Awd; Dean's List; Mem, Phi Theta Kappa; Nat Dean's List; W/W; g/Deg in Engrg.

LUNDY, RONALD TRACY oc/Student; b/Apr 21, 1965; h/Route 1, Box 1D, Havelock, NC 28532; ed/Havelock HS, 1983; Lenoir-Rhyne Col; cp/Varsity Ftball, Capt; Jr Varsity & Varsity Basketball, Capt; Track; r/Free Will Bapt; hon/All Conf, Varsity Ftball; All E; Hon Mention; All Conf Basketball, All Conf Track.

LUTZ, THOMAS LUTHER oc/Student; b/Mar 12, 1965; h/Route 3, Box 240, Lawndale, NC 28090; p/Mr and Mrs Marvin L Lutz, Lawndale, NC; ed/ HS, 1983; cp/Pres Classroom Scholar; Key Clb Pres; Beta Clb Pres; NHS; French Hon Soc; French Clb; Chess Clb; Sci Clb; Intramural Sports; Newspaper Corres; r/Meth, Ch Usher, Class Secy, Bd Yth Mem; Save the Lighthouse Drive; hon/Valedictorian, 1983; Barrier S'ship; Dover Foun S'ship; Commun & Ser Awd; Hist Awd; Key Clb Ser Awd; Dist Alt for Morehead S'ship; Gov's Hon Prog; Chief Jr Marshal; W/W; Commun Ldrs of Am; Nat Sci Merit Awd; g/Univ NC-Chapel Hill.

LYNCH, BETTY JEAN oc/Student; b/ Oct 19, 1964; h/Rural Route 2, South Haven, KS 67140; ba/Same; p/Mr and Mrs Robert Lynch, S Haven, KS; pa/ Dishwasher, 1980 Sum; Farm Wkr, Sums 1981-83; cp/FFA, Secy/Treas, 1979-83; FHA, Histn, Secy, 1979-83; Nat Hon Soc, 1979-83, Secy; Sr Class Secy, 1983; Jr Class Pres, 1982; Basketball & Volleyball, 1979-83; r/United Meth; hon/Nat Hon Soc, 1979; Basketball Homecoming Queen, 1983; KSHSAA Citizenship Awd; KU Hon Grad; W/W Am HS Students; g/Col, Acctg Maj, Minor in Computers.

LYNCH, KAREN BLAZINA oc/Associate Editor; b/Jul 30, 1957; h/3 Wintergreen Court, Woodridge, IL 60517; ba/ Downers Grove, IL; m/Kevin D; p/Mr and Mrs Frank Blazina, Hinsdale, IL; ed/ Campolindo HS, 1975; Baylor Univ, 1979; cp/Newspaper Editor; Author, Wkly Column for Local Paper; Student Cong Ofcr; Red Cross Vol; Girls Ath Assn; Orchesis Dance Clb; Tennis Team; CCD Aide; ALIVE Vol; Sigma Delta Chi; TX St Tchrs Assn; Debate Judge & Student Tchr; hon/Quill & Scroll; Hon Roll; Dean's List.

LYNN, MICHAEL A oc/Student; b/

May 23, 1963; h/160 Northeast 25 Court, Pompano Beach, FL 33064; ba/ Delray Beach, FL; p/Mr and Mrs R W Lynn, Pompano Beach, FL; ed/Pompano Bch HS, 1981; FL Atlantic Univ; pa/Asst Controller, Hardrives Inc, 1982-; cp/Nat Assn Accts; FL Atlantic Univ Circle K Clb Pres, 1982-83; Bd Mem, Ducks Unltd; r/Prot; hon/Outstg Clb in St, Pres, 1983; Pres, Number 2 Clb, 1983; HS Salutatorian; Dean's List; W/W Among Amg HS Students; g/MBA; CPA or Controller.

LYON, CHARLES ELIOT oc/Ophthalmology Resident; b/Jan 31, 1955; h/ Polk's Landing, Box 103, Chapel Hill, NC 27514; ba/Chapel Hill, NC; m/ Stephanie Delcombre; p/Mrs A D Lyon, Haynesville, LA; sp/Mr and Mrs Harry Landry, New Iberia, LA; ed/Haynesville HS, 1973; BS, NE LA Univ, 1976; MD, LA St Univ Med Sch; pa/Intern Internal Med, LA St Univ, 1981-82; Resident in Ophthal, Univ NC Med Ctr, 1982-; Am Med Assn; Am Acad Ophthal; cp/Nat Audubon Soc, Local Chapt New Hope Audubon Soc; Chapel Hill Bird Clb; Acacia Frat, 1974; r/Bapt; hon/Alpha Omega Alpha Hon Med Soc, 1979; Alpha Epsilon Delta Pre-Med Hon Soc, 1975; Phi Kappa Phi Hon Soc, 1976; Omicron Delta Kappa Soc, 1976; Phi Eta Sigma Freshman Hon Soc, 1976; g/ F'ship in Med & Surg Retina, Tulane Med Ctr.

LYSFORD, VERN oc/Student; b/Sep 29, 1960; h/Kennedy, MN 56733; m/Jill; p/Melvyn and Irene Lysford, Kennedy, MN; sp/Gordon and Kay Carlson, Hallock, MN; ed/Kennedy HS, 1979; BA, Univ MN, 1983; cp/Student Coun Pres, 1979; Lttrman's Clb Pres, 1979; NHS, 1979; Univ MN Morris Ftball Team, 1982; r/Cath; hon/Nat Hon Soc, 1979; Top of the St Ftball Conf Most Valuable Player, 1978; PTA S'ship, 1979; Hon Student; Dean's List; W/W; Intl Yth in Achmt; g/Corporate Controller.

713

M

MACARAGES, BRENDA JOYCE oc/ Student; b/Apr 26, 1956; h/2215 West-dale Drive, Fayetteville, NC; m/Sidney Jefferson Jr; p/Mr and Mrs Doyle M Stevens, Longmont, CO; ed/Dipl, Niwot HS, 1974; Cert of Completion, Med Spec Course, Ft Sam Houston, 1974; Cert of Completion, Allergy/ Immunol Course, Walter Reed Army Med Ctr, 1976; Univ of No CO, 1978; Pembroke St Univ, 1979-81; BSN, Univ of NC Chapel Hill, 1983; mil/AUS, 1974-76; USAR, 1978–; Med Secy, Dr Gary B Garison, 1979; Pt-time in Ob-Gyn Clin, Womack Army Hosp; Other Previous Positions; cp/Muscular Dystrophy Assn; NOW; March of Dimes; hon/Dean's List, Pembroke St Univ 1981 (Sprg), Univ of NC Chapel Hill 1981 (Fall), 1982 (Sprg and Fall); James M Johnston S'ship, 1982-83; Sigma Theta Tau Nsg Hon Soc, Alpha Alpha Chapt, 1983; g/To Wk as a Nurse in a Hosp Setting; To Enter the Army Nurse Corps; To Become More Involved in Commun Orgs; Master's Deg.

MacDONALD, MICHAEL JOSEPH oc/Student, Lifeguard; b/Aug 22, 1962; h/8651 Sylvan Drive, Melbourne, FL 32901; p/Hugh and Joan MacDonald, Melbourne, FL; ed/HS Grad, 1980; AA, Brevard Commun Col, 1982; pa/Life-guard, Brevard Co Bch, 1979-83; cp/ Space Coast Runners Assn; Harbor City Vol Ambulance Squad; Phi Theta Kappa Hon Frat, 1980-82; Alpha Epsilon Delta Pre-Med Soc, 1983; Varsity HS Track, Cross Country Capt; Symph Band; Marching Band; Spanish Clb; Key Clb; JV Wrestling; Coach, Commun Basket-ball; r/Cath; hon/Track and Cross Country S'ship to Brevard Commun Col, 1980-82; Marshal Hamilton S'ship to FSU, 1983-84; Acad All-Am Cross Country Team, 1980, 1981; Most Improved Cross Country Runner, 1979; W/W Among Am HS Students; Dist'd HS Students; Intl Yth in Achmt; Yg Personalities of S; Commun Ldrs of Am; g/MD.

MacDONALD, STEPHEN HUGH oc/ Student; b/Aug 22, 1962; h/8651 Sylvan Drive, Melbourne, FL 32901; p/Hugh and Joan MacDonald, Melbourne, FL; ed/Grad, Melbourne HS, 1980; AA, Brevard Commun Col, 1982; Att'g, FL St Univ; pa/Lifeguard, S Brevard Co Bch, 1979-83; cp/Space Coast Runner Assn; Harbor City Vol Ambulance Squad; Phi Theta Kappa Hons Frat, 1980-82; Alpha Epsilon Delta Pre-Med Hon Soc, 1983; Varsity HS Track; Capt, Varsity HS Cross Country Team; Symph Band; Spanish Clb; Marching Band; Key Clb; JV Wrestling; Coach, Commun Basketball; hon/Acad Excell Awd; Track and Cross Country S'ship to Brevard Commun Col, 1980-82; Marshal Hamilton S'ship to FSU, 1983-84; Acad All-Am Cross Country Team, 1980, 1981; Capt of Cross Country Team, 1979; W/W Among Am HS Students; Soc of Dist'd Am HS Students; Yth in Achmt; Intl Yth in Achmt; Yg Personalities of S; Commun Ldrs of Am; g/MD.

MACHEN, BILLY RANDALL oc/ Student; b/Jul 17, 1961; h/Route 1, Box 36, Magnolia, AR 71753; p/Billy Ray Machen, Magnolia, AR; Dorothy Machen, Magnolia, AR; ed/HS Grad,

1979; BS, Biol, So AR Univ, 1983; Att'g, Univ of TN Dental Sch at Memphis; cp/ Alpha Hon Soc, VP; Intramural Coun; Physics Clb; Biol Clb; r/Ch of Christ; hon/Alpha Hon Soc, 1981; g/Dentist.

MACK, LINDA DARLENE oc/Stu-dent; b/Jan 23, 1960; h/1331 Secession-ville Road, Charleston, SC; ba/Same; p/ Mr and Mrs Oliver Mack Sr, Charles-ton, SC; ed/Grad, Ft Johnson HS, 1978; SC St Col, 1978-82; MA, Univ of FL, 1984; pa/Student Spch, Lang and Hear-ing Assn; SC Spch, Lang and Hearing Assn; Soc for Autistic Chd; SC Soc for Autistic Chd; FL Spch and Hearing Assn; SEn Conf on Linguistics; Delta Sigma Theta Sorority Inc; hon/Alpha Kappa Mu Nat Hon Soc; Sigma Alpha Eta Hon Soc; 1st Attendant to Miss SC St Col, 1981-82; Beta Eta Sigma Hon Soc, 1984; Grad Minority F'ship, 1982-84; W/W Among Am HS Stu-dents; g/To Earn PhD in Spch Pathol and Aphasiology.

MACK, RALPH McDONALD oc/ Analytical Organic Chemist; b/May 24, 1955; h/152 Wade Lane, Oak Ridge, TN 37830; ba/Oak Ridge, TN; p/Ms Katie Mack, Holly Hill, SC; ed/Dipl, Holly Hill HS, 1973; BS, SC St Col, 1977; pa/ Chem, Union Carbide Nuclear Div, 1978–; Analytical Chem, Procter & Gamble, 1977; Ames Lab, IA St Univ, 1976; Chem, Celanese Fibers Indust, 1975; Am Enka, Doffer, 1974; NOBCChE, 1982; cp/Kappa Alpha Psi Frat Inc, 1975; Downtown Optimist Clb of Oak Ridge, 1978; SC St Col Alumni Assn, Oak Ridge/Knoxville Chapt, 1978; r/AME Ch; hon/MVP, HS Foot-ball Team, 1972-73; Dick Horne Foun S'ship, 1974; g/To Attain an Adv'd Deg in Analytical Chem and Become a Tech Mgr in Indust.

MACKAY, JULIE ANNE oc/Attorney at Law; b/Apr 9, 1956; h/2880 South Locust Street, Denver, CO 80222; p/ Robert and Joanne Mackay, Denver, CO; ed/Luth HS, 1974; BA, summa cum laude, Univ of Denver, 1978; JD, Stanford Law Sch, 1981; pa/Atty at Law; cp/Vol Chm, St Legis Campaign; Greenpeace; CO Soc Fund for Animals; Intl Fund for Animal Wel and Defenders of Wildlife; Repub Party Activ Mem; Cent Chm, Cong Campaign; Student Fellow, Cent CO Conf; r/Ascension Epis Ch; hon/Valedictorian, 1974; Univ of Denver Outstg Sr Wom; Phi Beta Kappa; AAUW Awd; g/Ptnr in Gen Corporate Law.

MacKNIGHT, MARK ALAN oc/ Salesclerk; b/Jul 16, 1963; h/PO Box 127, New Haven, WV 25265; p/John William and Sandra Lynn MacKnight, New Haven, WV; ed/Grad, Wahama HS, 1981; Mason Co Voc Tech Ctr; pa/ Salesclk; cp/Softball and Intramural Sports; r/Vicar, Acolyte & Usher, Zion Luth Ch; hon/W/W Among Am HS Students; Intl Yth in Achmt; Commun Ldrs of Am; Personalities of S.

MADDEN, GREGORY JOHN oc/ Director of National Advertising; b/ May 12, 1956; h/81 Middlesex Road, Chestnut Hill, MA 02167; ba/Same; p/ Frank and Anne Madden, Middlebury, CT; ed/Holy Cross HS, 1974; NEn Univ, 1979; pa/Dir of Nat Advtg, Amateur Hockey Assn of the US, 1981-82; Dir of Nat Advtg, Sports Concepts Inc, 1982–; Free-Lance Broadcaster; cp/ Huskey Key Soc, Pres 1977-79; Vol Fire

Dept; Cath Yth Org, Pres; Ch Folk Grp; Rel Instr, Tchr; hon/Dexter S Burnham Excell in Jour Awd; NEn Univ Dean's List, 1974-75; Outstg Contbn Awd, 1980; Intl Yth in Achmt; W/W Among Students in Am Cols and Univs; g/ Broadcasting; Films; Advtg.

MADISON, DEIRDRE LEA oc/Stu-dent; b/Oct 11, 1961; h/2810 Delano, Midland, TX 79701; p/Mr and Mrs George Madison; ed/Midland HS, 1980; BMus, Hardin-Simmons Univ; cp/HS Choir; NHS; Sigma Alpha Iota; Pres, Campus Bapt Yg Wom; Meals on Wheels Vol; Basketball; Volleyball; r/ Christian So Bapt; hon/DAR Awd; Achmt S'ship; Music S'ship; g/Christian Voc.

MADUCDOC, LURLEEN ROMERO oc/Student; b/May 6, 1966; h/2108 Willow Wood Road, Oak Hill, WV 25901; p/Dr and Mrs Serafino S Maduc-doc Jr, Oak Hill, WV; ed/Oak Hill HS, 1982; Att'g, WV Univ; pa/Receptionist, Dr S S Maducdoc Jr, 1980-83; cp/Vol, WV Univ Med Ctr Pediatrics Dept; Pi Beta Phi Sorority, Pledge Class VP; Mountaineer Wk Com; Sprg Hons Dinner Steering Com, Student Foun; Friends of WVU Hosp; Secy-Treas, Sr Class; Pres, Tri-Hi-Y Clb; French Clb; Pep Clb; Histn, Tri-Hi-Y; VP, 4-H Clb; Eng Bowl Team; Varsity Tennis Team; Student Coun; UMYF; Hi Teen Com; Yth in Govt Legis Del; r/Meth; hon/ Most Outstg Tri-Hi-Y Mem, 1982; I Dare You Awd Recip, 1982; Student Coun Ser Awd, 1982; Homecoming Ct, 1982; Proclamation of Mayor, Lurleen Maducdoc Day, May 31, 1982; Gov, Rhododendron Girls' St; Hon Student, Grad; Soc of Dist'd Am HS Students; Commun Ldrs of Am; g/Med Sch.

MADZUMA, KIMBERLY ANN MUL-HEREN oc/Language Arts and Science Teacher; b/Apr 8, 1957; h/#Q-5, Dutch Village Apartments, 1800 Grayland Street, Blacksburg, VA 24060; ba/ Pearisburg, VA; m/Stephen Dana; p/Mr and Mrs Clarence Mulheren Jr, Pearis-burg, VA; ed/Dipl, Giles HS, 1975; BS, Radford Col, 1979; pa/Title I Rdg Tchr, Grades 6 & 7; 6th Grade Lang Arts and Sci Tchr; VEA; NEA; cp/U Meth Home Missionary, Biloxi, MS, Served 2 Yrs; r/Chp for Missions, Mem of Coun on Mins, Adm Bd, 1st U Meth Ch; hon/ Pres Hon Frat in Col; Varsity Cheerldr, Col; Sr Hon Soc; Ed Hon Frat, Kappa Delta Phi; Intl Yth in Achmt; Person-alities of S; g/To Continue Tchg Sch and Eventually Have Chd and Raise Them w Husband.

MAGANDY, KATHLEEN MARIE oc/Student; b/Aug 3, 1962; h/1103 Pineville Road, Long Beach, MS 39560; ba/University, MS; p/Mr and Mrs John W Magandy, Long Beach, MS; ed/Long Bch HS, 1980; BA in Jour, Univ of MS, 1984; pa/Sports Editor, *The Daily Mis-sissippian*, 1983-84; Stringer, *Gulfport Star-Journal*, 1983; Asst Sports Editor 1982-83, Sports Writer 1982, *The Daily Mississippian*; Hall Pres, 1981-83; Resi-dent Advr, 1980-83; cp/Beta Clb, 1975-80; Spanish Clb, 1978-80; Debate Team, 1979-80; Residence Hall Assn, 1980-83; NROTC, 1982-83; Campus Daily Newspaper Staff; r/Rom Cath; hon/Outstg Jr Jour Student, Univ of MS, 1983; g/To Pursue a Career in Sports Jour.

MAHAFFEY, PATRICK B oc/Student; b/Mar 17, 1963; h/8027 East 20th, Indianapolis, IN 46219; ba/West Lafayette, IN; p/Jacqui Bridgeforth, Indianapolis, IN; ed/Grad, Warren Ctl HS, 1981; Att'g, Purdue Univ; pa/Field Engr, Bechtel Power Corp, 1982-85; Student Employee, Purdue Trans Ser, 1981-82; Bus Boy and Dishwasher, Choys Woks, 1981; Other Previous Positions; cp/Campus Life, Student Dir 1979-81; Student Body and Coun Pres, 1980-81; Purdue Soc of Constrn Engrs, 1982-; ASCE, 1982-; Wrestling, 1977-81; Football, 1979; Desegregation Com, 1980-81; hon/St Wrestling Champ (177 lbs), 1981; Nat Sr Hon Soc, 1980-81; Askren S'ship Recip, 1981; Kiwanis Student Coun Awd, 1981; MVP Awd, Wrestling, 1981; g/BS in Constrn Mgmt Engrg; Minor in Elect Engrg; Wk w Bechtel Power Corp.

MAHAN, KENNETH LYNN oc/Student; b/Dec 10, 1964; h/314 Wyman Drive, Salisbury, MD 21801; p/Grant and Louise Mahan, Salisbury, MD; ed/ Wicomico Sr High, 1982; Student, Salisbury St Col, 1982-; cp/Treas, Pres, Cnslr, UMYF; HS Basketball Stat, 1979-82; HS Tennis Mgr, 1979-82; r/ U Meth; Acolyte Crucifer and Adm Bd Mem, Ch; hon/Nat Hon Soc, 1979-80, 1980-81, 1981-82; Dean's List, SSC, Sprg 1983; W/W Among Am HS Students; Yg Commun Ldrs of Am; g/Bus Adm Maj; Go into Bus for Myself or w Friend; Go into Local or St Polit.

MAHER, MARY FRANCES oc/Attorney, Graduate Student; b/Apr 27, 1955; h/1501 Maple Avenue, #305, Evanston, IL 60201; ba/Glenview, IL; p/Mr and Mrs F J Maher, Birmingham, MI; ed/ BS/MA, NWn Univ, 1977; JD, Loyola Univ, 1980; PhD in Progress, NWn Univ; cp/Law Clk, Howington, Elworth, Osswald & Hough, 1979; Law Clk, Speranza & Veverka, 1979-81; Grad Student, Instr and Legal Rschr, NWn Univ, 1980-82; Atty, SFN Cos Inc, 1983-; ISBA, Copyright Com Chm; CBA, Intell Property Com, Copyright Subcom; AAP, Freedom to Read Com, Software Subcom of Copyright Com; ABA, Communs Law Forum, Com on Communs; ABA; ATLA; ISBA; CBA; Am Judic; SCA; ICA; CSSA; r/Rom Cath; hon/Grad Sch F'ship, NWn; Lewis Foun S'ship, Loyola; George M Sargent Prize; Hons in Communication Studies, 1975, 1976, 1977; World W/W Wom.

MAHER, TIMOTHY JOHN oc/Neuropharmacologist; b/Nov 24, 1953; h/63 Sumner Street, Milton, MA 02186; ba/ Boston, MA; m/Barbara Walz; c/ Andrew Michael, Matthew Edward; p/ Robert D and Veronica I Maher, Hyde Park, MA; ed/BS, Boston St Col, 1976; PhD, MA Col of Pharm, 1980; pa/Asst Prof, Pharm, MA Col of Pharm, 1980-83; Res Assoc, MIT, 1980-; Assoc Prof, Pharm, MA Col of Pharm, 1983-; Bd of Dirs, MA Soc for Med Res; r/Rom Cath; hon/Pub'd in *Journal of Neurochemistry*, *Life Sciences*, *Journal of Neural Transmission*, *Science*, *American Journal of Clinical Nutrition*, *Journal of Pharmaceutical Sciences*, *Biochemical Pharmacology*; Grad w Hons in Biol, 1976; Rho Chi; W/W Frontier Sci and Technol.

MAKARI, DORIS ANGELINA oc/ Student; b/Jun 26, 1958; h/88 Everett Road, Demarest, NJ 07627; p/Jack and Odette Makari, Demarest, NJ; ed/No Val Reg HS, 1976; Tufts Univ, 1980;

MD, Med Col of PA, 1984; pa/Phys for Social Responsibility; Am Acad of Fam Practitioners; Am Med Wom's Assn, Citywide Rep 1982; cp/Student Coor, MCP's Humanities Scholar Prog in Dept of Commun and Preven Med; Singing City Choir of PA; Soloist, Tufts Chorales; Musicals, Plays; hon/Rensselaer Polytechnic Inst Math and Sci Awd; Arion Awd for Music; Best Eng Student in HS Awd; Bergen Co and All-St Choirs of NJ; Intl Yth in Achmt; Commun Ldrs of Am; g/Fam Pract Practitioner.

MALONE, MICHAEL FRANK oc/ Medical Student; b/Dec 23, 1957; h/ 3526 Brisban Street, Harrisburg, PA 17111; p/Nada I Malone, Harrisburg, PA; ed/AA, Harrisburg Area Commun Col, 1980; BS, Psych, Univ of Scranton, 1980; DPM, OH Col of Podiatric Med, 1985; pa/Am Col of Foot Surgs, Student Chapt; Am Col of Podopediatrics; Sports Med Clb; Kappa Tau Epsilon Profl Podiatric Frat; r/Prot; hon/Eagle Scout, 1974; Order of the Arrow, 1973; Carlos Sheffield Meml Medal, 1970; Outstg Achmt in French, 1972.

MALOTT, HEATHER LEIGH oc/ Free-Lance Artist; b/Feb 10, 1961; h/ RR5, Wabash, IN; p/Roy and Marianne Malott, Wabash, IN; ed/Southwood HS, 1979; Louisville Sch of Art, 1980; pa/ Free-Lance Artist; cp/Nat Hon Soc; Public Donations, Hand Painted Murals, Signs to Schs, Ch; r/First Ch of God; hon/Voted Most Likely to Succeed; 1st, Best of Shows, Area and Statewide Art Competitions; Nat Scholastic Art Competition, Hallmark Awd S'ship; Nat Dean's List; Intl Yth in Achmt; Commun Ldrs of Am; g/Free-Lance Illustrative Artist.

MANDEVILLE, GLENN ARTHUR oc/Student; b/Nov 15, 1962; h/1941 South Glenwood, Springfield, IL 62704; ba/Quincy, IL; p/Robert Lee and Alma Gertrude Mandeville, Springfield, IL; ed/Griffin HS, 1980; Quincy Col, 1984; cp/Football; Cross Country; Track; Nat Hon Soc, Treas; Key Clb, Treas; Pastoral Adv Coun; Med Explorers, Treas; Intramurals; Campus Min Lay Min; Circle K Clb, VP, Lt Gov, Dist Treas; Bio Clb, Secy; Intramurals; r/Cath; hon/ Acad Achmt S'ship; James Mentesti Awd; Norman Anderson Awd; Emerson Awd; Nat Dean's List; Commun Ldrs of Am; Outstg Yg Men in Am; g/BS in Biol; BS in Chem; Med Sch.

MANGAL, RAKESH KUMAR oc/ Medical Student; b/Feb 5, 1962; h/2906 14th Street, Pascagoula, MS 39567; ba/ Pascagoula, MS; p/Dr and Mrs Keshav C Mangal, Pascagoula, MS; ed/Grad, Pascagoula HS, 1980; BS in Biol and Chem, Millsaps Col, 1984; cp/Pres, Theta Nu Sigma, 1983-84; Phi Eta Sigma Frat, 1980-84; Omicron Delta Kappa, 1983-84; Sigma Lambda, 1984; First VP, Student Body, 1983-84; Jackson Metro Intercol Coun, 1983-84; Pres, Student Affairs Com, 1983-84; Pres, Student Activs, 1983-84; Student Exec Bd, 1983-84; Peer Advr, 1982, 1983, 1984; Student Coun Mem, 1978, 1979, 1980; SPQR; JETS, 1980; Pres, Mu Alpha Theta; VP, Jr Class, 1978-79; VP, Sr Class, 1979-80; Millsaps Col Student Senate, 1980, 1981, 1982; Alpha Epsilon Delta, 1981, 1982; Phi Eta Sigma, 1981, 1982; Theta Nu Sigma, 1981, 1982; Tri Beta, 1982; Eta Sigma, 1982; Chm,

Student Test File Com; VP, Art Clb; VP, Mu Alpha and Theta; NHS; Beta Clb; r/Hindu; hon/Pres's List, 1980-84; Judge in MS St Sci Fair, 1983; Biol I Awd, 1978; Art I Awd, 1977; Latin II Awd,m 1979; 1st Place, Dist Sci Fair, 1978; MS Vet Med Awd, 1977, 1978; Med Tech Monotary Awd, 1980; AUS Bronze Medal at St 1978, Dist 1980; USAF Sci Awd, 1979; USN Sci Awd, 1979; 1st Place, Intl Wildlife Sci Awd, 1980; Susan Belcher Meml S'ship; Nat Latin II Exam cum laude; Pascagoula HS Hall of Fame; Marion L Smith S'ship, 1980; J B Price Gen Chem Awd, 1982; W/W Among Am HS Students; W/W Among Am Cols and Univs; g/Cardiovas Surg.

MANGRUM, SHELLEY SUZANNE oc/Fashion Merchandising Teacher; b/ Nov 3, 1960; h/5242 Trousdale Drive, Nashville, TN 37220; ba/Nashville, TN; p/Wade and Nancy Mangrum, Nashville, TN; ed/Grad, John Overton HS, 1978; BS, Broadcast Jour, Mid TN St Univ, 1982; Student of Comml Music, Belmont Col; pa/Fashion Msdg Tchr, Draughon's Jr Col, 1983-; Anchorwom, Spec Assignment Reporter, *Daily News Journal* and Murfreesboro Cable Co, 1982-83; Fashion Editor, *Merchants Advocate*, 1983; News Intern, WTVF-TV, 1981-82; Free-Lance Model, TV Commls, Photo, 1978-; Sigma Delta Chi, Profl Soc of Jour; cp/Gamma Beta Phi Hon Soc; Kappa Delta Social Sorority; Sigma Chi Frat; Am Lung Assn; Spec Olympics; r/Christian; hon/Dean's List and Hon Soc Mem, Col; Talent Winner and Top Ten Finalist, Miss TN Pageant, 1983; MTSU Calendar Girl, 1979, 1980; Miss W TN St Fair, 1983; g/MBA; To Become Successful in TV News Reporting w Ultimate Goal of Becoming an Anchorwom and Talk Show Hostess in a Maj Mkt.

MANHEIM, CHRIS JAMES oc/Public Management Consultant; b/Mar 6, 1954; h/201 South Pine Street, New Lenox, IL 60451; p/Casper F Sr and Angeline Manheim, New Lenox, IL; ed/ Lincoln-Way, 1972; Lewis Univ, 1975; En IL Univ, 1977; pa/Public Mgmt Conslt; ASPA; AGA; NESA; APSA; cp/ ARC; Dem Cand, IL Legis; Former Scoutmaster; hon/IL Legis Fellow; Scoutmaster Ser Awd of Apprec; Outstg Yg Men of Am; g/Rep, Dist of IL Legis; Consortium of Govtl Cnslrs.

MANSFIELD, TERRY WAYNE oc/ Student; b/Oct 8, 1964; h/111 Evergreen Street, Martin, TN 38237; p/Mr and Mrs Gary Mansfield, Martin, TN; ed/HS Grad, Westview, 1983; Student, Univ of TN Martin; pa/Stockman, Wal-Mart, 1983; Electronics Pers, Wal-Mart, 1983-; cp/Mu Alpha Theta, 1981-83; Soccer Clb, 1983; Band, 1975-83; Boy Scouts, 1975-81; UTM Rifle Clb; hon/Earl Knepp S'ship; Bkkpg (Acctg Awd); 3 Red Ribbons for Band and 4 Lttrs in Band; g/Maj in Aerospace Engrg; Employmt at NASA.

MANSMANN, LINDA ANN oc/Restaurant Shift Supervisor; b/Jul 26, 1958; h/18 North Lafayette Avenue, Ventnor, NJ 08406; ba/Atlantic City, NJ; p/ Thomas A and Ann Mansmann, St Albans, WV; ed/Cherry Hill E HS, 1976; Grad, Rutgers Univ, 1981; pa/Hostess 1981-82, Room Ser Supvr 1982, Restaurant Shift Mgr 1982-, Claridge Hotel and Casino; cp/Gamma Tau Chi Sorority Alumnae; Rutgers Univ Alumnae;

r/Rom Cath; hon/Nat Hon Soc Grad, HS; Sister of the Yr, Gamma Tau Chi Sorority, Rutgers Univ; W/W Am Cols and Univs; g/MBA in Mktg from Rutgers Univ; Career in Casino Mktg.

MANTANES, JOHN ANDREW oc/ Dental Student; b/Jan 12, 1960; h/ Mount Prospect, IL; p/Mike Mantanes, Mount Prospect, IL; ed/John Herset HS, 1978; BS in Biol, Lewis Univ, 1982; Student, Loyola Univ Dental Sch, 1983–; pa/Enterprise Co Inc, 1982–; Lewis Univ, 1981-82; Proctor Johnson Enterprises, 1981-82; Salesman, Windys Restaurant, 1980-81; cp/Chgo Traveling Soccer Clb; Hon Org, 1978-82; NHS, 1978-82; Hon Mem, Tau Kappa Epsilon, 1982; Greek Orthodox Yth Assn, 1974-82; Col Soccer Team, 1978-82; Nat Soccer Leag, 1974-82; r/ Greek Orthodox; hon/HS Sr Hon Roll; NHS; Hon Grad; Nat and Col Deans' Lists; Col Hon Grad; Hon Org; Acad and Ath S'ships; Emily Howe Fisk S'ship; Cert of Merit, IL St Scholar; W/ W; Am Biogl Inst; g/Oral Surg.

MARASZEK, LISA L oc/Student; b/ Apr 24, 1963; h/Route 1, Box 187, Loganville, WI 53943; ba/Same; p/Mr and Mrs Joe Maraszek, Loganville, WI; ed/Grad, Reedsburg HS, 1981; Student, Univ of WI Platteville, 1981-; pa/Viking Village Foods, 1981, 1982; cp/Beta Gamma Rho; Omicron Delta Epsilon; Acad Adv'g Coor'g Coun, 1983; r/Cath; hon/Freshman Engrg Awd, 1981; Reedsburg Bk S'ship, 1981; Nishan Awd, 1981, 1982; Rupert and Gurtrude Werth Meml S'ship, 1983; Nat Dean's List; g/Maj in Indust Technol and Bus Adm; Upper Level Mgmt Position in Mktg for an Indust Firm.

MARCELAIS, CYNTHIA SUSAN oc/Student; h/Pittsboro, NC; m/Ronald; c/Michael, Michelle; p/Francis and Elizabeth Durst, Richland Center, WI; ed/Ithaca HS; AA, Fayetteville Tech Inst; BS, Univ of WI Platteville; MBA, Univ of NC Chapel Hill, 1983; mil/Cash Control Ofcr, AUS; cp/Kappa Delta Pi; Beta Gamma Sigma; WI Ath and Rec Fdn of Col Wom, Exec Bd; hon/Dist'd Mil Grad of Both WAC Ofcr Basic Course and Fin Ofcr Basic Course; Nat Merit S'ship Finalist; Wurzburg Mil Commun Cert of Achmt; Financial Execs Inst Awd to Outstg Acctg Student, UNC; g/Staff Acct w Deloitte, Haskins & Sells.

MARCH, AMY CAROLYN oc/Student; b/Jan 28, 1966; h/Route 2, Box 22-B, Spring Hope, NC 27882; p/Jack and Carolyn March, Spring Hope, NC; ed/HS Student; cp/Student Coun, 1979-81; JETS Clb, 1981-82; Nat Hist Clb, 1982-83; Beta Clb, 1982-83; So Nash Firebird Marching Band, 1980-83; r/Prot; hon/Most Outstg, Sci, 1980; Ldrship Awd, 1980; Cert of Merit, French, 1982; Nom'd to Attend Gov's Sch, 1983; g/Maj in Psych at Appalachian St Univ.

MARCHBANKS, BECKY DARLENE oc/Student; b/Nov 30, 1965; h/1033 Townsend Drive, Easley, SC 29640; ba/ Greenville, SC; p/Wayne and Jean Marchbanks, Easley, SC; ed/Easley High; pa/Litchfield Theatre; hon/Sci; Miss Congeniality; Miss Sun Fun; g/To Enter the Field of Med.

MARCUM, DEBRA LYNN oc/Speech and Language Pathologist; h/208 Somerset Village, Somerset, KY 42501;

ba/Somerset, KY; p/Huston and Geneva Marcum, Greensburg, KY; ed/Greensburg HS; BA, MA, Wn KY Univ; pa/ Nat Com of Am Spch, Lang and Hearing Assn; KY Spch, Lang and Hearing Assn; N Am Rdg for the Handicapped Prog; Instrumental in Devel of BA and MA Prog in Spch/Lang Pathol at Univ; Developed Prog in Spch and Lang Pathol for 10 Co Area; Developed Prog for Horseback Riding for Handicapped; Instrumental in Developing Prog for Pet Therapy St-Wide and Developing Ch Camp for Handicapped; Co-Author, *Research in Speech Pathology and Audiology; Bibliography in Non-Verbal Communication*; r/Meth Ch; hon/Dean's List; Pres's List; Others; W/W S and SW.

MARCUS, CRAIG STUART oc/Pharmacist; b/Aug 21, 1960; h/1034 Court #202, Memphis, TN 38104; ba/Memphis, TN; m/Dorothy Ann; p/Charles and Anne Marcus, Memphis, TN; ed/ Sci Dipl, Harding Acad of Memphis, 1978; Pre-Pharm, Memphis St Univ, 1978-80; BS in Pharm, Univ of TN Ctr for Hlth Scis, 1983; pa/Pharm, Walgreen's, 1983; cp/Eagle Scout, BSA; r/ Ch of Christ; hon/MSU Freshman Hon Soc, Phi Eta Sigma, 1979; MSU Sophomore Hon Soc, Alpha Lambda Delta, 1980; Nat Hon Soc; g/Pharmacy Mgmt, Owner.

MARCUS, TRENT WRIGHT oc/ Student; b/Jul 20, 1963; h/555 McElroy, Memphis, TN 38119; p/Charles and Anne Marcus, Memphis, TN; ed/Sci Dipl, Harding Acad of Memphis; Pre-Profl Deg, Memphis St Univ; pa/ Best Locking Sys, 1981; Pharm Transporter 1982, 1983, Lab Data Clk 1983-, Meth Hosp; cp/BSA, Asst Scoutmaster; Gamma Beta Phi; Christian Student Ctr; NHS; Phi Eta Sigma; Biol Clb; Acappella Choir; Sci Fair; Track; Soccer; VBS Tchr; r/Pk Village Christian Ch; hon/Dean's List, 1982; Eagle Rank, BSA, 1981; Servant of Jesus Christ; St Champ, Soccer Team; Nat Dean's List; W/W Among Am HS Students; Commun Ldrs of Am; g/To Become a Med Dr Serving Some Mission Field.

MARKEY, EDWARD W oc/Sports Publicist; b/Nov 3, 1959; h/81 Middlesex Road, Chestnut Hill, MA 02167; ba/ Cambridge, MA; p/Mr and Mrs Edward Markey, Burlington, VT; ed/Grad, Rice Meml HS, 1977; BA, Eng, St Michael's Col, 1981; pa/Public Relats Intern, En Col Ath Conf, 1981-82; Asst Sports Info Dir, Harvard Univ, 1982-; Col Sports Info Dirs of Am, 1980-; Asst Editor of All Harvard Univ Ath Pubs, incl'g the Awd Winning *Harvard Football News* of 1982; cp/Nat Hon Soc, HS, 1977; hon/ Outstg Yg Men of Am; g/Involvement w Sports on TV (Especially Prodn).

MARKS, CONNIE RENEE oc/Registered Pharmacist; b/Sep 6, 1955; h/#915 30 Plaza Square, Saint Louis, MO 63103; ba/Saint Louis, MO; p/Cozy and Shirley Marks, Saint Louis, MO; ed/NW HS, 1973; BS in Pharm, Xavier Univ of NO, 1978; pa/Reg'd Pharm, Homer G Phillips Hosp 1978-79, Robert Koch Hosp 1979–, Mound City Pharm 1980–, Dome Pharm 1980–; Rho Chi Pharm Hon Soc; Nat Pharmaceutical Assn; Mound City Pharmaceutical Assn, Secy 1981-83; cp/U Negro Col Fund Vol; Girl Scout Coun of Gtr St Louis, Cadette Troop Ldr and Neighborhood Chm; r/ Bapt; hon/U Negro Col Fund Vol of the

Yr Awd, 1983; b/Master's in Hlth Adm/ Bus Adm.

MARKS, FRANCES oc/Resident; b/ Oct 1, 1956; h/New Rochelle, NY; ba/ Columbia Presbyterian Medical Center, New York, NY; m/Paul Steven Taxin DMD; p/Dr and Mrs Arthur Marks, New Rochelle, NY; ed/New Rochelle HS, 1974; BS, Fairleigh Dickinson Univ, 1978; MD, Columbia Univ Col of Phys and Surgs, 1982; pa/Resident, PGY II Dept Ob-Gyn; Sigma Xi; AMA; NY St Med Soc; Am Med Students Assn; Jr Fellow, Am Col of Obstetricians and Gynecologists; Am Med Wom's Assn; cp/US Tennis Assn; Am Mus of Natural Hist; Editor-in Chief, Sports Editor, Col Yrbook; Wom Varsity Tennis Team; Grad Com; Residence Life Coun; Organic Chem Recitation; Cnslg Ctr Tutor Prog; Cancer Res Ed Prog; Student Affil, Am Chem Soc; hon/ Sebrell F'ship, Columbia Univ Col of Phys and Surgs Inst of Human Nutrition, 1979; Grad, summa cum laude w Hons in Biol; Mennen S'ship, 1977; Thomas F Cock Prize, 1982; W/W Among HS Students; W/W Among Students in Am Univs and Cols; Intl Yth in Achmt; Commun Ldrs of Am; g/ Ob-Gyn: Res, Tchg and Pvt Pract.

MARKS, ROBERT DARRYL oc/ Student; b/Nov 26, 1960; h/608 North Cherry, Magnolia, MS 39652; p/Mr and Mrs Alphonse Marks, Magnolia, MS; ed/S Pike HS; MS St Univ; cp/Band; Biochem Clb, Pres; Alpha Phi Alpha; Alpha Zeta; Order of Omega; Capt, Basketball Team; Organist, Choir Ensemble; hon/Student Assn Senate; Pres, Coun of Black Student Org; Named "Dist'd Collegian," Body of Alpha Phi; g/Chem Engrg; Med Career.

MARLER, JOSEPH PAUL oc/Student; b/Jun 19, 1964; h/PO Box 623, Tracy City, TN 37387; p/Paul and Gayle Marler, Tracy City, TN; ed/Grundy Co HS, 1982; Att'g, Mid TN St Univ; cp/ CTO VP; Commun Basketball; HS Band; Sch Paper Staff; Lib Clb Sgt-at-Arms; Sportsman Clb; Archery Clb; Nat Hon Soc; Beta Clb; hon/ Percussion Awd; Percussion Ldr; Lib Aide; g/Maj in Pre-Law; Law Enforcement.

MAROULES, JEAN CHRISTY oc/ Student; b/Jul 19, 1960; h/2710 Carey Road, Kinston, NC 28501; p/Chris and Christine Maroules, Kinston, NC; ed/ Arendall Parrott Acad, 1978; cp/Student Govt Assn, Treas 1977; Epis Yth Grp, Secy, Treas, VP, Pres, 1973-77; Cheerldr, 1976; Intl Lang Org, Treas 1983; Phi Sigma Iota, 1983; r/Epis; hon/ Fleming S'ship Recip, 1983; Rotarian S'ship, 1978; Curric Bd Student Body Rep, 1982-83; Dean's List, 1980-83; g/ Career in Intl Commerce or Govt.

MARSHALL, BRENDA JOY oc/ Administrative Assistant, Sales Representative, Purchasing Agent; b/Jan 14, 1964; h/5411 Marsh Road, Haslett, MI 48840; ba/Okemos, MI; p/Dale and Patricia Marshall, Haslett, MI; ed/ Haslett HS, 1982; LPN, Lansing Commun Col, 1983; pa/Adm Asst, Sales Rep, Purchasing Agt, Bio-Gas Detector Corp, 1981-; cp/Cheerldr, Capt 1977-79; Marching Band, 1978-82; VP, Med Explorer Post #310, 1979-80; Secy, Explorers' Pres' Assn, 1979-81; Pres, Ch Yth Coun, 1979-81; Sum Missionary to AK, 1980; r/Bapt; hon/HS Valedictorian, 1982; Nat Hon Soc, 1980-82; MI Competitive S'ship, 1982; Phi Theta Kappa Jr Col Nat Hon Soc, 1983; W/W Among Am HS Students; g/To Attend Christian Col, Pursuing Bus and Adm.

MARSHALL, PAUL EUGENE oc/ Student; b/Jun 6, 1965; h/PO Box 700, Thoreau, NM 87323; p/Glenn E and Helen M Marshall, Thoreau, NM; cp/ NHS, 1982-83, VP 1982; Student Coun, Pres 1983; Ch Yth Coun, 1982-83; r/ Evangelical; hon/All-St Football, 1981; All-Dist Football, 1981-82; All-St Music, 1980-82; NMSU Sr Hon Band, 1983; Valedictorian, HS, 1983; W/W Music; g/Computer Engrg Deg from NM St Univ; Master's Deg; PhD.

MARSHALL, TODD EDSON oc/ Student; b/Apr 24, 1965; h/5411 Marsh Road, Haslett, MI 48840; p/Dale and Patricia Marshall, Haslett, MI; ed/ Haslett HS, 1983; cp/Football, 5 Yrs; Track, 4 Yrs; Pres, Ch Yth Coun, 1980-82; Sum Missionary to AK, 1980; Apple User Grp; r/Bapt; hon/Citizenship Awds, 6th, 8th and 12th Grades; Nat Hon Soc, 1981-83; All Leag, All Co Football Hons, Sr Yr, 1982; g/To Attend Christian Col, Pursuing Bus, Data Processing and Computers.

MARTIN, ANTHONY LEE oc/Student; b/Jul 2, 1968; h/Route 1, Box 162B, Estill Springs, TN 37330; p/James A and Judy K Childers, Estill Springs, TN; ed/ HS Student; cp/Sci Fair; Acad Bowl; Football Team; r/Bapt; hon/Nat Jr Hon Soc; Jr Beta Clb; Acad Bowl Mem, 3 Yrs; 2nd Place in Envir Scis, Chattanooga Reg Sci Fair; g/Biol Maj; Marine Oceanographer.

MARTIN, BRUCE ALBERT oc/Student; b/Jul 28, 1963; h/106 Garrell Street, Tabor City, NC 28463; p/Mr and Mrs Harry L Martin, Tabor City, NC; ed/HS Dipl, 1981; Att'd Col, 1981-82, 1983; pa/Asst Janitor, 1977-80; Asst Janitor, 1980-81; Asst Libn, 1981-82; Asst Vet, 1982-83; Asst Libn, 1983; r/ Bapt; hon/Sci and Math Awd, 1977; French Awd, 1980, 1981; W/W Among Am HS Students; Intl Yth in Achmt; g/To Receive a Deg in Jour; To Write a Book.

MARTIN, DENISE RITA oc/Teacher of the Learning Disabled; b/Oct 23, 1959; h/9637 South Kenton, Oak Lawn, IL 60453; ba/Hometown, IL; p/Charles and Blanche A Martin, Oak Lawn, IL; ed/Dipl, Mother McAuley HS, 1977; BS in Spec Ed and Early Childhood Ed, MS in Lng Disabilities, Chgo St Univ; pa/ Tchr of the Lng Disabled, Oak Lawn Hometown Sch Dist 123, 1982-; Instrnl Aide for Behavior Disordered, Ridgeland Sch Dist 122, 1980-82; CEC, 1981-; cp/Big Sister/Little Sister, HS; Campus Min, VP 1980-81; Coor, Newman Clb for Cath Students, 1980; Pres, Kappa Delta Pi, 1980-81; Co-Moderator, Cheerldrs, Hometown Sch, 1982-83; r/ Cath; hon/Kappa Delta Pi Awd, 1981; Bernadine Wash S'ship, 1981; Francis W Parker Awd for Excell in Tchg, 1981; CSU Grad S'ship, 1981; VP List; Dean's List, 1979, 1980; Nat Dean's List; Commun Ldrs of Am; W/W Am Cols and Univs; g/To Complete Doct Studies in Audiology; To Wk in Pvt Pract or in Hosps; To Open Own Sch for Hearing Impaired.

MARTIN, FRANCES YVONNE oc/ Student; b/Sep 22, 1964; h/Route 3,

White Horse Road, Greenville, SC 29609; ba/Greenville, SC; p/Frank and Frances Martin, Greenville, SC; ed/ Grad, Berea HS, 1982; Deg in Fashion Msdg, Anderson Jr Col, 1984; pa/ Pt-time Ofc Wkr, Elliott, Davis & Co, CPAs, 1983; Ch Day Camp Cnslr, Berea First Bapt Ch, 1981, 1982; cp/FBLA, 1980-82, VP 1982; FHA, 1978-80; OIK Frat, 1982-84, VP 1983-84; Ch Choir; Bapt Yg Wom; Phi Theta Kappa Frat, 1983-84; r/Bapt; hon/Hon Grad, 1982; Dean's List, 1983; Grad Marshal, 1983; Conf I Miss FBLA, 1982; W/W Am HS Students; Nat Dean's List; g/4-Yr Deg in Fashion Msdg and Mktg; Wk at a Maj Dept Store or Specialty Shop in a Position of Buyer.

MARTIN, MONICA LaCHELLE oc/Student; b/Jul 6, 1964; h/129 Wayne Drive, Gallatin, TN 37066; p/Mr and Mrs William D Martin, Gallatin, TN; ed/ Gallatin Sr HS; Student, Univ of TN Knoxville; pa/Filing, Gallatin C of C, 1980; Filing, Durham Mfg Co, 1980-81; Sales Clk, Store and Window Displays, The Peoples Store, 1980-83; cp/Gallatin Jr Girls' Cotillion Clb; Vol, Lib; Beta Clb; Tri-Hi-Y Reporter; Hist Soc; FCA; Basketball, Secy-Treas; Tennis Team; Cheerldr; Sch Newspaper Reporter; Student Coun; Art Clb; Teen Choir; Yth Coun; Yth Week Ofcr; Zeta Tau Alpha Sorority; Advtg Clb; r/Bapt; hon/ Sunland Plans Nat Mag Sales Winner; 2nd Place, Voice of Dem Spch Contest; 3rd Place, TN Wom Fdn Art Contest; Phi Eta Sigma; Dean's List w High Hons; Ranked 14th in Grad'g Class; W/W Among Am HS Students; g/Maj in Communs w Advtg Emphasis.

MARTIN, SANDRA ELIZABETH oc/ Student; b/Nov 21, 1965; h/Route 1, Box 341, Stantonville, TN 38379; p/Mr and Mrs Franklin Martin, Stantonville, TN; ed/McNairy Ctl HS; cp/Student Govt, 2nd VP 1983; Future Tchrs of Am, VP 1983; Mod Music Masters, Histn 1980; Asst Libn, Ch; r/So Bapt; hon/Class Favorite, 1983; Hall of Fame, 1983; Girls' St Del, 1983; Class Secy, 1982, 1983; W/W Among Am HS Students; g/Maj in Med, Memphis St Univ; Dr.

MARTIN, TIMOTHY EDWARD oc/ Student; h/Route 3, Box 462, Troutville, VA 24175; ba/Lexington, VA; p/Mr and Mrs Algie E Martin, Troutville, VA; ed/ Grad, Lord Botetourt HS; Grad, VA Mil Inst, 1985; mil/AFROTC; cp/Class Treas; Sci Clb Pres; Hon Soc; Nat Hon Soc VP; Wrestling Team, JV and Varsity; r/Prot; hon/Math Awd; Most Improved, Team Ldrship Awd, Wrestling; Am Legion Boys' St; AFROTC Navigator S'ship; g/Elect Engrg Maj; AF Navigator/Pilot.

MARTINSON, JOHANNA SHERRILL oc/Student; b/Sep 4, 1966; h/5310 North Powers Ferry, Atlanta, GA 30327; ba/Atlanta, GA; p/Robert W and Kathryn Smith, Atlanta, GA; ed/Dipl, Riverwood HS, 1984; pa/Sum Horse-Backriding Cnslr/Tchr, Little Hope Ranch, 1977-83; Barn Mgr and Tnr, Mt Vernon Stables, 1982-83; Sales Clk/Cashier, Barrett's Shoes, 1983-84; cp/Pres, Jr Key Clb, 1981-82; Pres, Interact Clb, 1983-84; Cross Country/ Track Mem, 1980-84; Drill Team Mem, 1982-83; Yg Life Secy, 1981-84; Nat Hon Soc, 1983-84; All-St Chorus, 1983; Fdg Lang Clb, 1981-83; Chorale/Girls' Chorus, 1982-83; Math Tutor, 1983-84;

r/Epis; hon/Gov's Hons Nom in Sci, 1983; Furman Scholar, Presb Col Jr Fellow, GA Cert of Merit, 1983; Tag Prog, 1978-84; Super Hon Roll, 1979-83; Yg Sports Personalities; g/To Attend Univ of VA or Duke Univ, and Pursue Biol Scis, Psych, Computer Sci and Marine Biol.

MASNERI, JOSEPH ARTHUR oc/ Student; b/Apr 27, 1960; h/442 Darlington Avenue, Darlington, SC 29532; p/ Mr and Mrs Ray Masneri, Darlington, SC; ed/Willington Acad, 1978; BS, Ec Zool, Clemson Univ, 1982; cp/Sigma Nu Frat, 1979-82; Capt, Intramural Sports, Football and Basketball, 1980; Key Clb Secy, 1977; HS Letterman, Football (4 Yrs), Basketball (3 Yrs); Capt, Track (2 Yrs), Tennis (1 Yr); HS Sr Class Ofcr, 1977 (Secy-Treas); r/Meth; hon/Boys' St, 1977; Basketball Tournament MVP, 1978; Graduation Marshall, 1977; Dean's List, Clemson, 1982; W/W Among Am HS Students; Soc of Dist'd HS Students; g/Pharm Sch at Med Univ of SC; Pharm Sales; Open Own Drugstore.

MASSEY, JACQUES ANTONIO oc/ Student; b/Mar 11, 1963; h/4528 South Roman Street, New Orleans, LA 70125; p/Mr and Mrs Louis L Massey, New Orleans, LA; ed/John F Kennedy HS, 1981; Currently Enrolled, So Univ in NO; pa/Pt-time Acctg Clk, NO Hilton Hotel and Towers; cp/Baseball Team, 1979; Homecoming Ct, 1979; DECA, 1980-81; Prom Night Com, 1981; Class Night Com, 1981; Freshman Class Senator and Dir of Pubs for Student Govt Assn, 1981-82; VP, Sophomore Class, 1982-83; VP, Jr Class and Bus Mgr for Student Govt Assn, 1983-84; W/W Com, 1981; Loan Com, 1982-83; NAACP; Alpha Phi Alpha Frat Inc, 1982; PAAC; Homecoming Ct, 1981, 1982, 1983; Disciplinary Bd, 1983-84; Homecoming Com, CoChm; r/Cath; hon/Chancellor's S'ship, 1983; So Univ Acad Hon Roll; Intl Yth in Achmt; g/ Deg in Acctg; Law Sch.

MASSINGILL, VONDA FRANCES oc/Student; b/Apr 21, 1967; h/140 Pine Street, Easley, SC 29640; p/Mr and Mrs Ray L Massingill, Easley, SC; ed/Grad, Easley Sr HS, 1985; cp/Nat Hon Soc, 1982, 1983, 1984; Sec-Treas, Homeroom, 1981-82, 1983-84; Touring Chorus, 1981-82, Music Coor 1981-82; Drama Clb, 1981-82, Play Participant 1983; Pep Clb, 1979-84; Girl Scouts, 1973-84; Jour Clb, Treas 1981-84; Treble Chorus, 1982-84; Acteens, 1979-84, Treas 1980-84; Spirit Com Mem, 1983-84; Newspaper Staff Mem, 1983-84; r/Pk St Bapt Ch, Wom's Softball Team 1981-84, Choir 1979-84; hon/Top 10% of Sophomore Class, 1983; Most Improved of Wom's Softball Team, 1982; Tuning In Participant, 1983; Studio '82 Participant, Breaker Block E, 1982; g/To Attend Furman Univ or Col of Charleston; Maj in Drama.

MASTERS, SUSAN BETH oc/Student; h/605 West Market, Taylorville, IL 62568; p/Mel and Ellen Masters, Taylorville, IL; ed/Taylorville HS, 1976; En IL Univ, 1976-77; BM in Applied Voice 1980, MM in Applied Voice 1982, Univ of IL; Staatliche Hochschule fuer Musik, Cologne, Germany, 1982-83; pa/ Tchg Asst, Voice, Univ of IL, 1981-82; Subst Tchr, Taylorville, IL, Public Schs,

1982; Self-Employed Voice Tchr, 1981-; Am Fdn of Musicians Union; Sigma Alpha Iota Music Frat; cp/Navigators, 1978-82; Taylorville Mun Band, 1973-; Alpha Omicron Pi Sorority; r/U Meth Ch; hon/Taylorville HS Sr Class Spkr, 1976; Talented Student Awd, En IL Univ, 1977; Bronze Tablet, Univ of IL, 1980; Yg Commun Ldrship Awd, 1982; Rotary Intl Ednl Awd, Grad S'ship, Staatliche Hochschule fuer Musik, 1982-83; W/W Among HS Students; W/ W Among Col Students; Col Register; g/Univ Music Prof.

MATHENY, HARVEY WILLIAMS oc/Student; b/Aug 8, 1962; h/2079 Highway 59 West, Covington, TN 38019; p/Mr and Mrs H W Matheny, Covington, TN; ed/Grad, Covington HS, 1980; Att'g, Memphis St Univ; cp/ Alpha Lambda Delta, 1981; Phi Eta Sigma, 1981; Tau Beta Pi, 1982-83; ASCE, 1982-83, VP 1983 (Sprg); Pres 1983 (Fall); r/Prot; hon/Dist'd Herff Engrg Scholar, 1980-83; Nat Dean's List; g/To Attend Grad Sch w Concentration in Envir Engrg.

MATTHEWS, JOYCE LYNN oc/ Student; b/Apr 21, 1961; h/1713 Kennedy Drive, Camden, SC 29020; p/ Mr and Mrs P M Matthews, Camden, SC; ed/BA, Eng, Columbia Col, 1983; Camden HS, 1979; pa/Clk, Camden Floral Co, 1980, 1981; cp/Columbia Col Wind Ensemble, 1979-82; Wesley F'ship, VP; Eng Majs' Clb, Secy-Treas 1982; *Columbian*, Sect Editor 1981, 1982; *Criterion*, Editor 1982-83; Student Senate, Coor'g Bd 1982-83; r/Meth; hon/Alpha Kappa Gamma, 1982; Grad, magna cum laude, 1983; Pres's List, 1982, 1983; Marshal, 1980, 1981, 1982, 1983; Ariail S'ship, Eng, 1981, 1982; Sigma Tau Delta, Eng Hon Awd, 1981, 1982; Eng Dept Awd, 1983; W/W Am Univs and Cols; g/Mag Copywriter or TV Writer.

MATTINA, RODNEY ANTHONY JR oc/Student; b/Oct 22, 1965; h/208 Spratley Avenue, Biloxi, MS 39531; ba/ University, MS; p/Mr and Mrs Rodney A Mattina Sr, Biloxi, MS; ed/Biloxi HS, 1983; Att'g, Univ of MS; cp/Nat Jr Hon Soc, 1980; Nat Hon Soc, 1982-83; Spanish Nat Hon Soc, 1982; Interact Clb, 1981; Key Clb, 1983; F'ship of Christian Aths, 1983; Football, 1981; Baseball, 1981-83; r/Rom Cath; hon/ MVP, Baseball, 1982-83; Mem, MS All-St Team for Baseball, 1983; Selected to Top 10 Baseball Players of Harrison Co, MS, 1983; Soc of Dist'd Am HS Students; g/Deg in Geol or Petro Engrg; Play Profl Baseball.

MAY, ARTHUR MICHAEL oc/Minister of Education; b/May 2, 1954; h/ 2174 Lynn, Freeport, IL 61032; ba/ Freeport, IL; m/Deborah Jane Ferrari, c/Jeramie Allen, Jason Matthew; p/ Delmar and Bertha May, Des Moines, IA; ed/Lincoln HS, 1972; BRE, BA (summa cum laude), Open Bible Col; MA, Assems of God Grad Sch; pa/Min of Ed; cp/Student Coun Rep; Pres, Sr Col Class; hon/Delta Epsilon Chi; W/ W Among Students in Am Univs and Cols; Intl Yth in Achmt; g/Doct in Ed/ Curric Theory; Col Tchr.

MAY, KEITH ALLEN oc/Student; b/ May 18, 1965; h/Route 1, Box 305, Bergton, VA 22811; ba/Blacksburg, VA; p/Mr and Mrs E A May Jr, Bergton, VA; ed/Grad, Broadway HS, 1983; Att'g, VA Polytechnic Inst; pa/Wk on Fam Farm; cp/FFA, Fdn Pres 1982-83, Chapt VP 1979, Reporter 1981, Treas 1982; Nat Hon Soc, VP 1983; Sci Clb, VP 1983; FCA, VP 1981-82; One Way Christian Clb, Secy-Treas 1981-82; Yth Grp, Treas 1980-82; Spanish Clb, 1980-82; Model UN Mem, 1982-83; Green Quill Reporter, 1981; Keep VA Green Mem, 1980-82; Academically Gifted Grp, 1982; Pop Quiz Team, 1982; HS Jour Mem, 1982; hon/En Reg Livestock Proficiency Winner, FFA, 1983; St Winner in Soil and Water Mgmt Proficiency, FFA, 1982; Star St Farmer in VA, 1982; Star Chapt Farmer, 1982; Sch Superlatives, Most Likely to Succeed, Best All Round, Most Thoughtful, Best Dressed, Most Common Sense, Most Studious; g/Animal Sci and Agri Ec.

MAYBEE, JANICE MARIE oc/Student; b/Oct 18, 1962; h/1565 North University Avenue, #149, Provo, UT 84604; p/Mr and Mrs William L Maybee, Green River, UT; ed/Green River HS, 1980; Att'g, Brigham Yg Univ; cp/ Cheerldr; LDS Sem Pres; Paper Co-Editor; Basketball Lttrman; Student Coun; Band; Chorus; Drill Team; Pep Clb; Drama; Jr Class VP; Secy, Prog for Single Adults; r/LDS; Sunday Sch Tchr; hon/Music Fest, Outstg Woodwind at Reg; Am's Outstg Names and Faces; W/ W Music; Soc of Dist'd Am HS Students; g/Maj in Sch Psych; Minor in Eng.

MAYFIELD, MICHAEL WADE oc/ Student; b/Oct 9, 1962; h/#1 Silly Sally Place, 1929 Honore Avenue, North Chicago, IL 60064; p/Mr and Mrs Hugh Mayfield, North Chicago, IL; ed/Grad, N Chgo Commun HS, 1981; Att'g, Wn IL Univ; cp/HS: Editor-in-Chief of Sch Paper, Bus Mgr for HS Yrbook, Cartoonist for Sch Paper, Sports Mgr for Football, Wrestling and Track, Varsity Clb Mem; r/Bapt; hon/1st Place, Floor Decorating Contest 1981, 1st Place, Pumpkin Carving Contest 1981, 3rd Place, Floor Mural Painting Contest 1982, 1st Place, Pumpkin Carving Contest 1982, 2nd Place, All-Univ Pumpkin Carving Contest 1982, 1st Place, Floor Decorating Contest 1982, 1st Place, Window Painting Contest 1982, All Sponsored by Weztel Hall, Wn IL Univ; Num Art Exhibs and Personal Achievements; Num HS Hons; W/W Among Am HS Students; Intl Yth in Achmt; Commun Ldrs of Am; g/To Pursue a Career as a Comml Artist w a Maj Firm, or Pursue a Career as a Cartoonist w a Metro Newspaper or Nat Mag.

MAYHAM, WADE GRANT JR oc/ Student, Program Assistant; b/Feb 20, 1963; h/4121 Shreve Avenue, Saint Louis, MO 63105; p/Wade G Mayham Sr, Saint Louis, MO; ed/Grad, Wm Beaumont HS, 1981; cp/Sr Class Bus Mgr, 1981; Nat Hon Soc; Treas, Student Coun; Past Pres, Antioch Dist Yth F'ship Yg Negro Musicians Assn (Hyden Wilson Music Guild), 1981; r/Bapt; hon/ Dist'd Am HS Roster, 1981; Outstg Student Awd, Phi Delta Kappa; g/Eng/ Math Maj; To Pursue a Career in Ed and Become a Prin.

MAYHEW, LEAH C oc/Student; b/ Nov 26, 1966; h/116 Windamere Road, Easley, SC 29640; ba/Easley, SC; p/Mr and Mrs Boyd R Mayhew, Easley, SC; ed/Student, Easley HS; cp/Hon Soc, 1983; Pep Clb, 1981-83; Homeroom Pres, 1982-83; Student Coun, 1982-83; French Clb, 1983; Latin Clb, 1981; Rich's Teen Bd, 1983; Handbell Choir, 1982-83; Band, 1977-81; Participant, HS Play, *L'il Abner*, 1983; Soccer Team, 1976-81; r/Prot; hon/Miss Sophomore, HS Pageant, 1982; Homecoming Ct, 1982; Participant in Miss 4th of July Pageant, 1983; Rated as Excell in En Shore Band Competition (Flute), 1981; Rated as Excell in SC Band Competition (Flute), 1982; g/To Attend Col and Maj in Computer Sci; To Pursue a Career in Modeling.

McCAGHREN, HOWELL KEITH oc/ Student; b/Dec 17, 1964; h/Route 3, Box 253, Danville, AL 35619; p/Mr and Mrs Howell McCashren, Danville, AL; ed/ HS Dipl, 1983; Student, Calhoun Commun Col, 1983-; cp/FFA, Chapt Pres 1983, Reporter 1982; HS Baseball and Basketball, 1979-83; r/Bapt; hon/Nat Eng Merit Awd, 1983; Nat Agri Merit Awd, 1983; Nat Beta Clb, 1983; Nat FFA Poultry Proficiency Contest Winner, 1983; Sr Class Pres, 1983; 12 Yrs Perfect Attendance at Sch, 1983; Dist Star Farmer, 1983; All-Co Baseball and Basketball, 1979-83; All-Area Basketball, 1982, 1983; g/Pursue a Career in Agri or Purchase a Farm and Become a Full-time Farmer.

McCAIN, LYNN CAROL oc/ Teacher, Librarian; b/Nov 14, 1960; h/ 7827 North Avenue, River Forest, IL 60305; ba/River Forest, IL; m/Paul Timothy; p/Dr and Mrs Robert A Grunow, Spring Hill, FL; ed/Lyman HS; Valparaiso Univ; BA in Elem Ed, Concordia Col, 1983; pa/Tchr/Libn, Roosevelt Jr HS, 1983-; AAUW; Roosevelt Sch Yrbook Advr; r/Luth; g/Continue in the Tchg Field.

McCAIN, PAUL TIMOTHY oc/Student; b/Feb 12, 1962; h/7827 North Avenue, River Forest, IL 60305; m/Lynn Carol Grunow; p/Paul and Jean McCain, Pensacola, FL; ed/Pensacola Cath HS; Student, Concordia Col; pa/Photog, Naval Air Rework Facility, US Govt; cp/ Phi Alpha Theta; r/Luth; hon/HS Top Ec Student, 1980; Top Social Studies Student, 1980; Nat Hon Soc, 1976-80; Jr Classical Leag; Hon Roll, 4 Yrs; Col Dean's List; Pres S'ship Recip; g/ Pre-Sem Study; Pastor in Luth Ch.

McCANN, KEVIN PATRICK oc/ Student; b/Aug 21, 1964; h/4520 A North Charles Street, Baltimore, MD 21210; p/Joseph V McCann, Liberia, Africa; Gaynel B McCann, San Anselmo, CA; ed/Our Lady of Good Counsel HS, 1982; Bus Adm Maj, Loyola Col; cp/Camp Good Counsel; BSA; Ch Wkr; Yth Retreat Ldr; Football; LaCrosse; Wrestling; Intramurals; Col Rugby; r/Cath; hon/W/W Among Am HS Students; g/Bus Adm Maj.

McCASLAND, GINA GILILLAND oc/Piano Teacher; b/Sep 22, 1959; h/812 Brett Drive, Edmond, OK 73034; m/ Ross D; p/Mr and Mrs Gary Gililland; ed/Grad, Midland HS, 1978; BMus, OK City Univ; pa/Piano Tchr; Am Guild of Organists, 1980-83; Sigma Alpha Iota Music Frat for Wom, 1981-83; Pi Kappa Lambda Hon Music Frat, 1983; hon/ Winner, Hemlee Organ S'ship, TX Tech Univ, 1978, 1979; Semi-Finalist, Am Guild of Organists Nat Student Competition, 1981; W/W Among Students in Am Univs and Cols; g/Continued Application of Deg in Area of Pvt Music

Tutoring.

McCAW, BRIAN PIERRE oc/Student; b/Nov 24, 1964; h/432 Plymouth Avenue, Charlotte, NC 28206; p/Mr and Mrs Albert McCaw, Charlotte, NC; ed/Grad, N Mecklenburg High; cp/Choir, 1979; Football, 1979; Track, 1978-79; Basketball Assn, 1978-83; Track Assn, 1982-83; Booster Clb, 1982-83; Media Assn, 1980-82; Newspaper Staff Sports Editor, 1982-83; r/Bapt; g/Computers; Jour; Media and TV; Acct.

McCLELLAN, CLARA ELIZABETH oc/Student; b/Nov 8, 1964; h/PO Box 395, Goodman, MS 39079; p/Mr and Mrs Henry B McClellan Jr, Goodman, MS; ed/Dipl, E Holmes Acad, 1982; Data Processing Deg, Holmes Jr Col, 1984; pa/Wk-Study, Holmes Jr Col's Bus Ofc, 1982-84; Rebecca's Drug Store, 1981-82; Joe's Drug Ctr, 1980-81; cp/Basketball and Track, 2 Yrs; Mem, *Signpost* and Annual Staff, 4 Yrs; Co-Editor of Annual, Jr Yr; Co-Editor, *Signpost*, Sr Yr; Sr Class Secy; Cheerldr; Basketball and Football Cheerldr, Col; Phi Beta Lambda, VP; Secy, Col Ser Clb; r/Bapt; hon/Bus Awd; One of 8 Campus Beauties; Freshman Class Favorite; Elected Homecoming Queen, 1983; g/Maj in Bus Adm, MS St Univ; Obtain a Job w a Corp.

McCONNELL, RACHEL ELIZABETH oc/Student; b/Sep 22, 1961; h/728 Wesley Drive, Atlanta, GA 30305; p/Mr and Mrs Harold S McConnell, Atlanta, GA; ed/The Westminster Schs, 1980; pa/Acctg Asst, Trust Co Bk of GA, 1983; cp/Student Admissions Rep, 1981-82; Exec Round Table, 1982-83; Bd of Student Activs; Student Govt Assn; Editor, *Agnes Scott Profile*; Gov's Intern, Public Relats Internship w the Leukemia Soc; r/Presb; g/Eng Maj; Possible Entry into the Fields of Communication, Both in Intercorporate Spheres as Well as Intracorporate in the Form of Public Relats.

McCORMACK, MARTHA LORENZO oc/Internal Auditor; b/Jul 19, 1959; h/6084 Hickory Station #1, Memphis, TN 38115; ba/Memphis, TN; m/James P; p/Oreol Lorenzo (dec); Judith Diaz Lorenzo, Ponce, Puerto Rico; ed/Master of Acctg, Univ of MS, 1982; BBA, Cath Univ, 1980; pa/Internal Auditor, Catherine's Stout Shoppe, 1983-; Audit Asst, Peat, Marwick, Mitchell & Co, 1982-83; Grad Asst, Univ of MS, 1981-82; cp/Mu Alpha Phi, Secy 1979, Amendment Com 1979, Ptnrs Com; Nat Bus Hon Soc; NHS; r/Cath; hon/Highest Acad Index in Acctg Dept, Cath Univ, 1981; Cert for Highest Hons in Bus Course, Nat Cath Bus Ed Assn, 1981; Grad, summa cum laude, Cath Univ, 1981; Nat Dean's List; Outstg Yth in Achmt; Am Biogl Inst; W/W Among Students in Am Univs and Cols; g/CPA.

McCOURRY, JOSEPH MICHAEL oc/Security Officer, Student; b/Jun 26, 1956; h/4628 North Ann Arbor, Oklahoma City, OK 73122; ba/Oklahoma City, OK; m/Patricia Sue; c/Joseph M II; p/Mr and Mrs T K McCourry, Oklahoma City, OK; ed/Grad, Putnam City HS, 1974; Student, Ctl St Univ, 1980-; Marine Security Guard Sch, 1977; mil/USMC 1975-80, Sgt (Hon Discharge); pa/Constrn Wkr, 1974-75; Marine Corps Audit and Fin Clk,

1975-77; Marine Embassy Guard, Accra, Ghana, W Africa, 1977-78; Marine Embassy Guard, Bonn, W Germany, 1978-80; Security Ofcr, J C Penney Co, 1980-; cp/OK Co Dpty Sheriff Vol, 1982-; Col Repubs, Secy-Treas 1981-82, Pres 1982-83; CSU Student Senate Pres, 1983; OK Intercol Legis, Senate Legal Advr 1982; OK Yg Repubs; Alpha Chi Hon Soc; Phi Eta Sigma Hon Soc; Ancient and Beneficent Order of the Red Red Rose; r/Meth; hon/W/W Am Cols and Univs; g/Polit Sci Maj w Emphasis on Intl Affairs (Wn Europe); Wk for the US Dept of St (Fgn Ser) and Become an Ambassador.

McCOWN, RICHARD H oc/Student; b/Sep 5, 1962; h/57 Charlesmeade Drive, Jackson, TN 38305; ba/Jackson, TN; p/Mr and Mrs Billy D Melton, Jackson, TN; ed/Hon Grad, N Side HS, 1980; BS, Ec and Fin, Union Univ, 1984; pa/Sales, Engraving, Shipping, Brodnax Jewelers; cp/Alpha Tau Omega Frat, Rush Chm 1983, Worthy Usher 1982; Intramural Sports; Bus Clb; Treas, Hist Clb; Peer Cnslr; Pre-Legal Soc; SGA Senator, 1981; Zeta Tau Alpha; r/So Bapt; Ch Basketball, Volleyball, Softball; Asst Sunday Sch Tchr; Asst Ch Tng Dir; hon/Zeta Tau Alpha Sorority, Zeta Man, 1981-; Dean's List; Nat Dean's List; g/Fed Job in Ec Area.

McCRAW, VICKY LYNN oc/Student; b/Apr 9, 1965; h/Route 1, Box 264, Elkin, NC 28621; p/Monroe and Vivian McCraw, Elkin, NC; ed/Surry Ctl HS, 1983; Student, Univ of NC Chapel Hill, 1983-; pa/Hlth Asst, Hugh Chatham Meml Hosp, 1981-82; cp/Hosp Vol, 1979-83; CPR/BLS Instr Aide, 1980-83; Chorus, FHA, 1979-80; HOSA, VP and Pres 1980-83; Tennis, 1980-82; Student Coun, Jr Class VP, Jr Grand Marshal 1981-82; NHS, 1981-83; Annual Staff, 1979-83, Class Editor; Med Explorer Post 580, Pres 1980-83; Christian Yth F'ship, Piedmont Dist VP 1981-82; CYF Coor, 1979-83; r/Salem Fork Christian Ch, Pianist, Choir Mem, Mem of 2 Separate Duets, CYF Coor, Preach a Wkly Chd's Sermonette, 1979-83; hon/Hlth/PE Awd, Algebra I, 1979-80; Biol, World Cultures, Geometry, HOE I Awd, 1980-81; Spanish I, HOE II Awd, 1981-82; Morehead Nom to Univ of NC Chapel Hill, 1982; St Rd Jaycettes Most Outstg Yth, 1983; W/W Surry Ctl; Soc of Dist'd Am HS Students; US Achmt Acad Nat Awds Yrbook; Intl Fgn Lang Awds Yrbook; W/W Among Am HS Students; g/PharmD; MBA; To Achieve an Exec Position in a Hosp Pharm.

McCRIMON, A DARLA oc/Student; b/Jul 3, 1962; h/Route 2, Box 32, Magnolia, MS 39652; p/Mr and Mrs Steve Flye, Magnolia, MS; ed/HS, 1980; BS, Psych, Univ of So MS, 1983; cp/Beta Clb; FHA; Spch Clb; Art Clb; Acteens; Yth Cong; VBS; Mission Friend Tchr; Choir; Homecoming Com Vol; Heart Fund Vol; March of Dimes Vol; MS Handicapped Vol; Campaigner for US Senate Cand; Residence Hall Desk Asst; Residence Hall Coun; Psi Chi, 1982-; Hillcrest Residence Hall Coun, Floor Rep 1980-81; Tutorial Intervention for Juv Delinquents, Vol Tutor 1982; Univ of So MS Alumni, 1983; Ch SS; Ch Tng; r/Bapt; hon/Beta and Hon Grad; Psych Awd; Hon Mention, Dist Mtl Hlth Essay, Ofc Aide; FHA Ldrship Awd; Home Ec Awd; 3rd

Place Ribbon, Art, MS Hist Fair; Univ of So MS Dean's List, 1981-83; W/W Among Am HS Students; Intl Biog Centre; Commun Ldrs of Am; Nat Dean's List; Am Biogl Inst; Intl Yth in Achmt; Dir of Dist'd Ams; g/PhD; Cnslg Psychol.

McCUE, DAVID J oc/Senior Management Consultant; b/Mar 28, 1956; h/2270 Whitehorse Hamilton Square Road, Hamilton Township, NJ 08690; m/Nicole E; p/Earl and Kathleen McCue, Trenton, NJ; ed/Steinert HS, 1974; BSC, summa cum laude, Rider Col, 1978; MBA, NY Univ, 1980; pa/Sr Mgmt Conslt, Arthur Andersen & Co, 1981-; Staff Conslt, HSI, 1980-81; Am Soc of Tng and Devel; Am Mgmt Assn; Assn of MBA Execs; cp/Rider Col Alumni Bd of Dirs, 1983-85; hon/Andrew J Rider Scholar, 1975, 1976, 1978; Intl Yth in Achmt; Outstg Yg Men of Am; W/W Among Students; Commun Ldrs of Am; Dir of Dist'd Ams.

McCULLOCH, WENDY JEANINE oc/Student; b/Oct 7, 1966; h/Route 4, Lakeview Heights, Loudon, TN 37774; ba/Same; p/Mr and Mrs Bob V McCulloch, Loudon, TN; ed/Grad, Loudon HS, 1984; Currently Enrolled, Univ of TN Knoxville; pa/Lifeguard, City Pool, 1982, 1983; Shirring Machine Operator, Union Carbide Corp, 1984; cp/HS Nat Hon Soc, Secy; Freshman Class Treas; Jr Class Treas; Yth Adv Coun Chp; Marching Band, Drum Majorette; Jazz Band; Concert Band; Student Coun; Red Cross Clb; Spanish Clb; Math and Sci Clb; Pep Clb; r/Bapt; hon/Am Legion Girls' St Rep, 1983; 1st Chair Flute, TN Tech Composers' Clin Hon Band, 1984; All-St E Hon Band, 1984; Homecoming Ct; Sr Superlatives, Most Talented and Best Personality; W/W Among Am HS Students; Acad All-Am; US Achmt Acad; g/Communs Maj.

McCURRY, CYNTHIA LENET oc/Graduate Student; b/Jul 2, 1957; h/1226 Fort Hill Drive, Humboldt, TN 38343; ba/Cookeville, TN; p/Cleveland and Flossie McCurry, Humboldt, TN; ed/Dipl, Humboldt High, 1975; AS, Jackson St Commun Col, 1977; BA, Lane Col, 1981; Student, TN Tech Univ; pa/Subst Tchr, Humboldt Sch Sys, 1981-83; Nurses' Asst, Nu-Care Convalescent Ctr, 1982; Reconciler, Third Nat Computer Ctr, 1980; Lib Asst, Humboldt Public Lib, 1974-80; Residential Asst, Lane Col, 1978-80; cp/Scholarly Affairs Clb, Secy 1978-79; Pre-Alumni Coun, Secy 1978-79; Student Govt Assn, Sr Rep 1980-81; Yth Dir, Brownsville Dyersburg Dist, 1982-83; Col Yg Dems, VP 1976-77; Third World Drama Clb, Co-Fdr; E TN Annual Conf Yg Adult Coun, Parliamentarian; Missionary Soc, Secy 1980-83; Christian Yth Org, Pres 1972-75; Brownsville Dyersburg Dist Christian Yth Org, Pres 1973-75; r/Lane Chapel CME Ch, Dir of Bd of Ed 1982; hon/Nat Dean's List, 1979; Actress of the Yr Awd, 1980; Grad, cum laude, 1981; W/W Among Students in Am Univs and Cols; Outstg Yg Wom of Am; Nat Scholastic Dean's List.

McDANIEL, MIMI EVELYN oc/Medical Secretary; b/Aug 8, 1960; h/119 Marable Drive, Tuskegee, AL 36083; ba/Montgomery, AL; p/Mr and Mrs William McDaniel, Tuskegee, AL; ed/Tuskegee Inst HS, 1978; AL St Univ, 1982; pa/Phlebotomist; Med Secy; cp/

Chief Copywriter, *Hornet* Yrbook, 1981-82; Alpha Kappa Mu, Secy; Beta Kappa Chi, Secy; Pres, Treas, Jud Coun Chm, Bessie Benson Hall; News Editor, *Hornet* Tribune; Pres, Spec Ser Clb; hon/ Hon Student; Miss AL St Univ; W/W Among Students in Am Univs and Cols; g/Hlth Adm.

McDANIEL, REGINALD DARYL oc/ Cameraman, Student; b/Jan 14, 1962; h/PO Box 22, Headland, AL 36345; p/ Carl and Evie McDaniel, Headland, AL; ed/Headland HS, 1980; BS, Eng, Miles Col, 1984; pa/IBM, 1983; Sports Photog, WVTM-13, 1983; cp/Student Govt; Freshman Class VP; Class Editor; Pres, Meth Clb; Jr Class Senator; Kappa Alpha Psi Frat; Polemarch, 1983-84; Keeper of Records, 1982-83; Ldg Scorer and Rebounder, 1982-83; Humanities Clb, 1983-84; Pres, Writer's Clb; r/Prot; hon/Pres Scholar's List, 1980, 1981, 1982, 1983 (Fall and Sprg); Hon Roll, 1981; Highest GPA, Delta Tau Chapt, Kappa Alpha Psi; W/W Among Students in Am Cols and Univs; Nat Dean's List; g/Editor of a Large Mag; Corporate Lwyr; US Senator.

McDANIEL, SHANNON KAYE oc/ Interior Designer; b/Nov 3, 1958; h/ 4401 Windsor Parkway, Dallas, TX 75205; ba/Dallas, TX; p/Mr and Mrs Charles R McDaniel, Canadian, TX; ed/ Canadian HS, 1977; BS, Interior Design, TX Wom's Univ, 1981; pa/Assoc Designer, Sally Johnson & Assocs, 1982-; Interior Designer, Design Plus Inc, 1981; Assoc Mem, Am Soc of Interior Designers; Univ Student Chapt Pres 1981, Affil Mem, Inst of Bus Designers; 500 Inc; cp/DAR; Daughts of the Republic of TX; Colonial Dames of the 17th Century; r/Bapt; hon/Delta Phi Delta, Pres 1981; Dean's List, 1980; TX Wom's Univ Redbud Princess, 1980, 1981; Am Petro Inst S'ship; Marian Corman Spillman Art S'ship, TWU.

McDANIEL, SHAWN MICHAEL oc/ Student; b/Feb 5, 1965; h/Box 52, 413 Panhandle Avenue, Canadian, TX 79014; p/Charles Raymond and Marjorie Wyvonne Clapp McDaniel, Canadian, TX; ed/Grad, Canadian HS, 1983; pa/Mechanic, J T Richardson Constrn, 1982, 1983; cp/Freshman Football Team, 1979; Jr Varsity Football Team, 1980; Varsity Football, 1981, 1982; All-Dist Both Offensive and Defensive Unanimous Choice; Capt of Football Team; Freshman Class Reporter; Freshman Basketball Team; Jr Varsity Basketball, 1981; Varsity Basketball Team, 1982-83; r/Bapt; hon/Fightness Wildcat Awd, 1983; Freshman Yr FFA Star Greenhand; Sophomore FFA Proficiency Awd; Star Chapt Farmer, Jr Yr; 1st Place, TSTI Agri Mech, Sr Yr; hon/ FHA Dream Beau, 1983; Basketball King, 1983; Voted Most All Around Student, 1983; g/Maj in Mktg at Tarleton St Univ.

McDOWELL, GERALD oc/Student; b/Dec 29, 1965; h/Route 1, Box 259, Hope Mills, NC 28348; p/Mr and Mrs Albert McDowell, Hope Mills, NC; ed/ S View Sr High; cp/Student Body Pres; Sci Clb; Christian F'ship Clb; Key Clb; Football; Basketball; Baseball; Fayetteville-Cumberland Co Yth Coun Mem; VP, Jr Beta Clb; Home Ec Clb; Jr Histn; Beta Clb; r/Bapt; hon/Cumberland Co's Student of the Yr; US Senate Prog Reg Finalist; g/4-Yr Col Grad; Maj

in Computer Sci; Computer Programmer.

McELROY, PAMELA KAY oc/Student; b/Mar 23, 1962; h/5202 Bryanhurst, Spring, TX 77373; p/Robert and Patsy McElroy, Spring, TX; ed/Klein HS, 1980; Univ of Houston; cp/Drill Team Capt, Maj; Japan and S Africa Perf Dance on Spec Tours; Tchr, Dance and Drill Team; Intl Drill Team and Dance Judge; Dance Cos Perf; hon/Miss Drill Team USA; Nat Hon Soc; W/W Among Am HS Students; g/Judge and Run Drill Team Pageants Internationally.

McFANN, KIMBERLY AILEEN oc/ Student; b/Jan 14, 1961; h/14 East Franklin Street, Baltimore, MD 21202; p/Charles and Mary Ellen McFann, Woodbine, MD; ed/Glenelg HS, 1979; AA, Howard Commun Col, 1981; BS, Univ of Balto, 1983; Att'g, Univ of Balto Grad and Law Sch; cp/SGA Coun Mem, Secy; Student Newspaper Reporter, Bus Mgr, Mng Editor, Editor-in-Chief; Secy Clb Reporter; Chamber Choir; Phi Theta Kappa; Internal Governance Commun Ed Com Student Rep; Commencement Com Student Rep; Student Senate Senator; Eng Clb; r/Christian; hon/Howard Commun Col Ed Foun Trustees S'ship Terry D Rippin Awd; SGA Awd; Dean's List; Outstg Achmt in Volleyball; Recog by MD Senate; Univ of Balto Awd of Merit; Intl Yth in Achmt; W/W Am Jr Cols; g/Complete MBA/JD Combined and Become a Corporate Atty, Preferably Abroad.

McFARLAND, JONI E oc/Evaluator; b/Oct 7, 1959; h/311 Tideway Drive, Alameda, CA 94501; ba/San Francisco, CA; p/Mr and Mrs Geo H McFarland, Nashville, TN; ed/Maplewood HS, 1977; BS, The Am Univ, 1981; MA, Georgetown Univ, 1983; pa/Aide to US Senator Jim Sasser, 1979-83; Evaluator, US Gen Acctg Ofc, 1983-; Am Planning Assn; Nashville Fdn of BPW Clb; cp/TN Fdn of Dem Wom; TN St Soc VP, Treas; hon/Outstg Undergrad S'ship Awd, Am Univ; Del-at-Large from TN, Dem Nat Conv; Pi Alpha Alpha; Pi Sigma Alpha; Phi Kappa Phi; Mortar Bd; g/Elected Public Ofc.

McGARY, JEFFREE LUCIEN oc/ Student; b/Jan 15, 1965; h/9041 North Alpine Road, Stockton, CA 95212; p/ Gerald and Donalee McGary, Stockton, CA; ed/Grad, Tokay HS, 1980; Student, Univ of So CA; cp/Cub Scouts; 4-H VP, Pres; Civitan St Rep; Student Senate; USC Water Polo; Innertube Water Polo Coach; Theta Xi; USC Squires, 1981; USC Knights, 1982; III FINA World Water Polo Cup Vol; McDonalds Intl Swim Meet Vol; USC Univ Events; hon/ San Joaquin Co Field Crops and Plant Sci Grand Champ Wool Breed Ram and Ewe of San Joaquin Co; Pres S'ship, USC; 4-H All-Star; USC JV Water Polo Capt, 1982; LAOOC Vol, 1983; W/W Am HS Students; Intl Yth in Achmt; Yg Commun Ldrs of Am; g/Med Sch; Phys.

McGEE, JANET M oc/Medical Records Administration, Quality Control; b/Jun 11, 1958; h/South 307 Lake Ferry Lane, Atlanta, GA 30339; ba/ Atlanta, GA; p/Mr and Mrs John P McGee, Portsmouth, NH; ed/Portsmouth High, 1976; AA 1979, AS 1980, BS 1981, Colby-Sawyer Col; Hlth Record Adm Prog, USPHS, 1981; pa/ Med Records Adm/Quality Control,

Computer Hlth Corp, 1983-; Claims Spec, Blue Cross and Blue Shield of Atlanta, 1982-83; Financial Cnslr/ Champus Hlth Benefits Advr, Wyman Pk Hlth Sys Inc, 1981-82; Reg'd Record Admr; Am Med Record Assn; GA Med Record Assn; cp/Student Govt Secy; Phi Theta Kappa, Pres, VP, Secy; Alpha Chi; Col Riding Team; hon/Undergrad Awd, 1978; Ranking Scholar; Pres S'ship, 1977; Nat Dean's List; Intl Yth in Achmt; Commun Ldrs of Am; g/Wkg towards Self-Employmt as Profl Image Conslt.

McGHEE, SEWARD MARVIN oc/ Student; b/Apr 3, 1951; h/PO Box 2112, Martinsville, VA 24112; ba/Harrisonburg, VA; p/Marvin P McGhee, Rocky Mount, VA; Peggy W McGhee, Martinsville, VA; ed/Col Preparatory Dipl, Hargrave Mil Acad, 1971; Assoc in Applied Sci Deg, Danville Commun Col, 1983; Student, Polit Sci, James Madison Univ; pa/Mgr and Mdse Buyer, Men's Dept, Leggett Dept Store, 1972-76; Patrol Ofcr, Breatholyzer Operator, Martinsville Police Dept, 1977-82; cp/ 1st Lt, Corp of Cadets, 1970-71; Pres, Radio Clb, 1971; Pres, Bd of Dirs, Southside Pool Inc, 1977; James Madison Univ Senate; James Madison Univ Jud Coun; r/Bapt; hon/Outstg Music Medal, 1971; Dean's List, 1971, 1970, 1969; Dean's List, Sprg, Sum and Fall 1982, Winter, Sprg and Sum 1983; Grad, magna cum laude, Danville Commun Col, 1983; g/BS in Polit Sci, James Madison Univ; Attend Univ of VA Law Sch; Practicing Atty at Law.

McGINNIS, BRETT NELSON oc/ Student; b/Apr 23, 1962; h/1 Pleasant Street, Oil City, PA 16301; ba/Same; p/ Mr and Mrs J Bruce McGinnis, Oil City, PA; ed/Dipl, Oil City Sr HS, 1980; BS, Bus Adm/Acctg, Clarion Univ, 1983; pa/ Asst Mgr, Bruce's Golden Dawn, 1980-84; Intern Student, Acctg, Oil City Hosp, 1983; Staff Acct, Coopers & Lybrand, 1984-; cp/Phi Beta Alpha, 1981-83; Acctg Clb Mem, 1982-83; YMCA Mem, 1978-84; r/Luth; hon/Phi Beta Alpha; Dean's List; Capt, HS Football and Basketball; W/W Among HS Students; g/Successful and Profl CPA; MBA.

McGINNIS, REBECCA ASHCRAFT oc/Student; b/Sep 21, 1962; h/47 Brighton Road, Atlanta, GA 30309; p/ Claude A and Jean M McGinnis, Atlanta, GA; ed/Grad, The Lovett Sch, 1981; BA, Broadcast Jour, So Meth Univ, 1985; pa/Gov's Intern Prog, 1983; Cnslr, The Lovett Sch Sum Camp, 1982; Other Previous Positions; r/Epis.

McINTOSH, SUSAN ELIZABETH oc/Physical Therapy Aide; b/Jan 11, 1961; h/111 Mayberry Court, Wilmington, NC 28403; ba/Wilmington, NC; p/ Mr and Mrs Henry L McIntosh, Fayetteville, NC; ed/Dipl, Terry Sanford HS, 1979; BA, Sociol, Univ of NC Wilmington, 1983; pa/Phy Therapy Aide, SEn Reg Rehab Ctr, 1980; Pulmonary Tech and Phy Therapy Aide, New Hanover Meml Hosp, 1980-82; Phy Therapy Aide, Comprehensive Home Hlth Care, 1983-; cp/Alpha Kappa Delta, 1983-; r/ Presb; hon/Alpha Kappa Delta, Intl Sociol Hon Soc, 1983; UNC-W Dean's List, 1981, 1982, 1983; g/To Attend Grad Sch to Receive Master's Deg in Phy Therapy; Lic'd Phy Therapist.

McKEE, BETH ANNE oc/Student; b/

Dec 1, 1965; h/PO Box 247, Boiling Springs, NC 28017; p/Harry and Margretta McKee, Boiling Springs, NC; ed/HS Grad; cp/Student Coun Secy, Senator; Beta Clb, Secy, VP; Nat Hon Soc; FCA, Pres; Hlth Occups Clb, VP; Cheerldg; French Clb; r/Bapt; hon/FCA Ser Awd; Homecoming Queen; French Medal; Biol Medal; Social Studies Medal; Algebra II Medal; Chem Awd; Girls' St; Jr Marshall; W/W Among Am HS Students.

McKINLEY, CONSTANCE ELAINE oc/Student; b/Jan 26, 1962; h/3131 Clearview Drive, Charlotte, NC 28216; c/C Xzavier; p/Mr and Mrs N L McKinley, Charlotte, NC; ed/W Charlotte HS, 1980; Johnson C Smith Univ, 1983-; Univ of NC Chapel Hill, 1982-83; Bennett Col, 1981-82; pa/Cashier, Harris Teeter, 1978-80; Nurse Asst, Charlotte Meml Hosp, 1980; Encoder, The Belk Ctr, 1980-81; Clerical, Ivey's, 1983-84; cp/AFS Exch Student, 1979; Red Cross Vol, 1982-83; Florence Crittenton Ser Vol, 1984-; Ob-Gyn Internship, 1978-79; r/Bapt; hon/Hon Roll, 1983; g/Maj in Chem/Math; Phys (Ob-Gyn).

McLAIN, JANET L oc/Student; b/Oct 12, 1965; h/Back Acres Country Club, Senatobia, MS 38668; p/Mr and Mrs Jimmy C McLain, Senatobia, MS; ed/Magnolia Hgts Sch, 1983; Currently Enrolled, Livingston Univ; cp/HS Class Pres, 1980-83; Jr Hist Soc, 1980; Lib Clb, 1980; Pep Squad, 1980-83; Hon Soc, 1980-83; Cheerldr, 1980-82; Chorus, 1981; Peace Pipes, 1981; Math Clb, 1982; F'ship of Christian Aths, 1982-83; Ofc Asst, 1982; Drama Clb, 1982-83; Editor of Yrbook, 1983; r/Bapt; hon/Citizenship Del in Wash, DC, 1981; Senatobia Garden Clb Student Rep, Hort Sum Sem, 1982; Semi-Finalist, Mid-S Fair Yth Talent Contest, 1981; Rotary Clb Citizenship Conf Del, 1983; Acad Betterment Competition, 1980, 1983; Class Favorite, 1981; Finalist, MHS Beauty Revue, 1981; Drama Awd, 1982-83; MHS Beauty, 1982; Fac Elite, 1982-83; Rotary Teenager of the Month, 1983; MHS Most Likely to Succeed, 1983; MHS Most Dependable, 1983; Gregg Mitchell Meml Bd of Dirs Awd, 1983; W/W Among Am HS Students; Soc of Dist'd Am HS Students; g/To Finish Col and Attend Med Sch; MD.

McLAIN, THOMAS JAMES oc/Student; b/Jul 16, 1964; h/Route 2, Box 166, Statesville, NC 28677; p/James and Ruby McLain, Statesville, NC; ed/N Iredell HS, 1982; Wingate Col, 1982-83; Mitchell Col, 1983-; pa/Nsg Asst, Iredell Meml Hosp, 1980-; Asst Dir, After Sch Day Care, 1983-84; Pianist, Troutman Bapt Ch, 1983-; Organist/Choir Dir, New Salem Meth Ch, 1983; Pianist, Monticello Bapt Ch, 1982; cp/Hlth Occups Students of Am, Pres 1982; Sci Clb, VP 1979; F'ship of Christian Students, VP 1982; r/Bapt; hon/HS Band Drum Maj, 1982; Outstg Concert Student, 1981; Beta Clb, 1982; Jr Marshal, 1981; Outstg Hlth Occups Student, 1981; g/Electronic Data Processing; Computer Programmer.

McLAMB, MELANIE LOU oc/Student; b/Mar 22, 1961; h/Route 6, Box 70, Dunn, NC 28334; p/Mr and Mrs Bobby B McLamb, Dunn, NC; ed/Midway HS, 1979; BS, Spec Ed, Appal-achian St Univ, 1983; pa/Intern, W Concord Sch, 1982; Intern, Wn Carolina Ctr for the Severely/Profoundly Retarded, 1982; Student Tchr, Hardin Pk Elem Sch, 1983; CEC, 1980-83; cp/Student's CEC, 1980-82; Chi Omega Wom's Frat, 1981-; Kappa Delta Pi, 1981-; Gamma Beta Phi, 1982-; French Clb, VP 1978-79; Nat Beta Clb, 1977-79; r/Bapt; hon/Induction into Kappa Delta Pi, Hon Soc in Ed, 1981; Induction into Gamma Beta Phi Nat Hon Soc, 1982; g/Tchg Position in the Field of Spec Ed; Tchg Lng Disabled, Mentally Handicapped or Emotionally Handicapped Chd.

McMACKLE, MARCHENA RENA oc/Student; b/Apr 20, 1962; h/5506 Simpson Avenue, Richmond, VA 23231; p/Mr and Mrs Marion McMackle Sr, Richmond, VA; ed/Armstrong HS, 1980; Old Dominion Univ; cp/VP, Nat Hon Soc; Pres, Y-Teens; Treas, Fgn Lang Clb; Tutor in Math; Math Soc; Parliamentarian, Student Coun; Drama Clb; Forensics Team; Pres, Sophomore and Jr Classes; r/Pres, Jr Usher Bd, Bapt Ch; hon/Dean's List, 1980, 1981, 1982, 1983; Salutatorian; Mayor's Complete Count Census Com; Social Studies Dept Choice to Rep Sch at Pres Classroom for Yg Am; g/Computer Analyst; Wk for Maj Corp.

McMAHON, BRENDA JEAN oc/Student; b/Apr 5, 1963; h/8405 Maryland Road, Pasadena, MD 21122; p/John and Catherine McMahon, Pasadena, MD; ed/Chesapeake HS; Univ of MD; cp/March of Dimes Vol; Cheerldg; Gymnastics Team; Toe Balley; Our Lady of the Chesapeake Parish Usher; SGA Secy; Varsity Clb; Ch Wom Sodality; UMBC Hon Clb; Ch Folk Grp; French Clb; SS Aide; Nat Hon Soc; hon/Miss Chesapeake HS; Salutatorian; MD Dist'd Scholar and S'ship; UMBC Chancellor's Merit S'ship; g/Deg in Fgn Lang and Eng.

McMAHON, MICHAEL INNO-CENZO oc/Student; b/Jan 25, 1962; h/2397 Valleybrook Road, Sumter, SC 29154; p/Mrs J T McMahon, Sumter, SC; ed/Hillcrest HS, 1980; BS, Ec, Clemson Univ, 1984; pa/Hd Lifeguard, Shaw AFB, 1976, 1977, 1978, 1979, 1980, 1981, 1982, 1983; McDonald's, 1977-84; cp/Vice-Wing Cmdr, Clemson Univ ROTC Det 770; Soc for the Advmt of Mgmt; Resv Ofcr Tng Corps; Scabbard and Blade Mil Frat; AF Assn; Red Cross Water Safety Instr; Student Pilot; Football, 1980; Track, 1980; r/Rom Cath; hon/Hon Roll, 1980, 1982; Acad Hons Ribbon, Dist'd Mil Grad, Superior Perf Awd, 1983; Pilot S'ship (USA-FROTC), Nat HS Awd for Excell, Palmetto Boys' St, 1979; W/W Among Am HS Students; g/Pilot, USAF; Master's Deg in Ec.

McMAIN, KEITH ALLEN oc/Student; b/Sep 15, 1961; h/3420 Terrace Drive, Erlanger, KY 41018; p/James and Carol McMain, Erlanger, KY; ed/Grad, St Henry HS, 1979; Att'g, No KY Univ (Mgmt Maj); Att'd, CA St Univ Northridge, 1½ Yrs; pa/Night Mgr, Burger Chef Restaurant, 1977-79; Asst Mgr, Ionna Tux, 1979-80; Mgr Trainee, Miller's Outpost, 1980-81; Frozen Foods, Thiftway Foods, 1981-83; cp/VP, No KY Univ Student Govt; Spec Projs Chm, Pi Kappa Alpha Frat; r/Cath; hon/St Champion, Cross Country Team, 1975; Nat Hon Soc, 4 Yrs; MVP, Track Team, 1979; Student Coun, 1979; No KY Univ Student Govt, VP 1983, Govt Affairs Chm 1982, Rep-at-Large 1982; Dean's S'ship, 1980; Miller's Outpost Employee S'ship, 1981; Dean's List, 1980, 1982, 1983; W/W Among Am HS Students; Dist'd Am HS Students; g/To Attend Yale Law Sch and Study Corporate Law.

McMILLAN, DARRYL JEROME oc/Student; b/Feb 1, 1966; h/PO Box 61, Shannon, NC 28386; p/Mr and Mrs Irvin McMillan, Shannon, NC; ed/Student, Red Sprgs HS, 1980-; cp/4-H, 1979-; Future Tchrs of Am, St Pres 1983-84; Reporter 1981-82; Beta Clb, 1982-84; French Clb; Annual Staff; r/Bapt; hon/Danforth "I Dare You" Awd, 1980; DAR Good Citizen, 1983-84; Hon Marshal, 1983; Nat Math Awd, 1981-83; Nat Ldrship and Ser Awd, 1983; g/To Attend Wake Forest Univ and Maj in Acctg.

McNEELY, KENNETH PERRY oc/Student; b/Apr 2, 1962; h/3629 Seaman Drive, Charlotte, NC 28210; p/Dolly E McNeely, Charlotte, NC; ed/S Mecklenburg HS, 1980; BA, Univ of NC, 1984; cp/Varsity Cheerldr, 1981-84; Sr Class, 1983-84; Secy, Dorm Govt; All-St Band; Most Valuable Shooter, UNC Pistol Team; r/Bapt; hon/Josephus Daniels Scholar; Morehead Finalist; Dean's List; g/Polit Sci Maj; Law Sch.

McNEILL, MICHAEL BRETT oc/Student; b/Feb 23, 1966; h/203 Ruth, Healdton, OK 73438; p/G T and Ruth Ann McNeill, Healdton, OK; ed/Healdton HS, 1984; Student, Abilene Christian Univ; pa/Self-Employed, Annual Fireworks Retailing Bus; Self-Employed, VideoImages, 1983; cp/Basketball, 1981-84; Baseball, 1982-84; Nat Hon Soc, 1980-84; OK Hon Soc, 1980-84; F'ship of Christian Aths, 1983-84; Healdton Prodn Co, Hon Choir, 1982-84; Bulldog Yrbook Staff, Photography Editor 1984; Jr and Sr Play Casts; Am Field Ser Host Fam, 1983-84; Ch Yth Grp; r/Ch of Christ; hon/Essay Contests: 2nd Place (OK Freedom Forum of Am Citizenship Ctr), 2nd in Area (DAR), 1st in Dist (Masonic Lodge); Valedictorian, 1984 (Perfect GPA); Masonic Student of Today Awd, 1981; OK Boys' St Del (Elected to 1st Ho of Reps 1983); Lion's Clb Student of the Month, 1983; Dist Hon Choir, 1983; Boys' Quartet and Mixed Ensemble, Superior at St Contest; 8 Outstg Class Awds, 1981-83; W/W Among Am HS Students; W/W Music; US Achmt Acad; Soc of Dist'd Am HS Students; g/Deg in Bus Field.

McPHILLIPS, LYNNE MARIE oc/Student; b/Mar 29, 1962; h/21709 Harney Street, Elkhorn, NE 68022; p/Mr and Mrs Jerome McPhillips, Elkhorn, NE; ed/Elkhorn Sr HS, 1980; Student, Sam Houston St Univ; pa/Sales Assoc in Retail Bus (Pt-time); cp/Golden Key Nat Hon Soc, 1983; Alpha Chi, 1982; HS Student Coun Rep; r/Cath; hon/Jesse H Jones S'ship, 1981, 1982; First Nat Bk of Huntsville S'ship, 1983; Nat Dean's List; g/Maj in Gen Bus Adm; Minor in Computer Sci; Career in Fashion Msdg.

McQUEEN, DENISE EVELYN oc/Office Assistant; b/Apr 30, 1963; h/19530 FM 2920, Tomball, TX 77375; ba/Houston, TX; m/James Michael; p/

Gerald and Evelyn Nichols, Tomball, TX; ed/Magnolia HS, 1981; pa/Accts Receivable Clk, M&R Utility, 1979-81; Clerical Asst II 1981-83; Ofc Asst I 1983-, Tenneco Oil Co P&M; cp/NHS, 1978-81; FBLA, 1980-81; DECA, 1981; OEA, 1980-81; HS Band, 1977-80; r/ Meth; hon/St Contestant in Typing, 1980; E TX Hon Band, 1979; Intl Yth in Achmt; W/W Among Am HS Students; Commun Ldrs of Am; g/Staff Supvr.

McWHORTER, JAMES MARK oc/ Student; b/May 18, 1959; h/Route 2, Box 64, Iowa Park, TX 76367; p/Mr and Mrs Milton McWhorter, Iowa Park, TX; ed/IA Pk HS; Studying for BBA, MWn St Univ; pa/Salesclk, Treasure City; Carpenter, Town and Country Mobile Homes; Other Previous Positions; cp/ Golf Team, IA Pk HS; Auto Mechs Clb, IA Pk HS; r/Ch of Christ; hon/W/W Among Am HS Students; g/CPA.

McWHORTER, TIMOTHY JOHN oc/Student; b/Mar 22, 1963; h/Route 2, Box 64, Iowa Park, TX 76367; p/Mr and Mrs Milton McWhorter, Iowa Park, TX; ed/IA Pk HS; pa/Clk, Target Stores; Sonic Drive In; r/Ch of Christ; hon/One of Top 10 Outstg Jr High Students in IA Pk Jr High, 1978; W/W Among Am HS Students; g/Acctg Maj, MWn St Univ.

MEACHAM, LILLIAN ROMINE oc/ Medical Student; b/Oct 12, 1957; h/815 Marstevan Drive, Atlanta, GA 30306; ba/Atlanta, GA; m/Daniel Weedon; p/ Mr and Mrs Ernest E Romine, Morrow, GA; ed/Morrow Sr High, 1975; BA, Converse Col, 1978; MMSc 1980, MD 1984, Emory Univ; pa/Respiratory Therapist, Egerston Hosp for Chd, 1980-84; Alpha Omega Alpha; Emory Med Wom's Assn; AMA, Student Mbrship; AMA; cp/High Mus of Art; Secy-Treas, Sr Class, Emory Univ Sch of Med; r/Active in Emory Presb Ch; hon/Alpha Omega Alpha, VP 1983; Converse Scholar, 1978; Grad, Gamma Sigma, 1984; g/Residency in Pediatrics.

MEADOR, ANNE CHARLENE oc/ Executive Secretary, Bookkeeper, Student; b/Jun 12, 1955; h/415-A Park Avenue, Florence, SC 29501; ba/Florence, SC; p/Herbert Lloyd Meador (dec); Elizabeth L Meador, Hardy, VA; ed/Hon Grad, Franklin Co HS, 1973; BS, Bus Adm, Francis Marion Col; pa/Modernization Secy, McKesson-Robbins Drug Co, 1973-74; Ofc Supvr/Bkkpr, Shore-Mount Corp, 1974-76; Exec Secy/ Bkkpr, TranSouth Financial Corp, 1976-; cp/U Way Acct Vol, 1981-83; March of Dimes, Team Capt 1982-83; r/Meth; hon/S'ship, Beasley Americanism Awd, Francis Marion Col, 1983; g/Mgmt Position in Bk Opers at NCNB.

MEADOWS, DAWN MICHELLE oc/ Underwriting Multi-Lines Policy Typist; b/Nov 6, 1963; h/415 31-W Highway, White House, TN 37188; ba/ Madison, TN; p/Mr and Mrs Sherman Meadows, White House, TN; ed/Grad, White House HS, 1982; pa/Pt-time Employee, Assorter, *The Bargain Browser*, 1978; Pt-time Cashier, Opryland USA, 1981; Multi-Lines Policy Typist, Mail and File Clk, St Automobile Mutual Ins Co, 1981-; Bus Ofc Ed Assn; Ofc Ed Assn; cp/Band; Chorus; Beta Clb Secy; OEA Secy; FHA; Student Coun; r/ Pleasant Val Bapt; Ch, Sunday Sch Tchr 1981-; hon/Recip, Awds from Ofc Ed

Assn: Exec Awd, Diplomat Awd, Stateswom Awd, Ambassador Awd, 1981-82; Salutatorian; Voted Most Dependable Sr Girl; W/W Among Am HS Students; g/Ofc Occup Career.

MEASURES, PAMELA ANN oc/ Public Relations Counselor; b/Mar 24, 1956; h/11870 Fairpoint, Houston, TX 77099; ba/Houston, TX; m/Mark C Thomasson; p/Mr and Mrs W Winston Measures, Fort Worth, TX; ed/SW HS, 1974; BS, Baylor Univ, 1978; Univ of Houston; pa/Public Relats Cnslr, Weekley & Penny; Winius-Brandon Advtg, 1981-83; Hermann Hosp, 1978-81; Public Relats Soc of Am, Public Relats Com Chm; cp/Houston Ballet Guild; Baylor Alumni Assn; Student Foun, Baylor; Public Relats Student Soc of Am, VP; hon/Outstg Sr in Public Relats; Kappa Omicron Phi; Dean's List; W/W SW; Intl Yth in Achmt; g/MBA; Own Public Relats Firm.

MEDCALF, ROBYN LYNNE oc/ Student; b/Aug 29, 1962; h/1878 Barton Street, Redwood City, CA 94061; ba/ Menlo Park, CA; p/Robert and Judith Medcalf, Redwood City, CA; ed/Dipl, Woodside HS; BA in Psych, Judson Col; Pursuing MSW Deg, Univ of CA Berkeley; pa/Asst Coor of Vol Sers, Americana Hlthcare Ctr, 1983; Asst Dir of Activs, Col Pk Convalescent Hosp, 1983-; cp/Pres, Sr High Grp, Bapt Ch; Pres, Sr High BYF; Debate Team; Swim Team; Track Team; Forever Fam Choir; Concert Choir; RA; r/Am Bapt; hon/ Pres S'ship, Judson Col; Most Inspirational Ath, Woodside Swim Team; Acad Hon Roll; Dean's List; g/Master's in Social Wel (Specialize in Direct Sers w the Elderly).

MEDCALF, TIMOTHY WAYNE oc/ Medical Student; b/Sep 28, 1960; h/710 Northeast 8 #124, Oklahoma City, OK 73104; m/Rhonda Sue; p/Dr and Mrs Winfred L Medcalf, Ardmore, OK; ed/ BS, Biol Scis, E Ctl Univ; Med Student, Univ of OK Col of Med (Class of '86); cp/VP, Class of '86, Univ of OK Col of Med; Tri Beta; Alpha Chi; Varsity Lttrman, Football; FCA; VP, Residence Hall Assn; hon/E Ctl Univ Gov George Nigh Hon Scholar, 1982; Univ of OK Col of Med, 1st Quartile Academically; E Ctl Univ Student of the Month; Fransisco Hatchett Achmt Awd; Pres Hon Roll; g/MD.

MEDFORD, MARGIE LYNN oc/ Marketing Representative; b/Jun 28, 1959; h/Route 1, Box 21-1A, Tifton, GA, 31794; p/Mr and Mrs H C Medford, Tifton, GA; ed/Tittarea Acad, 1977; Assoc Deg, Abraham Baldwin Agri Col, 1979; ABJ, Univ of GA, 1981; MBA w Mktg Concentration, GA St Univ, 1984; pa/Mktg Rep, Exec MBA Prog, GA St Univ; Public Relats Asst, Cable Am Inc, 1980-81; Am Mktg Assn, GA St Chapt; Energy/Impact Conf; ABAC Yrbook Editor; Off-Campus Senator, SGA; Chm, Lake Baldwin Renovation Proj; People to People Citizen Ambassador to Europe; Baldwin Players; hon/Salutatorian; P C F'ship; Superior Ldrship Awd, GA Agri-Bus Coun; Am Legion Ldrship Awd; Sr Eng Dept Awd; GA Key Awd; Commun Beautification Awd; 4-H Dist Winner; Lit Awds; Night Sch Merit Hon, GA St Univ, 1983; Grad, magna cum laude, Univ of GA, 1981; Dean's Awd for Acad Excell, 1981; Top 5% of Sr Class, Univ of GA, 1981; Phi Kappa

Phi; Phi Theta Kappa; Golden Key Nat Hon Soc; Kappa Tau Alpha; Outstg Yg Wom in Am; Yg Commun Ldrs of Am; W/W Among Am Jr Cols; g/VP of Mktg for a Medium-Sized Corp.

MEDLEY, CINDY MARIE oc/Student; b/Feb 23, 1962; h/1707 Longview Avenue, Tarboro, NC 27886; p/Mr and Mrs Robert K Medley, Tarboro, NC; ed/ Dipl, Tarboro Edgecombe Acad, 1981; AA, Louisburg Col, 1983; Student, E Carolina Univ; pa/Photog, Louisburg Col, 1981-83; cp/Louisburg Col Alumni Assn; r/Christian; hon/Photo Awd, 1983; Photo Awd, 1980; Drama Awd, 1978; g/BAD, Art, Photo, Communication Arts.

MEECE, BARRY DEWAYNE oc/ Student; b/Jun 5, 1966; h/Route 6, Box 659, Easley, SC 29640; ba/Easley, SC; p/Orbin and Sandra B Meece, Easley, SC; ed/HS Grad; pa/Pt-time Dishwasher 1980-82, Dishwasher and Cook 1983, Black's Fish Camp; r/Bapt; hon/Nat Jr Hon Soc, 1980-81; Nat Hon Soc, 1982, 1983; Top 10% of Class, 1981-82, 1983; Newberry Col Sum Scholar, 1983; Furman Scholar, 1983; Presb Col Jr Fellow, 1983; Invitation to 1983 Hon Sem at Univ of GA; g/To Attend Furman Univ or Clemson Univ and Maj in Mech Engrg.

MEIER, JANNINE ANN oc/Secretary; b/Jul 10, 1959; h/5009 Buffalo, Odessa, TX 79762; ba/Odessa, TX; m/ Joe Daniel; p/William and Judith Joyce, Noonan, ND; ed/BS, Minot St Col; pa/ Camp Cnslr 1978, 1979, Camp Dir 1980, 1981, ND Farmers Union; Resident Dorm Asst 1979-80, Asst Secy 1980-81, Minot St Col; Secy, Brannan & Co, 1982-84; Secy, Bk of the SW, 1984-; cp/JC Wom, Ofc of Internal Dir 1983-84; Beta Sigma Phi; Kappa Delta Pi; Pi Omega Pi, VP 1980, 1981; SNEA; Nat Bus Ed Assn; Farmer Union Activs on St and Nat Level; Phi Beta Lambda; r/Cath; hon/Minot St Col Outstg Bus Ed Student, 1981; Intl Yth in Achmt; Yg Commun Ldrs of Am; Outstg Yg Wom in Am; W/W Among Students in Am Univs and Cols; g/MBA.

MEINDERS, TERESA ANN oc/Registered Nurse, Law Student; b/Aug 3, 1959; h/2515 Boxwood, Norman, OK 73069; ba/Oklahoma City, OK; p/H C and Lois Meinders, Norman, OK; ed/ Norman High, 1977; BSN, Univ of OK, 1982; Student, OK Univ Col of Law; pa/RN, Critical Care, Presb Hosp, 1981-; Law Sch Student Cnslr, OK Univ Col of Law, 1983; cp/Concern for Dying, Am Bar Assn Law Student Div, 10th and 13th Circuits Rep; Yg Repubs; Legis Chm, OUSNA, 1981-82; Phi Delta Phi; Christian Med Soc, 1980-82; Christian Legal Soc, 1983; Student Govt Assn, 1981; Student Coun, 1978-82; Secy 1980; Panhellenic, Rush Chm 1980; HS Tennis; OSU Tennis Team; r/Epis; hon/Mortar Bd, 1981; Omicron Delta Kappa, 1981; Top Ten Freshmen Wom, 1978; Delta Delta Delta Social Sorority, Nat Model Pledge 1978; Law Sch Hon Roll; Yth Del, Repub Nat Conv, 1980; W/W Am Cols and Univs; g/ Atty-at-Law, Med Malpractice Def; Med Complex Med Law Prof.

MELHUISH, KIRK THOMAS oc/ Student; b/Mar 13, 1962; h/4635 North Le Claire, Chi, IL; p/Mr and Mrs Jack L Melhuish, Chi, IL; ed/Carl Schurz HS, 1980; Valparaiso Univ; pa/WVUR-FM,

WLJE-FM; WAKE-AM, 1980-; cp/ Co-Fdr, Vol Commun Ser, Fire Rescue Squad; Lit Mag; Q&S; Reporter, Newspaper; ROTC Sgt; 1st Class Radio Clb Mem; Commun, Polit Vol; CB Communication; Weather Forecaster, Severe Storm Spotter; Intramural Sports; Am Meteorological Soc; Nat Weather Assn; Col Jour Hon Soc, 1983; hon/Staff Meteorologist, Col Radio Sta; Intl Biogl Centre; W/W Among Am HS Students; g/Broadcast Meteorologist.

MENDEZ, MARCIA A oc/Student; b/ Sep 12, 1964; h/4055 Duryea Avenue, Bronx, NY 10466; ba/New York, NY; p/Daphne Mendez, Bronx, NY; ed/ Bklyn Tech HS; Att'g, Hofstra Univ; pa/ Day Camp Cnslr, Christ the King Sch, 1978, 1980; Salesperson, Fayva Shoe Store, 1981; Salesperson, Wendy's, 1981-82; Salesperson, Lerner Shop, 1982-83; cp/Hofstra's Org of Latin Ams, 1982-, Asst Secy; Gamma Dolls Inc, Alpha Gamma Omega Frat; r/Cath; hon/ARISTA, 1982; Ser Awd to HOLA, 1983; g/To Pursue a Career in Internal Bus.

MERRITT, DONNA BOLES oc/Business Dealer; b/Feb 26, 1963; h/13F Salem Garden Drive, Winston-Salem, NC 27107; ba/Same; m/Charles Lynn; c/Michael Ray, Kevin Lynn; p/Dolores T Boles, Winston-Salem, NC; ed/Dipl, Reynolds Sr HS, 1981; Multimedia Standard First Aid Course, 1982; pa/ Food Town, 1979-81; Made Rite Sandwich, 1981; Dealer, Friendly Home Parties/Prods; cp/Intramural Basketball; Jr Achmt; Y-Teens; Pep Clb; Band; GSA; Fire and Rescue Explorer; ARC Vol; Rainbow Girls; Latin Clb; Astra Clb; ARC Clb; Blood Donor; r/U Meth, Yth F'ship, Yth Choir, Treas; hon/First Class Girl Scout; Perfect Attendance, HS; Intl Yth in Achmt; W/W Among Am HS Students; Personalities of S; Biogl Roll of Hon; g/Undecided.

MERRITT, JAMES MITCHELL oc/ Student; b/Jul 16, 1961; h/PO Box 278, Rose Hill, NC 28458; p/Tom and Yvonne Merritt, Rose Hill, NC; ed/ Wallace Rose Hill HS, 1979; BS, Biol and Anthropology/Sociol, St Andrews Presb Col, 1983; Currently Enrolled, Univ of NC Chapel Hill Sch of Med; cp/Pres, St Andrews Hon Soc; Pres, Orange Dorm; Senator, St Andrews Student Govt Assn; Acad Affairs Hons Subcom; Hlth-Sci Clb; Rod-n-Reel Clb; Varsity Tennis; Intramural Basketball and Softball; hon/Grad w Hons, St Andrews Col, 1983; Hon Soc, St Andrews Col; Sophomore Hons; Hons S'ship; Armed Forces Hlth Professions S'ship; Yg Ldrs of Am; Soc of Dist'd Am HS Students; g/To Obtain Med Deg and Serve as a Phys in the USN.

MESEBERG, PATRICIA ANN oc/ Seamstress; b/Jun 17, 1961; h/Route 2, Box 18, LaFarge, WI 54639; ba/Ontario, WI; p/Ernie and Hope Meseberg, LaFarge, WI; ed/Grad, LaFarge HS, 1979; Univ of WI Platteville, 1979-80; AS, Univ of WI Richland, 1981; Clk-Typist Deg, Wn WI Tech Inst, 1982; pa/Seamstress; cp/GSA; Ch Involvement; Newspaper, Yrbook Staffs; Girls' Basketball, Softball Scorekeeper; Forensics; FHA; FFA; r/Meth; hon/Valedictorian of Grad'g Class, 1979; Dean's List, Univ of WI Platteville and Univ of WI Richland; Grad w Hons, Wn WI Tech Inst; W/W Am's Yth; Am Biogl Inst; g/

To Find a Job as a Clk-Typist; To Be Happy.

METCALF, DAVID WAYNE oc/ Student; b/Dec 20, 1962; h/2601 West Cumb Avenue, Middlesboro, KY; p/ William E and Wilma J Metcalf, Middlesboro, KY; ed/Middlesboro HS, 1981; Univ of KY; cp/Beta Clb; Key Clb; Jr Deacon, Ch; Basketball; Baseball; AFROTC; Arnold Soc; Vol, Med Ctr; hon/Selected to Participate in First Undergrad Wkshop of Ed Preparation Prog for Sum of 1983; Hon Roll; Lttrman; W/W Among Am HS Students; Commun Ldrs of Am; g/Phys Asst or MD.

METCALF, JOYCE ELAINE oc/Student; b/May 10, 1965; h/1635 Eastwood Drive, Kannapolis, NC 28081; p/Mr and Mrs Don E Metcalf, Kannapolis, NC; ed/A L Brown HS; Att'g, Univ of NC Chapel Hill; cp/Juniorettes, Home Life Com Chm; Nat Hon Soc; Omega Delta Pi, Sr Sorority, Pres; Sci Clb; Fgn Lang Clb; AFS; Hist Clb; Symphonic and Marching Bands; Bus and Mgmt Explorer's Post, VP 1982; r/Presb; hon/Gov's Sch Nom, 1981; Commun Schs Adv Coun, 1982-83; Cannon Mills S'ship for Computer Sci; Shelby Debutante, 1983; W/W Among Am HS Students; g/Study Computer Sci at Univ of NC Chapel Hill.

METCALF, ROLAND DEAN oc/ Student; b/Aug 14, 1960; h/107 Rankin Court, Wake Forest, NC 27587; m/ Arlene Dovie Young; p/L D and Jimmie Metcalf, Travelers Rest, SC; ed/Travelers Rest HS, 1978; AA in Gen Studies, N Greenville Col, 1980; BA in Rel, Mars Hill Col, 1982; pa/Machine Operator, Chandler's Reed Hooks, 1978-80; Observer of Large Ch Opers, Taylors First Bapt Ch, 1979; SC Bapt Student Union Sum Missionary to Juneau, AK, 1979; Yth Dir, Gowensville Bapt Ch, 1979-80; So Bapt Conv Home Mission Bd, Sum Missionary to Juneau, 1980; Pastor, Mid Fork Bapt Ch, 1980-83; cp/ Football, 1974, 1975; Track, 1975; Chorus, Mod Music Masters Nat Hon Soc; Pres, Pi Alpha Chapt of Phi Theta Kappa Nat Hon Soc, 1979-80; Pres, Ministerial Student Org, 1979-80; Served on Bapt Student Union Exec Coun as Campus Min, 1979-80; Mars Hill Col Alpha Chi Nat Hon Soc; Christian Student Movement; r/So Bapt; hon/Accepted Jesus Christ as Personal Saviour at Age 9; Accepted God's Call to Gospel Min, 1978; Lic'd to Preach, Walnut Grove Bapt Ch, 1978; Ordained, Walnut Grove Bapt Ch, 1981; Valedictorian, N Greenville Col; Grad, summa cum laude, Mars Hill Col; W/ W Among Am Jr Cols; Nat Dean's List; g/To Serve in the Pastoral and/or Evang Min Fields; To Be a Faithful and Effective Min of the Gospel of Jesus Christ.

METTEER, BRIAN LEE oc/Student; b/May 17, 1965; h/Route 10, Box 29-K, New Braunfels, TX 78130; p/Graham and Carol Lawrence, New Braunfels, TX; ed/Grad, Canyon HS, 1983; pa/TX Hwy Dept; cp/Varsity Swimming; Spanish Clb; hon/TX Tech Dean's S'ship, 1983-84; Am Legion Aux S'ship, 1983-84; Varsity Swimming Letter; W/ W Am Students; g/Computer Engrg, OR St Univ.

METTS, SELINA RENEE oc/Student; b/Jul 5, 1965; h/Route 2, Box 165,

Douglas, GA 31533; p/Russell L and Jo Ann Metts, Douglas, GA; ed/Grad, Coffee HS, 1983; Student, S GA Col; cp/4-H Clb, Pres 1982-83; Capt, Color Guard, Trojan Band, Coffee HS; Anchor Clb, Pres 1982-83; r/Bapt; hon/ Wash Citizenship Focus, 4-H, 1981; Key Awd, 4-H; W/W Among Am HS Students; US Achmt Acad; g/Career in Home Ec.

METZ, MARK ALAN oc/Student; h/ 1029 Indian Trail, Destin, FL 32541; p/ Dr and Mrs Gene A Metz, Destin, FL; ed/Grad, Ft Walton Bch HS, 1981; Grad, Furman Univ, 1985; pa/Sum Job as Swim Team Coach, Botany Woods Pool; cp/Phi Eta Sigma, Swim Team, Furman Univ; Key Clb; Playground Area YMCA Swim Team; r/Presb; hon/Salutatorian; Capt and High Point Winner, Ft Walton Bch HS Swim Team; Secy-Treas, HS Sr Class; Swimming and Hon S'ships to Furman Univ; Phi Eta Sigma, 1982; So Conf Male Swimmer of the Yr, 1982; Seahawk Invitational Best Male Swimmer, 1984; W/W Among Am HS Students; Intl Yth in Achmt; Yg Personalities of S; g/Maj in Computer Sci; Career in Computer Sci or Career as a Swim Team Coach.

MEYERS, MICHELE ROBIN oc/ Salesclerk; b/Nov 3, 1958; h/872 East 150th, Cleveland, OH 44110; ba/Cleveland Heights, OH; p/Mr and Mrs Francis R Meyers, Cleveland, OH; ed/Grad, Collinwood HS, 1976; BS, Chem, Heidelberg Col, 1980; pa/Student Helper 1977, Asst Supvr 1978, Nat Jr Tennis Leag of Cleveland; Sales Conslt, Higbee's Photo Studio, 1981; Sales Clk, Higbee's Dept Store, 1981-; cp/Tennis, 2-Yr Letterman 1975-76, 3-Yr Letterman 1977-78, 1980; Marching Band, HS, 4 Yrs; Student Affil, Am Chem Soc, 4 Yrs, Secy for 1 Yr; hon/Solo and Ensemble Contest of Cleveland, Clarinetist, 1975, 1976; NJTL of Cleveland Sportsmanship Awd, 1975; W/W Among Am HS Students; g/To Continue Studies in Bus Field, Combining This w Chem; To Wk in Sales in the Chem Field.

MEZZACAPPA, CAROL ANN oc/ Modern Dancer, Dance Instructor; b/ Dec 23, 1956; h/1830 63 Street, Brooklyn, NY 11204; ba/Brooklyn, NY; p/ Michael and Beatrice Mezzacappa, Brooklyn, NY; ed/BS, Bklyn Col, 1978; pa/Dancer, Bus Mgr, Deborah Carr Theatre Dance Ensemble Inc, 1979-, D Carr Artistic Dir; Dance Coor 1982-, Dance Instr 1979-, Bklyn Col Prep Ctr for the Perf'g Arts; HS of Perf'g Arts, 1980-82; Bklyn Col Adj Labanotation Instr, 1981; Mod Instr, Labanotation Instr, Stephens Col, CO, 1983; Guest Instr, Stephens Col, MO, 1983; Instr of Humphrey-Weidman Technique for the Charles Weidman Sch of Mod Dance Inc, NYC, 1983-84; Bd of Dirs, Charles Weidman Sch of Mod Dance Inc, 1982-; Co Rep, Deborah Carr Theatre Dance Ensemble Inc, 1979-; r/Cath; hon/ Eleanor D Kilcoyne Dance Awd, 1978; W/W Among Students in Am Univs and Cols; Commun Ldrs of Am; Intl Yth in Achmt.

MICHAEL, JEANNIE ANNETTE oc/ Secretary, Student; b/Jul 30, 1964; h/ 557 Old Hickory Boulevard, Apartment #5, Jackson, TN 38301; ba/Jackson, TN; p/Virgil and Judy Michael, Jackson, TN; ed/Att'd Freed-Hardeman Col 1982-83,

W TN Bus Col 1983-84; pa/Secy, Jackson Police Dept, Capt Crews, 1983-; pa/Pres, FHA-HERO, 1982; Spanish Clb, HS, 1982; Zeta Clb, 1982-83; hon/Dean's List, W TN Bus Col, 1983; Miss Northside's Miss Congeniality, 1981-82; Today's Girl St Miss Congeniality, 1980-81; Miss Pride of Am, 1982; Miss Independence, 1981; Miss Star of Tomorrow, 1981; Miss Casey Jones, 1983; g/Complete 4 Yrs at Freed-Hardeman Col, Obtain BS in Social Wk; Work w Child Abused Chd.

MICHAEL, TERESA PAULETTE oc/Student; b/Mar 13, 1970; h/557 Old Hickory Boulevard, Jackson, TN 38301; p/Virgil and Judy Michael, Jackson, TN; ed/Northside Jr High, 1982-83; Parkway Jr High, 1983-84; cp/4-H, 1982; Chorus, 1983-84; FHA, 1983; r/Ch of Christ; hon/Best Student Awd, 1980; Princess Miss Casey Jones, 1983; g/Career in Modeling.

MIDGETT, STEVEN RAY oc/Student; b/Jan 5, 1965; h/103 Quail Run, Elizabeth City, NC 27909; p/Ray and Sandra Midgett, Elizabeth City, NC; ed/HS, 1983; cp/Pres, VP, UMYF; Yth Rep, Ch Coun on Min and Adm Bd; Chm of Publicity, Dist UMYF; Tchr, Bible Sch; Heart Fund Vol; Albemarle Players; Choir Soloist; Pres, Student Govt; Chm, Jr-Sr Prom; Capt, Quiz Bowl Team; VP, Key Clb; VP, Jr Class; Announcer, Basketball Games; Senate Mem, Student Cong; Co-Editor, Yrbook; Pres, Spanish Clb; Pres, Student Coun; hon/Hons S'ship, Duke Univ; NC Sch of Math and Sci; John Motley Morehead S'ship, Dist Alt; Bus Dept Awd; HS Typewriting Contest, 4th in St Beginning Typing; Nat Hon Soc; Gov's Sch of NC; Hugh O'Brian Ldrship Foun Ambassador; Good Citizen of the Yr, DAR, 1982; W/W Among Am HS Students; g/Pre-Law Maj, Duke Univ.

MIEHE, ARNIE ALAN oc/High-School Health Instructor; b/Jul 23, 1955; h/204 Ravine Street, Darlington, WI 53530; p/Mr and Mrs E Charles Miehe, Belmont, WI; ed/HS, 1973; BS, 1979; pa/HS Hlth Instr; cp/Pres, Orgr, Redbird Running Clb; Author, Local Newspaper Column; SS Class Tchr; hon/Acad Hon Grad; Lttrman, Cross Country; W/W Among Students in Am Univs and Cols; g/Master's Deg in Hlth Ed.

MIFKA, JOHN FRANCIS oc/Attorney; b/Jul 15, 1957; h/Apartment #10, 2619 South 19th Street, Philadelphia, PA 19145; ba/Philadelphia, PA; p/Mary G Mifka, Scranton, PA; ed/Scranton Prep HS, 1975; Villanova Univ, 1975-76; BS, Crim Justice, cum laude, Univ of Scranton, 1979; Loyola Law Sch, 1979-80; JD, DE Law Sch, Widener Univ, 1982; pa/Assoc, Detweiler, Hughes & Kokonos, 1983-; Law Instr, Holmesburg Prison, Phila Bd of Ed, 1982-; Phila, PA, NJ, DC, Am Bar Assns; Admitted to Pract Law, PA, NJ, DC; cp/Mem, Bd of Dirs, Chm of Legal Affairs Com, World Tang Soo Do Assn; r/Cath; hon/Pi Gamma Mu Nat Social Sci Hon Soc, 1978; g/Trial Lwyr, Litigator; Juv Ct Judge.

MILAM, PATRICK DAVID oc/Student; b/Apr 24, 1965; h/401 Crosslake Drive, Tullahoma, TN 37388; p/Dr and Mrs William M Milam, Tullahoma, TN; ed/HS Grad; Att'g, Motlow St Col; pa/Pt-time Employmt, Harton Meml Hosp

Pharm, 1983-; cp/Forensics Clb; Editor of Echo; Press Clb; Nat Quill and Scroll Clb; Tennis Team; r/Bapt; hon/Jour Awds: Cert of Contbn to Echo as Asst Editor 1981-82, Hon Mention Awd for Competition (Univ of TN Knoxville) 1981-82, 3rd Place Edit Column Awd for St-Wide Competition (Univ of TN Knoxville) 1982-83, Tullahoma HS Letter for Participation on Echo Staff 1983, Quill and Scroll 1983, Cert of Awd from Staff at HS for Outstg Accomplishment and Excell in Editing the Echo 1983, Echo Received Excellent Rating from Judges at TN HS Press Assn Conv 1983; g/Career in Jour.

MILBY, LISA CAROLE oc/Student; b/Mar 9, 1965; h/416 York Road, Fayetteville, NC 28303; p/Holman and Emma Milby, Fayetteville, NC; ed/Grad, Westover Sr High, 1983; Presently Att'g, Univ of NC Chapel Hill; cp/Fayetteville-Cumberland Co Yth Coun; Teen Dem of Fayetteville; NC Yth Adv Coun; Keywanettes; Intl Clb; Pres, Treble Show Choir; Pres, Yth Coun of Ch; hon/Gubernatorial Appt to NC Yth Adv Coun; Gov Page; W/W Among Am HS Students; g/To Study Early Childhood Ed.

MILEN, LISA DENISE oc/Student; b/May 8, 1966; h/Route 1, Box 168, Old Fort, TN 37362; p/John D and Brenda Milen, Old Fort, TN; ed/Grad, Polk Co HS, 1984; cp/FFA, Chapt Secy 1981-83, Cherokee Dist Secy 1982-83, E TN Sweetheart 1983-84; 4-H Clbs, Student Coun Rep 1980-81, Secy 1981-82; Nat Hon Soc, Freshman Class Secy; r/Bapt; hon/Miss Photogenic, Fairest of the Fair Contest, 1982; 2nd Runner-Up, Miss Christmas Belle, 1982; Jr Class Beauty, 1982-83; Miss Polk Co, Top Ten, 1983; Nat Agri Awd, 1982; W/W Among Am HS Students; g/Radiol Technol, Chattanooga St Tech Commun Col.

MILES, SOLOMON THOMAS JR oc/Student; b/Sep 16, 1965; h/6426 6th Street, Northwest, Washington, DC 20012; p/Solomon T and Marion P Miles, Washington, DC; ed/McKinley HS; cp/Nat Holy Names Soc; Future Bus Ldrs of Am, VP; DC Yth Orch Prog; Jr HS Band; r/Cath; hon/Am Legion, All-City Music Fest; Perfect Attendance; Acad Hon Roll; Commun Ldrs of Am; US Achmt Acad; g/Career in Fin/Bkg.

MILLARD, CAROLYN DORIS oc/Graduate Student; b/Oct 22, 1960; h/Route 4, Box 247, Tullahoma, TN 37388; ba/Lexington, KY; p/Mr and Mrs William P Millard, Tullahoma, TN; ed/Dipl, Tullahoma HS, 1978; BS, Pharm, Univ of MS, 1983; pa/Lab Asst Trainee, Sverdrup Technol Envir Lab, 1980-83; Pharm Extern, Estill Sprgs Pharm, 1981-83; Grad Student in Toxicology, 1983-; Kappa Epsilon, 1981-83; Am Pharmaceutical Assn, 1981-; cp/Nat Rifle Assn, 1973-; Blackhawk Rifle Clb, 1975-; r/Luth; hon/Prone 3200 Reg Winner, 1975, 1978; TN St Prone Champion, 1975, 1977, 1980, 1981, 1982, 1983; Match Winner, Y Position Conventional Sectional, 1976, 1978; Intl Dewar Team, 1978, 1982, 1983; US Randall Team, 1977, 1978, 1980, 1981, 1982, 1983; g/To Attain a PhD in Envir Toxicology and Be Employed in That Field.

MILLENDER, MICHAEL JONATHAN oc/Student; b/Dec 4, 1966; h/

1295 Old Woodbine Road, Atlanta, GA 30319; p/Mr and Mrs Ivan Millender, Atlanta, GA; ed/The Paideia Sch, 1984; cp/Secy, U Synagogue Yth, 1981, VP 1983; Editor, HS Newspaper, 1984; Treas, Student Coun, 1984; r/Jewish; hon/1st Place, GA Hist Day, 1980, 1982; 2nd Place, GA Hist Day, 1981, 1983; Gov's Hon Prog Finalist, 1983; Gold Medal, Nat Latin Exam, 1980; g/Career in Law.

MILLER, GRETA EVANGELINE oc/Student; b/Apr 21, 1963; h/9117 Feldbank Drive, Charlotte, NC 28216; p/Rev and Mrs Robert Miller, Charlotte, NC; ed/Grad, N Mecklenburg Sr HS, 1981; Att'g, Winston-Salem St Univ; pa/Kroger Sav-On, 1980-; cp/Delta Sigma Theta Sorority Inc, Gamma Phi Chapt, Corresponding Secy and Chaplain 1983-84; NAACP; HS: Cheerldg Squad, NAACP, Monogram Clb, Red Cross Clb, Latin Clb; r/Bapt; hon/Beauty of the Week, Charlotte Post, 1983; Honoree of Acad Excell, Winston-Salem St Univ, 1983; HS Hon Roll, 1979-81; g/Maj in Bus Adm; Computer Programmer/Operator w So Bell or IBM.

MILLER, JOHN NORMAN oc/Student; b/Dec 22, 1961; h/100 Walnut, Berea, KY 40403; p/John E and Dorothy Miller, Berea, KY; ed/Berea Commun HS, 1980; BS, IN Univ, 1984; Cnslr, IN Sch for Gifted and Talented Yth, 1982; Archaeol Dept Rschr, ISU, 1983; cp/Red Cross Swim Instr, 1979, 1980, 1981; Nat Hon Soc, 1980; Beta Clb, Pres 1980; HS Swim Team; HS Soccer Team; Jazz Band, 1980; r/Luth; hon/Nat Merit Scholar, 1980; Nat Hon Soc, 1980; Beta Clb, 1979, 1980; John Philip Sousa Band Awd, 1980; Dean's List, IN Univ, 5 Semesters; Personalities of S; g/Master's Deg, NWn Univ; Archaeologist.

MILLER, LEONARD THEODORE oc/Student; b/Oct 24, 1961; h/1 Declaration Place, Washington Crossing, PA 18977; p/Mr and Mrs Leonard W Miller, Washington Crossing, PA; ed/Grad, The Hun Sch of Princeton, 1979; Student, Morehouse Col; cp/HS Basketball, Cross Country, Tennis; r/Prot; g/Deg in Bus Adm; To Be Employed by a Fortune 500 Co; To Become an Owner of Many Fast Food Franchises.

MILLER, LISA KAREN oc/Student; b/Sep 8, 1964; h/PO Box 36, Glendale Springs, NC 28629; p/Allen and Janet Miller, Glendale Springs, NC; ed/Ashe Ctl HS, 1982; cp/Pres, 4-H; Outstg 4-H'er; Ch Pianist; Ch Yth Rep; FBLA; FCA; French Clb; Beta Clb Secy; Blood Donor; Vol Fresco Guide; Capt, Girls' Ch Basketball Team; Scorekeeper, Ch Boys Basketball and Softball Teams; hon/Dean's List, Wake Forest Univ, 1983; Alt, NC Sch of Sci and Math; Ashe Ctl Hi-Q Team; Sch for Gifted Students in the Arts; W/W Among Am HS Students; g/Psych.

MILLER, MICHAEL TODD oc/Student; b/Apr 9, 1966; h/2004 Lakeshore Drive, Madisonville, KY; ba/Madisonville, KY; p/H Doug Miller, Madisonville, KY; ed/Grad, Madisonville-N Hopkins HS; Pt-time Student, Madisonville Commun Col; pa/Pres, The Connection, a JA Co, 1982-83; Food Distribution and Sales, Taco John's, 1983-; cp/Pres, Ec and Social Coun, 1983 KY UN Assem; Secy-Treas, Hopkins Co Achievers Assn; Student Coun Mem; VP, French

Clb; VP, MNHHS Parliamentary Procedure Team; Reporter, Spch and Drama Leag; r/So Bapt; hon/Civitan Citizenship Awd and S'ship; Litchfield Awd, Dist'd Del, KY Yth Assem; Ted Urban Debate Awd; 2-Yr Bronze Medal Recip, Wn KY Univ Hist Competition; W/W Among Am HS Students; g/Degs in Law, Polit Sci and Bus Adm.

MILLER, MICHAEL WARREN oc/Student; b/Dec 31, 1963; h/PO Box 176, Grandy, NC 27939; p/Mr and Mrs James K Miller, Grandy, NC; ed/Currituck Co HS, 1982; Campbell Univ, 1982-83; pa/Bus Owner; cp/Campbell Univ Choir, 1982-83; Campbell Players, 1982-83; Circle K, 1982-83; Freshman Class Rep; Chorus; Tennis Team; Jr Histn; FBLA; FCA; Drama Clb; Annual Staff; Jr Beta Clb; Spanish Clb; Prom Com; Mod Dance Clb; Christian F'ship Clb; r/Christian; hon/Sang for the Pres and Mrs Reagan at the Nat Prayer Breakfast, 1983; Hon Roll; Mod Music Masters; W/W Among Am HS Students; Yg Commun Ldrs of Am; g/To Become a Profl Actor and Singer; To Study at the Am Acad of Dramatic Arts.

MILLER, ROBIN ANN oc/Sales Assistant; b/Jun 3, 1961; h/Route 6, Box 535, Dickson, TN 37055; ba/Nashville, TN; p/George and Linda Miller, Dickson, TN; ed/Dipl, Dickson Co Sr High, 1979; BBA in Ofc Adm, Austin Peay St Univ, 1983; pa/Sales Asst, E F Hutton & Co Inc; TN Ofc Ed Clb, VP; Future Secys of Am; cp/Alpha Lambda Delta; Laurel Wreath; F'ship of Christian Aths; r/Sunday Sch Tchr, 1982-83; Secy, Ch of Christ Student Ctr, APSU; hon/AAUW Awd, 1982; Outstg Grad in the 4-Yr BBA Prog, 1983; Recognized from 1979-83 on Acad Hons Day, Austin Peay; Recognized in 1982 and 1983 on Acad Awds Day, Austin Peay; W/W Am HS Students; W/W Among Am Cols and Univs.

MILLER, SAMUEL ALLEN oc/Student; b/Nov 25, 1961; h/119 Oak Street, Darlington, SC 29532; p/Selma C Miller, Darlington, SC; ed/Dipl, St John's High, 1980; BA, Bus Adm, Erskine, 1984; cp/Pres, Key Clb, 1979-80; Football Team, 1977, 1979; Tennis Team, 1976-80; Band, 1976; Pep Clb, 1976-77; Audio Visual Clb, 1977-80; Capt of Tennis Team, 1981-84; VP, Philomathean Lit Soc, 1983; Treas, Student Govt Assn, 1983-84; r/Bapt; hon/MVP, Tennis Team, 1980; All Acad Tennis Team, 1983; g/Career in Bkg.

MILLER, SCOTT AARON oc/Student; b/Jan 17, 1962; h/10410 Albertsworth Lane, Los Altos Hills, CA 94022; p/Gary and Sylvia Miller, Los Altos Hills, CA; ed/Grad, Piedmont Hills HS, 1980; Att'd, Normandale Jr Col 1978-79, San Jose St Univ 1979-81; Att'g, Univ of MN, 1981-; pa/Sci-Cards Trainee, Sci Calculations; cp/Has Performed in Var Orchs (Cello), incl'g, San Jose Yth Symph 1979-80, and Bloomington Symph Orch 1977-79, 1981-; 100% Mem and Life Mem, CA S'ship Fdn; r/Luth; hon/Original Compositions Publicly Performed; CA S'ship Fdn; Bk of Am Achmt Awd, 1980; Superior Rating for HS Musicians Contest, MN St HS Leag, 1978 (Cello Solo); g/Music Maj (BMus in Composition and Cello); Profl Composer and/or Cellist; Music Edr.

MILLS, KIMBERLY LYNNE oc/Student; b/Aug 18, 1967; h/6060 Woodview Drive, Morrow, GA 30260; p/Charles and Jo Mills, Morrow, GA; ed/HS Student; cp/Beta Clb, Secy 1983-84; Chorus; Co-ed-Y; Jr Class Ofcr, Treas 1983-84; Show Choir; r/Bapt; hon/Most Talented in Chorus, 1980, 1983; Most Outstg Jr in Chorus, 1984; All-St Chorus, 1980-84; Gov's Hons, 1984; g/Maj in Music (Vocal).

MILLS, MYLA DAUNE oc/Student; b/Jan 8, 1967; h/1026 East Main Street, Winterville, NC 28590; ba/Greenville NC; p/Mr and Mrs Herman Don Mills Jr, Winterville, NC; ed/Student, D H Conley HS; Student, NC Acad of Dance Arts 1972-, Kajé's Sch of Modeling 1979-; cp/Cosmetic Model, Belk-Tyler, 1983; Salesperson, Cox Florist, 1982; Salesperson, T-Shirts +, 1982; Lifeguard for Area Pools, 1983; cp/Varsity Football Cheerldr, 1983; Reporter, Lit Clb, 1983; Secy, Pep Clb, 1983; Rep, Future Bus Ldrs of Am, 1983; Writer, *The Shield*, 1983-84; Stat for Baseball, 1983; Stat for Football, 1983-84; r/Christian; hon/Ideal Miss Pitt Co, 1983; Teen Miss Greenville, 1983; 2nd Runner-Up, Miss D H Conley HS Pageant, 1983; Outstg Choreographer of Musical, 1981; g/Attend Col and Maj in Dance; Establish Own Studio; Dance Professionally.

MILLS, TIMOTHY HOBART oc/Student; b/Aug 23, 1964; h/Highway 66, PO Box 199, Arjay, KY 40902; ba/Williamsburg, KY; p/Mr and Mrs James E Mills Sr, Arjay, KY; ed/Bell Co HS, 1983; Student, Cumberland Col; pa/DJ, WANO Radio (Fed Communs Lic 1979), 1977-83; Lic'd Min, 1st Bapt Ch, 1982; MC for Public Functions, 1979-; Entertainment, incl'g, the Music Man Show, 1978-; Performed at Super Dome, Kiwania Intl Conv, 1981; KY St Fair Chapel on the Circle Prog, 1980; Toured Holy Land w Choir, 1982; cp/4-H Involvement, 1975-84; Teen Clb, Orgr, Pres; Area, Coun St, Del to VA for KY; Wash Rep; WI Exch Student; Col Chorale Choir and Chamber Choir; Football, 1980, 1981, 1982; KY All-St Choir, 1981-83; r/Bapt; hon/1st Record, "Singing for the Lord," Released 1983; Hugh O'Brien Yth Ldrship Sem; Bell Co Vol Fire Dept Talent Contest Winner, 1980-83; KY House Page; En Univ Broadcasters Awd for HS Students, 1983; Outstg Names and Faces; W/W HS Students; g/Rel and Music Maj; Evang.

MILLS, VERNA THERESA oc/Student; b/Feb 5, 1966; h/62 U Street, Northwest, Washington, DC 20001; p/James Edward Mills, Washington, DC; ed/Grad, Immaculate Conception Acad; pa/Wk/Study Prog, St Mary's Ct, 1982-83; Pers Dept, St Mary's Ct, 1983; Assn of Trial Lwyrs of Am; cp/St Martin's Teen Clb; Yth Min, St Martin's; r/Cath; hon/Recip, 4 Separate Awds for Spch, VFW, Dept of DC, Ladies Aux, Am Acad of Achmt; g/To Go to Col and Maj in Communs (Film/TV) and Minor in Jour; Casting Dir or Journalist.

MILSTID, KATHY DIANE oc/Student; b/Nov 29, 1961; h/Star Route Box 449A, Bay Minette, AL 36507; p/Floyd Milstid Jr, Bay Minette, AL; ed/Baldwin Co HS, 1980; Chem Engrg Maj, Univ of S AL; pa/Sum Secy, Ins and Rlty Ofc; Pt-time Photog and Asst Sports Editor

for Newspaper; Cheerldr Instr, AL HS Ath Assn; cp/Pres, HS FCA, 1980; VP, Sr Class, 1980; NHS; Hostess for Univ of S AL Basketball Team, 1981; Varsity Cheerldr; r/Bapt; hon/Christian Ath of Yr, FCA, 1980; Softball All-Co Player; Runner-Up in Miss SW AL Pageant; Grad from HS in Top 10, 5th out of 270 Students; W/W Among Am HS Students; g/Deg in Chem Engrg.

MINER, SHAWN MITCHELL oc/Fiction Editor of Literary Magazine, Writer, Student; b/Apr 25, 1955; h/9102 East Berry Avenue, Englewood, CO 80111; ba/Denver, CO; p/Robert R Miner; ed/Philosophical Sems; Student, Metro St Univ; Has Structured and Participated in Var Forms of Alternative Ed; pa/Radio DJ, KWER-AM, 1974; Ward Clk, Craig Rehab Ctr, 1975-76; Writing Tutor, MSC Writing Ctr, 1975-76; Fiction Editor, *Metrosphere*, 1983-84; PSA Coor, *Metrosphere* Mag, 1983; Profile Coor of Adv Bd, *Metrosphere* Mag, 1984; r/Ch of Life; hon/VP's Hon Roll.

MINTER, JULIE MARIE oc/Accounts Manager; b/May 10, 1960; h/1244 Branchfield Court, Riverdale, GA 30296; ba/Atlanta, GA; p/Charles Minter, Riverdale, GA; Joan Fulgum, Greenville, SC; ed/Grad, J L Mann HS, 1978; Grad, cum laude, Univ of GA, 1982; pa/Record Bar, 1978-82; Accts Mgr, Silver Bear, 1982-; cp/Golden Key Nat Hon Soc, 1981; Phi Kappa Phi, 1982; Pi Sigma Epsilon, 1981; r/SDA; hon/Dean's List, Univ of GA, 1978-82.

MINTER, REGINA MARIA oc/Nursing Student; b/Jan 29, 1964; h/1244 Branchfield Court, Riverdale, GA 30296; ba/Riverdale, GA; p/Charles and Jimmie Minter, Riverdale, GA; ed/Grad, Forest Pk Christian Sch, 1981; Att'g, Clayton Jr Col; pa/Receptionist and Med Asst, Dr David L Cooper, 1981-; cp/HS Cheerldr, 1979-81; Hon Roll, 1978, 1979, 1980, 1981; Editor of HS Yrbook; Sr Class Treas; Perfect Attendance, 1979, 1981; r/Bapt; hon/Miss Nat So Belle, 1983; Miss Teen Riverdale, 1979; g/Bach Deg in Nsg.

MINTON, KIMBERLY ANN oc/PBX Operator, Admitting Clerk; b/Nov 8, 1964; h/Route 1, Box 165AA, Stantonville, TN 38379; p/Eugene and Virginia Minton, Stantonville, TN; ed/Adamsville HS, 1983; pa/PBX Operator, Admitting Clk, McNairy Co Gen Hosp, 1983-; cp/Beta Clb, 1981-83; Order of the Rainbow for Girls in the St of TN, 1980-84, Worthy Advr 1982-83, Grand Page 1982-83, Grand Nature 1983-84; r/Meth; hon/Top Ten of Grad'g Class, 1982-83; W/W Among Am HS Students; g/Maj in Info Processing, Jackson St Commun Col.

MINYARD, DONALD HOYT oc/Student; b/Apr 8, 1958; h/2501 Myers 2, Champaign, IL 61821; ba/Champaign, IL; p/Hoyt and Rachel Minyard, Gadsden, AL; ed/Southside HS, 1975; BSBA 1978, MBA 1979, Auburn Univ; PhD Cand, Univ of IL; pa/Instr, NW MO St Univ, 1979-; Tchg Asst, Univ of IL, 1982-; MO Soc of CPAs; Am Inst of CPAs; Beta Alpha Psi; Beta Gamma Sigma; Phi Kappa Phi; Am Acctg Assn; r/Bapt; hon/Pub, "Reporting Deferred Income Taxes on the Balance Sheet," 1981; Pres Cup, Gadsden St Jr Col, 1976; 7th Place, Phi Beta Lambda Nat Acctg Awd, 1976; AAA Doct F'ship

Winner, 1982, 1983; W/W HS; Soc of Outstg Am HS Students.

MIRACLE, JOE oc/Counselor; b/Jan 25, 1957; h/2550 West 8th, Apartment #40, Odessa, TX 79763; ba/Odessa, TX; ed/MEd, MS St Univ, 1980; BA, Social Wk, Lincoln Meml Univ, 1979; Voc Rehab Cnslr, TX Rehab Comm, 1981-; Col Instr, Psych, Odessa Col, 1982-; Voc Rehab Cnslr, Allied Enterprises, Div of Voc Rehab, 1980; Grad Asst, Triangle Frat, 1980-81; Grad Asst, Sigma Nu Frat, 1980; Relief Cnslr, Cumberland River Comprehensive Care, 1979; Other Previous Positions; APGA; Nat Rehab Assn; Nat Rehab Cnslg Assn; Alpha Chi; Phi Alpha Theta; hon/ Outstg Behavioral Sci Student, Lincoln Meml Univ, 1979; Vapor Trail Awd for Contbns in the Devel of Social Wk Prog and the Devel of Affirmative Action Progs, LMU, 1979; Red Cross Key to City of Middlesboro, KY, 1977; RSA S'ship for Grad Study in Voc Rehab Cnslg, 1979; Yg Commun Ldrs of Am; W/W; Yg Achievers and Ldrs in Am; g/ To Further Ed and Move Toward an Adm Position.

MITCHELL, JAMES WYETH oc/ Student; b/Nov 6, 1963; h/531 Crescent Road, Griffin, GA 30223; ed/Griffin HS; Student of Animal Sci, Univ of GA; Vet Asst, 1980-81; Egg Processor, Vaccinator, H&N Poultry Farm, 1981-82; In Charge of Herd Hlth, 300 Brood Sow Operation, 1983; Pt-time in Dairy Nutrition Lab and Univ Dairy, Univ of GA, 1982-83; cp/Interact Clb; Bapt Student Union, 1982; Ag-Hill Coun Rep, 1982; Block and Bridle Clb, 1982-84; UGA Ag-Alumni Bd of Dirs, 1983-84; Griffin High Tennis Team, 1980; UGA Col of Ag HS Recruiter; Alpha Gamma Rho Frat, Alumni Secy; GHS Swim Team, 1981; r/Presb; hon/ Interact Clb Pres, 1980; Alpha Zeta Agri Acad Hon Soc, 1983; g/Vet.

MITCHELL, JENI LYNN oc/Student; b/Mar 30, 1960; h/316 East Main Street, Perry, FL 32347; p/Rev and Mrs Douglas W Mitchell, Perry, FL; ed/Havana HS, 1978; AA, Tallahassee Commun Col, 1980; BS in Elem Ed, FL St Univ, 1982; Student, SWn Sem; pa/Title I 4th Grade Tchr, 1982-83; cp/Nat Hon Soc; Student Coun; Sch Chorus Pres; Valedictorian; Pres, Phi Theta Kappa; Col Chorale and Ensemble; Col Choir; Adult Choir, Ensemble; Sum Missionary; Vol Tchr; r/So Bapt; hon/I Dare You Awd; Acad Excell; W/W; g/Sem Master of Rel Ed, Ch Music Minor.

MITCHELL, LISA ANN oc/Student; b/Mar 11, 1965; h/Chester Street, Greenfield, TN 38230; p/Mr and Mrs Howard Mitchell, Greenfield, TN; ed/ Grad, Greenfield HS, 1983; Student, Univ of TN Martin; cp/HS Student Coun Secy and VP; Yth for Christ VP and Pres; FHA Treas and VP; Class Secy; Class Favorite; Miss GHS; Most Talented; HS Pubs; HS Band Drum Maj; Bapt Ch Pianist and Secy; Lions Clb Vol; r/Bapt; hon/Greenfield Bkg S'ship, 1983; Greenfield Lions Clb S'ship, 1983; g/Deg in Phy Therapy.

MITCHELL, MANDY CAROLINE oc/Buyer, Salesperson, Pharmacist Technician; b/Apr 9, 1961; h/815 Lynnbrook Drive, Selmer, TN 38375; ba/ Selmer, TN; p/Mr and Mrs Robert D Mitchell, Selmer, TN; ed/McNairy HS, 1975-79; BS in Communs, Univ of TN

Knoxville, 1983; pa/Buyer/Pharm Tech, Selmer Drug Co; cp/Merchandising Student Assn, 1982-83; Public Relats Student Soc of Am, 1982-83; Equestrian Clb, 1982-83; Campus Practitioners, Secy-Treas 1982; Campus Practitioners, VP 1983; r/Prot; hon/Nom'd, Outstg Yg Wom of the Yr, 1983; Dean's List, UTK; g/To Obtain a Pers/Public Relats Position w a Maj Corp and Later Wk for a Public Relats Agy.

MITCHELL, ROBIN COLLINS oc/ Student; b/Mar 22, 1959; h/4011 A Illinois, Midland, TX 79703; m/Carlton Lee; p/Dr and Mrs Reed Collins, Midland, TX; ed/HS Grad; BA, Spanish and Sociol, TX Tech, 1982; Student of Spanish, Univ of Los Andes, 1980; r/ Cath; g/RN; BS.

MITCHELL, STEVEN LESLIE oc/ Surgery Resident; b/Nov 9, 1955; h/717 North 8th Street, Fargo, ND 58102; ba/ Fargo, ND; p/Ronald and Lillian Mitchell, Fargo, ND; ed/BS 1977, BSMS 1980, MD 1982, Univ of ND; pa/Surg Resident, Univ of ND, 1982-83; Neurosurg Resident, The Neuropsychi Inst, Fargo, ND, 1983-; AMA; Phi Kappa Phi; cp/Order of DeMolay; Blue Key; hon/ Nat Merit Scholar, 1973; Phi Eta Sigma, 1974; Men of Achmt; Intl Yth in Achmt; W/W Among Am HS Students; W/W Among Students in Am Univs and Cols; g/Neurosurg.

MOBLEY, SARENA ANITA oc/Student; b/Dec 21, 1965; h/810 Archdale Drive, Charlotte, NC 28210; p/John Robert and Daisy Mobley, Charlotte, NC; ed/Grad, Olympic High, 1984; cp/ JV Cheerldr, 1981-82; Sophomore Class Secy, 1981-82; Varsity Cheerldr, 1982-83; Jr Class Pres, Sci Clb, Wn Piedmont Cheerldr, Interclb Coun, 1982-83; Exec Coun, 1983-84; Keywanettes, New Images Dance Grp, 1981-83; r/Bapt; hon/Beauty of the Week, *The Charlotte Post*, 1982; NC Sch of Sci and Math Hon Nom, 1981; NCA Spirit Stick; WPC Outstg Cheerldr, 1982; Pres Ldrship Sem, 1983; Hd Cheerldr, 1983-84; Belk Teen Bd, 1983-84; W/W; g/To Attend a 4-Yr Col and Maj in Computer Sci; To Model in Spare Time.

MONELL, NATHAN REED oc/Graduate Assistant, Student; b/Jan 9, 1957; h/2040 Chatham Village, 1980 Pauline Boulevard, Ann Arbor, MI 48103; ba/ Ann Arbor, MI; m/Jane Helen; p/Rev and Mrs Robert Monell, Kingston, PA; ed/Ross Corners Christian Acad, 1974; Word of Life Bible Inst, 1975; BA, Grand Rapids Bapt Col, 1978; MA, Univ of MI, 1984; pa/Zondervan Corp, 1978-79, 1981-82; Asst Pastor, Yth, Wealthy St Bapt Ch, 1979-81; Instr in Public Spkg, Univ of MI, 1982-; Lectr, Spch Fundamentals, Jackson Commun Col, 1983; cp/Big Brother, Washtenaw Juv Ct, 1983; Pres, Student Coun of Grand Rapids Bapt Col, 1976-77; r/Bapt; hon/ Pres's Awd for Ldrship, 1977; Alumni Tuition S'ship, 1976; Grad Tchg F'ship, 1982-83; W/W Am Cols and Univs; Outstg Am HS Students; Commun Ldrs of Am; g/Finish MA in Communication Studies; Intl Commerce w Sweden.

MONGELLUZZO, SUSAN MARIE oc/Accountant; b/May 2, 1958; h/107 Irene Avenue, Buena, NJ 08310; p/Mr and Mrs Tony Mongelluzzo, Buena, NJ; ed/Buena Reg HS, 1976; AS, Alt Commun Col, 1978; BS, Stockton St Col,

1980; pa/Acct, Edward L Avena, PA; Nat Soc of Public Accts; cp/Stockton St Fac Review Bd, Alumni Assn; Sr Class Pres; Spanish Clb Pres; Student Coun; Capt, Colorguard Squad; r/Minotola Meth Ch Sch Tchr, Choir Mem, Sunday Sch Supt, Yth Advr; hon/HS Student of the Month; Citizenship and S'ship Awds; Medals for Outstg Achmt in Num Areas; Dr J P Cleary Math S'ship; Grad, summa cum laude; Prog Distn Grad; Highest Hon Grad; Valedictorian; HS Hon Soc; Intl Yth in Achmt; W/W Among Students in Am Univs and Cols; Yg Commun Ldrs of Am; g/Build Own Personal Bus.

MONROE, ANN PATRICE oc/ Teacher; b/Feb 5, 1960; h/11-A West Humbird Street, Rice Lake, WI 54868; ba/Rice Lake, WI; p/Richard T and Mary E Monroe, Cleveland Heights, OH; ed/ Beaumont HS, 1978; BS in Exceptl Ed, Univ of WI Milwaukee, 1982; Master's Credits, NY Univ, 1983; pa/TMR Tchr, Rice Lake Area Schs, 1982-83, 1983-84; CEC; Assn for Severly Handicapped; Lib of Spec Ed; r/Cath; hon/Dean's Hon Roll, 1977, 1978; St Ed Dept Awd, Lois Plous, St Rep, 1978; g/Master's Deg in Exceptl Ed from NY Univ; PhD; Admr or Prof.

MONROE, DARREL GENE oc/Student; b/Jan 18, 1964; h/PO Box 102, Brenham, TX 77833; p/Mr and Mrs Bobby Gene Monroe, Brenham, TX; ed/ HS, 1982; Student, Aerospace Engrg, Univ of TX Austin; cp/AIAA; Univ of TX Longhorn Band; Alpha Lambda Delta Freshman Hon Soc; Phi Eta Sigma; Freshman Hon Soc; Tubists Universal Brotherhood Assn; Nat Hon Soc Pres; German Clb Pres; Jr Engrg Tech Soc VP; Band Brass Lt, Equip Lt; New Am Patriots; Blood Donor; Class Plays Student Dir; TX Boys' St; r/Luth; hon/Univ of TX Freshman Engrg Hons Prog, 1982-83; Engrg Hon Roll, 1982, 1983; Outstg Tuba Soloist, TX St Solo Contest; Nat Band Assn Nat Hon Band; TX All-St Grps; Symph Band; Philharm Orch; Nat Dean's List; W/W Music; W/ W Among Am HS Students; Commun Ldrs of Am; g/Obtain a Master's Deg in Aerospace Engrg; Wk for NASA.

MONTAGUE, DAVID FAIRFAX oc/ Research Engineer; b/Jan 27, 1956; h/ 9301 Collingwood Road, Knoxville, TN 37922; ba/Knoxville, TN; m/Diane Olivia Simcox; c/Nathaniel Fairfax; p/ Dr F E Montague, Palatka, FL; ed/ Palatka S HS, 1974; BNE, GA Inst of Technol, 1977; ME 1979, PhD 1984, Univ of TN; pa/Engr, FL Power and Light Co, 1976; Grad Res Asst, Univ of TN, 1977-79; VP, Tng, JBF Assocs Inc; Am Nuclear Soc, 1976-; IEEE, 1978-; ASQC, 1982-; Tau Beta Pi, 1976-; Phi Kappa Phi, 1976-; cp/Beta Clb, Pres 1970-74; Track Team, 1973-74; hon/Pub, "A Procedure to Calculate the Expected Number of Failures in a Phased Mission," 1979; Class Valedictorian, 1974; Grad 1st in Class w Highest Hons, 1977; Tau Beta Pi; Phi Kappa Phi; ANS Conf, 1979 (1st Place Paper); Phi Eta Sigma; Review Bd Mem, *IEEE Transactions on Reliability Journal*; Cert'd Reliability Engr, ASQC; g/Prof'ship at a Maj Univ.

MONTANEZ, ROSA MARIA oc/ Student; b/Aug 20, 1960; h/2601 West Occidental, Santa Ana, CA 92704; ba/ Santa Ana, CA; p/Mr and Mrs Eugenio

Montanez, Santa Ana, CA; ed/Orange Coast Col, 1981-; Santa Ana Col, 1979-81; pa/Asst Mgr, Carls Jr Restaurant; cp/Vol, Co of Orange Hlth Care Agy, 1982; Vol Cath Ch Rel Tchr, 1979-; CA S'ship Fdn; Soccer Clb; Girls' Leag; Spanish Clb Secy; r/Cath; hon/Dietetic Asst Cert, 1983; Intl Yth in Achmt; W/W Among Am HS Students; g/Dietitian.

MONTES, ALICIA ISABEL oc/Student, Education Assistant; b/Jan 7, 1962; h/5706 North Havana Avenue, Tampa, FL 33614; ba/Tampa, FL; p/Ramon and Alicia Montes; ed/Sch of Art and Design, 1976-78; Comml Art Deg, Tampa Bay Tech-Voc, 1978-80; AA, Bus, Hillsborough Commun Col, 1981; BS, Univ of Tampa, 1985; pa/Ed Asst, Tampa Mus, 1983-; Advtg Mgr, Hillsborough Commun Col Student Newspaper, 1981; cp/Tampa Mus; Lee Scarfune Gallery, Intern; Sch Plays; Jour Clb Rep to Student Govt; Student Newspaper, Layout Artist, Writer; Student Tchr, 1977-79; Red Cross; HS Rep, 4 Yrs; Mem, VICA; VP, Jour Clb; Secy-Treas, Beta Phi Gamma; hon/2nd Place Best Advtg Layout, Jr Col; Sci Awd, 1974; Citizenship Awd; W/W Among Am HS Students; g/Arts Admr for a Mus, Pvt or Public Indust and Govt.

MONTGOMERY, JAMES EDWARD oc/Student; b/Nov 24, 1965; h/Route 1, Boones Mill, VA 24065; p/Mr and Mrs James H Montgomery; ed/Grad, Franklin Co HS; cp/Future Bus Ldrs of Am, 1981-82, 1983-84; Latin Clb, 1982-83, 1983-84; Student Cooperative Assn, 1981-83, Com Mem 1984; Editor, *The Eagle*; hon/*Roanoke Times and World News*, Awd'd Grant to Attend Wkshop at VA Commonwealth Univ for Jour; Chosen to Attend VA HS Leag Wkshop for Jour; g/Maj in the Field of Mass Communs.

MOODISPAW, PAUL FRANKLIN oc/Student; b/Nov 26, 1962; h/PO Box 309, Neffs, OH 43940; p/William F and Irene V Moodispaw, Neffs, OH; ed/Bellaire HS, 1981; Att'g, OH St Univ; pa/Sum Camp Staff, BSA, 1978, 1979; Transport Orderly, City Hosp of Bellaire, 1979-81; cp/BSA, Troop 116, Asst Scoutmaster; Nat Eagle Scout Assn; Order of the Arrow, Advr; Nat Rifle Assn; r/U Meth Ch; hon/Tri-Valedictorian, 1981; Stadium S'ship; Dorm S'ship; Eagle Scout Awd; God and Country Awd; Vigil Hon Awd; W/W Among Am HS Students; Intl Biogl Centre; g/MD.

MOORE, AMY JO oc/Student; b/Oct 10, 1958; h/333 Charles Street, Blacksburg, VA 24060; ed/San Marcos HS, 1976; BA in Psych/Sociol, Austin Col, 1980; MS in Child Devel, VPI&SU, 1982; pa/Hd Tchr, 3-Yr Olds, Lab Sch, VPI&SU, 1981-82; Hd Tchr, Infant Room, VPI&SU, 1982-83; NAEYC; VAEYC; NCFR; SECFR; cp/Chief Justice, Grad Hon Sys; VP; Grad Rep, Student Budget Bd; Grad Student Assem; r/Christian; hon/Psi Chi; Pi Gamma; Selected as Chief Justice, Grad Hon Sys; g/PhD in Child Devel-Fam Devel.

MOORE, ANNE ELIZABETH oc/Student; b/Sep 19, 1966; h/105 South Swegles, St Johns, MI 48879; p/Mr and Mrs James Moore, St Johns, MI; ed/St Johns HS, 1984; pa/Employee, McDonalds; cp/VP, St Johns HS Student Coun; Capt, Swimming Team; Track

Team; Lions All-St Band; Orch; Class Secy, 1981; Student Coun Rep, 1982, 1983, 1984; r/Rom Cath; hon/Donna Carter Freshman Algebra Prize, 1981; Nat Hon Soc, 1983; g/To Attend the Univ of MI.

MOORE, BARRY RAY oc/Student; b/Jun 14, 1964; h/2608 Maxwell, Midland, TX 79701; ba/Lubbock, TX; p/Mr and Mrs Douglas R Moore, Bury St Edmunds, England; ed/Brit Adv'd Level Exams in Physics, Math, 1982; 7 Ordinary Level Exams, 1980; Student, TX Tech Univ; pa/Hwy Constrn Wkr, Clearwater Constructors Inc, 1982; cp/Phi Eta Sigma Hon Soc; r/Prot; hon/Dean's Hon List, Fall 1982; g/Maj in Indust Engrg; AF Pilot.

MOORE, DOREDA OPHELIA RENEE oc/Student; b/May 18, 1958; h/553 South 7th Avenue, Mount Vernon, NY 10550; p/Arthur (dec) and Evelyn Moore, Mount Vernon, NY; ed/BS in Computer Sci, Bowie St Col, 1983; pa/Asst Lab Tech, Dr D Council, 1982; Word Processing, Mr W Mumby, Mr J Dungy, Dr J Williams, Mr D Swift, 1979-81; cp/Nat Coun of Negro Wom, Dir of the Yg Adult Grp; NAACP, Life Mem; NCNW, Life Mem; Alpha Kappa Alpha Sorority Inc; Polit Canvassing Internally and Externally (Repub Party); Future Tchr; Keyette Clb; r/U Meth.

MOORE, JAMES HARRISON oc/Student; b/Dec 18, 1961; h/RFD #1, Box 157, New Market, VA 22844; p/J George and Virginia A Moore, New Market, VA; ed/Stonewall Jackson HS, 1980; Student, VA Mil Inst; mil/ROTC at VA Mil Inst; 2nd Lt, Army Reserves, 1984-; cp/Student Mem, ASCE; VMI Track Team; VMI Monogram Clb; r/Luth; g/Entry Level in Engrg w Future Goal of Higher Mgmt Position.

MOORE, KATHLEEN oc/Student; b/Oct 29, 1965; h/6111 Belgrade Drive, Huntsville, AL 35810; p/Samuel and Mary V Moore, Huntsville, AL; ed/Grad, J O Johnson HS, 1983; Att'g, AL A&M Univ; cp/Nat Hon Soc, 1981-83; Archonette Clb; Secy, SS Class; NAACP Yth Coun, Secy 1984; Math Clb; r/Bapt; hon/Hon Roll I, II, III, IV, 1979-83; Dean's List, 1984; Outstg Sr, 1983; Inductee of Zeta Yth Hall of Fame, 1983; First Class Girl Scout; Intl Yth in Achmt; Personalities of S; g/Maj in Computer Sci; To Obtain a Doct Deg in Computer Sci.

MOORE, KIMBERLY DIANNE oc/Student; b/Oct 9, 1961; h/129 Carol Lane, Red Oak, TX 75154; p/Herbert and Patricia Moore, Red Oak, TX; ed/Red Oak HS, 1979; AA, AS, Cedar Val Col, 1981; Student, Stephen F Austin St Univ; cp/Am Mktg Assn; SFA Mktg Clb; Nat Hon Soc; Ofc Ed Assn; Choir; Solo and Ensemble; UIL Participant; Phi Theta Kappa, Secy, Pres; Poetry Interpret; Selah Singers; hon/Student Del, Inauguration of Chancellor for Dallas; VP's Hon List; Nat Dean's List; Intl Yth in Achmt; g/BBA in Mktg.

MOORE, PHYLLIS DEANNA oc/Student; b/Mar 7, 1965; h/PO Box 364, Hampton, GA 30228; p/Larry and Yvonne Moore, Hampton, GA; ed/HS Grad; cp/Spec Activs for Gifted Ed; 3-Yr Drama Student; Vol Wkr, March of Dimes, Retarded Chd and the Elderly; Sum Camp Cnslr; r/Christian; hon/2nd Runner-Up, GA Miss Teen USA, 1979; Calendar Girl for Sch, 1980; 1st

Runner-Up, Geranium Fest Pageant, 1981; Dist Talent Winner, GA Miss TEEN, 1981; Dist Talent Winner, GA Miss TEEN, 1981; 3rd Runner-Up, GA Miss TEEN, 1981; Dist Talent and Vol Ser Winner, 1st Runner-Up, GA Miss TEEN, 1982; GA Miss TEEN, Dist Talent Vol Ser Winner, St Talent Winner, 1983; g/Maj in Drama and Theatre; Pursue Career in Perf'g Arts Field.

MOORE, ROBERT TRACY oc/Sales; b/May 9, 1960; h/333 Oberlin Court, Fayetteville, NC 28303; p/Mr and Mrs William T Moore, Fayetteville, NC; ed/E E Smith Sr High, 1978; Appalachian St Univ, 1978-80; Univ of NC Chapel Hill, 1981-82; pa/Cook, Peddler Steak House; Cook, White Horse Restaurant; Sales Rep, SWn Co; Cook, Spanky's Restaurant; Carpenter's Asst, D R Allen Constrn Co; cp/Key Clb, Sr Rep; High Y, Parliamentarian; Hon Roll; Fayetteville, Cumberland Co Yth Coun; Varsity Tennis Letterman; Phi Beta Lambda Bus Frat; Pi Kappa Phi Frat, Asst Social Chm and Interfrat Coun Rep; r/Bapt; hon/Dean's List; g/To Pursue Grad Sch (MBA); To Go into Bus for Self.

MOORE, SAMANTHA LYNN oc/Student; b/Sep 16, 1966; h/Route 3, Box 288, Adamsville, TN 38310; p/Mr and Mrs Kenneth S Moore, Adamsville, TN; ed/Grad, Adamsville HS, 1984; cp/Lib Clb, 1980; 4-H Clb Pres, 1983; 4-H Clb, 1975-84; FHA Subreg Secy, 1982-83; FHA Chapt Secy, 1982-83; FHA Chapt Pres, 1983-84; Student Coun Secy, 1983; AHS Chorus, 1983; *Cardinal Action* Staff, 1984; r/Bapt; hon/Girls' St Alternate, 1983; Voice of Dem 2nd Place, 1982, 1983; 4-H Co Public Spkg Winner, 1980, 1982, 1983; 2nd Place Civitan Clb Essay Contest, 1983; *Chapter Chatters* Editor, 1983; W/W Among Am HS Students; Soc of Dist'd HS Students; g/To Attend Univ of TN Martin and Maj in Communs w Emphasis on TV Jour.

MOORE, SHELLEY RENAE oc/Student; b/May 22, 1966; h/12626 East 137th Street, Broken Arrow, OK 74012; p/Mr and Mrs Ralph J Moore Jr, Broken Arrow, OK; ed/Student, Broken Arrow HS; cp/French Clb; Jr Exec Bd; Astronomy Clb; HS Track Team and Basketball Team; Yth Effectiveness Tng; Student Coun; r/Evang Tng at Immanuel Luth Ch; hon/Outstg Jour, 1980; Cert of Merit for Outstg Perf, NSU Interscholastic Hist Competition, 1982; Outstg Defensive Player, Basketball, 1982; HS Hon Roll, 1983; g/Deg in Theol Studies; Missionary and/or Musical Profession.

MOOREHEAD, PHYLLIS CLEMENT oc/Tutor, Hostess; h/215 North Pine Street, Seneca, SC 29678; m/Vincent DeWayne Moorehead; p/Johnnie M Clement, Seneca, SC; ed/Dipl, HS, 1979; BA Eng, Berea Col, KY, 1983; pa/Hostess/Waitress, Red Lobster, Sum & Fall 1984; Adm Secy, Col of Engrg, Clemson Univ, 1983; Eng Tutor & Revisor, Tri-Co Tech Col, 1983-84; Student Secy 1980-81 & 1982-83, Commun Cnslr 1981-82, Berea Col, KY; cp/VPres 1982-83, Bd Mem 1977-79, Chapel Choir, Berea Col, KY, 1979-84; Basketball, 1976-77; r/Christian Bapt; hon/Modified & Revised, *Annual Report for Industl Dept*, Tri-Co Tech Col; Am Legion Sch Achmt Awd S'ship, 1979; Most Talented Sr, Class of 1979; g/MA Communs; Career Cnslr.

MORELAND, ANITA SHVON oc/ Student; b/Jul 22, 1965; h/Route 1, Box 8-D, Rayle, GA 30660; p/Mr and Mrs Willie Joe Moreland, Rayle, GA; ed/ Berean Acad, 1983; Student, Huntingdon Col; cp/Sch Band and Choir, 4 Yrs; Basketball Team, 2 Yrs; Temperance Clb; Yrbook Editor and Newspaper Typist, Sr Yr; Student Coun Pres, and Social VP, 1 Yr; Sr Class VP; Hon Soc, 4 Yrs; Class Valedictorian; Girls' Quartet, 4 Yrs; r/SDA; hon/Typing Awd, 1983; Most Likely to Succeed, 1983; Most Studious, 1983; Most Cooperative, 1983; Math Awd, 1983; Ldrship Awd, 1983; US Achmt Acad; g/Maj in Acctg and Minor in Bus Adm; CPA.

MORLEY, MAUREEN JANE oc/Student; b/Aug 30, 1963; h/6619 South Kostner, Chicago, IL 60629; p/James J and Jane E Morley, Chicago, IL; ed/ Grad, Gurdon S Hubbard HS, 1981; Att'g, Columbia Col; pa/Salesperson, Winkelman's, 1981; Neighborhood Beautification, City of Chgo Sts of Sanitation Dept, 1982; cp/Nat Hon Soc, VP; Quill and Scroll, Secy; Newspaper Editor; Mu Alpha Theta; Sr Girls' Coun; Pom-Pon; Sophomore Sr Social Com; Civic Leag Del; Student Ath Assn; Parent Tchr Student Assn; Student Adv Bd, Constitutional Rights Foun, 1980-81; r/Cath; hon/Hubbard Class Salutatorian, 1981; Hon Roll, 1977-81; W/W Among Am HS Students; g/Maj in Arts Entertainment and Media Mgmt w an Emphasis on Music and Broadcasting.

MORRIS, CHARLES MICHAEL oc/ Student; b/Dec 17, 1964; h/2142 Loma Court, Morrow, GA 30260; p/Mr and Mrs H D Morris, Morrow, GA; ed/ Morrow Sr HS, 1983; Student, GA Inst of Technol; cp/Football; Basketball; Baseball; Track; Swimming; Nat Hon Soc; Key Clb; F'ship of Christian Aths, Nat; Close-Up; Model UN; Math Team; Gifted Minors Prog; Capt, Basketball, 1980; Capt, Baseball, 1983; Spec Olympics Vol, 1982-83; Beta Clb, 1979; r/ Bapt; hon/Most Outstg Student, 1979; Most Outstg French Student, 1980-81; Grad in Top 1%; All A Hon Roll, 1981-82, 1982-83; Mr Mustang, Baseball, 1981; GA Cert of Merit, 1982; Most Improved, Football, 1982-83; Acad Awds in Footall, Basketball, Baseball, 1981, 1982, 1983; US NLMA, 1983; J E Edmunds S'hip Recip, 1983; Lowry Meml S'hip, 1983; W/W Am HS Students; US Nat Ldrship Merit Awd; Soc of Dist'd HS Students; g/Deg in Elect Engrg; Grad Deg in Fin; Start Own Bus.

MORRIS, DONNA CAROLE oc/ Recent Graduate; b/Jun 24, 1961; h/201 Kenilworth Drive, Greenwood, SC 29646; p/Rev and Mrs F D Morris, Greenwood, SC; ed/Grad, Abbeville HS, 1979; BA, Columbia Col, 1983; pa/ Student Asst in Eng Dept, Columbia Col, 1979-83; Waitress, Pizza Inn, 1982; cp/*Criterion* Staff; *Columbian* Staff; Past Pres, Sigma Tau Delta, Nat Eng Frat; Editor, *Columbia Col Handbook*, 1982-83; Editor, *Campus Connection*; r/U Meth; hon/ Alpha Kappa Gamma, 1982-83; Order of the Purple Seal, 1981-83; Sigma Tau Delta, 1981, 1983; STD Hon Awd Recip, 1982; Trustee S'hip, 1979-83; Rollins S'ship, 1982; Pres's List, 1982-83; Dean's List, 1979-83; W/W Among Students in Am Univs and Cols; g/Edit or Public Relats Wk.

MORRIS, EDITH ANN oc/Student; b/May 7, 1964; h/PO Box 217, Friars Point, MS 38631; p/Mr Glynn Morris (dec); Mrs Glynn Morris, Friars Point, MS; ed/Lee Acad, 1982; Att'd, Coahoma Jr Col 1982, Phillips Co Commun Col 1982-83; cp/Gourmet Cooking Clb, 1979-81; Crafts and Needlework Clb, Secy-Treas 1980-81, 1981-82; Secys of Tommorrow, 1980-81; Chorus; Phi Theta Kappa, Phillips Col; r/Cath; hon/ Named Co-ed Correspondent, 1982; Named Most Courteous Sr Girl, 1982; Recip, Awd for Excell in Gen Psych, Coahoma Jr Col, 1983; Recip, Acad S'ship, Phillips Co Commun Col; g/Maj in Bus Adm, Delta St Univ.

MORRIS, LOWELL B oc/Student; b/ Aug 4, 1958; h/Route 1, Box 291, Cumberland City, TN 37050; ba/Knoxville, TN; p/Mr and Mrs Loriece Morris, Cumberland City, TN; ed/Dipl, Houston Co High; BS, Acctg, w High Hons, Univ of TN; Att'd, Université Laurentienne; Att'g, Université de Droit, d'Économie, et des Sciences d'Aix-Marseilles; pa/Catalog Sales Asst, Sears, Roebuck & Co, 1978-79; Sales Rep, World's Fair Souvenirs, 1982; Phys Asst and Receptionist, Ctl Vet Hosp, 1981-82; cp/Thornloe Players Theatrical Ensemble; Bus Students Adv Coun to the Dean; VP, Intl Students Org; Student Sers Com, Université Laurentienne; DeMolay; Pres, Alpha Kappa Psi; Beta Alpha Psi; Phi Kappa Phi; Beta Gamma Sigma; Omicron Delta Kappa; Del Square Psi; UMYF; r/Meth; hon/Intl Student Exch Prog; Golden Key Nat Hon Soc; Pres Scholar; Commun Ldrs of Am; Outstg Yg Man of Am; g/Intl Relats (US Fgn Ser).

MORRIS, PAUL WESLEY oc/Chiropractor; b/Oct 13, 1956; h/Route 2, Box 330, Chesnee, SC 29323; ba/Inman, SC; m/Susan Brown; c/Kristin Michelle; p/ Rev and Mrs John W Morris, Sebring, OH; ed/Hughesville HS, 1975; BA, Malone Col, 1979; Sherman Col of Straight Chiro, 1981; pa/Chiropractor; Palmetto Chiro Coun; cp/Right-to-Life; Spartansburg Citizens for Life; Spartansburg Animal Shelter; r/Beloit Friends Ch; hon/Intl Achmt Awd; W/ W Among Students in Am Univs and Cols; Outstg Yg Men of Am; Commun Ldrs of Am.

MORRIS, TEDDY JEFFERSON oc/ Student, Computer Operator; b/Jan 23, 1963; h/Route 9, Box 439, Salisbury, NC 28144; ba/Salisbury, NC; p/Mr and Mrs R G Morris, Salisbury, NC; ed/Grad, W Rowan HS, 1981; Att'd, NC St Univ, 1981-82; Att'g, Catawba Col (Maj in Intl Bus and Bus Adm); pa/Bus Driver, W Rowan HS, 1979-81; TV Repair Shop, 1981; Mech's Asst, Food Lion Truck Shop, 1982-83; Computer Operator, Food Lion Inc, 1983-; cp/Del, NC Gov's Sch; Chem Engrg Explorer's Post; Rowan Co 4-H Pres; Radio and TV Broadcasting Explorer's Post; Dist II Pres of NC Student Acad of Scis; Vol Bus Driver, Chapel Hill (Morehead Planetarium); 4-H Pres and Treas; VP of Bus Drivers Clb; NC St Col 4-H Clb Histn, Pres-Elect and Freshman of the Yr; Commerce Clb; Yg Ams for Freedom; Profl Bus Assn; YAF; Intl Bus Com; hon/NC Gov's Sch; I Dare You Awd Winner; Nat 4-H Cong in Chgo; Morehead Nom; NC 4-H Elect Winner; Nat 4-H Elect Winner; Intl Consltg Grp,

Nat 4-H Conf in Wash, DC; Recip, Johnston S'ship to Univ of NC Chapel Hill; Nat Elks S'ship; NC 4-H Devel Fund S'ship; NC Jr Sci and Humanities Symp Winner; Del to Nat Sci Symp; Freshman of the Yr Awd for NC St 4-H Col Clb; NC St Fellows Prog; Treas of Mktg Class; Host Com for Catawba Col Exec Symp; Rowan Co Kiwanis S'ship Winner; W/W; Personalities of S; Intl Yth in Achmt; g/To Get a Master's Deg in Intl Mgmt and Wk toward a Career as a Corporate Ofcr.

MORRISON, GERALD WILLIAM oc/Inventory Control; b/Mar 26, 1952; h/5490 South 670 West, Murray, UT 84107; p/Agnes Flower, Elma, WA; ed/ Tooele HS, 1970; Assoc Deg, UT Tech Col, 1980; Westminster Col; pa/Inventory Control; cp/VITA; DECA; hon/ Senator-at-Large; Photog Awds; W/W Am Jr Cols; g/Own Bus.

MORRISON, SHARON NANETTE oc/Student; b/Feb 8, 1963; h/1434 Rockbridge Road, Stone Mountain, GA 30087; p/John and Maria Morrison, Stone Mountain, GA; ed/Parkview HS, 1981; Att'g, GA So Col, 1981-; pa/Avon Rep, 1981; Arts and Crafts Cnslr, Camp Martha Johnston, 1983; cp/*Felis Concolor* Staff, Orgs Editor 1980, Fac Editor 1981; Beta Clb; Y-Clb, Scrapbook Chm 1980, VP 1981; French Clb; Mu Alpha Theta Hon Math Clb; Gamma Beta Phi Hon Soc; Phi Upsilon Omicron Hon Home Ec Frat; Am Soc of Interior Designers; r/Cath; hon/Hon Roll, 1978-81; PTSA Acad Awd, 1979, 1980, 1981; Statesboro Homebldrs Assn Awd, 1983; Dean's List, 1982; g/Maj in Interior Design; Deg in Arch.

MORTON, JENNIFER SUE oc/Student; b/Aug 17, 1966; h/2208 Millswood Road, Picayune, MS 39466; p/Clyde D and Jean S Morton, Picayune, MS; ed/ Carriere Christian Sch, 1983; Wkg on BS, Liberty Bapt Col; cp/Nat Home Ec Assn; r/Bapt; hon/Pub, *The Little Gnome, a Speller for Silent Letters*, 1984; Valedictorian of HS Grad'g Class, 1983.

MOSELEY, LORA EILEEN oc/Student; h/1612 Colony Drive, Tarboro, NC 27886; p/Mr and Mrs N C Moseley, Tarboro, NC; ed/HS Student; cp/Fine Arts and Lit Clb; Bible Clb, Secy; Am Field Ser Clb; Polit Sci Clb; French Clb, Secy; Student Coun; NC Student Acad of Sci Clb, Pres-Elect; Inter-Clb Coun; r/Bapt; Singer, Ch Yth Mission-Type Ensemble, Joy Explosion; hon/US Nat Sci Merit Awd Winner, 1982; NC Sch of Sci and Math Semi-Finalist, 1982; Participant in E Carolina Univ Math Contest, 1982; Nom for Gov's Sch of NC, 1983; Hon Roll and Prin's List, 1980-83; g/Career in the Field of Music (Organ) and/or Computer Programming.

MOSER, JEFFERY RICHARD oc/ Student; b/Feb 8, 1961; h/Star Route Box 19, Wessington, SD 57381; p/Mr and Mrs Richard Moser, Wessington, SD; ed/Grad w High Hons, Miller HS, 1979; BA, summa cum laude, Univ of MN, 1983; pa/Yth Adv Del, Gen Assem, U Presby Ch in USA, Phoenix AZ, 1984; cp/Eng Tutor Interview Com, Univ of MN Residence Hall, 1983; Coor, Christianity Sem Planning, Univ of MN Residence Hall, 1983; Hons Corp Roundtable, Norwest Corp & Univ of MN Hons Prog, 1983; Col of Liberal Arts Student Intermediary Bd (CLA-SI Bd),

Univ of MN, 1983, 1984; Review Com, Univ of MN Col of Liberal Arts, 1983; Miller County Theater, Ctl Plains Art Coun, 1983; Ad-Hoc Com on Res Investigations, Med Sci Panel, Student Rep, Univ of MN, 1983; Del, Golden Key Nat Hon Soc, Nat Convention, Atlanta, GA, 1983; US Capitol Hist Soc; Nat Geographic Soc; Farmers Union; 4-H Clb Foun of SD, Inc; Life Mem, Phi Beta Kappa, Alpha of MN Hon Soc, 1983; Life Mem, Omicron Delta Kappa; Circle of MN Hon Soc, 1983; Vol, Muscular Dystrophy Dance-A-Thon, Univ of MN, 1983; MW Writers Grp, 1982-83; Exec Com 1983, Pres 1983, Pioneer Resident Hall Assn; Intl Peace & Issues Forum; U Mins in Higher Ed, Univ of MN, 1981-82, 1982-83; Reception Coor, Golden Key NHS, 1983; Student Rep, Adv Com on Spec Lrng Opportunities, 1983; SD 4-H Foun; Nat Farmers Union; Fdr, Charter Mem, Pres, Golden Key Nat Hon Soc, 1983; Vol, Muscular Dystrophy Dance-a-Thon, 1983; Pres, Pioneer Residence Hall Assn, 1982-83; Col of Liberal Arts Student Intermediary Bd, 1983; Bd of Dirs, Intl Study and Travel Assn, 1982-83; Sum Internship for MN Col Srs; Hubert H Humphrey Inst of Public Affairs, 1982; Univ Com on Intl Ed, 1982-83; Univ Senate Com on Use of Human Subjects in Res, 1982-83; Asst Coor, All Campus Elections, 1983; Rep for Minorities and Wom, Col of Liberal Arts Assem, 1983; Univ Hlth Ser Com; Yth Activs Coor; 4-H Communs Internship; Univ Com on Use of Human Subjects in Res, St Rep 1980-81, 1981-82, 1982-83; Intl Student Study Sub-Com on Intl Students, Student Rep, Univ of MN, 1982; Rep to Pers Com, Intl Study & Travel Assn, Univ of MN, 1983; Del, St Conv, SD Farmers Union, 1981, 1982, 1983; Profl Rural Yth Ldrs Exch Prog; Univ Com on Intl Ed, 1981-82, 1982-83; Vol, Univ Hosp; r/Rose Hill Presb Ch; hon/Phi Beta Kappa, 1983; Omicron Delta Kappa, 1983; Sigma Tau Mortar Bd, 1982; Univ of MN Outstg Ser and Ldrship Awd, 1983; Univ of MN Hon Judge, Campus Carnival, 1983; Hons Corporate Roundtable, Univ of MN, 1983; Hons Rep, Spectrum Conf; Univ of MN Residence Hall Ldrship Awd, 1983; Nat Sr Yth Adv Coun, Nat Farmers Union; SD Superior Orator; DeKalb Agri Accomplishment Awd; First Bk Sys Nat S'ship; Intl Yth in Achmt; Yg Commun Ldrs of Am; W/W Among Am HS Students; g/Eng Maj/ Fam Sociol, German, Polit Sci Minors; Law/Grad Sch; Career in Public Affairs, Govt.

MOSES, ELIZABETH RENEE oc/ Student; b/Nov 18, 1961; h/Route 3, Box 119, Pittsboro, NC 27312; p/Mr and Mrs Thomas W Moses, Pittsboro, NC; ed/ Grad, Faith Christian Sch, 1980; BS in Exec Secretarial Sci w Minor in Polit Sci and Bus Adm, Liberty Bapt Col, 1984; pa/Waitress, Pizza Hut, 1982; Wk'd at Computer Terminal, Moral Majority, 1982-83; Internship in Wash, DC, The Conserative Caucus, 1983; cp/ Softball and Volleyball Teams, 1979; Class Treas; Yrbook Staff, 1977; Chorus, 1977, 1979; Ch Pianist, 1979-80; Soc for Advmt of Mgmt, 1983-; Yg Ams for Freedom, 1980-81; r/Meth; hon/HS Homecoming Queen Jr Rep, 1979; Hon

Roll; Chancellor's S'ship for Tuition, Liberty Bapt Col; Outstg Yg Wom of Am; g/Exec Secy in Polit Arena.

MOSES, MONICA TERESSA oc/ Graduate Student, Research Assistant; b/Nov 18, 1961; h/Route 2, Box 96, Newellton, LA 71357; ba/Monroe, LA; p/Mr and Mrs Leon K Moses Sr, Newellton, LA; ed/Newellton HS, 1979; BA, NE LA Univ, 1983; pa/Internship, Green Oaks Detention Home, 1983; Grad Asst in Crim Justice Dept, NE LA Univ, 1983; cp/Student Social Wk Assn, 1981-83; Student Correctional Assn, VP 1983; Phi Kappa Phi, 1983; HS Student Coun; FBLA; FHA; Hon Roll; Annual Staff; Alpha Phi Sigma (VP), 1981-83; hon/Paul Howard Kitchens Awd, 1981; Acad Hon Roll, 1980-83; Alpha Phi Sigma, 1981-83; Phi Kappa Phi, 1983; Grad, cum laude, 1983; HS Hon S'ship, 1979; Grad Asst'ship, 1983; W/W Among Am HS Students; Commun Ldrs of Am; g/Grad Student in Crim Justice; Law Sch.

MOSES, TAMRA LANE oc/Student; b/Jul 27, 1965; h/Route 3, Box 119, Pittsboro, NC 27312; p/Thomas W and Faye H Moses, Pittsboro, NC; ed/Grad, Faith Christian Sch, 1983; Ctl Carolina Tech Col, 1983; Student, Meredith Col; pa/Cashier, Byrd's Food Ctr, 1982-83; cp/Cheerldr, 1982; Freshman, Sophomore, Jr and Sr Class Ofcr, Treas; Yrbook Staff, 1983; HS Chorus; Ch Pianist; r/Meth; hon/Hon Roll, 1979-83; Jr Marshall; W/W Among Am HS Students; Soc of Dist'd Am HS Students; g/Bus Adm.

MOSS, SCARLETT JO oc/Student; b/Oct 29, 1963; h/702 Sandelwood, Midland, TX 79703; p/Cheryl Moss, Midland, TX; ed/Grad, Robert E Lee HS, 1982; Student, SWn Univ; cp/Nat Forensics Leag, 1st VP; Polit Sci Clb; U Girls' Softball; Debate; Hon Soc; Jr Engrg and Tech Soc; r/Meth; hon/HS Outstg Debater, 1982; Nat Forensics Leag Deg of Spec Recog, 1982; TX Girls' St, 1981; Nat Bicent Debates, 1982; UN Sem, NYC, 1983; Yth in Achmt; g/Polit Sci; Pract Law.

MOSS, SHARON AMELIA oc/Student; b/Nov 20, 1965; h/1708 West Wilson Street, Tarboro, NC 27886; p/ Mr and Mrs Reginald Moss, Tarboro, NC; ed/HS Student; pa/Page, Edgecombe Meml Lib, 1982-83; cp/Student Govt, 1981-83; Jr Ebonettes; Spanish Clb; Am Field Soc; Jr Class Secy-Treas; r/Epis; hon/NC Gov's Sch Nom, 1983; Hon Roll; Prin's List; g/Maj in Marine Biol, Minor in Music.

MOTOBU, CHANA CHIEMI oc/ Student; b/Jan 20, 1964; h/1695 Wailuku Drive, Hilo, HI 96720; p/Mr and Mrs Tsugio Motobu, Hilo, HI; ed/HI Prep Acad, 1981; Att'g, Wash Univ; cp/4-H Clb Pres, 1975-76; YMCA Clb Pres, 1975-76; Hilo Aquatic Clb Competitive Swimmer, 1973-79; Rainbow Girls 4, Worthy Advr, 1978-79; Nat Jr Hon Soc, 1976-78; cum laude Soc, 1980-81; Hilo Karate Assn, 1978-79; Student Body Govt Assn, VP 1976-77, Pres 1977-78; Sophomore Class Pres, 1978-79; Leo's Clb, 1978-79; HPA Girls' Tennis Team, 1979-80; Wash Univ Phonathon, 1981; Intramural Softball Team, 1982, 1983; r/Prot; hon/Ser Awd, 1976; Hon Awd and Pin and Ser Awd and Pin, 1978; Hon Awd, 1979-80; Hon Awd, 1980-81; Tennis Sportsmanship Awd, 1980-81;

Tennis Most Improved Awd, 1980-81; Rep HI St at Hugh O'Brian's Ldrship Sem, 1979; Rep Sophomore Class at Homecoming Activs, 1979; Brit Biogl Soc, 1980-81; Japanese Lang Spch Competition Awd and Pin, 1980, 1981; W/W Among Am HS Students; g/Math Maj; Med or Dentistry.

MOULDEN, REBECCA PAULINE oc/Elementary Reading Aide and Librarian; b/Feb 20, 1962; h/530 East Main Street, Elnora, IN 47529; p/Ray and Doris Moulden, Elnora, IN; ed/N Daviess Commun Sch, 1980; pa/Janitor; Elem Rdg Aide and Libn; cp/Vol, Right-to-Life, March of Dimes, Cerebral Palsy; CoChm, Co Fair Parade; Band; Beta Clb; Class Reporter; Lib Aides; Yrbook Editor; Jr Class VP; Hoosier Girls' St; Ch Secy; Chm, St Judes Bike-a-Thon, 1983; Girls' Basketball Coach; hon/Intl Yth in Achmt; W/ W Among Am HS Students; W/W IN and KY HS Fgn Langs; Commun Ldrs of Am; g/Re-Open Fam Grocery Store; Polit.

MOUNKES, RICHARD FRANKLIN oc/Assistant Manager; b/Oct 4, 1955; h/ RR #1, Box 187, Coppell, TX 75019; ba/ Irving, TX; p/Mr and Mrs John W Mounkes, Emporia, KS; ed/No Hgts HS, 1973; BS, w Hons, Emporia St Univ, 1980; pa/Customer Sers Supvr, SWn Bell Telephone Co, 1980-83; Asst Mgr, AT&T, 1983-; cp/JA Vol; Dem of Lyon Country VP; VP, Student Body, Emporia St Univ; Pres, Student Senate, Emporia St Univ; Heart Fund Vol; r/ Meth; hon/Xi Phi, 1980; Pi Gamma Mu, 1979; Scott Key Awd, 1980; Gamma Phi Alpha, 1980; Eagle Awd, 1982; W/W Among Students in Am Univs and Cols; Intl Yth in Achmt; Yg Commun Ldrs of Am; g/Higher Mgmt of AT&T.

MOWRY, FAITH RUTH oc/Student; h/PO Box 53-K105, Grand Prairie, TX 75053; p/Fran Probasco, Grand Prairie, TX; ed/Midland Lee HS; Student, TX Tech Univ; cp/Gamma Phi Beta, Histn 1982-83; Alpha Lambda Delta, 1983-; hon/Dean's List, 1983; Nat Hon Soc, 1980-82; g/Elem Ed Maj, Math.

MUELLER, NADEAN R oc/Graduate Student; b/Jan 8, 1959; h/1800 Polaris Drive, Bartlesville, OK 74003; p/Don and Naomi Mueller, Bartlesville, OK; ed/HS, 1977; Col, 1982; cp/Sigma Alpha Iota, Treas; Pres, Phi Eta Sigma; Treas, Wesleyan Yth Soc; hon/Nat Hon Soc; Tulsa Univ Pres S'ship; Tulsa Philharm S'ship; Manhattan Sch of Music S'ship; Dean's List; g/Orch and Chamber Music Player; Violin Tchr.

MUENCH, SHAREE ANN oc/Student, Waitress; b/Oct 3, 1964; h/701 Mayo Street, Shelby, NC 28150; ba/ Charlotte, NC; p/Mr and Mrs Rudolph Muench, Shelby, NC; ed/Shelby Sr HS, 1982; Student, Univ of NC Charlotte; pa/Cashier, Burger King, 1980-81; Waitress, Pizza Inn, 1981-82, 1982-; cp/ Civinettes, 1980-82; SHS Beta Clb, 1980-82; Pres, Nat Hon Soc, 1982; Spanish Clb, 1980-82; Latin Clb, 1980-81; Sr Class Homeroom Rep, 1982; Yg Life, 1980-82; F'ship of Christian Aths, 1978-82; FBLA, 1982; r/ Meth; hon/3rd in Class of 295 (Balfour S'ship Awd), 1982; Lutz-Yelton S'ship, St S'ship, 1982; PPG S'ship Finalist, 1982; Nat Merit Semi-Finalist, 1982; maxima cum laude on Nat Latin Exam, 1980; magna cum laude on Nat Latin

Exam, 1981; Hons Psych Class and Interdisciplinary Hons Sem; Chancellor's List; g/Double Maj in Bus Adm and Psych; Wk in the Area of Pers or Mktg.

MULLEN, BRUCE DIEDRICH oc/Student; b/Mar 6, 1962; h/705 Parish Road, Moreland, Charleston, SC 29407; p/Mr and Mrs Charles V Mullen Sr, Moreland, Charleston, SC; ed/Att'g, Col of Charleston; pa/Asst Mgr, Doscher's Supermkts Inc; cp/Ch Vol Wkr; Car Enthusiast; hon/W/W Among Am HS Students; Commun Ldrs of Am; Intl Yth in Achmt; Yg Personalities of S; Dir of Dist'd Ams; g/Career in Grocery Bus (Fam Owned Supermkt Chain).

MULLEN, TINA KAYE oc/Student; b/May 22, 1963; h/250 Andromeda Drive, Paducah, KY 42001; p/Mr and Mrs E D Mullen, Paducah, KY; ed/Dipl, HS, 1981; AS, Paducah Commun Col; Att'g, Murray St Univ (Ofc Adm and Word Processing Maj); pa/Pt-time Employee of Golf Course Pro Shop; cp/Varsity Basketball, 4 Yrs; Golf Team, 6 Yrs; Future Bus Ldrs of Am, 1 Yr; Softball Team Mem; Intramural Col Basketball; hon/Hon Grad, HS (Ranked 10th in Class); Acad S'ship; Hon Grad, Paducah Commun Col; Transfer Student S'ship to Murray St Univ; W/W Among Am HS Students; Intl Yth in Achmt; g/Med Asst.

MULLINS, GREGORY LEE oc/Graduate Student, PhD Candidate; b/Dec 12, 1955; h/4775 Jackson Highway, West Lafayette, IN 47906; ba/West Lafayette, IN; m/Iris Clay; c/Richard Tenil, Sarah Marie; p/Mrs Tenil Mullins, Clintwood, VA; ed/Clintwood HS, 1974; BS in Agri, Berea Col, 1979; MS in Agronomy, VPI&SU, 1981; pa/Berea Col Labor Prog, 1974-79; Student Trainee for Soil Conservationist, USDA Soil Conserv Ser, 1978; Res and Tchg Asst, VPI&SU, 1979-81; Res Asst, Purdue Univ, 1981-; Delta Tau Alpha, Chapt Pres 1978-79; Delta Tau Alpha; Gamma Sigma Delta; Phi Kappa Phi; Sigma Xi; Am Soc of Agronomy; Soil Sci Soc of Am; Coun for Agri Sci and Technol; cp/Football, All-Dist 1973; Intramural Football, Berea Col; FFA, Chapt VP 1972-73; Pres 1973-74; Berea Col Agri Union, Treas 1977-78, 1978-79; r/So Bapt; Sunday Sch Tchr, Grades 4-6; hon/Pubs, "Chemical Speciation of Leachates from Waste Disposal Sites" 1983, "Automated Analysis for Water Alkalinity" 1983, Others; FFA Deg of St Farmer, VA, 1974; Outstg FFA Chapt Mem, 1974; Nat Hon Soc; Agri Dept Labor Awd, Berea Col, 1979; Co-Recip, George D Scarseth Grad S'ship, 1983; Delta Tau Alpha; Gamma Sigma Delta; Phi Kappa Phi; Sigma Xi; Personalities of S; g/To Wk for a St Univ at the Level of Prof.

MULLINS, JEFFREY JAY oc/Joiner; b/Apr 8, 1964; h/302 Pinewood Drive, Ladson, SC 29456; p/Mr and Mrs Walter M Mullins, Ladson, SC; ed/Dipl, R B Stall HS, 1982; pa/Apprentice; cp/Boy Scouts, Asst Scoutmaster; r/Prot; g/To Attend a Tech Col to Further Ed.

MULLINS, TABITHA LYNNE oc/Student; b/Apr 14, 1966; h/113 Church Street, Whitesburg, KY 41858; p/Morris and Vernell Mullins, Whitesburg, KY; ed/HS Grad, 1984; cp/Beta Clb Pres, 1984; Quill and Scroll VP, 1984; French Clb, 1984; Meth Yth F'ship, 1984; Jr Handbell Choir, 1984;

r/Meth; hon/Valedictorian, 1984; Soil Conserv Essay Winner, 1984; US Achmt Acad Nat Awd Winner for Jour; Outstg Teens of Am.

MUNDY, LEA MARIE oc/Student; b/Nov 23, 1964; h/Route 1, Box 295, Buchanan, VA 24066; p/Mr and Mrs Charles S Mundy, Buchanan, VA; ed/James River HS, 1983; Att'g, Bridgewater Col; cp/Girls' Ath Assn, 1980-83, VP 1980-81, Pres 1982-83; F'ship of Christian Aths, 1982-83; Jr Class Secy; *Kanawhan* Annual, 1981-82, Editor-in-Chief 1982-83; r/Brethren; hon/Recip, Helen Waid Ednl Fund S'ship, 1983; W/W Among Am HS Students; Soc of Dist'd Am HS Students; g/Double Maj in Psych and Sociol; Wk w the Handicapped.

MURPHY, ANDREW THOMAS oc/Executive; b/Dec 14, 1959; h/3 Legged Farm, RD 1, Glen Mills, PA 19342; ba/Pasadena, CA; p/Thomas and Barbara Murphy, Philadelphia, PA; ed/Grad, St Joseph's Preparatory HS, 1978; AB, Physics, Occidental Col, 1982; Att'd, CA Inst of Technol, Pasadena City Col; pa/Pres, Murphy Technols, 1983; cp/Instr, Kubotan Inst, 1982-; Intl Karate Assn, 1978-; Phila Glider Coun, 1978-; Soaring Soc of Am, 1979-; Civil Air Patrol Ldr; Soc of Physics Students; AIAA; Ser Corps for 46th Intl Eucharistic Cong; Developer, HS Exch Prog w Sch in Germany; hon/Glider Solo, 1979; Eagle Scout; Alumni Awd for Achmt, Zeal, Ser; Amelia Earhart Awd; Nat Merit S'ship Semi-Finalist; Intl Yth in Achmt; W/W Among Am HS Students; Commun Ldrs of Am; Jane's W/W Aviation and Aerospace; g/Space Sci.

MURPHY, BYRON KEITH oc/Student; b/Sep 28, 1962; h/PO Box 267, Grayson, KY 41143; ba/Morehead, KY; p/Paul Jr and Louetta S Murphy, Grayson, KY; ed/Grad, E Carter Co HS, 1980; Ashland Commun Col, 1978-80; Grad, Morehead St Univ, 1984; pa/Announcer, Asst News Dir, WGOH-AM/WUGO-FM, 1978-81; Announcer, Newscaster, Sportscaster, Play-by-Play Man, Feature Prodr, Host of "Audiovisions," WMKY-FM, 1981-; cp/Morehead St Univ Spch Team (Individually 13th in Nation in Extemporaneous Spkg, 1983); NFA Championships (Team 4th in Nation, 1983); En KY Student Lib Assn Pres, 1979-80; Ath Tnr, E Carter HS, 1976-80; hon/2nd Place in KY for Documentary Reporting, KY UPI Awds, 1982; Most Helpful Affil, KY Radio Network, 1982; KY St Champion, Impromptu Spkg, 1983; Nat Dean's List; W/W Among Am HS Students; Intl Yth in Achmt; Commun Ldrs of Am; g/To Attend Grad Sch to Gain a Master's Deg in Communication; To Wk in Profl Communs.

MURPHY, MARGARET ELAINE oc/Student; b/Oct 5, 1966; h/25 East Fourth Street, PO Box 667, Maysville, KY 41056; p/Mr and Mrs William F Murphy, Maysville, KY; ed/Grad, St Patrick HS, 1984; pa/P J Murphy Jeweler, 1980-83; Limestone Square Tobacco Shop, 1983; Maysville-Mason Co Public Lib, 1983-; cp/Treas, St Patrick Spirit Clb, 1981-82, Pres 1983-84; 4-H, 1980-81, 1982-83, 1983-84; Stat, St Patrick Varsity and Jr Varsity Basketball Teams; Morehead St Univ Pres's Ldrship Clb; r/Rom Cath; hon/4-H Blue Ribbon, 1981; Citizenship

Awd, 1982-83; Nat Yth Foun "I Dare You" Awd for Qualities of Ldrship, 1982-83; Serra Clb Recog Awd, 1983-84; Century II Area Winner, 1983-84; g/To Attend Maysville Commun Col for 1 Yr and Then Transfer to Morehead St Univ.

MURPHY, MICHAEL FRANKLIN oc/Student; b/May 6, 1965; h/1131 Worden Southeast, Grand Rapids, MI 49507; p/Ernest and Carrie Murphy, Grand Rapids, MI; ed/HS Dipl w Hons; pa/Pt-time Maintenance, Meijer Inc, 1981-83; cp/Commun Parents and Students; Nat Hon Soc; Bus and Ofc Ednl Clb; Ofc Ed Assn; Calvinist Cadet Corps; UFCW Local 951; r/Pentecostal; hon/MI Competitive S'ship Recip; Afro-Am Lay Cath Caucus S'ship Recip; GRJC S'ship Recip.

MURPHY, MONTE JON oc/Band Teacher; b/Aug 13, 1960; h/Route 1, Box 58-3, Granbury, TX 76048; ba/Same; p/Pike C and Joyce L Murphy, Granbury, TX; ed/Dipl, Granbury HS, 1978; BMus, Univ of TX Arlington, 1982; mil/USAFR; pa/Kappa Kappa Psi, Nat Hon Band Frat, Secy 1979-80, VP 1980, Pres 1981-82; Phi Mu Alpha Sinfonia, Profl Music Frat, Treas 1980, VP 1981; cp/UTA Liberal Arts Constituency Coun, 1980-81; r/Prot; g/Band Dir in Public Schs.

MURRAY, MONICA DEE oc/Student; b/Oct 4, 1962; h/Route 2, Box 315, Burgaw, NC 28425; p/Mr and Mrs Winslor Murray, Burgaw, NC; ed/Pender HS, 1980; Att'g, Fayetteville Tech Inst; cp/Student Coun, Secy 1980; Guid Cnslr Asst, HS; Cheerldr, Sophomore Yr in HS; Paralegal Clb, Fayetteville Tech Inst; r/Bapt; hon/Fayetteville Tech Pres's List, 1981-82, 1982-83; g/To Wk as a Paralegal in the Area of Domestic Law.

MURRAY, RICHARD K oc/Recent Graduate; b/Jun 7, 1960; h/1036 William Street, Pittsfield, MA 01201; p/William and Sarah Murray, Pittsfield, MA; ed/Pittsfield HS, 1978; BS 1982, MA in Cnslg and Human Devel 1983, Bradley Univ; pa/Prodr, "The Renovation of Pittsfield High," 1977; Prodn Asst, "Life on the Mississippi," 1978; White House Advance, VP Mondale, 1980-81; Cnslt, Hamel-Somers Entertainment, LA; The Caruso Brothers, Detroit; Student Activs Ofc, Bradley Univ; cp/Bd Mem, NACA Ednl Foun; Carter-Mondale Pres Com Pres, Activs Coun; Bd Mem, Nat Entertainment and Campus Activs Assn; Cultural Affairs Com; Peoria Civic Ctr Grand Opening Com; r/Cath; hon/Pub, "Working with Special Constituencies," 1982; David Landa Meml S'ship; Olive B White S'ship; W/W Among Students in Am Univs and Cols; Outstg Yg Men of Am; Commun Ldrs of Am; g/Obtain a Managerial Position in the Entertainment Indust.

MURRAY, WILLIAM BATTLE oc/Student, Telephone Sales Representative; b/Mar 3, 1961; h/Route 5, Box 178-C1, Fayetteville, NC 28306; ba/Greensboro, NC; p/Mr and Mrs William B Murray Jr; ed/Douglas Byrd Sr High, 1979; BA in Theatre Arts Ed 1983, Enrolled in Grad Sch for EdM, Univ of NC Greensboro; pa/Waiter, Bantam Chef, 1976-79; Sales Clk, Telephone Sales Rep, Sears Roebuck & Co, 1981-83; cp/Intl Thespian Soc Troupe 3017, Pres 1978-79; Nat Beta Clb,

1978-79; Future Tchrs of Am, 1977-78; Elliott Univ Ctr, Univ of NC Greensboro, 1979-83, Pres 1981-83; Lambda Chi Alpha Frat, 1983; Masqueraders Drama Soc, 1980-83; r/Bapt; hon/HS Hon Grad, 1979; HS Merit Awd in Drama, 1979; UNC-G Outstg Student, 1983; UNC-G Outstg Sr, 1983; Hon Masquerader, 1983; g/To Obtain a EdM w a Concentration in Guid and Cnslg; To Wk as a Prog Dir for a Col Union; To Become a Profl Pianist for a Gospel Quartet.

MUSGROVE, DANETTE MILHOLLIN oc/Cashier; b/Apr 14, 1965; h/PO Box 313, Broxton, GA 31519; m/Jerry D; p/Mr and Mrs Dan Milhollin, Broxton, GA; ed/Broxton HS, 1972-83; pa/Cashier, McDonalds, 1983-; cp/Beta Clb Treas, 1983; Varsity Basketball, 1980-82; Student Coun, 1983; FFA, 1981-83; FHA, 1980; Annual Staff Editor, 1983; r/Bapt; hon/STAR Student of Broxton HS, 1983; Gov's Hons Prog, Nom 1981, Alt 1982; Valedictorian, 1983; W/W Among Am HS Students; g/To Attend S GA Col for 2 Yrs and Maj in Computer Programming.

MUSSO, MARK COLE oc/Self-Employed; b/Jan 22, 1957; h/2219 Jardine Drive, Wichita, KS 67219; p/Mrs Opal Crabaugh, Hutchinson, KS; ed/Hutchinson HS, 1975; AA, Hutchinson Commun Col, 1977; BBA 1979, MBA 1982, Wichita St Univ; pa/Asst to the Dean, Student Life and Sers, Wichita St Univ, 1981-82; Self-Employed Proj Coor, 1983-; cp/Circle K Intl, VP 1977-78, Pres 1979-80, Mbrship Chm of KS Dist and Conv Chm 1976-79; Conf on Vol Action, Chm 1981-; KS Spec Olympics, Asst Chm 1982; Toastmaster's Intl; r/Ecumenical; hon/W/W Among Students in Am Univs and Cols; W/W Among Students in Am Jr Cols; Intl Yth in Achmt; Outstg Yg Men of Am; Commun Ldrs of Am; Nat Dean's Hon Roll; g/Continue Vol Wk in the Commun; Public Ofc Candidacy.

MUUS, PAUL MAGNER oc/Architectural Student; b/Feb 8, 1961; h/500 8th Avenue Southeast, Minot, ND 58701; p/Magner and Marge Muus, Minot, ND; ed/Bishop Ryan HS, 1979; Att'd, Dakota NWn Univ, 1980, 1981, 1982; Student, ND St Univ; pa/Tchg Asst, NDSU, 1983-84; Self-Employed as Arch for Local Contractors, 1983; AIA, Student Chapt, 1981, 1982, 1983; Tau Sigma Delta, Arch Scholastic Soc, 1981, 1982, 1983; Tau Beta Pi; Phi Eta Sigma, 1979; Intl Solar Energy Soc; cp/Oceanic Soc; Cousteau Soc; Hon Soc; hon/Edison Scholar for St of ND; ND Brick Mason's Design Competition, 2nd Place, 1982; Mortar Bd Cand, 1982; Tau Sigma Delta Awd, Most Outstg 2nd Yr Designer, 1981; Knute Henning S'ship, Fac Selection to Student that Shows Most Promise in Design; Am Acad of Achmt Awd; Intl Yth in Achmt; Outstg Names and Faces; W/W MW; g/Complete 5th Yr of Arch and Then Study for a Master's Deg in Arch, Urban Design and Graphics.

MYERS, BRENDA CATHERINE oc/Secretary; b/Jun 7, 1958; h/209 Costello Street, Charleston, WV 25302; ba/South Charleston, WV; ed/Dipl, Honorarian of Class, Stonewall Jackson HS, 1976; BA, Oral Communs, magna cum laude, Univ of Charleston, 1980; pa/Stenographer 1980-81, Secy 1981-, Union Carbide Corp; U Talent Inc, 1976-80; cp/Friends of Messiah; Judge, 1983 Intl Yth Exhib Awds; Kanawha Val Chapt of Parents without Ptnrs; Var Vol Activs; hon/Alpha Lambda Delta, 1976 (VP); Pi Kappa Delta, 1977-80 (Pres); Kappa Delta Pi; Intl Yth in Achmt; Commun Ldrs of Am; g/Publish Photographs; Continue Grad Wk in Fields of Interest.

MYERS, DAVID SAMUEL JR oc/United States Marine Reservist, Notary Public, Tax Consultant; b/Sep 10, 1963; h/Route 2, Box 143, Hagerstown, MD 21740; m/Della Lucinda; p/Mrs David S Myers, Hagerstown, MD; ed/USMC Combat Engrg Sch, 1982; mil/USMC; pa/PFC 1982, L/Cpl 1983, USMC; cp/HS Marching Band, 1978-81; HS Concert Band, 1978-81; HS Pep Band, 1978-81; HS Bible Study, 199-81; French Clb, 1980-81; Latin Clb, 1979-81; Sr Boys' Clb, 1980-81; r/Prot; hon/Rdg Achmt Cert, 1973; Marine Corps Cert of Ath Accomplishment, 1974; Century 21 Typewriting Cert of Proficiency, 1981; W/W Among Am HS Students; Yg Commun Ldrs of Am; Intl Register of Profiles.

MYERS, DEANNA oc/Extension Agent; b/Jan 11, 1958; h/303 East 19th, Colorado City, TX 79512; p/Mr and Mrs J H Myers Jr, Snyder, TX; ed/Snyder HS, 1976; AA, Wn TX Col, 1978; BS, TX Tech Univ, 1980; MS, TX A&M Univ, 1981; pa/Ext Agt, Entomology (PM); Entomological Soc of Am; Alpha Zeta; Phi Theta Kappa; Phi Kappa Phi; Registry Assoc of the Am Registry of Profl Entomologists; Assn for Wom in Sci; BPW Org; hon/TX Tech Undergrad Res Awd; Farmland Indust S'ship; High GPA of Entomology Dept, TX Tech.

MYERS, WENDY SUE oc/Student; b/Oct 6, 1962; h/7504 Meri-Wood Drive, Fort Wayne, IN 46815; p/Paul and Marianne Matthews, Ft Wayne, IN; ed/Oral Roberts Univ; pa/Salesperson, Display Creator, Ladies Apparel Shop, Nobbson's, 1979-80; Salesperson, Bkkpr, Acct, Matthew's Sacred Music and Supply, 1980-81; Secy Position, ORU's Alumni Relats Ofc, 1981-82; Sales Rep, Soc Corp, 1982; cp/Am Mktg Assn, Bd Mem 1983-84, Secy 1982-83; Yrbook Staff Editor, ORU, 1983-84; Pres, Distribution Clbs of Am, 1980, 1981; Pres, Ser Clb of Commun, 1981; Spanish Clb, 1979-81; Puppet Team, Christian Ser Coun, 1981-82; Resident Advr 1983, Hd Resident Advr 1984, ORU; r/Prot; hon/E H Kilbarne Trust S'ship, 1981, 1982, 1983; 4-Yr Hon Roll Student; IN Hoosier Student, 1981; Intl Yth in Achmt; W/W Among Am HS Students; g/Advtg or Interior Design.

N

NABORS, JAMES HAROLD oc/ Ofcr, US Army; b/Jul 29, 1960; h/Box 314, Paron, AR 72122; ba/Ft Leavenworth, KS; p/Billy and Elizabeth Nabors, Paron, AR; ed/Paron HS, 1978; BS, Henderson St Univ, 1981; Univ Houston; Univ KS; mil/AUS, Signal Corps, 2nd Lt, 1982-; pa/2nd Lt, US Army Signal Corps; Chief, Proj Support Br, CECOM Software Devel Support Ctr; cp/BSA; Nat Hon Soc; Sigma Pi Sigma; Basketball; Varsity Rifle Marksmanship Team; Basketball HS; ROTC; Gamma Beta Phi; r/Bapt; hon/Eagle Scout w Double Silver Palms, 1973, 1976; Vigil Hon, 1976; Dist'd Mil Grad, 1982; Hon Grad, US Signal Ofcr Basic Course, 1982; W/W Among Am HS Students; AR Boys' St, 1977; 2nd Pl Sophomore, AR St Col Rifle Tour, 1980; God & Country, 1975; g/MS Computer Sci, MS Physics.

NAFF, NEAL JAMISON oc/Student; b/Aug 4, 1965; h/Route 1 Meadow Spring Farm, Boones Mill, VA 24065; p/Wesley Jr and Angelia Naff; ed/ Franklin Co HS; cp/Nat Hon Soc; Jr Classical Leag; FCA; Varsity Lttrman, Ftball, Wrestling; Pres, HS Student Body; r/Bretheren; hon/Recip of Paul Douglas Camp S'ship for Merit, VA Mil Inst; Army Resv Scholar/Ath Awd; Gov of Am Legion Boys' St of VA; VA Gov Sch for the Gifted; Southside Reg Rep to VA SCA; W/W; Commun Ldrs Am; g/MD; Mil Ofcr.

NAM, DAE HWAN oc/Student; b/Jun 20, 1961; h/6509 Cissna Drive, Fayetteville, NC 28303; ba/Lynchburg, VA; p/Dong Tak Nam, Fayetteville, NC; ed/ Westover Sr HS, 1980; NC St Univ, 1982; pa/Engrg Co-Op, 1982; Asst Design Engr, GE; cp/IEEE; Korean Student Assn; hon/Phi Eta Sigma; Alpha Lambda Delta; Nat Hon Soc; Tau Beta Pi; Eta Kappa Nu; Elect Engrg Hon Soc; Recip of NC St Alumni S'ship, 1981-83; g/Design Engr in Communication or Digital.

NAPIER, SUSAN JEAN oc/Student; h/3245 West 2nd, Apartment 3, Owensboro, KY 42301; p/Dr Merle Dean Napier (dec) and Mrs Jeanette Enot Napier Medley, Owensboro, KY; ed/ Apollo HS, 1977; Daviess Co St Voc Tech Sch, Cosmetology 1978, Bus & Ofc 1983; pa/Hairdresser, Regis Hairstylists, 1978; Hairdresser, Fantastic Sam's, 1979; Secy, Daviess Co SVTS, 1983; cp/Phi Beta Lambda, Parliamentn 1981-82, Pres 1982-83; St Exec Bd Rep, 1982-83; r/Cath; hon/Hon Soc St of KY, 1983; g/Career in the Secretarial Profession.

NAVIA, ALICIA STELLA oc/Admissions Counselor; h/594 Irving Street, Westbury, NY 11590; m/Dr Luis E; c/ Monica, Olga Lucia; p/Dr Santiago and Mariela Angel de Cadena, Flushing, NY; sp/Dr Jose Vicente and Juanita Navia, Flushing, NY; cp/Christian F'ship; NYIT; Col-Wide Cultural Com; Study Skills Ctr; Tutor; Freshman Orient Ldr; NY Chiro Col F'ship Cir; Nu Upsilon Tau; r/Cath; hon/Summa Cum Laude Grad; Fac Wom Assn of NYIT Awd in the Humanities; Alumni Awd; Nat Jr Hon Soc; Alumni Outstg Ser Awd; W/ W Among Students in Am Univs & Cols; Yg Commun Ldrship Awd; Commun Ldrs Am; Intl Yth in Achmt; g/

NEAL, SANDRA ANNITA oc/Student; b/Oct 26, 1964; h/Route 2, Box 11-A, Summit, MS 39666; p/Mr and Mrs Harold C Neal, Summit, MS; ed/ McComb HS, 1982; AA, SW MS Jr Col, 1984; cp/Bapt Student Union, Sum Missionary to AZ, 1984; SW MS Jr Col Concert Choir, Dynamics, Marching Band; Phi Theta Kappa; BSU Ensemble; BSU Coun Mem; r/Bapt, Summit Bapt Ch; hon/Dean's List; Hon Roll; Personalities of S; g/Career, Min of Music.

NEAL, TAMMY IRENE oc/Student; b/Dec 27, 1963; h/6427 Hidden Forest Drive, Charlotte, NC 28213; p/Ernest and Yun Pi Neal, Charlotte, NC; ed/ Myers Park Sr HS, 1983; Univ NC-Charlotte; cp/Nat Junior Hon Soc, 1979-80; JV & Varsity Cheerldr, 1978-80; Pres, Student Adv, 1979-80; VP, Fin, JA, 1981-82; Nat Hon Soc for Musicians, 1982-83; Student Exec Coun, 1979-80; Orch, 1980-83; Latin Clb, 1982-83; Med Exploring, 1980-81; r/Buddahist Bapt; hon/Num Articles in Pub; Ldrship Awd, 1979-80; Golden Eagle Awd, 1979-80; Carrousel Princess of Myers Park, 1982-83; Miss Univ NC-Charlotte, 1983-84; 1st Pl in Charlotte Fgn Lang Poster Awd, 1983; g/ CPA.

NEELY, HELEN FRANCES oc/Student; b/Oct 12, 1965; h/705 West Johnson, Osceola, AR 72370; p/Dewey and Helen Neely, Osceola, AR; ed/ Osceola HS, the Webb Sch; Univ AR; pa/Sales Clk, Merle Norman Cosmetics, 1981-82; Sales Clk, Newcomb's Drug Store, 1982; cp/Pres, Student Coun, 1980-81; Sci Clb, 1980-81; Chess Clb, 1980-81; Spanish Clb, 1980-82; Nat Jr Hon Soc, 1980-81; Future Phys Clb, 1981-82; Nat Hon Soc; Crown Clb, 1981-81; Pi Beta Phi Sorority, 1983-; r/ Presb; hon/Student Coun Awd, 1981; Spanish I Awd, 1981; Earth Sci Awd, 1981; Hon Roll; World Hist Awd, 1982; Spanish II Awd, 1982; Summa (A) Hon Roll; Magna (B) Hon Roll; g/Elem Ed, Tch 5th Grade.

NEELY, WILSON ALEXANDER IV oc/Carpenter; b/Dec 22, 1961; h/Route 2, Box 83-D, Lampasas, TX 76550; ba/ Same; p/Wilson and Barbara Neely, Lampasas, TX; ed/Lampasas HS, 1980; TSTI, Pvt Pilot & Instr, 1982; pa/Bldg Mfg, Lampasas Bldg Components, 1978-83; Bldg, Akin & Bryon Contractors, 1980; Bldg, Eaton Constrn, 1983; cp/HS Ftball; r/Ch of Christ; hon/Hon Roll HS, 1977-80; W/W.

NEGRI, ANNE MARIE oc/Student; b/May 1, 1962; h/59 Superior Street, Lyon, MA 01902; ba/Fitchburg, MA, p/ Ralph and Anne M Negri, Lynn, MA; ed/Fitchburg St Col; pa/Lab Asst, Salem Hosp, 1982; r/Cath; hon/Dean's List; Pres of Med Tech Class, 1983-84; g/Med Tech.

NELLA, MICHELLE RENEE oc/Secretary, Church Organist-Pianist; b/Jan 14, 1963; h/3125 Delaware Trail, Fort Worth, TX 76135; ba/Ft Worth, TX; p/ Mrs Henrietta Compton, Ft Worth, TX; ed/Lake Worth HS, 1981; Music Cert, Torrant Co Jr Col, 1982; Exec Legal Secy Deg, Ft Worth Sch Bus, 1982; pa/Editor of City Newspaper, 1980-82; Mfg Control Secy, Gen Dynamics/Ft Worth Div; cp/FTA, Pres & Sweetheart, Dist Histn; Band & Choir, Pres & Swee-

theart; Feature & Edit Writer for Sch Newspaper; r/So Bapt, First Bapt Ch of Lake Worth, Pianist-Organist; hon/ Num Articles; John Philip Sousa Awd, 1981; Band & Choir S'ships, 1981; Best Actress City, Dist, Reg, 1981; 1st Pl Feature Story Dist, 1980; W/W; g/Deg in Rel Music; Perform in Local Theatre.

NELLE, NANCY C oc/Public Relations Assitant ; b/Feb 23, 1961; h/822 Manor, Grand Prairie, TX 75050; p/Mr and Mrs Robert Nelle, Grand Prairie, TX; ed/Grand Prairie HS, 1979; Univ TX-Arlington, 1984; pa/Public Relats Asst, Liz Oliphant & Assoc Public Relats/Advtg Agy, 1983-84; cp/Public Relats Student Soc Am, Fundraising Com Chm, 1983-84; Sigma Delta Chi, Soc of Profl Jours, 1982-83; Talons, Spirit & Ser Org, PR Com, 1981-83; N TX St Univ Jazz String Ensemble, 1982; Metro Symph Orch, Violin, 1984; Grand Prairie Commun Theater Pit Orch, Violin, 1984; Dallas Sum Symph, 1979-81; Alpha Phi Omega, Secy, 1980-81; Biol Soc, 1979-81; Gymnastics Clb, 1980-81; Intramural Volleyball, 1980; All Reg Orch; r/Meth; hon/ PRSSA Excell Awd, Outstg Chapt Contbr, 1983-84; Dean's List; Riley Cross Jour, S'ship, 1983-84; PRIDE Cert, 1983; Pres Ldrship Awd; Hon Roll; Orch S'ship; Most Outstg Student; DAR Good Citizenship Awd; Outstg Orch Student; Eng Awd; Nat Hon Soc; Drill Team Awds; First Presb Ch S'ship; Viola Shoemake S'ship; W/W Among Am HS Students; Soc of Dist'd Am HS Students; g/Career w Public Relats.

NELSON, EMMA KAY oc/Clerk Typist; b/Jul 8, 1958; h/Post Office box 4704, Wilmington, NC 28406; ba/ Southport, NC; p/Mr and Mrs Lokie F Nelson, Conway, NC; ed/Northampton Co HS; AS Sci/Clerical, Chowan Col; BS, E Carolina Univ; pa/Secy, Chowan Col, 1976-78; Asst Bkkpr, Tarheel Bk & Trust Co, 1978-80; Secy, E Carolina Univ, 1979-80; Sci Tchr, NE Acad, 1981-82; Tchr, Northampton Co HS, 1982-83; Clk Typist, Carolina Power & Light Co, 1983; cp/Phi Theta Kappa, 1978; r/Bapt; hon/NC "A" Cert in Sci Ed, 1981; Internship in Microbiol, 1980; Best All-Around Student Awd, Chowan Col, 1978; Phi Theta Kappa, 1977-78; W/W: Among Am Jr Cols, Among Am HS Students; g/Computers.

NELSON, JOHN JENKINS oc/Student; b/Feb 22, 1966; h/208 Kent Drive, Greenville, NC 27834; p/Thurman and Cynthia Nelson, Greenville, NC; pa/ Bagboy, Krogers, 1982; Bagger, Perry's Peanut Co, 1982-83; Waiter, Parkers Barbeque Restaurant; cp/Nom for Hon Soc; Student Govt; Little Leag Coach Wrestling, 1979-81; Ftball, 1979; Gov's Page, 1979-83; r/Bapt; hon/Nom for Hon Soc; Most Dedicated on Wrestling Team; g/Attend US Naval Acad, Engrg Deg; Flight Sch.

NELSON, KIMBERLY CELESTE oc/ Runway Model; h/101 Longwood Street, Hartselle, AL 35640; p/Thomas and Shirley Nelson, Hartselle, AL; ed/ Hartselle HS; pa/Asst Bkkpr, Jim Cochrane Trucking Co; Runway Model, Choreographer, Beltline Mall; cp/Key Clb Sweetheart; Mem, Delta Sigma Phi; Girls' Chorus; Performing Arts Studio; Spch Secy; Annual Staff Copy Editor; hon/Winner of Essay Contest, 1983;

1982 Class Doubles Tennis Champ; Outstg Freshman Hist Student, 1983; NE AL Lovely Lady; Overall Dream Angel Talent Winner; Dream Angel, Most Beautiful, Best Model; Nums Awds; g/Doct in Child Psychol.

NELSON, SHARON ANNETTE oc/ Student; b/Mar 30, 1964; h/2024 Breezewood Drive, Charlotte, NC 28213; p/ Rev and Mrs Lazzell P Nelson, Charlotte, NC; ed/N Mecklenburg Sr HS, 1982; E Carolina Univ, 1982-83; Barber-Scotia Col; pa/File Clk, Allstate Ins, 1981-82; Pt-time Nurse's Asst, Huntersville Hosp, 1982-; Sales, Recording Clk, Barber-Scotia Col Bookstore, 1983; cp/Sch Booster Clb, 1979-82; Students in Action for Ed, 1978-82; Latin Clb, 1979-80; Gospel Choir, 1982; Residence Hall House Coun, 1982; VP Freshman Class, 1983-84; Features Page Editor, *Scotia Express*, 1983-; Student Govt Assn Senate, 1983-; Col Recruitment Prog, 1983-; r/Bapt; hon/Num Articles in Pub; Recip of Meml Fund S'ship, 1982; Cert in Outstg Ldrship Abilities, Omega Lambda Chapt of Alpha Kappa Alpha Sorority Inc, 1981; g/grad w BS in Med Technol.

NEUMANN, TERI BETH oc/Student; b/Sep 20, 1967; h/Route 1, Box 157-A, Estill Springs, TN 37330; p/Mark and Dolores Neumann, Estill Sprgs, TN; ed/ Franklin Co HS, 1985; cp/Nat Beta Clb, 1984; N Jr HS Yrbook Staff; Franklin Co HS Band; hon/2nd Pl in Biochem 1982, 1st Pl Biochem 1983, 1984, 2nd Grand Prize 1984, Chattanooga Reg Sci & Engrg Fair; Participant in 35th Intl Sci & Engrg Fair at Columbus OH, 1984; USAF Cit for Outstg Fair Proj, 1982-84; USMC Cit for Outstg Sci Fair Proj, 1983, 1984; AUS Cit for Outstg Sci Fair Proj, 1984; AUS Awd for Superior Achmt at Reg Sci Fair, 1984; 3397th AUS Garrison Cit for Outstg Sci Fair Proj, 1984; 3rd Pl Indiv, Webb Sch Hist Contest, 1981; Duck River Elect Mbrship Cooperation 1st Pl Awd for Class Sci Fair Proj, 1981; Top 5% of Freshman Class at N Jr HS, 1982; g/ Maj in Biochem; PhD; Res Biochemist.

NEUSTEDTER, JANICE ANN oc/ Stage Manager; b/Jan 25, 1961; Route 1, Box 44, Mukwonago, WI 53149; p/ Bill and Jane Neustedter, Mukwonago, WI; ed/Brookfield Ctl HS, 1978; BA, Beloit Col, 1982; pa/Stage Mgmt Intern, Actors Theatre of Louisville, 1982-83; cp/Vol Tutor; Yell Ldr; Gold Key Coor; Orient Ldr; Pi Beta Epsilon Pres, Rush & Social Chm, Treas; SS Tchr, Meth Ch; Pres, Med Outlooks Soc; Photog, Sch Newspaper; German Clb; r/United Meth; hon/Nat Col Players; Beloit Col Players; Omicron Delta Kappa; Mortar Bd; Nat Hon Soc; Recip of Delta Psi Delta Prize; Cum Laude Deg, Beloit Col, 1978; Recip of Lancer-Spartan S'ship, HS Hons Grad; Commun Ldrs Am; g/ Profl Stage Mgr &/or Drama Critic.

NEWBERRY, JAMES TAD oc/Student; b/Dec 22, 1962; h/9065 Southwest Monterey Place, Portland, OR 97225; p/Jim Newberry, Broken Arrow, OK, and Kitty Newberry, Portland, OR; ed/ Sunset HS, 1980; NW Nazarene Col; cp/ Circle K, Treas; Pres, Weightlifting/ Body Bldg Clb; hon/W/W Among Am HS Students; Intl Yth Achmt; Personalities of A; g/Write &/or Direct Movies.

NEWBY, DAREK LANE oc/Student; b/Feb 1, 1966; h/119 Sagewood Road,

Jamestown, NC 27282; p/Loy and Connie Newby, Jamestown, NC; pa/ Paper Carrier, Greensboro News Co, 1980-; Clk/Typist, Delman & Newby CPA's, 1982-; cp/Nat Beta Clb, 1982-83; r/Quaker; hon/2nd Deg Black Belt, Tae Kwon Do, 1981; g/Col Deg in Ec/Intl Relats.

NEWBY, MARLA LANETTE oc/ Student; b/Jun 2, 1962; h/Box 1, Fanshawe, OK 74935; p/Mr and Mrs Gene Newby, Fanshawe, OK; ed/Wister HS, 1980; Carl Albert Jr Col; BS, NEn St Univ; pa/Clerical Wkr, NEn St Univ, 1982-83; cp/Sigma Sigma Sigma Pledge, 1983; r/Assem God; hon/Outstg Student Hotel & Restaurant Awd; 3rd Runner-Up Homecoming Queen; NEn St Regents S'ship; Secy of Tourism Clb; Public Relats Chp, NEn Activs Bd; Kaleidoscope Com; Miss NEn, 1983; g/ Music Maj; Manage Recording Co; Own Recording Studio.

NEWMAN, STEVEN MICHAEL oc/ Student; b/Jul 9, 1967; h/744 Fawn Circle, Sumter, SC 29150; p/Mr and Mrs Rudy Newman, Sumter, SC; cp/VP, Key Clb; Octagon Clb; Jr Beta Clb; Sr Beta Clb; Pres, Jr Acad of Sci; St Cmdr, Sons of Am Legion; BSA; Yth Coun of Ch; Varsity Basketball Team; Volleyball Team; Crusader for Christ; Capt, JV Basketball Team, 1981-82; Student Coun, 1981-82, 1982-83; VP, Student Body, Secy 1982-83; Secy, F'ship of Christian Aths; Pres, Explorer's Grp; Secy of SC St Coun, 1981-82, 1982-83; hon/Biol Awd, 1983; Eng Awd, 1983; Eagle Scout; 1st Pl Sci Fair, 2nd Pl Essay Contest; g/Med.

NEWTON, DONALD ALVIN oc/ Student; b/Jan 16, 1956; h/1010 Paramount Circle, Gastonia, NC; p/Mr and Mrs Charles A Newton, Gastonia, NC; ed/Hunter Huss HS, 1974; Gardner-Webb Col; hon/Soph Scholastic Achmt Awd; Freshman Scholastic Achmt Awd; Hon Grad; Chem Awd; Physics Awd; g/Attend SEn Theol Sem; Enter the Pastorate.

NEWTON, ELIZABETH IRENE oc/ Student; b/Jan 25, 1964; h/Route 1, Box 276, Gibsonville, NC 27249; ba/Same; p/Mr and Mrs Darrell D Newton, Gibsonville, NC; ed/HS Dipl, 1982; Univ NC-Chapel Hill; cp/VP, UNC Formation Dance Team; Pres, UNC Ballroom Dance Clb; Solo Couple, Exhbn Dancer, 1982-83, 1983-84; French Soc Treas; Nat Hon Soc Chaplain; Homeroom Secy; SS Secy, Treas, Chaplain; HOSA; VBS Arts & Crafts Instr; Marching & Concert Band; Wind Ensemble; Pep Band; hon/Acad Achmt Awds; W/W Among Am HS Students; Commun Ldrs Am; g/Maj in Linguistics.

NG, JAMES BON oc/Student; b/May 27, 1962; h/3027 Kevin Lane, Houston, TX 77043; p/Mr and Mrs Tommy Ng, Houston, TX; ed/Spring Woods HS, 1980; Att'g Univ Houston; cp/Univ Houston Hons Prog; Jr Engrs & Tech Soc; Nat Hon Soc; IEEE; Mu Alpha Theta; hon/Jesse H Jones Scholar; Magna Cum Laude Grad; Dean's Hon List; Am's Outstg Names & Faces; W/ W Among Am HS Students; Intl Yth in Achmt; g/BSEE; Grad Sch.

NICHOLS, CONNIE oc/Student; b/ Jul 21, 1963; h/Route 1, Box 424, Saluda, SC 29138; ba/Rock Hill, SC; p/Jake and Trudie Nichols, Saluda, SC; ed/Saluda

HS, 1981; cp/Cloverleaf 4-H Teen Ldr; Dairy 4-H Clb; 4-H Camp Long Staff; Resident Life Staff; Co Ch Yth; Hons & Activs Chm, Alpha Delta Pi Sorority; Treas, Winhecon Clb; Band; Bus Drivers Clb; Art Clb; r/Luth; hon/Co, St, Nat 4-H Food Preserv Winner; SC Yth Power Winner; SC St 4-H Clothing Demonstration Winner; W/W; g/4-H Ext Agt; Deg in Home Ec Ed.

NICHOLSON, ANNE FULLER oc/ Student; b/Oct 10, 1964; h/300 Maple Street, Murfreesboro, NC 27855; p/D H and Carole Nicholson, Murfreesboro, NC 27855; ed/Murfreesboro HS, 1983; Wake Forest Univ; cp/Beta Clb; Math & Sci Clb; Polit Sci Clb; Drama Clb; Jour Clb; Lib Clb; Yrbook/Newspaper Asst Editor; Quiz Bowl Team; Varsity Cheerldr; r/Bapt; hon/US Hist, Eng, Geometry, Adv'd Biol, Adv'd Algebra Awds; Salutatorian HS, 1983; Exch Clb Student of Mo, 1982; Second Runner-Up Ahoskie Jr Miss Pageant, 1982; W/W Among Am HS Students; Soc of Dist'd Am HS Students; g/Lwyr.

NICHOLSON, FELECIA MARIE oc/ Student; b/May 31, 1961; h/319 Beechwood Drive, Akron, OH 44320; p/Mr and Mrs Frank W Nicholson, Akron, OH; ed/BA, Wilberforce Univ, 1983; EdM, Kent St Univ, 1984; pa/Work Aid Student, Wilberforce Univ, 1982; Outreach Asst, Golden Age Sr Citizens Ctr, 1981-82; Security Dispatcher, Wilberforce Univ, 1979, 1980, 1981, 1982; cp/ Groove Phi Groove Secy, 1979-80, VP 1980-81; Rehab Clb, 1981; Rho Chi Sigma Nat Hon Soc for Rehab Students, 1983; r/Pentecostal; hon/Alpha Kappa Mu, 1982; Buckeye Girls St Recip, 1978; g/BA in Rehab Cnslg Sociol.

NICKERSON, BEVERLY oc/Student; b/Apr 23, 1964; h/6117 Southwest 1st Street, Margate, FL 33068; ba/ Hanover, NH; p/Dennis D and Yuriko Nickerson, Margate, FL; ed/Claymont HS, 1982; Dartmouth Col; ba/Dartmouth Dining Assn, 1982-83; Cashier, Navy Exch-Phila, 1983; cp/Girls'Intramural Soccer, Volleyball, Basketball; Dartmouth Asian Am Assn, Secy; Dartmouth Dialectic Soc; Collis Gov'g Bd; Nat Forensic Leag; Nat Hon Soc, Secy; Mu Alpha Theta, VP; Rota Stamp & Coin Clb, Jr VP; Sch Newspaper, Reporter/Mng Editor; Awana; Student Coun; Orch; GSA; Yrbook Staff; r/Prot; hon/S'ship from Wilmington DE Br of Am Assn Univ Wom, 1982; 1982, 1983 S'ships from John B Lynch S'ship Foun; 1982, 1983 S'ships from the Milton & Hattie Kutz Foun; Nat Merit S'ship Semi-Finalist; W/W Among Am HS Students; Soc of Dist'd Am HS Students; g/Chem Maj.

NIEDOS, MARIA ANTOINETTE oc/Student; b/Mar 4, 1959; h/4559 South California Avenue, Chicago, IL 60632; p/Cosimir and Ann Marie Niedos, Chgo, IL; ed/Maria HS, 1977; BA, Univ Chgo, 1982; Master of Public Hlth Prog, Univ IL; pa/Pt-time Dance Instr, Lorraine Gray Dance Studio, 1977-; Specimen Control Tech 1981-, ECG Tech 1979, 1978, Patient Escort 1977, Michael Reese Hosp; cp/Christian Action Corp Pres; Nat Hon Soc; German Clb; Student Coun; Ath Clb; Thespians; Polish Rom Cath Am; IL Public Hlth Assn; Assoc Mem of Phys for Social Responsibility; Hon Mem of Brighton Pk C of C; r/Rom Cath; hon/

Essay "Of Beauty", Pub'd in the Annual Anthology of Am HS Essays, 1977; Dean's List; 2nd Runner-Up Miss Brighton Pk, 1976; Soc of Dist'd Am HS Students; W/W Among Am HS Students; g/Med Sch.

NINE, DIANE SIEGERT b/Apr 25, 1962; h/191 Lowell Court, Bloomfield Hills, MI 48013; p/Mr and Mrs Paul Nine, Bloomfield Hills, MI; ed/Kingswood Sch Cranbrook, 1980; BA, Denison Univ, 1984; pa/UPI Internship, 1982; Cable News Netwk Internship, 1983-; cp/Proj HOPE; Student Internship, Brit Parliament, US Senators Donald Riegle & Carl Levin; White House Info Ctr Internships; VP, Sr Class; Lit Symp; Sch Paper Writer; Varsity Clb Pres; Model UN; Tennis Competition; Editor, Dorm Newspaper; Delta Gamma; Am Lung Assn; Varsity Volleyball; Softball; Golf; Basketball; hon/Dean's List; W/W Among Am HS Students; Commun Ldrs Am; Intl Yth in Achmt.

NITTLER, LESLEY RENEE oc/Student; b/Jan 14, 1965; h/1605 Lexington, Garland, TX 75041; p/Ed and Gale Nittler, Garland, TX; cp/Student Coun, 1980-82, Pres 1982-83; Nat Hon Soc, Treas, 1982-83; Beta Clb, 1981-83; VP of Class, 1980-82; Latin Clb, 1981-83; Ldr in Yth Grp, 1980-83; r/Christian; hon/Nom'd for Golden Herald, Tact S'ships; All GHS, 1981-82; Student of Mo, 1982; Rotarian of Mo, 1982; Yth Apprec Wk for Garland Optimist Clb; g/OK Univ, Interior Design Maj & Computer Programming.

NORCROSS, JOHN C oc/Research Fellow; b/Aug 13, 1957; h/Curtis Corner Road, RD 3, Peacedale, RI 02879; m/Nancy A Caldwell; p/George and Carol Norcross, Merchantville, NJ; ed/Pennsauken HS, 1975; Rutgers Univ, 1979; MA 1981, PhD 1984, Univ RI; cp/En Psychol Assn; Am Psychol Assn; Assn for the Advmt of Psych; NE Psychol Assn; Psi Chi; Sigma Xi; hon/Num Articles Pub'd; Univ RI Grad F'ship, 1982-84; Athenaeum Hon Soc; Psi Chi Ser Awd, Cert of Recog; 3 Certs in Recog for Excell in Res; Intl Yth in Achmt; W/W Among Students in Am Univs & Cols; Commun Ldrs Am; g/Psychol; Academician.

NORCROSS, PHILIP A oc/Senatorial Staff Assistant; b/Jul 26, 1962; h/4001 Myrtle Avenue, Apartment F-1, Camden, NJ 08105; ba/Camden, NJ; p/George and Carol Norcross, Merchantville, NJ; ed/Pennsauken HS, 1980; Rutgers Univ, 1984; S Jersey Profl Sch of Bus, 1982; pa/Adm Asst, Co of Camden, 1979-81; Coor & Fundraising, Merlino Congl Campaign, 1982; Broker, Crump/Harris, 1982-83; cp/Pres, Rutgers Univ Polit Sci Soc, 1983-; Mem, Phi Sigma Alpha, 1982-; Mem, Fall Line Ski Clb, 1981-; r/Luth; hon/Rutgers Univ Dean's List; Polit Sci Hon Soc, 1982; Rutgers Hon Soc, 1983; g/Law Sch.

NORRIS, SARA BETH oc/Assistant Editor; b/Sep 24, 1958; h/6061 Village Bend, Number 202, Dallas, TX 75206; ba/Richardson, TX; p/Mr and Mrs Alton Norris, Longview, TX; ed/Longview HS, 1976; BS, Baylor Univ, 1980; MJourn, N TX St Univ, 1983; pa/Asst Editor, Soc of Petro Engrs, 1984-; Jour & Eng Instr, Mesquite HS, 1980-84; Grad Internships, Aerobics Ctr, *Dallas*

Times Herald; Undergrad Internship, *Longview Daily News*; cp/Baylor Univ Alumni Assn; Kilgore Jr Col Alumni Assn; Kilgore Jr Col Band Alumni Assn, Chp; Sigma Delta Chi Jour Soc; Public Relats Soc Am; Dallas Press Clb; Tau Beta Sigma Band Sorority; r/Bapt; hon/Articles in *Parkway Mag, Baylor Lariat, Longview Daily News*; Kappa Tau Alpha, Nat Jour Hon Soc, 1982; Nat Intercol Band, 1979; Jour S'ship, 1979.

NORTHCUTT, LEE EDWIN oc/Student, Church Organist, Bookkeeper; b/Jun 5, 1964; h/515 Lee Avenue, Wadesboro, NC 28170; p/Raymond and Doris Northcutt, Wadesboro, NC; ed/Southview Acad, 1982; Pfeiffer Col; cp/Sr Class Pres; Pres, Student Coun; Beta Clb; Civitan & Rotary Clb Wkr; Dir, Anson Chapt of Full Gospel Bus Men's F'ship; hon/US Achmt Acad, 1982-83; Nat Ldrship And Ser Awd, 1983; Nom for Sci Awd in Chem; Civitan Awd; Moorehead S'ship Nom; W/W Among Am HS Students; Soc of Dist'd Am HS Students; g/Doct of Ch Music & Organ; CPA.

NORTON, ELENA HOLLY oc/Student; b/Aug 19, 1963; h/632 Valley Brook Avenue, Lyndhurst, NJ 07071; p/Mary Ann Norton, Lyndhurst, NJ; ed/Lyndhurst HS, 1981; Brooks Col; Assoc Deg, Univ Bridgeport; Bach Prog, Univ Bridgeport; cp/Resident Aid, Univ Bridgeport; Ch Wkr; Commun Wkr; GSA; Hosp Aid; Lib Aid; Ofc Aid; Pep Clb; Red Cross; Baseball; Cheerldg; hon/Omega Sorority; Art Contest Winner; Cheerldg Tour Winner; Col S'ship; W/W; Intl Yth in Achmt; Commun Ldr; g/Advtg Layouts, Window Designing.

NOTARO, GIACOMO oc/Accountant; b/Jun 11, 1961; h/192 McAdoo Avenue, Hamilton Square, NJ 08619; p/Salvatore J and Mary J Notaro, Hamilton Square, NJ; ed/Hamilton HS, 1979; BS, Rider Col, 1983; pa/Acct, Louis H Linowitz & Co, CPA's, 1983-; Teller, Bk of Mid Jersey, 1981-83; Ofc Asst, Raymond Sayre Ins, 1981; Teller, Colonial First Nat Bk, 1979-81; Cashier/Clk, G C Murphy Co, 1978-79; cp/K of C; BPOE; Accts Clb; Rider Col Alumni; FBLA; Phi Beta Lambda Inc; Steinert Vol Internship Prog; Student Govt; Madrigal Singers; Sch Shows; r/Rom Cath; hon/Rider Col Dean's List; Intl Yth in Achmt; Yg Commun Ldrs Am; Accts Hon Soc; Omicron Delta Epsilon Hon Soc; Alpha Lambda Delta Hon Soc; FBLA Awds; K of C S'ship; Nat Hon Soc; g/Obtain Lic as CPA; Master's Deg in Acctg.

NOVAK, DARIA I oc/International Affairs Specialist; b/Feb 1, 1957; h/704 Seneca Road, Great Falls, VA 22066; ba/Washington, DC; ed/BA, Univ WY; Cert, Georgetown Univ Inst of Comparative Polit & Ec Sys; Grad Work Intl Affairs, George Washington Univ; pa/Employee, Dept of St Ofc of Chinese Affairs; Assn for Asian Studies; cp/Soc for Med Anthropolgy; Vol, Emer Med Tech on Ambulance; Vol Firefighter, Levels I, II, III, Great Falls VA Fire Dept; r/Rom Cath; hon/Co-Authored "China: The Rise to World Power", 1983; Dept of St, Awd for Excell Ser, 1981; Meritorious Hon Awd for Wk on US-China Jt Communique, 1982; Dept of St, Awd for Outstg Ser, 1982, 1983.

NOVAK, GEORGE DAVID II oc/

Student; b/Apr 29, 1963; h/Post Office Box 549, California, PA 15419; ba/Washington, PA; p/George David and Margaret Eileen Novak, California, PA; ed/California Area HS, 1981; Att'd CA St Col, 1977-82; BA, Washington & Jefferson Col, 1985; pa/Computer Programmer, CND Computer Sys, 1979-; Computer Programmer, Novak Assocs, 1979; Camp Assoc Instr, Sum 1980-82; Congl Intern, Sum 1982; Intern to US Dept of St, Bur of Info Sys, Sum 1983; cp/Citizen's Ambulance of CA, 1976-80; Alpha Pi Chapt of Alpha Tau Omega Frat, Secy, Public Relats Ofcr, 1982-; r/Rom Cath; hon/S'ship Awd of the Wash Co Alumni Assn of Wash & Jefferson Col, 1981; Acad Achmt Awd for ROTC, 1982; W/W Among Am HS Students; g/Polit Sci/Ec Maj; Career in Corporate or Intl Law.

NOVAK, SUZANNE CHRISTINA oc/Student; b/Aug 10, 1964; h/1216 East Vista Del Cerro, Number 2114, Tempe, AZ 85281; ba/Tempe, AZ; p/Joseph Novak, Alexandria, VA, and Irene Novak, Great Falls, VA; ed/the Madeira Sch, 1982; AZ St Univ; pa/Intern, Asst to Activs Dir, WI Ave Nsg Home, 1974-80; Congl Intern, Public Relats Asst, 1980-81; Student Tchr, Nat Chd's Ctr, 1981-82; Receptionist, Temporarily Yours, 1982; Financial Aids, Bk Loans Processor, AZ St Univ, 1982-; cp/Debate Clb, 1979-82; Model UN, 1979-82; St Press, HS Newspaper, 1979-82; AZ St Univ Hall Coun, 1982-83; Ed Com Chm, Residence Hall Assn Rep, VP Hall Coun; Little Sister to Alpha Epsilon Pi Frat, 1982-; Col Repubs, 1982-; r/Cath; hon/Del to Model UN Conf in Wash, DC, 1981; g/Communs Maj.

NOWLIN, ROBERT DOYNE oc/Student; b/Aug 10, 1957; h/513 Northwest Parkway, Blytheville, AR 72315; p/Bobby and Aleta Nowlin, Blytheville, AR; ed/Blytheville HS, 1975; AA, MS Co Commun Col, 1978; BFA, AR St Univ, 1980; Grad Prog at AR St Univ; pa/Freelance Floral Designer, 1975-; Pvt Art Instr, Dr Charlotte Jones Studio, 1983; Freelance Artist, NE AR Area; cp/Union Bd Com 1978-80, Art Student Unions 1983, AR St Univ; Blytheville Very Little Theatre, 1976-80; Am Thespian Assn, 1975; r/Bapt; hon/AR St Univ Creat Writing Mag, 1983-84; MS Co Commun Col Art Exhib, 2nd Pl, 1978; Student Art Show, AZ St Univ, 1980; Ritz Civic Ctr Pvt Exhbn, 1983.

NUNEZ, LOUIS EDWARD oc/Senior Underwriter; b/Jun 21, 1959; h/117 Bay 17th Street, Brooklyn, NY 11214; ba/New York, NY; p/Pedro and Juana Nunez; ed/Bishop Ford Ctl Cath, 1977; BBA 1982, MBA 1983, Col of Ins; pa/Comml Casualty Underwriter, Kemper Grp, 1981-83; Senior Underwriter, INA Spec Risk Facilities, 1983-; cp/Ins Soc NY; Col of Ins MBA Soc; Col of Ins Alumni Assn, Secy; Assn of MBA Execs; NY Chapt of CPCU; Notary Public; Assoc of Ins Inst of Am; r/Cath; hon/Ins Inst Am, Assoc in Underwriting, 1981; Assoc Mgmt, Assoc Risk Mgmt, 1982; Col of Ins, Profl Cert in Ins Bus Techniques, 1981; Risk & Mgmt Soc, Robert Spencer Meml S'ship; Dean's List; W/W; Intl Yth in Achmt; Nat Dean's List; g/Exec Career Level; JD; Aerospace Indust.

NUSSA, BARBARA LYNN b/Dec 19,

1962; h/1405 Estate Lane, Glenview, IL 60025; p/William and Dorothy Nussa, Glenview, IL; ed/R Nelson Snider HS, 1980; BS, Butler Univ, 1984; pa/Delta Gamma Field Conslt, 1984-85; Student Activs Ofc, Cont'g Ed Ofc, Butler Univ, 1983; cp/Delta Gamma, Pres, Corres'g Secy; Mortar Bd, 1983-84; Chimes, VP, 1982-83; Spurs, 1981-82, PR Mgr; Rho Lambda, 1983-84; r/Cath; hon/Butler

Univ Outstg Students, 1983-84; Alpha Tau Chapt of Delta Gamma Outstg Sr, 1983-84; g/Master's Deg in Student Pers, Wk in Univ Student Pers.

NUTTER, YUEH-MEI KIM oc/Student; b/Apr 26, 1963; h/321 Northeast 59 Court, Ft Lauderdale, FL 33334; p/Mr and Mrs Daniel Nutter, Ft Lauderdale, FL; ed/NE HS, 1981; FL Atlantic Univ; pa/Dental Asst, 1979-80; cp/Jr

Achmt, Treas, 1978-79; NE Hurricane Eye Newspaper, Photog 1978-79, Chief Photog 1979-80, Editor-in-Chief 1980-81; Adv Bd, 1980-81, Chm; NE Swim Team, Diver, 1978-80; AAU Diving Team, 1978-80; Circle K, 1981-83, 1983-84, Pres; hon/MVS NE Newspaper, 1981; Fac Scholar FL Atlantic Univ, 1981; Nat Hon Soc, 1979-81; g/Law Sch; Intl Lwyr.

O

O'DONNELL, CINDY L oc/Student; b/Oct 26, 1965; h/Route 1, Box 32F, Oologah, OK 74053; ed/Oologah HS, 1983; Student, OK Bapt Univ, 1982, 1983; Currently Enrolled, Univ of OK; cp/Chorus, 4 Yrs; Chorus Reporter, 1983; FCA, 2 Yrs; Beta Clb, 3 Yrs; Oologah Christian F'ship, 4 Yrs; Basketball, 2 Yrs; Track, 2 Yrs; Student Coun Mem, 2 Yrs; Jr Class Secy-Treas; Rogers Co Bk Jr Bd of Dirs; F'ship of Christian Musicians; Cheerldr, 3 Yrs; Pres's Hon Coun; Bisonettes; hon/ Supt's Hon Roll, 4 Yrs; St Hon Soc, 4 Yrs; Nat Merit Commended Student, 1983; Valedictorian; Algebra II Awd, 1981; Geometry Awd, 1982; Trigonometry Awd, 1983; Eng Awd, 1983; Track Awd, 1983; Elks Nat S'ship Recip; 4th Place in 800 Meter Run and 3,200 Meter Relay in 1983 St Track Meet; Pres's Hon Roll, 1982; g/Maj in Profl Jour; Write for Mags or Newspapers; Free-Lance Writer.

O'HAVER, PAMELA SUE oc/Secretary, Receptionist; b/Dec 9, 1961; h/RR #1, Hillsdale, IN 47854; m/Joe; p/Eugene and Roseann Giordano, Hillsdale, IN; ed/N Vermillion HS, 1980; AS, Vincennes Univ, 1982; Currently Enrolled, Wom's External Deg Prog, St Mary-of-the-Woods Col; pa/ Secy-Receptionist, Fountain Trust Co, 1982-; cp/Marching, Concert and Pep Bands, HS, 4 Yrs; OEA, VP; Drama Clb; Thespians; FHA; NHS; 4-H; Jazz, Concert and Pep Bands, Col, 1 Yr; r/St Joseph's Cath Ch; hon/Dean's List, 1980-82; Sch Winner, Century II Ldrs Awd, 1980; Outstg Sr Bus Student, 1980; W/W Among Am HS Students; Commun Ldrs of Am; g/BS in Acctg; CPA.

OLDHAM, LEWIS MARK oc/Student; b/Oct 12, 1960; h/Route 2, Box 207, Siler City, NC 27344; p/Mrs Lewis K Oldham, Siler City, NC; ed/Dipl, Jordan Matthews HS, 1978; BMus in Theory and Composition, Greensboro Col, 1983; pa/Organist and Asst Choir Dir, Hilcrest Bapt Ch, 1979-81; Pianist and Sanctuary Choir Accompanist, Allen Jay Bapt Ch, 1981-; Tchr, Elem Sch Students, 1982-; cp/Greensboro Col: Percussion Ensemble 1978-80, 1982-, Wind Ensemble 1978-81, Piano Ensemble 1981-82, Stage (Jazz) Band 1982-; Alpha Chi Acad Hon Soc, 1980-; VP, NC Xi Chapt of Alpha Chi, 1981-82; Student Del, SEn Reg, Nat Coun of Alpha Chi, 1981-84; Pres, NC Xi Chapt of Alpha Chi, 1982-; hon/Participant, Piano and Composition Progs of En Musical Fest 1980, Composition Master Classes of Composers James Drew and Dr John Boda 1980, 1981, Piano Master Classes of Pianists Frederick Moyer and Natalie Hinderas 1981, 1982; First Prize Winner, Col Div, NC Music Tchrs Assn Composition Contest, 1982; First Prize Winner, Col Div, So Div Composition Contest of Music Tchrs Nat Assn, 1983; Runner-Up, Col Div, Music Tchr's Nat Assn Inc, Nat Student Composition Contest, 1983; W/W Am Cols and Univs; g/DMus in Musical Composition and Music Theory; Career as Profl Musician, Composer, Tchr and Scholar in 20th Century Music.

OLEYAR, JUDITH LYNN oc/Housewife and Mother, Co-Manager; b/Jul 10,

1955; h/226 Wyleswood Drive, Berea, OH 44017; ba/Columbia Station, OH; m/Peter David; c/Lauren Elizabeth; p/ Mr and Mrs Robert Rewalt, Olmsted Falls, OH; ed/Olmsted Falls HS, 1973; Elem Ed Deg, W Liberty St Col, 1982; pa/Co-Mgr, Jaquay Lake Pk, 1984; cp/ Kappa Delta Pi Ednl Frat; Topperette Squad; Capt, Golden Bullet Drill Team Squad, 1972-73; r/Luth; hon/Grad w Hons, W Liberty St; Kappa Delta Pi Ednl Frat; Outstg Topperette, W Liberty St Col Squad, 1979; Capt, Topperette Squad, 1980; Personalities of S; Nat Dean's List.

OLIVAS, ADOLF oc/Attorney, Counselor at Law; b/Jan 31, 1956; h/Suite 88, 1385 Carriage Hill Lane, Hamilton, OH; ba/Hamilton, OH; p/Mr and Mrs Henry Olivas, Hamilton, OH; ed/BA, Univ of Cinc Col of Arts and Sci, 1974-78; JD, Univ of Cinc Col of Law, 1978-81; pa/ Assoc Atty, Holbrock, Jonson, Bressler and Houser, 1981-; Law Clk, US Dist Ct, En Dist of KY, 1981-; Elected Hamilton City Councilman, 1984-85; Res Asst, Col of Law, Univ of Cinc, 1980-81; Law Clk, US Dept of Treas, Ofc of Reg Coun, Bur of Alcohol, Tobacco and Fire Arms, 1980; Grad Asst to Vice Provost for Student Affairs, Univ of Cinc, 1978-81; Legal Res Asst for Dean, Col of Law, Univ of Cinc, 1979; Am Bar Assn; OH Acad of Trial Lwyrs; OH St Bar Assn; Cinc Bar Assn; Butler Co Bar Assn; Assn of Trial Lwyrs of Am; Phi Alpha Delta; cp/Student Body Pres, Univ of Cinc, 1977-78; Hamilton-Fairfield Chapt of US JCs; Dir of Govtl Affairs 1982-, Bd of Dirs 1982-, Hamilton-Fairfield JCs; Full Gospel Bus Men's F'ship Intl; Butler Co Dem Party, Prcnt Com'man 1980-83; Butler Co Campaign Coor, Celeste for OH Gov, 1982; Bd of Dirs, Hamilton Appalachian Peoples Ser Org, 1984-; Bd of Dirs, Open Door Food Pantry Inc, 1983-; Hamilton C of C; r/Rom Cath; hon/ Omicron Delta Kappa; Delta Tau Kappa; Col Register of Outstg Students, 1978; Metro Men's Hon Soc; Dean's List, Univ of Cinc, 1974-78; 1981; Freshman/Sophomore Hon Prog, 1974-76; Fraternal Order of Police Apprec Awd, 1983; Intl Yth in Achmt; Outstg Yg Men of Am; W/W Among Students in Am Univs and Cols; Commun Ldrs of Am.

OLIVER, CHARLES LINDBERGH oc/Educator, Student, Author, Poet; b/ Oct 1, 1956; h/1370 McMillan Street, Memphis, TN 38106; p/Charles and Daisy Oliver, Memphis, TN; ed/S Side HS, 1974; Univ of TN Knoxville, 1979; pa/Student Res, Ofc Asst, Black Cultural Ctr, Univ of TN Knoxville, 1975-79; Subst Tchr, Memphis City Schs, 1979-82; Chem Lab Clk and Helper, Reg Med Ctr at Memphis, 1983; Am Med Student Assn; Student Soc Am Med Technols; Am Med Technol Assn; AAAS; cp/Nat Assoc, Smithsonian Inst; Am Film Inst; Black Cultural Ctr Repertory Co Bd Mem; Student Lib Concert Choir; AASLF; Alpha Phi Alpha Sphinxmen; Alpha Phi Omega; r/Meth; hon/Author, Var Pubs; Vol Ser Awd, Memphis City Schs; The Col Register; Intl Yth in Achmt; Biogl Roll of Hon; Outstg Yg Men of Am; Yg Commun Ldrs of Am; Personalities of S; g/MD.

OLLIS, CLAYTON LLOYD oc/Stu-

dent; b/Dec 1, 1964; h/804 Rhodes Avenue, Kings Mountain, NC 28086; p/ Mr and Mrs Walter C Ollis, Kings Mountain, NC; ed/Grad, Kings Mtn Sr High, 1983; cp/Student Coun; Sophomore Class VP; Sr Class VP; Beta Clb; Nat Hon Soc; Drama Clb VP; French Clb; HS Chorale and Ensemble; Ch Yth Coun, Yth Pres 1980-83; Yth and Adult Choirs; r/Bapt; hon/Exch Clb Yth of the Month; Most Likely to Succeed; Hon S'ship from Mars Hill Col; Best Male Vocalist, 1980; W/W Among Am HS Students; g/To Attend Mars Hill Col and Maj in Ch Music (BMus); To Obtain a Full-time Position as Min of Music in a Bapt Ch.

OLSON, KIMBERLY ANN oc/Student; b/Sep 4, 1964; h/9 Cheyenne Court, Bryans Road, MD 20616; p/ Larry and Leone Olson, Bryans Road, MD; ed/La Plata HS, 1982; Charles Co Commun Col, 1982; Student, Univ of MD, 1983-; pa/Secy, D&D Copier Ser, 1982-83; cp/Cancer Soc Vol; Bloodmobile Vol; Nsg Home Vol; SS Aide; Bible Sch Aide; Danced for Bryans Rd Sr Citizens; Needy Fam Dr; Future Bus Ldrs of Am; Yrbook; Drama Clb; Student Guide; Student Coun; Math Competition Leag; Gymnastics Team, 1980-82; Prom Com, 1981; Majorette, Choir, 1979-80; Cheerldr, Pt Tobacco Players, 1978-79; Career Base Lng Ser, 1980-82; r/Meth; hon/NHS; Teen Model of the Month Winner for *Teen Magazine*; St Champ, MD Phy Fitness; Sci Fair Awds: 3rd Place-Sch Fair, 2nd Place-Co Fair, Hon Mention-Area Fair 1979, 2nd Place-Sch Fair, 2nd Place-Co Fair, Hon Mention-Area Fair 1980, 1st Place-Sch Fair, 3rd Place-Co Fair, Cert of Participation-Area Fair 1981; Queen Nicotina Ct, 1981; W/W Among Am HS Students; Yg Commun Ldrs of Am; g/ Bach Deg in Field of Communs w Concentration in Radio, TV and Film.

O'NEAL, DELAINE LYNETTE oc/ Student; b/Aug 7, 1963; h/RR #1, Box 92A, Satanta, KS 67870; p/Charles (dec) and Phyllis O'Neal, Satanta, KS; ed/ Grad, Satanta HS, 1981; Student, Gulf Coast Bible Col; cp/Volleyball; Basketball; Band; Debate; Forensics; Sch Plays; Pep Clb, VP Jr Yr; Kayettes; hon/ Satanta HS Co-Valedictorian, 1981; Rep of Satanta HS Debate Team which Earned Distn of 6th in KS St HS Championship Competition, 1980; Cert for Outstg Achmt, Forensic Team, KS St HS Championship Competition; Rep of Santanta HS Forensic Team; Nat Hon Soc; Outstg Novice Debater; KS Hon Student; Cert of Recog for Outstg Acad Achmt in the Eng Lang, 1981-82; Dean's List, 1981-82; g/Sec'dy Eng Tchr.

ONORATO, PATRICIA C oc/Student; b/Feb 19, 1966; h/7 Lee Shore, Hilton Head Island, SC 29928; p/Mr and Mrs Robert C Onorato, Hilton Head, SC; ed/Grad, May River Acad; cp/10th Grade: Varsity Football Cheerldr, Rep in Student Govt, Varsity Boys' Tennis Team, Varsity Girls' Basketball, Homecoming Ct, Coaches Ofc Secy; 11th Grade: Student Govt Treas, Jr Class VP, Varsity Football Cheerldr (Co-Capt), Homecoming Ct, Varsity Basketball Scorekeeper, Varsity Boys' Tennis Team, Coaches Ofc Secy, F'ship of Christian Aths; 12th Grade: Student Govt VP, VP of Sr Class, Varsity Football Cheerldg (Capt), F'ship of

Christian Aths, Interact Clb (Pres); r/ Presb; hon/Hon Roll, 9th, 10th and 11th Grades; Mathlete in Col of Charleston Math Meet; W/W Among Am HS Students; g/To Maj in Psych; To Attend Grad Sch to Earn a Deg in Indust Psych.

OPPERMAN, KIMBERLY ANN oc/ Student; b/May 24, 1966; h/101 Monte Video Drive, Seneca, SC 29678; p/Mr and Mrs Kenneth H Opperman, Seneca, SC; ed/HS Student; pa/Pt-time Wkr, Rose's Dept Store, 1982-; cp/Nat Beta Clb, 1982-83; Jr Beta Clb, 1980-82; Interact (Rotary) Clb, Treas 1983; Acteens, Pres 1982-83; Band, 1980-83; Teens for Christ, 1980, 1983; r/Bapt; hon/Rotary Scholar, 1983, 1982, 1981, 1979; Furman Scholar, 1983; PC Jr Fellow, 1983; Outstg French Student, 1982; Gov's Sch, 1983; Girls' St Alt, 1983; g/To Enter a Career in the Biol Field (Wildlife Biol or Genetic Engrg).

ORR, TRACY WALLBAUM oc/ Accountant; b/Apr 8, 1961; h/14 Sunset, Jacksonville, IL 62650; m/James Q; c/ Lisa Marie; p/Mr and Mrs John W Wallbaum, Murrayville, IL; ed/Grad, Routt HS, 1979; BA, IL Col, 1983; pa/ Hd Acct, Morgan-Scott, 1981-82; Bkkpr, Northernaire Aluminum, 1977-82; Delta Mu Delta Bus Hon Soc, 1981; cp/Softball; Math Clb; 4-H; Ch Choir; r/Cath; hon/Nat Hon Soc; Hart Sophomore Prize in Math, Thomas Smith Freshman Prize in Math, IL Col; Salutatorian, Routt HS; Dean's List; Elliot Math S'ship, 1982; Phi Beta Kappa, 1983; Grad, magna cum laude, 1983; g/CPA Exam.

OSBORNE, KAREN LYNN oc/Student; b/Mar 7, 1966; h/21790 East 67th, Broken Arrow, OK 74014; p/Howard and Cathy Osborne, Broken Arrow, OK; ed/Grad, Broken Arrow HS, 1984; Att'g, Univ of OK, 1984-; cp/Nat Hon Soc; Future Bus Ldrs of Am; F'ship of Christian Aths; Student Coun; Sr Class Pres; Tennis; r/Ch of Christ; hon/Miss Broken Arrow, 1983; Girls' St Del, 1983; Freedoms Foun to Val Forge, 1983; Sep Girl of Month, 1983; g/Maj in Acctg; To Have a Job Where I Can Grow as a Person and Grow in My Career as Well.

OSIGWEH, CHIMEZIE A B oc/University Professor; b/Nov 11, 1955; h/PO Box 932, Kirksville, MO 63501; ba/ Kirksville, MO; m/Brenda Jean; c/ Chinelo Amarachi-Genevieve Nkiruka, Chinenye Nkechinyere-Vivian Nneka; p/Mr and Mrs Joseph A A Osigweh, Owerri, Nigeria; ed/PhD 1982, MLHR 1981, MA 1980, OH St Univ; BSc w Hons, magna cum laude, E TN St Univ, 1978; pa/Asst Prof of Bus Adm, NW MO St Univ, 1982-; Res Assoc, Mershon Ctr for Res, 1982, 1979; Instr, Intl Relats, OH St Univ, 1981; Grad Tchg Assoc, Polit Sci, OH St Univ, 1979-81; Acad of Mgmt; Acad of Intl Bus; Am Inst for Decision Scis; Assn of Vol Action Scholars; Behavioral Scis Conf; Case Res Assn; MW Bus Adm Assn; r/ Christianity; hon/Pubs, *Improving Problem-Solving Participation* 1983, *Petals of Fire* 1984, Others; Author, Many Lnd Articles in the Areas of Indust Relats, Prob-Solving, Mgmt, Ec and Intl Bus; OH St Univ Nom for Morris Abrams Awd in Intl Relats, 1982; Dean's Lists, 1976-78; W/W Among Students in Am Univs and Cols; Intl Yth in Achmt.

OSTEEN, EDWARD POWELL JR oc/ Student; b/Nov 5, 1960; h/2410 Dawn Trail, Durham, NC 27712; p/Edward and Alice P Osteen, Durham, NC; ed/ No HS, 1979; BA, Duke Univ, 1982; Student, Duke Div Sch; pa/Intern, Metro U Meth Ch, 1983; Student Assoc, Trinity U Meth Ch, 1982-83; Coor, Duke Univ Precol Prog, 1982; Lab Tech, Cancer Immunol, Duke Med Ctr, 1979, 1980; cp/Duke Univ Bd of Trustees, 1981-84; Duke Univ Bus and Fin Com, 1981-84; Bd of Dirs, U Meth Campus Min, Duke Univ, 1979-83; Duke Campus Min Adv Coun, Fin Chp 1981-82; Duke Univ Chapel Choir, VP 1980-81; Yoke Fellow Prison Min; Rel Majs Com; Agape Bible Study; hon/A B Duke Meml S'ship, 1979-82; Phi Eta Sigma Hon Soc, 1980; Dean's List, Class Hons, magna cum laude, 1982; Pres's Sr Achmt Awd, Duke Univ, 1982; S'ship, King's Daughs and Sons, 1982, 1983; W/W Among Students in Am Univs and Cols; Outstg Yg Men of Am, 1983; Num HS Hons; g/Master of Div Deg; Local Ch Min in NC.

OTT, KENNETH DEAN oc/Student; b/Jun 21, 1962; h/811 Garden Grove, Yukon, OK 73099; p/Alveta M Ott, Yukon, OK; ed/BME, Ctl St Univ, 1986; Yukon HS, 1981; cp/Tau Kappa Epsilon; CSU Band, Drum Maj, Marching Dir 1982-83; Dorm Coun, 1982 (Wing Rep); Mktg Clb, Secy 1983; Univ Ctr Activs Bd, 1983; DeMolay, 1975; r/ Meth; hon/Dean's Hon Roll; Num Music Awds; Band S'ship.

P

PACE, FRANKLIN WAYNE oc/Student; b/Jun 27, 1960; h/Route 3, Box 515, Mineral, VA 23117; p/Mr and Mrs William J Pace, Mineral, VA; ed/Grad, Louisa Co HS, 1978; Assoc Deg, Ferrum Col, 1980; BS in Bus Adm, Old Dominion Univ, 1983; r/Bapt; hon/Yg Dist'd Ams; W/W Among Students in Am Jr Cols; Intl Yth in Achmt; Yg Commun Ldrs of Am; g/CPA.

PACE, KAREN ELISABETH oc/Student; b/Apr 13, 1961; h/483 Nova Scotia Hill Road, Watertown, CT 06795; p/Mr and Mrs Vincent Pace, Watertown, CT; ed/Watertown Sr HS, 1979; Mattatuck Commun Col, 1981; Student, WV Wesleyan Col; cp/Editor-in-Chief, Col Newspaper, 1983-84; Zeta Tau Alpha Sorority; Chp, Hlth Com, 1983-84; Student Govt; Alpha Phi Gamma; r/Cath; hon/Alpha Phi Gamma, Soc for Col Journalists, 1983; g/To Attend Law Sch and Pract Intl Law.

PADGETT, LORI SUE oc/Student; b/Jun 20, 1967; h/PO Box 216, Turkey, NC 28393; p/Rev and Mrs Larry D Padgett, Turkey, NC; ed/Student, Union HS; cp/Turkey Elem Sch Cheerldr, 1 Yr; Union Elem Sch Cheerldr, 1 Yr; Union HS Cheerldr, 2 Yrs; Union Elem Sch Volleyball, 1 Yr; Union Elem Sch Softball, 1 Yr; Turkey Elem Sch Softball, 1 Yr; Union HS Softball, 1 Yr; Class Pres, 10th Grade; Beta Clb; Hist Clb; Newspaper Staff; 4-H; Acteens; Chorus; Choir; r/Turkey Bapt Ch; hon/Softball, Most Valuable Player, 1980; Chief Marshall, 1980; Math Awd, 1982; Math Awd, 1983; Miss Union, 1983; Hon Roll Student; Student of the Month, 1983; Chd's Bible Drill St Winner, 1979; g/To Attend Col in Switzerland; To Become a Model; To Own a Bus.

PADGETTE, JACQUELINE ELLEN oc/Student; b/May 28, 1966; h/PO Box 364, Hobgood, NC 27843; p/Julian and Mary Ellen Padgette, Hobgood, NC; ed/Student, Hobgood Acad; cp/FHA; Monogram Clb; Sci Awd; Cheerldr; Class Secy; r/Bapt; hon/Miss Hobgood Acad, 1981; Homecoming Ct, 1981, 1983; Miss NC Hemisphere, 1982; Nat Hemisphere Finalist, 1982; Teen Model of the Month, 1982, 1983; Cheerldr, 1981, 1982, 1983; W/W Among Am HS Students; Soc of Dist'd Am HS Students; g/To Attend Col and Become a Fashion Designer.

PAFFENBARGER, JOHN ANDREW oc/Mechanical Engineer; b/Oct 12, 1959; ba/Bechtel Group Inc, PO Box 3965, San Francisco, CA 94119; p/George C Paffenbarger, Arden, NY; ed/AB, Dartmouth Col, 1981; MS, Mech Engrg, Stanford Univ, 1982; pa/Photo Asst, Sarah Lawrence Art Sch, 1978; Res Asst, Intl Paper Co Res Ctr, 1980; Engrg Apprentice, Elf-Aquitaine Res Ctr, 1981; Engr, Bechtel Grp Inc, 1982-; ASME; cp/Intl Visitors Ctr; hon/Valedictorian, Monroe Woodbury Sr HS, 1977; Dartmouth S'ships, 1978-81; Outstg Sr in Engrg Sci, Dartmouth, 1981; Phi Beta Kappa, Dartmouth, 1981; Stanford F'ship, 1981-82.

PAGE, CYNTHIA ANNETTE oc/Student; b/Nov 26, 1962; h/Route 2, Box 60, Apex, NC 27502; p/Mr and Mrs Zollie Moss, Apex, NC; ed/Grad, Apex Sr HS, 1981; cp/HS Student Coun VP, 1980-81; Hlth Occup Student of Am, Pres 1980-81; Ch Treas, 1980-81; Ch Choir, Secy 1979-81; Choir VP, Univ of NC Greensboro, 1983-84; AKA Debutante, 1981; r/Bapt; hon/S'ship from Alpha Kappa Alpha Debutante Ball; g/Nurse Anesthetist.

PAGE, DONNA RHEE oc/Secondary Educator; b/Nov 5, 1956; h/P107 Regency Park, Clarksville, TN 37043; ba/Ft Campbell, KY; p/Mr and Mrs William H Page, Clarksville, TN; ed/Grad, Clarksville HS, 1974; BSEE 1978, MAEd 1981, Austin Peay St Univ; pa/Edr, Ft Campbell HS; NEA; Alpha Phi Alumni Chapt; Alpha Phi Wom's Frat, Clarksville Chapt, Alumnae Pres; Kappa Delta Pi; cp/Am Heart Assn; r/U Meth Yth Sunday Sch Tchr; hon/Outstg Yg Wom of Am; W/W Among Students in Am Univs and Cols; Col Register; Intl Yth in Achmt; Personalities of S; g/Ed Spec Deg; BS in Computer Sci.

PAGE, SHERLON L oc/Branch Office Administrator; b/Oct 14, 1961; h/Route 1, Spring Hope, NC 27882; ba/Wilson, NC; p/Gerald and Peggy Page, Spring Hope, NC; ed/Hon Grad, So Nash Sr HS, 1980; Assoc in Applied Sci Deg in Acctg, Wilson Co Tech Inst, 1982; pa/Br Ofc Admr, Edward D Jones & Co, Mems of NY Stock Exch, 1982-; cp/Floods Chapel Commun Watch, Secy and Treas; r/Free-Will Bapt; Choir Mem, Asst Sunday Sch Tchr; hon/Nat Dean's List; Outstg Commun Ldrs of Am; W/W Among Students in Am Jr Cols; g/To Become More Knowledgable about the Stock Mkt.

PALANZO, DAVID ANTHONY oc/Chief Perfusionist; b/May 17, 1956; h/2540 Whippletree Drive, Harvey, LA 70058; ba/Marrero, LA; m/Jill Casper; p/Mr and Mrs Joseph Palanzo, Annville, PA; ed/Lebanon Cath HS, 1974; BS, Wilkes Col, 1977; Cert, Milton S Hershey Med Ctr, 1982; pa/Chief Perfusionist, O'Neill Surg Grp; cp/Bal Pres; Newspaper Page Editor; Class Pres; March of Dimes Walk-a-Thon; Human Ser Com; Jazz Band; hon/Bausch and Lomb Sci Awd; NHS; Dean's List; W/W Among Students in Am Cols and Univs; g/To Become a Mem of the Am Acad of Cardiovas Perfusionists.

PALERMO, FRANCIS ANTHONY oc/Student; b/Oct 13, 1957; h/1000 Walnut Street, Apartment 1400, Philadelphia, PA 19107; m/Sharon M; p/Joseph A and Anna C Palermo, Newport, DE; ed/St Marks HS, 1975; BA, Univ of DE, 1979; Jefferson Med Col, Class of 1984; pa/Respiratory Therapy, Wilmington Med Ctr 1979-80, Thomas Jefferson Univ Hosp 1981-82; Kappa Beta Phi; Phi Sigma Alpha; cp/Jefferson Shotokan Karate Clb; Baseball; Wrestling Capt; Marine Phy Fitness Team; Semi-Pro Baseball; Am Legion Baseball; Babe Ruth All-Star; Little Leag Baseball All-Star; Hon Soc Treas; Nat Soc of Student Ldrs; Col Register; Emer Care Unit; Resident Advr; Res, Med Examr for St of DE; hon/Hons in Sophomore Med Clerkship, 1982; Mortar Bd; Beta Beta Beta; Carl J Reese Alumni S'ship; Warrin Walker Acad Sch, Commrs of Newport as Outstg Newport HS Student; Dean's List Grad; W/W Among Am HS Students; g/Internal Med; Phys.

PALMER, LORI ANN oc/Student; b/Sep 12, 1963; h/12055 Charwick Drive, St Louis, MO 63128; p/Mr and Mrs Dean Lee Palmer, Baldwinsville, NY; ed/Grad, C W Baker HS, 1981; Student, St John Fisher Col; cp/Bal-on-Sen Triangle #65; Jr Advr of Onondaga Dist Org of Triangles Inc; 3rd Yr Varsity Wom's Volleyball Team at St John Fisher Col; hon/Most Improved Player, Coach Jim Pelcher Awd for Excell, Varsity Volleyball; Intl Yth in Achmt; W/W Among Am HS Students; g/Lwyr.

PALUMBO, R TODD oc/Student; b/Mar 8, 1963; h/RD #2, Box 29, Black Meadow Road, Chester, NY 10918; p/Mr and Mrs Robert Palumbo, Chester, NY; ed/NY St Regents Dipl, Warwick Val HS, 1981; BS in Computer Engrg, Boston Univ, 1985; cp/HS Band, Drum Maj 1979-81, Pres 1980-81; Drill Team; Rockland Defenders Drum and Bugle Corps, Drum Maj 1982; Boston Univ Band, Drum Maj 1982-; Kappa Kappa Psi Frat, Secy of BU Chapt; Col of Engrg Student Host and Orientation Ldr; HS Math Team Pres; US Col Wind Band European Concert Tour, 1980; All-Co Band, 1979; Area All-St Band, 1980; New England Intercol Band, 1983; r/Cath; hon/NY St Regents S'ship, 1981; Nat Hon Soc, 1981; All-Am Hall of Fame Band Awd; John Phillip Sousa Band Awd, 1981; US Nat Band Awd, 1980; HS Hon Roll, 1977-81; BU Col of Engrg Dean's List, 1981; Intl Yth in Achmt; W/W Music; W/W Among Am HS Students; Commun Ldrs of Am; g/BS in Computer Engrg.

PAMPLIN, CATHERINE LINDSAY oc/Student; b/Jan 10, 1959; h/813 Del Rio Pike, I-7, Franklin, TN 37064; ba/Nashville, TN; p/Mr and Mrs William A Pamplin, Winchester, TN; ed/Franklin Co HS; Pre-Nsg, Mid TN St Univ; BSN, Univ of TN Ctr for the Hlth Scis; pa/Grad Nurse, Bapt Hosp, 1983; r/Presb; hon/Tau Omicron, Hon Soc for Outstg Wom, 1979; Grad w Hons, Univ of TN Ctr for the Hlth Scis, 1983; Nat Dean's List for Profl Students, 1983; g/Master's Deg in Nsg.

PANDULLO, DAVID BRUCE oc/Electronics Engineer; b/May 23, 1957; h/11307 Grand Oak, Apartment 5, Grand Blanc, MI 48439; ba/Flint, MI; m/Joann Marie; p/Mrs Amy Pandullo, Scottdale, PA; ed/Southmoreland Sr HS; AAS, Electronics, Westmoreland Co Commun Col; BET, Electronics, PA St Univ; pa/Electronics Engr, AC Spark Plug, Div of Gen Motors Corp, 1981-; r/Cath; hon/Grad w Highest Hons, WCCC, 1979; g/Master's Deg in Computer Sci and Engrg.

PANKAU, VANESA ANN oc/Student; b/Jul 9, 1962; h/1710 Gardenia, New Braunfels, TX 78130; p/Melvin R and Betty H Pankau, New Braunfels, TX; ed/Pleasanton HS, 1980; BBA, Acctg, SW TX St Univ, 1983; pa/Grader, SW TX St Univ, 1981-; cp/Alpha Lambda Delta Nat Hon Soc for Wom, 1981-; Acctg Clb, 1983-; Annual Staff Editor, 1979-80; Luther Leag, 1976-80, Pres 1978-79; Nat Hon Soc, 1977-80; Band, 1976-80; Jr Class Rep, 1978-79; Sigma Mu Epsilon, 1976-80, Histn 1978-79; German Clb, 1978-79; FTA, 1977-78; r/Luth; hon/Davidson Fam Charitable Foun S'ship, 1980-; SW TX St Univ Freshman S'ship, 1980-81; Dean's List, 1980, 1981, 1982; Hon Roll, 1977-80; Top 10% of Grad'g Class, 1980; Citizenship Awd, 1979; Solo and Ensemble Awds, 1977-80; Co

Band Awds, 1977-80; Rotary Clb Duchess, 1978-79; C of C Duchess, 1979-80; W/W Among Am HS Students; Soc of Dist'd Am HS Students; g/To Grad w a BBA in Acctg and Become a CPA.

PANNELL, JAMES TIMOTHY oc/Professional Nurseryman, Student; b/Feb 28, 1963; h/PO Box 1868, Sylva, NC 28779; ba/Same; p/Mr and Mrs James P Pannell, Sylva, NC; ed/Grad, Sylva-Webster, 1981; Att'd, Wn Carolina Univ, 1981-82; Deg in Forest Mgmt, Haywood Tech Col, 1984; pa/Carpenters Helper, 1977-79; Asst Mgr, Christmas Tree Farm, 1979-80; Nurseryman, Tuckasegee Val Nursery, 1981-82; Profl Nurseryman, Country Roads Nursery, 1983-; Current Owner and Operator, Nursery which Produces Christmas Tree Seedlings, Groundcovers and Native Ornamentals; Jackson Co Nurserymans Assn, 1983-; cp/FFA, Secy 1978, VP 1980, Pres 1981; Beta Clb, 1979-81; VICA Clb, 1979-81, Secy 1980; r/Bapt; hon/1st Place in Area Forestry Contest, 1979; Winner in Soil Judging Contest, 1979; St Winner in Nursery Opers, 1981; 1st Place Winner in Hort Crops, 1981; Top Fifth of Sr Class; Recip, Am Hist Awd, Citizenship Awd, and Am Farmer Deg, 1983; Dean's List; W/W; g/To Continue Operating Nursery; To Wk for the Forest Ser as a Co Ranger; To Further Study in Hort and Forestry Field.

PAPAGEORGE, CHRISTINE L oc/Student; b/Dec 20, 1962; h/104 Rocky Hill Road, Hadley, MA 01035; ba/Amherst, MA; p/Mr and Mrs J C Papageorge, Hadley, MA; ed/Univ of MA Amherst, 1981-82; Grad, Greenfield Commun Col Nsg Prog; Barbizon Modeling Sch Grad, 1977; pa/Paper Girl, Hasting A J Inc, 1975-77; Laborer, Consolidated Cigar Corp, 1978; Sales Rep, Avon, 1978-80; Cashier, Niedbalas Mkt, 1978-81; Factory Laborer, Pro Corp, 1981; Sales Rep, Sarah Coventry, 1981-82; Nurses Aid, Amherst Nsg Home Inc, 1981-; cp/Elected to Greenfield Commun Col Senate as a Rep, Mem of Delta Zeta Sorority, 1981; HS Band, 1974-81; HS Marching Band, 1976-81; HS Stage Band, 1977-81; HS Soccer, 1977-81; HS Newspaper, 1977-81; Fgn Lang Clb, 1977-79; Future Nurses Clb, 1977-81, Pres; Art Wkshops, 1977; Photo Clb, 1977; Yrbook, 1978-81, VP 1981; 4-H, 1975-77; GSA, 1973-76; Vol, Cooley Dickinson Hosp; Teen Encounter Golf Team, 1981; hon/3 Varsity Lttrs in Soccer, 1978-81; 1 Varsity Lttr in Golf, 1981; Greg Typing Awd, 1977; Pres Phy Fitness Awd, 1977-79; Cooley Dickinson Hosp Vol Awd, 1977; Louis Armstrong Jazz Awd, 1981; Dir of Dist'd Ams; W/W Among Am HS Students; Intl Yth in Achmt; g/RN; Master's Deg in Psych.

PARAMORE, KENNETH DEAN oc/Student; b/Dec 1, 1960; h/102 Eagle Court, Greenville, NC 27834; p/Mrs Valerie J Paramore, Greenville, NC; ed/D H Conley HS, 1979; BS, Polit Sci, summa cum laude, E Carolina Univ, 1983; Att'g, Univ of NC Chapel Hill Sch of Law; cp/NC Polit Sci Assn, 1982; E Carolina Univ Law Soc, 1981; r/Free Will Bapt; hon/Phi Eta Sigma, 1980; Gamma Theta Upsilon, 1981; Pi Sigma Alpha, 1982; Phi Kappa Phi, 1982;

Selected Sr Hons Student by Phi Beta Kappa Alumni, 1983; NC Tuition S'ship, 1981-82; g/Lwyr.

PARHAM, FREDERICK MELVIN oc/Student; b/Sep 29, 1962; h/1210 Oakview Drive, Greenville, NC 27834; p/Mr and Mrs Frederick M Parham, Greenville, NC; ed/Grad, J H Rose HS, 1980; BS, Math and Computer Sci, Duke Univ, 1984; pa/Student Programmer, Duke Univ Computation Ctr, 1983; cp/HS Math Clb, 1977-80; Sci-Ecol Clb, 1977-79; Spanish Clb, 1977-78; Soc for Creat Anachronism, 1980-82; r/Greenville, NC, First Presb Ch Yth F'ship, 1977-80, Pres 1979; hon/Gov's Sch of NC, 1979; Inducted into Nat Hon Soc, 1979; Nat Merit S'ship, 1980-81; 1st Place in St Math Contest, 1980; NC Math Contest Awd (Duke S'ship); Inducted into Phi Beta Kappa, 1983; Julia Dale Prize for Excell in Math, Duke, 1983; g/PhD in Math; Career in Res or Tchg.

PARK, BLAKE STUART oc/Student; b/Feb 6, 1961; h/Dumbell Ranch, Alcova, WY 82620; p/Mr and Mrs Norman Park, Alcova, WY; ed/Natrona Co HS, 1979; Yale Univ, 1983; "Up with People" Cast E, 1979; cp/VChm, Residential Col Coun; Bd of Dirs, Yale Alumni Fund; Undergrad Schs Com; Yale Charities Dr; Yale Polit Union; Conserv Party Mem; Pres, Key Clb; Pres; Jr Civitan Clb; Polit Wkr, Rep Dick Cheney; hon/Gov-Appt'd Mem, WY Coun on Chd and Yth; Union Pacific WY Yth of the Yr; CARE Ldrship S'ship; W/W Among HS; Commun Ldrs of Am; g/JD; MBA; Law and Public Ser Career.

PARK, STEVEN HOWARD oc/Student; b/Aug 28, 1962; h/528 Northwest 15th Court, Boca Raton, FL 33432; p/Louis and Judy Park, Boca Raton, FL; ed/AA, Palm Bch Jr Col, 1982; Wkg towards BS, FL Atl Univ; cp/Phi Beta Lambda, PBJC, VP 1980-81; Pres, Student Govt, PBJC, 1981-82; Appt'd Student Rep for Admissions Appeals Com, PBJC, 1981-82; Appt'd Student Rep for Acad Appeals Com, PBJC, 1981-82; Student Senator, FL Atl Univ Student Govt, 1982; Appt'd Chm, Agencies and Progs Com, FL Atl Univ Student Govt, 1983; r/Jewish; hon/Participation Awd, PBJC, 1981-82; Dedicated Ser Awd, PBJC, 1981-82; Dedicated and Devoted Ser Awd to Student Govt, PBJC, 1981-82; FL Jr Col Student Govt Assn Ser Awd, 1982.

PARKER, DAVID ANDREW oc/Graduate Student; b/Jul 19, 1960; h/107 Thompson Street, McArthur, OH 45651; p/Carl and Louise Parker, McArthur, OH; ed/Vinton Co HS, 1978; BMus, magna cum laude, OH Univ, 1982; pa/Music Edrs Nat Conf; Percussive Arts Soc; Nat Assn of Jazz Edrs; cp/Jr and Sr Percussion Recitals; OH Univ Symph Orch; OH Univ Chamber Orch; Wind Ensemble; OH Univ Marching Band; Percussion Ensemble; Brass Choir; Jazz Ensemble; Concert Band; hon/Concerto II Contest Winner in Brass/Percussion Div; Phi Mu Alpha; Kappa Kappa Psi; Blue Key; Omicron Delta Kappa; Kappa Delta Pi; Hons Convocation; S'ships, 1979-; W/W Among Students in Am Cols and Univs; Nat Dean's List; Intl Yth in Achmt; Yg Commun Ldrs of Am; W/W in Music in Cols and Univs; g/To Receive a MMus; To Be a Percussionist (Marimba

Spec) in a Large Orch; To Get a Dr of Musical Arts Deg and Be a Col Prof.

PARKER, DONNA MARIE oc/Bookkeeper; b/Sep 10, 1961; h/616 F Street, Beckley, WV 25801; p/Mr and Mrs Fletcher J Parker, Beckley, WV; ed/Woodrow Wilson HS; Concord Col; pa/Bkkpr; cp/Delta Sigma Theta; Hon Soc; Marching Band; Concord Gospel Choir, Treas; Freshmen Orient Cnslr; Dorm Coun; UNICEF Vol; Am Cancer Soc Vol; Red Cross Vol; r/Ctl Bapt Ch; hon/Alpha Kappa Alpha Sorority S'ship; Beckley Citizen's S'ship; Yg Commun Ldrs of Am; Outstg Wom of Am; g/CPA; Pract in Beckley Area.

PARKER, DOUGLAS WILLIAM oc/Graduate Student; b/Jun 21, 1958; h/107 Thompson Street, McArthur, OH 45651; p/Carl and Louise Parker, McArthur, OH; ed/Vinton Co HS, 1976; BMus, summa cum laude 1980, MMus 1983, OH Univ; pa/Music Edrs Nat Conf; Tubists Universal Brotherhood Assn; Am Musicological Soc; MI Music Theory Soc; cp/OH Univ Symph Orch; Wind Ensemble; Brass Choir; Tuba Quartet; Brass Quintet; New Music Ensemble; Sr Recital; Grad Recital; Piano Accompanist, OH Univ Sch of Music; hon/Pi Kappa Lambda; Phi Mu Alpha; Kappa Kappa Psi; Omicron Delta Kappa; Phi Kappa Phi; Mortar Bd; Kappa Delta Pi; S'ships, 1976-79; Dean's List; Intl Yth in Achmt; W/W Among Students in Am Univs and Cols; Yg Commun Ldrs of Am; Nat Dean's List; W/W in Music in Cols and Univs; g/PhD; Col Prof of Music Theory.

PARKER, ELIZABETH ELLEN oc/Assistant Buyer; b/May 22, 1961; h/201 West Pine Street, Pine Level, NC 27568; p/Mr and Mrs B Benjamin Parker, Pine Level, NC; ed/Grad, N Johnston HS, 1979; BS, Bus Adm, Meredith Col, 1983; pa/Mgmt Devel Trainee, Branch Bk and Trust, 1983-84; Asst Buyer, Jo Mackie Inc, 1984-; cp/VP, Freshman Class, 1979; VP, Student Foun; Student Advr; Bus Clb; VP, CCA; Student Activs, Col; r/Pine Level Missionary Bapt Ch, Bus Adv Com; hon/Miss Johnston Co, 1984; Contestant in Miss NC Pageant, 1984; Miss Pine Level; Dist FFA Sweetheart, 1979; Dean's List; CoChm, Parents Weekend, Meredith Col; W/W Among Am HS Students; Intl Yth in Achmt; g/To Obtain an MBA from Univ of NC; To Open Own Bus; To Become Miss NC/Miss Am.

PARKER, GLADYS LaNELL oc/Student; b/Jul 4, 1965; h/1705 South Marshall, Midland, TX 79701; ba/Midland, TX; p/Robert and Gladys Parker, Midland, TX; ed/Grad, Midland Sr HS, 1983; pa/Cashier, Albertson; cp/Debutant, 1983; Treas, TAME Clb; r/Bapt; Active in Ch Activs; hon/Hon'd by Mrs Angevine for Being One of the Best Students at Midland Sr HS; g/To Attend Sch and Maj in Nsg.

PARKER, JACQUELYN SUSAN oc/T-38 Jet Pilot Instructor; b/Jul 4, 1960; h/PO Box 246, Boone, NC 28607; ba/Reece AFB, TX; p/Dr and Mrs W Dale Parker, Boone, NC; ed/Dipl, Colonial HS; AA, Univ of Ctl FL, 1977; BS in Computer Sci, Guilford Col, 1978; mil/USAF, 1st Lt; pa/Aerospace Scist Flight Controller, NASA, LBJ Space Ctr; Mem, Aerospace and Computer Sci Orgs; Charter Mem, Nat Space Inst; cp/Nat Hon Soc; Mensa Intl; hon/World's

739

Youngest Space Flight Controller (at Age 17); Cert of Merit in Ed, Cambridge, 1976; Golden Eagle Awd, Am Acad of Achmt, 1979; Kitty Hawk Awd, 1979; Mensa Register; Notable Ams of the Bicent Era; Personalities of S; Others; g/Astronaut.

PARKER, RUSSELL JAMES JR oc/Project Manager; b/Aug 14, 1955; h/1110 Fidler Lane 805, Silver Spring, MD 20910; ba/Silver Spring, MD; p/Mr and Mrs Russell J Parker Sr, Indianapolis, IN; ed/Brebeuf Prep Sch, 1973; BA, Dillard Univ, 1976; MBA, Atlanta Univ, 1980; pa/Proj Mgr, Prod Line Mgmt, C&P Telephone Co; Assn of MBA Execs; Am Mgmt Assn; cp/Beta Gamma Sigma; Psi Chi; Alpha Chi; Alpha Kappa Mu; Pres, Col Freshman Class; Dillard and Atlanta Univ Alumni Assns; VBS Tchr; r/U Meth; hon/Grad, summa cum laude, and 2nd Ranked Grad, Dillard Univ; Internship, Nationwide Mag Publishers Assn Winner; Top 5% of Grad'g Class, Atlanta Univ MBA Prog; Intl Yth in Review; Yg Commun Ldrs of Am; W/W in Am Cols and Univs; g/Excell in the Field of Mktg in Areas of Advtg and Promotion; Maintain a Well-Balanced Lifestyle.

PARKES, STANLEY MACK oc/Student; b/Jun 24, 1963; h/Route 2, Box 328, Louisville, MS 39339; ed/Grad, Noxapater HS, 1981; Att'g, E Ctl Jr Col; pa/Steel Wkr, Taylor Machine Wks, 1981-82; Sum Wk, Hamill Mfg Co, 1983; cp/Pres, Phi Theta Kappa Hon Soc; Pres, ROTC Cadet Assn; French Clb; Pres, Ch Yth Coun; VP, FFA; Beta Clb; Football; Track; r/Bapt; hon/Phi Theta Kappa; Dean's List; Football, All-Conf, 1979, 1980; Most Valuable Lineman, 1979, 1980; Track, St Class BB Pole Vault Champion, 1981; W/W Among Am Jr Col Students; Yth in Achmt; g/Deg in Geol; Comm'd Ofcr in AUS, Army Corp of Engrs Br.

PARKS, TRENT ALLEN oc/Student; b/Mar 12, 1963; h/837 North Maplewood Drive, Madison, SD 57042; p/Charles and Carolyn Parks, Madison, SD; ed/Lake Ctl HS, 1981; Student, Communs and Polit Sci, Univ of Las Vegas; cp/Legis Intern, SD Retailers Assn; Student Senate, Univ of Las Vegas; By-Laws Com, Radio Bd, Univ of Las Vegas; hon/Lttrman, Golf; Nat Forensics Leag Degs of Merit, Hon, Emerald; Intl Yth in Achmt; W/W Among Am HS Students; g/Bus Deg w Supermkgt Background; TV and Radio Wk.

PARNELL, JOYCE ANN oc/Insurance Clerk; b/Nov 16, 1962; h/State Route 1, Box 721, Andrews, TX 79714; ba/Andrews, TX; m/Rick; p/Mr and Mrs L E Gross, Andrews, TX; ed/Grad, Andrews HS, 1981; pa/Hairstylist, Lanita's Beauty Salon, 1981-83; Clk, Andrews Ins Agy, 1983-; cp/Nat Hon Soc, 1980-81; Cosmetology VICA, 1979-81, Treas; r/Nazarene; hon/Nat VICA TX Del, 1981; 1st Place, Iota Lambda Sigma Essay Contest, 1981; Acad Awd, 1978; Commun Ldrs of Am; g/To Further Ed in Bus and Get a Deg; To Wk in the Beauty Field.

PARROTT, TIMOTHY CHARLES oc/Self-Employed Translator; b/Jul 19, 1956; h/1128 Spruce Street, Iowa City, IA 52240; p/Charles F and Lois B Parrott, Iowa City, IA; ed/IA City HS, 1974; BA 1978, MA 1982, Univ of IA;

pa/Bkkpr, Parrott's Truck Painting Co Inc, 1975-; Res Asst, Univ of IA, 1979-82; Self-Employed Translator, 1979-; cp/Celtic Leag, Am Br; N Am Manx Assn; Yn Cheshaght Ghailckagh (Manx Gaelic Soc); Isle of Man Fam Hist Soc; PA German Soc; r/Cath; hon/Pub, "They Came from Bride," 1983; Nat Hon Soc; Scholastic Citation List, Univ of IA; Zertifikat Deutsch als Fremdsprache, Goethe-Institut; Commun Ldrs of Am; Intl Yth in Achmt; g/To Expand Present Translation Bus; To Continue Lng Addit Fgn Langs.

PARSON, AUBEDELLA oc/Student; b/Feb 8, 1963; h/4039 Ponca Street, memphis, TN 38109; p/Mrs Dorothy Parson, Memphis, TN; cp/Alpha Chi Scholastic Hon Soc, 1984; Alpha Kappa Alpha Sorority Inc, 1983-84; MARC Hon Student, 1983-84; Sr Class Senator; r/Bapt; g/Maj in Biol; Optom.

PARSONS, JOHN SCOTT oc/Student; b/Jun 19, 1962; h/PO Box 25, Beallsville, PA 15313; p/Ray W and Barbara J Parsons, Beallsville, PA; ed/Grad, Bethlehem-Ctr HS, 1980; BS, CA Univ of PA, 1984; cp/Explorers, 1978-80; HS Golf Team, 1978-79; Varsity Clb, 1979-80; JV Baseball, 1978-79; Math and Computer Sci Clb, 1981-, Pres 1981, 1983-84; Assn for Computing Machinery, 1981-; Secy-Treas of Student Chapt 1981, 1983-84; Ec Clb, 1983; Chi Gamma Psi, Math and Sci Hon, Histn 1983; r/Presb; hon/Salutatorian, HS Class, 1980; S'ship Awd, 1980; Lion's Clb Awd, 1980; Lion's Clb Boy of the Month, 1980; Most Intell of HS Class, 1980; Caddie S'ship, 1980; Am Legion Awd, 1977; Pres Scholar Awd, 1983; Soc of Dist'd Am HS Students; Intl Yth in Achmt; Yg Commun Ldrs of Am; W/W Among Am HS Students; g/Maj in Math and Computer Sci; Computer Programmer/Analyst.

PARSONS, KRISTINA DAWN oc/Student; b/Aug 19, 1963; h/129 South Florida Street, Buckhannon, WV 26201; p/Larry R and Carole J Parsons, Buckhannon, WV; ed/Buckhannon-Upshur HS; Att'g, WV Wesleyan Col; pa/Clk, Shop 'n' Save, 1980; Dr's Aid, Stephen M Smith MD, 1981-; Lib Wkr, WV Wesleyan Col, 1982-; cp/Choral Union; Hon Sect Ldr, Col Yrbook; Spec Activs Com; r/Meth; hon/Teenager of the Month, 1980; Teenager of the Yr, 1981; g/Maj in Public Relats; To Be Employed w a Hotel in the Public Relats Dept.

PASSARELLO, LAUREN CHRISTINE oc/Graduate; b/May 18, 1961; h/1720 Country Club Drive, Tullahoma, TN 37388; p/Col and Mrs Frank J Passarello, Tullahoma, TN; ed/HS Dipl, 1979; AA, Golden W Jr Col, 1981; BS in Home Ec, Dept of Child and Fam Studies, Univ of TN, 1983; pa/Res Asst in Proj for Autistic Chd, Univ of TN, 1982-83; cp/Phi Kappa Phi Hon Soc; Omicron Nu Hon Soc; Golden Key Hon Soc; r/Cath; hon/Highest Hons on Dean's List Every Quarter of Col, 1979-83; Most Outstg Jr in Col of Home Ec, 1982; Top Grad in Col of Home Ec; Voted Outstg Sr and Outstg Child and Fam Studies Student, 1983; g/Asst'ship to Continue Grad Wk.

PATE, ELIZABETH LORENE oc/Student; b/Dec 1, 1962; h/4644 Tara Drive, Nashville, TN 37215; p/Dr and Mrs A T Pate Jr, Nashville, TN; ed/Grad,

David Lipscomb HS, 1981; Att'g, David Lipscomb Col; cp/Civitan Clb; Chorus; Spanish Clb; Eng Translator for Fgn Refugees; Gamma Lambda; Heart Foun Vol; Commun Proj, Picnic; Musical Prodn; Am Psychol Assn, 1983-84; r/Ch of Christ; Bible Sch Tchr; hon/Spanish Awd; Beauty Contest Winner; Scholastic Ability and Ldrship S'ship; W/W Among Am HS Students; Intl Yth in Achmt; Commun Ldrs of Am; Personalities of S; Dist'd Ams; g/To Own Bus; To Be an Indep Businessperson.

PATE, TIMOTHY THOMAS oc/Music Teacher, Choral Director; b/Aug 29, 1960; h/Route 2, Box 218, Bell Buckle, TN 37020; ba/Unionville, TN; m/Joan M; p/Dr and Mrs A T Pate, Nashville, TN; ed/David Lipscomb HS, 1978; Grad, SEn Singing Sch, 1979; BS, Applied Voice/Music Ed, David Lipscomb Col, 1983; Currently Enrolled in Master's Prog, MTSU; pa/Song Dir, Neely's Berd Ch of Christ, 1978-82; Yth Min, Joywood Ch of Christ, 1982-; Tchr, Bedford Co Schs, 1983-; Songwriting Tchr, SEn Singing Sch, 1982-; Phi Mu Alpha, Chapt Pres 1980-81, 1981-82, Ofcr 1979-83; Music Edrs Nat Conf; NEA; cp/Civitans; David Lipscomb Col Chorale, 1978-83, Student Dir 1983; r/Ch of Christ; hon/HS TN All-St Chorus, 1976-77, 1977-78; TN Col All-St Chorus, 1981-82, 1982-83; David Lipscomb Col's Outstg Ser Awd, 1982; Dean's List, 1983; W/W Among Am HS Students.

PATERNO, C PETER oc/Student; b/Nov 2, 1962; h/5 Manor Road, Pawcatuck, CT 06379; p/Antonio and Lucia Paterno, Pawcatuck, CT; ed/Dipl, Stonington HS, 1980; BA, Ec, Eckerd Col, 1984; pa/Col Union Mgr 1983-84; Resident Advr 1981-82, 1983-84, Eckerd Col; Stone & Webster Engrg Corp Employee, 1982, 1983; Sales Rep, Grolier Interst Inc, 1981; Rec Dir, Town of Stonington, 1980; cp/Omicron Delta Kappa, 1982-; VP 1983-84, Eckerd Col Circle of ODK; Soc of Adv'd Mgmt, 1980-83, Co-Pres 1982-83; Org of World Concerns at Eckerd Col, 1981-82; r/Cath; hon/Invited by Fac to Do a Sr Thesis Proj in Ed, 1983-84; Boys' St Participant, 1978-79; Eckerd Col Hons S'ship, 1980-84; Eckerd Col Alumni Scholar, 1982-84; Dean's List, 1982-83; Selected to Participate in Eckerd's London Abroad Prog, 1982; Selected to Participate in 1983 Christian Faith and Ec Values Symp; Nat Dean's List; W/W Among Am HS Students; g/MBA or Master's in Fin/Ec; Career in Fin, Investmts or Bkg.

PATRIZI, LARRY ANTHONY oc/Student; b/Jun 11, 1959; h/250 Elmore Avenue, Trenton, NJ 08619; p/John and Dorothy Patrizi Sr, Trenton, NJ; ed/HS, 1977; cp/Editor, Sch Newspaper; YMCA Steering Com of Yth Adv Bd; Co Tennis Team; Racquetball Clb; Arabian Horse Registry of Am; Ch Yth Org; Am Heart Assn, Am Cancer Soc, Deborah Hosp Donator; hon/Hon by Local Bus; Hon For Tennis Abilities in Competition; Dean's List; g/Master's Deg Ldg to Mgmt Position w Multinational Firm.

PATTERSON, ELWYN KENNETH oc/Cash Management Officer; b/Nov 24, 1956; h/2571 South Candler Road, C-16, Decatur, GA 30032; p/E K and Juanita Patterson, Grambling, LA; ed/Grad, Grambling Col Lab HS, 1974; BS,

So IL Univ, 1977; MBA, Atlanta Univ Grad Sch of Bus Adm, 1980; pa/Cash Mgmt Ofcr, First Atlanta Corp; cp/US JCs Secy-Treas; Big Brothers, Atlanta Magnet Sch Prog; Placement Com; Toastmaster's Intl; hon/Valedictorian, 1974; Student Coun Pres, 1974; Beta Gamma Sigma; Intl Yth in Achmt; Outstg Yg Man of Am; W/W Among Students in Am Cols and Univs; Commun Ldrs of Am.

PATTON, EVELYN ROSE oc/Student; ba/Nov 2, 1962; h/Route 1, Box 279B, Winchester, TN 37398; p/Mr and Mrs Mark A Patton, Winchester, TN; ed/Franklin Co HS, 1981; Att'g, Mid TN St Univ; pa/Dietary Employee, Nat Hlth Corp, 1983; cp/Gamma Beta Phi, 1982-84; Alpha Delta Pi, 1981-84, Histn, Sophomore Mem at Large; Tau Omicron, 1983-84; Kappa Omicron Phi, 1982-84; Student Home Ec Assn, 1982-84; Jr Mem, Am Dietetic Assn, 1984; r/Bapt; hon/W/W Among Am Univs and Cols; Outstg Yg Wom of Am; Nat Dean's List; g/Maj in Foods and Nutrition; Complete Dietetic Internship; Wk as Reg'd Dietitian after Completing Registry Exam.

PAUL, ERIC GEORGE oc/Student; b/Sep 29, 1958; h/93 Hemlock Drive, West Seneca, NY 14224; p/George J and Helen M Paul, West Seneca, NY; ed/Orchard Pk Ctl HS, 1976; BA, St Univ of NY Albany, 1980; JD, Col of Law, OH No Univ, 1984; pa/Legis Aide, NY St Assem, Sessions 1977-80, Sums 1979-82; cp/Circle K Intl, Intl VP 1979-80, NY Gov 1978-79, NY Secy 1977-78, NY Adm Asst 1976-77; ONU Moot Ct, Presiding Judge 1983-84; Vol Fireman, W Seneca Fire Dist #3; r/Rom Cath; hon/2nd Place, ONU Anthony J Celebrezze Moot Ct Competition, 1983; Winning Team mem, ONU Moot Ct First Yr Competition, 1982; Outstg Yg Men of Am; W/W Am Law Students; W/W HS Students; g/Pract in Buffalo, NY, Area.

PAULUS, MICHAEL JOHN oc/Economist; h/312 West 98th Street, #GB, New York, NY; ba/New York, NY; p/Mr and Mrs John P Paulus, Port Washington, WI; ed/St Lawrence Sem, 1975; BA, Univ of WI, 1980; Master of Intl Affairs, Columbia Univ, 1982; pa/Economist, Fed Resv Bk of NY, 1982-; cp/Student Coun; Sr Class Pres; Varsity Football; Hon Mention All-Conf Defensive End; Sandburg Halls Adm Coun; Phi Sigma Alpha Asst Secy; Phi Alpha Theta; Mortar Bd; Nat Col Register; Lectr, Neuman Ctr; Intern w Congressman Michael J Harrington; r/Rom Cath; hon/Phi Beta Kappa; Phi Kappa Phi; Intl Fellow, Columbia Univ; Commun Ldrs of Am; Soc of Outstg Am HS Students.

PAWLAK, ROBERTA PAGE oc/Registered Professional Nurse; b/Jun 16, 1959; h/173 Commonwealth Avenue, Buffalo, NY 14216; ba/Buffalo, NY; m/Richard Edwin; p/Robert and Louise Page, Cassadaga, NY; ed/BSN, D'Youville Col, 1981; pa/Asst Hd Nurse, ICN, and Inser Edr, Chd's Hosp of Buffalo, 1983-84; Staff RN, Chd's Hosp of Buffalo, 1981-83; Sigma Theta Tau; Kappa Gamma Pi; cp/D'Youville Col Alumni Assn; r/Rom Cath; hon/W/W Among Students in Am Univs and Cols; Intl Yth in Achmt; g/MSN; MS, Nsg Adm.

PAWLUS, CHERRIE LYNN oc/Student; b/May 11, 1966; h/Route 1, Box 619, Scarbro, WV 25917; p/Mr and Mrs John Pawlus Jr, Scarbro, WV; ed/Grad, Oak Hill HS, 1984; cp/Pep Clb, Drama Clb, 1980-81; French Clb, 1981-82; Know Your Co Govt, 1982-83; Nat Hon Soc, 1982-84; Oak Hill HS Tennis Team, 1980-84; Feature Editor of OHHS Newspaper, 1982-83; r/Rom Cath; hon/Placed on Acad Hon Roll, 1980-83; Named to Nat Hon Soc, 1982-84; Lettered in Tennis, 1981-82; W/W Among Am HS Students; g/To Attend Either WVIT or WVU; To Study Med.

PAYNE, BRENDA B oc/Student, Pharmacy Technician; b/Jun 4, 1963; h/1921 Wadsworth Way, Baltimore, MD 21239; ba/Timonium, MD; p/Mr and Mrs Clarence R Payne, Baltimore, MD; ed/Dipl, Mercy HS, 1981; AA, Essex Commun Col, 1983; pa/Pharm Tech, Howard & Morris Pharm, 1983-; cp/Softball, 1972-81; Bowling, 1982-83; Intl Order of Job's Daughs, 1977-83, Hon'd Queen 1983; hon/Flame Awd, Jr and Sr Yrs of HS; Nat Hon Soc; Nat Hon Soc Sers Awd; Assoc'd Student Cong of Balto City Student Coun and Sch Ser Awds; Am Legion Awd; Student Coun Awd, HS; W/W Among Am HS Students; Yg Commun Ldrship; g/To Marry and Have a Fam.

PAYNE, JOHN FREDERICK oc/Student; b/Aug 7, 1966; h/Route 1, 30 Chinquapin Road, Travelers Rest, SC 29690; p/G Frederick and Kay M Payne, Tigerville, SC; ed/Blue Ridge HS, 1984; cp/Pres, Sr Class; Secy, Student Govt; Varsity Football; Varsity Baseball; Palmetto Boys' St; Furman Scholar; Erskine Scholar; Conserv Wkshop S'ship; Councilman, Greer Student in Govt Day; Pres, French Clb; Tiger Tales Newspaper Sports and Layout Editor; Greenville Co Yth Commr, Soil Conserv Dist; Beta Clb, Treas; Band; Acad Team; r/Bapt; hon/Biol Awd; Marshall; Salutatorian; Kennedy S'ship Finalist; Army ROTC S'ship Finalist; Sr Hall of Fame; g/Maj in Biol; Phys.

PAYNE, LISA LYNNE oc/Student; b/Dec 18, 1961; h/Route 6, Box 986, Beaumont, TX 77705; p/James L and Patricia G Payne, Beaumont, TX; ed/Grad, Evang Christian Sch, 1980; Baylor Univ; cp/Editor, Baylor Yrbook, 1983-84; Reporter, Alpha Delta Pi; Sigma Delta Chi; Student Govt; Intramurals; hon/Hyde Foun S'ship; W/W Among Am HS Students; Intl Yth in Achmt; Commun Ldrs of Am; Personalities of S; g/BA in Jour, Mktg Mgmt; To Wk in Advtg or w Yrbook Publishers.

PAYNE, MARGARET JEAN oc/Student; b/Oct 2, 1961; h/3226 East College, Jackson, LA 70748; p/Mr and Mrs Donald R Payne, Jackson, LA; ed/Silliman Inst, 1979; AA, SW MS Jr Col; Att'd, LA St Univ; Att'g, Univ of So MS; cp/Marching and Concert Band, Flute, Majorette; NHS; Commerce Clb, VP; St Hon Band; Beta Clb; BSU; r/1st Bapt Ch; hon/Grad w Hons, HS; Feliciana Farm Bur Queen and Talent Winner, 1981; Intl Yth in Achmt; W/W Music; W/W Among Am HS Students; Commun Ldrs of Am; g/BSN.

PAYNE, PATRICIA ALICE oc/Student; b/Jul 5, 1960; h/3226 East College, Jackson, LA 70748; p/Mr and Mrs Donald R Payne, Jackson, LA; ed/Silliman Inst, 1978; AA, SW MS Jr Col, 1980; Att'd, LA St Univ; BA, MS St

Univ, 1983; cp/HS Marching and Concert Band, Flute; St Hon Band; SW MS Jr Col and LA St Univ Marching Band, Flute; Ofcr in Social Wk Org; BSU; r/1st Bapt Ch; hon/Band Sweetheart; John Philip Sousa Awd; Intl Yth in Achmt; W/W Among Am HS Students; Commun Ldrs of Am; g/Master's Deg in Social Wk.

PEAKE, JANINE HILARY oc/Commercial Banking Officer; b/Nov 5, 1958; h/273 West 10th Street, #IRE, New York, NY 10014; ba/New York, NY; p/Merwin Wallace and Muriel May Peake, McLean, VA; ed/BA, Mary Wash Col, 1980; Oxford Univ External Sum Grad Sch, Univ Col, 1979; Master's Deg, Baylor Univ, 1981; pa/Comml Bkg Ofcr, Marine Midland Bk, 1983-; Loan Ofcr Trainee, Irving Trust Bk; Dir of Fin and Strategic Planning, Sunlight Corp, 1981-82; Res Asst, Baylor Univ Dept of Polit Sci, 1980-81; Res Asst, Irene and Ken Kohl, Authors, 1980; Legal Investigator, DC Public Defender Ser, Felony Div, 1978; Fin Mgmt Assn; Assn of MBA Execs; cp/Manhatten Grp; Big Sister for Disadvantaged Yth, 1977-80; Omicron Delta Epsilon, 1978-81; Chapt Fdr, Lt Gov, Pres, Circle K Clb, 1976-80; Editor, Circle K Tri-St Mag, 1979-80; No VA Spec Olympics Chmn, 1982; Co-Fdr, Wom's Crew Clb, 1978-80; Free-Lance Artist, *Bullet*, 1976-80; Secy, Pres, Inter-Clb Coun, 1978-80; VP, Intl Relats Clb, 1976-80; r/Epis; hon/Author of Num Pubs; Outstg Lt Gov, Cirlce K, 1979; Outstg Intl Editor, 1980; Omicron Delta Epsilon, 1981; Fin Mgmt Assn Hon Soc, 1981; Framar Hons House, 1979-80; Register of Outstg Col Srs, 1980; Circle K Gov's Awd for Outstg Yth Achmt, 1980; g/PhD in Polit Ec; IMF or Similar Org; Tng in Irving Trust's Intl Dept, European Opers Div.

PEAL, WILLA ANN oc/Student; b/Aug 25, 1963; h/Route 2, Box 344-A, Princeton, NC 27569; p/Mr and Mrs William R Peal, Princeton, NC; ed/Grad, Princeton HS, 1981; Att'g, Atl Christian Col; cp/Jr Ldr, 4-H; Senator, Student Govt Assn; r/Princeton Missionary Bapt Ch; hon/Nat 4-H Hon Soc Induction, 1983; Nat Jr Hort Assn Envir Beautification Winner, 1982; Music Student of Yr; 4-H'er of Yr, 2 Yrs; J B Coates Citizenship Awd; I Dare You Awd; Intl Yth in Achmt; Personalities of S; g/Maj in Rel/Psych; Rel Ed Dir.

PEARCE, AMBER LEIGH oc/Student, Salesclerk; b/Dec 14, 1963; h/19 Hillsboro Road, Clarksville, TN 37042; ba/Murfreesboro, TN; ed/NW HS, 1982; Att'g, Mid TN St Univ; cp/MTSU Assoc'd Student Body; Justice of Supr Ct, MTSU; TN Intercol St Legis Del; VP of Sophomore Class; NOW; Wom's Polit Caucus; r/Prot; hon/Most Dedicated, 1982; Most Likely to Succeed, 1982; W/W Among Am HS Students; g/Eng Maj/Pre-Law Student; To Attend Vanderbilt Law Sch and Become a Lwyr.

PEARL, GREGORY oc/Student; b/Mar 27, 1965; h/28 Two Johns Road, Preston, MD 21655; p/David and Joy Pearl, Preston, MD; ed/HS Grad; mil/NG, 1984-; pa/Laborer, Contractor, Keith Hildebrand, 1983; cp/Christian Ser Brigade Bat #6401, Bat Sgt; r/New Covenant Ch En Shore, Home Grp Ldr; hon/Nom'd Extraordinary Christian Sch Student, 1983; Bat #6401 Outstg Perf 1981; Dist'd Ldrship Perf 1983; g/

To Become a Part of the Full-time Ch Staff; To Become an Ofcr in the NG.

PEARSALL, ROXANE oc/Student; h/ East Southerland Street, Wallace, NC 28466; ed/HS Student; cp/4-H, Local Pres 1981, Local Reporter 1982, Co Reporter 1981-82, Co and Dist Rep 1981, 1982, 1983; Beta Clb; Math Clb; Student Coun; Hons Eng; Nat Piano Guild; Marching and Concert Band; Softball; Former Cheerldr; Stat, Basketball; Monogram Clb; r/Bapt; hon/ Superior Ratings in Nat Piano Guild, 1978-82; Nom, Sch of Sciand Math, NC; All-Co Band Mem, 1981-83; g/To Be Able to Solve Any Math Prob I am Given, or at Least Be Able to Give a Reason Why It Cannot Be Done; To Take as Many Courses in Algebra and Physics as Possible; To Become a Profl Public Spkr; To Become an Elect Engr w a PhD.

PEARSON, ROBERT RAY oc/Student; b/Dec 10, 1965; h/804 South Natchez Street, Kosciusko, MS 39090; p/Karen B Pearson, Kosciusko, MS; ed/ Student Kosciusko HS; cp/Math and Sci Clb, 1981-82; Beta Clb, 1982-83; Kosciusko HS Band, 1981, 1982, 1983; r/ First Bapt Ch Yth Choir, Handbell Choir; hon/World Hist Awd, KHS, 1981-82; Outstg Achmt Finalist in Our Am Heritage Hist Contest, MS St Univ; g/To Maj in Med at Univ of MS.

PECK, ANNA LAURA oc/Student; b/ Apr 28, 1965; h/Saint Andrews, TN 37372; p/Howard and Mary Preston Peck, Saint Andrews, TN; ed/HS Student; pa/Regency Hlth Care Ctr, 1983; cp/Vol, Emerald Hodgson Hosp, 1982; Wom's Sports Foun for Excell in Volleyball, 1983; Mid TN St Chorus, 1982-83; Dedication Com for Fdg of St Andrews-Sewanee Sch, 1982; Hon Roll, 1979-81; Dean's List, 1981-83; St Andrews-Sewanee Chorus Soloist, Wom's Mgr, Soprano Sect Ldr, 1981-83; Varsity Clb, 1983; Ath Com, 1982; Pres Phy Fitness Org, 1977-78; r/Meth; Dir of Music, UBS at Morton Meml U Meth Ch, 1981-83; hon/Allius Reid Scholar, 1979-81; Hon Student, 1979-83; Recip, Awds when Competing in AAU Jr Olympics, 1977; Latin Hons, 1980; Music Hons, Mid TN St Chorus for Vocal Excell, 1982, 1983; Named as 2-Yr MVP and Capt, Named to All-Dist Volleyball Team, Named as Mem in Wom's Sports Foun, 1982-83; Awd'd Medal for Being a Competent Yet Reasonable Wk Mgr; To Attend the Univ of the S Where I Can Expand My Musical Talent by Being in the Univ Chorus; To Wk toward a Career in Med; To Become the SE's Fifth Pediatric Neurological Surg.

PECK, MICHAEL STEVEN oc/Graduate Student in Nuclear Engineering; b/ Sep 30, 1956; h/Box 71, Crestvale Trail Court, Columbia, MO 65201; ba/Columbia, MO; m/Deborah Anne; c/Sarah Jean, Jessica Michael; p/Frank V Peck, Foristell, MO; ed/HS Grad, 1974; BS, Chem Engrg 1982, MS, Nuclear Engrg 1983, UMC; mil/Army, 1974-79; pa/Proj Engr, MO Mirror Engrg Fusion Proj, UMC, 1981-; Am Nuclear Soc, 1982; AICE, 1980; cp/Nat Rifle Assn, Life Mem; Noncomm'd Ofcrs Assn, 1976-79; hon/Author, Var Pubs; g/ Nuclear Power Prodn and Fusion Res.

PEELER, DAVID RANDOLPH oc/ Student; b/Dec 21, 1964; h/5832 Rose Valley Drive, Charlotte, NC 28210; p/ Donald Ray and Catherine Steagall Peeler, Charlotte, NC; ed/Grad, Olympic HS, 1983; Student, Duke Univ; cp/ Pres, Nat Hon Soc, 1982-83; Intl Pres, Jr Civitan, 1982-83; Dist Dpty Gov, Jr Civitan, 1981-82; Cross Country, 1981, 1982; Wrestling, 1981; Sophomore Exec Coun, 1980-81; Student Coun, 1981-82; Marching Band and Wind Ensemble, 1980-81; Boy Scouts, Troop Ldship Corps 1980, 1981, 1982, Sr Patrol Ldr 1980; Pres, Exec Coun, 1979-80; Pres, Jr Nat Hon Soc, 1979-80; French Clb, 1981-83; r/Epis; hon/Furman Scholar, 1982; Sledge Civitan Awd, 1983; T J Norman S'ship, 1983; W N Reynold's S'ship, 1983; Civitan Foun S'ship, 1983; Nat Merit Finalist; Eagle Scout Awd, 1983; God and Country Awd, 1981; DAR Citizenship Awd, 1980; NC Dist W Hon Key; Jr Civitan Intl Hon Key; Rotary Yth Merit Awd; Morehead S'ship Nom; W/W Am HS Students; Am's Outstg Names and Faces; g/ Double Maj in Ec and Polit Sci; Law Sch.

PELLETIER, HELEN E oc/Editor; b/ Jan 10, 1959; h/27 Federal Street, Apartment 5, Brunswick, ME 04011; ba/ Brunswick, ME; p/Mr and Mrs Robert G Pelletier, Sanford, ME; ed/Sanford HS, 1977; AB, cum laude, Bowdoin Col, 1981; pa/Editor, *Bowdoin Alumni Magazine*, Bowdoin Col, 1983-; Assoc Editor, *Bowdoin Alumnus*, Bowdoin Col, 1982-83; Writing Instr, Upward Bound, Bowdoin Col, 1982; Alumni Ofc Fellow, Bowdoin Col, 1981-82; Tchg Asst, The Sum Session, Phillips Andover, 1981; Bowdoin Col Alumni Coun, 1983-; cp/Track and Field Ofcl, 1981-.

PEMBERTON, TAMMY JO oc/Student; b/Jun 23, 1963; h/Route 2, Box 394A, LaFollette, TN 37766; ba/Cookeville, TN; p/Betty L Pemberton, LaFollette, TN; ed/Grad, Campbell Co HS, 1981; Att'g, TN Technological Univ; pa/Lab Asst, Chem Lab, TTU; cp/ 4-H Alumni; Bapt Student Union, F'ship Com; En Star; Chem-Med Clb; r/Bapt; hon/Vol-St; All-Star; 4-H Ldrship and Achmt; Intl Yth in Achmt; Yg Personalities of S; g/Pharm Deg.

PENA, ANTHONY LEE oc/Counselor, Student; b/Nov 20, 1953; h/4700 Humber Drive, B-1, Nashville, TN 37211; ba/Nashville, TN; p/Marjorie Pena, Clovis, NM; ed/Clovis HS, 1971; BS, En NM Univ, 1979; Grad Psych Studies, Mid TN St Univ; cp/Psi Chi; Nat Knife Collectors Assn; Drama Clb; Wesley Foun; Psych Clb; Student Action Assn; Yg Dems; ASB Ho of Reps; r/U Meth; hon/Nat Yth Min Org of UMC; Excell in Perf, Drama Theatre Dept; Commun Ldrs of Am; g/ Managerial-Adm Position in a Non-Profit Org.

PENNINGTON, ROBIN AMIE oc/ Student; b/Oct 31, 1964; h/211 North Avenue, #8, Athens, GA 30601; ba/ Athens, GA; p/John and Vicki Pennington, Gaffney, SC; ed/Gaffney Sr High, 1981; Student, Univ of GA, 1981-; cp/ UGA Wind Ensemble; Athens Symph; hon/SC Gov's Sch, 1981; All-St Band, 1981; All-St Hons Chorus, 1980, 1981; Dean's List, 1981-82; Hons Prog; Jr Cert; W/W Among Am HS Students; g/BS in Math, Music Minor; To Wk w Computers in a Math Orientation.

PEOPLES, JOHNNY RICHARD oc/ Student; b/Jan 21, 1969; h/32 Mar-Ree Drive, Laurel, MS 39440; p/Mr and Mrs William C Peoples, Laurel, MS; ed/ Student, R H Watkins HS; cp/Football; Tennis Team; Key Clb; r/Bapt; hon/US Achmt Acad Awd, 1984.

PEPPER, BRYAN WILLIAM oc/Student; b/Dec 18, 1962; h/PO Box 102, Selbyville, DE 19975; p/Mr and Mrs William C Pepper, Selbyville, DE; ed/ Indian River HS, 1981; Att'g, WV Wesleyan Col (Acctg Maj); pa/Asst Supvr of Stores, Pep-Up Dairy and Delis, 1982-; Owner, Pepper Brothers Distributors Inc, Cigarette Distributors; cp/Freshman Class Rep to Commun Coun, 1981-82, Sophomore Rep 1982-83; VP, Commun Coun, 1983-84; Theta Xi Frat, 1982-; Rep to Interfrat Coun, 1983; Student Mem, Acad Coun Bd of Trustees, 1983-84; Chm, Homecoming Parade, 1982; Dir of Fund Raising and Sr Class Overnight Trip to NYC; r/Meth; hon/Winner, I Dare You Awd; g/To Continue in the Cigarette Co.

PERCER, LEO RAINES oc/Student; b/Feb 14, 1960; h/4652 Doris Circle, Millington, TN 38053; p/Bobbie Sr and Donna F Percer, Millington, TN; ed/ Millington Ctl HS, 1978; BA, Union Univ, 1982; pa/Min of Yth, Hickory Ridge Bapt Ch, 1981-82; cp/Student Govt Assn, Senator 1980-81; Capt, HS Football Team, 1977-78; Nat Hon Soc, VP 1977-78; Physics Clb, VP 1977-78; Beta Clb, 1977-78; Key Clb, Treas 1977-78; Football, 1975-78; Wrestling, 1975-76, Track, 1975-78; Math Clb, 1975-78; M-Clb, 1975-78; Quiz 'em on the Air Team, 1977-78; Ministerial Assn, 1980-82; hon/Optimist Clb Achmt Awd, 1975-77; Most Likely to Succeed, 1978; Pres Preaching S'ship to So Sem, 1982; Am Bible Soc Awd for Biblical Studies, 1982; Acad Achmt Awds in Rel and Greek, 1982; Pi Gamma Mu Awd, 1982; Acad S'ship to Union Univ, 1979; Dean's List, 1979-82; Grad, magna cum laude, Union Univ, 1982; Hall of Fame, Union Univ, 1982; Commun Ldrs of Am; W/W Am Cols and Univs; W/W Am HS; g/Sem Study in Theol; Wk on Mission Field or as a Pastor.

PEREZ-VAZQUEZ, VERONICA oc/ Employee Relations Clerk; b/Aug 27, 1961; h/WC 57, Box 94, FBPO Norfolk, VA 23593; ba/Norfolk, VA; p/Nemesio and Emma Esther Perez, Norfolk, VA; ed/Wm T Sampson HS, 1979; Univ of NC Charlotte, 1983; pa/Employee Relats Clk, Civil Ser, 1983-; Gen Psych Lab Proctor, 1982-83; Clinician Asst, 1982; Student Intern for Mentally Retarded Adults Prog, 1982; Acctg Clk, 1981; cp/Govtl Wkshop Chp, Pres Classroom Chp, 1978-79; Sr Class Play, Walkathon, Powder Puff Football Game, 1978-79; Nat Hon Soc, Yrbook Staff, 1977-79; Girls' Ath Assn, Student Coun Rep, 1976-77; r/Rom Cath; hon/ Grad, cum laude, 1983; HS Nat Hon Soc, 1977-79; HS Salutatorian Grad, 1979; g/PhD in Psychopharmacology; Psychopharmacologist.

PERLMAN, SCOTT DAVID oc/Law Student; b/Mar 1, 1958; h/3062 Rosemont Drive, Sacramento, CA 95826; p/ Sanford Perlman, Los Angeles, CA; ed/ BA, Sonoma St Univ, 1981; McGeorge Sch of Law; cp/Assoc Students VP, Chm of Corp Bd of Dirs, 1981; CA St Student Assn Assoc Student Rep, 1980-81;

742

Assoc Students, Assem CoChm, 1980-81; Anti-Tuition Campaign, 1981; Nat Ed Moratorium Coor, 1981; Chartered Students Org Alliance Bd Mem, 1980-81; Sr Activs Coun, Coor 1980; Instructionally Related Activs Bd, VChm 1980; Assoc Students Fiscal Coor, 1979-80; Acad Senate, Student Rep, 1979-80; hon/Outstg Latin Student, 1975; Bk of Am Awd for Outstg Acad Achmt, 1976; NHS, 1976; W/W Among Students in Am Univs and Cols; Intl Yth in Achmt; Commun Ldrs of Am; g/Career in Polit via Law.

PERMENTER, GARY LAMAR oc/Student; b/Jan 11, 1965; h/1021 Hibbler Street, West Point, MS 39773; p/Mr and Mrs Donald Permenter, West Point, MS; ed/Grad, W Pt HS, 1983; Att'g, MS St Univ; pa/Pt-time Announcer, WROB-WKBB Radio Stas; cp/Nat Hon Soc; Pres, Mu Alpha Theta; Pres, Yth Choir; Sr Rep, Band Coun; Editor, HS Newspaper; r/So Bapt; hon/Valedictorian, 1983; MEC STAR Student; WPHS Hall of Fame; C of C Awd; Kathy Bryan Awd; Wal Mart S'ship Winner; Outstg Musician Awd; Gov's Scholar; g/Pre-Ministerial Maj; Pastor of So Bapt Ch.

PERRINE, ROBERT MATHEWS oc/Student; b/Dec 25, 1965; h/1302 6th Avenue, Jasper, AL 35501; p/Kenneth and Lynn Perrine, Jasper, AL; ed/Student, Walker HS; cp/Key Clb, Gov 1982-83; Secy 1981-82; Eagle Scout, 1983; Student Coun Delegation; Order of the Arrow; hon/Jr Nat Hon Soc, 1981-82; Nat Hon Soc, 1982-83; Beta Clb, 1982-83; Key Clb Dist'd Secy, 1981-82; Gov's Awd, Key Clb, 1981-82; g/To Attend Duke Univ and Study Law.

PERROTTA, LORI oc/Student; b/May 24, 1958; h/365 Bronx River Road, Yonkers, NY 10704; p/Mr and Mrs C Perrotta, Yonkers, NY; ed/Grad w Regents Dipl, St Barnabas HS; Grad w a Cert in the Exec Secretarial Prog, Berkley Bus Sch; Att'g, Mercy Col; cp/Advr, Soc for the Advmt of Mgmt; g/Mgmt/Mktg Maj; Wk in the Field of Advtg.

PERRY, RONALD BRYAN oc/Student; b/Oct 29, 1963; h/2626 Prairie Dunes Place, Ontario, CA 91761; ba/USAF Academy, CO; p/Mr and Mrs Ronald W Perry, Ontario, CA; Grad, Am Christian HS; Wkg on BS in Engrg Mechs, USAF Acad; mil/USAF Acad Cadet, 1982-84; pa/USAF Cadet, 1981-; cp/Student Body Pres, 1981; Basketball, 1978-80; Football, 1979-81; r/Prot; hon/Hon Roll; Grad, summa cum laude; Perfect GPA; Grad'd 1st in Class; Valedictorian, 1981; Eng Awd, 1978-81; Biol and Geometry Awd, 1979; Chem and Bible Awd, 1980; Am Govt, 1981; Bible, 1981; USAF Acad Dean's Hon List, 1982; Soc of Dist'd Am HS Students; W/W Among Am HS Students; DIB; Am Biogl Inst; g/BS, MA in Engrg Mechs, BS in Ed; Devel Engr.

PERRY, TIMOTHY PHILLIP oc/Finance Director; b/Apr 28, 1953; h/4312 Dehaven Drive, Chantilly, VA 22021; ba/Alexandria, VA; m/Marilyn N; p/B Ray and Grisilda Perry, Covington, VA; ed/Covington HS, 1971; BA, Wash and Lee Univ, 1975; MS, The Am Univ, 1984; mil/1975-80; pa/Fin Dir, Alexandria Re-Development and Housing Auth, 1980-; Financial Mgmt Assn; hon/Commerce Frat, 1974; Financial

Mgmt Assn Hon Soc, 1984; g/Position in Investmt Bkg.

PERSON, BRIAN DOUGLAS NIGHTINGALE oc/Assistant Pastor; b/Mar 24, 1957; h/4117 Stevenson Boulevard, #229, Fremont, CA 94538; m/Judy; p/Mary H Person, Santa Cruz, CA; ed/Santa Cruz HS, 1975; BA, Univ of CA Davis, 1979; MDiv w Concentration in Marriage and Fam Ministries, Fuller Theol Sem, 1983; pa/Ordained and Installed in Presb Ch, USA, 1983; Asst Pastor, Irvington Presb Ch; Christian Assn of Psychol Studies; Am Assn for Marriage and Fam Therapy; Evangelicals for Social Action; cp/Vol Week Long Camp Cnslr; Ticket Salesman, MS, March of Dimes Activs; Marcing Band; Football; Water Polo; Swimming; Soccer; Stage Band; Sr Class Pres; Fuller's Faith Renewal Team; Pledge Advr; hon/Theta Xi Outstg Grad Sr; Eagle Scout; Sportsmanship Awd; Boys' St Rep; Soroptimist Runner-Up; g/Wk w Yth and Fam in Presb Ch; Wk w Wife in Cnslg.

PESSAH, RUTH SUSAN oc/Administrative Assistant; b/Sep 5, 1960; h/2 Fairlane Drive, Shelton, CT 06484; p/Henry and Harriet Pessah, Shelton, CT; ed/Shelton HS, 1978; BA, Univ of Rochester, 1981; pa/Asst, Adm Ofc of Univ of Rochester; cp/Psychol Undergrad Coun; Marching and Concert Bands; Nat Hon Soc; Vol, Nsg Homes; hon/Univ of Rochester Alumni Reg S'ship; Cand for Rhodes, Fulbright, Luce, Marshall S'ships; Dean's List; CT St Scholar; Intl Yth in Achmt; Nat Dean's List; W/W Among Students in Am Cols and Univs; g/PhD in Clin Psych; Own Pract.

PETERSEN, ANNETTE JUANITA oc/Student; b/Aug 28, 1962; h/6-456 SR18 R1, Hamler, OH 43524; p/Mr and Mrs Alfred Petersen, Hamler, OH; ed/Patrick Henry HS, 1980; Bowling Green St Univ; pa/Internship, Buckingham, Knueven & Assocs, 1982; cp/Acctg Clb; 4-H Clb; Band; Orch; Choir; Pep Band; Swing Choir; Yrbook Editor and Bus Mgr; Farm Bur Yth; Local and Co 4-H Clbs Secy, Jr Ldr; READY Power Ldrs; Camp Cnslr; Dairy Judging Team; Shopping Bag Team; Jr Ldr Exch; Nat Luther Leag Gathering Del; 4-H Royal Ct; OH 4-H Cong Del; 4-H Clb Advr; BGSU Acctg Clb; BGSU 4-H Clb, Treas 1982-83, Histn 1981-82; r/Luth; Ch Choir; Sunday Sch Tchr; hon/Nat 4-H Dairy Conf Del, 1980; Mortar Bd, 1983; Beta Gamma Sigma, 1983; Beta Alpha Psi, 1982, Mbrship Dir 1983-84; Peat, Marwick, Mitchell & Co S'ship, 1983; Yg Commun Ldrs of Am; Intl Yth in Achmt; g/CPA.

PETERSEN, DENISE G oc/Office Manager; b/Dec 10, 1954; h/1936 Raulston, Poplar Bluff, MO 63901; ba/Poplar Bluff, MO; m/Glenn E Sr; c/Glenn E Jr; p/Mr and Mrs Sam Giambelluca, Poplar Bluff, MO; ed/Grad, Poplar Bluff Sr High, 1973; AA, Three Rivers Commun Col, 1975; BS, Murray St Univ, 1977; pa/Supvr, Capt D's, 1977; Asst Mgr, Sam's Shoes, 1977-82; Ofc Mgr, Poplar Bluff C of C, 1982-; cp/Xi Delta Xi Sorority, Treas 1981-83; March of Dimes, VP of the Bd 1982-83; Am Cancer Soc, Daffodil Chm 1983; Bluff Supper Clb, Treas 1981-83; WIBC, VP of Plantation Bowling Leag; Mayor's Com for the Jr Olympics, 1973-; Jr

Citizenship Clb, 1978-81; Butler Co Blood Chm, 1983; Dallas Days Com Person, 1980-; r/Cath; hon/Mayor Allen Awd for Contbns to the Jr Olympics, 1979; W/W Am Jr Cols; Outstg Yg Wom in Am.

PETERSON, KENNETH ALLEN JR oc/Student; b/Sep 14, 1966; h/3208 Phillips Avenue, Steger, IL 60475; p/Kenneth A and Marilyn M Peterson Sr, Steger, IL; ed/Bloom Trail HS; cp/Symphonic, Marching & Pep Band, 1980-; HS Wrestling Tm, 1981-82; BSA, Jr Asst Scout Master, 1982-; Sr Patrol Ldr 1980-82, Treas, Libn, Asst Patrol Ldr; Order of Arrow, BSA, Brotherhood Mem, Lodge Treas 1982-, Chapt Chief 1981-82; Luther Leag Mem; Acolyte, Crucifer; Little Leag, 1983-86; r/Luth; hon/Eagle Scout, BSA, 1980; Blue Buckeye Awd, 1981; Ctl Jr HS, High Hon, 1979, 1980; Sci Fair, Outstg Proj, 1980, 1981; HS Hon Soc, 1980, 1981, 1982; BSA Order of Arrow; IL Legis Proclamation Hon'g Achmts, 1980; Village of Steger Proclamation Hon'g Achmts, 1980; g/Pre-law Studies in Col Ldg to Becoming Lawyer.

PETERSON, MARK ALLEN oc/Student; b/Jan 3, 1964; h/Route 1, Box 21, Shannon, NC 28386; p/Cecile McNeill, Shannon, NC; ed/Grad, Magnolia HS; Att'g, Pembroke St Univ (Maj in Chem); pa/Canperter, B&B Constrn Co, 1982-83; Algebra Tutor, Robeson Tech Col; cp/Vol, ACLU; Pres, Student Coun; Beta Clb, Sgt-at-Arms; Treas, CECNC; Encampment of Citizenship; Chancellors Scholar, Pembroke St Univ; r/Bapt; hon/Am Civics, Eng I & II, Geometry, Bio, Hlth; Lttrs of Cit, NC NG; Smith S'ship; g/Maj in Chem.

PETITT, VICKI LYNN oc/Assistant Controller; b/Mar 23, 1960; h/9214 Ox Road, Lorton, VA 22079; ba/Falls Church, VA; p/Mr and Mrs Ernest A Petitt Jr, Lorton, VA; ed/BS Acctg, George Mason Univ, 1982; Passed Uniform CPA Exam, AICPA, 1982; pa/Clerk, Opers Ctr, Bk of VA, 1980; Auditor Trainee, Naval Audit Ser, 1981; Asst Controller, Technol Applications Inc; Secy, Beta Epsilon Phi, 1980-82; Alpha Chi Hon Soc, 1981-82; Univ Acctg Clb, 1981-82; Assn of Govt Accts, 1981-82; r/Meth; hon/HS Valedictorian, 1978; Univ Dean's List, 1978-82; Univ Grad w Distn, 1982; Assn of Govt Accts Acad S'ship, 1981; Fin Execs Inst Outstg Acctg Student, 1982; Nat Dean's List, 1978-82; g/Obtain MBA.

PETTIGREW, REGINA DEE oc/Student; b/Apr 19, 1964; h/4063 Muddy Creek Road, Harwood, MD; p/George and Edith Pettigrew, Harwood, MD; ed/S River Sr HS; Att'g Morgan St Univ; pa/Intern, Hist Annapolis, Inc; Tour Guide, Sum 1983; Intern, Anne Arundel Co Lib HQs, 1981-82; Secy, Harwood Homes Corp, Sum 1979-81; Gospel Pianist; French Clb; Reporter, Sch & Ch Newspapers; Band; Pres, Cercle Francais, Morgan St Univ Chapt; hon/Nat Dean's List; Phi Eta Sigma Nat Hon Soc; Promethean Kappa Tau Freshman/ Sophomore Hon Soc, Sprg 1983.

PETTY, TERESA DARLENE oc/Minister to Youth and Single Adults; b/May 15, 1956; h/2114 Highland Avenue, Shreveport, LA 71104; ba/Shreveport, LA; p/W E Petty, Tyler, TX; Mrs John Mosbaugh, Tyler, TX; ed/AA, Tyler Jr Col, 1976; Pvt Bus Dipl, Tyler Comml

Col, 1976; Att'd Stephen F Austin St Univ & Univ of HI; pa/Secy, Carlon Oil Co, 1977; Assoc Min to Yth, 1st Bapt Ch, Palestine, TX, 1978; Yth Dir, Waikiki Bapt Ch, Honolulu, HI, 1978-80; Min of Yth, Kailua Bapt Ch, 1980-82; Secy to Dean 1971-72, Adm Asst 1982, Wayland Bapt Univ; Min to Yth and Single Adults, Highland Bapt Ch, Shreveport, LA, 1983-; cp/St Yth Conslt for VBS, HI Bapt Conv, 1981; Bapt Yg Wom Dir, HI Bapt Conv, 1982; Camp Dir for St Older Yth Camp, HI Bapt Conv, 1980-82; Mem Nat Adv Coun for Evangelism to Wom for the Home Mission Bd, 1983; r/Bapt; hon/ Author, "Yth in HI: Isls of Love," *Event Mag*, 1980; Miss Congeniality, Miss Tyler Comml Col Contest, 1976; 3rd Runner-up, Miss Tyler Contest, 1977; "An Evening of Praise w Teresa" Concert, Kailua, HI, 1981; "Harmony & Understanding," 1974-75; g/Deg in Rel, Master's Deg in Rel Ed; Complete Christian Gospel Album.

PFEIFFER, ELOISE KIRBY b/Feb 25, 1964; h/Rt 1 Box 433, Shelby, NC 28150; p/Mr and Mrs A Graham Phifer, Shelby, NC; ed/HS, 1982; oc/Student; ca/Secy, Art Clb; Art Hon Soc; Pres, Spanish Clb; Spanish Hon Soc; Treas, FCA; Yrbk Staff Layout Editor; VP, Nat Hon Soc; Pres, Beta Clb; Quill & Scroll; Cheerldr; Debate Soc Pres; Pulpit Com; Asst Mbrship Chm, Kappa Kappa Gamma Sorority; Order of the Bell Tower; hon/Morehead S'ship; PPG S'ship; Cleveland Co Jr Miss; g/Univ NC-Chapel Hill Maj in Eng or Radio-TV-Motion Picture; Law Sch.

PHANSALKAR, KIRAN A oc/Student; ba/May 25, 1960; h/2112 Meadowbrook, Ponca City, OK 74601; ba/ Norman, OK; p/A K and Tara Phansalkar, Houston, TX; ed/BS, OK St Univ; JD (in progress), Univ of OK Col of Law; pa/Phi Kappa Phi, Phi Delta Phi Legal Frat; Nat Student Bar Assn; cp/ Delta Tau Delta Social Frat; YMCA, Student Govt Assn Ath Coun, All-Greek Ath; hon/Varsity Lttrs, Baseball, Basketball, Tennis, Volleyball; Pres's Hon Roll, 1982; Phi Kappa Phi, OK Law Review; Conoco Inc Nat S'ship; Wentz Ldrship S'ship; g/Sports Broadcaster for Radio Sta WBBZ, Ponca City, OK.

PHILLIPS, GLENN STEWART oc/ Student; b/Jul 23, 1964; h/Route 1 Box 230, Bear Creek, AL 35543; p/Stewart and Kellon Phillips, Bear Creek, AL; ed/ Grad, Phillips HS, 1982; cp/Cnslr, Upward Bound Prog, 1984; Photog, NW Jr Col Annual, *Viking II*; St 4-H Coun; Band, Drum Maj, 3 Yrs; Track; Basketball; Beta Clb; Sci Clb Pres; Student Govt; Pres, Co Coun 4-H; VP, Co St Ldrship; hon/St 4-H Elect Demo Winner, 1983; St 4-H Photo Exhib Winner, 1983; Most Creative Photo, *Viking II*, 1984; St 4-H Record Book Winner; Navy Superior Achmt Sci Awd, 3 Yrs; Sr Class Pres & Valedictorian; Most Valuable Player, Track; Superior Drum Maj Contest Rating; Sci & Energy Awds, NASA, USAF, Dept Energy & AL Power Co; W/W: Amg Am HS Students, Amg Dist'd Am HS Students, Music; Soc of Dist'd Am HS Students; Intl Yth in Achmt; g/Computer Engrg Deg, Auburn Univ; Career in Computer Field.

PHILLIPS, JEFFREY TAYLOR oc/

Professional Musician; b/May 22, 1961; h/202 Hurst Drive, Old Hickory, TN 37138; ba/Same; p/Clifford and Dottie Phillips, Old Hickory, TN; ed/BM Ed, Mid TN St Univ, 1984; Trombone Student of Brad Kinney, Horton Monroe, Horace Beasley, Roger Bissell; pa/ Instr of Music, MTSU Band Camps 1980, DuPont HS 1981, McGavock HS 1981, Madison HS 1983, Franklin HS 1983; Pvt Music Tchr, 1978-; Profl Musician, Num Wkshops, Bands, Ensembles, Orchs, 1982-; Musician, Knoxville Intl Energy Expo, 1982 World's Fair Band, 1982; Music Edrs Nat Conf; TN Music Edrs Assn; Intl Trombone Assn; Am Fdn of Musicians, Local 257 (AFL-CIO); cp/"Beau," Sisters of Delta Omicron Music Sorority; hon/ Music Compositions: "Ars Electra Asylum" 1982, "Echoes of '83" 1983; "A Game of Cards"; John Work III Music S'ship; Music & Acad S'ships to Mid TN St Univ; Elizabeth Shepherd S'ship; Mid TN St Univ Orch Soloist Competition, 2nd Place, 1982; Delta Omicron "Recital of the Year," 1983 (Soloist); g/Complete Bach of Music (Ed), Mid TN St Univ; Receive Master's of Music (Performance); Col Instr of Music/Freelance Profl Musician.

PHILLIPS, KELTON TOOLEY b/Jun 19, 1963; h/1524 Miller Street, Malvern, AR 72104; p/Mr and Mrs Bennie K Phillips, Malvern, AR; ed/Dipl, Malvern HS, 1981; BA (in progress), Hendrix Col; pa/Parliamentn 1979-80, Pres 1980-81, Future Bus Ldrs of Am; Pres, Sci Clb, 1980-81; Soc of Bus & Ec, 1982-83; Hendrix Student Host Com, 1983-85; r/Assem of God; hon/3rd Place Dist FBLA Conv, Acctg II, 1981; 4th Place, St FBLA Conv, Acctg II, 1981; 3rd Place, Sci Fair, 1981; Edward E Bailey Awd, 1981; Outstg Bus Ed Student, 1981; g/Receive Deg in Bus & Ec; Become Prominent & Respected Mem of Bus Commun.

PIANTADOSI, JEANETTE KEMCHICK oc/Corporate Executive; b/Sep 2, 1954; h/12115 San Vicente Boulevard, #311, Los Angeles, CA 90049; ba/ Los Angeles, CA; m/William J Collard; p/Patrick John Kmiechick, Gloria E Stensland, Bricktown, New Jersey; sp/ Wayne and Jennifer Collard, Northridge, CA; ed/BA Sociol magna cum laude 1977, M.Ed. Student Devel 1979, The Am Univ; Charles Revson Fellow, George Wash Univ, 1981; Computer Tng Course, Univ of CA-Los Angeles Ext, 1983; Att'd VA Polytechnic Inst & St Univ; pa/Dir Fin Aid, The Am Univ, 1977-81; Legis Aide, Rep Patricia Schroeder, Charles Revson Fellow, Wash DC, 1981-82; Dir Fed & St Relats, Sys Res Inc, Wash DC, 1981-; VP Mktg, Sigma Sys Inc, Los Angeles, CA, 1982-; Secy Designate 1980-81, Secy 1981-82, DE-DC-MD Assn of Student Fin Aid Admrs; DC Rep to Exec Bd 1978-81, Secy 1981-82, NE Assn of Student Employmt Admrs; Exec Coun ex-officio Mem, En Assn of Student Fin Aid Admrs, 1980-81; Nat Assn of Student Fin Aid Admrs, 1977-81; Chp Div of Govt/Agy Special Progs 1984, Nat Assn of Wom Deans, Admrs & Cnslrs; Liaison, Fdn of Orgs of Profl Wom, 1981-82; Nat Org for Wom, 1977-82; Am Assn of Univ Wom, 1980-82; Nat Assn of Col Admissions Cnslrs, 1979-81; cp/Cheerleading Coach, St

Dominic's Grammar Sch 1972-75, St Dominic's CYO 1972-75; Asst Cheerleading Coach, Sprg Lake Grammar Sch, 1971-72; r/Rom Cath; hon/Charles Revson Fellow, 1981-82; Outstg Yg Wom, 1979, 1981; Meritorious Ser, Am Univ, 1977, 1980; Gen Univ S'ship Recip, 1975-76; Mathas S'ship, 1975-76, 1976-77; Phi Theta Kappa, 1972-82; Phi Kappa Phi, 1972-82; W/W: W, Am Wom.

PIERSON, DEIRDRE KATHLEEN h/ 395-K Ridge Road, North Arlington, NJ 07032; p/Eilene C Pierson, Pompano, FL; ed/Grad, NE HS, Ft Lauderdale, FL; Boston Col; Sum Studies, Goethe Inst; pa/Freshman Asst, Boston Col Asst Prog; r/Cath; hon/Acad Hons, Freshman & Sophomore Yr, Boston Col; Dean's List; g/Attend Grad Sch, Become a Prof.

PIKE, MICKEY ROBERSON oc/ Instructor of Nursing; b/Jun 30, 1954; h/7822-B South Utica, Tulsa, OK 74136; ba/Tulsa, OK; m/Michael Alan Price; p/Mr and Mrs Roberson Sr, Gray, LA; sp/Dr and Mrs Roy E Pike, Jenks, OK; ed/AD Nsg, Nicholls St Univ, 1975; BS Nsg, NWn St Univ, 1979; Master's Deg Nsg, Oral Roberts Univ, 1983; pa/Charge Nurse & Staff Nurse, Terrebonne Gen Hosp (Louma, LA) 1975-77, Natchitoches Parish Hosp (Natchitoches, LA) 1978, Shumpert Med Ctr (Shreveport, LA) 1978-79; Actg Hd Nurse, Charge Nurse, Staff Nurse, Terrebonne Gen Hosp, 1980-82; Telephone Recruiter Grad Sch of Nsg 1981-83, Instr of Nsg 1983-, Oral Roberts Univ, Tulsa, OK; Alpha Lambda Delta, 1973; Phi Kappa Phi, 1979; Sigma Theta Tau, 1980; Am Nurses' Assn; r/Mem St James U Meth Ch; hon/Master's Thesis, "Influence of Personal Effects on Deg of Confusion in Hospitalized Elderly"; Nicholls St Univ Hon Soc; Oral Roberts Univ Anna Vaughn Sch of Nsg Hon Soc, 1983; Hon Grad, 1975, 1979, 1983; Acad S'ship, Oral Roberts Univ, 1981-83; g/Nurse Edr.

PILATE, PHIL (PRINCE MURRAY WHIPPER) oc/Philosopher; b/Mar 17, 1961; h/75 Brookfield Road, Mt Vernon, NY 10552; p/B J and Lucille Murray Whipper, Mt Vernon, NY; ed/Dipl, Mt Vernon HS, 1978; BA, Morehouse Col, 1982; Att'd Westchester Commun Col 1979, NY Univ 1980, Atlanta Univ 1981, 1982; mil/AUS, 1983; pa/News Libn, CBS, 1982; Lib Asst, Atlanta Univ, 1981-82; Lab Asst, Vick's Res & Devel, 1979, 1980; Lab Asst, Morehouse Col, 1979; Page, Mt Vernon Public Lib, 1976-77; Co-Editor, Morehouse Col *Catalyst*, 1979-80; cp/Psych Clb; Forensics Clb; Hlth Careers Soc; Morehouse Col Glee Clb; Atlanta Gospel Mvmt Choir; r/Moriah Bapt Ch, So Bapt Ch; hon/Mt Vernon Commun S'ship, 1979-81; So Bapt Ch S'ship, 1979-81; Dean's List, Hon Roll, 1978-79; NY Univ S'ship, 1980; TX So Univ S'ship, 1982; Hon Army Recruiter, 1983; g/Make Significant Intell Achmts.

PIPER, CHERYL LEA b/Mar 14, 1965; h/Unit Route Box 1, Harrison, NE 69346; p/Franklin Piper (dec); Marie Piper, Harrison, NE; ed/Grad, Sioux Co HS, 1983; cp/Band Mem, 1980-83; Chorus Mem, 1980-83; FBLA, 1981-83; FFA, 1980-82; FHA, 1982-83; Rodeo Clb, 1980-82; Basketball, 1980-83; Track, 1980-81; Track Mgr, 1983; 4-H

(10 Yrs), Reporter 1980, Secy-Treas 1981, VP 1982, Pres 1983; r/Cath; hon/ Math Hon for Straight A's, 1980, 1981, 1982; Perfect Attendance, 1980, 1982; FFA Ornamental Hort, Home & Farmstead Improvements, Livestock Prodn, 1981; FFA Chap S'ship for Highest Grades, 1980, 1981; Chorus & Band Hon, 1981; Home Ec Judging Pins, 1980, 1981, 1982; Judo White Belt w Blue Tabs; W/W Amg Am HS Students; g/ Earn BA Deg in Computer Sci; Become Computer Operator or Programmer.

PIPER, FRANKLIN JOSEPH b/Oct 31, 1963; h/Unit Route Box 1, Harrison, NE 69346; p/Franklin Piper (dec); Marie Piper, Harrison, NE; ed/Grad, Sioux Co HS, 1982; cp/FFA, 1980-82; Rodeo Clb, 1979, 1981; Chorus Mem 1979-81; Basketball, 1979, 1980, 1982; Track, 1980, 1982; Football, 1982; 4-H (10 Yrs), Pres 1981 & 1982, VP 1980, Reporter 1979; FFA, Parliamentn 1980-81, Sentinel 1981-82; Star Greenhand, Greenhand; hon/Track Hons, 1982; Soil & Water Conserv in FFA Hon Roll, 1981; g/Become a Mech Engr.

PITTMAN, PAULA KAY b/Jan 23, 1963; h/Route 1 Box 705, Harrah, Oklahoma 73045; p/Mr and Mrs Bryan W Pittman, Harrah, OK; ed/Grad, Harrah HS, 1981; cp/VP Communs Dept, Bapt Student Union; Alpha Lambda Delta; Kappa Delta Pi; Alpha Chi; Student Coun for Exceptl Chd; Sigma Alpha Eta; r/Bapt; hon/Recip Acad Tuition Waiver, 1981-84; Ctl St Univ Alumni S'ship; Dean's Hon Roll, 1981-84; g/Receive BS Spec Ed w Emphasis in Speech Pathol from Ctl St Univ & Wk in that Field.

PLAUTH, ANNA EARL b/Jun 4, 1966; h/1350 West Weoley Road, Atlanta, GA 30327; ba/Atlanta, GA; p/ Dr and Mrs William H Plauth, Atlanta, GA; ed/Att'd Westminster Schs, 1971-84; cp/Mem 1981-83, Girl's Co-Capt 1982-83, Debate Tm; Math Tm, 1980-84; Mgr JV Bseball Tm, 1981, 1983; Sch Chorale, 1980-84; Newspaper Staff, 1982-84; r/Presb; hon/Hon Roll, 1980-83; Harvard Bk Awd, 1983; #1 in Jr Class, 1982-83; Math & Sci Awd, Rensselaer Polytechnic Inst, 1983; Nat Merit Semi-Finalist, 1983; Awd of Excell from Nat Forensic Leag; g/Maj in Biol and/or Phil in Col, Continue on to Med Sch.

PLONK, JOHN OATES III oc/Sales Representative; b/Jun 29, 1959; h/118 North Piedmont Avenue, Kings Mountain, NC 28086; ba/Charlotte, NC; p/ John O Jr and Patricia N Plonk, Kings Mountain, NC; ed/Grad, Kings Mtn Sr HS, 1977; BA Ec & Bus Mgmt, NC St Univ, 1981; MBA, Wake Forest Univ, 1983; pa/Sales Rep, Metro Ins Cos, 1983-; cp/JCs; LUTC; NASD; r/Meth; hon/Dean's List; Career Success Sch Grad; g/Chm of the Bd, Metro Ins Cos.

PLUMB, RICHARD GEORGE oc/ Electrical Engineer; b/Jul 17, 1959; h/ G107 Cedarwood Drive, Baldwinsville, NY 13027; ba/Syracuse, NY; m/Mary; p/Michael Sr and Joan Plumb, Liverpool, NY; sp/Edward and Marget Lazarz, Liverpool, NY; ed/Grad, Liverpool HS, 1978; Adv'd Course in Engrg, Gen Elect; pa/Elect Engr, Gen Elect Co, 1982-; cp/ Eta Kappa Nu; IEEE; Tau Beta Pi; Syracuse Univ Crew Tm; Gen Elect Tchg Excell Com; Sr Events Planning Com; hon/Gen Motors Scholar Student;

Class Marshal for Grad Ceremony; Outstg Sr Elect Engr; Intl Yth in Achmt, Nat Dean's List, 1980-81, 1981-82; g/ PhD EE; Full-Time Col Prof.

PLUMMER, MARTIN F oc/Professional Photographer and Studio Partner; b/Apr 28, 1958; h/205 Princeton Drive, Tullahoma, TN 37388; ba/ Tullahoma, TN; p/Mr and Mrs R F Plummer, Tullahoma, TN; ed/Dipl, Tullahoma HS, 1976; AS Bus Mgmt, St Commun Col, 1981; AAS Photo Technol, Randolph Tech Col, 1983; pa/Profl Photog, Ptnr, Plummer's Studio, Portrait and Comml Photog; Profl Photogs of Am; TN Profl Photogs Assn; Softball Player; cp/HS Football, Baseball, Track Mgr; Coach, Yth Football Tm, 3 Yrs; Social Chm, Randolph Tech Col Alumni Assn, 1982-83; No St Student Govt Judiciary Ofcr, 1980-82; Randolph Tech Col SGA, 1982-83; r/Meth; hon/Pres's List, 4.0 GPA (2 times), Randolph Tech Col; Nom'd by Fac as Portrait Judge for Traveling Show of Photog at Randolph Tech Col; 5 Prints on Show in Traveling Show of Photog sponsored by Randolph Tech Col; g/To Be Financially Secure & Contribute to Commun through Needy Progs.

POIROT, MARY ELIZABETH oc/ Student; b/Jun 26, 1963; h/57 Glenwood Drive, Windsor, CT 06095; ba/W Hartford, CT; p/Mr and Mrs E J Poirot, Windsor, CT; ed/Grad, NW Cath HS, W Hartford, CT, 1981; Att'g St Joseph Col; pa/Salesperson (Old Saybrook Br) Sums 1980-83, Salesperson (Windsor Br) Winters 1982 & 1983, Sage-Allen; Waitress, S M DiCocco-St Joseph Col Pub, 1982, 1983; Aide to Handicapped Individual, 1982; cp/Girl's Ldr Clb, 1979-81; Hd, Student Coun Com, 1980-81; Vol Tutor for Inner-City Chd, 1982; Orgr Christmas Party for Chd's Orphanage, 1981; Delivered Thanksgiving Baskets to Poor in Hartford, CT, 1980, 1981; Vol Tchr's Aide, St Gabriel Sch, 1978, 1979, 1980; Pres 1981, Mem 1977-81, HS Pep Clb; HS French Clb, 1980-81; VP, Col French Clb, 1981-82; Col Student Affairs Com, 1981-82, 1982-83, 1983-84; VP 1982-83, Pres 1983-84, Col Student Govt Assn; Spec Ed Clb, 1983-84; Resident Asst Selection Com, 1981-82, 1982-83; W/W Selection Com, 1983; Participant, NACA Student Govt Wkshop, Charleston, IL, 1983; Participant, Gift-a-thon for Sr Citizens, 1983; Mem Ser Proj in Appalachian Mtns, Sutton, WV, 1983; Vol Tchr Sub, St Gabriel Sch, 1983; Vol Wk in Var Progs; r/Cath; hon/Nat Hon Soc; HS Grad w Hons, 1981; HS Student Coun Awd, 1980-81; HS French Cert Awd, 1978, 1979, 1980, 1981; Sr Rel Awd, 1981; Parents Clb Awd for Ser & Academics, 1981; Mem Hon Roll, NW, 4 Yrs; High Hons 8 Times; Smyth S'ship, 1982, 1983-84; Student Govt Assn S'ship, 1983-84; Cert of Recog as SGA Mem, 1983; Elected Pres of Student Govt Assn, 1983-84; g/Become Spec Ed Tchr & Obtain Master's Deg in Spec Ed.

POKLUDA, JAMIE ANN b/Mar 31, 1966; h/1102 North Red River, Mexia, TX 76667; p/Mr and Mrs James Pokluda, Mexia, TX; ed/HS; cp/JV Cheerleader, 1981-82; Varsity Tennis Tm, 1981-82; Student Coun Rep, 1981-84; Academic Sweater, 1982-83; Hon Roll, 1982-83; Band, 1978-84; Ofc Ed Assn, 1982-84;

Band Libn, 1983-84; r/Bapt; g/Bus Mgmt.

POLZIN, CAROL ANN oc/Counselor/Child Care Worker; b/Sep 23, 1960; h/723 Truax Boulevard, #2, Eau Claire, WI 54703; ba/Eau Claire, WI; p/Mr and Mrs Elmer Polzin, Peshtigo, WI; ed/ Grad, Peshtigo HS, 1978; BSW cum laude, Univ of WI-Eau Claire; pa/Exodus Prog as Cnslr/Child Care Wkr, Luth Social Sers of WI and Upper MI, 1982-; g/Become Cert'd Alcohol & Drug Cnslr within 2 Yrs.

POMARICO, CYNTHIA ANN oc/ Park Supervisor; b/Aug 25, 1963; h/58 North Chestnut Street, Beacon, NY 12508; p/Charles and Rosalie Pomarico, Beacon, NY; ed/Grad, Beacon HS, 1981; pa/Pk Supvr, Beacon Rec, 1981-83; cp/ Mem 1978-81, Pres 1981, Varsity Clb; GSA, 1973-; hon/BHS Hon Soc, 1980-81; NY St Wom's SP Class "B" MVP, 1979; MVP BHS Basketball, Softball, Volleyball, 1980; BHS Best Female Ath, 1980; Gutsy Awd, 1981; MVP Softball, 1981; BHS Best Female Ath, 1981; Recip 10 Varsity Lttrs; W/ W Amg Am HS Students; g/Elem PE Tchr, Coach, Phys Therapist.

PONDER, KATHRYN ANITA b/Jan 13, 1962; h/Route 2, Box 343A, Westminster, SC 29693; p/Charles Farrell and Joann Broome Ponder, Westminster, SC; ed/Grad, Seneca HS, 1980; Att'g Lander Col; pa/Hostess, Shoney's, 1983; Sales Clerk, Foxmoor, 1981-83; Sales Assoc, Gen Nutrition, 1980-82; Waitress, 12th Colony Restaurant, 1981; Nature Tchr, Unit Cnslr, St 4-H Camp Long, Sum 1980; cp/Pres, Aquarium Clb; Yth Commr, SC Land Resources Comm; Explorer Post #226; Cheerleader; Bus Demo Del to PA St Univ; Field Day Com, Lander Col, 1981; Student Govt, 1980-81; Expo Orientation Tm, 1980, 1983; Home Ec Clb, 1980-83; Home Ec Clb Outreach Dir, 1982-83; Kappa Sigma Frat Little Sister; Sigma Nu Little Sister, 1980; hon/4-H St Public Spkg Winner, Del to Nat Cong, Chicago, IL; Rep to Nat Inst of Coop Ed for SC; 1st Place, Talent Show/ Crosscreek Mall, 1982; Wn Yth Commr; Outstg Runner-up S'ship, 1980; Miss Lander, 1983; Talented Srs Spotlight, 1980; House Rep for St Student Govt; r/Bapt; g/Grad w Deg in Elem Ed, Obtain Master's Deg in Ed.

POOLE, JOSEPH BARRON oc/Student; b/Jan 30, 1966; h/Route 3, Benedict Road, Cedartown, GA 30125; p/Mr and Mrs Webb Wiggins, Cedartown, GA; ed/Att'g HS; pa/HS Chess Clb, Chaplain, Sci Clb; Envir Clb; Math Clb; Football, Wrestling, Tennis Tms; Hon Soc; Beta Clb; hon/1st Place in Algebra Competition, Berry Col, Freshman Yr; Outstg Student in Sci; Jr Awd from US Achmt Acad for Math; g/Become Computer Programmer, Attend Col.

POOLE, SHARON DENISE oc/Student, Child Care Worker; b/Sep 24, 1961; h/1004 Southeast 14th Street, Pryor, OK 74361; p/Harold and Rose Poole; ed/Grad, Pryor HS, 1979; Att'g Ctl St Univ; pa/Child Care Wkr, Pvt Home, 1982-; Tiarias JR Wom's Hon Soc, 1983-84; Wing Rep 1982-83, VP 1983-84, Murdaugh Dorm Coun; Treasurer 1983-84, St VP 1983-84, Student Coun of Exceptl Chd; Resident Hall Assn, 1982-84; Assn of Wom Students, 1982-84; Food Ser Com Rep'g Murdaugh Hall, 1982-83; cp/Aid, Underprivileged Chd's Christmas Party & Easter Egg Hunt, 1982-83; Collector, Heart & Lung Assn Rep'g Murdaugh Hall, 1982-83; hon/Dean's Hon Roll, 1981-; Nom'd W/W Am Cols & Univs; g/Grad from Ctl St Univ w Deg in Elem Ed; Teach Sch in Tulsa Area & Complete Master's Deg in Early Childhood Ed.

POOLE, VARQUELTA VENEE b/Aug 30, 1966; h/420 Highland Court, Tullahoma, TN 37388; ed/HS; pa/Zeta Lambda Chi Sorority; Varsity Basketball Tm; Varsity Track Tm; F'ship of Christian Aths; r/AME; g/Attend MTSU & Maj in Bus Mktg & Mgmt; Become Bus Owner.

POPE, ANNE LINDSAY oc/Student; b/Dec 25, 1962; h/1419 Lexington Road, Richmond, KY 40475; ba/Bowling Green, KY; p/Miles and Peggy Pope, Richmond, KY; ed/Grad, Model Lab Sch, 1980; Art Studies, Bregenz, Austria, Wagner College, Sum 1983; Att'g Wn KY Univ; pa/Ofc Clk, Census Counter, US Census Bur, 1980; Games Control, Beech Bend Amusement Pk, Bowling Green, KY, 1981; Applications Advisor, St Unemployment Ofc, 1982; pa/Ath Clb, 1976-80; Art Clb, 1976-79; Model Exemplar Advtg Staff, 1979-80; Advtg Clb, WKU, 1983; Diving Tm, 1974-76; Tennis Tm; Pep Clb, 1976-80; r/Bapt; hon/Nat Hon Soc, 1978-79, 1979-80; Varsity Lttr, Tennis Tm, 1976-78; W/W Am HS Students; g/Wk w Media Planning & Creation of Ads for Advtg Agy; Open Art Gallery w Father; Active in Bus.

POPE, RACHEL BELLE oc/Student; b/Jan 14, 1963; h/Route 1 Box 76, Spring Hope, NC 27882; ba/Elm City, NC; p/Mr and Mrs Daniel Lee Pope, Spring Hope, NC; ed/Grad, So Nash Sr HS, 1982; Att'g Edgecombe Tech Col; 2-Wk Prog, Halifax Commun Col; pa/FTA, 1982; SCA, 1980; Vocal Ensemble; Jr/Sr Dec Comm; Mixed Chorus; Annual Staff Artist; Track, 1979, 1980; r/Bapt; hon/Author, Articles Pub'd in Annual Book, 1980, 1981, 1982; Wilson Art S'ship, Track, 1979; SNSH Player of the Week for Track, 1980; Perfect Attendance Awd, 1980; 1st Pl Art Exhib, 1981; Hon Mention, Am Ed Wk Art Contest; Selected for Art Coun of Wilson Country Fair Contest; 1st & 2nd Pl, 3rd in So Flue-Cured Tobacco Art Contest, 1981; g/Maj as Cosmetologist & Become Fashion Designer & Model.

POPE, TAMERA ANNE oc/Student; b/Dec 7, 1964; h/Route 2 Box 99, Martin, TN 38237; p/Jerry Neal and Betty Pope, Martin, TN; ed/Grad, Westview HS; Att'g Univ of TN-Martin; pa/Typist, The Weakley Co Press, 1983-; Ofc Ed Assoc, 1981-83; FHA, 1979-82; Class Reporter, 1980-81; HS Annual Staff, 1981-83; Westview Aux Corps, 1980-83; r/Bapt; hon/Bus Filing Proficiency Cert; Ofc Ed Assn Stateswoman Awd; Pilot Clb S'ship; Martin Mfg Charitable Foun S'ship; City St Bk S'ship, 1983; g/Maj in Ofc Adm; Find Employmt in Ofc Job.

POPE, TOMMIE CLARE b/Sep 13, 1962; h/1610 Malibu Drive, Carrollton, TX 75006; p/Tommie Pope, Carrollton, TX; Joan M Pope, Carrollton, TX; ed/Newman Smith HS, 1981; S Plains Col; pa/Student Govt Rep, S Plains Col, 1982-83; Cheerldg Squad Ldr; Cheerldr,

1982-83; Cir K Secy; Drill Tm; Student Govt; Track Tm Varsity Lttr; hon/Contestant, S Plains Col Beauty Pageant; Contestant, Miss Cap Rock Beauty Pageant; Nom, Pres Hostess, S Plains Col; Wom of Yr Nom, S Plains Col, 1982-83; W/W S Plains Col; g/Fashion Mdse; Buy Clothes Store in Dallas Area.

PORTER, CINDY LOU oc/Law Student; b/Apr 1, 1960; h/Route 3, Box 272, Greenbrier, TN 37073; ba/Bloomington, IN; p/George S and Sigrid Porter, Greenbrier, TN; ed/Grad, Greenbrier HS, 1978; BA w Distn in Univ Hons, Mid TN St Univ, 1982; JD (in progress), IN Univ Sch of Law; pa/Sales Clk, J C Penney, Sums 1978-83; pa/MTSU Varsity Debate Tm, 1978-81; Hons Coun, 1981-82; ASB Sen, 1981-82; Pres, VP S'ship, Rush Chm, Alpha Gamma Delta, 1978-82; Hons Student Assn, 1981-82; Parliamentn, Gamma Beta Phi, 1979-82; Tau Omicron, 1980-82; Pres, Pi Gamma Mu, 1980-82; Pi Sigma Alpha, 1980-82; Delta Theta Phi Law Frat, 1982-83; Student Bar Assn, 1982-83; Wom's Caucus; r/Meth; hon/Hons Thesis, "Sentencing Reform: The Passage of Sen Bill 1484 in the TN Legis, 1982"; Law F'ship, 1983-84; Assoc, IN Law Jour, 1983-84; Distn in Univ Hons, 1982; Norman L Parks Awd, Outstg Pre-Law Student; Lower Div Hons Awd, 1980; Mid TN St Univ Deans List; Mid TN St Univ Hon Roll, 1978-82; Ldrship/Achmt S'ship; Debate S'ship; Atty Gen, ASB S'ship; W/W Amg Students in Am Univs & Cols; Yg Commun Ldrs of Am; Nat Dean's List; g/Atty.

POSEY, E PALMER II oc/Student, Machinist; b/Feb 15, 1962; h/Route 1, Box 599, Bremen, GA 30110; p/Erving P and Odell Clayton Posey, Bremen, GA; ed/Grad, Bremen HS, 1980; W GA Col; Att'g Carroll Co Area Voc Tech; pa/Stock Ck & Delivery, Clayton Pharm, 1979-80; Furn Finisher, Holcombe Enterprises; Machine Shop Computer Programmer & Operator, Neal Mfg Inc; Haralson Co Hist Soc; Caretaker Tower Clock & Bell, the Haralson Co Ct House; r/Mem Poseyville Meth Ch; hon/Author Articles on Hist of Bremen & Surrounding Co, *The Bremen Cent Book, Haralson Co Hist Book, The Bremen Gateway*.

POSEY, TAMERA HATCHETT oc/Medical Technologist; b/Dec 28, 1958; h/Route 2, Box 753, Madison, NC 27025; ba/Greensboro, NC; m/John Thomas Jr; p/John Lofton and Lenna Hughes Hatchett, Murphy, NC; sp/Edna Posey, Jamestown, NC; ed/Grad, Murphy HS, 1977; BS Med Technol, Wn Carolina Univ, 1983; pa/MT ASCP, Wesley Long Hosp, 1982-; Part-time MT, Humana Hosp, 1982-; Secy/Receptionist, Helen Lochaby Ins Agy, 1978-79; ASCP, 1983-; ASMT, 1982-; Alpha Delta Lambda Hon Soc, 1978; Med Technol Clb, 1982-83; Wesley Foun, 1977-83; Mgr, HS Jour Clb, 1976-77; VP, Beta Clb, 1975-77; Secy, Student Coun, 1976-77; Photog Clb, 1975-76; hon/Univ Scholar, 1983; Grad summa cum laude, 1983; Outstg Sr in Med Technol, 1983; Jr Marshal, 1976, 1982; Patrons of Quality S'ship, 1977, 1982; Hosp Aux S'ship, 1982; Outstg Freshman Wom, 1977; HS Valedictorian, 1977; 1st Pl in Speech Contest,

1975; W/W HS Students; g/Return to Sch & Complete Master's Prog in Biochem; Seek Employmt in Res Facility.

POSTON, JULIE ANN oc/Student; b/Dec 15, 1961; h/1242 Airport Road, Shelby, NC 28150; ba/Cullowhee, NC; p/Mr and Mrs I Dan Poston, Shelby, NC; ed/Grad w hon, Burns HS, 1980; Att'g Wn Carolina Univ; pa/Mem, Student Nat Edrs Assn; cp/Student Coun; Jr Coun; Sr Coun; Jr Class Treas; Sr Class Treas; Beta Clb; Pres, Histn, Future Homemakers Am; Future Bus Ldrs Am; HOSA; Color Guard; Band; Spanish Clb; Homecoming Sponsor; Keywanettes; Peer Tutor & Cnslr; HS Radio Show; Pep Clb; VP Pledge Class, Epsilon Gamma Chapt, Alpha Xi Delta Sorority; r/Bapt; hon/Beta Clb; Hon Student; Outstg Sr Awd; Outstg Home Ec Awd; Dean's List, Wn Carolina Univ; Dean's List; Cert of Academic Achmt, Wn Carolina Univ Panhellenic Assn, 1984; g/Deg in Early Childhood Ed, Become Tchr.

POTEET, JAMIE LOU oc/Teller; b/Mar 26, 1961; h/Post Office Box 182, Healdton, OK 73438; ba/Healdton, OK: p/Mr and Mrs D Adren Poteet, Healdton, OK; ed/Grad, Healdton HS, 1979; Att'd Ctl St Univ; pa/Waitress, Pizza Hut, Sum 1978; Waitress, Burger Supreme, Sum 1979; Census Taker, 1980; Sales Clerk, Lerner's Quail Springs Mall, OK City, Winter 1980; Drive-in Teller, Bk of Healdton, 1981-; cp/Healdton IPRA Kodiak Smokeless Tobacco Rodeo Queen, 1983; YMCA Wom's Basketball Leag, 1983; r/Meth; hon/1983 Rodeo Queen; Outstg Pledge for Alpha Gamma Delta, 1980.

PRATT, CAROL ANDREA oc/PFC Army Personnel; b/Aug 15, 1963; p/Nathaniel (dec) and Jean Pratt, Ahoskie, NC; ed/Grad, Ahoskie, NS, 1981; Chowan Col; mil/PFC Army Pers; pa/Sci Lab Asst; cp/Pep Clb; Varsity Clb; FHA; Prog Dir, Social Sci Clb; Bloodmobile Vol; Flag Guard, AHS Marching Band; Girls Basketball Tm Mgr; Hlth Occup Clb; NC Jr Miss Pageant; Usher in Ch Ser; g/MD; Cytotechnol or Lab Tech.

PRATT, NATHANIEL GLENN oc/Student, USMC Reserve; b/Oct 16, 1962; h/Route 3 Box 232H, Ahoskie, NC 27910; ba/Wash DC; p/Mrs Jean Pratt, Wash DC; ed/Dipl, Ahoskie HS, 1980; Att'd NC Ctl Univ, 1980-83; mil/USMC Res; pa/Part-time Clk through DECA; Harris Grocery, Ahoskie, 1979-80; Asst Ofc Mgr, CADA, Sum 1982; cp/Boy Scouts Alumni Assn, 1981-83; DECA, 1979-80; Secy, Sophisticated Gentlemen, 1981; g/Criminal Justice; Bus Adm.

PRESCOTT, KAREN ANNETTE oc/Speech Pathologist; b/Jan 27, 1960; h/1512 Bradbary Lane, Ponca City, OK 74601; ba/Pasadena, TX; p/Mr and Mrs Robert Prescott, Ponca City, OK; ed/Grad, Ponca City Sr HS, 1978; BS Ed, Baylor Univ, 1982; MA, Univ of Tulsa, 1983; pa/Speech Pathol, Pasadena Indep Sch Dist, 1983-; Am Speech, Lang & Hearing Assn; TX Speech, Lang & Hearing Assn; Zeta Tau Alpha; r/Luth; hon/Nat Merit Scholar; Mortar Bd; Omicron Delta Kappa; Grad summa cum laude, Baylor Univ; W/W Amg Am Col & Univ Students, 1982; g/Provide Speech & Lang Sers in Hosp or Clin Setting.

PREWETT, VICKI RENEE oc/Student; b/Jul 4, 1965; h/Route 1, Collard Valley Road, Cedartown, GA 30125; p/Mr and Mrs Gary Prewett, Cedartown, GA; ed/Grad, Cedartown HS, 1983; Att'g Coosa Valley Tech Col; pa/Travel Conslt, Steve Yoman, Travel Centre, Ltd, Cedartown, GA; pa/Chd's Ch, Sunbeam Ch, SS Tchr; Pres, Bapt Yth F'ship; CEF; Chd's Camp Helper; hon/Hon Roll; All Pageant Winning; Miss Polk Co, 1983; Miss Polk Co Fair Queen, 1983; Commun Ldrs of Am; g/Successful Model; Computer Work; Good Wife & Mother.

PRICE, MARVIN JR oc/Student; b/Jul 5, 1968; h/311 West Grandville Street, Dunn, NC 28334; p/Mr and Mrs Marvin Price; g/Maj in Art.

PRICE, RALPH DAVID oc/Student; b/Nov 7, 1959; h/423 Spruce, Fayetteville, AR 72701; ba/Fayetteville, AR; p/Mr and Mrs Ward Smith, Gassville, AR; ed/Grad, Mtn Home HS, 1978; BS Agri Engrg, Univ of AR, 1983; pa/Student-Asst, Univ of AR, Engrg Dept, 1982-; Stocker Clk, Harp's IGA, 1979-82; Spot-Welder, Whirlpool, 1979; Shop Asst, Univ of AR, Agri Engrg Dept, 1978-79; Stocker/Clk, Harp's Mkt, 1978-79; Pres, Alpha Epsilon, 1982-83; Tau Beta Pi, 1983; Mem 1979-83, Sgt-at-Arms 1981-82, Alpha Zeta; Secy 1982-83, Rep 1982-83, Mem 1980-83, Am Soc of Agri Engrg; Agri & HE Student Assn Exec Coun, 1981-83; Pres 1978-79, Secy/Treas 1979-81, Rep 1981-82, Mem 1978-83, Agri Mech Clb; hon/Outstg Sr in Agri Engrg, 1982-83; Outstg Jr Agri Mech, 1980-81; Outstg Sr Agri Mech, 1981-82; g/Study Field & Power Machinery; Career in Res & Devel.

PRICE, TODD DUNCAN oc/Aerospace Engineer; b/Aug 26, 1961; h/507 Forrest Road, Warsaw, NC 28398; ba/Cherry Point, NC; p/Mr and Mrs Carl D Price, Warsaw, NC; ed/Grad, James Kenan HS, 1976-79; BS Aerospace Engrg, NC St Univ, 1979-83; mil/NC Army NG, 1979-; pa/Aerospace Composite Structures Engr, Naval Air Rework Facility, 1983-; Nat Soc of Profl Engrs, 1980-; Am Inst of Aeronautics & Astronautics, 1981-; cp/BSA, 1971-77; Ch Yth Coun, 1977-78; Sch Rep to Pres Clrm for Yg Ams, 1978; Tennis Tm, 1977-79; Band, 1977-79; r/Bapt; hon/BSA Eagle Scout, 1977; I Dare You Ldrship Awd, 1978; Rotary Clb S'ship, 1979; Passing Score on Engr-in-Trng Test, 1983; g/Gain Addit Ed & Experience to Become Profl Engr; Continue Work & Study in Use of Adv'd Composite Structures for Aviational Use.

PRIDGEN, ALMA DELORES oc/Educator; b/Jun 29, 1961; h/Route 2 Box 93 B-7, Nashville, NC 27856; p/May Jr and Alma Jean Pridgen, Nashville, NC; ed/Dipl, 1979; Grad, St Augustine's Col, 1982; pa/2nd Grade Clrm Tchr, M B Hubbard Elem Sch; Pres, Assn Early Childhood Edrs; Pres, Kappa Delta Pi Hon Soc; Alpha Kappa Mu Hon Soc; Peer Cnslr; NCAE; cp/Jr Class, Miss UNCF; hon/Grad summa cum laude, St Augustines' Col; Dept'l Awd in Ed; VP Academic Affairs Awd; Sadie M Winslow S'ship; Letie-Pate-Whitehead S'ship; U Negro Col Fund Parcel S'ship; W/W Amg Students in Am Univs & Cols; Nat Dean's List; g/Master's Deg

in Early Childhood Ed.

PRIDGEN, BETTIE JEAN b/Jan 27, 1958; h/Route 2 Box 93-B7, Nashville, NC 27856; p/Mr and Mrs May Pridgen, Nashville, NC; ed/Grad, So Nash Sr HS, 1976; BA Intermediate Ed, St Augustine's Col, 1984; pa/Student Nat Ed Assn; Assn of Early Childhood Ed; Sr Class Treas; Reporter and Poetry Editor, Pen Sch Paper; r/Bapt; hon/Dean's List, 1982-84; Kappa Delta Pi Hon Soc; The Lettie Pate Whitehead S'ship, 1984; W/W Amg Col Students, 1984; g/Attend NC St Univ to Obtain Master's Deg in Area of Ed.

PRINCE, CHERYL P oc/Market Sales Manager; b/Mar 29, 1956; h/6710 Vernon Avenue South, #306, Edina, Minnesota 55436; ba/Minneapolis, MN; p/Mr and Mrs O G Prince, Atlanta, GA; ed/Grad, Northside HS, Atlanta, GA; AS 1977, BBA 1979, GA St Univ; BBA, Atlanta Univ, 1982; pa/Seasonal Stand Mgr 1973-75, Food Ser Supvr 1975-78, Six Flags Over GA; Customer Ser Rep 1978-79, Ser Sales Rep 1979-82, Mkt Sales Mgr 1983-, Honeywell, Inc; hon/Nat Dean's List, 1981-82; Beta Gamma Sigma, Atlanta Univ Sch of Bus, 1982; Outstg Yg Wom of Am.

PRINCE, TODD FRANKLIN oc/Computer Operator; h/148-C Route 2, Rutherfordton, NC 28137; ba/Rutherfordton, NC; m/Victoria D; p/Bill F and Helen M Prince, Spartanburg, SC; sp/Adrian and Jeri Packer, Elenboro, NC; ed/HS Dipl; Att'd N GA Mil Col; mil/SC NG; pa/Stockboy, White Auto Paint, 1977-81; Constrn Wkr, Metric Constrn, 1983-84; Computer Operator, Doncaster-Tanner, 1984-; r/Bapt.

PRINDLE, JOHN CARROLL JR oc/Graduate Student; b/Jun 9, 1960; h/2502 Terrace, Midland, TX 79701; p/Mr and Mrs John C Prindle Sr, Midland, TX; ed/Grad, Robert E Lee HS, 1978; BS Chem Engrg 1982, BS Math 1983, TX Tech Univ; Res Asst in Chem Engrg, Univ of WI; pa/Sum Engr, Shell Oil Co; Pres, Kappa Mu Epsilon, 1981-82; HS Recruiter & Charter Mem, Omega Chi Epsilon, 1981-82; Tau Beta Pi, 1980-82; Phi Kappa Phi, 1980-82; Phi Eta Sigma, 1978-79; Am Inst of Chem Engrg, 1980-82; hon/Outstg 1st & 2nd Yr Russian Lang Student, 1979, 1980; Recip, Alcoa S'ship, 1980; ARCS S'ship, 1981; Outstg Engrg Grad, 1982; g/Obtain PhD in Chem Engrg & Work as Conslt for R&D Div of Oil or Chem Corp.

PRISTER, JULIA EVELYN oc/Hearing Therapist/Consultant; b/Nov 16, 1960; h/638 Lee Street, Blacksburg, VA 24060; ba/Blacksburg, VA; p/Mr and Mrs Charles Prister, Rochester, NY; ed/Grad, Irondequoit HS, 1978; Interpreter Tng, Nat Tech Inst for the Deaf, Sum 1978; BA Ed of Hearing Impaired K-12 Intermediate Ed/Lang Arts, Lenoir-Rhyne Col, 1982; pa/Hearing Therapist/Conslt, Montgomery Co Schs, 1982-; Sum Sch Tchr, Rochester Sch for the Deaf, Sum, 1982, 1983, 1984; Free Univ Sign Lang Instr, YMCA, Sprg 1983-; Future Tchrs of Hearing Impaired; Sign Troupe; Peer Cnslr; Student Govt; Vol Residence Conslr & Rec Aide, Rochester Sch for the Deaf, 1975-78; r/Cath; hon/Dean's List, 4 Yrs; Mu Sigma Epsilon; Alhambra Musa Caravan S'ship; Upper 5%, HS Class; March of Dimes Hlth Careers

Awd; Yth Cares Awd; Nat Hon Soc; VFW Awd; Nat Dean's List; Intl Yth in Achmt; 1st Scholar, Lenior-Rhyne Col, 3.98 GPA; g/Lang Arts Edr in Resident Sch for the Deaf; Grad Sch Speech Pathol or Audiol.

PRUDHOMME, PENNY ANN oc/Student; b/Jul 2, 1965; h/2716 Carol, Big Spring, TX 79720; p/Lenace and Jean Prudhomme, Big Sprg, TX; ed/Grad, Big Sprg HS; Att'd Howard Col, 1982-83; pa/Treas, French Clb, 1982-83; Varsity Tennis, 1980-81; g/Attend TX Tech Univ; Become an Acct.

PRUITT, ANNISE DELAIN oc/Computer Systems Analyst; b/Dec 13, 1957; h/2509 Hoover Avenue, Dayton, OH 45407; ba/Dayton, OH; p/Robert and Mary L Pruitt, Dayton, OH; ed/Dipl, Belmont HS, 1976; BS Computer Sci, Ctl St Univ, 1980; pa/Data Processing Asst, Dayco, 1978, 1979; Computer Sys Analyst-3 1980-81, Computer Sys Analyst-2 1982-, Dayton Power & Light; cp/Ctl St Alumni; r/Tabernacle Bapt Ch, Christian Ed Bd Secy 1982, Tabernacle Tutorial Prog 1982; hon/Lizzie R Francis S'ship, 1976; Freshman Hons, 1977; Nat Dean's List, 1977, 1979, 1980; Intl Yth in Achmt; g/Receive Master's Deg in Computer Sci or MBA; Own Conslt Ser; Write Novels.

PRUITT, CHERYL LYNN oc/Student; b/Mar 17, 1963; h/2581 Monroe Street, Gary, IN 46407; ba/Holly Sprgs, MS; p/Mr and Mrs Robert Pruitt Jr, Gary, IN; ed/Grad, Roosevelt Sr HS, 1981; Att'g Rust Col; pa/Lab Tech, US Dept of Agri, 1983; Jewelry Clk, Zayres Dept Store, 1980-82; Secy, Madison & Madison's Intl, 1980; Cashier, Thrift-T-Mart Supermkt, 1980; Rec Supvr, Delaney U Meth Ch, 1979; cp/Pres, U Meth Yth; Xino Org; Bus Mgr, Exec Adults of Tomorrow; Miss E L Rust Hall, 1982; Sophomore Class Secy, 1981; Alpha Kappa Alpha Sorority Inc, Basileus (Theta Upsilon Chapt; HS Sr Class VP; hon/Info Newspaper, Outstg Citizen of NW IN Yth Awd, 1982; NHS; S'ship Awd; Miss Xino-Phi Delta Kappa, Beta Mu Chapt; W/W in Am; Soc of Dist'd Am HS Students; g/Biol, Pre-med, Med Sch.

PRUITT, CHERRY LEA oc/Secretary; b/Nov 3, 1961; h/8450 Cambridge, Apartment #1244, Houston, TX 77054; ba/Houston, TX; p/E B and Dessie Pruitt, Midland, TX; ed/Grad, Robert E Lee HS, 1980; Att'd Midland Jr Col, 1980-82; Maj Modeling Deg, Barbizon Sch of Modeling, 1982-83; pa/Gen Sales Mgr's Secy, Jimmie Green Chevrolet, 1983-; Data Processing Mgr, Specialty Res & Sales, Inc, 1980-82; Jobbership Clk, W TX Gas, 1979-80; Asst Sales Mgr, Austin Shoe Store, 1976-79; Pres, Ofc Ed Assn, 1979-80; Am Chem Assn; Artist Models Bur of Houston, 1983; cp/Midland Col Rodeo Assn, 1981-; Student Rep, 3 Yrs; hon/Miss Congeniality for Grad'g Class of Barbizon Sch of Modeling, 1983; 6th Pl at Regional OEA Conf in Job Interview II; Elected Sweetheart of Midland Col Rodio Clb, 1982; g/Further Ed & Strive for Maj in Communs; Further Advmt in Modeling Career through TV.

PRUITT, SHELLY APEL oc/Loan Officer; b/May 2, 1960; h/114 Northeast Taylor, Burleson, TX 76028; ba/Burleson, TX; m/Paul Eddie; p/Mr and Mrs Irvin Curt Apel, Burleson, TX; sp/

Winnia Bee Kocurek, Burleson, TX; ed/ Grad, Burleson HS, 1978; BFA Interior Design, N TX St Univ, 1982; pa/Interior Decorator, Montgomery Ward, 1982; Foster Mortgage Corp, 1982-83; Loan Ofcr, Ft Worth Mortgage, 1983-; hon/ Most Attractive, 1976 & 1978; Miss Burleson HS, 1978; Nat Hon Soc, 1976-78; Dean's List w Over GPA 3.5, 1980-81; g/Licensed Real Est Broker; Owner Bus in Interior Design.

PRYOR, LORENE oc/Executive Secretary; b/Jul 24, 1956; h/Post Office Box 635, Denmark, SC 29042; ba/ Denmark, SC; p/Wildon and Magalene Pryor, Summerville, SC; ed/Dipl, Summerville HS, 1974; Assoc Deg/Secretarial Sci, Denmark Tech Col, 1976; Att'g Voorhees Col; pa/Secy to Dean of Adult & Cont'g Ed 1976-79, Tchr Assoc Secretarial Sci Dept 1979-81, Exec Secy to the Pres 1981-, Denmark Tech Col; Editor-in-Chief, Col Yrbook, 1976; Denmark Tech Col Softball Tm Mem, 1975-76; Denmark Tech Col Advr; Student Govt Assn, 1979-80; Pep Clb, 1975-76; r/Bapt; hon/Hon Cert, Dean's List, Voorhees Col, 1982; Hon Cert, Pres's List, Voorhees Col, 1982; Art Achmt Awd, Summerville HS, 1974; Plaque for Sincere & Devoted Efforts in Secretarial Sci Dept, 1980; Trophy for Support & Appreciation to Student Govt Assn as Advr, 1979-80; g/Receive Bachelor's Deg in Bus Ed & Master's Deg; Tchg Career in Bus.

PRYZGODA, CRAIG ALAN oc/ Student; b/Oct 8, 1966; h/213 Cedarwood Drive, Jamestown, NC 27282; p/ Alan and Virginia Pryzgoda, Jamestown, NC; ed/Grad, SW Guilford HS, 1984; pa/HS Varsity Soccer & Varsity Baseball; SECME Clb; Tennis Tm; cp/ BSA; r/Cath; hon/NC Boys St, 1983; Yth Legis Assem, 1982.

PUGH, GREGORY TODD oc/Student; b/Apr 24, 1966; h/1306 Danny St, Claremore, OK 74017; p/Phillip and Shirley Pugh, Claremore, OK; pa/Pres, Future Bus Ldrs of Am; F'ship of Christian Aths; Spanish Clb; Golf; Tennis; Soccer; r/Cath; hon/Nat Hon Soc; OSU Hon Scholar; OSU Freshman S'ship; Hon Roll; Optimist's Honoree; Lttr Awds, Typing I, Hons Geometry, Hons Am Hist; 3-Yr Perfect Attendance; g/Attend OK St Univ & Maj in Aerospace Engrg.

PUGH, KIMBERLY CARZEL oc/ Student; b/Mar 23, 1966; h/330 East 2nd Street Northwest, Siler City, NC 27344; p/Jimmie C and Judy B Pugh, Siler City, NC; ed/Dipl, Jordan Matthews HS, 1984; pa/Treas 1983-84, Mem 1982-84, Beta Clb; VP of Freshmen, Sophomore

& Jr Classes; Pres, Durham Dist Yth Coun; Pres, Yg Adult Ch Choir; Upward Bound, UNC-Chapel Hill; hon/Girls St, UNC-G; W/W Amg Am HS Students; g/Attend NC A&T St Univ & Maj in Engrg.

PUGH, WILLIAM FRANKLIN oc/ Student and Legal Clerk; b/Jan 15, 1960; h/Post Office Box 56, Chilhowie, VA 24319; ba/Falls Ch, VA; p/Mr and Mrs Harry W Pugh, Chilhowie, VA; ed/ Grad, Chilhowie HS, 1978; BA, Oral Roberts Univ, 1982; JD (in progress), George Mason Univ Sch of Law; pa/ Legal Clk, Stuart B Mitchell & Assocs, Falls Ch, VA, 1984; Intern, US House of Reps, Agri Com; Vol Intern, US Cts Adm Ofc, Magistrates Div; cp/F'ship of Christian Aths; Christian Sers Coun, Oral Roberts Univ; Nat Hist Soc; hon/ Outstg Political Sci Student, Oral Roberts Univ, 1982; Nat Dean's List; Nat Hon Soc; Yg Personalities of the S; Intl Yth in Achmt; g/Legal Career.

PURVIS, WENDY KIM oc/Student; b/Aug 11, 1964; h/3205 Maxwell, Midland, TX 79701; p/James and Margaret Purvis, Midland, TX; ed/Grad, Robert E Lee HS, 1982; Att'g TX Christian Univ; pa/Secy, James H Purvis, 1979-81; Desk Clk, Saleslady, Julian Gold's, 1981; cp/Jr Engrg Tech Soc, 1981-82; Symph Debs, 1978-82; GSA, 1972-79; Jr Coun LHS, 1980-82; LHS 100 Clb Secy, 1979-80; LFS Flag Corps, 1978-79; Ch Choir, 1975-81; Ch F'ship, 1976-81; ASID, 1982-83; Wing Rep, Social Com, Programming Coun, Brachman Hall TCU, 1982-83; Explorers 1980-81, Post #299 1983-; Yg Life, 1978-82; LHS Gymnastics, 1979-80; Chi Omega, 1982-; LHS Rebelettes, 1979-81; Vol, Growth Ctr, Ft Worth; r/Presb; hon/1st Class Scout Awd, 1979; Midland 4-H Vaulting 1977-80, Bronze Medalist Awd 1977; g/TX Christian Univ Grad in Fashion Mdse & Minor in Mktg.

PURYEAR, PAULA LYNN oc/Student; b/Jun 22, 1967; h/3228 Constellation, Tallahassee, FL 32312; ba/ Tallahassee, FL; p/Ada Puryear, Tallahassee, FL; Paul Puryear, Charlottesville, VA; ed/Grad, Leon HS, 1983; pa/ Reg Chaplain, Jack & Jill of Am, Inc, 1982-; VP, Beta Clb, 1982-83, 1983-84; Hon Rebus Getis (Latin), 1982-; Santa-Gram Chm 1982-83, Chaplain 1983-84, Optimist Ser Clb; Charmrettes, 1982-; Explorer Post, Jour, 1982-; NAACP Yth Clb, 1982-; Trinity Ch Choir & Yth Grp, 1978-; Student Govt, 1983; Lemoyne Art Foun, 1979-82; Salters Dance Sch, 1981-82; Jr High Student Govt VP, 1979-80, 1980-81; 8th Grade Class Rep; Jr Varsity Cheerldr, 1980-81; Spanish Clb,

1982-83; Pep Clb, 1982-83; hon/Author Fiction, FL Hi Literary Mag 1981, Leon HS 1982; Poetry, Univ of Ctl FL; 2nd Pl 1982, 1st Pl 1983, FL A&M Univ; Tallahassee Democrat Lttr to Editor; Trinity Rep 1983, Harambie Fest Leon Rep 1983; cum laude Nat Latin, 1983; Most Valuable Optimist, 1983; Miss Jr Fashionette, 1981; Scholastic Art Contest Hon Mention, 1978; Gifted Prog, 1981-; Trinity Hons 11 AM Ser; Yth Spkr, 1982; Presiding Ofcr, 1983; 2nd Pl 1981 & 1983, 1st Pl 1982, Oratorical Contest Winner; Spkr at Black Hist Prog, Emancipation Day & Others; g/ Newspaper Jour, Become Pulitzer & Nobel Prize Winner.

PUYEAR, JILL BREWER oc/Student; b/Feb 6, 1961; h/226 River Valley Drive, Chesterfield, MO 63017; ba/Fayette, MO; p/Mr and Mrs R B Puyear, Chesterfield, MO; ed/Grad, Pkwy Ctl Sr HS, 1979; BS Ed, Ctl Meth Col, 1983; pa/ Social Pledge Capt, Social Chm, Secy, Zeta Psi Lambda, 1979-83; hon/Omicron Delta Kappa, 1982; Kappa Delta Pi, 1981; W/W; g/Elem Tchr.

PYLE, DAVID NELSON oc/Student; b/May 16, 1963; h/801 West 21st, Odessa, TX 79763; p/Mr and Mrs Joseph Pyle, Odessa, TX; ed/Grad, Odessa HS, 1981; Att'd Odessa Col, 1981-82, Sprg 1983; Univ of TX-Austin, Fall 1982; pa/ Am Chem Soc; VP, NJHS; NHS; German Clb; VP, Orch; FCA; cp/Football; Presb Yth Grp; VP, Hi-Y, 1981; Presb Yth Grp; hon/Acad Hon Roll; Nat Hon Soc; Jr Hon Soc; Hon Roll, 1977-81; Outstg Grad'g Sci Student, 1981; Lion's Clb Yg Texan of the Mo; Intl Rotary Yth Ldrship Awd, 1981; Grad cum laude 1982, Grad summa cum laude 1983; W/ W Amg HS Students; Commun Ldrs of Am; Intl Yth in Achmt; g/Obtain Bach's Deg in Biol; Enter Med Sch & Specialize in Anesth.

PYNE, PHILIP SCHUYLER oc/Sales Representative; b/Feb 11, 1956; h/3131 Meetinghouse Road, Apartment J-11, Boothwyn, Pennsylvania 19061; ba/ Fozcroft, PA; p/Charles Schuyler Pyne (dec); Virginia Smith Pyne, Fremont, IN; ed/Escola Graduada de Sao Paulo HS, 1975; Att'd Bowling Green St Univ, 1975-76; BS, Ball St Univ, 1981; mil/ ROTC, 2 Yrs; cp/Histn Gen, Descendants of the Signers of the Declaration of Independence; Capt, Basketball, Football Tms; Pres, Student Body; BSA Eagle Scout; VP, Col Repubs; Yg Repubs; Vestry Ad Hoc Com of Epis Ch; r/Epis; hon/Pi Sigma Gamma; Rep'd Ball St Univ at Model UN, 1980; All-Star Basketball Tm of Am Schs in S Am; Pi Sigma Alpha, 1978; Eagle Scout, 1974; g/MBA; Succeed in Bus, Run for Cong.

Q

QUIDD, DAVID ANDREW oc/ Paralegal; b/Sep 8, 1954; h/1141 Papworth Avenue, Metairie, LA 70005; ba/ New Orleans, LA; p/John and Mary Quidd, Metairie, LA; ed/Archbishop Rummel HS, 1972; BA, Univ New Orleans, 1976; pa/Paralegal, Philip L Kitchen Atty, 1983-; Paralegal, Kitchen & Montagnet, 1981-83; Paralegal, Elliot E Brown, 1981; St Vol Coor, Carter/ Mondale Re-Election Com, 1979-80; Law Clk, Bradley & Wall, 1979-80; cp/ Omicron Delta Kappa; Student Govt Pres, Univ New Orleans, 1975-76; Pres, LA Yg Dems, 1975-77; Pres, LA St Univ Dems, 1978; r/Cath; hon/Dist'd Polit Sci Grad, Polit Sci Dept, Univ New Orleans, 1976; Past Pres Awd, Alliance for Good Govt, 1983; W/W Am Polits, Personalities of S.

R

RADACK, PAUL CHESTER JR oc/ Student; b/Jul 4, 1963; h/1411 Pennell Drive, Morrow, GA 30260; p/Paul and Janet Radak, Morrow, GA; ed/Forest Pk Sr HS; Clayton Jr Col; Att'g Univ GA; cp/Alpha Hi-Y, 1976-77; Omega Hi-Y, Secy, 1977-78; Coed-Y 1978-81, Co-Commun Projs Chm 1979-80, Co-Pres 1980-81, NW Dist Pres St YMCA 1980-81; St YMCA Col Staff Mem, 1981-83; Spanish Clb 1979-81, VP 1980-81; Beta Clb 1978-81, VP 1980-81; Nat Hon Soc 1979-81, Co-Pres 1980-81; Interclb Rep Nat Hon Soc, 1980-81, Cross Country 1979-81; Math Team, 1979-80; Model UN Participant, 1979-80; Clayton Jr Col Fgn Lang Clb, Parliamentn 1982-83; Nat HS & Jr Col Math Clb, Mu Alpha Theta, 1982-83; Phi Theta Kappa, 1983; Varsity Track, 1978-80; Varsity Cross Country 1977-81, Capt 1979-81; Varsity Basket-ball, 1977-81; Jr Varsity Ftball 1979; Clayton Jr Col Intramural Horse Champ, 1983; r/Cath; hon/Cert of Acad Recog in Chem, 2nd Yr, 1st Pl Trophy, 1979-80; Cert of Acad Recog, Sci, Eng, World & Am Hist, Spanish, 1978-80; Spanish II Plaque, 1979-80; Lttr of Commend from Nat Merit S'ship, 1980-81; Cert of Merit Algebra 1978-79, Trigonometry 1979-80; Gov's Hons Nom, 1979-80; Nat Hon Soc Awd Winner, 1981; Valedictorian, 1981; John Ward West S'ship Recip, 1981-82, 1982-83; All-Am HS Student Ath, 1981; Clayton Jr Col Dean's List, 1981-83; Nat Dean's List, 1982-83; Recip of Clayton Jr Col Biol Awd, 1983; Recip of Clayton Jr Col Cash Awd for 4.0 GPA, 1983; Recip of Univ GA Transfer S'ship, 1983; W/W in Fgn Lang Students in GA & FL, 1979, 1980; g/Med Sch, Ortho Surge.

RAE, JANET SANDERSON b/Sep 14, 1962; h/600 John Street, Manhattan Beach, CA 90266; p/Matthew Jr and Janet Rae, Manhattan Beach, CA; ed/ Mira Costa HS, 1980; AB, Univ of MI; pa/Intern: *LA Times* Suburban Sects 1983, *LA Times* Wash Bur 1982, UPI-LA 1982, Bch Cities Newspapers 1981; Mng Editor, *The Michigan Daily*, 1983-; cp/ Alpha Phi Sorority; Histn, Adara Hon Soc; Golden Key Nat Hon Soc; CA Scholastic Press Assn; Pacific Coast Press Clb; VP, CSF; Night Editor, *Michigan Daily*; Rep, Inter-Sch Coun; Editor-in-Chief, Sch Newspaper; Prose Editor, Lit Mag; Jr Varsity Basketball; hon/1st Pl, News, Detroit Press Clb Foun Col Awds, 1982; Grad Best in Class, CA Scholastic Press Assn Wkshop; 1st Pl, News, El Camino Jr Col Press Day & So CA Jour Ed Assn Regs; Intl W/W Frats & Sororities; Intl Yth in Achmt; W/W Among Am HS Students; Am Outstg Names & Faces.

RAGAN, PAMELA DENISE b/Jan 29, 1961; h/Route 2 Box 37, Woods Valley Road, Cumberland Furnace, TN 37051; p/Mr and Mrs William Earl Ragan, Cumberland Furnace, TN; ed/Dickson Co Sr HS, 1979; Austin Peay St Univ; pa/Teller, No Bk of TN, 1983-; cp/Hon Prog Students Assn Pres; Phi Alpha Theta VP; John Jay Pre-Law Soc Pres; Pi Sigma Alpha, Pres; The Public Mgmt Soc; Laurel Wreath; Phi Kappa Phi; Gamma Beta Phi; Alpha Lambda Delta; SNEA; Omicron Delta Kappa; Student

Tchr Ed Assn; Secy, Jr Class; SGA Senator; Alpha Mu Gamma; hon/Social Studies Dept Awd; Top 5% of Grad'g Class; Del, Pres Classroom for Yg Ams; Hon mention, Fac Awds; 2nd Pl, Voice of Democracy Essay Contest; Future Tchrs Am S'ship; Pilot Clb S'ship; Pres Awd; Univ Ser S'ship; TN Hist Soc Awd for Most Outstg Graduating Sr Hist Maj; John Burgess Awd for Most Outstg Graduating Sr Polit Sci Maj; Havill Citizenship Awd Grad Asst'ship in Hist; g/Tch Am Hist at Col or Univ.

RAGLAND, LeANITA SHARME oc/ IBM Marketing Assistant; b/Aug 1, 1961; h/5470 Watercress Place, Colum-bia, MD 21045; ba/Balto, MD; ed/ Howard HS, 1979; BA, UMBC, 1983; pa/Asst Dir Arts/Crafts, Timber Ridge Camping Reservation, 1982-83; Merry-Go-Round, 1978-82; The Limited, 1983; Telephone Pollster, UMBC, 1979-83; cp/Phi Kappa Phi Hon Soc, 1983-; Las Caballeras, Fdr & Capt, 1977-78; r/Cath; hon/Miss MD, Nat Teen-Ager, 1978; Gov's Cert of Merit, 1978; Acad Achmt Awd, Col S'ship; Henry Callis Cup; Outstg Character in HS; MD Gifted & Talented Prog; Outstg Yg Ams; Intl Yth in Achmt; g/ to Run Own Bus.

RAGLAND, SHERMAN L II oc/ Student; b/Jul 4, 1962; h/5470 Water-cress Place, Columbia, MD 21045; p/Lt Col and Mrs S L Ragland, Columbia, MD; ed/Howard HS; BS, Towson St Univ, 1984; cp/IBM, Towson St Univ Student Govt Assn; Towson St Univ Residence Dept; Alpha Epsilon Rho Hon Broadcasting Soc; Student Ambassa-dors; Commun Asst; Soc for Advmt Mgmt; r/Cath; hon/Author of "The Use of Motivation, Org, Inspiration, Sales Technique, & PMA in Bldg An Effective Residence Envir"; W/W Among Am Col & Univ Students; W/W Among Am Biog Dist'd Ams; Personalities of Am; Biog of Outstg Yg Ams; W/W Among Am HS Students; Commun Ldrs Am; g/to become world's Greatest Philanthropist.

RAINS, REBECCA KAY oc/Student; b/May 19, 1962; h/340 North Walnut, Apartment 5, Cookeville, TN 38501; ed/ Pickett Co HS; Motlow St Commun Col; TN Technol Univ; cp/Soil Conserv Yth Bd; Kappa Delta Social Sorority, Chapt Ed Chm 1983, All-Sing Chm 1984; Gamma Beta Phi Hon Soc, 1981; Motlow St Lady Bucks Basketball Team, 1980-81; TN Tech Basketball Team, 1983; HS Basketball, Softball; Col Intramural Ftball, Softball & Volleyball; Acteens; Pep Clb; Beta Clb; FHA; Bapt Student Union, 1980-81; r/Bapt; hon/ Miss Pickett Co; Most Talented; Home-coming Ct, 1981; Homecoming Ct, 1983; All State in HS Basketball, 1978-80; All Dist 1978-79; All Reg 1977-80; All Tri Lakes Conf, 1977-80; Amateur Aths Am All Tourney; Ldrship Awd 1977-80, Gamma Beta Phi Hon soc; g/Mktg Maj; Advtg.

RAKES, MELANIE KAY oc/Student; b/Dec 12, 1963; h/Route 3, Box 176, Ferrum, VA 24088; ba/Same; p/Marvin R and Vivian M Rakes, Ferrum, VA; ed/ Franklin Co HS; Ferrum Col; pa/Fair-ystone Concessions Inc, Sum 1981; Seasonal Ranger, Fairystone St Pk, Sum 1982; Clerical Asst, Ferrum Col, Sum 1982; Employee Sum Progs, Ferrum Col, Sum 1983; cp/Phi Theta Kappa,

Secy, 1983-84; Ferrum Col Debate Clb, 1982-83; r/Assemblies of God; hon/ Author of "The Plane Crash", *The Chrysalis*; Freshman Eng Awd; Wn Civilization Awd; *Chrysalis* Awd; W/W Am Jr Cols; g/Biol Maj.

RAMEY, MELINDA LOUISE oc/ Teacher; b/Sep 30, 1961; h/2230 Rich-mond Avenue, Houston, TX 77098; ba/ Shreveport, LA; p/Mr and Mrs Horace E Hickman, Houston, TX; ed/Dipl of Vocal Music, St Dipl, 1979; BA in Music, 1983; cp/Omicron Delta Kappa; Phi Beta; Alpha Chi; Chi Omega Frat; Centenary Col Choir; hon/Nat Dean's List; Centenary Col Dean's List; Intl Yth in Achmt; Summa Cum Laude Grad; Outstg Sr Music Awd; Sue Solomon S'ship Awd; Hon Maroon Jacket; Not-able Wom of TX.

RAMIREZ, PETER PAUL oc/Student; b/Apr 29, 1964; h/7957 Cross Creek Drive, Glenburnie, MD; p/Jorge B and Adriana Ramirez, Glenburnie, MD; ed/ Martin Spolding HS, 1982; Loyola Col; cp/Varsity Soccer & LaCrosse, 1980-82; Sociedad Hon Hispanica Pres, 1979-82; NHS, 1979-82, Pres 1980-82; Sr Class Coun, 1981-82; r/Cath; hon/Outstg Soph, 1979-80; Soc Hon Hispanica Awd, 1980-81; Awds in biol, US Hist, Physics, Eng Lit, Am Lit, Chem, World Hist; MD Dist'd Scholar, 1982; Fac Awd, Sci Awd, 1982; g/MD.

RAMIS, ANTONIO FERNANDO oc/ Student; b/May 19, 1957; h/5604 Long-fellow Street, Number 201, Riverdale, MD 20737; m/Camille Irene; c/Angela Marie; p/Felipe and Maria Ramis, Mar-acay, Venezuela; ed/Elias Sanches Rubio, 1975; AA, Prince Georges Com-mun Col, 1983; BS, Univ MD, 1984; pa/ Engr, NIH, 1983-; cp/Am Soc Mech Engrs; Am Soc Heating, Refrigeration, & Air-Conditioning Engrs; r/Cath; hon/ Prince George Commun Col Dean's List; Nat Dean's List; Personalities of Am S; g/Career in Mech Engrg.

RAMSAY, ELIZABETH ANN oc/ Accountant; b/Jun 10, 1961; h/8633 Westglen, Dallas, TX 75228; ba/Dallas, TX; p/David and Charlene Ramsay, Dallas, TX; ed/Grad, Bryan Adams HS, 1979; BBA, Stephen F Austin St Univ, 1983; pa/Acct, Peak, Marwick, Mitchell & Co, 1983-; cp/Campus Crusade for Christ; Beta Alpha Psi, Reporting Secy; Phi Chi Theta, Treas; Phi Eta Sigma; Alpha Chi; Beta Gamma Sigma; Acctg Clb; r/Meth, Casa Linda U Meth Ch & Choir; hon/CPA Exam 1983; Tony Clifton Meml S'ship; YMCA Phillip Jonsson Foun S'ship; 1983 Outstg Student in Dept of Fin; 1983 Outstg Wom, Sch of Bus; Bryan Adams HS PTA S'ship; W/W Among Students in Am Cols & Univs; g/Career in Acctg & Obtain CPA; Grad Sch.

RAMSEY, JANET WOODY oc/Stu-dent; b/Jan 26, 1960; h/2902 Northwest 41st Avenue, Gainesville, FL 32605; m/ Bobby L Jr; p/Mr and Mrs George Walker Woody, Columbia, TN; sp/Mr and Mrs Bobby L Ramsey Sr, Spring Hill, TN; ed/Ctl HS, 1978; AS, Columbia St Commun Col, 1980; BA, Memphis St Univ, 1982; cp/Pvt Music Tutor; Phi Kappa Phi Hon Soc; Mortar Bd; Golden Key Nat Hon Soc; Chi Beta Phi Sci Hon Soc; Inter-Varsity Bible Study; Psychol Hons Prog, Memphis St Univ; Gamma Beta Phi; hon/Pres Awd for Top Grad, Columbia St Commun Col, 1980;

Golden Key Nat Hon Soc Sr S'ship Awd, 1981; W/W Among Students in Am Univs & Cols; g/Devel Psychol; Res w Gifted Chd & Creat.

RAMSEY, PATSY DARLENE oc/Student; b/Nov 8, 1962; h/200 55th Street Northeast, Washington, DC 20019; p/Betty L Ramsey, Wash, DC; ed/HD Woodson Sr HS, 1980; Univ SC; cp/Phi Beta Omega; Alpha Kappa Psi Bus Frat; Alpha Kappa Alpha Sorority; Rosa Hill Bapt Ch; Sr Class VP; Nat Hon Soc; r/Bapt; hon/Lyceum Lecture Awd, 1981; Nat Dean's List, 1980-81; W/W Among Am HS Students; Personalities of Am; Entrance into Fed Govt Jr F'ship Prog; Univ SC; g/Bus Adm Maj w Concentration in Mgmt.

RANDALL, NORRIS ASHLEY JR oc/Student; b/Aug 26, 1955; h/919 Lambeth Circle, Durham, NC 27705; ba/Durham, NC; m/Laine Austin; c/Laura Katherine; p/Norris A and Janet Randall, Phoenix City, AZ; sp/Laura C Austin, Amarillo, TX; ed/Glenwood Sch, 1973; BA, Huntingdon Col, 1977; MS, Univ NC-Greensboro, 1983; MDiv, Duke Div Sch, 1984; pa/Tech Dir, Springer Theatre Co, 1980-81; Prog Dir, Camp Chimney Rock, 1980; Tech Dir & Shop Steward, New Harmony Theatre Co, 1979; Aquatics Dir, YMCA, 1977; cp/Student Rep Assn of Duke Div Sch; Pres, Middler Class, 1982-83; Jr Class Rep, 1981-82; CoChm, Commun Life Com, 1983-84; Div Players, Prodr & Pres, 1982-84; r/United Meth; hon/Coloring Book Type, Exper & Chd's Divergent Pictorial Prodn, *Jour of Applied Devel Psychol*, 1981; Keller Small Grant for Res, 1980; Outstg Yg Men Am; W/W Am Cols; g/Min in Wn NC Conf of United Meth.

RANDOLPH, JOSEPH TODD oc/Student; b/Oct 26, 1966; h/Route 6, Box 317, Cookeville, TN 38501; p/Mr and Mrs John H Randolph, Cookeville, TN; ed/Rickman HS, 1984; cp/HS Basketall, Baseball, Jr Class Pres; hon/Alt Boys St, 1983; g/Attend TN Technol Univ, Crim Justice Maj.

RANDOLPH, KIMBERLY PHELPS oc/Customer Service Representative; b/Jun 6, 1963; h/Route 3, Box 705, Trinity, AL 35673; ba/Decatur, AL; m/Kelly Scott; p/Neal S and Theresa Phelps, Trinity, AL; sp/Jimmy and Dean Randolph, Bremen, AL; ed/W Morgan HS; Calhoun Commun Col; pa/First St Bk, 1981-83; Bk & Loan Teller, Pt-time Secy, Avco Financial Sers Inc, 1983-; Customer Ser Rep in Tng to become Adm Asst; cp/Majorette, 1981; Band Secy, 1981; Solo Ensemble, 1979-81; Pep Band; Jr Beta Clb Secy, 1977; Sr Beta Clb Pres, 1981; Yrbook Staff, 1980; Student Coun, 1978-80; Jr/Sr Class Pres, 1980-81; 1st Runner-up Miss Rebel, 1981; Miss Congeniality, 1981; "A" Hon Roll, 1981; Girls St Rep, 1980; r/So Bapt; hon/Homecoming Attendant, 1980, 1981; Soc Dist Am HS Students; W/W Among Am HS Students; Salutatorian; g/Mgmt.

RASEY, JEFFREY WATSON oc/Student; b/May 16, 1963; h/1811 Brightwood Drive, Hagerstown, MD 21740; p/Watson and Janice Rasey, Hagerstown, MD; ed/Att'd Parkway S HS, 1977-79; Grad, S Hagerstown HS, 1981; cp/Alpha Lambda Delta Hon Soc, Secy, 1982-83; Phi Eta Sigma Hon Soc, 1982-83; Am Mktg Assn, 1982-83;

Dorm Govt, Treas, 1982-83; Intramural Softball, Volleyball, Ftball, Soccer, Basketball, 1981-83; Yth Advr, MD Gov Coun; MD Boys St; Marching Concert & Pep Bands; Sr Boys Clb; Latin Clb; Drama Clb; Ski Clb; Track Team; Wrestling Team; Computer Clb; YMCA Yth & Govt; r/Prot; hon/Eagle Scout; Elks S'ship-Ldrship Awd; Nat Hon Soc; Outstg Latin Student; g/Law Sch.

RATCLIFFE, BARRY JOE oc/Student; b/Mar 6, 1962; h/Post Office Box 75, Glade Hill, VA 24092; p/Bernice A Ratcliffe, Glade Hill, VA; ed/Franklin Co HS, 1980; Cert, Carolina Sch Broadcasting, 1981; Radford Univ; cp/Student Coun Treas, 1975-80; Spanish Clb, 1978; Chess Clb, 1978; Photo Clb, 1979; Nat Assn Student Coun Treas, 1979; Basketball, 1976; IEEE, 1982; Chm of Plays & Shows Com, 1982; Pres of Student Life at Radford Univ, 1983; r/Bapt; hon/g/Communs Maj.

RATLEY, JEANIE RAY oc/Student; b/Aug 25, 1966; h/207 Stack Street, St Pauls, NC 28384; p/Jackie and Mildred Ratley, St Pauls, NC; cp/Secy, Treas, Pres, Sci Clb; Band Libn Secy, Capt; Jr Beta Clb, Pres; Jr Hons Soc, Pres; Student Govt Assn, Assem & Class Bds; French Clb; Leo Clb; PTSA, Student VP; Sophomore Homeroom Rep; Jr Class Treas; Jr Clb Reporter; Nat Hon Soc, Pres; Annual Staff, Bus Mgr; r/Bapt; hon/Reg Spelling Bee, 1979-80; All-St Band, 1980-81; WOW Hist Awd; Outstg Musicianship Awd; Perfect Attendance, 1981-82; Vol Ser Awd; Medals for Superior Ratings at Solo & Ensemble Contest; US Achmt Acad Nat Awd; W/W Among Am HS Students; Dist'd Am; Intl Yth in Achmt; g/attend Univ NC-Chapel Hill, Nsg Maj.

RAUNIKAR, ROBERT AUSTIN oc/Student; b/Aug 9, 1961; h/937 Springer Drive, Griffin, GA 30223; ba/Clinton, SC; p/Robert Raunikar, Griffin, GA; ed/BS, Presb Col, 1983; pa/Lab Asst 1980, 1981, Grad Level Rschr 1982, GA Exptl Sta; cp/Beta Clb; Key Clb, Histn; Med Internship; Med Explorers, Prog Chm; Am Chem Soc, VP, Pres; Am Inst Biol Sci; Tau Psi Chapt of Beta Beta Beta, Charter Mem & Second VP; Christians in Action (BSU), Newslttr Editor; Student Vol Sers, Hospice Coor; Staley Lecture Foun; Newlife Christian Singers; r/Prot; hon/Pubs; JROTC, Acad Excell Wreath & Ribbon, Superior Jr Cadet Decoration Awd; Univ GA Cert Merit; Freedom's Foun at Val Forge Participant; REA Yth Tour (Wash DC) Participant; Dillard-Elliott Scholar; Dean's List; Beta Beta Beta; W/W Among Students in Am Cols & Univs; W/W Among Am HS Students; g/MD.

RAY, ROBBIE LYNN oc/Secretary; b/Jun 13, 1961; h/Route 1, Box 251, Oglethorpe, GA 31068; p/Robert L Ray, Oglethorpe, GA, and Barbara A Ray, Montezuma, GA; ed/Macon Co HS, 1979; Brewton-Parker Col, 1979-81; BS, GA SWn Col, 1981-83; pa/Secy, Mayfair Indust Inc, 1983-; cp/Nsg & Allied Hlth Forum, Secy; Phi Theta Kappa, Pres; *Coronet*, Mng Editor, Editor-in-Chief; Bapt Student Union, Prog Chm; Puppet Team; Revival Team; Bapt Yg Wom; Asst Editor, Yearbook Staff; Pres, Tri-Hi-Y; Band; FTA, Pres; Sam Jones Hon Soc; Debate; Pep Clb; Student Coun; Art Editor, *Bow Wow*; Jour Clb; Vol for Am Cancer Soc; Ch

Pianist; r/Bapt; hon/Nat Dean's List; Yearbook Awd; Salutatorian of Class of 1979; Prin's Awd; Outstg Sci Student; Outstg Math Student; Univ of GA Cert of Merit; W/W Among Am Jr Cols; Intl Yth in Achmt; Home Ec Awd; Acad Bowl; Sci Team; Math Team; 4-Yr Perfect Attendance; Outstg Sr; "Most Intelligent"; "Most Likely to Succeed"; "Most Dependable"; Outstg Christian Ldrship; Crisco Awd, Outstg Home Ec Student; Cert for Math; Cert for Home Ec & FHA; Page in House of Reps; Salutatorian of 8th Grade Grad'g Class; Yg Personalities of S; g/Master's & Doct in Math.

RAY, RONA G oc/Student; b/Feb 5, 1962; h/233 South Porter Drive, Richmond, KY 40475; p/Harold Ray, Berea, KY, and Mary Plummer, Richmond, KY; ed/Madison Ctl HS, 1980; En KY Univ; pa/Sales Clk, Ken Car Clothing & Shoes, 1979-83; En KY Univ, 1983; cp/Kappa Delta Phi, 1983-84; 4-H Asst Dog Clb; Assn Ch'd Ed Intl; r/Bapt; g/Elem Ed; Adm Wk.

RAY, STEPHEN D oc/Student; b/Jun 24, 1965; h/Route 2, Box 402-B, Golden, MS 38847; p/Douglas and Rebecca Ray, Golden, MS; ed/Red Bay HS, 1983; NE MS Jr Col; cp/Beta Clb, 1980-83; HS Band, 1978-83; Col Band, Marching Band, Concert Band, Jazz Band, 1983-84; hon/US Achmt Acad Recog, 1983; Best All Around Bandsman, 1981, 1983; Mr Red Bay HS Bandsman, 1982; Business Awd, 1983-84; g/Dentistry.

RAYBURN, DOUGLASS MICHAEL oc/Student; b/Nov 11, 1966; h/5737 Buxbriar, Memphis, TN 38119; p/Dr and Mrs Mike Rayburn, Memphis, TN; ed/Memphis Univ; cp/Jr Varsity Basketball, 1982; Yg Life Meth Yth F'ship.

RAYFORD, CLEVELAND EUGENE oc/Resident Physician; b/Sep 29, 1955; h/411 Northeast Timber Creek Drive, Lee's Summit, MO 64063; m/Sherrill Y; c/Cleveland E II; p/Odell Rayford, Pine Bluff, AR; sp/Willie Mae Roberson, Rison, AR; ed/Watson Chapel HS, 1973; BSk, MD, Univ AR; pa/Resident Phy Internal Med, Univ MO-KC Affiliate Hosps, 1982; cp/Pres Student Coun, 1972-73; Treas, Local Br So Christian Ldrship, 1973-77; Pres, Alpha Kappa Mu Hon Soc, 1976-77; Pres, Student Nat Med Assn, Local Chapt, 1980-81; r/Bapt; hon/Boys St, 1976; Outstg HS Jr, 1971-72; Outstg HS Sr, 1972-73; Nat Sojourners Awd, 1973; Col S'ship; Alpha Kappa Mu Awd, 1977; Biol Awd, 1976, 1977; Nat Med Assn Awd, 1982; W/W: Among Am HS Students, Am Cols & Univs; Outstg Am HS Students.

RAYFORD, SHERRILL YVONNE oc/English Teacher; b/Mar 20, 1957; h/411 Northeast Timber Creek Drive, Lee's Summit, MO 64063; m/Cleveland E; c/Cleveland E II; p/Mrs Willie Roberson, Rison, AR; sp/Odell Rayford, Pine Bluff, AR; ed/BS, Univ AR, 1979; MA, Univ Ctl AR, 1983; pa/Lng Ctr Dir, Pioneer Commun Col, 1983; Devel Studies Instr, 1984; Pt-time Eng Instr, Penn Val Commun Col, 1983; Eng Tchr, Little Rock Public Schs, 1979-82; Clk-Typist, Univ AR, 1977-78; Cnslr, Univ AR, Upward Bound, 1977; Asst Secy, City Hall in Rison AR, 1976; cp/MO Voc Assn; MO Voc Special Needs Assn, 1933-84; Pioneer Fac Assn Mem, 1983-84; Nat Assn for Devel/Remedial Studies in Ed, 1983-84; Kappa Delta Pi,

1978; Sigma Tau Delta, 1977; Multi-Cultural Wkshop, 1981; CTA Fac Rep, 1980-81; NEA, 977-82; AR Ed Assn, 1979-82; AR Coun of Tchrs of Eng, 1981-82; r/Bapt; hon/Hist Plaque, 1977; Acad S'ship, 1975-77; Rockefeller S'ship, 1976-77; Dean's List, 1975, 1977, 1978; W/W: Among Am HS Students, Among Students in Am Univs & Cols.

READING, KAREN ELAINE oc/Student; b/Nov 10, 1962; h/Route 1, Box 215-A, Humboldt, KS 66748; ba/Lawrence, KS; p/Mr and Mrs Doyle Reading, Humboldt, KS; ed/KS Univ; cp/Nat Hon Soc; Phi Theta Kappa; Sigma Alpha; Fgn Lang Clb; Cheerldg; Student Coun; Clb for Christ; Keyettes; r/Bapt; hon/Poem in *KS Eng Tchrs*; Nat Hon Soc, 1981; Jr Miss of Woodson & Neosho Co; g/Chem.

RECHCIGL, JOHN EDWARD oc/Student; b/Feb 27, 1960; h/1703 Mark Lane, Rockville, MD 20852; m/Nancy Rechcigl; p/Dr and Mrs M Rechcigl, Rockville, MD; sp/Mr and Mrs J Palko; ed/Charles W HS, 1978; BS, Univ DE, 1978; MS, VA Polytechnic Inst & St Univ, 1982; cp/Am Soc Agronomy; Soil Sci Soc Am; Nat Eagle Scout Assn; US Figure Skating Assn; Czechoslovak Soc of Arts & Sci in Am; Hon Soc of Phi Sigma; Hon Soc of Sigma Xi; hon/Num Pubs; Undergrad Sigma Xi Res Awd, 1981; Undergrad Res Grant, 1981; Nom, DE-MD Plant Food Assn Awd, 1981; g/PhD in Agronomy.

REDDICK, M JAMES JR oc/Minister; b/Feb 24, 1957; h/1445 South Highland Park Drive, Lake Wales, FL 33853; p/Marvin J Reddick, Lake Wales, FL, and Exie L Reddick (dec); ed/AA, Oxford Col of Emory Univ, 1977; BA, Emory Col of Emory Univ, 1979; MDiv, NO Bapt Theol Sem, 1983; pa/Holy Trinity Epis Ch Decatur Ga, 1980; Airline Bapt Ch Metairie LA, 1980-81; First Bapt Ch, Hahnville LA, 1981; Hayne Blvd Bapt Ch MO LA, 1982; Beaumont Pl Bapt Ch, 1982; Praxis, NOBTS/Home Mission Bd of So Bapt Conv, Phoenix, AZ; Field Evang/Ch Planter, 1982; cp/Circle K Clb, CoFdr & VP; NOBTS; Gospel Quartet, 1981; Biblical Archeol Soc; The Statute of Liberty, Ellis Island Foun; Nat Geographic Soc; Key Clb Fin/Proj Chm, 1974-75; Men's Glee Clb & Wom Chorale, Emory Col Asst Student Conductor, 1978-79; Men's Glee Clb, Emory Col, Concert Soloist, 1977-79, Secy 1978-79; Barbershop Quartet, Emory Col, 1977-78; Oxford Chorus, Oxford Col, Concert Soloist, 1975-77; Gospel Quartet, 1981; Seminarians Concert Soloist, 1980-81, NOBTS; Christian Student Assn, 1975-77; Bapt Student F'ship, Emory Col, 1977-79; Emory Christian F'ship, Emory Col, 1977-79; r/So Bapt; hon/Personalities of Am; Dir of Dist'd Ams; g/Doct in Discipleship Evang; Pastor Dir in Ch Extension Div of Home Mission Bd of So Bapt Conv.

REDMAN, SHARON LYNN oc/Student; h/1830 Balla Way, Grand Prairie, TX 75051; p/Charles and Ernestine Redman, Grand Prairie, TX; ed/South Grand Prairie HS; BBA, McMurry Col; cp/Prom Com, 1981-82; Nat Hon Soc, 1982-83; FBLA, 1982-83; GSA; r/Bapt; hon/Hon Roll; Supt's Acad List; Evening Optimist Clb S'ship; Girl of Mo, 1979; Dist Level 3rd Pl, Shorthand Team, 1982-83; Freshman Volleyball, 1979-80,

Dist Champs; Chey-Anne Drill Team, 1981-83, Spirit Awd, 1981; Soc Dist'd Am HS Students; g/Career in Bkg Sers.

REDMON, SONIA MARLENE oc/Student; b/Oct 20, 1963; h/Route 2, Box B, Smithville, TN 37166; p/Mr and Mrs W L Redmon, Smithville, TN; ed/Dekalb Co HS, 1981; TN Tech Univ; cp/Chem-Med Clb, 1982; Am Chem Soc Affiliate Mem, 1982; Beta Clb; FBLA; FHA Reporter; Sci Clb; Ldrship Coun; Band; hon/Intl Yth in Achmt; Commun Ldrs Am; Highest Distn, HS; W/W Among Am HS Students; g/Pharm.

REECE, ANGELA (ANGIE) ELIZABETH oc/Student; b/Dec 10, 1963; h/Route 3, Box 562, Easley, SC 29640; p/Mr and Mrs Charles E Reece, Easley, SC; ed/Pickens HS, 1982; Furman Univ; cp/HS Student Govt Ofcr; Mem of Beta Clb, Ofcr for Jr & Sr Yr; r/Bapt; hon/Hon Grad; Co Winner of Hearst Found S'ship Awd; SC Bapt Acteens S'ship Recip; Furman's Commuter S'ship Recip; W/W Among Am HS Students; g/BS Biol, Genetic Cnslr.

REED, ALICIA R oc/Student; b/Apr 18, 1963; h/129, 55th Street, Fairfield, AL 35064; ba/Talladega, AL; p/Mrs Rose D Reed, Fairfield, AL; ed/Talladega Col; Miles Col, 1982; Fairfield HS, 1979-81; W A Berry HS, 1977-79; cp/Alpha Kappa Alpha, 1983; Beta Clb; Cultural Arts Devel Soc; r/Prot; Soc of Dist'd HS Students; Alpha Chi; Beta Kappa Chi; Nat Deans List; Nat Hon Roll; g/Biol Maj; Ob/Gyn.

REED, DONNA ANN oc/Student; b/Jan 9, 1968; h/Route 3, Box 267, Berea, KY 40403; p/Donald W and Irene A Reed, Berea, KY; ed/Berea Commun HS; pa/Swim Instr/Aide, Berea Swimming Pool, 1981, 1982; cp/Berea Commun HS Band; Concert Band, 1979-84; Marching Band, 1981-82; Flag Squad, 1982-84; Berea Commun HS Jr Beta Clb, 1982-83; Sr Beta clb, 1983-84; Jr HS Basketball Team, 1981-82; Pep Clb, 1981-84; r/Bapt; hon/1983 Cecilian Music Clb S'ship Essay Winner; 3 Superior Ratings from Ctl KY Music Edrs Assn Solo & Ensemble Fest; g/attend Col; Maj in Law &/or Music.

REED, TAMMY DIANE oc/Student; b/Mar 7, 1959; h/Post Office Box 2, Princeton, WV 24740; p/Bobby and Pearl Reed, Princeton, WV; ed/Lakenheath Am HS, 1977; BS-Travel Industry Mgmt, Concord Col, 1981; Word of Faith Bible & Ldrship Inst, 1983-; pa/Assoc, Rose's Dept Store, 1982; Leggett Store, 1982; Rep, Avon, 1982-; cp/Gamma Beta Phi; Hosp Vol; Secy-Treas, VP, Princeton Ch of God Chapt of Pioneers for Christ; Sounds of Conviction Musical Grp, Open Door F'ship; Assn w Yth Rehab Prog; r/Christian; hon/Cum Laude Grad, 1981; Nat Dean's List; Intl Yth in Achmt; Commun Ldrs Am; g/Yth & Evangelism Min.

REED, TAMMY MICHELLE oc/Student; b/Aug 13, 1966; h/Route 1, Box 170, Noxapater, MS 39346; p/Mr and Mrs D W Reed, Noxapater, MS; cp/Pres, FHA, 1983; Pianist Y-Teens, 1981-84; Beta Clb, 1980-84; r/Pentecostal; hon/Editor Sch Yrbook, 1984; Editor Sch Paper, 1982-83; 1st Alt to Winston Co Jr Miss, 1984; Math Awd, 1981; Eng Awd, 1983; Sci Awd, 1982; VFW Voice of Democracy Awd, 1st in Sch & Co, 2nd Runner-up in Dist, 1983; US Achmt Acad Nat Awds Yrbook; g/col.

REGISTER, JULIE LUMELLE oc/Student; b/Oct 14, 1968; h/Route 2, Box 170, Wallace, NC 28466; p/Mrs Lurine S Register, Wallace, NC; ed/E Duplin HS; cp/Volleyball; Tennis; Drama Clb; FTA; Sci Clb; F'ship of Christian Aths; Student Gov Assn; Secy, Freshman Class; VP, Sophomore Class; Nat Hon Soc; Hlth Occups Students Am; r/So Bapt; hon/Pub of Poetry in *New Demenstions*, 1984; Hugh O'Brian Yth Sem, 1984; NC Gov's Sch Nom; g/attend Univ NC-Chapel Hill.

REICH, MARK CARLTON oc/Student; b/Mar 4, 1964; h/Route 1, Box 64-A, Eagle Springs, NC 27242; p/Rev and Mrs Gaither B Reich, Eagle Sprgs, NC; ed/N Moore HS, 1982; King Col, 1981; Univ NC, 1982-83; Malone Col, 1983; cp/Nat Beta Clb; Spanish Clb; Annual Staff; Quiz Bowl Team; Student Coun; Baseball, Ftball, Track; Pres, Friends Yth Grp; r/Evang-Friends, Hd Usher, Rock Hill Evang Friends Ch; hon/Morehead Nom; King Fellow Prog; Century III Ldrship Awds, Sch Winner; W/W Among Am HS Students; Soc of Dist'd HS Students; Commun Ldrs Am; g/Bus Adm/Computer Sci.

REID, ANTHONY WAYNE oc/Real Estate Salesman; b/Jul 19, 1961; h/Route 1, Salem, SC 29676; ba/Fairplay, SC; p/Mr and Mrs James W Reid, Salem, SC; ed/Tamassee-Salem HS, 1979; BA, Erskine Col, 1983; pa/Real Est Salesman, Carolina Landing Inc; cp/Pres, Erskine Col SGA, 1982-83; Student Senate; Jud Coun; Phi Alpha Theta; r/Bapt; hon/1st Pl Res Paper, 1983; Reg Phi Alpha Theta Conv; g/Polits, Govt, Public Ser.

REID, CHARLES LEON oc/Student; b/May 14, 1953; h/104 Bishop House, Rutgers Col, New Brunswick, NJ 08903; ba/Same; p/Ollie M Reid, Washington, DC; ed/E C Glass HS, 1971; BS, VA Polytechnic Inst & St Univ, 1975; MA, Univ No Col, 1980; mil/USAF, 1st Lt; pa/Adm Ofcr, USAF-Bergstrom AFB; Mtl Hlth & Mtl Retard Spec I, Austin St Hosp, 1980-81; Adj Fac Psychol Instr, Bergstrom AFB Mil Resident Ctr Sys, 1981-82; Psychol Asst, Middlesex Co Dept of Adult Corrections, 1982-83; Residence Cnslr, Ofc of Dean of Students-Rutgers Col, 1982-; Am Psychol Assn; Assn of Black Psychol; hon/Nat Hon Soc; Num Mil Awds, 1971-75; Merit's W/W Among Am HS Students; W/W Among Students in Am Univs & Cols; g/Clin Psychol, Forensic Psychol.

REID, KRISTI TERESA oc/Student; b/Jun 24, 1964; h/Route 2, Box 357-A, Taylorsville, NC 28681; p/Mr and Mrs J Donald Reid, Taylorsville, NC; ed/Appalachian St Univ; Lenoir-Rhyne Col; pa/Child Devel Ctr, 1983; cp/Alpha Delta Pi; Student Coun; Jr Class Coun; Sr Class Coun Secy-Treas; Keywanettes Clb; Monogram Clb; Social Rec Clb Activs Dir; Tennis Team; Sun Sch Tchr; UMYF Treas; r/United Meth; hon/Intl Yth Achmt; Yg Commun Ldrs Am; W/W Among Am HS Students; g/Arts Mgmt.

REID, MONICA CAROLINE oc/Student; b/Jul 2, 1965; h/5309 Dayan Drive, Charlotte, NC 28216; ba/Durham, NC; p/Mr and Mrs Ervin D Reid, Charlotte, NC; ed/N Mecklenburg Sr HS, 1983; pa/Sum Helper, Moore & Van Allen Law Firm, 1983; cp/Pres, Student Govt, 1983; Pres, Inter-Clb Coun;

Charlotte-Mecklenburg Co Coun on Adolescent Pregnancy Bd of Dirs, 1981-83; Mem, Students in Action for Ed; r/Meth; hon/Salutatorian; Sr Fulfillment Awd, 1983; Sr of Yr, 1983; *Charlotte Observer* All-Star Scholar; *Charlotte Post* Top Sr of Yr; W/W Among Am HS Students; Soc of Dist'd Am HS Students; g/Maj in Polit Sci, Lwyr.

REID, RODNEY LEE oc/Student; b/May 12, 1966; h/338 Forrest Hill Lane, Grand Prairie, TX 75051; p/M L and Paulette Reid, Grand Prairie, TX; ed/S Grand Prairie HS, 1984; p/Telemktg, A J Woods Mktg Ser, 1983-; cp/Jr Bd of Dirs, Nat Bk of Grand Prairie; FBLA; Nat Hon Soc; Yrbook Staff, Commun & Bus Editor; r/Bapt; hon/Nat Merit Semi-Finalist; HS Hon Roll; W/W Among Am HS Students; g/Attend Col, Bus Deg, Start Ins & Travel Agy.

REILLY, CATHERINE ELIZABETH oc/Student; b/Jun 24, 1961; h/6233 Bridle Way, Norfolk, VA 23518; p/Capt & Mrs J D Reilly Jr, Norfolk, VA; ed/Norfolk Acad, 1973-79; BS, Lynchburg Col, 1979-84; cp/Alpha Sigma Pi, Treas, 1982-83; Lynchburg Col Student Nurses Assn, Treas, 1983-84; Student Nurses Assn of VA; Commun Hlth & Ed Com, Chp, 1983-84; Vol Wk at King's Daughs Hosp; Tutor at Orphanage; Student Activs Bd; Donated to St Jude's Hosp; hon/Dean's List, Lynchburg Col; Nat Dean's List; Hon Mention, 2 Times; g/Pediatric Oncology.

REIN, ROY OSCAR oc/Administrator; h/Post Office Box 10303, Atlanta, GA 30319; ba/Atlanta, GA; p/Leroy R Rein (dec) and Myra M Rein, Jackson, MS; ed/BS 1978, MBA 1979, MS St Univ; pa/Bd of Dirs, Dir of Legal Affairs, Thad Green Enterprises, Inc, 1981-; Dir of Fin, Thad Green Enterprises, 1980; Grad Asst, MS St Univ, 1978-79; cp/Delta Sigma Pi, VP 1979-80; Alpha Zeta Acting Pres, VP, 1977-78; MSU Hort Clb Pres, VP, 1976-78; Phi Kappa Phi Patron, 1981; Omicron Delta Kappa; Blue Key; Beta Gamma Sigma; Gamma Sigma Delta; Phi Eta Sigma; r/Luth; hon/MS St Univ Hall of Fame, 1978; 1st in Class, MS St Univ, 1978; Wingfield HS Hall of Fame, 1973; 1st in Class, Wingfield HS, 1973; Phi Kappa Phi Soph Awd, MS St Univ, 1974; Gamma Sigma Delta Soph & Sr Awds; Alpha Zeta Freshman Scholastic Awd, Best Key Awd, 1973; St of MS C of C STAR Student, 1973; L G Balfour Achmt Awd, 1973; Nat Exc Clbs Yth of the Yr Finalist, 1973; Jacksonians for Public Ed Ldrship Awd, 1973; *Reader's Digest* Valedictory Awd, 1973; Personalities of S; Men of Achmt; Intl Yth in Achmt; W/W Among Students in Am Univs & Cols; g/Corp Mgmt in Fortune 500 Firm.

REYNOLDS, STEPHANIE JEAN oc/Office Worker; b/Dec 12, 1963; h/Route 2, Box 324 Greenfield, TN 38230; ba/McKenzie, TN; p/Mr and Mrs Gerald Reynolds, Greenfield, TN; ed/Greenfield HS, 1982; Acctg Cert, McKenzie Voc Sch, 1983; pa/Inspector, Ofc Wk, Kellwood Co, 1982-83; Ofc Wk, Meth Hosp of McKenzie, 1983; cp/Beta Clb, 1981-82; G-Clb, 1981-82; FHA, 1980-82; Ofcr-Reporter, 1982; Yth for Christ, 1979-82; Lib Clb, 1979; r/Bapt; hon/HS Annual & Newspaper Staff, 1982; Top Ten of Class, 1982; Acad Dipl, 1982; UTM Math Contest, 1981; Bas-

ketball Team, 1981, 1982; g/Computer Field.

REZELMAN, JAN LYNN oc/Assistant Director of Campus Programs and Organizations; b/Jul 15, 1958; h/Twin Towers, Albion, MI 49224; ba/Albion, MI; p/Mr and Mrs A P Rezelman, Lapeer, MI; ed/Lapeer W Sr HS, 1976; BA, Olivet Col, 1980; MA, Bowling Green St Univ, 1982; pa/Asst Dir Campus Progs & Orgs, Residence Coor, Albion Col, 1982-; Hall Dir, Bluffton Col, 1980-82; cp/APGA; NACA; Omicron Delta Kappa; Psi Chi; r/Prot; g/PhD, Dean of Student Affairs.

RIAL, KERRY NELSON oc/Student; b/Mar 14, 1965; h/510 Fairview, Greenfield, TN 38230; p/Mr and Mrs Jerry Rial, Greenfield, TN; ed/Greenfield HS, 1983; Univ TN; cp/Student Coun, Sr Class Rep; Beta Clb; Lib Clb; G-Clb; Yth for Christ; Basketball; r/Bapt; hon/HS Newspaper; HS Annual; Ernest D & Fannie G Hedgecock S'ship; W/W; Most Likely to Succeed; g/Computer Programmer.

RICE, CHERYL LANETTE oc/Student; b/Nov 5, 1959; h/75 Henderson Road, Apartment 2-A, Newark, DE 19711; ba/Newark, DE; p/Dr and Mrs William J Rice, Winston-Salem, NC; ed/E Forsyth Sr HS, 1978; BA, NC Ctl Univ, 1982; MPA, Univ DE, 1984; pa/Motor Vehicle Mgmt Intern, FAA, 1981; Congressman Stephen L Neal, 1983; cp/NC Public Adm Soc, 1980-82; r/Meth; hon/Alpha Kappa Mu Hon Soc; NC Ctl Public Adm Hon Soc; Magna Cum Laude, 1982, NC Ctl Univ; g/Mgmt in Pers/Labor Relats.

RICH, ELIZABETH CAROL oc/Student; b/Jun 15, 1961; h/Post Office Box 328, Huntingdon, TN 38344; p/Mr and Mrs Harold Brewer, Huntingdon, TN; ed/Huntingdon HS, 1979; BS, Univ TN, 1983; cp/Phi Chi Theta, 1980-83; Interfaith Ctr, 1979-83, Editor of Newslttr 1982-83; Clement Hall Coun, 1979, 1983; Student TN Edrs Assn, 1981-83; Student Nat Edrs Assn, 1981-83; r/Meth; hon/Dean's List; g/Bus Ed Tchr.

RICH, FLORENCE MICHELLE oc/Student; b/Dec 21, 1966; h/Post Office Box 247, Kenansville, NC 28349; p/Mr and Mrs Craig Rich, Kenansville, NC; cp/Girl Scouts; Jr Beta Clb; Sr Beta Clb; Jr Varsity Cheerleading, Co-Capt, 1981-82; Varsity Cheerleading; Golf Team; r/Presb; hon/Nat Mem, Nat Piano Auditions, 1978, 1982; St Mem, Nat Piano Auditions, 1981.

RICHARD, JESSICA RENEE oc/Student; b/Jul 24, 1967; h/Route 2, Box 188-A, Pryor, OK 74361; p/Mr and Mrs Marion L Richard, Pryor, OK; ed/Adair HS; NEn Area Voc-Tech; cp/FFA, Reporter, 1984; Adair HS Band, Pres, 1984; Jr Class-VP, 1984; Sum Leag Softball, 1974-84; HS Stage Band, 1984; r/Bapt; hon/Top Awds for Spch Competitions in FFA; W/W Among HS Students; Nat Eng Merit Awd, 1984; g/Communs, Advtg.

RICHARDS, SCOTT MORGAN oc/Student; b/Jul 28, 1967; h/1920 Bethsaida Road, Riverdale, GA 30296; ba/Riverdale, Ga; p/Mr and Mrs R A Richards, Riverdale, GA; ed/N Clayton Sr HS, 1985; pa/Cashier, Big Star Foods, 1983-; cp/Nat Beta Clb, 1983-; Fgn Lang Clb, 1983; Quiz Bowl Team, 1983; UFCW Union Mem; r/Bapt; hon/Poem

in N Clayton Lit Mag, "Words in Print", 1984; Gov's Hons Alt, 1983, 1984; W/W Nom, 1984; Presb Col Jr Fellow, 1984; Univ GA Cert of Merit Winner, 1984; Outstg Participation, 1984, Acad Bowl; Hon Roll, 1980-84; W/W Among HS Seniors, 1984; g/Col, Engrg Deg.

RICHARDSON, ANNA CECILE oc/Student; b/Apr 15, 1964; h/1701 Fountainridge, Chapel Hill, NC 27514; p/Dr and Mrs Richard J Richardson, Chapel Hill, NC; ed/Chapel Hill HS, 1982; cp/Hosp Vol; Keywanettes VP, 1982; Nat Hon Soc; Pres, Spanish Hon Soc; r/Christian; hon/Elected Miss Chapel Hill HS, 1982; Priscilla Freeman Awd, 1982; Altrusa Clb S'ship; Outstg Spanish Student Awd; Univ NC Dean's List; Phi Eta Sigma Hon Soc, 1983; Soc of Dist'd Am HS Students; g/Elem Ed.

RICHARDSON, ELIZABETH ANNE oc/Cost Accountant; h/4774 Heath Hill Road, Columbia, SC; ed/BA, Converse Col; Middlebury Col French Sch; Certificat Superieur de la Langue Francaise, Sorbonne; pa/Eng Tchr, Lycie Fustel de Coulanges-Massy France, 1982-83; Cost Acct, Michelin Tire Corporation; cp/Jr Leag of Greenville; r/Epis.

RICHARDSON, JON MARK oc/Student; b/Nov 23, 1962; h/1701 Fountainridge, Chapel Hill, NC 27514; p/Dr and Mrs Richard J Richardson, Chapel Hill, NC; ed/Chapel Hill HS, 1981; Appalachian St Univ; pa/Finisher, Framemakers, 1978-80; Waiter, Carol Woods Retirement Commun, 1980; cp/Pres Class, 1976-78; Spanish Clb, Secy, 1978; Ftball, 1978; Track, 1979-80; r/Christian; hon/Outstg Marching Band Student, 1979; Teenage Mr NC Physique, 1982; Teenage Mr Tarheel, 1981; Mr Mountaineer, 1981; Col Mr Am, 3rd Lightweight, 1982; W/W Among Am HS Students.

RICHARDSON, GREG DREXEL oc/Attorney; b/Dec 22, 1955; h/207 East Irving Avenue, Number 204, Oshkosh, WI 54903; ba/Oshkosh, WI; m/Judy Lee Gross; p/H D and Katherine Richardson, Edgerton, WI; sp/Helen C Gross, Montebello, CA; ed/Edgerton Commun HS, 1974; BA, Univ of WI-Whitewater, 1978; JD, Univ of WI Law Sch, 1981; pa/Intern, LAIP, 1979; Asst to City Atty-Madison WI, 1980-81; Asst DA Grant Co WI, 1981-83; Asst DA Winnebago Co WI; cp/Handgun Control Inc; ABA-Crim Justice Sect; Nat Dist Attys Assn; St Bar of WI, Crim Law Sect; Govt Lwyrs Div; Dem Party of WI; St Hist Soc of WI; Student Body Pres; Notary Public; r/Presb Ch USA, Elder; hon/Phi Kappa Phi; Phi Alpha Theta; Intl Yth in Achmt; W/W Among Students in Am Univs & Cols; Commun Ldrs Am; g/Public Ser Career.

RICHARDSON, ORINTHIA FAY oc/Title IV-A Project Coordinator; b/Sep 7, 1959; h/Route 1, Box 17, Hollister, NC 27844; p/Eugene and Beatrice Richardson, Hollister, NC; ed/Eastman HS, 1977; BA, NC St Univ, 1982; AA, Halifax Commun Col, 1979; pa/Title IV-A Proj Coor, Halifax Co Sch Sys, 1982-83, 1983-84; cp/Haliwa Lib Com, 1983; Nat Indian Ed Assn, 1982-83; FFA; FHA; Bapt Ch Mem; Jr Choir; Bapt Yg Wom; Pioneers for Christ; Eng Clb; hon/Dean's List; Cert in Instrumental Mus; Rdg Tutor in Spec Ser Prog; g/Eng Tchr at HS Level.

RICHARDSON, TERRY WAYNE oc/

Minister; b/May 6, 1961; h/1638 Kirkwood, Garland, TX 75041; ba/Garland, TX; m/Bettina Jimise; c/Tiffany Renae; p/Mr and Mrs Wesley Richardson, San Antonio, TX; sp/Mr and Mrs Jimmy Williams, Maxwell AFB, AL; ed/John Jay HS, 1979; AA, BA SWn A/G God Col; Grad Wk at SWn Bapt Sem; pa/Min of Chd, Oak Cliff Assm of God, 1981-82; Assoc Paster, First Assem of God, 1982-83; Min Yth, Southside Assem of God, 1983-; cp/Mem, VP of Phi Theta Kappa, 1980-81; Delta Epsilon Chi, 1983-; Mem of Assem of God Mins, 1982-; r/Assem of God; hon/Pres' List; Nat Dean's List; Summa Cum Laude, SWn; Personalities of S; W/W Among Am Jr Col Students; W/W Among Am Col & Univ Students; Intl Yth in Achmt; g/Master's Deg in Rel Ed.

RICKS, ROBERT JR oc/Commercial Representative; b/Jul 3, 1959; h/419 Wagner Street, Tarboro, NC 27886; ba/Fayetteville, NC; p/Mr and Mrs Robert Ricks, Sr, Tarboro, NC; ed/Tarboro Sr HS, 1977; BS, St Augustine's Col, 1981; pa/Internship, Vol Action Ctr, 1981; Internship, Dept of Jails & Detention, 1981; Staff Asst 1981, Comml Rep 1982, Carolina Telephone & Telegraph; cp/Phi Beta Lambda Bus Clb, 1979; NAACP, 1975; St Augustines JCs, Treas, 1979; Nat Assn Black Accts, 1979; r/Bapt; hon/Most Valuable Weight Lifter, 1975-76; Sportsmanship Awd, 1976-77; Most Valuable Player Holy Hookskrit Basketball Leag, 1974; Tarboro All-AREA 165lb Weight Lifting Champ, 1979, 1980; St Augustine Col Intramural Weightlifting Champ, 1980; g/Master's in Bus, Dist Mgr for Carolina Telephone.

RICKS, STANLEY EARL oc/Student; b/Dec 24, 1963; h/523 North Monroe, Yazoo City, MS 39194; p/Mr and Mrs W D Ricks, Yazoo City, MS; ed/Yazoo City HS, 1982; Holmes Jr Col; cp/HS Ftball, 1980-82; FBLA, 1980-82, Pres 1981-82; Holmes Jr Col Dramatics Clb, Holme-Towne Players 1982-84; HTP Set Dir 1983-84; Nat Hon Dramatics Frat, Delta Psi Omega; Holmes Jr Col Marching Band, 1982-84; r/Meth; hon/Yazoo City Jr HS "B" Average, 1976-77; Overall "A" Average 1977-78; Best Prodn of a One-Act Play, 1984, Holmes Jr Col; Most Friendliest Male Student, Holmes Jr Col, 1983-84; g/Crim Justice; Law Enforcement Career.

RIDER, JON L II oc/Student; b/Sep 18, 1963; h/240 State, Millville, PA 17846; ba/University Park, PA; c/Rithman, Francis; p/Jon and Eunice, Millville, PA; ed/Millville HS, 1982; Penn St Univ; cp/Gamma Sigma Sigma; Yrbook Editor, Photo Editor; HS Senate; Life Scout; Explorer; Alpha Phi Omega; UMYF; Proj Spar; Band; Vol Fireman; Class Pres; Soccer, Wrestling, Chess, Baseball; Drama; Spanish; French; Quill & Scroll; Wrestling Capt; Booster & Pep Clb Treas; Class Histn; Prom & Float Chm; AFL; r/Hindu-Meth; hon/Penn St. Ice Cream Eating Champ, 1982, Runner-up 1983; Knighted by Govt of Lichtenstein; Intl Yth in Achmt; W/W Among Am HS Students; g/wk Overseas in Diplomatic Solution.

RIDOUT, TRACY M oc/Secondary, Special Education; b/Oct 23, 1958; h/353 State Highway, 12-1, Montesano, WA 98563; ba/Aberdeen, WA; m/Kristy Diane; c/Lynsey Briane; p/Floyd and Dorothy Ridout, Shelton, WA; sp/William and Joyce Jackstodt, Shelton, WA; cp/Twin Harbors Grp Home Assn; Grays Harbor Reg Planning Comm on Ed; Coun for Exceptl Chd; WA Ed Assn; NEA; Aberdeen Ed Assn; YMCA Swimming City-Rec Basketball, V'ball, Safeway Baseball; hon/1st Leag Swim Champ; Intl Yth in Achmt; W/W Among Students in Am Cols & Univs; Commun Ldrs Am; g/Master's Deg in Spec Ed; Adm Field of Ed.

RIES, NICOLE oc/Student, Gymnastics Coach, Model, Waitress; b/Jan 9, 1965; h/36 Livingston Road, Scarsdale, NY 10583; ba/Scarsdale, NY; p/Martin and Dianys Ries, Scarsdale, NY; ed/New Rochelle HS; C W Post Col; L I U; pa/Gym Instr, MW YM-YWHA, 1979-84; Model, L I Univ, 1977-78; Child Acrobatics, Ward Sch, 1981; Gymnastics Dir, Riverdale Day Camps, 1981-82; Waitress, Italian Vill Restaurant, 1983; Waitress, Texaco Corp, 1983; Gymnastics Class for Underpriviledged Chd, Pelham Bay Pk, Sum 1983; Waitress, Ground Round Restaurant, 1984; Gymnastics Instr, Bronxville Gymnastics Sch, 1983-84; Worked w A B Grossfeld Mens Olympic Coach; cp/Att'd the 3 I's Alt Prog at New Rochelle HS; HS Gymnastics Team, 1979-82; Swim Team & Diving Team, 1981-82; Mem, Mid-Westchester Gymnastics Team, 1975-83; r/Cath; hon/MVP Gymnastics Team Awd, Albert Leonard JHS, 1978; MVP, Gymnastics NRHS, 1979-82; MVP, Diving Team, 1981-82; NY St Champs, 1st Pl Medal, 1981; Class II Gym NY St Champs, 1st Pl Beam; g/Maj in Bus, Acctg; Career, Ofcl for Olympic Gymnastic.

RIGGS, ANGELA JO oc/Student; b/Oct 13, 1964; h/Route 3, Box 83, Inola, OK 74036; p/Mr and Mrs Finis Riggs Jr, Inola, OK; ed/Inola HS, 1982; pa/Oral Roberts Univ Student Wkr, 1981; Hostess, Fountains Restaurant, 1983; Secy, VSI Rltrs, 1983; cp/OK Hon Soc, 1982; Nat Hon Soc, 1982; F'ship Christian Aths, 1980-82; Cheerldr, 1979-82; Choir, 1980-82; Class Ofcr, 1979-82; Yrbook, 1981, 1982; March of Dimes Local Dir, 1981, 1982; Drama, 1979-82; OK Univ Choral, 1982, 1983; r/Bapt; hon/All-Dist Choir, 1981; Outstg Choral Mem, 1980, 1981; Yrbook-Editor, 1981-82; Yrbook Royalty, 1982; Ftball Homecoming Royalty, 1982; Miss TEEN OK, 1981; Little Miss, 1980; Miss Lake Oologah, 1982; W/W Among Am HS Students; g/Maj, Telecommuns.

RIHA, JANET KAY oc/Student; b/Apr 25, 1961; h/3734 FM Road 2218, Rosenberg, TX 77471; p/Mr and Mrs J L Riha, Rosenberg, TX; ed/Lamar Consolidated HS, 1979; Univ of TX at Austin; Our Lady of the Lake Univ; pa/Acapella Choir & Chamber Choir; Holy Rosary Cath CYO; UIL Spch Team Prose; Our Lady of the Lake Univ Student Govt, Dir of Student Rights Coun; Self Study Com; Beta Alpha; Univ Acctg Assn; Alpha Kappa Psi, Pres Pledge Class 1982, Pledge Tnr 1983; hon/TX All-St Choir; Am Legion Aux Girls St; HS Nat Hon Soc; Dean's List; Acad S'ship; Soc of Dist'd Am HS Students; W/W Among Am HS Students; g/CPA.

RILEY, BARBARA JO oc/Student; b/Dec 12, 1963; h/Route 3, Box 248, Bridgeport, WV 26330; p/J Victor and Betty Riley, Bridgeport, WV; ed/WV Univ; cp/Marching & Concert Band, 1979-82; Stage Band, 1981-82; Nat Jr Hon Soc, 1978-79; NHS, 1981-82; Vars Basketball Stat, 1981-82; Intl Order of Rainbow for Girls; r/Meth; hon/WVU Col of Agri & Forestry Pres' List, Dean's List; WV Golden Horseshoe Awd, 1978; No WV All-Fest Band, 1980; Nat Merit S'ship Finalist, 1982; WV Outstg Scholar, 1982; WV Achmt S'ship, 1982; W/W Among Am HS Students; Am Outstg Names & Faces; Yg Commun Ldrs of Am; Intl Yth in Achmt; g/Vet Med-Animal Sci.

RINCK, ROBERT PAUL JR oc/Student; b/Oct 5, 1965; h/Route 3, Box 364, Vine Grove, KY 40175; ba/Terre Haute, IN; p/Mr and Mrs Robert P Rinck, Sr, Vine Grove, KY; ed/N Hardion HS, 1983; Rose-Holman Inst of Technol; cp/Chess Clb, 1980-81; Sci Clb, 1981-83; Math Clb, 1982-83; Hist Clb, 1982-83; Girl's Basketball Mgr, Intramural Basketball, 1982-83; Pres, Nat Hon Soc; r/Bapt; hon/Rose Holman S'ship; Algebra II Awd, 1980-81; Trig/Analytic Awd, Typing I Awd, Adv'd Chem Awd, 1981-83; Valedictorian; Eng Awd; g/Maj in Computer Sci/Engrg.

RINGO, MICHAEL DAVID oc/Student; b/Aug 19, 1965; h/9203 Brave Court, Jonesboro, GA 30236; p/Dan and Linda Ringo, Jonesboro, GA; ed/Jonesboro Sr HS; pa/Cook, Edgewater Country Clb, 1982; Taco Bar Person, Del Taco, 1982-83; Dockman Receiving Dept, Richway Distbn Ctr, 1983-; cp/AFJROTC, 1980-83, Cadet Cmdr, Cadet Col; Sci Clb; Beta Clb; r/Prot; hon/AF Assn Awd, 1983; Various Other ROTC Ribbons & Awds, 1980-83; Navy 4 Yr S'ship; W/W Am HS Students; g/GA Tech; Pilot in Navy; Astronaut.

RITZ, DANIEL LAWRENCE oc/Student; b/Aug 28, 1963; h/295 Carling Road, Rochester, NY 14610; p/Lawrence A Ritz, Rochester, NY; ed/McQuaid Jesuit HS, 1981; BS, Fairfield Univ, 1985; cp/Alpha Mu Gamma; NHS; Fairfield Univ Glee Clb, Secy, 1983-84; Fairfield Univ Campus Tour Guides, Jr Coor, 1983-84; Nat Assn Accts; r/Cath; hon/Valedictorian, 1981; Gleason Meml Fund Spec S'ship, 1981; Fairfield Univ Pres S'ship, 1981; Awd from Phi Beta Kappa Iota; Rochester Jr Bowling S'ship; Fraternal Order of Eagles S'ship; W/W Among Am HS Students; g/Wk for Public Acctg Firm.

RIVERA, RUTH YVETTE oc/Student; b/Dec 22, 1964; h/2311 John Road, Killeen, TX 76541; ba/Dodge City, KS; p/Hector and Telma Rivera, Killeen, TX; ed/Killeen HS, 1982; St Mary of the Plain's Col; pa/Petronis & Petronis Law Firm; cp/Spanish Clb; French Clb; Drill Team Mem; r/Cath, Sunday Sch Tchr; hon/Best Indiv in ROTC, 1979; Best Staff Ofcr, 1980; St Finalist in May 1982 Vol Job Ed Job Manual Contest; 1st Pl in Dist Contest; W/W Am HS; g/FBI.

ROACH-JENNINGS, PAMELA FAY oc/Clinical Dietitian; b/Oct 10, 1959; h/7412 Northwest 23, Apartment 229, Bethany, OK 73008; ba/OKC, OK; m/Gary Lee; p/Charles and Joan Roach, Ada, OK; ed/HS, 1977; Sec'dy Sch Cert, Millicent, Australia, 1977; BS, Food Nutrit Inst Adm, 1981; Cert of Am Dietetic Assn, 1982; Reg'd Dietitian, 1983; pa/Clin Dietitian, RD, 1982-; cp/

Am Dietetic Assn; Omicron Mu; Phi Upsilon Omicron; *Candle* Reporter; FNIA Clb; Rep for Home Ec Student Coun, 1981; hon/Pres Hon Roll, 1978; Dean's Hon Roll, 1978-81; g/MS Deg.

ROAMER, KAREN oc/CPA; b/Jun 7, 1958; h/835-2 Ridgewood Drive, Sparks, NV 89431; ba/Reno, NV; m/James A; p/Mr and Mrs Alden Louden, Laguna Bch, CA; sp/Mr and Mrs James M Roamer Jr, Coronado, CA; ed/Laguna Bch HS, 1976; CA Bapt Col, 1981; pa/Staff Acct, CPA, McGladrey Hendrickson & Co, 1980-82; Staff Acct, Tax Dept, Kafoury, Armstrong & Co; cp/Alpha Chi Hon Soc, Treas, 1978-79; CA Bapt Col Bus Clb, Secy/Treas, 1978-79; r/Calvary Bible Ch, Treas; hon/Outstg Yg Wom Am; Bus Adm, Top Sr Awds, CA Bapt Col, 1979; Rotary Top Scholar, Top Sr, Ser Awd, 1976.

ROBBINS, BETSY CAROLINE oc/Student; b/Feb 25, 1964; h/404 Via Drive, Clarksville, TN 37043; ba/Clarksville, TN; p/Carlton and Helen Robbins, Clarksville, TN; ed/Clarksville HS, 1982; Austin Peay St Univ; cp/Alpha Lambda Delta Hon Soc, 1982, Editor, 1983; Bapt Student Union Mem, 1982, Pres 1983; r/So Bapt; hon/Undergrad Biol Hons Prog, 1983; Rec'd Acad Hons as a Freshman, 1982-83; Dean's List; g/BS Nsg, RN.

ROBERSON, LISA GAY oc/Student; b/Aug 3, 1961; h/Post Office Box 481, Douglas, GA 31533; p/Mr and Mrs Jimmy Roberson; ed/Coffee HS, 1979; AS, S GA Col, 1981; cp/Coffee HS Band; 4-H Pres, 1978; FHA, 1972-79; Student Coun, Treas, 1978-79; Bapt Student Union, VP, 1980-81; Student Govt, 1980-81; Am Home Ec Assn; Student Home Ec Assn; Phi Upsilon Omicron, Pres, 1983-84, Beta Mu Chapt; Gamma Beta Phi; r/Bapt; hon/Master 4-H'er, 1978; Flint River Mills S'ship, 1979; GSC Div of Home Ec S'ship, 1983; Rita Waters' S'ship, 1983; W/W Among Students in Am Cols & Univs; W/W Among Students in Am Jr Cols; g/Maj in Nutrition; Career in Ext.

ROBERTS, KAREN RUTH oc/Student; b/Oct 26, 1963; h/3121 North MacArthur, Oklahoma City, OK 73122; p/Coy and Mary Roberts, OKC, OK; ed/Putnam City W HS, 1981; cp/Active Cultural Ed for Students; OSU Cordell Hall, Co-Chm, 1981-82; OSU Rodeo Assn, Dir, 1983-84; hon/Nat Hon Soc; OSU Dean's Hon Roll; OSU Rodeo Assn Adv's Awd; OSU Rodeo Assn Spur Awd; World's Largest Jr Rodeo Queen, 1980; WLJR Horsemanship Winner, 1980; OK HS Rodeo Assn Queen, 1981; OHSRA Horsemanship Winner, 1981; OHSRA Girls Cutting Champ, 1981; Woodward Elk's Rodeo Queen, 1982; Rodeo of the Ozarks Horsemanship Winner, 1983; Miss Rodeo OK, 1984; MRO Pageant Horsemanship Winner, 1984; g/BS Agri Communication; Master's in Equine Technol.

ROBERTS, ROSA LYNN oc/Amway Distributor; b/Aug 26, 1961; h/HC 61, Box 15A, Whitney, NE 69367; m/Bruce J; c/Benjamin Joseph, Clinton James; p/Mr and Mrs Franklin Piper, Harrison, NE; sp/Charles Roberts, Whitney, NE; ed/Sioux Co HS, 1979; pa/Demonstrator, House of Lloyd, 1982; cp/Dawes Co Hist Soc; Earth Lodge Home Ext Clb, VP, 1984; r/Cath; hon/W/W Among Am HS Students; Intl Yth in Achmt; Com-

mun Ldrs of Am; Dir Dist'd Ams; Personalities of Am; g/Distbr in Am; Drafting, Arch.

ROBINSON, ANNIE LAURIE oc/Student; b/Feb 6, 1966; h/Post Office Drawer 737, West Point, MS 39773; ed/Oak Hill Acad, 1984; pa/Free-Lance Artist, 1981-; cp/Anchor Clb, Dir, 1982-84; Patriotic Am Yth, Chd of the Am Revolution, Registrar 1981-82, Pres 1982-83; MSCAR Studies Chm, 1983-84; Jr Classical Leag; Lib Clb, Reporter, 1981, r/Bapt; hon/USNMA Math Awd Book, 1983; "World's Great Contemp Poems", 1981; Hist ABC, 3rd in Dist, 1982; NEDT High Scorer, 1980; Hist Awd & WOW Awd; USNMA Math Awd, 1983; Wkshop at Memphis Acad Art, 1983; 17th Annual Jr Mid-St Art Comp, 1982; MS Model Security Coun, 1983; Rotary Yth Ldrship Conf, 1983; g/Comml Art, Advtg, Polit Sci.

ROBINSON, DeAUDRA SHERREL oc/Student; b/Sep 12, 1966; h/Route 1, Box 79, Wallace, NC 28466; p/Mrs Willie Mae Robinson, Wallace, NC; ed/Wallace-Rose Hill; cp/NHS; DECA; VICA; Math Clb; Spanish Clb, Pres; Chorus, All-Country; Student Council; Class Ofcr; 4-H Clb; r/Christian; hon/Marshall at 1983 Graduation; NC Scholastic Press Assn, 1983; Proj Uplift, 1983; Yth Involvement, 1983; Jr of the Mo, 1983; g/attend Univ NC-Chapel Hill.

ROBINSON, MICHAEL LEE oc/Student; b/Jul 9, 1965; h/Rural Route 1, Box 252, Liberty, IN 47353; ba/Liberty, IN; p/Mr and Mrs Ronald Robinson, Liberty, IN; ed/Union Co HS, 1983; cp/BSA, Life Scout; Drama Clb, 1979-83, VP 1983; Union Co Swing Choir, 1980-83, VP 1982, Pres 1983; Union Co HS Band, 1979-80; Nat Hon Soc, 1982-83; Union Co Musicals, 1979-83; Spch Team, 1982-83; r/Rom Cath; hon/IN Math Leag Awd, 1980; Dramatic Awd, 1981, 1982; Hon Roll, 1980, 1982; Barbershop Quartet Awd, 1982; IN St Music Assn Awds, 1980-83; W/W Among Am HS Students; g/Purdue Univ.

ROBINSON, PEGGY SUE SIMMONS oc/Para Professional; b/Dec 29, 1957; h/1409 Waterloo Drive, High Point, NC 27260; ba/High Point, NC; m/Gerald H; p/Helen P Simmons, Elliston, VA; sp/Howard Robinson, Camden, NJ, and Doris Robinson, Thomasville, NC; ed/Shawsville HS, 1976; BS, E TN St Univ, 1980; pa/Low Income Energy Asst Prog, Neighborhood Ser Ctr, 1980-81; High Point Public Schs, 1981-82; NC Assn Edrs; Coun Excptl Chd; Volleyball; Basketball; Track; Bowling Team; Softball; Pres, VP, Secy, FHA; Girls 4th Assn; SCEC, Secy, Newslttr Editor, TN SCEC; Yth Coor, Meth Ch; Asst, Spec Olympics; hon/DAR, 1976; W/W Among Am HS Students; W/W Among Students in Am Univs & Cols; Intl Yth in Achmt; Commun Ldrs Am; g/BS Deg in Phy Therapy.

ROBINSON, RENÉE LACHON oc/Student; b/Nov 1, 1966; h/4451 Victoria Drive, Nesbit, MS 38651; p/James and Thelma Robinson, Newbit, MS; ed/Hernando HS; cp/Spanish Clb, 1980-84; F'ship of Christian Aths, 1983-84; Nat Hon Soc, Treas/Secy, 1983-84; Quill & Scroll, VP, 1983-84; Yrbook Staff, 1982-84; Student Coun, 1982-83, Rep;

r/Ch of God hon/"The Tiger", 1983-84; Nat Hon Soc, 1983-84; Quill & Scroll, 1983-84; W/W Among Am HS Students; Soc Dist'd Am HS Students; Hall of Fame, Intell, US Achmt Awds; Jr Favorite; g/Maj Computer Sci; Career Computer Analyst.

RODRIGUEZ, ROSANNE oc/Student; b/Mar 16, 1966; h/1149 Panas Street, Nogales, AZ; p/Mr and Mrs Arnulfo Rodriguez, Nogales, AZ; ed/Nogales HS; cp/Band, VP; NHS; G & T Ed Sys; Powder Puff Ftball; Delta Leag Basketball, Softball; Band Treas; Jazz Band; Am Cancer Soc Bike-a-Thon; hon/Medal for Superior Solo Perf; 2nd Pl, Am Essay Contest; Medals for Highest Achmt in Spanish & Hlth Occups; Commun Ldrs of Am; g/Dentistry Deg, Spec in Orthodontia.

RODRIGUEZ, RUDY JR oc/Student; b/Aug 31, 1966; h/2308 Salado, Denton, TX 76201; p/Dr and Mrs Rudy Rodriguez Sr, Denton, TX; cp/Sr Class VP, 1983; Spanish Hon Soc Pres, 1983; Band Ofcr; Nat Hon Soc, 1982-83; Spanish Clb, 1980-83, Pres 1980; Whiz Quiz, 1983; All Reg Band, 1983; 1st Div Solo at UIL, 1980, 1982, 1983; Boy Scouts Sr Patrol Ldr, 1980-81; Cath Yth Worship Ldr, 1983; Ch Choir Mem; YMCA Yth in Govt, 1983; r/Cath; hon/Band Lttr for 4 Yrs; 3rd Pl Hist Fair, 1980; Boy Scouts "Best Swimmer" Awd, 1980; Outstg Achmt Awd, 1981; Regional 1st Pl in National Spanish Exam & Placed 2nd in St, 1982; Sum Enrichment Experience in Engrg, TX A & M Univ, 1982; Dr Scholl Fellow for Pres Classroom for Yg Ams, Wash DC, 1983; Intl Fgn Lang Awd, 1983; Am Outstg Names & Faces; US Achmt Acad Nat Awds Yrbook; g/Bioengrg Maj.

ROESNER, WAYNE DAVID oc/Manager; b/Jul 3, 1960; h/432 East North Street, Geneseo, IL 61254; ba/Atkinson, IL; m/Rebecca Jo; c/Emily Jo; p/Bernard F and Gladys M Roesner, Atkinson, IL; sp/Richard C and Mary Jo Kenady, Geneseo, IL; ed/Atkinson HS, 1978; AAS-Elects 1981, AAS-Computer Sci 1982, Black Hawk Col; pa/Co-Owner, Mgr of Computers Unltd, 1983-; Mgr Computer Software Dept, Archives Inc, 1982-83; Adm Trainee, Heeren Co; Instr, Black Hawk Col; cp/Fam Affair Bowling Leag, 1982-83; r/Cath; hon/Phi Theta Kappa; W/W Among Students in Am Jr Cols; Yg Commun Ldrship Awd; Intl Yth in Achmt; g/to become a Profitable Org.

ROGERS, ANNETTE CARLTON oc/Student; b/Jan 25, 1966; h/Post Office Box 167, Easley, SC 29641-0767; p/Dr and Mrs Dexter B Rogers, Easley, SC; ed/Easley HS; cp/Cross Country 1978-84; Track 1978-84; Basketball Scorekeeper 1981-84; Secy, Nat Hon Soc, 1982-83; Sec, Exec Bd of Student Coun, 1982-83; Interact Clb, 1981-84; Spanish Clb, 1984; r/Presb, 1st Presb Ch, Yth Adult & Handbell Choirs; hon/Rotary Scholar; Dist Chm of Nat Hon Soc; Graduation Marshall; Secy, Yth Com for Presb; Davidson July Experience, 1982; Pres Classroom for Yg Ams, 1983; g/Davidson Col.

ROGERS, DENIECE LYNN oc/Student, Consumer Research Interviewer; b/Jul 24, 1960; h/917 Kings Mill Rd, #216, Greenwood, IN 46142; ba/Indpls, IN; p/Rita June Ashby, Connersville, IN; ed/Connersville HS; BA, Wn KY Univ,

1982; IN Univ Sch Law; pa/Res Interviewer, Wallace Interviewing Ser, 1983-;Mgr, House of Beef, 1982; Waitress, Bill's Snowman 1980-82, KY Fried Chicken 1979; cp/Delta Sigma Rho; Tau Kappa Alpha; Spch, Debate Tm; Hall Coun; Writer for WKU *Talisman*; Student Bar Assn; hon/HS Yrbook Editor; Staff Mem, Student Newspaper; Nat Dean's List; Nom'd Omicron Delta Kappa; 3rd Pl Spch; Most Improved Spkr; g/Atty for Radio/TV Stas.

ROGERS, DONNA CAROL oc/Student b/Nov 6, 1962; h/Route 1, Box 43-A, Stephens, AR 71764; p/Mr and Mrs Don Rogers, Stephens, AR; ed/ Village HS, 1981; SAU-Tech, Profl Photo Associate's Deg, 1983; cp/Beta Clb, Secy/Treas; SGA Freshman Senator; r/Meth; hon/Salutatorian; W/W Among Am HS Students; W/W Among Jr Cols; g/Portrait Studio; Comml Advtg.

ROGERS, EDITH LYNN oc/Student; b/Apr 4, 1965; h/Rural Route 1, Box 43-A, Stephens, AR 71764; p/Mr and Mrs Don Rogers, Stephens, AR; ed/ Village HS, 1983; pa/Dairy Queen Braiser, Sum 1983; cp/Beta Clb, 1979-83; FCA, Pres, 1981; Tomahawk Staff, 1980-83; Village Sch Basketball Team, 1980-82; r/Meth; hon/Soc of Dist'd Am HS Students; Sci 1978; Hlth 1979; Math, 1979, 1980, 1981; Hist Citizenship, 1980; Home Ec, 1982; Eng, Hlth, Bkkpg, 1983; Valedictorian; Miss VHS, 1983; g/Col at SAU-TECH, Comml Advtg.

ROGERS, MARY KATHERINE oc/ Student; b/Jan 31, 1963; h/4711 Wrenwood Lane, Columbia, SC 29206; p/Mr and Mrs James L Rogers Jr, Columbia, SC; ed/Hammond Acad, 1981; cp/Pep Clb; Class Ofcr, Treas, Jr Class, 1979-80; Delta Delta Delta; r/Epis; hon/ W/W HS; g/Bus Deg.

ROGERS, PAMELA SUE oc/Student; b/May 7, 1963; h/483 Elaine Avenue, Camden, AR 71701; p/Owen and Bettie Rogers, Camden, AR; ed/Camden HS, 1981; So AR Univ; pa/Sales Clk, Dan Cook's Gifts & Ofc Supplies, 1980-82; Cashier, Andy's Hamburgers, 1981; Demonstrator 1983, Acctg File Clk 1983, First Nat Bk of Magnolia; cp/ Alpha Sigma Alpha Sorority, Treas, 1982-; Residence Hall Assn, Secy, 1982-; Heritage Singers, VP, 1981-; Concert Choir, 1981-; Student Foun, 1983-; r/ Bapt; hon/Dean's List; Acad S'ship; Choir S'ship; Alpha Hon Soc, Sec; Alpha Chi Hon Soc; Sigma Pi Orchid; g/CPA.

ROGERS, SUSAN GAYLE oc/Student; h/206 Troon Circle, Ocean Springs, MS 39564; ba/Univ MS; p/ LCDR H A Rogers, Mrs Shirley F Rogers, Ocean Springs, MS; ed/Princess Anne HS; W Orange HS, 1981; AA, Univ Ctl FL, 1982; Univ MS; pa/Lab Asst, Orlando Reg Med Ctr, 1980-81; Sales, Hammonds-Beck Enterprises Inc, 1982; cp/Nat Hon Soc; Mu Alpha Theta; Assoc of Wom Engrs; Am Inst Chem Engrs; Nat Sci Foun; Student Sci Tng Prog; r/Bapt; hon/Num Articles in Pub; Nat Hon Soc; Hon Dipl, W Orange HS; Freshman Acad Excell S'ship, Univ Ctl FL; Alumni S'ship, Univ MS; g/Chem Engrg; Grad Studies in Engrg & Mgmt.

ROGOWSKI, MICHAEL S oc/Territorial Manager; b/Mar 28, 1960; h/ 18040 Lorenz Avenue, Lansing, IL; p/ Stanley and Sophie Rogowski; ed/

Thorton Fractional S HS, 1978; BS, Bradley Univ, 1982; cp/Bradley Univ Student Body Pres; Bd of Trustees Student Rep; Student Senator; Deans Adv Coun; Interfrat Coun Rep; Delta Upsilon Frat VP; Exec Bd Pres; Chapt Relats Secy; Omicron Delta Kappa; hon/ Student Laureate Awd; Greek Student of the Yr; Outstg Yg Men of Am; W/ W Among Students in Am Univs & Cols.

ROHACK, J JAMES oc/Resident, Dept Internal Med, Univ TX Med Branch; b/Aug 22, 1954; h/104 Pompano, Galveston, TX; p/John and Margaret Rohack, E Rochester, NY; ed/ Lewis C Obourn HS, 1972; BS, Univ of TX at El Paso, 1976; MD, Univ of TX Med Br, 1980; cp/Psi Chi; Beta Beta Beta; Alpha Chi; Phi Kappa Phi; Alpha Omega Alpha; Galveston Co Med Soc; TX Med Assn Chm Residents Phys Sect; Am Med Assn Del to Res Phys Sec; So Med Assn; Phi Chi; Am Col of Phys; hon/Hon Mention, 1980 Gold Headed Cone Awd; Intl Yth in Achmt; Resident Rep to Nat Bd of Med Examrs; g/Role in Planning & Pract of Med in US.

ROHN, THOMAS GREG oc/Student; b/Aug 23, 1965; h/206 North 39th Street, Ft Pierce, FL 33450; p/Thomas and Saundra Rohn, Ft Pierce, FL; ed/ Westwood HS, 1983; Univ FL; cp/HS Basketball; Beta Clb, VP; Nat Hon Soc; Drama Clb, VP; Interclb Coun; Student Clb; r/Bapt; hon/Ft Pierce Exch Clb Student of Mo; US Achmt Acad, 1982-83; Pride Awd; Soc of Dist'd HS Students, 1982; Varsity Lttr Basketball; W/W; g/Univ FL, Pre-Vet, Vet.

ROMBERG, LEE ANNE oc/Vice President, Home Federal Savings & Loan; b/Jun 6, 1960; h/550 Ivey Terrace, Gainesville, GA 30501; ba/Gainesville, GA; p/Mr and Mrs Carl B Romberg II, Gainesville, GA; ed/Gainesville HS, 1978; BA, Brenau Col, 1982; pa/VP, Mktg Dir 1983-, Dir of Public Relats 1983, Home Fed S & L; Art Dir, Lockhart Graphics, 1982-83; cp/C of C; GA Mtns Jubilee Chp; Brenau Col Alumnae Coun; Alpha Chi Omega Rush Advr; Cancer Fund Capt; Friends of RR Soc; N GA Advtg Clb; Financial Insts Mktg Assn; Intl Assn Bus Communicators; GA Mtn Crafts; r/Meth; hon/ Articles in "The Crafts Report"; Designed & Produced, "The Vol Firemen"; Mary Mildred Sullivan Awd, 1982; W/W Am Col & Univs.

ROMIGUIERE, JEFFREY MICHAEL oc/Student; b/May 5, 1958; h/2854-B Golden Gate Avenue, San Francisco, CA 94118; ba/Hayward, CA; p/Ronald and Virginia Romiguiere, Castro Val, CA; ed/Canyon HS/Col Prep, 1976; BA, Cal St Univ, 1981; pa/Law Clk, Jensen, Jaquint, Cohn, 1983; Law Firm Employee, McCutchen, Doyle, Brown & Enersen, 1981-82; cp/Tutor, Lector in Operation SHARE Tutorial Prog, 1979-81; Acad Senator, 1980-81, in Univ Acad Senate; Univ Greepeace Assn, 1979-80; Pi Kappa Delta, 1979-80; Debate Team, 1979-80; Cross-Country Team, 1977-78; r/Rom Cath; hon/ Dean's List; Hon's List; W/W Among Students in Cols & Univs; g/Law Deg, JD, Career in Law.

ROMO, DEYANIRA oc/Student; b/ Sep 4, 1964; h/Post Office Box 862, Bandera, TX 78003; p/Mr and Mrs Joe Romo, Bandera, TX; ed/Bandera HS,

1983; TX A & M; cp/Nat Hon Soc, 1980-83, Secy 1982-83; Assn Legal Students, 1981-83, Pres 1982-83; Aths, 1979-83; Forensics, 1979-83; Cheerldr, 1980-83; Jour, 1980-83; Co-Editor, 1981-83; r/Cath; hon/All-Dist Basketball, 1981-83; Regional Qualifier in Forensics, 1979-83; Valedictorian, 1983; "A/B", Hon Roll, 1979-83; "A" Awd, 1983; Doane Scholar; Outstg Eng Student, 1983; g/Jour Maj; Write for Newspapers, Mags.

RONE, DEANNA LYNNE oc/Student; b/Jun 1, 1965; h/Route 1, Box 294, Burlison, TN 38015; p/James and Theta Rone, Burlison, TN; ed/Covington HS, 1983; cp/Student Coun, Treas; F'ship Christian Aths, Co-Capt; Pep Clb, Bd Dirs; Alpha Omega; Covington HS Band, Treas; Sr Class Play; Close-Up; Pres, Explorer Troop; 1st United Meth Ch Yth Grp; Pvt Tutor in Math; r/Bapt, Garland Bapt Ch, Subst Sunday Sch Tchr for Learner's Class, Asst Secy 1981-82; hon/Varsity Lttr in Softball, Volleyball, Track; Optimist Clb Awd, Outstg Sr Girl in Tipton Co HSs, 1982; Exch Clb Student of Mo, 1982; Girls' St Rep, 1982; Rep of Tipton Co Farm Bur to the Yth Citizenship Sem at Harding Univ, 1982; W/W: Miss Covington HS, 1983; Nat Hon Soc; Field Cmmdr of Covington HS Band, 1982; Superior Ratings at W TN Solo & Ensemble Contest, 1980-83; Outstg Jr Awd, Covington HS Band, 1982; Sr Class Treas, 1982-83; Jr Class VP, 1981-82; Sophomore Class Secy, 1980-81; Sophomore Class Favorite, 1981; Freshman Homecoming Rep, 1980; g/DM.

RONGSTAD, JAMES PAUL oc/ Accountant; b/Jul 16, 1958; h/3792 Oakridge Lane, White Bear Lake, MN 55110; ba/St Paul, MN; p/Norman and Gertrud Rongstad, St Paul, MN; ed/ Highland Park HS, 1976; BA, Augsburg Col, 1980; pa/Budgeting & Acctg Analyst II, Ramsey Co, 1980-; cp/Col Bus Team; Mun Fin Ofcrs Assn MN; Univ of MN Bus Games; Intramural Broomball Capt; Volleyball, Badminton; Campus Tour Guides; Freshman Student Advr; Staff Writer at Augsburg; hon/ Pi Gamma Mu; Dean's List; Cum Laude Grad; W/W Among Students in Am Univs & Cols; Intl Yth in Achmt; Commun Ldrs Am.

ROOF, COLETTE DENISE oc/Student; b/Sep 21, 1965; p/Mr and Mrs Phil Roof, Paducah, KY; ed/Saint Mary HS, 1983; William Woods Col; pa/Secy Hist Dept, William Woods Col; cp/Yrbook Editor; Pres Student Coun; Yth Grp; Secy, Math Clb; Beta Clb; Class VP; St Secy of KY Assn of Student Couns; Student Coun Rep; Baseball Stat; Ch Lector & Songldr; r/Rom Cath; hon/ Best Actress in Supporting & in Ldg Roles; Top 10% in NEDT; Alt to US-Japan Govtl Fgn Exch Prog; Reg 4-H Spch Winner; Spch Winner for Optimist KY & WV Dist; 2-Yr Winner of 6-St Reg in Nat Coun St Garden Clbs Spch Contest; Salutatorian; Outstg Sr Girl; Am Legion Awd; Christian Witness Awd; Prin's Awd for Attitude, Ser; Recip of 6 S'ships; Top 20% in Class; Pres' 20; Intl Studies Clb; Student Alumnae Assn; Student Alumnae Coun; Mng Editor of Newspaper; Student Life Comm Rep; Outstg Freshman Wom; Wk Pub'd in Campus Lit

Mag; Dean's List; Campus Christian F'ship; g/Radio/TV Maj; Reporter for Maj Broadcasting Co.

ROPER, LYDIA ANN oc/Student; b/ May 20, 1964; h/405 Cresent Drive, Seneca, SC 29678; ba/Greenville, SC; p/ Drs John and Ruth Roper, Seneca, SC; ed/Am Commun Sch, 1982; Furman Univ; pa/Camp Cnslr, Camp La Vida, 1983; cp/Basketball Team, 1978-79; Forensic Team, 1979-80; Track Team, 1977-81; Aide in Spec Ed Dept, 1981-82; Col Ednl Ser Corps, Vol; Ofc Coor for Hollis Ctr & Tutoring Prog, 1982-84; r/Bapt; hon/MVP for Track, 1980; g/ Psychol Maj; Grad Sch; Child Psychol.

ROPER, STEPHANIE JUSTYNE oc/ Student; b/May 1, 1962; h/2004 West Indiana, Midland, TX 79701; p/Mr and Mrs Fred T Roper, Midland, TX; ed/ Miramonte HS, 1976-79; Lee HS, 1980; pa/Tom Brown Inc, 1981; cp/Phi Theta Kappa; Annual Symp for the Pres, 1983; r/Meth; hon/Dean's List; Nat Dean's List; g/Interior Design.

RORRER, CARLA JEAN oc/Student, Public Relations Representative, b/Sep 12, 1964; h/14207 Cone Road, Maybee, MI 48159; ba/Milan, MI; p/Mr and Mrs G David Rorrer, Maybee, MI; ed/Milan HS, 1983; pa/Public Relats Rep, McDonald's Corporation, 1982-; cp/HS Student Coun Pres, 1982-83; Adv Com Rep, 1983; 4 Yrs Cross Country Team, 1979-83; Tae-Kwon-Do, 1978-82; Yth Coun Rep, 1981-83; r/Bapt.

ROSS, BRENDA JANE oc/Student; b/ May 23, 1963; h/Route 2, Box 217-T, Waverly, TN 37185; ba/Jackson, TN; p/ Mr and Mrs Rudy Ross, Waverly, TN; ed/Waverly Ctl HS, 1981; Union Univ; pa/Nurse's Aide, Hartsville Gen Hosp, 1982; Checker, Eddie's Foodtown, 1983; cp/Sci Clb, Secy 1980, Pres 1981; Mu Alpha Theta, 1980, 1981; Basketball Team, 1978-81; Sigma Zeta, 1983-84, Secy 1983-84; r/Missionary Bapt; hon/Kappa Mu Epsilon; Am Outstg Names & Faces; W/W Among Am HS Students; Nat Dean's List; One of Top Five Sci Papers, TN Jr Sci & Humanities Symp, 1979; Num Sports Awds & Hons incl'g MVP in Dist Tour & MVP on WCHS Team, TN Girls All Star Basketball Camp, Best Field Goal Percentage Student; Num Acad Hons incl'g WOW Outstg Hist Student, Westinghouse Hons Grp, Chem Rubber Co Outstg Freshman Chem Student Awd; incl'd in TN Jr Acad of Sci Annual Report, 1980; g/Med Sch.

ROSS, DANIEL EDMUND oc/Student; b/Dec 2, 1964; h/2414 Matilda Court, Warren, MI 48092; p/Anthony and Lois Ross, Warren, MI; ed/Bishop Foley HS, 1983; pa/Census Taker, Macomb Co, 1982-83; cp/HS Wrestling Team; Drama Clb; r/Cath; hon/W/W Among Am HS Students; Nat Merit S'ship Semi-Finalist, 1982-83; MI Competitive S'ship; g/Polit Sci at MI St Univ, Law Sch.

ROSS, JANET RHEA oc/Student; b/ Mar 20, 1965; h/Perkins Road, Adamsville, TN 38310; p/Mr and Mrs Tommy M Ross, Adamsville, TN 38310; ed/ Adamsville HS, 1983; Mid TN St Univ; pa/Pt-time Sales Clk, Pettigrew Rexall Drugs, 1980-82; Pt-time Employee, Pickwick Landing St Pk; cp/HS Freshman Class Pres, 1980; Sophomore Class Pres, 1981; Jr Class Pres, 1982; Sr Clas Pres, 1983; Beta Clb Pres, 1983;

Atlantic Clb Pres, 1983; HS Paper Editor, 1983; r/Meth; hon/Grad Top 20% of Class; HS Hon Roll; MVP in Basketball, 1982, 1983; MVP in Tennis, 1981-83; All-St in Basketball, 1983; W/ W Among Am HS Students; Soc of Dist'd HS Students; g/Master's Deg in Ed.

ROSS, TERRI LYNN oc/Student; b/ Oct 6, 1963; h/42 Orchard Street, Taunton, MA 02780; p/Edward and Jayne Ross, Taunton, MA; ed/Taunton HS, 1981; Fitchburg St Col; cp/Volleyball; Sr Class Rep; Yrbook Staff; Ch Yth Grp, CYO, Volleyball, Cheerldg; hon/ Magna Cum Laude Grad; Dean's List; Hon Roll; Nat Hon Soc; W/W Among Am HS Students; Intl Yth in Achmt; Yg Commun Ldrs; g/Med Tech.

ROSSIANNO, LORI ROBINSON oc/Telemarketing; b/Feb 19, 1962; h/324 West Kingston Avenue, Charlotte, NC 28203; m/Willie Lee Robinson; p/Lawrence and Patricia Rossiano, New York; sp/Louise Robinson, Charlotte, NC 28203; ed/Francis Lewis HS, 1980; BA, Johnson C Smith, 1984; r/Luth; hon/ Dean's List; Hon Roll; Duke S'ship; g/ Phd Clin Psychol.

ROTH, FREDERIC HULL III oc/ Student; b/Aug 23, 1963; h/30 Faculty Way, Bloomfield Hills, MI 48013; p/ Frederic Hull Jr and Kathleen Keady Roth, Bloomfield Hills, MI; ed/Yale Univ; cp/Hereditary Order of Founders & Patriots of Am; SAR; Yale Sons of Orpheus & Bacchus; Editor of Lit Mag, HS; Varsity Lttrs in Track, HS; r/Epis; hon/Social Register; Awd by Detroit Assn of Phi Beta Kappa; Yale Hon Hist Sem; Brown Univ Book Awd; Sr Hist Prize Awd, Cranbrook Hist Dept; Yg Commun Ldrs of Am; g/AB, MA, Yale Univ; MBA, Harvard Bus Sch; Mgmt or Mgmt Consltg.

ROUILLARD, KENNETH PAUL oc/ Student; b/May 16, 1966; h/2505 Southwest 84th, Oklahoma City, OK 73159; p/Mr and Mrs Richard Rouillard, OKC, OK; cp/Ch Yth Grp, 1980-84; Nat Hon Soc, 1980-84, Treas 1982; St Conv Del, 1982, Pres 1983; Math Clb, 1982; Model UN, 1982; Band, 1980-82; Track & Cross Country, 1981-83; r/Rom Cath; hon/Outstg Geometry Awd, 1982; Boys St Del, 1983; W/W Among Am HS Students; g/Undergrad, Grad Degs, Med, Gen Phys or Res Asst.

ROUSH, CLARK ALAN oc/Vocal Music Director; b/Sep 23, 1958; h/Post Office Box 671, Walnut, IA 51577; ba/ Walnut, IA; m/Sue Morris; p/Bob and Barb Roush, West Des Moines, IA; sp/ Elton and Orlia Morris, North Little Rock, AR; ed/Val HS, 1977; BA, Harding Univ, 1981; MA, Univ IA, 1982; pa/ Subst Tchr, Johnson Co Schs, 1981-82; Vocal Music Dir, Walnut Commun Schs, 1982-; cp/MENC; Am Choral Dirs Assn; IA Music Edrs Assn; IA Choral Dirs Assn; Gen Music Soc; Walnut Ed Assn; r/Ch of Christ; hon/Kappa Delta Pi, 1980; Alpha Chi, 1980; W/W Among Am Cols & Univs; Am Outstg Names & Faces; Intl Yth in Achmt; Commun Ldrs Am; g/PhD, Tch in Col or Univ.

ROWE, KAREN SUE oc/Student; b/ Jan 25, 1966; h/106 Millstone Drive, Richmond, KY 40475; p/William and Sarah Rowe, Richmond, KY; ed/Model Lab Sch, En KY Univ; cp/Model Key Clb, 1981-83; Pep Clb, 1980-81; Flag Corps, 1981-82; Track Team, 1981-84; Chorus,

1980-82; Nat Hon Soc, 1982-84; En KY Univ Dance Theater, 1983-84; r/Bapt; hon/USLMA Ldrship Merit Awd, 1983; USAA Awd, 1983; Soc of Dist'd Am HS Students, 1983; W/W Among Am HS Students; g/Deg in Aeronaut Engrg or Computer Sci.

ROY, JOHN THOMAS oc/Student; b/Jul 16, 1958; h/Route 1, Box 61, Philippi, WV 26416; ba/Blacksburg, VA; m/Julanne Michele Guild; p/Mr and Mrs Henry Thomas Roy, Philippi, WV; sp/ Mr and Mrs Walter E Guild, Penn Yan, NY; ed/Philip Barbour HS, 1976; BS, Alderson-Broaddus Col, 1980; VA Polytechnic Inst & St Univ; pa/Clk, Alderson-Broaddus Col, 1979-80; Tchg & Res Asst'ships, VA Polytechnic Inst & St Univ, 1980-; cp/Am Chem Soc, 1979-; Chi Beta Phi Sci Frat, 1979-80; Phi Lambda Upsilon Hon Soc, 1982-, Pres 1982-83; Silver Key Hon Soc, 1980; Explorer Post 99, 1973-80, Pres 1977-80; Col Golf Team, 1976-79; r/ Bapt; hon/Davis-Duncan Writing Awd, 1979; Bronze Big Horn Awd, BSA, 1980; Nat Sci Acad Awd, 1980; Outstg Male in Nat Sci, 1980; Second Pl Local Coun Winner, Nat Spkg Contest, BSA; Intl Yth in Achmt; W/W; g/Phd, Career in Chem.

ROY, JULANNE G oc/Special Assistant to Department Head, Virginia Tech; b/Sep 30, 1959; h/1600 H Terrace View, Blacksburg, VA 24060; ba/Blacksburg, VA; m/John Thomas; p/Mr and Mrs Walter E Guild Jr, Penn Yan, NY 14527; m/Mr and Mrs Henry Thomas Roy, Philippi, WV; ed/Penn Yan Acad, 1977; BS, Alderson-Broaddus Col, 1981; VPI & St Univ; pa/Student Asst Tech Sers, 1979-81; Clk B 1981-82, Data Entry Operator 1982-83; Spec Asst to Dept Hd 1983-, VPI & St Univ; cp/Pres of Yth Against Cancer; Mem of NY St Yth Against Cancer Com; Pres of Bapt Yth F'ship; Soccer Team; Alpha Omicron Pi; r/Bapt; hon/Finger Lakes Life Ins Underwriters Teenager of Yr, 1978; Yth Cares Awd, 1978; Dean's List; W/W Among HS Students.

ROYBAL, LAWRENCE oc/Chairman, International Center; b/Jun 6, 1962; h/Route 2, Box 41, Mountainair, NM 87036; ba/Albuquerque, NM; ed/ Mountainair HS; Univ NM-Communs w Intl Relats; Sch of Intl Mktg; Plaza Three Acad Fashion; pa/Chm, Pres Appts Com; Chm, Cultural Programming, Popejoy Hall; Chm, Intl Affairs Com; Asst Dir, Intl Ctr, Manzano Talent Agy; Public Relats; cp/ASUNM Senate; Fin Com; Pres Appts Com; Cultural Com; Intl Affairs Com; UN Assn; Mktg Assn; OEA Bus Assn; Steering Com; Lobby Com; Univ Band; Intl Horizons, Assoc Ed; The Branding Iron, Editor; r/Cath; hon/OEA Exec Awd; Diplomat Awd; Statesman Awd; Ambassador Awd; Nat Spch Del; St Spch Finalist; Outstg Student; Yg Am Citizens; W/W Among Univ & Col Students; Outstg Yth in Achmt; Outstg Yg Men Am; g/Grad Sch, Communs Maj/ Intl Relats.

RUBIO, IRMA MARIA oc/Student; b/Jul 22, 1960; h/8260 Northwest 185 Street, Miami, FL 33015; p/Irma Ricardo, Miami, FL; ed/Hialeah Miami Lakes Sr HS, 1978; Univ Miami; pa/ Secy, 1975-83; cp/Concert Choir, 1978-; MENC, 1979; r/Rom Cath; hon/Col

Register; Intl Yth in Achmt; Hon Roll; g/Music Ed Maj, Profl Singer.

RUDLOFF, DANIEL B oc/Student; b/ Feb 9, 1967; h/517 Ashmoor Drive, Bowling Green, KY 42101; p/William J and Rita Rudloff, Bowling Green, KY; ed/Bowling Green HS; pa/Newspaper Carrier, Pk City Daily News; r/Pres; hon/Nat Jr Hon Soc; HS Hon Roll.

RUDO, MICHELLE ARLENE oc/ Student; b/Sep 3, 1963; h/13 Deer Lodge Court, Owings Mills, MD 21117; p/ Myra Rudo, Owings Mills, MD; ed/ Owings Mills HS, 1981; Drexel Univ; pa/Computer Programmer, Dept Public Wks Engrg Anal, 1983; cp/Steering Com; Varsity Track; Mgr, Varsity Volleyball; Talent Shows; Sch Musicals; Alpha Sigma Alpha Sorority, 1982-; Drexel Dance Ensemble, 1981-; r/ Jewish; hon/Nat Hon Soc; W/W Among Am HS Students; Yg Commun Ldrs of Am; g/Computer Programmer.

RUDOLPH, ANGELA RENEE oc/ Student; b/Jun 8, 1965; h/80 Sunray Drive, Highland, IL 62249; ba/Lawrence, KS; p/Max and Marilyn Rudolph, Highland, IL; ed/Highland HS, 1983; Univ KS; pa/Waitress, Ken's Pizza Parlor, Sum 1981-83; cp/Student Occupl Therapy Assn, 1983/84; HS Varsity Cheerldr, 1980-83; VP of Class, 1980-83; Pres, Art Clb, 1982; Pres, Spanish Clb; HS Musicals; Drama Clb, 1980-83; hon/Dana Deibert S'ship Fund; Hon Student; W/W Among Am HS Students; g/Occupl Therapy.

RUDOLPH, JAMES ROBERT oc/ Student; b/Mar 1, 1957; h/13108 Turquoise NE, Albuquerque, NM; p/Mr and Mrs Robert Rudolph, Albuquerque, NM; ed/Manzano HS, 1975; BA 1980, MA 1981, Univ of NM; pa/Mgmt, Commonwealth Theatres Inc, 1975-79; Practicum Tchr, Chd's Psychi Ctr, 1981; Tchr, Albuquerque Public Schs, 1982; cp/Pi Kappa Alpha, Mbrship Ed Coor, Secy; Pi Lambda Theta, Pres, Prog Chm; Blue Key, Selections & Initiation Chm; Phi Alpha Theta; Delta Tau Kappa; Alpha Kappa Delta; Phi Sigma Tau; Phi Delta Kappa; Psi Chi Pres; Interfrat Coun VP; Univ NM Student Crisis Ctr Chm of the Bd; Las Campanas; hon/ Dean of Students Awd of Outstg Ser; Intl Yth in Achmt; W/W Among Students in Am Univs & Cols; Pi Kappa Alpha Frat Man of Yr, 1978; Univ NM Outstg Greek Man Nom, 1979; Pi Kappa Alpha Nat Outstg Undergrad Nom, 1979; Dean's Hon List; Commun Ldrs Am; g/EdD, Guid & Cnslg.

RUFF, CHARLES RICHARD oc/ Student; b/May 17, 1960; h/Route 2, Box 304, Newberry, SC 29108; p/Mr and Mrs Richard H Ruff, Newberry, SC; ed/Col Prep Dipl, Mid-Carolina HS, 1978; BS Poultry Sci, Summa Cum Laude 1982, MS Poultry Nutrition & Mgmt 1984, Clemson Univ; cp/Alpha Tau Omega Frat; Alpha Zeta, VP, Treas; Poultry Sci Clb; Dairy Sci Clb; Yrbook Editor; Tiger Brotherhood Hon Ser Frat; SC Jr Jersey Cattle Clb, Past Pres; Am Jr Jersey Cattle Clb; Clemson Poultry Judging Team, 3rd High Individual Nat Contest; Clemson Dairy Judging Team; Tiger Brotherhood Hon Ser Frat, Pres 1983-84, VP 1982-83; Blue Key Nat Hon Frat, Publicity Chm

for Tigerama, 1983; hon/Steve Hinson Awd; Tiger Brotherhood of Yr, 1984; Alpha Zeta Awd, Student of Yr Col of Agri, 1982; Gamma Sigma Delta Outstg Sr, 1982; Ralston Purina Res F'ship, 1982-83; SC Fam of Yr Reg Winner, 1983; Gamma Sigma Delta Outstg Sophomore; Nat Feedstuffs Scholar; Nat Alpha Zeta Scholar; Dean's List; Nat Dean's List; W/W Among Students in Am Cols & Univs; g/Nutrition Chem Sales or Tech Sers.

RUIZ, SOFIA CASTILLO oc/Student; b/Jul 25, 1965; h/411 North Dallas, Midland, TX 79701; p/Mr and Mrs Soloman Ruiz, Midland, TX; ed/Robert E Lee HS; cp/Pres of Ch Yth Clb, 1981-82; VP of Explorers Clb, 1981-82; Student Coun Rep, 1980-81; Student Coun Cabinet, 1979-80; French Clb, 1980-82; Geol Clb, 1982-83; r/Cath; hon/Miss Teen Pageant Contestant, 1982; Good Citizenship Awd, 1976; French Contest Awds; W/W Among Am HS Students; g/Baylor Univ.

RUMBOUGH, REBECCA ANN oc/ Secretary; b/Apr 20, 1958; h/2507 Spring Valley Road, Fayetteville, NC 28303; ba/Fayetteville, NC; p/Mr and Mrs R Albert Rumbough, Fayetteville, NC; ed/Terry Sanford Sr HS, 1976; Univ NC-Wilmington, 1978-81, BA 1982; pa/Gen Cinema Corp, 1980, 1982; Sales, Thalhimers, 1981; Secy, Riddle-Floyd-Godwin Rltrs, 1982-; cp/ Delta Zeta Sorority, Corres Secy; r/ Meth; g/Real Est, Bus, Computer.

RUSH, ELIZABETH THELMA oc/ Student; b/Nov 6, 1964; h/33877 County Road 34, Lajunta, CO 81050; p/Norris and Elizabeth J Rush, Lajunta, CO; ed/Cheraw HS, 1983; Tabor Col; cp/HS Volleyball; Lttrmans Clb; Cheerleader; Pep Clb; Student Coun; r/Meth; hon/Acctg Awd; Trigonometry Awd; Govt Awd; Good Samaritan Awd; Salutatorian; W/W Among Am HS Student; g/Deg in Computer Sci.

RUSSELL, DANA LA'RUE oc/Student; b/Nov 13, 1962; h/105 Don Drive, Greenville, SC 29607; ed/James L Mann HS; Columbia Col; pa/Hd of Promotions/Distbn, Flip/Side Record Prodns & Agy; cp/Secy of Columbia Col Concert Choir; Ofcr in Hi C's; r/Bapt; hon/Music Clb of Greenville Awd; Most Valuable Sr in Music HS; Columbia Col Music S'ship; Frank Z Harris Music Awd; Miss Golden Strip in Pageant; Friendship Awd; g/Master's Deg; Profl Entertainer.

RUSSELL, JEFFREY BILL oc/Student; b/Dec 9, 1960; h/3100 5th Street, 102, Sachse, TX 75098; m/Connie J; p/ Mr and Mrs Bill Russell, Garland, TX; sp/Mr and Mrs Thomas G Kirkpatrick, Sachse, TX; ed/Garland HS; BA, E TX St Univ, 1983; pa/Brass Instr, Paris Jr Col; cp/Alpha Chi Hon Soc; Phi Mu Alpha; Intl Trombone Assn; TX Music Edrs Assn; r/Saturn Road Ch of Christ; hon/FTA S'ship; Admiral Raphael Smith S'ship; W/W Among Am HS Students; Soc Dist'd Am HS Students; g/Teach in Public Schs; Master's in Ed.

RUSSELL, ROBERT FOSTER oc/ Student; b/Jun 16, 1959; h/526-A Georgetown Road, Charlottesville, VA 22901; m/Susan Kerley; p/Robert and Elizabeth Russell, Marion, VA 24354; sp/Mrs Gerry Kerly, Bristol, VA; ed/

Marion Sr HS, 1977; BA, Emory & Henry Col, 1981; MBA, Univ VA, 1984; pa/Land Mgr, Bartlett Energy Inc, 1982; Broker, Bartlett & Assocs, 1981; Internship-Pers, Brunswick Corporation, 1980; Rlty Stat 1980, Forestry Aide 1979, US Forest Ser; Investment Bkg, Scott Stringfellow Inc, 1983; cp/Col Jud Bd, Student Defender; Lacrosse; Blue Key; Acad Policies Com; Pre-Law Soc; Student Rep-Fac Meetings; Fin Com; VITA; Intramurals; Assn of MBA Execs; Jr Leag Basketball, Ftball Coach; Cert CPR; Rec Leag Softball; hon/Sr Achmt Awd, Psychol Dept; TN Eastman Kodak Corp S'ship; Dean's List; Magna Cum Laude; Sigma Nu; Intramural Ath of Yr; Intramural Champ, Wrestling, 2nd Racquetball; Nat Dean's List; Intl Yth in Achmt; g/Investment Bkg.

RUTLAND, CHARLES JR oc/CPA; b/ Jan 24, 1961; h/7735 Holland Court, Arvada, CO 80005; ba/Denver, CO; p/ Mr and Mrs Charles Rutland Sr, Warner Robins, GA; ed/Warner Robins Sr HS, 1978; BS, FL A & M Univ, 1982; pa/Staff Acct 1982, Sr Asst Acct 1983, Deloitte Haskins & Sells; cp/Recording Secy, Denver Chapt of the Nat Assn Black Accts; Jr Achmt Sponsor; Alpha Kappa Mu; Chief Justice, Student Supreme Court; Columnist, Sch Newspaper; r/Meth; hon/Nat Merit Scholar; Intl Yth in Achmt; W/W Among Am Students in Am Univs & Cols; Intl Yth in Excell; Yg Commun Ldrs Am.

RUTLAND, GRISELDA LATREASE oc/Student; b/Dec 19, 1965; h/1312 Moody Road, Warner Robins, GA 31093; p/Mr and Mrs Charles Rutland Sr, Warner Robins, GA; cp/Debate Team, 1981-84; Varsity Basketball Team, 1981-84; Essence Clb, Treas, 1982-84; Beta Clb, 1980-81; Jour & Yrbook Staff, 1980-81; Girls St Rep, 1983; r/Meth; hon/High Hon Roll Student, 1981-83; Most Likely to Succeed, 1980-81; Basketball MVP, 1980-81; Varisty Lttr & Hustler Awd, 1982-83; Sweetheart Queen for 1981; The Eng Awd, 1981; W/W Among Am HS Students; g/Attend Tuskegee Inst, Chem Engrg.

RYDER, JOHN HOYT oc/Electrical Engineer; b/Feb 25, 1960; h/2105 Adventure Trail, Durham, NC; p/John and Paige Ryder; ed/HS, 1978; NC St Univ; Wake Col, 1981; hon/Intl Yth in Achmt; W/W in Am Jr Cols.

RYVA, JEFFREY ALAN oc/ Attorney-at-Law; b/Nov 27, 1955; h/ 7150 North Terra Vista Drive, Peoria, IL 61614; m/Deborah Gaine Viring; p/ Mr and Mrs Jerry Ryva, Villa Park, IL; ed/Willowbrook HS, 1973; BA, Univ of IL, 1977; John Marshall Law Sch, 1980; cp/Am, IL, Chgo, Peoria Bar Assns; Editor-in-Chief, *John Marshall Law Review*; Pre-Law Clb; Rho Epsilon; HS Cross-Country, Track; hon/Casenote, *Hewitt v. Hewitt: Contract Cohabitation & Equitable Expectations Relief for Meretricious Spouses*, 1979; Comment, *Civil Aspects of Intrafamily Eavesdropping in Illinois: Caveats to Comprehensive Remedial Weaponry*, 1979; Scribes Awd of Mbrship in Am Soc of Writers on Legal Subjects; Order of John Marshall; Dean's List; Am Yth in Achmt; Commun Ldrs Am.

S

SACHTER, MELISSA BETH oc/ Primary/Junior Teacher; b/Aug 3, 1960; h/313 Glenayr Road, Toronto, Ontario, Canada M5P-3C6, p/Mr and Mrs R L Sachter, Toronto, Ontario; ed/Ontario Sec'dy Sch Hons Grad Dipl, Forest Hill Col Inst, 1979; BAECE, Ryerson Polytech Inst, 1983; BEd/Tchrs Cert, Univ Toronto, 1984; pa/Hd Presch Swim Prog, Forest Val Day Camp, 1984; Hd, Tri-Level Swim Sch, 1976-; Sales Clk, T Eaton Co, 1981-83; Asst Hd, Hd of Presch Swim Prog, Camp Robin Hood, 1976-79; cp/Mgr 1979-82, Competitor 1979-82, Ryerson Intercol Swim Team; Univ Toronto Intercol Swim Team, Mgr, 1983-84; Univ Toronto Swim Clb, Mgr, 1983-84; hon/Imperial Order of the Daugh's of the Empire Awd, 1981; Most Valuable Swimmer, Ryerson Polytech Inst, 1980-81.

SALZMAN, GENE RAINE JR oc/ Student, Part-time Custodian; b/Jul 13, 1960; h/2807 Riverview Drive, Fairbanks, AK 99701; p/Mr and Mrs Gene R Salzman, Fairbanks, AK; ed/Monroe HS, 1979; Hutchinson Career Ctr, Airframe & Power Plant, 1981; AAS, Univ AK-Fairbanks, 1982; pa/Airplane Mech's Helper, Wyatt's Air Ser, 1977-80; Custodian, Boiler Oper, Maintenance, Cath Schs of Fairbanks, 1980-; r/Rom Cath; hon/Citizen S'ship, 1977; Commun Ser S'ship, 1976, 1978; Intl Yth in Achmt; g/Return to Col.

SAMSON, RONALD PAMINTUAN oc/Student; b/Sep 8, 1963; h/1134 Denton Avenue, Hayward, CA 94545; ba/Hayward, CA; p/Mr and Mrs Wilfredo P Samson, Hayward, CA; ed/ George Cannon HS, 1978; Ctl Kitsap HS, 1980; Sunset HS, 1981; CA St Univ; pa/Floor Supvr, McDonald's Corporation, 1981-83; Sales Assoc, Emporium-Capwell, 1983-; cp/HS Assoc'd Student Body Coun; Chorus; Intl Thespian Soc; Key Clb; Spanish Clb; Filipino-Am Student Assn; Intl Clb; Quill & Scroll; CA S'ship Fdn; Ecol-Sci Clb; Ski Clb; Barbizon Modeling Agy; r/Rom Cath; hon/W/W Among Am HS Students; Personalities of Am; Intl Yth in Achmt; Commun Ldrs Am; Dir Dist'd Am.

SANABRIA, TERESITA LUCIA oc/ Student; b/Sep 1, 1965; h/401 69th Street, Guttenberg, NJ 07093; ba/West New York, NJ; p/Francisco and Arminda Sanabria, Guttenberg, NJ; ed/St Joseph of the Palisades HS, 1983; St Cecilia Music Acad, 1972-79; Sara Saltiel Music Acad, 1979-; NJ Scholars Prog at the Lawrenceville Sch, 1982; pa/Pt-time Receptionist, Bkkpr, Hygiene Instr, Oral Surg Asst, 1981-; Guest Lectr, St Peter's Col, 1982; cp/French Hon Soc; Nat Hon Soc, Com Coor 1981-; Parish Unity Proj, Coor 1982-; Christian Ldrship, Coor 1982-; r/Rom Cath; hon/ Author of "The Leaf", *Phoenix Lit Mag,* "Magic Windows", *Highlights,* 1983; hon/ Soc of Dist'd Am HS Students; NJ Scholar at the Lawrenceville Sch; Nat Hon Soc; First Hon Roll.

SANDEL, JANE MARIE oc/Student; b/Mar 3, 1962; h/Box 124, Centerville, TX 75833; ba/College Sta, TX; p/ Kenneth Wayne and Sandra Lynn Sandel, Centerville, TX; ed/Alexandria Sr HS; Centerville HS, 1980; TX A & M Univ; TX St Tech Inst; pa/Domestic

Sers, 1983; Leon Co Abstract Co, 1981; Halfway House Restaurant, 1980; Dairy Queen, 1979; Lawn Care Sers, 1978; Telephone Volunteer, 1978; cp/Cepheid Variable; Soc of Creat Anachronism; Aggie Allemanders; Russian Clb; Judo Clb; r/Meth; hon/*Forum,* Poetry, 1979; Valedictorian; 2nd Pl Lit Rally Interpretive Rdg; 1st Pl Solo & Ensemble/Piano Solo; 1st Pl Sci Fair/Math; W/W Among Am HS Students; Intl Yth in Achmt; Yg Commun Ldrs Am; g/Landscape Arch.

SANDERS, DORIL oc/Teacher/Coordinator; b/Aug 21, 1958; h/Post Office Box 6-A, 200 Downs Avenue, Mendenhall, MS 39114; ba/Magee, MS; p/Troy and Lexie Sanders, New Albany, MS; ed/New Albany W P Daniel HS, 1978; AA, NE MS Jr Col, 1978-81; BS, MS St Univ, 1981-83; pa/Cook, Shoney's, 1978-81; Bkstore Clk, Orient Ldr, Band Hall, NE MS Jr Col; Salesclk; Pay-N-Save, Sum 1980; Housing Maintenance Sum 1982, Resident Asst 1982-83, MS St Univ; Tchr/Coor, Magee HS, 1983-; cp/DECA-NEMJC, Pres; Reporter, MSU Pres, VP; Afro-Am Plus, Pres; Coun Black Student Orgs, Rep; Hamlin Hall Coun, VP; Phi Beta Lambda, Reporter, 1978-80; Student Govt Assn, 1980-81; Afro-Am Culture Soc, Pres, Sec; Tennis; Band; hon/W/W Among Am Jr Cols; Commun Ldrs Am; Intl Yth in Achmt; Sophomore Favorite NEMJC; g/Master's Deg in Student Pers Devel.

SANDERS, ELIZABETH MICHELLE oc/Student; b/Sep 28, 1968; h/Route 6, 607 Buckingham Road, Easley, SC 29640; p/Mrs Beth Sanders, Easley, SC; cp/Drama; Secy, Student Coun; Candystriper; Lib Vol; VP Yth Bible Grp; hon/1st Pl Duo Acting, 1981; 1st Pl Ensemble Theater, 1982; 1st Pl Lit Interpretation, 1983; Acad Excell in All Subjects, 1982, 1983; g/col, Maj in Computer Sci.

SANDERS, KEVIN SCHAUN oc/ Law Student; b/Jun 23, 1958; h/7381 Wending Court South, Jacksonville, FL 32244; p/Mr and Mrs Cledith A Sanders, Jacksonville, FL; ed/Nathan Bedford Forest HS, 1976; AA, FL Jr Col, 1979; BS, FL St Univ, 1981; pa/Asst Mgr of County Seat Inc; Asst Mgr, Regency Rlty Corp; Intern w St Rep Andy Johnson; Ser Sta Attendant; Constrn Wkr; cp/J'ville JCs; Alpha Tau Omega; Phi Theta Kappa; Zeta Tau Alpha Big Brother; Garnet & Gold Key Hon Soc; Student Govt Pres, 1977-79; Sr Class Pres, 1980-81; Union Bd Rep, 1980-81; Others; r/Epis; hon/Nat Hon Soc; Acad Recog from Harvard Clb of J'ville, 1975-76; Univ FL Blue Key Awd; Top Male of 15,000 Students, FL Jr Col; Union Prog Ofc "Friendship" Awd; Outstg Sr, FL St Univ; 1 of 8 Chosen from Class of 2200; Recog'd by Nat Exch Clb, DAR, Alumni Assn of Univ FL; W/ W: Among Am HS Students, Among Students in Am Jr Cols, Among Students in Am Univs & Cols; Outstg Yg Men Am; Outstg Yg Ldrs; Others; g/ To Achieve Success in Law & Polits.

SANDERS, MICHAEL JAMES oc/ Radiographer; b/Jan 4, 1963; h/395 Elm Street, Britton, MI 49229; p/Carlan and Barbara Sanders; Britton, MI; ed/ Britton-Macon HS, 1981; AAS, Ferris St Col, 1983; pa/Radiographer, Rogers City Hosp, 1983; Pt-time Non Grad

Radiographer, Towers Med Bldg, 1983; Short Order & Preparation Cook, Elias Brothers' Restaurant, 1978-81; cp/MI Soc of Radiologic Technologists; Lakeshore Soc of Radiologic Technologists; Org of Radiographic Interns, Butterworth Hosp; Ferris St Col X-Ray Clb; Ferris St Col Symphonic Band; Ferris St Col Marching Band; Blue Lake Intl Symphonic Band; HS Ftball, Basketball, Track; r/Cath; hon/Music S'ship, 1981-82; St of MI Competitive S'ship Prog Cert of Recog; Dean's List; Various HS Acad & Ath Awds incl'g Lttrs in Ftball, Track, & Basketball.

SANDERS, MICHELLE RENÉE oc/ Student; b/Feb 21, 1958; h/1047 Stratford, Wichita, KS 67206; ba/Wichita, KS; p/Vivian Sanders, Wichita, KS; ed/ BA, Wichita St Univ, 1980; cp/Biol Clb; Delta Gamma Sorority; Mtl Hlth Assn; SWn Psychol Assn; Div 38, APA; Ofcr, WSU Psych Grad Student Org, 1980; VP, Psych Clb, 1978-79; Vol, Wichita Wom's Crisis Ctr; Vol, Wesley Med Ctr; Student Govt; hon/BA magna cum laude, Wichita St Univ, 1980; Phi Kappa Phi; Psi Chi; Sr Hon Wom; Intl Yth in Achmt; W/W Among Am Univs & Cols; Commun Ldrs Am; g/Completion of 2nd Bach's Deg in Biol; Studies in Med.

SANDERS, TERRI SUE oc/Student; b/Jun 5, 1965; h/200 Woodward Avenue, Mingo Jct, OH 43938; p/Donna Sanders, Mingo Jct, OH; cp/Nat Hon Soc, Secy; Student Coun, VP; Med Careers Clb Pres; Pep Clb; Annual Staff Editor; Jefferson Co Yth Coor'g Coun; OH St Fair Band; hon/Jefferson Co Scholar, Silver Key, 1982; US Nat Band Awd, 1983; Buckeye Girls' St Rep, 1982; Hugh O'Brian Yth Ldrship Sem, 1980; g/Study Nsg, RN, become a Doctor.

SANDS, RAYMOND C III oc/Surveillance Systems Technician; h/1727 Haven Avenue, Ocean City, NJ 08226; p/Mrs Raymond C Sands Jr, Delran, NJ; ed/Holy Cross HS, 1975; BA, Rutgers Univ, 1980; Intl Assn Bomb Techs & Investigators Sch on Adv'd Explosives & Terrorist Activs, 1983; pa/Surveillance Sys Tech, Tropicana Hotel-Casino, 1983-; Security Computer Opers Sgt, 1982-83; cp/Kappa Sigma Upsilon Alumni Bd; Rutgers Univ Admissions Com, 1978; Rec'g Secy 1978, VP 1979, Inter-Frat Sorority Coun, Rutgers Univ; Rutgers Student Cong Rep, 1979-80, 1978-79; r/Cath; hon/W/W Among Students in Am Univs & Cols; Intl Yth in Achmt; Kappa Sigma Upsilon Scholastic Awd, 1979; g/to become a Spec Agt for the Drug Enforcement Adm, Dept of Justice.

SANFORD, SUZANNE ELIZABETH oc/Student, Bus Driver; b/Feb 15, 1965; h/Post Office Box 252, 106 Pinecrest Street, Boiling Springs, NC 28017; p/ Mr and Mrs John K Sanford, Boiling Springs, NC; ed/Crest Sr HS, 1983; Mars Hill Col; pa/Waitress, Movie House Restaurant, 1982; Bus Driver, 1982-; cp/Jr Beta Clb, 1979-80; Nat Hon Soc, 1982-83; 4-H; Girl Scouts; Ch Yth Choir Soc Chm, 1979-; Reflections Mem, 1982-; Yth Coun, Secy/Treas 1982, VP 1983; Evangelism Com; r/ Bapt; hon/Chem Awd, 1982; Typing Awd, 1982; Jr Marshall, 1982; 4-H Racking Horse Champ, 1979-80; 4-H Racking Horse Reserv Champ, 1980-81; Marshbanks-Anderson Scholar, 1982; Pres Scholar, 1982; 1st Runner-up

Crest Carousel Queen, 1982; g/Systems Analyst.

SANTOS, KELLI JOELLE oc/Student; b/Sep 13, 1962; h/3416 Norton Avenue, Modesto, CA 95351; p/Mr and Mrs Rufus Santos, Jr, Modesto, CA; ed/Modesto HS, 1980; AA, Modesto Jr Col, 1983; Stanislaus St; cp/Art Clb; Anelecta Clb, 1978-79; Softball, 1980; Basketball, 1976; VP, Freshman Class; Painted Murals in HS Gym, CA St Turlock; r/Cath; hon/Most Ser to Sch Awd; Bk Am S'ship Awd; Jr Achmt Awd; W/W Among Am HS Student; Art Clb S'ship; Intl Yth in Achmt; Commun Ldrs Am; Phy Fitness Awd; Annual Sch Traffic Safety Poster Contest; Hon Roll; g/BA Deg.

SAPAH-GULIAN, RANDOLPH VART oc/Finance Search Consultant; b/Apr 30, 1954; h/58 Gilmore Avenue, Cresskill, NJ 07626; ba/Same; p/Vart and Armenine Sapah-Guilan, Cresskill, NJ; ed/Grad, Armenian Lang Sch, 1968; Cresskill HS, 1972; BA, Rutgers Col, 1976; cp/Am Gen Benevolent Union, Exec Com Metro Chapt 1980-, Lead Soloist ANTRANIG Armenian Dance Ensemble 1969-, Artistic Dir/Choreographer 1979-, Creator/Dir "The Eternal Flame"; Zeta Psi, Delta Chapt; hon/Armenian Gen Benevolent Union S'ship for Study Abroad; Guest of Sch of Dance Choreography, Erevan, Armenia; Am Rep to Opening of Manoogian Armenian Cultural Ctr, Beirut, Lebanon; BSA Eagle Scout, 1969; Armenian Gen Ath Union Awd for Achmt in Fields of Wrestling Team; Lttrman, Wrestling, Track & Field; g/To Function as a Fin & Artistic Intermediary within the Entertainment Indust in Bringing Prods to the Stage.

SARKISS, CAROLYN JOAN oc/Student; b/Aug 9, 1960; h/10004 Minburn Street, Great Falls, VA 22066; ba/College Sta, TX; p/Col and Mrs Robert David Loe, Great Falls, Va; ed/J W Robinson Sec'dy; BBA 1982, MBA 1983, Univ GA; PhD Cand, TX A & M Univ; pa/Grad Asst, Res Tchr, 1983-84; Assn of MBA Execs; Omicron Delta Epsilon; Grad Bus Assn; Grad Bus Wom's Assn; Sponsor Liaison, Delta Delta Delta; Univ GA Ecs Clb; Communiversity; Athens Big Sister/Little Sister Prog; Am Cancer Soc Vol; Am Soc for Interior Design; Student Home Ecs Clb; Am Home Ecs Assn; r/Meth; hon/Dean's List; Panhellenic Dean's List; Nat Dean's List Nom; Personalities of S; Intl Yth in Achmt; g/Doct Deg & Tch, Res, Travel.

SARKOZI, ROBERT PAUL oc/Student; b/Oct 1, 1965; h/171 Louisiana Avenue, New Braunfels, TX 78130; p/Lewis Paul and Veronica Ann Sarkozi, New Braunfels; ed/HS Grad, 1984; cp/Nat Hon Soc; Mu Alpha Theta, Treas 1982-83, Pres 1983-84; Sci Clb, 1980-84; German Clb, 1982-84; Sci Team; Math Team; r/Cath; hon/Rotary Outstg Student, 1983; Elks Student of the Mo, 1983; Nat Merit Semi-Finalist; g/attend Rice Univ, Maj in Math.

SATTERFIELD, THOMAS ALBERT oc/Courtesy Clerk, Student; b/Mar 31, 1963; h/2589 Avalon Circle, Chattanooga, TN 37415; ba/Red Bank, TN; p/Mrs V E Satterfield, Chattanooga, TN; ed/Chattanooga HS, 1981; Univ TN-Chattanooga; pa/Courtesy Clk, Red Food Inc, 1981-; cp/BSA; Am Legion

Boys St; HS Student Coun; Nat Hon Soc; Treas, Fresh, Sophomore, Jr, & Sr Classes; Treas of Band; Treas of Math Clb; r/Seventh Day Adventist; hon/12 Years Perfect Attendance; Dean's List; Intl Yth in Achmt; Cread Bates Acad S'ship; W/W Among Am HS Students; Yg Personalities of S; Eagle Scout; g/BS in BA; CPA.

SAULS, CHARLES EDWIN oc/Student; b/May 22, 1961; h/109 West 7th Street, Tifton, GA 31794; ba/Augusta, GA; p/Mr and Mrs Frank Sauls, Tifton, GA; ed/Tift Co HS, 1979; Univ GA, Dental Sch-Med Col GA; cp/Pres of Freshman Class, Sch Dentistry; Am Dental Assn; St Ofcr, GA Jr Acad Sci; Beta Clb; Yth Leag for Christ; GA Entomological Soc; HS Yrbook Staff; Pres, Mu Alpha Theta; Interclb Coun; Treas, Alpha Lambda Delta; VP, Sigma Alpha Chi; Valdosta St Col Champ, Student Affil Am Chem Soc; Sophomore Senator at Large, Student Elections Com, Chm Allocations Com, Communs Bd, Student Govt Awareness Prog, Col Student Govt Assn; Selection Com, Annual Mac & Marga Awds for Outstg Grad'g Male & Female; Omicron Delta Kappa; r/Bapt; hon/Contbr 2 Sci Papers, *Jour of Chem Ecol*; Grand Awd in Life Scis, GA Sci & Engrg Fair, 2 Yrs; 2nd Awd in Zool, Intl Sci & Engrg Fair; First Hon Grad, Tift Co HS, 1979; 2nd Dist Tchrs Awd of Merit; Alpha Mu Epsilon Awd; AUS Awd of Excell; AUS Superior Awd; USAF 1st Pl Awd; Gov's Hons Finalist; Pres's Freshman Scholar, 1979-80; Exch Clbs' Yth of Yr; AUS Jr Sci & Humanities Symp; Intl Yth in Achmt; Am's Outstg Names & Faces; Personalities of S; g/Dentist.

SAUNDERS, ANDREA RENEÉ oc/Student; b/Jun 26, 1966; h/Route 1, Box 777, Spring Hope, NC 27882; p/Jerry Mac and Carole Ann Saunders, Spring Hope, NC; ed/So Nash Sr HS, 1984; cp/Freshman VP, SCA; Chp, Sophomore Pres of SCA; Quiz Bowl; NC Tarheels Jr Histn, 1981; Mars Hill Del; Hugh O'Brian St Level Conv; Math & Sci Fair Beta Clb, 1983; Homeroom Rep, 1983; r/Prot; hon/Commun Ldrs Am; W/W; US Achmt Awd; Semi-Finalist of NCSM, 1982; French I Awd; Plane Geometry Awd; Eng II Awd; Biol I Awd; Eng III Awd; Algebra II Awd; Chem I Awd; French II Awd; Danford I Dare You Awd; WOW Hist Awd; Chief Marshall; Intl Fgn Lang Awd; Gov's Page; g/Biol Maj; Wildlife Field Rschr.

SCADDEN, BRYAN FRED oc/Teacher, Coach; b/Jul 30, 1954; h/2622 East 12th Street, Cheyenne, WY 82001; ba/Cheyenne, WY; m/Gina D Stoll; c/Jennifer Deniece; p/Lawrence and Betty Scadden, North Salt Lake, UT; sp/Leroy and Gua Stoll, Cheyenne, WY; ed/Cheyenne Gast HS, 1972; AA, Laramie Co Commun Col, 1977; Bach, Univ WY, 1979; pa/Social Studies Tchr/Hd Volleyball Coach, Cheyenne Gast, 1979-; cp/NEA; WEA; CTEA; WY Coaches Assn; Nat Coaches Assn; Kappa Delta Pi; Local Close-up Sponsor; White House Conf on Chd/Yth; Nat Volleyball Coaches Assn; USVBA Coaches Assn; r/LDS; hon/Rotary Jr Col Student of Yr, 1976-77; Hon Grad, 1977; Hon Grad, Univ WY, 1979; Student Body Pres, 1975-76; Commun Ldrs Am; g/Masters & Doct of Ed; Teach at Maj Col.

SCANLON, JAMES JOSEPH III oc/

Student; b/Apr 12, 1962; h/227 Delsea Drive, Dept Ford, NJ 08096; p/James and Jacqueline Scanlon, Dept Ford, NJ; ed/Gloucester Cath HS, 1980; BS, VA Military Inst, 1984; mil/AF; pa/Field Tng Ofcr, McCord AFB, 1983; AFROTC Field Tng, Lackland AFB, 1982; Amusement Ride Operator, Hunt's Pier, 1981; cp/VMI Hon Court, 1983-; Yg Col Repubs, 1982-; VMI Ski Team, 1982-83; Marine Corps Marathon Team, 1982; Mem of IEEE, 1983-; r/Cath; hon/Etta Kappa Nu, 1982-; W/W Among Col Students in Am; Dean's List; Vice Commandant's Awd at AFROTC Field Tng, 1982; MVP in HS Golf, 1978-80; g/Space Technol in USAF.

SCARBORO, GARLAND oc/Student; b/Dec 24, 1964; h/Route 1, Box 152-A, Middlesex, NC 27557; p/Mr and Mrs Roosevelt Scarboro, Middlesex, NC 27557; ed/Smithfield-Selma Sr HS, 1983; Att'g Atlantic Christian Col; cp/Spanish Clb; Human Relat Clb, Treas; Nat Hon Soc; Chorus; r/Bapt; hon/Atlantic Christian Hons S'ship, 1983-84; Robert P Holdings S'ship, 1983-84; Alpha Merit Awd, 1983; W/W Among Am HS Students; g/Bus Maj; Computer Sci.

SCARBOROUGH, CHARLES JOSEPH oc/Student; b/Apr 9, 1963; h/3415 Brookshire Drive, Pensacola, FL 32503; p/Mr and Mrs George F Scarborough, Pensacola, FL; ed/Cath HS; Univ AL-Tuscaloosa; pa/Asst St Dir, Outstg Yg Ams; MC, Miss Am Coed Pageants; cp/VP Pledge Class, Pi Kappa Phi; Mayor's Adv Coun, Univ AL; r/First Bapt Ch, Pres Yth Coun; hon/All-Am Ath, 1980; Author & Perfr of Song Chosen as Sr Song, Cath HS Grad; S'ship, Outstg Hist Student, Univ AL; Outstg Yg Am; W/W Among Am HS Students; g/Atty.

SCARCELLA, VINCENT ANTHONY oc/Student; b/Nov 30, 1962; h/Shaughnessy Lane, Staten Island, NY 10305; p/Santi and Maria Scarcella, Staten Island, NY; ed/St Peter's Boys HS, 1980; Att'g Wagner Col; pa/Col Asst, Col of Staten Island Bursar/Bus Ofc, 1979-; cp/Pianist; Heyboardist; Singer; Songwriter; Composer (Has Composed Music & Songs); Pianist/Actor in Sch Musicals; Pianist/Actor in Sch Plays; Pianist at Sch Assems; Writer of Sch Plays; Dir of Sch Plays; Stage Crew; Band; Piano & Vocal Recitals at Wagner Col; Commun Concerts; Vol at Wagner Col Functions & Activs; Vol at Commun Functions & Activs; Altar Boy; Ch Organist; Ch Commentator; Ch Helper; St Peter's HS Tutor (Math, Eng, Acctg); St Peter's HS Nat Hon Soc; Lib Aide; Ofc Aide; St Peter's HS Newspaper Staff, Reporter, Writer, Sports Editor; Wagner Col Newspaper Staff, Writer, Entertainment Editor for *The Wagnerian*; Disc Jockey for WCBG-AM (Wagner Col Radio Sta); Played in 1st Annual WCBG Radio vs *The Wagnerian* Softball Game, 1983; Player for Staten Island Amusement Softball Team (Fed Div); Part in Intramural Sports, Ftball, Baseball, Softball, Basketball; Vol Helper, Annual Intl Fest; Part in Num Sporting Events; Appearances as Extra in Upcoming Motion Picture *Hlth Clb*; Mem, Wagner Col Acctg Soc; Mem, Wagner Col Yrbook Staff; Vol at Wagner Col Cent Celebration; Wagner Col Vol Income

Tax Asst Progr; r/Cath; hon/Sports Articles Pub'd in *The Staten Island Advance*; Pub'd in *The Wagnerian, The Eagle* (St Peter's HS Newspaper); Social Studies Awd, 1976; Farewell Address Reader, 1976; St Peter's HS Acad Hon Roll, 1976-80; St Peter's HS Hon Awds, Hon Certs, Lttrs of Achmt & Commend, 1976-80; St Peter's HS Nat Hon Soc; St Peter's HS Italian Hon Roll; Merit Achmt Awd, 1978-79; W/W Among Am HS Students 2nd Yr Awd, 1979-80; 1st Prize, CYO Talent Show (for Piano Perf), 1979; St Peter's HS Italian Awd, 1980; Rec'd Full S'ship to Wagner Col, 1980; Wagner Col Dean's List; Winner, Staten Island Advance Sports Lttr Contest (won twice for best lttr), 1981; W/W Among Am HS Students; Intl Yth in Achmt; Yg Commun Ldrs of Am; 2000 Notable Ams; Dir of Dist'd Ams; Intl Book of Hon; Biographical Roll of Hon; Commun Ldrs of World; Nat Dean's List; Men of Achmt; W/W Among Students in Am Univs & Cols; Intl W/W Intells; World Biographical Hall of Fame; g/Deg in Bus Adm/Acctg & to Obtain Success in all Endeavors.

SCHALDECKER, CARLA JEAN oc/ Student, Receptionist; b/Mar 6, 1963; h/1903 Grant, York, NE 68467; ba/ York, NE; p/Carl W Schaldecker (dec); Verna Jean Schaldecker, York, NE; ed/ York HS, 1981; York Col; cp/Tri Kappa Wom's Soc Clb York Col; 4-H, Secy; NE Yth Camp, Cnslr & Cook; VBS, Asst Tchr; Ch of Christ Joy Bus; Phi Beta Lambda; York Col Jog-a-Thon; Am Legion Aux; hon/W/W Among HS Students; Intl Yth in Achmt; g/BA Deg from Lubbock Christian Col, AA Deg from York Col.

SCHEFFEL, ROBIN GAYLE oc/Student; b/Dec 26, 1965; h/Route 2, Box 160, Pryor, OK 74361; p/Kenneth and Christine Scheffel, Pryor, OK; ed/Pryor HS, 1984; cp/Nat Hon Soc, Secy; Band; Mu Alpha Theta Math Clb; Biol Clb; Student Coun; Basketball; Softball; Tennis; r/Mennonite, Zion Mennonite Ch Choir, Yth F'ship Pres, Yth F'ship Secy/Treas, Softball Team; Girls Missionary Ser Aux Pres; hon/HS Valedictorian; US Nat Band Awd; Reg 3 All-Star Girls Softball Team; Reg Doubles Runner-ups in Tennis; Secy of St Awd for Excelling in OK Hist; Achmt Awd in Am Civics; Achmt Awd for Excelling in Typing; Bausch & Lomb Sci Awd; Basketball All-Tourney Team; Hon Memtion All-Conf Basketball; Best Girl Ath for Sch Yrbook; TULSA WORLD Hon Roll for Basketball; FFA Queen; US Achmt Acad; g/Attend Col; Nsg.

SCHLABACH, RONALD DEAN oc/ Medical Student; b/Mar 10, 1961; h/ 10214 North 39th Avenue, Phoenix, AZ 85021; m/Teresa Ann; p/Lee and Ada Schlabach, Phoenix, AZ; sp/Mr and Mrs R E Riggins, Bethany, OK; ed/Pueblo S HS, 1979; BS, Bethany Nazarene Col, 1983; MD, Univ OK Col Med, 1987; pa/ Orderly, Parkview Epis Hosp, 1978-79; Orderly, Deaconess Hosp, 1982-; cp/Am Med Student Assn; Student Mem of OK St Med Assn; BSA; Alpha Lambda Delta; Alpha Nu; Cardinal Key; HS Key Clb; r/Nazarene Ch; hon/Grad Summa Cum Laude, Bethany Nazarene Col, 1983; Col Marshal, Bethany Nazarene Col; HS Valedictorian; Eagle Scout, BSA; Pres's Hon Roll; Cardinal Key

Mbrship; Outstg Freshman in Biol, Bethany Nazarene Col; Nat Dean's List; W/W Among Students in Am Univ & Cols; Intl Yth in Achmt; g/Phys in Fam Pract.

SCHLIESSER, ANDREW WILEY oc/ Student; b/Aug 26, 1965; h/1909 Clubview Drive, Tyler, TX 75701; p/Luther M and Janet C Schliesser, Tyler, TX; ed/Robert E Lee HS, 1983; cp/Robert E Lee Cannoneers; Latin Clb; Nat Hon Soc; r/Prot; hon/Salutatorian, 1983; Recip of the Bausch & Lomb Hon Sci Awd, 1983; g/Pursue Chem Engrg Deg, Pre-Med Prog.

SCHMIDLEY, MARGUERITE oc/ Clinical Data Processor; b/Oct 19, 1961; h/1320 Azalea Street, Mobile, AL 36604; ba/Mobile, AL; p/Michael Finley and Frances Agatha Schmidley, Beloit, WI; ed/Beloit Meml HS, 1979; BS, Univ So MS, 1983; pa/Clin Data Processor, Mader Bearings, 1984-; cp/Yth in Govt, 1976-79; VP, AFS Clb, 1978-79; Beloit Yth Symph, 1977-79; WI Yth Symph Orch, 1977-79; Univ So MS Chamber Orch, 1979-83; Gulf Coast Symph, 1984; Pres Sigma Psi Alpha, 1983; Delta Sigma Pi, 1981-83; Resident Hall Coun, 1981; Resident Hall Assn, 1981; hon/ Hons Orch, 1978; Personalities of S; Outstg Mem Sigma Psi Alpha; 4-Yr Music Ser Awd S'ship; Dean's List, 1979-80; Nat Hon Soc, 1978-79; g/Deg in Acctg Data Processing; Data Processor.

SCHOBER, JEAN L oc/Dean of Students, University Administrator; b/Feb 20, 1947; h/1611 14th Avenue, Greeley, CO 80631; ba/Greeley, CO; p/Robert and Dondus Schober, Findlay, OH; BS 1969, MA 1974, Bowling Green St Univ; MAT, Oakland Univ, 1973; pa/Dean of Students 1980-, Dir Student Sers Ctr 1977-80, Asst Dean of Students 1974-77, Univ No CO; Asst Student Devel Spec, Bowling Green St Univ, 1973-74; cp/Dean of Students 1980-, Dir of Student Sers Ctr 1977-80, Asst Dean of Students 1974-77, Univ No CO; Asst Student Devel Spec, Bowling Green St Univ, 1973-74; Tchr, Lone Pine Elem Sch, 1969-73; Am Col Pers Assn; APGA; Nat Assn Wom Dean, Admrs & Cnslrs; cp/CO Wom Edrs Consortium; CO-WY Assn for Wom Admrs & Cnslrs, VP, Newslttr Editor, Recording Secy; Num Profl Activs; Num Civic Activs inc'g A Wom's Pl Inc; CO Luth Campus Min St Bd Dirs; Greeley Wom's Exch; CO Gov's Traffic Safety Adv Com; r/Am Luth; hon/Outstg Ser Awd, Univ No CO, 1979; Susan B Anthony Awd, 1979; KFKA Radio, Outstg Citizen Awd, 1979; Wom's Equality Day Awd for Contribution to Ed, 1977; KBTV Channel 9 Recip of "9 Who Care" Vol Awd, 1983; W/W W; Outstg Yg Wom Am; W/W Among Students in Am Univs & Cols; Dist'd Ser Awd.

SCHREIVER, ALBERT JOSEPH IV oc/Student, Bookkeeper; b/Oct 16, 1961; h/3108 Bernard Drive, Edgewood, KY 41017; ba/Erlanger, KY; p/Mr and Mrs Albert J Schreiver III, Edgewood, KY; ed/Covington Cath HS, 1979; BS, No KY Univ, 1983; pa/Bkkpr, Swan Floral & Gift Shop; cp/Student Govt, Rep-at-Large 1981-83; Chm, Grievance & Affirmative Action Com, 1982-83; Chm, Reorg Task Force, 1983; Dir, Student Forums, 1983; Student Book

Exch; Spec Activs Com, 1981-82; Nu Kappa Alpha Acctg Hon Soc, VP 1983; Newslttr Editor, 1983; Alpha Chi Nat Col Hon Soc, 1982-83; Student Bus Adv Coun, Ec Rep, 1981-83; Nomination & Selection Com, 1983; Peer Advising, 1983; Student Financial Aid Policy Com, 1982-83; UCB Org Funding Com, 1981-83; S'ship Policy Com, 1981-82; Freshman Orientation Tour Guide, 1982; Grad Marshall, 1982; hon/Nu Kappa Alpha Acctg Hon Soc's Newslttr, 1983, Editor; Covington Cath HS's *Colonel Courier*, 1978-79; Student Govt Outstg Rep Yr, 1983; NKU Paul J Sipes Awd Nom, 1983; Student Govt Ser Awd, 1983; Dean's List; Hon's List; Pres S'ship; Yg Commun Ldrs; W/W Among Students in Am Univs & Cols; g/ Position as a Staff Acct w CPA Firm.

SCHUESSLER, PAMELA BERNADETTE oc/Student; b/Mar 16, 1962; h/Box 616, Venice, FL 33595; p/Mr Raymond Schuessler, Venice, FL; ed/ Venice HS, 1980; BA, St Leo Col, 1984; pa/Editor, *The Encounter*, 1981-84; Arts Editor, *The Monarch*, 1981-84; cp/Nat Hon Soc, 1981-84; Lake Jovita Artist's Guild, 1981-84; Col Theater; r/Rom Cath; hon/Num Pubs in *The Encounter*; Hon S'ship for 4 Yrs; W/W Among Am Col Students; Summa Cum Laude Grad; Dean's List; g/PhD in Eng Lit; Tch on Col Level.

SCHUETZ, STEVEN EDWARD oc/ Grad Student; b/May 10, 1959; h/2300 Highland Avenue, Janesville, WI; p/ Alvin E and Janice M Schuetz, Janesville, WI; ed/George S Parker HS, 1977; BBA 1981, MBA 1983, Univ WI; pa/Utility Man, Beatrice Foods Co, 1983-80; Mason Tender, Worden Masonry, 1980-79; Doorman, Ch Key & Hdliners Night Clb, 1978; Assem Line & Maintenance, Gen Motors Assem Div, 1977-78; Whitewater Fin Assn, 1980-81; cp/Pres of Parker Lttrmen's Clb, 1976-77; Ftball, 1974-77; Wrestling, 1974-77; Intramural Sports; Boy Scouts, Sr Patrol Ldr, Eagle Scout; r/ Luth; hon/Nat Hon Soc; Janesville Parker HS; All Big Eight Conf Ftball; Capt of Parker Wrestling Team; Univ WI Alumni Assn S'ship; Nat Dean's List; g/Position w a Mgmt Consltg Firm.

SCHULMEYER, CYNTHIA ANN oc/ Student; b/May 12, 1962; h/230 Hunters Ridge Road, Timonium, MD 21093; p/Mr and Mrs G Stephen Schulmeyer, Timonium, MD; ed/Penncrest HS, 1980; BA-Psychol, BS-Spec Ed, Cabrini Col, 1983; pa/Camp Dir, Easter Seal Soc, 1983; cp/Pres, Cabrini Col CEC, 1983; Cabrini Col Theatre; Kappa Sigma Omega; Devereux Foun Day Sch; Easter Seals Camp; Math Hon Soc; Profl Ed Orgs; PSEA; hon/Cabrini Col Hon Soc, 1981-84; Cabrini Col Ser & Ldrship Awd, 1983; Jr Saturday Clb of Wayne Awd for Spec Ed, 1983; W/W Among Am HS Students; Nat Hon Soc; Yg Wom Am; g/Grad Sch for Clin Psychol.

SCHUSTER, BETTY LYNN oc/Student; b/Jun 11, 1960; h/913 Sam Houston, Dyersburg, TN 38024; p/Mr and Mrs Howard L Schuster Jr, D'burg, TN; ed/Grad, HS, 1978; BMus, 1981; Master of Music Therapy (in Progress); cp/Staff Asst, Freshman Dorm; Acad Life Com; Maryville Col Theater Assn; Tau Kappa Chi; SNEA; SMENC; r/Chd's Choir Dir, Asst Dir Handbell Choir; hon/Dean's List; Presser S'ship; Pres Scholar;

Student Foun; W/W Among Students in Am Univs & Cols; Outstg Yg Wom of Am; Intl Yth in Achmt; g/Finish Deg & Become Reg'd Music Therapist in Chd's Hosp.

SCHWARZ, PATRICIA ANN oc/Student; b/Dec 15, 1964; h/330 Kessler, New Braunfels, TX 78130; p/Alton and Irene Schwarz, New Braunfels, TX; ed/New Braunfels HS, 1983; Angelo St Univ; cp/Nat Hon Soc; German Clb; Band; Yg Dems; r/Prot; hon/W/W Among Am HS Students; Am Outstg Names & Faces; Am Achmt Acad; Nat Merit S'ship Fin; g/RN.

SCHWEIZER, F PETER oc/Student; b/Nov 24, 1964; h/26061 156th Avenue, Southeast, Kent, WA 98042; p/Erwin and Kerstin Schweizer, Kent, WA; cp/Nat Dir Yg Ams for Freedom, 1983-; Asst Supvr, King Co Repub Ctl Com; r/Luth; hon/Deg of Spec Distn; Nat Forensics Leag; US Govt Rep; US Study Tour of France.

SCILLEY, DAWN DENISE oc/Student; b/Apr 7, 1964; h/916 East Second Street, Maysville, KY 41056; p/Rev and Mrs Donald E Scilley, Maysville, KY; ed/Mason Co HS, 1982; Att'g Maysville Commun Col, Div of Univ KY; cp/Basketball; Pep Clb; French Clb; Sci Clb, Treas; Activs Clb; Mem of KY Assn Nsg Students; Student Coun; Band; Concert & Marching Band; Concert Choir; Adv Bd; Yth F'ship; Secy Yth F'ship; r/United Meth; hon/Salutatorian; Hon's Grad; Maysville Commun Col Homecoming Princess; g/Nsg Maj; RN.

SCIOLARO, CHARLES MICHAEL oc/Medical Student; b/Jul 5, 1958; h/8822 West 57th Street, Merriam, KS 66202; ba/KS City, KS; p/Gerald and Charleen Sciolaro, Merriam, KS; ed/Shawnee Mission N HS, 1976; BA, Mid-Am Nazarene Col, 1980; MD, KS Univ Med Ctr, 1984; cp/Am Acad of Fam Phys; AMA; Am Student Med Assn; r/Nazarene; hon/W/W Among Students in Am Univs & Cols; Nat Dean's List; Yg Commun Ldrs Am; Intl Yth in Achmt; g/Med Pract in Rural Area of KS.

SCOTT, JENNIFER MICHELE oc/Student and Research Technician; b/Sep 17, 1961; h/3507 Eratta Street, Jackson, MS 39213; p/Lula Scott, Jackson, MS; ed/Grad, Callaway HS, 1979; BS, Tougaloo Col, 1983; Att'g Emory Univ Grad Sch; cp/Alpha Lambda Delta; Swanza Scholars Hon Soc; Vol, Muscular Dystrophy; r/Bapt; hon/Co Author of "Changes in Components of the Calmodulin in Sys Rat Brain During Aging", *Mechanisms of Aging & Devel*; Magna Cum Laude, 1983; Pres's List; Dean's List; Nat Hon Soc; g/Attend Grad Sch in Microbiol & Become Parasitologist.

SCOTT, LISA DOWN oc/Student; b/Apr 18, 1965; h/Route 1, Box 15, Christiansburg, VA 24073; p/Mr and Mrs Arnold R Scott, Christiansburg, VA; ed/Christiansburg HS, 1983; VA Tech; cp/Band, Pres; FBLA; Latin Clb, Pres; Nat Hon Soc, VP; Beta Clb, Pres; Student Coun; Math Clb, Secy; Cheerldg; Monogram Clb; Baseball Stat; Chm, Yth Adv Coun; United Meth Yth F'ship, Treas; hon/Miss Christiansburg HS; John Philip Sousa Band Awd; Golden Eagle Cheerldg Awd; Lttr Band, Cheerldg, Baseball Stats; Alpha Delta

Kappa Tchg Awd; g/Elem Ed Maj.

SCOTT, MARGARET ELIZABETH oc/Student; b/Sep 19, 1966; h/105 Shalimar Heights, Senatobia, MS 38668; ba/Same; p/Mr and Mrs Clifford Scott, Senatobia, MS; ed/Magnolia Hgts Sch, 1984; cp/Sr Homecoming Maid, 1983; Basketball Team; Cheerldr; Math Clb; Annual Staff; Freshman Class Ofcr; r/Ch of Christ; hon/Soc of Dist'd Am HS Students; Gov's Yth Cong Del; W/W; g/Attend Delta St Univ; Maj in Ed.

SCOTT, MONTY KIM oc/Student; b/Oct 22, 1963; h/Route 2, Paradise Val, Hartshorne, OK 74547; ba/Talequah, OK; p/Richard and Myrna Scott, Hartshorne, OK; ed/HS, 1981; Assoc, En OK St Col, 1983; Att'g NEn St Univ; cp/Phi Beta Lambda, Pres, 1982-83; Ch Aide; Ofc Aide; FHA; Chorus; 4-H Clb; Red Cross Aide; hon/Acctg Awd; Home Ec Awd; W/W Among Am HS Students; W/W Among Am Jr Cols; Intl Yth in Achmt; g/CPA.

SCOTT, REBECCA LEE oc/Student; b/Apr 6, 1966; h/3067 Laughter Road South, Hernando, MS 38632; p/Mr and Mrs Morris Lee Scott, Hernando, MS; ed/Hernando HS; cp/FHA, Hero Clb, 1981-82; Spanish Clb, 1982-84; Yrbook Acads Editor, 1982-83, Co Editor Overall 1983-84; Meth; hon/Nat Hon Soc; Quill & Scroll, Treas 1983-84; W/W Among Am HS Students; US Nat Jour Awd, 1983-84; US Nat Ldrship Merit Awd, 1983-84; Soc Dist'd Am HS Students; Hall of Fame, 1984; Jr of the Mo, 1982; Sr of the Mo, 1983; Congl Page in Jackson, MS; Yrbook Jour Awd, 1983; Jr Sci & Humanities Symp Awd, 1984; g/Pharm.

SEAGLE, GARY DEAN oc/Student; b/Apr 11, 1964; h/310 1/2 Eleventh Street, Gaffney, SC 29340; ba/Spartanburg, SC; p/R J and Rosemary Seagle, Gaffney, SC; ed/Gaffney Sr HS, 1982; Wofford Col; cp/Nat Beta Clb, 1980-82; Quill & Scroll Hon Soc, 1981-82; Commun Relats Com, 1983; Student Recruitment Com, 1983; HS Newspaper Staff; Lit Mag Editor, 1981-82, 1983; The Wofford Singers, 1983; Glee Clb, 1983; Gaffney Little Theatre; r/Interdenominational; hon/Pubs in *The Pinnacle*, 1981, 1982, *The Jour*, 1983; Hons Grad, 1982; Outstg Sr, 1982; Sr Class Poet, 1982; Outstg Yg Ldr Am; Gov's Sch Alt; g/Maj in Eng & Ec; Career, Intl Corporate Lwyr.

SEARCY, KAREN RUTH oc/Student; b/Jun 9, 1953; h/Route 5, Box 226-B, Meadow Drive, Eufaula, AL 36027; p/Mrs E C Searcy, Eufaula, AL; ed/Eufaula HS, 1971; AAS, George C Wallace St Commun Col, 1980; Univ S AL; pa/Secy to Dir of Public Relats, Mann's Bait Mfg Co, 1972-78; Med Lab Tech, Brookwood Med Ctr, 1980-83; cp/Eufaula HS Band, 1966-71; Majorette, 1971; Music Libn, 1971; Phi Theta Kappa, 1978-; Assn Mem Am Soc of Clin Pathol, 1980-; Alpha Epsilon Delta, 1983; r/Meth; hon/Outstg Med Lab Technol Sch; CRC Freshman Chem Awd, 1982; Pres Acad S'ship, 1983-84; g/Maj, Biol.

SEASE, DENISE DIANNE oc/Student; b/Oct 11, 1964; h/1026 Cedar, Greenville, MS 38701; p/Mr and Mrs Elton Sease Jr, Greenville, MS; ed/Univ MS; pa/Salesperson, Mgr, Vil Players Tennis Shop; cp/Beta Clb; Drill Team;

Jr Cotillion Mem; Mu Alpha Theta; Delta Debutante Mem; Secy, Jr Cotillion Clb; r/Epis; hon/Hon Roll; Hon Grad; W/W Among Am Students; Share-a-Scholar Recip; g/to be a Doct.

SEAWRIGHT, SHERITA MOON oc/Analyst; b/Jul 19, 1958; h/3131 16th Street, NE, Washington, DC 20018; ba/Wash, DC; m/Rev Harry L; c/Shari Nicole; p/Rev and Mrs Peter Moon Sr, Clinton, SC; sp/Mrs Mary L Seawright, Swansea, SC; ed/Clinton HS, 1975; BA, Benedict Col, 1979; MA, OH St Univ, 1980; pa/Inst Planner, Benedict Col, 1980-82; AME Ch Missionary Soc, 1982; Agy for Intl Devel, 1982; cp/AME Mins Wives & Widows Alliance of Wash & Vicinity; r/AME; hon/BA, Summa Cum Laude; Strom Thurmond Foun S'ship, 1978-79; Master's F'ship, OH St Univ, 1979-80; Danisel Foun S'ship, 1977-79; W/W Among Students in Am Univs & Cols; Intl Yth in Achmt; Personalities of S; g/JD Deg.

SECRIST, DAVID EUGENE II oc/Student; b/Nov 27, 1965; h/Route 3, Box 376, Troutville, VA 24175; p/David E and Nancy M Secrist, Troutville, VA; ed/Lord Botetourt HS; r/Prot, Rainbow Forest Bapt Ch; hon/Nat Hon Soc, 1983; VA All St Chorus, 1983.

SEDDON, KAREN JUNE oc/Student; b/Jun 16, 1963; h/3509 J F K Boulevard, North Little Rock, AR 72116; p/Roy and Susan Snowden, Elaine, AR; ed/Elaine HS, 1981; Assoc Deg, Phillips Co Col, 1983; pa/Asst to Secy for Dean of Col Affairs, Phillips Col, 1981-83; cp/Phi Theta Kappa; Phi Beta Lambda; r/Bapt; hon/2nd Runner-up, Miss Teen USA, 1979; SEn Fair Queen, 1982; AR St Fair Queen, 1982; Miss Phillips Co, 1983; Rep Phillips Co in Glamour Mags, 1983; Top Ten Col Wom of Am; Finalist, Miss White River, 1982; g/BA Deg in Data Processing.

SEDRISH, ROBERT HOWARD oc/Executive Assistant; b/Apr 3, 1959; h/1 Deering Lane, East Rockaway, NY 11518; ba/New York, NY; m/Ivey L; p/Paul M Sedrish, E Rockaway, NY, and Rochelle Schwartz, Merrick, NY; ed/Lynbrook HS, 1977; BA, Hofstra Univ, 1981; MBA 1984, JD 1984, Am Univ; pa/Asst to Pres, Lincoln Capital Corporation; Legal Intern, Securities & Exch Comm Enforcement Div, 1983; Ptnr, Accts Investmt & Consltg Grp, 1980-; Acct, Norman J Rosenthal CPA, PC, 1980-81; cp/Financial Mgmt Assn; Nat Hon Soc; Phi Alpha Delta Intl Law Frat; Intl Law Soc; Beta Alpha Psi Hon Acctg Soc; hon/Dean's List; Provost Hons.

SEGLEM, SUSAN E oc/Vocal Music Teacher; b/May 23, 1960; h/Route 1, Box 45, Towanda, KS 67144; ba/El Dorado, KS; p/Clair and Betty Seglem, MW City, OK; ed/MW City HS, 1978; BMus, WI St Univ, 1983; pa/Music Tchr, El Dorado Public Sch Dist, 1984-; cp/Alpha Chi Omega, Pres, Del to Nat Conv, Rush Chm 2 Yrs, Warden, Songldr, Pledge Cl Pres; Sigma Alpha Iota; Yrbook Editor; Rush Skit Chm; Omicron Delta Kappa Ldrship Hon; SPURS, Sophomore Hon Org; Student Alumni Assn; Student MENC; KS Music Edrs Assn; Am Choral Dirs Assn; r/Meth; hon/Outstg Yg Wom of Am; W/W Among Students in Am Univs & Cols; Dean's Hon Roll; Sigma Phi Epsilon Golden Heart Girl; 3rd Runner-up to Miss KS; Debra Barnes

Instrumental Awd; Miss Butler Co, 1982; Sigma Alpha Iota Nat Outstg Yrbook Ed, 1981; Alpha Chi Omega Outstg Jr S'ship Awd, 1980; g/Masters of Ed Adm for Public Schs.

SEIBRING, MARK ALAN oc/Student; b/Aug 30, 1963; h/1817 Dodge Circle South, Melbourne, FL 32935; m/Angel; p/Mr and Mrs Marvin Seibring; sp/Sandra Farmer; ed/Eau Gallie HS, 1981; AA, Univ FL, 1984; cp/Mensa; Gold Key; Phi Eta Sigma Hon Frat; Nat Hon Soc; Math Clb; Spch & Debate Clb; Nat Beta Clb; Spanish Clb; Mu Alpha Theta; Nat Forensics Leag; Varsity Swim Team; BSA; Marching & Symph Bands; US Fencing Assn; hon/Pub'd in Driftwood III Lit Anthology; Eagle Scout, BSA; Melbourne Area C of C; Yg Adult of Yr Awd; John Philip Sousa Awd; I Dare You Ldrship Awd; Cliff Stiles Spch Ldrship Awd; Melbourne Exch Clb Boy of Yr; FL All-Star Marching Band; W/W; Personalities of S; Intl Yth in Achmt; Soc of Dist'd Am HS Students; g/Physics & Eng or Phil Degs; to Write Profly.

SEIDER, LYNN BETH oc/Computer Programmer; b/Feb 12, 1959; h/8434 West Lisbon Avenue, Apartment 1, Milwaukee, WI 53222; ba/Milwaukee, WI; m/Mark Steven; p/Mr and Mrs Hans Ziolkowski, Milwaukee, WI; sp/Mr and Mrs Virgil V Seider, Wauwatsoa, WI; ed/BBA 1980, MS 1984, Univ WI; pa/Computer Programmer, F W Woolworth Co, 1983-; Computer Conslt, Computing Sers Div, Univ WI, 1981-83; Salesperson, Bavarian Wursthaus, Milwaukee, WI Sausage Shop, 1977-80; cp/Beta Gamma Sigma VP, 1979-80; Initiation Parts, 1979-; Nom Com, 1981-83; Vol Adv'd Lifesaving Instr, Univ WI, 1978; Pi Sigma Epsilon, 1978-82, VP of Internal Affairs, 1980; Milwaukee Mortar Bd Alumni Soc, 1980-; Data Processing Mgmt Assn; 1980-; Fdg Mem, Vol Tutor, 1982; St Margaret Mary Yth Choir, 1974-77; K G Rheinischer Verein Gruen Weiss-Milwaukee, 1968-80; Flowergirl & Amazon, VP; r/Cath; hon/Univ WI Wom Swim Team Lttr Awd, 1976, 1977; Dean's List; Phi Kappa Phi, 1981; Beta Gamma Sigma, 1978; Sigma Epsilon Sigma, 1977; NHS, 1976; Phi Eta Sigma, 1977; Col Register; Commun Ldrs of Am; Intl Yth in Achmt; W/W Among Am HS Students; Dean's List; g/Mgmt; Computer Systems Anal.

SEIFARTH, MARK EVAN oc/Legislative Intern; b/Jul 5, 1957; h/1853 Solera Drive, Columbus, OH 43229; ba/Columbus, OH; p/Mr and Mrs John Paul Seifarth, Canfield, OH; ed/Canfield HS, 1975; BA Polit Sci, BA Public Relats, MA Polit Sci, Cert in Rel, Kent St Univ; pa/OH St Legis Ser Comm, 1983-; Kent St Univ Police Dept, 1983; Resident Dir 1979-, Resident Mgr/Asst Dir 1979, Resident Staff Advr 1977-79, Kent St Univ; Clk, Interviewer, Receptionist, Mehoning Co Bur of Child Support, Sums 1976, 1977, 1978; cp/Omicron Delta Kappa, Pres 1978-79, Treas 1977-78; Mortar Bd; Blue Key; Eta Sigma Phi; Kent St Univ Hons Col; r/Meth; hon/Commencement Address, 1979; Spkr, Omicron Delta Kappa Initiation Ceremony, 1981; Only Student to be Main Commencement Spkr, Kent St Univ, 1979; Outstg Sr, Kent St Univ, 1979; Pres, Omicron Delta

Kappa; Pi Sigma Alpha; W/W Among Students in Am Univs & Cols; Outstg Yg Men Am; Intl Yth in Achmt; g/Wk in Public Affairs or Bus Relats w Entry into Public Realm.

SEITER, PATRICIA A oc/Student; b/Aug 18, 1962; h/226 Riverside Parkway, Fort Thomas, KY 41075; p/Mr and Mrs William Seiter, Ft Thomas, KY; ed/Highlands HS, 1980; No KY Univ; pa/Asst to Supvr, Am Inst Plant Engrs, 1983-; Tchr's Aid/Tutor, Math Lng Ctr, 1982-; cp/Delta Zeta Sorority, Pres 1982-83, Treas 1981-82; Student Govt Jud Coun; Intramural Coun; r/Rom Cath, St Catherine of Siena Ch; hon/Dean's List; Delta Zeta "Sister of Yr", 1983; Best Treas in KY, 1982; Student Govt/Bookstore S'ship, 1982; g/Mgmt Position.

SELLERS, CRISTY JOY oc/Student; b/Apr 5, 1960; h/4453 England Drive, Shelbyville, MI 49344; ba/W Lafayette, IN; ed/Purdue Univ; Att'd MI Tech Univ, 1978-80; BS, GA Inst Technol, 1983; E Kentwood HS, 1978; pa/Applied Robotics 1983, Distbn Engr 1981, IBM; Proj Mgr, Kimberly Clark, 1982; Process Engr, Procter & Gamble, 1980; Mfg Engr, Oldsmobile, 1979; cp/Omicron Delta Kappa; Ramblin Reck Clb Mem; Ftball Com; Campus Spirit Com Mem; Traditions Night Com Mem; Mbrship Com Mem; Am Inst Indust Engrs; Soc Chm Alpha Gamma Delta; Exec Coun Mem; Campus Activs Com Mem; Pep Rally Com Mem; Secy of MTU Student Body; Secy of Ways & Means Bd; Student Rep on Campus Planning Com; Dir of Campus Cambodia Awareness Campaign-Altruism; Exec Caucus Mem; SGA Rep on Film Co-op Bd; Am Soc of Mech Engrs; hon/W/W Among Students in Am Univs & Cols; Intl Yth in Achmt; Outstg Yg Am; Yg Commun Ldr of Am; W/W Among Am HS Students; MI Competitive S'ship Awd; Dean's List; g/Complete Master's Deg.

SEWELL, BILLY C oc/Student; b/Oct 19, 1964; h/3209 Highsky, Midland, TX 79707; p/Bill and Betty Sewell, Midland, TX; cp/JETS, 1982-83; Chm of Publicity, 1982-83; Basketball, 1980-83; r/First Bapt Ch, Yth Coun Pres, Yth Coun Choir, Ofcr; hon/Nat Merit Finalist, 1983; PTA Awd, 1980-83; Acad Awd, 1980-83; Nat Merit Awd in Eng & Sci, 1982-83; g/Maj in Elect Engrg & Bus Mgmt, TX A & M Univ.

SEWELL, PATRICIA ANN oc/Summer Camp Counselor; b/Sep 30, 1965; h/128 Thompson Street, Cedartown, GA 30125; p/Mr and Mrs Roosevelt Sewell, Cedartown, GA; ed/Emory Univ; pa/Sum Camp Cnslr, Rock Eagle 4-H Ctr; cp/4-H Clb; FHA; Sci Clb; Hon Sci; Anglo-Afro Am Clbs, Secy; Band Mem; Yrbook Staff Mem; r/Bapt; hon/S'ship to Med Col of GA, 1982; Hall of Fame, 1983; Rec'd Grant from Emory Univ; g/Pre-Med Prog in Col; Biol Maj.

SEWELL, WENDOLYN Student; b/Jul 24, 1964; h/9155 Deadfall, Millington, TN 38053; p/Bill and Jackie Sewell, Millington, TN; ed/Rosemark Acad, 1982; Memphis St Univ; pa/Admissions Ofc, Pt-time, Memphis St Univ; cp/Phi Eta Sigma; Nat Col Dean's List; Nat Hon Soc; Beta Clb; Sci Clb, Pres; Pep Clb; R Clb; FCA; FBLA; Chorus; Thespians; W/W Among Am HS Students; Homecoming Queen, 1982; Cheerldg Nat Merit Winner; g/Bach Bus Maj; Career,

CPA.

SEXTON, JEFFREY LYNN oc/Student; b/Aug 24, 1967; h/Route 1, Box 223, Jenkins, KY 41537; p/Brenton and Paulette Sexton, Jenkins, KY; ed/Jenkins HS; cp/Varsity Ftball, Basketball; hon/En KY Mtn Conf Ftball Team 1983, Basketbll 1984; KET Scholastic Challenge, 1983; Jenkins Indep Sch Dist Spelling Champ, 1980; g/Attend Morehead St Univ; Math Maj.

SEXTON, KAREN BETH oc/Front Desk Clerk; b/Oct 2, 1961; h/Post Office Box 157, Freeman, WV 24724; ba/Bluefield, WV; p/Mr and Mrs R H Sexton, Freeman, WV; ed/Bramwell HS, 1979; BS, Concord Col, 1982; cp/Front Desk Clk, Sheraton Inn, 1983; cp/VP, Alpha Sigma Tau; Pi Kappa Alpha; Gamma Beta Phi; Proud Concordian; hon/Magna Cum Laude Grad, Concord Col; Valedictorian, HS Grad'g Class; Biol Awd; Algebra Awd; Band Awd; Choir Awd; Outstg Sophomore; All-Area & All-Co Band.

SEXTON, RONALD LYNN oc/Designer, Robot Development; b/Sep 7, 1961; h/6550 Murray Avenue, Cincinnati, OH 45227; ba/Cinc, OH; m/Rhonda Lynn; p/Berlon B Sexton, Williamsburg, OH; sp/Donald and Cleta Fields, Williamsburg, OH; ed/Williamsburg HS, 1979; Clemont Col; oc/Detailer, Robot Devel, Cinc Milacron; cp/Polits on Local Level; Tutor in Math; Promo of Res & Devel; Boys St Rep; Public Awareness; hon/4-Yr Math Awd, Williamsburg, HS; Nat Hon Soc; W/W Among Am HS Students; g/Deg in Mgmt & Mech Engrg; Career as Mgr of Engrg Firm Promoting Technol.

SEXTON, STEPHANIE LYNN oc/Student; b/Apr 21, 1968; h/General Delivery, Isom, KY 41824; p/Dan and Evelyn Taylor, Isom, KY; hon/Rec'd Awds in Volleyball, Basketball; All-Tour Trophy in Basketball, 1981; VP, Freshman Class; Nom for Homecoming Queen; Rec'd Awd for Att'g Computer Class, Sum 1982; Rec'd Good Attendance Cert; Selected Outstg Sophomore by Tchrs & Prin for Hugh O'Brian Sem; Hon Roll; g/Attend En KY Univ; Maj in Computer Sci.

SEYMORE, JOVON MARIE oc/Student; b/Aug 23, 1960; h/789 St Nicholas Avenue, Number 3, New York, NY 10031; p/Florene Wyche, New York, NY; ed/John F Kennedy HS, 1978; BA, Wilberforce Univ, 1983; pa/Pt-time, Warner Communs-Atlantic Records, 1977; cp/Alpha Kappa Mu Nat Hon Soc, 1982; Sigma Omega Hon Soc, 1982; Student Govt Secy, 1982-83; Bus Mgr of Univ Radio Sta, WURS, 1982-83, 1984; Reporter for Univ Newspaper, Mirror, 1981-82; r/Bapt; hon/Alpha Kappa Mu & Sigma Omega Hon Soc; WNOE/WTUE S'ship; Dean's List; W/W Among Students in Univs & Cols; g/TV or Radio Indust Profl.

SHADE, SHERRI LEVETTE oc/Student; b/Jan 9, 1966; h/Route 1, Box 80, Shelby, NC 28150; p/Perry and Barbara Shade, Shelby, NC; ed/Crest Sr HS, 1984; cp/Marching & Concert HS Band; French Clb; Hlth Occup Students of Am; Candystriper; Pres, Yth Choir; r/Meth; hon/Hon Roll; Second Pl Winner of IPBOE of W Oratorical Contest; Rec'd 17 Awds of Outstg Acads, incl'g Medals, Plaques, & Certs; g/Attend Univ NC-Charlotte; Hlth Field.

SHADOAN, DONNA GAIL oc/Student; b/May 20, 1961; h/116 Buckwood Drive, Richmond, KY 40475; ed/Model HS, 1979; BA, Asbury Col, 1983; pa/Thornberry's Super Value, 1979-83; cp/Dem Clb, 1982-83; Newspaper Staff 1979-80, Varsity Softball 1980-81, Asbury Col; Christian Assn Psychols, 1980-83; r/United Meth; hon/Soc Dist'd HS Students; g/Phd; Pvt Pract as Clin Psychol.

SHAMSIDDEEN, DORINDA MAHASIN oc/Student; b/Jun 26, 1962; h/113 West Desert Drive, Phoenix, AZ 85041; p/Abdur Rahim and Ummil Kheer Shamsiddeen, Phoenix, AZ; ed/S Mtn HS, 1980; AZ St Univ; cp/Secy/Treas of Black Bus Students Assn; Muslim Students Assn; Black Student Union; Am Mktg Assn; Asst Dir, Minority Affairs Bd of ASU; r/Al-Islam; hon/Pub'd Essay of Life of Prophet Muhammad, 1978; Wrote & Dir 3-Act Play that Ran for One Mo, was Filmed & Shown in Saudi Arabia; Dean's List, 1980-84; Intl Yth in Achmt; Outstg Muslim Yth of Yr; Yth of Yr Black C of C, AZ; Commun Ldrs Am; Dist'd Ams; g/Master's Deg in Intl Mktg.

SHARIFF, KAMAL A oc/Finance Analyst, Digital Equipment Corporation; b/Sep 18, 1958; h/70 Tennis Road, Mattapan, MA 02126; ba/Southboro, MA; p/Jesse and Edna Wright, Boston, MA; ed/BS, Bentley Col, 1983; cp/Chm, Bd Dirs, Capital Devel Economic Res Inst Inc; Treas, Bd Mem, FIRST Inc; Gov's Juv Justice Adv Com, 1976-77; hon/Commun Ldrs Am; Intl Yth in Achmt; g/MBA, JD; Career in Intl Bus, Ec, Law.

SHARP, TIMOTHY ALAN oc/Elementary School Music Teacher; b/Jul 19, 1960; h/3131 Northwest 151st Street, Opa-locka, FL 33054; ba/Miami, FL; p/Willie and Iwilla Pace, Opa-locka, FL; ed/Hialeah-Miami Lakes Sr HS, 1978; BA, Bethune-Cookman Col, 1982; MS, Univ IL, 1983; cp/Phi Delta Kappa; Kappa Delta Pi; r/Bapt; hon/FL Col Alpha of Yr, 1982; Alpha Man of Yr, Delta Beta Chapt, 1982; Cert of Apprec, Beta Delta Lambda Chapt, 1982; Outstg Yg Men of Am, 1982; g/Ofcrs Cand Sch, USN.

SHARPE, ALETHEA oc/Student; b/Jan 31, 1965; h/Post Office Box 806, Pinetops, NC 27864; p/William and Selma Sharpe, Pinetops, NC; ed/SW Edgecombe HS; cp/FBLA, Photog, Histn; FHA, Treas; SGA, Parliamentn; Pep Clb, Treas; DECA, Parliamentn; French Clb, VP; Monogram Clb; Mgr Baseball, Volleyball; r/Bapt; hon/Most Spirited Pep Clb Awd, 1982; 3rd Pl Dist Acctg I, 1982; 2nd Pl in St Acctg I, 1982; 1st Pl in St Acctg II, 1983; g/attend Col; Acctg & Bus Maj; CPA.

SHEKELL, CARMAN LYNN oc/Student; b/May 21, 1964; h/Route 1, Box 311, Cottage Grove, TN 38224; p/Mr and Mrs Jesse Kennedy, Cottage Grove, TN; ed/Henry Co HS, 1982; Univ TN-Knoxville, 1982; W TN Bus Col, 1982-83; pa/Bk Teller, Security Bk & Trust Co, 1981-82; Ofc Wkr & Adm Asst, United Way, 1982-83; cp/Beta Clb; ofc Ed Assn; FHA; Ch Wkr; Hon, Merit Rolls; r/Ch of Christ; hon/Dean's List; Ofc Ed Assn Exec Awd; FHA Encounter Level I Awd; W/W Among Am HS Students; Commun Ldrs Am; g/Data Processing Technol, Calhoun Commun Col.

SHELNUTT-LOFTIN, RITA JANE oc/Middle Grades, Music Teacher; b/Oct 30, 1960; h/Route 2, Box 109, Franklin, GA 30217; m/Richard C; p/Mr and Mrs Henry J Shelnutt, Franklin, GA; sp/Mr and Mrs Eley Loftin, Franklin, GA; ed/Heard Co HS, 1978; BMus 1982, MMus 1985, W GA Col; cp/VP, Omicron Delta Kappa; VP 1980-81, Pres 1981-82, W GA Col Chapt, Sigma Alpha Iota; Secy, Col Student Chapt, MENC; Delta Mu; Student Mem, Music Tchrs Nat Assn; Student Mem, GA Music Tchrs Assn; Musical Progs for Resident of Franklin Nsg Home; r/Centralhatchee Bapt Ch, Pianist, Organist, Ldr Chd's Choir, Pianist for Yth Choir, Vacation Bible Sch Music Dir, Ch Tng Ldr & Ch Tng Tchr; hon/Pres Scholar; Dean's List; Hons Recitals, 1978-79 & 1980-81; Hons Prog, 1978-82; Valedictorian; Don Staples Awd for Outstg Sr, 1978; Watson Awd for Outstg Student in Music, 1979; Gen S'ship for Scholastic Achmt, W GA Col; Atlanta Alumnae Chapt Sigma Alpha Iota Annual S'ship, 1981; 2nd Alt in Col Piano Auditions, GA Mus Tchrs Assn, 1979; Omicron Delta Kappa; Sigma Alpha Iota; Gov's Hons Prog in Eng, 1976; Phi Kappa Phi, 1983; Phi Kappa Phi Awd of Excell, Sch Arts & Sci, 1982-83; Summa Cum Laude Grad, 1982; W/W: Among Am HS Students, in Music in Am HS, Among Students in Am Univs & Cols; Commun Ldrs of Am; g/Continue Ed & Tchg.

SHELTON, MARCY ELIZABETH oc/Ladie's Shop Salesclerk; b/Jun 19, 1966; h/1727 Country Club Drive, Tullahoma, TN 37388; p/Mr and Mrs James L Shelton, Tullahoma, TN; cp/Secy of Class, 1980-81; VP of Student Coun, 1982-83; Pres of Student Coun, 1983-84; Freshman Cheerldr, 1980-81; Varsity Cheerldr, 1981-84; r/Bapt; hon/Jr Achmt, 1983; W/W Among Am HS Students; g/Corporate or Intl Law.

SHELTON, MARY NELL oc/Certified Medical Assistant; b/Sep 29, 1963; h/Route 1, Box 112, Ramer, TN 38367; ba/Corinth, MS; p/Willie A and Ruby Nell Shelton, Ramer, TN; ed/McNairy Ctl HS, 1981; AAS, NE MS Jr Col, 1983; pa/Med Asst-Opthalmologist, Pt-time Sum 1982; Med Asst-Gen Practitioner, 1982-; Med Asst-Gen Practitioner, 1983; cp/Phi Theta Kappa Hon Soc, Histn, 1982-83; Phi Beta Lambda Bus Clb, 1981-83, Secy 1982-83; Bapt Student Union, 1981-83; MCHS Beta Clb, 1978-81; Pep Clb, 1977-81, VP, 1980-81; TOEC, 1979-81, Chapt Treas, 1979-80; Pres TOEC Chapt, 1980-81; Student Coun, 1980-81; Softball, 1978-81; Basketball, 1977-79; Stat, 1980-81; Volleyball, 1979-80; r/So Bapt; hon/W/W Among Students in Am Jr Cols; Pres's List, 1983; Valedictorian, 1981; TOEC, 1st Pl; St Bus Math Contest, 1981; TOEC, 3rd Pl, St Gen Clerical II Contest; Students Excel 1981; Soc Dist'd Am HS Students.

SHEPARD, GARNET LEE JR oc/Salesman, Floresheim Shoe Store; b/Jul 26, 1962; h/Route 1, Box 244, Honaker, VA 24260; ba/Charlottesville, VA; p/Garnet and Helen Shepard Sr, Honaker, VA; ed/Honaker HS, 1981; AA, Lees-McRae Col, 1981-83; Univ VA, 1983; pa/Server, MacDonald's Cafeteria, 1981; Cashier, Druthers Restaurant, 1982; Door Voucher, Univ VA Intramural Dept, 1983; Salesman, Florsheim Shoe Store, 1983; cp/Band, 1973-82, Pres; Track, 1980; Jr Hi Clb & Sr Hi Clb, VP, 1979-81; r/So Bapt; hon/Kate Braley S'ship, 1981-83; W/W Among Am HS Students; g/attend Univ VA, Maj in Math; Law Sch.

SHEPARD, KAREN SCHREMPP oc/Director of Activities; b/Sep 21, 1957; h/1733 West Peralta, Mesa, AZ 85202; ba/Phoenix, AZ; m/William Robert Jr; p/John J Schrempp, and Ollie Mae Schrempp (dec); ed/Corona Sr HS, 1975; Inst for European Studies, 1978; BMus, Univ of Pacific, 1979; pa/Dir of Activs, Desert Terr Nsg Ctr, 1983; Reg'd Music Therapist, St Hosp, 1981-83; cp/Nat Assn Music Theory; AZ Assoc Music Therapy; AZ Assn Activ Coors; Elks Emblem Clb; Kappa Alpha Theta, VP 1977, Rush Chm 1979; Mu Phi Epsilon; Mortar Bd; Omega Phi Alpha "Little Sister", Pres 1978; r/Cath; hon/Co-Pub'd Song "Look at Me", 1981; Pres's Hons, Univ Pacific, 1975; Commun Ldrs Am; Nat Social Register of Prominent Col Students.

SHEPHERD, ELISSA CAROLE oc/Tax Auditor; b/Mar 15, 1958; h/Post Office Box 5, Dumas, AR 71639; p/Edwin Shepherd, Gould, AR; Nancy Raney, Pine Bluff, AR; ed/Gould Public Schs, 1976; BS, Univ of AR at Monticello, 1980; cp/Alpha Chi; Phi Beta Lambda; Univ AR-Monticello Bus Clb VP; Sigma Kappa Treas, Corres Secy, S'ship Chm; hon/Arthur Yg Acctg Awd; Intl Yth in Achmt; W/W Among Students in Am Univs & Cols; g/Pass CPA Exam.

SHEPPERD, REGINA LALAINE oc/Student; b/Sep 24, 1963; h/123 Reed Avenue, Louisville, MS 39339; p/Mr and Mrs Troy Shepperd, Louisville, MS; ed/Louisville HS, 1981; E Ctl Jr Col; pa/Cashier, Piggly Wiggly Grocery Store; cp/Mem of Players, Drama Clb at E Ctl; Instrumentalist for Collegians, Singing Grp at E Ctl; HS Band, Piano, Beta Clb, Math Clb, Sci Clb, Spanish Clb, FBLA; Basketball Mgr; Ch Ken SS Tchr; Asst Organist Ch; hon/Phi Theta S'ship, 1983-84; Band Ser Awd to Univ So; Jack B Mayo Meml Awd for Phi Theta Kappa; ACT Acad S'ship; Band S'ship; Intl Students Achmt; W/W Among Am HS Students; Yg Commun Ldrs; g/Attend Univ So, Bus Ed Deg.

SHERMAN, CYNTHIA JO oc/Student; b/Aug 7, 1961; h/Route 1, Box 139, Lexington, NE; p/Dale and Jo Sherman, Lexington, NE; ed/Lexington Sr HS, 1979; Univ NE, Grad Sch; Hastings Col; cp/Pres, Phi Upsilon Omicron; Secy, Am Home Ec Assn; Home Ec Adv Bd Mem; Student Host, UNL; Hlth Aide, Intramural Sports Chm, Songldr for Residence Hall; Bible Sch Tchr; Camp Cnslr; r/Presb; hon/Mortar Bd Notable Sr, 1983; Phi Upsilon Omicron Natl S'ship; Acad Hon Roll; Softball 5th in St; Outstg Thespian Awd; Pork Queen, Dawson Co, NE; Grace M Morton S'ship; Dawson Co Ext S'ship; Homecoming Queen Cand; g/Home Ec Maj in Fashion Mdse; Buyer for Retail Store; Master's Deg; Manage Own Store.

SHERRON, WILMA GAIL oc/Student; b/Dec 6, 1960; h/Route 2, Box 270, Bethpage, TN 37022; ba/Murfreesboro, TN; p/Mr and Mrs Eldridge Sherron, Bethpage, TN; ed/Westmoreland HS,

1979; AS, Vol St Commun Col, 1981; BBA, Mid TN St Univ, 1983; pa/Asst in Order Entry, Eaton Corp, 1979; VSCC Wk S'ship, 1979-81; MTSU Wk S'ship, 1982-; Acctg Internship, Acctg Clk, Ingram Book Co, 1982; cp/Gamma Beta Phi Hon Soc, 1981-; Wesley Foun Ch F'ship, 1982-; Am Soc Wom Accts, 1982-; r/Bapt; hon/Gamma Beta Phi Hon Soc; W/W Among Am HS Students; g/CPA.

SHIRVANI-SHAHENAYATI, MAHMOOD oc/Marriott Waiter, Student; b/Feb 18, 1958; h/900 West Second Street, Arlington, TX 76013; ba/Dallas, TX; p/Darous Hedayat, Tehran, Iran; ed/Azar HS; BS, Univ TX-Arlington; cp/Server, Marriott Hotel, 1982-; Cook, Grandy's Restaurant; Waiter, Intl House of Pancakes Inc; Mgr, Big "O" Restaurant; cp/Capt, Soccer Team; Pres, HS Class; hon/2 Nat Awds in HS Soccer; Intl Yth in Achmt; g/Degs in Elect Engrg, Math, Computer Sci.

SHIVELY, DONNA SUE oc/Student; b/Jan 15, 1964; h/Route 2, Box 128-A, Callaway, VA 24067; p/Mr and Mrs William Lee Shively, Callaway, VA; ed/Franklin Co HS; Ferrum Col; pa/Eli Lilly, Sum 1982; Wk Study, Ferrum Col Bookstore, 1982-83; r/Presb; hon/Ranked 19 out of 457 HS Students, 1982; Dean's List; Hon Student Mem of Pompeiiana Inc; Phi Theta Kappa; W/W Among Am HS Students; g/Deg in Pharm.

SHOOK, RODNEY GENE oc/Student; b/Jun 27, 1966; h/Route 1, Box 47, Milford, VA 22514; p/Ronnie and Mary Shook, Milford, VA; ed/Caroline HS; pa/Engr Apprentice, Naval Surface Weapons Ctr, Sum 1983; cp/Sci Clb, 1983; Nat Hon Soc, 1982-83; Spanish Clb, 1981-82; Band, 1981-83; r/Bapt; hon/Caroline Progress, 1983; Math Contest, 4th Pl, 1979; Chosen for Naval Surface Weapons Ctr Apprentice Prog, 1983; Cert for Nat Hon Soc; g/to Obtain a PhD in Elect Engrg.

SHUGAR, LORI ANN oc/Student; b/Aug 20, 1964; h/818 Hilman Circle, Tarboro, NC 27886; ba/Durham, NC; ed/Tarboro HS, 1982; Duke Univ; cp/Freshman Class Pres; HS Basketball; HS French Clb; Sci Clb; Fine Arts & Lit Clb; Envir Awareness Clb; Nat Hon Soc; B'nai Brith Yth Org; r/Jewish; hon/E Carolina Univ Annual Math Contests; NC St Math Contest; E Carolina Univ Sci Hons Sem; Jr Miss Pageant Contestant; Chief Marshal; Valedictorian; WOW Math Awd; Quigless Biol Awd; Math Awd; NC Student Acad of Sci Clb S'ship; W/W Among Am HS Students; g/Pre-Law.

SHULL, MIAH ELIZABETH oc/Student; b/Jan 31, 1966; h/604 Camelot Drive, College Park, GA 30349; ba/Atlanta, GA; p/Mr and Mrs Laird W Shull, Jr, Col Pk, GA; ed/M D Collins HS; Emory Univ; pa/Res Asst, Ctr for Disease Control, 1983; Cashier, Po Folks Restaurants, 1983-; Lifeguard, Woodruff Phy Ed Ctr, 1983-; cp/Drama Clb, VP 1981-82, Pres 1982-84; Adv'd Mixed Choir, Sect Ldr 1981-84; Student Coun, 1981-84; Track Team, 1982-84; Cheerldg, 1980-84; Jr Varsity Capt 1980-81, Varsity Capt 1982-83; Indep Study Team in Sci Res, 1981-84; Beta Clb, 1981-84; Nat Hon Soc, 1982-84; Talented & Gifted Soc, 1982-84; Atlanta

Symph Yth Choir, 1981-83; Teen Advrs Bd, 1980-84; r/Christian; hon/Super Hon Roll, 1979-84; Certs of Superior Achmt in Eng, Sci, Music, & Hist; GA Cert of Merit Winner, 1983; Presb Scholar, 1983; GA Gov's Hons Sci Participant, 1982; Talented & Gifted Awd for Superior Achmt, 1983; Nat Hon Soc Awd for Superior Sci Achmt, 1981; Emory Univ Early Acceptance Prog, 1983-84; Star Student Nom, 1983; Ctr for Disease Control Hi-Step Prog, 1983; Talented & Gifted Internship Prog, 1982; Westinghouse Talent Search Nom, 1983; Freshman Coun Nom, 1983; Bausch & Lomb Scholar for MD Collins HS, 1983; Fulton Co 1st Pl 1982, 1983, GA 1st Pl 1982, 1983, AUS 1983, GA Pharm Assn 1983, Med Assn GA 1983, Kodak Photo Studios 1982, Sci Fair Awds; AUS Sci & Humanities Symp Spkr 1982, 1983, Nat Rep, 1983; g/MD, PhD in Biol; Med Rschr Career.

SHUM, ALEX CHEUNG KEE oc/Student; b/Feb 10, 1956; h/800 McGuire Avenue, Apartment 3-B, Monroe, LA 71203; m/Connie; c/Kaulana; p/Mon Kee Shum and Mui Kuen Hung; ed/New Method Col, Hong Kong, 1975; BS, Brigham Yg Univ-HI, 1982; NE LA Univ; cp/Ch Work; Clk, Exec Secy, Mem Bishopric, Full-time Missionary; hon/Dean's Hon List; Cert'd Missionary of LDS Chi Acad S'ship; g/Pres of Corp or Mgr of Firm.

SIEGEL, RUTH VIVIAN oc/Lawyer, Educational Consultant; b/Sep 6, 1950; h/185 Levell Green Road, Brooktondale, NY 14817; ba/Ithaca, NY; p/Benjamin and Rachel Siegel, Ithaca, NY; ed/Ithaca HS, 1968; Ithaca Col, BA, 1974; St Univ NY-Buffalo, JD, 1976; Tchrs Col, Columbia Univ, EdM, 1982; pa/Lwyr, Pvt Pract, 1977-79; Legal & Ednl Conslt, 1979-; cp/Mem, Ithaca City Sch Dist Bd Ed, 1977-81; Mem, NY St Gov's Task Force on Domestic Violence, 1979-83; Bd Dirs, Offender Aid & Restoration of Tompkins Co 1978-80, Slaterville Vol Fire Co 1978-; Active Firefighter & EMT; hon/Author of "Ed for the Handicapped Creates Oppor for All", 1982; Commun Ldrs of Am.

SILLS, BONNIE LYNN oc/Student; b/Oct 21, 1965; h/Route 5, Box 52, Dunn, NC 28334; p/Mr and Mrs Morris B Sills, Dunn, NC 28334; ed/Midway HS; cp/Volleyball; Mem of FHA; Reach Out Clbs, 1980-84; French Clb; FBLA, 1983-84; Jr Beta Clb, 1982; Pres of Bethesda Friends Yth Grp, 1982; Mem of Bethesda Softball Team, 1979-82; r/Quaker; hon/Mem, Jr Beta Clb, 1982; US Hist Awd, 1982; Asst Editor of Sch Newspaper; Rander Round-up, 1984; g/to attend Campbell Univ; Sociol Deg; Social Wk.

SILVA, CARLA DENISE oc/Claims Analyst; b/May 4, 1958; h/1213 Kansas Avenue, Kansas City, KS 66105; p/Edith P Silva, Kansas City, KS; ed/J C Harmon HS, 1976; AA, Donnelly Col, 1980; BS, St Mary Col, 1982; pa/Customer Ser Coor, IBM, 1982-83; Claims Analyst, Ins Co of N Am, 1983-; cp/Donnelly Col Student Govt Rep-at-Large, Block Capt, Mayor's Re-election; 1st Christian Ch Yth Sponsor & Tchr; 2 + 2 Student Assn, VP; Per Mgmt Assn & Am Mktg Assn; hon/Poem Pub'd by Am Col Poetry, 1981; Elected to Alpha Lambda Chapt, Delta Epsilon Sigma, 1982; Elected to Kappa Gamma Pi Hon Soc,

1982; Phi Theta Kappa Nat Hon Soc; Nat Dean's List; Dean's Hon Roll; Outstg Yg Wom Am; Intl Yth in Achmt.

SILVER, MELANIE DAUN oc/Registered Nurse; b/Aug 10, 1960; h/Route 9, Box 261-T, New Braunfels, TX 78130; ba/New Braunfels, TX; p/Jerry L and Margaret C Silver, New Braunfels, TX; ed/I C Norcom HS, 1978; Portsmouth Sch of Practical Nsg, 1979; BS, Univ TX, 1983; pa/Staff LPN, Portsmouth Gen Hosp, 1977-79; Staff LPN, Richmond Metro Hosp, 1979-80; RN, McKenna Meml Hosp, 1980-; r/Bapt; hon/Career in Emer Nsg.

SILVERTOOTH, ABBY J oc/Child Care Worker; b/Dec 23, 1961; h/1120 Glendale Lane, Nashville, TN 37204; ed/Franklin Co HS, 1980; BS, David Lipscomb Col, 1982; MA, E TN St Univ, 1983; pa/Child Care Wkr, Monroe Harding Chd's Home, 1984-; Grad Asst, E TN St Univ, 1982-83; Cashier, Dobbs House, 1982-83; Cashier/Waitress, Saga Inc, 1982; Clk, Franklin Co Lib, 1975-79; cp/A Cappella Singers, David Lipscomb Col, 1980-82; Psi Chi, 1981-82; Am Psychol Assn, 1982; Alumni Chorus, 1984; r/Ch or Christ; hon/W/W Among Am HS Students; Valedictorian; Alpha Chi; g/Complete PhD in Child Psychol.

SIMMONS, ANGELA MAUREEN oc/Student; b/Feb 4, 1968; h/147 Patton Drive, Pearl, MS 39208; p/Ernest and Janice Simmons, Pearl, MS; ed/Pearl HS; cp/Mayor's Yth Coun; HS Choir; Chess Clb; Band; Tutor for Spec Chd; r/Bapt; hon/Selected for Mayor's Yth Coun, 1983; Most Spirited Sophomore, 1983; g/Col, Child Psychol.

SIMONTON, BONNIE oc/Student; b/Feb 20, 1961; h/228 Lamont Drive, Decatur, GA 30030; ba/Auburn, AL; p/John B Simonton, Decatur, GA; ed/Decatur HS, 1979; BS, Auburn Univ, 1984; cp/Student Am Pharm Assn, Chapt Pres 1982-84, Reg Ofc 1983; Phi Lambda Sigma, Nat Secy 1983-84; Rho Chi Scholastic Hon, 1983; Omicron Delta Kappa, 1983; Kappa Psi Pharm Frat, 1982; r/Meth; hon/Author of "A Taste for Knowledge", AL Pharm, 1983; McNeil Pharm Dean's Awd, 1984; McKesson Pharm Awd, 1983, 1984; Lemmon Pharm Awd, 1984; Phi Lambda Sigma Ldrship Awd, 1982; Intl W/W in Frats & Sororities; g/Grad Sch for Masters in Pharm Adm.

SIMS, ELTON HAROLD oc/CPA; b/Jan 21, 1961; h/4555 Holly Drive, L-6, Jackson, MS 39206; ba/Jackson, MS; p/Harold E and Agnes Yvonne Sims, Hattiesburg, MS; ed/Hattiesburg HS, 1979; BSBA, Univ So MS, 1983; pa/Staff Acct, Hagaman, Roper, Haddox, Reid, CPA's; cp/Phi Kappa Phi; Beta Alpha Psi; AICPA; MSCPA; r/First Bapt Ch of Jackson; hon/Highest Hon Grad 1983, Kennamond Theory Awd 1983, Univ So MS.

SIMS, JOHN SCOTT oc/Student; b/Dec 14, 1965; h/Route 1, Box 176, Parrish, AL 35580; p/John and Diane Sims, Parrish, AL; cp/Cross Country; Track; Basketball; Tennis; Yth Coun; Yth Assn Retarded Citizens; Pres, Student Coun, 1983-84; AL Dist Key Clb Gov, 1983-84; Key Clb Lt Gov Div III, 1982-83; K-Relats Chm for AL, 1981-82; Pres Key Clb, 1983-84, VP 1981-82; Pres, F'ship of Christian Aths; VP, Agape Clb; VP, Nat

Jr Hon Soc; First Mate of Anchor Clb; VP 1982-83, Pres 1983-84, Sci Clb; Nat Hon Soc; r/Bapt; hon/Boy's St, 1983; Outstg Lt Gov's Awd for AL Dist Key Clbs, 1983; Dist'd Ser Awd for Sci Clb, 1983; W/W Among Am HS Students; g/Law & Polits.

SINGLETON, JAMES RONALD oc/Student; b/Oct 3, 1961; h/Route 5, Easley, SC 29640; ba/Wake Forest, NC; p/Mr and Mrs H B Singleton, Easley, SC; ed/Pickens Sr HS, 1979; AA, N Greenville Col, 1981; BA, Furman Univ, 1983; r/Christian; hon/Nat 4-H Cong; Pickens HS Hon Grad, 1979; N Greenville Hon Grad, 1981; W/W Among Am Jr Col Students; g/MDiv; Chaplaincy, Mil or Hosp.

SISSOM, RITA LOU oc/Student; b/Apr 11, 1964; h/Route 6, Box 669, Manchester, TN 37355; p/Mr and Mrs Dwight Sissom, Manchester, TN; ed/Manchester Ctl HS, 1982; AS, Motlow St Commun, 1984; cp/VICA, Treas 1980-81, VP 1981-82; Motlow's Student Govt Assn, Class Senator, 1982-83; Spanish Clb, Secy 1982-83; Bapt Student Union, 1982-84; Ed Clb, 1982-84; Asst Editor of *Motlow Monitor*, 1982-83; Student Govt Pres, 1983-84; Motlow Student Ambassador, 1983-84; Mem of the 1983 Homecoming Ct; r/Bapt; hon/Coffee Co Ed Assn S'ship, 1982; Motlow Monitor S'ship, 1982; Am's Outstg Names & Faces; g/Deg in Elem Ed; Tch in a Christian Sch.

SISSON, DONNA DREW oc/Student; b/Nov 29, 1962; h/Route 1, Box 337, Fincastle, VA 24090; ba/Salem, VA; p/Mr and Mrs Beverly D Sisson, Fincastle, VA; ed/James River HS, 1980; BA, Roanoke Col, 1984; cp/Chi Omega Frat, Pledge Tnr 1982, VP 1983, Legal Aid Com 1983; Cardinal Key, 1982-; Alpha Lambda Delta, 1980-; Pi Gamma Mu, 1983; Alpha Kappa Delta, 1982; Student Asst, Ed Dept, 1982-83; Ch Organist; Phi Soc, 1982; Xi Theta Chi, 1982; r/Luth; hon/Jud Bd Mem, 1982, 1983; Botetourt Ct Junior Miss, 1980; Jr Scholar, 1982-83; Dean's List; Nat Dean's List; W/W Am HS Students; g/Maj in Crim Justice; Attend Law Sch.

SITES, CYNTHIA FAY oc/Pizza Den Employee; b/Dec 28, 1963; h/Post Office Box 185, Petersburg, WV 26847; ba/Petersburg, WV; m/Trenton Douglas; p/Irvin D and A Darlene Ullery, Cumberland, MD; sp/Jesse Sites (dec) and Georgianna Sites, Petersburg, WV; ed/Fort Hill HS, 1982; pa/Fox's Pizza Den, 1983; cp/Ullery Fam Gospel Singers; Co Store Opry, 1979; So Country, 1983; Sch Orch, Libn, Secy, VP; Sch Choir, Swing Choir, Jazz Band, Pit Band; r/Mem, Organist, Yth Ldr, Mt Horeb United Meth Ch; hon/Nat Hon Soc; Citizenship Awd, 1981; W/W Among Am HS Students; g/Bank Wk; Farm.

SKINNER, CERISE CEZANNE oc/Teacher; b/Apr 27, 1960; h/13000 Woodforest, Number 803, Houston, TX 77015; ba/Baytown, TX; m/Jerry Allan; p/Mr and Mrs C W Yeargain, Houston, TX; sp/Mr and Mrs F R Skinner, Houston, TX; ed/BS, Baylor Univ, 1982; Elem Tchr, Goose Creek CISD, 1982-; cp/Kappa Delta Pi, 1980-; r/Assem of God; hon/Lambda Chi Alpha Sweetheart, 1981; Dean's List, 1978-82; Magna Cum Laude Grad, 1982.

SLATER, MARK EDWARD oc/Student; b/Jan 23, 1965; h/12 Shore Drive,

Preston, MD 21655; p/Mr and Mrs Thomas J Slater, Preston, MD; ed/Colonel Richardson, 1980-82; New Covenant Christian Acad, 1982-84; pa/Field Test Tech, Black & Decker, 1981-84; Loader, United Parcel Ser, 1983; cp/2nd Lt of Battalion #6401 of the Christian Ser Brigade; Rhythm Guitar for New Covenant Ch Music Min; hon/Extraordinary Christian Sch Students of Am; Dedicated Ser & Support of Battalion #6401, 1984; g/BS Deg in Computer Sci; Computer Programmer.

SLAYDON, SUSAN GAIL oc/Student; b/Jan 15, 1965; h/2505 Culpeper, Midland, TX 79701; p/Mr and Mrs R E Slaydon Jr, Midland, TX; ed/Grad, Robert E Lee HS, 1983; cp/Rebelette Ofcr, Pep Squad; Yg Life; HECE; hon/Soc of Dist'd HS Students, 1983; Midland Downtown Lion's Clb Lioness of the Wk, 1983; Key Clb Calendar Girl, 1983; g/Attend TX Tech Univ & Maj in Bus; Become Real Est Broker & Owner of Real St Ofc.

SLEDGE, RICKEY LEE b/Oct 14, 1964; h/50 Lambert Drive, West Helena, AR 72390; p/Roy Zell Starks and Ella Mae, West Helena, AR; ed/Eliza Miller HS; pa/HS & Jr HS Football, Basketball & Track, 4 Yrs; FFA; FCA; r/Bapt; hon/MVP (2 times), Jr HS Football; HS Dream Tm; S'ship in Football, Holmes, MS.

SLOAN, MARJORIE ROYANNA oc/Student; b/Jan 5, 1963; h/3118 Bancroft Avenue, Fayetteville, NC 28301; p/Mr and Mrs Roy B Sloan, Fayetteville, NC; ed/Grad, Reid Ross HS, 1981; Att'g Univ of NC-Chapel Hill; pa/Cashier, Hardee's, 1981-82; Mgr, Ernest Roberts; Phi Eta Sigma; r/Bapt; hon/Dean's List, May 1982 & Dec 1982; Outstg HS Sr, 1981; Grad w Hons; W/W Amg Am HS Students; g/Maj in Pharm; Wk w Doctor after Graduation.

SLOAN, MARY-ELIZABETH oc/Student; b/May 15, 1965; h/1401 Roane Street, Covington, TN 38019; p/Mr and Mrs Tim Sloan, Covington, TN; ed/Grad, Covington HS, 1983; Att'g Memphis St Univ; pa/Part-time Cashier, McDonald's of Covington, 1981-83; Part-time Teller, 1st St Bk of Covington, 1983-; Student Coun, HS, 1981-82; VP, French Clb, 1980-81; Litarary Editor, HS Annual, 1982-83; r/Assem of God; hon/Soc of Dist'd Am HS Students, 1982; Nat Hon Soc, 1981-83; Winner St Bd of Regents S'ship to Memphis St Univ; Top 10 in HS Class, 1983; Voted Most Likely to Succeed by HS Sr Class; g/Maj in Mktg.

SLY, BRIAN NELSON oc/Financial Consultant; b/Oct 26, 1959; h/601 Stockton Street Apartment #4, San Francisco, CA 94108; p/Nelson Jr and Helen Sly, W Hartford, CT; ed/Grad, Kingswood-Oxford Sch, 1977; BS w distn, Univ VA McIntire Sch Commerce, 1981; pa/Fin Conslt, Merrill Lynch, 1983-; Credit Mgr, US Steel Corp; cp/Ranked in Top 8 Singles & Doubles, Col Intramurals; Top Seeded, Racquetball Doubles, Col Intramurals; hon/Intermediate Hons; Nat Hon Soc; g/Obtain Fin Independence through Entrepreneurial Effort and Travel; Photog Extensively Worldwide.

SLYE-ROTTER, BARBARA LINN b/May 21, 1956; h/404 S 8th Street, Escanaba, MI 49829; m/Gregory Rotter;

p/Mr and Mrs Allan Slye, Ontonagon, MI; sp/Mr and Mrs George Rotter, Holt, MI; ed/Ontonagon Area HS; BS, Lake Superior St Col, 1978; Univ WI-Madison; oc/Meteorologist; ca/Student Mem, Am Meteorol Soc; HS Intramurals, Band, Hon Soc, Sr Class Pres; Inter-Varsity Christian F'ship; hon/Class Commencement Spkr, Lake Superior St Col, 1978; BS magna cum laude, 1978; Lake Superior St Col Bd of Control Dist'd S'ship; Res Asst'ship, Univ WI-Madison; W/W Amg Students in Am Univs & Cols.

SMART, LAUREN TRACEY oc/Student; b/Mar 9, 1966; h/Route 1 Box 502, Walhalla, SC 29691; p/Mr and Mrs James Smart, Walhalla, SC; ed/Att'g HS; pa/Beta Clb; Anchor Clb; Order of the Rainbow; hon/Furman Scholar, 1983; All-St Orch, 1981; Wn Reg Orch, 1979, 1980; g/Col Maj in Chem Engrg.

SMELSER, SUE ELLEN b/Jun 3, 1966; h/Route 1, Box 50, Stephens, AR 71764; p/Mr and Mrs James L Smelser, Stephens, AR; ed/Grad, HS, 1984; pa/Concessions Sales, Magnolia Swimming Pool, 1982; Salesperson, Cato's, 1983; Cashier, Dairy Queen, 1983-; pa/Pres, Beta Clb; Pres, Jr Class; Yrbook Editor; hon/Soc of Dist'd Am HS Students; Eng Awd, 1981; Basketball Acad Awd; Home Ec Awd, 1982; Sci Awd; Basketball Most Valuable Player Awd; Acctg Awd, 1983; Hlth Awd; W/W Amg Dist'd Am HS Students; g/Attend So AR Univ for 2-Yr Course of Secretarial & Bus Mgmt.

SMITH, ABBIE JEANENE b/Mar 13, 1962; h/353 Grice Street, Shelby, NC 28150; p/Barbara A Smith, Shelby, NC; ed/Grad, Shelby HS, 1980; pa/Lifeguard; Windertender, Textile Co; hon/Winslow Foun S'ship, 1981, 1982; Am Bus-wom's S'ship, 1980-83; g/Maj in Animal Sci at NCSU; Attend NC St Univ's Vet Sch.

SMITH, ALISA FRANCES oc/Student; b/Aug 15, 1960; h/Route 2 Box 196, Wallace, NC 28466; p/Mr and Mrs William Ray Smith, Wallace, NC; ed/Dipl, E Duplin HS, 1974-78; BA Spanish, Univ of NC-Wilmington, 1982; Certs in Med Ofc Asst & Nurse Asst, Cape Fear Tech Inst, Wilmington, NC, 1983; pa/Records Maintenance Asst, Gen Elect Co, Wilmington, NC; Secy Asst, Univ of NC-Wilmington; NCAE; Spanish Nat Hon Soc; Spanish Clb, Univ of NC-Wilmington; hon/Nat Hon Soc; Spanish Nat Hon Soc; Best Typist Awd, 1978; Dean's List, Univ of NC-Wilmington; g/Sec'dy Ed Spanish & Eng Tchr.

SMITH, ALLISON BARKLEY oc/Student; b/Dec 20, 1963; h/1386 Hanover West Drive, Altanta, GA 30327; ba/Dallas, TX; p/Dr and Mrs Carter Smith Jr, Atlanta, GA; ed/Grad, Choate Rosemary Hall HS; Att'g So Meth Univ; pa/Asst Res Analyst for Stock Brokerage House, Robinson Humphrey/Am Express Inc, Sum 1983; Retail Sales, Brookstone, Inc, Sum 1982; Kappa Alpha So Belle Pledge Trainer, 1983-84; Kappa Alpha Omega-Altanta Rush Chm, 1983; Kappa Alpha So Belle; Varsity Lacrosse Tm; Varsity Downhill Ski Tm; Pres, Gold Key Soc, 1980-82; r/Epis; hon/Hon Coun, 1982-83; Hon Roll, 1978-82; MVP, Downhill Ski Tm, 1982; g/Intl Bus; Maj in Bus & Lang.

SMITH, ANGELA RENA oc/Student; b/Feb 28, 1968; h/Route 1, Box 63,

Bethel Springs, TN 38315; p/Mrs Loucille Smith, Bethel Sprgs, TN; ed/Att'g McNairy Ctl HS, 1982-83; pa/Drill Tm, Rifle Capt 1982-83; Chorus; Pep Clb, 1982-83; hon/Most Improved Rifle Line Mem, 1980-81; Most Outstg Rifle Line Mem, 1981-82; g/Marry; Pursue Career as Beautician.

SMITH, ANTHONY WAYNE oc/Chemist; b/Aug 14, 1954; h/3301 Ave D, Bay City, TX 77414; ba/Houston, TX; p/Lucinda Smith, Bay City, TX; ed/Bay City HS, 1972; AA, Wharton Co Jr Col, 1974; BS, TX So Univ, 1976; Grad Study, Univ Houston at Clear Lake; pa/Chem; cp/A G Hilliard Meml Commun Ctr; NAACP, Yth Coun Advr; Voter Registration Vol; 1st Sacred Meml Christian Ch Organist & Pianist; hon/TX Christian Missionary F'ship Man of the Yr; Grad magna cum laude in Chem, TX So Univ; Intl Yth in Achmt; g/MS in Chem.

SMITH, AUDREY MARIE oc/Student; b/Jul 29, 1961; h/Route 1, Box 594, Erwin, NC 28339; p/Ethelene Smith; ed/Grad Erwin HS, 1979; BBA, NC Ctl Univ; pa/Clk Typist, Hlth Care Fin'g Adm, Sum 1982; Phi Beta Lambda Bus Frat, 1981-83; Student Union Prog Bd; C T Will Bus Clb; hon/Dean's List, 1981-83; Nat Dean's List, 1982-83; Alpha Kappa Mu Hon Soc, 1982-83; Harnett Alumni S'ship, 1979; g/Computer Programmer, Am Telephone & Telegraph Co.

SMITH, CATHI A oc/Student; b/Oct 28, 1965; h/Route 2 Box 489, Selmer, TN 38375; ed/Grad, McNairy Ctl HS; Att'g Bethel Col; pa/Bethel Wom's Varsity; Lambda Sigma Sorority, Bethel Col, 1983-84; g/Maj in Pre-Vet Med.

SMITH, CINDY ANN oc/Electronic Salesperson; b/Jul 22, 1960; h/4055 Frankford Road, #921, Dallas, TX 75252; ba/Dallas, TX; p/Dr and Mrs R E Smith, Dallas, TX; ed/Grad, Justin F Kimball HS, 1978; BBA, Baylor Univ, 1982; pa/Inside Sales Rep, Motorola Semiconductor, 1982-84; Electronic Sales, Zeus Components, 1984-; pa/Am Mktg Assn; g/Deg in Elect Engrg.

SMITH, DENNIS WAYNE oc/Student; b/May 10, 1964; h/Route 1 Box 63, Bethel Springs, TN 38315; p/Mr and Mrs Loucille Smith, Bethel Sprgs, TN; ed/Grad, McNairy Ctl HS, 1982; Att'g Memphis St Univ; pa/Stocker, McNairy Co Bd of Ed, 1981; Photog Lab Supvr, Memphis St Univ Photo-Lab, 1982; cp/Vica, 1980; HS Drill Tm, 1981-82; Rifle Capt; Band Capt; Intl Clb; Copycats; Prom Deocration Com; Sch Musical; Ofcr, Chorus; Mod Music Masters (Tri-M); Pep Clb; hon/Band Lttr, 1981, 1982; 1st, 2nd, 3rd, Master, 1981, 1982; W/W Amg Am HS Students; W/W Music; Am's Outstg Names & Faces; g/Maj in Theatre to Become Profl Actor.

SMITH, DIANE MAIRE oc/Student; b/Aug 4, 1967; h/Mud Sand Route, Soper, OK 74759; p/Jonell and David Smith, Soper, OK; ed/Att'g Soper HS; cp/VP Co 4-H, Pres Soper 4-H, Mem Choctaw Co 4-H Clb; Pres, Local Sci Clb; Reporter, Choctaw Co Entomology Clb; r/Bapt; hon/Mem, OK St 4-H Nat Forestry Judging Tm; Att'd Wash DC Citizenship Short Course; Trip to Sweden for Stay with Host Fam; W/W Amg Am HS Students; g/Attend OSU to Study Bus.

SMITH, DWAYNE ARTHUR oc/

Public Relations Director; b/Feb 22, 1956; h/542-B North Eshelman, McPherson, KS 67460; ba/McPherson, KS; p/Arthur L Smith; ed/Grad, W Valley HS, 1974; BA Eng, Seattle Pacific Univ, 1978; pa/Sports Editor, Columbia Basin Herald, Moses Lake, WA; Editorial Asst, Light & Life Mag, Winona Lake, IN; Public Relations Dir, Ctl Col, McPherson, KS; r/Free Meth; hon/Staff Mem of 3 1st-Pl Pubs; W/W Am Univ & Cols; Intl Yth in Achmt; g/Own Newspaper or Public Relations Firm.

SMITH, GAIL ANN oc/Corporate Communications Assistant; b/Aug 21, 1981; h/474 Bridges Creek Trail, Northeast, Atlanta, GA 30328; p/Mr and Mrs C Dean Smith Jr, Atlanta, GA; ed/Grad, Ridgeview HS, 1979; BA, Brenau Col, 1983; pa/Corp Communs Asst, GA-Pacific Corp, Atlanta, GA; Public Relations Asst, Cargill, Wilson & Acree Advtg, Atlanta, 1983-84; Acctg Asst, Globe Oil Co, USA, Sums 1978-82; Wom in Communs; Class Ofcr, 1979-80, 1982-83; Secy, VP 1981-83, Student Govt Assn; Pres's Coun, 1980-83; Acad Affairs Com, 1979-80; Pres, Lit Clb, 1981-83; Layout Editor, Editor 1979-81, Yearbook Staff; WBCX Radio Staff, 1981-82; Newspaper Staff, 1982-83; Exec, VP, Treas, Chaplain, Marshal, Grad Cnslr, Delta Delta Delta; hon/HGH Sr Hon Soc, 1982-83; Pres, Alpha Lambda Delta, 1980-83; VP, Phi Beta Sigma, 1982-83; Trustee Merit Scholar, 1979-83; Joseph Worth Sharp Fellow, 1982-83; Most Outstg Humanities Student, 1981-82; Wom in Communs, 1981-83; Intl Yth in Achmt; g/Attend Grad Sch & Obtain Master's Deg in Bus Adm; Pursue a Career in Bus Communs.

SMITH, GINA FAYE oc/Student; b/Dec 31, 1964; h/Route 2 Box 60, Burkesville, KY 42717; p/Mr and Mrs Dennis Leon Smith, Burkesville, KY; ed/Grad, Cumberland Co HS, 1982; Att'g Wn KY Univ; pa/Camp Currie Cnslr, KY Dept of Fish & Wildlife, Aug 1983; Disc Jockey, WKYR Radio, 1983; Secy, Dyer Energy Conslts, 1982; Wn KY Univ Broadcasting Assn, 1982-83; Col Intramural Sports, 1982-83; Ofc of Admissions' Student Rep & Adv Bd, 1982-83; Local Pres 1980-81, Dist Pres 1981-82, Beta Clb; KY Assn of Pep Org Sponsors Judge, 1983; hon/Valedictorian, 1982; Wn KY Univ Awd of Excell S'ship, 1982-83; Sr Class Pres, 1982; Pres's Scholar, 1982-83; Dean's List, 1982-83; Sophomore Hons Convocation Honoree, 1982; g/Maj in Broadcast Communs, Minor in Govt/Writing; TV News Reporter/Anchor.

SMITH, GREGORY ERWIN oc/Graduate Student; b/Mar 31, 1961; h/3203 Mountain View Estates, Blacksburg, VA 24060; m/Tammy Jo; p/Mr and Mrs Russell Smith, Col Grove, TN; sp/Mr and Mrs Robert Sochurek, Mantua, NJ; ed/Grad, Franklin HS, 1979; BS, Mid TN St Univ, 1983; Att'g VA Polytechnic Inst & St Univ Grad Sch; pa/Physics Lab Instr 1981-83, Electronics Lab Asst 1982-83, TN St Univ; Electronics Salesman, Radio Shack, 1981-83; Grad Tchg Asst, VA Polytechnic Inst, 1983-; Assn of Computing Machinery; HS Band; cp/Presb Student F'ship; r/Presb; hon/Nat Hon Soc; Mid TN St Univ Faculty Achmt Awd in Physics, 1983; Dean's List, 8 Semesters; Gamma Beta Phi; Pi

Mu Epsilon; High Sch Top 20; Personalities of S; Nat Register of Outstg Col Grads, Nat Dean's List; g/Career in Elect Engrg.

SMITH, HEATHER RENEE oc/Student; b/Sep 9, 1966; h/6647 Wolf River Court, Riverdale, GA 30274; p/Mr and Mrs B J Smith, Riverdale, GA; ed/Grad, Riverdale Sr HS, 1984; pa/Reporter 1983-84, Mem 1981-84, FBLA; F'ship of Christian Students, 1981-84; Model UN, 1981-84; Am Red Cross Yth Vol, 1983-84; Nat Kidney Foun of GA, 1983-84; Sr Class Coun, 1983-84; Raider Review Newspaper Staff, 1983-84; Atlanta Chapt of Lupus Erythematosus Foun, 1983-84; Lupus Foun of Am, 1983-84; Tennis Tm, 1983-84; Nsg Home Vol, 1983-84; Parents-Tchrs-Students Assn, 1982-84; Co-Chm, Cystic Fibrosis Foun Dance-a-thon for Cystic Fibrosis Foun, 1983-84; Jr Class Coun, 1982-83; US Achmt Acad Nat Public Affairs Com, 1983; Close-Up Prog, 1983; Sci Clb, 1982-83; Varsity Softball Tm, 1981-82; Vol Usher, Civic Ctr, 1980-82; Lttr Clb, 1980-81; Pep Clb, 1980-81; Basketball Tm, 1980-81; Track Tm, 1980-81; Yth Adv Coun, 1980-81; Sts Softball Tm, 1980-81; r/Meth; hon/Pres 1983-84, Mem 1981-84, Nat Hon Soc; Nat Beta Clb, 1980-84; Sociedad Honoraria Hispánica; GA Cert of Merit, 1982-83; Best 9th Grade Student Awd, 1980-81; PTA Citizenship Awd, 1980-81; Optimist Clb's Most Outstg Student Awd, 1980; US Achmt Academy Nat Sci Awd,1981-82; Gov's Hons Prog Nominee in Sci, 1981-83; Intl Foreign Lang Awd, 1983-84; Clayton Jr Col Creative Arts Fest Hon Mention Awd in Poetry, 1981; Exploring the GA Coast Hons Prog, 1983; Biol Awd, 1981-82; Hon Roll, 1980-84; Perfect Attendance Awd, 1980-81; Cystic Fibrosis Foun Vol Ser Awd, 1982-84; Sr Superlative, Most Intellectual, 1983-84; FBLA 1983 Fall Ldrship Tng Conf Cert, 1983; Yth Appreciation Wk Cit, 1980; Varsity Lttr in Softball, 1981-82; 100% Awd, Basketball, 1980-81; Coach's Awd, Track, 1980-81; Expertise in Spanish Awd, 1983-84; Outstg Lit Student Awd, 1981-82; Atlanta Braves Straight "A" Prog, 1982-83; Eng Awd, 1982-83; Chem I Awd, 1982-83; Am Red Cross 1st Yr Ser Awd Pin, 1982-83; US Achmt Acad Nat Ldrship Ser Awd, 1984; Optimist Intl Yth Appreciation Wk Awd, 1980; 4.0 Grade Pt Average, 1980-84; W/W in Foreign Langs in GA & FL HS's; US Nat Sci Awd in US Achmt Academy Yearbook; US Achmt Academy Yearbook for Ldrship Ser Awd; W/W Amg Am HS Students; g/Attend Col & Maj in Jour & Eng.

SMITH, JEFFREY THOMAS (JT) oc/Student; b/May 4, 1964; h/307 Hawick Place, Louisville, KY 40243; ba/Louisville, KY; p/Tom and Suzanne Smith, Louisville, KY; ed/Grad, Male Traditional HS, 1982; Att'g Univ of Louisville Speed Sch; pa/Jr Achmt; Good News Clb; Univ of Louisville Ski Clb; r/Meth; hon/Photo on Cover of Achiever, Apr 1981; 7th VP of Prod Nationally, 1981; 3rd VP of Prod, 1982; Top Achmt, 1980-81; US Army Photog Awd; Kodak Photog Awd; g/Obtain Master's of Engrg & MBA.

SMITH, JOCELYN JEAN oc/Student; b/Apr 4, 1966; h/Star Route,

Richfield, KS 67953; p/Bob G and Elgy Smith, Richfield, KS; ed/HS Dipl, 1984; pa/Farming, Ranching, and Cattle Showing Asst, Sums 1981-84; Mem 11 Yrs, Co Coun Pres 1981-82, VP 1983, 4-H Clb; Dir, KS Jr Polled Hereford Assn; Volleyball, 1980-81; Track, 1980-82; Footbll Statistician, 1981-84; Pres 1981-84, Mem 1980-84, Meth Yth F'ship; Secy/Treas 1981-82, VP 1982-83, Pres 1983-84, Mem 1980-84, Pep Clb; Secy/Treas 1983-84, Mem 1981-84, Nat Hon Soc; VP 1983-84, Mem 1982-84, Student Coun; Freshman Class Pres, 1980-81; HS Choir 1980-84, 1st Div Rating St 1984; Show Choir, 1980-84; Madrigals 1980-84, 1st Div Rating St 1984; Girls Sextet, 1980-83; Girls Ensemble, 1980-81; Girls Glee Clb, 1983-84; Mixed Quartet 1983-84, 1st Div Rating St; Band, 1980-84; Vocal Soloist, 1st Div Rating St 1981; Trumpet Soloist, 1st Div Rating St 1981; hn/Hon Roll, 4 Yrs; Miss Aggie Princess, Panhandle St Univ, 1983; KS Polled Hereford Queen, 1983-84; Nat Polled Hereford Queen, 1984; Salutatorian of Sr Class, 1984; St Scholar by KS Bd of Regents, 1984; 4-H Champ Bull, 1974 Co Fair; 4-H Champ Heifer, 1975-83 Co Fairs; 4-H Champ Hereford Steer, 1977, 1980, 1981, 1982, 1983 Co Fairs; 4-H Champ Beef Showman, 1980, 1981, 1982 Co Fairs; 4-H Champ All- Around Showman, 1980, 1981, 1982 Co Fairs; 4-H Champ Heifer, 1980, 1981, 1982, 1983 Panhandle Expos; 4-H Champ Beef Showman, 1980, 1981, 1982; 4-H Champ Heifer Showman, 1978-83 Panhandle Expos; Make-It-Yourself-With-Wool Finalist, 1980; Dist Hon Choir, 1980, 1981, 1983; Trumpet 1st Div Rating Leag, 1981, 1983; Trumpet 1st Div Rating Reg, 1984; Vocal 1st Div Rating Leag 1981-84; Vocal 1st Div Rating Reg & St, 1984; Served as Page for KS Legis Session, 1984; Recip John Phillip Sousa Band Awd, 1984; Football & Basketball Homecoming Attendant, 1983-84; g/ Study Voice/Theatre, Poli Sci, Linguistics, Jour; Fgn Ser Wk; Theatre.

SMITH, JOHN HOBERT oc/Manufacturer's Representative; b/Aug 31, 1956; h/1979 Gurley Pike, Gurley, AL 35748; ba/Homewood, AL; p/Mr and Mrs Harry R Smith, Gurley, AL; ed/ Grad, Grissom HS, 1974; BSBA Mktg, Univ of AL-Huntsville; pa/Div Mgr, Sears, Roebuck & Co, 1975-79; Gen Mgr, Solar Unltd Inc, 1982-84; Mfr's Rep, Computer Site Support, Inc, 1984-; AL Solar Energy Assn; ASHRAE; ABC; cp/Past Mem, Huntsville JCs; Huntsville Home Bldrs; r/U Meth; hon/Nat Dean's List, 1979-80; Pres's Scholar, 1980; Hon Scholar, UAH, 1982; Personalities of the S; Yg Personalities of S.

SMITH, JOYCE IRENE oc/Data Entry Operator; b/Jul 28, 1957; h/Route 3 Box 397, London, KY 40741; p/Ruth E Bennett, Manchester, KY; ed/Grad, Clay Co HS, 1975; AA, Midway Col, 1978; BS, Union Col, 1980; cp/Sum Camp Asst, 3 Yrs; Phi Beta Lambda, Midway Col, 1 Yr; Cir K, Union Col, Mem 2 Yrs, Secy 1 Yr; r/Asst Bible Sch Tchr, 2 Yrs; hon/Hon Grad, Union Col 1980, Midway Col 1978, Clay Co HS 1975; Nat Dean's List; Intl Yth in Achmt; Commun Ldrs of Am; W/W Amg Students in Am Voc & Tech Schs; g/Career Related to Field of Study.

SMITH, KENNETH LEON oc/Student; h/603 Park Avenue, Copperas Cove, TX 76522; p/Robert A and Elke L Smith; ed/Copperas Cove HS, 1981; So Meth Univ; pa/Dallas Civic Symph; Harket Hgts Mun Band; J L Williams Jr HS Symph I Band; Copperas Cove HS Band; Copperas Cove HS Stage Band; Spanish Clb; Mustang Band; hon/ Dean's Hon S'ship; Nat Hon Roll; Nat Hon Soc; Acad Achmt Awd for Instrumental Music; John Philip Sousa Band Awd; Outstg Performer Awd for Solo at St Solo & Ensemble Contest; Meadows Artistic Achmt S'ship, Meadows Sch of the Arts, So Meth Univ, Dallas, 1983; Yth of the Month, 1981; Commun Ldrs of Am; Intl Yth in Achmt; g/Deg in Music Ed/Perf; Play Trombone for Maj Symph Orch.

SMITH, L MURPHY oc/Professor of Accountancy; b/Jul 20, 1957; h/3301 Whippoorwill Lane, Oxford, MS 38655; ba/Univ, MS; m/Katherine T; c/Tracy Rebecca; p/Dr and Mrs L C Smith, Jr, Ruston, LA; sp/Mr and Mrs Hubert Taken, Shreveport, LA; ed/HS Dipl, 1975; BBA, 1977; MBA, NE LA Univ, 1979; DBA Acctg, LA Tech Univ, 1973; pa/Asst Prof of Accountancy, Univ of MS, 1981-; Fac Resident, Arthur Andersen & Co, Houston, TX, 1982; Inst of Ec, LA Tech Univ, 1980-81; Am Inst of CPAs; Nat Assn of Accts; Am Acctg Assn; Fac VP, Alpha Theta Chapt, Beta Alpha Psi; Beta Gamma Sigma; Phi Kappa Phi; Omicron Delta Kappa; Omicron Delta Epsilon; Phi Eta Sigma; Dist Dir, Chapt Advr, Delta Sigma Pi; r/So Bapt; hon/Author, "EDP Auditors"; Co-author w Dr G L Porter, Mgmt Acctg, Aug 1983; Outstg Student in Col of Bus, NE LA Univ, 1977; So Reg of Delta Sigma Pi Undergrad of Yr, 1977; Grad summa cum laude, 1977; Outstg Yg Men of Am; W/W Students; g/Write a Book on Acctg/Ec; Attain Rank of Full Prof at Maj Univ.

SMITH, LILLIAN CATHERINE oc/ Student; b/May 12, 1965; h/8317 Quentin Street, New Carrollton, MD 20784; p/C Jasper Smith (dec); John R Jr and Doris Smith Webster, New Carrollton, MD; ed/Parkdale HS; pa/Asbury UMC; Del, Gov's Yth Adv Coun of MD; Pres, Nat Spanish Hon Soc at Parkdale HS; Pres, AFS; HS Concert Choir; Sr Girl Scout, Troop 2077, Girl Scout Coun of Nation's Capital; Chm, Page Com, Annual Meeting of Girl Scout Coun of Nation's Capital; Congl Aide in Ofc of Cong-man Baltasar Corrada, Sum 1981; Bus Mgr 1982-83, Mem 1980-81, 1981-82, Concert Choir, Parkdale; Am Field Ser/Intl, Pres Parkdale Clb 1981-82, 1982-83; Del, Gov's Yth Adv Coun, 1979-83; Yth Choir, Asbury U Meth Ch, Wash, DC; Yth F'ship; hon/ Part in Annual Christmas Pageant of Peace as Rep of GSA; Prince George's Co HS Hons Chorus, 1981-82,1982-83; MD All-St Chorus, 1982-83; MENC-All En Chorus, 1983; Nat Hon Soc, 1981-82, 1982-83; Pres, Spanish Hon Soc, 1981-82, 1982-83; Spanish Achmt Awd, 1980; Jesse J Warr Ldrship Awd, 1982; Spanish Awd of Hon, 1982, 1983; Girl's St, 1982; Red Lobster Student of the Mo, Sept 1982; Page to MD Assem, 1983; Supt's Awd, 1983; Susan Yohe Meml Awd, 1983; Yg Commun Ldrship Awd, 1982; US Achmt Academy Nat Awds, Hist & Fgn Lang, 1982; Soc of

Dist'd Am HS Students; W/W Amg Am HS Students; US Commun Ldrs of Am; g/Career in Jour/Communs.

SMITH, LINDA JEANETTE oc/Computer Programmer; b/Dec 21, 1960; h/ PO Box 67 Beech Bottom, WV 26030; ba/Wheeling, WV; p/Mr and Mrs Robert L Smith, Beech Bottom, WV; ed/Dipl, Brooke HS, 1979; BSBA, W Liberty St Col, 1983; pa/Computer Programmer, The Hlth Plan of the Upper OH Val, 1983-; Mem, Data Processing Mgmt Assn, 1983-; Life Mem, Alpha Kappa Psi; r/Indep Bapt; hon/Delta Mu Delta Hon Soc, 1982; Grad w Hons, W Liberty St Col, 1983; Nat Dean's List, 5 Sems; Soc for Dist'd Am HS Students; W/W Among Am HS Students; Intl Yth in Achmt; Personalities of S.

SMITH, LISA ANN oc/Student; b/ Nov 10, 1965; h/2326 SE 4th, Grand Prairie, TX 75051; p/Donald and Betty Smith, Grand Prairie, TX; ed/Dipl, S Grand Prairie HS, 1984; pa/Waitress, Pizza Hut Restaurant, Sum 1982; Cashier, Motts 5 & 10, 1983; cp/ Decorations Chm 1982-83, Agape Clb; Mu Alpha Theta, 1982-83; FCA, 1983; Yth Choir, Fairview Bapt Ch, 1979-83; r/Bapt; hon/Var Interviews for Volleyball Pub'd in Dallas Morning News & Grand Prairie Daily News, 1983; Hon Soc, 1982; Girl of the Mo, Sep 1983; 1st Tm All-Dist Volleyball, 3 Consecutive Yrs, 1981-83; Dallas Morning News All-Metro Tm Volleyball, 2 Consecutive Yrs, 1982-83; All-St Volleyball Tm, 1982; Homecoming Queen, 1983; Supt's Hon Roll; W/W Among Am HS Students; g/ Play on Olympic Volleyball Tm, Coach.

SMITH, MARK ALFRED oc/Marketing Representative; b/Aug 8, 1958; h/ 59 School Street, Northborough, MA 01532; ba/Boston, MA; m/Angela Ann Smith; p/Mr and Mrs Murray S Smith Jr, Fitchburg, MA; sp/Mr and Mrs Angelo Femino, Fitchburg, MA; ed/Dipl, Fitchburg HS, 1976; BS, NEn Univ, 1981; oc/Mktg Rep, C & F Underwriters Grp, 1983; Loss Control Rep, US Ins Grp; cp/Boston Bouve Col Hon Soc; Kappa Delta Pi; Eta Sigma Gamma; Am Soc of Safety Engrs; NH Soc of Ins Safety Profls; Nat Mem, Smithsonian Assocs; Faith U Parish Ch Yth Grp; r/ Prot; hon/NEn Univ Coop Ed Awd, 1981; Grad magna cum laude, Constance K Greene Awd for Outstg Field Experience, 1980-81; W/W Among Am HS Students; Intl Yth in Acht; Commun Ldrs of Am; Personalities of Am; g/ CPCU Deg in Ins, Obtaining Necessary Knowledge & Skills Needed to Progress into Mgmt Positions within a Large Corp.

SMITH, MICHAEL RAY oc/Student; b/Apr 18, 1961; h/447 South Main, Barberville, KY 40906; p/A J and Freda Smith, Barbourville, KY; ed/Att'g Col; cp/Gamma Beta Phi Nat Hon soc, 1981-84; Pres, Student Govt, 1983-84; Pres, Sci Soc, 1982-83; Capt, Swim & Tennis Tms, 1984; r/Christian; g/Maj in Biol, Chem, Physics & Math; Attend Med Sch.

SMITH, MICHEAL, J oc/Executive; b/Feb 11, 1954; h/607 Noth Douglas, Cleburne, TX 76031; p/Lindell and Barbara Smith, Lewisville, TX; ed/Dipl, Lewisville HS, 1972; BA & BS 1976, MS 1980, Abilene Christian Univ; Addit Study: Amber Univ; SWn Bapt Theol Sem; pa/Pres, Christian Ski Adventures, 1983-; Yth Min, 5 Yrs, 1978-82; Owner, Smith Cleaning Ser, 1978-83; cp/HS Track & Cross Country, 2 Yrs; Na Hon Soc; VFW Outstg Student Awd; Col: Dean's Hon Roll; Student Foun; Mu Sigma; Pres, Secy-Treas, Math Clb; Galaxy Social Clb; r/Ch of Christ.

SMITH, REGINALD K oc/Graduate Student; b/Mar 3, 1960; h/509 Woodlawn Avenue, Newark, DE 19711; ba/ Newark, DE; p/Mr and Mrs Rayford Smith, Kenansville, NC; ed/Dipl, James Kenan HS; Att'd NC Ctl Univ; Att'd James Sprunt Tech Col; Att'g Univ of DE; pa/St Food Sers Monitor/Supvr, DE Dept of Public Instrn, Sum 1983; Minority Affairs Asst, Govs Ofc for Minority Affairs, Sum 1982; Tech Asst, Sys Res & Devel Corp, Sep 1981; Prog Asst, Du-Penza Secy Inc, Sums 1980 & 1981; Public Hlth Analyst, Dept of Hlth & Human Sers, Sprg 1981; Mem: NC Spec Vol; Former Pres & VPres, NC Ctl Univ's Public Adm Clb; Am Soc for Public Adm (ASPA); Am Israel Public Affairs Com; Res Triangle Chapt, ASPA; DE Chapt, ASPA; cp/Dir of Yth for Energy Indep in St of DE; Yth Inst for Peace in Mid E; Ldrship Devel Mission to Israel, 1983; Appt'd, DE Energy Advy Com, 1983; Alpha Phi Alpha Frat; r/Meth; hon/Ranked 5th out of Class of 700, NC Ctl Univ, 1982; Recip, The 2nd Mile Awd for Outstg Ser in Public Adm, 1982; Recip, Ldrship Awd, Alpha Phi Alpha Frat, 1982; W/ W Among Students in Am Cols & Univs; Nat Register for Outstg Graduating Srs; g/Start Own Bus, Pursue JD Deg.

SMITH, SONELIUS LAREL JR oc/ Student; b/Mar 18, 1965; h/901 South Calhoun, Magnolia, AR 71753; p/S L Smith, NYC; Bernardine K Greer, Magnolia, AR; ed/Dipl, Magnolia HS, 1983; Att'g NWn St Univ-Natchitoches, LA; cp/Mem, Treas & Tutor for Sum Tutoring Prog, Actively Involved People (AIP); Senator, Boys' St; Nat Hon Soc; FTA; Yrbook Staff, Broadcaster, Newspaper Staff; Pres, Hist Clb; Rep, Student Coun; Magnolia HS Band; Treas, Spanish Clb; Homeroom Ofcr; Del, Laymen's Missionary Inst, Jackson, TN; Pres, Christain Yth F'ship; Reg'd CPR; Pres & Pianist, Yg Adult Choir, Trinity C M E; r/Meth; hon/All-Reg Band, Bassoon, 3 Yrs; All-St Band Bassoon, 2 Yrs (1st Chair, 1st Yr); Blue Medal, Hon Band, Flute; Tri-St Band/Orch Fest, Fayetteville; 2nd Place Winner, St Spanish Spch Fest; McDonald's All-Am HS Band Nom; Most Outstg Sr; Mem Am Yth Concert Band, Touring Nat's Capitol, Carnegie Hall & Europe; W/W Most Talented; g/Maj in Mass Communs.

SMITH, THOMAS MICHAEL oc/ Male Nurse; b/Nov 9, 1961; h/2329 Pleasant Avenue, Wellsburg, WV 26070; ba/Buckhannon, WV; p/Jack and Donna Smith, Wellsburg, WV; ed/Dipl, Brooke HS, 1980; Att'd Univ of Steubenville, 75 Nsg. WV Wesleyan Col, 1984; pa/Lifeguard, Wellsburg Pks & Brooke Hills Pk; Colorguard Instr, Wintersville HS; Nurse Extern, St Joseph's Hosp; cp/Pres, VPres Student Nurses of Wesleyan; Secy' Treas, Freshman Class; VPres, Sophomore Class; Secy, WV Student Nurses Assn; Beta Beta Beta; Benzene Ring; Commun Coun Rep; r/Cath; hon/Dean's List,

Sprg 1982 & 1983; Outstg Freshman, 1981; Claude Worthington Benedum Scholar, 1982-83; Elk's Student of the Mo, Nov 1981; W/W Among Music Students; g/Pursue Med Deg.

SMITH, TRACY JAN oc/Student; b/ Jun 9, 1966; h/Route 2, Box 26A, Valliant, OK 74764; p/Pete and Shirley Smith, Valliant, OK; ed/Dipl, HS; pa/ Cashier/Clk, S & S; cp/Student Coun; Annual Staff; Choir; Sci Clb; Ch Yth Grp; r/Assem of God; hon/Hon Soc, 1981-82; Supt's Hon Roll, 1983; Eng Medal, 1982; g/Become a Secy.

SMITH, WENDY DEE b/Feb 27, 1964; p/William and Wanda Smith, Penhook, VA; ed/Dipl, Franklin Co HS, 1982; Att'd Trade Sch Floral Desing, Northside Night Course, Roanoke, VA; pa/Energy Conslt, Am Energy Co; r/ Bapt; hon/2nd Place Talent Hunt, Omega Si Phi, 1981; Vocals, All-Reg Alto, 1981; Music Star of Mo, 4 Consecutive Months, 1980; Miss Apple Fes, 1983; W/W in Music; g/Attend Modeling Sch, Take Pvt Voice Lessons.

SMITHSON, ALYCE LOUISE oc/ Registered Nurse; b/Feb 2, 1958; h/422 Santa Fe Drive, Borger, TX 79007; ba/ Dallas, TX; p/Mr and Mrs Wiley Smithson Jr, Borger, TX; ed/Dipl, Borger HS, 1976; BSN, TX Wom's Univ, 1980; pa/ Critical Care & Trauma Nurse Intern, Parkland Hosp, 1981; Critical Care Reg'd Nurse, Currently; Mem: Am Assn of Critical Care Nurses; cp/ARC Nurse; Progs & Projs Dir 1978-79, Constl 1979-80, TX Nsg Students Assn; TX Nsg Assn Careers Com; hon/Sigma Theta Tau; Outstg Grad Nsg Student, Adult Nsg, 1983; Nat Dean's List; W/ W Among Students in Am Univs & Cols; Intl Yth in Achmt; Commun Ldrs of Am; g/Adv'd Study in Nsg, Tchr of Nsg in Undergrad Setting.

SNELL, JEFFREY GLYN oc/Student; b/Nov 5, 1962; h/HCR 5, Box 38, Lamesa, TX; ba/Hobbs, NM; p/Glyn and Wanda Snell, Lamesa, TX; ed/Dipl, HS, 1981; BS & BA, Col of SW, 1984; cp/ Intramural Sports; r/Bapt; hon/Dean's List, 1981-84; Acad S'ship, Col of SW, 1981-84; g/Masters Deg in Sociol.

SNELL, TAMI G oc/Student; b/Nov 17, 1967; h/HCR 5, Box 38, Lamesa, TX 79331; p/Glyn and Wanda Snell, Lamesa, TX; ed/Att'g HS; pa/Vol Sunday Night Tchr, Chd's Ch Class, Ages 3-6 Yrs Old; cp/Reporter, FHA, 1983-84; Varsity Basketball Tm, 1980-84; Most Improved Basketball Player, 1983-84; St Qualifier, Twirling, 1983-84; Hd Twirler, HS Band, 1984-85; 1st Dist, Girl's Doubles Tennis, 1981 & 1982; 3rd Dist Girls Doubles Tennis, 1982 & 1983; 4th Dist Girls Tennis, 1983 & 1984; r/Bapt; hon/I Rating in Twirling, UIL Dist Solo, 1983; 1st Place Winner, Feature Twirlng Solo, Class I-II & III A Schs, S Plains Commun Col, 1983; 2nd in Pageant & Twirling NBTA Contest, Rall's TX, 1984; 1st Beg Solo Twirling NBTA, Canyon, TX, 1984; W/W in Baton Twirling; g/Attend S Plains Jr Col, Maj in Phy Therapy, Minor in Math.

SNOW, FAYE ELAINE oc/Oct 18, 1961; h/PO Box 250, Mountain Home, AR 72653; p/Mr and Mrs William R Snow, Mtn Home, AR; ed/Dipl, Mtn Home HS, 1980; Att'g Univ of AR; pa/ Sales Clk, Mercy's Cards & Gifts, Sum 1979; Receptionist, Animal Hosp, Sum

1979 & 1980; Reporter, KTLO Radio, Sum 1982; New Dir, KUAF Radio, 1982-83; News Reporter, TV Sta H3; cp/Union Bd; Student Channel; Yg Dems, 1983; Anthropology Clb, 1982; Phi Eta Sigma; Nat Dean's List; Golden Key; Kappa Tau Alpha; KUAF News Dir; KUAF Sports Staff; AWS HS Newspaper Editor, 1980; HS FBLA, 1976-80; HS FTA, 1980; HS FHA, 1976; r/Bapt; hon/HS Hon Roll, 1976-80; HS Beta Clb, 1976-80; Univ of AR Acad S'ship, 1980; AHSPA Jour S'ship, 1980; AP Jour S'ship, 1983; Dean's List, 1980-83; g/Broadcast Jour, TV Sports Broadcaster.

SNOW, NANCY ELIZABETH oc/ Student; b/Feb 20, 1962; h/210 Hermitage Road, Greenville, SC 29615; p/Mr and Mrs Victor D Snow, Greenville, SC; ed/Dipl, Wade Hampton HS; Att'g Clemson Univ; cp/Men's Varsity Stat, Tennis Tm, 1981-82; Nom Rep, Bus Conf in Chgo; Clemson Lit Soc; Model UN; Sailing Clb; Debate Tm, 1982; Intern, Senator Strom Thurmond, SC; Nat Hon Soc, 1980-83; Omnibus Soc for Outstg Biol Students, 1980; Varsity Lttrs in Tennis; Grad w Hons, 1980; Student Govt Legal Advr, 1982-83; Sigma Tau Epsilon; Staff Writer, Sch Newspaper The Tiger, 1982-84; Poetry & Article Pub'd in Sch Lit Mag Chronicle; r/Christian Existentialist; hon/Phi Eta Sigma, 1981; Alpha Lambda Delta, 1981; Secy, Sigma Tau Epsilon, 1983-84; Phi Beta Phi; Phi Alpha Theta; Recip, Frank Gumby Meml S'ship for Outstg Acad Achmt, 1981-84; g/Master's Deg in Intl Mgmt or Hosp Mgmt.

SNYDER, AUDRA LYNN oc/Student; b/Jan 20, 1966; h/1271 Barnes Mill Road, Richmond, KY 40475; p/Burt and Wanda Snyder, Richmond, KY; ed/Dipl, Madison Ctl HS; cp/Varsity Golf Tm; FCA, 4 Yrs; CGAC, 3 Yrs; VPres, FHA 2 Yrs; Pep Clb, 4 Yrs; Beta Clb, 4 Yrs; Hlth Careers Clb, 1 Yrs; Jr Class Parliamentn; r/Bapt; hon/Hon Roll; Miss Madison Co Beauty Pageant, 1983; W/W Among Am HS Students.

SNYDER, KAREN DENISE oc/Student; b/Apr 18, 1966; h/106 San Fran Drive, Darlington, SC 29532; p/Mr and Mrs Charles E Snyder, Darlington, SC; ed/Dipl, St John's HS; cp/Asst Editor 1983-84, Staff 1982-83, HS Sch Newspaper; Treas 1982-83, 6th Dist Chm St Coun 1983-84, Student Coun; Pep Clb, 1980-84; Secy-Treas 1983-84, Block S J Clb; Co-Hd 1981-82, Jr Varsity Cheerldr; Hd Varsity Cheeldr, 1983-84; Spanish Clb, 1982-83; Jr/Sr Decorations Com, 1982-83; Powder Puff Football, 1982-83; ARC Vol, 1982-84; r/Bapt; hon/Selected to Serve on St Dept of Ed Student Coun, 1983-84; Sr of the Mo, Sep 1983; g/Maj in Bus.

SO, CATHERINE W H oc/Student; b/Sep 23, 1968; h/3283 Clearview Drive, Marietta, GA 30060; p/Mr and Mrs Andrew C K So, Marietta, GA; ed/Att'g Westminster Schs, Marietta, GA; cp/ Vol Prog, St JosephHosp, 1981-; Student Coun, 1982-83; Student Lecture Series Com, 1983-; Chorale, 1980-; Volleyball Mgr; Jr Varsity Co-Capt, Debate Tm, 1982-; r/Presb; hon/Hon Roll, 9th Grade; Old Testament Bible Awd, 1983; Eng Awd, 1983; Origins of Wn Soc Awd, 1983; 1st Place Extemporaneous Spkg in Reg, 1983; 2nd Place Extemporaneous Spkg, St, 1983; 1st

Place Extemporaneous Spkg, All-St; 1st Place Spkr, Mercer Univ Sum Tournament, 1982; g/Crim Lwyr or Free-lance Writer.

SOCKEL, CRAIG J oc/Assistant Manager; b/Dec 10, 1961; h/227 Belvedere Avenue, Reading, PA 19611; ba/ Reading, PA; p/Mr and Mrs Joseph R Sockel, Reading, PA; ed/Dipl, Holy Name HS; BS, Albright Col, 1983; pa/ Asst Mgr 1980-, Swing Mgr 1978-80, McDonald's, J R Mgmt Inc; Bkkpr, Perfect Lubrication, Sum 1982; Mem: Fund Raising Com, Acctg Bus Assn, 1980-; r/Rom Cath; g/Pvt Acctg Mgmt Position w Co.

SORENSON, SCOTT PAUL oc/ Instructor of Brass Instruments; b/Feb 16, 1954; h/1807 2nd Avenue So #24, Mpls, MN 55403; ba/Edina, MN; m/ Joyce Siu-Ping; p/Kenneth and Engeline Sorenson, Minnetonka, MN; ed/Dipl, Hopkins Lindbergh Sr HS; BA, Luther Col; MA, PhD, Univ of MN; oc/Instr of Brass Instruments, Schmitt Music Co, Edina, MN, 1983-; Tchg/Res Asst, Univ of MN, 1980-82; Asst Editor, Jour of Intl Trumpet Guild, 1982-; cp/Luth Ch of Am; Phi Kappa Phi; Pi Kappa Lambda; Pi Lambda Theta; hon/Author, "The 1982 & 1983 ITG Confs," "Valentine Snow, Handel's Trumpeter," in Jour of Intl Trumpet Guild; "An Ancient Confucian Record of Music," in MN Music Ed Res Review; Dir of Instrumental Music, Music Dept Chm, Hong Kong Intl Sch, 1978-80; g/Col Prof in Music/Music Ed.

SOUTHARD, LAURA ELLEN oc/ Engineer; b/Jun 29, 1961; h/2913 Larchmont, Ponca City, OK 74604; m/W Mark; p/Mr and Mrs Glen Brinson, Ponca City, OK; sp/Mr and Mrs William L Southard, Ponca City, OK; ed/Dipl, Ponca City HS, 1978; BS, Univ of OK, 1982; oc/Engr, Conoco Inc; Mem: Treas, Soc of Wom Engrs; Pres, Tau Beta Pi; Pres, Pi Mu Epsilon; AIChE; Desk & Derrick; cp/Public Lib Bd; Univ Jazz Ensemble; Engr's Clb; Campus Rel Orgs; Intramural Ath Tms; Vol Wkr in Chem Engrg Res Labs; hon/Outstg Sr in Col of Engrg, Univ of OK, 1981; Outstg Freshman at Univ of OK, 1979; Mortar Bd; g/Employmnt as Process Engr; Master's Deg.

SPARKMAN, JIMMY THOMAS oc/ Student; b/Jan 10, 1965; h/5640 Candies Creek Road, Cleveland, TN 37311; p/ Mr and Mrs Billie O Sparkman, Cleveland, TN; ed/Dipl, Bradley Ctl HS, 1983; Att'd Cleveland St Commun Col; cp/ UMYF; Dicie Boys' Baseball, 1978-81; Nat Hon Soc, 1981 & 1982; Beta Clb, 1981 & 1982; VPres 1982, Mem 1980-82, FFA; r/1st U Meth Ch; hon/ Am Legion Boys St Rep, 1982; FFA Parliamentary Procedure Tm, Nat Champs, 1982; 4-H Steer Calf Show, 1977-83; Wildlife Judging Tm, 1982; Soc of Dist'd Am HS Students; W/W Among Am HS Students; Yg Commun Ldrs of Am; g/Maj in Engrg.

SPARKS, TERESA LYNN oc/Student; b/Dec 30, 1966; h/Box 7, McRoberts, KY 41835; p/Bobby and Sue Sparks, McRoberts, KY; ed/Dipl, Fleming-Neon HS, 1984; Att'd Letcher Co Area Voc Ed Ctr; cp/Reporter, FBLA, 1982-84; HS Band, 1979-82; h/Superior Ensemble, Band, 1981; Hon Roll, 1981-84; W/W Among Am HS Students; g/Pursue Jour.

SPEAKE, CHERYL ATRINA oc/

Student; b/Nov 12, 1964; h/Route 1, Box 245, Mt Hope, AL 35651; p/James Coy Speake (dec); Clarion Lee Carroll, Mt Hope, AL; ed/Dipl, Hatto HS, 1983; Att'g Univ of N AL; cp/Reporter 1983, Devotion Ldr 1975-83, Co Coun VPres 1980, Co Coun Pres 1982-83, Chm Lawrence Co Dairy Foods Mo 1983, Lawrence Co Dist Rep 1983, 4-H; FHA, 1978-83; Hatton HS Marching & Concert Band, 1974-83; Pep Band, 1980-81; HS Volleyball Tm, 1982-83; Broadcasting Clb, Univ of N AL, 1983; r/Bapt; hon/Author of Articles on Food Nutrition, Dairy Foods & Food Presv Pub'd in The Moulton Advtr, 1979-84; S'ship, Ball Glass Co, 1983; Participant 4-H Nat Cong, Chgo, IL (sent by Kerr Glass Co), 1984; 1st Place St & Dist Winner, 4-H Food Presv, 1984; Recip, Trip to Wash DC 4-H Citizenship Conf, 1981; Recip, Trip to Fontana Village, NC for 4-H Conserv Conf, 1982; Lawrence Co Dairy Chm for Yth, 1983; Yth Tchr, OK Bapt Ch, 1982-84; Sum Bible Sch Tchr, 1982-83; 4-H Jr Ldr, 1980-83; Num Radio & TV Appearances; W/W Among Am HS Students; g/Dietitian Maj; Minor in Photog.

SPEAS, CYNTHIA KAY oc/Medical Student; b/Oct 10, 1960; h/Route 7, Box 333, Gainesville, GA 30506; ba/ Augusta, GA; p/Gary Lee Speas (dec); Melvin and Mary Catherine Kitchens, Gainesville, GA; ed/Dipl, N Hall HS, 1979; BS Chem, No GA Col, 1983; Att'g Med Col of GA; pa/Clk, Pharm Asst, Westside Pharm, 1978-82; Lab Phlebotomist, Lumpkin Co Hosp, 1981-83; cp/ HS: Drill Tm/Dance Corp, 1977-79; Sr Beta Clb, 1978-79; Jr & Sr Class Pres; Homecoming Ct, 1979; Most Likely to Succeed, 1979; Col: Sigma Chi Little Sister, 1982-83; Ideas & Issues Com, Rec Com, Union Bd, 1981-82; Fgn Lang Clb, 1981-82; Ofcr's Clb Sweetheart, 1983; Alpha Lambda, 1979-81; Phi Kappa Phi, 1983; Intro Ldr, 1979-83; Secy, S'ship Chm, Chapt Ed Chm, Rush Advr, 1981 Nat Conv Chapt Del, Kappa Delta Sorority, 1979-83; r/Luth; hon/ HS: I Dare You Awd, 1979; Valedictorian, 1979; Col: Paul M Hutcherson Outstg Student Awd, 1983; Sr Rep, Homecoming Ct, 1983; Dean's List, 4 Yrs; Pres's List, 4 Yrs; Hammock S'ship, 1979; Foun S'ship, 1979-83; Grad F'ship, Nat Kappa Delta Sorority, 1983; Miss N GA Col, 1983; Grad magna cum laude, N GA Col, 1983; Steele S'ship, Med Col of GA, 1983; W/W Among Am HS Students; Intl Yth in Achmt; Outstg Yg Wom; g/Obtain MD.

SPEARS, DAVID MICHAEL oc/ Student, Salesman; b/Sep 13, 1963; h/ 3425 South Willis, Abilene, TX 79605; p/Donald E and Dorothy D Spears, Abilene, TX; ed/Dipl, Cooper HS, 1981; Att'g Hardin-Simmons Univ; pa/Salesman, Cameras & Assocs, 1984-; cp/ Editor, Jr HS Newspaper; Football; Photog, Sch Newspaper & Yrbook, 3 Yrs; Editor-in-Chief, Yrbook, 2 Yrs; Pres, Film Soc, 2 Yrs; Homeroom VPres, 1 Yr; Treas, Kappa Phi Omega, 1984-85; hon/Jr Nat Hon Soc; Yth Apprec Awd, Optimists; Outstg Jour Student Awd, Abilene Reports News Merit Awd; Dept Awd for Pub, 1979-81; Dist'd Ser Awd; W/W Among Am HS Students; Intl Yth in Achmt; g/Deg in Bus Adm, Mktg.

SPELL, MARGARET ANN oc/Student; b/Nov 24, 1961; h/919 West

Richardson Avenue, Summerville, SC 29483; p/Mr and Mrs W T Spell, Summerville, SC; ed/Dipl, Summerville HS, 1980; Att'd Col of Charleston, 1980-82; Att'g Univ of SC; cp/HS: Beta Clb; Nat Hon Soc; Quill & Scroll Soc; Mu Alpha Theta; French Clb; Summerville HS Band; Col: Psych Clb, Col of Charleston; Assn of Hons Students, Univ of SC; hon/Gov's Sch, Sum 1979; Foun S'ship, Col of Charleston, 1980-82; Nat Dean's List; g/PhD in Psych.

SPENCER, SHANNON KAREL oc/ Student; b/Aug 21, 1962; h/216 Oakdale, Bastrop, LA 71220; p/Mr and Mrs Bobby J Spencer, Bastrop, LA; ed/Dipl, Prairie View Acad, 1980; BS Radiologic Technol, NE LA Univ, 1984; cp/Nat Hon Soc; Pres, Freshman & Jr Classes; Drill Tm; Pep Clb; Student Coun; Ballet Jazz, Tap; Spch Rally Contestant; Lit Rally; Staff 4 Yrs, Editor 2 Yrs, HS Annual; Bayou Radiers; Orienteering Clb; Chi Beta Gamma; r/Meth; hon/Soc of Dist'd Am HS Students; Sweepstakes Winner, NE LA Univ Sci Fair; Nav Sci Awd; St Rep, Intl Sci Fair; St Rep, Nat Yth Sci Fair; 2nd Place, Parish Voice of Dem; W/W Among Am HS Students; Intl Yth in Achmt; Commun Ldrs of Am; g/ Further Deg in Nuclear Med & Radiation Therapy.

SPIELBERGER, JOAN ELLEN oc/ Law Student; b/Mar 31, 1960; h/6308 Barrister Place, Alexandria, VA 22307; ba/Williamsburg, VA; p/Adele D Spielberger, Alexandria, VA; ed/Dipl, Devel Res Sch HS; BA, Tufts Univ; Att'g Marshall-Wytne Sch of Law, Col of Wm & Mary; pa/Law Clk, Douglass, Davey, Cooper & Coppins, Attys at Law, Tallahassee, FL, Currently; cp/Vice Justice, Phi Alpha Delta Legal Frat; r/ Jewish; hon/Grad cum laude, Tufts Univ, 1982; W/W Among Am HS Students; g/Gen Pract Atty.

SPILLER, KATHERINE QUESNEY oc/English Teacher; b/Jun 26, 1957; h/ 211 Rue Orleans Baytown, TX 77520; m/Marc Gordon; c/Justine; p/Sam and Ellen Spiller, Baytown, TX; sp/Lance and Ellie Gordon; ed/Dipl, Ross S Sterling HS; AA, Lee Jr Col; BA, SW TX St Univ; MA Cand, Univ of Houston/CLC; pa/Tchr, Sharpstown HS, 1980-81; 9th Grade Eng Tchr, Sterling HS, 1983-84; Mem: Houston Area Coun Tchrs of Eng (HACTE), 1983-; r/Jewish; hon/Phi Theta Kappa, 1976-78; Nat Eng Hon Soc, 1979-80; Dean's List, Lee Col, 1976-78; Dean's List, SW TX St Univ, 1979-81.

SPRINGER, JUSTIN KEITH oc/Student; b/Nov 25, 1965; h/5901 Southest 10th, Midwest City, OK 73110; p/W G and Faye Springer, Midwest City, OK; ed/Dipl, Midwest City HS; cp/HS Football, Baseball & Weightlifting; OK Boys St; Am Ldrship Sem Del; Nat Hon Soc; St Hon Soc; r/Ch of Christ; hon/OK Boys St, 1983; g/Deg in Math Ed; Become a Tchr.

STADIUS, RUTH NAOMI oc/Computer Operator, Legislative Correspondent; b/Jul 22, 1959; h/19-8th Street Northeast, Apartment 1, Washington, DC 20002; ba/Wash, DC; p/Mrs Ardelle Stadius, Hancock, MI; ed/Dipl, Hancock HS, 1977; AA, Suomi Col, 1979; Att'd Univ of Helsinki, Finland, 1 Yr; BA, Univ of Ctl MI, 1982; pa/Legis Corres, US Cong-man Bob Davis, MI 11th Dist,

Currently; Mem: VPres, Pres, Nat Soc of Profl Jours (Sigma Delta Phi), 1981-82; cp/Editor, Sch Newspaper, 1978-79; Mem & VPres, Student Coun, 1977-79; Majorette, 1975-77; Nat Hon Soc, 1977; Theatre, 1976-79; hon/HS Nat Hon Soc; Sports Lttr Track & Swimming Hon Student, 1977-79; Samso Soc Awd; Delta Psi Omega Theatre Awd; Most Outstg Student Coun Mem, 1981, Ctl MI Univ; W/W: Among Am HS Students, Among Students in Am Jr Cols; g/Maj in Jour w Emphasis in Public Relats, Minor in Polit Sci; Newspaper Jour.

STAFFORD, RONALD JAY oc/Professional Musician, Instructor; b/Jul 11, 1957; h/4126 North Belmont, Kansas City, MO 6417; p/Mr and Mrs Harold F Stafford, Kansas City, KS; ed/Dipl, J C Harmon HS, 1975; BMus, Univ of MO-KC, 1979; pa/Adj Instr of Percussion, MO Wn St Col; Profl Musician, Student; cp/VPres, Social Chm, Sr Marshall, Sigma Phi Epsilon; Phi Kappa Phi; Pi Kappa Lambda; Mortar Bd; KC Fedn of Musicians Local 34-627; Percussive Arts Soc; Student Rep, MO PAS St Bd; Nat Hon Soc; hon/V Chancellor for Student Affairs Hon Awd; Nat Dean's List; Col Register; g/MBA, Profl Musician, Sales Rep or Mktg Mgmt for Major Drum Co.

STAGNOLIA, CAROLE ANN oc/Information Systems Mgmt; b/Dec 11, 1961; h/1304 Fairchild Street, Cumberland, KY 40823; ba/L'ville, KY; p/Reecie Stagnolia, Cumberland, KY; ed/Dipl, Cumberland HS, 1979; BS, En KY Univ, 1983; pa/Cnslr, Harlan Co Commun Action Agy, Sum 1980; Algebra Lab Instr, Mat Sci Dept, En KY Univ, Fall 1982; Info Sys Mgmt Prog, Gen Elect Co, 1983-; cp/HS: King's Chd, Bapt Yth Grp, 1975-79; Beta Clb, 1977-79; Nat Hon Soc, 1977-79; Yrbook Staff Photog, 1979; Col: Secy 1982-83, Kappa Mu Epsilon; Phi Kappa Phi, 1983; r/So Bapt; hon/HS: Valedictorian; DAR Citizenship Awd, 1979; Eng, Jour & Sch Spirit Awds, 1979; Col: Pres S'ship, En KY Univ, 1979-83; Georgia-Pacific S'ship, 1979-83; Dean's List, 1979-83; Grad w High Distn, 1983; g/Pursue Master's Deg in Computer Sci.

STALLWORTH, EUNICE HARTENSE oc/Graduate Student in Children's Theatre; b/Jan 24, 1959; h/521 North Bethel Street, Hartselle, AL 35640; ba/Lawrence, KS; p/l F Stallworth (dec); Eva L Stallworth, Hartselle, AL; ed/Dipl, Morgan Co HS; BFA, KS Univ, 1981; pa/Staff Asst, Wlms Ednl Fund, 1978-81; Archery Supvr/Gymnastics Coach, Rock Chalk Ranch, 1978; Resident Asst, MWn Music & Art Camp, KS Univ, 1978-79; Archery Supvr, KS Univ, 1981-; Resident Asst, Naismith Hall, 1981-; KS Univ-TYP Tour Tech, 1984; Adm Asst, KS Univ Alumni Ctr, 1984; Media Model, Centron Films, 1979-; cp/Nat Archery Assn, 1972-; Am Film Inst, 1979-; Am Theatre Assn, 1982-; Lawrence Arts Ctr, 1983-; r/Judah-Christian; hon/Co-Dir, NCAA Vols for Yth, 1979-81; Coor, Intl Yr of the Child Activs, 1979; Nat Hon soc, 1975-77; Post-Baccalaureate S'ship, 1983-84; One-Wom Show (Images) MA Proj, 1981; W/W Among Am HS Students; g/MA Deg in Chd's Theatre; Chd's Theatre Perf.

STAMPER, MARCIE LYNN oc/Student; b/Sep 15, 1964; h/Rural Route 2, Box 12, Plainville, KS 67663; ba/Manhattan, KS; p/E Kent and Bette Stamper, Plainville, KS; ed/Dipl, Plainville HS, 1983; pa/Employeed by U Sch Dist # 270, 1982-83; cp/Nat Hon Soc, 1981-83; The Enterainment Com, 1979-83; Christian Ch Yth Grp, 1979-80; Lttrman's Clb (Track), 1982-83; Pres 1981-83, Mem 1979-83, Pep Clb; Forensics Tm, 1979-83; Col Chorale, 1983-; r/Christian; hon/Editor-in-Chief, Sch Newspaper; Author of Var 4-H Articles; HS Valedictorian, 1983; 4-H Key Awd & Gold Key Awd, 1981; St Forensics, 1979-83; Girl's St Del, 1982; Farm Bur Citizenship Camp Del, 1981; St Hanson S'ship Winner; W/W Among Am HS Students; g/Maj in Interior Design/Bus.

STANBACK, ROSALIND MARIE oc/Student; b/Apr 9, 1965; h/1240 Bilmark Avenue, Charlotte, NC 28213; p/Mrs Annette L Stanback, Charlotte, NC; ed/Dipl, Myers Park, 1980-83; cp/NJROTC Drill Tm, 1980-81; Capt, JV Basketball, 1980-81; Capt, Girl's Track Tm, 1980-82; NAACP, 1980-83; Jr Rep 1981-82, Sr Rep 1983, Student Coun; Latin Clb, 1981-83; VPres, Y-Teens, 1982-83; Sgt of Arms, Keyettes, 1982-83; Volleyball Tm, 1982; Co-Capt, Varsity Basketball, 1981-83; Spirit Clb, 1983; Big Sister, 1983; Computer Clb, 1983; Flag Corp, 1983; Homecoming Queen, 1983; r/Bapt; hon/Nat Beta Clb, 1981-83; Latin Hon Soc, 1981-83; Outstg Sportsmanship Awd, 1982; *The Charlotte Post* Outstg Sr, 1983; g/Attend Univ of NC-Greensboro; Maj in Bus Data Processing, Minor in Acctg.

STANOS, PETER PARDEE oc/Research Assistant; b/Feb 1, 1963; h/3661 Barber Drive, Canfield, OH 44406; p/Mr and Mrs Pardee P Stans, Canfield, OH; ed/Dipl, Canfield HS, 1981; Att'd OH Wesleyan Univ; Att'g Ygstown St Univ; pa/Concessions Mgr, Br Co-mgr, Antones Restaurant, 1979-82; Resr & Res Asst, Ygstown St Univ, 1981-; cp/HS Student Coun, 1980; Pres, VPres, Grk Orthodox Yth of Am; Hd Altar Boy & Super Rdr of Ch; Ch Yth Basketball; Ygstown CoChm & HS Chm, ACS Gt Am Smoke-Out; HS Varsit Tennis, Bowling; Hd Lab Asst; Biol Tutor; French Clb; Prom Photo Chm; BSA; Ygstown St Univ: Soccer Referee; Acad Status Com & Acad Policy Com, 1982-83; Med & Zool Couns, 1982-83; Ch Phi Frat; OH Acad of Sci Med Div; hon/Author of Pub'd Res: "Regeneration of Amputated Finger Tips," 1981 "Hormonal Effects on Sexual Discrimination," 1982; AHEPA Medal for Scholastic Excell; Nat Hon Soc; Rep, Mahoning Co at 14th Annual Yth & Sci Cong; HS Hon Roll, 4 Yrs; Spec St Dipl, 1981; W/W Among Am HS Students; Intl Yth in Achmt; Commun Ldrs of Am; g/Career in Med, Ob-Gyn.

STARKS, CLARISSA HOLLY oc/Student; b/Apr 11, 1968; h/Route 5 Box 439, Moss Chapel Road, Hartselle, AL 35640; p/Virgil Starks Jr (dec); Mr and Mrs William Glenn, Hartselle, AL; ed/Att'g Hartselle HS; cp/Delta Sigma Phi, 1983-84; Key Clb Sweethearts, 1983-84; Sr Girl Scout, Troop #155, 5 Yrs; HS Cheerldr, 1982-84; HS Girls Chorus Ensemble, 1982-84; Mt Pleasant Yg Adult Choir, 1984; r/Meth; hon/Cert of Attendance, 1979-80 & 1980-81; Gov's Phy Fitness Awd, 1982; Cheerldrs

Awd, 1983-84; g/Attend Grambling St Univ; Data Processing Sys Analyst.

STARKS, TIMOTHY LARMONT oc/Student; b/Feb 7, 1963; h/5922 South Laflin, Chicago, IL 60636; ba/Holly Springs, MS; p/Ms Mabel L Starks, Chgo, IL; ed/Dipl, Robert Lindblom Tech HS, 1981; Att'g Rust Col; cp/Alpha Phi Alpha Frat; Men Senate; Hon Roll, NAACP; r/A M E Zion; hon/Dean's List, 1982; Hon Roll, 1983; Chgo Conf S'ship, A M E Zion Ch; g/Pursue Grad Deg in Chem; Physician.

STARR, ROBIN JEANINE oc/Student; b/Apr 4, 1962; h/Route 1, Box 136, Kings Mountain, NC 28086; p/Robert Marshall Starr (dec); Grace B Starr, Kings Mtn, NC; ed/Dipl, Hunter Huss HS, 1980; Att'g, Talladega Col; cp/Tchr's Aide, 1980; Sum Intern, The Equitable Life Assurance Soc of US, 1983; cp/Treas, Allpha Kappa Alpha Sorority; r/Meth; hon/Pres S'ship, 19080-81; Dean's List, 1980-83; VPres's List, 1980-83; Alpha Chi, 1983; Beta Kappa Chi, 1983; French Awd, 1980-81; g/Pursue Master's Deg in Math.

STEELE, DEBORAH FAY oc/Student; b/Dec 5, 1964; h/803 Sinclair, Midland, TX 79701; ba/Midland, TX; p/Mr and Mrs Luther E Steele, Midland, TX; ed/Dipl, Midland HS, 1983; Att'g Mc Murry Col, 1983; pa/Pt-time Filing Secy, W S Gesell & Co, Midland, TX; cp/Sr Luther Leag; r/Luth; hon/Pres S'ship, McMurry Col, 1983; 2nd Place Typing, 1980; All-Star Cast, in One-act Play, 1981; Girls Basketball, 1980; g/Maj in Mgmt, Minor in Computer Sci; Own Retail Clothing Store.

STEELE, GINA MARLENE B oc/Executive Legal Secretary; b/Jul 7, 1961; h/2448 Laughlin #125, Dallas, TX 75228; ba/Dallas, TX; m/James; p/Monte and Katha Berry, Ennis, TX; sp/Jimmy and Johnnie Steele, Houston, TX; ed/Dipl, Ennis HS, 1979; Att'd Exec Secy Sch, 1980; pa/Exec Legal Secy: Thompson & Knight Attys-at-Law, Scotta E McFarland Esq, Brad E Mahon Esq, 1980-; cp/Social Chm, FBLA, 1979; Editorial Editor, *The Dandee Lion*, 1978-79; Perf'g Arts Clb, 1979; Twirler, Ennis HS Band, 1977-79; Hd Twirler, 1979; NIKE, 1977-78; Jets Sci Clb, 1977-79; Secy, Joy Bus, 1981-82; Var Ch Activs; r/Ch of Christ; hon/8th in St, UIL Editorial Writing, 1978; Reg UIL Competition Headline Writing, 1979; Num 1st & 2nd Hons in UIL Competition & Saxophone, 1974-79; Thespians, 1979; W/W Among Am HS Students; Intl Yth in Achmt; Yg Commun Ldrs of Am; g/Ext Study in Voice & Music; Sign Lang Courses.

STEFANSKY, TRACY LYNNE b/Oct 31, 1960; h/4332 Lakeside Drive, Fayetteville, NC 28301; p/Mr and Mrs Henry C Stefansky Fayetteville, NC; ed/Dipl, Pine Forest sR HS, 1979; BA Spch Commun, Univ of NC-Wilmington, 1983; pa/Col Intern, The March of Dimes Org, 1983; Salesperson & Shirt Printer, Artshirts, LSum 1980; Salesperson, *The Fayetteville Times & Observer*, Sum 1979; cp/HS Basketball, Tennis & Softball; Pres, HS Tri-Hi-Y; VPres, The Commun Clb (Col); The Am Mktg Assn; r/Bapt; hon/Dean's List; VA S'ship; Creat Arts Acad S'ship; Phi Kappa Phi; Grad magna cum laude, 1983; g/Public Relats Wk for Non-profit Orgs.

STEFANYSHYN, HEIDEMARIE MARTHA oc/Student; b/Feb 7, 1965; h/98 Garfield, St Paul, MN 55102; ba/Cambridge, MA; p/Mr and Mrs Michael Stefanyshyn, St Paul, MN; ed/Dipl, Derham Hall HS, 1980; BSME, MA Inst of Technol (MIT), 1984; mil/ROTC-Nav; USN, Ensign, 1984-; cp/Explorers; Ukranian Folk Dancing; HS Track; Jr Yrbook Prodn Editor; Nat Hon Soc; PLAST, Ukranian Clb; Spanish Clb; MIT Varsity Crew Tm; r/Cath; hon/MVP, MIT Wom's Varsity Crew; Nav Salutatorian; 4-Yrs Nav ROTC S'ship; Jr Achmt; W/W Among Am HS Students; Commun Ldrs of Am.

STEGENGA, SUSAN JAYNE oc/Art Educator; b/Jun 11, 1957; h/545 Mills Road, Sacramento, CA 95825; ba/Garden Grove, CA; p/Mr and Mrs Preston J Stegenga, Sacramento, CA; ed/Dipl, Encina HS, 1975; BA, Univ of Pacific, 1978; Grad Intern in Art Ed, Kennedy Ctr, Wash DC, 1979; MA, SF St Univ, 1983; pa/Art Tchr, Crystal Cathedral Acad, 1983-; Envir Sci Tchr, San Juan Unified Sch Dist, Sacramento, CA, 1982-83; 6th Grade Tchr, Melvin-Smith Prep Sch, Sacramento, CA, 1979-81; Puppetry Tchr, Kids-on-Kampus, 1981-82; Chd's TV Puppet Show Intern; cp/Panel Mem, Alliance for Arts Ed Conf; Puppetry Guild; Chd's TV Emmy Awds Judge (SF 1982); Univ of Pacific Alumni Coun; VPres, Child Advocates; Sch of Ed Spec Events Com; r/Prot; hon/TV Interviews: "Arts Alive"; "Romper Rm"; "Creativity"; Author, "The Ednl Values of Puppetry"; "Using Puppetry w Lrng Disabled Chd"; "Puppets to Tch Hlth"; Grad summa cum laude, Univ of Pacific; Phi Kappa Phi; Mortar Bd; Dean's Hon Rolls; Soroptimist Yth Citizenship Awd & 1st Place Trophy; W/W Among Am HS Students; Yg Commun Ldrs of Am; g/Univ Prof of Arts Ed; Arts Ed In-ser Dir.

STEGGEMAN, JAMES J oc/Graduate Student; b/Sep 20, 1961; h/244 Applewood Drive, Ft Mitchell, KY 41017; p/Theodore and Mary Louise Steggeman, Ft Mitchell, KY; ed/Dipl, Covington Cath HS, 1979; BS, No KY Univ, 1983; Hosp Adm Cand, Tulane Univ; pa/Centrex Operator 1979-Sprg 1982 & Oct-Dec 1982, Groundskeeping/Maintenance Sums 1982 & 1983, St Elizabeth Med Ctr S, Edgewood, KY; Machine Operator, Husky Prods Inc, Florence, KY, May-Oct 1979; cp/No KY Univ: Student Govt Rep; Univ Affairs Chm for Student Govt; Soc for the Advmt of Mgmt; Intramural Softball, Football, Volleyball, Basketball & Tennis; Commun Activs: Covington-Kenton JC's; Tulane: PRes, Sch of Public Hlth & Tropical Med; r/Rom Cath; hon/No KY Univ: Hons List, Sprg & Fall 1980; Dean's List, Sprg 1981 & 1983; Achmt S'ship, Soc for the Advmt of Mgmt; g/Grad Deg in Sys Hlth Mgmt; Hosp Adm & CEO; Adm in Nat Hospice Org.

STEIN, SUSAN ALYSON oc/Research Assistant; b/Jan 23, 1956; h/15 Walters Place, Great Neck, NY 11023; ba/New York, NY; p/Estelle Stein, Great Neck, NY; ed/Dipl, John L Miller-Great Neck N Sr HS, 1974; BA, Harpur Col, SUNY—Binghamton, 1978; MA, SUNY-Binghamton, 1980; oc/Res Asst, European Paintings Dept,

The Metro Mus of Art, NYC, 1981-; Grad Asst 1978-79, Tchg Asst 1979-80, Art Hist Dept, SUNY-Binghamton; Res Asst Curatorial Intern Sum 1977, Hilla Rebay Fellow Sum 1980, Solomon R Guggenheim Mus; cp/Col Art Assn; hon/Author, "Kandinsky & Abstract Stage Composition: Pract & Theory 1909-1912," in Art Jour, 1983; Catalogue Texts & Chronology in Vasily Kandinsky: A Selection from the Solomon R Guggenheim Mus & The Hilla von Rebay Foun, 1982; "Vasily Kandinsky Chronology," in Kandinsky Watercolors, 1980; "Edward Hopper: The Uncrossed Threshold," in Arts Mag, 1980; Essays on Burchfield, Chamberlain, Hopper and Sheeler, in The Sara Roby Collection Catalogue, 1979; hon/Phi Beta Kappa; Creat Wk in the Fine Arts Awd, 1978; Lathrop V Beale Prize in Sociol, 1978; Grad w Highest hons in Art Hist, 1978; W/W: Among Am HS Students, Among Students in Am Univs & Cols; Intl Yth in Achmt; g/Art Histn, Am & European Art, 19th & 20th Cent.

STEINER, BARBARA A oc/Promotions Coordinator; b/Dec 29, 1958; h/10401 Grosvenor Place #1423, Rockville, MD 20852; ba/Bethesda, MD; p/Mr and Mrs Louis A Steiner, Ligonier, PA; ed/Dipl, Ligonier Val Sr HS, 1976; Att'd Khema Siri Sch, Bangkok, 1977; BA, Hood Col, 1981; pa/Asst to Registrar 1981, Asst Registrar 1982, Promotions Coor 1982-, The Am Col of Cardiol; r/Epis; hon/W/W Among Students in Am Cols & Univs.

STEITZ, DAVID LEE oc/Student; b/Mar 23, 1965; h/3418 Hayman Drive, Garland, TX 75043; p/Walter and Elaine Steitz, Garland, TX; ed/Dipl, HS, 1983; cp/Nat Hon Soc; Beta Clb; Mu Alpha Theta; r/Christian; hon/Nat Coun of Tchrs of Eng Achm in Writing Awd, 1982; HS Sr of Mo Awd, Jan 1983; W/W Among Am HS Students; g/Attend Baylor Univ; Maj in Pre-Med.

STENGL, BURGESS HAGAN oc/Student; b/Jan 9, 1962; h/6001 Leisure Run, Austin, TX 78745; m/Angela T; c/Shara Anne; p/Jerry Stengl, Midland, TX; sp/Francis G Tompkins, Midland, TX; ed/Dipl, Midland HS, 1980; Att'd Midland Col; Att'd TX Tech Univ; Attg, Univ of TX; cp/Epis Yg Chmen; German Clb; TAGS; hon/Nat Hon Soc; Intl Yth in Achmt; W/W Among Am HS Students; g/BS Deg in Geology, MS Deg in Energy.

STENNER, VICKI McCABE oc/Elementary Teacher; b/Jan 4, 1956; h/305 East Waco Street, Broken Arrow, OK 74011; m/Timothy H; p/Edwin E and Gladys McCabe, Plain City, OH; sp/Charles and Patricia Stenner, Plain City, OH; ed/Dipl, Jonathan Alder HS, 1974; BSEd, Bowling Green St Univ, 1979; pa/Lrng Disabilities Tchr, Plain City, OH, 1979; Lrng Disabilites & Elem Tchr, Sapulpa, OK, 1979-82; Elem Tchr, Bixby, OK, 1982-; Mem: Assn for Chd w Lrng Disabilities; hon/Human Relats Awd 1980, Tchr of Yr Awd 1981, Wash Elem Sch; Outstg Yg Wom of Am; W/W Among Students in Am Cols & Univs; Commun Ldrs of Am.

STEPHENS, DARLENE RENEE oc/Registered Staff Nurse; b/Jan 2, 1959; h/3507-L North Elm Street, Greensboro, NC 27405; ba/Greensboro, NC; p/James and Kay Stephens, Natick, MA; ed/Dipl, Satellite HS, 1977; BS summa

cum laude, NC A&T St Univ Sch of Nsg, 1981; pa/Staff Nurse, Med/Surg Floor; RN, Staff Nurse Level I, Wesley Long Commun Hosp, 1981-; Mem: Sigma Chi Beta Chapt of Chi Eta Phi Inc, 1981-; r/Bapt; hon/Nat Hon Soc, 1975-77; Hon Awd for Most Promising Student from Moses Cone Hosp, 1980; Alpha Lambda Delta, 1978; Alpha Chi, 1980; Nat Dean's List; Intl Yth in Achmt.

STEPHENS, JOSEPH RALPH oc/Student; b/Jan 10, 1965; h/528 East Union, Magnolia, AR 71753; p/Jimmy Stephens, Barling, AR; Gloria Stephens, Magnolia, AR; ed/Dipl, Magnolia HS, 1983; Att'g So AR Univ; pa/Paper Carrier, Banner News, 1979-81; CETA, Sum 1981; cp/Magnolia HS Band, 1980-83; Mu Alpha Theta, 1981-83; Nat Hon Soc, 1982-83; Magnolia HS French Clb, 1980-82; Magnolia Jr HS Band, 1977-79; HS Pep Band, 1980-83; Tubists Universal Brotherhood Assn, 1983-; r/Prot; hon/Poems Pub's in Campus Cub Jr HS Newspaper; & Poems in HS Anthology, 1982-83; Jr HS All-Reg 2nd Band; Jr HS All-Reg 1st Band; All-Reg st Band, 3 Yrs; AR All-St Orch; AR All-St 2nd Band, 2 Yrs; Nom'd McDonald's All-Am HS Band; 1st Band in 4 Sts Bandmasters Assn; g/BA Music Ed, Band Director or Profl Musician.

STEPHENSON, ELWYN BART oc/Student; b/Jan 7, 1966; h/Route 1, Box 89, Mt Hope, AL 35651; p/Elwyn and Melba Stephenson, Mt Hope, AL; ed/Attg Sr HS; cp/HS Football, Baseball & Basketball, 1980-84; r/Presb; hon/Featured in Bama Mag; All-Area, All-Co, All-St & All-S in Football, 1983; MVP, Baseball, 1981-83; All-St, Basketball, 1983; W/W Among Am HS Students; g/Attend Col to Play Football or Baseball.

STERLING, DAVID MANN oc/Accountant; b/Sep 15, 1961; h/2075 Cabana Circle S #6, Memphis, TN 38107; ba/Memphis, TN; p/Mr and Mrs JH Sterling, Atoka, TN; ed/Dipl, Rosemark Acad HS, 1979; BS Acctg, Christian Brothers Col, 1983; pa/Fed Express, 1981-83; Acct, Deloitte, Haskins & Sells, 1983-; cp/Treas 1982, Sr VPres 1983, Delta Sigma Pi; Sr Class VPres 1983, Christian Brothers Col; Student Ct Justice; Student Discipline Com; Intramurals; Delta Sigma Pi Baseball Tm; r/Bapt; hon/HS Most Likely to Succeed & Best All Around; Delta Sigma Pi Best Pledge, Sprg 1980; Grad cum laude, Christian Brothers Col, 1983; W/W: Among Am HS Students, in Am Cols & Univs; Outstg Yg Men of Am; g/CPA, MBA, Spec in Agri-bus & EDP Acctg.

STERLING, RICHARD MAURY oc/Student; b/Jan 15, 1964; h/Route 2, Atoka, TN 38004; ed/Dipl, Rosemark Acad HS, 1982; Att'g Univ of TN-Knoxville; pa/Entrepreneur of Produce Bus, Overseeing Truck Crop Opers & Mktg; cp/Pres, Beta Clb; Pres, HS Freshman Class; VPres, HS Sophomore & Jr Class; Treas, HS Sr Class; Nat Hon Soc; FCA; Basketball; Baseball; Pep Clb; r/Presb; hon/Recip, Callie, Wood, Ross Bus S'ship to Univ of TN, 1982; W/W: Among Am HS Students, Among Am Bus Students; g/Maj in Mktg, Commodity Broker.

STEVENS, JAMES ALLEN oc/Student; b/Jul 29, 1965; h/202 Buckingham Road, Easley, SC 29640; ba/Easley, SC; p/Mr and Mrs Roy Allen Stevens,

Easley, SC; ed/Dipl, HS, 1984; Att'g Clemson Univ; r/Christian; hon/Top 10% of Class, 1981; Top 10% of Class, 1982; Palmetto Boys St Citizen, 1983; Selected as Bapt Col Scholar; W/W Among Am HS Students; g/BS Deg in Pre-Dentistry; Attend Dental & Orthodontics Sch.

STEVENSON, DANIEL CARROLL oc/Student; b/Sep 29, 1966; h/34 Monument Avenue, Bennington, VT 05201; p/Charles L Stevenson (dec); Nora C Stevenson, Bennington, VT; ed/Dipl, Inerlocken Arts Acad, MI, 1984; hon/ Piano Solo w VT Symph Orch, 1977; Winner for Compositions: "Quintet" 1977, "6 Inventions for Piano" 1978 & "Piano Quintet" 1981, Music Tchrs Nat Assn Contest, St of VT; En Div Winner for Composition "Rustic Celebration," 1979; Perf'd, Interlochen Arts Acad Piano Tour, 1983; Composition "Twilight Image for String & Orch" Perf'd at Inerlochen, 1983; Commun Ldrs of Am; g/Career in Piano Performance, Music Composition.

STEVENSON, LAURA ANN oc/ Student; b/Nov 6, 1964; h/Route 8, Box 8718 Manchester, TN 37355; p/Mr and Mrs C W Stevenson, Manchester, TN; ed/Dipl, Ctl HS, 1983; Att'g Univ of TN-Knoxville; cp/4—H Clb, 1975-83; HS Yrbook Staff, 1981-83; Student Mem, Am Home Ec Assn, 1984; Alpha Lambda Delta; Phi Eta Sigma, 1984; Active in Campus Wesley Foun; r/ Christian; hon/HS Valedictorian, 1983; Nat 4-H Dairy Foods Winner, 1983; Earned Highest Hons during Fall Qtr 1983 & Winter Qtr 1984; W/W Among Am HS Students; g/Deg in Nutrition-Food Sc, Reg'd Dietitian.

STEWART, JAMES RODNEY oc/ Student; b/Aug 20, 1966; h/209 East Petty Lane, Winchester, TN 37398; p/ Mr and Mrs Billy H Stewart, Winchester, TN; ed/Dipl, Franklin Co HS, 1984; Att'g Motlow Commun Col; cp/Nat Beta Clb, 1981-84; FCA, 1981; VPres, VICA, 1981-84; VPres, Student Coun, 1981; r/Bapt; hon/Recip of Awds from Chattanooga Reg Sci Fair: 1st Place Awd Microbiol 1981-84, Kodak Awd 1982, AF Awd 1982-84, AUS Awd 1982-84, Nav Sci Awd 1983 & 1984, USMC Best of Show Awd 1984, ASM Awd 1984, Best of Show Awd 1980, Am Dental Soc Awd 1984; HS Citizenship Awd; W/W Among Am HS Students; g/Deg in Elect Engrg, Univ of TN.

STEWART, JOHN SIDNEY oc/Student; b/Aug 26, 1964; h/Rural Route 1, Box 13-F, West Liberty, KY 41472; ba/ Morehead, KY; p/Sidney and Mary Stewart, West Liberty, KY; ed/Dipl, Morgan Co HS, 1982; Att'g Morehead St Univ; cp/Nat Hon Soc, 1978-82; Morgan Co Varsity Basketball Capt, 1980-82; Morehead St Univ Hons Prog, 1982-84; Nat Dean's List, 1982-84; Gamma Beta Phi Soc, 1983; hon/ All-NEKC Tour Selection, 1980-82; Pres S'ship to Morehead St Univ, 1982; Pres List, 1982-83; Salutatorian, Morgan Co HS, 1982; Active Page, St Senate, 1976; g/BS Deg in Elect Technol & Engrg Deg in Elect Technol.

STEWART, JULIE ANN oc/Process Chemical Engineer; b/Oct 26, 1961; h/ 181 Cascabel, Los Alamos, NM 87544; ba/Kekaha, Kauai HI; p/Mr and Mrs John N Stewart Jr, Los Alamos, NM; ed/Dipl, Los Alamos HS, 1979; BSChE,

Univ of CA-Davis, 1983; pa/Process Chem Engr, Kekaha Sugar Co, Amfac Sugar Refinery. Kauai, HI, 1983-; Engrg Asst, Gen Elect, Sum 1982; Asst Pool Mgr Sum 1981, Lifeguard 1980, Barranca Mesa Pool Assn; Engrg Asst, Univ of CA-Davis Phy Plant, Sprg 1981; Mem: Pres 1982-83, Sem Chm & Industl BBQ Chm 1981-82, AIChE; Activs Fund Chm, Oper Chm for Rush, Delta Delta Delta; Univ of CA-Davis Wom's Swim Tm; Student Chapt, AIChE; SWE HS Swim Tm; Band & Marching Band; Treas, Sophomore Class; Secy, Student Coun; Student Coun Rep; AAU Swimming; Teen-age Repubs; GSA; r/Prot; hon/Frank Gannett Newspaper Carriers S'ship; Pres Awd, Delta, Delta, Delta; Girls St, 1978; Outstg Sr Awd, 1983; W/W Among Am HS Students; Intl Yth in Achmt; Commun Ldrs of Am; Commun Ldrs of Am; g/MBA or MA in Process Control/Chem Engrg.

STEWART, KAREN ANN oc/Student; b/Sep 6, 1961; h/1217 Burleson Grand Prairie, TX 75050; p/Harrison A Stewart (dec); Bettye R Stewart, Grand Prairie, TX; ed/Dipl, Grand Prairie HS, 1980; Pvt Lessons in Modeling, Dancing, Twirling & Drama; Att'g Univ of TX-Arlington; pa/Sales Clk & Inventory, Sanger Harris Dept Store, 1980-83; Fin Aid Ofc Asst, Univ of TX-Arlington, 1983-; cp/Phi Eta Sigma, 1981; Alpha Chi, 1983; Bapt Ch Yth Choir; Hosp Vol; Polit Campaign Vol; Perf'd in Shows for Charities, Benefits for ARC, March of Dimes; hon/Dean's List, 1981; Hon Soc, 1982-83; Govt Awd, 1980; Pres Ldrship Awd, 1980; Am Pageant Awd, 1980-81; Yg Texanne Declaration of Merit, 1980; Fed of Wom's Clb Lindership S'ship, 1980-81; Panhandlenic Merit Awd, 1980; Sanger Harris Golden Awd, 1980; Tell Holder, Nat Am Sweetheart; Wom Local, St Nat Titles; 1st Female to be Elected HS Student Body Pres; HS Student Coun Del; Nat Hon Soc; Outstg Yg Wom of Am, 1983; Yg Personalities of Am; Commun Ldrs of Am; Dist'd Am HS Students; Intl Yth in Achmt; W/W Among Am HS Students; g/Career in Bus.

STEWART, LAWRENCE KEVIN oc/ Engineer; b/Dec 4, 1957; h/1212 Chadford Road, Irmo, SC 29063; ba/Columbia, SC; m/Shirley Gale; p/Mr and Mrs Leslie B Stewart, Clover, SC; Mr and Mrs Thurman Short, Clover, SC; ed/ Dipl, Clover HS, 1976; BSCE, The Citadel, 1980; mil/SC AUS Resv NG; pa/Engr, So Bell Telephone Co, 1980-; Mem: Tau Beta Pi; ASCE; SCARING; cp/Jr Employees of the Telephone Sys; Ancient Free Masons; r/Bapt; hon/Pres, Clas of 1980, The Citadel; Dist'd Mil Grad; Summerall Guards, Elite Sr Platoon, 1980; Outstg Yg Bus-man of Am; Intl Yth in Achmt; W/W Among Students in Am Univs & Cols; g/Profl Engrg Lic, MBA, Own Large Bus.

STEWART, ROSALIND A oc/Student; b/Route 1, Box 344, Atoka, TN 38004; ed/Dipl, Munford HS, 1980; BA Pre-Law, Univ of TN-Martin, 1984; cp/ Black Student Assn; Pres, Alpha Kappa Alpha Sorority; Pre-Legal Soc; Polit Sci CLb & Yg Dems; Congperson in Student Govt Assn; r/Bapt; hon/Miss Black Student Assn, 1981-83; Selected to be Student Recruiter, Univ of TN-Martin; g/Attend Memphis St Law Sch.

STIGALL, JACQULYN VAUNELL oc/Student; b/Dec 29, 1962; h/Box 8, Gleason, TN 38229; p/Mr and Mrs Billy Stigall, Gleason, TN; ed/Dipl, HS, 1981; Att'g Univ of TN-Martin; pa/Asst In Bus Affairs Dept, Univ of TN-Martin; cp/HS: Class Ofcr, 3 Yrs; Capt & Best Offense (Sr Yr), Basketball, 4 Yrs; WCMT's MVP, Sr Yr; G-Clb, 3 Yrs; Secy (Sr), Treas (Jr), Beta Clb, 3 Yrs; Pres (Jr), Sub-Reg Ofcr (Sr), FHA, 4 Yrs; Secy (Sr), Student Coun, 2 Yrs; Col: Editor, Col Yrbook; Treas 1983, Ritual Chm 1984, Zeta Tau Alpha; Little Sister, Alpha Gamma Rho Frat; Phi Chi Theta; r/Bapt; hon/HS: Ms Sr; Salutatorian; Ms Gleason Royalty; DAR Citizenship Awd; Girls St; Col: Dean's List; g/Deg in Mktg & Mdsg.

STINNETT, TERESA LYNN oc/ Admissions Secretary; b/Dec 21, 1959; h/Route 6, Box 375, Athens, AL 35611; ba/Athens, AL; p/Zane and Millanee Stinnett, Athens, AL; ed/Dipl, W Limestone HS, 1978; Att'd Calhoun Commun Col, 1978-80; BSBA, Athens St Col, 1982; pa/Wk-study Student, Calhoun Commun Col, 1978-80; Wk-Study Student, Athens St Col, 1980-82; Admissions Secy, Athens St Col, 1982-; cp/Athens St Col Clb, 1983-84; Citizens Advy Coun, Am Inst for Cancer Res; Repub Pres Task Force; US Senatorial Clb; Phi Theta Kappa; Pres, Civitans; Libn, Athens St Col Singers; Hostess for Belgian Students, Calhoun Commun Col; r/Ch of Christ; hon/Grad cum laude, 1982; Phi Theta Kappa 1979; Pi Tau Chi, 1982; Hon Prog, Calhoun Commun Col; Highest Eng Avg & Shorthand Awd, W Limestone HS, 1978; Nat Dean's List; Intl Yth in Achmt; g/Wk at Athens St Col, MBA, Pers Dir or Mgr for Small Firm.

STOCKTON, STEPHANIE KAY oc/ Student; b/Dec 1, 1965; h/Route 5, Livingston, TN 38570; p/Mr and Mrs Keith Stockton, Livingston, TN; ed/ Dipl, Livingston Acad HS, 1984; cp/HS Freshman Class Secy; FHA; Sci Clb; Beta Clb; Spanish Clb; r/Meth; hon/Ms Congeniality, Overton Co Fairest of the Fair Contest, 1983; W/W Among Am HS Students; g/Maj in Bus Mgmt & Sys Anal.

STODDARD, DARIN WESLEY oc/ Warehouseman; b/Sep 1, 1965; h/819 5000 West, West Point, UT 84015; ba/ Ogden, UT; p/James F Stoddard, West Point, UT; Justine Wilson, Ogden, UT; ed/Dipl, Ben Lomand HS, 1983; Att'g UT St Univ; pa/Warehouseman, 1981-82; Lot Boy, Mt Ogden Porsche & Audi, Sprg 1982; Warehouseman, Jasckson Dist, 1982-; cp/Nat Audubon Soc; BSA; UT Golf Assn; UT St Fish & Game; US Golf Assn; LDS Sports; r/LDS; hon/3rd Place, UT Reg Sci Fair; 1st Place, Ogden HS Sci Fair; 1st Place, Ben Lomand HS Sci Fair; High Hon Roll, Moun Ft Jr HS; Hon Roll, Ben Lomand HS; g/Deg in Wildlife Sci &/or Zool, UT St Univ.

STOKES, BRENDAN D oc/Computer Support; b/Jul 31, 1957; h/20 Northern Boulevard, Plum Island, Newbury, MA 01950; ba/Newburyport, MA; m/ Hannah-Martha; p/Mr and Mrs John F Stokes, Newburyport, MA; sp/Mr and Mrs I R Webster Jr, Newburyport, MA; ed/Dipl, Triton Reg HS, 1976; Atted, SEn MA Univ; pa/Mgr Stokes Enterprises Inc; Computer Support, Elect

Circuit Protection Div, Gould Inc, 1983-; cp/Student Trustee, Advy Coun of Exec Ofc of Ednl Affairs of Commonwlth of MA; Para-Profl Career Cnslr; St Bd of Dirs, MA Public Interest Res Grp; hon/SEn MA Univ Bd of Trustees; W/W Among Students in Am Univs & Cols; g/MBA w Concentration in Computer Sci.

STONE, LISA CAROL oc/Student, Assistant Manager; b/Jun 3, 1962; h/216 Dunstone Drive, Oroville, CA 95965; ba/Chico, CA; p/James R Stone and Carol J Gray, Oroville, CA; ed/Dipl, Las Plumas HS; Att'g CA St Univ-Chico; pa/ Exec Coor & Prodr of Musical, "Godspell," Stevenson Theatre Guild of Univ of CA-Santa Cruz, 1980-81; Asst Mgr, Shoe Stop, 1982-; Bkkpr, Conslt, Personal Rep, Inadequate Investments Co, 1982-; cp/Chapel of Faith Deliverance Ch, 1978-; Interdenom Bible Study, 1978-; Pres, Keywanettes, 1980; Life Mem, CA S'ship Fedn, 1980; Top 10, 1977 & 1980; Tennis Tm, 1977-80; Student Body, 1977-79; Class VPres, 1976 & 1978; Secy, Block LP, 1978; Ath Clb; r/Christian; hon/Jim Hastie S'ship, 1980; CA S'ship Fedn S'ship, 1980; Top 10 S'ship, 1980; Valedictorian, 1980; Exceptl Achmt Awd & S'ship, 1976; Commun Achmt Awd, 1977 & 1980; W/ W Among Am HS Students; g/BS Computer Sci & BA in Bus Adm; Sys Anal.

STORMES, TY oc/Student; b/May 31, 1962; h/Route 1, Box 530 Hackett, AR 72937; p/Buddy and Sharon Stormes, Hackett, AR; ed/Att'g Hackett Sch; cp/Hon Student; Def Capt, Football, 1983; Ch Leag Baseball, 1982-83; Co-Reporter 1984, Photogr 1983, 4-H; r/Prot; hon/Co 4-H Barbeque Winner, 1983-84; 1st Alt, 4-H St Barbeque, 1983; Gold Medal, Rdg Olympics, 1982; MVP, Football, 1982; All-Star Tm, Baseball, 1979-83; Co 4-H Record Bk Winner for Elect Proj; g/Finish HS; Become a Profl Cowboy.

STREPEK, EUGENE E oc/Banker; b/ Jan 1, 1962; h2123 W Augusta Boulevard, Chicago, IL 60622; ba/Chgo, IL; p/Edward and Rose Strepek, Chgo, IL; ed/HS Dipl, 1980; pa/Bkr, 1st Nat Bk of Chgo; cp/chgo Coun on Fgn Relats; Nat Res & Def Coun; Shedd Aquarium; Smithsonian Instn; Am Mus of Natural Hist; The Planetary Soc; Lincoln Pk Zoo Soc; Am Space Foun, Nat Space Inst; Field Mus of Natural Hist; Nat Wildlife Fedn; AAAS; hon/Nat Hon Soc, 1980; W/W Among Am HS Students.

STRICKLAND, WILLIAM GARRISON oc/Student; b/Apr 16, 1956; h/ 2703-B Wenst Linden Avenue, Nashville, TN 37212; m/Gina Sheppard; c/ William Garrison Jr; p/Mr and Mrs A L Strickland, Scottsboro, AL; sp/Mr and Mrs R M Sheppard, Scottsboro, AL; ed/ Dipl, Scottsboro HS, 1974; BS, Univ of AL-Tuscaloosa, 1978; MD, PhD, Vanderbilt Univ Sch of Med, 1984; pa/ Intern; Mem: AMA; So Med Assn; N'ville Acad of Med; cp/Vanderbilt Rep to Org of Student Reps of the Assn of Am Med Cols; Pres, Alpha Epsilon Delta, 1977; Gamma Sigma Epsilon; Pi Mu Epsilon; Phi Beta Kappa; Phi Eta Sigma; MD/PhD Com of Vanderbilt Med Sch; r/Tchr, Ch of Christ; hon/Nat Res Ser Awd, Med Scist Tng Prog; Merck Awd for Most Outstg Sr in Chem, Univ of AL-Tuscaloosa; Nat

Merit S'ship; g/Res in Hormonal Regulation of Metabolism & Mechanism of Hormone Action.

STROM, NANCY FAYE oc/Student; b/Jan 17, 1966; h/102 Winchester Court Clemson, SC 29631; p/Mr and Mrs James L Strom, Clemson, SC; ed/Dipl, D W Daniel HS, 1984; cp/Acad Editor Jr Yr, Editor-in-Chief Sr Yr, *Summit*, Yrbook; Jr Class Pres; VPres, Mu Alpha Theta, Jr Yr; Chm, Jr/Sr Planning Com; Pres, Clemson Ldrs Clb, Jr Yr; Secy-Treas, Clemson Area Yth Coun, Sophomore Yr; r/So Bapt; hon/F'ship Awd for Highest Scholastic Avg for 3 Yrs, 1981; French Excell Awd, 1981 & 1983; 1st Place, Clemson Biol Merit Exam, 1982; 3rd Place, Presb Col Math Contest, 1983; Presb Col Jr Fellow, 1983; Furman Scholar, 1983; SC Girls St, 1983; g/Deg in Engrg.

STUBBS, WILLIAM BENJAMIN III oc/Graduate Assistant; b/Jul 6, 1961; h/ 4165 Bordeaux Drive, Kenner, LA 70062; ba/Waco, TX; ed/Dipl, Bonnabel HS, 1979; BA, LA Col, 1983; MA Cand in Communs, Baylor Univ; pa/Pt-time Teller, 1st Metro Bk, 1979-83; Disc Jockey, KSYL-AM Radio, 1982-83; Asst Dorm Dir, LA Col, 1980-81; Tech Dir, Miss LA Col, 1982; Grad Asst, Baylor Univ, Currently; c/HS: Treas 1977, VPres 1978, Key Clb; Pres, Photo Clb, 1978; LA Col: Athenian Lit Soc; Alph Psi Omega; r/So Bapt; hon/LA Col Student Union Outstg Mem, 1980 & 1983; LA Student Merit Ct; Nat Dean's List; g/Wk in Public Relats.

SUFFA, NEIL FREDERICK oc/Student; b/May 22, 1964; h/7816 Accotink Place, Alexandria, VA 22308; p/Mr and Mrs Frederick W Suffa, Alexandria, VA; ed/Dipl, Ft Hunt HS, 1982; Att'g Univ of Richmond; pa/Cook & crew Chief, Ponderosa Steak house, 1980-81; Trumpet Tchr, Elem Sch Chd, 1981-82; Lifeguard & Mgr, Hamilton Pool Ser, 1982; Mgr, Ft Ellsworth Condominium Pool, Atlantic Pool Co, 1983; cp/Sr Patrol Ldr 1977-82, BSA; Ft Hunt Math Tm, 1979-81; HS Marching & Symph Bands, 1978-82; Fairfax Yth Symph, 1981-82; Reg Band (Top Band), 1980-82; Mt Vernon Swim Tm, 1970-82; r/Epis; hon/USMC Semper Fidelis Awd, 1982; Eagle Scout, 1982; Order of the Arrrow, 1981; 4th Place Backstroke, NVSL Div VI, 1981; Supts Awd for Acad Achmt, 1980; Usher, Inauguration, 1980; g/Acctg Maj; CPA.

STUTTS, PRESSLEY CAVIN JR oc/ Pastor; b/Feb 3, 1957; h/Route 1, Box 307, Shelby, NC 28150; ba/Shelby, NC; m/Jeanna Fisher; c/Pressley Cavin III; p/ James E Fisher (dec); Katherine I Benton, Flint, MI; ed/Dipl, Durand Area HS, 1975; BA, Gardner-Webb Col, 1978; MDiv, SWn Bapt Theol Sem, 1981; mil/Chaplain, USNR; pa/Pastor, New Prospect Bapt Ch, Shelby, NC, 1982-; Assoc Chaplain, Cleveland Meml Hosp, Shelby, NC, 1982-; Cert'd SS Enlargement Campaign Dir, 1983-; Preacher, Home Mission Bd, 1977; Yth Dir, 1st Bapt Ch, Salisbury, NC, 1978; Cnslr, Camp Caraway, 1976; cp/Eagle Scout, BSA, 1973; FCA, 1973-77; HS & Col, Nat Hon Soc; Chm, World Hunger Action Com, 1978-81; Pres, Student Body, Gardner-Webb Col, 1977-78; Student Govt in HS, Col & Grad Sch; Theol F'ship, 1978-81; r/So Bapt; hon/Pressley Stutts Day, City of

Durand, MI, Sep 18, 1973; 1st Place Oral Presentation Contest, Rotary Clb, 1974; Cnslr of Yr, Camp Carraway, 1976; W/ W: Among Am HS Students, Among Students in Am Univs & Cols; Intl Yth in Achmt; Personalities of S; Outstg Yg Men of Am; g/Doct of Min Deg.

SUGG, LaREE PEARL oc/Student; b/ Nov 11, 1969; h/21305 Sparta Drive, Petersburg, VA 23803; p/Cynthia Nelson Sugg, Petersburg VA; ed/Att'g Matoaca HS; cp/Pres, 9-12 Age Grp, Reporter Teen-Grp 1983, Jack & Jill of Am; Student Coun Assn; Band; Am Jr Golf Assn; US Golf Assn; hon/Most Talented, Matoaca Mid Sch, 1983; hon/ 1981 *Golf Mag*, Jr All-Am Tm; 1981 World of Jr Golf All-Am Tm; Ping Jr Golf Champ, 1981; VA St Unit of SCLA & Play Maker Fellows LTD Awd for Achmt in Excell on Nat Level, Golf, 1981; Delta Sigma Theta Petersburg Chapt Awd for Spec Hon & Recog for Outstg Achmt in Aths; 1st Place, Sprg Am-Am Golf Tourn; 1st Place, PH St Jr Class, Woodland, Golf & Country Clb; Other Golf Awds; Featured on WXEX-TV Sports, "PM Mag," WHUR-FM "Wom in Sports," *Ebony Mag*; g/Play on LPGA Tour.

SUMILAT, JAMES MARTHIN oc/ Medical Technologist, Student; b/Sep 15, 1957; h/25219 Davidson Street, San Bernardino, CA 92408; p/John and Mary Sumilat, San Bernardino, CA; ed/ HS Dipl, 1976; BS Med Technol, Loma Linda Univ, 1981; pa/Med Technol, Loma Linda Univ Med Ctr, 1981-; Vol, Set up a Lab in Belize, Ctl Am, Oct & Nov 1983; cp/Loma Linda Univ Med Technol Alumni Assn; Spritual Growth Grp; Am Soc of Clin Pathol; r/7th Day Adventist; hon/Bk of Am Math Awd, 1976; Bausch & Lomb Sci Awd, 1976; Dean's List, 1980; Grad w High Hons, 1976 & 1981; g/Lrn a Maual Skill (Mechanics); Vol Tchr.

SUNGHERA, GILBERT oc/Student; b/Sep 27, 1961; h/20682 Chaucer Lane, Huntington Beach, CA 92646; ed/Dipl, Edison HS, 1979; Att'g Univ of CA-Irvine; cp/Campus Rep/Tour Guide; Commuter Clb Advr; Interfaith Folk Choir-Dir; Acting Chm, Interfaith Liturgical Com; Interim Ofcr, Mid Earth Legis Coun; Dorm Pres; Grad Recors/ Yrbook Staff-Sect Editor; BACCHUS (Alcohol Awareness Com); Social Ecol Review Com; Social Ecol Majs Assn; Univ of CA—Irvine Alumni Assn; ACE; Assn of Envir Profls; HS Yrbook Staff; HS Marching Band; SS Simon & Jude Folk Choir; CSF Sealbearer; Quill & Scroll; ASCE; Edison Ho of Reps; hon/ Yth of Mo, Oct, 1978; Intl Yth in Achmt; W/W: Among Am HS Students, Among Students in Am Univs & Cols; Yg Commun Ldrs of Am; g/Position as Urban Planner.

SUTTON, MARY ELIZABETH oc/ Student; b/Jun 13, 1964; h/115 Southland Drive, Richmond, KY 40475; ba/ Winston-Salem, NC; p/William and Dorothy Sutton, Richmond, KY; ed/ Dipl, Model Lab Sch, 1982; Att'g Wake Forest Univ; pa/Chd's Tennis Tchr, Arlington Country Clb, Sum 1983; cp/ Fideles Soc, Wake Forest Univ, 1983; HS Newspaper Editor, 1980-82; Varsity Tennis Tm, 1979-82; Capt & MVP, Tennis, 1981 & 1982; Pres, Nat Hon Soc, 1981-82; Jr & Sr Class VPres, 1981-82; r/Presb; hon/Short Story

"Secrets," Pub'd in KCTE Essay Contest, 1982; Winner of LDC Short Story Contest, 1982; Essay Pub'd in *Footprints*, 1982; Jr Ms Scholastic Awd, 1981; 2nd Runner-up, Ch Bell Choir, Treble Choir Yth Grp, 1979-82; Optimist Yth, 1981; Chem Awd, 1981; Eng Awd, 1981-82; Jour Awd, 1981-82; I Dare You Awd, 1981; Biol Awd, 1980; Am Hist Awd, 1979; En KY Univ Achmt, 1982; Student of Mo, Mar 1981; Dean's List, Wake Forest Univ, Fall 1981 & Sprg 1983; W/ W Among Am HS Students; g/Eng Maj; Attend Law Sch.

SUTTON, MICHAEL BRENT oc/ Student; b/Sep 25, 1960; h/713 Edgewood Drive, Murfreesboro, NC 27855; p/Ben C Sutton, Murfreesboro, NC; Minnie F Branch, Sylva, NC; ed/Dipl, Sanderson HS, 1979; AA Printing Technol, Chowan Col, 1984; Att'g Rochester Inst of Technol; pa/Pt-time Produce Clk, Full-time Clk, Asst Produce Mgr 1977-82, Big Star; cp/VPres Iota Delta Chapt, Phi Theta Kappa; VICA; Chm Chowan Chapt, Data Processing Mgmt Assn; hon/Featured in *Chowanian* & *Smoke Signals*; Dean's List, 1st Sem 1982; Hon List 2nd & 3rd Sem, 1983; W/W of Am Jr Col Students; g/ Master's Deg in Printing Technol.

SUTTON, NANCY PARKS oc/Student; b/Aug 12, 1963; h/PO Box 975, Cullowhee, NC 28723; p/Mr and Mrs Lewis F Sutton, Cullowhee, NC; ed/ Dipl, Cullowhee HS, 1981; Att'g Wn Carolina Univ; r/Prot; hon/Grad HS w Hons, 1981; Kappa Delta Pi, Wn Carolina Univ; g/Maj in PE, Minor in Spanish; Tch in Public Schs; Coach Wom's Sports.

SWALLOW, CRAIG DANIEL oc/ Student; b/Apr 15, 1963; h/Rural Route 2, Box 37, LeRoy, IL 61752; p/Carl and Myrna Swallow, LeRoy, IL; ed/Dipl, LeRoy HS, 1981; Att'g IL St Univ; cp/ Treas, Pres, Student Coun; VPres, Nat Hon Soc; Secy, FFA; Soc of Acad Achmt; Drum Maj, Band; Chorus; Madrigals; MVP, Spch Tm; Football; Drum Maj, Nat FFA Band; IL St Univ Big Red Marching Machine; Knights Drum & Bugle Corps; hon/HS Valedictorian; McLean Co 4-H King; IL St Scholar; Sect 16 Star St Farmer, FFA; W/W: Among Am HS Students, in Music; Intl Yth in Achmt; g/Dir of Bands on a Sec'dy Level.

SWEAT, S SABRINA oc/Emergency Loan Assistant; h/Route 1, Box 140A, Stantonville, IN 38379; ba/Dyersburg,

TN; p/Mr and Mrs Carthel, Stantonville, TN; ed/HS Dipl, 1979; BS, Univ of TN-Martin, 1983; pa/Emer Loan Asst, Farmers Home Adm, 1983-; Trainee, McNairy Farmers Coop, Sum 1982; Farm Labor, John W Case Farm, Sprg & Sum 1981; cp/Pres 1981-82, Alpha Gamma Rho Little Sister, 1970-83; VPres 1982-83, Alpha Zeta; Agri Clb; FFA; Resource Mgmt Leag; hon/Durens Supply Co S'ship, 1979; Alpha Zeta Awd for Outstg Freshman Student, 1980; Dean's Hon List, 1979-83; Alpha Gamma Rho Sweetheart, 1982; Sam & Gladys Seigal Awd for Outstg Agri Student, 1983; W/W Among Am Col Students; g/Career w FmHA, Asst Co Supvr.

SWEENEY, AUDREY VALACENIA oc/Student; b/Aug 3, 1964; h/705 South Fairfield Road, Greenville, SC 29605; p/ Mr and Mrs Fred L Sweeney, Greenville, SC; ed/Dipl, Laurel HS, 1981; Att'g Erskine Col; cp/Pres, Yg Disciples of Christ, 1983; Recording Secy 1983-84, Student Govt Assn; Parliamentn 1983-84, Erskine Black Student Union; *The Review*, 1983-84; r/Bapt; hon/ Beta Clb, 1976-77; The Soc of Dist'd Am HS Students, 1981; Dr and Mrs James Boyce S'ship, 1983; g/Maj in Eng; Attend Law Sch; Enter Politics.

SWENSON, MAREN JOYCE oc/ Student; b/Apr 20, 1963; h/818 Avenue C West, Bismarck, ND 58501; ba/ Northfield, MN; p/Mr and Mrs Wayne Swenson, Bismarck, ND; ed/Dipl, Bismarck HS; Att'd ND St Univ, 1 Yr; Att'd ND St Univ Sum Study at Augsburg Col, Norway; Att'g Carleton Col; pa/ Norwegian Lang Instr, Concordia Lang Villages, Skogfjorden, Norway, Aug 1979 & Sum 1980; ND Chd's Theatre, "Plain People," Sum 1982; cp/Local Unge Venner Dir 1981-82, Dist #4 Secy-Treas, Sons of Norway; Nat Hon Soc; r/Luth; hon/Golden Scroll Awd, Am Acad of Achmt, 1981; Gold Cup for 9 Superior Ratings in Piano, Am Fedn of Music; Alumni S'ship, ND St Univ; g/French or Eng Maj; Grad Sch in Theatre Arts.

SWITZER, JANET DIANNE oc/Unit Secretary; b/May 4, 1964; h/2629 East 14th, Ada, OK 74820; ba/Ada, OK; p/ Mrs Gwen Switzer, Ada, OK; ed/Dipl, Ada HS, 1982; Att'g E Ctl Univ; pa/ Cashier, Long John Silvers, 1981-82; Univ Secy, Val View Hosp, Ada, OK, 1982-; cp/Contnahomas, 1979-81; Pres, Mat Maids (Wrestling), 1980-82; Rebels

Softball & Volleyball Tm, 1979-82; Hon Soc, 1979-81; FCA, 1979-80; Yrbook Staff, 1982; Ch Choir; Basketball; r/ Nazarene; hon/Mat Maid of Yr, 1979-80; Outstg Mat Maid, 1981; Typing Awd, 1979; 2nd Interscholastic Meet in Spelling, 1980; Nat Hon Roll; g/Maj in Basic Ed, Minor in Psych & Bus.

SWOOPE, SUSAN ELIZABETH oc/ Student; b/Sep 17, 1964; h/Route 3, Box 230F, Columbus, MS 39773; p/Mr and Mrs Frank G Swoope Sr, Columbus, MS; ed/Dipl, Oak Hill Acad, 1982; Att'g MS St Univ; pa/Jr Cnslr Sum 1978, Sr Cnslr Sum 1980, Assts Prog Dir Sum 1981, YMCA Camp Henry Pratt; Sales Clk, Rebecca's, Winter-Sum 1982; Sales Clk, W Point Jewelry, Christmas 1980 & 1981 & Sum 1982; c/Secy & Treas, Anchor Clb, 1979-82; Secy, Beta Clb, 1979-82; Pres & VPres, Patriotic Am Yth, 1979-82; Rep & Reporter, Student Govt, 1978-82; Panhellenic Rep, Kappa Delta Sorority, 1982-; Roadrunners Recruiting Org, 1983-; Class Ofcr, 1977-83; Campus Crusade for Christ; Newswriter, *Emphasis*, HS Paper, 1978-82; r/Presb; hon/Biol Awd, 1980; Homecoming Maid, l978 & 1980; Homecoming Queen, 1981; OHA's Jr Miss; Jr Miss Scholastic Awd; Class Favorite, 1978 & 1981; Beauty, 1982; 3rd Hon Grad Deb, So Deb Assem, 1983; Miss Jr HS of OHA, 1979; Kappa Alpha Little Sister, 1982-; W/W: Hall of Fame, Among Am HS Students; g/Maj in Eng; Tchg Cert in Eng & Spch; MA & PhD Degs; Enter Pub'g & Editing Field.

SYKES, STEPHEN McKENZIE JR oc/ Singer, Entertainer; b/Aug 24, 1960; h/ 3305 Buckeye Lane, Temple, TX 76502; ba/Sandusky, OH; p/Mr and Mrs S M Sykes, Temple, TX; ed/Dipl, Temple HS, 1978; Att'd Univ of Mary Hardin Baylor, 1979-80; Att'd Temple Jr Col, 1982; pa/ Sales Clk, H J Wilsons Sporting Goods, 1977-78; Singer, New Edition, Univ of Mary Hardin Baylor, 1978-80; Singer, Fred Waring Show, 1980-81; Singer, Amazement Pk Revue, Cedar Pt Amusement Pk Inc, 1982-; cp/Pres, Freshman Class, 1978-79; Pres, Circle K Clb, 1978-79; Mem, New Edition Contemp Christian Singing Grp; Mem of "Fred Waring's Yg Pennsylvanians," on Farewell Tour of USA, 1980-81; r/Meth; hon/ Most Talented Sr Boy, 1977-78; Sr Choir Pres, 1978; g/Finish Col Deg in Psych & Polit Sci; Continue to Pursue Career in Music & Entertainment.

T

TACKETT, DARREL S oc/High School Student; b/Jun 22, 1968; h/Box 22, Burdine, KY 41517; p/Jackie and Deanna Tackett, Burdine, KY; ed/Att'g Jenkins HS; cp/Jenkins Track Tm; Jenkins Varsity Basketball; Jenkins Varsity Football; People's Fundamental Bapt Yth Leag; Former Mem, Royal Ambassadors; Former Mem, BSA; The Explorers Clb; r/Fundamental Bapt; g/ Study Law or Computer Technol.

TANGNEY, JOAN CAROL WHITE oc/Registered Nurse; b/May 16, 1954; h/10 Woodlawn Terrace, Meriden, CT 06450; ba/Mieriden, CT; m/Alfred J; p/ Mr and Mrs Abbott W White, Norwalk, CT; sp/Mr and Mrs Walter P Tangney, Wallingford, CT; ed/Dipl, Norwalk HS, 1972; RN, Meriden-Wallingford Hosp Sch of Nsg, 1975; AS, Middlesex Commun Col, 1980; Cert in Human Sers, Tunxis Commun Col, 1981; BA Sociol, Ctl CT St Univ, 1984; pa/Reg'd Nurse; cp/Nat Hon Soc; Grace Epis Ch Basketball Tm; Pres, Future Med Corps; Alumnae Mem, Phi Theta Kappa; Unit Dose Com, Meriden-Wallingford Hosp Sch of Nsg; Sociol Clb; hon/Phi Theta Kappa; Grad w High Hons, Middlesex Commun Col, 1980; Nat Dean's List; Intl Yth in Achmt; Personalities of Am; g/Advmt in Nsg Ser Adm; Master's Deg.

TANNER, TONJA TIRESE oc/University Student; b/Feb 28, 1963; h/1505 Tanner Drive, Hartselle, AL 35640; ba/ FL, AL; p/Mr and Mrs Jeff Tanner, Hartselle, AL; ed/Dipl, Decatur HS, 1981; Att'd Calhoun Commun Col, 1981-82 & 1982-83; Att'g, Univ of N AL; pa/Pt Mallard Mini Golf, Sum 1979-83; Decatur Pk & Rec, Sums; Country Store in Hartselle, Christmas Time, 1982; cp/Student Govt Senator, 1980-82; Secy, Student Govt, 1981-82; Tau Beta Sigma Music Sorority, 1983-84; Phi Beta Lambda Bus Sorority, 1983-84; Circle-K, 1980-84; Fashion Forum, 1983-84; Drama Clb, 1983-84; Eng Clb, 1983-84; Blood Drive Chm, 1982; Chm, Jump Rope for Heart, 1983; Phi Mu Social Sorority, 1983-84; Sigma Tau Delta, 1983-84; HS Student Coun, 4 Yrs; HS Majorette (Hd Majorette Sr Yr), 4 Yrs; r/Mem, 1st U Meth Ch; hon/ Majorette, Univ of N AL, 1983-84; Homecoming Queen, 1981-82; Beauty Walk Winner, 1982-83; Miss Agri Queen, 1983-84; Dream Angel, 1983; Marching Queen, 1980; g/Maj in Fashion Mdsg, Minor in Bus & Eng.

TART, MARY KATHLEEN oc/University Student; b/Jan 13, 1963; h/730 Lockner, New Braunfels, TX 78130; ba/ Austin, TX; p/William and Genevieve Tart, New Braunfels, TX; ed/Dipl, New Braunfels HS, 1981; Att'g Univ of TX-Austin; pa/Pt-time Wk, Fam Credit Corp; cp/Beta Gamma Sigma, 1983; Alpha Lambda Delta, 1981; VPres, Phi Beta, Kinsolving, 1982-83; Nat Hon Soc, 1980-81; HS Newspaper Editor; Varsity Lttr in HS Basketball & Voleyball; Secy-Treas, FCA, 1980-81; r/Luth; hon/ Hon Roll, Fall 1981, Sprg 1982, Fall 1982; Grad summa cum laude, HS; g/ Deg in Acctg.

TATE, JAMES GREGORY oc/University Student; b/Jul 2, 1961; h/914 Speed, Memphis, TN 38107; ba/Knoxville, TN; p/Mr and Mrs Willie J Tate, Memphis, TN; ed/Dipl, Memphis Cath HS, 1980; Att'g, Univ of TN—Knoxville; pa/Pt-time Wk, WUTK-FM, Campus Radio Sta, 1982-83; cp/VPres, Assn of Black Commrs; Announcer, Campus Radio Sta, WUTK-FM; Appeared in Univ Prodn of "Streamers"; Mem, Love U Gospel Choir, Univ of TN; HS: Spch Clb; Jazz Band, 3 Yrs; Gospel Choir; r/ Bapt; g/Pursue Master's Deg in Mass Communs; TV Prodr.

TATE, SONJA LORRAINE b/Jul 1, 1958; h/622 School Street, Jefferson, MO 65101; p/Rosie L Tate, St Louis, MO; ed/Dipl, SW HS; BA Stephens Col, 1980; oc/IBM Corp; cp/Nat Hon Soc; Mem HS Track Tm; Student Coun; Jefferson City C of C; St Paul AME Ch Choir; Hypathia Hexagon, 1978-80; Resident Student Asst, 1978-80; Yth Motivation Wkshop, 1982; BPW Clb; 1st VPres, Capitol Wom's Polit Caucus, 1982-; Vol, MO Correctional Instns, 1982-; Am Public Welfare Assn, 1982-83; hon/Nat Hon Soc; Outstg Yg Wom of Am; W/W Among Students in Am Univs & Cols; g/Pursue MBA & PhD Degs.

TAYLOR, BEVERLY ANN oc/University Student; b/Nov 13, 1962; h/ Route 1, Box 211, Trezevant, TN 38258; p/Early and Mattie Taylor, Trezevant, TN; ed/Dipl, Trezevant HS, 1981; Att'g, Univ of TN—Martin; cp/Cheerldr, 1978-80; Class Pres, Hom Ec, 1980-81; Annual Staff, 1980-81; Black Student Assn, Univ of TN—Martin, 1982-83; U Collegiate Chorus, 1982 & 1983; AHEA-SMS, 1983; r/Bapt; hon/Beta Clb, 1980-81; Carroll Co Black Hon Students, 1980-81; Rehab Corp S'ship Fall, 1983; W/W Among Am HS Students, 1980-81; g/Deg in Childhood Devel Enrichment, Home Ec.

TAYLOR, BRADLEY DOUGLAS oc/ Naval Officer; b/Aug 9, 1958; h/1446 W Stuart, Fresno, CA 93711; p/Mr and Mrs Phillip O Taylor, Fresno, CA; ed/ Dipl, Bullard HS, 1976; BSEE, US Nav Acad, 1980; Grad, Nav Nuclear Power Sch, 1981-; Qualified for Supvn of Nav Nuclear Power Plant, Nav Prototype Tng Univ, 1981; mil/USN, Nuclear Submarines, Sonar Ofcr, 1st Lt, Reactor Controls Asst, Elect Ofcr, Interior Communs Ofcr; Mem: Omicron Delta Epsilon; Prodr, USNA Musical "Damn Yankees," 1980; VPres, USNA Glee Clb, 1980; USNA Prot Antiphonal Choir, 1976-80; YP Sqdrn, 1976-80; cp/Chm 1975-76, Student Advy Bd, Fresno Bd of Ed; Forensics Tm, 1973-76; CSF, 1973-76; Yth for Christ; hon/Cmdg Ofcr, USNA YP Craft; 1st USNA Class to Qualify as Ofcr of Deck of Ship of the Line; Life Mem, CSF; Deg of Excell, Nat Forensics Soc, 1975; g/Qualify as Submarine as Nuclear Engr Ofcr, Cmdg Ofcr of Nuclear Submarine; Further Grad Ed in Tech Design & Mgmt.

TAYLOR, BRETT S oc/University Student; b/Sep 30, 1965; h/154 Scarsdale Drive, Riverdale, GA 30274; ba/ Forest Park, GA; p/Mr and Mrs C M Taylor Jr, Riverdale, GA; ed/Dipl, Riverdale HS, 1983; Att'g, GA Inst of Technol; pa/Pt-time Swimming Isntr, City of Forest Pk, GA, 1982; Pt-time Clk, J C Penney, 1983; cp/Nat Hon Soc, 1982-83; Beta Clb, 1982-83; HS Cross Country, Track & Swimming Tms; hon/ J E Edwards S'ship, 1983; Most Valuable Swimmer, HS Swim Tm, 1982 & 1983; Outstg Algebra II, Trigonometry &

Calculus Awds, HS; Acad Avg Awd, HS; W/W Among Am HS Students; g/Deg in Elect Engrg.

TAYLOR, BRIAN KEITH b/Feb 24, 1962; h/11053 Roane Drive, Knoxville, TN 37922; p/Mr and Mrs James C Taylor, Knoxville, TN; ed/Dipl, Farragut HS, 1980; BA, Emory & Henry Col, 1984; pa/Dir of Mtn TO P Camp, Sum 1983; Asst in Min, Emory U Meth Ch, l1983-84; Asst in Min, Concord U Meth Ch, Sum 1982; r/U Meth; cp/HS: Pres Sophomore, Jr & Sr Classes; Col: Class Coun, 1980-84; Blue Key Hon Frat, 1982-84; VPres, Kergyma, 1983; Chp, Emphasis, 1984; hon/Acad Hon Roll, 1982-84; Armbrister Meml S'ship for Christian Character & S'ship, 1983; Clarence Hadon Strinder Awd for S'ship in Rel, 1983; U Meth Scholar, 1983; W/W Among Am HS Students.

TAYLOR, CASSANDRA ANN oc/ Music Instructor, Speech and Drama Coach; b/Dec 15, 1961; h/Route 1, Box 360, Cadiz, KY 42211; ba/Washington Col, TN; p/Wallace W Taylor (dec); Elizabeth Carr Taylor, Cadiz, KY; ed/ Dipl, Trigg Co HS, 1979; BME, Murray St Univ, 1983; pa/Music Instr, Spch & Drama Coach, Wash Col Acad, 1983-84; Mem: Bd Mem, So KY Indep Theatre; Sigma Alpha Iota; KY Ed Assn; Nat Conf of KY Music Tchrs Assn; Nat Assn of Dancers & Artists Affil'd; cp/Trigg Co Hist Soc; r/Bapt; hon/Murray St Music Dept S'ship, 1979-83; Bea Farrell Music S'ship, 1983; Roy McDonald S'ship, 1979; HS Hon Grad, 1979; FHA St Ofcr, 1978-79; Col Hon Grad 3.4 of a Possible 4.0 GPA; Outstg Yg Am; g/ To Tch the Joy & Apprec of Music to Students; Pursue Master's Deg.

TAYLOR, MARY LYNNETTE oc/ College Student; b/Oct 1, 1966; h/Route 1, Box 147-A, Double Springs, AL 35553; p/Lonnie H and Rosemary Taylor, Double Springs, AL; ed/Dipl, Winston Co HS, 1984; Att'g, Walker Col; cp/Beta Clb; Student Action for ed; Student Govt Assn; Students for Christ; Lib Clb; Sci Clb; Winston Co HS Band; r/Bapt; hon/Princess of Hearts, 1981; Miss Cent, 1983; Typing II Awd & Perfect Attendance Awd, Grades 1-11 (Except for 3rd & 4th); Participant, Miss AL Agri, 1983; g/Attend Univ of AL; Pursue Maj in Law, Minor in Drafting.

TAYLOR, MICHAEL LOUIS oc/ College Student; b/Mar 26, 1960; h/ Route 7, Box 677, Easley, SC 29640; ba/ Same; p/Reside in N Wilkesboro, NC; ed/Dipl, Cary HS, 1978; AA, Anderson Col, 1982; Att'g, Furman Univ, Greenville, SC; Siloam Bapt Ch, Powdersville, SC; r/Bapt; hon/Phi Theta Kappa; Gamma Beta Phi; g/Deg in Phil; Attend Law Sch; Write A Book of Phil.

TAYLOR, NANCY ALINE oc/Student; b/Sep 23, 1957; h/4600 Jackson Boulevard # 178, Columbia, SC 29209; ba/Columbia, SC; p/K W And Elizabeth Taylor, Sumter, SC; ed/Dipl, Sumter HS, 1975; Att'g, Millie Lewis Modeling Sch, Columbia, SC; Att'g, Bailey Fine Arts (Dancing), Columbia; Att'd, Sumter Area Tech, 1981; Bus Deg Cand, Midlands Tech, Columbia; pa/Asst Cashier 1983, Loan Admr 1981, Bkkpr, Collection Dept, Installment Loans Receptions, Adm Asst 1974-81, SC Nat Bk; Mem: Columbia Fin Assn; Am Inst of Bkg; VPres, Sumter Credit Wom, 1981; cp/Sumter YMCA; Sumter Little

Theatre; Columbia Ath Clb; r/Luth; hon/Cheerldrs, Sumter HS, 1970-75; g/ Pursue Ed; Complete Bus Deg; Modeling & Dancing.

TAYLOR, TERESA GAIL oc/University Student; b/Oct 9, 1964; h/220 West South, Dyer, TN 38330; p/Mr and Mrs Philip Taylor, Dyer, TN; ed/Dipl, Gibson Co HS, 1983; pa/Wk Study Employee in Intl Progs, Univ of TN-Martin; cp/Student TN Edn Assn; Treas (Sr Yr), Beta Clb, 4 Yrs HS; Editor, *Pioneer*, Gibson Co HS Yrbook, 1982-83; r/Bapt; hon/Del, Vol Girls St, 1982; Miss Gibson Co HS, 1983; Most Likely to Succeed & Most Dependable, HS Sr Yr; Recip, 2 US Nat S'ships; Soc of Dist'd HS Students; W/W Among Am HS Students; g/Maj in Elem Ed; Tchr.

TEAGUE, ALANA DELISE (DEESE) oc/University Student; b/Jan 3, 1963; h/ Route 2, Box 263C, Ramer, TN 38367; ba/Blue Mtn, MS; p/Mr and Mrs Benny H Teague, Ramer, TN; ed/Dipl, McNairy Ctl HS, 1981; Att'g, Blue Mtn Col; pa/YMCA, Corinth, MS; Clk, Teague's Grocery; Cnslr, Blue Mtn Col Basketball Camp; Ofc Wkr, Patrick Home Ctr Inc; cp/Beta Clb, 6 Yrs; Pres, Pep Clb, Christian Yth Org; Pres, FTA; VPres, BMC Sophomore Class; Exec Coun, Bapt Student Union; Gtr Coun; PEMM Clb; Eng Clb; Treas, Student Govt Assn; r/Bapt, Ramer Bapt Ch; hon/ Ideal Student, 1980; Eng Awd, 1980 & 1981; Drama Awd, 1981; Algebra Awd, 1979; World Hist Awd, 1981; Homecoming Rep, 1978-80; Acctg Awd, 1980; Adv'd Acctg Awd, 1981; Sprg Fest Maid & Field Day Maid, 1983; Most Ath & Class Favorite, 1981-82; Hall of Fame, 1981; Top 10 GPA, 1981; Outstg Softball Player, 1978; Basketball Awds, 1976-83; Softball Awds, 1975-83;; Best All-around 4th Awd, 1977; Pres List, 1982-83; Full Basketball & Softball S'ship, Blue Mtn Col, 1982-85; Soc of Dist'd Am HS Students; W/W Among Am HS Students; g/Maj in Eng, Minor in Bus Adm; Attend Grad Sch in Acctg; CPA.

TEDDER, STEPHEN DAVID oc/Golf Shop Assistant; b/Sep 13, 1966; h/3414 Old Onslow Rd, Greensboro, NC 27407; ba/Greensboro, NC; p/Dewey and Dora Tedder, Greensboro, NC; ed/ Dipl, HS; pa/Grill Person, Bojangle's Inc, 1982; Bag Boy, Bestway Inc, 1982-83; Golf Shop Asst, Sedgefield Country Clb, 1983-; cp/Pres, Nat Hon Soc, 1983-84; Beta Clb; Pres, French Clb, 1983-84; French Nat Hon Soc; Jr Civitans; High IQ Tm; Meth Yth F'ship; Teen-age Repubs; Sect Editor, HS Yrbook Staff; NC Leag of Math; Continental Math Leag; Meth; hon/Acad Achmt Awd, NC A&T Univ, 1982-83; Achmt Awd, St Andrews Col Sci Olympiad, 1982-83; Achmt Awd, Appalachian St Univ Sum Sci Prog, 1982; NC Gov's Sch, 1983; Sch Rep to NC Close-up & YLA 1982-83; Chief Marshall, 1983; Semi-finalist, NC Sch of Sci & Math, 1982; W/W Among Greensboro Yth; g/ Maj in Chem, Attend Med Sch, MD.

TEEL, JOE DEWAYNE oc/University Student; b/Mar 24, 1963; h/PO Box 21, Wayne, OK 73095; p/Mr and Mrs Elva D Teel, Wayne, OK; ed/Dipl, Wayne High, 1981; Att'g, OK St Univ, 1981-; pa/Printer's Asst, Tyler & Simpson Co, Norman, OK, Sums 1982 & 83; cp/ Treas, Alpha Tu Alpha, 1984; Treas

1983, Pres 1984, OK St Univ FFA; Chm, Nat Col FFA Wkshop, 1984; r/Ch of Christ; hon/Pub'd in *Gtr Nat Soc of Poets Inc*, 1981; Outstg Col FFA, OK St Univ, 1984; Royal Blue Awd: A Commitment to Excell, OK St Univ, 1984; Cert of Apprec, Nat FFA Ofcr Tm, 1984; Nom for Outstg Men of Am, US JC's, 1984; Ldrship Devel Awd, OK St Univ, 1982; Hon Page, OK Senate, 1981; FFA Star Chapt Farmer Deg 1979-81, FFA St Farmer Deg 1981, OK FFA; W/W Among Am HS Students; Outstg Names & Faces; Intl Yth in Achmt; Yg Personalities of S; g/Complete BS Deg in Agri Ed & Animal Sci; HS Agri Tchr.

TEICHMILLER, CHRIS DEWAYNE oc/Student-Athlete; b/Sep 24, 1962; h/ Route 6, Box 412, Hartselle, AL 35640; ba/Birmingham, AL; p/Jerry and Betty Teichmiller, Hartselle, AL; ed/Dipl, Morgan Co HS, 1980; BS, Univ of AL-B'ham, 1984; pa/Res Asst, Dept of Biol, Sum 1982 & 1983; cp/Pitcher, Univ of AL-B'ham Baseball Tm, 1980-84; AL Chapt, Alpha Epsilon Delta, 1983-84; Omicron Delta Kappa, 1983-84; Pi Kappa Phi, 1983-84; r/U Meth; hon/ Univ of AL-B'ham S'ship, 1980-82 & 1982-84; Ath S'ship in Baseball, 1980-84; Hon Mention, Acad All-Am, Col Sports Info Dirs of Am, 1983; Soc of Dist'd Am HS Students; Hon Roll, 1979-80; W/W Among Am HS Students.

TEMPLE, JOHN (JAY) WALTER III oc/University Student; b/Oct 5, 1961; h/900 West Pearsall, Dunn, NC 28334; ba/Chapell Hill, NC; p/Mr and Mrs J W Temple Jr, Dunn, NC; ed/Dipl, Dunn HS, 1980; Att'g, Univ of NC-Chapel Hill; pa/Sum Employmnt, Dunn Auto Parts Co Inc; cp/Univ of NC Pre-Law Clb; Student Coun Pres, Dunn HS; Editor-in-Chief, Dunn HS *Echo*; Jr Clas Pres; Harnett Co Student Advy Coun Chm; Pres, Dunn Yth Advy Coun; Pres, Key Clb; CYF; hon/Morehead Merit S'ship; HSS Valedictorian; Rotary Intl Study Abroad Nom; Gov's Sch; Boys St; Univ of NC London Study Abroad Prog; Whitfield Intl S'ship Nom, Wesley Foun; W/W; Intl Yth Achmt; g/Grad from Law Sch & Become an Atty in NC.

TERRY, KAREN MICHELLE oc/ Doctoral Candidate; b/Feb 9, 1960; h/ 104 Bennett Drive, Darlington, SC 29532; p/Amos and Helen Terry Jr, Darlington, SC; ed/Dipl, Walter E Stebbins HS, 1977; BS, TN St Univ, 1981; MA, OH St Univ, 1983; Doct Cand in Clin Psych; mil/USAF, 2nd Lt; pa/Ofce Aid, TN St Univ, 1977-78, 1978-79; Adm Wkr, Wright-Patterson AFB, 1978; Cnslr, US Dept of Agri, 1980; Grad Tchg Asst Psych Dept 1982-, Ofc Asst 1983-, OH St Univ; Mem: Mem 1977-, Pres 1978-79, Alpha Lambda Delta; Pres 1980-81, Treas 1979-80, Gamma Beta Phi; VPres 1980-81, Alpha Kappa Mu; Sect Editor, TN St Univ Yrbook Staff, 1979-80; Treas 1981-82, VPres 1982-83, OH St Univ Black Grad Students in Psych; r/ U Meth; Alpha Kappa Mu Grad Sch S'ship, 1981; USAF Dist'd Mil Grad, 1981; Dean's List, 1980; OH St Univ Grad Fellow, 1981; W/W Among Students in Am Univs & Cols; Outstg Yg Wom of Am; g/Clin Psych USAF.

THARRINGTON, VICKI LYNNE oc/University Student; b/May 7, 1963; h/106 Castle Drive, Smithfield, NC

27577; ba/Greenville, NC; p/Harold & Carolyn Tharrington; ed/Dipl, Smithfield-Selma Sr HS; Att'g E Carolina Univ; cp/Mem, Perf'g Arts Dept; Ofcr, Keywanettes; Nat Hon Soc; Feature Twirler & Hd Majorette, Smithfield-Selma Sr HS; Ofc Asst; SS Acteens, Yth Grp & Choir, Sharon Bapt Ch; Performer, Neuse Little Theatre; Nat Dance & Twirl Tm; Vol Performer at Rest Homes; Civic Grps; Cablerama March of Dimes TV; Instr, Wheel Chair Dance Therapy at Nsg Ctr; Former Mem Juniorettes; Wk w Retarded Chd; r/Att'd Gov's Sch of NC in Dance, Sum 1980; Nat Hon Soc; Crowned Miss NC Chamr, 1982; Recip Num Awds for Baton & Dance; Highest Awd, "Ser Aide," for Mision Wk; Instr of Baton & Dance for Lane Dance Acad; Homecoming Ct, Smithfield-Selma Sr HS; Dean's List; Gamma Beta Phi; Miss Johnston Co, 1982-83; 4th Runner-up, Miss NC Pageant & Preliminary Swinsuit Winner, 1983; g/Deg in Elem Ed, Tch in Public Schs, Tch & Own Dance Studio.

THELEN, TEDD M oc/Cast Member; b/Jun 1, 1962; h/1912 Sergeant, Joplin, MO 64801; p/Mrs and Mrs Charles Thelon, Joplin, MO; ed/Dipl, Meml HS, 1980; Att'g, MO So St Col; pa/Cast Mem, "Up with People,"; Ofce of Career Planning & Placement, MO So St Col, 1980-83; cp/VPres, Student Senate, 1983; Campus Activs Bd; Computer Sci Leag; Marching & Concert Bands; VPres Wesley Foun 1983, Chancel Choir, 1st U Meth Ch; r/U Meth; hon/ Kiwanis S'ship; Dean's List; Now Crusade Mission Trip to Colombia, S Am; Cast of "Up w People," 1983-84; W/W Among Students in Am Cols & Univs; g/Career in Travel Indust or Computer Sci.

THELEN, TODD S oc/Cast Member; b/Jun 1, 1962; h/1912 Sergeant, Joplin, MO 64801; p/Mr and Mrs Charles Thelen, Joplin, MO; ed/Dipl, Meml HS, 1980; Att'g, MO So St Col; pa/Cast Mem, "Up with People," 1983-84; Computer Ctr, MO So St Col, 1980-82; Contract Freighters Inc, Joplin, MO, 1982-83; cp/Pres, MO So St Col, Computer Sci Leag, 1982-83; Student Senate; Campus Activs Bd; Marching & Concert Bands; Wesley Foun, Ch Chancel Choir, U Meth Ch; r/U Meth; hon/ Outstg Computer Sci Student, 1982-83; Regents S'ship; Dean's List; Now Crusade Mission Trip to Colombia, S Am, 1980; Cast of "Up w People," 1983-84; W/W Among Students in Am Cols & Univs; g/Grad Wk in Computer Sci Field.

THERIAULT, CARLA MARIE oc/ University Student, Real Estate; b/Sep 15, 1961; h/14 Page Avenue, Caribou, ME 04736; ba/Bangor, ME; ed/Dipl, Caribou HS, 1979; AS, Endicott Col, 1981; Fundamentals of Profl Selling Sem, 1982; Att'g Univ of ME—Orono; pa/Queen City Cent 21; Brokerage Wk, Securities & Real Est; cp/HS Class Rep; Key Clb; Nat Hon Soc; Drama Clb; Vol for Blood Drives, Muscular Dystrophy & Heart Fund; Phi Theta Kappa; Col Blood Drives; Globe Players; YMCA Nursery Sch Aid; Biblical Res; hon/ Dean's List; Nat Dean's List; Intl Yth in Achmt; Commun Ldrs of Am; g/To Own a Small Fashion Boutique for Ladies Apparel.

THESENVITZ, MICHAEL DEAN oc/ Student; b/Oct 7, 1966; h/Route 2, Box 62, Inola, OK 74036; ba/Inola, OK; p/ Mr and Mrs Larrie Thesenvitz, Inola, OK; ed/Dipl, Inola HS; cp/Nat Hon Soc; St Hon Soc; German Clb; hon/Nat Merit Semifinalist, 1983; Rep to Gov's Day of Ldrship, 1981; Soc of Dist'd Am HS Students; Intl Fgn Lang Awds; W/W Among Am HS Students; g/Maj in Info Sys.

THOMAS, CHERYL JANINE oc/ University Student; b/Sep 28, 1961; h/ 3906 Village Drive, Fayetteville, NC 28304; p/Sam H Thomas, Fayetteville, NC; Peggy W Edge, Fayetteville, NC; ed/Dipl, Douglas Byrd Sr HS, 1979; Att'g Appalachian St Univ; pa/Pt-tme Waitress, Chestnut Mill Seaford Rest, Fayetteville, NC; cp/Student Govt Assn Senator, 1980-81; People Editor, Douglas Byrd Sr HS Annual, *The Aquila"*; *Crim Justice Clb; Charter Mem, Appalachian Chapt of Crim Just Hon Soc; Instrnl Asst Devel Math, 1982; r/Bapt; hon/Dean's List, Fall 1981, Sprg 1982; Charter Mem Appalachian St, Nat Crim Justice Hon Soc; g/Pract Crim Law or Corp Law.

THOMAS, CHRISTY LYN oc/Student; b/Jun 4, 1968; h/1738 East North Street, Greenville, SC 29607; p/Mr and Mrs David C Thomas, Greenville, SC; ed/Att'g, J L Mann HS; cp/Chd's Choir Pianist; Acteens; Pres & VPres of Mktg 1982-83; Jr Achmt; Jr Civitan Chaplain, 1983-84; Nat Jr Hon Soc; Volleyball Tm, 1982-83; r/So Bapt; hon/S Carolina St Yth Bible Drill Winner, 1983; Top 10 in Sewing Contest at Anderson Col, 1981-83; Outstg Home Ec Student, 1983; Superior Rating, Nat Piano Tchrs' Guild, 1983; Participant, Duke Univ Talent Search, 1981; 50 Hr Pin, Candystriping, 1982; g/Pursue Deg in Home Ec; Homemaker.

THOMAS, DERRICK LeROY oc/ University Student; b/Mar 8, 1965; h/ Route 2, Rebecca Drive, Paducah, KY 42001; p/Charles and Mary Anna Thomas, Paducah, KY; ed/Dipl, HS; cp/ NAACP Yth Branch; Student Coun VPres; FCA; Yg Men's Usher Bd (Ch); r/Bapt; hon/All St Linebacker, 1981-82 & 1982-83; Atty Gen, Boy's St, 1982; Edwin T Gunter Acad Awd, Basketball, 1983; Gus Hank IV Meml Awd in Track, 1983; 1st Place in St Shot Put, 1982 & 1983; Yth Salute Awd for Recog of Scholastic & Ldrship Ability; The Sullivan MVP Awd for Football, 1982; Soc of Dist'd Am HS Students; Outstg HS Aths in Am; Am Outstg Names & Faces; g/Deg in Bus Adm & DPQA.

THOMAS, JOHN CHARLES oc/ Crisis Line Counselor; b/Oct 14, 1959; h/Lot 56 501 Trailer Court, Lynchburg, VA 24501; ba/Lynchburg, VA; p/Clyde M Thomas Sr, Myrtle Beach, SC; ed/ Dipl, Roxbury HS, 1977; BS 1981, MA 1984, Libery Bapt Sem; Evangel Tchr Tng Assn, 1984; pa/Crisis Line Cnslr; Security Ofcr, 1981-83, Cook, Bonanza, 1979-81; cp/VPres, Student Govt Assn, Liberty Bapt Sem; Student Mem, VA Psychol Assn, 1980-81; Evangel Tchr Tngl Clb; r/Bapt; hon/Nat Hon Soc, 1981; Dean's List, 1981-84; Cand, Outstg Yg Men in Am; g/Pursue PhD, Start Pvt Pract Cnslg Ctr.

THOMAS, LAWRENCE DALE oc/ Electronics Engineer; b/Jun 26, 1959; h/ Huntsville, AL; ba/MSFC, AL; p/Mr and Mrs L D Thomas, Albertville, AL; ed/

Dipl, Albertville HS, 1977; BSE, Univ of AL-Huntsville, 1981; MSIE, NC St Univ, 1983; pa/Elects Engr, NASA, MSFC, AL, 1983-; Mem: IEEE; IIE; Phi Kappa Phi; Tau Beta Pi; cp/Deacon, Alder Sprgs Presb Ch; r/Presb; hon/ Author, "Enhanced Automatic Spch Recog Reliability Through the Use of Aided Vocab Selection," in *Proceedings of Voice Data Entry Sys Applications Conf*, 1983; Soc of Mfg Engrs Grad F'ship; Werner von Braun S'ship, 1981; Engrg Student of Yr, Univ of AL-Huntsville; W/W in Am Cols & Univs; Intl Yth in Achmt; g/PhD in Elect Engrg; Pursue Career in Acad Res & Tchg.

THOMAS, LINDA FAYE oc/Medical Secretary/Receptionist; b/May 21, 1963; h/Route 2, Box 652, Troutville, VA 24175; ba/Buchanon, VA; p/Charles Walter and Linda Ruff Thomas, Troutville, VA; ed/Dipl, James River HS, 1981; AA, Nat Bus Col, 1983; pa/Med Secy/ Receptionist, Dr Margaret Hagan, 1983-; cp/Former Pres, Future Secys Intl; r/Bapt; hon/Cert of Dean's List, Nat Bus Col; Pin, ARC Vols; Pin, Future Secys Intl; Plaques, Nat Dean's List; W/ W Among Students in Am Jr Cols; g/ Become a Cert'd Profsl Secy.

THOMAS, LYLE BLAINE oc/Student; b/Sep 16, 1966; h/441 Walnut Street, Cedartown, GA 30125; p/John and Sara Anne Thomas, Cedartown, GA; pa/Trombone Player in Profl Dance Band; cp/Treas, Ch Yth Grp, 1982-83; Treas, German Clb, 1981-82; Sci Clb, 1980-83; Math Clb & Math Tm, 1980-83; Drama Clb, 1982-83; r/Meth; hon/Excell Awds: Algebra, 1981; Geometry, World Hist, German I, 1982; Band & German II, 1983; Att'd, Brevard Music Ctr, 1982; Gov's Hon Prog, 1983; g/Pursue Study in Math &/or Music.

THOMAS, NICHOLAS P oc/Project Engineer; b/Jun 26, 1958; h/3650 East 1st Street #5, Long Beach, CA 90803; ba/La Habra, CA; p/G P Thomas, Ft Collins, CO; Lucinda Thomas, Ft Collins, CO; ed/Dipl, Poudre HS, 1976; BS, CO St Univ, 1981; 1 Yr Study, ITESM, Monterey, NL, Mexico; oc/Project Engr, Chevron, USA, 1982-; Mem: Soc of Petro Engrs; cp/Spks Spanish, Russian, Portugues; Plays French Horn, Ft Collins Symph Orch & CO St Univ Brass Quintet; Nat Ski Patrol; Pres, AIAA & Engrg Sci Soc, CO St Univ; Perf'g Arts Coun; hon/Voted Outstg Sr in Engrg Sci; Tau Beta Pi; Creat & Perf'g Arts S'ship; Dept of Engrg S'ship for Study in Mexico; g/Career in Engrg.

THOMAS, NINA NICHELLE oc/ Student; b/Jul 29, 1967; h/1744 West 79th Street, Chicago, IL 60620; p/Willie and Katie Thomas, Chgo, IL; ed/Att'g, Acad of Our Lady HS; cp/Student Coun; Mu Alpha Theta; French Clb; Treas, Blue Magic 4-H Clb; Sr Homecoming Pom Pom; Attendance Ofc Aid; Concert Choir; r/Bapt; g/Pursue Career in Math, Engrg, Computer Programming or Acctg.

THOMAS, REGINALD C oc/University Student; b/Sep 26, 1963; h/Route 3, Box 215, Huntington, TN 38344; ba/ Jackson, TN; p/Mr and Mrs James L Thomas, Huntington, TN; ed/Dipl, Huntington HS, 1981; Att'g Union Univ; cp/Pres Student Body, Union Univ, 1983-84; Pres Freshman Class, 1981-82; Pres Sophomore Class, 1982-83; VChm Existing Indust Com,

Town of Huntington, TN, 1981; Union Univ Student Foun; Andrew T Tip Taylor Pre-Legal Soc; Min Assn; Student Govt Assn; r/Bapt; hon/Rotary Clb Sers Awd, 1981; Good Citizenship Awd, 1981; Selected, Campus Favorite, Union Univ; Intl Yth In Achmt; g/Attend Seminary & Pursue MA & Doct; Become Pastor of Large Urban Ch.

THOMAS, SABRINA BABETTE oc/ Junior Analyst; b/Feb 19, 1961; h/200 North Negley Avenue, Apartment G47, Pittsburgh, PA 15206; ba/Pgh, PA; p/ Joshua Jr and Rose Lee Thomas, Northport, AL; ed/Dipl, Summerville, HS, 1979; BBA Computer Based Info Sys, Howard Univ, 1983; pa/Jr Analyst, Alcoa, 1983-; Mem: Assn for Computing Machinery; Computer Based Info Sys Soc; cp/Mu Alpha Theta; Beta Clb; Nat Hon Soc; Marching Band; Color Guard; Beta Gamma Sigma; r/Bapt; hon/Beta Gamma Sigma; GEICP Achmt Awd; Nat Dean's List; g/Position as Sr Sys Analyst in Computer Firm.

THOMAS, VICKI LYNN oc/University Student; b/Dec 8, 1961; h/118 West Van Burne, Centerville, IA 52544; p/ Ernest Thomas, Centerville, IA; Marion Thomlinson, Summersville, MO; ed/ Dipl, Centerville HS, 1980; AA, Indian Hills Commun Col, 1982; Att'g NE MO St Univ; pa/Pt-time Acctg Clk, IA So Utilities; cp/HS Track & Volleyball Tms; Ofc Ed Assn; hon/Homemaking Cert; Cert of Proficiency, Typing; Shorthand Proficiency Cert; Gregg Shorthand Awd; W/W Among Am HS Students; Intl Yth in Achmt; Commun Ldrs of Am; g/Degs in Data Processing & Acctg.

THOMASON, ANITA LYNN oc/ Nursing Student; b/Jul 27, 1965; h/ Route 2, Box 130, Mooresboro, NC 28114; p/Mr and Mrs Buddy Thomason, Mooresboro, NC; ed/Dipl, Chase HS; Att'g, Gardner-Webb Col; cp/Mem 1980, VPres 1981, Treas 1982, Keywanettes; Mem 1980-82, Pres 1981, Band; Mem 1981-82, Treas 1982, Jr Civitan Clb; Sr Rep 1982, Mem 1981-82, Beta Clb; French Clb, 1981; r/Prot; hon/ French I Awd, 1980; World Cultures Awd, 1980; Outstg Sophomore in Band, 1980; French II Awd, 1981; John Phillip Sousa Aws, 1981; UNC Book Awd, 1981; Jr Marshall, 1981; Adv'd Biol Awd, 1981; Acad Awd, 1982; Outstg Sr in Band, 1982; Grad Spkr, 1982; W/W in Am HS Students; g/BS Deg in Nsg.

THOMPSON, AMANDA YVETTE oc/Student; b/Mar 3, 1967; h/2500 Linkwood Place, Charlotte, NC 28208; p/Mr and Mrs Woodrow Thompson, Charlotte, NC; ed/Att'g Harding HS; cp/ Student Class PRes, 1983-84; Hon Soc Pres, 1984-85; Student Class Rep, 1982-84; Red Cross Clb, 1982-84; French Clb, 1982-85; Keylite, 1983-85; Imperatore, 1984-85; Ass Chief Marshall, 1983-84; Chief Flag Girl, 1982-85; Homecoming Attendant, 1983; Softball Tm, 1982-84; Flag Squad, 1982-85; Band, 1982-85; Basketball, 1982-83; Debate Tm, 1982-84; Close-up Org, 1984; Student Coun, 1982-84; Big Brother & Sisters, 1983-84; Sci Clb, 1983-84; r/Presb; hon/Gov's Sch, 1983; Mem & Citizenship Awd, DAR, 1984; Carolina Book Awd, 1984; Hon Soc, 1984-85; I Dare You Book Awd, 1984; Att'd "Med as a Career" Session, Bowman Gray, 1984; Hugh O'Brien Ldrship Awd, 1983; Recip, 2 Lttrs in

Softball, 1983-84; g/Maj in Child Psych, Univ of NC-Chapel Hill.

THOMPSON, BOBBY GAINES JR oc/University Student; b/Nov 28, 1962; h/15 Post Oak Road, Greenville, SC 29605; p/Mr and Mrs Bobby G Thompson Sr, Greenville, SC; ed/Dipl, Greenville HS, 1981; Att'd GA Inst of Technol, 1982; Att'g Univ of GA; pa/Pt-time Cut-off Saw Operator, Steel Heddle Mfg Co, 1981; Pt-time Landscaper, 1983; r/Prot; cp/BIFTAD (Outstg Overall Achmt); Alpha Epsilon Delta; Phi Eta Sigma; Gamma Beta Phi; Tau Kappa Epsilon; HS Student Coun; Student Body VPres, 1981; HS Inter-High Coun; HS Band; HS Football, Tennis & Wrestling Tms; Nat Hon Soc; HS Math & Sci Tm; SC Wn Reg Band; Greenville All-Co Band; Jr Engrg Tech Soc; FCA; Horticulture Clb; HS Pep Clb; r/Prot; hon/Hon Prog, Univ of GA; Nat Merit Commend Student, 1980; Salute to Ed Awd, 1981; Palmetto Boy's St, 1980; Gov's Sch Alt, 1980; Nat Sci Essay Contest Runner-up, 1980; Wofford Col Scholar, 1980; Presb Jr Col Fellow, 1980; HS Hall of Fame, 1981; Highest GPA Among HS Aths; Earned 6 Block Lttrs, 1978-81; SC Solo & Ensemble Superior Rating (Trumpet), 1978-79; J E Sirrine S'ship, 1982-85; W/W Among Am HS Students; Intl Yth of Achmt; g/Pursue Grad Studies in Med; Become a Phys.

THOMPSON, BRETRAN R oc/Law Student; b/Dec 12, 1958; h/1824 Walker Avenue, Memphis, TN 38114; ed/Dipl, Whitchaven HS; Att'g Univ of TN; pa/Policy Planner, TN Val Auth; Ast Hd Resident Univ of TN; Bk, Nat Bk of Commerce; Law Clk, Schledwitz, Crow, Beliles, Bearman, Butler & Washington; cp/Phi Beta Sigma; Pi Eta Sigma; r/Bapt; hon/Mortarboard; Most Outstg Yg Men of Am; g/Atty.

THOMPSON, DANA LYNN oc/Accountant; b/Apr 5, 1959; h/4109 South 19th Street #922, Tacoma, WA 98405; ba/Tacoma, WA; p/Mr and Mrs Glenn R Thompson, Castle Rock, WA; ed/Dipl, Toledo HS, 1977; Dipl, Longview Bus Col, 1978; BS, LA Col, 1982; pa/Staff Acct, Dwyer, Pemberton & Coulson, CPA's, Tacoma, WA, 1984-; Staff Acct, Lord & Nelson, CPA's, Tacoma, WA 1983; Staff Acct, Knight, Masden, Easterling & Marler, CPA's, Sum 1981; Acctg Lab Instr, LA Col, 1979-82; Sales Clk, Cowlitz Cableview, Sum 1979; Bkkpr, RGA Cable TV, 1977-78; Mem: Am Soc of Wom Accts; Acctg & Auditing Roundtable; Christian Bus & Profl Wom; Pres 1980-82, Secy-Treas 1979-80, Bus Adm Soc; cp/Gamma Theta Sigma, 1981-82; Secy Treas, 1980-82, Food Se Com 1980-81, Alpha Chi; HS Band, 1973-77; Mem 1973-77, VPres 1975-76, Dir of Public Relats 1974-75, FHA; r/So Bapt; hon/Essay, "Human Relats," Pub'd in Campus Lit Mag, 1979; Passed CPA Exam 1st Sitting, 1982; Outstg Sr Acctg Maj, 1981-82; HS Citizenship Awd, 1977; Grad summa cum laude, 1982; Nat Dean's List; Intl Yth in Achmt; Commun Ldrs of Am; Dir of Dist'd Ams; g/CPA.

THOMPSON, DEBRA INEZ oc/Student; b/Sep 3, 1961; h/503 Fairwood Avenue, Charlotte, NC 28203; ba/Charlotte, NC; p/Mr and Mrs John L Thompson, Charlotte, NC; ed/Dipl, Myers Pk HS, 1979; BA Bus Adm, Univ

of NC-Charlotte, 1983; MBA Cand; pa/Bk Teller, Student Fin Sers, Univ of NC-Charlotte, 1982; Bk Teller, NC Nat Bk, Charlotte, Sum 1980-82; cp/Col: Chm, Student Activ Fees Comm; VPres, Alpha Kappa Alpha Sorority, 1982-83; Chm Ways & Means Com, Student Legis; Bus Adm Rep to Student Legis; r/Friendship Bapt; hon/Alumni Merit S'ship Recip, Univ of NC-Charlotte; S'ship Recip, NCNB, Sum 1982; Chancellor's Commend, Univ of NC-Charlotte, 6 Sems; Pres, Omicron Delta Kappa Ldrship Hon Soc; S'ship Recip, NC Lions Assn for the Blind; Tate-Culbertson S'ship Recip; g/MBA; Mgmt Position.

THOMPSON, DONALD EUGENE oc/Student; b/Oct 25, 1961; h/2500 Linkwood Place, Charlotte, NC 28208; p/Mr and Mrs Woodrow Thompson, Charlotte, NC; ed/Dipl, Harding HS, 1980; Att'g Johnson C Smith Univ; pa/Utility Maintenance, K-Mart, 1981-82; Custodian/Maintenance, Queens Pk Cinema, 1983-; cp/Mem: NC Alliance for Hlth, PE, Rec & Dance, 1983-; Metro Phillies, 1983-84; Mets, 1980-83; PE & Hlth Clb, Johnson C Smith Univ, 1983-; Ch Yth Org, 1980-82; r/Presb; hon/Recip, Duke S'ship; Dean's List; VPres, PE & Hlth Clb; g/Maj in Phy Therapy & Rec Sports.

THOMPSON, DONALD LEE oc/Biologist; b/Mar 4, 1956; h/16 Valley View Drive, Vienna, WV 26105; ba/Huntington, WV; p/Ezra A and Bobbie A Thompson, Vienna WV; ed/Dipl, Parkersburg, HS, 1974; AAS, Parkersburg Commun Col, 1977; BS, Marshall Univ, 1981; pa/Anal Chem, IHI Kemron, Wmsburg, WV, 1982; Biol, VA Med Ctr, Huntington, WV, 1983-; Mem: Am Chem Soc, 1981-; Am Soc of Clin Pathols, 1977-; Gamma Beta Phi; r/Bapt; hon/Author, "Vitamin A Attenuates Streptozotocin-Induced Diabetes Millitus in the Rat," 1983; VA Spec Contribution Awd, 1983; Nat Dean's List; Intl Yth in Achmt; Commun Ldrs of Am; Dir of Dist'd Ams; Med Lab Res; Biochem.

THOMPSON, KELLY NELON oc/Singer; b/Dec, 1, 1959; h/3355 Sir Lancelot Place, Marietta, GA 30060; ba/Smyrna, GA; m/Jerry L Thompson; p/Rex and Shirley Nelon, Smyrna, GA; sp/Clarence and Alice Thompson, Englewood, TN; ed/Dipl, Campbell HS, 1977; Am Sch of Corres, 1977; Att'd Univ of TN; pa/Singer, Rex Nelon Singers (Gospel), 1976-; cp/Gospel Music Assn; Sponsored Calvary Chd's Home; Vol, Cobb Gen Hosp; r/Bapt, Vinnings Bapt Ch; hon/Solo Album, "Her Father's Child"; Queen of Gospel Music, Singing News Fan Awds, 1980-83; Bride of Yr, Smyrna GA, 1979; g/To Spread the Word of God Through Gospel Music.

THOMPSON, LISA KIMBERLY oc/Student; b/Jan 24, 1964; h/3300 Elbert Street, Baltimore, MD 21229; p/Alma T Bell; ed/Dipl, Wn HS, 1982; Att'g Vassar Col; pa/Ec Res Asst Ec Dept, Vassar Col, 1982-83; Sum Employee, Provident Savs Bk of Balto, 1983; cp/Vassar Clb of MD Student Recruiter; Art Chp; French Clb; Fdrs Day Com; Vol Freshman & Sophomore Class Coun; Vol & Netwking Com, SAS; Vol, Citizens for Mayor Shaefer Com; Assoc'd Student Cong of Balto Alumni Clb; r/Epis; hon/Recip, Vassar Col

S'ship; Commend, Citizens for Mayor Shaefer; W/W Among Outstg HS Students; Commun Ldrs of Am; g/Cognitive Sci Maj; Law Sch.

THOMPSON, MICHAEL RICHARD oc/Student, Minister of Music; b/Mar 31, 1961; h/Route 1, Box 112, State Road, NC 28676; p/Mr and Mrs Richard Thompson, State Road, NC; ed/Dipl, E Wilkes HS; AB, Gardner-Webb Col, 1983; Att'g Grad Sch in Music; pa/Min of Music, Allen Meml Bapt Ch, 1982-; Mem, Contemp Christian Grp, 1983-; Higher Power, 1983-; cp/HS: Band, Chorus, Tennis Tm; Col: Mem 1979-83, Ofcr 1982, Music Edrs Nat Conf; SNEA; r/Christian-Bapt; hon/Gov's Sch Nom, 1978; Most Improved, Tennis, 1979; All-Conf Hon Mention, Tennis, 1979; Col Hon Roll, 1982-83; Best Instrumentalist, Gardner-Webb Col, 1982; W/W Among Am HS Students; g/Grad Deg in Music (Perf).

THOMPSON, PERRY WALLACE oc/Student; b/Jan 7, 1964; h/15 Post Oak Road, Greenville, SC 29605; p/Mr and Mrs Bobby G Thompson, Greenville, SC; ed/Dipl, Greenville HS, 1982; Att'g, Univ of SC; pa/Pt-time Clk & Stocker, Fam Mart Inc, 1981-84; cp/HS Marching, Concert & Jazz Bands (Corp 1980); HS Tennis (Conf Champs 1982); Eastlan Bapt Ch Basketball Tm (St Champs 1982); Univ Water Ski Clb; Univ Intramural Tennis, Basketball, Soccer; r/Prot; hon/Citadel Scholar; Outstg French Student Awd, 1982; Acad Hon Roll, 1982; Greenville All-Co Band, 1979-80; SC Solo & Ensemble Superior Rating, 1979-80; Conf Runner-up in Flight 3 Singles, Tennis, 1982; Block Lttr (Band 1980, Tennis 1982); Participant, Gov's Inaugural Parade, 1979; Dir of Dist'd Ams; g/BA Bus Adm Deg w Minor in Computer Sci.

THOMPSON, ROOSEVELT L oc/Law Intern; b/Jan 28, 1962; h/1924 Allis Street, Little Rock, AR 72204; p/ C R and Dorothy L Thompson; ed/Dipl, Little Rock Ctl HS, 1980; Att'g Yale Univ; pa/Intern, Gov Bill Clinton (D-AR), Sum 1980 & Sum 1983; Copy Boy, AR Gazette, 1978-79 & Sum 1980; Intern, Senator David Pryor (D-AR), Sum 1981; Intern Clk, Rose Law Firm, Little Rock, AR, Sum 1982; Wk/Study Intern, New Haven Ofc of Housing & Neighborhood Devel, 1981-; cp/Chm 1982-83, Calhoun Col Coun; Mgr 1983, Calhoun Cabaret; Varsity Football Tm, Yale Univ; Coor 1981-82, Troup Mid Sch Tutoring Proj, Calhoun Col; Secy 1982-83, Black Aths of Yale; Parliamentn 1978-82, Nat Christian Yth Coun, AME Zion Ch; Undergrad Fin Aid Advy Com; Dem Party; HS: Student Coun, Sophomore Senator; Jr VPres; Sr Student Body Pres; Mng Editor Jr Yr, Asst Editor, HS Newspaper; HS Football Tm; hon/Phi Beta Kappa, 1982; Hart Lymon Prize, 1983; Harry S Truman Scholar, 1982; Hd Advr, Pres Scholars, 1982; Pres Scholar, US Senate Yth Scholar, 1980; Nat Finalist, Cent III Ldrs Scholars; Nat Merit & Nat Achmt Finalist, 1979; AR AAAAA All-St Football Tm; Intl Yth In Achmt; Personalities of S; Commun Ldrs of Am; g/Maj in Hist & Ec-Polit Sci; Pursue Joint Degs in Law & Public Policy or Govt; Career in Law & Polits.

THOMPSON, SUSAN CAROL oc/

Student; b/Nov 9, 1961; h/Route 4, Box 83, Tullahoma, TN 37388; ba/Nashville, TN; p/Mr and Mrs Raymond Thompson, Tullahoma, TN; ed/Dipl, Tullahoma HS, 1980; BBA, Belmont Col, 1984; pa/Micro-film-Fesh Operator, Harton Hosp, Sum 1980; Missionary to MT, Home Mission Bd (Bapt), Sum 1981; Sum Missionary to World's Fair (Puppet Min), TN Bapt Conv, Knoxville, TN, 1982; Country Music Assn, 1982-83; cp/Pres, BSU, 1982-83; Secy, Jr Class, 1982-83; Secy, Assn of Christian Musicians & Artists, 1981-83; Legis Coun 1980-83, Wom's Student Govt Assn; Chi Alpha Nu Sorority, 1980-83; Chaplain, BSU Puppet Tm, 1980-83; BSU Ensemble, 1980-82; r/So Bapt; hon/ Sophomore Class Favorite 1981-82; Jr Class Favorite, 1982-83; Holland S'ship, 1980-82; g/Attend Sem; Mission Wk.

THORNBURG, TAMARA LYNN oc/Student; b/Mar 20, 1966; h/8061 Stringtown, Ripley, OH 45167; p/David and Barbara Thornburg, Ripley, OH; ed/ Dipl, St Patrick's HS, 1984; cp/Com Hd, Spirit Clb; Trinity Luth Wom's Guild; r/Luth; hon/Author, of Stories Pub'd in *Leprechaun* the Sch Newspaper, 1983-84; Nat Hon Soc; Nat Hon Roll; Soc of Dist'd HS Students; W/W of Am HS Students; g/Maj in Early Ed w Minor in Bus.

THRASH, WILLARD MARK oc/ Assistant Pastor; b/Jul 18, 1956; h/4200 14th Way Northeast, St Petersburg, FL 33703; ba/St Petersburg, FL; p/Willard Thrash, St Petersburg, FL; Sara Arline Thrash, St Petersburg, FL; ed/Dipl, Northeast, HS, 1974; BA 1979, MA 1980, Stetson Univ; MDiv, So Bapt Theol Sem, 1982; pa/Asst Pastor, 1st Bapt Ch, St Petersburg, FL, 1982-; Hosp Chaplain, L'ville Gen & Ctl St Hosp, 1981-82; Meat Cutter, Deland, FL, 1977-80; Mem: AAPS, 1982-; ACPE, 1982-; cp/So Bapt Hist Soc, 1982-; r/So Bapt; hon/Dean's List Throughout Col; Chi Chapt S'ship Awd, Pi Kappa Phi, 1980; Ath of Yr, 1978-80; Pres, Pi Kappa Phi (Stetson Univ), 1979; g/Obtain Doct in Rel/Psych; Earn Law Deg.

THROWER, ANGELA SUE oc/Student; b/Aug 15, 1965; h/Route 1, Box 63, Lynchburg, TN 37352; ba/Tullahoma, TN; p/Nolan and Barbara Thrower, Lynchburg, TN; ed/Dipl, Moore Co HS, 1983; Att'g, Motlow St Commun Col; pa/Cashier, Ed's Bi-Rite, Lynchurg, TN, 1982; cp/Beta Clb, 4 Yrs; Student Body Pres, Moore Co HS, 1983; Secy-Treas, Sr Class, 1983; hon/Miss Moore Co HS, 1983; USS Acad of Achmt AWd, 1983; W/W Among Am HS Students; g/Maj in Computer Sci, Minor in Hist; Wk in Mid TN Area.

THROWER, SHEILA GAYE oc/Student, Loan Clerk; b/Oct 15, 1964; h/511 Auburn Street, Tuskegee, AL 36083; p/ Mr and Mrs J W Thrower Jr; ed/Dipl, Macon Acad, 1982; Att'd Troy St Univ-Montgomery, 1982-83; pa/Loan Clk, Farmers Home Adm, Tuskegee, AL, 1983-; Pt-time Law Clk, Firm of Baxley, Beck & Dillard, Montgomery, AL, 1982; Pt-time Sales Clk, Macong Drugs, Tuskegee, AL; cp/HS: Treas 1981-82, Beta Clb, Mem 3 Yrs; Editor, HS Yrbook, 1981-82; VPres Sr Class, 1981-82; Student Coun Rep; MA Clb, 3 Yrs; Student Libn; Typist for Knights Light Staff; Girls Softball Tm, 3 Yrs; Girls Basketball Tm, 3 Yrs; Adult Ch

Choir; Nursery SS Tchr; Assisted w Mother & Sister in Dir'g Miss AL World Pageant, 1979; Assisted w Vacation Bible Sch; hon/Beta Clb S'ship, 1982; HS Annual Awd, 1982; Most Dependable & Best Dressed; Calendar Girl, 1980-81 & 1981-82; Runner-up, Sp Pageantry Christmas Competition, 1980; Winner, DAR Essay Contest; Best Prog Participant, Miss AL US Teen Pageant, 1979; W/W Among Am HS Students; Intl Yth in Achmt; Commun Ldrs of Am; Outstg Yg Wom of Am.

THURMON, KIMBERLY BOOTH oc/Student; b/Aug 6, 1962; h/PO Box 9, Walthourville, GA 31333; m/Mark Edward; p/Everette & Faye Booth, Walthourville, GA; sp/Bill and Evelyn Thurmon; ed/Dipl, Bradwen Inst, 1980; Att'g Ga So Col; cp/HS: Band Student; French Clb; Secy, Sci Clb; FBLA; Col; Beta Phi Hon Soc, GA So Col; r/Prot; hon/Bicent Essay Contest; W/W Amog Am HS Stuents; Intl Yth in Achmt; Commun Ldrs of Am; W/W Among Wom.

TIDWELL, MELANIE DAWN oc/ Student; b/Nov 19, 1964; h/Route 1, Box 501, Burns, TN 37029; p/J C and Maxine Tidwell, Burns, TN; ed/Dipl, HS, 1983; cp/Pres, FHA Chapt, 1982-83; FTA Clb, 1982-83; Photog Clb; Drama Clb; Lit Clb; Leo Clb; Sci Clb; Newspaper & Annual Staff, 1982-83; r/Ch of Christ; hon/Poems Pub'd in *Israfel* the Sch Mag , 1981-82; Stories for Sch Newspaper, 1982-83; 2nd Place, Grand Nat Baton Competition; W/W Among Am HS Students; Yg Commun Ldrs of Am; g/ Maj in Med Technol.

TIERNEY, TIMOTHY JOHN PATRICK oc/Engineer; b/Jan 2, 1957; h/2045 South La Rosa Drive, Tempe, AZ 85282; ba/ Holmdel, NJ; p/John H and Ruth C Tierney, Tempe, AZ; ed/ Dipl, Tempe Union HS, 1975; BSEE, BS Computer Sci, No AZ Univ, 1981; MSEE, Purdue Univ, 1982; oc/Engr, Bell Labs; IEEE; IEEE Computer Soc; Phi Kappa Phi; Pres, VPres, Pledge Tnr, S'ship Chm, Intramural Chm, Corres'g Secy, Recording Secy, Sigma Chi; By-laws Com Chm, Tau Beta Pi; hon/ Sigma Chi SE Province Balfour Awd, 1981; No AZ Univ Gold Axe Awd, 1981; Archons, Greek Ldrship Hon Soc, NAU.

TIESMAN, JAY PATRICK b/May 21, 1963; h/Rural Route 4, Sterling, IL 61081; p/Mr and Mrs Roland Jay Tiesman, Sterling, IL; ed/Dipl, Newman Ctl Cath HS, 1981; Att'd Sauk Val Col; Att'd Creighton Univ; cp/Phys for Social Responsibility; Creighton Univ Phil Soc; Nat Hon Soc; Am Legion Premier Boys St; Chess Clb; Computer Clb; Spch Tm; Drama Clb; Band; Choral Music; HS Newspaper & Annual Staff; hon/IL St Scholar; Nat Merit S'ship Qualifier; W/ W Among Am HS Students; g/Career in Med or Dentistry, Spec'g in Temporomandibular Joint Disorders.

TIGUE, ANNIE MARIE oc/Student, Part-time Audit Worker; b/Apr 19, 1961; h/458 Florida Street, Clarksdale, MS 38614; ba/Jackson, MS; p/Mrs Brize Tigue, Clarksdale, MS; ed/Dipl, Coahoma Co HS, 1979; BS Acctg, Jackson St Univ, 1983; pa/Audit Clerical Asst, Sears, Roebuck & Co, 1981; cp/Fin Secy, Delta Sigma Theta Sorority Inc, 1982-83; Yg Dems; NAACP; Parliamentn, SGA Legis Coun; MS Soc of Wom Accts; Nat Assn of Black Accts;

Delta Mu Delta Bus Frat, 1981; Alpha Chi Hon Soc; Pres, Phi Beta Lambda, 1981-82; VPres, Acctg Soc, 1981-82; VPres, Delta Sigma Pi, 1981-82; Alpha Lambda Delta Hon Soc, 1980; r/Bapt; hon/Fannie Pitts Awd, 1982; Most Dependable Mem Awd, Phi Beta Lambda, 1982; AICPA S'ship, 1980-83; Pres List; Nat Dean's List; Others; W/ W Among Students in Am Cols & Univs; g/CPA.

TILBURY, KATHLEEN MARTHA oc/Student; b/Mar 31, 1963; h/Rural Route 1, Box 215, Hudson, IN 46747; ba/Lake Forest, IL; p/Mr and Mrs Ervin E Tilbury, Hudson, IN; ed/Dipl, Prairie Hgts HS, 1981; Att'g Lake Forest Col; pa/Secy, Lake Forest Col, 1982-; CETA, Angola Occupl Devel Ctr, Sums 1977, 1978 & 1981; cp/Nat Hon Soc; Pres, Fgn Lang Clb; VPres, Stamp & Coin Clb; IFEA; FFA; Student Coun; Swing Choir; Yrbook Staff; VPres, Spanish Clb, 1983-84; Campus Life; Orientation Ldr; VPres 1983-84, Gamma Rho Delta; Prods Com, Secy, WMXM Col Radio Sta; Garrick Players; Tri-Beta; Choir Mem; Ambassadors; hon/Poetry Pub'd in *The World of Poetry*; Essay Pub'd in the *Steuben-Repub* Newspaper; Att'd 1st Annual Presb Ch Yth Triennium at IN Univ; Att'd 2 Wk Sem, Ball St Univ; Winner, Local Essay Contest, Sponsored by Elks Clb; Band & Vocal Medals for Solos & Duets; IN Hoosier Scholar; W/W Among Am HS Students; Intl Yth in Achmt; g/Receive Distn in Biol Field.

TILSON, E VINCENT oc/Associate Director of Development; b/Dec 18, 1955; h/4626 Long Leaf Hills Drive, Wilmington, NC 28403; p/Mr and Mrs Charles Vincent Tilson Jr, Wilmington, NC; ed/Dipl, John T Hoggard HS, 1974; BA, Univ of NC-Wilmington, 1978; MDiv, So Bapt Theol Sem, 1981; pa/ Assoc Dir of Devel, Chowan Col; Prof & Admr, So Bapt Theol Sem; cp/VPres, Student Govt Assn, So Bapt Theol Sem, 1980-81; Chp & Lectr on Prog of Pop Culture Assn of S, 1980; Bd of Dirs, U Christian Campus Mins, Univ of NC—Wilmington, 1975-77; r/Bapt; hon/Grad w Hons & cum laude Distn, Univ of NC-Wilmington, 1978.

TIMMER, STEPHEN BLAINE oc/ Student; b/May 19, 1962; ba/St Petersburg, FL; p/Blaine E and Nancy J M Timmer, Holland, MI; ed/Dipl, Lake Brantley HS, 1980; BA, Eckerd Col, 1984; pa/Intl Editor, Eckerd Col *Eckspress*, 1982-83; Coor, Intl Yth Campt WERA Inc, 1982; Coor, Sprg Val Yth Camp, Sprg Val Assn, 1981; Legal Asst, Rumberger, Kirk & Caldwell, 1980; cp/ Sailing Tm, 1980-82; Ldrship Core 1981-83, Mem 1980-83, Org of World Concerns; Dorm Advr for Intl Students, 1981-83; Student Ct, 1981-83; Chief Justice, 1982-83; VPres, Circle K 1981-82; Intl Students Assn, 1980-83; Salvador Dali Mus Activ Guild, 1982-83; Campus Min, 1980-83; Intramural Sports, 1980-83; Mem 1981-84, Pres 1982-84, Omicron Delta Kappa; Pres, Jr Achmt Co, 1978; Co-Capt 1980, Swim Tm, 1977-80; Num Public Spkg Presentations; Var Others; r/Presb; hon/Author, "What's Wrong w Boating," *The Boating Indust*, 1982; Christian Aths Awd, 1980; Coaches Achmt Awd, 1980; Intl Students Ser Awd, 1983; Outstg Resident Advr Awd, 1982, 1983; W/W Among Am HS Students; Nat

Dean's List; g/Attend Law Sch, Spec in Intl Law & Diplomacy.

TINGELSTAD, CATHERINE JANE oc/Student; b/Dec 8, 1965; h/208 Chowan Road, Greenville, NC 27834; p/Mr and Mrs Jon B Tingelstad, Greenville, NC; ed/Dipl, J H Rose HS, 1984; pa/Lab Asst, Pitt Co Meml Hosp, Sum 1982; cp/Sr Rep 1983-84, Mem 1981-84, Anchor Clb; Pres 1983-84, Mem 1983, Juniorettes; Student Govt Rep, 1982-83; Nat Hon Soc, 1983; "Rampart Lines" Editor, Newspaper Staff, 1983-84; r/Luth; hon/NC Gov's Sch, Sum 1983; Marshall, 1983.

TINGEN, TIMOTHY A oc/Student; b/Feb 26, 1961; h/Route 7, Box 480, Greenville, NC 27834; ba/Springfield, OH; p/C Aubrey Tingen (dec); Revalene Tingen Bartlett, Greenville, NC; ed/Dipl, Ridgefield HS (CT), 1979; BA, Wittenberg Univ, 1983; cp/HS Theatre Roles in: *All My Sons; The Odd Couple; The Importance of Being Earnest;* Commun Theatre: *My Fair Lady;* Col Theatre Roles in: *Pvt Ear; Man & Superman; The Runner Stumbles; The Miser; Sam Time Next Yr; All My Sons;* Disc Jockey, Radio Sta WUSO, Wittenberg Univ, 1983; r/Prot; h/Drama Awd, Nagoza Intl HS, Japan; g/Continue to Wk in Theatre.

TIPTON, STEPHANIE ELISABETH oc/Student; b/Sep 10, 1065; h/Route 4, Box 682, Easley, SC 29640; ba/Brevard, NC; ed/Dipl, Wren HS, 1983; cp/Wren HS Concert & Marching Bands, 6 Yrs; HS Chorus, 2 Yrs; Horn, Carolina Yth Symph, 2 Yrs; Studied Piano, 7 Yrs; Studied Voice 1 Yr; Studied Horn, 1 Yr; Sch Musical, 1982; Att'd Furman Band Camp, 1981; Secy 1983, Chm Nom'g Com 1982-83, Fairview U Meth Ch Yth Grp; Num Music, Singing & Dance Charity Activs; r/Meth; hon/Nat Fed of Music Clbs, 1982; Rated II for Horn Duet, Rated II for Horn Solo, Rated I for Voice Solo, SC Solo & Ensemble Fest for Voice & Band, 1983; J H Nichols S'ship; Brevard Col Trustee Grant, 1983; g/Deg in Music; Tch Chd w Lrng Disabilities; Dir Ch Choirs/Perform.

TOLNAS, CAROL LEE oc/Student; b/Mar 30, 1964; h/1801 Oxford Drive, Maryville, TN 37801; p/Mr and Mrs T J Tolnas, Maryville, TN; ed/Dipl, Maryville HS, 1982; Att'g Univ of TN; cp/Corres'g Secy, Kappa Alpha Theta; Secy-Treas, VPres, Pres, Explorer Post 684; Editor, HS Yrbook; Nat Hon Soc; Mu Alpha Theta; Jr & Sr Planning Coms, HS; Great Decisions; hon/Sci Ser Awd, 1982; Maryville HS Scholar, 1982; Alcoa Foun S'ship, 1982; Freshman Alumni S'ship, Univ of TN; Fred M Foun S'ship; Del to Girl's St & Girl's Co; Top 10% of Class, HS; Bell Bocker Algebra II Awd, HS; W/W Among Am HS Students; g/Deg in Bus Mgmt.

TONEY, JACQUELINE J oc/Student; b/Mar 29, 1962; h/Route 2, Box 401 Forrest City, AR 72335; p/Mr and Mrs J A Toney, Forrest City, AR; ed/Dipl, Forrest City HS, 1980; Att'g Henderson St Univ; cp/Henderson St Univ: Music Therapy Clb; Concert Choir; Dir, Gospel Choir; Senator, Student Govt Assn; Alpha Kappa Alpha Sorority; Treas, Panhellenic Coun, 1982-83; HS: Recording Secy, Student Coun, 1980; Hd Accompanist of Mustang Concert Choir, 1979-80; VPres, FBLA, 1979-80; FHA, 1978-80; Pianist/Organist, Salem Missionary Bapt Ch; Pianist, Gtr Plea-

sant Hill Bapt Ch, 1980-83; r/Bapt; hon/ Girl Giving Most Ser to Sch Awd, 980; W/W: Among Am HS Students, Among Am Cols & Univs; g/Deg in Music Therapy w Emphasis in Spec Ed.

TORRES, ALFRED J oc/Student; b/ Dec 24, 1961; h/5204 Palisade Avenue, West New York, NJ 07093; p/Guillermo and Gladys Alonso, West New York, NJ; ed/Dipl, Meml HS, 1980; Grad, Columbia Col, Columbia Univ, 1984; cp/Exec Com, HS Student Govt; Col Crew Tm; Student Advr; Alpha Delta Phi; hon/HS Acad Achmt Awd; Columbia Crew Tms Numerals; Intl Yth in Achmt; Commun Ldrs of Am; g/Wk in Computer Sci Field.

TOYAMA, LISA M oc/Student; b/ Oct 7, 1964; h/2905 Lake Forest Drive, Greensboro, NC 27408; ba/Durham, NC; p/Mr and Mrs Philip Toyama, Greensboro, NC; ed/Dipl, W H Page HS, 1982; Att'g, Duke Univ; pa/Vol, Duke Primate Ctr; Pt-tme, Univ of NC-Greensboro Biol Dept, 1983; Pt-tme, Duke DownUnder Tavern, 1982-83; Pt-time, Greensboro Nat Sci Ctr, 1981-82; cp/Kappa Delta Sorority; Inter-Varsity Christian F'ship; Freshman Advy Coun; Con of Freshman Pres; Jarvis House Pres; Duke Ski Devils; Duke IM Tennis Tm; Hlth for Life Chm; Tutor; r/Presb; hon/NC Gov's Sch; Secy of St, Am Legion Aux Tar Heel Girl's St; Gov's Page; W/W Among Am HS Students; Intl Yth in Achmt; g/BS Deg in Zool.

TREAT, DENNIS LEE oc/Student, Farmer; b/Mar 31, 1960; h/Route 1, Box 143, Warden, WA 98857; p/Ronald and Delores Treat, Warden, WA; ed/Dipl, Warden HS, 1978; AA, Big Bend Commun Col, 1982; Att'g Walla Walla Col; cp/Pres 1977-78, Nat Hon Soc, 1976-78; HS Football, 1976-78; HS Wrestling, 1976-77; Pres 1977-78, Treas 1976-77, FFA; VPres, ASB, 1977-78; Big Brothers/Big Sisters; Hosts Tutoring Prog, 1982; Deacon, 7th Day Adventist Ch; Ch Leag Basketball & Softball Tm; City Leag Volleyball Tm; Mem, Columbia Basin Allied Arts; r/7th Day Adventist; hon/Star Chapt Farmer FFA, 1978; Hon Roll, Warden HS, 1976-78; Hon Roll, Big Bend Commun Col, 1980-82; Grad w Highest Hons, Big Bend Commun Col; W/W Among Am HS Students; c/ Deg in Elem Ed.

TREAT, TAMMY ANNE oc/Student; b/OCt 5, 1961; h/Route 1, Box 143, Warden, WA 98857; p/Ron and Delores Treat, Warden, WA; ed/Dipl, Warden HS, 1980; AA, Big Bend Commun Col, 1982; Att'g WA St Univ; cp/Brig Brothers/Big Sisters; Hd Secy, 7th Day Adventist Ch, 1980-81; Pres 1980, Secy 1978-79, Sentinel 1977-78, FFA; Asst Treas 1979-80, ASB; HS Volleyball & Basketball Tm; City Leag Volleyball, 1982-83; hon/Hon Roll, Warden HS, 1977-80; Hon Roll, Big Bend Commun Col, 1980-82; W/W Among Am HS Students; Yg Commun Ldrs of Am; g/ Maj in Comml Rec, Bus Minor.

TREFTS, DEBORAH CAMPBELL oc/Student; b/Feb 6, 1958; h/2722 10th Avenue East, Seattle, WA 98102; ba/ Seattle, WA; p/Albert Sharpe and Joan Landenberger Trefts, Shaker Heights, OH; ed/BA, Wellesley Col, 1980; MSL, VT Law Sch, 1982; MMA, Univ of WA, 1984; pa/Univ of WA F'ships: World Fisheries Proj Inst of Marine Studies, 1983-84; Inst for Envir Mediation, Sum

1983; Coastal Resources Prog Inst for Marine Studies, 1982-83; Affil to 3rd UN Conf on Law of the Sea, 1979-81; Congl Internships; Policy Analyst for Boston Cnsltg Firm; Courier for Frontier Nsg Ser; Tech Intern, Boston Public Interest Envir Law Org; cp/Grad Assocs Prog Schof Intl Studies, Univ of WA, 1983-84; Wom's Fisheries Netwk, Seattle, WA; DAR; Colonial Dames of 17th Cent; VT Law Sch Student Bar Assn; r/Presb; hon/3 Papers to be Pub'd on Var Aspects of Law & the Oceans; Cert in Bus Adm, Sum Prog in Adm, 1983; Mortar Bd S'ship, Univ of WA, 1983-84; Grad w Hons (magna cum laude), Wellesley Col; W/W Among Am HS Students; Commun Ldrs of Am; g/Intl Marine Resources Mgmt/Negotiations.

TRESSLER, RICHARD W JR oc/ Student; b/Jan 19, 1963; h/1046 Sun Villa Drive, Vero Beach, FL 32960; p/ Richard W and Patricia Tressler, Vero Beach, FL; ed/Dipl, Vero Bch HS, 1981; AA, Univ of FL, 1983; cp/Vero Bch Surf Clb, 1981; Beta Theta Pi Frat, 1982-83; VPres 1980, Mem 1979-81, FBLA; HS Sr Class Treas; HS Student Coun; Pres, HS Math Clb; r/Cath; hon/4th Place FBLA Dist Acctg I, 1979; 2nd Place FBLA St Contest Acctg I, 1979; 1st Place, FBLA Dist Contest Acctg II, 1981; g/CPA.

TROLLINGER, JEFFREY BRUCE oc/ Student; b/Mar 23, 1964; h/2937 Maple Drive, Fairfax, VA 22031; ba/Vienna, VA; p/Haywood J and Rebecca M Trollinger, Fairfax, VA; ed/Dipl, HS, 1982; cp/Pres, VPres, Histn, FBLA; Meth Yth F'ship; Ch Softball Tm; Walk for Mankind, 3 Yrs; Cystic Fibrosis Bike-a-thon; Astronomy Clb; Jr Achmt; Student Rep, Fairfax Co Bus Adv Comm; Mgr, Varsity Football & Track; hon/Lttr'd as Mgr, Varsity Football & Track; W/W Among Am HS Students; Yg Commun Ldrs of Am; g/Deg in Aerospace Engrg from VA Polytech Inst & St Univ; Career w NASA.

TRUJILLO, CYNDI H oc/Student; b/ Apr 8, 1965; h/PO Box 1335 Ozona, TX 76943; p/Felix and Evelyn Rodriguez Trujillo, Ozona, TX; ed/Dipl, Ozona HS, 1983; Att'd, Wn TX Col, 1983-85; Att'g SW TX St Univ; pa/Secy in Jour Dept, Wn TX Col, 1983-85; Desk Clk, Ozona Inn of the W, Sum 1984; cp/Col 1983-84: Student Senate; Spec Effects Com; Phi Theta Kappa; Press Clb; HS: Co-editor of Yrbook; Track Mgr; HS Newspaper Staff, *The Lion's Roar;* Clarinet, HS Band, 4 Yrs; Participant, UIL Writing Events (News, Feature & Readywriting); r/ Cath; hon/Author of Var Articles, Assoc Editor & Bus/Circulation Mgr, for Campus Newspaper, *The Wn Texan,* Wn TX Col, 1983-84; Outstg Jour Student, Wn TX Col, 1983-84; Dean's List, Wn TX Col, 1984; Recip Jour S'ship; Wn TX Col, 1983-84; g/Deg in Jour; Reporter for a City Newspaper.

TRUMBO, SANDRA M oc/Student; b/Sep 15, 1968; h/Rural Delivery 2, Box 1064, Schuylkill Haven, PA 17972; p/ Mr and Mrs Henry L Trumbo, Schuylkill Haven, PA; ed/Att'g HS; cp/Patrol Ldr, GSA; Pres, Jr Choir; Pres/Chm, Fund Raising; Secy, Ch Yth Grp; Chorus, Ensemble; Drama Clb; Part in Musical, "Anything Goes"; Student of Piano, 19 Yrs; Student of Ballet & Tap Dance; hon/Essay Winner, "Why I Love Am"; Del, Spelling Bee; US Nat Ldrship

Merit Awd Winner; g/Studies in Bus or Acctg.

TRUSS, SUSAN KIM oc/Student; b/ Aug 26, 1963; h/Foxglen, 98 Village Drive, Shelton, CT 06484; p/Mr and Mrs Colin Truss, Shelton, CT; ed/Dipl, Shelton HS, 1981; Att'g Fairfield Univ; cp/Secy 1982-83, Pres 1983-84, Univ Intl Relats Clb; HS Debate Tm; French Clb; Nat Hon Soc; Chorus; Ofc & Lib Aide; Class Rep; Univ Tour Guide; hon/ Dean's List; Manitoba Tchrs Assn Math Awd, 1978; Cert of Merit, French, 1979; HS Hon Roll; W/W Among Am HS Students; Intl Yth in Achmt; Commun Ldrs of Am; g/Career in Hist Res, Archaeol.

TRYBUL, ADRIENNE LEIGH oc/ Student, Receptionist; b/Jul 31, 1964; h/ 9543 Saluda Court, Lorton, VA 22079; ba/McLean, VA; p/Mr and Mrs Theodore Trybul, Lorton, VA; ed/Dipl, Hayfield Sec'dy, 1982; Att'g No VA Commun Col; pa/Telecommuns Attendant 1982-83, Pt-time Variable Programmer (Trainee), Planning Res Corp; Rececptionist, Joint Tactical Fusion Prog Mgr's Ofc, 1983-; cp/Pres 1980-82, VPres 1979, Keyettes; Big Sister; Mtl Hlth Assn of No VA, 1983; r/Cath; hon/ W/W Among Am HS Jrs & Srs; g/Deg in Bus Adm; Design & Implement Computer Progs.

TSUKAMOTO, LISA YURIKO oc/ Student; b/Jun 8, 1962; h/225 Hanamaulu Street, Honolulu, HI 96825; p/ George K and Sachiko Tsukamoto, Honolulu, HI; ed/Dipl, Sacrd Hearts Acad, 1980; Att'g Univ of HI; pa/ Salesperson, Liberty House of HI, 1979-80; Sr Sales Staff, Baskin-Robbins Ice Cream, 1980; Student Clk, Dept of Rel, Univ of HI, 1982; cp/Pres, Waialae Strike & Spare Bowling Leag, 1981-82; Phi Eta Sigma, 1981-82; Univ of HI Pre-Law Soc, 1982; Secy, Aha Ekalesia HI, 1982; hon/Dean's List, 1982; Phi Kappa Phi Awd for Acad Achmt, 1982; HS Nat Hon Soc; Var Acad & Ldrship Awds in HS; Soc of Dist'd Am HS Students; W/W Among Am HS Students; Intl Yth in Achmt; Commun Ldrs of Am; g/Polit Sci/Hist Maj; Attend Law Sch & Pract Corp Law.

TUCK, EDGAR ROLAND oc/Student; b/Nov 6, 1966; h/Route 1, Box 176, Moneta, VA 24121; p/Billy R and Marie M Tuck, Moneta, VA; ed/Attg, Staunton River HS; cp/HS Band; Basketball; French Clb; Nat Forensic Leag; Reporter, Newspaper Staff; Sch Musical; Sci Clb; Student Coun; 4-H Clb; VPres, Redford Co Hon Clb; r/Bapt; hon/Acad Awds; All-Co Awd; All-Dist Awd; All-Star Awd; Citizenship Awd; Danforth (I Dare You) Awd; Lion's Clb Awd; 4-H Awds; US Nat Band Awd, 1982; Lynchburg Fine Arts Ctr Awds; g/ Attend James Madison Univ.

TUCKER, BETTY ELAINE oc/Kindergarten Teacher; b/Mar 22, 1960; h/ 6310 Ella Lee, Houston, TX 77057; ba/ Katy, TX; p/Mr and Mrs Robert A Tucker, Shreveport, LA; ed/Dipl, 1st Bapt Ch Sch, 1978; BS, Baylor Univ, 1982; pa/Kgn Tchr, Zelma Hutsell Elem Sch, Katy ISD, Katy, TX, 1982-; Mem:

Baylor Alumni Assn; Houston-Baylor Alumni Assn; Kay Ed Assn; TX St Tchrs Assn; NEA; Gtr Houston Area Rdg Coun; r/Bapt; hon/HS Class Valedictorian, 1978; Dean's List & Dean's Dist'd List, Col; Alpha Lambda Delta Hon Soc, 1979; Alpha Chi Hon Soc, 1981; Kappa Delta Pi Ed Hon Soc, 1982; Grad magna cum laude, Baylor Univ, 1982; W/W Among Am HS Students.

TUCKER, DANNY LEO oc/Corrections Officer, Minister; b/Sep 7, 1955; h/20885 River Terrace Road, Ettrick, VA 23803; ba/St Farm, VA; m/Donna Jackson; c/Amber Chamone, Danny Jr; p/John R and Corrine Tucker, Prince George, VA; sp/Carl L and Pansy Jackson, Ettrick, VA; ed/Dipl, Prince George HS; BS, VA St Univ, 1978; Att'd Univ of KS; pa/Lic'd Min, Providence Bapt Ch, 1980-; Corrections Ofcr; cp/ Tchr Cert, St of VA, 1978; Bible Study Tchr, Petersburg City Jail; Dist Pres, VPres, Mem-at-Large, Kappa Kappa Psi; hon/Phi Mu Alpha; Kappa Delta Pi; W/W Among Students in Am Cols & Univs; Intl Yth in Achmt; g/MDiv Deg; Ordained Min; Wk as Prison Chaplain.

TUCKER, DUANE HAIMES JR oc/ Research Technician; b/Sep 30, 1960; h/ 155 Woodlake Place, Athens, GA 30605; ba/Athens, GA; p/Mr and Mrs D H Tucker, Starkville, MS; ed/Dipl, Starkville Acad, 1978; BS 1982, MS 1984, MS St Univ; pa/Res Tech III, Univ of GA Coop Ext Ser, 1983-; MS St Univ Res Assoc, 1982-83; Mem: Am Phytopathol Soc, 1980; So Div Am Phytopathol Soc, 1982; MS Assn of Plant Pathols & Nematologists, 1983; cp/Treas 1981-82, Mem 1978-82, Pi Kappa Alpha Frat; Treas 1982-83, Mem 1979-82, Acting Pres 1982, Inter Frat Coun; U Way Fundraiser, 1980-81; Fundraiser, Muscular Dystrophy Assn, 1980; Usher, Meadowview Bapt Ch; r/Bapt; hon/ Author of Article & Abstract Pub'd in *Phytopathol*; Most Outstg Pike on Campus, Local Chapt, Pi Kappa Alpha, 1982; Ldrship Awd, Nat Pi Kappa Alpha, 1982; Pres Scholar, MS St Univ, 1978, 1981-83; Most Outstg Pledge, Pi Kappa Alpha, 1979; Outstg Yg Men of Am; g/PhD in Plant Pathol; Employed in Ext Ser or Indust.

TUPINO, NORA ELIZABETH oc/ Registered Nurse; b/Dec 18, 1949; h/6 North Stevens Place, Hazlet, NJ 07730; ba/Holmdel, NJ; m/James; c/James John, Christopher Joseph; p/Simon and Maria Ramos, Bivona, NY; sp/Serapio and Esther Tupino, Key West, FL; ed/AAS, Bronx Commun Col, 1969; BA, Queens Col, 1977; MEd, Rutgers Univ, 1984; pa/ Hd Nurse, Jacobi Hosp, NYC, 1969-74; Staff Nurse, Bayshore Commun Hosp, 1979-83; Mem: NJ St Nurses Assn; NJ St Assn of Allied Hlth Profls; r/Christian; g/Hlth Edr, Tchg in Allied Hlth Field.

TURBA, JOYCE ADELINE oc/Elementary School Teacher; b/Oct 11, 1957; h/200 East Kirych Street, Thorp, WI 54771; ba/Stanley, WI; p/Mr and Mrs Kenneth Turba, Elkhart Lake, WI; ed/ Dipl, New Holstein HS, 1976; Att'd, Univ of WI-Fond Du Lac, 1976-77; BS

Elem & Spec Ed, Univ of WI-Eau Claire, 1981; pa/2nd Grade Tchr, Holy Fam Sch, 1981-; Hd Cook, Camp Evergreen for Handicapped People, Sum 1981-83; Nurses Aid, Eau Claire Manor, 1980; Concession Stand Wkr, Gemeni Theatre, Eure Claire, Sum 1980; Child Care Wkr, Eau Claire Acad, 1978-79; Tutor, Yth Ctr Wkr (VISTA), Kansas City, 1977-78; Other Employmnt; Mem: NEA, 1981-; cp/Adolescent Companion, 1979-80; Vol Camp Cnslr for Retarded Citizens, 1974-78; Yth Assn for Retarded Citizens, 1973-77; Girls Ath Assn, 1972; Forensics, 1975-76; r/Cath; g/Wk in Field of Spec Ed, w Mtl Retard or Lrng Disabilities.

TURLEY, KATHY ELAINE oc/Special Education Secretary, Student; b/Sep 28, 1956; h/Route 2, Box 502-A, Albertville AL 35950; ba/Guntersville, AL; m/ Aubrey Dale; c/Keri LeeAnn; p/Mr and Mrs Walter L Smith, Crossville, AL; sp/ Mr and Mrs J R Turley, Albertville, AL; ed/Dipl, Crossville HS, 1974; BS Elem Ed, Jacksonville St Univ, 1984; pa/Bkkg Dept & Teller, Albertville Nat Bk, 1974-78; Aide in Deaf Ed Class, Marshall Co Bd of Ed, 1978-79; Spec Ed Secy, Marshall Co Bd of Ed, 1979-; Pvt, Music Tchr, 1972-79; cp/Organist 1975-82, Pianist 1982-, White Oak Ch; AEA-ESPO, 1978; SS Tchr Primary Class, White Oak Ch, 1982-; Yth Activs Com, Yth Activs Com, 1977-79; r/Prot; hon/Valedictorian, Crossville HS, 1974; Miss FHA, 1974; W/W Among Am HS Students, 1974; g/Tchr in Grades 1-6.

TURNER, GLENN RAY oc/Student; b/May 27, 1966; h/Route 1, Box 69, Belvidere, TN 37306; p/Richard and Alice Turner, Belvidere, TN; ed/Dipl, Huntland Sch, 1984; Att'g, Univ of TN-Knoxville, TN; cp/Basketball & Baseball Tms in HS; Beta Clb; FFA; VICA; Pep Clb; Varsity Clb; Harmony C P Ch Softball; r/Presb, Cumberland Presb Ch; hon/Salutatorian; Class Pres; Most Likely to Succeed; Most Studious Sr; g/Elect Engrg Deg.

TURNER, MARY LYNN oc/Student; b/Sep 15, 61; h/Route 3, Box 361, Cherryville, NC 28021; p/Jim L Turner (dec); Mrs Jim L Turner, Cherryville, NC; ed/Dipl, Cherryville Sr HS, 1979; Att'g Gardner-Webb Col; cp/Music Edrs of NC; Student Nat Ed Assn; r/Bapt; Outstg Commun Ldrs of Am; g/Tch Public Sch Music; Pvt Instrn in Piano & Voice.

TURNLEY, ROBERT LEE oc/Student; b/Dec 5, 1964; p/PO Box 1765, Ozona, TX 76943; p/Mr and Mrs Ted Turnley, Ozona, TX; ed/Dipl, Ozona HS; Att'd, Wn TX Col, 1983-84; Att'g, Angela St Univ; cp/Chm, Bapt Student Union, 1983-84; Intramural Football & Basketball, 1983-84; Phi Theta Kappa, 1983-84; r/So Bapt; hon/Sports Editor, *Lion's Roar* & the *Lion*; hon/US Nat Jour Awd, 1983; Nat Hon Soc, 1983; The Soc of Dist'd Am HS Students; W/W Among Am HS Students; g/Maj in Jour; Jour Tchr or Prin.

TURPIN, LEANDRA KAY oc/Student; b/Dec 5, 1961; h/103 McWhorter Court, Richmond, KY 40475; p/Rosemary Turpin, Richmond, KY; ed/Att'd Model Lab Sch; Att'g En KY Univ; cp/ Student Activs Chm, Kappa Alpha Theta; Kappa Delta Pi; Mortor Bd; Collegiate Pentacle; VPres, ACE, 1982-83; r/Christian; hon/HS Nat Hon Soc, 1978-80; Dean's List, En KY Univ, 1981-83; Kappa Delta Pi; Collegiate

Pentacle; Nat Dean's List, 1983; W/W Among Am HS Students; g/Teach Kgn.

TWILLIE, CYNTHIA LORRAINE oc/Student; b/May 1, 1963; h/701 West Sharpe, Forrest City, AR 72335; p/Mr and Mrs Cecil B Twillie, Forrest City, AR; ed/Dipl, Forrest City HS, 1981; Att'g Univ of MO-Columbia; cp/Beta

Clb; Mu Alpha Theta; Student Coun; FHA; Concert Choir; Student Dietetics Assn; r/Bapt; hon/PRes, AR Fedn XI FHA, 1980-81; Forrest City HS Campus Personality, 1981; Soc of Dist'd Am HS Students; W/W Among Am HS Students; g/Become a Reg'd Adm Dietician.

U

UHRICH, CRAIG EDWARD oc/ Graduate Student; b/Sep 29, 1958; h/ 4283 George Avenue, San Mateo, CA 94403; p/Mr and Mrs Bernard Finkelstein, San Mateo, CA; ed/Grad, San Carlos HS, 1976; San Diego St Univ, 1981; cp/Peace Corps Vol, Physics Instr, Ghana, 1981-83; HS Sr Class VP; HS Track Team; Coordinated Studies Assn; r/Col Ave Bapt Ch; hon/Grad'd, summa cum laude; Outstg Student Awd, Physics Dept, 1981; Phi Kappa Phi; Phi Eta Sigma; Univ Dean's List all Semesters; Intl Yth in Achmt; Commun Ldrs of Am; g/Studies in Physics/Optics w Focus on Laser Technol in Med Communication and Entertainment.

ULEP, STACEY JON oc/Football Coach; b/Jul 30, 1961; p/Carole A Ulep, Waialua, HI; ed/Waialua High and Intermediate Sch, 1979; Fire Protection Sch, 1980; EMT Sch, 1981; NCO Ldrship Sch, 1983; Firefighter Rescueman Sch, 1982; Hurst Rescue Tool Course, 1982; mil/USAF, 1980-83; pa/ Firefighter 1980, Firetruck Driver/ Operator 1981, Firefighter Rescueman/ EMT 1982, USAF; Asst Football Coach, Waialua HS, 1983; cp/Quill and Scroll, 1979; MacDill Powerlifting, 1982; Sch Yrbook Artist, 1979; Football Team, 1975-79; Wrestling Team, 1976-79; Judo Team, 1978-79; Campus Police Ofcr, 1976-79; Sophomore Class Treas; r/Christian; hon/Outstg Wrestler, 1978-79; Best All Around, 1979; Outstg

Artist, 1979; PTA Outstg Ath, 1979; Outstg Electronics Student, 1979; One of 12 Outstg Srs, 1979; W/W Among Am HS Students; Yth in Achmt; g/Fire Protection Engr Specializing in Petro, or Marine Biologist.

UNDERWOOD, MARY ANN oc/ Restaurant Lead Person; b/Feb 14, 1961; h/1412 Nisson Road, #9, Tustin, CA 92680; ba/Tustin, CA; m/Stephen; p/ John and Gertrude Sysak, Oceanside, CA; ed/BA, Psych, Univ of CA Irvine, 1981; AA, Saddleback Commun Col, 1980; Mission Viejo HS, 1979; cp/Vol, Saddleback Commun Hosp, 1980-81; Univ of CA Irvine Commun Concern, 1981; USC Newman Ctr Extended Staff, 1979; Saddleback Col Spch Team, 1980; r/Cath; Ch Rel Class Aide; Sponsor of Jr High Yth Grp; HS Retreat Team; hon/Dean's Hon List, Saddleback Commun Col and Univ of CA Irvine; Commun Ser Awd, Commun Concern, 1981; g/Multisubject Tchg Credential; Wk as Elem Tchr.

UNDERWOOD, SUSAN ERIKA oc/ Student; b/Dec 26, 1968; h/6646 Peacock Boulevard, Morrow, GA 30260; p/ James E and Erika K Underwood, Morrow, GA; ed/HS Student; cp/Intl Order of Rainbow for Girls, Worthy Advr 1983; Beta Clb, 1983; Nat Hon Soc, 1984; Drama Clb, 1983-84; Acad Bowl Team, 1983-84; Quiz Bowl Team, 1982-83; r/Bapt; hon/French Superlative, 1983; Best Communicator, 1984; AB Hon Roll; Outstg Sci Awd, 184; Hugh O'Brian Ldrship Awd; g/To Maj

in Crim Justice in Col and Go on to Wk for an Agy Such as the GBI.

UPCHURCH, SHEILA SUSAN oc/ Student; b/Aug 19, 1963; h/2201 Redstone Drive, Fayetteville, NC 28306; ba/ Winston-Salem, NC; p/John Charles and Ernestine Upchurch, Fayetteville, NC; ed/S View Sr High, 1981; AA, Peace Col, 1983; Att'g, Salem Col; cp/Spanish Clb, Pres; FBLA; Bible Clb; Treas, Histn, French Clb; Lib Clb; Sci Clb; FHA; Keywanettes; Pep Clb; Student Govt; r/Presb-Bapt; hon/Fgn Lang and Mgmt Maj, Salem Col; BA; Career in Intl Bus and Ec.

URIBE, GEORGE oc/Student; b/Mar 22, 1962; h/11036 Avenue B, Chicago, IL 60617; p/Mr and Mrs Ulysses Uribe, Chicago, IL; ed/George Wash HS, 1980; Att'g, DePaul Univ; cp/AV Clb; Spanish Clb; Jr Achmt, VP of Mktg; Alpha Clb; Hon Roll; hon/Leag of U Latin Am Citizen S'ship, 1980; W/W Among Am HS Students; Intl Yth in Achmt; Commun Ldrs of Am; g/Deg in Fin and Mktg.

UTZIG, MARK DAVID oc/Assistant Manager; b/Oct 7, 1958; h/Route 4, 4839 Highway 11, Janesville, WI 53545; ba/Janesville, WI; p/Mr and Mrs David Utzig, Janesville, WI; ed/George S Parker HS, 1977; BBA, Gen Mgmt, Univ of WI Whitewater, 1981; pa/Asst Mgr, Utzig Body Shop Inc, 1981-; cp/4-H, Nat 4-H Cong 1977; Janesville JCs, Commun Devel VP 1983; HS Football; r/ Christian; hon/Sigma Iota Epsilon; Nat Dean's List, 1979-80, 1980-81; Commun Ldrs of Am; Intl Yth in Achmt; g/To Own and Operate a Small Bus.

V

VAKACEGU, ILIESA LEDUA oc/
Student; ba/Aug 23, 1960; h/3554
Dalebranch Number 2, Memphis, TN
38116; p/Mr and Mrs Aisake Vakacegu,
Fiji Islands; ed/Grad, Whitehaven HS,
1981; Att'd, Shelby St Commun Col,
1981-82; Studying for BS in Mech
Engrg, Memphis St Univ; cp/Intl Grp
of Memphis; Beta Clb; Future Tchrs of
Am; Key Clb; Lang Translator, ARC
and Memphis Public Lib; hon/Grad w
Acad Hons, HS; Supt's Awd for Acad
Hons; Hist Day Awd; g/BS in Mech
Engrg, Memphis St Univ; Wk as a Mech
Engr.

VAN CANAGAN, JAMIE LYNN oc/
Graduate Student; b/May 9, 1959; h/433
North El Molino #4, Pasadena, CA
91101; ba/Pasadena, CA; p/Paul and
Beverly Van Canagan, Missoula, MT;
ed/Grad, Sentinel HS, 1977; Att'd,
Whitman Col, 1977-79; BA in Sociol,
Univ of WA Seattle, 1981; cp/HS: Nat
Hon Soc, Sr Class Pres, Student Senate,
Class Coun; Vol Aide, Missoula
Crippled Chd's Bazaar and Rehab Ctr;
Vol Wk, Wn MT Reg Commun Mtl Hlth
Prog; Whitman Col: Kappa Kappa
Gamma, Ofcr; Student Affairs Coun,
Spec Events Com Coor; Univ of WA:
Sorority (First and Second VP Coms),
Congreg Ch (Yth Grp Ldr 1980-81),
Presb Ch (Univ Intern 1981-82), Cnslr
for SW Yth Ser Bur 1981-82, Cnslr for
Reality Therapy (Cert'd Reality Ther-
apist 1982), Female Rep for Col Bound;
Fuller Theol Sem: VP of All-Sem Coun,
Marriage and Fam Ministries Prog
Student, Cnslr at Azusa Pacific Col for
Univ Students, Cnslr Trainee Selected
at Christian Inst for Fam Cnslg; hon/
HS: Sci Fair Awds, Band Awds, Outstg
Teenager of the Month Awd (Elks Clb),
Chosen as Tchr's Aid, Cert of Excell
from Mod Bus Col, Flight of the Altus
Writing Awd from MN Mining and Mfg
Co, High Hon Roll, MT Bd of Ed Hon
S'ship Relinquished to Attend Whitman
Col; Whitman Col: Clair Sherwood
S'ship, Tau Kappa Epsilon Frat Swee-
theart 1977-78, Music S'ship; g/MDiv;
To Counsel and Teach Pt-time and Wk
in a Wholistic Hlth Ctr.

**VANDENBRANDEN, MONICA
LYNN** oc/Student; b/Nov 19, 1961; h/
827 Westbrook, West Point, MS 39773;
ba/Columbus, MS; p/Marvin J and
Catherine C Vandenbranden, West
Point, MS; ed/W Pt HS, 1979; Grad, MS
Univ for Wom, 1984; pa/Prodn Artist,
Sullivan's Printing, 1977-81; Illustrator,
ADIMAGE; Free-Lance for Var Other
Firms and Cos; cp/Prairie Arts Coun,
Art Dir; Harmon Robinson's Campaign
Art Dir; Highlander Social Clb; Black
List; SEA Student Entertainment Assn;
SGA Student Govt Assn, Election
Commr; Student Art Leag; Kappa Pi;
r/Cath; hon/Art Wk for Var Mags; Dist
Winner, FBLA Poster Contest, 1978;
MUW's Sch Mascot Design, 1983; Copy
Cat, 1982-83; Blacklist Hon, 1983-84;
Bryan Public Lib Solo Art Display; g/
Comml Art Maj w a Minor in Art Hist;
Job in Advtg.

VAN DER VEER, VANESSA GAYLE
oc/Church Youth Director; b/Nov 30,
1956; h/Route 2, Box 175, Bon Aqua,
TN 37025; ba/Dickson, TN; p/Mr and
Mrs Gaylord M Van Der Veer, Bon
Aqua, TN; ed/Boca Raton Sr HS, 1974;

BS, Nazarene Col, 1979; Grad, The
Success Acad, Boca Raton, FL and TN
Real Est Ednl Sys; pa/Ofc Mgr, Bkkpr,
Secy, Knob Hill Devel Co and Commun
Constrn, 1980-81; Pt-time, Rose Martin
Rltrs, 1981; Tchg Position, Dickson,
TN, 1981-82; Yth Dir, First Ch of the
Nazarene, 1982-; Zone Pres, Nazarene
Yth Intl; Sunday Sch Tchr, First Ch of
the Nazarene; Ch Bd, Ch of the Naz-
arene, 1981, 1982-83; Notary Public, FL;
Real Est Lic, FL; cp/Juniorettes Ser Clb;
Future Tchrs Am; FHA; Pep Clb; Music
Clb; Student Activs Com; Intramural
Aths; Cheerldr; All-St Vocal Rep; St
Vocal Solo and Ensemble Competition;
Lead Role in HS Musical; Col Chapel
Choir, Concert Choir, Choral Soc;
STEA; Vol Tchg Asst, Harris Hillman
Sch for the Mtly Retarded and Handi-
capped; r/Nazarene; hon/1st Place
Winner, Talent Awd, Miss Dickson
Pageant; Exceeded Goals in Ch and Yth
Wk; Num Music and Ath Awds; 3rd
Place, Nat Quartet Conv Vocal Com-
petition, 1977; Pres Phy Fitness Awd;
Miss Dickson, *The Dickson Herald* 1983,
Nashville Banner 1983, *Dickson Free Press*
1983, *Hickman County Times* 1983, *The
Dickson Herald* 1983; Finalist, Miss TN
Pageant, 1983; Yg Commun Ldrs of Am;
Num Other Hons; g/Further Ed in
Music/Music Perf.

VANN, ANGELA LEVELLE oc/Devel-
opmental Technician; b/May 12, 1959;
h/1742 Englewood Drive, Apartment
D-1, Staunton, VA 24401; ba/Staunton,
VA; p/Mr and Mrs Lonnie Vann, Fayet-
teville, NC; ed/HS Dipl, Cape Fear Sr
HS; BA, Psych, Catawba Col; EdS, Sch
Psych, James Madison Univ; pa/Devel-
opmental Tech, DeJarnette Ctr, 1982-;
Psychi Tech, Cumberland Psychi Hosp,
1981-82; Records Clk, Salisbury Police
Dept, 1980-81; Avon Rep, Fayetteville,
1980-81; Cnslr, Cumberland Co Mtl Htl
Ctr, 1980; r/Prot; hon/Life Dynamics
F'ship, Assoc Mem; Intl Yth in Achmt;
Commun Ldrs of Am; Dir of Dist'd
Ams; g/To Complete Sch Psych Grad
Studies at James Madison Univ and To
Establish a Pvt Pract in Psychotherapy.

VAN PATTEN, CHARLENE ANNIE
oc/Student; b/Aug 10, 1962; h/101
Abbotsford Drive, Simpsonville, SC
29681; p/Mr and Mrs Charles H Van
Patten, Simpsonville, SC; ed/Hillcrest
HS, 1980; Grad, Univ of SC, 1983; cp/
Phi Beta Kappa Nat Hon Soc; Gamma
Beta Phi Hon Soc; Golden Key Nat Hon
Soc; Kappa Phi Kappa Nat Ednl Frat;
hon/J McTyeire Daniel S'ship, 1982-83;
Nat Dean's List, 1981, 1982, 1983; W/
W Am HS Students; g/Maj in Ed; To
Teach HS Hist and Eng.

VANTURE, HOLLY FROST oc/Legis-
lative Aide; b/Oct 15, 1957; h/1451
Lamia Court, Orlando, FL 32822; ba/
Orlando, FL; m/Homer S Jr; p/Mr and
Mrs Thomas N Frost, Jacksonville, FL;
ed/Robert E Lee HS, 1975; BA, Univ of
FL, 1979; pa/Legis Aide, FL Ho of Reps,
1979-; Computer Analyst, FL Dept of
Commerce, 1978-79; Am Soc of Public
Admrs; cp/FL Blue Key; Col Ath Assn
Bd of Dirs; Kappa Kappa Gamma, Exec
Bd of Alumni Grp, Chapt Advr; Ctl FL
Panhellenic; Ctl FL Yg Dems; Ctl FL
Gator Clb; Univ of FL Nat Alumni Assn
Bd of Dirs, 1981-82; r/Epis; hon/Apprec
Awd, Univ of FL Ath Assn; Gov for Bd
of Regents Nom; W/W Among Students
in Am Cols and Univs; Dir of Dist'd

Ams; 5,000 Personalities of World;
Outstg Yg Wom of Am; World W/W
Wom; Personalities of S; g/MPA; Posi-
tion in Mgmt; Computer Sci Deg.

**VAN VELDHUIZEN, VARINA JOLI
ELIZABETH** oc/Student; b/Jan 4, 1962;
h/PO Box 81577, ½ Mile Gilmore Trail,
Fairbanks, AK 99708; p/Mr and Mrs
Philip A Van Veldhuizen, Fairbanks,
AK; ed/HS, 1980; cp/Campus Yth
F'ship, Prog Com Chm; Col of ID Rep
to Val Rdg Assn; W Val Key Clb, Secy;
4-H, Pres, Jr Ldr, Secy, Reporter, Histn;
hon/Truman Scholar, 1981; Col of ID
Dean's List; Nat Dean's List; W/W
Among Am HS Students; Intl Yth in
Achmt; g/Deg in Elem Ed; Rdg Minor;
Tchr of Handicapped Chd.

**VATANDOOST, LALEH DEBORA-
LEE** oc/Student; b/Feb 22, 1967; h/105
Country Club Estates, Hendersonville,
TN 37075; p/Ira and Nossi Vatandoost,
Hendersonville, TN; ed/Student, Hen-
dersonville HS; cp/Tennis Team; Com-
mandos Soccer Team; Newspaper Staff;
Sci Clb; Battalion-Pep Clb; F'ship of
Christian Aths; FHA; Serteen; hon/Cert
of Hon in Editing Sch Newspaper, 1982;
DAR Awd for Outstg Wk in Am Hist,
1979; Ath Awd for Soccer Participation,
1983; g/Majs in Jour and Law, Minor
in Psych; Newscaster, Legal Journalist.

VEAL, TRACEY YVONNE oc/Stu-
dent; b/Mar 16, 1962; h/3511 Eisenhower Circle, Atlanta, GA 30354; ba/
Decatur, GA; p/Jonas H and Lavada M
Veal, Decatur, GA; ed/Gordon HS,
1980; Univ of Marburg Sum Study
Abroad, 1981; Att'g, Agnes Scott Col;
pa/Asst to Curator of Art Galleries
1980-82, Dept of Sociol Student Asst
1982-83, Lib Asst 1983, Asst to Dir of
Student Hlth Sers 1982-84, Agnes Scott
Col; Intern, Emory Univ Sum Fam
Planning Prog, 1982; Intern, Continuum Alliance for Human Devel, 1983;
cp/Kappa Clb Pres, 1979-80; Math Clb,
1978-80; Student Govt Mem, 1979-80;
Atlanta Journal Constitution HS Sports
Correspondent, 1978-79; Col German
Clb, 1980; Pres, Black Student Org,
1981-82; Student Admissions Rep,
1980-84; Campus Newspaper, Hlth and
Sci Columnist and Writer 1982-84;
Public Relats Dir, Multi-Cultural
Awareness Symp, 1983-84; Big Sister,
1981-82; Pres, Sociol Clb, 1983-84; Sr
Cnslr, 1983-84; Vol, Planned Parent-
hood of Atlanta, 1982-83; Vol, Grady
Meml Hosp, 1982-83; hon/PTA S'ship
Recip, 1980; Gifted Student Awd, 1980;
Hon Roll, 1978-80; Nat Hon Soc,
1979-80; Beta Clb, 1978-80; Student
Coun Ldrship Awd, 1980; Kappa Clb
Ser Awd, 1980; Soc of Wom Engrs Excell
Awd, 1980; WSB Yg Am, 1980; *Atlanta
Journal Constitution* Cup, 1980; Am Soci-
ological Assn Hon Scholar, 1983; W/W
Am HS Students; g/Majs in Sociol,
Anthropol and Psych; PhD in Sociol,
Specializing in Hlth and Med Res and
Adm.

VELEHRADSKY, NANCY JO oc/
Elementary Music Instructor; b/Jan 22,
1958; h/556 North Absaroka, Powell,
WY 82435; ba/Powell, WY; p/Joseph and
Ina Velehradsky, Bellevue, NE; ed/
Bellevue HS, 1976; BMus, NE Wesleyan
Univ, 1980; pa/Elem Music Instr, Powell
Public Schs, 1982-; Elem Music Instr,
Harlan Commun Schs, 1980-82; Secy,
Rocky Ridge Music Ctr, 1978-80; Other
Previous Positions; AAUW; Beta Sigma

Phi; NEA; ISEA; HEA; WSEA; PEA; MENC; hon/Kappa Delta Pi; Mu Phi Epsilon; Ionians; Cardinal Key; Outstg Sr, 1980; Griggs and Bennett S'ship, Music; Pres's S'ship, Acad; Miss So Kol S Omaha Czech Queen, 1980; Miss NE Czech Queen, 1980; 4th Runner-Up, Miss NE Pageant, 1981; WY Girls' St Music Dir, 1982; Miss Pk Co, 1983; Miss Congeniality, 1983; W/W Am HS and Cols; g/To Teach Music Overseas.

VERBA, DAVID C oc/Student; b/Mar 5, 1954; h/1152 East 176 Street, Cleveland, OH 44119; p/Steve and Isebel Verba, Cleveland, OH; ed/Collinwood HS, 1972; Dipl, Cooper Sch of Art, 1976; BFA, The Cleveland Inst of Art, 1980; Student, Kent St Univ; pa/Eng Instr, Cities of Yonago and Matsue, Japan, 1981-82; Instr, Cooper Sch of Art, 1980-81; r/Buddhist; hon/Cert of Recog, 28th Annual Art Show, 1982; Helen Green Perry Traveling S'ship, Cleveland Inst of Art, 1980; Henry Keller Meml Drawing Awd, Cleveland Inst of Art, 1978, 1979; Clarence T Reinbeger Meml S'ship, Cleveland Inst of Art, 1979; Hon S'ship, Cleveland Inst of Art, 1978; Hon Mention in Painting, Cleveland Inst of Art, 1978; Hon S'ship, Cooper Sch of Art, 1972; Martha Holden Jennings Foun S'ship Awd, 1970; Yg Commun Ldrs of Am; Intl Yth in Achmt; Nat Dean's List; g/To Finish Grad Sch; To Gain Employmt as an Instr in Japan.

VERRETTE, CRAIG JAMES oc/Outside Equipment Salesman; b/Jul 3, 1955; h/186 East Oakland Drive, St Rose, LA 70087; ba/New Orleans, LA; m/Jane Hazlitt; c/Adam James; p/Mr and Mrs Davis A Verrette, Metairie, LA; ed/Archbishop Rummel HS, 1973; Univ of NO, 1973-75; BA, Loyola Univ, 1978; pa/Parts Mgr, Exxon Co, 1974-76; Salesman, Exec Trainee, Genuine Parts, 1976-78; Mgr, Purchasing Agt, Raceland Ace Hardware, 1978-80; Parts Sales, Purchasing Agt, Inventory Control Mgr, Shipping and Receiving Mgr, Parts Mgr, Outside Sales, Ser Engrg Co, 1980-; c/Loyola Alumni Assn; Metairie JC's, 1980; r/Cath; hon/Nat Hon Soc, 1982-83; Outstg CYO, 1971; VP, Loyola City Col Student Union, 1976; Dean's List, Loyola Univ, 1975-76; W/W Among Students in Am Univs and Cols; Intl Yth in Achmt.

VICKERS, MARK STEPHEN oc/Executive Director; b/Sep 11, 1957; h/1060 Elm Street #11, Glendale, CA 91201; ba/Burbank, CA; p/John and Anne Vickers, Vallejo, CA; ed/St Patrick HS, 1975; BA, Bus Adm, Azusa Pacific Univ, 1979; pa/Copywriter, Pennington Ad Agy, 1978; Communs Dir, Glendora C of C, 1979; Dir, Public Relats/Asst Mgr 1979-82, Exec Dir 1982-, Burbank C of C; Pres-Elect, So CA Assn of C of C Execs; cp/Pres-Elect, San Fernando Val Press Clb; Burbank Adult Basic Ed Adv Com; Friends of Burbank Airport; r/Christian; hon/Bk of Am Bus Awd, 1975; Eagle Scout; W/W W; Outstg Yg Men in Am.

VILLANUEVA, MARY HELEN TORRES oc/Social Worker; b/Oct 21, 1960; h/2608 Auburn Street, Lubbock, TX 79415; ba/Lubbock, TX; m/Ramiro; p/Mrs Maria S Torres; ed/Dipl, Lubbock HS; BA in Sociol, Lubbock Christian Col; pa/Social Wkr/Patient Rep, Highland Hosp, 1982-84; Social Ser Dir,

Highland Hosp, 1984-; Med Social Wkr; Cert'd Social Wkr, TX; hon/Dean's Awd; Grad, summa cum laude; Dean's List All Semesters at Col; W/W Among Outstg Yg Wom; g/MSW.

VILLARREAL, RENE oc/Meat Lab Supervisor; b/Mar 8, 1962; h/629 West Durham, Raymondville, TX 78580; ba/Alpine, TX; p/Ruben and Edelmira M Villarreal, Raymondville, TX; ed/Raymondville HS, 1980; AAS Deg, Meat Technol, Sul Ross St Univ, 1982; Bach, Meat Sci, Sul Ross St Univ, 1984; pa/Meat Lab Hd Processor; TX OK Meat Packers Assn; cp/Livestock Judging Team; Meat Judging Team; 4-H; FFA; Football; Track; Swimming; Diving; hon/Delta Tau Alpha, Pres; Nat Hon Soc; g/Meat Lab Supvr.

VINCENT, MARK LA VAL oc/Student; b/Oct 4, 1961; h/Route 4, Box 89, Kershaw, SC 29067; p/Mr and Mrs Curtis Vincent; ed/Mt Pisgah HS; Bapt Col at Charleston; cp/Student Govt Treas, Activs Bd; Psi Kappa Phi, Com for Orientation; Men's Tennis; Jr and Sophomore Class Senator; Senate Com Chm; Tri Psi Chi; Senate Chaplain; Cnslg Asst; Others; hon/Commencement Marshal; Christian Ldrship Scholar; HS Salutatorian; g/Master's Deg.

VINCIGUERRA, AMELIA MARIA oc/Student; b/Mar 14, 1964; h/6018 Suzanne Road, Waldorf, MD 20601; p/Anthony and Amelia Vinciguerra, Waldorf, MD; ed/Thomas Stone HS, 1982; Att'g, Frostburg St Col; cp/Cross Country, HS Capt, 4 Yrs; HS Track, 4 Yrs, Capt 1980-82; Col Cross Country; Col Radio Sta, Bus Mgr 1982-84; Bd of Dirs, WFNR, 1983-84; Nat Hons Prog, 1982-84; FSC Escort Ser, 1983; r/Cath; hon/Hon Roll, 1983; Nat Hon Soc, 1980-82; MVP, Track, 1980; Century II Sch Ldr, 1982; Finalist, Miss MD TEEN Pageant, 1981-82; Female Ath of the Yr Nom, 1982; Christian Ath Awd, 1982; W/W Among Am HS Students; Nat Hon Roll; Intl Yth in Achmt; g/Deg in Bus Adm; Financing; Stockbroker.

VITE, BRADLEY SCOTT oc/Executive; b/Aug 6, 1955; h/1838 Greenleaf Boulevard, Elkhart, IN 46514; ba/Elkhart, IN; p/Mr and Mrs Frank A Vite, Elkhart, IN; ed/WaWaSee Prep Sch, 1973; BLS, Hillsdale Col, 1980; Cert'd Real Est Course, IN Univ S Bend; pa/Pres, Bradley Vite Fine Arts; cp/Pres and Fdg Father, Alpha Kappa Chapt, Sigma Chi; Pres, Men's Coun, Jud Body on Campus; Dean's List Student; Internship, The Hillsdale Daily News, 1978; Res Advr, 1978; Varsity Golf; Intramural Sprots; Elk; C of C; Vol w Mtly Retarded; Bd of Dirs, AIEC; PBS, Art Chm of Channel 34, Auction Cabinet; hon/Omicron Delta Kappa; W/W Among Students in Am Univs and Cols; Intl Yth in Achmt; g/Career Involving Deg in Commun Arts Media.

VITULLI, PAIGE ANN oc/Student; b/Oct 8, 1963; h/2025 Maryknoll Court, Mobile, AL 36609; p/Dr and Mrs William F Vitulli, Mobile, AL; ed/HS Grad; Att'g, Univ of S AL; pa/Salesperson, Page 1 Ltd, 1982-; cp/Ath Org; HS Cheerldr, 1979-82; hon/HS Hon Roll, 1982; W/W Among Am HS Students; g/Maj in Early Childhood Ed; Elem Sch Tchr.

VLIEG, RONALDO ANTONIO oc/Student; b/Mar 23, 1958; h/PO Box 398, Hope, AR 71801; ba/Hope, AR; m/Judith

Lynn; p/Olga Maria Santos-Vleig; ed/BS in Biol and Chem, Henderson St Univ; BA in Polit Sci, So AR Univ; mil/USAR; pa/Lab Asst, Biol Dept, Henderson St Univ; Info Conslt, Howard Co Migrant Ednl Sers; cp/ROTC Cadet; Scabbard and Blade; Cadet Soc; Leag of U Latin Am Citizens; Henderson St Univ Alumni; r/Rom Cath; hon/Outstg Achmt Awd, So AR Univ, 1982; ROTC Awd, 1982; Dist'd Mil Student, Dept of the Army Awd, 1983; g/Comm'd 2nd Lt, AUS; Med Sch.

VON KALOW, DANA SUSAN oc/Student; b/Aug 2, 1963; h/8427 Greenstone Drive, Dallas, TX 75243; p/Mr and Mrs Billy Von Kalow, Dallas, TX; ed/Lake Highlands HS, 1981; Att'g, N TX St Univ; pa/Spec Ed Aide, Pre-Sch and Elem Sch Level; cp/Hosp Vol, Pre-Employmt Lab Ed; Spirit Team Lt; Pre-Employmt Lab Ed; hon/Commun Ldrs of Am; Intl Yth in Achmt; W/W Among Am HS Students; g/Doctrine in Tchrs of Yg Chd; Psych; Own and Run Sch for Yg Chd.

VOSLER, DEBORAH LYNN oc/Biology Instructor, Coach; b/Mar 16, 1957; h/3306 Bevans, Cheyenne, WY 82001; ba/Cheyenne, WY; p/Robert C Vosler, Rock River, WY; A Eileen Vosler, Guernsey, WY; ed/Cheyenne E HS, 1975; AA, E WY Col; BSEd, Cameron Univ, 1979; MA, Ed, SWn OK St Univ, 1980; pa/Biol Instr, Varsity Volleyball and Basketball Coach, E HS; WY Coaches Assn; Nat and WY Sci Tchrs Assns; NEA; CTEA; cp/Student Missionary Internship; Phi Kappa Phi; Nat Hon Soc; Sigma Tau Delta; CPR Instr, ARC and Am Heart Assn; HS Sr Class Pres; Varsity Volleyball; hon/Grad w Highest Hons, 1979; SWOSU Hons Fellow; Hd Volleyball Coach, OK St Volleyball Champions Div III, 1979-80; Intl Yth in Achmt; Nat Dean's List; Commun Ldrs of Am; g/Doct Deg in PE/Coaching; Position as Phy Edr and Hd Volleyball Coach at Maj Col or Univ.

VOSLER, TAMRA LYN oc/Student; b/May 8, 1967; h/2949 Henderson Drive, Cheyenne, WY 82001; p/Charles and Linda Vosler, Cheyenne, WY; ed/Student, E HS; cp/E-Clb; Pep Clb; Am Field Ser; Christian Yth F'ship; F'ship of Christian Aths; Intramural Participant, 20 Activs; r/First Christian; hon/Runner-Up, Intramural Sports, 1983-84; Coaches Awd, Volleyball, 1983-84; Volleyball, All Conf, All Reg Team, All St Tournament Team, All St Player, 1983-84; Basketball Player of the Wk, 2 Times, 1983-84; Volleyball Player of the Wk, 7 Times, 1983-84; Meet of Champs Medalist for Track, 1983-84; All Reg, All St Track Mem, 1983-84; All Reg Track Mem, 1982-83; Lettered in Track, 1983-84, 1982-83; Lettered in Basketball, 1983-84, 1982-83; Lettered in Volleyball, 1983-84, 1982-83; Other Ath Hons; g/To Participate on a Nat Volleyball Team; Elem Spec Ed Tchr; Vet Tech.

VRSIC, PAVLA GABRIEL FRANK oc/Student; b/May 30, 1964; N/Jarvis Christian College, Hawkins, TX 75765; p/Prof and Mrs G Frank Vrsic, Hawkins, TX; ed/Hawkins HS, 1981; Att'g, Brigham Young Univ; pa/Data-Entry Typist, Computer Tchg Sers, 1983-; Geriatrics, Roger's Residential Care Facility, 1983-; Psychol Tech, UT St Prison, 1983; Hostess, JCC Catering,

1983; Transcriber, BYU German and French Depts, 1983; cp/HS Band, 1976-80; Jarvis Col Band, 1980-81; FTA, 1977-81; FHA, 1977-80; Spch and Drama Clb, 1979-81; Nat Hon Soc, Secy 1979-81; Yrbook Staff, 1978-79, 1980-81; Spch and Drama Teams, 1977-81; UIL Play Cast, 1980-81; MENSA, 1980-; Slavic Clb, 1982-; Brigham Yg Univ Hon Prog, 1981-82; French Clb; Tommorrow's Treasures Photo Org; New England Hist Geneal Soc; r/LDS; hon/Poetry Pub'd in *Dreams, Yearbook of Modern Poetry, Poetry Anthology,* *Eternal Echoes, Trouvere's Annual Unknown Poem & Short Story Book, Images of the Mystic Truth, Poetry of Love;* Rdg Trophy, 1980; Best Rdr Trophy, 1981; Nat Merit Letter of Commend for High Score on NMSQ/PSAT Test, 1980; Superior Ratings at UIL Contests for Poetry and Prose, 1980; Superior Ratings at UIL Contests for Poetry, Prose, Vocal Solos, 1981; 3rd Place, Miss FTA, 1981; 2nd Place, Rotary Spkg Contest, 1981; Rotary Student of the Month, 1981; 4th Place, UIL Spelling and Poetry, 1981; UIL All-Star Cast, 1981; Hon Mention, Nat Poetry Contest, 1981; Pres S'ship for Tuition to Brigham Yg Univ, 1981; HS Salutatorian, 1981; Eng and Hist Awd, 1981; Christian Wom's S'ship, 1981; 1st Place, MS Read-A-Thon, 1977-78; 2nd Place, Rotary Spkg Contest, 1978-79; Rdg Awds, 1978-80; W/W; Intl Yth in Achmt; Commun Ldrs of Am; Personalities of S; 2,000 Notable Ams; Intl Book of Hon; W/W Among Am HS Students; Dir of Dist'd Ams; Personalities of W and MW; Biogl Roll of Hon; Intl W/W Intells; World Biogl Hall of Fame.

W

WADE, DEBRA ANN oc/Student; b/ Mar 21, 1963; h/122 East Washington Street, Poynette, WI 53955; p/Royce and Corrine Wade, Poynette, WI; ed/ Grad, Poynette HS, 1981; Student, Univ of WI Whitewater; pa/Cashier, KY Fried Chicken, 1981; Boxer, Trimmer and Inspector, AMPI, 1982; cp/UMYF, 1975-79, Secy 1979; Nat Hon Soc, 1977-81, VP 1981; Annual Staff, 1977-81; Varsity Clb, 1979-81; Hall Coun, 1981-83, Wing Social Rep; r/ Meth; hon/DAR Awd, 1981; Badger Girls' St, 1980; Tallman Scholar, 1981-82; Dean's List, 1981-82; Phi Eta Sigma, 1982; g/Bus Career.

WADE, JAMES ANTHONY oc/Engineering Assistant; b/Apr 13, 1963; h/ 11 Hickory Lane, Dover, DE 19901; p/ Mr and Mrs Frank J Wade, Dover, DE; ed/Grad, Caesar Rodney HS, 1981; Univ of DE; pa/Engrg Asst, Dover AFB; cp/ Nat Hon Soc; German Clb; BSA; hon/ Fed Jr F'ship Prog; Records S'ship, Univ of DE; Intl Yth in Achmt; W/W Among Am HS Students; g/Elect Engr.

WADE, SAMANTHA oc/Student; b/ Aug 14, 1967; h/Route 5, Box 279, Alexander City, AL 35010; p/Mr and Mrs Donald G Wade, Alexander City, AL; ed/Benjamin Russell HS; cp/Campfire Girl; HS Band; Math Clb; Nat Jr Hon Soc; r/Comer Meml Bapt Ch, Yth Choir; Pres, SS Class; hon/Band Awds: 9 Solo Medals, 1 Medal for Band Requirements, 2 Lttrs, 1979-80; Recip of Trophy for Being 1st Place in Math Tournament, 1980; 3 First Place Ribbons for Alexander City Jr HS Math Tournament, 1980; Nat Jr Hon Soc, 1981; US Nat Math Awd, 1982; Beauty Pageant, 1982; Math Clb, 1982; Spanish Hon Soc, 1983; Nat Hon Soc, 1983; Nat Ednl Devel Tests Awd, 1983; Yg Commun Ldrship Awd, Comer Meml Bapt Ch Yth Choir, 1983; g/Study Math; Computer Sci Career.

WAITE, DENISE C oc/Student; b/ Mar 7, 1963; h/7 Meadow Lane, Walpole, MA 02081; p/Lana D Waite, Walpole, MA; ed/Bishop Feehan HS, 1981; Att'g, Emmanuel Col, 1981-; pa/ Cashier, Heartland Drug, 1979-; Secretarial Wk 1981-82, Math Tutor 1982-, Emmanuel Col; cp/Student Govt, Student Rep 1981-82, Treas 1982-83, VP 1983-; Resident Asst, 1983-; Cheerldg, 1977-79; Travel Abroad, 1979; Spanish Hon Soc, 1978-80; Hon Soc, 1978-81; r/Rom Cath; hon/Dean's List, 1981-; Heartland Drug S'ship, 1983; W/W Among Am HS Students; g/To Wk in a Math-Oriented Field.

WALKER, ANDREW WADE oc/Student; b/Oct 3, 1966; h/2807 Raquet, Nacoqdoches, TX 75961; p/Dr and Mrs Larry L Walker, Nacoqdoches, TX; ed/ Student, Nacoqdoches HS; cp/Eagle Scout, 183; Nacoqdoches Key Clb, 1981-83; TX-OK Dist Lt Gov, Key Clb Intl, 1982-83; Student Coun Del, 1983; French Clb; NHS; Capt, JV Football; r/ Presb; hon/Outstg Freshman, Nacoqdoches Key Clb, 1981-82; Nacoqdoches Kiwanis Sophomore of the Yr, 1983; Outstg Sophomore, 1983; g/To Attend Col and Maj in Pre-Law.

WALKER, CYNTHIA ANN (CINDY) oc/Student; b/Sep 3, 1963; h/1816 Pocahontas Trail, Lebanon, TN 37087; p/Mr and Mrs Richard Walker,

Lebanon, TN; ed/Grad, Lebanon HS, 1981; AS, Cumberland Col, 1983; Student, Mid TN St Univ; cp/Capt, Wrestling Cheerldrs, Sr Yr; Co-Editor-in-Chief, *Devil's Advocate*, Student Coun; HS and Col F'ship of Christian Aths; HS and Col Pep Clb; Drama Clb; Quill and Scroll; Col Cheerldr; Phi Beta Lambda; Outdoor Clb, Pres; Pep Clb; Gamma Beta Phi; r/Ch of Christ; hon/Basketball Homecoming Queen, Sr Yr HS; Jour Awd; HS Grad; Pres's Awd, Cumberland Col, 1983; Ms Cumberland, 1983; C of C Awd in Bus Adm; Banker's Awd in Acctg; Basketball Homecoming Queen, 1981; W/W Jr Cols; Soc of Dist'd Am HS Students; g/Maj in Bus Ed; To Teach Bus in Sec'dy Sch.

WALKER, DUNCAN HUGHITT oc/ Student; b/Oct 25, 1962; h/200 Laurel Forest Circle, Atlanta, GA 30342; p/Mr and Mrs Marvin H Walker, Atlanta, GA; ed/Grad, Mt Vernon Christian Acad, 1981; BA in Hist, The Citadel, 1985; mil/ Midshipman 2/C, USNR; cp/Drama Clb; Basketball, Lettered; Sgt, SC Corps of Cadets; Hist Clb; r/Christian; hon/ Hustle and Desire Awd, Basketball; Dean's List, May 1982, Dec 1982, May 1983; Gold Stars, 1983; Citadel Devel Foun S'ship, 1981; Navy CNET 3-Yr S'ship, 1982; g/To Attend Grad Sch w the Goal of an MA in Hist; Career in the Navy.

WALKER, GORDON THOMAS oc/ Student; b/Aug 3, 1964; h/205 Eleanor Street, Greenville, NC 27834; ba/Buies Creek, NC; p/Mr and Mrs Edward M Walker, Greenville, NC; ed/J H Rose HS; E Carolina Univ; Campbell Univ; pa/ Supvr, Overton's Inc; cp/Key Clb; VP, Spanish Clb; Pres, VICA; Boys' St; Col Repubs; Freshman SGA Rep; Trust Majors Clb; VP, Sophomore Class; Sophomore SGA Rep; Rules Com, Campbell Univ; r/Bapt; hon/Pres Scholar, Campbell Univ, 1982; Phi Eta Sigma, 1983; W/W Among HS Students; g/Ec Maj at Wake Forest Univ; Law Sch; Some Field of Law in the Financial Realm.

WALKER, KAY LYNNE oc/Student; b/Jul 25, 1967; h/Route 1, Box 140, Pryor, OK 74361; p/Carl T and Dorthy Walker, Pryor, OK; ed/HS Student; cp/ Green Country Girls' Softball Org; CSRA; OCA; AQHA; MQHA; Pryor 4 Way Assn; St Congl Page, Rep J D Whorton, 1981; FFA, Treas 1981, Reporter; Softball; Basketball; Band, 1977-; Jr Mem, N Am S Devon Assn, 1980-; r/Bapt; hon/Won Over 100 Ribbons and Trophys at Rodeos; Taught Over 27 Col Students How to Feed, Groom, Ride and Properly Care for Horses, 1982; FFA Awds: Soil and Water Mgmt, Landscape, Extemporaneous Public Spkg; Recognized, OK St Univ Col of Agri for Outstg Achmts in Dairy Products Judging; Nom'd for St Farmer, FFA; Lettered in Band; g/Archaeologist; Interpreter.

WALKER, TISH oc/Student; b/Apr 30, 1963; h/24 Cumberland Circle, El Paso, TX 79903; p/Col W A Walker Jr (dec); Mrs W A Walker Jr, El Paso, TX; ed/Burges HS; Student, Columbia Col, 1980-; cp/Student Govt Pres, 1983-84; 2nd VP, SGA, 1982-83; Bd of Dirs, SC Student Assn, 1983-84; SC St Student Legis, Asst Lt Gov 1983; r/Meth; hon/ Columbia Col Trustee Scholar,

1980-84; Top Acad Marshal at Columbia Col, 1982-83; Acad Marshal, 1980-83; Columbia Col Pres's List and Dean's List; Nancy Moore S'ship, 1981-82; g/Law Sch.

WALLACE, KAREN GAYE oc/Student; ba/Jan 15, 1965; h/Route 1, Box 151, Kenansville, NC 28349; p/Mr and Mrs E G Wallace, Kenansville, NC; ed/ HS Dipl, 1983; cp/Stat, Boys' Basketball, 1981-82; Scorekeeper, Girls' Basketball, 1981-82; Pres, Beta Clb, 1979-80; Co-Pres, Chorus, 1979-80; VP, Student Coun, 1979-80; Yth Adv Coun on Lunches, 1979-80; Quiz Bowl Team, 1981, 1982, 1983; Co-Pres, Sophomore Class, 1980-81; Pep Clb Treas, 1981-82; Prom Com, 1983; Drama Clb Adv Coun, 1983; Editor of HS Annual, 1982-83; r/ Meth; hon/One of 5 Outstg Srs, Goldsboro Dist of the U Meth Ch; Freshman Hist Awd; Freshman Consumer and Homemaking Home Ec Awd; Rotary Student of the Month, 1983; S'ship to Queens Col; g/To Study Nsg at Queens Col; BS; To Be Involved in Student Govt.

WALLACE, SUSAN CLARA oc/Student; b/Mar 15, 1960; h/Route 2, Box 305, Cherryville, NC 28021; p/Mr and Mrs William Warren Wallace Sr, Cherryville, NC; ed/Burns Sr HS, 1978; BA, Gardner-Webb Col, 1982; cp/FHA; FFA; Art Clb; Band; Orch; Chorus Accompanist, 1981-82; Music Edrs Nat Conf, VP 1980-81, Pres 1981-82; Am Choral Dir's Assn Inter-Clb Coun, 1980-81; Accompanist, 2 Opera Prodns; Jr and Sr Piano Recitals; Focus Team to Catawba, NC; Asst Pianist/Organist, First Wesleyan Ch of Cherryville; In-Grp Yg Believers; Girls' Quartet; hon/Awd in Ornamental Hort, 1977; Hon Roll; Recog'd by Sr Class; Tied for 2nd, Yth Talent Contest; Spangler Music S'ship; Campbell Music Achmt Awd; g/BA in Sacred Music; Min of Music in Ch; Mission Wk in Tulsa, OK.

WALSH, KIMBERLY ANITA oc/ Product Development Engineer; b/Apr 21, 1957; h/14744 Tutwiler Avenue, Memphis, TN 38107; ba/Memphis, TN; p/Fondren and Eva Walsh, Biloxi, MS; ed/Dipl w High Hons, D'Iberville, HS, 1975; BS in Biol Engrg, MS St Univ, 1981; MS in Biomed Engrg, Tulane Univ, 1983; Att'g, Memphis St Univ; pa/ Prod Devel Engr, Richards Med Co, 1983-; Biomats Res Assoc, Tulane Med Ctr, 1981-83; Biomed Res Asst, Biol Engrg Dept, MS St Univ, 1979-81; MS Soc of Biol Engrs, VP 1980-81; Engrg Student Coun, 1980-81; Soc of Wom Engrs, 1980-82; r/Prot; hon/Pub, "Variables Affecting the Interface Mechanics of Porous Co-Cr-Mo Systems," 1983; Pres's and Dean's Acad List, 1976-81; Carbomedics F'ship, 1982; g/To Attain MBA; To Wk in High Tech Mktg.

WALTERS, JAMES TODD oc/Student; b/Nov 3, 1964; h/116 Woodford Street, Versailles, KY 40383; p/ Anthony Wayne and Elizabeth Stith Walters, Versailles, KY; ed/Elizabethtown HS; Att'g, Univ of KY Col of Bus and Ec; cp/Elizabethtown Chapt Nat Beta Clb; Hardin Co Jr Achmt, VP of Fin, VP of Mktg; ARC Vol Swim Aide; St James Sch of Rel Vol; Elizabethtown HS Intramural Sports; Spanish Clb; hon/Nat Merit Commended Student; Math Student of Yr, HS, 1980, 1981; 99 Percentile, ACT; 4 Acad Lttrs, 3 Yrs;

Dean's List, Fall 1982, Sprg 1983; g/Bus Adm Maj; Earn MBA at Univ of KY; Attend Law Sch; Corporate Lwyr.

WALTON, ELMILA DAISETTA oc/Student; b/Dec 24, 1960; h/1400 First Street, Bay City, TX 77414; p/Mr and Mrs John Walton, Bay City, TX; ed/Dipl, Bay City HS, 1979; AA, Wharton Co Jr Col, 1982; Att'g, Lamar Univ; pa/Receptionist, Celanese Chem Corp, 1978-79; Census Ennumerator, US Govt, 1979; Student Aide for Sum Sch, Bay City ISD, 1980, 1981; Student Aide in Communs Dept, Lamar Univ, 1982; Record and Document Control, Bechtel Energy Corp, 1983; cp/Yg Am Clb Com Chm, 1980-81; Ebony Clb, Secy; All St Choir, 1980, 1981; Delta Psi Omega, Dramatic Frat; Green Room Players, 1980-81; Psalms 150 Gospel Chorus; GSU Adversary Tng Prog; r/Prot; hon/Dean's List, 1980, 1981, 1982; Outstg Sr Spch Student, 1983; W/W Among Jr Cols; g/BA in Spch Communication, Lamar Univ; Teach Spch on Univ Level While Wkg on Master's Deg.

WALTON, MARY JOYCE oc/Student; b/Jun 15, 1967; h/Route 2, Box 106, Fayette, AL 35555; p/Howard and Mary Lee Walton, Fayette, AL; ed/Fayette HS, 1985; cp/Debate, Spanish, Sci Clbs; Student Coun; Hon Soc; Tiger Rag Staff; Stage Band; Melody Jr Music; Organ Clb; Donations to MS Soc; Marching Band; Hon Roll; r/Pisgue Bapt Ch; hon/All-St Clarinet; 2 Gold Cups, Piano Perf; Gold Cup, Organ Perf; Jr Nat Hon Soc; Class Rep, Most Handsome/Most Beautiful Contest; g/Deg in Aeronautical Engrg; Career w NASA.

WALZ, JEFF L oc/Principal; b/Apr 14, 1957; h/Box 104, Clearwater, NE 68726; ba/Clearwater, NE; ed/Grad, Valentine HS, 1975; BA, Chadron St Col, 1978; MS, Wayne St Col, 1981; pa/Tchr/Coach, Clearwater HS; Current Prin, Clearwater Public Schs; Am Assn Physics Tchrs; NE Coaches Assn; cp/Yg Men's Clb; r/Lay Min and Rel Ed Tchr, St Wms Ch; hon/Top Grad, Chadron St Col; Appt'd Res Asst, Argonne Nat Lab; Res Asst, IA St Univ; g/PhD in Ed, Univ of NE; Col Tchr.

WARD, ANDRA R oc/Student; b/Jul 5, 1963; h/3654 Forest Park Drive, Cincinatti, OH 45229; p/Henry Jr and Gloria Ward, Cincinatti, OH; ed/Cinc Sch for Creat and Perf'g Arts; Att'g, No KY Univ; pa/Nat Christian Yth Coun; Coor'g Com Bd of Dirs, Black Achievers Prog, YMCA, 1981; hon/Black Yth Achiever 1979, Outstg Black Yth Achiever, Cinc 1982, YMCA; Bd of Trustees, Cinc Sch for Creat and Perf'g Arts; Awd of Outstg Acad Achmt, Pres Black U Students, No KY Univ; Commun Ldrs of Am; g/Corporate Mgmt in Telecommuns Enterprises.

WARD, TAMMY LYNN BREWINGTON oc/Student; b/Oct 14, 1964; h/Route 3, Paragould, AR 72450; m/Mark; p/Bill and Beverly Brewington, Paragould, AR; ed/Oak Grove HS; Att'g, AR St Univ; cp/4-H, 2 Yrs; Beta Clb, 4 Yrs; FHA, 3 Yrs; Future Tchrs of Am, 3 Yrs; Sci Clb, 3 Yrs; Photo Clb, 2 Yrs; Drama Clb, 2 Yrs; Basketball, 6 Yrs; hon/Best Freethrow Shooter, 2 Yrs; Capt, Jr HS Basketball Team, 1 Yr; Capt, Sr HS Basketball Team, 2 Yrs; Biol I Awd, 1981; Biol II Awd, 1982; Eng II Awd, 1982; g/To Make a Career in the Med Field.

WARE, MARTHA JO oc/Student; b/Feb 1, 1963; h/1302 Clayton, Borger, TX 79007; p/Jack D and Betty Fletcher Ware, Borger, TX; ed/Grad, Borger HS, 1981; Att'g, Xavier Univ; cp/Pres, Med Explorer Post 507, 1980-81; Histn, JCL, 1980-81; Vol, ARC; Big Sister; Treas, Xavier Players, 1982-83, VP 1983-84; r/SS Tchr; hon/W/W Among Am HS Students; Other Biogl Listings; g/Clin Psychol.

WARE, THOMAS R oc/Student; b/May 10, 1964; h/3045 Brookwood Drive, Edgewood, KY 41017; p/Mr and Mrs Thomas E Ware, Edgewood, KY; ed/Grad, Dixie Hgts HS, 1982; Att'g, No KY Univ; pa/Mgr, Small Recording Ser, Tom Ware Prodns; Piano Tchr; cp/Staff Writer, NKU Student Newspaper; KY All-St Chorus; hon/NKU Pres 4-Yr S'ship, 1982; Salutatorian, HS; Dean's List, NKU; 1st Place, KFWC St Piano Competition, 1982; 11 Consecutive Superior Ratings in Nat Fdn of Music Clbs (Piano) Contest; W/W Among Am HS Students; W/W Music; Commun Ldrs of Am; g/Pre-Med Biol Maj, NKU; Phys.

WASHINGTON, HALIE MARIE oc/Student; b/Apr 7, 1961; h/812 Vagabond Drive, Fayetteville, NC 28304; p/Mrs Lorene Washington, Fayetteville, NC; ed/E E Smith Sr HS, 1979; BA in Psych and Sociol, Univ of NC Chapel Hill, 1983; pa/Tutor, E E Smith Sr High, 1978-79; Pers Asst, UNC-CH, 1981-83; cp/Orientation Cnslr, 1980, 1982; Proj Uplift Cnslr, 1981; Big Buddy, 1982-83; Chp, Campus Commun Link, 1982-83; Lady of Black and Gold, 1981-83; Pre-Orientation Cnslr, 1981, 1982; Nsg Home Vol, 1981; Student Cnslr Rep, 1977; r/Meth; hon/Nat Hon Soc; Dean's List, 1982; W/W Among NC HS Srs; g/PhD in Gerontology.

WASHINGTON, JOYCE DENISE oc/Student; b/Jan 22; h/201 Northwest Street, Lompoc, CA 93436; p/Mr and Mrs Arvan Washington Jr, Lompoc, CA; ed/Lompoc Sr HS, 1980; Naval Acad Prep Sch, 1981; USAF Acd; cp/GSA; Track, Prep Sch, HS and Intercol; Secy, Pres, HS Forensics Clb; Cheerldr, Prep Sch; r/Lector, Usher, SS Tchr, Parish Coun Mem'-at-Large, Ch; hon/First Class Girl Scout, GSA; Intl W/W; W/W Among Am HS Students.

WATKINS, JOHN ANDREW oc/Student; b/Feb 6, 1965; h/123 Baker Road, Martin, TN 38237; p/Dr and Mrs Phillip W Watkins, Martin, TN; ed/Westview HS; Att'g, Univ of TN Martin; pa/Paint Crew, UTM, 1980-82; Asst Chef, 4UR Ranch, CO, 1983; cp/Football, 4 Yrs; Basketball, 4 Yrs; Student Coun Pres; Key Clb Secy; Jr Class Pres; Pi Kappa Alpha Frat; r/Meth; hon/Student Coun Pres S'ship, 1983; Am Legion Boys' St, 1982; g/Maj in Plant and Soil Sci.

WATSON, MARGARET FORD oc/Student; b/Sep 28, 1964; h/PO Box E, Farmville, VA 23901; p/Mr and Mrs W A Watson III, Farmville, VA; ed/Grad w Hons, Prince Edward Acad, 1981; Deg in Fin, VA Polytechnic Inst and St Univ, 1986; pa/Cnslr, VA Tech All-Sports Camp, 1983; cp/Circle K, Com Chp 1983, Outstg Mem 1983; Vatico, Pep Clb, 1983; r/Bapt; hon/Nat Hon Soc; Deg of Distn, Nat Forensics Leag; W/W Among Am HS Students; Soc of Dist'd HS Students; Yg Commun Ldrs;

g/Maj in Fin; Career in Investmts.

WATTS, KAREN LYNN oc/Student; b/Nov 19, 1964; h/PO Box 17, Buchanan, VA 24066; ba/Lynchburg, VA; p/Mr and Mrs L N Watts Jr, Buchanan, VA; ed/HS Dipl, 1983; Att'g, Randolph-Macom Wom's Col; cp/FHA, Pres 1982-83, Secy 1981-82, Treas 1980-81; FHA Star Fdn, 2nd VP 1980-81, 1st VP 1981-82, Treas 1982-83; Drama Clb; Sch Musicals; Wrestling Stat; NHS; Lang Clb, VP 1982-83; Chorus; r/Presb; Sunday Sch Tchr; hon/Chorus Letter, 1982; Hon Chord, 1983; FHA Jr Deg of Achmt, 1979; FHA Chapt Deg, 1980; FHA St Deg, 1983; Botetourt Assn for Retarded Citizens S'ship, 1983; Botetourt Ed Assn S'ship, 1983; Intl Fgn Lang Awd, 1982; W/W Among Am HS Students; Intl Fgn Lang Acad; g/To Earn MA in Psych; To Wk as a Child Psychol.

WATTS, MARIE ELIZABETH oc/Interior Designer, Manager; b/Oct 12, 1960; h/1053 Papermill Court, Washington, DC 20007; ba/Washington, DC; ed/Ursuline Acad; SMU; BA, Mt Vernon Col; pa/Designer, Ofc Mgr, Am Interiors Inc; Assoc, ASID, 1984-; cp/DAR, 1984; Active in Repub Party; Intl Clb, 1979-81; Vol, Chd's Med Ctr, 1979-80; Dallas N Jr Achmt, Treas 1975; Spanish Clb Treas, 1977; Dallas Cotillion, Dallas Country Clb, 1972-79; Perf'g Spch Clb, 1974-76; hon/2nd Prize, TX St Fair (Painting), 1972; 1st Prize, TX St Fair (Original), 1976; First Prize, Four St Fair (Art), 1968; W/W E; g/Own Bus (Intl Design Firm).

WAYNE, BRYAN MATTHEW oc/Student; b/Aug 9, 1957; h/6718 Callaghan #312, San Antonio, TX 78229; p/Lloyd G and Sandra L Wayne, Albuquerque, NM; ed/Sandia HS, 1975; BS, cum laude, Baylor Univ, 1979; Univ of TX San Antonio; pa/AMA; TX Med Assn; Delta Tau Chi Med Frat; Med Admissions Com; Med Athletics Com; Alpha Omega Alpha Nat Med Hon Soc; cp/Nat Hon Soc; Lttr Clb; Yg Life; Football; Wrestling; Baseball; Track; Track and Field Ath of Yr, 1975; Navigators; Spurr Nat Hon Soc; Tri-Beta Nat Biol Hon Soc; Pres, VP, Esquire Frat; Soccer; Rugby; DCD Track Clb; ITA Clb; Vol HS Track Coach; Little Leag Coach; Soccer Coach; Intramural Football, Softball, Soccer, Weightlifting, Track; Res Asst; Emer Room Orderly; hon/Alpha Omega Alpha Nat Med Hon Soc; Gamma Beta Phi Nat Hon Soc; Dist'd Dean's List; Dean's List; Rugby Player of the Yr, 1982; W/W Among Students in Am Univs and Cols; Commun Ldrs of Am; g/Orthopedic Surg.

WEAVER, CARA LYNNE oc/Student; b/Oct 11, 1964; h/326 Smith Avenue Ext, Darlington, SC 29532; p/Mr and Mrs Billy B Weaver, Darlington, SC; ed/St John's HS, 1982; Att'g, Chris Logan's Beauty Col; pa/Belk's Dept Store, Pt-time 1979-82, Full-time 1982-83; Piano Tchr; cp/Student Coun, 1982; Sr Class Secy, 1981-82; Pres, Leo Clb, 1981-82; Band, 1979-82; St John's Singers, 1979-82; Orch, 1980-82; r/Epis; hon/Superior Awd, Flute, All-St Band, 1981, 1982; Govs All-Star Band, 1981, 1982; Talent Awd, Miss Darlington, 1981; John Phillip Sousa Awd, Flute, 1982; Cnslr of the Sum, Camp Love, 1982.

WEBB, BRENDA SUE oc/Bank Teller, Student; b/Aug 16, 1960; h/Route 3, Box 305, Rocky Mount, VA 24151; ba/Rocky Mount, VA; ed/Franklin Co HS, 1978; AA, Bus Ed, Ferrum Col, 1980; BS, Bus Adm, Univ of MD En Shore, 1982; pa/ Bk Teller, First VA Bk, 1983-; Secy, Franklin Co Clks Ofc, 1983; Other Previous Positions; cp/Pres, Kappa Queens, 1982; SGA, Cabinet Mem; Phi Beta Lambda, 1980-82, Secy; Vol Recruiter for Admissions Ofc, 1980-82; Secy, Martinsville Clb; Miss Sr, 1982; Secy for Pigg River Bapt Jr Assn; Hostess for Chancellor of the Univ; hon/Acad S'ship, Univ of MD En Shore, 1981; W/W Among Students in Am Jr Cols; g/Master's Deg in Bus Adm; Become an Exec.

WEBB, LINDA LOU oc/Admissions Representative; b/Aug 16, 1960; h/ Route 3, Box 305, Rocky Mount, VA 24151; p/Tommy and Virginia Webb, Rocky Mount, VA; ed/Dipl, Franklin Co HS, 1978; AA, Bus Ed, Ferrum Col, 1980; BS, Bus Adm, Univ of MD En Shore, 1982; pa/Admissions Rep, Nat Bus Col, 1983; Secy, Univ of MD En Shore, 1982; Other Previous Positions; cp/Sweetheart, Omega Psi Phi Frat, 1981-82; Phi Beta Lambda, 1981-82; Vol Recruiter for Admissions, 1981; Secy, Student Govt Assn, 1981-82; Hostess for Chancellor's Reception at Univ of MD; r/Bapt; hon/Intl Yth Awd, 1982; g/To Wk on Master's Deg in Bus Adm and Be a Successful Bus-wom.

WEBB, STEPHANIE KRISTEN oc/ Student; b/Apr 4, 1966; h/PO Box 827, Bay Springs, MS 39422; p/Mr and Mrs Ray Robinson, Bay Springs, MS; pa/ Lifeguard, Bay Sprgs Country Clb, 1982; cp/Y-Teens, 1980-81; Cloc Clb, 1980-81; Secy, Drama Clb, 1982-83; Pres, Acteens, 1982-83; Pres, Band, 1983-84; Flag Capt, 1983-84; Reporter, Sci Clb, 1983-84; Reporter, Sr Class, 1983-84; Reporter, SGA, 1983-84; r/ Bapt; hon/Band; Pres, BSHS Band, 1983-84; Flag Capt, 1983-84; Most Outstg Band Mem, 1982-83; Sopho-more Homecoming Maid, 1981-82; Most Attractive, 1981-82; Class Favor-ite and Most Attractive, 1982-83; Homecoming Queen, 1983-84; St Band Clin, 1983; US Nat Achmt Awd for Band; W/W Among Am HS Students; g/To Attend the Univ of So MS; Maj in Interior Design.

WEBB-EARNEST, MELISSA LEE oc/ Clerk, Typist; b/Dec 4, 1958; h/1309 Carroll Drive, Northwest, Lawton, OK 73501; ba/Ft Sill, OK; m/John W Jr; c/ Amanda Jo; p/Janet F Webb, Princeton, KY; ed/Caldwell Co HS, 1977; BS, Computer Sci and Hist, Austin Peay St Univ, 1982; pa/Clk/Typist, Civilian Pers Ofc; cp/Jr Girl Scout Co-Ldr, 1982-83; Driver for Meals on Wheels, 1982-83; Ofcrs' Wives' Clb; Organist, First Christian Ch; Pres, Rush Chm, Pledge Tnr, Song Ldr, Marshall, Alpha Phi Wom's Frat; Alpha Tau Omega Little Sister; Secy-Treas, Omicron Delta Kappa; Laurel Wreath Hon Soc; Alpha Lambda Delta; Assn Computing Machinery; Brownie Troop Aide, 1982; Intl Wildlife Fdn; hon/Valedictorian, 1977; Dean's List; Outstg Yg Wom of Am; W/W Among Am Univs and Cols; g/Computer Sci Career in Sys Mgmt and Programming.

WEBBER, JO E oc/Student; b/Dec 12,

1963; h/2700 Cross Street, Little Rock, AR 72206; p/Mr and Mrs E J Webber, Little Rock, AR; ed/Dipl, Hall HS, 1982; Att'g, Philander Smith Col (Bus Adm Maj); cp/Phi Beta Lambda, Chapt Secy 1982-83; HS Nat Hon Soc; HS Nat Beta Clb; Future Bus Ldrs of Am, Chapt Pres 1980-82; Friends of St Jude Clb; Red Cross Clb; r/U Meth; hon/Alpha Phi Alpha Debutante, 1982-83; Runner-Up for the Bus Career Devel Prog Awd, 1982; Outstg Voc Ed Student Awd, 1982; Ms FBLA-City Conf 1st Place Awd; Hon Roll; W/W in FBLA; W/W Among Am HS Students; g/Deg in Bus Adm.

WEBER, SELENA MARIE oc/Stu-dent, Part-time Secretary; b/Mar 15, 1966; h/300 Timberland Trail, River-dale, GA 30274; ba/Forest Park, GA; p/ Herbert and Ann Weber, Riverdale, GA; ed/Grad, Riverdale Sr HS, 1984; pa/ Pt-time Secy, Century 21 Arbor Rlty; cp/Student Coun; Beta Clb; Future Bus Ldrs of Am, Reporter 1984; Drill Team, 1981-84; Cheerldr, 1980-81; Band, 1981-82; hon/Superlative, 1980-81; Lettered in Drill Team, 1981-84; Let-tered in Band, 1981-82; Sr Favorite, 1984; Guest Performer w the Chonta Jazz Theatre, 1982; Recip, Num Awds for Dancing; g/To Attend Col and Maj in Perf'g Arts/Computer Sci.

WEBSTER, F ELAINE oc/Student; b/ Jan 7, 1964; h/PO Box 366, Winfield, AL 35594; p/Betty J Harris, Winfield, AL; ed/Winfield City HS, 1981; AS in Bus Adm, Brewer St Jr Col, 1983; pa/ Secy, Estes Hlth Care Ctr, 1981; cp/ Basketball; Volleyball; Softball; Track; Annual Staff, Bus Mgr 1980, Editor 1981; Student Coun; Future Bus Ldrs of Am; F'ship of Christian Aths, Jr Class VP; Newspaper Staff, Sports Editor 1980, Assoc Bus Mgr 1981; Nat Hon Soc; SGA, Freshman Rep 1982, Pres 1983; Cheerldr, 1982; Softball, 1982, 1983; Phi Theta Kappa Hon Frat, 1982, 1983; Circle K Civic Org, 1983, Secy 1983; Pres, Fayette Co Yth Assn for Retarded Citizens, 1982; Adm Affairs Com; r/Meth; hon/Basketball, Capt's Awd 1981, Most Points per Game 1980, 1981, Most Assists per Game 1981; Volleyball, Most Improved 1979, Hustle Awd 1980, 1981; Univ of AL Ldrship Conf, 1981; Most Outstg Shorthand Student, 1981; Most Athletic, 1981; Mod Culture Clb S'ship, 1981; Softball S'ship, 1982, 1983; All-Star St Softball Team, 1982; Nov Brewer Beauty, 1981, 1982; Homecoming Rep, 1982; Roy S Martin Student Ath Awd, 1982; Fall Favorite, 1983; Most Outstg Student, 1983; Miss Brewer St Acad Awd, 1983; Dean's List, 3 Quarters; Pres's List, 1 Quarter; g/Deg in Acctg.

WEBSTER, SUZANNE MAE oc/Reg-istered Nurse; b/Oct 24, 1960; h/2208 South 93rd Street, Apartment 3, West Allis, WI 53227; ba/Milwaukee, WI; m/ Thomas James; p/Mr and Mrs Royce A Wade, Poynette, WI; ed/Poynette HS, 1978; BS, Univ of WI Eau Claire, 1982; pa/RN, St Luke's Hosp, 1982-; Nsg Assem of Am Lung Assn of WI; r/U Meth; hon/Alpha Lambda Delta, 1979; Sigma Theta Tau, 1981; Univ of WI Hon Roll, 1978-82; Univ of WI Dean's List, 1981; Outstg Sr, 1982; W/W Among Students in Am Univs and Cols; Nat Register of Outstg Col Grads; W/W Among Am HS Students; g/RN in OB

Nsg.

WEEKS, KARI CAROLYN oc/Stu-dent; b/Mar 31, 1964; h/Box 1559, Willis, TX 77378; ba/Willis, TX; p/Bill and Betty Weeks, Willis, TX; ed/HS Grad, Schreiner Col, 1982; Assoc of Liberal Arts Deg, Schreiner Col, 1983; Att'g, TX A&M Univ; pa/Reporter and Composing Room Wkr, Kerrville Daily Times, 1982-83; Real Est Salesperson, Walnut Cove Subdivision, 1983; Scho-lastic Newspaper Editor, Tyler County Booster, 1979-80; cp/HS: Band 1978-81, Twirler 1979-80, Treas of Christian Aths 1979-80, FCA 1978-80, Volleyball Team 1978-79, Varsity Basketball Mgr 1978-79, Flag Corps 1980-81, Yrbook and Newspaper Staffs 1979-81, Staff of Sophomore Lit Mag 1979, Co-Editor of Yrbook 1980-81, FHA 1978-81 (VP 1980-81), Tennis Team 1980-81, Nat Hon Soc 1980-81; Col: Repub Clb 1982, Pres and Charter Mem of Demetrian Social Clb 1982-83, German Clb 1982, Schreiner Ambassadors 1982-83, News-paper Staff 1983, Performer in Sprg Dance Concert 1982; Hike-Bike-A-Thon for Muscular Dystrophy; Mtl Hlth and Mtl Retard Assn; Num Other Orgl Activs; r/Bapt; hon/St Hon Band, 1980; UIL Solo, Ensemble, and Twirling Awds, 1978-80; Winner of First Annual Dogwood Marathon Div 15 and Under; UIL Dist Winner, Feature Writing, 1980-81; A's Awd, 1980-81; Prog for Accelerated Col Entrance, Schreiner Col; Hon Grad, Schreiner Col, 1983; Awd for Acad Achmt as the Most Outstg Student in Liberal Arts, 1983; W/W Among Am HS Students; g/Study Law; Continue Writing.

WEEMSTRA, JANET MARIE oc/ Student, Pt-time Dental Hygienist; b/ Jun 27, 1963; h/RD #2, Box 33A, Sussex, NJ 07461; p/Albert and Margaret Weem-stra, Sussex, NJ; ed/High Pt Reg HS, 1981; AS in Dental Hygiene, Fairleigh Dickinson Univ Sch of Dentistry, 1983; Att'g, Montclair St Col, 1983-; cp/Field Hockey, 1977-78, 1978-79; Alpha Chi Rho Little Sister, 1982-; Student Chapt of Am Dental Hygienists Assn, 1981-; Student Coun Rep, 1977-78, 1980-81; Yrbook Sr Editor, 1980-81; Nat Hon Soc, 1980; r/Prot; hon/Hon Roll, 1977-81; Hon's List, 1981-82; Alpha Chi Rho Little Sister of the Yr, 1982-83; Dean's List, 1983; AS w Hons, FDU, 1983; W/W Among Am HS Students; g/BS in Allied Hlth, Montclair St Col, 1985; Career as Dental Hygienist.

WEGTER, JAMES JOHN oc/Explor-atory and Research Geologist; b/Apr 19, 1957; h/W10544 Highway C, Deer-brook, WI 54424; ba/Deerbrook, WI; ed/ Antigo Sr HS, 1975; BS, Univ of WI Oshkosh, 1980; pa/Badger Mining Corp, Lab Tech 1980, Hd of QC 1981, Exploratory and Res Geol 1982-; Lab Tech, Amron Corp, 1981; cp/Geog Clb; Intramural Sports; Oshkosh City Leag Football; r/Luth; hon/Cert'd Soil Tester; Nat Merit S'ship Prog Commend Stu-dent, 1975; Hon Roll, 1975; Dean's List; Grad, cum laude; Delta Tau Kappa; W/ W Among Students in Am Univs and Cols; Intl Yth in Achmt; Commun Ldrs of Am; g/Wk w Environment and Wisely Use Our Natural Resources.

WEIDER, LEW AARON oc/Student; b/Oct 5, 1962; h/1150 East Beech, Alliance, OH 44601; p/Mr and Mrs Alfred R Weider, Alliance, OH; ed/

Alliance HS, 1981; Att'g, Liberty Bapt Col; pa/Adm Asst Christian Ser Dir, Liberty Bapt Col; cp/BSA, Ldrship Corps 1978-80; Liberty Bapt Col Phil Clb, VP 1983-84; Yth F'ship, VP 1980; r/Bapt; hon/Eagle Scout, 1980; God and Country, 1980; Madrigal and Solo, Excell Rating at HS Singing Competition, 1978, 1979, 1980; g/BS in Pastoral Mins; MDiv; Start a Ch in New England States Area.

WEINGART, JERRY STUART oc/Sales Representative; b/May 6, 1960; h/755 West California Avenue, Sebring, OH 44672; ba/Alliance, OH; m/Karen Scott; c/Shawn Michael; p/Claire and Celesta Weingart, North Benton, OH; ed/W Br HS, 1978; BS in Bus Adm, Ashland Col, 1982; pa/Mgr Trainee (Sales Assoc), 84 Lumber, 1982-83; Sales Rep, Damon Chem Co Inc, 1983-; cp/Football, Basketball and Baseball Co-Capt, HS; Pres, Student Coun; Jr and Sr Class VP; Treas, Sophomore Class; Nat Hon Soc; Boys' St Del; Latin Clb; Co-Capt of Baseball, Bus Clb, Math Clb, Col; hon/Canton Class A All-Star, Baseball, 1983; Dist 4 All-Acad; George Donges Meml S'ship; 1st Team, Mahoning Val Conf; Intl Yth in Achmt; g/Sales Rep w a Future in Mktg Res.

WELCH, TERESA MARIE oc/Student; b/Jun 29, 1964; h/Bandera, TX 78003; p/Walter W and Lorena Welch, Bandera, TX; ed/Grad, Bandera HS, 1983; cp/Bandera HS Band Twirler; Cross Country, 4 Yrs; Volleyball, 3 Yrs; Basketball, 4 Yrs; Track, 4 Yrs; All-Dist 1st Team, Volleyball; Basketball; Regs in Track, 3 Yrs; Nat Hon Soc, 3 Yrs; 4-H, 10 Yrs; Teens for Christ; r/Bapt; hon/Most Outstg Ath, Sr Yr; Miss BHS; Class VP, 3 Yrs; Class Favorite; g/Phy Therapist.

WELKER, LINDA KAY oc/Student; b/Sep 17, 1961; h/1808 Willow Springs, Nashville, TN 37216; ba/Nashville, TN; p/Mr and Mrs Allen R Welker, Dickson, TN; ed/Grad, Dickson Co Sr HS; Att'g, David Lipscomb Col and Nashville St Tech Inst; pa/Prof's Asst, David Lipscomb Col, 1979-82; Area Lead, Mdse Dept, Opryland USA, 1980-; cp/Nat Ed Assn, 1980-; Vol, Vanderbilt Univ Hosp, 1982-; STEA, 1980-; HS: Sci Clb, Pep Clb, Beta Clb, Math Clb, Future Tchrs of Am 1978-79, Sci Fairs; r/Ch of Christ; hon/S'ship to David Lipscomb Col; 1st Place, Sci Fair in Biol; Del to Nat Sci Symp; Hon Roll, DLC; W/W; g/Maj in Elem Ed, DLC; Maj in Computer Programming, Nashville Tech; To Design Ednl Packets for Computers to Use in Sch.

WELLER, STACEY ANN oc/Sales Clerk; b/Aug 6, 1964; h/13229 Creagerstown Road, Thurmont, MD 21788; p/Mr and Mrs Roland E Weller, Thurmont, MD; ed/Catoctin HS; pa/Sales Clerk; cp/Adv'd Biol Clb; Computer Clb; Student Coun; Pep Clb; Marching Band; Concert Band; Orch; Pit Band; Basketball Stat; SS Class Treas; hon/Inductee, Nat Hon Soc; All-Co Band; W/W; g/Math Deg; Tchr.

WELLS, BERRI ANN oc/Student; b/Aug 30, 1963; h/2440 North El Molino Avenue, Altadena, CA 91001; p/Charles W Peters; Thelma M Wells, Altadena, CA; ed/John Muir HS, 1981; AFS Cultural Exch Student, Ancona, Italy; Howard Univ (Expected Graduation, 1986); cp/Candy Striper, W Adams

Hosp; John Muir HS Yrbook Staff, 1981; Assoc'd Student Coun, Publicity Chm 1981; r/Christ the Shepherd Luth Ch, Yth Grp Pres; hon/AFS Intl Exch Student; Pasadena Urban Coalition Achmt Awd, 1980; John Robert Powers Most Improved Student Awd, 1981; Intl Yth in Achmt; g/Atty, Intl Bus Law.

WELLS, DANNY JOE oc/Student, Part-time Preacher; b/Aug 26, 1959; h/Route 14, Box 116, Crossville, TN 38555; p/Mrs Moses Wells, Crossville, TN; ed/Cumberland Co HS, 1977; Ext Courses, Harding Univ; TN Technol Univ; cp/Band, Beta Clb, HS; Christian Student Ctr, TN Technol Univ; Chs of Christ Exhib Wkr, World's Fair, 1982; r/Ch of Christ; hon/Biblical Scholar Awd, TN Technol Univ Christian Student Ctr, 1980; Del, Am Legion Boys' St, 1976; A Pres Classroom for Yg Ams, 1977; W/W Among Am HS Students; g/BS in Indust Technol; Preaching.

WELLS, JOHNNA MARLENE oc/Student; b/Oct 6, 1962; h/RR 1, Raleigh, IL 62977; p/John W and Wilma M Wells, Raleigh, IL; ed/Edorado HS, 1980; McKendree Col; cp/McKendree Col; Varsity Basketball, Softball and Volleyball 1980-81, Varsity Volleyball, Softball and Basketball 1981-82, Varsity Basketball and Softball 1982-83; Co Ofcr, Clb Ofcr, 4-H; Sum Softball; Cancer Dr Fund; Wom's Sum Volleyball; F'ship of Christian Aths; hon/Sr Class Pres, HS, 1980; Most Improved Player, Volleyball, McKendree Col 1980-81; St and Co Hons, 4-H; All-Star Team, Wom's Sum Softball; W/W Among Am HS Students; g/Maj in PE/Tchg, Minor in Biol/Coaching.

WELLS, LOU ALLEN oc/Student; b/Nov 16, 1965; h/Route 2, Fuquay Varina, NC 27526; ba/Willow Springs, NC; p/Bailey and Dot Wells, Fuquay Varina, NC; ed/HS Student; pa/Lifeguard; cp/Spanish Hon Soc; Beta Clb; Boys Golf Team; Tchr, Swimming and Golf Lessons; r/Presb; hon/Spanish Hon Soc, 1982; Beta Clb, 1982; g/To Attend Univ of NC Chapel Hill for Pharm Deg.

WELLS, STEPHEN D oc/Student; b/Jun 21, 1960; h/3220 Bayberry Circle, Florence, SC 29501; p/Larry L and Sandra L Wells, Florence, SC; ed/S Mecklenburg HS, 1978; BA, Pfeiffer Col, Univ of NC Charlotte, 1983; cp/Pres and Capt, Univ of NC Charlotte Debate Team; Elected Mem, Phi Kappa Phi, Omicron Delta Kappa and Pi Sigma Alpha Hon Socs; Student Marshall, 1982 Commencement Ceremonies; hon/Spkr Trophies and Mun Debating Awds; Grad w Perfect Cumulative GPA; g/Harvard Law Sch; JD.

WENDEL, ELIZABETH DAWN oc/Student; b/Jan 22, 1962; h/115 Chase Drive, Portland, TX 78374; p/Mr and Mrs Halley B Wendel, Portland, TX; ed/Grad, Gregory Portland HS, 1980; BA, Mass Communs and Adm Mgmt, TX Luth Col, 1984; pa/Sports Reporter, *Corpus Christi Caller Times*, 1983 (Internship); Internship, San Antonio Spurs Basketball Org, 1983; Other Previous Positions; cp/Alpha Chi Hon Soc, 1982-84, Pres 1983-84; Alpha Lambda Delta Hon Soc, 1981-84, Secy 1981-82; TX Luth Col Scholar's Prog, 1981-84, Exec Com 1982-84; Dean's List, 1980-83; Varsity Basketball Team, 1980-84, Capt 1983-84; F'ship of Chris-

tian Aths, 1980-84, Treas 1981-82, Secy 1982-84; Beta Alpha Sigma Social Sorority, 1981-84; Luth Student Movement, USA, 1981-84; Campus Min Coun, 1981-84; Student Newspaper, 1980-83, Sports Editor 1982-83; Camp Fire Girls; r/Luth; hon/Camp Fire Wo-He-Lo Medallion, 1979; Dean's List, 1980-83; TAIAW-TFIAW Awd of Acad Achmt, 1980-83; Ath Advmt Assn Merit Awd, 1980-83; Big St Conf Dist'd Achmt Awd, 1982-83; W/W Among Am HS Students; Nat Dean's List; g/To Attend Grad Sch at the Univ of TX Austin.

WENTZ, DAVID NORTHROP oc/Student, Pastor; b/Feb 12, 1954; h/5923 Woodville Road, Mount Airy, MD 21771; ba/Same; m/Paula McKay Wentz; c/Joshua David, John Emerald, Jeremiah James; p/George Robinson and Flonell Northrop Wentz; ed/Severna Pk HS, 1972; BS, magna cum laude, Univ of VA Sch of Engrg and Applied Sci, 1976; MDiv, summa cum laude, Melodyland Sch of Theol, 1981; Grad Wk, Wesley Theol Sem; pa/Res Asst, Univ of VA Res Labs for Engrg Scis, 1975-76; Adv'd Safety Engr, Ford Motor Co, 1976-78; Conslttg Engr in Energy Mgmt, 1978-81; Pastor, U Meth Ch; Announcer, Rel Music Radio Show, 1974-76; cp/MD Right to Life; Local UNICEF Coor, 1981; Sect Ldr, Univ of VA Marching Band, 1975-76; Worship Ldr, Melodyland Sch of Theol, 1978-81; Coach, Wom's Softball Team, 1977; hon/Tau Beta Pi Engrg Hon Soc; Nat Dean's List; W/W Among Students in Am Univs and Cols; g/Ordination w U Meth Ch; ThD in Biblical Interpretation; Sem Prof.

WENZEL, SUZANNE LISA oc/Student; b/Jan 16, 1963; h/671 Cross Street, New Braunfels, TX 78130; p/Marcus Wenzel, New Braunfels, TX; ed/Grad, New Braunfels HS, 1981; Att'g, SW TX St Univ (Geog and Planning Maj); pa/Asst Wallpaper Hanger to Profl in LA, 1982; Pt-time Employee, Jack-in-the-Box, 1983; cp/HS: Band, Art Clb, German Clb, Eng Clb; hon/Phi Eta Sigma Freshman Hon Soc, 1982; Golden Key Nat Hon Soc, 1983; Liberal Arts Awd of Acad Excell, 1984; Alfred Nolle Meml S'ship, SW TX St Univ, 1984-85; Pi Gamma Mu, Intl Social Sci Hon Soc, 1984; W/W Among Am HS Students; g/To Study Geog or Urban Planning in Grad Sch.

WESLEY, ELIZABETH ANN oc/Production Secretary; b/Apr 1, 1961; h/PO Drawer D, Whitehouse, TX 75791; ba/Tyler, TX; p/Mr and Mrs Robert L Wesley; ed/Whitehouse HS; Legal Secy Deg, Tyler Comml Col; pa/Prodn Secy; cp/FTA; FHA; Troupe 296, Intl Thespian Soc; Band; Spch and Drama Clb; r/Friendly Bapt Ch; hon/W/W Among Am HS Students; Intl Yth in Achmt; g/Photog.

WESSON, THOMAS DAVID oc/Assistant Manager; g/Aug 30, 1960; h/35 Fickling Drive, Lancaster, SC 29720; ba/Lancaster, SC; m/Ellen Hooker; c/Shannon Marie, Christina Leigh; p/Mr and Mrs Thomas R Wesson Jr, Hamlet, NC; ed/Grad, Richmond Sr HS, 1978; NC St Univ; pa/Dishwasher, Wn Sizzlin, 1979; Cook 1980-82, Relief Mgr 1982-83, Shoney's; Asst Mgr, The Sirloin, 1983-; cp/VP, Future Tchrs of Am, 1978; Beta Clb, 1978; r/Bapt; hon/

Nom'd to US Naval Acad, USAF Acad, USCG Acad, 1978; Intl Yth in Achmt; Commun Ldrs of Am; g/Indust Engrg Deg; Ofcrs Tng Sch; Ofcr, USN.

WEST, DEBORAH LILLIAN oc/Student; b/Oct 21, 1965; h/Route 1, Box 223E, Warsaw, NC 28398; p/Mr and Mrs James W West, Warsaw, NC; ed/James Kenan HS, 1984; cp/FHA, Pres 1981; Hist Clb, Pres 1981; Beta Clb, 1981; Pep Clb, 1982-84; Monogram Clb, 1982-84; Nat Hon Soc, 1983-84; Drama Clb, 1983-84; Student Coun, Class Rep 1982-84; Basketball Mgr/Scorekeeper, 1982-84; Softball, 1981, 1982; Tennis, 1982; Cheerldg, 1983, 1984, Co-Capt 1984; Wash Close-Up Prog, 1983; Meth Yth F'ship, 1981, 1982, 1983, 1984, Pres 1983; r/Meth; hon/Student of the Month, 1981; Student of the Yr, 1981; Algebra I Awd, 1981; Hons Eng II Awd, 1983; Elect Mbrship Corp Essay Contest Runner-Up, 1983; Marshal, 1983; Rotary Clb Student of the Month, 1984; Nat Sci Merit Awd, Physics, 1984; Morehead S'ship Nom, Co, 1984; g/Attend a 4-Yr Col.

WEST, TAMMY MELISA oc/Student; b/Apr 19, 1967; h/Route 3, Box 814, Waynesboro, MS 39367; p/Mr and Mrs Marlon West, Waynesboro, MS; ed/Student, Clara HS; cp/Beta Clb; FHA; Class Secy and Treas; Basketball Cheerldr; Homecoming Ct, Jr Maid; Most Beautiful, CHS; YLA's; r/Clara Ch of God Yth Choir; hon/Hon Roll; Nat Math Awd; NEMA Awd; g/To Attend Col and Maj in Ed or Communs.

WESTERVELT, MARGARET MARY oc/Teacher; b/Aug 17, 1956; h/333 Fairmount Avenue, Jersey City, NJ 07306; ba/Jersey City, NJ; p/John and Mary Westervelt, Jersey City, NJ; ed/St Dominic Acad, 1974; BA, Caldwell Col, 1978; MA, Jersey City St Col, 1981; pa/CYO Camp Dir, 1981-; Tchr, 1978-; cp/Social Concerns Del for St Aedan's Parish Coun; Yth Rep, Chp, Hudson Co Yth Com, Com of Archdiocese Priority, Newark, NJ; Chp, Jersey City Cheerldg Competition, 1982, 1983; Coor'g Com, Hudson Co Vicariate Conf, 1983; Public Sch #39, Sch Effectiveness Tng Coor'g Coun, 1981-; hon/W/W Among Students in Am Univs and Cols; Intl Yth in Achmt; Commun Ldrs of Am; g/PhD in Curric Devel.

WEYAND, SUSAN CHARLYN oc/Assistant Cashier and Teller; b/Aug 23, 1960; h/Route 1, Box 5, Round Top, TX 78954; ba/Round Top, TX; m/Roy Gene, c/Kevin Ross; p/Mr and Mrs August Aschenbeck Jr, Brenham, TX; ed/Grad, Brenham HS, 1978; BAA, Blinn Jr Col, 1980; pa/Asst Cashier and Teller, Round Top St Bk; r/Ch, Dir of Wom's Choir; hon/Nat Hon Soc; Hon Grad, Blinn Jr Col; Phi Theta Kappa; Mu Alpha Theta; Intl Yth in Achmt; g/Career in Bus or Bkg.

WHEAT, PANSY ELIZABETH oc/Student; b/Jan 8, 1962; h/PO Box 937, Roanoke Rapids, NC 27870; ba/Greenville, SC; p/Rev and Mrs Maurice F Wheat, Roanoke Rapids, NC; ed/Att'd, Roanoke Rapids HS; Grad, Roanoke Christian Sch, 1979; BS in Math Ed, Bob Jones Univ, 1984; Camp Cnslr, The Wilds, 1982, 1983; Dorm Monitor, Bob Johns Univ, 1980-83; Libn, Bob Jones Univ, 1980; Salesperson, Roses Dept Store, 1978-80; cp/Keywanettes, 1978; Sigma Lambda Delta, Treas 1980-81,

**VP 1982; Secy of Jr Class, 1981-82; r/Indep Bapt; hon/Valedictorian of Sr Class in HS, 1979; W/W Among Am Univs and Cols; g/Postgrad Wk in Computer Sci at Bob Jones Univ; Tchr of Math and Eng in a Christian HS.

WHITACRE, AMANDA P oc/Travel Agent and Consultant, Student; b/Mar 30, 1964; h/Bloomery Route Box 94, Winchester, VA 22601; p/Mr and Mrs Richard P Whitacre Sr, Winchester, VA; ed/Grad, James Wood HS, 1982; Lord Fairfax Commun Col; Grad, Intl Travel Tng Courses Inc, 1983; pa/Intl Travel Soc; cp/Sky Forest Phantasy (Theatre Grp); Nat Hon Soc; Student Coun Assn Senator; Pres, Commun Nat Energy Ed Day; FBLA; Spanish Clb; Spec Tng for Care of SIDS Babies; Pres, Investmt Clb; hon/1st Place, Prose Rdg; Miss Gainesboro Hon Fire Chief; W/W Among Am HS Students; Commun Ldrs of Am; g/Communs Deg; Public Relats.

WHITAKER, DAYNA KIMBERLY oc/Student; b/Jun 23, 1966; h/117 Edgewater, New Braunfels, TX 78130; p/William W and Katrina Joy Whitaker, New Braunfels, TX; ed/Student, New Braunfels HS; r/Christian; hon/Winner, Num Track Meets, incl'g, St (2-Mile), 1982, 1983; Broke Nat Record in 3,200 Meter, 1983; US Achmt Acad; g/To Attend Rice Univ and Study Sports Med.

WHITE, AVIS HUNTER oc/Teacher of the Emotionally Handicapped; b/Oct 19, 1956; h/Route 2, Box 156E, Spartanburg, SC 29302; ba/Spartanburg, SC; m/Scott Manuel; p/Mr and Mrs Jones Thomas Hunter Jr, Marion, SC; ed/Dipl, James F Byrnes Acad, 1974; Spec Ed, Elem Ed, George Peabody Col for Tchrs, 1974-78; Ed Adm, Univ of SC, 1984; pa/Ednl Therapist, Charles Lea Ctr, 1978-82; Coor of Vol Prog, Autistic Prog, Charles Lea Ctr, 1979-80; Tchr of the Emotionally Handicapped, McCracken Jr HS, 1982-; r/Bapt; g/Ed Adm.

WHITE, EMILY ANN oc/Transportation Industry Analyst; b/Aug 6, 1956; h/1600 South Eads Street, #613-S, Arlington, VA 22202; ba/Washington, DC; p/Mr and Mrs Ralph T White, Florence, AL; ed/Mars Hill HS, 1974; BA 1977, MBA 1979, Univ of AL; pa/Trans Indust Analyst, Interst Commerce Comm; cp/Pi Sigma Alpha Polit Sci Hon Soc; Chi Delta Phi Eng Hon Soc; Computer Hons Prog; Alpha Lambda Delta; Phi Eta Sigma Freshmen Hon Soc; Adv Bd, Col of Arts and Scis; Chm, Pre-Legal Soc, Ath Ticket Comm; Student Mem, Task Force on SEn Conf Sports; Corolla Yrbook Sports Editor; hon/Interst Commerce Comm Merit Awd; Intl Yth in Achmt; W/W Among Students in Am Univs and Cols; g/Law Sch; Top-Level Mgmt, Bus Firm or Intl Affairs Agy.

WHITE, FRANK NORRIS oc/Student; b/Dec 30, 1963; h/5180 Highpoint Road, Norhteast, Atlanta, GA 30342; p/Mr and Mrs Frank D White, Atlanta, GA; ed/Grad, Ridgeview HS, 1982; Att'g, Duke Univ; cp/Kappa Sigma Frat; Key Clb; Student Coun; Sr Coun; Ofcr, Kappa Sigma Exec Coun; Big Ch Student Radio, WXDU; r/Prot; hon/Nat Merit Scholar; Dean's List, Duke; Harvard Book Awd; Sr Superlative, HS; Editor-in-Chief, HS Newspaper; Vale-

dictorian, HS Class; Atlanta Journal Cup, Best All-Around Sr; Most Likely to Succeed; g/Double Maj in Polit Sci and Psych, Duke Univ; Law Sch.

WHITE, GERRY DAVID oc/Student; b/Apr 6, 1963; h/821 Wood Street, Brookston, IN 47923; p/Mr and Mrs David S White, Brookston, IN; ed/Twin Lakes HS, 1981; Currently Enrolled, Liberty Bapt Col, 1981-; pa/Adm Asst, Christian Ser Dir, Liberty Bapt Col; cp/HS Basketball, 1977; Most Competitive Singing Grp in HS, Golden Throats, 1980-81; r/Bapt; hon/Indust Arts Awd, 1981; Golden Throats, 1980-81; g/BS in Pastoral Studies, Liberty Bapt Col; Asst Christian Ser Dir, Liberty Bapt Col.

WHITE, JAMES R JR oc/Student; b/Jan 25, 1966; h/8909 South Kentucky, Oklahoma City, OK 73159; p/James and Willa White, Oklahoma City, OK; ed/HS Student; r/Bapt; hon/OK Am Legion Boys' St Del, 1983; Outstg Jr Citizen, Civitan Awd, 1983; Nat and St Hon Socs, 1981-83; Pres, Ch Yth Coun; Varsity Letter in Basketball, 1982; Varsity Letter in Baseball, 1983; Scholastic Medals in Eng and Govt; Soc of Dist'd Am HS Students; W/W Among Am HS Students; g/Dr.

WHITE, JEREMY LEE oc/Student; b/Jul 3, 1966; h/1013 Payne, Murray, KY 42071; p/Dr and Mrs Jerrell G White, Murray, KY; ed/HS Dipl; cp/Tennis Team; Latin Clb, Pres; FBLA, Reporter; Math Team; Student Coun; Hi-Y, Chaplain; Spanish Clb, Treas; Spch Clb; Yth Coun, Pres; Computer Clb; Swim Team; r/Bapt; hon/Salutatorian, 1984; DAR Good Citizen, 1984; Sr Superlative, Most Dependable; Area Yth Salute; 1st Place in Ec Competition; 1st Place in Dist Hist Essay Contest; Soc of Dist'd Am HS Students; g/To Attend Col and Maj in Fin and Acctg.

WHITE, JOLETTA VICTOREEN oc/Student; b/Mar 14, 1967; h/9007 Oden Court, Brentwood, TN 37027; ed/Student, Brentwood HS; cp/Nat Piano Auditions, 1977-80; Nat Hon Roll of Am Col of Musicians, 1977-80; Student Adv Secy, Jr HS, 1980-81; St and Reg Rhoer Secy; Jack and Jill of Am, Williamson Co Chapt VP 1981-82, Secy 1982-83; Rhoer Pres, 1982-83; ARC Vol Ser, 1981; 4-H Clb, 1976-80; GSA, 1975-81; r/Bapt; Ch Choir and Usher Bd, 1980-83; Yth Secy, Gtr Pleasant View Ch, 1981, 1983; hon/SE Reg Winner, George W Carver Essay Contest, 1981; Jack and Jill Oratorical Contest Winner, St and Reg, 1981, 1982; Northside Jr High Hall of Fame, 1982; USAA Finalist in S'ship, 1982; SE Reg Voting Del in Jack and Jill of Am, 1982, 1983; Jr Achmt Awds, Best VP of Mktg, 1982-83; Jr Achmt, Secretarial Awd, 1982-83; TN Hugh O'Brian Yth Sem Ambassador, 1982-83; Constant Acad Hon Roll Student; 2nd Runner-Up, Miss TN Teen, 1980; g/To Receive a Bach and a Master's Deg in Bus Adm and/or Computer Sci; To Own and Manage a Bus.

WHITE, KAREN LYNN oc/Student; b/Jun 22, 1964; h/1010 Thompson Avenue, Moundsville, WV 26041; ba/Morgantown, WV; p/Mr and Mrs James E White Sr, Moundsville, WV; ed/Grad, John Marshall HS, 1982; Att'g, WV Univ; cp/Band, 1974-82; French Clb, 1979-82, Pres 1978-79, VP 1980-81; Nat Maids, 1979; Newspaper, 1979-81,

Picture Editor 1980-81; Nat Hon Soc, 1981-82; Student Coun, 1981-82; Civil Air Patrol, 1979-; r/Meth; hon/1st Runner-Up in Miss Teenworld Spch Contest, 1982; Chosen to Participate in Miss U Teenager; Billy Mitchell Awd, 1983; Cadet Adv Coun, Recorder 1982, Chm 1983; W/W Among Am HS Students; g/Maj in Polit Sci, WV Univ; Law Sch; Polits.

WHITE, LINDA MARIE oc/Student; b/Oct 30, 1962; h/RR 3, Storm Lake, IA 50588; p/Mr and Mrs Russell K White, Storm Lake, IA; ed/Albert City-Truesdale HS, 1981; Assoc Deg in Acctg, SWn Commun Col, 1983; cp/ Choir, Col; HS: Choir for 4 Yrs, Band for 5 Yrs, Soloist, Baseball Mgr, Track, Spanish Clb, Dir of Sch Play, Art Clb; Ch Soloist, Grps; hon/Highest Hons, Hon Roll; Soc of Dist'd Am HS Students; W/W Among Am HS Students; Intl Yth in Achmt; g/Bus Ed.

WHITE, MELINDA CAROL oc/Nursing Student; b/Apr 29, 1961; h/837 East Main Street, Shelby, NC; p/Bobby E and Nellie P White, Shelby, NC; ed/Dipl, Crest Sr HS, 1979; BSN, Univ of NC Charlotte, 1983; pa/Student Asst III, Cleveland Meml Hosp, 1980-; cp/French Clb, 1975-79; Beta Clb, 1975-79; Scorekeeper, Basketball and Baseball Teams, 1975-79; Intl Order of Rainbow for Girls, 1973-; OES, 1979-; Student Nurses Assn, 1982-; Sigma Theta Tau, 1983-; r/Meth; hon/Grand Ofcr, Intl Order of Rainbow for Girls for St of NC, 1978; Nat Nsg Hon Soc, Sigma Theta Tau, 1983; g/Wk in a Hosp Setting; Continue Ed.

WHITE, SCOTT RAY oc/Student; b/ Feb 14, 1963; h/300 West Wall, Harrisonville, MO 64701; p/Raymond W and Connie Kay White, Harrisonville, MO; ed/Harrisonville HS, 1981; Student of Mech Engrg, Univ of MO Rolla; cp/Soc of Automotive Engrs, Pres 1983; MO Miner, Sports Editor 1983; Pi Kappa Alpha Frat, Treas 1983; UMR Student Coun, Com Chm 1983; UMR Varsity Cross Country, 1983; Phi Eta Sigma Acad Hons Frat; r/Bapt; hon/Curators S'ship, 1981-85; Runner-Up, Freshman of the Yr, 1982; GMC Scholars Finalist; Acad Hon Roll; W/W Among HS Students; Intl W/W HS Students; g/Doct in Mech Engrg; Own Engrg Conslt Firm.

WHITE, SONYA CORDELIA oc/ Student; b/Jul 2, 1966; h/15 Bayou Auguste Homes, Biloxi, MS 39530; p/ Ms Melinda White, Biloxi, MS; ed/Dipl, Biloxi HS, 1984; cp/Homecoming Queen, 1983; Co-Capt, Football Cheerldg Squad, 1983; Homecoming Maid, 1981-82; Hd Football Cheerldr, Jr HS, 1980; r/Bapt; hon/Voted Most Athletic Girl, Jr HS, 1980; Voted Most Valuable Basketball Player, Jr HS, 1980; Chosen Dist Pt Guard Player, 1980; Set Jr High Dist High Jump Record, 1980; g/4 Yrs of Col as a Computer Sci Maj, Psych Minor; 2 Yrs of Perf'g Art Sch.

WHITE, STEVEN JOHN oc/Student; b/Apr 6, 1962; h/Route 2, Box 166C, Killeen, TX 76541; p/Mrs Roswitha A White, Killeen, TX; ed/Grad, C E Ellison HS, 1980; BS in Biol, Baylor Univ, 1984; pa/Col Sum Prog in Biomed Scis 1981, Med Tech 1982, UT Sys Cancer Res Ctr, M D Anderson Hosp; Denton A Cooley Cardiovas Surg Prog, TX Heart Inst, 1983; cp/Student Coun, Pres 1980, VP

1979; Nat Hon Soc, VP; Key Clb, Reporter, Histn; Student Body Treas; Baylor Ambassador; Coor, Omicron Delta Kappa, 1983; Men and Wom of Merit Wk; Mortar Bd; Kappa Omega Tau Social Ser Frat, S'ship Chm; Student Cong; Leakey Ldrship Lab; Security Adv Com; r/Rom Cath; hon/Valedictorian, 1980; Dean's Dist'd List; Hons Prog; Hon Socs: Alpha Lambda Delta, Gamma Beta Phi, Alpha Chi, Omicron Delta Kappa, Mortar Bd; Intl Yth in Achmt; Yg Commun Ldrs of Am; W/ W Among Students in Am Univs and Cols; W/W Among Am HS Students; Soc of Dist'd Am HS Students; g/MD.

WHITFORD, ELAINE MOYE oc/ Student; b/Feb 26, 1964; h/1006 Wickliff Avenue, High Point, NC 27262; p/Mr and Mrs Howard N Whitford, High Point, NC; ed/Grad, High Pt Ctl HS, 1982; Currently Att'g, Univ of NC Chapel Hill; cp/Lifeguard, Swim Instr, Red Cross; Chapel Hill Civic Ballet Co, 1982-83; Pres, Nat Forensics Leag, 1981-82; High Pt Ctl Exec Bd, 1981-82; r/Christianity; hon/Dean's List, UNC, 1983; Outstg Ser Awd for Nat Forensics Leag, HS, 1982; St Debutante for NC 1983; Nat Hon Soc, 1981; W/W Among Am HS Students; Commun Ldrs of Am; g/Ec Maj; Grad Deg in Bus Adm.

WHITLOCK, DAVID BRIAN oc/ Student; b/Nov 7, 1955; h/490 Plaza Boulevard, E47, Morrisville, PA 19067; m/Katri Hudspeth; p/Dr and Mrs L D Whitlock, Altus, OK; ed/Grad, Altus HS, 1975; BA, Greek and Eng, Baylor Univ, 1979; MDiv, Theol, SWn Bapt Theol Sem, 1982; MTh, Ch Hist, Princeton Theol Sem, 1983; pa/Salesperson, Surrey Shop, 1973-75; Sales, Rosewood Meml Pk, 1976-79; Assoc Pastor, Min to Yth, Northside Bapt Ch, 1981-82; Security Pers, Firestone Lib, Princeton Univ, 1983-; Sigma Chi Frat; Gamma Beta Phi, Hon Scholastic; r/So Bapt; hon/W/W Among Am Cols and Univs; g/PhD in Area of Ch Hist; To Teach in a Univ.

WHITMAN, DAWN MARIE oc/Student; b/May 25, 1964; h/Route 3, Box 895, Selmer, TN 38375; p/James and Barbara Whitman, Selmer, TN; ed/ McNairy Ctl, 1981; Savannah St Area Voc-Tech Sch, 1982; Att'g, W TN Bus Col; cp/VP, Selmer Jaycettes, 1982-83, Treas 1983-84; Softball, 1985-; Basketball, 1977-78; Sch Newspaper, 1980-81; r/Luth; hon/Dean's List, Roosevelt High, Fresno, CA; Dean's List, W TN Bus Col; g/Wk in a Hosp or Dr's Ofc as a Med Secy.

WHITNEY, DONALD HOWARD JR oc/Student; b/Dec 9, 1962; h/2208 Maplecrest Drive, Charlotte, NC 28212; p/Mr and Mrs Donald Whitney Sr, Charlotte, NC; ed/Att'g, Liberty Bapt Col; Grad, Independence Sr HS, 1981; cp/AF Jr ROTC; Nat Rifle Assn; r/Bapt; hon/ROTC Awd from Am Legion, 1981; g/Maj in Polit Sci.

WHITNEY, G WARREN oc/Student; b/Nov 10, 1962; h/PO Box 60489, Fairbanks, AK 99706; p/Guy W and Anita J Whitney, Fairbanks, AK; ed/ Lathrop HS, 1980; AZ St Univ, Tempe; cp/Treas, Student Coun; Photog, Yrbook; Swim Team; Softball Team; Wrestling Team; Trans-AK Pipeline; Prot; hon/S'ship, Univ of AZ Local #375; W/W Among Am HS Students; Intl Yth in Achmt; Commun Ldrs of Am; g/

Engrg Deg.

WHITSON, MARY ANTOINETTE oc/Student; b/Mar 9, 1966; h/Route 1, Box 163, Berry, AL 35546; p/Mr and Mrs Nathaniel Whitson, Berry, AL; ed/ Berry HS; Fayette Co Area Voc Ctr (HOE); cp/Hlth Occup Students of Am, Local Pres 1982-83; 4-H, Pres 1982-83; Cheerldr; r/Bapt; hon/4-H: Sr Girls' Public Spkg, 1980 (1st), 1982 (1st), 1981 (3rd), 1983 (1st), Best Non-Sr Sr Girls' 4-H Awd 1981, 1982; g/To Become an RN.

WHITTAKER, M JILL oc/Student; b/ Aug 5, 1962; h/113 Hammons Drive, Richmond, KY 40475; p/Mr and Mrs Jimmy Whittaker, Richmond, KY; ed/ Madison Ctl HS, 1980; Att'g, En KY Univ; pa/Registrar Wkr, En KY Univ, 1980-81, 1981-82, 1982-83; cp/Beta Clb, 1977, 1978, 1979; Mgr, Track, 1977, 1978, 1979; Mgr, Cross Country, 1978, 1979; Basketball Scorekeeper, 1978, 1979; Pep Clb, 1979; Ctl Girls' Ath Clb, 1977, Secy 1978, VP 1979; Bell Choir, 1980, 1981; 1982; r/Union City Christian Ch Softball Team, 1983; hon/110% Awd, Ctl Girls' Ath Clb; Sr Awd, Ctl Girls' Ath Clb; Hon Roll, HS; Dean's List, EKU; W/W Among Am HS Students; Soc of Dist'd Am HS Students; g/Maj in Elem Ed; To Teach in the Madison Co Sch Sys.

WHITTEN, MICAH DWAYNE oc/ Student; b/Jan 1, 1963; h/Route 1, Box 233A, Stantonville, TN 38379; p/Preston and Norma Whitten, Stantonville, TN; ed/McNairy Ctl HS, 1981; Att'd, NE MS Jr Col; Att'g, St Tech at Memphis; cp/Band Pres, Dist Ed Clbs of Am Treas, HS; Phi Beta Lambda, Col; r/Falcon Bapt Ch; hon/Tri-M, Modern Music Masters Alumni; Nat Hon Roll Soc; Most Talented, Student Excell, Band MVP, HS; W/W in Music Among Am HS Students; g/AS in Electronic Data Processing; Cert'd Data Processor.

WICE, TINA IRIS oc/Student; b/Jan 17, 1962; h/PO Box 607, Nortonville, KY 42442; ba/Murray, KY; p/Col and Mrs L Paul Wice, Nortonville, KY; ed/ Grad, C E Ellison HS, 1980; Att'd, TX A&M Univ, 1980-81; BS, Clothing, Textiles and Fashion, Murray St Univ, 1984; pa/Sales Clk, J C Penny, 1983-84; Sales Clk, Cherry's, 1983; Student Wkr, Murray St Univ, 1982; Resident Advr, Murray St Univ, 1982; Other Previous Positions; cp/Secy, Clothing, Fashion and Textiles Clb, 1983-84; Initiated Campus-Wide Fashion Show; Coor, Fashion Show for Wellness Fest, MSU; hon/Dean's List, 1981-84; g/To Obtain a Position in an Exec Devel Prog.

WIESTLING, YVONNE MARIE oc/ Student; b/Dec 27, 1963; h/122 Holly Street, Hummelstown, PA 17036; p/ Wallace S Wiestling, Hummelstown, PA; Barbara A Wiestling, Hummelstown, PA; ed/Lower Dauphin HS, 1982; No Burlington Co Reg HS, 1978-80; Att'd, Hood Col, 1982-83; Att'g, Millersville Univ, 1983-; pa/Acctg Dept Aide, Everite Knitting Mills, 1983-; Ofc Aide, Hood Col Biol Dept, 1983; Other Previous Positions; cp/ Student Social Wk Org, 1983-, Secy 1982-83; Nat Spanish Hon Soc, 1979-; Hood Col Paper, 1982-83; Spanish Clb, 1980-82, Pres 1981-82; Debate Team, 1981-82; Tennis Team, 1980-81; Student Govt, 1978-80; Longitudinal Studies Grp I, Limestone, 1980-81; r/Cath;

hon/Nat Spanish Hon Soc, 1979; Quarterly Excell Hons, 1977-82; Class Coun Awd, 1978-79; McGuire AFB Open House Plaque of Apprec, 1979; Dean's List, 1982; Miss TEEN PA Contestant, 1982; g/Deg in Social Wk and Cert of Proficiency in Spanish; Assist and Benefit the Commun.

WIGGINS, CHARLES EDWARD oc/Student; b/Nov 22, 1959; h/1600 South Mount Pleasant, Apartment B-9, Monroeville, AL 26460; ba/Monroeville, AL; p/Allie Mae Richardson, Monroeville, AL; ed/Monroe Co HS, 1978; AA, Patrick Henry St Jr Col, 1980; Att'g, Livingston Univ; pa/Owner, Freebirds Investmts; Nsg Attendant, Monroe Hosp; Receptionist, Livingston Univ; Legal Advr, Monroe Co; cp/Owens Love Bus Assn, 1982; Intl Students Friendship Assn, 1982; Freebirds Preliminary Frat, 1982; Col Civitan Intl, 1980; r/Bapt; hon/Alumni S'ship Recip, 1978; Commun Ldrship S'ship Recip, 1978; Dean's List, 1978; Outstg Perf Awd in Varsity Football, 1977; W/W Among Students in Am Jr Cols; Intl Yth in Achmt; Am Yg Commun Ldrs; g/BS in Bus Mgmt, Livingston Univ; Public Relats in Grad Sch; Transform Freebirds Investmts into Corp.

WILEY, GAIL LISETTE oc/Teacher; b/May 15, 1954; h/2008 Queen Mary Court, #2, Virginia Beach, VA 23454; ba/Virginia Beach, VA; p/Ruth M Wiley, Madison, NC; ed/Madison-Mayodan HS, 1972; BA, Spec Ed, Bennett Col, 1981; pa/Tchr, Lng Disabilities; NEA; VBEA; CEC; cp/NAACP, 1981; Pres, VP, Delta Sigma Theta Sorority; Pres, Interdorm Coun; Student Asst, Freshman Studies; Parliamentarian, Student Union Bd; Student Mem, NTE Bd; r/Bapt; hon/Dean's List; Outstg Bennett Belle, 1980-81; W/W Among Students in Am Cols and Univs; Intl Yth in Achmt; g/MA in Spec Ed; Own Kgn for Handicapped.

WILKERSON, DEBORAH DENISE oc/Fashion Coordinator, Student; b/Oct 23, 1959; h/1641 Old Rex Morrow Road, Morrow, GA 30260; p/Mr and Mrs Homer L Wilkerson Jr, Morrow, GA; ed/Morrow Sr High, 1977; Att'd, Univ of GA, 1977-79; GA St Univ, 1983-; pa/Fashion Coor, Richs-Lenox; Med Sales Rep, Life Line Technols; Other Previous Positions; cp/Zeta Tau Alpha Sorority; r/Bapt; hon/Miss Atlanta, 1983-84; 1st Runner-Up, Miss Clayton Co, 1978-80; Gov's Hon Prog; Guest Vocalist, Nat Anthem, Braves Games; W/W Among Outstg Choral Students; Outstg Yg Wom of Am; g/To Complete BA Deg in Jour; TV/Radio Commentating; Public Spkg.

WILKERSON, SHERRI LYNN oc/Student; b/Sep 29, 1962; h/Route 2, Box 97, Belvidere, TN 37306; ba/Cookeville, TN; p/Mr and Mrs Prentice Wilkerson, Belvidere, TN; ed/HS Dipl; AS, Motlow St; Wkg toward BS in Ed, TN Technological Univ; cp/Gamma Beta Phi; Phi Kappa Phi; Mortar Bd; Kappa Delta Pi; Intermurals; Bapt Student Union, Secy 1981, Pres 1982; Missions, 1983; Sum Missionary 1981; r/Bapt; hon/Gamma Beta Phi, 1981; Kappa Delta Pi, 1982; Mortar Bd, 1982; Phi Kappa Phi, 1982; Gwendolyn Boyette Button S'ship; g/Elem Ed Tchr; MDiv in Cnslg or Social Wk; Start or Wk in an Orphanage.

WILKES, JACKIE JR oc/Student; b/Jun 28, 1965; h/1000 Yuma Street, Charlotte, NC 28213; p/Jackie and Lucinda Wilkes, Charlotte, NC; ed/HS Student; cp/Order of the Lion, 1982; Beta Clb, 1979; Basketball; W Charlotte HS Sports Prog; r/Mt Olive U Presb Ch, Softball Team; hon/Citizenship Awd, 1980; Most Improved, Baseball, 1981; MVP Lineman, 1980; Outstg Def, Baseball, 1980; All-Conf Football Team, 1981; Lion Sports Awd, Baseball, 1982; All-St Team, Football, 1982; All-Conf Football Team, 1982; Most Athletic, Sr Superlatives, 1982-83; All-Mecklenburg Def, Football, 1982; Second Team Offense, 1982; All-St Hon Mention, 1982; g/To Play Profl Football; To Wk in the Computer Field in Bus.

WILKINS, CATHERINE ELAINE oc/Part-time Fashion Consultant, Student; b/Oct 18, 1964; h/3610 Galaxie, Garland, TX 75041; ba/Mesquite, TX; p/John M and Martha Wilkins, Garland, TX; ed/Grad, S Garland, HS, 1983; pa/Fashion Conslt, Casual Corner, 1982-; cp/Capt, So Belles, 1982-83; Strutters; Pres's Coun; Belle Coun; All-City Drill Team, 1981-83; Bus Ldrs of S Garland, 1982-83; r/Cath; hon/3rd Runner-Up, Miss Garland Pageant, 1982; Nat Superstar Drill Team, 1982; Miss USA Girl, 1982; Superstar Girl at Sum Camp, Line and Ofcr Camps, 1982.

WILKINS, MICHAEL DWAYNE oc/Student; b/Oct 4, 1960; h/Route 1, Box 249, La Crosse, VA 23950; p/Mr and Mrs Sollie Wilkins Sr, La Crosse, VA; ed/Dipl, Pk View Sr HS, 1978; Dipl, Cinc Col of Mortuary Sci, 1980; BS, Bus Adm/Mgmt, St Paul's Col, 1984; pa/Maintenance Wkr, St Paul's Col, 1983; 2-Yr Apprenticeship, Oris P Jones Funeral Home, 1980-82; Morgue Attendant, Cinc Col of Mortuary Sci, 1979-80; r/Reformed Zion Union Apostolic; Pres, Reformed Zion Union Yg People's Conf, 1976, 1978, 1980, 1982, 1984; VP, Annual Sunday Sch Conv; hon/Hon Roll throughout HS; Jr Beta Clb; Former DJ, WSHV, 1977-78; Cert of Awd for Phy Sci, 1975; Recip, Funeral Dirs and Embalmers Lic, VA St Bd of Funeral Dirs and Embalmers, 1984; g/To Serve the Public w the Best in Funeral Customs.

WILKINSON, M LANCE oc/Student; b/Aug 10, 1955; h/PO Box 576, Rusk, TX 75785; c/Arleta Muriel Starr; p/Mr and Mrs R L Wilkinson, Rusk, TX; ed/GED, 1973; AA, 1983; pa/Foreman, Brown & Root, 1979; r/Meth; hon/Outstg Acad Achmt, 1983; Outstg Computer Sci Student, 1982-83; Dean's Hon List, 1981, 1982, 1983; Dean's List, 1982; Nat Dean's List; g/Bach Degs in Mech Engrg and Computer Sci; Law Sch.

WILKINSON, MARGARET ELIZABETH oc/Student; b/Jan 25, 1965; h/Route 1, Box 70, Alligator, MS 38720; p/Mr and Mrs E L Wilkinson, Alligator, MS; ed/Grad, Clarksdale HS, 1983; cp/Distributive Ed Clbs of Am, Pres 1983; Cath Yth Org, 1979-81; Student Coun, 1981-82; Pres, Jr-Sr Social Clb, 1982-83; r/Cath; hon/VFW S'ship Awd, 1983; Tom Edmundson Meml Awd, 1983; Student Coun Ofcr, 1981-82; Nat Hon Roll, 1982-83; Rotary Clb Del to Ldrship Conf; g/Maj in Nsg (Anesthesiology).

WILLHITE, LYNN ELAINE oc/Sales Coordinator, Student; b/Oct 21, 1957; h/201 Cedarwood Drive, Jamestown,

NC 27282; ba/High Point, NC; p/Charlotte Willhite, Jamestown, NC; ed/HS Grad, 1975; Real Est Cert, 1981; Att'g, High Pt Col (BA in Bus Adm); mil/Marine Corps, 1981-82; pa/Waitress, Grants Bradford House, 1975; Sales and Hd of Stock, Thalhimers, 1977-78; Billing Clk and Supvr, Stuart Circle Hosp, 1978-80; Asst Mgr, Ormond, 1980-81; Marine Corps Mil Police, 1981-82; Mgmt of Accts Receivable, Piedmont Wholesale Co, 1982-83; r/Christian; g/Mgr of Own Co.

WILLIAMS, CANDACE MAE oc/Student; b/Oct 7, 1964; h/Route 1, Steadman Road, Tallapoosa, GA 30176; p/Chester Jr and Katherine Williams, Tallapoosa, GA; ed/Grad, Haralson Co HS; cp/Chorus; FHA; 4-H; FFA; Voc Clb; r/Epis; hon/1st Place, 4-H Co Awd in Human Devel; 3 2nd Place Awds, Spec Olympics; 2nd Place, City Swim Meet; Camp Alamisco for the Blind, 3rd Place in Horse Show; Trophy for Most Helpful Camper; g/To Attend Voc Sch at GA or AL Sch for the Blind.

WILLIAMS, CHRISTOPHER DALE oc/Student; b/Aug 3, 1964; h/315 Florence Drive, Selmer, TN 38375; ba/Jackson, TN; p/Johnny and Sue Williams, Selmer, TN; ed/Grad, McNairy Ctl HS; Att'g, Union Univ; cp/Asst Dir of Student Activs, Union Univ, 1982; Chm of Fund Raiser to Aid Carl Perkins Child Abuse Ctr, 1983; Yg Repubs; Pres, Col Freshman and Sophomore Classes; Student Univ Affairs Com; Univ Planning Com; Sigma Alpha Epsilon; Student Govt Exec and Planning Com; Student Founs Recruiter for Univ; Univ Senator; HS Bk, 1979-81; r/So Bapt; hon/1 Yr Contract for Promotion w Hollywood N Talent Promotions, NBC; Commentary on Capital Punishment; Intl Clb; Sociol Awd; 3 1st Place Medals for Musical Achmt; Feature Spkr for Univ Rising Sr Day; Intern for ABC-TV; Congl Intern in Wash, DC, for Congressman Don Sundquist, 1984; Commun Ldrs of Am; Intl W/W Yth in Achmt; g/Maj in Communs and Eng-Jour, Minor in Spch; TV Public Relats or Music Promotion Position.

WILLIAMS, DARYL VANCE oc/Director; b/Oct 1, 1956; h/1406-H Clarkson Road, Richmond, VA 23224; ba/Richmond, VA; m/Sharon McDaniel; p/Hattie N Williams, Portsmouth, VA; ed/Manor HS, 1974; BA, cum laude, Shaw Univ, 1978; pa/Dir, K L Johnson Ctr, 1982; Coor of Student Activs, Fisher Elem Sch, 1980-82; Tchr's Aide, Richmond Public Schs, 1978-80; cp/Alpha Phi Alpha Inc, Dir of Ednl Activs 1978; r/Apostolic; hon/Hon Grad, 1978; W/W Among Students in Am Univs and Cols; Intl Yth in Achmt; Dist'd Collegians; Commun Ldrs of Am; g/PhD in Ed Adm and Supvn.

WILLIAMS, DEBBIE KAY oc/Housewife; b/Mar 6, 1963; h/117 South Lincoln, Hobart, OK 73651; m/Eddie; c/Brandon David; p/Mr and Mrs Richard G Benefield, Anadarko, OK; ed/Grad, Anadarko HS, 1981; BA, Sociol, Univ Sci and Arts OK; cp/Shortgrass Theatre Co, 1983; Future Bus Ldrs of Am; Nat Hon Soc; St Hon Soc; Drama Clb; Reporter, Chem Clb; VP, Student Union Activs Bd; Pres, Biol-Pre-Hlth Sci Clb; Student Union Renovations Com; hon/Pi Gamma Mu Hon Soc; Full Chem S'ship; Hon Roll; Ranked 4th, HS Grad'g

Class; Bausch and Lomb Sci Awd; Sci, Drama and 3 Ec Awds; HS Acad Awd, OK St Univ; Intl Yth in Achmt; g/BS in Chem; Become a Pharm; JD.

WILLIAMS, GARRETT OWEN oc/Student; b/Dec 15, 1960; h/Apartment 1-A Farmwood Garden, Kernersville, NC 27284; p/Elaine M Holbrook, Kernersville, NC; ed/E Forsyth Sr High, 1979; BS in Polit Sci and Indust Relats, Univ of NC Chapel Hill, 1983; pa/Acctg Tech, UNC Ctr for Public TV, 1980-; Hotel Auditor, Winston-Salem Holiday Inn Ctl, 1980; Chaperone and Conductor, Winston-Salem Tours Inc, 1982; cp/ Atkins HS: Tennis, 1975-77, Team Capt 1976-77; E Forsyth Sr High: Key Clb 1978-79, Baseball 1977-79 (Team Capt 1978-79), F'ship of Christian Aths 1977-79; Univ of NC Chapel Hill: Co-Capt of Jr Varsity Baseball 1979-81, Chi Psi Frat (Pres of Fall 1980 Pledge Class, Alumni Coor 1982), Intervarsity Christian F'ship 1977-79 (Bible Study Grp Ldr 1981, Billy Graham Lecture Series Follow-Up Ldr 1982), Interfrat Coun 1982; Winston-Salem Giants, Semi-Profl Baseball Team, 1980-83, Capt 1982; hon/MVP, Tennis, Atkins HS, 1976-77; Nat Hon Soc, E Forsyth Sr High, 1979; Wk-Study S'ship, Univ of NC Chapel Hill, 1980-82; g/Entry into Bkg (Mgmt Tng); MBA.

WILLIAMS, JACQUELINE RHODEMA oc/Student; b/Sep 6, 1962; h/ Route 2, Box 254-A, North Wilkesboro, NC 28659; p/Jack M Williams, Fredricksburg, VA; ed/Dipl, N Wilkes HS, 1980; Att'g, Univ of NC Greensboro; pa/Col Wk-Study, Gen Ofc Wk, Info Sers, UNC-G, 1982-83; Other Previous Positions; cp/Vol for ARC, 1981-82; r/ Bapt; hon/Pres of Student Coun, 1979-80; VP, Band Coun; Lead Drummer for Marching Band; Parliamentarian for Christian Yth Org; HS Spanish Awd; Hubbard S'ship for Nsg, 1980-84; Disciplinary Mem of Hawkins Dorm, UNC-G, 1982-83; W/W; g/Wk in a Lexington Based Hosp as a Surg Scrub Nurse.

WILLIAMS, JOSEPH EVERETTE JR oc/Director of Special Services; h/PO 1354, Livingston, AL 35470; ba/Livingston, AL; p/Joseph E and Thelma E Williams; ed/MA, Delta St Univ, 1979; BA, Jackson St Univ, 1976; St Aloysius HS, 1971; pa/Dir of Spec Sers, Livingston Univ, 1982-; Prog Asst 1979-81, Resident Cnslr 1977-79, MS Val St Univ; Subst Tchr, Vicksburg Public Schs, 1976; MS Assn of Ednl Opport Prog Pers, VP 1981-82; Nat Tchrs Assn; cp/YMCA; hon/Outstg Yg Man of Am, 1982; YMCA Outstg Girls' Basketball Coach, 1978; St Aloysius HS Football and Basketball Awds, 1970, 1971; g/ Advance Deg at Livington Univ.

WILLIAMS, JOSEPH MAXWELL oc/ Student; b/Oct 30, 1953; h/1026 Ingraham Street #104, Los Angeles, CA 90017; p/Robert (dec) and Inez Williams, Los Angeles, CA; ed/Ctl HS, 1970; Queen's Col, 1972; BS 1979, BSC 1980, Woodbury Univ; Master's Deg, Univ of CA LA, 1983; cp/Pres, VP, Treas, Lion's Clb; Coor'g Chm, Leo Clbs, Guyana; Ednl Com Chm, Sch Org; Pres, VP, Woodbury Univ Student Body; Ldr, St George's Folk Grp; Ldr, African Caribbean Students; Editor, Campus Newspaper; Commun Involvement, Ch Yth Org; hon/Phi Gamma Kappa Awd,

Communs 1980, Mktg 1979; Floyd Kirby Awd for Col Citizenship; Best Debating Team Ldr; Grad, summa cum laude, 1979; Grad, magna cum laude, 1980; g/Commun and Bus Involvement.

WILLIAMS, KATHY JOHNSON oc/ Sales Manager; b/Mar 31, 1959; h/619 University Avenue, Building 6, Apartment 4, Oxford, MS 38655; p/Mr and Mrs Harold G Williams, Water Valley, MS; ed/Grad, Col Hill Acad, 1976; BPA, Univ of MS, 1980; pa/Williams' Sales Mgr, 1983-; Frito-Lay Sales Mgr, 1982-83; Procter & Gamble, 1980-82; cp/Area Coor, Phi Mu Frat, 1983; VP, Assoc'd Student Body; Pres, MS St Univ Rush Advr and Chapt Advr, Chapt Advr, Phi Mu; Treas, Assn Wom Students; Campus Favorite; Campus Senator; Pres, Campus Senate; Chancellor, Standing Com; Chm, Welcoming Com; Freshman Orientation Com; Sect Editor, The Ole Miss; Adv Com, Daily MS; Chm, Code Revision Com; Chm, Panhellenic Bylaws Com; Panhellenic Del; Omicron Delta Kappa; hon/Hall of Fame; Omicron Delta Kappa; Mortar Bd; Rho Lambda; Watermelon Carnival Queen; Outstg Alum, Collegian MS, Phi Mu; Gov, Am Legion Aux Girls' St; Alpha Lambda Delta; Phi Kappa Phi Freshman Awd; Delta Debutante; Outstg Yg Wom of Am; Intl Yth in Achmt; W/W Among Students in Am Univs and Cols; Nat Dean's List; Personalities of S; Outstg Yg Wom of Am.

WILLIAMS, LINETHA FAYE oc/ Student; b/Sep 4, 1967; h/1702 Dee Street, Douglas, GA 31533; p/Linda M Williams, Douglas, GA; ed/HS Student; cp/Letter Clb; Pep Clb; Fgn Lang Clb; Varsity Cheerldr; Anchor Clb; Student Coun Rep; Sect Ldr in Chorus, 1981-83; r/Deliverance Ctrs of GA; hon/All-St Chorus, 1980-81, 1981-82; Gov's Hon Alternate, 1982, 1983; Hon of Achmts in Chorus, 1981-83; European Tour w Sound of Am, 1984; g/To Attend Col and Maj in Computer Sci.

WILLIAMS, LORELEI ANNE oc/ Student; b/Jul 19, 1958; h/Route 2, Box 254-A, North Wilkesboro, NC 28659; p/Savannah Williams, North Wilkesboro, NC; ed/N Wilkes HS; Att'g, Wilkes Commun Col; pa/Waitress, 1968-79; Purchasing Asst, Lowes Co Inc, 1976-81; cp/BSU Pres at Wilkes Commun Col; Editor of The Cougar, WCC; Student Govt Assn, WCC; r/Dir of Yth Choir, Oak Grove Bapt; hon/Dean's List, WCC, 1982-83; Homecoming Ct, WCC, 1983; Chosen to Wk at Gov's Banquet, WCC, 1983; g/To Receive an AS at WCC; BS; To Wk w Computers.

WILLIAMS, MARVIN JR oc/Office Clerk; b/Jun 29, 1966; h/5016 Brookdale Drive, Oklahoma City, OK 73115; p/ Marvin and Nam Williams, Oklahoma City, OK; pa/Ofc Clk at Grocery Store; cp/Drama Clb, Pres; Yrbook Staff; Tennis Team; r/Bapt; hon/W/W Clb, 1983; Boys' St Del, 1983; Hugh O'Brian Ldrship Awd, 1982; Ch Yth Grp Pres, 1983; Drama VP, 1983; g/Study at OK Univ; Become a Dr.

WILLIAMS, RACHEL ELIZABETH oc/Student, Part-time Typesetter; b/ Nov 18, 1963; h/5225 Wendy Street, Paragould, AR 72450; ba/Paragould, AR; p/V L Williams, Paragould, AR; Willodine Williams, Inglewood, CA; ed/ Grad, Crowley's Ridge Acad, 1981; AA, Crowley's Ridge Col, 1983; Att'g, OK

Christian Col; pa/Cashier, Taco Hut, 1980; Pt-time Typesetter, Crowley's Ridge Col Bookstore and Press, 1981-; cp/Am Legion AR Girls' St Del; Nat Hon Soc; Yrbook Staff; FHA; Col Intramurals; Ambassadors and Choralaires Music Grps; Alpha Chi, 1984; OCC Chorale, 1983-84; Delta Tau Omega Social Clb, 1983-84; Gleaners, 1983-84; r/Ch of Christ; hon/CRC's Best All Around Female, 1981-83; Personalities of S; W/W Among Students in Am Jr Cols; Intl Yth in Achmt; Commun Ldrs of Am; W/W Among Am HS Students; g/Double Maj in Math Ed and Computer Sci; Tchr.

WILLIAMS, REGINALD ROMERO oc/College Student; b/May 12, 1961; h/ 610 Gainesville, Memphis, TN 38109; ba/Martin, TN; p/Mr and Mrs Willie Williams, Memphis, TN; ed/Westwood HS, 1979; Att'g, Univ of TN Martin (Maj in Geo-Sci and Physics Meteorology); cp/Black Students Assn, 4 Yrs; Univ Coun Mem; Geo-Sci and Physics Mem; SGA Registration Com; Dorm Hall Mem; Co-Capt, Badminton Team; March of Dimes Superwalk, 1981-83; Chm, Frat Thanksgiving Can Food Drive, 2 Yrs; Campus-Wide Blood Drive, 1980-83; Parent/Student Sem, 2 Yrs; Frat Easter Seals (Nat Proj); Jerry Lewis Annual Muscular Dystrophy Telethon, 1981-82; SGA, Congl Rep 1980-81, Movie Com 1981-82, Secy of Communs 1982-83, Pres 1983-84; Chm, Pub and Publicity Coms, 1982-83; Alpha Phi Alpha Frat, Histn 1981-82, Editor of the Sphinxman 1981-82, Dir of Ednl Affairs 1981-82, Corresponding Secy 1982-83, Dean of Steps 1982-83, 1983-84; Asst St Dir of TN, Alpha Phi Alpha Frat, 1983-84; Pep Ldr, 1982-84; Chp of Pageant, 1982-83; Student Writer, Pacer, 1981-82; Visitor, Hillsview Nsg Home, 1981-83; r/Bapt; hon/ Delta Sigma Theta S'ship; Dean's List Hons, 1980-82; Certs of Merit in Participation, Attendance and Var Recog Awds; Most Outstg Mem, Pilgrim Rest Bapt Ch, 1980-81; TN Col Brother of the Yr, 1982-83; Cand for Dist'd Collegian of the Yr, 1982-83; Recip, Am Legion Awd, 1979; Recip, Hons and Certs for 3 Yrs of Participation on UTM Badminton Team; W/W Among Col Freshmen; g/To Attend Grad Sch at St Louis Univ or FL St Univ.

WILLIAMS, SHEPHARD FRED oc/ Student; b/Oct 15, 1962; h/1678 Country Club Road, Elberton, GA 30635; p/ Rev and Mrs Lougene Williams Sr, Elberton, GA; ed/AA, Bus Adm, 1982; cp/Beta Clb; Mu Alpha Theta; Ofcr, Reporter, FTA; FBLA; Delta Psi Omega; Christian Ser Org; Salvation Army Vol; Big Brothers Org; r/Yth VP, Freewill Missionary BTU; SS Pianist; Primary SS Tchr; hon/W/W Among Am HS Students; Intl Yth in Achmt; g/Bus Adm/ Acctg Deg.

WILLIAMS, UTONA LYNN oc/Student; b/Dec 26, 1965; h/415 Berkley Court, Radcliff, KY 40160; p/Roy E Williams, Tallahassee, FL; Billie A Williams, Radcliff, KY; ed/HS Student; cp/Class Rep; Flag Corps; Student Coun; Pep Clb; Treas, Teens Who Care Clb; German Clb; FHA; Secy, Band; Chorus; Marching and Concert Band; Wom's Clb Dist Talent Show; Vol Wkr, Nsg Homes and Handicapped; Yth Chm, ARC; Sunny Side Up Gospel Singing

Grp; Wom's Softball; Order of the Rainbow for Girls; Wrestling Cheerldr; Secy, Student Coun; Participant, Jump for Heart; Math Bowl Team; Basketball, Fencing, Soccer, Bowling Teams; March of Dimes Jogathon Participant; r/Prot; hon/Miss Ctl KY Teen Charm, 1982; St Sci Fair Awd; Miss Freshman, 1981; Pres, Beta Clb; Yg Commun Ldrs of Am; g/Dental or Med Field; Wk w Handicapped and Elderly; Help and Serve People and God.

WILLIAMSON, AMY GAIL oc/Student; b/Sep 4, 1963; h/17 Omar Circle, Jackson, TN 38301; ba/Martin, TN; p/ Rev and Mrs B L Gaddie, Jackson, TN; ed/Grad, Jackson Ctl-Merry HS, 1981; Grad, Univ of TN Martin, 1985; pa/ Waitress, Holiday Inn, 1982-; cp/Zeta Tau Alpha, 1st VP 1983; U Meth Yth F'ship; r/Meth; hon/Nat Hon Soc, 1981; All-W TN Choir, 1980; W/W Among Am HS Students; g/Communs Maj; Career in Public Relats.

WILLIAMSON, DAYNA RENEE oc/ Student; b/Nov 16, 1964; h/Route 1, Box 33, Philadelphia, MS 39350; p/Mr and Mrs Samuel Lee Williamson, Philadelphia, MS; ed/Grad, Phila HS, 1982; AA, E Ctl Jr Col, 1983; cp/Basketball, E Ctl Jr Col; HS Basketball and Track; r/Ch of Christ; hon/HS: Friendliest Girl, Best All-Around Girl, Sr Homecoming Maid, MVP in Basketball, 4-Yr Hon Student; Jr Col: Homecoming Queen, Secy of Sophomore Class, VP of ROTC Cadet Assn, Treas of Student Body Assn, VP of French Clb, Pres of F'ship of Christian Aths, Secy of Dorm Coun; W/W Among Am HS Students; Soc of Dist'd Am HS Students; g/Maj in Computer Sci.

WILLIAMSON, LAURA JEANICE oc/Student; b/Jun 15, 1963; h/PO Box 802, Perry, FL 32347; p/Mr and Mrs F L Williamson, Perry, FL; ed/Taylor Co HS; Att'g, Flagler Col; pa/Cnslr/Lifeguard, GA/Acteens Camps for FL Bapt Conv, 1980-83; Waitress/Clk, Bakery/ Coffee Shop, 1982; Customer Ser Wkr, KY Fried Chicken (Present); cp/HS Band, Capt; Class Treas; NHS VP; Little Wom VP and Pres; FSU Marching Chiefs, 2 Yrs; Tau Beta Sigma; FSU BCM; BCM Singers; r/Bapt; hon/Rotary Clb S'ship, 1981; FL Acad Scholar's Fund Awd, 1982; So S'ship Foun, 1981; USMC Awd, 1981; Salutatorian, summa cum laude Grad, 1981; g/Deaf Ed/Elem Ed Deg, Flagler Col; Early Childhood Cert; Tchr of Presch Deaf Chd.

WILLIAMSON, TAMMY RENA oc/ Student; b/Dec 19, 1966; h/Route 3, Box 147B, Louisville, MS 39339; p/Mrs Billy Heard, Louisville, MS; ed/HS Student; cp/Cheerldr; Beta Clb; NW Clb; Ch Choir; Softball; r/Bapt; hon/W/W Among Am HS Students; g/To Attend MS St Univ and Maj in Bus w the Intention of Going to Law Sch.

WILLRICH, CANDACE YVETTE oc/ Student; b/Mar 26, 1965; h/701 Manning Road, Grand Prairie, TX 75051; ba/ Austin, TX; p/Mr and Mrs Theodis Willrich, Grand Prairie, TX; ed/Sam Houston HS, 1983; Att'g, Univ of TX Austin; cp/Nat Forensic Leag, 1983; Spanish Clb, Treas 1982-83; Nat Hon Soc, 1982-83; Newcomers Clb; Ebony Eight Plus, 1983-84; r/Ch of God in Christ; hon/C of C Girl of the Month, 1982-83; Arlington Assn of Concerned

Citizens S'ship; TX Coalition of Black Dems S'ship; TX Achmt Awd; PSAT Commended Student; W/W Among Am HS Students; g/Deg in Computer Sci or Engrg.

WILLS, CHRISTY LYNN oc/Assembly Worker; b/Dec 26, 1959; h/Route 1, Box 229, Barboursville, VA 22923; ba/ Charlottesville, VA; p/Mr and Mrs Samuel Lee Wills, Barboursville, VA; ed/ Wm Monroe HS, 1978; Att'g, Piedmont, VA, Commun Col; pa/Assem Wkr, Comdial Telephone Sys; cp/Vol, Am Cancer Soc, Am Heart Fund; Ladies Aux, Ruckersville Fire Dept; Vacation Bible Sch Tchr, 1978-84; Future Bus Ldrs of Am, 1976-78; Pres, FHA, 1976-77; Histn, SAE, 1974-75; Newspaper Staff Editor; Yrbook Editor; Sunday Sch Tchr, K-1, 1980-84; Softball, 1972-78; Capt, Softball, 1977; Ch Softball Team; r/Bapt; hon/Little Miss Greene Co, 1967; Del, Am Legion Aux Girls' St, 1976-77; Beta Clb, 1977-78; Miss Nat Teenager Pageant, 1977-78; Hon Roll, 8th through 12th Grade; Outstg Yg Ams; W/W Among Am HS Students; Yg Personalities of S; g/ Career as Computer Programmer; Bus and Computer Sci.

WILROY, LOU ANN oc/Student; b/ Dec 21, 1964; h/PO Box 187, Hernando, MS 38632; p/Mr and Mrs William Wilroy Jr, Hernando, MS; ed/Hernando HS; Att'd, Millsaps Col; Att'g, Univ of TN; pa/Hernando Bk, 1982, 1983; cp/ Quill and Scroll, 1981-83; Girls' St Del; hon/Poetry in *Illusions*, 1981, 1982; Lady of the Realm, Memphis Cotton Carnival; Hall of Fame, 1982; Intells, 1982; Creat Writing Awd, 1982; g/Comml Artist w a Mag.

WILSON, BARON R oc/Student; b/ Apr 18, 1960; h/Midland, TX; p/Buck Wilson, Midland, TX; Mrs Irby L Dyer, Midland, TX; ed/Midland HS, 1978; Midland Col, 1981-83; TX Tech Univ, 1983; r/Cath; hon/Nat Dean's List; Pres's List, 1983; Indust Arts St Competition, 1978; g/BArch, TX Tech Univ.

WILSON, DANIEL KEVIN oc/Student; b/Sep 9, 1958; h/Star Route, Rew, PA 16744; ba/Same; p/Richard A and Carol Wilson, Rew, PA; ed/Smethport Area Jr-Sr HS, 1976; BS, Alderson Broaddus Col, 1980; WV Sch of Osteopathic Med; cp/Band, Nat Hon Soc Pres, Drama, HS; Concert Band, Brass Choir, Chapel Choir, Drama Clb, Chi Beta Phi Sci Frat Local Chapt Pres, Zeta Alpha Gamma Sci Clb, Silverkey Soc, Col; Bible Study Ldr; Student Mem, AOA; Christian Med Soc; hon/HS Awd, Col; Outstg Jr Chem Awd, Am Chem Soc; W/W Among Students in Am Univs and Cols; Nat Register of Outstg Col Grads; Am's Outstg Names and Faces; g/ Osteopathic Phys in Fam Pract.

WILSON, DAVID BARRETT oc/ Student; b/Mar 21, 1967; h/3100 Eastwood Court, Boulder, CO 80302; p/Mr and Mrs Thomas E Jones, Boulder, CO; ed/Grad, Boulder HS, 1985; pa/Royalty Dept (Typing), Westview Press, 1982; Sales, Left Hand Bookstore, 1984; Dir, Safe Ride Prog, Boulder HS, 1983-84; cp/Capt, Boulder Val Lacrosse Clb, 1982-83, 1983-84; Students for a Positive Future, 1983-84; Latin Clb, 1983-84; Cross Country Team, Boulder HS, 1983-84; People Involved in Ctl Am, 1984; Christmas Proj, 1983; Peer Cnslr, Base Line Jr High, 1980-82; Hons Prog,

1979-84; hon/Finalist, Freedoms Foun Essay Contest, 1984; Finalist, CO Lang Arts Position Paper Competition, 1984; 1st Place, Life Sci Div, Boulder Val Sci Fair, 1980; Base Line Citizenship Awd, 1980-81; Base Line Ldrship Awd, 1980-81; Base Line S'ship Awd (Straight A Average), 1981-82; g/Polit Sci, Phil.

WILSON, GLENN GRAYBILL JR oc/ Student; b/Dec 8, 1962; h/209 McArthur Street, Galax, VA 24333; p/Mr and Mrs Glenn Graybill Wilson; ed/Galax HS, 1981; Emory and Henry Col, 1981-; cp/Pres, 9th Grade Homeroom; Exec Coun, Student Coun Assn; Band, 5 Yrs; Jazz Band, 5 Yrs; Football and Basketball, 8th Grade; Varsity Football, 4 Yrs; Track, 4 Yrs; Ch Yth Grp, 5 Yrs, Pres for 1 Yr; Varsity Clb, 3 Yrs; Ch Yth Choir, 4 Yrs; VP, Yg Dems, Col; Polit Vol; Del, Boys' St; US JCs, Galax Chapt; Circle K; r/First U Meth Ch; hon/Prin's Awd, Am Legion Citizenship Awd, HS Graduation; Most Outstg Band Sr; Arion Awd; Sportsmanship Awd, Football; Treas, VA Col Yg Dems, 1981-82; VChm, VA Col Yg Dems, 1982-83; Soc of Dist'd Am HS Students; W/W Among Am HS Students; g/BS in Hist and Govt; Tchr and Football Coach, HS.

WILSON, KELLI TAYLOR oc/Student; b/Jul 19, 1966; h/Route 3, Box 717-A, Shelby, NC 28150; p/Knox Wilson, Jax, FL; Rachel Wilson, Shelby, NC; ed/Grad, Crest Sr HS, 1984; cp/ Sci Clb, 1980-82, Pres 1982; Student Coun, 1980-83; Band, 1980-83; French Clb, 1981-82; Busdriver, 1983; Beta Clb, 1983; Scorekeeper, Baseball and Basketball, 1981-83; r/Poplar Sprgs Bapt Ch Mission Team, Yth Choir, 1982-83; hon/Nom for Gov's Sch, 1983; Girls' St, 1983; g/Psych; Med Career; Law.

WILSON, MARCUS DEAN oc/Student; b/Dec 12, 1962; h/5100 D Foxridge Apartments, Blacksburg, VA 24060; p/ Mr and Mrs Gerald L Wilson, Ridgeway, VA; ed/Dreway Mason HS; Att'g, VA Tech; pa/Clk, Winn-Dixie; Clk, The Peanut Shack; Dispatcher, The Pillsbury Co-Miller Brewery; cp/Mu Alpha Theta, Nat Math Soc, Secy-Treas; Football, 5 Yrs; BSA; r/Bapt; hon/W/W; g/To Go to a Profl Sch and Become a Dentist.

WILSON, MARIANNE CHI oc/Student; b/Aug 5, 1957; h/602 Washington Street, #4, Blacksburg, VA 24060; p/Mr and Mrs John Leslie Wilson, New Castle, PA; ed/HS, 1975; BS, WV Wesleyan Col, 1979; cp/Chief Justice, Grad Hon Sys, VPI&SU, 1980-82; WV Wesleyan Home Ec Assn, Secy & Fin Funds Chp; WV St Home Assn Student Mem Secy, Parliamentarian; Kappa Phi Wom's Christian Org, Pledgemaster and Rep to Rel Life Coun; Campus Commun Prog Bd, Fine Arts Com; *Pharos* Student Weekly Newspaper, Layout and Reporter, Experiment in Intl Living, Homestay Prog, Barnstaple, N Devon, England, 1979; Intl Order Of Rainbow for Girls, Worthy Advr 1976, PA St Rep to WV 1975-76; hon/Kappa Omicron Phi Nat Home Ec Hon Soc, Secy; Silver Joan of Arc Medallion for Outstg Commun Ser and Ldrship, St Lucy's Aux Guild to the Blind; g/Reg'd Dietitian; MS in Human Nutrition and Foods.

WILSON, MARJORIE DENISE oc/ Graduate Student; b/Jul 3, 1960; h/2401 Barclay Place, Ponca City, OK 74601;

p/Mr and Mrs Ronald Wilson, Ponca City, OK; ed/Ponca City Sr HS, 1978; BS, OK St Univ, 1982; cp/Phi Theta Kappa; Marching Band; Concert Band; Phi Beta Lambda; Beta Alpha Psi; Delta Sigma Pi, Pledge Pres; Chi Alpha; Residence Hall Pres; IRS Vol, Income Tax Asst Prog; Yth Grp, VP; Yth Newspaper Editor; hon/Jr Univ Scholar; Residence Hall Assn Meritorious Ser Awd; 1st Place St, 2nd Place Reg, Ch Music Contest; W/W Among Students in Am Univs and Cols; Commun Ldrs of Am; g/MBA.

WILSON, MICHAEL DEWAYNE oc/Student; b/Aug 19, 1968; h/95 West Calaveras, Altadena, CA 91001; p/Sandra Elaine Wilson Thomas, Altadena, CA; ed/Student, Pasadena HS; pa/Staff, Camp Waswagen Sum Camp; cp/Pasadena Boys' Clb; Jr C of C, VP 1979; Jr Achmt, CA, VP of Mktg; r/Lincoln Ave Bapt Ch, Yth Dept and Choir; hon/Nat Hon Soc, 1980-81; Capt, Varsity Basketball Team, 1981-82; Mentally Gifted Minor Acad Soc, 1978-82; MVP, KC Little Leag Baseball Tour, 1977.

WILSON, PATRICIA AILENE oc/Student; b/Feb 5, 1964; h/810 Kay Circle, Chattanooga, TN 37421; p/Mr and Mrs W B Wilson; ed/Tyner HS, 1982; cp/Bd of Dirs, Anchor Clb; FHA; Beta Clb; TN Ofc Ed Clb; r/Outreach Ldr, SS Class, Concord Bapt Ch; Homecoming Activs, 1980; Newspaper Staff, 1981; Perfect Attendance Awd, 1981; Mng Editor, Sch Newspaper, 1981-82; hon/W/W Among Am HS Students; g/Med Technol Deg, Univ of TN Chattanooga.

WILSON, ROBIN LYNN oc/Student; b/Sep 19, 1959; h/11 Willowdale Court, Montclair, NJ 07042; p/Robert and Juanita Wilson, Montclair, NJ; ed/BA, Dickinson, 1981; MA, Adelphi Univ, 1984; pa/Crisis Intervention Cnslr, 1981-83; Minority Recruiter in Admissions, Dickinson Col, 1980-81; Tutorial Coor, 1980-81; cp/Coor of Girls' Acad and Rec Prog, Pres of Single's Grp 1983; Pres, Black Student Union, 1980; Bd Mem, Yth on the Move for Christ Mins; hon/Acad F'ship, Adelphi Univ, 1983.

WILSON, TAMMIE RENE oc/Student; b/Jan 1, 1965; h/Route 1, Box 130, Guys, TN 38339; p/Dwight and Sarah Wilson, Guys, TN; ed/Grad, McNairy Ctl HS, 1983; cp/Beta, 1980-83; Student Govt, 1980-83; Secy, Distributive Ed, 1982-83; Secy, FHA, 1980-83; VP, Pres, and Sub-Reg Pres, Pep Clb, 1980-83; Jr Keyboard Clb, 1982, 1983; r/So Bapt; hon/Hall of Fame, 1983; Students Excel, 1983; Outstg Mem of DECA, 1982; FHA, 1980, 1981; Student Govt, 1980, 1981, 1982; Miss McNairy Ctl, 1983; W/W Among Am HS Students; h/To Attend Memphis St Univ and Maj in Fashion Mdsg/Bus Mgmt.

WILSON, VINCENT CHARLES oc/Student; b/Jul 1, 1963; h/95 West Calaveras, Altadena, CA 91001; p/Sandra E Wilson Thomas, Altadena, CA; ed/Pasadena HS; Sumner Acad of Arts and Scis; Att'g, Pomona Pitzer Acad Col; pa/Cnslr, Camp Waswagen, Camp Fire Girls, 1981-82; Basketball Coach, Pasadena Boys Clb, 1979-81; cp/Pasadena HS Varsity Basketball, 1979-80; Pómona Pitzer Varsity Basketball; Acad Hon Roll; Boys' St VP, 1980; Student Body Pres, 1980; r/Lincoln Ave Bapt Ch; hon/Nat Hon Soc, 1978-80;

VP, Sr Class, 1980; MVP, Pacific Coast Basketball Tour, 1981; Pitzer Acad S'ship; Kappa Phi Acad S'ship, 1980; Delta S'ship, 1980; W/W Among Am HS Students; Intl Yth in Achmt; Nat HS Ath W/W.

WINANS, CHRISTOPHER E oc/Student; b/May 7, 1959; h/Route 7, Box 242, Fairview, NC 28730; p/Mr and Mrs Homer Sales, Fairview, NC; ed/Hartford HS, 1977; BA, Gardner-Webb Col, 1983; cp/Gardner-Webb Chamber Chorus, 3 Yrs, Asst Conductor 1980-83; Am Choral Dirs Assn, 1981-83, Mem at Large of Col Br 1983; Opera Theatre, 1982, 1983; r/So Bapt; hon/Voted Best Male Vocalist and Best All-Around Male Musician, Music Students at Gardner-Webb, 1982; W/W Among Students in Am Cols and Univs; g/To Be a Music/Yth Dir at a Ch; Deg in Christian Cnslg.

WINN, ALLICYN CHARISSE oc/Insurance Representative, Student; b/Aug 16, 1963; h/487 Section Line Road, Gurley, AL 35748; ba/Huntsville, AL; p/Mr and Mrs Robert H Winn, Gurley, AL; ed/Dipl, Madison Co HS; Att'g, AL Agri and Mech Univ; pa/Supvr of Madison Co Welcome Sta, Madison Co Travel and Tourism Bd, 1981-82; Ins Rep, Intergraph Corp; cp/Class Pres, 1978-81; Homecoing Maid, 1978-81; Cheerldr, 1978-81, Capt 1978, 1981; Sci Clb, 1979-81, Treas of Class 1981; Pres of Yth Dept of Mud Creek N AL and TN Ch Assn, 1980-83; Softball Catcher, 1980-81; Student Govt Assn Secy, 1980; Math Clb, 1980; VIP Clb, 1980; Student Govt Assn Pres, 1981; Secy of Ch Choir, 1981; Most Dependable of 1981 Grad'g Class; Treas of Class, 1981; Student Govt Assn Rep of AL Agri and Mech Univ, 1981; AL Agri and Mech Marching Band, 1982-83; r/Missionary Bapt; hon/Delta Phi Epsilon Awd, 1980-81; Sigma Xi Awd, 1981; Outstg Ldrship Awd, 1981; Pres S'ship, 1981; Recip, Hon Roll and Dean's List, AL Agri and Mech Univ, 1983; Debutante, 1981; W/W Among All-Am Students; g/To Receive a Master's in Psych and Become an Indust or Clin Psychol.

WINSKI, PAUL J oc/Student; b/Jun 4, 1964; h/4365 Edgemont Street, Philadelphia, PA 19137; p/Mr and Mrs Walter Winski, Philadelphia, PA; ed/Grad, W B Saul HS of Agri Sci, 1982; Att'g, DE Val Col of Sci and Agri; cp/VP, HS Nat Hon Soc, 1982; PA Hort Soc, 1982-83; Cath Yth Org, 1981-82; HS FFA, Phila Chapt, 1979-82; r/Rom Cath; hon/Valedictorian, 1982; Jr Horticulturist Awd, PA Hort Soc, 1982; Col Dean's List, 1982-83; Nat Dean's List; g/Maj in Ornamental Hort; To Enter the Res Area of Plant Physiol.

WINTERS, MARK CREAMER oc/Student; b/Oct 2, 1965; h/206 Orville, Potean, OK 74953; ba/Norman, OK; p/Dr and Mrs Richard L Winters, Potean, OK; cp/Lambda Chi Alpha Frat; OU Pres's Ldrship Class; HS Student Coun; Nat Hon Soc; r/Prot; hon/All-Dist and All-Conf Football, 1982-83; OU Alumni Scholar, 1983-84; Potean High Valedictorian, 1982-83; g/To Earn Degs in Mech and Chem Engrg; Med Sch.

WIPF, SHERYL MICHELLE oc/Student; b/Sep 11, 1965; h/101 Walnut Street, Freeman, SD 57029; p/Mr and Mrs Orville D Wipf, Freeman, SD; ed/Freeman Jr/Sr HS, 1983; cp/Nat Hon

Soc; Pep Clb; Ch Organist; SS and Bible Sch Tchr; Choir Accompanist; Yth Grp Secy-Treas; Yth Choir; Town Organist; Vol at Rehab Home; Progs for Home Big Sister Prog; hon/All-St MTNA Piano Winner, 3 Yrs; All-St Band, Basoonist; All-St Orch; All-St Chorus; Hons Choir; Bassoonist, John Phillips Intl HS Hons Band; Paderewski Gold Medal Winner, AMTA; Am's Outstg Names and Faces; Commun Ldrs of Am; W/W Among Am HS Students; g/To Study Chem Engrg as a Prerequisite to Med Sch at Univ of MN's Inst of Technol.

WISE, BRENDA A oc/Substitute Teacher, Resident Assistant; b/Feb 25, 1960; h/2313 Fairland Drive, West Des Moines, IA 50265; ba/Des Moines, IA; p/Mr and Mrs J J Marvin, West Des Moines, IA; ed/HS Dipl, Val High; BS in Ed, Drake Univ; Grad Wk, NY Univ; cp/CEC, Student Chapt, Secy; Vol, Pre-Sch Handicapped Prog; IA Spec Olympics Helper; hon/Kappa Delta Pi Hon Soc; Pres's Hon Roll; Dean's List; Nat Hon Soc; Intl Yth in Achmt; g/Tchr of Mentally Retarded Chd; Further Ed in Disability Areas.

WITTMAN, CURTIS DALE oc/Owner of Advertising Agency; b/May 27, 1954; h/PO Box 401854, Dallas, TX 75240; ba/Dallas, TX; m/Kelly A; c/Blake A; p/Leroy and Laverne Wittmann, L Grange, TX; ed/La Grange HS, 1972; AA, TSTI, 1977; pa/Foreman of Punch Press Dept, Welder, Hurricane Steel, 1972-75; Advtg Asst, Hurricane Steel, 1976; Art Dir, Visador Co, 1977-80; Owner, CWITT Advtg, 1980-; cp/Adv Com, TSTI, 1980-; Pres, Comml Art Class, TSTI, 1977; Student Coun, TSTI, 1976-77; r/Luth; hon/1st Place for Booth Design, NSDJA, 1978, (Nat Sash and Doors Jobbers Assn); Dependable Am I Awd, Visador Co, 1979; g/To Be One of the First in-House Computer Graphics Agys.

WLODARCZYK, DEBRA J MEATH oc/Medical Technologist; b/Apr 9, 1958; oc/Medical Technologist; b/Apr 9, 1958; h/110 Andes Avenue, Geneva, NY; ba/Geneva, NY; m/Stephan John; p/Mr and Mrs James T Meath Sr, Newark, NY; ed/Newark HS, 1976; Keuka Col, 1980, 1982; USPHS Sch of Med Technol, 1981; pa/Med Tech, CHS, 1981-82; Med Tech, Chem, GGH, 1982-; cp/GAC; WAA; Secy, Sr Class; Tennis Team; Intramural Sports; hon/Harriet Loomis Biol Awd; Chi Beta Phi; Alpha Sigma; Am's Outstg Names and Faces; W/W Among Students in Am Univs and Cols; g/Master's Deg in Biol.

WLODARCZYK, STEPHAN JOHN oc/Photographer, Clerk, Student; b/Apr 28, 1958; h/110 Andes Avenue, Geneva, NY 14456; ba/Lyons, NY; m/Debra Jeanne; p/Mr and Mrs Stanley Wlodarczyk, Newark, NY; ed/Newark Sr HS, 1976; BS in Music, Nazareth Col, 1982; Att'g, Nazareth Col (Master's in Elem Ed); pa/Accompanist for Ballet Class, Lyons Commun Ctr, 1982-83; Pvt Piano Tchr, 1979-83; Cashier/Clk, True Value Hardware Store, 1976-83; Cashier/Clk, Fox's News, 1976-83; Profl Photographer, Santelli Studio, 1976-83; Music Edrs Nat Conf, 1981-82; Treas, Music Tchrs Nat Assn, 1978-81; cp/Nazareth Col Piano Ensemble, 1978; Nazareth Col Concert Choir, 1978-82; New Student Orientation, 1979; Student Senate, 1981; St Michael's Adult

Choir, 1975-83; r/Cath.

WOHLSTEIN, KATHY LYNN oc/ Student; b/May 22, 1961; h/146 Whitman Avenue, West Hartford, CT 06107; ba/West Hartford, CT; m/Robert J Ashens III; p/Mr and Mrs Richard Wohlstein, Athens, OH; ed/Athens HS, 1979; GSG Atheneum 5VWO, Eindhoven, Netherlands, 1979-80; Hartt Sch of Music; cp/HS Track; HS Student Coun; HS Band Pres; HS Choir Accompanist; YFU Exch Student to Holland; Hartt Chorale Pres; Hartt Opera Asst Coach; hon/Alpha Chi, 1982; Arion Foun and John Philip Sousa Awd; Nat Hon Soc; Dean's List; Intl Yth in Achmt; W/W Among Am HS Students; g/Profl Coach/Accompanist; Maj Contbn to Arts.

WOMACK, ROBERT W oc/Student; b/Oct 14, 1964; h/7715 Ciboney Drive, Jonesboro, GA 30236; ba/Jonesboro, GA; p/Orval and Barbara Womack, Jonesboro, GA; ed/Grad, Jonesboro Sr High; Att'g, Devry Inst of Technol; mil/AF Jr ROTC, HS, 3 Yrs; r/Bapt; hon/Silver Medal of Valor, AF Jr ROTC, 1982; Dean's List for 2 Trimesters; Proclamation from Clayton Co Bd of Commrs, 1982; Heart Fund Cert, 1979, 1980; W/W Among Am Students; g/Complete Bach Deg in Computer Sci; Obtain a Job in the Computer Indust and Eventually Wk in the NASA Prog.

WONG, CAROL JOAN MARIE oc/Student; b/Nov 5, 1964; h/23 Cardamon Drive, Orlando, FL 32817; p/Bertie and Olga Wong, Orlando, FL; ed/Grad, Colonial HS, 1981; BA, Cornell Univ, 1985; cp/Biomed and Technol Assn; Pre-Profl Med Soc; Ethos Yrbook; Treas, Sci Clb; Chinese Students Assn; Commun and Ch Wkr; Math Clb; hon/Nat Hon Soc; Hon Roll; Commun Ldrs of Am; Intl Yth in Achmt; W/W Among Am HS Students; Personalities of S; g/Asian Studies Deg; Career in Med Field.

WOOD, RAYMOND DEAN oc/Student; b/Mar 24, 1959; h/Route 2, Box 386-EEE, Springfield, LA; p/Roxford and Elaine Wood, Springfield, LA; ed/Grad, Elkhart HS, 1977; Grad, SEn LA Univ, 1983; pa/Equip Control Supvr, Good Hope Energies; Traveling Expeditor and Communs Liaison Ofcr, Good Hope Energies; cp/Student Govt, VChm; Am Student Assn, Reg 9 Bd Mem; Student Rep, Ethics Com; SLU Rugby Team Capt; Soccer Team; Fdr, SLU Spirit Com; Student Rep, Orgs and Activs Com; SLU RFC, VP; hon/Green S Awd, SLU, 1982; Aide-de-Camp, Gov's Staff of David Treen, St of LA; Apprec Awd, SGA, 1982; W/W; g/To Attend Tulane Law Sch; To Actively Participate in St and Nat Govt.

WOODARD, JANET oc/Student; b/Nov 14, 1962; h/PO Box 203, Chatom, AL 36518; p/John H Woodard, Chatom, AL; ed/Grad, Wash Co HS, 1980; BS, Bus Adm, Miles Col, 1984; cp/Alpha Kappa Alpha, Treas 1982-84; Sr Class, VP 1983-84; Student Govt Assn, Senator 1983-84; r/Meth; hon/UNCF S'ship, 1983-84; W/W Among Students in Am Univs and Cols; Nat Dean's List; g/To Further Ed in the Field of Acctg; CPA.

WOODBY, DAVID EDWARD oc/Student; b/Aug 18, 1958; h/Route 1, Box 897, Bristol, TN 37620; p/Mr and Mrs Ernest E Woodby, Bristol, TN; ed/Grad, Sullivan E HS, 1976; BS, E TN St Univ; Att'g Law Sch; cp/Cartoonist, East

Tennessean Student Newspaper; hon/Nat Col Register; Intl Yth in Achmt; g/Comml Artist or Profl Cartoonist; PhD in Hist.

WOODFIN, ELEANOR KATHERINE oc/Student; b/Aug 11, 1964; h/Route 1, Box 66, Tullahoma, TN 37388; p/M Clarke Woodfin Jr, Tullahoma, TN; ed/Clarksville HS; Att'g, Maryville Col; cp/Maryville Col Playhouse, 1982-; Intervarsity Christian F'ship, 1982-; Sign Lang Clb, 1982-; Outdoor Clb, 1982-; Delta Omicron, 1983-; Student Foun, Student Coor 1983-; Residence Hall Staff Mem, 1983-; All-Col Coun, 1983-; Freshman Class Secy, 1982-83; Choir Dept Pres, 1981-82; Choir Dept VP, 1980-81; Concert Choir, 1980-82; Madrigals, 1981-82; Crusaders, 1979-82, Pres for 2 Yrs; Yth Grp Pres, 1980-81; Spch and Drama Clb Pres, 1981-82; FHA, 1981-82; Beginning Choir, 1979-80; 9th Grade Chorus, 1978-79; hon/Pres Scholars, 1982-; TN All-St Choir, 1981, 1982; TN All-Mid-St Choir, 1982; Mid TN St Univ Hon Chorus, 1982; Quad St Hon Chorus, 1982; Nat Hon Soc, 1982; Danforth Awd, 1982; Vol Girls' St, 1981; W/W Among Am HS Students; Am's Outstg Names and Faces; g/Sign Lang Interpreting Deg; Eng Deg; Grad Sch; Career in Interpreting for the Deaf and/or Blind/Deaf People.

WOODS, BARBARA GENNICE oc/Student; b/Jul 15, 1965; h/2310 South Marshall, Little Rock, AR 72206; p/Dorothy J Mitchell, Little Rock, AR; ed/Little Rock Ctl HS, 1983; Att'g, Univ of AR Fayetteville; cp/Nat Hon Soc; Beta Clb; Mu Alpha Theta, Treas; Latin Clb; Sci Clb; Drill Team; Track Mgr; Gymnastics Mgr, 1983; r/Holiness; hon/Cert for Perf on Nat Latin Exam, 1982, 1983; Nat Achmt S'ship, 1983; March of Dimes Walk-a-Thon, 1980, 1981, 1982; g/Pre-Med Maj; Obstetrician.

WOODWARD KAREN oc/Student; b/Oct 5, 1960; h/1075 East 400 North, Orem, UT 84057; p/Joyce W Woodward, Orem, UT; ed/Orem HS, 1978; Assoc's Deg, Ricks Col; BS, Brigham Yg Univ, 1982; cp/Phi Kappa Phi Hon Soc, 1981-82; Pres, Future Edrs of Am, 1979-80; Student NEA, 1978-79; LDS Ch Relief Soc, Compassionate Ser Ldr 1979-80, Homemaking Tchr 1978-79; Pianist 1980-; hon/Outstg Jr, Brigham Yg Univ Col of Ed, 1981; Intl Yth in Achmt; Nat Dean's List; Commun Ldrs of Am; g/Tchr; Instill in Students a Desire to Learn and Provide Positive Experiences.

WOODY, LINDA PRICE oc/Student; b/Jun 18, 1962; h/Route 2, Box 107, Rocky Mount, VA 24151; p/Mr and Mrs Dennis T Woody; ed/Grad, Franklin Co HS, 1980; BBA, James Madison Univ, 1984; pa/Student Asst in Govt Documents Sect, Madison Meml Lib, JMU, 1980-84; Ofc Helper, Franklin Co Pks and Rec Dept, Sums 1982, 1983; Other Previous Positions; cp/Col: Carman Blough Student Affil Chapt of Nat Assn of Accts; Paralegal Studies Clb, JMU Col 4-H Clb (Secy and Fundraising Chm); HS: Franklin Co 4-H Hon Clb (Secy-Treas), Future Bus Ldrs of Am, Nat Hon Soc, Tri-Hi-Y 1977-80; r/So Bapt, Beulah Bapt Ch; hon/Grad'd 7th Out of 430, HS; Ranked 635th Out of 2,006 at JMU, 1983; VA Chapt, 4-H All-Stars; Dean's List, HS and JMU; W/

W Among HS Students; g/Acctg Maj; Minors in Paralegal Studies and Ec; Acct.

WOODY, PAMELA DENISE oc/Student; b/Jun 30, 1966; h/Route 2, Box 107, Rocky Mount, VA 24151; p/Dennis T and Mary Elizabeth Woody, Rocky Mount, VA; ed/Grad, Franklin Co HS, 1984; cp/Pres, Yth Com, 1983, Secy 1980-82; Pres, Acteens, 1982; Basketball, 1979-84; F'ship of Christian Aths, 1980-84; Latin Clb, 1980-82; Future Bus Ldrs of Am, 1981-83; Ch Yth Choir, 1978-84; 4-H, 1976-83; Brownies, 1973-75; r/Bapt; hon/Outstg Jr 4-H'er, 1980; Co-Capt, 9th Grade Girls' Basketball Team, 1979, Capt 1980; Capt, Varsity Girls' Basketball, 1983; MVP, 1980; Prin's Hon Roll, 1978-83; W/W Among Am HS Students; g/Child Psychol or Elem Sch Tchr.

WOOSLEY, ROBERT STEVEN oc/Accountant; b/Jan 12, 1961; h/9 Castle Hill Court, Little Rock, AR 72207; ba/Little Rock, AR; p/Mr and Mrs Robert C Woosley, Little Rock, AR; ed/BA, Ouachita Bapt Univ; pa/Internal Auditor, Fairfield Communities Inc, 1983-; Asst to the Pres, Envir Sers Co Inc, 1979-82; Other Previous Positions; cp/Acctg Clb, 1981-82; r/Bapt; hon/4-Yr Ath S'ship, 1979-82; Jerry Forehand Ath Ldrship Awd, 1983; Nat Assn of Intercol Aths Div I All-Am Football Team Hon Mention, 1982; Assoc'd Press Little All-Am Team Hon Mention, 1982; Nat Assn of Intercol Aths Dist 17 All-Dist, 1982; AR Intercol Conf All-Conf, 1982; Personalities of S; g/CPA.

WOOTTON, MICHAEL J oc/Student; b/Dec 1, 1965; h/301 Section Line, Plainville, KS 67663; p/Calvin R and Linda J Wootton; ed/Grad, Plainville HS, 1984; pa/Shophand, Tom's Machine and Welding, 1983-; cp/U Meth Yth F'ship, 1980-84; Plainville Lettermen's Clb, 1981-84; Jazz Band, 1981-84; Concert Band, 1980-84; Football, 1980-84; Basketball, 1980-84; Track, 1981, 1982; All-Sch Play, 1983-84; Forensics, 1981; Plainville High Booster Staff, 1983-84; Boys' St Del, 1983; Hon Roll, 1981-84; r/Meth; hon/1st Place, KS Scholastic Press Assn Regs, Sports Writing, 1983; Emporia S'ship Tests, 1st Place, St Contest, Plane Geometry; Nat Merit Test, Commended Student, 1983; g/To Attend KS St Univ and Maj in Engrg w a Possible Slant towards Electronics and Computers.

WORLEY, DEMETRICE ANNTIA oc/Graduate Student; b/Apr 24, 1960; h/RR 1, Box 49B, Secor, IL 61771; p/Thomas D and Ernestine Worley, Peoria, IL; ed/Att'g, Univ of IL Champaign/Urbana, 1982-; BA, cum laude, Bradley Univ, 1982; Grad, Peoria HS, 1978; pa/Tchg Asst, Univ of IL, 1983-; Draftsman, Caterpillar Tractor Co, 1977-82; cp/Sigma Tau Delta, Pres 1981-82; Sigma Silhouettes, Pres 1980-81; Merri-n-ettes, 1978-79; Hospitality Corps, 1978-79; Univ of IL: Wom in Eng 1982-83, Eng Grad Students Assn 1982-83, Black Grad Students Assn 1982-83; hon/Poetry Pub'd in Var Periodicals; Sigma Tau Delta, 1980; Mortar Bd, 1981-82; Outstg Yg Wom in Am; Commun Ldrs of Am; Nat Dean's List; W/W Among Students in Am Univs and Cols.

WORTHINGTON, AL MOYE oc/Student; h/306 Kenansville, NC 28349;

p/Robert and Alice Worthington, Kenansville, NC; ed/Student, Harrells Christian Acad; pa/Duplin Gen Hosp, 1981, 1982; cp/4-H, 1974-82; Beta Clb, 1981-; hon/Co Winner in 4-H Safety, 1975-81, Dist Winner 1977-81; Co Public Spkg Runner-Up, 1979, 1980; W/ W Among Am HS Students; g/MA in Bus Adm to Prepare for Wk w Ins Co.

WRENTMORE, R JAYNE oc/Programmer and Analyst; b/Jun 1, 1960; h/ 5045 Dierker Road, Apartment B3, Columbus, OH 43220; ba/Columbus, OH; p/Mr and Mrs Lloyd Wrentmore, Logan, OH; ed/Logan HS, 1978; BS, summa cum laude, OH Univ, 1982; pa/ Staff Programmer 1982-83, Applications Programmer 1983, Programmer/ Analyst 1983-, Chem Abstracts Ser; Assn for Computing Machinery, Ctl OH Chapt; cp/Kappa Phi Christian Wom's Clb; Venus Chapt #76, OES; Scandinavian Hlth Spa; r/Prot; hon/Phi Kappa Phi; Phi Beta Kappa; Intl Yth in Achmt; World W/W Wom; Commun Ldrs of Am.

WRIGHT, CAROL D oc/Student; b/ Jul 8, 1961; h/Route 2, Box 48, Penhook, VA 24137; ed/Franklin Co High, 1979; AA 1981, BSW 1983, Ferrum Col; pa/ Asst Secy, 1979-83; Resident Asst, 1983; Visiting Social Wkr/Cnslr, 1982; Tutoring Coor, 1983; cp/Spanish Clb, 1979; FHA, Pres 1979; Voices of Hope Choral Grp, Asst Dir 1982; Black Student Union, Pres 1982-83; Hall Coun, 1983; French Clb, 1982; r/Bapt; hon/Dean's List, 1981-83; Pageant Runner-Up, 1979; Fashion Show Winner, 1978; Nat Hon Soc, 1981; NAACP Awd, 1979; g/To Do Field Wk in the Area of Social Wk; MSW.

WRIGHT, CAROL RENE oc/Recent Graduate; b/Dec 15, 1960; h/Route 2, Box 159, Troutville, VA 24175; p/Earl G (dec) and Sarah O Wright, Troutville, VA; ed/BS in Communication Arts, cum laude, James Madison Univ, 1983; Hon Grad, Lord Botetourt HS, 1979; cp/ News Reporter, Anchor, Bluegrass DJ, WMRA, 1983; News Reporter, WTON,. 1983; Bluegrass DJ, FM Mag Feature Reporter, WMRA, 1982-83; Other Previous Positions; Assoc Mem, VA Assn of Broadcasters, 1983-; cp/Alpha Epsilon Rho, 1981-84, Secy 1982-83; JMU Jazz Spectrum, 1982-83; Sigma Phi Lambda, 1981-82; Phi Theta Kappa, 1980-81; r/Bapt; hon/WWBT-TV $1,000 Broadcasting S'ship, 1983; Alpha Epsilon Rho S'ship, 1982; Pres Awd, 1983; Sigma Phi Lambda Col Bowl Team, 1981; Outstg Composer, 1977; 2nd Place, Yamaha Electrone Organ Fest, 1977; W/W Am Cols and Univs; g/Broadcast Journalist.

WRIGHT, CARRIE LEE oc/Student; b/Jun 2, 1966; cp/Latin I Rep to Student Coun; Student Coun VP; Chm for Sch Dance Com; Latin Clb VP; CoChm for St Latin Conv; Pres, Pep Clb; Jazz Choir,

2 Yrs; The Grp; Jog-a-Thon for Latin Clb and Choral Music Dept; r/First Bapt Ch; Pres of Yth Choir; Handbells Choir, 3 Yrs; Vacation Bible Sch Tchr; hon/ OK Hon Soc, 4 Yrs; Nat Hon Soc, 2 Yrs; Supt's Hon Roll, 3 Yrs; NEMA, Senator Boren Govt Awd; Eng II Awd; Sweepstakes in Choral, 4 Yrs; Superior Awds in Ensembles, Trios, Quartets; 1st and 2nd Place, So Choral Music Fest, FL; Adv'd Choir, 1st Place; 2nd Place Awd and Medal for Latin Curric Contest; Best Entertainer Awd; Rotary Student of the Month; Jazz Choir Contest, Superiors; Piano Awds in Debussy Contests, St and Dist Contests; 7th Place in Nat Latin Exam; Hon Roll, 4 Yrs; IFLA; USBEA; Best Supporting Actress, *South Pacific*; Most Outstg Student, 1983-84; Soc of Dist'd Am HS Students; W/W Latin; W/W Among Am HS Students; g/To Attend Col; To Do the Best I Can in Whatever I Am Doing; To Be an Asset to Society Instead of a Hindrance.

WRIGHT, ROBIN L oc/Mathematics Teacher; b/Oct 6, 1960; h/72 Congress Street, Beaufort, SC 29902; ba/Beaufort, SC; p/Mr and Mrs Emory L Wright, Winfield, WV; ed/Col Preparatory Dipl, Winfield HS; BA in Math, BA in Elem Ed, Berea Col; pa/Math Tchr, 1983-; r/ U Meth; hon/Mortar Bd, 1982-83; KY Wom's Intercol Conf for Field Hockey, 1982-83; Wom of the Dorm, 1981-83; Am's Yth in Concert Orch, 1978; W/ W Am Yth; g/To Receive Master's Deg and Doct Deg in the Hist of Math.

WRIGHT, STEPHEN WAYNE oc/ Student, Farmer; b/Feb 11, 1964; h/1101 Main Street, Murray, KY 42071; ba/ Murray, KY; p/Mr and Mrs Bennett·R Wright, Marion, KY; ed/Crittenden Co HS; Murray St Univ; pa/Farmer; MSU Security; cp/Pres, Reg Reporter, FFA; Pres, Student Coun, Indust Arts Clb; Yg Farmers, Local Chapt; MSU Agri Clb; hon/Hon Commr Agri; KY St Farmer Deg, FFA; W/W Among Am HS Students; g/BS in Agri.

WYATT, CLARENCE RAY oc/Student; b/Nov 21, 1956; h/457 High Street, Danville, KY 40422; p/Eva R Wyatt, Hopkinsville, KY; ed/Grad, Christian Co HS, 1974; AB, Centre Col, KY, 1978; MA, Univ of KY, 1984; pa/ Res Assoc, Centre Col, 1979-82; Tchg Asst, Univ of KY, 1982-; cp/Co Com, Dem Party; VP, Hist Grad Students Assn, Univ of KY; hon/Phi Alpha Theta; W/W Among Students in Am Univs and Cols; g/PhD in Am Hist; Career in Col Tchg.

WYER, ROBERT BOYNTON oc/ Student; b/Dec 26, 1962; h/70 Des Plaines Lane, Hoffman Estates, IL 60194; p/John U and Katherine Wyer, Hoffman Estates, IL; ed/James B Conant HS, 1981; Att'g, USC; cp/Concert and Marching Bands, 1977-81; Brass Sect Ldr, Prin Trumpet and Soloist for Wind

Ensemble, 1980-81; Prin Trumpet and Soloist for Symphonic Band, 1977-79; Prin Trumpet of Conant Brass Quintet, 1980-81; Conant's Sum Nat Champ Band, 1980; Reporter, *The Crier*, Feature Sect Editor 1979-80; Math Clb; Choir, 1980-81; Participant, *Li'l Abner*, 1978; Brass Sect Ldr, Pit Band, *The King & I*, 1981; Drum and Bugle Corps, 1980; r/ Prot; hon/IL St Scholar, 1981; Hon Roll, 1977-81; 1981 Conant Cougar Band Awd; Dean's List, 1982; 1st Div Rating in Brass Quintet Contests Entered, 1980-81; Cert of Outstg Reporting, 1978-79; Math Clb Contest Winner, 1977-78; W/W Among Am HS Students; Intl Yth in Achmt; g/Film Dir.

WYNN, KAREN ARLENE oc/Student; b/Jun 19, 1964; h/Route 3, Rutledge Lake Road, Greenville, SC 29611; p/Mr and Mrs J Randall Wynn, Greenville, SC; ed/Travelers Rest HS, 1982; Att'g, Erskine Col; cp/Epsilon Sigma Tau, 1983-84; Campus Ministries, 1982-84; Student Christian Assn, 1982-84, Secy 1984-85; r/Forestville Bapt Ch; hon/Valedictorian of Travelers Rest HS, 1982; Dean's List, Fall 1982, Sprg 1983, Fall 1983, Sprg 1984; Garnet Circle, 1983-84; Grad Marshal, 1984; g/ BA in Eng; Tchr Cert in Sec'dy Ed.

WYRICK, KIMBERLY DIANE oc/ Student; b/Aug 7, 1965; h/Box 292A, Bradford, TN 38316; p/Johnny and Diane Wyrick, Bradford, TN; ed/Bradford Sr High; Att'g, Univ of TN Martin; cp/Basketball; Home Ec, VP; Sci Clb; Pep Clb; B-Clb; *Beacon* Staff; Campus Action Clb; r/Bapt; hon/Freshman of the Yr Awd; Most Beautiful of Sr Class; Miss Bradford and Miss Christmas Awds; Miss TN Nat Royalty; Miss TN Dixie Royalty; Miss Doodle Soup Royalty; g/ Study of Ed (Childhood Devel).

WYSOCK, ELIZABETH ANNE oc/ Student; b/Jun 21, 1962; h/PO Box 34, 663 Camp Wawa Road, Lederach, PA 19450; p/Mr and Mrs Edward T Wysock, Lederach, PA; ed/Souderton Area HS, 1980; BA, Eng Lit, St Joseph's Univ, 1984; cp/Residence Jud Bd, 1980-83; Hand-in-Hand, Fest for Mentally Handicapped, 1981; Intramural Volleyball, 1980-81; r/Lector, St Mary's Rom Cath Ch, St Joseph's Univ, 1979-83; hon/Intl Yth in Achmt; g/Law Sch.

WYTTENBACH, ROBERT ALAN oc/Student; b/Aug 8, 1961; h/1640 Cambridge Road, Lawrence, KS 66044; p/Charles R and Ellen G Wyttenbach, Lawrence, KS; ed/Lawrence HS, 1979; Att'g, Univ of KS; pa/Tchrs Asst, Chd's Sch of Sci, Woods Hole, MA, 1977; Apparatus Asst, Marine Biol Lab, Woods Hole, MA, 1981, 1982; cp/Owl Soc, 1980; Phi Kappa Phi, 1981; Phi Beta Kappa, 1981; Phi Sigma, 1981; Upsilon Pi Epsilon, 1982; hon/Nat Merit S'ship, 1979; Summerfield S'ship, 1979; Outstg Sr in Computer Sci, 1982; Hon Roll, 1979-82; g/PhD in Biol; Univ Tchg and Res in Neurophysiol and Behavior.

Y

YAKLIN, JAMES JOHN oc/Student; b/Jun 29, 1962; h/7887 North Vernon Road, New Lothrop, MI 48460; ba/Flint, MI; p/James T and Joan F Yaklin, New Lothrop, MI; ed/Grad, New Lothrop HS, Gen Motors Inst; pa/Coop Student, Buick Motor Div; cp/HS Baseball, Basketball; FFA; Pres, Nat Hon Soc; Freshman Class Pres; r/Rom Cath; hon/ John Philip Sousa Band Awd; FFA St Farmer Deg; Salutatorian; g/Deg in Indust Adm; Cont'd Wk w Buick Motor Div.

YARBROUGH, KONRAD STAN-TON oc/Student; b/Aug 17, 1964; h/PO Box 429, Chouteau, OK; ba/ Stillwater, OK; p/Larry S and Elizabeth F Yarbrough, Chouteau, OK; ed/Chouteau HS, 1980; Att'g, OK St Univ; cp/ Student Coun, Jr Rep 1981-82, Reporter and Sr Rep 1982-83; Sr Class Reporter, 1982-83; Tulsa Computer Soc, 1982-; Uncle Fester Fan Clb, Pres 1983-; OK Boys' St Del, 1981-82; hon/$1,000 S'ship, A P Green, 1983; Valedictorian of HS Grad'g Class, 1983; Freshman Regents' Dist'd S'ship, OSU, 1983; HS Hon Roll, 4 Yrs; Elks Clb Yth Achmt Awd, 1983; W/W Am HS Students; g/ Deg in Computer Sci; To Write Progs in the Chem Field and the Gaming Field; To Write and Publish a Series of Books.

YEADON, SLOANE JOINER oc/ Student; b/Dec 5, 1961; h/1818 North Rock Springs Road, Northeast, Atlanta, GA 30324; p/Mr and Mrs Gordon D Yeadon, Atlanta, GA; ed/Grad, summa cum laude, Woodward Acad, 1980; AB, Sweet Briar Col, 1984; cp/Nat Hon Soc; Woodward Fest Chorale; Interact Clb; Col Collegium; Chp, Yg Repub Clb; Italian Clb; Intervarsity Clb; r/ Second-Ponce de Leon Bapt Ch; Perf w Chapel Choir and Revelation; hon/ Recip, 4 Gold Eagle Awds for Highest Acad Standing, Woodward Acad; Freshman Hons, 1980-81; Dean's List, 1981-82; Sweet Briar Scholar, 1982-83; Jr Hons, 1982-83; Helen F Young Music S'ship, 1982-83; St of GA Gov's Internship Prog, 1982; Applicant to Sam A Nunn Senate Internship Prog, 1983; g/ Study of Voice; Law Sch w Preparation toward a Career in US Fgn Ser and/or Other Related St and Fed Agys.

YERACARIS, ANTHONY MICHAEL CONSTANTINE oc/Design Engineer; b/Jul 12, 1960; h/485 Norwood Avenue, Buffalo, NY 14222; ba/ Palo Alto, CA; p/C A and B L Yeracaris, Buffalo, NY; ed/Pk Sch of Buffalo, 1977; BS, Cornell Univ, 1981; pa/Design Engr, The Wollongong Grp, 1983-; Software Engr, Digital Equip Corp, 1981-82; cp/ MENSA; Am Field Ser S'ship to Costa Rica; hon/BS w Distn (cum laude); Dean's List; NY St Regents S'ships Awd, 1977; Math Assn of Am Awd, 1976, 1977; Commun Ldrs of Am; g/MS, Stanford Univ.

YONELUNAS, RUTH-MARIE MAR-GARET oc/Reserve Librarian; b/Sep 16, 1960; h/4 Forest Row, Great Neck, NY 11023; p/Eugene P and Noreene B Yonelunas, Great Neck, NY; ed/Grad,

Maria Regina Diocean HS, 1978; BA, Univ of Charleston, 1982; Presently Enrolled in Grad Prog, C W Post Col; pa/Camp Cnslr, Nassau Coun of Girl Scouts, 1976-80; Lifeguard, Great Neck Pk Dist, 1981, 1982; Resident Asst, Hd Resident Asst, Univ of Charleston, 1979-82; Rec Asst, Great Neck Pk Dist, 1982; Reserve Libn, Great Neck Lib; cp/ Nassau Coun of Girl Scouts; Volleyball, Softball, Univ of Charleston; Student Adv Coun, Social Sers Dept, Univ of Charleston; CYO Ath and Coaching; r/ Rom Cath; hon/Res Wk; Rdgs in Hons Eng, Univ of Charleston, 1978-82; Intl Yth in Achmt; W/W Among Am HS Students; World W/W of Wom; g/Grad Deg in Lib Sci.

YONGUE, CHARLES JEFFREY oc/ Student; b/Oct 22, 1962; h/1804 LaSalle Street, Charlotte, NC 28216; p/Charles and Vaughn Yongue; ed/Grad, Independence Sr HS, 1981; Student of Communication Arts, Johnson C Smith Univ, 1981-; cp/Black Media Assn; Student Adv Coun for Communication Arts Dept; IRA Aldridge Drama Guild; Bowling; HS: NAACP (Treas), Track Team, FHA (Pres), ICC Clb, Hlth Clb; hon/Dean's List, 1983-84; Alpha Psi Omega Nat Hon Frat; WSOC Radio and TV S'ship Recip.

YORK, BRENDA GAYLE oc/Student; b/Dec 10, 1962; h/124 Moss Hill Lane, Conroe, TX 77303; p/Ervin and Bonita York, Conroe, TX; ed/Conroe HS, 1981; Student, Evangel Col; pa/ Pt-time, Sales, Seven Coves, 1981-83; cp/Col Class Treas, 1982-83, 1983-84; Pres, VP, Capt, Bowling Leag; Camp Cnslr; Chd Ch Wkr; Yth Counsel; hon/ Camp Queen for Christian Example; HS Queen Cand, 1981; Num Art and Bowling Awds; Col Freshman Class Treas, 1981-83; Col Sophomore Class Treas, 1983-84; Congratulatory Letter from Ronald Reagan, 1981; W/W Among Am HS Students; Intl Yth in Achmt; Commun Ldrs of Am; g/Maj in Bus (Computers); Travel Agt.

YOUNG, ERIC EMMANUEL oc/ Student; b/Mar 2, 1965; h/603 Depot Street, Seneca, SC 29679; p/Carrie S Young, Seneca, SC; ed/Seneca HS, 1983; Att'g, Newberry Col; cp/Freshman Class Secy-Treas; Mtl Awareness Soc, Secy-Treas; Intervarsity Christian F'ship; Freshman Class Rep; Col Yrbook and Lit Mag; HS Lit Mag; hon/All-St Band, 1980; Beta Clb; Grad w Hons; Student Marshall; Newberry Col Deptl S'ship; Boys' St; Gov's Sch; W/W Among Am HS Students; g/Music Edr.

YOUNG, HEIDI SAMUELS oc/Student; b/May 17, 1963; h/304 Cherokee Drive, Jasper, AL 35501; p/Mr and Mrs W B Young Jr, Jasper, AL; ed/Dipl, Walker HS, 1981; Att'g, Walker Jr Col; cp/Pres of Local Chapt, Yth Assn for Retarded Citizens; Secy, Circle K Clb; Sports Editor, *The Viking*, HS; Activs Chp, Jr Class, 1979-80; Track and Cross Country; French Clb; Pep Clb; r/Pres of Yth, Christ U Meth Ch; hon/Offered Ldrship S'ship to Livingston Univ; Elected Homecoming Queen, Walker Col, 1983; Maj Role in Col Presentation

of *The Good Doctor*, 1982; Role in *Hello Dolly*, 1983; Treas of Sr Class; Elected Miss Walker HS, 1981; Pres of Quest Clb, 1981; Quill and Scroll, 1981; Key Clb Favorite, 1980-81; Named Top Teen and Fairest of the Fair, 1981; g/To Become an Activs Dir in a Hlth Care Ctr; Maj in Rec Therapy.

YOUNG, LYNDA RUTH oc/Student; b/Mar 19, 1964; h/2213 Collins Boulevard, Gulfport, MS 39501; p/Mr and Mrs William E Young, Gulfport, MS; ed/Grad, Gulfport HS; pa/Financial Aid Secy, MGCJC, Jefferson Davis Campus, 1982-84; cp/Majorette Capt, 1980-82; Student Exch to Sioux Falls, SD, 1982; Band, 1980-82; Freshman Student Coun Rep, 1982; Student Body Pres, 1983-84; MGCJC Tri-Campus Student Body Pres, 1983-84; r/So Bapt; hon/ Student Coun Assn of MS, 1983; Jefferson Davis Hall of Fame, 1983; Most Outstg Aux-Majorette Capt, 1982; Finalist, Miss U Teenage Pageant; W/W Among Am Jr Col Students; Soc of Dist'd Am HS Students; g/To Attend the Univ of So MS and Receive a Deg in Med Adm.

YOUNG, MELODY SUE oc/Student; b/Mar 11, 1965; h/504 South Avery, Moore, OK 73160; p/Mr and Mrs Billy G Young, Moore, OK; ed/Grad, Moore HS, 1983; pa/Counter Help, Orange Julius, 1981; Counter Help, McDonalds, 1983-; cp/Nat Hon Soc, 1981-83; Nat Jr Hon Soc, 1979-81; Band, 1977-83; Math Clb, 1980-81; Intl Clb, 1980-81; hon/Phillips Petro S'ship, 1983; Ctl St Univ Hons S'ship Prog, 1983; OU and OSU Jr Hons Scholars, 1982; W/W Among Am HS Students; Soc of Dist'd Am HS Students; g/Master's Deg in Math Ed; Teach Sec'dy Sch Math.

YOUNGBLOOD, KATHERINE LORAINE oc/Student; h/Route 7, Box 20, South Rugby Road, Hendersonville, NC 28739; p/Mr and Mrs Kenneth Ray Youngblood, Hendersonville, NC; ed/ Hendersonville HS, 1980; Att'g, Wn Carolina Univ; pa/Receptionist, Fletcher Motor Co, 1982-83; Clk, Sports Cellar, 1980-82; Waitress, Clifton's Cafeteria, 1977-80; cp/Student Body VP, 1979; Student Body Pres, 1980; Softball Team, 1977-80; Symphonic Band; WCU Delta Zeta Sorority, 1983-84; WCU Wom's Ath Tnr, 1982-83; Justice, Supr Ct, WCU, 1984; r/Fletcher U Meth Ch Yth Grp Pres, 1979-80; hon/Carolina Theatre Cup, 1980; Sertoma Ser to Mankind Awd, 1980; R Hugh Lockaby Awd, 1980; Citizen of the Yr, HS, 1980; Homecoming Ct, 1980; WCU Homecoming Queen, 1983; Sigma Phi Epsilon Golden Heart, 1984; g/Maj in Social Scis; To Teach HS Hist and Coach.

YOW, KIM ANGOLA oc/Student; b/ Mar 29, 1959; h/2412 Ivy Street, Roosevelt City, AL 35020; p/Rev and Mrs Hasty Kim Yow Jr, Roosevelt City, AL; ed/Adv'd Acad Dipl, Shades Val Resource Lng Ctr, 1977; BA, NWn Univ, 1981; Laval Univ, 1981; JD, IN Univ Sch of Law, 1985; cp/Phi Alpha Delta, Black Law Student Assn; Civil Air Patrol; French Clb; Student Coun; Hon Soc; Theater Black Admissions Adv

Bd; Hosp Vol; Tchr's Aide; hon/IN Univ Law Sch F'ship; Frederick Douglas Moot Ct Competition; Dean's List; Nat Achmt Scholar; W/W Among Am HS Students; Intl Yth in Achmt; g/Atty.

YURI-LUNA, LUIS ENRIQUE oc/ Electrical Engineer; b/Mar 17, 1961; h/ 373 Ferrer Street, Santurce, Puerto Rico 00915; ba/Humacao, Puerto Rico; p/ Antonio Yuri, Santurce, Puerto Rico; Estela Luna, Santurce, Puerto Rico; ed/ San Vicente De Paul HS, 1978; BSEE, Univ of Puerto Rico, Mayaguez Campus, 1982; pa/Test Engr, Qume Caribe; Quality Engr, Intel Caribbean; IEEE; Colegio de Ingenieros y Agrimensores de Puerto Rico; cp/Cursillo; Alumni Assn, Univ of Puerto Rico; Student Cnslr; Student Coun of Sch of Engrg, 1980-81; Acad Senator, 1981-82; VP, CECIAPR; Pres and VP, Grupo Apostodado Catolico, 1979-80, 1981-82; r/ Cath; g/MBA.

Z

ZABEL, KENNETH MICHAEL oc/
Student; b/Oct 25, 1961; h/710 Village
Drive, Pittsburg, KS 66762; p/Dr and
Mrs Kenneth P Zabel, Pittsburg, KS;
ed/Grad, Pittsburg HS, 1980; BS in
Chem and Biol, Graceland Col, 1984;
pa/Lab Asst, Graceland Col, 1982-84;
Res Asst, KS Univ Sch of Med, 1983;
Computer Operator, Pittsburg Med
Complex, 1977-80; cp/Pres, Graceland
Student Govt, 1983-84; Co-Pres, Grace-
land Pre-Med Clb, 1982-83; House Pres,
Graceland Col, 1982-83; Senator, Spkr
pro-tem of Senate, Chm of Elections
Com, 1981-82; Boy Scout, 1972-78; r/
RLDS; hon/Eagle Scout, 1974; Outstg
Freshman Chem Student Awd, 1981;
Pres's List; Hugh O'Brian Ldrship Awd,
1978; Univ of KS Summerfield Scholar,
1980; g/To Attend Med Sch; Phys.
ZALAR, MYLENE GUDRUN oc/
Student; b/Jul 8, 1961; h/841 Kentwood
Drive, Riverside, CA 92507; ba/River-
side, CA; p/Joseph S Zalar (dec); Anne-
lore Gurdun Zalar, Riverside, CA; ed/
Grad, John Wesley N HS, 1980; AA,
Riverside City Col, 1982; Att'g, Univ of
CA Riverside; pa/Relief Sta Mgr
1977-79, Asst Circulation Area Supvr
1979-82, Asst Dock Supvr (Present),
Press-Enterprise Newspaper Co; cp/Life
Mem, CA S'ship Fdn, 1980; Perm Mem,
Alpha Gamma Sigma, 1982; Treas,
Alpha Gamma Sigma Clb, 1982; r/Luth;
hon/Paper Carrier of the Wk, 1977; Cert
of Achmt for 2 Yrs of Perfect Ser on
Paper Route, 1978; Hon Guard for
Graduation, 1979; Outstg Ser Awd,
Alpha Gamma Sigma Clb, 1982; W/W
Among Am HS Students; Commun
Ldrs of Am; Intl Yth in Achmt; g/Deg
in Biochem at Univ of CA Riverside.
ZANNINI, GIAVANNA oc/Student;
b/Oct 18, 1962; h/442 Charlotte Circle,
Jackson, AL 36545; p/Rev and Mrs
James N Love, Jackson, AL; Col Robert
H Zannini, Montgomery, AL; ed/Chi-
pley HS, 1980; Huntingdon Col; cp/
Campus Ministries Assn, Pres 1983-84,
Publicity Chm 1982-83; SGA, 1983-84;
Homecoming Com, Sets Chm 1983; Psi
Chi Hon Soc, 1982-83; Nat Hon Soc;
Student Coun Rep, 1977-78; FL Dist II
Hon Band, 1979, 1980; Band Clb; Jr Red
Cross Clb, VP; ARC Vol; Art Clb;
Artist, HS Yrbook, Newspaper; Little
Wom; Hon Roll; UMYF; Liberty Yth
Camp Cnslr; Huntingdon Col Wind
Ensemble; "Joyful Noises!" Musical
Revue and Singing Co; Oil Paintings
and Drawings; r/Yth Dir, Liberty Ch;
hon/1st Runner-Up, Miss Huntingdon,
1982; Homecoming Ct, 1982; Hon Grad,
1980; John Philip Sousa Band Awd,
1980; Sr Hall of Fame, 1980; Most
Outstg Sr Band Mem, 1980; W/W
Among Am HS Students; g/Bach's Deg
in Christian Ed/Sociol; Master's Deg in
Yth Min/Evangelism; Career in Yth
Evangelism.
ZELEI, BERNADETTE VERONICA
oc/Student; b/May 4, 1962; h/1019
Silvercrest Avenue, Southwest, Akron,
OH 44314; p/Dr Rita A Zelei, Akron,
OH; ed/Dipl, St John HS, 1980; Att'g,
OH St Univ; pa/Res, St Luke Hosp,
1983; cp/Delta Omega Kappa Sorority,
Secy of Pledge Class 1982; Newman
Ctr; Soc of Am Magicians, 1978; Intram-
ural Softball, 1982; OSU Block O Pep
Clb, 1982-83; Band Pres, HS, 1979-80;

Sr Yrbook Editor, 1979-80; Lib Aide,
1976-79; Drama Clb, 1976-80; Latin
Clb, 1976-78; Pep Clb, 1977-79; Sci Clb,
1977-80; Bowling, 1978-80; Med Explor-
ers, 1977-80; r/Cath; hon/Nat Hon Soc,
1979; Perfect Attendance for 12 Yrs of
Sch, 1968-80; Number Awds from Sch,
Cong, Pres Carter, Pope Paul; John
Philip Sousa Awd, 1980; Commun Ldrs
of Am; Intl Yth in Achmt; W/W Among
Am HS Students; g/Career as a Phys,
Specializing in Surg.
ZEMPLENY, KALMAN STEPHEN II
oc/Student, Reservations Agent; b/Dec
29, 1964; h/3842 Ventura Canyon
Avenue, Sherman Oaks, CA 91423; ba/
Sherman Oaks, CA; p/Kalman Stephen
and June Louise Zempleny, Sherman
Oaks, CA; ed/Notre Dame HS; LA Val
Col; Grad, Loyola Marymount Univ,
1984; pa/Reservations Agt, Sheraton
Plaza La Reina Hotel; Yth News Editor
and Advtg Acct Exec, Assoc'd Val Pubs
Inc; Intern/Asst to Dir of Ofc of Public
Affairs, US Dept of the Interior; Dpty
to the Dir, Ofc of Public Relats, King
Tut Exhbn, LA Co Mus of Art; Pres
and CEO, Wiz Communs; cp/LA World
Affairs Coun; Ec Soc; US Def Com;
Dept of St Confs/Sems; Pi Kappa Alpha
Frat; Repub Nat Com; Nat Repub Congl
Com; CA Repub Party; Native Sons of
the Golden W, Hon Mem; Bd of Dirs,
Loyola Marymount Univ; LA Olympic
Citizens Adv Comm, Adv Com on Yth
Activs; Asst to the Dean of Men and
to the Adm Secy to the Prin, Notre
Dame HS; Yth Chm, Representing all
LA Schs for LA Bicent; Fdr,
Student-Commun Activs Netwk; Asst
to Dr Richard E Ferraro, Sr Mem of LA
Bd of Ed; Yth Chm, Representing all
LA Schs, San Fernando Val Beautiful;
US Def Com; hon/Outstg Yth Awd, San
Fernando Val Repub Bus Wom's Fdn,
1983; Pres Achmt Awd, Pres Ronald
Reagan, 1982; Awd, LA Sch Bd of Ed
in Recog for Dedication to Yth and
Their Var Activs, 1981; Awd, LA C of
C, 1981 Salute to Yth in Vol Ser 1st
Place Awd; St Awd Winner, Elk's Nat
Foun Ldrship S'ship, 1981; Wash
Wkshops Foun Merit Awd Winner,
1981; Secy, Ec Soc, 1981; Yth of Yr,
Soroptomist Intl, 1979; Num Other
Hons; Intl Yth in Achmt; Yg Commun
Ldrs of Am; W/W Am; W/W Among Am
HS Students; g/Bus Adm Deg (Intl Bus);
MBA; Law Deg.
ZENNER, CLARA JO oc/Student; b/
Mar 25, 1964; h/PO Box 160, LaVernia,
TX 78121; p/Mr and Mrs Carl M
Zenner, LaVernia, TX; pa/Waitress,
Hi-Way Haus Cafe, 1980-82; Pt-time
Waitress, TX Dancehall, 1983; cp/HS Jr
Class Pres; HS Sr Class VP; Basketball;
Softball; Track; Tennis; Volleyball; HS
4-H; HS FHA; HS Band; HS Student
Coun; UIL Typing; r/Cath; hon/HS Reg
Track, 1980; Basketball All-Dist First
Team, 1981, 1982; Volleyball 2nd Team
All-Dist, 1982; g/Maj in Acctg; CPA.
ZENOBIANS, ARA oc/Student; b/
Aug 18, 1960; h/6805 Golden West
Avenue, Arcadia, CA 91006; p/Haik and
Irma Zenobians, Arcadia, CA; ed/Dipl
in Armenian Studies, 1974; HS Dipl,
Don Bosco Col, 1978; Univ of La Verne,
1979-81; Att'g, Univ of So CA; r/
Christian; hon/Awd of Commend, First
Annual USC-ASU Student Design
Competition, 1982; Dean's List Awd for
7 Semesters; Hon Awd Recog, Nat

Dean's List; Intl Yth in Achmt; Yg
Commun Ldrs of Am; g/BA in Arch,
1985.
ZEPH, CYNTHIA MARIE oc/Stu-
dent; b/Dec 4, 1961; h/Route 12, Box
634, Laurel Drive, Sanford, NC 27330;
ba/Charlotte, NC; p/Mr and Mrs J David
Zeph, Sanford, NC; ed/Dipl, Page HS,
1980; BA, Eng, Univ of NC Charlotte,
1984; pa/Bookstore Cashier, Univ Book-
store, UNCC Sta; cp/Delta Zeta Soror-
ity, Courtesy Chm 1980-81, 1st VP
1981-82, Ways and Means 1982-83;
Campus Guide, 1982-83; Rehab Hosp
Vol in Spch and Audiology Dept, 1983;
Editor-in-Chief, *Buccaneer* Yrbook, HS,
1979-80; r/Cath; hon/Sister of the
Month, Delta Zeta Sorority; g/Master's
Deg in Jour-Advtg, Univ of NC Chapel
Hill; Spch Career in Advtg; Bkg;
Audiology.
ZIMMERMAN, SCOTT ALAN oc/
Loan Officer; b/Mar 5, 1957; h/3108
Canterbury Lane, Janesville, WI 53545;
ba/Janesville, WI; p/Irving and Margaret
Zimmerman, Darlington, WI; ed/Dar-
lington HS; BS, Dairy Sci, Univ of WI
Madison; 1979; pa/Loan Ofcr, Prodn
Credit Assn of Janesville, 1979-; Profl
Ag Coun; cp/Pres, Janesville JCs, 1983;
Commun VP, Janesville JCs, 1982; Frat
of Alpha Zeta; Former FFA and 4-H
Mem; Dairy Sci Clb, Univ of WI; Saddle
and Sirloin Clb, Univ of WI; hon/JCs
Armbruster Awd, 1982; Outstg Ofcr,
Janesville JCs, 1982; Outstg Commun
Devel VP, WI JCs; Baseball Capt and
MVP, HS, 1975; Alpha Zeta Hon Frat,
1978; Hon Student, HS; Hon Student,
Univ of WI; Yth in Achmt; g/A Position
in Mid to Upper Mgmt.
ZIRBEL, JAN MARIE oc/Health Care
Financing and Administrative Assist-
ant; b/Aug 14, 1962; h/10 Elm Street,
Everett, MA 02149; ba/Boston, MA; p/
Mr and Mrs Ralph Zirbel, Sturgeon Bay,
WI; ed/Assoc Deg, Data Processing, NE
WI Tech Inst, 1983; HS Dipl, Sturgeon
Bay HS, 1980; pa/Hlth Care Financing/
Adm Asst, Suburban Mortgage Assocs;
Computer Programmer, Distribution
Mgmt Sers, 1982-83; Profl Org of
Programmers; cp/Pres, Future Tchrs of
Am, 1979-80; Vol, NEn Med Ctr; r/
Cath; hon/Grad w Highest Hons, 1983;
POP Clb S'ship, 1982; Grad'd 3rd in
Class, 1980; Cmdr Cunningham Sci and
Math Awd, 1980; g/Career in Hlth Care
Field.
ZOPF, ERIC PAUL oc/Student; b/
Nov 15, 1962; h/815 George White
Road, Greensboro, NC 27410; p/Dr and
Mrs Paul Zopf Jr, Greensboro, NC; ed/
Dipl, New Garden Friends Sch, 1981;
Att'g, Guilford Col; r/Quaker; hon/
Awd'd S'ship for Study at the Patterson
Sch, Lenoir, NC, 1978; Cert from US
Yth Conserv Corps in Envir Studies,
1978; Cert from US Yth Conserv Corps
in Wilderness Survival, 1979; Intl Yth
in Achmt; Commun Ldrs of Am; Yg
Personalities of S; g/To Wk w the US
Pk Ser.
ZOPPO, ADRIANA oc/Student,
Free-Lance Musician; b/Mar 8, 1961; h/
12451 Deerbrook Lane, Los Angeles,
CA 90049; p/Ciro E and Rosemary
Zoppo, Los Angeles, CA; ed/Palisades
HS, 1978; BA 1982, BMus 1982, Univ
of So CA; pa/Free-Lance Violinist and
Violist in CA, 1974-; First Violinist,
Debut Orch 1980-82, Am Yth Symph
1981-82, Univ of So CA Symph

1978-82, LA Philharm Inst Orch 1981, Santa Monica Yth Orch 1976-78, LA Yth Symph 1983, Univ of So CA Contemp Music Ensemble 1982; Mem of Num Commun Orchs, 1974-; Played for Masquer's Clb, 1981; cp/Creat Writing Clb, 1977-78; hon/First Place Solo/Ensemble Fest, 1975; Awd of

Merit, Co Supvr Dean Dana, 1981; W/ W Music; g/Violinist in a Maj Orch in US or Abroad; Violinist in a Chamber Ensemble.

ZUAZUA, MARIA KATHY oc/Student; b/Dec 28, 1961; h/2238 Grand Avenue, San Diego, CA 92109; m/Lai Ngai Chin; p/Xuan Zuazua, San Anto-

nio, TX; ed/Nuernberg Am HS, 1979; Our Lady of the Lake Univ, 1982; pa/ Cashier, 1975-78; Asst Secy, 1979-82; cp/Kappa Pi Sigma; Intl Clb; Soc for Advmt of Mgmt; r/Cath; hon/Yg Commun Ldrs of Am; g/To Wk in Pers Ofc as a Pers Mgr.

Appendix I

Dr. GEORGE BRUCE
25 Warriston Crescent, Edinburgh, EH3 5LB Scotland
Lecturer in Extra-Mural Studies, Edinburgh University, Scotland; Writer, Broadcaster

SYLVIA LEIGH BRYANT, F.I.B.A., A.M.A.B.I.
Route 5, Box 498A, Madison Heights, Virginia 24572 USA
Editor-Publisher, The Anthology Society; Poet, Free-lance Writer, Consultant

JUAN B. CALATAYUD, M.D., F.A.C.A.
1712 Eye Street, NW, Suite 1004, Washington, D.C. 20006 USA
Professor, George Washington University School of Medicine, Private Physician

JOSEPH PETER CANGEMI, Ed.D, F.A.C.A.
Psychology Department, Western Kentucky University, Bowling Green, Kentucky 42101 USA
Professor of Psychology, Western Kentucky University; Management Consultant, Researcher, Educator

C. EUGENE COKE, Ph.D., F.R.S.C., F.A.I.C., F.A.B.I., F.S.D.C., F.T.I., F.C.I.C.
26 Aqua Vista Drive, Ormond Beach, Florida 32074 USA
Chairman, Coke and Associate Consultants; Scientist, Author, Educator, International Authority on Man-Made Fibers

GROVER F. DAUSSMAN, P.E., Ph.D.
1910 Colice Road, SE, Huntsville, Alabama 35801 USA
Engineering Consultant; Former United States Government Engineer

GARTH WILFRED PRYCE DAVIES
11 Rue Charles De Gaulle, Cappellen/Olm 8322, Luxembourg
Head, European Networks Service, Commission of the European Communities

ELIAS D. DEKAZOS, Ph.D.
408 Sandstone Drive, Athens, Georgia 30605 USA
Plant Physiologist, R. Russell Agriculture Research Center

BERNARD T. DELOFFRE
2 Bis Villa Mequillet, 92200 Neuilly, France
Director General, Satel Conseil, Paris; Executive Secretary, European Consulting Satellite Organization, Paris

The Hon. Mr. Justice R. ELSE-MITCHELL, C.M.G.
2nd Floor, Northbourne House, 219 Northbourne Avenue, Canberra, ACT 2600 Australia
Chairman, Commonwealth Grants Commission

Mr. INGEMAR ESSEN
Eriksbergsgatan 16, S-114 30 Stockholm, Sweden
President, Swedish Federation of Trades, Industries and Family Enterprises

SANDRA FOWLER, F.A.B.I., L.A.A.B.I.
West Columbia, West Virginia 25287 USA
Associate Editor, Ocarina and The Album; Editor, Publisher

LORRAINE S. GALL, Ph.D., F.A.B.I.
Sandpiper Village, 1049 Anna Knapp Boulevard, Mt. Pleasant, South Carolina 29464 USA
President, Bacti-Consult Associates; Senior Microbiological Consultant, Private Business; Researcher, Space Scientist, Educator

JOSEPH B. GAVIN, Ph.D., S.J.
Campion College, University of Regina, 3769 Winnipeg Street, Regina S4S 0A2 Canada
President, Campion College, University of Regina, Regina, Canada

CARRIE LEIGH GEORGE, Ph.D., M.Div., Ed.S., M.A., D.Rel.
1652 Detroit Avenue, NW, Atlanta, Georgia 30314 USA
Research Associate and Assistant Professor of Curriculum and Instruction, Georgia State University; Ordained Clergywomen, Consultant, Researcher, Educator

ANTONIO GIRAUDIER, F.A.B.I., L.P.A.B.I.
215 East 68th Street, New York City, New York 10021 USA
Writer, Author, Poet, Artist, Musician

LEWIS DANIEL HOUCK, JR., Ph.D., L.F.I.B.A., F.A.B.I.
11111 Woodson Avenue, Kensington, Maryland 20795 USA
Project Leader for Economic Research Service, United States Department of Agriculture; Management Consultant, Author, Educator, Businessman

MOZELLE BIGELOW KRAUS, Ed.D., L.A.A.B.I.
The Willoughby, No. 925N, 5500 Friendship Blvd., Chevy Chase, Maryland 20815 USA
Private Psychology Practice, Psychotherapist

JOHN F. KURTZKE, M.D., F.A.C.P.
7509 Salem Road, Falls Church, Virginia 22043 USA
Vice Chairman and Professor of Nuerology, Georgetown Medical School, Washington D.C.; Neurologist, Epidemiologist, Consultant, Author

ENRIQUE ROBERTO LARDE, M.G.A., F.A.B.I.
Post Office Box 2922, Old San Juan, Puerto Rico 00903 USA
Director, South Continental Insurance Agency, Inc.; Director and President, Corporacion Insular de Seguros; Researcher, Business Executive

RUBY STUTTS LYELLS, L.H.D.
1116 Isiah Montgomery Street, Jackson, Mississippi 39203 USA
Federal Jury Commissioner, United States District Court, Southern District of Mississippi; Trustee, Prentiss Institute; Writer, Researcher, Librarian

KRISHNA SHANKAR MANUDHANE, Ph.D., F.A.B.I.
5211 Meadowview Avenue, North Bergen, New Jersey 07047 USA
Director of Technical Services, Zenith Laboratories, Inc., Northvale, New Jersey; Researcher

ROBERT C. McGEE, JR., F.A.B.I.
Box 29540, Richmond, Virginia 23229 USA
President, Swan Industries, Inc.; Business Executive, Aeronautical Engineer, Consultant, Administrator

ROD McKUEN
Post Office Box G, Beverly Hills, California 90213 USA
Poet, Composer-Lyricist, Author, Performer; President, Stanyan Records, Discus New Gramophone Society, Mr. Kelly Productions, Montcalm Productions, Stanyan Books, Cheval Books, Biplane Books, Rod McKuen Enterprises

HERBERT B. MOBLEY, Ph.D., D.D., S.T.D., L.P.A.B.I.
Post Office Box 165, Summit Station, Pennsylvania 17979 USA
Pastor Emeritus, St. Mark's (Brown's) United Church of Christ, Summit Station; Acting Pastor, St. Peter's United Church of Christ, Frackville, Pennsylvania

MAKIO MURAYAMA, Ph.D.
5010 Benton Avenue, Bethesda, Maryland 20814 USA
Research Biochemist, National Institute of Health

VIRGINIA SIMMONS NYABONGO, Ph.D.
935 34th Avenue North, Nashville, Tennessee 37209 USA
Professor Emeritus of French, Research, Tennessee State University; Researcher, Author, Educator

MIHAIL PROTOPAPADAKIS
Square Ambidrix 32, 1040 Brussels, Belgium
Deputy, European Parliament

ROLAND B. SCOTT, M.D.
1723 Shepherd Street, NW, Washington, DC 20011 USA
Distinguished Professor of Pediatrics and Child Health and Director, Sickle Cell Disease Center, Howard University; Educator, Administrator

SIR JAMES SIDNEY RAWDON SCOTT-HOPKINS, M.E.P.
2, Queen Anne's Gate, London, SW1H 9AA England
Member of the European Parliament

DR. CHOOMPOL SWASDIYAKORN
196 Phaholyothin Road, Bangkhen, Bangkok 10900 Thailand
Secretary-General, National Research Council of Thailand

HERBERT H. TARSON, Ph.D., F.A.B.I.
4611 Denwood Rod, La Mesa, California 92041 USA
Senior Vice President, National University, San Diego, California; Researcher, Educator

ANDREW B. THOMPSON, JR., F.A.B.I., L.P.A.B.I., L.F.I.B.A.
Post Office Box 3008, Montgomery, Alabama 36109 USA
President, National Pricing Service, Inc.

BASIL P. TOUTORSKY, D.Mus., L.P.A.B.I., F.A.B.I., L.F.I.B.A.
1720 16th Street, NW, Washington DC 20009 USA
Director, Toutorsky Academy of Music; Professor, Composer, Pianist

WALTER E. ULRICH
8 Pasadena Drive, Hamilton Township, New Jersey 08619 USA
Deputy Commissioner, New Jersey State Department of Human Services

AYIYAH W.M. VON NUSSBAUMER, Ph.D., D.Th.
11110 Hazen Road, Houston, Texas 77072 USA
Research Librarian, Published Author, Educator

ROGER LODGE WOLCOTT
4796 Waterloo Road, Atwater, Ohio 44201 USA
Former Specialist in Aeromechanical Research and Development; Engineering Department, Goodyear Aerospace Corporation, Akron; Secretary, The Lighter Than Air Society; Aviation Pioneer, Inventor, Association Executive

Appendix II

Roster of Life and Annual Members
The American Biographical Institute
Research Association

LIFE PATRONS

Allison, Frank
Aly, Said
Anderson, Vivian
Aragona, Guylaine
Aragona, Ronald
Au, Chang-Hung
Ayers, Anne
Barbour, Judy
Barcynski, Leon
Barnes, Melver
Barr, Nona
Baruwa, Abraham
Batal, A.
Baxter, Ruth
Bebawi, Girgis
Belisle, Lenore
Bell, Deanne
Benner, Richard
Benskina, Margarita
Berkey, Maurice
Blakely, Martha
Bohmfalk, Johnita
Bomkamp, Loraine
Boulton, Shauna
Break, Virginia
Carnevale, Dario
Carver, George
Cecconi-Bates, Augusta
Chambers, Lois
Chilton, Howard
Chin, Sue
Christensen, R.
Clark, James
Cole, Eddie-Lou
Collier, Richard
Cook, David
Cook, J.
Coriaty, George
Crause, Herman
Crihan, Herman
Croxton, Thomas
Dansby, Huddie
Davis, Alexander
Davis, Gordon
Davis, Robert
Dennison, Jerry
Denton, Thomas
Di Ponio, Concetta
DuBroff, Diana
Dumouchel, Anne
Duncan, Dyna
Duncan, Gertrude
Ellerbee, Estelle
Erwin, Jean
Everett, Thelma
Farmakis, George
Fergus, Patricia
Ferguson, Harry

Fisher, Mary
Follingstad, Henry
Ford, Gordon
Fox, Pauline
Fox, Vivian Estelle
Freeze, Elizabeth
Freund, E.
Gebo, Robert
Gershowitz, Sonya
Ghattas, Sonia
Giraudier, Antonio
Goh, Han
Gomez, Nelida
Goodman, Jess
Goulding, C.
Griffith, Reginald
Haas, Arthur
Hackett, William
Hanns, Christian
Hanson, Freddie
Harbani, Suharnoko
Harpster, V.
Harris, Louise
Harris, Thomas
Harrison, Winnie
Harz, Frances
Hatajack, Frank
Headlee, William
Heckart, Robert
Hendricks, Robert
Herren, Peter
Holland, Ray
Hornsby, J.
Houseal, Reuben
Houseal, Ruth
Howard, Adeline
Hubbard, L.
Huff, Cherry
Huff, Norman
Huraj, Helen
Ilo, Moses
Johnson, Rufus
Jordan, Lan
Kagey, F.
Kales, Robert
Karpen, Marian
Kaufman, Irene
Kerr, Catherine
King, Joseph
Kjartansson, Kristjan
Ko, Yih-Song
Kokenzie, Henry
Larde, Enrique
Laudenslager, Wanda
Leavitt, Charles
Lewis, Loraine
Long, Shirley
Lowry, Dolores

Malone, June
Manogura, Ben
Marchetti, Jean
Martin, Deborah Louise
Mashhour, Abdel-Hay
Mason, Madeline
Mathewson, Hugh
McCoy, Patricia
McCullough, Constance
McLaughlin, Sybil
Michna, Marienka
Miller, Virginia
Mills, George
Mills, William
Mitra, Gopal
Mobley, Herbert
Mollenhauer, Bernhard
Mooney, John
Moore, Dalton
Morahan, Daniel
Morgan, Branch
Mori, Marianne
Morrison, Francine
Music, Edward
Nazareno, Jose
Nicholls, James
Nikolai, Lorraine
Ogden, R.
O'Malley, William
O'Neal, Robert
Overby, George
Overby-Dean, Talulah
Pace, Jon
Parks, Anna
Payton, Ralph
Peachey, Christine
Pearson, Norman
Phillips, Karen
Phillips, Virginia
Pirkle, Estus
Plewinski, Gustaw
Plewinski, Teresa
Pollack, Stephen
Powell, Russell
Prichard, Thora
Puh, Chiung
Purvis, Mary
Puskarich, Michael
Raatz, Sherry
Rahımtoola, S.
Rasmussen, Helen
Rex, Lonnie
Reyman, Maria
Rhemann, Eugene
Richmond, John
Riemann, Wilhelmina
Roberts-Wright, Bessie
Robeson, Lillyan

Robinson, Ralph
Rodkiewicz, Czeslaw
Rodriguez, Beatriz
Rosenberg, Claire
Rowe, Iris
Rubly, Lucille
Sabella, Emmanuel
Savard, Lorena
Sawyer, Joseph
Seale, Ruth
Shah, Shirish
Sharif, Mohammed
Sheh, Violet
Simeck, Clyde
Smith, Norvel
Stein, David

Stevens, Myrtle
Stimach, Janet
Straub, Nellie
Stueber, Gustav
Sutton, Doris
Sweeney, James
Switaj, Lawrence
Szegho, Emeric
Tashiro, Noboru
Tekle, Afewerk
Thomas, William
Thompson, Andrew
Torres-Aybar, Francisco
Toutorsky, Basil
Urry, Vern
Van der Kuyp, Edwin

Vaughn, Pearl
Volpert, Don
Wainwright, Mary
Walden, Kathryn
Wlaker, Glynda
Waters, Raymond
Waters, Rowena
Webb, Rozana
Weinbaum, Eleanor
Whisenant, Mary
Wiemann, Marion
Williams, Annie
Williams, Melva
Williams, Yvonne
Wolanin, Sophie
Wolf, Joseph
Woods, Willie
Young, James

LIFE FELLOWS

Abba, Hilda
Abba, Raymond
Abrell, Ronald
Adetoro, J.
Al Bahar, Adnan
Al Seif, Khaled
Allen, Edgard
Allison, William
Ames, John
Amir-Moez, Ali
Anderson, Gordon
Anderson, Thelma
Anderson, Ursula
Aston, Katherine
Atkinson-Killian, Hulda
Attiah, Hassan
Averhart, Lula
Ayim, Emmanuel
Babajide, Solomon

Bair, Mary
Baker, Elsworth
Barbachano, Don
Bare, Jean
Baum, Carl
Beardmore, Glenn
Benebig, Roger
Bennett, Stefanie
Benson, Opral
Besche-Wadish, Pamela
Bethell, M.
Binford, Linwood
Bitters, Robert
Black, Larry
Blakeney, Roger
Bolton, Douglas
Bossert, Michael
Bourne, Geoffrey
Boyer, Theodore
Brame, Arden
Brown, Earle
Brown, F.
Bullard, Ethel
Bunnag, Srichitra
Burgess, Caroline
Burley-Allen, Madelyn
Burns, Maretta
Bush, Wendell
Bushbaum, Marianne
Campbell, Caroline
Carpenter, Charles
Carroll, Beatrice
Carson, William

Castro, Manfredo
Cauthen, Deloris
Chan, Kum Peng
Chang, Hong-Lou
Chang, Woo Joo
Char, Wai
Chisholm, William
Chretien, LaVerne
Chun, Sae-il M.D.
Ciancone, Lucy
Cintron, Emma
Clark, Fred
Clemente, Patrocinio
Cleveland, Hattye
Clift, Annie
Cohen, Irwin
Corniffe, Doris
Corsello, Lily
Couch, M.
Cullingford, Ada
D'Agostino, Ralph
Davis, Evelyn
Delphin, Jacques
Dillon, Robert
Doelle, Horst
Doherty, Elizabeth
Dolezal, Henry
Dorion, Robert
Dow, Marguerite
Drummond, Malcolm
D'Silva, Roby
Dunn, Helen
Dyer, Eileen
Eastland, Mary
Edwards, Angela
El-Sayeh, Ramzy
Emrick, Raymond
Enyi, Brown
Errazuriz, Rafael
Essenwanger, Oskar
Evans, Roymond
Fadahunsi, Samuel
Fairweather, Gladstone
Farley, Dorothy
Farrar, Margaret
Fawcett, James
Feist, Marian
Field, Elizabeth
Fink, Aaron
Francis, Mabel
Fries, Herluf
Frym, Janet

Fuchs, Helmuth
Gambrell, Mildred
Gan, Woon
Garcia, Henry
Gardine, Juanita
Garrison, Patricia
Gausman, Harold
Gauthier, Thomas
German, Fin
Gibson, Curtis
Gibson, Weldon
Glaze, Diana
Goerigk, Wolfgang
Goodman, Julius
Gospodaric, Mimi
Gossge-Blue, Edna
Gray, Dora
Greene, Sharon
Groeber, Richard
Guest, Bernette
Guyton, Suzanne
Haastrup, Adedokun
Hackney, Howard
Hale, Arnold
Hall, Wilfred
Hamilton, Madrid
Hammer, Jane
Hammons, Thomas
Hanf, James
Hanif, Akhtar
Hansen, Kathryn
Haritun, Rosalie
Hearn, Charles
Hedtke, Delphine
Hobdy, Frances
Holland, Ruby
Holmstrom, Gustaf
Hooper, Marjorie
Huck, Larry
Hui, Stephen
Hunter, Cannie
Huq, Syed
Hussaini, Hisham Rushdi
Huzurbazar, Vasant
Jacobsen, Parley
Jacobsen, William
Javed, Muhammad
Jensen, Helen
Johnston, Ruth
Jones, Bernard
Jordan, W.
Kaltenbach, Anneliese

Kanagawa, Robert
Kar, Anil
Karl, Dorothy
Kellogg, Bruce
Kelly, John
Kemp, Dorothy
Khan, Muzaffar
Kiehm, Tae M.D.
Kim, Un
King, Edwin
King, Helen
Kitada, Shinichi
Knaebel, Jeff
Knelson, Nelda
Koch, Frances
Kolb, Florence
Kolman, Laurence
Kong, Lim
Kraus, Pansy
Kritjanson, Harold
La Claustra, Vera
Landers, Newlin
Landers, Vernette
Le Cocq, Rhoda
Leeds, Sylvia
Lennox, William
Lim, Phillip
Lindberg, Elayne
Little, Florence
Littlejohn, Joan
Loening, Sarah
Long, Leonard
Lonneker, Arleen
Loper, Marilyn
Luahiwa, Judith
Lundell, Frederick
Lutzker, Edythe
Maass, Vera
Mabe, Ruth
MacLennan, Beryce
Magargal, Larry
Maigida, Umaru-Sanda
Malami, Alhaji
Malin, Howard
Manahan, Manny
Marais, Jan
Martin, James
Mason, Aretha
Massier, Paul
Masuda, Gohta
Matsumoto, Junji
McAdoo, Phyllis
McAvoy, Joseph
McCoin, John
McCormack, Grace
McNabb, Sue
Meldrum, Alex
Mellichamp, Josephine
Mello, Henry
Meskell, Una
Mestnik, Irmtraut
Meyer, G.
Miller, C.
Miller, Laverne
Miller, Robert
Mills, Rosemary
Min, Frank
Morler, Edward
Morris, Rich
Moseley, Laurice
Moses, Elbert
Mosonyi, Emil

Murayama, Makio
Naidu, Shrinivas
Naylor, Pleas
NeSmith, Vera
Nevel, Eva
Newbern, Captolia
Newman, Michele
Nichols, Thomas
Njoku, Rose
Norby, Alice
Northup, William
Novak, Lela
Nwankwo, Ochia
O'Dougherty, Pascual
Oh, May
Oien, Arthur
Okafor, Andrew
Okigbo, Pius
Oloruntoba, Barnabas
Opalka, Joyce
Osborn, Prime
Owelle, Frank
Oyeleye, Victor
Pai, Chung-Ruei
Pak, Chan
Palombo, Thomas
Parker, Lucy
Pasricha, Manohar
Pastor, Lucille
Perks, Barbara
Perry, Emma
Persch, Ruth
Peterson, Daniel
Philpott, Emalee
Pine, Charles
Pirs, Joze
Pollard, Joseph
Polley, Elizabeth
Porter, Michael
Prentice, Sartell
Price, Thomas
Putnam, Michael
Raddatz, Otto
Ragan, Bryant
Ramovs, Primoz
Regan, Helene
Reinhardt, Siegfried
Reynolds, Clayton
Richards, John
Richards, Novelle
Rifaat, Alsayed
Roberts, C.
Roberts, Josephine
Rodenburg, Carl
Rodkiewicz, Czeslaw
Rogers, Gayle
Rogers, Gifford
Roode, Johanna
Roth, Frederic
Rozenbaum, Najman
Ruas, Vitoriano
Rubly, Grant
Rutledge, Varian
Saheed, Mohammed
Sanders, Frances
Santiago, Margaret
Saxton, Beryl
Schabbel, Helen
Schirripa, Dennis
Schliephake, Erwin
Schwarzott, Wilhelm
Scott, Wilton

Sealy, Vernol
Sebastianelli, Mario
Seegar, Charlon
Segan, B.
Sewer, Pauline
Silvers, Morgan
Simpson, Jack
Singer, Jeanne
Slack, Florence
Slowik, Richard
Smith, Cecile
Snookal, Donald
Snyder, John
Soekanto, R.
Southward, B.
Speir, Kenneth
Sreenivas, Nanjappa
Steiner, A.
Stevens, Ben
Stewart, Elizabeth
Stewart, Roberta
Stilgenbauer, Robert
Stockton, Barbara
Stonebridge, Jerry
Stromillo, Mario
Stuhl, Oskar
Suleiman, Suleiman
Swamy, M.
Tabuena, Romeo
Talley-Morris, Neva
Tanzil, H. O. K.
Terao, Toshio
Tew, E.
Thomas, K.
Thomas, V.
Thomasson, Raymond
Todd, Vivian
Todres, Bernice
Torres, Rafael
Towne, Dorothea
Toyomura, Dennis
Tran, Quang
Tsau, Wen
Tulong, Joseph
Tung, Rosalie
Turk, Oscar
Turkay, Osman
Turyahikayo-Rugyema, Benon
Tyson, Helen
Umber, Anna
Vlachos, Estella
Voss, Arthur
Vukovic, Drago
Wallis, Ben
Walters, Helen
Walters-Godfree, Dorothy
Wanderman, Richard
Ward, William
Weber, Gertrude
Webster, Burnice
Welsh, Carol June
Whitfield, Vallie Jo
Wilhelm, Willa
Williams, Harvey
Willoughby, Clarice
Wilson, Jeanne
Woo, Po-Shing
Wrentmore, Anita
Wright, Jean
Wyslotsky, Ihor
Yee, Phillip
Yopconka, Natalie

LIFE ASSOCIATES

Breazeale, Morris
Dunlap, Estelle
Gaither, Dorothy
James, Shaylor
Lauer, Frances
McDowell, Margaret
Meeks, Elsie
Overton, Dean
Pasternak, Eugenia
Purcell, George
Sliwinski, M.
Small, Fay
Weaton, George

ANNUAL ASSOCIATES

Adewole, Olufunmilayo
Aldrich, Stephanie
Alexander, Samuel
Allen, Johnny
Amer, Nabil
Angus, J.
Baily, Doris
Banik, Sambhu
Basu, Debatosh
Beaman, Margarine
Bera, Sudhir
Bernard, Jonathan
Berresford, Brady
Bjornsson, Petur
Bjornsson, Sigurjon
Boim, Leon
Bomberger, Audrey
Bothwell, Shirley
Boykin, Frances
Bradley, Ramona
Brady, Bryan
Britton, Michael
Brod, Joseph
Brost, Eileen
Brott, Alexander
Brown, Edward
Brunale, Vito
Bryant, Sylvia
Burns, Marjorie
Campazzi, Betty
Capitol, Viola
Carter, Marion
Cassidy, Virginia
Cellini, William
Chappell, Mae
Chesney, Rose
Chor Fook Sin, Bill
Choun, Robert
Christensen, Don
Christias, Christos
Clark, Richard
Colston, Freddie
Corey, Margaret
Crafton-Masterson, Adrienne
Cucin, Robert
Dabbousi, M.
Davidson, Mabel
de Bettencourt Barbosa, Maria
de Brault, E.
Dean, Lloyd

DeJoia, Ruth
Dell, Margaret
Denktas, Raul
Deyton, Camilla
Dixon, Lawrence
Dossett, Betty
Downing, Everett
Drake, Josephine
Durbney, Clydrow
Dwyer, Marie
Engle, Patricia
Ester, Mary
Fales, DeCoursey
Fehrman, Cherie
Fenske, Virginia
Filos, Alberto
Forman, Ruth
Fuertes, Abelardo
Fuller, James
Fulling, Kay
Galamaga, Donald
Gallipeau, Joan
Garcia Olivero, Carmen
Gardner, Nord
Garnham, Frank
Gary, Gayle
Gibson, Jacquelyn
Gil del Real, Maria
Golton, Margaret
Goodstone, Geraldine
Gregory, Calvin
Groesbeck, E.
Gruber, Rosalind
Gugl, Wolfgang
Guy, Edward
Hagan, Paul
Hain, Violet
Hardy, Carole
Harris, Vander
Hartmann-Johnsen, Olaf
Hasumi, Toshimitsu
Havilland, Ben
Helgi, Johannes
Hemenway, Dorothy
Herring, Michael
Horswell-Chambers, Margaret
Howell, James
Hsu, Wen-ying
Hu, John
Hulsey, Ruth

Hunt, Edward
Ijiri, Yutaka
Jackson, Linda
Jamison, Maggie
Jeffrey, Margie
JemmottWilliams, Maxwell
Joannou, Michael
Jones, Myrtle
Joseph, Cuthbert
Kachel, Henry
Kane, Flora
Kang, Byung-Kyu
Kaplan, Richard
Kawano, Ietoshi
Keenan, Retha
Keroher, Grace
Kiddell, Sidney
Kihlstenius, Alf-Roger
Kjoss-Hansen, Bente
Kline, Tex
Klit, Erik
Knauf, Janine
Knepper, Eugene
Koehler, Isabel
Kopfler, Judith
Kraus, Mozelle
Ksiazek, Marilyn
Lair, Helen
Lane, Cynthia
Lang, Helmer
Larkin, Gertie
Lauterbach, Kathryn
Lawrie, Eileen
Leader, Harry
Learnard, James
Leba, Samuel
Lemire, David
Lester, William
Levandowski, Dr. Barbara
Lewis, Cecelia
Lim, Ho-Peng
Lim-Quek, Muriel
Littell, Bertha
Loret de Mola, Maria
MacLellan, Helen
Mader, Eileen
Mahaffey, Joan
Makinen, Kauko
Mallon, Thomas
Marcucci, Silvestro

Marshall, Patricia
Martin, Chippa
Martins, Micael
Masse, Louis
Mavros, Constantin
Mayer, Jacob
McCabe, Donald
McCune, Weston
McDowell, A.
Meghji, Mohamed
Melton, Ira
Mendieta, Marcelo
Messerlian, Zaven
Moore, Martha
Morgan, Clyde
Morris, William
Morse, Genevieve
Moutote, Daniel
Moya, Aury
Mozingo, Margaret
Muhlanger, Erich
Munson, Norma
Muss, Peter
Naouri, Issa
Neeper, Ralph
Nelson, Lorraine
Nelson, Robert
Nelson, Thomas
Newell, Virginia
Ney, Judy
Nicholson, Rosemary
Nicklin, Helen
Nicole, Christopher
Nohe, B.
Norby, Alice
Norton, Alan
Nozaki, Masako
Nzegwu, Ifeanyi
Olsen, Virginia
Orata, Pedro
Oswald, Roy
Ovenstone, Irene
Papamichael, Anna
Parson, Erwin
Paschall, Amy
Patten, Clara
Patterson, E.
Perate, Hannah
Peterson, Constance
Peterson, Mary

Pilioko, Aloi
Pizer, Elizabeth
Poehner, Raymond
Posta, Elaine
Prydz, Svein
Pulliainen, Erkki
Pulliam, Paul
Rahming, Philip
Rao, A.
Reicher, Arthur
Reichle, Frederick
Reid, Douglas
Reifler, Henrietta
Reinl, Harry
Ringsdorf, W.
Ritter, Olive
Rogell, Irma
Rogers, Carol
Roney, Alice
Rughani, M.
Saleh, Mohamad
Salsbury, Barbara
Salter, Margaret
Sanchez, Juan
Sanford, Paul
Snataella, Irma
Schioldborg, Ragnhild
Scott, J.
Seltzer, Ronni
Seppala, Arvo
Shaw, Imara
Sheetz, Ralph
Shelton, Bessie
Shiffman, Max
Shragai, E.
Simmons, Troy
Slappey, Mary
Smith, Mary
Smythe-Wood, Ian
Sperry, S.
Sproll, Heinz
Staffeld-Madsen, Alfred
Stanat, Ruth
Stankovic, Milorad
Stanley, Sandra
Stephens, Rupert
Stevens, Grace
Stewart, Joan
Stiefel, Betty
Stoeger, Keith

Stottsberry, Teresa
Studley, Helen
Stuhl, Johannes
Sulaiman, Suliantono
Takino, Masiuchi
Tamari, Moshe
Tan, It-Koon
Taylor, John
Tekelioglu, Meral
Terpening, Virginia
Thomas, Peggy
Tipton, Dorothy
Tipton, Rains
Tisch, J.
Tompkins, James
Touw, J.
Tunick, Phyllis
Turner, Terrance
Tzafestas, S.
Ulrich, Walter
Varner, Barbara
Vilgrain, Jacques
Vinokooroff, Leonide
Waddington, Bette
Walker, Lorna
Wallace, Betty
Wallace, Deborah
Walton, Fernie
Warner, J.
Way, Tsung-To
Wayne, David
Webb, William
Welch, Fern
Wells, Marrion
White, Margaret
Wierbicki, Eugen
Wilford, Rowland
Wilkinson, George
Wilson, Reba
Winston, William
Wolfe, Janet
Womack, William
Wong, Robert
Wood, Sandra
Wright, Dana
Yanosko, Elizabeth
Yap, Meow
Zelner, Estelle
Zibrun, S.
Zimmerman, Richard

ABIRA FOUNDING MEMBERS

Acker, Louise
Bardis, Panos
Benton, Suzanne
Brownell, Daphne
Kalvinskas, John
Westerfield, Hilda
Williams, Patrick

Aero, Fellow, SAE, 1936; Hon Fellow, AIAA; ASME; Quiet Birdmen; VPres, FL Aero Clb, 1936; Exptl Aircraft Assn; AOPA; Life Mem, TX Aerial Applicators Assn; Hon Life Mem, Flying Engrs; U Flying Octogenarians; Tau Beta Pi; Sigma Zi; Pi Tau Sigma; Phi Kappa Phi; Sigma Gamma Tau; cp/Rotary Clb, 1939-; Pres, Vero Bch Clb, 1961-62; hon/Author, *Aircraft Propeller Design*, 1930; Over 60 NACA Tech Reports & Notes; Num Tech Aeronaut Articles Pub'd; Sylvanus Albert Reed Awd, 1944; Fawcett Aviation Awd, 1945; Puffer Awd, Nat Agri Aviations Assn, 1972; Laura Tabor Barber Air Safety Awd, 1975; Listed as Significant Contbr to Flight Technol, Nat Air & Space Mus of Smithsonian Instn; W/W in Aviation.

WEIDA, DONNA LEE oc/Computer Company Executive; b/Oct 29, 1939; h/ 14241 Utrillo Drive, Irvine, CA 97714; ba/Irvine, CA; c/Mark, Traci, Teri; p/ Donald L and Leila J (Sweet) Klackner; ed/AA, Orange Coast Col and Saddleback Col, 1980; BS, Bus Adm & Computer Info Sys, CA St Univ-Fullerton, 1983; pa/Secy, K L K Mfg Co, Logansport, IN, 1957-60, 1963-65; Secy, Sch of Ed, MI St Univ, 1962-63; Secy, Sch of Fine Arts, Univ of CA-Irvine, 1966-69; Co-orgr, Plaza Vet Clin, Upland, CA, 1969-70; Mgr, Bob Bondurant Sch H Perf Driving, Ontario Motor Speedway, CA, 1970-73; Chuck Jones Racing, Costa Mesa, CA, 1973; Exec Secy, Dana Steel, Newport Bch, CA, 1974; Estimator/Ofc Mgr, Hardy & Harper, Tustin, CA, 1975-76; Controller/Mgr, Gillen/Kloss Advtg , Newport Bch, 1977-78; Purchasing Admr, Butler Housing, Irvine, CA, 1979; Controller, X Mark Corp, Costa Mesa, 1980-81; Corp Secy, Adm Mgr, Pers Sys Tech Inc, Irvine, CA, 1982; Fdr, Owner, Numbers & Words, Irvine, CA, 1982-; Mem: Nat Assn Female Execs; Am Soc Profl & Exec Wom; Beta Sigma Phi; cp/ Repub; r/Epis; hon/W/W of Am Wom; Personalities of W & MW.

WEINSTOCK, HELENE SUZETTE (KARLIN) oc/Psychotherapist and Marriage, Family, Child Counselor; b/Apr 26, 1935; h/Fountain Valley, CA; ba/ Huntington Bch, CA; m/Donald J(ay); p/Bernard L Karlin (dec); Betty E (Balter) Karlin, Canoga Pk, CA; sp/ Irving A and Rose (Primack) Weinstock, Camarillo, CA; ed/AA 1954, AB 1955, MA 1958, CPhil in Hist 1969, Univ of CA-LA; MA Psych, CA St Univ-LA, 1980; pa/Tchr, Mt Vernon Jr HS, LA City Schs, 1958-61; Public & Profl Ed Coor, Riverside, CA Mtl Hlth Assn, 1967-73; Psych Asst, Leonard I Schneider PhD & Assocs, Newport Bch, CA, 1976-78; Psych Cnsltr, Huntington Bch, CA Commun Clin, 1978-80; Psych Cnslr, Non-profit W Co Cnslg Ctr, 1980-81; Conslt & Supvr of Interns & Trainees, W Co Cnslg Ctr, 1981-; Pvt Pract Psychotherapist & Marriage, Fam & Child Cnslr, Huntington Bch, CA, 1981-; Mem: Am Assn for Marriage & Fam Therapy; So CA Assn for Marriage & Fam Therapy; CA Assn of Marriage & Fam Therapists; Orange Co Chapt, CAMFT; Am Psych Assn; Wn Psychol Assn; CA St Psychol Assn; Nat Assn for Poetry Therapy; Coor Com for Wom in Hist Prof; Wn Assn of Wom Histns; Phi Beta Kappa; Psi Chi; Pi Gammu Mu; Phi Alpha Theta; Pi Sigma Alpha; Alpha

Mu Gamma; Alpha Lambda Delta; cp/ Mem, Bd of Dirs & Num Coms, Riverside Mtl Hlth Assn; Var Coms, Riverside Co Mtl Hlth Advy Bd; Riverside Co Mtl Hlth Action Com, 1968-72; Riverside Co/Commun Drug-Abuse Action Com, 1970; Riverside Co Mtl Hlth & Mtl Retard Com, 1972; Num Other Coms in Riverside Co, CA; r/Judaism; hon/Author of Pub'd Poems & Articles, *Voices: The Art & Sci of Psychotherapy*, Jour of Am Acad of Psychotherapists; *Pudding Mag*, Nat Assn for Poetry Therapy; Nat Def Fgn Lang F'ships in Afrikaans, Sum 1964, 1964-65, 1965-66; Mabel Wilson Richards Grad Scholar in Polit Sci, Univ of CA-LA, 1955-56; Mem, Num Hon Socs; W/W: in W, in CA.

WEISHEIT, RICHARD LANE oc/ Certified Public Accountant, Executive; b/Jan 27, 1951; h/10210 Chisholm Trail, Dallas, TX 75243; ba/Dallas, TX; m/ Margaret Lynette; p/Mr and Mrs O G Weisheit Jr, Tyler, TX; sp/Nancille Willis, Dallas, TX; ed/BBA, TX Tech Univ, 1973; CPA, 1978; pa/Staff Acct, Frank Began CPA, 1973-77; Sr Acct, Isham P Nelson CPA's, 1977-78; Pres, Richard L Weisheit PC, CPA's, 1978-; Mem: Public Relats Com & Taxpayer Ed Com, Dallas Chapt of CPA's, 1979-81; Dallas Discussion Ldr, Peer Grp of CPA's, 1982; cp/Yg Repubs; Treas, 500 Inc of Dallas, 1981-82, 1982-83; r/Meth; hon/Author of Article on Tax Equity & Fiscal Responsibility Act of 1982 in *Big B Acctg & Tax Manual*; Outstg Yg CPA's in Dallas, 1979-80; W/ W in S & SW.

WEISSINGER, MARY HAZEL MATTINGLY oc/Teacher; b/Nov 4, 1927; h/ Georgiana Plantation Box 333, Cary, MS 39054; m/Charles Hyde; c/Charles Hyde Jr, Guy Mattingly, MaryAnne W Smith, Elizabeth Hansford, Thomas Leland, Hazel Shanahan; p/Guy Leland Mattingly, Greenville, MS; Hazel Shanahan Mattingly (dec); sp/Harry McElroy Weissinger (dec); Ethel Powers Weissinger, Cary, MS; ed/BS, MS Univ for Wom, 1949; Grad Study: Univ of AL; Univ of MS; MS St Univ; pa/Clrm Tchr; cp/Pres, MS Soc Colonial Dames XVII Cent, 1977-79; Sr Pres 1974-80, Sr Chaplain 1978-81, MS River Soc Chd of Am Revolution; Libn, St Soc DAC, 1978-81; Libn, James McBride Chapt, DAC, 1981-85; 1st V Regent, Belvidere Chapt, DAR, 1980-83; Gov Thomas Welles Chapt, Colonial Dames XVII Cent, 1983-85; r/Rom Cath; hon/Wom of Achmt, BPW Clb, 1969; Dream Girl, Pi Kappa Alpha; Other Hons; W/W of Wom; Personalities of S; The Hereditary Register of US.

WELCH, FERN STEWART oc/Public Relations Consultant, Writer; b/Aug 13, 1934; h/7511 East Berridge Lane, Scottsdale, AZ 85253; ba/Phoenix, AZ; m/ Kenneth A; c/Joni Stewart Olsen, Susan Stewart Caldwell, John D Stewart; p/ Mrs E L DeMente Phoenix AZ; ed/AA, Phoenix Col, 1953; Att'd: AZ St Univ, 1965; Bellevue Commun Col, 1967; Lake Wash Commun Col, 1968; pa/ Writer, Reporter, Columnist, *Sammamish Val News*, Redmond, WA, 1967-71; Staff Writer, Asst Public Relats Dir, The 1st Nat Bk OR, Portland, 1971-72; Asst Public Relats Dir 1972-73, Public Relats Dir 1973-77, The AZ Bk, Phoenix; Fdr & Pres, Fern Stewart & Assoc, 1977-;

Mem: Nat & Phoenix Chapts, Public Relats Soc of Am; Intl Assn of Bus Commrs; Wom in Commun Inc; Arizonians for Cultural Devel; cp/Scottsdale Ctr for the Arts; Val Shakespearel; AZ Hist Soc; Friends of Channel 8 (PBS); Phoenix Country Clb & the Plaza Clb; Bd of Dirs, Ctl AZ & Maricopa Co Chapts, ARC; Bd of Dirs, Compas; Scottsdale Girls Clb; r/Presb; hon/ Author, Num Bus-related & Freelance Articles Pub'd in Maj Nat Newspapers & Mags Incl'g: *LA Times*; *Seattle Times*; *Am Bkr*; *Phoenix Mag*; *Wn Bkr*; *Entree Mag*; *AZ Living*; Others; Awds of Merit & Excel, Intl Assn Bus Commrs, 1975-77; Merit & Best of Indust Awds, Fin World, 1975; Awds for Excel in Public Relats Vol Efforts During Floods, ARC, 1980 & 1981; W/W in W.

WELLS, VALDA E oc/Management Services; b/Jun 23, 1935; h/36-19 Bowne Street, Flushing, NY 11354; ba/Flushing, NY; p/William F and Valda Baldwin Wells; ed/BA Ec, New Sch for Social Res, 1967; Addit Grad Studies; pa/Edit, Layout & Copy Editing, Subscription Fulfillment, w Prentice-Hall, Harcourt Brace & *Saturday Review*, 1964-67; Res Assoc Trade Policy 1967-73, Conslt Trade Policy Devel 1973-75, Mgr Intl Res Progs 1975-80, Gen Elect Co, NYC; Pres, Wellspring (Mgmt Consltg Co), NYC, 1980-; Co-Dir, CW Assocs (Mgmt Sers Co), NYC, 1983-; Mem: Nat Assn of Female Execs; Am Soc of Profl & Exec Wom; AAUW; Intl Platform Assn; Indep Citizens Res Foun; r/Presb; hon/Author & Co-Author Over 15 Articles Incl'g: "Polit & Mil Strategy in WW III," 1981; "Effect of Exch Rates on Dollar Valuation of World Exports," 1980; 'The Generalized Sys of Preferances," 1980; "Progress in Intl Trade Documentation," 1979; "Opports for the 1980's (Intl Trade Negotiations)," 1978; Others; W/W of Am Wom.

WELSCH, JAMES LESTER oc/Municipal Judge; b/Oct 2, 1917; h/707 North Frontier Street, Bloomfield, NM 87413; ba/Bloomfield, NM; m/Grace Warner; p/ W F Welsch (dec); sp/W F Warner (dec); ed/BS, Purdue Univ, 1942; MA, LA St Col, 1954; Addit Grad Study; mil/USN, US & PTO, 1942-46, Lt (JG); Korean Police Action, 1951-52, Lt; USNR, Lt; Cmdr, USNR Unit, Fairbanks, AK, 1949-50; Cmdr, US Coast Guard Aux, Farmington, NM, 1969-72; pa/Safety & Plant Protection Ofcr, Alumninum Co of Am, Lafayette, IN, 1940-42; Safety Mgr, Vigo Ordinance Plant, Esslinger-Misch Contracting Corp, Terre Haute, IN, 1942; Instr, Purdue Univ, W Lafayette, IN, 1940-42; Instr, DePauw Univ, Greencastle, IN, 1943; Br Mgr & Asst Secy Nat City Br, San Diego Pacific Title Co, San Diego, CA, 1946-49; Dir of Athletics & Hd of PE Dept, Univ of AK, 1949-50; Dir of Industl Relats Elects Div, The Nat Cash Register Co, Hawthorne, CA, 1952-55; Dir Industl Relats & Acting Prodn Mgr Mercast Mfg Corp La Verne 1955-56, Dir Industl Relats La Verne 1956-57, Plant Sers Mgr Sums Gyroscope Corp Santa Monica 1958, The Atlas Corp of NY; Safety Mgr, Kaise Aluminum & Chem Corp, Halethorpe, MD, 1956; Asst Prof Bus & Ec, En NM Univ, 1957-58; Asst Prof Industl Mgmt, CA Wn Univ, San Diego, CA, 1958-63; Prin, Chilchinbeto Day Sch, US Bur of Indian

Affairs, Chilchinbeta, AZ 1963-66; Sci Tchr, Hermosa Jr HS, Farmington, NM, 1966; Supt, Dolores Public Schs, Dolores, CO, 1967-68; Proj Dir, Montelores Multicultural Ctr, Cortez, CO, 1968-69; Asst Prin, Farmington HS, Farmington, NM, 1970-71; Real Est Salesman, Foutz Real Est, Farmington, NM, 1971-73; Asst Prin, Bloomfield HS, Bloomfield, NM, 1971-74; Realtor, Broker, Co-Owner, Realty 1, Bloomfield, NM, 1973-; Guid Cnslr, Dzilth-na-odith-hle Commun Sch, US Bur of Indian Affairs, Bloomfield, NM, 1974-76; Supvry Guid Cnslr, Huerfano Dorm, US Bur of Indian Affairs, 1976-80; Realty Spec, Rts Protection Jun Area Ofc 1980-81, & Supvry Realty Spec, AK Native Claims Settlement Act (ANCSA) Projs Ofc, Juneau Area Ofc, Anchorage, 1981-83; Mun Judge, Bloomfield, NM, 1984-; Mem: AK Chapt, Am Soc of Safety Engrs, 1982-; Mesa Verde Chapt, CO Pres 1979-80, Life Mem, Phi Delta Kappa; Nat Assn of Realtors Wash DC, 1971; Ed Com 1979-80, Realtors Assn of NM, Santa Fe, 1971-; San Juan Co Bd of Realtors, 1971-; NM Sch Admrs Assn, Santa Fe, 1971; NM Pers & Guid Assn, Albuquerque, 1974; cp/ Dir San Juan Co Chapt, ARC, 1980; Dir, San Juan Co Mus Assn, 1977-79; Dir, Bloomfield C of C, 1977-79; Spec Dpty Sheriff, San Juan Co, 1974-; Chm 74th Precinct, San Juan Co, Repub Party, 1973, 1974 & 1984; Mason; K Templar; OES; Nav Resv Assn; Ret'd Ofcrs Assn; Am Legion; VFW; Lions Clb; Rotary Intl; Kiwanis Intl; FFA; Rainbow for Girls; BSA; Num Other Commun Activs; r/Prot; hon/Var Pubs, "Industl Mgmt Ed-Present and Future"; *Col News & Views*; Cert of Ser, US Dept of Interior, 1983; Admiral, The TX Nav, St of TX, Galveston; Spec Act Awd, Navajo Areas, US Dept of Indian Affairs, Dept of Interior; Order of Red Cross of Constantine, St Sophia Conclave, NM; Others; W/W in W.

WELTERS, GWENDOLYN HEASTIE oc/Elementary Assistant Principal; b/Apr 30, 1924; h/2900 Northwest 50th Street, Miami, FL 33142; ba/Miami, FL; m/Warren W Sr; c/Bernard C, Martha A, Warren W III; p/Raymond C Heastie (dec); Lena H Heastie, Miami, FL; sp/ Peter and Martha Welters, Key West FL; ed/BS, FL A&M Col, 1943; MA, Columbia Univ, 1962; pa/Secy 1943-57, Elem Tchr 1957-59, Douglas Elem Sch; Elem Tchr 1959-63, Rdg Tchr 1963-65, Bethune Elem; Elem Tchr, W Lab Sch, 1965-68; PLATS Tchr, Johnson Elem, 1968-69; Elem Tchr, Olinda Elem, 1969-70; Rdg Tchr, Bright Elem, 1970-74; Adm Asst, Westview Elem, 1974-77; Mem: Past Mem, Basileus, Alpha Kappa Alpha, 1976-77; Nat Dir, Intl Trends & Sers 1982-84, Treas Gtr Miami Chapt 1978-81, The Links Inc; Local Chm, Alpha Kappa Alpha Nat Conv, 1974; Chm Wom's Activs, Alpha Phi Alpha Nat Conv, 1975; FL Assn of Sch Admrs; Assn for Supvn & Curric Devel; r/Cath; hon/25 Yr Soror 1976, Soror of Yr 1977, Alpha Kappa Alpha; W/W in S & SW.

WENBERG, BURNESS G oc/Professor; b/Jul 14, 1927; h/2608 Rockwood, East Lansing, MI 48823; ba/Lansing, MI; p/Mrs H L Wenberg, Beach, ND; ed/BS Dietetics & Home Ec, Univ of ND, 1949; MS Nutritional Ed, OH St Univ, 1957;

Cert Dietetic Intern, VA Hosp Hines, IL, 1949-50; pa/Assoc Prof & Coor Undergrad Dietetic Curric Dept of Food Sci & Human Nutrition, MI St Univ, E Lansing, 1973-; Assoc Prof & Dir Dietetic Intern Sch of Home Ec, Univ of WA, Seattle, 1970-72; Asst Prof Med Dietetics 1968-69, Asst Dir Sch of Allied Med Profs 1966-68, Asst Prof Med Dietetics 1961-66, Instr 1957-59, OH St Univ, Columbus; Asst Prof, SD St Col, Brookings, 1959-61; Tchr Cut Bk HS, Cut Bank, MT, 1954-56; Staff & Head Dietition, Kammehameha Schs, Honolulu, HI, 1952-54; Staff & Hd Dietitian, VA Hosp, LA, CA, 1950-52; Dietetics Conslt, Var Univs, Towns & Projs; Mem: Am, MI & Lansing Dietetic Assns; Am & MI Home Ecs Assns; Am Soc of Allied Hlth Profs; Am Ed Res Assn; Am Assn on Higher Ed; Nutrition Today Soc; Soc for Nutrition Ed; MI Public Hlth Assn; MI League for Human Sers; Secy 1963-65, Pres-elect & Pres 1965-67, Columbus (OH) Dietetic Assn; Secy, OH Dietetic Assn, 1968-70; Var Coms, Am Dietetic Assn; Var Coms, Am Diabetes Assn; Nutrition Com, MI Diabetes Assn, 1976-; Var Coms, MI Dietetic Assn; Other Commun Activs; Num Orgl Presentations; r/U Ch of Christ; hon/Author, *Intro to Hlth Professions*, 1972; *Dynamics of Clin Dietetics*, 1982; 2 Book Chapts & 4 Monographs; Over 10 Articles Pub'd in Profl Jours; Phi Upsilon Omicron, Univ of ND; Delta Kappa Gamma Awd for Outstg Grad Sr in Ed, Univ of ND, 1949; Phi Kappa Phi, MI St Univ, 1980.

WERNER, JANE BROOK oc/Tibetan Specialist, Asian Art Consultant; b/Oct 14, 1931; h/61 Grove Street, New York, NY 10014; ba/Same; m/Lobsang Nyima Aye; p/June McCallen, Bronxville, NY; sp/Wangchuk Dolma Aye (dec); pa/Asst Dir, YLHS India, 1963; Asst Dir, Am Emer Com for Tibetan Refugees, NY, 1962; Dir of Asian Dept ACEP, NY, 1968; Dir of Public Relats to His Holiness the Dalai Lama, Ofc of Tibet, NY, 1970; Fdr & Dir, Tibetan Cultural Inst, 1976-; Former Curator, Jacques Marchais Mus, SI, NY, 1972; Mus Conslt, Newark Mus, 1974; Christie's Spec in Tibetan & Himalayan Art, London, Paris, Brussels & Amsterdam, 1980; Mem: Appraiser's Assn of Am; Himalayan Coun of the Asia Soc, NY; r/Mahayana Buddhist; hon/Translations of Medieval Tibetan; Author, "An Hist Outline of the Sakyapa Sect," 1963; "The Jalsey Lalay of the Sakya Pandita," 1974.

WERT, JONATHAN MAXWELL JR oc/Management Consultant; b/Nov 8, 1939; h/916 Town Lane, Port Royal, PA 17082; ba/Harrisburg, PA; m/Monica Kay Manbeck; c/Jonathan Maxwell III, Kimberly Dee; p/Jonathan and Helen Wert, Port Royal, PA; sp/Miriam Manbeck, Mifflintown, PA; ed/BS 1966, MS 1968, Austin Peay St Univ; PhD, Univ of AL, 1974; mil/USMC, 1958-61; pa/ Energy Conslts Inc, 1983-; PA Dept of Commun Affairs, 1982-83; PA St Univ, 1977-81; Energy/Envir Conslt, 1975-77; TN Val Auth, 1971-75; Bays Mtn Pk, Envir Ctr, 1969-71; PA Dept of Forests & Waters, 1968-69; Mem: Num Profl Assns, Advy Couns & Coms; r/Luth; hon/Author, Over 40 Pubs on Envir Quality, Planning, Mgmt & Conserv; Am Motors Conserv Awd, 1976; W/W:

in World, in Am, in E, in S & SW; Men of Achmt; DIB; Commun Ldrs & Noteworthy Ams.

WESLEY, JANICE MARION oc/ Administrative Assistant; b/Mar 16, 1943; h/Middleburg Road, Liberty, KY 42539; ba/Camden, NJ; p/Charles E Wesley, Liberty, KY; ed/AA, Lindsey Wilson Jr Col, 1964; AB, En KY Univ, 1966; Att'd: Spalding Col 1973-78; Univ of L'ville 1979; Univ of KY 1980; pa/ Elem Tdchr, Liberty, 1962-68; Social Wkr, Liberty, 1968-78; Adm Asst, Watson Lumber Co Inc, 1978-79; Disaster Loan Asst, Mobile, AL, 1978-80; Asst Loan Ofcr & Documents Examr, NO, LA, 1980-81; Legal Documents Examr & Asst Loan Ofcr, Denver, CO, 1981-; Document Examr, Fargo, ND & Sioux Falls, 1982; Adm Asst, Respond Inc, Camden, NJ, 1982-83; cp/Wom's Repub Clb; VPres, Woms Clb of Ctl KY; Sierra Clb; Casey Co War Meml Hosp Aux; U Way; r/Meth.

WESLEY, THERESSA GUNNELS oc/ Writer, Director of Writing Lab; b/Sep 2, 1945; h/14508 Sara Lynn Drive, Little Rock, AR 72206; ba/Pine Bluff, AR; m/ John W; c/Dwayne, Rashida, Kameelah, Jameel, Crystal; p/Fred Gunnels, Morrilton, AR; Florence Gunnels (dec); sp/ Walter Wesley, Springfield, AR; Carries Wesley (dec); ed/BA, Philander Smith Col, 1962; MA, Kent St Univ, 1972; pa/ 9th & 10th Grades Eng Tchr, Springfield Public Schs, 1967-69; 7th & 10th Grades Eng Tchr, Pulaske Co Sch Sys, Little Rock, AR, 1969-70; Eng Instr, Univ of WI, 1972-74; Dir of Career Devel, Philander Smith Col, Little Rock, AR, 1975-78; Eng Tchr, Little Rock Public Schs, 1980-83; Writer, Dir of Writing Lab, Univ of AR-Pine Bluff, 1983-; cp/Zeta Phi Beta Sorority; 1st Bapt Ch-Highland Pk; r/Bapt; hon/ Author, *Black Am Writers Past & Present: A Biogl & Bibliogl Dir*, 1975; Outstg Ref Book, Select Co, of Am Lib Assn, 1975; Personalities of S & SW; 2000 Notable Ams; Book of Hon; Other Biogl Listings.

WEST, BILL GRAYUM oc/Professional Speaker; b/May 24, 1930; h/2138 Park Willow, Katy, TX 77450; ba/ Houston, TX; m/Ann; c/Jason; p/Mr and Mrs Kade West, Vernon, TX; sp/Mrs Dorthy Radnor, Houston, TX; ed/BA, 1951; ThD, 1957; pa/Pastor, 1st Bapt Ch, Alamulgee, 1958-65; Pastor, River Oaks Bapt Ch, Houston, 1965-72; Assoc Prof, Houston Bapt Univ, 1972-75; Profl Spkr, 1975-; Mem: Am Soc for Tng & Devel; Nat Spkrs Assn; hon/Author, 4 Books: *Free To Be Me*, 1971; *How To Survive Stress*, 1981; *Platform To Sucess*, 1982; *Successful Supvn Step By Step*, 1982; Over 100 Articles in Nat Pubs; W/W: in S & SW, in Fin & Indust; Intl Authors & Writers W/W.

WEST, DOROTHY ANNE oc/Speech Pathologist and Educational Consultant; b/Mar 21, 1936; h/976 Baird Drive, Baton Rouge, LA 70808; ba/Baton Rouge, LA; c/Jeffrey W Freeman; p/ Philip W West, Baton Rouge, LA; ed/ BS 1958, MEd 1973, LA St Univ; pa/ Spch & Hearing Therapist, St Helena Parish Schs, 1959-61; Asst to Dean of Wom, LA St Univ, 1961-66; Spch & Hearing Therapist, E Baton Rouge Parish Schs, 1966-82; Compliance Conslt & Spch Pathol/Ednl Conslt, E Baton Rouge Parish Schs, 1982-; Mem: Pres, Mortar Bd Alumnae Assn,

1960-62; Bd of Dirs, Diamondhead Commun Assn, 1980-81; Bd of Dirs 1978-82, Secy-Treas 1978 & 1979, Pres 1980, 1981 & 1982, Lakeside Villa Condominium Assn; Phi Delta Kappa; S'ship Chm 1965-69, Nom'g Com 1968-70, Povince IX Col Chm 1970-75, Awds Chm 1975-79, Gamma Zeta Chapt' Pledge Advr 1959-60, Advy Bd Chm 1960-61 & 1979-82, S'ship Advr 1978-79, Baton Rouge Alumnae Chapt Panhellenic Del 1969-70, Pres 1982-, Delta Gamma Frat; hon/Delta Gamma Cable Awd, 1980; Delta Gamma Foun Name Grant; Outstg Yg Wom of Am; W/W in S & SW; Commun Ldrs of Am; Other Biogl Listings.

WEST, EARL IRVIN oc/Minister, Teacher; b/May 18, 1920; h/722 North Payton Road, Indianapolis, IN 46219; c/ Robert Earl, Timothy Eugen; p/Tena West, Indianapolis, IN; ed/BA, George Pepperdine Col, 1943; MA 1945, BD 1948, ThM 1950, Butler Univ Sch of Rel; PhD, IN Univ, 1968; pa/Min, Franklin Rd Ch of Christ, Indianapolis, IN, 1957-; Tchr Harding Grad Sch of Rel, 1968-; r/Ch of Christ; hon/Author, *Life & Times of David Lipscomb*, 1953; *Search For Ancient Order* Vol I 1949, Vol II 1953 & Vol III, 1975; *Elder Ben Franklin: Eye of the Storm*, 1983; Apprec Dinner, By AL Christ Sch of Rel, 1983; Personalities of S.

WEST, JOHN C oc/Attorney; b/Aug 27, 1922; h/176 Mooring Buoy, Hilton Head Island, SC 29928; ba/Hilton Head Isl, SC; m/Lois Rhame; c/John Carl Jr, Douglas Allen, Shelton Simmons; ed/ BA, The Citadel, 1942; LLB, Univ of SC, 1948; mil/AUS, 1942-46, Maj; pa/Ptnr, Law Firm of West, Holland, Furman & Cooper, Camden, SC, 1947-70; Ptner, Law Firm of West, Cooper, Bowen, Beard & Smoot, Camden, SC, 1975-77; Law Firm, John C West, PA, Hilton Head Isl, SC, 1981-; Dist'd Prof of Med E Studies, Univ of SC, 1981; St Senator, St of SC, 1954-66; Lt Govr, St of SC, 1966-70; Gov, St of SC, 1971-75; Ambassador to Saudi Arabia, 1977-81; Mem: Phi Beta Kappa; Bd of Trustees, So Ctr for Intl Studies; Bd of Dirs, Donaldson, Lufkin & Jenrette; Bd of Dirs, Whittaker Corp; Bd of Dirs, Circle "S" Industs Inc; Bd of Dirs, Vinnell Corp; cp/Dem; r/Presb; hon/AUS Commend Medal; K Cmdr, Order of Mert, Fed Repub of Germany.

WEST, KENNETH LAFE oc/Alcohol and Drug Counselor; b/Aug 15, 1939; h/Box 446, Mackay, ID 83251; ba/Elko, NV; c/Jeri Diane; p/Mr and Mrs Lafe West (dec); ed/AA Elects, Col So ID, 1971; AA Cnslg, Otero Jr Col, 1979; Att'd ID St Univ-Pocatello; mil/AUS, 1957-58; mil/USAF, 1962-65; pa/Vol Probation/Parole Ofcr, Elko, NV; Alcohol/Drug Cnslr, 1983-; Owner, Wn Silver Inc, Mining Co; Owner/Ptner, Gen Mgr, Moonwalker Inc, 1981, 1983; Gen Mgr, Owner, Dir, Attitude Awareness Ctr, 1979-81; Secy, Moonwalker Foun, 1981-83; Probation Ofcr, Custer Co, ID, 1981; Newspaper Columnist, *The Post Register*; Guest Columnist, *ID St Jour*; cp/Am Legion; DAV; Lions Intl; Masonic Lodge #19 (Mackay, ID); Edr, ID St Univ, 1980-81; Host, Radio Show, KID Radio, Idaho Falls; Num Guest Appearances on KID-TW; hon/ Congl Nom to West Point, 1957; W/W in W.

WESTBROOK, VIRGINIA GRAY oc/Retired English Teacher; b/Jan 30, 1916; h/8116 Eastern Avenue Northwest, Washington, DC 20012; m/Fred E; c/Anita W McClendon, Fred E Jr; p/Lula Hammond Gray, Washington DC; sp/ Mr and Mrs A W Westbrook (dec); ed/ BA, Lane Col, 1938; MS 1956, Linguistic Spec 1963, TN St Univ; Adv'd Study, Univ of TN; pa/Eng & Music Tchr, Memphis & Shelby Co Bd of Ed, 1938-45; Eng Tchr, Bd of Ed, Nashville, TN, 1946-73; Mem: Secy, Chm Ed Com, 1974, AAUW; Bd Mem, Ed Ch, Dir 1980 Census Contest for DC Students, DC Leag of Wom Voters; Secy 1976, Ch Wom U; Life Mem, Anti Basileus, Reporter, Public Relats Chm, Chm Music Com, Alpha Kappa Alpha Sorority, 1944-; Spiritual Editor of Epistle Newslttr, Deaconess Bapt Ch; Focus Bd, Wide Horizon Support Grp for DC Schs; Vol Tutor in Eng Skills, Operation Rescue for DC Elem Pupils; r/ Christian-Bapt; hon/Author, Units (Unipacs) on Eng Grammar; Editorials; Poems; Outstg Contributions to Sorority, Xi Omega & Alpha Delta Omega Chapts, Alpha Kappa Alpha.

WESTERFIELD, WILLIAM (BO) A oc/University Professor and Administrator; b/Mar 1, 1947; h/376 Milagra Drive, Pacifica, CA 94044; ba/San Francisco, CA; p/Richard A and LaValle Slater Westerfield, Overlea, MD; ed/BA 1970, MA 1971, Univ of MD; PhD, Wayne St Univ, 1976; pa/Acting Chair Theatre Arts Dept 1983-, Assoc Prof 1974-, SF St Univ; Pres, BOWEST Talent & Modeling Agy, 1979-82; Mng Dir, Chd's Theatre Wing, Santa Rosa Sum Theatre, 1977; Exec Dir, No CA Chd's Theatre Fest, 1976 & 1977; Asst to Dir of Public Relats, Wayne St Univ, 1972-74; Other Previous Positions; Mem: URTA Fellow 1972-74, Mem 1968-, Am Theatre Assn; Gov Reg 8 1978-80, Mem-at-Large 1977-78, Nat Awds Com 1979 & 1984, Mem 1974-, Chd's Theatre Assn of Am; US Del to Intl Cong in Madrid 1978, Mem 1976-, (ASSITEJ) Intl Chd's Theatre Assn; cp/ Wk w Num Adult & Chd's Theatre Arts Progs & Orgs; r/Luth; hon/Assoc Editor, *Chd's Theatre Review*, 1980-; Author of Var Articles Pub'd in *Chd's Theatre Review*; Contbg Author, *How to Produce a Succesful Chd's Theatre Fest*, 1976; *Training the Actor for Participation Theatre*, 1977; *Emergence of An Americanized Form of Theatre-in-Ed*, 1977; Co-Author, *A Kidsum Night's Dream*; Hilberry F'ship, Wayne St Univ, 1972-74; Acting S'ship, Univ of SC, Sum 1968; Grant, Arts AK Artist-in Residence Prog, 1980; Others; W/W: in Am, in W; Outstg Yg Men of Am; Noteworthy Ams of Bicent Era; DIB.

WESTON, J FRED oc/Professor; b/ Feb 6, 1916; h/258 Tavistock, Los Angeles, CA 90049; ba/LA, CA; m/June Mildred; c/Kenneth F, Byron L, Ellen J; p/David and Bertha (Schwartz) Weston (dec); sp/Charles and Mildred Sherman (dec); ed/BA 1937, MBA 1942, PhD 1948, Univ of Chgo; mil/AUS, 1943-45; pa/Instr 1940-42, Asst Prof 1945-48, Sch of Bus, Univ of Chgo; Ec Conslt to Pres, Am Bkrs Assn, 1945-46; Prof Mgrl Ec & Fin, Grad Sch of Mgmt, Univ of CA-LA, 1949-; Mem: Pres, Am Fin Assn, 1966; Pres, Wn Ec Assn, 1960; Am Ec Assn; Econometric Soc; Am Statl Assn; Royal Ec Soc; Fin Analysts Soc;

Pres, Fin Mgmt Assn, 1980-81; r/Presb; hon/Author, Books: *Mgrl Fin*, 1981; *The Impact of Large Firms in the US Economy*, 1973; *Scope & Methodology of Fin*, 1968; *Essentials of Mgrl Fin*, 1979; *Intl Mgrl Fin*, 1972; *Fin Theory & Corp Policy*, 1979; Ford Foun Res F'ship, 1961-62; McKinsey Foun Grant, 1965-68; Gen Elect Foun Grant, 1972-82; Pres, Am Fin Assn, 1966; Pres, Wn Ec Assn, 1959-60; Pres, Fin Mgmt Assn, 1979-80; W/W in CA.

WESTOVER, DAVID ARTHUR oc/ Executive; b/Apr 13, 1950; h/Kingsbury Road, Walpole, NH 03608; ba/Keene, NH; m/Cynthia; c/Robert; p/Arthur Westover, Port St Lucie, FL; Edna Westover (dec); sp/Robert and May Graves, Walpole, NH; ed/BA Psych, Keene St Col, 1972; Cert'd Ins Cnslr, 1976; pa/Underwriter, Peerless Ins Co, 1972-75; Treas and Comml Accts Spec, Clark Ins Agy, 1975-; cp/Bd of Dirs, Big Brothers & Big Sisters Monadnock Reg; Bd of Dirs, Monadnock U Way; Bd of Dirs, Keene Day Care Ctr; Past Pres, Keene JCs; Past St Treas, NJ JCs; r/Luth; hon/NH JC of Yr, 1977; Clint Dunagan Meml Awd, US JCs, 1980; Outstg Yg Men of Am.

WETHINGTON, THOMAS DEWEY oc/Engineer; b/Dec 5, 1926; h/1305 Melmart Drive Bartlesville, OK 74003; ba/Bartlesville, OK; m/Jennevieve Laverne Rieke; c/Lynette Diane, Susan Marie, David Thomas, Karen Rae; p/ Herbert Omer and Jenny Marie Smith Wethington (dec); sp/Ray Enos and Esther G Schmidt Rieke (dec); ed/BSME, Univ of CO, 1950; MSEngrg, TX Tech Univ, 1971; mil/USAAF, 1945; pa/ Inspector, Cadillac Motor Div, Gen Motor Corp, Detroit, MI, 1950; Wholesale Clk, Crane-O-Fallon Co, Pueblo, CO, 1950-51; Time Study & Methods Engr, Gates Rubber Co, Denver, CO, 1951-57; Assoc Design Engr Waco, TX 1957, Assoc Design & Maintenance Engr 1958-60, Sr Mech Engr 1960-63, Chief Mech Engr 1963-72, Chief Maintenance Planner 1972-75, Maintenance & Sers Supt Borger, TX 1975-78, Phillips Petro Co, Phillips, TX; Prin Constrn Planning Engr, Philips Petro Co, Bartlesville, OK, 1978-; ASME, 1949-51; AIIE, 1954-57; Bartlesville Engrs Clb, 1981-82; cp/Dir, VPres & Pres, Borger JC's, 1958-62; Borger C of C, 1972-78; Co Conv Del, Dem Party, 1958-72; St Conv Del, Repub Party, 1976; CoChm Pubs & Recogs Coms, TX Tech Dad's Assn, 1972-82; Bartlesville Geneal Soc, 1981-82; Com Mem to Estab Voc Tech Sch, Pt-time Fluid Mechs Instr 1972-76, Frank Phillips Jr Col r/Prot; hon/W/W in S & SW.

WEWER, DEE J oc/Executive; b/Apr 27, 1948; h/0226 Kings Row, Carbondale, CO 81623; ba/Aspen, CO; m/Ira E Litke; p/Gene and Juanita Wewer, San Antonio, TX; sp/Mae Litke, Miami, FL; ed/BS, Univ of So MS, 1969; MA, Am Univ, 1974; Doct Wk, Georgetown Univ, 1981-82; PhD Cand, The Union Univ; pa/Employee w Dixie Press, Biloxi, MS, 1968-70; Tchr, St Martin Public Sch, Biloxi, 1970; Editor, Newspaper of Nat War Col, Ft McNair, Wash DC, 1971-73; Press & Scheduling Assoc & Coor, Nat Fedn St Chm, Ofc of Chm, Repub Nat Com, Wash DC, 1972-73; Conslt, Nat Wom's Ed Fund, Nat Wom's Polit Caucus, 1973-74; Gen Mgr, Treas, Printing Sers Unltd, Wash DC, 1975;

Instr, Inst of Polits, Harvard Univ, Boston, 1976; Media Dir/Prodn, Mgr/Creat Grp Hd, Bailey, Deardourff & Assocs, Wash DC, 1975-76; Dir Mktg/Acct Supvr, Weitzman & Assocs, Wash DC, 1976-78; Dir Mktg, Britches of Georgetown, Wash DC, 1978-79; Instr, Col of Bus Mgmt, Univ of MD, Col Pk, 1980-; VPres Public Affairs, AMF Hd Sports Wear, Columbia, MD, 1979-81; Exec VPres, Sport-Obermeyer, Aspen, CO, 1982-; Conslt in Field; Mem: Ski Industs of Am; Wom in Advtg & Mktg; Am Wom in Radio & TV; Am Mgmt Assn; Advtg Clb; Art Dirs Clb; NOW; hon/Author of Poems Pub'd in *Am Poet's Anthology*; Recip, Creat Design Distn, Andy, Printing Industs Am, 1981; Dist Merit Awd, Advtg Clb of NY, 1980; Arts Dirs Clb of Met, Wash DC, 1980; Cleo Awds, 1979; Outstg Wkg Wom, *Glamour Mag*, 1978; Nat Newspaper Nat Creat Awd, 1974; W/W: of Am Wom, in W.

WHEELER, BEVERLY GAIL oc/Medical Doctor, Psychiatrist; b/Jul 15, 1952; h/2552 Madison Road #4, Cincinnati, OH 45208; ba/Cincinnati, OH; p/Mr and Mrs Jesse L Wheeler, Springfield, VA; ed/BS, Emory Univ, 1974; MD, Med Col of VA, 1978; Postgrad Med Tng in Psychi 1978-82, F'ship in Geriatric Psychi 1982-84, Univ of Cinc Med Ctr; pa/Admitting Psych, Rollman's Psychi Inst, 1980-; Adj Clin Instr, Dept of Psychi 1982-83, F'ship in Geriatric Psychi Dept of Psychi 1982-84, Univ of Cin Med Ctr; Staff Psychi in Conslt Liaison Psychi, Cinc VA Hosp, 1982-83; Mem: AMA; Am Med Wom's Assn; Am Psychi Assn; OH Psychi Assn; Cinc Acad of Med; Assn for Advmt of Psychi; r/Presb; hon/Phi Sigma Hon Soc for Biol Res, 1973; Hon Res in Biol, Emory Univ, 1973-74; Upjohn Achmt Awd for Most Outstg Intern, Univ of Cinc Med Ctr, 1979; Chief Resident in Psychi, Univ of Cinc Hosp, 1982; W/W in Am Wom.

WHEELOCK, SHARON MARIE oc/Newspaper Publisher; b/Jun 23, 1938; h/Box 134, Hyannis, NE 69350; ba/Hyannis, NE; c/Robyn Reneé, James Sidney, Londa Sue, Chris Marie, Lance Michael; p/Milton D Thomas, Englewood, CA; Lois Mae (Jone) Thomas Mansfield, No Platte, NE; ed/PublicSchs in Denver, CO & Hyannis, NE; pa/Writer 1957, Chief Reporter 1962, Mgr & Editor 1974, Owner, Pubr & Editor, 1976-, Grnat Co News; Mem: NE Writers Guild; Nat Fedn of Press Wom; NE Pres Assn; Intl Clover Poetry Assn; Soc of Am Poets Sigma Delta Chi; r/Bapt; hon/Author of Wkly Newspaper Column, "Sass & Sentiments"; Poetry Pub'd in *Clover Collections & Verse; 20th Cent Poets & Their Poems*; 3rd Prize, Clover Poetry Contest; W/W of Am Wom.

WHELAN, PAUL ANDREW oc/Clinical Psychologist; b/Dec 12, 1943; h/PO Box 592, Monticello, IN 47960; ba/Monticello, IN; m/Karen Mary Hammill; p/Alden and Lucille Whelan (dec); sp/Frank and Margaret Hammill, Kalamazoo, MI; ed/BA, Lawrence Univ, 1966; MA, Wn MI Univ, 1969; PhD, Univ of UT, 1974; pa/Parole Agt, Dept of Corrections, Milwaukee, WI, 1966-67; Asst Prof, Buffalo St Col, Buffalo, NY, 1973-76; Dir Clin Psych, Smoky Mtn Area Mtl Hlth Ctr, Bryson City, NC, 1976-82; Dir Clin Psych, Carroll-White Mtl Hlth Ctr, Monticello,

IN, 1982-; Mem: Bd of Dirs, Autistic Soc of Wn NY, 1974-75; Bd of Dirs, IN Psych Assn Polit Action Com, 1982; cp/Chm, Commun Schs Com, 1976-82; Swain Co/Bryson City Planning Bd, 1980-82; Bd of Dirs, Tecumseh Area Planned Parenthood, 1982; Pres, Bryson City Rotary Clb, 1981; r/Meth; hon/Phi Kappa Phi, 1973; Outstg Edrs of Am; W/W in S & SW.

WHIPPLE, CAROL OWEN oc/Ranching and Business Consultant; b/Apr 11, 1940; h/Route 2, Box 370 Canyon, TX 79015; ba/Amarillo, TX; m/Gordon; c/Laura, Randall, Katherine; p/Wiley Ducoe Owen (dec); Mrs W D Owen, Amarillo, TX; sp/Floyd Whipple (dec); Mrs Floyd Whipple, Waynoka, OK; ed/Undergrad Wk: Univ of AZ & W TX St Univ; pa/Owner-Operator, Creekwood Ranch (Horses & Cattle), 1960-; Corp Dir 1976-78, Corp Secy 1978-80, OK Stud Inc (Horsebreeding), Purcell, OK; Corp Secy 1975-79, Pres 1979-, Rowel Inc (Small Comml Bldgs & Property Mgmt); Owner & Operator, A New Idea Furniture Leasing, 1979-80; Pres, Sun Tans Unltd Inc, 1979-81; Ptnr, Whipple Assocs (Bus & Mgmt Consltg Ser), 1981-; Mem: Nat Assn of Female Execs; Am Soc of Profl & Exec Wom; Intl Entreprenuer Assn; Fedn of Indep Bus; Am Qtr Horse Assn; Appaloosa Horse Clb Inc; cp/Kappa Alpha Theta; Pres, Amarillo Girl Scout Coun, 1974-84; r/Presb; hon/Thanks Badge, Highest Hon Given Vols by GSA, 1978; W/W of Am Wom; World W/W of Wom.

WHITE, CALVIN EDDY oc/Research Animal Scientist; b/Jul 17, 1943; h/Route 2, Box 2280, Live Oak, FL 32060; ba/Live Oak, FL; m/Patricia Parker; c/Emily Elizabeth; p/James A White Sr, Scott, AR; ed/BS 1970, MS 1972, PhD 1978, Univ of AR; mil/USAF, 1961-65; Capt, USAR; pa/Res Animal Sci, Univ of FL, IFAS—AREC, Live Oak, 1978-; Grad Asst, Univ of AR, Fayetteville, AR, 1975-78; Ecologist II, AR Dept of Pollution Control & Ecol, Little Rock, AR, 1972-75; Mem: Am Soc of Animal Sci; Sigma Xi; Gamma Sigma Delta; r/Ch of Christ; hon/Author, Num Sci Articles Pub'd in Profl Jours & Num Experiment Reports; Var Pop Articles; Contbg Author, Chapt in Toxicological Textbook; Pres Outstg Unit Awd, 1963; AUS Commend Medal, 1983; Nat Def Ser Medal, 1965.

WHITE, GERALD E oc/Safety-Health Manager; b/Sept 1, 1923; h/1 Hearthstone Drive Reading, PA 19606; ba/Boyertown, PA; m/Betty A; c/Barry Lee, Nancy Jean; p/LeRoy J and Miriam White, Shillington, PA; ed/BS Chem, Albright Col, 1948; Postgrad, Temple Univ, 1954; Participant Textile Machine Wks Coop Prog, WY Polytech Inst, 1946; mil/AUS, 1943-46, ETO; pa/Chem, Foreman Safety Engr, Safety-Hlth Mgr, Beryllium Corp & Succesor Firms: Kaweck Berylco Indust Inc & Divof Cabot Corp, Reading, PA; Mem: Am Soc of Safety Engrs; Nat Safety Coun; Bekrs Co Mfg Assn Safety-Hlth Grp; cp/Advy Bd, Hawk Mtn BSA, 1960-; Bd of Dir 1968-, Pres 1975-81, Hope Rescue Mission; Bd of Dirs 1954-58, St Safety Chm 1956, Jr C of C; Pres, James U Ch of Christ, 1980-82; Other Commun Activs; r/Prot; hon/Recip, Commun Ser Cit, PA Acad of Opthol & Otolaryngology,

1967.

WHITE, IRMA REED oc/Librarian Assistant for International Law Firm; h/4000 Massachusetts Avenue Northwest, Apartment 331, Washington, DC; ba/Washington, DC; m/Wilford L (dec); p/Eustace Glen and Martha Soper Reed (dec); ed/BA, Univ of CP, 1919; pa/Eng Instr, Univ of CO, 1922-24; Report Writing Instr, Harvard Sch of Bus Adm, 1926-28; Asst Chief Field Sect, Edit Rationed Foods Lttr, Ofc Price Adm, 1943-47; Public Info Spec, Bur of Census & Ofc Secy of Commerce, 1958-71; Dir Press Room, Cost of Living Coun, 1971-74; Libn Asst, Mayer, Brown & Platt, 1975-; Mem: Nat Press Clb; Nat Leag of Am Pen Wom; Am News Wom's Clb; Intl Coun Smal Bus; hon/Author, "Do You Know Your Economic ABC's?," Dept of Commerce Best Seller Series; Articles Pub'd in: *Am Heritage; Ency Brittanica; Ency Americana; Christian Sci Monitor; London Times*; Awd for Outstg Achm, Ofc Price Adm, 1945; Meritious Ser Awd, Bur of Census, 1959; Silver Medal for Dist'd Ser, 1964; Awd for Creat Commun, Dept of Commerce, 1965; 3 Awds for Excell in Commun, Fed Edits Assn, 1965, 1966, 1970; Cert of Merit, Patent Law Assn of SF, 1966; Nat Achmt Awd, Nat Leag of Am Pen Wom, 1966; Outstg Ser Awd, Cost of Living Coun, 1972, 1973; Public Ser Awd, Small Bus Adm, 1978; Intl Coun Small Bus, 1978; W/W: of Am Wom, in E; World W/W of Wom; DIB; 2000 Wom of Achmt.

WHITE, JACK LESLIE III oc/Executive; b/Mar 4, 1948; h/2202 Surrey Lane, Bossier City, LA 71111; ba/Bossier City, LA; m/Joanne Marie; c/Jocelyn Marie; p/Ellen Mae White, Republic, PA; sp/John Russi, Brownsville, PA; ed/BS, Cornell Univ, 1970; MA, Bowling Green St Univ, 1974; MA, Harvard Univ, 1980; mil/USAR, 1966-71, 1st Lt; pa/Salesman 1970-72, Sales Mgr 1972-74, Fin Analyst 1974-76, W R Grace & Co; Dir of Mktg, Bird & Son Inc, 1976-80; VPres Mktg & Sales, McElroy Metal Mills Inc, 1980-; Mem: Am Mgmt Assm, 1976-; AMBA, 1974; Bd of Dir, Quadco, Boston, MA, 1980-; Bd of Dirs, Expansil Inc, NYC, 1981-; Planning Execs of Am, 1979-; cp/Diplomat, Shreveport C of C; r/Rom Cath; hon/Author of Num Articles Pub'd in: *Metal Bldg News; Farm Bldg News; Am Economist*; Var Local Newspapers & Reg Trade Pubs; Top 10 Outstg Ldrs in Metal Bldg Indust, 1981; W/W in Am.

WHITE, LAWANDA JEANNE oc/Animal Control Officer and Pound Master; b/Jan 18, 1945; h/Route 10, Box 73 Claremore, OK 74017; ba/Claremore, OK; m/Stanley R; c/Kimberley Gail Engel, Keith Robert Engel, Karl Gorden Engel; p/Calvin Edwards, Jay, OK; Jessie M Phillips (dec); sp/Mr and Mrs George White, Vinita, OK; ed/Cake Decorating & Baking & Adv'd Sewing, Kirkwood Col, Cedar Rapids, IA; pa/Collins Radio & Gen Mdse Mgr, Warehouse Mkt, Cedar Rapids, IA; Newspaper Columnist, Mays Co, OK; Cake Decorator, Tiffney's Bakery, Tulsa, OK; Cake Decorator, Warehouse Mkt, Claremore, OK; Baker & Cake Decorator, Safeway Bakery, Claremore, OK; Pound Master, Police Dept, Claremore, OK; Mem: Humane Soc, Rogers Co, 1981; Am Kennel Clb, 1983; Assem of

God Ch, 1979; r/Prot.

WHITE, LOUISE HUMPHRIES oc/
Writer and Publisher; b/Mar 30, 1926;
h/3286 Wetherbyrne Road, Kennesaw,
GA 30144; ba/Kennesaw, GA; m/Verlin
Ralph; c/Carol L W Kelly, V Ralph Jr;
p/Ernest Christ and Mary Elder Humph-
ries (dec); sp/Guy L White (dec); Gladys
Hefley White, Prague, OK; ed/BA Eng,
Centenary Col of LA, 1962; MEd Cnslg,
GA St Univ, 1971; pa/Employmnt Cnslr,
Yt Opport Ctr, LA St Employmnt Ser,
1965-68; Master Cnslr GA St Bur of
Employmnt Security, Dept of Labor,
1968-78; Owner, Cnslg Assocs Profl
Ofc; Atlanta, GA, 1978-80; Writer &
Pubr of Hist Pubs, Archive Press,
Kennesaw, 1982-; cp/Treas 1980-83,
Kennesaw Hist Soc; GA Trust for Hist
Presv; Northside Wom's Clb; Chm Arts
Dept, GEWC, 1979-80; Daughs of King,
Cathedral of St Philip Epis Ch; hon/
Writer & Pubr of Book on Early Hist
of Kennesaw GA & Its Fdrs; Jongleurs
Dramatic Awd, Shreveport, LA, 1962;
US Cath Conf for Selfish Devotion to
Resettlement of Indo-Chinese Refu-
gees, 1975-77; W/W in S & SE; DIB.

WHITE, MARGARET ELIZABETH
oc/Insurance Agent; b/Dec 23, 1920; h/
4305 Pensacola Court, Dallas, TX
75211; ba/Dallas, TX; m/Femme Sole;
p/Russel Worley White (dec); Margaret
McGaha White, Dallas, TX; ed/Dipl,
Metro Bus Col, 1940; Cert of Achmt,
Dallas Col of So Meth Univ, 1955, 1956;
Cert of Achmt, El Centro Commun Col,
1973; pa/Secy-Ins Solicitor,
Cairns-Blakeley & Co, Dallas, TX,
1959-62; Ins Agt, Asst to Pres, Gen
Aviation Underwriting Corp, Dallas,
TX, 1936-64; Sole Owner & Agt, Fire
& Casualty/Personal, Margaret E White
Ins Co, 1964-; Ofcr Mgr, Asa Hunt Inc,
Dallas, TX, 1978-82; Mem: Pres, SW
BPW Clbs, 1977-78; Chm Hallmark Art
Contest, Dallas Fdn of Wom's Clbs,
1970-71; Former Mem: Zeta Gamma
Chi; Beta Sigma Phi; Dallas Assn of Ins
Wom; cp/Pres, Wom's C of C, Dallas,
1967-68; Spec Advr, Dallas Public Lib
Lrng Prog, "Remembering and Writ-
ing," 1980; Dallas Comm on Status of
Wom, 1979; VPres, Cliff Hills Repub
Wom's Clb, 1979; Charter Mem,
Kessler Pk Repub Wom's Clb, 1983; Oak
Cliff Soc of Fine Arts; Oak Cliff C of
C, Dallas; Meth Hosps of Dallas "Life-
line"; Dallas Coun on World Affairs
Wom's Grp; Sponsor, Lone Star Coun
of Camp Fire Girls Inc, Dallas, 1981; r/
Meth; hon/Wom of Yr, SW BPW Clb,
Dallas, 1978; W/W of Am Wom.

WHITE, ROBERT EDWARD oc/
Manager & Supervisor; b/Nov 27, 1928;
h/7614 Southwest 7th Place, North
Lauderdale, FL 33068; ba/Ft Lauderdale,
FL; m/Betty Lucille Tice; c/Walter Reed,
Robert E; p/Francis Wheaton White
(dec); Katherine Rankin Rowton White
Smith, N Lauderdale, FL; sp/Glen
Aldrich and Ethel Lawrence Rumery
Tice (dec); ed/USAF Sr NCO Acad,
1960; Courses in Mgmt & Elects, Dept
of Def; Radio Communs Technol,
Commun Col of the AF, l977; Minicom-
puter & Microprocessor Technol,
Capitol Radio Engrg Inst, 1982; mil/
USAF, 1946-77, Ret'd Chief Master Sgt;
pa/Var Positions as Elects Tech & Shop
Supvr 1946-56, Sr Tech Advr Directo-
rate of Sys Eval, HQ's of AF Communs
Ser 1966-77, USAF; Sr Engr, Harris

Corp R F Commun Div, Rochester, NY,
1977-78; Mgr/Supvr, OKI Elects of Am
Inc, 1978-; Mem: IEEE, 1977-; Armed
Forces Communs & Elects Assn, 1976-;
VFW, 1979-; AF Sgts Assn, 1974-; NCO
Assn, 1977-; cp/Treas, Palm Bch Soc of
Am Inventors, 1982; r/Prot; hon/Patent:
Co-Inventor "Improvements in & Relat-
ing to Teleprinter Apparatus"; Bronze
Star Medal, 1972; Meritorious Ser
Medal w OLC, 1972, 1977; W/W: in S
& SW, in Aviation & Aerospace.

WHITEHAIR, CHESTER LOUIS oc/
Aerospace Engineering Executive; b/Jan
28, 1936; h/8681 Shannon River Circle,
Fountain Valley, CA 92708; ba/El
Segundo, CA; m/Mary Kathryn Hors-
ney; c/Anne Michele, Robert Scott; p/
Berry Morgan Whitehair, St Peters-
berg, FL; Margaret Beatrice (Fairfax)
Whitehair, San Leandro, CA; sp/
Andrew Jr and Anna Teresa (Stydahar)
Horsney; ed/BS Aeronaut Engrg, Univ
of WV-Morgantown, 1959; Addit Engrg
& Mgmt Study: Univ of CA-LA, Pep-
perdine Univ, The Aerospace Corp; mil/
USMCR, E4, 1956-62; pa/Mech
Designer, Whitehair's Machine Shop,
Clarksburg, WV, 1956-59; Instr Air-
craft Detail Design, WV Univ-
Morgantown, 1958-59; Missile Propul-
son Design Engr (Thor, Sky Bolt & Nike
Zeus), Douglas Aircraft Co, Santa
Monica, CA, 1959-62; Designer 1st
Semi-submerged Solid Rocket Nozzle
for Skybolt, 1960; Chief Design Engr
Metals Div, SuperTemp Corp, Santa Fe
Springs, CA, 1962-63; Var Tech &
Mgmt Positions, Space Launch Vehi-
cles, The Aerospace Corp 1963-78, Prin
Dir of Intertial Upper Stage 1978-, El
Segundo, CA; Advr, USAF Space Div
on Titan III Space Launch Vehicle, 1963-
73 & Space Shuttle Inertial Upper Stage
1973-; Mem: AIAA, 1959-; AF Assn,
1984; cp/Repub; r/Rom Cath; hon/
Author of The Aerospace Corp Report
"Titan IIIC SSLV-5 # 12 Payload Fairing
Failure Report," 1969; Lucy Bailey
S'ship, 1954; Am Legion Student
Ldrship Awd, 1954; Inst of Aeronaut
Scis Best Student Paper Awd, 1959;
USAF Sys Command Outstg Achmt
Awd, 1966; USAF Commend Lttrs,
1975, 1978, 1980, 1981 & 1982; W/W:
in W, in Aviation & Aerospace.

**WHITELEY, MARILYNN MAX-
WELL** oc/Educator; b/Apr 17, 1929; h/
971 Linden Hall Road, Chattanooga, TN
37415; ba/Chattanooga, TN; m/William
K Whitley (dec); c/Margaret K, Janet W
Sullivan, Kenneth M; p/M W Maxwell,
Greenville, NC; Thelma M Maxwell
(dec); sp/Kenneth F Whiteley (dec); Jean
E Whiteley, Greenville, NC; ed/BS, E
Carolina Univ, 1949; MEd 1975, EdD
1981, Univ of TN; pa/Tchr, S Edge-
combe HS, Tarboro, NC, 1949-51; Tchr,
Chattanooga & Hamilton Co Schs,
1966-74; Rdg Spec in Fed Progs, Chat-
tanooga Public Schs, 1974-; Adj Prof in
Curric & Instrn, Univ of TN-
Chattanooga, 1980-; Mem: Phi Delta
Kappa; Delta Kappa Gamma; IRA;
NCTE; Assn for Supvn & Curric Devel;
AAUW; U Tchg Prof; r/Meth; hon/
Author, "A Semantic Description of
Selected 1st Grade Basal Rdg Textbooks
Using Case Grammar," 1981; Alpha
Chapt S'ship, Delta Kappa Gamma,
1975; Sabbatical Leave, 1978-79; W/W:
in S & SW, in Chattanooga.

WHITEMAN, BETTY B oc/Retired

Teacher, Museum Attendant; b/Jun 2,
1914; h/Box 218 Richey, MT 59259; m/
George D (dec); c/Dewey Dean, Peggy
Louise W Ganzeveld, Sharon Elizabeth
W Canfield, Janice K W Louser; ed/
Grad, St Normal Sch, 1937; Elem Life
Cert, 1942; BS, Wn MT Col, 1976; pa/
Tchr, Richland & Dawson Cos, MT,
1933-42 & 1955-57; Tchr, Richey Elem
Sch, 1950-54 & 1957-78; Collector of
Info & Photos of Area Homesteaders
for, Mus Archives, Richey; cp/
Secy-Treas, Richey Hist Soc, 1970-84;
Treas, Richey Hlth Ctr, 1975-79; VPres,
Richey Sr Citizens, 1980-84; Chaplain
1978-80, VPres 1980-83, Am Legion
Aux; Secy, U Meth Ch, 1981-84; r/
Meth; hon/Author, Honyacker's Heritage-
A Hist of Richey, MT, 1981; Richey's
Outstg Citizen, 1974-75; Runner-up
1979, Cand 1980, (DIANA) Dist'd Intl
Acad of Noble Achmt; W/W: of Wom,
of Intells.

WHITFIELD, BRIAN THOMAS oc/
Chiropractor; b/Jul 9, 1952; h/13 Chapel
Hill Drive, Plymouth, MA 02360; ba/
Plymouth, MA; p/Frederick Arthur
Whitfield, Eufaula, OK; Phyllis Inez
Whitfield, San Diego, CA; ed/BS, 1981;
Doct of Chiro, 1981; pa/Section Player,
Fresno Philharm, 1974-78; Doct of
Chiro, 1981-; Mem: Linus Pauling Inst,
1979-; MA Chiro Soc, 1982; Am Chiro
Assn, 1982; cp/Class Pres 1978-81;
Delta Tau Alpha, 1979-81; Pres 1981,
Mem 1978-81, Toastmaster Intl; Ply-
mouth C of C, 1982; r/Christian; hon/
Band Am Awd in Art, 1970; Class Pres
Plaque, 1981; Outstg Student Awd,
1981; Clin Lecture Series, 1981; W/W:
Among Am HS Students, Among Am
Cols & Univs.

WHITLEY, ONA RUTH oc/Retired
Emeritus Bacteriologist; b/Dec 6, 1898;
h/1000 East Franklin Street, Monroe,
NC 28110; p/Amis David N and Eliza-
beth (Belle) Whitley (dec); ed/BA,
Queens Col, 1920; AB 1924, Postgrad
Study in Botany 1926-27, Univ of
NC-Chapel Hill; MSc, Sch of Hygiene
& Public Hlth, Johns Hopkins Univ,
1934; pa/HS Sci Tchr, 1920-23; Hd Sci
Dept, Chapel Hill HS, 1924-29; Botany
& Biol Instr, Univ of NC-Chapel Hill,
Sums 1924-27; Asst Bacteriologist,
Cultural Lab, MD St Dept of Hlth,
1930-36; Assoc Bacteriologist &
Bacteriologist-in-charge, St Br Lab,
Hagerstown, MD, 1936-39; Sr Bacteri-
ologist & Mycologist, Montgomery, AL,
1942-46; Sr Bacteriologist & Mycolo-
gist, Dir of Diphtheria & Mycology
Labs, IN St Bd of Hlth, Indianapolis, IN,
1946-61; Mem: Secy & Treas IN Br
1952-54, Soc of Am Bacteriologists; NY
Acad of Sci; AAAS; APHA; Fellow,
Royal Soc of Hlth; cp/Wom's Rotary Clb
of Indianapolis; hon/Author of Var
Articles Pub'd in Profl Jours Incl'g: Jour
of Sab & Clin Med, 1934 & 1935; Am Jour
of Hygiene, 1936; Public Hlth Reports, 1949;
Gold Medal in NC St Spelling Contest,
Davidson Col, 1916; Rep Queen's Col,
at Inauguration of Russel J Humbert as
Pres of DePauw Univ, Greencastle, IN,
1952; Cit, IN St Bd of Hlth, 1961; Rep
Univ of NC-Chapel Hill, at Inaugura-
tion of Thomas E Corts as Pres of
Wingate Col, 1974; Outstg Alumna
Awd, Queen's Col, 1975; Hon Fellow,
Anglo-Am Acad of Cambridge, Eng-
land, 1980; W/W: in S & SW, in MW,
of Am Wom, of Intells; Ldrs in Am Sci;

NC Lives; DIB; Notable Ams of Bicent Era; Men & Wom of Distn; Num Other Biogl Listings.

WHITLOCK, RUTH H S oc/Professor, Choral Music Educator; b/May 10, 1934; h/2712 6th Avenue, Fort Worth, TX 76110; ba/Ft Worth, TX; m/Robert Edward; c/Karen W Williams, Robert Edward III, Harold McIntosh Summers; p/Harold G Hendricks (dec); Lucile McKee Hendricks, McAllen, TX; sp/R E Whitlock (dec); Mrs R E Whitlock, Austin, TX; ed/BA, Newcomb Col of Tulane Univ, 1955; MA, Occidental Col, 1970; PhD, N TX St Univ, 1981; pa/TX Choral Music Tchr: Georgetown ISD, 1955-58; Austin ISD, 1958-59; Edinburg Co ISD, 1959-67; McAllen ISD, 1970-72; Carrollton-Farmers Br ISD 1972-73; Assoc Prof Choral Music Ed, N TX St Univ, 1973-; Mem: Kappa Alpha Theta; Music Edrs Nat Conf; TX Music Edrs Conf; TX Music Edrs Assn; Am Choral Dirs Assn; TX Choral Dirs Assn; Mu Phi Epsilon; r/Epis; hon/Author, *Choral Insights* Gen Edition & Renaissance Edition, 1982; Var Articles Pub'd in Profl Jours; Theodore Presser S'ship, 1953; Alpha Sigma Sigma, 1953; Outstg Fac Awd, 1980; Mu Phi Epsilon Doct Grant, 1980; Pi Kappa Lambda, 1979; W/W: in Am Univs & Cols, in Am, in Music; TX Wom of Distn.

WHITNEY, MYRNA-LYNNE oc/ Integrated Logistics Support Engineer; ba/Canoga Park, CA; m/Richard Abbott; p/Edmund and Sylvia Prasloski, Ventura, CA; ed/BA, CA St Univ-Northridge, 1971; MS, Ctl MO St Univ, 1975; mil/USAF, 1971-74; USAFR, Maj, 1975-; pa/Secy 1962-69, Methods & Procedures Analyst 1976-77, Envir Hlth & Safety Engr 1977-79, Sys Safety Engr 1979-81, Integrated Logistics Support Engr 1981-, Rocketdyne, Rockwell Intl, Canoga Pk, CA; Mem: Am Soc of Safety Engrs; Sys Safety Soc; Phi Kappa Phi; Resv Ofcrs Assn; r/Rel Sci; hon/Meritorious Ser Medal, USAF, 1974; 1st OLC to Meritorious Ser Medal, 1984; W/W: in W, in Am.

WHITNEY, VIRGINIA K oc/Educator; b/Feb 6, 1927; h/502 Orchard St, Aztec, NM 87410; c/Barbara Peterson, James Thomas; p/Clare V Koogler, Aztec, NM; ed/BS 1959, MEd 1965, Adams St Col; pa/Sci Tchr 1959-62, Libn 1962-, K Jr HS, Aztec, NM; Mem: Pres, NM Sch Libns, 1972-73; Pres, NM Media Assn, 1982-; NM St Legis Com, NEA, 1973-79; St Pres, Kappa Kappa Iota Ednl Sorority, 1962-65; cp/St Ctl Com 4 Yrs, Del to Nat Conv 1984, Repub Party; Pres, San Juan Co Repub Wom, 1984; r/Meth; hon/Author, *Wom in Ed in NM*, 1977; *Koogler Fam of VA*, 1969; Westinghouse Sci S'ship, 1944; Fellow, NM Acad of Sci, 1973; Delta Kappa Gamma St Awd, 1982; W/W: of Am Wom, in Polits; DIB; Other Biogl Listings.

WHITTEMORE, EDWARD WILLIAM oc/Executive; b/Dec 25, 1922; h/ 22 Flying Cloud Road, Dolphin Cove, Stamford, CT 06092; ba/New York, NY; m/Jeanne McConnochie; c/Edward William Jr, Jeannette L; p/Harold Clifton Whittemore (dec); Florence Veronica (Stratton) Whitemore; ed/BA, Columbia Col, Columbia Univ, 1947; mil/ USAF, 1943-45; pa/Var Positions 1947-72, Exec VPres 1970-72, Wilson

Jones Co, Chgo; Exec VPres 1972-75, Pres & COO 1975-77, Pres & CEO 1977-78, Swingline Inc, NYC; Dir 1977-, VPres Sub Adm 1978-79, Exec VPres Opers 1979-80, Chm & CEO 1981-, Am Brands Inc, NYC; Mem: Chm Res Com 1968-70, VPres & Chm Mfrs Div 1969-70, Nat Ofc Prods Assn; Dir, Wholesale Stationers Assn, 1970-72; Pres, Bus Records Mfrs Assn, 1971-72; cp/Exec Com, The Pres's Pvt Sector Survey on Cost Control, 1982-; 1st VChm Bd of Visitors, Columbia Col, Columbia Univ; Dir & Chm of Exec & Fin Coms, Police Ath Leag Inc; The Ec Clb of NY; NY Yacht Clb; hon/Patentee, Binder & Compression Mechanism; John Jay Awd for Dist'd Profl Achmt, Columbia Col, Columbia Univ, 1982; W/ W: in Am, in Fin & Indust; Other Biogl Listings.

WHITTINGTON, MARGARET ANN oc/Executive; b/Aug 3, 1948; h/ 14972 Paddock Street, Sylmar CA 91342; ba/Valencia, CA; m/Edward A Wagner; p/David Kelsey Whittington, Gibsonia, PA; sp/Ruth M Wagner Bridgeville, PA; ed/Att'd Blackburn Col, 1967-68; Att'd Commun Col of Allegheny Co, 1971-72; pa/Student Employmnt Coor, Carnegie-Mellon Univ, Pgh, PA, 1975-77; Admissions Asst, CA Inst of Arts, Valencia, CA, 1977-80; Adm Mgr, G W Smith & Assocs Inc, Valencia, CA, 1980-82; Exec VPres & Controller, US Fin Conslts Inc, Valencia, CA, 1983-; Mem: Trustee on Bd of Trustees, CA Inst of Arts, 1978-79, 1979-80; VPres, SCV Career Wom's Netwk, 1983-84; NOW, 1973-; r/Presb; hon/Spec Cert, Grad Sch of Photog, CA Inst of Arts, 1979; Spec Recog/Student Coun, CA Inst of Arts, 1980; W/W: in CA, in W.

WICKWIRE, PATRICIA JOANNE NELLOR oc/Consultant; h/2900 Amby Place, Hermosa Bch, CA 90254; ba/ Same; m/Robert James; c/William James; p/William McKinley Nellor (dec); Clara Pautsch Nelor, Charter Oak, IA; ed/BA, Univ of No IA, 1951; MA, Univ of IA, 1959; PhD, Univ of TX-Austin, 1971; Addit Grad Studies; pa/Tchr, Ricketts ISD, IA, 1946-48; Tchr & Cnslr, Waverly-Shell Rock ISD, IA, 1951-55; Rdg Conslt, Hd Dorm Cnslr, Univ of IA, 1955-57; Tchr, Sch Psychol, Coor of Psychol Sers, Dir of Student Sers & Spec Ed, S Bay Union HS Dist, CA, 1962-82; Lectr, Loyola-Marrymount Univ, CA, 1980-; Conslt, CA St Dept of Ed; Indep Const in Mgmt & Ed; Mem: Pres, Exec Bd, CA Assn for Measurement & Eval in Guid, 1981-; Exec Bd, CA Assn of Sch Psychols, 1981-83; Exec Bd, Assn of CA Sch Admrs, 1977-81; Exec Bd, CA Pers & Guid Assn, 1977-78; Pres, LA Co Admrs of Pupil Sers, 1974-79; Pres, Exec Bd, LA Co Pers & Guid Assn, 1977-80; Pres, LA Co SW Admrs of Spec Ed, 1976-81; CA Exec Bd, AAUW, 1965-70; Chm of Bd, CA St Univ-Dominguez Hills, 1981-; Exec Bd, CA Interagy Mtl Hlth Coun, 1968-72; World Future Soc; Nat Assn of Female Execs; Am Psychol Assn; Am Pers & Guid Assn; Am Assn of Sch Admrs; Am Assn for Measurement & Eval in Guid; cp/Exec Bd, VPres, Bch Cities Symph Assn, 1970-82; r/Luth; hon/Author, *The Acad Achmt & Lang Devel of Am Chd of Latin Heritage*, 1971; Contbr, Num Articles to Profl Jours, Mags &

Newspapers; Achmt Awd in Jour, 1950; Achmt Awd in Eng, 1951; S Bay Wom of Yr, 1978; Pi Lambda Theta; Psi Chi; Sigma Alpha Iota; Kappa Delta Pi; Alpha Phi Gamma; W/W: in CA, in W, of Am Wom, Among Sch Dist Ofcls; DIB; Other Biogl Listings.

WIDISS, ALAN I oc/Lawyer, Educator; b/Sep 28, 1938; h/316 Kimball Road, Iowa City, IA 52240; ba/Iowa City, IA; m/Ellen Louise Magaziner; c/Benjamin L, Deborah Anne, Rebecca Elizabeth; p/ Al and Rose H (Sobole) Widiss; ed/BS 1960, LLB 1963, Univ of So CA; LLM, Harvard Univ, 1964; Admitted to CA Bar, 1963; pa/Tchg Fellow, Harvard Univ, 1964-65; Asst Prof Law 1965-68, Assoc Prof 1968-69, Prof 1969-78, Joseph R Witte Prof 1978-, Univ of IA; Vis'g Prof, Univ of So CA & Univ of San Diego; Dir, CLRS Mass No-Fault Auto Ins Study, 1971-76; Trustee, Univ of IA Sch of Rel, 1976-; Chm, Johnson Co Citizens Advy Com for Reg Trans Study, 1971-75; Mem: ABA; CA Bar Assn; Am Law Inst; Am Assn of Law Schs; Order of Coif; Phi Kappa Phi; Delta Sigmga Rho; hon/Author, Editor (w Others), *Arbitration: Comml Disputes, Ins & Tort Claims*, 1979; *No-Fault Auto Ins in Action: The Experiences in MA, IL, DE & NY*, 1977; *A Guide to Uninsured Motorist Coverage*, 1969; *Uninsured & Underinsured Motorist Ins, Volume I*, 1984; Contbr, Num Articles to Law Jours; W/W in World.

WIEGLER, BARRY ALLAN oc/Consulting Firm Executive; b/Jun 17, 1938; h/6162 Pat Avenue, Woodland Hills, CA 91367; ba/Santa Monica, CA; m/ Deanna; c/Laurie, David, Michael, Lisa, Shera; p/Paul Wiegler (dec); Marie Wiegler, LA, CA; sp/Mr and Mrs Robert Hamilton, Pilot Rock, OR; ed/Att'd Santa Monica Col, 1956-59; BBA, Woodbury Univ, 1965; MBA, CA St Univ-LA, 1967; mil/USAFR, 1956-65; pa/Assoc VPres, Security Pacific Nat Bk, LA, CA, 1961-69; Mgr Fin Indust Planning, Gen Elect Computer Div, Phoenix, AZ, 1969-71; Dir Res & Planning, MSI Dat Corp, Costa Mesa CA, 1971-72; VPres in SF1973-80, VPres in LA 1980-81, Sr VPres 1981-82, Gottfried Conslts Inc, CA; Pres, Bd of Dirs & Co-Fdr, Key Consltg Grp Inc, Santa Monica, CA, 1983-; Mem: Trustee & Chm of Bd, EDP Steering Com; Ofc Automation Advy Com, Woodbury Univ, LA; cp/Rotary Clb of SF; r/Jewish; hon/Phi Gamma Kappa, 1964; Ctl Data Processor, 1965; Jr Col Tchg Credential, 1965; W/W: in CA, in W.

WIEMANN, MARION R JR oc/Biologist and Microscopist; b/Sept 7, 1929; h/PO Box E, Chesterton, IN 46304; ba/ Chesterton, IN; c/Tamara Lee; p/Marion R and Verda Peek Wiemann Sr, Chesterton, IN; ed/BS, IN Univ, 1959; Course Completion Certs 1967, 1968, 1970, 1971, Formal Tng Microscopy, McCrone Res Inst, Chgo, IL; AN(P), Na Tech Tng Ctr, Jacksonville, FL, 1952; AD "A", Na Tech Tng Ctr, Memphis, TN, 1952; mil/USN, 1951-53; pa/ Histo-Res Tech 1959, Res Asst 1959-62, Res Tech 1962-64, Res Tech 1965-67, Sr Res Tech 1967-70, Res Technol 1970-79, Univ Chgo; Sci Tchr, Westchester Twp Sch, Chesterton, IN, 1964-66; Prin, Marion Wieman & Assocs, Consltg, Res & Devel, Chesterton, IN, 1979-; Mem: VPres 1969-70, Pres 1970-71, St Microscopal Soc of IL;

AAAS, 1983-; Intl Platform Assn, 1983-; Life Mem, Field Mus of Natural Hist, 1967-; Other Sci Socs; cp/Former Commr, BSA; Life Mem, ABIRA, 1983-; hon/Contbr, Num Articles to Profl Jours Incl'g: *Am Biol Tchr; Jour Dental Res, Jour Periodontol; Oral Med; Oral Pathol; The Microscope;* Photomicrographs Pub'd in *Ency Britanica; TransVision Atlas of Hlth; Sci Yr; World Book Sci Annual;* Num Others; Scouters Key 1968, Arrowhead Hon 1968, BSA; Awd of Merit, Soc for Tech Commun, 1973; Dist'd Tech Communr, 1974; S'ships, McCrone Res Inst, 1968; Dean's Hon List, High Scholastic Achmt, 1952, 1956; Fellow, Royal Microscopical Soc, 1971; Nat Advr, ABIRA, 1982-; Cit, Marquis W/W, 1981; W/W in MW; Awd of Merit, ABI, 1982; Dedication of Intl Book of Hon, 1983; Notable Am Awd, 1983; Cert of Merit, Intl Biogl Ctr, 1983; Commun Ldrs of World; W/W of Intell; Dir of Dist'd Ams; World Biogl Hall of Fame; Num Other Biogl Listings.

WIER, RAYMOND DAVID JR oc/ Certified Public Accountant; b/Aug 25, 1947; h/1449 Richland, Abilene, TX 79603; ba/Abilene, TX; m/Cindy Harrison Wier; c/John Matthew, Jordan Leigh; p/Mr and Mrs Raymond D Wier, Odessa, TX; sp/Mr and Mrs Earl P Harrison, Abilene, TX; ed/BA, Baylor Univ, 1969; MS, Abilene Christian Univ, 1979; mil/USAF, 1969-81, Capt; pa/Intell Ofcr 1969-73, Navigator C130 1973-81, USAF; CPA Budget & Forecasting Acct, W TX Utilites Co, Abilene, TX, 1982-; Mem: Am Inst of CPA's; TX Soc of CPA's; Nat Assn of Accts; Soc of Petro Accts; cp/Kiwanis; r/Bapt; hon/ AF Commend Medal for Combat is SE Asia, 1973; God & Country Awd, BSA, 1964.

WIEWIOROWSKI, EDWARD IGNACY oc/Chemical Engineer; b/May 10, 1931; h/3620 Rue Andree, New Orleans, LA 70114; ba/Braithwaite, LA; m/Irena Sobolewska; c/Martin Charles, Maria Gertruda; p/Karol Ignacy and Gertruda (Pluszkiewicz) Wiewicrowski (dec); sp/Franciszek Sobolewska (dec); Maria (Urbanek) Sobolewska; ed/ BSChE, MSChE 1956, PhD Chem Engrg 1965, Gdansk Inst of Technol, Poland; pa/Asstship 1954-63, Fac Mem 1963-72, Gdansk Inst of Technol, Gdansk, Poland; Pvt Pract in Chem Engrg & Consltg, Gdansk & Warsaw Poland, 1964-72; Sr Res & Dev Engr, Amax Nickel, Braithwaite, LA, 1973-; Mem: Lic'd Profl Engr, LA, 1980; Nat Soc of Profl Engrs; LA Engrg Soc; Am Inst of Metal Engrs; Am Chem Soc; AIChE; Polish Chem Soc; Assn Engrg Polish Chem Indust; r/Cath; hon/ Author, 50 Papers Pub'd in Profl Jours; US & Europe Patents in Field of Chem Engrg & Hydrometallurgy; Naturalized Citizen, 1978; W/W in S & SW.

WIGGINS-JONES, KATHLYN YVETTE oc/Communications Systems Representative; b/Dec 16, 1950; h/22 University, Buffalo, NY 14214; ba/ Buffalo, NY; m/Young B Jones; c/ Anayet; p/Mack C Sr and Texana R Wiggins, Memphis, TN; sp/Willis Jones, Lake Providence, LA; Katie Howard (dec); ed/BS, 1972; MS, 1974; Doct Cand; pa/Communs Sys Rep 1981-, Mktg Adm 1977-81, Commun Conslt 1974-77, NY Telephone Co; Mem: Am Mktg Assn; Curric Devel & Instrnl

Media Clb; Nat Assn of Female Execs; Exec Urban Leag; NAACP; Alpha Kappa Alpha; r/Bapt; hon/Author, *Telecommuns Info for the Blind & Visually Impaired,* 1981; Video: "Intro to Bell Mktg Dept," 1981; W/W of Am Wom.

WIGLEY, JEAN M oc/Homemaker, Volunteer, Fiber Artist; b/Apr 4, 1931; h/5735 Westbrook Road, Minneapolis, MN 55422; m/Robert J; c/Michael, Thomas, Kristin (dec); p/K O Christianson (dec); Marian Christianson, Decorah, IA; sp/M R Wigley (dec); Myrtle Wigles, Mpls, MN; ed/Att'd Mankata St, 1949-51; Grad in Related Art, Univ of MN, 1967; pa/ Self-employed Fiber Artist & Tchr, Vol, Currently; Home Economist, Pillsbury Co, 196-68; Ofc Mgr, Water Prods Co; Mem: Pres Bd of Dirs 1981-83, Bd of Dirs 1978-84, Mem Num Coms, Mmpls Area YWCA; Pres Ch Coun 1983, VPres 1980-82, Calvary Luth Ch of Golden Val; Nat Trainer, YWCA; Secy & one of Fdrs, Twin City Chapt, The Compassionate Friends (A Support Grp for Bereaved Parents); Vol Trainer, "I Can" Trainer (a Nat Interagy Collaboration for Vol Devel; Funding Com, Vols for MN; Past Pres, PEO Chapt DJ; cp/Mem Num Arts & Wom's Orgs; r/Luth.

WILBER, DONALD BLAINE oc/ Minister/Pastoral Counselor; b/Oct 5, 1952; h/1006 Burgundy Place, Prosser, WA 99350; ba/Prosser, WA; m/Janet M; c/Eric, Charles, Ty; p/M Blaine and S June Wilber, Ontario, OR; sp/Lester and Mary Scott, Ontario, OR; ed/BA, NW Nazarene Col, 1976; MA Cnslg, Col of ID, 1980; PhD Cnslg Psych, Columbia Pacific Univ, 1982; pa/Min & Pastoral Cnslr, Ch of Nazarene, Harper, OR, 1976-79; Yth Min & Cnslr, Ontario, OR, 1975-76; Min & Pastoral Cnslr Coun, ID, 1979-80; Hlth Crisis Cnslr Intern, Mtn States Tumor Inst, Boise, ID, 1980; Pvt Pract Cnslg, Ontario, OR, 1980-82; Min/Pastoral Cnslr in Pvt Pract, Prosser, WA, 1982-; Mem: Christian Assn of Psychol Studies; Am Orthopsyci Assn; Am Assn of Cnslg & Devel; Am Mtl Hlth Cnslrs Assn; VPres, Coun Min Assn, 1979; Prosser Min Assn; r/Nazarene; hon/Author, Var "Insight" Column Articles for Local Newspaper; Ordained Min, 1978; W/W in W.

WILDER, LISA FAYE oc/Certified Public Accountant; b/Aug 18, 1956; ba/ Blytheville, AR; c/Misty L Eubanks; p/ John Wilder Sr, Kennet, MO; Suzanne Garrett, Nashville, TN; ed/BS Acctg, AR St Univ, 1981; pa/CPA, Sr Acct, Block, Kelly & Co, Currently; Jr Acct, Robert Stiles & Co, 1981; Mem: AICPA; ASCPA; AWSCPA; r/Meth; hon/Dean's List, AR St Univ; NHS, Kennet HS; Cert of Recog, Univ of MO.

WILDMAN, SUZANNE BLANCHARD oc/Composer, Educator; b/Jan 4, 1940; h/27 Pine Street, Manchester, MA 01944; ba/Manchester, MA; c/ Helen LeRoy, Ben H II; p/Helen L Pirnie, Manchester, MA; ed/AB Classics, Stanford Univ, 1958; AB, SF Conservatory of Music, 1957; Att'd Am Sch of Music, Fontainbleau, France, 1965; pa/Tchr of Elem Piano, SF Conservatory, 1963-64; Pt-time Sales Clk, Macy's, SF, CA; Inventory Taker, The Emporium; Mem: Leag of Wom Voters of SF; Met Opera Raffle; UNICEF; Am Security Coun; Stanford Univ Alumni Assn; Repub

Town Com, Manchester, MA; Foster Parent "Happy Child" Taiwan, 1975-81; cp/Pebble Bch Clb, Carmel, CA; Bath & Tennis Clb, Manchester, MA; Revolutionary Ridge Book Clb, Concord, MA; Advry Mem, Marquis Biogl Lib Soc; r/Christian Sci; hon/Music Compositions Incl: "Preludes 1 & 2" Perf'd at Palace fo Legion of Hon, SF, 1961; "Prelude 3 & Fugue" Perf'd at Temple Emmanuel, SF, 1961; "The Gov Proposes," 1962; "5 Christmas Duets for Tchr & Beginner," 1968.

WILDS, BOBBY oc/Branch Director of Club; b/Sep 22, 1947; h/2509 Pine Street, Tampa, FL 33607; ba/Tampa, FL; c/Darrolyn, Michelle, Bobby Jr; p/Jettie B and Minnie Wilds, Tampa, FL; ed/ Att'd FL A&M Univ, 1966-68; Addit Tng; mil/AUS, 1968-70, Supply Sgt; pa/ Tng & Job Experience Spec, Tampa Concentrated Employmnt Prog (TECEP), 1970-71; Pre-Trial Spec & Cnslr, A L Nellum & Assocs, 1971-72; Job Develr, Human Resources Devel Prog, 1972-74; Job Develr/Cnslr 1974-75, Chief Cnslr Ctl Intake 1975, Prog Dir Chemotreatment Ctr 1975, Drug Abuse Comprehensive Coor'g Ofc (DACCO); Investigator, Ofc of Public Defender Hillsborough Co, 1975-78; Dir Jose Llaneza Br, Boys & Gils Clb of Gtr Tampa, 1978-; Mem: Cert'd Instr, Am Coaching Effectiveness Prog, 1982; Cert'd Instr, Nat Yth Sports Coaching Assn, 1983; cp/Football Coach, Police Ath Leag, 6 Yrs; Ath Dir, Tampa Eagles Football Inc, 8 Yrs; Cert'd Notary Public, 19 Yrs; Proj Ldr, FL Dem Party, 1974; Dept Supvr Election Ofc, Hills Co, 1974; Treas, Police Advy Com, 1975; Tampa JC's, 1977; Asst Varsity Football Coach, Tampa Bay Tech, 1980; Num Spkg Presentations; hon/Tampa Bay Blacks Most Influential, 1983; Coach of Yr, Ath Dir of Yr, Tampa Eagles; Coach of Yr, PAL; Awd for Devel of Black Talent, Tampa Urban Leag; Awd for Ser to Commun in Yth Football, Tampa Golf Clb; Awd for Dedication, Tampa Eagles; Awd for Ser on Oratorical Contest, Optimist Clb of Ybor City; Ser Awd, HRS, 1982; Ser Awd, Belmont Hgts Little Leag Nat Champs, 1981; Ser Awd, Coop Ed Clb, Robinson HS, 1980; Cert of Apprec for Outstg Ser, 5th Annual KY Sch of Alcohol Studies; Citizen of Day, Citizens Fed Savs & Ln Assn & WPLP/Talk Radio 57.

WILES, MICHAEL ROBERT oc/ Chiropractic Educator; b/Feb 15, 1951; h/Rural Route 1, Locust Hill, Ontario, Canada L0H1JU; ba/Toronto, Ontario, Canada; m/Janice Isobel; c/Timothy Matthew; ed/Doct of Chiro, CMCC, 1976; BSc, Univ of Toronto, 1979; Med, Brock Univ, 1983; pa/Asst Dean 1982-, Chm Dept of Chiro Sci 1978-, Resident Chiro Sci 1976-78, CMCC; Assoc Editor, *Jour of Canadian Chiro Assn,* 1978-83; Mem: Am Chiro Assn; Canadian Chiro Assn; AAHM; hon/Author, Num Profl Papers, Edits & Lttrs Pub'd in *Jour of CCA, Jour of MPT* & Other Profl Jours; Jack Nosle Prize (Highest Acad Standing in Med Class), Brock Univ, 1983; W/W: in Chiro, in Commonwlth; Intl Book of Hon.

WILHELM, WILLA METTA oc/ Retired Educator; b/Sep 10, 1912; h/ 85501 Jasper Pk Road, Pleasant Hill, OR 97455; m/George A; c/Daren Lyle (dec);

p/Charles and Margaret Logsdon (dec); sp/George and Amelia Wilhelm, Junction City, OR; ed/BS 1933, MEd 1941, Univ of OR; pa/Jr HS Instr, Sprague River, OR, 1934-35; Instr, Canyonville HS, OR, 1935-37; Instr, Junction City HS, OR, 1937-41; Bus Ofc, Corvair Corp, San Diego, CA, 1942-45; Instr 1945-46, Supt 1946-47, Riddle HS, OR; Instr 1947-61, Media Spec 1961-77, Lowell HS, OR; r/Cath; hon/Recip Int 1st Place Awd, Lowell HS Newspaper Broadcaster; Quill & Scroll Awds, 1948-49, 1949-50; Personalities of W & MW; Commun Ldrs of World.

WILKINS, ROBERT MASON oc/Physician, Rancher; b/Apr 18, 1937; h/Route 4, Dry Lake Road, Nampa, ID 83651; ba/Nampa, ID; m/Gloria (Jaci); c/Robert Bruce, Marguerite Davis; p/Robert Bruce Wilkins (dec); Marguerit Edwards, Durham, NC; sp/Mr and Mrs Frederick Heil (dec); ed/AB Eng, Univ of NC, 1959; MD, Bowman-Gray Sch of Med, Wake Forest Univ, 1963; Intern, Univ of CO, 1963-64; F'ship in Gastroenterology 1964-65, Resident in Med 1977-78, Duke Univ Med Ctr; mil/USN, 1965-67; pa/Pvt Pract Gastroenterology, Durham, NC, 1969, 1972; Conslt Gastroenterologist, VA Hosp, Fayetteville, NC, 1969-71; Assoc Commun Hlth Scis, Duke Univ Med Ctr, 1969-72; Pvt Pract Gastroenterology, Med Ctr Phys, PA, Nampa, ID, 1972-; Clin Asst Prof of Med, Univ of WA, Seattle, 1977-; Mem: Fellow, Gov for ID 1984-88, Am Col of Phys; Diplomate, Am Bd of Internal Med; Fellow, Am Col of Gastroenterology; Am Gastroenterology Assn; AMA; So Med Assn; SW Dist ID Med Soc; ID Med Assn; ID Soc of Internal Med; Pres, Wn Sts Angus Assn; Pres, ID Angus Assn; Others; r/Epis; hon/Author, Over 10 Papers Pub'd in Profl Jours & Presented at Assn Meetings; Morehead Scholar, Univ of NC, 1955-59; W/W in W.

WILKINSON, THOMAS LLOYD JR oc/Materials Engineering; b/Dec 14, 1939; h/6908 Park Avenue, Richmond, VA 23226; ba/Richmond, VA; m/Maxine Doyle; c/Margaret Carter, Thomas Douglas; p/Gladys M Wilkinson, Lynchburg, VA; sp/Mr and Mrs M E Doyle, McKinnley, VA; ed/BS, VA Commonwlth Univ, 1963; MC, Univ of Richmond, 1976; pa/Sr Devel Proj Dir 1980-, Proj Dir 1973-80, Sr Devel Engr 1967-73, Devel Engr 1966-67, Test Engr 1963-66, Reynolds Metals Co; Mem: Soc for Advmt of Material & Process Engrg; Adhesives Coun Soc of Mfrg Engrs; VChm Richmond Chapt, Am Soc for Metals; Secy, Am Soc for Testing & Mats Adhesives Com; Modern Plastics Mgmt Advy Coun, 1979-81; cp/Theta Chi; Pres, Duntreath Civic Assn, 1979; Precinct Capt, 1980; r/Presb; hon/Author, 4 Books: *Aluminum Assn Booklet T17 "Weldbonding—An Alternative Joining Method for Aluminum Auto Body Alloys",* 1978; *Aluminum Assn Booklet T14,* 1975; *Reynolds Metals Co Tech Bltn,* 1981; *Reynolds Co Tech Handbook,* 1966; Over 15 Articles & Papers Pub'd in Profl Jours & Presented at Assn Meetings; W/W in S & SW.

WILKS, JACQUELIN H oc/Counselor; b/Jan 18, 1950; h/Route 3, Shawnee, OK 74801; ba/Shawnee, OK; m/Tom; c/David, Brian; sp/Milton and Bernice Wilks, Bastrop, LA; ed/BS, LA Col,

1972; Att'd So Bapt Theol Sem, 1974; Att'd SE MO St Univ, 1977; MAT, OK City Univ, 1982; Adv'd Reality Therapy Cnslg, OK Univ, 1982; Cnslg Cert, Ctl St Univ, OK, 1982-83; pa/Coor of Student Pers, Gordon Cooper Voc-Tech, Shawnee, OK, 1982-; Dir of Tutorial Prog, Instr 1980-82, Dir of Admissions & Fin Aid 1979-80, OK Bapt Univ, Shawnee, OK; 6th Grade Sci Tchr A D Simpson Sch 1976, 1st Grade Tchr Bertrand Elem Sch 1975, Charleston R-1 Sch Dist, Charleston, MO; Kgn Tchr Doyle Elem Sch 1974, E Prairie R-2 Sch Dist, E Prairie, MO; Eng & Rdg Tchr, Pine Bluff HS, AR, 1972; Secy to VPres Installment Ln Dept, Nat Bk of Commerce, Pine Bluff, AR, 1972; Singer & Spkr in Foun Singers, LA Moral & Civic Foun, Baton Rouge, LA, 1970; Instr, Triple D Guest Ranch, 1969; Secy to Admr, Allen Parish Hosp, Kinder, LA, 1968; cp/Tutor, Prog in Own Home for Chd under Juris of Juv Ct, Jefferson Co, AR; Grp Cnslg Session Ldr, Juv Ct, Jefferson Co, AR; Repub; Mini Basketball Clin, Charleston, MO Girls Basketball Tm; r/Bapt; hon/Superior Sum Student, Hd Cheerldrs, Miss LA Col Finalist, Homecoming Ct, May Ct Finalist, Campus Favorite, LA Col.

WILLIAMS, ANNIE RUTH oc/Executive; b/Dec 24, 1934; h/13068 Sutton, Cerritos, CA 90701; ba/Cerritos, CA; p/Erwin Stevens, Atlanta, GA; Rosie Sturns, Long Beach, CA; ed/BS 1971, MS 1972, Fresno St Univ; MS, CA St Univ-LA, 1976; pa/Pres, Owner, Rehab Mgmt Spec Inc, 1978-; Supvr, Profl Cnslr Inc, 1977-78; Fac/Asst Prof, CA St Univ-LA, 1975-77; Inser Instr, VA Hosp, 1972-75; Asst Prof, Fresno St Univ, 1971-72; Mem: Ed Chp, CARP, 1980-82; Com Chp, CPGA, 1980-82; Ad Hoc Minority Exec Secy, 1974-77; Dir, CA St Retention Prog; Chm, Ethnic Ed Com; r/Prot; hon/Author, *Nurses Attitude toward Therapeutic Abortion Patients;* Grad magna cum laude, Fresno St Univ, 1972; Best Oratory Awd, HS; W/W: of Am Wom, Among Black Wom in CA.

WILLIAMS, BARBARA ELIZABETH WOMACK oc/Guidence Counselor, Licensed Professional; b/Feb 4, 1938; h/5556 McVitty Road, Roanoke, VA 24018; ba/Roanoke, VA; m/Leon Franklin; c/Mark Franklin, Alice Kathleen, Stephanie Todd; p/William A and Margaret K Womack, Huntsville, AL; sp/Frank and Louise Williams, Callao, VA; ed/BA 1966, MEd 1968, Am Univ; Postgrad Studies, Univ of VA, VA Polytech Inst & St Univ, Radford Univ; pa/Mil & Security Ofc HQs, Redstone Arsenal, Huntsville, AL, 1956-57; In Charge of Maintenance of Fgn Students, US Dept of Agri, Wash DC, 1957-59; Tchr Eng, Humanities & Psychol, Glenvar HS, Roanoke, VA, 1968-72; Guidance Cnslr, Hidden Valley Jr HS, 1972-; Lic'd Profl Cnslr, 1974-; NEA; VA Ed Assn; Secy, VA Assn of Tchrs of Eng; Chm Profl Ser, Roanoke Co Ed Assn; Roanoke Valley Mtl Hlth Assn; Roanoke Area Personnel & Guid Assn; Nat Coun Tchrs of Eng; VA Personnel & Guid Assn; cp/Fdr, Farmingdale Civic Leag; hon/Americanism Awd, Nat Sojourners; Lrdship Awd, Elks Clb; Cited by Secy of Agri for Outstg Ser to Attache Commun; Personalities of S; W/W: Am Wom, S & SW; 2000 Notable Ams; Intl W/W Wom.

WILLIAMS, BETTY C oc/Ranch Owner and Investor; ba/The Triple "W" Ranch, Route 3, Box 260, Lindale, TX 75771; c/Joy Lynne Williams; p/William Purvis Cox (dec); Jewel Lena Hering George, Hawkins, TX; pa/Owner/Mgr, Triple "W" Ranch, near Tyler, TX; Investor in Comml Real Est Incl'g Ofc Bldgs & Land; Dir, Bk of E TX; r/Meth; Mem: Am Mgmt Assn; Nat Assn of Female Execs; cp/Dallas Coun on World Affairs; Les Femmes du Monde, Dallas; Timberlawn Foun, Dallas; Fdg Patron, TX Bus Hall of Fame, Tyler, TX; Holly Tree Country Clb, Tyler; Willow Brook Country Clb, Tyler; Plaza Clb, Tyler; Petro Clb, Tyler; The Listeners Book Clb, Dallas.

WILLIAMS, CHARLES MOLTON oc/Mortgage Banking Executive; b/Jun 21, 1930; h/3924 Royal Oak Drive, Birmingham, AL 35243; ba/Birmingham, AL; m/Hope; c/Charles Molton Jr, John Thomas Hunter, John White, Kate Hope; p/Elliot Tuttle and Gertrude Molton Williams (dec); sp/John M and Kate Hope White, Uniontown, AL; ed/BS, Wash & Lee Univ, 1952; Grad Wk, Univ of AL; mil/AUS, 1952-54; pa/Var Ofcs, Ins VPres 1954-68, Pres & CEO 1968-78, Chm of Bd 1978-, Molton, Allen & Williams Inc; Mem: Bd of Dirs, The Bapt Hosp Foun of Birmingham Inc; Dir, Nat Bk of Commerce, 1980-; Mortgage Bkrs Assn of Am & AL; Past Pres, Mrtgage Bkrs Assn of AL; Yg Pres' Org, 1972-80; Dir Edward Lee Norton Ctr for Cont'g Ed, Birmingham-So Co, 1979-; cp/Pres, Birmingham Fest of Arts Assn, 1979; Bd of Visitors, Montreat-Anderson Col, 1981-; Advy Coun, Salvation Army Home & Hosp, 1978-; Exec Bd Birmingham Area Coun, BSA, 1979-; Dir, Birmingham Boys' Clb, 1979-; Kiwanis Clb; Redstone Clb; Newcomen Soc of Am; Relay House; Jefferson Clb; Country Clb of Birmingham; Shoal Creek Country Clb; Quarterback Clb; The Clb; r/Presb; hon/W/W: in S & SW, in Fin & Indust, in the World; The Am Bkr; Dir of US Bkg Execs; Men of Achmt; Other Biogl Listings.

WILLIAMS, CHERIE DAWSON oc/Professor; b/Mar 1, 1947; h/5420 East 113th Place South, Tulsa, OK 74136; ba/Tulsa, OK; m/Eddie Anthony; p/Dona M Dawson, Tulsa, OK; ed/BS 1968, MA 1970, EdD 1972, Univ of Tulsa; pa/Instr 1971-72, Asst Prof 1972-81, Assoc Prof 1982-, Oral Roberts Univ; Mem: Phi Gamma Kappa; Kappa Delta Pi; NEA; OK Ed Assn; Secy-Treas, OK Assn of Tchr Edrs; Intl Acad of Preven Med; Secy, Oral Roberts Univ Fac Senate; Pres Tenured Fac, Oral Roberts Univ, 1981-83; Am Assn of Tchr Edrs; OCCETE; AERA; r/Pentecostal; hon/Author, "The Commun as a Sci Resource," in *Sci & Chd,* 1982; F B Parriott Fellow, 1969-70; Univ Scholar, 1964-68; Outstg Edr of Am, 1974.

WILLIAMS, CLARKSTON GUSTAV oc/Author and Tax Accountant; b/Dec 11, 1940; h/Route 1, Box 532, West Point, MS 39773; ba/West Point, MS; c/Christian Eric, Victory Rene; p/Daniel Abel Williams (dec); Inse Virginia (Hazelwood) Williams, West Point, MS; ed/Grad, AUS Engr Sch, 1960; BSBA, MS St Univ, 1968; Grad, H & R Block Tax Sch, 1974; mil/AUS, 1958, 1960-61, 1975; pa/Chief Ofc Clk, IL Ctl RR,

Jackson, MS, 1968-69; Hist Tchr, Canton, MS Acad, 1969-70; Hist & Ec Tchr, Faith Christian HS, Collingwood, NJ, 1970-72; Social Studies Tchr, Greenville MS Christian Sch, 1972-73; Owner, The Tax Man, West Point, MS, 1973-; Owner, The Book Hut, West Point, MS, 1973-; Owner, Paul Revere Press, 1975-; Mem: Soc for the Admvt of Mgmt, 1964-68; Alpha Phi Omega, 1965-; Nat Hist Soc, 1972-74; r/Pentecostal Ch of God; hon/Pubr & Compiler: *Handbook on God & Country*, 1975; *Handbook on Liberty*, 1976; Author, *How to Fail in Marriage: Be the Ruler of the Roost & Your Wife Might Become Your Ex*, 1981; Cong of Freedom Liberty Awd, 1975 & 1976; W/W in S & SW.

WILLIAMS, DENNIS BUCHER oc/ Actor; b/Aug 21, 1944; h/11684 Ventura Boulevard, Ste 124, Studio City, CA 91604; ba/Beverly Hills, CA; p/Mr and Mrs A W Bird, Stilwell, KS; ed/Att'd Shawnee Mission W Jr Col; Att'd Kansas City Jr Col; BA Theatre & Drama, Univ of KS; pa/Motion Pictures: "Synthetic Fuel Conspiracy"; "Silent Movie"; "Truce in the Forest"; "Paved w Gold"; "Born of Water"; TV: "Gypsy Warriors"; "Operation Petticoat"; "Bionic Wom"; "Mary Hartman, Mary Hartman"; "Maude"; "Nancy Walker Show"; Movies of the Wk: "Spec Olympics Spec"; "Jour From Darkness"; "Halls of Anger"; "Dennis Williams Show"; Theatre: "Spec Olympics"; "Beautiful People of Am"; "Star Spangled Girl"; "Oklahoma"; "Hope Sch"; "Fantastiks"; Mem: Screen Actors Guild; AFTRA; AEA; AGVA; Spec Olympics; Christian Chds Fund; Actors & Others for Animals; Am Film Inst; Hollywood Heritage; Motion Picture Relief Fund; Permanent Charities Com; Nat Screen Coun; hon/Author of Screenplay, "Sunset Heaven," 1978; Presv of Arts Awd, Am Film Inst, 1976; Cert of Apprec, Anaheim C of C, 1977; Nat Gold Key for Art, 1963; Nat Gold Key for Art, 1963; Kennedy Foun Spec Awd, 1983; Golden Eagle Best Actor Awd, Munich Film Fest, 1978; Bronze Halo Awd, So CA Motion Picture Coun, 1983; W/W in Theatre; Personalities of W & MW; Noteworthy Ams.

WILLIAMS, DOUGLAS oc/Management Consultant; b/Oct 13, 1912; h/7612 Horizon Drive, PO Box 941, Carefree, AZ 85377; ba/Carefree, AZ; m/Esther Grant; c/Penelope W Winters, Grant T; p/Marjorie T Williams, Greenwich, CT; ed/AB, Cornell Univ, 1934; MBA, Harvard Univ, 1936; mil/AUS, WW II, Lt Col; pa/Air Reduction Co, 1936-37; Stat, Am Inst of Public Opinion, 1938; Mkt Res Consult, Elmo Roper Co, 1939-40; Assoc Dir, Nat Opinion Res Ctr, Univ of Denver, 1940-42; Pres, Douglas Williams Assocs, NYC & AZ, 1948-; Mem: Pres, Commun Chest, 1939-40; Bd of Mgrs, West Side YMCA, NYC, 1957-60; cp/Larchmonst Yacht Clb; Winged Foot Golf Clb; Union Leag; Desert Forest Golf Clb; AZ Harvard Bus Sch; r/Epis; hon/Author, "The Ed of Employees," for Am Mgmt Assn, 1953; *Survey of Small Bus*, US Dept of Commerce, 1957; "Employee Attitude Surveys," Sect in *Handbook of Bus Adm*, 1967; *Cornell Univ Survey*, 1969; Num Other Articles Pub'd in Profl Jours & Bus Mags; W/W: in W, in Fin & Indust.

WILLIAMS, EDDIE ANTHONY oc/

Business Systems Manager; b/Oct 2, 1947; h/5420 East 113th Place South, Tulsa, OK 74136; ba/Tulsa, OK; m/Cherie Anna; p/Mr and Mrs Eddie Ray Williams, Tyler, TX; sp/Mrs Dona Dawson, Tulsa, OK; ed/BS, Univ of TX-Arlington, 1970; MBA, Univ of Tulsa, 1978; pa/Programmer, Standard Oil of IN, Tulsa, OK, 1970-73; Sr Programmer Analyst, The Mentor Corp, Tulsa, 1973-75; Sr LSys Analyst, The Williams Cos, Tulsa, 1975-79; Mgr Bus Sys, C—E NATCO, Tulsa, 1979-; Mem: Lic'd Sales Assoc, OK Real Est Comm; Assn for Sys Mgmt, 1976-; cp/Conserv Dem; r/Pentecostal; hon/Sigma Iot Epsilon; Dean's List, Univ of TX-Arlington; W/W in S & SW.

WILLIAMS, GLORIA LOUISE oc/ Communication & Government Security Officer; b/May 31, 1932; h/304 Emma Jane, Rockwall, TX 75087; ba/Garland, TX; p/Lonnie and Louise Williams (dec); ed/Att'd Prairie View A&M Univ, 1950-51 & 1953-54; pa/Maid 1960-63, Mail Clk 1963-66, Pers Clk 1966-68, Security Admr 1968-71, Security Ofcr 1971-77, Varo Inc, Garland, TX; Communs & Govt Security Ofcr, EEO/Affirmative Action Prog, 1977-80; cp/Bd of Dirs, Rockwall YMCA, 1977-81; Rockwall Growth Com, 1977-78; Tour Guide for Ch Tours; r/Bapt; hon/Active in Getting Swimming Pool for Black Commun, 1960's; Recip James S Cogswell Awd, Varo Inc, 1975 & 1981.

WILLIAMS, MAMIE ALETHIA oc/ Pastor; b/Aug 13, 1950; h/1031 East Monument Street, Baltimore, MD 21202; ba/Balto, MD; p/John W Williams, Sumter, SC; Mrs John W Williams (dec); ed/BA, Claflin Col, 1972; MDiv, Wesley Theol Sem, 1978; pa/Pastor, Cent U Meth Ch, 1982-; Pastor, Calvary U Meth Ch, 1977-82; Sum Investment Wkr, SC Annual Conf, 1983; Coor, NW Parish Ed Min WA Ctl Dist, 1976-77; Other Previous Employmnt; Mem: Steering Com, Balto Conf Bd of Pensions, 1982; Balto Clergy & Laity Concerned, 1982; Nat Bd of Black Meths for Ch Renewal, 1976-80; Gen Bd of Ch & Soc, 1976-80; Ordained Elder, 1979; Ordained Deacon, 1976; Lic'd to Preach, 1974 & 1975; Other U Meth Ch Coms; cp/Balto Br, NAACP; Pres, Bd of Dirs, Wash Innner City Self-Help, 1979-; Pres, Bd of Dirs, Common Capital Fund, 1980-; Co-Convener Wash Br, Wom's Intl Leag for Peace & Freedom, 1980-82; Bd of Dirs, Metro Wash Planning & Housing Assn, 1981-82; Interim Dir 1980-82, Pres, Bd of Dirs 1981-82, Calvary Bilingual Day Care Lrng Ctr; Nat Black Hook-up of Black Wom Inc, 1979-80; Convenor, Multi-ethnic Task Force on the ERA, 1979-80; 14th Street Proj Area Proj, 1977-80; African Am Wom's Assn, 1979-80; Bd of Dirs, Planned Parenthood of Wash, 1979-80; DC Cong of Parents & Tchrs Assn, 1978-79; Num Public, Radio & TV Appearances; r/U Meth; hon/Mamie A Williams Day, Wash DC City Coun Resolution, Jun 6, 1982; Las Amigas' Ser Awd, 1982; Columbia Hgts Commun Ser Awd, 1977-78; WISH, 1982; Crusade Scholar, 1976, 1978; Choir Recog 4 Yrs in Col; Am Legion Awd, 1972; Plaque, UNCF Ser Awd, 1970; Simon P Montgomery Awd, 1970; Pres S'ship, 1970; Dean's

List, 1970; Cent Medallion, 1968; Am Ledion Medallion, 1968; Outstg Yg Wom in Am; Other Awds & Hons.

WILLIAMS, PEGGY FOWLER oc/ Management Consultant; b/May 8, 1933; ba/PO Box 7173, Dallas, TX 75209; c/Leigh Ann, Walter Lochran; p/Leon Dockrey Fowler (dec); Annie Bell (Williams) Dodd, Baylor Co, TX; ed/BS, N TX St Univ, 1954; MBA, Rollins Col, 1963; Cert of Adv'd Study, Am Grad Sch of Intl Mgmt, 1980; pa/Mgmt Consltg, Owner, Williams Consltg Sers (Formerly Moranz Consltg), 1963-; Employed w TX Instruments, 1957-58; w Temco Aircraft, Dallas, TX, 1951-53 & 1955-57; HS Math Tchr, Arlington, TX, 1953-54; Mem: Nat Assn of Female Execs; Am Mgmt Assn; AAUW; cp/Listeners Clb; Bonnie Blue Flag Chapt, UDC; Dallas Hist Soc; r/Epis; hon/CPS Designation Awd, Nat Secys Assn Intl, 1965; GRI Designation Awd, TX Assn of Realtors, 1978; W/W of Am Wom.

WILLIAMS, PEGGY LENORE oc/ Assistant Performance Director; b/Nov 5, 1948; h/1909 Jefferson Street, Madison, WI 53711; ba/Washington, DC; p/Madison, WI; ed/Att'd Univ of WI-Madison, 1970; Grad, Ringling Bros & Barnum & Bailey Circus Clown Col, 1970; pa/Positions w Ringling Bros & Barnum & Bailey Circus (RBBB): Profl Circus Clown RBBB, 1970-79; Staff Instr, RBBB Clown Col, 1973-; Advance Clown (Public Relats), 1973-80; Coor Ednl Sers Dept, RBBB Circus, 1980-81; Asst Perf Dir Blue Unit, RBBB Circus, 1981-; Mem: Nat Asns Female Execs, 1980-; Circus Fans of Am, 1977-; r/Ch of Jesus Christ of LDS; hon/Appearances on Over 100 Local & Nat TV Shows & in Num Mags; 1st Female Asst Perf Dir in Circus Hist; 1st Female Grad of RBBB Clown Col; W/W of Am Wom.

WILLIAMS, RICHARD LEE JR oc/ Business Executive, Psychologist; b/Sep 13, 1943; h/425½ East 4th Claremore, OK 74017; ba/Same; c/Richard, Tracey, Michael; p/C L and Julie Williams, Ocean Springs, MS; ed/BA, Univ of W FL, 1969; MS 1972, PhD 1979, Univ of So MS; mil/AUS, 1961-64; pa/Nuclear Test Tech 1964-69, Sys & Test Engr Nuclear Power Div 1972, Litton Industs; Engr Nuclear Power Div, Westinghouse Col, 1969-71; Conslt, St of MS, Jackson, 1972-74; Pvt Pract Industl Conslt, Employee Asst Progs, Jackson, 1974-; Pres, Williams Oil, Gas & Mining Corp, Tulsa, OK, 1980-; Pres, Williams Fgn Mining Opers Inc, Tulsa, 1980-; Psych Lectr, NE St Univ, Tahlequah, OK, 1980-; Hypnosis/Psych Lectr, Claremore, Jr Col, OK, 1980-; Diplomate, Am Acad Behavioral Med; Am Psychol Assn; OK Psychol Assn; Tulsa Psychol Assn; cp/Meth Clb; Elks; r/Meth; hon/Author (w Gutsch & Sizemore) *Sys of Psychotherapy*, 1978; Sr Editor, *Occupl Alcoholism Progs*, 1974; Grad Fellow, Univ So MS, 1969-72, 1977-79; W/W in S & SW.

WILLIAMS, ROBERT BRUCE oc/ Library Director; b/Oct 21, 1942; h/107 South 8th Street, Williamsburg, KY 40769; ba/Williamsburg, KY; p/Bruce V Williams (dec); Ada Gillian Williams, Williamsburg, KY; ed/BA Cumberland Col; AM George Peabody Col for Tchrs, EdD Cand, Vanderbilt Univ; pa/Dir, Public Lib, Corbin, KY, 1965-74; Fellow, Grad Sch of Lib Sci, George Peabody

Col for Tchrs, 1975-76; Hd Ref Dept, Univ of TN-Nashville, 1976-79; Hd Libn & Dir Lib Sers, Cumberland Col, 1979-; Mem: Am Lib Assn; KY Lib Assn; TN Lib Assn; SEn Lib Assn; Am Soc for Info Sci; AAUP; Coun of Indep Am Cols & Univ Libns; KY Bapt Col Lib Netwk; Bet Phi Mu; r/Disciple of Christ; hon/ Editor, *KY Rel Heritage Series*, Cumberland Col; Editor, Peabody Lib Sch *Forum*; T J Roberts Ldrship Prize, Cumberland Col; George Peabody Fellow; Andrew Mellon Foun Grantee; Outstg Fac Awd, Cumberland Col Student Govt Assn; W/W in S & SW.

WILLIAMS, ROSE A oc/Marketing, Public Relations, Special Productions; b/ Sep 24, 1949; h/3129 West Flournoy, Chicago, IL 60612; ba/Chgo, IL; p/Bealie and Louise Williams (dec); BS Ed, 1971; pa/Sr Proj Mgr, Spec Mkt Sers Inc, 1982-; Pres, Rose & Assocs, 1980-; Dr of Mkgtg, Chgo Defender Newspaper, 1979-80; Ecec Asst, Bk Mktg Assn, 1974-79; Mdsg Mgr, Playboy Enterprises, 1970-73; Mem: Publicity Clb of Chgo; Am Mgmt Assn; Nat Assn of Media Wom; Chgo Fashion Exch; Netwk Dir, Nat Assn for Female Execs; Chm Publicity, Spkrs Bur; cp/Undergrad Advr, Delta Sigma Theta, 1978-80; Chgo PBS Sta WTTW; Provident Hosp Wom's Aux, 1980-83; NAACP, 1977-; 1992 World's Fair Com; r/Cath; hon/ Govs Awd, 1981; Public Ser Awd, Nat Coun Negro Wom, 1978; Chgo Black Gold Recip, 1983; Dept of Labor Wom's Bur, 1981 & 1982; Nat Assn of Female Execs, 1982; Outstg Yg Wom of Am; W/W of Am Wom.

WILLIAMS, SHIRLEY ANN oc/ Teacher; b/May 10, 1954; h/4006 Tiffin Street, Houston, TX 77026; ba/Houston, TX; p/Mrs Blossom H Williams, Houston, TX; ed/BS 1975, MS 1978, Pairie View A&M Univ; PhD, Pacific Wn Univ, 1981; pa/Art Instr, Cit Houston, YMCA, 1973-74; Asst to Dean of Sch of Agri, Prairie View A&M Univ, 1978; Tchr, Conslt-Facilitator, Houston ISD, 1976-; Mem: Parliamentn, Phi Delta Kappa; Intl Human Relats Assn; Houston Assn for Supvn & Curric Devel; Houston Coun of Ed; Houston Tchrs Assn; PTA; r/Meth; hon/Author, *A Study of Sibling Attitudes Toward the Mtly Retarded Child*; W/W of Am Wom.

WILLIAMS, VERNON B JR oc/ Retired Urban Consultant; b/Jul 17, 1908; h/7026 South Saint Lawrence Avenue, Chicago, IL 60637; ba/Chgo, IL; m/Naomi S; c/Vernon B III; p/Vernon B and Edith S Williams (dec); sp/ Jeremiah P and Lena G Williams (dec); ed/BS, IL Inst of Technol, 1937; MA Ednl Adm, Univ of Chgo, 1939; pa/ Telephone Supvr, 1941-45; Telephone Mgr, 1945-49; Ofc Mgr, 1949-53; Comml Mgr, Comml Engr Rate Analyst; Asst Staff Supvr; Public Relats Asst; Commun Relats Mgr & Pers Supvr; cp/Past Pres, Frontiers Intl; Lions Intl; Past Pres, Chatham Lions; Chgo Area Proj; Beatric Caffrey Yth Ser; Halfway House Com & Intl Visitors Ctr; Chm, Wash Pk Fund Drive; South Side Div, March of Dimes; Num Other Commun Activs; r/Jewish; hon/Invited Participant, Joint Civilian Orientation Conf #39, 1969.

WILLIAMS, WILBUR E oc/Sales and Marketing Director, Lawyer; b/Oct 2, 1947; h/Urb. Ponce de León, Calle 20 #308, Guaynabo, PR 00657; ba/San Juan, PR; m/Myriam Capó; c/Mayrim M, Bilmarie, Wilbur G; p/Wilber E and Matilde Ortíz Williams; sp/Aristides and Margarita Martir Capó; ed/BBA, 1969; JD, 1972; mil/PR Army NG; pa/Profl Med Rep, Upjohn Intl, 1965; Profl Hosp Prods Rep 1972, Dist Sales Mgr 1975, Div Mgr Hosp Prods Div 1979, Abbott Labs; Sales & Mktg Dir, PR & Caribbean, Schering del Caribe Inc, 1982-; Mem: Past Pres PR Chapt, Am Mktg Assn, 1981-82; Am Mgmt Assn, 1979-; Past Pres, Nu Sigma Beta Frat; Isla Verde, PR; Clb Deportivo de Ponce; Lions Clb; r/Cath; hon/Ser Awd, PR NG, 1964.

WILLIAMS, WILLA ETTA MITCHELL oc/Elementary Teacher; b/Apr 17, 1934; h/7900 Crenshaw Boulevard, Apartment D, Inglewood, CA 90305; ba/LA, CA; p/Lucille Williams, LA, CA; ed/AA, LA City Col, 1954; BA, CA St Univ-LA, 1958; MA, Azusa Pacific Col, 1979; pa/Grades 2 & 3 Tchr, 75th St Sch, LA Unified Sch Dist, 1958-64; Spec Ed Tchr, Parmalee Avenue Sch, LA Sch Dist, 1965-67; Tchr, Raymond Ave Sch, LA Unified Sch Dist, 1968-71; Tng Tchr for Pepperdine Univ, 1968-71; Hoffman Rdg Lab Tchr, 59th St Sch, LA Unified Sch Dist, 1972-76; Grade 4 Tchr 1977-80, Bilingual Grade 4 Tchr 1981-84, Marvin Ave Sch, LA Unified Sch Dist; Mem: NEA; CA Tchrs Assn; U Tchrs of LA; Alpha Kappa Alpha; Nat Assn of Col Wom; Phi Delta Kappa; Intl Toastmistress; Nat Assn of Supvn & Curric Devel; cp/Las Comunicadores; LA Music Assn; Marvin Ave PTA; Marvin Ave Advy Coun; LA In-School Scouting; Num Guest Spkg Presentations; Num Other Sch & Commun Coms & Activs; r/U Meth, St Mark's U Meth Ch; hon/Author, Poetry; U Way Ser Awd, 1983; Phi Delta Kappa Ser Awd, 1983; Marvin Ave PTA Ser Awd, 1982; Coor, Urban Impacted Sch Activs; Num Other Hons & Awds.

WILLIAMS, YVONNE ELAINE oc/ Home Economics Teacher; b/Oct 13, 1944; h/1720 Applewood Ridge Court, Colorado Springs, CO 80907; ba/Colorado Springs, CO; m/Lawrence Richard; c/Jeremy Za; p/William Dean and Martha LaVerne Sams, Rush, CO; sp/Vearl and Josephine Williams (dec); ed/BS, Bob Jones Univ, 1966; MA, Univ of No CO, 1968; Postgrad Wk, Univ of CO-Colorado Springs, 1980 & 1983; pa/ Home Ec Tchr, Kit Carson Sch Dist, Kit Carson, CO, 1966-68; Hom Ec Tchr, Elkhart HS, Elkhart, KS, 1968-73; Home Ec Tchr, Russell Jr HS Colorado Springs, CO, 1974-75; Hom Ec Tchr & Dept Chm, Doherty HS, Colorado Springs, CO, 1975-; 2nd VPres Rho Chapt, Delta Kappa Gamma, 1980-84; cp/Judge, CO Beef Cook-Off, Local & Dist Competions; Judge, Clothing Exhibits, El Paso Co Fair; Gifted & Talented Parent Grp, Lincoln Elem Sch, 1980-83; Asst Cub Scout Den Mother, BSA; Bible Sch Tchr, Calvary Bapt Ch, 1982-83; r/Prot; hon/Recip, Bob Jones Univ Outstg Achm in Home Ec Awd, 1966; Yg Career Wom of Elkhart, KS, 1969; Outstg Yg Wom of Am; W/W: Among Students in Am Cols & Univs, in W.

WILLIAMSON, NANCY D oc/Nurse Educator & Clinical Nurse Coordinator; b/Sep 26, 1944; h/1725 Sourwood Place, Charlottesville, VA 22901; ba/Charlottesville, VA; m/John Rollen; c/John Russell, Jennifer Leigh, Jessica Marie; p/ Elmer Charles and Agnes Marie Onten Burk, McDonald, KS; sp/John Russell Williamson (dec); Lois Foshee Williamson, Augusta, GA; ed/Dipl in Nsg, Wichita St Joseph Sch of Nsg, 1965; BSN 1977, MSN 1979, Med Col of GA; pa/ Clin Nurse Coor & Asst Prof 1983-, Instr Sch of Nsg 1980-83, Relief Nsg Supvr Univ Hosp, 1981-82, Univ of VA Hosps, Blue Ridge Gerontology/Oncology Unit & Univ of VA Sch of Nsg, Charlottesville, VA; Nsg Instr, Johnson Co Commun Col, Overland Pk, KS, 1979-80; Nsg Instr, Augusta Area Tech Sch, 1975-76; Staff Nurse Intensive Care & Coronary Care Unit, St Joseph Hosp, Augusta, GA; 1969 & 1975; Charge Nurse ER, St John's Hosp, Salina, KS, 1970-71; Staff Nurse ER, Monmouth Med Ctr, Eatontoron, NJ, 1970; Charge Nurse Intensive Care & Coronary Care Unit, Commanchee Co Hosp, Lawton, OK, 1969; Designed, Estab'd & Hd Nurse Coronary Care Unit 1967-69, Hd Nurse Intensive Care Univ 1966-67, Charge Nurse Med-Surg Unit 1965-66, Asst Nurse ORN 1963-65, St Joseph Hosp, Wichita, KS; Nurse Aide, Med-Surg-Ob Unit, St Anthony's Hosp, Dodge City, KS, 1962-63; Mem: Num Univ, Nsg & Hosp Coms; ANA; VA Nurses Assn; Var Positions w Beta Kappa Chapt, Sigma Theta Tau; Cert'd CPR Instr, Am Heart Assn, 1980-; cp/Sustaining Mbrship Chp, Girl Scout Troop 401, 1981; Conductor Vol, Adult Diet Clin for Overweight Clients, Karlsruhe, Germany, 1973-74; Vol Cnslg Ser, AUS Ser-men, Karlsruhe, Germany, 1973-74; Num Other Ser Activs; r/ Cath; hon/Author, *Handbook for Univ of VA Sch of Nsg Students in Albemarle Co Schs*, 1981 & 1982; Co-Author, "Factors Affecting Employmnt of Grads of Univ of VA Sch of Nsg from 1978-80," 1982; Author, Var Wkshop Presentations, Nsg Assessment Tools & Other Orgl Paper Presentations; Sigma Theta Tau, 1979; 100 Hours Pin, ARC, 1973; Career Girl, Bus & Profl Wom's Assn, 1967; 2nd VPres, KS St Student Nurses' Assn, 1964-65; W/W of Am Wom.

WILLIS, JOHN PATRICK oc/Chemical Research Manager; b/Mar 10, 1947; h/101 Brimstone Lane, Sudbury, MA 01776; ba/Same; m/Tientje Jane; p/Mary C Willins, Albany, NY; sp/Hans H Dirzuweit, Rensselaer, NY; ed/BS, Iona Col, 1969; MS, SUNY-Oswego, 1974; PhD, Univ of CT, 1977; pa/Mgr of Chem Research, Nova Biomed Corp, 1980-; Postdoct Resr, Univ of MN, 1979-80; Res Chem, Uniroyal Inc, 1977-79; Res Chem, Winthrop Labs, 1970-72; Mem: Fellow, Am Inst of Chems, 1982-; Am Chem Soc, 1970-; Electrochem Soc, 1975; Am Assn of Clin Chem, 1982-; NY Acad of Sci, 1981; hon/Author, Num Profl Pubs in Field, Patentee in Field, 1982; Res Foun Fellow, Univ of CT, 1976; Sigma Xi, 1976; Phi Kappa Phi, 1976; Phi Lambda Upsilon, 1974; W/W in E.

WILSON, ARTHUR JESS oc/Clinical Psychologist; b/Oct 25, 1910; h/487 Park Avenue, Yonkers, NY 10703; ba/ Same; m/Lillian; c/Warren David, Anton Francis; p/Samuel Louis and Ann Gilbert Wilson (dec); ed/BS 1935, MA 1949,

PhD 1961, NY Univ; LLB, St Lawrence Univ, 1940; JD Bklyn Law Sch, 1967; mil/USN, 1944-46, Classification Spec; pa/Pvt Pract Clin Psych, 1973-; Clin Psychol, VA Hosp, Montrose, NY, 1968-73; Dir, Manhattan Narcotic Rehab Ctr, NYC, 1967-68; Dir of Rehab, Westchester Co Med Ctr, Valhalla, NY, 1948-67; Supvr of Voc Rehab, NY St Ed Dept, NYC, 1942-44; Mem: Am Psychol Assn; NY St Psychol Assn; Kappa Delta Pi; Phi Delta Kappa; Epsilon Pi Tau; hon/Author, *The Emotional Life of the Ill & Injured*, 1950; *A Guide to the Genius of Cardozo*, 1939; *The Wilson Tchg Inventory*, 1941; Contbr, Num Articles to Profl Jours; Elected, NY Acad of Scis; Fdrs Day Awd for Achmt, NY Univ, 1961; Hon Mem, Intl Mark Twain Soc, 1950; Westchester Author, Westchester Co Hist Soc, 1957; W/W in E, in Am Ed; Am Men of Sci; DIB.

WILSON, BRENDA COKER oc/ Attorney; b/Jun 25, 1952; h/Apartment 45B, 4259 22nd Avenue Southwest, Naples, FL 33999; ba/Naples, FL; m/ George A II; p/Paul and Helen Coker, Naples, FL; sp/Mr and Mrs George Wilson, Cinc, OH; ed/BA, Univ of No IA, 1974; JD, Univ of Tulsa, 1977; pa/ Sole Pract'g Atty, The Legal Ctr, Naples, FL, 1980-; Assoc Atty, Firm of Rhodes & Tucker, Marco Isl FL, 1978-80; Legal Intern, Tulsa Co Legal Aid Soc, Tulsa, OK, 1976-78; Mem: Yg Lwyrs Div, FL Bar Assn; ABA; Collier Co Bar Assn, 1978-83; Co-Chm Law Day Com 1981, Bd of Dirs 1981-83, Treas 1981-83, Nat & FL Assn of Wom Lwyrs; cp/Bd of Dirs 1979-83, VPres 1982-83, Abuse of Naples Inc; Past Pres, Sun Coast Chapt, Am Bus-wom's Assn; Leag of Wom Voters; Zonta Intl Inc; Co-Fdr, Naples Profl Wom's Netwk; Dem Wom's Clb; Orig'g Mem, Collier Co Rape Crisis Prog; Bd of Dirs, Planned Parenthood; Co-Chm, Com to Re-elect the Gov, 1982; Num Orgl Spkg Presentations; Other Commun Activs; r/ Presb; hon/Jaycettes Outstg Yg Wom of Marco, 1981; Exec Dir's Awd, Cath Ser Bur, 1981; Salute to Wom, Wom Achiever of Collier Co, 1983; W/W: of Wom, in Am Law; Personalities of S.

WILSON, BYRDIE BRUNER oc/ Executive Director; b/Sep 13, 1922; h/ 78 Country Club Boulevard, Town House 244, Worcester MA 01605; ba/ Marlboro, MA; p/Joseph M and Mary Luther Bruner (dec); ed/BS, NC Clt Univ, 1944; Nsg Dipl, Harlem Hosp Sch of Nsg, 1951; MSN, NY Univ Dept of Nsg Ed, 1959; pa/Exec Dir, Assabet Val Home Hlth Assoc Inc (Non-profit Commun Hlth Agy), Marlboro, MA, 1976-; Adm Supvr & Conslt, Webster-Dudley Samaritan Assoc Inc, MA, 1976; Prog Dir, Fam Nurse Practitioner Prog, Worcester Hahnemann Hosp, MA, 1974-75; Dir Nsg, Maternity & Fam Planning Ctr, Bronx, NY, 1970-74; Adm Supvr 1959-70, Staff Nurse 1953-58, Vis'g Nurse Ser of NY; Staff Nurse, Newborn Nursery, Harlem Hosp, 1951-52; Mem: APHA; ANA; Bd of Dirs, Pres, Baypath Sr Citizens Sers, Framingham, MA, 1980-; Profl Advy Com, Hahnemann Rehab Ctr, 1980-; r/ Prot; hon/W/W: of Wom, in Hlth Care.

WILSON, CHARLES WILLIAM oc/ Physician, Psychiatrist; b/Aug 12, 1916; h/4655 Basque Drive, Santa Maria, CA 93455; ba/Same; m/Frances Preshia Stephenson; c/Charles William II, Walter Stephen, Cherrie, James Robin; p/ Jacob Resor and Estella Cherrie Wilson (dec); ed/BA, Wichita Univ, 1938; MD, Kansas Univ, 1942; Intern, Harper Hosp, Detroit, MI, 1942-43; Resident Phys Neurology, Univ Hosps, Iowa City, IA, 1946-47; Resident Phys Psychi, Ctl St Hosp, Norman, OK, 1964-67; mil/ USN, 1943-46, Lt (Sgt), MC; pa/Pvt Pract Psychi & Med Hypnosis: Ponca City, OK 1967-71 & Santa Maria, CA 1971-; Psychi Dir, Mtl Hlth Ctr for Students, OK St Univ, Stillwater, OK, 1968-71; Staff Psychi at Commun Mtl Hlth Ctrs: Attascadero St Hosp 1975-79, San Luis Obispo, CA 1973-75, Santa Maria, CA 1971-72, Ponca City, OK 1967-71, Gen Pract & Pvt Pract Phys & Psychi: La Crosse, KS 1962-64; St Francis, KS 1947-62; Mem: Am Psychi Assn; So CA Psychi Soc; Acad of Parapsychol & Med; The Soc for Clin & Exptl Hypnosis; Intl Soc of Hypnosis; AMA; Var St & Co Med Socs in KS, OK & CA; Charter Mem, The Am Soc of Clin Hypnosis; Pres, NW KS Med Soc, 1951; cp/Scoutmaster, Explorer Ldr, Scouter Tnr & Other Positions, BSA, 23 Yrs; Pres St Francis, KS 1955, Ponca City, OK, Rotary Intl, 19 Yrs; Lions Clb; Elem Sch Bd, St Francis, KS; Am Legion; Masonic Lodge; OES; Men of Webster; Phi Lambda Psi; Delta Upsilon; Phi Beta Pi; Toastmaster Intl; AAAS; r/Meth; Lay Ldr, Meth Ch, La Crosse, KS; Com Mem 1st Meth Ch, Norman, OK, SS Tchr, Meth Ch, Ponca City, OK; hon/Author, *Stop Bedwetting!*, 1979; Cit, Nat PTA; Eagle Scout Awd, Silver Explorer Awd, Scoutmasters Key & Wood Badge, BSA; Ext Prof, CA Polytech St Univ, San Louis Obispo, CA; Instr, Allan Hancock Col, Santa Maria, CA; The Intl Platform Assn; Resr & Develr of 4 Rapid Psychotherapies; W/W: in CA, in W, in Am, in World, of Intells, of Commun Ser, of Contemp Achmt; Men of Achmt; Men & Wom of Distn; Intl Dir of Dist'd Psychotherapists; Inl Book of Hon; DIB; Num Other Biogl Listings.

WILSON, CLARENCE JR oc/Personnel Manager; b/Sep 19, 1952; h/D-4 Bellwood Apartments, Laurel, MS 39440; ba/Taylorsville, MS; m/Phyllis Beatrice Williams; c/Caralisa, Carmen; p/Clarence and Maggie Wilson, Talladega, AL; sp/Williams & Louvenia Gilmore, B'ham, AL; ed/BA, B'ham So Col, 1975; pa/Measurer & Lister, H L Yoh Appraisal Co, 1975-76; Social Wkr, Dept of Pensions & Security, 1976-78; Asst Pers Dir, Crown Textile Co, 1978-83; Pers Mgr, GA Pacific Corp, 1983; cp/ Div Chm 1979-83, Bd of Dirs 1981, U Way; Chm, U Meth Men's Grp, 1983; Treas, Kappa Alpha Psi Frat Inc; Talladega Alumni Assn, 1982-83; Bd Mem, Pittard Voc Sch, 1982; r/Meth; hon/ Outstg Yg Men Nom, Talladega JC's, 1981; Outstg Yg Man of Am, US JC's, 1983.

WILSON, DEIRDRE oc/Theatre/ Dance Education, Drama Therapist, Counselor, Choreographer & Performer; b/Feb 21, 1945; h/Northeast 1050 "B" Street, Pullman, WA 99163; m/Douglas John Hammel; c/Devon; p/ Joseph H Wilson; Audrie Ilene Branin (dec); sp/John and Norma Hammel; ed/ AA, Grossmont Col, 1977; BA, Antioch Univ, 1979; MEd 1983, MA Theatre 1983, Doct Cand Cnslg, WA St Univ; Addit Tng & Study; pa/Perf'g Experience: Ballet Soloist, SF Opera, 1972-75; Ballet Soloist, SF Sprg Opera Theatre, 1974-75; SF Ballet, 1972-74; Demi-Soloist, Dance Spectrum, SF, 1974-75; Soloist, SF Dance Theatre, 1973-75; Prin Dancer "Tommy," Seattle Opera Co, Seattle, 1972-; Opera Ballet, Pasadina Opera Co, Pasadina, 1970-; Am Consert Ballet, LA, 1967-70; Musical Theatre/Theatre Experience: Prin Dance/Featured Vocalist, "Tommy," Seattle Opera Co, 1972; Co-star in "Showboat" Supporting Role in "Carousel," Louis & Yg Prodns, Intl St Dept Goodwill Tour of S Am, 1967; Supporting Role in "Carousel," Sacramento Music Circus, 1967-; Supporting Role in "Carousel," Fresno Music Circus, 1967-; Ensemble & Featured Dancer in Var Prodns, Val Music Theatre, Woodland Hills, CA, 1965-66; Ensemble Var Prodns, Carousel Theatre, West Covina, CA, 1965-; Dancer in "Here's Love," San Bernadino Civic Light Opera, 1964-; Dancer & Featured Performer Var Prodns, San Diego Civic Light Opera, 1961-64; "Galileo," Old Globe Theatre, San Diego, CA, 1964-; Films: "How To Succeed in Bus w/o Really Trying," 1967; "Hold On," 1967; Tchg Experience: ½-time Grad Tchg Asst, Dept of Spch/Theatre Arts Current, Dept of PE 1980, Dept of Ed Sum 1980, WA St Univ; Dir, Owner & Admr, Acad of Ballet, Pullman, WA, Currently; Instr, Ballert Folk, Moscow, ID, 1980-; Instr, SF Dance Theatre, 1974-75; Instr, Ed Mock Studios, SF, 1974-75; Num Courses & Wkshops in Drama Therapy; Choreography: Dir & Choreographer, WA Jr Concert Ballet, Currently; Var Prodns w WA St Univ & SF Opera; Mem: Actor's Equity Assn; Am Guild of Musical Artists; Nat Assn for Drama Therapy; Am Pers & Guid Assn; Phi Delta Kappa; cp/Dir, Pocket Players, 1983-; Chm, Disabled Sers Advy Coun, 1978; Advy Bd, Exploring Fam Sch, 1977-78; Senate (Grad Rep), WA St Univ Senate, 1980; Others; hon/ Author, *Intro to Theatre for the Aged Disabled*, 1977; *Adaptive Theatre: Theory & Methods*; Fed Grant Recip, to Devel & Dir the San Diego Theatre for the Disabled, 1978; Grante, RA From the Ofc of Grants, Res & Devel, WA St Univ, 1982; Grantee, WA Comm for the Humanities; W/W in W.

WILSON, FRANCES PRESHIA oc/ Psychiatric Nurse and Homemaker; b/ Mar 13, 1919; h/4655 Basque Drive, Santa Maria, CA 93455; ba/Santa Maria, CA; m/Charles W; c/Charles William II, Walter Stephen, Cherrie W Pedigo, James Robin; sp/Walter P Stephenson (dec); Grace M Stephenson, Menlo Pk, CA; ed/BS, RN, Univ of KS, 1940; pa/Instr & Asst Dir, Sch Nsg, Axtell Christian Hosp, Newton, KS, 1940-41; Admr & Chp Student Hlth Prog, Grace Hosp, Detroit, MI, 1941-43; Ofcr Nurse, Norton, KS, 1944-46; Instr Psychi Nsg, Ctl St Hosp, Norman, OK, 1964-67; 1st Chp Geriatric Nsg Div, OK St Nurses Assn, 1964-67; Psychi Nurse, Co-Cnslr & Receptionist for Psychi (Husband), 1971-; Mem: AAUW; Alpha Chi Omega; ANA; Nat Leag for Nsg Ed; ARC Nsg Ser; KS St Nsg Assn, 1960-64; MI St Nurses Assn, 1941-43; OK St Nurses Assn, 1964-71; Pres

1951-53, Mem 1947-62, NW KS Nurses Aux; cp/Water Safety Instr & Chp Water Safety Prog, Cheyenne Co, KS, 1948-62; Key Tnr, Brownie Ldr, Camp Nurse, GSA; OES; Rotary Anns; Am Legion Aux; PTA; Fellow, Intl Platform Assn; Others; r/Prot; Life Mem & Pres, Wom's Soc Christian Ser; SS Tchr; Ordained Min; hon/Co-Resr & Co-Develr (w Husband), 4 Very Rapid Psychotherapies; Hon DDiv; Nat Hon Soc; Sigma Theta Tau Nat Nsg Frat; Most Outstg Girl Scouter Cheyenne Co, St Francis, KS; W/W of Wom; Dir of Dist'd Ams.

WILSON, LOWELL HENRY oc/Real Estate Developer and Insurance Marketing; b/May 24, 1932; h/217 Fairway West, Tequesta, FL 33458; ba/Miami, FL; m/Joan Ann; c/Joel, Jeff; p/Harry W Wilson (dec); sp/Henrietta Cloase, Hobe Sound, FL; ed/Att'd Drake Univ; pa/Self-employed in Cnstrn Bus, 1953-58; Pres & Prin Var Real Est Corps in IA, MO, KY & VA, 1958-; Fdr & VPres, Life Ins Mktg Corp, Ofcs in 15 Sts, 1972-; Past Pres, JJAA; cp/Blue Lodge, York Rite, Scottish Rite, Masons; Charter Mem & Past Potentate, AMARA Shrine Temple; r/Presb; hon/ Var W/W & Other Biogl Listings.

WILSON, THOMAS JOSEPH JR oc/ Optometrist; b/Dec 28, 1916; h/202 Canebreak Lane, Simpsonville, SC 29681; ba/Simpsonville, SC; m/Doris An (Bender); c/Maureen Louis (W) Wersinger, Thomas Joseph III, John Romuald, James Michael; p/Thomas Joseph Sr and Rose Esther (Solari) Wilson (dec); Leslie Colby and Miriam Gertrude (Michael) Bender (dec); ed/BS, Univ of PA, 1960; OD, So Col of Optometry, 1963; mil/USN, 1938-60, Med Dept; pa/Pvt Pract Optom, Charleston, SC, 1963-74; Dept Hd & Prof of Optom Technol, Greenville Tech Col, Greenville, SC, 1974-79; Pvt Prac Optom, Simpsonville, SC, 1979-; Mem: Am Optom Assn; SC Optom Assn; Appalachian Optom Soc; Optom Ext Prog; Optom Foun; Omega Delta Optom Frat; cp/US Nav Inst; FRA; Am Legion; r/Rom Cath; hon/Author, Num Articles Pub'd in Profl Optom Pubs; Pres, Charleston Co Optom Assn, 1964-66; Chm, Armed Sers Com, SC Optom Assn, 1967-70; Frs, Dept of Optom Technol, Greenville Tech Col, Greenville, SC, 1974; Optom Conslt, USAF Base Hosp, Charleston, 1964-68; Subnormal Vision Conslt, VA Hosp, Columbia, SC, 1977-79; Gov's Comm for Consolidated Govt Charleston Co, 1964-66; Recip Dedicated Public Ser Awd 1974, Outstg Ser to Profession of Optom Awd 1979, SC Optom Assn; VPres, Alpha Chapt, Omega Delta Intl Frat, 1963; W/W in S & SW.

WILSON-THOMAS, SANDRA ELAINE oc/Circuit Designer; b/Feb 11, 1943; h/95 West Calaveras, Altadena, CA 91007; ba/LA, CA; m/A Douglas Thomas; c/Vincent Charles, Michael DeWayne, Rosalyn Walker; p/Mr and Mrs Harry M Jackson, Kansas City, KS; Mrs Aline Sloan, Kansas City, KS; sp/ Mr and Mrs L T Thomas (dec); ed/AA, Kansas City Col, 1962; BA Bus, BA Psych, Univ of KS, 1978; pa/Supvr, Nat Bellas Hess, 1964-65; Engrg Aid, AT&T, 1964-77; Circuit Designer, Pacific T&T, 1978-; Mem: Pres, Ctl Coun, Telephone Pioneers of Am; cp/Music Coor, Lincoln

Avenue Bapt Ch, 1979-84; Wom's Aux; Pasadena Boys Clb; r/Bapt; hon/Outstg Wom of Am; W/W: in W, of Am Wom.

WILTSE, CHLORYCE J oc/Computer Software Programmer, Marketer and Speaker; b/Nov 25, 1933; ba/ Volberg, MT; m/Gary L Wiltse; c/Mark Wiltse, Lynn Braswell; p/Carl Ode and Leila Gibbs Ode, Tempe, AZ; sp/Earle Wiltse, DeKalb, IL; Erma Wiltse (dec); ed/BS, Univ of NE-Lincoln, 1955; Adv'd Wk: IA St Univ; Univ of MT; Mt St Univ; pa/Home Ec Instr, Osceola HS, Osceola, NE, 1955-57; Rural Tchr, Billup Sch, Powder River Co, MT, 1957-58; Home Ec & Computer Sci Instr, Powder River HS, Broadus, MT, 1964-83; Computer Software Prodr, Tchr & Spkr, Clo's----Line, Volberg, MT, 1982-; Mem: Am Home Ec Assn; Treas 1980-82, MT Home Ec Assn; Phi Upsilon Omicron; Omicron Nu; Gamma Alpha Chi; Delta Kappa Gamma; Kappa Delta; Wm 1977, OES; WIFE; Mortar Bd; Alpha Lambda Delta; Phi Sigma Chi; r/Luth; hon/Author, Computer Software under Clo's----Line Copyright: "The Cost Study Prog," "The Calorie Study Prog," "Recipe Search," "The Two-Income Lifestyle Study," "Clrm Potpourri"; Book/Software: *Apples for the Tchrs*; MT Hom Ec Tchr of Yr, 1975; Outstg Sec'dy Edr of Am, 1974; Broadus Outstg Yg Edr of Yr, 1976; Tchr, Nat Winning Class of Fleischmann Yeast Menu Planning Contest, 1969; Nat Runner-up, Share-the-Hlth Contest, 1980; Top FHA Chapt in MT, 1968 & 1973; W/W in W.

WIMMER, GLEN ELBERT oc/Professional Engr and Management Consultant; b/Feb 16, 1903; h/3839-48 Vista Campana South, Oceanside, CA 92056; ba/Same; m/Mildred G McCullough; c/ Frank Thomas; ed/BSME 1925, MSME 1933, IA St Univ; MBA NWn Univ, 1935; mil/USAR, Ofcr Active 1925-28, Inactive to 1938; pa/Draftsman, GE Co, Ft Wayne, IN, 1925-29; Asst Engr, Wn Elect Co, Chgo, IL, 1929-32; Mech Engr Instr, MI Col Mining & Technol, 1936-37; Machine Designer, Firestone Tire & Rubber Co, Akron, OH, 1937-38; Engr in Charge of Design, Ditto Inc, Chgo, 1938-39; Asst to Chief Engr, Victorgraph Corp, Chgo, 1939-40; Designer of Tools & Machinery, Pioneer Engrg & Mfg Co, Detroit, MI, l940-41; Designer & Checker, Assoc Designers, Detroit, MI, 1941-42; Designer & Checker, Engrg Ser Corp, Detroit, MI, 1942; Checker & Asst Supt, Design for Norman E Miller & Assocs, Detroit, MI, 1942; Engrg Checker, Lee Engrg Co, Detroit, MI, 1942-45; Hd Design & Devel Dept, Cummins Perforator Co, Chgo, 1943-45; Staff Engr Charge of Design & Devel, Tammen & Denison Inc, Chgo, 1945-58; Instr of Cost Anal, Evening Course, IL Inst of Technol, Chgo, 1946-47; Engr, Barnes & Reinick Inc, Chgo, 1958-60, 1961-68; Devel Engr, B H Bunn Co, Chgo, 1960-61; Pvt Pract, 1968-; Mem: Dir, IL Engrg Coun, 1958-66; Soc of Automotive Engrs; Soc Mfg Engrs; Computer & Automated Sys Assn; IPA; Delta Chi; Cert'd, Nat Bur Engrg Bds; cp/Am Def Preparedness Assn; Life Mem, IBA; r/Meth; hon/W/W: in Engrg, in MW, W, in CA, in Technol Today; Ldrs in Am Sci; Intl Blue Book World Notables; Nat Social Dir; Soc Dirs of US & CA;

The Blue Book; IL Lives; 2000 Men of Achmt; 2000 Notable Ams; Dir of Dist'd Ams; DIB; Intcontl Biog Assn; Men of Achmt; Personalities of W & MW; CA Register; Intl Register of Profiles; Intl W/W of Intells, Commun Ser; Commun Ldrs of Am; Am Patriots of the 1980's; Am Registry; CA W/W in Bus & Fin; Notable Ams; Commun Ldrs & Noteworthy Ams; Notables of the Bicent Era; Profiles of Freedom (Impressions of the Am Hist Soc); Men & Wom of Distn; Book of Hon.

WINBORN, LOIS DIANE MOYER oc/Principal; b/May 7; h/5390 Sherwood Drive, Katy, TX 77449; ba/Katy, TX; c/ Wendy Diane, Rebecca Marie; p/George and Lois Moyer, La Marque, TX; ed/BS, Univ of TX; MEd, Univ of Houston, 1973; pa/Tchr, Houston ISD; Tchr, Alief ISD, 1971-76; Asst Prin 1976-78, Prin 1978-, Katy ISD; Mem: TX Elem Prins & Supvrs Assn; TX Assn for Curric & Devel; cp/DAR; Daugh of Am Colonists; Colonial Dames of XVII Cent; Descendents of Colonial Clergy; Order of Huguenots; r/Epis; hon/W/W in S & SW; The Balliet Fam; Soc of Discendents of Colonial Clergy.

WINFIELD, ARLEEN DENT oc/Public Administration; b/Jul 14, 1932; h/ 3512 Jeff Road, Landover, MD 20785; ba/Washington, DC; m/Emeile I Jr; c/ Tawana Tolson Hinton; p/Emily F Dent, Forestville, MD; sp/Lillie G Winfield, Norfolk, VA; ed/BS, Hampton Inst, 1965; Addit Study: George Wash Univ & NIH Grad Sch in Immunology/ Virology, 1965-68; Bus Adm, Univ of MD, 1971-73; Num Certs for Def Intell, Profl, Mgrl & Exec Courses, 1967-80; pa/Microbiol Intell Analyst 1965-68, Microbiol 1968-70, Dept of AUS; Sci/ Math Tchr, Prince George's Co, MD Schs, 1970-71; Social Sci Res Analyst 1971-75, Social Sci Advr 1975-79, Career Devel Advr, Social Sci Advr 1979-, Wom's Bur, US Dept of Labor; Mem: Leag of Wom Votes, 1966-67; Am Pers & Guid Assn, 1974-77; Chair, Dept of Labor Employee Awds Com, 1975-77; Bus & Profl Wom's Assn, 1975-79; cp/ Chair, Civic Assn Planning Com, 1975-78; Co Civic & Coun Rep for Budget, Assessment & Tax Com; Study Dir, Pres Carter's Task Force on Wom Bus Owners, 1977-78; Wash DC Hampton Inst Alumni Assn; Bd of Dirs, Interfaith Commnuns Cable Netwk, 1982-83; r/Meth; hon/Author, *Careers for Wom in the '70s*, 1972; "Engrg Today & Tomorrow: Wom Needed Too," in *Proceedings of Engrg Foun Conf*, 1973; *Facilitating Career Devel for Wom & Girls*, 1973; "The Bottom Line: Unequal Enterprise in Am," Sect of Pres Report, 1978; Co-Author, *Wom in Apprenticeship: A Tng Wkshop*, 1980; Num Other Articles Pub'd in Profl Jours & Newspapers; Num Radio, TV & Public Spkg Presentations; Deptl Hons, 1965; Spec Achmt Awd, Dept of Labor, 1978; Num Certs, Lttrs of Apprec from Var Orgs Incl'g: Dept of AF, Dept of AUS, NASA, GSA; Invited Spkr, NC Tar Heel Girls St, Univ of NC-Greensboro, Am Legion Aux, 1972-82; Legal Def Fund Wash Com; Hampton Inst Alumni Dir.

WINKLEMAN, GLORIA PAULINE oc/Teacher and Private Elementary Grade Tutor; b/Nov 18, 1944; h/88 Coachman Drive South, Freehold Township, NJ 07728; ba/Perth Amboy, NJ; m/

Edward M Jr; p/Richard and Minnie Santillo, Pompton Plains, NJ; sp/Edward W Winkleman Sr, Garwood, NJ; Marguerite Winkleman (dec); ed/BA, Paterson St Col, 1966; Tchg Related Courses & Sems on Cont'g Ed Basis; pa/1st Grade Tchr, Perth Amboy Bd of Ed, 1966-; Elem Rdg & Math Tutor, 1966-; Mem: NJ Ed Asn; Am Fedn Tchrs, AFL-CIO #857, 1966-; cp/Mbrship Chp, Sea Rayders Inc; Downs Collectors Clb, 1981; Goebel Collectors Clb, 1978-81; r/Cath; hon/Musical Participant, World Music Fest, Kerkrade, Netherlands, 1962.

WINSKI, LOUISE F oc/Staff Biologist; b/Jun 20, 1950; h/1090 Bayless Place, Engleville, PA 19403; ba/West Point, PA; p/Ladislaus and Florence Winski, Phila, PA; ed/BSc in Med Technol, Phi Col of Pharm & Sci, 1972; pa/Staff Biol, Merck, Sharp & Donne, 1975-; Med Technol, Lower Bucks Hosp, 1972-75; Mem: Am Soc of Clin Pathols; Reg'd Med Technol & Affil Mem; cp/Exec Coun, Polish Intercol Clb of Phila, 1983; Bd of Dirs, Alumni Assn of Phil Col of Pharm & Sci, 1983-84; r/Rom Cath; hon/W/W: Among Students in Am Cols & Univs; Among Am Wom.

WIRTHS, WALLACE RICHARD oc/ Executive; b/Jul 7, 1921; h/Wantage House, Compton Road, Rural Delivery 3, Sussex, NJ 07461; ba/Same; c/Harold John, Ung N Le; p/Rudolph and Dorothy Wirths (dec); ed/BS, Lehigh Univ, 1942; Att'd Fordham Law Sch, 1943; Addit Courses: NY Univ, Stevens Inst, Rutgers Univ, Upsala Col; mil/USNR, 1950-54; pa/Aluminum Co of Am, 1943-54; Sylvania Elect Co, 1954-56; Westinghouse Elect Corp, 1956-81; Pres, Wantage Galleries Inc, 1981-; cp/ Nat Coun on Crime & Delinq, 1966-; Past Chm Essex Co Chapt, NJ Employers Legis Com, 1959-; VPres of Wantage Township Com, Sussex Co Repub Com, 1962-; Sussex Co Soil Conserv Dist, 1967-; NJ Farm Bur, 1960-; NJ Agri Soc, 1969-; Life Mem, Sussex Co Hist Soc; Sussex Co SPCA, 1974-; Exec Com, Sussex Co Arts Coun, 1973-; Pres, Unique Homeowners, 1973-; Life Mem, Alexander Linn Hosp Assn; KY Col, 1973-; No NJ Lehigh Alumni Clb, 1964-; Repub Congl Clb, 1972-; Sustaining Mem, Repub Party, 1970-; Reg Hlth Planning Coun, 1979-; Pres Advy Bd, Upsala Co, 1980-; Num Other Coms & Commun Activs; r/Prot; hon/Author of Newspaper Column, "Candidly Spkg," 1970-82; Book: Candidly Spkg, 1982; Conserv Farmer of Yr, Sussex Co Soil Conserv Dist, 1975; Host for the Pres, 1972; Fund Raising Prog Awd, Sussex Co Cancer Soc, 1975; Ortho Nat Commun Ser AWd, Chevron, 1976; Commun Ser Awd, Westinghouse Corp, 1976; Donated 1 Million Dollar Sussex Campus to Upala Col, 1978; Sussex Co Citizen of Yr, Radio Sta WSUS, 1979; Outstg Big Brother of Yr, 1978; Outstg Commun Ser Cit, Wantage Twnship, 1978; Hon Doc of Laws, Upsala Col, 1981; Cert of Recog, Nat Repub Congl Com, 1982; Nat Repub Victory Cert, 1979; Awd of Apprec, Repub Nat Com, 1982; Others; W/W: in E, in World, in Fin & Indust, in Commun Ser, of Intells; Men of Achmt; DIB; Other Biogl Listings.

WISE, JANIE DENISE oc/Executive;

b/Dec 15, 1945; h/5020 Puritan Circle, Tampa, FL 33617; ba/Tampa, FL; p/ Joseph W Wise (dec); Kathryn S Wise, Lakeland, FL; ed/BA, Univ of KY, 1970; MA, Univ of L'ville, 1972; pa/Pres, Effective Communs (Exec Conslt'g Firm), 1980-; Communs Spec, Sales-Mktg, 3M Co, 1978-80; Communs Spec, Public Affairs, Tri-Co Alcoholism Sers, 1975-78; Pvt Pract Psychol, 1973-75; Cnslr, Public Affairs, Hillsborough Co Alcoholism Sers, 1972-73; Commun Relats Spec, L'ville, KY, 1971-72; Tchr, 1970-71; Nat Mgmt Conslt; Guest Spkr in Field; FL Rep, Nat Cong for Ofc of Wom, Wash DC; Dir, FL Task Force on Wom & Alcohol; cp/ Pilot; hon/"People on the Move," Tampa Bay Area, 1982; Outstg Yg Wom of Yr, St of KY; W/W in Am Wom.

WISEMAN, JAY DONALD oc/Executive and Business Owner; b/Dec 23, 1952; h/6429 South 300 East, Murray, UT 84107; ba/Bountiful, UT; m/Barbara Taylor; c/Jill Reva, Steve Jay; p/Donald Wiseman; Reva Wiseman Peterson, Provo, UT; sp/L Eugene and Helen Taylor, Midvale, UT; ed/Att'd UT St Univ, 197-72; Att'd Univ of UT, 1975-77; pa/Estimator 1976-81, VPres 1981-, A&T Heating; Pres, Owner, Jay Wiseman Photo, 1977-; Mem: IPPA; RMPP of Am; PP of Am; PSA; r/LDS, Mormon, Missionary in Finland; hon/ Recog of Photos in The Profl Photog, Jul, Oct & Nov, 1983; 1st Place, RMPPA, 1982; 1st Place, IPPA, 1981, 1982 & 1983; Best of Show, IPPA, 1982; Masters Trophy, IPPA, 1982; 75% of Prints Entered Accepted, PP of Am Intl; 88% of Prints Entered Accepted & 3 Hon Mentions, TCC Intl Salon, 1983; W/W in W.

WISLER, NORMAN E oc/Marketing Communications Executive; b/Mar 26, 1943; h/2139 Clay Street, Phila, PA 19130; ba/North Wales, PA; m/Marcia; p/Norman Wisler, Phila, PA; sp/Rose Rosen, W Palm Bch, FL; ed/BS, Temple Univ, 1964; Dipl, Charles Morris Price Sch of Advtg & Jour, 1965; pa/Copy Contact, Tricebock Advtg, Huntington Val, PA, 1965; Advtg Asst, KSM Div, Omark Industs, Morrestown, NJ, 1965-67; Advtg Mgr, Amchem Prods Inc, Ambler, PA, 1967-73; Reg Mktg Mgr, Hitchcock Pub'g Co, Wheaton, IL, 1973-83; Advtg Acct Mgr, Leeds & Northrop Instruments, N Wales, PA, 1983-; Mem: Asst Treas 1972-73, Treas 1973-74, Chm Clins & Sems 1968-70, Dir 1968-72, Hospitality Chm 1978-80, Auditing Chm 1973-75, CBC Com Chm 1980-83, Dir 1980-82, Secy 1983-, Bus Profl Advtg Assn; r/Rom Cath; hon/ Contbr, Var Bus-Related Articles to Trade Pubs, 1967-73; Cert'd Bus Communr (CBC) Designation; Bus Profl Advtg Assn, 1980; Alumnus Awd, Charles Morris Price Sch of Advtg & Jour, 1965; W/W: in World, in Fin & Indust.

WITCHER, SETH LAMAR JR oc/ Surgeon; b/Mar 28, 1950; h/101 Pompano, Galveston, TX 77550; ba/Galveston, TX; m/Martha Jane; c/Jennifer, Trey; p/Mr and Mrs S L Witcher, Clifton, TX; sp/Mr and Mrs M E Keath, Sabinal, TX; ed/BA 1972, BS 1974, Baylor Univ; Doct of Dental Surg, Univ of TX Dental Sch, 1979; pa/Yth Dir 1970-71, Interim Pastor 1971-72, Kopperl Bapt Ch, TX; Resident, Audie

Murphy VA Hosp, San Antonio, TX, 1979-80; Pvt Pract Gen Dentistry, Hondo, TX, 1980-82; Resident, Oral & Maxillofacial Surg, Galveston,TX, 1982-; Mem: Am Dental Assn; TX Dental Assn; Xi Psi Phi, 1975-79; Univ of TX Dental Sch-San Antonio Alumni Assn; Life Mem, Baylor Alumni Assn; Baylor Lttrman's Assn, 1972-; cp/Asst Scoutmaster Troop 376, Clifton, TX, BSA; Baylor Univ C of C, 1970-74; Coach, Clifton Little Leag Baseball; Pres, Hondo Little Leag, 1981-82; Hondo C of C, 1980-; A Capella Choir, Baylor Univ, 1968-72; r/Mem 1970-75, Mid-wk Meal Com 1974-75, Fin Com 1974-75, SS Tchr for 4 & 5 Yr Olds 1974-75, 7th & James Bapt Ch; Mem 1975-80; Yth (11th & 12th Grades) SS Tchr 1976-78, Manor Bapt Ch, San Antonio; Mem 1980-82, Deacon Selection Com 1980-81, Pastor Search Com 1981-82, 1st Bapt Ch, Hondo; Ch Choirs, 1972-80; Current Mem, 1st Bapt Ch, Galveston; hon/Author of Var Dental Surg Articles Pub'd in Profl Jours; NHS, 1965-68; Eagle Scout 1967, God & Country Awd 1968, BSA; TX Yth Safety Coun, 1967; All-Dist Band, 1967-68; All-Reg Band, 1968; Reg Qualifier, Ready Writing, 1966-68; St Alt, Ready Writing, 1968; Reg Qualifier, Persuasive Spkg, 1968; Hon Grad, 1968; St Qualifier, Solo & Ensemble Contest, 1967; Mosby S'ship Awd, 1979; Dental Mgmt Mag Advy Staff, 1983.

WITTELES, ELEONORA MEIRA oc/ Physicist; b/Jul 14, 1938; h/4714 Browndeer Lane, Palos Verdes, CA 90274; ba/ LA, CA; p/Salomon and Rivka Komornik Witteles (dec); ed/BS 1962, MS 1963, Fordham Univ; MS, NY Univ, 1965; PhD, Yeshiv Univ, 1969; pa/Asst Prof, Bar-Ilan Univ, Israel, 1970-72; Indep Conslt, 1972-80; Sr Res Sci, Atlantic Richfield Co, 1980-; Mem: Am Phy Soc; AAAS; IEEE; IEEE Engrg in Med & Biol Soc; IEEE Magnetics Soc; The Com on the Status of Wom in Physics; hon/ Author, Inventions in Med Instrumentation & Cryogenic Instrumentation; Num Articles Pub'd in Profl Jours in Field of: Solid St Physics, Applied Mat Sci & Superconductivity; Post Doct F'ship, Bar-Ilan Univ, 1969-70; Res F'ship, Yeshiva Univ, 1967-69; W/W of Am Wom.

WOECKENER, JAME M PACHURA oc/Registered Dietician; b/Dec 15, 1949; h/3405 La Selva Drive, San Mateo, CA 94403; ba/Stanford, CA; m/Michael C (dec); p/Edward P Pachura (dec); Helen (Grabski) Pachura, Mosinee, WI; ed/BS, Univ of WI, 1972; MS, Univ of IA, 1976; Dietetic Intern, Univ of IA Hosp & Clins, 1972-73; Reg'd Dietician, 1973-; pa/Reg'd Dietician, Univ of IA Hosp & Clins, 1973-76; Conslt Dietician for Nsg Homes, IA, 1974-76; Clin Instr in Dietetics Sch of Home Ec, Univ of WI-Stevens Point, 1976-77; Food Ser Admr I & Dir of Dietetic Interns, Univ of WI Hosp-Madison, 1977-80; Asst Dir of Dietetics/Nutritional Sers, Stanford Univ Hosp, Stanford, CA, 1980-; Mem: Am Dietetic Assn; Am Hosp Assn; Am Soc for Parenteral & Enteral Nutrition; CA Dietetic Assn; Chm Quality Assurance Com, San Jose Peninsula Dist Dietetic Assn, 1982-84; Clin Nutrition Mgmt Pract Grp; Am Soc for Hosp Food Ser Admrs; Omicron Nu; Sigma Zeta; Other Previous Profl Assns; r/Rom Cath; hon/Co-Author, "Urinary

Urea-Nitrogen Ratio as an Index of Protein Nutrition in Diabetic Pregnancy," in *Jour of OB & Gyn*, 1978; Internship, S'ship, WI Dietetic Assn, 1972; S'ship, Alpha Delta Alpha Dietetics Clb, 1972; Traineeship Grant, Dept of Hlth, Ed & Welfare, 1973-76; W/W in W.

WOHL, EMANUEL oc/Insurance Broker; b/Oct 11, 1920; h/3150 Rochambeau Avenue, New York, NY 10467; ba/New York, NY; p/Samuel and Fannie Wohl (dec); ed/BS, Col of City of NY, 1943; MS, NY Univ, 1948; Bus Adm, Alexander Hamilton Inst, 1954; LLB, LaSalle Ext Univ, 1969; pa/Chemist, Keto Chem Co, LI, NY, 1943-44; Chem, Radio Receptor Co Inc, NYC, 1944-48; Res Chem, Sylvania Elect Prods Inc, Boston, MA, 1948-49; Sr Chem, Galvanic Prods Corp, Val Stream, NY, 1952-53; Ptner, Riviera Wine & Liquor Co, Bronx, NY, 1954-61; Abstractor, Chem Abstracts Sers, Am Chem Soc, Columbus, OH, 1963-64; Reg'd Rep, Becker, Nagler & Weisman Inc, Bronx, NY, 1963-67; Ins Broker-Agt, Securities Broker-Dealer, Paramount Brokerage Co, Bronx, NY 1969-; Mem: Nat Assn of Securities Dealers Inc; Am Chem Soc; cp/Dem Co Com, 1967 & 1968; Participant, White House Conf on Small Bus, 1979; Bd of Dirs, NY Univ Gard Sch of Arts & Sci Alumni; Intl Clarinet Soc; hon/Author, "Studies w N-Acetyl Phenylisopropylamine Derivatives (Olefin-Nitrile Condensation)"; W/W in Fin & Indust.

WOJCIECHOWSKA, CÉCILE CLOUTIER oc/Professor and Writer; b/Jun 13, 1930; h/44 Farm Greenway, Don Mills, Ontario, Canada, M2A 3M2; ba/Toronto, Ontario, Canada; m/Jerry; c/Maria, Eve; ed/BA 1951, MA 1953, Licence es Lettres 1953, Dipl d'Etudes Supérieures 1954, Laval Univ; Doct in Esthétique, Univ of Paris, The Sorbonne, 1962; MPh, McMaster Univ, 1978; MTh, Univ of Toronto, 1981; pa/Prof of Latin, Greek, Spanish & Fr Lit, Marymount Col, Quebec, 1955-58; Prof of Fr & Quebec Lit, Univ of Ottawa, 1958-64; Prof Aesthetics, Fr & Quebec Lit, Univ of Toronto, 1965-; Guest Prof, Laval Univ, Sums 1969-72; Vis'g Prof, Queen's Univ, Fall Sem 1980; Mem: MLA; Am Assn of Tchrs of French; Assn Canadienne des Professeurs de Francais; Société des Ecrivains Canadiens; Sociéte des Poetes; Pen Clb; Assn des Anciens de l'Université de Paris; Sociéte d'Esthétique de Paris; Am Soc of Aesthetics; Brit Soc of Aesthetics; Assn des Ecrivains de Langue Francais; Intl Platform Assn; cp/Participant in Num Confs; Num Lectr & Spkg Presentations; r/Cath; hon/Author, Books of Poetry Incl: *Mains de Sable*, 1960; *Cuivre Et Oies*, 1964; *Cannelles Et Craie*, 1969; *Paupieres*, 1970; *Cablegrammes*, 1972; *Chalevils*, 1979; *Springtime of Spoken Words*, 1979; Num Articles, Reviews & Wks of Translations;. Médaille D'argent de la Société des Écrivains Francais, Paris, 1960 (Prix Jugé par Jean Cocteau); Prix du Concours de la Comm du Centenaire, Ottawa, 1967; Others.

WOLAVER, LYNN E oc/Dean for Research; b/Mar 10, 1924; h/1380 Timberwyck Court, Fairborn, OH 45324; ba/Wright-Patterson AFB, OH; m/Arah-Dean S; c/Stephen A, Rick S; p/Mr and Mrs Lendle H Wolaver (dec);

sp/Mrs Arthur H Scheele, Springfield, IL; ed/BS 1949, MS 1950, Univ of IL; PhD, Univ of MI, 1964; mil/USAAC, 1944-46; pa/Positions at Wright-Patterson AFB, OH: Engr, Wright Air Devel Ctr, USAF, 1950-56; Applied Math 1956-65, Dir 1966-71, Aerospace Res Labs, USAF; Dean for Res, AF Inst of Technol, USAF, 1971-; Mem: Soc of Industl & Applied Math (SIAM); IEEE; Biofeedback Soc; Fellow, Brit Interplanetary Soc; MWn Simulation Coun; AAAS; Am Soc for Engrg Ed; cp/Fairborn, OH Planning Bd; r/Luth; hon/Author, *Mod Techniques in Astrodynamics*, 1970; Over 60 Papers in Field of Navigatin, Astrodynamics, Nonlinear Sys, Modeling Physiol Sys, 1950-80; Meritorious Civilian Ser Awd, USAF, 1979; Eta Kappa Nu, 1949; Tau Beta Pi, 1970; Sigma Xi, 1974; Outstg Tchr, 1978-82; W/W: in MW, in Govt; Am Men & Wom of Sci; DIB; Ldrs in Am Sci; Outstg Ldrs in Ed.

WOLENS, MICKEY EARL oc/Corporate Purchasing Manager; b/Jan 6, 1937; h/3500 Williams & Mary Road, Birmingham, AL 35216; ba/B'ham, AL; m/Mary Bobbie Wolens; c/Jason Zachary, Heather Lynne; p/Cyril Wolens (dec); Elaine Wolens, Corsicana, TX; ed/BBA 1982, MBA 1982, Pacific Wn Univ; Att'd Num Mgmt Sems, 1974-80; mil/AUS Armored Div, 1958-61, SP4 (CPL); pa/Purchasing Mgr 1979 & 1982-, Asst Mgr of Purchasing 1980-82, B E & K Constrn Co, B'ham, AL; Procurement Mgr 1976-79 & 1979-80, The Litwin Corp, Houston, TX; Purchasing Mgr 1974-76, Mgr of Inspection, Expediting & Traffic 1974, Proj Purchasing Agt 1973-74, Davy Powergas Inc, Lakeland, FL; Sr Buyer, Hess Oil Virgin Isl Corp, St Croix, Virgin Isl, 1973; Purchasing Agt 1970-73, Supvr of Field Inspectors/Expeditors 1969-70, Asst Purchasing Agt 1967-69, The M W Kellogg Co, Houston, TX; Sr Buyer, Trinity Industs Inc, Dallas, TX; Cert'd Purchasing Mgr (CPM), Nat Assn of Purchasing Mgmt Inc; Purchasing Mgmt Assn of AL Inc; Chm Mbrship Com 1983, Assoc'd Bldrs & Contractors of AL Inc (ABC); W/W in S & SW.

WOLF, JACK oc/Insurance and Financial Planning; b/Nov 9, 1934; h/2927 Robinson Road, Missouri City, TX 77459; ba/Houston, TX; m/Marlene; c/David, Michael, Stephen; p/Joseph Wolf (dec); Mary Wolf, Kansas City, MO; ed/BA, Univ of MO, 1956; Chartered Life Underwriter (CLU), Am Col of Life Ins, 1972; mil/AUS; pa/Agt & Gen Mgr, Jack Wolf, CLU Ins, 1967-; Mem: Am Soc of CLU, 1972-; Million Dollar Round Table, 1980-; cp/VPres 1983-84, E Ft Bend Kiwanis Clb; Life Master, Am Contract Bridge Leag, 1959-; Qualifying Mem, Million Dollar Round Table, 1980-84; TX Ldr's Round Table, Lone Star Ldr, 1983; W/W in SW.

WOLF, SEYMOUR SY oc/Executive; b/May 12, 1921; h/2245 Vistact, Northbrook, IL 60062; ba/Northfield, IL; m/Ellie; c/Susan, Stephen, Charles; p/Charles and Mae Wolf (dec); sp/David & Gussie Schreiber (dec); ed/LLB, NWn Univ, 1948; Att'd Col of Pacific; mil/AUS, 1941-45; pa/VPres, Selected Brands Inc; Pres, Ceramic World; Pres, S C Ltd; cp/Magistrate, Niles Twnship; Staff Profl, US Golf Acad; World Golf Hall of Fame; Canadian Football Assn;

r/Jewish; hon/Ideaism Awd, City Hope; Cert of Apprec, City Hope; W/W; W/W in MW; Personalities of MW.

WOLFE, CHARLES EDWARD oc/Methodist Clergyman; b/Nov 7, 1931; h/3100 Shiloh Road, Hampstead, MD 21074; ba/Same; m/Helen Bickel; c/Christian, Hawley, Lewis, David; p/Mrs Harley Strawer, Zephyrhills, FL; ed/BA, No IA Univ, 1952; BD, Austin Presb Theol Sem, 1958; DMin, Wesley Theol Sem, 1977; mil/AUS, 1966-69, Chaplain, VietNam Ser 1967-68; AUS Command & Gen Staff Col; DC NG Chaplain Corps, Lt Col Ret'd; pa/Adj Prof, Wn MD Col, Current; Bible Instr, Course of Study, Wesley Theol Sem, Current; Pastor, Shiloh Meth Ch, Hampstead, MD, 1977-; Pastor, W End Presb Ch, Albany, NY, 1971-76; Pastor, 1st Presb Ch, Killeen, TX, 1960-66; Assoc Pastor, Delmar Meth Ch, NY, 1968-69; Chaplain, AUS, 1966-69; Mem: Soc Biblical Lit; r/Meth; hon/Presenter of Scholarly Papers at Nat & Reg Meetings; Author, *Homecoming: 1st Person Sermons*, 1979; *The 7 Words From the Cross: A Commentary*, 1981; *Exegesis of the Biblical Texts for the Spec Days Exegetical Resource*, 1982; "Exegetical Resource," for *Pulpit Resource*; Scholarly Jour Awd 1983, Fac Book Awd 1980, Wn MD Col; W/W in Rel; NG Register; DIB; Commun Ldrs of Am; Men of Achmt.

WONG, BETTY JEAN oc/Educatinal Administrator; b/Mar 15, 1949; h/1137 Woodfield Drive, Jackson, MS 39211; ba/Jackson, MS; pa/Mr and Mrs Henry Wong, Greenville, MS; ed/BS Ednl Psych, MS St Univ, 1971; MEd Guid & Cnslg, Delta St Univ, 1973; pa/Career Devel Spec, Greenville mun Separate Sch Dist, 1973-74; Instnl Mats Spec for Career Ed 1974-76, Res Spec 1976-77, Res Curric Spec, Res/Curric Unit 1977-79, MS St Univ; Coor of Res, Curricula, Tchr Ed 1979-80, Asst Dir Supportive Sers Sect Voc Div 1980-, St Dept of Ed; Mem: St Exec Bd, MS Pers & Guid Assn; Am Pers & Guid Assn; MS Voc Assn; Nat Policy Bd Guid Sect 1982-84, Planning Com for Nat Conv 1984, Am Voc Assn; Handbook Chp 1976, AAUW; Nat Voc Guid Assn; MS Voc Cnslrs Assn; cp/Jackson Symph Leag; Jackson Arts Alliance; New Stage Theatre; r/Bapt; hon/Author of Career Ed Mats & the Job Placement Handbook for Voc Cnslrs in MS; Commun Advy Coun, EBCE Itawamba Jr Col; One of 15 Outstg Wom in US in Voc Ed, Am Voc Assn, 1983; W/W: in S, of Wom; Personalities of S; Notable Ams.

WONG, OTTO oc/Epidemiologist/Biostatistician; b/Nov 14, 1947; h/111 Clyde Drive, Walnut Creek, CA 94598; ba/Berkeley, CA; m/Betty; c/Elaine, Jonathan; p/K Wong, Toronto, Canada; sp/B Yeung, Tucson, AZ; ed/BS, Univ of AZ, 1970; MS, Carnegie-Mellon Univ, 1972; MS 1973, ScD 1975, Univ of Pgh; pa/Sr Epidemioligist, Envir Hlth Assocs, 1981-; Dir of Occupl Res, Biometric Res Inst, Wash DC 1980-81; Dir of Epidemiology, Tabershaw Occupl Med Assocs, 1978-80; Asst Prof Epidemiology, Georgetown Univ Sch of Med, 1975-78; Mem: Am Col of Epidemiology; Am Statl Assn; Biometric Soc; Soc for Epidemiol Res; APHA; Soc for Clin Trial; Soc for Occupl & Envir Hlth; hon/Author, Num Articles Pub'd in Profl Jours Incl'g: *Intl Jour of Epidemiology*; *Jour* of Occupl Med; Jour of Chronic Diseases; Am Jour of Clin Nutrition; Brit Jour of Industl Med; Intl S'ship Recip, Univ Scholar, Univ of AZ; Pi Mu Epsilon; Phi Beta Kappa; Grad BS magna cum laude; W/ W: in CA, in W.

WOOD, ARLETTA RENEE oc/Executive; b/Apr 19, 1945; h/2418 Homestead Drive, Silver Spring, MD 20902; ba/Washington, DC; ed/BSBA, Howard Univ, 1967; Att'd Spec Courses, Montgomery Col, 1977-78; pa/Exec Secy to Dept Hd, OH Dept of Ed, 1963-64; Adm Secy to Hd Botany Dept, Howard Univ, 1964-66; Adm Asst, Exec & Adm Secy Var Locations, 1967-79; Adm Secy, Air Trans Assn of Am, Wash DC, 1979; Fdr & Pres, Affil Enterprises Inc (Artists Mgmt & Fin Brokerage), Silver Spring, MD, 1967-; Pres, B I Prodns, 1971-79; Pres Renee's Beauty Boutique, 1974-79; Mem: Air Transport Assn; Pres 1980-81, Am Employees Assn; Am Soc Profl & Exec Wom; UN Assn US Pres's Assn; Am Mgmt Assn; Intl Platform Assn; Am Lyceum Assn; Am Film Inst; Am Fedn of Musicians; cp/Nat Trust Hist Presv; Smithsonian Instn; Spiritualist Clb; Toastmasters Intl; hon/ "Arletta Renee Day," Proclamation by Mayor Marion Bradley of Wash DC, Jan 8, 1982; W/W: in S, in A, in World, of Wom, Among Black Ams, in Fin & Indust; Dir Dist'd Ams; 2000 Notable Am Personalities.

WOOD, CHARLES NEWBOLD oc/ Self-Employed; b/Jan 16, 1943; h/Mill House Farm, 31 West Fourbridges Road, Long Valley, NJ 07853; ba/Same; p/ Wilfrid and Charlotte Wood (dec); ed/ Att'd St Bernards Col; BA, MA, PhD, Yale Univ, 1966; pa/Self-Employed, Mill House Farm & Horse Farm (Cedar Hill Farm); Doct of Psych; r/High Espc; hon/ Racing, Riding & Sailing; NY Social Register.

WOOD, FAY S oc/National Sales Manager; b/Aug 22, 1945; h/61-20 Grand Ctl Parkway, Forest Hills, NY 11375; ba/New York, NY; c/Deborah S, Esther L; p/Paul H Wiener, Phila, PA; sp/Dorothy B Berkowitz (dec); BA, PA St Univ, 1967; Grad Exec Mgmt Courses RCA Corp, 1977; pa/Nat Sales Mgr 1982-, Quantech Corp; Pres, Full Line Repairs Ctrs Inc, 1979-82; Reg Sales Mgr RCA Ser Co, 1976-79; VPres Sales, P H D Hearing Ctrs Inc, 1972-76; Dist Sales Mgr, Beltone Hearing Aid Ctrs, 1970-72; Sales Rep, Real Est of PA, 1968-70; Mem: AAUW; Bus & Profl Wom; NAFE; Wom Bus Owners; Leag of Wom Voters; cp/B'nai B'rith; NYC Comm on the Status of Wom; r/Jewish; hon/Articles Pub'd in HFD Retailing Hom Furnishings; Sales & Mktg Mgmt Mag; Master Conslt Awd, 1975; Reg Mgr of Yr Awd, 1979; 1st Deg Black Belt, Tae Kwan Do, Karate, 1975; W/W of Am Wom.

WOOD, KATHERINE E oc/Social Worker; b/Jul 4, 1950; h/331 North Hass, Frankenmuth, MI 48734; ba/Bay City, MI; m/Michael (dec); c/Jared M Wood; p/Maurice and June Finger, Frankenmuth, MI; sp/Harold Wood and Cynthia Rose, Rose City and Clio, MI; ed/BA, Valparaiso Univ, 1971; MSW, Wayne St Univ, 1976; pa/Tchr's Aide, Nursery for Emotionally Impaired Chd, S Bend, IN, 1971; Sch Social Wkr, Caroad Blanc & Goodrich Sch Dists, MI, 1972; Subst Tchr, Frankenmuth, Clio & Birch

Run Sch Dists, MI, 1973-74; Clin Social Wkr & Pre-intake Wkr, Bay Area Guid Ctr, Bay City, MI 1976-81; Pvt Pract Cert'd Social Wkr, Bay City, MI, 1982-; Mem: Nat Assn of Social Wkrs, 1971-; Wom's Chair 1982-84, VPres in Charge of Programming 1983-85, AAUW; r/ Prot; hon/Play & Observation Rms Dedicated in Her Name, Bay Area Guid Ctr, MI, 1981; W/W: in Am Wom, in World of Wom.

WOOD, LARRY (MARYLAIRD) oc/ Journalist, Educator; h/6161 Castle Drive, Oakland, CA 94611; c/Mary, Marcia, Barry; p/Edward Hayes and Alice (McNeel) Small; ed/BA 1938, MA 1940, Univ of WA-Seattle; Postgrad Study 1941-42, Cert in Photo 1971, Stanford Univ; Postgrad Wk in Jour: Univ of WI, 1971-72; Univ of MN 1971-72; Univ of GA 1972-73; Univ of CA-Santa Cruz, 1974-76; pa/By-line Columnist, Oakland Tribune, SF Chronicle, 1946-; Contbg Editor: Mech Illus, 1946-; Popular Mech, 1948-; Feature Writer Wn Reg: Christian Sci Monitor, CSM Radio Syn & Intl News, 1973-; Des Moines Register & Tribune Syn, 1973-; Contbg Editor, Travelday Mag, 1976-; Author, Contbg Editor: Fodor Guides, David McKay Co, NYC, 1982; (Book) SF, 1982; Charles Merrill Co Sci Series 1982-83; Bell & Howell (Charles Merrill, USA) Worldwide Editions of Focus On Sci, 4 Books, 1983-; Reg Corres: Spokane Mag; CA Corres, Money Mag; Portland Oregonian; Seattle Times Sunday Mag; Far W Contbg Editor, Fashion Showcase, Dallas; Byline Feature Writer, Photog, Parade Mag, 1960-; Feature Writer Industl Progress: CA Today, 1977-; E/W Netwk, 1982-; Feature Writer, Chevron USA, 1982; Feature Writer Motorland Pubs: AAA Travel Mag-No CA & AAA Travel Mag-So CA; Wk for Syn Feature Synopses on Radio Stas, CSM Radio News Ser; Freelance Writer Var Mags Incl'g: Times Mirror Co Syn; Knight Ridder Syn; Linguapress France; Parents; Sports Illus'd; Ocean & Seas Frontiers; Accent; People on Parade; House Beautiful; Am Home; Others; Dir Public Relats, No CA Assn Phi Beta Kappa, 1969-; Asst Prof Jour, Envir Sci & Pub Relats, San Diego St Univ, 1975-; Other Positions; Mem: Intl Assn of Bus Commrs; Coun for Advmt in Sci Writing; Nat Acad of TV Arts & Scis; CA Press Wom; Public Relats Soc of Am; Am Mgmt Assn; Nat Exec Bd Mag Div 1979-, Nat Chm Travel Writing Contest for Am Univ Students 1978-, Am Assn Edn in Jour; Advtg & Mktg Assn; Nat Assn Sci Writers; Travel Writers of Am; Soc Profl Jours; Nat Press Clb; Sigma Delta Chi; CA Writers Clb; Num Other Orgs; cp/Secy, Oakland Jr Arts Ctr, 1962-; Trustee, CA St Pks Foun, 1976-; Other Commun Activs; hon/Author, Eng for Social Living: Tell the Town; Principles of Sci Series (4 Books); Feature Writer (Bus & Sci) Honoree, Chevron USA & Oakland C of C, 1983; Cit, Nat Pk Ser, 1976; Nat Headline Awd, Mercury News, 1979 & 1980; NOAA Cit, 1981 & 1982; Wks Selected for CA Rm, Oakland Public Lib & NW Rm, Univ of WA Lib; Num Other Hons & Awds; W/W of World.

WOOD, LINCOLN JACKSON oc/ Aerospace Engineer and University Professor; b/Sep 30, 1947; ba/Jet Propulsion Lab, 4800 Oak Grove Drive, Pasadena, CA 91109; p/William Hulbert

and Sarah Brock (Strumsky) Wood; ed/ BS, Cornell Univ, 1968; MS 1969, PhD 1972, Stanford Univ; pa/Bechtel Instr in Engrg 1972-74, Lectr in Sys Engrg 1975-76, Vis'g Asst Prof of Sys Engrg 1976-78, Vis'g Assoc Prof of Sys Engrg 1978-, CA Inst of Technol, Pasadena CA; Staff Engr, Sys Anal Lab, Space & Communs Grp, Hughes Aircraft Co, El Segundo, CA, 1974-77; Tech Staff 1977-81, Tech Grp Supvr (Future Mission Studies Grp) 1981-, Navigation Sys Sect, Jet Propulsion Lab, CA Inst of Technol; Conslt to Var Aerospace Cos, 1972-74 & 1979; Mem: Sr Mem, Space Flight Mech Com 1980-, Am Astronaut Soc; AIAA; AAAS; IEEE; Assoc Editor, Jour of the Astronaut Scis, 1980-83; Jour of Guid, Control & Dynamics, 1983-; cp/Del, CA Dem Coun Conv, 1978; VPres & Dir 1980-, LA Stanford Bachelors; Pres, Seal & Serpent Soc, 1967-68; LA Co Mus of Art; Cornell & Stanford Alumni Assns; hon/Author & Co-Author Over 30 Tech Papers on Interplanetary Navigation, Trajectory Optimization, Gravity Field Estimation & Control Theory; Sigma Xi; Tau Beta Pi; Phi Kappa Phi; Phi Eta Sigma; Dean's List, 1964-68; NSF Trainee, 1968-72; W/ W: in CA, in W, in Aviation & Aerospace; Men of Achmt; Commun Ldrs of Am; DIB; Dir of Dist'd Ams; Num Other Biogl Listings.

WOOD, RONALD WILSON oc/ Engineering Management; b/Nov 17, 1943; h/6267 North Lausanne Drive, Mobile, AL 36608; ba/Pascagoula, MS; m/Janith Carolyn; c/Christopher Darby, Heather Michelle; p/Frank W and Renee S Wood, Farmington, NH; sp/Harold W and Freta Maine, Kinsington, CA; ed/ BSME, Worcester Polytech Inst, 1965; MBA, Univ of S AL, 1976; pa/Staff Asst to Dir of Design Engrg 1982-, MGR US Nav Res & Devel Studies 1980-82, Proj Mgr 1978-80, Sec Mgr 1974-78, Sr Engr 1969-74, Ingalls Shipbldg Co, Pascagoula, MS; Engr, Elect Boat Co, 1965-69; Mem: Local Coun, Am Soc of Nav Engrs; ASME; Soc of Nav Archs & Marine Engrs; Am Def Preparedness Assn; cp/Coach & Bd Mem, Springhill Dixie Boys Baseball; r/Epis; hon/W/W in S & SW.

WOOD, SANDRA E oc/Systems Analyst Programmer; b/Jun 27, 1944; h/ PO Box 303, Big Island, VA 24526; ba/ Big Island, VA; p/Mr and Mrs W L Wood Dr, Big Isl, VA; ed/Exec Secy Cert 1970, Cert'd Profl Secy 1972, Phillips Bus Col; BA 1982, MBA Cand, Lynchburg Col; pa/Sales Clk, G C Murphy, 1962; Sales Clk, Baldwin's, 1962-63; Secy, Schewels Furn Co, 1963-64; Secy, C W Hancock & Sons Inc, 1964-66; Secy in Var Positions 1966-74, Data Processing Supvr/Programmer 1974-76, Sys Anal Programmer 1977-, Owens IL Inc; Mem: Secy, Exec VPres, Pres, Data Processing Mgmt Assn, 1977-; CRS Assocs, 1972-; Chapt Treas, Chapt 1st VPres, Chapt Pres, Sem Chm, Chapt Conv Del, Div Com Chm, Coor 1982 SE Dist Conf, Profl Secys Assn; Participant, Wom's Focus, 1983; cp/Secy, Bedford Co Trans Safety Comm, 1974-; r/Meth; hon/Interviewed in Data Mgmt Mag, 1981; Valedictorian HS Sr Class; Chapt Secy of Yr, 1970; Outstg Alumni, Phillips Bus Col, 1972; Gold Key Hon Soc 1982, Grad cum laude, Lynchburg Col; Beta Clb, 1961-62; NHS; Outstg

Yg Wom of Am; W/W of Am Wom.

WOODARD, MARSHA BROWN oc/ Minister of Christian Education; b/Mar 22, 1949; h/5610 Enright Apartment 108, St Louis, MO 63112; ba/St Louis, MO; p/Mr Portia Brown, Univ City, MO; Mrs Laura Brown, St Louis, MO; ed/BA, Ottawa Univ (KS), 1971; MDiv, Eden Theol Sem, 1980; pa/Tchr, Franklin Co Day Care, Ottawa, KS, 1971-73; Tchr, Webster Groves Day Care, 1973-76; Dir Acad of Urban Sers, Child Devel Ctr, 1976-77; Dir, James E Cook Nursery, 1977-80; Min of Christian Ed, Antioch Bapt Ch, 1980-; Mem: Exec Coun 1981-85, Ch Wom St Metro St Louis; 2nd VPres, Metro Min Alliance, 1983; Secy 1982, Bd Mem, Early Child Care Devel Corp; Nat Coun of Christians & Jews; Clergy Support Com, The Opports Industrialization Corp; cp/ YWCA; r/Bapt; hon/Author of Var Articles Pub'd in *Ch Wom Mag*, 1983; *Chd's Tchr SS Pub'g Bd*, 1983; Commun Ser Awd, OES, 1982; Outstg Yg Wom of Am.

WOODS, GLORIA JEAN SUGGS oc/ Administrative Assistant; b/Dec 19, 1948; h/5601 Hamil Road #227, Houston, TX 77039; ba/Houston, TX; m/ Arthur Allen; p/George Lee and Clarice (Cassidy) Suggs, Durham, NC; sp/Uhl and Marcella Woods, Ooltewah, TX; ed/ BA, NC Ctl Univ, 1971; MA, Howard Univ, 1972; EdD 1982 & Current Postgrad Wk, TX So Univ; pa/Tchr, Bd of Ed, Norwalk, CT, 1973-76; Tchr 1976-80, Adm Asst for Asst Supt of Pers 1980-, N Forest ISD, TX; Mem: TX Assn of Sch Pers Admrs; TX ST Tchrs Assn; Assn of Supvn & Curric Devel; Nat Assn Female Execs; Am Assn of Sch Pers Admrs; r/Bapt; hon/Outstg Fac Rep, N Forest ISD, 1980; Ms NC Ctl Univ Band, 1970; W/W of Am Wom.

WOODS, JONATHAN CARL oc/ Engineer, Executive; b/Aug 11, 1939; h/ Two Breakers Isle, Laguna Niguel, CA 92677; ba/Huntington Bch, CA; m/Janet Sue Parker; c/Christine, Nicola, Jonathan; p/Carl S Woods, Gallipolis, OH; Rugh C Woods, San Gabriel, CA; sp/ Helen Parker, Mission Viejo, CA; ed/ Cert in Paint Technol, LA City Col, 1962; AA, E LA Col, 1962; BS, Univ of Redlands, 1980; mil/USMC, 1962-65; pa/Fdr & Pres, Engard Coatings Corp, Huntington Bch, CA, 1964-; Formulating Coating Chem, Mobil Chem Corp, Azusa, CA, 1963-64; Formulating Coating Chem, Magna Corp, Santa Fe Springs, CA, 1961-63; Mem: Nat Assn of Corrosion Engrs; Am Soc for Testing & Mats; Nat Paint & Coatings Assn; LA Soc for Coating Technol; Am Water Wkrs Assn; cp/Reg Comm, Coach & Referee, Am Yth Soccer Org; Mission Viejo Gymnastics Acad Booster Clb; Poorer Man's Poker Clb of Laguna Bch; r/Luth; hon/Active Mem of ASTM Subcom Do1-43 which Prepared the *Manual of Coating Wk for Light-Water Nuclear Power Plant Primary Containment & Other Safety Related Facilities*, 1979; W/W: in CA, in W.

WOODS, POWELL oc/Lawyer; b/Jan 19, 1922; h/411 South Britt, Siloam Springs AR 72761; ba/Siloam Springs, AR; m/Lola Lavoy Keener; c/Lola Lavoy (Mrs Steve Walthour), John Powell III; p/John Powell and Mabel Fairfax Hon Woods (dec); sp/Orlando Roswell and Myrtle Harris Keener (dec); ed/BS, Univ

of AR-Fayetteville, 1948; LLB, AR Law Sch-Little Rock, 1950; mil/AUS, 1943-45; pa/City Atty, Siloam Springs, 1960-62 & 1973-75; Mun Judge, Siloam Springs, 1963-64; Gen Pract, Currently; Mem: ABA; Benton Co Bar Assn; AR Bar Assn; Comml Law Leag; cp/ Secy-Treas, Siloam Springs Salvation Army, 1962-81; Rotary Clb; Isaac Walton Leag; Am Legion; NW AR Geol Soc; Benton Co Hist Assn; r/Meth; W/ W in S & SW; AR Lives.

WOODWORTH, GENE BOSWELL oc/Teacher; b/Oct 11, 1926; h/704 Madison Street, Manchester, TN 37355; ba/Tullahoma, TN; c/Jill, Camille, Patricia, John; p/Carl and Vida Langford Boswell, Manchester, TN; ed/ BS 1968, MA 1975, Mid TN St Univ; pa/Tchr, Tullahoma TN Sch Sys, 1968-; Mem: Assn for Supvn & Curric Devel; NEA; TN Ed Assn; Med TN Ed Assn; Past Pres, Tullahoma Ed Assn; cp/ Tullahoma Hist Assn; Bus & Profl Wom Manchester; r/Meth; hon/S'ship, Freedom Foun, 1979-80; S'ship, NSF, 1978 & 1981; Panel Mem, NSF Grant Awds, 1980; W/W: in S & SW, in Am; Personalities of S.

WOOLARD, GILBERT GARLAND JR oc/Educator, School Administrator; b/Sep 23, 1929; h/108 Valley Court, Camden, SC 29020; ba/Camden, SC; m/ Betty Heath; c/Garland, Becky, David; p/G G and Inez Woolard (dec); sp/Henry and Lilian Heath (dec); ed/BS, MA, E Carolina Univ, 1951; EdD (EPDA Fellow), NC St Univ, 1973; Postgrad Wk: Univ of CA; Univ of SC; Clemson Univ; Ball St Univ; mil/USAF, 1951-56, Jet Fighter Pilot/Instr, Korea; pa/Prin, Bushy Fork Sch, 1951; Mgr, Woolard Furniture Co, Williamston, NC, 1956-63; Mgr, Kimbrell's Furniture Col, Camden, SC, 1964-68; Dir, Kershaw Co Voc Ctr & Dist Voc & Adult Ed Progs, Camden, SC, 1968-; Ednl Conslt & Adj Prof: Univ of SC & Var Gvt Agys & Fgn Countries; Mem: AASA; AVA; AEA; NAPCAE; Phi Delta Kappa; ACE; Camden Merchs Coun, 1967; SC Voc Dirs Assn, 1974; SC Voc Assn, 1979; Former Commandant of Cadets, SC Civil Air Patrol, 1968-72; Num Other Ednl & Aviation Coms & Orgs; cp/Past Pres: Williamston Kiwanis, U Fund, C of C, 1960; Scoutmaster; Commr; Ch Bd & Tchr, Williamston, 7 Yrs; r/Meth; hon/Author, *Master Craftsman-Master Techr, Some Got To Fly*, Num Other Ednl Articles; Yg Man of Yr, Williamston JC's, 1960; Silver Beaver Awd, BSA, 1963; Num Dist'd Sers Awds; SC Legis Commend, 1976; SC Voc Edr, 1979; W/ W: in S & SW, in Aviation, in Ed.

WOOLLIAMS, KEITH RICHARD oc/Arboretum and Botanical Garden Director; b/Jul 17, 1940; h/47-722J Ahuimanu Loop, Kaneohe, HI 96744; ba/Haleiwa, HI; m/Akiko; c/Frank Hiromi, Angela Misako; p/Gordon and Margaret Woolliams, England; sp/ Toshio and Nobuko Narita, Japan; ed/ Grad, Royal Botanic Gardens, Kew, UK, 1963; Var Certs in Horticulture, Royal Horticulture Soc; Cert of Arborculture, Royal Forestry Soc of England & Wales; pa/Hd Res Sta, Univ of London, UK, 1963-65; Horticulturist, Hotel Grp, Bermuda, 1965-67; Curator, Botanic Garden, Dept of Forests, Div of Botany, Lae, Papua, New Guinea, 1967-68; Studied Horticulture/Botany in Japan,

1969-70; Horticulturist & Supt, Pacific Tropical Botanical Garden, Kauai, HI, 1971-74; Horticulturist 1974-80, Dir 1980-, Waimea Arboretum & Botanical Graden, Oahu, HI; Mem: Res Affil, Bishop Mus (Botany), Honolulu, HI; Am Assn Botanic Gradens & Arboreta; Am Horticulture Soc; Royal Horticulture Soc, London; Pres 1980, HI Botanical Soc; hon/Editor 1973-, *Notes From Waimea Arboretum* 10 Volumes to Date; Author, Var Horticulture Articles Pub'd in Profl Jours & Pub'd Ednl Series: "Waimea Arboretum Foun (HI Plants for Cultivation)"; W/W in W.

WOOTEN, JOAN GUYMON oc/ Elementary Instructor; b/Dec 14, 1949; h/Route 8, 112 North Kerns Drive, Gulfport, MS 39503; ba/Gulfport, MS; m/Michael Lynn; c/Jeffrey Michael; p/ Mr and Mrs Martin L "Bud" Watson, Wesson, MS; sp/Roy L Wooten, Brittany, LA; Sally Wooten, Collin, MS; ed/ AA, Copiah-Lincoln Jr Col, 1969; BS, Univ of So MS, 1971; MA 1979, AAA 1980, Wm Carey Col; Extended Studies, Gulf Park, 1980; pa/Tchr, Harrison Ctl Elem Sch 1971-75; Tchr, Bel-Aire Elem Sch, 1975-; Hd Tchr, Title I, 1979; Adult Ed Tchr, 1981-; Mem: NEA; MS Ed Assn; Harrison Co Tchr Assn; Assn Supvn & Curric Devel; Nat Math for Elem Tchrs; FTA; Phi Delta Kappa; cp/ Grade Chm 1972-75, Hospitality Chm 1972-75, Wesley Foun; r/Meth; hon/ Author, "A Study of the Effects of Adding Phonetic Instrn to a Basal Rdg Prog"; Moose Lodge S'ship, 1967; W/ W: in S & SW, in Am Ed.

WORD, AMOS JARMAN III oc/ Architect; b/Mar 10, 1949; h/101 Gillon Drive, Birmingham, AL 35209; ba/ B'ham, AL; p/Mary David Word, Inverness, MS; ed/Att'd Univ of MS, 1967-69; Att'd Delta St Univ, Sum 1969; BA, Auburn Univ, 1973; pa/Grad & Arch, Brewer Godbold & Assoc, Clarksdale, MS 1973-78; Arch, Blondheim, Williams & Golson, B'ham, AL, 1978-79; Assoc, The Ritchie Org, B'ham, AL, 1979-; Mem: AIA, 1978-; Cert, Nat Coun of Arch Registration Bd; r/Bapt; hon/AIA Cert of Recog, Participation in Cont'g Ed; W/W in S & SW; Personalities of S.

WORDELL, EDWIN HOWLAND oc/ Artist; b/Aug 27, 1927; h/6251 Lorea Drive, San Diego, CA 92115; ba/Same; m/Marie C; c/Cathryn L (W) Murduck, Thomas A; p/Edwin H Wordell (dec); Cathryn Burns, Largo, FL; sp/Josephine D Cunningham, San Diego, CA; ed/BS, San Diego St Univ; mil/USN, 1945-49; pa/Journeyman Meat Cutter, 1949-61; Crim Invest, IRS, 1961-82; Artist, 1956-; Mem: Beta Gamma Sigma; Nat Watercolor Soc; Rocky Mtn Watermedia Soc Watercolor W; Pres 1975-76, San Diego Watercolor Soc; Pres, San Diego Art Inst, 1978-79; hon/Wks in Permanent Collection, UT St Univ, Logan, UT, 1982; Wk Exhibns: Missoula Mus of Arts, Missoula, MT, Aug 1982; Univ of WI, Whitewater, WI, May 1982; Westmoreland Co Mus of Art, Greensburg PA, Sum 1982; San Bernardinao Co Mus, San Bernardino, CA, Oct 1982; Nat Arts Clb, NYC, Mar-Apr 1983; FL A&M Univ, Tallahassee, FL, Jun 1983; Atlanta Meml Arts Ctr, Atlanta, GA, Jul-Aug, 1983; Owensboro Mus of Fine Art, Owensboro, KY, Aug-Sep 1983; Salmagundi Clb, NYC, Nov 1983;

Greenville Mus of Art, Greenville, SC, Jan-Feb 1984; hon/Hon Mention Awd, Traditional Show, Fine Arts Inst, San Bernardino Co Mus, CA, 1983; Invitation, W Pub'g Co's "W's/83 Art & the Law," Nat Traveling Exhibit, 1983-84; 1st Awd, San Diego Watercolor Soc Mbrship Exhibit, CA, 1982; Hn Mention Awd, Wn Fedn 7, Pueblo Grand Mus, Phoenix, AZ, 1982; 1st Awd, San Diego Watercolor Soc Mbrship Exhibn, CA, 1981; 1st Awd, St Mark's Lenten Art Fest, San Diego, CA, 1981; Painting Selected for Nat Traveling Exhibit, Nat Watercolor Soc's Open Annual Show, 1980; 2nd Awd, Nat Watercolor Soc Mbrship Exhibit, St Mary's Col, LA, CA, 1980; Juror's Cash Awd, San Diego Watercolor Soc, CA, 1979; Nat Watercolor Soc Cash Awd, Watercolor W XI Exhibit, Riverside, CA, 1979; W/W: in W, in Am.

WORK, WILLIAM ALEC oc/Professional Artist; b/Nov 21, 1951; h/304 Ridgewood Drive, Tullahoma, TN 37388; ba/Same; m/Linda Carolyn; c/ Matthew Peter, Benjamin Andrew, Seth Adam; ed/Att'd Motlow St Commun Co, 1980-81; pa/Profl Artist, 1974-; Mem: Tullahoma Fine Art Ctr, Tullahoma, TN, 1983; Assoc Mem, So Watercolor Soc, 1983; Intl Assn of Quality Circles, 1983; Gamma Beta Phi Hon Soc, 1980-81; cp/Num Public Spkg Presentations; r/Christian; hon/Wk in Exhibns: 83rd Annual Open Watercolor Exhibn, Nat Arts Clb, NYC; 10th Ihntl Dogwood Fest Art Show, Atlanta, GA.

WORRELL, GAIL G oc/Medical Illustrator; b/Apr 11, 1946; h/3850 Clifton Avenue, Cincinnati, OH 45220; ba/ Cinc, OH; m/Bruce S; p/Wayne and Gloria Garrett, Amelia, OH; sp/Charles and Lee Worrell, Lehigh Acres, FL; ed/ BS in Design, Univ of Cinc, 1969; pa/ Graphic Designer, Alpha Designs Inc, 1969-73; Med Illustr Supvr, Good Samaritan Hosp, 1973-; Freelance Designer; cp/Soroptimist Intl of Cinc, OH; hon/Illustr, *Vascular Surg*, Volume 2; Contbg Illustr to Num Med Textbooks; 2nd Prize, OH Med Assn Exhibit, 1977; Bronze Plaque, OH Med Assn, 1978; Hull Awd, AMA, 1980; Tulsa Art Dir Show, 1977; 1st Prize, Am Occupl Med Assn Exhibit, 1976; W/W of Am Wom.

WORTHAM, JEANETTE STRATTON PORTER oc/Mathematics and Curriculum Specialist; b/Apr 3, 1931; h/ 1902 Warrington Way, Louisville, KY 40222; ba/L'ville, KY; m/1st, L Glenn Collins (dec); 2nd, Francis L; c/Patrick Glenn Collins, Susan Jean Collins; p/ Herbert and Ethel Thomas Russell, Liberty, KY; sp/Fonrose Wortham (dec); Eva Decker Wortham, L'ville, KY; ed/ AA, Lindsey Wilson Col, 1950; BS 1952, MA 1953, En KY Univ; NSF Grants: Univ of ID, 1958-59; Ctl WA Univ, 1964; Univ of Puget Sound, 1965; Univ of L'ville, 1980; pa/Elem Tchr, Casey Co, KY Schs, 1949; Math Tchr, Versailles HS, KY, 1952-56; Math Tchr, San Diego Unified Schs, 1957; Mat & Hist Tchr, Moscow HS, ID, 1957-60; Math Tchr, Clover Pk HS, Tacoma, WA, 1960-65; Math Tchr, Jefferson Co, KY Schs, 1966-69; Math Conslt/Spec, Jefferson Co Schs, 1969-; Elem Math Instr, Univ of L'ville, 1974-80; Mem: Life Mem, NEA; Pres 1981, Gtr L'ville Chapt, En KY Univ Alumni Assn; Pres 1982, Gtr

L'ville Coun of Tchrs of Math; Pres Xi Chapt 1982-84, Delta Kappa Gamma; KY Coun & Nat Coun of Tchrs of Math; Nat Coun of Supvrs of Math; KY Assn of Ednl Supvrs Exec Bd, 1981-83; KY & Jefferson Co Assn of Sch Admrs; ASCD; CUE; NSDAR; cp/Filson Clb; Casey Co Hist Socs; hon/W/W: in KY, in S & SW; Personalities of S.

WORTHEN, BLAINE RICHARD oc/ Professor; b/Oct 10, 1936; h/175 Quarter Circle Drive, Logan Rural Free Delivery, UT 84321; ba/Logan, UT; m/ Barbara Allen; c/Jeffrey Allen, Lynette (W) Penrod, Bradley Wade; p/Grace M Worthen; ed/BS 1960, MS 1965, Univ of UT; PhD, OH St Univ, 1968; pa/Prof & Hd Dept of Psych, UT St Univ, Currently; Dir, Wasatch Inst for Res & Eval, Currently; Dir Div of Eval, Res & Assessment 1975-78, Dir Ofc Res & Eval Sers 1973-75, NW Reg Ed Lab; Asst & Assoc Prof Ednl Psych & Co-dir Lab of Ednl Res, Univ of CO, 1969-73; Asst Prof Ednl Res & Devel 1968-69, Assoc Dir Eval Ctr 1967-69, OH St Univ; Mem: Am Ednl Res Assn, 1965-; Am Psychol Assn, 1969-; Interam Soc of Psych, 1983-; Nat Wkg Grp on Eval, 1968-; Nat Eval Netwk, 1975-; Rocky Mtn Psychol Assn, 1983-; UT Psychol Assn, 1980-; r/LDS (Mormon); hon/ Co-Author of 4 Books Incl'g: *Ednl Eval: Theory & Pract*, 1973; *Measurement & Eval in the Schs*; Author of Over 11 Pub'd Book Chapts Incl'g: "Jour Entries of an Eclectic Evalr," in *Applied Strategies for Curric Eval*, 1981; "Prog Eval," in *Intl Ency of Ed: Res & Studies*, 1983; Author of Over 23 Articles & 3 Reviews Pub'd in Profl Jours Incl'g: *Contemp Psych; Ednl Eval & Policy Anal; Ednl Ldrship; Ednl Resr; Ednl & Psychol Measurement; Jour of Ednl Measurement; Jour of Ednl Res; Jour of Higher Ed; Jour of Sch Psych; Jour of Tchr Ed; Res in Higher Ed*; Other Pubs Incl: 11 Set of Media or Print Tng Mats; 5 Tests or Test Reviews; 67 Res & Eval Reports or Tech Papers; Flesher Fellow for Outstg Grad Student in Ed, OH St Univ, 1968; Awd for Best Eval Study (Eval of HS 3-2-1 Prog), Am Ednl Res Assn, 1977; Outstg Conslt Awd, Assn for Supvn & Curric Devel, 1982; W/W in W; Contemp Authors.

WRENTMORE, ANITA KAY oc/ Lecturer of Mathematics; b/Dec 3, 1955; h/103 Ramona Avenue, Newark, OH 43055; ba/Newark, OH; p/Mr and Mrs Lloyd Wrentmore, Logan, OH; ed/BS 1978, MS 1979, OH Univ; pa/Instr of Math 1983-, Guest Lecturer of Math & Computer Sci 1981-, Ctl OH Tech Col; Instr of Math, OH St Univ-Newark, 1980-83; Guest Lectr of Math & Computer Sci, Denison Univ, 1980; Mem: Phi Kappa Phi; Delta Pi; VPres, Publicity Chm, Newark Coun Tchrs of Math; Nat Coun Tchrs of Math; OH Coun of Tchrs of Math; Math Assn of Am; Am Math Soc; Sch Sci & Math Assn; OH Math Assn of 2-yr Cols; Ctl OH Chapt, Assn for Computing Machinery; Assn for Individually Guided Ed; Coun for Basic Ed; OH Assn for Supvn & Curric Devel; Assn of Tchr Edrs; Nat Ret'd Tchrs Assn; OH Assn of 2-yr Cols; AAUW; cp/Licking Co BPW Clb; YWCA; Venus Chapt #76, OES; W/W: in MW; 2000 Notable Ams; Commun Ldrs of World; Dir of Dist'd Ams; DIB; Personalities of MW.

WRIGHT, ESTELLE VIOLA oc/ Artist, Sculptor; b/Sep 28, 1905; h/226 West 138th Street, New York, NY 10030; ba/Same; m/William McKinley Wright (dec); p/Elijah and Elicia (Butler) Harrison (dec); sp/Thomas and Augusta Wright (dec); ed/Att'd Art Student Leag of NYC; Nat Acad of Design; Newark Mus S'ship; Nat Acad Sch of Fin Arts: Studied w Carl Schmitz & Ellen Kay-O-Berg; pa/Pvt Modelling Monitors of Mbrship Class, Art Student Leag, 1955-79; ARC Metro Area, 1950-67; Chd's Aid Soc Tchr, 1948-50; Spec Tchr, Bd of Ed, 1970-72; Art Wks Incl: Relief of Ethel Morgan, Designer & Singer, 1979-80; Bas-relief of Christ & His Disciples, The Commun Ch, Lake Placid, NY; Bronze Bust of Eubie Blake in Schomberg Collection, Mus of City of NY, 1960; Bronze Bust of Dr Adolphous Anderson, Sch of Podiatry, Temple Univ, Phila, PA, 1966; Portrait Bust of Mary McClod Bethune, Public Sch 92; Bust of Hippocrates, 1961; Bust of Noble Sissle, 1960; Wk Included in Num Exhibits Incl'g: "Forever Free" Art by African Am Wom 1862-1980, IL St Univ; Lever House Black Hist Mo, 1981; Others; cp/Mem Frederick Douglas Chapt, John Beoron Meml Assn; Wom's Coun of Bklyn; r/Rosicrucian Anthroposophic Leag; hon/Author of 4 Articles & Lttrs to Students of the Rosicrucian Anthroposophic Leag; Meritorious Ser Cert, Bklyn Wom's Coun, 1963; Sculptor S'ship, NY Acad of Design, 1962; Nat Sculptor S'ship, 1962; W/W: in E, of Wom; DIB.

WRIGHT, LANCE SANDERS oc/ Psychiatrist, Psychoanalyst, Child Psychiatry; b/Mar 9, 1923; h/4028 Filbert Street, Philadelphia, PA 19104; ba/Phila, PA; m/Barbara Ramsay; c/Deborah Jean, Rebecca Ann, Lance S III, Wayne Arthur; ed/BC, MS St Univ, 1943; MD, Univ of TN, 1946; MED, Univ of MI, 1948; mil/USPHS, 1951-52; pa/Dir Tng Child Psychi, Devereux Sch, 1957-60; Dir Child Psychi, Montgomery Co Mtl Hlth Clin, 1959-61; Sr Att'g Psychi, Psychi Institute, PA Hosp, 1961-; Assoc Prof Child Psychi, Hahnamann Med Univ, 1970-; Assoc Dir, Grp Psychotherapy, Phila Guid Hosp, 1956-76; Dir, Psychi Sers Inc, 1970-; Mem: Pres, Phil Assn of Adolescent Psychi, 1968; Pres, DE Val Grp Psychotherapy Assn, 1974; Med Dir, Tri-Co Foun Ctr, 1960-76; Fdg Mem, Assn of Holistic Hlth; Fdg Mem, Am Holistic Med Assn; Fdg Mem, Am Soc Adolescent Psychi; Fellow, Am Psychi Assn; Fellow, Am Grp Psychotherapy Assn; Fellow, Am Orthopsychi Assn; Pres, N Am Reg Col, World Univ; r/Prot; hon/Author, *Silva Mind Control*, 1976; Conslt, *Aftermath of Rape*, 1978; *Grp Psychotherapy Probational Sex Offender*, 1974; *Talking Grp Therapy 11 Yr Old Boys*; DLit, World Acad of Arts & Culture, 1981; Fellow, Am Psychi Assn, 1966; Fellow, Am Grp Psychotherapy Assn, 1981; Res Fellow, World Univ, 1978; 2000 Notable Ams.

WRIGHT, LINDA J oc/Executive; b/ Dec 14, 1949; h/8360 Greensboro Drive, Rotunda 3-118, McLean, VA 22102; ba/ Falls Ch, VA; m/Kelly W Jr; p/Eugene F and Rosemary M Kemph, Chgo, IL; sp/Mr and Mrs Kelly W Wright Sr, Swordscreek, VA; ed/Att'd Loretto Hgts Col, 1967-69; Att'd Univ of IL, 1970-71; pa/Asst to VPres, Busey 1st

Nat Bk, Urbana, IL, 1969-72; Spa Mgr, Sales Tng Supvr, Venus & Apollo Hlth Clb, 1973-76; Owner, Retail Plant Store, 1967-77; Sr VPres Comml Lending, Town & Country Bk & Trust Co, 1977-; Mem: Secy of Bd of Dirs, Town & Country Bk & Trust Co; Chm No VA Grp 1981, Nat Assn of Bk Wom; cp/Dir & Treas, No VA Local Devel Corp; Dir & VPres, Fairfax Co C of C; Exec Com, Fairfax/Falls Ch U Way; Mem, Fairfax Hunt; Pvt Pilot; r/Rom Cath; hon/W/W: in S & SW, of Am Wom.

WRIGHT, MARY L oc/Educator; b/Jul 26, 1947; h/11930 Midlake Drive, Dallas, TX 75218; ba/Dallas, TX; p/Giles C and Nancy Van Sant Wright, Dallas, TX; ed/BA 1972, MEd, So Meth Univ; EdD Cand, E TX St Univ; pa/Art Tchr, Dallas ISD, 1973-74; Art & Remedial Rdg Tchr, Dallas ISD, 1974-76; Rdg Resource Tchr, Dallas ISD, 1976-79; Intern Ldrship Tng Prog, Dallas ISD, 1976; Lang Arts, Social Studies Tchr, Dallas ISD, 1979-82; Rdg Clin Tchr, Sums, 1975-77 & 1979-80; Mem: Phi Delta Kappa; IRA; Assn of Supvn & Curric Devel; r/Epis; W/W in S & SW; Personalities of S.

WRIGHT, RICHARD A oc/Professor; b/Jan 16, 1953; h/751 East Euclid Street, McPherson, KS 67460; ba/McPherson, KS; m/Sharon Bowman; c/William; p/Ruth Wright Kite, McPherson, KS; sp/Mr and Mrs L E Bowman, Vienna, VA; ed/BS, James Madison Univ, 1973; MA, OH Univ, 1975; Addit Grad Study: PA St Univ & IN Univ; pa/Asst Instr, IN Univ, 1976-78; Asst Prof Sociol, McPherson Col, 1979-; Mem: Am Sociol Assn; MW Sociol Soc; Am Soc of Criminology; hon/Author, 1 Book, 3 Chapts in Books; 15 Articles & 25 Book Reviews in Profl Jours; Prof of Yr Awd for Excell in Tchg, McPherson Col, 1983; 1st Prize Winner, No Ctl Sociol Assn Grad Student Paper Competition, 1976; Var Biogl Listings.

WRIGHT, WILBUR ERNEST oc/Administrator; b/Jul 23, 1932; b/Stanford University Medical Center, Stanford, CA 94305; c/Diane, Stephen, Jeanine, Brian; p/Wilbur Samual and Marie Ernestine (Clarke) Wright, Rockledge, FL; ed/BS, St Peter's Col, 1955; MSS, Fordham Univ, 1958; Public Hlth Adm, Univ of OK, 1965; JD, SF Law Sch, 1984; mil/AUS, 1st Lt; USPHS, Comdr; pa/Mtl Dept of Clin Social Wk, Stanford Univ Med Ctr, 1982-; Public Hlth Social Wk Conslt, CA Dept of Hlth Sers, 1981-82; Mtl Hlth Admr, SF Coun of Chs, 1980-81; Secy Gen Coun of Intl Progs, US St Dept, Wash DC, 1978-80; Exec Dir, Mtl Hlth Bd of Ctl FL Inc, Orlando, FL, 1975-78; Hd Dept of Social Wk, Royal Perth Hosp, Wn Australia, 1974-75; Dpty Hd Dept of Social Wk, Alfred-Monash Univ Hosp Dept of Preven & Social Med, Fawkner Pk Commun Hlth Ctr, Prahran, Victoria, Australia, 1973-74; Conslt/Dir of Resource Devel, OBECA/Arriba Juntos- Commun Devel Corp, Cath Charities (Archdiocese of SF), 1972-73; Dir of Ser & Rehab, CA Div of Am Cancer Soc, SF, 1968-72; Dir of Social Wk, Scripps Meml Hosp, LaJolla, CA, 1966-68; Sr Med Social Wkr, Univ of CA-San Diego & San Diego Co Hosp, 1965-66; Conslt/Hlth Ser Ofcr 1962-65, Med Ser Corp Ofcr 1959-62, USPHS,

Wash DC; Fam Cnslr, U Fam & Chd's Soc, Plainfield, NJ, 1958-59; Mem: Fellow, APHA; Fellow, Royal Soc of Hlth, UK; Fellow, Soc for Clin Social Wk; Assn of Mtl Hlth Adm; Am Hosp Assn; Soc for Hosp Social Wk Dirs; Others; Conslt & Guest Lectr in Field; cp/Participant on Num Local Coms & Bds; r/Anglican; hon/Author, Var Articles Pub'd in Profl Jours; Var Reports, Prog & Ser Guides, Handbook & Manual for Profl Socs & Govt Agys; W/W: in CA, in S & SW, in MW, in Hlth Care; in Commun Ser; Commun Ldrs & Noteworthy Ams.

WRUSCH, MICHAEL MANFRED oc/Interior Designer; b/Oct 26, 1957; ba/Palos Verdes Estates, CA 90274; p/Gerhard and Margot Wrusch, Utica, MI; ed/BA, MI St Univ, 1980; Interior Designer, Martha Shinn Interiors, Okemos, MI, 1978-80; Sr Interior Designer, Carlton Wagner Designer, Palos Verdes, CA, 1980-81; Prin Designer, Michael Wrusch Designs, Palos Verdes Ests, CA, 1981-; Mem: Am Soc of Interior Designers (ASID), 1981-; cp/Nat Trust for Hist Presv, 1984; r/Luth; hon/Author of Articles Pub'd in "MI Lifestyle," Detroit Free Press, 1981; "Home Sect," LA Times, 1981; Decorative Arts & Arch S'ship, MI St Univ, 1979; Omicron Nu Ldrship Awd, 1979; Sandpiper Awd for Dist'd Ser, 1982; Mem, Phi Kappa Phi, 1980; Mem, Omicron Nu 1978; W/W in W.

WU, TSE CHENG oc/Research Associate; b/Aug 21, 1923; h/14-E Dorado Drive, Morristown, NJ 07960; ba/Morristown, NJ; m/Janet Ling; c/Alan Leo, Anna Mae, Bernard Jay; ed/BS, Yenching Univ, 1946; MS, Univ of IL, 1948; PhD, IA St Univ, 1952; pa/Res Chem, E I DuPont De Nemour & Co, 1953-60; Res Chem, Gen Elect Co, 1960-71; Sr Res Chem, Arbor Inc, 1971-77; Res Assoc, Allied Corp, 1977-; Mem: Am Chem Soc; Alpha Chi Sigma; cp/Troy Arts Guild; Morris Co Art Assn; hon/Author of Over 21 Articles Pub'd in Sci & Tech Jours; Holder of 30 US Patents in Field; Gold Medallion Awd for Inventions, Gen Elect Corp, 1967; Phi Kappa Phi; Phi Lambda Upsilon; Sigma Xi; W/W: in E, Technol; DIB.

WYATT, WILSON W SR oc/Attorney; b/Nov 21, 1905; h/The 1400 Willow Apartment 1205, Louisville, KY 40204; ba/L'ville, KY; m/Anne K Duncan; c/Wilson W Jr, Mary Anne, Nancy (W) Zorn; p/Richard H and Mary (Watkins) Wyatt (dec); ed/Att'd, Bellarmine Col & Univ of L'ville; pa/Atty, Law Firm of Wyatt, Tarrant & Combs; Mayor, City of L'ville, 1941-45; Housing Expediter & Admr, Nat Housing Agy, 1946; Chm Bd of Trustees, Univ of L'ville, 1951-55; Lt Gov, St of KY, 1959-63; Mem: ABA; KY Bar Assn; L'ville Bar Assn; cp/Pres, L'ville C of C, 1972; Pres 1973-75, Chm Nat Conf on Govt 1976-78, Nat Mun Leag; Chm US Sts Circuit Judge Nom'g Comm, 6th Circuit Panel, 1977-80; Chm of Bd, Reg Cancer Ctr Corp, 1977-84; Chm Bd of Trustees, Bellarmine Col, 1979-82; Chm, Ldrship L'ville Foun, 1979-81; VChm, KY Ec Devel Corp, 1984-; Chm, L'ville Commun Foun, 1984-; Chm, Ldrship KY, 1984-; r/Presb; hon/Personal Campaign Mgr of Adlai E Stevenson Pres Campaigns; Pres Emissary, From Pres Kennedy to Pres

Sukarno, Indonesian Oil Negotiations, Tokyo, 1963; Man of Yr, Advtg Clb of L'ville, 1973; Lwyr of Yr, KY Bar Assn 1976; Lwyr of Yr, L'ville Bar Assn, 1981; W/W in Am; Best Lwyrs in Am; Num Other Biogl Listings.

WYCKOFF, CHARLOTTE oc/Educational Administrator; b/Oct 8, 1934; h/5333 Amethyst Alta Loma, CA 91701; ba/Cucamonga, CA; m/Bill; c/Robert, Shir, Paul, Brandy, Joseph; p/Ray L and Ruth Charlotte (McLain) Murphy; ed/BA, LaVerne Col, 1974; MA, CA St Univ-San Bernardino, 1977; Postgrad Study US Intl Univ-San Diego; pa/Fdr & Dir, CA Lrng Ctrs, Rancho Cucamonga, 1967-; Prof, Chaffey Commun Col, Rancho Cucamonga, 1973-; Coor Tng Progs, Casa Colina Hosp, Pomona, CA, 1975-76; Advy Bd, Bonita HS, San Dimas, CA, 1975-77 & Pomona HS, 1975-77; Admr, Claremont (CA) Collegiate Sch, 1977-; Mem: Advy Bd, Pomona HS & Bonita HS; Am Pers & Guid Assn; Nat Soc Autistic Chd; Nat Assn Edn of Yg Chd Assn; Humanistic Psychols; CA Assn of Spec Schs; Nat Assn for Edn Yg Chd; Pre Sch Assn; CA Assn Sch Psychols & Psychometrists; CA St Psychol Assn; CA Assn Neurol Handicapped Chd; Doctorial Soc Clb; Altrusa Clb.

WYDLER, HANS ULRICH oc/Intl Lawyer; b/Nov 11, 1923; h/945 5th Avenue, New York, NY 10021; ba/Same; m/Susan Hart; c/Hans Laurence, Steven Courtney; p/Grethe A Wydler, Baker, OR; sp/Marjorie E Hart, NYC; ed/BS 1944, BME 1947, BIE 1949, OH St Univ; MS, MA Inst of Technol, 1948; LLB, Harvard Law Sch, 1951; mil/USN, 1944-46; pa/Intl Lwyr, Conslt, Hans U Wydler, 1966-; Sr VPres, Security Nat Bk, Huntington, NY, 1973-74; VPres, Mfrs Nat Bk of Detroit, Detroit, MI, 1964-65; Ass VPres, Chem Bk, NYC, 1958-64; Atty, Fin Conslt, Trustee, Louis J Hunter Assocs, Boston, MA, 1951-57; Mem: MA Bar Assn; ABA; NY Co Lwyrs' Assn; Reg'd Profl Engr; US Treas Dept (Tax) Pract; Life Mem, Acad of Polit Sci; ASME; Nat Soc of Profl Engrs; Dir, Buning Intl Inc; Dir, Volume Mdse Inc; r/Rom Cath; W/W: in E, in Fin & Indust; DIB; Royal Blue Book.

WYERS, MARY ELLEN oc/University Dean; b/May 15, 1938; h/3405 Ashford, Ft Worth, TX 76133; ba/Arlington, TX; m/Patrick Z; c/Randolph Zane, Suzanee Abell; p/Hazel M Abell, Charlottesville, VA; sp/Ruth O Wyers, Ft Worth, TX; ed/BSN, Univ of VA, 1959; MEd, TX Christian Univ, 1972; MSN, Univ of TX-Austin, 1981; EdD, Nova Univ, 1976; pa/Hd Nurse, Univ of VA Hosp, 1961-62; Med-Surg Coor, So Bapt Hosp Sch of Nsg, 1963-66; Asst Nurse Admr, John Peter Smith Hosp Sch of Nsg, 1967-71; Asst Prof & Dir of Cont'g Ed 1971-76, Assoc Prof & Assoc Dean Sch of Nsg 1976-, Univ of TX-Arlington; Mem: ANA; Dist #3 Secy & Exec Bd 1982-84, TX Nurses Assn; NLN; Com of Nom, TX LN; Univ Orgs: Eval Com, Undergrad Curric Com, Grad Progs Com, Grad Studies Com, Interprog Coun, Adm Coun, NLN Self Study Steering Com, Asst Dean Search Com; cp/Allocation Sub-com, U Way of Gtr Tarrant Co, 1981-; Bd Mem, Pres Elect 1983-84, Arlington Div, Am Heart Assn; Bd of Dirs, ARC, 1983-84; Mayor's Com on Employmnt of the

Handicapped, 1983-84; Forum Ft Worth; r/Meth; hon/Author, Var Articles, Prog Reports, Studies & Res Presentations Pub'd in Profl Pubs & Presented to Profl Orgs; Sigma Theta Tau; Hazel M Jay Res Awd, 1983; Univ of TX Res Awd, 1983; Ldrship Ft Worth, 1980; Site Visitor, CBHDP, 1982-.

WYMAN, RICHARD H oc/Property Management/Leasing; b/Aug 5, 1946; h/206 Prospect Street, Framingham, MA 01701; ba/Boston, MA; m/Mary Ellen; c/Michelle, Christine; p/Majorie Wyman, Winchester, MA; sp/Mr and Mrs Joseph Stanley, Framingham, MA; ed/BA, Univ of ME, 1969; MBA Babson Col, 1973; Fellow, Life Mgmt Inst Ins Ed Prog, 1979; Cert'd Life Underwriter Prog; pa/Property Mgmt/Leasing 1982-, Property Mgmt/Leasing 1979-82, Investmnt Acctg 1977-78, Computer Sys Devel & Var Positions 1969-76, Prudential Ins Co, Boston, MA; Ptnr, RELM Income Properties, 1982-; Pt-time Broker Comml Div, Dallamora Realtors, Framingham, MA, 1982-; Mem: N Eng Coun Shopping Mall Mgrts, 1979-; MA Property Investors; cp/Fin Advr, Jr Achmt; Boston C of C; Gov King's Mgmt Task Force 1979, Adv Com, Dept of Revenue; Ins Acctg Instr; Auction Fundraiser Com (Chm for Prudential Ctr/Back Bay 1981), Channel 2; W/W: in World, in Fin & Indust; The Am Registry.

WYNDEWICKE, KIONNE ANNETTE oc/Teacher; b/Mar 28; h/533 East 33rd Street, Chicago, IL 60610; ba/Chgo, IL; p/Clifton Thomas and Missouria Jackson Johnson (dec); ed/BS, IL St Univ, 1960; MEd, Nat Col of Ed, 1982; pa/Casewkr, Cook Co Dept of Public Aid, 1960; Tchr, Chgo Bd of Ed, 1961-; Mem: CARA; ISTA; Spch Commun Assn; CABSE; IPA; Corres'g Secy, Installation Co-chm, Ad-book Co-chm, Publicity Chm & Co-chm, Vol Ser, Dinner Dance, PWA of Provident Hosp; cp/Luth Ch Wom; r/Luth; hon/One of 25 Black Wom in Chgo to Receive a Kizzy Awd from Womafest, Beatrice Caffney Yth Ser Inc, 1978; Outstg Commun Ser Awd; W/W: in MW, of Am Wom, World of Wom, of Commun Ser; 2000 Notable Ams; Intl Register of Profiles; Book of Hon; Personalities of W & MW; DIB.

WYNNE, RICHARD THOMAS oc/Agricultural Meteorologist; b/Jul 31, 1951; h/104 Pleasant Apartment 217, Bryan, TX 77801; ba/College Sta, TX; p/Walter David (dec); Ethel Elizabeth (Lauffer) Wynne, Minooka, IL; ed/BS, No IL Univ, 1973; MS, IA St Univ, 1976; pa/Agri Meteorologist, NOAA/Nat Weather Ser, 1976-; Mem: Am Agron-omy Soc; Soil Sci Soc of Am; Am Meteorological Soc; Nat Weather Assn; Toastmaters Intl; cp/TX A&M Sailing Clb; Brazos Sailing Clb; r/Rom Cath; hon/SAR Awd, 1969; W/W in S & SW.

WYSZYNSKI, VALENTINE ADAM oc/Executive; b/Dec 24, 1941; h/PO Box 1558, Belen, NM 87002; ba/PO Box 2012, Las Cruces, NM 88004; m/Elizabeth Kathleen DeWitt; c/Brian Lee DeWitt, Tonia Rae DeWitt; p/Genevieve Wyszynski, Cicero, IL; sp/Lenora Robinson, Las Cruces, NM; ed/BSEE, NM St Univ, 1980; mil/USAF, 1964-70, S/Sgt; pa/Pres, Tierra Communs Sys, 1980-; Graphics Conslt, Nifty-Five Pubs, 1983-; Sound-Video Designer, NM St Univ Drama Dept, 1977-81; Reg Sales Mgr, Combined Ins Co, 1973-76; Ldr of the "Majestics" Rock n' Roll Grp, 1959-64; Mem: Soc of Broadcast Engrs, 1981-; Satellite Antenna Spec Assn, 1982-; Nat Assn of Christains in Social Wk, 1980-; cp/St Dir, Newslttr Editor, Romeoville/IL JCs, 1969-73; r/7th Day Adventist; hon/Orig Music Composed for: Tony Awd Winner "Chd of a Lesser God," 1980; The "Majestic Kid," 1981 (written by Mark Medoff); "Nightlife" Columnist Entertainment Guide, 1982-83; Spoke Awd 1970, Best Newslttr 1971, IL JCs; 500 Clb, Ford Motor Co, 1971; W/W in SW.

Y

YAMANASHI, WILLIAM SOIC-HIRO oc/Associate Professor Radiology; b/Jul 12, 1943; h/107 East G Street, Jenks, OK 74037; ba/Tulsa, OK; m/Sandra L; c/Allison S; p/Minoru and Fuyo Yamanashi, Tokyo, Japan; sp/Calvin Noltee (dec) and Eula Mae Atkins; ed/BA, Andrews Univ, 1966; PhD, MIT, 1969; pa/Sr NMR Physicist & Assoc Prof, Radiol, City of Faith Med & Res Ctr, Oral Roberts Univ Sch Med, 1983-; Asst Prof, Asst Biomed Engr, MD, Anderson Hosp & Tumor Inst, Univ TX, 1980-83; Asst Prof Adj, Physiol, Baylor Col Med, 1982-; AAAS; Soc Magnetic Resonance Med; Soc Magnetic Resonance Imaging; IEEE; Radiation Res Soc; Assn Univ Radiologists; Am Assn Physicists Med; Bioelectromagnetic Soc; Am Phy Soc; Am Chem Soc; r/Christian Ch; hon/Author of Num Pubs; Cum Laude, Andrews Univ, 1966; Phi Lambda Upsilon; W/W Am Col & Univs.

YAO, CHRISTOPHER KANG-LOH oc/System Engineer, Audio Distribution Systems, IBM; b/Apr 4, 1941; h/885 Windsor Trail, Roswell, GA 30076; ba/Atlanta, GA; m/Becky J; c/Jenney, Mary; p/Huang-Jui (dec) and Shu-Mei Yao, Roswell, GA; sp/David and Phoebe Jung, Indpls, IN; ed/BS, Univ KS, 1966; MS, Union Col, 1978; pa/Jr Metallurgist, Mat Engr, Mfg Quality Engr, Prod Devel Engr, Mat Mgmt Programmer, Facility Sys Analyst, Audio Sys Engr, IBM, 1967; Sys Engr, 1981-82, Audio Dist Sys; Am Soc Metals; Am Soc Ceramics; cp/Pres, Atlanta Chapt, Nat Assn Chinese-Ams, 1979; hon/Author of "Gen Purpose Automation Exec" 1981.

YASSA, GUIRGUIS F oc/Senior Analyst Systems, Chase Manhattan Bank; b/Oct 1, 1930; h/RD 1, Box 178, Sussex, NJ 07461; ba/New York, NY; m/Laila; c/Elham, Medhat, Magdi, Laura Marie; p/Fahmy Yassa (dec); sp/Naguib Nosseir (dec); ed/B Eng 1951, MSc 1964, Dipl Stats 1966, Cairo Univ; ITC Photogrammetric Eng, Netherlands, 1956; PhD, Cornell Univ, 1973; pa/Topographic Engr 1951-53, Photogrammetric Engr 1953-65, Hd Photogrammetric Sect 1965-67, Survey Egypt; Sr Lectr, Intl Inst Aerial Survey, 1967-69; Tchg Asst, Cornell, 1962-72; Systems Analyst, Dir Mapping, Robinson Aerial Surveys, 1973-79; Sr Programmer, Analyst, Chase Manhattan Bk, 1980-; Am Soc Photogrammetry; Am Soc Civil Engrs; Sigma Xi; r/Coptic Orthodox; hon/Author of Num Pubs; Talbert Abrams Awd, Am Soc Photogrammetry, 1979; W/W E.

YATES, EDWARD CARSON JR oc/Aerospace Engineer; b/Nov 3, 1926; h/3800 Chesapeake Avenue, Hampton, VA 23669; ba/Hampton, VA; m/Carleen Wells; c/Barry Wells; p/Edward Carson and Estelle Yarborough Yates (dec); sp/Roy Leon and Eula Simpson Wells, Altavista, VA; ed/BS 1948, MS 1949, NC St Univ; MS, 1953, Univ VA; PhD, VA Polytechnic Inst, St Univ, 1959; pa/Aerospace Engr, NASA/NACA Langley Res Ctr, 1949-; Lctr Physics, VA Polytechnic Inst & St Univ, 1959-67; Adj Assoc Prof, NC St Univ, 1964-75; Professorial Lectr, George Wash Univ,

1968-; Assoc Editor, Jour Aircraft, 1972-78; Assoc Fellow, Am Inst Aeronautics & Astronautics; hon/Author of Num Pubs; Phi Eta Sigma; Phi Kappa Phi; Sigma Xi; Num S'ships, 1947, 1948; NASA Perf Awd, 1964; Fed Aviation Adm Cit, 1964; NASA Grp Achmt Awd, 1967; NASA Apollo Achmt Awd, 1969; NASA Spec Achmt Awd, 1982; NASA Exceptl Ser Medal, 1982; W/W: S & SW, Govt, Technol Today, Aviation & Aerospace, Aviation, Frontier Sci & Tech; Am Men & Wom Sci; Men Achmt; Dict Biography; Intl W/W Engrg.

YEARGAIN, BETTY JAN oc/Banker; b/Jul 20, 1942; h/13723 Woodthrush, Choctaw, OK 73020; ba/Midwest City, OK; m/Virgil L; c/Marvie Allen Dunn III; p/Edgar J and Audrey B Fisher, Walnut Grove, MS; sp/Virgil E Yeargain (dec) and Marilee Yeargain Walters; pa/Sr VP & Cashier, Security Bank & Trust Co, 1983-; Sr VP, Cashier, Adv Dir, So Bk & Trust Co, 1978-83; Opers Ofcr, Choctaw St Bk, 1977-78; Asst VP, Employmt Mgr, Fidelity Bk NA, 1969-77; Exec Secy, Security Bk, 1968-69; Am Inst Bkg; Nat Assn Bk Wom; Ctl OK Clearinghouse Assn; r/Bapt; hon/Bkr Yr, 1975, Am Inst Bkg; W/W: Am Wom, Intl Intells.

YEN, PETER T oc/Professor and Director, International Business Institute; b/Sep 22, 1937; ba/Saint Bonaventure, NY; ed/BA, NCU; MA, CA St Univ; PhD, Univ SF; Post Doct, Univ CA-LA; mil/AUS; pa/Prof, Sch Bus, St Bonaventure Univ; Exch Prof, Univ W FL, 1980; Vis'g Scholar, Grad Sch Mgmt, Univ CA-LA, 1979; Prof Mktg & Mgmt, NCU, 1976-79; Asst Prof Mgmt, HD Devel, VA Polytechnic Inst, 1975-76; Am Mktg Assn; Mgmt Sci Assn; Mem & Bd Dir, Mktg Res Assn; Acad Mgmt; Acad Intl Bus; Fellow, Intl Acad Mgmt; r/Cath; hon/Author of Num Pubs; Grant Nat Behavior Sci Coun; Hon Citizen, Pensacola FL; Cultural Exch Awd; Intl W/W Intell; Men Dist'd; W/W Ed.

YODER, DAVID HARVEY oc/Housing and Real Estate Development; b/Oct 10, 1931; h/Winona Court, Morgantown, WV 26505; ba/Morgantown, WV; m/Ruby Jeanelle Shenk; c/Jon David, Robert Eliott; p/G Ernest Yoder, Salisbury, PA; sp/C W Shenk, Elida, OH; ed/BA, Goshen Col, 1957; MA, WV Univ, 1965; PhD Cand, Univ Vienna, 1965; Vienna Acad of Music, 1962; Vis'g Scholar, Univ of Graz, Vienna, 1965; pa/Dean of Students, Wn Mennonite Prep Sch, 1953-54; Student Asst, Goshen Col, 1956-57; Grad Asst, WV Univ, 1963-64; Designer, Housing Constrn, 1966-; Supvr, Real Est Mktg & Sales; Bd of Dirs, N Ctl WV Home Bldrs Assn, 1976-; 1st VP 1976, Pres 1977-80; Chm Com on Legis & Govtl Affairs, Home Bldrs of WV, 1978-80; Bd Dirs, Nat Assn of Homes Bldrs, 1978-; St Home Bldrs Rep, House & Senate of WV, 1978-80, Rep to US Cong, 1979; 1st VP 1979-82, Pres 1983-84, WV Home Bldrs Assn; Chm Com on Mortgage Fin, 1980-; Expert Conslt for Home Bldg Indust to US Cong, 1979; Appt'd by WV Legis to its Task Force on Housing, 1981; Pres, Pineview Rlty Inc; Exec VP, Allegheny Devel Corp; Secy/Treas, Pineview Supply Corp; Treas, Allegheny Real Est Sales Inc; cp/C of C; hon/

Bldr of the Month Awd, 1972; Outstg Bldr of the Yr, 1973; Cert of Merit for Outstg Contbns to Bldg Indust, 1976; Mbr of the Yr Awd, WV Home Bldrs Assn, 1980; W/W: Fin & Indust, S & SW; Men of Achmt.

YODER, PAUL TIMOTHY oc/Physician, Family Practice, District Overseer-10 Churches; b/Feb 24, 1928; h/1047 Stuart Street, Harrisonburg, VA 22801; ba/Harrisonburg, VA; m/Daisy Agnes Byler; c/Debra Ann, Daniel Wayne, Paul Timothy Jr, Judith Carol; p/David Samuel and Savilla Bender Yoder; sp/Jesse D (dec) and Agnes Gunden Byler, Topeka, IN; ed/BS, 1950, En Mennonite Col, 1950; MD, George Wash Univ Med Sch, 1955; Att'd En Bapt Sem, 1968; MPH, Johns Hopkins Univ Sch Public Hlth & Hygiene, 1972; pa/Phys, 1977-; Med Missionary, En Mennonite Bd Missions & Charities, 1956-77; Proj Dir, Awash Commun Hlth Sers, 1972-77; Med Ofcr, Med Secy, 1968-72; Med Dir 1962-63, 1968-71, Staff Phys 1957-60, Acting Med Dir 1956-57, Haile Mariam Mammo Meml Hosp; Med Dir, 1963-66; Med Dir, Deder Hosp-Ethiopia, 1960-61; Staff Phys, Blue Ridge 1961-62; Med Soc VA; Rockingham Co Med Soc; Am Acad Fam Phys; Christian Med Soc; Mennonite Med Assn; Diplomate Am Bd Fam Pract; Mennonite Hlth Assn; cp/George Wash Gen Alumni Assn; Alumni Assn Johns Hopkins Univ; r/Prot; hon/Author of Num Pubs; Alumnus (w Wife) of Yr, En Mennonite Col, 1982; Am Med Assn Phys' Recog Awd, 1980, 1983; Election to King-Kane Obstetrical Soc.

YONKERS, WINIFRED FRANCES oc/Reading Specialist; b/Sep 30, 1939; h/2011 Hannon Street, Hyattsville, MD 20783; ba/Washington, DC; m/Mervyn Leroy; c/Pamela Marie, Vernon Lee; p/Wilfred Lawrence (dec) and Mary Frances Haddock, Pittsburgh, PA; sp/Earl H and Isabella Yonkers, Pittsburgh, PA; ed/BS, Univ Pgh, 1961; MA, George Wash Univ, 1967; pa/Elem Tchr, Pgh Public Schs, 1961-63; Elem Tchr, DC Public Schs, 1963-67; Rdg Spec, DC Public Schs, 1967-; Curric Writer, DC Public Schs, Sum 1982; IRA; cp/Alpha Kappa Alpha; Pi Lambda Theta; Lewisdale Civic Assn; Lewisdale, Univ PK Boys & Girls Clb; r/Prot.

YOO, JANG HEE oc/Professor of Economics, Economic Analyst; b/Feb 11, 1941; h/3219 Nuttree Woods Drive, Midlothian, VA 23113; ba/Richmond, VA; m/Chong Cha; c/Alex, Kenneth; p/Jong Ja Jung, McLean, VA; sp/Mr and Mrs Changsop Song, Gwachon, Korea; ed/BA, Seoul Nat Univ, 1963; MA, Univ CA-LA, 1969; PhD, TX A & M Univ, 1973; Spec Prog in Public Ec, MIT, 1979; mil/ROKA, Lt, (Korea); pa/Res Asst, Ec Res Ctr 1963-65, Prof 1981-82, Seoul Nat Univ; Res Assoc, Human Resource Res Ctr, USC, 1969-70; Asst Prof Ec, Clark Univ, 1972-76; Assoc Prof 1976-81, Prof 1981-, VA Commonwealth Univ; Am Ec Assn; Prog Com Mem, Nat Tax Assn; Assoc Mng Editor of Jour Ec Devel; Chm Sessions, Nat Tax Assn Conv, Wn Ec Assn Conv, SWn Soc Sci Assn Conv, Korean Economists Assn Meeting; r/Presb; hon/Author of Num Pubs incl'g "Macro Cross Elasticities in Disequilibrium Adjustments" *Korean Economic Review* 1976; Grantee of Soc Sci

Res Coun & Am Coun of Learned Soc, NSF, Am Coun Life Ins, Economic Planning Bd; W/W S & SW; Am Economic Assn Listings.

YORK, GEORGE WOLTZ oc/Sales Executive; b/Sep 2, 1940; h/714 Enchanted River, Spring, TX 77373; ba/ Houston, TX; m/Emily Miriam Slayton; c/Janet Lyn, William Tuck; p/Mr and Mrs Guy Aytca York, Atlanta, GA; sp/ Mrs Olive Dixon Philpot, Memphis, TN; ed/Univ GA, 1958-59; BIE, GA Inst Technol, 1966; Postgrad, Univ Houston, 1968-69; pa/Tech Sales Rep 1969-, Area Mgr 1980-, Tech Conslt 1980-, York Div Borg Warner Corp; ASME; ASHRAE; cp/GA Tech Alumni Assn; Sigma Nu; US JCs; Num Sports & Social Clbs; r/Presb; hon/Provided Tech Asst for "Design of Mech Refrigeration Sys" 1967; York Div, Borg Warner Sales Hall of Fame; Pres' Hon Clb Awd; Salesman of Yr Awd; Spec Recog Awd; W/W in S & SW.

YOUNG, EULALIE BARNES oc/ Social Services Consultant; b/Oct 24, 1942; h/4157 Brookfield Drive, Sacramento, CA 95823; ba/San Bernardino, CA; m/James Leonard; c/Shawn Arlene McGee, Darren Lance McGee, Jayanna; p/Roy and Lucille Woods Barnes, New Orleans, LA; ed/BA, So Univ, 1966; MS, St Univ NY, 1976; pa/Supervisory Rec Spec, Dept Army, Fort Polk, 1967-72; Prog Coor, YMCA/Model Cities Teen Ctr, 1972-74; Student Intern, VA Hosp, 1974-76; Prog Coor, BUILD Wk Assessmt Ctr, 1976-77; Sr Rehab Cnslr, CA St Dept Rehab, 1978-80; Soc Ser

Conslt, CA St Dept Social Sers, 1980-; Am Pers & Guid Assn; Nat Rehab Assn; Assn Black Psychol; cp/CA Coor, Nat Hook-up Black Wom; Aware of Wom; r/Bapt; hon/Outstg Achmt Awd, CA St Dept Rehab, 1980; W/W of Am Wom.

YOUNG, LEO F oc/Mail Order Dist; b/Nov 20, 1944; h/8319 South Breeze, Houston, TX 77071; ba/Houston, TX; m/Willie C; c/Tyrone, Elisabeth, Bruce; ed/AA Electroncis; mil/USCG Resv; pa/ Gen Mgr, Williams & Son Inc, 1974-82; Owner, Baabys Ltd Record Sales, 1970-74; Clk, A & P Supermkt, 1970; cp/Chm, Riceville Civic Assn Inc; r/Bapt; hon/Author of "Breath Freshener", " Hlthy Pets" 1981; Gulf Coast Commun Ser Awd; Dept Energy Cert 1981; W/ W in Business.

YOUSSEF, KAMAL A oc/Physician, Laboratory Executive; b/Sep 15, 1933; h/Sorter 6548, West Palm Beach, FL 33405; p/A M and L Y Mansour Youssef; ed/MD, Cairo Univ, 1957; DMSc, 1964; Intern, Min of Hlth Hosps, Egypt, 1958-59; pa/Med Tech, Manhattan Med & Dental Assist Sch, NYC, 1969-70; Res Assoc, So Bio-Res, FL So Col, Lakeland, 1970-71; Resident in Pathol, Bapt Meml Hosp, Jacksonville, 1971-72; Resident in Pathol, Misericordia & Meth Hosp, 1972-74; Fdr, Pres, Mycogel Labs Inc, Bkly, 1975-; Am Soc for Microbiol; Nat Soc for Human & Animal Mycology; Med Mycological Soc of the Ams; Med Mycological Soc of NY; Fdr, Pres, World Nutrition Islamic Foun; hon/Presentation to Egyptian Med Assn Clin Soc, 1957; Discovered 7 Novel Species of

Amoeba; 33 Patents Worldwide; Presentation, Nat Cancer inst, 1973; Recip, Sci Achmt Awd from U Scists & Inventors of the US; World W/W; W/W in Fin & Indust.

YUGOVICH, JOHN oc/Electrical Designer; b/May 12, 1952; h/30900 Ridgeway, Farmington Hills, MI 48018; b/Same; p/Mr and Mrs Michael Yugovich, Dearborn, MI; ed/Henry Ford Commun Col, 1972; Lawrence Inst Technol; pa/Elect Designer, Diclemente-Siegel Engrg Co, 1970-79; Pres, Yugovich Enterprises, 1979-83; cp/Mem, Detroit Bldrs Exchg Vol Wkr for Sarah Fisher Home for Underpriviledged Chd, 1982-; r/Cath; hon/Pres Elect, Dale Carnegie Class, 1981; Cert Merit for Training & Employing the Handicapped.

YUNICE, ANDY ANIECE oc/ Research Scientist and Associate Professor; b/Jan 2, 1925; h/2325 Morgan Drive, Norman, OK 73039; ba/Oklahoma City, OK; m/Lillian; c/Carla, Paula, and Laurie; p/Asad and Mona Yunice, Lebanon; sp/Mitchel and Najla Saleeby; ed/BA, Am Univ Beirut, 1948; MS, Wayne St Univ, 1958; PhD, OK Univ, 1971; pa/Res Instr, WA Univ, 1958-69; Asst Prof Med & Physiol, 1971-77, OKC, OK; Assoc Prof & Dir Trace Metal Lab, 1977-, OK Univ & VAMC; Am Physiol Soc; Am & Intl Soc Nephrology; Sigma Xi; r/Christian; hon/ Author of Num Pubs; Awd for Graduate Studies, 1969; W/W in S & SW; Am Men & Women of Science.

Z

ZAJICEK, BARBARA J oc/Vice President-Business Manager Health Care, Medical Management; b/Jan 12, 1932; h/619 Hillside Road, Glenview, IL 60025; ba/Des Plaines, IL; m/Albert F; c/Gregg Hahn, Lisa Jeffries, Dana Hahn; p/Gale E (dec) and Thelma B Allen, Ft Myers, FL; sp/Rudy and Anastasia Zajicek (dec); pa/Ofc Supvr, Asst to Pres, Larry Smith & Co, 1970-74, 1976-77; Asst to Pres, Devel Control Corporation, 1974-76; Bus Mgr, EMSCO Ltd, 1978-; VP, MW Med Mgmt Inc, 1982-; Sr VP 1983-84, Emer Med Mgmt Assn, 1978-; Nat Assn Freestanding Emer Ctrs, 1982-; r/Luth; hon/Pres' Scholar, Oakton Commun Col, 1980; W/W Am Wom.

ZALESKI, MAREK BOHDAN oc/Immunologist, University Professor; b/Oct 18, 1936; h/95 Willow Green, Tonawanda, NY 14150; ba/Buffalo, NY; p/Stanislaw and Jadwiga Zaleski; ed/MD 1960, DMS 1963, Med Acad-Warsaw Poland; mil/Polish Army Resv, 1st Lt Med Corp; pa/Instr 1955-60, Asst Prof 1960-69, Dept Histology, Sch Med Warsaw; Res Asst Prof 1969-72, Assoc Prof 1976-78, Prof 1978-, Dept Microbiol, St Univ NY; Asst Prof 1972-75, Assoc Prof 1975-76, Dept Anatomy, MI St Univ; Vis'g Scist 1965, Inst Exptl Biol Genetics, Czechoslovak Acad Sci; Brit Coun Scholar, 1966-67, Queen Victoria Hosp-England; Polish Anatomic Soc; Transplantation Soc; Intl Soc Exptl Hematology; Am Assn Immunologists; NY Acad Sci; Buffalo Collegium Immunol; Ernest Witebski Ctr Immunol; Edit Com, Immunological Communs; cp/Solidarity & Human Right Assn; r/Rom Cath; hon/Author of Num Pubs; Recip Num Grants incl'g NIH, 1976-; W/W: Am, World, Technol Today; Men Achmt; Dic Bibliog.

ZAMONSKI, STANLEY WALTER oc/Museum Director and Curator; b/Aug 7, 1919; h/800 South Vellejo, Denver, CO 80223; ba/Golden, OH; m/Barbara Helen; p/Stanley W and Cecilia (Zamojski) Zamonski (dec); sp/Forrest I Stewart (dec); Mildred K Stewart, Dallas, TX; ed/Att'd N Eng Aircraft-Wentworth Inst, 1940-42; Att'd MIT, 1942-43; Addit Study, Georgetown Univ; mil/USAAC, Pilot, 2nd Lt, B-24 Bomber, PTO; pa/Engrg-Draftsman, Airway Manual, 1946-47; Engrg-Draftsman, CO Dept of Hwys, 1947-55; Free Lance Photog-writer, 1950-70; Photog, Jefferson Sentinal Press, 1955-70; Prof of Photo-jour, Instituto Allenda, San Miguel Allenda, Mexico, 1970-72; Engrg-Draftsman, Denver Planning Dept, 1973-78; Curator, Buffalo Bill Meml Mus, Golden, CO, 1978-; Mem: Nat Writers Clb; Polish Inst of Arts & Scis; CO Authors Leag; CO—WY Assn of Mus; Am Assn of St & Local Hist; Wn Hist Assn; Denver Press Clb; Am Coun of Polish Culture; cp/Dpty Sheriff, Denver Wnrs, 1982; Treas, Denver Art Clb, 1950; CO Hist Assn; Denver Hist Assn; Indust Jefferson Co; Chm of Comm Lakewood; hon/Author of Over 100 Articles Pub'd in Newspapers & Mags; Books Incl: The 59'ers, Roaring Denver, 1961-83; The Westernaires, 1967; Buffalo Bill- His Life & Legend, 1981; Grunwald, 1982; Denver City, 1982;

Gentleman Rogue, 1984; Padre Polaco, 1984; Decorated Air Medal w 2 OLC; Braum Awd, Denver Art Dirs & Advtg Assn, 1959; CO Press Photog, 1965-67; Nat Press, 1967; Buffalo Bill Tent Awd, 1982; W/W: in W, of Wn Histns, of Contemp Authors.

ZAMPIELLO, RICHARD SIDNEY oc/Executive, Copper Industry; b/May 7, 1933; h/Woodbury Road, Washington, CT 06793; ba/Waterbury, CT; m/Helen Shirley Palsa; c/Geoffrey R; p/Sidney and Louise Zampiello, Hamden, CT; sp/Anna Palsa, Washington, CT; ed/Bach, Trinity Col, 1955; MBA, Univ Bridgeport, 1961; pa/Westinghouse Elect Corp, 1955-64; Exec VP, Ullrich Copper Inc, 1964-71; Sr VP, Gerald Metals Inc; GMP Div; ASME; AIME; SME; cp/Mining Clb; Yale Club; Copper Clb; Wash Clb; Delta Kappa Epsilon Clb; r/Cath; hon/Author of Num Pubs; W/W E.

ZEHEL, WENDELL EVANS oc/General Surgeon; b/Mar 6, 1934; h/553 Harrogate Road, Pittsburgh, PA 15241; ba/Pittsburgh, PA; m/Joan; c/Lori, Wendell; ed/BA, Wash & Jefferson Col, 1956; MD, Univ Pgh, 1960; mil/USAF, 1961-63, Capt; pa/Gen Surg, 1968-82; Am Col Surgs; AMA; Nat Adv Bd Am Biographic Inst; NY Acad Sci; Assn Advmt Med Instrumentation; AAAS; hon/W/W E; Noble Personalities Am; Dir Dist'd Ams; 2000 Noble Ams; Intl Register Profiles; Intl W/W: Intells, Commun Ser.

ZEITCHICK, ABRAHAM A oc/Security Director; h/1280 East 86th Street, Brooklyn, NY 11236; Married; 2 Chd; pa/Dir of Security Guards; Lic'd Pvt Investigator; Employed w Kings Co Dist Atty's Ofc; Ins Broker; Mutual Fund Salesman; cp/Commun Planning Bd; Bklyn Jewish Coun; VP, Flatbush Commun Coun; Chm, W Remsen Civic Assn; Pres, Remsen Hgts Jewish Ctr; VP, Jewish Nat Fund; Dir, Child Guild Clinic; B'nai B'rith; K of P; Others; hon/Man of the Month, Holy Fam PTA; BSA; Oscar, Dist Commr's Key, Scouters Key, Order of Arrow, Silver Beaver; Appt'd to Am Fdn Police; Others.

ZELAZO, NATHANIEL K oc/President and Chief Executive Office; b/Sep 28, 1918; h/1610 North Prospect Avenue, Milwaukee, WI 53202; ba/Milwaukee, WI; m/Helene Fishbein-Ret; c/Ronald E, Annette R; p/Morris (dec) and Ida Zelazo, Queens, NY; sp/David and Rose Mihaly Fishbein-Ret; ed/BS, City Univ NY, 1940; MSME, Univ WI, 1957; Postgrad Studies, Columbia Univ; Hon Doct Engrg Deg, Milwaukee Sch Engrg; mil/USN Dept; pa/Pres & CEO, Astronautics Corporation Am, 1959-; Dir Res, Devel Avionics Div, 1955-59; VP, United Aircraft Corporation, 1952-55; Regent & Mem Corporate Bd, 1979-, Milwaukee Sch Engrg; Chm, 1983-84, WI Elect Assn; Milwaukee Sch Engrg, Elect Engrg Technol Indust Adv Com, 1983-84; Assoc Fellow, AIAA; St Mem, IEEE; Nat Soc Profl Engrs; Am Soc Nav Engrs; Am Helicopter Soc; Navy Leag US; AF Assn; Engrs & Scist Milwaukee Inc; Physics Clb Milwaukee; Armed Forces Communs & Elects Assn; hon/IEEE, Cent Medal; Milwaukee Sch Engrg, Hon Deg; Albert Einstein Awd, 1982, Am Technion Soc; Employer of Yr Awd, Dept Def; Billy Mitchell Awd, AF Assn; Small Businessman Yr WI,

Small Bus Adm; W/W: Aviation, Fin & Indust, Technol Today, Am; WI Men Achmt; Biographical Dir Computer Graphics Indust.

ZELLER, VIRGINIA G M oc/Public Relations, Real Estate Investments; h/1701 Park Avenue, Baltimore, MD 21217; m/Leon H (dec); p/John Gordon Mitchell (dec) and Mrs J Gordon Mitchell, Charlotte, NC; ed/BS; MS, 1983, Johns Hopkins Univ; pa/Fdg Pres, Advtg Assn of Balto; cp/Past Pres, Balto Opera Guild Inc; Fdg Pres, MD Action for Foster Chd Inc; hon/1st Nat Awd for Org'g MD Action for Foster Chd "Model" for the Country, HEW, 1974; J Hochreiter Awd for Foster Chd Commun Ser.

ZEMEL, HELENE LEVEY oc/Association Executive; b/Jan 3, 1947; h/102-40 67th Road, Apartment 3W, Forest Hills, NY 11375; ba/New York, NY; m/Leonard S; p/Theodore (dec) and Sylvia Levey, Rosedale, NY; sp/Abraham and Sandra Zemel, Delray Beach, FL; ed/BA, Hofstra Univ, 1968; MA, Queens Col, 1972; MBA Cand, NY Inst Technol; pa/Piano Instr & Concert Pianist, 1968-77; Asst Admr Soc/Coun Adm 1977-78; Admr Conf Activs 1978-, IEEE; Recording Secy 1981-82, Treas 1982-83, Bd Dirs 1983-85, Del NY St Conv 1983, NY Leag BPW; Budget & Fin Com Mem, 1982-83, Meeting Planners Intl; r/Jewish; hon/Piano Recitals incl'g Lincoln Ctr; Sigma Kappa Alpha; Tchg F'ship, Queens Col; Cum Laude, Hofstra Univ; W/W Am Wom.

ZERR, RITA GREGORIO oc/Director, Teaching Assistantship Program Elementary Schools; b/Jun 9, 1928; h/4759 Knight Drive, New Orleans, LA 70127; ba/New Orleans, LA; m/George James; c/Jeanne Rita, Gary George; p/Fred (dec) and Clothilde Gregorio, New Orleans, LA; sp/George B Zerr, Metairie, LA, and Ida B Piro (dec); ed/BA, Newcomb Col, 1948; MA, Tulane Univ, 1959; PhD, Univ So MS, 1970; pa/Food Chem, Charles Dennery Inc, 1948; Elem Tchr, New Orleans Public Schs, 1948-66; Adj Fac, Ctr Tchr Ed, Tulane Univ, 1961-67; Instr, Newcomb Col, 1967-71; Assoc Dir 1967-68, Dir 1968-, Coor Elem Ed, Asst Prof 1971-, Tchg Asst'ship Prog Elem Schs, Tulane; VP 1976-77, Pres-Elect 1977-78, Pres 1978-79, LA Coun Social Studies; Res Editor, 1983-84, Intl Assn Pupil Pers Wkrs; Nat Coun Social Studies, Prog Com, 1974-75; Assoc Curric & Supvn; Am Ednl Res Assn; cp/Fac Sponsor, Nominations Com 1982-84, Chm Nominations Com 1984-86, Kappa Delta Pi; r/Rom Cath; hon/Author of Num Pubs incl'g "The Mid Sch Potential Dropout: A Proactive Approach" Jour Intl Assn Pupil Pers Wkrs 1983; Pres Cit, Nat Soc Perf & Instrn, 1972; Personalities of S; DIB; World W/W Wom; W/W Social Studies.

ZIBRUN, STEPHEN MICHAEL oc/President, Telemarketing Consultancy Firm; b/Aug 1, 1945; h/346 South 48th Avenue, Bellwood, IL 60104; ba/Bellwood, IL; m/Carol Ann Salerno; c/Michael, Jennifer; p/Stephen John and Elizabeth Behrendt Zibrun, New Port Richey, FL; sp/Dominic and Mary Salerno, River Forest, IL; ed/BA, Bus Adm, 1968; MBA, IL Benedictine Col, 1982; mil/USNR, 1968-70; pa/Pres, S Michael Assocs, 1981-; Mgr, Corporate Communs, Mark Controls Corporation, 1980-81; Advtg Dir, Patten Indust Inc, 1979-80; Advtg Mgr, 1968-79; Cert'd Bus Communicator, Bus/Profl Advtg Assn; cp/Bellwood C of C; Bellwood Zoning Bd Appeals; r/Rom Cath; hon/Author of Num Pubs; W/W: in MW, in Consltg.

ZIMBAL, CAMILLA K oc/US Probation Officer; b/Jun 25, 1949; h/1679 State Highway 121, Apartment 801, Lewisville, TX 75067; ba/Dallas, TX; p/Mr and Mrs Ray W Zimbal, May, TX; ed/BS, Howard Payne Univ, 1971; MS, Abilene Christian Univ, 1980; PhD, TX Wom's Univ; mil/AUS, 1st Lt; pa/US Probation Ofcr, Mtl Hlth Spec, US Probation No Dist TX, 1979-; St Parole Ofcr, St Bd Pardons & Parole, 1977-79; Adjutant & Chief Alcohol/Drug Mgmt Preven & Control Prog, US Army, 1975-77; Adj Fac Criminal Justice, TX Wom's Univ, 1982-; Instr, Dallas Commun Col Prog, 1979-80; Tnr, St Parole Ofc, 1978-79; Instr, US Army, 1975-77; Eng Tchr, Bangs HS, Bangs, TX, 1972-75; TX St Tchrs Assn; TX Correctional Assn; Am Correctional Assn; Fed Probation Ofcrs Assn; Fed Law Enforcement Ofcrs Assn; Am Sociological Assn; TX Mtl Hlth Assn; TX Profl Cnslrs; cp/Public Spkr, Rape Crisis Ctr, 1979-; Commun Ed, Dallas Public Sch Sys Corrections, 1979-; Coun Govts, Public Spkr Crim Aspects & Progs of Rehab, 1980-; Dallas Coun Alcoholism, Commun Treatment Prog, 1980-; Dallas Mtl Hlth Assn, Public Spkr Mtl Illness Corrections, 1981-; r/Ch of Christ; hon/Author of Num Pubs incl'g "Hiring Wom Ex-Offenders: What We Can Do", Fed Probation, 1983.

ZIMMER, THERESA MAGDALENA oc/Assistant Professor in College of Business; b/Dec 16, 1951; h/239 Arlington Drive, Lake Charles, LA 70605; ba/Lake Charles, LA; p/George C (dec) and Florence C Zimmer, Arabi, LA; ed/BS 1973, MEd 1977, Univ of New Orleans; PhD, N TX St Univ, 1981; pa/Secy, LSUNO, 1971-73; Secy, Blue Plate Foods, 1973-74; Bus Tchr, Andrew Jackson HS, 1974-81; Asst Prof, McNeese St Univ, 1981-; St Bernard Assn Edrs, Sch Rep, 1975-77; LA Assn Bus Ed, St Treas, 1982-84; Nat Bus Ed Assn; AAUW; cp/Phi Chi Theta, Pres, 1973; Delta Pi Epsilon; Phi Kappa Phi; Phi Delta Kappa, Nat Col Assn of Secy; Kappa Delta Pi; SASA; LVA; r/Cath; hon/Author of "Tchg the Alphabet & Num Keys Concurrently in HS Typewriting Classes" Alpha Epsilon Res 1983; Outstg FBLA Advr; Conslt & Spkr, Word Processing & Ofc Sys.

ZIMMERMAN, FRANCIS ADDIE oc/Training Instructor, Public Relations Department of Labor; b/Oct 10, 1924; h/9706 Hayes, Overland Park, KS 66212; ba/Kansas City, MO; m/Eugene R (dec); c/Donald E, Nancy C Giller, Robert J, Laura L; p/Dewey J (dec) and Louise F Howell, Kansas City, KS; ed/Park Col, 1941-44; Rockhurst Col, 1972;

Univ of MI; Univ of Houston; pa/Dir Public Relats & Co Orgr, Am Gancer Soc, 1959-60; Public Relats, MO Employmt Ser, 1962-75; Instr & Art Dir, Reg Tng Ctr, US Dept Labor, 1975-80; Employer Coor, 1980-; Intl Assn Pers; Mgr, Employmt Security; Am Soc Tnrs; Nat Assn Female Execs; cp/Nelson Gallery Art; Kansas City C of C; Urban Leag Gtr KC; Personal Dynamics Assn; Pk Col Alumni Assn; Art Dirs Clb KC; Lioness; KC PTA Bd; Bd Dirs, Shawnee Mission HS; r/Unity; hon/W/W of Am Wom.

ZINIAK, MADELINE oc/Television Producer, Journalist; b/Jun 2, 1956; h/24 Tarlton Road, Toronto M5P 2M4, Ontario; ba/Don Mills, Ontario; p/Mr and Mrs M Ziniak, Toronto, Ontario; ed/BA, Univ of Toronto, 1979; Ryerson Polytech Inst, 1980; Royal Conservatory Music; Cable TV, 1980-; cp/Ontario Adv Coun, Multiculturalism & Citizenship, Chp Media & Communs Com; Canadian Ethnic Jour & Writers Clb; Byelorussian Wom's Com; r/Byelorussian Orthodox; hon/Author of "Don't Overlook Mkt Served by Ethnic Media" 1980; The Canadian Acad Cultural Exch, 1980; Canadian Ethnic Jour Awd, 1982; World W/W of Wom.

ZOOK, MARTHA HARRIS oc/Director Nursing; b/Nov 15, 1921; h/1109 Johnson Street, Larned, KS 67550; ba/Larned, KS; m/Paul W; c/Mark Warren, Mary Elizabeth Hughey; p/Dwight Thacher and Helen Houston Harris; sp/Elizabeth Zook, Larned, KS; ed/Dipl, Meriden Hosp Sch Nsg, 1947; BA, Stephens Col, 1977; mil/Cadet Nurse Corps; pa/Staff Nurse, Watkins Meml Hosp, 1948-49; Nsg Supvr, Larned St Hosp, 1949-53; Sect Supvr, 1956-57; Dir Nsg, 1958-61; Sect Nurse Sedgwick Sect, 1961-76; Clin Instr, Nsg Ed, 1976-77; Dir Nsg Ed, 1977-83; Dir Nsg, 1983-; Clin Nurse for Podiatrist, 1953; Sect Supvr Dillon Bldg, Larned, KS, 1957-58; ANA; KS Nurses Assn; Nat Leag Nsg; KS Leag Nsg; St Bd Nsg (Mtl Hlth Tech Exam Com); Nat Assn Human Ser Edrs; AAUW; r/Cath; hon/W/W of Am Wom.

ZUCKERMAN, STUART oc/Medical Director, Clinical Professor; b/Feb 18, 1933; h/6700 Atlantic Avenue, Ventnor, NJ 08406; ba/Ventnor, NJ; p/George Zuckerman, Atlantic City, NJ, and Cassie Zuckerman (dec); ed/BS, Univ Al, 1954; DO, Phila Col Osteopathic Med, 1958; Rotating Intern, 1958-59; p/Psychi Fellow, Resident, Phila Mtl Hlth Clin, 1959-62; Psychoanal Studies Inst 1959-62, Chief Resident 1962; Chief Div Neuropsychi, Grandview Hosp, Dayton, OH, 1962-65; Asst Med Dir, Chief Chd's & Adolescents Unit, NJ St Hosp, Ancora, 1967-70, Chief Outpatient Dept, Atlantic City, 1970-72; Pract in Neuropsychi, 1965-76; Fdg Prof Psychi, Sch Med, Marshall Univ, 1977-78, Clin Prof 1979-; Chief Mtl Hygiene, VA Hosp, Huntington, WV,

1978-79; Liaison Psychi, VA Med Ctr, Perry Pt, MD, 1979-; Med Dir, Mtl Hygiene Clin Ocean Co, Toms River, NJ 1980-; Consltg Psychi, 1977-; Conslt, Chd Study, Spec Sers, S Jersey Sch Sys; Nom Com, Mtl Hlth Assn Atlantic Co, 1972-75; Hosp Insp Team, Am Osteopathic Assn, 1971-75; Bd Dirs, Atlantic Co Fam Sers Assn, 1968-74; Cape May Co Drug Abuse Coun; Diplomate, Am Osteopathic Bd Neurol & Psychi; Am Nat Bd Psychi; Fellow, Royal Soc Hlth; Intl, Am, MD, Psychi Assns; Am NJ Public Hlth Assns; Am Osteopathic Assn; AAUP; Am Soc for Law & Med; Am Acad Forensic Scis; Am Assn Acad Psychi; Am Col Emer Phys; Am Acad Psychotherapists; Am Assn on Mtl Deficiency; Acad Psychosomatic Med; NJ, CA Assns Osteopathic Phys & Surgs; NJ Hosp Assn; Am Voc Assn; Am Assn Grp Therapy; Assn Mil Surgs US; Am Assn Psychi Admrs; Am Assn Adolescent Psychi; World Med Assn; Am Assn Mtl Hlth Admrs; Am Assn Gen Hosp Psychis; Am Phys F'ship Assn for Res Nervous & Mtl Diseases; Atlantic Co Osteopathic Med Soc, Pres 1970-72; Assoc Editor, Bulletin of Am Col Neuropsychis, 1963-70; hon/Author of Num Profl Pubs; W/W: in Am, in E, in MW; World W/W.

ZYBINE, ALEK oc/Choreographer, Ballet Master; b/Jun 2, 1934; h/Av San Francisco 3388, Col, Chapalita, Guadalajara, Jal, Mexico; ba/Same; m/Violette; c/Nadya, Olivia; p/Lilia Zybina, Great Barrington, MA; sp/Uros and Zora Zelich, Daytona Beach, FL; ed/Universidad Autonoma de Mexico; Dance Studies w Hypolite Zybine, Anatole Vilzac, Edward Caton, Anthony Tudor, Matt Mattox; pa/Danced, Choreographed for TV & Movies, 1951-55; Danced w Ballet Russe de Montecarlo in USA, 1956-58; Soloist, Metro Opera NYC, 1958-60; Ldg Dancer Dallas Liric Opera, 1961; Ldg Dancer, Kovach, Rabowsky Co, 1961-62; Assoc Dir, Choreographer, Tchr & Dancer, Nassau Civic Ballet, 1962-70; Headed Creation & Dir of Folklore Grp Sent to Olympic Games in Mexico, 1968; Guest Leading Dancer in Port Au Prince under Lavinia Williams, 1972; Dir, Fdr, "New Breed Dancers Ltd", 1973-75; Headed the Dance Dept for Min of Ed in Bahamas, 1973-75; Choreographed "Misa Caribe" 1975; Est'd Academia del Ballet Guadalajara, AC, 1975; Dance Tchr, Folklorie Grp of Univ Guadalajara, 1975; Dir, Dance Dept, Bellas Artes, Jalisco, 1982; Dir, Official Dance Co, Jalisco, 1983; r/Russian Orthodox; hon/1st Prize Dance Contest, Instituto Nacional de la Juventud Mexicana, 1952; Presented to Queen Elizabeth II as Pres of Festival of Arts & Crafts in Nassau, 1966; 1st Father/Daughter Team, Intl Ballet Competition in Varna, Bulgaria; Men of Achmt; Intl W/W of Intells; Dic of Intl Biography.

PERSONALITIES OF AMERICA

ADDENDUM

ASHTON, KATE PEGGY oc/Editor, Professor, Speech Consultant; b/Sep 11, 1948; h/5046 Ducos Place, San Diego, CA 92124; ba/San Diego, CA; p/Lester Leopold, Boca Raton, FL; Louise Monroe, Hartwood, VA; ed/BS in Spch Communication 1970, MA in Platform Arts 1972, Bob Jones Univ; MA in Spch Communication, San Diego St Univ, 1979; pa/Instr, Bob Jones Univ, 1970-72; Asst Prof, Christian Heritage Col, 1972-76; Prof, San Diego City Col, 1976-83; Editor, *Where* Mag, 3M, 1980-83; Spch Conslt, Marine Corps, San Diego Gas & Elect & Pacific Telephone; Wn Spch Assn, 1985; Communicating Arts Grp, 1982; r/Prot; Hon/Pubs, "Take Home Pictures" in *Where* Mag, 1982; "Coping w Student Criticism" in *Guide* 1977; & *Emily* 1972; W/W: Am Wom, Among Cols & Univs.

BURKES, DORIS S HAMILTON oc/ Retired Educator; b/Apr 23, 1914; h/ Route 3, Box 255, Laurel, MS 39440; m/Grady B (dec); p/Oscar D and Era Magee Simmons (dec); ed/BS 1937, MA 1954, Univ of So MS; pa/Civilian Employeee, USAAC, 1944-45; Tchr, Voc Home Ec, Moselle 1937-40, Brandon 1940-41, Hattiesburg 1941-42, Jones Co Schs 1945-54, Laurel City Schs 1954-71; Supervisory Tchr, Univ of So MS, 1941-42, 1947-71; Jones Co Tchrs Assn, Pres 1953-54; MS Home Ec Assn, Treas 1964; Delta Kappa Gamma Soc, Zeta St Pres 1965-67; BPW Clb; Laurel Clrm Tchr; Laurel Ed Assn, Pres; Pres, MS Voc Home Ec Tchrs, 1968-70; MS Voc Assn, 1970-71; MS Ret'd Tchrs, 1982-83; cp/MS 4-H Adult Ldrs Coun, Pres 1952-53; Altrusa Clb, Pres, Laurel 1957-58, 1970-73; Red Cross Bd & Tchr, 1946-; MS Chgo Clb, 1983-84; Farm Bur, Bd & Wom's Chair; Coun of Aging, Chair, Adv Com 1982; SS Tchr; hon/ Articles in Newslttrs as St Pres; 4-H Ldrship Awd, 1953; MS 4-H Alumni Recog Awd, 1954; Named Wom of Achmt, BPW Clb, 1975; Diana Awd, 1978; Zeta St Delta Kappa Gamma Outstg Sers Awd, 1979; W/W: in Am Ed, of Am Wom, in S & SW, in US; Commun Ldrs of Am; DIB.

586

YOUNG PERSONALITIES OF AMERICA

A

AARON, GRACE A oc/Graduate Student; b/Feb 9, 1961; h/11622 Pawnee Drive Southwest, Tacoma, WA 98499; p/Mr and Mrs Russell K Aaron, Tacoma, WA; ed/Grad, Clover Park HS; BA, MS Univ for Wom, 1983; Att'g MS St Univ, MPPA expected 1984; cp/MS Univ for Wom Student Govt VP; Phi Kappa Phi; Student Senate Pres, MS Univ for Wom; Mng Editor, MS Univ Wom Newspaper; MS Univ for Wom Literary Mag Editor; Sigma Delta Chi, Soc for Profl Jour, Pres; Wom in Communs, VP; Gamma Beta Phi, Pres; Mortar Bd; Treas, Jr Class Honorary; Sigma Tau Delta, English Hon Soc; r/Meth; hon/Dean's & Pres' List, MS Univ for Wom; Grad magna cum laude, 1983; F'ship to MS St Univ, 1983-84; HS Hon Grad; Ray A Furr Jour S'ship; W/W Among Students in Am Univs & Cols; Intl Youth in Achmt; Commun Ldrs Am; Nat Dean's List; g/MPPA, 1984; Position in St or Fed Govt.

ABEL, MICHAEL A oc/Chef; b/Jan 17, 1965; h/Route 4, Box 74-D, Piedmont, AL 36272; ba/Gadsden, AL; p/James B Jr and Rachel F Abel, Piedmont, AL; ed/Sprg Garden HS; ba/Dock Instr, Browns Transport Co, 1979-80; Hdchef, Asst Mgr, The Other Office, 1981-84; Pres, FFA, 1980-83; Lib Asst, 1982-83; HS Ftball; Jr HS & HS Basketball; HS Class Treas; r/Bapt; hon/ FFA Pres; Chapt Farmer, 1982; Greenhand Awd, 1980; Lib Asst Awd, 1983; g/Computer Programmer & Repair.

ABELE, KAREN ANN oc/Student; b/May 17, 1962; h/3223 Ramsgate Road, Augusta, GA 30909; p/Dr and Mrs Donald C Abele, Augusta, GA; ed/BA, Converse Col, 1984; cp/Crescent Pres, 1981-82; Yrbk Editor, 1982-83; Alpha Lambda Delta, VP 1981-82; Mortar Bd, VP 1983-84; House Bd, Dorm Pres 1982-83; Chm of House Bd, 1983-84; Student Gov't VP, 1983-84; r/Presb; hon/Milliken Scholar, 1980-84; CRC Freshman Chem Awd, 1981; Fac S'ship, 1982-84; Converse Scholar, 1982-84; Jr Marshal, 1982-83; W/W; Nat Dean's List; g/Med Sch of the Med Col of GA.

ABNER, TROY ALLEN oc/Student, Part-time Photographer; b/Jan 21, 1963; h/General Delivery, Kay Jay, KY 40906; p/Troy and Phyllis Abner, Kay Jay, KY; ed/Knox Central HS, 1981; Eastern KY Univ, 1981-82; Union Col, 1982-84; pa/ Ofc Asst, John C Dixon, Atty, 1980-81; Ofc Asst, Milton Townsend, VP, Union Col, 1982-83; Photog, Union Col, 1983-; cp/Treas 1980, VP 1981, Future Bus Ldrs of Am; Barrister's Soc, Pre-Law Org, 1981-82; Treas 1982, VP 1983, Phi Beta Lambda Pre-Profl Bus Org; Student Governing Bd, 1982-83; Acad Policy Comm, 1982-83; Gamma Beta Phi Nat Hon, Mem 1982-83, Reporter 1982; St VP 1983; Commmun Registry for Sharing Sers, 1982-83; r/Bapt; hon/ Eng Composition Awd, 1983; Phi Beta Lambda Outstg Mem Awd, 1983; St and Reg Awds in Bus Law, 1980-81; Sr Bus Student Awd, 1981; Hon Roll, 1979-81; Dean's List, 1981-83; W/W; Am's Outstg Names and Faces; Nat Dean's List; Soc for Dist'd Am Students; g/Degs in Bus, Psych, and Sociol; Attend Law Sch; Return to Appalachia for Practice.

ABNEY, CARRIE GAIL oc/Student; b/Jan 13, 1966; h/Kaye Street, Route 5, Berea, KY 40403; p/Mr and Mrs William E Abney, Berea, KY; ed/Att'g HS; pa/ Cashier, Druther's Restaurant, 1983; cp/Nat Hon Soc, Reporter 1983; Sr Beta Clb, VP 1982-83; FHA, Treas, Pres, 1980-83; Student Govt VP, 1982-83; Sr Class Secy, 1983; Pep Clb, Treas 1980-84; Future Bus Ldrs of Am, Secy 1983; Colorguard Squad Co-Capt, Capt, 1980-84; *The Pirate* Monthly HS Newspaper; HS Yrbook; r/Bapt; hon/HS Health Awd; Jr HS Math Bowl Team, 1983; Homecoming Court 1st Runner-up; FHA Sophomore Sweetheart Attendant; Del to KY Girls' St, 1983; W/W Among Am HS Students; g/Attend Col with Major in Home Ec to become Teacher.

ABRAHAM, MARTIN A oc/Graduate Student; b/Feb 18, 1961; h/14-3A Cheswold Boulevard, Newark, DE 19713; p/Sam and Barbara Abraham, Levittown, NY; ed/Gen Douglas MacArthur HS, 1978; BSChE, Rensselaer Polytechnic Inst, 1982; Att'g Univ of DE; pa/Co-op Student, ARCO Chem Co, 1980-81; Summer Intern, Stauffer Chem Co, 1982-83; cp/AIChE; ACS; Colburn Clb; hon/Tau Beta Pi, 1981-; Phi Lambda Upsilon, 1981-; Univ of DE F'ship, 1982-; W/W in Am Cols and Univs; Commun Ldrs of Am; g/PhD, Chem Engrg at Major Univ.

ABRAMS, MARY TOMMIE oc/Student; b/Nov 13, 1960; h/732 Amelia Street, Newberry, SC 29108; p/Mr and Mrs George Carter Abrams, Newberry, SC; ed/Newberry HS, 1979; BA, Newberry Col, 1982; pa/Middle Sch Drama Tchr, 1982-83; cp/Alpha Psi Omega Hist; Phi Gamma Nu Editor; Intervarsity Christian F'ship Prog Coor; Christian Coun; Presb Ch SS Tchr; DAR; Bus Mgr *The Indian*; hon/Cardinal Key; Outstg Theatre Freshman/Sr On-Stage/Off-Stage Supporting Awds; W/W in Am Cols and Univs; g/Grad Study, Presb Sch of Christian Ed, Christian Edr.

ADAIR, DENNIS W oc/Senior Internal Auditor; b/Jan 4, 1955; h/4436 Pasture Drive, Elizabethtown, PA 17022; ba/Hershey, PA; m/Bonnie L; c/ Matthew C; p/William and Alma Adair, Ephrata, PA; sp/Theodore and Mildred Dietrich, Akron, PA; ed/Att'd PA St Univ, 1973-75; BS, Elizabethtown Col, 1977; pa/Auditor 1977-80, Sr Info Conslt 1980-81, Arthur Andersen & Co; Sr Internal Auditor, Hershey Foods Corporation, 1981-; Am Inst CPAs; PA Inst CPAs; r/United Ch Christ; hon/ Acad S'ship, Elizabethtown, 1976, 1977; PA Inst CPAs S'ship, 1977; Investmt Awd, Wall St Jour, 1977; Elected as Cand for Sch Dir, 1983.

ADAMEC, JAMES C oc/Student, Electrician; b/Feb 1, 1957; h/c/o Forte Certland Home, Apt 5A, Lexington Avenue, Mohegan, NY 10547; m/Margaret; p/Kenneth E Adamec, Stamford, CT; Joan C Gall Adamec, Danberry, CT; sp/Charles Sammann Jr, Katonah, NY; ed/John Jay Sr HS, 1975; AAS, Westchester Commun Col, 1982; Fordham Univ, 1978-80; cp/HS Varsity Ftball; Fordham Univ Student Govt; IEEE; HS Varsity Ski Racing Tm; hon/Dean's List; W/W Among Students in Am Cols & Univs; Commun Ldrs of Am; g/BSEE, PE, R&D Eng.

ADAMIK, JASON MICHAEL oc/Student; b/May 16, 1962; h/3309 Oak Hill Drive, Garland, TX 75043; p/Wayne and Joan Adamik, Garland, TX; ed/S Garland HS, 1980; Att'd TX A&M Univ, 1980; Att'g N TX St Univ, Music Major; cp/HS Band, 1976-80; Key Clb, Treas 1978; Chem Clb, 1977-80; French Clb, 1978-79; Beta Clb, 1978-80; Math Tm, 1979; Biol Clb, 1976-79; Active in Cath Student Commun of N TX St Univ & TWU, 1981-83; Soc for Creative Anachronism, NTSU, 1982; r/Cath; hon/ Illustrated Book on Early Am Hist; Illustrated 3 Annual HS Literary Mags; HS Sr Class Pres, 1980; Highest Score in HS, Nat Math Exam, 1980; All-City Band, 1979-80; Medals in UIL Music, 1979-80; Art Editor of *Libertas*; Art & Lit Pub, 1978-79; Rotary Clb Student of the Month, Twice, 1980; N TX St Univ First Freshman Classical Guitar Major, 1981; g/Bach's Deg in Art or Chem; Use Scientific & Artistic Abilities in Career in Scientific Res.

ADAMS, ALESIA SUZANNE oc/ Student; b/Mar 15, 1964; h/Route 2, Box 2, Clover, SC 29710; p/George S Adams, Gastonia, NC; Brenda M Burgin, Clover, SC; ed/Att'g E Carolina Univ; cp/Ch Choir; SS Pres; UMYF; 4-H Reporter; Varsity Basketball, Volleyball; hon/Scholar/Ath Awd; Outstg Sr S'ship; g/Vet Med.

ADAMS, AMY R oc/Sales Representative; b/May 10, 1960; h/2011 Estrada Parkway #134, Irving, TX 75061; p/Mr and Mrs Richard D Adams, Orange, TX; ed/Little Cypress-Mauriceville HS, 1978; BBA Fin, TX A&M Univ, 1982; pa/Student Asst, TX A&M Univ Lib Circulation Div, 1979-82; Aquatics Dir & Swim Instr, YMCA of Orange, TX, 1979-80; Sales Rep, CompuShop, 1983-; cp/Teens Aid Retarded, Pres 1978; Spec Olympics; Nat Hon Soc; Cath Yth Org; HS Tennis Tm; Student Govt; Fin Assn; Lib Staff Assn; Intramural Sports; Little Sister, Pi Kappa Phi Frat; r/Cath; hon/ Hon Grad; Am Legion Citizenship Awd, 1978; Ath Boosters Clb S'ship, 1978; Dist'd Student, TX A&M, 1982; g/Store Mgr, CompuShop; MBA, Bus Computing Sci.

ADAMS, LESTER LEE oc/Student; b/ Jan 25, 1963; h/905 Wall Street, Galena, KS 66739; p/Lester L and Doris L Adams, Galena, KS; ed/Galena HS, 1981; Pgh St Univ; cp/Order of DeMolay, Past Master Cnslr; Jr Class VP; Sr Class Pres; Yrbook Co-Bus Mgr; Sigma Phi Alpha Pres; Boy's St Supr Ct Justice; Cherokee Co Repub Ctl Com-man; Yg Repub Party Secy/Treas; Straight A Hon Roll; KU Hon Student; hon/St Scholar of KS; St of KS St Scholar S'ship; Lambda Sigma; Kappa Mu Epsilon; Alpha Mu Gamma; Dean's Hon Roll; Math S'ship, David Wright Meml S'ship; W/W Amg Am HS Students; Intl Yth In Achmt; Yg Commun Ldrs of Am.

ADAMS, MARY CAROLYN oc/Student; b/Oct 17, 1966; h/Box 121A, Jeremiah, KY 41826; p/Jimmy Ray and Jean Adams, Jeremiah, KY; ed/Att'g Letcher HS and Letcher Co Area Voc Ed Center, Bus Ofc Dept; cp/Future Bus Ldrs of Am, 1982-84 (Pres, 1983-84); r/Bapt; hon/Hon Roll, 1980-84; Write Articles for Sch Newspaper, 1983-84; g/Attend Col, Bus Adm; Manage Own Bus Firm.

ADAMS, PENELOPE RENEE oc/ Student; b/Sep 25, 1963; h/4 Trailridge

Lane, Route 7, Edwardsville, IL 61761; p/Mr and Mrs Luther Holst, Edwardsville, IL; ed/Collinsville HS, 1981; Att'd Greenville Col, Psych; Att'd IL St Univ, Music Therapy; pa/Clerical Secy, May Dept Stores, 1981; Secy, McDonnell Douglas, 1982; Recreational Aide, Music Tchr, Huddleson Bapt Chd's Home, 1983; cp/Collinsville HS Band, Bassoon Player; Flag Corps, Capt; Newspaper, Yrbook, Staff Mem; Greenville Col, Singing Gp, Cornerstone, Pianist; Yrbook, Staff Mem; Il St Univ, Student Christian F'ship; Music Therapy Clb; Alpha Gamma Delta Sorority; Ch Organist; r/Bapt; hon/Miss Collinsville, 1983; running, Miss IL, 1984; g/ BS, Employmt, Music/Music Therapy.

ADAMS, RUTHIE COLEMAN oc/ Nursing Supervisor; b/Mar 6, 1957; h/ Post Office Box 2148, Natchez, MS 39120; ba/Natchez, MS; m/Johnny E III; p/Joe and Rosie Shepherd, Macon, MS; sp/Luther and Willie Adams, Shubuta, MS; ed/BSN, 1979; pa/GN Staff Nurse, St Dominic Hosp, 1979; RN Staff Nurse, Hinds Gen Hosp, 1979; RN Instr, Alcorn St Univ, 1981-82; RN Nsg Supvr, Humana Hosp, 1981-; MS Nurse Assn; ANA; Chi Beta Phi Hon Sci Frat; r/ Meth; hon/Deans List, MS St Univ, 1976; Sr Campus Beauty, William Carey Col Sch Nsg, 1978-79.

ADAMS, SHEILA DAWN oc/Spanish Teacher; b/Nov 20, 1962; h/1400 West Blue Starr, #1-J, Claremore, OK 74053; p/John and Pat Adams, Oologah, OK; ed/Oologah HS, 1980; BA Spanish, OK St Univ, 1983; pa/Spanish Tchr, Oologah HS, 1983-; cp/Oologah Clrm Tchrs Assn; OK Ed Assn; Nat Ed Assn; OK Fgn Lang Tchrs Assn.

ADAMS, SHIRLEY LORRAINE (LORI) oc/Student; b/Jul 7,1962; h/74 Bahama Circle, Tampa, FL 33606; p/ Bruce Waldo and Shirley Bowman Adams, Tampa, FL; ed/Grad, Tampa Prep Sch; Att'd Yale Univ; cp/Asst Num Plays, Artist for Sets & Playbills, Yale Univ; HS Student Coun; Spec Olympics Asst; Piano, Bach Fests, Yrly; GSA; r/ Prot; hon/Valedictorian; Scholastic Art Awd, Gold Key; Nat Merit Scholar; Most Valuable Tennis Player, 4 Yrs; Full S'ship (declined), Eckerd Col; Intl Yth in Achmt; W/W Amg Am HS Students.

ADAMSON, ANGELA ALLYN oc/ Student; b/Mar 20, 1961; h/375 Dundee Road, Glencoe, IL 60022; p/R Christina Adamson, Glencoe, IL; ed/New Trier Twp HS E, 1970; Univ of Notre Dame; cp/Fdr, Dir, Abiogenesis Dance Collective; Photo Editor, Scholastic Mag; Pres, Photo Clb; Newspaper Art Columnist; Arts & Lttrs Student Adv Coun to the Dean; Staff Asst, Notre Dame/St Mary's Theatre; hon/Notre Dame Scholar; Dean's List; W/W Amg Am HS Students; g/MFA or MA in Dance or Arts Adm.

ADAMSON, TERRIE ELAINE oc/ Teacher, Coach; b/Aug 5, 1953; h/1419 Shady Lane, #403, Bedford, TX 76021; p/Mrs T J Adamson, Jr, Brenham, TX; ed/ HS, Brenham, TX, 1971; BS, TX Christian Univ, 1975; Att'd Univ of Salzburg, Austria, 1979-80; Att'd Univ of St Andrews, Scotland, 1982; pa/ Teacher, Coach, Richland HS, 1976-; Cnslr, Am Inst for Fgn Studies, 1978-; cp/Ch Choir; Softball Leag; r/Epis; hon/ HS Tennis Tm, 1967-71; First Dist Doubles, Jr. Davis Cup Tour Invitation,

Reg Finalist 1968, Dist Finalist 1971; HS Basketball Tm, 1968-71; St Quarterfinalist, 1971; Col Tennis Tm, 1971-74; Conf Conslt, 1972; Col Basketball Tm, 1973-75; Commun Ldrs of Am; g/Write Best-selling Book.

ADKINS, CARL EDWARD oc/Student; b/Jul 30, 1965; h/319 Kennedy, Middleton, TN 38052; p/Mr and Mrs Larry C Adkins, Middleton, TN; ed/ Middleton HS, 1983; Att'g Memphis St Univ; pa/Sta Attendant, Vicker's Delta Ser Ctr, 1981-82; Factory Worker, Dover Elevator Corp, 1983; cp/HS Beta Clb, Mem 1980-83, Pres, 1983; HS Basketball Scorekeeper, 1980-83; Sr Class Pres; Selected Most Likely to Succeed; r/Bapt; hon/Hugh O'Brian Yth Ldrship Foun Rep, 1980; First Pl Acctg 1982, Mr Future Bus Exec, Top 10% of Class 1977-83, Bus Day Conf, Freed-Hardeman Col; g/Maj in Acctg, CPA.

ADKINS, CURTIS ELWOOD oc/ Student; b/Sep 29, 1960; h/6451 Naldo Lane, Franklin, OH 45005; p/Curtis and Audrey Adkins, Franklin, OH; ed/HS, 1978; BA, Warner So Col, 1982; pa/Yth Pastor, First Ch of God, 1979; Yth Pastor, Chapelwood Ch of God, 1980-81; Yth Pastor, First Ch of God, 1982; Yth Pastor, Helm St Ch of God, 1983; cp/BSA Jr Asst Scoutmaster; NHS; Nu Alpha Theta; German Clb; Pres, Ch Yth F'ship; Chm, Acad Excell Com; Fund Raising Com; Student Body Pres; Varsity Soccer; hon/Nat Dean's List; Intl Yth in Achmt; W/W in Am Cols & Univs; Commun Ldrs of Am; Outstg Col Grads; g/Biblical Studies; Pastoral Min; Psychol; Christian Ed; Master's Deg; MDiv.

AGEE, CONNIE LYNN oc/Sr Secy, Dean of Col of Social and Behavioral Sci in Bus 1974; b/Aug 20, 1956; h/ Route 6, Frazerwood, Richmond, KY 40475; p/W J and Nannie Agee, Richmond, KY; ed/Madison Ctl HS, 1974; En KY Univ; Madison Co Voc Sch in Bus, 1974; cp/Pres, Reg Treas, FBLA; Beta Clb; Madison Co Voc Sch FBLA Clb; hon/Cert of Recog; Secretarial-Stenographic Awd; Intl Yth in Achmt; Phi Kappa Phi Awd for High Scholastic Achmt, 1982; Yg Personalities of the S; Commun Ldrs of Am; g/ Bus Adm Deg.

AGEE, DAWN LYNN oc/Student; b/ Jun 27, 1964; h/Rural Route #3, Richmond, KY 40475; p/Donald and Jeanette Agee, Richmond, KY; ed/Madison Ctl HS, Att'g En KY Univ; pa/Telephone Conslt, Olan Mills Studio, 1981; Clothing Clk, Heck's Dept Store, 1981-82; Shoe Salesperson, Adams Shoe Store, 1982-83; cp/Jr Beta Clb; Sr Beta Clb; Hlth Careers Clb; Pep Clb; FBLA; ARC Vol; Cancer Crusade and Mar of Dimes; Bapt Ch Yth Grp; Assn'l Yth Grp; 4-H Clb, Choral Grp; Ch Choir; Pres, Bapt Ch Yth Grp; r/So Bapt; hon/Eng Merck Awd; Hon for Dist'n, HS; Acad Excell Awd; Baton Twirling Hon Awd, 1975; Third Runner-Up Twirling Contest, 1976; March of Dimes Yth Participation Awd; St Finalist, Miss Teen Pageant; St Finalist, Miss U Teenager Pageant; g/ Maj in Bus Adm; Work for Maj Corp.

AGEE, NANCY DENISE oc/Student; Part-time Cashier; b/Dec 12, 1964; h/ 1505 Randy Drive, Cookeville, TN 38501; p/Don and Irene Agee, Cookeville, TN 38501; ed/Cookeville HS,

1983; Att'g, TN Tech; pa/Arts and Crafts Tchr, Parks and Rec, 1978-80; Salesperson, Don's Antiques, 1980-82; Salesperson, Armand's Dept Store, 1983; Cashier, Food Town Grocery Store, 1983; cp/Basketball, 1976-83, Capt 1978-79, 1983; Softball, 1976-83, Capt 1978-79, 1983; FHA Clb; Secy, DECA; Secy, Jr and Sr HS Classes; C Clb, Sigma Delta Sigma Soriorty; g/Maj in Home Ec; Own Real Est Ofc.

AGUILERA, RAYMOND OTTO oc/ Student; b/Jul 13, 1963; h/1724 West Melrose Street, Chicago, IL 60657; p/ Ramon and Margot Aguilera; ed/St Patrick HS, 1981; Lewis Univ; pa/ Firefighter, Tri-St Fire Dept; Admissions Peer Cnslr, Orientation Ldr Incoming Freshmen Prog, Resident Asst, Lewis Univ; cp/Nat Jr Hon Soc; Nat Hon Soc; Key Clb VP; Student Coun VP & Pres; Wrestling; Ftball; Spanish Nat Hon Soc; Curric Com; Yth Grp Secy; Ch Folk Grp; Candy Stripers-IL Masonic ER; Singer, Westmont Hlth Ctr; Diplomat, Mid-W Model UN, 1983; Communs Chp, Student Govt, 1983; hon/Nat Dean's List, 1983; Univ Dean's List, Hon Roll, 1983; W/ W Among Am HS Students; Cambridge Student Search; Kiwanis Citizenship Awd; Commun Ldrs of Am; Intl Students in Achmt; g/Majs in Polit Sci, Public Adm; Intl Polit.

AHO, KATHERINE WINDSOR oc/ Graphic Designer; b/Jul 5, 1961; h/B-3 Sturbridge Square, Blacksburg, VA 24060; m/David; ed/Dipl, HS, 1979; BFA, VA Commonwealth Univ, 1983; pa/Graphic Designer, Advantage Advertising Agy, 1983-; cp/Pres, Inter-Varsity Christian F'ship, VA Commonwealth Univ Chapt 1980-81, Missions Coor 1981-82; Sum Mission Wk in Philippines, 1981; hon/Ruth Hibbs Hyland Awd; g/Overseas Mission Wk.

AKAR, NABIH NABIH b/Jan 12, 1959; h/22087 Barton Road, Grand Terrace, CA 92334; p/Nabih and Nadia Akar, Grand Terrace, CA; ed/Univ So MS; BS 1981, MA 1983, Univ CA; pa/ Internship, Dept Finance, Riverside, CA; Pres, Chm Publicity for Soc Advmt Mgmt, 1980-82; Mem, Am Prodn & Inventory Control Soc, 1980-82; hon/ Nat Dean's List, 1981; Cert Achmt, Soc Advmt Mgmt, 1981; London Awd, Inst Anglo-Am Studies, 1981; g/PhD in Fin; Ldg Ofcr in Bkg Indus.

AKERS, BRENDA LACHELLE oc/ Student; b/Mar 18, 1964; h/209 Cindy Place, Goodlettsville, TN 37072; p/Mr and Mrs Akers, Goodlettsville, TN; ed/ Goodlettsville HS, 1982; Att'g Univ TN, 1982; pa/Full-time Student, Univ TN; FFA St Farmer, 1982; Secy 1983-84; r/ Bapt; hon/FFA St Farmer 1982; FFA Star Chapt Farmer Awd, 1982; W/W Among Am HS Students; Commun Ldrs Am; g/Marketing Major.

AKIYAMA, JULIE S oc/Graduate Student; b/Jan 17, 1957; h/1147 South Windsor Boulevard, Los Angeles, CA 90019; p/John and Dorothy Akiyama, LA, CA; ed/LA HS, 1975; BA, CA St Univ-LA, 1980; MA, Pepperdine Univ, 1983; PhD Prog, St Louis Univ; pa/ Psych Intern, Asian Pacific Cnslg & Treatment Ctr, Hollywood Mtl Hlth, 1982; Tchr's Asst, Pepperdine Univ, 1981-83; Therapeutic Intern, Beverlywood Mtl Hlth Ctr, 1982-83; r/Christian; hon/Nat Dean's List, 1980; Ephebian Soc, 1975; g/PhD in Clin Psychol; Child Psychol.

ALDERMAN, LOUIS CLEVELAND III oc/Computer Sys Tech Support Engineer; b/Oct 7, 1955; h/3011 Falling Brook Drive, Kingwood, TX 77339; p/ Louis C Jr and Anne A W Alderman, Cochran, GA; ed/Cochran HS, 1973; AS, Mid GA Col, 1975; BEE, GA Inst Tech, 1977; pa/TX Reg'd Profl Engr; Chd of Am Revolution, Charter Pres; SAR; Nat Assn of Eagle Scouts; Magna Charter Barons; hon/Eagle Scout; STAR Student; Salutatorian; Hon Grad; Beta Clb; Phi Theta Kappa; Wallace Harris Meml S'ship; Burgoyne Gibson Moors Meml S'ship; Dean's List; St of GA, Univ GA Cert of Merit; St of GA Gov Hon Prog, Math; W/W Am Jr Cols; g/MBA.

ALDRIDGE, SABRINA KAYE oc/ Student; b/May 18, 1960; h/Route 2, Box 224A, Moulton, AL 35650; p/ Hansel and Martha Aldridge, Moulton, AL; ed/Lawrence Co HS, 1978; BA, Univ AL, 1982; Att'g Athens St Col for BS Ed; pa/Reporter, *The Moulton Advertiser*, 1984; Secy, Calhoun Commun Col, 1984; Reporter, *The Huntsville News*, 1982; Sigma Delta Chi; Soc Profl Journalists; r/Ch of Christ; hon/Athens St, Miss Merry Christmas, 1983; Outstg Yg Ams, 1979; Nat Dean's List, 1979; US Senate Yth Prog, 1978; g/ Master's Deg, Tchg.

ALEMAR, DEBRA CARTER oc/ Switchboard Operator; b/Mar 5, 1959; h/3325 Galindo Street, Oakland, CA 94601; m/Carlos R; p/Mr and Mrs B J Carter; ed/HS Dipl, Patten Acad of Christian Ed, 1977; BA, Patten Col, 1981; ETTA Cert, 1981; pa/Registrar, Patten Col, 1980-82; Switchboard Operator, Retirement Home, 1983-; Food Sers Cashier, 1983; cp/VP, HS; VP, Secy, Col; Symphonette; Co-Editor of Sch Paper; Sunday Sch Tchr; Tchr's Asst; AACRAO; Col Singers Orch II; r/Christian Evang; hon/Nat Dean's List, 1981; Grad, cum laude; Gold "P"; Silver and Gold "A," 1977; W/W Among Sudent in Am Univs and Cols; W/W Among Dist'd HS Students.

ALEXANDER, ALPHA VERNELL oc/ Associate Athletic Director; b/Jun 9, 1954; h/870 North 28th Street, Apartment 216, Philadelphia, PA 19130; p/Mr and Mrs Alexander (dec); ed/Jefferson Sr HS, 1972; BA, Col of Wooster, 1976; Master's Deg 1978, Doct Deg 1981, Temple Univ; pa/Assoc Ath Dir 1983-, Acting Wom's Ath Dir 1982-83, Temple Univ; AAHPER; PA AHPER; Nat Assn for Girls and Wom in Sport; Black Interested Coaches; Psycho/Sociol Sport Interactions Lab, Temple Univ; Wom Sport Foun; Site Dir, USFHA Olympic "D" Camp, Temple Univ; Ad Hoc Com Wom Ath; Search Com, HPERD Outdoor Facilities Coor; Pers Com Mem Wom Ath; Grad Student Rep, Dean's Search Com; Records Custodian of Wom Intercol Ath Pers Com; Chm of Wom Intercol Ath Pers Com; Wom Intercol Ath Res Coun; Dir of Grad Student Assn Coffee Shop; Participant, EAIAW Reg 1-B Basketball Tourn; Minority Recruitment Prog for PE; Full-time Wom SportsInfo Dir; hon/ Pub, *Black Women in Sport*, 1981; Outstg Wooster Student; Martindale Compton S'ship; Outstg Yg Wom of Am; Intl Yth Achmt; Basketball Awd; Dir of Dist'd

Ams; g/To Help Minority Wom.

ALEXANDER, ANDREA ALICIA oc/ Student; b/Jul 23, 1967; h/204 Edgemont Street, Easley, SC 29640; p/ Barron and Lynn Alexander, Easley, SC; ed/Easley HS; cp/French Clb, Secy 1983-84; Jr Class Secy, 1983-84; Student Coun, 1983-84; Student Coun-Homeroom Pres, 1982-83; r/ Presb; Interact Handbell Choir at Ch, 4 Yrs; hon/Participant in Clemson Univ Biol Merit Exam, 1983; Participant in Miss Teen of SC Pageant, 1983; g/To Attend Either the Univ of AL or Clemson Univ and Maj in Bus Adm or Computer Sci.

ALEXANDER, CAROLYN JEAN oc/ Student; b/Dec 21, 1960; h/1524 Dade Street, Augusta, GA 30904; p/Ms Agnes Alexander, Augusta, GA; ed/Dipl, Acad of Richmond Co, 1978; BS, Biol, Clark Col, 1982; Student, NC A&T Univ, 1983-; pa/Subst Tchr, Acad of Richmond Co, 1982-83; Res, "Invivo Location of R6K Plasmids in *E coli*," Morehouse Col, 1981-82; Res, "Regulation of Phosphotidylcholine Biosynthesis," Purdue Univ, Sum 1981; Beta Kappa Chi Sch Hon Soc, Secy; cp/Acad of Richmond Co, Exec Coun Secy 1977; Red Cross Vol, 1973-; Vol Tutor, 1982-; r/Born Again Christian; Ch Pianist, 1976-81; hon/Undergrad Access to Res Careers S'ship, 1980-82; Alpha Kappa Mu Hon Soc, 1980; Beta Kappa Chi Sci Hon Soc, 1981; g/To Attain PhD in Biol and Become a Biomed Scist/Rschr.

ALEXANDER, DON L oc/Associate Professor of Mathematics; b/Feb 22, 1948; h/582 Ashville Road, Montevallo, AL 35115; ba/Montevallo, AL; p/Dr and Mrs W A Alexander, Covington, TN; ed/BS 1970, MA 1972, PhD 1979, Univ of AL; pa/Asst Prof of Math 1974, Assoc Prof of Math 1981, Univ of Montevallo; AL Tchrs of Col Math; Univ of Montevallo Fac Coun, Secy; cp/Bd of Dirs, AL Soccer Leag; Montgomery Caps Soccer Team; Univ of Montevallo Ultimate Frisbee Team, Fac Advr; Univ of Montevallo Soccer Clb, Fac Advr; B'ham Track Clb; Porsche Clb of Am; hon/Pubs, "Concerning Equivalences of Almost Continuous and Connectivity Functions of Baire Class I on Peano Continua" 1979, "Blocking Sets and Almost Continuous Functions" 1979; Univ of Montevallo Merit Awd Recip, 1982.

ALEXANDER, FRED JR oc/Student; b/Mar 28, 1965; h/2307 Briargrove Drive, Charlotte, NC 28215; p/Fred and Dilsie Alexander, Charlotte, NC; ed/ Grad, Garinger HS, 1983; cp/Student Body Pres, 1982-83; Nat Hon Soc, 1982-83; Math Hon Soc, 1982-83; Treas, Exec Com, 1981-83; Pres, Bible I, 1982-83; Pres, French Clb, 1980-81; Sophomore Class Treas, 1981-82; Jr Marshall, 1981-82; Sci Clb, 1982-83; Varsity Baseball, 1980-81, 1981-83, 1982-83; Band, 1980-81, 1981-82, 1982-83; Coun of Concerned Citizens, 1982-83; Master Knight, Knights of Pythagoras, 1982-83; hon/Civitan Awd, 1983; Grad Panhellenic Coun Outstg Sr, 1983; Charlotte Post Top 10 Srs, 1983; Mr Garinger, 1983; Garinger Super Sr, 1983; Voted Most Intellectual, 1983; Highest Batting Average Awd, 1982; Proj Excell at Davidson Col, 1982; INROADS Prog, 1983; Ranked 10th of 484, 1983; W/W Academics; W/W

Music; g/To Attend NC St Univ.

ALEXANDER, RONALD EDDIE oc/ Student; b/Mar 28, 1962; h/Route 2, Box 48, Salem, SC 29676; p/Mr and Mrs Bea Alexander Jr, Salem, SC; ed/ Tamassee-Salem HS; BA, Furman Univ, 1984; pa/Govt Relats Intern at 70,001 LTD, Wash Ctr Internship Prog, Sprg Term, 1983; Sum Yth Employmt Cnslr, Pre-Employmt Coor, Field Coor, CETA-Share, Sums 1982-83; Yth Dir, Salem Bapt Chm, Sums 1981-82; cp/Vol Wk in Var Polit Campaigns; Col Ednl Ser Corps, 1980-84, Div Hd 1982-84, May Play Day CoChp 1982, Coor 1981-84; Yg Dems Clb, 1984; Reorg'd Clb and Served as Pres 1982-84; Bapt Student Union, 1980-84, Prog Chm 1983-84, Min Chm 1982-83; Col Bowl Team Mem, 1982-84; Bread for the World, 1980-84; Furman Univ Hunger Alliance, 1982-84; r/So Bapt; hon/Voted the Alfred S Reid Outstg Jr Male, 1983; Elected Mem, Quaternion Clb, 1983-84; Recip, Doyle Meml S'ship, 1980-84; Recip, Furman Scholar S'ship, 1980-84; Recip, Class of 1965 S'ship, 1983-84; Dean's List Each Term; Omicron Delta Kappa Ldrship Hon, 1983; Dist'd Ams; W/W Among Students in Am Cols and Univs; g/To Attend Law Sch and Become Involved in Politics.

ALEXANDER, RUTH ANN oc/Student; b/Jan 6, 1965; h/Route 1, Box 47, Mt Crawford, VA 22841; p/R V and Phyllis L Alexander, Mt Crawford, VA; ed/Sch Dipl, 1983; Assoc of Fine Arts, So Sem Jr Wom's Col, 1985; pa/Stage Mgr, Shenendoah Val Choral Soc, 1983; cp/Turner Ashby Concert Choir, 1979-83, Libn 1981-83, Secy 1982-83; Turner Ashby Band, 1979-83, Libn 1982-83; Turner Ashby Forensic Team, 1974-83; Turner Ashby Drama Clb, 1979-83; So Sem Drama Clb, 1983-84; r/Luth; hon/Turner Ashby Outstg Vocal Music Student Awd, 1983; Music Hon Awd, 1980-83; VA Lions Clb Band S'ship Contest, Vocal Div, 1st Place Awd, 1981-83; W/W Am HS Students; g/To Attain a BA in Music Ed at Bridgewater Col.

ALEXANDER, THEODORE M III oc/Computer Operations Intern; b/Sep 15, 1961; h/3148 Kingsdale Drive, Atlanta, GA 30311; ba/Hapeville, GA; p/T M Jr (dec) and Janis B Alexander, Atlanta, GA; ed/HS, The Westminster Sch, 1980; Seeking Deg in Computer Sci w a Bus Minor, Morehouse Col; Subsequently Seeking an MBA at Emory or Stanford; pa/Salesman, Programmer, Datamart Inc, 1979; Computer Sci Apprentice, Res Ctr for Sci and Engrg, 1980; Computer Reservationist, The Day Co, 1981; Computer Opers Intern, First Atlanta Bk, 1982-; Alpha Phi Alpha Frat, Chapt Treas 1982-83; cp/NAACP, Life Mem; Jack & Jill of Am Inc, Chapt Secy 1980; Engrg Clb at Morehouse, Com Chp 1980; HS: Tennis Team 1977-79, Chess Team 1977-78, Computer Sci Clb 1977-80; Col: Tennis Team 1980; r/Congregational; hon/Hon Roll at Morehouse, Fall Semester 1980 and Sprg Semester 1981; Dean's List, Sprg Semester 1981; NAACP, Act-So Sci Awd, 1979; g/To Own or Co-Own a Fortune 500 Co in the Area of Computer Applications and to Further His Investmt Skills and Knowledge.

ALEXANDER, YOLETTE UDA oc/ Unemployed; b/Mar 23, 1958; h/3616

7th Court, Wylam, Birmingham, AL 35224; p/Lloyd L and Emma Alexander, Birmingham, AL; ed/Ensley HS, 1976; Miles Col, 1976-78; BA, Social Wk, Univ of Montevallo, 1981; cp/NASW; Social Wk Clb; Afro-Am Soc; Sociol Clb; Am JA Soc; Electron Clb Treas; Acad Hon Roll; Bapt Ch SS Tchr; Asst Yth Dir; Yg Adult Usher Bd, Secy; Girl Scout Ldr, Cahaba Girl Scout Coun, 1982-83 (Troop #229, Jrs); hon/Friends of Miles Col S'ship Awd; Nat Dean's List; Outstg Yg Wom of Am; Commun Ldrs of Am; g/Master's Deg in Social Wk; Social Wkr.

ALFORD, KEITH ANTHONY oc/Salesperson; b/Dec 6, 1961; h/815 Pine Street, Columbia, SC 29205; ba/Florence, SC; p/Ethel J Finley, Columbia, SC; ed/HS Dipl, Dreher HS, 1979; BA, Hist and Sociol, Coker Col, 1983; pa/Columnist, *Black News*, 1977-79; Intern, Darlington Co Dept of Social Sers, 1980; Intern, SC St Dept of Social Sers, 1981; Intern, Midlands Human Resources Devel Comm, 1982; Practicum in Social Sers, Darlington Co Dept of Social Sers, 1983; Salesperson, Belk Dept Store, Magnolia Mall; cp/Coker Col: Commr Ser Org, F'ship of Christian Students, Student Admissions Com, Coker Singers, Student Rep to Lib Com, Student Rep to Acad Standards Com, Publicity and Calendar Chp, Sophomore Class Pres 1980-81, Student Govt Assn Pres 1981-82, 1982-83, Coker Col Union Exec Bd Mem, Bd of Govs Mem; r/Bapt; hon/Charles Kirkland Dunlap Scholar, 1982-83; Coker Col Dean's List, Sprg 1980, Fall 1980, Fall 1982, Sprg 1983; W/W Among Students in Am Univs and Cols; Nat Dean's List; Intl Biogl Centre; g/To Earn a Master's Deg in Social Wk; To Wk as a Protective Sers Wkr in the Fam Sers/Protective Ser Div of the Dept of Social Sers.

ALGARY, KATHRYN ELIZABETH oc/Student; b/Aug 18, 1962; h/20 Stonehaven Drive, Greenville, SC 29607; p/Dr and Mrs William P Algary, Greenville, SC; ed/Grad, J L Mann HS, 1980; BS, Winthrop Col, 1984; pa/Co-op Position at Bigelow-Sanford Inc; Full-time Employee, Pers Dept, Bigelow-Sanford Inc, Sum 1983; cp/Social Chm, Panhellenic Coun, Winthrop Col, 1982; Pres, Delta Zeta Sorority, Winthrop Col, 1983; Alpha Kappa Psi Bus Frat; r/Presb; hon/Dean's List, Winthrop Col, 1983; Recip, Homes Key in HS; g/To Attain an MBA Deg.

ALLEGRETTI, EDWARD PHILIP oc/Student; b/Jan 31, 1962; h/12500 Poppy Lane, San Jose, CA 95127; p/Mr and Mrs John M Allegretti, San Jose, CA; ed/Grad, Piedmont Hills HS, 1980; Student, San Jose St Univ; pa/Res Asst, NASA/Ames, Sum 1980; Asst Mgr, Wilson's Suede and Leather, Sum 1982; Asst Supvr, Nat Communs Inc, Sum 1983; cp/Phi Alpha Theta, Intl Hon Soc in Hist; Alpha Lambda Delta, Nat Hon Soc; Soc for Advmt of Mgmt; Italian-Am Heritage Foun; Sec and Treas Univ's Bd of Gen Studies, 1981-83; Fdr and Pres, Yth Grp, Italian-Am Heritage Foun, 1982; r/Trustees Bd, Hd Usher, Alum Rock Covenant Ch, 1983; hon/Dean's Hon List, 1982, 1983; Alumni Assn Dean's S'ship, 1981; Commends from Mayor Hayes of San Jose and Congressman Mineta; Intl Yth in

Achmt; W/W Commun Ldrs; g/Fin Maj w Career Goal of Bus Mgmt.

ALLEN, BONNIE ROSE oc/Farmer; b/Mar 14, 1958; h/Route 1, Box 202, Pinetops, NC 27864; ba/Macclesfield, NC; p/James and Mildred Allen, Pinetops, NC; ed/Grad, S Edgecombe HS, Pinetops, 1976; Att'd, E Carolina Univ, 1976-78; pa/Asst Mgr, Deena Casuals Clothing Store, Tarboro, NC, 1978-79; Farmer, 1979-; Floor Mgr, B&F Tobacco Warehouse, Rocky Mount, NC, 1983-; NC Farm Bur (Yg Farmers) St Adv Com Mem, 1982-83; cp/HS Beta Clb, 1973-76; HS Math Clb, Secy 1975-76; r/Bapt; W/W Among Am HS Students; g/To Attend USDA Tobacco Grading Sch; To Attend Ednl Farming Progs in Near Future.

ALLEN, BRONWYN JAYE oc/Student; b/Jun 25, 1966; h/Lynn at 25th Street, Big Spring, TX 79720; p/Mr and Mrs Robert J Allen, Big Spring, TX; ed/HS Grad, 1984; cp/Pres, Nat Jr Hon Soc, 1980; Nat Hon Soc, 1982-83; Student Coun, 1981, 1984; Class Treas, 1981, 1982; Girl's Choir Treas, 1981; French Clb Treas, 1981, 1982; Tri-Hi-Y Yth in Govt Treas and Publicity Chm, 1981, 1982, 1983; Basic Jr C of C, 1982-83, 1983-84; Hosp Jr Vol (Candy Striper), 1981, 1982; Baseball Home Run Honeys, 1982, 1983; r/1st Christian Ch; Ch Handbell Choir, 1978-83; Ch Chancel Choir, 1980, 1981; Christian Yth F'ship, 1981-83; Chi Rho (Jr High Ch Yth Grp), 1978-80; hon/Am Legion Awd, 1980; Soc of Dist'd Am HS Students, 1981, 1982, 1983; US Achmt Acad Awd in French, 1982; Quaternion 1st Place in French, 1983; Sum Sci Sem, USAF Acad, 1983; Jr Statesmen Foun Sum Sch, Wash, DC, 1983; Oddfellows UN Pilgrimage for Yth, 1983; Tri-Hi-Y Dist and St Convs, 1981, 1982, 1983; W/W Big Sprg HS; W/W Among Am HS Students.

ALLEN, ELIZABETH HOPE oc/Student; b/Nov 22, 1960; h/3905 Third Place, Northwest, Rochester, MN 55901; p/Paul and Beverly Allen, Rochester, MN; ed/Grad, John Marshall HS, 1979; BA, Carleton Col, 1983; pa/Pt-time, Sum Help Positions; cp/Sierra Clb, 1982-; AAU Swim Team, 1976-78; Student Coun Rep; Hosp Vol; r/Meth; hon/Nat Hon Soc, 1978-; Nat Merit Commend, 1979; Mortar Bd, 1982-; #1 in Class; Dean's List; Cross Country Team; W/W Among Am HS Students; Commun Ldrs of Am; g/To Attend Div Sch and Study Comparative Rels at the Grad Level; To Attain an MDiv and PhD.

ALLEN, FREDERICK LEWIS oc/Part-Owner of Business; b/Feb 25, 1957; h/PO Box 264, Polson, MT 59860; ba/Polson, MT; p/Warren G and Marjorie H Allen, Minot, ND; ed/Minot Sr HS, 1975; BCS 1978, BS 1980, Minot St Col; MA in Eng, Univ of ID, 1983; pa/Sales/Stock, Sharks Clothiers, 1975-76; Sales, Yg Am Inc, 1976-80; Eng Instr, Cambridge HS, 1980-81; Tchg Asst, Univ of ID, 1981-83; Pt-Owner, Recording Studio; cp/NHS; Gov's Coun on Yth in ND; hon/Mng Editor, Cartoonist, *Rock* (Student Pub); Assn Pres, HS; Pres's Hon Roll; Nat Dean's List; W/W Am Cols and Univs; g/PhD in Eng.

ALLEN, JEAN RENEE oc/Head Waitress; b/Sep 13, 1963; h/Route 654

Birchwood Apartments, Apartment 13-H, Cloverdale, VA 24077; ba/Daleville, VA; p/Mr and Mrs Calvin R Allen, Monroe, VA; ed/Adv'd Dipl, Amherst Co HS, 1981; Dipl, Wilma Boyd Career Sch, 1982; Att'd, Ctl VA Commun Col, 1981; pa/Waitress, Madison Hgts Pizza Hut; Hd Waitress, Daleville Pizza Hut; cp/March of Dimes Walkathon, 1978-79; Am Cancer Soc, 1980; Lynchburg Tng Sch and Hosp Vol; Amherst Co Jr High Softball, 1977; Pep, Spanish, Tri-Hi-Y Clbs, 1979; Pep Clb, Tri-Hi-Y (Secy), 1980; Pep, Tri-Hi-Y (Secy), Varsity Clbs, 1981; Band, Clarinet, 1976-81; Rifles, 1979-81; Co-Capt 1980, Capt 1981, Sabre; Drill Team, 1981; r/U Meth Yth F'ship, Secy; hon/Miss U VA Teenager Articles, 1979; Miss Botetourt Pageant Articles, 1981; Adv'd Dipl, 1981; Perfect Attendance, 9 Out of 12 Yrs of Sch; 4-H Hons, Blue Ribbons, 1974 (1), 1975 (3), 1976 (3), 1974 (Red, 2), 1975 (1), 1976 (Purple, 1); Miss U VA Teenager, 1980 (3rd Runner-Up); Miss Botetourt, 1981 (1st Runner-Up); g/To Attend Cosmotology Sch.

ALLEN, LISA CORBETT oc/Student; b/Feb 13, 1965; h/3309 Evans Street, Greenville, NC 27834; p/Mr and Mrs Kenneth Allen Sr, Greenville, NC; ed/Grad, D H Conley HS, 1983; Student, Math Ed, Campbell Univ; pa/Var Farm Jobs for Kenneth Allen & Son Farms, 1977-82; Cashier/Hostess, Jack's Steak House, 1981-82; cp/HS Chorus, 1979-80; Student Coun Assn, 1979-80; Lit Clb, 1979-80, 1981-82; Nat Hon Soc, 1981-83; Mu Alpha Theta, 1981-83; Future Bus Ldrs of Am, 1980-81, 1982-83; Bi-Chem-Phy, 1980-81; Spanish Clb, Pres 1982-83; Quill and Scroll, 1982-83; r/Free-Will Bapt; Ch Yth Grp, Secy and Treas 1981-82; hon/Pres S'ship to Campbell Univ; Recip, Prospective Tchr S'ship; Loan Fund Recip, Marshal, 1982-83; Hon Sr; g/To Become a Math Tchr.

ALLEN, ROBERT EARL oc/Student; b/Feb 9, 1960; h/Route 1, Box 350 C, Drummonds, TN 38023; p/Robert and Sue Allen, Drummonds, TN; ed/Millington HS, 1978; Assoc in Applied Sci (Drafting and Design Technol), NW MS Jr Col, 1982; Current Student, Univ of TN Martin; cp/MCHS, Rodeo Clb Pres 1976-77, 1977-78; NWJC, Tech Soc 1980-81, Pres 1981-82; AG Clb, 1980-81, 1981-82; Rodeo Team, 1980-81; Phi Theta Kappa, Pres 1981-82; UP Senate, 1981-82; UTM Rodeo Clb, 1982-83, 1983-84; IEEE, 1983-84; r/Bapt; hon/Pres Lists, NWJC, Fall 1981; Grad'd on Dean's List, 1982; Rodeo S'ship, NWJC, 1980-81, 1981-82; Rodeo S'ship, UTM, 1983; g/Deg, Elect Engr in Technol.

ALLEN, RODNEY HOLT oc/Student; b/Oct 22, 1952; h/207 Truman Drive, Fayetteville, NC; p/J T Allen Jr, Fayetteville, NC; ed/Pine Forest Sr HS, 1970; NC St Univ, 1970-72; Baylor Univ, 1976; Hlth Ser Command Phys Subst Course; cp/Sponsor, WUNC TV and Radio Repub Nat Com; AUS Spec Forces; Hon Grad, Phys Subst Course; Pershing Rifles; Bsn; hon/Author, USASF Phys Subs Tests and Ref Volumes; Army Meritorious Ser; Army Commend; Eagle Awd, BSA; g/MD Deg w Ob-Gyn.

ALLEN, SUSAN KAY oc/Registered

Nurse; b/Jun 22, 1959; h/5018 11th Avenue, Northeast, Seattle, WA 98105; p/Mr and Mrs Richard G Allen, Redding, CA; ed/Los Altos HS, 1977; BSN, Pacific Luth Univ, 1981; pa/Med-Surg Staff Nurse, VA Mason Hosp, 1981-; Hosp Quality Assurance Com; WA St Nurses Assn; ANA; cp/Univ Singers; r/ Luth Ch Choir; hon/Grad, summa cum laude; Nat Dean's List; Am Biogs; g/ Adult Practitioner or Instr in Nsg.

ALLEN, WILLIAM RICHARD oc/ Student; b/Oct 18, 1957; h/130 South Estes Drive, Chapel Hill, NC 27514; p/ Mr and Mrs Junior R Allen, Abingdon, VA; ed/Chilhowie HS, 1976; BS, Emory and Henry Col, 1980; Univ of NC Chapel Hill; cp/Basketball; Track; Hi-Y; Beta Clb; NHS; Band; Monogram Clb; Sigma Mu; Am Phy Soc; hon/Grad, magna cum laude; Nat Merit Scholar; Col Phy Awd; Nat Dean's List; Intl Yth in Achmt; Soc of Dist'd Am HS Students; g/Doct in Physics.

ALLENSWORTH, DEANETTE FAYE oc/Student; b/Oct 20, 1962; h/PO Box 123, Plainville, IL 62365; p/John and Betty Stout, Plainville, IL; ed/Seymour HS, 1980; NE MO St Univ; pa/Univ Res Asst, NM St Univ, Sprg 1983; cp/Pep Clb Band; All-St Band; Band Pres; Student Coun; Elem Ed Clb; Intramural V'ball, Softball, Basketball; HS Lttrman's Clb; Girl's Ath Assn; Basketball Capt; Track; Softball; V'ball; Pep Clb Pres; Elem Ed Clb, Treas; Floor Pres, NM St Univ, 1983-84; Alpha Phi Sigma Hon Frat; Campus Vols; r/Akers Chapel Christian Ch; hon/HS Student of the Yr; HS Co-Valedictorian; Univ Dean's List, 1983-84; Intl Yth in Achmt; Yg Commun Ldrs of Am; g/Elem Tchr.

ALLISON, LESA HOKE oc/Student; b/Mar 7, 1961; h/1405 Stadium View Drive, Murray, KY 42071; m/Doug; p/ Charles Robert and Peggy Beale Hoke, Almo, KY; ed/Calloway Co HS, 1979; BA, Radio-TV, Murray St Univ, 1983; pa/Customer Ser Dir, K-Mart Corp, 1979-83; Student Wkr, Murray St Univ Extended Ed Ofc, 1980; cp/Newswriter for Murray St Univ TV 11 News; Calloway Spch Team, 1978 St Champs, VP 1979; Nat Forensic Leag, 1976-79; Students in Action for Ed, 1977-79; Alpha Delta Pi Social Sorority; Sigma Chi Little Sisters; Hostess for "Friday Magazine" Prog for Murray St Univ-TV 11 News; FCC 3rd Class Lic; hon/4th KY St Spch Team, 1978; Dean's List, 1979; Calloway Spch Team Hall of Fame, 1979; hon/W/W Among HS Students; g/To Become a Broadcast Journalist, and Then a Reporter-Anchor.

ALLISON, DONALD HALASZ oc/ World Bank Official; b/Mar 29, 1955; h/1623 33rd Street, Northwest, Washington, DC 20007; ba/Washington, DC; p/Harry and Agnes Allison; ed/BA, Ec, Univ of CA Berkeley, 1977; MBA, Harvard Bus Sch, 1979; Dipl in Devel Ec, Oxford Univ, 1980; pa/Assoc, Lewis Bouley & Assocs, 1979-81; Financial Analyst, US Synthetic Fuels Corp, 1981; World Bk Ofcl, 1981-; hon/Co-Author, *The Real World War*, 1982; Phi Beta Kappa, 1977; Baker Scholar, Harvard Bus Sch, 1979; Grad w Distn, Oxford Univ, 1980; Former Eagle Scout; Outstg Yg Men of Am Awd, 1983.

ALLISON, LYNDA M oc/Student; b/

Oct 27, 1961; h/1005 Buckingham Circle, Atlanta, GA 30327; p/Mrs W F Eve, Atlanta, GA; ed/The Lovett Sch; BA in Communs and Jour, Brenau Col, 1983; pa/Free-Lance Writer and Photog; Equestrian Sci Instr for Brenau Col, 1981-82; cp/Brenau Nom'g Com, 1979-80; Alpha Chi Omega Sorority, VP of the Pledge Class; Brenau Rec Assn; Exec Bd, Brenau F'ship Assn; Exec Cabinet, Annual and Newspaper Staff; Phoenix Soc Debutante, 1980-81; Brenau Panhellenic Assn, Secy; r/Rom Cath; hon/Author, Articles in *Georgia Journal*, 1981, 1982; HGH Sr Hon Soc, 1983; W/W in Am Cols and Univs; W/ W Intl Frats and Sororities.

ALLOWAY, JAMES EUGENE oc/ Student; h/821 North Central, Parsons, KS 67357; p/William S Fouts, Parsons, KS; ed/Parsons HS, 1982; Student of Hist and German, Univ of KS; cp/Nat Hon Soc, 1981-82; Pres of PHS Chess Clb, 1981-82; Nat Forensic Leag, 1979-82; Student Coun Rep at Large, 1981-82; Jud Bd of Battenfeld S'ship Hall, 1983; r/Bapt; Bapt Yth F'ship, 1979-82; hon/Outstg Hist Student, PHS, 1982; Recip, Caroline B Spongler German S'ship, 1983; Bd of Regents Scholar, 1982; Dewey S'ship Recip, 1982-83; Anschutz S'ship Recip, 1982-83; KU S'ship Hall Mem, 1982-84; W/W Am HS Students; g/To Work in Archives.

ALSOBROOK, ALICE E oc/Student, Secretary; b/Apr 5, 1963; h/Box 132, Highway 55, Cusseta, AL 36852; ba/ Troy, AL; p/Mrs John N Alsobrook, Cusseta, AL; ed/HS Dipl, Lee Acad; AA, Troy St Univ; pa/Secy, E AL Med Ctr, 1980; Secy, Bill Fuller, Atty at Law, 1981, 1982; Bkkpg Clk, Farmers and Merchants Bk, 1982; Secy, Botts & Ray Inc, Civil Engrs and Surveyors, 1982-; cp/Alpha Gamma Delta Social Sorority; Sigma Chi Social Frat, Little Sister; Gamma Beta Phi Hon Soc; r/Prot; hon/ Alpha Gamma Delta, Pledge of Yr 1981; W/W; g/Secy/Paralegal.

ALSOBROOK, MARY ANNE oc/ Student in Graduate School; b/Apr 6, 1961; h/PO Box 26, Cusseta, AL 36852; ed/HS, Lee Acad; Bach Deg, Early Childhood Ed, Univ of AL, 1982; pa/ Proof Operator, Auburn Nat Bk, 1983-; Teller, Bkkpr, F&M Bk, 1979-82; Cnslr, Camp ASCCA for E AL Mtl Hlth, 1978; Secy, Country and Comml Properties; cp/Kappa Delta Pi, Ed Hon; Assn for Chd Intl; Beta Clb; Anchor Clb; Delta Zeta Sorority, Asst Treas; r/Bapt; Inducted, Kappa Delta Pi, 1983; Dean's List, Univ of AL; Miss Lee Acad, 1979; W/W Among Am HS Students; Commun Ldrs of Am; g/To Teach Kgn or First Grade.

ALSTON, WARREN DELANO oc/ Student; b/Apr 5, 1962; h/RR 1, Box 28-A, Awendaw, SC 29429; p/Mr and Mrs Timothy Alston Sr, Awendaw, SC; ed/Lincoln HS, 1981; Univ; cp/Basketball; Ftball; Gov Scholar; hon/Valedictorian; NHS; Best All-Around Student; Spkg Contest Awd; 1st Place, Math Fair; W/W Among Am HS Students; Soc of Dist'd Am HS Students; g/Law, Math, Sci, Phil, Engrg.

ALTENHOF, SHIRLEY ELAINE oc/ Student; b/Oct 30, 1960; h/Route 2, Box 687, New Braunfels, TX 78130; p/Mr and Mrs Howard A Altenhof, New Braunfels, TX; ed/Seguin HS, 1979; BS

cum laude in Agri Ec; TX A&M Univ, 1983; pa/Sum Intern, TX Bk for Cooperatives, 1981; Ofc Asst, Prodrs Cooperative Mktg Assn, 1980; cp/Bd of Trustees, Nat Alpha Zeta Foun, 1982-83; TAMU Placement Adv Coun and Student Orgs Bd, 1981-83; TAMU Col of Agri Student Coun, 1982-83; Pres 1982-83, Treas 1981-82, TAMU Agri Ec Clb; Secy, TAMU Nat Agri-Mktg Assn, 1980-81; Histn, Photog, TAMU Jr Hon, 1981-82; Phi Kappa Phi Scholastic Hon; Gamma Sigma Delta Agri Hon, 1983-; Mortar Bd Sr Hon, 1982; Lambda Sigma Sophomore Hon, 1980; Alpha Lambda Delta Freshmen Hon, 1980; r/Luth; hon/Nat Alpha Zeta Agri Hon Top S'ship Recip, 1982-83; TAMU Spirit Awd, 1983; TAMU Undergrad Fellow, 1982-83; TAMU Col of Agri Sr Merit Awd, 1983; TAMU Dept of Agri Ec Fac and Student Outstg Sr Awd, 1983; W/W Among Students in Univs and Cols; Outstg Yg Ams; g/Law Sch.

ALTICE, TAMMI LYNN oc/Student; b/Mar 23, 1963; h/Route 1, Box 475, Wirtz, VA 24184; ba/Radford, VA; p/ Wilford and Betty Altice, Wirtz, VA; ed/ HS, 1981; Student, Radford Univ; pa/ Post Ofc Clk, Radford Univ (Wk/Study S'ship for 2 Yrs); CRT Operator, Blue Cross and Blue Shield; cp/Nat Hon Soc; Spanish Clb; FBLA; Math Clb; Alpha Lambda Delta; Kappa Mu Epsilon; r/ Meth; hon/Alpha Lambda Delta, 1982; Kappa Mu Epsilon, 1983; Spanish Clb S'ship, 1981; Local S'ships, 1981, 1982, 1983; Nat Hon Soc; W/W; Intl Yth in Achmt; g/To Be a Computer Programmer or Analyst.

ALVAREZ, GIL oc/Manager for Sistemas de Riego; b/Nov 5, 1954; h/Calle Terrazas #4, Colonia Juarez 31857, Chihuahua, Mexico; ba/Chihuahua, Mexico; p/Mr and Mrs David Alvarez, Chihuahua, Mexico; ed/Academia Juarez AC, 1973; BS 1979, MS 1981, Sul Ross St Univ; pa/Br Mgr for Intl Commerce Corp; Mgr for Sistemas de Riego, JEFE; cp/Student Govt Ofc; Delta Tau Alpha, Pres; Alpha Chi; Rodeo Clb; Interviewed as Example Student in Documentary TV Film about Sul Ross Univ; r/Ch of Christ of LDS; hon/Intl Yth in Achmt; Nat Dean's List; W/W Am Cols and Univs; g/Ranch Operation.

ANCHELL, THEODORE JAMES JR oc/Electrical Engineer; b/Oct 5, 1961; h/ 8485 San Rafael, Charlack, MO 63114; ba/St Louis, MO; ed/Luth HS W; Valparaiso Univ; Enrolled in Wash Univ Grad Engrg Prog (Wkg toward MSEE Deg); pa/Engr, McDonnell Douglas Aircraft Co, 1983-; IEEE; cp/Phi Sigma Epsilon; Choral Soc; Alpha Lambda Delta; Overseas Study Prog; hon/Phi Beta Kappa Awd; Dean's List; Valparaiso Univ Sr Hons; Valparaiso Univ High Hons; g/Elect Engrg Deg.

ANDERBERG, MICHELLE RENEE oc/Student; b/Feb 12, 1961; h/1825 Route 20 West, Galena, IL 61036; p/Mr and Mrs Richard Anderberg, Galena, IL; ed/Galena HS, 1979; Coe Col; cp/Pres, GSA Troop; Q&S; Delta Delta Delta; Track; Band; hon/W/W Among Am HS Students; g/RN; BSN; Wk in Neonatal ICU.

ANDERSON, DALYN DEE oc/Graduate Student; b/Mar 4, 1960; h/3804 Booth #11, Kansas City, KS 66103; p/ Mr and Mrs David B Anderson, Drexel,

MO; ed/Shawnee Mission NW HS, 1978; Bach Deg, KS St Univ, 1982; Grad Student, Spch Pathol, KS Univ; cp/AKL Little Sister; Spch Pathol Clb; Boyd Hall Bible Study, Publicity Ofcr; Univ Prog Coun; 4-H Camp Cnslr, Adv Bd Mem, Oil Painting Ldr; Designed, Painted Nursery Mural for Ch; AFS Host; Student Govt Elections Helper; Kappa Alpha Theta, Rush Advr 1983; Dancer, *Hello Dolly*, Theatre in the Pk; hon/1978 Miss Bo Peep; 1978 Miss 4-H; Phi Kappa Phi; Nat 4-H Sheep Winner S'ship; Golden Key Hon; Kappa Alpha Theta Grad S'ship Winner, 1982; Selected for UAF, Grad Stipend; g/Spch Pathol Deg.

ANDERSON, GRAHAM THOMAS oc/Flight Test Analysis Engineer; b/Oct 22, 1961; h/5503 Mesagrove Avenue, Whittier, CA 90601; ba/PO Box 2507, Pomona, CA 91766; ed/AS, Don Bosco Tech Inst, 1980; BS, Engrg Technol, CA St Polytechnic Univ, 1982; pa/Flight Test Anal Engr, Gen Dynamics, Pomona Div, 1982-; cp/1st Trombonist in Col Band; Pks and Rec; Hosp; Yth Grp; hon/Tau Alpha Pi, 1982.

ANDERSON, JUDY PAGE oc/Student; b/Jan 15, 1962; h/632 Wilson Street, Roanoke Rapids, NC 27870; p/Rev and Mrs Austin Anderson, Roanoke Rapids, NC; ed/Roanoke Rapids HS, 1980; BA, Psych, Meredith Col, 1984; pa/Psych Prof's Asst, Meredith Col, 1982; Reservation and Sales Agt, World-Wide Sheraton Reservations, 1982; NC Dept of Adm Intern, NC St Govt, 1983; cp/HS: Drum Majorette 1980, Keywanettes (Treas 1980), French Hon Soc; Col: Meredith Christian Assn 1980-81, Psych Clb 1980-83, VP of Psych Clb, Co-Chair of Carolinas Psych Conf 1983; Am Psychol Assn, 1983; r/Christian; hon/Pubs, "Teacher's Reading Patterns to Children 2 & 4 Yrs" 1983, "Effects of Stimulus Familiarity on Semantic Memory" 1982; Psi Chi Induction, 1983; Kappa Nu Sigma Induction, 1983; g/To Attend Grad Sch; To Wk w Inmates in Correctional Instns.

ANDERSON, KAREN RENEE oc/Student; b/Apr 14, 1963; h/Box 27, Jackson, MN 56143; p/Harold and Helen Anderson, Jackson, MN; ed/Jackson HS, 1983; Student, Mankato St Univ; cp/Co 4-H Fdn Treas; German Clb; Sch Newspaper, Annual Staff; Chorus Declamation; Alpha Chi Omega Asst Rush Chm and Histn; Col Flag Corps, 1982, 1983; Little Sister to Alpha Tau Omega, 1982; hon/Lions Clb "Extra Curric Activs Student of the Yr"; MN 4-H Key Clb Awd; Intl Yth in Achmt; W/W Among HS Students; g/To Complete Course Wk in Scandinavian Studies, and Find Suitable Career in It.

ANDERSON, KATHY LYNNETTE oc/Student; b/Mar 30, 1967; h/Route 2, Box 300-A, Fuquay-Varina, NC 27526; p/Leon and Teresa Anderson, Fuquay-Varina, NC; ed/Student, HS; cp/Basketball; Softball; Tennis; French Clb; Pep Clb; FBLA; Class Ofcr; Beta Clb; Cheerldr; Monogram Clb; Student Coun Ofcr; hon/Intl Fgn Lang Awd, 1982; Hist Awd, 1982; Geometry Awd, 1982; Typing I Awd, 1983; AG Eng II Awd, 1983; Algebra II Awd, 1983; Perfect Attendance Awd, 1980-83; Nat Ldrship and Ser Awd, 1983; US Achmt Acad; Commun Ldrs of Am; g/RN.

ANDERSON, KRISTEN DAWN oc/

Student; h/Route 10, Box 372, Morganton, NC; p/Mr and Mrs Charles W Anderson, Morganton, NC; ed/Freedom HS, 1981; Appalachian St Univ; cp/Anchor Clb Pres; NHS; Mar Band; ASU Mar Band; Gamma Beta Phi, 1982, 1983; Compass Clb, Pres (Charter Clb) 1983; r/U Meth Ch F'ship Secy; hon/Valedictorian, Freedom HS, 1981; Yth Apprec Wk Awd, Breakfast Optimists; Hon'd as One of Top 10 Students in Jr Class at ASU, 1983; g/To Become a Tchr of Spec Students; To Share My Humanity w Others to Make the World Better for Them.

ANDERSON, LAURA KAY oc/Teacher; b/May 23, 1961; h/RR #1, Box 21, Gladstone, IL 61437; ba/Wellsville, MO; p/Mr and Mrs L A Anderson, Gladstone, IL; ed/Grad, Union HS, 1979; BS, Elem Ed, Culver-Stockton Col, 1983; pa/3rd Grade Tchr, Wellsville-Middletown Schs, 1983-; cp/Student SMSTA; AWS, Treas and Pres; Student Intramural Dir, 2 Yrs; Ball Girl for Men's Basketball Team; Alpha Chi, Hon Scholastic Frat, VP; McDonald Hall Secy, 2 Yrs; Acad Coun Mem; Cross Country Team; hon/Col Homecoming Queen, 1982; 2nd in Dist in Cross-Country, 1982; I Dare You, 1979; Soc of Am Dist'd HS Students, 1979; Most Served Points in Volleyball, 1977; Coaches Attitude Awd, 1978; Valedictorian, 1979; Grad, magna cum laude, 1983; Outstg Female of Col Sr Class, 1983; Wood Citizenship Awd, 1983; W/W Am Cols and Univs; W/W Among HS Students; g/Grad Wk.

ANDERSON, LEROY JR oc/National Direct Student Loan Operations Manager, Business Owner; b/Apr 14, 1960; h/2608 La Salle Street, Charlotte, NC 28216; ba/Winston Salem, NC; p/Mr and Mrs Leroy Anderson Sr, Charlotte, NC; ed/Dipl, W Charlotte Sr HS, 1978; BA in Bus Adm, Morehouse Col, 1982; pa/Nat Direct Student Loan Operations Mgr, Wachovia Sers Inc, 1983-; Bus Owner, Synergy Intl, 1980-; cp/BSA, Troop 107, Scoutmaster (Univ Pk Bapt Ch); Morehouse Col Nat Alumni Assn; Metrolina Morehouse Alumni Clb; NC Yg Dems; r/Bapt; hon/Morehouse Col, Hon Roll 1979-82, Dean's List 1979-82, Dept of Ec and Bus Adm Hons 1982, Morehouse Aux Prize 1982; W/W Among Students in Am Univs and Cols; Outstg Yg Men of Am; Yg Commun Ldrs of Am; Intl Yth in Achmt; Nat Dean's List; g/Cert'd Financial Planner; MBA Deg (Mgmt).

ANDERSON, LORI CHOYCE oc/Student; b/Oct 25, 1963; h/Route 2, Box 67, Indian Trail, NC 28079; p/George Thomas and Margaret Jean Wyatt Anderson; ed/Sun Val HS; BA in Human Sers w Double Emphasis in French and Sociol, Wingate Col; Wkg on Master's Deg in Clin Cnslg, The Citadel; cp/Rainbow Girls Past Worthy Adv, Grand Cross of Color Bearer; Past Grand Page; Spec Recog for Wk; Jr Civitans, Civitan of the Yr 1979, Miss Civitan for Sun Val, 3rd Runner-Up at Miss NC Jr Civinette; Spec Olympics; Gov Sch; Spec Ldrship Conf; U Co Quiz Bowl Team; High Q Bowl Team; Homecoming Ct; Yrbook Staff; Pep Clb; French Clb; Math Clb; Sci Clb; Passed Cecchetti Grade V; TV Appearances; Charlotte Ballet Theatre; r/Prot; hon/Marshal, Wingate's 1983 Graduation;

NHS; French NHS; Nat Ed Devel Tests Awd; Cert of Excell in Adv'd Placement Calculus and Eng; Num S'ships for Var Sources; Lttrs of Congratulations from U Co Supt B Paul Hammack and Congressman Bill Hefner; Outstg Sr in Acad; Valedictorian; Personalities of S; Commun Ldrs of Am; Intl Yth in Achmt; g/To Incorporate the Uses of Self-Expression and Humor w Cnslg.

ANDERSON, PAMELA YVONNE oc/Student; b/Aug 3, 1962; h/230 Keowee Trail, Seneca, SC 29678; ba/Greenville, SC; p/Mr and Mrs James M Anderson, Seneca, SC; ed/Grad, Seneca HS, 1980; Student, Furman Univ; cp/Beta Chi Biol Clb, 1981-83; Alpha Epsilon Delta, 1982-83; All Committed Together, 1981-83; Girl's Soc, Rush Chm 1983; Inter Clb Coun, 1981-83, VP 1982-83; Montague Living Lng Ctr, 1981-83; Ser Corp CESC, 1981-83; Jr Acad of Sci, 1977-80, Pres 1979-80; Student Coun, 1978-80; Beta Clb, 1976-80; Debating Clb, 1976-80; r/Bapt; hon/Dean's List, Furman Univ, 1980-83; Salutatorian, HS, 1980; Rotary Scholar, 1976, 1977, 1979, 1980; Sci Awd, 1980; Math Awd, 1980; Furman Scholar, 1979; Gov's Scholar, 1979; PC Jr Fellow, 1979; Beta Chord, 1980; g/BS in Biol; BS in Pharm; PharmD.

ANDERSON, PATRICK DEAN oc/Student; b/Nov 25, 1960; h/1278 Briarwood Drive, San Luis Obispo, CA 93401; p/Regina Anderson, San Luis Obispo, CA; ed/San Luis Obispo Sr HS; BS, Food Sci, CA Polytechnic St Univ; pa/Lab Tech, Sum Wk; cp/Food Sci Clb, Polyroyal Chm, Clb Photg, 1980-; Order of the Arrow, 1976-; r/Cath; hon/Boys' St, Hon Scout; W/W Among HS Students; Commun Ldrs of Am; g/MBA.

ANDERSON, PAUL LEON oc/Student; b/Mar 17, 1962; h/2608 La Salle Street, Charlotte, NC 28216; p/Leroy Sr and Veola C Anderson; ed/Dipl, W Charlotte Sr High, 1980; BBA, NC Ctl Univ; DTh, Theol Sem; Received Lic, The Gospel Min, 1983; cp/Bus Mgr, Sch Newspaper, 1983-84; Reporter/Writer/Columnist, Sch Newspaper; Pres, Jr Ushers; Bus Dr; MVP Basketball; Var Tennis, Soccer; Asst Coach, Var Basketball; r/Christian; hon/Jr HS Citizenship Hon; Outstg Christian Ser Awd; g/MBS.

ANDERSON, ROBERT JOSEPH oc/Student; b/Aug 8, 1960; h/1525 Robert Hardeman Road, Winterville, GA 30683; p/Dr and Mrs James L Anderson, Winterville, GA; Mrs G L Anderson, Lawrence, KS; ed/Grad, Cedar Shoals HS, 1979; Grad, Univ of GA, 1983; cp/Pianist, GA Jazzband II; Campus/Commun Relats Chm, Phi Gamma Delta; Phi Eta Sigma, Freshman Hon; Kappa Delta Big Brother; Univ of GA Karate Clb; Beta Clb; Nat Hon Soc; Initiations Chm, Jr Classical Leag; Lttr, Swimming; Cedar Shoals Jazzband; hon/Biftad, Highest Hon for Freshman or Sophomore Male, Univ of GA; Phi Eta Sigma; Nat Hon Soc; Dean's List; 3rd in Latin Derivation, St Competition; Hons Prog Participant, Univ of GA; Outstg Commun Ldrs; Personalities of S; g/BBA and MBA in Mgmt Info Sys.

ANDERSON, TRACY KAY oc/Student; b/Aug 9, 1960; h/15 Capri Drive, Mankato, MN 56001; ba/Same; p/John R and Judith M Anderson, Abaco,